W9-ASC-556

Presented to

By

On

This Certifies That

AND

WERE UNITED IN

Holy Matrimony

ON THE

DAY OF A.D.

AT

IN ACCORDANCE WITH THE LAWS OF

OFFICIATING

WITNESS

WITNESS

Special Occasions to Remember

EVENT

PLACE DATE

EVENT

PLACE DATE

EVENT

PLACE DATE

EVENT

PLACE DATE

EVENT

PLACE DATE

EVENT

PLACE DATE

EVENT

PLACE DATE

Family Record

Births

NAME BORN TO DATE

NAME BORN TO DATE

NAME BORN TO DATE

NAME BORN TO DATE

Baptisms

NAME MINISTER DATE

NAME MINISTER DATE

NAME MINISTER DATE

NAME MINISTER DATE

Marriages

HUSBAND WIFE DATE

HUSBAND WIFE DATE

HUSBAND WIFE DATE

HUSBAND WIFE DATE

Deaths

NAME DATE

NAME DATE

NAME DATE

NAME DATE

The MacArthur Study Bible

John MacArthur
AUTHOR AND GENERAL EDITOR

NEW KING JAMES VERSION

WORD BIBLES
Nashville • London • Vancouver • Melbourne

THE MACARTHUR STUDY BIBLE

The text of the *New King James Version* (NKJV) may be quoted or reprinted without prior written permission with the following qualifications:
(1) up to and including 1,000 verses may be quoted in printed form as long as the verses quoted amount to less than 50 percent of a complete book of the Bible and make up less than 50 percent of the total work in which they are quoted;
(2) all NKJV quotations must conform accurately to the NKJV text.

Any use of the NKJV text must include a proper acknowledgment as follows:
Scripture take from the *New King James Version.* Copyright © 1979, 1980, 1982 by Thomas Nelson, Inc. Used by permission. All rights reserved.

However, when quotations from the NKJV text are used in church bulletins, orders of service, Sunday school lessons, church newsletters and similar works in the course of religious instruction or services at a place of worship or other religious assembly, the following notice may be used at the end of each quotation: "NKJV."

For quotation requests not covered by the above guidelines, write to Nelson/Word Publishing Group, Attn: Bible Rights and Permissions, P. O. Box 14100, Nashville, Tennessee 37214-1000.

Interior charts and maps used by permission. Copyright © Thomas Nelson, Inc., Nashville, Tennessee.

Chronological charts on pages 2,3,10,11,1370,1371,1376,1377 are used by permission of John C. Whitcomb, Jr. and James L. Boyer.

"Jerusalem in Jeremiah's Time" on page 662 is taken from *The Illustrated Bible Dictionary* and is used by permission. Copyright © 1980 by The Universities and Colleges Christian Fellowship.

"Second Kings, Jeremiah, and Lamentations Compared" on page 1139 is taken from *A Biblical Approach to Personal Suffering* by Walter C. Kaiser, Jr. and is used by permission. Copyright © 1982 by The Moody Bible Institute of Chicago.

"A Harmony of the Gospels" on pages 1378–84 is taken from *A Harmony of the Gospels With Explanations and Essays* by Robert L. Thomas and Stanley N. Gundry and is used by permission. Copyright © 1978 by Robert L. Thomas and Stanley N. Gundry.

Cover art and design by The Puckett Group, Atlanta, Georgia.

Typesetting, final interior design, and production done by Multnomah Graphics, Troutdale, Oregon.

Hardcover: ISBN 0-8499-1222-9
Bonded Leather: ISBN 0-8499-1223-7 (black); 0-8499-1536-8 (indexed black); 0-8499-1537-6 (burgundy); 0-8499-1538-4 (indexed burgundy).
Genuine Leather: ISBN 0-8499-1539-2 (black); 0-8499-1540-6 (indexed black); 0-8499-1541-4 (burgundy); 0-8499-1542-2 (indexed burgundy).

97 98 99 00 01 QKP 9 8 7 6 5 4 3 2 1
Published by Word Publishing

Table of CONTENTS

Index of

CHARTS AND MAPS

Introduction to the BIBLE

The Bible is a collection of 66 documents inspired by God. These documents are gathered into two testaments, the Old (39) and the New (27). Prophets, priests, kings, and leaders from the nation of Israel wrote the OT books in Hebrew (with two passages in Aramaic). The apostles and their associates wrote the NT books in Greek.

The OT record starts with the creation of the universe and closes about 400 years before the first coming of Jesus Christ.

The flow of history through the OT moves along the following lines:

- Creation of the universe
- Fall of man
- Judgment flood over the earth
- Abraham, Isaac, Jacob (Israel)—fathers of the chosen nation
- The history of Israel
  - Exile in Egypt—430 years
  - Exodus and wilderness wanderings—40 years
  - Conquest of Canaan—7 years
  - Era of Judges—350 years
  - United Kingdom—Saul, David, Solomon—110 years
  - Divided Kingdom—Judah/Israel—350 years
  - Exile in Babylon—70 years
  - Return and rebuilding the land—140 years

The details of this history are explained in the 39 books divided into 5 categories:

- The Law—5 (Genesis—Deuteronomy)
- History—12 (Joshua—Esther)
- Wisdom—5 (Job—Song Of Solomon)
- Major Prophets—5 (Isaiah—Daniel)
- Minor Prophets—12 (Hosea—Malachi)

After the completion of the OT, there were 400 years of silence, during which God did not speak or inspire any Scripture. That silence was broken by the arrival of John the Baptist announcing that the promised Lord Savior had come. The NT records the rest of the story from the birth of Christ to the culmination of all history and the final eternal state; so the two testaments go from creation to consummation, eternity past to eternity future.

While the 39 OT books major on the history of Israel and the promise of the coming Savior, the 27 NT books major on the person of Christ and the establishment of the church. The 4 gospels give the record of His birth, life, death, resurrection, and ascension. Each of the 4 writers views the greatest and most important event of history, the coming of the God-man, Jesus Christ, from a different perspective. Matthew looks at Him through the perspective of His kingdom; Mark through the perspective of His servanthood; Luke through the perspective of His humanness; and John through the perspective of His deity.

The book of Acts tells the story of the impact of the life, death, and resurrection of Jesus Christ, the Lord Savior—from His ascension, the consequent coming of the Holy Spirit, and the birth of the church, through the early years of gospel preaching by the apostles and their associates. Acts records the establishment of the church in Judea, Samaria, and into the Roman Empire.

The 21 epistles were written to churches and individuals to explain the significance of the person and work of Jesus Christ, with its implications for life and witness until He returns.

The NT closes with Revelation, which starts by picturing the current church age, and culminates with Christ's return to establish His earthly kingdom, bringing judgment on the ungodly and glory and blessing for believers. Following the millennial reign of the Lord Savior will be the last judgment, leading to the eternal state. All believers of all history enter the ultimate eternal glory prepared for them, and all the ungodly are consigned to hell to be punished forever.

To understand the Bible, it is essential to grasp the sweep of that history from creation to consummation. It is also crucial to keep in focus the unifying theme of Scripture. The one constant theme unfolding throughout the whole Bible is this: God for His own glory has chosen to create and gather to Himself a group of people to be the subjects of His eternal kingdom, to praise, honor, and serve Him forever and through whom He will display His wisdom, power, mercy, grace, and glory. To gather His chosen ones, God must redeem them from sin. The Bible reveals God's plan for this redemption from its inception in eternity past to its completion in eternity future. Covenants, promises, and epochs are all secondary to the one continuous plan of redemption.

There is one God. The Bible has one Creator. It is one book. It has one plan of grace, recorded from initiation, through execution, to consummation. From predestination to glorification, the Bible is the story of God redeeming His chosen people for the praise of His glory.

As God's redemptive purposes and plan unfold in Scripture, 5 recurring motifs are constantly emphasized:

- the character of God
- the judgment for sin and disobedience
- the blessing for faith and obedience
- the Lord Savior and sacrifice for sin
- the coming kingdom and glory

Everything revealed on the pages of both the OT and NT is associated with those 5 categories. Scripture is always teaching or illustrating: 1) the character and attributes of God; 2) the tragedy of sin and disobedience to God's holy standard; 3) the blessedness of faith and obedience to God's standard; 4) the need for a Savior by whose righteousness and substitution sinners can be forgiven, declared just, and transformed to obey God's standard; and 5) the coming glorious end of redemptive history in the Lord Savior's earthly kingdom and the subsequent eternal reign and glory of God and Christ. It is essential as one studies Scripture to grasp these recurring categories like great hooks on which to hang the passages. While reading through the Bible, one should be able to relate each portion of Scripture to these dominant topics, recognizing that what is introduced in the OT is also made more clear in the NT.

Looking at these 5 categories separately gives an overview of the Bible.

1. The Revelation of the Character of God

Above all else, Scripture is God's self-revelation. He reveals Himself as the sovereign God of the universe who has chosen to make man and to make Himself known to man. In that self-revelation is established His standard of absolute holiness. From Adam and Eve through Cain and Abel and to everyone before and after the law of Moses, the standard of righteousness was established and is sustained to the last page of the NT. Violation of it produces judgment, temporal and eternal.

In the OT, it is recorded that God revealed Himself by the following means:

- creation—primarily through man—who was made in His image
- angels
- signs, wonders, and miracles
- visions
- spoken words by prophets and others
- written Scripture (OT)

In the NT, it is recorded that God revealed Himself again by the same means, but more clearly and fully:

- creation—the God-man, Jesus Christ, who was the very image of God
- angels
- signs, wonders, and miracles
- visions
- spoken words by apostles and prophets
- written Scripture (NT)

2. The Revelation of Divine Judgment for Sin and Disobedience

Scripture repeatedly deals with the matter of man's sin, which leads to divine judgment. Account after account in Scripture demonstrates the deadly effects in time and eternity of violating God's standard. There are 1,189 chapters in the Bible. Only 4 of them don't involve a fallen world: the first 2 and the last 2—before the Fall and after the creation of the new heaven and new earth. The rest is the chronicle of the tragedy of sin.

In the OT, God showed the disaster of sin—starting with Adam and Eve, to Cain and Abel, the patriarchs, Moses and Israel, the kings, priests, some prophets, and Gentile nations. Throughout the OT is the relentless record of continual devastation produced by sin and disobedience to God's law.

In the NT, the tragedy of sin becomes more clear. The preaching and teaching of Jesus and the apostles begin and end with a call to repentance. King Herod, the Jewish leaders, and the nation of Israel—along with Pilate, Rome, and the rest of the world—all reject the Lord Savior, spurn the truth of God, and thus condemn themselves. The chronicle of sin continues unabated to the end of the age and the return of Christ in judgment. In the NT, disobedience is even more flagrant than OT disobedience because it involves the rejection of the Lord Savior Jesus Christ in the brighter light of NT truth.

3. The Revelation of Divine Blessing for Faith and Obedience

Scripture repeatedly promises wonderful rewards in time and eternity that come to people who trust God and seek to obey Him. In the OT, God showed the blessedness of repentance from sin, faith in Himself, and obedience to His Word—from Abel, through the patriarchs, to the remnant in Israel—and even Gentiles who believed (such as the people of Nineveh).

God's standard for man, His will, and His moral law were always made known. To those who faced their inability to keep God's standard, recognized their sin, confessed their impotence to please God by their own effort and works, and asked Him for forgiveness and grace—there came merciful redemption and blessing for time and eternity.

In the NT, God again showed the full blessedness of redemption from sin for repentant people. There were those who responded to the preaching of repentance by John the Baptist. Others repented at the preaching of Jesus. Still others from Israel obeyed the gospel through the apostles' preaching. And finally, there were Gentiles all over the Roman Empire who believed the gospel. To all those and to all who will believe through all of history, there is blessing promised in this world and the world to come.

4. The Revelation of the Lord Savior and Sacrifice for Sin

This is the heart of both the OT, which Jesus said spoke of Him in type and prophecy, and the NT, which gives the biblical record of His coming. The promise of blessing is dependent on grace and mercy given to the sinner. Grace means that sin is not held against the sinner. Such forgiveness is dependent on a payment of sin's penalty to satisfy holy justice. That requires a substitute—one to die in the sinner's place. God's chosen substitute—the only one who qualified—was Jesus. Salvation is always by the same gracious means, whether during OT or NT times. When any sinner comes to God, repentant and convinced he has no power to save himself from the deserved judgment of divine wrath, and pleads for mercy, God's promise of forgiveness is granted. God then declares him righteous because the sacrifice and obedience of Christ is put to his account. In the OT, God justified sinners that same way, in anticipation of Christ's atoning work. There is, therefore, a continuity of grace and salvation through all of redemptive history. Various covenants, promises, and epochs do not alter that fundamental continuity, nor does the discontinuity between the OT witness nation, Israel, and the NT witness people, the church. A fundamental continuity is centered in the cross, which was no interruption in the plan of God, but the very thing to which all else points.

Throughout the OT, the Savior and sacrifice are promised. In Genesis, He is the seed of the woman who will destroy Satan. In Zechariah, He is the pierced one to whom Israel turns and by whom God opens the fountain of forgiveness to all who mourn over their sin. He is the very One symbolized in the sacrificial system of the Mosaic law. He is the suffering substitute spoken of by the prophets. Throughout the OT, He is the Messiah who would die for the transgressions of His people; from beginning to end in the OT, the theme of the Lord Savior as a sacrifice for sin is presented. It is solely because of His perfect sacrifice for sin that God graciously forgives repentant believers.

In the NT, the Lord Savior came and actually provided the promised sacrifice for sin on the cross. Having fulfilled all righteousness by His perfect life, He fulfilled justice by His death. Thus God Himself atoned for sin, at a cost too great for the human mind to fathom. Now He graciously supplies on their behalf all the merit necessary for His people to be the objects of His favor. That is what Scripture means when it speaks of salvation by grace.

5. The Revelation of the Kingdom and Glory of the Lord Savior

This crucial component of Scripture brings the whole story to its God-ordained consummation. Redemptive history is controlled by God, so as to culminate in His eternal glory. Redemptive history will end with the same precision and exactness with which it began. The truths of eschatology are neither vague nor unclear—nor are they unimportant. As in any book, how the story ends is the most crucial and compelling part—so with the Bible. Scripture notes several very specific features of the end planned by God.

In the OT, there is repeated mention of an earthly kingdom ruled by the Messiah, Lord Savior, who will come to reign. Associated with that kingdom will be the salvation of Israel, the salvation of Gentiles, the renewal of the earth from the effects of the curse, and the bodily resurrection of God's people who have died. Finally, the OT predicts that there will be the "uncreation" or dissolution of the universe, and the creation of a new heaven and new earth—which will be the eternal state of the godly—and a final hell for the ungodly.

In the NT, these features are clarified and expanded. The King was rejected and executed, but He promised to come back in glory, bringing judgment, resurrection, and His kingdom for all who believe. Innumerable Gentiles from every nation will be included among the redeemed. Israel will be saved and grafted back into the root of blessing from which she has been temporarily excised.

Israel's promised kingdom will be enjoyed, with the Lord Savior reigning on the throne, in the renewed earth, exercising power over the whole world, having taken back His rightful authority, and receiving due honor and worship. Following that kingdom will come the dissolution of the renewed, but still sin-stained creation, and the subsequent creation of a new heaven and new earth—which will be the eternal state, separate forever from the ungodly in hell.

Those are the 5 topics that fill up the Bible. To understand them at the start is to know the answer to the question that continually arises—Why does the Bible tell us this? Everything fits into this glorious pattern. As you read, hang the truth on these 5 hooks and the Bible will unfold, not as 66 separate documents, or even two separate testaments—but one book, by one divine Author, who wrote it all with one overarching theme.

My prayer is that the magnificent and overwhelming theme of the redemption of sinners for the glory of God will carry every reader with captivating interest from beginning to end of the story. Christian—this is your story. It is from God for you—about you. It tells what He planned for you, why He made you, what you were, what you have become in Christ, and what He has prepared for you in eternal glory.

John MacArthur

Personal Notes

Why write a study Bible? The answer to that question comes in a conversation between Philip and an Ethiopian recorded in Acts 8:30,31:

> So Philip ran to him, and heard him reading the prophet Isaiah, and said, "Do you understand what you are reading?" And he said, "How can I, unless someone guides me?" And he asked Philip to come up and sit with him.

As Philip did with the eunuch, I want to sit with you and explain the Scripture. This Study Bible allows me that intimate opportunity.

Although I personally bear full responsibility for all the notes in *The MacArthur Study Bible* because they all have come from me and through me, a work of this magnitude with the responsibility to be so accurate could only have been done with a team of supportive co-workers who committed themselves to assist me by arduous labor with loving devotion and commitment to excellence. Many friends have participated in the team—all of whom deserve to be commended and thanked.

My highest gratitude belongs to my friend and ministry partner, Dr. Richard Mayhue, Senior Vice President and Dean of The Master's Seminary. He has worked next to me through the whole project, laboring beyond anyone while serving as project manager, OT and NT researcher, editor, and counselor. His exceptional gift for management, along with his vast knowledge of Scripture and doctrine, coupled with our one-mindedness theologically, plus his writing skill, have made for a most effective partnership.

Gratitude in abundance must be given to the faculty of The Master's Seminary for their assistance in original research and carefully prepared first draft material for the study notes on the Old Testament. Using the foundation of that original research and material, I worked and re-worked the study notes into their final form.

Thank you to Dr. Irv Busenitz, Dr. Trevor Craigen, Prof. Dave Deuel, Prof. Keith Essex, Dr. Richard Mayhue, Dr. Larry Pettegrew, Dr. Jim Rosscup, Prof. Jim Stitzinger, Dr. Bob Thomas, and Dr. George Zemek.

Because over the last 28 years I have studied and expositionally preached through nearly all the New Testament, my own original research was available to be summarized into the NT study notes. A team composed of The Master's Seminary faculty and editors at Grace to You, who work regularly editing my books, accepted the task of spending long hours culling the salient features from my research into study note form. Likewise, from that first draft, I worked to bring the material to its final form.

Thank you to Dr. Bill Barrick, Dave Douglass, Dave Enos, Dr. David Farnell, Phil Johnson, Garry Knussman, Dr. Richard Mayhue, Tom Pennington, Dr. Larry Pettegrew, and Mike Taylor.

It was also essential to have readers who carefully scrutinized all the material for accuracy and checked all Scripture references. My gratitude goes to them for their faithful effort at a tedious task. My thanks to Dennis Swanson and Bob White at The Master's Seminary; to Dave Enos and Allacin Morimizu at Grace to You; and to June Gunden and her team of readers at Peachtree Editorial and Proofreading Service.

The nearly 2,400 pages of single-spaced notes had to be entered into computers and repeatedly edited and corrected after each of the six occasions when everything was reworked. A team of loyal and diligent secretaries from The Master's Seminary, Grace Community Church, and Grace to You worked on that formidable task inside a confining schedule to meet endless deadlines in the process. Since I write in longhand, most of the material was a combination of print and longhand that called for difficult deciphering of my marginally legible writing. Along with their other duties, they graciously took on this task, as did all the rest of the team.

My thanks to Dr. Mayhue's secretary, Cindy Gehman (OT Coordinator) and my personal secretary, Pat Rotisky (NT Coordinator) who labored with Amy Brandenstein, Rhonda Connor, Louise Essex, Marilyn Foster, Marcia Griffiths, Carol Smith, Diane Haschak, Pam Leopold, Willa Loveless, Dareth Luna, Wilma Miller, Joyce Modert, Susan Rogers, Patti Schott, and Teri White.

All the above mentioned friends made this effort a joyous marathon for me to run. I pray God's blessing on them all in response to their devotion to the Word of God.

Finally, I offer great appreciation to David Moberg, my publisher at Word Publishing, who exhibited vision, confidence, patience, and expertise through the relentless complexities of the project. He proved to be both a friend and guide.

Never have I been so challenged and blessed at the same time as during the two intense years of this work. Studying alone in my private place, perusing every word of Scripture, plus being challenged to understand each phrase and verse has yielded richness to my life and ministry like nothing I have undertaken before.

I have always been committed to the Scripture as inspired, inerrant, infallible, sufficient, and eternal. I have always preached the Bible expositionally, verse by verse, book by book. After this enterprise, I feel even more strongly about the necessity of preaching every pure word of Scripture (Ps. 12:6). I have been profoundly enriched in my own life, as never before, because of the sheer force of so much divine truth pouring through me daily. For many months I spent eight or more hours every day working in the Word, not so much because I had to, but because I could not leave the text—its riches held me captive.

Most especially, my thanks to you, the reader, for loving Scripture enough to be a serious student. This work is an additional way of fulfilling my calling as a pastor-teacher mandated "for the equipping of the saints for the work of ministry, for the edifying of the body of Christ" (Eph. 4:12).

With gratitude most of all to our glorious God who gave us His precious Word, do I pray that He will be honored by this effort to explain what His Word means by what it says.

JOHN MACARTHUR

How We Got
THE BIBLE

Ever since Eve encountered Satan's barrage of doubt and denial (Gen. 3:1-7), mankind has continued to question God's Word. Unfortunately, Eve had little or no help in sorting through her intellectual obstacles to full faith in God's self-disclosure (Gen. 2:16,17).

Now the Scripture certainly has more than enough content to be interrogated, considering that it's comprised of 66 books, 1,189 chapters, 31,173 verses, and 774,746 words. When you open your English translation to read or study, you might have asked in the past or are currently asking, "How can I be sure this is the pure and true Word of God?"

A question of this kind is not altogether bad, especially when one seeks to learn with a teachable mind (Acts 17:11). The Scripture invites the kinds of queries that a sincere student asks. A whole host of questions can flood the mind, such as:

- Where did the Bible come from?
- Whose thinking does it reflect?
- Did any books of the Bible get lost in time past?
- What does the Scripture claim for itself?
- Does it live up to its claims?
- Who wrote the Bible—God or man?
- Has Scripture been protected from human tampering over the centuries?
- How close to the original manuscripts are today's translations?
- How did the Bible get to our time and in our language?
- Is there more Scripture to come, beyond the current 66 books?
- Who determined, and on what basis, that the Bible would be composed of the traditional list of 66 books?
- If the Scriptures were written over a period of 1,500 years (ca. 1405 B.C. to A.D. 95), passed down since then for almost 2,000 years, and translated into several thousand languages, what prevented the Bible from being changed by the carelessness or ill motives of men?
- Does today's Bible really deserve the title "The Word of God"?

Undoubtedly, these questions have bombarded the minds of many. A study of the Scriptures alone settles all questions to the extent that there is no need to be bothered by them again. Scripture gives this assurance.

Scriptures' Self Claims

Take the Bible and let it speak for itself. Does it claim to be God's Word? Yes! Over 2,000 times in the Old Testament alone, the Bible asserts that God spoke what is written within its pages. From the beginning (Gen. 1:3) to the end (Mal. 4:3) and continually throughout, this is what Scripture claims.

The phrase "the Word of God" occurs over 40 times in the New Testament. It is equated with the Old Testament (Mark 7:13). It is what Jesus preached (Luke 5:1). It was the message the apostles taught (Acts 4:31; 6:2). It was the Word the Samaritans received (Acts 8:14) as given by the apostles (Acts 8:25). It was the message the Gentiles received as preached by Peter (Acts 11:1). It was the word Paul preached on his first missionary journey (Acts 13:5,7,44,48,49; 15:35,36). It was the message preached on Paul's second missionary journey (Acts 16:32; 17:13; 18:11). It was the message Paul preached on his third missionary journey (Acts 19:10). It was the focus of Luke in the book of Acts in that it spread rapidly and widely (Acts 6:7; 12:24; 19:20). Paul was careful to tell the Corinthians that he spoke the Word as it was given from God, that it had not been adulterated, and that it was a manifestation of truth (2 Cor. 2:17; 4:2). Paul acknowledged that it was the source of his preaching (Col. 1:25; 1 Thess. 2:13).

Psalms 19 and 119, plus Proverbs 30:5-6, make powerful statements about God's Word which set it apart from any other religious instruction ever known in the history of mankind. These passages make the case for the Bible being called "sacred" (2 Tim. 3:15) and "holy" (Rom. 1:2).

The Bible claims ultimate spiritual authority in doctrine, reproof, correction, and instruction in righteousness because it represents the inspired Word of Almighty God (2 Tim. 3:16,17). Scripture asserts its spiritual sufficiency, so much so that it claims exclusivity for its teaching (cf. Is. 55:11; 2 Pet. 1:3,4).

God's Word declares that it is *inerrant* (Pss. 12:6; 119:140; Prov. 30:5a; John 10:35) and *infallible* (2 Tim. 3:16, 17). In other words, it is true and therefore trustworthy. All of these qualities are dependent on the fact that the Scriptures are God-given (2 Tim. 3:16; 2 Pet. 1:20,21), which guarantees its quality at the Source and at its original writing.

In Scripture, the person of God and the Word of God are everywhere interrelated, so much so that whatever is true about the character of God is true about the nature of God's Word. God is true, impeccable, and reliable; therefore, so is His Word. What a person thinks about God's Word, in reality, reflects what a person thinks about God.

Thus, the Scripture can make these demands on its readers.

> So He humbled you, allowed you to hunger, and fed you with manna which you did not know nor did your fathers know, that He might make you know that man shall not live by bread alone; but man lives by every *word* that proceeds from the mouth of the LORD.
>
> Deut. 8:3

> I have not departed from the commandment of His lips; I have treasured the words of His mouth more than my necessary *food*.
>
> Job 23:12

The Publishing Process

The Bible does not expect its reader to speculate on how these divine qualities were transferred from God to His Word, but rather anticipates the questions with convincing answers. Every generation of skeptics has assailed the self-claims of the Bible, but its own explanations and answers have been more than equal to the challenge. The Bible has gone through God's publishing process in being given to and distributed among the human race. Its several features are discussed below.

Revelation

God took the initiative to disclose or reveal Himself to mankind (Heb. 1:1). The vehicles varied; sometimes it was through the created order, at other times through visions/dreams or speaking prophets. However, the most complete and understandable self-disclosures were through the propositions of Scripture (1 Cor. 2:6-16). The revealed and written Word of God is unique in that it is the only revelation of God that is complete and that so clearly declares man's sinfulness and God's provision of the Savior.

Inspiration

The revelation of God was captured in the writings of Scripture by means of "inspiration." This has more to do with the process by which God revealed Himself than the fact of His self-revelation. "All Scripture *is* given by inspiration of God..." (2 Tim. 3:16) makes the claim. Peter explains the process, "... knowing this first, that no prophecy of Scripture is of any private interpretation, for prophecy never came by the will of man, but holy men of God spoke *as they were* moved by the Holy Spirit" (2 Pet. 1:20,21). By this means, the Word of God was protected from human error in its original record by the ministry of the Holy Spirit (cf. Deut. 18:18; Matt. 1:22). A section of Zech. 7:12 describes it most clearly, "... the law and the words which the LORD of hosts had sent by His Spirit through the former prophets." This ministry of the Spirit extended to both the part (the words) and to the whole in the original writings.

Canonicity

We must understand that the Bible is actually one book with one Divine Author, though it was written over a period of 1,500 years through the pens of almost 40 human writers. The Bible began with the creation account of Genesis 1,2, written by Moses about 1405 B.C., and extends to the eternity future account of Revelation 21,22, written by the Apostle John about A.D. 95. During this time, God progressively revealed Himself and His purposes in the inspired Scriptures. But this raises a significant question: "How do we know what supposed sacred writings were to be included in the canon of Scripture and which ones were to be excluded?"

Over the centuries, 3 widely recognized principles were used to validate those writings which came as a result of divine revelation and inspiration. First, the writing had to have a recognized prophet or apostle as its author (or one associated with them, as in the case of Mark, Luke, Hebrews, James, and Jude). Second, the writing could not disagree with or contradict previous Scripture. Third, the writing had to have general consensus by the church as an inspired book. Thus, when various councils met in church history to consider the canon, they did not vote for the canonicity of a book but rather recognized, after the fact, what God had already written.

With regard to the Old Testament, by the time of Christ all of the Old Testament had been written and accepted in the Jewish community. The last book, Malachi, had been completed about 430 B.C. Not only does the Old Testament canon of Christ's day conform to the Old Testament which has since been used throughout the centuries, but is does not contain the uninspired and spurious Apocrypha, that group of 14 rogue writings which were written after Malachi and attached to the Old Testament about 200–150 B.C. in the Greek translation of the Hebrew Old Testament called the Septuagint (LXX), appearing to this very day in some versions of the Bible. However, not one passage from the Apocrypha is cited by any New Testament writer, nor did Jesus affirm any of it as He recognized the Old Testament canon of His era (cf. Luke 24:27,44).

By Christ's time, the Old Testament canon had been divided up into two lists of 22 or 24 books respectively, each of which contained all the same material as the 39 books of our modern versions. In the 22 book canon, Jeremiah and Lamentations were considered as one, as were Judges and Ruth. Here is how the 24 book format was divided.

The Hebrew Old Testament

Law	Prophets	Writings
1. Genesis	A. *Former Prophets*	A. *Poetical Books*
2. Exodus	6. Joshua	14. Psalms
3. Leviticus	7. Judges	15. Proverbs
4. Numbers	8. Samuel (1 & 2)	16. Job
5. Deuteronomy	9. Kings (1 & 2)	
	B. *Latter Prophets*	B. *Five Rolls (Megilloth)*
	10. Isaiah	17. Song of Solomon
	11. Jeremiah	18. Ruth
	12. Ezekiel	19. Lamentations
	13. The Twelve (minor prophets)	20. Ecclesiastes
		21. Esther
		C. *Historical Books*
		22. Daniel
		23. Ezra-Nehemiah
		24. Chronicles (1 & 2)

The same 3 key tests of canonicity that applied to the Old Testament also applied to the New Testament. In the case of Mark and Luke/Acts, the authors were considered to be, in effect, the penmen for Peter and Paul respectively. James and Jude were written by Christ's half-brothers. While Hebrews is the only New Testament book whose authorship is unknown for certain, its content is so in line with both the Old Testament and New Testament, that the early church concluded it must have been written by an apostolic associate. The 27 books of the New Testament have been universally accepted since ca. A.D. 350–400 as inspired by God.

Preservation

How can one be sure that the revealed and inspired, written Word of God, which was recognized as canonical by the early church, has been handed down to this day without any loss of material? Furthermore, since one of the Devil's prime concerns is to undermine the Bible, have the Scriptures survived this destructive onslaught? In the beginning, he denied God's Word to Eve (Gen. 3:4). Satan later attempted to distort the Scripture in his wilderness encounter with Christ (Matt. 4:6,7). Through King Jehoiakim, he even attempted to literally destroy the Word (Jer. 36:23). The battle for the Bible rages, but Scripture has and will continue to outlast its enemies.

God anticipated man's and Satan's malice towards the Scripture with divine promises to preserve His Word. The very continued existence of Scripture is guaranteed in Isaiah 40:8, "The grass withers, the flower fades, but the word of our God stands forever" (cf. 1 Pet. 1:25). This even means that no inspired Scripture has been lost in the past and still awaits rediscovery.

The actual content of Scripture will be perpetuated, both in heaven (Ps. 119:89) and on earth (Is.

59:21). Thus the purposes of God, as published in the sacred writings, will never be thwarted, even in the least detail (cf. Matt. 5:18; 24:25; Mark 13:3; Luke 16:17).

So shall My word be that goes forth from My mouth; it shall not return to Me void, but it shall accomplish what I please, and it shall prosper *in the thing* for which I sent it.

Is. 55:11

Transmission

Since the Bible has frequently been translated into multiple languages and distributed throughout the world, how can we be sure that error has not crept in, even if it was unintentional? As Christianity spread, it is certainly true that people desired to have the Bible in their own language which required translations from the original Hebrew and Aramaic languages of the Old Testament and the Greek of the New Testament. Not only did the work of translators provide an opportunity for error, but publication, which was done by hand copying until the printing press arrived ca. A.D. 1450, also afforded continual possibilities of error.

Through the centuries, the practitioners of textual criticism, a precise science, have discovered, preserved, catalogued, evaluated, and published an amazing array of biblical manuscripts from both the Old and New Testaments. In fact, the number of existing biblical manuscripts dramatically outdistances the existing fragments of any other ancient literature. By comparing text with text, the textual critic can confidently determine what the original prophetic/apostolic, inspired writing contained.

Although existing copies of the main, ancient Hebrew text (Masoretic) date back only to the tenth century A.D., two other important lines of textual evidence bolster the confidence of textual critics that they have reclaimed the originals. First, the tenth century A.D. Hebrew Old Testament can be compared to the Greek translation called the Septuagint or LXX (written ca. 200–150 B.C.; the oldest existing manuscripts dates to ca. A.D. 325). There is amazing consistency between the two, which speaks of the accuracy in copying the Hebrew text for centuries. Second, the discovery of the Dead Sea Scrolls in 1947–1956 (manuscripts that are dated ca. 200–100 B.C.) proved to be monumentally important. After comparing the earlier Hebrew texts with the later ones, only a few slight variants were discovered, none of which changed the meaning of any passage. Although the Old Testament had been translated and copied for centuries, the latest version was essentially the same as the earlier ones.

The New Testament findings are even more decisive because a much larger amount of material is available for study; there are over 5,000 Greek New Testament manuscripts that range from the whole testament to scraps of papyri which contain as little as part of one verse. A few existing fragments date back to within 25–50 years of the original writing. New Testament textual scholars have generally concluded that 1) 99.99 percent of the original writings have been reclaimed, and 2) of the remaining one hundredth of one percent, there are no variants substantially affecting any Christian doctrine.

With this wealth of biblical manuscripts in the original languages and with the disciplined activity of textual critics to establish with almost perfect accuracy the content of the autographs, any errors which have been introduced and/or perpetuated by the thousands of translations over the centuries can be identified and corrected by comparing the translation or copy with the reassembled original. By this providential means, God has made good His promise to preserve the Scriptures. We can rest assured that there are translations available today which indeed are worthy of the title, The Word of God.

The history of a full, English translation Bible essentially began with John Wycliffe (ca. A.D. 1330–1384), who made the first English translation of the whole Bible. Later, William Tyndale was associated with the first complete, printed New Testament in English, ca. A.D. 1526. Myles Coverdale followed in A.D. 1535, by delivering the first complete Bible printed in English. By A.D. 1611, the King James Version (KJV) had been completed. Since then, hundreds of translations have been made—some better, some worse. Today, the better English translations of the Hebrew and Greek Scriptures include: 1) New King James Version (NKJV); 2) New International Version (NIV); and 3) New American Standard Bible (NASB).

Summing It Up

God intended His Word to abide forever (preservation). Therefore His written, propositional, self disclosure (revelation) was protected from error in its original writing (inspiration) and collected in 66 books of the Old and New Testaments (canonicity).

Through the centuries, tens of thousands of copies and thousands of translations have been made (transmission) which did introduce some error. Because there is an abundance of existing ancient Old Testament and New Testament manuscripts, however, the exacting science of textual criticism has been able to reclaim the content of the original writings (revelation and inspiration) to the extreme degree of 99.99 percent, with the remaining one hundredth of one percent having no effect on its content (preservation).

The sacred book which we read, study, obey, and preach deserves to unreservedly be called The Bible or "The Book without peer," since its author is God and it bears the qualities of total truth and complete trustworthiness as also characterizes its divine source.

Is There More To Come?

How do we know that God will not amend our current Bible with a 67th inspired book? Or, in other words, "Is the canon forever closed?"

Scripture texts warn that no one should delete from or add to Scripture (Deut. 4:2; 12:32; Prov. 30:6). Realizing that additional canonical books actually came after these words of warning, we can only conclude that while no deletions whatsoever were permitted, in fact, authorized, inspired writings were permitted to be added in order to complete the canon protected by those passages.

The most compelling text on the closed canon is the Scripture to which nothing has been added for 1,900 years.

> For I testify to everyone who hears the words of the prophecy of this book: If anyone adds to these things, God will add to him the plagues that are written in this book; and if anyone takes away from the words of the book of this prophecy, God shall take away his part from the Book of Life, from the holy city, and *from* the things which are written in this book.
>
> Rev. 22:18,19

Several significant observations, when taken together, have convinced the church over the centuries that the canon of Scripture is actually closed, never to be reopened.

1. The book of Revelation is unique to the Scripture in that it describes with unparalleled detail the end-time events which precede eternity future. As Genesis began Scripture by bridging the gap from eternity past into our time/space existence with the only detailed creation account (Gen. 1, 2), so there was a parallel silence after John delivered Revelation. This also leads to the conclusion that the New Testament canon was then closed.

2. Just as there was prophetic silence after Malachi completed the Old Testament canon, so there was a parallel silence after John delivered Revelation. This leads to the conclusion that the New Testament canon was then closed also.

3. Since there have not been, nor now are, any authorized prophets or apostles in either the Old Testament and New Testament sense, there are not any potential authors of future inspired, canonical writings. God's Word, "once for all delivered to the saints," is never to be added to, but to be earnestly contended for (Jude 3).

4. Of the 4 exhortations not to tamper with Scripture, only the one in Revelation 22:18,19 contains warnings of severe Divine judgement for disobedience. Further, Revelation is the only book of the New Testament to end with this kind of admonition and was written over 20 years after any other New Testament book. Therefore, these facts strongly suggest that Revelation was the last book of the canon and that the Bible is complete; to either add or delete would bring God's severe displeasure.

5. Finally, the early church, those closest in time to the apostles, believed that Revelation concluded God's inspired writings, the Scriptures.

So we can conclude, based on solid Biblical reasoning, that the canon is and will remain closed. There will be no future 67th book of the Bible.

Where Do We Stand?

In April, 1521, Martin Luther appeared before his ecclesiastical accusers at the Diet of Worms. They had given him the ultimatum to repudiate his unwavering faith in the sufficiency and perspicuity of the Scriptures. Luther is said to have responded, "Unless I am convicted by Scripture and plain reason—I do not accept the authority of popes and councils, for they have contradicted each other—my conscience is captive to the Word of God. . . . God help me! Here I stand."

Like Martin Luther, may we rise above the doubts within and confront the threats without when God's Word is assailed. God help us to be loyal contenders of the faith. Let us stand with God and the Scripture alone.

The Bible

This book contains: the mind of God, the state of man, the way of salvation, the doom of sinners, and the happiness of believers.

Its doctrine is holy, its precepts are binding, its histories are true, and its decisions are immutable. Read it to be wise, believe it to be saved, and practice it to be holy.

It contains light to direct you, food to support you, and comfort to cheer you. It is the traveler's map, the pilgrim's staff, the pilot's compass, the soldier's sword, and the Christian's charter. Here heaven is open, and the gates of hell are disclosed.

Christ is the grand subject, our good its design, and the glory of God its end. It should fill the memory, rule the heart, and guide the feet.

Read it slowly, frequently, and prayerfully. It is a mine of wealth, health to the soul, and a river of pleasure. It is given to you here in this life, will be opened at the judgment, and is established forever.

It involves the highest responsibility, will reward the greatest labor, and condemn all who trifle with its contents.

For this reason we also thank God without ceasing, because when you received the word of God which you heard from us, you welcomed *it* not *as* the word of men, but as it is in truth, the word of God, which also effectively works in you who believe.

1 Thess. 2:13

How to Study

THE BIBLE

Here are tips on how to get the most out of the study of this "divine handbook." These pointers will help answer the most crucial question of all, "How can a young man cleanse his way?" The psalmist responds, "By taking heed according to Your Word" (Ps. 119:9).

Why is it Important to Study the Bible?

Why is God's Word so important? Because is contains God's mind and will for your life (2 Tim. 3:16, 17). It is the only source of absolute divine authority for you as a servant of Jesus Christ.

It is infallible in its totality: "The law of the LORD is perfect, converting the soul; the testimony of the LORD is sure, making wise the simple" (Ps. 19:7).

It is inerrant in its parts: "Every word of God is pure; He *is* a shield to those who put their trust in Him. Do not add to His words, lest He rebuke you, and you be found a liar" (Prov. 30:5,6).

It is complete: "For I testify to everyone who hears the words of the prophecy of this book: If anyone adds to these things, God will add to him the plagues that are written in this book; and if anyone takes away from the words of the book of this prophecy, God shall take away his part from the Book of Life, from the holy city, and *from* the things which are written in this book" (Rev. 22:18,19).

It is authoritative and final: "Forever, O Lord, Your word is settled in heaven" (Ps. 119:89).

It is totally sufficient for your needs: ". . . that the man of God may be complete, thoroughly equipped for every good work" (2 Tim. 3:16,17).

It will accomplish what it promises: "So shall My word be that goes forth from My mouth; it shall not return to Me void, but it shall accomplish what I please, and it shall prosper *in the thing* for which I sent it" (Is. 55:11).

It provides the assurance of your salvation: "He who is of God hears God's words . . ." (John 8:47; 20:31).

How Will I Benefit from Studying the Bible?

Millions of pages of material are printed every week. Thousands of new books are published each month. This would not be surprising to Solomon who said, ". . . be admonished . . . Of making many books *there is* no end" (Eccl. 12:12).

Even with today's wealth of books and computer helps, the Bible remains the only source of divine revelation and power that can sustain Christians in their "daily walk with God." Note these significant promises in the Scripture.

The Bible is the source of truth: "Sanctify them by Your truth; Your word is truth" (John 17:17).

The Bible is the source of God's blessing when obeyed: "But He said, 'More than that, blessed *are* those who hear the word of God and keep it'" (Luke 11:28).

The Bible is the source of victory: ". . . the sword of the Spirit, which is the word of God" (Eph. 6:17).

The Bible is the source of growth: "As newborn babes, desire the pure milk of the word, that you may grow thereby" (1 Pet. 2:2).

The Bible is the source of power: "For I am not ashamed of the gospel of Christ, for it is the power of God to salvation for everyone who believes, for the Jew first and also for the Greek" (Rom. 1:16).

The Bible is the source of guidance: "Your word *is* a lamp to my feet and a light to my path" (Ps. 119:105).

What Should Be My Response to the Bible?

Because the Bible is so important and because it provides unparalleled eternal benefits, then these should be your responses:

Believe it (John 6:68,69)
Honor it (Job 23:12)
Love it (Ps. 119:97)
Obey it (1 John 2:5)

Guard it (1 Tim. 6:20)
Fight for it (Jude 3)
Preach it (2 Tim. 4:2)
Study it (Ezra 7:10)

Who Can Study the Bible?

Not everyone can be a Bible student. Check yourself on these necessary qualifications for studying the Word with blessing:

- Are you saved by faith in Jesus Christ (1 Cor. 2:14-16)?
- Are you hungering for God's Word (1 Pet. 2:2)?
- Are you searching God's Word with diligence (Acts 17:11)?
- Are you seeking holiness (1 Pet. 1:14-16)?
- Are you Spirit-filled (Col. 3:16)?

The most important question is the first. If you have never invited Jesus Christ to be your personal Savior and the Lord of your life, then your mind is blinded by Satan to God's truth (2 Cor. 4:4).

If Christ is your need, stop reading right now and, in your own words with prayer, turn away from sin and turn toward God: "For by grace you have been saved through faith, and that not of yourselves; *it is* the gift of God, not of works, lest anyone should boast" (Eph. 2:8,9).

What Are the Basics of Bible Study?

Personal Bible study, in precept, is simple. I want to share with you 5 steps to Bible study which will give you a pattern to follow.

STEP 1—Reading. Read a passage of Scripture repeatedly until you understand its theme, meaning the main truth of the passage. Isaiah said, "Whom will he teach knowledge? And whom will he make to understand the message? Those *just* weaned from milk? Those *just* drawn from the breasts? For precept *must be* upon precept, precept upon precept, line upon line, here a little, there a little" (Is. 28:9,10).

Develop a plan on how you will approach reading through the Bible. Unlike most books, you will probably not read it straight through from cover to cover. There are many good Bible reading plans available, but here is one that I have found helpful.

Read through the Old Testament at least once a year. As you read, note in the margins any truths you particularly want to remember, and write down separately anything you do not immediately understand. Often as you read you will find that many questions are answered by the text itself. The questions to which you cannot find answers become the starting points for more in-depth study using commentaries or other reference tools.

Follow a different plan for reading the New Testament. Read one book at a time repetitiously for a month or more. This will help you to retain what is in the New Testament and not always have to depend on a concordance to find things.

If you want to try this, begin with a short book, such as 1 John, and read it through in one sitting every day for 30 days. At the end of that time, you will know what is in the book. Write on index cards the major theme of each chapter. By referring to the cards as you do your daily reading, you will begin to remember the content of each chapter. In fact, you will develop a visual perception of the book in your mind.

Divide longer books into short sections and read each section daily for 30 days. For example, the gospel of John contains 21 chapters. Divide it into 3 sections of 7 chapters. At the end of 90 days, you will finish John. For variety, alternate short and long books, and in less than 3 years you will have finished the entire New Testament—as you will really know it!

STEP 2—Interpreting. In Acts 8:30, Philip asked the Ethiopian eunuch, "Do you understand what you are reading?" Or put another way, "What does the Bible mean by what it says?" It is not enough to read the text and jump directly to the application; we must first determine what it means, otherwise the application may be incorrect.

As you read Scripture, always keep in mind one simple question: "What does this mean?" To answer that question requires the use of the most basic principle of interpretation, called the analogy of faith, which tells the reader to "interpret the Bible with the Bible." Letting the Holy Spirit be your teacher (1 John 2:27), search the Scripture He has authored, using cross references, comparative passages, concordances, indexes, and other helps. For those passages that yet remain unclear, consult your pastor or godly men who have written in that particular area.

Errors to Avoid

As you interpret Scripture, several common errors should be avoided.

1. Do not draw any conclusions at the price of proper interpretation. That is, do not make the Bible say what you want it to say, but rather let it say what God intended when He wrote it.

2. Avoid superficial interpretation. You have heard people say, "To me, this passage means," or "I feel it is saying. . . ." The first step in interpreting the Bible is to recognize the four gaps we have to bridge: language, culture, geography, and history (see below).

3. Do not spiritualize the passage. Interpret and understand the passage in its normal, literal, historical, grammatical sense, just like you would understand any other piece of literature you were reading today.

Gaps to Bridge

The books of the Bible were written many centuries ago. For us to understand today what God was communicating then, there are several gaps that need to be bridged: the language gap, the cultural gap, the geographical gap, and the historical gap. Proper interpretation, therefore, takes time and disciplined effort.

1. *Language*. The Bible was originally written in Greek, Hebrew, and Aramaic. Often, understanding the meaning of a word or phrase in the original language can be the key to correctly interpreting a passage of Scripture.

2. *Culture*. The culture gap can be tricky. Some people try to use cultural differences to explain away the more difficult biblical commands. Realize that Scripture must first be viewed in the context of the culture in which it was written. Without an understanding of first-century Jewish culture, it is difficult to understand the gospel. Acts and the epistles must be read in light of the Greek and Roman cultures.

3. *Geography*. A third gap that needs to be closed is the geography gap. Biblical geography make the Bible come alive. A good Bible atlas is an invaluable reference tool that can help you comprehend the geography of the Holy Land.

4. *History*. We must also bridge the history gap. Unlike the scriptures of most other world religions, the Bible contains the records of actual historical persons and events. An understanding of Bible history will help us place the people and events in it in their proper historical perspective. A good Bible dictionary or Bible encyclopedia is useful here, as are basic historical studies.

Principles to Understand

Four principles should guide us as we interpret the Bible: literal, historical, grammatical, and synthesis.

1. *The Literal Principle*. Scripture should be understood in its literal, normal, and natural sense. While the Bible does contain figures of speech and symbols, they were intended to convey literal truth. In general, however, the Bible speaks in literal terms, and we must allow it to speak for itself.

2. *The Historical Principle*. This means that we interpret in its historical context. We must ask what the text meant to the people to whom it was first written. In this way we can develop a proper contextual understanding of the original intent of Scripture.

3. *The Grammatical Principle*. This requires that we understand the basic grammatical structure of each sentence in the original language. To whom do the pronouns refer? What is the tense of the main verb? You will find that when you ask some simple questions like those, the meaning of the text immediately becomes clearer.

4. *The Synthesis Principle*. This is what the Reformers called the *analogia scriptura*. It means that the Bible does not contradict itself. If we arrive at an interpretation of a passage that contradicts a truth taught elsewhere in the Scriptures, our interpretation cannot be correct. Scripture must be compared with Scripture to discover its full meaning.

STEP 3—Evaluating. You have been reading and asking the question, "What does the Bible say?" Then you have interpreted, asking the question, "What does the Bible mean?" Now it is time to consult others to insure that you have the proper interpretation. Remember, the Bible will never contradict itself.

Read Bible introductions, commentaries, and background books which will enrich your thinking through that illumination which God has given to other men and to you through their books. In your evaluation, be a true seeker. Be one who accepts the truth of God's Word even though it may cause you to change what you always have believed, or cause you to alter your life pattern.

STEP 4—Applying. The next question is: "How does God's truth penetrate and change my own life?" Studying Scripture without allowing it to penetrate to the depths of your soul would be like preparing a banquet without eating it. The bottom-line question to ask is, "How do the divine truths and principles contained in any passage apply to me in terms of my attitude and actions?"

Jesus made this promise to those who would carry their personal Bible study through to this point: "If you know these things, blessed are you if you do them" (John 13:17).

Having read and interpreted the Bible, you should have a basic understanding of what the Bible says, and what it means by what it says. But studying the Bible does not stop there. The ultimate goal should be to let it speak to you and enable you to grow spiritually. That requires personal application.

Bible study is not complete until we ask ourselves, "What does this mean for my life and how can I practically apply it?" We must take the knowledge we have gained from our reading and interpretation and draw out the practical principles that apply to our personal lives.

If there is a command to be obeyed, we obey it. If there is a promise to be embraced, we claim it. If there is a warning to be followed, we heed it. This is the ultimate step: we submit to Scripture and let it transform our lives. If you skip this step, you will never enjoy your Bible study and the Bible will never change your life.

STEP 5—Correlating. This last stage connects the doctrine you have learned in a particular passage or book with divine truths and principles taught elsewhere in the Bible to form the big picture. Always keep in mind that the Bible is one book in 66 parts, and it contains a number of truths and principles, taught over and over again in a variety of ways and circumstances. By correlating and cross-referencing, you will begin to build a sound doctrinal foundation by which to live.

What Now?

The psalmist said, "Blessed *is* the man who walks not in the counsel of the ungodly, nor stands in the path of sinners, nor sits in the seat of the scornful; But his delight *is* in the law of the Lord, and in His law he meditates day and night" (Ps. 1:1,2).

It is not enough just to study the Bible. We must meditate upon it. In a very real sense we are giving our brain a bath; we are washing it in the purifying solution of God's Word.

> This Book of the Law shall not depart from your mouth, but you shall meditate in it day and night, that you may observe to do according to all that is written in it. For then you will make your way prosperous, and then you will have good success.
>
> Josh. 1:8

Here is the spring where waters flow,
To quench our heat of sin:
Here is the tree where truth doth grow,
To lead our lives therein:
Here is the judge that stints the strife,
When men's devices fail:
Here is the bread that feeds the life
That death cannot assail.
The tidings of salvation dear,
Comes to our ears from hence:
The fortress of our faith is here,
And shield of our defense.
Then be not like the swine that hath
A pearl at his desire,
And takes more pleasure from the trough
And wallowing in the mire.
Read not this book in any case,
But with a single eye:
Read not but first desire God's grace,
To understand thereby.
Pray still in faith with this respect,
To bear good fruit therein,
That knowledge may bring this effect,
To mortify thy sin.
Then happy you shall be in all your life,
What so to you befalls:
Yes, double happy you shall be,
When God by death you calls.

(From the first Bible printed in Scotland—1576)

Preface to the NEW KING JAMES VERSION

Purpose

In the preface to the 1611 edition, the translators of the Authorized Version, known popularly as the King James Bible, state that it was not their purpose "to make a new translation . . . but to make a good one better." Indebted to the earlier work of William Tyndale and others, they saw their best contribution to consist in revising and enhancing the excellence of the English versions which had sprung from the Reformation of the sixteenth century. In harmony with the purpose of the King James scholars, the translators and editors of the present work have not pursued a goal of innovation. They have perceived the Holy Bible, New King James Version, as a continuation of the labors of the earlier translators, thus unlocking for today's readers the spiritual treasures found especially in the Authorized Version of the Holy Scriptures.

A Living Legacy

For nearly four hundred years, and throughout several revisions of its English form, the King James Bible has been deeply revered among the English-speaking peoples of the world. The precision of translation for which it is historically renowned, and its majesty of style, have enabled that monumental version of the word of God to become the mainspring of the religion, language, and legal foundations of our civilization.

Although the Elizabethan period and our own era share in zeal for technical advance, the former period was more aggressively devoted to classical learning. Along with this awakened concern for the classics came a flourishing companion interest in the Scriptures, an interest that was enlivened by the conviction that the manuscripts were providentially handed down and were a trustworthy record of the inspired Word of God. The King James translators were committed to producing an English Bible that would be a precise translation, and by no means a paraphrase or a broadly approximate rendering. On the one hand, the scholars were almost as familiar with the original languages of the Bible as with their native English. On the other hand, their reverence for the divine Author and His Word assured a translation of the Scriptures in which only a principle of utmost accuracy could be accepted.

George Bernard Shaw became a literary legend in our century because of his severe and often humorous criticisms of our most cherished values. Surprisingly, however, Shaw pays the following tribute to the scholars commissioned by King James: "The translation was extraordinarily well done because to the translators what they were translating was not merely a curious collection of ancient books written by different authors in different stages of culture, but the Word of God divinely revealed through His chosen and expressly inspired scribes. In this conviction they carried out their work with boundless reverence and care and achieved a beautifully artistic result." History agrees with these estimates. Therefore, while seeking to unveil the excellent *form* of the traditional English Bible, special care has also been taken in the present edition to preserve the work of *precision* which is the legacy of the 1611 translators.

Complete Equivalence in Translation

Where new translation has been necessary in the New King James Version, the most complete representation of the original has been rendered by considering the history of usage and etymology of words in their contexts. This principle of complete equivalence seeks to preserve *all* of the information in the text, while presenting it in good literary form. Dynamic equivalence, a recent procedure in Bible translation, commonly results in paraphrasing where a more literal rendering is needed to reflect a specific and vital sense. For example, complete equivalence truly renders the original text in expressions such as "lifted her voice and wept" (Gen. 21:16); "I gave you cleanness of teeth" (Amos 4:6); "Jesus met them, saying, 'Rejoice!'" (Matt. 28:9); and "Woman, what does your concern have to do with Me?" (John 2:4). Complete equivalence translates fully, in order to provide an English text that is both accurate and readable.

In keeping with the principle of complete equivalence, it is the policy to translate interjections which are commonly omitted in modern language renderings of the Bible. As an example, the interjection *behold,* in the older King James editions, continues to have a place in English usage, especially in dramatically calling attention to a spectacular scene, or an event of profound importance such as the Immanuel prophecy of Isaiah 7:14. Consequently, *behold* is retained for these occasions in the present edition. However, the Hebrew and Greek originals for this word can be translated variously, depending on the circumstances in the passage. Therefore, in addition to *behold*, words such as *indeed, look, see*, and *surely* are also rendered to convey the appropriate sense suggested by the context in each case.

In faithfulness to God and to our readers, it was deemed appropriate that all participating scholars sign a statement affirming their belief in the verbal and plenary inspiration of Scripture, and in the inerrancy of the original autographs.

Devotional Quality

The King James scholars readily appreciated the intrinsic beauty of divine revelation. They accordingly disciplined their talents to render well-chosen English words of their time, as well as a graceful, often musical arrangement of language, which has stirred the hearts of Bible readers through the years. The translators, the committees, and the editors of the present edition, while sensitive to the late-twentieth-century English idiom, and while adhering faithfully to the Hebrew, Aramaic, and Greek texts, have sought to maintain those lyrical and devotional qualities that are so highly regarded in the Authorized Version. This devotional quality is especially apparent in the poetic and prophetic books, although even the relatively plain style of the Gospels and Epistles cannot strictly be likened, as sometimes suggested, to modern newspaper style. The Koine Greek of the New Testament is influenced by the Hebrew background of the writers, for whom even the gospel narratives were not merely flat utterance, but often sung in various degrees of rhythm.

The Style

Students of the Bible applaud the timeless devotional character of our historic Bible. Yet it is also universally understood that our language, like all living languages, has undergone profound change since 1611. Subsequent revisions of the King James Bible have sought to keep abreast of changes in English speech. The present work is a further step toward this objective. Where obsolescence and other reading difficulties exist, present-day vocabulary, punctuation, and grammar have been carefully integrated. Words representing ancient objects, such as *chariot* and *phylactery*, have no modern substitutes and are therefore retained.

A special feature of the New King James Version is its conformity to the thought flow of the 1611 Bible. The reader discovers that the sequence and selection of words, phrases, and clauses of the new edition, while much clearer, are so close to the traditional that there is remarkable ease in listening to the reading of either edition while following with the other.

In the discipline of translating biblical and other ancient languages, a standard method of transliteration, that is, the English spelling of untranslated words, such as names of persons and places, has never been commonly adopted. In keeping with the design of the present work, the King James spelling of untranslated words is retained, although made uniform throughout. For example, instead of the spellings *Isaiah* and *Elijah* in the Old Testament, and *Esaias* and *Elias* in the New Testament, *Isaiah* and *Elijah* now appear in both Testaments.

King James doctrinal and theological terms, for example, *propitiation, justification*, and *sanctification*, are generally familiar to English-speaking peoples. Such terms have been retained except where the original language indicates need for a more precise translation.

Readers of the Authorized Version will immediately be struck by the absence of several pronouns: *thee, thou*, and *ye* are replaced by the simple *you*, while, *your*, and *yours* are substituted for *thy* and *thine* as applicable. *Thee, thou, thy*, and *thine* were once forms of address to express a special relationship to human as well as divine persons. These pronouns are no longer part of our language. However, reverence for God in the present work is preserved by capitalizing pronouns, including *You, Your*, and *Yours*, which refer to Him. Additionally, capitalization of these pronouns benefits the reader by clearly distinguishing divine and human persons referred to in a passage. Without such capitalization the distinction is often obscure, because the antecedent of a pronoun is not always clear in the English translation.

In addition to the pronoun usages of the seventeenth century, the *-eth* and *-est* verb endings, so familiar in the earlier King James editions, are now obsolete. Unless a speaker is schooled in these verb endings, there is common difficulty in selecting the correct form to be used with a given subject of the verb in vocal prayer. That is, should we use *love, loveth*, or *lovest*? *do, doeth, doest*, or *dost*? *have, hath*, or *hast*? Because these forms are obsolete, contemporary English usage has been substituted for the previous verb endings.

In older editions of the King James Version, the frequency of the connective *and* far exceeded the limits of present English usage. Also, biblical linguists agree that the Hebrew and Greek original words for this conjunction may commonly be translated otherwise, depending on the immediate context. Therefore, instead of *and*, alternatives such as *also, but, however, now, so, then*, and *thus* are accordingly rendered in the present edition, when the original language permits.

The real character of the Authorized Version does not reside in its archaic pronouns or verbs or other grammatical forms of the seventeenth century, but rather in the care taken by its scholars to impart the letter and spirit of the original text in a majestic and reverent style.

The Format

The format of the New King James Version is designed to enhance the vividness and devotional quality of the Holy Scriptures:

- Subject headings assist the reader to identify topics and transitions in the biblical content.
- Words or phrases in *italics* indicate expressions in the original language which require clarification by additional English words, as also done throughout the history of the King James Bible.
- Verse numbers within a paragraph are easily distinguishable.
- *Oblique type* in the New Testament indicates a quotation from the Old Testament.
- Prose is divided into paragraphs to indicate the structure of thought.
- Poetry is structured as contemporary verse to reflect the poetic form and beauty of the passage in the original language.
- The covenant name of God was usually translated from the Hebrew as "LORD" or "GOD" (using capital letters as shown) in the King James Old Testament. This tradition is maintained. In the present edition the name is so capitalized whenever the covenant name is quoted in the New Testament from a passage in the Old Testament.

The Old Testament Text

The Hebrew Bible has come down to us through the scrupulous care of ancient scribes who copied the original text in successive generations. By the sixth century A.D. the scribes were succeeded by a group known as the Masoretes, who continued to preserve the sacred Scriptures for another five hundred years in a form known as the Masoretic Text. Babylonia, Palestine, and Tiberias were the main centers of Masoretic activity; but by the tenth century A.D. the Masoretes of Tiberias, led by the family of ben Asher, gained the ascendancy. Through subsequent editions, the ben Asher text became in the twelfth century the only recognized form of the Hebrew Scriptures.

Daniel Bomberg printed the first Rabbinic Bible in 1516–17; that work was followed in 1524–25 by a second edition prepared by Jacob ben Chayyim and also published by Bomberg. The text of ben Chayyim was adopted in most subsequent Hebrew Bibles, including those used by the King James translators. The ben Chayyim text was also used for the first two editions of Rudolph Kittel's *Biblia Hebraica* of 1906 and 1912. In 1937 Paul Kahle published a third edition of Biblia Hebraica. This edition was based on the oldest dated manuscript of the ben Asher text, the Leningrad Manuscript B19a (A.D. 1008), which Kahle regarded as superior to that used by ben Chayyim.

For the New King James Version the text used was the 1967/1977 Stuttgart edition of the Biblia Hebraica, with frequent comparisons being made with the Bomberg edition of 1524–25. The Septuagint (Greek) Version of the Old Testament and the Latin Vulgate also were consulted. In addition to referring to a variety of ancient versions of the Hebrew Scriptures, the New King James Version draws on the resources of relevant manuscripts from the Dead Sea caves. In the few places where the Hebrew was so obscure that the 1611 King James was compelled to follow one of the versions, but where information is now available to resolve the problems, the New King James Version follows the Hebrew text.

The New Testament Text

There is more manuscript support for the New Testament than for any other body of ancient literature. Over five thousand Greek, eight thousand Latin, and many more manuscripts in other languages attest the integrity of the New Testament. There is only one basic New Testament used by Protestants, Roman Catholics, and Orthodox, by conservatives and liberals. Minor variations in hand copying have appeared through the centuries, before mechanical printing began about A.D. 1450.

Some variations exist in the spelling of Greek words, in word order, and in similar details. These ordinarily do not show up in translation and do not affect the sense of the text in any way.

Other manuscript differences such as omission or inclusion of a word or a clause, and two paragraphs in the Gospels, should not overshadow the overwhelming degree of agreement which exists among the ancient records. Bible readers may be assured that the most important differences in English New Testaments of today are due, not to manuscript divergence, but to the way in which translators view the task of translation: How literally should the text be rendered? How does the translator view the matter of biblical inspiration? Does the translator adopt a paraphrase when a literal rendering would be quite clear and more to the point? The New King James Version follows the historic precedent of the Authorized Version in maintaining a literal approach to translation, except where the idiom of the original language cannot be translated directly into our tongue.

The King James New Testament was based on the traditional text of the Greek-speaking churches, first published in 1516, and later called the Textus Receptus or Received Text. Although based on the relatively few available manuscripts, these were representative of many more which existed at the time but only became known later. In the late nineteenth century, B. Westcott and F. Hort taught that this text had been officially edited by the fourth-century church, but a total lack of historical evidence for this event has forced a revision of the theory. It is now widely held that the Byzantine Text that largely supports the Textus Receptus has as much right as the Alexandrian or any other tradition to be weighed in determining the text of the New Testament. Those readings in the Textus Receptus which have weak support are indicated in the side reference column as being opposed by both Critical and Majority Texts (see "Center-Column Notes").

Since the 1880s most contemporary translations of the New Testament have relied upon a relatively few manuscripts discovered chiefly in the late nineteenth and early twentieth centuries. Such translations depend primarily on two manuscripts, Codex Vaticanus and Codex Sinaiticus, because of their greater age. The Greek text obtained by using these sources and the related papyri (our most ancient manuscripts) is known as the Alexandrian Text. However, some scholars have grounds for doubting the faithfulness of Vaticanus and Sinaiticus, since they often disagree with one another, and Sinaiticus exhibits excessive omission.

A third viewpoint of New Testament scholarship holds that the best text is based on the consensus of the majority of existing Greek manuscripts. This text is called the Majority Text. Most of these manuscripts are in substantial agreement. Even though many are late, and none is earlier than the fifth century, usually their readings are verified by papyri, ancient versions, quotations from the early church fathers, or a combination of these. The Majority Text is similar to the Textus Receptus, but it corrects those readings which have little or no support in the Greek manuscript tradition.

Today, scholars agree that the science of New Testament textual criticism is in a state of flux. Very few scholars still favor the Textus Receptus as such, and then often for its historical prestige as the text of Luther, Calvin, Tyndale, and the King James Version. For about a century most have followed a Critical Text (so called because it is edited according to specific principles of textual criticism) which depends heavily upon the Alexandrian type of text. More recently many have abandoned this Critical Text (which is quite similar to the one edited by Westcott and Hort) for one that is more eclectic. Finally, a small but growing number of scholars prefer the Majority Text, which is close to the traditional text except in the Revelation.

In light of these facts, and also because the New King James Version is the fifth revision of a historic document translated from specific Greek texts, the editors decided to retain the traditional text in the body of the New Testament and to indicate major Critical and Majority Text variant readings in the center reference column. Although these variations are duly indicated in the center-column notes of the present edition, it is most important to emphasize that fully eighty-five percent of the New Testament text is the same in the Textus Receptus, the Alexandrian Text, and the Majority Text.

Center-Column Notes

Significant explanatory notes, alternate translations, and cross-references, as well as New Testament citations of Old Testament passages, are supplied in the center reference column.

Important textual variants in the Old Testament are identified in a standard form.

The textual notes in the present edition of the New Testament make no evaluation of readings, but do clearly indicate the manuscript sources of readings. They objectively present facts without such tendentious remarks as "the best manuscripts omit" or "the most reliable manuscripts read." Such notes are value judgments that differ according to varying viewpoints on the text. By giving a clearly defined set of variants the New King James Version benefits readers of all textual persuasions.

Where significant variations occur in the New Testament Greek manuscripts, textual notes are classified as follows:

1. NU-Text

   These variations from the traditional text generally represent the Alexandrian or Egyptian type of text described previously in "The New Testament Text." They are found in the Critical Text published in the twenty-seventh edition of the Nestle-Aland Greek New Testament (N) and in the United Bible Societies' fourth edition (U), hence the acronym, "NU-Text."

2. M-Text

   This symbol indicates points of variation in the Majority Text from the traditional text, as also previously discussed in "The New Testament Text." It should be noted that M stands for whatever reading is printed in the published *Greek New Testament According to the Majority Text*, whether supported by overwhelming, strong, or only a divided majority textual tradition.

The textual notes reflect the scholarship of the past 150 years and will assist the reader to observe the variations between the different manuscript traditions of the New Testament. Such information is generally not available in English translations of the New Testament.

The CENTER REFERENCE COLUMN

The unequaled accuracy, beauty, and completeness of the New King James Version makes it a most suitable translation for Bible study. The text of *The MacArthur Study Bible* is separated into paragraphs, as well as verses, allowing the reader to quickly group Scriptures according to content. Subject headings further organize the Bible text, summarizing the essential content and religious significance of major sections of the Bible.

law through faith? Certainly not! On the
contrary, we establish the law.

Abraham Justified by Faith

4 What then shall we say that [a]Abraham
our [b]father[1] has found according to
the flesh? 2 For if Abraham was [c]justified
by works, he has *something* to boast about,

Study of the Bible text is enhanced by information in the center reference column that is keyed to specific words and phrases:

A *superior letter* (usually preceding the referenced word or phrase in the text) indicates a cross-reference. *Square brackets* around a cross-reference in the center column mark it as a conceptual cross-reference, which identifies a passage similar in *concept* to the referenced passage in the text.

A *superior numeral* indicates and alternate translation, equivalent translation, literal translation, explanatory note, language note, or textual note.

11 [n] [Ps. 2:7]; Is. 42:1; Matt. 3:17; 12:18; Mark 9:7; Luke 3:22
12 [o] Matt. 4:1-11; Luke 4:1-13 [5] *sent Him out*

12 [o]Immediately the Spirit [5]drove Him
into the wilderness. 13 And He was there
in the wilderness forty days, tempted by
Satan, and was with the wild beasts; [p]and
the angels ministered to Him.

An *Alternate Translation* is *different* in meaning from the words in the text, but is justified by the original languages. That is, the translators could have understood the original word or phrase this way, although they felt their choice was more appropriate.

17 [i] [Eccl. 5:4, 5] [6] *Pay*
18 [j] Matt. 22:23-33; Luke 20:27-38 [k] Acts 23:8
19 [l] Deut. 25:5
24 [7] *Or deceived*

24 Jesus answered and said to them,
"Are you not therefore [7]mistaken, because
you do not know the Scriptures nor the
power of God? 25 For when they rise from
the dead, they neither marry nor are given

An *Equivalent Translation* is *similar* in meaning to the translation in the text. It helps you understand the text by showing you a synonym.

17 [i] [Eccl. 5:4, 5] [6] *Pay* **18** [j] Matt. 22:23-33; Luke 20:27-38 [k] Acts 23:8 **19** [l] Deut. 25:5 **24** [7] Or *deceived*	and inscription *is* this?" They said to Him, "Caesar's." **17** And Jesus answered and said to them, [6]"Render to Caesar the things that are Caesar's, and to [i]God the things that are God's."

A *Literal Translation* gives the literal meaning of the word or phrase.

13 [f] Matt. 22:15-22; Luke 20:20-26 **14** [g] Acts 18:26 [4] Court no man's favor [5] Lit. *look at the face of men*	in *His* words. **14** When they had come, they said to Him, "Teacher, we know that You are true, and [4]care about no one; for You do not [5]regard the person of men, but teach the [g]way of God in truth. Is it lawful

An *Explanatory Note* explains the word or phrase in the text. Words set in roman type in translation notes are explanatory only and are not translated from the original languages.

[5] *for appearance' sake* **41** [g] Luke 21:1-4 [h] 2 Kin. 12:9 **42** [6] Gr. *lepta*, very small copper coins [7] A Roman coin	in much. **42** Then one poor widow came and threw in two [6]mites, which make a [7]quadrans. **43** So He called His disciples to *Himself* and said to them, "Assuredly, I say to you that [i]this poor widow has put in

A *Language Note* gives the Hebrew, Greek, or Aramaic word or phrase that underlies the English translation.

43 [l] [Deut. 13:6]; Matt. 5:29, 30; 18:8, 9 [1] *crippled* [2] Gr. *Gehenna* **44** [m] Is. 66:24 [3] NU omits v. 44.	into the sea. **43** [l]If your hand causes you to sin, cut it off. It is better for you to enter into life [1]maimed, rather than having two hands, to go to [2]hell, into the fire that shall never be quenched— **44** [3]where

A *Textual Note* points out one or more significant textual variants. The sources of the variant readings are identified by abbreviations listed on page xxix. (See also Preface, "Center-Column Notes.")

44 [m] Is. 66:24 [3] NU omits v. 44. **45** [4] Gr. *Gehenna* [5] NU omits the rest of v. 45 and all of v. 46.	**45** And if your foot causes you to sin, cut it off. It is better for you to enter life lame, rather than having two feet, to be cast into [4]hell, [5]into the fire that shall never be quenched— **46** where

Table of ABBREVIATIONS

A.D.	in the year of our Lord
a.k.a.	also known as
a.m.	midnight to noon
ANE	Ancient Near Eastern
Arab.	Arabic
Aram.	Aramaic
B.C.	before Christ
Bg.	the 1524–25 edition of the Hebrew Old Testament published by Daniel Bomberg (see Preface, "The Old Testament Text")
ca.	about, approximately
cf.	compare
chap., chaps.	chapter, chapters
contra.	contrast
DOL	Day of the Lord
DSS	Dead Sea Scrolls
E	East
e.g.	for example
et al.	and others
etc.	and so forth
fem.	feminine
f., ff.	following verse, following verses
Gr.	Greek
Heb.	Hebrew
i.e.	that is
Kt.	Kethib (literally, in Aramaic, "written")—the written words of the Hebrew Old Testament preserved by the Masoretes (see "Qr.")
Lat.	Latin
lit.	literally
LXX	Septuagint—an ancient translation of the Old Testament into Greek
M	Majority Text (see Preface, "The New Testament Text")
masc.	masculine
mi.	mile/miles
ms., mss.	manuscript, manuscripts
Mt.	mount
MT	Masoretic Text—the traditional Hebrew Old Testament (see Preface, "The Old Testament Text")
N	North
NT	New Testament
NU	the most prominent modern Critical Text of the Greek New Testament, published in the twenty-seventh edition of the Nestle-Aland *Greek New Testament* and in the fourth edition of the United Bible Societies' *Greek New Testament* (see Preface, "The New Testament Text")
OT	Old Testament
pl.	plural
p.m.	noon to midnight
Qr.	Qere (literally, in Aramaic, "read")—certain words read aloud, differing from the written words, in the Masoretic tradition of the Hebrew Old Testament (see "Kt.")
S	South
Sam.	Samaritan Pentateuch—a variant Hebrew edition of the books of Moses, used by the Samaritan community
sing.	singular
Syr.	Syriac
Tg.	Targum—an Aramaic paraphrase of the Old Testament
TR	Textus Receptus or Received Text (see Preface, "The New Testament Text")
v., vv.	verse, verses
vss.	versions—ancient translations of the Bible
Vg.	Vulgate—an ancient translation of the Bible into Latin, translated and edited by Jerome
W	West

Books of the Bible

ABBREVIATIONS

The Old Testament

Genesis	Gen.	2 Chronicles	2 Chr.	Daniel	Dan.
Exodus	Ex.	Ezra	Ezra	Hosea	Hos.
Leviticus	Lev.	Nehemiah	Neh.	Joel	Joel
Numbers	Num.	Esther	Esth.	Amos	Amos
Deuteronomy	Deut.	Job	Job	Obadiah	Obad.
Joshua	Josh.	Psalms	Ps.	Jonah	Jon.
Judges	Judg.	Proverbs	Prov.	Micah	Mic.
Ruth	Ruth	Ecclesiastes	Eccl.	Nahum	Nah.
1 Samuel	1 Sam.	Song of Solomon	Song	Habakkuk	Hab.
2 Samuel	2 Sam.	Isaiah	Is.	Zephaniah	Zeph.
1 Kings	1 Kin.	Jeremiah	Jer.	Haggai	Hag.
2 Kings	2 Kin.	Lamentations	Lam.	Zechariah	Zech.
1 Chronicles	1 Chr.	Ezekiel	Ezek.	Malachi	Mal.

The New Testament

Matthew	Matt.	Ephesians	Eph.	Hebrews	Heb.
Mark	Mark	Philippians	Phil.	James	James
Luke	Luke	Colossians	Col.	1 Peter	1 Pet.
John	John	1 Thessalonians	1 Thess.	2 Peter	2 Pet.
Acts	Acts	2 Thessalonians	2 Thess.	1 John	1 John
Romans	Rom.	1 Timothy	1 Tim.	2 John	2 John
1 Corinthians	1 Cor.	2 Timothy	2 Tim.	3 John	3 John
2 Corinthians	2 Cor.	Titus	Titus	Jude	Jude
Galatians	Gal.	Philemon	Philem.	Revelation	Rev.

Key to Parenthetical Reference

( )	exact text
(cf.)	corroborative text
(see)	amplifying/clarifying text
(contra.)	contrasting text

The Progress of Revelation

OLD TESTAMENT

	Book	Approximate Writing Date	Author
1.	Job	Unknown	Anonymous
2.	Genesis	1445–1405 B.C.	Moses
3.	Exodus	1445–1405 B.C.	Moses
4.	Leviticus	1445–1405 B.C.	Moses
5.	Numbers	1445–1405 B.C.	Moses
6.	Deuteronomy	1445–1405 B.C.	Moses
7.	Psalms	1410–450 B.C.	Multiple Authors
8.	Joshua	1405–1385 B.C.	Joshua
9.	Judges	ca. 1043 B.C.	Samuel
10.	Ruth	ca. 1030–1010 B.C.	Samuel (?)
11.	Song of Solomon	971–965 B.C.	Solomon
12.	Proverbs	971–686 B.C.	Solomon primarily
13.	Ecclesiastes	940–931 B.C.	Solomon
14.	1 Samuel	931–722 B.C.	Anonymous
15.	2 Samuel	931–722 B.C.	Anonymous
16.	Obadiah	850–840 B.C.	Obadiah
17.	Joel	835–796 B.C.	Joel
18.	Jonah	ca. 775 B.C.	Jonah
19.	Amos	ca. 750 B.C.	Amos
20.	Micah	735–710 B.C.	Micah
21.	Hosea	750–710 B.C.	Hosea
22.	Isaiah	700–681 B.C.	Isaiah
23.	Nahum	ca. 650 B.C.	Nahum
24.	Zephaniah	635–625 B.C.	Zephaniah
25.	Habakkuk	615–605 B.C.	Habakkuk
26.	Ezekiel	590–570 B.C.	Ezekiel
27.	Lamentations	586 B.C.	Jeremiah
28.	Jeremiah	586–570 B.C.	Jeremiah
29.	1 Kings	561–538 B.C.	Anonymous
30.	2 Kings	561–538 B.C.	Anonymous
31.	Daniel	536–530 B.C.	Daniel
32.	Haggai	ca. 520 B.C.	Haggai
33.	Zechariah	480–470 B.C.	Zechariah
34.	Ezra	457–444 B.C.	Ezra
35.	1 Chronicles	450–430 B.C.	Ezra (?)
36.	2 Chronicles	450–430 B.C.	Ezra (?)
37.	Esther	450–331 B.C.	Anonymous
38.	Malachi	433–424 B.C.	Malachi
39.	Nehemiah	424–400 B.C.	Ezra

The Progress of Revelation

NEW TESTAMENT

	Book	Approximate Writing Date	Author
1.	James	A.D. 44–49	James
2.	Galatians	A.D. 49–50	Paul
3.	Matthew	A.D. 50–60	Matthew
4.	Mark	A.D. 50–60	Mark
5.	1 Thessalonians	A.D. 51	Paul
6.	2 Thessalonians	A.D. 51–52	Paul
7.	1 Corinthians	A.D. 55	Paul
8.	2 Corinthians	A.D. 55–56	Paul
9.	Romans	A.D. 56	Paul
10.	Luke	A.D. 60–61	Luke
11.	Ephesians	A.D. 60–62	Paul
12.	Philippians	A.D. 60–62	Paul
13.	Colossians	A.D. 60–62	Paul
14.	Philemon	A.D. 60–62	Paul
15.	Acts	A.D. 62	Luke
16.	1 Timothy	A.D. 62–64	Paul
17.	Titus	A.D. 62–64	Paul
18.	1 Peter	A.D. 64–65	Peter
19.	2 Timothy	A.D. 66–67	Paul
20.	2 Peter	A.D. 67–68	Peter
21.	Hebrews	A.D. 67–69	Unknown
22.	Jude	A.D. 68–70	Jude
23.	John	A.D. 80–90	John
24.	1 John	A.D. 90–95	John
25.	2 John	A.D. 90–95	John
26.	3 John	A.D. 90–95	John
27.	Revelation	A.D. 94–96	John

The OLD TESTAMENT

Introduction to the PENTATEUCH

The first 5 books of the Bible (Genesis, Exodus, Leviticus, Numbers, Deuteronomy) form a complete literary unit called the Pentateuch, meaning "five scrolls." The 5 independent books of the Pentateuch were written as an unbroken unity in content and historical sequence, with each succeeding book beginning where the former left off.

Genesis' first words, "In the beginning God created . . ." (Gen. 1:1) imply the reality of God's eternal or "before time" existence and announce the spectacular transition to time and space. While the exact date of creation cannot be determined, it certainly would be estimated to be thousands of years ago, not millions. Starting with Abraham (ca. 2165–1990 B.C.) in Gen. 11, this book of beginnings spans over 300 years to the death of Joseph in Egypt (ca. 1804 B.C.). There is then another gap of almost 300 years until the birth of Moses in Egypt (ca. 1525 B.C.; Ex. 2).

Exodus begins with the words "Now these *are* the names" (Ex. 1:1), listing those of the family of Jacob who went down to Egypt to be with Joseph toward the end of Gen. (Gen. 46ff.). The second book of the Pentateuch, which records the escape of the Israelites from Egypt, concludes when the cloud which led the people through the wilderness descends upon the newly constructed tabernacle.

The first Hebrew words of Leviticus may be translated, "Now the LORD called to Moses" (Lev. 1:1). From the cloud of God's Presence in the tabernacle of meeting (Lev. 1:1), God summons Moses in order to prescribe to him the ceremonial law which told Israel how they must approach their Holy Lord. Leviticus concludes with, "These *are* the commandments which the LORD commanded Moses for the children of Israel on Mount Sinai" (Lev. 27:34).

Numbers, much like Leviticus, commences with God commissioning Moses at the tabernacle of meeting, this time to take a census in preparation for war against Israel's enemies. The book's title in the Hebrew Bible accurately represents the content—"Wilderness." Due to lack of trust in God, Israel did not want to engage its enemies militarily in order to claim the Promised Land. After 40 additional years in the wilderness for their rebellion, Israel arrived on the plains of Moab.

Despite the fact that "*It is* eleven days' *journey* from Horeb by way of Mount Seir to Kadesh Barnea" (Deut. 1:2), the journey took Israel 40 years due to their rebellion against God. Moses preached the book of Deuteronomy as a sermon on the Plains of Moab in preparation for God's people to enter the land of covenant promise (Gen. 12:1-3). The title Deuteronomy is from the Gr. phrase *deuteros nomos,* meaning "second law." The book focuses on the restatement and, to some extent, the reapplication of the law to Israel's new circumstances.

Moses was the human author of the Pentateuch (Ex. 17:14; 24:4; Num. 33:1,2; Deut. 31:9; Josh. 1:8; 2 Kin. 21:8); thus, another title for the collection is "The Books of Moses." Through Moses, God revealed Himself, His former works, Israel's family history, and its role in His plan of redemption for mankind. The Pentateuch is foundational to all the rest of Scripture.

Quoted or alluded to thousands of times in the OT and in the NT, the Pentateuch was Israel's first inspired body of Scripture. For many years, this alone was Israel's Bible. Another common title for this section of Scripture is *Torah* or Law, nomenclature which looks at the didactic nature of these books. The Israelites were to meditate upon it (Josh. 1:8), teach it to their children (Deut. 6:4-8), and read it publicly (Neh. 8:1ff.). Just before his death and Israel's move into the Promised Land, Moses set forth the process by which public reading would make its way into human hearts and change their relationship with God, and ultimately their conduct:

> Gather the people together, men and women and little ones, and the stranger who *is* within your gates, that they may hear and that they may learn to fear the LORD your God and carefully observe all the words of this law. Deut. 31:12

The relationships between the commands is important. The people must: 1) gather to hear the law in order to learn what is required of them and what it has to say about God; 2) learn about the Lord in order to fear Him based on a correct understanding of who He is; and 3) fear God in order to be correctly motivated to obedience and good works. Good works performed for any other reason will be improp-

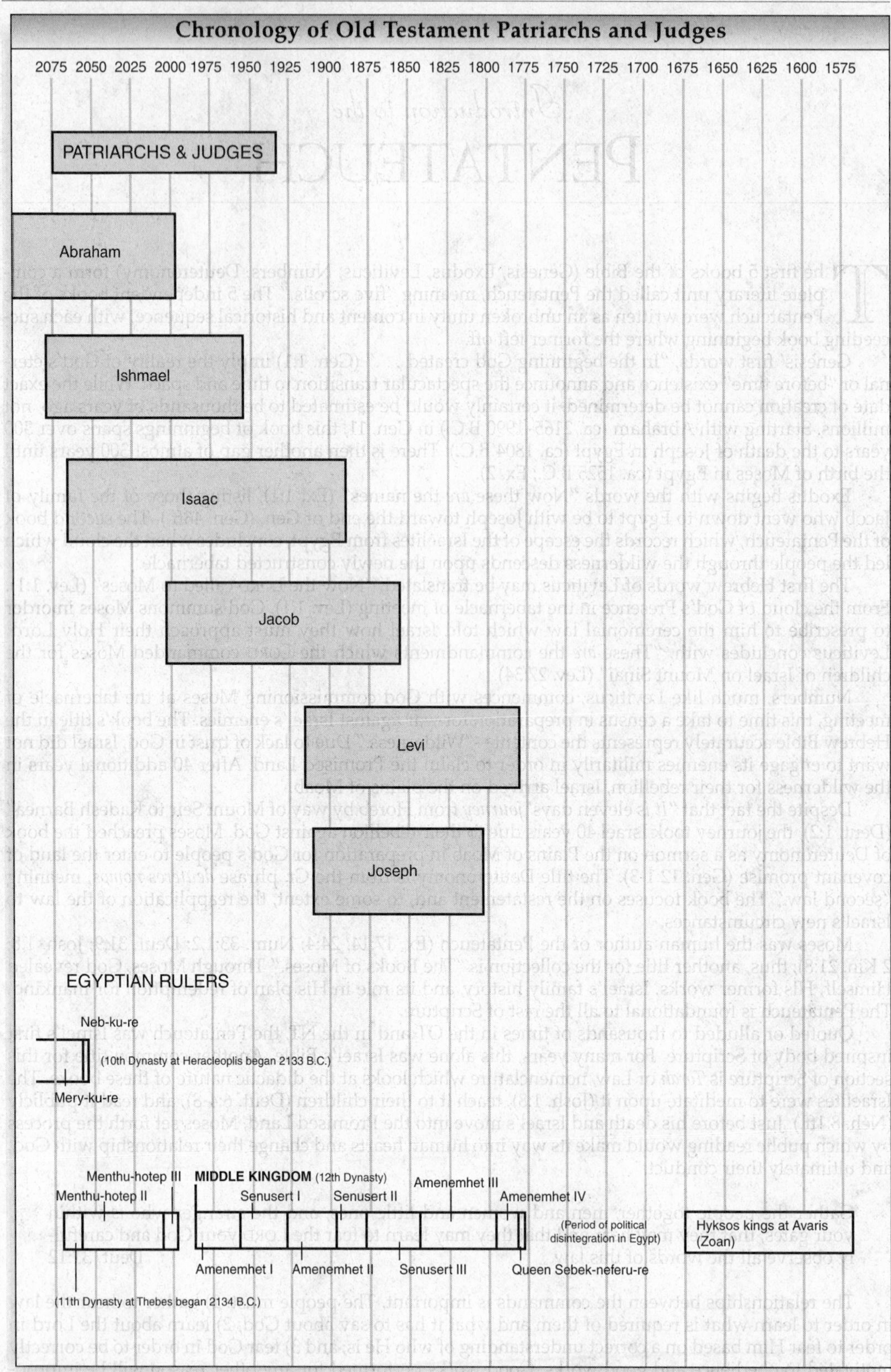
Chronology of Old Testament Patriarchs and Judges
2075 2050 2025 2000 1975 1950 1925 1900 1875 1850 1825 1800 1775 1750 1725 1700 1675 1650 1625 1600 1575
PATRIARCHS & JUDGES
Abraham
Ishmael
Isaac
Jacob
Levi
Joseph
EGYPTIAN RULERS
Neb-ku-re
(10th Dynasty at Heracleopolis began 2133 B.C.)
Mery-ku-re
Menthu-hotep III
MIDDLE KINGDOM (12th Dynasty)
Menthu-hotep II
Senusert I
Senusert II
Amenemhet III
Amenemhet IV
(Period of political disintegration in Egypt)
Hyksos kings at Avaris (Zoan)
Amenemhet I
Amenemhet II
Senusert III
Queen Sebek-neferu-re
(11th Dynasty at Thebes began 2134 B.C.)

Chronology of Old Testament Patriarchs and Judges

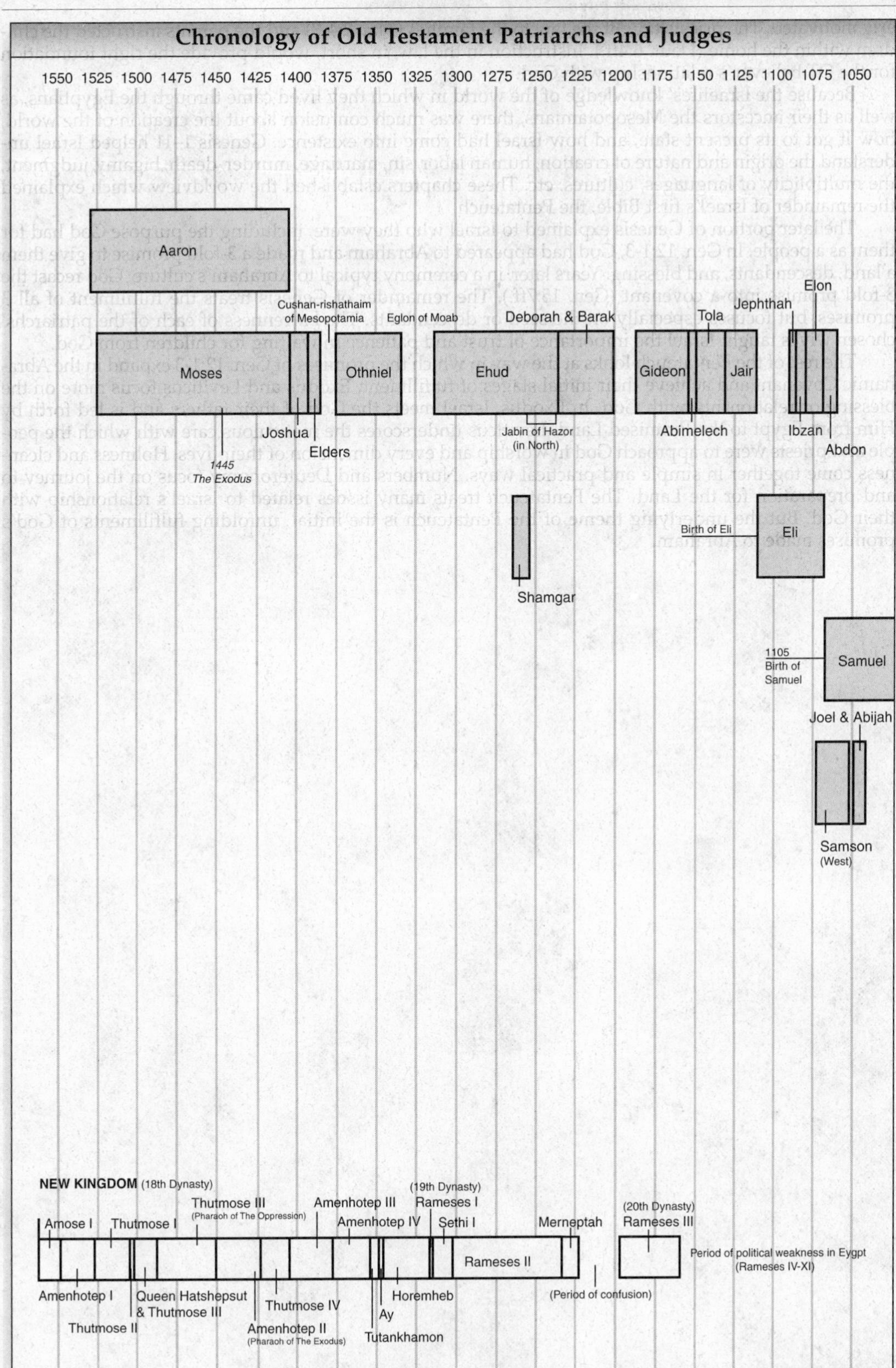
1550 1525 1500 1475 1450 1425 1400 1375 1350 1325 1300 1275 1250 1225 1200 1175 1150 1125 1100 1075 1050
Aaron
Cushan-rishathaim of Mesopotamia
Eglon of Moab
Deborah & Barak
Tola
Jephthah
Elon
Moses
Othniel
Ehud
Gideon
Jair
Joshua
Elders
1445
The Exodus
Jabin of Hazor (in North)
Abimelech
Ibzan
Abdon
Birth of Eli
Eli
Shamgar
1105
Birth of Samuel
Samuel
Joel & Abijah
Samson (West)
NEW KINGDOM (18th Dynasty)
(19th Dynasty)
Rameses I
Thutmose III
(Pharaoh of The Oppression)
Amenhotep III
Amose I
Thutmose I
Amenhotep IV
Sethi I
Merneptah
(20th Dynasty)
Rameses III
Rameses II
Period of political weakness in Eygpt (Rameses IV-XI)
Amenhotep I
Queen Hatshepsut & Thutmose III
Thutmose IV
Horemheb
(Period of confusion)
Thutmose II
Amenhotep II
(Pharaoh of The Exodus)
Ay
Tutankhamon

erly motivated. The priests taught the law to the families (Mal. 2:4-7) and the parents instructed the children within the home (Deut. 6:4ff.). Instruction in the law, in short, would provide the right foundation for the OT believer's relationship with God.

Because the Israelites' knowledge of the world in which they lived came through the Egyptians, as well as their ancestors the Mesopotamians, there was much confusion about the creation of the world, how it got to its present state, and how Israel had come into existence. Genesis 1–11 helped Israel understand the origin and nature of creation, human labor, sin, marriage, murder, death, bigamy, judgment, the multiplicity of languages, cultures, etc. These chapters established the worldview which explained the remainder of Israel's first Bible, the Pentateuch.

The later portion of Genesis explained to Israel who they were, including the purpose God had for them as a people. In Gen. 12:1-3, God had appeared to Abraham and made a 3-fold promise to give them a land, descendants, and blessing. Years later, in a ceremony typical to Abraham's culture, God recast the 3-fold promise into a covenant (Gen. 15:7ff.). The remainder of Genesis treats the fulfillment of all 3 promises, but focuses especially on the seed or descendants. The barrenness of each of the patriarchs' chosen wives taught Israel the importance of trust and patience in waiting for children from God.

The rest of the Pentateuch looks at the way in which the promises of Gen. 12:1-3 expand in the Abrahamic Covenant and achieve their initial stages of fulfillment. Exodus and Leviticus focus more on the blessing or relationship with God. In Exodus, Israel meets the God of their fathers and is led forth by Him from Egypt to the Promised Land. Leviticus underscores the meticulous care with which the people and priests were to approach God in worship and every dimension of their lives. Holiness and cleanness come together in simple and practical ways. Numbers and Deuteronomy focus on the journey to and preparation for the Land. The Pentateuch treats many issues related to Israel's relationship with their God. But the underlying theme of the Pentateuch is the initial, unfolding fulfillments of God's promises made to Abraham.

A Harmony of the Books of SAMUEL, KINGS, AND CHRONICLES

I. THE KINGSHIP OF GOD (1 Sam. 1:1–7:17; 1 Chr. 1:1–9:44)

A. Genealogical Tables (1 Chr. 1:1–9:44)
1. Genealogies of the Patriarchs (1 Chr. 1:1–2:2)
2. Genealogies of the Tribes of Israel (1 Chr. 2:3–9:44)

B. The Close of the Theocracy (1 Sam. 1:1–7:17)
1. The Early Life of Samuel (1 Sam. 1:1–4:1a)
   a. Samuel's birth and infancy (1 Sam. 1:1–2:11)
   b. Samuel at Shiloh (1 Sam. 2:12–4:1a)
2. The Period of National Disaster (1 Sam. 4:1b–7:2)
   a. Israel's defeat and loss of the ark (1 Sam. 4:1b-11a)
   b. Fall of the house of Eli (1 Sam. 4:11b-22)
   c. The ark of God (1 Sam. 5:1–7:2)
3. Samuel, the Last of the Judges (1 Sam. 7:3-17)

II. THE KINGSHIP OF SAUL (1 Sam. 8:1–31:13; 1 Chr. 10:1-14)

A. Establishment of Saul as First King of Israel (1 Sam. 8:1–10:27)

B. Saul's Reign until His Rejection (1 Sam. 11:1–15:35)

C. The Decline of Saul and the Rise of David (1 Sam. 16:1–31:13)
1. David's Early History (1 Sam. 16:1-23)
2. David's Advancement and Saul's Growing Jealousy (1 Sam. 17:1–20:42)
   a. David and Goliath (1 Sam. 17:1-51)
   b. David at the court of Saul (1 Sam. 18:1–20:42)
3. David's Life of Exile (1 Sam. 21:1–28:2)
   a. David's flight (1 Sam. 21:1–22:5)
   b. Saul's vengeance on the priests of Nob (1 Sam. 22:6-23)
   c. David rescue of Keilah (1 Sam. 23:1-13)
   d. David's last meeting with Jonathan (1 Sam. 23:14-18)
   e. David's betrayal by the Ziphites (1 Sam. 23:19-24a)
   f. David's escape from Saul in the Wilderness of Maon (1 Sam. 23:24b-28)
   g. David's flight from Saul; David's mercy on Saul's life in the cave (1 Sam. 23:29–24:22)
   h. Samuel's death (1 Sam. 25:1)
   i. David wedding to Abigail (1 Sam. 25:2-44)
   j. David's mercy on Saul's life again (1 Sam. 26:1-25)
   k. David's joining with the Philistines (1 Sam. 27:1–28:2)
4. Saul's Downfall in War with the Philistines (1 Sam. 28:3–31:13; 1 Chr. 10:1-14)
   a. Saul's fear of the Philistines (1 Sam. 28:3-6)
   b. Saul's visit to the witch of Endor (1 Sam. 28:7-25)
   c. David leaves the Philistines; defeats the Amalakites (1 Sam. 29:1–30:31)
   d. Saul and his sons slain (1 Sam. 31:1-13; 1 Chr. 10:1-14)

III. THE KINGSHIP OF DAVID (2 Sam. 1:1–24:25; 1 Kin. 1:1–2:11; 1 Chr. 10:14–29:30)

A. David's Victories (2 Sam. 1:1–10:19; 1 Chr. 10:14–20:8)
  1. The Political Triumphs of David (2 Sam. 1:1–5:25; 1 Chr. 10:14–12:40)
    a. David is king of Judah (2 Sam. 1:1–4:12; 1 Chr. 10:1–12:40)
    b. David is king over all Israel (2 Sam. 5:1–5:25)
  2. The Spiritual Triumphs of David (2 Sam. 6:1–7:29; 1 Chr. 13:1–17:27)
    a. The ark of the covenant (2 Sam. 6:1-23; 1 Chr. 13:1–16:43)
    b. The temple and the Davidic Covenant (2 Sam. 7:1-29; 1 Chr. 17:1-27)
  3. The Military Triumphs of David (2 Sam. 8:1–10:19; 1 Chr. 18:1–20:8)

B. David's Sins (2 Sam. 11:1-27)
  1. David's Adultery with Bathsheba (2 Sam. 11:1-5)
  2. David's Murder of Uriah the Hitite (2 Sam. 11:6-27)

C. David's Problems (2 Sam. 12:1–24:25; 1 Chr. 21:1–27:34)
  1. David's House Suffers (2 Sam. 12:1–13:36)
    a. Nathan's prophecy against David (2 Sam. 12:1-14)
    b. David's son dies (2 Sam. 12:15-25)
    c. Joab's loyalty to David (2 Sam. 12:26-31)
    d. Amnon's incest (2 Sam. 13:1-20)
    e. Amnon's murder (2 Sam. 13:21-36)
  2. David's Kingdom Suffers (2 Sam. 13:37–24:25; 1 Chr. 21:1–27:34)
    a. Absalom's rebellion (2 Sam. 13:37–17:29)
    b. Absalom's murder (2 Sam. 18:1-33)
    c. David's restoration as king (2 Sam. 19:1–20:26)
    d. David's kingship evaluated (2 Sam. 21:1–23:39)
    e. David's numbering of the people (2 Sam. 24:1–24:25; 1 Chr. 21:1-30)

D. David's Preparation and Organization for the Temple (1 Chr. 22:1–27:34)

E. David's Last Days (1 Kin. 1:1–2:11; 1 Chr. 28:1–29:30)
  1. David's Failing Health: Abishag the Shunammite (1 Kin. 1:1-4)
  2. Adonijah's Attempt to Seize the Kingdom (1 Kin. 1:5-9)
  3. Solomon's Anointing as King (1 Kin. 1:10-40; 1 Chr. 29:20-25)
  4. Adonijah's Submission (1 Kin. 1:41-53)
  5. David's Last Words (1 Kin. 2:1-9; 1 Chr. 28:1–29:25)
    a. David's words for Israel (1 Chr. 28:1-8)
    b. David's words for Solomon (1 Kin. 2:1-9; 1 Chr. 28:9–29:19)
  6. David's Death (1 Kin. 2:10,11; 1 Chr. 29:26-30)

IV. THE KINGSHIP OF SOLOMON (1 Kin. 2:12–11:43; 1 Chr. 29:20-30; 2 Chr. 1:1–9:31)

A. Solomon's Kingship Begins (1 Kin. 2:12–4:34; 1 Chr. 29:20-30; 2 Chr. 1:1-17)
  1. Solomon's Kingship Established (1 Kin. 2:12; 1 Chr. 29:20–2 Chr. 1:1)
  2. Solomon's Adversaries Removed (1 Kin. 2:13-46)
  3. Solomon's Wedding to Pharaoh's Daughter (1 Kin. 3:1)
  4. Solomon's Spiritual Condition (1 Kin. 3:2,3)
  5. Solomon's Sacrifice at Gibeon (1 Kin. 3:4; 2 Chr. 1:2-6)
  6. Solomon's Dream and Prayer for Wisdom (1 Kin. 3:5-15; 2 Chr. 1:7-12)
  7. Solomon's Judging of the Harlots with God's Wisdom (1 Kin. 3:16-28)
  8. Solomon's Officers, His Power, Wealth, and Wisdom (1 Kin. 4:1-34; 2 Chr. 1:13-17)

B. Solomon's Splendor (1 Kin. 5:1–8:66; 2 Chr. 2:1–7:22)
  1. Preparations for the Building of the Temple (1 Kin. 5:1-18; 2 Chr. 2:1-18)
  2. The Building of the Temple (1 Kin. 6:1-38; 2 Chr. 3:1-14)

3. The Building of the Royal Palace (1 Kin. 7:1-12)
4. The Making of the Vessels for the Temple (1 Kin. 7:13-51; 2 Chr. 3:15–5:1)
5. The Dedication and Completion of the Temple (1 Kin. 8:1-66; 2 Chr. 5:2–7:22)

C. Solomon's Demise (1 Kin. 9:1–11:43; 2 Chr. 8:1–9:31)
1. Davidic Covenant Repeated (1 Kin. 9:1-9)
2. Solomon's Disobedience to the Covenant (1 Kin. 9:10–11:8; 2 Chr. 8:1–9:12)
3. Solomon's Chastening for Breaking the Covenant (1 Kin. 11:9-40; 2 Chr. 9:13-28)
4. Solomon's Death (1 Kin. 11:41-43; 2 Chr. 9:29-31)

V. THE KINGDOM DIVIDED (1 Kin. 12:1–22:53; 2 Kin. 1:1–17:41; 2 Chr. 10:1–28:27)

A. The Kingdom Divides (1 Kin. 12:1–14:31; 2 Chr. 10:1–28:27)
1. The Division's Cause (1 Kin. 12:1-24)
2. Jeroboam, King of Israel (1 Kin. 12:25–14:20; 2 Chr. 10:1–13:22)
3. Rehoboam, King of Judah (1 Kin. 14:21-31; 2 Chr. 10:1–12:16)

B. Judah's Two Kings (1 Kin. 15:1-24; 2 Chr. 13:1–16:14)
1. Abijam, a.k.a. Joram, King of Judah (1 Kin. 15:1-8; 2 Chr. 13:1-22)
2. Asa, King of Judah (1 Kin. 15:9-24; 2 Chr. 14:1–16:14)

C. Israel's Five Kings (1 Kin. 15:25–16:28; 2 Chr.16:1-6)
1. Nadab, King of Israel (1 Kin. 15:25-31)
2. Baasha, King of Israel (1 Kin. 15:32–16:7; 2 Chr. 16:1-6)
3. Elah, King of Israel (1 Kin. 16:8-14)
4. Zimri, King of Israel (1 Kin. 16:15-20)
5. Omri, King of Israel (1 Kin. 16:21-28)

D. Ahab, King of Israel (1 Kin. 16:29–22:40; 2 Chr. 16:1-34)
1. Ahab's Sin (1 Kin. 16:29-34)
2. Elijah the Prophet (1 Kin. 17:1–19:21; 2 Chr. 16:1-34)
3. Wars with Syria (1 Kin. 20:1-43)
4. Naboth Swindled and Killed (1 Kin. 21:1-16)
5. Ahab's Death (1 Kin. 21:17–22:40)

E. Jehoshaphat, King of Judah (1 Kin. 22:41-50; 2 Chr. 17:1–21:3)
F. Ahaziah, King of Israel (1 Kin. 22:51-53; 2 Kin. 1:1-18; 2 Chr. 20:35-37)
G. Jehoram, a.k.a. Joram, King of Israel (2 Kin. 2:1–8:15; 2 Chr. 22:5-7)
H. Jehoram, King of Judah (2 Kin. 8:16-24; 2 Chr. 21:4-20)
I. Ahaziah, King of Judah (2 Kin. 8:25–9:29; 2 Chr. 22:1-9)
J. Jehu, King of Israel (2 Kin. 9:30–10:36; 2 Chr. 22:7-12)
K. Athaliah, Queen of Judah (2 Kin. 11:1-16; 2 Chr. 22:10–23:21)
L. Joash, King of Judah (2 Kin. 11:17–12:21; 2 Chr. 24:1–24:27)
M. Jehoahaz, King of Israel (2 Kin. 13:1-9)
N. Jehoash, a.k.a. Joash, King of Israel (2 Kin. 13:10-25; 2 Chr. 25:17-24)
O. Amaziah, King of Judah (2 Kin. 14:1-22; 2 Chr. 25:1-28)
P. Jeroboam II, King of Israel (2 Kin. 14:23-29)
Q. Uzziah, a.k.a., Azariah, King of Judah (2 Kin. 15:1-7; 2 Chr. 26:1-23)
R. Zechariah, King of Israel (2 Kin. 15:8-12)
S. Shallum, King of Israel (2 Kin. 15:13-15)
T. Menahem, King of Israel (2 Kin. 15:16-22)
U. Pekahiah, King of Israel (2 Kin. 15:23-26)
V. Pekah, King of Israel (2 Kin. 15:27-31)
W. Jotham, King of Judah (2 Kin. 15:32-38; 2 Chr. 27:1-9)
X. Ahaz, King of Judah (2 Kin. 16:1-20; 2 Chr. 28:1-27)
Y. Hoshea, King of Israel (2 Kin. 17:1-41)

VI. THE SURVIVING KINGDOM OF JUDAH (2 Kin. 18:1–25:30; 2 Chr. 29:1–36:23)

A. Hezekiah, King of Judah (2 Kin. 18:1–20:21; 2 Chr. 29:1–32:33; Is. 36–39)
B. Manasseh, King of Judah (2 Kin. 21:1-18; 2 Chr. 33:1-20)
C. Amon, King of Judah (2 Kin. 21:19-26; 2 Chr. 33:21-25)
D. Josiah, King of Judah (2 Kin. 22:1–23:30; 2 Chr. 34:1–35:27)
E. Jehoahaz, King of Judah (2 Kin. 23:31-34; 2 Chr. 36:1-4)
F. Jehoiakim, King of Judah (2 Kin. 23:35–24:7; 2 Chr. 36:4-8)
G. Jehoiachin, King of Judah (2 Kin. 24:8-16; 2 Chr. 36:9,10)
H. Zedekiah, King of Judah (2 Kin. 24:17–25:21; 2 Chr. 36:11-21)
I. Gedaliah, Governor of Judah (2 Kin. 25:22-26)
J. Jehoiachin Released in Babylon (2 Kin. 25:27-30)
K. Cyrus Decrees Rebuilding in Jerusalem (2 Chr. 36:22,23)

Introduction to the

PROPHETS

The writing prophets of the OT fall into two groups: the 4 major prophets—Isaiah, Jeremiah, Ezekiel, and Daniel—and the 12 minor prophets—Hosea, Joel, Amos, Obadiah, Jonah, Micah, Nahum, Habakkuk, Zephaniah, Haggai, Zechariah, and Malachi. Lamentations falls into the major-prophet grouping because of its connection with Jeremiah.

Besides these, the OT regarded others as prophets. Such prophets as Gad, Nathan, Elijah, and Elisha were typical of the nonwriting prophets. In a sense, John the Baptist as a forerunner of Jesus was a prophet who belonged to the OT era.

The following table gives the sequence and approximate dates and direction of ministry for the writing prophets, with "Israel" designating the northern kingdom and "Judah" the southern:

Prophets Organized by Date and Direction of Ministry

Prophet	Ministered To	In the Years
Obadiah	Edom	850–840 B.C.
Joel	Judah	835–796 B.C.
Jonah	Ninevah	784–774 B.C.
Amos	Israel	763–755 B.C.
Hosea	Israel	755–710 B.C.
Isaiah	Judah	739–680 B.C.
Micah	Judah	735–710 B.C.
Nahum	Ninevah	650–630 B.C.
Zephaniah	Judah	635–625 B.C.
Jeremiah	Judah	627–570 B.C.
Habakkuk	Judah	620–605 B.C.
Daniel	Babylon	605–536 B.C.
Ezekiel	Babylon	593–570 B.C.
Haggai	Judah	520–505 B.C.
Zechariah	Judah	520–470 B.C.
Malachi	Judah	437–417 B.C.

Another way of categorizing the writing prophets relates them chronologically to the captivities of Israel (ca. 722 B.C.) and Judah (ca. 586 B.C.):

Prophets Organized by Writing Date and Captivity

Pre-Exilic		Exilic	Post-Exilic
Obadiah	Micah	Daniel	Haggai
Joel	Nahum	Ezekiel	Zechariah
Jonah	Zephaniah		Malachi
Amos	Jeremiah		
Hosea	Habakkuk		
Isaiah			

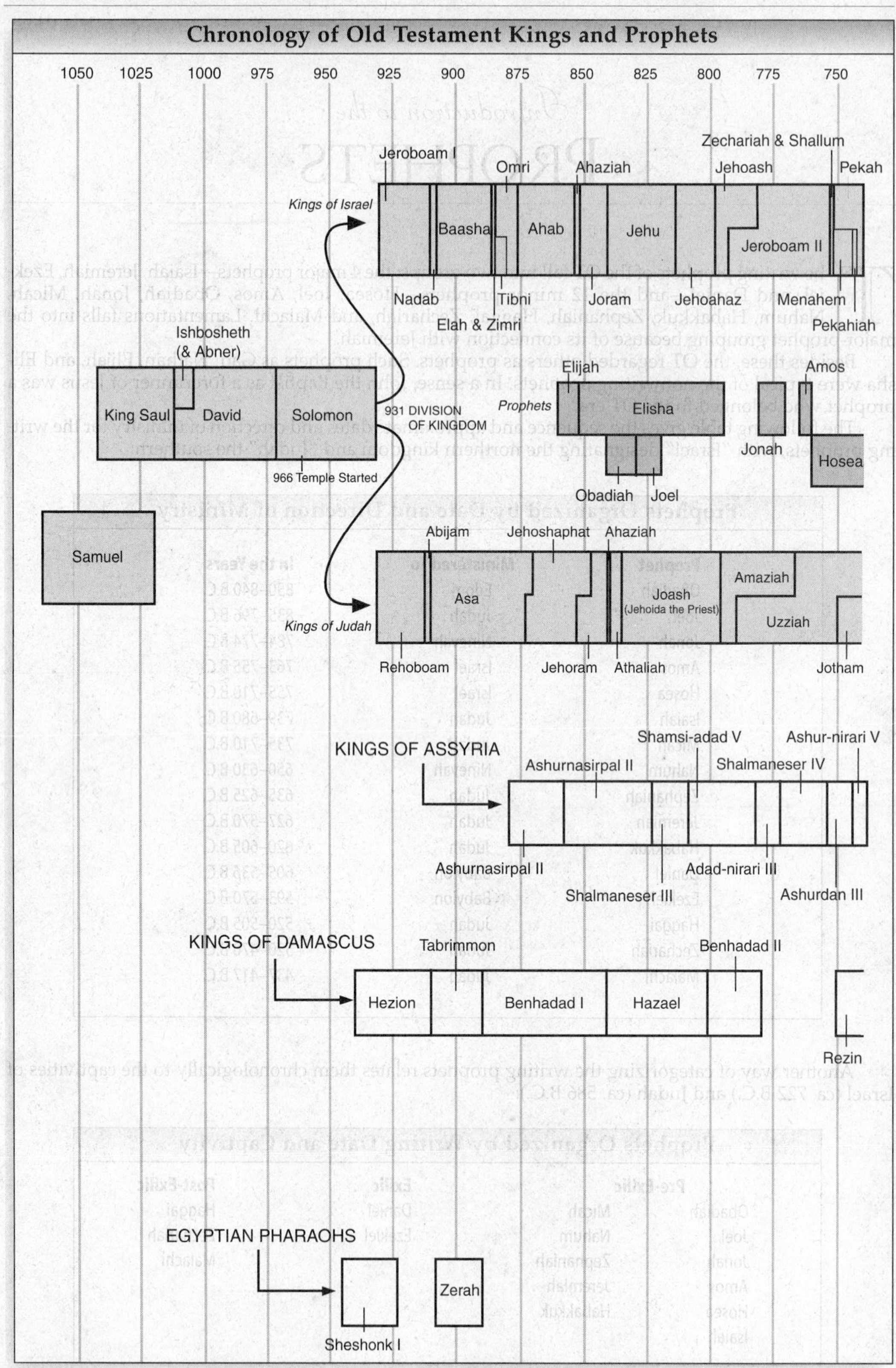
Chronology of Old Testament Kings and Prophets
1050
1025
1000
975
950
925
900
875
850
825
800
775
750
Kings of Israel
Jeroboam I
Omri
Ahaziah
Zechariah & Shallum
Jehoash
Pekah
Baasha
Ahab
Jehu
Jeroboam II
Nadab
Tibni
Elah & Zimri
Joram
Jehoahaz
Menahem
Pekahiah
Ishbosheth
(& Abner)
King Saul
David
Solomon
931 DIVISION
OF KINGDOM
966 Temple Started
Prophets
Elijah
Elisha
Amos
Jonah
Hosea
Obadiah
Joel
Samuel
Kings of Judah
Abijam
Jehoshaphat
Ahaziah
Asa
Joash
(Jehoida the Priest)
Amaziah
Uzziah
Rehoboam
Jehoram
Athaliah
Jotham
KINGS OF ASSYRIA
Shamsi-adad V
Ashur-nirari V
Ashurnasirpal II
Shalmaneser IV
Ashurnasirpal II
Adad-nirari III
Shalmaneser III
Ashurdan III
KINGS OF DAMASCUS
Tabrimmon
Benhadad II
Hezion
Benhadad I
Hazael
Rezin
EGYPTIAN PHARAOHS
Zerah
Sheshonk I

Chronology of Old Testament Kings and Prophets

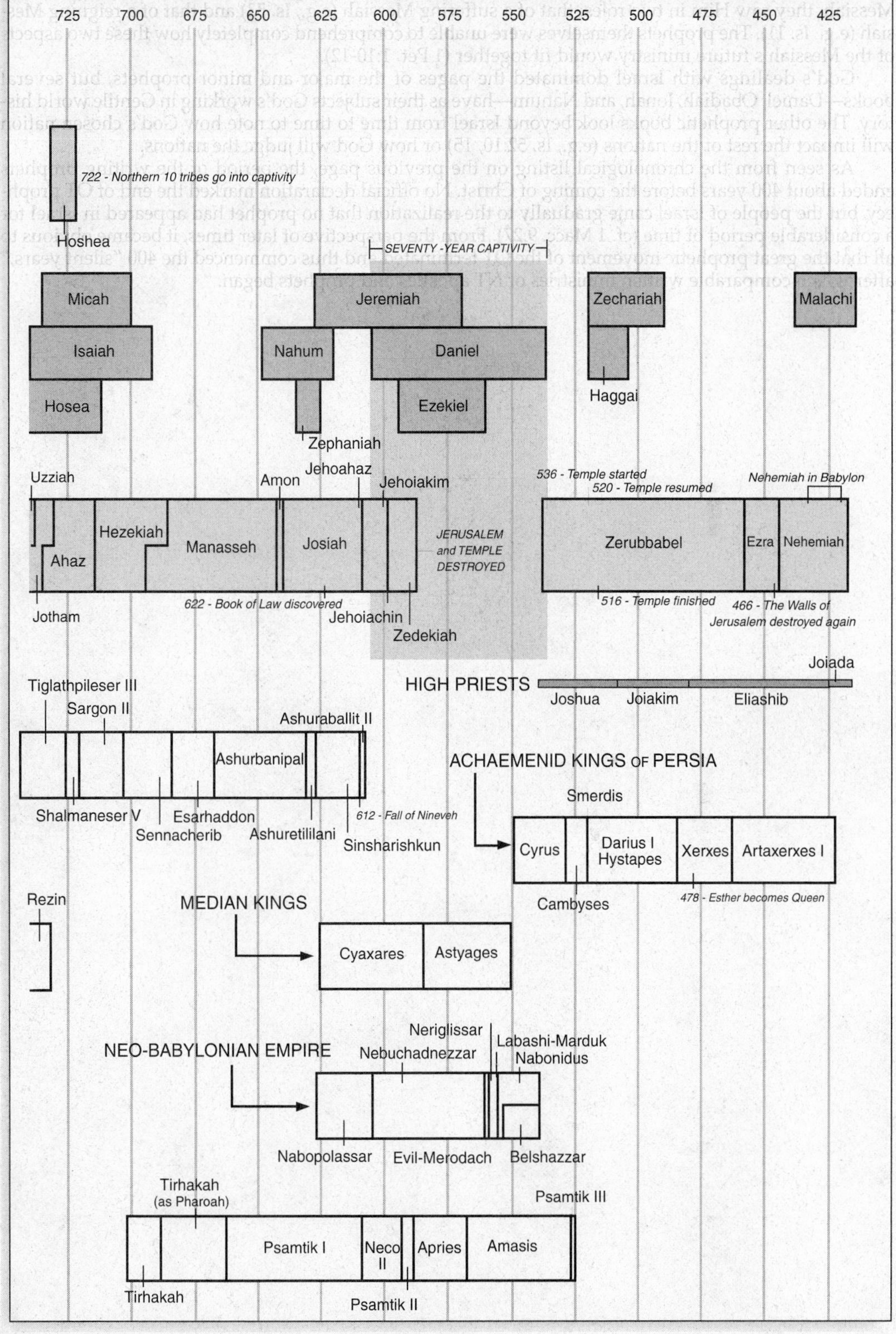

725 700 675 650 625 600 575 550 525 500 475 450 425

722 - Northern 10 tribes go into captivity
Hoshea
SEVENTY -YEAR CAPTIVITY

Micah
Isaiah
Hosea
Jeremiah
Nahum
Daniel
Ezekiel
Zephaniah
Zechariah
Haggai
Malachi

Uzziah
Amon
Jehoahaz
Jehoiakim
Hezekiah
Ahaz
Manasseh
Josiah
JERUSALEM and TEMPLE DESTROYED
Jotham
622 - Book of Law discovered
Jehoiachin
Zedekiah

536 - Temple started
520 - Temple resumed
Nehemiah in Babylon
Zerubbabel
Ezra
Nehemiah
516 - Temple finished
466 - The Walls of Jerusalem destroyed again

HIGH PRIESTS
Joshua
Joiakim
Eliashib
Joiada

Tiglathpileser III
Sargon II
Ashuraballit II
Ashurbanipal
Shalmaneser V
Sennacherib
Esarhaddon
Ashuretililani
612 - Fall of Nineveh
Sinsharishkun

ACHAEMENID KINGS OF PERSIA
Smerdis
Cyrus
Darius I Hystapes
Xerxes
Artaxerxes I
Cambyses
478 - Esther becomes Queen

Rezin

MEDIAN KINGS
Cyaxares
Astyages

NEO-BABYLONIAN EMPIRE
Neriglissar
Nebuchadnezzar
Labashi-Marduk
Nabonidus
Nabopolassar
Evil-Merodach
Belshazzar

Tirhakah (as Pharoah)
Psamtik III
Psamtik I
Neco II
Apries
Amasis
Tirhakah
Psamtik II

Messages of the writing prophets sometimes related to the prophet's immediate future (e.g., Is. 7:1-11) and sometimes to the distant future (e.g., Is. 7:12-14). In their frequent predictions about the coming Messiah, they saw Him in two roles: that of a suffering Messiah (e.g., Is. 53) and that of a reigning Messiah (e.g., Is. 11). The prophets themselves were unable to comprehend completely how these two aspects of the Messiah's future ministry would fit together (1 Pet. 1:10-12).

God's dealings with Israel dominated the pages of the major and minor prophets, but several books—Daniel, Obadiah, Jonah, and Nahum—have as their subjects God's working in Gentile world history. The other prophetic books look beyond Israel from time to time to note how God's chosen nation will impact the rest of the nations (e.g., Is. 52:10, 15) or how God will judge the nations.

As seen from the chronological listing on the previous page, the period of the writing prophets ended about 400 years before the coming of Christ. No official declaration marked the end of OT prophecy, but the people of Israel came gradually to the realization that no prophet had appeared in Israel for a considerable period of time (cf. 1 Macc. 9:27). From the perspective of later times, it became obvious to all that the great prophetic movement of the OT terminated and thus commenced the 400 "silent years," after which comparable written ministries of NT apostles and prophets began.

The First Book of Moses Called
GENESIS

Title

The English title, Genesis, comes from the Greek translation (Septuagint, LXX) meaning "origins"; whereas, the Hebrew title is derived from the Bible's very first word, translated "in the beginning." Genesis serves to introduce the Pentateuch (the first 5 books of the OT) and the entire Bible. The influence of Genesis in Scripture is demonstrated by its being quoted over 35 times in the NT and hundreds of allusions appearing in both Testaments. The story line of salvation which begins in Gen. 3 is not completed until Rev. 21,22 where the eternal kingdom of redeemed believers is gloriously pictured.

Author and Date

While 1) the author does not identify himself in Genesis and 2) Genesis ends almost 3 centuries before Moses was born, both the OT (Ex. 17:14; Num. 33:2; Josh. 8:31; 1 Kin. 2:3; 2 Kin. 14:6; Ezra 6:18; Neh. 13:1; Dan. 9:11,13; Mal. 4:4) and the NT (Matt. 8:4; Mark 12:26; Luke 16:29; 24:27,44; John 5:46; 7:22; Acts 15:1; Rom. 10:19; 1 Cor. 9:9; 2 Cor. 3:15) ascribe this composition to Moses, who is the fitting author in light of his educational background (cf. Acts 7:22). No compelling reasons have been forthcoming to challenge Mosaic authorship. Genesis was written after the Exodus (ca. 1445 B.C.), but before Moses' death (ca. 1405 B.C.). For a brief biographical sketch of Moses read Ex. 1–6.

Background and Setting

The initial setting for Genesis is eternity past. God then, by willful act and divine Word, spoke all creation into existence, furnished it, and finally breathed life into a lump of dirt which He fashioned in His image to become Adam. God made mankind the crowning point of His creation, i.e., His companions who would enjoy fellowship with Him and bring glory to His name.

The historical background for the early events in Genesis is clearly Mesopotamian. While it is difficult to pinpoint precisely the historical moment for which this book was written, Israel first heard Genesis sometime prior to crossing the Jordan River and entering the Promised Land (ca. 1405 B.C.).

Genesis has 3 distinct, sequential geographical settings: 1) Mesopotamia (chaps. 1–11); 2) the Promised Land (chaps. 12–36); and 3) Egypt (chaps. 37–50). The time frames of these 3 segments are: 1) Creation to ca. 2090 B.C.; 2) 2090–1897 B.C.; and 3) 1897–1804 B.C. Genesis covers more time than the remaining books of the Bible combined.

Historical and Theological Themes

In this book of beginnings, God revealed Himself and a worldview to Israel which contrasted, at times sharply, with the worldview of Israel's neighbors. The author made no attempt to defend the existence of God or to present a systematic discussion of His person and works. Rather, Israel's God distinguished Himself clearly from the alleged gods of her neighbors. Theological foundations are revealed which include God the Father, God the Son, God the Holy Spirit, man, sin, redemption, covenant, promise, Satan and angels, kingdom, revelation, Israel, judgment, and blessing.

Genesis 1–11 (primeval history) reveals the origins of the universe, i.e., the beginnings of time and space and many of the firsts in human experience, such as marriage, family, the Fall, sin, redemption, judgment, and nations. Genesis 12–50 (patriarchal history) explained to Israel how they came into existence as a family whose ancestry could be traced to Eber (hence the "Hebrews"; Gen. 10:24,25) and even more remotely to Shem, the son of Noah (hence the "Semites"; Gen. 10:21). God's people came to understand not only their ancestry and family history, but also the origins of their institutions, customs, languages, and different cultures, especially basic human experiences such as sin and death.

Because they were preparing to enter Canaan and dispossess the Canaanite inhabitants of their homes and properties, God revealed their enemies' background. In addition, they needed to understand the actual basis of the war they were about to declare in light of the immorality of killing, consistent with the other 4 books that Moses was writing (Exodus, Leviticus, Numbers, and Deuteronomy). Ultimately, the Jewish nation would understand a selected portion of preceding world history and the inaugural background of Israel as a basis by which they would live in their new beginnings under Joshua's leadership in the land which had previously been promised to their original patriarchal forefather, Abraham.

Genesis 12:1-3 established a primary focus on God's promises to Abraham. This narrowed their view from the entire world of peoples in Gen. 1–11 to one small nation, Israel, through whom God would progressively accomplish His redemptive plan. This underscored Israel's mission to be "a light to the Gentiles" (Is. 42:6). God promised land, descendants (seed), and blessing. This 3-fold promise became, in turn, the basis of the covenant with Abraham (Gen. 15:1-20). The rest of Scripture bears out the fulfillment of these promises.

On a larger scale, Gen. 1–11 set forth a singular message about the character and works of God. In the sequence of accounts which make up these chapters of Scripture, a pattern emerges which reveals God's abundant grace as He responded to the willful disobedience of mankind. Without exception, in each account God increased the manifestation of His grace. But also without exception, man responded in greater sinful rebellion. In biblical words, the more sin abounded the more did God's grace abound (cf. Rom. 5:20).

One final theme of both theological and historical significance sets Genesis apart from other books of Scripture, in that the first book of Scripture corresponds closely with the final book. In the book of Revelation, the paradise which was lost in Genesis will be regained. The apostle John clearly presented the events recorded in his book as future resolutions to the problems which began as a result of the curse in Gen. 3. His focus is upon the effects of the Fall in the undoing of creation and the manner in which God rids His creation of the curse effect. In John's own words, "And there shall be no more curse" (Rev. 22:3). Not surprisingly, in the final chapter of God's Word, believers will find themselves back in the Garden of Eden, the eternal paradise of God, eating from the tree of life (Rev. 22:1-14). At that time, they will partake, wearing robes washed in the blood of the Lamb (Rev. 22:14).

Interpretive Challenges

Grasping the individual messages of Genesis which make up the larger plan and purpose of the book presents no small challenge since both the individual accounts and the book's overall message offer important lessons to faith and works. Genesis presents creation by divine fiat, *ex nihilo*, i.e., "out of nothing." Three traumatic events of epic proportions, namely the Fall, the universal Flood, and the Dispersion of nations are presented as historical backdrop in order to understand world history. From Abraham on, the pattern is to focus on God's redemption and blessing.

The customs of Genesis often differ considerably from those of our modern day. They must be explained against their ancient Near Eastern background. Each custom must be treated according to the immediate context of the passage before any attempt is made to explain it based on customs recorded in extrabiblical sources or even elsewhere in Scripture.

Outline

Genesis by content is comprised of two basic sections: 1) Primitive history (Gen. 1–11) and 2) Patriarchal history (Gen. 12–50). Primitive history records 4 major events: 1) Creation (Gen. 1,2); 2) the Fall (Gen. 3–5); 3) the Flood (Gen. 6–9); and 4) the Dispersion (Gen. 10,11). Patriarchal history spotlights 4 great men: 1) Abraham (Gen. 12:1–25:8); 2) Isaac (Gen. 21:1–35:29); 3) Jacob (Gen. 25:21–50:14); and 4) Joseph (Gen. 30:22–50:26).

The literary structure of Genesis is built on the frequently recurring phrase "the history/genealogy of" and is the basis for the following outline.

Outline

I. The Creation of Heaven and Earth (1:1–2:3)

II. The Generations of the Heavens and the Earth (2:4–4:26)
- A. Adam and Eve in Eden (2:4-25)
- B. The Fall and Its Outcomes (chap. 3)
- C. Murder of a Brother (4:1-24)
- D. Hope in the Descendants of Seth (4:25,26)

III. The Generations of Adam (5:1–6:8)
- A. Genealogy—Seth to Noah (chap. 5)
- B. Rampant Sin Prior to the Flood (6:1-8)

IV. The Generations of Noah (6:9–9:29)
- A. Preparation for the Flood (6:9–7:9)
- B. The Flood and Deliverance (7:10–8:19)
- C. God's Noahic Covenant (8:20–9:17)

D. The History of Noah's Descendants (9:18-29)

V. The Generations of Shem, Ham, and Japheth (10:1–11:9)

A. The Nations (chap. 10)

B. Dispersion of the Nations (11:1-9)

VI. The Generations of Shem: Genealogy of Shem to Terah (11:10-26)

VII. The Generations of Terah (11:27–25:11)

A. Genealogy (11:27-32)

B. The Abrahamic Covenant: His Land and People (12:1–22:19)

1. Journey to the Promised Land (12:1-9)
2. Redemption from Egypt (12:10-20)
3. Division of the land (chap. 13)
4. Victory over the kings (chap. 14)
5. The covenant ratified (chap. 15)
6. Rejection of Hagar and Ishmael (chap. 16)
7. The covenant confirmed (chap. 17)
8. Birth of Isaac foretold (18:1-15)
9. Sodom and Gomorrah (18:16–19:38)
10. Philistine encounter (chap. 20)
11. Isaac's birth (chap. 21)
12. Abraham's act of faith with Isaac (22:1-19)

C. Abraham's Promised Seed (22:20–25:11)

1. Rebekah's background (22:20-24)
2. Death of Sarah (chap. 23)
3. Isaac's marriage to Rebekah (chap. 24)
4. Isaac the only heir (25:1-6)
5. Death of Abraham (25:7-11)

VIII. The Generations of Ishmael (25:12-18)

IX. The Generations of Isaac (25:19–35:29)

A. Competition Between Esau and Jacob (25:19-34)

B. Covenant Blessings to Isaac (chap. 26)

C. Jacob's Deception for the Blessing (27:1-40)

D. Blessing on Jacob in a Foreign Land (27:41–32:32)

1. Jacob sent to Laban (27:41–28:9)
2. Angel at Bethel (28:10-22)
3. Disagreements with Laban (29:1-30)
4. Promised seed (29:31–30:24)
5. Departure from Aram (30:25–31:55)
6. Angels at Mahanaim and Penuel (chap. 32)

E. Esau's Reunion and Reconciliation with Jacob (33:1-17)

F. Events and Deaths from Shechem to Mamre (33:18–35:29)

X. The Generations of Esau (36:1–37:1)

XI. The Generations of Jacob (37:2–50:26)

A. Joseph's Dreams (37:2-11)

B. Family Tragedy (37:12–38:30)

C. Vice Regency over Egypt (chaps. 39–41)

D. Reunion with Family (chaps. 42–45)

E. Transition to Exodus (chaps. 46–50)

1. Journey to Egypt (46:1-27)
2. Occupation in Goshen (46:28–47:31)
3. Blessings on the twelve tribes (48:1–49:28)
4. Death and burial of Jacob in Canaan (49:29–50:14)
5. Death of Joseph in Egypt (50:15-26)

The History of Creation

1 In the [a]beginning [b]God created the
heavens and the earth. 2 The earth was
[c]without form, and void; and darkness
[1]*was* on the face of the deep. [d]And the Spirit of God was hovering over the face of the
waters.
3 [e]Then God said, [f]"Let there be [g]light";
and there was light. 4 And God saw the
light, that *it was* good; and God divided
the light from the darkness. 5 God called
the light Day, and the [h]darkness He called
Night. [2]So the evening and the morning
were the first day.
6 Then God said, [i]"Let there be a [3]firma-
ment in the midst of the waters, and let it
divide the waters from the waters." 7 Thus
God made the firmament, [j]and divided the
waters which *were* under the firmament
from the waters which *were* [k]above the firmament; and it was so. 8 And God called
the firmament Heaven. So the evening and
the morning were the second day.
9 Then God said, [l]"Let the waters under
the heavens be gathered together into one
place, and [m]let the dry *land* appear"; and it
was so. 10 And God called the dry *land*
Earth, and the gathering together of the
waters He called Seas. And God saw that *it
was* good.
11 Then God said, "Let the earth [n]bring
forth grass, the herb *that* yields seed, *and* the
[o]fruit tree *that* yields fruit according to its
kind, whose seed *is* in itself, on the earth";
and it was so. 12 And the earth brought forth
grass, the herb *that* yields seed according to
its kind, and the tree *that* yields fruit, whose
seed *is* in itself according to its kind. And
God saw that *it was* good. 13 So the evening
and the morning were the third day.
14 Then God said, "Let there be [p]lights in

CHAPTER 1

1 [a] Ps. 102:25; Is. 40:21; [John 1:1-3; Heb. 1:10] [b] Gen. 2:4; [Ps. 8:3; 89:11; 90:2]; Is. 44:24; Acts 17:24; Rom. 1:20; [Heb. 1:2; 11:3]; Rev. 4:11
2 [c] Jer. 4:23 [d] [Gen. 6:3]; Job 26:13; Ps. 33:6; 104:30; Is. 40:13, 14 [1] Words in italic type have been added for clarity. They are not found in the original Hebrew or Aramaic.
3 [e] Ps. 33:6, 9 [f] 2 Cor. 4:6 [g] [Heb. 11:3]
5 [h] Job 37:18; Ps. 19:2; 33:6; 74:16; 104:20; 136:5; Jer. 10:12 [2] Lit. *And evening was, and morning was, a day, one.*
6 [i] Job 37:18; Jer. 10:12; 2 Pet. 3:5 [3] *expanse*
7 [j] Job 38:8-11; Prov. 8:27-29 [k] Ps. 148:4
9 [l] Job 26:10; Ps. 104:6-9; Prov. 8:29; Jer. 5:22; 2 Pet. 3:5 [m] Ps. 24:1, 2; 33:7; 95:5
11 [n] Ps. 65:9-13; 104:14; Heb. 6:7 [o] 2 Sam. 16:1; Luke 6:44
14 [p] Deut. 4:19; Ps. 74:16; 136:5-9

1:1–2:3 This description of God creating heaven and earth is understood to be: 1) recent, i.e., thousands not millions of years ago; 2) *ex nihilo,* i.e., out of nothing; and 3) special, i.e., in 6 consecutive 24 hour periods called "days" and further distinguished as such by this phrase, "the evening and the morning." Scripture does not support a creation date earlier than about 10,000 years ago. **In the beginning.** While God exists eternally (Ps. 90:2), this marked the beginning of the universe in time and space. In explaining Israel's identity and purpose to her on the plains of Moab, God wanted His people to know about the origin of the world in which they found themselves. **God.** Elohim is a general term for deity and a name for the True God, though used also at times for pagan gods (31:30), angels (Ps. 8:5), men (Ps. 82:6), and judges (Ex. 21:6). Moses made no attempt to defend the existence of God, which is assumed, or explain what He was like in person and works which is treated elsewhere (cf. Is. 43:10,13). Both are to be believed by faith (cf. Heb. 11:3,6). **created.** This word is used here of God's creative activity alone, although it occasionally is used elsewhere of matter which already existed (Is. 65:18). Context demands in no uncertain terms that this was a creation without preexisting material (as does other Scripture: cf. Is. 40:28; 45:8,12,18; 48:13; Jer. 10:16; Acts 17:24). **the heavens and the earth.** All of God's creation is incorporated into this summary statement which includes all 6, consecutive days of creation.

1:2 without form, and void. This means "not finished in its shape and as yet uninhabited by creatures" (cf. Is. 45:18,19; Jer. 4:23). God would quickly (in 6 days) decorate His initial creation (1:2–2:3). **deep.** Sometimes referred to as primordial waters, this is the term used to describe the earth's water-covered surface before the dry land emerged (1:9,10). Jonah used this word to describe the watery abyss in which he found himself submerged (Jon. 2:5). **Spirit of God.** Not only did God the Holy Spirit participate in creation, but so did God the Son (cf. John 1:1-3; Col. 1:16; Heb. 1:2).

1:3 God said. God effortlessly spoke light into existence (cf. Pss. 33:6; 148:5). This dispelled the darkness of v. 2. **light.** The greater and lesser lights (the sun and moon) were created later (1:14-19) on the fourth day. Here, God was the provider of light (2 Cor. 4:6) and will in eternity future be the source of light (cf. Rev. 21:23).

1:4 good. Good for the purposes it was intended to serve (cf. 1:31).

1:4,5 divided...called. After the initial creation, God continued to complete His universe. Once God separated certain things, He then named them. Separating and naming were acts of dominion and served as a pattern for man, who would also name a portion of God's creation over which God gave him dominion (2:19,20).

1:5 first day. God established the pattern of creation in 7 days which constituted a complete week. "Day" can refer to: 1) the light portion of a 24 hour period (1:5,14); 2) an extended period of time (2:4); or 3) the 24 hour period which basically refers to a full rotation of the earth on its axis, called evening and morning. This cannot mean an age, but only a day, reckoned by the Jews from sunset to sunset (vv. 8,13,19,23,31). "Day" with numerical adjectives in Hebrew always refers to a 24 hour period. Comparing the order of the week in Ex. 20:8-11 with the creation week confirms this understanding of the time element. Such a cycle of light and dark means that the earth was rotating on its axis, so that there was a source of light on one side of the earth, though the sun was not yet created (v. 16).

1:6 firmament. The portion of God's creation named "heavens," that which man saw when he looked up, i.e., the atmospheric and stellar heaven.

1:7 under the firmament. Refers to subterranean reservoirs (cf. 7:11). **above the firmament.** This could possibly have been a canopy of water vapor which acted to make the earth like a hothouse, provided uniform temperature, inhibited mass air movements, caused mist to fall, and filtered out ultraviolet rays, thus extending life.

1:9,10 dry *land*. This was caused by a tremendous, cataclysmic upheaval of the earth's surface, and the rising and sinking of the land, which caused the waters to plunge into the low places, forming the seas, the continents and islands, the rivers and lakes (cf. Job 38:4-11; Ps. 104:6-9).

1:11 whose seed *is* in itself. The principle of reproduction that marks all life (cf. vv. 22,24,28).

1:11,12 according to its kind. God set in motion a providential process whereby the vegetable kingdom could reproduce through seeds which would maintain each one's unique characteristics. The same phrase is used to describe the perpetuating reproduction of animals within their created species (vv. 21,24,25), and indicates that evolution, which proposes reproduction across species lines, is a false explanation of origins.

1:14 lights. Cf. v. 16. For 3 days there had been light (v. 4) in the day as though there were a sun, and lesser light at night as though there

the firmament of the heavens to divide the
day from the night; and let them be for
signs and [q]seasons, and for days and years;
15 and let them be for lights in the firmament of the heavens to give light on the
earth"; and it was so. 16 Then God made
two great [4]lights: the [r]greater light to rule
the day, and the [s]lesser light to rule the
night. *He made* [t]the stars also. 17 God set
them in the firmament of the [u]heavens to
give light on the earth, 18 and to [v]rule over
the day and over the night, and to divide
the light from the darkness. And God saw
that *it was* good. 19 So the evening and the
morning were the fourth day.
20 Then God said, "Let the waters
abound with an abundance of living [5]crea-
tures, and let birds fly above the earth
across the face of the [6]firmament of the
heavens." 21 So [w]God created great sea
creatures and every living thing that
moves, with which the waters abounded,
according to their kind, and every winged
bird according to its kind. And God saw
that *it was* good. 22 And God blessed them,
saying, [x]"Be fruitful and multiply, and fill
the waters in the seas, and let birds multiply on the earth." 23 So the evening and the
morning were the fifth day.
24 Then God said, "Let the earth bring
forth the living creature according to its
kind: cattle and creeping thing and beast of
the earth, *each* according to its kind"; and it
was so. 25 And God made the beast of the
earth according to its kind, cattle according
to its kind, and everything that creeps on
the earth according to its kind. And God
saw that *it was* good.
26 Then God said, [y]"Let Us make man in
Our image, according to Our likeness; [z]let
them have dominion over the fish of the sea,
over the birds of the air, and over the cattle,
over [7]all the earth and over every creeping
thing that creeps on the earth." 27 So God
created man [a]in His *own* image; in the image
of God He created him; [b]male and female
He created them. 28 Then God blessed them,
and God said to them, [c]"Be fruitful and
multiply; fill the earth and [d]subdue it; have
dominion over the fish of the sea, over the
birds of the air, and over every living thing
that [8]moves on the earth."
29 And God said, "See, I have given you
every herb *that* yields seed which *is* on the
face of all the earth, and every tree whose
fruit yields seed; [e]to you it shall be for
food. 30 Also, to [f]every beast of the earth,
to every [g]bird of the air, and to everything
that creeps on the earth, in which *there is*
[9]life, *I have given* every green herb for
food"; and it was so. 31 Then [h]God saw
everything that He had made, and indeed
it was very good. So the evening and the
morning were the sixth day.

14 [q]Ps. 104:19
16 [r]Ps. 136:8 [s]Deut. 17:3; Ps. 8:3 [t]Deut. 4:19; Job 38:7; Is. 40:26 [4]*luminaries*
17 [u]Gen. 15:5; Jer. 33:20, 25
18 [v]Jer. 31:35
20 [5]*souls* [6]*expanse*
21 [w]Ps. 104:25-28
22 [x]Gen. 8:17
26 [y]Gen. 9:6; Ps. 100:3; Eccl. 7:29; [Eph. 4:24]; James 3:9 [z]Gen. 9:2; Ps. 8:6-8 [7]Syr. *all the wild animals of*
27 [a]Gen. 5:2; 1 Cor. 11:7 [b]Matt. 19:4; [Mark 10:6-8]
28 [c]Gen. 9:1, 7; Lev. 26:9 [d]1 Cor. 9:27 [8]*moves about on*
29 [e]Gen. 9:3; Ps. 104:14, 15
30 [f]Ps. 145:15 [g]Job 38:41 [9]*a living soul*
31 [h][Ps. 104:24; 1 Tim. 4:4]

were the moon and stars. God could have left it that way, but did not. He created the "lights, sun, moon, and stars," not for light, but to serve as markers for signs, seasons, days, and years. **signs.** Certainly to include: 1) weather (Matt. 16:2,3); 2) testimony to God (Pss. 8,19; Rom. 1:14-20; 3) divine judgment (Joel 2:30,31; Matt. 24:29); and 4) navigation (Matt. 2:1,2). **seasons.** It is the earth's movement in relation to the sun and moon that determines the seasons and the calendar.

1:15-19 two great lights...to divide the light from the darkness. It was God (not some other deity) who created the lights. Israel had originally come from Mesopotamia, where the celestial bodies were worshiped, and more recently from Egypt, where the sun was worshiped as a primary deity. God was revealing to them that the very stars, moons, and planets which Israel's neighbors had worshiped were the products of His creation. Later, they became worshipers of the "host of heaven" (*see note on 2 Kin. 17:16*), which led to their being taken captive out of the Promised Land.

1:20 living creatures. These creatures, including the extraordinarily large ones, included all sorts of fish and mammals, even dinosaurs (*see notes on Job 40:15–41:34*).

1:22 blessed. This is the first occurrence of the word "bless" in Scripture. God's admonition to "be fruitful and multiply" was the substance of the blessing.

1:24,25 cattle...beast. This probably represents all kinds of large, four-legged animals.

1:24 beast of the earth. Different from and larger than the clan of cattle, this would include dinosaurs like Behemoth (Job 40:15ff.).

1:26 Us...Our. The first clear indication of the triunity of God (cf. 3:22; 11:7). The very name of God, Elohim (1:1), is a plural form of El. **man.** The crowning point of creation, a living human, was made in God's image to rule creation. **Our image.** This defined man's unique relation to God. Man is a living being capable of embodying God's communicable attributes (cf. 9:6; Rom. 8:29; Col. 3:10; James 3:9). In his rational life, he was like God in that he could reason and had intellect, will, and emotion. In the moral sense, he was like God because he was good and sinless.

1:26-28 have dominion...subdue. This defined man's unique relation to creation. Man was God's representative in ruling over the creation. The command to rule separated him from the rest of living creation and defined his relationship as above the rest of creation (cf. Ps. 8:6-8).

1:27 male and female. Cf. Matt. 19:4; Mark 10:6. While these two persons equally shared God's image and together exercised dominion over creation, they were by divine design physically diverse in order to accomplish God's mandate to multiply, i.e., neither one could reproduce offspring without the other.

1:28 blessed. This second blessing (cf. 1:22) involved reproduction and dominion. **"Be fruitful and multiply; fill the earth and subdue it..."** God, having just created the universe, created His representative (dominion) and representation (cf. image and likeness). Man would fill the earth and oversee its operation. "Subdue" does not suggest a wild and unruly condition for the creation because God Himself pronounced it "good." Rather, it speaks of a productive ordering of the earth and its inhabitants to yield its riches and accomplish God's purposes.

1:29,30 for food...for food. Prior to the curse (3:14-19), both mankind and beasts were vegetarians.

1:31 very good. What had been pronounced good individually (vv. 4,10,12,18,21,25) was now called "very good" collectively. The words anticipated God's conclusion that it was "not good" for a man to be alone (2:18), which occurred on the sixth day.

2 Thus the heavens and the earth, and
[a]all the host of them, were finished.
2 [b]And on the seventh day God ended His
work which He had done, and He rested
on the seventh day from all His work
which He had done. 3 Then God [c]blessed
the seventh day and sanctified it, because
in it He rested from all His work which
God had created and made.

4 [d]This *is* the [1]history of the heavens and
the earth when they were created, in the
day that the LORD God made the earth and
the heavens, 5 before any [e]plant of the field
was in the earth and before any herb of the
field had grown. For the LORD God had not
[f]caused it to rain on the earth, and *there was*
no man [g]to till the ground; 6 but a mist
went up from the earth and watered the
whole face of the ground.

7 And the LORD God formed man *of* the
[h]dust of the ground, and [i]breathed into his
[j]nostrils the breath of life; and [k]man became a living being.

Life in God's Garden

8 The LORD God planted [l]a garden [m]east-
ward in [n]Eden, and there He put the man
whom He had formed. 9 And out of the
ground the LORD God made [o]every tree
grow that is pleasant to the sight and good
for food. [p]The tree of life *was* also in the
midst of the garden, and the tree of the
knowledge of good and [q]evil.

10 Now a river went out of Eden to
water the garden, and from there it parted
and became four riverheads. 11 The name
of the first *is* Pishon; it *is* the one which
skirts [r]the whole land of Havilah, where
there is gold. 12 And the gold of that land *is*
good. [s]Bdellium and the onyx stone *are*
there. 13 The name of the second river *is*
Gihon; it *is* the one which goes around the
whole land of Cush. 14 The name of the
third river *is* [t]Hiddekel;[2] it *is* the one
which goes toward the east of [3]Assyria.
The fourth river *is* the Euphrates.

15 Then the LORD God took [4]the man
and put him in the garden of Eden to [5]tend
and keep it. 16 And the LORD God commanded the man, saying, "Of every tree of
the garden you may freely eat; 17 but of the
tree of the knowledge of good and evil

CHAPTER 2
1 [a]Ps. 33:6
2 [b]Ex. 20:9-11; 31:17; Heb. 4:4, 10
3 [c][Is. 58:13]
4 [d]Gen. 1:1; Ps. 90:1, 2 [1]Heb. *toledoth*, lit. *generations*
5 [e]Gen. 1:11, 12 [f]Gen. 7:4; Job 5:10; 38:26-28 [g]Gen. 3:23
7 [h]Gen. 3:19, 23; Ps. 103:14 [i]Job 33:4 [j]Gen. 7:22 [k]1 Cor. 15:45
8 [l]Is. 51:3 [m]Gen. 3:23, 24 [n]Gen. 4:16
9 [o]Ezek. 31:8 [p][Gen. 3:22; Rev. 2:7; 22:2, 14] [q][Deut. 1:39]
11 [r]Gen. 25:18
12 [s]Num. 11:7
14 [t]Dan. 10:4 [2]Or *Tigris* [3]Heb. *Ashshur*
15 [4]Or *Adam* [5]*cultivate*

2:1-3 These words affirm that God had completed His work. Four times it is said that He finished His work, and 3 times it is said that this included all His work. Present processes in the universe reflect God sustaining that completed creation, not more creation (cf. Heb. 1:3).

2:2 ended...rested. God certainly did not rest due to weariness; rather, establishing the pattern for man's work cycle, He only modeled the need for rest. Later, the Sabbath ordinance of Moses found its basis in the creation week (cf. Ex. 20:8-11). The Sabbath was God's sacred ordained day in the weekly cycle. Jesus said, "The Sabbath was made for man..." (Mark 2:2) and Gen. 2:3 stated that God "sanctified" or set apart the Sabbath day because He rested in it. Later, it was set aside for a day of worship in the Mosaic law (*see notes on Ex. 20:8-11*). Hebrews 4:4 distinguishes between physical rest and the redemptive rest to which it pointed. Colossians 2:16 makes it clear that the Mosaic "Sabbath" has no symbolic or ritual place in the New Covenant. The church began worshiping on the first day of the week to commemorate the resurrection of Christ (Acts 20:7).

2:4–4:26 The history of the heavens and the earth (v. 4).

2:4-25 the history of. Genesis 2:4-25 fills in details, especially of the sixth day, which were not included in 1:1–2:3. How did Moses obtain this account, so different from the absurd fictions of the pagans? Not from any human source, for man was not in existence to witness it. Not from the light of reason, for though intellect can know the eternal power of the Godhead (Rom. 1:18-20) and that God made all things, it cannot know how. None but the Creator Himself could give this data and, therefore, it is through faith that one understands that the worlds were formed by the Word of God (Heb. 11:3).

2:4,5 before any plant. Verse 4 gives a summary of days one and two, before the vegetation of day 3.

2:6 mist went up. A very heavy mist or vapor which characterized the earth at the end of day two (cf. 1:6-8). The change in temperature between day and night was sufficient to cause daily evaporation from the bodies of water and condensation into dew and fog. This was in place on days two and three, before the plants were created.

2:7-25 This account details day 6 (cf. 1:24-31).

2:7 formed. Many of the words used in this account of the creation of man picture a master craftsman at work shaping a work of art to which he gives life (1 Cor. 15:45). This adds detail to the statement of fact in 1:27 (cf. 1 Tim. 2:13). Cf. Ps. 139:14. Made from dirt, a man's value is not in the physical components that form his body, but in the quality of life which forms his soul (see Job 33:4).

2:8 garden...Eden. The Babylonians called the lush green land from which water flowed *edenu;* today, the term "oasis" describes such a place. This was a magnificent garden paradise, unlike any the world has seen since, where God fellowshiped with those He created in His image. The exact location of Eden is unknown; if "eastward" was used in relationship to where Moses was when he wrote, then it could have been in the area of Babylon, the Mesopotamian Valley.

2:9 tree of life. A real tree, with special properties to sustain eternal life. It was placed in the center of the garden, where it must have been observed by Adam, and its fruit perhaps eaten by him, thus sustaining his life (2:16). Such a tree, symbolic of eternal life, will be in the new heavens and new earth (*see notes on Rev. 22:2,14*). **tree...knowledge.** Cf. 2:16; 3:1-6,11,22. It was perhaps given that title because it was a test of obedience by which our first parents were tried, whether they would be good or bad—obey God or disobey His command.

2:10 out of. That is to say "the source," and likely refers to some great spring gushing up inside the garden from some subterranean reservoir. There was no rain at that time.

2:11 Pishon...Havilah. Locations are uncertain. This represents pre-Flood geography, now dramatically altered.

2:12 Bdellium. A gum resin. This refers more to appearance than color, i.e., it had the appearance of a pale resin.

2:13 Gihon...Cush. The river location is uncertain. Cush could be modern-day Ethiopia.

2:14 Hiddekel...Assyria. The post-Flood Tigris River runs NW to SE east of the city of Babylon through the Mesopotamian Valley. **Euphrates.** A river that runs parallel (NW to SE) to the Tigris and empties into the Persian Gulf after joining the Tigris.

2:15 tend and keep it. Work was an important and dignified part of representing the image of God and serving Him, even before the Fall. Cf. Rev. 22:3.

[u]you shall not eat, for in the day that you
eat of it [v]you[6] shall surely [w]die."
18 And the LORD God said, "*It is* not
good that man should be alone; [x]I will
make him a helper comparable to him."
19 [y]Out of the ground the LORD God
formed every beast of the field and every
bird of the air, and [z]brought *them* to
[7]Adam to see what he would call them.
And whatever Adam called each living
creature, that *was* its name. **20** So Adam
gave names to all cattle, to the birds of the
air, and to every beast of the field. But for
Adam there was not found a helper
comparable to him.
21 And the LORD God caused a [a]deep
sleep to fall on Adam, and he slept; and He
took one of his ribs, and closed up the flesh
in its place. **22** Then the rib which the LORD
God had taken from man He [8]made into a
woman, [b]and He [c]brought her to the man.

23 And Adam said:

"This *is* now [d]bone of my bones
And flesh of my flesh;
She shall be called [9]Woman,
Because she was [e]taken out of
[1]Man."

24 [f]Therefore a man shall leave his father
and mother and [g]be[2] joined to his wife,
and they shall become one flesh.
25 [h]And they were both naked, the man
and his wife, and were not [i]ashamed.

The Temptation and Fall of Man

3 Now [a]the serpent was [b]more cunning
than any beast of the field which the
LORD God had made. And he said to the
woman, "Has God indeed said, 'You shall
not eat of every tree of the garden'?"
2 And the woman said to the serpent,

17 [u]Gen. 3:1, 3, 11, 17 [v]Gen. 3:3, 19; [Rom. 6:23] [w]Rom. 5:12; 1 Cor. 15:21, 22 [6]Lit. *dying you shall die*
18 [x]1 Cor. 11:8, 9; 1 Tim. 2:13
19 [y]Gen. 1:20, 24 [z]Ps. 8:6 [7]Or *the man*
21 [a]Gen. 15:12; 1 Sam. 26:12
22 [b]Gen. 3:20; 1 Tim. 2:13 [c]Heb. 13:4 [8]Lit. *built*
23 [d]Gen. 29:14; Eph. 5:28-30 [e]1 Cor. 11:8, 9 [9]Heb. *Ishshah* [1]Heb. *Ish*
24 [f]Matt. 19:5; Eph. 5:31 [g]Mark 10:6-8; 1 Cor. 6:16 [2]Lit. *cling*
25 [h]Gen. 3:7, 10 [i]Is. 47:3

CHAPTER 3

1 [a]1 Chr. 21:1; [Rev. 12:9; 20:2, 10] [b]2 Cor. 11:3

2:17 surely die. To "die" has the basic idea of separation. It can mean spiritual separation, physical separation, and/or eternal separation. At the moment of their sin, Adam and Eve died spiritually, but because God was merciful they did not die physically until later (5:5). There is no reason given for this prohibition, other than it was a test (*see note on v. 9*). There was nothing magical about that tree, but eating from it after it had been forbidden by God would indeed give man the knowledge of evil—since evil can be defined as disobeying God. Man already had the knowledge of good.

2:18 not good. When God saw His creation as very good (1:31), He viewed it as being to that point the perfect outcome to His creative plan. However, in observing man's state as not good, He was commenting on his incompleteness before the end of the sixth day because the woman, Adam's counterpart, had not yet been created. The words of this verse emphasize man's need for a companion, a helper, and an equal. He was incomplete without someone to complement him in fulfilling the task of filling, multiplying, and taking dominion over the earth. This points to Adam's inadequacy, not Eve's insufficiency (cf. 1 Cor. 11:9). Woman was made by God to meet man's deficiency (cf. 1 Tim. 2:14).

2:19 This was not a new creation of animals. They were created before man on the fifth and sixth days (1:20-25). Here the Lord God was calling attention to the fact that He created them "out of the ground" as He did man, but man, who was a living soul in the image of God was to name them, signifying his rule over them.

2:20 gave names to. Naming is an act of discerning something about the creature so as to appropriately identify it and also an act of leadership or authority over that which was named. There is no kinship with any animal since none was a fitting companion for Adam.

2:21 one of his ribs. This could also be "sides," including surrounding flesh ("flesh of my flesh," v. 23). Divine surgery by the Creator presented no problems. This would also imply the first act of healing in Scripture.

2:23 bone of my bones. Adam's poem focuses on naming the delight of his heart in this newly found companion. The man (ish) names her "woman" (isha) because she had her source in him (the root of the word "woman" is "soft"). She truly was made of bone from his bones and flesh from his flesh. Cf. 1 Cor. 11:8. The English words man/woman sustain the same relationship as the Hebrew words, hinting at that original creation.

2:24 leave...be joined to. The marital relationship was established as the first human institution. The responsibility to honor one's parents (Ex. 20:12) does not cease with leaving and the union of husband with wife (Matt. 19:5; Mark 10:7,8; 1 Cor. 6:16; Eph. 5:31), but does represent the inauguration of a new and primary responsibility. "Joined" carries the sense of a permanent or indissoluble union, so that divorce was not considered (cf. 2:16). "One flesh" speaks of a complete unity of parts making a whole, e.g., one cluster, many grapes (Num. 13:23) or one God in 3 persons (Deut. 6:4); thus this marital union was complete and whole with two people. This also implies their sexual completeness. One man and one woman constitute the pair to reproduce. The "one flesh" is primarily seen in the child born of that union, the one perfect result of the union of two. Cf. uses of this verse in Matt. 19:5,6; Mark 10:8; 1 Cor. 6:16; Eph. 5:31. Permanent monogamy was and continues to be God's design and law for marriage.

2:25 both naked...not ashamed. With no knowledge of evil before the Fall, even nakedness was shameless and innocent. They found their complete gratification in the joy of their one union and their service to God. With no inward principle of evil to work on, the solicitation to sin had to come from without, and it did.

3:1 the serpent. The word means "snake." The apostle John identified this creature as Satan (cf. Rev. 12:9; 20:2) as did Paul (2 Cor. 11:3). The serpent, a manifestation of Satan, appears for the first time before the Fall of man. The rebellion of Satan, therefore, had occurred sometime after 1:31 (when everything in creation was good), but before 3:1. Cf. Ezek. 28:11-15 for a possible description of Satan's dazzling beauty and Is. 14:13,14 for Satan's motivation to challenge God's authority (cf. 1 John 3:8). Satan, being a fallen archangel and, thus, a supernatural spirit, had possessed the body of a snake in its pre-Fall form (cf. 3:14 for post-Fall form). **more cunning.** Deceitful; cf. Matt. 10:16. **to the woman.** She was the object of his attack, being the weaker one and needing the protection of her husband. He found her alone and unfortified by Adam's experience and counsel. Cf. 2 Tim. 3:6. Though sinless, she was temptable and seducible. **Has God... said...?** In effect Satan said, "Is it true that He has restricted you from the delights of this place? This is not like one who is truly good and kind. There must be some mistake." He insinuated doubt as to her understanding of God's will, appearing as an angel of light (2 Cor. 11:14) to lead her to the supposed true interpretation. She received him without fear or surprise, but as some credible messenger from heaven with the true understanding, because of his cunning.

3:2,3 In her answer, Eve extolled the great liberty that they had; with only one exception, they could eat all the fruit.

"We may eat the [c]fruit of the trees of the
garden; 3 but of the fruit of the tree which
is in the midst of the garden, God has said,
'You shall not eat it, nor shall you [d]touch it,
lest you die.' "
4 [e]Then the serpent said to the woman,
"You will not surely die. 5 For God knows
that in the day you eat of it your eyes will
be opened, and you will be like God,
knowing good and evil."
6 So when the woman [f]saw that the tree
was good for food, that it *was* [1]pleasant to
the eyes, and a tree desirable to make *one*
wise, she took of its fruit [g]and ate. She also
gave to her husband with her, and he ate.
7 Then the eyes of both of them were
opened, [h]and they knew that they *were*
naked; and they sewed fig leaves together
and made themselves [2]coverings.
8 And they heard [i]the [3]sound of the
LORD God walking in the garden in the
[4]cool of the day, and Adam and his wife
[j]hid themselves from the presence of the
LORD God among the trees of the garden.
9 Then the LORD God called to Adam
and said to him, "Where *are* you?"
10 So he said, "I heard Your voice in the
garden, [k]and I was afraid because I was
naked; and I hid myself."
11 And He said, "Who told you that you
were naked? Have you eaten from the tree
of which I commanded you that you
should not eat?"
12 Then the man said, [l]"The woman
whom You gave *to be* with me, she gave me
of the tree, and I ate."
13 And the LORD God said to the woman,
"What *is* this you have done?"
The woman said, [m]"The serpent deceived me, and I ate."
14 So the LORD God said to the serpent:

"Because you have done this,
You *are* cursed more than all cattle,
And more than every beast of the
field;
On your belly you shall go,
And [n]you shall eat dust
All the days of your life.
15 And I will put enmity
Between you and the woman,
And between [o]your seed and [p]her
Seed;
[q]He shall bruise your head,
And you shall bruise His heel."

2 [c]Gen. 2:16, 17
3 [d]Ex. 19:12, 13; Rev. 22:14
4 [e]John 8:44; [2 Cor. 11:3; 1 Tim. 2:14]
6 [f]1 John 2:16 [g]1 Tim. 2:14 [1]Lit. *a desirable thing*
7 [h]Gen. 2:25 [2]*girding coverings*
8 [i]Job 38:1 [j]Job 31:33; Jer. 23:24 [3]Or *voice* [4]Or *wind, breeze*
10 [k]Gen. 2:25; Ex. 3:6; Deut. 9:19; 1 John 3:20
12 [l][Prov. 28:13]
13 [m]Gen. 3:4; 2 Cor. 11:3; 1 Tim. 2:14
14 [n]Deut. 28:15-20; Is. 65:25; Mic. 7:17
15 [o]John 8:44; Acts 13:10; 1 John 3:8 [p]Is. 7:14; Luke 1:31, 34, 35; Gal. 4:4 [q]Rom. 16:20; [Rev. 12:7, 17]

3:3 nor shall you touch it. An addition to the original prohibition as recorded (cf. Gen. 2:17). Adam may have so instructed her for her protection.

3:4,5 not...die. Satan, emboldened by her openness to him, spoke this direct lie. This lie actually led her and Adam to spiritual death (separation from God). So, Satan is called a liar and murderer from the beginning (John 8:44). His lies always promise great benefits (as in v. 5). Eve experienced this result—she and Adam did know good and evil; but by personal corruption, they did not know as God knows in perfect holiness.

3:6 good...pleasant...desirable. She decided that Satan was telling the truth and she had misunderstood God, but she didn't know what she was doing. It was not overt rebellion against God, but seduction and deception to make her believe her act was the right thing to do (cf. v. 13). The NT confirms that Eve was deceived (2 Cor. 11:3; 1 Tim. 2:14; Rev. 12:9). **he ate.** A direct transgression without deception (*see note on 1 Tim. 2:13,14*).

3:7 opened...knew...sewed. The innocence noted in 2:25 had been replaced by guilt and shame (vv. 8-10), and from then on they had to rely on their conscience to distinguish between good and their newly acquired capacity to see and know evil.

3:8 God appeared, as before, in tones of goodness and kindness, walking in some visible form (perhaps Shekinah light as He later appeared in Ex. 33:18-23; 34:5-8,29; 40:34-38). He came not in fury, but in the same condescending way He had walked with Adam and Eve before.

3:9 "Where *are* you?" The question was God's way of bringing man to explain why he was hiding, rather than expressing ignorance about man's location. Shame, remorse, confusion, guilt, and fear all led to their clandestine behavior. There was no place to hide; there never is. See Ps. 139:1-12.

3:10 Your voice. The sound of 3:8, which probably was God calling for Adam and Eve. Adam responded with the language of fear and sorrow, but not confession.

3:11 Adam's sin was evidenced by his new knowledge of the evil of nakedness, but God still waited for Adam to confess to what God knew they had done. The basic reluctance of sinful people to admit their iniquity is here established. Repentance is still the issue. When sinners refuse to repent, they suffer judgment; when they do repent, they receive forgiveness.

3:12 The woman whom You gave. Adam pitifully put the responsibility on God for giving him Eve. That only magnified the tragedy in that Adam had knowingly transgressed God's prohibition, but still would not be open and confess his sin, taking full responsibility for his action, which was not made under deception (1 Tim. 2:14).

3:13 The serpent deceived me. The woman's desperate effort to pass the blame to the serpent, which was partially true (1 Tim. 2:14), did not absolve her of the responsibility for her distrust and disobedience toward God.

3:14 to the serpent. The cattle and all the rest of creation were cursed (see Rom. 8:20-23; cf. Jer. 12:4) as a result of Adam and Eve's eating, but the serpent was uniquely cursed by being made to slither on its belly. It probably had legs before this curse. Now snakes represent all that is odious, disgusting, and low. They are branded with infamy and avoided with fear. Cf. Is. 65:25; Mic. 7:17.

3:15 After cursing the physical serpent, God turned to the spiritual serpent, the lying seducer, Satan, and cursed him. **bruise your head...bruise His heel.** This "first gospel" is prophetic of the struggle and its outcome between "your seed" (Satan and unbelievers, who are called the Devil's children in John 8:44) and her seed (Christ, a descendant of Eve, and those in Him), which began in the garden. In the midst of the curse passage, a message of hope shone forth—the woman's offspring called "He" is Christ, who will one day defeat the Serpent. Satan could only "bruise" Christ's heel (cause Him to suffer), while Christ will bruise Satan's head (destroy him with a fatal blow). Paul, in a passage strongly reminiscent of Gen. 3, encouraged the believers in Rome, "And the God of peace will crush Satan under your feet shortly" (Rom. 16:20). Believers should recognize that they participate in the crushing

16 To the woman He said:

"I will greatly multiply your sorrow
and your conception;
[r]In pain you shall bring forth
children;
[s]Your desire *shall be* [5]for your
husband,
And he shall [t]rule over you."

17 Then to Adam He said, [u]"Because you
have heeded the voice of your wife, and
have eaten from the tree [v]of which I commanded you, saying, 'You shall not eat of it':

[w]"Cursed *is* the ground for your sake;
[x]In toil you shall eat *of* it
All the days of your life.
18 Both thorns and thistles it shall
[6]bring forth for you,
And [y]you shall eat the herb of the
field.
19 [z]In the sweat of your face you shall
eat bread
Till you return to the ground,
For out of it you were taken;
[a]For dust you *are*,
And [b]to dust you shall return."

20 And Adam called his wife's name
[c]Eve,[7] because she was the mother of all
living.
21 Also for Adam and his wife the LORD
God made tunics of skin, and clothed
them.
22 Then the LORD God said, "Behold, the
man has become like one of Us, to know
good and evil. And now, lest he put out his
hand and take also of the tree of life, and
eat, and live forever"— 23 therefore the
LORD God sent him out of the garden of
Eden [d]to till the ground from which he was
taken. 24 So [e]He drove out the man; and
He placed [f]cherubim [g]at the east of the
garden of Eden, and a flaming sword
which turned every way, to guard the way
to the tree of [h]life.

Cain Murders Abel

4 Now Adam knew Eve his wife, and
she conceived and bore [1]Cain, and
said, "I have acquired a man from the
LORD." 2 Then she bore again, this time his
brother [2]Abel. Now [a]Abel was a keeper of
sheep, but Cain was a tiller of the ground.
3 And [3]in the process of time it came to
pass that Cain brought an offering of the
fruit [b]of the ground to the LORD. 4 Abel
also brought of [c]the firstborn of his flock
and of [d]their fat. And the LORD [e]respected

16 [r]Is. 13:8; John 16:21 [s]Gen. 4:7 [t]1 Cor. 11:3; Eph. 5:22; 1 Tim. 2:12,15 [5]Lit. *toward*
17 [u]1 Sam. 15:23 [v]Gen. 2:17 [w]Gen. 5:29; Rom. 8:20-22; Heb. 6:8 [x]Job 5:7; 14:1; Eccl. 2:23
18 [y]Ps. 104:14 [6]*cause to grow*
19 [z]2 Thess. 3:10 [a]Gen. 2:7; 5:5 [b]Job 21:26; Eccl. 3:20
20 [c]2 Cor. 11:3; 1 Tim. 2:13 [7]Lit. *Life* or *Living*
23 [d]Gen. 4:2; 9:20
24 [e]Ezek. 31:3, 11 [f]Ex. 25:18-22; Ps. 104:4; Ezek. 10:1-20; Heb. 1:7 [g]Gen. 2:8 [h]Gen. 2:9; [Rev. 22:2]

CHAPTER 4

1 [1]Lit. *Acquire*
2 [a]Luke 11:50,51 [2]Lit. *Breath* or *Nothing*
3 [b]Num. 18:12 [3]Lit. *at the end of days*
4 [c]Num. 18:17 [d]Lev. 3:16 [e]Heb. 11:4

of Satan because, along with their Savior and because of His finished work on the cross, they also are of the woman's seed. For more on the destruction of Satan, see Heb. 2:14,15; Rev. 20:10.

3:16 conception...pain. This is a constant reminder that a woman gave birth to sin in the human race and passes it on to all her children. She can be delivered from this curse by raising godly children, as indicated in 1 Tim. 2:15 (*see note there*). **Your desire...he shall rule.** Just as the woman and her seed will engage in a war with the serpent, i.e., Satan and his seed (v. 15), because of sin and the curse, the man and the woman will face struggles in their own relationship. Sin has turned the harmonious system of God-ordained roles into distasteful struggles of self-will. Lifelong companions, husbands and wives, will need God's help in getting along as a result. The woman's desire will be to lord it over her husband, but the husband will rule by divine design (Eph. 5:22-25). This interpretation of the curse is based upon the identical Heb. words and grammar being used in 4:7 (*see note there*) to show the conflict man will have with sin as it seeks to rule him.

3:17 Because you have heeded. The reason given for the curse on the ground and human death is that man turned his back on the voice of God, to follow his wife in eating that from which God had ordered him to abstain. The woman sinned because she acted independently of her husband, disdaining his leadership, counsel, and protection. The man sinned because he abandoned his leadership and followed the wishes of his wife. In both cases, God's intended roles were reversed.

3:17,18 Cursed *is* the ground for your sake. God cursed the object of man's labor and made it reluctantly, yet richly, yield his food through hard work.

3:19 return to the ground. I.e., to die (cf. 2:7). Man, by sin, became mortal. Although he did not die the moment he ate (by God's mercy), he was changed immediately and became liable to all the sufferings and miseries of life, to death, and to the pains of hell forever. Adam lived 930 years (5:5).

3:21 tunics of skin. The first physical deaths should have been the man and his wife, but it was an animal—a shadow of the reality that God would someday kill a substitute to redeem sinners.

3:22 like one of Us. *See note on 1:26.* This was spoken out of compassion for the man and woman, who only in limited ways were like the Trinity, knowing good and evil—not by holy omniscience, but by personal experience (cf. Is. 6:3; Hab. 1:13; Rev. 4:8).

3:22,23 and live forever. *See note on 2:9.* God told man that he would surely die if he ate of the forbidden tree. But God's concern may also have been that man not live forever in his pitifully cursed condition. Taken in the broader context of Scripture, driving the man and his wife out of the garden was an act of merciful grace to prevent them from being sustained forever by the tree of life.

3:24 cherubim. Later in Israel's history, two cherubim or angelic figures guarded the ark of the covenant and the Holy of Holies in the tabernacle (Ex. 25:18-22), where God communed with His people. **flaming sword.** An unexplainable phenomenon, perhaps associated directly with the cherubim or the flaming, fiery Shekinah presence of God Himself.

4:1 Adam knew Eve his wife. The act of sexual intercourse was considered only the means by which God Himself gave children. He was acknowledged as the sovereign giver of all life.

4:2 she bore again. Some think the boys may have been twins, since no time element intervenes between vv. 1,2. **keeper of sheep...tiller of the ground.** Both occupations were respectable; in fact, most people subsisted through a combination of both. God's focus was not on their vocation, but on the nature of their respective offerings.

4:3 fruit of the ground. Produce in general.

4:4 firstborn...fat. The best animals.

Abel and his offering, 5 but He did not respect Cain and his offering. And Cain was
very angry, and his countenance fell.
6 So the LORD said to Cain, "Why are you
angry? And why has your countenance
fallen? 7 If you do well, will you not be accepted? And if you do not do well, sin lies
at the door. And its desire *is* [4]for you, but
you should rule over it."
8 Now Cain [5]talked with Abel his
[6]brother; and it came to pass, when they
were in the field, that Cain rose up against
Abel his brother and [f]killed him.
9 Then the LORD said to Cain, "Where *is*
Abel your brother?"
He said, [g]"I do not know. *Am* I [h]my
brother's keeper?"
10 And He said, "What have you done?
The voice of your brother's blood [i]cries out
to Me from the ground. 11 So now [j]you *are*
cursed from the earth, which has opened
its mouth to receive your brother's blood
from your hand. 12 When you till the
ground, it shall no longer yield its strength
to you. A fugitive and a vagabond you
shall be on the earth."
13 And Cain said to the LORD, "My [7]pun-
ishment *is* greater than I can bear! 14 Surely You have driven me out this day from
the face of the ground; [k]I shall be [l]hidden
from Your face; I shall be a fugitive and a
vagabond on the earth, and it will happen
that [m]anyone who finds me will kill me."
15 And the LORD said to him, [8]"Therefore, whoever kills Cain, vengeance shall
be taken on him [n]sevenfold." And the
LORD set a [o]mark on Cain, lest anyone finding him should kill him.

The Family of Cain

16 Then Cain [p]went out from the [q]pres-
ence of the LORD and dwelt in the land of
[9]Nod on the east of Eden. 17 And Cain knew
his wife, and she conceived and bore Enoch.
And he built a city, [r]and called the name of
the city after the name of his son—Enoch.
18 To Enoch was born Irad; and Irad begot
Mehujael, and Mehujael begot Methushael,
and Methushael begot Lamech.
19 Then Lamech took for himself [s]two
wives: the name of one *was* Adah, and the
name of the second *was* Zillah. 20 And
Adah bore Jabal. He was the father of those
who dwell in tents and have livestock.
21 His brother's name *was* Jubal. He was
the father of all those who play the harp
and [1]flute. 22 And as for Zillah, she also
bore Tubal-Cain, an instructor of every
craftsman in bronze and iron. And the sister of Tubal-Cain *was* Naamah.
23 Then Lamech said to his wives:

"Adah and Zillah, hear my voice;
Wives of Lamech, listen to my
speech!

7 [4] Lit. *toward*
8 [f] Matt. 23:35; Luke 11:51; [1 John 3:12-15]; Jude 11 [5] Lit. *said to* [6] Sam., LXX, Syr., Vg. add *"Let us go out to the field."*
9 [g] John 8:44 [h] 1 Cor. 8:11-13
10 [i] Num. 35:33; Deut. 21:1-9; Heb. 12:24; Rev. 6:9, 10
11 [j] Gen. 3:14; Deut. 11:28; 28:15-20; Gal. 3:10
13 [7] *iniquity*
14 [k] Ps. 51:11 [l] Deut. 31:18; Is. 1:15 [m] Gen. 9:6; Num. 35:19, 21, 27
15 [n] Gen. 4:24; Ps. 79:12 [o] Gen. 9:6; Ezek. 9:4, 6 [8] So with MT, Tg.; LXX, Syr., Vg. *Not so;*
16 [p] 2 Kin. 13:23; 24:20; Jer. 23:39; 52:3 [q] Jon. 1:3 [9] Lit. *Wandering*
17 [r] Ps. 49:11
19 [s] Gen. 2:24; 16:3; 1 Tim. 3:2
21 [1] *pipe*

4:4,5 Abel's offering was acceptable (cf. Heb. 11:4), not just because it was an animal, nor just because it was the very best of what he had, nor even that it was the culmination of a zealous heart for God; but, because it was in every way obediently given according to what God must have revealed (though not recorded in Genesis). Cain, disdaining the divine instruction, just brought what he wanted to bring: some of his crop.

4:5,6 angry. Rather than being repentant for his sinful disobedience, he was hostile toward God, whom he could not kill, and jealous of his brother, whom he could kill (cf. 1 John 3:12; Jude 11).

4:7 do well...be accepted. God reminded Cain that if he had obeyed God and offered the animal sacrifices God had required, his sacrifices would have been acceptable. It wasn't personal preference on God's part, or disdain for Cain's vocation, or the quality of his produce that caused God to reject his sacrifice. **sin lies at the door.** God told Cain that if he chose not to obey His commands, ever-present sin, crouched and waiting to pounce like a lion, would fulfill its desire to overpower him (cf. 3:16).

4:8 The first murder in Scripture (cf. Matt. 23:35; Luke 11:51; Heb. 12:24). Cain rejected the wisdom spoken to him by God Himself, rejected doing well, refused to repent, and thus crouching sin pounced and turned him into a killer. Cf. 1 John 3:10-12.

4:9 *Am* I my brother's keeper? Cain's sarcasm was a play on words, based on the fact that Abel was the "keeper" of sheep. Lying was the third sin resulting from Cain's attitude of indifference to God's commands. Sin was ruling over him (v. 7).

4:10 voice...blood. A figure of speech to indicate that Abel's death was well known to God.

4:11 cursed from the earth. A second curse came from God affecting just the productivity of the soil Cain would till. To a farmer like Cain, this curse was severe, and meant that Cain would all his life be a wanderer, "a fugitive and a vagabond" (vv. 12, 14).

4:14 anyone...kill me. This shows that the population of the earth was, by then, greatly increased. As a wanderer and scavenger in an agrarian world, Cain would be easy prey for those who wanted his life.

4:15 mark. While not described here, it involved some sort of identifiable sign that he was under divine protection which was mercifully given to Cain by God. At the same time, the mark that saved him was the lifelong sign of his shame.

4:16 Nod. An unknown location.

4:17 Cain knew his wife. Cain's wife obviously was one of Adam's later daughters (5:4). By Moses' time, this kind of close marriage was forbidden (Lev. 18:7-17), because of genetic decay. **Enoch.** His name means "initiation," and was symbolic of the new city where Cain would try to mitigate his curse.

4:19 two wives. No reason is given on Lamech's part for the first recorded instance of bigamy. He led the Cainites in open rebellion against God (cf. 2:24) by his violation of marriage law.

4:20 Jabal. He invented tents and the nomadic life of herdsmen so common in the Middle East and elsewhere.

4:21 Jubal. He invented both stringed and wind instruments.

4:22 Tubal-Cain. He invented metallurgy.

4:23,24 Lamech killed someone in self-defense. He told his wives that they need not fear any harm coming to them for the killing because if anyone tried to retaliate, he would retaliate and kill them. He

For I have [2]killed a man for
wounding me,
Even a young man [3]for hurting me.
24 [t]If Cain shall be avenged sevenfold,
Then Lamech seventy-sevenfold."

A New Son

25 And Adam knew his wife again, and
she bore a son and [u]named him [4]Seth, "For
God has appointed another seed for me instead of Abel, whom Cain killed." 26 And
as for Seth, [v]to him also a son was born;
and he named him [5]Enosh. Then *men*
began [w]to call on the name of the LORD.

The Family of Adam

5 This is the book of the [a]genealogy of
Adam. In the day that God created
man, He made him in [b]the likeness of God.
2 He created them [c]male and female, and
[d]blessed them and called them Mankind in
the day they were created. 3 And Adam
lived one hundred and thirty years, and
begot *a son* [e]in his own likeness, after his
image, and [f]named him Seth. 4 After he
begot Seth, [g]the days of Adam were eight
hundred years; [h]and he had sons and
daughters. 5 So all the days that Adam
lived were nine hundred and thirty years;
[i]and he died.
6 Seth lived one hundred and five years,
and begot [j]Enosh. 7 After he begot Enosh,
Seth lived eight hundred and seven years,
and had sons and daughters. 8 So all the
days of Seth were nine hundred and
twelve years; and he died.
9 Enosh lived ninety years, and begot
[1]Cainan. 10 After he begot Cainan, Enosh
lived eight hundred and fifteen years, and
had sons and daughters. 11 So all the days
of Enosh were nine hundred and five
years; and he died.
12 Cainan lived seventy years, and begot
Mahalalel. 13 After he begot Mahalalel,
Cainan lived eight hundred and forty
years, and had sons and daughters. 14 So
all the days of Cainan were nine hundred
and ten years; and he died.
15 Mahalalel lived sixty-five years, and
begot Jared. 16 After he begot Jared, Mahalalel lived eight hundred and thirty years,
and had sons and daughters. 17 So all the
days of Mahalalel were eight hundred and
ninety-five years; and he died.
18 Jared lived one hundred and sixty-
two years, and begot [k]Enoch. 19 After he
begot Enoch, Jared lived eight hundred
years, and had sons and daughters. 20 So
all the days of Jared were nine hundred
and sixty-two years; and he died.
21 Enoch lived sixty-five years, and
begot Methuselah. 22 After he begot
Methuselah, Enoch [l]walked with God
three hundred years, and had sons and
daughters. 23 So all the days of Enoch were
three hundred and sixty-five years. 24 And
[m]Enoch walked with God; and he *was* not,
for God [n]took him.
25 Methuselah lived one hundred and
eighty-seven years, and begot Lamech.
26 After he begot Lamech, Methuselah
lived seven hundred and eighty-two years,
and had sons and daughters. 27 So all the
days of Methuselah were nine hundred
and sixty-nine years; and he died.
28 Lamech lived one hundred and
eighty-two years, and had a son. 29 And he
called his name [o]Noah,[2] saying, "This *one*

23 [2] *slain a man for my wound* [3] *for my hurt*
24 [t] Gen. 4:15
25 [u] Gen. 5:3 [4] Lit. *Appointed*
26 [v] Gen. 5:6 [w] Gen. 12:8; 26:25; 1 Kin. 18:24; Ps. 116:17; Joel 2:32; Zeph. 3:9; 1 Cor. 1:2 [5] Gr. *Enos,* Luke 3:38

CHAPTER 5

1 [a] Gen. 2:4; 6:9; 1 Chr. 1:1; Matt. 1:1 [b] Gen. 1:26; 9:6; [Eph. 4:24; Col. 3:10]
2 [c] Gen. 1:27; Deut. 4:32; Matt. 19:4; Mark 10:6 [d] Gen. 1:28; 9:1
3 [e] 1 Cor. 15:48, 49 [f] Gen. 4:25
4 [g] 1 Chr. 1:1-4; Luke 3:36-38 [h] Gen. 1:28; 4:25
5 [i] Gen. 2:17; 3:19; 6:17; [Heb. 9:27]
6 [j] Gen. 4:26
9 [1] Heb. *Qenan*
18 [k] Jude 14, 15
22 [l] Gen. 6:9; 17:1; 24:40; 48:15; 2 Kin. 20:3; Ps. 16:8; [Mic. 6:8]; Mal. 2:6; 1 Thess. 2:12; [Heb. 11:39]
24 [m] 2 Kin. 2:11; Jude 14 [n] 2 Kin. 2:10; Ps. 49:15; 73:24; Heb. 11:5
29 [o] Luke 3:36; Heb. 11:7; 1 Pet. 3:20 [2] Lit. *Rest*

---

thought that if God promised 7-fold vengeance on anyone killing Cain, He would give 77-fold vengeance on anyone attacking Lamech.

4:25 Seth. With Cain removed as the older brother and heir of the family blessing, and with Abel dead, God graciously gave Adam and Eve a godly son through whom the seed of redemption (3:15) would be passed all the way to Jesus Christ (Luke 3:38).

4:26 *men* began to call on the name of the LORD. As men realized their inherent sinfulness with no human means to appease God's righteous indignation and wrath over their multiplied iniquities, they turned to God for mercy and grace in hopes of a restored personal relationship.

5:1–6:8 the genealogy of Adam. Ten specific families are mentioned. Most likely, in accord with other biblical genealogies, this listing is representative rather than complete (cf. Ruth 4:18-22).

5:1-32 Adam…Noah. The genealogy connects Adam to the Noahic family which not only survived the Flood, but also became first in God's re-creation. Two recurring phrases carry redemption history forward: "…and he had sons and daughters," "…and he died." These lines, which get repeated for each successive descendant of Adam, echo two contrasting realities; God had said "you shall surely die," (2:17) but He had also commanded them to "Be fruitful and multiply" (1:28).

5:1 the likeness of God. *See notes on 1:26.*

5:2 called them Mankind. In naming man, God declared His own dominion over all creation (Matt. 19:4; Mark 10:6).

5:3 in his own likeness, after his image. The human image and likeness in which God created mankind was procreatively passed to the second generation and to all generations which follow.

5:5 nine hundred and thirty years. These are literal years marking unusual length of life which are accounted for by the pre-Flood environment provided by the earth being under a canopy of water, filtering out the ultraviolet rays of the sun and producing a much more moderate and healthful condition. *See notes on 1:7; 2:6.* **and he died.** God told Adam that if he ate of the tree he would surely die (2:17). It included spiritual death immediately and then physical death later.

5:24 walked with God…*was* not, for God took him. Enoch is the only break in the chapter from the incessant comment, "and he died." Cf. 4:17,18; 1 Chr. 1:3; Luke 3:37; Heb. 11:5; Jude 14. Only one other man is said to have enjoyed this intimacy of relationship in walking with God, Noah (6:9). Enoch experienced being taken to heaven alive by God, as did Elijah later (2 Kin. 2:1-12).

5:25-27 Methuselah. The man who lived the longest life on record. He died the year of the flood judgment (cf. 7:6).

will comfort us concerning our work and
the toil of our hands, because of the
ground [p]which the LORD has cursed."
30 After he begot Noah, Lamech lived five
hundred and ninety-five years, and had
sons and daughters. 31 So all the days of
Lamech were seven hundred and seventy-
seven years; and he died.
32 And Noah was five hundred years
old, and Noah begot [q]Shem, Ham, [r]and
Japheth.

The Wickedness and Judgment of Man

6 Now it came to pass, [a]when men
began to multiply on the face of the
earth, and daughters were born to them,
2 that the sons of God saw the daughters of
men, that they *were* beautiful; and they
[b]took wives for themselves of all whom
they chose.
3 And the LORD said, [c]"My Spirit shall
not [d]strive[1] with man forever, [e]for he *is* indeed flesh; yet his days shall be one hundred and twenty years." 4 There were [2]gi-
ants on the earth in those [f]days, and also
afterward, when the sons of God came in
to the daughters of men and they bore *children* to them. Those *were* the mighty men
who *were* of old, men of renown.
5 Then [3]the LORD saw that the wickedness of man *was* great in the earth, and *that*

29 [p]Gen. 3:17-19; 4:11
32 [q]Gen. 6:10; 7:13 [r]Gen. 10:21

CHAPTER 6

1 [a]Gen. 1:28
2 [b]Deut. 7:3, 4
3 [c]Gen. 41:38; [Gal. 5:16, 17]; 1 Pet. 3:19, 20 [d]2 Thess. 2:7 [e]Ps. 78:39 [1]LXX, Syr., Tg., Vg. *abide*
4 [f]Num. 13:32, 33; Luke 17:27 [2]Heb. *nephilim, fallen* or *mighty ones*
5 [g]Gen. 8:21; Ps. 14:1-3; Prov. 6:18; Matt. 15:19; Rom. 1:28-32 [3]So with MT, Tg.; Vg. *God;* LXX *LORD God* [4]*thought* [5]*all the day*
6 [h]Gen. 6:7; 1 Sam. 15:11, 29; 2 Sam. 24:16; Jer. 18:7-10; Zech. 8:14 [i]Ps. 78:40; Is. 63:10; Eph. 4:30 [j]Mark 3:5
7 [k]Gen. 7:4, 23; Deut. 28:63; 29:20; Ps. 7:11
8 [l]Gen. 19:19; Ex. 33:12, 17; Luke 1:30; Acts 7:46
9 [m]Gen. 7:1; Ezek. 14:14, 20; Heb. 11:7; 2 Pet. 2:5 [n]Gen. 5:22, 24; 2 Kin. 23:3 [6]*blameless* or *having integrity*

every [g]intent[4] of the thoughts of his heart
was only evil [5]continually. 6 And [h]the LORD
was sorry that He had made man on the
earth, and [i]He was grieved in His [j]heart.
7 So the LORD said, "I will [k]destroy man
whom I have created from the face of the
earth, both man and beast, creeping thing
and birds of the air, for I am sorry that I
have made them." 8 But Noah [l]found
grace in the eyes of the LORD.

Noah Pleases God

9 This is the genealogy of Noah. [m]Noah
was a just man, [6]perfect in his generations.
Noah [n]walked with God. 10 And Noah
begot three sons: [o]Shem, Ham, and Japheth.
11 The earth also was corrupt [p]before
God, and the earth was [q]filled with violence. 12 So God [r]looked upon the earth,
and indeed it was corrupt; for [s]all flesh
had corrupted their way on the earth.

The Ark Prepared

13 And God said to Noah, [t]"The end of
all flesh has come before Me, for the earth
is filled with violence through them; [u]and
behold, [v]I will destroy them with the earth.
14 Make yourself an ark of gopherwood;

10 [o]Gen. 5:32; 7:13 11 [p]Deut. 31:29; Judg. 2:19; Rom. 2:13 [q]Ezek. 8:17 12 [r]Ps. 14:2; 53:2, 3 [s]Ps. 14:1-3; Is. 28:8 13 [t]Is. 34:1-4; Jer. 51:13; Ezek. 7:2, 3; Amos 8:2; 1 Pet. 4:7 [u]Gen. 6:17 [v]2 Pet. 2:4-10

5:29 This *one* will comfort us. Comfort would come through the godly life of Noah, who is an "heir of the righteousness" which is according to faith (Heb. 11:7).

6:1-4 The account that follows records an act of degradation that reveals the end-point of God's patience.

6:1 Such long lifespans as indicated in the record of chap. 5 caused massive increase in earth's population.

6:2 the sons of God saw the daughters of men. The sons of God, identified elsewhere almost exclusively as angels (Job 1:6; 2:1; 38:7), saw and took wives of the human race. This produced an unnatural union which violated the God-ordained order of human marriage and procreation (Gen. 2:24). Some have argued that the sons of God were the sons of Seth who cohabited with the daughters of Cain; others suggest they were perhaps human kings wanting to build harems. But the passage puts strong emphasis on the angelic vs. human contrast. The NT places this account in sequence with other Genesis events and identifies it as involving fallen angels who indwelt men (*see notes on 2 Pet. 2:4,5; Jude 6*). Matthew 22:30 does not necessarily negate the possibility that angels are capable of procreation, but just that they do not marry. To procreate physically, they had to possess human, male bodies.

6:3 My Spirit. Cf. Gen. 1:2. The Holy Spirit played a most active role in the OT. The Spirit had been striving to call men to repentance and righteousness, especially as Scripture notes, through the preaching of Enoch and Noah (1 Pet. 3:20; 2 Pet. 2:5; Jude 14). **one hundred and twenty.** The span of time until the Flood (cf. 1 Pet. 3:20), in which man was given opportunity to respond to the warning that God's Spirit would not always be patient.

6:4 giants. The word *nephilim* is from a root meaning "to fall," indicating that they were strong men who "fell" on others in the sense of overpowering them (the only other use of this term is in Num. 13:53). They were already in the earth when the "mighty men" and "men of renown" were born. The fallen ones are not the offspring from the union in 6:1,2.

6:5 his heart *was* only evil continually. This is one of the strongest and clearest statements about man's sinful nature. Sin begins in the thought-life (*see notes on James 1:13-15*). The people of Noah's day were exceedingly wicked, from the inside out. Cf. Jer. 17:9,10; Matt. 12:34,35; 15:18,19; Mark 7:21; Luke 6:45.

6:6 sorry...grieved. Sin sorrowed God who is holy and without blemish (Eph. 4:30). Cf. Ex. 32:14; 1 Sam. 15:11; Jer. 26:3.

6:7 God promised total destruction when His patience ran out (cf. Eccl. 8:11).

6:8 But Noah found grace. Lest one believe that Noah was spared because of his good works alone (cf. Heb. 11:7), God makes it clear that Noah was a man who believed in God as Creator, Sovereign, and the only Savior from sin. He found grace for himself, because he humbled himself and sought it (cf. 4:26). *See notes on Is. 55:6,7;* he was obedient, as well (6:22; 7:5; James 4:6-10).

6:9–9:29 The generations of Noah.

6:9 a just man...perfect...walked. Cf. Ezek. 14:14,20; 2 Pet. 2:5. The order is one of increasing spiritual quality before God: "just" is to live by God's righteous standards; "perfect" sets him apart by a comparison with those of his day; and that he "walked with God" puts him in a class with Enoch (5:24).

6:11 corrupt...filled with violence. Cf. 6:3,5. The seed of Satan, the fallen rejectors of God, deceitful and destructive, had dominated the world.

6:13 I will destroy them with the earth. Destroy did not mean annihilation, but rather referred to the flood judgment, both of the earth and its inhabitants.

6:14 ark. A hollow chest, a box designed to float on water (Ex.

make [7]rooms in the ark, and cover it inside
and outside with pitch. 15 And this is how
you shall make it: The length of the ark
shall be three hundred [8]cubits, its width
fifty cubits, and its height thirty cubits.
16 You shall make a window for the ark,
and you shall finish it to a cubit from
above; and set the door of the ark in its
side. You shall make it *with* lower, second,
and third *decks.* 17 [w]And behold, I Myself
am bringing [x]floodwaters on the earth, to
destroy from under heaven all flesh in
which *is* the breath of life; everything that
is on the earth shall [y]die. 18 But I will establish My [z]covenant with you; and [a]you
shall go into the ark—you, your sons, your
wife, and your sons' wives with you.
19 And of every living thing of all flesh you
shall bring [b]two of every *sort* into the ark,
to keep *them* alive with you; they shall be
male and female. 20 Of the birds after their
kind, of animals after their kind, and of
every creeping thing of the earth after its
kind, two of every *kind* [c]will come to you
to keep *them* alive. 21 And you shall take
for yourself of all food that is eaten, and
you shall gather *it* to yourself; and it shall
be food for you and for them."
22 [d]Thus Noah did; [e]according to all that
[f]God commanded him, so he did.

The Great Flood

7 Then the [a]LORD said to Noah, [b]"Come
into the ark, you and all your household, because I have seen *that* [c]you *are*
righteous before Me in this generation.
2 You shall take with you seven each of
every [d]clean animal, a male and his female;
[e]two each of animals that *are* unclean, a
male and his female; 3 also seven each of
birds of the air, male and female, to keep
[1]the species alive on the face of all the
earth. 4 For after [f]seven more days I will
cause it to rain on the earth [g]forty days and
forty nights, and I will [2]destroy from the
face of the earth all living things that I have
made." 5 [h]And Noah did according to all
that the LORD commanded him. 6 Noah
was [i]six hundred years old when the
floodwaters were on the earth.
7 [j]So Noah, with his sons, his wife, and
his sons' wives, went into the ark because
of the waters of the flood. 8 Of clean animals, of animals that *are* unclean, of birds,
and of everything that creeps on the earth,
9 two by two they went into the ark to
Noah, male and female, as God had commanded Noah. 10 And it came to pass after
seven days that the waters of the flood
were on the earth. 11 In the six hundredth
year of Noah's life, in the second month,
the seventeenth day of the month, on [k]that
day all [l]the fountains of the great deep
were broken up, and the [m]windows of
heaven were opened. 12 [n]And the rain was
on the earth forty days and forty nights.
13 On the very same day Noah and
Noah's sons, Shem, Ham, and Japheth, and

14 [7]Lit. *compartments* or *nests*
15 [8]A cubit is about 18 inches.
17 [w]Gen. 7:4, 21-23; 2 Pet. 2:5 [x]2 Pet. 3:6 [y]Luke 16:22
18 [z]Gen. 8:20–9:17; 17:7 [a]Gen. 7:1, 7, 13; 1 Pet. 3:20; 2 Pet. 2:5
19 [b]Gen. 7:2, 8, 9, 14-16
20 [c]Gen. 7:9, 15
22 [d]Gen. 7:5; 12:4, 5; Heb. 11:7 [e]Gen. 7:5, 9, 16 [f][1 John 5:3]

CHAPTER 7

1 [a]Matt. 11:28 [b]Matt. 24:38; Luke 17:26; Heb. 11:7; 1 Pet. 3:20; 2 Pet. 2:5 [c]Gen. 6:9; Ps. 33:18; Prov. 10:9; 2 Pet. 2:9
2 [d]Lev. 11; Deut. 14:3-20 [e]Lev. 10:10; Ezek. 44:23
3 [1]Lit. *seed*
4 [f]Gen. 7:10; Ex. 7:25 [g]Gen. 7:12, 17 [2]Lit. *blot out*
5 [h]Gen. 6:22
6 [i]Gen. 5:4, 32
7 [j]Gen. 6:18; 7:1, 13; Matt. 24:38; Luke 17:27
11 [k]Matt. 24:39; Luke 17:27; 2 Pet. 2:5; 3:6 [l]Gen. 8:2; Prov. 8:28; Is. 51:10; Ezek. 26:19 [m]Gen. 8:2; Ps. 78:23
12 [n]Gen. 7:4, 17; 1 Sam. 12:18

2:3). **gopherwood.** Probably cedar or cypress trees, abundant in the mountains of Armenia.

6:15,16 While the ark was not designed for beauty or speed, these dimensions provided extraordinary stability in the tumultuous floodwaters. A cubit was about 18 inches long, making the ark 450 feet long, 75 feet wide, and 45 feet high. A gigantic box of that size would be very stable in the water, impossible to capsize. The volume of space in the ark was 1.4 million cubic feet, equal to the capacity of 522 standard railroad box cars, which could carry 125,000 sheep. It had 3 stories, each 15 feet high; each deck was equipped with various rooms (lit. "nests"). "Pitch" was a resin substance to seal the seams and cracks in the wood. The "window" may have actually been a low wall around the flat roof to catch water for all on the ark.

6:17 floodwaters. Other notable Scriptures on the worldwide flood brought by God include: Job 12:15; 22:16; Pss. 29:10; 104:6-9; Is. 54:9; Matt. 24:37-39; Luke 17:26,27; Heb. 11:7; 1 Pet. 3:20; 2 Pet. 2:5; 3:5,6.

6:18 But I will establish My covenant with you. In contrast with the rest of the created order which God was to destroy, Noah and his family were not only to be preserved, but they were to enjoy the provision and protection of a covenant relationship with God. This is the first mention of "covenant" in Scripture. This pledged covenant is actually made and explained in 9:9-17 (*see notes there*).

6:19,20 There are less than 18,000 species living on earth today. This number may have been doubled to allow for now extinct creatures. With two of each, a total of 72,000 creatures is reasonable as indicated in the note on 6:15,16; the cubic space could hold 125,000 sheep, and since the average size of land animals is less than a sheep, perhaps less than 60 percent of the space was used. The very large animals were surely represented by young. There was ample room also for the one million species of insects, as well as food for a year for everyone (v. 21).

7:1 righteous. Cf. 6:9; Job 1:1.

7:2,3 seven...seven. The extra 5 pairs of clean animals and birds would be used for sacrifice (8:20) and food (9:3).

7:3 to keep the species alive. So that God could use them to replenish the earth.

7:4 God allowed one more week for sinners to repent. **rain...forty days and forty nights.** A worldwide rain for this length of time is impossible in post-Flood atmospheric conditions, but not then. The canopy that covered the whole earth (*see note on 1:7*), a thermal water blanket encircling the earth, was to be condensed and dumped all over the globe (v. 10).

7:11 month...day. The calendar system of Noah's day is unknown, although it appears that one month equaled 30 days. If calculated by the Jewish calendar of Moses' day, it would be about May. This period of God's grace was ended (cf. 6:3,8; 7:4). **all the fountains of the great deep were broken up.** The subterranean waters sprang up from inside the earth to form the seas and rivers (1:10; 2:10-14), which were not produced by rainfall (since there was none), but by deep fountains in the earth. **the windows of heaven.** The celestial waters in the canopy encircling the globe were dumped on the earth and joined with the terrestrial and the subterranean waters (cf. 1:7). This ended the water canopy surrounding the earth and unleashed the water in the earth; together these phenomena began the new system of hydrology that has since characterized the earth (see

Noah's wife and the three wives of his sons
with them, entered the ark— 14 [o]they and
every beast after its kind, all cattle after
their kind, every creeping thing that creeps
on the earth after its kind, and every bird
after its kind, every bird of every [p]sort.
15 And they [q]went into the ark to Noah, two
by two, of all flesh in which *is* the breath of
life. 16 So those that entered, male and female of all flesh, went in [r]as God had commanded him; and the LORD shut him in.

17 [s]Now the flood was on the earth forty
days. The waters increased and lifted up
the ark, and it rose high above the earth.
18 The waters prevailed and greatly increased on the earth, [t]and the ark moved
about on the surface of the waters. 19 And
the waters prevailed exceedingly on the
earth, and all the high hills under the
whole heaven were covered. 20 The waters
prevailed fifteen cubits upward, and the
mountains were covered. 21 [u]And all flesh
died that moved on [3]the earth: birds and
cattle and beasts and every creeping thing
that creeps on the earth, and every man.
22 All in [v]whose nostrils *was* the breath [4]of
the spirit of life, all that *was* on the dry *land,*
died. 23 So He destroyed all living things
which were on the face of the ground: both
man and cattle, creeping thing and bird of
the air. They were destroyed from the
earth. Only [w]Noah and those who *were*
with him in the ark remained *alive.* 24 [x]And
the waters prevailed on the earth one hundred and fifty days.

Noah's Deliverance

8 Then God [a]remembered Noah, and
every living thing, and all the animals
that *were* with him in the ark. [b]And God
made a wind to pass over the earth, and the
waters subsided. 2 [c]The fountains of the
deep and the windows of heaven were also
[d]stopped, and [e]the rain from heaven was
restrained. 3 And the waters receded continually from the earth. At the end [f]of the
hundred and fifty days the waters decreased. 4 Then the ark rested in the seventh month, the seventeenth day of the
month, on the mountains of Ararat. 5 And

14 [o]Gen. 6:19 [p]Gen. 1:21
15 [q]Gen. 6:19, 20; 7:9
16 [r]Gen. 7:2, 3
17 [s]Gen. 7:4, 12; 8:6
18 [t]Ps. 104:26
21 [u]Gen. 6:7, 13, 17; 7:4 [3]*the land*
22 [v]Gen. 2:7 [4]LXX, Vg. omit *of the spirit*
23 [w]Matt. 24:38, 39; Luke 17:26, 27; Heb. 11:7; 1 Pet. 3:20; 2 Pet. 2:5
24 [x]Gen. 8:3, 4

CHAPTER 8

1 [a]Gen. 19:29; Ex. 2:24; 1 Sam. 1:19; Ps. 105:42; 106:4 [b]Ex. 14:21; 15:10; Job 12:15; Ps. 29:10; Is. 44:27; Nah. 1:4
2 [c]Gen. 7:11 [d]Deut. 11:17 [e]Gen. 7:4, 12; Job 38:37
3 [f]Gen. 7:24

Job 26:8; Eccl. 1:7; Is. 55:10; Amos 9:6). The sequence in this verse, indicating that the earth's crust breaks up first, then the heavens drop their water, is interesting because the volcanic explosions that would have occurred when the earth fractured would have sent magma and dust into the atmosphere, along with gigantic sprays of water, gas, and air—all penetrating the canopy triggering its downpour.

7:16 the LORD shut him in. No small event is spared in the telling of this episode, although the details are sparse.

7:19 all the high hills. This describes the extent of the Flood as global. Lest there be any doubt, Moses adds "under the whole heaven" (cf. 2 Pet. 3:5-7). There are over 270 flood stories told in cultures all over the earth, which owe their origin to this one global event.

7:20 The highest mountains were at least 22.5 feet under water, so that the ark floated freely above the peaks. This would include the highest peak in that area, Mt. Ararat (8:4), which is ca. 17,000 feet high. That depth further proves it was not a local flood, but a global one.

7:24 one hundred and fifty days. These days included the 40 day and night period of rain (7:12,17). The Flood rose to its peak at that point (cf. 8:3). It then took over 2½ months before the water receded to reveal other mountain peaks (8:4,5), over 4½ months before the dove could find dry land (8:8-12), and almost 8 months before the occupants could leave the ark (8:14).

8:1 Then God remembered Noah. God's covenant with Noah brought provision and protection in the midst of severe judgment. The remnant was preserved and God initiated steps toward reestablishing the created order on earth. **the waters subsided.** God used the wind to dry the ground; evaporation returned water to the atmosphere.

8:4 the mountains of Ararat. These were in the region of the

The Flood Chronology

1. In the 600th year of Noah (second month, tenth day), Noah entered the ark (Gen. 7:4,10,11).
2. In the 600th year of Noah (second month, seventeenth day), the flood began (Gen. 7:11).
3. The waters flooded the earth for 150 days (5 months of 30 days each), including the 40 days and 40 nights of rain (Gen. 7:12,17,24; 8:1).
4. In the 600th year of Noah (seventh month, seventh day), the waters began to recede (7:24; 8:1).
5. The waters later receded to the point that (600th year, seventh month, seventeenth day) the ark rested on Ararat (Gen. 8:3,4).
6. The waters continued to abate so that (600th year, tenth month, first day) the tops of the mountains were visible (Gen. 8:5).
7. Forty days later (600th year, eleventh month, tenth day) Noah sent out a raven and a dove (Gen. 8:6). Over the next 14 days, Noah sent out two more doves (Gen. 8:10,12). In all, this took 61 days or two months and one day.
8. By Noah's 601st year on the first month, the first day, the water had dried up (Gen. 8:12,13).
9. Noah waited one month and twenty-six days before he disembarked in the second month, the 27th day of his 601st year. From beginning to end, the Flood lasted one year and ten days from Gen. 7:11 to Gen. 8:14.

the waters decreased continually until the
tenth month. In the tenth *month,* on the first
day of the month, the tops of the mountains
were seen.
6 So it came to pass, at the end of forty
days, that Noah opened [g]the window of
the ark which he had made. 7 Then he sent
out a raven, which kept going to and fro
until the waters had dried up from the
earth. 8 He also sent out from himself a
dove, to see if the waters had receded from
the face of the ground. 9 But the dove
found no resting place for the sole of her
foot, and she returned into the ark to him,
for the waters *were* on the face of the whole
earth. So he put out his hand and took her,
and drew her into the ark to himself.
10 And he waited yet another seven days,
and again he sent the dove out from the
ark. 11 Then the dove came to him in the
evening, and behold, a freshly plucked
olive leaf *was* in her mouth; and Noah
knew that the waters had receded from the
earth. 12 So he waited yet another seven
days and sent out the dove, which did not
return again to him anymore.

6 [g] Gen. 6:16
16 [h] Gen. 7:13
17 [i] Gen. 1:22, 28; 9:1, 7
20 [j] Gen. 12:7; Ex. 29:18, 25

13 And it came to pass in the six hundred
and first year, in the first *month,* the first
day of the month, that the waters were
dried up from the earth; and Noah removed the covering of the ark and looked,
and indeed the surface of the ground was
dry. 14 And in the second month, on the
twenty-seventh day of the month, the
earth was dried.
15 Then God spoke to Noah, saying,
16 "Go out of the ark, [h]you and your wife,
and your sons and your sons' wives with
you. 17 Bring out with you every living
thing of all flesh that *is* with you: birds and
cattle and every creeping thing that creeps
on the earth, so that they may abound on
the earth, and [i]be fruitful and multiply on
the earth." 18 So Noah went out, and his
sons and his wife and his sons' wives with
him. 19 Every animal, every creeping
thing, every bird, *and* whatever creeps on
the earth, according to their families, went
out of the ark.

God's Covenant with Creation

20 Then Noah built an [j]altar to the LORD,

Caucuses, also known as ancient Urartu, where the elevation exceeded 17,000 feet.

8:7-12 a raven…a dove. Ravens survive on a broad range of food types. If any food was available outside the ark, the raven could survive. In contrast, a dove is much more selective in its food choices. The dove's choice of food would indicate that new life had begun to grow; thus Noah and his family could also survive outside the ark.

8:14-16 Noah and his family had been in the ark for 378 days (cf. 7:4,10,11).

8:17-19 be fruitful and multiply. In the process of replenishing the created order that He had judged with destruction, God repeated the words of the blessing which He had put upon non-human creatures (1:22). Noah faced a new world where longevity of life began to decline immediately; the earth was subject to storms and severe weather, blazing heat, freezing cold, seismic action, and natural disasters.

8:20 built an altar. This was done as an act of worship in response to God's covenant faithfulness in sparing him and his family.

Major Mountains of the Bible

Mt. Ararat (in modern Turkey), where Noah's ark came to rest (Gen. 8:4).

Mt. Carmel, where Elijah was victorious over the prophets of Baal (1 Kin. 18:9-42).

Mt. Ebal (opposite Mt. Gerizim), where Moses commanded that an altar be built after the Hebrews entered the Promised Land (Deut. 27:4).

Mt. Gerizim where Jesus talked with the Samaritan woman at the well (John 4:20).

Mt. Gilboa, where King Saul and his sons were killed in a battle with the Philistines (1 Chr. 10:1,8).

Mt. Hermon, a mountain range that marked the northern limit of the conquest of Canaan (Josh. 11:3,17).

Mt. Lebanon, the source of cedar wood for Solomon's temple in Jerusalem (1 Kin. 5:14,18).

Mt. Moriah, where Abraham brought Isaac for sacrifice (Gen. 22:2) and the location of Solomon's temple (2 Chr. 3:1).

Mt. Olivet, or Mt. of Olives, where Jesus gave the discourse on His Second Coming (Matt. 24:3).

Mt. Pisgah, or Nebo, where Moses viewed the Promised Land (Deut. 34:1).

Mt. Seir, south of the Dead Sea, the location to which Esau moved after Isaac's death (Gen. 36:8).

Mt. Sinai, or Horeb (near Egypt), where the law was given to Moses (Ex. 19:2-25).

Mt. Tabor, 6 miles east of Nazareth, served as a boundary between Issachar and Zebulun; also Barak launched his attack on Sisera from Tabor (Judg. 4:6-15).

Mt. Zion, originally limited to the SW sector (2 Sam. 5:7), was later used of all Jerusalem (Lam. 1:4).

and took of [k]every clean animal and of
every clean bird, and offered [l]burnt offerings on the altar. 21 And the LORD smelled
[m]a soothing aroma. Then the LORD said in
His heart, "I will never again [n]curse the
ground for man's sake, although the
[o]imagination[1] of man's heart *is* evil from
his youth; [p]nor will I again destroy every
living thing as I have done.

22 "While the earth [q]remains,
Seedtime and harvest,
Cold and heat,
Winter and summer,
And [r]day and night
Shall not cease."

9 So God blessed Noah and his sons, and
said to them: [a]"Be fruitful and multiply, and fill the earth. 2 [b]And the fear of
you and the dread of you shall be on every
beast of the earth, on every bird of the air,
on all that move *on* the earth, and on all the
fish of the sea. They are given into your
hand. 3 [c]Every moving thing that lives
shall be food for you. I have given you [d]all
things, even as the [e]green herbs. 4 [f]But you
shall not eat flesh with its life, *that is,* its
blood. 5 Surely for your lifeblood I will demand *a reckoning;* [g]from the hand of every
beast I will require it, and [h]from the hand
of man. From the hand of every [i]man's
brother I will require the life of man.

6 "Whoever [j]sheds man's blood,
By man his blood shall be shed;
[k]For in the image of God
He made man.

7 And as for you, [l]be fruitful and
multiply;
Bring forth abundantly in the earth
And multiply in it."

8 Then God spoke to Noah and to his
sons with him, saying: 9 "And as for Me,
[m]behold, I establish [n]My covenant with
you and with your [1]descendants after you,
10 [o]and with every living creature that *is*
with you: the birds, the cattle, and every
beast of the earth with you, of all that go
out of the ark, every beast of the earth.
11 Thus [p]I establish My covenant with you:
Never again shall all flesh be cut off by the
waters of the flood; never again shall there
be a flood to destroy the earth."
12 And God said: [q]"This *is* the sign of the
covenant which I make between Me and
you, and every living creature that *is* with
you, for perpetual generations: 13 I set [r]My
rainbow in the cloud, and it shall be for the
sign of the covenant between Me and the
earth. 14 It shall be, when I bring a cloud
over the earth, that the rainbow shall be
seen in the cloud; 15 and [s]I will remember
My covenant which *is* between Me and
you and every living creature of all flesh;
the waters shall never again become a
flood to destroy all flesh. 16 The rainbow
shall be in the cloud, and I will look on it to
remember [t]the everlasting covenant between God and every living creature of all
flesh that *is* on the earth." 17 And God said
to Noah, "This *is* the sign of the covenant
which I have established between Me and
all flesh that *is* on the earth."

20 [k]Gen. 7:2; Lev. 11 [l]Gen. 22:2; Ex. 10:25
21 [m]Ex. 29:18, 25; Lev. 1:9; Ezek. 20:41; 2 Cor. 2:15; Eph. 5:2 [n]Gen. 3:17; 6:7, 13, 17; Is. 54:9 [o]Gen. 6:5; 11:6; Job 14:4; Ps. 51:5; Jer. 17:9; Rom. 1:21; 3:23; Eph. 2:1-3 [p]Gen. 9:11, 15 [1]*intent or thought*
22 [q]Is. 54:9 [r]Ps. 74:16; Jer. 33:20, 25

CHAPTER 9

1 [a]Gen. 1:28, 29; 8:17; 9:7, 19; 10:32
2 [b]Gen. 1:26, 28; Ps. 8:6
3 [c]Deut. 12:15; 14:3, 9, 11; Acts 10:12, 13 [d]Rom. 14:14, 20; 1 Cor. 10:23, 26; Col. 2:16; [1 Tim. 4:3, 4] [e]Gen. 1:29
4 [f]Lev. 7:26; 17:10-16; 19:26; Deut. 12:16, 23; 15:23; 1 Sam. 14:33, 34; Acts 15:20, 29
5 [g]Ex. 21:28 [h]Gen. 4:9, 10; Ps. 9:12 [i]Acts 17:26
6 [j]Ex. 21:12-14; Lev. 24:17; Num. 35:33; Matt. 26:52 [k]Gen. 1:26, 27
7 [l]Gen. 9:1, 19
9 [m]Gen. 6:18 [n]Is. 54:9 [1]Lit. *seed*
10 [o]Ps. 145:9
11 [p]Gen. 8:21; Is. 54:9
12 [q]Gen. 9:13, 17; 17:11
13 [r]Ezek. 1:28; Rev. 4:3
15 [s]Lev. 26:42, 45; Deut. 7:9; Ezek. 16:60
16 [t]Gen. 17:13, 19; 2 Sam. 23:5; Is. 55:3; Jer. 32:40; Heb. 13:20

8:21 smelled a soothing aroma. God accepted Noah's sacrifice. **curse...destroy.** Regardless of how sinful mankind would become in the future, God promised not to engage in global catastrophe by flood again (cf. 9:11). *See notes on 2 Pet. 3:3-10* for how God will destroy the earth in the future.

8:22 While the earth remains. With many alterations from the global flood, God reestablished the cycle of seasons after the catastrophic interruption.

9:1 blessed Noah.... Be fruitful and multiply, and fill the earth. God blessed Noah and recommissioned him to fill the earth (cf. 1:28).

9:2,3 the fear of you. Man's relationship to the animals appears to have changed, in that man is free to eat animals for sustenance (v. 3).

9:4 blood. Raw blood was not to be consumed as food. It symbolically represented life. To shed blood symbolically represented death (cf. Lev. 17:11). The blood of animals, representing their life, was not to be eaten. It was, in fact, that blood that God designed to be a covering for sin (Lev. 17:11).

9:5 beast...man. Capital punishment was invoked upon every animal (Ex. 21:28) or man who took human life unlawfully. Cf. John 19:11; Acts 25:11; Rom. 13:4 for clear NT support for this punishment.

9:6 For in the image of God. The reason man could kill animals, but neither animals nor man could kill man, is because man alone was created in God's image.

9:7-17 This is the first covenant God made with man, afterwards called the Noahic Covenant.

9:9,10 with you...with your descendants,...with every living creature. The covenant with Noah included living creatures as was first promised in 6:18.

9:11 by the waters. The specific promise of this covenant, never to destroy the world again by water, was qualified by the means, for God has since promised to destroy the earth with fire one day (2 Pet. 3:10,11; Rev. 20:9; 21:1).

9:12 the sign of the covenant. The rainbow is the perpetual, symbolic reminder of this covenant promise, just as circumcision of all males would be for the Abrahamic Covenant (17:10,11).

9:15 I will remember. Not simple recognition, but God's commitment to keep the promise.

9:16 the everlasting covenant. This covenant with Noah is the first of 5 divinely originated covenants in Scripture explicitly described as "everlasting." The other 4 include: 1) Abrahamic (Gen. 17:7); 2) Priestly (Num. 25:10-13); 3) Davidic (2 Sam. 23:5); and 4) New (Jer. 32:40). The term "everlasting" can mean either 1) to the end of time and/or 2) through eternity future. It never looks back to eternity past. Of the 6 explicitly mentioned covenants of this kind in Scripture, only the Mosaic or Old Covenant was nullified.

Noah and His Sons

18 Now the sons of Noah who went out
of the ark were Shem, Ham, and Japheth.
[u]And Ham *was* the father of Canaan.
19 [v]These three *were* the sons of Noah,
[w]and from these the whole earth was populated.
20 And Noah began *to be* [x]a farmer, and
he planted a vineyard. 21 Then he drank of
the wine [y]and was drunk, and became
uncovered in his tent. 22 And Ham, the father of Canaan, saw the nakedness of his
father, and told his two brothers outside.
23 [z]But Shem and Japheth took a garment,
laid *it* on both their shoulders, and went
backward and covered the nakedness of
their father. Their faces *were* [2]turned away,
and they did not see their father's nakedness.
24 So Noah awoke from his wine, and
knew what his younger son had done to
him. 25 Then he said:

[a]"Cursed *be* Canaan;
A [b]servant of servants
He shall be to his brethren."

26 And he said:

[c]"Blessed *be* the LORD,
The God of Shem,
And may Canaan be his servant.
27 May God [d]enlarge Japheth,
[e]And may he dwell in the tents of
Shem;
And may Canaan be his servant."

28 And Noah lived after the flood three
hundred and fifty years. 29 So all the days
of Noah were nine hundred and fifty
years; and he died.

Nations Descended from Noah

10 Now this *is* the genealogy of the
sons of Noah: Shem, Ham, and
Japheth. [a]And sons were born to them
after the flood.
2 [b]The sons of Japheth *were* Gomer,
Magog, Madai, Javan, Tubal, Meshech, and
Tiras. 3 The sons of Gomer *were* Ashkenaz,
[1]Riphath, and Togarmah. 4 The sons of
Javan *were* Elishah, Tarshish, Kittim, and
[2]Dodanim. 5 From these [c]the coastland
peoples of the Gentiles were separated into
their lands, everyone according to his language, according to their families, into
their nations.
6 [d]The sons of Ham *were* Cush, Mizraim,
[3]Put, and Canaan. 7 The sons of Cush *were*
Seba, Havilah, Sabtah, Raamah, and
Sabtechah; and the sons of Raamah *were*
Sheba and Dedan.
8 Cush begot [e]Nimrod; he began to be a
mighty one on the earth. 9 He was a
mighty [f]hunter [g]before the LORD; therefore
it is said, "Like Nimrod the mighty hunter
before the LORD." 10 [h]And the beginning of
his kingdom was [i]Babel, Erech, Accad, and
Calneh, in the land of Shinar. 11 From that
land he went [j]to Assyria and built Nineveh, Rehoboth Ir, Calah, 12 and Resen be-

18 [u] Gen. 9:25-27; 10:6
19 [v] Gen. 5:32 [w] Gen. 9:1, 7; 10:32; 1 Chr. 1:4
20 [x] Gen. 3:19, 23; 4:2; Prov. 12:11; Jer. 31:24
21 [y] Prov. 20:1; Eph. 5:18
23 [z] Ex. 20:12; Gal. 6:1 [2] Lit. *backwards*
25 [a] Deut. 27:16; Josh. 9:23, 27 [b] Josh. 9:23; 1 Kin. 9:20, 21
26 [c] Gen. 14:20; 24:27; Ps. 144:15; Heb. 11:16
27 [d] Gen. 10:2-5; 39:3; Is. 66:19 [e] Luke 3:36; John 1:14; Eph. 2:13, 14; 3:6

CHAPTER 10
1 [a] Gen. 9:1, 7, 19
2 [b] 1 Chr. 1:5-7
3 [1] *Diphath*, 1 Chr. 1:6
4 [2] Sam. *Rodanim* and 1 Chr. 1:7
5 [c] Gen. 11:8; Ps. 72:10; Jer. 2:10; 25:22
6 [d] 1 Chr. 1:8-16 [3] Or *Phut*
8 [e] Mic. 5:6
9 [f] Jer. 16:16; Mic. 7:2 [g] Gen. 21:20
10 [h] Mic. 5:6 [i] Gen. 11:9
11 [j] Gen. 25:18; 2 Kin. 19:36; Mic. 5:6

9:18 Ham *was* the father of Canaan. Canaan's offspring, the idolatrous enemies of Israel whose land Abraham's descendants would later take (15:13-16), became a primary focus in chap. 10. This notation is important since Moses was writing the Pentateuch just before the Israelites took Canaan (see Introduction: Author and Date, Background and Setting).

9:19 from these the whole earth. All men who have ever lived since the Flood came from these 3 sons of Noah (cf. 10:32). The "one blood" of Acts 17:26 is that of Noah through his sons. All physical characteristics of the whole race were present in the genetics of Noah, his sons, and their wives.

9:21 was drunk. Fermentation, which leads to drunkenness, may have been caused by changed ecological conditions as a result of the Flood. He may have taken off his clothes because of the heat, or been involuntarily exposed due to his drunkenness.

9:22 saw the nakedness. There is no reasonable support for the notion that some perverse activity, in addition to seeing nakedness, occurred. But clearly, the implication is that Ham looked with some sinful thought, if only for a while until he left to inform his brothers. Perhaps he was glad to see his father's dignity and authority reduced to such weakness. He thought his brothers might share his feelings so he eagerly told them. They did not, however, share his attitude (v. 23).

9:25-27 Cursed *be* Canaan. The shift from Ham to his son Canaan established the historic legitimacy of Israel's later conquest of the Canaanites. These were the people with whom Israel had to do battle shortly after they first heard Moses' reading of this passage. Here, God gave Israel the theological basis for the conquest of Canaan. The descendants of Ham had received a sentence of judgment for the sins of their progenitor. In 10:15-20, the descendants of Canaan are seen to be the earlier inhabitants of the land later promised to Abraham.

9:26 may Canaan be his servant. Conquered peoples were called servants, even if they were not household or private slaves. Shem, the ancestor of Israel, and the other "Semites" were to be the masters of Ham's descendants, the Canaanites. The latter would give their land to the former.

9:27 dwell in the tents. This means that spiritual blessings would come to the Japhethites through the God of Shem (v. 26) and the line of Shem from which Messiah would come.

10:1–11:9 The genealogy of Shem, Ham, and Japheth (v. 1).

10:1-32 See the map "The Nations of Genesis 10" for the locations of Noah's descendants.

10:5 were separated...according to his language. This act describes the situation after the Tower of Babel account in chap. 11.

10:6-20 The sons of Ham. Many of whom were Israel's enemies.

10:8-10 Nimrod. This powerful leader was evidently the force behind the building of Babel (see 11:1-4).

10:10 Babel. The beginning of what later would prove to be Babylon, the destroyer of God's people and His city Jerusalem (ca. 605–539 B.C.).

10:11 to Assyria and built Nineveh. This was Israel's primary enemy from the East. Nimrod was Israel's prototypical ancient enemy warrior, whose name in Heb. means "rebel" (cf. Mic. 5:6).

tween Nineveh and Calah (that *is* the principal city).
13 Mizraim begot Ludim, Anamim,
Lehabim, Naphtuhim, 14 Pathrusim, and
Casluhim [k](from whom came the Philistines and Caphtorim).
15 Canaan begot Sidon his firstborn, and
[l]Heth; 16 [m]the Jebusite, the Amorite, and
the Girgashite; 17 the Hivite, the Arkite,
and the Sinite; 18 the Arvadite, the Zemarite, and the Hamathite. Afterward the
families of the Canaanites were dispersed.
19 [n]And the border of the Canaanites was
from Sidon as you go toward Gerar, as far
as Gaza; then as you go toward Sodom,
Gomorrah, Admah, and Zeboiim, as far as
Lasha. 20 These *were* the sons of Ham, according to their families, according to their
languages, in their lands *and* in their nations.
21 And *children* were born also to Shem,
the father of all the children of Eber, [4]the
brother of Japheth the elder. 22 The [o]sons of
Shem *were* Elam, Asshur, [p]Arphaxad, Lud,
and Aram. 23 The sons of Aram *were* Uz,
Hul, Gether, and [5]Mash. 24 [6]Arphaxad
begot [q]Salah, and Salah begot Eber. 25 [r]To
Eber were born two sons: the name of one
was [7]Peleg, for in his days the earth was divided; and his brother's name *was* Joktan.
26 Joktan begot Almodad, Sheleph, Hazarmaveth, Jerah, 27 Hadoram, Uzal, Diklah,
28 [8]Obal, Abimael, Sheba, 29 Ophir, Havilah, and Jobab. All these *were* the sons of
Joktan. 30 And their dwelling place was
from Mesha as you go toward Sephar, the
mountain of the east. 31 These *were* the
sons of Shem, according to their families,
according to their languages, in their
lands, according to their nations.
32 [s]These *were* the families of the sons of
Noah, according to their generations, in
their nations; [t]and from these the nations
were divided on the earth after the flood.

14 [k] 1 Chr. 1:12
15 [l] Gen. 23:3
16 [m] Gen. 14:7; 15:19-21; Deut. 7:1; Neh. 9:8
19 [n] Gen. 13:12, 14, 15, 17; 15:18-21; Num. 34:2-12
21 [4] *Or the older brother of Japheth*
22 [o] Gen. 11:10-26; 1 Chr. 1:17-28 [p] Gen. 10:24; 11:10; Luke 3:36
23 [5] LXX *Meshech* and 1 Chr. 1:17
24 [q] Gen. 11:12; Luke 3:35 [6] So with MT, Vg., Tg.; LXX *Arphaxad begot Cainan, and Cainan begot Salah* (cf. Luke 3:35, 36)
25 [r] 1 Chr. 1:19 [7] Lit. *Division*
28 [8] *Ebal*, 1 Chr. 1:22
32 [s] Gen. 10:1 [t] Gen. 9:19; 11:8

10:15-19 Canaan. A notable shift occurs in this section away from place names to the inhabitants themselves (note the "ite" ending). These are not only the cursed people of Canaan's curse for the scene at Noah's drunkenness, but also they are those who possess the Promised Land which Israel as a nation needed to conquer. But the Noahic curse alone did not determine their guilt, for God said to Abram that the iniquity of the Amorites must first be complete before his descendants could occupy the Promised Land (15:16).

10:21-31 The sons of Shem, i.e., Semitic people.

10:21 Japheth the elder. The marginal variant is correct which would make Shem the oldest of Noah's 3 sons.

10:25 the earth was divided. This looks ahead to the dispersion of nations at Babel (11:1-9).

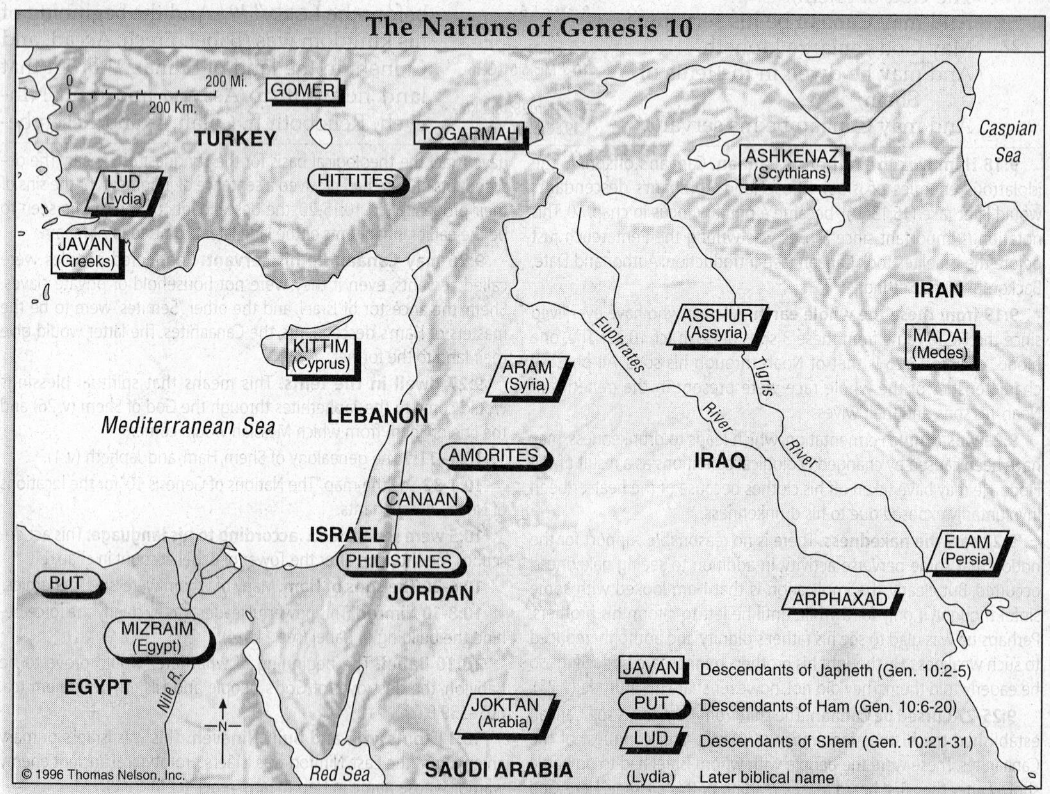

The Tower of Babel

11 Now the whole earth had one language and one [1]speech. **2** And it
came to pass, as they journeyed from the
east, that they found a plain in the land [a]of
Shinar, and they dwelt there. **3** Then they
said to one another, "Come, let us make
bricks and [2]bake *them* thoroughly." They
had brick for stone, and they had asphalt
for mortar. **4** And they said, "Come, let us
build ourselves a city, and a tower [b]whose
top *is* in the heavens; let us make a [c]name
for ourselves, lest we [d]be scattered abroad
over the face of the whole earth."
5 [e]But the LORD came down to see the
city and the tower which the sons of men
had built. **6** And the LORD said, "Indeed
[f]the people *are* one and they all have [g]one
language, and this is what they begin to
do; now nothing that they [h]propose to do
will be withheld from them. **7** Come, [i]let
Us go down and there [j]confuse their language, that they may not understand one
another's speech." **8** So [k]the LORD scattered
them abroad from there [l]over the face of all
the earth, and they ceased building the
city. **9** Therefore its name is called [3]Babel,
[m]because there the LORD confused the language of all the earth; and from there the
LORD scattered them abroad over the face
of all the earth.

Shem's Descendants

10 [n]This *is* the genealogy of Shem: Shem
was one hundred years old, and begot
Arphaxad two years after the flood. **11** After
he begot Arphaxad, Shem lived five hundred years, and begot sons and daughters.
12 Arphaxad lived thirty-five years, [o]and
begot Salah. **13** After he begot Salah,
Arphaxad lived four hundred and three
years, and begot sons and daughters.
14 Salah lived thirty years, and begot
Eber. **15** After he begot Eber, Salah lived
four hundred and three years, and begot
sons and daughters.
16 [p]Eber lived thirty-four years, and
begot [q]Peleg. **17** After he begot Peleg, Eber
lived four hundred and thirty years, and
begot sons and daughters.
18 Peleg lived thirty years, and begot
Reu. **19** After he begot Reu, Peleg lived two
hundred and nine years, and begot sons
and daughters.
20 Reu lived thirty-two years, and begot
[r]Serug. **21** After he begot Serug, Reu lived
two hundred and seven years, and begot
sons and daughters.
22 Serug lived thirty years, and begot
Nahor. **23** After he begot Nahor, Serug
lived two hundred years, and begot sons
and daughters.
24 Nahor lived twenty-nine years, and
begot [s]Terah. **25** After he begot Terah,
Nahor lived one hundred and nineteen
years, and begot sons and daughters.
26 Now Terah lived seventy years, and
[t]begot [4]Abram, Nahor, and Haran.

Terah's Descendants

27 This *is* the genealogy of Terah: Terah
begot [u]Abram, Nahor, and Haran. Haran
begot Lot. **28** And Haran died before his fa-

CHAPTER 11

1 [1] Lit. *lip*
2 [a] Gen. 10:10; 14:1; Dan. 1:2
3 [2] Lit. *burn*
4 [b] Deut. 1:28; 9:1; Ps. 107:26 [c] Gen. 6:4; 2 Sam. 8:13 [d] Deut. 4:27
5 [e] Gen. 18:21; Ex. 3:8; 19:11, 18, 20
6 [f] Gen. 9:19; Acts 17:26 [g] Gen. 11:1 [h] Deut. 31:21; Ps. 2:1
7 [i] Gen. 1:26 [j] Gen. 42:23; Ex. 4:11; Deut. 28:49; Is. 33:19; Jer. 5:15
8 [k] Gen. 11:4; Deut. 32:8; Ps. 92:9; [Luke 1:51] [l] Gen. 10:25, 32
9 [m] 1 Cor. 14:23 [3] Lit. *Confusion*, Babylon
10 [n] Gen. 10:22–25; 1 Chr. 1:17
12 [o] Luke 3:35
16 [p] 1 Chr. 1:19 [q] Luke 3:35
20 [r] Luke 3:35
24 [s] Gen. 11:31; Josh. 24:2; Luke 3:34
26 [t] Josh. 24:2; 1 Chr. 1:26 [4] *Abraham*, Gen. 17:5
27 [u] Gen. 11:31; 17:5

11:1 one language and one speech. God, who made man as the one creature with whom He could speak (1:28), was to take the gift of language and use it to divide the race, for the apostate worship at Babel indicated that man had turned against God in pride (11:8,9).

11:2 as they journeyed from the east. God had restated His commission for man to "be fruitful and multiply and fill the earth" (9:7). It was in the course of spreading out that the events of this account occurred.

11:3,4 let us make bricks...build ourselves a city, and a tower...make a name for ourselves. While dispersing, a portion of the post-Flood group, under the leading of the powerful Nimrod (10:8-10), decided to stop and establish a city as a monument to their pride and for their reputation. The tower, even though it was a part of the plan, was not the singular act of rebellion. Human pride was, which led these people to defy God. They were refusing to move on, i.e., scattering to fill the earth as they had been instructed. In fact, this was Nimrod's and the people's effort to disobey the command of God in 9:1, and thus defeat the counsel of heaven. They had to make bricks, since there were few stones on the plain.

11:4 whose top *is* in the heavens. Not that the tower would actually reach to the abode of God and not that the top would represent the heavens. They wanted it to be a high tower as a monument to their abilities, one that would enhance their fame. In this endeavor, they disobeyed God and attempted to steal His glory.

11:6 nothing...withheld. They were so united that they would do all they desired to do.

11:7 let Us. *See note on 1:26* (cf. 3:22).

11:8 scattered them abroad. God addressed their prideful rebellion at the first act. They had chosen to settle; He forced them to scatter. This account tells how it was that the families of the earth "were separated, everyone according to his language" (10:5) and "were divided on the earth after the flood" (10:32).

11:9 its name is called Babel. This is linked to a Heb. word meaning "to confuse." From this account, Israel first understood not only how so many nations, peoples, and languages came about, but also the rebellious origins of their archetypal enemy, Babylon (cf. 10:5,20,31). **scattered them.** Because they would not fill the earth as God had commanded them, God confused their language so that they had to separate and collect in regions where their own language was spoken.

11:10-26 Shem...Abram. The genealogy of Shem (v. 10). Israel, upon hearing this section read, learned how the generation who survived the Flood related to their own father, Abram (v. 26), later known as Abraham (cf. 17:5). The shortening of lifespans was in effect.

11:14 Eber. Progenitor of the Hebrews (i.e., Eber's descendants).

11:26 seventy years. The age that Terah began to father children. Abram was born later when Terah was 160 (ca. 2165 B.C.). Cf. 11:32 with 12:4.

11:27–25:11 The genealogy of Terah (v. 27).

11:27 Abram. The name means "exalted father." Cf. 17:5.

ther Terah in his native land, in Ur of the
Chaldeans. 29 Then Abram and Nahor
took wives: the name of Abram's wife *was*
[v]Sarai,[5] and the name of Nahor's wife,
[w]Milcah, the daughter of Haran the father
of Milcah and the father of Iscah. 30 But
[x]Sarai was barren; she had no child.

31 And Terah [y]took his son Abram and
his grandson Lot, the son of Haran, and his
daughter-in-law Sarai, his son Abram's
wife, and they went out with them from
[z]Ur of the Chaldeans to go to [a]the land of
Canaan; and they came to Haran and
dwelt there. 32 So the days of Terah were
two hundred and five years, and Terah
died in Haran.

Promises to Abram

12 Now the [a]LORD had said to Abram:

"Get [b]out of your country,
From your family
And from your father's house,
To a land that I will show you.
2 [c]I will make you a great nation;
[d]I will bless you
And make your name great;
[e]And you shall be a blessing.
3 [f]I will bless those who bless you,
And I will curse him who curses
you;
And in [g]you all the families of the
earth shall be [h]blessed."

4 So Abram departed as the LORD had
spoken to him, and Lot went with him. And
Abram *was* seventy-five years old when he
departed from Haran. 5 Then Abram took
Sarai his wife and Lot his brother's son, and
all their possessions that they had gathered,
and [i]the [1]people whom they had acquired
[j]in Haran, and they [k]departed to go to the
land of Canaan. So they came to the land of
Canaan. 6 Abram [l]passed through the land
to the place of Shechem, [m]as far as [2]the terebinth tree of Moreh. [n]And the Canaanites
were then in the land.

7 [o]Then the LORD appeared to Abram
and said, [p]"To your [3]descendants I will
give this land." And there he built an [q]altar

29 [v] Gen. 17:15; 20:12 [w] Gen. 22:20, 23; 24:15 [5] *Sarah,* Gen. 17:15
30 [x] Gen. 16:1, 2; Luke 1:36
31 [y] Gen. 12:1 [z] Gen. 15:7; Neh. 9:7; Acts 7:4 [a] Gen. 10:19

CHAPTER 12

1 [a] Gen. 15:7; Acts 7:2, 3; [Heb. 11:8] [b] Gen. 13:9
2 [c] [Gen. 17:4-6]; 18:18; 46:3; Deut. 26:5; 1 Kin. 3:8 [d] Gen. 22:17; 24:35 [e] Gen. 28:4; Zech. 8:13; Gal. 3:14
3 [f] Gen. 24:35; 27:29; Ex. 23:22; Num. 24:9 [g] Gen. 18:18; 22:18; 26:4; 28:14; Ps. 72:17; Matt. 1:1; Luke 3:34; Acts 3:25; [Gal. 3:8] [h] Is. 41:27
5 [i] Gen. 14:14 [j] Gen. 11:31 [k] Gen. 13:18 [1] Lit. *souls*
6 [l] Heb. 11:9 [m] Deut. 11:30; Judg. 7:1 [n] Gen. 10:18, 19 [2] Heb. *Alon Moreh*
7 [o] Gen. 17:1; 18:1 [p] Gen. 13:15; 15:18; 17:8; Deut. 34:4; Ps. 105:9-12; Acts 7:5; Gal. 3:16 [q] Gen. 13:4, 18; 22:9 [3] Lit. *seed*

11:28 Ur of the Chaldeans. A prosperous, populous city in Mesopotamia.

11:31 from Ur...to Haran. Cf. Acts 7:2-4; Heb. 11:8-10. Abram traveled along the Euphrates to Haran, a crossroads trading town in northern Mesopotamia or Syria, the best route from which to come down into Canaan and avoid crossing the great desert with all his people and animals (see 12:4).

12:1-3 the LORD...to Abram. This passage is the promise whose fulfillment extends all through Scripture (either in fact or in expectation) to Rev. 20. The actual Abrahamic Covenant is introduced in 12:1-3, actually made in 15:18-21, reaffirmed in 17:1-21, then renewed also with Isaac (26:2-5) and Jacob (28:10-17). It is an everlasting covenant (17:7,8; 1 Chr. 16:17; Ps. 105:7-12; Is. 24:5) which contains 4 elements: 1) seed (17:2-7; cf. Gal. 3:8,16 where it referred to Christ); 2) land (15:18-21; 17:8); 3) a nation (12:2; 17:4); plus 4) divine blessing and protection (12:3). This covenant is unconditional in the sense of its ultimate fulfillment of a kingdom and salvation for Israel (*see notes on Rom. 11:1-27*), but conditional in terms of immediate fulfillment (cf. 17:4). Its national importance to Israel is magnified by its repeated references and point of appeal throughout the OT (cf. 2 Kin. 13:23; 1 Chr. 16:15-22; Neh. 9:7,8). Its importance spiritually to all believers is expounded by Paul (*see notes on Gal. 3, 4*). Stephen quoted 12:1 in Acts 7:31.

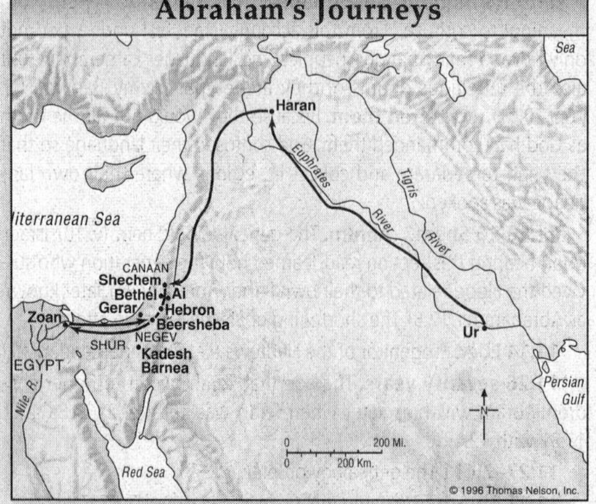

12:1 To a land. Abram was still in Haran (11:31) when the call was repeated (Acts 7:2) to go to Canaan.

12:2 name great. Abram's magnificent reputation and legacy was fulfilled materially (13:2; 24:35), spiritually (21:22), and socially (23:6).

12:3 I will curse him who curses you. Those who "curse" Abram and his descendants are those who treat him lightly, despise him, or treat him with contempt. God's curse for such lack of respect and disdain was to involve the most harsh of divine judgments. The opposite was to be true for those who bless him and his people. **in you all the families of the earth shall be blessed.** Paul identified these words as "the gospel to Abraham beforehand" (Gal. 3:8).

12:4 Haran. *See note on 11:31.* They must have been there for some time because they accumulated a group of people (probably servants).

12:5 they came to...Canaan. Ca. 2090 B.C.

12:6 Shechem. A Canaanite town located in the valley between Mt. Ebal and Mt. Gerizim (cf. Deut. 27:4,12) W of the Jordan about 15 mi. and N of Jerusalem about 30 mi. Moreh was most likely a resident of the area for whom the tree was named. **Canaanites *were* then in the land.** Moses was writing approximately 700 years after Abram entered the land (ca. 1405 B.C.). The Canaanites, of whom he wrote, were soon to be the opponents of Israel as they entered Canaan.

12:7 I will give this land. Cf. 13:15; 15:18; 17:7,8; Gal. 3:16. God was dealing with Abram, not in a private promise, but with a view toward high and sacred interests long into the future, i.e., the land which his posterity was to inhabit as a peculiar people. The seeds of divine truth were to be sown there for the benefit of all mankind. It was chosen as the most appropriate land for the coming of divine revelation and salvation for the world. **altar to the LORD.** By this act, Abram made an open confession of his religion, established worship of the true God, and declared his faith in God's promise. This was the first true place of

to the LORD, who had appeared to him.
8 And he moved from there to the mountain east of Bethel, and he pitched his tent
with Bethel on the west and Ai on the east;
there he built an altar to the LORD and
[r]called on the name of the LORD. 9 So
Abram journeyed, [s]going on still toward
the [4]South.

Abram in Egypt

10 Now there was [t]a famine in the land,
and Abram [u]went down to Egypt to dwell
there, for the famine *was* [v]severe in the
land. 11 And it came to pass, when he was
close to entering Egypt, that he said to
Sarai his wife, "Indeed I know that you
are [w]a woman of beautiful countenance.
12 Therefore it will happen, when the
Egyptians see you, that they will say, 'This
is his wife'; and they [x]will kill me, but they
will let you live. 13 [y]Please say you *are* my
[z]sister, that it may be well with me for your
sake, and that [5]I may live because of you."
14 So it was, when Abram came into
Egypt, that the Egyptians saw the woman,
that she *was* very beautiful. 15 The princes
of Pharaoh also saw her and commended
her to Pharaoh. And the woman was taken
to Pharaoh's house. 16 He [a]treated Abram
well for her sake. He [b]had sheep, oxen,
male donkeys, male and female servants,
female donkeys, and camels.
17 But the LORD [c]plagued Pharaoh and
his house with great plagues because of
Sarai, Abram's wife. 18 And Pharaoh called
Abram and said, [d]"What *is* this you have
done to me? Why did you not tell me that
she *was* your wife? 19 Why did you say,
'She *is* my sister'? I might have taken her
as my wife. Now therefore, here is your
wife; take *her* and go your way." 20 [e]So
Pharaoh commanded *his* men concerning
him; and they sent him away, with his wife
and all that he had.

Abram Inherits Canaan

13 Then Abram went up from Egypt,
he and his wife and all that he had,
and [a]Lot with him, [b]to the [1]South.
2 [c]Abram *was* very rich in livestock, in silver, and in gold. 3 And he went on his journey [d]from the South as far as Bethel, to the
place where his tent had been at the beginning, between Bethel and Ai, 4 to the [e]place
of the altar which he had made there at
first. And there Abram [f]called on the name
of the LORD.
5 Lot also, who went with Abram, had
flocks and herds and tents. 6 Now [g]the
land was not able to [2]support them, that
they might dwell together, for their possessions were so great that they could not
dwell together. 7 And there was [h]strife between the herdsmen of Abram's livestock
and the herdsmen of Lot's livestock. [i]The
Canaanites and the Perizzites then dwelt
in the land.
8 So Abram said to Lot, [j]"Please let there

8 [r] Gen. 4:26; 13:4; 21:33
9 [s] Gen. 13:1, 3; 20:1; 24:62 [4] Heb. *Negev*
10 [t] Gen. 26:1 [u] Ps. 105:13 [v] Gen. 43:1
11 [w] Gen. 12:14; 26:7; 29:17
12 [x] Gen. 20:11; 26:7
13 [y] Gen. 20:1-18; 26:6-11 [z] Gen. 20:12 [5] Lit. *my soul*
16 [a] Gen. 20:14 [b] Gen. 13:2
17 [c] Gen. 20:18; 1 Chr. 16:21; [Ps. 105:14]
18 [d] Gen. 20:9, 10; 26:10
20 [e] [Prov. 21:1]

CHAPTER 13

1 [a] Gen. 12:4; 14:12, 16 [b] Gen. 12:9 [1] Heb. *Negev*
2 [c] Gen. 24:35; 26:14; Ps. 112:3; Prov. 10:22
3 [d] Gen. 12:8, 9
4 [e] Gen. 12:7, 8; 21:33 [f] Ps. 116:17
6 [g] Gen. 36:7 [2] Lit. *bear*
7 [h] Gen. 26:20 [i] Gen. 12:6; 15:20, 21
8 [j] 1 Cor. 6:7; [Phil. 2:14, 15]

---

worship ever erected in the Promised Land. Isaac would later build an altar also to commemorate the Lord's appearance to him (26:24,25), and Jacob also built one in Shechem (33:18-20).

12:8 Bethel...Ai. Bethel, 7 mi. N of Jerusalem, was named later by Abraham (28:19). Ai was 2 mi. E of Bethel, where Joshua later fought (Josh. 7, 8).

12:9 toward the South. Abram moved toward the Negev into a less desirable area for raising crops but better for his vocation as a herdsman, perhaps engaging also in merchant activity.

12:10 a famine in the land. Famine was not an unusual phenomenon in Canaan; two other major food shortages also occurred during the patriarchal period (26:1; 41:56). The severity and timing of this one forced Abram, soon after his arrival and travel in the Promised Land (vv. 5-9), to emigrate to Egypt, where food was usually in abundant supply. Still holding to God's promise, he did not return to Ur, though matters were extremely difficult (cf. Heb. 11:15).

12:11 woman...beautiful. At 65, she was still young and exceptionally attractive, being only half the age she was to be when she died (127). The patriarchs lived long; Abram was 175 when he died.

12:12,13 Abram's fear of Sarai being taken to Pharaoh's harem and him being killed led him to disguise his true relationship to her (cf. 20:13). Abram sought on his own initiative to take care of his future, thinking to assist God in fulfilling His promises.

12:13 sister. This was a lying half-truth, since Sarai was Abram's half-sister (20:12).

12:15 taken to Pharaoh's house. Egyptian officials did take notice of Sarai and informed their monarch of her beauty. The result was not unexpected; she ended up in Pharaoh's harem!

12:17 the LORD plagued Pharaoh...with great plagues. The separation of Abram and Sarai was critical enough to evoke the Lord's personal and dramatic intervention. Abram engineered the ruse to protect himself (v. 13, "that I may live") apparently without too much thought being given to Sarai; but God's reaction focused upon the protection of Sarai ("because of Sarai").

12:18,19 What *is* this you have done to me?...take *her* and go. Somehow, and it remains unexplained, the plagues uncovered the deceit of Abram for Pharaoh. The monarch of Egypt humiliated Abram with his questions, showing more character than Abram gave him credit for and sending Abram out of his country.

12:20 sent him away. Abram's lie brought him and his extended family to an ignominious exit from Egypt—one which the servants must have talked about among themselves, with some loss to Abram's integrity and reputation in their eyes. *See note on 13:9.*

13:1-4 Significantly, after the disastrous situation in Egypt, Abram journeyed back to where he had erected an altar and there he again worshiped (see 12:8).

13:5 flocks and herds. Wealth in the ancient world was measured, not by land owned, but by the size of one's herds and the possession of silver, gold, and jewels (cf. v. 2; Job 1:1-3).

13:6,7 Not unexpectedly, conflict occurred because of crowded conditions and limited grazing space. Both uncle and nephew had accrued much on the slow trip from Ur via Haran and Egypt to the Bethel/Ai region.

13:7 Perizzites. A Canaanite tribe. Cf. 34:30; Deut. 7:1; Judg. 1:4; 3:5,6; 1 Kin. 9:20,21; Ezra 9:1.

be no strife between you and me, and between my herdsmen and your herdsmen;
for we *are* brethren. 9 [k]*Is* not the whole land
before you? Please [l]separate from me. [m]If
you take the left, then I will go to the right;
or, if *you go* to the right, then I will go to the
left."
10 And Lot lifted his eyes and saw all
[n]the plain of Jordan, that it *was* well watered everywhere (before the LORD [o]de-
stroyed Sodom and Gomorrah) [p]like the
garden of the LORD, like the land of Egypt
as you go toward [q]Zoar. 11 Then Lot chose
for himself all the plain of Jordan, and Lot
journeyed east. And they separated from
each other. 12 Abram dwelt in the land of
Canaan, and Lot [r]dwelt in the cities of the
plain and [s]pitched *his* tent even as far as
Sodom. 13 But the men of Sodom [t]*were* exceedingly wicked and [u]sinful against the
LORD.
14 And the LORD said to Abram, after Lot
[v]had separated from him: "Lift your eyes
now and look from the place where you
are—[w]northward, southward, eastward,
and westward; 15 for all the land which
you see [x]I give to you and [y]your [3]descen-
dants forever. 16 And [z]I will make your descendants as the dust of the earth; so that if
a man could number the dust of the earth,
then your descendants also could be numbered. 17 Arise, walk in the land through
its length and its width, for I give it to
you."

9 [k]Gen. 20:15; 34:10 [l]Gen. 13:11, 14 [m][Rom. 12:18]
10 [n]Gen. 19:17-29; Deut. 34:3 [o]Gen. 19:24 [p]Gen. 2:8, 10; Is. 51:3 [q]Gen. 14:2, 8; 19:22; Deut. 34:3
12 [r]Gen. 19:24, 25, 29 [s]Gen. 14:12; 19:1
13 [t]Gen. 18:20, 21; Ezek. 16:49; 2 Pet. 2:7, 8 [u]Gen. 6:11; 39:9; Num. 32:23
14 [v]Gen. 13:11 [w]Gen. 28:14
15 [x]Gen. 12:7; 13:17; 15:7, 18; 17:8; Deut. 34:4; Acts 7:5 [y]2 Chr. 20:7; Ps. 37:22 [3]Lit. *seed*
16 [z]Gen. 22:17; Ex. 32:13; Num. 23:10
18 [a]Gen. 26:17 [b]Gen. 14:13 [c]Gen. 23:2; 35:27 [d]Gen. 8:20; 22:8, 9 [4]Heb. *Alon Mamre*

CHAPTER 14

1 [a]Gen. 10:10; 11:2 [b]Is. 11:11; 21:2; Dan. 8:2 [1]Heb. *goyim*
2 [c]Gen. 10:19; Deut. 29:23 [d]Gen. 13:10; 19:22
3 [e]Num. 34:12; Deut. 3:17; Josh. 3:16
4 [f]Gen. 9:26
5 [g]Gen. 15:20 [h]Deut. 2:20 [i]Num. 32:37; Deut. 2:10
6 [j]Gen. 36:20; Deut. 2:12, 22
7 [k]2 Chr. 20:2

18 [a]Then Abram moved *his* tent, and
went and [b]dwelt by [4]the terebinth trees of
Mamre, [c]which *are* in Hebron, and built an
[d]altar there to the LORD.

Lot's Captivity and Rescue

14 And it came to pass in the days of
Amraphel king [a]of Shinar, Arioch
king of Ellasar, Chedorlaomer king of
[b]Elam, and Tidal king of [1]nations, 2 *that*
they made war with Bera king of Sodom,
Birsha king of Gomorrah, Shinab king of
[c]Admah, Shemeber king of Zeboiim, and
the king of Bela (that is, [d]Zoar). 3 All these
joined together in the Valley of Siddim
[e](that is, the Salt Sea). 4 Twelve years [f]they
served Chedorlaomer, and in the thirteenth year they rebelled.
5 In the fourteenth year Chedorlaomer
and the kings that *were* with him came and
attacked [g]the Rephaim in Ashteroth Karnaim, [h]the Zuzim in Ham, [i]the Emim in
Shaveh Kiriathaim, 6 [j]and the Horites in
their mountain of Seir, as far as El Paran,
which *is* by the wilderness. 7 Then they
turned back and came to En Mishpat (that
is, Kadesh), and attacked all the country of
the Amalekites, and also the Amorites who
dwelt [k]in Hazezon Tamar.
8 And the king of Sodom, the king of Gomorrah, the king of Admah, the king of Zeboiim, and the king of Bela (that *is*, Zoar)
went out and joined together in battle in
the Valley of Siddim 9 against Chedor-

13:8 we *are* brethren. Abram's whole reaction in resolving the strife between the two households and their personnel portrayed a different Abram than seen in Egypt; one whose attitude was not self-centered. Waving his right to seniority, he gave the choice to his nephew, Lot.

13:9 *Is* not the whole land before you? Abram gladly called on Lot to select for himself (vv. 10,11) what he desired for his household and flocks. After Lot's choice had been exercised, then Abram would accept what was left for him. Perhaps this did much to restore, in the eyes of the servants, Abram's integrity and reputation (*see note on 12:20*).

13:10 before the LORD destroyed Sodom and Gomorrah. When Moses was writing (700 years after Abram came to Canaan) the devastation of that region had long before occurred by divinely initiated catastrophe (19:23-29), totally obliterating any evidence of its agricultural richness. **like the garden of the LORD...like... Egypt.** This two-fold appraisal of the Jordan Valley, with its meadows on either side of the river to which Lot was so strongly attracted, highlighted its lush and fertile nature. Moses, reading this to the Jews about to enter Canaan and likening it to the Garden of Eden, referred hearer and reader to God's revelatory description of it (Gen. 2:8-15). Likening it to an obviously well known and well irrigated region of Egypt referred them to a place the Jews had likely known well in their sojourn in Egypt. **Zoar.** Cf. 4:2. A town located at the S end of the Dead Sea, whose name means "small place" (see 19:22).

13:11,12 An excellent yet selfish choice, from a worldly point of view, but disastrous spiritually because it drew him into the wickedness of Sodom (v. 13).

13:13 the men of Sodom *were* exceedingly wicked. Lot's decisions put him in dangerous proximity to those cities whose names would become a byword for perversion and unbridled wickedness. Their evil is the theme of chap. 19.

13:14-17 With Lot gone, the Lord reaffirmed His covenant promise with Abram (Gen. 12:1-3). Strikingly and unmistakably, the Lord deeded the Land (v. 14—look in all directions, and v. 17—walk in all directions) in perpetuity to Abram and his descendants, whom He declared would be definitely innumerable (v. 16—as the dust).

13:18 the terebinth trees of Mamre. A distinctively large grove of trees owned by Mamre the Amorite (14:13) located ca. 19 mi. SW of Jerusalem at Hebron whose elevation exceeds 3,000 feet. **built an altar.** Cf. 12:7,8; 13:4. He was devoted to the worship of God.

14:1-12 Raiding, conquering, and making other kings and city-states subservient vassals were all part of the world of the Fertile Crescent in Abraham's day. These locations mentioned range from Shinar in the east (the region of Babylon in Mesopotamia) to the region S of the Salt Sea (Dead Sea) to the Jordan Valley, to the land of Moab, SW of the Dead Sea to Mt. Seir (later Edom). Amalekites (*see note on Ex. 17:8*) did not yet exist in Abram's time (cf. 36:12), but they did when Moses wrote. Amorites scattered throughout Palestine became Canaanites. Vassal states, when they thought they could throw off the yoke of their suzerain with impunity, rebelled by not paying the assessed tribute and waited for any military response. This time rebellion evoked a major military excursion by the offended suzerain Chedorlaomer and his allies (vv. 5-7); in the ensuing confrontation with Sodom and Gomorrah and their allies (vv. 8-10), the vassals miscalculated and they lost. Lot, by then a resident of Sodom, was taken captive.

laomer king of Elam, Tidal king of [2]na-
tions, Amraphel king of Shinar, and Arioch
king of Ellasar—four kings against five.
10 Now the Valley of Siddim *was full of* [l]as-
phalt pits; and the kings of Sodom and Gomorrah fled; *some* fell there, and the remainder fled [m]to the mountains. 11 Then
they took [n]all the goods of Sodom and Gomorrah, and all their provisions, and went
their way. 12 They also took Lot, Abram's
[o]brother's son [p]who dwelt in Sodom, and
his goods, and departed.
13 Then one who had escaped came and
told Abram the [q]Hebrew, for [r]he dwelt by
[3]the terebinth trees of Mamre the Amorite,
brother of Eshcol and brother of Aner; [s]and
they *were* allies with Abram. 14 Now [t]when
Abram heard that [u]his brother was taken
captive, he armed his three hundred and
eighteen trained *servants* who were [v]born
in his own house, and went in pursuit [w]as
far as Dan. 15 He divided his forces against
them by night, and he and his servants [x]at-
tacked them and pursued them as far as
Hobah, which *is* [4]north of Damascus. 16 So
he [y]brought back all the goods, and also
brought back his brother Lot and his goods,
as well as the women and the people.
17 And the king of Sodom [z]went out to
meet him at the Valley of Shaveh (that *is,*
the [a]King's Valley), [b]after his return from
[5]the defeat of Chedorlaomer and the kings
who *were* with him.

Abram and Melchizedek

18 Then [c]Melchizedek king of Salem
brought out [d]bread and wine; he *was* [e]the
priest of [f]God Most High. 19 And he
blessed him and said:

[g]"Blessed be Abram of God Most
High,
[h]Possessor of heaven and earth;
20 And [i]blessed be God Most High,
Who has delivered your enemies
into your hand."

And he [j]gave him [6]a tithe of all.
21 Now the king of Sodom said to
Abram, "Give me the [7]persons, and take
the goods for yourself."
22 But Abram [k]said to the king of
Sodom, "I [l]have raised my hand to the
LORD, God Most High, [m]the Possessor of
heaven and earth, 23 that [n]I *will take* nothing, from a thread to a sandal strap, and
that I will not take anything that *is* yours,
lest you should say, 'I have made Abram
rich'— 24 except only what the young men
have eaten, and the portion of the men

9 [2] Heb. *goyim*
10 [l] Gen. 11:3 [m] Gen. 19:17,30
11 [n] Gen. 14:16,21
12 [o] Gen. 11:27; 12:5 [p] Gen. 13:12
13 [q] Gen. 39:14; 40:15 [r] Gen. 13:18 [s] Gen. 14:24; 21:27,32 [3] Heb. *Alon Mamre*
14 [t] Gen. 19:29 [u] Gen. 13:8; 14:12 [v] Gen. 12:5; 15:3; 17:27; Eccl. 2:7 [w] Deut. 34:1; Judg. 18:29; 1 Kin. 15:20
15 [x] Is. 41:2,3 [4] Lit. *on the left hand of*
16 [y] Gen. 31:18; 1 Sam. 30:8,18,19
17 [z] 1 Sam. 18:6 [a] 2 Sam. 18:18 [b] Heb. 7:1 [5] Lit. *striking*
18 [c] Ps. 110:4; Heb. 7:1-10 [d] Gen. 18:5; Ex. 29:40; Ps. 104:15 [e] Ps. 110:4; Heb. 5:6 [f] Acts 16:17
19 [g] Ruth 3:10 [h] Gen. 14:22; Matt. 11:25
20 [i] Gen. 24:27 [j] Gen. 28:22; Heb. 7:4 [6] *one-tenth*
21 [7] Lit. *souls*
22 [k] Gen. 14:2,8,10 [l] Dan. 12:7 [m] Gen. 14:19
23 [n] 2 Kin. 5:16; Esth. 9:15,16

14:10 Valley of Siddim. Perhaps this was the large peninsula that comes out into the Dead Sea from the eastern shore. In Abram's time, it may have come all the way across to the western shore (near Masada), so the bottom third of the current Dead Sea formed this dry valley. **asphalt pits.** Tar pits which provided sealants for all sorts of uses.

14:13 one who had escaped. One of the survivors who had fled from the invaders to the mountains (v. 10) went further and located Lot's uncle (the people knew who was related to whom). One as wealthy as Abram would not be hard to find, and was obviously thought to be one who could do something about the crisis which had affected his own close relatives. **the Hebrew.** For the first time in the biblical record, this ethnic appellation, "descended from Eber" (cf. 11:15-17), is accorded to Abram. Foreigners used it of Israelites and Israelites used it of themselves in the presence of foreigners (cf. 34:14; 40:15; 43:32). **trees of Mamre.** *See note on 13:18.*

14:14 trained *servants.* Abram's private militia, members of his extended family ("born in his house") totaling 318, were highly skilled bodyguards and the protective force for his possessions. These, together with the trained men of his allies (vv. 13,24), were mustered and set off in pursuit of the military kidnappers, lest their captives be taken away to the E, to Shinar (the early name for Mesopotamia) or further E, to Elam.

14:15,16 divided...attacked...pursued...brought back. A battle-wise Abram, no stranger to military strategy, pursued the enemy for over 150 mi. (N of Damascus) and defeated the marauding consortium, being totally successful in his objective.

14:17 the Valley of Shaveh. *See note on 2 Sam. 18:18.* The liberated king of Sodom went to meet Abram near Jerusalem.

14:18 Melchizedek king of Salem. The lack of biographical and genealogical particulars for this ruler, whose name meant "righteous king" and who was a king-priest over ancient Jerusalem, allowed for later revelation to use him as a type of Christ (cf. Ps. 110:4; Heb. 7:17,21). His superior status in Abram's day is witnessed 1) by the king of Sodom, the first to meet Abram returning in victory, deferring to Melchizedek before continuing with his request (vv. 17,21) and 2) by Abram, without demur, both accepting a blessing from and also giving a tithe to this priest-king (vv. 19,20). Cf. Heb. 7:1,2. **priest of God Most High.** The use of El Elyon (Sovereign Lord) for God's name indicated that Melchizedek, who used this title two times (vv. 18,19), worshiped, served, and represented no Canaanite deity, but the same one whom Abram also called Yahweh El Elyon (v. 22). That this was so is confirmed by the added description, "Possessor of heaven and earth," being used by both Abram and Melchizedek (vv. 19,22).

14:20 Who has delivered your enemies into your hand. Credit for victory over a superior military coalition correctly went to the Sovereign Lord (El Elyon) and not to Abram's prowess (*see note at vv. 15,16*). To Melchizedek, and to Abram too, this amounted to true worship of the true God. **a tithe.** This is the first mention in Scripture of giving 10 percent (cf. 28:22). This 10-percent offering was purely voluntary, and may only have been a tenth of the best, not a tenth of the total (*see note on Heb. 7:4*). This tenth is not like the required tenths given to Israel in the Mosaic law (*see notes on Num. 18:21-28; Deut. 14:22; 26:12*).

14:21-24 If Abram acceded to the king of Sodom's request, he would have allowed that wicked king to attribute Abram's wealth to the king's generosity, thus distorting the clear testimony of the Lord's blessings on his life. To accept such payment would belie his trust in God! Such a personal commitment would not be foisted upon his allies, who could make their own decisions. As for his own servants, their meals taken from the spoils was sufficient compensation. Undoubtedly, the servants remembered their master's reaction and testimony; it overcame much of the negative aspects in the memory of the earlier exit from Egypt (see 12:20).

who went with me: Aner, Eshcol, and
Mamre; let them take their portion."

God's Covenant with Abram

15 After these things the word of the
LORD came to Abram [a]in a vision,
saying, [b]"Do not be afraid, Abram. I *am*
your [c]shield, [1]your exceedingly [d]great reward."
2 [e]But Abram said, "Lord GOD, what will
You give me, [f]seeing I [2]go childless, and
the heir of my house *is* Eliezer of Damascus?" 3 Then Abram said, "Look, You have
given me no offspring; indeed [g]one[3] born
in my house is my heir!"
4 And behold, the word of the LORD *came*
to him, saying, "This one shall not be your
heir, but one who [h]will come from your
own body shall be your heir." 5 Then He
brought him outside and said, "Look now
toward heaven, and [i]count the [j]stars if you
are able to number them." And He said to
him, [k]"So shall your [l]descendants be."
6 And he [m]believed in the LORD, and He
[n]accounted it to him for righteousness.
7 Then He said to him, "I *am* the LORD,
who [o]brought you out of [p]Ur of the
Chaldeans, [q]to give you this land to inherit it."
8 And he said, "Lord GOD, [r]how shall I
know that I will inherit it?"
9 So He said to him, "Bring Me a three-
year-old heifer, a three-year-old female
goat, a three-year-old ram, a turtledove,
and a young pigeon." 10 Then he brought
all these to Him and [s]cut them in two,
down the middle, and placed each piece
opposite the other; but he did not cut [t]the
birds in two. 11 And when the vultures
came down on the carcasses, Abram drove
them away.
12 Now when the sun was going down,
[u]a deep sleep fell upon Abram; and behold, horror *and* great darkness fell upon
him. 13 Then He said to Abram: "Know
certainly [v]that your descendants will be
strangers in a land *that is* not theirs, and
will serve them, and [w]they will afflict them
four hundred years. 14 And also the nation
whom they serve [x]I will judge; afterward
[y]they shall come out with great possessions. 15 Now as for you, [z]you shall [4]go [a]to
your fathers in peace; [b]you shall be buried
at a good old age. 16 But [c]in the fourth generation they shall return here, for the iniquity [d]of the Amorites [e]*is* not yet complete."
17 And it came to pass, when the sun
went down and it was dark, that behold,
there appeared a smoking oven and a
burning torch that [f]passed between those
pieces. 18 On the same day the LORD [g]made
a covenant with Abram, saying:
[h]"To your descendants I have given this
land, from the river of Egypt to the great
river, the River Euphrates— 19 the Kenites,

CHAPTER 15

1 [a] Gen. 15:4; 46:2; 1 Sam. 15:10; Dan. 10:1 [b] Gen. 21:17; 26:24; Is. 41:10; Dan. 10:12 [c] Deut. 33:29; Ps. 3:3; 84:11; 91:4 [d] Num. 18:20; Ps. 58:11; Prov. 11:18 [1] *Or your reward shall be very great*
2 [e] Gen. 17:18 [f] Acts 7:5 [2] *am childless*
3 [g] Gen. 14:14 [3] *a servant*
4 [h] 2 Sam. 7:12; Gal. 4:28
5 [i] Gen. 22:17; 26:4; Deut. 1:10; Ps. 147:4 [j] Jer. 33:22 [k] Ex. 32:13; Rom. 4:18; Heb. 11:12 [l] Gen. 17:19
6 [m] Gen. 21:1; Rom. 4:3, 9, 22; Gal. 3:6; James 2:23 [n] Ps. 32:2; 106:31
7 [o] Gen. 12:1 [p] Gen. 11:28, 31 [q] Gen. 13:15, 17; Ps. 105:42, 44
8 [r] Gen. 24:13, 14; Judg. 6:36-40; 1 Sam. 14:9, 10; Luke 1:18
10 [s] Gen. 15:17; Jer. 34:18 [t] Lev. 1:17
12 [u] Gen. 2:21; 28:11; Job 33:15
13 [v] Ex. 1:11; Acts 7:6 [w] Ex. 12:40
14 [x] Ex. 6:6 [y] Ex. 12:36
15 [z] Job 5:26 [a] Gen. 25:8; 47:30 [b] Gen. 25:8 [4] Die and join your ancestors
16 [c] Gen. 15:13; Ex. 12:41 [d] Gen. 48:22; Lev. 18:24-28; 1 Kin. 21:26 [e] 1 Kin. 11:12; Matt. 23:32
17 [f] Jer. 34:18, 19
18 [g] Gen. 24:7 [h] Gen. 12:7; 17:8; Ex. 23:31; Num. 34:3; Deut. 11:24; Josh. 1:4; 21:43; Acts 7:5

15:1 I *am* your shield. God served Abram as his divine protector (cf. Pss. 7:10; 84:9).

15:2 I go childless. In response to God's encouragement and admonition (v. 1), Abram showed what nagged at him. How could God's promise of many descendants (13:16) and of being a great nation (12:2) come about when he had no children? **Eliezer of Damascus.** To Abram, God's promise had stalled; so adoption of a servant as the male heir—a well known contemporary Mesopotamian custom—was the best officially recognizable arrangement to make it come to pass, humanly speaking.

15:3-5 The question, "What will You give me?" (v. 2) became an accusation, "You have not given me!" (v. 3). The Lord's rejection of Abram's solution (v. 4) preceded God's reiterated promise of innumerable descendants (v. 5).

15:5 Cf. Rom. 4:18.

15:6 believed...accounted...for righteousness. The Apostle Paul quoted these words as an illustration of faith over and against works (Rom. 4:3,9,22; Gal. 3:6; James 2:23). Abram was regenerated by faith! *See notes on Rom. 4 and Gal. 3* for a fuller discussion of justification by faith.

15:7 to give you this land to inherit it. That a specifically identifiable land (see vv. 18-21) was intimately linked with Abram's having many descendants in God's purpose and in the Abrahamic Covenant was clearly revealed and, in a formal ceremony (vv. 9-21), would be placed irrevocably beyond dispute.

15:8 how shall I know that I will inherit it? A question not of veiled accusation at the delayed fulfillment but of genuine request for information and assurance. In response, God affirmed His covenant with Abram in a remarkable ceremony (vv. 9-21).

15:9,10 cut them in two. The sign of ancient covenants often involved the cutting in half of animals, so that the pledging parties could walk between them, affirming that the same should happen to them if they broke the covenant (see Jer. 34:18,19).

15:12 sleep. God put him to sleep, because the covenant did not involve any promise on his part. He would not walk through the pieces as a pledge (see v. 17).

15:13,14 The words of God in the covenant ceremony assured Abram that his descendants would definitely be in the land, although a painful detour into Egypt would delay fulfillment until long after his demise. Cf. Acts. 7:6,7.

15:13 four hundred years. This represents an approximated number which is precisely 430 years (cf. Ex. 12:40).

15:16 the iniquity of the Amorites *is* not yet complete. A delay in judgment occasioned the delay in covenant fulfillment. Judgment on Egypt (v. 14) would mark the departure of Abram's descendants for their Land, and judgment on the Canaanites (broadly defined ethnically as Amorites) would mark their entrance to that Land.

15:17 smoking oven...burning torch. Cf. Ex. 13:21. These items symbolized the presence of God, who solemnly promised by divine oath to fulfill His promises to Abram by alone passing through the animal pieces (vv. 9-11).

15:18-21 river of Egypt to the...Euphrates. Scripture records both general (Ex. 23:31; Num. 13:21; Deut. 11:24; 1 Kin. 8:65; 2 Kin. 14:25; Is. 27:12) and specific (Num 14:1-12; Josh. 15:1,2; Ezek. 47:15-20

the Kenezzites, the Kadmonites, 20 the Hittites, the Perizzites, the Rephaim, 21 the
Amorites, the Canaanites, the Girgashites,
and the Jebusites."

Hagar and Ishmael

16 Now Sarai, Abram's wife, [a]had
borne him no *children*. And she had
[b]an Egyptian maidservant whose name
was [c]Hagar. 2 [d]So Sarai said to Abram,
"See now, the LORD [e]has restrained me
from bearing *children*. Please, [f]go in to my
maid; perhaps I shall [1]obtain children by
her." And Abram [g]heeded the voice of
Sarai. 3 Then Sarai, Abram's wife, took
Hagar her maid, the Egyptian, and gave
her to her husband Abram to be his wife,
after Abram [h]had dwelt ten years in the
land of Canaan. 4 So he went in to Hagar,
and she conceived. And when she saw that
she had conceived, her mistress became
[i]despised in her [2]eyes.
5 Then Sarai said to Abram, [3]"My wrong
be upon you! I gave my maid into your embrace; and when she saw that she had conceived, I became despised in her eyes. [j]The
LORD judge between you and me."
6 [k]So Abram said to Sarai, "Indeed your
maid *is* in your hand; do to her as you
please." And when Sarai dealt harshly
with her, [l]she fled from her presence.
7 Now the [m]Angel of the LORD found her
by a spring of water in the wilderness, [n]by
the spring on the way to [o]Shur. 8 And He
said, "Hagar, Sarai's maid, where have you
come from, and where are you going?"
She said, "I am fleeing from the presence
of my mistress Sarai."
9 The Angel of the LORD said to her, "Return to your mistress, and [p]submit yourself under her hand." 10 Then the Angel of
the LORD said to her, [q]"I will multiply your
descendants exceedingly, so that they shall
not be counted for multitude." 11 And the
Angel of the LORD said to her:

"Behold, you *are* with child,
[r]And you shall bear a son.
You shall call his name [4]Ishmael,
Because the LORD has heard your
affliction.
12 [s]He shall be a wild man;
His hand *shall be* against every
man,
And every man's hand against him.
[t]And he shall dwell in the presence
of all his brethren."

13 Then she called the name of the LORD
who spoke to her, You-Are-[5]the-God-Who-
Sees; for she said, "Have I also here [6]seen
Him [u]who sees me?" 14 Therefore the well
was called [v]Beer Lahai Roi;[7] observe, *it is*
[w]between Kadesh and Bered.
15 So [x]Hagar bore Abram a son; and
Abram named his son, whom Hagar bore,
Ishmael. 16 Abram *was* eighty-six years old
when Hagar bore Ishmael to Abram.

CHAPTER 16

1 [a]Gen. 11:30; 15:2, 3 [b]Gen. 12:16; 21:9 [c]Gal. 4:24
2 [d]Gen. 30:3 [e]Gen. 20:18 [f]Gen. 30:3, 9 [g]Gen. 3:17 [1]Lit. *be built up from*
3 [h]Gen. 12:4, 5
4 [i]1 Sam. 1:6, 7; [Prov. 30:21, 23] [2]*sight*
5 [j]Gen. 31:53; Ex. 5:21 [3]*The wrong done to me be*
6 [k]1 Pet. 3:7 [l]Gen. 16:9; Ex. 2:15
7 [m]Gen. 21:17, 18; 22:11, 15; 31:11 [n]Gen. 20:1; 25:18 [o]Ex. 15:22
9 [p][Titus 2:9]
10 [q]Gen. 17:20
11 [r]Luke 1:13, 31 [4]Lit. *God Hears*
12 [s]Gen. 21:20; Job 24:5; 39:5-8 [t]Gen. 25:18
13 [u]Gen. 31:42 [5]Heb. *El Roi* [6]Seen the back of
14 [v]Gen. 24:62 [w]Gen. 14:7; Num. 13:26 [7]Lit. *Well of the One Who Lives and Sees Me*
15 [x]Gal. 4:22

cf. Ezek. 48:1,28) descriptions of the Promised Land, centering on the ancient land of Canaan. Such precise geographic demarcation will not allow for any redefinitions which would emasculate God's promise of its specificity. The river of Egypt was most probably what became known as the Wadi El Arish, the southern border of Judah. **Ken-ites...Jebusites.** The various peoples who inhabited the land are named. Such precise detailing of the nations in the land of Canaan attests again to the specificity of the Promised Land in God's promises.

16:1 See Gal. 4:21-31, where Paul uses Hagar as an illustration.

16:3 gave her to her husband. After 10 childless years (cf. 12:4), Sarai resorted to the custom of the day by which a barren wife could get a child through one of her own maidservants (v. 2, "I shall obtain children by her"). Abram, ignoring divine reaction and assurance in response to his earlier attempt to appoint an heir (cf. 15:2-5), sinfully yielded to Sarai's insistence, and Ishmael was born (v. 15).

16:5 My wrong *be* upon you!...I became despised. Sarai, not anticipating contemptuous disregard by Hagar (v. 4) as the result of her solution for barrenness, blamed Abram for her trouble and demanded judgment to rectify the broken mistress-servant relationship. Abram transferred his responsibility to Sarai, giving her freedom to react as she wished (v. 6, "your maid is in your hand..."). Sarai treated her so badly, she left.

16:7 the Angel of the LORD. This special individual spoke as though He were distinct from Yahweh, yet also spoke in the first person as though He were indeed to be identified as Yahweh Himself, with Hagar recognizing that in seeing this Angel, she had seen God (v. 13). Others had the same experience and came to the same conclusion (cf. Gen 22:11-18; 31:11-13; Ex. 3:2-5; Num. 22:22-35; Judg. 6:11-23; 13:2-5; 1 Kin. 19:5-7). The Angel of the Lord, who does not appear after the birth of Christ, is often identified as the pre-incarnate Christ. *See note on Ex. 3:2.* **Shur.** South of Palestine and east of Egypt, which meant that Hagar attempted to return home to Egypt.

16:8 Hagar, Sarai's maid. Both the salutation and the instruction (v. 9, "Return...submit...") given by the Angel and the response by Hagar treated the mistress-servant relationship as if it were still intact. Rebelling and absconding was not the solution (v. 9)!

16:10 I will multiply. A servant she might have been, but mother of many she would also become, thus making Abram the father of two groups of innumerable descendants (see 13:16; 15:5).

16:11 call his name Ishmael. With her son's name meaning "God hears," Hagar the servant could not ever forget how God had heard her cry of affliction.

16:12 a wild man...against every man. The untameable desert onager (wild donkey) best described the fiercely aggressive and independent nature Ishmael would exhibit, along with his Arabic descendants.

16:13 You-Are-the-God-Who-Sees. Recognizing the Angel as God and ascribing this new name to Him arose from Hagar's astonishment at having been the object of God's gracious attention. The theophany and revelation led her to call Him also "The One Who Lives and Sees Me" (v. 14).

16:15 his son...Ishmael. Ca. 2079 B.C.

16:16 eighty-six years old. Abram was 75 when he left Haran (12:4). There would be a 13 year interval until 17:1 picks up the narrative again.

The Sign of the Covenant

17 When Abram was ninety-nine years
old, the LORD [a]appeared to Abram
and said to him, [b]"I *am* [1]Almighty God;
[c]walk before Me and be [d]blameless. 2 And
I will make My [e]covenant between Me and
you, and [f]will multiply you exceedingly."
3 Then Abram fell on his face, and God
talked with him, saying: 4 "As for Me, behold, My covenant is with you, and you
shall be [g]a father of [2]many nations. 5 No
longer shall [h]your name be called [3]Abram,
but your name shall be [4]Abraham; [i]for I
have made you a father of [5]many nations.
6 I will make you exceedingly fruitful; and
I will make [j]nations of you, and [k]kings
shall come from you. 7 And I will [l]establish
My covenant between Me and you and
your descendants after you in their generations, for an everlasting covenant, [m]to be
God to you and [n]your descendants after
you. 8 Also [o]I give to you and your descendants after you the land [p]in[6] which
you are a stranger, all the land of Canaan,
as an everlasting possession; and [q]I will be
their God."
9 And God said to Abraham: "As for
you, [r]you shall keep My covenant, you and
your descendants after you throughout
their generations. 10 This *is* My covenant
which you shall keep, between Me and you
and your descendants after you: [s]Every
male child among you shall be circumcised;
11 and you shall be circumcised in the flesh
of your foreskins, and it shall be [t]a sign of
the covenant between Me and you. 12 He
who is eight days old among you [u]shall be
circumcised, every male child in your generations, he who is born in your house or
bought with money from any foreigner
who is not your descendant. 13 He who is
born in your house and he who is bought
with your money must be circumcised, and
My covenant shall be in your flesh for an
everlasting covenant. 14 And the uncircumcised male child, who is not circumcised in
the flesh of his foreskin, that person [v]shall
be cut off from his people; he has broken
My covenant."
15 Then God said to Abraham, "As for
Sarai your wife, you shall not call her name
Sarai, but [7]Sarah *shall be* her name. 16 And
I will bless her [w]and also give you a son by
her; then I will bless her, and she shall be *a
mother* [x]*of* nations; [y]kings of peoples shall
be from her."
17 Then Abraham fell on his face [z]and
laughed, and said in his heart, "Shall *a*

CHAPTER 17

1 [a]Gen. 12:7; 18:1 [b]Gen. 28:3; 35:11; Ex. 6:3; Job 42:2 [c]2 Kin. 20:3 [d]Gen. 6:9; Deut. 18:13 [1]Heb. *El Shaddai*
2 [e]Gen. 15:18; Ex. 6:4; [Gal. 3:19] [f]Gen. 12:2; 13:16; 15:5; 18:18
4 [g][Rom. 4:11, 12, 16] [2]Lit. *multitude of nations*
5 [h]Neh. 9:7 [i]Rom. 4:17 [3]Lit. *Exalted Father* [4]Lit. *Father of a Multitude* [5]*a multitude of*
6 [j]Gen. 17:16; 35:11 [k]Matt. 1:6
7 [l][Gal. 3:17] [m]Gen. 26:24; 28:13; Lev. 11:45; 26:12, 45; Heb. 11:16 [n]Rom. 9:8; Gal. 3:16
8 [o]Gen. 12:7; 13:15, 17; Acts 7:5 [p]Gen. 23:4; 28:4 [q]Ex. 6:7; 29:45; Lev. 26:12; Deut. 29:13; Rev. 21:7 [6]Lit. *of your sojournings*
9 [r]Ex. 19:5
10 [s]John 7:22; Acts 7:8
11 [t]Ex. 12:13, 48; [Rom. 4:11]
12 [u]Lev. 12:3
14 [v]Ex. 4:24-26

15 [7]Lit. *Princess* **16** [w]Gen. 18:10 [x]Gen. 35:11; Gal. 4:31; 1 Pet. 3:6 [y]Gen. 17:6; 36:31; 1 Sam. 8:22 **17** [z]Gen. 17:3; 18:12; 21:6

17:2 My covenant between Me and you. Another reaffirmation of His unilateral covenant with Abram, which did not mean that there would be no responsibilities falling upon its recipients. *See notes on vv. 7-9 below and on 12:1-3; 15:13-18.*

17:4 many nations. The 3-fold reaffirmation of the divine promise of many descendants, perhaps including Isaac's and Ishmael's, brackets the change of name (vv. 4-6), giving it significant emphasis.

17:5 your name shall be Abraham. Cf. 11:27. The name meaning "father of many nations" reflected Abraham's new relationship to God as well as his new identity based on God's promise of seed. Cf. Rom. 4:17.

17:6 kings shall come from you. This promise highlights the reality of more than one people group, or nation in its own right, coming from Abraham.

17:7 I will establish My covenant. This relationship was set up at God's initiative and also designated as an "everlasting covenant" (v. 7), thus applying to Abraham's posterity with equal force and bringing forth the declaration "I will be their God" (v. 8). This pledge became the dictum of the covenant relationship between Yahweh, i.e., Jehovah, and Israel.

17:8 all the land of Canaan. God's reaffirmation of His covenant promises to Abraham did not occur without mention of the land being deeded by divine right to him and his descendants as "an everlasting possession." Cf. Acts 7:5.

17:9 you shall keep My covenant. Despite repeated disobedience by the patriarchs and the nation, God's faithfulness to His covenant commitment never wavered (e.g., Deut. 4:25-31; 30:1-9; 1 Chr. 16:15-18; Jer. 30:11; 46:27,28; Amos 9:8; Luke 1:67-75; Heb. 6:13-18). Divine attestations of Abraham's obedience (22:16-18; 26:3-5) were pronounced years after the formal establishment of His covenant (12:1-3; 15:12-18). Though the nation was apostate, there was always an obedient remnant of faithful Israelites (see Zeph. 3:12,13).

17:11 a sign of the covenant. Circumcision (cutting away the male foreskin) was not entirely new in this period of history, but the special religious and theocratic significance then applied to it was entirely new, thus identifying the circumcised as belonging to the physical and ethnical lineage of Abraham (cf. Acts 7:8; Rom. 4:11). Without divine revelation, the rite would not have had this distinctive significance, thus it remained a theocratic distinctive of Israel (cf. v. 13). There was a health benefit, since disease could be kept in the folds of the foreskin, so that removing it prevented that. Historically, Jewish women have had the lowest rate of cervical cancer. But the symbolism had to do with the need to cut away sin and be cleansed. It was the male organ which most clearly demonstrated the depth of depravity because it carried the seed that produced depraved sinners. Thus, circumcision symbolized the need for a profoundly deep cleansing to reverse the effects of depravity.

17:12 eight days old. This same time frame was repeated in Lev. 12:3.

17:14 shall be cut off from his people. Being cut off from the covenant community meant loss of temporal benefits stemming from being part of the special, chosen, and theocratic nation, even to the point of death by divine judgment.

17:15 Sarai...Sarah. Fittingly, since Sarai ("my princess") would be the ancestress of the promised nations and kings, God changed her name to Sarah, taking away the limiting personal pronoun "my," and calling her "princess" (v. 16).

17:16 *mother of* nations. Cf. 17:5.

17:17 fell on his face and laughed, and said in his heart. A proper reaction of adoration over God's promises was marred by the incredulity of Abraham. He knew he was to be a father (12:2; 15:4), but this was the first mention that his barren, old wife was to be the mother.

child be born to a man who is one hundred
years old? And shall Sarah, who is ninety
years old, bear *a child?*" **18** And Abraham
[a]said to God, "Oh, that Ishmael might live
before You!"
19 Then God said: "No, [b]Sarah your wife
shall bear you a son, and you shall call his
name Isaac; I will establish My [c]covenant
with him for an everlasting covenant, *and*
with his descendants after him. **20** And as
for Ishmael, I have heard you. Behold, I
have blessed him, and will make him fruitful, and [d]will multiply him exceedingly. He
shall beget [e]twelve princes, [f]and I will make
him a great nation. **21** But My [g]covenant I
will establish with Isaac, [h]whom Sarah shall
bear to you at this [i]set time next year."
22 Then He finished talking with him, and
God went up from Abraham.
23 So Abraham took Ishmael his son, all
who were born in his house and all who
were bought with his money, every male
among the men of Abraham's house, and
circumcised the flesh of their foreskins that
very same day, as God had said to him.
24 Abraham *was* ninety-nine years old
when he was circumcised in the flesh of his
foreskin. **25** And Ishmael his son *was* thirteen years old when he was circumcised in
the flesh of his foreskin. **26** That very same
day Abraham was circumcised, and his
son Ishmael; **27** and [j]all the men of his
house, born in the house or bought with
money from a foreigner, were circumcised
with him.

The Son of Promise

18 Then the LORD appeared to him by
[1]the [a]terebinth trees of Mamre, as
he was sitting in the tent door in the heat of
the day. **2** [b]So he lifted his eyes and looked,
and behold, three men were standing by
him; [c]and when he saw *them,* he ran from
the tent door to meet them, and bowed
himself to the ground, **3** and said, "My
Lord, if I have now found favor in Your
sight, do not pass on by Your servant.
4 Please let [d]a little water be brought, and
wash your feet, and rest yourselves under
the tree. **5** And [e]I will bring a morsel of
bread, that [f]you may refresh your hearts.
After that you may pass by, [g]inasmuch as
you have come to your servant."
They said, "Do as you have said."
6 So Abraham hurried into the tent to Sarah and said, "Quickly, make ready three
measures of fine meal; knead *it* and make
cakes." **7** And Abraham ran to the herd, took
a tender and good calf, gave *it* to a young
man, and he hastened to prepare it. **8** So [h]he
took butter and milk and the calf which he
had prepared, and set *it* before them; and he
stood by them under the tree as they ate.
9 Then they said to him, "Where *is* Sarah
your wife?"
So he said, "Here, [i]in the tent."
10 And He said, "I will certainly return
to you [j]according to the time of life, and
behold, [k]Sarah your wife shall have a son."
(Sarah was listening in the tent door
which *was* behind him.) **11** Now [l]Abraham
and Sarah were old, well advanced in age;
and [2]Sarah [m]had passed the age of
childbearing. **12** Therefore Sarah [n]laughed
within herself, saying, [o]"After I have
grown old, shall I have pleasure, my [p]lord
being old also?"
13 And the LORD said to Abraham, "Why
did Sarah laugh, saying, 'Shall I surely
bear *a child,* since I am old?' **14** [q]Is anything
too hard for the LORD? [r]At the appointed
time I will return to you, according to the
time of life, and Sarah shall have a son."
15 But Sarah denied *it,* saying, "I did not
laugh," for she was afraid.
And He said, "No, but you did laugh!"

18 [a]Gen. 18:23
19 [b]Gen. 18:10; 21:2; [Gal. 4:28] [c]Gen. 22:16; Matt. 1:2; Luke 3:34
20 [d]Gen. 16:10 [e]Gen. 25:12-16 [f]Gen. 21:13, 18
21 [g]Gen. 26:2-5 [h]Gen. 21:2 [i]Gen. 18:14
27 [j]Gen. 18:19

CHAPTER 18

1 [a]Gen. 13:18; 14:13 [1]Heb. *Alon Mamre*
2 [b]Gen. 18:16, 22; 32:24; Josh. 5:13; Judg. 13:6-11; Heb. 13:2 [c]Gen. 19:1; 1 Pet. 4:9
4 [d]Gen. 19:2; 24:32; 43:24
5 [e]Judg. 6:18, 19; 13:15, 16 [f]Judg. 19:5; Ps. 104:15 [g]Gen. 19:8; 33:10
8 [h]Gen. 19:3
9 [i]Gen. 24:67
10 [j]2 Kin. 4:16 [k]Gen. 17:19, 21; 21:2; Rom. 9:9
11 [l]Gen. 17:17; Luke 1:18; Rom. 4:19; Heb. 11:11, 12, 19 [m]Gen. 31:35 [2]Lit. *the manner of women had ceased to be with Sarah*
12 [n]Gen. 17:17 [o]Luke 1:18 [p]1 Pet. 3:6
14 [q]Num. 11:23; Jer. 32:17; Zech. 8:6; Matt. 3:9; 19:26; Luke 1:37; Rom. 4:21 [r]Gen. 17:21; 18:10; 2 Kin. 4:16

17:18 Oh, that Ishmael might live before You! Abraham's plea for a living son to be the designated beneficiary of God's promises betrayed just how impossible it was for he and Sarah to have children (cf. Rom. 4:17).

17:19-21 Again, patiently but firmly rejecting Abraham's alternative solution, God emphatically settled the matter by bracketing His gracious bestowal of much posterity to Ishmael (see 25:12-18) with affirmations that indeed Sarah's son would be the heir of the "everlasting covenant." For the first time God named the son.

17:19 call his name Isaac. The name of the promised son meant "he laughs," an appropriate reminder to Abraham of his initial, faithless reaction to God's promise.

17:23-27 that very same day. Without delay, Abraham fully carried out God's command on himself, on "every male," and on "all the men of his house" (vv. 23,27).

18:1 the LORD appeared. Another instance of a theophany, although Abraham perhaps did not recognize at first that one of his visitors, whom he humbly greeted and entertained (vv. 2-8) and properly sent on their way (v. 16), was Yahweh. **trees of Mamre.** *See note on 13:18.*

18:3 My Lord. Although perhaps first used as the customary respectful address of a host to a visitor, later in their interchange it was used knowingly by Abraham of his true and sovereign Lord, whom he addressed as "Master" (vv. 22,30-32), and whom he must have recognized when the visitor spoke of Himself as "LORD" (v. 14).

18:9-13 Despite a promise clearly reminiscent of God's words to Abraham, Sarah reacted with similar incredulity as her husband had done (cf. 17:17). She was not thinking of divine miracle but of divine providence working only within the normal course of life, being convinced that, at their age, bearing children was just not naturally possible.

18:10,14 Cf. Rom. 9:9.

18:14,15 A rhetorical question ("Is anything too hard...?) and divine declaration ("At the appointed time..."), coupled with obvious knowledge of her thoughts ("laughed within herself"), made Sarah fearfully perceive her total misperception of God's working.

Abraham Intercedes for Sodom

16 Then the men rose from there and
looked toward Sodom, and Abraham went
with them [s]to send them on the way.
17 And the LORD said, [t]"Shall I hide from
Abraham what I am doing, 18 since Abraham shall surely become a great and
mighty nation, and all the nations of the
earth shall be [u]blessed in him? 19 For I
have known him, in order [v]that he may
command his children and his household
after him, that they keep the way of the
LORD, to do righteousness and justice, that
the LORD may bring to Abraham what He
has spoken to him." 20 And the LORD said,
"Because [w]the outcry against Sodom and
Gomorrah is great, and because their [x]sin
is very grave, 21 [y]I will go down now and
see whether they have done altogether according to the outcry against it that has
come to Me; and if not, [z]I will know."
22 Then the men turned away from there
[a]and went toward Sodom, but Abraham
still stood before the LORD. 23 And Abraham [b]came near and said, [c]"Would You
also [d]destroy the [e]righteous with the
wicked? 24 Suppose there were fifty righteous within the city; would You also destroy the place and not spare *it* for the fifty
righteous that were in it? 25 Far be it from
You to do such a thing as this, to slay the
righteous with the wicked, so [f]that the
righteous should be as the wicked; far be it
from You! [g]Shall not the Judge of all the
earth do right?"
26 So the LORD said, [h]"If I find in Sodom
fifty righteous within the city, then I will
spare all the place for their sakes."
27 Then Abraham answered and said,
"Indeed now, I who *am* [i]*but* dust and ashes
have taken it upon myself to speak to the
Lord: 28 Suppose there were five less than
the fifty righteous; would You destroy all
of the city for *lack of* five?"
So He said, "If I find there forty-five, I
will not destroy *it*."
29 And he spoke to Him yet again and
said, "Suppose there should be forty found
there?"
So He said, "I will not do *it* for the sake
of forty."
30 Then he said, "Let not the Lord be
angry, and I will speak: Suppose thirty
should be found there?"
So He said, "I will not do *it* if I find thirty there."
31 And he said, "Indeed now, I have
taken it upon myself to speak to the Lord:
Suppose twenty should be found there?"
So He said, "I will not destroy *it* for the
sake of twenty."
32 Then he said, [j]"Let not the Lord be
angry, and I will speak but once more: Suppose ten should be found there?"
[k]And He said, "I will not destroy *it* for
the sake of ten." 33 So the LORD went His
way as soon as He had finished speaking
with Abraham; and Abraham returned to
his place.

Sodom's Depravity

19 Now [a]the two angels came to
Sodom in the evening, and [b]Lot was
sitting in the gate of Sodom. When Lot saw
them, he rose to meet them, and he bowed
himself with his face toward the ground.
2 And he said, "Here now, my lords, please
[c]turn in to your servant's house and spend

16 [s] Acts 15:3; Rom. 15:24
17 [t] Gen. 18:22, 26, 33; Ps. 25:14; Amos 3:7; [John 15:15]
18 [u] [Gen. 12:3; 22:18]; Matt. 1:1; Luke 3:34; [Acts 3:25, 26; Gal. 3:8]
19 [v] [Deut. 4:9, 10; 6:6, 7]
20 [w] Gen. 4:10; 19:13; Ezek. 16:49, 50 [x] Gen. 13:13
21 [y] Gen. 11:5; Ex. 3:8; Ps. 14:2 [z] Deut. 8:2; 13:3; Josh. 22:22; Luke 16:15; 2 Cor. 11:11
22 [a] Gen. 18:16; 19:1
23 [b] [Heb. 10:22] [c] Ex. 23:7; Num. 16:22; 2 Sam. 24:17; Ps. 11:4-7 [d] Job 9:22 [e] Gen. 20:4
25 [f] Job 8:20; Is. 3:10, 11 [g] Deut. 1:16, 17; 32:4; Job 8:3, 20; 34:17; Ps. 58:11; 94:2; Is. 3:10, 11; Rom. 3:5, 6
26 [h] Jer. 5:1; Ezek. 22:30
27 [i] [Gen. 3:19]; Job 4:19; 30:19; 42:6; [1 Cor. 15:47, 48]
32 [j] Judg. 6:39 [k] James 5:16

CHAPTER 19

1 [a] Gen. 18:2, 16, 22 [b] Gen. 18:1-5
2 [c] Gen. 24:31; [Heb. 13:2]

18:17 Shall I hide from Abraham what I am doing, since...? The Lord's reason for permitting Abraham to know of judgment in advance underscored his special role in the plan of God and the certain outcome of His covenant with Abraham—many offspring and great blessing.

18:18 Cf. Gal. 3:8.

18:19 For I have known him, in order that he may command. An expression of divine confidence, i.e., a tribute to faithfulness, obedience, and consistency.

18:20 Because the outcry...is great. The iniquity of the two cities, by then complete (cf. 15:16), had reached the point of no return before the Lord, who demonstrated before Abraham how justly He assessed the time for judgment (v. 21, "I will go down now and see...").

18:23 Would You also destroy the righteous with the wicked? The intercession for the two wicked cities began with a question that portrayed Abraham's acute awareness of God's mercy toward the righteous and the distinction He made between the good and the bad (v. 25).

18:24 fifty righteous. Among the righteous was Lot (see 2 Pet. 2:7,8).

18:25 Shall not the Judge of all the earth do right? Abraham's clear understanding of God's character being able only to do what is good and totally above reproach was affirmed with this rhetorical question.

18:27 I who *am but* dust and ashes. Abraham's negotiation, far from being crassly or selfishly manipulative, humbly and compassionately expressed his concern for people (cf. 13:8,9) and particularly interceded for the place where his nephew Lot and his family lived. Neither did he intend to anger the Lord by his repeated requests (vv. 28,30,32).

18:32 for the sake of ten. That the number of righteous people necessary to forestall judgment had been reduced from 50 to 10 may have reflected Abraham's awareness both of the intense wickedness of the cities as well as Lot's ineffective witness there. Abraham probably had the whole of Lot's family in mind.

18:33 the LORD went His way...Abraham returned to his place. Nothing more could be done; the judgment was inevitable!

19:1 two angels. These were the angels who, with God, had visited Abraham (18:22). They had taken human form (v. 10; called "men"). **Lot was sitting in the gate.** Since city officials and other prominent citizens conducted the community's affairs at the gate, Lot participated there as a judge (v. 9).

19:2 please turn in to your servant's house. Lot's invitation to the two angels (vv. 1-3) to partake themselves of his hospitality was

the night, and [d]wash your feet; then you
may rise early and go on your way."
And they said, [e]"No, but we will spend
the night in the open square."
3 But he insisted strongly; so they turned
in to him and entered his house. [f]Then he
made them a feast, and baked [g]unleavened
bread, and they ate.
4 Now before they lay down, the men of
the city, the men of Sodom, both old and
young, all the people from every quarter,
surrounded the house. 5 [h]And they called
to Lot and said to him, "Where are the men
who came to you tonight? [i]Bring them out
to us that we [j]may know them *carnally.*"
6 So [k]Lot went out to them through the
doorway, shut the door behind him, 7 and
said, "Please, my brethren, do not do so
wickedly! 8 [l]See now, I have two daughters
who have not known a man; please, let me
bring them out to you, and you may do to
them as you wish; only do nothing to these
men, [m]since this is the reason they have
come under the shadow of my roof."
9 And they said, "Stand back!" Then
they said, "This one [n]came in to [1]stay *here,*
[o]and he keeps acting as a judge; now we
will deal worse with you than with them."
So they pressed hard against the man Lot,
and came near to break down the door.
10 But the men reached out their hands and
pulled Lot into the house with them, and
shut the door. 11 And they [p]struck the men
who *were* at the doorway of the house with
blindness, both small and great, so that
they became weary *trying* to find the door.

Sodom and Gomorrah Destroyed

12 Then the men said to Lot, "Have you
anyone else here? Son-in-law, your sons,
your daughters, and whomever you have
in the city—[q]take *them* out of this place!
13 For we will destroy this place, because
the [r]outcry against them has grown great
before the face of the LORD, and [s]the LORD
has sent us to destroy it."
14 So Lot went out and spoke to his sons-
in-law, [t]who had married his daughters,
and said, [u]"Get up, get out of this place;
for the LORD will destroy this city!" [v]But to
his sons-in-law he seemed to be joking.
15 When the morning dawned, the angels urged Lot to hurry, saying, [w]"Arise,
take your wife and your two daughters
who are here, lest you be consumed in the
punishment of the city." 16 And while he
lingered, the men [x]took hold of his hand,
his wife's hand, and the hands of his two
daughters, the [y]LORD being merciful to
him, [z]and they brought him out and set
him outside the city. 17 So it came to pass,
when they had brought them outside, that
[2]he said, [a]"Escape for your life! [b]Do not
look behind you nor stay anywhere in the
plain. Escape [c]to the mountains, lest you
be [3]destroyed."
18 Then Lot said to them, "Please, [d]no,
my lords! 19 Indeed now, your servant has
found favor in your sight, and you have in-

2 [d]Gen. 18:4; 24:32 [e]Luke 24:28
3 [f]Gen. 18:6-8; Ex. 23:15; Num. 9:11; 28:17 [g]Ex. 12:8
5 [h]Is. 3:9 [i]Judg. 19:22 [j]Gen. 4:1; Rom. 1:24, 27; Jude 7
6 [k]Judg. 19:23
8 [l]Judg. 19:24 [m]Gen. 18:5
9 [n]2 Pet. 2:7, 8 [o]Ex. 2:14 [1]As a resident alien
11 [p]Gen. 20:17, 18
12 [q]Gen. 7:1; 2 Pet. 2:7, 9
13 [r]Gen. 18:20 [s]Lev. 26:30-33; Deut. 4:26; 28:45; 1 Chr. 21:15
14 [t]Matt. 1:18 [u]Num. 16:21, 24, 26, 45; Rev. 18:4 [v]Ex. 9:21; Jer. 43:1, 2; Luke 17:28; 24:11
15 [w]Ps. 37:2; Rev. 18:4
16 [x]Deut. 5:15; 6:21; 7:8; 2 Pet. 2:7 [y]Ex. 34:7; Ps. 32:10; 33:18, 19; Luke 18:13 [z]Ps. 34:22
17 [a]1 Kin. 19:3; Jer. 48:6 [b]Gen. 19:26; Matt. 24:16-18; Luke 9:62; Phil. 3:13, 14 [c]Gen. 14:10 [2]LXX, Syr., Vg. *they* [3]Lit. *swept away*
18 [d]Acts 10:14

most likely not just courtesy, but an effort to protect them from the known perversity of the Sodomites (cf. v. 8, "this is the reason").

19:3 he insisted strongly. Such was Lot's concern for these strangers that their stated preference to pass the night in the town square could not be permitted.

19:4 the men of the city…all the people. Both the size of the lustful mob of men boisterously milling around Lot's house and the widespread nature of Sodom's moral perversion received emphasis both from the additional qualifiers used ("all the people from every quarter" and "both old and young") and the request made (v. 5, "know them *carnally*"). Even acknowledging legitimate exaggeration in this use of "all" would not detract from this emphasis—this was indeed a wicked city!

19:5 know them *carnally.* They sought homosexual relations with the visitors. God's attitude toward this vile behavior became clear when He destroyed the city (vv. 23-29). Cf. Lev. 18:22, 29; 20:13; Rom. 1:26; 1 Cor. 6:9; 1 Tim. 1:10 where all homosexual behavior is prohibited and condemned by God.

19:6-8 Lot's response betrayed tension in his ethics; his offer to gratify their sexual lust contradicted his plea not to act "so wickedly." Such contradiction made clear also the vexation of spirit under which he lived in wicked Sodom (cf. 2 Pet. 2:6, 7).

19:8 do to them as you wish. The constraints of Eastern hospitality and the very purpose for which Lot had invited the visitors in (vv. 2, 3), compelled Lot to offer his daughters for a less deviant (*see notes on Rom. 1:24-27*) kind of wickedness, so as to protect his guests. This foolish effort shows that while Lot was right with God (2 Pet. 2:7, 8), he had contented himself with some sins and weak faith rather than leaving Sodom. But God was gracious to him because he was righteous, by faith, before God.

19:9 keeps acting as a judge. Their accusation suggests Lot had made moral pronouncements before, but his evaluation was no longer tolerable. **pressed hard.** Homosexual deviation carries an uncontrollable lust that defies restraint. Even when blinded, they tried to fulfill their lust (v. 11).

19:10, 11 Lot was now being protected by those whom he had earlier sought to protect!

19:13 the LORD has sent us to destroy it. With the wickedness of the city so graphically confirmed (vv. 4-11), divine judgment was the only outcome, but Lot's family could escape it (vv. 12, 13). Cf. Jude 7.

19:14 seemed to be joking. Lot's warning of imminent judgment fell within the category of jesting, so concluded his sons-in-law (or perhaps his daughters' fiancés).

19:16 the LORD being merciful to him. This reason, elsewhere described as God having remembered Abraham (v. 29), is why, in the face of Lot's seeming reluctance to leave ("lingered"), the angels personally and forcefully escorted him and his family beyond the city's precincts.

19:17-21 An urbanized lifestyle was apparently superior to a lonely one in the mountains and might be why Lot, playing upon the mercy already shown him, negotiated for an alternative escape destination—another city! The angel's reply (v. 21) indicated that this city was included in the original judgment plan, but would be spared for Lot's sake.

creased your mercy which you have
shown me by saving my life; but I cannot
escape to the mountains, lest some evil
overtake me and I die. 20 See now, this city
is near *enough* to flee to, and it *is* a little one;
please let me escape there (*is* it not a little
one?) and my soul shall live."
21 And he said to him, "See, [e]I have favored you concerning this thing also, in that
I will not overthrow this city for which you
have spoken. 22 Hurry, escape there. For [f]I
cannot do anything until you arrive there."
Therefore [g]the name of the city was
called [4]Zoar.
23 The sun had risen upon the earth
when Lot entered Zoar. 24 Then the LORD
rained [h]brimstone and [i]fire on Sodom and
Gomorrah, from the LORD out of the heavens. 25 So He [5]overthrew those cities, all
the plain, all the inhabitants of the cities,
and [j]what grew on the ground.
26 But his wife looked back behind him,
and she became [k]a pillar of salt.
27 And Abraham went early in the
morning to the place where [l]he had stood
before the LORD. 28 Then he looked toward
Sodom and Gomorrah, and toward all the
land of the plain; and he saw, and behold,
[m]the smoke of the land which went up like
the smoke of a furnace. 29 And it came to
pass, when God destroyed the cities of the
plain, that God [n]remembered Abraham,
and sent Lot out of the midst of the overthrow, when He overthrew the cities in
which Lot had dwelt.

The Descendants of Lot

30 Then Lot went up out of Zoar and
[o]dwelt in the mountains, and his two
daughters were with him; for he was afraid
to dwell in Zoar. And he and his two
daughters dwelt in a cave. 31 Now the firstborn said to the younger, "Our father *is* old,
and *there is* no man on the earth [p]to come in
to us as is the custom of all the earth.
32 Come, let us make our father drink wine,
and we will lie with him, that we [q]may preserve the [6]lineage of our father." 33 So they
made their father drink wine that night.
And the firstborn went in and lay with her
father, and he did not know when she lay
down or when she arose.
34 It happened on the next day that the
firstborn said to the younger, "Indeed I lay
with my father last night; let us make him
drink wine tonight also, and you go in *and*
lie with him, that we may preserve the
[7]lineage of our father." 35 Then they made
their father drink wine that night also. And
the younger arose and lay with him, and
he did not know when she lay down or
when she arose.
36 Thus both the daughters of Lot were
with child by their father. 37 The firstborn
bore a son and called his name Moab; [r]he
is the father of the Moabites to this day.
38 And the younger, she also bore a son
and called his name Ben-Ammi; [s]he *is* the
father of the people of Ammon to this day.

Abraham and Abimelech

20 And Abraham journeyed from
[a]there to the South, and dwelt between [b]Kadesh and Shur, and [c]stayed in
Gerar. 2 Now Abraham said of Sarah his
wife, [d]"She *is* my sister." And Abimelech
king of Gerar sent and [e]took Sarah.
3 But [f]God came to Abimelech [g]in a
dream by night, and said to him, [h]"Indeed
you *are* a dead man because of the woman
whom you have taken, for she *is* [1]a man's
wife."

21 [e]Job 42:8, 9; Ps. 145:19
22 [f]Ex. 32:10; Deut. 9:14 [g]Gen. 13:10; 14:2 [4]Lit. *Little* or *Insignificant*
24 [h]Deut. 29:23; Ps. 11:6; Is. 13:19; Jer. 20:16; 23:14; 49:18; 50:40; Ezek. 16:49, 50; Hos. 11:8; Amos 4:11; Zeph. 2:9; Matt. 10:15; Mark 6:11; Luke 17:29; Rom. 9:29; 2 Pet. 2:6; Jude 7; Rev. 11:8 [i]Lev. 10:2
25 [j]Ps. 107:34 [5]*devastated*
26 [k]Gen. 19:17; Luke 17:32
27 [l]Gen. 18:22
28 [m]Rev. 9:2; 18:9
29 [n]Gen. 8:1; 18:23; Deut. 7:8; 9:5, 27
30 [o]Gen. 19:17, 19
31 [p]Gen. 16:2, 4; 38:8, 9; Deut. 25:5
32 [q][Mark 12:19] [6]Lit. *seed*
34 [7]Lit. *seed*
37 [r]Num. 25:1; Deut. 2:9
38 [s]Num. 21:24; Deut. 2:19

CHAPTER 20

1 [a]Gen. 18:1 [b]Gen. 12:9; 16:7, 14 [c]Gen. 26:1, 6
2 [d]Gen. 12:11-13; 26:7 [e]Gen. 12:15
3 [f]Ps. 105:14 [g]Job 33:15 [h]Gen. 20:7 [1]Lit. *married to a husband*

19:24 brimstone...from the LORD out of the heavens. When morning came (v. 23) judgment fell. Any natural explanation, about how the Lord used combustible sulfur deposits to destroy that locale, falters on this emphatic indication of miraculous judgment. "Brimstone" could refer to any inflammable substance; perhaps a volcanic eruption and an earthquake with a violent electrical storm "overthrew" (v. 25) the area. That area is now believed to be under the south end of the Dead Sea. Burning gases, sulfur, and magma blown into the air all fell to bury the region.

19:26 his wife looked back. Lot's wife paid the price of disregarding the angelic warning to flee without a backward glance (v. 17). In so doing, she became not only encased in salt, but a poignant example of disobedience producing unwanted reaction at judgment day (cf. Luke 17:29-32), even as her home cities became bywords of God's judgment on sin (cf. Is. 1:9; Rom. 9:29; 2 Pet. 2:5,6).

19:29 the cities of the plain. The best archeological evidence locates Sodom and Gomorrah at the south of the Dead Sea region, i.e., in the area south of the Lisan Peninsula that juts out on the east (*see note on 14:10*). **God remembered Abraham.** Cf. 18:23-33.

19:30 afraid to dwell in Zoar. Perhaps because the people there felt he was responsible for all the devastation, or he feared more judgment on the region might hit the city (vv. 17-23).

19:31-36 The immoral philosophy of Sodom and Gomorrah had so corrupted the thinking of Lot's daughters that they unhesitatingly contrived to be impregnated by their own father! They were virgins (v. 8), the married daughters were dead (v. 14) and there were no men left for husbands (v. 25). In fearing they would have no children, they conceived the gross iniquity.

19:37,38 The two sons born of incest became the progenitors of Moab and Ammon, Israel's longstanding enemies.

20:1 Gerar. A Philistine city on the border between Palestine and Egypt, about 10 mi. S of Gaza.

20:2 She *is* my sister. Twenty-five years after leaving Egypt in disgrace because of lying about his wife (12:10-20), Abraham reverted to the same ploy. **Abimelech.** This king who took Sarah into his harem was most likely the father or grandfather of the Abimelech encountered by Isaac. *See note on 26:1.*

20:3 God came...in a dream. Again Abraham's Lord intervened to protect Sarah, who had joined in the lie of her husband (v. 5), deceiving a king who earnestly protested his innocence and integrity

4 But Abimelech had not come near her;
and he said, "Lord, [i]will You slay a righteous nation also? 5 Did he not say to me,
'She *is* my sister'? And she, even she herself said, 'He *is* my brother.' [j]In the [2]integ-
rity of my heart and innocence of my
hands I have done this."
6 And God said to him in a dream, "Yes,
I know that you did this in the integrity of
your heart. For [k]I also withheld you from
sinning [l]against Me; therefore I did not let
you touch her. 7 Now therefore, restore the
man's wife; [m]for he *is* a prophet, and he
will pray for you and you shall live. But if
you do not restore *her,* [n]know that you
shall surely die, you [o]and all who *are*
yours."
8 So Abimelech rose early in the morning, called all his servants, and told all
these things in their hearing; and the men
were very much afraid. 9 And Abimelech
called Abraham and said to him, "What
have you done to us? How have I [3]of-
fended you, [p]that you have brought on me
and on my kingdom a great sin? You have
done deeds to me [q]that ought not to be
done." 10 Then Abimelech said to Abraham, "What did you have in view, that you
have done this thing?"
11 And Abraham said, "Because I
thought, surely [r]the fear of God *is* not in
this place; and [s]they will kill me on account of my wife. 12 But indeed [t]*she is* truly
my sister. She *is* the daughter of my father,
but not the daughter of my mother; and
she became my wife. 13 And it came to
pass, when [u]God caused me to wander
from my father's house, that I said to her,
'This *is* your kindness that you should do
for me: in every place, wherever we go,
[v]say of me, "He *is* my brother." ' "
14 Then Abimelech [w]took sheep, oxen,
and male and female servants, and gave
them to Abraham; and he restored Sarah
his wife to him. 15 And Abimelech said,
"See, [x]my land *is* before you; dwell where
it pleases you." 16 Then to Sarah he said,
"Behold, I have given your brother a thousand *pieces* of silver; [y]indeed this [4]vindi-
cates you [z]before all who *are* with you and
before everybody." Thus she was [5]re-
buked.
17 So Abraham [a]prayed to God; and God
[b]healed Abimelech, his wife, and his female servants. Then they bore *children;*
18 for the LORD [c]had closed up all the
wombs of the house of Abimelech because
of Sarah, Abraham's wife.

Isaac Is Born

21 And the LORD [a]visited Sarah as He
had said, and the LORD did for Sarah [b]as He had spoken. 2 For Sarah [c]con-
ceived and bore Abraham a son in his old
age, [d]at the set time of which God had spoken to him. 3 And Abraham called the
name of his son who was born to him—
whom Sarah bore to him—[e]Isaac.[1] 4 Then
Abraham [f]circumcised his son Isaac when
he was eight days old, [g]as God had commanded him. 5 Now [h]Abraham was one
hundred years old when his son Isaac was
born to him. 6 And Sarah said, [i]"God has
[2]made me laugh, *and* all who hear [j]will
laugh with me." 7 She also said, "Who
would have said to Abraham that Sarah
would nurse children? [k]For I have borne
him a son in his old age."

Hagar and Ishmael Depart

8 So the child grew and was weaned.
And Abraham made a great feast on the
same day that Isaac was weaned.
9 And Sarah saw the son of Hagar [l]the
Egyptian, whom she had borne to Abraham, [m]scoffing.[3] 10 Therefore she said to

4 [i] Gen. 18:23-25; Num. 16:22
5 [j] 1 Kin. 9:4; 2 Kin. 20:3; Ps. 7:8; 26:6 [2] *innocence*
6 [k] Gen. 31:7; 35:5; Ex. 34:24; 1 Sam. 25:26, 34 [l] Gen. 39:9; 2 Sam. 12:13
7 [m] 1 Sam. 7:5; 2 Kin. 5:11; Job 42:8; James 5:14, 15 [n] Gen. 2:17 [o] Num. 16:32, 33
9 [p] Gen. 26:10; 39:9; Ex. 32:21; Josh. 7:25 [q] Gen. 34:7 [3] *sinned against*
11 [r] Gen. 42:18; Neh. 5:15; Ps. 36:1; Prov. 16:6 [s] Gen. 12:12; 26:7
12 [t] Gen. 11:29
13 [u] Gen. 12:1-9, 11; [Heb. 11:8] [v] Gen. 12:13; 20:5
14 [w] Gen. 12:16
15 [x] Gen. 13:9; 34:10; 47:6
16 [y] Gen. 26:11 [z] Mal. 2:9 [4] Lit. *is a covering of the eyes for you to all* [5] Or *justified*
17 [a] Num. 12:13; 21:7; Job 42:9; [James 5:16] [b] Gen. 21:2
18 [c] Gen. 12:17

CHAPTER 21

1 [a] 1 Sam. 2:21 [b] Gen. 17:16, 19, 21; 18:10, 14; [Gal. 4:23, 28]
2 [c] Acts 7:8; Gal. 4:22; Heb. 11:11, 12 [d] Gen. 17:21; 18:10, 14; Gal. 4:4
3 [e] Gen. 17:19, 21 [1] Lit. *Laughter*
4 [f] Acts 7:8 [g] Gen. 17:10, 12; Lev. 12:3
5 [h] Gen. 17:1, 17
6 [i] Gen. 18:13; Ps. 126:2; Is. 54:1 [j] Luke 1:58 [2] Lit. *made laughter for me*
7 [k] Gen. 18:11, 12
9 [l] Gen. 16:1, 4, 15 [m] [Gal. 4:29] [3] Lit. *laughing*

before God (vv. 4-6) and who, together with his aides, demonstrated proper submission to the warning of God (v. 8).

20:6 withheld you from sinning. Notwithstanding God's restraint of Abimelech, he was still required to restore Sarah to forestall judgment.

20:7 he *is* a prophet. Abraham, in spite of his lie, still served as God's intermediary and intercessor for Abimelech (cf. vv. 17,18). This is the first time the Hebrew term for "prophet" is used in Scripture. Here it identified Abraham as recognized by God to speak to Him on behalf of Abimelech. Usually it is used to describe, not one who speaks to God on behalf of someone, but one who speaks to someone on behalf of God.

20:9 deeds...not to be done. The confrontation between prophet and king attested the grievous nature of Abraham's actions. How humiliating for the prophet of God to be so rebuked by a heathen king.

20:11-13 Abraham offered 3 reasons for his lie: 1) his perception from the horrible vices in Sodom that all other cities had no fear of God, including Gerar; 2) his fear of death as a mitigating factor for what he had done; and 3) his wife actually being his half-sister as justification for lying and hiding their marital status. Abraham didn't need fraud to protect himself. God was able to provide safety for him.

20:16 rebuked. This is better translated "justified" (cf. margin).

21:1 the LORD visited Sarah. To the aged couple (vv. 2,5,7), exactly as promised, a son was born and the 25 year suspense was finally over with the laughter of derision turning to rejoicing (v. 6). The barrenness of Sarah (11:26) had ended.

21:4 circumcised. *See note on 17:11.*

21:5 Isaac...born to him. Ca. 2065 B.C. God fulfilled His promise to Abraham (12:2; 15:4,5; 17:7).

21:8 weaned. This usually occurred in the second or third year.

21:9 the son of Hagar...scoffing. The celebration of Isaac's passage from infancy to childhood witnessed the laughter of ridicule (an intensive form of the Hebrew for laughing) and offended Sarah, causing her to demand the expulsion of Ishmael and his mother from the encampment (v. 10).

Abraham, [n]"Cast out this bondwoman
and her son; for the son of this bondwoman shall not be heir with my son,
namely with Isaac." 11 And the matter was
very [4]displeasing in Abraham's sight [o]be-
cause of his son.
12 But God said to Abraham, "Do not let
it be displeasing in your sight because of
the lad or because of your bondwoman.
Whatever Sarah has said to you, listen to
her voice; for [p]in Isaac your seed shall be
called. 13 Yet I will also make [q]a nation of
the son of the bondwoman, because he *is*
your [5]seed."
14 So Abraham rose early in the morning, and took bread and [6]a skin of water;
and putting *it* on her shoulder, he gave *it*
and the boy to Hagar, and [r]sent her away.
Then she departed and wandered in the
Wilderness of Beersheba. 15 And the water
in the skin was used up, and she placed the
boy under one of the shrubs. 16 Then she
went and sat down across from *him* at a
distance of about a bowshot; for she said to
herself, "Let me not see the death of the
boy." So she sat opposite *him*, and lifted
her voice and wept.
17 And [s]God heard the voice of the lad.
Then the [t]angel of God called to Hagar out
of heaven, and said to her, "What ails you,
Hagar? Fear not, for God has heard the
voice of the lad where he *is*. 18 Arise, lift up
the lad and hold him with your hand, for
[u]I will make him a great nation."
19 Then [v]God opened her eyes, and she
saw a well of water. And she went and
filled the skin with water, and gave the lad
a drink. 20 So God [w]was with the lad; and
he grew and dwelt in the wilderness, [x]and
became an archer. 21 He dwelt in the
Wilderness of Paran; and his mother [y]took
a wife for him from the land of Egypt.

10 [n]Gen. 25:6; 36:6, 7; Gal. 3:18; 4:30
11 [o]Gen. 17:18 [4]*distressing*
12 [p]Matt. 1:2; Luke 3:34; [Rom. 9:7, 8]; Heb. 11:18
13 [q]Gen. 16:10; 17:20; 21:18; 25:12-18 [5]*descendant*
14 [r]John 8:35 [6]A water bottle made of skins
17 [s]Ex. 3:7; Deut. 26:7; Ps. 6:8 [t]Gen. 22:11
18 [u]Gen. 16:10; 21:13; 25:12-16
19 [v]Gen. 3:7; Num. 22:31; 2 Kin. 6:17; Luke 24:31
20 [w]Gen. 28:15; 39:2, 3, 21 [x]Gen. 16:12
21 [y]Gen. 24:4
22 [z]Gen. 20:2, 14; 26:26 [a]Gen. 26:28; Is. 8:10
23 [b]Josh. 2:12; 1 Sam. 24:21 [7]*take an oath*
25 [c]Gen. 26:15, 18, 20-22
27 [d]Gen. 26:31; 31:44; 1 Sam. 18:3 [8]*treaty*
29 [e]Gen. 33:8
30 [f]Gen. 31:48, 52
31 [g]Gen. 21:14; 26:33 [9]Lit. *Well of the Oath* or *Well of the Seven*
33 [h]Gen. 4:26; 12:8; 13:4; 26:25 [i]Gen. 35:11; Ex. 15:18; Deut. 32:40; 33:27; Ps. 90:2; 93:2; Is. 40:28; Jer. 10:10; Hab. 1:12; Heb. 13:8

A Covenant with Abimelech

22 And it came to pass at that time that
[z]Abimelech and Phichol, the commander
of his army, spoke to Abraham, saying,
[a]"God *is* with you in all that you do.
23 Now therefore, [b]swear[7] to me by God
that you will not deal falsely with me, with
my offspring, or with my posterity; but
that according to the kindness that I have
done to you, you will do to me and to the
land in which you have dwelt."
24 And Abraham said, "I will swear."
25 Then Abraham rebuked Abimelech
because of a well of water which Abimelech's servants [c]had seized. 26 And Abimelech said, "I do not know who has done
this thing; you did not tell me, nor had I
heard *of it* until today." 27 So Abraham
took sheep and oxen and gave them to
Abimelech, and the two of them [d]made a
[8]covenant. 28 And Abraham set seven ewe
lambs of the flock by themselves.
29 Then Abimelech asked Abraham,
[e]"What *is the meaning of* these seven ewe
lambs which you have set by themselves?"
30 And he said, "You will take *these*
seven ewe lambs from my hand, that [f]they
may be my witness that I have dug this
well." 31 Therefore he [g]called that place
[9]Beersheba, because the two of them swore
an oath there.
32 Thus they made a covenant at Beersheba. So Abimelech rose with Phichol, the
commander of his army, and they returned
to the land of the Philistines. 33 Then *Abraham* planted a tamarisk tree in Beersheba,
and [h]there called on the name of the LORD,
[i]the Everlasting God. 34 And Abraham
stayed in the land of the Philistines many
days.

21:10 Cast out...not be heir. Legal codes of Abraham's day—e.g., of Nuzi and of Hammurabi—forbade the putting out of a handmaiden's son if a rightful, natural heir was born. Sarah's request, thus, offended social law, Abraham's sensibilities, and his love for Ishmael (v. 11). Abraham, however, was given divine approval and assurances to overcome his scruples before sending Hagar and Ishmael out into the wilderness (vv. 12-15). Cf. Gal. 4:22-31.

21:12 Cf. Rom. 9:7; Heb. 11:18.

21:13 Cf. v. 18; *see notes on 16:11,12.* Ishmael was about 17 years old, a customary time for sons to go out to set up their own lives.

21:14 Wilderness of Beersheba. A wide, extensive desert on the southern border of Palestine.

21:17 God heard the voice of the lad. When desperation turned the lad's voice of scoffing into a cry of anguish at probable death from thirst (vv. 15,16), God heard him whose name had been given years before when God had heard Hagar's cries (16:11). It reminded the mother of the promise made to Abraham about her son (17:20). **angel of God.** Same person as the Angel of the Lord. *See note on Ex. 3:2.*

21:18 *See note on v. 13.*

21:21 Wilderness of Paran. Located in the NE section of the Sinai peninsula, the area called Arabia.

21:22-34 A parity treaty formally struck between Abimelech and Abraham guaranteed the proper control and sharing of the region's limited water resources and also assured the king of the patriarch's fair and equitable treatment for years to come.

21:31 Beersheba. This site is about 45 mi. SW of Jerusalem.

21:32 The land of the Philistines. Abraham had contact with early migrations of Aegean traders who settled along the SW coastal regions of Canaan and who were the predecessors of the 12th century B.C. influx of Philistines, the future oppressors of Israel.

21:33 tamarisk tree. This tree functioned as a reminder of the treaty concluded between two well known contemporaries, and also as a marker of one of Abraham's worship sites. **the Everlasting God.** A divine name appropriately signifying to Abraham the unbreakable and everlasting nature of the covenant God had made with him, notwithstanding his being only a resident alien and a sojourner in the Land (cf. 23:3).

Abraham's Faith Confirmed

22 Now it came to pass after these
things that [a]God tested Abraham,
and said to him, "Abraham!"
And he said, "Here I am."
2 Then He said, "Take now your son,
[b]your only *son* Isaac, whom you [c]love, and
go [d]to the land of Moriah, and offer him
there as a [e]burnt offering on one of the
mountains of which I shall tell you."
3 So Abraham rose early in the morning
and saddled his donkey, and took two of
his young men with him, and Isaac his son;
and he split the wood for the burnt offering, and arose and went to the place of
which God had told him. 4 Then on the
third day Abraham lifted his eyes and saw
the place afar off. 5 And Abraham said to
his young men, "Stay here with the donkey; the [1]lad and I will go yonder and worship, and we will [f]come back to you."
6 So Abraham took the wood of the
burnt offering and [g]laid *it* on Isaac his son;
and he took the fire in his hand, and a
knife, and the two of them went together.
7 But Isaac spoke to Abraham his father
and said, "My father!"
And he said, "Here I am, my son."
Then he said, "Look, the fire and the
wood, but where *is* the [2]lamb for a burnt
offering?"
8 And Abraham said, "My son, God will
provide for Himself the [h]lamb for a [i]burnt
offering." So the two of them went together.
9 Then they came to the place of which
God had told him. And Abraham built an
altar there and placed the wood in order;
and he bound Isaac his son and [j]laid him
on the altar, upon the wood. 10 And Abraham stretched out his hand and took the
knife to slay his son.
11 But the [k]Angel of the LORD called to
him from heaven and said, "Abraham,
Abraham!"
So he said, "Here I am."
12 And He said, [l]"Do not lay your hand
on the lad, or do anything to him; for
[m]now I know that you fear God, since you
have not [n]withheld your son, your only
son, from Me."
13 Then Abraham lifted his eyes and
looked, and there behind *him was* a ram
caught in a thicket by its horns. So Abraham went and took the ram, and offered it
up for a burnt offering instead of his son.
14 And Abraham called the name of the
place, [3]The-LORD-Will-Provide; as it is said
to this day, "In the Mount of the LORD it
shall be provided."
15 Then the Angel of the LORD called to
Abraham a second time out of heaven,
16 and said: [o]"By Myself I have sworn, says
the LORD, because you have done this
thing, and have not withheld your son,
your only *son*— 17 blessing I will [p]bless
you, and multiplying I will multiply your
descendants [q]as the stars of the heaven
[r]and as the sand which *is* on the seashore;
and [s]your descendants shall possess the
gate of their enemies. 18 [t]In your seed all
the nations of the earth shall be blessed,
[u]because you have obeyed My voice."
19 So Abraham returned to his young men,
and they rose and went together to [v]Beer-
sheba; and Abraham dwelt at Beersheba.

The Family of Nahor

20 Now it came to pass after these things
that it was told Abraham, saying, "Indeed

CHAPTER 22

1 [a]Deut. 8:2, 16; 1 Cor. 10:13; Heb. 11:17; [James 1:12-14; 1 Pet. 1:7]
2 [b]Gen. 22:12, 16; John 3:16; Heb. 11:17; 1 John 4:9 [c]John 5:20 [d]2 Chr. 3:1 [e]Gen. 8:20; 31:54
5 [f][Heb. 11:19] [1]Or *young man*
6 [g]John 19:17
7 [2]Or *goat*
8 [h]John 1:29, 36 [i]Ex. 12:3-6
9 [j][Heb. 11:17-19; James 2:21]
11 [k]Gen. 16:7-11; 21:17, 18; 31:11
12 [l]1 Sam. 15:22 [m]Gen. 26:5; James 2:21, 22 [n]Gen. 22:2, 16; John 3:16
14 [3]Heb. *YHWH Yireh*
16 [o]Ps. 105:9; Luke 1:73; [Heb. 6:13, 14]
17 [p]Gen. 17:16; 26:3, 24 [q]Gen. 15:5; 26:4; Deut. 1:10; Jer. 33:22; Heb. 11:12 [r]Gen. 13:16; 32:12; 1 Kin. 4:20 [s]Gen. 24:60
18 [t]Gen. 12:3; 18:18; 26:4; Matt. 1:1; Luke 3:34; [Acts 3:25, 26]; Gal. 3:8, 9, 16, 18 [u]Gen. 18:19; 22:3, 10; 26:5
19 [v]Gen. 21:31

22:1 God tested Abraham. This was not a temptation; rather God examined Abraham's heart (cf. James 1:2-4,12-18).

22:2 Take...your son...and offer him. These startling commands activated a special testing ordeal for Abraham, i.e., to sacrifice his "only son" (repeated 3 times by God, vv. 2,12,16). This would mean killing the son (over 20 years old) and with that, ending the promise of the Abrahamic Covenant. Such action would seem irrational, yet Abraham obeyed (v. 3). **Moriah.** Traditionally associated with Jerusalem, and the site on which Solomon's temple would be built later (cf. 2 Chr. 3:1).

22:4 third day. With no appearance of reluctance or delay, Abraham rose early (v. 3) for the two day trip from Beersheba to Moriah, one of the hills around Jerusalem.

22:5 the lad and I will go...we will come back. The 3-day journey (v. 4) afforded much time of reflection upon God's commands but, without wavering or questioning the morality of human sacrifice or the purposes of God, Abraham confidently assured his servants of his and Isaac's return and went ahead with arrangements for the sacrifice (v. 6). Hebrews 12:17-19 reveals that he was so confident in the permanence of God's promise, that he believed if Isaac were to be killed, God would raise him from the dead (*see notes*), or God would provide a substitute for Isaac (v. 8).

22:9,10 Abraham's preparations to kill his only son could not have placed his trust in God in sharper focus. Cf. Heb. 11:17-19.

22:11 Angel of the LORD. *See note on Ex. 3:2.*

22:12 now I know. Abraham passed the test (v. 1). He demonstrated faith that God responds to with justification. *See note on James 2:21.*

22:13 instead of his son. The idea of substitutionary atonement is introduced, which would find its fulfillment in the death of Christ (Is. 53:4-6; John 1:29; 2 Cor. 5:21).

22:15-18 In this formal reaffirmation of His Abrahamic Covenant, the Lord mentioned the 3 elements of land, seed, and blessing, but with attention directed graphically to the conquest of the Land promised (v. 17, "shall possess the gate of their enemies").

22:16,17 Cf. 12:1-3; 15:13-18; 17:2,7,8,9; Heb. 6:13,14.

22:17 possess the gate of their enemies. Cf. 24:60. Refers to conquering enemies, so as to control their city.

22:18 Cf. Acts 3:25.

22:20-24 it was told. This is clear indication that, despite geographical separation, information about family genealogies flowed back and forth in the Fertile Crescent region. This update advised most notably of a daughter, Rebekah, born to Isaac's cousin, Bethuel

[w]Milcah also has borne children to your
brother Nahor: 21 [x]Huz his firstborn, Buz
his brother, Kemuel the father [y]of Aram,
22 Chesed, Hazo, Pildash, Jidlaph, and
Bethuel." 23 And [z]Bethuel begot [4]Rebekah.
These eight Milcah bore to Nahor, Abraham's brother. 24 His concubine, whose
name was Reumah, also bore Tebah,
Gaham, Thahash, and Maachah.

Sarah's Death and Burial

23 Sarah lived one hundred and twenty-seven years; *these were* the years
of the life of Sarah. 2 So Sarah died in [a]Kir-
jath Arba (that *is*, [b]Hebron) in the land of
Canaan, and Abraham came to mourn for
Sarah and to weep for her.
3 Then Abraham stood up from before
his dead, and spoke to the sons of [c]Heth,
saying, 4 [d]"I *am* a foreigner and a visitor
among you. [e]Give me property for a burial
place among you, that I may bury my dead
out of my sight."
5 And the sons of Heth answered Abraham, saying to him, 6 "Hear us, my lord:
You *are* [f]a [1]mighty prince among us; bury
your dead in the choicest of our burial
places. None of us will withhold from you
his burial place, that you may bury your
dead."
7 Then Abraham stood up and bowed
himself to the people of the land, the sons
of Heth. 8 And he spoke with them, saying,
"If it is your wish that I bury my dead out
of my sight, hear me, and [2]meet with
Ephron the son of Zohar for me, 9 that he
may give me the cave of [g]Machpelah
which he has, which *is* at the end of his
field. Let him give it to me at the full price,
as property for a burial place among you."
10 Now Ephron dwelt among the sons of
Heth; and Ephron the Hittite answered
Abraham in the presence of the sons of
Heth, all who [h]entered at the gate of his
city, saying, 11 [i]"No, my lord, hear me: I
give you the field and the cave that *is* in it;
I give it to you in the presence of the sons
of my people. I give it to you. Bury your
dead!"
12 Then Abraham bowed himself down
before the people of the land; 13 and he
spoke to Ephron in the hearing of the people of the land, saying, "If you *will give it*,
please hear me. I will give you money for
the field; take *it* from me and I will bury
my dead there."
14 And Ephron answered Abraham, saying to him, 15 "My lord, listen to me; the
land *is worth* four hundred [j]shekels of silver. What *is* that between you and me? So
bury your dead." 16 And Abraham listened to Ephron; and Abraham [k]weighed
out the silver for Ephron which he had
named in the hearing of the sons of Heth,
four hundred shekels of silver, currency of
the merchants.
17 So [l]the field of Ephron which *was* in
Machpelah, which *was* before Mamre, the
field and the cave which *was* in it, and all
the trees that *were* in the field, which *were*
within all the surrounding borders, were
deeded 18 to Abraham as a possession in
the presence of the sons of Heth, before all
who went in at the gate of his city.
19 And after this, Abraham buried Sarah
his wife in the cave of the field of Machpelah, before Mamre (that *is*, Hebron) in

20 [w]Gen. 11:29; 24:15
21 [x]Job 1:1 [y]Job 32:2
23 [z]Gen. 24:15 [4]*Rebecca,* Rom. 9:10

CHAPTER 23

2 [a]Gen. 35:27; Josh. 14:15; 15:13; 21:11 [b]Gen. 13:18; 23:19
3 [c]Gen. 10:15; 15:20; 2 Kin. 7:6
4 [d][Gen. 17:8]; Lev. 25:23; 1 Chr. 29:15; Ps. 39:12; 105:12; 119:19; [Heb. 11:9, 13] [e]Acts 7:5, 16
6 [f]Gen. 13:2; 14:14; 24:35 [1]Lit. *prince of God*
8 [2]*entreat*
9 [g]Gen. 25:9
10 [h]Gen. 23:18; 34:20, 24; Ruth 4:1, 4, 11
11 [i]2 Sam. 24:21-24
15 [j]Ex. 30:13; Ezek. 45:12
16 [k]2 Sam. 14:26; Jer. 32:9, 10; Zech. 11:12
17 [l]Gen. 25:9; 49:29-32; 50:13; Acts 7:16

(v. 23). It also reminds the readers that Abraham and Sarah had not lost all ties with their original home. Abraham's brother, Nahor, still lived back in Mesopotamia, though he had not seen him for about 60 years.

23:1,2 Although Sarah's age—the only woman's age at death recorded in Scripture—might suggest her importance in God's plan, it more importantly reminds of the birth of her only son well beyond childbearing age (at 90 years of age, cf. 17:17) and of God's intervention to bring about the fulfillment of His word to her and Abraham. Sarah's death occurred ca. 2028 B.C.

23:2 Hebron. *See note on 13:18.*

23:3 the sons of Heth. A settlement of Hittites whose original home was in Anatolia (modern-day Turkey), who had already been established in Canaan far from their homeland.

23:4 Give me property. Negotiations for the purchase ("give" signifies here "sell") of Hittite property was properly conducted in accordance with contemporary Hittite custom, with Abraham wanting to pay the market value for it (v. 9).

23:6 a mighty prince among us. Rank and reputation accorded Abraham a place of leadership and respect, leading his neighbors (the Hittites) to freely offer their best sepulchers to him. They went on and arranged for Abraham to purchase a cave that belonged to a wealthy neighbor called Ephron (vv. 7-9), unknown to Abraham.

23:10 dwelt. Lit. "was sitting," perhaps at the city gate where business was usually transacted.

23:11 I give you the field. This suggests not that Ephron felt generous, but that he was constrained by Hittite feudal polity, which tied ownership of land with service to the ruler. Passing the land to Abraham would pass also feudal responsibilities to Abraham, making him liable for all taxes and duties. This Ephron was apparently anxious to do, thus the offer to give the land.

23:14,16 shekels of silver, currency of the merchants. Precious metals were not made into coins for exchange until centuries later. Merchants maintained the shekel as the standard weight of value for business transactions. A shekel weighed less than one half ounce.

23:17,18 With the words of the transaction, the careful description of the property, and the payment of the stated price all done before witnesses and at the proper place of business, ownership of the land officially passed to Abraham. It was still binding years later in the time of Jacob (49:29-32; 50:12,13).

23:19 after this. Once the purchase had been made, Abraham buried Sarah. Moses notes the place is Hebron in Canaan, to which his initial readers were soon headed.

the land of Canaan. 20 So the field and the
cave that *is* in it [m]were deeded to Abraham
by the sons of Heth as property for a burial place.

A Bride for Isaac

24 Now Abraham [a]was old, well advanced in age; and the LORD [b]had
blessed Abraham in all things. 2 So Abraham said [c]to the oldest servant of his
house, who [d]ruled over all that he had,
"Please, [e]put your hand under my thigh,
3 and I will make you [f]swear[1] by the LORD,
the God of heaven and the God of the
earth, that [g]you will not take a wife for my
son from the daughters of the Canaanites,
among whom I dwell; 4 [h]but you shall go
[i]to my country and to my family, and take
a wife for my son Isaac."
5 And the servant said to him, "Perhaps
the woman will not be willing to follow me
to this land. Must I take your son back to
the land from which you came?"
6 But Abraham said to him, "Beware that
you do not take my son back there. 7 The
LORD God of heaven, who [j]took me from
my father's house and from the land of my
family, and who spoke to me and swore to
me, saying, [k]'To your [2]descendants I give
this land,' [l]He will send His angel before
you, and you shall take a wife for my son
from there. 8 And if the woman is not willing to follow you, then [m]you will be released from this oath; only do not take my
son back there." 9 So the servant put his
hand under the thigh of Abraham his master, and swore to him concerning this matter.
10 Then the servant took ten of his master's camels and departed, [n]for all his master's goods *were in* his hand. And he arose
and went to Mesopotamia, to [o]the city of
Nahor. 11 And he made his camels kneel
down outside the city by a well of water at
evening time, the time [p]when women go
out to draw *water.* 12 Then he [q]said, "O
LORD God of my master Abraham, please
[r]give me success this day, and show kindness to my master Abraham. 13 Behold,
here [s]I stand by the well of water, and [t]the
daughters of the men of the city are coming out to draw water. 14 Now let it be that
the young woman to whom I say, 'Please
let down your pitcher that I may drink,'
and she says, 'Drink, and I will also give
your camels a drink'—*let* her *be the one* You
have appointed for Your servant Isaac.
And [u]by this I will know that You have
shown kindness to my master."
15 And it happened, [v]before he had finished speaking, that behold, [w]Rebekah,[3]
who was born to Bethuel, son of [x]Milcah,
the wife of Nahor, Abraham's brother,
came out with her pitcher on her shoulder.
16 Now the young woman [y]*was* very beautiful to behold, a virgin; no man had
known her. And she went down to the
well, filled her pitcher, and came up.
17 And the servant ran to meet her and
said, "Please let me drink a little water
from your pitcher."
18 [z]So she said, "Drink, my lord." Then
she quickly let her pitcher down to her
hand, and gave him a drink. 19 And when
she had finished giving him a drink, she
said, "I will draw *water* for your camels
also, until they have finished drinking."
20 Then she quickly emptied her pitcher

20 [m] Jer. 32:10, 11

CHAPTER 24

1 [a] Gen. 18:11; 21:5 [b] Gen. 12:2; 13:2; 24:35; Ps. 112:3; Prov. 10:22; [Gal. 3:9]
2 [c] Gen. 15:2 [d] Gen. 24:10; 39:4-6 [e] Gen. 47:29; 1 Chr. 29:24
3 [f] Gen. 14:19, 22 [g] Gen. 26:35; 28:2; Ex. 34:16; Deut. 7:3; 2 Cor. 6:14-17 [1] *take an oath*
4 [h] Gen. 28:2 [i] Gen. 12:1; Heb. 11:15
7 [j] Gen. 12:1; 24:3 [k] Gen. 12:7; 13:15; 15:18; 17:8; Ex. 32:13; Deut. 1:8; 34:4; Acts 7:5 [l] Gen. 16:7; 21:17; 22:11; Ex. 23:20, 23; 33:2; Heb. 1:4, 14 [2] Lit. *seed*
8 [m] Josh. 2:17-20
10 [n] Gen. 24:2, 22 [o] Gen. 11:31, 32; 22:20; 27:43; 29:5
11 [p] Ex. 2:16; 1 Sam. 9:11
12 [q] Gen. 24:27, 42, 48; 26:24; 32:9; Ex. 3:6, 15 [r] Gen. 27:20; Neh. 1:11; Ps. 37:5
13 [s] Gen. 24:43 [t] Ex. 2:16
14 [u] Judg. 6:17, 37; 1 Sam. 14:10; 16:7; 20:7; 2 Kin. 20:9; Prov. 16:33; Acts 1:26
15 [v] Is. 65:24 [w] Gen. 24:45; 25:20 [x] Gen. 22:20, 23 [3] *Rebecca,* Rom. 9:10
16 [y] Gen. 12:11; 26:7; 29:17
18 [z] Gen. 24:14, 46; [1 Pet. 3:8, 9]

23:20 So the field and the cave…were deeded. This is an important summary, because finally, after years of nomadic wandering, Abraham owned a small piece of real estate in the midst of all the land divinely promised to him and his descendants. The cave also became many years later the family burial plot for Abraham, Isaac, Rebekah, Leah, and Jacob (cf. 25:9; 49:31; 50:13), with Rachel being the exception (35:19).

24:2 the oldest servant…who ruled. Eliezer, at 85 years of age, had risen to steward, or "chief of staff," a position of substantial authority (indicated in v. 10). He would have received all Abraham's wealth if he had no son (see 15:1,2), yet when Isaac was born the inheritance became Isaac's. So, not only had he loyally served his master despite having been displaced by another heir (cf. 15:2-4), but he also faithfully served that heir (v. 67).

24:2-4 put your hand under my thigh…and…swear. *See note on v. 9.* A solemn pledge mentioning the Lord's name and formalized by an accepted customary gesture indicated just how serious an undertaking this was in Abraham's eyes. At his age (v. 1), Abraham was concerned to perpetuate his people and God's promise through the next generation, so he covenanted with his servant to return to Mesopotamia and bring back a wife for Isaac.

24:3,4 Matrimonial arrangements were made by parents, and chosen partners were to come from one's own tribe. It was apparently customary to marry one's first cousin. But Abraham's higher motive was to prevent Isaac from marrying a Canaanite pagan after Abraham's death, thus possibly leading the people away from the true God.

24:6,7 do not take my son back there. Should the expected scenario not materialize (v. 5) then the dictates of the oath were lifted (v. 8), but the option of Isaac going was summarily rejected because it suggested a nullification of God's promise and calling for the land of promise (v. 7).

24:7 He will send His angel before you. A statement of Abraham's faith that the 450 mile expedition to Mesopotamia was clearly under divine oversight.

24:9 his hand under the thigh. An ancient Near Eastern custom by which an intimate touch affirmed an oath (cf. 47:29).

24:10 city of Nahor. No doubt the home of Abraham's brother, Nahor (22:20).

24:12-14 The steward's prayer manifests not only his trust in God to direct affairs but also the selflessness with which he served Abraham. His patience after prayer (v. 21), his worship at answered prayer (v. 26), and his acknowledgment of divine guidance (v. 27) also portrayed his faith.

24:14 camels a drink. Hospitality required giving water to a thirsty stranger, but not to animals. A woman who would do that was

into the trough, ran back to the well to
draw *water,* and drew for all his camels.
21 And the man, wondering at her, remained silent so as to know whether [a]the
LORD had made his journey prosperous or
not.
22 So it was, when the camels had finished drinking, that the man took a golden
[b]nose ring weighing half a shekel, and two
bracelets for her wrists weighing ten
shekels of gold, 23 and said, "Whose daughter *are* you? Tell me, please, is there room *in*
your father's house for us [4]to lodge?"
24 So she said to him, [c]"I *am* the daughter of Bethuel, Milcah's son, whom she
bore to Nahor." 25 Moreover she said to
him, "We have both straw and feed
enough, and room to lodge."
26 Then the man [d]bowed down his head
and worshiped the LORD. 27 And he said,
[e]"Blessed *be* the LORD God of my master
Abraham, who has not forsaken [f]His
mercy and His truth toward my master. As
for me, being on the way, the LORD [g]led me
to the house of my master's brethren."
28 So the young woman ran and told her
mother's household these things.
29 Now Rebekah had a brother whose
name *was* [h]Laban, and Laban ran out to the
man by the well. 30 So it came to pass,
when he saw the nose ring, and the
bracelets on his sister's wrists, and when
he heard the words of his sister Rebekah,
saying, "Thus the man spoke to me," that
he went to the man. And there he stood by
the camels at the well. 31 And he said,
"Come in, [i]O blessed of the LORD! Why do
you stand outside? For I have prepared the
house, and a place for the camels."
32 Then the man came to the house. And
he unloaded the camels, and [j]provided
straw and feed for the camels, and water to
[k]wash his feet and the feet of the men who
were with him. 33 *Food* was set before him
to eat, but he said, [l]"I will not eat until I
have told about my errand."
And he said, "Speak on."
34 So he said, "I *am* Abraham's servant.
35 The LORD [m]has blessed my master greatly, and he has become great; and He has
given him flocks and herds, silver and
gold, male and female servants, and
camels and donkeys. 36 And Sarah my
master's wife [n]bore a son to my master
when she was old; and [o]to him he has
given all that he has. 37 Now my master
[p]made me swear, saying, 'You shall not
take a wife for my son from the daughters
of the Canaanites, in whose land I dwell;
38 [q]but you shall go to my father's house
and to my family, and take a wife for my
son.' 39 [r]And I said to my master, 'Perhaps
the woman will not follow me.' 40 [s]But he
said to me, 'The LORD, [t]before whom I
walk, will send His angel with you and
[5]prosper your way; and you shall take a
wife for my son from my family and from
my father's house. 41 [u]You will be clear
from this oath when you arrive among my
family; for if they will not give *her* to you,
then you will be released from my oath.'
42 "And this day I came to the well and
said, [v]'O LORD God of my master Abraham, if You will now prosper the way in
which I go, 43 [w]behold, I stand by the well
of water; and it shall come to pass that
when the virgin comes out to draw *water,*
and I say to her, "Please give me a little
water from your pitcher to drink," 44 and
she says to me, "Drink, and I will draw for
your camels also,"—*let* her *be* the woman
whom the LORD has appointed for my
master's son.'
45 [x]"But before I had finished [y]speaking
in my heart, there was Rebekah, coming
out with her pitcher on her shoulder; and
she went down to the well and drew *water.*
And I said to her, 'Please let me drink.'
46 And she made haste and let her pitcher
down from her *shoulder,* and said, 'Drink,
and I will give your camels a drink also.'
So I drank, and she gave the camels a drink
also. 47 Then I asked her, and said, 'Whose
daughter *are* you?' And she said, 'The
daughter of Bethuel, Nahor's son, whom
Milcah bore to him.' So I put the nose ring
on her nose and the bracelets on her wrists.
48 [z]And I bowed my head and worshiped
the LORD, and blessed the LORD God of my
master Abraham, who had led me in the
way of truth to [a]take the daughter of my
master's brother for his son. 49 Now if you
will [b]deal kindly and truly with my mas-

21 [a]Gen. 24:12-14, 27, 52
22 [b]Gen. 24:47; Ex. 32:2, 3; Is. 3:19-21
23 [4]*to spend the night*
24 [c]Gen. 22:23; 24:15
26 [d]Gen. 24:48, 52; Ex. 4:31
27 [e]Gen. 24:12, 42, 48; Ex. 18:10; Ruth 4:14; 1 Sam. 25:32, 39; 2 Sam. 18:28; Luke 1:68 [f]Gen. 32:10; Ps. 98:3 [g]Gen. 24:21, 48
29 [h]Gen. 29:5, 13
31 [i]Gen. 26:29; Judg. 17:2; Ruth 3:10; Ps. 115:15
32 [j]Gen. 43:24; Judg. 19:21 [k]Gen. 19:2; John 13:5, 13-15
33 [l]Job 23:12; John 4:34; Eph. 6:5-7
35 [m]Gen. 13:2; 24:1
36 [n]Gen. 21:1-7 [o]Gen. 21:10; 25:5
37 [p]Gen. 24:2-4
38 [q]Gen. 24:4
39 [r]Gen. 24:5
40 [s]Gen. 24:7 [t]Gen. 5:22, 24; 17:1; 1 Kin. 8:23 [5]*make your way successful*
41 [u]Gen. 24:8
42 [v]Gen. 24:12
43 [w]Gen. 24:13
45 [x]Gen. 24:15 [y]1 Sam. 1:13
48 [z]Gen. 24:26, 52 [a]Gen. 22:23; 24:27; Ps. 32:8; 48:14; Is. 48:17
49 [b]Gen. 47:29; Josh. 2:14

unusually kind and served beyond the call of duty. Rebekah's servant attitude was revealed (vv. 15-20) as was her beauty and purity (v. 16).

24:20 all his camels. A single camel can hold up to 25 gallons and he had 10 of them. Serving them was a great task as she filled them all (v. 22).

24:22 shekel. *See note on 23:14,16.*

24:24 I *am* the daughter of. In formal introductions, an abbreviated genealogy provided for specific identification (cf. 22:23). She was Isaac's cousin.

24:29-31 Laban. From what is revealed about his character (chap. 29), there is reason to believe that his sight of all the presents and the camels generated the welcome.

24:33 I will not eat until. The first order of business was to identify his master and to explain his assignment, but not without stressing the blessings of God upon his master and upon his trip (vv. 34-48) and also not without immediately seeking to conclude his task and return home (vv. 49,54-56). This is the portrait of a committed, faithful, and selfless servant!

ter, tell me. And if not, tell me, that I may
turn to the right hand or to the left."
50 Then Laban and Bethuel answered
and said, [c]"The thing comes from the
LORD; we cannot [d]speak to you either bad
or good. 51 [e]Here *is* Rebekah before you;
take *her* and go, and let her be your master's son's wife, as the LORD has spoken."
52 And it came to pass, when Abraham's
servant heard their words, that [f]he worshiped the LORD, *bowing himself* to the
earth. 53 Then the servant brought out
[g]jewelry of silver, jewelry of gold, and
clothing, and gave *them* to Rebekah. He
also gave [h]precious things to her brother
and to her mother.
54 And he and the men who *were* with
him ate and drank and stayed all night.
Then they arose in the morning, and he
said, [i]"Send me away to my master."
55 But her brother and her mother said,
"Let the young woman stay with us *a few*
days, at least ten; after that she may go."
56 And he said to them, "Do not [6]hinder
me, since the LORD has prospered my way;
send me away so that I may go to my master."
57 So they said, "We will call the young
woman and ask her personally." 58 Then
they called Rebekah and said to her, "Will
you go with this man?"
And she said, "I will go."
59 So they sent away Rebekah their sister
[j]and her nurse, and Abraham's servant
and his men. 60 And they blessed Rebekah
and said to her:

"Our sister, *may* you *become*
[k]*The mother of* thousands of ten
thousands;
[l]And may your descendants possess
The gates of those who hate them."

61 Then Rebekah and her maids arose,
and they rode on the camels and followed
the man. So the servant took Rebekah and
departed.
62 Now Isaac came from the way of
[m]Beer Lahai Roi, for he dwelt in the South.
63 And Isaac went out [n]to meditate in the
field in the evening; and he lifted his eyes
and looked, and there, the camels *were*
coming. 64 Then Rebekah lifted her eyes,
and when she saw Isaac [o]she dismounted
from her camel; 65 for she had said to the
servant, "Who *is* this man walking in the
field to meet us?"
The servant said, "It *is* my master." So
she took a veil and covered herself.
66 And the servant told Isaac all the
things that he had done. 67 Then Isaac
brought her into his mother Sarah's tent;
and he [p]took Rebekah and she became his
wife, and he loved her. So Isaac [q]was comforted after his mother's *death*.

Abraham and Keturah

25 Abraham again took a wife, and her
name *was* [a]Keturah. 2 And [b]she
bore him Zimran, Jokshan, Medan, Midian, Ishbak, and Shuah. 3 Jokshan begot
Sheba and Dedan. And the sons of Dedan
were Asshurim, Letushim, and Leummim.
4 And the sons of Midian *were* Ephah,
Epher, Hanoch, Abidah, and Eldaah. All
these *were* the children of Keturah.
5 And [c]Abraham gave all that he had to
Isaac. 6 But Abraham gave gifts to the sons
of the concubines which Abraham had;
and while he was still living he [d]sent them

50 [c] Ps. 118:23; Matt. 21:42; Mark 12:11 [d] Gen. 31:24, 29
51 [e] Gen. 20:15
52 [f] Gen. 24:26, 48
53 [g] Gen. 24:10, 22; Ex. 3:22; 11:2; 12:35 [h] 2 Chr. 21:3; Ezra 1:6
54 [i] Gen. 24:56, 59; 30:25
56 [6] *delay*
59 [j] Gen. 35:8
60 [k] Gen. 17:16 [l] Gen. 22:17; 28:14
62 [m] Gen. 16:14; 25:11
63 [n] Josh. 1:8; Ps. 1:2; 77:12; 119:15, 27, 48; 143:5; 145:5
64 [o] Josh. 15:18
67 [p] Gen. 25:20; 29:20; Prov. 18:22 [q] Gen. 23:1, 2; 38:12

CHAPTER 25

1 [a] 1 Chr. 1:32, 33
2 [b] 1 Chr. 1:32, 33
5 [c] Gen. 24:35, 36
6 [d] Gen. 21:14

24:49 right...left. An expression indicating the matter of which way to go next.

24:50,51 The servant's conviction and focus was obvious and intense, precluding anything but immediate acknowledgment of God's leading and anything less than a full compliance with his request from Rebekah's father and brother (vv. 50,51).

24:53 By this dowry, Rebekah was betrothed to Isaac.

24:54 Send me away to my master. Protocol and courtesy demanded a messenger be dismissed by the addressee.

24:57,58 Will you go with this man? Commendably, Rebekah concurred with an immediate departure, and showed her confident acceptance of what was providentially coming about in her life.

24:59 her nurse. See 35:8.

24:60 they blessed Rebekah and said. Little did they realize that their conventional prayer wishing numerous offspring to Rebekah fitted in nicely with God's promises of many descendants to Abraham through Sarah and Isaac. They also wished for her offspring to be victorious over their enemies ("possess their gates"), perhaps echoing God's promises of possession of the land of the Canaanites (13:17; 15:7,16; 17:8).

24:62 Beer Lahai Roi. See 16:14. Located on the Palestine-Egypt border, about 25 mi. NW of Kadesh Barnea. Isaac lived there after Abraham's death (25:11).

24:63 to meditate. How God drew Isaac from home to where Hagar encountered the Angel of the Lord (cf. 16:14) remains unknown, but he was in the right place to meet the caravan returning with his fiancée. Perhaps he was prayerfully contemplating the circumstances of his life and the void left by his mother's death (v. 67), as well as thinking about and hoping the steward would not return from a failed mission.

24:65 she took a veil and covered herself. Convention demanded the designated bride veil her face in the presence of her betrothed until the wedding day.

24:67 his mother Sarah's tent. He thus established his acceptance of her as his wife before he had seen her beauty. When he did see her, "he loved her."

25:1-4 Abraham's sons through Keturah, (a concubine, cf. v. 6; 1 Chr. 1:32) a wife of lower status than Sarah, became the progenitors of various Arab tribes to the east of Canaan.

25:5,6 Conferring gifts upon these other sons, then sending them away, and also conferring the estate upon Isaac ensured that Isaac would be considered as the rightful heir without competition or

eastward, away from Isaac his son, to [e]the
country of the east.

Abraham's Death and Burial

7 This *is* the sum of the years of Abraham's life which he lived: one hundred
and seventy-five years. 8 Then Abraham
breathed his last and [f]died in a good old
age, an old man and full *of years,* and [g]was
gathered to his people. 9 And [h]his sons
Isaac and Ishmael buried him in the cave
of [i]Machpelah, which *is* before Mamre, in
the field of Ephron the son of Zohar the
Hittite, 10 [j]the field which Abraham purchased from the sons of Heth. [k]There Abraham was buried, and Sarah his wife.
11 And it came to pass, after the death of
Abraham, that God blessed his son Isaac.
And Isaac dwelt at [l]Beer Lahai Roi.

The Families of Ishmael and Isaac

12 Now this *is* the [m]genealogy of Ishmael, Abraham's son, whom Hagar the
Egyptian, Sarah's maidservant, bore to
Abraham. 13 And [n]these *were* the names of
the sons of Ishmael, by their names, according to their generations: The firstborn
of Ishmael, Nebajoth; then Kedar, Adbeel,
Mibsam, 14 Mishma, Dumah, Massa,
15 [1]Hadar, Tema, Jetur, Naphish, and
Kedemah. 16 These *were* the sons of Ishmael and these *were* their names, by their
towns and their [2]settlements, [o]twelve
princes according to their nations. 17 These
were the years of the life of Ishmael: one
hundred and thirty-seven years; and [p]he
breathed his last and died, and was gathered to his people. 18 [q](They dwelt from
Havilah as far as Shur, which *is* east of
Egypt as you go toward Assyria.) He [3]died
[r]in the presence of all his brethren.
19 This *is* the [s]genealogy of Isaac, Abraham's son. [t]Abraham begot Isaac. 20 Isaac
was forty years old when he took Rebekah
as wife, [u]the daughter of Bethuel the Syrian of Padan Aram, [v]the sister of Laban the
Syrian. 21 Now Isaac pleaded with the
LORD for his wife, because she *was* barren;
[w]and the LORD granted his plea, [x]and Rebekah his wife conceived. 22 But the children struggled together within her; and
she said, "If *all is* well, why *am I like* this?"
[y]So she went to inquire of the LORD.
23 And the LORD said to her:

[z]"Two nations *are* in your womb,
Two peoples shall be separated
from your body;
One people shall be stronger than
[a]the other,
[b]And the older shall serve the
younger."

24 So when her days were fulfilled *for her*
to give birth, indeed *there were* twins in her
womb. 25 And the first came out red. *He was*
[c]like a hairy garment all over; so they called
his name [4]Esau. 26 Afterward his brother
came out, and [d]his hand took hold of Esau's
heel; so [e]his name was called [5]Jacob. Isaac
was sixty years old when she bore them.
27 So the boys grew. And Esau was [f]a
skillful hunter, a man of the field; but Jacob
was [g]a [6]mild man, [h]dwelling in tents.

6 [e]Judg. 6:3
8 [f]Gen. 15:15; 47:8, 9 [g]Gen. 25:17; 35:29; 49:29, 33
9 [h]Gen. 35:29; 50:13 [i]Gen. 23:9, 17; 49:30
10 [j]Gen. 23:3-16 [k]Gen. 49:31
11 [l]Gen. 16:14
12 [m]Gen. 11:10, 27; 16:15
13 [n]1 Chr. 1:29-31
15 [1]MT *Hadad*
16 [o]Gen. 17:20 [2]*camps*
17 [p]Gen. 25:8; 49:33
18 [q]Gen. 20:1; 1 Sam. 15:7 [r]Gen. 16:12 [3]*fell*
19 [s]Gen. 36:1, 9 [t]Matt. 1:2
20 [u]Gen. 22:23; 24:15, 29, 67 [v]Gen. 24:29
21 [w]1 Sam. 1:17; 1 Chr. 5:20; 2 Chr. 33:13; Ezra 8:23; Ps. 127:3 [x]Rom. 9:10-13
22 [y]1 Sam. 1:15; 9:9; 10:22
23 [z]Gen. 17:4-6, 16; 24:60; Num. 20:14; Deut. 2:4-8 [a]2 Sam. 8:14 [b]Gen. 27:29, 40; Mal. 1:2, 3; Rom. 9:12
25 [c]Gen. 27:11, 16, 23 [4]Lit. *Hairy*
26 [d]Hos. 12:3 [e]Gen. 27:36 [5]*Supplanter* or *Deceitful*, lit. *One Who Takes the Heel*
27 [f]Gen. 27:3, 5 [g]Job 1:1, 8 [h]Heb. 11:9 [6]Lit. *complete*

threat from his half-brothers. The steward, Eliezer, had informed Rebekah's relatives that all of Abraham's estate was Isaac's (cf. 24:36).

25:8 gathered to his people. A euphemism for death, but also an expression of personal continuance beyond death, which denoted a reunion with previously departed friends (ca. 1990 B.C.). Cf. Matt. 8:11; Luke 16:22,23.

25:9,10 his sons…buried him. Abraham's funeral brought together two sons who would perhaps otherwise have remained somewhat estranged from each other (cf. 35:29). He was buried in the place which he had purchased at Hebron (chap. 23).

25:12-18 the genealogy of Ishmael. With the death of Abraham and the focus shifting to Isaac, the record confirms God's promise of 12 princes to Ishmael (cf. 17:20,21).

25:13-16 Arab tradition has it that these are their earliest ancestors.

25:16 by their towns and their settlements. In addition to serving as a testimony to God's promises (17:20), information such as this genealogy helped Israel to understand the origins of their neighbors in central and northern Arabia.

25:19–35:29 The genealogy of Isaac.

25:20 Padan Aram. The "plain of Aram" in upper Mesopotamia near Haran to the NNE of Canaan.

25:21 she *was* barren. Confronted by 20 years of his wife's barrenness (vv. 19,26), Isaac rose to the test and earnestly turned to God in prayer, obviously acknowledging thereby God's involvement and timing in the seed-promise.

25:22 struggled together within her. The very uncomfortable condition of her pregnancy ("why *am I like* this?") prompted Rebekah, undoubtedly following the example of her husband, to turn earnestly to God in prayer. She learned directly from the Lord that the severe jostling in her womb prefigured the future antagonism between the two nations to arise from her twin sons (v. 23).

25:23 the older shall serve the younger. This was contrary to the custom in patriarchal times when the elder son enjoyed the privileges of precedence in the household and at the father's death received a double share of the inheritance and became the recognized head of the family (cf. Ex. 22:29; Num 8:14-17; Deut. 21:17). Grave offenses could annul such primogeniture rights (cf. Gen. 35:22; 49:3,4; 1 Chr. 5:1) or the birthright could be sacrificed or legally transferred to another in the family, as in this case (vv. 29-34). In this case, God declared otherwise since His sovereign elective purposes did not necessarily have to follow custom (cf. Rom. 9:10-14, esp. v. 12).

25:24 days were fulfilled. Esau and Jacob were born ca. 2005 B.C.

25:25 red. This would be the linguistic basis for calling Esau's country "Edom" (cf. v. 30).

25:27,28 The difference between the two sons manifested itself in several areas: 1) as progenitors—Esau of Edom and Jacob of Israel; 2) in disposition—Esau a rugged, headstrong hunter preferring the

28 And Isaac loved Esau because he [i]ate *of*
his game, [j]but Rebekah loved Jacob.

Esau Sells His Birthright

29 Now Jacob cooked a stew; and Esau
came in from the field, and he *was* weary.
30 And Esau said to Jacob, "Please feed me
with that same red *stew,* for I *am* weary."
Therefore his name was called [7]Edom.
31 But Jacob said, "Sell me your
birthright as of this day."
32 And Esau said, "Look, I *am* about to
die; so [k]what *is* this birthright to me?"
33 Then Jacob said, [8]"Swear to me as of
this day."
So he swore to him, and [l]sold his
birthright to Jacob. 34 And Jacob gave Esau
bread and stew of lentils; then [m]he ate and
drank, arose, and went his way. Thus Esau
[n]despised *his* birthright.

Isaac and Abimelech

26 There was a famine in the land, besides [a]the first famine that was in
the days of Abraham. And Isaac went to
[b]Abimelech king of the Philistines, in
Gerar.
2 Then the LORD appeared to him and
said: [c]"Do not go down to Egypt; live in
[d]the land of which I shall tell you. 3 [e]Dwell
in this land, and [f]I will be with you and
[g]bless you; for to you and your descendants [h]I give all these lands, and I will perform [i]the oath which I swore to Abraham
your father. 4 And [j]I will make your descendants multiply as the stars of heaven; I
will give to your descendants all these
lands; [k]and in your seed all the nations of
the earth shall be blessed; 5 [l]because Abraham obeyed My voice and kept My charge,
My commandments, My statutes, and My
laws."
6 So Isaac dwelt in Gerar. 7 And the men
of the place asked about his wife. And [m]he
said, "She *is* my sister"; for [n]he was afraid
to say, "*She is* my wife," *because he thought,*
"lest the men of the place kill me for Rebekah, because she *is* [o]beautiful to behold." 8 Now it came to pass, when he had
been there a long time, that Abimelech
king of the Philistines looked through a
window, and saw, and there was Isaac,
[1]showing endearment to Rebekah his wife.
9 Then Abimelech called Isaac and said,
"Quite obviously she *is* your wife; so how
could you say, 'She *is* my sister'?"
Isaac said to him, "Because I said, 'Lest I
die on account of her.' "
10 And Abimelech said, "What *is* this
you have done to us? One of the people
might soon have lain with your wife, and
[p]you would have brought guilt on us."
11 So Abimelech charged all *his* people,
saying, "He who [q]touches this man or his
wife shall surely be put to death."
12 Then Isaac sowed in that land, and
reaped in the same year [r]a hundredfold;
and the LORD [s]blessed him. 13 The man
[t]began to prosper, and continued prospering until he became very prosperous; 14 for
he had possessions of flocks and possessions of herds and a great number of servants. So the Philistines [u]envied him.
15 Now the Philistines had stopped up all
the wells [v]which his father's servants had
dug in the days of Abraham his father, and

28 [i] Gen. 27:4, 19, 25, 31 [j] Gen. 27:6-10
30 [7] Lit. *Red*
32 [k] Matt. 16:26; Mark 8:36, 37
33 [l] Heb. 12:16 [8] *Take an oath*
34 [m] Eccl. 8:15; Is. 22:13; 1 Cor. 15:32 [n] Heb. 12:16, 17

CHAPTER 26

1 [a] Gen. 12:10 [b] Gen. 20:1, 2
2 [c] Gen. 12:7; 17:1; 18:1; 35:9 [d] Gen. 12:1
3 [e] Gen. 20:1; Ps. 39:12; Heb. 11:9 [f] Gen. 28:13, 15 [g] Gen. 12:2 [h] Gen. 12:7; 13:15; 15:18 [i] Gen. 22:16; Ps. 105:9
4 [j] Gen. 15:5; 22:17; Ex. 32:13 [k] Gen. 12:3; 22:18; Gal. 3:8
5 [l] Gen. 22:16, 18
7 [m] Gen. 12:13; 20:2, 12, 13 [n] Prov. 29:25 [o] Gen. 12:11; 24:16; 29:17
8 [1] *caressing*
10 [p] Gen. 20:9
11 [q] Ps. 105:15
12 [r] Matt. 13:8, 23; Mark 4:8 [s] Gen. 24:1; 25:8, 11; 26:3; Job 42:12; Prov. 10:22
13 [t] Gen. 24:35; [Prov. 10:22]
14 [u] Gen. 37:11; Eccl. 4:4
15 [v] Gen. 21:25, 30

outdoors and Jacob a plain, amiable man preferring the comforts of home; and 3) in parental favoritism—Esau by his father and Jacob by his mother. These were the ingredients for conflict and heartache!

25:30 Edom. In a play upon words to forever recall that Esau was born red and hairy (v. 25) and had sold his birthright for red stew, he was also named Edom, i.e., "Red."

25:31 birthright. A double portion of the inheritance (Deut. 21:17) and the right to be family chief and priest (Ex. 4:22).

25:34 despised *his* birthright. The final evaluation of the verbal tussle and bartering which took place between the twins, all of which was indicative of prior discussions or arguments sufficient for Jacob to conclude how little Esau valued it. He became, therefore, known as irreligious, i.e., "a profane person" (Heb. 12:16).

26:1 a famine in the land. Once again the land of promise forced the beneficiaries of the covenant to move so as to escape the effects of a famine. **Abimelech.** Most probably a Philistine dynastic title, with this being a different king from the one who had met Abraham (chap. 20). *See note on 20:2.* **Philistines.** This tribe of people who originally sailed the Mediterranean Sea became fierce enemies of Israel when they settled along the SW coast of Palestine. Friendly to Isaac, they were forerunners of hostile descendant enemies.

26:2-11 Obedience and deceit were in juxtaposition. Obeying God to dwell in the land (vv. 2,3,6), yet lying about his wife to the people of the land (vv. 7-11) reflected familiar shades of Abraham's strategy for survival (see 12:10-14; 20:1-4).

26:3-5 God confirmed the Abrahamic Covenant with Isaac, stressing the same 3 elements as before: land, seed, and blessing. He appended specific honorable mention of Abraham's obedient response to all of God's words. *See notes on 12:1-3; 15:13-18; 17:2,7,8,9.* Although Isaac was commended for his deeds, the Abrahamic Covenant was an unconditional covenant grounded in God's sovereign will (cf. Lev. 26:44,45).

26:4 Cf. Acts 3:25.

26:6-9 Unlike his ancestor to whom God sovereignly revealed the relationship between Abraham and Sarah (20:3), this king providentially discovered Rebekah's relationship to Isaac by just happening to look out of a window and witnessing caresses indicative of marriage and intimacy.

26:11 charged all *his* people…put to death. A pagan king imposing the death penalty on anyone troubling Isaac or Rebekah suggests God was at work to preserve His chosen seed (cf. vv. 28,29). Cf. Ps. 105:14,15.

26:12-14 Isaac was content to stay in that place and farm some land. His efforts were blessed by God, but envied by the Philistines!

26:15 stopped up all the wells. Water was so precious in that desert land that wells were essential. Plugging someone's well was

they had filled them with earth. 16 And
Abimelech said to Isaac, "Go away from
us, for [w]you are much mightier than we."
17 Then Isaac departed from there and
[2]pitched his tent in the Valley of Gerar, and
dwelt there. 18 And Isaac dug again the
wells of water which they had dug in
the days of Abraham his father, for the
Philistines had stopped them up after the
death of Abraham. [x]He called them by
the names which his father had called them.
19 Also Isaac's servants dug in the valley,
and found a well of running water there.
20 But the herdsmen of Gerar [y]quarreled
with Isaac's herdsmen, saying, "The water
is ours." So he called the name of the well
[3]Esek, because they quarreled with him.
21 Then they dug another well, and they
quarreled over that *one* also. So he called
its name [4]Sitnah. 22 And he moved from
there and dug another well, and they did
not quarrel over it. So he called its name
[5]Rehoboth, because he said, "For now the
LORD has made room for us, and we shall
[z]be fruitful in the land."
23 Then he went up from there to Beersheba. 24 And the LORD [a]appeared to him
the same night and said, [b]"I *am* the God of
your father Abraham; [c]do not fear, for [d]I
am with you. I will bless you and multiply
your descendants for My servant Abraham's sake." 25 So he [e]built an altar there
and [f]called on the name of the LORD, and
he pitched his tent there; and there Isaac's
servants dug a well.
26 Then Abimelech came to him from
Gerar with Ahuzzath, one of his friends,
[g]and Phichol the commander of his army.
27 And Isaac said to them, "Why have you
come to me, [h]since you hate me and have
[i]sent me away from you?"
28 But they said, "We have certainly seen
that the LORD [j]is with you. So we said, 'Let
there now be an oath between us, between
you and us; and let us make a [6]covenant
with you, 29 that you will do us no harm,
since we have not touched you, and since
we have done nothing to you but good and
have sent you away in peace. [k]You *are* now
the blessed of the LORD.' "
30 [l]So he made them a feast, and they ate
and drank. 31 Then they arose early in the
morning and [m]swore an oath with one another; and Isaac sent them away, and they
departed from him in peace.
32 It came to pass the same day that
Isaac's servants came and told him about
the well which they had dug, and said to
him, "We have found water." 33 So he
called it [7]Shebah. [n]Therefore the name of
the city *is* [8]Beersheba to this day.
34 [o]When Esau was forty years old, he
took as wives Judith the daughter of Beeri
the Hittite, and Basemath the daughter of
Elon the Hittite. 35 And [p]they were a grief
of mind to Isaac and Rebekah.

Isaac Blesses Jacob

27 Now it came to pass, when Isaac
was [a]old and [b]his eyes were so dim
that he could not see, that he called Esau
his older son and said to him, "My son."
And he answered him, "Here I am."
2 Then he said, "Behold now, I am old. I
[c]do not know the day of my death. 3 [d]Now
therefore, please take your weapons, your
quiver and your bow, and go out to the
field and hunt game for me. 4 And make
me [1]savory food, such as I love, and bring

16 [w] Ex. 1:9
17 [2] *camped*
18 [x] Gen. 21:31
20 [y] Gen. 21:25 [3] Lit. *Quarrel*
21 [4] Lit. *Enmity*
22 [z] Gen. 17:6; 28:3; 41:52; Ex. 1:7 [5] Lit. *Spaciousness*
24 [a] Gen. 26:2 [b] Gen. 17:7, 8; 24:12; Ex. 3:6; Acts 7:32 [c] Gen. 15:1 [d] Gen. 26:3, 4
25 [e] Gen. 12:7, 8; 13:4, 18; 22:9; 33:20 [f] Gen. 21:33; Ps. 116:17
26 [g] Gen. 21:22
27 [h] Judg. 11:7 [i] Gen. 26:16
28 [j] Gen. 21:22, 23 [6] *treaty*
29 [k] Gen. 24:31; Ps. 115:15
30 [l] Gen. 19:3
31 [m] Gen. 21:31
33 [n] Gen. 21:31; 28:10 [7] Lit. *Oath* or *Seven* [8] Lit. *Well of the Oath* or *Well of the Seven*
34 [o] Gen. 28:8; 36:2
35 [p] Gen. 27:46; 28:1, 8

CHAPTER 27

1 [a] Gen. 35:28 [b] Gen. 48:10; 1 Sam. 3:2
2 [c] [Prov. 27:1; James 4:14]
3 [d] Gen. 25:27, 28
4 [1] *tasty*

ruinous to them and constituted serious aggression, often leading to war. Isaac could have retaliated, but he did not; rather he dug new wells (vv. 16-19).

26:22 Rehoboth. The word means "room enough." Finally a well was dug without a quarrel erupting (vv. 20,21). Now that they were no longer perceived as encroaching upon another's territory, Isaac selected an appropriate place-name which reflected how he saw God providentially working out their situation.

26:24,25 This abbreviated reaffirmation of the Abrahamic Covenant was designed to assuage Isaac's anxiety at facing envy, quarrels, and hostility (vv. 14,20,27), and to assure Isaac that he had reasoned right—fruitfulness in posterity would prevail. That it was a significant reminder to Isaac is seen in a response reminiscent of his father—he built an altar of worship to mark the spot of God's appearance to him (12:7).

26:26 Abimelech...and Phichol. Because 90 years had passed since Abraham was visited by men with the same names, they must have been titles rather than proper names (cf. 21:22). *See note on v. 1.*

26:28 an oath...a covenant. In a mirror image of a former occasion (21:22-32), Abimelech in the company of a friend and the highest ranking officer in his army (v. 26) sought after a treaty with one they estimated to be superior and stronger than themselves and a possible threat (v. 29). Isaac, on the other hand, perceived them as hostile (v. 27). The outcome was most desirable for both—peace between them (v. 31).

26:30 Ratification of a covenant often involved a banquet.

26:33 Beersheba. Lit. "the well of the oath." The very place where his father Abraham had made an oath with another Abimelech and Phichol (*see note on v. 26*) and which Abraham had named Beersheba (21:32).

26:35 grief of mind. Esau's choice of wives from among neighboring Hittite women saddened his parents. His action had deliberately ignored the standard set by Abraham for Isaac (24:3). Cf. 27:46.

27:1 Isaac was old. Blind Isaac evidently thought he was near death (v. 2) and would not live much beyond his current 137 years, which was the age of Ishmael when he died (25:17). He certainly did not expect to live another 43 years as he actually did (35:28; cf. 30:24,25; 31:41; 41:46,47; 45:6; 47:9 to calculate Isaac's age at 137 and his twin sons' ages at 77 years old).

27:4 my soul may bless you. Ignoring the words of God to Rebekah (25:23), forgetting Esau's bartered birthright (25:33), and overlooking Esau's grievous marriages (26:35), Isaac was still intent on

it to me that I may eat, that my soul [e]may
bless you before I die."
5 Now Rebekah was listening when
Isaac spoke to Esau his son. And Esau
went to the field to hunt game and to bring
it. 6 So Rebekah spoke to Jacob her son,
saying, "Indeed I heard your father speak
to Esau your brother, saying, 7 'Bring me
game and make [2]savory food for me, that I
may eat it and bless you in the presence of
the LORD before my death.' 8 Now therefore, my son, [f]obey my voice according to
what I command you. 9 Go now to the
flock and bring me from there two choice
kids of the goats, and I will make [g]savory
food from them for your father, such as he
loves. 10 Then you shall take *it* to your father, that he may eat *it*, and that he [h]may
bless you before his death."
11 And Jacob said to Rebekah his mother, "Look, [i]Esau my brother *is* a hairy man,
and I *am* a smooth-*skinned* man. 12 Perhaps
my father will [j]feel me, and I shall seem to
be a deceiver to him; and I shall bring [k]a
curse on myself and not a blessing."
13 But his mother said to him, [l]"*Let* your
curse *be* on me, my son; only obey my
voice, and go, get *them* for me." 14 And he
went and got *them* and brought *them* to his
mother, and his mother [m]made [3]savory
food, such as his father loved. 15 Then Rebekah took [n]the choice clothes of her elder
son Esau, which *were* with her in the house,
and put them on Jacob her younger son.
16 And she put the skins of the kids of the
goats on his hands and on the smooth part
of his neck. 17 Then she gave the savory
food and the bread, which she had prepared, into the hand of her son Jacob.

4 [e] Gen. 27:19, 25, 27, 31; 48:9, 15, 16; 49:28; Deut. 33:1; Heb. 11:20
7 [2] *tasty*
8 [f] Gen. 27:13, 43
9 [g] Gen. 27:4
10 [h] Gen. 27:4; 48:16
11 [i] Gen. 25:25
12 [j] Gen. 27:21, 22 [k] Gen. 9:25; Deut. 27:18
13 [l] Gen. 43:9; 1 Sam. 25:24; 2 Sam. 14:9; Matt. 27:25
14 [m] Prov. 23:3; Luke 21:34 [3] *tasty*
15 [n] Gen. 27:27

18 So he went to his father and said, "My
father."
And he said, "Here I am. Who *are* you,
my son?"
19 Jacob said to his father, "I *am* Esau
your firstborn; I have done just as you told
me; please arise, sit and eat of my game,
[o]that your soul may bless me."
20 But Isaac said to his son, "How *is it*
that you have found *it* so quickly, my
son?"
And he said, "Because the LORD your
God brought *it* to me."
21 Isaac said to Jacob, "Please come near,
that I [p]may feel you, my son, whether you
are really my son Esau or not." 22 So Jacob
went near to Isaac his father, and he felt
him and said, "The voice *is* Jacob's voice,
but the hands *are* the hands of Esau."
23 And he did not recognize him, because
[q]his hands were hairy like his brother
Esau's hands; so he blessed him.
24 Then he said, "*Are* you really my son
Esau?"
He said, "I *am*."
25 He said, "Bring *it* near to me, and I
will eat of my son's game, so [r]that my soul
may bless you." So he brought *it* near to
him, and he ate; and he brought him wine,
and he drank. 26 Then his father Isaac said
to him, "Come near now and kiss me, my
son." 27 And he came near and [s]kissed
him; and he smelled the smell of his clothing, and blessed him and said:

"Surely, [t]the smell of my son
Is like the smell of a field
Which the LORD has blessed.
28 Therefore may [u]God give you
Of [v]the dew of heaven,

19 [o] Gen. 27:4
21 [p] Gen. 27:12
23 [q] Gen. 27:16
25 [r] Gen. 27:4, 10, 19, 31
27 [s] Gen. 29:13 [t] Song 4:11; Hos. 14:6
28 [u] Heb. 11:20 [v] Gen. 27:39; Deut. 33:13, 28; 2 Sam. 1:21; Ps. 133:3; Prov. 3:20; Mic. 5:7; Zech. 8:12

treating Esau as the eldest and granting him the blessing of birthright, and so arranged for his favorite meal before bestowing final fatherly blessing on his favorite son.

27:5 Now Rebekah was listening. Desperation to secure patriarchal blessing for Jacob bred deception and trickery, with Rebekah believing her culinary skills could make goat's meat taste and smell like choice venison (vv. 8-10) and make Jacob seem like Esau (vv. 15-17).

27:12 I shall seem to be a deceiver to him. To his credit, Jacob at first objected. The differences between him and Esau would surely not fool his father and might result in blessing being replaced with a curse as a fitting punishment for deception.

27:13 *Let* your curse *be* on me. With his mother accepting full responsibility for the scheme and bearing the curse should it occur, Jacob acquiesced and followed Rebekah's instructions.

27:15 choice clothes of her elder son. Esau, having been married for 37 years (cf. v 1; 26:35), would have had his own tents and his own wives to do for him; so how and why Rebekah came by some of his best clothes in her tent is unknown. Perhaps these garments were the official robes associated with the priestly functions of the head of the house, kept in her house until passed on to the oldest son. Perhaps Esau had, on occasion, worn them, thus their smell of the field (v. 27).

27:20 Because the LORD your God brought *it* to me. Isaac's perfectly legitimate question in v. 20 (hunting took time and Jacob had come so quickly with goats from the pen) afforded Jacob an escape route—confess and stop the deceit! Instead, Jacob, with consummate ease, knowing he needed Isaac's irrevocable confirmation even though he had bought the birthright, ascribed success in the hunt to God's providence. A lie had to sustain a lie, and a tangled web had begun to be woven (vv. 21-24). Although Jacob received Isaac's blessing that day, the deceit caused severe consequences: 1) he never saw his mother after that; 2) Esau wanted him dead; 3) Laban, his uncle, deceived him; 4) his family life was full of conflict; and 5) he was exiled for years from his family. By the promise of God he would have received the birthright (25:23). He didn't need to scheme this deception with his mother.

27:27-29 Finally, with all lingering doubts removed, Isaac pronounced the blessing upon Jacob, although the opening words show he thought the one receiving it was Esau, the man of the field. His prayer-wish called for prosperity and superiority and ended with a repeat of God's words to Abraham (v. 29c; cf. 12:1-3). The words indicated that Isaac thought the covenantal line should have continued through his eldest son, Esau.

Of [w]the fatness of the earth,
And [x]plenty of grain and wine.
29 [y]Let peoples serve you,
And nations bow down to you.
Be master over your brethren,
And [z]let your mother's sons bow
down to you.
[a]Cursed *be* everyone who curses
you,
And blessed *be* those who bless
you!"

Esau's Lost Hope

30 Now it happened, as soon as Isaac
had finished blessing Jacob, and Jacob had
scarcely gone out from the presence of
Isaac his father, that Esau his brother came
in from his hunting. 31 He also had made
[4]savory food, and brought it to his father,
and said to his father, "Let my father arise
and [b]eat of his son's game, that your soul
may bless me."
32 And his father Isaac said to him,
"Who *are* you?"
So he said, "I *am* your son, your firstborn, Esau."
33 Then Isaac trembled exceedingly, and
said, "Who? Where *is* the one who hunted
game and brought *it* to me? I ate all *of it* before you came, and I have blessed him—
[c]*and* indeed he shall be blessed."
34 When Esau heard the words of his father, [d]he cried with an exceedingly great
and bitter cry, and said to his father, "Bless
me—me also, O my father!"
35 But he said, "Your brother came with
deceit and has taken away your blessing."
36 And *Esau* said, [e]"Is he not rightly
named [5]Jacob? For he has supplanted me
these two times. He took away my
birthright, and now look, he has taken
away my blessing!" And he said, "Have
you not reserved a blessing for me?"
37 Then Isaac answered and said to
Esau, [f]"Indeed I have made him your master, and all his brethren I have given to him
as servants; with [g]grain and wine I have
[6]sustained him. What shall I do now for
you, my son?"
38 And Esau said to his father, "Have
you only one blessing, my father? Bless
me—me also, O my father!" And Esau lifted up his voice [h]and wept.
39 Then Isaac his father answered and
said to him:

"Behold, [i]your dwelling shall be of
the [7]fatness of the earth,
And of the dew of heaven from
above.
40 By your sword you shall live,
And [j]you shall serve your brother;
And [k]it shall come to pass, when
you become restless,
That you shall break his yoke from
your neck."

Jacob Escapes from Esau

41 So Esau [l]hated Jacob because of the
blessing with which his father blessed him,
and Esau said in his heart, [m]"The days of
mourning for my father [8]are at hand;
[n]then I will kill my brother Jacob."
42 And the words of Esau her older son
were told to Rebekah. So she sent and
called Jacob her younger son, and said to
him, "Surely your brother Esau [o]comforts
himself concerning you *by intending* to kill
you. 43 Now therefore, my son, obey my
voice: arise, flee to my brother Laban [p]in
Haran. 44 And stay with him a [q]few days,
until your brother's fury turns away, 45 until your brother's anger turns away from
you, and he forgets what you have done to
him; then I will send and bring you from
there. Why should I be bereaved also of
you both in one day?"
46 And Rebekah said to Isaac, [r]"I am
weary of my life because of the daughters
of Heth; [s]if Jacob takes a wife of the daugh-

28 [w]Gen. 45:18; Num. 18:12 [x]Deut. 7:13; 33:28
29 [y]Gen. 9:25; 25:23; Is. 45:14; 49:7; 60:12, 14 [z]Gen. 37:7, 10; 49:8 [a]Gen. 12:2, 3; Zeph. 2:8, 9
31 [b]Gen. 27:4 [4]*tasty*
33 [c]Gen. 25:23; 28:3, 4; Num. 23:20; Rom. 11:29
34 [d][Heb. 12:17]
36 [e]Gen. 25:26, 32-34 [5]*Supplanter* or *Deceitful,* lit. *One Who Takes the Heel*
37 [f]2 Sam. 8:14
[g]Gen. 27:28, 29 [6]*provided support for*
38 [h]Heb. 12:17
39 [i]Gen. 27:28; Heb. 11:20 [7]*fertility*
40 [j]Gen. 25:23; 27:29; 2 Sam. 8:14; [Obad. 18-20] [k]2 Kin. 8:20-22
41 [l]Gen. 26:27; 32:3-11; 37:4, 5, 8 [m]Gen. 50:2-4, 10 [n]Obad. 10 [8]*are soon here*
42 [o]Ps. 64:5
43 [p]Gen. 11:31; 25:20; 28:2, 5
44 [q]Gen. 31:41
46 [r]Gen. 26:34, 35; 28:8 [s]Gen. 24:3

27:33 Isaac trembled exceedingly. Visibly shocked when the scandal was uncovered by the entrance of Esau, the father, remembering the Lord's words to Rebekah (25:23), refused to withdraw the blessing and emphatically affirmed its validity—"indeed he shall be blessed" and a little later "indeed I have made him your master" and also "you shall serve your brother" (vv. 37,40). Sudden realization at having opposed God's will all those years likely made the shock more severe.

27:34 Bless me—me also. Esau fully expected to receive the blessing, for he had identified himself to his father as the firstborn (v. 32). Anguished at losing this important paternal blessing and bitterly acting as the innocent victim (v. 36), Esau shifted the blame for the loss of birthright and blessing to Jacob and pleaded for some compensating word of blessing from his father (vv. 36,38).

27:39,40 The prayer-wish called for prosperity and inferiority, i.e., maintaining the validity of the words to Jacob and replacing "be master over your brethren" with "you shall serve your brother" (vv. 29,40). This secondary blessing would not and could not undo the first one.

27:40 you shall break his yoke from your neck. In later history, the Edomites, who descended from the line of Esau, fought time and again with Israel and shook off Israelite control on several occasions (2 Kin. 8:20; 2 Chr. 21:8-10; 28:16,17).

27:41 The days of mourning for my father. Evidently Esau also thought his father was on the verge of death (27:1) and so, out of respect for his aged father, he postponed murder. Esau lived another 43 years (*see note on 27:1*).

27:45 bereaved also of you both in one day. Rebekah understood she stood to lose both her sons since, after the murder of Jacob, the avenger of blood, i.e., the next nearest relative, would track down and execute Esau.

27:46 daughters of Heth. Local Hittite women. *See note on 26:35.*

ters of Heth, like these *who are* the daughters of the land, what good will my life be
to me?"

28

Then Isaac called Jacob and
[a]blessed him, and [1]charged him,
and said to him: [b]"You shall not take a wife
from the daughters of Canaan. 2 [c]Arise, go
to [d]Padan Aram, to the house of [e]Bethuel
your mother's father; and take yourself a
wife from there of the daughters of [f]Laban
your mother's brother.

3 "May [g]God Almighty bless you,
And make you [h]fruitful and
multiply you,
That you may be an assembly of
peoples;
4 And give you [i]the blessing of
Abraham,
To you and your descendants with
you,
That you may inherit the land
[j]In[2] which you are a stranger,
Which God gave to Abraham."

5 So Isaac sent Jacob away, and he went to
Padan Aram, to Laban the son of Bethuel
the Syrian, the brother of Rebekah, the
mother of Jacob and Esau.

Esau Marries Mahalath

6 Esau saw that Isaac had blessed Jacob
and sent him away to Padan Aram to take
himself a wife from there, *and that* as he
blessed him he gave him a charge, saying,
"You shall not take a wife from the daughters of Canaan," 7 and that Jacob had
obeyed his father and his mother and had
gone to Padan Aram. 8 Also Esau saw [k]that
the daughters of Canaan did not please his
father Isaac. 9 So Esau went to Ishmael and
[l]took [m]Mahalath the daughter of Ishmael,
Abraham's son, [n]the sister of Nebajoth, to
be his wife in addition to the wives he had.

Jacob's Vow at Bethel

10 Now Jacob [o]went out from Beersheba
and went toward [p]Haran. 11 So he came to
a certain place and stayed there all night,
because the sun had set. And he took one
of the stones of that place and put it at his
head, and he lay down in that place to
sleep. 12 Then he [q]dreamed, and behold, a
ladder *was* set up on the earth, and its top
reached to heaven; and there [r]the angels of
God were ascending and descending on it.

13 [s]And behold, the LORD stood above it
and said: [t]"I *am* the LORD God of Abraham
your father and the God of Isaac; [u]the land
on which you lie I will give to you and
your descendants. 14 Also your [v]descen-
dants shall be as the dust of the earth; you
shall spread abroad [w]to the west and the
east, to the north and the south; and in you
and [x]in your seed all the families of the
earth shall be blessed. 15 Behold, [y]I *am*
with you and will [z]keep[3] you wherever
you go, and will [a]bring you back to this
land; for [b]I will not leave you [c]until I have
done what I have spoken to you."

16 Then Jacob awoke from his sleep and
said, "Surely the LORD is in [d]this place, and

CHAPTER 28
1 [a]Gen. 27:33 [b]Gen. 24:3 [1]*commanded*
2 [c]Hos. 12:12 [d]Gen. 25:20 [e]Gen. 22:23 [f]Gen. 24:29; 27:43; 29:5
3 [g]Gen. 17:16; 35:11; 48:3 [h]Gen. 26:4, 24
4 [i]Gen. 12:2, 3; 22:17; Gal. 3:8 [j]Gen. 17:8; 23:4; 36:7; 1 Chr. 29:15; Ps. 39:12 [2]Lit. *Of your sojournings*
8 [k]Gen. 24:3; 26:34, 35; 27:46
9 [l]Gen. 26:34, 35 [m]Gen. 36:2, 3 [n]Gen. 25:13
10 [o]Gen. 26:23; 46:1; Hos. 12:12 [p]Gen. 12:4, 5; 27:43; 29:4; 2 Kin. 19:12; Acts 7:2
12 [q]Gen. 31:10; 41:1; Num. 12:6 [r]John 1:51; Heb. 1:4, 14
13 [s]Gen. 35:1; 48:3; Amos 7:7 [t]Gen. 26:24 [u]Gen. 13:15, 17; 26:3; 35:12
14 [v]Gen. 13:16; 22:17 [w]Gen. 13:14, 15; Deut. 12:20 [x]Gen. 12:3; 18:18; 22:18; 26:4; Matt. 1:2; Luke 3:34; Gal. 3:8
15 [y]Gen. 26:3, 24; 31:3 [z]Gen. 48:16; Num. 6:24; Ps. 121:5, 7, 8 [a]Gen. 35:6; 48:21; Deut. 30:3 [b]Lev. 26:44; Deut. 7:9; 31:6, 8; Josh. 1:5; 1 Kin. 8:57; Heb. 13:5 [c]Num. 23:19 [3]*protect*
16 [d]Ex. 3:5; Josh. 5:15; Ps. 139:7-12

28:1,2 take yourself a wife from there. Anxious for the safety of her son, Rebekah easily convinced her husband that the time had come for him to seek a non-Canaanite wife back in their homeland and preferably from near kinsmen (vv. 2,5), just as Rebekah had been sought for Isaac (see 24:1-4).

28:2 Padan Aram. *See note on 25:20.*

28:3,4 This extra patriarchal blessing unveiled where Isaac was in his thinking. He had come to understand that the divine blessings would go through Jacob, to whom the Abrahamic Covenant promises of posterity and land also applied—quite the reversal of prior wishes and understanding (cf. 27:27-29). The lack of land possession at that time, described by the phrase "in which you are a stranger," did not deter at all from the certainty of God's promise.

28:3 God Almighty. Significantly, El Shaddai was the name Isaac chose to employ when blessing Jacob. It was the name of sovereign power with which God had identified Himself to Abraham in covenant reaffirmation (17:1) which must have been an encouraging factor to both him and his son.

28:5 Isaac sent Jacob away. Ca. 1928 B.C. This must have been a hard departure for the domestic Jacob.

28:9 So Esau went to Ishmael. Marrying back into the line of Abraham through the family of Ishmael seemed to have been a ploy to gain favor with his father (vv. 6,8), and show an obedience similar to his brother's (v. 7). He hoped by such gratifying of his parents to atone for past delinquencies, and maybe have his father change the will. He actually increased iniquity by adding to his pagan wives (26:34,35) a wife from a family God had rejected.

28:10-15 For the first time, and significantly while Jacob was on his way out of the land of Canaan, God revealed Himself to Jacob and confirmed the Abrahamic Covenant with him in all of its 3 elements of land, seed, and blessing (vv. 13,14). Later, God would remind Jacob of this event when He instructed him to return to the land (31:13) and Jacob would remind his household of it when he instructed them to cleanse their homes before they could return to Bethel (35:3).

28:10 Haran. *See note on 11:31.*

28:11 a certain place. Identified in v. 19 as Bethel, about 50 mi. N of Beersheba, and about 6 mi. N of Jerusalem. There he spent the night in an open field.

28:12 a ladder...angels of God were ascending and descending. A graphic portrayal of the heavenly Lord's personal involvement in the affairs of earth, and here especially as they related to divine covenant promises in Jacob's life (vv. 13-15). This dream was to encourage the lonely traveler. God's own appointed angelic messengers ensured the carrying out of His will and plans. More than likely, the angels traversed a stairway rather than a ladder.

28:15 will keep you...will bring you back. A most timely, comforting, and assuring promise which remained engraved on Jacob's heart during his sojourn in Haran (see 30:25). His forced departure from Canaan did not and would not abrogate any of God's promises to him.

I did not know *it*." 17 And he was afraid
and said, "How awesome *is* this place!
This *is* none other than the house of God,
and this *is* the gate of heaven!"
18 Then Jacob rose early in the morning,
and took the stone that he had put at his
head, [e]set it up as a pillar, [f]and poured oil
on top of it. 19 And he called the name of
[g]that place [4]Bethel; but the name of that
city had been Luz previously. 20 [h]Then Jacob made a vow, saying, "If [i]God will be
with me, and keep me in this way that I am
going, and give me [j]bread to eat and clothing to put on, 21 so that [k]I come back to my
father's house in peace, [l]then the LORD
shall be my God. 22 And this stone which I
have set as a pillar [m]shall be God's house,
[n]and of all that You give me I will surely
give a [5]tenth to You."

Jacob Meets Rachel

29 So Jacob went on his journey [a]and
came to the land of the people of the
East. 2 And he looked, and saw a [b]well in
the field; and behold, there *were* three
flocks of sheep lying by it; for out of that
well they watered the flocks. A large stone
was on the well's mouth. 3 Now all the
flocks would be gathered there; and they
would roll the stone from the well's
mouth, water the sheep, and put the stone
back in its place on the well's mouth.
4 And Jacob said to them, "My brethren,
where *are* you from?"
And they said, "We *are* from [c]Haran."
5 Then he said to them, "Do you know
[d]Laban the son of Nahor?"
And they said, "We know him."
6 So he said to them, [e]"Is he well?"
And they said, "*He is* well. And look, his
daughter Rachel [f]is coming with the
sheep."
7 Then he said, "Look, *it is* still [1]high
day; *it is* not time for the cattle to be gathered together. Water the sheep, and go and
feed *them*."
8 But they said, "We cannot until all the
flocks are gathered together, and they have
rolled the stone from the well's mouth;
then we water the sheep."
9 Now while he was still speaking with
them, [g]Rachel came with her father's
sheep, for she was a shepherdess. 10 And it
came to pass, when Jacob saw Rachel the
daughter of Laban his mother's brother,
and the sheep of Laban his mother's brother, that Jacob went near and [h]rolled the
stone from the well's mouth, and watered
the flock of Laban his mother's brother.
11 Then Jacob [i]kissed Rachel, and lifted up
his voice and wept. 12 And Jacob told Rachel that he *was* [j]her father's relative and
that he *was* Rebekah's son. [k]So she ran and
told her father.
13 Then it came to pass, when Laban
heard the report about Jacob his sister's
son, that [l]he ran to meet him, and embraced him and kissed him, and brought
him to his house. So he told Laban all these
things. 14 And Laban said to him, [m]"Surely
you *are* my bone and my flesh." And he
stayed with him for a month.

Jacob Marries Leah and Rachel

15 Then Laban said to Jacob, "Because
you *are* my relative, should you therefore
serve me for nothing? Tell me, [n]what
should your wages *be?*" 16 Now Laban had
two daughters: the name of the elder *was*
Leah, and the name of the younger *was* Rachel. 17 Leah's eyes *were* [2]delicate, but Ra-

18 [e]Gen. 31:13, 45 [f]Lev. 8:10-12
19 [g]Judg. 1:23, 26 [4]Lit. *House of God*
20 [h]Gen. 31:13; Judg. 11:30; 2 Sam. 15:8 [i]Gen. 28:15 [j]1 Tim. 6:8
21 [k]Judg. 11:31; 2 Sam. 19:24, 30 [l]Deut. 26:17; 2 Sam. 15:8
22 [m]Gen. 35:7, 14 [n]Gen. 14:20; [Lev. 27:30]; Deut. 14:22 [5]*tithe*

CHAPTER 29

1 [a]Gen. 25:6; Num. 23:7; Judg. 6:3, 33; Hos. 12:12
2 [b]Gen. 24:10, 11; Ex. 2:15, 16
4 [c]Gen. 11:31; 28:10
5 [d]Gen. 24:24, 29; 28:2
6 [e]Gen. 43:27 [f]Gen. 24:11; Ex. 2:16, 17
7 [1]*early in the day*
9 [g]Ex. 2:16
10 [h]Ex. 2:17
11 [i]Gen. 33:4; 45:14, 15
12 [j]Gen. 13:8; 14:14, 16; 28:5 [k]Gen. 24:28
13 [l]Gen. 24:29-31; Luke 15:20
14 [m]Gen. 2:23; 37:27; Judg. 9:2; 2 Sam. 5:1; 19:12, 13
15 [n]Gen. 30:28; 31:41
17 [2]*Or weak*

28:18-21 a pillar. Marking a particular site as of special religious significance by means of a stone pillar was a known practice. A libation offering, a change of place-name, and a vow of allegiance to the Lord in exchange for promised protection and blessing completed Jacob's ceremonial consecration of Bethel, i.e., "House of God."

28:22 a tenth. Tithing, though not commanded by God, was obviously already known and voluntarily practiced, and served to acknowledge God's providential beneficence in the donor's life (*see note on 14:20*). Jacob may have been bargaining with God, as if to buy His favor rather than purely worshiping God with his gift, but it is best to translate the "if" (v. 20) as "since" and see Jacob's vow and offering as genuine worship based on confidence in God's promise (vv. 13-15).

29:1-4 Conveniently meeting at his destination, shepherds who knew both Laban and Rachel reflected the directing hand of God upon his life, just as promised (28:15).

29:2,3 A large stone. Perhaps due to the fact that this well of precious stored water could evaporate rapidly in the sun, or be filled with blowing dust, or used indiscriminately, it had been covered and its use regulated (vv. 7,8).

29:5 Laban the son of Nahor. Genealogical fluidity in the use of "son," meaning male descendant, occurred in Jacob's inquiry after Laban, for he was actually Nahor's grandson (cf. v. 2; 22:20-23).

29:6-8 It appears that Jacob was trying to get these men to water their sheep immediately and leave, so he could be alone with Rachel for the meeting.

29:9 speaking with them. The language of Haran was Aramaic or Chaldee and evidently was known by Abraham and his sons. There is no comment on how these patriarchs spoke with the Canaanites and Egyptians in their travels, but it is reasonable to assume they had become skilled linguists, knowing more than Hebrew and Aramaic.

29:10-14 Customary greetings and personal introductions ended 97 years of absence since Rebekah had left (*see notes on 25:21; 27:1*), and Laban's nephew was welcomed home.

29:14 a month. Tradition in that ancient area allowed a stranger to be cared for 3 days. On the fourth he was to tell his name and mission. After that he could remain if he worked in some agreed-upon way (v. 15).

29:17 eyes *were* delicate. Probably means that they were a pale color rather than the dark and sparkling eyes most common. Such paleness was viewed as a blemish.

chel was [o]beautiful of form and appearance.
18 Now Jacob loved Rachel; so he said,
[p]"I will serve you seven years for Rachel
your younger daughter."
19 And Laban said, "*It is* better that I
give her to you than that I should give her
to another man. Stay with me." 20 So Jacob
[q]served seven years for Rachel, and they
seemed *only* a few days to him because of
the love he had for her.
21 Then Jacob said to Laban, "Give *me*
my wife, for my days are fulfilled, that I
may [r]go in to her." 22 And Laban gathered
together all the men of the place and
[s]made a feast. 23 Now it came to pass in the
evening, that he took Leah his daughter
and brought her to Jacob; and he went in to
her. 24 And Laban gave his maid [t]Zilpah to
his daughter Leah *as* a maid. 25 So it came
to pass in the morning, that behold, it *was*
Leah. And he said to Laban, "What is this
you have done to me? Was it not for Rachel
that I served you? Why then have you [u]de-
ceived me?"
26 And Laban said, "It must not be done
so in our [3]country, to give the younger before the firstborn. 27 [v]Fulfill her week, and
we will give you this one also for the service which you will serve with me still another seven years."
28 Then Jacob did so and fulfilled her
week. So he gave him his daughter Rachel
as wife also. 29 And Laban gave his maid
[w]Bilhah to his daughter Rachel as a maid.
30 Then *Jacob* also went in to Rachel, and he
also [x]loved Rachel more than Leah. And he
served with Laban [y]still another seven
years.

The Children of Jacob

31 When the LORD [z]saw that Leah *was*
[4]unloved, He [a]opened her womb; but Rachel *was* barren. 32 So Leah conceived and
bore a son, and she called his name [5]Reu-
ben; for she said, "The LORD has surely
[b]looked on my affliction. Now therefore,
my husband will love me." 33 Then she
conceived again and bore a son, and said,
"Because the LORD has heard that I *am* [6]un-
loved, He has therefore given me this *son*
also." And she called his name [7]Simeon.
34 She conceived again and bore a son, and
said, "Now this time my husband will become attached to me, because I have borne
him three sons." Therefore his name was
called [8]Levi. 35 And she conceived again
and bore a son, and said, "Now I will
praise the LORD." Therefore she called his
name [c]Judah.[9] Then she stopped bearing.

30 Now when Rachel saw that [a]she
bore Jacob no children, Rachel [b]en-
vied her sister, and said to Jacob, "Give me
children, [c]or else I die!"
2 And Jacob's anger was aroused against
Rachel, and he said, [d]"*Am* I in the place of
God, who has withheld from you the fruit
of the womb?"
3 So she said, "Here is [e]my maid Bilhah;
go in to her, [f]and she will bear *a child* on
my knees, [g]that I also may [1]have children
by her." 4 Then she gave him Bilhah her
maid [h]as wife, and Jacob went in to her.
5 And Bilhah conceived and bore Jacob a
son. 6 Then Rachel said, "God has [i]judged
my case; and He has also heard my voice
and given me a son." Therefore she called
his name [2]Dan. 7 And Rachel's maid Bilhah conceived again and bore Jacob a sec-

17 [o] Gen. 12:11, 14; 26:7
18 [p] Gen. 31:41; 2 Sam. 3:14; Hos. 12:12
20 [q] Gen. 30:26; Hos. 12:12
21 [r] Judg. 15:1
22 [s] Judg. 14:10; John 2:1, 2
24 [t] Gen. 30:9, 10
25 [u] Gen. 27:35; 31:7; 1 Sam. 28:12
26 [3] Lit. *place*
27 [v] Gen. 31:41; Judg. 14:2
29 [w] Gen. 30:3-5
30 [x] Gen. 29:17-20; Deut. 21:15-17 [y] Gen. 30:26; 31:41; Hos. 12:12

31 [z] Ps. 127:3 [a] Gen. 30:1 [4] Lit. *hated*
32 [b] Gen. 16:11; 31:42; Ex. 3:7; 4:31; Deut. 26:7; Ps. 25:18 [5] Lit. *See, a Son*
33 [6] Lit. *hated* [7] Lit. *Heard*
34 [8] Lit. *Attached*
35 [c] Gen. 49:8; Matt. 1:2 [9] Lit. *Praise*

CHAPTER 30

1 [a] Gen. 16:1, 2; 29:31 [b] Gen. 37:11 [c] 1 Sam. 1:5, 6; [Job 5:2]
2 [d] Gen. 16:2; 1 Sam. 1:5
3 [e] Gen. 16:2 [f] Gen. 50:23; Job 3:12 [g] Gen. 16:2, 3 [1] Lit. *be built up by her*
4 [h] Gen. 16:3, 4
6 [i] Gen. 18:25; Ps. 35:24; 43:1; Lam. 3:59 [2] Lit. *Judge*

29:18-30 Love and working to provide his service as a dowry (vv. 18-20) combined to make Jacob happily remain during the first 7 years in Laban's household, almost as an adopted son rather than a mere employee. But Jacob, the deceiver (27:1-29), was about to be deceived (vv. 22-25). Local marriage customs (v. 26), love for Rachel, and more dowry desired by Laban (vv. 27-30) all conspired to give Jacob, not only 7 more years of labor under Laban, but two wives who were to become caught up in jealous childbearing competition (30:1-21).

29:23 The deception was possible because of the custom of veiling the bride and the dark of the night (v. 24).

29:23,30 went in to. This is a euphemism for consummating marriage.

29:27,30 It appears that Laban agreed to give Jacob Rachel after the week of wedding celebration for Leah's marriage to him, and before the 7 years of labor.

29:28 Rachel as wife also. Such consanguinity was not God's will (*see note on Gen. 2:24*), and the Mosaic code later forbade it (Lev. 18:18). Polygamy always brought grief, as in the life of Jacob.

29:31 Leah *was* unloved...Rachel *was* barren. There was quite a contrast when the one dearly beloved (vv. 18,20,30) had no children, whereas the one rejected did. Jacob might have demoted Leah, but God took action on her behalf. Leah had also prayed about her husband's rejection (v. 33) and had been troubled by it, as seen in the names given to her first 4 sons (vv. 32-35).

30:1 or else I die! A childless woman in ancient Near Eastern culture was no better than a dead wife and became a severe embarrassment to her husband (see v. 23).

30:2 *Am* I in the place of God...? Although spoken in a moment of frustration with Rachel's pleading for children and the envy with which it was expressed, Jacob's words do indicate an understanding that ultimately God opened and closed the womb.

30:3 on my knees. When the surrogate gave birth while actually sitting on the knees of the wife, it symbolized the wife providing a child for her husband.

30:1-21 The competition between the two sisters/wives is demonstrated in using their maids as surrogate mothers (vv. 3,7,9,12), in declaring God had judged the case in favor of the plaintiff (v. 6), in bartering for time with the husband (vv. 14-16), in accusing one of stealing her husband's favor (v. 15), and in the name given to one son—"wrestled with my sister" (Naphtali, v. 8). The race for children was also accompanied by prayers to the Lord or by acknowledgment of His providence (vv. 6,17,20,22; also 29:32,33,35). This bitter and intense rivalry, all the more fierce though they were sisters, and even though they occupied different dwellings with their children as

ond son. 8 Then Rachel said, "With [3]great
wrestlings I have wrestled with my sister,
and indeed I have prevailed." So she called
his name [4]Naphtali.
9 When Leah saw that she had stopped
bearing, she took Zilpah her maid and
[j]gave her to Jacob as wife. 10 And Leah's
maid Zilpah bore Jacob a son. 11 Then Leah
said, [5]"A troop comes!" So she called his
name [6]Gad. 12 And Leah's maid Zilpah
bore Jacob a second son. 13 Then Leah said,
"I am happy, for the daughters [k]will call
me blessed." So she called his name
[7]Asher.
14 Now Reuben went in the days of
wheat harvest and found mandrakes in the
field, and brought them to his mother
Leah. Then Rachel said to Leah, [l]"Please
give me *some* of your son's mandrakes."
15 But she said to her, [m]"*Is it* a small matter that you have taken away my husband?
Would you take away my son's mandrakes
also?"
And Rachel said, "Therefore he will lie
with you tonight for your son's mandrakes."
16 When Jacob came out of the field in
the evening, Leah went out to meet him
and said, "You must come in to me, for I
have surely hired you with my son's mandrakes." And he lay with her that night.
17 And God listened to Leah, and she
conceived and bore Jacob a fifth son.
18 Leah said, "God has given me my
wages, because I have given my maid to
my husband." So she called his name [8]Is-
sachar. 19 Then Leah conceived again and
bore Jacob a sixth son. 20 And Leah said,
"God has endowed me *with* a good endowment; now my husband will dwell
with me, because I have borne him six
sons." So she called his name [9]Zebulun.
21 Afterward she bore a [n]daughter, and
called her name [1]Dinah.
22 Then God [o]remembered Rachel, and
God listened to her and [p]opened her
womb. 23 And she conceived and bore a
son, and said, "God has taken away [q]my
reproach." 24 So she called his name [2]Jo-
seph, and said, [r]"The LORD shall add to me
another son."

Jacob's Agreement with Laban

25 And it came to pass, when Rachel had
borne Joseph, that Jacob said to Laban,
[s]"Send me away, that I may go to [t]my own
place and to my country. 26 Give *me* my
wives and my children [u]for whom I have
served you, and let me go; for you know
my service which I have done for you."
27 And Laban said to him, "Please *stay,* if
I have found favor in your eyes, *for* [v]I have
learned by experience that the LORD has
blessed me for your sake." 28 Then he said,
[w]"Name me your wages, and I will give
it."
29 So *Jacob* said to him, [x]"You know how
I have served you and how your livestock
has been with me. 30 For what you had before I *came was* little, and it has increased to
a great amount; the LORD has blessed you
[3]since my coming. And now, when shall I
also [y]provide for my own house?"
31 So he said, "What shall I give you?"
And Jacob said, "You shall not give me
anything. If you will do this thing for me, I

8 [3] Lit. *wrestlings of God* [4] Lit. *My Wrestling*
9 [j] Gen. 30:4
11 [5] So with Qr., Syr., Tg.; Kt., LXX, Vg. *in fortune* [6] Lit. *Troop* or *Fortune*
13 [k] Prov. 31:28; Luke 1:48 [7] Lit. *Happy*
14 [l] Gen. 25:30
15 [m] [Num. 16:9, 13]
18 [8] Lit. *Wages*
20 [9] Lit. *Dwelling*
21 [n] Gen. 34:1 [1] Lit. *Judgment*
22 [o] Gen. 19:29; 1 Sam. 1:19, 20 [p] Gen. 29:31
23 [q] 1 Sam. 1:6; Is. 4:1; Luke 1:25
24 [r] Gen. 35:16-18 [2] Lit. *He Will Add*
25 [s] Gen. 24:54, 56 [t] Gen. 18:33
26 [u] Gen. 29:18-20, 27, 30; Hos. 12:12
27 [v] Gen. 26:24; 39:3; Is. 61:9
28 [w] Gen. 29:15; 31:7, 41
29 [x] Gen. 31:6, 38-40; Matt. 24:45; Titus 2:10
30 [y] [1 Tim. 5:8] [3] Lit. *at my foot*

customary, shows that the evil lay in the system itself (bigamy), which as a violation of God's ordinance (Gen. 2:24) could not yield happiness.

30:14 mandrakes. Jacob had 8 sons by then from 3 women and about 6 years had elapsed since his marriages. The oldest son, Reuben, was about 7. Playing in the field during wheat harvest, he found this small, orange-colored fruit and "brought them to his mother Leah." These were superstitiously viewed in the ancient world as "love-apples," an aphrodisiac or fertility-inducing narcotic.

30:15,16 This odd and desperate bargain by Rachel was an attempt to become pregnant with the aid of the mandrakes, a fable which failed to understand that God gives children (vv. 6,17,20,22).

30:20 now my husband will dwell with me. The plaintive cry of one still unloved (cf. 29:31) as confirmed by Jacob's frequent absence from her home. She hoped that having 6 children for Jacob would win his permanent residence with her. **Zebulun.** The name means "dwelling," signifying her hope of Jacob's dwelling with her.

30:21 Dinah. Although not the only daughter to be born to Jacob (cf. 37:35; 46:7), her name is mentioned in anticipation of the tragedy at Shechem (chap. 34).

30:22 Then God remembered Rachel. All the desperate waiting (see 30:1) and pleading climaxed at the end of 7 years with God's response. Then Rachel properly ascribed her delivery from barrenness to the Lord, whom she also trusted for another son (vv. 23,24).

30:24 Joseph. Ca. 1914 B.C. His name means "he will add" or "may he add," indicating both her thanks and her faith that God would give her another son.

30:25 Send me away...to my country. Fourteen years of absence had not dulled Jacob's acute awareness of belonging to the land God had given to him. Since Mesopotamia was not his home and his contract with Laban was up, he desired to return to "my own place" and "my country." Jacob's wish to return to Canaan was not hidden from Laban (v. 30).

30:27 by experience. Lit. "by divination." *See note on Deut. 18:9-12.*

30:28 Name me your wages. On the two occasions that Laban asked this of Jacob it was to urge him to stay. The first time (29:15) Laban had sought to reward a relative, but this time it was because he had been rewarded since "the LORD has blessed me for your sake" (v. 27). Jacob readily confirmed Laban's evaluation in that "little" had indeed become "a great amount" (v. 30) since he had come on the scene. Laban's superficial generosity should not be mistaken for genuine goodness (see 31:7). He was attempting to deceive Jacob into staying because it was potentially profitable for him.

30:31-36 What shall I give you? Laban wanted Jacob to stay and asked what it would take for him to do so. Jacob wanted nothing except to be in a position for God to bless him. He was willing to stay,

will again feed and keep your flocks: 32 Let
me pass through all your flock today, removing from there all the speckled and
spotted sheep, and all the brown ones
among the lambs, and the spotted and
speckled among the goats; and [z]*these* shall
be my wages. 33 So my [a]righteousness will
answer for me in time to come, when the
subject of my wages comes before you:
every one that *is* not speckled and spotted
among the goats, and brown among the
lambs, will be considered stolen, if *it is*
with me."

34 And Laban said, "Oh, that it were according to your word!" 35 So he removed
that day the male goats that were [b]speck-
led and spotted, all the female goats that
were speckled and spotted, every one that
had *some* white in it, and all the brown
ones among the lambs, and gave *them* into
the hand of his sons. 36 Then he put three
days' journey between himself and Jacob,
and Jacob fed the rest of Laban's flocks.

37 Now [c]Jacob took for himself rods of
green poplar and of the almond and chestnut trees, peeled white strips in them, and
exposed the white which *was* in the rods.
38 And the rods which he had peeled, he set
before the flocks in the gutters, in the watering troughs where the flocks came to
drink, so that they should conceive when
they came to drink. 39 So the flocks conceived before the rods, and the flocks
brought forth streaked, speckled, and spotted. 40 Then Jacob separated the lambs, and
made the flocks face toward the streaked
and all the brown in the flock of Laban; but
he put his own flocks by themselves and
did not put them with Laban's flock.

41 And it came to pass, whenever the
stronger livestock conceived, that Jacob
placed the rods before the eyes of the livestock in the gutters, that they might conceive among the rods. 42 But when the
flocks were feeble, he did not put *them* in;
so the feebler were Laban's and the
stronger Jacob's. 43 Thus the man [d]became
exceedingly prosperous, and [e]had large
flocks, female and male servants, and
camels and donkeys.

Jacob Flees from Laban

31 Now *Jacob* heard the words of
Laban's sons, saying, "Jacob has
taken away all that was our father's, and
from what was our father's he has acquired all this [a]wealth." 2 And Jacob saw
the [b]countenance of Laban, and indeed it
was not [c]*favorable* toward him as before.
3 Then the LORD said to Jacob, [d]"Return to
the land of your fathers and to your family, and I will [e]be with you."

4 So Jacob sent and called Rachel and
Leah to the field, to his flock, 5 and said to
them, [f]"I see your father's [1]countenance,
that it *is* not *favorable* toward me as before;

32 [z]Gen. 31:8
33 [a]Ps. 37:6
35 [b]Gen. 31:9-12
37 [c]Gen. 31:9-12
43 [d]Gen. 12:16; 30:30 [e]Gen. 13:2; 24:35; 26:13, 14

CHAPTER 31
1 [a]Ps. 49:16
2 [b]Gen. 4:5 [c]Deut. 28:54
3 [d]Gen. 28:15, 20, 21; 32:9 [e]Gen. 46:4
5 [f]Gen. 31:2, 3 [1]Lit. *face*

but not be further indebted to the scheming and selfish Laban. He offered Laban a plan that could bless him while costing Laban nothing. He would continue to care for Laban's animals, as he had been doing. His pay would consist of animals not yet born, animals which would seem the less desirable to Laban because of their markings and color. None of the solid color animals would be taken by Jacob, and if any were born into Jacob's flocks, Laban could take them (they were considered as stolen). Only those animals born speckled, spotted, striped, or abnormally colored would belong to Jacob. Evidently, most of the animals were white (sheep), black (goats), and brown (cattle). Few were in the category of Jacob's request. Further, Jacob would not even use the living speckled or abnormally colored animals to breed more like them. He would separate them into a flock of their own kind, apart from the normally colored animals. Only the spotted and abnormally colored offspring born in the future to the normally colored would be his. Since it seemed to Laban that the birth of such abnormally marked animals was unlikely to occur in any significant volume from the normally colored, he agreed. He believed this a small and favorable concession on his part to maintain the skills of Jacob to further enlarge his herds and flocks. Jacob, by this, put himself entirely in God's hands. Only the Lord could determine what animals would be Jacob's. To make sure Jacob didn't cheat on his good deal, Laban separated the abnormally marked from the normal animals in Jacob's care (v. 34-36).

30:37-42 rods. Jacob was knowledgeable about sheep, goats, and cattle, having kept his father's animals for most of his 90 years, and Laban's for the last 14 years. He knew that when one uncommonly marked animal was born (with a recessive gene), he could then begin to breed that gene selectively to produce flocks and herds of abnormally marked animals, which were in no way inferior physically to the normally marked. Once he began this breeding process, he sought to stimulate it by some methods that may appear superstitious and foolish to us (as the mandrakes in v. 14). But it is most likely that he had learned that, when the bark was peeled, there was some stimulant released into the water that stimulated the animals to sexual activity. In v. 38, the word "conceive" is literally, in Heb., "to be hot," or as is said of animals "to be in heat." His plan was successful (v. 39) and kept his own flock separate from the abnormally colored ones of Laban. His system worked to his own advantage, not that of Laban (v. 42) who had for years taken advantage of him. Jacob gave God the credit for the success of his efforts (31:7,9).

31:1,2 Of materialistic bent and envious at Jacob's success, Laban's sons grumbled at what they saw as the depleting of their father's assets, thus hurting their own inheritance. If Jacob heard of this, so did Laban, and that knowledge rankled him to the point of surliness toward his son-in-law (cf. 31:20). Profiting from God's blessings through Jacob (30:27,30) was one thing, but seeing only Jacob blessed was quite another matter and elicited no praise or gratitude to God from Laban.

31:3 Return to the land. When Jacob sought to leave at the end of his contract (30:25), God's timing was not right. Now it was, so God directed Jacob's departure, and in confirmation assured him of His presence. So, after another 6 years, it was time to go (vv. 38-41).

31:4 called...to the field. In the privacy of the open field, Jacob's plans could be confidentially shared with his wives.

31:5 your father's...my father. A contrast, perhaps not intentional, but nevertheless noticeable since their father signaled rejection toward him, whereas the God of his father had accepted him.

but the God of my father [g]has been with me. 6 And [h]you know that with all my might I have served your father. 7 Yet your father has deceived me and [i]changed my wages [j]ten times, but God [k]did not allow him to hurt me. 8 If he said thus: [l]'The speckled shall be your wages,' then all the flocks bore speckled. And if he said thus: 'The streaked shall be your wages,' then all the flocks bore streaked. 9 So God has [m]taken away the livestock of your father and given *them* to me.

10 "And it happened, at the time when the flocks conceived, that I lifted my eyes and saw in a dream, and behold, the rams which leaped upon the flocks *were* streaked, speckled, and gray-spotted. 11 Then [n]the Angel of God spoke to me in a dream, saying, 'Jacob.' And I said, 'Here I am.' 12 And He said, 'Lift your eyes now and see, all the rams which leap on the flocks *are* streaked, speckled, and gray-spotted; for [o]I have seen all that Laban is doing to you. 13 I *am* the God of Bethel, [p]where you anointed the pillar *and* where you made a vow to Me. Now [q]arise, get out of this land, and return to the land of your family.' "

14 Then Rachel and Leah answered and said to him, [r]"Is there still any portion or inheritance for us in our father's house? 15 Are we not considered strangers by him? For [s]he has sold us, and also completely consumed our money. 16 For all these riches which God has taken from our father are *really* ours and our children's; now then, whatever God has said to you, do it."

17 Then Jacob rose and set his sons and his wives on camels. 18 And he carried away all his livestock and all his possessions which he had gained, his acquired livestock which he had gained in Padan Aram, to go to his father Isaac in the land of [t]Canaan. 19 Now Laban had gone to shear his sheep, and Rachel had stolen the [u]household[2] idols that were her father's. 20 And Jacob stole away, unknown to Laban the Syrian, in that he did not tell him that he intended to flee. 21 So he fled with all that he had. He arose and crossed the river, and [v]headed[3] toward the mountains of Gilead.

Laban Pursues Jacob

22 And Laban was told on the third day that Jacob had fled. 23 Then he took [w]his brethren with him and pursued him for seven days' journey, and he overtook him in the mountains of Gilead. 24 But God [x]had come to Laban the Syrian in a dream by night, and said to him, "Be careful that you [y]speak to Jacob neither good nor bad."

25 So Laban overtook Jacob. Now Jacob had pitched his tent in the mountains, and Laban with his brethren pitched in the mountains of Gilead.

26 And Laban said to Jacob: "What have you done, that you have stolen away unknown to me, and [z]carried away my daughters like captives *taken* with the sword? 27 Why did you flee away secretly, and steal away from me, and not tell me;

[g] Gen. 21:22; 28:13, 15; 31:29, 42, 53; Is. 41:10; Heb. 13:5
6 [h] Gen. 30:29; 31:38-41
7 [i] Gen. 29:25; 31:41 [j] Num. 14:22; Neh. 4:12; Job 19:3; Zech. 8:23 [k] Gen. 15:1; 20:6; 31:29; Job 1:10; Ps. 37:28; 105:14
8 [l] Gen. 30:32
9 [m] Gen. 31:1, 16
11 [n] Gen. 16:7-11; 22:11, 15; 31:13; 48:16
12 [o] Gen. 31:42; Ex. 3:7; Ps. 139:3; Eccl. 5:8
13 [p] Gen. 28:16-22; 35:1, 6, 15 [q] Gen. 31:3; 32:9
14 [r] Gen. 2:24
15 [s] Gen. 29:15, 20, 23, 27; Neh. 5:8
18 [t] Gen. 17:8; 33:18; 35:27
19 [u] Gen. 31:30, 34; 35:2; Judg. 17:5; 1 Sam. 19:13; Hos. 3:4 [2] Heb. *teraphim*
21 [v] Gen. 46:28; 2 Kin. 12:17; Luke 9:51, 53 [3] Lit. *set his face toward*
23 [w] Gen. 13:8
24 [x] Gen. 20:3; 31:29; 46:2-4; Job 33:15; Matt. 1:20 [y] Gen. 24:50; 31:7, 29
26 [z] 1 Sam. 30:2

31:6-9 As Jacob explained it, his unstinting service to their father had been met by Laban with wage changes intended to cripple his son-in-law's enterprise, but God had intervened by blocking the intended hurt (v. 7) and overriding the wage changes with great prosperity (v. 9).

31:10-12 *See notes on 30:37-42.*

31:11 the Angel of God. Cf. 21:17. The same as the Angel of the Lord (16:11; 22:11,15). *See note on Ex. 3:2.*

31:13 I *am* the God of Bethel. The Angel of God (v. 11) clearly identified Himself as the Lord, pointing back as He did so to the earlier critical encounter with God in Jacob's life (28:10-22).

31:14-16 The two wives concurred that, in the context of severely strained family relationships, their inheritance might be in question since the ties that bind no longer held them there. They also agreed that God's intervention had, in effect, refunded what their father had wrongfully withheld and spent.

31:19 household idols. Lit., teraphim (cf. 2 Kin. 23:24; Ezek. 21:21). These images or figurines of varying sizes, usually of nude goddesses with accentuated sexual features, either signaled special protection for, inheritance rights for, or guaranteed fertility for the bearer. Or, perhaps possession by Rachel would call for Jacob to be recognized as head of the household at Laban's death. *See notes on vv. 30,44.*

31:20 stole away. Because of fear at what Laban might do (v. 31), Jacob dispensed with the expected courtesy he had not forgotten before (30:25) and clandestinely slipped away at an appropriate time (v. 19). With all his entourage, this was not a simple exit. Laban's gruffness (vv. 1,2) exuded enough hostility for Jacob to suspect forceful retaliation and to react by escaping what danger he could not know for sure.

31:21 the river...mountains of Gilead. The Euphrates River and the area S of Galilee to the E of the Jordan River respectively.

31:23 seven days' journey. That it took so long for Laban's band to catch up with a much larger group burdened with possessions and animals indicates a forced march was undertaken by Jacob's people, probably motivated by Jacob's fear.

31:24 Be careful...neither good nor bad. God again sovereignly protected, as He had done for Abraham and Isaac (12:17-20; 20:3-7; 26:8-11), to prevent harm coming to His man. In a proverbial expression (cf. Gen. 24:50; 2 Sam. 13:22) Laban is cautioned not to use anything in the full range of options open to him, "from the good to the bad," to alter the existing situation and bring Jacob back.

31:26 my daughters like captives. Laban evidently did not believe that his daughters could have possibly agreed with the departure and must have left under duress.

31:27-29 Laban's questions protested his right to have arranged a proper send-off for his family and functioned as a rebuke of Jacob's thoughtlessness toward him.

for I might have sent you away with joy
and songs, with timbrel and harp? **28** And
you did not allow me [a]to kiss my sons and
my daughters. Now [b]you have done foolishly in *so* doing. **29** It is in my power to do
you harm, but the [c]God of your father
spoke to me [d]last night, saying, 'Be careful
that you speak to Jacob neither good nor
bad.' **30** And now you have surely gone because you greatly long for your father's
house, *but* why did you [e]steal my gods?"
31 Then Jacob answered and said to
Laban, "Because I was [f]afraid, for I said,
'Perhaps you would take your daughters
from me by force.' **32** With whomever you
find your gods, [g]do not let him live. In the
presence of our brethren, identify what I
have of yours and take *it* with you." For Jacob did not know that Rachel had stolen
them.
33 And Laban went into Jacob's tent, into
Leah's tent, and into the two maids' tents,
but he did not find *them.* Then he went out
of Leah's tent and entered Rachel's tent.
34 Now Rachel had taken the [4]household
idols, put them in the camel's saddle, and
sat on them. And Laban [5]searched all
about the tent but did not find *them.* **35** And
she said to her father, "Let it not displease
my lord that I cannot [h]rise before you, for
the manner of women *is* with me." And he
searched but did not find the [6]household
idols.
36 Then Jacob was angry and rebuked
Laban, and Jacob answered and said to
Laban: "What *is* my [7]trespass? What *is* my
sin, that you have so hotly pursued me?
37 Although you have searched all my
things, what part of your household things
have you found? Set *it* here before my
brethren and your brethren, that they may
judge between us both! **38** These twenty
years I *have been* with you; your ewes and
your female goats have not miscarried
their young, and I have not eaten the rams
of your flock. **39** [i]That which was torn *by*
beasts I did not bring to you; I bore the loss
of it. [j]You required it from my hand,
whether stolen by day or stolen by night.
40 *There* I was! In the day the drought consumed me, and the frost by night, and my
sleep departed from my eyes. **41** Thus I

28 [a] Gen. 31:55; Ruth 1:9, 14; 1 Kin. 19:20; Acts 20:37 [b] 1 Sam. 13:13
29 [c] Gen. 28:13; 31:5, 24, 42, 53 [d] Gen. 31:24
30 [e] Gen. 31:19; Josh. 24:2; Judg. 17:5; 18:24
31 [f] Gen. 26:7; 32:7, 11
32 [g] Gen. 44:9
34 [4] Heb. *teraphim*
[5] Lit. *felt*
35 [h] Ex. 20:12; Lev. 19:32 [6] Heb. *teraphim*
36 [7] *transgression*
39 [i] Ex. 22:10 [j] Ex. 22:10-13

31:30 why…steal my gods? Longing to return to Canaan (cf. 30:25) might excuse his leaving without notice, but it could not excuse the theft of his teraphim (31:19). Laban's thorough search for these idols (vv. 33-35) also marked how important they were to him as a pagan worshiper. *See notes on vv. 19,44.*

31:31 afraid. A reasonable fear is experienced by Jacob, who had come to find a wife and stayed for at least 20 years (v. 38) under the selfish compulsions of Laban.

31:34,35 One dishonest deed needed further dishonesty and trickery to cover it up.

31:35 the manner of women. Rachel claimed she was having her menstrual period.

31:37 judge between us both. Rachel's theft and dishonest cover-up had precipitated a major conflict between her father and her husband which could only be resolved by judicial inquiry before witnesses.

31:38-42 Jacob registered his complaint that he had unfairly borne the losses normally carried by the owner and had endured much discomfort in fulfilling his responsibility. Jacob also delivered his conclusion that except for the oversight of God, Laban may very well have fleeced him totally.

False Gods in the Old Testament

1. Rachel's household gods (Gen. 31:19)
2. The golden calf at Sinai (Ex. 32)
3. Nanna, the moon god of Ur, worshiped by Abraham before his salvation (Josh. 24:2)
4. Asherah, or Ashtaroth, the chief goddess of Tyre, referred to as the lady of the sea (Judg. 6:24-32)
5. Dagon, the chief Philistine agriculture and sea god and father of Baal (Judg. 16:23-30; 1 Sam. 5:1-7)
6. Ashtoreth, a Canaanite goddess, another consort of Baal (1 Sam. 7:3,4)
7. Molech, the god of the Ammonites and the most horrible idol in the Scriptures (1 Kin. 11:7; 2 Chr. 28:14; 33:6)
8. The two golden images made by King Jeroboam, set up at the shrines of Dan and Bethel (1 Kin. 12:28-31)
9. Baal, the chief deity of Canaan (1 Kin. 18:17-40; 2 Kin. 10:28; 11:18)
10. Rimmon, the Syrian god of Naaman the leper (2 Kin. 5:15-19)
11. Nishroch, the Assyrian god of Sennacherib (2 Kin. 19:37)
12. Nebo, the Babylonian god of wisdom and literature (Is. 46:1)
13. Merodach, also called Marduk, the chief god of the Babylonian pantheon (Jer. 50:2)
14. Tammuz, the husband and brother of Ishtar (Asherah), goddess of fertility (Ezek. 8:14)
15. The golden image in the plain of Dura (Dan. 2)

have been in your house twenty years; I
[k]served you fourteen years for your two
daughters, and six years for your flock,
and [l]you have changed my wages ten
times. 42 [m]Unless the God of my father, the
God of Abraham and [n]the Fear of Isaac,
had been with me, surely now you would
have sent me away empty-handed. [o]God
has seen my affliction and the labor of my
hands, and [p]rebuked *you* last night."

Laban's Covenant with Jacob

43 And Laban answered and said to Jacob, "*These* daughters *are* my daughters,
and *these* children *are* my children, and *this*
flock *is* my flock; all that you see *is* mine.
But what can I do this day to these my
daughters or to their children whom they
have borne? 44 Now therefore, come, [q]let
us make a [8]covenant, [r]you and I, and let it
be a witness between you and me."
45 So Jacob [s]took a stone and set it up *as*
a pillar. 46 Then Jacob said to his brethren,
"Gather stones." And they took stones and
made a heap, and they ate there on the
heap. 47 Laban called it [9]Jegar Sahadutha,
but Jacob called it [1]Galeed. 48 And Laban
said, [t]"This heap *is* a witness between you
and me this day." Therefore its name was
called Galeed, 49 also [u]Mizpah,[2] because
he said, "May the LORD watch between
you and me when we are absent one from
another. 50 If you afflict my daughters, or if
you take *other* wives besides my daughters, *although* no man *is* with us—see, God
is witness between you and me!"
51 Then Laban said to Jacob, "Here is this
heap and here is *this* pillar, which I have
placed between you and me. 52 This heap *is*
a witness, and *this* pillar *is* a witness, that I
will not pass beyond this heap to you, and
you will not pass beyond this heap and this
pillar to me, for harm. 53 The God of Abraham, the God of Nahor, and the God of
their father [v]judge between us." And Jacob
[w]swore by [x]the [3]Fear of his father Isaac.
54 Then Jacob offered a sacrifice on the
mountain, and called his brethren to eat
bread. And they ate bread and stayed all
night on the mountain. 55 And early in the
morning Laban arose, and [y]kissed his sons
and daughters and [z]blessed them. Then
Laban departed and [a]returned to his place.

Esau Comes to Meet Jacob

32 So Jacob went on his way, and [a]the
angels of God met him. 2 When Jacob saw them, he said, "This *is* God's
[b]camp." And he called the name of that
place [1]Mahanaim.
3 Then Jacob sent messengers before him
to Esau his brother [c]in the land of Seir, [d]the
[2]country of Edom. 4 And he commanded
them, saying, [e]"Speak thus to my lord
Esau, 'Thus your servant Jacob says: "I
have dwelt with Laban and stayed there
until now. 5 [f]I have oxen, donkeys, flocks,
and male and female servants; and I have
sent to tell my lord, that [g]I may find favor
in your sight."'"
6 Then the messengers returned to Jacob,
saying, "We came to your brother Esau, and
[h]he also is coming to meet you, and four
hundred men *are* with him." 7 So Jacob was
greatly afraid and [i]distressed; and he divided the people that *were* with him, and the
flocks and herds and camels, into two companies. 8 And he said, "If Esau comes to the
one company and [3]attacks it, then the other
company which is left will escape."
9 [j]Then Jacob said, [k]"O God of my father
Abraham and God of my father Isaac, the

41 [k]Gen. 29:20, 27-30 [l]Gen. 31:7
42 [m]Gen. 31:5, 29, 53; Ps. 124:1, 2 [n]Gen. 31:53; Is. 8:13 [o]Gen. 29:32; Ex. 3:7 [p]Gen. 31:24, 29; 1 Chr. 12:17
44 [q]Gen. 21:27, 32; 26:28 [r]Josh. 24:27 [8]*treaty*
45 [s]Gen. 28:18; 35:14; Josh. 24:26, 27
47 [9]Lit., in Aram., *Heap of Witness* [1]Lit., in Heb., *Heap of Witness*
48 [t]Josh. 24:27
49 [u]Judg. 10:17; 11:29; 1 Sam. 7:5, 6 [2]Lit. *Watch*
53 [v]Gen. 16:5 [w]Gen. 21:23 [x]Gen. 31:42 [3]A reference to God
55 [y]Gen. 29:11, 13; 31:28, 43 [z]Gen. 28:1 [a]Gen. 18:33; 30:25; Num. 24:25

CHAPTER 32

1 [a]Num. 22:31; 2 Kin. 6:16, 17; [Ps. 34:7; 91:1; Heb. 1:14]
2 [b]Josh. 5:14; Ps. 103:21; 148:2; Luke 2:13 [1]Lit. *Double Camp*
3 [c]Gen. 14:6; 33:14, 16 [d]Gen. 25:30; 36:6-9; Deut. 2:5; Josh. 24:4 [2]Lit. *field*
4 [e]Prov. 15:1
5 [f]Gen. 30:43 [g]Gen. 33:8, 15
6 [h]Gen. 33:1
7 [i]Gen. 32:11; 35:3
8 [3]Lit. *strikes*
9 [j][Ps. 50:15] [k]Gen. 28:13; 31:42

31:42 Fear of Isaac. Also see "the Fear of his father Isaac" (v. 53). This was another divine name, signifying Jacob's identification of the God who caused Isaac to reverence Him.

31:43 Laban pled his case, amounting to nothing more than the manifestation of his grasping character, by claiming everything was his.

31:44 let us make a covenant. Although Laban did regard all in Jacob's hands as his—after all Jacob had arrived 20 years before with nothing—nevertheless, the matter was clearly ruled in Jacob's favor, since Laban left with nothing. A treaty was struck in the customary fashion (vv. 45-51) in which they covenanted not to harm one another again (v. 52). With heaps of stones as testaments to the treaty named and in place (vv. 47-49), with the consecration meals having been eaten (vv. 46,54), and with the appropriate oaths and statements made in the name of their God (vv. 50,53), the agreement was properly sanctioned and concluded and thus they parted company. All contact between Abraham's kin in Canaan and Mesopotamia appears to have ended at this point.

31:47-49 Jegar Sahadutha...Galeed...Mizpah. The first two words mean in Aramaic and also Hebrew, "heap of witnesses." The third word means "watchtower."

31:53 God of Nahor. Laban's probable syncretistic paralleling of the God of Abraham with that of Nahor and Terah, his brother and father respectively, elicited Jacob again using "the Fear of Isaac," a reference to the true God (v. 42), for he certainly could not give credence to any of Laban's syncretistic allusions.

32:1 The angels of God. With one crisis behind him and before him the suspense of having to face Esau, Jacob was first met by an angelic host, who must have reminded him of Bethel, which served also as a timely reminder and encouragement of God's will being done on earth (28:11-15).

32:2 God's camp...Mahanaim. Meaning "double camp," i.e., one being God's and one being his own. It was located E of the Jordan River in Gilead near the River Jabbok.

32:3 Seir...Edom. The territory of Esau S of the Dead Sea.

32:7 greatly afraid and distressed. He had sought reconciliation with Esau (vv. 4,5), but the report of the returning envoys (v. 6) only confirmed his deepest suspicions that Esau's old threat against him (27:41,42) had not abated over the years, and his coming with force betokened only disaster (vv. 8,11). He prepared for the attack by dividing his company of people and animals.

LORD [l]who said to me, 'Return to your
country and to your family, and I will deal
well with you': 10 I am not worthy of the
least of all the [m]mercies and of all the truth
which You have shown Your servant; for I
crossed over this Jordan with [n]my staff,
and now I have become two companies.
11 [o]Deliver me, I pray, from the hand of my
brother, from the hand of Esau; for I fear
him, lest he come and [4]attack me *and* [p]the
mother with the children. 12 For [q]You said,
'I will surely treat you well, and make your
descendants as the [r]sand of the sea, which
cannot be numbered for multitude.' "

13 So he lodged there that same night,
and took what [5]came to his hand as [s]a
present for Esau his brother: 14 two hundred female goats and twenty male goats,
two hundred ewes and twenty rams,
15 thirty milk camels with their colts, forty
cows and ten bulls, twenty female donkeys
and ten foals. 16 Then he delivered *them* to
the hand of his servants, every drove by itself, and said to his servants, "Pass over
before me, and put some distance between
successive droves." 17 And he commanded
the first one, saying, "When Esau my
brother meets you and asks you, saying,
'To whom do you belong, and where are
you going? Whose *are* these in front of
you?' 18 then you shall say, 'They *are* your
servant Jacob's. It *is* a present sent to my
lord Esau; and behold, he also *is* behind
us.' " 19 So he commanded the second, the
third, and all who followed the droves,
saying, "In this manner you shall speak to
Esau when you find him; 20 and also say,
'Behold, your servant Jacob *is* behind us.' "
For he said, "I will [t]appease him with the
present that goes before me, and afterward
I will see his face; perhaps he will accept
me." 21 So the present went on over before
him, but he himself lodged that night in
the camp.

9 [l]Gen. 31:3, 13
10 [m]Gen. 24:27 [n]Job 8:7
11 [o]Ps. 59:1, 2 [p]Hos. 10:14 [4]Lit. *strike*
12 [q]Gen. 28:13-15 [r]Gen. 22:17
13 [s]Gen. 43:11 [5]*he had received*

Wrestling with God

22 And he arose that night and took his
two wives, his two female servants, and
his eleven sons, [u]and crossed over the ford
of Jabbok. 23 He took them, sent them
[6]over the brook, and sent over what he
had. 24 Then Jacob was left alone; and [v]a
Man wrestled with him until the [7]breaking
of day. 25 Now when He saw that He did
not prevail against him, He [8]touched the
socket of his hip; and [w]the socket of Jacob's
hip was out of joint as He wrestled with
him. 26 And [x]He said, "Let Me go, for the
day breaks."

But he said, [y]"I will not let You go unless
You bless me!"

27 So He said to him, "What *is* your
name?"

He said, "Jacob."

20 [t][Prov. 21:14]
22 [u]Num. 21:24; Deut. 3:16; Josh. 12:2
23 [6]*across*
24 [v]Josh. 5:13-15; Hos. 12:2-4 [7]*dawn*
25 [w]Matt. 26:41; 2 Cor. 12:7 [8]*struck*
26 [x]Luke 24:28 [y]Hos. 12:4

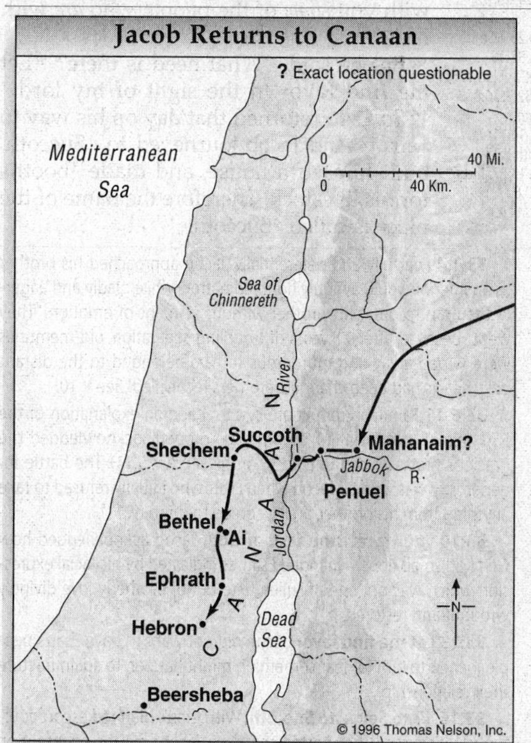

The route of Jacob's journey from Padan Aram to Canaan (Gen. 31–33).

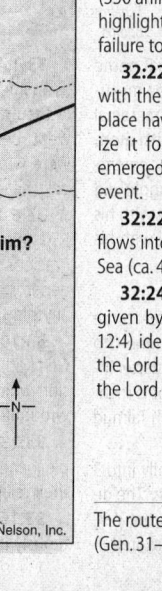

32:9-12 Commendably, notwithstanding the plans to appease his brother (vv. 13-21), Jacob prayed for deliverance, rehearsing God's own commands and covenant promise (v. 12; see 28:13-15), acknowledging his own anxiety, and confessing his own unworthiness before the Lord. This was Jacob's first recorded prayer since his encounter with God at Bethel en route to Laban (28:20-22).

32:13-21 The logistics of Jacob's careful appeasement strategy (550 animals Esau would prize) may highlight his ability to plan but it highlights even more, given the goal statement at the end (v. 20), his failure to pray and believe that God would change Esau's heart.

32:22-32 This unique, nightlong wrestling match at Peniel ends with the 97 year old Jacob having a change of name (v. 28) and the place having a new name assigned to it (v. 30) in order to memorialize it for Jacob and later generations. The limp with which he emerged from the match (vv. 25,31) also served to memorialize this event.

32:22 Jabbok. A stream, 60-65 mi. long, E of the Jordan which flows into that river midway between the Sea of Galilee and the Dead Sea (ca. 45 mi. S of the Sea of Galilee).

32:24 a Man wrestled. The site name, Peniel, or "face of God," given by Jacob (v. 30) and the commentary given by Hosea (Hos. 12:4) identifies this Man with whom Jacob wrestled as the Angel of the Lord who is also identified as God, a pre-incarnate appearance of the Lord Jesus Christ. *See note on Ex. 3:2.*

28 And He said, [z]"Your name shall no
longer be called Jacob, but [9]Israel; for you
have [a]struggled with God and [b]with men,
and have prevailed."
29 Then Jacob asked, saying, "Tell *me*
Your name, I pray."
And He said, [c]"Why *is* it *that* you ask
about My name?" And He [d]blessed him
there.
30 So Jacob called the name of the place
[1]Peniel: "For [e]I have seen God face to face,
and my life is preserved." 31 Just as he
crossed over [2]Penuel the sun rose on him,
and he limped on his hip. 32 Therefore to
this day the children of Israel do not eat the
muscle that shrank, which *is* on the hip
socket, because He [3]touched the socket of
Jacob's hip in the muscle that shrank.

Jacob and Esau Meet

33 Now Jacob lifted his eyes and
looked, and there, [a]Esau was coming, and with him were four hundred men.
So he divided the children among Leah,
Rachel, and the two maidservants. 2 And
he put the maidservants and their children
in front, Leah and her children behind, and
Rachel and Joseph last. 3 Then he crossed
over before them and [b]bowed himself to
the ground seven times, until he came near
to his brother.
4 [c]But Esau ran to meet him, and embraced him, [d]and fell on his neck and
kissed him, and they wept. 5 And he lifted
his eyes and saw the women and children,
and said, "Who *are* these with you?"
So he said, "The children [e]whom God
has graciously given your servant." 6 Then
the maidservants came near, they and their
children, and bowed down. 7 And Leah
also came near with her children, and they
bowed down. Afterward Joseph and Rachel came near, and they bowed down.
8 Then Esau said, "What *do* you *mean by*
[f]all this company which I met?"
And he said, "*These are* [g]to find favor in
the sight of my lord."
9 But Esau said, "I have enough, my
brother; keep what you have for yourself."
10 And Jacob said, "No, please, if I have
now found favor in your sight, then receive my present from my hand, inasmuch
as I [h]have seen your face as though I had
seen the face of God, and you were pleased
with me. 11 Please, take [i]my blessing that is
brought to you, because God has dealt
[j]graciously with me, and because I have
[1]enough." [k]So he urged him, and he took
it.
12 Then Esau said, "Let us take our journey; let us go, and I will go before you."
13 But Jacob said to him, "My lord
knows that the children *are* weak, and the
flocks and herds which are nursing *are*
with me. And if the men should drive
them hard one day, all the flock will die.
14 Please let my lord go on ahead before his
servant. I will lead on slowly at a pace
which the livestock that go before me, and
the children, [2]are able to endure, until I
come to my lord [l]in Seir."
15 And Esau said, "Now let me leave
with you *some* of the people who *are* with
me."
But he said, "What need is there? [m]Let
me find favor in the sight of my lord."
16 So Esau returned that day on his way to
Seir. 17 And Jacob journeyed to [n]Succoth,
built himself a house, and made [3]booths
for his livestock. Therefore the name of the
place is called [4]Succoth.

28 [z]Gen. 35:10; 1 Kin. 18:31; 2 Kin. 17:34 [a]Hos. 12:3, 4 [b]Gen. 25:31; 27:33 [9]Lit. *Prince with God*
29 [c]Judg. 13:17, 18 [d]Gen. 35:9
30 [e]Gen. 16:13; Ex. 24:10, 11; 33:20; Num. 12:8; Deut. 5:24; Judg. 6:22; Is. 6:5; [Matt. 5:8; 1 Cor. 13:12] [1]Lit. *Face of God*
31 [2]Lit. *Face of God;* same as *Peniel,* v. 30
32 [3]*struck*

CHAPTER 33

1 [a]Gen. 32:6
3 [b]Gen. 18:2; 42:6
4 [c]Gen. 32:28 [d]Gen. 45:14, 15
5 [e]Gen. 48:9; [Ps. 127:3]; Is. 8:18
8 [f]Gen. 32:13-16 [g]Gen. 32:5
10 [h]Gen. 43:3; 2 Sam. 3:13; 14:24, 28, 32
11 [i]Judg. 1:15; 1 Sam. 25:27; 30:26 [j]Gen. 30:43; Ex. 33:19 [k]2 Kin. 5:23 [1]Lit. *all*
14 [l]Gen. 32:3; 36:8 [2]*can stand*
15 [m]Gen. 34:11; 47:25; Ruth 2:13
17 [n]Josh. 13:27; Judg. 8:5; Ps. 60:6 [3]*shelters* [4]Lit. *Booths*

32:28 no longer...Jacob, but Israel. Jacob's personal name changed from one meaning "heel-catcher" or "deceiver" to one meaning "God's fighter" or "he struggles with God" (cf. 35:10). The marginal reading "Prince with God" is not preferred. **with God and with men.** An amazing evaluation of what Jacob had accomplished, i.e., emerging victorious from the struggle. In the record of his life, "struggle" did indeed dominate: 1) with his brother Esau (chaps. 25–27); 2) with his father (chap. 27); 3) with his father-in-law (chaps. 29–31); 4) with his wives (chap. 30); and 5) with God at Peniel (v. 28).

32:30 Peniel. *See note on v. 24.*

32:32 not eat the muscle that shrank. This might refer to the sciatic muscle/tendon. The observation that up to Moses' time ("to this day") the nation of Israel did not eat this part of a hindquarter intrigues because it bears no mention elsewhere in the OT, nor is it enshrined in the Mosaic law. It does find mention in the Jewish Talmud as a sacred law.

33:1,2 Esau was coming. Jacob hastily divided his family into 3 groups (cf. 31:7) and went ahead of them to meet his brother. The division and relative location of his family in relationship to the perceived danger gives tremendous insight into whom Jacob favored.

33:3,4 Fearfully and deferentially, Jacob approached his brother as an inferior would a highly honored patron, while gladly and eagerly, Esau ran to greet his brother without restraint of emotion. "They wept" because, after 21 years of troubling separation, old memories were wiped away and murderous threats belonged to the distant past; hearts had been changed, brothers reconciled! See v. 10.

33:5-11 Family introductions (vv. 5-7) and an explanation of the 550 animals gift (vv. 8-10; cf. 32:13-21) properly acknowledged the gracious provision of the Lord upon his life (vv. 5,11). The battle for generosity was won by Jacob when Esau, who initially refused to take anything from his brother, finally agreed to do so (v. 11).

33:10 your face...the face of God. Jacob acknowledged how God had so obviously changed Esau, as indicated by his facial expression which was not one of sullen hate but of brotherly love divinely wrought and restored.

33:15 Let me find favor. Jacob did not want to have Esau's people loaned to him for fear something might happen to again fracture their relationship.

33:16,17 to Seir...to Succoth. With Esau's planned escort courteously dismissed, they parted company. Jacob's expressed intention

Jacob Comes to Canaan

18 Then Jacob came [5]safely to [o]the city of
[p]Shechem, which *is* in the land of Canaan,
when he came from Padan Aram; and he
pitched his tent before the city. 19 And [q]he
bought the parcel of [6]land, where he had
pitched his tent, from the children of
Hamor, Shechem's father, for one hundred
pieces of money. 20 Then he erected an
altar there and called it [r]El[7] Elohe Israel.

The Dinah Incident

34 Now [a]Dinah the daughter of Leah,
whom she had borne to Jacob, went
out to see the daughters of the land. 2 And
when Shechem the son of Hamor the
Hivite, prince of the country, saw her, he
[b]took her and lay with her, and violated
her. 3 His soul [1]was strongly attracted to
Dinah the daughter of Jacob, and he loved
the young woman and spoke [2]kindly to
the young woman. 4 So Shechem [c]spoke to
his father Hamor, saying, "Get me this
young woman as a wife."
5 And Jacob heard that he had defiled
Dinah his daughter. Now his sons were
with his livestock in the field; so Jacob
[d]held[3] his peace until they came. 6 Then
Hamor the father of Shechem went out to
Jacob to speak with him. 7 And the sons of
Jacob came in from the field when they
heard *it;* and the men were grieved and
very angry, because he [e]had done a disgraceful thing in Israel by lying with Jacob's daughter, [f]a thing which ought not to
be done. 8 But Hamor spoke with them,
saying, "The soul of my son Shechem
longs for your daughter. Please give her to
him as a wife. 9 And make marriages with
us; give your daughters to us, and take our
daughters to yourselves. 10 So you shall
dwell with us, and the land shall be before
you. Dwell and trade in it, and acquire
possessions for yourselves in it."
11 Then Shechem said to her father and
her brothers, "Let me find favor in your
eyes, and whatever you say to me I will
give. 12 Ask me ever so much [g]dowry[4] and
gift, and I will give according to what you
say to me; but give me the young woman
as a wife."
13 But the sons of Jacob answered
Shechem and Hamor his father, and spoke
[h]deceitfully, because he had defiled Dinah
their sister. 14 And they said to them, "We
cannot do this thing, to give our sister to
one who is [i]uncircumcised, for [j]that *would
be* a reproach to us. 15 But on this *condition*
we will consent to you: If you will become
as we *are,* if every male of you is circumcised, 16 then we will give our daughters to
you, and we will take your daughters to
us; and we will dwell with you, and we
will become one people. 17 But if you will
not heed us and be circumcised, then we
will take our daughter and be gone."
18 And their words pleased Hamor and

18 [o] John 3:23 [p] Gen. 12:6; 35:4; Josh. 24:1; Judg. 9:1; Ps. 60:6 [5] Or *to Shalem, a city of*
19 [q] Josh. 24:32; John 4:5 [6] Lit. *the field*
20 [r] Gen. 35:7 [7] Lit. *God, the God of Israel*

CHAPTER 34

1 [a] Gen. 30:21
2 [b] Gen. 20:2
3 [1] Lit. *clung to* [2] *tenderly*
4 [c] Judg. 14:2
5 [d] 2 Sam. 13:22 [3] *kept silent*
7 [e] Deut. 22:20-30; Josh. 7:15; Judg. 20:6 [f] Deut. 23:17; 2 Sam. 13:12
12 [g] Ex. 22:16, 17; Deut. 22:29 [4] *bride-price*
13 [h] Gen. 31:7; Ex. 8:29
14 [i] Ex. 12:48 [j] Josh. 5:2-9

to meet again in Seir (*see note on 32:3*), for whatever reason, did not materialize. Instead, Jacob halted his journey first at Succoth, then at Shechem (v. 18). Succoth is E of the Jordan River, 20 mi. E of Shechem, which is 65 mi. N of Jerusalem, located between Mts. Ebal and Gerizim.

33:18 came safely. Ca. 1908 B.C. A reference to the fulfillment of Jacob's vow made at Bethel when, upon departure from Canaan, he looked to God for a safe return. Upon arrival in Canaan, he would tithe of his possessions (28:20-22). Presumably Jacob fulfilled his pledge at Shechem or later at Bethel (35:1).

33:19 bought the parcel of land. This purchase became only the second piece of real estate legally belonging to Abraham's line in the Promised Land (cf. 23:17,18; 25:9,10). However, the land was not Abraham's and his descendants simply because they bought it, but rather because God owned it all (Lev. 25:23) and gave it to them for their exclusive domain (*see notes on 12:1-3*).

33:20 erected an altar. In the place where Abraham had first built an altar (12:6,7), Jacob similarly marked the spot with a new name, incorporating his own new name (32:28), "God, the God of Israel," declaring that he worshiped the "Mighty One." "Israel" perhaps foreshadowed its use for the nation with which it rapidly became associated, even when it consisted of not much more than Jacob's extended household (34:7).

34:1-31 The tawdry details of the abuse of Dinah and the revenge of Levi and Simeon are recounted in full, perhaps in order to highlight for the readers about to enter Canaan how easily Abraham's descendants might intermingle and marry with Canaanites, contrary to patriarchal desires (cf. 24:3; 27:46; 28:1) and God's will (Ex. 34:6; Deut. 7:3; Josh. 23:12,13; Neh. 13:26,27).

34:1 to see the daughters. Little did Dinah (see 30:20,21) realize that her jaunt to the nearby city to view how other women lived would bring forth such horrific results.

34:2 saw...took...violated. Scripture classifies Shechem's action as forcible rape, no matter how sincerely he might have expressed his love for her afterwards (v. 3) and desire for marriage (vv. 11,12). Other expressions in the account underscore the clearly unacceptable nature of this crime, e.g. "defiled" (vv. 5,13), "grieved and very angry" (v. 7), "a disgraceful thing...which ought not to be done" (v. 7), and "treat our sister like a harlot" (v. 31).

34:5 Jacob held his peace. In the absence of further data, Jacob's reticence to respond should not be criticized. Wisdom dictated that he wait and counsel with his sons, but their reaction, grief, anger, and vengeance hijacked the talks between Jacob and Hamor (v. 6) and led finally to Jacob's stern rebuke (v. 30).

34:6-10 The prince of Shechem painted a picture of harmonious integration (v. 16, "become one people"). However, Shechemite self-interest and enrichment actually prevailed (v. 23).

34:7 in Israel. Already Jacob's household is being called by the name God had given him as father of the coming nation (32:28).

34:13-17 Feigning interest in the proposals put forward and misusing, if not abusing, the circumcision sign of the Abrahamic Covenant (*see notes on 17:11-14*), Jacob's sons conned both father and son into convincing all the men to submit to circumcision because the outcome would be to their favor with marriages (v. 9) and social, economic integration (v. 10).

Shechem, Hamor's son. 19 So the young man did not delay to do the thing, because he delighted in Jacob's daughter. He *was* [k]more honorable than all the household of his father.

20 And Hamor and Shechem his son came to the [l]gate of their city, and spoke with the men of their city, saying: 21 "These men *are* at peace with us. Therefore let them dwell in the land and trade in it. For indeed the land *is* large enough for them. Let us take their daughters to us as wives, and let us give them our daughters. 22 Only on this *condition* will the men consent to dwell with us, to be one people: if every male among us is circumcised as they *are* circumcised. 23 *Will* not their livestock, their property, and every animal of theirs *be* ours? Only let us consent to them, and they will dwell with us." 24 And all who went out of the gate of his city heeded Hamor and Shechem his son; every male was circumcised, all who [m]went out of the gate of his city.

25 Now it came to pass on the third day, when they were in pain, that two of the sons of Jacob, [n]Simeon and Levi, Dinah's brothers, each took his sword and came boldly upon the city and killed all the males. 26 And they [o]killed Hamor and Shechem his son with the edge of the sword, and took Dinah from Shechem's house, and went out. 27 The sons of Jacob came upon the slain, and plundered the city, because their sister had been defiled. 28 They took their sheep, their oxen, and their donkeys, what *was* in the city and what *was* in the field, 29 and all their wealth. All their little ones and their wives they took captive; and they plundered even all that *was* in the houses.

30 Then Jacob said to Simeon and Levi, [p]"You have [q]troubled me [r]by making me obnoxious among the inhabitants of the land, among the Canaanites and the Perizzites; [s]and since I *am* few in number, they will gather themselves together against me and kill me. I shall be destroyed, my household and I."

31 But they said, "Should he treat our sister like a harlot?"

Jacob's Return to Bethel

35 Then God said to Jacob, "Arise, go up to [a]Bethel and dwell there; and make an altar there to God, [b]who appeared to you [c]when you fled from the face of Esau your brother."

2 And Jacob said to his [d]household and to all who *were* with him, "Put away [e]the foreign gods that *are* among you, [f]purify yourselves, and change your garments. 3 Then let us arise and go up to Bethel; and I will make an altar there to God, [g]who answered me in the day of my distress [h]and has been with me in the way which I have gone." 4 So they gave Jacob all the foreign [1]gods which *were* in their hands, and the [i]earrings which *were* in their ears; and Jacob hid them under [j]the terebinth tree which *was* by Shechem.

5 And they journeyed, and [k]the terror of God was upon the cities that *were* all around them, and they did not pursue the sons of Jacob. 6 So Jacob came to [l]Luz (that *is*, Bethel), which *is* in the land of Canaan, he and all the people who *were* with him. 7 And he [m]built an altar there and called

19 [k] 1 Chr. 4:9
20 [l] Gen. 19:1; 23:10; Ruth 4:1, 11; 2 Sam. 15:2
24 [m] Gen. 23:10, 18
25 [n] Gen. 29:33, 34; 42:24; 49:5-7
26 [o] Gen. 49:5, 6
30 [p] Gen. 49:6 [q] Josh. 7:25 [r] Ex. 5:21; 1 Sam. 13:4; 2 Sam. 10:6 [s] Gen. 46:26, 27; Deut. 4:27; 1 Chr. 16:19; Ps. 105:12

CHAPTER 35

1 [a] Gen. 28:19; 31:13 [b] Gen. 28:13 [c] Gen. 27:43
2 [d] Gen. 18:19; Josh. 24:15 [e] Gen. 31:19, 30, 34; Josh. 24:2, 14, 23 [f] Ex. 19:10, 14; Lev. 13:6
3 [g] Gen. 32:7, 24; Ps. 107:6 [h] Gen. 28:15, 20; 31:3, 42
4 [i] Hos. 2:13 [j] Josh. 24:26; Judg. 9:6 [1] *idols*
5 [k] Ex. 15:16; 23:27; [Deut. 2:25; 11:25]; Josh. 2:9; 1 Sam. 14:15
6 [l] Gen. 28:19, 22; 48:3
7 [m] Gen. 33:20; 35:3; Eccl. 5:4

34:19 He *was* more honorable. Meaning that the men agreed to such an excruciating surgery (vv. 24,25) because they had so much respect for him and because they anticipated mercenary benefit (v. 23).

34:20 gate of their city. The normal place for public gatherings.

34:25-29 A massacre of all males and the wholesale plunder of the city went way beyond the reasonable, wise, and justly deserved punishment of one man; this was a considerably more excessive vengeance than the Mosaic law would later legislate (cf. Deut. 22:28,29).

34:27 The sons of Jacob. Simeon and Levi set in motion the barbarity of that day and attention validly falls upon them in the narrative (vv. 25,30; cf. 49:5-7), but their brothers joined in the looting, thereby approving murder and mayhem as justifiable retribution for the destroyed honor of their sister (v. 31).

34:30 You have troubled me. Vengeance exacted meant retaliation expected. Total loss of respect ("making me obnoxious") and of peaceful relations (v. 21) put both him and them in harm's way with survival being highly unlikely. This threat tested God's promise of safety, giving Jacob cause for great concern (28:15; 32:9,12). **Perizzites.** *See note on 13:7.*

35:1 Bethel. This was the place where God confirmed the Abrahamic Covenant to Jacob (28:13-15).

35:2-4 Put away the foreign gods. Moving to Bethel necessitated spiritual preparation beyond the level of an exercise in logistics. Possession of idolatrous symbols such as figurines, amulets, or cultic charms (v. 4, "earrings") were no longer tolerable, including Rachel's troubling teraphim (31:19). Idols buried out of sight, plus bathing and changing to clean clothes, all served to portray both cleansing from defilement by idolatry and consecration of the heart to the Lord. It had been 8 or 10 years since his return to Canaan and, appropriately, time enough to clean up all traces of idolatry.

35:4 terebinth tree...Shechem. Possibly this was the same tree as in Abraham's day (12:6).

35:5 the terror of God. A supernaturally induced fear of Israel rendered the surrounding city-states unwilling and powerless to intervene and made Jacob's fear of their retaliation rather inconsequential (34:30).

35:7 built an altar there. Through this act of worship, fulfillment of his vow (28:20-22), and renaming the site, Jacob reconfirmed his allegiance to God, who also affirmed His commitment to Jacob by reappearing to him, repeating the change of name (v. 10; cf. 32:28), and rehearsing the Abrahamic promises (vv. 11,12). In response, Jacob also repeated the rite he had performed when he first met God at Bethel (v. 14) and reaffirmed its name (v. 15).

the place [2]El Bethel, because [n]there God
appeared to him when he fled from the
face of his brother.
8 Now [o]Deborah, Rebekah's nurse, died,
and she was buried below Bethel under
the terebinth tree. So the name of it was
called [3]Allon Bachuth.
9 Then [p]God appeared to Jacob again,
when he came from Padan Aram, and
[q]blessed him. **10** And God said to him,
"Your name *is* Jacob; [r]your name shall not
be called Jacob anymore, [s]but Israel shall
be your name." So He called his name Israel. **11** Also God said to him: [t]"I *am* God
Almighty. [u]Be fruitful and multiply; [v]a nation and a company of nations shall proceed from you, and kings shall come from
your body. **12** The [w]land which I gave
Abraham and Isaac I give to you; and to
your descendants after you I give this
land." **13** Then God [x]went[4] up from him in
the place where He talked with him. **14** So
Jacob [y]set up a pillar in the place where He
talked with him, a pillar of stone; and he
poured a drink offering on it, and he
poured oil on it. **15** And Jacob called the
name of the place where God spoke with
him, [z]Bethel.

Death of Rachel

16 Then they journeyed from Bethel.
And when there was but a little distance to
go to Ephrath, Rachel labored *in childbirth,*
and she had hard labor. **17** Now it came to
pass, when she was in hard labor, that the
midwife said to her, "Do not fear; [a]you will
have this son also." **18** And so it was, as her
soul was departing (for she died), that she
called his name [5]Ben-Oni; but his father
called him [6]Benjamin. **19** So [b]Rachel died
and was buried on the way to [c]Ephrath
(that *is,* Bethlehem). **20** And Jacob set a pillar on her grave, which *is* the pillar of Rachel's grave [d]to this day.
21 Then Israel journeyed and pitched his
tent beyond [e]the tower of Eder. **22** And it
happened, when Israel dwelt in that land,
that Reuben went and [f]lay with Bilhah his
father's concubine; and Israel heard *about it.*

Jacob's Twelve Sons

Now the sons of Jacob were twelve:
23 the sons of Leah *were* [g]Reuben, Jacob's
firstborn, and Simeon, Levi, Judah, Issachar, and Zebulun; **24** the sons of Rachel
were Joseph and Benjamin; **25** the sons of
Bilhah, Rachel's maidservant, *were* Dan
and Naphtali; **26** and the sons of Zilpah,
Leah's maidservant, *were* Gad and Asher.
These *were* the sons of Jacob who were
born to him in Padan Aram.

Death of Isaac

27 Then Jacob came to his father Isaac at
[h]Mamre, or [i]Kirjath Arba[7] (that *is,* Hebron), where Abraham and Isaac had
dwelt. **28** Now the days of Isaac were one
hundred and eighty years. **29** So Isaac
breathed his last and died, and [j]was [8]gath-
ered to his people, *being* old and full of
days. And [k]his sons Esau and Jacob buried
him.

The Family of Esau

36 Now this *is* the genealogy of Esau,
[a]who is Edom. **2** [b]Esau took his
wives from the daughters of Canaan: Adah
the daughter of Elon the [c]Hittite; [d]Aholi-
bamah[1] the daughter of Anah, the daughter of Zibeon the Hivite; **3** and [e]Basemath,
Ishmael's daughter, sister of Nebajoth.
4 Now [f]Adah bore Eliphaz to Esau, and

7 [n]Gen. 28:13 [2]Lit. *God of the House of God*
8 [o]Gen. 24:59 [3]Lit. *Terebinth of Weeping*
9 [p]Josh. 5:13; Dan. 10:5 [q]Gen. 32:29; Hos. 12:4
10 [r]Gen. 17:5 [s]Gen. 32:28
11 [t]Gen. 17:1; 28:3; 48:3, 4; Ex. 6:3 [u]Gen. 9:1, 7 [v]Gen. 17:5, 6, 16; 28:3; 48:4
12 [w]Gen. 12:7; 13:15; 26:3, 4; 28:13; 48:4; Ex. 32:13
13 [x]Gen. 17:22; 18:33 [4]*departed*
14 [y]Gen. 28:18, 19; 31:45
15 [z]Gen. 28:19
17 [a]Gen. 30:24; 1 Sam. 4:20
18 [5]Lit. *Son of My Sorrow* [6]Lit. *Son of the Right Hand*
19 [b]Gen. 48:7 [c]Ruth 1:2; 4:11; Mic. 5:2; Matt. 2:6
20 [d]1 Sam. 10:2
21 [e]Mic. 4:8
22 [f]Gen. 49:4; 1 Chr. 5:1
23 [g]Gen. 29:31-35; 30:18-20; 46:8; Ex. 1:1-4
27 [h]Gen. 13:18; 18:1; 23:19 [i]Josh. 14:15 [7]Lit. *Town* or *City of Arba*
29 [j]Gen. 15:15; 25:8; 49:33 [k]Gen. 25:9; 49:31 [8]Joined his ancestors

CHAPTER 36

1 [a]Gen. 25:30
2 [b]Gen. 26:34; 28:9 [c]2 Kin. 7:6 [d]Gen. 36:25 [1]Or *Oholibamah*
3 [e]Gen. 28:9
4 [f]1 Chr. 1:35

35:11 kings shall come from your body. God's words, here included for the first time since His promises at Abraham's circumcision (17:6,16), served as a reminder of future royalty.

35:13 went up. The presence of God was there in some visible form.

35:14 A commonly done way to make a covenant (*see note on 28:18-21*).

35:16 Ephrath. A more ancient name for Bethlehem (v. 19; 48:7; cf. 5:2).

35:18 Ben-Oni...Benjamin. The dying mother appropriately named her newly born son "Son of my sorrow," but the grieving father named him "Son of my right hand," thus assigning him a place of honor in the home. Her prayer at the birth of her firstborn was answered (30:24).

35:20 The memorial to Rachel could still be seen in Moses' day, about one mi. N of Bethlehem.

35:21 tower of Eder. Likely a watchtower for shepherds, near Bethlehem.

35:22 the sons of Jacob. The birth of Benjamin in Canaan (v. 18) furnished reason to simply review the sons born outside of Canaan, with only one sad note preceding it, i.e., the sin of Reuben, which tainted the qualifier "Jacob's firstborn" in the listing (see 49:3,4; Deut. 22:30; 1 Chr. 5:1,2).

35:27 Mamre...Hebron. *See note on 13:18.*

35:29 his sons Esau and Jacob. Ca. 1885 B.C. Isaac's funeral brought his two sons back together, as Abraham's funeral had done for Isaac and Ishmael (25:9). Jacob, back in the land before his father's death, fulfilled yet another part of his Bethel vow (28:20, "come back to my father's house in peace").

36:1–37:1 The genealogy of Esau (v. 1).

36:1-19 The taking up of "the history of Jacob" (37:2), the next patriarch, is preceded by a fairly detailed genealogy of Esau, to which is appended both the genealogy of Seir the Horite, whose descendants were the contemporary inhabitants of Edom and a listing of Edomite kings and chiefs. Jacob's and Esau's posterities, as history would go on to show, would not be in isolation from each other as originally intended (vv. 6-8). They were to become bitter enemies engaged with each other in war.

36:1 Edom. Cf. v. 8; *see note on 25:30;* see Introduction to Obadiah.

Basemath bore Reuel. 5 And [2]Aholibamah
bore Jeush, Jaalam, and Korah. These *were*
the sons of Esau who were born to him in
the land of Canaan.
6 Then Esau took his wives, his sons, his
daughters, and all the persons of his
household, his cattle and all his animals,
and all his goods which he had gained in
the land of Canaan, and went to a country
away from the presence of his brother Jacob. 7 [g]For their possessions were too great
for them to dwell together, and [h]the land
where they were strangers could not support them because of their livestock. 8 So
Esau dwelt in [i]Mount Seir. [j]Esau *is* Edom.
9 And this *is* the genealogy of Esau the
father of the Edomites in Mount Seir.
10 These *were* the names of Esau's sons:
[k]Eliphaz the son of Adah the wife of Esau,
and Reuel the son of Basemath the wife of
Esau. 11 And the sons of Eliphaz were
Teman, Omar, [3]Zepho, Gatam, and Kenaz.
12 Now Timna was the concubine of
Eliphaz, Esau's son, and she bore [l]Amalek
to Eliphaz. These *were* the sons of Adah,
Esau's wife.
13 These *were* the sons of Reuel: Nahath,
Zerah, Shammah, and Mizzah. These were
the sons of Basemath, Esau's wife.
14 These were the sons of [4]Aholibamah,
Esau's wife, the daughter of Anah, the
daughter of Zibeon. And she bore to Esau:
Jeush, Jaalam, and Korah.

The Chiefs of Edom

15 These *were* the chiefs of the sons of
Esau. The sons of Eliphaz, the firstborn *son*
of Esau, were Chief Teman, Chief Omar,
Chief Zepho, Chief Kenaz, 16 [5]Chief
Korah, Chief Gatam, *and* Chief Amalek.
These *were* the chiefs of Eliphaz in the land
of Edom. They *were* the sons of Adah.
17 These *were* the sons of Reuel, Esau's
son: Chief Nahath, Chief Zerah, Chief
Shammah, and Chief Mizzah. These *were*
the chiefs of Reuel in the land of Edom.
These *were* the sons of Basemath, Esau's
wife.
18 And these *were* the sons of [6]Aholi-
bamah, Esau's wife: Chief Jeush, Chief
Jaalam, and Chief Korah. These *were* the
chiefs *who descended* from Aholibamah,
Esau's wife, the daughter of Anah.
19 These *were* the sons of Esau, who is
Edom, and these *were* their chiefs.

The Sons of Seir

20 [m]These *were* the sons of Seir [n]the
Horite who inhabited the land: Lotan,
Shobal, Zibeon, Anah, 21 Dishon, Ezer, and
Dishan. These *were* the chiefs of the
Horites, the sons of Seir, in the land of
Edom.
22 And the sons of Lotan were Hori and
[7]Hemam. Lotan's sister *was* Timna.
23 These *were* the sons of Shobal: [8]Alvan,
Manahath, Ebal, [9]Shepho, and Onam.
24 These *were* the sons of Zibeon: both
Ajah and Anah. This *was the* Anah who
found the [1]water in the wilderness as he
pastured [o]the donkeys of his father
Zibeon. 25 These *were* the children of Anah:
Dishon and [2]Aholibamah the daughter of
Anah.
26 These *were* the sons of [3]Dishon:
[4]Hemdan, Eshban, Ithran, and Cheran.
27 These *were* the sons of Ezer: Bilhan, Zaa-
van, and [5]Akan. 28 These *were* the sons of
Dishan: [p]Uz and Aran.
29 These *were* the chiefs of the Horites:
Chief Lotan, Chief Shobal, Chief Zibeon,
Chief Anah, 30 Chief Dishon, Chief Ezer,
and Chief Dishan. These *were* the chiefs of
the Horites, according to their chiefs in the
land of Seir.

The Kings of Edom

31 [q]Now these *were* the kings who
reigned in the land of Edom before any
king reigned over the children of Israel:
32 Bela the son of Beor reigned in Edom,
and the name of his city *was* Dinhabah.
33 And when Bela died, Jobab the son of
Zerah of Bozrah reigned in his place.
34 When Jobab died, Husham of the land of
the Temanites reigned in his place. 35 And
when Husham died, Hadad the son of
Bedad, who attacked Midian in the field of

5 [2] Or *Oholibamah*
7 [g] Gen. 13:6, 11 [h] Gen. 17:8; 28:4; Heb. 11:9
8 [i] Gen. 32:3; Deut. 2:5; Josh. 24:4 [j] Gen. 36:1, 19
10 [k] 1 Chr. 1:35
11 [3] *Zephi*, 1 Chr. 1:36
12 [l] Ex. 17:8-16; Num. 24:20; Deut. 25:17-19; 1 Sam. 15:2, 3
14 [4] Or *Oholibamah*
16 [5] Sam. omits *Chief Korah*
18 [6] Or *Oholibamah*
20 [m] 1 Chr. 1:38-42 [n] Gen. 14:6; Deut. 2:12, 22
22 [7] *Homam*, 1 Chr. 1:39
23 [8] *Alian*, 1 Chr. 1:40 [9] *Shephi*, 1 Chr. 1:40
24 [o] Lev. 19:19 [1] So with MT, Vg. (*hot springs*); LXX *Jamin*; Tg. *mighty men*; Talmud *mules*
25 [2] Or *Oholibamah*
26 [3] Heb. *Dishan* [4] *Hamran*, 1 Chr. 1:41
27 [5] *Jaakan*, 1 Chr. 1:42
28 [p] Job 1:1
31 [q] Gen. 17:6, 16; 35:11; 1 Chr. 1:43

36:7 too great for them to dwell together. Crowded grazing and living conditions finally clinched the decision by Esau to move permanently to Edom, where he had already established a home (cf. 32:3; 33:14,16). Since it was Abraham's descendants through Isaac and Jacob who would possess the land, it was fitting for God to work out the circumstances providentially of keeping Jacob's lineage in the land and moving Esau's lineage out. It is not revealed if Esau had understood and come to accept the promises of God to Jacob, although his descendants surely sought to deny Israel any right to their land or their life.

36:8 Mount Seir. This was divinely assigned as Esau's place (Deut. 2:5; Josh. 24:4).

36:10-14 Cf. 1 Chr. 1:35-37.

36:15 the chiefs. This term, "ruler of a thousand," apart from one exception (Zech. 12:5,6), is used exclusively for the tribal princes or clan leaders, the political/military leaders in Edom. It may suggest a loosely formed tribal confederacy.

36:20-28 Cf. 1 Chr. 1:38-42.

36:31-39 kings...before any king...of Israel. Sandwiched in the genealogical details of Edom is a statement prophetically pointing to kingship in Israel (17:6,16; 35:11; 49:10; Num. 24:7,17,18; Deut. 17:14-20). The kings' list does not introduce a dynasty, each ruler not being the son of his predecessor. "Kings" more likely suggests rule over a more settled people than tribal groups.

Moab, reigned in his place. And the name
of his city *was* Avith. 36 When Hadad died,
Samlah of Masrekah reigned in his place.
37 And when Samlah died, Saul of [r]Re-
hoboth-*by*-the-River reigned in his place.
38 When Saul died, Baal-Hanan the son of
Achbor reigned in his place. 39 And when
Baal-Hanan the son of Achbor died,
[6]Hadar reigned in his place; and the name
of his city *was* [7]Pau. His wife's name *was*
Mehetabel, the daughter of Matred, the
daughter of Mezahab.

The Chiefs of Esau

40 And these *were* the names of the chiefs
of Esau, according to their families and
their places, by their names: Chief Timnah,
Chief [8]Alvah, Chief Jetheth, 41 Chief
[9]Aholibamah, Chief Elah, Chief Pinon,
42 Chief Kenaz, Chief Teman, Chief
Mibzar, 43 Chief Magdiel, and Chief Iram.
These *were* the chiefs of Edom, according to
their dwelling places in the land of their
possession. Esau *was* the father of [1]the
Edomites.

Joseph Dreams of Greatness

37 Now Jacob dwelt in the land
[a]where his father was a [1]stranger, in
the land of Canaan. 2 This *is* the history of
Jacob.
Joseph, *being* seventeen years old, was
feeding the flock with his brothers. And
the lad *was* with the sons of Bilhah and the
sons of Zilpah, his father's wives; and Joseph brought [b]a bad report of them to his
father.
3 Now Israel loved Joseph more than all
his children, because he *was* [c]the son of his
old age. Also he [d]made him a tunic of *many*
colors. 4 But when his brothers saw that
their father loved him more than all his
brothers, they [e]hated him and could not
speak peaceably to him.
5 Now Joseph had a dream, and he told *it*
to his brothers; and they hated him even
more. 6 So he said to them, "Please hear this
dream which I have dreamed: 7 [f]There we
were, binding sheaves in the field. Then behold, my sheaf arose and also stood upright; and indeed your sheaves stood all
around and bowed down to my sheaf."
8 And his brothers said to him, "Shall
you indeed reign over us? Or shall you indeed have dominion over us?" So they
hated him even more for his dreams and
for his words.
9 Then he dreamed still another dream
and told it to his brothers, and said, "Look,
I have dreamed another dream. And this
time, [g]the sun, the moon, and the eleven
stars bowed down to me."
10 So he told *it* to his father and his
brothers; and his father rebuked him and
said to him, "What *is* this dream that you
have dreamed? Shall your mother and I
and [h]your brothers indeed come to bow
down to the earth before you?" 11 And [i]his
brothers envied him, but his father [j]kept
the matter *in mind.*

Joseph Sold by His Brothers

12 Then his brothers went to feed their
father's flock in [k]Shechem. 13 And Israel
said to Joseph, "Are not your brothers
feeding *the flock* in Shechem? Come, I will
send you to them."
So he said to him, "Here I am."
14 Then he said to him, "Please go and
see if it is well with your brothers and well

37 [r]Gen. 10:11
39 [6]Sam., Syr. *Hadad* and 1 Chr. 1:50 [7]*Pai,* 1 Chr. 1:50
40 [8]*Aliah,* 1 Chr. 1:51
41 [9]Or *Oholibamah*
43 [1]Heb. *Edom*

CHAPTER 37

1 [a]Gen. 17:8; 23:4; 28:4; 36:7; Heb. 11:9 [1]*sojourner,* temporary resident
2 [b]Gen. 35:25, 26; 1 Sam. 2:22-24
3 [c]Gen. 44:20 [d]Gen. 37:23, 32; Judg. 5:30; 1 Sam. 2:19
4 [e]Gen. 27:41; 49:23; 1 Sam. 17:28; John 15:18-20
7 [f]Gen. 42:6, 9; 43:26; 44:14
9 [g]Gen. 46:29; 47:25
10 [h]Gen. 27:29
11 [i]Matt. 27:17, 18; Acts 7:9 [j]Dan. 7:28; Luke 2:19, 51
12 [k]Gen. 33:18-20

36:43 father of the Edomites. The closing title of the genealogy calls attention to the Lord's words to Rebekah at the birth of her sons, "two nations are in your womb" (25:23); here was the nation from the older.

37:1 father was a stranger. This by-line into the story of Jacob's son, Joseph, informs the reader that Jacob's father, Isaac, hence his sons as well, though in the land, had not yet entered into possession of their inheritance. They were still alien residents.

37:2–50:26 The genealogy of Jacob (v. 2).

37:1 land of Canaan. Actually Jacob and his family were in Hebron (v. 14). *See note on 13:18.*

37:2 Joseph, *being* seventeen years old. Eleven years had passed since he had entered the land of Canaan with his family (cf. 30:22-24), since Joseph was born 6 years before departing from Haran. **a bad report.** Whether Joseph brought this at his own initiative or reported back at the father's demand on 4 of his brothers (e.g., v. 14) is not elaborated upon, nor specifically cited as the cause of the brothers' intense dislike of Joseph (cf. 4,5,8,11,18,19).

37:3,4 Overt favoritism of Joseph and tacit appointment of him as the primary son by the father (*see note on 37:3*) conspired to estrange him from his brothers. They hated and envied him (vv. 4,5,10) and could not interact with him without conflict and hostility. Joseph must have noticed the situation.

37:3 tunic of *many* colors. The Septuagint (LXX) favored this translation of the Heb. phrase used by Moses, although some prefer "a long-sleeved robe" or "an ornamented tunic." It marked the owner as the one whom the father intended to be the future leader of the household, an honor normally given to the firstborn son.

37:5-10 The content of the dreams which Joseph recounted exacerbated fraternal hostility, with the second one also incurring paternal rebuke. The dream symbolism needed no special interpretation to catch its significant elevation of the favored son to ruling status over his brothers (vv. 8-10).

37:11 kept the matter *in mind.* Unlike the brothers, who immediately rejected any meaning to Joseph's words yet still allowed the dream to sorely irritate them into greater resentment of their brother (v. 19), the father, notwithstanding his public admonishment of Joseph, continued to ponder the meaning of the dreams.

37:12-17 The assignment to Shechem brought Joseph providentially to Dothan, a site more convenient for contact with merchants using the main trade route on their way to Egypt.

with the flocks, and bring back word to
me." So he sent him out of the Valley of
[l]Hebron, and he went to Shechem.
15 Now a certain man found him, and
there he was, wandering in the field. And
the man asked him, saying, "What are you
seeking?"
16 So he said, "I am seeking my brothers.
[m]Please tell me where they are feeding
their flocks."
17 And the man said, "They have departed from here, for I heard them say, 'Let
us go to Dothan.' " So Joseph went after his
brothers and found them in [n]Dothan.
18 Now when they saw him afar off,
even before he came near them, [o]they conspired against him to kill him. 19 Then they
said to one another, "Look, this [2]dreamer
is coming! 20 [p]Come therefore, let us now
kill him and cast him into some pit; and we
shall say, 'Some wild beast has devoured
him.' We shall see what will become of his
dreams!"
21 But [q]Reuben heard *it,* and he delivered him out of their hands, and said, "Let
us not kill him." 22 And Reuben said to
them, "Shed no blood, *but* cast him into
this pit which *is* in the wilderness, and do
not lay a hand on him"—that he might deliver him out of their hands, and bring him
back to his father.
23 So it came to pass, when Joseph had
come to his brothers, that they [r]stripped
Joseph *of* his tunic, the tunic of *many* colors
that *was* on him. 24 Then they took him and
cast him into a pit. And the pit *was* empty;
there was no water in it.
25 [s]And they sat down to eat a meal.
Then they lifted their eyes and looked, and
there was a company of [t]Ishmaelites, coming from Gilead with their camels, bearing
spices, [u]balm, and myrrh, on their way to
carry *them* down to Egypt. 26 So Judah said
to his brothers, "What profit *is there* if we
kill our brother and [v]conceal his blood?
27 Come and let us sell him to the Ishmaelites, and [w]let not our hand be upon
him, for he *is* [x]our brother *and* [y]our flesh."
And his brothers listened. 28 Then [z]Midi-
anite traders passed by; so *the brothers*
pulled Joseph up and lifted him out of the
pit, [a]and sold him to the Ishmaelites for
[b]twenty *shekels* of silver. And they took Joseph to Egypt.
29 Then Reuben returned to the pit, and
indeed Joseph *was* not in the pit; and he
[c]tore his clothes. 30 And he returned to his
brothers and said, "The lad [d]*is* no *more;*
and I, where shall I go?"
31 So they took [e]Joseph's tunic, killed a
kid of the goats, and dipped the tunic in
the blood. 32 Then they sent the tunic of
many colors, and they brought *it* to their father and said, "We have found this. Do you

14 [l] Gen. 13:18; 23:2, 19; 35:27; Josh. 14:14, 15; Judg. 1:10
16 [m] Song 1:7
17 [n] 2 Kin. 6:13
18 [o] 1 Sam. 19:1; Ps. 31:13; 37:12, 32; Matt. 21:38; 26:3, 4; 27:1; Mark 14:1; John 11:53; Acts 23:12
19 [2] Lit. *master of dreams*
20 [p] Gen. 37:22; Prov. 1:11
21 [q] Gen. 42:22
23 [r] Matt. 27:28
25 [s] Prov. 30:20 [t] Gen. 16:11, 12; 37:28, 36; 39:1 [u] Jer. 8:22
26 [v] Gen. 37:20
27 [w] 1 Sam. 18:17 [x] Gen. 42:21 [y] Gen. 29:14
28 [z] Gen. 37:25; Judg. 6:1-3; 8:22, 24 [a] Gen. 45:4, 5; Ps. 105:17; Acts 7:9 [b] Matt. 27:9
29 [c] Gen. 37:34; 44:13; Job 1:20
30 [d] Gen. 42:13, 36
31 [e] Gen. 37:3, 23

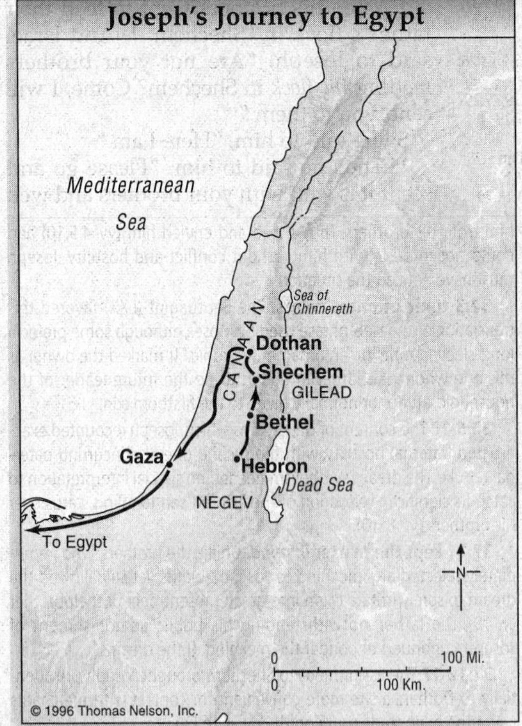

37:12,14 Shechem...Hebron. Shechem (*see note on 12:6*) was located ca. 50 mi. N of Hebron (*see note on 13:18*).

37:17 Dothan. Almost 15 mi. N of Shechem.

37:18-27 The brothers' plans for murder and cover-up, the fruit of hate and envy, were forestalled by two brothers: first by Reuben, who intended to affect a complete rescue (vv. 21,22), and then by Judah who, prompted by a passing merchants' caravan, proposed a profitable alternative to fratricide (vv. 25-27).

37:25 Ishmaelites. Also known as Midianites (cf. vv. 28,36; 39:1). The descendants of Ishmael and of Abraham through Keturah and Midian (25:1,2) were sufficiently intermarried or were such inveterate travelers and traders, that they were viewed as synonymous groups. These were coming W from Gilead. **Gilead.** *See note on 31:21.*

37:27 This criminal behavior would later be prohibited by the Mosaic legislation (Ex. 21:16; Deut. 24:7)

37:28 twenty *shekels* of silver. This was the average price of a slave at that time in the second millennium B.C. Although most slaves were part of the booty of military conquest, private and commercial slave-trading was also common. Joseph was sold into slavery ca. 1897 B.C.

37:29 Reuben...tore his clothes. Although he was absent at the time of the sale, he would be held responsible for the treachery, and so joined in the cover-up (vv. 30-35). His grief manifested how much he had actually wanted to rescue Joseph (see 42:22).

37:31-35 The deceiver of Isaac (27:18-29) was deceived by his own sons' lie. Sin's punishment is often long delayed.

know whether it *is* your son's tunic or
not?"
33 And he recognized it and said, "*It is*
my son's tunic. A [f]wild beast has devoured
him. Without doubt Joseph is torn to
pieces." 34 Then Jacob [g]tore his clothes, put
sackcloth on his waist, and [h]mourned for
his son many days. 35 And all his sons and
all his daughters [i]arose to comfort him; but
he refused to be comforted, and he said,
"For [j]I shall go down into the grave to my
son in mourning." Thus his father wept for
him.
36 Now [k]the [3]Midianites had sold him in
Egypt to Potiphar, an officer of Pharaoh
and captain of the guard.

Judah and Tamar

38 It came to pass at that time that Judah departed from his brothers,
and [a]visited a certain Adullamite whose
name *was* Hirah. 2 And Judah [b]saw there a
daughter of a certain Canaanite whose
name *was* [c]Shua, and he married her and
went in to her. 3 So she conceived and bore
a son, and he called his name [d]Er. 4 She
conceived again and bore a son, and she
called his name [e]Onan. 5 And she conceived yet again and bore a son, and called
his name [f]Shelah. He was at Chezib when
she bore him.
6 Then Judah [g]took a wife for Er his firstborn, and her name *was* [h]Tamar. 7 But [i]Er,
Judah's firstborn, was wicked in the sight
of the LORD, [j]and the LORD killed him.
8 And Judah said to Onan, "Go in to [k]your
brother's wife and marry her, and raise up
an heir to your brother." 9 But Onan knew
that the heir would not be [l]his; and it came
to pass, when he went in to his brother's
wife, that he emitted on the ground, lest he
should give an heir to his brother. 10 And
the thing which he did [1]displeased the
LORD; therefore He killed [m]him also.
11 Then Judah said to Tamar his daughter-in-law, [n]"Remain a widow in your father's house till my son Shelah is grown."
For he said, "Lest he also die like his brothers." And Tamar went and dwelt [o]in her father's house.
12 Now in the process of time the daughter of Shua, Judah's wife, died; and Judah
[p]was comforted, and went up to his
sheepshearers at Timnah, he and his friend
Hirah the Adullamite. 13 And it was told
Tamar, saying, "Look, your father-in-law is
going up [q]to Timnah to shear his sheep."
14 So she took off her widow's garments,
covered *herself* with a veil and wrapped
herself, and [r]sat in an open place which
was on the way to Timnah; for she saw
[s]that Shelah was grown, and she was not
given to him as a wife. 15 When Judah saw
her, he thought she *was* a harlot, because
she had covered her face. 16 Then he
turned to her by the way, and said, "Please
let me come in to you"; for he did not
know that she *was* his daughter-in-law.

33 [f]Gen. 37:20
34 [g]Gen. 37:29; 2 Sam. 3:31 [h]Gen. 50:10
35 [i]2 Sam. 12:17 [j]Gen. 25:8; 35:29; 42:38; 44:29, 31
36 [k]Gen. 39:1 [3]MT *Medanites*

CHAPTER 38

1 [a]2 Kin. 4:8
2 [b]Gen. 34:2 [c]1 Chr. 2:3
3 [d]Gen. 46:12; Num. 26:19
4 [e]Gen. 46:12; Num. 26:19
5 [f]Num. 26:20
6 [g]Gen. 21:21 [h]Ruth 4:12
7 [i]Gen. 46:12; Num. 26:19 [j]1 Chr. 2:3
8 [k]Deut. 25:5, 6; Matt. 22:24
9 [l]Deut. 25:6
10 [m]Gen. 46:12; Num. 26:19 [1]Lit. *was evil in the eyes of*
11 [n]Ruth 1:12, 13 [o]Lev. 22:13
12 [p]2 Sam. 13:39
13 [q]Josh. 15:10, 57; Judg. 14:1
14 [r]Prov. 7:12 [s]Gen. 38:11, 26

37:35 grave. This is the first OT use of this term for the abode of the dead (in 35:20 it is used to refer to an earthly burial plot). It is a general Hebrew term meaning the place of the dead (*Sheol*—used 65 times in the OT), referring to either the body in its decaying form or the soul in its conscious afterlife.

37:36 Potiphar. He was a prominent court official and high-ranking officer in Egypt, perhaps captain of the royal bodyguard (cf. 40:3,4). His name, a most unusual grammatical form for that period, either meant "the one whom the god Ra has given" or "the one who is placed on earth by Ra," making it a descriptive epithet more than a personal name. *See note on 40:3,4.*

38:1-30 The Judah-Interlude, as it is sometimes known, is bracketed by references to the sale of Joseph to Potiphar (37:36; 39:1). Such a parenthesis in the Joseph story demands some reason why a chapter laced with wickedness, immorality, and subterfuge should of necessity be placed in this spot. The answer is that the events recorded are chronologically in the right place, being contemporary with the time of Joseph's slavery in Egypt (v. 1, "at that time"). The account is also genealogically in the right place, i.e., with Joseph gone (seemingly for good), with Reuben, Simeon, and Levi out of favor (for incest and for treachery), Judah would most likely accede to firstborn status. It provides a contrast because it also demonstrates the immoral character of Judah, as compared with the virtue of Joseph. Canaanite syncretistic religion and inclusivism threatened to absorb the fourth and later generations of Abraham's heirs, but Egyptian exile and racial exclusivism produced not loss of their ethnic identity, but preservation of it.

38:1 Adullamite. Adullam was a town about 1 mi. NW of Hebron.

38:2-5 Judah's separation from his brethren was marked by more than the geographical; it involved integration. His Canaanite wife had 3 sons for his family line.

38:6-10 Two sons were executed by the Lord, one for unspecified wickedness and one for deliberate and rebellious rejection of the duty to marry a relative's widow, called a levirate marriage. This was a rather dubious distinction for the line of Judah to gain. For details on levirate marriage according to later Mosaic law, *see notes on Deut. 25:5-10;* see Introduction to Ruth.

38:11 Remain a widow...till my son. Taking her father-in-law at his word and residing at her father's household as a widow would do, Tamar vainly waited for Judah's third son to protect the inheritance rights of her deceased husband (v. 14) and finally resorted to subterfuge to obtain her rights (vv. 13-16). In so doing, she may have been influenced by Hittite inheritance practices which wickedly called the father-in-law into levirate marriage in the absence of sons to do so.

38:12 Timnah. The specific location in the hill country of Judah is unknown. Cf. Samson, Judg. 14:1.

38:13 shear his sheep. Such an event was frequently associated, in the ancient world, with festivity and licentious behavior characteristic of pagan fertility-cult practices.

38:14,15 Feeling that no one was going to give her a child, Tamar resorted to disguising herself as a prostitute, obviously knowing she could trap Judah, which says little for his moral stature in her eyes. Judah's Canaanite friend, Hirah (vv. 1,20), called her a shrine-prostitute (v. 21), which made Judah's actions no less excusable just because cultic prostitution was an accepted part of Canaanite culture. He solicited the iniquity by making the proposal to her (v. 16), and she played the role of a prostitute, negotiating the price (v. 17).

So she said, "What will you give me,
that you may come in to me?"
17 And he said, [t]"I will send a young
goat from the flock."
So she said, [u]"Will you give *me* a pledge
till you send *it?*"
18 Then he said, "What pledge shall I
give you?"
So she said, [v]"Your signet and cord, and
your staff that *is* in your hand." Then he
gave *them* to her, and went in to her, and
she conceived by him. 19 So she arose and
went away, and [w]laid aside her veil and
put on the garments of her widowhood.
20 And Judah sent the young goat by the
hand of his friend the Adullamite, to receive *his* pledge from the woman's hand,
but he did not find her. 21 Then he asked
the men of that place, saying, "Where is the
harlot who *was* [2]openly by the roadside?"
And they said, "There was no harlot in
this *place*."
22 So he returned to Judah and said, "I
cannot find her. Also, the men of the place
said there was no harlot in this *place*."
23 Then Judah said, "Let her take *them* for
herself, lest we be shamed; for I sent this
young goat and you have not found her."
24 And it came to pass, about three
months after, that Judah was told, saying,
"Tamar your daughter-in-law has [x]played
the harlot; furthermore she *is* [3]with child
by harlotry."
So Judah said, "Bring her out [y]and let
her be burned!"
25 When she *was* brought out, she sent to
her father-in-law, saying, "By the man to
whom these belong, I *am* with child." And
she said, [z]"Please determine whose these
are—the signet and cord, and staff."
26 So Judah [a]acknowledged *them* and
said, [b]"She has been more righteous than I,
because [c]I did not give her to Shelah my
son." And he [d]never knew her again.
27 Now it came to pass, at the time for
giving birth, that behold, twins *were* in her
womb. 28 And so it was, when she was giving birth, that *the one* put out *his* hand; and
the midwife took a scarlet *thread* and
bound it on his hand, saying, "This one
came out first." 29 Then it happened, as he
drew back his hand, that his brother came
out unexpectedly; and she said, "How did
you break through? *This* breach *be* upon
you!" Therefore his name was called
[e]Perez.[4] 30 Afterward his brother came out
who had the scarlet *thread* on his hand.
And his name was called [f]Zerah.

Joseph a Slave in Egypt

39 Now Joseph had been taken [a]down
to Egypt. And [b]Potiphar, an officer
of Pharaoh, captain of the guard, an Egyptian, [c]bought him from the Ishmaelites
who had taken him down there. 2 [d]The
LORD was with Joseph, and he was a successful man; and he was in the house of his
master the Egyptian. 3 And his master saw
that the LORD *was* with him and that the
LORD [e]made all he did [1]to prosper in his
hand. 4 So Joseph [f]found favor in his sight,
and served him. Then he made him [g]over-
seer of his house, and all *that* he had he put
[2]under his authority. 5 So it was, from the
time *that* he had made him overseer of his
house and all that he had, that [h]the LORD
blessed the Egyptian's house for Joseph's
sake; and the blessing of the LORD was on
all that he had in the house and in the field.
6 Thus he left all that he had in Joseph's

17 [t]Judg. 15:1; Ezek. 16:33 [u]Gen. 38:20
18 [v]Gen. 38:25; 41:42
19 [w]Gen. 38:14
21 [2]*in full view*
24 [x]Judg. 19:2 [y]Lev. 20:14; 21:9; Deut. 22:21 [3]*pregnant*
25 [z]Gen. 37:32; 38:18
26 [a]Gen. 37:33 [b]1 Sam. 24:17 [c]Gen. 38:14 [d]Job 34:31, 32
29 [e]Gen. 46:12; Num. 26:20; Ruth 4:12; 1 Chr. 2:4; Matt. 1:3 [4]Lit. *Breach* or *Breakthrough*
30 [f]Gen. 46:12; 1 Chr. 2:4; Matt. 1:3

CHAPTER 39

1 [a]Gen. 12:10; 43:15 [b]Gen. 37:36; Ps. 105:17 [c]Gen. 37:28; 45:4
2 [d]Gen. 26:24, 28; 28:15; 35:3; 39:3, 21, 23; 1 Sam. 16:18; 18:14, 28; Acts 7:9
3 [e]Ps. 1:3 [1]*to be a success*
4 [f]Gen. 18:3; 19:19; 39:21 [g]Gen. 24:2, 10; 39:8, 22; 41:40 [2]Lit. *in his hand*
5 [h]Gen. 18:26; 30:27; 2 Sam. 6:11

38:18 signet and cord, and your staff. A prominent man in the ancient Near East endorsed contracts with the cylinder seal he wore on a cord around his neck. Her request for the walking stick suggests it also had sufficient identifying marks on it (cf. v. 25, "please determine whose these are . . ."). The custom of using 3 pieces of identification is attested to in Ugaritic (Canaanite) literature.

38:20-23 It was not good for one's reputation to keep asking for the whereabouts of a prostitute.

38:24 let her be burned! Double standards prevailed in that Judah, no less guilty than Tamar, commanded her execution for immorality. Later Mosaic legislation would prescribe this form of the death penalty for a priest's daughter who prostituted herself or for those guilty of certain forms of incest (Lev. 20:14; 21:9).

38:26 more righteous than I. This was not an accolade for her moral character and faith, but a commendation by Judah for her attention to inheritance rights of her family line and his shameful neglect thereof. Her death sentence was rescinded.

38:29 Perez. This first of the twins, born of prostitution and incest to Tamar, nevertheless came into the messianic line, which went through Boaz and Ruth to King David (Ruth 4:18-22; Matt. 1:3). His name means "breach" or "pushing through."

39:1 Potiphar. *See note on 37:36.* **Ishmaelites.** *See note on 37:25.*

39:2 The LORD was with Joseph. Any and all ideas that Joseph, twice a victim of injustice, had been abandoned by the Lord are summarily banished by the employment of phrases highlighting God's oversight of his circumstances, e.g. "with him" (vv. 3,21), "made all he did prosper" (vv. 3,23), "found/gave him favor" (vv. 4,21), "blessed/blessing" (v. 5), and "showed him mercy" (v. 21). Neither being unjustly sold into slavery and forcibly removed from the Land (37:28), nor being unjustly accused of sexual harassment and imprisoned (vv. 13-18) were events signaling even a temporary loss of divine superintendence of Joseph's life and God's purpose for His people, Israel.

39:2-4 successful . . . overseer of his house. This involved the authority and trust as the steward of the whole estate (v. 5, "house and field" and v. 9, "no one greater"), one of the criteria for which was trust. No doubt Joseph was conversant in the Egyptian language (*see note on 29:9*).

39:5 blessing of the LORD. Joseph was experiencing fulfillment of the Abrahamic Covenant, even at that time before Israel was in the Land (see 12:1-3).

39:6 except for the bread which he ate. Since Joseph proved trustworthy enough to need no oversight, his master concerned him-

[3]hand, and he did not know what he had
except for the [4]bread which he ate.
Now Joseph [i]was handsome in form and
appearance.
7 And it came to pass after these things
that his master's wife [5]cast longing eyes on
Joseph, and she said, [j]"Lie with me."
8 But he refused and said to his master's
wife, "Look, my master does not know
what *is* with me in the house, and he has
committed all that he has to my hand.
9 *There is* no one greater in this house than
I, nor has he kept back anything from me
but you, because you *are* his wife. [k]How
then can I do this great wickedness, and
[l]sin against God?"
10 So it was, as she spoke to Joseph day
by day, that he [m]did not heed her, to lie
with her *or* to be with her.
11 But it happened about this time, when
Joseph went into the house to do his work,
and none of the men of the house *was* inside, 12 that she [n]caught him by his garment, saying, "Lie with me." But he left his
garment in her hand, and fled and ran outside. 13 And so it was, when she saw that
he had left his garment in her hand and
fled outside, 14 that she called to the men
of her house and spoke to them, saying,
"See, he has brought in to us a [o]Hebrew to
[6]mock us. He came in to me to lie with me,
and I cried out with a loud voice. 15 And it
happened, when he heard that I lifted my
voice and cried out, that he left his garment with me, and fled and went outside."
16 So she kept his garment with her until
his master came home. 17 Then she [p]spoke
to him with words like these, saying, "The
Hebrew servant whom you brought to us
came in to me to mock me; 18 so it happened, as I lifted my voice and cried out,
that he left his garment with me and fled
outside."
19 So it was, when his master heard the
words which his wife spoke to him, saying, "Your servant did to me after this
manner," that his [q]anger was aroused.
20 Then Joseph's master took him and [r]put
him into the [s]prison, a place where the
king's prisoners *were* confined. And he was
there in the prison. 21 But the LORD was
with Joseph and showed him mercy, and
He [t]gave[7] him favor in the sight of the
keeper of the prison. 22 And the keeper of
the prison [u]committed to Joseph's hand all
the prisoners who *were* in the prison; whatever they did there, it was his doing. 23 The
keeper of the prison did not look into anything *that was* under [8]*Joseph's* authority, because [v]the LORD was with him; and whatever he did, the LORD made *it* prosper.

The Prisoners' Dreams

40 It came to pass after these things
that the [a]butler and the baker of the
king of Egypt offended their lord, the king
of Egypt. 2 And Pharaoh was [b]angry with
his two officers, the chief butler and the
chief baker. 3 [c]So he put them in custody in
the house of the captain of the guard, in the
prison, the place where Joseph *was* confined. 4 And the captain of the guard
charged Joseph with them, and he served
them; so they were in custody for a while.

6 [i]Gen. 29:17; 1 Sam. 16:12 [3]Care [4]Food
7 [j]2 Sam. 13:11 [5]Lit. *lifted up her eyes toward*
9 [k]Lev. 20:10; Prov. 6:29, 32 [l]Gen. 20:6; 42:18; 2 Sam. 12:13; Ps. 51:4
10 [m]Prov. 1:10
12 [n]Prov. 7:13
14 [o]Gen. 14:13; 41:12 [6]*laugh at*
17 [p]Ex. 23:1; Ps. 120:3; Prov. 26:28
19 [q]Prov. 6:34, 35
20 [r]Ps. 105:18; [1 Pet. 2:19] [s]Gen. 40:3, 15; 41:14
21 [t]Gen. 39:2; Ex. 3:21; Ps. 105:19; [Prov. 16:7]; Dan. 1:9; Acts 7:9, 10 [7]Caused him to be viewed with favor by
22 [u]Gen. 39:4; 40:3, 4
23 [v]Gen. 39:2, 3 [8]Lit. *his hand*

CHAPTER 40

1 [a]Gen. 40:11, 13; Neh. 1:11
2 [b]Prov. 16:14
3 [c]Gen. 39:1, 20, 23; 41:10

self only with his own meals or his very own personal affairs. Joseph himself remarked that Potiphar had delegated to him so much, that he no longer knew the full extent of his own business affairs (v. 8); in fact, he knew only what was set before him (v. 6).

39:9 this great wickedness. Joseph explained, when first tempted, that adultery would be a gross violation of his ethical convictions which demanded 1) the utmost respect for his master and 2) a life of holiness before his God. Far more was involved than compliance with the letter of an ancient Near Eastern law-code, many of which did forbid adultery, but rather obedience to the moral standards belonging to one who walked with God, and that long before Mosaic law-code prescriptions applied (cf. Ps. 51:4).

39:10-18 Her incessant efforts to seduce Joseph failed in the face of his strong convictions not to yield nor be compromised. At flashpoint, Joseph fled! Based on false accusations, Joseph was deemed guilty and imprisoned. Cf. 2 Tim. 2:22 for a NT picture of Joseph's attitude.

39:12 his garment. See 37:31-35 for the other time one of Joseph's cloaks was used in a conspiracy against him.

39:17 Hebrew servant. This term was used by Potiphar's wife as a pejorative, intended to heap scorn upon someone considered definitely unworthy of any respect. Its use may also suggest some latent attitudes toward dwellers in Canaan, which could be aggravated to her advantage. Potiphar's wife also neatly shifted the blame onto her husband for having hired the Hebrew in the first place (vv. 16-18) and stated this also before the servants (v. 14).

39:19,20 The death penalty for adultery may not have applied to a charge of attempted adultery, attempted seduction or rape (cf. vv. 14,18), so Potiphar consigned Joseph to the prison reserved for royal servants, from where, in the providence of God, he would be summoned into Pharaoh's presence and begin the next stage of his life (cf. chaps. 40,41). *See note on 40:3,4.*

39:21 showed him mercy. God did not permit this initial painful imprisonment to continue (cf. Ps. 105:18,19).

39:22,23 Once again Joseph, though in circumstances considerably less comfortable than Potiphar's home, rose to a position of trust and authority and proved to be trustworthy enough not to need any oversight.

40:1 the king of Egypt. To be identified as Senusert II, ca. 1894–1878 B.C.

40:2 the chief butler and the chief baker. Both these occupations and ranks in Pharaoh's court are attested in existing ancient Egyptian documents. The "butler" was the king's cupbearer, who gave him his drinks. The baker cooked his bread. Both had to be trustworthy and beyond the influence of the monarch's enemies.

40:3,4 captain of the guard. *See note on 37:36.* If this was Potiphar, the captain of the guard, then Joseph's former master directed him to attend to the two royal servants remanded into his custody until sentence was past. This prison was also called "the house of the captain of the guard" (v. 3), "his lord's house" (v. 7), and "dungeon" (40:15; 41:14), unless Joseph had been moved to another penal facility.

5 Then the butler and the baker of the
king of Egypt, who *were* confined in the
prison, [d]had a dream, both of them, each
man's dream in one night *and* each man's
dream with its *own* interpretation. 6 And
Joseph came in to them in the morning and
looked at them, and saw that they *were*
[1]sad. 7 So he asked Pharaoh's officers who
were with him in the custody of his lord's
house, saying, [e]"Why do you look *so* sad
today?"
8 And they said to him, [f]"We each have
had a dream, and *there is* no interpreter of
it."
So Joseph said to them, [g]"Do not interpretations belong to God? Tell *them* to me,
please."
9 Then the chief butler told his dream to
Joseph, and said to him, "Behold, in my
dream a vine *was* before me, 10 and in the
vine *were* three branches; it *was* as though it
budded, its blossoms shot forth, and its
clusters brought forth ripe grapes. 11 Then
Pharaoh's cup *was* in my hand; and I took
the grapes and pressed them into Pharaoh's cup, and placed the cup in Pharaoh's hand."
12 And Joseph said to him, [h]"This *is* the
interpretation of it: The three branches [i]*are*
three days. 13 Now within three days Pharaoh will [j]lift up your head and restore you
to your [2]place, and you will put Pharaoh's
cup in his hand according to the former
manner, when you were his butler. 14 But
[k]remember me when it is well with you,
and [l]please show kindness to me; make
mention of me to Pharaoh, and get me out
of this house. 15 For indeed I was [m]stolen
away from the land of the Hebrews; [n]and
also I have done nothing here that they
should put me into the dungeon."
16 When the chief baker saw that the interpretation was good, he said to Joseph, "I
also *was* in my dream, and there *were* three
[3]white baskets on my head. 17 In the uppermost basket *were* all kinds of baked
goods for Pharaoh, and the birds ate them
out of the basket on my head."
18 So Joseph answered and said, [o]"This
is the interpretation of it: The three baskets
are three days. 19 [p]Within three days Pharaoh will lift [4]off your head from you and
[q]hang you on a tree; and the birds will eat
your flesh from you."
20 Now it came to pass on the third day,
which was Pharaoh's [r]birthday, that he
[s]made a feast for all his servants; and he
[t]lifted up the head of the chief butler and
of the chief baker among his servants.
21 Then he [u]restored the chief butler to his
butlership again, and [v]he placed the cup in
Pharaoh's hand. 22 But he [w]hanged the
chief baker, as Joseph had interpreted to
them. 23 Yet the chief butler did not remember Joseph, but [x]forgot him.

Pharaoh's Dreams

41 Then it came to pass, at the end of
two full years, that [a]Pharaoh had a
dream; and behold, he stood by the river.
2 Suddenly there came up out of the river
seven cows, fine looking and fat; and they
fed in the meadow. 3 Then behold, seven
other cows came up after them out of the
river, ugly and gaunt, and stood by the
other cows on the bank of the river. 4 And
the ugly and gaunt cows ate up the seven
fine looking and fat cows. So Pharaoh
awoke. 5 He slept and dreamed a second
time; and suddenly seven heads of grain
came up on one stalk, plump and good.
6 Then behold, seven thin heads, blighted

5 [d]Gen. 37:5; 41:1
6 [1]*dejected*
7 [e]Neh. 2:2
8 [f]Gen. 41:15 [g][Gen. 41:16; Dan. 2:11, 20-22, 27, 28, 47]
12 [h]Gen. 40:18; 41:12, 25; Judg. 7:14; Dan. 2:36; 4:18, 19 [i]Gen. 40:18; 42:17
13 [j]2 Kin. 25:27; Ps. 3:3; Jer. 52:31 [2]*position*
14 [k]1 Sam. 25:31; Luke 23:42 [l]Gen. 24:49; 47:29; Josh. 2:12; 1 Sam. 20:14, 15; 2 Sam. 9:1; 1 Kin. 2:7
15 [m]Gen. 37:26-28 [n]Gen. 39:20
16 [3]Or *baskets of white bread*
18 [o]Gen. 40:12
19 [p]Gen. 40:13 [q]Deut. 21:22 [4]Lit. *up*
20 [r]Matt. 14:6-10 [s]Mark 6:21 [t]Gen. 40:13, 19; 2 Kin. 25:27; Jer. 52:31; Matt. 25:19
21 [u]Gen. 40:13 [v]Neh. 2:1
22 [w]Gen. 40:19; Deut. 21:23; Esth. 7:10
23 [x]Job 19:14; Ps. 31:12; Eccl. 9:15, 16; Is. 49:15; Amos 6:6

CHAPTER 41

1 [a]Gen. 40:5; Judg. 7:13

40:5 dream. Oneiromancy, the science or practice of interpreting dreams, flourished in ancient Egypt because dreams were thought to determine the future. Both Egypt and Babylon developed a professional class of dream interpreters. Deuteronomy 13:1-5 shows that such dream interpreters were part of ancient false religion and to be avoided by God's people. By some 500 years later, a detailed manual of dream interpretation had been compiled. Unlike Joseph, neither butler nor baker understood the significance of their dreams (cf. 37:5-11).

40:8 interpretations belong to God. Joseph was careful to give credit to his Lord (cf. 41:16). Daniel, the only other Hebrew whom God allowed to accurately interpret revelatory dreams, was just as careful to do so (Dan. 2:28). Significantly, God chose both men to play an important role for Israel while serving pagan monarchs and stepping forward at the critical moment to interpret their dreams and reveal their futures.

40:9-13 the chief butler. Consistent with his duty as the cupbearer to the king, he dreamed of a drink prepared for Pharaoh. It was a sign that he would be released and returned to his position (v. 13).

40:14,15 remember me. A poignant appeal to the butler, whose future was secure, to speak a word for Joseph's freedom, because he knew butlers had the ear of kings. The butler quickly forgot Joseph (v. 23) until his memory was prompted just at the right moment two years later (41:1,9).

40:15 the land of the Hebrews. Giving this designation to the land of Canaan indicates that Joseph understood the land promise of the Abrahamic Covenant.

40:16 the interpretation was good. The chief baker, noting some similarity in the dreams, was encouraged to request interpretation of his dream. Joseph's words employ a subtle play upon words: the butler's head would be "lifted up" (v. 13) but the baker's would be "lifted off" (v. 18).

40:20 Pharaoh's birthday. The Rosetta Stone (discovered in A.D. 1799, this is a trilingual artifact from Egyptian antiquity, ca. 196 B.C., whose Greek inscription enabled linguists to understand the language of hieroglyphics) records a custom of releasing Pharaoh's prisoners, but at this party held for his servants, Pharaoh rendered two very different kinds of judgment (vv. 21,22).

41:1 the river. Probably the Nile River, which dominated Egyptian life.

by the [b]east wind, sprang up after them.
7 And the seven thin heads devoured the
seven plump and full heads. So Pharaoh
awoke, and indeed, *it was* a dream. 8 Now
it came to pass in the morning [c]that his
spirit was troubled, and he sent and called
for all [d]the magicians of Egypt and all its
[e]wise men. And Pharaoh told them his
dreams, but *there was* no one who could interpret them for Pharaoh.
9 Then the [f]chief butler spoke to Pharaoh, saying: "I remember my faults this
day. 10 When Pharaoh was [g]angry with his
servants, [h]and put me in custody in the
house of the captain of the guard, *both* me
and the chief baker, 11 [i]we each had a
dream in one night, he and I. Each of us
dreamed according to the interpretation of
his *own* dream. 12 Now there *was* a young
[j]Hebrew man with us there, a [k]servant of
the captain of the guard. And we told him,
and he [l]interpreted our dreams for us; to
each man he interpreted according to his
own dream. 13 And it came to pass, just [m]as
he interpreted for us, so it happened. He
restored me to my office, and he hanged
him."
14 [n]Then Pharaoh sent and called Joseph, and they [o]brought him quickly [p]out
of the dungeon; and he shaved, [q]changed
his clothing, and came to Pharaoh. 15 And
Pharaoh said to Joseph, "I have had a
dream, and *there is* no one who can interpret it. [r]But I have heard it said of you *that*
you can understand a dream, to interpret
it."
16 So Joseph answered Pharaoh, saying,
[s]"*It is* not in me; [t]God will give Pharaoh an
answer of peace."
17 Then Pharaoh said to Joseph: "Behold, [u]in my dream I stood on the bank of
the river. 18 Suddenly seven cows came up
out of the river, fine looking and fat; and
they fed in the meadow. 19 Then behold,
seven other cows came up after them, poor
and very ugly and gaunt, such ugliness as
I have never seen in all the land of Egypt.
20 And the gaunt and ugly cows ate up the
first seven, the fat cows. 21 When they had
eaten them up, no one would have known
that they had eaten them, for they *were* just
as ugly as at the beginning. So I awoke.
22 Also I saw in my dream, and suddenly
seven [1]heads came up on one stalk, full
and good. 23 Then behold, seven heads,
withered, thin, *and* blighted by the east
wind, sprang up after them. 24 And the
thin heads devoured the seven good
heads. So [v]I told *this* to the magicians, but
there was no one who could explain *it* to
me."
25 Then Joseph said to Pharaoh, "The
dreams of Pharaoh *are* one; [w]God has
shown Pharaoh what He *is* about to do:
26 The seven good cows *are* seven years,
and the seven good [2]heads *are* seven years;
the dreams *are* one. 27 And the seven thin
and ugly cows which came up after them
are seven years, and the seven empty heads
blighted by the east wind are [x]seven years
of famine. 28 [y]This *is* the thing which I
have spoken to Pharaoh. God has shown
Pharaoh what He *is* about to do. 29 Indeed
[z]seven years of great plenty will come
throughout all the land of Egypt; 30 but
after them seven years of famine will
[a]arise, and all the plenty will be forgotten
in the land of Egypt; and the famine [b]will
deplete the land. 31 So the plenty will not
be known in the land because of the
famine following, for it *will be* very severe.
32 And the dream was repeated to Pharaoh
twice because the [c]thing *is* established by
God, and God will shortly bring it to pass.
33 "Now therefore, let Pharaoh select a
discerning and wise man, and set him over
the land of Egypt. 34 Let Pharaoh do *this*,
and let him appoint [3]officers over the land,
[d]to collect one-fifth *of the produce* of the
land of Egypt in the seven plentiful years.
35 And [e]let them gather all the food of
those good years that are coming, and
store up grain under the [4]authority of
Pharaoh, and let them keep food in the
cities. 36 Then that food shall be as a [5]re-
serve for the land for the seven years of
famine which shall be in the land of Egypt,

6 [b] Ex. 10:13; Ezek. 17:10
8 [c] Dan. 2:1, 3; 4:5, 19 [d] Ex. 7:11, 22; Is. 29:14; Dan. 1:20; 2:2; 4:7 [e] Matt. 2:1
9 [f] Gen. 40:1, 14, 23
10 [g] Gen. 40:2, 3 [h] Gen. 39:20
11 [i] Gen. 40:5; Judg. 7:15
12 [j] Gen. 39:14; 43:32 [k] Gen. 37:36 [l] Gen. 40:12
13 [m] Gen. 40:21, 22
14 [n] Ps. 105:20 [o] Dan. 2:25 [p] [1 Sam. 2:8] [q] 2 Kin. 25:27-29
15 [r] Gen. 41:8, 12; Dan. 5:16
16 [s] Dan. 2:30; Acts 3:12; [2 Cor. 3:5] [t] Gen. 40:8; 41:25, 28, 32; Deut. 29:29; Dan. 2:22, 28, 47
17 [u] Gen. 41:1
22 [1] Heads of grain
24 [v] Gen. 41:8; Ex. 7:11; Is. 8:19; Dan. 4:7
25 [w] Gen. 41:28, 32; Dan. 2:28, 29, 45; Rev. 4:1
26 [2] Heads of grain
27 [x] 2 Kin. 8:1
28 [y] [Gen. 41:25, 32; Dan. 2:28]
29 [z] Gen. 41:47
30 [a] Gen. 41:54, 56 [b] Gen. 47:13; Ps. 105:16
32 [c] Gen. 41:25, 28; Num. 23:19; Is. 46:10, 11
34 [d] [Prov. 6:6-8] [3] *overseers*
35 [e] Gen. 41:48 [4] Lit. *hand*
36 [5] Lit. *supply*

41:8 no one who could interpret. The combined expertise of a full council of Pharaoh's advisers and dream experts, all of whom had been summoned into his presence, failed to provide an interpretation of the two disturbing dreams. Without knowing it, they had just set the stage for Joseph's entrance on the scene of Egyptian history.

41:9 Then the chief butler spoke. With memory suitably prompted, the butler apologized for his neglect ("I remember my faults"), and apprised Pharaoh of the Hebrew prisoner and his accurate interpretation of dreams two years earlier (vv. 10-13).

41:14 Then Pharaoh sent and called Joseph. The urgent summons had Joseph in front of Pharaoh with minimum delay, in prized, clean-shaven Egyptian style for a proper appearance.

41:16 *It is* not in me; God will give. Deprecating any innate ability, Joseph advised at the very outset that the answer Pharaoh desired could only come from God.

41:25 God has shown. Joseph's interpretation kept the focus fixed upon what God had determined for Egypt (vv. 28,32).

41:33-36 After interpreting the dream, Joseph told Pharaoh how to survive the next 14 years. Incongruously, Joseph, a slave and a prisoner, appended to the interpretation a long-term strategy for establishing reserves to meet the future need, and included advice on the quality of the man to head up the project. Famines had ravaged Egypt before, but this time divine warning permitted serious and sustained advance planning.

that the land [f]may not [6]perish during the
famine."

Joseph's Rise to Power

37 So [g]the advice was good in the eyes of
Pharaoh and in the eyes of all his servants.
38 And Pharaoh said to his servants, "Can
we find *such a one* as this, a man [h]in whom
is the Spirit of God?"
39 Then Pharaoh said to Joseph, "Inasmuch as God has shown you all this, *there*
is no one as discerning and wise as you.
40 [i]You shall be [7]over my house, and all
my people shall be ruled according to your
word; only in regard to the throne will I be
greater than you." 41 And Pharaoh said to
Joseph, "See, I have [j]set you over all the
land of Egypt."
42 Then Pharaoh [k]took his signet ring off
his hand and put it on Joseph's hand; and
he [l]clothed him in garments of fine linen
[m]and put a gold chain around his neck.
43 And he had him ride in the second
[n]chariot which he had; [o]and they cried out
before him, "Bow the knee!" So he set him
[p]over all the land of Egypt. 44 Pharaoh also
said to Joseph, "I *am* Pharaoh, and without
your consent no man may lift his hand or
foot in all the land of Egypt." 45 And Pharaoh called Joseph's name [8]Zaphnath-
Paaneah. And he gave him as a wife [q]Ase-
nath, the daughter of Poti-Pherah priest of
On. So Joseph went out over *all* the land of
Egypt.
46 Joseph was thirty years old when he
[r]stood before Pharaoh king of Egypt. And

36 [f]Gen. 47:15, 19 [6]*be cut off*
37 [g]Ps. 105:19; Acts 7:10
38 [h]Num. 27:18; [Job 32:8; Prov. 2:6]; Dan. 4:8, 9, 18; 5:11, 14; 6:3
40 [i]Ps. 105:21; Acts 7:10 [7]In charge of
41 [j]Gen. 42:6; Ps. 105:21; Dan. 6:3; Acts 7:10
42 [k]Esth. 3:10 [l]Esth. 8:2, 15 [m]Dan. 5:7, 16, 29
43 [n]Gen. 46:29 [o]Esth. 6:9 [p]Gen. 42:6
45 [q]Gen. 46:20 [8]Probably Egyptian for *God Speaks and He Lives*
46 [r]1 Sam. 16:21; 1 Kin. 12:6, 8; Dan. 1:19
47 [9]Lit. *by handfuls*
49 [s]Gen. 22:17; Judg. 7:12; 1 Sam. 13:5
50 [t]Gen. 46:20; 48:5
51 [u]Ps. 45:10 [1]Lit. *Making Forgetful*
52 [v]Gen. 17:6; 28:3; 49:22 [2]Lit. *Fruitfulness*
54 [w]Ps. 105:16; Acts 7:11 [x]Gen. 41:30
55 [y]John 2:5
56 [z]Gen. 42:6 [3]Lit. *all that was in them*
57 [a]Ezek. 29:12

Joseph went out from the presence of Pharaoh, and went throughout all the land of
Egypt. 47 Now in the seven plentiful years
the ground brought forth [9]abundantly.
48 So he gathered up all the food of the
seven years which were in the land of
Egypt, and laid up the food in the cities; he
laid up in every city the food of the fields
which surrounded them. 49 Joseph gathered very much grain, [s]as the sand of the
sea, until he stopped counting, for *it was*
immeasurable.
50 [t]And to Joseph were born two sons
before the years of famine came, whom
Asenath, the daughter of Poti-Pherah
priest of On, bore to him. 51 Joseph called
the name of the firstborn [1]Manasseh: "For
God has made me forget all my toil and all
my [u]father's house." 52 And the name of
the second he called [2]Ephraim: "For God
has caused me to be [v]fruitful in the land of
my affliction."
53 Then the seven years of plenty which
were in the land of Egypt ended, 54 [w]and
the seven years of famine began to come,
[x]as Joseph had said. The famine was in all
lands, but in all the land of Egypt there
was bread. 55 So when all the land of Egypt
was famished, the people cried to Pharaoh
for bread. Then Pharaoh said to all the
Egyptians, "Go to Joseph; [y]whatever he
says to you, do." 56 The famine was over
all the face of the earth, and Joseph opened
[3]all the storehouses and [z]sold to the Egyptians. And the famine became severe in the
land of Egypt. 57 [a]So all countries came to

41:37-41 To Pharaoh and his royal retinue, no other candidate but Joseph qualified for the task of working out this good plan, because they recognized that he spoke God-given revelation and insight (v. 39). Joseph's focus on his Lord had taken him from prison to the palace quickly (v. 41).

41:38 Spirit of God. The Egyptians did not understand about the third person of the triune Godhead. They merely meant that God had assisted Joseph, thus "spirit" would be more appropriate than "Spirit."

41:41 set you over all the land of Egypt. The country-wide jurisdiction accorded to Joseph receives frequent mention in the narrative (vv. 43, 44, 46, 55; 42:6; 45:8).

41:42 signet ring…garments…gold chain. Emblems of office and a reward of clothing and jewelry suitable to the new rank accompanied Pharaoh's appointment of Joseph as vizier, or prime minister, the second-in-command (v. 40; 45:8, 26). Joseph wore the royal seal on his finger, authorizing him to transact the affairs of state on behalf of Pharaoh himself.

41:43-45 Other awards appropriate to promotion were also bestowed upon Joseph, namely official and recognizable transportation (v. 43), an Egyptian name (v. 45), and an Egyptian wife (v. 45). Further, the populace was commanded to show deference for their vizier (v. 43, "bow the knee"). All these dreams had been revealed by God, in a rare display of manifesting truth through pagans, so that Joseph would be established in Egypt as a leader and, thus elevated, could be used for the preservation of God's people when the famine came to Canaan. Thus, God cared for His people and fulfilled His promises (*see note on 45:1-8*).

41:43 the second chariot. This signified to all that Joseph was second-in-command.

41:45 Zaphnath-Paaneah. This name probably means "The Nourisher of the Two Lands, the Living One" but various other proposals have also been suggested (see marginal note); certainty of that meaning still eludes scholars. Foreigners are known to have been assigned an Egyptian name.

41:46 thirty years old. Ca. 1884 B.C. Only 13 years had elapsed since his involuntary departure from "the land of the Hebrews" (cf. 40:15). Joseph had been 17 when the narrative commenced (37:2).

41:50 On. One of the 4 great Egyptian cities, also called Heliopolis, which was known as the chief city of the sun god, Ra. It was located ca. 19 mi. N of ancient Memphis.

41:51,52 Manasseh…Ephraim. The names, meaning "forgetful" and "fruitful," assigned to his sons together with their explanations depict the centrality of God in Joseph's worldview. Years of suffering, pagan presence, and separation from his own family had not harmed his faith.

41:54-57 Use of hyperbole with "all" (vv. 54, 56, 57) emphatically indicates the widespread ravaging impact of famine far beyond Egypt's borders. She had become indeed the "breadbasket" of the ancient world.

41:55,56 Go to Joseph. After 7 years, Joseph's authority re-

Joseph in Egypt to [b]buy *grain,* because the
famine was severe in all lands.

Joseph's Brothers Go to Egypt

42 When [a]Jacob saw that there was
grain in Egypt, Jacob said to his
sons, "Why do you look at one another?"
2 And he said, "Indeed I have heard that
there is grain in Egypt; go down to that
place and buy for us there, that we may
[b]live and not die."
3 So Joseph's ten brothers went down to
buy grain in Egypt. 4 But Jacob did not
send Joseph's brother Benjamin with his
brothers, for he said, [c]"Lest some calamity
befall him." 5 And the sons of Israel went
to buy *grain* among those who journeyed,
for the famine was [d]in the land of Canaan.
6 Now Joseph *was* governor [e]over the
land; and it was he who sold to all the people of the land. And Joseph's brothers
came and [f]bowed down before him with
their faces to the earth. 7 Joseph saw his
brothers and recognized them, but he
acted as [g]a stranger to them and spoke
[1]roughly to them. Then he said to them,
"Where do you come from?"
And they said, "From the land of
Canaan to buy food."
8 So Joseph recognized his brothers, but
they did not recognize him. 9 Then Joseph
[h]remembered the dreams which he had
dreamed about them, and said to them,
"You *are* spies! You have come to see the
[2]nakedness of the land!"
10 And they said to him, "No, my lord,
but your servants have come to buy food.
11 We *are* all one man's sons; we *are* honest
men; your servants are not spies."

57 [b]Gen. 27:28, 37; 42:3

CHAPTER 42

1 [a]Acts 7:12
2 [b]Gen. 43:8; Ps. 33:18, 19; Is. 38:1
4 [c]Gen. 42:38
5 [d]Gen. 12:10; 26:1; 41:57; Acts 7:11
6 [e]Gen. 41:41, 55 [f]Gen. 37:7-10; 41:43; Is. 60:14
7 [g]Gen. 45:1, 2 [1]*harshly*
9 [h]Gen. 37:5-9 [2]Exposed parts

12 But he said to them, "No, but you have
come to see the nakedness of the land."
13 And they said, "Your servants *are*
twelve brothers, the sons of one man in the
land of Canaan; and in fact, the youngest *is*
with our father today, and one [i]*is* no more."
14 But Joseph said to them, "It *is* as I
spoke to you, saying, 'You *are* spies!' 15 In
this *manner* you shall be tested: [j]By the life
of Pharaoh, you shall not leave this place
unless your youngest brother comes here.
16 Send one of you, and let him bring your
brother; and you shall be [3]kept in prison,
that your words may be tested to see
whether *there is* any truth in you; or else,
by the life of Pharaoh, surely you *are*
spies!" 17 So he [4]put them all together in
prison [k]three days.
18 Then Joseph said to them the third
day, "Do this and live, [l]*for* I fear God: 19 If
you *are* honest *men,* let one of your brothers be confined to your prison house; but
you, go and carry grain for the famine of
your houses. 20 And [m]bring your youngest
brother to me; so your words will be verified, and you shall not die."
And they did so. 21 Then they said to
one another, [n]"We *are* truly guilty concerning our brother, for we saw the anguish of
his soul when he pleaded with us, and we
would not hear; [o]therefore this distress has
come upon us."
22 And Reuben answered them, saying,
[p]"Did I not speak to you, saying, 'Do not
sin against the boy'; and you would not listen? Therefore behold, his blood is now
[q]required of us." 23 But they did not know
that Joseph understood *them,* for he spoke
to them through an interpreter. 24 And he
turned himself away from them and

13 [i]Gen. 37:30; 42:32; 44:20; Lam. 5:7
15 [j]1 Sam. 1:26; 17:55
16 [3]Lit. *bound*
17 [k]Gen. 40:4, 7, 12 [4]Lit. *gathered*
18 [l]Gen. 22:12; 39:9; Ex. 1:17; Lev. 25:43; Neh. 5:15; Prov. 1:7; 9:10
20 [m]Gen. 42:34; 43:5; 44:23
21 [n]Gen. 37:26-28; 44:16; 45:3; Job 36:8, 9; Hos. 5:15 [o]Prov. 21:13; Matt. 7:2
22 [p]Gen. 37:21, 22, 29 [q]Gen. 9:5, 6; 1 Kin. 2:32; 2 Chr. 24:22; Ps. 9:12; Luke 11:50, 51

mained intact, and Pharaoh still fully trusted his vizier. He dispensed the food supplies by sale to Egyptians and others (v. 47).

42:1-3 Jacob's sons were paralyzed in the famine, and Jacob was reluctant to let his family return to Egypt, not knowing what would happen to them (v. 4). But, with no other choice left, he dispatched them to buy grain in Egypt (v. 2).

42:4 Benjamin. See 35:16-19. He was the youngest of all, the second son of Rachel, Jacob's beloved, and the favorite of his father since he thought Joseph was dead.

42:6 bowed down. Without their appreciating it at the time, Joseph's dream became reality (37:5-8). Recognition of Joseph was unlikely because: 1) over 15 years had elapsed and the teenager sold into slavery had become a mature adult; 2) he had become Egyptian in appearance and dress; 3) he treated them without a hint of familiarity (vv. 7,8); and 4) they thought he was dead (v. 13).

42:9-22 The brothers' final evaluation after being imprisoned for 3 days, after protesting the charge of espionage, and after hearing the royal criterion for establishing their innocence (vv. 15,20), revealed their guilty conscience and their understanding that vengeance for their wrongdoing to Joseph had probably arrived (vv. 21,22). Calling themselves "honest men" (v. 10) was hardly an accurate assessment.

42:9 remembered the dreams. Joseph remembered his boyhood dreams about his brothers bowing down to him (37:9) as they were coming true.

42:15 By the life of Pharaoh. Speaking an oath in the name of the king would most likely have masked Joseph's identity from the brothers. Perhaps it also prevented them from grasping the significance of his declaration, "I fear God" (v. 18). **unless your youngest brother comes.** Joseph wanted to find out if they had done the same or a similar thing to Benjamin as to himself.

42:19,20 If you *are* honest *men.* Joseph took their assessment of themselves at face value when exhorting them to respond to his proposals, but still asked for a hostage.

42:21 anguish of his soul. The brothers had steeled their hearts when selling Joseph to the Midianites (37:28,29), but they could not forget the fervent pleading and terror-filled voice of the teenager dragged away as a slave from home. Reuben reminded them of his warning at that time and the consequence.

42:22 blood…required of us. This declaration referred to the death penalty (9:5).

[r]wept. Then he returned to them again, and talked with them. And he took [s]Simeon from them and bound him before their eyes.

The Brothers Return to Canaan

25 Then Joseph [t]gave a command to fill their sacks with grain, to [u]restore every man's money to his sack, and to give them provisions for the journey. [v]Thus he did for them. 26 So they loaded their donkeys with the grain and departed from there. 27 But as [w]one *of them* opened his sack to give his donkey feed at the encampment, he saw his money; and there it was, in the mouth of his sack. 28 So he said to his brothers, "My money has been restored, and there it is, in my sack!" Then their hearts [5]failed *them* and they were afraid, saying to one another, "What *is* this *that* God has done to us?"

29 Then they went to Jacob their father in the land of Canaan and told him all that had happened to them, saying: 30 "The man *who is* lord of the land [x]spoke [6]roughly to us, and took us for spies of the country. 31 But we said to him, 'We *are* honest *men;* we are not spies. 32 We *are* twelve brothers, sons of our father; one *is* no *more,* and the youngest *is* with our father this day in the land of Canaan.' 33 Then the man, the lord of the country, said to us, [y]'By this I will know that you *are* honest *men:* Leave one of your brothers *here* with me, take *food for* the famine of your households, and be gone. 34 And bring your [z]youngest brother to me; so I shall know that you *are* not spies, but *that* you *are* honest *men.* I will grant your brother to you, and you may [a]trade in the land.' "

35 Then it happened as they emptied their sacks, that surprisingly [b]each man's bundle of money *was* in his sack; and when they and their father saw the bundles of money, they were afraid. 36 And Jacob their father said to them, "You have [c]bereaved me: Joseph is no *more,* Simeon is no *more,* and you want to take [d]Benjamin. All these things are against me."

37 Then Reuben spoke to his father, saying, "Kill my two sons if I do not bring him *back* to you; put him in my hands, and I will bring him back to you."

38 But he said, "My son shall not go down with you, for [e]his brother is dead, and he is left alone. [f]If any calamity should befall him along the way in which you go, then you would [g]bring down my gray hair with sorrow to the grave."

Joseph's Brothers Return with Benjamin

43 Now the famine *was* [a]severe in the land. 2 And it came to pass, when they had eaten up the grain which they had brought from Egypt, that their father said to them, "Go [b]back, buy us a little food."

3 But Judah spoke to him, saying, "The man solemnly warned us, saying, 'You shall not see my face unless your [c]brother *is* with you.' 4 If you send our brother with us, we will go down and buy you food. 5 But if you will not send *him,* we will not go down; for the man said to us, 'You shall not see my face unless your brother *is* with you.' "

6 And Israel said, "Why did you deal *so* [1]wrongfully with me *as* to tell the man whether you had still *another* brother?"

7 But they said, "The man asked us pointedly about ourselves and our family, saying, '*Is* your father still alive? Have you *another* brother?' And we told him according to these words. Could we possibly have known that he would say, 'Bring your brother down'?"

8 Then Judah said to Israel his father, "Send the lad with me, and we will arise and go, that we may [d]live and not die, both we and you *and* also our little ones. 9 I myself will be surety for him; from my hand you shall require him. [e]If I do not bring him *back* to you and set him before you, then let me bear the blame forever. 10 For if we had not lingered, surely by now we would have returned this second time."

11 And their father Israel said to them, "If *it must be* so, then do this: Take some of the best fruits of the land in your vessels

24 [r]Gen. 43:30; 45:14, 15 [s]Gen. 34:25, 30; 43:14, 23
25 [t]Gen. 44:1 [u]Gen. 43:12 [v][Matt. 5:44; Rom. 12:17, 20, 21; 1 Pet. 3:9]
27 [w]Gen. 43:21, 22
28 [5]*sank*
30 [x]Gen. 42:7 [6]*harshly*
33 [y]Gen. 42:15, 19, 20
34 [z]Gen. 42:20; 43:3, 5 [a]Gen. 34:10
35 [b]Gen. 43:12, 15, 21
36 [c]Gen. 43:14 [d]Gen. 35:18; [Rom. 8:28, 31]
38 [e]Gen. 37:22; 42:13; 44:20, 28 [f]Gen. 42:4; 44:29 [g]Gen. 37:35; 44:31

CHAPTER 43

1 [a]Gen. 41:54, 57; 42:5; 45:6, 11
2 [b]Gen. 42:2; 44:25
3 [c]Gen. 42:20; 43:5; 44:23
6 [1]Lit. *wickedly*
8 [d]Gen. 42:2; 47:19
9 [e]Gen. 42:37; 44:32; Philem. 18, 19

42:24 took Simeon. He kept hostage not Reuben the firstborn, but Simeon, the oldest brother, who willingly participated in the crime against Joseph (37:21-31).

42:28 God has done. Their guilty conscience and fear of vengeance from God surfaced again in this response to the money with which they had purchased the grain being returned and found in the one sack which had been opened. Later, upon discovering all their money had been returned, their fear increased even further (v. 35).

42:36 Jacob could not handle the prospect of losing another son, and didn't trust the brothers who had already divested him of two sons by what he may have thought were their intrigues. **All... against me.** The whole situation overwhelmed Jacob who complained against his sons (cf. 43:6) and would not release Benjamin (v. 38).

42:37 The always salutary Reuben generously made his father an offer easy to refuse—killing his grandsons!

43:3 solemnly warned us. The seriousness of Joseph's words portended failure for another mission to buy food, unless the criterion he had set down was strictly met.

43:9 I myself will be surety for him. Reuben's offer to guarantee the safety of Benjamin had been rejected (42:37,38), but Judah's was accepted (v. 11) because of the stress of the famine and the potential death of all (v. 8) if they waited much longer (v. 10).

43:11 a little. Likely, this was a significant present because they

and [f]carry down a present for the man—a
little [g]balm and a little honey, spices and
myrrh, pistachio nuts and almonds.
12 Take double money in your hand, and
take back in your hand the money [h]that
was returned in the mouth of your sacks;
perhaps it was an oversight. 13 Take your
brother also, and arise, go back to the man.
14 And may God [i]Almighty [j]give you
mercy before the man, that he may release
your other brother and Benjamin. [k]If I am
bereaved, I am bereaved!"

15 So the men took that present and Benjamin, and they took double money in
their hand, and arose and went [l]down to
Egypt; and they stood before Joseph.
16 When Joseph saw Benjamin with them,
he said to the [m]steward of his house, "Take
these men to my home, and slaughter [2]an
animal and make ready; for *these* men will
dine with me at noon." 17 Then the man
did as Joseph ordered, and the man
brought the men into Joseph's house.

18 Now the men were [n]afraid because
they were brought into Joseph's house;
and they said, "*It is* because of the money,
which was returned in our sacks the first
time, that we are brought in, so that he
may [3]make a case against us and seize us,
to take us as slaves with our donkeys."

19 When they drew near to the steward
of Joseph's house, they talked with him at
the door of the house, 20 and said, "O sir,
[o]we indeed came down the first time to
buy food; 21 but [p]it happened, when we
came to the encampment, that we opened
our sacks, and there, *each* man's money *was*
in the mouth of his sack, our money in full
weight; so we have brought it back in our
hand. 22 And we have brought down other
money in our hands to buy food. We do
not know who put our money in our
sacks."

11 [f]Gen. 32:20; 33:10; 43:25, 26; [Prov. 18:16] [g]Gen. 37:25; Jer. 8:22; Ezek. 27:17
12 [h]Gen. 42:25, 35; 43:21, 22
14 [i]Gen. 17:1; 28:3; 35:11; 48:3 [j]Gen. 39:21; Ps. 106:46 [k]Gen. 42:36; Esth. 4:16
15 [l]Gen. 39:1; 46:3, 6
16 [m]Gen. 24:2; 39:4; 44:1 [2]Lit. *a slaughter*
18 [n]Gen. 42:28 [3]Lit. *roll himself upon us*
20 [o]Gen. 42:3, 10
21 [p]Gen. 42:27, 35
23 [q]Gen. 42:24
24 [r]Gen. 18:4; 19:2; 24:32
26 [s]Gen. 37:7, 10; 42:6; 44:14
27 [t]Gen. 29:6; 42:11, 13; 43:7; 45:3; 2 Kin. 4:26
28 [u]Gen. 37:7, 10
29 [v]Gen. 35:17, 18 [w]Gen. 42:13
30 [x]1 Kin. 3:26 [y]Gen. 42:24; 45:2, 14, 15; 46:29
31 [z]Gen. 43:25
32 [a]Gen. 41:12; Ex. 1:15 [b]Gen. 46:34; Ex. 8:26
33 [c]Gen. 27:36; 42:7; Deut. 21:16, 17

23 But he said, "Peace *be* with you, do
not be afraid. Your God and the God of
your father has given you treasure in your
sacks; I had your money." Then he brought
[q]Simeon out to them.

24 So the man brought the men into Joseph's house and [r]gave *them* water, and
they washed their feet; and he gave their
donkeys feed. 25 Then they made the present ready for Joseph's coming at noon, for
they heard that they would eat bread there.

26 And when Joseph came home, they
brought him the present which *was* in their
hand into the house, and [s]bowed down before him to the earth. 27 Then he asked
them about *their* well-being, and said, "*Is*
your father well, the old man [t]of whom
you spoke? *Is* he still alive?"

28 And they answered, "Your servant
our father *is* in good health; he *is* still
alive." [u]And they bowed their heads down
and prostrated themselves.

29 Then he lifted his eyes and saw his
brother Benjamin, [v]his mother's son, and
said, "*Is* this your younger brother [w]of
whom you spoke to me?" And he said,
"God be gracious to you, my son." 30 Now
[x]his heart yearned for his brother; so Joseph made haste and sought *somewhere* to
weep. And he went into *his* chamber and
[y]wept there. 31 Then he washed his face
and came out; and he restrained himself,
and said, "Serve the [z]bread."

32 So they set him a place by himself,
and them by themselves, and the Egyptians who ate with him by themselves; because the Egyptians could not eat food
with the [a]Hebrews, for that *is* [b]an
abomination to the Egyptians. 33 And they
sat before him, the firstborn according to
his [c]birthright and the youngest according
to his youth; and the men looked in astonishment at one another. 34 Then he took

had little left. But there was no future at all past the little if they did not get grain in Egypt.

43:14 Jacob's acquiescence to let Benjamin go (v. 13) ended with prayer for the brothers' and Benjamin's safety and with a cry of being a helpless victim of circumstances. Pessimism had apparently set into his heart and deepened after the loss of Joseph.

43:23 Your God...has given. An indication of Joseph's steward either having come to faith in God or having become very familiar with how Joseph talked of his God and life. So concerned were the brothers to protest their ignorance of the means of the money being returned and to express their desire to settle this debt (vv. 20-22), that they missed the steward's clear reference to the God of Israel ("the God of your father") and his oversight of events in which he had played a part ("I had your money").

43:26 bowed down. Again, Joseph's boyhood dream (37:5-8) had become reality (cf. 42:6).

43:29 God be gracious. Joseph easily used the name of God in his conversation, but the brothers did not hear the name of their own covenant God being spoken by one who looked just like an Egyptian (cf. 42:18).

43:30 to weep. Joseph was moved to tears on several occasions (42:24; 45:2, 14, 15; 46:29).

43:32 not eat food with the Hebrews. Exclusivism kept the Egyptians sensitive to the social stigma attached to sharing a meal table with foreigners (cf. 46:34). Discrimination prevailed at another level too: Joseph ate alone, his rank putting him ahead of others and giving him his own meal-table and setting.

43:33 the firstborn...the youngest. To be seated at the table in birth order in the house of an Egyptian official was startling—how did he know this of them? Enough clues had been given in Joseph's previous questions about the family and his use of God's name for them to wonder about him and his personal knowledge of them. Obviously, they simply did not believe Joseph was alive (44:20) and certainly not as a personage of such immense influence and authority. They had probably laughed through the years at the memory of Joseph's dreams of superiority.

servings to them from before him, but Benjamin's serving was [d]five times as much as
any of theirs. So they drank and were
merry with him.

Joseph's Cup

44 And he commanded [1]the [a]steward
of his house, saying, [b]"Fill the men's
sacks with food, as much as they can carry,
and put each man's money in the mouth of
his sack. 2 Also put my cup, the silver cup,
in the mouth of the sack of the youngest,
and his grain money." So he did according
to the word that Joseph had spoken. 3 As
soon as the morning dawned, the men
were sent away, they and their donkeys.
4 When they had gone out of the city, *and*
were not *yet* far off, Joseph said to his steward, "Get up, follow the men; and when
you overtake them, say to them, 'Why have
you [c]repaid evil for good? 5 *Is* not this *the*
one from which my lord drinks, and with
which he indeed practices divination? You
have done evil in so doing.' "
6 So he overtook them, and he spoke to
them these same words. 7 And they said to
him, "Why does my lord say these words?
Far be it from us that your servants should
do such a thing. 8 Look, we brought back
to you from the land of Canaan [d]the
money which we found in the mouth of
our sacks. How then could we steal silver
or gold from your lord's house? 9 With
whomever of your servants it is found, [e]let
him die, and we also will be my lord's
slaves."
10 And he said, "Now also *let* it *be* according to your words; he with whom it is
found shall be my slave, and you shall be
blameless." 11 Then each man speedily let
down his sack to the ground, and each
opened his sack. 12 So he searched. He
began with the oldest and [2]left off with the
youngest; and the cup was found in Benjamin's sack. 13 Then they [f]tore their clothes,
and each man loaded his donkey and returned to the city.
14 So Judah and his brothers came to Joseph's house, and he *was* still there; and
they [g]fell before him on the ground.
15 And Joseph said to them, "What deed *is*
this you have done? Did you not know
that such a man as I can certainly practice
divination?"
16 Then Judah said, "What shall we say
to my lord? What shall we speak? Or how
shall we clear ourselves? God has [h]found
out the iniquity of your servants; here [i]we
are, my lord's slaves, both we and *he* also
with whom the cup was found."
17 But he said, [j]"Far be it from me that I
should do so; the man in whose hand the
cup was found, he shall be my slave. And
as for you, go up in peace to your father."

Judah Intercedes for Benjamin

18 Then Judah came near to him and
said: "O my lord, please let your servant
speak a word in my lord's hearing, and [k]do
not let your anger burn against your servant; for you *are* even like Pharaoh. 19 My
lord asked his servants, saying, 'Have you
a father or a brother?' 20 And we said to
my lord, 'We have a father, an old man,
and [l]a child of *his* old age, *who is* young; his
brother is [m]dead, and he [n]alone is left of
his mother's children, and his [o]father loves
him.' 21 Then you said to your servants,
[p]'Bring him down to me, that I may set my
eyes on him.' 22 And we said to my lord,
'The lad cannot leave his father, for *if* he
should leave his father, *his father* would

34 [d]Gen. 35:24; 45:22

CHAPTER 44

1 [a]Gen. 43:16 [b]Gen. 42:25 [1]Lit. *the one over*
4 [c]1 Sam. 25:21
8 [d]Gen. 43:21
9 [e]Gen. 31:32
12 [2]*finished with*
13 [f]Gen. 37:29, 34; Num. 14:6; 2 Sam. 1:11
14 [g]Gen. 37:7, 10
16 [h][Num. 32:23] [i]Gen. 44:9
17 [j]Prov. 17:15
18 [k]Gen. 18:30, 32; Ex. 32:22
20 [l]Gen. 37:3; 43:8; 44:30 [m]Gen. 42:38 [n]Gen. 46:19 [o]Gen. 42:4
21 [p]Gen. 42:15, 20

43:34 Benjamin's serving. Favoritism shown to Rachel's son silently tested their attitudes; any longstanding envy, dislike, or animosity could not be easily masked. None surfaced.

44:2 my cup, the silver cup. Joseph's own special cup, also described as one connected with divination (vv. 5,15) or hydromancy (interpreting the water movements), was a sacred vessel symbolizing the authority of his office of Egyptian vizier. Mention of its superstitious nature and purpose need not demand Joseph be an actual practitioner of pagan religious rites. *See note on v. 15.*

44:5 divination. *See note on Deut. 18:9-12.*

44:7-9 The brothers, facing a charge of theft, protested their innocence by pointing first to their integrity in returning the money from the last trip, and then by declaring death on the perpetrator and slavery for themselves.

44:12 began with the oldest. Again, there was a display of inside knowledge of the family, which ought to have signaled something to the brothers. *See note on 43:33.*

44:13 tore their clothes. A well known ancient Near Eastern custom of visibly portraying the pain of heart being experienced. They were very upset that Benjamin might become a slave in Egypt (v. 10). Benjamin appears to have been speechless. They had passed a second test of devotion to Benjamin (the first in v. 34).

44:14 fell before him. Again the dream had become reality (cf. 37:5-8; 42:6); but now prostrate before him, they had come to plead for mercy both for their youngest brother Benjamin and for their father Jacob (vv. 18-34).

44:15 practice divination. *See notes on vv. 2,5.* Joseph, still disguising himself as an Egyptian official before his brothers, permitted them to think it so.

44:16 Then Judah said. Judah stepped forward as the family spokesman since it was he who came with his brothers to Joseph's house and he who pled with him (cf. vv. 14,18); Reuben, the firstborn, had been eclipsed. **God has found out the iniquity.** Judah, showing how his heart had changed, acknowledged the providence of God in uncovering their guilt (note the "we" in the questions), and did not indulge in any blame shifting, even onto Benjamin.

44:18-34 An eloquent and contrite plea for mercy, replete with reference to the aged father's delight in and doting upon the youngest son (vv. 20,30) and the fatal shock should he be lost (vv. 22,29,31,34). Judah's evident compassion for Jacob and readiness to

die.' 23 But you said to your servants, [q]'Unless your youngest brother comes down
with you, you shall see my face no more.'
24 "So it was, when we went up to your
servant my father, that we told him the
words of my lord. 25 And [r]our father said,
'Go back *and* buy us a little food.' 26 But we
said, 'We cannot go down; if our youngest
brother is with us, then we will go down;
for we may not see the man's face unless
our youngest brother *is* with us.' 27 Then
your servant my father said to us, 'You
know that [s]my wife bore me two sons;
28 and the one went out from me, and I
said, [t]"Surely he is torn to pieces"; and I
have not seen him since. 29 But if you [u]take
this one also from me, and calamity befalls
him, you shall bring down my gray hair
with sorrow to the grave.'
30 "Now therefore, when I come to your
servant my father, and the lad *is* not with
us, since [v]his life is bound up in the lad's
life, 31 it will happen, when he sees that the
lad *is* not *with us,* that he will die. So your
servants will bring down the gray hair of
your servant our father with sorrow to the
grave. 32 For your servant became surety
for the lad to my father, saying, [w]'If I do
not bring him *back* to you, then I shall bear
the blame before my father forever.'
33 Now therefore, please [x]let your servant
remain instead of the lad as a slave to my
lord, and let the lad go up with his brothers. 34 For how shall I go up to my father if
the lad *is* not with me, lest perhaps I see the
evil that would [3]come upon my father?"

Joseph Revealed to His Brothers

45 Then Joseph could not restrain himself before all those who stood by
him, and he cried out, "Make everyone go
out from me!" So no one stood with him
[a]while Joseph made himself known to his
brothers. 2 And he [b]wept aloud, and the
Egyptians and the house of Pharaoh heard
it.
3 Then Joseph said to his brothers, [c]"I *am*
Joseph; does my father still live?" But his
brothers could not answer him, for they
were dismayed in his presence. 4 And Joseph said to his brothers, "Please come
near to me." So they came near. Then he
said: "I *am* Joseph your brother, [d]whom
you sold into Egypt. 5 But now, do not
therefore be grieved or angry with yourselves because you sold me here; [e]for God
sent me before you to preserve life. 6 For
these two years the [f]famine *has been* in the
land, and *there are* still five years in which
there will be neither plowing nor harvesting. 7 And God [g]sent me before you to preserve a [1]posterity for you in the earth, and
to save your lives by a great deliverance.
8 So now *it was* not you *who* sent me here,
but [h]God; and He has made me [i]a father to
Pharaoh, and lord of all his house, and a
[j]ruler throughout all the land of Egypt.
9 "Hurry and go up to my father, and
say to him, 'Thus says your son Joseph:
"God has made me lord of all Egypt; come
down to me, do not [2]tarry. 10 [k]You shall
dwell in the land of Goshen, and you shall
be near to me, you and your children, your
children's children, your flocks and your
herds, and all that you have. 11 There I will
[l]provide for you, lest you and your household, and all that you have, come to poverty; for *there are* still five years of famine."'
12 "And behold, your eyes and the eyes
of my brother Benjamin see that *it is* [m]my
mouth that speaks to you. 13 So you shall
tell my father of all my glory in Egypt, and
of all that you have seen; and you shall
hurry and [n]bring my father down here."
14 Then he fell on his brother Benjamin's
neck and wept, and Benjamin wept on his
neck. 15 Moreover he [o]kissed all his brothers and wept over them, and after that his
brothers talked with him.
16 Now the report of it was heard in Pharaoh's house, saying, "Joseph's brothers
have come." So it pleased Pharaoh and his
servants well. 17 And Pharaoh said to Joseph, "Say to your brothers, 'Do this: Load

23 [q]Gen. 43:3, 5
25 [r]Gen. 43:2
27 [s]Gen. 30:22-24; 35:16-18; 46:19
28 [t]Gen. 37:31-35
29 [u]Gen. 42:36, 38; 44:31
30 [v][1 Sam. 18:1; 25:29]
32 [w]Gen. 43:9
33 [x]Ex. 32:32
34 [3]Lit. *find*

CHAPTER 45

1 [a]Acts 7:13
2 [b]Gen. 43:30; 46:29
3 [c]Gen. 43:27; Acts 7:13
4 [d]Gen. 37:28; 39:1; Ps. 105:17
5 [e]Gen. 45:7, 8; 50:20; Ps. 105:16, 17
6 [f]Gen. 43:1; 47:4, 13
7 [g]Gen. 45:5; 50:20 [1]*remnant*
8 [h][Rom. 8:28] [i]Judg. 17:10; Is. 22:21 [j]Gen. 41:43; 42:6
9 [2]*delay*
10 [k]Gen. 46:28, 34; 47:1, 6; Ex. 9:26
11 [l]Gen. 47:12
12 [m]Gen. 42:23
13 [n]Gen. 46:6-28; Acts 7:14
15 [o]Gen. 48:10

substitute himself for Benjamin in slavery finally overwhelmed Joseph—these were not the same brothers of yesteryear (45:1).

45:1-8 Stunned by the revelation of who it really was with whom they dealt, the brothers then heard expressed a masterpiece of recognition of and submission to the sovereignty of God, i.e., His providential rule over the affairs of life, both good and bad. *See note on 41:43-45.*

45:6 these two years. Joseph would have been 39 years old and away from his brothers for 22 years (37:2).

45:7 to preserve a posterity. Words reflecting, on Joseph's part, an understanding of the Abrahamic Covenant and its promise of a nation (cf. chaps. 12; 15; 17).

45:8 father to Pharaoh. A title which belonged to viziers and which designated one who, unrelated to Pharaoh, nevertheless performed a valuable function and held high position, which in Joseph's case was "lord of all Egypt" (v. 9). A new and younger Pharaoh now reigned, Senusert III, ca. 1878–1841 B.C.

45:10 land of Goshen. This area, located in the NE section of the Egyptian Delta region, was appropriate for grazing the herds of Jacob (cf. 47:27; 50:8). Over 400 years later, at the time of the Exodus, the Jews still lived in Goshen (cf. Ex. 8:22; 9:26).

45:14,15 Reconciliation was accomplished with much emotion, which clearly showed that Joseph held no grudges and had forgiven them, evidencing the marks of a spiritually mature man. *See note on 50:15-18.* It had been 22 years since the brothers sold Joseph into slavery.

45:16 So it pleased Pharaoh. The final seal of approval for Joseph's relatives to immigrate to Egypt came unsought from Pharaoh (vv. 17-20).

your animals and depart; go to the land of
Canaan. 18 Bring your father and your
households and come to me; I will give
you the best of the land of Egypt, and you
will eat [p]the [3]fat of the land. 19 Now you
are commanded—do this: Take carts out of
the land of Egypt for your little ones and
your wives; bring your father and come.
20 Also do not be concerned about your
goods, for the best of all the land of Egypt
is yours.' "

21 Then the sons of Israel did so; and Joseph gave them [q]carts,[4] according to the
command of Pharaoh, and he gave them
provisions for the journey. 22 He gave to all
of them, to each man, [r]changes of garments; but to Benjamin he gave three hundred *pieces* of silver and [s]five changes of
garments. 23 And he sent to his father these
things: ten donkeys loaded with the good
things of Egypt, and ten female donkeys
loaded with grain, bread, and food for his
father for the journey. 24 So he sent his
brothers away, and they departed; and he
said to them, "See that you do not become
troubled along the way."

25 Then they went up out of Egypt, and
came to the land of Canaan to Jacob their
father. 26 And they told him, saying, "Joseph *is* still alive, and he *is* governor over
all the land of Egypt." [t]And Jacob's heart
stood still, because he did not believe
them. 27 But when they told him all the
words which Joseph had said to them, and
when he saw the carts which Joseph had
sent to carry him, the spirit [u]of Jacob their
father revived. 28 Then Israel said, "*It is*
enough. Joseph my son *is* still alive. I will
go and see him before I die."

Jacob's Journey to Egypt

46 So Israel took his journey with all
that he had, and came to [a]Beershe-
ba, and offered sacrifices [b]to the God of his
father Isaac. 2 Then God spoke to Israel [c]in
the visions of the night, and said, "Jacob,
Jacob!"
And he said, "Here I am."
3 So He said, "I *am* God, [d]the God of
your father; do not fear to go down to
Egypt, for I will [e]make of you a great nation there. 4 [f]I will go down with you to
Egypt, and I will also surely [g]bring you up
again; and [h]Joseph [1]will put his hand on
your eyes."

5 Then [i]Jacob arose from Beersheba; and
the sons of Israel carried their father Jacob,
their little ones, and their wives, in the
[2]carts [j]which Pharaoh had sent to carry
him. 6 So they took their livestock and
their goods, which they had acquired in
the land of Canaan, and went to Egypt, [k]Ja-
cob and all his descendants with him. 7 His
sons and his sons' sons, his daughters and
his sons' daughters, and all his descendants he brought with him to Egypt.

8 Now [l]these *were* the names of the children of Israel, Jacob and his sons, who
went to Egypt: [m]Reuben *was* Jacob's firstborn. 9 The [n]sons of Reuben *were* Hanoch,
Pallu, Hezron, and Carmi. 10 [o]The sons of
Simeon *were* [3]Jemuel, Jamin, Ohad,
[4]Jachin, [5]Zohar, and Shaul, the son of a
Canaanite woman. 11 The sons of [p]Levi
were Gershon, Kohath, and Merari. 12 The
sons of [q]Judah *were* [r]Er, Onan, Shelah,
Perez, and Zerah (but Er and Onan died in
the land of Canaan). [s]The sons of Perez
were Hezron and Hamul. 13 The sons of Issachar *were* Tola, [6]Puvah, [7]Job, and Shimron. 14 The [t]sons of Zebulun *were* Sered,
Elon, and Jahleel. 15 These *were* the [u]sons
of Leah, whom she bore to Jacob in Padan
Aram, with his daughter Dinah. All the
persons, his sons and his daughters, *were*
thirty-three.

16 The sons of Gad *were* [8]Ziphion,
Haggi, Shuni, [9]Ezbon, Eri, [1]Arodi, and
Areli. 17 [v]The sons of Asher *were* Jimnah,
Ishuah, Isui, Beriah, and Serah, their sister.
And the sons of Beriah *were* Heber and
Malchiel. 18 [w]These *were* the sons of Zil-
pah, [x]whom Laban gave to Leah his

18 [p]Gen. 27:28; 47:6; Deut. 32:9-14 [3]The choicest produce
21 [q]Gen. 45:19; 46:5 [4]*wagons*
22 [r]2 Kin. 5:5 [s]Gen. 43:34
26 [t]Job 29:24; Ps. 126:1; Luke 24:11, 41
27 [u]Judg. 15:19; Is. 40:29

CHAPTER 46

1 [a]Gen. 21:31, 33; 26:32, 33; 28:10 [b]Gen. 26:24, 25; 28:13; 31:42; 32:9
2 [c]Gen. 15:1; 22:11; 31:11; Num. 12:6; Job 33:14, 15
3 [d]Gen. 17:1; 28:13 [e]Gen. 12:2; Ex. 1:9; 12:37; Deut. 26:5
4 [f]Gen. 28:15; 31:3; 48:21; Ex. 3:12 [g]Gen. 15:16; 50:12, 24, 25; Ex. 3:8 [h]Gen. 50:1 [1]Will close your eyes when you die
5 [i]Gen. 47:9; Acts 7:15 [j]Gen. 45:19-21 [2]*wagons*
6 [k]Deut. 26:5; Josh. 24:4; Ps. 105:23; Is. 52:4; Acts 7:15
8 [l]Ex. 1:1-4 [m]Num. 26:4, 5; 1 Chr. 2:1
9 [n]Ex. 6:14
10 [o]Ex. 6:15; Num. 26:12 [3]*Nemuel,* 1 Chr. 4:24 [4]*Jarib,* 1 Chr. 4:24 [5]*Zerah,* 1 Chr. 4:24
11 [p]Ex. 6:16, 17; 1 Chr. 6:1, 16
12 [q]Num. 26:19, 20; 1 Chr. 2:3; 4:21 [r]Gen. 38:3, 7, 10 [s]Gen. 38:29
13 [6]*Puah,* Num. 26:23; 1 Chr. 7:1 [7]*Jashub,* Num. 26:24; 1 Chr. 7:1
14 [t]Num. 26:26
15 [u]Gen. 35:23; 49:31
16 [8]Sam., LXX *Zephon* and Num. 26:15 [9]*Ozni,* Num. 26:16 [1]*Arod,* Num. 26:17
17 [v]Num. 26:44-47; 1 Chr. 7:30
18 [w]Gen. 30:10; 37:2 [x]Gen. 29:24

45:24 troubled along the way. A needed admonition because they would have so much sin to think about as they readied their confession to their father.

45:26 Jacob's heart stood still. Like his sons (v. 3), Jacob was stunned by the totally unexpected good news. Even though the record is silent on the matter, this was the appropriate occasion for the sons to confess their crime to their father.

46:1 offered sacrifices. The route to Egypt for Jacob went via Beersheba, a notable site about 25 mi. SW of Hebron and favorite place of worship for both Abraham and Isaac (21:33; 26:25).

46:2-4 God spoke...in the visions. Jacob's anxiety about his departure to Egypt was allayed by the Lord's approval and confirmation of his descendants returning as a nation. God had previously appeared/spoken to Jacob in 28:10-17; 32:24-30; 35:1,9-13.

46:4 hand on your eyes. A promise of dying peacefully in the presence of his beloved son (cf. 49:33).

46:6 went to Egypt. Ca. 1875 B.C. They remained 430 years (Ex. 12:40) until the Exodus in 1445 B.C.

46:8 the children of Israel. This was the first time that author Moses referred to the family as a whole in this way, although "in Israel" had been used by the sons of Jacob before (cf. 34:7).

46:8-27 The genealogical register, separately listing and totaling the sons per wife and handmaid, is enveloped by notification that it records the sons/persons of Jacob who went to Egypt (vv. 8,27). Ancient Near Eastern genealogies could include historical notes as is true here, namely the death of Er and Onan (v. 11), and that Laban gave the handmaids to his daughters (vv. 18,25).

daughter; and these she bore to Jacob: sixteen persons.
19 The [y]sons of Rachel, [z]Jacob's wife,
were Joseph and Benjamin. 20 [a]And to Joseph in the land of Egypt were born Manasseh and Ephraim, whom Asenath, the
daughter of Poti-Pherah priest of On, bore
to him. 21 [b]The sons of Benjamin *were*
Belah, Becher, Ashbel, Gera, Naaman, [c]Ehi,
Rosh, [d]Muppim, [2]Huppim, and Ard.
22 These *were* the sons of Rachel, who were
born to Jacob: fourteen persons in all.
23 The son of Dan *was* [3]Hushim. 24 [e]The
sons of Naphtali *were* [4]Jahzeel, Guni, Jezer,
and [5]Shillem. 25 [f]These *were* the sons of Bilhah, [g]whom Laban gave to Rachel his
daughter, and she bore these to Jacob:
seven persons in all.
26 [h]All the persons who went with Jacob
to Egypt, who came from his body, [i]be-
sides Jacob's sons' wives, *were* sixty-six
persons in all. 27 And the sons of Joseph
who were born to him in Egypt *were* two
persons. [j]All the persons of the house of
Jacob who went to Egypt were seventy.

Jacob Settles in Goshen

28 Then he sent Judah before him to Joseph, [k]to point out before him *the way* to
Goshen. And they came [l]to the land of
Goshen. 29 So Joseph made ready his
[m]chariot and went up to Goshen to meet
his father Israel; and he presented himself
to him, and [n]fell on his neck and wept on
his neck a good while.
30 And Israel said to Joseph, [o]"Now let
me die, since I have seen your face, because you *are* still alive."
31 Then Joseph said to his brothers and
to his father's household, [p]"I will go up
and tell Pharaoh, and say to him, 'My
brothers and those of my father's house,
who *were* in the land of Canaan, have come
to me. 32 And the men *are* [q]shepherds, for
their occupation has been to feed livestock;
and they have brought their flocks, their
herds, and all that they have.' 33 So it shall
be, when Pharaoh calls you and says,
[r]'What is your occupation?' 34 that you
shall say, 'Your servants' [s]occupation has
been with livestock [t]from our youth even
till now, both we *and* also our fathers,' that
you may dwell in the land of Goshen; for
every shepherd *is* [u]an[6] abomination to the
Egyptians."

47

47 Then Joseph [a]went and told Pharaoh, and said, "My father and my
brothers, their flocks and their herds and
all that they possess, have come from the
land of Canaan; and indeed they *are* in [b]the
land of Goshen." 2 And he took five men
from among his brothers and [c]presented
them to Pharaoh. 3 Then Pharaoh said to
his brothers, [d]"What *is* your occupation?"
And they said to Pharaoh, [e]"Your servants *are* shepherds, both we *and* also our
fathers." 4 And they said to Pharaoh, [f]"We
have come to dwell in the land, because
your servants have no pasture for their
flocks, [g]for the famine *is* severe in the land
of Canaan. Now therefore, please let your
servants [h]dwell in the land of Goshen."
5 Then Pharaoh spoke to Joseph, saying,
"Your father and your brothers have come
to you. 6 [i]The land of Egypt *is* before you.
Have your father and brothers dwell in the
best of the land; let them dwell [j]in the land
of Goshen. And if you know *any* competent men among them, then make them
chief herdsmen over my livestock."
7 Then Joseph brought in his father
Jacob and set him before Pharaoh; and Jacob [k]blessed Pharaoh. 8 Pharaoh said to
Jacob, "How old *are* you?"
9 And Jacob said to Pharaoh, [l]"The days
of the years of my [1]pilgrimage *are* [m]one

19 [y]Gen. 35:24 [z]Gen. 44:27
20 [a]Gen. 41:45, 50-52; 48:1
21 [b]1 Chr. 7:6; 8:1 [c]Num. 26:38 [d]Num. 26:39; 1 Chr. 7:12 [2]*Hupham*, Num. 26:39
23 [3]*Shuham*, Num. 26:42
24 [e]Num. 26:48 [4]*Jahziel*, 1 Chr. 7:13 [5]*Shallum*, 1 Chr. 7:13
25 [f]Gen. 30:5, 7 [g]Gen. 29:29
26 [h]Ex. 1:5 [i]Gen. 35:11
27 [j]Ex. 1:5; Deut. 10:22; Acts 7:14
28 [k]Gen. 31:21 [l]Gen. 47:1
29 [m]Gen. 41:43 [n]Gen. 45:14, 15
30 [o]Luke 2:29, 30
31 [p]Gen. 47:1
32 [q]Gen. 47:3
33 [r]Gen. 47:2, 3
34 [s]Gen. 47:3 [t]Gen. 30:35; 34:5; 37:17 [u]Gen. 43:32; Ex. 8:26 [6]*loathsome*

CHAPTER 47

1 [a]Gen. 46:31 [b]Gen. 45:10; 46:28; 50:8
2 [c]Acts 7:13
3 [d]Gen. 46:33; Jon. 1:8 [e]Gen. 46:32, 34; Ex. 2:17, 19
4 [f]Gen. 15:13; Deut. 26:5; Ps. 105:23 [g]Gen. 43:1; Acts 7:11 [h]Gen. 46:34
6 [i]Gen. 20:15; 45:10, 18; 47:11 [j]Gen. 47:4
7 [k]Gen. 47:10; 48:15, 20; 2 Sam. 14:22; 1 Kin. 8:66; Heb. 7:7
9 [l]Ps. 39:12; [Heb. 11:9, 13] [m]Gen. 47:28 [1]Lit. *sojourning*

46:26 sixty-six persons. The total of vv. 8-25 is 70, from which Er, Onan, Manasseh, and Ephraim need to be deleted.

46:27 seventy. Jacob, Joseph, Manasseh, and Ephraim should be added to the 66. The 75 of Acts 7:14 included an additional 5 people, born in the land, which were added in the LXX reading of 46:8-25 (cf. Ex. 1:5; Deut. 10:22). These 5 included two sons of Manasseh, two sons of Ephraim, and one grandson of the latter. *See note on Ex. 1:5.*

46:28 sent Judah before him. Once again Judah was the leader going ahead as Jacob's representative, not Reuben. *See note on 44:16.* **Goshen.** *See note on 45:10.*

46:31-34 Joseph's instructions about his preparatory interview with Pharaoh were designed to secure his relatives a place somewhat separate from the mainstream of Egyptian society. The social stigma regarding the Hebrews (43:32), who were shepherds also (v. 34), played a crucial role in protecting Israel from intermingling and losing their identity in Egypt. *See notes on 43:32; 47:1.*

47:1-6 in the land of Goshen. By informing Pharaoh of where he had located his family (cf. 45:10; 46:28) and then by having the family's 5 representatives courteously request permission to reside in Goshen (vv. 2,4), Joseph, wise to court procedures, paved the way for Pharaoh's confirmation and approval (v. 6).

47:7,10 Jacob blessed Pharaoh. The aged patriarch's salutations pronounced, undoubtedly in the name of God, a benediction on Pharaoh Senusert III (*see note on 45:8*) for his generosity and his provision of a safe place for Jacob's family. Though Senusert III had ascended to the throne before the famine ended, he honored his father's commitments.

47:9 my pilgrimage…few and evil. Since neither Jacob nor his fathers had actually possessed the land of Canaan, describing life as a pilgrimage was a fitting evaluation to give. In addition, his years seemed few in contrast to those of the two who had visited Egypt long before him, Abraham and Isaac (175 and 180 years respectively). And still overshadowed with pessimism, the days were "evil," in the sense of toil and trouble, of many sorrows, distresses, and crises. *See note on 48:15.*

hundred and thirty years; [n]few and evil have been the days of the years of my life, and [o]they have not attained to the days of the years of the life of my fathers in the days of their pilgrimage." 10 So Jacob [p]blessed Pharaoh, and went out from before Pharaoh.

11 And Joseph situated his father and his brothers, and gave them a possession in the land of Egypt, in the best of the land, in the land of [q]Rameses, [r]as Pharaoh had commanded. 12 Then Joseph provided [s]his father, his brothers, and all his father's household with bread, according to the number in *their* families.

Joseph Deals with the Famine

13 Now *there was* no bread in all the land; for the famine *was* very severe, [t]so that the land of Egypt and the land of Canaan languished because of the famine. 14 [u]And Joseph gathered up all the money that was found in the land of Egypt and in the land of Canaan, for the grain which they bought; and Joseph brought the money into Pharaoh's house.

15 So when the money failed in the land of Egypt and in the land of Canaan, all the Egyptians came to Joseph and said, "Give us bread, for [v]why should we die in your presence? For the money has failed."

16 Then Joseph said, "Give your livestock, and I will give you *bread* for your livestock, if the money is gone." 17 So they brought their livestock to Joseph, and Joseph gave them bread *in exchange* for the horses, the flocks, the cattle of the herds, and for the donkeys. Thus he [2]fed them with bread *in exchange* for all their livestock that year.

18 When that year had ended, they came to him the next year and said to him, "We will not hide from my lord that our money is gone; my lord also has our herds of livestock. There is nothing left in the sight of my lord but our bodies and our lands. 19 Why should we die before your eyes, both we and our land? Buy us and our land for bread, and we and our land will be servants of Pharaoh; give *us* seed, that we may [w]live and not die, that the land may not be desolate."

20 Then Joseph [x]bought all the land of Egypt for Pharaoh; for every man of the Egyptians sold his field, because the famine was severe upon them. So the land became Pharaoh's. 21 And as for the people, he [3]moved them into the cities, from *one* end of the borders of Egypt to the *other* end. 22 [y]Only the land of the [z]priests he did not buy; for the priests had rations *allotted to them* by Pharaoh, and they ate their rations which Pharaoh gave them; therefore they did not sell their lands.

23 Then Joseph said to the people, "Indeed I have bought you and your land this day for Pharaoh. Look, *here is* seed for you, and you shall sow the land. 24 And it shall come to pass in the harvest that you shall give one-fifth to Pharaoh. Four-fifths shall be your own, as seed for the field and for your food, for those of your households and as food for your little ones."

25 So they said, "You have saved [a]our lives; let us find favor in the sight of my lord, and we will be Pharaoh's servants." 26 And Joseph made it a law over the land of Egypt to this day, *that* Pharaoh should have one-fifth, [b]except for the land of the priests only, *which* did not become Pharaoh's.

Joseph's Vow to Jacob

27 So Israel [c]dwelt in the land of Egypt, in the country of Goshen; and they had possessions there and [d]grew and multi-

9 [n][Job 14:1] [o]Gen. 5:5; 11:10, 11; 25:7, 8; 35:28
10 [p]Gen. 47:7
11 [q]Ex. 1:11; 12:37 [r]Gen. 47:6, 27
12 [s]Gen. 45:11; 50:21
13 [t]Gen. 41:30; Acts 7:11
14 [u]Gen. 41:56; 42:6
15 [v]Gen. 47:19
17 [2]*supplied*

19 [w]Gen. 43:8
20 [x]Jer. 32:43
21 [3]So with MT, Tg.; Sam., LXX, Vg. *made the people virtual slaves*
22 [y]Lev. 25:34; Ezra 7:24 [z]Gen. 41:45
25 [a]Gen. 33:15
26 [b]Gen. 47:22
27 [c]Gen. 47:11 [d]Gen. 17:6; 26:4; 35:11; 46:3; Ex. 1:7; Deut. 26:5; Acts 7:17

47:11 land of Rameses. An alternative designation for Goshen (cf. 46:24; 47:1,6), with this name perhaps used later to more accurately describe the region for Moses' contemporary readers. *See note on Ex. 1:11* regarding the name Rameses ("Raamses" being the alternate spelling in Exodus). This region is also called Zoan elsewhere (cf. Ps. 78:12,43).

47:12 according to the number in *their* families. A rationing system was evidently in operation.

47:13-24 When the famine finally exhausted the Egyptians' supply of money, Joseph accepted animals in exchange for grain (v. 17). After the animals ran out, the people were desperate enough to exchange their land (vv. 19,20). Eventually, Pharaoh owned all the land, except what was the priests' (v. 22), though the people were allowed to work the land and pay one-fifth of its yield to Pharaoh (v. 24). Whatever may have been the land tenure system at that time, some private land ownership did at first exist, but finally, as in a feudal system, all worked their land for Pharaoh. Landed nobility did lose out and declined during major social reforms undertaken under Senusert III. This is the first record in Scripture of a national income tax, and the amount was 20 percent. Later, after the Exodus, God would prescribe tithes for Israel as national income taxes to support the theocracy (see Mal. 3:10).

47:15 when the money failed. The severity of the famine finally bankrupted all in Egypt and Canaan. With no monetary instruments available as a medium of exchange, a barter system was established (vv. 16-18).

47:16-18 Land soon replaced animals as the medium of exchange.

47:25,26 The extra measures imposed by Joseph to control the impact of the famine, i.e., moving parts of the population into cities (v. 21) and demanding a one-fifth tax on crop yields (v. 24), did not affect his approval ratings (v. 25). Whatever the gain to Pharaoh, the people obviously understood that Joseph had not enriched himself at their expense.

47:27,28 grew and multiplied. For 17 years, Jacob was witness to the increase; he had a glimpse of God's promise to Abraham, Isaac, and himself in the process of being fulfilled.

plied exceedingly. 28 And Jacob lived in the
land of Egypt seventeen years. So the
length of Jacob's life was one hundred and
forty-seven years. 29 When the time [e]drew
near that Israel must die, he called his son
Joseph and said to him, "Now if I have
found favor in your sight, please [f]put your
hand under my thigh, and [g]deal kindly
and truly with me. [h]Please do not bury me
in Egypt, 30 but [i]let me lie with my fathers;
you shall carry me out of Egypt and [j]bury
me in their burial place."

And he said, "I will do as you have
said."

31 Then he said, "Swear to me." And he
swore to him. So [k]Israel bowed himself on
the head of the bed.

Jacob Blesses Joseph's Sons

48 Now it came to pass after these
things that Joseph was told,
"Indeed your father *is* sick"; and he took
with him his two sons, [a]Manasseh and
Ephraim. 2 And Jacob was told, "Look,
your son Joseph is coming to you"; and Israel [1]strengthened himself and sat up on
the bed. 3 Then Jacob said to Joseph: "God
[b]Almighty appeared to me at [c]Luz in the
land of Canaan and blessed me, 4 and said
to me, 'Behold, I will [d]make you fruitful
and multiply you, and I will make of you a
multitude of people, and [e]give this land to
your descendants after you [f]*as* an everlasting possession.' 5 And now your [g]two
sons, Ephraim and Manasseh, who were
born to you in the land of Egypt before I
came to you in Egypt, *are* mine; as Reuben
and Simeon, they shall be mine. 6 Your
[2]offspring [3]whom you beget after them
shall be yours; they will be called by the
name of their brothers in their inheritance.
7 But as for me, when I came from Padan,
[h]Rachel died beside me in the land of
Canaan on the way, when *there was* but a
little distance to go to Ephrath; and I
buried her there on the way to Ephrath
(that is, Bethlehem)."

8 Then Israel saw Joseph's sons, and
said, "Who *are* these?"

9 Joseph said to his father, "They *are* my
sons, whom God has given me in this *place*."

And he said, "Please bring them to me,
and [i]I will bless them." 10 Now [j]the eyes of
Israel were dim with age, *so that* he could
not see. Then Joseph brought them near
him, and he [k]kissed them and embraced
them. 11 And Israel said to Joseph, [l]"I had
not thought to see your face; but in fact,
God has also shown me your offspring!"

12 So Joseph brought them from beside
his knees, and he bowed down with his
face to the earth. 13 And Joseph took them
both, Ephraim with his right hand toward
Israel's left hand, and Manasseh with his
left hand toward Israel's right hand, and
brought *them* near him. 14 Then Israel
stretched out his right hand and [m]laid *it* on
Ephraim's head, who *was* the younger, and
his left hand on Manasseh's head, [n]guid-
ing his hands knowingly, for Manasseh
was the [o]firstborn. 15 And [p]he blessed Joseph, and said:

"God, [q]before whom my fathers
Abraham and Isaac walked,
The God who has fed me all my
life long to this day,
16 The Angel [r]who has redeemed me
from all evil,
Bless the lads;
Let [s]my name be named upon them,
And the name of my fathers
Abraham and Isaac;
And let them [t]grow into a
multitude in the midst of the
earth."

29 [e] Deut. 31:14; 1 Kin. 2:1 [f] Gen. 24:2-4 [g] Gen. 24:49; Josh. 2:14 [h] Gen. 50:25
30 [i] 2 Sam. 19:37 [j] Gen. 49:29; 50:5-13; Heb. 11:21
31 [k] Gen. 48:2; 1 Kin. 1:47; Heb. 11:21

CHAPTER 48

1 [a] Gen. 41:51, 56; 46:20; 50:23; Josh. 14:4
2 [1] Collected his strength
3 [b] Gen. 43:14; 49:25 [c] Gen. 28:13, 19; 35:6, 9
4 [d] Gen. 46:3 [e] Gen. 35:12; Ex. 6:8 [f] Gen. 17:8
5 [g] Gen. 41:50; 46:20; 48:8; Josh. 13:7; 14:4
6 [2] *children* [3] Who are born to you
7 [h] Gen. 35:9, 16, 19, 20
9 [i] Gen. 27:4; 47:15
10 [j] Gen. 27:1; 1 Sam. 3:2 [k] Gen. 27:27; 45:15; 50:1
11 [l] Gen. 45:26
14 [m] Matt. 19:15; Mark 10:16 [n] Gen. 48:19 [o] Gen. 41:51, 52; Josh. 17:1
15 [p] Gen. 47:7, 10; 49:24; [Heb. 11:21] [q] Gen. 17:1; 24:40; 2 Kin. 20:3
16 [r] Gen. 22:11, 15-18; 28:13-15; 31:11; [Ps. 34:22; 121:7] [s] Amos 9:12; Acts 15:17 [t] Num. 26:34, 37

47:29 your hand under my thigh. Cf. Abraham and Eliezer in Gen. 24:9. **do not bury me in Egypt.** With the customary sign of an oath in that day, Joseph sincerely promised to bury Jacob, at his request, in the family burial cave in Canaan (cf. 49:29-32).

47:31 Cf. Heb. 11:21.

48:3-6 After summarizing God's affirmation of the Abrahamic Covenant to himself, Jacob/Israel, in gratitude for Joseph's great generosity and preservation of God's people, formally proclaimed adoption of Joseph's sons on a par with Joseph's brothers in their inheritance, thus granting to Rachel's two sons (Joseph and Benjamin) 3 tribal territories in the Land (cf. v. 16). This may explain why the new name, Israel, was used throughout the rest of the chapter.

48:4 Cf. Acts 7:5.

48:8 Who *are* these? Blind Jacob asked for identification of Joseph's sons before he would pronounce their blessings. Perhaps, at this point, he recollected the time of blessing before his own father and the trick played on blind Isaac (27:1-29).

48:14 guiding his hands knowingly. Intentionally crossing his hands, Jacob altered what Joseph expected to happen and placed his right hand on the youngest, not on the firstborn. When Joseph attempted to correct Jacob's mistake (vv. 17,18), he learned that Jacob knew exactly what he was doing (vv. 19,20). The patriarchal blessing took on prophetic significance with such action and words, since Ephraim would be the most influential of the two to the extent that Ephraim would become a substitute name for Israel (*see note on 48:19*).

48:15 blessed Joseph. With hands on the sons' heads, Jacob uttered the prayer-wish for Joseph, which indicated by his wording that these two would be taking his son's place under Abraham and Isaac. *See note on vv. 3-6.*

48:15,16 Pessimism no longer overshadowed Jacob's testimony; he recognized that every day had been under God's hand or that of His Angel (*see note on 16:13*). This was a different evaluation of his life than previously given (47:9).

48:16 redeemed me. This is the first mention of God as redeemer, deliverer, or Savior.

17 Now when Joseph saw that his father
[u]laid his right hand on the head of
Ephraim, it displeased him; so he took
hold of his father's hand to remove it from
Ephraim's head to Manasseh's head.
18 And Joseph said to his father, "Not so,
my father, for this *one is* the firstborn; put
your right hand on his head."
19 But his father refused and said, [v]"I
know, my son, I know. He also shall become a people, and he also shall be great;
but truly [w]his younger brother shall be
greater than he, and his descendants shall
become a multitude of nations."
20 So he blessed them that day, saying,
[x]"By you Israel will bless, saying, 'May
God make you as Ephraim and as Manasseh!' " And thus he set Ephraim before
Manasseh.
21 Then Israel said to Joseph, "Behold, I
am dying, but [y]God will be with you and
bring you back to the land of your fathers.
22 Moreover [z]I have given to you one [4]por-
tion above your brothers, which I took
from the hand [a]of the Amorite with my
sword and my bow."

Jacob's Last Words to His Sons

49 And Jacob called his sons and said,
"Gather together, that I may [a]tell
you what shall befall you [b]in the last days:

2 "Gather together and hear, you sons
of Jacob,
And listen to Israel your father.

3 "Reuben, you are [c]my firstborn,
My might and the beginning of my
strength,
The excellency of dignity and the
excellency of power.
4 Unstable as water, you shall not
excel,
Because you [d]went up to your
father's bed;
Then you defiled *it*—
He went up to my couch.

5 "Simeon and Levi *are* brothers;
Instruments of [1]cruelty *are in* their
dwelling place.
6 [e]Let not my soul enter their council;
Let not my honor be united [f]to
their assembly;
[g]For in their anger they slew a man,
And in their self-will they
[2]hamstrung an ox.
7 Cursed *be* their anger, for *it is* fierce;
And their wrath, for it is cruel!
[h]I will divide them in Jacob
And scatter them in Israel.

8 "Judah, [i]you *are he* whom your
brothers shall praise;
[j]Your hand *shall be* on the neck of
your enemies;
[k]Your father's children shall bow
down before you.
9 Judah *is* [l]a lion's whelp;
From the prey, my son, you have
gone up.

17 [u]Gen. 48:14
19 [v]Gen. 48:14 [w]Num. 1:33, 35; Deut. 33:17
20 [x]Ruth 4:11, 12
21 [y]Gen. 28:15; 46:4; 50:24
22 [z]Gen. 14:7; Josh. 24:32; John 4:5 [a]Gen. 34:28 [4]Lit. *shoulder*

CHAPTER 49

1 [a]Deut. 33:1, 6-25; [Amos 3:7] [b]Num. 24:14; [Deut. 4:30]; Is. 2:2; 39:6; Jer. 23:20; Heb. 1:2
3 [c]Gen. 29:32
4 [d]Gen. 35:22; Deut. 27:20; 1 Chr. 5:1
5 [1]*violence*
6 [e]Ps. 64:2; Prov. 1:15, 16 [f]Ps. 26:9; Eph. 5:11 [g]Gen. 34:26 [2]*lamed*
7 [h]Num. 18:24; Josh. 19:1, 9; 21:1-42; 1 Chr. 4:24-27
8 [i]Deut. 33:7; Rev. 5:5 [j]Ps. 18:40 [k]Gen. 27:29; 1 Chr. 5:2
9 [l]Deut. 33:22; Ezek. 19:5-7; Mic. 5:8; [Rev. 5:5]

48:19 younger brother shall be greater. Ephraim did indeed become the dominant tribe of the 10 northern tribes, eventually being used as the national designate for the 10 tribes in the prophets (Is. 7:2,5,9,17; Hos. 9:3-16).

48:21 bring you back. Dying Jacob gave voice to his undying trust in God's taking his descendants back to Canaan.

48:22 one portion…with my sword. Jacob's history does not record any conquest of Amorite land. He did purchase property from the children of Hamor (Gen. 33:19) but that was not by conquest. At some time this military event had actually occurred, but for some unknown reason it finds no other mention in God's revelation.

49:1-28 With Judah and Joseph receiving the most attention (vv. 8-12,22-26), the father's blessing portrayed the future history of each son, seemingly based upon their characters up to that time. The cryptic nature of the poetry demands rigorous analysis for correlating tribal history with Jacob's last word and testament. See Moses' blessing on the tribes in Deut. 33, ca. 1405 B.C.

49:1 in the last days. The key expression leading into the poetic content of Jacob's prediction for each son often signifies the last days in prophetic literature (Is. 2:2; Ezek. 38:16) or points more generally to "the latter days" (Deut. 4:30; 31:29), i.e., in the sense of "in subsequent days."

49:2-27 The names of the sons are not given in birth order (cf. 29:32–30:24; 35:18), nor in the pattern of wife, then handmaid (cf. 46:8-25). The order is as per the mother: 1) the 6 sons of Leah; 2) one son of Bilhah; 3) two sons of Zilpah; 4) one son of Bilhah; and 5) the two sons of Rachel. Other than the reversal of Leah's fifth and sixth sons, the others remain in chronological order in relation to their mothers. No other pattern is discernible. It may have been nothing more than a mnemonic device, or just how Jacob personally had come to recall them to mind.

49:3,4 The seriousness of Reuben's sin (35:22) was not forgotten. Its consequences erased his birthright (1 Chr. 5:1-3), and whatever dignity and majesty he might have had, his tribe received scant mention in Israelite history and produced not one judge, prophet, military leader, or other important person (cf. Judg. 5:15; 1 Chr. 5:1). Moses prayed for this tribe not to die out (Deut. 33:6). "Unstable as water" lit. means "boiling" and shows instability.

49:5-7 The cruelty and anger of Simeon and Levi at Shechem was not forgotten (34:25). Its consequences affected Simeon who: 1) became the smallest tribe in the second census of Moses (Num. 26:14); 2) was omitted from the blessing of Moses (Deut. 33:8); and 3) later shared territory with Judah (Josh. 19:1-9). Levi was "scattered" (v. 7) throughout Israel; they became, by God's grace and through their loyalty to God (Ex. 32:26), the priestly tribe and residents of the cities of refuge. Neither possessed their own designated region in the Land, although Levi's priestly position was certainly a privileged one (cf. Deut. 33:8-11; Josh. 21:1-3). "Hamstrung" means to cut the leg tendons as a means of destroying the animal's usefulness.

49:8-12 As strong as a young lion and entrenched as an old lion, to Judah's line belonged national prominence and kingship, including David, Solomon, and their dynasty (640 years after this), as well as "the one to whom the scepter belongs," i.e., Shiloh, the cryptogram for the Messiah, the one also called the "Lion of the Tribe of Judah" (Rev. 5:5).

[m]He [3]bows down, he lies down as a
lion;
And as a lion, who shall rouse him?
10 [n]The [4]scepter shall not depart from
Judah,
Nor [o]a lawgiver from between his
feet,
[p]Until Shiloh comes;
[q]And to Him *shall be* the obedience
of the people.
11 Binding his donkey to the vine,
And his donkey's colt to the choice
vine,
He washed his garments in wine,
And his clothes in the blood of
grapes.
12 His eyes *are* darker than wine,
And his teeth whiter than milk.

13 "Zebulun[r] shall dwell by the haven
of the sea;
He *shall become* a haven for ships,
And his border shall [s]adjoin Sidon.

14 "Issachar[t] is a strong donkey,
Lying down between two burdens;
15 He saw that rest *was* good,
And that the land *was* pleasant;
He bowed [u]his shoulder to bear *a
burden,*
And became a band of slaves.

9 [m] Num. 23:24; 24:9 [3] *couches*
10 [n] Num. 24:17; Jer. 30:21; Matt. 1:3; 2:6; Luke 3:33; Rev. 5:5 [o] Ps. 60:7 [p] Is. 11:1; [Matt. 21:9] [q] Deut. 18:15; Ps. 2:6-9; 72:8-11; Is. 42:1, 4; 49:6; 60:1-5; [Luke 2:30-32] [4] A symbol of kingship
13 [r] Deut. 33:18, 19; Josh. 19:10, 11 [s] Gen. 10:19; Josh. 11:8
14 [t] 1 Chr. 12:32
15 [u] 1 Sam. 10:9
16 [v] Gen. 30:6; Deut. 33:22; Judg. 18:26, 27
17 [w] Judg. 18:27
18 [x] Ex. 15:2; Ps. 25:5; 40:1-3; 119:166, 174; Is. 25:9; Mic. 7:7
19 [y] Gen. 30:11; Deut. 33:20; 1 Chr. 5:18 [5] Lit. *Troop* [6] Lit. *raid*
20 [z] Deut. 33:24; Josh. 19:24-31
21 [a] Deut. 33:23
23 [b] Gen. 37:4, 24; Ps. 118:13
24 [c] Job 29:20; Ps. 37:15 [d] Ps. 132:2, 5; Is. 1:24; 49:26 [7] Or *supple*

16 "Dan[v] shall judge his people
As one of the tribes of Israel.
17 [w]Dan shall be a serpent by the way,
A viper by the path,
That bites the horse's heels
So that its rider shall fall backward.
18 [x]I have waited for your salvation,
O LORD!

19 "Gad,[y] [5]a troop shall [6]tramp upon
him,
But he shall [6]triumph at last.

20 "Bread from [z]Asher *shall be* rich,
And he shall yield royal dainties.

21 "Naphtali[a] *is* a deer let loose;
He uses beautiful words.

22 "Joseph *is* a fruitful bough,
A fruitful bough by a well;
His branches run over the wall.
23 The archers have [b]bitterly grieved
him,
Shot *at him* and hated him.
24 But his [c]bow remained in strength,
And the arms of his hands were
[7]made strong
By the hands of [d]the Mighty *God* of
Jacob

On the march through the wilderness, Judah went first (Num. 10:14) and had the largest population in Moses' census (cf. Num. 1:27; 26:22). This language (vv. 11,12) describes prosperity so great that people will tie a donkey to a choice vine, letting it eat because there is such abundance; wine will be as plentiful as water and everyone will be healthy. This is likely a millennial prophecy.

49:13 Although Zebulun's territory did not border the Mediterranean nor the Sea of Galilee, the tribe was situated to benefit from the important trade route, the Via Maris, traversed by sea traders moving through her territory.

49:14,15 Issachar, an industrious, robust, hardy, and stalwart tribe, lived up to the name of their founder whose name meant "man of wages" (cf. 1 Chr. 7:1-5; 12:32).

49:16-18 Dan, whose name meant "Judge," fathered an aggressive tribe that would also judge in the nation but would not be known for moral stature or religious faithfulness (cf. Judg. 13:2; 18:1ff.; 1 Kin. 12:28-30; 2 Kin. 10:29). Dan would later abandon its land allotment (Josh 19:40-48) and migrate to the extreme north of Israel (Judg. 18:1-31). Jacob's closing cry expressed hope for Dan in the day when salvation would indeed come to Israel. Dan, however, is omitted in the list of tribes in Rev. 7:4-8.

49:19 Settling in Transjordan exposed Gad's people to invasions, making them valiant fighters worthy of victory and commendation (cf. 1 Chr. 5:18-22; 12:8-15).

49:20 Asher benefited much from occupying the agriculturally rich coastal region N of Carmel, and provided gourmet delights for the palace. Cf. Josh. 19:24-31.

49:21 Deer-like speed and agility marked Naphtali's military prowess (cf. Judg. 4:6; 5:18). The song of Deborah and Barak, who hailed from Naphtali (Judg. 4:6), is representative of his eloquent words (Judg. 5).

49:22-26 Addressed to Joseph, but applicable to his two sons (cf. 48:15-20), these words thrust forth a contrasting experience of growth and prosperity alongside of hostility and conflict. Verses 23,24 may be a biography of Joseph. No other tribe had such direct refer-

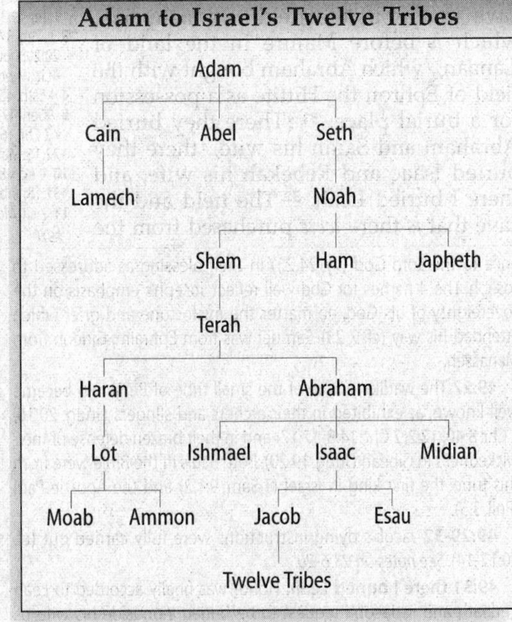

Adam to Israel's Twelve Tribes

[e](From there [f]*is* the Shepherd, [g]the
Stone of Israel),
25 [h]By the God of your father who
will help you,
[i]And by the Almighty [j]who will
bless you
With blessings of heaven above,
Blessings of the deep that lies
beneath,
Blessings of the breasts and of the
womb.
26 The blessings of your father
Have excelled the blessings of my
ancestors,
[k]Up to the utmost bound of the
everlasting hills.
[l]They shall be on the head of Joseph,
And on the crown of the head of
him who was separate from
his brothers.

27 "Benjamin is a [m]ravenous wolf;
In the morning he shall devour the
prey,
[n]And at night he shall divide the
spoil."

28 All these *are* the twelve tribes of Israel,
and this *is* what their father spoke to them.
And he blessed them; he blessed each one
according to his own blessing.

Jacob's Death and Burial

29 Then he charged them and said to
them: "I [o]am to be gathered to my people;
[p]bury me with my fathers [q]in the cave that
is in the field of Ephron the Hittite, 30 in the
cave that *is* in the field of Machpelah,
which *is* before Mamre in the land of
Canaan, [r]which Abraham bought with the
field of Ephron the Hittite as a possession
for a burial place. 31 [s]There they buried
Abraham and Sarah his wife, [t]there they
buried Isaac and Rebekah his wife, and
there I buried Leah. 32 The field and the
cave that *is* there *were* purchased from the
sons of Heth." 33 And when Jacob had finished commanding his sons, he drew his
feet up into the bed and breathed his last,
and was gathered to his people.

50 Then Joseph [a]fell on his father's face
and [b]wept over him, and kissed
him. 2 And Joseph commanded his servants the physicians to [c]embalm his father.
So the physicians embalmed Israel. 3 Forty
days were required for him, for such are the
days required for those who are embalmed;
and the Egyptians [d]mourned[1] for him seventy days.

4 Now when the days of his mourning
were past, Joseph spoke to [e]the household
of Pharaoh, saying, "If now I have found
favor in your eyes, please speak in the hearing of Pharaoh, saying, 5 [f]'My father made
me swear, saying, "Behold, I am dying; in
my grave [g]which I dug for myself in the
land of Canaan, there you shall bury me."
Now therefore, please let me go up and
bury my father, and I will come back.' "

6 And Pharaoh said, "Go up and bury
your father, as he made you swear."

7 So Joseph went up to bury his father;
and with him went up all the servants of
Pharaoh, the elders of his house, and all
the elders of the land of Egypt, 8 as well as
all the house of Joseph, his brothers, and
his father's house. Only their little ones,
their flocks, and their herds they left in the
land of Goshen. 9 And there went up with
him both chariots and horsemen, and it
was a very great gathering.

10 Then they came to the threshing floor
of Atad, which *is* beyond the Jordan, and
they [h]mourned there with a great and very
solemn lamentation. [i]He observed seven
days of mourning for his father. 11 And
when the inhabitants of the land, the
Canaanites, saw the mourning at the
threshing floor of Atad, they said, "This *is*
a deep mourning of the Egyptians." Therefore its name was called [2]Abel Mizraim,
which *is* beyond the Jordan.

24 [e]Gen. 45:11; 47:12 [f][Ps. 23:1; 80:1] [g][Ps. 118:22]; Is. 28:16; [1 Pet. 2:6-8] **25** [h]Gen. 28:13; 32:9; 35:3; 43:23; 50:17 [i]Gen. 17:1; 35:11 [j]Deut. 33:13 **26** [k]Deut. 33:15; Hab. 3:6 [l]Deut. 33:16 **27** [m]Judg. 20:21, 25 [n]Num. 23:24; Esth. 8:11; Ezek. 39:10; Zech. 14:1 **29** [o]Gen. 15:15; 25:8; 35:29 [p]Gen. 47:30; 2 Sam. 19:37 [q]Gen. 23:16-20; 50:13 **30** [r]Gen. 23:3-20 **31** [s]Gen. 23:19, 20; 25:9 [t]Gen. 35:29; 50:13

CHAPTER 50

1 [a]Gen. 46:4, 29 [b]2 Kin. 13:14 **2** [c]Gen. 50:26; 2 Chr. 16:14; Matt. 26:12; Mark 16:1; Luke 24:1; John 19:39, 40 **3** [d]Gen. 37:34; Num. 20:29; Deut. 34:8 [1]Lit. *wept* **4** [e]Esth. 4:2 **5** [f]Gen. 47:29-31 [g]2 Chr. 16:14; Is. 22:16; Matt. 27:60 **10** [h]Acts 8:2 [i]1 Sam. 31:13; Job 2:13 **11** [2]Lit. *Mourning of Egypt*

ence to the Lord God (vv. 24,25) in their blessing as addressed to Joseph. The 4 names for God well reflect Joseph's emphasis on the sovereignty of his God, no matter the misfortune and grief which attended his way (cf. v. 23). Samuel was from Ephraim, Gideon from Manasseh.

49:27 The warlike nature of the small tribe of Benjamin became well known, as exhibited in their archers and slingers (Judg. 20:16; 1 Chr. 8:40; 12:2; 2 Chr. 14:8; 17:17) and in their brazen defense of their wickedness in Gibeah (Judg. 19,20). Both Sauls in the Bible were from this tribe: the first king in Israel (1 Sam. 9:1,2) and the Apostle Paul (Phil. 3:5).

49:29-32 Jacob's dying instructions were fully carried out (cf. 50:12-14). *See notes on 23:6-20.*

49:31 there I buried Leah. Honor was finally accorded to Leah in death and in Jacob's request to be buried alongside his wife, as were his fathers. Burial alongside Rachel, the beloved wife, was not requested.

49:33 Jacob...breathed his last. Ca. 1858 B.C. **gathered to his people.** *See note on 25:8.*

50:2,3 physicians to embalm. Joseph summoned medical men, who were fully capable of embalming, rather than the religious embalmers in order to avoid the magic and mysticism associated with their practices. Usually in Egypt, mummifying was a 40 day process, which included gutting the body, drying it, and wrapping it.

50:3-6 Once normal embalming and mourning had been properly observed according to Egyptian custom, Joseph was free to seek permission to conduct a funeral in Canaan.

50:7-11 Out of respect for Joseph, a substantial escort accompanied him and all his relatives into the land of Canaan. This extraordinary event gave assurance to later generations because the bodies of

12 So his sons did for him just as he had
commanded them. 13 For [j]his sons carried
him to the land of Canaan, and buried him
in the cave of the field of Machpelah, before Mamre, which Abraham [k]bought with
the field from Ephron the Hittite as property for a burial place. 14 And after he had
buried his father, Joseph returned to
Egypt, he and his brothers and all who
went up with him to bury his father.

Joseph Reassures His Brothers

15 When Joseph's brothers saw that their
father was dead, [l]they said, "Perhaps Joseph will hate us, and may [3]actually repay
us for all the evil which we did to him."
16 So they sent *messengers* to Joseph, saying, "Before your father died he commanded, saying, 17 'Thus you shall say to Joseph: "I beg you, please forgive the
trespass of your brothers and their sin;
[m]for they did evil to you."' Now, please,
forgive the trespass of the servants of [n]the
God of your father." And Joseph wept
when they spoke to him.
18 Then his brothers also went and [o]fell
down before his face, and they said, "Behold, we *are* your servants."
19 Joseph said to them, [p]"Do not be
afraid, [q]for *am* I in the place of God? 20 [r]But
as for you, you meant evil against me; *but*
[s]God meant it for good, in order to bring it
about as *it is* this day, to save many people
alive. 21 Now therefore, do not be afraid; [t]I
will provide for you and your little ones."
And he comforted them and spoke [4]kind-
ly to them.

Death of Joseph

22 So Joseph dwelt in Egypt, he and his
father's household. And Joseph lived one
hundred and ten years. 23 Joseph saw
Ephraim's children [u]to the third *generation.*
[v]The children of Machir, the son of Manasseh, [w]were also brought up on Joseph's
knees.
24 And Joseph said to his brethren, "I am

13 [j]Gen. 49:29-31; Acts 7:16 [k]Gen. 23:16-20
15 [l][Job 15:21] [3]*fully*
17 [m][Prov. 28:13] [n]Gen. 49:25
18 [o]Gen. 37:7-10; 41:43; 44:14
19 [p]Gen. 45:5 [q]Gen. 30:2; 2 Kin. 5:7
20 [r]Gen. 45:5, 7; Ps. 56:5 [s][Acts 3:13-15]
21 [t][Matt. 5:44] [4]Lit. *to their hearts*
23 [u]Gen. 48:1; Job 42:16 [v]Num. 26:29; 32:39 [w]Gen. 30:3

the 3 patriarchs were in Canaan and Joseph's bones awaited transport there when, as per Joseph's last words, God's promises to the 3 began to be fulfilled.

50:15-18 The brothers' guilty consciences reasserted themselves and caused them to seriously underestimate the genuineness of Joseph's forgiveness and affection for them. Jacob's concern to plead on his sons' behalf equally underestimated Joseph's words and actions toward his brethren.

50:19 *am* I in the place of God? This concise question tweaked their memory of his explanation of how God had put him where he was (cf. 45:3-8), in the place God intended him to be at that time.

50:20 *but* God meant it for good. Joseph's wise, theological answer has gone down in history as the classic statement of God's sovereignty over the affairs of men. *See note on 45:1-8.*

Joseph—A Type of Christ

Joseph	Parallels	Jesus
37:2	A shepherd of his father's sheep.	John 10:11,27-29
37:3	His father loved him dearly.	Matt. 3:17
37:4	Hated by his brothers.	John 7:4, 5
37:13,14	Sent by father to brothers.	Hebrews 2:11
37:20	Others plotted to harm them.	John 11:53
37:23	Robes taken from them.	John 19:23,24
37:26	Taken to Egypt.	Matt. 2:14, 15
37:28	Sold for the price of a slave.	Matt. 26:15
39:7	Tempted.	Matt. 4:1
39:16-18	Falsely accused.	Matt. 26:59,60
39:20	Bound in chains.	Matt. 27:2
40:2, 3	Placed with two other prisoners, one who was saved and the other lost.	Luke 23:32
41:41	Exalted after suffering.	Phil. 2:9-11
41:46	Both 30 years old at the beginning of public recognition.	Luke 3:23
42:24; 45:2,14,15; 46:29	Both wept.	John 10:35
45:1-15	Forgave those who wronged them.	Luke 23:34
45:7	Saved their nation.	Matt. 1:21
50:20	What men did to hurt them, God turned to good.	1 Cor. 2:7,8

dying; but [x]God will surely visit you, and
bring you out of this land to the land [y]of
which He swore to Abraham, to Isaac, and
to Jacob." 25 Then [z]Joseph took an oath
from the children of Israel, saying, "God
will surely [5]visit you, and [a]you shall carry
up my [b]bones from here." 26 So Joseph
died, *being* one hundred and ten years old;
and they embalmed him, and he was put
in a coffin in Egypt.

24 [x]Gen. 15:14; 46:4; 48:21; Ex. 3:16, 17; Josh. 3:17; Heb. 11:22 [y]Gen. 26:3; 35:12; 46:4; Ex. 6:8
25 [z]Gen. 47:29, 30; Ex. 13:19; Josh. 24:32; Acts 7:15, 16; Heb. 11:22 [a]Gen. 17:8; 28:13; 35:12; Deut. 1:8; 30:1-8 [b]Ex. 13:19 [5]*give attention to*

50:24 God will surely visit you. Joseph died just as he had lived, firmly trusting in God to carry out His promises (cf. Heb. 11:22). Almost 4 centuries later, Moses took Joseph's remains out of Egypt (Ex. 13:19) and Joshua buried them at Shechem (Josh. 24:32). **to Abraham, to Isaac, and to Jacob.** The death of Jacob had finally allowed for the 3 patriarchs to be mentioned together.

50:26 one hundred and ten years old. Ca. 1804 B.C. Joseph's span of life was considered, at that time in Egypt, an ideal lifespan. Amenemhet III (ca. 1841–1792 B.C.) was the reigning Pharaoh. Exodus picked up the historical narrative, after a 280 year silence, ca. 1525 B.C. with the birth of Moses. *See note on Ex. 1:6-8.*

The Second Book of Moses Called
EXODUS

Title

The Greek Septuagint (LXX) and the Latin Vulgate versions of the OT assigned the title "Exodus" to this second book of Moses, because the departure of Israel from Egypt is the dominant historical fact in the book (19:1). In the Hebrew Bible, the opening words, "And (or Now) these *are* the names," served as the title of the book. The opening "And" or "Now" in the Hebrew title suggests that this book was to be accepted as the obvious sequel to Genesis, the first book of Moses. Hebrews 11:22 commends the faith of Joseph who, while on his deathbed (ca. 1804 B.C.), spoke of the "departure" or the "exiting" of the sons of Israel, looking ahead over 350 years to the Exodus (ca. 1445 B.C.).

Author and Date

Mosaic authorship of Exodus is unhesitatingly affirmed. Moses followed God's instructions and "wrote all the words of the LORD" (24:4), which included at the least the record of the battle with Amalek (17:14), the Ten Commandments (34:4,27-29), and the Book of the Covenant (20:22–23:33). Similar assertions of Mosaic writing occur elsewhere in the Pentateuch: Moses is identified as the one who recorded the "starting points of their journeys" (Num. 33:2) and who "wrote this law" (Deut. 31:9).

The OT corroborates Mosaic authorship of the portions mentioned above (see Josh. 1:7,8; 8:31,32; 1 Kin. 2:3; 2 Kin. 14:6; Neh. 13:1; Dan. 9:11-13; and Mal. 4:4). The NT concurs by citing Ex. 3:6 as part of "the book of Moses" (Mark. 12:26), by assigning Ex. 13:2 to "the law of Moses," which is also referred to as "the law of the Lord" (Luke 2:22,23), by ascribing Ex. 20:12 and 21:17 to Moses (Mark 7:10), by attributing the law to Moses (John 7:19; Rom. 10:5), and by Jesus' specifically declaring that Moses had written of Him (John 5:46,47).

At some time during his 40 year tenure as Israel's leader, beginning at 80 years of age and ending at 120 (7:7; Deut. 34:7), Moses wrote down this second of his 5 books. More specifically, it would have been after the Exodus and obviously before his death on Mt. Nebo in the plains of Moab. The date of the Exodus (ca. 1445 B.C.) dictates the date of the writing in the 15th century B.C.

Scripture dates Solomon's fourth year of reign, when he began to build the temple (ca. 966/65 B.C.), as being 480 years after the Exodus (1 Kin. 6:1), establishing the early date of 1445 B.C. Jephthah noted that, by his day, Israel had possessed Heshbon for 300 years (Judg. 11:26). Calculating backward and forward from Jephthah, and taking into account different periods of foreign oppression, judgeships and kingships, the wilderness wanderings, and the initial entry and conquest of Canaan under Joshua, this early date is confirmed and amounts to 480 years.

Scripture also dates the entry of Jacob and his extended family into Egypt (ca. 1875 B.C.) as being 430 years before the Exodus (12:40), thus placing Joseph in what archeologists have designated as the 12th Dynasty, the Middle Kingdom period of Egyptian history, and placing Moses and Israel's final years of residence and slavery in what archeologists have designated as the 18th Dynasty, or New Kingdom period. Further, Joseph's stint as vizier over all of Egypt (Gen. 45:8) precludes his having served under the Hyksos (ca. 1730–1570 B.C.), the foreign invaders who ruled during a period of confusion in Egypt and who never controlled all of the country. They were a mixed Semitic race who introduced the horse and chariot as well as the composite bow. These implements of war made possible their expulsion from Egypt.

Background and Setting

Eighteenth Dynasty Egypt, the setting for Israel's dramatic departure, was not a politically or economically weak and obscure period of Egyptian history. Thutmose III, for example, the Pharaoh of the Oppression has been called the "Napoleon of Ancient Egypt," the sovereign who expanded the boundaries of Egyptian influence far beyond natural borders. This was the dynasty which over a century before, under the leadership of Amose I, had expelled the Hyksos kings from the country and redirected the country's economic, military, and diplomatic growth. At the time of the Exodus, Egypt was strong, not weak.

Moses, born in 1525 B.C. (80 years old in 1445 B.C.), became "learned in all the wisdom of the Egyptians" (Acts 7:22) while growing up in the courts of Pharaohs Thutmose I and II and Queen Hatshepsut for his first 40 years (Acts 7:23). He was in self-imposed, Midianite exile during the reign of Thutmose III for another 40 years (Acts 7:30), and returned at God's direction to be Israel's leader early in the reign of Amenhotep II, the pharaoh of the Exodus. God used both the educational system of Egypt and his exile in Midian to prepare Moses to represent his people before a powerful pharaoh and to guide his people through the wilderness of the Sinai peninsula during his final 40 years (Acts 7:36). Moses died on Mt. Nebo when he was 120 years old (Deut. 34:1-6), as God's judgment was on him for his anger and disrespect (Num. 20:1-3). While he looked on from afar, Moses never entered the Promised Land. Centuries later he appeared to the disciples on the Mt. of Transfiguration (Matt. 17:3).

Historical and Theological Themes

In God's timing, the Exodus marked the end of a period of oppression for Abraham's descendants (Gen. 15:13), and constituted the beginning of the fulfillment of the covenant promise to Abraham that his descendants would not only reside in the Promised Land, but would also multiply and become a great nation (Gen. 12:1-3,7). The purpose of the book may be expressed like this: To trace the rapid growth of Jacob's descendants from Egypt to the establishment of the theocratic nation in their Promised Land.

At appropriate times, on Mt. Sinai and in the plains of Moab, God also gave the Israelites that body of legislation, the law, which they needed for living properly in Israel as the theocratic people of God. By this, they were distinct from all other nations (Deut. 4:7,8; Rom. 9:4,5).

By God's self-revelation, the Israelites were instructed in the sovereignty and majesty, the goodness and holiness, and the grace and mercy of their Lord, the one and only God of heaven and earth (see especially Ex. 3,6,33,34). The account of the Exodus and the events that followed are also the subject of other major biblical revelation (cf. Pss. 105:25-45; 106:6-27; Acts 7:17-44; 1 Cor. 10:1-13; Heb. 9:1-6; 11:23-29).

Interpretive Challenges

The absence of any Egyptian record of the devastation of Egypt by the 10 plagues and the major defeat of Pharaoh's elite army at the Red Sea should not give rise to speculation on whether the account is historically authentic. Egyptian historiography did not permit records of their pharaohs' embarrassments and ignominious defeats to be published. In recording the Conquest under Joshua, Scripture specifically notes the three cities which Israel destroyed and burned (Josh. 6:24; 8:28; 11:11-13). The Conquest, after all, was one of takeover and inhabitation of property virtually intact, not a war designed to destroy. The date of Israel's march into Canaan will not be confirmed, therefore, by examining extensive burn levels at city-sites of a later period.

Despite the absence of any extrabiblical, ancient Near Eastern records of the Hebrew bondage, the plagues, the Exodus, and the Conquest, archeological evidence corroborates the early date. All the pharaohs, for example, of the 15th century left evidence of interest in building enterprises in Lower Egypt. These projects were obviously accessible to Moses in the Delta region near Goshen.

The typological significance of the tabernacle has occasioned much reflection. Ingenuity in linking every item of furniture and every piece of building material to Christ may appear most intriguing, but if NT statements and allusions do not support such linkage and typology then hermeneutical caution must rule. The tabernacle's structure and ornamentation for efficiency and beauty are one thing, but finding hidden meaning and symbolism is unfounded. How the sacrificial and worship system of the tabernacle and its parts meaningfully typify the redeeming work of the coming Messiah must be left to those NT passages which treat the subject.

Outline

Israel's Suffering in Egypt

1 Now [a]these *are* the names of the children of Israel who came to Egypt; each
man and his household came with Jacob:
2 Reuben, Simeon, Levi, and Judah; 3 Issachar, Zebulun, and Benjamin; 4 Dan,
Naphtali, Gad, and Asher. 5 All those [1]who
were descendants of Jacob were [b]seventy[2]
persons (for Joseph was in Egypt *already*).
6 And [c]Joseph died, all his brothers, and all
that generation. 7 [d]But the children of Israel were fruitful and increased abundantly, multiplied and [3]grew exceedingly
mighty; and the land was filled with them.
8 Now there arose a new king over
Egypt, [e]who did not know Joseph. 9 And
he said to his people, "Look, the people of
the children of Israel *are* more and [f]might-
ier than we; 10 [g]come, let us [h]deal shrewdly with them, lest they multiply, and it happen, in the event of war, that they also join
our enemies and fight against us, and *so* go
up out of the land." 11 Therefore they set
taskmasters over them [i]to afflict them with
their [j]burdens. And they built for Pharaoh
[k]supply cities, Pithom [l]and Raamses. 12 But
the more they afflicted them, the more they
multiplied and grew. And they were in
dread of the children of Israel. 13 So the
Egyptians made the children of Israel
[m]serve with [4]rigor. 14 And they [n]made
their lives bitter with hard bondage—[o]in
mortar, in brick, and in all manner of service in the field. All their service in which
they made them serve *was* with rigor.
15 Then the king of Egypt spoke to the
[p]Hebrew midwives, of whom the name of
one *was* Shiphrah and the name of the
other Puah; 16 and he said, "When you do
the duties of a midwife for the Hebrew
women, and see *them* on the birthstools, if
it *is* a [q]son; then you shall kill him; but if it
is a daughter, then she shall live." 17 But
the midwives [r]feared God, and did not do
[s]as the king of Egypt commanded them,
but saved the male children alive. 18 So the
king of Egypt called for the midwives and
said to them, "Why have you done this
thing, and saved the male children alive?"
19 And [t]the midwives said to Pharaoh,
"Because the Hebrew women *are* not like
the Egyptian women; for they [5]*are* lively
and give birth before the midwives come
to them."

CHAPTER 1

1 [a] Gen. 46:8-27; Ex. 6:14-16
5 [b] Gen. 46:26,27; [Deut. 10:22] [1] Lit. *who came from the loins of* [2] DSS, LXX *seventy-five;* cf. Acts 7:14
6 [c] Gen. 50:26; Acts 7:15
7 [d] Gen. 12:2; 28:3; 35:11; 46:3; 47:27; 48:4; Num. 22:3; Deut. 1:10,11; 26:5; Ps. 105:24; Acts 7:17 [3] *became very numerous*
8 [e] Acts 7:18,19
9 [f] Gen. 26:16
10 [g] Ps. 83:3,4 [h] Ps. 105:25; [Prov. 16:25]; Acts 7:19
11 [i] Gen. 15:13; Ex. 3:7; 5:6 [j] Ex. 1:14; 2:11; 5:4-9; 6:6 [k] 1 Kin. 9:19; 2 Chr. 8:4 [l] Gen. 47:11
13 [m] Gen. 15:13; Ex. 5:7-19 [4] *harshness*
14 [n] Ex. 2:23; 6:9; Num. 20:15; [Acts 7:19,34] [o] Ps. 81:6
15 [p] Ex. 2:6
16 [q] Matt. 2:16; Acts 7:19
17 [r] Ex. 1:21; Prov. 16:6 [s] Dan. 3:16,18; Acts 4:18-20; 5:29
19 [t] Josh. 2:4; 2 Sam. 17:19,20 [5] *have vigor of life,* bear quickly, easily

1:1–12:36 This section recounts Israel's final years in Egypt before the Exodus.

1:1-5 Genesis also reported the names and the number of Jacob's descendants who came to Egypt (Gen. 35:23; 46:8-27).

1:5 seventy persons. Cf. Gen. 46:8-27. Acts 7:14 reports 75 with the addition of 5 relatives of Joseph included in the LXX, but not the Heb. text.

1:6-8 This summary of a lengthy period of time moves the record from the death of Joseph (ca. 1804 B.C.), the last recorded event in Genesis, to the radical change in Israel's history, i.e., from favor before Egypt's pharaoh to disfavor and enslavement (ca. 1525–1445 B.C.).

1:7 The growth of the nation (cf. 12:37) was phenomenal! It grew from 70 men to 603,000 males, 20 years of age and older, thus allowing for a total population of about 2 million (Num. 1:46) departing from Egypt. The seed of Abraham was no longer an extended family, but a nation. The promise that his descendants would be fruitful and multiply (Gen. 35:11,12) had indeed been fulfilled in Egypt.

1:8 there arose a new king. This king is either to be identified as one of the Hyksos kings (see Introduction) during a period of political disintegration, or as Pharaoh Amose I, founder of what archeologists have designated as the 18th Dynasty of the New Kingdom period in Egyptian history. It is probably best to take this new king, who knew not Joseph, as a Hyksos ruler. Furthermore, the term "arose" signifies "rose against," which accords well with a foreign seizure of the Egyptian throne. The Hyksos (ca. 1730–1570 B.C.) came from outside Egypt (cf. Acts 7:18).

1:9-12 Another summary of a fairly lengthy period of time, as indicated by the population continuing to grow in spite of increasing hardship imposed on Israel.

1:9 the people. An Egyptian pharaoh designated Israel as a nation, marking the first time the term "people" or "nation" is used of them.

1:10,11 join our enemies...set taskmasters over them. Israel was assessed both as a threat to national security and as an economic asset—slavery would, therefore, control the danger and maximize their usefulness.

1:11 supply cities, Pithom and Raamses. Places where both provisions and military hardware were stored. Archeological identification has not been finally definitive, with some 3 to 5 options being put forward for them. Pithom is usually taken as a center of solar worship in northern Egypt, and Raamses as Qantir in the eastern delta region. In addition, the city might very well have been re-named under the reign of the later, powerful pharaoh, and that name was better known to Israel later on (cf. the case of Laish, or Leshem, renamed Dan in Gen. 14:14, Josh. 19:47, and Judg. 18:29).

1:13 the Egyptians. The native inhabitants continued to enslave Israel. Between vv. 12 and 13 a major change in Egyptian history took place—the Hyksos were driven out (ca. 1570 B.C.).

1:14 hard bondage—in mortar, in brick. Archeologists have uncovered reliefs and paintings confirming the Egyptian practice of imposing forced labor on prisoners and slaves. These paintings also show foremen and guards watching construction work while scribes registered data on tablets.

1:15-17 the midwives feared God. These brave, older women reverenced their God and thus obeyed Him and not man. They obviously understood that children were a gift from God and that murder was wrong. The two midwives mentioned by name were probably the leading representatives of their profession, for it is unlikely that such a burgeoning population had only two midwives to deal with all the births.

1:15,16 The failure of rigorous bondage to suppress population growth necessitated that different measures be taken; hence, the royal order to the Hebrew midwives to murder male infants at birth.

1:16 birthstools. Lit. "two stones" on which the women sat to deliver.

1:19,20 Rather than trying to argue for a justifiable lie on the part of midwives seeking to protect God's people, take it as a statement of what was true: God was directly involved in this affair of birth and na-

20 [u]Therefore God dealt well with the
midwives, and the people multiplied and
[6]grew very mighty. 21 And so it was, because the midwives feared God, [v]that He
[7]provided households for them.
22 So Pharaoh commanded all his people, saying, [w]"Every son who is [8]born you
shall cast into the river, and every daughter you shall save alive."

Moses Is Born

2 And [a]a man of the house of Levi went
and took *as wife* a daughter of Levi.
2 So the woman conceived and bore a son.
And [b]when she saw that he *was* a beautiful
child, she hid him three months. 3 But
when she could no longer hide him, she
took an ark of [c]bulrushes for him, daubed
it with [d]asphalt and [e]pitch, put the child in
it, and laid *it* in the reeds [f]by the river's
bank. 4 [g]And his sister stood afar off, to
know what would be done to him.
5 Then the [h]daughter of Pharaoh came
down to bathe at the river. And her maidens walked along the riverside; and when
she saw the ark among the reeds, she sent
her maid to get it. 6 And when she opened
it, she saw the child, and behold, the baby
wept. So she had compassion on him, and
said, "This is one of the Hebrews' children."
7 Then his sister said to Pharaoh's
daughter, "Shall I go and call a nurse for

20 [u]Gen. 15:1; Ruth 2:12; [Prov. 11:18]; Eccl. 8:12; [Is. 3:10]; Heb. 6:10 [6]*became very numerous*
21 [v]1 Sam. 2:35; 2 Sam. 7:11, 13, 27, 29; 1 Kin. 2:24; 11:38; [Ps. 127:1] [7]*gave them families*
22 [w]Acts 7:19 [8]Sam., LXX, Tg. add *to the Hebrews*

CHAPTER 2

1 [a]Ex. 6:16–20; Num. 26:59; 1 Chr. 23:14
2 [b]Acts 7:20; Heb. 11:23
3 [c]Is. 18:2 [d]Gen. 14:10 [e]Gen. 6:14; Is. 34:9 [f]Is. 19:6
4 [g]Ex. 15:20; Num. 26:59
5 [h]Ex. 7:15; Acts 7:21
10 [i]Acts 7:21 [1]Heb. *Mosheh,* lit. *Drawn Out*
11 [j]Acts 7:23, 24; Heb. 11:24–26
12 [k]Acts 7:24, 25
13 [l]Acts 7:26–28 [m]Prov. 25:8
14 [n]Gen. 19:9; Acts 7:27, 28 [o]Judg. 6:27; Heb. 11:27

you from the Hebrew women, that she
may nurse the child for you?"
8 And Pharaoh's daughter said to her,
"Go." So the maiden went and called the
child's mother. 9 Then Pharaoh's daughter
said to her, "Take this child away and
nurse him for me, and I will give *you* your
wages." So the woman took the child and
nursed him. 10 And the child grew, and she
brought him to Pharaoh's daughter, and he
became [i]her son. So she called his name
[1]Moses, saying, "Because I drew him out
of the water."

Moses Flees to Midian

11 Now it came to pass in those days,
[j]when Moses was grown, that he went out
to his brethren and looked at their burdens. And he saw an Egyptian beating a
Hebrew, one of his brethren. 12 So he
looked this way and that way, and when
he saw no one, he [k]killed the Egyptian and
hid him in the sand. 13 And [l]when he went
out the second day, behold, two Hebrew
men [m]were fighting, and he said to the one
who did the wrong, "Why are you striking
your companion?"
14 Then he said, [n]"Who made you a
prince and a judge over us? Do you intend
to kill me as you killed the Egyptian?"
So Moses [o]feared and said, "Surely this
thing is known!" 15 When Pharaoh heard
of this matter, he sought to kill Moses. But

tional growth. That's the key to understanding why no decree of Pharaoh's would work out as he intended it, and why Hebrew women were so healthy and gave birth with ease.

1:22 The failure of the extermination program demanded of the midwives finally caused Pharaoh to demand that all his subjects get involved in murdering newborn boys.

2:1,2 Since Moses was born soon after the general decree of 1:22 was given (ca. 1525 B.C.), the issuer of the decree was Thutmose I.

2:3,4 The careful actions of Moses' mother to construct the ark of bulrushes, to set Moses afloat close to the royal bathing place, and to have his sister watch to see what would happen, indicate a hope that something would work out right for the child.

2:5 the daughter of Pharaoh. Identified possibly as Hatshepsut or another princess; in either case a princess whom God providentially used to override Pharaoh's death decree and protect the life of His chosen leader for the Israelites.

2:10 became her son. The position of "son" undoubtedly granted Moses special privileges belonging to nobility, but none of these persuaded Moses to relinquish his native origin. Rather, as the NT advises, his spiritual maturity was such that when he came of age, "he refused to be called the son of Pharaoh's daughter" (Heb. 11:24). The formal education in the court of that time meant that Moses would have learned reading, writing, arithmetic, and perhaps one or more of the languages of Canaan. He would also have participated in various outdoor sports, e.g., archery and horseback riding, two favorites of the 18th Dynasty court.

2:11 when Moses was grown. The narrative skips over all details of Moses' life as the adopted son of a princess prior to the event which led to his flight into Midian.

2:11,12,16-21 Two injustices aroused Moses' indignation with different consequences: one resulted in his leaving home, having killed an Egyptian who beat an Israelite; the other resulted in his finding a new home as an Egyptian who helped the Midianite daughters of Reuel, and in his finding a wife. Undoubtedly, Reuel and his family soon discovered Moses was not really an Egyptian.

2:14 Cf. Acts 7:27,28,35.

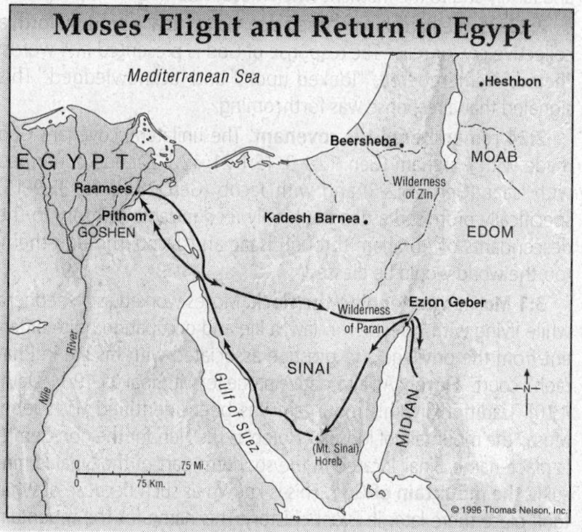

[p]Moses fled from [2]the face of Pharaoh and
dwelt in the land of [q]Midian; and he sat
down by [r]a well.
16 [s]Now the priest of Midian had seven
daughters. [t]And they came and drew
water, and they filled the [u]troughs to water
their father's flock. 17 Then the [v]shepherds
came and [w]drove them away; but Moses
stood up and helped them, and [x]watered
their flock.
18 When they came to [y]Reuel[3] their father, [z]he said, "How *is it that* you have
come so soon today?"
19 And they said, "An Egyptian delivered us from the hand of the shepherds,
and he also drew enough water for us and
watered the flock."
20 So he said to his daughters, "And
where *is* he? Why *is* it *that* you have left the
man? Call him, that he may [a]eat bread."
21 Then Moses was content to live with
the man, and he gave [b]Zipporah his
daughter to Moses. 22 And she bore *him* a
son. He called his name [c]Gershom,[4] for he
said, "I have been [d]a [5]stranger in a foreign
land."
23 Now it happened [e]in the process of
time that the king of Egypt died. Then the
children of Israel [f]groaned because of the
bondage, and they cried out; and [g]their cry
came up to God because of the bondage.
24 So God [h]heard their groaning, and God
[i]remembered His [j]covenant with Abraham, with Isaac, and with Jacob. 25 And

15 [p] Acts 7:29; Heb. 11:27 [q] Ex. 3:1 [r] Gen. 24:11; 29:2; Ex. 15:27 [2] *the presence of Pharaoh*
16 [s] Ex. 3:1; 4:18; 18:12 [t] Gen. 24:11, 13, 19; 29:6-10; 1 Sam. 9:11 [u] Gen. 30:38
17 [v] Gen. 47:3; 1 Sam. 25:7 [w] Gen. 26:19-21 [x] Gen. 29:3, 10
18 [y] Num. 10:29 [z] Ex. 3:1; 4:18 [3] *Jethro,* Ex. 3:1
20 [a] Gen. 31:54; 43:25
21 [b] Ex. 4:25; 18:2
22 [c] Ex. 4:20; 18:3, 4 [d] Gen. 23:4; Lev. 25:23; Acts 7:29; Heb. 11:13, 14 [4] Lit. *Stranger There* [5] *sojourner,* temporary resident
23 [e] Acts 7:34 [f] Deut. 26:7 [g] Ex. 3:7, 9; James 5:4
24 [h] Ex. 6:5; Acts 7:34 [i] Gen. 15:13; 22:16-18; 26:2-5; 28:13-15; Ps. 105:8, 42 [j] Gen. 12:1-3; 15:14; 17:1-14
25 [k] Ex. 4:31; Luke 1:25; Acts 7:34 [l] Ex. 3:7

CHAPTER 3

1 [a] Ex. 4:18 [b] Ex. 2:16 [c] Ex. 17:6; 1 Kin. 19:8 [d] Ex. 18:5

God [k]looked upon the children of Israel,
and God [l]acknowledged *them.*

Moses at the Burning Bush

3 Now Moses was tending the flock of
[a]Jethro his father-in-law, [b]the priest of
Midian. And he led the flock to the back
of the desert, and came to [c]Horeb, [d]the
mountain of God. 2 And [e]the Angel of the
LORD appeared to him in a flame of fire
from the midst of a bush. So he looked, and
behold, the bush was burning with fire,
but the bush *was* not consumed. 3 Then
Moses said, "I will now turn aside and see
this [f]great sight, why the bush does not
burn."
4 So when the LORD saw that he turned
aside to look, God called [g]to him from the
midst of the bush and said, "Moses, Moses!"
And he said, "Here I am."
5 Then He said, "Do not draw near this
place. [h]Take your sandals off your feet, for
the place where you stand *is* holy ground."
6 Moreover He said, [i]"I *am* the God of your
father—the God of Abraham, the God of
Isaac, and the God of Jacob." And Moses
hid his face, for [j]he was afraid to look upon
God.
7 And the LORD said: [k]"I have surely seen
the oppression of My people who *are* in

2 [e] Deut. 33:16; Mark 12:26; Luke 20:37; Acts 7:30 **3** [f] Acts 7:31 **4** [g] Ex. 4:5; Deut. 33:16 **5** [h] Josh. 5:15; Acts 7:33 **6** [i] Gen. 28:13; Ex. 3:16; 4:5; [Matt. 22:32; Mark 12:26, 27; Luke 20:37, 38]; Acts 7:32 [j] 1 Kin. 19:13 **7** [k] Ex. 2:23-25; Neh. 9:9; Ps. 106:44

2:15 Midian. The Midianites, who were descendants of Abraham and Keturah (Gen. 25:1-4), settled in the Arabian Peninsula along the eastern shore of the Gulf of Aqabah.

2:18 Reuel. He was also known as Jethro (3:1), who may very well have been a worshiper of the true God (cf. 18:12-23), notwithstanding his being also the priest of Midian.

2:21-23 The narrative skips over the unimportant details of this 40 year period and moves the record quickly to the finding of a new home and family and to the moment when Moses returned to his people.

2:23-25 The hardship imposed upon Israel finally brought forth a collective cry for relief. The response of God is presented in 4 words: "heard," "remembered," "looked upon," and "acknowledged." This signaled that a response was forthcoming.

2:24 remembered His covenant. The unilateral covenant God made with Abraham (Gen. 12:1-3; 15:1-21; 17:1-22) and confirmed with Isaac (Gen. 26:2-5) and with Jacob (Gen. 28:10-15; 35:9-15) specifically promised a geographically recognizable territory to the descendants of Abraham through Isaac and Jacob. Through them, too, the world would be blessed.

3:1 Moses was tending the flock. Moses worked as a shepherd while living with his father-in-law; a life and occupation quite different from the privilege and prestige associated with his life in Pharaoh's court. **Horeb.** An alternative name for Mt. Sinai (cf. 19:11; Deut. 4:10). Traditionally, this mountain has been identified with Jebel Musa, "the mountain of Moses." "Horeb" is the Heb. for the non-Semitic place-name, Sinai, located in the southern part of the Sinai Peninsula. **the mountain of God.** This is known as such because of what took place there later in Israel's history. This name for the mountain suggests that the book of Exodus was written by Moses after the events at Sinai. Others suggest that it was already known as a sacred mountain prior to the call of Moses; but it seems best to relate the name to what God did for Israel there.

3:2 The Angel of the LORD. Lit. "messenger of Yahweh" who, in context, turns out to be the Lord Himself talking to Moses (cf. Acts 7:30).

3:2-4 Moses' attention was drawn to a most unusual sight, that of a burning bush which was not being consumed by the fire within. A supernatural event is the only viable explanation. Natural explanations of certain types of flowers with gaseous pods or oil glands fail, in that, after 40 years of work in the desert, Moses would surely have ignored something normal. This was so different that it aroused his curiosity and demanded further examination. God was in the bush speaking, clearly a miraculous event.

3:5-10 Cf. Acts 7:33,34.

3:5 Do not draw near this place. Take your sandals off. A sign of reverence in a holy place, one set apart from the norm because God was present there. These commands prevented Moses from rashly intruding, unprepared, into God's presence.

3:6 I *am* the God of your father. God's opening words, although important for Moses to hear, point the reader back to 2:24—showing that the God of Israel has remembered His people and has begun to take action (cf. Matt. 22:32; Mark 12:26; Luke 20:37; Acts 3:13; 7:32). **Moses hid his face.** A fitting reaction of reverent fear in the presence of the Divine was modeled by Moses.

3:7,8 I have surely seen...have heard. An emphasis on God's having been well aware of the desperate situation of Israel. The result:

Egypt, and have heard their cry [l]because of
their taskmasters, [m]for I know their [1]sor-
rows. 8 So [n]I have come down to [o]deliver
them out of the hand of the Egyptians, and
to bring them up from that land [p]to a good
and large land, to a land [q]flowing with milk
and honey, to the place of [r]the Canaanites
and the Hittites and the Amorites and the
Perizzites and the Hivites and the Jebusites.
9 Now therefore, behold, [s]the cry of the children of Israel has come to Me, and I have
also seen the [t]oppression with which the
Egyptians oppress them. 10 [u]Come now,
therefore, and I will send you to Pharaoh
that you may bring My people, the children
of Israel, out of Egypt."

11 But Moses said to God, [v]"Who *am* I
that I should go to Pharaoh, and that I
should bring the children of Israel out of
Egypt?"

12 So He said, [w]"I will certainly be with
you. And this *shall be* a [x]sign to you that I
have sent you: When you have brought the
people out of Egypt, you shall serve God
on this mountain."

13 Then Moses said to God, "Indeed,
when I come to the children of Israel and
say to them, 'The God of your fathers has
sent me to you,' and they say to me, 'What
is His name?' what shall I say to them?"

14 And God said to Moses, "I AM WHO
I AM." And He said, "Thus you shall say to
the children of Israel, [y]'I AM has sent me to
you.'" 15 Moreover God said to Moses,
"Thus you shall say to the children of Israel: 'The LORD God of your fathers, the
God of Abraham, the God of Isaac, and the
God of Jacob, has sent me to you. This *is*
[z]My name forever, and this *is* My memorial to all generations.' 16 Go and [a]gather the
elders of Israel together, and say to them,
'The LORD God of your fathers, the God of
Abraham, of Isaac, and of Jacob, appeared
to me, saying, [b]"I have surely visited you
and *seen* what is done to you in Egypt;
17 and I have said [c]I will bring you up out
of the affliction of Egypt to the land of the
Canaanites and the Hittites and the Amorites and the Perizzites and the Hivites and
the Jebusites, to a land flowing with milk
and honey."' 18 Then [d]they will heed your
voice; and [e]you shall come, you and the elders of Israel, to the king of Egypt; and you
shall say to him, 'The LORD God of the He-

7 [l]Ex. 1:11 [m]Gen. 18:21; Ex. 2:25 [1]*pain*
8 [n]Gen. 15:13-16; 46:4; 50:24, 25 [o]Ex. 6:6-8; 12:51 [p]Num. 13:27; Deut. 1:25; 8:7-9; Josh. 3:17 [q]Ex. 3:17; 13:5; Jer. 11:5; Ezek. 20:6 [r]Gen. 15:19-21; Josh. 24:11
9 [s]Ex. 2:23 [t]Ex. 1:11, 13, 14
10 [u]Gen. 15:13, 14; Ex. 12:40, 41; [Mic. 6:4]; Acts 7:6, 7
11 [v]Ex. 4:10; 6:12; 1 Sam. 18:18
12 [w]Gen. 31:3; Ex. 4:12, 15; 33:14-16; Deut. 31:23; Josh. 1:5; Is. 43:2; Rom. 8:31 [x]Ex. 4:8; 19:3
14 [y][Ex. 6:3; John 8:24, 28, 58; Heb. 13:8; Rev. 1:8; 4:8]
15 [z]Ps. 30:4; 97:12; 102:12; 135:13; [Hos. 12:5]
16 [a]Ex. 4:29 [b]Gen. 50:24; Ex. 2:25; 4:31; Ps. 33:18; Luke 1:68
17 [c]Gen. 15:13-21; 46:4; 50:24, 25
18 [d]Ex. 4:31 [e]Ex. 5:1, 3

He promised to deliver them from Egyptian oppression. Here, and in the next two verses, the repetitive manner in describing what God saw and would do, served to underscore all the more His personal involvement in the history of His people whom He had sent into Egypt.

3:8 to a good and large land, to a land...to the place. Three descriptions of the land to which Israel was going to be taken emphatically underscored the land promise of the Abrahamic Covenant. **flowing with milk and honey.** A formal and graphic way of describing a fertile land of bounteous provision. **of the Canaanites and the Hittites.** A specific identification of the territory to which Israel was going; her Promised Land was currently inhabited by other peoples.

3:10 I will send you. The divine summons made Moses both leader/deliverer of Israel and ambassador of God before Pharaoh.

3:11 Who *am* I...? The first response is an objection from Moses to the divine summons, an expression of inadequacy for such a serious mission. It sounded reasonable, for after 40 years of absence from Egypt, what could he, a mere shepherd in Midian, do upon return?

3:12 I will certainly be with you. The divine promise, one given also to the patriarchs, Abraham, Isaac, and Jacob, should have been sufficient to quell all the chosen agent's fears and sense of inadequacy for the task. **you shall serve God on this mountain.** A second divine promise signified the future success of the mission, suggesting that Israel would not be delivered simply out of bondage and oppression, but rescued to worship! (Cf. Acts 7:7).

3:13 Then Moses said. Was Moses at this point crossing the line from reasonable inquiry to unreasonable doubt? God's patient replies instructing Moses on what He would do and what the results would be, including Israel's being viewed with favor by the Egyptians (3:21), ought to caution the reader from hastily classifying Moses' attitude as altogether wrong from the very beginning of the interaction between him and the Lord. A response of divine anger comes only in 4:14 at the very end of Moses' questions and objections. *See note at 4:1.* **What *is* His name?** Moses raised a second objection. Israel might ask for God's name in validation of Moses' declaration that he had been sent by the God of their fathers. Significantly, the question was not "Who is this God?" The Hebrews understood the name Yahweh had been known to the patriarchs (which Genesis well indicates). Asking "what" meant they sought for the relevancy of the name to their circumstances. "Who?" sought after title, name, and identity, whereas "What?" inquired into the character, quality, or essence of a person.

3:14 I AM WHO I AM. This name for God points to His self-existence and eternality; it denotes "I am the One who is/will be," which is decidedly the best and most contextually suitable option from a number of theories about its meaning and etymological source. The significance in relation to "God of your fathers" is immediately discernible: He's the same God throughout the ages! The consonants from the Heb. word *Yhwh,* combined with the vowels from the divine name *Adonai* (Master or Lord), gave rise to the name "Jehovah" in English. Since the name *Yahweh* was considered so sacred that it should not be pronounced, the Massoretes inserted the vowels from *Adonai* to remind themselves to pronounce it when reading instead of saying *Yahweh.* Technically, this combination of consonants is known as the "tetragrammaton."

3:15-22 Having provided Moses with His name in response to his second inquiry, God then furnished him with two speeches, one for Israel's elders (vv. 16,17) and one for Pharaoh (v. 18b). Also included was notification of the elders' positive response to Moses' report (v. 18a), of Pharaoh's refusal to grant them their request (v. 19), of God's miraculous, judgmental reaction (v. 20), and of Israel's plundering of the Egyptians, who found themselves responding favorably to the departing nation's request for silver, gold, and clothing (vv. 21,22). The last of these harkens back to God's promise to Abraham that his descendants would come out of the land of their affliction with great possessions (Gen. 15:14).

3:15 Cf. Matt. 22:23; Mark 12:26; Acts 3:13.

3:16 elders. Lit. "bearded ones," which indicated the age and wisdom needed to lead.

3:17 land of. *See notes on 3:8.*

brews has [f]met with us; and now, please,
let us go three days' journey into the
wilderness, that we may sacrifice to the
LORD our God.' 19 But I am sure that the
king of Egypt [g]will not let you go, no, not
even by a mighty hand. 20 So I will [h]stretch
out My hand and strike Egypt with [i]all My
wonders which I will do in its midst; and
[j]after that he will let you go. 21 And [k]I will
give this people favor in the sight of the
Egyptians; and it shall be, when you go,
that you shall not go empty-handed.
22 [l]But every woman shall ask of her
neighbor, namely, of her who dwells near
her house, [m]articles of silver, articles of
gold, and clothing; and you shall put *them*
on your sons and on your daughters. So
[n]you shall plunder the Egyptians."

Miraculous Signs for Pharaoh

4 Then Moses answered and said, "But
suppose they will not believe me or listen to my voice; suppose they say, 'The
LORD has not appeared to you.' "
2 So the LORD said to him, "What *is* that
in your hand?"
He said, "A rod."
3 And He said, "Cast it on the ground."
So he cast it on the ground, and it became a
serpent; and Moses fled from it. 4 Then the
LORD said to Moses, "Reach out your hand
and take *it* by the tail" (and he reached out
his hand and caught it, and it became a rod
in his hand), 5 "that they may [a]believe that
the [b]LORD God of their fathers, the God of
Abraham, the God of Isaac, and the God of
Jacob, has appeared to you."
6 Furthermore the LORD said to him,
"Now put your hand in your bosom." And
he put his hand in his bosom, and when he
took it out, behold, his hand *was* leprous,
[c]like snow. 7 And He said, "Put your hand
in your bosom again." So he put his hand
in his bosom again, and drew it out of his
bosom, and behold, [d]it was restored like his
other flesh. 8 "Then it will be, if they do not
believe you, nor heed the message of the
[e]first sign, that they may believe the message of the latter sign. 9 And it shall be, if
they do not believe even these two signs, or
listen to your voice, that you shall take
water from [1]the river and pour *it* on the dry
land. [f]The water which you take from the
river will become blood on the dry *land.*"
10 Then Moses said to the LORD, "O my
Lord, I *am* not eloquent, neither before nor
since You have spoken to Your servant; but
[g]I *am* slow of speech and [2]slow of tongue."
11 So the LORD said to him, [h]"Who has
made man's mouth? Or who makes the
mute, the deaf, the seeing, or the blind?
Have not I, the LORD? 12 Now therefore, go,
and I will be [i]with your mouth and teach
you what you shall say."
13 But he said, "O my Lord, [j]please send
by the hand of whomever *else* You may
send."
14 So [k]the anger of the LORD was kindled
against Moses, and He said: "Is not Aaron
the Levite your [l]brother? I know that he
can speak well. And look, [m]he is also coming out to meet you. When he sees you, he
will be glad in his heart. 15 Now [n]you shall
speak to him and [o]put the words in his
mouth. And I will be with your mouth and
with his mouth, and [p]I will teach you what

18 [f] Num. 23:3, 4, 15, 16
19 [g] Ex. 5:2
20 [h] Ex. 6:6; 9:15 [i] Deut. 6:22; Neh. 9:10; Ps. 105:27; 135:9; Jer. 32:20; Acts 7:36 [j] Ex. 11:1; 12:31-37
21 [k] Ex. 11:3; 12:36; 1 Kin. 8:50; Ps. 105:37; 106:46; [Prov. 16:7]
22 [l] Ex. 11:2 [m] Ex. 33:6 [n] Job 27:17; Prov. 13:22; [Ezek. 39:10]

CHAPTER 4

5 [a] Ex. 4:31; 19:9 [b] Gen. 28:13; 48:15; Ex. 3:6, 15
6 [c] Num. 12:10; 2 Kin. 5:27
7 [d] Num. 12:13-15; Deut. 32:39
8 [e] Ex. 7:6-13
9 [f] Ex. 7:19, 20 [1] The Nile
10 [g] Ex. 3:11; 4:1; 6:12; Jer. 1:6 [2] *heavy* or *dull of tongue;* cannot talk very well
11 [h] Ps. 94:9; 146:8; Matt. 11:5; Luke 1:20, 64
12 [i] Ex. 4:15, 16; Deut. 18:18; Is. 50:4; Jer. 1:9; [Matt. 10:19; Mark 13:11; Luke 12:11, 12; 21:14, 15]
13 [j] Jon. 1:3
14 [k] Num. 11:1, 33 [l] Num. 26:59 [m] Ex. 4:27; 1 Sam. 10:2, 3, 5
15 [n] Ex. 4:12, 30; 7:1, 2 [o] Num. 23:5, 12; Deut. 18:18; 2 Sam. 14:3, 19; Is. 51:16; 59:21; Jer. 1:9 [p] Deut. 5:31

3:18 three days' journey. The request for a 3 day journey to worship, in the light of 1) direct promises of deliverance from Egypt, 2) worship at Horeb, and 3) entrance into Canaan, was not a ruse to get out and then not return, but an initial, moderate request to highlight the intransigence of Pharaoh—he just would not let these slaves leave under any conditions (v. 19)!

3:22 *See note on 12:36.*

4:1 Then Moses answered and said. In a third objection, Moses gave an unworthy response, after the lengthy explanation by God to Moses in 3:14-22. At this point, the hypothetical situation proposed became more objection than reasonable inquiry.

4:2-9 In response to the hypothetical situation of Israel's rejecting God as having appeared to him, Moses was given 3 signs to accredit him as the chosen spokesman and leader. Note the purpose stated: "That they may believe that the LORD God…appeared to you" (v. 5). Two of these signs personally involved Moses right then and there—the rod to snake and back, the hand leprous and healed. No matter what the situation Moses could envision himself facing, God had sufficient resources to authenticate His man, and Moses was not to think otherwise.

4:10 I *am* not eloquent. With his fourth argument, Moses focused on his speech disability, describing himself lit. as not being "a man of words," as being "heavy in mouth and heavy in tongue," i.e., unable to articulate his thoughts in fluent, flowing speech. An ancient document, *The Tale of the Eloquent Peasant,* suggests that eloquence was important in Egyptian culture, something which Moses would have well known from his time in the court. **neither before nor since You have spoken.** This is a pointed and inappropriate, if not impolite, criticism that somehow in all the discussion God had overlooked Moses' speech disability. Unless this disability changed, Moses believed that he could not undertake the assigned task (cf. 6:12).

4:11,12 Who has made man's mouth? Three rhetorical questions from God shut the door on any complaints or criticisms about being clumsy of speech. The follow-up command, "Therefore, go!" including its promise of divine help in speech forbade all such objections.

4:13-16 Moses' fifth and final statement, notwithstanding the opening supplication, "O my Lord," was a polite way of bluntly saying, "Choose someone else, not me!" The anger of God toward this overt expression of reluctance was appropriate, yet the Lord still provided another way for His plan to move forward unhindered. Providentially (v. 27), Aaron would meet his brother Moses, and positively respond to being the spokesman.

4:15 and I will teach you. The plural pronoun "you" means that God had promised to assist both of them in their newly appointed duties.

you shall do. 16 So he shall be your
spokesman to the people. And he himself
shall be as a mouth for you, and [q]you shall
be to him as God. 17 And you shall take
this rod in your hand, with which you
shall do the signs."

Moses Goes to Egypt

18 So Moses went and returned to
[r]Jethro his father-in-law, and said to him,
"Please let me go and return to my
brethren who *are* in Egypt, and see
whether they are still alive."
And Jethro said to Moses, [s]"Go in peace."
19 Now the LORD said to Moses in [t]Midi-
an, "Go, return to [u]Egypt; for [v]all the men
who sought your life are dead." 20 Then
Moses [w]took his wife and his sons and set
them on a donkey, and he returned to the
land of Egypt. And Moses took [x]the rod of
God in his hand.
21 And the LORD said to Moses, "When
you go back to Egypt, see that you do all
those [y]wonders before Pharaoh which I
have put in your hand. But [z]I will harden
his heart, so that he will not let the people
go. 22 Then you shall [a]say to Pharaoh,
'Thus says the LORD: [b]"Israel *is* My son,
[c]My firstborn. 23 So I say to you, let My son
go that he may serve Me. But if you refuse
to let him go, indeed [d]I will kill your son,
your firstborn." ' "

24 And it came to pass on the way, at the
[e]encampment, that the LORD [f]met him and
sought to [g]kill him. 25 Then [h]Zipporah
took [i]a sharp stone and cut off the foreskin
of her son and [3]cast *it* at [4]*Moses'* feet, and
said, "Surely you *are* a husband of blood to
me!" 26 So He let him go. Then she said,
"*You are* a [5]husband of blood!"—because
of the circumcision.
27 And the LORD said to Aaron, "Go into
the wilderness [j]to meet Moses." So he
went and met him on [k]the mountain of
God, and kissed him. 28 So Moses [l]told
Aaron all the words of the LORD who had
sent him, and all the [m]signs which He had
commanded him. 29 Then Moses and
Aaron [n]went and gathered together all the
elders of the children of Israel. 30 [o]And
Aaron spoke all the words which the LORD
had spoken to Moses. Then he did the
signs in the sight of the people. 31 So the
people [p]believed; and when they heard
that the LORD had [q]visited the children of
Israel and that He [r]had looked on their affliction, then [s]they bowed their heads and
worshiped.

First Encounter with Pharaoh

5 Afterward Moses and Aaron went in
and told Pharaoh, "Thus says the LORD

16 [q] Ex. 7:1, 2
18 [r] Ex. 2:21; 3:1; 4:18 [s] Gen. 43:23; Judg. 18:6
19 [t] Ex. 3:1; 18:1 [u] Gen. 46:3, 6 [v] Ex. 2:15, 23; Matt. 2:20
20 [w] Ex. 18:2-5; Acts 7:29 [x] Ex. 4:17; 17:9; Num. 20:8, 9, 11
21 [y] Ex. 3:20; 11:9, 10 [z] Ex. 7:3, 13; 9:12, 35; 10:1, 20, 27; 14:4, 8; Deut. 2:30; Josh. 11:20; 1 Sam. 6:6; Is. 63:17; John 12:40; Rom. 9:18
22 [a] Ex. 5:1 [b] Is. 63:16; 64:8; Hos. 11:1; [Rom. 9:4; 2 Cor. 6:16, 18] [c] Jer. 31:9; [James 1:18]
23 [d] Ex. 11:5; 12:29; Ps. 105:36; 135:8; 136:10
24 [e] Gen. 42:27 [f] Ex. 3:18; 5:3; Num. 22:22 [g] Gen. 17:14
25 [h] Ex. 2:21; 18:2 [i] Gen. 17:14; Josh. 5:2, 3 [3] Lit. *made it touch* [4] Lit. *his*
26 [5] *bridegroom*
27 [j] Ex. 4:14 [k] Ex. 3:1; 18:5; 24:13
28 [l] Ex. 4:15, 16 [m] Ex. 4:8, 9
29 [n] Ex. 3:16; 12:21
30 [o] Ex. 4:15, 16
31 [p] Ex. 3:18; 4:8, 9; 19:9 [q] Gen. 50:24; Ex. 3:16 [r] Ex. 2:25; 3:7 [s] Gen. 24:26; Ex. 12:27; 1 Chr. 29:20

4:16 you shall be to him as God. Aaron would speak to the people for Moses, even as Moses would speak to Aaron for the Lord.

4:17 this rod…with which you shall do the signs. Moses, despite God's anger at his unwillingness, retained superiority in that he had the instrument by which miracles would be done so that it was identified as "the rod of God" (v. 20).

4:18 Please let me go. Courtesy toward the father-in-law for which he worked was not overlooked because of the divine call to service as national leader. Exactly how much was explained of the encounter at the burning bush remains unknown, but the purpose for the return, "and see whether they are still alive," suggests that specific details of the call for him to be leader/deliverer were left unsaid, in contrast to the full explanation given to Aaron (v. 28).

4:20 sons. Gershom (2:22) and Eliezer (18:4).

4:21 I will harden his heart. The Lord's personal and direct involvement in the affairs of men so that His purposes might be done is revealed as God informed Moses what would take place. Pharaoh was also warned that his own refusal would bring judgment on him (v. 23). Previously Moses had been told that God was certain of Pharaoh's refusal (3:19). This interplay between God's hardening and Pharaoh's hardening his heart must be kept in balance. Ten times (4:21; 7:3; 9:12; 10:1,20,27; 11:10; 14:4,8,17) the historical record notes specifically that God hardened the king's heart, and ten times (7:13,14,22; 8:15,19,32; 9:7,34,35; 13:15) the record indicates the king hardened his own heart. The Apostle Paul used this hardening as an example of God's inscrutable will and absolute power to intervene as He chooses, yet obviously never without loss of personal responsibility for actions taken. The theological conundrum posed by such interplay of God's acting and Pharaoh's acting can only be resolved by accepting the record as it stands and by taking refuge in the omniscience and omnipotence of the God who planned and brought about His deliverance of Israel from Egypt, and in so doing also judged Pharaoh's sinfulness. *See note at 9:12.*

4:22 My son, My firstborn. To the ancient Egyptians, the firstborn son was special and sacred, and the Pharaoh considered himself the only son of the gods. Now he heard of a whole nation designated as God's firstborn son, meaning "declared and treated as first in rank, preeminent, with the rights, privileges, and responsibilities of being actually the firstborn." The Lord pointedly referred to the nation collectively in the singular in order to show that He was a father in what He would do, i.e., bring a nation into existence, then nurture and lead him (cf. Deut. 14:1,2). Divine sonship, as in the pagan world's perverted concept of a sexual union between the gods and women, was never so much as hinted at in the way God used the term to express His relationship with Israel, who were His people, a treasured possession, a kingdom of priests, and a holy nation (cf. 6:7; 19:4-6).

4:24-26 The presence of Zipporah's name indicates that the personal pronouns refer to Moses. She, judging by her action of suddenly and swiftly circumcising her son, understood that the danger to her husband's life was intimately connected to the family's not bearing the sign of the covenant given to Abraham for all his descendants (Gen. 17:10-14). Her evaluation, "*You are* a husband of blood to me," suggests her own revulsion with this rite of circumcision, which Moses should have performed. The result, however, was God's foregoing the threat and letting Moses go (v. 26a). The reaction of God at this point dramatically underscored the seriousness of the sign He had prescribed. *See note on Jer. 4:4.*

4:29,30 The "leadership team" functioned as instructed: Aaron told all and Moses performed all the signs given to him (vv. 2-9).

4:31 So the people believed…then they bowed…and

God of Israel: 'Let My people go, that they
may [1]hold [a]a feast to Me in the wilderness.' "
2 And Pharaoh said, [b]"Who *is* the LORD,
that I should obey His voice to let Israel
go? I do not know the LORD, [c]nor will I let
Israel go."
3 So they said, [d]"The God of the Hebrews
has [e]met with us. Please, let us go three
days' journey into the desert and sacrifice
to the LORD our God, lest He fall upon us
with [f]pestilence or with the sword."
4 Then the king of Egypt said to them,
"Moses and Aaron, why do you take the
people from their work? Get *back* to your
[g]labor." 5 And Pharaoh said, "Look, the
people of the land *are* [h]many now, and you
make them rest from their labor!"
6 So the same day Pharaoh commanded
the [i]taskmasters of the people and their officers, saying, 7 "You shall no longer give
the people straw to make [j]brick as before.
Let them go and gather straw for themselves. 8 And you shall lay on them the
quota of bricks which they made before.
You shall not reduce it. For they are idle;
therefore they cry out, saying, 'Let us go
and sacrifice to our God.' 9 Let more work
be laid on the men, that they may labor in
it, and let them not regard false words."
10 And the taskmasters of the people
and their officers went out and spoke to
the people, saying, "Thus says Pharaoh: 'I
will not give you straw. 11 Go, get yourselves straw where you can find it; yet
none of your work will be reduced.' " 12 So
the people were scattered abroad throughout all the land of Egypt to gather stubble
instead of straw. 13 And the taskmasters
forced *them* to hurry, saying, "Fulfill your
work, *your* daily quota, as when there was
straw." 14 Also the [k]officers of the children
of Israel, whom Pharaoh's taskmasters had
set over them, were [l]beaten *and* were
asked, "Why have you not fulfilled your
task in making brick both yesterday and
today, as before?"
15 Then the officers of the children of Israel came and cried out to Pharaoh, saying,
"Why are you dealing thus with your servants? 16 There is no straw given to your
servants, and they say to us, 'Make brick!'
And indeed your servants *are* beaten, but
the fault *is* in your *own* people."
17 But he said, "You *are* idle! Idle! Therefore you say, 'Let us go *and* sacrifice to the
LORD.' 18 Therefore go now *and* work; for
no straw shall be given you, yet you shall
deliver the quota of bricks." 19 And the officers of the children of Israel saw *that* they
were in trouble after it was said, "You shall
not reduce *any* bricks from your daily
quota."
20 Then, as they came out from Pharaoh,
they met Moses and Aaron who stood
there to meet them. 21 [m]And they said to
them, "Let the LORD look on you and
judge, because you have made [2]us abhorrent in the sight of Pharaoh and in the sight
of his servants, to put a sword in their
hand to kill us."

Israel's Deliverance Assured

22 So Moses returned to the LORD and
said, "Lord, why have You brought trouble
on this people? Why *is* it You have sent
me? 23 For since I came to Pharaoh to
speak in Your name, he has done evil to
this people; neither have You delivered
Your people at all."

CHAPTER 5

1 [a] Ex. 3:18; 7:16; 10:9 [1] *keep a pilgrim-feast*
2 [b] 2 Kin. 18:35; 2 Chr. 32:14; Job 21:15 [c] Ex. 3:19; 7:14
3 [d] Ex. 3:18; 7:16 [e] Ex. 4:24; Num. 23:3 [f] Ex. 9:15
4 [g] Ex. 1:11; 2:11; 6:6
5 [h] Ex. 1:7, 9
6 [i] Ex. 1:11; 3:7; 5:10, 13, 14
7 [j] Ex. 1:14
14 [k] Ex. 5:6 [l] Is. 10:24
21 [m] Ex. 6:9; 14:11; 15:24; 16:2 [2] Lit. *our scent to stink before*

worshiped. Just as God predicted, they responded in belief at the signs and in worship at the explanation of God's awareness of their misery.

5:1 Let My people go. With this command from Israel's Lord, the confrontation between Pharaoh and Moses, between Pharaoh and God, commenced. It was a command Pharaoh would hear often in the days leading up to the Exodus.

5:2 Who *is* the LORD...? In all likelihood Pharaoh knew of Israel's God, but his interrogative retort insolently and arrogantly rejected Him as having any power to make demands of Egypt's superior ruler.

5:3-5 As a follow-up to Pharaoh's rejection, the spokesmen rephrase more specifically their request, together with a warning of possible divine judgment upon Israel for their failure to obey their God. Pharaoh saw this simply as a ruse to reduce the hours put in by his slave work force.

5:6-9 Showing his authority to give orders to Israel, Pharaoh immediately increased their workload and the severity of their bondage. By adding, "let them not regard false words," he showed his negative evaluation of God's words.

5:10 taskmasters...and their officers. When combined with "officers of the children of Israel" (v. 15), a 3-level command structure is seen to have been in place—Egyptian section leaders and labor gang bosses, and Israelite foremen.

5:11 straw. Ancient documents from Egypt show that straw was used as a necessary component of bricks—it helped bind the clay together.

5:15-19 The formal labor complaint at the highest level was rejected with an emphatic evaluation of laziness on the part of Israel and a demand that production not slack.

5:20-21 The leadership team evidently knew of the lodging of the formal labor complaint and waited outside the royal hall in order to meet Israel's representatives. The meeting was definitely not a cordial one, with accusations raised both about the propriety of and the authority of the words and actions of Aaron and Moses toward Pharaoh.

5:22,23 Moses returned to the LORD. Whether Moses and his brother remonstrated with the foremen about their strong and wrong evaluation remains a moot point. Rather, the focus is upon Moses, who remonstrated with the Lord in prayer. Evidently, Moses did not anticipate what effect Pharaoh's refusal and reaction would have upon his own people. Confrontation with Pharaoh so far had provoked both angry resentment of Israel by the Egyptians and of Moses by Israel—this was not the expected scenario!

6 Then the LORD said to Moses, "Now
you shall see what I will do to Pharaoh. For [a]with a strong hand he will let
them go, and with a strong hand [b]he will
drive them out of his land."
2 And God spoke to Moses and said to
him: "I *am* [1]the LORD. 3 [c]I appeared to
Abraham, to Isaac, and to Jacob, as [d]God
Almighty, but *by* My name [e]LORD[2] I was
not known to them. 4 [f]I have also [3]estab-
lished My covenant with them, [g]to give
them the land of Canaan, the land of their
[4]pilgrimage, [h]in which they were [5]strang-
ers. 5 And [i]I have also heard the groaning
of the children of Israel whom the Egyptians keep in bondage, and I have remembered My covenant. 6 Therefore say to the
children of Israel: [j]'I *am* the LORD; [k]I will
bring you out from under the burdens of
the Egyptians, I will [l]rescue you from their
bondage, and I will redeem you with [6]an
outstretched arm and with great judgments. 7 I will [m]take you as My people,
and [n]I will be your God. Then you shall
know that I *am* the LORD your God who
brings you out [o]from under the burdens of
the Egyptians. 8 And I will bring you into
the land which I [p]swore[7] to give to Abraham, Isaac, and Jacob; and I will give it to
you *as* a heritage: I *am* the LORD.' " 9 So Moses spoke thus to the children of Israel;
[q]but they did not heed Moses, because of
[r]anguish[8] of spirit and cruel bondage.
10 And the LORD spoke to Moses, saying,
11 "Go in, tell Pharaoh king of Egypt to let
the children of Israel go out of his land."
12 And Moses spoke before the LORD,
saying, "The children of Israel have not
heeded me. How then shall Pharaoh heed
me, for [s]I *am* [9]of uncircumcised lips?"
13 Then the LORD spoke to Moses and
Aaron, and gave them a [t]command[1] for
the children of Israel and for Pharaoh king
of Egypt, to bring the children of Israel out
of the land of Egypt.

The Family of Moses and Aaron

14 These *are* the heads of their fathers'
houses: [u]The sons of Reuben, the firstborn
of Israel, *were* Hanoch, Pallu, Hezron, and
Carmi. These are the families of Reuben.
15 [v]And the sons of Simeon *were* [2]Jemuel,
Jamin, Ohad, Jachin, Zohar, and Shaul the
son of a Canaanite woman. These *are* the
families of Simeon. 16 These *are* the names
of [w]the sons of Levi according to their generations: Gershon, Kohath, and Merari.
And the years of the life of Levi *were* one
hundred and thirty-seven. 17 [x]The sons of
Gershon *were* Libni and Shimi according to
their families. 18 And [y]the sons of Kohath
were Amram, Izhar, Hebron, and Uzziel.
And the years of the life of Kohath *were*
one hundred and thirty-three. 19 [z]The sons
of Merari *were* Mahli and Mushi. These *are*
the families of Levi according to their generations.
20 Now [a]Amram took for himself
[b]Jochebed, his father's sister, as wife; and
she bore him [c]Aaron and Moses. And the
years of the life of Amram *were* one hundred and thirty-seven. 21 [d]The sons of
Izhar *were* Korah, Nepheg, and Zichri.
22 And [e]the sons of Uzziel *were* Mishael,
Elzaphan, and Zithri. 23 Aaron took to
himself Elisheba, daughter of [f]Ammina-
dab, sister of Nahshon, as wife; and she
bore him [g]Nadab, Abihu, [h]Eleazar, and

CHAPTER 6

1 [a]Ex. 3:19 [b]Ex. 12:31, 33, 39
2 [1]Heb. *YHWH*
3 [c]Gen. 17:1; 35:9; 48:3 [d]Gen. 28:3; 35:11 [e]Ex. 3:14, 15; 15:3; Ps. 68:4; 83:18; Is. 52:6; Jer. 16:21; Ezek. 37:6, 13; John 8:58 [2]Heb. *YHWH*, traditionally *Jehovah*
4 [f]Gen. 12:7; 15:18; 17:4, 7, 8; 26:3; 28:4, 13 [g]Gen. 47:9; Lev. 25:23 [h]Gen. 28:4 [3]*made* or *ratified* [4]*sojournings* [5]*sojourners*, temporary residents
5 [i]Ex. 2:24; [Job 34:28]; Acts 7:34
6 [j]Ex. 13:3, 14; 20:2; Deut. 6:12 [k]Ex. 3:17; 7:4; 12:51; 16:6; 18:1; Deut. 26:8; Ps. 136:11 [l]Ex. 15:13; Deut. 7:8; 1 Chr. 17:21; Neh. 1:10 [6]Mighty power
7 [m]Ex. 19:5; Deut. 4:20; 7:6; 2 Sam. 7:24 [n]Gen. 17:7; Ex. 29:45, 46; Lev. 26:12, 13, 45; Deut. 29:13; Rev. 21:7 [o]Ex. 5:4, 5
8 [p]Gen. 15:18; 26:3; Num. 14:30; Neh. 9:15; Ezek. 20:5, 6 [7]*promised*, lit. *lifted up My hand*
9 [q]Ex. 5:21 [r]Ex. 2:23; Num. 21:4 [8]Lit. *shortness*
12 [s]Ex. 4:10; 6:30; Jer. 1:6 [9]One who does not speak well
13 [t]Num. 27:19, 23; Deut. 31:14 [1]*charge*
14 [u]Gen. 46:9; Num. 26:5-11; 1 Chr. 5:3
15 [v]Gen. 46:10; Num. 26:12-14; 1 Chr. 4:24 [2]*Nemuel*, Num. 26:12
16 [w]Gen. 46:11; Num. 3:17; 1 Chr. 6:16-30 17 [x]1 Chr. 6:17
18 [y]1 Chr. 6:2, 18 19 [z]1 Chr. 6:19; 23:21 20 [a]Ex. 2:1, 2; Num. 3:19 [b]Num. 26:59 [c]Num. 26:59 21 [d]Num. 16:1; 1 Chr. 6:37, 38
22 [e]Lev. 10:4 23 [f]Ruth 4:19, 20; 1 Chr. 2:10; Matt. 1:4 [g]Lev. 10:1; Num. 3:2; 26:60 [h]Ex. 28:1

6:1 Now you shall see. The Lord announced in response to Moses' prayer that finally the stage had been set for dealing with Pharaoh, who, in consequence, would only be able to urge Israel to leave.

6:2-5 God spoke to Moses and reminded him of His promises to the patriarchs. Once again the focal point of the covenant was the land of Canaan deeded to their descendants by divine decree. The fact that this covenant was remembered meant obvious removal from Egypt!

6:2,3 I *am* the LORD. The same self-existent, eternal God, Yahweh, had been there in the past with the patriarchs; no change had occurred in Him, either in His covenant or promises.

6:3 God Almighty...LORD...not known. Since the name Yahweh was spoken before the Flood (Gen. 4:26) and later by the patriarchs (Gen. 9:26; 12:8; 22:14; 24:12), the special significance of Yahweh, unknown to them, but to be known by their descendants, must arise from what God would reveal of Himself in keeping the covenant and in redeeming Israel. *See notes on 3:13,14.*

6:4 My covenant. The Abrahamic Covenant (cf. Gen. 15:1-21; 17:1-8).

6:6-8 God instructed Moses to remind Israel of what they had previously been told: of God's remembering the covenant with Abraham, of His seeing their misery, of His delivering them from it, of His granting to them the land of Canaan, and thus taking them there. The repetitive "I will" (7 times) marked God's personal, direct involvement in Israel's affairs. Bracketed, as they were, by the declaration, "I am Yahweh," denoted certainty of fulfillment.

6:9 because of anguish of spirit. The bondage was so great that it blocked out even the stirring words Moses had just delivered to them (vv. 6-8).

6:12 uncircumcised lips? *See notes on 4:10.*

6:14-27 The genealogical information formally identified Moses and Aaron as descendants of Levi, third son of Jacob by Leah. It also listed Aaron's son, Eleazar, and grandson, Phinehas, both of whom would become Israel's High-Priests. Mention of Levi in company with Reuben and Simeon recalled, perhaps, the unsavory background belonging to these three tribal fathers (Gen. 49:3-7) and emphasized that the choice of Moses and Aaron was not due to an exemplary lineage. This is intended to be a representative genealogy, not a complete one.

Ithamar. 24 And [i]the sons of Korah *were* Assir, Elkanah, and Abiasaph. These are the families of the Korahites. 25 Eleazar, Aaron's son, took for himself one of the daughters of Putiel as wife; and [j]she bore him Phinehas. These *are* the heads of the fathers' houses of the Levites according to their families.

26 These *are the same* Aaron and Moses to whom the LORD said, "Bring out the children of Israel from the land of Egypt according to their [k]armies."[3] 27 These *are* the ones who spoke to Pharaoh king of Egypt, [l]to bring out the children of Israel from Egypt. These *are the same* Moses and Aaron.

Aaron Is Moses' Spokesman

28 And it came to pass, on the day the LORD spoke to Moses in the land of Egypt, 29 that the LORD spoke to Moses, saying, "I *am* the LORD. [m]Speak to Pharaoh king of Egypt all that I say to you."

30 But Moses said before the LORD, "Behold, [n]I *am* [4]of uncircumcised lips, and how shall Pharaoh heed me?"

7 So the LORD said to Moses: "See, I have made you [a]*as* God to Pharaoh, and Aaron your brother shall be [b]your prophet. 2 You [c]shall speak all that I command you. And Aaron your brother shall tell Pharaoh to send the children of Israel out of his land. 3 And [d]I will harden Pharaoh's heart, and [e]multiply My [f]signs and My wonders in the land of Egypt. 4 But [g]Pharaoh will not heed you, so [h]that I may lay My hand on Egypt and bring My [1]armies *and* My people, the children of Israel, out of the land of Egypt [i]by great judgments. 5 And the Egyptians [j]shall know that I *am* the LORD, when I [k]stretch out My hand on Egypt and [l]bring out the children of Israel from among them."

6 Then Moses and Aaron [m]did *so;* just as the LORD commanded them, so they did. 7 And Moses *was* [n]eighty years old and [o]Aaron eighty-three years old when they spoke to Pharaoh.

Aaron's Miraculous Rod

8 Then the LORD spoke to Moses and Aaron, saying, 9 "When Pharaoh speaks to you, saying, [p]'Show a miracle for yourselves,' then you shall say to Aaron, [q]'Take your rod and cast *it* before Pharaoh, *and* let it become a serpent.' " 10 So Moses and Aaron went in to Pharaoh, and they did so, just [r]as the LORD commanded. And Aaron cast down his rod before Pharaoh and before his servants, and it [s]became a serpent.

11 But Pharaoh also [t]called the wise men and [u]the [2]sorcerers; so the magicians of Egypt, they also [v]did in like manner with their [3]enchantments. 12 For every man threw down his rod, and they became serpents. But Aaron's rod swallowed up their rods. 13 And Pharaoh's heart grew hard, and he did not heed them, as the LORD had said.

The First Plague: Waters Become Blood

14 So the LORD said to Moses: [w]"Pharaoh's heart *is* hard; he refuses to let the

24 [i]Num. 26:11
25 [j]Num. 25:7, 11; Josh. 24:33
26 [k]Ex. 7:4; 12:17, 51; Num. 33:1 [3]*hosts*
27 [l]Ex. 6:13; 32:7; 33:1; Ps. 77:20
29 [m]Ex. 6:11; 7:2
30 [n]Ex. 4:10; 6:12; Jer. 1:6 [4]One who does not speak well

CHAPTER 7

1 [a]Ex. 4:16; Jer. 1:10 [b]Ex. 4:15, 16
2 [c]Ex. 4:15; Deut. 18:18
3 [d]Ex. 4:21; 9:12 [e]Ex. 11:9; Acts 7:36 [f]Ex. 4:7; Deut. 4:34
4 [g]Ex. 3:19, 20; 10:1; 11:9 [h]Ex. 9:14 [1]*hosts* [i]Ex. 6:6; 12:12
5 [j]Ex. 7:17; 8:22; 14:4, 18; Ps. 9:16 [k]Ex. 9:15 [l]Ex. 3:20; 6:6; 12:51
6 [m]Ex. 7:2
7 [n]Deut. 29:5; 31:2; 34:7; Acts 7:23, 30 [o]Num. 33:39
9 [p]Ex. 10:1; Is. 7:11; John 2:18; 6:30 [q]Ex. 4:2, 3, 17
10 [r]Ex. 7:9 [s]Ex. 4:3
11 [t]Gen. 41:8 [u]Dan. 2:2; 2 Tim. 3:8 [v]Ex. 7:22; 8:7, 18; 2 Tim. 3:9; Rev. 13:13, 14 [2]*soothsayers* [3]*secret arts*
14 [w]Ex. 8:15; 10:1, 20, 27

6:28–7:5 A summary of the mission to Egypt resumes the narrative after the genealogical aside on Moses and Aaron.

7:1 *as* God to Pharaoh. Moses, as the spokesman and ambassador for God, would speak with authority and power. **your prophet.** Aaron, as the divinely appointed spokesman for Moses, would forthrightly deliver the message given to him. Cf. Acts 14:11-13, where Barnabas and Paul were so perceived in a similar situation.

7:4 My armies *and* My people. The first term in this double-barreled designation of Israel occurred originally in 6:26. The nation was seen as organized like an army with its different divisions (its tribes) and also as God's military instrument upon the Canaanites. The second term with its possessive pronoun revealed the incongruity of Pharaoh's acting as though these people belonged to him.

7:5 know that I *am* the LORD. This purpose of the Exodus finds repeated mention in God's messages to Pharaoh and in God's descriptions of what He was doing (cf. 7:16; 8:10,22; 9:14,16,29; 14:4,18). Some of the Egyptians did come to understand the meaning of the name Yahweh, for they responded appropriately to the warning of the seventh plague (9:20), and others accompanied Israel into the wilderness (12:38). In the final analysis, Egypt would not be able to deny the direct involvement of the God of Israel in their rescue from bondage and the destruction of Egypt's army.

7:9 Show a miracle. Pharaoh's desire for accreditation would not go unanswered. That which God had done for Moses with the rod (4:2-9), and Moses had copied for Israel (4:30,31), also became the sign of authority before Pharaoh (cf. 7:10).

7:11 magicians. Magic and sorcery played a major role in the pantheistic religion of Egypt. Its ancient documents record the activities of the magicians, one of the most prominent being the charming of serpents. These men were also styled "wise men" and "sorcerers," i.e., the learned men of the day and the religious as well (the word for sorcery being derived from a word meaning "to offer prayers"). Two of these men were named Jannes and Jambres (cf. 2 Tim. 3:8). Any supernatural power came from Satan (cf. 2 Cor. 11:13-15). **enchantments.** By means of their "secret arts" or "witchcraft," the wise men, sorcerers, and magicians demonstrated their abilities to perform a similar feat. Whether by optical illusion, sleight of hand, or learned physical manipulation of a snake, all sufficiently skillful enough to totally fool Pharaoh and his servants, or by evil supernaturalism, the evaluation given in the inspired record is simply "they also did in like manner." However, the turning of rods into snakes, and later turning water into blood (7:22) and calling forth frogs (8:7), were not the same as trying to create lice from inanimate dust (8:18-19). At that point, the magicians had no option but to confess their failure.

7:12 Aaron's rod swallowed up their rods. The loss of the magicians' rods in this fashion gave evidence of the superiority of God's power when Aaron's rod gulped down theirs.

7:14–10:29 The obvious miraculous nature of the 10 plagues cannot be explained by identifying them with natural occurrences to which Moses then applied a theological interpretation. The specific prediction of, as well as the intensity of, each plague moved it beyond being normal, natural phenomena. The notification of the specific dis-

people go. 15 Go to Pharaoh in the morning, when he goes out to the [x]water, and
you shall stand by the river's bank to meet
him; and [y]the rod which was turned to a
serpent you shall take in your hand.
16 And you shall say to him, [z]'The LORD
God of the Hebrews has sent me to you,
saying, "Let My people go, [a]that they may
[4]serve Me in the wilderness"; but indeed,
until now you would not hear! 17 Thus
says the LORD: "By this [b]you shall know
that I *am* the LORD. Behold, I will strike the
waters which *are* in the river with the rod
that *is* in my hand, and [c]they shall be
turned [d]to blood. 18 And the fish that *are* in
the river shall die, the river shall stink, and
the Egyptians will [e]loathe[5] to drink the
water of the river." ' "

19 Then the LORD spoke to Moses, "Say to
Aaron, 'Take your rod and [f]stretch out your
hand over the waters of Egypt, over their
streams, over their rivers, over their ponds,
and over all their pools of water, that they
may become blood. And there shall be
blood throughout all the land of Egypt,
both in *buckets of* wood and *pitchers of*
stone.' " 20 And Moses and Aaron did so,
just as the LORD commanded. So he [g]lifted
up the rod and struck the waters that *were*
in the river, in the sight of Pharaoh and in
the sight of his servants. And all the [h]wa-
ters that *were* in the river were turned to
blood. 21 The fish that *were* in the river died,
the river stank, and the Egyptians [i]could
not drink the water of the river. So there
was blood throughout all the land of Egypt.

22 [j]Then the magicians of Egypt did [k]so
with their [6]enchantments; and Pharaoh's
heart grew hard, and he did not heed
them, [l]as the LORD had said. 23 And Pharaoh turned and went into his house. Neither was his heart moved by this. 24 So all
the Egyptians dug all around the river for
water to drink, because they could not
drink the water of the river. 25 And seven
days passed after the LORD had struck the
river.

The Second Plague: Frogs

8 And the LORD spoke to Moses, "Go to
Pharaoh and say to him, 'Thus says the
LORD: "Let My people go, [a]that they may

15 [x]Ex. 2:5; 8:20 [y]Ex. 4:2, 3; 7:10
16 [z]Ex. 3:13, 18; 4:22 [a]Ex. 3:12, 18; 4:23; 5:1, 3; 8:1 [4]*worship*
17 [b]Ex. 5:2; 7:5; 10:2; Ps. 9:16; Ezek. 25:17 [c]Ex. 4:9; 7:20 [d]Rev. 11:6; 16:4, 6
18 [e]Ex. 7:24 [5]*be weary of drinking*
19 [f]Ex. 8:5, 6, 16; 9:22; 10:12, 21; 14:21, 26
20 [g]Ex. 17:5 [h]Ps. 78:44; 105:29, 30
21 [i]Ex. 7:18
22 [j]Ex. 7:11 [k]Ex. 8:7 [l]Ex. 3:19; 7:3 [6]*secret arts*

CHAPTER 8

1 [a]Ex. 3:12, 18; 4:23; 5:1, 3

criminatory nature of some of the plagues, distinguishing between Hebrew and Egyptian (cf. 8:23; 9:4,6; 10:23), or Goshen and the rest of the land (cf. 8:22; 9:26), as they did, also marks the supernatural nature of these events.

7:15 in the morning. Apparently, Pharaoh habitually went to the river for washing or, more likely, for the performance of some religious rite. Three times Moses would meet him at this early morning rendezvous to warn of plagues, i.e., the first, fourth, and seventh (8:20; 9:13). **by the river's bank.** The first confrontation of the plague cycle took place on the banks of the Nile, the sacred waterway of the land, whose annual ebb and flow contributed strategically and vitally to the agricultural richness of Egypt. Hymns of thanksgiving were often sung for the blessings brought by the Nile, the country's greatest, single economic resource.

7:17 blood. The Heb. word does not denote red coloring such as might be seen when red clay is washed downstream, but denotes actual substance, i.e., blood.

7:19,20 the waters...all the waters. The use of different words, "waters, streams, rivers, ponds, and pools," indicates graphically the extent of the plague. Even buckets of wood and stone filled with water and kept inside the homes could not escape the curse of their contents being turned into blood.

7:22 the magicians...did so with their enchantments. How ludicrous and revealing that the magicians resorted to copycat methodology instead of reversing the plague. What they did, bringing just more blood, did serve, however, to bolster Pharaoh's stubbornness.

7:24 dug all around the river. The only recourse was to tap into the natural water table, the subterranean water supply. Evidently this was the water which was available to the magicians to use (v. 22).

7:25 seven days. An interval of time occurred before another warning was delivered, indicating that the plagues did not occur rapidly in uninterrupted succession.

8:1 Go to Pharaoh. The warning for the second plague was de-

The Ten Plagues on Egypt

The Plague	Egyptian Deity	The Effect
1. Blood (7:20)	Hapi	Pharaoh hardened (7:22)
2. Frogs (8:6)	Heqt	Pharaoh begs relief, promises freedom (8:8), but is hardened (8:15)
3. Lice (8:17)	Hathor, Nut	Pharaoh hardened (8:19)
4. Flies (8:24)	Shu, Isis	Pharaoh bargains (8:28), but is hardened (8:32)
5. Livestock diseased (9:6)	Apis	Pharaoh hardened (9:7)
6. Boils (9:10)	Sekhmet	Pharaoh hardened (9:12)
7. Hail (9:23)	Geb	Pharaoh begs relief (9:27), promises freedom (9:28), but is hardened (9:35)
8. Locusts (10:13)	Serapis	Pharaoh bargains (10:11), begs relief (10:17), but is hardened (10:20)
9. Darkness (10:22)	Ra	Pharaoh bargains (10:24), but is hardened (10:27)
10. Death of firstborn (12:29)		Pharaoh and Egyptians beg Israel to leave Egypt (12:31-33)

serve Me. 2 But if you [b]refuse to let *them*
go, behold, I will smite all your territory
with [c]frogs. 3 So the river shall bring forth
frogs abundantly, which shall go up and
come into your house, into your [d]bed-
room, on your bed, into the houses of your
servants, on your people, into your ovens,
and into your kneading bowls. 4 And the
frogs shall come up on you, on your people, and on all your servants." ' "
5 Then the LORD spoke to Moses, "Say to
Aaron, [e]'Stretch out your hand with your
rod over the streams, over the rivers, and
over the ponds, and cause frogs to come
up on the land of Egypt.' " 6 So Aaron
stretched out his hand over the waters of
Egypt, and [f]the frogs came up and covered
the land of Egypt. 7 [g]And the magicians
did so with their [1]enchantments, and
brought up frogs on the land of Egypt.
8 Then Pharaoh called for Moses and
Aaron, and said, [h]"Entreat[2] the LORD that
He may take away the frogs from me and
from my people; and I will let the people
[i]go, that they may sacrifice to the LORD."
9 And Moses said to Pharaoh, "Accept
the honor of saying when I shall intercede
for you, for your servants, and for your
people, to destroy the frogs from you and
your houses, *that* they may remain in the
river only."
10 So he said, "Tomorrow." And he said,
"*Let it be* according to your word, that you
may know that [j]*there is* no one like the
LORD our God. 11 And the frogs shall depart from you, from your houses, from
your servants, and from your people. They
shall remain in the river only."
12 Then Moses and Aaron went out from
Pharaoh. And Moses [k]cried out to the LORD
concerning the frogs which He had
brought against Pharaoh. 13 So the LORD
did according to the word of Moses. And
the frogs died out of the houses, out of the
courtyards, and out of the fields. 14 They
gathered them together in heaps, and the
land stank. 15 But when Pharaoh saw that
there was [l]relief, [m]he hardened his heart
and did not heed them, as the LORD had
said.

The Third Plague: Lice

16 So the LORD said to Moses, "Say to
Aaron, 'Stretch out your rod, and strike the
dust of the land, so that it may become
[3]lice throughout all the land of Egypt.' "
17 And they did so. For Aaron stretched
out his hand with his rod and struck the
dust of the earth, and [n]it became lice on
man and beast. All the dust of the land became lice throughout all the land of Egypt.
18 Now [o]the magicians so worked with
their [4]enchantments to bring forth lice, but
they [p]could not. So there were lice on man
and beast. 19 Then the magicians said to
Pharaoh, "This *is* [q]the[5] finger of God." But
Pharaoh's [r]heart grew hard, and he did not
heed them, just as the LORD had said.

2 [b] Ex. 7:14; 9:2 [c] Rev. 16:13
3 [d] Ps. 105:30
5 [e] Ex. 7:19
6 [f] Ps. 78:45; 105:30
7 [g] Ex. 7:11, 22 [1] *secret arts*
8 [h] Ex. 8:28; 9:28; 10:17; Num. 21:7; 1 Kin. 13:6 [i] Ex. 10:8, 24 [2] *Pray to, Make supplication to*
10 [j] Ex. 9:14; 15:11; Deut. 4:35, 39; 33:26; 2 Sam. 7:22; 1 Chr. 17:20; Ps. 86:8; Is. 46:9; [Jer. 10:6, 7]
12 [k] Ex. 8:30; 9:33; 10:18; 32:11; [James 5:16-18]
15 [l] Eccl. 8:11 [m] Ex. 7:14, 22; 9:34; 1 Sam. 6:6
16 [3] *gnats*
17 [n] Ps. 105:31
18 [o] Ex. 7:11, 12; 8:7 [p] Dan. 5:8; 2 Tim. 3:8, 9 [4] *secret arts*
19 [q] Ex. 7:5; 10:7; 1 Sam. 6:3, 9; Ps. 8:3; Luke 11:20 [r] Ex. 8:15 [5] *An act of God*

livered to Pharaoh, presumably at his palace. Warnings for the fifth (9:1) and eighth (10:1) plagues also occurred at the palace.

8:2 smite. The verb God used also meant "to plague." Various terms (lit. from the Heb.), namely "plagues" (9:14), "strike" (12:13), and "pestilence" (9:3,15), were employed to impress them with the severity of what was happening in Egypt. **frogs.** That Egyptians favored frogs was seen in the wearing of amulets in the shape of a frog and in the prohibition against intentionally killing frogs, who were considered sacred animals. The croaking of frogs from the river and pools of water signaled to farmers that the gods who controlled the Nile's flooding and receding had once again made the land fertile. The god Hapi was venerated on this occasion because he had caused alluvial deposits to come downstream. Further, the frog was the representation, the image, of the goddess Heqt, the wife of the god Khum, and the symbol of resurrection and fertility. The presence of frogs in such abundance, all over everywhere outside and inside the houses (vv. 3,13), however, brought only frustration, dismay, and much discomfort, rather than the normal signal that the fields were ready for cultivating and harvesting.

8:7 the magicians did so. Once again, instead of reversing the plague, the magicians in demonstrating the power of their secret arts only appeared to increase the frog population to the added discomfort of the people. Their power was not sufficient enough to do more than play "copycat." That the magicians could duplicate but not eradicate the problem was, however, sufficient to solidify royal stubbornness.

8:8 Entreat the LORD. Using the Lord's name and begging for relief through His intervention was more a point in negotiation and not a personal or official recognition of Israel's Lord.

8:9 remain in the river only. A specific detail like this in Moses' question indicates that the Nile and the waters had returned to normal and again continued to support life.

8:10 Tomorrow. Having been granted the privilege to set the time when the Lord would answer Moses' prayer for relief, Pharaoh requested a cessation only on the next day. Presumably he hoped something else would happen before then so that he would not have to acknowledge the Lord's power in halting the plague, nor be obligated to Moses and his God. But God answered the prayer of Moses, and Pharaoh remained obstinate (v. 15).

8:16 Without prior warning, the third plague descended on the country. The same absence of warning occurred for the sixth (9:8,9) and the ninth (10:21) plagues. A 3-fold pattern surfaces: prior warning at the river, then at the palace, and then no warning given. **lice.** The Heb. term is preferably taken to designate tiny, stinging gnats barely visible to the naked eye. Those priests, who fastidiously kept themselves religiously pure by frequent washing and by shaving off body hair, were afflicted and rendered impure in their duties.

8:17 All the dust of the land...throughout all the land. The record stresses by its repetition of "all" and "land" the tremendous extent and severity of this pestilence.

8:19 This *is* the finger of God. The failure of the magicians to duplicate this plague elicited from them this amazing evaluation, not only among themselves, but publicly before Pharaoh, who nevertheless remained recalcitrant, unwilling to acknowledge the power of God.

The Fourth Plague: Flies

20 And the LORD said to Moses, [s]"Rise
early in the morning and stand before Pharaoh as he comes out to the water. Then say
to him, 'Thus says the LORD: [t]"Let My people go, that they may serve Me. 21 Or else,
if you will not let My people go, behold, I
will send swarms *of flies* on you and your
servants, on your people and into your
houses. The houses of the Egyptians shall
be full of swarms *of flies,* and also the
ground on which they *stand.* 22 And in that
day [u]I will set apart the land of [v]Goshen,
in which My people dwell, that no swarms
of flies shall be there, in order that you may
[w]know that I *am* the LORD in the midst of
the [x]land. 23 I will [6]make a difference between My people and your people. Tomorrow this [y]sign shall be."'" 24 And the
LORD did so. [z]Thick swarms *of flies* came
into the house of Pharaoh, *into* his servants' houses, and into all the land of
Egypt. The land was corrupted because of
the swarms *of flies.*
25 Then Pharaoh called for Moses and
Aaron, and said, "Go, sacrifice to your God
in the land."
26 And Moses said, "It is not right to do
so, for we would be sacrificing [a]the
abomination of the Egyptians to the LORD
our God. If we sacrifice the abomination of
the Egyptians before their eyes, then will
they not [7]stone us? 27 We will go [b]three
days' journey into the wilderness and sacrifice to the LORD our God as [c]He will command us."
28 So Pharaoh said, "I will let you go,
that you may sacrifice to the LORD your
God in the wilderness; only you shall not
go very far away. [d]Intercede for me."
29 Then Moses said, "Indeed I am going
out from you, and I will entreat the LORD,
that the swarms *of flies* may depart tomorrow from Pharaoh, from his servants, and
from his people. But let Pharaoh not [e]deal
deceitfully anymore in not letting the people go to sacrifice to the LORD."
30 So Moses went out from Pharaoh and
[f]entreated the LORD. 31 And the LORD did
according to the word of Moses; He removed the swarms *of flies* from Pharaoh,
from his servants, and from his people.
Not one remained. 32 But Pharaoh [g]hard-
ened his heart at this time also; neither
would he let the people go.

The Fifth Plague: Livestock Diseased

9 Then the LORD said to Moses, [a]"Go in
to Pharaoh and tell him, 'Thus says the
LORD God of the Hebrews: "Let My people
go, that they may [b]serve Me. 2 For if you
[c]refuse to let *them* go, and still hold them,
3 behold, the [d]hand of the LORD will be on
your cattle in the field, on the horses, on

20 [s]Ex. 7:15; 9:13 [t]Ex. 3:18; 4:23; 5:1, 3; 8:1
22 [u]Ex. 9:4, 6, 26; 10:23; 11:6, 7; 12:13 [v]Gen. 50:8 [w]Ex. 7:5, 17; 10:2; 14:4 [x]Ex. 9:29
23 [y]Ex. 4:8 [6]Lit. *set a ransom,* Ex. 9:4; 11:7
24 [z]Ps. 78:45; 105:31
26 [a]Gen. 43:32; 46:34; [Deut. 7:25, 26; 12:31]

[7]Put us to death by stoning
27 [b]Ex. 3:18; 5:3 [c]Ex. 3:12
28 [d]Ex. 8:8, 15, 29, 32; 9:28; 1 Kin. 13:6
29 [e]Ex. 8:8, 15
30 [f]Ex. 8:12
32 [g]Ex. 4:21; 8:8, 15; Ps. 52:2

CHAPTER 9
1 [a]Ex. 4:23; 8:1 [b]Ex. 7:16
2 [c]Ex. 8:2
3 [d]Ex. 7:4; 1 Sam. 5:6; Ps. 39:10; Acts 13:11

8:21 swarms. The LXX translates "swarms" as "dog-fly," a blood-sucking insect. The ichneumon fly, which deposited its eggs on other living things so the larvae could feast upon it, was considered the manifestation of the god Uatchit. "The land was corrupted because of the swarms" (v. 24) is hardly an evaluation propitious for any insect-god! Whatever the specific type of fly might have been, the effect of the plague was intense and distressful.

8:22 set apart the land of Goshen. For the first time in connection with the plagues, God specifically noted the discrimination to be made—Israel would be untouched! The term "sign" (v. 23) describes the distinction which was being drawn and which was also specifically noted for the fifth, seventh, ninth, and tenth plagues. Coupled with the repeated emphasis on "My people" in God's pronouncements, the specific distinguishing between Israel in Goshen and Egypt itself highlighted both God's personal and powerful oversight of His people.

8:23 Tomorrow. The plague-warning on this occasion stated exactly when it would strike, giving Pharaoh and his people opportunity to repent or yield. "Tomorrow" was also the due time for the fifth, seventh, and eighth plagues (9:5,18; 10:4), and "about midnight" was the stated time for the ninth plague to commence (11:4). *See note on 11:4.*

8:26 sacrificing the abomination of the Egyptians. An attempt at appeasement by compromise on the part of Pharaoh—"Go, sacrifice…in the land"—was countered by Moses' pointing out that Israel's sacrifices would not be totally acceptable to the Egyptians, who might even react violently—"will they not stone us?" This evaluation Pharaoh immediately understood. Either their strong dislike of shepherds and sheep (Gen. 46:34) or Israel's sacrificial animals being sacred ones in their religion brought about Egyptian aversion to Israel's sacrifices.

8:27-29 We will go…I will let you go. The first declaration showed the decision to travel no less than 3 days beyond Egyptian borders was a non-negotiable item. The second declaration showed Pharaoh trying to keep that decision to travel and sacrifice strictly under his authority and not as a response to the Lord's request for His people.

8:28 Intercede for me. An abbreviated request, applying not only to himself but also for the removal of the plague as previously asked in connection with the second plague (8:8).

8:29 let Pharaoh not deal deceitfully. Moses' closing exhortation underscored the deceptive nature of the king's words.

8:31 Not one remained. This declaration of the total divine removal of the flies—a demonstration of God's answering Moses' entreaty—did not persuade Pharaoh at all. Once again, removed from the humiliating effects of a plague, his stubborn resistance resurfaced (v. 32).

9:3 horses…camels. Horses, which were common in the period, had been brought into military service by the Hyksos. See Introduction: Author and Date. Camels were a domesticated animal by this time in the 15th century B.C. **a very severe pestilence.** In listing the different kinds of livestock, the severe nature of the plague was emphatically underscored as one which would for the first time target personal property. Egyptian literature and paintings substantiate how valuable livestock was to them. Whatever the exact nature of this pestilence—anthrax, murrain, or other livestock disease—it was clearly contagious and fatal. Religious implications were obvious: Egypt prized the bull as a sacred animal with special attention and worship being given to the Apis bull, the sacred animal of the god Ptah. Heliopolis venerated the bull, Mnevis. Further, the goddess Hathor, represented by a cow, or a cow-woman image, was worshiped in several cities. **in the field.** Apparently stabled livestock did

the donkeys, on the camels, on the oxen,
and on the sheep—a very severe pestilence. 4 And [e]the LORD will make a difference between the livestock of Israel and
the livestock of Egypt. So nothing shall die
of all *that* belongs to the children of Israel.”’” 5 Then the LORD appointed a set
time, saying, “Tomorrow the LORD will do
this thing in the land.”
6 So the LORD did this thing on the next
day, and [f]all the livestock of Egypt died;
but of the livestock of the children of Israel,
not one died. 7 Then Pharaoh sent, and indeed, not even one of the livestock of the
Israelites was dead. But the [g]heart of Pharaoh became hard, and he did not let the
people go.

The Sixth Plague: Boils

8 So the LORD said to Moses and Aaron,
“Take for yourselves handfuls of ashes from
a furnace, and let Moses scatter it toward
the heavens in the sight of Pharaoh. 9 And it
will become fine dust in all the land of
Egypt, and it will cause [h]boils that break out
in sores on man and beast throughout all
the land of Egypt.” 10 Then they took ashes
from the furnace and stood before Pharaoh,
and Moses scattered *them* toward heaven.
And *they* caused [i]boils that break out in
sores on man and beast. 11 And the [j]magi-
cians could not stand before Moses because
of the [k]boils, for the boils were on the magicians and on all the Egyptians. 12 But the
LORD hardened the heart of Pharaoh; and he
[l]did not heed them, just [m]as the LORD had
spoken to Moses.

The Seventh Plague: Hail

13 Then the LORD said to Moses, [n]“Rise
early in the morning and stand before Pharaoh, and say to him, ‘Thus says the LORD
God of the Hebrews: “Let My people go,
that they may [o]serve Me, 14 for at this time
I will send all My plagues to your very
heart, and on your servants and on your
people, [p]that you may know that *there is*
none like Me in all the earth. 15 Now if I

4 [e] Ex. 8:22
6 [f] Ex. 9:19, 20, 25; Ps. 78:48, 50
7 [g] Ex. 7:14; 8:32
9 [h] Deut. 28:27; Rev. 16:2
10 [i] Deut. 28:27
11 [j] [Ex. 8:18, 19; 2 Tim. 3:9] [k] Deut. 28:27; Job 2:7; Rev. 16:1, 2
12 [l] Ex. 7:13 [m] Ex. 4:21
13 [n] Ex. 8:20 [o] Ex. 9:1
14 [p] Ex. 8:10; Deut. 3:24; 2 Sam. 7:22; 1 Chr. 17:20; Ps. 86:8; Is. 45:5-8; 46:9; Jer. 10:6, 7

not succumb to the pestilence. Although incredibly severe, some animals were still alive afterwards for Egypt to continue without total loss to an economy which depended upon domesticated animals. A few months later, when the seventh plague struck, there were still some cattle, which, if left in the field, would have died (9:19).

9:4 nothing shall die. The additional declaration on the safety of Israel's livestock graphically underscored the miraculous nature of what God was about to do as He declared for the second time the distinction being made between Israel and Egypt. It underscored Israel's protection and to whom she really belonged.

9:5 appointed a set time. The prophetic and miraculous nature of this plague is highlighted by stating "tomorrow" and, by noting "on the next day," it happened as predicted (v. 6).

9:6 of the livestock...of Israel, not one died. The distinction being made received added emphasis with this double declaration that Israelites suffered absolutely no loss in livestock.

9:7 Then Pharaoh sent. This time the king had to check on the veracity of the protection afforded Israel. Whatever his own rationalizations or theories about it might have been, they only confirmed him in his resistance and disobedience, despite finding out that it was true, "indeed, not even one...was dead."

9:9 boils that break out in sores on man and beast. For the first time human health was targeted.

9:10 ashes from the furnace. Aaron and Moses took two handfuls of ash, not just from any furnace, but from a lime-kiln or brickmaking furnace. That which participated so largely in their oppressive labor became the source of a painful health hazard for the oppressors!

9:11 magicians could not stand. A side comment indicates that these men (who in Egyptian eyes were men of power) had been so sorely afflicted that they could not stand, either physically or vocationally, before God's spokesmen. Although they are not mentioned after the third plague, they apparently had continued to serve before Pharaoh and were undoubtedly there when plagues 4 and 5 were announced. Their powerlessness had not been sufficient as yet for Pharaoh to dispense with their services—an outward symbol, perhaps, of Pharaoh's unwillingness to grant the God of Israel total sovereignty.

9:12 the LORD hardened. For the first time, apart from the words to Moses before the plagues began (cf. Ex. 4:21; 7:3), the statement is made that God hardened Pharaoh's heart. In the other instances, the record observes that Pharaoh hardened his own heart. Each instance records "as the Lord commanded," so what happened did so from two closely related perspectives: 1) God was carrying out His purpose through Pharaoh, and 2) Pharaoh was personally responsible for his actions as the command of v. 13 implies. *See note on 4:21.*

9:14 My plagues. God's use of the possessive pronoun specified what should have become abundantly clear to Pharaoh by then, namely, that these were God's own workings. **to your very heart.** "To send to the very heart" was apparently a colloquial expression denoting someone's being made to feel the full force of an act, to feel it strike home!

9:14-19 After sounding again the customary demand to release God's people for worship (v. 13), and after delivering a warning of how His plagues would really have an impact (v. 14), God provided more information and issued certain preliminary instructions:

(1) A 3-fold purpose pertained to the plagues, namely, the Egyptians would recognize that Yahweh was incomparable, that His power would be demonstrated through them, and that His name, character, attributes, and power, would be known everywhere. Egypt could not keep from other nations her humiliation by the plagues of Israel's Lord.

(2) A declaration that whatever royal authority Pharaoh had, it had been because of God's sovereign and providential control of world affairs, which included putting Pharaoh on his throne. This was a telling reminder that He was what He declared Himself to be, the one and only true and immanent Lord.

(3) A reminder of the worst scenario for Egypt if Yahweh had chosen, in lieu of the preceding plagues, to strike the people first—they would have perished. In other words, God had been gracious and longsuffering in the progression of the plagues.

(4) A declaration that the weather about to be unleashed by the incomparable God was unlike anything previously recorded in Egypt's entire history, or "since its founding" or "since it became a nation."

(5) An instruction as to how the Egyptians could avoid severe storm damage and loss of property. Grace again was afforded them!

had [q]stretched out My hand and struck you
and your people with [r]pestilence, then you
would have been cut off from the earth.
16 But indeed for [s]this *purpose* I have raised
you up, that I may [t]show My power *in* you,
and that My [u]name may be declared in all
the earth. 17 As yet you exalt yourself
against My people in that you will not let
them go. 18 Behold, tomorrow about this
time I will cause very heavy hail to rain
down, such as has not been in Egypt since
its founding until now. 19 Therefore send
now *and* gather your livestock and all that
you have in the field, for the hail shall come
down on every man and every animal
which is found in the field and is not
brought home; and they shall die." ' "
20 He who [v]feared the word of the LORD
among the [w]servants of Pharaoh made his
servants and his livestock flee to the houses. 21 But he who did not regard the word
of the LORD left his servants and his livestock in the field.
22 Then the LORD said to Moses, "Stretch
out your hand toward heaven, that there
may be [x]hail in all the land of Egypt—on
man, on beast, and on every herb of the
field, throughout the land of Egypt."
23 And Moses stretched out his rod toward
heaven; and [y]the LORD sent thunder and
hail, and fire darted to the ground. And the
LORD rained hail on the land of Egypt.
24 So there was hail, and fire mingled with
the hail, so very heavy that there was none
like it in all the land of Egypt since it became a nation. 25 And the [z]hail struck
throughout the whole land of Egypt, all
that *was* in the field, both man and beast;
and the hail struck every herb of the field
and broke every tree of the field. 26 [a]Only
in the land of Goshen, where the children
of Israel *were*, there was no hail.
27 And Pharaoh sent and [b]called for Moses and Aaron, and said to them, [c]"I have
sinned this time. [d]The LORD *is* righteous,
and my people and I *are* wicked. 28 [e]En-
treat[1] the LORD, that there may be no *more*
[2]mighty thundering and hail, for *it is*
enough. I will let you [f]go, and you shall
stay no longer."
29 So Moses said to him, "As soon as I
have gone out of the city, I will [g]spread out
my hands to the LORD; the thunder will
cease, and there will be no more hail, that
you may know that the [h]earth *is* the LORD's.
30 But as for you and your servants, [i]I know
that you will not yet fear the LORD God."
31 Now the flax and the barley were
struck, [j]for the barley *was* in the head and
the flax *was* in bud. 32 But the wheat and the
spelt were not struck, for they *are* [3]late crops.
33 So Moses went out of the city from
Pharaoh and [k]spread out his hands to the
LORD; then the thunder and the hail
ceased, and the rain was not poured on the
earth. 34 And when Pharaoh saw that the
rain, the hail, and the thunder had ceased,
he sinned yet more; and he hardened his
heart, he and his servants. 35 So [l]the heart
of Pharaoh was hard; neither would he let
the children of Israel go, as the LORD had
spoken by Moses.

The Eighth Plague: Locusts

10 Now the LORD said to Moses, "Go
in to Pharaoh; [a]for I have hardened
his heart and the hearts of his servants,
[b]that I may show these signs of Mine before him, 2 and that [c]you may tell in the
hearing of your son and your son's son the
mighty things I have done in Egypt, and

15 [q]Ex. 3:20; 7:5 [r]Ex. 5:3
16 [s]Ex. 14:17; Prov. 16:4; [Rom. 9:17, 18; 1 Pet. 2:8, 9]
16 [t]Ex. 7:4, 5; 10:1; 11:9; 14:17 [u]1 Kin. 8:43
20 [v]Ex. 1:17; 14:31; [Prov. 13:13] [w]Ex. 8:19; 10:7
22 [x]Rev. 16:21
23 [y]Gen. 19:24; Josh. 10:11; Ps. 18:13; 78:47; 105:32; 148:8; Is. 30:30; Ezek. 38:22; Rev. 8:7
25 [z]Ex. 9:19; Ps. 78:47, 48; 105:32, 33
26 [a]Ex. 8:22, 23; 9:4, 6; 10:23; 11:7; 12:13; Is. 32:18, 19
27 [b]Ex. 8:8 [c]Ex. 9:34; 10:16, 17 [d]2 Chr. 12:6; Ps. 129:4; 145:17; Lam. 1:18
28 [e]Ex. 8:8, 28; 10:17; Acts 8:24 [f]Ex. 8:25; 10:8, 24 [1]*Pray to, Make supplication to* [2]Lit. *voices of God* or *sounds of God*
29 [g]1 Kin. 8:22, 38; Ps. 143:6; Is. 1:15 [h]Ex. 8:22; 19:5; 20:11; Ps. 24:1; 1 Cor. 10:26, 28
30 [i]Ex. 8:29; [Is. 26:10]
31 [j]Ruth 1:22; 2:23
32 [3]Lit. *darkened*
33 [k]Ex. 8:12; 9:29
35 [l]Ex. 4:21

CHAPTER 10

1 [a]Ex. 4:21; 7:14; 9:12; 10:27; 11:10; 14:4; Josh. 11:20; John 12:40; Rom. 9:18 [b]Ex. 7:4; 9:16
2 [c]Ex. 12:26; 13:8, 14; Deut. 4:9; 6:7; 11:19; Ps. 44:1; 78:5; Joel 1:3

9:16 See Rom. 9:17 where Paul indicates God's sovereignty over Pharaoh.

9:20,21 who feared...who did not regard. Some heard the instruction and obeyed; others, like their national leader, did not "regard the word of the LORD," a graphic expression of refusal to heed divine instruction.

9:23,24 fire darted...fire mingled. The violent, electrical thunderstorm brought with it unusual lightning, or "fireballs," which zigzagged (lit. "fire taking hold of itself") to and fro on the ground with the hail.

9:26 Only in the land of Goshen. The discriminatory nature of this plague was unannounced beforehand, but the national distinction previously declared and observed again prevailed. Although unstated, those who were in the strife-torn regions and who obeyed instructions obviously found their livestock equally safe and sound.

9:27 I have sinned this time. Any improvement in Pharaoh's theological understanding, notwithstanding the following confession of a righteous Lord and of a wicked people, was rendered suspect by the face-saving caveat "this time." Lacking repentance, it brushed aside all previous reaction and disobedience as having no significance.

9:28 *it is* enough. Moses' reply (v. 30) indicated that such an evaluation was not one of repentance nor one of fearing the Lord and acknowledging His power.

9:31,32 flax and the barley were struck...the wheat and the spelt were not struck. A very brief bulletin on which crops were damaged and which were not placed this plague in Feb. All 4 crops mentioned were important economic resources. Wheat would be harvested only a month later than flax and barley together with the aftercrop "spelt" or "rye." God's timing of the disaster to two crops left room for Pharaoh to repent before the other crops might be destroyed.

9:34 sinned yet more. Pharaoh's culpability increased because when he saw God answer Moses' prayer—an entreaty he had requested (v. 28)—still all his admissions and promises were promptly swept aside. **he and his servants.** For the first time mention is made of the stubborn resistance of Pharaoh's entourage, all of whom had hardened their hearts. The striking contrast emerges in God's directions to Moses for the next plague: He had hardened their hearts for a purpose (10:1).

10:2 that you may tell...that you may know. The release from Egypt, accompanied by these great acts of God, was designed to be-

My signs which I have done among them,
that you may [d]know that I *am* the LORD."
3 So Moses and Aaron came in to Pharaoh and said to him, "Thus says the LORD
God of the Hebrews: 'How long will you
refuse to [e]humble yourself before Me? Let
My people go, that they may [f]serve Me.
4 Or else, if you refuse to let My people go,
behold, tomorrow I will bring [g]locusts into
your territory. 5 And they shall cover the
face of the earth, so that no one will be able
to see the earth; and [h]they shall eat the
residue of what is left, which remains to
you from the hail, and they shall eat every
tree which grows up for you out of the
field. 6 They shall [i]fill your houses, the
houses of all your servants, and the houses
of all the Egyptians—which neither your
fathers nor your fathers' fathers have seen,
since the day that they were on the earth to
this day.' " And he turned and went out
from Pharaoh.
7 Then Pharaoh's [j]servants said to him,
"How long shall this man be [k]a snare to
us? Let the men go, that they may serve the
LORD their God. Do you not yet know that
Egypt is destroyed?"
8 So Moses and Aaron were brought
again to Pharaoh, and he said to them,
"Go, serve the LORD your God. Who *are* the
ones that are going?"
9 And Moses said, "We will go with our
young and our old; with our sons and our
daughters, with our flocks and our herds
we will go, for [l]we must hold a feast to the
LORD."
10 Then he said to them, "The LORD had
better be with you when I let you and your
little ones go! Beware, for evil is ahead of
you. 11 Not so! Go now, you *who are* men,
and serve the LORD, for that is what you
desired." And they were driven [m]out from
Pharaoh's presence.
12 Then the LORD said to Moses, [n]"Stretch
out your hand over the land of Egypt for the
locusts, that they may come upon the land
of Egypt, and [o]eat every herb of the land—
all that the hail has left." 13 So Moses
stretched out his rod over the land of Egypt,
and the LORD brought an east wind on the
land all that day and all *that* night. When it
was morning, the east wind brought the locusts. 14 And [p]the locusts went up over all
the land of Egypt and rested on all the territory of Egypt. *They were* very severe; [q]previ-
ously there had been no such locusts as
they, nor shall there be such after them.
15 For they [r]covered the face of the whole
earth, so that the land was darkened; and
they [s]ate every herb of the land and all the
fruit of the trees which the hail had left. So
there remained nothing green on the trees
or on the plants of the field throughout all
the land of Egypt.
16 Then Pharaoh called [t]for Moses and
Aaron in haste, and said, [u]"I have sinned
against the LORD your God and against
you. 17 Now therefore, please forgive my
sin only this once, and [v]entreat[1] the LORD

2 [d] Ex. 7:5, 17; 8:22
3 [e] [1 Kin. 21:29; 2 Chr. 34:27]; Job 42:6; [James 4:10; 1 Pet. 5:6] [f] Ex. 4:23; 8:1; 9:1
4 [g] Prov. 30:27; Rev. 9:3
5 [h] Ex. 9:32; Joel 1:4; 2:25
6 [i] Ex. 8:3, 21
7 [j] Ex. 7:5; 8:19; 9:20; 12:33 [k] Ex. 23:33; Josh. 23:13; 1 Sam. 18:21; Eccl. 7:26; 1 Cor. 7:35
9 [l] Ex. 5:1; 7:16
11 [m] Ex. 10:28
12 [n] Ex. 7:19 [o] Ex. 10:5, 15
14 [p] Deut. 28:38; Ps. 78:46; 105:34 [q] Joel 1:4, 7; 2:1-11; Rev. 9:3
15 [r] Ex. 10:5 [s] Ps. 105:35
16 [t] Ex. 8:8 [u] Ex. 9:27
17 [v] Ex. 8:8, 28; 9:28; 1 Kin. 13:6 [1] *make supplication to*

come an important and indelible part in recounting the history of Israel to succeeding generations. It would tell just who their God was and what He had done. **the mighty things...done.** Lit. "to deal harshly with" or "to make sport of," and describing an action by which shame and disgrace is brought upon its object.

10:3 How long will you refuse...? The question asked of Pharaoh struck a contrast with the opening words of God to Moses (v. 1), "I have hardened his heart." What God did cannot erase personal responsibility from Pharaoh to hear, repent, and submit. Under the cumulative weight of 7 plagues, the time had come to deliver a challenge to reconsider and obey. This is God's grace operating parallel with His own sovereign purposes.

10:4-6 The extent and intensity of the locust plague was such that it would be unique in Egyptian history—nothing like any locust problem during the previous two generations, nor like any locust swarm in the future (v. 14). Locust invasions were feared in Egypt, to the point that the farmers often prayed to the locust god to ensure the safety of their crops. The humiliation of their god was total, as was the damage: "There remained nothing green..." (v. 15).

10:7 How long shall this man...? The first "How long?" question in this encounter dealt with the desired response from Pharaoh (v. 3), whereas this second "How long?" question pointed out their impatience at Pharaoh's intransigence. Their advice—to give in—was the best choice. **Egypt is destroyed.** The advisers negatively evaluated the state of the country after 7 plagues, and suggested that Pharaoh was refusing to acknowledge how desperate the situation really was even before the agriculture was completely destroyed. Stubborn resistance did not necessarily rob them of all reason, and the better part of wisdom this time demanded acquiescence to Moses' request.

10:8 Who *are* the ones that are going? For the first time Pharaoh tried to negotiate a deal before the threatened plague struck. Adroitly, he suggested in his question that only representatives of Israel, perhaps only the men (v. 11), need go out to worship.

10:10 The LORD had better be with you. Sarcastic threats demonstrated the unyielding and unreasonable obstinacy of Pharaoh. Egyptian women did accompany their men in religious celebration, but in Israel's case if the men went out then the women and children were in effect hostages bidding them return.

10:11 driven out. For the first time, God's two spokesmen were angrily dismissed from the throne room.

10:12 all that the hail has left. This reminder of the previous plague in which God had graciously restrained the extent of agricultural damage appeared also in the warning of the plague given to Pharaoh and his advisers (v. 5) and in the description of the damage done by the locusts (v. 15).

10:13 an east wind. God used natural means, most probably the spring hot wind, or "sirocco," to bring the locusts into the country from the Arabian peninsula.

10:16 in haste. A recognition on the part of Pharaoh that his country now faced a crisis brought forth a hurried confession to Aaron and Moses, which again was merely an expedient course of action.

10:17 forgive my sin. Again, an attempt to sound earnest in his response, and again with an appeal for Moses to pray for removal of

your God, that He may take away from me
this death only." **18** So he [w]went out from
Pharaoh and entreated the LORD. **19** And
the LORD turned a very strong west wind,
which took the locusts away and blew
them [x]into the Red Sea. There remained not
one locust in all the territory of Egypt.
20 But the LORD [y]hardened Pharaoh's heart,
and he did not let the children of Israel go.

The Ninth Plague: Darkness

21 Then the LORD said to Moses,
[z]"Stretch out your hand toward heaven,
that there may be darkness over the land of
Egypt, [2]darkness *which* may even be felt."
22 So Moses stretched out his hand toward
heaven, and there was [a]thick darkness in
all the land of Egypt [b]three days. **23** They
did not see one another; nor did anyone
rise from his place for three days. [c]But all
the children of Israel had light in their
dwellings.

24 Then Pharaoh called to Moses and
[d]said, "Go, serve the LORD; only let your
flocks and your herds be kept back. Let
your [e]little ones also go with you."

25 But Moses said, "You must also give
[3]us sacrifices and burnt offerings, that we
may sacrifice to the LORD our God. **26** Our
[f]livestock also shall go with us; not a hoof
shall be left behind. For we must take some
of them to serve the LORD our God, and
even we do not know with what we must
serve the LORD until we arrive there."

27 But the LORD [g]hardened Pharaoh's
heart, and he would not let them go.
28 Then Pharaoh said to him, [h]"Get away
from me! Take heed to yourself and see my
face no more! For in the day you see my
face you shall die!"

29 So Moses said, "You have spoken
well. [i]I will never see your face again."

Death of the Firstborn Announced

11 And the LORD said to Moses, "I will
bring one more plague on Pharaoh
and on Egypt. [a]Afterward he will let you
go from here. [b]When he lets *you* go, he will
surely drive you out of here altogether.
2 Speak now in the hearing of the people,
and let every man ask from his neighbor
and every woman from her neighbor, [c]arti-
cles of silver and articles of gold." **3** [d]And
the LORD gave the people favor in the sight
of the Egyptians. Moreover the man [e]Mo-
ses *was* very great in the land of Egypt, in
the sight of Pharaoh's servants and in the
sight of the people.

4 Then Moses said, "Thus says the LORD:
[f]'About midnight I will go out into the

18 [w] Ex. 8:30
19 [x] Joel 2:20
20 [y] Ex. 4:21; 10:1; 11:10
21 [z] Ex. 9:22 [2] Lit. *that one may feel the darkness*
22 [a] Ps. 105:28; Rev. 16:10 [b] Ex. 3:18
23 [c] Ex. 8:22, 23
24 [d] Ex. 8:8, 25; 10:8 [e] Ex. 10:10
25 [3] Lit. *into our hands*
26 [f] Ex. 10:9
27 [g] Ex. 4:21; 10:1, 20; 14:4, 8
28 [h] Ex. 10:11
29 [i] Ex. 11:8; Heb. 11:27

CHAPTER 11

1 [a] Ex. 12:31, 33, 39 [b] Ex. 6:1; 12:39
2 [c] Ex. 3:22; 12:35, 36
3 [d] Ex. 3:21; 12:36; Ps. 106:46 [e] Deut. 34:10-12; 2 Sam. 7:9; Esth. 9:4
4 [f] Ex. 12:12, 23, 29

the plague. He referred to it this time as "this death," or "deadly plague," phrases which highlighted the severity of Egypt's condition.

10:19 west wind. In answer to prayer, wind direction reversed as the Lord caused the locusts to be blown eastward out of the country. The completeness of their removal received emphasis. That none remained in the country was apparently something unusual, perhaps somewhat distinct from previously known locust invasions. The absence of locusts was a challenging reminder of the power of the Lord who had brought it all to pass.

10:21,22 darkness…felt…thick darkness. Such a description of the ninth plague, which occurred without warning, pointed to the most unusual nature of the three-day darkness that now prevented any from leaving their homes. That Israel had light in their dwellings and went about their normal activity stresses the supernatural nature of this plague. It takes attention away from trying to explain the darkness solely in terms of the Khamsin, the swirling sandstorms of the day. The LXX did, however, string together 3 Gr. words, two for darkness and one for storm, to portray the nuance of the Heb. In so doing, it may unwittingly have given some credence to a severe sandstorm. Theologically, such thick darkness directly challenged the faithfulness of the sun god, Ra, to provide warmth and sunshine from day to day, and also prevented any daily worship rituals from taking place.

10:24 Go…Let your little ones also go with you. Pharaoh's deceitful and manipulative negotiating skills rose to the occasion: Let the people go but keep back their livestock as the hostage forcing their return. He had not yet understood that partial obedience to the Lord's directions was unacceptable.

10:25 See 3:18 for remarks on the request to leave for worship suggesting something less than permanent departure.

10:28 Get away from me!…you shall die! Pharaoh's obstinacy and resistance reached a new height when he summarily dismissed Moses and Aaron and this time added a death threat.

10:29 never see your face again. Moses concurred, but from another perspective than that of Pharaoh. All negotiations and requests ceased immediately. Moses would be summoned to see Pharaoh again after the tenth plague (12:31), but that would be to hear him finally concede defeat.

11:1-3 And the LORD said. Read as "the LORD had said." In a parenthetical paragraph, the narrative recorded that which God had already said to Moses during the 3 days of darkness, priming him for Pharaoh's summons, and priming Israel to receive Egyptian jewelry and other goods. An aside explained Egyptian generosity as occasioned by divine intervention (cf. 12:35,36). This also included a healthy respect by Egypt's leaders and people for Israel's leader.

11:4-8 Then Moses said. Moses' response to Pharaoh's threat continued with his giving warning of the final plague and leaving with great indignation. The death threat delivered by Pharaoh evoked one from God. The "get out!" from Pharaoh to Israel's and God's spokesmen would be met by the "get out" from the Egyptians to Israel.

11:4 About midnight. The day was not specified, as in previous plagues by "tomorrow." It took place either the same day of the final confrontation with Pharaoh or a few days later. If the instructions for the Passover (12:1-20) were not given during the days of darkness, then 4 days minimum would be required to set the stage for that special feast day, i.e., from the tenth to the fourteenth day (12:3,6). *See note on 8:23.* **I will go out.** God was, of course, involved in all previous plagues through whatever means He chose to use, but this time, to warrant personal attention, God stated that He Himself (emphatic personal pronoun used) would march throughout the land. Note the repeated "I will" statements in the Passover instructions (12:12,13).

midst of Egypt; 5 and [g]all the firstborn in
the land of Egypt shall die, from the firstborn of Pharaoh who sits on his throne,
even to the firstborn of the female servant
who *is* behind the handmill, and all the
firstborn of the animals. 6 [h]Then there shall
be a great cry throughout all the land of
Egypt, [i]such as was not like it *before,* nor
shall be like it again. 7 [j]But against none of
the children of Israel [k]shall a dog [1]move its
tongue, against man or beast, that you may
know that the LORD does make a difference
between the Egyptians and Israel.' 8 And
[l]all these your servants shall come down to
me and bow down to me, saying, 'Get out,
and all the people who follow you!' After
that I will go out." [m]Then he went out from
Pharaoh in great anger.
9 But the LORD said to Moses, [n]"Pharaoh
will not heed you, so that [o]My wonders
may be multiplied in the land of Egypt."
10 So Moses and Aaron did all these wonders before Pharaoh; [p]and the LORD hardened Pharaoh's heart, and he did not let
the children of Israel go out of his land.

The Passover Instituted

12 Now the LORD spoke to Moses and
Aaron in the land of Egypt, saying,
2 [a]"This month *shall be* your beginning of
months; it *shall be* the first month of the
year to you. 3 Speak to all the congregation
of Israel, saying: 'On the [b]tenth of this
month every man shall take for himself a
lamb, according to the house of *his* father, a
lamb for a household. 4 And if the household is too small for the lamb, let him and
his neighbor next to his house take *it* according to the number of the persons; according to each man's need you shall make
your count for the lamb. 5 Your lamb shall
be [c]without[1] blemish, a male [2]of the first
year. You may take *it* from the sheep or
from the goats. 6 Now you shall keep it
until the [d]fourteenth day of the same
month. Then the whole assembly of the
congregation of Israel shall kill it at twilight. 7 And they shall take *some* of the
blood and put *it* on the two doorposts and
on the lintel of the houses where they eat it.
8 Then they shall eat the flesh on that
[e]night; [f]roasted in fire, with [g]unleavened
bread *and* with bitter *herbs* they shall eat it.
9 Do not eat it raw, nor boiled at all with
water, but [h]roasted in fire—its head with
its legs and its entrails. 10 [i]You shall let
none of it remain until morning, and what
remains of it until morning you shall burn
with fire. 11 And thus you shall eat it: [3]*with
a belt on your waist, your sandals on your
feet, and your staff in your hand.* So you
shall eat it in haste. [j]It *is* the LORD's
Passover.
12 'For I [k]will pass through the land of
Egypt on that night, and will strike all the
firstborn in the land of Egypt, both man
and beast; and [l]against all the gods of
Egypt I will execute judgment: [m]I *am* the

5 [g] Ex. 4:23; 12:12, 29; Ps. 78:51; 105:36; 135:8; 136:10; Amos 4:10
6 [h] Ex. 12:30; Amos 5:17 [i] Ex. 10:14
7 [j] Ex. 8:22 [k] Josh. 10:21 [1] *sharpen*
8 [l] Ex. 12:31-33 [m] Ex. 10:29; Heb. 11:27
9 [n] Ex. 3:19; 7:4; 10:1 [o] Ex. 7:3; 9:16
10 [p] Ex. 7:3; 9:12; 10:1, 20, 27; Josh. 11:20; Is. 63:17; John 12:40; Rom. 2:5

CHAPTER 12

2 [a] Ex. 13:4; 23:15; 34:18; Deut. 16:1
3 [b] Josh. 4:19
5 [c] Lev. 22:18-21; 23:12; Mal. 1:8, 14; [Heb. 9:14; 1 Pet. 1:19] [1] *perfect* or *sound* [2] *a year old*
6 [d] Ex. 12:14, 17; Lev. 23:5; Num. 9:1-3, 11; 28:16; Deut. 16:1, 4, 6
8 [e] Ex. 34:25; Num. 9:12 [f] Deut. 16:7 [g] Deut. 16:3, 4; 1 Cor. 5:8
9 [h] Deut. 16:7
10 [i] Ex. 16:19; 23:18; 34:25
11 [j] Ex. 12:13, 21, 27, 43 [3] Made ready to travel
12 [k] Ex. 11:4, 5 [l] Num. 33:4 [m] Ex. 6:2

11:5 the firstborn. The firstborn held a particularly important position in the family and society, not only inheriting a double portion of the father's estate, but also representing special qualities of life and strength (cf. Gen. 49:3). In Egypt, the firstborn would ascend to the throne and continue the dynasty. Whatever significance might have been attached religiously, politically, dynastically, and socially, it was all stripped away by the extent and intensity of the plague—namely the execution of all the firstborn of all classes of the population including their animals.

11:6 So drastic was this plague that its uniqueness in Egypt's history, already past and yet to come, was noted in the warning.

11:7 In contrast to the turmoil and grief experienced in Egyptian territory, all remained tranquil in Israelite territory—so much so that not even a dog barked. That the Lord had made and was making a sharp distinction between the two peoples was a fact to which none could be blind.

12:1 the LORD spoke. Most probably, the instructions on the Passover (vv. 1-20) were also given during the 3 days of darkness in order to fully prepare Israel for the grand finale, their Exodus from Egypt. **in the land.** Later, while Israel was in the wilderness, Moses wrote (23:14-17; Deut. 16:1-8) and indicated that the detailed instructions for this very special feast day in Israel's religious calendar were not like those of the other special days, all which were given after the nation had already left Egypt. This one, the Passover, was inextricably linked to what took place in the Exodus, and that connection was never to be forgotten. It became indelibly entrenched in Israel's tradition and has always marked the day of redemption from Egypt.

12:2 This month. The month of Abib (Mar./Apr.) by divine decree became the beginning of the religious calendar, marking the start of Israel's life as a nation. Later in Israel's history, after the Babylonian captivity, Abib would become Nisan (cf. Neh. 2:1; Esth. 3:7).

12:3-14 The detailed instructions for the Passover included what animal to select, what to do with its blood, how to cook it, what to do with leftovers, how to dress for the meal, the reason why it was being celebrated "in haste," and what the shed blood signified.

12:5 Your lamb shall be without blemish. A kid goat was an alternative choice. Any flaw would render it unfit to represent a pure, wholesome sacrifice given to Yahweh.

12:6 at twilight. Lit. "between the two evenings." Since the new day was reckoned from sunset, the sacrificing of the lamb or kid was done before sunset while it was still day 14 of the first month. "Twilight" has been taken to signify either that time between sunset and the onset of darkness, or from the decline of the sun until sunset. Later Moses would prescribe the time for the sacrifice as "at twilight, at the going down of the sun" (Deut. 16:6). According to Josephus, it was customary in his day to slay the lamb at about 3:00 p.m. This was the time of day that Christ, the Christian's Passover lamb (1 Cor. 5:7), died (Luke 23:44-46).

12:9 Do not eat it raw. A prohibition with health implications which also distinguished them from pagan peoples who often ate raw flesh in their sacred festivals.

12:12 against all the gods. The tenth plague was a judgment against all Egyptian deities. The loss of the firstborn of men and beasts had far-reaching theological implications, namely, the impotence of the pagan deities, many of whom were represented by ani-

LORD. 13 Now the blood shall be a sign for
you on the houses where you *are.* And
when I see the blood, I will pass over you;
and the plague shall not be on you to destroy *you* when I strike the land of Egypt.
14 'So this day shall be to you [n]a memorial; and you shall keep it as a [o]feast to the
LORD throughout your generations. You
shall keep it as a feast [p]by an everlasting
ordinance. 15 [q]Seven days you shall eat unleavened bread. On the first day you shall
remove leaven from your houses. For whoever eats leavened bread from the first day
until the seventh day, [r]that [4]person shall
be [5]cut off from Israel. 16 On the first day
there shall be [s]a holy convocation, and on
the seventh day there shall be a holy convocation for you. No manner of work shall
be done on them; but *that* which everyone
must eat—that only may be prepared by
you. 17 So you shall observe *the Feast of* Unleavened Bread, for [t]on this same day I
will have brought your [6]armies [u]out of the
land of Egypt. Therefore you shall observe
this day throughout your generations as an
everlasting ordinance. 18 [v]In the first
month, on the fourteenth day of the month
at evening, you shall eat unleavened
bread, until the twenty-first day of the
month at evening. 19 For [w]seven days no
leaven shall be found in your houses, since
whoever eats what is leavened, that same
person shall be cut off from the congregation of Israel, whether *he is* a stranger or a
native of the land. 20 You shall eat nothing
leavened; in all your dwellings you shall
eat unleavened bread.' "
21 Then [x]Moses called for all the [y]elders
of Israel and said to them, [z]"Pick out and
take lambs for yourselves according to
your families, and kill the Passover *lamb.*
22 [a]And you shall take a bunch of hyssop,
dip *it* in the blood that *is* in the basin, and
[b]strike the lintel and the two doorposts
with the blood that *is* in the basin. And
none of you shall go out of the door of his
house until morning. 23 [c]For the LORD will
pass through to strike the Egyptians; and
when He sees the [d]blood on the [7]lintel and
on the two doorposts, the LORD will pass
over the door and [e]not allow [f]the destroyer to come into your houses to strike *you.*
24 And you shall [g]observe this thing as an
ordinance for you and your sons forever.

14 [n]Ex. 13:9 [o]Lev. 23:4, 5; 2 Kin. 23:21 [p]Ex. 12:17, 24; 13:10
15 [q]Ex. 13:6, 7; 23:15; 34:18; Lev. 23:6; Num. 28:17; Deut. 16:3, 8 [r]Gen. 17:14; Ex. 12:19; Num. 9:13 [4]*soul* [5]*Put to death*
16 [s]Lev. 23:2, 7, 8; Num. 28:18, 25
17 [t]Ex. 12:14; 13:3, 10 [u]Num. 33:1 [6]*hosts*
18 [v]Ex. 12:2; Lev. 23:5-8; Num. 28:16-25
19 [w]Ex. 12:15; 23:15; 34:18
21 [x][Heb. 11:28] [y]Ex. 3:16 [z]Ex. 12:3; Num. 9:4; Josh. 5:10; 2 Kin. 23:21; Ezra 6:20; Mark 14:12-16
22 [a]Heb. 11:28 [b]Ex. 12:7
23 [c]Ex. 11:4; 12:12, 13 [d]Ex. 24:8 [e]Ezek. 9:6; Rev. 7:3; 9:4 [f]1 Cor. 10:10; Heb. 11:28 [7]Crosspiece at top of door
24 [g]Ex. 12:14, 17; 13:5, 10

mals, to protect their devotees from such nationwide tragedies. The great cry of grief (11:6; 12:30) may also have bemoaned the incapability of the nation's gods.

12:14 a memorial. The details of how this Passover Day was to be memorialized in future years were laid down (vv. 14-20), and then repeated in the instructions to the elders (vv. 21-27). Prescribing the eating of unleavened bread for 7 days, demanding a thorough house-cleaning from leaven (v. 15), issuing a stern warning of banishment for eating leaven (v. 15), and bracketing the 7 days with special holy days (v. 16), served to proclaim the high importance of the nation's remembering this event.

12:16 prepared by you. *See note on v. 46.*

12:19 a stranger. Provision was made right at the beginning for non-Israelites to be included in the nation's religious festivals. Failure to comply with the regulations on leaven would result in banishment for the alien as well.

12:22 bunch of hyssop. Certain identification is impossible, but this could be the jarjoram plant. **lintel...the two doorposts.** The top and two sides of the doorway.

12:23 the destroyer. This is most likely the Angel of the Lord (cf. 2 Sam. 24:16; Is. 37:36). *See note on 3:2.*

Chronology of the Exodus

Date	Event	Reference
Fifteenth day, first month, first year	Exodus	Exodus 12
Fifteenth day, second month, first year	Arrival in Wilderness of Sin	Exodus 16:1
Third month, first year	Arrival in Wilderness of Sinai	Exodus 19:1
First day, first month, second year	Erection of Tabernacle	Exodus 40:1,17
	Dedication of Altar	Numbers 7:1
	Consecration of Levites	Numbers 8:1-26
Fourteeneth day, first month, second year	Passover	Numbers 9:5
First day, second month, second year	Census	Numbers 1:1,18
Fourteeneth day, second month, second year	Supplemental Passover	Numbers 9:11
Twentieth day, second month, second year	Departure from Sinai	Numbers 10:11
First month, fortieth year	In Wilderness of Zin	Numbers 20:1,22-29; 33:38
First day, fifth month, fortieth year	Death of Aaron	Numbers 20:22-29; 33:38
First day, eleventh month, fortieth year	Moses' Address	Deuteronomy 1:3

25 It will come to pass when you come to
the land which the LORD will give you,
[h]just as He promised, that you shall keep
this service. 26 [i]And it shall be, when your
children say to you, 'What do you mean
by this service?' 27 that you shall say, [j]'It *is*
the Passover sacrifice of the LORD, who
passed over the houses of the children of
Israel in Egypt when He struck the Egyptians and delivered our households.'" So
the people [k]bowed their heads and worshiped. 28 Then the children of Israel went
away and [l]did *so;* just as the LORD had
commanded Moses and Aaron, so they
did.

The Tenth Plague: Death of the Firstborn

29 [m]And it came to pass at midnight that
[n]the LORD struck all the firstborn in the
land of Egypt, from the firstborn of Pharaoh who sat on his throne to the firstborn
of the captive who *was* [8]in the dungeon,
and all the firstborn of [o]livestock. 30 So
Pharaoh rose in the night, he, all his servants, and all the Egyptians; and there was
a great cry in Egypt, for *there was* not a
house where *there was* not one dead.

The Exodus

31 Then he [p]called for Moses and Aaron
by night, and said, "Rise, go out from
among my people, [q]both you and the children of Israel. And go, serve the LORD as
you have [r]said. 32 [s]Also take your flocks
and your herds, as you have said, and be
gone; and bless me also."

33 [t]And the Egyptians [u]urged the people,
that they might send them out of the land

25 [h] Ex. 3:8, 17
26 [i] Ex. 10:2; 13:8, 14, 15; Deut. 32:7; Josh. 4:6; Ps. 78:6
27 [j] Ex. 12:11 [k] Ex. 4:31
28 [l] [Heb. 11:28]
29 [m] Ex. 11:4, 5 [n] Num. 8:17; 33:4; Ps. 135:8; 136:10
[o] Ex. 9:6 [8] *in prison*
31 [p] Ex. 10:28, 29 [q] Ex. 8:25; 11:1 [r] Ex. 10:9
32 [s] Ex. 10:9, 26
33 [t] Ex. 10:7 [u] Ex. 11:8; Ps. 105:38

12:25 The promise of entering the land again received emphasis. Israel was not to think of the Exodus as merely a departure from Egypt, but rather as a departure from one land in order to enter another land, which would be their own, in strict accordance with the specifics of the Abrahamic Covenant for his descendants through Isaac and Jacob (cf. Gen. 17:7,8).

12:26,27 In the annual commemoration of the Passover, parents were obligated to teach their children its meaning. It became customary for the youngest child of a Jewish family to elicit the father's formal explanation of what happened in connection with the original observance of the meal in Egypt.

12:31 Rise, go out…serve the LORD. Finally, Pharaoh's response to the repeated "Let My people go!" became "Leave my people!" with no attempt at further negotiation, but total acquiescence. His subjects, fearing more deaths, concurred and hastened Israel's departure (v. 33), driving them out with no time wasted (v. 39).

12:32 bless me also. Undoubtedly, this final request from Pharaoh, whose heart was certainly not repentant (14:8), temporarily conceded defeat and acknowledged Moses and his God as the victors and as those who had the power and resources to bless him.

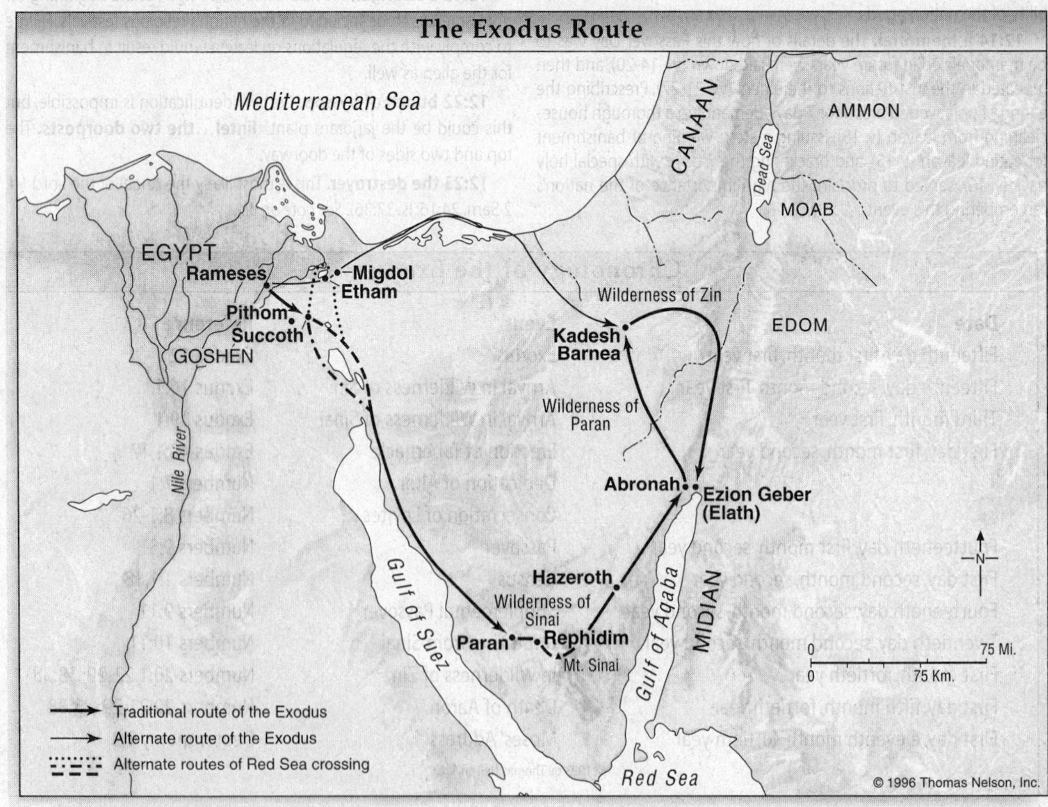

in haste. For they said, "We *shall* all *be*
dead." 34 So the people took their dough
before it was leavened, having their kneading bowls bound up in their clothes on
their shoulders. 35 Now the children of Israel had done according to the word of Moses, and they had asked from the Egyptians
[v]articles of silver, articles of gold, and clothing. 36 [w]And the LORD had given the people
favor in the sight of the Egyptians, so that
they granted them *what they requested.* Thus
[x]they plundered the Egyptians.
37 Then [y]the children of Israel journeyed
from [z]Rameses to Succoth, about [a]six hundred thousand men on foot, besides children. 38 A [b]mixed multitude went up with
them also, and flocks and herds—a great
deal of [c]livestock. 39 And they baked unleavened cakes of the dough which they
had brought out of Egypt; for it was not
leavened, because [d]they were driven out of
Egypt and could not wait, nor had they
prepared provisions for themselves.
40 Now the [9]sojourn of the children of Israel who lived in [1]Egypt *was* [e]four hundred and thirty years. 41 And it came to
pass at the end of the four hundred and
thirty years—on that very same day—it
came to pass that [f]all the armies of the
LORD went out from the land of Egypt. 42 It
is [g]a [2]night of solemn observance to the
LORD for bringing them out of the land of
Egypt. This *is* that night of the LORD, a
solemn observance for all the children of
Israel throughout their generations.

Passover Regulations

43 And the LORD said to Moses and
Aaron, "This *is* [h]the ordinance of the
Passover: No foreigner shall eat it. 44 But
every man's servant who is bought for
money, when you have [i]circumcised him,
then he may eat it. 45 [j]A sojourner and a
hired servant shall not eat it. 46 In one
house it shall be eaten; you shall not carry
any of the flesh outside the house, [k]nor
shall you break one of its bones. 47 [l]All the
congregation of Israel shall keep it. 48 And
[m]when a stranger [3]dwells with you *and*
wants to keep the Passover to the LORD, let
all his males be circumcised, and then let
him come near and keep it; and he shall be
as a native of the land. For no uncircumcised person shall eat it. 49 [n]One law shall
be for the native-born and for the stranger
who dwells among you."
50 Thus all the children of Israel did; as
the LORD commanded Moses and Aaron,
so they did. 51 [o]And it came to pass, on
that very same day, that the LORD brought
the children of Israel out of the land of
Egypt [p]according to their armies.

The Firstborn Consecrated

13 Then the LORD spoke to Moses, saying, 2 [a]"Consecrate[1] to Me all the
firstborn, whatever opens the womb
among the children of Israel, *both* of man
and beast; it is Mine."

35 [v]Ex. 3:21, 22; 11:2, 3; Ps. 105:37
36 [w]Ex. 3:21 [x]Gen. 15:14
37 [y]Num. 33:3, 5 [z]Gen. 47:11; Ex. 1:11; Num. 33:3, 4 [a]Gen. 12:2; Ex. 38:26; Num. 1:46; 2:32; 11:21; 26:51
38 [b]Num. 11:4 [c]Ex. 17:3; Num. 20:19; 32:1; Deut. 3:19
39 [d]Ex. 6:1; 11:1; 12:31-33
40 [e]Gen. 15:13, 16; Acts 7:6; Gal. 3:17 [9]Length of the stay [1]Sam., LXX *Egypt and Canaan*
41 [f]Ex. 3:8, 10; 6:6; 7:4
42 [g]Ex. 13:10; 34:18; Deut. 16:1, 6 [2]*night of vigil*
43 [h]Ex. 12:11; Num. 9:14
44 [i]Gen. 17:12, 13; Lev. 22:11
45 [j]Lev. 22:10
46 [k]Num. 9:12; Ps. 34:20; [John 19:33, 36]
47 [l]Ex. 12:6; Num. 9:13, 14
48 [m]Num. 9:14 [3]As a resident alien
49 [n]Lev. 24:22; Num. 15:15, 16; [Gal. 3:28]
51 [o]Ex. 12:41; 20:2 [p]Ex. 6:26

CHAPTER 13

2 [a]Ex. 13:12, 13, 15; 22:29; Lev. 27:26; Num. 3:13; 8:16; 18:15; Deut. 15:19; Luke 2:23 [1]*Set apart*

12:36 they plundered the Egyptians. Cf. Gen. 15:14; Ex. 3:20,21. This was not done with deceit, but rather a straightforward request (cf. 11:2,3).

12:37–18:27 This section recounts the march of the Israelites from Egypt to Mt. Sinai.

12:37 Rameses to Succoth. One of the cities Israel built (1:11) headed up the itinerary for the journey through the wilderness to Canaan. Succoth is first mentioned in Gen. 33:17 as an encampment designated by the word *Succoth*, which means "booth." Although there is later a town by that name E of the Jordan (cf. Judg. 8:5-16), this is rather a place near Egypt (cf. 13:20; Num. 33:5,6). **six hundred thousand men on foot.** A conservative estimate based on the number of men, probably the fighting men 20 years of age and above, would give a population of 2 million. Israel's population had exploded from the 70 who entered with Jacob in 1875 B.C. to the 2 million who left with Moses in 1445 B.C. *See note on 1:7.*

12:38 A mixed multitude. Other Semitic peoples, other races, and perhaps some native Egyptians accompanied the departing nation. They preferred to be identified with the victorious nation and Jehovah God. Later, some of these became the troublemakers with whom Moses had to deal (Num 11:4).

12:40,41 four hundred and thirty years. Abraham had been told that his descendants would be aliens mistreated in a foreign land for 400 years, using a figure rounded to hundreds (Gen. 15:13).

12:43-51 Additional regulations given for the holding of the Passover contained prohibitions on any uncircumcised foreigner, stranger, or hired servant being a valid participant. To partake of this meal, non-Israelites had to be "as a native of the land" (v.48). *See note on Jer. 4:4.*

12:46 break...bones. Christ, the Christian's Passover lamb (1 Cor. 5:7), had no bones broken (John 19:36).

12:50 so they did. On two occasions (see also v. 28) Moses emphasized the complete obedience of the nation in response to the Lord's commands to them: a contrast to the disobedience they would demonstrate in the very near future.

12:51 on that very same day. What would be for the nation in their new Land a special Sabbath day, was for them at that time the day on which their journey began.

13:2-10 Further explanation tied their departure to the divine promise of entrance and residence in a new land where commemoration of the Exodus would occur through annual observance of this 7 day feast. Again the pedagogical opportunity afforded was not to be overlooked (vv. 8,16).

13:2 Consecrate to Me all the firstborn. Since the firstborn of Israel, of both man and animal, were untouched by the tenth plague, it was fitting that they be set aside as special unto God. Note the closing emphasis: "it is Mine." Further instruction followed on the law relating to the firstborn males once they were in their assigned territory (vv. 11-16). This divine demand was closely linked to the day of departure (12:51, "on that very same day") and the Feast of Unleavened Bread (v. 3, "this day" and v. 4, "on this day...in the month of Abib"). See Luke 2:7, where Christ was referred to as Joseph and Mary's firstborn.

The Feast of Unleavened Bread

3 And Moses said to the people: [b]"Remember this day in which you went out of
Egypt, out of the house of [2]bondage; for
[c]by strength of hand the LORD brought you
out of this *place.* [d]No leavened bread shall
be eaten. 4 [e]On this day you are going out,
in the month Abib. 5 And it shall be, when
the LORD [f]brings you into the [g]land of the
Canaanites and the Hittites and the Amorites and the Hivites and the Jebusites,
which He [h]swore to your fathers to give
you, a land flowing with milk and honey,
[i]that you shall keep this service in this
month. 6 [j]Seven days you shall eat unleavened bread, and on the seventh day *there*
shall be a feast to the LORD. 7 Unleavened
bread shall be eaten seven days. And [k]no
leavened bread shall be seen among you,
nor shall leaven be seen among you in all
your quarters. 8 And you shall [l]tell your
son in that day, saying, '*This is done* because of what the LORD did for me when I
came up from Egypt.' 9 It shall be as [m]a
sign to you on your hand and as a memorial between your eyes, that the LORD's law
may be in your mouth; for with a strong
hand the LORD has brought you out of
Egypt. 10 [n]You shall therefore keep this
[3]ordinance in its season from year to year.

The Law of the Firstborn

11 "And it shall be, when the LORD
[o]brings you into the land of the [p]Canaan-
ites, as He swore to you and your fathers,
and gives it to you, 12 [q]that you shall [4]set
apart to the LORD all that open the womb,
that is, every firstborn that comes from an
animal which you have; the males *shall be*
the LORD's. 13 But [r]every firstborn of a donkey you shall redeem with a lamb; and if
you will not redeem *it,* then you shall break
its neck. And all the firstborn of man among
your sons [s]you shall redeem. 14 [t]So it shall
be, when your son asks you in time to come,
saying, 'What *is* this?' that you shall say to
him, [u]'By strength of hand the LORD
brought us out of Egypt, out of the house of
bondage. 15 And it came to pass, when Pharaoh was stubborn about letting us go, that
[v]the LORD killed all the firstborn in the land
of Egypt, both the firstborn of man and the
firstborn of beast. Therefore I sacrifice to the
LORD all males that open the womb, but all
the firstborn of my sons I redeem.' 16 It shall
be as [w]a sign on your hand and as frontlets
between your eyes, for by strength of hand
the LORD brought us out of Egypt."

The Wilderness Way

17 Then it came to pass, when Pharaoh
had let the people go, that God did not
lead them *by* way of the land of the Philistines, although that *was* near; for God
said, "Lest perhaps the people [x]change
their minds when they see war, and [y]re-
turn to Egypt." 18 So God [z]led the people
around *by* way of the wilderness of the Red
Sea. And the children of Israel went up in
orderly ranks out of the land of Egypt.
19 And Moses took the [a]bones of [b]Joseph
with him, for he had placed the children of
Israel under solemn oath, saying, [c]"God
will surely [5]visit you, and you shall carry
up my bones from here with you."

3 [b] Ex. 12:42; Deut. 16:3 [c] Ex. 3:20; 6:1 [d] Ex. 12:8, 19 [2] Lit. *slaves*
4 [e] Ex. 12:2; 23:15; 34:18; Deut. 16:1
5 [f] Ex. 3:8, 17; Josh. 24:11 [g] Gen. 17:8; Deut. 30:5 [h] Ex. 6:8 [i] Ex. 12:25, 26
6 [j] Ex. 12:15-20
7 [k] Ex. 12:19
8 [l] Ex. 10:2; 12:26; 13:14; Ps. 44:1
9 [m] Ex. 12:14; 13:16; 31:13; Deut. 6:8; 11:18; Matt. 23:5
10 [n] Ex. 12:14, 24 [3] *regulation*
11 [o] Ex. 13:5 [p] Num. 21:3
12 [q] Ex. 13:1, 2; 22:29; 34:19; Lev. 27:26; Num. 18:15; Ezek. 44:30; Luke 2:23 [4] Lit. *cause to pass over*
13 [r] Ex. 34:20; Num. 18:15 [s] Num. 3:46, 47; 18:15, 16
14 [t] Ex. 10:2; 12:26, 27; 13:8; Deut. 6:20; Josh. 4:6, 21 [u] Ex. 13:3, 9
15 [v] Ex. 12:29
16 [w] Ex. 13:9; Deut. 6:8
17 [x] Ex. 14:11; Num. 14:1-4 [y] Deut. 17:16
18 [z] Ex. 14:2; Num. 33:6
19 [a] Gen. 50:24, 25; Josh. 24:32 [b] Ex. 1:6; Deut. 33:13-17 [c] Ex. 4:31 [5] *give attention to*

13:8 for me when I. A personalized application of God's working belonged to the first generation who experienced the Exodus. Later generations could only say "for us, when we…" in the sense of "our nation," but without loss to the significance of how God had brought about such an important day in the nation's history. Note the personalized application of the law of the firstborn as well (v. 15, "I sacrifice…my sons I redeem").

13:9 Later generations would translate this figurative and proverbial expression (cf. Prov. 3:3; 6:21) into the physical reality of phylacteries—the leather prayer-boxes which were strapped on the left arm and on the forehead. Four strips of parchment inscribed with certain words (13:1-16; Deut. 6:4-9; 11:13-21) were placed inside these boxes. The imagery of the proverbial mode of speech signified that their conduct was to be that of someone who could verbally recall what God's law demanded of them. Yahweh who had rescued them had also provided the standards of life for them!

13:12,15 See Luke 2:23.

13:17 *by* way of the land of the Philistines. Travelers going E and NE out of Egypt had two good options: "the way of the sea," or "the way of Shur." The first route, the most direct and shortest, was dotted with Egyptian fortresses which monitored arrivals and departures to and from Egypt. A little further N, Philistine territory also presented a military threat. The lack of battle-readiness on Israel's part deleted the first option, and God chose the second option (v. 18; 15:22). In any case, God had told Moses to lead the people to Horeb or Sinai, the mountain of God (3:1), and not to take them immediately into Canaan (3:12).

13:18 the Red Sea. An alternative designation, quite in accord with the Heb. term, would be "Sea of Reeds," or perhaps "of papyrus marshes." The difficulty of precisely locating other names associated with the crossing of the Red Sea (see 14:2) has occasioned much debate on the location of the crossing. Four views have generally emerged: It was located 1) in the northeastern region of the delta—but this would have been in effect "the way of the sea" and would not have been 3 days' journey from Marah (15:22,23); 2) in the northern end of the Gulf of Suez—but this rules out entry into the wilderness of Shur (15:22); 3) in the vicinity of Lake Timsah or the southern extension of present day Lake Menzaleh—but probably more than 3 days from Marah; and 4) in the Bitter Lakes region, satisfying, in terms of geography and time, all objections to the other options.

13:19 the bones of Joseph. In fulfillment of their solemnly sworn duty and responsibility (Gen. 50:24-26), the Israelites took Joseph's coffin with them. Some 360 years earlier he had foreseen the day when God would bring about the Exodus, and his instructions about his bones being carried to the Promised Land indicated just how certain he was of Israel's departure for Canaan (cf. Gen. 50:24-26; Heb. 11:22). After the years of wilderness wanderings, Joseph's remains reached their final resting place in Shechem (Josh. 24:32).

20 So [d]they took their journey from [e]Suc-
coth and camped in Etham at the edge of
the wilderness. 21 And [f]the LORD went before them by day in a pillar of cloud to lead
the way, and by night in a pillar of fire to
give them light, so as to go by day and
night. 22 He did not take away the pillar of
cloud by day or the pillar of fire by night
from before the people.

The Red Sea Crossing

14 Now the LORD spoke to Moses, saying: 2 "Speak to the children of Israel, [a]that they turn and camp before [b]Pi
Hahiroth, between [c]Migdol and the sea,
opposite Baal Zephon; you shall camp before it by the sea. 3 For Pharaoh will say of
the children of Israel, [d]'They *are* bewildered by the land; the wilderness has
closed them in.' 4 Then [e]I will harden Pharaoh's heart, so that he will pursue them;
and I [f]will gain honor over Pharaoh and
over all his army, [g]that the Egyptians may
know that I *am* the LORD." And they did so.
5 Now it was told the king of Egypt that
the people had fled, and [h]the heart of Pharaoh and his servants was turned against
the people; and they said, "Why have we
done this, that we have let Israel go from
serving us?" 6 So he [1]made ready his chariot and took his people with him. 7 Also, he
took [i]six hundred choice chariots, and all
the chariots of Egypt with captains over
every one of them. 8 And the LORD [j]hard-
ened the heart of Pharaoh king of Egypt,
and he pursued the children of Israel; and
[k]the children of Israel went out with boldness. 9 So the [l]Egyptians pursued them, all
the horses *and* chariots of Pharaoh, his
horsemen and his army, and overtook
them camping by the sea beside Pi Hahiroth, before Baal Zephon.
10 And when Pharaoh drew near, the
children of Israel lifted their eyes, and behold, the Egyptians marched after them.
So they were very afraid, and the children
of Israel [m]cried out to the LORD. 11 [n]Then
they said to Moses, "Because *there were* no
graves in Egypt, have you taken us away
to die in the wilderness? Why have you so
dealt with us, to bring us up out of Egypt?
12 [o]*Is* this not the word that we told you in
Egypt, saying, 'Let us alone that we may
serve the Egyptians'? For *it would have been*
better for us to serve the Egyptians than
that we should die in the wilderness."
13 And Moses said to the people, [p]"Do
not be afraid. [q]Stand still, and see the [r]sal-
vation[2] of the LORD, which He will accomplish for you today. For the Egyptians
whom you see today, you shall [s]see again
no more forever. 14 [t]The LORD will fight for
you, and you shall [u]hold[3] your peace."
15 And the LORD said to Moses, "Why do

20 [d] Num. 33:6-8 [e] Ex. 12:37
21 [f] Ex. 14:19, 24; 33:9, 10; Num. 9:15; 14:14; Deut. 1:33; Neh. 9:12; Ps. 78:14; 99:7; 105:39; [Is. 4:5]; 1 Cor. 10:1

CHAPTER 14

2 [a] Ex. 13:18 [b] Num. 33:7 [c] Jer. 44:1
3 [d] Ps. 71:11
4 [e] Ex. 4:21; 7:3; 14:17 [f] Ex. 9:16; 14:17, 18, 23; Rom. 9:17, 22, 23 [g] Ex. 7:5; 14:25
5 [h] Ps. 105:25
6 [1] *harnessed*
7 [i] Ex. 15:4
8 [j] Ex. 14:4 [k] Ex. 6:1; 13:9; Num. 33:3; Acts 13:17
9 [l] Ex. 15:9; Josh. 24:6
10 [m] Josh. 24:7; Neh. 9:9; Ps. 34:17; 107:6
11 [n] Ex. 5:21; 15:24; 16:2; 17:3; Num. 14:2, 3; 20:3; Ps. 106:7, 8
12 [o] Ex. 5:21; 6:9
13 [p] Gen. 15:1; 46:3; Ex. 20:20; 2 Chr. 20:15, 17; Is. 41:10, 13, 14 [q] Ps. 46:10, 11 [r] Ex. 14:30; 15:2 [s] Deut. 28:68 [2] *deliverance*
14 [t] Ex. 14:25; 15:3; Deut. 1:30; 3:22; Josh. 10:14, 42; 23:2; 2 Chr. 20:29; Neh. 4:20; Is. 31:4 [u] [Is. 30:15] [3] Lit. *be quiet*

13:20 Etham at the edge of the wilderness. The Heb. name of this place may be a transliteration of the Egyptian *Khetem* meaning "fortress." A line of fortresses (*see note on v. 17*) stretched from the Mediterranean Sea to the Gulf of Suez. Even if the site remains unknown so that pinpointing it is not possible, it was surely a place bordering on the desert area to the E of Egypt.

13:21 a pillar of cloud...a pillar of fire. This was the means by which God led the people. It was a single column, being cloud by day and fire by night (cf. 14:24) and was associated with the Angel of God (14:19; 23:20-23) or the Angel of God's presence (Is. 63:8,9). *See note on 3:2.* It was the pillar from which the Lord also spoke to Moses (33:9-11).

14:3,4 Pharaoh will say...I will harden. Pharaoh was kept abreast of Israelite progress and when he heard of the change of direction, he assumed they were lost in unfamiliar territory and were trapped, closed in by desert, sea, and marsh. God intervened again and the stage was set for the final confrontation and final display of divine power.

14:5 Why have we done this...? Hardened hearts lost all sensitivity to the recent tragedy and focused instead on the loss of the economic benefit Israel's enslavement had provided. Those who had urged the Israelites to quickly leave now had the urge to force them to return!

14:7 six hundred choice chariots. Chariots, introduced by the Hyksos (see Introduction: Author and Date), featured prominently in the army of Egypt, and these "choice" ones belonged to an elite, specialized unit.

14:8 Israel went out with boldness. The confidence shown by Israel in their departure is in sharp contrast to the fear they exhibited when they became aware of the pursuing force (v. 10).

14:10 cried out to the LORD. The initial reaction of the people on seeing the approach was to turn to the Lord in anxious prayer. But prayer soon turned to complaints with Moses as the target of their dismay.

14:11 no graves in Egypt. In the light of Egypt's excessive preoccupation with death and various funerary and mortuary rituals, the bitter irony of Israel's questions marked how easily they had forgotten both bondage and rescue.

14:12 serve the Egyptians? Just how much they conveniently forgot the degree of enslavement came out in their "We told you so" attitude. The comment of being better off living and serving than dying perhaps summarized their earlier reaction to Moses and Aaron outside the royal chambers (5:20,21).

14:13 Do not be afraid. Moses' exhortation turned attention to the Lord, whose power they had already seen dramatically in action, and whose deliverance they were about to witness and personally experience. All they needed to do was stand by and watch their God at work, fighting on their side. Euphemistically, Moses informed his people of the certain death of the Egyptian soldiers—you will not see them again! Expressing and experiencing fear did not mean Israel was less than 600,000 fighting men in number, as some have objected. The poorly trained, inadequately equipped, militarily unprepared, and inexperienced Israelites (13:17) were no match for Pharaoh's experienced troops and his highly trained and mobilized chariot force.

14:14 The LORD will fight. This has been and will be true throughout the history of Israel (cf. 1 Sam. 17:47; 2 Chr. 14:10,11; 20:15; Ps. 24:8; Zech. 14:3).

14:15 Why do you cry to Me?...go forward. The Lord's promise of deliverance overruled all despair and sense of hopelessness.

you cry to Me? Tell the children of Israel to
go forward. 16 But [v]lift up your rod, and
stretch out your hand over the sea and divide it. And the children of Israel shall go
on dry *ground* through the midst of the sea.
17 And I indeed will [w]harden the hearts of
the Egyptians, and they shall follow them.
So I will [x]gain honor over Pharaoh and
over all his army, his chariots, and his
horsemen. 18 Then the Egyptians shall
know that I *am* the LORD, when I have
gained honor for Myself over Pharaoh, his
chariots, and his horsemen."
19 And the Angel of God, [y]who went before the camp of Israel, moved and went behind them; and the pillar of cloud went
from before them and stood behind them.
20 So it came between the camp of the Egyptians and the camp of Israel. Thus it was a
cloud and darkness *to the one,* and it gave
light by night *to the other,* so that the one did
not come near the other all that night.
21 Then Moses stretched out his hand
over the sea; and the LORD caused the sea to
go *back* by a strong east wind all that night,
and [z]made the sea into dry *land,* and the waters were [a]divided. 22 So [b]the children of Israel went into the midst of the sea on the dry
ground, and the waters *were* [c]a wall to them
on their right hand and on their left. 23 And
the Egyptians pursued and went after them
into the midst of the sea, all Pharaoh's horses, his chariots, and his horsemen.
24 Now it came to pass, in the morning
[d]watch, that [e]the LORD looked down upon
the army of the Egyptians through the pillar
of fire and cloud, and He [4]troubled the army
of the Egyptians. 25 And He [5]took off their
chariot wheels, so that they drove them with
difficulty; and the Egyptians said, "Let us
flee from the face of Israel, for the LORD
[f]fights for them against the Egyptians."
26 Then the LORD said to Moses, "Stretch
out your hand over the sea, that the waters
may come back upon the Egyptians, on
their chariots, and on their horsemen."
27 And Moses stretched out his hand over
the sea; and when the morning appeared,
the sea [g]returned to its full depth, while
the Egyptians were fleeing into it. So the
LORD [h]overthrew[6] the Egyptians in the
midst of the sea. 28 Then [i]the waters returned and covered the chariots, the horsemen, *and* all the army of Pharaoh that came
into the sea after them. Not so much as one
of them remained. 29 But [j]the children of
Israel had walked on dry *land* in the midst
of the sea, and the waters *were* a wall to
them on their right hand and on their left.
30 So the LORD [k]saved[7] Israel that day
out of the hand of the Egyptians, and Israel
[l]saw the Egyptians dead on the seashore.
31 Thus Israel saw the great [8]work which
the LORD had done in Egypt; so the people
feared the LORD, and [m]believed the LORD
and His servant Moses.

The Song of Moses

15 Then [a]Moses and the children of Israel sang this song to the LORD, and
spoke, saying:

"I will [b]sing to the LORD,
For He has triumphed gloriously!

16 [v]Ex. 4:17, 20; 7:19; 14:21, 26; 17:5, 6, 9; Num. 20:8, 9, 11; Is. 10:26
17 [w]Ex. 14:8 [x]Ex. 14:4
19 [y]Ex. 13:21, 22; [Is. 63:9]
21 [z]Ps. 66:6; 106:9; 136:13, 14 [a]Ex. 15:8; Josh. 3:16; 4:23; Neh. 9:11; Ps. 74:13; 78:13; 114:3, 5; Is. 63:12, 13
22 [b]Ex. 15:19; Josh. 3:17; 4:22; Neh. 9:11; Ps. 66:6; 78:13; Is. 63:13; 1 Cor. 10:1; Heb. 11:29 [c]Ex. 14:29; 15:8; Hab. 3:10
24 [d]Judg. 7:19 [e]Ex. 13:21 [4]*confused*
25 [5]Sam., LXX, Syr. *bound* [f]Ex. 7:5; 14:4, 14, 18
27 [g]Josh. 4:18 [h]Ex. 15:1, 7; Deut. 11:4; Neh. 9:11; Ps. 78:53; Heb. 11:29 [6]Lit. *shook off*
28 [i]Ps. 78:53; 106:11
29 [j]Ex. 14:22; Ps. 66:6; 78:52, 53; Is. 11:15
30 [k]Ex. 14:13; Ps. 106:8, 10; Is. 63:8, 11 [l]Ps. 58:10; 59:10 [7]*delivered*
31 [m]Ex. 4:31; 19:9; Ps. 106:12; John 2:11; 11:45 [8]Lit. *hand with which the LORD worked*

CHAPTER 15

1 [a]Ps. 106:12; Rev. 15:3 [b]Is. 12:1-6

14:16,17 lift up your rod. For the grand, triumphant finale, the rod which had previously been used to bring in different plagues on the Egyptians now divided the water, opening up a valley through which Israel would walk and in which Egypt's army would drown.

14:19 stood behind them. The Angel of the Lord, and the pillar of cloud and fire, moved from being advance guard to being rear guard, from leading to protecting. *See note on 3:2.*

14:21 strong east wind. God's use of natural phenomena does not detract in any way from the miraculous nature of what took place that night. The psalmist recorded this event as the Lord dividing the sea by His strength (Ps. 74:13). The wind walled up the waters on either side of the pathway then opened (v. 22; 15:8; Ps. 78:13).

14:24 the morning watch. The last of three 4-hour night watches (2:00–6:00 a.m.) ended about sunrise.

14:24,25 the LORD looked down…and He troubled. Not only was the Lord fully aware of exactly what was happening—after all, He hardened Egyptian hearts to pursue Israel—He also brought havoc among them. Entrapped in the valley between the walls of water and in total disarray, they acknowledged that the Lord was fighting for their enemy. Not only were they swept aside by the returning waters (vv. 26-28), they were also hindered from driving their chariots forward by a sudden cloudburst (Ps. 77:17-19).

14:29-31 The stark difference between Israel and Egypt is again rehearsed: One nation is obstinate and defeated, their dead on the shores of the sea, having acknowledged the Lord victorious; the other nation is alive on the shores, having traversed the sea on dry ground, acknowledging the work of the Lord, reverencing and believing Him and His servant, Moses.

15:1-18 The structure of the song now sung by the nation contains 4 stanzas (vv. 1-5; 6-10; 11-13; and 14-17) and a one-line closing declaration (v. 18). Stanzas one and two end with "They sank…," a refrain emphasizing the finality of the enemy army's defeat. Stanzas three and four end with reference to God's Holy Place (vv. 13 and 17). More is involved than in easily observing these break points of the song. The flow of thought and emphasis is also interesting. Stanza one briefly introduces God's powerful victory (vv. 1-5). Stanza two graphically repeats the victory and then inserts the arrogant and vengeful assertions of victory by the enemy to show how puny they were (vv. 6-10). Stanza three concisely summarizes the victory after asking an appropriate question (vv. 11-13). Further, since the victory was essential for Israel's rescue, the stanza also introduces them. Stanza four picks up and expands on Yahweh's leading His people to their divinely assigned home and the consequent fear by other nations as they hear of Israel's dramatic rescue from such a powerful enemy nation (vv. 14-17). The closing line sums it all up: The Lord reigns! A narrative interlude (vv. 19,20) reminds of the theme behind the song, and introduces the antiphonal response of Miriam and her band of women (v. 21).

15:1 I will sing. The Israelites began their song in the first per-

The horse and its rider
He has thrown into the sea!
2 The LORD *is* my strength and [c]song,
And He has become my salvation;
He *is* my God, and [d]I will praise
Him;
My [e]father's God, and I [f]will exalt
Him.
3 The LORD *is* a man of [g]war;
The LORD *is* His [h]name.
4 [i]Pharaoh's chariots and his army
He has cast into the sea;
[j]His chosen captains also are
drowned in the Red Sea.
5 The depths have covered them;
[k]They sank to the bottom like a
stone.

6 "Your [l]right hand, O LORD, has
become glorious in power;
Your right hand, O LORD, has
dashed the enemy in pieces.
7 And in the greatness of Your
[m]excellence
You have overthrown those who
rose against You;
You sent forth [n]Your wrath;
It [o]consumed them [p]like stubble.
8 And [q]with the blast of Your
nostrils
The waters were gathered together;
[r]The floods stood upright like a
heap;
The depths [1]congealed in the heart
of the sea.
9 [s]The enemy said, 'I will pursue,
I will overtake,
I will [t]divide the spoil;
My desire shall be satisfied on
them.
I will draw my sword,
My hand shall destroy them.'
10 You blew with Your wind,
The sea covered them;
They sank like lead in the mighty
waters.

11 "Who[u] *is* like You, O LORD, among
the [2]gods?
Who *is* like You, [v]glorious in
holiness,
Fearful in [w]praises, [x]doing
wonders?
12 You stretched out Your right hand;
The earth swallowed them.
13 You in Your mercy have [y]led forth
The people whom You have
redeemed;
You have guided *them* in Your
strength
To [z]Your holy habitation.

14 "The [a]people will hear *and* be
afraid;
[b]Sorrow [3] will take hold of the
inhabitants of Philistia.
15 [c]Then [d]the chiefs of Edom will be
dismayed;
[e]The mighty men of Moab,
Trembling will take hold of them;
[f]All the inhabitants of Canaan will
[g]melt away.
16 [h]Fear and dread will fall on them;
By the greatness of Your arm
They will be [i]*as* still as a stone,
Till Your people pass over, O LORD,
Till the people pass over
[j]Whom You have purchased.
17 You will bring them in and [k]plant
them
In the [l]mountain of Your
inheritance,
In the place, O LORD, *which* You
have made
For Your own dwelling,
The [m]sanctuary, O LORD, *which*
Your hands have established.

18 "The[n] LORD shall reign forever and
ever."

19 For the [o]horses of Pharaoh went with
his chariots and his horsemen into the sea,
and [p]the LORD brought back the waters of
the sea upon them. But the children of Israel went on dry *land* in the midst of the
sea.

The Song of Miriam

20 Then Miriam [q]the prophetess, [r]the sister of Aaron, [s]took the timbrel in her hand;
and all the women went out after her [t]with

2 [c] Ps. 18:1, 2; Is. 12:2; Hab. 3:18, 19 [d] Gen. 28:21, 22 [e] Ex. 3:6, 15, 16 [f] 2 Sam. 22:47; Ps. 99:5; Is. 25:1
3 [g] Ex. 14:14; Rev. 19:11 [h] Ex. 3:15; 6:2, 3, 7, 8; Ps. 24:8; 83:18
4 [i] Ex. 14:28 [j] Ex. 14:7
5 [k] Ex. 15:10; Neh. 9:11
6 [l] Ex. 3:20; Ps. 17:7; 118:15
7 [m] Deut. 33:26 [n] Ps. 78:49, 50 [o] Ps. 59:13 [p] Deut. 4:24; Is. 5:24; Heb. 12:29
8 [q] Ex. 14:21, 22, 29 [r] Ps. 78:13 [1] *became firm*
9 [s] Judg. 5:30 [t] Is. 53:12
11 [u] Ex. 8:10; 9:14; Deut. 3:24; 2 Sam. 7:22; 1 Kin. 8:23; Ps. 71:19; 86:8; Mic. 7:18 [2] *mighty ones* [v] Ps. 68:35; Is. 6:3; Rev. 4:8
[w] 1 Chr. 16:25 [x] Ex. 3:20; Ps. 77:11, 14
13 [y] Neh. 9:12; [Ps. 77:20] [z] Ex. 15:17; Deut. 12:5; Ps. 78:54
14 [a] Josh. 2:9 [b] Ps. 48:6 [3] *Anguish*
15 [c] Gen. 36:15, 40 [d] Deut. 2:4 [e] Num. 22:3, 4 [f] Josh. 5:1 [g] Josh. 2:9-11, 24
16 [h] Ex. 23:27; Deut. 2:25; Josh. 2:9 [i] 1 Sam. 25:37 [j] Ex. 15:13; Ps. 74:2; Is. 43:1; Jer. 31:11; [Titus 2:14]; 2 Pet. 2:1
17 [k] Ps. 44:2; 80:8, 15 [l] Ps. 2:6; 78:54, 68 [m] Ps. 68:16; 76:2; 132:13, 14
18 [n] 2 Sam. 7:16; Ps. 10:16; 29:10; Is. 57:15
19 [o] Ex. 14:23 [p] Ex. 14:28
20 [q] Judg. 4:4 [r] Ex. 2:4; Num. 26:59; 1 Chr. 6:3; Mic. 6:4 [s] 1 Sam. 18:6; 1 Chr. 15:16; Ps. 68:25; 81:2; 149:3; Jer. 31:4 [t] Judg. 11:34; 21:21; 2 Sam. 6:16; Ps. 30:11; 150:4

son, effectively personalizing the community's song as individually relevant, each person heralding Yahweh's victory and declaring who and what He was to them (note the possessive pronouns in v. 2).

15:6 O LORD. The forthright declarations of the opening stanza (vv. 1-5) are most appropriately followed by this vocative form of address in the rest of the song (vv. 6, 11, 16, 17), since the focus of attention is on His working and intervention.

15:15 Edom...Moab...Canaan. Edom and Moab were on the eastern border of the Jordan; Canaan or Palestine is to the west.

15:16,17 An expression of confidence in the promises that God had made to Abraham 700 years earlier (see Gen. 12, 15, 17).

15:18 reign forever. This speaks of the eternal, universal Kingship of the Lord (cf. Ps. 145:13).

15:20 the prophetess. Miriam was the first woman to be given this honor. She herself claimed the Lord had spoken through her (Num. 12:2). She apparently played an important role in these rescue events because the prophet Micah states that God delivered Israel by the hand of Moses, Aaron, and Miriam (Mic. 6:4). Other women to receive this rare honor were Deborah (Judg. 4:4); Huldah (2 Kin. 22:14);

timbrels and with dances. 21 And Miriam
[u]answered them:

[v]"Sing to the LORD,
For He has triumphed gloriously!
The horse and its rider
He has thrown into the sea!"

Bitter Waters Made Sweet

22 So Moses brought Israel from the Red
Sea; then they went out into the Wilderness of [w]Shur. And they went three days in
the wilderness and found no [x]water.
23 Now when they came to [y]Marah, they
could not drink the waters of Marah, for
they *were* bitter. Therefore the name of it
was called [4]Marah. 24 And the people
[z]complained against Moses, saying, "What
shall we drink?" 25 So he cried out to the
LORD, and the LORD showed him a tree.
[a]When he cast *it* into the waters, the waters
were made sweet.

There He [b]made a statute and an [5]ordi-
nance for them, and there [c]He tested them,
26 and said, [d]"If you diligently heed the
voice of the LORD your God and do what is
right in His sight, give ear to His commandments and keep all His statutes, I
will put none of the [e]diseases on you
which I have brought on the Egyptians.
For I *am* the LORD [f]who heals you."

27 [g]Then they came to Elim, where there
were twelve wells of water and seventy

21 [u] 1 Sam. 18:7 [v] Ex. 15:1
22 [w] Gen. 16:7; 20:1; 25:18; Num. 33:8 [x] Ex. 17:1; Num. 20:2
23 [y] Num. 33:8; Ruth 1:20 [4] Lit. *Bitter*
24 [z] Ex. 14:11; 16:2; Ps. 106:13
25 [a] 2 Kin. 2:21 [b] Josh. 24:25 [c] Ex. 16:4; Deut. 8:2, 16; Judg. 2:22; 3:1, 4; Ps. 66:10 [5] *regulation*
26 [d] Ex. 19:5, 6; Deut. 7:12, 15 [e] Deut. 28:27, 58, 60 [f] Ex. 23:25; Deut. 32:39; Ps. 41:3, 4; 103:3; 147:3
27 [g] Num. 33:9

CHAPTER 16

1 [a] Num. 33:10, 11; Ezek. 30:15 [b] Ex. 12:6, 51; 19:1
2 [c] Ex. 14:11; 15:24; Ps. 106:25; 1 Cor. 10:10
3 [d] Ex. 17:3; Num. 14:2, 3; 20:3; Lam. 4:9 [e] Num. 11:4, 5
4 [f] Neh. 9:15; Ps. 78:23–25; 105:40; [John 6:31–35]; 1 Cor. 10:3 [g] Ex. 15:25; Deut. 8:2, 16 [h] Judg. 2:22 [1] Lit. *the portion of a day in its day*
5 [i] Ex. 16:22, 29; Lev. 25:21
6 [j] Ex. 6:7

palm trees; so they camped there by the
waters.

Bread from Heaven

16 And they [a]journeyed from Elim,
and all the congregation of the children of Israel came to the Wilderness of
Sin, which is between Elim and [b]Sinai, on
the fifteenth day of the second month after
they departed from the land of Egypt.
2 Then the whole congregation of the children of Israel [c]complained against Moses
and Aaron in the wilderness. 3 And the
children of Israel said to them, [d]"Oh, that
we had died by the hand of the LORD in the
land of Egypt, [e]when we sat by the pots of
meat *and* when we ate bread to the full! For
you have brought us out into this wilderness to kill this whole assembly with
hunger."

4 Then the LORD said to Moses, "Behold,
I will rain [f]bread from heaven for you. And
the people shall go out and gather [1]a certain quota every day, that I may [g]test them,
whether they will [h]walk in My law or not.
5 And it shall be on the sixth day that they
shall prepare what they bring in, and [i]it
shall be twice as much as they gather
daily."

6 Then Moses and Aaron said to all the
children of Israel, [j]"At evening you shall
know that the LORD has brought you out of
the land of Egypt. 7 And in the morning

Isaiah's wife (Is. 8:3); Anna (Luke 2:36); and Philip's four daughters (Acts 21:9).

15:24 complained against Moses. Israelite memory of victory displayed a remarkable brevity. The personalized declarations of their ode to the Lord sung 3 days earlier vanished into thin air. Their belief of Moses faded out of the picture (14:31). Their question about drinking water roughly brushed aside all recent affirmations of God's being worthy of praise because He had done wonders and was clearly taking them to their land.

15:25 waters were made sweet. Since there is no known tree which would naturally make unpalatable water drinkable, this must have been a miracle by which God demonstrated His willingness and ability to look after His people in a hostile environment. Marah is usually associated with modern day Ain Hawarah, where the waters still remain brackish and unpleasant. **tested them.** "To subject to difficulty in order to prove the quality of someone or something" is one way to explain the meaning of the Heb. word used. Later, at Rephidim (17:1-7), at Sinai (20:20), and at Taberah (Num. 11:1-3; 13:26-33), God did just that to Israel. This is something which no one can do to God Himself (Deut. 6:16)—He needs no testing in character or deed, but man certainly does need proving.

15:26 the LORD who heals. Since this is what He is, Jehovah-Rapha, obedience to divine instruction and guidance will obviously bring healing, not the consequence of plagues like those visited upon Egypt. This promise is limited in context to Israel, most likely for the duration of the Exodus only.

15:27 Elim. The next stopping place, most probably in modern day Wadi Garandel, had an abundant water supply—God would and did lead them aright!

16:1 Wilderness of Sin. More details of the camp sites in the journey from Rameses to Succoth and beyond are found in Num. 33:5-11. That itinerary also lists the next stop as having been Dophkah (Num. 33:12). Identifying it with modern Debbet er Ramleh locates it in the SW of the Sinai peninsula on a direct line between Elim and Sinai. **fifteenth day...second month.** Thirty days after their departure from Rameses.

16:2 the whole congregation...complained. What characterized them as a whole was this attitude of negativism. Faced with the scarcity of resources in the wilderness, they hankered after the abundant resources they had experienced in Egypt. The country which had enslaved them looked good in comparison to the wilderness. Again, their complaining so soon after benefiting from the miracles done by the Lord on their behalf points only to their short-term memory and self-centeredness.

16:3 died by the hand of the LORD. Incredibly, Israel's complaint still acknowledged the intervention of the Lord in their affairs. Sarcastically, they voiced a preference for dying in Egypt. The hand of the Lord which they had glorified in song (15:6) only a month beforehand, they now pretended would have been better used to kill them in Egypt.

16:4 I will rain bread. God's gracious answer to their complaining was to promise an abundance of the bread they missed. God's directions on how to gather it would also test their obedience to Him (vv. 4,5,16,26-28). *See note on 16:31.*

16:5 The same principle on a larger scale would feed the nation during and after the sabbatical year (cf. Lev. 25:18-22).

16:6 you shall know. Israel's short-term memory loss would be short-lived because that very day of complaint would witness not

you shall see [k]the glory of the LORD; for He
[l]hears your complaints against the LORD.
But [m]what *are* we, that you complain
against us?" 8 Also Moses said, "*This shall*
be seen when the LORD gives you meat to
eat in the evening, and in the morning
bread to the full; for the LORD hears your
complaints which you make against Him.
And what *are* we? Your complaints *are* not
against us but [n]against the LORD."
9 Then Moses spoke to Aaron, "Say to all
the congregation of the children of Israel,
[o]'Come near before the LORD, for He has
heard your complaints.' " 10 Now it came
to pass, as Aaron spoke to the whole congregation of the children of Israel, that they
looked toward the wilderness, and behold,
the glory of the LORD [p]appeared in the
cloud.
11 And the LORD spoke to Moses, saying,
12 [q]"I have heard the complaints of the
children of Israel. Speak to them, saying,
[r]'At twilight you shall eat meat, and [s]in the
morning you shall be filled with bread.
And you shall know that I *am* the LORD
your God.' "
13 So it was that [t]quails came up at
evening and covered the camp, and in the
morning [u]the dew lay all around the camp.
14 And when the layer of dew lifted, there,
on the surface of the wilderness, was [v]a
small round [w]substance, *as* fine as frost on
the ground. 15 So when the children of Israel saw *it,* they said to one another, "What
is it?" For they did not know what it *was.*
And Moses said to them, [x]"This *is* the
bread which the LORD has given you to eat.
16 This is the thing which the LORD has
commanded: 'Let every man gather it [y]ac-
cording to each one's need, one [z]omer for
each person, *according to the* number of persons; let every man take for *those* who *are*
in his tent.' "
17 Then the children of Israel did so and
gathered, some more, some less. 18 So
when they measured *it* by omers, [a]he who
gathered much had nothing left over, and
he who gathered little had no lack. Every
man had gathered according to each one's
need. 19 And Moses said, "Let no one
[b]leave any of it till morning." 20 Notwithstanding they did not [2]heed Moses. But
some of them left part of it until morning,
and it bred worms and stank. And Moses
was angry with them. 21 So they gathered
it every morning, every man according to
his need. And when the sun became hot, it
melted.
22 And so it was, on the sixth day, *that*
they gathered twice as much bread, two
omers for each one. And all the rulers of the
congregation came and told Moses. 23 Then
he said to them, "This *is what* the LORD has
said: 'Tomorrow *is* [c]a Sabbath rest, a holy
Sabbath to the LORD. Bake what you will
bake *today,* and boil what you will boil; and
lay up for yourselves all that remains, to be
kept until morning.' " 24 So they laid it up
till morning, as Moses commanded; and it
did not [d]stink, nor were there any worms in
it. 25 Then Moses said, "Eat that today, for
today *is* a Sabbath to the LORD; today you
will not find it in the field. 26 [e]Six days you
shall gather it, but on the seventh day, the
Sabbath, there will be none."
27 Now it happened *that some* of the people went out on the seventh day to gather,
but they found none. 28 And the LORD said
to Moses, "How long [f]do you refuse to
keep My commandments and My laws?
29 See! For the LORD has given you the Sabbath; therefore He gives you on the sixth
day bread for two days. Let every man remain in his place; let no man go out of his
place on the seventh day." 30 So the people
rested on the seventh day.
31 And the house of Israel called its
name [3]Manna. And [g]it *was* like white coriander seed, and the taste of it *was* like
wafers *made* with honey.

7 [k] Ex. 16:10, 12; Is. 35:2; 40:5; John 11:4, 40 [l] Num. 14:27; 17:5 [m] Num. 16:11
8 [n] 1 Sam. 8:7; Luke 10:16; [Rom. 13:2]; 1 Thess. 4:8
9 [o] Num. 16:16
10 [p] Ex. 13:21; 16:7; Num. 16:19; 1 Kin. 8:10
12 [q] Ex. 16:8; Num. 14:27 [r] Ex. 16:6 [s] Ex. 16:7; 1 Kin. 20:28; Joel 3:17
13 [t] Num. 11:31; Ps. 78:27-29; 105:40 [u] Num. 11:9
14 [v] Ex. 16:31; Num. 11:7, 8; Deut. 8:3; Neh. 9:15; Ps. 78:24; 105:40 [w] Ps. 147:16
15 [x] Ex. 16:4; Neh. 9:15; Ps. 78:24; [John 6:31, 49, 58]; 1 Cor. 10:3
16 [y] Ex. 12:4 [z] Ex. 16:32, 36
18 [a] 2 Cor. 8:15
19 [b] Ex. 12:10; 16:23; 23:18
20 [2] *listen to*
23 [c] Gen. 2:3; Ex. 20:8-11; 23:12; 31:15; 35:2; Lev. 23:3; Neh. 9:13, 14
24 [d] Ex. 16:20
26 [e] Ex. 20:9, 10
28 [f] 2 Kin. 17:14; Ps. 78:10; 106:13
31 [g] Num. 11:7-9; Deut. 8:3, 16 [3] Lit. *What?* Ex. 16:15

only God's provision for them but also would powerfully remind them of who had brought them out of Egypt, namely, the Lord their God (cf. v. 11,12).

16:7 the glory of the LORD. In seeing the start of the provision of daily bread on the next day, Israel would also see the Lord's glory, an appropriate term to use because what He did showed His presence with them. "Glory" typically refers to God's manifested presence, which makes Him impressive and leads to worship. **your complaints.** Set in the context of instruction on how the Lord would act to provide for them, the 4-fold repetition of this phrase (vv. 6-9) served to highlight God's gracious response in contrast to their ungracious grumbling against Him. For an effective poetic presentation of this contrast, refer to Ps. 78:17-25.

16:13 quails. The psalmist removed all doubt about whether these birds of the partridge family were not real birds but something else, for he called them "feathered fowl" and in the preceding line of the parallelism referred to the coming of the quails as God having "rained meat" on them (Ps. 78:27). Upon return to their former habitat, these migratory birds would often fall to the ground, exhausted from prolonged flight. In ancient Egyptian paintings, people were shown catching quails by throwing nets over the brush where they were nesting.

16:16,32 Omer. Slightly more than two quarts.

16:18 See 2 Cor. 8:15, where Paul applies this truth to Christian giving.

16:22-30 The provision of manna on 6 days only but none on the seventh was a weekly lesson on the nature of the Sabbath as a different day. It taught the people to keep the Sabbath properly, and acted as a challenge to obey God's commands.

16:31 Manna. The arrival of the quails in much quantity (v. 13) was totally overshadowed by the arrival of manna the next morning. Despite the different descriptions given for its form and taste (vv.

32 Then Moses said, "This *is* the thing
which the LORD has commanded: 'Fill an
omer with it, to be kept for your generations, that they may see the bread with
which I fed you in the wilderness, when I
brought you out of the land of Egypt.' "
33 And Moses said to Aaron, [h]"Take a pot
and put an omer of manna in it, and lay it
up before the LORD, to be kept for your
generations." 34 As the LORD commanded
Moses, so Aaron laid it up [i]before the Testimony, to be kept. 35 And the children of
Israel [j]ate manna [k]forty years, [l]until they
came to an inhabited land; they ate manna
until they came to the border of the land of
Canaan. 36 Now an omer *is* one-tenth of an
ephah.

Water from the Rock

17 Then [a]all the congregation of the
children of Israel set out on their
journey from the Wilderness of [b]Sin, according to the commandment of the LORD,
and camped in Rephidim; but *there was* no
water for the people to [c]drink. 2 [d]Therefore
the people contended with Moses, and
said, "Give us water, that we may drink."
So Moses said to them, "Why do you
contend with me? Why do you [e]tempt the
LORD?"
3 And the people thirsted there for
water, and the people [f]complained against
Moses, and said, "Why *is* it you have
brought us up out of Egypt, to kill us and
our children and our [g]livestock with
thirst?"
4 So Moses [h]cried out to the LORD, saying, "What shall I do with this people?
They are almost ready to [i]stone[1] me!"
5 And the LORD said to Moses, [j]"Go on
before the people, and take with you some
of the elders of Israel. Also take in your
hand your rod with which [k]you struck the
river, and go. 6 [l]Behold, I will stand before
you there on the rock in Horeb; and you
shall strike the rock, and water will come
out of it, that the people may drink."
And Moses did so in the sight of the elders of Israel. 7 So he called the name of the
place [m]Massah[2] and [3]Meribah, because of
the contention of the children of Israel, and
because they [4]tempted the LORD, saying,
"Is the LORD among us or not?"

Victory over the Amalekites

8 [n]Now Amalek came and fought with
Israel in Rephidim. 9 And Moses said to
Joshua, "Choose us some men and go out,
fight with Amalek. Tomorrow I will stand
on the top of the hill with [o]the rod of God

33 [h] Heb. 9:4; Rev. 2:17
34 [i] Ex. 25:16, 21; 27:21; 40:20; Num. 17:10
35 [j] Deut. 8:3, 16 [k] Num. 33:38; John 6:31, 49 [l] Josh. 5:12; Neh. 9:20, 21

CHAPTER 17

1 [a] Ex. 16:1 [b] Num. 33:11-15 [c] Ex. 15:22; Num. 20:2
2 [d] Ex. 14:11; Num. 20:2, 3, 13 [e] [Deut. 6:16]; Ps. 78:18, 41; [Matt. 4:7]; 1 Cor. 10:9
3 [f] Ex. 16:2, 3 [g] Ex. 12:38
4 [h] Ex. 14:15 [i] John 8:59; 10:31 [1] Put me to death by stoning
5 [j] Ezek. 2:6 [k] Num. 20:8
6 [l] Num. 20:10, 11; Deut. 8:15; Neh. 9:15; Ps. 78:15; 105:41; 114:8; [1 Cor. 10:4]
7 [m] Num. 20:13, 24; 27:14; Ps. 81:7 [2] Lit. *Tempted* [3] Lit. *Contention* [4] tested
8 [n] Gen. 36:12; Num. 24:20; Deut. 25:17-19; 1 Sam. 15:2
9 [o] Ex. 4:20

14,31), the name chosen for it derived from the question they asked. "Manna" was an older form of their question, "What is it?" The psalmist referred to manna as the "bread of heaven" and "angels' food" which rained down after God had opened the windows of heaven (Ps. 78:23-25). Natural explanations for the manna, such as lichen growing on rocks or insect-excreted granules on tamarisk thickets, are totally inadequate to explain its presence in sufficient quantity on the ground under the dew every day except the Sabbath for the next 40 years (v. 35) to satisfy every family's hunger. It was supernaturally produced and supernaturally sustained to last for the Sabbath!

16:32-36 lay it up before the LORD. Provision was made for memorializing the giving of the manna. When the tabernacle was finally constructed, the pot of manna was placed inside the ark. Succeeding generations would be reminded, when they came for worship, of the faithfulness of the Lord in caring for His people (cf. Heb. 9:4).

17:1 Rephidim. To be identified as modern day Wadi Refayid.

17:2 the people contended. This time the people, reacting to Moses' leading them to a waterless site, quarreled with him or laid a charge against him. So intense was their reaction that Moses thought he was about to be stoned (v. 4). Significantly, the nation had not come to Rephidim without divine guidance (v. 1), portrayed by the column of fire and cloud. The people, in the midst of their emotional response, simply could not see that right before their eyes was the evidence of God's leading.

17:4 Moses cried out to the LORD. The leader turned to God in prayer, whereas the people, instead of following his example, turned on their leader. Moses' petition was not an isolated incident. His life was characterized by prayer (cf. 15:25; 32:30-32; Num. 11:2,11; 12:13; 14:13,19) and by turning to God for solutions to problems and crises.

17:5,6 Go on before…I will stand before. By these words in His instructions to Moses, the Lord reinforced both the position of Moses as leader and Himself as present to act. He answered the people's charge against Moses and their underlying challenge of His presence (v. 7). In fact, He intervened miraculously!

17:7 Massah and Meribah. Appropriate names, "Testing" and "Contending," were assigned to this place; a disappointing culmination to all they had experienced of God's miraculous care and guidance (cf. Ps. 95:7,8; Heb. 3:7,8).

17:8 Amalek came and fought. The Amalekites took their name from Amalek, the grandson of Esau, and dwelt as a nomadic people in the Negev. Israel first encountered their military at Rephidim in the wilderness (Ex. 17:8-13; Deut. 25:17,18). As a result, the Amalekites were doomed to annihilation by God (17:14; Num. 24:20; Deut. 25:19) but it would not be immediate (17:16). The Amalekites defeated disobedient Israel at Hormah (Num. 14:43-45). Saul failed to destroy them as God ordered (1 Sam. 15:2,3,9). David later fought and defeated the Amalekites (1 Sam. 30:1-20). In Hezekiah's day, the Amalekite remnant in the land was finally destroyed by Hezekiah (ca. 716-687 B.C.). The final descendants of Agag (Esth. 3:1), the Amalekite king in Saul's day, were destroyed in Persia at the time of Esther and Mordecai (ca. 473 B.C.; Esth. 2:5,8-10).

17:9-13 Through the circumstances they experienced, Israel had learned how God provided food and water. They had to learn through warfare that God would also bring about defeat of hostile neighbors.

17:9 Joshua. The name of Moses' aide-de-camp, or personal minister (24:13; 33:11; Josh. 1:1) appears here for the first time in Exodus. His assignment to muster a task force was part of his being groomed for military leadership in Israel. Actually, at this stage his name was still Hoshea, which later changed to Joshua at Kadesh just before the reconnaissance mission in Canaan (Num. 13:16). At this stage, Israel could not be described as a seasoned army and was not even militarily well prepared and trained. See Introduction to Joshua. **the rod of God.** The staff which Moses held up in his hands was no magic wand.

in my hand." 10 So Joshua did as Moses
said to him, and fought with Amalek. And
Moses, Aaron, and Hur went up to the top
of the hill. 11 And so it was, when Moses
[p]held up his hand, that Israel prevailed;
and when he let down his hand, Amalek
prevailed. 12 But Moses' hands *became*
[5]heavy; so they took a stone and put *it*
under him, and he sat on it. And Aaron
and Hur supported his hands, one on one
side, and the other on the other side; and
his hands were steady until the going
down of the sun. 13 So Joshua defeated
Amalek and his people with the edge of
the sword.
14 Then the LORD said to Moses, [q]"Write
this *for* a memorial in the book and recount
it in the hearing of Joshua, that [r]I will utterly blot out the remembrance of Amalek
from under heaven." 15 And Moses built
an altar and called its name, [6]The-LORD-Is-
My-Banner; 16 for he said, "Because [7]the
LORD has [s]sworn: the LORD *will have* war
with Amalek from generation to generation."

Jethro's Advice

18 And [a]Jethro, the priest of Midian,
Moses' father-in-law, heard of all
that [b]God had done for Moses and for Israel His people—that the LORD had
brought Israel out of Egypt. 2 Then Jethro,
Moses' father-in-law, took [c]Zipporah, Moses' wife, after he had sent her back, 3 with
her [d]two sons, of whom the name of one
was [1]Gershom (for he said, [e]"I have been a
[2]stranger in a foreign land") 4 and the
name of the other *was* [3]Eliezer (for *he said,*
"The God of my father *was* my [f]help, and
delivered me from the sword of Pharaoh");
5 and Jethro, Moses' father-in-law, came
with his sons and his wife to Moses in the
wilderness, where he was encamped at
[g]the mountain of God. 6 Now he had said
to Moses, "I, your father-in-law Jethro, am
coming to you with your wife and her two
sons with her."
7 So Moses [h]went out to meet his father-
in-law, bowed down, and [i]kissed him. And
they asked each other about *their* well-being, and they went into the tent. 8 And Moses told his father-in-law all that the LORD
had done to Pharaoh and to the Egyptians
for Israel's sake, all the hardship that had
come upon them on the way, and *how* the
LORD had [j]delivered them. 9 Then Jethro
rejoiced for all the [k]good which the LORD
had done for Israel, whom He had delivered out of the hand of the Egyptians.
10 And Jethro said, [l]"Blessed *be* the LORD,
who has delivered you out of the hand of
the Egyptians and out of the hand of Pharaoh, *and* who has delivered the people
from under the hand of the Egyptians.

11 [p][James 5:16]
12 [5]Weary of being held up
14 [q]Ex. 24:4; 34:27; Num. 33:2 [r]Deut. 25:19; 1 Sam. 15:3; 2 Sam. 1:1; 1 Chr. 4:43
15 [6]Heb. *YHWH Nissi*
16 [s]Gen. 22:14-16 [7]Lit. *a hand is upon the throne of the LORD*

CHAPTER 18

1 [a]Ex. 2:16, 18; 3:1 [b][Ps. 106:2, 8]
2 [c]Ex. 2:21; 4:20-26
3 [d]Ex. 2:20; 4:20; Acts 7:29 [e]Ex. 2:22 [1]Lit. *Stranger There* [2]*sojourner,* temporary resident
4 [f]Gen. 49:25 [3]Lit. *My God Is Help*
5 [g]Ex. 3:1, 12; 4:27; 24:13
7 [h]Gen. 18:2 [i]Gen. 29:13; Ex. 4:27
8 [j]Ex. 15:6, 16; Ps. 81:7
9 [k][Is. 63:7-14]
10 [l]Gen. 14:20; 2 Sam. 18:28; 1 Kin. 8:56; Ps. 68:19, 20

Rather it had been previously used to initiate, via His chosen leader, the miracles which God did and about which He had informed Moses in advance. It became, therefore, the symbol of God's personal and powerful involvement, with Moses' outstretched arms perhaps signifying an appeal to God. The ebb and flow of battle in correlation with Moses' uplifted or drooping arms imparted more than psychological encouragement as the soldiers looked up to their leader on the hilltop, and more than Moses' interceding for them. It demonstrated and acknowledged their having to depend upon God for victory in battle and not upon their own strength and zeal. It also confirmed the position of Moses both in relation to God and the nation's well-being and safety. They had angrily chided him for their problems, but God confirmed his appointment as leader.

17:10 Hur. Caleb's son and the grandfather of Bezalel, the artisan (cf. 31:2-11; 1 Chr. 2:19,20).

17:14 Write this *for* a memorial...and recount *it*. Moses would have learned writing and record-keeping in Pharaoh's school of government. Official Hebrew records other than Scripture were also to be kept, and in this case especially for the purpose of remembering the victory in the very first battle in which they nationally engaged. God referred to "the book," so Moses had evidently already begun it. This was not, then, the initial entry into what perhaps became known as "The Book of the Wars of Yahweh" (Num. 21:14). Writing it was essential, so the facts could be verified and needed not to depend upon human memory or solely oral tradition. **blot out the remembrance.** The sentence of national extinction which the Amalekites proclaimed for Israel (cf. Ps. 83:4-7) passed by divine decree upon the Amalekites. The sentence was partially realized in Saul's and David's day (cf. 1 Sam. 15:1-9 and 2 Sam. 1:1; 8:11,12), after which it is scarcely mentioned again. However, due to Saul's disobedience in sparing Agag, the Amalekite king and some of his people (1 Sam. 15:7-9), he lost his throne (v. 23). Samuel killed Agag (v. 33), but some Amalekites remained to return a few years later to raid Israel's southern territory, even capturing David's family (1 Sam. 30:1-5). David killed all but 400 (v. 16,17) who escaped. It was a descendant of Agag, Haman, who tried to exterminate the Jews later in Esther's day (cf. Esth. 3:1,6).

17:15 The-LORD-Is-My-Banner. By titling the altar with this designation for the Lord, Yahweh-Nissi, Moses declared the Lord Himself to be the Standard of His people.

17:16 The LORD has sworn. The difficulty of the Heb. text permits an alternative translation: "a hand is upon/toward/against the throne/banner of Yahweh," with the sense of supplication, or of taking an oath. Contextually, the significance is clear, whatever the translation adopted: The ongoing problem with Amalek was not merely one nation hostile toward another, it was a war between God and Amalek.

18:1 Jethro...heard of all. The intelligence-gathering ability of ancient peoples should not be underestimated. Quickly and thoroughly the news of significant events in other lands passed from one place to another, very often via the merchant caravans which traversed the Fertile Crescent, or through ambassadors and other official contacts between nations. In Jethro's case, whatever knowledge he had gleaned of Israel's progress had been supplemented with information from Zipporah and her sons after Moses sent them ahead to her home (v. 2).

18:7-12 Moses' testimony elicited responses of praise and sacrifice from Jethro; evidence of his belief. Further, he understood fully the incomparability of Yahweh (v. 11). The priest of Midian (v. 1) was surely no worshiper of Midian's gods! Since Midianites were generally regarded as idolaters (cf. Num. 25:17,18; 31:2,3,16), Jethro must be viewed as remarkably different from his contemporaries; a difference

11 Now I know that the LORD *is* [m]greater
than all the gods; [n]for in the very thing in
which they [4]behaved [o]proudly, *He was*
above them." 12 Then Jethro, Moses' father-in-law, [5]took a burnt [p]offering and
other sacrifices *to offer* to God. And Aaron
came with all the elders of Israel [q]to eat
bread with Moses' father-in-law before
God.
13 And so it was, on the next day, that
Moses [r]sat to judge the people; and the
people stood before Moses from morning
until evening. 14 So when Moses' father-in-
law saw all that he did for the people, he
said, "What *is* this thing that you are doing
for the people? Why do you alone [6]sit, and
all the people stand before you from morning until evening?"
15 And Moses said to his father-in-law,
"Because [s]the people come to me to inquire of God. 16 When they have [t]a [7]diffi-
culty, they come to me, and I judge between one and another; and I make known
the statutes of God and His laws."
17 So Moses' father-in-law said to him,
"The thing that you do *is* not good. 18 Both
you and these people who *are* with you
will surely wear yourselves out. For this
thing *is* too much for you; [u]you are not
able to perform it by yourself. 19 Listen
now to my voice; I will give you [8]counsel,
and God will be with you: Stand [v]before
God for the people, so that you may [w]bring
the difficulties to God. 20 And you shall
[x]teach them the statutes and the laws, and
show them the way in which they must
walk and [y]the work they must do. 21 Moreover you shall select from all the people
[z]able men, such as [a]fear God, [b]men of

11 [m]Ex. 12:12; 15:11; 2 Chr. 2:5; Ps. 95:3; 97:9; 135:5 [n]Ex. 1:10, 16, 22; 5:2, 7 [o]Luke 1:51 [4]*acted presumptuously*
12 [p]Ex. 24:5 [q]Gen. 31:54; Deut. 12:7 [5]So with MT, LXX; Syr., Tg., Vg. *offered*
13 [r]Deut. 33:4, 5; Matt. 23:2
14 [6]*Sit as judge*
15 [s]Lev. 24:12; Num. 9:6, 8; 27:5; Deut. 17:8-13
16 [t]Ex. 24:14; Deut. 19:17 [7]*dispute*
18 [u]Num. 11:14, 17; Deut. 1:12
19 [v]Ex. 4:16; 20:19 [w]Num. 9:8; 27:5 [8]*advice*
20 [x]Deut. 5:1 [y]Deut. 1:18
21 [z]Ex. 18:24, 25; Deut. 1:13, 15; 2 Chr. 19:5-10; Ps. 15:1-5; Acts 6:3 [a]Gen. 42:18; 2 Sam. 23:3 [b]Ezek. 18:8
[c]Deut. 16:19
22 [d]Lev. 24:11; Deut. 1:17 [e]Num. 11:17
23 [f]Ex. 16:29
25 [g]Ex. 18:21; Deut. 1:15
26 [h]Job 29:16 [9]*difficult matters*
27 [i]Num. 10:29, 30

CHAPTER 19

1 [a]Num. 33:15
2 [b]Ex. 17:1 [c]Ex. 3:1, 12; 18:5
3 [d]Acts 7:38 [e]Ex. 3:4
4 [f]Deut. 29:2 [g]Deut. 32:11; Is. 63:9; Rev. 12:14 [1]*sustained*

truth, [c]hating covetousness; and place *such*
over them *to be* rulers of thousands, rulers
of hundreds, rulers of fifties, and rulers of
tens. 22 And let them judge the people at
all times. [d]Then it will be *that* every great
matter they shall bring to you, but every
small matter they themselves shall judge.
So it will be easier for you, for [e]they will
bear *the burden* with you. 23 If you do this
thing, and God *so* commands you, then
you will be able to endure, and all this people will also go to their [f]place in peace."
24 So Moses heeded the voice of his father-in-law and did all that he had said.
25 And [g]Moses chose able men out of all Israel, and made them heads over the people:
rulers of thousands, rulers of hundreds,
rulers of fifties, and rulers of tens. 26 So
they judged the people at all times; the
[h]hard [9] cases they brought to Moses, but
they judged every small case themselves.
27 Then Moses let his father-in-law depart, and [i]he went his way to his own land.

Israel at Mount Sinai

19 In the third month after the children
of Israel had gone out of the land of
Egypt, on the same day, [a]they came *to* the
Wilderness of Sinai. 2 For they had departed from [b]Rephidim, had come *to* the
Wilderness of Sinai, and camped in the
wilderness. So Israel camped there before
[c]the mountain.
3 And [d]Moses went up to God, and the
LORD [e]called to him from the mountain,
saying, "Thus you shall say to the house of
Jacob, and tell the children of Israel: 4 [f]'You
have seen what I did to the Egyptians, and
how [g]I [1]bore you on eagles' wings and

highlighted by Aaron and the elders worshiping and fellowshiping together with him (v. 12).

18:12 to God. Since the name Yahweh is always used in connection with sacrifices prescribed for Israel in the Pentateuch, the switch to Elohim must have some significance here, particularly after Jethro had himself used the name of Yahweh in his response to Moses. Despite the strong declaration of his faith and understanding, Jethro was a believing Gentile, therefore, a proselyte, and an alien. In this situation the Lord was relating to the Israelite and Gentile world simultaneously, thus the use of Elohim rather than Yahweh, the unique covenant name for Israel.

18:13-27 Jethro's practical wisdom was of immense benefit to Moses and Israel, and has been lauded as an example of delegation and management organization by efficiency experts for centuries—and still is. Woven into Jethro's advice were statements about God and the virtues of godly men that cause one to respect this man as having his newfound faith well integrated into his thinking. Indeed, he fully recognized that Moses needed divine permission to enact his advice (v. 23). Moses apparently did not immediately implement Jethro's solution, but waited until the law had been given (cf. Deut. 1:9-15).

18:21 These same spiritual qualities were required of NT leaders (see Acts. 6:3; 1 Tim. 3:1-7; Titus 1:6-9).

19:1–40:38 This section outlines Israel's activities during their approximately 11 month stay at Sinai (cf. 19:1 with Num. 10:11).

19:3-8 The Israelites discerned the familiar pattern, in shortened form, of a suzerainty (superior-subordinate relationship) treaty in God's words: a preamble (v. 3), a historical prologue (v. 4), certain stipulations (v. 5a), and blessings (vv. 5b-6a). The acceptance in solemn assembly would normally be recorded in the final treaty document. Here it follows upon presentation of the treaty to them (vv. 7, 8). *See note on 24:7.*

19:3 from the mountain. The sign which the Lord had given particularly to Moses when he was still in Midian (3:12), that God had indeed sent him, was now fulfilled; he was with the people before the mountain of God. **house of Jacob...children of Israel.** In employing this dual designation for the nation, the Lord reminded them of their humble beginnings as descendants of Abraham through Isaac and Jacob, who had been with them in Egypt, and of their status now as a nation (children = people).

19:4 bore you on eagles' wings. With a most appropriate metaphor, God described the Exodus and the journey to Sinai. Eagles were known to have carried their young out of the nests on their wings and taught them to fly, catching them when necessary on their outspread wings. Moses, in his final song, employed this metaphor of

brought you to Myself. 5 Now [h]therefore, if
you will indeed obey My voice and [i]keep
My covenant, then [j]you shall be a special
treasure to Me above all people; for all the
earth *is* [k]Mine. 6 And you shall be to Me a
[l]kingdom of priests and a [m]holy nation.'
These *are* the words which you shall speak
to the children of Israel."

7 So Moses came and called for the [n]el-
ders of the people, and [2]laid before them
all these words which the LORD commanded him. 8 Then [o]all the people answered together and said, "All that the LORD has
spoken we will do." So Moses brought
back the words of the people to the LORD.
9 And the LORD said to Moses, "Behold, I
come to you [p]in the thick cloud, [q]that the
people may hear when I speak with you,
and believe you forever."

So Moses told the words of the people to
the LORD.

10 Then the LORD said to Moses, "Go to
the people and [r]consecrate them today and
tomorrow, and let them wash their clothes.
11 And let them be ready for the third day.
For on the third day the LORD will come
down upon Mount Sinai in the sight of all
the people. 12 You shall set bounds for the
people all around, saying, 'Take heed to
yourselves *that* you do *not* go up to the
mountain or touch its base. [s]Whoever
touches the mountain shall surely be put to
death. 13 Not a hand shall touch him, but
he shall surely be stoned or shot *with an*
arrow; whether man or beast, he shall not
live.' When the trumpet sounds long, they
shall come near the mountain."

14 So Moses went down from the mountain to the people and sanctified the people, and they washed their clothes. 15 And
he said to the people, "Be ready for the
third day; [t]do not come near *your* wives."

16 Then it came to pass on the third day,
in the morning, that there were [u]thunder-
ings and lightnings, and a thick cloud on
the mountain; and the sound of the trumpet was very loud, so that all the people
who *were* in the camp [v]trembled. 17 And
[w]Moses brought the people out of the
camp to meet with God, and they stood at
the foot of the mountain. 18 Now [x]Mount
Sinai *was* completely in smoke, because the
LORD descended upon [y]it in fire. [z]Its
smoke ascended like the smoke of a furnace, and [3]the [a]whole mountain quaked
greatly. 19 And when the blast of the trumpet sounded long and became louder and
louder, [b]Moses spoke, and [c]God answered
him by voice. 20 Then the LORD came down
upon Mount Sinai, on the top of the mountain. And the LORD called Moses to the top
of the mountain, and Moses went up.

21 And the LORD said to Moses, "Go
down and warn the people, lest they break
through [d]to gaze at the LORD, and many of
them perish. 22 Also let the [e]priests who
come near the LORD [f]consecrate themselves,
lest the LORD [g]break out against them."

23 But Moses said to the LORD, "The people cannot come up to Mount Sinai; for
You warned us, saying, [h]'Set bounds
around the mountain and consecrate it.'"

24 Then the LORD said to him, "Away!
Get down and then come up, you and
Aaron with you. But do not let the priests
and the people break through to come up

5 [h] Ex. 15:26; 23:22 [i] Deut. 5:2; Ps. 78:10 [j] Deut. 4:20; 7:6; 14:2; 26:18; 1 Kin. 8:53; Ps. 135:4; Titus 2:14; 1 Pet. 2:9 [k] Ex. 9:29; Deut. 10:14; Job 41:11; Ps. 50:12; 1 Cor. 10:26
6 [l] Deut. 33:2-4; [1 Pet. 2:5, 9; Rev. 1:6; 5:10] [m] Deut. 7:6; 14:21; 26:19; Is. 62:12; [1 Cor. 3:17]
7 [n] Ex. 4:29, 30 [2] *set*
8 [o] Ex. 4:31; 24:3, 7; Deut. 5:27; 26:17
9 [p] Ex. 19:16; 20:21; 24:15; Deut. 4:11; Ps. 99:7; Matt. 17:5 [q] Deut. 4:12, 36; John 12:29, 30
10 [r] Lev. 11:44, 45; [Heb. 10:22]
12 [s] Ex. 34:3; Heb. 12:20
15 [t] [1 Cor. 7:5]
16 [u] Heb. 12:18, 19 [v] Heb. 12:21
17 [w] Deut. 4:10
18 [x] Deut. 4:11; Judg. 5:5; Ps. 104:32; 144:5 [y] Ex. 3:2; 24:17; Deut. 5:4; 2 Chr. 7:1-3; Heb. 12:18 [z] Gen. 15:17; 19:28; Rev. 15:8 [a] Ps. 68:8; 1 Kin. 19:12; Jer. 4:24; [Heb. 12:26] [3] LXX *all the people*
19 [b] Heb. 12:21 [c] Neh. 9:13; Ps. 81:7
21 [d] 1 Sam. 6:19
22 [e] Ex. 19:24; 24:5 [f] Lev. 10:3; 21:6-8 [g] 2 Sam. 6:7, 8
23 [h] Ex. 19:12

God's care for Israel and especially noted that there was only one Lord who did this (Deut. 32:11-12).

19:5,6 Three titles for Israel, "a special treasure," "a kingdom of priests," and "a holy nation," were given by the Lord to the nation, contingent upon their being an obedient and covenant-keeping nation. These titles summarized the divine blessings which such a nation would experience: belonging especially to the Lord, representing Him in the earth and being set apart unto Him for His purposes. These expanded ethnically and morally what it meant to have brought them to Himself. "For all the earth is mine," in the midst of the titles, laid stress upon the uniqueness and sovereignty of the Lord and had to be understood as dismissing all other claims by so-called other gods of the nations. It was more than the power of one god over another in Israel's situation; it was the choice and power of the only Lord! See 1 Pet. 2:9, where Peter uses these terms in the sense of God's spiritual kingdom of the redeemed.

19:8 Then all the people answered together. Presented with the details of God's bilateral, conditional covenant (note the "if you will obey…then you shall be" in v. 5), the people, briefed by their elders, responded with positive enthusiasm. The Lord's response to them does not take it as a rash promise by the people (cf. Deut. 5:27-29).

19:9 and believe you forever. The Lord designed the upcoming encounter with Him so as to forestall any later accusation that Moses had himself compiled the law and had not met with the Lord on the mountain. It would also lead to great deference being accorded Moses by the people.

19:10 consecrate them. How serious this step was for the nation was emphasized for them by two days of special preparation. The inward preparation for meeting with God was mirrored in the outward actions of maintaining bodily cleanliness.

19:12,13 The proper approach to a holy God could not have been better stressed than by imposing a death penalty upon those who violated the arbitrary boundaries which God had set around the mountain. Even animals could not encroach upon this sacred area (cf. Heb. 12:20).

19:15 do not come near *your* wives. This was so they would be ceremonially clean (see Lev. 15:16-18).

19:16 thunderings and lightnings. The dramatic visual presentation of God's presence on the mountain, accompanied by thick cloud and trumpet blast, more than impressed the onlookers with God's majesty and power—they trembled, but so did Moses (Heb. 12:21). The unusual was happening, not the usual phenomena from volcanic activity, as some writers have proposed.

19:24 the priests. With the law still to be given, no priesthood had been established in Israel. These priests must have been the first-born in each family who served as family priests because they had

to the LORD, lest He break out against them." 25 So Moses went down to the people and spoke to them.

The Ten Commandments

20 And God spoke [a]all these words, saying:
2 [b]"I *am* the LORD your God, who brought you out of the land of Egypt, [c]out of the house of [1]bondage.
3 [d]"You shall have no other gods before Me.
4 [e]"You shall not make for yourself a carved image—any likeness *of anything* that *is* in heaven above, or that *is* in the earth beneath, or that *is* in the water under the earth;
5 [f]you shall not bow down to them nor [2]serve them. [g]For I, the LORD your God, *am* a jealous God, [h]visiting[3] the iniquity of the fathers upon the children to the third and fourth *generations* of those who hate Me,
6 but [i]showing mercy to thousands, to those who love Me and keep My commandments.
7 [j]"You shall not take the name of the LORD your God in vain, for the LORD [k]will not hold *him* guiltless who takes His name in vain.

CHAPTER 20
1 [a]Deut. 5:22
2 [b]Hos. 13:4 [c]Ex. 13:3; Deut. 7:8 [1]slaves
3 [d]Deut. 6:14; 2 Kin. 17:35; Jer. 25:6; 35:15
4 [e]Lev. 19:4; 26:1; Deut. 4:15-19; 27:15
5 [f]Is. 44:15, 19 [g]Ex. 34:14; Deut. 4:24; Josh. 24:19; Nah. 1:2 [h]Num. 14:18, 33; Deut. 5:9, 10; 1 Kin. 21:29; Ps. 79:8; Jer. 32:18 [2]worship [3]punishing
6 [i]Deut. 7:9; Rom. 11:28
7 [j]Lev. 19:12; Deut. 6:13; 10:20; [Matt. 5:33-37] [k]Mic. 6:11

been dedicated to the Lord (cf. 13:2; 24:5). Their place would be taken over later by the Levites (Num. 3:45).

20:1 all these words. This general description of the commands to follow also received from Moses the title "Ten Commandments" (34:28; Deut. 4:13). By this emphasis on God Himself speaking these words (cf. Deut. 5:12,15,16,22,32,33), all theories on Israel's borrowing legal patterns or concepts from the nations around them are unacceptable.

20:3-17 The Ten Commandments, also known as the Decalogue, which follow upon the opening historical prologue (v. 2), are formed as a precept or direct command given in the second person. This form was something rather uncommon in that day. Ancient Near Eastern law codes for the most part were casuistic, or case-law, in form, i.e., an "if…then" construction written in the third person wherein a supposed offense was followed by a statement of the action to be taken or penalty to be exacted. The Ten Commandments may also be grouped into two broad categories: the vertical, namely man's relationship to God (vv. 2-11), and the horizontal, namely man's relationship to the community (vv. 12-17). Concisely listed prohibitions mark the second category, with only one exception—an imperative plus its explanation (v. 12). Explanation or reason appended to a prohibition marks the first category. By these Ten Commandments, true theology and true worship, the name of God and the Sabbath, family honor, life, marriage, and property, truth and virtue are well protected. *See note on 24:7.*

20:3 before Me. Meaning "over against Me," a most appropriate expression in the light of the next few verses. All false gods stand in opposition to the true God, and the worship of them is incompatible with the worship of Yahweh. When Israel departed from the worship of the only one and true God, she plunged into religious confusion (Judg. 17,18).

20:4-6 The mode or fashion of worship appropriate to only one Lord forbids any attempt to represent or caricature Him by use of anything He has made. Total censure of artistic expression was not the issue; the absolute censure of idolatry and false worship was the issue. Violation would seriously affect succeeding generations because the Lord demanded full and exclusive devotion, i.e., He is a jealous God (cf. 34:14; Deut. 4:24; 5:9). The worship of man-made representations was nothing less than hatred of the true God.

20:5,6 to the third and fourth *generations* . . . thousands. Moses had made it clear that children were not punished for the sins of their parents (Deut. 24:16; see Ezek. 18:19-32), but children would feel the impact of breaches of God's law by their parents' generation as a natural consequence of its disobedience, its hatred of God. Children reared in such an environment would imbibe and then practice similar idolatry, thus themselves expressing hateful disobedience. The difference in consequence served as both a warning and a motivation. The effect of a disobedient generation was to plant wickedness so deeply that it took several generations to reverse.

20:7 take the name…in vain. To use God's name in such a way as to bring disrepute upon His character or deeds was to irreverently misuse His name. To fail to perform an oath in which His name had been legitimately uttered (cf. 22:10,11; Lev. 19:12; Deut. 6:13) was to call into question His existence, since the guilty party evidently had no further thought of the God whose name he had used to improve his integrity. For the believer in the church age, however, the use of the name of God is not a needed verification of his intention and trust-

The Ten Commandments

Commandment	O.T. Statement	O.T. Death Penalty	N.T. Restatement
1st Polytheism	Ex. 20:3	Ex. 22:20; Deut. 6:13-15	Acts 14:15
2nd Graven Images	Ex. 20:4	Deut. 27:15	1 John 5:21
3rd Swearing	Ex. 20:7	Lev. 24:15,16	James 5:12
4th Sabbath	Ex. 20:8	Num. 15:32-36	Col 2:16 nullifies
5th Obedience to parents	Ex. 20:12	Ex. 21:15-17	Eph. 6:1
6th Murder	Ex. 20:13	Ex. 21:12	1 John 3:15
7th Adultery	Ex. 20:14	Lev. 20:10	1 Cor 6:9,10
8th Theft	Ex. 20:15	Ex. 21:16	Eph. 4:28
9th False Witness	Ex. 20:16	Deut. 18:16-21	Col. 3:9,10
10th Coveting	Ex. 20:17	———	Eph. 5:3

8 [l]"Remember the Sabbath day, to keep
it holy. 9 [m]Six days you shall
labor and do all your work, 10 but
the [n]seventh day *is* the Sabbath of
the LORD your God. *In it* you shall
do no work: you, nor your son,
nor your daughter, nor your male
servant, nor your female servant,
nor your cattle, [o]nor your stranger who *is* within your gates.
11 For [p]*in* six days the LORD made
the heavens and the earth, the
sea, and all that *is* in them, and
rested the seventh day. Therefore
the LORD blessed the Sabbath day
and hallowed it.
12 [q]"Honor your father and your mother, that your days may be [r]long
upon the land which the LORD
your God is giving you.
13 [s]"You shall not murder.
14 [t]"You shall not commit [u]adultery.
15 [v]"You shall not steal.

8 [l]Ex. 23:12; 31:13-16; Lev. 26:2; Deut. 5:12
9 [m]Ex. 34:21; 35:2, 3; Lev. 23:3; Deut. 5:13; Luke 13:14
10 [n]Gen. 2:2, 3 [o]Neh. 13:16-19
11 [p]Gen. 2:2, 3; Ex. 31:17
12 [q]Lev. 19:3; Deut. 27:16; Matt. 15:4; 19:19; Mark 7:10; 10:19; Luke 18:20; Eph. 6:2 [r]Deut. 5:16, 33; 6:2; 11:8, 9
13 [s][Matt. 5:21, 22]; 19:18; Mark 10:19; Luke 18:20; Rom. 13:9; [1 John 3:15]
14 [t]Matt. 5:27; Mark 10:19; Luke 18:20; Rom. 13:9; James 2:11 [u]Lev. 20:10; Deut. 5:18
15 [v]Ex. 21:16; Lev. 19:11, 13; Matt. 19:18; Rom. 13:9
16 [w]Ex. 23:1, 7; Deut. 5:20; Matt. 19:18

16 [w]"You shall not bear false witness
against your neighbor.
17 [x]"You shall not covet your neighbor's
house; [y]you shall not covet your
neighbor's wife, nor his male servant, nor his female servant, nor
his ox, nor his donkey, nor anything that *is* your neighbor's."

The People Afraid of God's Presence

18 Now [z]all the people [a]witnessed the
thunderings, the lightning flashes, the
sound of the trumpet, and the mountain
[b]smoking; and when the people saw *it,*
they trembled and stood afar off. 19 Then
they said to Moses, [c]"You speak with us,
and we will hear; but [d]let not God speak
with us, lest we die."
20 And Moses said to the people, [e]"Do
not fear; [f]for God has come to test you, and

17 [x][Luke 12:15]; Rom. 7:7; 13:9; [Eph. 5:3, 5]; Heb. 13:5 [y]2 Sam. 11:2; [Matt. 5:28] 18 [z]Heb. 12:18, 19 [a]Rev. 1:10, 12 [b]Ex. 19:16, 18 19 [c]Gal. 3:19; Heb. 12:19 [d]Deut. 5:5, 23-27 20 [e]Ex. 14:13; [Is. 41:10, 13] [f]Ex. 15:25; [Deut. 13:3]

worthiness since his life is to exhibit truth on all occasions, with his "yes" meaning "yes" and his "no" meaning "no" (Matt. 5:37; James 5:12).

20:8 Sabbath. Cf. 31:12-17. Each seventh day belonged to the Lord and would not be a work day but one set apart (i.e., holy) for rest and for time devoted to the worship of Yahweh. The term "Sabbath" is derived from "to rest or cease from work." The historical precedent for such a special observance was the creation week; a span of time equal to what man copied in practice. Each Sabbath day should have reminded the worshiper that the God whom he praised had indeed made everything in both realms of existence in 6 twenty-four hour days. The Sabbath would also stand, therefore, as a counter to evolutionary ideas prevalent in false religion. Moses, in the review of the Decalogue, also linked the observance of the Sabbath with Israel's exodus from Egypt and specified that this was why Israel was to keep it (Deut. 5:12-15). Significantly, the command for the Sabbath is not repeated in the NT, whereas the other 9 are. In fact, it is nullified (cf. Col. 2:16,17). Belonging especially to Israel under the Mosaic economy, the Sabbath could not apply to the believer of the church age, for he is living in a new economy.

20:12-16 Cf. Matt. 19:18-19; Mark 10:19; Luke 18:20.

20:12 Honor your father and your mother. The key to societal stability is reverence and respect for parents and their authority. The appended promise primarily related the command to life in the Promised Land and reminded the Israelite of the program God had set up for him and his people. Within the borders of their territory, God expected them not to tolerate juvenile delinquency, which at heart is overt disrespect for parents and authority. Severe consequences, namely capital punishment, could apply (cf. Deut. 21:18-21). One of the reasons for the Babylonian exile was a failure to honor parents (Ezek. 22:7,15). The Apostle Paul individualized this national promise when he applied the truth to believers in his day (cf. Matt. 15:4; Mark 7:10; Eph. 6:1-3).

20:13-15 Cf. Rom. 13:9.

20:13 murder. The irreversible nature of the divinely imposed sentence of death on every manslayer who killed another intentionally (cf. 21:12; Num. 35:17-21) stands without parallel in ancient Near Eastern literature and legal codes (cf. Gen. 9:5,6). Further, the sacredness of human life stands out in the passages dealing with unintentional manslaughter. The accident of death still carried with it a penalty of banishment to the city of refuge until the death of the High-Priest for the one who killed but not with intent. Careful appraisal of the word Moses used (one of 7 different Heb. words for killing, and one used only 47 times in the OT) suggests a broad translation of "to kill, slay" but denoting the taking of life under a legal system where he would have to answer to the stipulations of a legal code, no matter whether he killed unintentionally or intentionally. By this command, men would be reminded and exhorted to strive after carefulness in the affairs of life so that on the person-to-person level no one would die by their hand. *See note on 21:12-14* (cf. Matt. 5:21; James 2:11).

20:14 adultery. Applicable to both men and women, this command protected the sacredness of the marriage relationship. God had instituted marriage at the creation of man and woman (Gen. 2:24) and had blessed it as the means of filling the earth (Gen. 1:28). The penalty for infidelity in the marital relationship was death (Lev. 20:10). Adultery was also referred to as "a great sin" (Gen. 20:9) and a "great wickedness and sin against God" (cf. Gen. 39:9; Matt. 5:27; James 2:11).

20:15 steal. Any dishonest acquiring of another's goods or assets greatly disturbs the right to ownership of private property, which is an important principle for societal stability.

20:16 false witness. Justice is not served by any untruthful testimony. Practically all societies have recognized this principle and adjure all witnesses in courts to tell the truth and nothing but the truth.

20:17 covet. The thoughts and desires of the heart do not escape attention. A strong longing to have what another has is wrong. This tenth command suggests that none of the previous 9 commandments are only external acts with no relation to internal thoughts (cf. Matt. 15:19; Rom. 7:7; 13:9).

20:18 trembled and stood afar off. The people fearfully withdrew from the cluster of phenomena accompanying this theophany, this appearance of God on the mountain. They instinctively placed Moses in the position of mediator between them and God, because such was the gap between them and their holy God that they feared they were not fit to live in His presence (v. 19).

20:19 let not God speak. Fearing for their lives, the nation asked Moses to be their mediator (cf. Heb. 12:18-21).

20:20 Instructed not to respond to the phenomena with fear, they

[g]that His fear may be before you, so that
you may not sin." 21 So the people stood
afar off, but Moses drew near [h]the thick
darkness where God *was*.

The Law of the Altar

22 Then the LORD said to Moses, "Thus
you shall say to the children of Israel: 'You
have seen that I have talked with you
[i]from heaven. 23 You shall not make *anything to be* [j]with Me—gods of silver or
gods of gold you shall not make for yourselves. 24 An altar of [k]earth you shall make
for Me, and you shall sacrifice on it your
burnt offerings and your peace offerings,
[l]your sheep and your oxen. In every
[m]place where I [4]record My name I will
come to you, and I will [n]bless you. 25 And
[o]if you make Me an altar of stone, you
shall not build it of hewn stone; for if you
[p]use your tool on it, you have profaned it.
26 Nor shall you go up by steps to My
altar, that your [q]nakedness may not be exposed on it.'

The Law Concerning Servants

21 "Now these *are* the [1]judgments
which you shall [a]set before them:
2 [b]If you buy a Hebrew servant, he shall
serve six years; and in the seventh he shall
go out free and pay nothing. 3 If he comes
in by himself, he shall go out by himself; if
he *comes in* married, then his wife shall go
out with him. 4 If his master has given him
a wife, and she has borne him sons or
daughters, the wife and her children shall
be her master's, and he shall go out by himself. 5 [c]But if the servant plainly says, 'I love
my master, my wife, and my children; I will
not go out free,' 6 then his master shall
bring him to the [d]judges. He shall also
bring him to the door, or to the doorpost,
and his master shall pierce his ear with an
awl; and he shall serve him forever.
7 "And if a man [e]sells his daughter to be
a female slave, she shall not go out as the
male slaves do. 8 If she [2]does not please her
master, who has betrothed her to himself,
then he shall let her be redeemed. He shall
have no right to sell her to a foreign people,
since he has dealt deceitfully with her.
9 And if he has betrothed her to his son, he
shall deal with her according to the custom
of daughters. 10 If he takes another *wife*, he
shall not diminish her food, her clothing,
[f]and her marriage rights. 11 And if he does
not do these three for her, then she shall go
out free, without *paying* money.

The Law Concerning Violence

12 [g]"He who strikes a man so that he
dies shall surely be put to death. 13 However, [h]if he did not lie in wait, but God [i]de-
livered *him* into his hand, then [j]I will appoint for you a place where he may flee.
14 "But if a man acts with [k]premedita-
tion against his neighbor, to kill him by
treachery, [l]you shall take him from My
altar, that he may die.
15 "And he who strikes his father or his
mother shall surely be put to death.
16 [m]"He who kidnaps a man and [n]sells
him, or if he is [o]found in his hand, shall
surely be put to death.
17 "And [p]he who curses his father or his
mother shall surely be put to death.
18 "If men contend with each other, and
one strikes the other with a stone or with
his fist, and he does not die but is confined
to *his* bed, 19 if he rises again and walks
about outside [q]with his staff, then he who
struck *him* shall be [3]acquitted. He shall
only pay *for* the loss of his time, and shall
provide *for him* to be thoroughly healed.

20 [g] Deut. 4:10; 6:24; Prov. 3:7; 16:6; Is. 8:13
21 [h] Ex. 19:16; Deut. 5:22
22 [i] Deut. 4:36; 5:24, 26; Neh. 9:13
23 [j] Ex. 32:1, 2, 4; Deut. 29:17
24 [k] Ex. 20:25; 27:1-8 [l] Ex. 24:5; Lev. 1:2 [m] Deut. 12:5; 16:6, 11; 1 Kin. 9:3; 2 Chr. 6:6 [n] Gen. 12:2 [4] *cause My name to be remembered*
25 [o] Deut. 27:5 [p] Josh. 8:30, 31
26 [q] Ex. 28:42, 43

CHAPTER 21

1 [a] Ex. 24:3, 4; Deut. 4:14; 6:1 [1] *ordinances*
2 [b] Lev. 25:39-43; Deut. 15:12-18; Jer. 34:14
5 [c] Deut. 15:16, 17
6 [d] Ex. 12:12; 22:8, 9
7 [e] Neh. 5:5
8 [2] *Lit. is evil in the eyes of*
10 [f] [1 Cor. 7:3, 5]
12 [g] Gen. 9:6; Lev. 24:17; Num. 35:30; [Matt. 26:52]
13 [h] Deut. 19:4, 5 [i] 1 Sam. 24:4, 10, 18 [j] Num. 35:11; Deut. 19:3; Josh. 20:2
14 [k] Deut. 19:11, 12; [Heb. 10:26] [l] 1 Kin. 2:28-34
16 [m] Deut. 24:7 [n] Gen. 37:28 [o] Ex. 22:4
17 [p] Lev. 20:9; Prov. 20:20; Matt. 15:4; Mark 7:10
19 [q] 2 Sam. 3:29 [3] *exempt from punishment*

were also told that proper fear, i.e., awe and reverence of God, deterred sin.

20:22-26 Sacrifices, offerings, and altars were not unknown to Israel and were already part of certain worship ceremonies. Neither the earthen nor stone altars would have even a hint of being shaped to represent something more specific, so the restrictions on the form and the method of building would ensure the appropriateness and propriety of their worship. Leviticus 1–7 outlines the Mosaic sacrifices.

21:1 judgments. A combination of casuistic (case-law) and apodictic (direct command) precepts laid down, as a detailed enlargement of the Decalogue, the framework for judging and resolving civil disputes in Israel. Such a combination continued to confirm the uniqueness of Israel's law among the different ancient Near Eastern law-codes. Later in a special ceremony, God entitled these precepts "The Book of the Covenant" (24:7).

21:2-11 The law of the slave guaranteed freedom after a specified period of 6 years unless the slave himself elected permanent servitude, but this would be service in a context not of abuse but of love (v. 5). Any permanent, involuntary servitude for a Hebrew slave to a Hebrew master was obviously undesirable for Israelite society and was unknown in Israel (cf. Lev. 25:39-55). Provision was also made to ensure the proper treatment of female slaves, who could not deliberately be left destitute by wrongful action on the part of their master.

21:12-14 The laws relating to personal injury (vv. 15-36) from man or animal were preceded by the most serious of injuries, homicide. The death penalty was prescribed for intentional homicide only (see 20:13), whereas for unintentional homicide the penalty was banishment to an appointed place, which later God revealed were the cities of refuge (cf. Num. 35:6-24; Deut. 19:1-13). No degree of sanctuary applied to one guilty of premeditated murder. Death by accident at the hand of another is something unplanned by man but which God let happen. The law did afford sanctuary but away from home and vengeful relatives, often for life because there the one guilty of involuntary manslaughter remained until the death of the High-Priest (Num. 35:25,28).

21:15,17 Disrespect for parents seen in physical and verbal abuse of them by their children was so serious it was designated a capital offense. Commandment 5 was a serious matter! Other ancient law-

20 "And if a man beats his male or female servant with a rod, so that he dies
under his hand, he shall surely be punished. 21 Notwithstanding, if he remains
alive a day or two, he shall not be punished; for he *is* his [r]property.
22 "If men [4]fight, and hurt a woman
with child, so that [5]she gives birth prematurely, yet no harm follows, he shall surely
be punished accordingly as the woman's
husband imposes on him; and he shall
[s]pay as the judges *determine.* 23 But if *any*
harm follows, then you shall give life for
life, 24 [t]eye for eye, tooth for tooth, hand
for hand, foot for foot, 25 burn for burn,
wound for wound, stripe for stripe.
26 "If a man strikes the eye of his male or
female servant, and destroys it, he shall let
him go free for the sake of his eye. 27 And
if he knocks out the tooth of his male or female servant, he shall let him go free for
the sake of his tooth.

Animal Control Laws

28 "If an ox gores a man or a woman to
death, then [u]the ox shall surely be stoned,
and its flesh shall not be eaten; but the
owner of the ox *shall be* [6]acquitted. 29 But if
the ox [7]tended to thrust with its horn in
times past, and it has been made known to
his owner, and he has not kept it confined,
so that it has killed a man or a woman, the
ox shall be stoned and its owner also shall
be put to death. 30 If there is imposed on
him a sum of money, then he shall pay [v]to
redeem his life, whatever is imposed on
him. 31 Whether it has gored a son or gored
a daughter, according to this judgment it
shall be done to him. 32 If the ox gores a
male or female servant, he shall give to
their master [w]thirty shekels of silver, and
the [x]ox shall be stoned.
33 "And if a man opens a pit, or if a man

21 [r]Lev. 25:44-46
22 [s]Ex. 18:21, 22; 21:30; Deut. 22:18 [4]*struggle* [5]Lit. *her children come out*
24 [t]Lev. 24:20; Deut. 19:21; [Matt. 5:38-44; 1 Pet. 2:19-21]
28 [u]Gen. 9:5 [6]*exempt from punishment*
29 [7]*was inclined*
30 [v]Ex. 21:22; Num. 35:31
32 [w]Zech. 11:12, 13; Matt. 26:15; 27:3, 9 [x]Ex. 21:28

digs a pit and does not cover it, and an ox
or a donkey falls in it, 34 the owner of the
pit shall make *it* good; he shall give money
to their owner, but the dead *animal* shall be
his.
35 "If one man's ox hurts another's, so
that it dies, then they shall sell the live ox
and divide the money from it; and the
dead *ox* they shall also divide. 36 Or if it
was known that the ox tended to thrust in
time past, and its owner has not kept it
confined, he shall surely pay ox for ox, and
the dead animal shall be his own.

Responsibility for Property

22 "If a man steals an ox or a sheep,
and slaughters it or sells it, he shall
[a]restore five oxen for an ox and four sheep
for a sheep. 2 If the thief is found [b]breaking
in, and he is struck so that he dies, *there
shall be* [c]no guilt for his bloodshed. 3 If the
sun has risen on him, *there shall be* guilt for
his bloodshed. He should make full restitution; if he has nothing, then he shall be
[d]sold[1] for his theft. 4 If the theft is certainly [e]found alive in his hand, whether it is an
ox or donkey or sheep, he shall [f]restore
double.
5 "If a man causes a field or vineyard to
be grazed, and lets loose his animal, and it
feeds in another man's field, he shall make
restitution from the best of his own field
and the best of his own vineyard.
6 "If fire breaks out and catches in thorns,
so that stacked grain, standing grain, or the
field is consumed, he who kindled the fire
shall surely make restitution.
7 "If a man [g]delivers to his neighbor
money or articles to keep, and it is stolen
out of the man's house, [h]if the thief is
found, he shall pay double. 8 If the thief is
not found, then the master of the house
shall be brought to the [i]judges *to see*

CHAPTER 22
1 [a]2 Sam. 12:6; Prov. 6:31; Luke 19:8
2 [b]Job 24:16; Matt. 6:19; 24:43; 1 Pet. 4:15 [c]Num. 35:27
3 [d]Ex. 21:2; Matt. 18:25 [1]Sold as a slave
4 [e]Ex. 21:16 [f]Prov. 6:31
7 [g]Lev. 6:1-7 [h]Ex. 22:4
8 [i]Ex. 21:6, 22; 22:28; Deut. 17:8, 9; 19:17

codes, e.g., the Code of Hammurabi, also respected parental authority and prescribed severe consequences, although not the death penalty.

21:17 Cf. Matt. 15:4; Mark 7:10.

21:20,21,26,27 Punishment of slaves was considered the right of the owner (Prov. 10:13; 13:24), but did not allow for violence. Judges were to decide the appropriate punishment if the slave died (v. 20). If the slave lived a few days it was evidence that the owner had no intent to kill, and the loss of the slave was punishment enough (v. 21). A beating without death immediately ensuing was construed as a disciplinary matter not a homicidal one. Any permanent personal injury brought freedom and loss of a master's investment. The master's power over the slave was thus limited, which made this law unprecedented in the ancient world.

21:22 Compensation was mandatory for accidentally causing a premature birth, even if no injury resulted to either mother or child. Judges were brought into the legal process so that damages awarded were fair and were not calculated out of vengeance.

21:23,24 Cf. Lev. 24:19,20; Deut. 19:21. The principle of retaliation, or *lex taliones,* applied if injury did occur to either mother or child. The punishment matched, but did not exceed, the damage done to the victim. The welfare of a pregnant woman was protected by this law so that unintentional maltreatment constituted culpable negligence. Significantly for the abortion debate, the fetus was considered a person; thus, someone was held accountable for its death or injury.

21:24 Cf. Matt. 5:38.

21:30 Animal owners were held responsible for death or injuries caused by their animals. Since the owner was guilty of negligence and not of an intentional crime, he was able to make payment to escape the death penalty. Again, judges are brought into the process to ensure that no vengeful decisions are made.

21:32 shekels. A shekel weighs .4 oz.; 30 shekels would weigh 12 oz. Christ was betrayed for the price of a slave (Zech. 11:12,13; Matt. 26:14,15).

22:3 If the sun has risen on him. The culpability of a householder's actions against an intruder depended on whether the break-in (lit. "digging through" the mud walls) was at night or in the daytime.

whether he has put his hand into his neighbor's goods.
9 "For any kind of trespass, *whether it*
concerns an ox, a donkey, a sheep, or clothing, *or* for any kind of lost thing which *an-*
other claims to be his, the [j]cause of both
parties shall come before the judges; *and*
whomever the judges condemn shall pay
double to his neighbor. 10 If a man delivers
to his neighbor a donkey, an ox, a sheep, or
any animal to keep, and it dies, is hurt, or
driven away, no one seeing *it*, 11 *then* an
[k]oath of the LORD shall be between them
both, that he has not put his hand into his
neighbor's goods; and the owner of it shall
accept *that*, and he shall not make *it* good.
12 But [l]if, in fact, it is stolen from him, he
shall make restitution to the owner of it.
13 If it is [m]torn to pieces *by a beast*, *then* he
shall bring it as evidence, *and* he shall not
make good what was torn.
14 "And if a man borrows *anything* from
his neighbor, and it becomes injured or
dies, the owner of it not *being* with it, he
shall surely make *it* good. 15 If its owner
was with it, he shall not make *it* good; if it
was hired, it came for its hire.

Moral and Ceremonial Principles

16 [n]"If a man entices a virgin who is not
betrothed, and lies with her, he shall surely pay the bride-price for her *to be* his wife.
17 If her father utterly refuses to give her to
him, he shall pay money according to the
[o]bride-price of virgins.
18 [p]"You shall not permit a sorceress to
live.
19 [q]"Whoever lies with an animal shall
surely be put to death.
20 [r]"He who sacrifices to *any* god, except
to the LORD only, he shall be utterly destroyed.
21 [s]"You shall neither mistreat a [2]strang-
er nor oppress him, for you were strangers
in the land of Egypt.
22 [t]"You shall not afflict any widow or
fatherless child. 23 If you afflict them in
any way, *and* they [u]cry at all to Me, I will
surely [v]hear their cry; 24 and My [w]wrath
will become hot, and I will kill you with
the sword; [x]your wives shall be widows,
and your children fatherless.
25 [y]"If you lend money to *any of* My people *who are* poor among you, you shall not
be like a moneylender to him; you shall not
charge him [z]interest. 26 [a]If you ever take
your neighbor's garment as a pledge, you
shall return it to him before the sun goes
down. 27 For that *is* his only covering, it *is*
his garment for his skin. What will he sleep
in? And it will be that when he cries to Me,
I will hear, for I *am* [b]gracious.
28 [c]"You shall not revile God, nor curse a
[d]ruler of your people.
29 "You shall not delay *to offer* [e]the first
of your ripe produce and your juices. [f]The
firstborn of your sons you shall give to Me.
30 [g]Likewise you shall do with your oxen
and your sheep. It shall be with its mother
[h]seven days; on the eighth day you shall
give it to Me.
31 "And you shall be [i]holy men to Me:
[j]you shall not eat meat torn *by beasts* in the
field; you shall throw it to the dogs.

Justice for All

23 "You [a]shall not circulate a false report. Do not put your hand with the
wicked to be an [b]unrighteous witness.
2 [c]You shall not follow a crowd to do evil;
[d]nor shall you testify in a dispute so as to
turn aside after many to pervert *justice*.

9 [j] Deut. 25:1; 2 Chr. 19:10
11 [k] Heb. 6:16
12 [l] Gen. 31:39
13 [m] Gen. 31:39
16 [n] Deut. 22:28, 29
17 [o] Gen. 34:12; 1 Sam. 18:25
18 [p] Lev. 19:31; 20:6, 27; Deut. 18:10, 11; 1 Sam. 28:3-10; Jer. 27:9, 10
19 [q] Lev. 18:23; 20:15, 16; Deut. 27:21
20 [r] Ex. 32:8; 34:15; Lev. 17:7; Num. 25:2; Deut. 17:2, 3, 5; 1 Kin. 18:40; 2 Kin. 10:25
21 [s] Ex. 23:9; Deut. 10:19; Zech. 7:10 [2] *sojourner*
22 [t] Deut. 24:17, 18; Prov. 23:10, 11; Jer. 7:6, 7; [James 1:27]
23 [u] [Luke 18:7] [v] Deut. 10:17, 18; Ps. 18:6
24 [w] Ps. 69:24 [x] Ps. 109:9
25 [y] Lev. 25:35-37 [z] Deut. 23:19, 20; Neh. 5:1-13; Ps. 15:5; Ezek. 18:8
26 [a] Deut. 24:6, 10-13; Job 24:3; Prov. 20:16; Amos 2:8
27 [b] Ex. 34:6, 7
28 [c] Eccl. 10:20 [d] Acts 23:5
29 [e] Ex. 23:16, 19; Deut. 26:2-11; Prov. 3:9 [f] Ex. 13:2, 12, 15
30 [g] Deut. 15:19 [h] Lev. 22:27
31 [i] Ex. 19:6; Lev. 11:44; 19:2 [j] Lev. 7:24; 17:15; Ezek. 4:14

CHAPTER 23

1 [a] Ex. 20:16; Lev. 19:11; Deut. 5:20; Ps. 101:5; [Prov. 10:18] [b] Deut. 19:16-21; Ps. 35:11; [Prov. 19:5]; Acts 6:11
2 [c] Gen. 7:1 [d] Lev. 19:15

At night quick evaluation of an intruder's intentions was not as clear as it might be in daytime, nor would someone be awake and on hand to help.

22:11 an oath of the LORD. Presumably an oath of innocence which would bind the two parties to a dispute over lost goods and preclude any further legal action being taken.

22:16 If a man entices…pay the bride-price. The male was held accountable for premarital intercourse and the victim was seen as having been exploited by him, for which he paid a price (cf. Deut. 22:22-29).

22:18 sorceress. A woman who practices occultism.

22:19 The degree of sexual perversion in Canaanite culture was such that bestiality was fairly commonplace (cf. Lev. 18:23,24). Hittite laws, for example, even permitted cohabitation with certain animals.

22:20 utterly destroyed. Lit. meaning "put to the ban" or "devoted to sacred use," which in this case meant death (cf. Josh. 7:2ff.).

22:22 widow or fatherless child. God reserved His special attention for widows and orphans who often had no one to care for them. He also reserved a special reaction, His wrath, for those abusing and exploiting them. This wrath would work out in military invasions as the sword reduced the abusers' families to the same status of being without spouse or parents.

22:25 interest. One way in which the people showed their concern for the poor and needy was to take no business advantage of them. Charging interest was allowable (Lev. 25:35-37; Deut. 23:19,20), but not when it was exorbitant or worsened the plight of the borrower. The psalmist identified a righteous man as one who lends money without interest (Ps. 15:5).

22:28 See Acts 23:5, where Paul apparently violated this law, not knowing to whom he spoke.

22:31 holy men to Me. All these laws and regulations caused Israel to be set apart in conduct, not just in name. The special calling as Yahweh's firstborn son (4:22) and as His treasured possession, a kingdom of priests and a holy nation (19:5,6) mandated ethical uprightness. **eat meat torn.** Flesh of an animal killed by another and lying in the field became unclean by coming into contact with unclean carnivores and insects and with putrefaction by not having had the

3 You shall not show partiality to a [e]poor
man in his dispute.
4 [f]"If you meet your enemy's ox or his
donkey going astray, you shall surely bring
it back to him again. 5 [g]If you see the donkey of one who hates you lying under its
burden, and you would refrain from helping it, you shall surely help him with it.
6 [h]"You shall not pervert the judgment
of your poor in his dispute. 7 [i]Keep yourself far from a false matter; [j]do not kill the
innocent and righteous. For [k]I will not justify the wicked. 8 And [l]you shall take no
bribe, for a bribe blinds the discerning and
perverts the words of the righteous.
9 "Also [m]you shall not oppress a [1]strang-
er, for you know the heart of a stranger, because you were strangers in the land of
Egypt.

The Law of Sabbaths

10 [n]"Six years you shall sow your land
and gather in its produce, 11 but the seventh *year* you shall let it rest and lie fallow,
that the poor of your people may eat; and
what they leave, the beasts of the field may
eat. In like manner you shall do with your
vineyard *and* your [2]olive grove. 12 [o]Six
days you shall do your work, and on the
seventh day you shall rest, that your ox
and your donkey may rest, and the son of
your female servant and the stranger may
be refreshed.
13 "And in all that I have said to you, [p]be
circumspect and [q]make no mention of the
name of other gods, nor let it be heard
from your mouth.

3 [e]Ex. 23:6; Lev. 19:15; Deut. 1:17; 16:19
4 [f][Rom. 12:20]
5 [g]Deut. 22:4
6 [h]Eccl. 5:8
7 [i]Ex. 20:16; Ps. 119:29; Eph. 4:25 [j]Matt. 27:4 [k]Ex. 34:7; Deut. 25:1; Rom. 1:18
8 [l]Deut. 10:17; 16:19; Prov. 15:27; 17:8, 23; Is. 5:22, 23
9 [m]Ex. 22:21; Lev. 19:33; Deut. 24:17; 27:19 [1]*sojourner*
10 [n]Lev. 25:1-7
11 [2]*olive yards*
12 [o]Luke 13:14
13 [p]Deut. 4:9, 23; 1 Tim. 4:16 [q]Josh. 23:7; Ps. 16:4; Hos. 2:17
14 [r]Ex. 23:17; 34:22-24; Deut. 16:16
15 [s]Ex. 12:14-20; Lev. 23:6-8; Num. 28:16-25 [t]Ex. 22:29; 34:20
16 [u]Ex. 34:22; Lev. 23:10; Num. 28:26 [v]Deut. 16:13
17 [w]Ex. 23:14; 34:23; Deut. 16:16 [3]Heb. *YHWH*, usually translated *LORD*
18 [x]Ex. 34:25; Lev. 2:11 [y]Ex. 12:10; Lev. 7:15; Deut. 16:4 [4]*feast*
19 [z]Ex. 22:29; 34:26; Deut. 26:2, 10; Neh. 10:35; Prov. 3:9 [a]Deut. 14:21
20 [b]Ex. 3:2; 13:15; 14:19; Josh. 5:14
21 [c]Num. 14:11; Deut. 9:7; Ps. 78:40, 56 [d]Deut. 18:19; 1 John 5:16 [e]Is. 9:6; Jer. 23:6

Three Annual Feasts

14 [r]"Three times you shall keep a feast to
Me in the year: 15 [s]You shall keep the Feast
of Unleavened Bread (you shall eat unleavened bread seven days, as I commanded you, at the time appointed in the month
of Abib, for in it you came out of Egypt;
[t]none shall appear before Me empty);
16 [u]and the Feast of Harvest, the firstfruits
of your labors which you have sown in the
field; and [v]the Feast of Ingathering at the
end of the year, when you have gathered in
the fruit of your labors from the field.
17 [w]"Three times in the year all your
males shall appear before the Lord [3]GOD.
18 [x]"You shall not offer the blood of My
sacrifice with leavened [y]bread; nor shall
the fat of My [4]sacrifice remain until morning. 19 [z]The first of the firstfruits of your
land you shall bring into the house of the
LORD your God. [a]You shall not boil a
young goat in its mother's milk.

The Angel and the Promises

20 [b]"Behold, I send an Angel before you
to keep you in the way and to bring you
into the place which I have prepared. 21 Beware of Him and obey His voice; [c]do not
provoke Him, for He will [d]not pardon your
transgressions; for [e]My name *is* in Him.
22 But if you indeed obey His voice and do
all that I speak, then [f]I will be an enemy to
your enemies and an adversary to your adversaries. 23 [g]For My Angel will go before
you and [h]bring you in to the Amorites and
the Hittites and the Perizzites and the

22 [f]Gen. 12:3; Num. 24:9; Deut. 30:7; Jer. 30:20 23 [g]Ex. 23:20 [h]Josh. 24:8, 11

blood drained properly from it. A set apart lifestyle impacted every area of life, including from where one collected his meat.

23:1-9 A list of miscellaneous laws, which includes the protection of equitable and impartial justice for all. False testimony, undiscerningly following a majority, favoring one over another, and accepting bribes, all contribute to the perversion of true justice. The attitude of impartiality was to include the helping of another with his animals regardless of whether he be friend or foe. If no help was given, his livelihood could very well be adversely affected, which was a situation others in the community could not allow to happen.

23:10,11 seventh *year*. A sabbatical year of rest after 6 years of farming benefited both the land and the poor. This pattern of letting a field lie fallow appears to have been unique with Israel.

23:13 Idolatry was to be avoided right down to the level of not causing the name of other deities to be remembered. This perhaps served also as a prohibition of intermarriage with other nations, for in the marriage contract recognition was given to the deities of the parties involved, which would have had the effect of putting God on a par with pagan gods.

23:14-19 Requiring all males to be present for 3 specified feasts at a central sanctuary would have had a socially and religiously uniting effect on the nation. The men must trust the Lord to protect their landholdings while on pilgrimage to the tabernacle (cf. 34:23,24). All 3 feasts were joyful occasions, being a commemoration of the Exodus (the Feast of Unleavened Bread), an expression of gratitude to God for all the grain He had provided (the Feast of Harvest), and a thanksgiving for the final harvest (the Feast of Ingathering). Alternative names appear in the biblical record for the second and third feasts: the Feast of Weeks (34:22) or Firstfruits (34:22; Acts 2:1), and the Feast of Tabernacles or Booths (Lev. 23:33-36). For additional discussions, see, Lev. 23:1–24:9; Num. 28,29; Deut. 16.

23:19 not boil a young goat. Canaanite ritual, according to excavations at Ras Shamra (ancient Ugarit), called for sacrificial kids to be boiled in milk, but the damaged Ugaritic text does not clearly specify mother's milk. If it were so, then it is understandable that Israel was being prevented from copying pagan idolatrous ritualism. Another option suggests that the dead kid was being boiled in the very substance which had sustained its life; hence the prohibition. Until more archeological information comes to light, the specific religious or cultural reason remains as supposition.

23:23 My Angel. Usually taken to be a reference to the Angel of Yahweh, who is distinguished from the Lord who talks about Him as another person. *See note on 3:2.* Yet, He is identified with Him by reason of His forgiving sin and the Lord's name being in Him (v. 21). Neither Moses nor some other messenger or guide qualify for such descriptions. The key to victory in the upcoming takeover of the Land

Canaanites and the Hivites and the Jebusites; and I will [5]cut them off. **24** You shall
not [i]bow down to their gods, nor serve
them, [j]nor do according to their works;
[k]but you shall utterly overthrow them and
completely break down their *sacred* pillars.
25 "So you shall [l]serve the LORD your
God, and [m]He will bless your bread and
your water. And [n]I will take sickness away
from the midst of you. **26** [o]No one shall suffer miscarriage or be barren in your land; I
will [p]fulfill the number of your days.
27 "I will send [q]My fear before you, I will
[r]cause confusion among all the people to
whom you come, and will make all your
enemies turn *their* backs to you. **28** And [s]I
will send hornets before you, which shall
drive out the Hivite, the Canaanite, and
the Hittite from before you. **29** [t]I will not
drive them out from before you in one
year, lest the land become desolate and the
beasts of the field become too numerous
for you. **30** Little by little I will drive them
out from before you, until you have increased, and you inherit the land. **31** And
[u]I will set your [6]bounds from the Red Sea
to the sea, Philistia, and from the desert to
the [7]River. For I will [v]deliver the inhabitants of the land into your hand, and you
shall drive them out before you. **32** [w]You
shall make no [8]covenant with them, nor
with their gods. **33** They shall not dwell in
your land, lest they make you sin against
Me. For *if* you serve their gods, [x]it will
surely be a snare to you."

23 [5] *annihilate them*
24 [i] Ex. 20:5; 23:13, 33 [j] Deut. 12:30, 31 [k] Ex. 34:13; Num. 33:52; Deut. 7:5; 12:3; 2 Kin. 18:4
25 [l] Deut. 6:13; [Matt. 4:10] [m] Deut. 28:5 [n] Ex. 15:26; Deut. 7:15
26 [o] Deut. 7:14; 28:4; Mal. 3:11 [p] 1 Chr. 23:1
27 [q] Gen. 35:5; Ex. 15:16; Deut. 2:25; Josh. 2:9 [r] Deut. 7:23
28 [s] Deut. 7:20; Josh. 24:12
29 [t] Deut. 7:22
31 [u] Gen. 15:18; Deut. 1:7, 8; 11:24; 1 Kin. 4:21, 24 [v] Josh. 21:44 [6] *boundaries* [7] Heb. *Nahar,* the Euphrates
32 [w] Ex. 34:12, 15; Deut. 7:2 [8] *treaty*
33 [x] Ex. 34:12; Deut. 12:30; Josh. 23:13; Judg. 2:3; 1 Sam. 18:21; Ps. 106:36

CHAPTER 24

1 [a] Ex. 6:23; 28:1; Lev. 10:1, 2 [b] Ex. 1:5; Num. 11:16
3 [c] Ex. 19:8; 24:7; Deut. 5:27; [Gal. 3:19] [1] *ordinances*
4 [d] Ex. 17:14; 34:27; Deut. 31:9 [e] Gen. 28:18
5 [f] Ex. 18:12; 20:24
6 [g] Ex. 29:16, 20; Heb. 9:18
7 [h] Ex. 24:4; Heb. 9:19

Israel Affirms the Covenant

24 Now He said to Moses, "Come up
to the LORD, you and Aaron,
[a]Nadab and Abihu, [b]and seventy of the elders of Israel, and worship from afar.
2 And Moses alone shall come near the
LORD, but they shall not come near; nor
shall the people go up with him."
3 So Moses came and told the people all
the words of the LORD and all the [1]judg-
ments. And all the people answered with
one voice and said, [c]"All the words which
the LORD has said we will do." **4** And Moses [d]wrote all the words of the LORD. And
he rose early in the morning, and built an
altar at the foot of the mountain, and
twelve [e]pillars according to the twelve
tribes of Israel. **5** Then he sent young men
of the children of Israel, who offered [f]burnt
offerings and sacrificed peace offerings of
oxen to the LORD. **6** And Moses [g]took half
the blood and put *it* in basins, and half the
blood he sprinkled on the altar. **7** Then he
[h]took the Book of the Covenant and read in
the hearing of the people. And they said,
"All that the LORD has said we will do, and
be obedient." **8** And Moses took the blood,
sprinkled *it* on the people, and said, "This
is [i]the blood of the covenant which the
LORD has made with you according to all
these words."

8 [i] Zech. 9:11; [Matt. 26:28; Mark 14:24; Luke 22:20; 1 Cor. 11:25; Heb. 9:19, 20; 13:20; 1 Pet. 1:2]

would not be Israel's military skill but the presence of this Angel, who is the pre-incarnate Christ.

23:24 *sacred* pillars. Stone markers of pagan shrines were absolutely intolerable once the Land had been taken from the tribes just mentioned in the previous verse.

23:25,26 Proper worship brought with it due rewards, not only good harvests and a good water supply, but also physical health, including fertility and safe pregnancies.

23:28 hornets. This figurative expression of the panic-producing power of God parallels "My fear" (v. 27), which was the obvious effect of "My Angel" having been the advance guard to the conquest (v. 23). In anticipation of the conquest of their Land, Israel was being given another reminder that victory depended on God and not their own efforts alone. Fear and panic did play a strategic role in the victories in Transjordan and Canaan (Num. 22:3; Josh. 2:9,11; 5:1; 9:24). An alternative non-figurative view is based upon the bee or wasp being a heraldic symbol of Egyptian pharaohs whose steady succession of military strikes into Canaan year after year God providentially used to weaken Canaan prior to the invasion by Israel.

23:29,30 The occupation would be a gradual but effective process taking longer than a year to accomplish, but ensuring full control of a land in good condition and not left desolate by a sweeping and destructive warfare. The reference to the multiplication of wild beasts if the land was desolated underscores the fertility of the land and its ability to support life.

23:31 I will set your bounds. God gave both broad and more detailed geographic descriptions of the Land. Even limited demarcation of borders was sufficient to lay out the extent of their possession. It would extend from the Gulf of Aqabah to the Mediterranean and from the desert in the Negev to the river of the northern boundary.

23:32 make no covenant. International diplomacy, with its parity or suzerainty treaties, was not an option open to Israel in dealing with the tribes living within the designated borders of the Promised Land (Deut. 7:1,2). All these treaties were accompanied by the names of the nations' gods, so it was fitting to deliver a charge not to make a treaty (covenant) with them, nor to serve their pagan gods. The situation with other nations outside the land being given to Israel was different (cf. Deut. 20:10-18).

24:4 twelve pillars. Unlike pagan stone markers (23:24), these were built to represent the 12 tribes and were placed alongside the altar Moses had erected in preparation for a covenant ratification ceremony. They did not mark the worship site of a pagan deity.

24:5 young men. Most probably a reference to firstborn children who officiated until the law appointed the Levites in their place.

24:7 the Book of the Covenant. Civil, social, and religious laws were received by Moses on Mt. Sinai, orally presented (v. 3), then written down (v. 4), and read to the people. This Book contained not only this detailed enlargement of the Decalogue (20:22–23:33), but also the Ten Commandments themselves (20:1-17) and the preliminary abbreviated presentation of the treaty (19:3-6). *See notes on 19:3-8; 20:3-17.*

24:8 sprinkled *it* on the people. By this act, Moses, in response to the positive acceptance and assertion of obedience by the people after hearing the Book of the Covenant read to them, officially sealed

On the Mountain with God

9 Then Moses went up, also Aaron,
Nadab, and Abihu, and seventy of the elders of Israel, 10 and they [j]saw the God of
Israel. And *there was* under His feet as it
were a paved work of [k]sapphire stone, and
it was like the [l]very [2] heavens in *its* clarity.
11 But on the nobles of the children of Israel He [m]did not [3]lay His hand. So [n]they
saw God, and they [o]ate and drank.
12 Then the LORD said to Moses, [p]"Come
up to Me on the mountain and be there;
and I will give you [q]tablets of stone, and
the law and commandments which I have
written, that you may teach them."
13 So Moses arose with [r]his assistant
Joshua, and Moses went up to the mountain of God. 14 And he said to the elders,
"Wait here for us until we come back to
you. Indeed, Aaron and [s]Hur *are* with you.
If any man has a difficulty, let him go to
them." 15 Then Moses went up into the
mountain, and [t]a cloud covered the mountain.
16 Now [u]the glory of the LORD rested on
Mount Sinai, and the cloud covered it six
days. And on the seventh day He called to
Moses out of the midst of the cloud. 17 The
sight of the glory of the LORD *was* like [v]a
consuming fire on the top of the mountain
in the eyes of the children of Israel. 18 So
Moses went into the midst of the cloud and
went up into the mountain. And [w]Moses
was on the mountain forty days and forty
nights.

Offerings for the Sanctuary

25 Then the LORD spoke to Moses, saying: 2 "Speak to the children of Israel, that they bring Me an [1]offering.
[a]From everyone who gives it willingly
with his heart you shall take My offering.
3 And this *is* the offering which you shall
take from them: gold, silver, and bronze;
4 blue, purple, and scarlet *thread,* fine linen,
and goats' *hair;* 5 ram skins dyed red, [2]bad-
ger skins, and acacia wood; 6 [b]oil for the
light, and [c]spices for the anointing oil and
for the sweet incense; 7 onyx stones, and
stones to be set in the [d]ephod and in the

10 [j] Ex. 24:11; Num. 12:8; Is. 6:5; [John 1:18; 6:46]; 1 John 4:12 [k] Ezek. 1:26; Rev. 4:3 [l] Matt. 17:2 [2] Lit. *substance of heaven*
11 [m] Ex. 19:21 [n] Gen. 32:30; Judg. 13:22 [o] 1 Cor. 10:18 [3] *stretch out His*
12 [p] Ex. 24:2, 15 [q] Ex. 31:18; 32:15; Deut. 5:22
13 [r] Ex. 32:17
14 [s] Ex. 17:10, 12
15 [t] Ex. 19:9; Matt. 17:5
16 [u] Ex. 16:10; 33:18; Num. 14:10
17 [v] Ex. 3:2; Deut. 4:26, 36; 9:3; Heb. 12:18, 29
18 [w] Ex. 34:28; Deut. 9:9; 10:10

CHAPTER 25

2 [a] Ex. 35:4-9, 21; 1 Chr. 29:3, 5, 9; Ezra 2:68; Neh. 11:2; [2 Cor. 8:11-13; 9:7] [1] *heave offering*
5 [2] Or *dolphin*
6 [b] Ex. 27:20 [c] Ex. 30:23
7 [d] Ex. 28:4, 6-14

the treaty with blood; a not uncommon custom (cf. Gen. 15:9-13,17). Half of the blood used had been sprinkled on the altar as part of the consecration ceremony. The representatives of Israel were thereby qualified to ascend the mountain and participate in the covenant meal with Yahweh (24:11; cf. Heb. 9:20).

24:9,11 they saw God. The representatives accompanying Moses up the mountain, as per God's instructions, were privileged to have seen God without being consumed by His holiness. Precisely what they saw must remain a moot point and must stay within the description given, which focuses only on what was under His feet. This perhaps indicates that only a partial manifestation took place such as would occur before Moses (33:20), or that the elders, in the presence of divine majesty, beauty, and strength (cf. Ps. 96:6), did not dare raise their eyes above His footstool.

24:10 paved work of sapphire stone. The description sounds like a comparison with lapis lazuli, an opaque blue precious stone much used in Mesopotamia and Egypt at that time.

24:12 tablets of stone. For the first time, mention is made of what form the revelation of the law would take: tablets of stone. They were also called the "tablets of the Testimony" (31:18) and the "tablets of the covenant" (Deut. 9:9).

24:14 Hur. *See note on 17:10.*

24:16-18 This was the first (ending in 32:6) of two (40 days and 40 nights each) trips to Sinai (cf. 34:2-28). The awe-inspiring sight of God's glory cloud, the Shekinah, resting on the mountain and into which Moses disappeared for 40 days and nights, impressed everyone with the singular importance of this event in Israel's history. During these days Moses received all the instructions on the tabernacle and its furnishings and accoutrements (chaps. 25–31). The settling of the Shekinah upon the tabernacle at its completion impressed the Israelites with the singular importance of this structure in Israel's worship of and relationship to Yahweh (40:34-38).

25:1–40:38 The primary focus of attention in the closing chapters is upon the design and construction of the central place of worship for the nation. In preparation for occupation of their Land, they had been given a system of law to regulate individual and national life, to prevent exploitation of the poor and the stranger, and to safeguard against polytheism and idolatry. That these safeguards were needed was confirmed by the idolatrous golden calf incident (32:1-35). The very detailed and divinely given blueprint of the tabernacle removes all speculation about whether it has any comparison with, or was somehow derived from, the little portable sanctuaries belonging to various tribal deities. The origin of the tabernacle was found in God and delivered to Moses by special revelation (cf. 25:9,40; 26:30; Heb. 8:5).

25:2 an offering...willingly. Voluntarily and freely the people were given opportunity to personally contribute to the nation's worship center from the list of 14 components and materials needed to build the tabernacle. One wonders how much of their contribution came originally from Egyptian homes and had been thrust into the hands of the Israelites right before the Exodus (cf. 12:35,36). The people so responded with joy and enthusiasm that they finally had to be restrained from bringing any more gifts (35:21-29; 36:3-7). A similar response occurred centuries later, when King David requested gifts to build the temple (1 Chr. 29:1-9).

25:4 blue, purple, and scarlet *thread.* These colors were produced by dying the thread: blue from a shellfish, purple from the secretion of a murex snail, and crimson from powdered eggs and bodies of certain worms, which attached themselves to holly plants. Deriving different colored dyes from different natural sources demonstrates a substantial degree of technical sophistication with textiles and fabrics. **fine linen.** Egypt had a reputation for excellence in producing finely twined linens.

25:5 ram skins dyed red. With all the wool removed and then dyed, it resembled moroccan leather. **acacia wood.** A hard, durable, close-grained, and aromatic desert wood avoided by wood-eating insects. It was considered good for cabinet making, and could also be found in sufficient quantities in the Sinai peninsula.

25:6 spices. For the many years of Bible history, Arabia was highly respected for the variety of balsams she exported.

25:7 onyx stones. Sometimes thought to be chrysoprase quartz, a product known to the Egyptians and with which Israel was no doubt familiar. The LXX translated it as beryl.

breastplate. 8 And let them make Me a
[e]sanctuary,[3] that [f]I may dwell among
them. 9 According to all that I show you,
that is, the pattern of the tabernacle and the
pattern of all its furnishings, just so you
shall make *it.*

The Ark of the Testimony

10 [g]"And they shall make an ark of acacia wood; two and a half cubits *shall be* its
length, a cubit and a half its width, and a
cubit and a half its height. 11 And you shall
overlay it with pure gold, inside and out
you shall overlay it, and shall make on it a
molding of [h]gold all around. 12 You shall
cast four rings of gold for it, and put *them*
in its four corners; two rings *shall be* on one
side, and two rings on the other side.
13 And you shall make poles *of* acacia
wood, and overlay them with gold. 14 You
shall put the poles into the rings on the
sides of the ark, that the ark may be carried
by them. 15 [i]The poles shall be in the rings
of the ark; they shall not be taken from it.
16 And you shall put into the ark [j]the Testimony which I will give you.

17 [k]"You shall make a mercy seat of pure
gold; two and a half cubits *shall be* its
length and a cubit and a half its width.
18 And you shall make two cherubim of
gold; of hammered work you shall make
them at the two ends of the mercy seat.
19 Make one cherub at one end, and the
other cherub at the other end; you shall
make the cherubim at the two ends of it *of
one piece* with the mercy seat. 20 And [l]the
cherubim shall stretch out *their* wings
above, covering the mercy seat with their
wings, and they shall face one another; the
faces of the cherubim *shall be* toward the
mercy seat. 21 [m]You shall put the mercy
seat on top of the ark, and [n]in the ark you
shall put the Testimony that I will give
you. 22 And [o]there I will meet with you,
and I will speak with you from above the
mercy seat, from [p]between the two cherubim which *are* on the ark of the Testimony,
about everything which I will give you in
commandment to the children of Israel.

The Table for the Showbread

23 [q]"You shall also make a table of acacia
wood; two cubits *shall be* its length, a cubit
its width, and a cubit and a half its height.
24 And you shall overlay it with pure gold,
and make a molding of gold all around.
25 You shall make for it a frame of a handbreadth all around, and you shall make a
gold molding for the frame all around.
26 And you shall make for it four rings of
gold, and put the rings on the four corners
that *are* at its four legs. 27 The rings shall be
close to the frame, as holders for the poles
to bear the table. 28 And you shall make
the poles of acacia wood, and overlay them
with gold, that the table may be carried
with them. 29 You shall make [r]its dishes, its
pans, its pitchers, and its bowls for pouring. You shall make them of pure gold.
30 And you shall set the [s]showbread on the
table before Me always.

The Gold Lampstand

31 [t]"You shall also make a lampstand of
pure gold; the lampstand shall be of hammered work. Its shaft, its branches, its

8 [e]Ex. 36:1, 3, 4; Lev. 4:6; 10:4; 21:12; Heb. 9:1, 2 [f]Ex. 29:45; 1 Kin. 6:13; [2 Cor. 6:16; Heb. 3:6; Rev. 2:13] [3] *sacred place*
10 [g]Ex. 37:1-9; Deut. 10:3; Heb. 9:4
11 [h]Ex. 37:2; Heb. 9:4
15 [i]Num. 4:6; 1 Kin. 8:8
16 [j]Ex. 16:34; 31:18; Deut. 10:2; 31:26; 1 Kin. 8:9; Heb. 9:4
17 [k]Ex. 37:6; Heb. 9:5
20 [l]1 Kin. 8:7; 1 Chr. 28:18; Heb. 9:5
21 [m]Ex. 26:34; 40:20 [n]Ex. 25:16
22 [o]Ex. 29:42, 43; 30:6, 36; Lev. 16:2; Num. 17:4 [p]Num. 7:89; 1 Sam. 4:4; 2 Sam. 6:2; 2 Kin. 19:15; Ps. 80:1; Is. 37:16
23 [q]Ex. 37:10-16; 1 Kin. 7:48; 2 Chr. 4:8; Heb. 9:2
29 [r]Ex. 37:16; Num. 4:7
30 [s]Ex. 39:36; 40:23; Lev. 24:5-9
31 [t]Ex. 37:17-24; 1 Kin. 7:49; Zech. 4:2; Heb. 9:2; Rev. 1:12

25:8 I may dwell. The tabernacle, a noun derived from the verb "to dwell," was an appropriate designation for that which was to be the place of God's presence with His people. His presence would be between the cherubim and from there He would meet with Moses (v. 22).

25:9 tabernacle. The Pentateuch records 5 different names for the tabernacle: 1) "sanctuary," denoting a sacred place or set apart, i.e., holy, place; 2) "tent," denoting a temporary or collapsible dwelling; 3) "tabernacle," from "to dwell," denoting the place of God's presence (as well as other titles); 4) "tabernacle of the congregation, or meeting"; and 5) "tabernacle of the testimony."

25:11 pure gold. The technology of the day was sufficient to refine gold.

25:16 the Testimony. This designation for the two tablets of stone containing the Ten Commandments which were placed inside the ark explains why it was also called "the ark of the Testimony" (v. 22), and shows why it was appropriate to call the whole structure "the tabernacle" or "the Tent of the Testimony." "The ark of the covenant of the Lord of all the earth" (Josh. 3:11) and "the holy ark" (2 Chr. 35:3) were alternative designations.

25:17 mercy seat. The lid or cover of the ark was the "mercy seat" or the place at which atonement took place. Between the Shekinah glory cloud above the ark and the tablets of law inside the ark was the blood-sprinkled cover. Blood from the sacrifices stood between God and the broken law of God!

25:18 cherubim. Forged as one with the golden cover of the ark were two angelic beings rising up on each end and facing one another, their wings stretching up and over forming an arch. Cherubim, associated with the majestic glory and presence of God (cf. Ezek. 10:1-22), were appropriately woven into the tabernacle curtains and the veil for the Holy of Holies (26:1,31), for this place was where God was present with His people. Scripture reveals them as the bearers of God's throne (1 Sam. 4:4; Is. 37:16) and the guardians of the Garden of Eden and the Tree of Life (Gen. 3:24).

25:30 showbread. Each week a new batch of 12 loaves of bread was laid on a table on the N side of the Holy Place. The utensils for this table were also made of refined gold (v. 29). This "Bread of His Presence" was not set out in order to feed Israel's God, unlike food placed in pagan shrines and temples, but to acknowledge that the 12 tribes were sustained constantly under the watchful eye and care of their Lord. The bread was eaten in the Holy Place each Sabbath by the priests on duty (Lev. 24:5-9). The showbread is understood to typify the Lord Jesus Christ as the Bread which came from heaven (John 6:32-35).

25:31 lampstand. Situated opposite the table of showbread on the S side of the Holy Place stood an ornate lampstand, or menorah,

bowls, its *ornamental* knobs, and flowers shall be *of one piece.* 32 And six branches shall come out of its sides: three branches of the lampstand out of one side, and three branches of the lampstand out of the other side. 33 [u]Three bowls *shall be* made like almond *blossoms* on one branch, *with* an *ornamental* knob and a flower, and three bowls made like almond *blossoms* on the other branch, *with* an *ornamental* knob and a flower—and so for the six branches that come out of the lampstand. 34 [v]On the lampstand itself four bowls *shall be* made like almond *blossoms, each with* its *ornamental* knob and flower. 35 And *there shall be* a knob under the *first* two branches of the same, a knob under the *second* two branches of the same, and a knob under the *third* two branches of the same, according to the six branches that extend from the lampstand. 36 Their knobs and their branches *shall be of one piece;* all of it *shall be* one hammered piece of pure gold. 37 You shall make seven lamps for it, and [w]they shall arrange its lamps so that they [x]give light in front of it. 38 And its wick-trimmers and their trays *shall be* of pure gold. 39 It shall be made of a talent of pure gold, with all these utensils. 40 And [y]see to it that you make *them* according to the pattern which was shown you on the mountain.

The Tabernacle

26 "Moreover [a]you shall make the tabernacle *with* ten curtains *of* fine woven linen and blue, purple, and scarlet *thread;* with artistic designs of cherubim you shall weave them. 2 The length of each curtain *shall be* twenty-eight cubits, and the width of each curtain four cubits. And every one of the curtains shall have [1]the same measurements. 3 Five curtains shall be coupled to one another, and *the other* five curtains *shall be* coupled to one another. 4 And you shall make loops of blue *yarn* on the edge of the curtain on the selvedge of *one* set, and likewise you shall do on the outer edge of *the other* curtain of the second set. 5 Fifty loops you shall make in the one curtain, and fifty loops you shall make on the edge of the curtain that *is* on the end of the second set, that the loops may be clasped to one another. 6 And you shall make fifty clasps of gold, and couple the curtains together with the clasps, so that it may be one tabernacle.

7 [b]"You shall also make curtains of goats' *hair,* to be a tent over the tabernacle. You shall make eleven curtains. 8 The length of each curtain *shall be* thirty cubits, and the width of each curtain four cubits; and the eleven curtains shall all have the same measurements. 9 And you shall couple five curtains by themselves and six curtains by themselves, and you shall double over the sixth curtain at the forefront of the tent. 10 You shall make fifty loops on the edge of the curtain that is outermost in *one* set, and fifty loops on the edge of the curtain of the second set. 11 And you shall make fifty bronze clasps, put the clasps into the loops, and couple the tent together, that it may be one. 12 The remnant that remains of the curtains of the tent, the half curtain that remains, shall hang over the back of the tabernacle. 13 And a cubit on one side and a cubit on the other side, of what remains of the length of the curtains of the tent, shall hang over the sides of the tabernacle, on this side and on that side, to cover it.

14 [c]"You shall also make a covering of ram skins dyed red for the tent, and a covering of badger skins above that.

15 "And for the tabernacle you shall [d]make the boards of acacia wood, standing upright. 16 Ten cubits *shall be* the length of a board, and a cubit and a half *shall be* the width of each board. 17 Two [2]tenons *shall be* in each board for binding one to another. Thus you shall make for all the boards of the tabernacle. 18 And you shall make the boards for the tabernacle, twenty boards for the south side. 19 You shall make forty sockets of silver under the twenty boards: two sockets under each of the boards for its two tenons. 20 And for the second side of the tabernacle, the north side, *there shall be* twenty boards 21 and their forty sockets of silver: two sockets under each of the boards. 22 For the far side of the tabernacle, westward, you shall

33 [u]Ex. 37:19
34 [v]Ex. 37:20-22
37 [w]Ex. 27:21; 30:8; Lev. 24:3, 4; 2 Chr. 13:11 [x]Num. 8:2
40 [y]Ex. 25:9; 26:30; Num. 8:4; 1 Chr. 28:11, 19; Acts 7:44; [Heb. 8:5]

CHAPTER 26

1 [a]Ex. 36:8-19
2 [1]Lit. *one measure*
7 [b]Ex. 36:14
14 [c]Ex. 35:7, 23; 36:19
15 [d]Ex. 36:20-34
17 [2]Projections for joining, lit. *hands*

patterned after a flowering almond tree. It provided light for the priests serving in the Holy Place. Care was taken, according to God's instructions (27:20,21; 30:7,8; Lev. 24:1-4), to keep it well supplied with pure olive oil so that it would not be extinguished. The lampstand is seen as typifying the Lord Jesus Christ, who was the true Light which came into the world (John 1:6-9; 8:12).

25:39 talent. Approximately 75 pounds.

25:40 Cf. Heb. 8:5.

26:1 ten curtains. The beauty of these curtains could be seen only from the inside, the thick outer protective covering of goats' hair drapes, and ram and badger skins (v. 14) hiding them from the view of anyone except the priests who entered.

26:7 eleven curtains. The extra length of the outer drapes doubled as a covering for the front and back of the tabernacle structure (vv. 9-13).

26:15-29 The frame or trellis work, on which the curtains and outer coverings were draped also received precise instructions. The portability of the whole structure was obvious. Throughout the wilderness wanderings, it could be quickly dismantled and readied for transport, and just as rapidly re-erected.

make six boards. 23 And you shall also
make two boards for the two back corners
of the tabernacle. 24 They shall be [3]coupled
together at the bottom and they shall be
coupled together at the top by one ring.
Thus it shall be for both of them. They shall
be for the two corners. 25 So there shall be
eight boards with their sockets of silver—
sixteen sockets—two sockets under each of
the boards.
26 "And you shall make bars of acacia
wood: five for the boards on one side of the
tabernacle, 27 five bars for the boards on
the other side of the tabernacle, and five
bars for the boards of the side of the tabernacle, for the far side westward. 28 The
[e]middle bar shall pass through the midst
of the boards from end to end. 29 You shall
overlay the boards with gold, make their
rings of gold *as* holders for the bars, and
overlay the bars with gold. 30 And you
shall raise up the tabernacle [f]according to
its pattern which you were shown on the
mountain.

24 [3] Lit. *doubled*
28 [e] Ex. 36:33
30 [f] Ex. 25:9, 40; 27:8; 39:32; Num. 8:4; Acts 7:44; [Heb. 8:2, 5]
31 [g] Ex. 27:21; 36:35-38; Lev. 16:2; 2 Chr. 3:14; Matt. 27:51; Heb. 9:3; 10:20
33 [h] Ex. 25:10-16; 40:21 [i] Lev. 16:2; Heb. 9:2, 3
34 [j] Ex. 25:17-22; 40:20; Heb. 9:5
35 [k] Ex. 40:22; Heb. 9:2 [l] Ex. 40:24
36 [m] Ex. 36:37
37 [n] Ex. 36:38

31 [g]"You shall make a veil woven of
blue, purple, and scarlet *thread,* and fine
woven linen. It shall be woven with an
artistic design of cherubim. 32 You shall
hang it upon the four pillars of acacia *wood*
overlaid with gold. Their hooks *shall be*
gold, upon four sockets of silver. 33 And
you shall hang the veil from the clasps.
Then you shall bring [h]the ark of the Testimony in there, behind the veil. The veil
shall be a divider for you between [i]the
holy *place* and the Most Holy. 34 [j]You shall
put the mercy seat upon the ark of the Testimony in the Most Holy. 35 [k]You shall set
the table outside the veil, and [l]the lampstand across from the table on the side of
the tabernacle toward the south; and you
shall put the table on the north side.
36 [m]"You shall make a screen for the
door of the tabernacle, *woven of* blue, purple, and scarlet *thread,* and fine woven
linen, made by a weaver. 37 And you shall
make for the screen [n]five pillars of acacia
wood, and overlay them with gold; their

26:30 pattern. Again (cf. 25:40) the warning was sounded that the blueprint must be carefully followed. Nothing was to be left to human guesswork, no matter how skilled the craftsmen might have been.

26:31-34 A veil, similar in design to the inner curtains (*see note on 26:1*), divided the tabernacle into the Holy Place and the Most Holy, or lit. the Holy of Holies.

26:36 screen. Another curtain or veil, without the embroidered cherubim motif, was made to cover the entrance way into the Holy Place.

The Plan of the Tabernacle

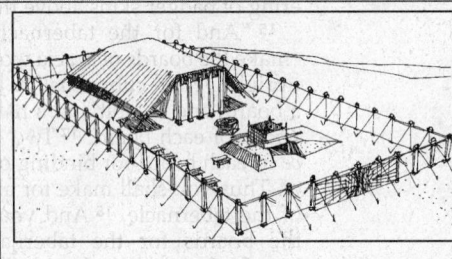

The tabernacle was to provide a place where God might dwell among His people. The term *tabernacle* sometimes refers to the tent, including the Holy Place and the Most Holy Place, which was covered with embroidered curtains. But in other places it refers to the entire complex, including the curtained court in which the tent stood.

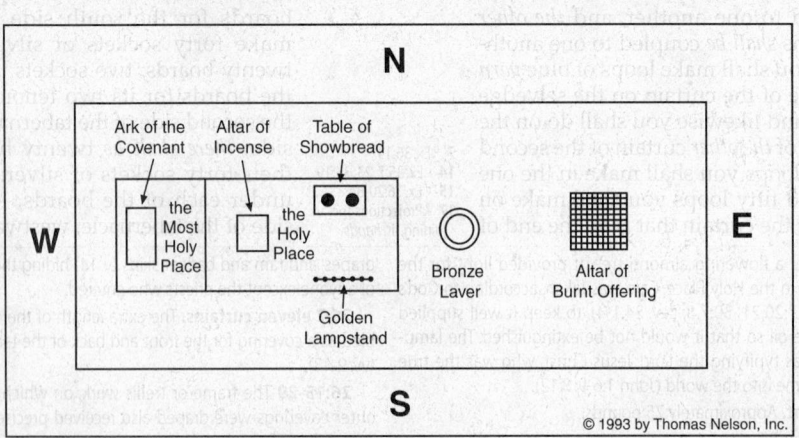

This illustration shows relative positions of the tabernacle furniture used in Israelite worship. The tabernacle is enlarged for clarity.

hooks *shall be* gold, and you shall cast five
sockets of bronze for them.

The Altar of Burnt Offering

27 "You shall make [a]an altar of acacia
wood, five cubits long and five cubits wide—the altar shall be square—and
its height *shall be* three cubits. 2 You shall
make its horns on its four corners; its horns
shall be of one piece with it. And you shall
overlay it with bronze. 3 Also you shall
make its pans to receive its ashes, and its
shovels and its basins and its forks and its
firepans; you shall make all its utensils of
bronze. 4 You shall make a grate for it, a
network of bronze; and on the network
you shall make four bronze rings at its four
corners. 5 You shall put it under the rim of
the altar beneath, that the network may be
midway up the altar. 6 And you shall make
poles for the altar, poles of acacia wood,
and overlay them with bronze. 7 The poles
shall be put in the rings, and the poles shall
be on the two sides of the altar to bear it.
8 You shall make it hollow with boards; [b]as
it was shown you on the mountain, so
shall they make *it.*

The Court of the Tabernacle

9 [c]"You shall also make the court of the
tabernacle. For the south side *there shall be*
hangings for the court *made of* fine woven
linen, one hundred cubits long for one
side. 10 And its twenty pillars and their
twenty sockets *shall be* bronze. The hooks
of the pillars and their bands *shall be* silver.
11 Likewise along the length of the north
side *there shall be* hangings one hundred *cubits* long, with its twenty pillars and their
twenty sockets of bronze, and the hooks of
the pillars and their bands of silver.
12 "And along the width of the court on
the west side *shall be* hangings of fifty cubits, with their ten pillars and their ten
sockets. 13 The width of the court on the
east side *shall be* fifty cubits. 14 The hangings on *one* side *of the gate shall be* fifteen cubits, *with* their three pillars and their three
sockets. 15 And on the other side *shall be*
hangings of fifteen *cubits, with* their three
pillars and their three sockets.
16 "For the gate of the court *there shall be*
a screen twenty cubits long, *woven of* blue,
purple, and scarlet *thread,* and fine woven
linen, made by a weaver. It *shall have* four
pillars and four sockets. 17 All the pillars
around the court shall have bands of silver;
their [d]hooks *shall be* of silver and their sockets of bronze. 18 The length of the court
shall be one hundred cubits, the width fifty
throughout, and the height five cubits,
made of fine woven linen, and its sockets of
bronze. 19 All the utensils of the tabernacle
for all its service, all its pegs, and all the
pegs of the court, *shall be* of bronze.

The Care of the Lampstand

20 "And [e]you shall command the children of Israel that they bring you pure oil
of pressed olives for the light, to cause the
lamp to [1]burn continually. 21 In the tabernacle of meeting, [f]outside the veil which *is*
before the Testimony, [g]Aaron and his sons
shall tend it from evening until morning
before the LORD. [h]*It shall be* a statute forever to their generations on behalf of the children of Israel.

Garments for the Priesthood

28 "Now take [a]Aaron your brother,
and his sons with him, from among
the children of Israel, that he may minister
to Me as [b]priest, Aaron *and* Aaron's sons:
[c]Nadab, Abihu, [d]Eleazar, and Ithamar.
2 And [e]you shall make [1]holy garments for
Aaron your brother, for glory and for

CHAPTER 27

1 [a]Ex. 38:1; Ezek. 43:13
8 [b]Ex. 25:40; 26:30; Acts 7:44; [Heb. 8:5]
9 [c]Ex. 38:9-20
17 [d]Ex. 38:19
20 [e]Ex. 35:8, 28; Lev. 24:1-4 [1]Lit. *ascend*
21 [f]Ex. 26:31, 33 [g]Ex. 30:8; 1 Sam. 3:3; 2 Chr. 13:11 [h]Ex. 28:43; 29:9; Lev. 3:17; 16:34; Num. 18:23; 19:21; 1 Sam. 30:25

CHAPTER 28

1 [a]Num. 3:10; 18:7 [b]Ps. 99:6; Heb. 5:4 [c]Ex. 24:1, 9; Lev. 10:1 [d]Ex. 6:23; Lev. 10:6, 16
2 [e]Ex. 29:5, 29; 31:10; 39:1-31; Lev. 8:7-9, 30 [1]*sacred*

27:1 altar. The largest piece of equipment, also known as the "altar of burnt offering" (Lev. 4:7,10,18), was situated in the courtyard of the tabernacle. It was covered, not in gold as the items inside the Holy Place, but in bronze. Like the other pieces of furniture and equipment, it was also built to be carried by poles (vv. 6,7).

27:3 All the altar's utensils and accessories were also made of bronze, not gold.

27:9 the court of the tabernacle. The dimensions of the rectangular courtyard space, bordered by curtains and poles around the tabernacle were also precisely given (vv. 9-19; 150 ft. by 75 ft.). The outer hangings were high enough, 5 cubits or 7.5 ft., to block all view of the interior of the courtyard (v. 18). Entry into the courtyard of God's dwelling place was not gained just generally and freely from all quarters.

27:16 gate of the court. The curtain forming the covering for the entrance way into the courtyard was colored differently from that which surrounded the oblong courtyard. Clearly there was only one way to enter this very special place where God had chosen to place the evidence of His dwelling with His people.

27:20,21 pure oil of pressed olives. The clear oil from crushed unripened olives granted almost a smoke-free light. The people were to provide the fuel to maintain the light needed by the High-Priest and his priestly staff in the Holy Place.

28:1 minister to Me as priest. The 3-fold repetition of this phrase in the opening words about Aaron's priestly wardrobe would appear to stress the importance of his role in the religious life of the nation. Aaron's sons were part of the priesthood being set up. The Heb. text groups the sons in two pairs, the first pair being Nadab and Abihu, both of whom died because of wanton disregard of God's instructions (Lev. 10:1,2). Aaron and his descendants, as well as the tribe of Levi, were selected by God to be Israel's priests—they did not appoint themselves to the position. The law clearly defined their duties for worship and the sacrifices in the tabernacle and for the individual worshiper and the nation's covenantal relationship to God.

28:2 for glory and for beauty. The garments were designed to exalt the office and function of the priesthood, vividly marking out

beauty. 3 So [f]you shall speak to all *who are*
gifted artisans, [g]whom I have filled with
the spirit of wisdom, that they may make
Aaron's garments, to consecrate him, that
he may minister to Me as priest. 4 And
these *are* the garments which they shall
make: [h]a breastplate, [i]an [2]ephod, [j]a robe,
[k]a skillfully woven tunic, a turban, and [l]a
sash. So they shall make holy garments for
Aaron your brother and his sons, that he
may minister to Me as priest.

The Ephod

5 "They shall take the gold, blue, purple,
and scarlet *thread,* and the fine linen,
6 [m]and they shall make the ephod of gold,
blue, purple, *and* scarlet *thread,* and fine
woven linen, artistically worked. 7 It shall
have two shoulder straps joined at its two
edges, and *so* it shall be joined together.
8 And the [3]intricately woven band of the
ephod, which *is* on it, shall be of the same
workmanship, *made of* gold, blue, purple,
and scarlet *thread,* and fine woven linen.
9 "Then you shall take two onyx [n]stones
and engrave on them the names of the sons
of Israel: 10 six of their names on one stone
and six names on the other stone, in order
of their [o]birth. 11 With the work of an [p]en-
graver in stone, *like* the engravings of a
signet, you shall engrave the two stones
with the names of the sons of Israel. You
shall set them in settings of gold. 12 And
you shall put the two stones on the shoulders of the ephod *as* memorial stones for
the sons of Israel. So [q]Aaron shall bear
their names before the LORD on his two
shoulders [r]as a memorial. 13 You shall also
make settings of gold, 14 and you shall
make two chains of pure gold like braided
cords, and fasten the braided chains to the
settings.

The Breastplate

15 [s]"You shall make the breastplate of
judgment. Artistically woven according to
the workmanship of the ephod you shall
make it: of gold, blue, purple, and scarlet
thread, and fine woven linen, you shall
make it. 16 It shall be doubled into a
square: a span *shall be* its length, and a span
shall be its width. 17 [t]And you shall put settings of stones in it, four rows of stones:
The first row *shall be* a [4]sardius, a topaz,
and an emerald; *this shall be* the first row;
18 the second row *shall be* a turquoise, a
sapphire, and a diamond; 19 the third row,
a [5]jacinth, an agate, and an amethyst;
20 and the fourth row, a [6]beryl, an [7]onyx,
and a jasper. They shall be set in gold settings. 21 And the stones shall have the
names of the sons of Israel, twelve according to their names, *like* the engravings of a
signet, each one with its own name; they
shall be according to the twelve tribes.
22 "You shall make chains for the breastplate at the end, like braided cords of pure
gold. 23 And you shall make two rings of
gold for the breastplate, and put the two
rings on the two ends of the breastplate.
24 Then you shall put the two braided
chains of gold in the two rings which are on
the ends of the breastplate; 25 and the *other*
two ends of the two braided *chains* you
shall fasten to the two settings, and put
them on the shoulder straps of the ephod
in the front.
26 "You shall make two rings of gold,
and put them on the two ends of the
breastplate, on the edge of it, which is on
the inner side of the ephod. 27 And two
other rings of gold you shall make, and put
them on the two shoulder straps, underneath the ephod toward its front, right at
the seam above the [8]intricately woven
band of the ephod. 28 They shall bind the
breastplate by means of its rings to the
rings of the ephod, using a blue cord, so
that it is above the intricately woven band
of the ephod, and so that the breastplate
does not come loose from the ephod.
29 "So Aaron shall [u]bear the names of
the sons of Israel on the breastplate of
judgment over his heart, when he goes into
the holy *place,* as a memorial before the
LORD continually. 30 And [v]you shall put in
the breastplate of judgment the [9]Urim and
the Thummim, and they shall be over Aar-

3 [f]Ex. 31:6; 36:1 [g]Ex. 31:3; 35:30, 31; Is. 11:2; Eph. 1:17
4 [h]Ex. 28:15 [i]Ex. 28:6 [j]Ex. 28:31 [k]Ex. 28:39 [l]Lev. 8:7
[2]Ornamented vest
6 [m]Ex. 39:2-7; Lev. 8:7
8 [3]*ingenious work of*
9 [n]Ex. 35:27
10 [o]Gen. 29:31–30:24; 35:16-18
11 [p]Ex. 35:35
12 [q]Ex. 28:29, 30; 39:6, 7 [r]Lev. 24:7; Num. 31:54; Josh. 4:7; Zech. 6:14; 1 Cor. 11:24
15 [s]Ex. 39:8-21
17 [t]Ex. 39:10 [4]Or *ruby*
19 [5]Or *amber*
20 [6]Or *yellow jasper* [7]*Or carnelian*
27 [8]*ingenious work of*
29 [u]Ex. 28:12
30 [v]Lev. 8:8; Num. 27:21; Deut. 33:8; 1 Sam. 28:6; Ezra 2:63; Neh. 7:65 [9]Lit. *Lights and the Perfections*

Aaron as a special person playing a special mediatorial role—they were "holy" vestments. In the OT priestly system for the nation of Israel, such dress maintained the priest-laity distinction.

28:3 gifted artisans. This was the first reference in God's instructions to Moses that certain men would be especially empowered by Him to work skillfully on this construction project.

28:5-13 ephod. Whenever Aaron entered the sanctuary, he carried with him on his shoulders the badge and the engraved stones that were representative of the 12 tribes.

28:15-30 the breastplate of judgment. The 12 precious stones, each engraved with a tribe's name, colorfully and ornately displayed Aaron's representative role of intercession for the tribes before the Lord. The breastplate was to be securely fastened to the ephod so as not to come loose from it (v. 28 and 39:21). Thus, to speak of the ephod after this was done would be to speak of the whole ensemble.

28:30 Urim and the Thummim. The etymological source of these two terms, as well as the material nature of the objects represented by them, cannot be established with any degree of finality. Clearly two separate objects were inserted into the breastplate and became thereby an essential part of the High-Priest's official regalia. Aaron and his successors bore over their heart "the judgment of the children of Israel," i.e., "judgment" in the sense of giving a verdict or decision. The passages in which the terms appear (Lev. 8:8; Num. 27:21; Deut. 33:8; 1 Sam 28:6; Ezra 2:63; Neh. 7:65) and those which

on's heart when he goes in before the
LORD. So Aaron shall bear the judgment of
the children of Israel over his heart before
the LORD continually.

Other Priestly Garments

31 [w]"You shall make the robe of the
ephod all of blue. 32 There shall be an
opening for his head in the middle of it; it
shall have a woven binding all around its
opening, like the opening in a coat of mail,
so that it does not tear. 33 And upon its
hem you shall make pomegranates of blue,
purple, and scarlet, all around its hem, and
bells of gold between them all around: 34 a
golden bell and a pomegranate, a golden
bell and a pomegranate, upon the hem of
the robe all around. 35 And it shall be upon
Aaron when he ministers, and its sound
will be heard when he goes into the holy
place before the LORD and when he comes
out, that he may not die.
36 [x]"You shall also make a plate of pure
gold and engrave on it, *like* the engraving
of a signet:

HOLINESS TO THE LORD.

37 And you shall put it on a blue cord, that
it may be on the turban; it shall be on the
front of the turban. 38 So it shall be on Aaron's forehead, that Aaron may [y]bear the iniquity of the holy things which the children of Israel hallow in all their [1]holy gifts;
and it shall always be on his forehead, that
they may be [z]accepted before the LORD.
39 "You shall [a]skillfully weave the tunic
of fine linen *thread,* you shall make the turban of fine linen, and you shall make the
sash of woven work.
40 [b]"For Aaron's sons you shall make tunics, and you shall make sashes for them.
And you shall make [2]hats for them, for
glory and [c]beauty. 41 So you shall put them
on Aaron your brother and on his sons
with him. You shall [d]anoint them, [e]conse-
crate them, and [3]sanctify them, that they
may minister to Me as priests. 42 And you
shall make [f]for them linen trousers to
cover their [4]nakedness; they shall [5]reach
from the waist to the thighs. 43 They shall
be on Aaron and on his sons when they
come into the tabernacle of meeting, or
when they come near [g]the altar to minister
in the holy *place,* that they [h]do not incur
[6]iniquity and die. [i]*It shall be* a statute forever to him and his descendants after him.

Aaron and His Sons Consecrated

29 "And this is what you shall do to
them to hallow them for minister-
ing to Me as priests: [a]Take one young bull
and two rams without blemish, 2 and [b]un-
leavened bread, unleavened cakes mixed
with oil, and unleavened wafers anointed
with oil (you shall make them of wheat
flour). 3 You shall put them in one basket
and bring them in the basket, with the bull
and the two rams.
4 "And Aaron and his sons you shall
bring to the door of the tabernacle of meeting, [c]and you shall wash them with water.
5 [d]Then you shall take the garments, put
the tunic on Aaron, and the robe of the
ephod, the ephod, and the breastplate, and
gird him with [e]the intricately woven band
of the ephod. 6 [f]You shall put the turban on
his head, and put the holy crown on the
turban. 7 And you shall take the anointing
[g]oil, pour *it* on his head, and anoint him.
8 Then [h]you shall bring his sons and put
tunics on them. 9 And you shall gird them
with sashes, Aaron and his sons, and put
the hats on them. [i]The priesthood shall be
theirs for a perpetual statute. So you shall
[j]consecrate Aaron and his sons.
10 "You shall also have the bull brought
before the tabernacle of meeting, and

31 [w]Ex. 39:22-26 **36** [x]Ex. 39:30, 31; Lev. 8:9; Zech. 14:20 **38** [y]Ex. 28:43; Lev. 10:17; 22:9, 16; Num. 18:1; [Is. 53:11]; Ezek. 4:4-6; [John 1:29; Heb. 9:28; 1 Pet. 2:24] [z]Lev. 1:4; 22:27; 23:11; Is. 56:7 [1]*sacred* **39** [a]Ex. 35:35; 39:27-29 **40** [b]Ex. 28:4; 39:27-29, 41; Ezek. 44:17, 18 [c]Ex. 28:2 [2]*headpieces* or *turbans*

41 [d]Ex. 29:7-9; 30:30; 40:15; Lev. 10:7 [e]Ex. 29:9; Lev. 8; Heb. 7:28 [3]*set them apart* **42** [f]Ex. 39:28; Lev. 6:10; 16:4; Ezek. 44:18 [4]*bare flesh* [5]Lit. *be* **43** [g]Ex. 20:26 [h]Lev. 5:1, 17; 20:19, 20; 22:9; Num. 9:13; 18:22 [i]Ex. 27:21; Lev. 17:7 [6]*guilt*

CHAPTER 29

1 [a]Lev. 8; [Heb. 7:26-28] **2** [b]Lev. 2:4; 6:19-23 **4** [c]Ex. 40:12; Lev. 8:6; [Heb. 10:22] **5** [d]Ex. 28:2; Lev. 8:7 [e]Ex. 28:8 **6** [f]Ex. 28:36, 37; Lev. 8:9 **7** [g]Ex. 25:6; 30:25-31; Lev. 8:12; 10:7; 21:10; Num. 35:25; Ps. 133:2 **8** [h]Ex. 28:39, 40; Lev. 8:13 **9** [i]Ex. 40:15; Num. 3:10; 18:7; 25:13; Deut. 18:5 [j]Ex. 28:41; Lev. 8

record inquiries of the Lord when a High-Priest with the ephod was present (Josh. 9:14; Judg. 1:1,2; 20:18; 1 Sam. 10:22; 23:2,4,10-12; 1 Chr. 10:14) allow for the following conclusions: 1) that these two objects represented the right of the High-Priest to request guidance for the acknowledged leader who could not approach God directly, as Moses had done, but had to come via the God-ordained priestly structure, and 2) that the revelation then received gave specific direction for an immediate problem or crisis, and went beyond what could be associated with some sort of sacred lots providing merely a wordless "yes" and "no" response.

28:31-35 robe. The priest's outer garment.

28:32 coat of mail. A flexible metal covering used by the Egyptians for protection in battle.

28:33 bells of gold. The sound of the tinkling bells sewn on the hem of the High-Priest's robe signaled those waiting outside the Holy Place that their representative ministering before the Lord was still alive and moving about, fulfilling his duties.

28:36-38 turban. The headdress carried the declaration essential to worship and priestly representation, namely the holiness of the Lord, and in so doing reminded the High-Priest and all others that their approach to God must be done with reverence.

28:39 tunic...sash. An undergarment.

28:40-43 The rest of the priests also had distinctive dress to wear, visually setting them apart from the ordinary citizen. Failure to comply with the dress regulations when serving in the sanctuary brought death. Such a severe consequence stressed the importance of their duties and should have motivated the priests not to consider their priestly role as a mundane, routine, and thankless task.

29:1-18 hallow. The ones chosen to begin the priesthood could not enter into office without Moses' conducting a solemn, 7-day investiture (vv. 4-35 and Lev. 8:1-36), involving washing, dressing, anointing, sacrificing, daubing and sprinkling with blood, and eating.

[k]Aaron and his sons shall put their hands
on the head of the bull. 11 Then you shall
kill the bull before the LORD, *by* the door of
the tabernacle of meeting. 12 You shall take
some of the blood of the bull and put *it* on
[l]the horns of the altar with your finger, and
[m]pour all the blood beside the base of the
altar. 13 And [n]you shall take all the fat that
covers the entrails, the fatty lobe *attached* to
the liver, and the two kidneys and the fat
that *is* on them, and burn *them* on the altar.
14 But [o]the flesh of the bull, with its skin
and its offal, you shall burn with fire outside the camp. It *is* a sin offering.

15 [p]"You shall also take one ram, and
Aaron and his sons shall [q]put their hands
on the head of the ram; 16 and you shall kill
the ram, and you shall take its blood and
[r]sprinkle *it* all around on the altar. 17 Then
you shall cut the ram in pieces, wash its entrails and its legs, and put *them* with its
pieces and with its head. 18 And you shall
burn the whole ram on the altar. It *is* a
[s]burnt offering to the LORD; it *is* a sweet
aroma, an offering made by fire to the
LORD.

19 [t]"You shall also take the other ram,
and Aaron and his sons shall put their
hands on the head of the ram. 20 Then you
shall kill the ram, and take some of its
blood and put *it* on the tip of the right ear
of Aaron and on the tip of the right ear of
his sons, on the thumb of their right hand
and on the big toe of their right foot, and
sprinkle the blood all around on the altar.
21 And you shall take some of the blood
that is on the altar, and some of [u]the
anointing oil, and sprinkle *it* on Aaron and
on his garments, on his sons and on the
garments of his sons with him; and [v]he
and his garments shall be hallowed, and
his sons and his sons' garments with him.

22 "Also you shall take the fat of the ram,
the fat tail, the fat that covers the entrails,
the fatty lobe *attached to* the liver, the two
kidneys and the fat on them, the right
thigh (for it *is* a ram of consecration),
23 [w]one loaf of bread, one cake *made with*
oil, and one wafer from the basket of the
unleavened bread that *is* before the LORD;
24 and you shall put all these in the hands
of Aaron and in the hands of his sons, and
you shall [x]wave them *as* a wave offering
before the LORD. 25 [y]You shall receive them
back from their hands and burn *them* on
the altar as a burnt offering, as a sweet
aroma before the LORD. It *is* an offering
made by fire to the LORD.

26 "Then you shall take [z]the breast of the
ram of Aaron's consecration and wave it *as*
a wave offering before the LORD; and it
shall be your portion. 27 And from the ram
of the consecration you shall consecrate
[a]the breast of the wave offering which is
waved, and the thigh of the heave offering
which is raised, of *that* which *is* for Aaron
and of *that* which is for his sons. 28 It shall
be from the children of Israel *for* Aaron and
his sons [b]by a statute forever. For it is a
heave offering; [c]it shall be a heave offering
from the children of Israel from the sacrifices of their peace offerings, *that is,* their
heave offering to the LORD.

29 "And the [d]holy garments of Aaron
[e]shall be his sons' after him, [f]to be anointed in them and to be consecrated in them.
30 [g]That son who becomes priest in his
place shall put them on for [h]seven days,
when he enters the tabernacle of meeting
to minister in the [1]holy *place.*

31 "And you shall take the ram of the
consecration and [i]boil its flesh in the holy
place. 32 Then Aaron and his sons shall eat
the flesh of the ram, and the [j]bread that *is*
in the basket, *by* the door of the tabernacle
of meeting. 33 [k]They shall eat those things
with which the atonement was made, to
consecrate *and* to sanctify them; [l]but an
outsider shall not eat *them,* because they
are holy. 34 And if any of the flesh of the
consecration offerings, or of the bread, remains until the morning, then [m]you shall
burn the remainder with fire. It shall not be
eaten, because it *is* holy.

35 "Thus you shall do to Aaron and his
sons, according to all that I have commanded you. [n]Seven days you shall consecrate them. 36 And you [o]shall offer a bull
every day *as* a sin offering for atonement.
[p]You shall cleanse the altar when you
make atonement for it, and you shall
anoint it to sanctify it. 37 Seven days you
shall make atonement for the altar and
sanctify it. And the altar shall be most holy.
[q]Whatever touches the altar must be holy.

The Daily Offerings

38 "Now this *is* what you shall offer on
the altar: [r]two lambs of the first year, [s]day
by day continually. 39 One lamb you shall
offer [t]in the morning, and the other lamb
you shall offer [2]at twilight. 40 With the one
lamb shall be one-tenth *of an ephah* of flour

10 [k]Lev. 1:4; 8:14
12 [l]Lev. 8:15 [m]Ex. 27:2; 30:2; Lev. 4:7
13 [n]Lev. 1:8; 3:3, 4
14 [o]Lev. 4:11, 12, 21; Heb. 13:11
15 [p]Lev. 8:18 [q]Lev. 1:4-9
16 [r]Ex. 24:6; Lev. 1:5, 11
18 [s]Ex. 20:24
19 [t]Lev. 8:22
21 [u]Ex. 30:25, 31; Lev. 8:30 [v]Ex. 28:41; 29:1; [Heb. 9:22]
23 [w]Lev. 8:26
24 [x]Lev. 7:30; 10:14
25 [y]Lev. 8:28
26 [z]Lev. 7:31, 34; 8:29
27 [a]Lev. 7:31, 34; Num. 18:11, 18; Deut. 18:3
28 [b]Lev. 10:15 [c]Lev. 3:1; 7:34
29 [d]Ex. 28:2 [e]Num. 20:26, 28 [f]Ex. 28:41; 30:30; Num. 18:8
30 [g]Num. 20:28 [h]Lev. 8:35 [1]*sanctuary*
31 [i]Lev. 8:31
32 [j]Matt. 12:4
33 [k]Lev. 10:14, 15, 17 [l]Ex. 12:43; Lev. 22:10
34 [m]Ex. 12:10; 23:18; 34:25; Lev. 7:18; 8:32
35 [n]Lev. 8:33-35
36 [o]Heb. 10:11 [p]Ex. 30:26-29; 40:10, 11
37 [q]Num. 4:15; Hag. 2:11-13; Matt. 23:19
38 [r]Num. 28:3-31; 29:6-38; 1 Chr. 16:40; Ezra 3:3 [s]Dan. 12:11
39 [t]Ezek. 46:13-15 [2]Lit. *between the two evenings*

29:19,20 Daubing blood on the right ear, hand, and big toe symbolically sanctified the ear to hear the Word of God, the hand to do the work of God, and the foot to walk in the way of God.

29:27,28 wave offering...heave offering. *See note on Lev. 7:30.*

29:40 *ephah*...hin. Four to six gallons and six to eight pints respectively.

mixed with one-fourth of a hin of pressed
oil, and one-fourth of a hin of wine *as* a
drink offering. 41 And the other lamb you
shall [u]offer [3]at twilight; and you shall offer
with it the grain offering and the drink offering, as in the morning, for a sweet
aroma, an offering made by fire to the
LORD. 42 *This shall be* [v]a continual burnt offering throughout your generations *at* the
door of the tabernacle of meeting before
the LORD, [w]where I will meet you to speak
with you. 43 And there I will meet with the
children of Israel, and *the tabernacle* [x]shall
be sanctified by My glory. 44 So I will consecrate the tabernacle of meeting and the
altar. I will also [y]consecrate both Aaron
and his sons to minister to Me as priests.
45 [z]I will dwell among the children of Israel and will [a]be their God. 46 And they
shall know that [b]I *am* the LORD their God,
who [c]brought them up out of the land of
Egypt, that I may dwell among them. I *am*
the LORD their God.

The Altar of Incense

30 "You shall make [a]an altar to burn incense on; you shall make it of acacia
wood. 2 A cubit *shall be* its length and a cubit
its width—it shall be square—and two cubits *shall be* its height. Its horns *shall be* of
one piece with it. 3 And you shall overlay its
top, its sides all around, and its horns with
pure gold; and you shall make for it a
[1]molding of gold all around. 4 Two gold
rings you shall make for it, under the molding on both its sides. You shall place *them* on
its two sides, and they will be holders for
the poles with which to bear it. 5 You shall
make the poles of acacia wood, and overlay
them with gold. 6 And you shall put it before the [b]veil that *is* before the ark of the Testimony, before the [c]mercy seat that *is* over
the Testimony, where I will meet with you.
7 "Aaron shall burn on it [d]sweet incense
every morning; when [e]he tends the lamps,
he shall burn incense on it. 8 And when
Aaron lights the lamps [2]at twilight, he
shall burn incense on it, a perpetual incense before the LORD throughout your
generations. 9 You shall not offer [f]strange
incense on it, or a burnt offering, or a grain
offering; nor shall you pour a drink offering on it. 10 And [g]Aaron shall make atonement upon its horns once a year with the
blood of the sin offering of atonement;
once a year he shall make atonement upon
it throughout your generations. It *is* most
holy to the LORD."

The Ransom Money

11 Then the LORD spoke to Moses, saying:
12 [h]"When you take the census of the children of Israel for their number, then every
man shall give [i]a [3]ransom for himself to the
LORD, when you number them, that there
may be no [j]plague among them when *you*
number them. 13 [k]This is what everyone
among those who are numbered shall give:
half a shekel according to the shekel of the
sanctuary [l](a shekel *is* twenty gerahs).
[m]The half-shekel *shall be* an offering to the
LORD. 14 Everyone included among those
who are numbered, from twenty years old
and above, shall give an [4]offering to the
LORD. 15 The [n]rich shall not give more and
the poor shall not give less than half a
shekel, when *you* give an offering to the
LORD, to make atonement for yourselves.
16 And you shall take the atonement
money of the children of Israel, and [o]shall
[5]appoint it for the service of the tabernacle
of meeting, that it may be [p]a memorial for
the children of Israel before the LORD, to
make atonement for yourselves."

The Bronze Laver

17 Then the LORD spoke to Moses, saying:
18 [q]"You shall also make a [6]laver of bronze,

41 [u] 1 Kin. 18:29, 36; 2 Kin. 16:15; Ezra 9:4, 5; Ps. 141:2 [3] Lit. *between the two evenings*
42 [v] Ex. 30:8 [w] Ex. 25:22; 33:7, 9; Num. 17:4
43 [x] Ex. 40:34; 1 Kin. 8:11; 2 Chr. 5:14; Ezek. 43:5; Hag. 2:7, 9
44 [y] Lev. 21:15
45 [z] Ex. 25:8; Lev. 26:12; Num. 5:3; Deut. 12:11; Zech. 2:10; [John 14:17, 23; Rev. 21:3] [a] Gen. 17:8; Lev. 11:45
46 [b] Ex. 16:12; 20:2; Deut. 4:35 [c] Lev. 11:45

CHAPTER 30

1 [a] Ex. 37:25-29
3 [1] *border*
6 [b] Ex. 26:31-35 [c] Ex. 25:21, 22
7 [d] Ex. 30:34; 1 Sam. 2:28; 1 Chr. 23:13; Luke 1:9 [e] Ex. 27:20, 21
8 [2] Lit. *between the two evenings*
9 [f] Lev. 10:1
10 [g] Lev. 16:3-34
12 [h] Ex. 38:25, 26; Num. 1:2; 26:2; 2 Sam. 24:2 [i] Num. 31:50; [Matt. 20:28; 1 Pet. 1:18, 19] [j] 2 Sam. 24:15 [3] *the price of a life*
13 [k] Matt. 17:24 [l] Lev. 27:25; Num. 3:47; Ezek. 45:12 [m] Ex. 38:26
14 [4] *contribution*
15 [n] Job 34:19; Prov. 22:2; [Eph. 6:9]
16 [o] Ex. 38:25-31 [p] Num. 16:40 [5] *give*
18 [q] Ex. 38:8; 1 Kin. 7:38 [6] *basin*

29:42 throughout your generations. Perhaps this phrase intends a prophetic reminder or confirmation of a long history for Israel.

29:45 I will dwell. That He would be their God and they would be His people was one thing, but that He would also dwell or tabernacle with them was a very important reality in the experience of the new nation. They were to understand not only the transcendence of their God, whose dwelling place was in the heaven of heavens, but also the immanence of their God, whose dwelling place was with them. Their redemption from Egypt was for this purpose (v. 46).

30:1-10 altar...incense. The design for this piece of furniture for the Holy Place was not given with the other two (25:23-40) but follows the instructions about the priesthood perhaps because it was the last piece to which the High-Priest came before he entered the Holy of Holies once a year. Right after Aaron's consecration ceremony had been noted, his duties of 1) ensuring proper incense was offered continually upon this altar and that 2) he was also once a year to cleanse it with blood from the atonement offering (v. 10) received attention.

30:6 before the veil. This places the altar outside of the "Holy of Holies" in the Holy Place. Heb. 9:3,4 speaks of the altar in the "Holy of Holies" in the sense of its proximity to the ark and in relation to its cleansing on the Day of Atonement. The priests could not go beyond it on any other day.

30:9 strange incense. See v. 38.

30:12 census. The reason for the numbering of all males of military age (v. 14) was not stated, but its seriousness surfaces in the dire warning given about a plague and the use of the term "ransom" in connection with it (cf. 1 Chr. 21).

30:13 shekel of the sanctuary. A shekel weighed about .4 oz. (cf. Lev. 5:15; 27:3,25; Num. 3:47; 7:13ff.).

30:18-21 laver of bronze. The washing of hands and feet was mandatory before engaging in priestly duties. Again, the seriousness

with its base also of bronze, for washing.
You shall [r]put it between the tabernacle of
meeting and the altar. And you shall put
water in it, 19 for Aaron and his sons [s]shall
wash their hands and their feet in water
from it. 20 When they go into the tabernacle
of meeting, or when they come near the
altar to minister, to burn an offering made
by fire to the LORD, they shall wash with
water, lest they die. 21 So they shall wash
their hands and their feet, lest they die.
And [t]it shall be a [7]statute forever to them—
to him and his descendants throughout
their generations."

The Holy Anointing Oil

22 Moreover the LORD spoke to Moses,
saying: 23 "Also take for yourself [u]quality
spices—five hundred *shekels* of liquid
[v]myrrh, half as much sweet-smelling cinnamon (two hundred and fifty *shekels*), two
hundred and fifty *shekels* of sweet-smelling
[w]cane, 24 five hundred *shekels* of [x]cassia,
according to the shekel of the sanctuary,
and a [y]hin of olive oil. 25 And you shall
make from these a holy anointing oil, an
ointment compounded according to the art
of the perfumer. It shall be [z]a holy anointing oil. 26 [a]With it you shall anoint the
tabernacle of meeting and the ark of the
Testimony; 27 the table and all its utensils,
the lampstand and its utensils, and the
altar of incense; 28 the altar of burnt offering with all its utensils, and the laver and
its base. 29 You shall consecrate them, that
they may be most holy; [b]whatever touches
them must be holy. 30 [c]And you shall
anoint Aaron and his sons, and consecrate
them, that *they* may minister to Me as
priests.
31 "And you shall speak to the children
of Israel, saying: 'This shall be a holy
anointing oil to Me throughout your generations. 32 It shall not be poured on man's
flesh; nor shall you make *any other* like it,
according to its composition. [d]It *is* holy,
and it shall be holy to you. 33 [e]Whoever
[8]compounds *any* like it, or whoever puts
any of it on an outsider, [f]shall be [9]cut off
from his people.' "

18 [r] Ex. 40:30
19 [s] Ex. 40:31, 32; Ps. 26:6; Is. 52:11; John 13:8, 10; Heb. 10:22
21 [t] Ex. 28:43 [7] *requirement*
23 [u] Song 4:14; Ezek. 27:22 [v] Ps. 45:8; Prov. 7:17 [w] Song 4:14; Jer. 6:20
24 [x] Ps. 45:8 [y] Ex. 29:40
25 [z] Ex. 37:29; 40:9; Lev. 8:10; Num. 35:25; Ps. 89:20; 133:2
26 [a] Ex. 40:9; Lev. 8:10; Num. 7:1
29 [b] Ex. 29:37; Num. 4:15; Hag. 2:11-13
30 [c] Ex. 29:7; Lev. 8:12
32 [d] Ex. 30:25, 37
33 [e] Ex. 30:38 [f] Gen. 17:14; Ex. 12:15; Lev. 7:20, 21 [8] *mixes* [9] Put to death

34 [g] Ex. 25:6; 37:29
35 [h] Ex. 30:25
36 [i] Ex. 29:42; Lev. 16:2 [j] [Ex. 29:37; 30:32]; Lev. 2:3
37 [k] Ex. 30:32 [1] Lit. *proportion*
38 [l] Ex. 30:33

CHAPTER 31

2 [a] Ex. 35:30–36:1 [b] 1 Chr. 2:20
3 [c] Ex. 28:3; 35:31; 1 Kin. 7:14; Eph. 1:17
6 [d] Ex. 35:34 [e] Ex. 28:3; 35:10, 35; 36:1
7 [f] Ex. 36:8 [g] Ex. 37:1-5 [h] Ex. 37:6-9
8 [i] Ex. 37:10-16 [j] Ex. 37:17-24; Lev. 24:4
9 [k] Ex. 38:1-7 [l] Ex. 38:8
10 [m] Ex. 39:1, 41 [1] Or *woven garments*
11 [n] Ex. 30:23-33 [o] Ex. 30:34-38

The Incense

34 And the LORD said to Moses: [g]"Take
sweet spices, stacte and onycha and gal-
banum, and pure frankincense with *these*
sweet spices; there shall be equal amounts
of each. 35 You shall make of these an incense, a compound [h]according to the art of
the perfumer, salted, pure, *and* holy. 36 And
you shall beat *some* of it very fine, and put
some of it before the Testimony in the
tabernacle of meeting [i]where I will meet
with you. [j]It shall be most holy to you.
37 But *as for* the incense which you shall
make, [k]you shall not make any for yourselves, according to its [1]composition. It
shall be to you holy for the LORD. 38 [l]Who-
ever makes *any* like it, to smell it, he shall
be cut off from his people."

Artisans for Building the Tabernacle

31 Then the LORD spoke to Moses, saying: 2 [a]"See, I have called by name
Bezalel the [b]son of Uri, the son of Hur, of
the tribe of Judah. 3 And I have [c]filled him
with the Spirit of God, in wisdom, in understanding, in knowledge, and in all *manner of* workmanship, 4 to design artistic
works, to work in gold, in silver, in bronze,
5 in cutting jewels for setting, in carving
wood, and to work in all *manner of* workmanship.
6 "And I, indeed I, have appointed with
him [d]Aholiab the son of Ahisamach, of the
tribe of Dan; and I have put wisdom in the
hearts of all the [e]gifted artisans, that they
may make all that I have commanded you:
7 [f]the tabernacle of meeting, [g]the ark of the
Testimony and [h]the mercy seat that *is* on it,
and all the furniture of the tabernacle—
8 [i]the table and its utensils, [j]the pure *gold*
lampstand with all its utensils, the altar of
incense, 9 [k]the altar of burnt offering with
all its utensils, and [l]the laver and its base—
10 [m]the [1]garments of ministry, the holy
garments for Aaron the priest and the garments of his sons, to minister as priests,
11 [n]and the anointing oil and [o]sweet incense for the holy *place*. According to all
that I have commanded you they shall do."

of being ceremonially purified is seen in the warning of death if this washing is neglected. Nothing casual was being done in the sanctuary or out in the courtyard!

30:22-33 Nothing was left to chance or to human ingenuity. The ingredients for making the anointing oil were carefully spelled out. Anything different was totally unacceptable and brought with it the penalty of death (v. 33). This was to be a unique blend! Using it for any other purpose also erased its holy status as set apart for use in the tabernacle and made it no different from the ordinary and the mundane.

30:25,35 art of the perfumer. The skill of the perfumer was obviously already well known in Israel, a trade which they undoubtedly observed in Egypt.

30:34-38 incense. God also listed the ingredients for the unique blend of incense prescribed for use at the altar of incense. Making anything different would have been to make "strange incense" (v. 9) and would also result in death (v. 38). Personal use rendered its holy status null and void. Nadab and Abihu were executed for violating this command (cf. Lev. 10:1,2).

31:1-11 God identified two men by name as specially chosen and divinely endued with ability, or Spirit-filled, to make all He had revealed to Moses (cf. 28:3; 36:1). None of the craftsmen were left un-

The Sabbath Law

12 And the LORD spoke to Moses, saying,
13 "Speak also to the children of Israel, saying: [p]'Surely My Sabbaths you shall keep,
for it *is* a sign between Me and you
throughout your generations, that *you* may
know that I *am* the LORD who [q]sanctifies[2]
you. 14 [r]You shall keep the Sabbath, therefore, for *it is* holy to you. Everyone who
[3]profanes it shall surely be put to death;
for [s]whoever does *any* work on it, that person shall be cut off from among his people.
15 Work shall be done for [t]six days, but the
[u]seventh *is* the Sabbath of rest, holy to the
LORD. Whoever does *any* work on the Sabbath day, he shall surely be put to death.
16 Therefore the children of Israel shall
keep the Sabbath, to observe the Sabbath
throughout their generations *as* a perpetual covenant. 17 It *is* [v]a sign between Me and
the children of Israel forever; for [w]*in* six
days the LORD made the heavens and the
earth, and on the seventh day He rested
and was refreshed.'"
18 And when He had made an end of
speaking with him on Mount Sinai, He
gave Moses [x]two tablets of the Testimony,
tablets of stone, written with the finger of
God.

The Gold Calf

32 Now when the people saw that Moses [a]delayed coming down from the
mountain, the people [b]gathered together
to Aaron, and said to him, [c]"Come, make
us [1]gods that shall [d]go before us; for *as for*
this Moses, the man who [e]brought us up
out of the land of Egypt, we do not know
what has become of him."
2 And Aaron said to them, "Break off the
[f]golden earrings which *are* in the ears of
your wives, your sons, and your daughters, and bring *them* to me." 3 So all the
people broke off the golden earrings which
were in their ears, and brought *them* to
Aaron. 4 [g]And he received *the gold* from
their hand, and he fashioned it with an engraving tool, and made a molded calf.
Then they said, "This *is* your god, O Israel, that [h]brought you out of the land of
Egypt!"
5 So when Aaron saw *it,* he built an altar
before it. And Aaron made a [i]proclamation
and said, "Tomorrow *is* a feast to the
LORD." 6 Then they rose early on the next
day, offered burnt offerings, and brought
peace offerings; and the people [j]sat down
to eat and drink, and rose up to play.
7 And the LORD said to Moses, [k]"Go, get
down! For your people whom you brought
out of the land of Egypt [l]have corrupted
themselves. 8 They have turned aside quickly out of the way which [m]I commanded
them. They have made themselves a molded calf, and worshiped it and sacrificed to
it, and said, [n]'This *is* your god, O Israel,
that brought you out of the land of
Egypt!' " 9 And the LORD said to Moses, [o]"I
have seen this people, and indeed it *is* a
[2]stiff-necked people! 10 Now therefore, [p]let
Me alone, that [q]My wrath may burn hot
against them and I may [3]consume them.
And [r]I will make of you a great nation."
11 [s]Then Moses pleaded with [4]the LORD
his God, and said: "LORD, why does Your
wrath burn hot against Your people whom
You have brought out of the land of Egypt
with great power and with a mighty hand?
12 [t]Why should the Egyptians speak, and
say, 'He brought them out to harm them, to

13 [p]Ex. 31:17; Lev. 19:3, 30; 26:2; Ezek. 20:12, 20 [q]Lev. 20:8 [2]*consecrates*
14 [r]Ex. 20:8; Deut. 5:12 [s]Ex. 31:15; 35:2; Num. 15:32-36; John 7:23 [3]*defiles*
15 [t]Ex. 20:9-11; Lev. 23:3; Deut. 5:12-14 [u]Gen. 2:2; Ex. 16:23; 20:8; 35:2
17 [v]Ex. 31:13; Ezek. 20:12 [w]Gen. 1:31; 2:2, 3; Ex. 20:11
18 [x][Ex. 24:12; 32:15, 16; Deut. 4:13; 5:22; 2 Cor. 3:3]

CHAPTER 32

1 [a]Ex. 24:18; Deut. 9:9-12 [b]Ex. 17:1-3 [c]Acts 7:40 [d]Ex. 13:21 [e]Ex. 32:8 [1]Or *a god*
2 [f]Ex. 11:2; 35:22; Judg. 8:24-27
4 [g]Ex. 20:3, 4, 23; Deut. 9:16; Judg. 17:3, 4; 1 Kin. 12:28; Neh. 9:18; Ps. 106:19; Acts 7:41 [h]Ex. 29:45, 46
5 [i]Lev. 23:2, 4, 21, 37; 2 Kin. 10:20; 2 Chr. 30:5
6 [j]Ex. 32:17-19; Num. 25:2; 1 Cor. 10:7
7 [k]Deut. 9:8-21; Dan. 9:14 [l]Gen. 6:11, 12
8 [m]Ex. 20:3, 4, 23; Deut. 32:17 [n]1 Kin. 12:28
9 [o]Ex. 33:3, 5; 34:9; Deut. 9:6; 2 Chr. 30:8; Is. 48:4; [Acts 7:51] [2]*stubborn*
10 [p]Deut. 9:14, 19 [q]Ex. 22:24 [r]Num. 14:12 [3]*destroy*
11 [s]Deut. 9:18, 26-29 [4]Lit. *the face of the LORD*
12 [t]Num. 14:13-19; Deut. 9:28; Josh. 7:9

touched by divinely bestowed understanding in the intricacy of their work. They were called "gifted artisans," suggesting previously developed skill. They were to make all that is prescribed in Ex. 25–30.

31:12-17 *See note on 20:8.*

31:18 two tablets of the Testimony. *See note on 25:16.* **written with the finger of God.** A figurative way of attributing the law to God.

32:1 make us gods. Such was the influence of the polytheistic world in which they lived that the Israelites, in a time of panic or impatience, succumbed to a pagan world view. What made it even more alarming was the rapidity with which pagan idolatry swept in despite recent real-life demonstrations of God's greatness and goodness toward them. But they weren't just requesting gods, but gods to lead them forward—"that shall go before us." The pagan world view had robbed them of seeing God as having led them out of Egypt and instead they scornfully attributed the Exodus to Moses (cf. Acts. 7:40).

32:4 a molded calf. The young bull, which Aaron caused to be fashioned, was a pagan religious symbol of virile power. A miniature form of the golden calf, although made of bronze and silver, was found at the site of the ancient Philistine city of Ashkelon. Since it dates to about 1550 B.C. it indicates that calf worship was known not only in Egypt, but also in Canaan prior to the time of Moses. In worshiping the calf, the Israelites violated the first 3 commandments (20:3-7).

32:5 feast to the LORD. Syncretism brought about the ludicrous combination of an idol, an altar, and a festal celebration held in a bizarre attempt to honor the true God.

32:6 rose up to play. The Heb. word allows for the inclusion of drunken and immoral activities so common to idolatrous fertility cults in their revelry (see the description in vv. 7,25). Syncretism had robbed the people of all ethical alertness and moral discernment (cf. 1 Cor. 10:7).

32:7 your people. In alerting Moses to the trouble in the camp, God designated Israel as Moses' people, a change of possessive pronoun Moses could not have missed. Beforehand God had acknowledged them as "My people." In pleading with God for Israel and in responding to God's offer to make of him a great nation (v. 10), Moses maintained what he knew to be true, given the Exodus and the divine promises to the patriarchs (vv. 12,13), and designated them correctly as "Your people" (v. 11).

32:10 make of you a great nation. God could have consumed all the people and started over again with Moses, just like he had earlier with Abraham (Gen. 12).

kill them in the mountains, and to consume them from the face of the earth'? Turn from Your fierce wrath, and [u]relent from this harm to Your people. 13 Remember Abraham, Isaac, and Israel, Your servants, to whom You [v]swore by Your own self, and said to them, [w]'I will multiply your descendants as the stars of heaven; and all this land that I have spoken of I give to your descendants, and they shall inherit *it* forever.' " 14 So the LORD [x]relented from the harm which He said He would do to His people.

15 And [y]Moses turned and went down from the mountain, and the two tablets of the Testimony *were* in his hand. The tablets *were* written on both sides; on the one *side* and on the other they were written. 16 Now the [z]tablets *were* the work of God, and the writing *was* the writing of God engraved on the tablets.

17 And when Joshua heard the noise of the people as they shouted, he said to Moses, "*There is* a noise of war in the camp."

18 But he said:

"*It is* not the noise of the shout of victory,
Nor the noise of the cry of defeat,
But the sound of singing I hear."

19 So it was, as soon as he came near the camp, that [a]he saw the calf *and* the dancing. So Moses' anger became hot, and he cast the tablets out of his hands and broke them at the foot of the mountain. 20 [b]Then he took the calf which they had made, burned *it* in the fire, and ground *it* to powder; and he scattered *it* on the water and made the children of Israel drink *it.* 21 And Moses said to Aaron, [c]"What did this people do to you that you have brought *so* great a sin upon them?"

22 So Aaron said, "Do not let the anger of my lord become hot. [d]You know the people, that they *are set* on evil. 23 For they said to me, 'Make us gods that shall go before us; *as for* this Moses, the man who brought us out of the land of Egypt, we do not know what has become of him.' 24 And I said to them, 'Whoever has any gold, let them break *it* off.' So they gave *it* to me, and I cast it into the fire, and this calf came out."

25 Now when Moses saw that the people *were* [e]unrestrained (for Aaron [f]had not restrained them, to *their* shame among their enemies), 26 then Moses stood in the entrance of the camp, and said, "Whoever *is* on the LORD's side—*come* to me!" And all the sons of Levi gathered themselves together to him. 27 And he said to them, "Thus says the LORD God of Israel: 'Let every man put his sword on his side, and go in and out from entrance to entrance throughout the camp, and [g]let every man kill his brother, every man his companion, and every man his neighbor.' " 28 So the sons of Levi did according to the word of Moses. And about three thousand men of the people fell that day. 29 [h]Then Moses said, [5]"Consecrate yourselves today to the LORD, that He may bestow on you a blessing this day, for every man has opposed his son and his brother."

30 Now it came to pass on the next day that Moses said to the people, [i]"You have committed a great sin. So now I will go up to the LORD; [j]perhaps I can [k]make atonement for your sin." 31 Then Moses [l]returned to the LORD and said, "Oh, these people have committed a great sin, and have [m]made for themselves a god of gold! 32 Yet now, if You will forgive their sin—but if not, I pray, [n]blot me [o]out of Your book which You have written."

12 [u]Ex. 32:14
13 [v]Gen. 22:16-18; [Heb. 6:13] [w]Gen. 12:7; 13:15; 15:7, 18; 22:17; 26:4; 35:11, 12; Ex. 13:5, 11; 33:1
14 [x]2 Sam. 24:16
15 [y]Deut. 9:15
16 [z]Ex. 31:18
19 [a]Deut. 9:16, 17
20 [b]Num. 5:17, 24; Deut. 9:21
21 [c]Gen. 26:10
22 [d]Ex. 14:11; Deut. 9:24
25 [e]Ex. 33:4, 5 [f]2 Chr. 28:19
27 [g]Num. 25:5-13
29 [h]Ex. 28:41; 1 Sam. 15:18, 22; Prov. 21:3; Zech. 13:3 [5]Lit. *Fill your hand*
30 [i]1 Sam. 12:20, 23 [j]2 Sam. 16:12 [k]Num. 25:13
31 [l]Deut. 9:18 [m]Ex. 20:23
32 [n]Ps. 69:28; Is. 4:3; Mal. 3:16; Rom. 9:3 [o]Dan. 12:1; Phil. 4:3; Rev. 3:5; 21:27

32:13 Israel. Another name for Jacob, which means "one who strives with God" (cf. Gen. 32:28).

32:14 the LORD relented from the harm. Moses' appeal for God to change His mind, to relent, succeeded because God had only threatened judgment, not decreed it. A divine intention is not an unchangeable divine decree. Decrees or sworn declarations (cf. Gen. 22:16-18; Ps. 110:4) or categorical statements of not changing or relenting (cf. Jer. 4:28; Ezek. 24:14; Zech. 8:14,15) are unconditional and bind the speaker to the stated course of action regardless of the circumstances or reactions of the listeners. Intentions retain a conditional element and do not necessarily bind the speaker to a stated course of action (cf. Jer. 15:6; 18:8-10; 26:3,13,19; Joel 2:13; Jon. 3:9,10; 4:2).

32:19 broke them. Moses pictured the nation breaking God's commandments by actually breaking the tablets on which they were written.

32:22-24 Aaron, held responsible by Moses for what had taken place in the camp (vv. 21,25), endeavored to avoid responsibility for the people's actions by shifting the blame to their propensity to do evil, and also for the presence of the golden calf by ridiculously representing it as having just popped out of the fire all by itself!

32:23 See Acts. 7:40.

32:26 Whoever *is* on the LORD's side. Only the tribe of Levi responded to the call to take action in response to this situation which demanded judgment be inflicted. They had understood that neutrality could not exist in the open confrontation between good and evil. Family and national ties were superseded by submission to the Lord to do His will, which in this situation was to wield the sword of God's judgment to preserve His honor and glory.

32:28 They apparently killed those who persisted in idolatry and immorality (cf. Num. 25:6-9).

32:32 blot me out of Your book. Nothing more strongly marked the love of Moses for his people than his sincere willingness to offer up his own life rather than see them disinherited and destroyed. The book to which Moses referred, the psalmist entitled "the book of the living" (Ps. 69:28). Untimely or premature death would constitute

33 And the LORD said to Moses, [p]"Whoever has sinned against Me, I will [q]blot
him out of My book. 34 Now therefore, go,
lead the people to *the place* of which I have
[r]spoken to you. [s]Behold, My Angel shall
go before you. Nevertheless, [t]in the day
when I [u]visit for punishment, I will visit
punishment upon them for their sin."
35 So the LORD plagued the people because of [v]what they did with the calf
which Aaron made.

The Command to Leave Sinai

33 Then the LORD said to Moses, "Depart *and* go up from here, you [a]and
the people whom you have brought out of
the land of Egypt, to the land of which I
swore to Abraham, Isaac, and Jacob, saying, [b]'To your descendants I will give it.'
2 [c]And I will send *My* Angel before you,
[d]and I will drive out the Canaanite and the
Amorite and the Hittite and the Perizzite
and the Hivite and the Jebusite. 3 *Go up* [e]to
a land flowing with milk and honey; for I
will not go up in your midst, lest [f]I [1]con-
sume you on the way, for you *are* a [g]stiff-
necked[2] people."
4 And when the people heard this bad
news, [h]they mourned, [i]and no one put on
his ornaments. 5 For the LORD had said to
Moses, "Say to the children of Israel, 'You
are a stiff-necked people. I could come up
into your midst in one moment and consume you. Now therefore, take off your
[3]ornaments, that I may [j]know what to do
to you.'" 6 So the children of Israel
stripped themselves of their ornaments by
Mount Horeb.

Moses Meets with the LORD

7 Moses took his tent and pitched it outside the camp, far from the camp, and
[k]called it the tabernacle of meeting. And it
came to pass *that* everyone who [l]sought
the LORD went out to the tabernacle of
meeting which *was* outside the camp. 8 So

33 [p] Lev. 23:30; [Ezek. 18:4; 33:2, 14, 15] [q] Ex. 17:14; Deut. 29:20; Ps. 9:5; Rev. 3:5; 21:27
34 [r] Ex. 3:17 [s] Ex. 23:20; Josh. 5:14 [t] Deut. 32:35; Rom. 2:5, 6 [u] Ps. 89:32
35 [v] Neh. 9:18

CHAPTER 33

1 [a] Ex. 32:1, 7, 13; Josh. 3:17 [b] Gen. 12:7
2 [c] Ex. 32:34; Josh. 5:14 [d] Ex. 23:27-31; Josh. 24:11
3 [e] Ex. 3:8 [f] Num. 16:21, 45 [g] Ex. 32:9; 33:5 [1] *destroy* [2] *stubborn*
4 [h] Num. 14:1, 39 [i] Ezra 9:3; Esth. 4:1, 4; Ezek. 24:17, 23
5 [j] [Ps. 139:23] [3] *jewelry*
7 [k] Ex. 29:42, 43 [l] Deut. 4:29
8 [m] Num. 16:27
9 [n] Ex. 25:22; 31:18; Ps. 99:7
10 [o] Ex. 4:31
11 [p] Num. 12:8; Deut. 34:10 [q] Ex. 24:13
12 [r] Ex. 3:10; 32:34 [s] Ex. 33:17; John 10:14, 15; 2 Tim. 2:19
13 [t] Ex. 34:9 [u] Ps. 25:4; 27:11; 86:11; 119:33 [v] Ex. 3:7, 10; 5:1; 32:12, 14; Deut. 9:26, 29
14 [w] Ex. 3:12; Deut. 4:37; Is. 63:9 [x] Deut. 12:10; 25:19; Josh. 21:44; 22:4
15 [y] Ex. 33:3
16 [z] Num. 14:14 [a] Ex. 34:10; Deut. 4:7, 34
17 [b] [James 5:16]
18 [c] Ex. 24:16, 17; [1 Tim. 6:16]

it was, whenever Moses went out to the
tabernacle, *that* all the people rose, and
each man stood [m]*at* his tent door and
watched Moses until he had gone into the
tabernacle. 9 And it came to pass, when
Moses entered the tabernacle, that the pillar of cloud descended and stood *at* the
door of the tabernacle, and *the* LORD
[n]talked with Moses. 10 All the people saw
the pillar of cloud standing *at* the tabernacle door, and all the people rose and [o]wor-
shiped, each man *in* his tent door. 11 So
[p]the LORD spoke to Moses face to face, as a
man speaks to his friend. And he would return to the camp, but [q]his servant Joshua
the son of Nun, a young man, did not depart from the tabernacle.

The Promise of God's Presence

12 Then Moses said to the LORD, "See,
[r]You say to me, 'Bring up this people.' But
You have not let me know whom You will
send with me. Yet You have said, [s]'I know
you by name, and you have also found
grace in My sight.' 13 Now therefore, I
pray, [t]if I have found grace in Your sight,
[u]show me now Your way, that I may know
You and that I may find grace in Your
sight. And consider that this nation *is*
[v]Your people."
14 And He said, [w]"My Presence will go
with you, and I will give you [x]rest."
15 Then he said to Him, [y]"If Your Presence does not go *with us,* do not bring us
up from here. 16 For how then will it be
known that Your people and I have found
grace in Your sight, [z]except You go with
us? So we [a]shall be separate, Your people
and I, from all the people who *are* upon the
face of the earth."
17 So the LORD said to Moses, [b]"I will
also do this thing that you have spoken; for
you have found grace in My sight, and I
know you by name."
18 And he said, "Please, show me [c]Your
glory."

being blotted out of the book. The Apostle Paul displayed a similar passionate devotion for his kinsmen (Rom. 9:1-3).

33:2-6 Good news included bad news! Entry into the Promised Land was not forfeited, but God's presence on the way was withdrawn. What was a sworn covenant-promise to the patriarchs just could not be broken: what was assured—the divine presence on the way—could be set aside because of sin (cf. 23:20-23). Removal of their jewelry depicted outwardly the people's sorrow of heart. It was a response analogous to donning sackcloth and ashes.

33:2 *See notes on 3:8.*

33:7 the tabernacle of meeting. In the time prior to the construction of the tabernacle, Moses' tent became the special meeting place for Moses to talk intimately, "face to face" (v. 11), with God. No doubt the people watching from afar were reminded of the removal of God's immediate presence.

33:12-17 Again Moses entered earnestly and confidently into the role of intercessor before God for the nation whom he again referred to as "Your people" (vv. 13,16). Moses clearly understood that without God's presence they would not be a people set apart from other nations, so why travel any further? Moses' favored standing before the Lord comes out in the positive response to his intercession (v. 17).

33:18-23 Cautionary measures were needed for God to respond only in part to Moses' request to see more of Him than he was already experiencing (cf. Num. 12:8)—otherwise he would die. Notwithstanding God's being gracious and compassionate to whomever He chose, Moses could not see God's face and live. Whatever he saw of God's nature transformed into blazing light is referred to as "God's back" and was never subsequently described by Moses (cf. John 1:18; 1 John 4:12).

19 Then He said, "I will make all My
[d]goodness pass before you, and I will proclaim the name of the LORD before you. [e]I
will be gracious to whom I will be [f]gra-
cious, and I will have compassion on
whom I will have compassion." 20 But He
said, "You cannot see My face; for [g]no man
shall see Me, and live." 21 And the LORD
said, "Here is a place by Me, and you shall
stand on the rock. 22 So it shall be, while
My glory passes by, that I will put you [h]in
the cleft of the rock, and will [i]cover you
with My hand while I pass by. 23 Then I
will take away My hand, and you shall see
My back; but My face shall [j]not be seen."

Moses Makes New Tablets

34 And the LORD said to Moses, [a]"Cut
two tablets of stone like the first
ones, and [b]I will write on *these* tablets the
words that were on the first tablets which
you broke. 2 So be ready in the morning,
and come up in the morning to Mount Sinai, and present yourself to Me there [c]on
the top of the mountain. 3 And no man
shall [d]come up with you, and let no man
be seen throughout all the mountain; let
neither flocks nor herds feed before that
mountain."
4 So he cut two tablets of stone like the
first *ones.* Then Moses rose early in the
morning and went up Mount Sinai, as the
LORD had commanded him; and he took in
his hand the two tablets of stone.
5 Now the LORD descended in the [e]cloud
and stood with him there, and [f]proclaimed
the name of the LORD. 6 And the LORD
passed before him and proclaimed, "The
LORD, the LORD [g]God, merciful and gracious, longsuffering, and abounding in
[h]goodness and [i]truth, 7 [j]keeping mercy
for thousands, [k]forgiving iniquity and
transgression and sin, [l]by no means clearing *the guilty,* visiting the iniquity of the fathers upon the children and the children's
children to the third and the fourth generation."
8 So Moses made haste and [m]bowed his
head toward the earth, and worshiped.
9 Then he said, "If now I have found grace
in Your sight, O Lord, [n]let my Lord, I pray,
go among us, even though we *are* a [o]stiff-
necked[1] people; and pardon our iniquity
and our sin, and take us as [p]Your inheritance."

The Covenant Renewed

10 And He said: "Behold, [q]I make a
covenant. Before all your people I will [r]do
[2]marvels such as have not been done in all
the earth, nor in any nation; and all the
people among whom you *are* shall see the
work of the LORD. For it *is* [s]an awesome
thing that I will do with you. 11 [t]Observe
what I command you this day. Behold, [u]I
am driving out from before you the Amorite and the Canaanite and the Hittite and
the Perizzite and the Hivite and the Jebusite. 12 [v]Take heed to yourself, lest you
make a covenant with the inhabitants of
the land where you are going, lest it be a
snare in your midst. 13 But you shall [w]de-
stroy their altars, break their *sacred* pillars,
and [x]cut down their wooden images 14 (for
you shall worship [y]no other god, for the
LORD, whose [z]name *is* Jealous, *is* a [a]jealous
God), 15 lest you make a covenant with the
inhabitants of the land, and they [b]play the
harlot with their gods and make sacrifice
to their gods, and *one of them* [c]invites you
and you [d]eat of his sacrifice, 16 and you
take of [e]his daughters for your sons, and
his daughters [f]play the harlot with their
gods and make your sons play the harlot
with their gods.
17 [g]"You shall make no molded gods for
yourselves.
18 "The Feast of [h]Unleavened Bread you
shall keep. Seven days you shall eat unleavened bread, as I commanded you, in
the appointed time of the month of Abib;
for in the [i]month of Abib you came out
from Egypt.
19 [j]"All [3]that open the womb *are* Mine,
and every male firstborn among your livestock, *whether* ox or sheep. 20 But [k]the firstborn of a donkey you shall redeem with a
lamb. And if you will not redeem *him,* then
you shall break his neck. All the firstborn
of your sons you shall redeem.
"And none shall appear before Me
[l]empty-handed.

19 [d] Ex. 34:6, 7 [e] [Rom. 9:15, 16, 18] [f] [Rom. 4:4, 16]
20 [g] [Gen. 32:30]
22 [h] Song 2:14; Is. 2:21 [i] Ps. 91:1, 4; Is. 49:2; 51:16
23 [j] Ex. 33:20; [John 1:18]

CHAPTER 34

1 [a] [Ex. 24:12; 31:18; 32:15, 16, 19; Deut. 4:13] [b] Deut. 10:2, 4
2 [c] Ex. 19:11, 18, 20
3 [d] Ex. 19:12, 13; 24:9-11
5 [e] Ex. 19:9 [f] Ex. 33:19
6 [g] Num. 14:18; Deut. 4:31; Neh. 9:17; Joel 2:13 [h] Rom. 2:4 [i] Ps. 108:4
7 [j] Ex. 20:6 [k] Ps. 103:3, 4; Dan. 9:9; Eph. 4:32; 1 John 1:9 [l] Josh. 24:19; Job 10:14; Mic. 6:11; Nah. 1:3
8 [m] Ex. 4:31
9 [n] Ex. 33:12-16 [o] Ex. 33:3 [p] Ps. 33:12; 94:14 [1] *stubborn*
10 [q] Ex. 34:27, 28; Deut. 5:2 [r] Deut. 4:32; Ps. 77:14 [s] Ps. 145:6 [2] *wonderful acts*
11 [t] Deut. 6:25 [u] Ex. 23:20-33; 33:2; Josh. 11:23
12 [v] Ex. 23:32, 33
13 [w] Ex. 23:24; Deut. 12:3 [x] Deut. 16:21; Judg. 6:25, 26; 2 Kin. 18:4; 2 Chr. 34:3, 4
14 [y] [Ex. 20:3-5] [z] [Is. 9:6; 57:15] [a] [Ex. 20:5; Deut. 4:24]
15 [b] Judg. 2:17 [c] Num. 25:1, 2; Deut. 32:37, 38 [d] 1 Cor. 8:4, 7, 10
16 [e] Gen. 28:1; Deut. 7:3; Josh. 23:12, 13; 1 Kin. 11:2; Ezra 9:2; Neh. 13:25 [f] Num. 25:1, 2; 1 Kin. 11:4
17 [g] Ex. 20:4, 23; 32:8; Lev. 19:4; Deut. 5:8
18 [h] Ex. 12:15, 16 [i] Ex. 12:2; 13:4
19 [j] Ex. 13:2; 22:29 [3] *the firstborn*
20 [k] Ex. 13:13 [l] Ex. 22:29; 23:15; Deut. 16:16

33:19 See Rom. 9:15.

34:1 Cut two tablets of stone. Renewal of the covenant meant replacement of the broken original tablets on which God had personally written the Ten Commandments (cf. 32:19).

34:2-28 Moses' second period of 40 days and nights on Mt. Sinai (cf. 25-32).

34:6,7 Here is one of the testimonies to the character of God.

34:7 *See note on 20:5,6.*

34:11 *See note on 3:8.*

34:12-17 *See note on 23:32.* This time the admonition on international treaties included a warning of how idolatry could easily ensnare them by seemingly innocent invitations to join the festivities like a good neighbor or by intermarriage, because these events would require recognition of the contracting parties' deities. Their future history demonstrated the urgency of such instruction and the disaster of disobeying it.

34:18 *See note on 12:14.*

34:19,20 *See note on 13:1.*

21 [m]"Six days you shall work, but on the
seventh day you shall rest; in plowing time
and in harvest you shall rest.
22 "And you shall observe the Feast of
Weeks, of the firstfruits of wheat harvest,
and the Feast of Ingathering at the year's
end.
23 [n]"Three times in the year all your men
shall appear before the Lord, the LORD God
of Israel. 24 For I will [o]cast out the nations
before you and enlarge your borders; neither will any man covet your land when
you go up to appear before the LORD your
God three times in the year.
25 "You shall not offer the blood of My
sacrifice with leaven, [p]nor shall the sacrifice of the Feast of the Passover be left until
morning.
26 [q]"The first of the firstfruits of your
land you shall bring to the house of the
LORD your God. You shall not boil a young
goat in its mother's milk."
27 Then the LORD said to Moses, "Write
[r]these words, for according to the tenor of
these words I have made a covenant with
you and with Israel." 28 [s]So he was there
with the LORD forty days and forty nights;
he neither ate bread nor drank water. And
[t]He wrote on the tablets the words of the
covenant, the [4]Ten Commandments.

The Shining Face of Moses

29 Now it was so, when Moses came
down from Mount Sinai (and the [u]two
tablets of the Testimony *were* in Moses'
hand when he came down from the mountain), that Moses did not know that [v]the
skin of his face shone while he talked with
Him. 30 So when Aaron and all the children of Israel saw Moses, behold, the skin
of his face shone, and they were afraid to
come near him. 31 Then Moses called to
them, and Aaron and all the rulers of the
congregation returned to him; and Moses
talked with them. 32 Afterward all the children of Israel came near, [w]and he gave
them as commandments all that the LORD
had spoken with him on Mount Sinai.
33 And when Moses had finished speaking
with them, he put [x]a veil on his face. 34 But
[y]whenever Moses went in before the LORD
to speak with Him, he would take the veil
off until he came out; and he would come
out and speak to the children of Israel
whatever he had been commanded.
35 And whenever the children of Israel saw
the face of Moses, that the skin of Moses'
face shone, then Moses would put the veil
on his face again, until he went in to speak
with Him.

Sabbath Regulations

35 Then Moses gathered all the congregation of the children of Israel
together, and said to them, [a]"These *are* the
words which the LORD has commanded
you to do: 2 Work shall be done for [b]six
days, but the seventh day shall be a holy
day for you, a Sabbath of rest to the LORD.
Whoever does any work on it shall be put
to [c]death. 3 [d]You shall kindle no fire
throughout your dwellings on the Sabbath
day."

Offerings for the Tabernacle

4 And Moses spoke to all the congregation of the children of Israel, saying, [e]"This
is the thing which the LORD commanded,
saying: 5 'Take from among you an offering to the LORD. [f]Whoever *is* of a willing
heart, let him bring it as an offering to the
LORD: [g]gold, silver, and bronze; 6 [h]blue,
purple, and scarlet *thread,* fine linen, and
[i]goats' *hair;* 7 ram skins dyed red, badger
skins, and acacia wood; 8 oil for the light,
[j]and spices for the anointing oil and for the
sweet incense; 9 onyx stones, and stones to
be set in the ephod and in the breastplate.

Articles of the Tabernacle

10 [k]'All *who are* gifted artisans among
you shall come and make all that the LORD
has commanded: 11 [l]the tabernacle, its tent,
its covering, its clasps, its boards, its bars,
its pillars, and its sockets; 12 [m]the ark and
its poles, *with* the mercy seat, and the veil of

21 [m]Ex. 20:9; 23:12; 31:15; 35:2; Lev. 23:3; Deut. 5:13
23 [n]Ex. 23:14-17
24 [o][Ex. 33:2]; Josh. 11:23; 1 Kin. 4:21; 2 Chr. 36:14-16; Ps. 78:55
25 [p]Ex. 12:10
26 [q]Ex. 23:19; Deut. 26:2
27 [r]Ex. 17:14; 24:4; Deut. 31:9
28 [s]Ex. 24:18 [t]Ex. 34:1, 4; Deut. 4:31; 10:2, 4 [4]Lit. *Ten Words*
29 [u]Ex. 32:15 [v]Matt. 17:2; 2 Cor. 3:7
32 [w]Ex. 24:3
33 [x][2 Cor. 3:13, 14]
34 [y][2 Cor. 3:13-16]

CHAPTER 35

1 [a]Ex. 34:32
2 [b]Ex. 20:9, 10; Lev. 23:3; Deut. 5:13 [c]Num. 15:32-36
3 [d]Ex. 12:16; 16:23
4 [e]Ex. 25:1, 2
5 [f]Ex. 25:2; 1 Chr. 29:14; Mark 12:41-44; 2 Cor. 8:10-12; 9:7 [g]Ex. 38:24
6 [h]Ex. 36:8 [i]Ex. 36:14
8 [j]Ex. 25:6; 30:23-25
10 [k]Ex. 31:2-6; 36:1, 2
11 [l]Ex. 26:1, 2; 36:14
12 [m]Ex. 25:10-22

34:21 *See note on 20:8.*

34:22,23,26 *See note on 23:14-19.*

34:29-35 The first time on the mount (24:12–32:14), unlike the second, had not left Moses with a face which was reflecting some radiance associated with being in the presence of the Lord for an extended period of time. On the first occasion, mere mention was made of Moses' being gone 40 days and nights (24:18). On the second, mention was made of the 40 day and night absence but adding that Moses had been there with the Lord, neither eating nor drinking (v. 28), appears to draw attention to the different nature of the second visit. It, in comparison with the first, was not interrupted by the Lord's sending Moses away because of sin in the camp (32:7-10). A compliant and not defiant people feared the evidence of God's presence. When not speaking to the Lord or authoritatively on His behalf to the people, Moses veiled his face. The Apostle Paul advised that the veil prevented the people from seeing a fading glory and related it to the inadequacy of the old covenant and the blindness of the Jews in his day (*see notes on 2 Cor. 3:7-18*).

35:1–40:38 In this section, the Israelites constructed the tabernacle as God so prescribed in 25:1–31:18.

35:1-3 *See notes on 20:8; 31:12-17.* This time, however, an extra admonition forbids the making of a fire on the Sabbath.

35:4-9 *See note on 25:2.*

35:10-19 *See all the notes on 25:11–28:43.*

the covering; 13 the [n]table and its poles, all
its utensils, [o]and the showbread; 14 also
[p]the lampstand for the light, its utensils, its
lamps, and the oil for the light; 15 [q]the incense altar, its poles, [r]the anointing oil, [s]the
sweet incense, and the screen for the door
at the entrance of the tabernacle; 16 [t]the
altar of burnt offering with its bronze grating, its poles, all its utensils, *and* the laver
and its base; 17 [u]the hangings of the court,
its pillars, their sockets, and the screen for
the gate of the court; 18 the pegs of the
tabernacle, the pegs of the court, and their
cords; 19 [v]the [1]garments of ministry, for
ministering in the holy *place*—the holy garments for Aaron the priest and the garments of his sons, to minister as priests.' "

The Tabernacle Offerings Presented

20 And all the congregation of the children of Israel departed from the presence
of Moses. 21 Then everyone came [w]whose
heart [2]was stirred, and everyone whose
spirit was willing, *and* they [x]brought the
LORD's offering for the work of the tabernacle of meeting, for all its service, and for
the holy garments. 22 They came, both men
and women, as many as had a willing
heart, *and* brought [y]earrings and nose
rings, rings and necklaces, all [z]jewelry of
gold, that is, every man who *made* an offering of gold to the LORD. 23 And [a]every
man, with whom was found blue, purple,
and scarlet *thread,* fine linen, goats' *hair,* red
skins of rams, and [3]badger skins, brought
them. 24 Everyone who offered an offering
of silver or bronze brought the LORD's offering. And everyone with whom was
found acacia wood for any work of the service, brought *it.* 25 All the women *who were*
[b]gifted artisans spun yarn with their
hands, and brought what they had spun,
of blue, purple, *and* scarlet, and fine linen.
26 And all the women whose hearts
[4]stirred with wisdom spun yarn of goats'
hair. 27 [c]The rulers brought onyx stones,
and the stones to be set in the ephod and in
the breastplate, 28 and [d]spices and oil for
the light, for the anointing oil, and for the
sweet incense. 29 The children of Israel
brought a [e]freewill offering to the LORD, all
the men and women whose hearts were
willing to bring *material* for all kinds of
work which the LORD, by the hand of Moses, had commanded to be done.

The Artisans Called by God

30 And Moses said to the children of Israel, "See, [f]the LORD has called by name
Bezalel the son of Uri, the son of Hur, of
the tribe of Judah; 31 and He has filled him
with the Spirit of God, in wisdom and understanding, in knowledge and all manner
of workmanship, 32 to design artistic
works, to work in gold and silver and
bronze, 33 in cutting jewels for setting, in
carving wood, and to work in all manner
of artistic workmanship.
34 "And He has put in his heart the ability to teach, *in* him and [g]Aholiab the son of
Ahisamach, of the tribe of Dan. 35 He has
[h]filled them with skill to do all manner of
work of the engraver and the designer and
the tapestry maker, in blue, purple, and
scarlet *thread,* and fine linen, and of the
weaver—those who do every work and
those who design artistic works.

36 "And Bezalel and Aholiab, and
every [a]gifted artisan in whom the
LORD has put wisdom and understanding,
to know how to do all manner of work for
the service of the [b]sanctuary,[1] shall do according to all that the LORD has commanded."

The People Give More than Enough

2 Then Moses called Bezalel and Aholiab, and every gifted artisan in whose heart
the LORD had put wisdom, everyone
[c]whose heart [2]was stirred, to come and do
the work. 3 And they received from Moses
all the [d]offering which the children of Israel [e]had brought for the work of the service of making the sanctuary. So they continued bringing to him freewill offerings
every morning. 4 Then all the craftsmen
who were doing all the work of the sanctuary came, each from the work he was
doing, 5 and they spoke to Moses, saying,
[f]"The people bring much more than
enough for the service of the work which
the LORD commanded *us* to do."
6 So Moses gave a commandment, and
they caused it to be proclaimed throughout
the camp, saying, "Let neither man nor
woman do any more work for the offering
of the sanctuary." And the people were restrained from bringing, 7 for the material
they had was sufficient for all the work to
be done—indeed too [g]much.

13 [n] Ex. 25:23 [o] Ex. 25:30; Lev. 24:5, 6
14 [p] Ex. 25:31
15 [q] Ex. 30:1 [r] Ex. 30:25 [s] Ex. 30:34-38
16 [t] Ex. 27:1-8
17 [u] Ex. 27:9-18
19 [v] Ex. 31:10; 39:1, 41 [1] Or *woven garments*
21 [w] Ex. 25:2; 35:5, 22, 26, 29; 36:2 [x] Ex. 35:24 [2] Lit. *lifted him up*
22 [y] Ex. 32:2, 3 [z] Ex. 11:2
23 [a] 1 Chr. 29:8 [3] Or *dolphin*
25 [b] Ex. 28:3; 31:6; 36:1
26 [4] Lit. *lifted them up*
27 [c] 1 Chr. 29:6; Ezra 2:68
28 [d] Ex. 30:23
29 [e] Ex. 35:5, 21; 36:3; 1 Chr. 29:9
30 [f] Ex. 31:1-6
34 [g] Ex. 31:6
35 [h] Ex. 31:3, 6; 35:31; 1 Kin. 7:14; 2 Chr. 2:14; Is. 28:26

CHAPTER 36

1 [a] Ex. 28:3; 31:6; 35:10, 35 [b] Ex. 25:8 [1] *holy place*
2 [c] Ex. 35:21, 26; 1 Chr. 29:5, 9, 17 [2] *lifted him up*
3 [d] Ex. 35:5 [e] Ex. 35:27
5 [f] 2 Chr. 24:14; 31:6-10; [2 Cor. 8:2, 3]
7 [g] 1 Kin. 8:64

35:20-29 *See note on 25:2.*

35:30–36:1 The Lord also gave the two named artisans skill in teaching their trades. This substantiates that they were most probably the supervisors or leaders of the construction teams. *See notes on 28:3; 31:1-11.*

36:2-7 The people, stubborn and disobedient at times, nevertheless rose to the occasion and voluntarily brought much more than was needed for the building of the tabernacle. *See note on 25:2.*

36:8–39:43 The report of the work done is repeated in the past tense. This report also highlighted how careful the workers were in

Building the Tabernacle

8 [h]Then all the gifted artisans among them who worked on the tabernacle made ten curtains woven of fine linen, and of blue, purple, and scarlet thread; *with* artistic designs of cherubim they made them. 9 The length of each curtain *was* twenty-eight cubits, and the width of each curtain four cubits; the curtains *were* all the same size. 10 And he coupled five curtains to one another, and *the other* five curtains he coupled to one another. 11 He made loops of blue *yarn* on the edge of the curtain on the selvedge of one set; likewise he did on the outer edge of *the other* curtain of the second set. 12 [i]Fifty loops he made on one curtain, and fifty loops he made on the edge of the curtain on the end of the second set; the loops held one *curtain* to another. 13 And he made fifty clasps of gold, and coupled the curtains to one another with the clasps, that it might be one tabernacle.

14 [j]He made curtains of goats' *hair* for the tent over the tabernacle; he made eleven curtains. 15 The length of each curtain *was* thirty cubits, and the width of each curtain four cubits; the eleven curtains *were* the same size. 16 He coupled five curtains by themselves and six curtains by themselves. 17 And he made fifty loops on the edge of the curtain that is outermost in one set, and fifty loops he made on the edge of the curtain of the second set. 18 He also made fifty bronze clasps to couple the tent together, that it might be one. 19 [k]Then he made a covering for the tent of ram skins dyed red, and a covering of [3]badger skins above *that*.

20 For the tabernacle [l]he made boards of acacia wood, standing upright. 21 The length of each board *was* ten cubits, and the width of each board a cubit and a half. 22 Each board had two [4]tenons [m]for binding one to another. Thus he made for all the boards of the tabernacle. 23 And he made boards for the tabernacle, twenty boards for the south side. 24 Forty sockets of silver he made to go under the twenty boards: two sockets under each of the boards for its two tenons. 25 And for the other side of the tabernacle, the north side, he made twenty boards 26 and their forty sockets of silver: two sockets under each of the boards. 27 For the west side of the tabernacle he made six boards. 28 He also made two boards for the two back corners of the tabernacle. 29 And they were coupled at the bottom and [5]coupled together at the top by one ring. Thus he made both of them for the two corners. 30 So there were eight boards and their sockets—sixteen sockets of silver—two sockets under each of the boards.

31 And he made [n]bars of acacia wood: five for the boards on one side of the tabernacle, 32 five bars for the boards on the other side of the tabernacle, and five bars for the boards of the tabernacle on the far side westward. 33 And he made the middle bar to pass through the boards from one end to the other. 34 He overlaid the boards with gold, made their rings of gold *to be* holders for the bars, and overlaid the bars with gold.

35 And he made [o]a veil of blue, purple, and scarlet *thread,* and fine woven linen; it was worked *with* an artistic design of cherubim. 36 He made for it four pillars of acacia *wood,* and overlaid them with gold, with their hooks of gold; and he cast four sockets of silver for them.

37 He also made a [p]screen for the tabernacle door, of blue, purple, and scarlet *thread,* and fine woven linen, made by a [6]weaver, 38 and its five pillars with their hooks. And he overlaid their capitals and their rings with gold, but their five sockets *were* bronze.

Making the Ark of the Testimony

37 Then [a]Bezalel made [b]the ark of acacia wood; two and a half cubits *was* its length, a cubit and a half its width, and a cubit and a half its height. 2 He overlaid it with pure gold inside and outside, and made a molding of gold all around it. 3 And he cast for it four rings of gold *to be set* in its four corners: two rings on one side, and two rings on the other side of it. 4 He made poles of acacia wood, and overlaid them with gold. 5 And he put the poles into the rings at the sides of the ark, to bear the ark. 6 He also made the [c]mercy seat of pure gold; two and a half cubits *was* its length and a cubit and a half its width. 7 He made two cherubim of beaten gold; he made them of one piece at the two ends of the mercy seat: 8 one cherub at one end on this side, and the other cherub at the *other* end on that side. He made the cherubim at the two ends *of one piece* with the mercy seat. 9 The cherubim spread out *their* wings above, *and* covered the [d]mercy seat with their wings. They faced one an-

8 [h]Ex. 26:1-14
12 [i]Ex. 26:5
14 [j]Ex. 26:7
19 [k]Ex. 26:14 [3]Or *dolphin*
20 [l]Ex. 26:15-29
22 [m]Ex. 26:17 [4]Projections for joining, lit. *hands*

29 [5]Lit. *doubled*
31 [n]Ex. 26:26-29
35 [o]Ex. 26:31-37
37 [p]Ex. 26:36 [6]Lit. *variegator,* a weaver in colors

CHAPTER 37

1 [a]Ex. 35:30; 36:1 [b]Ex. 25:10-20
6 [c]Ex. 25:17
9 [d]Ex. 25:20

carrying out the instructions and blueprints received. Note the repeated refrain on doing all just as the Lord had commanded Moses (39:1,5,7,21,26,29,31,32,42,43 and 40:19,21,23,25,27,29,32).

36:8-37 *See all notes on chap. 26.*

37:1-9 *See notes on 25:16,17,18.*

other; the faces of the cherubim were toward the mercy seat.

Making the Table for the Showbread

10 He made [e]the table of acacia wood;
two cubits *was* its length, a cubit its width,
and a cubit and a half its height. 11 And he
overlaid it with pure gold, and made a
molding of gold all around it. 12 Also he
made a frame of a handbreadth all around
it, and made a molding of gold for the
frame all around it. 13 And he cast for it
four rings of gold, and put the rings on the
four corners that *were* at its four legs.
14 The rings were close to the frame, as
holders for the poles to bear the table.
15 And he made the poles of acacia wood
to bear the table, and overlaid them with
gold. 16 He made of pure gold the utensils
which were on the table: its [f]dishes, its
cups, its bowls, and its pitchers for pouring.

Making the Gold Lampstand

17 He also made the [g]lampstand of pure
gold; of hammered work he made the
lampstand. Its shaft, its branches, its
bowls, its *ornamental* knobs, and its flowers
were of the same piece. 18 And six branches came out of its sides: three branches of
the lampstand out of one side, and three
branches of the lampstand out of the other
side. 19 There were three bowls made like
almond *blossoms* on one branch, with an *ornamental* knob and a flower, and three
bowls made like almond *blossoms* on the
other branch, with an *ornamental* knob and
a flower—and so for the six branches coming out of the lampstand. 20 And on the
lampstand itself *were* four bowls made like
almond *blossoms, each with* its *ornamental*
knob and flower. 21 *There was* a knob under
the *first* two branches of the same, a knob
under the *second* two branches of the same,
and a knob under the *third* two branches of
the same, according to the six branches extending from it. 22 Their knobs and their
branches were of one piece; all of it *was* one
hammered piece of pure gold. 23 And he
made its seven lamps, its [h]wick-trimmers,
and its trays of pure gold. 24 Of a talent of
pure gold he made it, with all its utensils.

Making the Altar of Incense

25 [i]He made the incense altar of acacia
wood. Its length *was* a cubit and its width
a cubit—*it was* square—and two cubits *was*
its height. Its horns were *of one piece* with it.
26 And he overlaid it with pure gold: its
top, its sides all around, and its horns. He
also made for it a molding of gold all
around it. 27 He made two rings of gold for
it under its molding, by its two corners on
both sides, as holders for the poles with
which to bear it. 28 And he [j]made the poles
of acacia wood, and overlaid them with
gold.

Making the Anointing Oil and the Incense

29 He also made [k]the holy anointing oil
and the pure incense of sweet spices, according to the work of the perfumer.

Making the Altar of Burnt Offering

38 He made [a]the altar of burnt offering
of acacia wood; five cubits *was* its
length and five cubits its width—*it was*
square—and its height *was* three cubits.
2 He made its horns on its four corners; the
horns were *of one piece* with it. And he
overlaid it with bronze. 3 He made all the
utensils for the altar: the pans, the shovels,
the basins, the forks, and the firepans; all
its utensils he made of bronze. 4 And he
made a grate of bronze network for the
altar, under its rim, midway from the bottom. 5 He cast four rings for the four corners of the bronze grating, *as* holders for
the poles. 6 And he made the poles of acacia wood, and overlaid them with bronze.
7 Then he put the poles into the rings on
the sides of the altar, with which to bear it.
He made the altar hollow with boards.

Making the Bronze Laver

8 He made [b]the laver of bronze and its
base of bronze, from the bronze mirrors of
the serving women who assembled at the
door of the tabernacle of meeting.

Making the Court of the Tabernacle

9 Then he made [c]the court on the south
side; the hangings of the court *were of* fine
woven linen, one hundred cubits long.
10 There *were* twenty pillars for them, with
twenty bronze sockets. The hooks of the
pillars and their bands *were* silver. 11 On
the north side *the hangings were* one hundred cubits *long,* with twenty pillars and
their twenty bronze sockets. The hooks of
the pillars and their bands *were* silver.
12 And on the west side *there were* hangings
of fifty cubits, with ten pillars and their ten
sockets. The hooks of the pillars and their

10 [e] Ex. 25:23-29
16 [f] Ex. 25:29
17 [g] Ex. 25:31-39
23 [h] Num. 4:9
25 [i] Ex. 30:1-5
28 [j] Ex. 30:5
29 [k] Ex. 30:23-25

CHAPTER 38

1 [a] Ex. 27:1-8
8 [b] Ex. 30:18
9 [c] Ex. 27:9-19

37:10-16 *See note on 25:30.*
37:17-24 *See note on 25:31.*
37:25-28 *See note on 30:1.*
37:29 *See notes on 30:22-33,34-38.*
38:1-7 *See note on 27:1.*
38:8 *See note on 30:18-21.*

bands *were* silver. 13 For the east side *the*
hangings were fifty cubits. 14 The hangings
of one side *of the gate were* fifteen cubits
long, with their three pillars and their three
sockets, 15 and the same for the other side
of the court gate; on this side and that *were*
hangings of fifteen cubits, *with* their three
pillars and their three sockets. 16 All the
hangings of the court all around *were of*
fine woven linen. 17 The sockets for the pillars *were* bronze, the hooks of the pillars
and their bands *were* silver, and the overlay
of their capitals *was* silver; and all the pillars of the court had bands of silver. 18 The
screen for the gate of the court *was* woven
of blue, purple, and scarlet *thread,* and of
fine woven linen. The length *was* twenty
cubits, and the height along its width *was*
five cubits, corresponding to the hangings
of the court. 19 And *there were* four pillars
with their four sockets of bronze; their
hooks *were* silver, and the overlay of their
capitals and their bands *was* silver. 20 All
the [d]pegs of the tabernacle, and of the
court all around, *were* bronze.

Materials of the Tabernacle

21 [1]This is the inventory of the tabernacle, [e]the tabernacle of the Testimony, which
was counted according to the commandment of Moses, for the service of the
Levites, [f]by the hand of [g]Ithamar, son of
Aaron the priest.
22 [h]Bezalel the son of Uri, the son of Hur,
of the tribe of Judah, made all that the
LORD had commanded Moses. 23 And with
him *was* [i]Aholiab the son of Ahisamach, of
the tribe of Dan, an engraver and [2]de-
signer, a weaver of blue, purple, and scarlet *thread,* and of fine linen.
24 All the gold that was used in all the
work of the holy *place,* that is, the gold of
the [j]offering, was twenty-nine talents and
seven hundred and thirty shekels, according to [k]the shekel of the sanctuary. 25 And
the silver from those who were [l]numbered
of the congregation *was* one hundred talents and one thousand seven hundred and
seventy-five shekels, according to the
shekel of the sanctuary: 26 [m]a bekah for
[3]each man (*that is,* half a shekel, according
to the shekel of the sanctuary), for everyone included in the numbering from twenty years old and above, for [n]six hundred
and three thousand, five hundred and fifty
men. 27 And from the hundred talents of
silver were cast [o]the sockets of the sanctuary and the bases of the veil: one hundred
sockets from the hundred talents, one talent for each socket. 28 Then from the one
thousand seven hundred and seventy-five
shekels he made hooks for the pillars, overlaid their capitals, and [p]made bands for
them.
29 The offering of bronze *was* seventy talents and two thousand four hundred
shekels. 30 And with it he made the sockets
for the door of the tabernacle of meeting,
the bronze altar, the bronze grating for it,
and all the utensils for the altar, 31 the
sockets for the court all around, the bases
for the court gate, all the pegs for the tabernacle, and all the pegs for the court all
around.

Making the Garments of the Priesthood

39 Of the [a]blue, purple, and scarlet
thread they made [b]garments[1] of
ministry, for ministering in the [2]holy *place,*
and made the holy garments for Aaron, [c]as
the LORD had commanded Moses.

Making the Ephod

2 [d]He made the [e]ephod of gold, blue,
purple, and scarlet *thread,* and of fine
woven linen. 3 And they beat the gold into
thin sheets and cut *it into* threads, to work
it in *with* the blue, purple, and scarlet
thread, and the fine linen, *into* artistic designs. 4 They made shoulder straps for it to
couple *it* together; it was coupled together
at its two edges. 5 And the intricately
woven band of his ephod that *was* on it *was*
of the same workmanship, *woven of* gold,
blue, purple, and scarlet *thread,* and of fine
woven linen, as the LORD had commanded
Moses.
6 [f]And they set onyx stones, enclosed in
[3]settings of gold; they were engraved, as
signets are engraved, with the names of

20 [d]Ex. 27:19
21 [e]Num. 1:50, 53; 9:15; 10:11; 17:7, 8; 2 Chr. 24:6; Acts 7:44 [f]Num. 4:28, 33 [g]Ex. 28:1; Lev. 10:6, 16 [1]Lit. *These are the things appointed for*
22 [h]Ex. 31:2, 6; 1 Chr. 2:18-20
23 [i]Ex. 31:6; 36:1 [2]*skillful workman*
24 [j]Ex. 35:5, 22 [k]Ex. 30:13, 24; Lev. 5:15; 27:3, 25; Num. 3:47; 18:16
25 [l]Ex. 30:11-16; Num. 1:2
26 [m]Ex. 30:13, 15 [n]Ex. 12:37; Num. 1:46; 26:51 [3]Lit. *a head*
27 [o]Ex. 26:19, 21, 25, 32
28 [p]Ex. 27:17

CHAPTER 39

1 [a]Ex. 25:4; 35:23 [b]Ex. 31:10; 35:19 [c]Ex. 28:4 [1]Or *woven garments* [2]*sanctuary*
2 [d]Ex. 28:6-14 [e]Lev. 8:7
6 [f]Ex. 28:9-11 [3]*plaited work*

38:9-20 *See notes on 27:9,16.*

38:21-31 The inventory taken calculates out at half a shekel (cf. 30:13-16) per man 20 years old and up to equal 603,550 men (cf. Num. 1:46 and the first census). Talents were about 75 pounds and shekels about half an ounce.

39:1,2 they made...He made. The third-person plural, "they," dominating the manufacturing report (vv. 2-31), is interrupted 4 times by the singular "he" (vv. 2,7,8,22). The plural undoubtedly refers to Bezalel and/or his associates in operation, whereas the singular marks out what Bezalel worked on by himself.

39:1 as the LORD had commanded Moses. This repetitive refrain (vv. 1,5,7,21,26,29,31), a quality-control statement, signals to the reader of every age, or to the listener in Israel back then, that God's detailed instructions to Moses on the fabricating of the ephod (vv. 2-7), breastplate (vv. 8-21), and priestly garments (vv. 22-31) were followed to the letter. Obedience in every detail was taken seriously by Israel's artisans.

39:2 He made the ephod. *See note on 28:5-13.*

39:3 They beat the gold into thin sheets and cut *it into* threads. The process adopted to get the delicate strips for braided chains or gold embroidery work conformed well with contemporary Egyptian methods of gold-working.

the sons of Israel. 7 He put them on the
shoulders of the ephod *as* [g]memorial
stones for the sons of Israel, as the LORD
had commanded Moses.

Making the Breastplate

8 [h]And he made the breastplate, artistically woven like the workmanship of the
ephod, of gold, blue, purple, and scarlet
thread, and of fine woven linen. 9 They
made the breastplate square by doubling
it; a span *was* its length and a span its
width when doubled. 10 [i]And they set in it
four rows of stones: a row with a sardius, a
topaz, and an emerald was the first row;
11 the second row, a turquoise, a sapphire,
and a diamond; 12 the third row, a jacinth,
an agate, and an amethyst; 13 the fourth
row, a beryl, an onyx, and a jasper. *They*
were enclosed in settings of gold in their
mountings. 14 *There were* [j]twelve stones according to the names of the sons of Israel:
according to their names, *engraved like* a
signet, each one with its own name according to the twelve tribes. 15 And they made
chains for the breastplate at the ends, like
braided cords of pure gold. 16 They also
made two settings of gold and two gold
rings, and put the two rings on the two
ends of the breastplate. 17 And they put the
two braided *chains* of gold in the two rings
on the ends of the breastplate. 18 The two
ends of the two braided *chains* they fastened in the two settings, and put them on
the shoulder straps of the ephod in the
front. 19 And they made two rings of gold
and put *them* on the two ends of the breastplate, on the edge of it, which *was* on the
inward side of the ephod. 20 They made
two *other* gold rings and put them on the
two shoulder straps, underneath the
ephod toward its front, right at the seam
above the intricately woven band of the
ephod. 21 And they bound the breastplate
by means of its rings to the rings of the
ephod with a blue cord, so that it would be
above the intricately woven band of the
ephod, and that the breastplate would not
come loose from the ephod, as the LORD
had commanded Moses.

Making the Other Priestly Garments

22 [k]He made the [l]robe of the ephod of
woven work, all of blue. 23 And *there was*
an opening in the middle of the robe, like
the opening in a coat of mail, *with* a woven
binding all around the opening, so that it
would not tear. 24 They made on the hem
of the robe pomegranates of blue, purple,
and scarlet, and of fine woven *linen.*
25 And they made [m]bells of pure gold, and
put the bells between the pomegranates on
the hem of the robe all around between the
pomegranates: 26 a bell and a pomegranate, a bell and a pomegranate, all around
the hem of the robe to [4]minister in, as the
LORD had commanded Moses.
27 [n]They made tunics, artistically woven
of fine linen, for Aaron and his sons, 28 [o]a
turban of fine linen, exquisite hats of fine
linen, [p]short trousers of fine woven linen,
29 [q]and a sash of fine woven linen with
blue, purple, and scarlet *thread,* made by a
weaver, as the LORD had commanded Moses.
30 [r]Then they made the plate of the holy
crown of pure gold, and wrote on it an inscription *like* the engraving of a signet:

[s]HOLINESS TO THE LORD.

31 And they tied to it a blue cord, to fasten
it above on the turban, as the LORD had
commanded Moses.

The Work Completed

32 Thus all the work of the tabernacle of
the tent of meeting was [t]finished. And the
children of Israel did [u]according to all that
the LORD had commanded Moses; so they
did. 33 And they brought the tabernacle to
Moses, the tent and all its furnishings: its
clasps, its boards, its bars, its pillars, and
its sockets; 34 the covering of ram skins

7 [g] Ex. 28:12, 29; Josh. 4:7
8 [h] Ex. 28:15-30
10 [i] Ex. 28:17
14 [j] Rev. 21:12

22 [k] Ex. 28:31-35 [l] Ex. 29:5; Lev. 8:7
25 [m] Ex. 28:33
26 [4] *serve*
27 [n] Ex. 28:39, 40
28 [o] Ex. 28:4, 39; Lev. 8:9; Ezek. 44:18 [p] Ex. 28:42; Lev. 6:10
29 [q] Ex. 28:39
30 [r] Ex. 28:36, 37 [s] Zech. 14:20
32 [t] Ex. 40:17 [u] Ex. 25:40; 39:42, 43

39:8 he made the breastplate. *See notes on 28:15,30.* The Urim and Thummim were inserted into the breastplate and became an essential part of it, or were seen as a permanent connection with it.

39:22 He made the robe of the ephod. *See note on 28:31-35.*

39:27 They made tunics…for Aaron and his sons. *See notes on 28:39-43.*

39:30 they made the plate of the holy crown. *See note on 28:36-38* on this special plate engraved with its message of God's purity and separation from all the profane and impure.

39:32 Thus all the work…was finished. Finally the moment arrived when all the different tasks assigned to different artisans was all completed, and the great task on which they embarked was ready for formal presentation to Israel's leader. **And the children of Israel.** No individual artisan is singled out for special mention or award; instead the whole nation was represented as doing everything in accordance with the Lord's instructions to Moses. **so they did.** In what is almost an offhanded aside, emphasis is placed on the strict attention paid to the official, divine specifications for all parts of the work for the tabernacle.

39:33 And they brought the tabernacle to Moses. Attestations of obedience and accuracy provide, as it were, an envelope (vv. 32,42,43) for the concise inventory of all the parts included in that presentation to Moses. None of the individual parts listed, nor the sum of them, reflect just human ingenuity in designing something they wanted to have, but reflect instead just what their Lord required them to have. It was fully His architecture and His design at every level of the undertaking.

dyed red, the covering of badger skins,
and the veil of the covering; **35** the ark of
the Testimony with its poles, and the
mercy seat; **36** the table, all its utensils, and
the [v]showbread; **37** the pure *gold* lampstand with its lamps (the lamps set in
order), all its utensils, and the oil for light;
38 the gold altar, the anointing oil, and the
sweet incense; the screen for the tabernacle
door; **39** the bronze altar, its grate of
bronze, its poles, and all its utensils; the
laver with its base; **40** the hangings of the
court, its pillars and its sockets, the screen
for the court gate, its cords, and its pegs; all
the utensils for the service of the tabernacle, for the tent of meeting; **41** and the [5]gar-
ments of ministry, to [6]minister in the holy
place: the holy garments for Aaron the
priest, and his sons' garments, to minister
as priests.
42 According to all that the LORD had
commanded Moses, so the children of Israel [w]did all the work. **43** Then Moses
looked over all the work, and indeed they
had done it; as the LORD had commanded,
just so they had done it. And Moses
[x]blessed them.

The Tabernacle Erected and Arranged

40 Then the LORD [a]spoke to Moses,
saying: **2** "On the first day of the
[b]first month you shall set up [c]the tabernacle of the tent of meeting. **3** [d]You shall put
in it the ark of the Testimony, and [1]parti-
tion off the ark with the veil. **4** [e]You shall
bring in the table and [f]arrange the things
that are to be set in order on it; [g]and you
shall bring in the lampstand and [2]light its
lamps. **5** [h]You shall also set the altar of gold
for the incense before the ark of the Testimony, and put up the screen for the door of
the tabernacle. **6** Then you shall set the [i]al-
tar of the burnt offering before the door of
the tabernacle of the tent of meeting. **7** And
[j]you shall set the laver between the tabernacle of meeting and the altar, and put
water in it. **8** You shall set up the court all
around, and hang up the screen at the
court gate.
9 "And you shall take the anointing oil,
and [k]anoint the tabernacle and all that *is*
in it; and you shall hallow it and all its
utensils, and it shall be holy. **10** You shall
[l]anoint the altar of the burnt offering and
all its utensils, and consecrate the altar.
[m]The altar shall be most holy. **11** And you
shall anoint the laver and its base, and consecrate it.
12 [n]"Then you shall bring Aaron and his
sons to the door of the tabernacle of meeting and wash them with water. **13** You shall
put the holy [o]garments on Aaron, [p]and
anoint him and consecrate him, that he
may minister to Me as priest. **14** And you
shall bring his sons and clothe them with
tunics. **15** You shall anoint them, as you
anointed their father, that they may minister to Me as priests; for their anointing
shall surely be [q]an everlasting priesthood
throughout their generations."
16 Thus Moses did; according to all that
the LORD had commanded him, so he did.
17 And it came to pass in the first month
of the second year, on the first *day* of the
month, *that* the [r]tabernacle was [3]raised
up. **18** So Moses raised up the tabernacle,
fastened its sockets, set up its boards, put
in its bars, and raised up its pillars. **19** And
he spread out the tent over the tabernacle
and put the covering of the tent on top of
it, as the LORD had commanded Moses.
20 He took [s]the Testimony and put *it* into
the ark, inserted the poles through the
rings of the ark, and put the mercy seat on
top of the ark. **21** And he brought the ark
into the tabernacle, [t]hung up the veil of
the covering, and partitioned off the ark of
the Testimony, as the LORD had commanded Moses.
22 [u]He put the table in the tabernacle of

36 [v]Ex. 25:23-30
41 [5]Or *woven garments* [6]*serve*
42 [w]Ex. 35:10
43 [x]Lev. 9:22, 23; Num. 6:23-26; Josh. 22:6; 2 Sam. 6:18; 1 Kin. 8:14; 2 Chr. 30:27

CHAPTER 40

1 [a]Ex. 25:1–31:18
2 [b]Ex. 12:2; 13:4 [c]Ex. 26:1, 30; 40:17
3 [d]Ex. 26:33; 40:21; Lev. 16:2; Num. 4:5 [1]*screen*
4 [e]Ex. 26:35; 40:22 [f]Ex. 25:30; 40:23 [g]Ex. 40:24, 25 [2]*set up*
5 [h]Ex. 40:26
6 [i]Ex. 39:39
7 [j]Ex. 30:18; 40:30
9 [k]Ex. 30:26; Lev. 8:10
10 [l]Ex. 30:26-30 [m]Ex. 29:36, 37
12 [n]Ex. 29:4-9; Lev. 8:1-13
13 [o]Ex. 29:5; 39:1, 41 [p][Ex. 28:41]; Lev. 8:12
15 [q]Ex. 29:9; Num. 25:13
17 [r]Ex. 40:2; Num. 7:1 [3]*erected*
20 [s]Ex. 25:16; Deut. 10:5; 1 Kin. 8:9; 2 Chr. 5:10; Heb. 9:4
21 [t]Ex. 26:33
22 [u]Ex. 26:35

39:42,43 The double repetition of the same quality-control refrain found earlier in the chapter together with the 3 additional phrases emphasizing exact conformity (note "indeed," or "behold," and "just so") to all specifications combine to formally mark the closing of these great God-initiated preparations for the place of His presence and the site of their worship. Israel's skillful artisans had done their work with zero tolerance for error in mind!

39:43 Then Moses looked over all the work. Fittingly enough, the one who had been with God on the mount and had passed on to the people the blueprints for everything connected with the Lord's tabernacle personally inspected the work and confirmed its successful completion. The term "work" is to be taken as "the end result of professional and skilled craftsmen." **And Moses blessed them.** By this act, Moses set his final and formal seal of approval on the outcome of their earnestness and diligence, and expressed his prayer-wish that good would result to them from their God. This is the only instance recorded in Exodus of Moses' pronouncing a blessing upon his people. The other appearances of the verb "to bless" occur 3 times with God as the subject of the verb (20:11,24; 23:25) and one time with Pharaoh requesting Moses to bless him (12:32).

40:1-33 Finally the time arrived for the tabernacle to be erected with the Holy of Holies and its accompanying Holy Place to the W, and the courtyard entrance to the E. In terms of pagan religions and their worship of the sun god, some polemic significance might be seen in the High-Priest worshiping God with his back to the rising sun. All who entered the courtyard also turned their backs to the rising sun as they came in to sacrifice and worship.

40:17 The tabernacle was completed almost one year after the Exodus from Egypt. The people were at the foot of Mt. Sinai at that time, where the book of Leviticus was given in the first month of that second year. The record of Numbers begins with the people still at Mt. Sinai in the second month of that second year after leaving Egypt (cf. Num. 1:1).

meeting, on the north side of the tabernacle, outside the veil; 23 [v]and he set the
bread in order upon it before the LORD, as
the LORD had commanded Moses. 24 [w]He
put the lampstand in the tabernacle of
meeting, across from the table, on the
south side of the tabernacle; 25 and [x]he lit
the lamps before the LORD, as the LORD had
commanded Moses. 26 [y]He put the gold
altar in the tabernacle of meeting in front
of the veil; 27 [z]and he burned sweet incense on it, as the LORD had commanded
Moses. 28 [a]He hung up the screen *at* the
door of the tabernacle. 29 [b]And he put the
altar of burnt offering *before* the door of the
tabernacle of the tent of meeting, and [c]of-
fered upon it the burnt offering and the
grain offering, as the LORD had commanded Moses. 30 [d]He set the laver between the
tabernacle of meeting and the altar, and
put water there for washing; 31 and Moses,
Aaron, and his sons would [e]wash their
hands and their feet *with water* from it.
32 Whenever they went into the tabernacle
of meeting, and when they came near the
altar, they washed, [f]as the LORD had commanded Moses. 33 [g]And he raised up the
court all around the tabernacle and the
altar, and hung up the screen of the court
gate. So Moses [h]finished the work.

The Cloud and the Glory

34 [i]Then the [j]cloud covered the tabernacle of meeting, and the [k]glory of the LORD
filled the tabernacle. 35 And Moses [l]was
not able to enter the tabernacle of meeting,
because the cloud rested above it, and the
glory of the LORD filled the tabernacle.
36 [m]Whenever the cloud was taken up
from above the tabernacle, the children of
Israel would [4]go onward in all their journeys. 37 But [n]if the cloud was not taken up,
then they did not journey till the day that
it was taken up. 38 For [o]the cloud of the
LORD *was* above the tabernacle by day, and
fire was over it by night, in the sight of all
the house of Israel, throughout all their
journeys.

23 [v] Ex. 40:4; Lev. 24:5, 6
24 [w] Ex. 26:35
25 [x] Ex. 25:37; 30:7, 8; 40:4; Lev. 24:3, 4
26 [y] Ex. 30:1, 6; 40:5
27 [z] Ex. 30:7
28 [a] Ex. 26:36; 40:5
29 [b] Ex. 40:6 [c] Ex. 29:38-42
30 [d] Ex. 30:18; 40:7
31 [e] Ex. 30:19, 20; John 13:8
32 [f] Ex. 30:19
33 [g] Ex. 27:9-18; 40:8 [h] [Heb. 3:2-5]
34 [i] Ex. 29:43; Lev. 16:2; Num. 9:15; 2 Chr. 5:13; Is. 6:4 [j] 1 Kin. 8:10, 11 [k] Lev. 9:6, 23
35 [l] [Lev. 16:2]; 1 Kin. 8:11; 2 Chr. 5:13, 14
36 [m] Ex. 13:21, 22; Num. 9:17; Neh. 9:19 [4] *journey*
37 [n] Num. 9:19-22
38 [o] Ex. 13:21; Num. 9:15; Ps. 78:14; Is. 4:5

40:34 the cloud covered…the glory of the LORD filled. This was the final confirmation for Moses and the people that all the work for setting up God's dwelling place had been properly done and all the tedious instructions obediently followed.

40:36 taken up. This first occurred (as recorded in Num. 10:11) 50 days after the tabernacle was finished and erected.

The Third Book of Moses Called

LEVITICUS

Title

The original Hebrew title of this third book of the law is taken from the first word, translated "And He called." Several OT books derive their Hebrew names in the same manner (e.g., Genesis, "In the beginning"; Exodus, "Now these are the names"). The title "Leviticus" comes from the Latin Vulgate version of the Greek OT (LXX) *Leuitikon* meaning "matters of the Levites" (25:32,33). While the book addresses issues of the Levites' responsibilities, much more significantly, all the priests are instructed in how they are to assist the people in worship, and the people are informed about how to live a holy life. New Testament writers quote the book of Leviticus over 15 times.

Author and Date

Authorship and date issues are resolved by the concluding verse of the book, "These *are* the commandments which the LORD commanded Moses for the children of Israel on Mount Sinai" (27:34; cf. 7:38; 25:1; 26:46). The fact that God gave these laws to Moses (cf. 1:1) appears 56 times in Leviticus' 27 chapters. In addition to recording detailed prescriptions, the book chronicles several historical accounts relating to the laws (see 8–10; 24:10-23). The Exodus occurred in 1445 B.C. (see Introduction to Exodus: Author and Date) and the tabernacle was finished one year later (Ex. 40:17). Leviticus picks up the record at that point, probably revealed in the first month (Abib/Nisan) of the second year after the Exodus. The book of Numbers begins after that in the second month (Ziv; cf. Num. 1:1).

Background and Setting

Before the year that Israel camped at Mt. Sinai: 1) the presence of God's glory had never formally resided among the Israelites; 2) a central place of worship, like the tabernacle, had never existed; 3) a structured and regulated set of sacrifices and feasts had not been given; and 4) a High-Priest, a formal priesthood, and a cadre of tabernacle workers had not been appointed. As Exodus concluded, features one and two had been accomplished, thereby requiring that elements three and four be inaugurated, which is where Leviticus fits in. Exodus 19:6 called Israel to be "a kingdom of priests and a holy nation." Leviticus in turn is God's instruction for His newly redeemed people, teaching them how to worship and obey Him.

Israel had, up to that point, only the historical records of the patriarchs from which to gain their knowledge of how to worship and live before their God. Having been slaves for centuries in Egypt, the land of a seemingly infinite number of gods, their concept of worship and the godly life was severely distorted. Their tendency to hold on to polytheism and pagan ritual is witnessed in the wilderness wanderings, e.g., when they worshiped the golden calf (cf. Ex. 32). God would not permit them to worship in the ways of their Egyptian neighbors, nor would He tolerate Egyptian ideas about morality and sin. With the instructions in Leviticus, the priests could lead Israel in worship appropriate to the Lord.

Even though the book contains a great deal of law, it is presented in a historical format. Immediately after Moses supervised the construction of the tabernacle, God came in glory to dwell there; this marked the close of the book of Exodus (40:34-38). Leviticus begins with God calling Moses from the tabernacle and ends with God's commands to Moses in the form of binding legislation. Israel's King had occupied His palace (the tabernacle), instituted His law, and declared Himself a covenant partner with His subjects.

No geographical movement occurs in this book. The people of Israel stay at the foot of Sinai, the mountain where God came down to give His law (25:1; 26:46; 27:34). They were still there one month later when the record of Numbers began (cf. Num. 1:1).

Historical and Theological Themes

The core ideas around which Leviticus develops are the holy character of God and the will of God for Israel's holiness. God's holiness, mankind's sinfulness, sacrifice, and God's presence in the sanctuary are the book's most common themes. With a clear, authoritative tone, the book sets forth instruction toward personal holiness at the urging of God (11:44,45; 19:2; 20:7,26; cf. 1 Pet. 1:14-16). Matters pertaining to Israel's life of faith tend to focus on purity in ritual settings, but not to the exclusion of concerns regarding Israel's personal purity. In fact, there is a continuing emphasis on personal holiness in response to the holiness of God (cf. this emphasis in chaps. 17–27). On over 125 occasions, Leviticus indicts mankind for uncleanness and/or instructs on how to be purified. The motive for such holiness is stated in two repeated phrases: "I am the LORD" and "I am holy." These are used over 50 times. *See note on 11:44,45.*

The theme of the conditional Mosaic Covenant resurfaces throughout the book, but particularly in chap. 26. This contract for the new nation not only details the consequences for obedience or disobedience to the covenant stipulations, but it does so in a manner scripted for determining Israel's history. One cannot help but recognize prophetic implications in the punishments for disobedience; they sound like the events of the much later Babylonian deportment, captivity, and subsequent return to the land almost 900 years after Moses wrote Leviticus (ca. 538 B.C.). The eschatological implications for Israel's disobedience will not conclude until Messiah comes to introduce His kingdom and end the curses of Lev. 26 and Deut. 28 (cf. Zech. 14:11).

The 5 sacrifices and offerings were symbolic. Their design was to allow the truly penitent and thankful worshiper to express faith in and love for God by the observance of these rituals. When the heart was not penitent and thankful, God was not pleased with the ritual. Cf. Amos 5:21-27. The offerings were burnt, symbolizing the worshiper's desire to be purged of sin and sending up the fragrant smoke of true worship to God. The myriad of small details in the execution of the rituals was to teach exactness and precision that would extend to the way the people obeyed the moral and spiritual laws of God and the way they revered every facet of His Word.

Interpretive Challenges

Leviticus is both a manual for the worship of God in Israel and a theology of Old Covenant ritual. Comprehensive understanding of the ceremonies, laws, and ritual details prescribed in the book is difficult today because Moses assumed a certain context of historical understanding. Once the challenge of understanding the detailed prescriptions has been met, the question arises as to how believers in the church should respond to them, since the NT clearly abrogates OT ceremonial law (cf. Acts 10:1-16; Col. 2:16,17), the levitical priesthood (cf. 1 Pet. 2:9; Rev. 1:6; 5:10; 20:6), and the sanctuary (cf. Matt. 27:51), as well as instituting the New Covenant (cf. Matt. 26:28; 2 Cor. 3:6-18; Heb. 7–10). Rather than try to practice the old ceremonies or look for some deeper spiritual significance in them, the focus should be on the holy and divine character behind them. This may partly be the reason that explanations which Moses often gave in the prescriptions for cleanness offer greater insight into the mind of God than do the ceremonies themselves. The spiritual principles in which the rituals were rooted are timeless because they are embedded in the nature of God. The NT makes it clear that from Pentecost forward (cf. Acts 2), the church is under the authority of the New Covenant, not the Old (cf. Heb. 7–10).

The interpreter is challenged to compare features of this book with NT writers who present types or analogies based on the tabernacle and the ceremonial aspects of the law, so as to teach valuable lessons about Christ and New Covenant reality. Though the ceremonial law served only as a shadow of the reality of Christ and His redemptive work (Heb. 10:1), excessive typology is to be rejected. Only that which NT writers identify as types of Christ should be so designated (cf. 1 Cor. 5:7, "Christ our Passover").

The most profitable study in Leviticus is that which yields truth in the understanding of sin, guilt, substitutionary death, and atonement by focusing on features which are not explained or illustrated elsewhere in OT Scripture. Later OT authors, and especially NT writers, build on the basic understanding of these matters provided in Leviticus. The sacrificial features of Leviticus point to their ultimate, one-time fulfillment in the substitutionary death of Jesus Christ (Heb. 9:11-22).

Outline

Leviticus 1–16 explains how to have personal access to God through appropriate worship and Leviticus 17–27 details how to be spiritually acceptable to God through an obedient walk.

Outline

- I. Laws Pertaining to Sacrifice (1:1–7:38)
  - A. Legislation for the Laity (1:1–6:7)
    1. Burnt offerings (chap. 1)
    2. Grain offerings (chap. 2)
    3. Peace offerings (chap. 3)
    4. Sin offerings (4:1–5:13)
    5. Trespass offerings (5:14–6:7)
  - B. Legislation for the Priesthood (6:8–7:38)
    1. Burnt offerings (6:8-13)
    2. Grain offerings (6:14-23)
    3. Sin offerings (6:24-30)
    4. Trespass offerings (7:1-10)
    5. Peace offerings (7:11-36)
    6. Concluding remarks (7:37,38)
- II. Beginnings of the Priesthood (8:1–10:20)
  - A. Ordination of Aaron and His Sons (chap. 8)
  - B. First Sacrifices (chap. 9)
  - C. Execution of Nadab and Abihu (chap. 10)
- III. Prescriptions for Uncleanness (11:1–16:34)
  - A. Unclean Animals (chap. 11)
  - B. Uncleanness of Childbirth (chap. 12)
  - C. Unclean Diseases (chap. 13)
  - D. Cleansing of Diseases (chap. 14)
  - E. Unclean Discharges (chap. 15)
  - F. Purification of the Tabernacle from Uncleanness (chap. 16)
- IV. Guidelines for Practical Holiness (17:1–27:34)
  - A. Sacrifice and Food (chap. 17)
  - B. Proper Sexual Behavior (chap. 18)
  - C. Neighborliness (chap. 19)
  - D. Capital/Grave Crimes (chap. 20)
  - E. Instructions for Priests (chaps. 21,22)
  - F. Religious Festivals (chap. 23)
  - G. The Tabernacle (24:1-9)
  - H. An Account of Blasphemy (24:10-23)
  - I. Sabbatical and Jubilee Years (chap. 25)
  - J. Exhortation to Obey the Law: Blessings and Curses (chap. 26)
  - K. Redemption of Votive Gifts (chap. 27)

The Burnt Offering

1 Now the LORD [a]called to Moses, and
spoke to him [b]from the tabernacle of
meeting, saying, 2 "Speak to the children
of Israel, and say to them: [c]'When any one
of you brings an offering to the LORD, you
shall bring your offering of the livestock—
of the herd and of the flock.
3 'If his offering *is* a burnt sacrifice of the
herd, let him offer a male [d]without blemish; he shall offer it of his own free will at
the door of the tabernacle of meeting before the LORD. 4 [e]Then he shall put his
hand on the head of the burnt offering,
and it will be [f]accepted on his behalf [g]to
make atonement for him. 5 He shall kill
the [h]bull before the LORD; [i]and the priests,
Aaron's sons, shall bring the blood [j]and
sprinkle the blood all around on the altar
that *is by* the door of the tabernacle of
meeting. 6 And he shall [k]skin the burnt offering and cut it into its pieces. 7 The sons
of Aaron the priest shall put [l]fire on the
altar, and [m]lay the wood in order on the
fire. 8 Then the priests, Aaron's sons, shall
lay the parts, the head, and the fat in order
on the wood that *is* on the fire upon the
altar; 9 but he shall wash its entrails and
its legs with water. And the priest shall
burn all on the altar as a burnt sacrifice, an

CHAPTER 1

1 [a]Ex. 19:3; 25:22; Num. 7:89 [b]Ex. 40:34
2 [c]Lev. 22:18, 19
3 [d]Ex. 12:5; Lev. 22:20-24; Deut. 15:21; Eph. 5:27; Heb. 9:14; 1 Pet. 1:19
4 [e]Ex. 29:10, 15, 19; Lev. 3:2, 8, 13; 4:15 [f][Rom. 12:1]; Phil. 4:18 [g]Lev. 4:20, 26, 31; 2 Chr. 29:23, 24
5 [h]Mic. 6:6 [i]2 Chr. 35:11 [j]Lev. 1:11; 3:2, 8, 13; [Heb. 12:24; 1 Pet. 1:2]
6 [k]Lev. 7:8
7 [l]Lev. 6:8-13; Mal. 1:10 [m]Gen. 22:9

1:1–7:38 This section provides laws pertaining to sacrifice. For the first time in Israel's history, a well defined set of sacrifices were given to them, although people had offered sacrifices since the time of Abel and Cain (cf. Gen. 4:3,4). This section contains instructions for the people (1:1–6:7) and the priests (6:8–7:38). For a comparison with the millennial kingdom sacrifices, *see notes on Ezek. 45,46.*

1:1–6:7 God had taken the nation at its word, "All that the LORD has spoken we will do" (Ex. 19:8; 24:3-8) and gave detailed instructions as to how they were to sacrifice to Him. Five sacrifices were outlined: the first 3 were voluntary, the last 2 compulsory. They were: 1) burnt offering (1:1-17); 2) grain offering (2:1-16); 3) peace offering (3:1-17); 4) sin offering (4:1–5:13); and 5) trespass offering (5:14–6:7). All these offerings were forms of worship to God, to give expression of the penitent and thankful heart. Those who were truly God's by faith gave these offerings with an attitude of worship; for the rest, they were external rituals only.

1:1 Now the LORD called to Moses. Leviticus begins where Exodus left off (See Introduction: Author and Date; Background and Setting). No sooner did the glory cloud come down to rest on the tabernacle in the concluding verses of Exodus, than God instructed Moses with the content in Leviticus. The question of how to use the tabernacle in worship is answered here by an audible voice from the Divine Glory over the ark in the Holy of Holies (cf. Ex. 40:34; Num. 7:89; Ps. 80:1). **tabernacle of meeting.** This is so named since it was the place where Israel would gather to meet the Lord (cf. Ex. 25:8,22; 26:1-37). See Ex. 25–32 for a detailed description of the tabernacle.

1:2 Speak to the children of Israel. This is essential revelation, with reference to their spiritual life, for all the descendants of Jacob, who was also called Israel (cf. Gen. 32:28). **When any one of you brings.** These were completely voluntary and freewill offerings with no specific number or frequency given (1:3). The regulation excluded horses, dogs, pigs, camels, and donkeys, which were used in pagan sacrifices, as well as rabbits, deer, beasts, and birds of prey. The sacrifice had to be from the offerer's herd or he had to purchase it. **an offering.** The Pharisees manipulated this simple concept so that adult children could selfishly withhold the material goods which would help their parents, under the guise of *Corban*, that it was dedicated to the Lord (cf. Mark 7:8-13). **herd...flock.** These terms refer to the cattle (1:3), sheep, or goats (1:10) respectively. Only domestic animals could be sacrificed.

1:3-17 See 6:8-13 for the priests' instructions. The burnt offerings were the first sacrifices revealed because these were the ones to be most frequently offered: every morning and evening (Num. 28:1-8), every Sabbath (Num. 28:9,10), the first day of each month (Num. 28:11-15), and at the special feasts (Num. 28:16–29:40). This offering signified voluntary and complete dedication and consecration to the Lord. It was an offering of repentance for sins committed, with the desire to be purged from the guilt of sinful acts. Designed to demonstrate the sinner's penitence and obedience, it indicated his self-dedication to the worship of God. The most costly animal was mentioned first; the least costly last. The singing of psalms later became a part of this ritual (cf. Pss. 4; 5; 40; 50; 66).

1:3-9 This section describes the sacrifice of bulls (1:5).

1:3 burnt sacrifice. This offering is so called because it required that the animal be completely consumed by the fire, except for the crop of feathers of a bird (1:16) or skin of the bull, which went to the priest (1:6; 7:8). **a male without blemish.** Since no animal with any deformity or defect was permitted, the priests would inspect each animal, perhaps using a method which the Egyptians employed in their sacrifices, calling for all inspected and approved animals to have a certificate attached to the horns and sealed with wax. A male without blemish was required, as it was the choicest offering of the flock. **at the door...before the LORD.** This entrance to the courtyard around the tabernacle where the altar of burnt offering stood (Ex. 40:6) would place the one offering a sacrifice on the N side of the altar (cf. 1:11). God's presence in the cloud rested upon the mercy seat of the ark in the Holy of Holies inside the tabernacle proper (*see note on 1:1*). The offering was brought to and offered before the Lord, not before man.

1:4 put his hand on the head. This symbolic gesture pictured the transfer of the sacrificer's sin to the sacrificial animal and was likely done with a prayer of repentance and request for forgiveness (cf. Ps. 51:18,19). **on his behalf.** This was a substitutionary sacrifice that prefigured the ultimate substitute—Jesus Christ (cf. Is. 53; *see note on 2 Cor. 5:21*). **make atonement.** The word means "cover." The psalmist defines it by saying, "Blessed is *he whose* transgression *is* forgiven, *whose* sin *is* covered" (Ps. 32:1). Theologically, the "atonement" of the OT covered sin only temporarily, but it did not eliminate sin or later judgment (Heb. 10:4). The one time sacrifice of Jesus Christ fully atoned for sin, thus satisfying God's wrath forever and insuring eternal salvation (cf. Heb. 9:12; 1 John 2:2), even to those who put saving faith in God for their redemption before Christ's death on the cross (cf. Rom. 3:25,26; Heb. 9:15).

1:5 He shall kill. Making vivid and dramatic the consequences of sin, the person offering the sacrifice slew and butchered the animal (cf. v. 6). **Aaron's sons.** This refers to the immediate descendants of Aaron, i.e., Nadab, Abihu, Eleazar, and Ithamar (cf. Ex. 28:1). In the beginning, there were 5 priests, including Aaron, who served as the High-Priest. **shall bring...sprinkle the blood.** The priest had to collect the blood in a basin and then offer it to God as a sacrifice to indicate that a life had been taken, i.e., death occurred (cf. 17:11,14). The price of sin is always death (cf. Gen. 2:17; Rom. 6:23). **the altar.** The altar of burnt offering (cf. Ex. 27:1-8; 38:1-7), which is in the courtyard outside of the tabernacle proper. The prototype experience, before the tabernacle was constructed, is remembered in Ex. 24:1-8.

1:9 wash. This allowed the one sacrificing to cleanse the animal of excrement and thus make it clean. **a sweet aroma.** The pleasant

offering made by fire, a [n]sweet[1] aroma to
the LORD.
10 'If his offering *is* of the flocks—of the
sheep or of the goats—as a burnt sacrifice,
he shall bring a male [o]without blemish.
11 [p]He shall kill it on the north side of the
altar before the LORD; and the priests, Aaron's sons, shall sprinkle its blood all
around on the altar. 12 And he shall cut it
into its pieces, with its head and its fat; and
the priest shall lay them in order on the
wood that *is* on the fire upon the altar;
13 but he shall wash the entrails and the
legs with water. Then the priest shall bring
it all and burn *it* on the altar; it *is* a burnt
sacrifice, an [q]offering made by fire, a sweet
aroma to the LORD.
14 'And if the burnt sacrifice of his offering to the LORD *is* of birds, then he shall
bring his offering of [r]turtledoves or young
pigeons. 15 The priest shall bring it to the
altar, [2]wring off its head, and burn *it* on the
altar; its blood shall be drained out at the
side of the altar. 16 And he shall remove its
crop with its feathers and cast it [s]beside the
altar on the east side, into the place for
ashes. 17 Then he shall split it at its wings,
but [t]shall not divide *it* completely; and the
priest shall burn it on the altar, on the
wood that *is* on the fire. [u]It *is* a burnt sacrifice, an offering made by fire, a [3]sweet
aroma to the LORD.

9 [n] Gen. 8:21; [Ezek. 20:28, 41; 2 Cor. 2:15] [1] *soothing* or *pleasing aroma*
10 [o] Ex. 12:5; Lev. 1:3; Ezek. 43:22; [1 Pet. 1:19]
11 [p] Ex. 24:6; 40:22; Lev. 1:5; Ezek. 8:5
13 [q] Num. 15:4-7; 28:12-14
14 [r] Gen. 15:9; Lev. 5:7, 11; 12:8; Luke 2:24
15 [2] Lit. *nip* or *chop off*
16 [s] Lev. 6:10
17 [t] Gen. 15:10; Lev. 5:8 [u] Lev. 1:9, 13 [3] *soothing* or *pleasing aroma*

CHAPTER 2

1 [a] Lev. 6:14; 9:17; Num. 15:4 [b] Lev. 5:11
2 [c] Lev. 2:9; 5:12; 6:15; 24:7; Acts 10:4
3 [d] Lev. 7:9 [e] Lev. 6:6; 10:12, 13 [f] Ex. 29:37; Num. 18:9
4 [g] Ex. 29:2 [1] *spread*
5 [2] *flat plate or griddle*
7 [h] Lev. 7:9
9 [i] Lev. 2:2, 16; 5:12; 6:15 [j] Ex. 29:18
10 [k] Lev. 2:3; 6:16

The Grain Offering

2 'When anyone offers [a]a grain offering
to the LORD, his offering shall be *of* fine
flour. And he shall pour oil on it, and put
[b]frankincense on it. 2 He shall bring it to
Aaron's sons, the priests, one of whom
shall take from it his handful of fine flour
and oil with all the frankincense. And the
priest shall burn [c]*it as* a memorial on the
altar, an offering made by fire, a sweet
aroma to the LORD. 3 [d]The rest of the grain
offering *shall be* Aaron's and his [e]sons'. [f]*It*
is most holy of the offerings to the LORD
made by fire.
4 'And if you bring as an offering a grain
offering baked in the oven, *it shall be* unleavened cakes of fine flour mixed with oil,
or unleavened wafers [g]anointed[1] with oil.
5 But if your offering *is* a grain offering
baked in a [2]pan, *it shall be of* fine flour, unleavened, mixed with oil. 6 You shall break
it in pieces and pour oil on it; it *is* a grain
offering.
7 'If your offering *is* a grain offering
baked in a [h]covered pan, it shall be made *of*
fine flour with oil. 8 You shall bring the
grain offering that is made of these things
to the LORD. And when it is presented to
the priest, he shall bring it to the altar.
9 Then the priest shall take from the grain
offering [i]a memorial portion, and burn *it*
on the altar. *It is* an [j]offering made by fire,
a sweet aroma to the LORD. 10 And [k]what is

smell of burning meat signified the sacrifice of obedience which was pleasing to the Lord. While the costly ritual recognized God's anger for sin committed (cf. 1:13,17), the penitent heart behind the sacrifice made it acceptable. That was far more significant than the sacrifice itself (cf. Gen. 8:21; 1 Sam. 15:23). This is the first of 3 freewill offerings to please the Lord; cf. the grain offering (2:2) and the peace offering (3:5).

1:10-13 of the flocks. This section describes the sacrifice of sheep and goats.

1:11 north side. This placed the one sacrificing in front of the tabernacle door (cf. 1:3).

1:14-17 of birds. This section describes the sacrifice of birds. God does not ask the poor to bring the same burnt offering as those financially well off because the relative cost to the one sacrificing was an important factor. This is the kind of sacrifice brought by Joseph and Mary on the eighth day after Christ's birth for Mary's purification (cf. 12:8; Luke 2:22-24).

1:15 The priest...wring off. Unlike the livestock being killed by the one offering the sacrifice, the bird was killed by the priest.

1:16 crop...feathers. This refers to the neck or gullet of a bird, where food was stored. **east side...place for ashes.** This was the closest side to the entrance of the tabernacle compound and provided for the easiest removal of the ashes outside (cf. 6:10-11).

2:1-16 See 6:14-23 for the priests' instructions. The grain offering signified homage and thanksgiving to God as a voluntary offering which was offered along with a burnt offering and a drink offering at the appointed sacrifices (cf. Num. 28:1-15). Three variations were prescribed: 1) uncooked flour (2:1-3); 2) baked flour (2:4-13); or 3) roasted firstfruit grain from the harvest (2:14-16). This was the only non-animal sacrifice of the 5 and shows that there was a place for offering from the fruit of the soil (as in the case of Cain in Gen. 4).

2:1-3 fine flour. The first variation consisted of uncooked flour whose quality of "fine" paralleled the "unblemished" animal in the burnt offering. A portion of this offering was to support the priests (v. 3). Like the drink offering or "libation," the grain offering was added to the burnt offering (cf. Num. 28:1-15).

2:1 oil. *See note on 2:4.* **frankincense.** *See note on 2:15.*

2:2 handful. Unlike the whole burnt offering (1:9), only a representative or memorial portion was given to the Lord. **sweet aroma.** *See note on 1:9.*

2:3 Aaron's and his sons'. Unlike the burnt offering (cf. 1:9,13,17), this offering supplies provision for the priests. **most holy.** This was unique from the others because it was not limited to God alone, like the burnt offering, nor eaten in part by the worshiper, like the peace offering. Only the priest could eat the portion not burned (see 7:9). The sin offering (6:17,25) and the trespass offering (6:17; 7:1) are also called "most holy."

2:4-13 This variation of the grain offering involved baked flour. The kinds of containers discussed are: 1) oven (2:4); 2) griddle (2:5,6); and 3) covered pan (2:7-10). The manner of preparation is discussed in 2:11-13.

2:4 unleavened cakes. The notion of leaven as a symbol representing the presence of sin remains valid beyond the context of the Passover and continues to the NT (cf. Matt. 16:6; 1 Cor. 5:6,7). **anointed with oil.** Anointing is usually reserved for human appointments by God. Here, it was applied to the preparation of a holy sacrifice, set apart as a memorial to the Lord.

left of the grain offering *shall be* Aaron's
and his sons'. *It is* most holy of the offerings to the LORD made by fire.
11 'No grain offering which you bring to
the LORD shall be made with [l]leaven, for
you shall burn no leaven nor any honey in
any offering to the LORD made by fire.
12 [m]As for the offering of the firstfruits,
you shall offer them to the LORD, but they
shall not be burned on the altar for a sweet
aroma. 13 And every offering of your grain
offering [n]you shall season with salt; you
shall not allow [o]the salt of the covenant of
your God to be lacking from your grain offering. [p]With all your offerings you shall
offer salt.
14 'If you offer a grain offering of your
firstfruits to the LORD, [q]you shall offer for
the grain offering of your firstfruits green
heads of grain roasted on the fire, grain
beaten from [r]full heads. 15 And [s]you shall
put oil on it, and lay frankincense on it. It
is a grain offering. 16 Then the priest shall
burn [t]the memorial portion: *part* of its
beaten grain and *part* of its oil, with all the
frankincense, as an offering made by fire to
the LORD.

11 [l]Ex. 23:18; 34:25; Lev. 6:16, 17; [Matt. 16:12; Mark 8:15; Luke 12:1; 1 Cor. 5:8; Gal. 5:9] **12** [m]Ex. 22:29; 34:22; Lev. 23:10, 11, 17, 18 **13** [n][Mark 9:49, 50; Col. 4:6] [o]Num. 18:19; 2 Chr. 13:5 [p]Ezek. 43:24 **14** [q]Lev. 23:10, 14 [r]2 Kin. 4:42 **15** [s]Lev. 2:1 **16** [t]Lev. 2:2

CHAPTER 3

1 [a]Lev. 7:11, 29 [b]Lev. 1:3; 22:20-24 [1]*imperfection or defect* **2** [c]Ex. 29:10, 11, 16, 20; Lev. 1:4, 5; 16:21 [d]Lev. 1:5 **3** [e]Ex. 29:13, 22; Lev. 1:8; 3:16; 4:8, 9 **5** [f]Ex. 29:13; Lev. 6:12; 7:28-34 [g]2 Chr. 35:14 [h]Num. 28:3-10 [i]Num. 15:8-10 **6** [j]Lev. 3:1; 22:20-24 **7** [k]Num. 15:4, 5 [l]1 Kin. 8:62 [m]Lev. 17:8, 9

The Peace Offering

3 'When his offering *is* a [a]sacrifice of a
peace offering, if he offers *it* of the
herd, whether male or female, he shall
offer it [b]without [1]blemish before the
LORD. 2 And [c]he shall lay his hand on the
head of his offering, and kill it *at* the door
of the tabernacle of meeting; and Aaron's
sons, the priests, shall [d]sprinkle the blood
all around on the altar. 3 Then he shall
offer from the sacrifice of the peace offering an offering made by fire to the LORD.
[e]The fat that covers the entrails and all the
fat that *is* on the entrails, 4 the two kidneys and the fat that *is* on them by the
flanks, and the fatty lobe *attached* to the
liver above the kidneys, he shall remove;
5 and Aaron's sons [f]shall burn it on the
altar upon the [g]burnt sacrifice, which *is*
on the wood that *is* on the fire, *as* an [h]of-
fering made by fire, a [i]sweet aroma to the
LORD.
6 'If his offering as a sacrifice of a peace
offering to the LORD *is* of the flock, *whether*
male or female, [j]he shall offer it without
blemish. 7 If he offers a [k]lamb as his offering, then he shall [l]offer it [m]before the
LORD. 8 And he shall lay his hand on the

2:11 This applies to the offerings of 2:4-10, all of which were to be burned on the altar. **no leaven nor any honey.** Both yeast and honey were edible foods, but were never to be used with a grain offering, since both could induce fermentation, which symbolized sin (*see note on 2:4*).

2:12 This applies to the offering of 2:14-16, which was not to be burned on the altar, but rather roasted by the worshiper (v. 14) before going to the tabernacle.

2:13 the salt of the covenant. This was included in all of the offerings in 2:4-10,14-16 since salt was emblematic of permanence or loyalty to the covenant.

2:14 firstfruits. These would be offered at the Feast of Firstfruits (23:9-14) and the Feast of Weeks (23:15-22).

2:15 frankincense. A gum resin with a pungent, balsamic odor, used for the incense in the tabernacle sacrifices (cf. Ex. 30:34).

3:1-17 See 7:11-36 for the priests' instructions. The peace offering symbolizes the peace and fellowship between the true worshiper and God (as a voluntary offering). It was the third freewill offering resulting in a sweet aroma to the Lord (3:5), which served as the appropriate corollary to the burnt offering of atonement and the grain offering of consecration and dedication. It symbolized the fruit of redemptive reconciliation between a sinner and God (cf. 2 Cor. 5:18).

3:1-5 Pertains to cattle, i.e., the herd, used in the peace offering.

3:1,2 male or female. This is similar to the burnt offering in manner of presentation (cf. 1:3-9), but different in that a female was allowed.

3:4 the fat. All of the fat was dedicated to the Lord (3:3-5,9-11,14-16).

3:6-11 Pertains to sheep used in the peace offering.

Christ in the Levitical Offerings

Offering	Christ's Provision	Christ's Character
1. Burnt Offering (Lev. 1:3-17; 6:8-13)	atonement	Christ's sinless nature
2. Grain Offering (Lev. 2:1-16; 6:14-23)	dedication/consecration	Christ was wholly devoted to the Father's purposes
3. Peace Offering (Lev. 3:1-17; 7:11-36)	reconciliation/fellowship	Christ was at peace with God
4. Sin Offering (Lev. 4:1–5:13; 6:24-30)	propitiation	Christ's substitutionary death
5. Trespass Offering (Lev. 5:14–6:7; 7:1-10)	repentance	Christ paid it all for redemption

head of his offering, and kill it before the
tabernacle of meeting; and Aaron's sons
shall sprinkle its blood all around on the
altar.
9 'Then he shall offer from the sacrifice
of the peace offering, as an offering made
by fire to the LORD, its fat *and* the whole fat
tail which he shall remove close to the
backbone. And the fat that covers the entrails and all the fat that *is* on the entrails,
10 the two kidneys and the fat that *is* on
them by the flanks, and the fatty lobe *attached* to the liver above the kidneys, he
shall remove; 11 and the priest shall burn
them on the altar *as* [n]food, an offering
made by fire to the LORD.
12 'And if his [o]offering *is* a goat, then
[p]he shall offer it before the LORD. 13 He
shall lay his hand on its head and kill it before the tabernacle of meeting; and the
sons of Aaron shall sprinkle its blood all
around on the altar. 14 Then he shall offer
from it his offering, as an offering made by
fire to the LORD. The fat that covers the entrails and all the fat that *is* on the entrails,
15 the two kidneys and the fat that *is* on
them by the flanks, and the fatty lobe *attached* to the liver above the kidneys, he
shall remove; 16 and the priest shall burn
them on the altar *as* food, an offering made
by fire for a sweet aroma; [q]all the fat *is* the
LORD's.
17 '*This shall be* a [r]perpetual[2] statute
throughout your generations in all your
dwellings: you shall eat neither fat nor
[s]blood.' "

11 [n] Lev. 21:6, 8, 17, 21, 22; 22:25; Num. 28:2; [Ezek. 44:7; Mal. 1:7, 12]
12 [o] Num. 15:6-11 [p] Lev. 3:1, 7
16 [q] Lev. 7:23-25; 1 Sam. 2:15; 2 Chr. 7:7
17 [r] Lev. 6:18; 7:36; 17:7; 23:14 [s] Gen. 9:4; Lev. 7:23, 26; 17:10, 14; 1 Sam. 14:33 [2] *everlasting* or *never-ending*

CHAPTER 4

2 [a] Lev. 5:15-18; Num. 15:22-30; 1 Sam. 14:27; Acts 3:17 [1] *through error*
3 [b] Ex. 40:15; Lev. 8:12 [c] Lev. 3:1; 9:2 [d] Lev. 9:7
4 [e] Lev. 1:3, 4; 4:15; Num. 8:12
5 [f] Lev. 16:14; Num. 19:4
6 [g] Ex. 40:21, 26
7 [h] Lev. 4:18, 25, 30, 34; 8:15; 9:9; 16:18 [i] Ex. 40:5, 6; Lev. 5:9
10 [j] Lev. 3:3-5

The Sin Offering

4 Now the LORD spoke to Moses, saying,
2 "Speak to the children of Israel, saying: [a]'If a person sins [1]unintentionally
against any of the commandments of the
LORD *in anything* which ought not to be
done, and does any of them, 3 [b]if the
anointed priest sins, bringing guilt on the
people, then let him offer to the LORD for
his sin which he has sinned [c]a young bull
without blemish as a [d]sin offering. 4 He
shall bring the bull [e]to the door of the
tabernacle of meeting before the LORD, lay
his hand on the bull's head, and kill the
bull before the LORD. 5 Then the anointed
priest [f]shall take some of the bull's blood
and bring it to the tabernacle of meeting.
6 The priest shall dip his finger in the blood
and sprinkle some of the blood seven times
before the LORD, in front of the [g]veil of the
sanctuary. 7 And the priest shall [h]put some
of the blood on the horns of the altar of
sweet incense before the LORD, which is in
the tabernacle of meeting; and he shall
pour [i]the remaining blood of the bull at the
base of the altar of the burnt offering,
which is at the door of the tabernacle of
meeting. 8 He shall take from it all the fat
of the bull as the sin offering. The fat that
covers the entrails and all the fat which *is*
on the entrails, 9 the two kidneys and the
fat that *is* on them by the flanks, and the
fatty lobe *attached* to the liver above the
kidneys, he shall remove, 10 [j]as it was
taken from the bull of the sacrifice of the
peace offering; and the priest shall burn
them on the altar of the burnt offering.

3:11 *as* food. The sacrifice was intended to symbolize a meal between God and the one offering it, where peace and friendship were epitomized by sharing that meal together.

3:12-16 Pertains to goats used in the peace offering.

3:17 neither fat nor blood. The details given in the chapter distinctly define which fat was to be burned and not eaten, so that whatever adhered to other parts or was mixed with them might be eaten. As with many facets of the Mosaic legislation, there were underlying health benefits also.

4:1–6:7 The sin (4:1–5:13) and trespass (5:14–6:7) offerings differed from the previous 3 in that the former were voluntary and these were compulsory. The sin offering differed from the trespass offering in that the former involved iniquity where restitution was not possible, while in the latter it was possible.

4:1–5:13 See 6:24-30 for the priests' instructions. The sin offering atoned for sins committed unknowingly where restitution was impossible. This was a required sacrifice, as was the trespass offering (5:14–6:7). Unintentional sins of commission (4:1-35) and unintentional sins of omission (5:1-13) are discussed. Leviticus 4:1-35 indicates the person committing the sin: 1) the High-Priest (vv. 3-12); 2) the congregation (vv. 13-21); 3) a leader (vv. 22-26); and 4) an individual (vv. 27-35). Leviticus 5:1-13 unfolds according to the animal sacrificed: 1) lamb/goat (vv. 1-6); 2) bird (vv. 7-10); and 3) flour (vv. 11-13).

4:2 unintentionally. The intended meaning is to stray into a sinful situation, but not necessarily to be taken completely by surprise. Num. 15:30,31 illustrates the defiant attitude of intentional sin. **ought not…does any.** Sins of commission.

4:3-12 Sacrifices for the sin of the High-Priest are given.

4:3 the anointed priest. See Ex. 29:29 and Lev. 16:32, which defined this person as the High-Priest. **bringing guilt on the people.** Only the High-Priest, due to his representative position, was capable of this type of guilt infusion. For example, Achan had brought about the defeat of Israel when he held back the spoils, but the entire nation was not executed, as was his family (cf. Josh. 7:22-26).

4:5 to the tabernacle. He actually went into the Holy Place.

4:6 seven times. The number of completion or perfection, indicating the nature of God's forgiveness (Ps. 103:12). **the veil of the sanctuary.** The veil marked the entry into the very presence of God in the Holy of Holies.

4:7 altar of sweet incense. See Ex. 30:1-10. This altar was in the tabernacle proper before the veil. It was so close to the ark that Hebrews speaks of it as actually being in the Holy of Holies (Heb. 9:4). This altar was also sprinkled with blood on the Day of Atonement (Ex. 30:10). **altar…burnt offering.** The altar in the courtyard on which blood was normally splashed.

4:10 peace offering. *See note on 3:1-17.*

11 [k]But the bull's hide and all its flesh, with
its head and legs, its entrails and offal—
12 the whole bull he shall carry outside the
camp to a clean place, [l]where the ashes are
poured out, and [m]burn it on wood with
fire; where the ashes are poured out it shall
be burned.
13 'Now [n]if the whole congregation of Israel sins unintentionally, [o]and the thing is
hidden from the eyes of the assembly, and
they have done *something against* any of the
commandments of the LORD *in anything*
which should not be done, and are guilty;
14 when the sin which they have committed becomes known, then the assembly
shall offer a young bull for the sin, and
bring it before the tabernacle of meeting.
15 And the elders of the congregation
[p]shall lay their hands on the head of the
bull before the LORD. Then the bull shall be
killed before the LORD. 16 [q]The anointed
priest shall bring some of the bull's blood
to the tabernacle of meeting. 17 Then the
priest shall dip his finger in the blood and
sprinkle *it* seven times before the LORD, in
front of the veil. 18 And he shall put *some* of
the blood on the horns of the altar which *is*
before the LORD, which *is* in the tabernacle
of meeting; and he shall pour the remaining blood at the base of the altar of burnt
offering, which is at the door of the tabernacle of meeting. 19 He shall take all the fat
from it and burn *it* on the altar. 20 And he
shall do [r]with the bull as he did with the
bull as a sin offering; thus he shall do with
it. [s]So the priest shall make [2]atonement for
them, and it shall be forgiven them.
21 Then he shall carry the bull outside the
camp, and burn it as he burned the first
bull. It *is* a sin offering for the assembly.
22 'When a [3]ruler has sinned, and [t]done
something unintentionally *against* any of
the commandments of the LORD his God *in*
anything which should not be done, and is
guilty, 23 or [u]if his sin which he has committed [4]comes to his knowledge, he shall
bring as his offering a kid of the goats, a
male without blemish. 24 And [v]he shall lay
his hand on the head of the goat, and kill it
at the place where they kill the burnt offering before the LORD. It *is* a sin offering.
25 [w]The priest shall take some of the blood
of the sin offering with his finger, put *it* on
the horns of the altar of burnt offering, and
pour its blood at the base of the altar of
burnt offering. 26 And he shall burn all its
fat on the altar, like [x]the fat of the sacrifice
of the peace offering. [y]So the priest shall
make [5]atonement for him concerning his
sin, and it shall be forgiven him.
27 [z]'If [6]anyone of the [7]common people
sins unintentionally by doing *something*
against any of the commandments of the
LORD *in anything* which ought not to be
done, and is guilty, 28 or [a]if his sin which
he has committed comes to his knowledge,
then he shall bring as his offering a kid of
the goats, a female without blemish, for his
sin which he has committed. 29 [b]And he
shall lay his hand on the head of the sin offering, and kill the sin offering at the place
of the burnt offering. 30 Then the priest

11 [k]Ex. 29:14; Lev. 9:11; Num. 19:5
12 [l]Lev. 4:21; 6:10, 11; 16:27 [m][Heb. 13:11, 12]
13 [n]Num. 15:24-26; Josh. 7:11 [o]Lev. 5:2-4, 17
15 [p]Lev. 1:3, 4
16 [q]Lev. 4:5; [Heb. 9:12-14]
20 [r]Lev. 4:3 [s]Lev. 1:4; Num. 15:25 [2]Lit. *covering*
22 [t]Lev. 4:2, 13, 27 [3]*leader*
23 [u]Lev. 4:14; 5:4 [4]*is made known to him*
24 [v]Lev. 4:4; [Is. 53:6]
25 [w]Lev. 4:7, 18, 30, 34
26 [x]Lev. 3:3-5 [y]Lev. 4:20; Num. 15:28 [5]Lit. *covering*
27 [z]Lev. 4:2; Num. 15:27 [6]Lit. *any soul* [7]Lit. *people of the land*
28 [a]Lev. 4:23
29 [b]Lev. 1:4; 4:4, 24

4:11 offal. This term identifies the major internal organs of an animal.

4:12 carry outside the camp. This was a symbolic gesture of removing the sin from the people (cf. Heb. 13:11-13 in reference to Christ).

4:13-21 Sacrifices for the sin of the congregation were to follow essentially the same procedure as that for the sin of priests (4:3-12).

4:16 The anointed priest. *See note on 4:3.*

4:22-26 These are sacrifices for the sin of a ruler. The blood of the sacrifice was not sprinkled in the Holy Place, as for the priest or congregation (4:6,17), but only on the altar of burnt offering.

4:27-35 These are sacrifices for the sin of an individual. Either a goat (4:27-31) or a lamb (4:32-35) could be sacrificed in much the same manner as the offering for a ruler (4:22-26).

Old Testament Sacrifices Compared to Christ's Sacrifice

Leviticus		Hebrews
1. Old Covenant (temporary)	Heb. 7:22; 8:6,13; 10:20	1. New Covenant (permanent)
2. Obsolete promises	Heb. 8:6-13	2. Better promises
3. A shadow	Heb. 8:5; 9:23,24; 10:1	3. The reality
4. Aaronic priesthood (many)	Heb. 6:19–7:25	4. Melchizedekian priesthood (one)
5. Sinful priesthood	Heb. 7:26,27; 9:7	5. Sinless priest
6. Limited-by-death priesthood	Heb. 7:16,17,23,24	6. Forever priesthood
7. Daily sacrifices	Heb. 7:27; 9:12,25,26; 10:9,10,12	7. Once-for-all sacrifice
8. Animal sacrifices	Heb. 9:11-15,26; 10:4-10,19	8. Sacrifice of God's Son
9. Ongoing sacrifices	Heb. 10:11-14,18	9. Sacrifices no longer needed
10. One year atonement	Heb. 7:25; 9:12,15; 10:1-4,12	10. Eternal propitiation

shall take *some* of its blood with his finger,
put *it* on the horns of the altar of burnt offering, and pour all *the remaining* blood at
the base of the altar. 31 [c]He shall remove all
its fat, [d]as fat is removed from the sacrifice
of the peace offering; and the priest shall
burn it on the altar for a [e]sweet aroma to
the LORD. [f]So the priest shall make atonement for him, and it shall be forgiven him.
32 'If he brings a lamb as his sin offering,
[g]he shall bring a female without blemish.
33 Then he shall [h]lay his hand on the head
of the sin offering, and kill it as a sin offering at the place where they kill the burnt
offering. 34 The priest shall take *some* of the
blood of the sin offering with his finger,
put *it* on the horns of the altar of burnt offering, and pour all *the remaining* blood at
the base of the altar. 35 He shall remove all
its fat, as the fat of the lamb is removed
from the sacrifice of the peace offering.
Then the priest shall burn it on the altar,
[i]according to the offerings made by fire to
the LORD. [j]So the priest shall make atonement for his sin that he has committed, and
it shall be forgiven him.

The Trespass Offering

5 'If a person sins in [a]hearing the utterance of an oath, and *is* a witness,
whether he has seen or known *of the matter*—if he does not tell *it*, he [b]bears [1]guilt.
2 'Or [c]if a person touches any unclean
thing, whether *it is* the carcass of an unclean beast, or the carcass of unclean livestock, or the carcass of unclean creeping
things, and he is unaware of it, he also
shall be unclean and [d]guilty. 3 Or if he
touches [e]human uncleanness—whatever
uncleanness with which a man may be defiled, and he is unaware of it—when he realizes *it*, then he shall be guilty.
4 'Or if a person [2]swears, speaking
thoughtlessly with *his* lips [f]to do evil or [g]to
do good, whatever *it is* that a man may
pronounce by an oath, and he is unaware
of it—when he realizes *it*, then he shall be
guilty in any of these *matters*.
5 'And it shall be, when he is guilty in
any of these *matters*, that he shall [h]confess
that he has sinned in that *thing*; 6 and he
shall bring his trespass offering to the LORD
for his sin which he has committed, a female from the flock, a lamb or a kid of the
goats as a sin offering. So the priest shall
make atonement for him concerning his
sin.
7 [i]'If he is not able to bring a lamb, then
he shall bring to the LORD, for his trespass
which he has committed, two [j]turtledoves
or two young pigeons: one as a sin offering
and the other as a burnt offering. 8 And he
shall bring them to the priest, who shall
offer *that* which *is* for the sin offering first,
and [k]wring off its head from its neck, but
shall not divide *it* [3]completely. 9 Then he
shall sprinkle *some* of the blood of the sin
offering on the side of the altar, and the
[l]rest of the blood shall be drained out at
the base of the altar. It *is* a sin offering.
10 And he shall offer the second *as* a burnt
offering according to the [m]prescribed manner. So [n]the priest shall make atonement
on his behalf for his sin which he has committed, and it shall be forgiven him.
11 'But if he is [o]not able to bring two turtledoves or two young pigeons, then he
who sinned shall bring for his offering
one-tenth of an ephah of fine flour as a sin
offering. [p]He shall put no oil on it, nor
shall he put frankincense on it, for it *is* a sin
offering. 12 Then he shall bring it to the
priest, and the priest shall take his handful
of it [q]as a memorial portion, and burn *it* on
the altar [r]according to the offerings made
by fire to the LORD. It *is* a sin offering.
13 [s]The priest shall make atonement for
him, [4]for his sin that he has committed in
any of these matters; and it shall be forgiv-
en him. [t]*The rest* shall be the priest's as a
grain offering.' "

Offerings with Restitution

14 Then the LORD spoke to Moses, saying: 15 [u]"If a person commits a trespass,
and sins unintentionally in regard to the

31 [c]Lev. 3:14 [d]Lev. 3:3, 4 [e]Gen. 8:21; Ex. 29:18; Lev. 1:9, 13; 2:2, 9, 12 [f]Lev. 4:26
32 [g]Lev. 4:28
33 [h]Lev. 1:4; Num. 8:12
35 [i]Lev. 3:5 [j]Lev. 4:26, 31

CHAPTER 5

1 [a]Prov. 29:24; [Jer. 23:10] [b]Lev. 5:17; 7:18; 17:16; 19:8; 20:17; Num. 9:13 [1]*his iniquity*
2 [c]Lev. 11:24, 28, 31, 39; Num. 19:11-16; Deut. 14:8 [d]Lev. 5:17
3 [e]Lev. 5:12, 13, 15
4 [f]1 Sam. 25:22; Acts 23:12 [g][Matt. 5:33-37]; Mark 6:23; [James 5:12] [2]*vows*
5 [h]Lev. 16:21; 26:40; Num. 5:7; Ezra 10:11, 12; Ps. 32:5; Prov. 28:13
7 [i]Lev. 12:6, 8; 14:21 [j]Lev. 1:14
8 [k]Lev. 1:15-17 [3]Lit. *apart*
9 [l]Lev. 4:7, 18, 30, 34
10 [m]Lev. 1:14-17 [n]Lev. 4:20, 26; 5:13, 16
11 [o]Lev. 14:21-32 [p]Lev. 2:1, 2; 6:15; Num. 5:15
12 [q]Lev. 2:2 [r]Lev. 4:35
13 [s]Lev. 4:26 [t]Lev. 2:3; 6:17, 26 [4]*concerning his sin*
15 [u]Lev. 4:2; 22:14; Num. 5:5-8

5:1-13 Dealing with unintentional sins continues with an emphasis on sins of omission (vv. 1-4). Lambs/goats (v. 6), birds (vv. 7-10), or flour (vv. 11-13) were acceptable sacrifices.

5:1-5 This call to confession named a few examples of violations for which penitence was the right response: 1) withholding evidence (v. 1); 2) touching something unclean (vv. 2-4); and 3) rash oath making (v. 5).

5:1 oath…witness. A witness who did not come forward to testify was sinning when he had actually seen a violation or had first-hand knowledge, such as hearing the violator confess to the sin.

5:4 swears. "Speaking thoughtlessly" suggests a reckless oath for good or bad, i.e., an oath the speaker should not or could not keep.

5:5 he shall confess. Confession must accompany the sacrifice as the outward expression of a repentant heart which openly acknowledged agreement with God concerning sin. Sacrifice minus true faith, repentance, and obedience was hypocrisy (cf. Ps. 26:4; Is. 9:17; Amos 5:21-26).

5:7 burnt offering. *See notes on 1:3-17.*

5:11 ephah. About 6 gallons. **no oil…frankincense.** Contrast the grain offering (2:2).

5:13 grain offering. *See notes on 2:1-16.*

5:14–6:7 See 7:1-10 for the priests' instructions. The trespass offering symbolized an atonement for sin unknowingly committed where restitution was possible. Like the sin offering (4:1–5:13), this one was compulsory. For sins against the Lord's property, restitution was made to the priest (5:14-19), while restitution was made to the person who suffered loss in other instances (6:1-7).

holy things of the LORD, then [v]he shall
bring to the LORD as his trespass offering a
ram without blemish from the flocks, with
your valuation in shekels of silver according to [w]the shekel of the sanctuary, as a
trespass offering. 16 And he shall make
restitution for the harm that he has done in
regard to the holy thing, [x]and shall add
one-fifth to it and give it to the priest. [y]So
the priest shall make atonement for him
with the ram of the trespass offering, and it
shall be forgiven him.

17 "If a person sins, and commits any of
these things which are forbidden to be
done by the commandments of the LORD,
[z]though he does not know *it,* yet he is
[a]guilty and shall bear his [5]iniquity.
18 [b]And he shall bring to the priest a ram
without blemish from the flock, with your
valuation, as a trespass offering. So the
priest shall make atonement for him regarding his ignorance in which he erred
and did not know *it,* and it shall be forgiv-
en him. 19 It is a trespass offering; [c]he has
certainly trespassed against the LORD."

6 And the LORD spoke to Moses, saying:
2 "If a person sins and [a]commits a trespass against the LORD by [b]lying[1] to his
neighbor about [c]what was delivered to him
for safekeeping, or about [2]a pledge, or
about a robbery, or if he has [d]extorted from
his neighbor, 3 or if he [e]has found what was
lost and lies concerning it, and [f]swears
falsely—in any one of these things that a
man may do in which he sins: 4 then it shall
be, because he has sinned and is guilty, that
he shall [3]restore [g]what he has stolen, or the
thing which he has extorted, or what was
delivered to him for safekeeping, or the lost
thing which he found, 5 or all that about
which he has sworn falsely. He shall [h]re-
store its full value, add one-fifth more to it,
and give it to whomever it belongs, on the
day of his trespass offering. 6 And he shall
bring his trespass offering to the LORD, [i]a
ram without blemish from the flock, with
your [4]valuation, as a trespass offering, to
the priest. 7 [j]So the priest shall make atonement for him before the LORD, and he shall
be forgiven for any one of these things that
he may have done in which he trespasses."

The Law of the Burnt Offering

8 Then the LORD spoke to Moses, saying,
9 "Command Aaron and his sons, saying,
'This *is* the [k]law of the burnt offering: The
burnt offering *shall be* on the hearth upon
the altar all night until morning, and the fire
of the altar shall be kept burning on it.
10 [l]And the priest shall put on his linen garment, and his linen trousers he shall put on
his body, and take up the ashes of the burnt
offering which the fire has consumed on the
altar, and he shall put them [m]beside the
altar. 11 Then [n]he shall take off his garments, put on other garments, and carry the
ashes outside the camp [o]to a clean place.
12 And the fire on the altar shall be kept
burning on it; it shall not be put out. And
the priest shall burn wood on it every
morning, and lay the burnt offering in order
on it; and he shall burn on it [p]the fat of the
peace offerings. 13 A fire shall always be
burning on the [q]altar; it shall never go out.

The Law of the Grain Offering

14 'This *is* the law of the grain offering:
The sons of Aaron shall offer it on the altar
before the LORD. 15 He shall take from it his
handful of the fine flour of the grain offering, with its oil, and all the frankincense
which *is* on the grain offering, and shall
burn *it* on the altar *for* a sweet aroma, as a
memorial to the LORD. 16 And the remainder of it Aaron and his sons shall eat; with
unleavened bread it shall be eaten in a holy
place; in the court of the tabernacle of

15 [v] Ezra 10:19 [w] Ex. 30:13; Lev. 27:25
16 [x] Lev. 6:5; 22:14; 27:13, 15, 27, 31; Num. 5:7 [y] Lev. 4:26
17 [z] Lev. 4:2, 13, 22, 27 [a] Lev. 5:1, 2 [5] *punishment*
18 [b] Lev. 5:15
19 [c] Ezra 10:2

CHAPTER 6

2 [a] Num. 5:6 [b] Lev. 19:11; Acts 5:4; Col. 3:9 [c] Ex. 22:7, 10 [d] Prov. 24:28 [1] *deceiving his associate* [2] *an entrusted security*
3 [e] Ex. 23:4; Deut. 22:1-4 [f] Ex. 22:11; Lev. 19:12; Jer. 7:9; Zech. 5:4
4 [g] Lev. 24:18, 21 [3] *return*
5 [h] Lev. 5:16; Num. 5:7, 8; 2 Sam. 12:6
6 [i] Lev. 1:3; 5:15 [4] *appraisal*
7 [j] Lev. 4:26
9 [k] Ex. 29:38-42; Num. 28:3-10
10 [l] Ex. 28:39-43; Lev. 16:4; Ezek. 44:17, 18 [m] Lev. 1:16
11 [n] Ezek. 44:19 [o] Lev. 4:12
12 [p] Lev. 3:3, 5, 9, 14
13 [q] Lev. 1:7

5:15 shekel of the sanctuary. This amounted to 20 gerahs (Ex. 30:13; Lev. 27:25; Num. 3:47) or 2 bekahs (Ex. 38:26), which is the equivalent of four-tenths of one ounce. God fixed the value of a shekel.

5:16 one-fifth. The offender was required to make a 120 percent restitution, which was considerably lower than that prescribed elsewhere in the Mosaic law, e.g., Ex. 22:7,9. Perhaps this is accounted for by a voluntary confession in contrast to an adjudicated and forced conviction.

6:1-7 While all sins are against God (cf. Ps. 51:4), some are direct (5:14-19) and others are indirect, involving people (6:1-7), as here. These violations are not exhaustive, but representative samples used to establish and illustrate the principle.

6:6 your valuation. The priest served as an appraiser to give appropriate value to the goods in question.

6:8–7:38 These were laws of sacrifice for the priesthood. Leviticus 1:1–6:7 has dealt with 5 major offerings from the worshiper's perspective. Here instructions for the priests are given, with special attention to the priests' portion of the sacrifice.

6:8-13 The burnt offering. *See notes on 1:3-17.*

6:9 on the hearth upon the altar all night. This resulted in the complete incineration of the sacrifice, picturing it as totally given to the Lord, with the smoke arising as a sweet aroma to Him (1:7,13,17).

6:10,11 ashes. This described both the immediate (v. 10) and final (v. 11) disposition of the ash remains, i.e., that which is worthless.

6:12 fat...peace offerings. *See note on 3:4.*

6:13 always be burning. The perpetual flame indicated a continuous readiness on the part of God to receive confession and restitution through the sacrifice.

6:14-23 The grain offering. *See notes on 2:1-16.*

6:15 handful. *See note on 2:2.*

6:16-18 Unlike the burnt offering, the grain offering provided food for the priests and their male children, i.e., future priests.

6:16 in a holy place. This was to be eaten only in the courtyard of the tabernacle.

meeting they shall eat it. 17 It shall not be
baked with leaven. I have given it *as* their
[5]portion of My offerings made by fire; it *is*
most holy, like the sin offering and the
[r]trespass offering. 18 [s]All the males among
the children of Aaron may eat it. [t]*It shall be*
a statute forever in your generations concerning the offerings made by fire to the
LORD. [u]Everyone who touches them must
be holy.' "
19 And the LORD spoke to Moses, saying,
20 [v]"This *is* the offering of Aaron and his
sons, which they shall offer to the LORD, *beginning* on the day when he is anointed:
one-tenth of an [w]ephah of fine flour as a
daily grain offering, half of it in the morning and half of it at night. 21 It shall be
made in a [x]pan with oil. *When it is* mixed,
you shall bring it in. The baked pieces of
the grain offering you shall offer *for* a
[6]sweet aroma to the LORD. 22 The priest
from among his sons, [y]who is anointed in
his place, shall offer it. *It is* a statute forever to the LORD. [z]It shall be [7]wholly burned.
23 For every grain offering for the priest
shall be wholly burned. It shall not be
eaten."

The Law of the Sin Offering

24 Also the LORD spoke to Moses, saying,
25 "Speak to Aaron and to his sons, saying,
'This *is* the law of the sin offering: [a]In the
place where the burnt offering is killed, the
sin offering shall be killed before the LORD.
It *is* most holy. 26 [b]The priest who offers it
for sin shall eat it. In a holy place it shall be
eaten, in the court of the tabernacle of
meeting. 27 [c]Everyone who touches its
flesh [8]must be holy. And when its blood is
sprinkled on any garment, you shall wash
that on which it was sprinkled, in a holy
place. 28 But the earthen vessel in which it
is boiled [d]shall be broken. And if it is
boiled in a bronze pot, it shall be both
scoured and rinsed in water. 29 All the
males among the priests may eat it. It *is*
most holy. 30 [e]But no sin offering from
which *any* of the blood is brought into the
tabernacle of meeting, to make atonement
in [9]the holy [f]*place*, shall be [g]eaten. It shall
be [h]burned in the fire.

The Law of the Trespass Offering

7 'Likewise [a]this *is* the law of the trespass offering (it *is* most holy): 2 In the
place where they kill the burnt offering
they shall kill the trespass offering. And its
blood he shall sprinkle all around on the
altar. 3 And he shall offer from it all its fat.
The fat tail and the fat that covers the entrails, 4 the two kidneys and the fat that *is*
on them by the flanks, and the fatty lobe *attached* to the liver above the kidneys, he
shall remove; 5 and the priest shall burn
them on the altar *as* an offering made by
fire to the LORD. It *is* a trespass offering.
6 [b]Every male among the priests may eat it.
It shall be eaten in a holy place. [c]It *is* most
holy. 7 [d]The trespass offering *is* like the sin
offering; *there is* one law for them both: the
priest who makes atonement with it shall
have *it*. 8 And the priest who offers anyone's burnt offering, that priest shall have
for himself the skin of the burnt offering
which he has offered. 9 Also [e]every grain
offering that is baked in the oven and all
that is prepared in the covered pan, or [1]in
a pan, shall be the priest's who offers it.
10 Every grain offering, *whether* mixed with
oil or dry, shall belong to all the sons of
Aaron, to one *as much* as the other.

The Law of Peace Offerings

11 [f]'This *is* the law of the sacrifice of
peace offerings which he shall offer to the
LORD: 12 If he offers it for a thanksgiving,
then he shall offer, with the sacrifice of
thanksgiving, unleavened cakes mixed
with oil, unleavened wafers [g]anointed
with oil, or cakes of blended flour mixed

17 [r] Lev. 7:7 [5] *share*
18 [s] Lev. 6:29; 7:6; Num. 18:10; 1 Cor. 9:13 [t] Lev. 3:17 [u] Ex. 29:37; Lev. 22:3-7; Num. 4:15; Hag. 2:11-13
20 [v] Ex. 29:2 [w] Ex. 16:36
21 [x] Lev. 2:5; 7:9 [6] *pleasing*
22 [y] Lev. 4:3 [z] Ex. 29:25 [7] *completely*
25 [a] Lev. 1:1, 3, 5, 11
26 [b] [Lev. 10:17, 18]; Num. 18:9, 10; [Ezek. 44:28, 29]
27 [c] Ex. 29:37; Num. 4:15; Hag. 2:11-13 [8] Lit. *shall*
28 [d] Lev. 11:33; 15:12
30 [e] Lev. 4:7, 11, 12, 18, 21; 10:18; 16:27; [Heb. 13:11, 12] [f] Ex. 26:33 [g] Lev. 6:16, 23, 26 [h] Lev. 16:27 [9] The Most Holy Place when capitalized

CHAPTER 7

1 [a] Lev. 5:14–6:7
6 [b] Lev. 6:16-18, 29; Num. 18:9 [c] Lev. 2:3
7 [d] Lev. 6:24-30; 14:13
9 [e] Lev. 2:3, 10; Num. 18:9; Ezek. 44:29 [1] *on a griddle*
11 [f] Lev. 3:1; 22:18, 21; Ezek. 45:15
12 [g] Lev. 2:4; Num. 6:15

6:19-23 Aaron, as High-Priest, was to make a daily grain offering at morning and night on behalf of his priestly family.

6:20 ephah. *See note on 5:11.* **he is anointed.** See 8:7-12.

6:22 The priest...in his place. The High-Priests who succeed Aaron are in view here. **wholly burned.** The priests' offering was to be given completely, with nothing left over.

6:24-30 The sin offering. *See notes on 4:1–5:13.*

6:25 burnt offering. *See notes on 1:3-17.* **most holy.** *See note on 2:3.*

6:26 priest...eat. The priest putting the offering on the brazen altar could use it for food, if the sacrifice was for a ruler (4:22-26) or the people (4:27-35).

6:27,28 Instructions on the cleanness of the priest's garments as they relate to blood.

6:30 no sin offering...eaten. Those sacrifices made on behalf of a priest (4:3-12) or the congregation (4:13-21) could be eaten.

7:1-10 The trespass offering. *See notes on 5:14–6:7.* Verses 7-10 provide a brief excursus on what may be eaten by the priests.

7:1 most holy. *See note on 2:3.*

7:7 *See note on 6:26.*

7:10 mixed with oil or dry. Both were acceptable options.

7:11-36 The peace offering. *See notes on 3:1-17.* The purposes for the peace offering are given in vv. 11-18. Special instructions which prevented a priest from being "cut off" (vv. 19-27) and the allotment to Aaron and his sons (vv. 28-36) are enumerated.

7:11-15 A peace offering for thanksgiving shall also be combined with a grain offering (see 2:1-16). The meat had to be eaten that same day, probably for the reason of health since it would rapidly spoil and for the purpose of preventing people from thinking that such meat had some spiritual presence in it, thus developing some superstitions.

with oil. 13 Besides the cakes, *as* his offering he shall offer [h]leavened bread with the
sacrifice of thanksgiving of his peace offering. 14 And from it he shall offer one cake
from each offering *as* a heave offering to
the LORD. [i]It shall belong to the priest who
sprinkles the blood of the peace offering.
15 [j]'The flesh of the sacrifice of his peace
offering for thanksgiving shall be eaten the
same day it is offered. He shall not leave
any of it until morning. 16 But [k]if the sacrifice of his offering *is* a vow or a voluntary
offering, it shall be eaten the same day that
he offers his sacrifice; but on the next day
the remainder of it also may be eaten;
17 the remainder of the flesh of the sacrifice
on the third day must be burned with fire.
18 And if *any* of the flesh of the sacrifice of
his peace offering is eaten at all on the
third day, it shall not be accepted, nor shall
it be [l]imputed to him; it shall be an [m]abom-
ination *to* him who offers it, and the person
who eats of it shall bear [2]guilt.
19 'The flesh that touches any unclean
thing shall not be eaten. It shall be burned
with fire. And as for the *clean* flesh, all who
are [3]clean may eat of it. 20 But the person
who eats the flesh of the sacrifice of the
peace offering that *belongs* to the [n]LORD,
[o]while he is unclean, that person [p]shall be
cut off from his people. 21 Moreover the
person who touches any unclean thing,
such as [q]human uncleanness, *an* [r]unclean
animal, or any [s]abominable[4] unclean
thing, and who eats the flesh of the sacrifice of the peace offering that *belongs* to the
LORD, that person [t]shall be cut off from his
people.' "

Fat and Blood May Not Be Eaten

22 And the LORD spoke to Moses, saying,
23 "Speak to the children of Israel, saying:
[u]'You shall not eat any fat, of ox or sheep
or goat. 24 And the fat of an animal that
dies *naturally*, and the fat of what is torn by
wild beasts, may be used in any other way;
but you shall by no means eat it. 25 For
whoever eats the fat of the animal of which
men offer an offering made by fire to the
LORD, the person who eats *it* shall be cut off
from his people. 26 [v]Moreover you shall
not eat any blood in any of your dwellings,
whether of bird or beast. 27 Whoever eats
any blood, that person shall be cut off from
his people.' "

The Portion of Aaron and His Sons

28 Then the LORD spoke to Moses, saying, 29 "Speak to the children of Israel, saying: [w]'He who offers the sacrifice of his
peace offering to the LORD shall bring his
offering to the LORD from the sacrifice of
his peace offering. 30 [x]His own hands shall
bring the offerings made by fire to the
LORD. The fat with the breast he shall
bring, that the [y]breast may be waved *as* a
wave offering before the LORD. 31 [z]And the
priest shall burn the fat on the altar, but the
[a]breast shall be Aaron's and his sons'.
32 [b]Also the right thigh you shall give to
the priest *as* a heave offering from the sacrifices of your peace offerings. 33 He
among the sons of Aaron, who offers the
blood of the peace offering and the fat,
shall have the right thigh for *his* part. 34 For
[c]the breast of the wave offering and the
thigh of the heave offering I have taken
from the children of Israel, from the sacrifices of their peace offerings, and I have
given them to Aaron the priest and to his
sons from the children of Israel by a statute
forever.' "
35 This *is* the consecrated portion for
Aaron and his sons, from the offerings
made by fire to the LORD, on the day when
Moses presented them to [5]minister to the
LORD as priests. 36 The LORD commanded
this to be given to them by the children of
Israel, [d]on the day that He anointed them,
by a statute forever throughout their generations.
37 This *is* the law [e]of the burnt offering,
[f]the grain offering, [g]the sin offering, [h]the
trespass offering, [i]the consecrations, and
[j]the sacrifice of the peace offering,
38 which the LORD commanded Moses on

13 [h] Lev. 2:12; 23:17, 18; Amos 4:5
14 [i] Num. 18:8, 11, 19
15 [j] Lev. 22:29, 30
16 [k] Lev. 19:5-8
18 [l] Num. 18:27 [m] Lev. 11:10, 11, 41; 19:7; [Prov. 15:8] [2] *his iniquity*
19 [3] *pure*
20 [n] [Heb. 2:17] [o] Lev. 5:3; 15:3; 22:3-7; Num. 19:13; [1 Cor. 11:28] [p] Gen. 17:14; Ex. 31:14
21 [q] Lev. 5:2, 3, 5 [r] Lev. 11:24, 28 [s] Ezek. 4:14 [t] Lev. 7:20 [4] So with MT, LXX, Vg.; Sam., Syr., Tg. *swarming thing* (cf. 5:2)
23 [u] Lev. 3:17; 17:10-15; Deut. 14:21; Ezek. 4:14; 44:31
26 [v] Gen. 9:4; Lev. 3:17; 17:10-16; 19:26; Deut. 12:23; 1 Sam. 14:33; Ezek. 33:25; Acts 15:20, 29
29 [w] Lev. 3:1; 22:21; Ezek. 45:15
30 [x] Lev. 3:3, 4, 9, 14 [y] Ex. 29:24, 27; Lev. 8:27; 9:21; Num. 6:20
31 [z] Lev. 3:5, 11, 16 [a] Num. 18:11; Deut. 18:3
32 [b] Ex. 29:27; Lev. 7:34; 9:21; Num. 6:20
34 [c] Ex. 29:28; Lev. 10:14, 15; Num. 18:18, 19; Deut. 18:3
35 [5] *serve*
36 [d] Ex. 40:13-15; Lev. 8:12, 30
37 [e] Lev. 6:9 [f] Lev. 6:14 [g] Lev. 6:25 [h] Lev. 7:1 [i] Ex. 29:1; Lev. 6:20 [j] Lev. 7:11

7:13 leavened bread. Contrast the unleavened grain offering (see 2:11).

7:16-18 vow...voluntary offering. The priest could eat the meat the same day or next day, but eating on the third day brought punishment.

7:19-21 cut off. Uncleanness was punishable by death. See chap. 22 for more details.

7:22-27 *See note on 3:17.*

7:27 cut off. *See note on 7:19-21.*

7:29 offering...sacrifice. The worshiper made a peace offering from his sacrifice so that the Lord received the blood (v. 33) and the fat (v. 33). The priests received the breast (vv. 30,31) and right thigh (v. 33). The worshiper could use the rest for himself.

7:30-32 wave offering...heave offering. These were symbolic acts indicating the offering was for the Lord. Bread (Ex. 29:23-24), meat (Ex. 29:22-24), gold (Ex. 38:24), oil (Lev. 14:12), and grain (Lev. 23:11) all served as wave offerings. Heave offerings are far less numerous (see Ex. 29:27-28 and Deut. 12:6,11,17). Jewish tradition portrayed the wave offering as being presented with a horizontal motion and the heave offering with a vertical motion, as suggested by Lev. 10:15. Leviticus 9:21 refers to both as a wave offering.

7:36 He anointed them. See 8:30.

7:37,38 Moses gives a summary conclusion of 1:3–7:36.

7:37 the consecrations. This refers to the offerings at the ordination of Aaron and his sons (see 8:14-36; Ex. 29:1-46).

Mount Sinai, on the day when He commanded the children of Israel [k]to offer
their offerings to the LORD in the Wilderness of Sinai.

Aaron and His Sons Consecrated

8 And the LORD spoke to Moses, saying:
2 [a]"Take Aaron and his sons with him,
and [b]the garments, [c]the anointing oil, a
[d]bull as the sin offering, two [e]rams, and a
basket of unleavened bread; 3 and gather
all the congregation together at the door of
the tabernacle of meeting."
4 So Moses did as the LORD commanded
him. And the congregation was gathered
together at the door of the tabernacle of
meeting. 5 And Moses said to the congregation, "This *is* what the LORD commanded
to be done."
6 Then Moses brought Aaron and his
sons and [f]washed them with water. 7 And
he [g]put the tunic on him, girded him with
the sash, clothed him with the robe, and
put the ephod on him; and he girded him
with the intricately woven band of the
ephod, and with it tied *the ephod* on him.
8 Then he put the breastplate on him, and
he [h]put the [1]Urim and the Thummim in
the breastplate. 9 [i]And he put the turban
on his head. Also on the turban, on its
front, he put the golden plate, the holy
crown, as the LORD had commanded Moses.
10 [j]Also Moses took the anointing oil,
and anointed the tabernacle and all that
was in it, and consecrated them. 11 He
sprinkled some of it on the altar seven
times, anointed the altar and all its utensils, and the laver and its base, to [2]conse-
crate them. 12 And he [k]poured some of the
anointing oil on Aaron's head and anointed him, to consecrate him.
13 [l]Then Moses brought Aaron's sons
and put tunics on them, girded them with
sashes, and put [3]hats on them, as the LORD
had commanded Moses.
14 [m]And he brought the bull for the sin
offering. Then Aaron and his sons [n]laid
their hands on the head of the bull for the
sin offering, 15 and Moses killed *it*. [o]Then
he took the blood, and put *some* on the
horns of the altar all around with his finger, and purified the altar. And he poured
the blood at the base of the altar, and consecrated it, to make [4]atonement for it.
16 [p]Then he took all the fat that *was* on the
entrails, the fatty lobe *attached to* the liver,
and the two kidneys with their fat, and
Moses burned *them* on the altar. 17 But the
bull, its hide, its flesh, and its offal, he
burned with fire outside the camp, as the
LORD [q]had commanded Moses.
18 [r]Then he brought the ram as the burnt
offering. And Aaron and his sons laid their
hands on the head of the ram, 19 and Moses killed *it*. Then he sprinkled the blood
all around on the altar. 20 And he cut the
ram into pieces; and Moses [s]burned the
head, the pieces, and the fat. 21 Then he
washed the entrails and the legs in water.
And Moses burned the whole ram on the
altar. It *was* a burnt sacrifice for a [5]sweet
aroma, an offering made by fire to the
LORD, [t]as the LORD had commanded Moses.
22 And [u]he brought the second ram, the
ram of consecration. Then Aaron and his
sons laid their hands on the head of the
ram, 23 and Moses killed *it*. Also he took
some of [v]its blood and put it on the tip of
Aaron's right ear, on the thumb of his right
hand, and on the big toe of his right foot.
24 Then he brought Aaron's sons. And Moses put *some* of the [w]blood on the tips of
their right ears, on the thumbs of their
right hands, and on the big toes of their
right feet. And Moses sprinkled the blood
all around on the altar. 25 [x]Then he took
the fat and the fat tail, all the fat that *was* on
the entrails, the fatty lobe *attached to* the
liver, the two kidneys and their fat, and the
right thigh; 26 [y]and from the basket of unleavened bread that was before the LORD
he took one unleavened cake, a cake of

38 [k] Lev. 1:1, 2; Deut. 4:5

CHAPTER 8

2 [a] Ex. 29:1-3 [b] Ex. 28:2, 4 [c] Ex. 30:24, 25 [d] Ex. 29:10 [e] Ex. 29:15, 19
6 [f] Ex. 30:20; Heb. 10:22
7 [g] Ex. 39:1-31
8 [h] Ex. 28:30; Num. 27:21; Deut. 33:8; 1 Sam. 28:6; Ezra 2:63; Neh. 7:65 [1] Lit. *Lights and the Perfections*, Ex. 28:30
9 [i] Ex. 28:36, 37; 29:6
10 [j] Ex. 30:26-29; 40:10, 11; Lev. 8:2
11 [2] *set them apart for the LORD*
12 [k] Ex. 29:7; 30:30; Lev. 21:10, 12; Ps. 133:2
13 [l] Ex. 29:8, 9 [3] *headpieces*
14 [m] Ex. 29:10; Ps. 66:15; Ezek. 43:19

[n] Lev. 4:4
15 [o] Ex. 29:12, 36; Lev. 4:7; Ezek. 43:20, 26; [Heb. 9:22] [4] Lit. *covering*
16 [p] Ex. 29:13; Lev. 4:8
17 [q] Ex. 29:14; Lev. 4:11, 12
18 [r] Ex. 29:15
20 [s] Lev. 1:8
21 [t] Ex. 29:18 [5] *pleasing*
22 [u] Ex. 29:19, 31; Lev. 8:2
23 [v] Ex. 29:20, 21; Lev. 14:14
24 [w] [Heb. 9:13, 14, 18-23]
25 [x] Ex. 29:22
26 [y] Ex. 29:23

8:1–10:20 Beginnings of the Aaronic priesthood are discussed in this section. Before the time of Aaron, the patriarchs (Gen. 4:3,4) and the fathers (Job 1:5) had offered sacrifices to God, but with Aaron came the fully prescribed priestly service.

8:1-36 Aaron and his sons were consecrated before they ministered to the Lord. The consecration of Aaron and his sons had been ordered long before (*see notes on Ex. 29:1-37*), but is here described with all the ceremonial details as it was done after the tabernacle was completed and the regulations for the various sacrifices enacted.

8:2 the garments. *See notes on Ex. 28:1-43.* **the anointing oil.** Oil was used for ceremonial anointing (8:12,30). **sin offering.** *See notes on 4:1–5:13, esp. 4:3-12.*

8:6-9 *See notes on Ex. 28:1-43.*

8:8 the Urim and the Thummim. A feature on the breastplate of the High-Priest by which God's people were given His decision on matters which required a decision. *See note on Ex. 28:30.*

8:11 seven times. *See note on 4:6.*

8:12 to consecrate him. This act was to ceremonially set Aaron apart from the congregation to be a priest unto God, and from the other priests to be High-Priest.

8:14-17 *See notes on 4:3-12.*

8:17 offal. *See note on 4:11.*

8:18-21 *See notes on 1:3-17.*

8:23,24 right ear...right hand...right foot. Using a part to represent the whole, Aaron and his sons were consecrated to listen to God's holy Word, to carry out his holy assignments, and to live holy lives.

bread *anointed with* oil, and one wafer, and put *them* on the fat and on the right thigh; 27 and he put all *these* [z]in Aaron's hands and in his sons' hands, and waved them *as* a wave offering before the LORD. 28 [a]Then Moses took them from their hands and burned *them* on the altar, on the burnt offering. They *were* consecration offerings for a sweet aroma. That *was* an offering made by fire to the LORD. 29 And [b]Moses took the [c]breast and waved it *as* a wave offering before the LORD. It was Moses' [d]part of the ram of consecration, as the LORD had commanded Moses.

30 Then [e]Moses took some of the anointing oil and some of the blood which *was* on the altar, and sprinkled *it* on Aaron, on his garments, on his sons, and on the garments of his sons with him; and he consecrated Aaron, his garments, his sons, and the garments of his sons with him.

31 And Moses said to Aaron and his sons, [f]"Boil the flesh *at* the door of the tabernacle of meeting, and eat it there with the bread that *is* in the basket of consecration offerings, as I commanded, saying, 'Aaron and his sons shall eat it.' 32 [g]What remains of the flesh and of the bread you shall burn with fire. 33 And you shall not go outside the door of the tabernacle of meeting *for* seven days, until the days of your consecration are ended. For [h]seven days he shall consecrate you. 34 [i]As he has done this day, *so* the LORD has commanded to do, to make atonement for you. 35 Therefore you shall stay *at* the door of the tabernacle of meeting day and night for seven days, and [j]keep the [6]charge of the LORD, so that you may not die; for so I have been commanded." 36 So Aaron and his sons did all the things that the LORD had commanded by the hand of Moses.

The Priestly Ministry Begins

9 It came to pass on the [a]eighth day that Moses called Aaron and his sons and the elders of Israel. 2 And he said to Aaron, "Take for yourself a young [b]bull as a sin offering and a ram as a burnt offering, without blemish, and offer *them* before the LORD. 3 And to the children of Israel you shall speak, saying, [c]'Take a kid of the goats as a sin offering, and a calf and a lamb, *both* of the first year, without blemish, as a burnt offering, 4 also a bull and a ram as peace offerings, to sacrifice before the LORD, and [d]a grain offering mixed with oil; for [e]today the LORD will appear to you.' "

5 So they brought what Moses commanded before the tabernacle of meeting. And all the congregation drew near and stood [1]before the LORD. 6 Then Moses said, "This *is* the thing which the LORD commanded you to do, and the glory of the LORD will appear to you." 7 And Moses said to Aaron, "Go to the altar, [f]offer your sin offering and your burnt offering, and make atonement for yourself and for the people. [g]Offer the offering of the people, and make atonement for them, as the LORD commanded."

8 Aaron therefore went to the altar and killed the calf of the sin offering, which *was* for himself. 9 Then the sons of Aaron brought the blood to him. And he dipped his finger in the blood, put *it* on the horns of the altar, and poured the blood at the base of the altar. 10 [h]But the fat, the kidneys, and the fatty lobe from the liver of the sin offering he burned on the altar, as the LORD had commanded Moses. 11 [i]The flesh and the hide he burned with fire outside the camp.

12 And he killed the burnt offering; and Aaron's sons presented to him the blood, [j]which he sprinkled all around on the altar. 13 [k]Then they presented the burnt offering to him, with its pieces and head, and he burned *them* on the altar. 14 [l]And he washed the entrails and the legs, and burned *them* with the burnt offering on the altar.

15 [m]Then he brought the people's offering, and took the goat, which *was* the sin offering for the people, and killed it and offered it for sin, like the first one. 16 And he brought the burnt offering and offered it [n]according to the [2]prescribed manner. 17 Then he brought the grain offering, took a handful of it, and burned *it* on the altar, [o]besides the burnt sacrifice of the morning.

18 He also killed the bull and the ram *as* [p]sacrifices of peace offerings, which *were*

27 [z] Ex. 29:24; Lev. 7:30, 34
28 [a] Ex. 29:25
29 [b] Ps. 99:6 [c] Ex. 29:27 [d] Ex. 29:26
30 [e] Ex. 29:21; 30:30; Num. 3:3
31 [f] Ex. 29:31, 32
32 [g] Ex. 29:34
33 [h] Ex. 29:30, 35; Lev. 10:7; Ezek. 43:25, 26
34 [i] [Heb. 7:16]
35 [j] Num. 1:53; 3:7; 9:19; Deut. 11:1; 1 Kin. 2:3; Ezek. 48:11 [6] *office*

CHAPTER 9

1 [a] Ezek. 43:27
2 [b] Ex. 29:21; Lev. 4:1-12
3 [c] Lev. 4:23, 28; Ezra 6:17; 10:19
4 [d] Lev. 2:4 [e] Ex. 29:43; Lev. 9:6, 23
5 [1] *in the presence of*
7 [f] Lev. 4:3; 1 Sam. 3:14; [Heb. 5:3-5; 7:27] [g] Lev. 4:16, 20; Heb. 5:1
10 [h] Ex. 23:18; Lev. 8:16
11 [i] Lev. 4:11, 12; 8:17
12 [j] Lev. 1:5; 8:19
13 [k] Lev. 8:20
14 [l] Lev. 8:21
15 [m] [Is. 53:10; Heb. 2:17; 5:3]
16 [n] Lev. 1:1-13 [2] *ordinance*
17 [o] Ex. 29:38, 39
18 [p] Lev. 3:1-11

8:29 wave offering. *See note on 7:30-32.*

8:35 keep the charge of the LORD. The commandment of God ordered Aaron and his sons to do exactly as the Lord had spoken through Moses. Disobedience would meet with death.

9:1-24 Since the priests had been consecrated and appropriate sacrifices offered on their behalf, they were prepared to fulfill their priestly duties on behalf of the congregation as they carried out all of the prescribed sacrifices in Lev. 1–7 and rendered them to the Lord.

9:2-4 sin…burnt…peace…grain offering. *See notes on 4:1–5:13; 1:3-17; 3:1-17; and 2:1-16* respectively.

9:4,6 the glory of the LORD. The Lord's manifestation or presence was going to appear to them to show acceptance of the sacrifices. *See notes on vv. 23,24,* where that appearance is recorded.

9:8-21 Aaron presented sacrifices on his own behalf (vv. 8-14) and on behalf of the people (vv. 15-21).

9:17 burnt sacrifice…morning. See Ex. 29:41; Num. 28:4.

for the people. And Aaron's sons presented to him the blood, which he sprinkled all
around on the altar, 19 and the fat from the
bull and the ram—the fatty tail, what covers *the entrails* and the kidneys, and the
fatty lobe *attached to* the liver; 20 and they
put the fat on the breasts. [q]Then he burned
the fat on the altar; 21 but the breasts and
the right thigh Aaron waved [r]*as* a wave offering before the LORD, as Moses had commanded.
22 Then Aaron lifted his hand toward the
people, [s]blessed them, and came down
from offering the sin offering, the burnt offering, and peace offerings. 23 And Moses
and Aaron went into the tabernacle of
meeting, and came out and blessed the
people. Then the glory of the LORD appeared to all the people, 24 and [t]fire came
out from before the LORD and consumed
the burnt offering and the fat on the altar.
When all the people saw *it,* they [u]shouted
and fell on their [v]faces.

The Profane Fire of Nadab and Abihu

10 Then Nadab[a] and Abihu, the sons
of Aaron, [b]each took his censer
and put fire in it, put incense on it, and
offered [c]profane fire before the LORD,
which He had not commanded them. 2 So
[d]fire went out from the LORD and devoured them, and they died before the
LORD. 3 And Moses said to Aaron, "This
is what the LORD spoke, saying:

'By those [e]who come near Me
I must be regarded as holy;
And before all the people
I must be glorified.' "

So Aaron held his peace.
4 Then Moses called Mishael and Elzaphan, the sons of Uzziel the uncle of
Aaron, and said to them, "Come near,
[f]carry your brethren from [1]before the sanctuary out of the camp." 5 So they went near
and carried them by their tunics out of the
camp, as Moses had said.
6 And Moses said to Aaron, and to Eleazar and Ithamar, his sons, "Do not [2]un-
cover your heads nor tear your clothes, lest
you die, and [g]wrath come upon all the
people. But let your brethren, the whole
house of Israel, [3]bewail the burning which
the LORD has kindled. 7 [h]You shall not go
out from the door of the tabernacle of
meeting, lest you die, [i]for the anointing oil
of the LORD *is* upon you." And they did according to the word of Moses.

Conduct Prescribed for Priests

8 Then the LORD spoke to Aaron, saying:
9 [j]"Do not drink wine or intoxicating
drink, you, nor your sons with you, when
you go into the tabernacle of meeting, lest

20 [q] Lev. 3:5, 16
21 [r] Ex. 29:24, 26, 27; Lev. 7:30-34
22 [s] Num. 6:22-26; Deut. 21:5; Luke 24:50
24 [t] Gen. 4:4; Judg. 6:21; 2 Chr. 7:1; Ps. 20:3 [u] Ezra 3:11 [v] 1 Kin. 18:38, 39

CHAPTER 10

1 [a] Ex. 24:1, 9; Num. 3:2-4; 1 Chr. 24:2 [b] Lev. 16:12 [c] Ex. 30:9; 1 Sam. 2:17
2 [d] Gen. 19:24; Num. 11:1; 16:35; Rev. 20:9
3 [e] Ex. 19:22; Lev. 21:6; Is. 52:11; Ezek. 20:41
4 [f] Acts 5:6, 10 [1] *in front of*
6 [g] Num. 1:53; 16:22, 46; 18:5; Josh. 7:1; 22:18, 20; 2 Sam. 24:1 [2] An act of mourning [3] *weep bitterly*
7 [h] Lev. 8:33; 21:12 [i] Lev. 8:30
9 [j] Gen. 9:21; [Prov. 20:1; 31:5]; Is. 28:7; Ezek. 44:21; Hos. 4:11; Luke 1:15; [Eph. 5:18]; 1 Tim. 3:3; Titus 1:7

9:21 wave offering. *See note on 7:30-32.*

9:22 lifted his hand toward the people. The High-Priest gave a symbolic gesture for blessing, perhaps pronouncing the priestly blessing (Num. 6:24-26; cf. 2 Cor. 13:14).

9:23 the glory of the LORD appeared. The Bible speaks often of the glory of God—the visible appearance of His beauty and perfection reduced to blazing light. His glory appeared to Moses in a burning bush in Midian (Ex. 3:1-6), in a cloud on Mt. Sinai (Ex. 24:15-17), and in a rock on Mt. Sinai (Ex. 33:18-23). The glory of God also filled the tabernacle (Ex. 40:34), led the people as a pillar of fire and cloud (Ex. 40:35-38), and also filled the temple in Jerusalem (1 Kin. 8:10,11). When Aaron made the first sacrifice in the wilderness, as a priest, the "glory of the Lord appeared to all the people." In these manifestations, God was revealing His righteousness, holiness, truth, wisdom, and grace—the sum of all He is. However, nowhere has God's glory been more perfectly expressed than in His Son, the Lord Jesus Christ (John 1:14). It will be seen on earth again when He returns (Matt. 24:29-31; 25:31).

9:24 fire came out…consumed. This fire miraculously signified that God had accepted their offering (cf. 1 Kin. 18:38,39), and the people shouted for joy because of that acceptance and worshiped God.

10:1 Nadab and Abihu. These were the two oldest sons of Aaron. **censer.** The vessel in which the incense was burned in the Holy Place (its features are unknown) was to be used only for holy purposes. **profane fire.** Though the exact infraction is not detailed, in some way they violated the prescription for offering incense (cf. Ex. 30:9,34-38), probably because they were drunk (see vv. 8,9). Instead of taking the incense fire from the brazen altar, they had some other source for the fire and thus perpetrated an act, which, considering the descent of the miraculous fire they had just seen and their solemn duty to do as God told them, betrayed carelessness, irreverence, and lack of consideration for God. Such a tendency had to be punished for all priests to see as a warning.

10:2 fire went out. The same divine fire that accepted the sacrifices (9:24) consumed the errant priests. That was not unlike the later deaths of Uzzah (2 Sam. 6:6,7) or Ananias and Sapphira (Acts 5:5,10).

10:3 regarded as holy…be glorified. Nadab and Abihu were guilty of violating both requirements of God's absolute standard. The priests had received repeated and solemn warnings as to the necessity of reverence before God (see Ex. 19:22; 29:44). **Aaron held his peace.** In spite of losing his two sons, he did not complain, but submitted to the righteous judgment of God.

10:4 Mishael…Elzaphan. See Ex. 6:22 for their lineage. This procedure prevented the priests from defiling themselves by handling the dead bodies (Lev. 21:1), and allowed the whole congregation to see the result of such disregard for the holiness of God. **out of the camp.** As this was done with the ashes of sacrificed animals (6:11), so it was done with the remains of these two priests who received God's wrath.

10:6 Eleazar and Ithamar. Aaron's youngest sons who yet lived. Later, the line of Eleazar would be designated as the unique line of the High-Priest (cf. Num. 25:10-13).

10:6,7 This prohibition against the customary signs of mourning was usually reserved for the High-Priest only as prescribed in 21:10-12. Here, Moses applies it to Eleazar and Ithamar also.

10:8,9 not drink wine or intoxicating drink. Taken in its context, this prohibition suggests that intoxication led Nadab and Abihu to perform their blasphemous act. Cf. Prov. 23:20-35; 1 Tim. 3:3; Titus 1:7.

you die. *It shall be* a statute forever
throughout your generations, 10 that you
may [k]distinguish between holy and unholy, and between unclean and clean,
11 [l]and that you may teach the children of
Israel all the statutes which the LORD has
spoken to them by the hand of Moses."

12 And Moses spoke to Aaron, and to Eleazar and Ithamar, his sons who were left:
[m]"Take the grain offering that remains of
the offerings made by fire to the LORD, and
eat it without leaven beside the altar; [n]for
it *is* most holy. 13 You shall eat it in a [o]holy
place, because it *is* your [4]due and your
sons' due, of the sacrifices made by fire to
the LORD; for [p]so I have been commanded.
14 [q]The breast of the wave offering and the
thigh of the heave offering you shall eat in
a clean place, you, your sons, and your
[r]daughters with you; for *they are* your due
and your sons' [s]due, *which* are given from
the sacrifices of peace offerings of the children of Israel. 15 [t]The thigh of the heave offering and the breast of the wave offering
they shall bring with the offerings of fat
made by fire, to offer *as* a wave offering before the LORD. And it shall be yours and
your sons' with you, by a statute forever,
as the LORD has commanded."

16 Then Moses made careful inquiry
about [u]the goat of the sin offering, and
there it was—burned up. And he was
angry with Eleazar and Ithamar, the sons
of Aaron *who were* left, saying, 17 [v]"Why
have you not eaten the sin offering in a
holy place, since it *is* most holy, and *God*
has given it to you to bear [w]the guilt of the
congregation, to make atonement for them
before the LORD? 18 See! [x]Its blood was not
brought inside [5]the holy *place;* indeed you
should have eaten it in a holy *place,* [y]as I
commanded."

19 And Aaron said to Moses, "Look,
[z]this day they have offered their sin offering and their burnt offering before the
LORD, and such things have befallen me! *If*
I had eaten the sin offering today, [a]would
it have been accepted in the sight of the
LORD?" 20 So when Moses heard *that,* he
was content.

Foods Permitted and Forbidden

11 Now the LORD spoke to Moses and
Aaron, saying to them, 2 "Speak to
the children of Israel, saying, [a]'These *are*
the animals which you may eat among
all the animals that *are* on the earth:
3 Among the animals, whatever divides
the hoof, having cloven hooves *and* chewing the cud—that you may eat. 4 Nevertheless these you shall [b]not eat among those
that chew the cud or those that have
cloven hooves: the camel, because it chews
the cud but does not have cloven hooves,
is [1]unclean to you; 5 the [2]rock hyrax, because it chews the cud but does not have
cloven hooves, *is* [3]unclean to you; 6 the
hare, because it chews the cud but does not
have cloven hooves, *is* unclean to you;
7 and the swine, though it divides the hoof,
having cloven hooves, yet does not chew
the cud, [c]*is* unclean to you. 8 Their flesh
you shall not eat, and their carcasses you
shall not touch. [d]They *are* unclean to you.

10 [k]Lev. 11:47; 20:25; Ezek. 22:26; 44:23
11 [l]Deut. 24:8; Neh. 8:2, 8; Jer. 18:18; Mal. 2:7
12 [m]Num. 18:9 [n]Lev. 21:22
13 [o]Num. 18:10 [p]Lev. 2:3; 6:16 [4]*portion*
14 [q]Ex. 29:24, 26, 27; Lev. 7:30-34; Num. 18:11 [r]Lev. 22:13 [s]Num. 18:10
15 [t]Lev. 7:29, 30, 34
16 [u]Lev. 9:3, 15
17 [v]Lev. 6:24-30 [w]Ex. 28:38; Lev. 22:16; Num. 18:1
18 [x]Lev. 6:30 [y]Lev. 6:26, 30 [5]The Most Holy Place when capitalized
19 [z]Lev. 9:8, 12 [a][Is. 1:11-15]; Jer. 6:20; 14:12; Hos. 9:4; [Mal. 1:10, 13; 3:1-4]

CHAPTER 11

2 [a]Deut. 14:4; Ezek. 4:14; Dan. 1:8; [Matt. 15:11]; Acts 10:12, 14; [Rom. 14:14; Heb. 9:10; 13:9]
4 [b]Acts 10:14 [1]*impure*
5 [2]*rock badger* [3]*impure*
7 [c]Is. 65:4; 66:3, 17; Mark 5:1-17
8 [d]Is. 52:11; [Mark 7:2, 15, 18]; Acts 10:14, 15; 15:29

10:11 that you may teach the children of Israel. It was essential that alcohol not hinder the clarity of their minds, since the priests were to teach God's law to all of Israel. They were the expositors of the Scripture, alongside the prophets who generally received the Word directly from the Lord. Ezra would become the supreme example of a commendable priest (Ezra 7:10).

10:12-15 *See notes on the peace offering in 3:1-17; 7:11-36.*

10:16-20 The sin offering had not been eaten as prescribed in 6:26, but rather it was wholly burned. It was the duty of the priests to have eaten the meat after the blood was sprinkled on the altar, but instead of eating it in a sacred feast, they had burned it outside the camp. Moses discovered this disobedience, probably from a dread of some further judgment, and challenged, not Aaron, whose heart was too torn in the death of his sons, but the two surviving sons in the priesthood to explain their breach of ritual duty. Aaron, who heard the charge, however, and by whose direction the violation had occurred, gave the explanation. His reason was that they had done all the ritual sacrifice correctly up to the point of eating the meat, but omitted eating because he was too dejected for a feast in the face of the appalling judgments that had fallen. He was wrong, because God had specifically commanded the sin offering to be eaten in the Holy Place. God's law was clear and it was sin to deviate from it at all. Moses sympathized with Aaron's grief, however, and having made his point, dropped the issue.

11:1–16:34 Prescriptions for uncleanness are covered in this section. God used the tangible issues of life which He labeled clean/unclean to repeatedly impress upon Israel the difference between what was holy and unholy. "Clean" means acceptable to God; "unclean" means unacceptable to God. Leviticus 11–15 details the code of cleanness; Lev. 16 returns to sacrifices on the Day of Atonement.

11:1-47 This section contains further legislation on the consumption of animals. Abel's offering hints at a "post-Fall/pre-Flood" diet of animals (Gen. 4:4). After the Noahic flood, God specifically had granted man permission to eat meat (Gen. 9:1-4), but here spelled out the specifics as covenant legislation. All of the reasons for the prohibitions are not specified. The major points were: 1) that Israel was to obey God's absolute standard, regardless of the reason for it, or the lack of understanding of it; and 2) such a unique diet was specified that Israel would find it difficult to eat with the idolatrous people around and among them. Their dietary laws served as a barrier to easy socialization with idolatrous peoples. Dietary and hygienic benefits were real, but only secondary to the divine purposes of obedience and separation.

11:3-23 This section is repeated in Deut. 14:3-20 in almost exact wording. The subject matter includes animals (vv. 3-8), water life (vv. 9-12), birds (vv. 13-19), and insects (vv. 20-23).

11:4 camel. The camel has a divided foot of two large parts, but the division is not complete and the two toes rest on an elastic pad.

11:5,6 rock hyrax...hare. While not true ruminating animals, the manner in which these animals processed their food gave the distinct appearance of "chewing the cud."

9 [e]'These you may eat of all that *are* in
the water: whatever in the water has fins
and scales, whether in the seas or in the
rivers—that you may eat. 10 But all in the
seas or in the rivers that do not have fins
and scales, all that move in the water or
any living thing which *is* in the water, they
are [4]an [f]abomination to you. 11 They shall
be an abomination to you; you shall not eat
their flesh, but you shall regard their carcasses as an abomination. 12 Whatever in
the water does not have fins or scales—
that *shall be* an abomination to you.
13 [g]'And these you shall regard as an
abomination among the birds; they shall
not be eaten, they *are* an abomination: the
eagle, the vulture, the buzzard, 14 the kite,
and the falcon after its kind; 15 every raven
after its kind, 16 the ostrich, the short-eared
owl, the sea gull, and the hawk after its
kind; 17 the little owl, the fisher owl, and
the screech owl; 18 the white owl, the jackdaw, and the carrion vulture; 19 the stork,
the heron after its kind, the hoopoe, and
the bat.
20 'All flying insects that creep on *all*
fours *shall be* an abomination to you. 21 Yet
these you may eat of every flying insect
that creeps on *all* fours: those which have
jointed legs above their feet with which to
leap on the earth. 22 These you may eat:
[h]the locust after its kind, the destroying locust after its kind, the cricket after its kind,
and the grasshopper after its kind. 23 But
all *other* flying insects which have four feet
shall be an abomination to you.

Unclean Animals

24 'By these you shall become [5]unclean;
whoever touches the carcass of any of
them shall be unclean until evening;
25 whoever carries part of the carcass of
any of them [i]shall wash his clothes and be
unclean until evening: 26 *The carcass* of any
animal which divides the foot, but is not
cloven-hoofed or does not chew the cud, *is*
unclean to you. Everyone who touches it
shall be unclean. 27 And whatever goes on
its paws, among all kinds of animals that
go on *all* fours, those *are* unclean to you.
Whoever touches any such carcass shall be
unclean until evening. 28 Whoever carries
any such carcass shall wash his clothes and
be unclean until evening. It *is* unclean to
you.
29 'These also *shall be* unclean to you
among the creeping things that creep on
the earth: the mole, [j]the mouse, and the
large lizard after its kind; 30 the gecko, the
monitor lizard, the sand reptile, the sand
lizard, and the chameleon. 31 These *are* unclean to you among all that creep. Whoever [k]touches them when they are dead shall
be unclean until evening. 32 Anything on
which *any* of them falls, when they are
dead shall be [6]unclean, whether *it is* any
item of wood or clothing or skin or sack,
whatever item *it is*, in which *any* work is
done, [l]it must be put in water. And it shall
be unclean until evening; then it shall be
clean. 33 Any [m]earthen vessel into which
any of them falls [n]you shall break; and
whatever *is* in it shall be unclean: 34 in such
a vessel, any edible food upon which water
falls becomes unclean, and any drink that
may be drunk from it becomes unclean.
35 And everything on which *a part* of *any
such* carcass falls shall be unclean; *whether
it is* an oven or cooking stove, it shall be
broken down; *for* they *are* unclean, and
shall be unclean to you. 36 Nevertheless a
spring or a cistern, *in which there is* plenty
of water, shall be clean, but whatever
touches any such carcass becomes unclean.
37 And if a part of *any such* carcass falls on
any planting seed which is to be sown, it
remains clean. 38 But if water is put on the
seed, and if *a part* of *any such* carcass falls
on it, it *becomes* [7]unclean to you.
39 'And if any animal which you may eat
dies, he who touches its carcass shall be
[o]unclean until evening. 40 [p]He who eats of
its carcass shall wash his clothes and be
unclean until evening. He also who carries
its carcass shall wash his clothes and be
unclean until evening.
41 'And every creeping thing that creeps
on the earth *shall be* [8]an abomination. It
shall not be eaten. 42 Whatever crawls on
its belly, whatever goes on *all* fours, or
whatever has many feet among all creeping things that creep on the earth—these
you shall not eat, for they *are* an abomination. 43 [q]You shall not make [9]yourselves

9 [e]Deut. 14:9
10 [f]Lev. 7:18, 21; Deut. 14:3 [4]*detestable*
13 [g]Deut. 14:12-19; Is. 66:17
22 [h]Matt. 3:4; Mark 1:6
24 [5]*impure*
25 [i]Lev. 14:8; 15:5; Num. 19:10, 21, 22; 31:24; Zech. 13:1; [Heb. 9:10; 10:22; Rev. 7:14]
29 [j]Is. 66:17
31 [k]Hag. 2:13
32 [l]Lev. 15:12 [6]*impure*
33 [m]Lev. 6:28 [n]Lev. 15:12; Ps. 2:9; Jer. 48:38; [2 Tim. 2:21]; Rev. 2:27
38 [7]*impure*
39 [o]Hag. 2:11-13
40 [p]Ex. 22:31; Lev. 17:15; 22:8; Deut. 14:21; Ezek. 4:14; 44:31
41 [8]*detestable*
43 [q]Lev. 20:25 [9]Lit. *your souls*

11:9 fins and scales. Much like the cud and hoof characteristics, the "no fin and scales" guidelines ruled out a segment of water life commonly consumed by ancient people.

11:13 among the birds. Rather than unifying characteristics as in the hoof-cud and no fin-scales descriptions, the forbidden birds were simply named.

11:21 This describes the locust (v. 22), which was allowed for food.

11:24-43 This section deals with separation from other defiling things.

11:26,27 These prohibited animals would include horses and donkeys, which have a single hoof, and lion and tigers, which have paws.

11:30 gecko. A type of lizard.

11:36 a spring or a cistern. The movement and quantity of water determined the probability of actual contamination. Water was scarce also, and it would have been a threat to the water supply if all water touched by these prohibited carcasses were forbidden for drinking.

[1]abominable with any creeping thing that
creeps; nor shall you make yourselves unclean with them, lest you be defiled by
them. **44** For I *am* the LORD your [r]God. You
shall therefore consecrate yourselves, and
[s]you shall be holy; for I *am* holy. Neither
shall you defile yourselves with any creeping thing that creeps on the earth. **45** [t]For I
am the LORD who brings you up out of the
land of Egypt, to be your God. [u]You shall
therefore be holy, for I *am* holy.
46 'This *is* the law [2]of the animals and
the birds and every living creature that
moves in the waters, and of every creature
that creeps on the earth, **47** [v]to distinguish
between the unclean and the clean, and between the animal that may be eaten and
the animal that may not be eaten.' "

The Ritual After Childbirth

12 Then the LORD spoke to Moses, saying, **2** "Speak to the children of Israel, saying: 'If a [a]woman has conceived,
and borne a male child, then [b]she shall be
[1]unclean seven days; [c]as in the days of her
customary impurity she shall be unclean.
3 And on the [d]eighth day the flesh of his
foreskin shall be circumcised. **4** She shall
then continue in the blood of *her* purification thirty-three days. She shall not touch
any [2]hallowed thing, nor come into the
sanctuary until the days of her purification
are fulfilled.
5 'But if she bears a female child, then she
shall be unclean two weeks, as in her customary impurity, and she shall continue in
the blood of *her* purification sixty-six days.
6 [e]'When the days of her purification are
fulfilled, whether for a son or a daughter,
she shall bring to the priest a [f]lamb [3]of the
first year as a burnt offering, and a young
pigeon or a turtledove as a [g]sin offering, to
the door of the tabernacle of meeting.
7 Then he shall offer it before the LORD, and
make [4]atonement for her. And she shall be
clean from the flow of her blood. This *is* the
law for her who has borne a male or a female.
8 [h]'And if she is not able to bring a lamb,
then she may bring two turtledoves or two
young pigeons—one as a burnt offering
and the other as a sin offering. [i]So the
priest shall make atonement for her, and
she will be [5]clean.' "

The Law Concerning Leprosy

13 And the LORD spoke to Moses and
Aaron, saying: **2** "When a man has
on the skin of his body a swelling, [a]a scab,
or a bright spot, and it becomes on the skin
of his body *like* a [1]leprous sore, [b]then he
shall be brought to Aaron the priest or to
one of his sons the priests. **3** The priest
shall examine the sore on the skin of the
body; and if the hair on the sore has turned
white, and the sore appears *to be* deeper

43 [1] *impure*
44 [r] Ex. 6:7; Lev. 22:33; 25:38; 26:45 [s] Ex. 19:6; Lev. 19:2; 20:7, 26; [Amos 3:3]; Matt. 5:48; 1 Thess. 4:7; 1 Pet. 1:15, 16; [Rev. 22:11, 14]
45 [t] Ex. 6:7; 20:2; Lev. 22:33; 25:38; 26:45; Ps. 105:43-45; Hos. 11:1 [u] Lev. 11:44
46 [2] *concerning*
47 [v] Lev. 10:10; Ezek. 44:23; Mal. 3:18

CHAPTER 12

2 [a] Lev. 15:19; [Job 14:4; Ps. 51:5] [b] Ex. 22:30; Lev. 8:33; 13:4; Luke 2:22 [c] Lev. 18:19 [1] *impure*
3 [d] Gen. 17:12; Luke 1:59; 2:21; John 7:22, 23; Gal. 5:3
4 [2] *consecrated*
6 [e] Luke 2:22 [f] [John 1:29; 1 Pet. 1:18, 19] [g] Lev. 5:7 [3] Lit. *a son of his year*
7 [4] Lit. *covering*
8 [h] Lev. 5:7; Luke 2:22-24 [i] Lev. 4:26 [5] *pure*

CHAPTER 13

2 [a] Deut. 28:27; Is. 3:17 [b] Deut. 17:8, 9; 24:8; Mal. 2:7; Luke 17:14 [1] Heb. *saraath*, disfiguring skin diseases, including leprosy, and so in vv. 2-46 and 14:2-32

11:44,45 consecrate yourselves...be holy; for I *am* holy. In all of this, God is teaching His people to live antithetically. That is, He is using these clean and unclean distinctions to separate Israel from other idolatrous nations who have no such restrictions, and He is illustrating by these prescriptions that His people must learn to live His way. Through dietary laws and rituals, God is teaching them the reality of living His way in everything. They are being taught to obey God in every seemingly mundane area of life, so as to learn how crucial obedience is. Sacrifices, rituals, diet, and even clothing and cooking are all carefully ordered by God to teach them that they are to live differently from everyone else. This is to be an external illustration for the separation from sin in their hearts. Because the Lord is their God, they are to be utterly distinct. In v. 44, for the first time the statement "I am the LORD your God" is made, as a reason for the required separation and holiness. After this verse, that phrase is mentioned about 50 more times in this book, along with the equally instructive claim, "I am holy." Because God is holy and is their God, the people are to be holy in outward ceremonial behavior as an external expression of the greater necessity of heart holiness. The connection between ceremonial holiness carries over into personal holiness. The only motivation given for all these laws is to learn to be holy because God is holy. The holiness theme is central to Leviticus (see 10:3; 19:2; 20:7,26; 21:6-8).

12:1-8 Uncleanness is related to the mother's afterbirth, not the child.

12:2 customary impurity. This refers to her monthly menstruation cycle (see 15:19-24).

12:3 eighth day. Joseph and Mary followed these instructions at the birth of Christ (Luke 2:21). **circumcised.** The sign of the Abrahamic (Gen. 17:9-14) Covenant was incorporated into the laws of Mosaic cleanness. Cf. Rom. 4:11-13. (For a discussion on circumcision, *see note on Jer. 4:4.*)

12:5 two weeks...sixty-six days. Apparently mothers were unclean twice as long (80 days) after the birth of a daughter as a son (40 days), which reflected the stigma on women for Eve's part in the Fall. This stigma is removed in Christ (*see note on 1 Tim. 2:14,15*).

12:6 burnt offering...sin offering. Though the occasion was joyous, the sacrifices required were to impress upon the mind of the parent the reality of original sin and that the child had inherited a sin nature. The circumcision involved a cutting away of the male foreskin, which could carry infections and diseases in its folds. This cleansing of the physical organ so as not to pass on disease (Jewish women have historically had the lowest incidence of cervical cancer), was a picture of the deep need for cleansing from depravity, which is most clearly revealed by procreation, as men produce sinners and only sinners. Circumcision points to the fact that cleansing is needed at the very core of a human being, a cleansing God offers to the faithful and penitent through the sacrifice of Christ to come.

12:8 turtledoves...pigeons. Cf. Lev. 1:14-17; 5:7-10. These were the offerings of Joseph and Mary after Christ's birth (cf. Luke 2:24), when they presented Jesus as their firstborn to the Lord (Ex. 13:2; Luke 2:22). Birds, rather than livestock, indicated a low economic situation, though one who was in total poverty could offer flour (5:11-14).

13:1–14:57 This section covers laws pertaining to skin diseases.

13:2 bright spot. This probably refers to inflammation. **a leprous sore.** This is a term referring to various ancient skin disorders that were sometimes superficial, sometimes serious. It may have in-

than the skin of his body, it *is* a leprous
sore. Then the priest shall examine him,
and pronounce him [2]unclean. 4 But if the
bright spot *is* white on the skin of his body,
and does not appear *to be* deeper than the
skin, and its hair has not turned white,
then the priest shall isolate *the one who has*
the sore [c]seven days. 5 And the priest shall
examine him on the seventh day; and indeed *if* the sore appears to be as it was, *and*
the sore has not spread on the skin, then
the priest shall isolate him another seven
days. 6 Then the priest shall examine him
again on the seventh day; and indeed *if* the
sore has faded, *and* the sore has not spread
on the skin, then the priest shall pronounce
him clean; it *is only* a scab, and he [d]shall
wash his clothes and be clean. 7 But if the
scab should at all spread over the skin,
after he has been seen by the priest for his
cleansing, he shall be seen by the priest
again. 8 And *if* the priest sees that the scab
has indeed spread on the skin, then the
priest shall pronounce him [3]unclean. It *is*
leprosy.
9 "When the leprous sore is on a person,
then he shall be brought to the priest.
10 [e]And the priest shall examine *him;* and
indeed *if* the swelling on the skin *is* white,
and it has turned the hair white, and *there*
is a spot of raw flesh in the swelling, 11 it *is*
an old leprosy on the skin of his body. The
priest shall pronounce him [4]unclean, and
shall not isolate him, for he *is* unclean.
12 "And if leprosy breaks out all over the
skin, and the leprosy covers all the skin of
the one who has the sore, from his head to
his foot, wherever the priest looks, 13 then
the priest shall consider; and indeed *if* the
leprosy has covered all his body, he shall
pronounce *him* clean *who has* the sore. It
has all turned [f]white. He *is* clean. 14 But
when raw flesh appears on him, he shall be
unclean. 15 And the priest shall examine
the raw flesh and pronounce him to be unclean; *for* the raw flesh *is* unclean. It *is* leprosy. 16 Or if the raw flesh changes and
turns white again, he shall come to the
priest. 17 And the priest shall examine him;
and indeed *if* the sore has turned white,
then the priest shall pronounce *him* clean
who has the sore. He *is* clean.
18 "If the body develops a [g]boil in the
skin, and it is healed, 19 and in the place of
the boil there comes a white swelling or a
bright spot, reddish-white, then it shall be
shown to the priest; 20 and *if,* when the
priest sees it, it indeed *appears* deeper than
the skin, and its hair has turned white, the
priest shall pronounce him unclean. It *is* a
leprous sore which has broken out of the
boil. 21 But if the priest examines it, and indeed *there are* no white hairs in it, and it *is*
not deeper than the skin, but has faded,
then the priest shall isolate him seven
days; 22 and if it should at all spread over
the skin, then the priest shall pronounce
him unclean. It *is* a [5]leprous sore. 23 But if
the bright spot stays in one place, *and* has
not spread, it *is* the scar of the boil; and the
priest shall pronounce him clean.
24 "Or if the body receives a [h]burn on its
skin by fire, and the raw *flesh* of the burn becomes a bright spot, reddish-white or white,
25 then the priest shall examine it; and indeed *if* the hair of the bright spot has turned
white, and it appears deeper than the skin, it
is leprosy broken out in the burn. Therefore
the priest shall pronounce him unclean. It *is*
a leprous sore. 26 But if the priest examines
it, and indeed *there are* no white hairs in the
bright spot, and it *is* not deeper than the
skin, but has faded, then the priest shall isolate him seven days. 27 And the priest shall
examine him on the seventh day. If it has at
all spread over the skin, then the priest shall
pronounce him unclean. It *is* a leprous sore.
28 But if the bright spot stays in one place,
and has not spread on the skin, but has
faded, it *is* a swelling from the burn. The
priest shall pronounce him clean, for it *is* the
scar from the burn.
29 "If a man or woman has a sore on the
head or the beard, 30 then the priest shall
examine the sore; and indeed if it appears
deeper than the skin, *and there is* in it thin
yellow hair, then the priest shall pronounce
him unclean. It *is* a scaly leprosy of the
head or beard. 31 But if the priest examines
the scaly sore, and indeed it does not ap-

3 [2] *defiled*
4 [c] Lev. 14:8
6 [d] Lev. 11:25; 14:8; [John 13:8, 10]
8 [3] *defiled*
10 [e] Num. 12:10, 12; 2 Kin. 5:27; 2 Chr. 26:19, 20
11 [4] *defiled*
13 [f] Ex. 4:6
18 [g] Ex. 9:9; 15:26
22 [5] *infection*
24 [h] Is. 3:24

cluded modern leprosy (Hansen's disease). The symptoms described in vv. 2,6,10,18,30, and 39 are not sufficient for a diagnosis of the clinical condition. For the protection of the people, observation and isolation were demanded for all suspected cases of what could be a contagious disease. This biblical leprosy involved some whiteness (v. 3; Ex. 4:6), which disfigured its victim but did not disable him. Naaman was able to exercise his functions as general of Syria's army, although a leper (2 Kin. 5:1,27). Both OT and NT lepers went almost everywhere, indicating that this disease was not the leprosy of today that cripples. A victim of this scaly disease was unclean as long as the infection was partial. Once the body was covered with it, he was clean and could enter the place of worship (see vv. 12-17). Apparently the complete covering meant the contagious period was over. The allusion to a boil (vv. 18-28) with inflamed or raw areas and whitened hairs may refer to a related infection that was contagious. When lepers were cured by Christ, they were neither lame nor deformed. They were never brought on beds. Similar skin conditions are described in vv. 29-37 and vv. 38-44 (some inflammation from infection). The aim of these laws was to protect the people from disease, but more importantly, to inculcate into them by vivid object lessons how God desired purity, holiness, and cleanness among His people.

pear deeper than the skin, and *there is* no
black hair in it, then the priest shall isolate
the one who has the scale seven days. 32 And
on the seventh day the priest shall examine
the sore; and indeed *if* the scale has not
spread, and there is no yellow hair in it,
and the scale does not appear deeper than
the skin, 33 he shall shave himself, but the
scale he shall not shave. And the priest
shall isolate *the one who has* the scale another seven days. 34 On the seventh day the
priest shall examine the scale; and indeed *if*
the scale has not spread over the skin, and
does not appear deeper than the skin, then
the priest shall pronounce him clean. He
shall wash his clothes and be clean. 35 But if
the scale should at all spread over the skin
after his cleansing, 36 then the priest shall
examine him; and indeed *if* the scale has
spread over the skin, the priest need not
seek for yellow hair. He *is* unclean. 37 But if
the scale appears to be at a standstill, and
there is black hair grown up in it, the scale
has healed. He *is* clean, and the priest shall
pronounce him clean.

38 "If a man or a woman has bright spots
on the skin of the body, *specifically* white
bright spots, 39 then the priest shall look;
and indeed *if* the bright spots on the skin of
the body *are* dull white, it *is* a white spot
that grows on the skin. He *is* clean.

40 "As for the man whose hair has fallen
from his head, he *is* bald, *but* he *is* clean.
41 He whose hair has fallen from his forehead, he *is* bald on the forehead, *but* he *is*
clean. 42 And if there is on the bald head or
bald [i]forehead a reddish-white sore, it *is*
leprosy breaking out on his bald head or
his bald forehead. 43 Then the priest shall
examine it; and indeed *if* the swelling of
the sore *is* reddish-white on his bald head
or on his bald forehead, as the appearance
of leprosy on the skin of the body, 44 he is a
leprous man. He *is* unclean. The priest
shall surely pronounce him [6]unclean; his
sore *is* on his [j]head.

45 "Now the leper on whom the sore *is*,
his clothes shall be torn and his head [k]bare;
and he shall [l]cover his mustache, and cry,
[m]'Unclean! Unclean!' 46 He shall be unclean. All the days he has the sore he shall
be unclean. He *is* unclean, and he shall
[7]dwell alone; his dwelling *shall be* [n]outside
the camp.

The Law Concerning Leprous Garments

47 "Also, if a garment has a [8]leprous
plague in it, *whether it is* a woolen garment
or a linen garment, 48 whether *it is* in the
warp or woof of linen or wool, whether in
leather or in anything made of leather,
49 and if the plague is greenish or reddish
in the garment or in the leather, whether in
the warp or in the woof, or in anything
made of leather, it *is* a leprous [9]plague and
shall be shown to the priest. 50 The priest
shall examine the plague and isolate *that
which has* the plague seven days. 51 And he
shall examine the plague on the seventh
day. If the plague has spread in the garment, either in the warp or in the woof, in
the leather *or* in anything made of leather,
the plague *is* [o]an active leprosy. It *is* unclean. 52 He shall therefore burn that garment in which is the plague, whether warp
or woof, in wool or in linen, or anything of
leather, for it *is* an active leprosy; *the garment* shall be burned in the fire.

53 "But if the priest examines *it*, and indeed the plague has not spread in the garment, either in the warp or in the woof, or
in anything made of leather, 54 then the
priest shall command that they wash *the
thing* in which *is* the plague; and he shall
isolate it another seven days. 55 Then the
priest shall examine the plague after it has
been washed; and indeed *if* the plague has
not changed its color, though the plague
has not spread, it *is* unclean, and you shall
burn it in the fire; it continues eating away,
whether the damage *is* outside or inside.
56 If the priest examines *it*, and indeed the
plague has faded after washing it, then he
shall tear it out of the garment, whether
out of the warp or out of the woof, or out
of the leather. 57 But if it appears again in
the garment, either in the warp or in the
woof, or in anything made of leather, it *is* a
spreading *plague*; you shall burn with fire
that in which is the plague. 58 And if you
wash the garment, either warp or woof, or
whatever is made of leather, if the plague
has disappeared from it, then it shall be
washed a second time, and shall be clean.

59 "This *is* the law of the leprous plague
in a garment of wool or linen, either in the
warp or woof, or in anything made of
leather, to pronounce it clean or to pronounce it unclean."

42 [i] 2 Chr. 26:19
44 [j] Is. 1:5
[6] *altogether defiled*
45 [k] Lev. 10:6; 21:10
[l] Ezek. 24:17, 22; Mic. 3:7 [m] Is. 6:5; 64:6; Lam. 4:15; Luke 5:8
46 [n] Num. 5:1-4; 12:14; 2 Kin. 7:3; 15:5; 2 Chr. 26:21; Ps. 38:11; Luke 17:12
[7] *live alone*

47 [8] A mold, fungus, or similar infestation, and so in vv. 47-59
49 [9] *mark*
51 [o] Lev. 14:44

13:45 'Unclean! Unclean!' Here are the symbols of grief and isolation. This same cry is heard from the survivors of Jerusalem's destruction (cf. Lam. 4:15).

13:47-59 Deals with garments worn by infected persons.

13:59 to pronounce it clean or…unclean. The primary purpose of this legislation was to assist the priest in determining the presence of contagious skin disease. The language of the passage indicates disease that affects the clothes as it did the person. This provided more illustrations of the devastating infection of sin and how essential cleansing was spiritually.

The Ritual for Cleansing Healed Lepers

14 Then the LORD spoke to Moses, saying, 2 "This shall be the law of the
[1]leper for the day of his cleansing: He
[a]shall be brought to the priest. 3 And the
priest shall go out of the camp, and the
priest shall examine *him;* and indeed, *if*
the [2]leprosy is healed in the leper, 4 then
the priest shall command to take for him
who is to be cleansed two living *and* clean
birds, [b]cedar wood, [c]scarlet, and [d]hyssop.
5 And the priest shall command that one of
the birds be killed in an earthen vessel over
running water. 6 As for the living bird, he
shall take it, the cedar wood and the scarlet and the hyssop, and dip them and the
living bird in the blood of the bird *that was*
killed over the running water. 7 And he
shall [e]sprinkle it [f]seven times on him who
is to be cleansed from the leprosy, and shall
pronounce him clean, and shall let the living bird loose in the open field. 8 He who is
to be cleansed [g]shall wash his clothes,
shave off all his hair, and [h]wash himself in
water, that he may be clean. After that he
shall come into the camp, and [i]shall stay
outside his tent seven days. 9 But on the
[j]seventh day he shall shave all the hair off
his head and his beard and his eyebrows—
all his hair he shall shave off. He shall
wash his clothes and wash his body in
water, and he shall be clean.
10 "And on the eighth day [k]he shall take
two male lambs without blemish, one ewe
lamb of the first year without blemish,
three-tenths *of an ephah* of fine flour mixed
with oil as [l]a grain offering, and one log of
oil. 11 Then the priest who makes *him* clean
shall present the man who is to be made
clean, and those things, before the LORD, *at*
the door of the tabernacle of meeting.
12 And the priest shall take one male lamb
and [m]offer it as a trespass offering, and the
log of oil, and [n]wave them *as* a wave offering before the LORD. 13 Then he shall kill
the lamb [o]in the place where he kills the sin
offering and the burnt offering, in a holy
place; for [p]as the sin offering *is* the priest's,
so *is* the trespass offering. [q]It *is* most holy.
14 The priest shall take *some* of the blood of
the trespass offering, and the priest shall
put *it* [r]on the tip of the right ear of him
who is to be cleansed, on the thumb of his
right hand, and on the big toe of his right
foot. 15 And the priest shall take *some* of the
log of oil, and pour *it* into the palm of his
own left hand. 16 Then the priest shall dip
his right finger in the oil that *is* in his left
hand, and shall [s]sprinkle some of the oil
with his finger seven times before the
LORD. 17 And of the rest of the oil in his
hand, the priest shall put *some* on the tip of
the right ear of him who is to be cleansed,
on the thumb of his right hand, and on the
big toe of his right foot, on the blood of the
trespass offering. 18 The rest of the oil that
is in the priest's hand he shall put on the
head of him who is to be cleansed. [t]So the
priest shall make [3]atonement for him before the LORD.
19 "Then the priest shall offer [u]the sin offering, and make atonement for him who
is to be cleansed from his uncleanness. Afterward he shall kill the burnt offering.
20 And the priest shall offer the burnt offering and the grain offering on the altar.
So the priest shall make atonement for
him, and he shall be [v]clean.
21 "But [w]if he *is* poor and cannot afford
it, then he shall take one male lamb *as* a
trespass offering to be waved, to make
atonement for him, [4]one-tenth *of an ephah*
of fine flour mixed with oil as a grain offering, a log of oil, 22 [x]and two turtledoves
or two young pigeons, such as he is able to
afford: one shall be a sin offering and the
other a burnt offering. 23 [y]He shall bring
them to the priest on the eighth day for his
cleansing, to the door of the tabernacle of
meeting, before the LORD. 24 [z]And the

CHAPTER 14

2 [a]Matt. 8:2, 4; Mark 1:40, 44; Luke 5:12, 14; 17:14 [1]See note at 13:2
3 [2]Heb. *saraath,* disfiguring skin diseases, including leprosy, and so in vv. 2-32
4 [b]Lev. 14:6, 49, 51, 52; Num. 19:6; Heb. 9:19 [c]Ex. 25:4 [d]Ex. 12:22; Ps. 51:7
7 [e]Num. 19:18, 19; [Heb. 9:13, 21; 12:24] [f]2 Kin. 5:10, 14; Ps. 51:2
8 [g]Lev. 11:25; 13:6; Num. 8:7 [h]Lev. 11:25; [Eph. 5:26; Heb. 10:22; Rev. 1:5, 6] [i]Lev. 13:5; Num. 5:2, 3; 12:14, 15; 2 Chr. 26:21
9 [j]Num. 19:19
10 [k]Matt. 8:4; Mark 1:44; Luke 5:14 [l]Lev. 2:1; Num. 15:4
12 [m]Lev. 5:6, 18; 6:6; 14:19 [n]Ex. 29:22-24, 26
13 [o]Ex. 29:11; Lev. 1:5, 11; 4:4, 24 [p]Lev. 6:24-30; 7:7 [q]Lev. 2:3; 7:6; 21:22
14 [r]Ex. 29:20; Lev. 8:23, 24
16 [s]Lev. 4:6
18 [t]Lev. 4:26; 5:6; Num. 15:28; [Heb. 2:17] [3]Lit. *covering*
19 [u]Lev. 5:1, 6; 12:7; [2 Cor. 5:21]
20 [v]Lev. 14:8, 9
21 [w]Lev. 5:7, 11; 12:8; 27:8 [4]Approximately two dry quarts
22 [x]Lev. 12:8; 15:14, 15
23 [y]Lev. 14:10, 11
24 [z]Lev. 14:12

14:1-32 This section explains the cleansing ritual for healed persons.

14:2 the law of the leper. The sense of this law is a prescription, not for healing from leprosy and other such diseases, but rather for the ceremonial cleansing, which needed to be performed after the person was declared clean.

14:3 out of the camp. The leper was not allowed to return to society immediately. Before the person could enter the camp, some priest skilled in the diagnoses of disease needed to examine him and assist with the ritual of the two birds (vv. 4-7).

14:4-7 The bundle of cedar and hyssop tied with scarlet included the living bird. It was all dipped 7 times into the blood of the killed bird mixed with water to symbolize purification. The bird was then set free to symbolize the leper's release from quarantine.

14:4 hyssop. *See note on Ex. 12:22* (cf. Lev. 14:6,49,51).

14:8 outside his tent. The movement was progressive until finally he could enter and dwell in his own tent, giving dramatic indication of the importance of thorough cleansing for fellowship with God's people. This was a powerful lesson from God on the holiness He desired for those who lived among His people. This has not changed (see 2 Cor. 7:1).

14:10-20 As part of the leper's ceremonial cleansing ritual, trespass (5:14–6:7), sin (4:1–5:13), burnt (1:3-17), and grain (2:1-16) offerings were to be made.

14:10 one log of oil. Less than one pint.

14:12 wave offering. *See note on 7:30-32.*

14:17 right ear...right hand...right foot. *See note on 8:23,24.*

14:18 put on the head. This would not have been understood as an anointing for entry into an office, but rather a symbolic gesture of cleansing and healing. There could be a connection with the NT directive to anoint the sick for healing (Mark 6:13; 16:18; James 5:14).

priest shall take the lamb of the trespass offering and the log of oil, and the priest shall wave them *as* a wave offering before the LORD. 25 Then he shall kill the lamb of the trespass offering, [a]and the priest shall take *some* of the blood of the trespass offering and put *it* on the tip of the right ear of him who is to be cleansed, on the thumb of his right hand, and on the big toe of his right foot. 26 And the priest shall pour some of the oil into the palm of his own left hand. 27 Then the priest shall sprinkle with his right finger *some* of the oil that *is* in his left hand seven times before the LORD. 28 And the priest shall put *some* of the oil that *is* in his hand on the tip of the right ear of him who is to be cleansed, on the thumb of the right hand, and on the big toe of his right foot, on the place of the blood of the trespass offering. 29 The rest of the oil that *is* in the priest's hand he shall put on the head of him who is to be cleansed, to make atonement for him before the LORD. 30 And he shall offer one of [b]the turtledoves or young pigeons, such as he can afford— 31 such as he is able to afford, the one *as* a sin offering and the other *as* a burnt offering, with the grain offering. So the priest shall make atonement for him who is to be cleansed before the LORD. 32 This *is* the law *for one* who had a leprous sore, who cannot afford [c]the usual cleansing."

The Law Concerning Leprous Houses

33 And the LORD spoke to Moses and Aaron, saying: 34 [d]"When you have come into the land of Canaan, which I give you as a possession, and [e]I put the [5]leprous plague in a house in the land of your possession, 35 and he who owns the house comes and tells the priest, saying, 'It seems to me that *there is* [f]some plague in the house,' 36 then the priest shall command that they empty the house, before the priest goes *into it* to examine the plague, that all that *is* in the house may not be made unclean; and afterward the priest shall go in to examine the house. 37 And he shall examine the plague; and indeed *if* the plague *is* on the walls of the house with ingrained streaks, greenish or reddish, which appear to be [6]deep in the wall, 38 then the priest shall go out of the house, to the door of the house, and [7]shut up the house seven days. 39 And the priest shall come again on the seventh day and look; and indeed *if* the plague has spread on the walls of the house, 40 then the priest shall command that they take away the stones in which *is* the plague, and they shall cast them into an unclean place outside the city. 41 And he shall cause the house to be scraped inside, all around, and the dust that they scrape off they shall pour out in an unclean place outside the city. 42 Then they shall take other stones and put *them* in the place of *those* stones, and he shall take other mortar and plaster the house.

43 "Now if the plague comes back and breaks out in the house, after he has taken away the stones, after he has scraped the house, and after it is plastered, 44 then the priest shall come and look; and indeed *if* the plague has spread in the house, it *is* [g]an active leprosy in the house. It *is* unclean. 45 And he shall break down the house, its stones, its timber, and all the plaster of the house, and he shall carry *them* outside the city to an unclean place. 46 Moreover he who goes into the house at all while it is shut up shall be [8]unclean [h]until evening. 47 And he who lies down in the house shall [i]wash his clothes, and he who eats in the house shall wash his clothes.

48 "But if the priest comes in and examines *it,* and indeed the plague has not spread in the house after the house was plastered, then the priest shall pronounce the house clean, because the plague is healed. 49 And [j]he shall take, to cleanse the house, two birds, cedar wood, scarlet, and hyssop. 50 Then he shall kill one of the birds in an earthen vessel over running water; 51 and he shall take the cedar wood, the hyssop, the scarlet, and the living bird, and dip them in the blood of the slain bird and in the running water, and sprinkle the house seven times. 52 And he shall [9]cleanse the house with the blood of the bird and the running water and the living bird, with the cedar wood, the hyssop, and the scarlet. 53 Then he shall let the living bird loose outside the city in the open field, and [k]make atonement for the house, and it shall be clean.

54 "This *is* the law for any [l]leprous sore and scale, 55 for the [m]leprosy of a garment [n]and of a house, 56 [o]for a swelling and a

25 [a] Lev. 14:14, 17
30 [b] Lev. 14:22; 15:14, 15
32 [c] Lev. 14:10
34 [d] Gen. 12:7; 13:17; 17:8; Num. 32:22; Deut. 7:1; 32:49 [e] [Prov. 3:33] [5] Decomposition by mildew, mold, dry rot, etc., and so in vv. 34-53
35 [f] [Ps. 91:9, 10; Prov. 3:33; Zech. 5:4]
37 [6] Lit. *lower than the wall*
38 [7] *quarantine*
44 [g] Lev. 13:51; [Zech. 5:4]
46 [h] Lev. 11:24; 15:5 [8] *defiled*
47 [i] Lev. 14:8
49 [j] Lev. 14:4
52 [9] *ceremonially cleanse*
53 [k] Lev. 14:20
54 [l] Lev. 13:30; 26:21
55 [m] Lev. 13:47-52 [n] Lev. 14:34
56 [o] Lev. 13:2

14:33-57 This section covers contaminated houses which most likely involved some kinds of infectious bacteria, fungus, or mold.

14:34 I put the leprous plague. God's sovereign hand is acknowledged in the diseases that were in Canaan (cf. Ex. 4:11; Deut. 32:39). He had His purposes for these afflictions, as He always does. Uniquely, in Israel's case, they allowed for object lessons on holiness.

14:37 ingrained streaks, greenish or reddish. The disease would appear to be some sort of contagious mildew. Leprosy (Hansen's disease), as we know it today, is not the problem here since it is a disease related to the human senses, i.e., the destruction of feeling due to the dysfunction of the nerves. It is not known to be contagious either, and it couldn't be developed in a house. The matter of cleansing such houses is delineated in vv. 38-53.

scab and a bright spot, 57 to [p]teach when *it*
is unclean and when *it is* clean. This *is* the
law of leprosy."

The Law Concerning Bodily Discharges

15 And the LORD spoke to Moses and
Aaron, saying, 2 "Speak to the children of Israel, and say to them: [a]'When any
man has a discharge from his body, his discharge *is* unclean. 3 And this shall be his
uncleanness in regard to his discharge—
whether his body runs with his discharge,
or his body is stopped up by his discharge,
it *is* his uncleanness. 4 Every bed is [1]un-
clean on which he who has the discharge
lies, and everything on which he sits shall
be unclean. 5 And whoever [b]touches his
bed shall [c]wash his clothes and [d]bathe in
water, and be unclean until evening. 6 He
who sits on anything on which he who has
the [e]discharge sat shall wash his clothes
and bathe in water, and be unclean until
evening. 7 And he who touches the body of
him who has the discharge shall wash his
clothes and bathe in water, and be unclean
until evening. 8 If he who has the discharge
[f]spits on him who is clean, then he shall
wash his clothes and bathe in water, and be
unclean until evening. 9 Any saddle on
which he who has the discharge rides shall
be unclean. 10 Whoever touches anything
that was under him shall be unclean until
evening. He who carries *any of* those things
shall wash his clothes and bathe in water,
and be unclean until evening. 11 And
whomever the one who has the discharge
touches, and has not rinsed his hands in
water, he shall wash his clothes and bathe
in water, and be unclean until evening.
12 The [g]vessel of earth that he who has the
discharge touches shall be broken, and
every vessel of wood shall be rinsed in
water.
13 'And when he who has a discharge is
cleansed of his discharge, then [h]he shall
count for himself seven days for his cleansing, wash his clothes, and bathe his body
in running water; then he shall be clean.
14 On the eighth day he shall take for himself [i]two turtledoves or two young pigeons, and come before the LORD, to the
door of the tabernacle of meeting, and give
them to the priest. 15 Then the priest shall
offer them, [j]the one *as* a sin offering and
the other *as* a burnt offering. [k]So the priest
shall make [2]atonement for him before the
LORD because of his discharge.
16 [l]'If any man has an emission of
semen, then he shall wash all his body in
water, and be unclean until evening.
17 And any garment and any leather on
which there is semen, it shall be washed
with water, and be unclean until evening.
18 Also, when a woman lies with a man,
and *there is* an emission of semen, they
shall bathe in water, and [m]be unclean until
evening.
19 [n]'If a woman has a discharge, *and* the
discharge from her body is blood, she shall
be [3]set apart seven days; and whoever
touches her shall be unclean until evening.
20 Everything that she lies on during her
impurity shall be unclean; also everything
that she sits on shall be unclean. 21 Whoever touches her bed shall wash his clothes
and bathe in water, and be unclean until
evening. 22 And whoever touches anything that she sat on shall wash his clothes
and bathe in water, and be unclean until
evening. 23 If *anything* is on *her* bed or on
anything on which she sits, when he
touches it, he shall be unclean until
evening. 24 And [o]if any man lies with her
at all, so that her impurity is on him, he
shall be [4]unclean seven days; and every
bed on which he lies shall be unclean.
25 'If [p]a woman has a discharge of blood
for many days, other than at the time of
her *customary* impurity, or if it runs beyond
her *usual time of* impurity, all the days of
her unclean discharge shall be as the days
of her *customary* impurity. She *shall be* unclean. 26 Every bed on which she lies all the
days of her discharge shall be to her as the
bed of her impurity; and whatever she sits
on shall be unclean, as the uncleanness of
her impurity. 27 Whoever touches those
things shall be unclean; he shall wash his
clothes and bathe in water, and be unclean
until evening.
28 'But [q]if she is cleansed of her discharge, then she shall count for herself
seven days, and after that she shall be
clean. 29 And on the eighth day she shall

57 [p] Lev. 11:47; 20:25; Deut. 24:8; Ezek. 44:23

CHAPTER 15

2 [a] Lev. 22:4; Num. 5:2; 2 Sam. 3:29
4 [1] *defiled*
5 [b] Lev. 5:2; 14:46 [c] Lev. 14:8, 47 [d] Lev. 11:25; 17:15
6 [e] Lev. 15:10; Deut. 23:10
8 [f] Num. 12:14
12 [g] Lev. 6:28; 11:32, 33
13 [h] Lev. 14:8; 15:28; Num. 19:11, 12
14 [i] Lev. 14:22, 23, 30, 31
15 [j] Lev. 14:30, 31 [k] Lev. 14:19, 31 [2] Lit. *covering*
16 [l] Lev. 22:4; Deut. 23:10, 11
18 [m] [Ex. 19:15; 1 Sam. 21:4; 1 Cor. 6:18]
19 [n] Lev. 12:2 [3] Lit. *in her impurity*
24 [o] Lev. 18:19; 20:18 [4] *defiled*
25 [p] Matt. 9:20; Mark 5:25; Luke 8:43
28 [q] Lev. 15:13-15

14:57 to teach when *it is* unclean and when *it is* clean. The priest needed instruction in identifying and prescribing the course for disease such as that described herein, to teach people the importance of distinguishing holy things.

15:1-33 This section deals with purification for bodily discharges. Several types of discharges by men (vv. 1-18) and women (vv. 19-30) are identified and given prescribed treatment.

15:2-15 These verses describe secretions related to some disease of the male sexual organs. After he became well, he was required to make both a sin and a burnt offering (v. 15).

15:16-18 These verses refer to natural sexual gland secretions for which no offerings were required.

15:19-24 These verses concern the natural menstrual discharge of a woman for which no offerings were required.

15:25-30 These verses deal with some secretion of blood indicating disease, not menstruation, requiring a sin and burnt offering after she is well.

take for herself two turtledoves or two
young pigeons, and bring them to the
priest, to the door of the tabernacle of
meeting. **30** Then the priest shall offer the
one *as* a sin offering and the other *as* a
[r]burnt offering, and the priest shall make
atonement for her before the LORD for the
discharge of her uncleanness.
31 'Thus you shall [s]separate the children
of Israel from their uncleanness, lest they
die in their uncleanness when they [t]defile
My tabernacle that *is* among them. **32** [u]This
is the law for one who has a discharge,
[v]and *for him* who emits semen and is unclean thereby, **33** [w]and for her who is indisposed because of her *customary* impurity,
and for one who has a discharge, either
man [x]or woman, [y]and for him who lies
with her who is unclean.' "

The Day of Atonement

16 Now the LORD spoke to Moses
after [a]the death of the two sons of
Aaron, when they offered *profane fire* before the LORD, and died; **2** and the LORD
said to Moses: "Tell Aaron your brother
[b]not to come at *just* any time into the
Holy *Place* inside the veil, before the
mercy seat which *is* on the ark, lest he die;
for [c]I will appear in the cloud above the
mercy seat.
3 [1]"Thus Aaron shall [d]come into the
Holy *Place:* [e]with *the blood of* a young bull
as a sin offering, and *of* a ram as a burnt offering. **4** He shall put the [f]holy linen tunic
and the linen trousers on his body; he shall
be girded with a linen sash, and with the
linen turban he shall be attired. These *are*
holy garments. Therefore [g]he shall wash
his body in water, and put them on. **5** And
he shall take from [h]the congregation of the
children of Israel two kids of the goats as a
sin offering, and one ram as a burnt offering.
6 "Aaron shall offer the bull as a sin offering, which *is* for himself, and [i]make
atonement for himself and for his house.
7 He shall take the two goats and present
them before the LORD *at* the door of the
tabernacle of meeting. **8** Then Aaron shall

30 [r] Lev. 5:7
31 [s] Lev. 11:47; 14:57; 22:2; Deut. 24:8; Ezek. 44:23; [Heb. 12:15] [t] Lev. 20:3; Num. 5:3; 19:13, 20; Ezek. 5:11; 23:38; 36:17
32 [u] Lev. 15:2 [v] Lev. 15:16
33 [w] Lev. 15:19 [x] Lev. 15:25 [y] Lev. 15:24

CHAPTER 16

1 [a] Lev. 10:1, 2; 2 Sam. 6:6-8
2 [b] Ex. 30:10; Lev. 16:34; 23:27; [Heb. 6:19; 9:7, 8, 12; 10:19] [c] Ex. 25:21, 22; 40:34; 1 Kin. 8:10-12
3 [d] Lev. 4:1-12; 16:6; [Heb. 9:7, 12, 24, 25] [e] Lev. 4:3 [1] Lit. *With this*
4 [f] Ex. 28:39, 42, 43; Lev. 6:10; Ezek. 44:17, 18 [g] Ex. 30:20; Lev. 8:6, 7
5 [h] Lev. 4:14; Num. 29:11; 2 Chr. 29:21; Ezra 6:17; Ezek. 45:22, 23
6 [i] Lev. 9:7; [Heb. 5:3; 7:27, 28; 9:7]

15:31-33 In all these instructions, God was showing the Israelites that they must have a profound reverence for holy things; and nothing was more suited to that purpose than to bar from the tabernacle all who were polluted by any kind of uncleanness, ceremonial as well as natural, physical as well as spiritual. In order to mark out His people as dwelling before Him in holiness, He required of them complete purity and didn't allow them to come before Him when defiled, even by involuntary or secret impurities. And when one considers that God was training a people to live in His presence, it becomes apparent that these rules for the maintenance of personal purity, pointing to the necessity of purity in the heart, were neither too stringent nor too minute.

16:1-34 This section covers the Day of Atonement (cf. Ex. 30:10; Lev. 23:26-32; Num. 29:7-11; Heb. 9:1-28), which was commanded to be observed annually (v. 34) to cover the sins of the nation, both corporately and individually (v. 17). Even with the most scrupulous observance of the required sacrifices, many sins and defilements still remained unacknowledged and, therefore, without specific expiation. This special inclusive sacrifice was designed to cover all that (v. 33). The atonement was provided, but only those who were genuine in faith and repentance received its benefit, the forgiveness of God. That forgiveness was not based on any animal sacrifice, but on the One all sacrifices pictured—the Lord Jesus Christ and His perfect sacrifice on the cross (cf. Heb. 10:1-10). This holiest of all Israel's festivals occurred in Sept./Oct. on the tenth day of the seventh month (v. 29). It anticipated the ultimate High-Priest and the perfect sacrificial Lamb.

16:1 The death of the two sons of Aaron. Cf. 10:1-3.

16:2 Common priests went every day to burn incense on the golden altar in the part of the tabernacle sanctuary outside the veil, where the lamp stand, table, and show bread were. None except the High-Priest was allowed to enter inside the veil (cf. v. 12), into the Holy Place, actually called the Holy of Holies, the Most Holy (Ex. 26:33), or the Holiest of All (Heb. 9:3,8), where the ark of the covenant rested. This arrangement was designed to inspire a reverence for God at a time when His presence was indicated by visible symbols. **appear in the cloud.** This cloud was likely the smoke of the incense which the High-Priest burned on his annual entrance into the Most Holy Place. It was this cloud that covered the mercy seat on the ark of the covenant (see v. 13). **the mercy seat.** See Ex. 25:17-22. It lit. means "place of atonement" and referred to the throne of God between the cherubim (cf. Is. 6). It is so named because it was where God manifested Himself for the purpose of atonement.

16:3 sin…burnt offering. For these offerings brought by Aaron the High-Priest, *see notes on 4:1–5:13; 6:24-30 and 1:3-17; 6:8-13,* respectively. The bull was sacrificed first as a sin offering (16:11-14) and later the ram as a burnt offering (16:24).

16:4 For a description of the priests' normal clothing see Ex. 28:1-43 and Lev. 8:6-19. He wore them later for the burnt offering (cf. v. 24). These humbler clothes were less ornate, required for the Day of Atonement to portray the High-Priest as God's humble servant, himself in need of atonement (vv. 11-14).

16:5 two…goats. See 16:7-10,20-22. One animal would be slain to picture substitutionary death and the other sent to the wilderness to represent removal of sin. **one ram.** Along with the High-Priest's ram (v. 3), these were to be offered as burnt offerings (v. 24).

16:6-28 The following sequence describes the activities of the High-Priest and those who assisted him on the Day of Atonement: 1) The High-Priest (HP) washed at the laver in the courtyard and dressed in the tabernacle (v. 4). 2) The HP offered the bull as a sin offering for himself and his family (vv. 3,6,11). 3) The HP entered the Holy of Holies (HH) with the bull's blood, incense, and burning coals from the altar of burnt offering (vv. 12,13). 4) The HP sprinkled the bull's blood on the mercy seat 7 times (v. 14). 5) The HP went back to the courtyard and cast lots for the two goats (vv. 7,8). 6) The HP sacrificed one goat as a sin offering for the people (vv. 5,9,15). 7) The HP reentered the HH to sprinkle blood on the mercy seat and also the Holy Place (cf. Ex. 30:10; vv. 15-17). 8) The HP returned to the altar of burnt offering and cleansed it with the blood of the bull and goat (vv. 11,15,18,19). 9) The scapegoat was dispatched to the wilderness (vv. 20-22). 10) Afterward, the goatkeeper cleansed himself (v. 26). 11) The HP removed his special Day of Atonement clothing, rewashed, and put on the regular HP clothing (vv. 23,24). 12) The HP offered two rams as burnt offerings for himself and the people (vv. 3,5,24). 13) The fat of the sin offering was burned (v. 25). 14) The bull-and-goat sin offerings were carried outside the camp to be burned (v. 27). 15) The one who burned the sin offering cleansed himself (v. 28).

cast lots for the two goats: one lot for the
LORD and the other lot for the scapegoat.
9 And Aaron shall bring the goat on which
the LORD's lot fell, and offer it *as* a sin offering. 10 But the goat on which the lot fell
to be the scapegoat shall be presented alive
before the LORD, to make [j]atonement upon
it, *and* to let it go as the scapegoat into the
wilderness.
11 "And Aaron shall bring the bull of the
sin offering, which is for [k]himself, and
make atonement for himself and for his
house, and shall kill the bull as the sin offering which *is* for himself. 12 Then he shall
take [l]a censer full of burning coals of fire
from the altar before the LORD, with his
hands full of [m]sweet incense beaten fine,
and bring *it* inside the veil. 13 [n]And he
shall put the incense on the fire before the
LORD, that the cloud of incense may cover
the [o]mercy seat that *is* on the Testimony,
lest he [p]die. 14 [q]He shall take some of the
blood of the bull and [r]sprinkle *it* with his
finger on the mercy seat on the east *side;*
and before the mercy seat he shall sprinkle
some of the blood with his finger seven
times.
15 [s]"Then he shall kill the goat of the sin
offering, which *is* for the people, bring its
blood [t]inside the veil, do with that blood
as he did with the blood of the bull, and
sprinkle it on the mercy seat and before the
mercy seat. 16 So he shall [u]make atonement for the Holy *Place,* because of the
uncleanness of the children of Israel, and
because of their transgressions, for all their
sins; and so he shall do for the tabernacle
of meeting which remains among them in
the midst of their uncleanness. 17 There
shall be [v]no man in the tabernacle of meeting when he goes in to make atonement in
the Holy *Place,* until he comes out, that he
may make atonement for himself, for his
household, and for all the assembly of Israel. 18 And he shall go out to the altar that
is before the LORD, and make atonement
for [w]it, and shall take some of the blood of
the bull and some of the blood of the goat,
and put it on the horns of the altar all
around. 19 Then he shall sprinkle some of
the blood on it with his finger seven times,
cleanse it, and [x]consecrate[2] it from the
[3]uncleanness of the children of Israel.
20 "And when he has made an end of
atoning for the Holy *Place,* the tabernacle
of meeting, and the altar, he shall bring the
live goat. 21 Aaron shall lay both his hands
on the head of the live goat, [y]confess over
it all the iniquities of the children of Israel,
and all their transgressions, concerning all
their sins, [z]putting them on the head of the
goat, and shall send *it* away into the
wilderness by the hand of a suitable man.
22 The goat [4]shall [a]bear on itself all their
iniquities to an [5]uninhabited land; and he
shall [b]release the goat in the wilderness.
23 "Then Aaron shall come into the
tabernacle of meeting, [c]shall take off the
linen garments which he put on when he
went into the Holy *Place,* and shall leave
them there. 24 And he shall wash his body
with water in a holy place, put on his garments, come out and offer his burnt offering and the burnt offering of the people,
and make [6]atonement for himself and for
the people. 25 [d]The fat of the sin offering he
shall burn on the altar. 26 And he who released the goat as the scapegoat shall wash
his clothes [e]and bathe his body in water,
and afterward he may come into the camp.
27 [f]The bull *for* the sin offering and the goat
for the sin offering, whose blood was
brought in to make atonement in the Holy
Place, shall be carried outside the camp.

10 [j] [Is. 53:5, 6; Rom. 3:25; Heb. 7:27; 9:23, 24; 1 John 2:2]
11 [k] [Heb. 7:27; 9:7]
12 [l] Lev. 10:1; Num. 16:7, 18; Is. 6:6, 7; Rev. 8:5 [m] Ex. 30:34-38
13 [n] Ex. 30:7, 8; Num. 16:7, 18, 46 [o] Ex. 25:21 [p] Ex. 28:43; Lev. 22:9; Num. 4:15, 20
14 [q] Lev. 4:5; [Heb. 9:25; 10:4] [r] Lev. 4:6, 17
15 [s] [Heb. 2:17] [t] [Heb. 6:19; 7:27; 9:3, 7, 12]
16 [u] Ex. 29:36; 30:10; Ezek. 45:18; [Heb. 9:22-24]
17 [v] Ex. 34:3; Luke 1:10
18 [w] Ex. 29:36
19 [x] Lev. 16:14; Ezek. 43:20 [2] *set it apart* [3] *impurity*
21 [y] Lev. 5:5; 26:40 [z] [Is. 53:6]
22 [a] Lev. 8:14; [Is. 53:6, 11, 12; John 1:29; Heb. 9:28; 1 Pet. 2:24] [b] Lev. 14:7 [4] *shall carry* [5] *solitary land*
23 [c] Lev. 6:11; 16:4; Ezek. 42:14; 44:19
24 [6] Lit. *covering*
25 [d] Lev. 1:8; 4:10
26 [e] Lev. 15:5
27 [f] Lev. 4:12, 21; 6:30; Heb. 13:11

16:8 cast lots. *See note on Prov. 16:33.* **the scapegoat.** Cf. vv. 10,26. This goat (lit. *Azazel* or "escape goat") pictured the substitutionary bearing and total removal of sin which would later be fully accomplished by Jesus Christ (cf. Matt. 20:28; John 1:29; 2 Cor. 5:21; Gal. 1:4; 3:13; Heb. 9:28; 10:1-10; 1 Pet. 2:24; 1 John 2:2). *See notes on vv. 20-22.*

16:9,10 *See notes on vv. 20-22.*

16:12 inside the veil. *See note on v. 2.* The veil separated all from the holy and consuming presence of God. It was this veil in Herod's temple that was torn open from top to bottom at the death of Christ, signifying access into God's presence through Jesus Christ (see Matt. 27:51; Mark 15:38; Luke 23:45).

16:13 cloud. *See note on v. 2.* **on the Testimony.** The Testimony included the tablets of stone, upon which were written the Ten Commandments (Ex. 25:16; 31:18), located in the ark under the mercy seat.

16:14 seven times. This number symbolically indicated completion or perfection (cf. v. 19).

16:16 atonement for the Holy *Place*. The object of this solemn ceremony was to impress the minds of the Israelites with the conviction that the whole tabernacle was stained by the sins of a guilty people. By those sins, they had forfeited the privileges of the presence of God and worship of Him, so that an atonement had to be made for their sins as the condition of God remaining with them.

16:17 himself...household...assembly. The Day of Atonement was necessary for everyone since all had sinned, including the High Priest.

16:20-22 This "sin offering of atonement" (Num. 29:11) portrayed Christ's substitutionary sacrifice (vv. 21,22) with the result that the sinner's sins were removed (v. 22). *See notes on Is. 52:13–53:12* for another discussion of these truths. Christ lived out this representation when He cried from the cross, "My God, My God, why have You forsaken Me?" (Matt. 27:46).

16:21,22 putting them on the head of the goat. This act was more than a symbolic gesture; it was a picture of the ultimate "substitutionary atonement" fulfilled by the Lord Jesus Christ (cf. Is. 53:5,6; 10:12; *see note on 2 Cor. 5:21*).

16:27 outside the camp. This represents the historical reality of Christ's death outside of Jerusalem (cf. Heb. 13:10-14).

And they shall burn in the fire their skins,
their flesh, and their offal. 28 Then he who
burns them shall wash his clothes and
bathe his body in water, and afterward he
may come into the camp.
29 "*This* shall be a statute forever for you:
[g]In the seventh month, on the tenth *day* of
the month, you shall [7]afflict your souls,
and do no work at all, *whether* a native of
your own country or a stranger who
[8]dwells among you. 30 For on that day *the
priest* shall make [9]atonement for you, to
[h]cleanse you, *that* you may be clean from
all your sins before the LORD. 31 [i]It *is* a sabbath of solemn rest for you, and you shall
afflict your souls. *It is* a statute forever.
32 [j]And the priest, who is anointed and
[k]consecrated to minister as priest in his father's place, shall make atonement, and
put on the linen clothes, the holy garments;
33 then he shall make [1]atonement for [2]the
Holy Sanctuary, and he shall make atonement for the tabernacle of meeting and for
the altar, and he shall make atonement for
the priests and for all the people of the assembly. 34 [l]This shall be an everlasting
statute for you, to make atonement for the
children of Israel, for all their sins, [m]once a
year." And he did as the LORD commanded
Moses.

The Sanctity of Blood

17 And the LORD spoke to Moses, saying, 2 "Speak to Aaron, to his sons,
and to all the children of Israel, and say to
them, 'This *is* the thing which the LORD
has commanded, saying: 3 "Whatever
man of the house of Israel who [a]kills an ox
or lamb or goat in the camp, or who kills *it*
outside the camp, 4 and does not bring it
to the door of the tabernacle of meeting to
offer an offering to the LORD before the
tabernacle of the LORD, the guilt of bloodshed shall be [b]imputed to that man. He
has shed blood; and that man shall be [1]cut
off from among his people, 5 to the end
that the children of Israel may bring their
sacrifices [c]which they offer in the open
field, that they may bring them to the
LORD at the door of the tabernacle of meeting, to the priest, and offer them *as* peace
offerings to the LORD. 6 And the priest
[d]shall sprinkle the blood on the altar of the
LORD *at* the door of the tabernacle of meeting, and [e]burn the fat for a sweet aroma to
the LORD. 7 They shall no more offer their
sacrifices [f]to [2]demons, after whom they
[g]have played the harlot. This shall be a
statute forever for them throughout their
generations." '
8 "Also you shall say to them: 'Whatever
man of the house of Israel, or of the strangers who dwell among you, [h]who offers a
burnt offering or sacrifice, 9 and does not
[i]bring it to the door of the tabernacle of
meeting, to offer it to the LORD, that man
shall be [3]cut off from among his people.
10 [j]'And whatever man of the house of
Israel, or of the strangers who dwell
among you, who eats any blood, [k]I will set
My face against that person who eats
blood, and will cut him off from among his
people. 11 For the [l]life of the flesh *is* in the
blood, and I have given it to you upon the
altar [m]to make atonement for your souls;
for [n]it *is* the blood *that* makes atonement
for the soul.' 12 Therefore I said to the children of Israel, 'No one among you shall eat
blood, nor shall any stranger who dwells
among you eat blood.'
13 "Whatever man of the children of Israel, or of the strangers who dwell among
you, who [o]hunts and catches any animal or
bird that may be eaten, he shall [p]pour out

29 [g] Ex. 30:10; Lev. 23:27-32; Num. 29:7 [7] *humble yourselves* [8] As a resident alien
30 [h] Ps. 51:2; Jer. 33:8; [Eph. 5:26; Heb. 9:13, 14; 1 John 1:7, 9] [9] Lit. *covering*
31 [i] Lev. 23:27, 32; Ezra 8:21; Is. 58:3, 5; Dan. 10:12
32 [j] Lev. 4:3, 5, 16; 21:10 [k] Ex. 29:29, 30; Num. 20:26, 28
33 [1] Lit. *covering* [2] *The Most Holy Place*
34 [l] Lev. 23:31; Num. 29:7 [m] Ex. 30:10; [Heb. 9:7, 25, 28]

CHAPTER 17

3 [a] Deut. 12:5, 15, 21
4 [b] Rom. 5:13 [1] Put to death
5 [c] Gen. 21:33; 22:2; 31:54; Deut. 12:1-27; Ezek. 20:28
6 [d] Lev. 3:2 [e] Ex. 29:13, 18; Num. 18:17
7 [f] Ex. 22:20; 32:8; 34:15; Deut. 32:17; 2 Chr. 11:15; Ps. 106:37; 1 Cor. 10:20 [g] Ex. 34:15; Deut. 31:16; Ezek. 23:8 [2] Having the form of a goat or satyr
8 [h] Lev. 1:2, 3; 18:26
9 [i] Lev. 14:23 [3] Put to death
10 [j] Gen. 9:4; Lev. 3:17; 7:26, 27; Deut. 12:16, 23-25; 15:23; 1 Sam. 14:33 [k] Lev. 20:3, 5, 6
11 [l] Gen. 9:4; Lev. 17:14 [m] [Matt. 26:28; Rom. 3:25; Eph. 1:7; Col. 1:14, 20; 1 Pet. 1:2; 1 John 1:7] [n] [Heb. 9:22]
13 [o] Lev. 7:26 [p] Deut. 12:16, 24

16:29 seventh month. Tishri is Sept./Oct. **afflict your souls.** This act of denying oneself was probably with respect to food, making the Day of Atonement the only day of prescribed fasting in Israel's annual calendar.

16:30 clean from all your sins. See Ps. 103:12; Is. 38:17; Mic. 7:19. This day provided ceremonially cleansing for one year, and pictured the forgiveness of God available to all who believed and repented. Actual atonement was based on cleansing through the sacrifice of Christ (cf. Rom. 3:25,26; Heb. 9:15).

16:34 once a year. The better sacrifice of Jesus Christ was offered once-for-all, never to be repeated (cf. Heb. 9:11–10:18). Upon that sacrifice all forgiveness of sin is based, including that of OT believers.

17:1–27:34 Guidelines for practical holiness are detailed throughout this section.

17:1–22:33 Holiness issues that pertain to the individual are enumerated.

17:1-16 Miscellaneous laws relating to sacrifice are discussed.

17:1-9 The Lord warns against sacrificing anywhere other than at the door of the tabernacle of meeting (cf. vv. 5-7).

17:4 guilt of bloodshed. An unauthorized sacrifice could result in death.

17:5 peace offerings. *See notes on 3:1-17; 7:11-34.*

17:10-16 Warnings against the misuse of blood are issued (cf. 7:26,27; Deut. 12:16,23-25; 15:23; 1 Sam. 14:32-34).

17:11 life of the flesh *is* in the blood. This phrase is amplified by "its blood sustains its life" (17:14). Blood carries life-sustaining elements to all parts of the body; therefore it represents the essence of life. In contrast, the shedding of blood represents the shedding of life, i.e., death (cf. Gen. 9:4). NT references to the shedding of the blood of Jesus Christ are references to His death. **blood *that* makes atonement.** Since it contains the life, blood is sacred to God. Shed blood (death) from a substitute atones for or covers the sinner, who is then allowed to live.

17:13,14 It was customary with heathen hunters, when they killed any game, to pour out the blood as an offering to the god of the hunt. The Israelites, to the contrary, were enjoined by this directive and banned from all such superstitious acts of idolatry.

its blood and [q]cover it with dust; 14 [r]for *it*
is the life of all flesh. Its blood sustains its
life. Therefore I said to the children of Israel, 'You shall not eat the blood of any
flesh, for the life of all flesh is its blood.
Whoever eats it shall be cut off.'
15 [s]"And every person who eats what
died *naturally* or what was torn *by beasts,*
whether he is a native of your own country
or a stranger, [t]he shall both wash his
clothes and [u]bathe in water, and be unclean until evening. Then he shall be clean.
16 But if he does not wash *them* or bathe his
body, then [v]he shall bear his [4]guilt."

Laws of Sexual Morality

18 Then the LORD spoke to Moses, saying, 2 "Speak to the children of Israel, and say to them: [a]'I am the LORD your
God. 3 [b]According to [1]the doings of the
land of Egypt, where you dwelt, you shall
not do; and [c]according to the doings of the
land of Canaan, where I am bringing you,
you shall not do; nor shall you walk in
their [2]ordinances. 4 [d]You shall observe My
judgments and keep My ordinances, to
walk in them: I *am* the LORD your God.
5 You shall therefore keep My statutes and
My judgments, which if a man does, he
shall live by them: I *am* the LORD.
6 'None of you shall approach anyone
who is near of kin to him, to uncover his
nakedness: I *am* the LORD. 7 The nakedness
of your father or the nakedness of your
mother you shall not uncover. She *is* your
mother; you shall not uncover her nakedness. 8 The nakedness of your [e]father's wife
you shall not uncover; it *is* your father's
nakedness. 9 [f]The nakedness of your sister,
the daughter of your father, or the daughter
of your mother, *whether* born at home or
elsewhere, their nakedness you shall not
uncover. 10 The nakedness of your son's
daughter or your daughter's daughter,
their nakedness you shall not uncover; for
theirs *is* your own nakedness. 11 The
nakedness of your father's wife's daughter,
begotten by your father—she *is* your sister—you shall not uncover her nakedness.
12 [g]You shall not uncover the nakedness of
your father's sister; she *is* near of kin to
your father. 13 You shall not uncover the
nakedness of your mother's sister, for she *is*
near of kin to your mother. 14 [h]You shall
not uncover the nakedness of your father's
brother. You shall not approach his wife;
she *is* your aunt. 15 You shall not uncover
the nakedness of your daughter-in-law—
she *is* your son's wife—you shall not uncover her nakedness. 16 You shall not uncover the nakedness of your brother's wife;
it *is* your brother's nakedness. 17 You shall
not uncover the nakedness of a woman and
her [i]daughter, nor shall you take her son's
daughter or her daughter's daughter, to
uncover her nakedness. They *are* near of
kin to her. It *is* wickedness. 18 Nor shall you
take a woman [j]as a rival to her sister, to uncover her nakedness while the other is
alive.
19 'Also you shall not approach a
woman to uncover her nakedness as [k]long
as she is in her [l]*customary* impurity.
20 [m]Moreover you shall not lie carnally
with your [n]neighbor's wife, to defile yourself with her. 21 And you shall not let any
of your descendants [o]pass through [p]*the fire*

13 [q]Ezek. 24:7
14 [r]Gen. 9:4; Lev. 17:11; Deut. 12:23
15 [s]Ex. 22:31; Lev. 7:24; 22:8; Deut. 14:21; Ezek. 4:14; 44:31 [t]Lev. 11:25 [u]Lev. 15:5
16 [v]Lev. 5:1 [4]*iniquity*

CHAPTER 18
2 [a]Ex. 6:7; Lev. 11:44, 45; 19:3; Ezek. 20:5, 7, 19, 20
3 [b]Josh. 24:14; Ezek. 20:7, 8 [c]Ex. 23:24; Lev. 18:24-30; 20:23; Deut. 12:30, 31 [1]*what is done in* [2]*statutes*
4 [d]Ezek. 20:19
8 [e]Gen. 35:22
9 [f]Lev. 18:11; 20:17; Deut. 27:22
12 [g]Lev. 20:19
14 [h]Lev. 20:20
17 [i]Lev. 20:14
18 [j]1 Sam. 1:6, 8
19 [k]Ezek. 18:6 [l]Lev. 15:24; 20:18
20 [m][Prov. 6:25-33] [n]Ex. 20:14; Lev. 20:10; [Matt. 5:27, 28; 1 Cor. 6:9; Heb. 13:4]
21 [o]Lev. 20:2-5; Deut. 12:31 [p]2 Kin. 16:3

17:15,16 This cleansing was necessary because these animals would not have had the blood drained properly. Cf. Ex. 22:31; Deut. 14:21.

18:1-30 Laws are given, relating to sexual practices, which would eliminate the abominations being practiced by the heathen in the land (18:27; cf. Lev. 20:10-21; Deut. 22:13-30). These specific laws assume the general prohibition of adultery (Ex. 20:14) and a father incestuously engaging his daughter. They do not necessarily invalidate the special case of a levirate marriage (cf. Deut. 25:5). The penalties for such outlawed behavior are detailed in 20:10-21.

18:3 doings. Repeating the sexual practices or customs of the Egyptians and Canaanites was forbidden by God.

18:4 I *am* the LORD your God. This phrase, used over 50 times, asserts the uniqueness of the One True and Living God, who calls His people to holiness as He is holy, and calls them to reject all other gods.

18:5 if a man does, he shall live by them. Special blessing was promised to the Israelites on the condition of their obedience to God's law. This promise was remarkably verified in particular eras of their history, in the national prosperity they enjoyed when pure and undefiled religion prevailed among them. Obedience to God's law always insures temporal blessings, as this verse indicates. But these words have a higher reference to spiritual life as indicated by the Lord (cf. Luke 10:28) and Paul (cf. Rom. 10:5). Obedience does not save from sin and hell, but it does mark those who are saved (cf. Eph. 2:8,9; *see notes on Rom. 2:6-10*).

18:6-18 This section deals with consanguinity, i.e., the sins of incest.

18:6 uncover his nakedness. This is a euphemism for sexual relations.

18:8 your father's wife. Actually a stepmother is in mind here (cf. v. 7).

18:11 your sister. Here he is forbidden to marry a stepsister.

18:18 while the other is alive. The principle on which the prohibitions are made changes slightly. Instead of avoiding sexual involvement because it would violate a relational connection, this situation defaults to the principle of one person at a time, or while the other is still alive, i.e., it forbids polygamy. Commonly in Egyptian, Chaldean, and Canaanite culture, sisters were taken as wives in polygamous unions. God forbids such, as all polygamy is forbidden by the original law of marriage (see Gen. 2:24,25). Moses, because of hard hearts, tolerated it, as did others in Israel in the early stages of that nation. But it always led to tragedy.

18:19 *customary* impurity. This refers to her menstrual period (cf. 15:24).

to [q]Molech, nor shall you profane the
name of your God: I *am* the LORD. 22 You
shall not lie with [r]a male as with a woman.
It *is* an abomination. 23 Nor shall you mate
with any [s]animal, to defile yourself with it.
Nor shall any woman stand before an animal to mate with it. It *is* perversion.
24 [t]'Do not defile yourselves with any of
these things; [u]for by all these the nations
are defiled, which I am casting out before
you. 25 For [v]the land is defiled; therefore I
[w]visit[3] the punishment of its iniquity upon
it, and the land [x]vomits out its inhabitants.
26 [y]You shall therefore [4]keep My statutes
and My judgments, and shall not commit
any of these abominations, *either* any of
your own nation or any stranger who
dwells among you 27 (for all these
abominations the men of the land have
done, who *were* before you, and thus the
land is defiled), 28 lest [z]the land vomit you
out also when you defile it, as it vomited
out the nations that *were* before you. 29 For
whoever commits any of these abominations, the persons who commit *them* shall
be [5]cut off from among their people.
30 'Therefore you shall keep My [6]ordi-
nance, so [a]that *you* do not commit *any* of
these abominable customs which were
committed before you, and that you do not
defile yourselves by them: [b]I *am* the LORD
your God.' "

Moral and Ceremonial Laws

19 And the LORD spoke to Moses, saying, 2 "Speak to all the congregation
of the children of Israel, and say to them:
[a]'You shall be holy, for I the LORD your God
am holy.
3 [b]'Every one of you shall revere his
mother and his father, and [c]keep My Sabbaths: I *am* the LORD your God.
4 [d]'Do not turn to idols, [e]nor make for
yourselves [1]molded gods: I *am* the LORD
your God.
5 'And [f]if you offer a sacrifice of a peace
offering to the LORD, you shall offer it of
your own free will. 6 It shall be eaten the
same day you offer *it*, and on the next day.
And if any remains until the third day, it
shall be burned in the fire. 7 And if it is
eaten at all on the third day, it *is* an
abomination. It shall not be accepted.
8 Therefore *everyone* who eats it shall bear
his iniquity, because he has profaned the
hallowed *offering* of the LORD; and that person shall be cut off from his people.
9 [g]'When you reap the harvest of your
land, you shall not wholly reap the corners
of your field, nor shall you gather the
gleanings of your harvest. 10 And you shall
not glean your vineyard, nor shall you
gather *every* grape of your vineyard; you
shall leave them for the poor and the
stranger: I *am* the LORD your God.
11 [h]'You shall not steal, nor deal falsely,
[i]nor lie to one another. 12 And you shall
not [j]swear by My name falsely, [k]nor shall
you profane the name of your God: I *am*
the LORD.
13 [l]'You shall not cheat your neighbor,
nor rob *him*. [m]The wages of him who is
hired shall not remain with you all night
until morning. 14 You shall not curse the
deaf, [n]nor put a stumbling block before
the blind, but shall fear your God: I *am* the
LORD.
15 'You shall do no injustice in [o]judgment.
You shall not [p]be partial to the poor, nor
honor the person of the mighty. In righteousness you shall judge your neighbor.

21 [q] 1 Kin. 11:7, 33; Acts 7:43
22 [r] Lev. 20:13; Rom. 1:27
23 [s] Ex. 22:19; Lev. 20:15, 16; Deut. 27:21
24 [t] Matt. 15:18-20; 1 Cor. 3:17 [u] Lev. 18:3; 20:23; Deut. 18:12
25 [v] Num. 35:33, 34; Ezek. 36:17 [w] Is. 26:21; Jer. 5:9 [x] Lev. 18:28; 20:22 [3] *bring judgment for*
26 [y] Lev. 18:5, 30 [4] *obey*
28 [z] Jer. 9:19
29 [5] Put to death
30 [a] Lev. 18:3; 22:9 [b] Lev. 18:2 [6] *charge*

CHAPTER 19

2 [a] Ex. 19:6; Lev. 11:44; 20:7, 26; [Eph. 1:4]; 1 Pet. 1:16
3 [b] Ex. 20:12; Deut. 5:16; Matt. 15:4; Eph. 6:2 [c] Ex. 16:23; 20:8; 31:13
4 [d] Ex. 20:4; Ps. 96:5; 115:4-7; 1 Cor. 10:14; [Col. 3:5] [e] Ex. 34:17 [1] *molten*
5 [f] Lev. 7:16
9 [g] Lev. 23:22; Deut. 24:19-22
11 [h] Ex. 20:15, 16 [i] Jer. 9:3-5; Eph. 4:25
12 [j] Ex. 20:7; Deut. 5:11; [Matt. 5:33-37; James 5:12] [k] Lev. 18:21
13 [l] Ex. 22:7-15, 21-27; Mark 10:19 [m] Deut. 24:15; Mal. 3:5; James 5:4
14 [n] Deut. 27:18
15 [o] Deut. 16:19 [p] Ex. 23:3, 6; Deut. 1:17; 10:17; Ps. 82:2

18:21 Molech. This Semitic false deity (god of the Ammonites) was worshiped with child sacrifice (cf. Lev. 20:2-5; 1 Kin. 11:7; 2 Kin. 23:10; Jer. 32:35). Since this chapter deals otherwise with sexual deviation, there is likely an unmentioned sexual perversion connected with this pagan ritual. Jews giving false gods homage gave foreigners occasion to blaspheme the true God.

18:22 not lie with a male. This outlaws all homosexuality (cf. 20:13; Rom. 1:27; 1 Cor. 6:9; 1 Tim. 1:10). *See notes on Gen. 19:1-29.*

18:23 mate with any animal. This outlaws the sexual perversion of bestiality.

18:29 cut off. All the sexual perversions discussed in this chapter were worthy of death, indicating their loathsomeness before God.

18:30 were committed before you. Not in their presence, but by the people who inhabited the Land before them in time (cf. v. 27), were such sins committed.

19:1-37 Here are practical applications of holy conduct in society.

19:2 I the LORD your God *am* holy. This basic statement, which gives the reason for holy living among God's people, is the central theme in Leviticus (cf. 20:26). *See note on 11:44,45.* Cf. 1 Pet. 1:16. Israel had been called to be a holy nation, and the perfectly holy character of God (cf. Is. 6:3) was the model after which the Israelites were to live (cf. 10:3; 20:26; 21:6-8).

19:3 revere his mother and his father. The fifth commandment (cf. Ex. 20:12) to honor one's father and mother is amplified by the use of a different word, "revere." Because they revered (an attitude), they could then honor (an action).

19:3,4 In addition to the fifth commandment, the fourth (19:3b), the first (19:4a), and the second (19:46) were commanded as illustrations of holy behavior (cf. Ex. 20:3-6,8-11).

19:5-8 peace offering. *See notes on 3:1-17; 7:11-34.*

19:9,10 This was the law of gleaning (cf. 23:22; Deut. 24:19-22), a practice seen in Ruth 2:8-23.

19:11 Commandments from Ex. 20 are again repeated.

19:12 Cf. Matt. 5:33.

19:13 wages...shall not remain with you all night. Hired workers were to be paid at the end of a work day. Unsalaried day workers depended on pay each day for their sustenance. *See notes on Matt. 20:1,2.*

19:14 the deaf...the blind. Israel's God of compassion always demonstrated a concern for the disabled.

16 You shall not go about *as* a [q]talebearer
among your people; nor shall you [r]take a
stand against the life of your neighbor: I *am*
the LORD.
17 [s]'You shall not hate your brother in
your heart. [t]You shall surely [2]rebuke your
neighbor, and not bear sin because of him.
18 [u]You shall not take vengeance, nor bear
any grudge against the children of your
people, [v]but you shall love your neighbor
as yourself: I *am* the LORD.
19 'You shall keep My statutes. You shall
not let your livestock breed with another
kind. You shall not sow your field with
mixed seed. Nor shall a garment of mixed
linen and wool come upon you.
20 'Whoever lies carnally with a woman
who *is* [w]betrothed to a man as a concubine,
and who has not at all been redeemed nor
given her freedom, for this there shall be
[3]scourging; *but* they shall not be put to
death, because she was not free. 21 And he
shall bring his trespass offering to the
LORD, to the door of the tabernacle of meeting, a ram as a trespass offering. 22 The
priest shall make [4]atonement for him with
the ram of the trespass offering before the
LORD for his sin which he has committed.
And the sin which he has committed shall
be forgiven him.
23 'When you come into the land, and
have planted all kinds of trees for food,
then you shall count their fruit as [5]uncir-
cumcised. Three years it shall be as uncircumcised to you. *It* shall not be eaten.
24 But in the fourth year all its fruit shall be
holy, a praise to the LORD. 25 And in the
fifth year you may eat its fruit, that it may
yield to you its increase: I *am* the LORD
your God.
26 'You shall not eat *anything* with the
blood, nor shall you practice divination or
soothsaying. 27 You shall not shave around
the sides of your head, nor shall you disfigure the edges of your beard. 28 You shall
not [x]make any cuttings in your flesh for
the dead, nor tattoo any marks on you: I
am the LORD.
29 [y]'Do not prostitute your daughter, to
cause her to be a harlot, lest the land fall
into harlotry, and the land become full of
wickedness.
30 'You shall [6]keep My Sabbaths and
[z]reverence My sanctuary: I *am* the LORD.
31 'Give no regard to mediums and familiar spirits; do not seek after [a]them, to be
defiled by them: I *am* the LORD your God.
32 [b]'You shall [7]rise before the gray headed and honor the presence of an old man,
and [c]fear your God: I *am* the LORD.
33 'And [d]if a stranger dwells with you in
your land, you shall not mistreat him.
34 [e]The stranger who dwells among you
shall be to you as [8]one born among you,
and [f]you shall love him as yourself; for
you were strangers in the land of Egypt: I
am the LORD your God.
35 'You shall do no injustice in judgment,
in measurement of length, weight, or volume. 36 You shall have [g]honest scales, honest weights, an honest ephah, and an honest hin: I *am* the LORD your God, who
brought you out of the land of Egypt.
37 [h]'Therefore you shall observe all My
statutes and all My judgments, and perform them: I *am* the LORD.' "

16 [q] Prov. 11:13; 18:8; 20:19 [r] Ex. 23:7; Deut. 27:25; 1 Kin. 21:7-19
17 [s] [1 John 2:9, 11; 3:15] [t] Matt. 18:15; [Luke 17:3]; Eph. 5:11 [2] *reprove*
18 [u] [Deut. 32:35; 1 Sam. 24:12; Rom. 12:19; Heb. 10:30] [v] Matt. 5:43; 19:19; Mark 12:31; Luke 10:27; [Rom. 13:9; Gal. 5:14]; James 2:8
20 [w] Deut. 22:23-27 [3] *punishment*
22 [4] Lit. *covering*
23 [5] *unclean*
28 [x] 1 Kin. 18:28; Jer. 16:6
29 [y] Lev. 21:9; Deut. 22:21; 23:17, 18
30 [z] Lev. 26:2; Eccl. 5:1 [6] *observe*
31 [a] Lev. 20:6, 27; Deut. 18:11; 1 Sam. 28:3; Is. 8:19
32 [b] Prov. 23:22; Lam. 5:12; 1 Tim. 5:1 [c] Lev. 19:14 [7] *rise to give honor*
33 [d] Ex. 22:21; Deut. 24:17, 18
34 [e] Ex. 12:48 [f] Deut. 10:19 [8] *native among you*
36 [g] Deut. 25:13-15; Prov. 20:10
37 [h] Lev. 18:4, 5; Deut. 4:5, 6; 5:1; 6:25

19:16 take a stand against the life. This refers to doing anything that would wrongfully jeopardize the life of a neighbor.

19:18 This, called the second great commandment, is the most often quoted OT text in the NT (Matt. 5:43; 19:19; 22:39; Mark 12:31,33; Luke 10:27; Rom. 13:9; Gal. 5:14; James 2:8).

19:19 These mixtures may have been characteristic of some idolatrous practices.

19:20-22 In the case of immorality with a betrothed slave, the couple was to be punished (possibly by scourging), but not killed. Afterward, a trespass offering (*see notes on 5:14–6:7*) was to be rendered with appropriate reparation. This is an exception to the norm (cf. Deut. 22:23,24).

19:23-25 uncircumcised. They could not eat from the fruit trees of Canaan for 4 years after entering the Land because the fruit of the first 3 years was to be considered unclean, and the fourth year the fruit was to be offered to the Lord. Some gardeners say preventing a tree from bearing fruit in the first years, by cutting off the blossoms, makes it more productive.

19:26 divination...soothsaying. Attempting to tell the future with the help of snakes and clouds was a common ancient way of foretelling good or bad future. These were forbidden forms of witchcraft which involved demonic activity. *See note on Deut. 18:9-12.*

19:27,28 These pagan practices were most likely associated with Egyptian idolatry and were therefore to be avoided. The practice of making deep gashes on the face and arms or legs, in times of grief, was universal among pagans. It was seen as a mark of respect for the dead, as well as a sort of propitiatory offering to the gods who presided over death. The Jews learned this custom in Egypt and, though weaned from it, relapsed into the old superstition (cf. Is. 22:12; Jer. 16:6; 47:5). Tattoos also were connected to names of idols, and were permanent signs of apostasy.

19:29 prostitute your daughter. Even the pagans of ancient Assyria at this time forbade such horrendous means of monetary gain.

19:30 Sabbaths. *See note on 19:3,4.*

19:31 mediums...familiar spirits. Mediums are humans who act as "go-betweens" to supposedly contact/communicate with the spirits of the dead, who are actually impersonated by demons. Cf. 20:6,27.

19:32 rise...honor. Showing respect for the older man acknowledged God's blessing of long life and the wisdom that comes with it (cf. Is. 3:5).

19:33,34 stranger. Cf. Ex. 22:21.

19:36 ephah...hin. These dry and liquid measures respectively were equal approximately to 4 to 6 gallons and 6 to 8 pints.

Penalties for Breaking the Law

20 Then the LORD spoke to Moses, saying, 2 [a]"Again, you shall say to the
children of Israel: [b]'Whoever of the children of Israel, or of the strangers who
[1]dwell in Israel, who gives *any* of his descendants to Molech, he shall surely be put
to death. The people of the land shall
[c]stone him with stones. 3 [d]I will set My
face against that man, and will [2]cut him off
from his people, because he has given *some*
of his descendants to Molech, to defile My
sanctuary and profane My holy name.
4 And if the people of the land should in
any way [3]hide their eyes from the man,
when he gives *some* of his descendants to
Molech, and they do not kill him, 5 then I
will set My face against that man and
against his family; and I will cut him off
from his people, and all who prostitute
themselves with him to commit harlotry
with Molech.
6 'And [e]the person who turns to mediums and familiar spirits, to prostitute himself with them, I will set My face against
that person and cut him off from his people. 7 [f]Consecrate[4] yourselves therefore,
and be holy, for I *am* the LORD your God.
8 And you shall keep [g]My statutes, and
perform them: [h]I *am* the LORD who [5]sancti-
fies you.
9 'For [i]everyone who curses his father or
his mother shall surely be put to death. He
has cursed his father or his mother. [j]His
blood *shall be* upon him.
10 [k]'The man who commits adultery
with *another* man's wife, *he* who commits
adultery with his neighbor's wife, the
adulterer and the adulteress, shall surely
be put to death. 11 The man who lies with
his [l]father's wife has uncovered his father's nakedness; both of them shall surely
be put to death. Their blood *shall be* upon
them. 12 If a man lies with his [m]daughter-
in-law, both of them shall surely be put to
death. They have committed perversion.
Their blood *shall be* upon them. 13 [n]If a
man lies with a male as he lies with a
woman, both of them have committed an
abomination. They shall surely be put to
death. Their blood *shall be* upon them. 14 If
a man marries a woman and her [o]mother,
it *is* wickedness. They shall be burned with
fire, both he and they, that there may be no
wickedness among you. 15 If a man mates
with an [p]animal, he shall surely be put to
death, and you shall kill the animal. 16 If a
woman approaches any animal and mates
with it, you shall kill the woman and the
animal. They shall surely be put to death.
Their blood *is* upon them.
17 'If a man takes his [q]sister, his father's
daughter or his mother's daughter, and sees
her nakedness and she sees his nakedness, it
is a wicked thing. And they shall be [6]cut off
in the sight of their people. He has uncovered his sister's nakedness. He shall bear his
[7]guilt. 18 [r]If a man lies with a woman during
her [8]sickness and uncovers her nakedness,
he has [9]exposed her flow, and she has
uncovered the flow of her blood. Both of
them shall be [1]cut off from their people.
19 'You shall not uncover the nakedness
of your [s]mother's sister nor of your [t]fa-
ther's sister, for that would uncover his near
of kin. They shall bear their guilt. 20 If a man
lies with his [u]uncle's wife, he has uncovered his uncle's nakedness. They shall bear
their sin; they shall die childless. 21 If a man
takes his [v]brother's wife, it *is* an [2]unclean
thing. He has uncovered his brother's
nakedness. They shall be childless.
22 'You shall therefore keep all My [w]stat-
utes and all My judgments, and perform
them, that the land where I am bringing
you to dwell [x]may not vomit you out.
23 [y]And you shall not walk in the statutes
of the nation which I am casting out before
you; for they commit all these things, and
[z]therefore I abhor them. 24 But [a]I have said
to you, "You shall inherit their land, and I
will give it to you to possess, a land flowing with milk and honey." I *am* the LORD
your God, [b]who has separated you from
the peoples. 25 [c]You shall therefore distinguish between clean animals and unclean,
between unclean birds and clean, [d]and you
shall not make yourselves [3]abominable by
beast or by bird, or by any kind of living
thing that creeps on the ground, which I
have separated from you as [4]unclean.

CHAPTER 20

2 [a]Lev. 18:2 [b]Lev. 18:21; 2 Kin. 23:10; 2 Chr. 33:6; Jer. 7:31 [c]Deut. 17:2-5 [1]As resident aliens
3 [d]Lev. 17:10 [2]Put him to death
4 [3]*disregard*
6 [e]Lev. 19:31; 1 Sam. 28:7-25
7 [f]Lev. 19:2; Heb. 12:14 [4]*Set yourselves apart* for the LORD
8 [g]Lev. 19:19, 37 [h]Ex. 31:13; Deut. 14:2; Ezek. 37:28 [5]*sets you apart*
9 [i]Ex. 21:17; Deut. 27:16; Prov. 20:20; Matt. 15:4 [j]2 Sam. 1:16
10 [k]Ex. 20:14; Lev. 18:20; Deut. 5:18; 22:22; John 8:4, 5
11 [l]Lev. 18:7, 8; Deut. 27:20
12 [m]Lev. 18:15
13 [n]Lev. 18:22; Deut. 23:17; Judg. 19:22
14 [o]Lev. 18:17
15 [p]Lev. 18:23; Deut. 27:21
17 [q]Lev. 18:9; Deut. 27:22 [6]Put to death [7]*iniquity*
18 [r]Lev. 15:24; 18:19 [8]Or *customary impurity* [9]Lit. *made bare* [1]*Put to death*
19 [s]Lev. 18:13 [t]Lev. 18:12
20 [u]Lev. 18:14
21 [v]Lev. 18:16; Matt. 14:3, 4 [2]*indecent, impure*
22 [w]Lev. 18:26; 19:37 [x]Lev. 18:25, 28; 2 Chr. 36:14-16
23 [y]Lev. 18:3, 24 [z]Deut. 9:5
24 [a]Ex. 3:17; 6:8; 13:5; 33:1-3 [b]Ex. 19:5; 33:16; Lev. 20:26; Deut. 7:6; 14:2; 1 Kin. 8:53
25 [c]Lev. 10:10; 11:1-47; Deut. 14:3-21 [d]Lev. 11:43 [3]*detestable* or *loathsome* [4]*defiled*

20:1-27 Here capital and other grave crimes are discussed. Many of the same issues from chap. 18,19 are elaborated, with the emphasis on the penalty paid for the violation.

20:2 gives *any* of his descendants to Molech. Molech (Moloch), the Ammonite god of the people surrounding Israel, required human (especially child) sacrifice. *See note on 18:21.*

20:5,6 cut him off. This means to kill. It is synonymous with "put to death" in v. 9.

20:5 prostitute themselves. This speaks figuratively of spiritual harlotry.

20:6 medium...familiar spirits. *See note on 19:31.* "Familiar spirits" refers to demons (cf. 20:27).

20:9 curses his father or his mother. Doing the very opposite of the command to honor or to revere (cf. 19:3) had fatal consequences. See Mark 7:10, where Jesus referred to this text.

20:10-21 Here are the punishments for violating the prohibitions of sexual sins detailed in 18:1-30; see Deut. 22:13-30.

20:22 may not vomit you out. God told Israel repeatedly that remaining in the Land required obedience to the Mosaic Covenant (cf. 18:25,28).

26 And you shall be holy to Me, [e]for I the
LORD *am* holy, and have separated you
from the peoples, that you should be Mine.
27 [f]'A man or a woman who is a medium,
or who has familiar spirits, shall surely be
put to death; they shall stone them with
stones. Their blood *shall be* upon them.' "

Regulations for Conduct of Priests

21 And the LORD said to Moses,
"Speak to the priests, the sons of
Aaron, and say to them: [a]'None shall defile
himself for the dead among his people,
2 except for his relatives who are nearest to
him: his mother, his father, his son, his
daughter, and his brother; 3 also his virgin
sister who is near to him, who has had no
husband, for her he may defile himself.
4 *Otherwise* he shall not defile himself, *be-*
ing a [1]chief man among his people, to profane himself.
5 [b]'They shall not make any bald *place* on
their heads, nor shall they shave the edges
of their beards nor make any cuttings in
their flesh. 6 They shall be [c]holy to their
God and not profane the name of their
God, for they offer the offerings of the
LORD made by fire, *and* the [d]bread of their
God; [e]therefore they shall be holy. 7 [f]They
shall not take a wife *who is* a harlot or a defiled woman, nor shall they take a woman
[g]divorced from her husband; for [2]*the priest*
is holy to his God. 8 Therefore you shall
[3]consecrate him, for he offers the bread of
your God. He shall be holy to you, for [h]I
the LORD, who [i]sanctify you, *am* holy. 9 The
daughter of any priest, if she profanes herself by playing the harlot, she profanes her
father. She shall be [j]burned with fire.
10 '*He who is* the high priest among his
brethren, on whose head the anointing oil
was [k]poured and who is consecrated to
wear the garments, shall not [l]uncover[4] his
head nor tear his clothes; 11 nor shall he go
[m]near any dead body, nor defile himself
for his father or his mother; 12 [n]nor shall he
go out of the sanctuary, nor profane the
sanctuary of his God; for the [o]consecration
of the anointing oil of his God *is* upon him:
I *am* the LORD. 13 And he shall take a wife
in her virginity. 14 A widow or a divorced
woman or a defiled woman *or* a harlot—
these he shall not marry; but he shall take
a virgin of his own people as wife. 15 Nor
shall he profane his posterity among his
people, for I the LORD sanctify him.' "
16 And the LORD spoke to Moses, saying,
17 "Speak to Aaron, saying: 'No man of
your descendants in *succeeding* generations, who has *any* defect, may approach to
offer the bread of his God. 18 For any man
who has a [p]defect shall not approach: a
man blind or lame, who has a marred *face*
or any *limb* [q]too long, 19 a man who has a
broken foot or broken hand, 20 or is a
hunchback or a dwarf, or *a man* who has
a defect in his eye, or eczema or scab, or is
a eunuch. 21 No man of the descendants of
Aaron the priest, who has a defect, shall
come near to offer the offerings made by
fire to the LORD. He has a defect; he shall
not come near to offer the bread of his God.
22 He may eat the bread of his God, *both*
the most holy and the holy; 23 only he shall
not go near the [r]veil or approach the altar,
because he has a defect, lest [s]he profane
My sanctuaries; for I the LORD sanctify
them.' "
24 And Moses told *it* to Aaron and his
sons, and to all the children of Israel.

22 Then the LORD spoke to Moses, saying, 2 "Speak to Aaron and his sons,
that they [a]separate[1] themselves from the
holy things of the children of Israel, and that
they [b]do not profane My holy name *by* what
they [c]dedicate to Me: I *am* the LORD. 3 Say to

26 [e] Lev. 19:2; 1 Pet. 1:16
27 [f] Lev. 19:31; 1 Sam. 28:9

CHAPTER 21

1 [a] Lev. 19:28; Ezek. 44:25
4 [1] Lit. *master* or *husband*
5 [b] Lev. 19:27; Deut. 14:1; Ezek. 44:20
6 [c] Ex. 22:31 [d] Lev. 3:11 [e] Is. 52:11
7 [f] Ezek. 44:22 [g] Deut. 24:1,2 [2] Lit. *he*
8 [h] Lev. 11:44,45 [i] Lev. 8:12,30 [3] *set him apart*
9 [j] Deut. 22:21
10 [k] Lev. 8:12 [l] Lev. 10:6,7 [4] In mourning
11 [m] Num. 19:14
12 [n] Lev. 10:7 [o] Ex. 29:6,7
18 [p] Lev. 22:19-25 [q] Lev. 22:23
23 [r] Lev. 16:2 [s] Lev. 21:12

CHAPTER 22

2 [a] Num. 6:3 [b] Lev. 18:21 [c] Ex. 28:38; Lev. 16:19; 25:10; Num. 18:32; Deut. 15:19 [1] *keep themselves apart from*

20:27 medium...familiar spirits. *See note on 19:31.*

21:1-24 Laws for the priests are given, which demanded a higher standard of holy conduct than for the general Israelite.

21:1 defile himself. Coming into contact with a corpse (Num. 19:11) or being in the same room with one (Num. 19:14) made one unclean. The exceptions were the dead from the priest's own family (vv. 2-4).

21:5 bald *place*...edges...cuttings in their flesh. These were the superstitious marks of grief. *See note on 19:27,28.* Cf. 1 Kin. 18:28.

21:6 the bread of their God. This phrase appears 5 times in Lev. 21 (cf. vv. 8,17,21,22). It most likely refers to the bread of the Presence in the Holy Place (cf. Ex. 25:30; 39:36; 40:23; Lev. 24:5-9).

21:7,8 The priest was allowed to marry, but only in the purest of circumstances. A holy marriage union pictured the holy union between God and His people. See 21:13,14. The priests were to be living models of that holy union. Cf. Paul's words regarding pastors in 1 Tim. 3:2,4; Titus 1:6.

21:9 The priests' children were to live a holy life. The common punishment of stoning (cf. Deut. 22:21) is replaced with burning by fire. Cf. 1 Tim. 3:4; Titus 1:6.

21:10-15 Here is a summary of the standards for the High-Priest which were the highest and most holy in accord with his utmost sacred responsibility.

21:10 shall not uncover his head nor tear his clothes. Acts associated with mourning or anguish (cf. the violation in Christ's trial, Matt. 26:65; Mark 14:63).

21:16-23 defect. Just as the sacrifice had to be without blemish, so did the one offering the sacrifice. As visible things exert strong impressions on the minds of people, any physical impurity or malformation tended to distract from the weight and authority of the sacred office, failed to externally exemplify the inward wholeness God sought, and failed to be a picture of Jesus Christ, the Perfect High-Priest to come (cf. Heb. 7:26).

22:1-33 These are additional instructions on ceremonial cleanness for the priests, beginning with a death threat (v. 3, "cut off") to those who might violate these rules.

them: 'Whoever of all your descendants
throughout your generations, who goes
near the holy things which the children of Israel dedicate to the LORD, [d]while he has [2]un-
cleanness upon him, that person shall be cut
off from My presence: I *am* the LORD.
4 'Whatever man of the descendants of
Aaron, who *is* a [e]leper or has [f]a discharge,
shall not eat the holy offerings [g]until he is
clean. And [h]whoever touches anything
made unclean *by* a corpse, or [i]a man who
has had an emission of semen, 5 or [j]who-
ever touches any creeping thing by which
he would be made unclean, or [k]any person
by whom he would become unclean, whatever his uncleanness may be— 6 the person who has touched any such thing shall
be unclean until evening, and shall not eat
the holy *offerings* unless he [l]washes his
body with water. 7 And when the sun goes
down he shall be clean; and afterward he
may eat the holy *offerings,* because [m]it *is* his
food. 8 [n]Whatever dies *naturally* or is torn
by beasts he shall not eat, to defile himself
with it: I *am* the LORD.
9 'They shall therefore keep [o]My [3]ordi-
nance, [p]lest they bear sin for it and die
thereby, if they profane it: I the LORD sanctify them.
10 [q]'No outsider shall eat the holy *offering;*
one who [4]dwells with the priest, or a hired
servant, shall not eat the holy thing. 11 But if
the priest [r]buys a person with his money, he
may eat it; and one who is born in his house
may eat his food. 12 If the priest's daughter
is married to an outsider, she may not eat of
the holy offerings. 13 But if the priest's
daughter is a widow or divorced, and has
no child, and has returned to her father's
house as in her youth, she may eat her father's food; but no outsider shall eat it.
14 'And if a man eats the holy *offering*
unintentionally, then he shall restore a holy
offering to the priest, and add one-fifth to it.
15 They shall not profane the [s]holy *offerings*
of the children of Israel, which they offer to
the LORD, 16 or allow them to bear the guilt
of trespass when they eat their holy *offerings;* for I the LORD sanctify them.' "

Offerings Accepted and Not Accepted

17 And the LORD spoke to Moses, saying,
18 "Speak to Aaron and his sons, and to all
the children of Israel, and say to them:
[t]'Whatever man of the house of Israel, or
of the strangers in Israel, who [5]offers his
sacrifice for any of his vows or for any of
his freewill offerings, which they offer to
the LORD as a burnt offering— 19 [u]*you shall
offer* of your own free will a male without
blemish from the cattle, from the sheep, or
from the goats. 20 [v]Whatever has a defect,
you shall not offer, for it shall not be
acceptable on your behalf. 21 And [w]who-
ever offers a sacrifice of a peace offering to
the LORD, [x]to fulfill *his* vow, or a freewill
offering from the cattle or the sheep, it
must be perfect to be accepted; there shall
be no defect in it. 22 [y]Those *that are* blind or
broken or maimed, or have an [6]ulcer or
eczema or scabs, you shall not offer to the
LORD, nor make [z]an offering by fire of
them on the altar to the LORD. 23 Either a
bull or a lamb that has any limb [a]too long
or too short you may offer *as* a freewill
offering, but for a vow it shall not be accepted.
24 'You shall not offer to the LORD what
is bruised or crushed, or torn or cut; nor
shall you make *any offering of them* in your
land. 25 Nor [b]from a foreigner's hand shall
you offer any of these as [c]the bread of your
God, because their [d]corruption *is* in them,
and defects *are* in them. They shall not be
accepted on your behalf.' "
26 And the LORD spoke to Moses, saying:
27 [e]"When a bull or a sheep or a goat is
born, it shall be seven days with its mother; and from the eighth day and thereafter
it shall be accepted as an offering made by
fire to the LORD. 28 *Whether it is* a cow or
ewe, do not kill both her [f]and her young
on the same day. 29 And when you [g]offer a
sacrifice of thanksgiving to the LORD, offer
it of your own free will. 30 On the same day
it shall be eaten; you shall leave [h]none of it
until morning: I *am* the LORD.
31 [i]"Therefore you shall keep My commandments, and perform them: I *am* the
LORD. 32 [j]You shall not profane My holy
name, but [k]I will be [7]hallowed among the
children of Israel. I *am* the LORD who [l]sanc-
tifies you, 33 [m]who brought you out of the
land of Egypt, to be your God: I *am* the
LORD."

3 [d] Lev. 7:20, 21; Num. 19:13 [2] *defilement*
4 [e] Num. 5:2 [f] Lev. 15:2 [g] Lev. 14:2; 15:13 [h] Lev. 11:24-28, 39, 40; Num. 19:11 [i] Lev. 15:16, 17
5 [j] Lev. 11:23-28 [k] Lev. 15:7, 19
6 [l] Lev. 15:5
7 [m] Lev. 21:22; Num. 18:11, 13
8 [n] Ex. 22:31; Lev. 7:24; 11:39, 40; 17:15; Ezek. 44:31
9 [o] Lev. 18:30 [p] Ex. 28:43; Lev. 22:16; Num. 18:22 [3] *charge*
10 [q] Ex. 29:33; Lev. 22:13; Num. 3:10 [4] *As a visitor*
11 [r] Ex. 12:44
15 [s] Num. 18:32
18 [t] Lev. 1:2, 3, 10 [5] *brings his offering*
19 [u] Lev. 1:3; Deut. 15:21
20 [v] Deut. 15:21; 17:1; Mal. 1:8, 14; [Eph. 5:27; Heb. 9:14; 1 Pet. 1:19]
21 [w] Lev. 3:1, 6 [x] Num. 15:3, 8; Ps. 61:8; 65:1; Eccl. 5:4, 5
22 [y] Lev. 22:20; Mal. 1:8 [z] Lev. 1:9, 13; 3:3, 5 [6] *running sore*
23 [a] Lev. 21:18
25 [b] Num. 15:15, 16 [c] Lev. 21:6, 17 [d] Mal. 1:14
27 [e] Ex. 22:30
28 [f] Deut. 22:6, 7
29 [g] Lev. 7:12; Ps. 107:22; 116:17; Amos 4:5
30 [h] Lev. 7:15
31 [i] Lev. 19:37; Num. 15:40; Deut. 4:40
32 [j] Lev. 18:21 [k] Lev. 10:3; Matt. 6:9; Luke 11:2 [l] Lev. 20:8 [7] *treated as holy*
33 [m] Lev. 19:36, 37; Num. 15:40; Deut. 4:40

22:4 leper. *See 13:1–14:32 and note on 13:2.* **discharge.** *See notes on 15:1-33.*

22:5 creeping thing. See 11:29-38.

22:7 he shall be clean. In the same manner, much water is not made unclean by a small contamination. Time was essential for ceremonial purification.

22:10,11 buys a person with his money. This portion of the sacrifice assigned to the support of the priests was restricted to the use of his family. However, an indentured servant was to be treated as one of the priest's family, pertaining to eating the consecrated food. See the laws of release, which show this to be a temporary indenture (25:10; Ex. 21:2-11; Deut. 15:12-18).

22:17-30 This section describes the unacceptable and acceptable sacrifices.

22:31-33 The motive behind obedience to God was His holy nature and grace in delivering the nation.

Feasts of the LORD

23 And the LORD spoke to Moses, saying, 2 "Speak to the children of Israel, and say to them: 'The feasts of the
LORD, which you shall proclaim *to be* [a]holy
convocations, these *are* My feasts.

The Sabbath

3 [b]'Six days shall work be done, but the
seventh day *is* a Sabbath of solemn rest, a
holy convocation. You shall do no work *on
it;* it *is* the Sabbath of the LORD in all your
dwellings.

The Passover and Unleavened Bread

4 [c]'These *are* the feasts of the LORD, holy
convocations which you shall proclaim at
their appointed times. 5 [d]On the fourteenth
day of the first month at twilight *is* the
LORD's Passover. 6 And on the fifteenth
day of the same month *is* the Feast of Unleavened Bread to the LORD; seven days
you must eat unleavened bread. 7 [e]On the
first day you shall have a holy convocation; you shall do no [1]customary work on
it. 8 But you shall offer an offering made by
fire to the LORD for seven days. The seventh day *shall be* a holy convocation; you
shall do no customary work *on it.*' "

The Feast of Firstfruits

9 And the LORD spoke to Moses, saying,
10 "Speak to the children of Israel, and say
to them: [f]'When you come into the land
which I give to you, and reap its harvest,
then you shall bring a sheaf of [g]the firstfruits of your harvest to the priest. 11 He
shall [h]wave the sheaf before the LORD, to
be accepted on your behalf; on the day
after the Sabbath the priest shall wave it.
12 And you shall offer on that day, when
you wave the sheaf, a male lamb of the first
year, without blemish, as a burnt offering
to the LORD. 13 Its grain offering *shall be*

CHAPTER 23
2 [a]Ex. 12:16
3 [b]Ex. 20:9; 23:12; 31:15; Lev. 19:3; Deut. 5:13, 14; Luke 13:14
4 [c]Ex. 23:14-16; Lev. 23:2, 37
5 [d]Ex. 12:1-28; Num. 9:1-5; 28:16-25; Deut. 16:1-8; Josh. 5:10
7 [e]Ex. 12:16; Num. 28:18, 25
[1]*occupational*
10 [f]Ex. 23:19; 34:26
[g][Rom. 11:16]; James 1:18; Rev. 14:4
11 [h]Ex. 29:24

23:1–27:34 Holiness issues that pertain to the nation collectively are outlined.

23:1–24:9 The special feasts of Israel are explained. Cf. Ex. 23:14-17; Num. 28:1–29:40; Deut. 16:1-17.

23:1-44 This section points to days which are sacred to the Lord. After the Sabbath (v. 3), the feasts are given in the order of the calendar (vv. 4-44).

23:2 proclaim *to be* holy convocations. These festivals did not involve gatherings of all Israel in every case. Only the feasts of 1) Unleavened Bread; 2) Weeks; and 3) Tabernacles required that all males gather in Jerusalem (cf. Ex. 23:14-17; Deut. 16:16,17).

23:3 Sabbath of solemn rest. The Mosaic ordinance of the fourth commandment came first (cf. Gen. 2:1-3; Ex. 20:8-11).

23:4-22 Three events were commemorated in Mar./Apr.: 1) Passover on the 14th (v. 5); 2) Feast of Unleavened Bread on the 15th–21st (vv. 6-8); and Feast of Firstfruits on the day after the Sabbath of Unleavened Bread week (vv. 9-14).

23:5 the LORD's Passover. The festival commemorated God's deliverance of Israel from Egypt (cf. Ex. 12:1-14,43-49; Num. 28:16; Deut. 16:1,2).

23:6-8 Feast of Unleavened Bread. This festival connected with the Passover, commemorated Israel's hurried departure from Egypt and the associated hardships (cf. Ex. 12:15-20; 13:3-10; Num. 28:17-25; Deut. 16:3-8).

23:9-14 the firstfruits of your harvest. This festival dedicated the initial part of the barley harvest in Mar./Apr. and was celebrated on the day after the Sabbath of Unleavened Bread week. It involved presenting to the Lord a sheaf of barley (cf. 23:10,11) accompanied by burnt, grain, and drink offerings (cf. Ex. 29:40). Firstfruits symbolized the consecration of the whole harvest to God, and was a pledge of the whole harvest to come (cf. Rom. 8:23; 11:16; 1 Cor. 15:20; James 1:18).

Jewish Feasts

Feast of	Month on Jewish Calendar	Day	Corresponding Month	References
Passover	Nisan	14	Mar.-Apr.	Ex. 12:1-14; Matt. 26:17-20
*Unleavened Bread	Nisan	15-21	Mar.-Apr.	Ex. 12:15-20
Firstfruits	Nisan	16	Mar.-Apr.	Lev. 23:9-14
	or Sivan	6	May-June	Num. 28:26
*Pentecost (Harvest or Weeks)	Sivan	6 (50 days after barley harvest)	May-June	Deut. 16:9-12; Acts 2:1
Trumpets, Rosh Hashanah	Tishri	1, 2	Sept.-Oct.	Num. 29:1-6
Day of Atonement, Yom Kippur	Tishri	10	Sept.-Oct.	Lev. 23:26-32; Heb. 9:7
*Tabernacles (Booths or Ingathering)	Tishri	15-22	Sept.-Oct.	Neh. 8:13-18; John 7:2
Dedication (Lights), Hanukkah	Chislev	25 (8 days)	Nov.-Dec.	John 10:22
Purim (Lots)	Adar	14, 15	Feb.-Mar.	Esth. 9:18-32

*The three major feasts for which all males of Israel were required to travel to the temple in Jerusalem (Ex. 23:14-19).

two-tenths *of an ephah* of fine flour mixed
with oil, an offering made by fire to the
LORD, for a [2]sweet aroma; and its drink offering *shall be* of wine, one-fourth of a hin.
14 You shall eat neither bread nor parched
grain nor fresh grain until the same day
that you have brought an offering to your
God; *it shall be* a statute forever throughout
your generations in all your dwellings.

The Feast of Weeks

15 'And you shall count for yourselves
from the day after the Sabbath, from the
day that you brought the sheaf of the wave
offering: seven Sabbaths shall be completed. 16 Count [i]fifty days to the day after the
seventh Sabbath; then you shall offer [j]a
new grain offering to the LORD. 17 You shall
bring from your dwellings two wave *loaves*
of two-tenths *of an ephah.* They shall be of
fine flour; they shall be baked with leaven.
They are [k]the firstfruits to the LORD. 18 And
you shall offer with the bread seven lambs
of the first year, without blemish, one
young bull, and two rams. They shall be *as*
a burnt offering to the LORD, with their
grain offering and their drink offerings, an
offering made by fire for a sweet aroma to
the LORD. 19 Then you shall sacrifice [l]one
kid of the goats as a sin offering, and two
male lambs of the first year as a sacrifice of
a [m]peace offering. 20 The priest shall wave
them with the bread of the firstfruits *as* a
wave offering before the LORD, with the
two lambs. [n]They shall be holy to the LORD
for the priest. 21 And you shall proclaim on
the same day *that* it is a holy convocation
to you. You shall do no customary work *on
it. It shall be* a statute forever in all your
dwellings throughout your generations.

13 [2] *pleasing*
16 [i] Acts 2:1 [j] Num. 28:26
17 [k] Ex. 23:16, 19; Num. 15:17-21
19 [l] Lev. 4:23, 28; Num. 28:30; [2 Cor. 5:21] [m] Lev. 3:1
20 [n] Lev. 14:13; Num. 18:12; Deut. 18:4
22 [o] Lev. 19:9, 10; Deut. 24:19-22; Ruth 2:2, 15
24 [p] Num. 29:1 [q] Lev. 25:9
27 [r] Lev. 16:1-34; 25:9; Num. 29:7
28 [s] Lev. 16:34
29 [t] Is. 22:12; Jer. 31:9; Ezek. 7:16 [u] Gen. 17:14; Lev. 13:46; Num. 5:2
30 [v] Lev. 20:3-6
32 [3] *humble yourselves* [4] *observe your sabbath*

22 [o]'When you reap the harvest of your
land, you shall not wholly reap the corners
of your field when you reap, nor shall you
gather any gleaning from your harvest.
You shall leave them for the poor and for
the stranger: I *am* the LORD your God.' "

The Feast of Trumpets

23 Then the LORD spoke to Moses, saying, 24 "Speak to the children of Israel, saying: 'In the [p]seventh month, on the first *day*
of the month, you shall have a sabbath-*rest*,
[q]a memorial of blowing of trumpets, a holy
convocation. 25 You shall do no customary
work *on it;* and you shall offer an offering
made by fire to the LORD.' "

The Day of Atonement

26 And the LORD spoke to Moses, saying:
27 [r]"Also the tenth *day* of this seventh
month *shall be* the Day of Atonement. It
shall be a holy convocation for you; you
shall afflict your souls, and offer an offering made by fire to the LORD. 28 And you
shall do no work on that same day, for it *is*
the Day of Atonement, [s]to make atonement for you before the LORD your God.
29 For any person who is not [t]afflicted *in
soul* on that same day [u]shall be cut off from
his people. 30 And any person who does
any work on that same day, [v]that person I
will destroy from among his people. 31 You
shall do no manner of work; *it shall be* a
statute forever throughout your generations in all your dwellings. 32 It *shall be* to
you a sabbath of *solemn* rest, and you shall
[3]afflict your souls; on the ninth *day* of the
month at evening, from evening to
evening, you shall [4]celebrate your sabbath."

23:15-22 fifty days. The Feast of Weeks (May/June) dedicated the firstfruits of the wheat harvest (cf. Ex. 23:16; Num. 28:26-31; Deut. 16:9-12). It occurred on the 50th day after the Sabbath preceding the Feast of Firstfruits. It is also known as the Feast of Harvest (Ex. 23:16) and Pentecost, Gr. for 50 (Acts. 2:1).

23:23-43 Three events were commemorated in Sept./Oct.: 1) Feast of Trumpets on the 1st (vv. 23-25); 2) Day of Atonement on the 10th (vv. 26-32); and 3) Feast of Tabernacles on the 15th-21st (vv. 33-43).

23:23-25 memorial of blowing of trumpets. This feast, called the Feast of Trumpets, consecrated the seventh month (Sept./Oct.) as a sabbatical month (cf. Num. 29:1-6).

23:26-32 Day of Atonement. The annual Day of Atonement pointed to the forgiveness and cleansing of sin for the priests, the nation, and the tabernacle (*see notes on 16:1-34; Num. 29:7-11*).

Christ Fulfills Israel's Feasts

The Feasts (Lev. 23)	Christ's Fulfillment
Passover (March/April)	Death of Christ (1 Cor. 5:7)
Unleavened Bread (March/April)	Sinlessness of Christ (1 Cor. 5:8)
Firstfruits (March/April)	Resurrection of Christ (1 Cor. 15:23)
Pentecost (May/June)	Outpouring of Spirit of Christ (Acts 1:5; 2:4)
Trumpets (Sept./Oct.)	Israel's Regathering by Christ (Matt. 24:31)
Atonement (Sept./Oct.)	Substitutionary Sacrifice by Christ (Rom. 11:26)
Tabernacles (Sept./Oct.)	Rest and Reunion with Christ (Zech. 14:16-19)

The Feast of Tabernacles

33 Then the LORD spoke to Moses, saying, 34 "Speak to the children of Israel, saying: [w]'The fifteenth day of this seventh
month *shall be* the Feast of Tabernacles *for*
seven days to the LORD. 35 On the first day
there shall be a holy convocation. You shall
do no customary work *on it*. 36 *For* seven
days you shall offer an [x]offering made by
fire to the LORD. [y]On the eighth day you
shall have a holy convocation, and you
shall offer an offering made by fire to the
LORD. It *is* a [z]sacred[5] assembly, *and* you
shall do no customary work *on it*.
37 [a]'These *are* the feasts of the LORD
which you shall proclaim *to be* holy convocations, to offer an offering made by fire to
the LORD, a burnt offering and a grain offering, a sacrifice and drink offerings,
everything on its day— 38 [b]besides the
Sabbaths of the LORD, besides your gifts,
besides all your vows, and besides all your
freewill offerings which you give to the
LORD.
39 'Also on the fifteenth day of the seventh month, when you have [c]gathered in
the fruit of the land, you shall keep the
feast of the LORD *for* seven days; on the first
day *there shall be* a sabbath-*rest*, and on the
eighth day a sabbath-*rest*. 40 And [d]you
shall take for yourselves on the first day
the [6]fruit of beautiful trees, branches of
palm trees, the boughs of leafy trees, and
willows of the brook; [e]and you shall rejoice
before the LORD your God for seven days.
41 [f]You shall keep it as a feast to the LORD
for seven days in the year. *It shall be* a
statute forever in your generations. You
shall celebrate it in the seventh month.
42 [g]You shall dwell in [7]booths for seven
days. [h]All who are native Israelites shall
dwell in booths, 43 [i]that your generations
may [j]know that I made the children of Israel dwell in booths when [k]I brought them
out of the land of Egypt: I *am* the LORD
your God.' "
44 So Moses [l]declared to the children of
Israel the feasts of the LORD.

34 [w] Ex. 23:16; Num. 29:12; Deut. 16:13-16; Ezra 3:4; Neh. 8:14; Zech. 14:16-19; John 7:2
36 [x] Num. 29:12-34 [y] Num. 29:35-38; Neh. 8:18; John 7:37 [z] Deut. 16:8; 2 Chr. 7:8 [5] *solemn*
37 [a] Lev. 23:2, 4
38 [b] Num. 29:39
39 [c] Ex. 23:16; Deut. 16:13
40 [d] Neh. 8:15 [e] Deut. 12:7; 16:14, 15 [6] *foliage*
41 [f] Num. 29:12; Neh. 8:18
42 [g] [Is. 4:6] [h] Neh. 8:14-16 [7] *tabernacles; shelters made of boughs*
43 [i] Ex. 13:14; Deut. 31:13; Ps. 78:5 [j] Ex. 10:2 [k] Lev. 22:33
44 [l] Lev. 23:2

CHAPTER 24

2 [a] Ex. 27:20, 21
4 [b] Ex. 25:31; 31:8; 37:17 [1] *arrange* or *set in order*
5 [c] Ex. 25:30; 39:36; 40:23
6 [d] Ex. 25:23, 24; 1 Kin. 7:48; 2 Chr. 4:19; 13:11; Heb. 9:2
7 [e] Lev. 2:2, 9, 16
8 [f] Num. 4:7; 1 Chr. 9:32; 2 Chr. 2:4; Matt. 12:4, 5
9 [g] 1 Sam. 21:6; Matt. 12:4; Mark 2:26; Luke 6:4 [h] Ex. 29:33; Lev. 8:31
11 [i] Ex. 22:28 [j] Job 1:5, 11, 22; Is. 8:21 [k] Ex. 18:22, 26
12 [l] Num. 15:34 [m] Num. 27:5 [2] *under guard* [3] Lit. *it might be declared to them from the mouth of the LORD*
14 [n] Deut. 13:9; 17:7

Care of the Tabernacle Lamps

24 Then the LORD spoke to Moses, saying: 2 [a]"Command the children of
Israel that they bring to you pure oil of
pressed olives for the light, to make the
lamps burn continually. 3 Outside the veil
of the Testimony, in the tabernacle of meeting, Aaron shall be in charge of it from
evening until morning before the LORD
continually; *it shall be* a statute forever in
your generations. 4 He shall [1]be in charge
of the lamps on [b]the pure *gold* lampstand
before the LORD continually.

The Bread of the Tabernacle

5 "And you shall take fine flour and
bake twelve [c]cakes with it. Two-tenths *of
an ephah* shall be in each cake. 6 You shall
set them in two rows, six in a row, [d]on the
pure *gold* table before the LORD. 7 And you
shall put pure frankincense on *each* row,
that it may be on the bread for a [e]memo-
rial, an offering made by fire to the LORD.
8 [f]Every Sabbath he shall set it in order before the LORD continually, *being taken* from
the children of Israel by an everlasting
covenant. 9 And [g]it shall be for Aaron and
his sons, [h]and they shall eat it in a holy
place; for it *is* most holy to him from the offerings of the LORD made by fire, by a perpetual statute."

The Penalty for Blasphemy

10 Now the son of an Israelite woman,
whose father *was* an Egyptian, went out
among the children of Israel; and this Israelite *woman's* son and a man of Israel
fought each other in the camp. 11 And the
Israelite woman's son [i]blasphemed the
name *of the LORD* and [j]cursed; and so they
[k]brought him to Moses. (His mother's
name *was* Shelomith the daughter of Dibri,
of the tribe of Dan.) 12 Then they [l]put him
[2]in custody, [m]that [3]the mind of the LORD
might be shown to them.
13 And the LORD spoke to Moses, saying,
14 "Take outside the camp him who has
cursed; then let all who heard *him* [n]lay

23:33-43 Feast of Tabernacles. This festival commemorated God's deliverance, protection, and provision during the wilderness wanderings of the Exodus (cf. Ex. 23:16; Num. 29:12-38; Deut. 16:13-15). It is also known as the Feast of Booths (Deut. 16:13) and Feast of Ingathering (Ex. 23:16). The people lived in booths or huts made from limbs (cf. Neh. 8:14-18), remembering their wilderness experience. It also celebrated the autumn harvest and will be celebrated in the Millennium (cf. Zech. 14:16).

24:1-9 These are additional instructions for the tabernacle relating to the lamps (vv. 1-4) and the bread (vv. 5-9). See Ex. 25:31-40; 27:20,21; 37:17-24 and Ex. 25:23-30; 39:36; 40:23, respectively.

24:5 Each loaf was made with 4 quarts of flour.

24:10-23 This portion relates to the sin of blasphemy. Cf. Ex. 20:7; 22:28.

24:10-14,23 Now the son. Here is another historical example of blasphemy along similar lines as the Nadab and Abihu account (10:1,2). The blasphemer was one of the "many other people." The people transferred the guilt of them all to him.

24:12 put him in custody. There were no jails in Israel since incarceration was not a penalty for crime. They had merely restrained him, probably in a pit of some sort, until they could establish his punishment. Punishments were corporal, banishment, or, in severe cases, death. Those who lived through the punishment worked to secure restitution for those they had violated.

their hands on his head, and let all the congregation stone him.
15 "Then you shall speak to the children
of Israel, saying: 'Whoever curses his God
[o]shall [4]bear his sin. 16 And whoever [p]blas-
phemes the name of the LORD shall surely
be put to death. All the congregation shall
certainly stone him, the stranger as well as
him who is born in the land. When he blasphemes the name *of the LORD*, he shall be
put to death.
17 [q]'Whoever kills any man shall surely
be put to death. 18 [r]Whoever kills an animal shall make it good, animal for animal.
19 'If a man causes disfigurement of his
neighbor, as [s]he has done, so shall it be
done to him— 20 fracture for [t]fracture,
[u]eye for eye, tooth for tooth; as he has
caused disfigurement of a man, so shall it
be done to him. 21 And whoever kills an
animal shall restore it; but whoever kills a
man shall be put to death. 22 You shall
have [v]the[5] same law for the stranger and
for one from your own country; for I *am*
the LORD your God.' "
23 Then Moses spoke to the children of
Israel; and they took outside the camp him
who had cursed, and stoned him with
stones. So the children of Israel did as the
LORD commanded Moses.

The Sabbath of the Seventh Year

25 And the LORD spoke to Moses on
Mount [a]Sinai, saying, 2 "Speak to
the children of Israel, and say to them:
'When you come into the land which I give
you, then the land shall [b]keep a sabbath to
the LORD. 3 Six years you shall sow your
field, and six years you shall prune your
vineyard, and gather its fruit; 4 but in the
[c]seventh year there shall be a sabbath of
solemn [d]rest for the land, a sabbath to the
LORD. You shall neither sow your field nor
prune your vineyard. 5 [e]What grows of its
own accord of your harvest you shall not
reap, nor gather the grapes of your untended vine, *for* it is a year of rest for the
land. 6 And the sabbath *produce* of the land
shall be food for you: for you, your male
and female servants, your hired man, and
the stranger who dwells with you, 7 for
your livestock and the beasts that *are* in
your land—all its produce shall be for
food.

The Year of Jubilee

8 'And you shall count seven sabbaths of
years for yourself, seven times seven years;
and the time of the seven sabbaths of years
shall be to you forty-nine years. 9 Then you
shall cause the trumpet of the Jubilee to
sound on the tenth *day* of the seventh
month; [f]on the Day of Atonement you
shall make the trumpet to sound throughout all your land. 10 And you shall consecrate the fiftieth year, and [g]proclaim liberty throughout *all* the land to all its
inhabitants. It shall be a Jubilee for you;
[h]and each of you shall return to his possession, and each of you shall return to his
family. 11 That fiftieth year shall be a Jubilee to you; in it [i]you shall neither sow
nor reap what grows of its own accord, nor
gather *the grapes* of your untended vine.
12 For it *is* the Jubilee; it shall be holy to
you; [j]you shall eat its produce from the
field.
13 [k]'In this Year of Jubilee, each of you
shall return to his possession. 14 And if
you sell anything to your neighbor or buy
from your neighbor's hand, you shall not
[l]oppress one another. 15 [m]According to
the number of years after the Jubilee you
shall buy from your neighbor, and according to the number of years of crops he
shall sell to you. 16 According to the multitude of years you shall increase its price,
and according to the fewer number of
years you shall diminish its price; for he
sells to you *according* to the number *of the
years* of the crops. 17 Therefore [n]you shall
not [1]oppress one another, [o]but you shall
fear your God; for I *am* the LORD your
God.

15 [o]Lev. 20:17; Num. 9:13 [4]*be responsible for*
16 [p]Ex. 20:7; 1 Kin. 21:10, 13; [Matt. 12:31; Mark 3:28, 29]
17 [q]Gen. 9:6; Ex. 21:12; Num. 35:30, 31; Deut. 19:11, 12; 27:24
18 [r]Lev. 24:21
19 [s]Ex. 21:24
20 [t]Ex. 21:23; Deut. 19:21 [u][Matt. 5:38, 39]
22 [v]Ex. 12:49; Lev. 19:33-37; Num. 9:14; 15:15, 16, 29 [5]*one standard of judgment*

CHAPTER 25

1 [a]Lev. 26:46
2 [b]Lev. 26:34, 35
4 [c]Deut. 15:1; Neh. 10:31 [d][Heb. 4:9]
5 [e]2 Kin. 19:29
9 [f]Lev. 23:24, 27
10 [g]Is. 61:2; 63:4; Jer. 34:8, 15, 17; [Luke 4:19] [h]Lev. 25:13, 28, 54; Num. 36:4
11 [i]Lev. 25:5
12 [j]Lev. 25:6, 7
13 [k]Lev. 25:10; 27:24; Num. 36:4
14 [l]Lev. 19:13
15 [m]Lev. 27:18, 23
17 [n]Lev. 25:14; Prov. 14:31; 22:22; Jer. 7:5, 6; 1 Thess. 4:6 [o]Lev. 19:14, 32; 25:43 [1]*mistreat*

24:20 Cf. Matt. 5:38. This law of retaliation established the principle that the punishment should fit the crime, but not go beyond it.

25:1-55 Proper care for the Lord's property is prescribed for the sabbatical year (25:1-7) and the Jubilee year (25:8-55).

25:1-7 This involves revitalization of the land. The seventh year of rest would invigorate and replenish the nutrients in the soil. Whatever grew naturally was free to all for the taking (vv. 6,7).

25:8-55 The Year of Jubilee involved a year of release from indebtedness (vv. 23-38) and bondage of all sorts (vv. 39-55). All prisoners and captives were set free, slaves released, and debtors absolved. All property reverted to original owners. This plan curbed inflation and moderated acquisitions. It also gave new opportunity to people who had fallen on hard times.

25:8-17 These are general instructions for Jubilee.

25:9 Jubilee. This lit. means "ram's horn," which was blown on the tenth day of the seventh month to start the 50th year of universal redemption.

25:10 proclaim liberty. Not only must they let the land lie fallow, but the people were allowed a one-year break from their labor. Those bound by a work contract were released from their commitments and there was the release of indentured servants.

25:14-16 The Jubilee year had an effect on the value of land, which was to be considered in all transactions.

25:17 you shall not oppress one another. No one should take advantage of or abuse another person, because cruelty is against the very character of God. Penalties for crime were to be swift and exact.

Provisions for the Seventh Year

18 [p]'So you shall observe My statutes
and keep My judgments, and perform
them; [q]and you will dwell in the land in
safety. 19 Then the land will yield its fruit,
and [r]you will eat your fill, and dwell there
in safety.
20 'And if you say, [s]"What shall we eat in
the seventh year, since [t]we shall not sow
nor gather in our produce?" 21 Then I will
[u]command My blessing on you in the
[v]sixth year, and it will bring forth produce
enough for three years. 22 [w]And you shall
sow in the eighth year, and eat [x]old produce until the ninth year; until its produce
comes in, you shall eat *of* the old *harvest.*

Redemption of Property

23 'The land shall not be sold permanently, for [y]the land *is* Mine; for you *are*
[z]strangers and sojourners with Me. 24 And
in all the land of your possession you shall
grant redemption of the land.
25 [a]'If one of your brethren becomes
poor, and has sold *some* of his possession,
and if [b]his redeeming relative comes to redeem it, then he may redeem what his
brother sold. 26 Or if the man has no one to
redeem it, but he himself becomes able to
redeem it, 27 then [c]let him count the years
since its sale, and restore the remainder to
the man to whom he sold it, that he may
return to his possession. 28 But if he is not
able to have *it* restored to himself, then
what was sold shall remain in the hand of
him who bought it until the Year of Jubilee;
[d]and in the Jubilee it shall be released, and
he shall return to his possession.
29 'If a man sells a house in a walled city,
then he may redeem it within a whole year
after it is sold; *within* a full year he may redeem it. 30 But if it is not redeemed within
the space of a full year, then the house in
the walled city shall belong permanently
to him who bought it, throughout his generations. It shall not be released in the Jubilee. 31 However the houses of villages
which have no wall around them shall be
counted as the fields of the country. They
may be redeemed, and they shall be released in the Jubilee. 32 Nevertheless [e]the
cities of the Levites, *and* the houses in the
cities of their possession, the Levites may
redeem at any time. 33 And if a man purchases a house from the Levites, then the
house that was sold in the city of his possession shall be released in the Jubilee; for
the houses in the cities of the Levites *are*
their possession among the children of Israel. 34 But [f]the field of the common-land
of their cities may not be [g]sold, for it *is*
their perpetual possession.

Lending to the Poor

35 'If one of your brethren becomes poor,
and [2]falls into poverty among you, then
you shall [h]help him, like a stranger or a sojourner, that he may live with you. 36 [i]Take
no usury or interest from him; but [j]fear
your God, that your brother may live with
you. 37 You shall not lend him your money
for usury, nor lend him your food at a profit. 38 [k]I *am* the LORD your God, who brought
you out of the land of Egypt, to give you
the land of Canaan *and* to be your God.

The Law Concerning Slavery

39 'And if *one of* your brethren *who dwells*
by you becomes poor, and sells himself to
you, you shall not compel him to serve as
a slave. 40 As a hired servant *and* a sojourner he shall be with you, *and* shall
serve you until the Year of Jubilee. 41 And
then he shall depart from you—he and his
children [l]with him—and shall return to his
own family. He shall return to the possession of his fathers. 42 For they *are* [m]My servants, whom I brought out of the land of
Egypt; they shall not be sold as slaves.
43 [n]You shall not rule over him [o]with
[3]rigor, but you [p]shall fear your God.

18 [p] Lev. 19:37 [q] Lev. 26:5; Deut. 12:10; Ps. 4:8; Jer. 23:6
19 [r] Lev. 26:5; Ezek. 34:25
20 [s] Matt. 6:25, 31 [t] Lev. 25:4, 5
21 [u] Deut. 28:8 [v] Ex. 16:29
22 [w] 2 Kin. 19:29 [x] Lev. 26:10; Josh. 5:11
23 [y] Ex. 19:5; 2 Chr. 7:20 [z] Gen. 23:4; Ex. 6:4; 1 Chr. 29:15; Ps. 39:12; Heb. 11:13; 1 Pet. 2:11
25 [a] Ruth 2:20; 4:4, 6 [b] Num. 5:8; Ruth 3:2, 9, 12; [Job 19:25]; Jer. 32:7, 8
27 [c] Lev. 25:50-52
28 [d] Lev. 25:10, 13
32 [e] Num. 35:1-8; Josh. 21:2
34 [f] Num. 35:2-5 [g] Acts 4:36, 37
35 [h] Deut. 15:7-11; 24:14, 15; Luke 6:35; 1 John 3:17 [2] Lit. *his hand fails*
36 [i] Ex. 22:25; Deut. 23:19, 20 [j] Neh. 5:9
38 [k] Lev. 11:45; 22:32, 33
41 [l] Ex. 21:3
42 [m] Lev. 25:55; [Rom. 6:22; 1 Cor. 7:22, 23]
43 [n] Eph. 6:9; Col. 4:1 [o] Ex. 1:13, 14; Lev. 25:46, 53; Ezek. 34:4 [p] Ex. 1:17; Deut. 25:18; Mal. 3:5 [3] *severity*

25:18-22 God's provision in the year of no planting was given, which on a smaller scale had been true for the Sabbath day during the Exodus (cf. Ex. 16:5).

25:20,21 enough for three years. When the important query was asked, God responded by promising to supply enough to last.

25:23-34 Various regulations regarding real estate are outlined.

25:23 the land *is* Mine. God owns the earth and all that is in it (cf. Ps. 24:1). The people of Israel were, in fact, only tenants on the land by the Lord's grace. Therefore ownership of property was temporary, not permanent.

25:33 cities of the Levites. Cf. Num. 35:1-8; Josh. 21.

25:34 common-land. These were fields that the village/city-at-large used to grow crops.

25:35-38 Instructions on dealing with the poor are outlined.

25:35 like a stranger or a sojourner. The law required gleanings (leftovers after harvest) for the Israelite as well as the stranger (cf. 19:9,10; 23:22; Deut. 24:19-21).

25:36 usury or interest. Usury or excessive interest was prohibited for all (Ps. 15:5). Even fair interest was otherwise prohibited in dealing with the poor (*see notes on Deut. 23:19,20; 24:10-13*). The basics of life were to be given, not loaned, to the poor.

25:38 to give you the land of Canaan. The Lord cites His generosity in giving them a land that was not theirs as a motive for their generosity toward their countrymen.

25:39-55 The principles for dealing with slavery are laid out.

25:42 For they *are* My servants. The spirit of OT slavery is revealed in these words. God, in effect, ordered that slaves be treated like family, i.e., better than employees, because they are His slaves which He redeemed out of the slave markets of Egypt. God owned not only the land (v. 23), but also the people.

44 And as for your male and female slaves
whom you may have—from the nations
that are around you, from them you may
buy male and female slaves. 45 Moreover
you may buy [q]the children of the strangers
who dwell among you, and their families
who are with you, which they beget in
your land; and they shall become your
property. 46 And [r]you may take them as an
inheritance for your children after you, to
inherit *them as* a possession; they shall be
your permanent slaves. But regarding
your brethren, the children of Israel, you
shall not rule over one another with rigor.
47 'Now if a sojourner or stranger close
to you becomes rich, and *one of* your
brethren *who dwells* by him becomes poor,
and sells himself to the stranger *or* sojourner close to you, or to a member of the
stranger's family, 48 after he is sold he may
be redeemed again. One of his brothers
may redeem him; 49 or his uncle or his
uncle's son may redeem him; or *anyone*
who is near of kin to him in his family may
redeem him; or if he is able he may redeem
himself. 50 Thus he shall reckon with him
who bought him: The price of his release
shall be according to the number of years,
from the year that he was sold to him until
the Year of Jubilee; *it shall be* [s]according to
the time of a hired servant for him. 51 If
there are still many years *remaining*, according to them he shall repay the price of his
redemption from the money with which he
was bought. 52 And if there remain but a
few years until the Year of Jubilee, then he
shall reckon with him, *and* according to his
years he shall repay him the price of his redemption. 53 He shall be with him as a
yearly hired servant, and he shall not rule
with rigor over him in your sight. 54 And if
he is not redeemed in these *years*, then he
shall be released in the Year of Jubilee—he
and his children with him. 55 For the children of Israel *are* servants to Me; they *are*
My servants whom I brought out of the
land of Egypt: I *am* the LORD your God.

45 [q] [Is. 56:3, 6, 7]
46 [r] Is. 14:2
50 [s] Job 7:1; Is. 16:14

Promise of Blessing and Retribution

26 'You shall [a]not make idols for yourselves;
neither a carved image nor a *sacred* pillar shall you rear up for yourselves;
nor shall you set up an engraved stone in your land, to bow down to it;
for I *am* the LORD your God.
2 [b]You shall [1]keep My Sabbaths and reverence My sanctuary:
I *am* the LORD.

3 [c]'If you walk in My statutes and keep My commandments, and perform them,
4 [d]then I will give you rain in its season, [e]the land shall yield its produce, and the trees of the field shall yield their fruit.
5 [f]Your threshing shall last till the time of vintage, and the vintage shall last till the time of sowing;
you shall eat your bread to the full, and [g]dwell in your land safely.
6 [h]I will give peace in the land, and [i]you shall lie down, and none will make *you* afraid;
I will rid the land of [j]evil[2] beasts, and [k]the sword will not go through your land.
7 You will chase your enemies, and they shall fall by the sword before you.
8 [l]Five of you shall chase a hundred, and a hundred of you shall put ten thousand to flight;
your enemies shall fall by the sword before you.

CHAPTER 26

1 [a] Ex. 20:4, 5; Deut. 4:15-18; 5:8
2 [b] Lev. 19:30 [1] *observe*
3 [c] Deut. 28:1-14
4 [d] Is. 30:23 [e] Ps. 67:6
5 [f] Deut. 11:15; Joel 2:19, 26; Amos 9:13 [g] Lev. 25:18, 19; Ezek. 34:25
6 [h] Is. 45:7 [i] Job 11:19; Ps. 4:8; Zeph. 3:13 [j] 2 Kin. 17:25; Hos. 2:18 [k] Ezek. 14:17 [2] *wild beasts*
8 [l] Deut. 32:30; Judg. 7:7-12

25:44-46 from the nations. These slaves included people whom Israel was to either drive out or destroy (i.e., slavery was a humane option) and those who came to Israel in the Exodus from Egypt.

25:47-55 This section deals with an alien who has an Israelite slave.

25:48 redeemed. Redemption, a contractual agreement which existed in the slave culture, offered the potential for emancipation to indentured individuals under certain conditions. Slaves could be bought out of slavery or some other sort of indentured status by family members or other interested parties who would pay the ransom price.

25:51-54 the price of his redemption. The cost of buying him out of slavery was affected by the Jubilee year, when he could be set free.

25:55 The Israelites emancipated from Egypt by God were all God's servants; therefore, they were to treat their own slaves with the same grace and generosity as God had granted them.

26:1-46 The covenant blessings for obedience (26:3-13) and curses for disobedience (26:14-39) are elaborated (cf. Deut. 28). A provision for repentance is also offered (26:40-45).

26:1,2 A representative summary of the Ten Commandments (Ex. 20:3-17) was set forth as the standard by which Israel's obedience or disobedience would be measured.

26:1 image...pillar...engraved stone. Israel's neighbors used all of these devices for the worship of their gods.

26:3-13 These blessings will reward obedience.

26:4 rain in its season. If the rains did not come at the right times, the people experienced crop failure and famine (cf. 1 Kin. 17,18).

26:6 evil beasts. Dangerous animals such as lions and bears existed in that area. Joseph's brothers claimed that such an animal had killed him (Gen. 37:20).

26:7 chase your enemies. God provided victories repeatedly in the conquest of Canaan (cf. Josh. 8–12).

9 'For I will [m]look on you favorably
and [n]make you fruitful, multiply you and confirm My [o]cov-
enant with you.
10 You shall eat the [p]old harvest, and
clear out the old because of the
new.
11 [q]I will set My [3]tabernacle among
you, and My soul shall not
abhor you.
12 [r]I will walk among you and be your
God, and you shall be My peo-
ple.
13 I *am* the LORD your God, who
brought you out of the land of
Egypt, that *you* should not be
their slaves;
I have broken the bands of your
[s]yoke and made you walk [4]up-
right.

14 'But if you do not obey Me, and do
not observe all these commandments,
15 and if you despise My statutes, or if
your soul abhors My judgments,
so that you do not perform all
My commandments, *but* break
My covenant,
16 I also will do this to you:
I will even appoint terror over you,
[t]wasting disease and fever
which shall [u]consume the eyes
and [v]cause sorrow of heart.
And [w]you shall sow your seed [5]in
vain, for your enemies shall eat
it.
17 I will [6]set [x]My face against you, and
[y]you shall be defeated by your
enemies.
[z]Those who hate you shall reign
over you, and you shall [a]flee
when no one pursues you.

18 'And after all this, if you do not obey
Me, then I will punish you
[b]seven times more for your sins.

9 [m] Ex. 2:25; 2 Kin. 13:23 [n] Gen. 17:6, 7; Ps. 107:38 [o] Gen. 17:1-7
10 [p] Lev. 25:22
11 [q] Ex. 25:8; 29:45, 46; Josh. 22:19; Ps. 76:2; Ezek. 37:26; Rev. 21:3 [3] *dwelling place*
12 [r] Deut. 23:14; [2 Cor. 6:16]
13 [s] Gen. 27:40 [4] *erect*
16 [t] Deut. 28:22 [u] 1 Sam. 2:33 [v] Ezek. 24:23; 33:10 [w] Judg. 6:3-6; Job 31:8; Mic. 6:15 [5] *without profit*
17 [x] Ps. 34:16 [y] Deut. 28:25; 1 Sam. 4:10; 31:1 [z] Ps. 106:41 [a] Prov. 28:1 [6] *oppose you*
18 [b] 1 Sam. 2:5

19 [c] Is. 25:11 [d] Deut. 28:23
20 [e] Ps. 127:1; Is. 17:10, 11; 49:4; Jer. 12:13 [f] Gen. 4:12; Deut. 11:17
22 [g] Deut. 32:24; Ezek. 14:21 [h] Judg. 5:6; 2 Chr. 15:5; Zech. 7:14
23 [i] Jer. 2:30; Amos 4:6-12
24 [j] Lev. 26:28, 41; Ps. 18:26
25 [k] Ezek. 5:17 [l] Num. 16:49; Deut. 28:21; 2 Sam. 24:15
26 [m] Ps. 105:16; Is. 3:1; Ezek. 4:16, 17; 5:16 [n] Mic. 6:14; Hag. 1:6

19 I will [c]break the pride of your
power;
I [d]will make your heavens like iron
and your earth like bronze.
20 And your [e]strength shall be spent in
vain;
for your [f]land shall not yield its
produce, nor shall the trees of
the land yield their fruit.

21 'Then, if you walk contrary to Me,
and are not willing to obey Me, I
will bring on you seven times
more plagues, according to your
sins.
22 [g]I will also send wild beasts among
you, which shall rob you of your
children, destroy your livestock,
and make you few in number;
and [h]your highways shall be desolate.

23 'And if [i]by these things you are not
reformed by Me, but walk contrary to Me,
24 [j]then I also will walk contrary to
you, and I will punish you yet
seven times for your sins.
25 And [k]I will bring a sword against
you that will execute the vengeance of the covenant;
when you are gathered together
within your cities [l]I will send
pestilence among you;
and you shall be delivered into the
hand of the enemy.
26 [m]When I have cut off your supply of
bread, ten women shall bake
your bread in one oven, and
they shall bring back your bread
by weight, [n]and you shall eat
and not be satisfied.

27 'And after all this, if you do not obey
Me, but walk contrary to Me,
28 then I also will walk contrary to you
in fury;

26:9 make you fruitful, multiply you and confirm My covenant with you. What God commanded at Creation and repeated after the Flood was contained in the covenant promise of seed (Gen. 12:1-3), which He will fulfill to the nation of Israel as promised to Abraham (Gen. 15:5,6).

26:12 your God...My people. The promise of an intimate covenant relationship with the God of the universe is given (cf. 2 Cor. 6:16).

26:14-39 These punishments will repay disobedience.

26:15 break My covenant. By disobeying the commandments and the various laws of the Mosaic Covenant, Israel broke this conditional covenant. Unlike the ultimate provisions of the unconditional covenant made with Abraham, all blessings in the covenant of Mosaic law were conditioned upon obedience (cf. Lev. 26:25).

26:16 wasting disease. Perhaps tuberculosis or leprosy is in view (the subject of much legislation in Lev. 13,14), but no certain identification is possible. **your enemies shall eat it.** They will be conquered by their enemies at a time when those enemies will enjoy Israel's harvest.

26:22 highways shall be desolate. The activity on a nation's roadway, i.e., messengers, merchants, and people traveling, reflected the well-being of that country. This is a picture of extreme economic siege.

26:25 the vengeance of the covenant. God's retribution for Israel's breaking the conditional Mosaic Covenant is pledged.

and I, even I, will chastise you seven
times for your sins.
29 [o]You[7] shall eat the flesh of your sons,
and you shall eat the flesh of
your daughters.
30 [p]I will destroy your high places, cut
down your incense altars, and
cast your carcasses on the lifeless forms of your idols;
and My soul shall abhor you.
31 I will lay your [q]cities waste and
[r]bring your sanctuaries to desolation, and I will not [s]smell the
fragrance of your [8]sweet aromas.
32 [t]I will bring the land to desolation,
and your enemies who dwell in
it shall be astonished at it.
33 [u]I will scatter you among the nations
and draw out a sword after you;
your land shall be desolate and
your cities waste.
34 [v]Then the land shall enjoy its sabbaths as long as it lies desolate
and you *are* in your enemies'
land;
then the land shall rest and enjoy its
sabbaths.
35 As long as *it* lies desolate it shall
rest—
for the time it did not rest on your
[w]sabbaths when you dwelt in it.

36 'And as for those of you who are left,
I will send [x]faintness[9] into their
hearts in the lands of their enemies;
the sound of a shaken leaf shall
cause them to flee;
they shall flee as though fleeing
from a sword, and they shall fall
when no one pursues.
37 [y]They shall stumble over one another, as it were before a sword,
when no one pursues;
and [z]you shall have no *power* to
stand before your enemies.
38 You shall [a]perish among the nations, and the land of your enemies shall eat you up.

29 [o] Deut. 28:53; 2 Kin. 6:28, 29 [7] In time of famine
30 [p] 1 Kin. 13:2; 2 Chr. 34:3; Is. 27:9; Ezek. 6:3-6, 13
31 [q] 2 Kin. 25:4, 10 [r] 2 Chr. 36:19; Ps. 74:7 [s] Is. 1:11-15 [8] *pleasing*
32 [t] Jer. 9:11; 18:16
33 [u] Deut. 4:27; Ps. 44:11; Ezek. 12:15; 20:23; 22:15; Zech. 7:14
34 [v] Lev. 26:43; 2 Chr. 36:21
35 [w] Lev. 25:2
36 [x] Is. 30:17; Lam. 1:3, 6; 4:19; Ezek. 21:7, 12, 15 [9] *fear*
37 [y] Judg. 7:22; 1 Sam. 14:15, 16; Is. 10:4 [z] Josh. 7:12, 13; Judg. 2:14
38 [a] Deut. 4:26

39 [b] Deut. 28:65; Ezek. 4:17; 33:10; Zech. 10:9 [c] Ex. 34:7 [1] *rot away*
40 [d] Num. 5:7; 1 Kin. 8:33, 34; Neh. 9:2; Luke 15:18; [1 John 1:9]
41 [e] Acts 7:51; Rom. 2:29 [f] 2 Chr. 12:6, 7, 12; 1 Pet. 5:5, 6 [g] Ps. 39:9; 51:3, 4; Dan. 9:7
42 [h] Ex. 2:24; 6:5; Ps. 106:45; Ezek. 16:60 [i] Ps. 136:23
43 [j] Lev. 26:34, 35 [k] Lev. 26:15
44 [l] Deut. 4:31; 2 Kin. 13:23; Jer. 30:11; [Rom. 11:1-36]
45 [m] [Rom. 11:28] [n] Lev. 22:33; 25:38 [o] Ps. 98:2; Ezek. 20:9, 14, 22
46 [p] Lev. 27:34; Deut. 6:1; 12:1; [John 1:17]

39 And those of you who are left [b]shall
[1]waste away in their iniquity in
your enemies' lands;
also in their [c]fathers' iniquities,
which are with them, they shall
waste away.

40 '*But* [d]if they confess their iniquity
and the iniquity of their fathers,
with their unfaithfulness in
which they were unfaithful to
Me, and that they also have
walked contrary to Me,
41 and *that* I also have walked contrary to them and have brought
them into the land of their enemies;
if their [e]uncircumcised hearts are
[f]humbled, and they [g]accept their
guilt—
42 then I will [h]remember My covenant
with Jacob, and My covenant
with Isaac and My covenant with
Abraham I will remember;
I will [i]remember the land.
43 [j]The land also shall be left empty by
them, and will enjoy its sabbaths
while it lies desolate without
them;
they will accept their guilt, because
they [k]despised My judgments
and because their soul abhorred
My statutes.
44 Yet for all that, when they are in the
land of their enemies, [l]I will not
cast them away, nor shall I abhor
them, to utterly destroy them
and break My covenant with
them;
for I *am* the LORD their God.

45 But [m]for their sake I will remember
the covenant of their ancestors,
[n]whom I brought out of the land
of Egypt [o]in the sight of the nations, that I might be their God:
I *am* the LORD.' "
46 [p]These *are* the statutes and judgments
and laws which the LORD made between

26:29 eat the flesh. There will be widespread famine in the land and thus the people will even resort to cannibalism, which actually came to pass (cf. 2 Kin. 6:28,29; Jer. 19:9; Lam. 2:20; 4:10).

26:30 high places. These were natural shrines for the worship of idols. Solomon disobeyed God by worshiping Him on the high places (1 Kin. 3:4), and not long afterward, he was serving the gods of his foreign wives (1 Kin. 11:1-9).

26:31-35 All this occurred in the terrible invasion of the northern kingdom of Israel in 722 A.D. by the Assyrians and the destruction of the southern kingdom of Judah in 605–586 B.C. by the Babylonians. In the case of Judah, it was a 70-year captivity to rest the Land for all the Sabbath years that had been violated. See 2 Chr. 36:17-21.

26:35 the time it did not rest. By implication, because they had violated the Sabbath repeatedly. This violation became the basis of the later 70-year Babylonian captivity (cf. 2 Chr. 36:20-21).

26:38 The 10 tribes of the northern kingdom of Israel never returned directly from captivity. See 2 Kin. 17:7-23; *see note on Acts 26:7*.

26:40-42 if they confess,...I will remember My covenant. God's covenant was rooted in the relationship He had initiated with His people. True repentance would be honored by Him.

26:42 Jacob...Isaac...Abraham. The reverse order is a look in retrospect as opposed to the actual historical sequence.

26:46 Much of the content of Leviticus came during Moses' two

Himself and the children of Israel [q]on Mount Sinai by the hand of Moses.

Redeeming Persons and Property Dedicated to God

27 Now the LORD spoke to Moses, saying, 2 "Speak to the children of Israel, and say to them: [a]'When a man [1]consecrates by a vow certain persons to the LORD, according to your [2]valuation, 3 if your valuation is of a male from twenty years old up to sixty years old, then your valuation shall be fifty shekels of silver, [b]according to the shekel of the sanctuary. 4 If it *is* a female, then your valuation shall be thirty shekels; 5 and if from five years old up to twenty years old, then your valuation for a male shall be twenty shekels, and for a female ten shekels; 6 and if from a month old up to five years old, then your valuation for a male shall be five shekels of silver, and for a female your valuation shall be three shekels of silver; 7 and if from sixty years old and above, if *it is* a male, then your valuation shall be fifteen shekels, and for a female ten shekels.

8 'But if he is too poor to pay your valuation, then he shall present himself before the priest, and the priest shall set a value for [c]him; according to the ability of him who vowed, the priest shall value him.

9 'If *it is* an animal that men may bring as an offering to the LORD, all that *anyone* gives to the LORD shall be holy. 10 He shall not substitute it or exchange it, good for bad or bad for good; and if he at all exchanges animal for animal, then both it and the one exchanged for it shall be [d]holy. 11 If *it is* an unclean animal which they do not offer as a sacrifice to the LORD, then he shall present the animal before the priest; 12 and the priest shall set a value for it, whether it is good or bad; as you, the priest, value it, so it shall be. 13 [e]But if he *wants* at all *to* redeem it, then he must add one-fifth to your valuation.

14 'And when a man [3]dedicates his house *to be* holy to the LORD, then the priest shall set a value for it, whether it is good or bad; as the priest values it, so it shall stand. 15 If he who dedicated it *wants to* [4]redeem his house, then he must add one-fifth of the money of your valuation to it, and it shall be his.

16 'If a man [5]dedicates to the LORD *part* of a field of his possession, then your valuation shall be according to the seed for it. A homer of barley seed *shall be valued* at fifty shekels of silver. 17 If he dedicates his field from the Year of Jubilee, according to your valuation it shall stand. 18 But if he dedicates his field after the Jubilee, then the priest shall [f]reckon to him the money due according to the years that remain till the Year of Jubilee, and it shall be deducted from your valuation. 19 And if he who dedicates the field ever wishes to redeem it, then he must add one-fifth of the money of your valuation to it, and it shall belong to him. 20 But if he does not want to redeem the field, or if he has sold the field to another man, it shall not be redeemed anymore; 21 but the field, [g]when it is released in the Jubilee, shall be holy to the LORD, as a [h]devoted field; it shall be [i]the possession of the priest.

22 'And if a man dedicates to the LORD a field which he has bought, which is not the field of [j]his possession, 23 then the priest shall reckon to him the worth of your valuation, up to the Year of Jubilee, and he shall give your valuation on that day *as* a holy *offering* to the LORD. 24 [k]In the Year of Jubilee the field shall return to him from whom it was bought, to the one who *owned* the land as a possession. 25 And all your valuations shall be according to the shekel of the sanctuary: [l]twenty gerahs to the shekel.

26 'But the [m]firstborn of the animals, which should be the LORD's firstborn, no man shall dedicate; whether *it is* an ox or sheep, it *is* the LORD's. 27 And if *it is* an unclean animal, then he shall redeem *it* according to your valuation, and [n]shall add one-fifth to it; or if it is not redeemed, then it shall be sold according to your valuation.

28 [o]'Nevertheless no [6]devoted *offering* that a man may devote to the LORD of all that he has, *both* man and beast, or the field of his possession, shall be sold or redeemed; every devoted *offering is* most holy to the LORD. 29 [p]No person under the ban, who may become doomed to destruction among men, shall be redeemed, *but* shall surely be put to death. 30 And [q]all the tithe of the land, *whether* of the seed of the land *or* of the fruit of the tree, *is* the LORD's.

46 [q] Lev. 25:1

CHAPTER 27

2 [a] Lev. 7:16; Num. 6:2; Deut. 23:21-23; Judg. 11:30, 31, 39 [1] *Or makes a difficult or extraordinary vow* [2] *appraisal*
3 [b] Ex. 30:13; Lev. 27:25; Num. 3:47; 18:16
8 [c] Lev. 5:11; 14:21-24
10 [d] Lev. 27:33
13 [e] Lev. 6:5; 22:14; 27:15, 19
14 [3] *sets apart*
15 [4] *buy back*
16 [5] *sets apart*
18 [f] Lev. 25:15, 16, 28
21 [g] Lev. 25:10, 28, 31 [h] Lev. 27:28 [i] Num. 18:14; Ezek. 44:29
22 [j] Lev. 25:10, 25
24 [k] Lev. 25:10-13, 28
25 [l] Ex. 30:13; Lev. 27:3; Num. 3:47; 18:16; Ezek. 45:12
26 [m] Ex. 13:2, 12; 22:30
27 [n] Lev. 27:11, 12
28 [o] Lev. 27:21; Num. 18:14; Josh. 6:17-19 [6] Given exclusively and irrevocably
29 [p] Num. 21:2
30 [q] Gen. 28:22; Num. 18:21, 24; 2 Chr. 31:5, 6, 12; Neh. 13:12; Mal. 3:8

"forty day and night" visits to Sinai (cf. Ex. 24:16–32:6; 34:2-28; Lev. 7:37,38; 25:1; 27:34).

27:1-34 Standard legislation is given for dedicated persons, animals, houses, and lands.

27:2-7 consecrates by a vow. This sets the gift apart from the rest of his household and possessions as a gift to the Lord and His service.

27:3 the shekel of the sanctuary. *See note on 5:15.*

27:26 the firstborn. The firstborn already belonged to the Lord (Ex. 13:2), so the worshiper could not dedicate it a second time.

27:29 person under the ban. Like Achan in Josh. 7.

27:30-32 tithe. This general tithe was given to the Levites. Cf. Num. 18:21-32. This is the only mention of tithe or 10-percent in

It *is* holy to the LORD. 31 [r]If a man wants at
all to redeem *any* of his tithes, he shall add
one-fifth to it. 32 And concerning the tithe
of the herd or the flock, of whatever [s]pass-
es under the rod, the tenth one shall be
holy to the LORD. 33 He shall not inquire
whether it is good or bad, [t]nor shall he exchange it; and if he exchanges it at all, then
both it and the one exchanged for it shall
be holy; it shall not be redeemed.' "

34 [u]These *are* the commandments which
the LORD commanded Moses for the children of Israel on Mount [v]Sinai.

31 [r] Lev. 27:13
32 [s] Jer. 33:13; Ezek. 20:37; Mic. 7:14
33 [t] Lev. 27:10
34 [u] Lev. 26:46; Deut. 4:5; Mal. 4:4 [v] Ex. 19:1-6, 25; [Heb. 12:18-29]

Leviticus. However, along with this offering, there were two other OT tithes which totaled about 23 percent annually (cf. the second tithe—Deut. 14:22; and the third tithe every 3 years—Deut. 14:28,29; 26:12).

The Fourth Book of Moses Called
NUMBERS

Title

The English title "Numbers" comes from the Greek (LXX) and Latin (Vg.) versions. This designation is based on the numberings that are a major focus of chaps. 1–4 and 26. The most common Hebrew title comes from the fifth word in the Hebrew text of 1:1, "in the wilderness [of]." This name is much more descriptive of the total contents of the book, which recount the history of Israel during almost 39 years of wandering in the wilderness. Another Hebrew title, favored by some early church Fathers, is based on the first word of the Hebrew text of 1:1, "and He spoke." This designation emphasizes that the book records the Word of God to Israel.

Author and Date

The first 5 books of the Bible, called the Law, of which Numbers is the fourth, are ascribed to Moses throughout Scripture (Josh. 8:31; 2 Kin. 14:6; Neh. 8:1; Mark 12:26; John 7:19). The book of Numbers itself refers to the writing of Moses in 33:2 and 36:13.

Numbers was written in the final year of Moses' life. The events from 20:1 to the end occur in the 40th year after the Exodus. The account ends with Israel poised on the eastern side of the Jordan River across from Jericho (36:13), which is where the conquest of the land of Canaan began (Josh. 3–6). The book of Numbers must be dated ca. 1405 B.C., since it is foundational to the book of Deuteronomy, and Deuteronomy is dated in the 11th month of the 40th year after the Exodus (Deut. 1:3).

Background and Setting

Most of the events of the book are set "in the wilderness." The word "wilderness" is used 48 times in Numbers. This term refers to land that contains little vegetation or trees, and because of a sparsity of rainfall, it cannot be cultivated. This land is best used for tending flocks of animals. In 1:1–10:10, Israel encamped in "the wilderness in Sinai." It was at Sinai that the Lord had entered into the Mosaic Covenant with them (Ex. 19–24). From 10:11–12:16, Israel traveled from Sinai to Kadesh. In 13:1–20:13, the events took place in and around Kadesh, which was located in "the wilderness of Paran" (12:16; 13:3,26), "the wilderness of Zin" (13:21; 20:1). From 20:14–22:1, Israel traveled from Kadesh to the "plains of Moab." All the events of 22:2–36:13 occurred while Israel was encamped in the plain to the N of Moab. That plain was a flat and fertile piece of land in the middle of the wasteland (21:20; 23:28; 24:1).

The book of Numbers concentrates on events that take place in the second and fortieth years after the Exodus. All incidents recorded in 1:1–14:45 occur in 1444 B.C., the year after the Exodus. Everything referred to after 20:1 is dated ca. 1406/1405 B.C., the 40th year after the Exodus. The laws and events found in 15:1–19:22 are undated, but probably all should be dated ca. 1443 to 1407 B.C. The lack of material devoted to this 37 year period, in comparison with the other years of the journey from Egypt to Canaan, communicates how wasted these years were because of Israel's rebellion against the Lord and His consequent judgment.

Historical and Theological Themes

Numbers chronicles the experiences of two generations of the nation of Israel. The first generation participated in the Exodus from Egypt. Their story begins in Ex. 2:23 and continues through Leviticus and into the first 14 chapters of Numbers. This generation was numbered for the war of conquest in Canaan (1:1-46). However, when the people arrived at the southern edge of Canaan, they refused to enter the Land (14:1-10). Because of their rebellion against the Lord, all the adults 20 and over (except Caleb and Joshua) were sentenced to die in the wilderness (14:26-38). In chaps. 15–25, the first and second generations overlap; the first died out as the second grew to adulthood. A second numbering of the people commenced the history of this second generation (26:1-56). These Israelites did go to war (26:2) and inherited the land (26:52-56). The story of this second generation, beginning in Numbers 26:1, continues through the books of Deuteronomy and Joshua.

Three theological themes permeate Numbers. First, the Lord Himself communicated to Israel through Moses (1:1; 7:89; 12:6-8), so the words of Moses had divine authority. Israel's response to Moses mirrored her obedience or disobedience to the Lord. Numbers contains three distinct divisions based on Israel's response to the word of the Lord: obedience (chaps. 1–10), disobedience (chaps. 11–25), and renewed obedience (chaps. 26–36). The second theme is that the Lord is the God of judgment. Throughout Numbers, the "anger" of the Lord was aroused in response to Israel's sin (11:1,10,33; 12:9; 14:18; 25:3,4; 32:10,13,14). Third, the faithfulness of the Lord to keep His promise to give the seed of Abraham the land of Canaan is emphasized (15:2; 26:52-56; 27:12; 33:50-56; 34:1-29).

Interpretive Challenges

Four major interpretive challenges face the reader of Numbers. First, is the book of Numbers a separate book, or is it a part of a larger literary whole, the Pentateuch? The biblical books of Genesis, Exodus, Leviticus, Numbers, and Deuteronomy form the Torah. The remainder of the Scripture always views these 5 books as a unit. The ultimate meaning of Numbers cannot be divorced from its context in the Pentateuch. The first verse of the book speaks of the Lord, Moses, the tabernacle and the Exodus from Egypt. This assumes that the reader is familiar with the 3 books that precede Numbers. Still, every Hebrew manuscript available divides the Pentateuch in exactly the same way as the present text. In them the book of Numbers is a well defined unit, with a structural integrity of its own. The book has its own beginning, middle, and ending, even as it functions within a larger whole. Thus, the book of Numbers is also to be viewed with singular identity.

The second interpretive question asks, "Is there a sense of coherence in the book of Numbers?" It is readily evident that Numbers contains a wide variety of literary materials and forms. Census lists, genealogies, laws, historical narratives, poetry, prophecy, and travel lists are found in this book. Nevertheless, they are all blended to tell the story of Israel's journey from Mt. Sinai to the Plains of Moab. The coherence of Numbers is reflected in the outline that follows.

A third issue deals with the large numbers given for the tribes of Israel in 1:46 and 26:51. These two lists of Israel's men of war, taken 39 years apart, both put the number over 600,000. These numbers demand a total population for Israel in the wilderness of around 2.5 million at any one time. From a natural perspective, this total seems too high for the wilderness conditions to sustain. However, it must be recognized that the Lord supernaturally took care of Israel for 40 years (Deut. 8:1-5). Therefore, the large numbers must be accepted at face value (*see note on 1:46*).

The fourth interpretive challenge concerns the heathen prophet Balaam, whose story is recorded in 22:2–24:25. Even though Balaam claimed to know the Lord (22:18), Scripture consistently refers to him as a false prophet (2 Pet. 2:15,16, Jude 11). The Lord used Balaam as His mouthpiece to speak the true words He put in his mouth (*see notes on 22:2–24:25*).

Outline

- I. The Experience of the First Generation of Israel in the Wilderness (1:1–25:18)
  - A. The Obedience of Israel toward the Lord (1:1–10:36)
    1. The organization of Israel around the tabernacle of the Lord (1:1–6:27)
    2. The orientation of Israel toward the tabernacle of the Lord (7:1–10:36)
  - B. The Disobedience of Israel toward the Lord (11:1–25:18)
    1. The complaining of Israel on the journey (11:1–12:16)
    2. The rebellion of Israel and its leaders at Kadesh (13:1–20:29)
       - a. The rebellion of Israel and the consequences (13:1–19:22)
       - b. The rebellion of Moses and Aaron and the consequences (20:1-29)
    3. The renewed complaining of Israel on the journey (21:1–22:1)
    4. The blessing of Israel by Balaam (22:2–24:25)
    5. The final rebellion of Israel with Baal of Peor (25:1-18)
- II. The Experience of the Second Generation of Israel in the Plains of Moab: The Renewed Obedience of Israel toward the Lord (26:1–36:13)
  - A. The Preparations for the Conquest of the Land (26:1–32:42)
  - B. The Review of the Journey in the Wilderness (33:1-49)
  - C. The Anticipation of the Conquest of the Land (33:50–36:13)

The First Census of Israel

1 Now the LORD spoke to Moses [a]in the
Wilderness of Sinai, [b]in the tabernacle
of meeting, on the [c]first *day* of the second
month, in the second year after they had
come out of the land of Egypt, saying:
2 [d]"Take a census of all the congregation of
the children of Israel, by their families, by
their fathers' houses, according to the
number of names, every male [e]individu-
ally, 3 from [f]twenty years old and above—
all who *are able to* go to war in Israel. You
and Aaron shall number them by their
armies. 4 And with you there shall be a
man from every tribe, each one the head of
his father's house.
5 "These are the names of the men who
shall stand with you: from Reuben, Elizur
the son of Shedeur; 6 from Simeon, Shelumiel the son of Zurishaddai; 7 from Judah, Nahshon the son of Amminadab;
8 from Issachar, Nethanel the son of Zuar;
9 from Zebulun, Eliab the son of Helon;
10 from the sons of Joseph: from Ephraim,
Elishama the son of Ammihud; from Manasseh, Gamaliel the son of Pedahzur;
11 from Benjamin, Abidan the son of Gideoni; 12 from Dan, Ahiezer the son of Ammishaddai; 13 from Asher, Pagiel the son of
Ocran; 14 from Gad, Eliasaph the son of
[g]Deuel;[1] 15 from Naphtali, Ahira the son of
Enan." 16 [h]These *were* [i]chosen[2] from the
congregation, leaders of their fathers'
tribes, [j]heads of the divisions in Israel.
17 Then Moses and Aaron took these
men who had been [3]mentioned [k]by name,
18 and they assembled all the congregation
together on the first *day* of the second
month; and they recited their [l]ancestry by
families, by their fathers' houses, according to the number of names, from twenty
years old and above, each one individually. 19 As the LORD commanded Moses, so
he numbered them in the Wilderness of
Sinai.
20 Now the [m]children of Reuben, Israel's
oldest son, their genealogies by their families, by their fathers' house, according to
the number of names, every male individually, from twenty years old and above, all
who *were able to* go to war: 21 those who
were numbered of the tribe of Reuben *were*
forty-six thousand five hundred.
22 From the [n]children of Simeon, their
genealogies by their families, by their fathers' house, of those who were numbered,
according to the number of names, every
male individually, from twenty years old
and above, all who *were able to* go to war:
23 those who were numbered of the tribe of
Simeon *were* fifty-nine thousand three hundred.
24 From the [o]children of Gad, their genealogies by their families, by their fathers'

CHAPTER 1

1 [a] Ex. 19:1; Num. 10:11, 12 [b] Ex. 25:22 [c] Ex. 40:2, 17; Num. 9:1; 10:11
2 [d] Ex. 30:12; Num. 26:2, 63, 64; 2 Sam. 24:2; 1 Chr. 21:2 [e] Ex. 30:12, 13; 38:26
3 [f] Ex. 30:14; 38:26
14 [g] Num. 7:42 [1] *Reuel,* Num. 2:14
16 [h] Ex. 18:21; Num. 7:2; 1 Chr. 27:16-22 [i] Num. 16:2 [2] *called*
[j] Ex. 18:21, 25; Jer. 5:5; Mic. 3:1, 9; 5:2
17 [k] Is. 43:1 [3] *designated*
18 [l] Ezra 2:59; Heb. 7:3
20 [m] Num. 2:10, 11; 26:5-11; 32:6, 15, 21, 29
22 [n] Num. 2:12, 13; 26:12-14
24 [o] Gen. 30:11; Num. 26:15-18; Josh. 4:12; Jer. 49:1

1:1–10:36 The first 10 chapters of Numbers record the final preparations of Israel necessary for their conquest of the land of Canaan. In this section, the Lord spoke to Israel through Moses (1:1; 2:1; 3:1,5,11,14,44; 4:1,17,21; 5:1,5,11; 6:1,22; 7:4; 8:1,5,23; 9:1,9; 10:1), and Moses and Israel responded with obedience (1:19,54; 2:33,34; 3:16,42,51; 4:49; 7:2,3; 8:3; 9:5,18,23; 10:13,14-28 [in accordance with 2:34]). These chapters divide into two parts (1:1–6:27 and 7:1–10:36), which both end with an invocation of the Lord's blessing on Israel (6:22-27 and 10:35,36).

1:1–6:27 These 6 chapters chronologically follow the events recorded in 7:1–10:10. The ordering of Israel around the tabernacle (1:1–4:49) and the purity of the camp of Israel (5:1–6:27) were the final results of the Lord's commands that began in Ex. 25:1. Obeying God's instructions transformed an impure (Ex. 32:7,8) and disorderly (Ex. 32:25) Israel into a people ready to march into Canaan.

1:1 Now the LORD spoke to Moses. This connects the revelation given here by the Lord with Ex. 25:1ff. and Lev. 1:1ff. The Word from God directed everything that was done by Israel. **the Wilderness of Sinai.** Israel had been encamped there for 11 months. See Ex. 19:1. **the tabernacle of meeting.** The tabernacle, where the Lord's glory resided in the cloud, had been erected one month earlier (Ex. 40:17). This was God's dwelling place in the midst of his people. In Num. 1:1–6:27, Israel was organized with the tabernacle as the central feature. **the second year.** Numbers begins in the 14th month (377 days) after the Exodus from Egypt.

1:2 a census. In Ex. 30:11-16, the Lord had commanded that a census of the males in Israel over 20 (excluding the Levites) be taken for the purpose of determining the ransom money for the service of the tabernacle. The result of that census is recorded in Ex. 38:25-28. The total number, 603,550 (Ex. 38:26), equals the number in 1:46.

1:3 go to war. The purpose of this census was to form a roster of fighting men. The book of Numbers looks ahead to the invasion of the land promised to Abraham (cf. Gen. 12:1-3).

1:4 a man. One leader from each of the 12 tribes was to assist Moses and Aaron in the numbering of the men. These same leaders are mentioned in Num. 2:1-34 and 10:14-28 as the heads of tribes and in 7:1-88 they bring gifts to the tabernacle.

1:17-46 The numbers from the tribes were:

Reuben	46,500	(v. 21)
Simeon	59,300	(v. 23)
Gad	45,650	(v. 25)
Judah	74,600	(v. 27)
Issachar	54,400	(v. 29)
Zebulun	57,400	(v. 31)
Ephraim	40,500	(v. 33)
Manasseh	32,200	(v. 35)
Benjamin	35,400	(v. 37)
Dan	62,700	(v. 39)
Asher	41,500	(v. 41)
Naphtali	53,400	(v. 43)
Total	603,550	(v. 46)

The tribal order follows the pattern of Jacob's wives: first, the sons of Leah; second, the sons of Rachel; and third, the sons of the maids, except Gad (born of Leah's maid), who replaced Levi in the third-born position (cf. Gen. 29:31–30:24; 35:16-20).

house, according to the number of names, from twenty years old and above, all who *were able to* go to war: 25 those who were numbered of the tribe of Gad *were* forty-five thousand six hundred and fifty.

26 From the [p]children of Judah, their genealogies by their families, by their fathers' house, according to the number of names, from twenty years old and above, all who *were able to* go to war: 27 those who were numbered of the tribe of Judah *were* [q]seventy-four thousand six hundred.

28 From the [r]children of Issachar, their genealogies by their families, by their fathers' house, according to the number of names, from twenty years old and above, all who *were able to* go to war: 29 those who were numbered of the tribe of Issachar *were* fifty-four thousand four hundred.

30 From the [s]children of Zebulun, their genealogies by their families, by their fathers' house, according to the number of names, from twenty years old and above, all who *were able to* go to war: 31 those who were numbered of the tribe of Zebulun *were* fifty-seven thousand four hundred.

32 From the sons of Joseph, the [t]children of Ephraim, their genealogies by their families, by their fathers' house, according to the number of names, from twenty years old and above, all who *were able to* go to war: 33 those who were numbered of the tribe of Ephraim *were* forty thousand five hundred.

34 From the [u]children of Manasseh, their genealogies by their families, by their fathers' house, according to the number of names, from twenty years old and above, all who *were able to* go to war: 35 those who were numbered of the tribe of Manasseh *were* thirty-two thousand two hundred.

36 From the [v]children of Benjamin, their genealogies by their families, by their fathers' house, according to the number of names, from twenty years old and above, all who *were able to* go to war: 37 those who were numbered of the tribe of Benjamin *were* thirty-five thousand four hundred.

38 From the [w]children of Dan, their genealogies by their families, by their fathers' house, according to the number of names, from twenty years old and above, all who *were able to* go to war: 39 those who were numbered of the tribe of Dan *were* sixty-two thousand seven hundred.

40 From the [x]children of Asher, their genealogies by their families, by their fathers' house, according to the number of names, from twenty years old and above, all who *were able to* go to war: 41 those who were numbered of the tribe of Asher *were* forty-one thousand five hundred.

42 From the children of Naphtali, their genealogies by their families, by their fathers' house, according to the number of names, from twenty years old and above, all who *were able to* go to war: 43 those who were numbered of the tribe of Naphtali *were* fifty-three thousand four hundred.

44 [y]These are the ones who were numbered, whom Moses and Aaron numbered, with the leaders of Israel, twelve men, each one representing his father's house. 45 So all who were numbered of the children of Israel, by their fathers' houses, from twenty years old and above, all who *were able to* go to war in Israel— 46 all who were numbered were [z]six hundred and three thousand five hundred and fifty.

47 But [a]the Levites were not numbered among them by their fathers' tribe; 48 for the LORD had spoken to Moses, saying: 49 [b]"Only the tribe of Levi you shall not number, nor take a census of them among the children of Israel; 50 [c]but you shall appoint the Levites over the tabernacle of the Testimony, over all its furnishings, and over all things that belong to it; they shall carry the tabernacle and all its furnishings; they shall attend to it [d]and camp around the tabernacle. 51 [e]And when the tabernacle is to go forward, the Levites shall take it down; and when the tabernacle is to be set up, the Levites shall set it [f]up. [g]The outsider who comes near shall be put to death. 52 The children of Israel shall pitch their tents, [h]everyone by his own camp, everyone by his own standard, according to their armies; 53 [i]but the Levites shall camp around the tabernacle of the Testimony,

26 [p] Gen. 29:35; Num. 26:19-22; 2 Sam. 24:9; Ps. 78:68; Matt. 1:2
27 [q] 2 Chr. 17:14
28 [r] Num. 2:5, 6
30 [s] Num. 2:7, 8; 26:26, 27
32 [t] Gen. 48:1-22; Num. 26:28-37; Deut. 33:13-17; Jer. 7:15; Obad. 19
34 [u] Num. 2:20, 21; 26:28-34
36 [v] Gen. 49:27; Num. 26:38-41; 2 Chr. 17:17; Rev. 7:8
38 [w] Gen. 30:6; 46:23; Num. 2:25, 26; 26:42, 43
40 [x] Num. 2:27, 28; 26:44-47
44 [y] Num. 26:64
46 [z] Ex. 12:37; 38:26; Num. 2:32; 26:51, 63; Heb. 11:12; Rev. 7:4-8
47 [a] Num. 2:33; 3:14-22; 26:57-62; 1 Chr. 6:1-47; 21:6
49 [b] Num. 2:33; 26:62
50 [c] Ex. 38:21; Num. 3:7, 8; 4:15, 25-27, 33 [d] Num. 3:23, 29, 35, 38
51 [e] Num. 4:5-15; 10:17, 21 [f] Num. 10:21 [g] Num. 3:10, 38; 4:15, 19, 20; 18:22
52 [h] Num. 2:2, 34; 24:2
53 [i] Num. 1:50

1:46 six hundred and three thousand five hundred and fifty. This number, combined with the 22,000 Levite males a month old and above (3:39), allows for a total population of over 2,000,000 Israelites. Since this number seems too high for the wilderness conditions and relatively few firstborn sons (3:43), some have reinterpreted the plain meaning of the text by 1) saying "thousand" means "clan" or "chief" here, or 2) stating the numbers are symbolic. However, if "thousand" is not the meaning in this chapter, 1:46 would read 598 "clans" or "chiefs" with only 5,500 individuals. Thus, the meaning "thousand" must be retained. Further, there is no textual indication that these numbers are symbolic. The only conclusion is that God took care of over 2,000,000 people in the wilderness during the period of 40 years (cf. Deut. 8:3,4). Tampering with the number is tampering with God's purpose for these numbers—to show His power in behalf of Israel.

1:50 appoint the Levites. The tribe of Levi, including Moses and Aaron, was not included in this census because it was exempt from military service. The Levites were to serve the Lord by carrying and attending to the tabernacle (cf. 3:5-13; 4:1-33,46-49).

1:51 The outsider. This word often refers to the "alien" or "stranger." The non-Levite Israelite was like a "foreigner" to the transporting of the tabernacle and had to keep his distance lest he die.

that there may be no [j]wrath on the congregation of the children of Israel; and the
Levites shall [k]keep[4] charge of the tabernacle of the Testimony."
54 Thus the children of Israel did; according to all that the LORD commanded
Moses, so they did.

The Tribes and Leaders by Armies

2 And the LORD spoke to Moses and
Aaron, saying: 2 [a]"Everyone of the
children of Israel shall camp by his own
[1]standard, beside the emblems of his father's house; they shall camp [b]some distance from the tabernacle of meeting. 3 On
the [c]east side, toward the rising of the sun,
those of the standard of the forces with Judah shall camp according to their armies;
and [d]Nahshon the son of Amminadab *shall*
be the leader of the children of Judah."
4 And his army was numbered at seventy-
four thousand six hundred.
5 "Those who camp next to him *shall be*
the tribe of Issachar, and Nethanel the son
of Zuar *shall be* the leader of the children of
Issachar." 6 And his army was numbered
at fifty-four thousand four hundred.
7 "Then *comes* the tribe of Zebulun, and
Eliab the son of Helon *shall be* the leader of
the children of Zebulun." 8 And his army
was numbered at fifty-seven thousand
four hundred. 9 "All who were numbered
according to their armies of the forces with
Judah, one hundred and eighty-six thousand four hundred—[e]these shall [2]break
camp first.
10 "On the [f]south side *shall be* the standard of the forces with Reuben according
to their armies, and the leader of the children of Reuben *shall be* Elizur the son of
Shedeur." 11 And his army was numbered
at forty-six thousand five hundred.
12 "Those who camp next to him *shall be*
the tribe of Simeon, and the leader of the
children of Simeon *shall be* Shelumiel the son
of Zurishaddai." 13 And his army was numbered at fifty-nine thousand three hundred.
14 "Then *comes* the tribe of Gad, and the
leader of the children of Gad *shall be* Eliasaph the son of [3]Reuel." 15 And his army

53 [j] Lev. 10:6; Num. 8:19; 16:46; 18:5; 1 Sam. 6:19 [k] Num. 8:24; 18:2-4; 1 Chr. 23:32 [4] *have in their care*

CHAPTER 2

2 [a] Num. 1:52; 24:2 [b] Josh. 3:4 [1] *banner*
3 [c] Num. 10:5 [d] Num. 1:7; 7:12; 10:14; Ruth 4:20; 1 Chr. 2:10; Matt. 1:4; Luke 3:32, 33
9 [e] Num. 10:14 [2] Lit. *set forth*
10 [f] Num. 10:6
14 [3] *Deuel,* Num. 1:14; 7:42

1:53 no wrath. The purpose of setting the Levites apart and arranging them around the tabernacle was to keep the wrath of the Lord from consuming Israel (cf. Ex. 32:10,25-29).

2:2 standard...emblems. The emblems were flags identifying the individual tribes (probably with some sort of insignia). The standards were flags marking each of the 4 encampments of 3 tribes each. **tabernacle of meeting.** For details see Ex. 25–30.

2:3 On the east side...Judah. Judah occupied the place of honor to the E. Genesis 49:8-12 highlights the role and centrality Judah would have in the defeat of Israel's enemies. Judah was the tribe through which the Messiah would be born. **Nahshon.** Nahshon appears in the later genealogies of the messianic line (cf. Ruth 4:20; Matt. 1:4).

2:14 Reuel. See marginal note. The letters R and D are similar in Heb. and were easily confused by the scribes who copied the text.

The Placement of Israel's Tribes

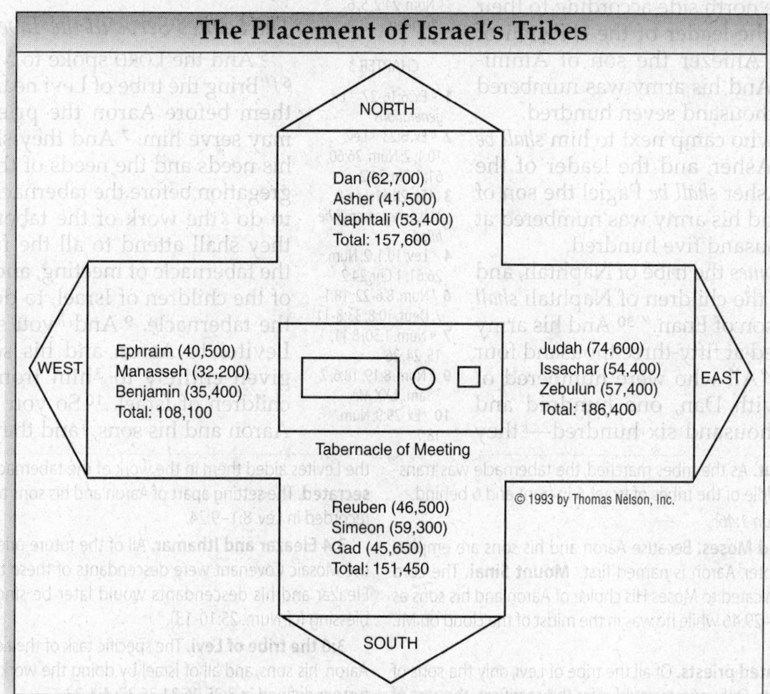

was numbered at forty-five thousand six
hundred and fifty. 16 "All who were numbered according to their armies of the
forces with Reuben, one hundred and
fifty-one thousand four hundred and
fifty—[g]they shall [4]be the second to break
camp.
17 [h]"And the tabernacle of meeting shall
move out with the [5]camp of the Levites [i]in
the middle of the [6]camps; as they camp, so
they shall move out, everyone in his place,
by their [7]standards.
18 "On the west side *shall be* the standard
of the forces with Ephraim according to
their armies, and the leader of the children
of Ephraim *shall be* Elishama the son of
Ammihud." 19 And his army was numbered at forty thousand five hundred.
20 "Next to him *comes* the tribe of Manasseh, and the leader of the children of
Manasseh *shall be* Gamaliel the son of Pedahzur." 21 And his army was numbered
at thirty-two thousand two hundred.
22 "Then *comes* the tribe of Benjamin,
and the leader of the children of Benjamin
shall be Abidan the son of Gideoni." 23 And
his army was numbered at thirty-five
thousand four hundred. 24 "All who were
numbered according to their armies of the
forces with Ephraim, one hundred and
eight thousand one hundred—[j]they shall
[8]be the third to break camp.
25 "The [9]standard of the forces with Dan
shall be on the north side according to their
armies, and the leader of the children of
Dan *shall be* Ahiezer the son of Ammishaddai." 26 And his army was numbered
at sixty-two thousand seven hundred.
27 "Those who camp next to him *shall be*
the tribe of Asher, and the leader of the
children of Asher *shall be* Pagiel the son of
Ocran." 28 And his army was numbered at
forty-one thousand five hundred.
29 "Then *comes* the tribe of Naphtali, and
the leader of the children of Naphtali *shall
be* Ahira the son of Enan." 30 And his army
was numbered at fifty-three thousand four
hundred. 31 "All who were numbered of
the forces with Dan, one hundred and
fifty-seven thousand six hundred—[k]they
shall [1]break camp last, with their [2]stan-
dards."
32 These *are* the ones who were numbered of the children of Israel by their fathers' houses. [l]All who were numbered
according to their armies of the forces
were six hundred and three thousand five
hundred and fifty. 33 But [m]the Levites
were not numbered among the children
of Israel, just as the LORD commanded
Moses.
34 Thus the children of Israel [n]did according to all that the LORD commanded
Moses; [o]so they camped by their [3]stan-
dards and so they broke camp, each one
by his family, according to their fathers'
houses.

The Sons of Aaron

3 Now these *are* the [a]records[1] of Aaron
and Moses when the LORD spoke with
Moses on Mount Sinai. 2 And these *are* the
names of the sons of Aaron: Nadab, the
[b]firstborn, and [c]Abihu, Eleazar, and Ithamar. 3 These *are* the names of the sons of
Aaron, [d]the anointed priests, [2]whom he
consecrated to minister as priests.
4 [e]Nadab and Abihu had died before the
LORD when they offered profane fire before
the LORD in the Wilderness of Sinai; and
they had no children. So Eleazar and Ithamar ministered as priests in the presence of
Aaron their father.

The Levites Serve in the Tabernacle

5 And the LORD spoke to Moses, saying:
6 [f]"Bring the tribe of Levi near, and present
them before Aaron the priest, that they
may serve him. 7 And they shall attend to
his needs and the needs of the whole congregation before the tabernacle of meeting,
to do [g]the work of the tabernacle. 8 Also
they shall attend to all the furnishings of
the tabernacle of meeting, and to the needs
of the children of Israel, to do the work of
the tabernacle. 9 And [h]you shall give the
Levites to Aaron and his sons; they *are*
given entirely to [3]him from among the
children of Israel. 10 So you shall appoint
Aaron and his sons, [i]and they shall attend

16 [g]Num. 10:18 [4]Lit. *set forth second*
17 [h]Num. 10:17, 21 [i]Num. 1:53 [5]*company* [6]*whole company* [7]*banners*
24 [j]Num. 10:22 [8]Lit. *set forth third*
25 [9]*banner*
31 [k]Num. 10:25 [1]Lit. *set forth last* [2]*banners*
32 [l]Ex. 38:26; Num. 1:46; 11:21
33 [m]Num. 1:47; 26:57-62
34 [n]Num. 1:54 [o]Num. 24:2, 5, 6 [3]*banners*

CHAPTER 3

1 [a]Ex. 6:16-27 [1]Lit. *generations*
2 [b]Ex. 6:23 [c]Lev. 10:1, 2; Num. 26:60, 61; 1 Chr. 24:2
3 [d]Ex. 28:41; Lev. 8 [2]Lit. *whose hands he filled*
4 [e]Lev. 10:1, 2; Num. 26:61; 1 Chr. 24:2
6 [f]Num. 8:6-22; 18:1-7; Deut. 10:8; 33:8-11
7 [g]Num. 1:50; 8:11, 15, 24, 26
9 [h]Num. 8:19; 18:6, 7 [3]Sam., LXX *Me*
10 [i]Ex. 29:9; Num. 18:7

2:17 move out. As the tribes marched, the tabernacle was transported in the middle of the tribes of Israel, 6 in front and 6 behind.

2:32 *See note on 1:46.*

3:1 Aaron and Moses. Because Aaron and his sons are emphasized in this chapter, Aaron is named first. **Mount Sinai.** The Lord had first communicated to Moses His choice of Aaron and his sons as priests in Ex. 28:1–29:46 while he was in the midst of the cloud on Mt. Sinai (Ex. 24:18).

3:3 the anointed priests. Of all the tribe of Levi, only the sons of Aaron were priests. Only priests could offer the sacrifices; the rest of the Levites aided them in the work of the tabernacle (cf. 3:7-9). **consecrated.** The setting apart of Aaron and his sons to the priesthood is recorded in Lev. 8:1–9:24.

3:4 Eleazar and Ithamar. All of the future priests of Israel under the Mosaic Covenant were descendants of these two sons of Aaron. Eleazar and his descendants would later be singled out for great blessing (cf. Num. 25:10-13).

3:6 the tribe of Levi. The specific task of the Levites was to serve Aaron, his sons, and all of Israel by doing the work of the tabernacle, further defined in 3:25,26,31,36,37; 4:4-33.

to their priesthood; [j]but the outsider who
comes near shall be put to death."
11 Then the LORD spoke to Moses, saying: 12 "Now behold, [k]I Myself have taken
the Levites from among the children of Israel instead of every firstborn who opens
the womb among the children of Israel.
Therefore the Levites shall be [l]Mine, 13 because [m]all the firstborn *are* Mine. [n]On the
day that I struck all the firstborn in the
land of Egypt, I sanctified to Myself all the
firstborn in Israel, both man and beast.
They shall be Mine: I *am* the LORD."

Census of the Levites Commanded

14 Then the LORD spoke to Moses in the
Wilderness of Sinai, saying: 15 "Number
the children of Levi by their fathers' houses, by their families; you shall number
[o]every male from a month old and above."
16 So Moses numbered them according
to the [4]word of the LORD, as he was commanded. 17 [p]These were the sons of Levi
by their names: Gershon, Kohath, and Merari. 18 And these *are* the names of the sons
of [q]Gershon by their families: [r]Libni and
Shimei. 19 And the sons of [s]Kohath by
their families: [t]Amram, Izehar, Hebron,
and Uzziel. 20 [u]And the sons of Merari by
their families: Mahli and Mushi. These *are*
the families of the Levites by their fathers'
houses.
21 From Gershon *came* the family of the
Libnites and the family of the Shimites;
these *were* the families of the Gershonites.
22 Those who were numbered, according
to the number of all the males from a
month old and above—of those who were
numbered *there were* seven thousand five
hundred. 23 [v]The families of the Gershonites were to camp behind the tabernacle
westward. 24 And the leader of the father's
house of the Gershonites *was* Eliasaph the
son of Lael. 25 [w]The duties of the children
of Gershon in the tabernacle of meeting *included* [x]the tabernacle, [y]the tent with [z]its
covering, [a]the screen for the door of the
tabernacle of meeting, 26 [b]the screen for the
door of the court, [c]the hangings of the
court which *are* around the tabernacle and
the altar, and [d]their cords, according to all
the work relating to them.
27 [e]From Kohath *came* the family of the
Amramites, the family of the Izharites, the
family of the Hebronites, and the family of
the Uzzielites; these *were* the families of the
Kohathites. 28 According to the number of
all the males, from a month old and above,
there were eight thousand [5]six hundred
[6]keeping charge of the sanctuary. 29 [f]The
families of the children of Kohath were to
camp on the south side of the tabernacle.
30 And the leader of the fathers' house of
the families of the Kohathites *was* Elizaphan the son of [g]Uzziel. 31 [h]Their duty
included [i]the ark, [j]the table, [k]the lampstand, [l]the altars, the utensils of the sanctuary with which they ministered, [m]the
screen, and all the work relating to them.
32 And Eleazar the son of Aaron the
priest *was to be* chief over the leaders of the
Levites, *with* oversight of those who kept
charge of the sanctuary.
33 From Merari *came* the family of the
Mahlites and the family of the Mushites;
these *were* the families of Merari. 34 And
those who were numbered, according to
the number of all the males from a month
old and above, *were* six thousand two hundred. 35 The leader of the fathers' house of
the families of Merari *was* Zuriel the son of
Abihail. [n]These *were* to camp on the north
side of the tabernacle. 36 And [o]the appointed duty of the children of Merari *included*
the boards of the tabernacle, its bars, its
pillars, its sockets, its utensils, all the work
relating to them, 37 and the pillars of the
court all around, with their sockets, their
pegs, and their cords.
38 [p]Moreover those who were to camp
before the tabernacle on the east, before the
tabernacle of meeting, *were* Moses, Aaron,
and his sons, [q]keeping charge of the sanctuary, [r]to meet the needs of the children of

10 [j]Num. 1:51; 3:38; 16:40
12 [k]Num. 3:41; 8:16; 18:6 [l]Ex. 13:2; Num. 3:45; 8:14
13 [m]Ex. 13:2; Lev. 27:26; Num. 8:16, 17; Neh. 10:36; Luke 2:23 [n]Ex. 13:12, 15; Num. 8:17
15 [o]Num. 3:39; 26:62
16 [4]Lit. *mouth*
17 [p]Gen. 46:11; Ex. 6:16-22; Num. 26:57; 1 Chr. 6:1, 16; 23:6
18 [q]Num. 4:38-41 [r]Ex. 6:17
19 [s]Num. 4:34-37 [t]Ex. 6:18
20 [u]Ex. 6:19; Num. 4:42-45
23 [v]Num. 1:53
25 [w]Num. 4:24-26 [x]Ex. 25:9 [y]Ex. 26:1 [z]Ex. 26:7, 14 [a]Ex. 26:36
26 [b]Ex. 27:9, 12, 14, 15 [c]Ex. 27:16 [d]Ex. 35:18
27 [e]1 Chr. 26:23
28 [5]Some LXX mss. *three* [6]*taking care of*
29 [f]Ex. 6:18; Num. 1:53
30 [g]Lev. 10:4
31 [h]Num. 4:15 [i]Ex. 25:10 [j]Ex. 25:23 [k]Ex. 25:31 [l]Ex. 27:1; 30:1 [m]Ex. 26:31-33
35 [n]Num. 1:53; 2:25
36 [o]Num. 4:31, 32
38 [p]Num. 1:53 [q]Num. 18:5 [r]Num. 3:7, 8

3:10 the outsider. Laymen or strangers (cf. 1:51) would die if they participated in priestly activities (cf. 3:38; 16:40).

3:12 firstborn. At the Exodus, the Lord claimed for Himself the firstborn of Israel's males (cf. Ex. 13:1,2). The firstborn was to act as the family priest. But when the full ministry of the Mosaic economy came in, God transferred the priestly duties to the Levites, perhaps partly because of their holy zeal in the golden calf incident (cf. Ex. 32:29). The Levites substituted for the firstborn.

3:15 Number. Moses took a census of every Levite male who was at least one month old. This included Moses and Aaron and their sons, because they descended from Amram (3:19; cf. Ex. 6:20).

3:21-26 Gershon. The Gershonites numbered 7,500 males and were responsible for the coverings of the tabernacle. They were to camp W of the tabernacle.

3:27-32 Kohath. The Kohathites probably numbered 8,300 males. (See the marginal note on 3:28; the addition of one Hebrew letter changes the "six" to a "three." This letter was dropped very early in the copying of the text.) They were responsible for the holy objects of the tabernacle (including transporting the ark) and were to camp S of the tabernacle.

3:33-37 Merari. The Merarites numbered 6,200 males and were responsible for the wooden framework of the tabernacle. They were to camp N of the tabernacle.

3:38 Moses, Aaron. Moses and Aaron and his sons were given the place of honor on the east of the tabernacle and gave overall supervision to the Levites. Eleazar oversaw the Kohathites (3:32), and Ithamar oversaw the Gershonites and Merarites (4:28,33).

Israel; but [s]the outsider who came near
was to be put to death. 39 [t]All who were
numbered of the Levites, whom Moses
and Aaron numbered at the commandment of the LORD, by their families, all the
males from a month old and above, *were*
twenty-two thousand.

Levites Dedicated Instead of the Firstborn

40 Then the LORD said to Moses: [u]"Number[7] all the firstborn males of the children
of Israel from a month old and above, and
take the number of their names. 41 [v]And
you shall take the Levites for Me—I *am* the
LORD—instead of all the firstborn among
the children of Israel, and the livestock of
the Levites instead of all the firstborn
among the livestock of the children of Israel." 42 So Moses numbered all the firstborn among the children of Israel, as the
LORD commanded him. 43 And all the firstborn males, according to the number of
names from a month old and above, of
those who were numbered of them, were
twenty-two thousand two hundred and
seventy-three.

44 Then the LORD spoke to Moses, saying: 45 [w]"Take the Levites instead of all the
firstborn among the children of Israel, and
the livestock of the Levites instead of their
livestock. The Levites shall be Mine: I *am*
the LORD. 46 And for [x]the redemption of
the two hundred and seventy-three of the
firstborn of the children of Israel, [y]who are
more than the number of the Levites,
47 you shall take [z]five shekels for each one
[a]individually; you shall take *them* in the
currency of the shekel of the sanctuary,
[b]the shekel of twenty gerahs. 48 And you
shall give the money, with which the excess number of them is redeemed, to
Aaron and his sons."

49 So Moses took the redemption money
from those who were over and above those
who were redeemed by the Levites.
50 From the firstborn of the children of Israel he took the money, [c]one thousand
three hundred and sixty-five *shekels*, according to the shekel of the sanctuary.
51 And Moses [d]gave their redemption
money to Aaron and his sons, according to
the word of the LORD, as the LORD commanded Moses.

Duties of the Sons of Kohath

4 Then the LORD spoke to Moses and
Aaron, saying: 2 "Take a census of the
sons of [a]Kohath from among the children
of Levi, by their families, by their fathers'
house, 3 [b]from thirty years old and above,
even to fifty years old, all who enter the
service to do the work in the tabernacle of
meeting.

4 [c]"This *is* the service of the sons of Kohath in the tabernacle of meeting, *relating
to* [d]the most holy things: 5 When the camp
prepares to journey, Aaron and his sons
shall come, and they shall take down [e]the
covering veil and cover the [f]ark of the Testimony with it. 6 Then they shall put on it a
covering of badger skins, and spread over
that a cloth entirely of [g]blue; and they shall
insert [h]its poles.

7 "On the [i]table of showbread they shall
spread a blue cloth, and put on it the dishes, the pans, the bowls, and the [1]pitchers
for pouring; and the [j]showbread[2] shall be
on it. 8 They shall spread over them a scarlet cloth, and cover the same with a covering of badger skins; and they shall insert
its poles. 9 And they shall take a blue cloth
and cover the [k]lampstand of the light,
[l]with its lamps, its wick-trimmers, its
trays, and all its oil vessels, with which
they service it. 10 Then they shall put it
with all its utensils in a covering of badger
skins, and put *it* on a carrying beam.

11 "Over [m]the golden altar they shall
spread a blue cloth, and cover it with a
covering of badger skins; and they shall insert its poles. 12 Then they shall take all the
[n]utensils of service with which they minister in the sanctuary, put *them* in a blue
cloth, cover them with a covering of badger skins, and put *them* on a carrying
beam. 13 Also they shall take away the
ashes from the altar, and spread a purple
cloth over it. 14 They shall put on it all its
implements with which they minister
there—the firepans, the forks, the shovels,
the [3]basins, and all the utensils of the
altar—and they shall spread on it a covering of badger skins, and insert its poles.
15 And when Aaron and his sons have finished covering the sanctuary and all the
furnishings of the sanctuary, when the

38 [s] Num. 3:10
39 [t] Num. 3:43; 4:48; 26:62
40 [u] Num. 3:15 [7] *Take a census of*
41 [v] Num. 3:12, 45
45 [w] Num. 3:12, 41
46 [x] Ex. 13:13, 15; Num. 18:15, 16 [y] Num. 3:39, 43
47 [z] Lev. 27:6; Num. 18:16 [a] Num. 1:2, 18, 20 [b] Ex. 30:13
50 [c] Num. 3:46, 47
51 [d] Num. 3:48

CHAPTER 4
2 [a] Num. 3:27-32
3 [b] Num. 4:23, 30, 35; 8:24; 1 Chr. 23:3, 24, 27; Ezra 3:8
4 [c] Num. 4:15 [d] Num. 4:19
5 [e] Ex. 26:31; Heb. 9:3 [f] Ex. 25:10, 16
6 [g] Ex. 39:1 [h] Ex. 25:13; 1 Kin. 8:7, 8
7 [i] Ex. 25:23, 29, 30 [j] Lev. 24:5-9 [1] *jars for the drink offering* [2] Lit. *continual bread*
9 [k] Ex. 25:31 [l] Ex. 25:37, 38
11 [m] Ex. 30:1-5
12 [n] Ex. 25:9; 1 Chr. 9:29
14 [3] *bowls*

3:43 twenty-two thousand two hundred and seventy-three. This was the total number of Gershonite, Kohathite, and Merarite males born in the 12½ months since the Exodus. The Levites took the place of the first 22,000 firstborns and the rest (273) were redeemed with 1,365 silver shekels (about 170 lbs.).

4:1-49 For a discussion of the tabernacle and contents, *see notes on Ex. 25–30.*

4:3 thirty...to fifty. This second census of the Levites determined those who would carry the tabernacle on the coming journey to Canaan. Only those between the ages of 30 and 50 were called by the Lord for this task (*see note on 8:24*).

4:4-16 Kohath. The Kohathites carried the furnishings of the tabernacle only after they had been covered by Aaron and his sons. If the Kohathites touched (4:15) or saw (4:20) any of the holy things, they would die.

camp is set to go, then [o]the sons of Kohath
shall come to carry *them;* [p]but they shall
not touch any holy thing, lest they die.
[q]"These *are* the things in the tabernacle
of meeting which the sons of Kohath are to
carry.
16 "The appointed duty of Eleazar the
son of Aaron the priest *is* [r]the oil for the
light, the [s]sweet incense, [t]the daily grain
offering, the [u]anointing oil, the oversight
of all the tabernacle, of all that *is* in it, with
the sanctuary and its furnishings."
17 Then the LORD spoke to Moses and
Aaron, saying: 18 "Do not cut off the tribe
of the families of the Kohathites from
among the Levites; 19 but do this in regard
to them, that they may live and not die
when they approach [v]the most holy things:
Aaron and his sons shall go in and [4]ap-
point each of them to his service and his
task. 20 [w]But they shall not go in to watch
while the holy things are being covered,
lest they die."

Duties of the Sons of Gershon

21 Then the LORD spoke to Moses, saying:
22 "Also take a census of the sons of [x]Ger-
shon, by their fathers' house, by their families. 23 [y]From thirty years old and above,
even to fifty years old, you shall number
them, all who enter to perform the service,
to do the work in the tabernacle of meeting.
24 This *is* the [z]service of the families of the
Gershonites, in serving and carrying:
25 [a]They shall carry the [b]curtains of the
tabernacle and the tabernacle of meeting
with its covering, the covering of [c]badger
skins that *is* on it, the screen for the door of
the tabernacle of meeting, 26 the screen for
the door of the gate of the court, the hangings of the court which *are* around the
tabernacle and altar, and their cords, all the
furnishings for their service and all that is
made for these things: so shall they serve.
27 "Aaron and his sons shall [5]assign all
the service of the sons of the Gershonites,
all their tasks and all their service. And
you shall [6]appoint to them all their tasks as
their duty. 28 This *is* the service of the families of the sons of Gershon in the tabernacle of meeting. And their duties *shall be*
[d]under the [7]authority of Ithamar the son of
Aaron the priest.

Duties of the Sons of Merari

29 "*As for* the sons of [e]Merari, you shall
number them by their families and by their
fathers' house. 30 [f]From thirty years old
and above, even to fifty years old, you
shall number them, everyone who enters
the service to do the work of the tabernacle
of meeting. 31 And [g]this *is* [h]what they must
carry as all their service for the tabernacle
of meeting: [i]the boards of the tabernacle,
its bars, its pillars, its sockets, 32 and the
pillars around the court with their sockets,
pegs, and cords, with all their furnishings
and all their service; and you shall [j]assign
to each man by name the items he must
carry. 33 This *is* the service of the families of
the sons of Merari, as all their service for
the tabernacle of meeting, under the [8]au-
thority of Ithamar the son of Aaron the
priest."

Census of the Levites

34 [k]And Moses, Aaron, and the leaders
of the congregation numbered the sons of
the Kohathites by their families and by
their fathers' house, 35 from thirty [l]years
old and above, even to fifty years old,
everyone who entered the service for work
in the tabernacle of meeting; 36 and those
who were numbered by their families were
two thousand seven hundred and fifty.
37 These *were* the ones who were numbered of the families of the Kohathites, all
who might serve in the tabernacle of meeting, whom Moses and Aaron numbered
according to the commandment of the
LORD by the hand of Moses.
38 And those who were numbered of the
sons of Gershon, by their families and by
their fathers' house, 39 from thirty years
old and above, even to fifty years old,
everyone who entered the service for work
in the tabernacle of meeting— 40 those
who were numbered by their families, by
their fathers' house, were two thousand six
hundred and thirty. 41 [m]These *are* the ones
who were numbered of the families of the
sons of Gershon, of all who might serve in
the tabernacle of meeting, whom Moses
and Aaron numbered according to the
commandment of the LORD.
42 Those of the families of the sons of
Merari who were numbered, by their families, by their fathers' [9]house, 43 from thirty years old and above, even to fifty years
old, everyone who entered the service for
work in the tabernacle of meeting—
44 those who were numbered by their families were three thousand two hundred.
45 These *are* the ones who were numbered

15 [o] Num. 7:9; 10:21; Deut. 31:9; Josh. 4:10; 2 Sam. 6:13; 1 Chr. 15:2, 15 [p] 2 Sam. 6:6, 7; 1 Chr. 13:9, 10 [q] Num. 3:31
16 [r] Ex. 25:6; Lev. 24:2 [s] Ex. 30:34 [t] Ex. 29:38 [u] Ex. 30:23-25
19 [v] Num. 4:4 [4] *assign*
20 [w] Ex. 19:21; 1 Sam. 6:19
22 [x] Num. 3:22
23 [y] Num. 4:3; 1 Chr. 23:3, 24, 27
24 [z] Num. 7:7
25 [a] Num. 3:25, 26 [b] Ex. 36:8 [c] Ex. 26:14
27 [5] *command* [6] *assign*
28 [d] Num. 4:33 [7] Lit. *hand*
29 [e] Num. 3:33-37
30 [f] Num. 4:3; 8:24-26
31 [g] Num. 3:36, 37 [h] Num. 7:8 [i] Ex. 26:15
32 [j] Ex. 25:9; 38:21
33 [8] Lit. *hand*
34 [k] Num. 4:2
35 [l] Num. 4:47
41 [m] Num. 4:22
42 [9] *household*

4:21-28 Gershon. *See note on 3:21-26.*

4:29-33 Merari. *See note on 3:33-37.*

4:34-49 numbered. The Kohathites totaled 2,750 (4:36), the Gershonites 2,630 (4:40), the Merarites 3,200 (4:44). All the Levites from 30-50 years old in service added up to 8,580 (4:48).

of the families of the sons of Merari,
whom Moses and Aaron numbered [n]ac-
cording to the word of the LORD by the
hand of Moses.
46 All who were [o]numbered of the
Levites, whom Moses, Aaron, and the
leaders of Israel numbered, by their families and by their fathers' houses, 47 [p]from
thirty years old and above, even to fifty
years old, everyone who came to do the
work of service and the work of bearing
burdens in the tabernacle of meeting—
48 those who were numbered were eight
thousand five hundred and eighty.
49 According to the commandment of
the LORD they were numbered by the hand
of Moses, [q]each according to his service
and according to his task; thus were they
numbered by him, [r]as the LORD commanded Moses.

Ceremonially Unclean Persons Isolated

5 And the LORD spoke to Moses, saying:
2 "Command the children of Israel that
they put out of the camp every [a]leper,
everyone who has a [b]discharge, and whoever becomes [c]defiled [1]by a corpse. 3 You
shall put out both male and female; you
shall put them outside the camp, that they
may not defile their camps [d]in the midst of
which I dwell." 4 And the children of Israel
did so, and put them outside the camp; as
the LORD spoke to Moses, so the children of
Israel did.

Confession and Restitution

5 Then the LORD spoke to Moses, saying,
6 "Speak to the children of Israel: [e]'When a
man or woman commits any sin that men
commit in unfaithfulness against the LORD,
and that person is guilty, 7 [f]then he shall
confess the sin which he has committed.

45 [n]Num. 4:29
46 [o]Num. 3:39; 26:57-62; 1 Chr. 23:3-23
47 [p]Num. 4:3, 23, 30
49 [q]Num. 4:15, 24, 31 [r]Num. 4:1, 21

CHAPTER 5

2 [a]Lev. 13:3, 8, 46; Num. 12:10, 14, 15 [b]Lev. 15:2 [c]Lev. 21:1; Num. 9:6, 10; 19:11, 13; 31:19 [1]*by contact with*
3 [d]Lev. 26:11, 12; Num. 35:34; [2 Cor. 6:16]
6 [e]Lev. 5:14–6:7
7 [f]Lev. 5:5; 26:40, 41; Josh. 7:19; Ps. 32:5; 1 John 1:9
[g]Lev. 6:4, 5
8 [h]Lev. 5:15; 6:6, 7; 7:7 [2]*redeemer,* Heb. *goel*
9 [i]Ex. 29:28; Lev. 6:17, 18, 26; 7:6-14 [j]Lev. 7:32-34; 10:14, 15 [3]*heave offering*
10 [k]Lev. 10:13 [4]*consecrated*
13 [l]Lev. 18:20; 20:10 [m]John 8:4
14 [n]Prov. 6:34; Song 8:6
15 [o]Lev. 5:11 [p]1 Kin. 17:18; Ezek. 29:16; Heb. 10:3

He shall make restitution for his trespass
[g]in full, plus one-fifth of it, and give *it* to
the one he has wronged. 8 But if the man
has no [2]relative to whom restitution may
be made for the wrong, the restitution for
the wrong *must go* to the LORD for the
priest, in addition to [h]the ram of the atonement with which atonement is made for
him. 9 Every [i]offering[3] of all the holy
things of the children of Israel, which they
bring to the priest, shall be [j]his. 10 And
every man's [4]holy things shall be his;
whatever any man gives the priest shall be
[k]his.' "

Concerning Unfaithful Wives

11 And the LORD spoke to Moses, saying,
12 "Speak to the children of Israel, and say
to them: 'If any man's wife goes astray and
behaves unfaithfully toward him, 13 and a
man [l]lies with her carnally, and it is hidden
from the eyes of her husband, and it is concealed that she has defiled herself, and
there was no witness against her, nor was
she [m]caught— 14 if the spirit of jealousy
comes upon him and he becomes [n]jealous
of his wife, who has defiled herself; or if
the spirit of jealousy comes upon him and
he becomes jealous of his wife, although
she has not defiled herself— 15 then the
man shall bring his wife to the priest. He
shall [o]bring the offering required for her,
one-tenth of an ephah of barley meal; he
shall pour no oil on it and put no frankincense on it, because it *is* a grain offering of
jealousy, an offering for remembering, for
[p]bringing iniquity to remembrance.
16 'And the priest shall bring her near,
and set her before the LORD. 17 The priest
shall take holy water in an earthen vessel,
and take some of the dust that is on the
floor of the tabernacle and put *it* into the

5:1-4 These verses deal with outward, visible defects.

5:2 leper. One having an infectious skin disease (cf. Lev. 13:1–14:57). **discharge.** A bodily emission indicative of disease, primarily from the sex organs (cf. Lev. 15:1-33).

5:2 corpse. Physical contact with a dead body (cf. Lev. 21:11). All of these prohibitions had sensible health benefits as well as serving to illustrate the need for moral cleanliness when approaching God.

5:3 outside the camp…in the midst of which I dwell. God's holy presence in the cloud in the tabernacle demanded cleanness. Therefore, all the unclean were barred from the encampment of Israel.

5:5-10 These verses deal with personal sins, which are not as outwardly visible as the uncleanness of 5:1-4.

5:6 against the LORD. A sin committed against God's people was considered a sin committed against God Himself. There was a need for confession and restitution in addition to the trespass offering (cf. Lev. 5:14–6:7).

5:8 no relative. A supplement to Lev. 6:1-7. If the injured party had died and there was no family member to receive the restitution called for in v. 7, it was to go to the priest as the Lord's representative.

5:11-31 These verses deal with the most intimate of human relationships and the most secret of sins. Adultery was to be determined and dealt with to maintain the purity of the camp. To accomplish that purity, God called for a very elaborate and public trial. If adultery was proven, it was punished with death, and this ceremony made guilt or innocence very apparent. It was not a trial with normal judicial process, since such sins are secret and lack witnesses, but it was effective. The ceremony was designed to be so terrifying and convicting that the very tendencies of human nature would make it clear if the person was guilty.

5:14 the spirit of jealousy. A mood of suspicion came over the husband that his wife had defiled herself with another man. The accuracy of the suspicion was determined to be right or wrong.

5:15 for bringing iniquity to remembrance. The purpose of the husband's offering was to bring the secret iniquity (if it was present) to light. How this was done is explained in 5:18,25-26.

water. 18 Then the priest shall stand the
woman before the [q]LORD, uncover the
woman's head, and put the offering for remembering in her hands, which *is* the
grain offering of jealousy. And the priest
shall have in his hand the bitter water that
brings a curse. 19 And the priest shall put
her under oath, and say to the woman, "If
no man has lain with you, and if you have
not gone astray to uncleanness *while* under
your husband's *authority,* be free from this
bitter water that brings a curse. 20 But if
you have gone astray *while* under your
husband's *authority,* and if you have defiled yourself and some man other than
your husband has lain with you"— 21 then
the priest shall [r]put the woman under the
oath of the curse, and he shall say to the
woman—[s]"the LORD make you a curse and
an oath among your people, when the
LORD makes your thigh [5]rot and your belly
swell; 22 and may this water that causes
the curse [t]go into your stomach, and make
your belly swell and *your* thigh rot."

[u]'Then the woman shall say, "Amen, so
be it."

23 'Then the priest shall write these curses in a book, and he shall scrape *them* off
into the bitter water. 24 And he shall make
the woman drink the bitter water that
brings a curse, and the water that brings
the curse shall enter her *to become* bitter.
25 [v]Then the priest shall take the grain offering of jealousy from the woman's hand,
shall [w]wave the offering before the LORD,
and bring it to the altar; 26 and the priest
shall take a handful of the offering, [x]as its
memorial portion, burn *it* on the altar, and
afterward make the woman drink the
water. 27 When he has made her drink the
water, then it shall be, if she has defiled
herself and behaved unfaithfully toward
her husband, that the water that brings a
[y]curse will enter her *and become* bitter, and
her belly will swell, her thigh will rot, and
the woman [z]will become a curse among
her people. 28 But if the woman has not defiled herself, and is clean, then she shall be
free and may conceive children.

29 'This *is* the law of jealousy, when a
wife, *while* under her husband's *authority,*
[a]goes astray and defiles herself, 30 or when
the spirit of jealousy comes upon a man,
and he becomes jealous of his wife; then he
shall stand the woman before the LORD,
and the priest shall execute all this law
upon her. 31 Then the man shall be free
from [6]iniquity, but that woman [b]shall bear
her [7]guilt.' "

The Law of the Nazirite

6 Then the LORD spoke to Moses, saying,
2 "Speak to the children of Israel, and
say to them: 'When either a man or woman
[1]consecrates an offering to take the vow of
a Nazirite, [a]to separate himself to the
LORD, 3 [b]he shall separate himself from
wine and *similar* drink; he shall drink neither vinegar made from wine nor vinegar
made from *similar* drink; neither shall he
drink any grape juice, nor eat fresh grapes
or raisins. 4 All the days of his [2]separation
he shall eat nothing that is produced by the
grapevine, from seed to skin.

5 'All the days of the vow of his separation no [c]razor shall come upon his head;
until the days are fulfilled for which he
separated himself to the LORD, he shall be
holy. *Then* he shall let the locks of the hair
of his head grow. 6 All the days that he separates himself to the LORD [d]he shall not go
near a dead body. 7 [e]He shall not [3]make
himself unclean even for his father or his
mother, for his brother or his sister, when
they die, because his separation to God *is*

18 [q]Heb. 13:4
21 [r]Josh. 6:26; 1 Sam. 14:24; Neh. 10:29 [s]Jer. 29:22 [5]Lit. *fall away*
22 [t]Ps. 109:18 [u]Deut. 27:15-26
25 [v]Lev. 8:27 [w]Lev. 2:2, 9
26 [x]Lev. 2:2, 9
27 [y]Deut. 28:37; Is. 65:15; Jer. 24:9; 29:18, 22; 42:18 [z]Num. 5:21
29 [a]Num. 5:19
31 [b]Lev. 20:17, 19, 20 [6]*guilt* [7]*iniquity*

CHAPTER 6

2 [a]Lev. 27:2; Judg. 13:5; [Lam. 4:7; Amos 2:11, 12]; Acts 21:23; Rom. 1:1 [1]Or *makes a difficult vow*
3 [b]Lev. 10:9; Amos 2:12; Luke 1:15
4 [2]Separation as a Nazirite
5 [c]Judg. 13:5; 16:17; 1 Sam. 1:11
6 [d]Lev. 21:1-3, 11; Num. 19:11-22
7 [e]Lev. 21:1, 2, 11; Num. 9:6 [3]By touching a dead body

5:18 before the LORD. The woman was brought to a priest at the tabernacle. There she was in the presence of the Lord, who knew her guilt or innocence. **uncover the woman's head.** Lit. "unbind the head." In Lev. 10:6; 13:45; 21:10, this phrase signifies mourning. This seems to signify the expectation of judgment and consequent mourning if the woman was proven to be guilty. **the bitter water.** This water included dust from the tabernacle floor (5:17) and the ink used to write the curses (5:23). The woman was to drink the water (5:26). If the woman was guilty, the water would make her life bitter by carrying out the curse of making her thigh rot and her belly swell (5:21,27). The public, frightening nature of this test could not fail to make guilt or innocence appear when the conscience was so assaulted.

5:28 conceive children. The penalty for the guilty wife was obvious, since the death penalty was called for. In contrast, the innocent wife was assured she would live to bring forth children.

6:1-21 Whereas 5:1-31 dealt with the cleansing of the camp by dealing with the unclean and sinful, 6:1-21 showed how consecration to the Lord was possible for every Israelite. Although only the family of Aaron could be priests, any man or woman could be "priestly" (i.e., dedicated to God's service) for a time (from a month to a lifetime) by means of the vow of a Nazirite. Such a vow was made by people unusually devout toward God and dedicated to His service.

6:2 the vow of a Nazirite. The word "vow" here is related to the word "wonder," which signifies something out of the ordinary. "Nazirite" transliterates a Heb. term meaning "dedication by separation." The Nazirite separated himself to the Lord by separating himself from 1) grape products (6:3,4), 2) the cutting of one's hair (6:5), and 3) contact with a dead body (6:6,7). The High-Priest was also forbidden 1) to drink wine while serving in the tabernacle (Lev. 10:9), and 2) to touch dead bodies (Lev. 21:11). Further, both the High-Priest's crown (Ex. 29:6; 39:30; Lev. 8:9) and the Nazirite's head (6:9,18) are referred to by the same Heb. word. The Nazirite's hair was like the High-Priest's crown. Like the High-Priest, the Nazirite was holy to the Lord (6:8; cf: Ex. 28:36) all the days (6:4,5,6,8) of his vow.

on his head. 8 [f]All the days of his separation he shall be holy to the LORD.
9 'And if anyone dies very suddenly beside him, and he defiles his consecrated
head, then he shall [g]shave his head on the
day of his cleansing; on the seventh day he
shall shave it. 10 Then [h]on the eighth day
he shall bring two turtledoves or two
young pigeons to the priest, to the door of
the tabernacle of meeting; 11 and the priest
shall offer one as a sin offering and *the*
other as a burnt offering, and make atonement for him, because he sinned in regard
to the corpse; and he shall sanctify his head
that same day. 12 He shall consecrate to the
LORD the days of his separation, and bring
a male lamb in its first year [i]as a trespass
offering; but the former days shall be [4]lost,
because his separation was defiled.
13 'Now this *is* the law of the Nazirite:
[j]When the days of his separation are fulfilled, he shall be brought to the door of the
tabernacle of meeting. 14 And he shall present his offering to the LORD: one male
lamb in its first year without blemish as a
burnt offering, one ewe lamb in its first
year without blemish [k]as a sin offering,
one ram without blemish [l]as a peace offering, 15 a basket of unleavened bread,
[m]cakes of fine flour mixed with oil, unleavened wafers [n]anointed with oil, and
their grain offering with their [o]drink offerings.
16 'Then the priest shall bring *them* before
the LORD and offer his sin offering and his
burnt offering; 17 and he shall offer the ram
as a sacrifice of a peace offering to the LORD,
with the basket of unleavened bread; the
priest shall also offer its grain offering and
its drink offering. 18 [p]Then the Nazirite
shall shave his consecrated head *at* the door
of the tabernacle of meeting, and shall take
the hair from his consecrated head and put
it on the fire which is under the sacrifice of
the peace offering.
19 'And the priest shall take the [q]boiled
shoulder of the ram, one [r]unleavened cake
from the basket, and one unleavened
wafer, and [s]put *them* upon the hands of the
Nazirite after he has shaved his consecrated *hair,* 20 and the priest shall wave them
as a wave offering before the LORD; [t]they
are holy for the priest, together with the
breast of the wave offering and the thigh of
the heave offering. After that the Nazirite
may drink wine.'
21 "This is the law of the Nazirite who
vows to the LORD the offering for his separation, and besides that, whatever else his
hand is able to provide; according to the
vow which he takes, so he must do according to the law of his separation."

The Priestly Blessing

22 And the LORD spoke to Moses, saying:
23 "Speak to Aaron and his sons, saying,
'This is the way you shall bless the children of Israel. Say to them:

24 "The LORD [u]bless you and [v]keep
you;
25 The LORD [w]make His face shine
upon you,
And [x]be gracious to you;
26 [y]The LORD [5]lift up His countenance
upon you,
And [z]give you peace."'

27 [a]"So they shall [6]put My name on the
children of Israel, and [b]I will bless them."

Offerings of the Leaders

7 Now it came to pass, when Moses had
finished [a]setting up the tabernacle, that
he [b]anointed it and consecrated it and all its
furnishings, and the altar and all its utensils; so he anointed them and consecrated

8 [f][2 Cor. 6:17, 18]
9 [g]Lev. 14:8, 9; Acts 18:18; 21:24
10 [h]Lev. 5:7; 14:22; 15:14, 29
12 [i]Lev. 5:6 [4]*void*
13 [j]Acts 21:26
14 [k]Lev. 4:2, 27, 32 [l]Lev. 3:6
15 [m]Lev. 2:4 [n]Ex. 29:2 [o]Num. 15:5, 7, 10
18 [p]Num. 6:9; Acts 21:23, 24
19 [q]1 Sam. 2:15 [r]Ex. 29:23, 24 [s]Lev. 7:30
20 [t]Ex. 29:27, 28
24 [u]Deut. 28:3-6 [v]Ps. 121:7; John 7:11
25 [w]Ps. 31:16; 67:1; 80:3, 7, 19; 119:135; Dan. 9:17 [x]Gen. 43:29; Ex. 33:19; Mal. 1:9
26 [y]Ps. 4:6; 89:15 [z]Lev. 26:6; Is. 26:3, 12; John 14:27; Phil. 4:7 [5]Look upon you with favor
27 [a]Deut. 28:10; 2 Sam. 7:23; 2 Chr. 7:14; Is. 43:7; Dan. 9:18, 19 [b]Ex. 20:24; Num. 23:20; Ps. 5:12; 67:7; 115:12, 13; Eph. 1:3 [6]*invoke*

CHAPTER 7

1 [a]Ex. 40:17-33 [b]Lev. 8:10, 11

6:9 dies...suddenly. If the Nazirite inadvertently came in contact with a dead body, he was to shave his head, on the eighth day bring the prescribed offerings, and begin the days of his vow again. This is a good illustration of the fact that sin can become mingled with the best intentions, and is not always premeditated. When sin is mixed with the holiest actions, it calls for a renewed cleansing.

6:13 fulfilled. At the end of the determined time, the Nazirite was released from his vow through offerings and the shaving of his head. His hair was to be brought to the sanctuary at the time of those offerings (cf. Acts 18:18).

6:22-27 Obedient Israel, organized before and consecrated to the Lord, was the recipient of God's blessing (i.e., His favor) pronounced by the priests.

6:24 bless. The Lord's blessing was described as His face (i.e., His presence) shining on His people (v. 25) and looking at them (v. 26). God shone forth in benevolence on Israel and looked on them for good. **keep.** The results of the Lord's blessing were His preservation of Israel ("keep"), His kindness toward her ("be gracious," v. 25), and her total well-being ("peace," v. 26).

6:27 put My name. The name of the Lord represented His person and character. The priests were to call for God to dwell among His people and meet all their needs.

7:1–10:36 These 4 chapters show how the Lord spoke to Moses (7:89) and led Israel (9:22; 10:11,12) from the tabernacle. As Israel was properly oriented toward the Lord and obeyed His word, God gave them victory over their enemies (10:35).

7:1-89 As the people of Israel had been generous in giving to the construction of the tabernacle (see Ex. 35:4-29), they showed the same generosity in its dedication.

7:1 finished setting up the tabernacle. According to Ex. 40:17, the tabernacle was raised up on the first day of the first month of the second year. Thus the tabernacle was set up 11½ months after the Exodus from Egypt.

them. 2 Then [c]the leaders of Israel, the
heads of their fathers' houses, who *were* the
leaders of the tribes [1]and over those who
were numbered, made an offering. 3 And
they brought their offering before the LORD,
six covered carts and twelve oxen, a cart for
every two of the leaders, and for each one
an ox; and they presented them before the
tabernacle.
4 Then the LORD spoke to Moses, saying,
5 "Accept *these* from them, that they may
be used in doing the work of the tabernacle of meeting; and you shall give them to
the Levites, *to* every man according to his
service." 6 So Moses took the carts and the
oxen, and gave them to the Levites. 7 Two
carts and four oxen [d]he gave to the sons of
Gershon, according to their service; 8 [e]and
four carts and eight oxen he gave to the
sons of Merari, according to their service,
under the [2]authority of Ithamar the son of
Aaron the priest. 9 But to the sons of Kohath he gave none, because theirs *was* [f]the
service of the holy things, [g]*which* they carried on their shoulders.
10 Now the leaders offered [h]the dedication *offering* for the altar when it was
anointed; so the leaders offered their offering before the altar. 11 For the LORD said to
Moses, "They shall offer their offering, one
leader each day, for the dedication of the
altar."
12 And the one who offered his offering
on the first day *was* [i]Nahshon the son of
Amminadab, from the tribe of Judah.
13 His offering *was* one silver platter, the
weight of which *was* one hundred and thirty *shekels,* and one silver bowl of seventy
shekels, according to [j]the shekel of the
sanctuary, both of them full of fine flour
mixed with oil as a [k]grain offering; 14 one
gold pan of ten *shekels,* full of [l]incense;
15 [m]one young bull, one ram, and one male
lamb [n]in its first year, as a burnt offering;
16 one kid of the goats as a [o]sin offering;
17 and for [p]the sacrifice of peace offerings:
two oxen, five rams, five male goats, and
five male lambs in their first year. This *was*
the offering of Nahshon the son of Amminadab.
18 On the second day Nethanel the son
of Zuar, leader of Issachar, presented *an of-*
fering. 19 *For* his offering he offered one silver platter, the weight of which *was* one
hundred and thirty *shekels,* and one silver
bowl of seventy shekels, according to the
shekel of the sanctuary, both of them full of
fine flour mixed with oil as a grain offering; 20 one gold pan of ten *shekels,* full of incense; 21 one young bull, one ram, and one
male lamb in its first year, as a burnt offering; 22 one kid of the goats as a sin offering;
23 and as the sacrifice of peace offerings:
two oxen, five rams, five male goats, and
five male lambs in their first year. This *was*
the offering of Nethanel the son of Zuar.
24 On the third day Eliab the son of
Helon, leader of the children of Zebulun,
presented an offering. 25 His offering *was* one
silver platter, the weight of which *was* one
hundred and thirty *shekels,* and one silver
bowl of seventy shekels, according to the
shekel of the sanctuary, both of them full of
fine flour mixed with oil as a grain offering; 26 one gold pan of ten *shekels,* full of incense; 27 one young bull, one ram, and one
male lamb in its first year, as a burnt offering; 28 one kid of the goats as a sin offering;
29 and for the sacrifice of peace offerings:
two oxen, five rams, five male goats, and
five male lambs in their first year. This *was*
the offering of Eliab the son of Helon.
30 On the fourth day [q]Elizur the son of
Shedeur, leader of the children of Reuben,
presented an offering. 31 His offering *was* one
silver platter, the weight of which *was* one
hundred and thirty *shekels,* and one silver
bowl of seventy shekels, according to the
shekel of the sanctuary, both of them full of
fine flour mixed with oil as a grain offering; 32 one gold pan of ten *shekels,* full of incense; 33 one young bull, one ram, and one
male lamb in its first year, as a burnt offering; 34 one kid of the goats as a sin offering;
35 and as the sacrifice of peace offerings:
two oxen, five rams, five male goats, and
five male lambs in their first year. This *was*
the offering of Elizur the son of Shedeur.
36 On the fifth day [r]Shelumiel the son of
Zurishaddai, leader of the children of
Simeon, *presented an offering.* 37 His offering *was* one silver platter, the weight of
which *was* one hundred and thirty *shekels,*
and one silver bowl of seventy shekels, according to the shekel of the sanctuary, both
of them full of fine flour mixed with oil as
a grain offering; 38 one gold pan of ten
shekels, full of incense; 39 one young bull,
one ram, and one male lamb in its first
year, as a burnt offering; 40 one kid of the

2 [c]Num. 1:4 [1]Lit. *who stood over*
7 [d]Num. 4:24-28
8 [e]Num. 4:29-33 [2]Lit. *hand*
9 [f]Num. 4:15 [g]Num. 4:6-14
10 [h]Num. 7:1; Deut. 20:5; 1 Kin. 8:63; 2 Chr. 7:5, 9; Ezra 6:16; Neh. 12:27
12 [i]Num. 2:3
13 [j]Ex. 30:13 [k]Lev. 2:1
14 [l]Ex. 30:34, 35
15 [m]Lev. 1:2 [n]Ex. 12:5
16 [o]Lev. 4:23
17 [p]Lev. 3:1
30 [q]Num. 1:5; 2:10
36 [r]Num. 1:6; 2:12; 7:41

7:2 the leaders of Israel. The leaders of the 12 tribes were those named in 1:5-15 who oversaw the numbering of the people. The order of the presentation by tribe of their offerings to the tabernacle was the same as the order of march given in 2:3-32.

7:6 the carts and the oxen. These were to be used in the transportation of the tabernacle. According to v. 9, the sons of Kohath did not receive a cart because they were to carry the holy things of the tabernacle on their shoulders.

7:12 the first day. I.e., the first day of the first month. The gifts of the leaders to the tabernacle were given over 12 successive days.

goats as a sin offering; 41 and as the sacrifice of peace offerings: two oxen, five rams,
five male goats, and five male lambs in
their first year. This *was* the offering of Shelumiel the son of Zurishaddai.
42 On the sixth day [s]Eliasaph the son of
[3]Deuel, leader of the children of Gad, *presented an offering.* 43 His offering *was* one
silver platter, the weight of which *was* one
hundred and thirty *shekels,* and one silver
bowl of seventy shekels, according to the
shekel of the sanctuary, both of them full of
fine flour mixed with oil as a grain offering; 44 one gold pan of ten *shekels,* full of incense; 45 one young bull, one ram, and one
male lamb in its first year, as [t]a burnt
offering; 46 one kid of the goats as a sin offering; 47 and as the sacrifice of peace
offerings: two oxen, five rams, five male
goats, and five male lambs in their first
year. This *was* the offering of Eliasaph the
son of Deuel.
48 On the seventh day [u]Elishama the son
of Ammihud, leader of the children of
Ephraim, *presented an offering.* 49 His offering *was* one silver platter, the weight of
which *was* one hundred and thirty *shekels,*
and one silver bowl of seventy shekels, according to the shekel of the sanctuary, both
of them full of fine flour mixed with oil as
a grain offering; 50 one gold pan of ten
shekels, full of incense; 51 one young bull,
one ram, and one male lamb in its first
year, as a burnt offering; 52 one kid of the
goats as a sin offering; 53 and as the sacrifice of peace offerings: two oxen, five rams,
five male goats, and five male lambs in
their first year. This *was* the offering of
Elishama the son of Ammihud.
54 On the eighth day [v]Gamaliel the son
of Pedahzur, leader of the children of Manasseh, *presented an offering.* 55 His offering
was one silver platter, the weight of which
was one hundred and thirty *shekels,* and
one silver bowl of seventy shekels, according to the shekel of the sanctuary, both of
them full of fine flour mixed with oil as a
grain offering; 56 one gold pan of ten
shekels, full of incense; 57 one young bull,
one ram, and one male lamb in its first
year, as a burnt offering; 58 one kid of the
goats as a sin offering; 59 and as the sacrifice of peace offerings: two oxen, five rams,
five male goats, and five male lambs in
their first year. This *was* the offering of Gamaliel the son of Pedahzur.
60 On the ninth day [w]Abidan the son of
Gideoni, leader of the children of Benjamin, *presented an offering.* 61 His offering
was one silver platter, the weight of which
was one hundred and thirty *shekels,* and
one silver bowl of seventy shekels, according to the shekel of the sanctuary, both of
them full of fine flour mixed with oil as a
grain offering; 62 one gold pan of ten
shekels, full of incense; 63 one young bull,
one ram, and one male lamb in its first
year, as a burnt offering; 64 one kid of the
goats as a sin offering; 65 and as the sacrifice of peace offerings: two oxen, five rams,
five male goats, and five male lambs in
their first year. This *was* the offering of Abidan the son of Gideoni.
66 On the tenth day [x]Ahiezer the son of
Ammishaddai, leader of the children of
Dan, *presented an offering.* 67 His offering
was one silver platter, the weight of which
was one hundred and thirty *shekels,* and
one silver bowl of seventy shekels, according to the shekel of the sanctuary, both of
them full of fine flour mixed with oil as a
grain offering; 68 one gold pan of ten
shekels, full of incense; 69 one young bull,
one ram, and one male lamb in its first
year, as a burnt offering; 70 one kid of the
goats as a sin offering; 71 and as the sacrifice of peace offerings: two oxen, five rams,
five male goats, and five male lambs in
their first year. This *was* the offering of Ahiezer the son of Ammishaddai.
72 On the eleventh day [y]Pagiel the son of
Ocran, leader of the children of Asher, *presented an offering.* 73 His offering *was* one
silver platter, the weight of which *was* one
hundred and thirty *shekels,* and one silver
bowl of seventy shekels, according to the
shekel of the sanctuary, both of them full of
fine flour mixed with oil as a grain offering; 74 one gold pan of ten *shekels,* full of incense; 75 one young bull, one ram, and one
male lamb in its first year, as a burnt offering; 76 one kid of the goats as a sin offering;
77 and as the sacrifice of peace offerings:
two oxen, five rams, five male goats, and
five male lambs in their first year. This *was*
the offering of Pagiel the son of Ocran.
78 On the twelfth day [z]Ahira the son of
Enan, leader of the children of Naphtali,
presented an offering. 79 His offering *was* one
silver platter, the weight of which *was* one
hundred and thirty *shekels,* and one silver
bowl of seventy shekels, according to the
shekel of the sanctuary, both of them full of
fine flour mixed with oil as a grain offering; 80 one gold pan of ten *shekels,* full of incense; 81 one young bull, one ram, and one
male lamb in its first year, as a burnt offering; 82 one kid of the goats as a sin offering;
83 and as the sacrifice of peace offerings:
two oxen, five rams, five male goats, and
five male lambs in their first year. This *was*
the offering of Ahira the son of Enan.

42 [s]Num. 1:14; 2:14; 10:20 [3]*Reuel,* Num. 2:14
45 [t]Ps. 40:6
48 [u]Num. 1:10; 2:18; 1 Chr. 7:26
54 [v]Num. 1:10; 2:20
60 [w]Num. 1:11; 2:22
66 [x]Num. 1:12; 2:25
72 [y]Num. 1:13; 2:27
78 [z]Num. 1:15; 2:29

84 This *was* [a]the dedication *offering* for
the altar from the leaders of Israel, when it
was anointed: twelve silver platters,
twelve silver bowls, and twelve gold pans.
85 Each silver platter *weighed* one hundred
and thirty *shekels* and each bowl seventy
shekels. All the silver of the vessels *weighed*
two thousand four hundred *shekels*, according to the shekel of the sanctuary.
86 The twelve gold pans full of incense
weighed ten *shekels* apiece, according to the
shekel of the sanctuary; all the gold of the
pans *weighed* one hundred and twenty
shekels. 87 All the oxen for the burnt offering *were* twelve young bulls, the rams
twelve, the male lambs in their first year
twelve, with their grain offering, and the
kids of the goats as a sin offering twelve.
88 And all the oxen for the sacrifice of
peace offerings were twenty-four bulls, the
rams sixty, the male goats sixty, and the
lambs in their first year sixty. This *was* the
dedication *offering* for the altar after it was
[b]anointed.

89 Now when Moses went into the tabernacle of meeting [c]to speak with Him, he
heard [d]the voice of One speaking to him
from above the mercy seat that *was* on the
ark of the Testimony, from [e]between the
two cherubim; thus He spoke to him.

Arrangement of the Lamps

8 And the LORD spoke to Moses, saying:
2 "Speak to Aaron, and say to him,
'When you [a]arrange the lamps, the seven
[b]lamps shall give light in front of the lampstand.' " 3 And Aaron did so; he arranged
the lamps to face toward the front of the
lampstand, as the LORD commanded Moses. 4 [c]Now this workmanship of the lampstand *was* hammered gold; from its shaft to
its flowers it *was* [d]hammered work. [e]Ac-
cording to the pattern which the LORD had
shown Moses, so he made the lampstand.

Cleansing and Dedication of the Levites

5 Then the LORD spoke to Moses, saying:
6 "Take the Levites from among the children of Israel and cleanse them *ceremonially.* 7 Thus you shall do to them to cleanse
them: Sprinkle [f]water of purification on
them, and [g]let[1] them shave all their body,
and let them wash their clothes, and *so*
make themselves clean. 8 Then let them
take a young bull with [h]its grain offering of
fine flour mixed with oil, and you shall
take another young bull as a sin offering.
9 [i]And you shall bring the Levites before
the tabernacle of meeting, [j]and you shall
gather together the whole congregation of
the children of Israel. 10 So you shall bring
the Levites before the LORD, and the children of Israel [k]shall lay their hands on the
Levites; 11 and Aaron shall [2]offer the
Levites before the LORD *like* a [l]wave offering from the children of Israel, that they
may perform the work of the LORD.
12 [m]Then the Levites shall lay their hands
on the heads of the young bulls, and you
shall offer one as a sin offering and the
other as a burnt offering to the LORD, to
make atonement for the Levites.

13 "And you shall stand the Levites before Aaron and his sons, and then offer
them *like* a wave offering to the LORD.
14 Thus you shall [n]separate the Levites
from among the children of Israel, and the
Levites shall be [o]Mine. 15 After that the
Levites shall go in to service the tabernacle
of meeting. So you shall cleanse them and
[p]offer them *like* a wave offering. 16 For they
are [q]wholly given to Me from among the
children of Israel; I have taken them for
Myself [r]instead of all who open the womb,
the firstborn of all the children of Israel.
17 [s]For all the firstborn among the children
of Israel *are* Mine, *both* man and beast; on
the day that I struck all the firstborn in the
land of Egypt I [3]sanctified them to Myself.
18 I have taken the Levites instead of all the
firstborn of the children of Israel. 19 And [t]I
have given the Levites as a gift to Aaron
and his sons from among the children of
Israel, to do the work for the children of Israel in the tabernacle of meeting, and to
make atonement for the children of Israel,

84 [a] Num. 7:10
88 [b] Num. 7:1, 10
89 [c] [Ex. 33:9, 11]; Num. 12:8 [d] Ex. 25:21, 22 [e] Ps. 80:1; 99:1

CHAPTER 8

2 [a] Lev. 24:2-4 [b] Ex. 25:37; 40:25
4 [c] Ex. 25:31 [d] Ex. 25:18 [e] Ex. 25:40; Acts 7:44
7 [f] Num. 19:9, 13, 17, 20; Ps. 51:2, 7; [Heb. 9:13, 14] [g] Lev. 14:8, 9 [1] Heb. *let them cause a razor to pass over*
8 [h] Lev. 2:1; Num. 15:8-10
9 [i] Ex. 29:4; 40:12 [j] Lev. 8:3
10 [k] Lev. 1:4
11 [l] Num. 18:6 [2] *present*
12 [m] Ex. 29:10
14 [n] Num. 16:9 [o] Num. 3:12, 45; 16:9
15 [p] Num. 8:11, 13
16 [q] Num. 3:9 [r] Ex. 13:2; Num. 3:12, 45
17 [s] Ex. 12:2, 12, 13, 15; Num. 3:13; Luke 2:23 [3] *set them apart*
19 [t] Num. 3:9

7:84-88 Each of the leaders gave the same offerings to the tabernacle. Here the total of all the gifts was given.

7:89 He spoke to him. With the completion of the tabernacle, the Lord communicated His Word to Moses from the mercy seat in the Holy of Holies (see Lev. 1:1, Num. 1:1).

8:1-4 Exodus 25:32-40 recorded the instructions for the making of the golden lampstand and Ex. 37:17-24 reported its completion. Here, as a part of the dedication of the tabernacle, the 7 lamps of the lampstand were lit.

8:5-26 This ceremony set apart the Levites to the service of the Lord. Their dedication was a feature of the overall description of the dedication of the tabernacle.

8:6 cleanse. In contrast to the priests who were consecrated (Ex. 29:1,9), the Levites were cleansed. According to v. 7, this cleansing was accomplished by first, the sprinkling of water; second, the shaving of the body; and third, the washing of the clothes. This cleansing of the Levites made them pure so they might come into contact with the holy objects of the tabernacle. Similar requirements were given for the cleansing of the leper in Lev. 14:8,9.

8:9 the whole congregation. Since the Levites took the place of the firstborn, who had acted as family priests among the people of Israel (see vv. 16-18), all of the congregation of Israel showed their identification with the Levites by the laying on of their hands.

8:19 a gift to Aaron. The Levites were given by God to assist the priests.

[u]that there be no plague among the children of Israel when the children of Israel
come near the sanctuary."
20 Thus Moses and Aaron and all the
congregation of the children of Israel did
to the Levites; according to all that the
LORD commanded Moses concerning the
Levites, so the children of Israel did to
them. 21 [v]And the Levites purified themselves and washed their clothes; then
Aaron presented them *like* a wave offering
before the LORD, and Aaron made atonement for them to cleanse them. 22 [w]After
that the Levites went in to do their work in
the tabernacle of meeting before Aaron
and his sons; [x]as the LORD commanded
Moses concerning the Levites, so they did
to them.
23 Then the LORD spoke to Moses, say-
ing, 24 "This *is* what *pertains* to the Levites:
[y]From twenty-five years old and above
one may enter to perform service in the
work of the tabernacle of meeting; 25 and
at the age of fifty years they must cease
performing this work, and shall work no
more. 26 They may minister with their
brethren in the tabernacle of meeting, [z]to
attend to needs, but they *themselves* shall
do no work. Thus you shall do to the
Levites regarding their duties."

The Second Passover

9 Now the LORD spoke to Moses in the
Wilderness of Sinai, in the first month
of the second year after they had come out
of the land of Egypt, saying: 2 "Let the children of Israel keep [a]the Passover at its appointed [b]time. 3 On the fourteenth day of
this month, [1]at twilight, you shall [2]keep it
at its appointed time. According to all its
[3]rites and ceremonies you shall keep it."
4 So Moses told the children of Israel that
they should keep the Passover. 5 And [c]they
kept the Passover on the fourteenth day of
the first month, at twilight, in the Wilderness of Sinai; according to all that the LORD
commanded Moses, so the children of Israel did.
6 Now there were *certain* men who were
[d]defiled by a human corpse, so that they
could not keep the Passover on that day;
[e]and they came before Moses and Aaron
that day. 7 And those men said to him, "We
became defiled by a human corpse. Why are
we kept from presenting the offering of the
LORD at its appointed time among the children of Israel?"
8 And Moses said to them, "Stand still,
that [f]I may hear what the LORD will command concerning you."
9 Then the LORD spoke to Moses, saying, 10 "Speak to the children of Israel,
saying: 'If anyone of you or your [4]poster-
ity is unclean because of a corpse, or *is* far
away on a journey, he may still keep the
LORD's Passover. 11 On [g]the fourteenth
day of the second month, at twilight, they
may keep it. They shall [h]eat it with unleavened bread and bitter herbs. 12 [i]They
shall leave none of it until morning, [j]nor
break one of its bones. [k]According to all
the [5]ordinances of the Passover they shall
keep it. 13 But the man who *is* clean and is
not on a journey, and ceases to keep the
Passover, that same person [l]shall be cut
off from among his people, because he
[m]did not bring the offering of the LORD at
its appointed time; that man shall [n]bear
his sin.
14 'And if a stranger [6]dwells among you,
and would keep the LORD's Passover, he
must do so according to the rite of the
Passover and according to its ceremony;
[o]you shall have one [7]ordinance, both for
the stranger and the native of the land.' "

The Cloud and the Fire

15 Now [p]on the day that the tabernacle
was raised up, the cloud [q]covered the
tabernacle, the tent of the Testimony; [r]from

19 [u]Num. 1:53; 16:46; 18:5; 2 Chr. 26:16
21 [v]Num. 8:7
22 [w]Num. 8:15 [x]Num. 8:5
24 [y]Num. 4:3; 1 Chr. 23:3, 24, 27
26 [z]Num. 1:53

CHAPTER 9

2 [a]Ex. 12:1-16; Lev. 23:5; Num. 28:16; Deut. 16:1, 2 [b]2 Chr. 30:1-15; Luke 22:7; [1 Cor. 5:7, 8]
3 [1]Lit. *between the evenings* [2]*observe* [3]*statutes*
5 [c]Josh. 5:10
6 [d]Num. 5:2; 19:11-22; John 18:28 [e]Ex. 18:15, 19, 26; Num. 27:2
8 [f]Ex. 18:22; Num. 27:5
10 [4]*descendants*
11 [g]2 Chr. 30:2, 15 [h]Ex. 12:8
12 [i]Ex. 12:10 [j]Ex. 12:46; [John 19:36] [k]Ex. 12:43 [5]*statutes*
13 [l]Gen. 17:14; Ex. 12:15, 47 [m]Num. 9:7 [n]Num. 5:31
14 [o]Ex. 12:49; Lev. 24:22; Num. 15:15, 16, 29 [6]As a resident alien [7]*statute*
15 [p]Ex. 40:33, 34; Neh. 9:12, 19; Ps. 78:14 [q]Is. 4:5 [r]Ex. 13:21, 22; 40:38

8:19 no plague. *See note on 1:53.*

8:24 twenty-five years old. The Levites were to begin their service in helping the priests at age 25. However, in 4:3 the age of commencement is 30. A rabbinic suggestion was that the Levites were to serve a 5-year apprenticeship. A better solution can be discovered by noting the differing tasks in the two chapters. Numbers 4 dealt with the carrying of the tabernacle, while here they helped in the service in the tabernacle. A Levite began serving in the tabernacle at 25 and carrying the tabernacle at 30. In both cases, his service ended at age 50. David later lowered the age to 20 (see 1 Chr. 23:24,27; cf. Ezra 3:8).

9:1-14 The call from the Lord to keep the Passover led to an inquiry from those whose uncleanness kept them from obeying. This request led to an amplification of the requirement by the Lord. This was the second Passover.

9:1 the first month. The events recorded in these verses precede the beginning of the census in chap. 1, but follow the dedication of the tabernacle in chap. 7.

9:3 twilight. The time between the end of one day and the beginning of the next. See Ex. 12:6.

9:6 defiled. Ceremonially unclean because of contact with a dead body. *See note on 5:2.*

9:10 posterity. This word from the Lord was not only for the current situation, but it was a continuing ordinance for Israel. If a man was unable to eat the Passover because of uncleanness or because he was away from the land, he could partake of the Passover on the fourteenth day of the second month.

9:12 This text is alluded to in John 19:36.

9:13 cut off. If any Israelite did not keep the Passover at the appointed time and was not unclean or away from the land, he was to be "cut off," which implies that he was to be killed.

9:14 one ordinance. A non-Israelite who wished to participate in the Passover would be required to be circumcised.

evening until morning it was above the
tabernacle like the appearance of fire. 16 So
it was always: the cloud covered it *by day,*
and the appearance of fire by night.
17 Whenever the cloud [s]was [8]taken up
from above the tabernacle, after that the
children of Israel would journey; and in
the place where the cloud settled, there the
children of Israel would pitch their tents.
18 At the [9]command of the LORD the children of Israel would journey, and at the
command of the LORD they would camp;
[t]as long as the cloud stayed above the
tabernacle they remained encamped.
19 Even when the cloud continued long,
many days above the tabernacle, the children of Israel [u]kept the charge of the LORD
and did not journey. 20 So it was, when the
cloud was above the tabernacle a few days:
according to the command of the LORD
they would remain encamped, and according to the command of the LORD they
would journey. 21 So it was, when the
cloud remained only from evening until
morning: when the cloud was taken up in
the morning, then they would journey;
whether by day or by night, whenever the
cloud was taken up, they would journey.
22 *Whether it was* two days, a month, or a
year that the cloud remained above the
tabernacle, the children of Israel [v]would
remain encamped and not journey; but
when it was taken up, they would journey.
23 At the command of the LORD they remained encamped, and at the command of
the LORD they journeyed; they [w]kept the
charge of the LORD, at the command of the
LORD by the hand of Moses.

Two Silver Trumpets

10 And the LORD spoke to Moses, saying: 2 "Make two silver trumpets
for yourself; you shall make them of hammered work; you shall use them for [a]call-
ing the congregation and for directing the
movement of the camps. 3 When [b]they
blow both of them, all the congregation
shall gather before you at the door of the
tabernacle of meeting. 4 But if they blow
only one, then the leaders, the [c]heads of the
divisions of Israel, shall gather to you.
5 When you sound the [d]advance, [e]the
camps that lie on the east side shall then
begin their journey. 6 When you sound the
advance the second time, then the camps
that lie [f]on the south side shall begin their
journey; they shall sound the call for them
to begin their journeys. 7 And when the assembly is to be gathered together, [g]you
shall blow, but not [h]sound the advance.
8 [i]The sons of Aaron, the priests, shall blow
the trumpets; and these shall be to you as
an [1]ordinance forever throughout your
generations.
9 [j]"When you go to war in your land
against the enemy who [k]oppresses you,
then you shall sound an alarm with the
trumpets, and you will be [l]remembered
before the LORD your God, and you will be
saved from your enemies. 10 Also [m]in the
day of your gladness, in your appointed
feasts, and at the beginning of your
months, you shall blow the trumpets over
your burnt offerings and over the sacrifices
of your peace offerings; and they shall be
[n]a memorial for you before your God: I *am*
the LORD your God."

Departure from Sinai

11 Now it came to pass on the twentieth
day of the second month, in the second
year, that the cloud [o]was taken up from
above the tabernacle of the Testimony.
12 And the children of Israel set out from

17 [s] Ex. 40:36-38; Num. 10:11, 12, 33, 34; Ps. 80:1 [8] *lifted up*
18 [t] 1 Cor. 10:1 [9] Lit. *mouth*
19 [u] Num. 1:53; 3:8
22 [v] Ex. 40:36, 37
23 [w] Num. 9:19

CHAPTER 10

2 [a] Is. 1:13
3 [b] Jer. 4:5; Joel 2:15
4 [c] Ex. 18:21; Num. 1:16; 7:2
5 [d] Joel 2:1 [e] Num. 2:3
6 [f] Num. 2:10
7 [g] Num. 10:3 [h] Joel 2:1
8 [i] Num. 31:6; Josh. 6:4; 1 Chr. 15:24; 2 Chr. 13:12 [1] *statute*
9 [j] Num. 31:6; Josh. 6:5; 2 Chr. 13:14 [k] Judg. 2:18; 4:3; 6:9; 10:8, 12 [l] Gen. 8:1; Ps. 106:4
10 [m] Lev. 23:24; Num. 29:1; 1 Chr. 15:24; 2 Chr. 5:12; Ps. 81:3 [n] Lev. 23:24; Num. 10:9
11 [o] Num. 9:17

9:15-23 See Ex. 40:34-38. The cloud, the visible symbol of the Lord's presence, was continually sitting above the tabernacle. The movement of the cloud was the signal to Israel that they were to travel on their journey.

9:15 tabernacle...raised up. The presence of the Lord arrived when the tabernacle was completed and erected on the first day of the first month of the second year after they had come out of Egypt.

9:16 cloud...fire. The presence of the Lord which was seen in the cloud by day became a fire that was seen at night (cf. Lev. 16:2).

9:23 command...command. The text emphasizes that Israel obeyed the Lord at this point in her experience. Throughout the wilderness wanderings, the Israelites could only journey as the cloud led them. When it did not move, they stayed encamped where they were.

10:1-10 Israel was also to be guided by the blowing of the two silver trumpets made by Moses. Both a call to gather and a call to march were communicated with the trumpets.

10:2 trumpets. According to a Jewish tradition, these instruments were between 12 and 20 in. long and had a narrow tube that was flared at the end. **hammered work.** The same description is given concerning the cherubim above the mercy seat. See Ex. 25:18; 37:7.

10:3,4 both...one. The first function of the trumpets was to gather the people to the tabernacle. When both trumpets were blown, all adult males of the congregation were to gather. If only one trumpet was blown, the leaders were to come.

10:5 advance. The second purpose of the trumpets was to give a signal indicating that the tribes were to set out on their march. The exact difference between the blowing for the gathering at the tabernacle and for the march is not known. Jewish tradition said the convocation sound was a long steady blast, while the advance signal was a succession of 3 shorter notes.

10:8 an ordinance forever. The blowing of the horns was to be a perpetual ordinance in Israel, calling the people to worship or to war.

10:11-36 Finally, in an orderly and obedient fashion, Israel departed from Sinai as the Lord commanded through Moses.

10:11 ***day...month...year.*** Only 13 months after the Exodus

the [p]Wilderness of Sinai on [q]their journeys;
then the cloud settled down in the [r]Wilder-
ness of Paran. 13 So they started out for the
first time [s]according to the command of
the LORD by the hand of Moses.
14 The [2]standard of the camp of the children of Judah [t]set out first according to
their armies; over their army was
[u]Nahshon the son of Amminadab. 15 Over
the army of the tribe of the children of
Issachar *was* Nethanel the son of Zuar.
16 And over the army of the tribe of the
children of Zebulun *was* Eliab the son of
Helon.
17 Then [v]the tabernacle was taken down;
and the sons of Gershon and the sons of
Merari set out, [w]carrying the tabernacle.
18 And [x]the standard of the camp of
Reuben set out according to their armies;
over their army *was* Elizur the son of
Shedeur. 19 Over the army of the tribe of
the children of Simeon *was* Shelumiel the
son of Zurishaddai. 20 And over the army
of the tribe of the children of Gad *was* Eliasaph the son of Deuel.
21 Then the Kohathites set out, carrying
the [y]holy things. (The tabernacle would be
[3]prepared for their arrival.)
22 And [z]the standard of the camp of the
children of Ephraim set out according to
their armies; over their army *was* Elishama the son of Ammihud. 23 Over the
army of the tribe of the children of Manasseh *was* Gamaliel the son of Pedahzur.
24 And over the army of the tribe of the
children of Benjamin *was* Abidan the son
of Gideoni.
25 Then [a]the standard of the camp of the
children of Dan (the rear guard of all the
camps) set out according to their armies;
over their army *was* Ahiezer the son of
Ammishaddai. 26 Over the army of the
tribe of the children of Asher *was* Pagiel the
son of Ocran. 27 And over the army of the
tribe of the children of Naphtali *was* Ahira
the son of Enan.
28 [b]Thus *was* the order of march of the
children of Israel, according to their
armies, when they began their journey.
29 Now Moses said to [c]Hobab the son of
[d]Reuel[4] the Midianite, Moses' father-in-
law, "We are setting out for the place of
which the LORD said, [e]'I will give it to you.'
Come with us, and [f]we will treat you well;
for [g]the LORD has promised good things to
Israel."
30 And he said to him, "I will not go, but
I will depart to my *own* land and to my relatives."
31 So *Moses* said, "Please do not leave,
inasmuch as you know how we are to
camp in the wilderness, and you can [5]be
our [h]eyes. 32 And it shall be, if you go with
us—indeed it shall be—that [i]whatever
good the LORD will do to us, the same we
will do to you."
33 So they departed from [j]the mountain
of the LORD on a journey of three days;
and the ark of the covenant of the LORD
[k]went before them for the three days'
journey, to search out a resting place for
them. 34 And [l]the cloud of the LORD *was*
above them by day when they went out
from the camp.
35 So it was, whenever the ark set out,
that Moses said:

[m]"Rise up, O LORD!
Let Your enemies be scattered,
And let those who hate You flee
before You."

36 And when it rested, he said:

"Return, O LORD,
To the many thousands of Israel."

12 [p]Ex. 19:1; Num. 1:1; 9:5 [q]Ex. 40:36 [r]Gen. 21:21; Num. 12:16; Deut. 1:1
13 [s]Num. 10:5, 6
14 [t]Num. 2:3-9 [u]Num. 1:7 [2]*banner*
17 [v]Num. 1:51 [w]Num. 4:21-32; 7:7-9
18 [x]Num. 2:10-16
21 [y]Num. 4:4-20; 7:9 [3]*Prepared by the Gershonites and the Merarites*
22 [z]Num. 2:18-24
25 [a]Num. 2:25-31; Josh. 6:9
28 [b]Num. 2:34
29 [c]Judg. 4:11 [d]Ex. 2:18; 3:1; 18:12 [e]Gen. 12:7; Ex. 6:4-8 [f]Judg. 1:16 [g]Gen. 32:12; Ex. 3:8 [4]*Jethro,* Ex. 3:1; LXX *Raguel*
31 [h]Job 29:15 [5]*Act as our guide*
32 [i]Ex. 18:9; Lev. 19:34; Judg. 1:16
33 [j]Ex. 3:1; Deut. 1:6 [k]Deut. 1:33; Josh. 3:3-6; Ezek. 20:6
34 [l]Ex. 13:21; Neh. 9:12, 19
35 [m]Ps. 68:1, 2; 132:8; Is. 17:12-14

from Egypt and 11 months after the arrival at Sinai, Israel began to march toward Canaan.

10:12 the Wilderness of Paran. According to 13:26, Kadesh was in the Wilderness of Paran, probably at its northern border. This verse gives a summary of God's leading from Sinai to Kadesh.

10:14-28 The order of march followed by Israel in these verses is in exact conformity to the details given in 2:1-34.

10:14 standard. *See note on 2:2.* **Nahshon.** For the fourth, and final time in the book of Numbers, the 12 leaders of the first generation of Israel were noted (see chaps. 1,2 and 7). In accordance with Gen. 49:8-12, the tribe of Judah was given preeminence as the ruling tribe. It led the march into the Promised Land.

10:29 Hobab. As the son of Reuel, Hobab was Moses' brother-in-law. **Reuel.** Reuel was the father-in-law of Moses (see Ex. 2:18). **Come with us.** Moses sought Hobab's help in leading Israel through the wilderness. He promised Hobab a portion of the inheritance of Israel within the Land if he would come. The text of Numbers does not explicitly state whether Hobab responded to Moses or not. But Judg. 1:16 implies that Hobab agreed to Moses' request. Later, he joined with Judah in the conquest of the Land and did receive the blessing of dwelling in the land.

10:33 journey…three days. The Israelites traveled for 3 days from Sinai before they encamped for more than one night.

10:35,36 As Israel traveled and encamped, Moses prayed that the Lord would give victory and that His presence would be among her.

11:1–25:18 In contrast to Num. 1–10, a major change takes place at 11:1. Obedient Israel became complaining (11:1; 14:2,27,29,36; 16:1-3,41; 17:5) and rebellious (14:9; 17:10) Israel. Ultimately, Moses and Aaron rebelled against the Lord as well (20:10,24). In response to Israel's disobedience, the Lord's anger was aroused (11:1,10,33; 12:9; 14:18; 25:3,4) and He plagued His people (14:37; 16:46,47,48,49,50; 25:8,9,18) as He had Pharaoh and the Egyptians (Ex. 9:14; 12:13; 30:12). Nevertheless, even though God judged that generation of Israel, He will still fulfill His promises to Abraham in the future (23:5–24:24).

The People Complain

11 Now [a]*when* the people complained, it displeased the LORD; [b]for the LORD heard *it,* and His anger was aroused. So the [c]fire of the LORD burned among them, and consumed *some* in the outskirts of the camp. 2 Then the people [d]cried out to Moses, and when Moses [e]prayed to the LORD, the fire was [1]quenched. 3 So he called the name of the place [2]Taberah, because the fire of the LORD had burned among them.

4 Now the [f]mixed multitude who were among them [3]yielded to [g]intense craving; so the children of Israel also wept again and said: [h]"Who will give us meat to eat? 5 [i]We remember the fish which we ate freely in Egypt, the cucumbers, the melons, the leeks, the onions, and the garlic; 6 but now [j]our whole being *is* dried up; *there is* nothing at all except this manna *before* our eyes!"

7 Now [k]the manna *was* like coriander seed, and its color like the color of bdellium. 8 The people went about and gathered *it,* ground *it* on millstones or beat *it* in the mortar, cooked *it* in pans, and made cakes of it; and [l]its taste was like the taste of pastry prepared with oil. 9 And [m]when the dew fell on the camp in the night, the manna fell on it.

10 Then Moses heard the people weeping throughout their families, everyone at the door of his tent; and [n]the anger of the LORD was greatly aroused; Moses also was displeased. 11 [o]So Moses said to the LORD, "Why have You afflicted Your servant? And why have I not found favor in Your sight, that You have laid the [4]burden of all these people on me? 12 Did I conceive all these people? Did I beget them, that You should say to me, [p]'Carry them in your bosom, as a [q]guardian carries a nursing child,' to the land which You [r]swore[5] to their fathers? 13 [s]Where am I to get meat to give to all these people? For they weep all over me, saying, 'Give us meat, that we may eat.' 14 [t]I am not able to bear all these people alone, because the burden *is* too heavy for me. 15 If You treat me like this, please kill me here and now—if I have found favor in Your sight—and [u]do not let me see my wretchedness!"

The Seventy Elders

16 So the LORD said to Moses: "Gather to Me [v]seventy men of the elders of Israel, whom you know to be the elders of the people and [w]officers over them; bring them to the tabernacle of meeting, that they may stand there with you. 17 Then I will come down and talk with you there. [x]I will take of the Spirit that *is* upon you and will put *the same* upon them; and they shall bear the burden of the people with you, that you may not bear *it* yourself alone. 18 Then you shall say to the people, [6]'Consecrate yourselves for tomorrow, and you shall eat meat; for you have wept [y]in the hearing of the LORD, saying, "Who will give us meat to eat? For *it was* well with us in Egypt." Therefore the LORD will give you meat, and you shall eat. 19 You shall eat, not one day, nor two days, nor five days, nor ten days, nor twenty days, 20 [z]but *for* a whole month, until it comes out of your nostrils and becomes loathsome to you, because you have [a]despised the LORD who is among you, and have wept before Him, saying, [b]"Why did we ever come up out of Egypt?" ' "

21 And Moses said, [c]"The people whom I *am* among *are* six hundred thousand men on foot; yet You have said, 'I will give them meat, that they may eat *for* a whole month.' 22 [d]Shall flocks and herds be slaughtered for them, to provide enough for them? Or shall all the fish of the sea be gathered together for them, to provide enough for them?"

23 And the LORD said to Moses, [e]"Has[7] the LORD's arm been shortened? Now you shall see whether [f]what I say will happen to you or not."

CHAPTER 11

1 [a] Num. 14:2; 16:11; 17:5; Deut. 9:22 [b] Ps. 78:21 [c] Lev. 10:2; 2 Kin. 1:12
2 [d] Num. 12:11, 13; 21:7 [e] [James 5:16] [1] *extinguished*
3 [2] Lit. *Burning*
4 [f] Ex. 12:38 [g] 1 Cor. 10:6 [h] [Ps. 78:18] [3] Lit. *lusted intensely*
5 [i] Ex. 16:3
6 [j] Num. 21:5
7 [k] Ex. 16:14, 31
8 [l] Ex. 16:31
9 [m] Ex. 16:13, 14
10 [n] Ps. 78:21
11 [o] Ex. 5:22; Deut. 1:12 [4] *responsibility*
12 [p] Is. 40:11 [q] Is. 49:23; 1 Thess. 2:7 [r] Gen. 26:3 [5] *solemnly promised*
13 [s] Matt. 15:33; Mark 8:4
14 [t] Ex. 18:18; Deut. 1:12
15 [u] Rev. 3:17
16 [v] Ex. 18:25; 24:1, 9 [w] Deut. 16:18
17 [x] 1 Sam. 10:6; 2 Kin. 2:15; [Joel 2:28]
18 [y] Ex. 16:7 [6] *Set yourselves apart*
20 [z] Ps. 78:29; 106:15 [a] 1 Sam. 10:19 [b] Num. 21:5
21 [c] Gen. 12:2; Ex. 12:37; Num. 1:46; 2:32
22 [d] 2 Kin. 7:2
23 [e] Is. 50:2; 59:1 [f] Num. 23:19 [7] Is the LORD's power limited?

11:1–12:16 The complaining of the people and leaders began on the journey from Sinai to Kadesh.

11:1 the LORD heard *it.* Their complaining was outward and loud. **the outskirts of the camp.** God in His grace consumed only those who were on the very edges of the encampment of Israel.

11:4 the mixed multitude. The word only occurs here in the OT. However, another word, "mixed company," was used in Ex. 12:38. The "mixed multitude" here are non-Israelites who left Egypt with Israel in the Exodus. **meat.** After over a year of eating manna in the wilderness, the mixed multitude wanted the spicy food of Egypt once again.

11:7 manna. See Ex. 16:14. **bdellium.** This refers more to appearance than color, i.e., it had the appearance of a pale resin.

11:13,14 Moses confessed to God that he was not able to provide meat for the people as they demanded. Their complaining was discouraging him so that because of this great burden, Moses desired death from the hand of the Lord.

11:16-30 In response to Moses' despair in leading the people, the Lord gave him 70 men to help.

11:16 seventy men. These aides to Moses might be the same 70 referred to in Ex. 18:21-26.

11:17 the Spirit. This refers to the Spirit of God. It was by means of the Holy Spirit that Moses was able to lead Israel. In v. 25, the Lord gave the Spirit to the 70 men in fulfillment of the Word He gave to Moses.

11:21 six hundred thousand. Moses rounded off the 603,550 of 1:46; 2:32.

11:23 Has the LORD's arm been shortened? A figure of speech

24 So Moses went out and told the people the words of the LORD, and he [g]gath-
ered the seventy men of the elders of the
people and placed them around the tabernacle. 25 Then the LORD came down in the
cloud, and spoke to him, and took of the
Spirit that *was* upon him, and placed *the*
same upon the seventy elders; and it happened, [h]when the Spirit rested upon them,
that [i]they prophesied, [8]although they
never did *so* again.
26 But two men had remained in the
camp: the name of one *was* Eldad, and the
name of the other Medad. And the Spirit
rested upon them. Now they *were* among
those listed, but who [j]had not gone out to
the tabernacle; yet they prophesied in the
camp. 27 And a young man ran and told
Moses, and said, "Eldad and Medad are
prophesying in the camp."
28 So Joshua the son of Nun, Moses' assistant, *one* of his choice men, answered
and said, "Moses my lord, [k]forbid them!"
29 Then Moses said to him, "Are you
[9]zealous for my sake? [l]Oh, that all the
LORD's people were prophets *and* that the
LORD would put His Spirit upon them!"
30 And Moses returned to the camp, he
and the elders of Israel.

The LORD Sends Quail

31 Now a [m]wind went out from the
LORD, and it brought quail from the sea
and left *them* fluttering near the camp,
about a day's journey on this side and
about a day's journey on the other side, all
around the camp, and about two cubits
above the surface of the ground. 32 And
the people stayed up all that day, all night,
and all the next day, and gathered the quail
(he who gathered least gathered ten [n]ho-
mers); and they spread *them* out for themselves all around the camp. 33 But while
the [o]meat *was* still between their teeth, before it was chewed, the wrath of the LORD
was aroused against the people, and the
LORD struck the people with a very great
plague. 34 So he called the name of that
place [1]Kibroth Hattaavah, because there
they buried the people who had yielded to
craving.
35 [p]From Kibroth Hattaavah the people
moved to Hazeroth, and camped at Hazeroth.

Dissension of Aaron and Miriam

12 Then [a]Miriam and Aaron [1]spoke
[b]against Moses because of the
[2]Ethiopian woman whom he had married;
for [c]he had married an Ethiopian woman.
2 So they said, "Has the LORD indeed spoken only through [d]Moses? [e]Has He not
spoken through us also?" And the LORD
[f]heard *it*. 3 (Now the man Moses *was* very
humble, more than all men who *were* on
the face of the earth.)
4 [g]Suddenly the LORD said to Moses,
Aaron, and Miriam, "Come out, you three,
to the tabernacle of meeting!" So the three
came out. 5 [h]Then the LORD came down in
the pillar of cloud and stood *in* the door of
the tabernacle, and called Aaron and Miriam. And they both went forward. 6 Then
He said,

"Hear now My words:
If there is a prophet among you,
I, the LORD, make Myself known to
him [i]in a vision;
I speak to him [j]in a dream.

24 [g] Num. 11:16
25 [h] 2 Kin. 2:15 [i] 1 Sam. 10:5, 6, 10; Joel 2:28; Acts 2:17, 18; 1 Cor. 14:1 [8] Tg., Vg. *and they did not cease*
26 [j] Jer. 36:5
28 [k] [Mark 9:38-40; Luke 9:49]
29 [l] 1 Cor. 14:5 [9] *jealous*
31 [m] Ex. 16:13; Ps. 78:26-28; 105:40
32 [n] Ex. 16:36; Ezek. 45:11
33 [o] Ps. 78:29-31; 106:15
34 [1] Lit. *Graves of Craving*
35 [p] Num. 33:17

CHAPTER 12

1 [a] Ex. 15:20, 21; Num. 20:1 [b] Num. 11:1 [c] Ex. 2:21 [1] *criticized* [2] *Cushite*
2 [d] Num. 16:3 [e] Ex. 15:20; Mic. 6:4 [f] Gen. 29:33; Num. 11:1; 2 Kin. 19:4; Is. 37:4; Ezek. 35:12, 13
4 [g] [Ps. 76:9]
5 [h] Ex. 19:9; 34:5; Num. 11:25; 16:19
6 [i] Gen. 46:2; 1 Sam. 3:15; Job 33:15; Ezek. 1:1; Dan. 8:2; Luke 1:11; Acts 10:11, 17; 22:17, 18 [j] Gen. 31:10; 1 Kin. 3:5, 15; Matt. 1:20

indicating that the Lord was able to do as He had said and provide meat for the 600,000 men of Israel and their families for one month.

11:25 prophesied. Here the prophesying refers to the giving of praise and similar expressions of worship to the Lord without prior training. The text is clear that this was a one-time event as far as these men were concerned.

11:29 that the LORD would put His Spirit upon them. Moses desired and anticipated the day when all of God's people would have His spirit within them. By this, he looked forward to the New Covenant. See Ezek. 36:22-27; Jer. 31:31ff.; Joel 2:28.

11:31 a day's journey. The Lord, using a wind, brought a great quantity of quail that surrounded the encampment within one day's journey. **about two cubits above the…ground.** The birds flew at a height of about 3 ft. where they were able to be easily captured or clubbed to the ground by the people.

11:32 ten homers. About 60-70 bu.

12:1-16 The brother and sister of Moses opposed his leadership. The immediate occasion was the prophesying of the elders. Moses' position as the spokesman for God to Israel was called into question.

12:1 Ethiopian. Ethiopia, S of Egypt, was inhabited by the descendants of Cush, the firstborn son of Ham (Gen. 10:6,7). Although the term "Ethiopian" could have been used concerning Zipporah, Moses' first wife, it seems more likely that Moses had remarried after the death of Zipporah. The marriage to the Ethiopian woman had been recent and furnished the pretext for the attack of Miriam and Aaron. Since Miriam is mentioned first, she probably was the instigator of the attack against Moses.

12:2 spoken only through Moses. Miriam and Aaron asserted that God had spoken to them in the same way that He had spoken to Moses.

12:3 very humble. This statement is often cited as evidence that Moses could not have written the book of Numbers, for he would not have boasted in his own humility. However, the Holy Spirit certainly could inspire Moses to make an accurate statement about himself, probably against his own natural inclination. In this context, Moses was asserting there was nothing that he had done to provoke this attack by Miriam and Aaron.

12:5 the LORD came down. As in Gen. 11:5, this clause states that the Lord knows and deals with situations on earth. Here the Lord came down and, in v. 10, departed. This was God's answer to the attack against Moses.

7 Not so with [k]My servant Moses;
[l]He *is* faithful in all [m]My house.
8 I speak with him [n]face to face,
Even [o]plainly,[3] and not in [4]dark
sayings;
And he sees [p]the form of the LORD.
Why then [q]were you not afraid
To speak against My servant
Moses?"

9 So the anger of the LORD was aroused
against them, and He departed. 10 And
when the cloud departed from above the
tabernacle, [r]suddenly Miriam *became* [s]lep-
rous, as *white as* snow. Then Aaron turned
toward Miriam, and there she was, a leper.
11 So Aaron said to Moses, "Oh, my lord!
Please [t]do not lay [5]*this* sin on us, in which
we have done foolishly and in which we
have sinned. 12 Please [u]do not let her be as
one dead, whose flesh is half consumed
when he comes out of his mother's
womb!"
13 So Moses cried out to the LORD, saying, "Please [v]heal her, O God, I pray!"
14 Then the LORD said to Moses, "If her
father had but [w]spit in her face, would she
not be shamed seven days? Let her be
[x]shut[6] out of the camp seven days, and afterward she may be received *again*." 15 [y]So
Miriam was shut out of the camp seven
days, and the people did not journey till
Miriam was brought in *again*. 16 And afterward the people moved from [z]Hazeroth
and camped in the Wilderness of Paran.

Spies Sent into Canaan

13 And the LORD spoke to Moses, saying, 2 [a]"Send men to spy out the
land of Canaan, which I am giving to the
children of Israel; from each tribe of their
fathers you shall send a man, every one a
leader among them."
3 So Moses sent them [b]from the Wilderness of Paran according to the command of
the LORD, all of them men who *were* heads
of the children of Israel. 4 Now these *were*
their names: from the tribe of Reuben,
Shammua the son of Zaccur; 5 from the
tribe of Simeon, Shaphat the son of Hori;
6 [c]from the tribe of Judah, [d]Caleb the son
of Jephunneh; 7 from the tribe of Issachar,
Igal the son of Joseph; 8 from the tribe of
Ephraim, [1]Hoshea the son of Nun; 9 from
the tribe of Benjamin, Palti the son of
Raphu; 10 from the tribe of Zebulun,
Gaddiel the son of Sodi; 11 from the tribe of
Joseph, *that is,* from the tribe of Manasseh,
Gaddi the son of Susi; 12 from the tribe of
Dan, Ammiel the son of Gemalli; 13 from
the tribe of Asher, Sethur the son of Michael; 14 from the tribe of Naphtali, Nahbi
the son of Vophsi; 15 from the tribe of Gad,
Geuel the son of Machi.
16 These *are* the names of the men whom
Moses sent to [2]spy out the land. And Moses called [e]Hoshea[3] the son of Nun,
Joshua.
17 Then Moses sent them to spy out the
land of Canaan, and said to them, "Go up
this *way* into the South, and go up to [f]the
mountains, 18 and see what the land is like:
whether the people who dwell in it *are*
strong or weak, few or many; 19 whether
the land they dwell in *is* good or bad;
whether the cities they inhabit *are* like
camps or strongholds; 20 whether the land
is [4]rich or poor; and whether there are
forests there or not. [g]Be of good courage.
And bring some of the fruit of the land."
Now the time *was* the season of the first
ripe grapes.

7 [k]Josh. 1:1; Ps. 105:26 [l]Heb. 3:2, 5 [m]1 Tim. 1:12
8 [n]Ex. 33:11; Deut. 34:10; Hos. 12:13 [o][1 Cor. 13:12] [p]Ex. 33:19-23 [q]2 Pet. 2:10; Jude 8 [3]*appearing* [4]*riddles*
10 [r]Deut. 24:9 [s]Ex. 4:6; 2 Kin. 5:27; 15:5; 2 Chr. 26:19, 20
11 [t]2 Sam. 19:19; 24:10 [5]*the penalty for this*
12 [u]Ps. 88:4
13 [v]Ps. 103:3
14 [w]Deut. 25:9; Job 30:10; Is. 50:6 [x]Lev. 13:46; Num. 5:1-4 [6]*exiled*
15 [y]Deut. 24:9; 2 Chr. 26:20, 21
16 [z]Num. 11:35; 33:17, 18

CHAPTER 13

2 [a]Num. 32:8; Deut. 1:22; 9:23
3 [b]Num. 12:16; 32:8; Deut. 1:19; 9:23
6 [c]Num. 34:19 [d]Num. 14:6, 30; Josh. 14:6, 7; Judg. 1:12; 1 Chr. 4:15
8 [1]LXX, Vg. *Oshea*
16 [e]Ex. 17:9; Deut. 32:44 [2]*secretly search* [3]LXX, Vg. *Oshea*
17 [f]Judg. 1:9
20 [g]Deut. 31:6, 7, 23 [4]*fertile or barren*

12:7 My servant Moses. This phrase is also repeated in v. 9. A servant of the Lord in the OT is one who responded in faith by obedience to the Word of the Lord. **faithful in all My house.** A reference to Moses' loyal performance of his role as covenant mediator between the Lord and Israel.

12:8 face to face. God spoke to Moses without mediation. Also the Lord did not speak to Moses through visions and dreams, but plainly. It was not that Moses saw the full glory of God (cf. John 1:18), but rather that he had the most explicit, intimate encounters (cf. Deut. 34:10). **the form of the LORD.** This is the likeness or representation of the Lord which Moses was privileged to see. See Ex. 33:23.

12:10 leprous. In judgment of Miriam's opposition to Moses, the Lord struck her with leprosy. For the treatment of a leper, see Lev. 13–14. A public sin required a public response from the Lord.

12:16 Wilderness of Paran. *See note on 10:12.*

13:1–14:45 These chapters record the massive failure of Israel at Kadesh. The people failed to believe the Lord (14:11) and take the Promised Land. Their lack of faith was open rebellion against the Lord (14:9). The NT looks back to these times as an illustration of apostasy (cf. 1 Cor. 10:5; Heb. 3:16-19).

13:1 the LORD spoke to Moses. According to Deut. 1:22,23, the people had first requested the spies be sent out after Moses challenged them to take the land. Here, the Lord affirmed the peoples' desire and commanded Moses to send them.

13:2 spy out the land of Canaan. The spies were specifically called to explore the Land that God had promised to Israel. This exploration gave valuable information to Moses for the conquest of the Land.

13:3 heads of the children of Israel. These leaders were different than those mentioned in Num. 1,2,7,10. Presumably the tribal leaders in the 4 earlier lists were older men. The task for the spies called for some leaders who were younger, probably about 40 years of age, based on the ages of Caleb and Joshua.

13:16 Hoshea...Joshua. For reasons not made clear, Moses changed the name of Hoshea, meaning "desire for salvation," to Joshua, meaning "the Lord is salvation."

13:17-20 The spies were to determine the nature of the Land itself, as well as the strengths and weaknesses of the people.

13:20 the season of the first ripe grapes. Mid-summer (mid to late July).

21 So they went up and spied out the land [h]from the Wilderness of Zin as far as [i]Rehob, near the entrance of [j]Hamath. 22 And they went up through the South and came to [k]Hebron; Ahiman, Sheshai, and Talmai, the descendants of [l]Anak, *were* there. (Now Hebron was built seven years before Zoan in Egypt.) 23 [m]Then they came to the [5]Valley of Eshcol, and there cut down a branch with one cluster of grapes; they carried it between two of them on a pole. *They* also *brought* some of the pomegranates and figs. 24 The place was called the Valley of [6]Eshcol, because of the cluster which the men of Israel cut down there. 25 And they returned from spying out the land after forty days.

26 Now they departed and came back to Moses and Aaron and all the congregation of the children of Israel in the Wilderness of Paran, at [n]Kadesh; they brought back word to them and to all the congregation, and showed them the fruit of the land. 27 Then they told him, and said: "We went to the land where you sent us. It truly [7]flows with [o]milk and honey, [p]and this *is* its fruit. 28 Nevertheless the [q]people who dwell in the land *are* strong; the cities *are* fortified *and* very large; moreover we saw the descendants of [r]Anak there. 29 [s]The Amalekites dwell in the land of the South; the Hittites, the Jebusites, and the Amorites dwell in the mountains; and the Canaanites dwell by the sea and along the banks of the Jordan."

30 Then [t]Caleb quieted the people before Moses, and said, "Let us go up at once and take possession, for we are well able to overcome it."

31 [u]But the men who had gone up with him said, "We are not able to go up against the people, for they *are* stronger than we." 32 And they [v]gave the children of Israel a bad report of the land which they had spied out, saying, "The land through which we have gone as spies *is* a land that devours its inhabitants, and [w]all the people whom we saw in it *are* men of *great* stature. 33 There we saw the [8]giants ([x]the descendants of Anak came from the giants); and we were [y]like[9] grasshoppers in our own sight, and so we were [z]in their sight."

Israel Refuses to Enter Canaan

14 So all the congregation lifted up their voices and cried, and the people [a]wept that night. 2 [b]And all the children of Israel complained against Moses and Aaron, and the whole congregation said to them, "If only we had died in the land of Egypt! Or if only we had died in this wilderness! 3 Why has the LORD brought us to this land to [1]fall by the sword, that our wives and [c]children should become victims? Would it not be better for us to return to Egypt?" 4 So they said to one another, [d]"Let us select a leader and [e]return to Egypt."

5 Then Moses and Aaron [2]fell on their faces before all the assembly of the congregation of the children of Israel.

6 But Joshua the son of Nun and Caleb the son of Jephunneh, *who were* among those who had spied out the land, tore their clothes; 7 and they spoke to all the congregation of the children of Israel, saying: [f]"The land we passed through to spy out *is* an exceedingly good land. 8 If the LORD [g]delights in us, then He will bring us into this land and give it to us, [h]'a land which flows with milk and honey.' 9 Only [i]do not rebel against the LORD, [j]nor fear the people of the land, for [k]they[3] *are* our bread;

21 [h]Num. 20:1; 27:14; 33:36; Josh. 15:1 [i]Josh. 19:28 [j]Num. 34:8; Josh. 13:5
22 [k]Josh. 15:13, 14; Judg. 1:10 [l]Josh. 11:21, 22
23 [m]Gen. 14:13; Num. 13:24; 32:9; Deut. 1:24, 25 [5]*Wadi*
24 [6]Lit. *Cluster*
26 [n]Num. 20:1, 16; 32:8; 33:36; Deut. 1:19; Josh. 14:6
27 [o]Ex. 3:8, 17; 13:5; 33:3 [p]Deut. 1:25 [7]Has an abundance of food
28 [q]Deut. 1:28; 9:1, 2 [r]Josh. 11:21, 22
29 [s]Ex. 17:8; Judg. 6:3
30 [t]Num. 14:6, 24
31 [u]Num. 32:9; Deut. 1:28; 9:1-3; Josh. 14:8
32 [v]Num. 14:36, 37; Ps. 106:24 [w]Amos 2:9
33 [x]Deut. 1:28; 9:2; Josh. 11:21 [y]Is. 40:22 [z]1 Sam. 17:42 [8]Heb. *nephilim* [9]As mere insects

CHAPTER 14

1 [a]Num. 11:4; Deut. 1:45
2 [b]Ex. 16:2; 17:3; Num. 16:41; Ps. 106:25; 1 Cor. 10:10
3 [c]Num. 14:31; Deut. 1:39 [1]*be killed in battle*
4 [d]Neh. 9:17 [e]Deut. 17:16; Acts 7:39
5 [2]*prostrated themselves*
7 [f]Num. 13:27; Deut. 1:25
8 [g]Deut. 10:15; 2 Sam. 15:25, 26; 1 Kin. 10:9; Ps. 147:11 [h]Ex. 3:8; Num. 13:27
9 [i]Deut. 1:26; 9:7, 23, 24; 1 Sam. 15:23 [j]Deut. 7:18 [k]Num. 24:8 [3]They shall be as food for our consumption.

13:21 from the Wilderness of Zin as far as Rehob. These were the southernmost and northernmost borders of the land.

13:22 Hebron. The first major city the spies came to in Canaan. Abram had earlier built an altar to the Lord here (cf. Gen. 13:18). Abraham and Isaac were buried here (Gen. 49:31). The city had been fortified at about 1730 B.C., 7 years before the building of Zoan in Egypt, and later became the inheritance of Caleb (Josh. 14:13-15) and then David's capital when he reigned over Judah (2 Sam. 2:1-4). **the descendants of Anak.** Cf. 13:28. Anak was probably the ancestor of Ahiman, Sheshiai, and Talmai, who were living at Hebron. They were noted for their height (Deut. 2:21; 9:2).

13:23 the Valley of Eshcol. Eshcol means "cluster."

13:28 the people...*are* strong. The spies reported that the Land was good; however, the people were too strong to be conquered.

13:30 Caleb quieted the people. The verb "quieted" usually occurs in the form of the interjection "hush!" This implies that the spies report evoked a vocal reaction from the people. Caleb concurred with the report of the other spies, but called the people to go up and take the Land, knowing that with God's help they were able to overcome the strong people.

13:32 a bad report. The report of the 10 spies was evil because it exaggerated the dangers of the people in the Land, sought to stir up and instill fear in the people of Israel and, most importantly, it expressed their faithless attitude toward God and His promises.

13:33 giants. This term was used in Gen. 6:4 for a group of strong men who lived on the earth before the Flood. The descendants of Anak were, in exaggeration, compared to these giants, which led the spies to view themselves as grasshoppers before them.

14:1 all the congregation...wept. All of Israel bewailed the circumstances.

14:2 complained. The term means "to murmur." Specifically they wished they had died in Egypt or the wilderness.

14:4 select a leader and return to Egypt. The faithless people were ready to reject God's leader, Moses.

14:6 tore their clothes. This was an indication of distress (see Gen. 37:29).

14:7-9 Joshua and Caleb reaffirmed their appraisal that the Land

their protection has departed from them,
[l]and the LORD *is* with us. Do not fear
them."
10 [m]And all the congregation said to
stone them with stones. Now [n]the glory of
the LORD appeared in the tabernacle of
meeting before all the children of Israel.

Moses Intercedes for the People

11 Then the LORD said to Moses: "How
long will these people [o]reject[4] Me? And
how long will they not [p]believe Me, with
all the [5]signs which I have performed
among them? 12 I will strike them with the
pestilence and disinherit them, and I will
[q]make of you a nation greater and mightier than they."
13 And [r]Moses said to the LORD: [s]"Then
the Egyptians will hear *it,* for by Your
might You brought these people up from
among them, 14 and they will tell *it* to the
inhabitants of this land. They have [t]heard
that You, LORD, *are* among these people;
that You, LORD, are seen face to face and
Your cloud stands above them, and You go
before them in a pillar of cloud by day and
in a pillar of fire by night. 15 Now *if* You
kill these people as one man, then the nations which have heard of Your fame will
speak, saying, 16 'Because the LORD was
not [u]able to bring this people to the land
which He swore to give them, therefore
He killed them in the wilderness.' 17 And
now, I pray, let the power of my Lord be
great, just as You have spoken, saying,
18 [v]'The LORD is longsuffering and abundant in mercy, forgiving iniquity and
transgression; but He by no means clears
the guilty, [w]visiting the iniquity of the fathers on the children to the third and
fourth *generation.*' 19 [x]Pardon the iniquity
of this people, I pray, [y]according to the
greatness of Your mercy, just [z]as You have
forgiven this people, from Egypt even
until now."

20 Then the LORD said: "I have pardoned,
[a]according to your word; 21 but truly, as I
live, [b]all the earth shall be filled with the
glory of the LORD— 22 [c]because all these
men who have seen My glory and the
signs which I did in Egypt and in the
wilderness, and have put Me to the test
now [d]these ten times, and have not heeded
My voice, 23 they certainly shall not [e]see
the land of which I [6]swore to their fathers,
nor shall any of those who rejected Me see
it. 24 But My servant [f]Caleb, because he has
a different spirit in him and [g]has followed
Me fully, I will bring into the land where
he went, and his descendants shall inherit
it. 25 Now the Amalekites and the Canaanites dwell in the valley; tomorrow turn and
[h]move out into the wilderness by the Way
of the Red Sea."

Death Sentence on the Rebels

26 And the LORD spoke to Moses and
Aaron, saying, 27 [i]"How long *shall I bear*
with this evil congregation who complain
against Me? [j]I have heard the complaints
which the children of Israel make against
Me. 28 Say to them, [k]'As I live,' says the
LORD, 'just as you have spoken in My hearing, so I will do to you: 29 The carcasses of
you who have complained against Me
shall fall in this wilderness, [l]all of you who
were numbered, according to your entire
number, from twenty years old and above.
30 [m]Except for Caleb the son of Jephunneh
and Joshua the son of Nun, you shall by no
means enter the land which I [7]swore I
would make you dwell in. 31 [n]But your little ones, whom you said would be victims,
I will bring in, and they shall [8]know the
land which [o]you have despised. 32 But *as*
for you, [p]your[9] carcasses shall fall in this
wilderness. 33 And your sons shall [q]be
[1]shepherds in the wilderness [r]forty years,
and [s]bear the brunt of your infidelity, until
your carcasses are consumed in the wilder-

9 [l]Gen. 48:21; Ex. 33:16; Deut. 20:1, 3, 4; 31:6-8; Josh. 1:5; Judg. 1:22; 2 Chr. 13:12; Ps. 46:7, 11; Zech. 8:23; Matt. 28:20; Heb. 13:5
10 [m]Ex. 17:4 [n]Ex. 16:10; Lev. 9:23
11 [o]Ps. 95:8; Heb. 3:8 [p]Deut. 9:23; [John 12:37] [4]*despise* [5]*miraculous signs*
12 [q]Ex. 32:10
13 [r]Ps. 106:23 [s]Ex. 32:12; Deut. 9:26-28; 32:27
14 [t]Deut. 2:25
16 [u]Deut. 9:28
18 [v]Ex. 34:6, 7; Deut. 5:10; 7:9; Ps. 103:8; 145:8; Jon. 4:2 [w]Ex. 20:5; Deut. 5:9
19 [x]Ex. 32:32; 34:9 [y]Ps. 51:1; 106:45 [z]Ps. 78:38
20 [a]2 Sam. 12:13; Mic. 7:18-20; [1 John 5:14-16]
21 [b]Ps. 72:19; Is. 6:3; 66:18, 19; Hab. 2:14
22 [c]Deut. 1:35; 1 Cor. 10:5; Heb. 3:17 [d]Gen. 31:7
23 [e]Num. 26:65; 32:11; Heb. 3:18 [6]*solemnly promised*
24 [f]Josh. 14:6, 8, 9 [g]Num. 32:12
25 [h]Num. 21:4; Deut. 1:40
27 [i]Ex. 16:28 [j]Ex. 16:12
28 [k]Deut. 1:35; 2:14, 15; Heb. 3:16-19
29 [l]Num. 1:45, 46; 26:64; Josh. 5:6
30 [m]Num. 26:65; 32:12; Deut. 1:36-38; Josh. 14:6-15 [7]*solemnly promised*
31 [n]Num. 14:3; Deut. 1:39 [o]Ps. 106:24 [8]*be acquainted with*
32 [p]Num. 26:64, 65; 32:13; 1 Cor. 10:5 [9]You shall die.
33 [q]Num. 32:13; Ps. 107:40 [r]Deut. 2:14 [s]Ezek. 23:35 [1]Vg. *wanderers*

was good and their confidence that the Lord would deliver it and its people into their hands.

14:10 the glory of the LORD appeared. In response to the people's violent rejection of Joshua and Caleb's challenge, God appeared.

14:11 reject...not believe Me. They had refused to trust or rely on God and His power to give them the land of Canaan in spite of the signs that He had done in their midst.

14:12 I will make of you a nation. As in Ex. 32:9,10, God threatened to wipe out the people and start over again with Moses' "son." This justifiable threat showed the seriousness with which God took rebellion on the part of His people.

14:13-19 As in Ex. 32:11-13, Moses interceded for Israel to protect the Lord's reputation with the Egyptians, who would charge the Lord with inability to complete His deliverance of Israel and thus deny His power. Second, the Lord's loyal love was the basis on which the Lord could forgive His people.

14:22 ten times. Taken literally this includes: 1) Ex. 14:10-12; 2) Ex. 15:22-24; 3) Ex. 16:1-3; 4) Ex. 16:19,20; 5) Ex. 16:27-30; 6) Ex. 17:1-4; 7) Ex. 32:1-35; 8) Num. 11:1-3; 9) Num. 11:4-34; 10) Num. 14:3.

14:24 My servant Caleb. Since Caleb was recognized as one who feared and trusted the Lord, He later rewarded his faith (cf. Josh. 14).

14:25 turn and move out into the wilderness. Because of Israel's refusal to enter the Land, instead of continuing northward, God commanded they move southward toward the Gulf of Aqabah.

14:26-35 The Lord granted the Israelites their wish, i.e., their judgment was that they would die in the wilderness (vv. 29,35: cp. v. 2). Their children, however, whom they thought would become victims (v. 3), God would bring into the land of Canaan (vv. 30-32). The present generation of rebels would die in the wilderness until 40 years were completed. The 40 years were calculated as one year for each day the spies were in Canaan.

ness. 34 [t]According to the number of the days in which you spied out the land, [u]forty days, for each day you shall bear your [2]guilt one year, *namely* forty years, [v]and you shall know My [3]rejection. 35 [w]I the LORD have spoken this. I will surely do so to all [x]this evil congregation who are gathered together against Me. In this wilderness they shall be consumed, and there they shall die.' "

36 Now the men whom Moses sent to spy out the land, who returned and made all the congregation complain against him by bringing a bad report of the land, 37 those very men who brought the evil report about the land, [y]died by the plague before the LORD. 38 [z]But Joshua the son of Nun and Caleb the son of Jephunneh remained alive, of the men who went to spy out the land.

A Futile Invasion Attempt

39 Then Moses told these words to all the children of Israel, [a]and the people mourned greatly. 40 And they rose early in the morning and went up to the top of the mountain, saying, [b]"Here we are, and we will go up to the place which the LORD has promised, for we have sinned!"

41 And Moses said, "Now why do you [4]transgress the command of the LORD? For this will not succeed. 42 [c]Do not go up, lest you be defeated by your enemies, for the LORD *is* not among you. 43 For the Amalekites and the Canaanites *are* there before you, and you shall fall by the sword; [d]because you have turned away from the LORD, the LORD will not be with you."

44 [e]But they presumed to go up to the mountaintop. Nevertheless, neither the ark of the covenant of the LORD nor Moses departed from the camp. 45 Then the Amalekites and the Canaanites who dwelt in that mountain came down and attacked them, and drove them back as far as [f]Hormah.

Laws of Grain and Drink Offerings

15 And the LORD spoke to Moses, saying, 2 [a]"Speak to the children of Israel, and say to them: 'When you have come into the land you are to inhabit, which I am giving to you, 3 and you [b]make an offering by fire to the LORD, a burnt offering or a sacrifice, [c]to fulfill a vow or as a freewill offering or [d]in your appointed feasts, to make a [e]sweet[1] aroma to the LORD, from the herd or the flock, 4 then [f]he who presents his offering to the LORD shall bring [g]a grain offering of one-tenth *of an ephah* of fine flour mixed [h]with one-fourth of a hin of oil; 5 [i]and one-fourth of a hin of wine as a drink offering you shall prepare with the burnt offering or the sacrifice, for each [j]lamb. 6 [k]Or for a ram you shall prepare as a grain offering two-tenths *of an ephah* of fine flour mixed with one-third of a hin of oil; 7 and as a drink offering you shall offer one-third of a hin of wine as a sweet aroma to the LORD. 8 And when you prepare a young bull as a burnt offering, or as a sacrifice to fulfill a vow, or as a [l]peace offering to the LORD, 9 then shall be offered [m]with the young bull a grain offering of three-tenths *of an ephah* of fine flour mixed with half a hin of oil; 10 and you shall bring as the drink offering half a hin of wine as an offering made by fire, a sweet aroma to the LORD.

11 [n]'Thus it shall be done for each young bull, for each ram, or for each lamb or young goat. 12 According to the number that you prepare, so you shall do with everyone according to their number. 13 All who are native-born shall do these things in this manner, in presenting an offering made by fire, a sweet aroma to the LORD. 14 And if a stranger [2]dwells with you, or whoever *is* among you throughout your generations, and would present an offering made by fire, a sweet aroma to the LORD, just as you do, so shall he do. 15 [o]One [3]ordinance *shall be* for you of the assembly and for the stranger who dwells *with you,* an ordinance forever throughout your generations; as you are, so shall the stranger be before the LORD. 16 One law and one custom shall be for you and for the stranger who dwells with you.' "

17 Again the LORD spoke to Moses, saying, 18 [p]"Speak to the children of Israel,

34 [t]Num. 13:25 [u]Ps. 95:10; Ezek. 4:6 [v]1 Kin. 8:56; [Heb. 4:1] [2]*iniquity* [3]*opposition*
35 [w]Num. 23:19 [x]1 Cor. 10:5
37 [y]Num. 16:49; [1 Cor. 10:10]; Heb. 3:17, 18
38 [z]Josh. 14:6, 10
39 [a]Ex. 33:4
40 [b]Deut. 1:41-44
41 [4]*overstep*
42 [c]Deut. 1:42; 31:17
43 [d]2 Chr. 15:2
44 [e]Deut. 1:43
45 [f]Num. 21:3

CHAPTER 15

2 [a]Lev. 23:10; Num. 15:18; Deut. 7:1
3 [b]Lev. 1:2, 3 [c]Lev. 7:16; 22:18, 21 [d]Lev. 23:2, 8, 12, 38; Num. 28:18, 19, 27; Deut. 16:10 [e]Gen. 8:21; Ex. 29:18; Lev. 1:9 [1]*pleasing*
4 [f]Lev. 2:1; 6:14 [g]Ex. 29:40; Lev. 23:13 [h]Lev. 14:10; Num. 28:5
5 [i]Num. 28:7, 14 [j]Lev. 1:10; 3:6; Num. 15:11; 28:4, 5
6 [k]Num. 28:12, 14
8 [l]Lev. 7:11
9 [m]Num. 28:12, 14
11 [n]Num. 28
14 [2]As a resident alien
15 [o]Ex. 12:49; Num. 9:14; 15:29 [3]*statute*
18 [p]Num. 15:2; Deut. 26:1

14:37 died by the plague. As an indication of the certainty of the coming judgment, the 10 spies who undermined the people's faith were struck by the plague and died.

14:44 they presumed to go up to the mountaintop. With characteristic obstinacy, the people rejected Moses' counsel and the Lord's command and went to attack the Amalekites in the hill country. Since the Lord was not with them, they were defeated.

15:1-41 Even though the Israelites had rebelled against the Lord and were under his judgment, the Lord still planned to give the land of Canaan to them. These laws assumed Israel's entrance into the Land (15:2,17).

15:1-16 The law of the grain offering recorded here differs from that given in Lev. 2. The grain offerings in Leviticus were offered separately as a gift to the Lord. Here, for the first time, grain and drink offerings were allowed to be offered along with either a burnt or a peace offering.

15:4 *ephah*...hin. Measurements equal to 4 to 6 gallons and 6 to 8 pints.

15:17-21 This regulation pertained to the offering of the firstfruits of the harvest. When the people entered the land of Canaan and began to enjoy its produce, they were to show their devotion to the Lord by presenting to Him a cake baked from the first cuttings of the grain.

and say to them: 'When you come into the
land to which I bring you, 19 then it will be,
when you eat of [q]the bread of the land, that
you shall offer up a heave offering to the
LORD. 20 [r]You shall offer up a cake of the
first of your ground meal *as* a heave offering; as [s]a heave offering of the threshing
floor, so shall you offer it up. 21 Of the first
of your ground meal you shall give to the
LORD a heave offering throughout your
generations.

Laws Concerning Unintentional Sin

22 [t]'If you sin unintentionally, and do
not observe all these commandments
which the LORD has spoken to Moses—
23 all that the LORD has commanded you
by the hand of Moses, from the day the
LORD gave commandment and onward
throughout your generations— 24 then it
will be, [u]if it is unintentionally committed,
[4]without the knowledge of the congregation, that the whole congregation shall
offer one young bull as a burnt offering, as
a sweet aroma to the LORD, [v]with its grain
offering and its drink offering, according
to the ordinance, and [w]one kid of the goats
as a sin offering. 25 [x]So the priest shall
make atonement for the whole congregation of the children of Israel, and it shall be
forgiven them, for it was unintentional;
they shall bring their offering, an offering
made by fire to the LORD, and their sin offering before the LORD, for their unin-
tended sin. 26 It shall be forgiven the
whole congregation of the children of Israel and the stranger who dwells among
them, because all the people *did it* unintentionally.

27 'And [y]if a person sins unintentionally,
then he shall bring a female goat in its first
year as a sin offering. 28 [z]So the priest shall
make atonement for the person who sins
unintentionally, when he sins unintentionally before the LORD, to make atonement for him; and it shall be forgiven him.
29 [a]You shall have one law for him who
sins unintentionally, *for* him who is native-
born among the children of Israel and for
the stranger who dwells among them.

19 [q] Josh. 5:11, 12
20 [r] Ex. 34:26; Lev. 23:10, 14, 17; Deut. 26:2, 10; Prov. 3:9, 10 [s] Lev. 2:14; 23:10, 16
22 [t] Lev. 4:2
24 [u] Lev. 4:13 [v] Num. 15:8-10 [w] Lev. 4:23 [4] Lit. *away from the eyes*
25 [x] Lev. 4:20; [Heb. 2:17]
27 [y] Lev. 4:27-31
28 [z] Lev. 4:35
29 [a] Num. 15:15
30 [b] Num. 14:40-44; Deut. 1:43; 17:12; Ps. 19:13; Heb. 10:26 [5] *defiantly*, lit. *with a high hand* [6] *blasphemes* [7] *Put to death*
31 [c] 2 Sam. 12:9; Prov. 13:13 [8] *iniquity*
32 [d] Ex. 31:14, 15; 35:2, 3
34 [e] Lev. 24:12
35 [f] Ex. 31:14, 15 [g] Lev. 24:14; Deut. 21:21; 1 Kin. 21:13; Acts 7:58
38 [h] Deut. 22:12; Matt. 23:5
39 [i] Ps. 103:18 [j] Deut. 29:19 [k] Ps. 73:27; 106:39; James 4:4
40 [l] [Lev. 11:44, 45; Rom. 12:1; Col. 1:22; 1 Pet. 1:15, 16]

CHAPTER 16
1 [a] Ex. 6:21

Law Concerning Presumptuous Sin

30 [b]'But the person who does *anything*
[5]presumptuously, *whether he is* native-born
or a stranger, that one [6]brings reproach on
the LORD, and he shall be [7]cut off from
among his people. 31 Because he has [c]de-
spised the word of the LORD, and has broken His commandment, that person shall
be completely cut off; his [8]guilt *shall be*
upon him.' "

Penalty for Violating the Sabbath

32 Now while the children of Israel were
in the wilderness, [d]they found a man gathering sticks on the Sabbath day. 33 And
those who found him gathering sticks
brought him to Moses and Aaron, and to
all the congregation. 34 They put him [e]un-
der guard, because it had not been explained what should be done to him.

35 Then the LORD said to Moses, [f]"The
man must surely be put to death; all the
congregation shall [g]stone him with stones
outside the camp." 36 So, as the LORD commanded Moses, all the congregation
brought him outside the camp and stoned
him with stones, and he died.

Tassels on Garments

37 Again the LORD spoke to Moses, saying, 38 "Speak to the children of Israel: Tell
[h]them to make tassels on the corners of
their garments throughout their generations, and to put a blue thread in the tassels
of the corners. 39 And you shall have the
tassel, that you may look upon it and [i]re-
member all the commandments of the
LORD and do them, and that you [j]*may* not
[k]follow the harlotry to which your own
heart and your own eyes are inclined,
40 and that you may remember and do all
My commandments, and be [l]holy for your
God. 41 I *am* the LORD your God, who
brought you out of the land of Egypt, to be
your God: I *am* the LORD your God."

Rebellion Against Moses and Aaron

16 Now [a]Korah the son of Izhar, the
son of Kohath, the son of Levi, with

15:22 sin unintentionally. Sin offerings were prescribed whenever any of the Lord's commands were unwittingly disobeyed, i.e., by unintentional neglect or omission. In vv. 24-26, the offerings for the whole community were given. In vv. 27-29, the offerings for the individual person who sinned unintentionally were stated.

15:30 does *anything* presumptuously. Lit. "with a high hand." These sins, committed knowingly and deliberately were described as blasphemous because they were an arrogant act of insubordination against the Lord. Anyone guilty of presumptuous sin was to be excommunicated from Israel and put to death.

15:32-36 This was an illustration of defiant sin. When it was determined that there was a premeditated violation of the Sabbath law, death was required.

15:37,38 tassels. These blue tassels were in the form of a flower or petal and were attached to the garments of the Israelites to remind them of their need to trust and obey God's commands.

15:41 the LORD. This reminder harkens back to Moses' first encounter with the Lord in the desert (Ex. 3:13-22).

16:1–18:32 In 16:1-40, Korah (a Levite), allied with some Reubenites and other leaders of Israel, instigated an organized opposition to the authority of Aaron and the priests. Their argument against Moses and Aaron was that by claiming the unique right and

[b]Dathan and Abiram the sons of Eliab, and
On the son of Peleth, sons of Reuben, took
men; 2 and they rose up before Moses with
some of the children of Israel, two hundred
and fifty leaders of the congregation, [c]rep-
resentatives of the congregation, men of
renown. 3 [d]They gathered together against
Moses and Aaron, and said to them, "*You*
[1]*take* too much upon yourselves, for [e]all
the congregation *is* holy, every one of
them, [f]and the LORD *is* among them. Why
then do you exalt yourselves above the assembly of the LORD?"
4 So when Moses heard *it,* he [g]fell on his
face; 5 and he spoke to Korah and all his
company, saying, "Tomorrow morning the
LORD will show who *is* [h]His and *who is*
[i]holy,[2] and will cause *him* to come near to
Him. That one whom He chooses He will
cause to [j]come near to Him. 6 Do this: Take
censers, Korah and all your company;
7 put fire in them and put incense in them
before the LORD tomorrow, and it shall be
that the man whom the LORD chooses *is* the
holy one. *You take* too much upon yourselves, you sons of Levi!"
8 Then Moses said to Korah, "Hear now,
you sons of Levi: 9 *Is it* [k]a small thing to
you that the God of Israel has [l]separated
you from the congregation of Israel, to
bring you near to Himself, to do the work
of the tabernacle of the LORD, and to stand
before the congregation to serve them;
10 and that He has brought you near *to
Himself,* you and all your brethren, the sons
of Levi, with you? And are you seeking the
priesthood also? 11 Therefore you and all
your company *are* gathered together
against the LORD. [m]And what *is* Aaron that
you complain against him?"
12 And Moses sent to call Dathan and
Abiram the sons of Eliab, but they said,
"We will not come up! 13 *Is it* a small thing
that you have brought us up out of [n]a land
flowing with milk and honey, to kill us in
the wilderness, that you should [o]keep acting like a prince over us? 14 Moreover [p]you
have not brought us into [q]a land flowing
with milk and honey, nor given us inheritance of fields and vineyards. Will you put
out the eyes of these men? We will not
come up!"
15 Then Moses was very angry, and said
to the LORD, [r]"Do not [3]respect their offering. [s]I have not taken one donkey from
them, nor have I hurt one of them."
16 And Moses said to Korah, "Tomorrow, you and all your company be present
[t]before the LORD—you and they, as well as
Aaron. 17 Let each take his censer and put
incense in it, and each of you bring his
censer before the LORD, two hundred and
fifty censers; both you and Aaron, each
with his censer." 18 So every man took his
censer, put fire in it, laid incense on it, and
stood at the door of the tabernacle of meeting with Moses and Aaron. 19 And Korah
gathered all the congregation against them
at the door of the tabernacle of meeting.
Then [u]the glory of the LORD appeared to all
the congregation.
20 And the LORD spoke to Moses and
Aaron, saying, 21 [v]"Separate yourselves
from among this congregation, that I may
[w]consume them in a moment."
22 Then they [x]fell[4] on their faces, and
said, "O God, [y]the God of the spirits of all
flesh, shall one man sin, and You be angry
with all the [z]congregation?"
23 So the LORD spoke to Moses, saying,
24 "Speak to the congregation, saying, 'Get
away from the tents of Korah, Dathan, and
Abiram.' "
25 Then Moses rose and went to Dathan
and Abiram, and the elders of Israel followed him. 26 And he spoke to the congregation, saying, [a]"Depart now from the
tents of these wicked men! Touch nothing
of theirs, lest you be consumed in all their
sins." 27 So they got away from around the
tents of Korah, Dathan, and Abiram; and
Dathan and Abiram came out and stood at

1 [b] Num. 26:9; Deut. 11:6
2 [c] Num. 1:16; 26:9
3 [d] Num. 12:2; 14:2; Ps. 106:16 [e] Ex. 19:6 [f] Ex. 29:45 [1] *assume too much for*
4 [g] Num. 14:5; 20:6
5 [h] [2 Tim. 2:19] [i] Lev. 21:6-8, 12 [j] Ezek. 40:46; 44:15, 16 [2] *set aside* for His use only
9 [k] 1 Sam. 18:23; Is. 7:13 [l] Num. 3:41, 45; 8:13-16; Deut. 10:8
11 [m] Ex. 16:7, 8
13 [n] Ex. 16:3; Num. 11:4-6 [o] Ex. 2:14; Acts 7:27, 35
14 [p] Num. 14:1-4 [q] Ex. 3:8; Lev. 20:24
15 [r] Gen. 4:4, 5 [s] 1 Sam. 12:3; Acts 20:33 [3] *graciously regard*
16 [t] 1 Sam. 12:3, 7
19 [u] Ex. 16:7, 10; Lev. 9:6, 23; Num. 14:10
21 [v] Gen. 19:17; Jer. 51:6 [w] Ex. 32:10; 33:5
22 [x] Num. 14:5 [y] Num. 27:16; Job 12:10; Eccl. 12:7; Heb. 12:9 [z] Gen. 18:23-32; 20:4 [4] *prostrated themselves*
26 [a] Gen. 19:12, 14, 15, 17

responsibility to represent the people before God, they took "too much upon themselves" based on the promise that "all the congregation *is* holy, every one of them, and the LORD *is* among them" (16:3). The Lord dealt with these rebels (16:4-40) and reaffirmed His choice of Aaron (16:41–17:13). Finally, the Lord restated the duties and support of both the priests and Levites (18:1-32). These events took place at some unidentified place and time during Israel's wilderness wanderings.

16:1 Korah. Korah was descended from Levi through Kohath. Being a son of Kohath, he already had significant duties at the tabernacle (see 4:1-20). However, he desired further to be a priest (see v. 10).

16:8 sons of Levi. Other Levites were involved in this rebellion with Korah.

16:12 Dathan and Abiram. These two men of the tribe of Reuben despised Moses, blaming him for taking Israel out of the land of Egypt and failing to bring them into the land of Canaan. Because of Moses' perceived failure, they attacked him, joining with Korah in the rebellion against Moses and Aaron.

16:15 nor have I hurt one of them. Moses pled his innocence before the Lord, claiming to have been a true servant-leader. This confirms that Num. 12:3 could have been written by Moses.

16:16-35 God judged those who rebelled against Moses and Aaron by putting them to death.

16:21 The Lord answered Moses' intercession by calling the people to depart from the tents of the rebels so that only they would be judged.

16:22 the God of the spirits of all flesh. This phrase appears only here and in 27:16. Moses called on omniscient God who knows the heart of everyone to judge those who had sinned, and those only.

the door of their tents, with their wives,
their sons, and their little [b]children.
28 And Moses said: [c]"By this you shall
know that the LORD has sent me to do all
these works, for *I have* not *done them* [d]of my
own will. 29 If these men die naturally like
all men, or if they are [e]visited by the common fate of all men, *then* the LORD has not
sent me. 30 But if the LORD creates [f]a new
thing, and the earth opens its mouth and
swallows them up with all that belongs to
them, and they [g]go down alive into the pit,
then you will understand that these men
have rejected the LORD."
31 [h]Now it came to pass, as he finished
speaking all these words, that the ground
split apart under them, 32 and the earth
opened its mouth and swallowed them up,
with their households and [i]all the men
with Korah, with all *their* goods. 33 So they
and all those with them went down alive
into the pit; the earth closed over them,
and they perished from among the assembly. 34 Then all Israel who *were* around
them fled at their cry, for they said, "Lest
the earth swallow us up *also!*"
35 And [j]a fire came out from the LORD
and consumed the two hundred and fifty
men who were offering incense.
36 Then the LORD spoke to Moses, saying:
37 "Tell Eleazar, the son of Aaron the priest,
to pick up the censers out of the blaze, for
[k]they are holy, and scatter the fire some distance away. 38 The censers of [l]these men
who sinned [5]against their own souls, let
them be made into hammered plates as a
covering for the altar. Because they presented them before the LORD, therefore they are
holy; [m]and they shall be a sign to the children of Israel." 39 So Eleazar the priest took
the bronze censers, which those who were
burned up had presented, and they were
hammered out as a covering on the altar,
40 *to be* a [6]memorial to the children of Israel
[n]that no outsider, who *is* not a descendant
of Aaron, should come near to offer incense
before the LORD, that he might not become
like Korah and his companions, just as the
LORD had said to him through Moses.

Complaints of the People

41 On the next day [o]all the congregation
of the children of Israel complained
against Moses and Aaron, saying, "You
have killed the people of the LORD."
42 Now it happened, when the congregation had gathered against Moses and
Aaron, that they turned toward the tabernacle of meeting; and suddenly [p]the cloud
covered it, and the glory of the LORD appeared. 43 Then Moses and Aaron came before the tabernacle of meeting.
44 And the LORD spoke to Moses, saying,
45 "Get away from among this congregation, that I may consume them in a moment."
And they fell on their faces.
46 So Moses said to Aaron, "Take a
censer and put fire in it from the altar, put
incense *on it,* and take it quickly to the congregation and make [7]atonement for them;
[q]for wrath has gone out from the LORD.
The plague has begun." 47 Then Aaron
took *it* as Moses commanded, and ran into
the midst of the assembly; and already the
plague had begun among the people. So he
put in the incense and made atonement for
the people. 48 And he stood between the
dead and the living; so [r]the plague was
stopped. 49 Now those who died in the
plague were fourteen thousand seven hundred, besides those who died in the Korah
incident. 50 So Aaron returned to Moses at
the door of the tabernacle of meeting, for
the plague had stopped.

The Budding of Aaron's Rod

17 And the LORD spoke to Moses, saying: 2 "Speak to the children of Israel, and get from them a rod from each father's house, all their leaders according to
their fathers' houses—twelve rods. Write
each man's name on his rod. 3 And you
shall write Aaron's name on the rod of
Levi. For there shall be one rod for the
head of *each* father's house. 4 Then you
shall place them in the tabernacle of meeting before [a]the Testimony, [b]where I meet

27 [b] Ex. 20:5; Num. 26:11
28 [c] Ex. 3:12; John 5:36 [d] Num. 24:13; John 5:30
29 [e] Ex. 20:5; Job 35:15; Is. 10:3
30 [f] Job 31:3; Is. 28:21 [g] [Ps. 55:15]
31 [h] Num. 26:10; Ps. 106:17
32 [i] Num. 26:11; 1 Chr. 6:22, 37
35 [j] Lev. 10:2; Num. 11:1–3; 26:10; Ps. 106:18
37 [k] Lev. 27:28
38 [l] Prov. 20:2; Hab. 2:10 [m] Num. 17:10; Ezek. 14:8 [5] *Or at the cost of their own lives*
40 [n] Num. 3:10; 2 Chr. 26:18 [6] *reminder*
41 [o] Num. 14:2; Ps. 106:25
42 [p] Ex. 40:34
46 [q] Lev. 10:6; Num. 18:5 [7] *Lit. covering*
48 [r] Num. 25:8; Ps. 106:30

CHAPTER 17

4 [a] Ex. 25:16 [b] Ex. 25:22; 29:42, 43; 30:36; Num. 17:7

16:30 a new thing. This supernatural opening of the earth to swallow the rebels was a sign of God's wrath and the vindication of Moses and Aaron.

16:32 their households. Numbers 26:11 indicates that this did not include their children.

16:36-40 The 250 leaders of Israel had brought censers filled with fire before the Lord (16:17,18). The censers were holy to the Lord since they had been used in the tabernacle. Therefore, Eleazar was commanded to hammer out the metal censers into a covering for the altar. That covering was to be a perpetual reminder that God had chosen Aaron and his descendants for the priesthood.

16:41-50 Instead of bringing about the repentance of the people, the Lord's wrath only led to more complaining. Though the children of Israel held Moses and Aaron accountable for the people who had been killed by the Lord, it was the intervention of Moses and Aaron for the entire nation that saved them from destruction because of their opposition to God.

16:46 incense. Incense was symbolic of prayer. Aaron interceded in prayer and the plague stopped (v. 48).

16:49 fourteen thousand seven hundred. See 1 Cor. 10:10.

17:2 twelve rods. These sticks of wood were to bear the names of the 12 tribes, with the tribe of Levi replaced by the name Aaron.

17:4 before the Testimony. The Testimony is the Ten Commandments written on two stone tablets kept in the ark of the covenant.

with you. 5 And it shall be *that* the rod of
the man [c]whom I choose will blossom;
thus I will rid Myself of the complaints of
the children of Israel, [d]which they make
against you."
6 So Moses spoke to the children of Israel, and each of their leaders gave him a
rod apiece, for each leader according to
their fathers' houses, twelve rods; and the
rod of Aaron *was* among their rods. 7 And
Moses placed the rods before the LORD in
[e]the tabernacle of witness.
8 Now it came to pass on the next day
that Moses went into the tabernacle of witness, and behold, the [f]rod of Aaron, of the
house of Levi, had sprouted and put forth
buds, had produced blossoms and yielded
ripe almonds. 9 Then Moses brought out
all the rods from before the LORD to all the
children of Israel; and they looked, and
each man took his rod.
10 And the LORD said to Moses, "Bring
[g]Aaron's rod back before the Testimony, to
be kept [h]as a sign against the rebels, [i]that
you may put their complaints away from
Me, lest they die." 11 Thus did Moses; just
as the LORD had commanded him, so he
did.
12 So the children of Israel spoke to Moses, saying, "Surely we die, we perish, we
all perish! 13 [j]Whoever even comes near
the tabernacle of the LORD must die. Shall
we all utterly die?"

Duties of Priests and Levites

18 Then the LORD said to Aaron: [a]"You
and your sons and your father's
house with you shall [b]bear the [1]iniquity *re-*
lated to the sanctuary, and you and your
sons with you shall bear the iniquity *asso-*
ciated with your priesthood. 2 Also bring
with you your brethren of the [c]tribe of
Levi, the tribe of your father, that they may
be [d]joined with you and serve you while
you and your sons *are* with you before the
tabernacle of [2]witness. 3 They shall attend
to your [3]needs and [e]all the needs of the
tabernacle; [f]but they shall not come near
the articles of the sanctuary and the altar,
[g]lest they die—they and you also. 4 They
shall be joined with you and attend to the
needs of the tabernacle of meeting, for all
the work of the tabernacle; [h]but an outsider shall not come near you. 5 And you
shall attend to [i]the duties of the sanctuary
and the duties of the altar, [j]that there *may*
be no more wrath on the children of Israel.
6 Behold, I Myself have [k]taken your
brethren the Levites from among the children of Israel; [l]*they are* a gift to you, given
by the LORD, to do the work of the tabernacle of meeting. 7 Therefore [m]you and your
sons with you shall attend to your priesthood for everything at the altar and [n]be-
hind the veil; and you shall serve. I give
your priesthood *to you* as a [o]gift for service,
but the outsider who comes near shall be
put to death."

Offerings for Support of the Priests

8 And the LORD spoke to Aaron: "Here,
[p]I Myself have also given you [4]charge of
My heave offerings, all the holy gifts of the
children of Israel; I have given them [q]as a
portion to you and your sons, as an ordinance forever. 9 This shall be yours of the
most holy things *reserved* from the fire:
every offering of theirs, every [r]grain offering and every [s]sin offering and every [t]tres-
pass offering which they render to Me,
shall be most holy for you and your sons.
10 [u]In a most holy *place* you shall eat it;
every male shall eat it. It shall be holy to
you.
11 "This also *is* yours: [v]the heave offering of their gift, with all the wave offerings
of the children of Israel; I have given them
to you, and your sons and daughters with
you, as an ordinance forever. [w]Everyone
who is [5]clean in your house may eat it.
12 [x]"All the [6]best of the oil, all the best of
the new wine and the grain, [y]their firstfruits which they offer to the LORD, I have
given them to you. 13 Whatever first ripe

5 [c]Num. 16:5 [d]Num. 16:11
7 [e]Ex. 38:21; Num. 1:50, 51; 9:15; 18:2; Acts 7:44
8 [f][Ezek. 17:24]; Heb. 9:4
10 [g]Heb. 9:4 [h]Num. 16:38; Deut. 9:7, 24 [i]Num. 17:5
13 [j]Num. 1:51, 53; 18:4, 7

CHAPTER 18

1 [a]Num. 17:13 [b]Ex. 28:38; Lev. 10:17; 22:16 [1]*guilt*
2 [c]Gen. 29:34; Num. 1:47 [d]Num. 3:5-10 [2]*testimony*
3 [e]Num. 3:25, 31, 36 [3]*service* [f]Num. 16:40 [g]Num. 4:15
4 [h]Num. 3:10
5 [i]Ex. 27:21; 30:7; Lev. 24:3 [j]Num. 8:19; 16:46
6 [k]Num. 3:12, 45 [l]Num. 3:9
7 [m]Num. 3:10; 18:5 [n]Heb. 9:3, 6 [o]Matt. 10:8; 1 Pet. 5:2, 3
8 [p]Lev. 6:16, 18; 7:28-34; Num. 5:9 [q]Ex. 29:29; 40:13, 15 [4]*custody*
9 [r]Lev. 2:2, 3; 10:12, 13 [s]Lev. 6:25, 26 [t]Lev. 7:7; Num. 5:8-10
10 [u]Lev. 6:16, 26
11 [v]Ex. 29:27, 28; Deut. 18:3-5 [w]Lev. 22:1-16 [5]*purified*
12 [x]Ex. 23:19; Neh. 10:35, 36 [y]Ex. 22:29; Lev. 23:20 [6]Lit. *fat*

The phrase "before the Testimony" is synonymous with "before the ark."

17:8 the rod of Aaron. God had stated that the stick of the man He had chosen would blossom (17:5). The stick of Aaron had not only blossomed, but had yielded ripe almonds. Thus God had exceeded the demands of the test, so there would be no uncertainty of the fact that Aaron had been chosen as High-Priest.

17:10 a sign. Aaron's rod that blossomed and brought forth fruit was to be kept as an indication of God's choice in order to permanently stop the murmuring of the rebellious Israelites.

17:12 Surely we die. Finally, the people realized their sin in challenging Aaron's role.

17:13 comes near. The people's fear of going near to God led to a reaffirmation of the priesthood of Aaron and his sons in chap. 18.

18:1-7 Only Aaron and his family could minister with the holy articles of the sanctuary of God.

18:1 the LORD said to Aaron. Only here in vv. 1-25 and in Lev. 10:8 does the Lord speak directly to Aaron alone. **bear the iniquity.** Aaron and his sons from this point forward were responsible for any offense against the holiness of the tabernacle or violations of the rules of priesthood.

18:7 a gift for service. Even though the priesthood demanded much, the priests were to view it as a gift from the Lord.

18:8-20 In return for their service to the Lord, the priests were to receive a portion of the offerings which the people presented in worship. They could keep all of the parts of the sacrifices not consumed on the altar by fire. Also, the offerings of firstfruits and everything devoted to the Lord were theirs as well.

fruit is in their land, [z]which they bring to
the LORD, shall be yours. Everyone who is
clean in your house may eat it.
14 [a]"Every [7]devoted thing in Israel shall
be yours.
15 "Everything that first opens [b]the
womb of all flesh, which they bring to the
LORD, whether man or beast, shall be
yours; nevertheless [c]the firstborn of man
you shall surely redeem, and the firstborn
of unclean animals you shall redeem.
16 And those redeemed of the devoted
things you shall redeem when one month
old, [d]according to your valuation, for five
shekels of silver, according to the shekel of
the sanctuary, which *is* [e]twenty gerahs.
17 [f]But the firstborn of a cow, the firstborn
of a sheep, or the firstborn of a goat you
shall not redeem; they *are* holy. [g]You shall
sprinkle their blood on the altar, and burn
their fat *as* an offering made by fire for a
sweet aroma to the LORD. 18 And their flesh
shall be yours, just as the [h]wave[8] breast
and the right thigh are yours.
19 "All the heave offerings of the holy
things, which the children of Israel offer to
the LORD, I have given to you and your
sons and daughters with you as an ordinance forever; [i]it *is* a covenant of salt forever before the LORD with you and your
descendants with you."
20 Then the LORD said to Aaron: "You
shall have [j]no inheritance in their land, nor
shall you have any portion among them; [k]I
am your portion and your inheritance
among the children of Israel.

Tithes for Support of the Levites

21 "Behold, [l]I have given the children of
Levi all the tithes in Israel as [9]an inheritance in return for the work which they
perform, [m]the work of the tabernacle of
meeting. 22 [n]Hereafter the children of Israel shall not come near the tabernacle of
meeting, [o]lest they bear sin and die. 23 But
the Levites shall perform the work of the
tabernacle of meeting, and they shall bear
their iniquity; *it shall be* a statute forever,
throughout your generations, that among
the children of Israel they shall have no inheritance. 24 For the tithes of the children
of Israel, which they offer up *as* a heave offering to the LORD, I have given to the
Levites [1]as an inheritance; therefore I have
said to them, 'Among the children of Israel
they shall have no inheritance.' "

The Tithe of the Levites

25 Then the LORD spoke to Moses, saying, 26 "Speak thus to the Levites, and say
to them: 'When you take from the children
of Israel the tithes which I have given you
from them as your inheritance, then you
shall offer up a heave offering of it to the
LORD, [p]a tenth of the tithe. 27 And your
heave offering shall be reckoned to you as
though *it were* the grain of the [q]threshing
floor and as the fullness of the winepress.
28 Thus you shall also offer a heave offering to the LORD from all your tithes which
you receive from the children of Israel, and
you shall give the LORD's heave offering
from it to Aaron the priest. 29 Of all your
gifts you shall offer up every heave offering due to the LORD, from all the [2]best of
them, the consecrated part of them.'
30 Therefore you shall say to them: 'When
you have lifted up the best of it, then *the
rest* shall be accounted to the Levites as the
produce of the threshing floor and as the
produce of the winepress. 31 You may eat it
in any place, you and your households, for
it *is* [r]your [3]reward for your work in the
tabernacle of meeting. 32 And you shall
[s]bear no sin because of it, when you have
lifted up the best of it. But you shall not
[t]profane the holy gifts of the children of Israel, lest you die.' "

Laws of Purification

19 Now the LORD spoke to Moses and
Aaron, saying, 2 "This *is* the [1]ordi-
nance of the law which the LORD has commanded, saying: 'Speak to the children of
Israel, that they bring you a red heifer
without [2]blemish, in which there *is* no
[a]defect [b]*and* on which a yoke has never
come. 3 You shall give it to Eleazar the
priest, that he may take it [c]outside the
camp, and it shall be slaughtered before

13 [z]Ex. 22:29; 23:19; 34:26
14 [a]Lev. 27:1-33 [7]*consecrated*
15 [b]Ex. 13:2 [c]Ex. 13:12-15; Num. 3:46; Luke 2:22-24
16 [d]Lev. 27:6 [e]Ex. 30:13
17 [f]Deut. 15:19 [g]Lev. 3:2, 5
18 [h]Ex. 29:26-28; Lev. 7:31-36 [8]*breast of the wave offering*
19 [i]Lev. 2:13; 2 Chr. 13:5; [Mark 9:49, 50]
20 [j]Deut. 10:8, 9; 12:12; 14:27-29; 18:1, 2; Josh. 13:14, 33 [k]Ps. 16:5; Ezek. 44:28
21 [l]Lev. 27:30-33; Deut. 14:22-29; Neh. 10:37; 12:44; Mal. 3:8-10; [Heb. 7:4-10] [m]Num. 3:7, 8 [9]*a possession*
22 [n]Num. 1:51 [o]Lev. 22:9
24 [1]*for a possession*
26 [p]Neh. 10:38
27 [q]Num. 15:20; [2 Cor. 8:12]
29 [2]Lit. *fat*
31 [r][Matt. 10:10; Luke 10:7]; 1 Cor. 9:13; [1 Tim. 5:18] [3]*wages*
32 [s]Lev. 19:8; 22:16; Ezek. 22:26 [t]Lev. 22:2, 15

CHAPTER 19

2 [a]Lev. 22:20-25 [b]Deut. 21:3; 1 Sam. 6:7 [1]*statute* [2]*defect*
3 [c]Lev. 4:12, 21; Num. 19:9; Heb. 13:11

18:19 a covenant of salt forever. Salt, which does not burn, was a metaphor to speak of durability. As salt keeps its flavor, so the Lord's covenant with the priesthood was durable. The Lord would provide through the offerings of His people for His priests forever.

18:21-24 The Levites received the tithes from the people. This was their source of income and compensation for their tabernacle service.

18:25-32 As the Levites themselves received the tithe, they were also required to present a tithe (a tenth) of what they received to the Lord.

19:1-22 Over a period of 38½ years, over 1.2 million people died in the wilderness because of God's judgment. The Israelites were continually coming into contact with dead bodies, which led to ceremonial uncleanness. Therefore, the Lord provided a means of purification so that those who came into contact with dead bodies might be cleansed.

19:1-10 The provision given for the preparation of the "water of purification" (cf. Lev. 12–15).

19:2 a red heifer. A reddish brown cow, probably young since no yoke had been laid on it. This cow was burned and its ashes were used as the agent of purification (see v. 9).

19:3 Eleazar. The son of Aaron was a deputy High-Priest who was in charge of the slaughter of the red cow. **outside the camp.** The

him; 4 and Eleazar the priest shall take
some of its blood with his finger, and
[d]sprinkle some of its blood seven times directly in front of the tabernacle of meeting.
5 Then the heifer shall be burned in his
sight: [e]its hide, its flesh, its blood, and its
offal shall be burned. 6 And the priest
shall take [f]cedar wood and [g]hyssop and
scarlet, and cast *them* into the midst of the
fire burning the heifer. 7 [h]Then the priest
shall wash his clothes, he shall bathe in
water, and afterward he shall come into
the camp; the priest shall be unclean until
evening. 8 And the one who burns it shall
wash his clothes in water, bathe in water,
and shall be unclean until evening. 9 Then
a man *who is* clean shall gather up [i]the
ashes of the heifer, and store *them* outside
the camp in a clean place; and they shall
be kept for the congregation of the children of Israel [j]for the water of [3]purifica-
tion; it *is* for purifying from sin. 10 And the
one who gathers the ashes of the heifer
shall wash his clothes, and be unclean
until evening. It shall be a statute forever
to the children of Israel and to the stranger
who dwells among them.
11 [k]'He who touches the dead [4]body of
anyone shall be unclean seven days. 12 [l]He
shall purify himself with the water on the
third day and on the seventh day; *then* he
will be clean. But if he does not purify himself on the third day and on the seventh
day, he will not be clean. 13 Whoever
touches the body of anyone who has died,
and [m]does not purify himself, [n]defiles the
tabernacle of the LORD. That person shall
be cut off from Israel. He shall be unclean,
because [o]the water of purification was not
sprinkled on him; [p]his uncleanness *is* still
on him.
14 'This *is* the law when a man dies in a

4 [d]Lev. 4:6; Heb. 9:13
5 [e]Ex. 29:14; Lev. 4:11, 12; 9:11
6 [f]Lev. 14:4, 6, 49 [g]Ex. 12:22; 1 Kin. 4:33
7 [h]Lev. 11:25; 15:5; 16:26, 28
9 [i][Heb. 9:13, 14] [j]Num. 19:13, 20, 21 [3]Lit. *impurity*
11 [k]Lev. 21:1, 11; Num. 5:2; 6:6; 9:6, 10; 31:19; Lam. 4:14; Hag. 2:13 [4]Lit. *soul of man*
12 [l]Num. 19:19; 31:19
13 [m]Lev. 22:3-7 [n]Lev. 15:31 [o]Num. 8:7; 19:9 [p]Lev. 7:20; 22:3
15 [q]Lev. 11:32; Num. 31:20
16 [r]Num. 19:11; 31:19
17 [s]Num. 19:9 [5]Lit. *living*
18 [t]Ps. 51:7
19 [u]Lev. 14:9
20 [v]Num. 19:13
22 [w]Hag. 2:11-13 [x]Lev. 15:5

CHAPTER 20
1 [a]Num. 13:21; 33:36 [b]Num. 13:26 [c]Ex. 15:20; Num. 26:59

tent: All who come into the tent and all
who *are* in the tent shall be unclean seven
days; 15 and every [q]open vessel, which has
no cover fastened on it, *is* unclean.
16 [r]Whoever in the open field touches one
who is slain by a sword or who has died,
or a bone of a man, or a grave, shall be unclean seven days.
17 'And for an unclean *person* they shall
take some of the [s]ashes of the heifer burnt
for purification from sin, and [5]running
water shall be put on them in a vessel. 18 A
clean person shall take [t]hyssop and dip *it*
in the water, sprinkle *it* on the tent, on all
the vessels, on the persons who were there,
or on the one who touched a bone, the
slain, the dead, or a grave. 19 The clean *person* shall sprinkle the unclean on the third
day and on the seventh day; [u]and on the
seventh day he shall purify himself, wash
his clothes, and bathe in water; and at
evening he shall be clean.
20 'But the man who is unclean and does
not purify himself, that person shall be cut
off from among the assembly, because he
has [v]defiled the sanctuary of the LORD. The
water of purification has not been sprinkled on him; he *is* unclean. 21 It shall be a
perpetual statute for them. He who sprinkles the water of purification shall wash his
clothes; and he who touches the water of
purification shall be unclean until evening.
22 [w]Whatever the unclean *person* touches
shall be unclean; and [x]the person who
touches *it* shall be unclean until evening.' "

Moses' Error at Kadesh

20 Then[a] the children of Israel, the
whole congregation, came into the
Wilderness of Zin in the first month, and
the people stayed in [b]Kadesh; and [c]Miriam
died there and was buried there.

red cow was killed outside the camp of Israel and its ashes were stored there as well (see v. 9). Hebrews 13:11-13 picks up the image of "outside the camp" as it relates to Christ's death outside of Jerusalem.

19:6 cedar wood and hyssop and scarlet. The cow was totally consumed by the fire along with these 3 materials, which were also used in the ritual of purification of skin disease (Lev. 14:1-9). The ashes of all these and the cow were mixed to make the agent by which cleansing could take place.

19:11-22 A general statement regarding the use of the "water of purification" (vv. 11-13) is followed by a more detailed explanation of the procedure to be followed.

19:18 A clean person. Any clean person, not just priests, could sprinkle the unclean with the water of purification.

20:1–22:1 These chapters record the beginning of the transition from the old generation (represented by Miriam and Aaron) to the new generation (represented by Eleazar). Geographically, Israel moves from Kadesh (20:1) to the plains of Moab (22:1) from where the conquest of the Land would be launched. There is an interval of 37 years between 19:22 and 20:1.

20:1-13 Just as the children of Israel failed to trust in the Lord (14:11) and thus were not allowed to go into the Promised Land (14:30), Israel's leaders, Moses and Aaron, would also not go into the Land because of failure to trust in the Lord.

20:1 the first month. The year is not stated. However, at the end of this chapter, there is a report of the death of Aaron. According to Num. 33:38, Aaron died on the first day of the fifth month of the fortieth year after the Exodus from Egypt. Thus, the first month here must be of the fortieth year. Most of the older generation had died in the wilderness. **Kadesh.** As the people had begun their wilderness wanderings at Kadesh (13:26), so they ended them there. Kadesh was located on the northern boundary of the Wilderness of Paran (13:26) and on the SE border of the Wilderness of Zin. **Miriam died.** Miriam, who led Israel in celebrating the victory over Egypt at the Red Sea (Ex. 15:20,21), also led the attack against Moses recorded in Num. 12:1-15. Her death served as a symbol that the old generation would not enter Canaan.

2 [d]Now there was no water for the congregation; [e]so they gathered together
against Moses and Aaron. 3 And the people [f]contended with Moses and spoke, saying: "If only we had died [g]when our
brethren died before the LORD! 4 [h]Why
have you brought up the assembly of the
LORD into this wilderness, that we and our
animals should die here? 5 And why have
you made us come up out of Egypt, to
bring us to this evil place? It *is* not a place
of grain or figs or vines or pomegranates;
nor *is* there any water to drink." 6 So Moses and Aaron went from the presence of
the assembly to the door of the tabernacle
of meeting, and [i]they [1]fell on their faces.
And [j]the glory of the LORD appeared to
them.

7 Then the LORD spoke to Moses, saying,
8 [k]"Take the rod; you and your brother
Aaron gather the congregation together.
Speak to the rock before their eyes, and it
will yield its water; thus [l]you shall bring
water for them out of the rock, and give
drink to the congregation and their animals." 9 So Moses took the rod [m]from before the LORD as He commanded him.

10 And Moses and Aaron gathered the
assembly together before the rock; and he
said to them, [n]"Hear now, you rebels!
Must we bring water for you out of this
rock?" 11 Then Moses lifted his hand and
struck the rock twice with his rod; [o]and
water came out abundantly, and the congregation and their animals drank.

12 Then the LORD spoke to Moses and
Aaron, "Because [p]you did not believe Me,
to [q]hallow Me in the eyes of the children of
Israel, therefore you shall not bring this assembly into the land which I have given
them."

13 [r]This *was* the water of [2]Meribah, because the children of Israel contended with
the LORD, and He was hallowed among
them.

Passage Through Edom Refused

14 [s]Now Moses sent messengers from
Kadesh to the king of [t]Edom. [u]"Thus says
your brother Israel: 'You know all the
hardship that has befallen us, 15 [v]how our
fathers went down to Egypt, [w]and we
dwelt in Egypt a long time, [x]and the Egyptians [3]afflicted us and our fathers.
16 [y]When we cried out to the LORD, He
heard our voice and [z]sent the Angel and
brought us up out of Egypt; now here we
are in Kadesh, a city on the edge of your
border. 17 Please [a]let us pass through your
country. We will not pass through fields or
vineyards, nor will we drink water from
wells; we will go along the King's Highway; we will not turn aside to the right
hand or to the left until we have passed
through your territory.' "

18 Then [b]Edom said to him, "You shall
not pass through my *land*, lest I come out
against you with the sword."

19 So the children of Israel said to him,
"We will go by the Highway, and if I or my
livestock drink any of your water, [c]then I
will pay for it; let me only pass through on
foot, nothing *more*."

20 Then he said, [d]"You shall not pass
through." So Edom came out against them
with many men and with a strong hand.
21 Thus Edom [e]refused to give Israel passage through his territory; so Israel [f]turned
away from him.

Death of Aaron

22 Now the children of Israel, the whole

2 [d]Ex. 17:1 [e]Num. 16:19, 42
3 [f]Ex. 17:2; Num. 14:2 [g]Num. 11:1, 33; 14:37; 16:31-35, 49
4 [h]Ex. 17:3
6 [i]Num. 14:5; 16:4, 22, 45 [j]Num. 14:10 [1]*prostrated themselves*
8 [k]Ex. 4:17, 20; 17:5, 6 [l]Neh. 9:15; Ps. 78:15, 16; 105:41; Is. 43:20; 48:21; [1 Cor. 10:4]
9 [m]Num. 17:10
10 [n]Ps. 106:33
11 [o]Ex. 17:6; Deut. 8:15; Ps. 78:16; Is. 48:21; [1 Cor. 10:4]
12 [p]Num. 20:28; 27:14; Deut. 1:37; 3:26, 27; 34:5 [q]Lev. 10:3; Ezek. 20:41; 36:23; 1 Pet. 3:15
13 [r]Deut. 33:8; Ps. 106:32 [2]Lit. *Contention*
14 [s]Judg. 11:16, 17 [t]Gen. 36:31-39 [u]Deut. 2:4; Obad. 10-12
15 [v]Gen. 46:6; Acts 7:15 [w]Ex. 12:40 [x]Ex. 1:11; Deut. 26:6; Acts 7:19 [3]*did evil to*
16 [y]Ex. 2:23; 3:7 [z]Ex. 3:2; 14:19
17 [a]Num. 21:22
18 [b]Num. 24:18; Ps. 137:7; Ezek. 25:12, 13; Obad. 10-15
19 [c]Deut. 2:6, 28
20 [d]Judg. 11:17
21 [e]Deut. 2:27, 30 [f]Deut. 2:8; Judg. 11:18

20:2 no water. During Israel's 40 years in the wilderness, water was their greatest physical need. The Lord had provided it continually, beginning at Horeb (Ex. 17:1-7). The present lack of water stirred the people to contend with Moses.

20:3 If only we had died when our brethren died. The situation was so desperate in the people's mind, that they wished they had been among those who died in Korah's rebellion (16:41-50).

20:6 fell on their faces. As he had done in the past, Moses sought the Lord's counsel (see 14:5; 16:4).

20:8 Speak to the rock. Though God told Moses to take his rod with which He had performed many wonders in the past (Ex. 4:1-5; 7:19-21; 14:16; 17:5,6), he was only to speak to the rock for it to yield water.

20:10 you rebels. Instead of speaking to the rock, Moses spoke to the people, accusing them of being rebels against God. By his actions, Moses joined the people in rebellion against God (see 27:14).

20:12 you did not believe Me. The Lord's evaluation of Moses was that he failed to take God at His Word and thus to treat Him as holy to the people. Moses here failed in the same way as Israel had at Kadesh 38 years previously (14:11). **you shall not bring this assembly into the land.** God's judgment upon Moses for his sin of striking the rock was that he would not take Israel into the land of Canaan. The inclusion of Aaron demonstrated his partnership with Moses in the action against the Lord.

20:13 Meribah. Lit. "contention, quarreling." The same name was used earlier at the first occasion of bringing water from the rock (Ex. 17:7).

20:14-21 Moses' attempt to pass through the territory of Edom was rejected by the king.

20:14 your brother Israel. The people of Edom were descended from Esau, the brother of Jacob (see Gen. 36:1).

20:17 the King's Highway. The major N-S trade route from the Gulf of Aqabah N to Damascus, which passed through the Edomite city of Sela.

20:20 with many men and with a strong hand. The king of Edom sent out his army to intercept Israel. Since Israel was forbidden by the Lord to engage in warfare with Edom (Deut. 2:4-6), they turned away from Edom's border.

20:22-29 Eleazar succeeded his father Aaron as High-Priest. Aaron's death further marked the passing of the first generation.

congregation, journeyed from [g]Kadesh
[h]and came to Mount Hor. 23 And the LORD
spoke to Moses and Aaron in Mount Hor
by the border of the land of Edom, saying:
24 "Aaron shall [4]be [i]gathered to his people,
for he shall not enter the land which I have
given to the children of Israel, because you
rebelled against My word at the water of
Meribah. 25 [j]Take Aaron and Eleazar his
son, and bring them up to Mount Hor;
26 and strip Aaron of his garments and put
them on Eleazar his son; for Aaron shall be
gathered *to his people* and die there." 27 So
Moses did just as the LORD commanded,
and they went up to Mount Hor in the sight
of all the congregation. 28 [k]Moses stripped
Aaron of his garments and put them on Eleazar his son; and [l]Aaron died there on the
top of the mountain. Then Moses and Eleazar came down from the mountain.
29 Now when all the congregation saw that
Aaron was dead, all the house of Israel
mourned for Aaron [m]thirty days.

Canaanites Defeated at Hormah

21 The [a]king of Arad, the Canaanite,
who dwelt in the South, heard that
Israel was coming on the road to Atharim.
Then he fought against Israel and took
some of them prisoners. 2 [b]So Israel made a
vow to the LORD, and said, "If You will indeed deliver this people into my hand,
then [c]I will utterly destroy their cities."
3 And the LORD listened to the voice of Israel and delivered up the Canaanites, and
they utterly destroyed them and their
cities. So the name of that place was called
[1]Hormah.

The Bronze Serpent

4 Then they journeyed from Mount Hor
by the Way of the Red Sea, to [d]go around
the land of Edom; and the soul of the people became very [2]discouraged on the way.
5 And the people [e]spoke against God and
against Moses: "Why have you brought us
up out of Egypt to die in the wilderness?
For *there is* no food and no water, and our
soul [3]loathes this worthless bread." 6 So
[f]the LORD sent [g]fiery serpents among the
people, and they bit the people; and many
of the people of Israel died.
7 [h]Therefore the people came to Moses,
and said, "We have [i]sinned, for we have
spoken against the LORD and against you;
[j]pray to the LORD that He take away the
serpents from us." So Moses prayed for the
people.
8 Then the LORD said to Moses, [k]"Make a
[l]fiery *serpent,* and set it on a pole; and it
shall be that everyone who is bitten, when
he looks at it, shall live." 9 So [m]Moses
made a bronze serpent, and put it on a
pole; and so it was, if a serpent had bitten
anyone, when he looked at the bronze serpent, he lived.

From Mount Hor to Moab

10 Now the children of Israel moved on
and [n]camped in Oboth. 11 And they journeyed from Oboth and camped at [4]Ije Abarim, in the wilderness which *is* east of
Moab, toward the sunrise. 12 [o]From there
they moved and camped in the Valley of
Zered. 13 From there they moved and
camped on the other side of the Arnon,
which *is* in the wilderness that extends
from the border of the Amorites; for [p]the
Arnon *is* the border of Moab, between
Moab and the Amorites. 14 Therefore it is
said in the Book of the Wars of the LORD:

[5]"Waheb in Suphah,
The brooks of the Arnon,

22 [g] Num. 33:37 [h] Num. 21:4
24 [i] Gen. 25:8; Deut. 32:50 [4] Die and join his ancestors
25 [j] Num. 33:38; Deut. 32:50
28 [k] Ex. 29:29, 30; Deut. 10:6 [l] Num. 33:38
29 [m] Gen. 50:3, 10; Deut. 34:8

CHAPTER 21

1 [a] Num. 33:40; Josh. 12:14; Judg. 1:16
2 [b] Gen. 28:20; Judg. 11:30 [c] Deut. 2:34
3 [1] Lit. *Utter Destruction*
4 [d] Judg. 11:18 [2] *impatient*
5 [e] Num. 20:4, 5 [3] *detests*
6 [f] 1 Cor. 10:9 [g] Deut. 8:15
7 [h] Num. 11:2; Ps. 78:34; Is. 26:16; Hos. 5:15 [i] Lev. 26:40 [j] Ex. 8:8; 1 Sam. 12:19; 1 Kin. 13:6; Acts 8:24
8 [k] [John 3:14, 15] [l] Is. 14:29; 30:6
9 [m] 2 Kin. 18:4; John 3:14, 15
10 [n] Num. 33:43, 44
11 [4] Lit. *The Heaps of Abarim*
12 [o] Deut. 2:13
13 [p] Num. 22:36; Judg. 11:18
14 [5] Ancient unknown places; Vg. *What He did in the Red Sea*

20:22 Mount Hor. Likely a mountain to the NE of Kadesh on the border of Edom.

20:24 because you rebelled against My word. Aaron had joined Moses in rebellion against God (v. 12). Aaron's death foreshadowed the death of Moses.

20:29 mourned…thirty days. This was the same mourning period as for Moses (Deut. 34:8). Since the normal time for mourning was 7 days (see Gen. 50:10), the length of this mourning showed the importance of Aaron and the loss to Israel.

21:1-3 Israel's first victory over the Canaanites occurred at Hormah, the place they had previously been defeated (see 14:45).

21:1 king of Arad. This raiding king came from a Canaanite city in the S (i.e., the Negev).

21:3 they utterly destroyed them. Israel vowed to the Lord that if He would give them victory over Arad, they would completely destroy them, not claiming the spoils of victory for themselves. The Lord responded to this vow and gave victory.

21:4-9 After their victory over Arad, Israel showed again their lack of obedience toward the Lord.

21:4 by the Way of the Red Sea. Cf. Deut. 2:1. Since the way through Edom was barred, Moses turned to the S to take Israel around Edom. Thus, Israel journeyed toward Elath on the coast of the Gulf of Aqabah. This long, circuitous route led to impatience and frustration on the part of Israel.

21:5 this worthless bread. The people's impatience led them to despise the manna (see 11:6).

21:6 fiery serpents. So called because these snake bites inflicted a fiery inflammation.

21:7 We have sinned. The people confessed their iniquity and asked that they might be released from the judgment God had sent.

21:9 a bronze serpent. One had to fix his gaze upon this snake, a definite act of the will, if he wanted to be healed and live. See the typological use of this incident in John 3:14,15.

21:10-20 Israel circled around both Edom and Moab and encamped on the N side of the Arnon River in the territory of the Amorites.

21:14 the Book of the Wars of the LORD. This was apparently a

15 And the slope of the brooks
That reaches to the dwelling of [q]Ar,
And lies on the border of Moab."

16 From there *they went* [r]to Beer, which *is*
the well where the LORD said to Moses,
"Gather the people together, and I will
give them water." 17 [s]Then Israel sang this
song:

"Spring up, O well!
All of you sing to it—
18 The well the leaders sank,
Dug by the nation's nobles,
By the [t]lawgiver, with their
staves."

And from the wilderness *they went* to
Mattanah, 19 from Mattanah to Nahaliel,
from Nahaliel to Bamoth, 20 and from
Bamoth, *in* the valley that *is* in the [6]coun-
try of Moab, to the top of Pisgah which
looks [u]down on the [7]wasteland.

King Sihon Defeated

21 Then [v]Israel sent messengers to Sihon
king of the Amorites, saying, 22 [w]"Let me
pass through your land. We will not turn
aside into fields or vineyards; we will not
drink water from wells. We will go by the
King's Highway until we have passed
through your territory." 23 [x]But Sihon
would not allow Israel to pass through his
territory. So Sihon gathered all his people
together and [8]went out against Israel in
the wilderness, [y]and he came to Jahaz and
fought against Israel. 24 Then [z]Israel defeated him with the edge of the sword, and
took possession of his land from the Arnon
to the Jabbok, as far as the people of
Ammon; for the border of the people of
Ammon *was* fortified. 25 So Israel took all
these cities, and Israel [a]dwelt in all the
cities of the Amorites, in Heshbon and in
all its villages. 26 For Heshbon *was* the city
of Sihon king of the Amorites, who had
fought against the former king of Moab,
and had taken all his land from his hand as
far as the Arnon. 27 Therefore those who
speak in [9]proverbs say:

"Come to Heshbon, let it be built;
Let the city of Sihon be repaired.

28 "For [b]fire went out from Heshbon,
A flame from the city of Sihon;
It consumed [c]Ar of Moab,
The lords of the [d]heights of the
Arnon.
29 Woe to you, [e]Moab!
You have perished, O people of
[f]Chemosh!
He has given his [g]sons as
fugitives,
And his [h]daughters into captivity,
To Sihon king of the Amorites.

30 "But we have shot at them;
Heshbon has perished [i]as far as
Dibon.
Then we laid waste as far as
Nophah,
Which *reaches* to [j]Medeba."

31 Thus Israel dwelt in the land of the
Amorites. 32 Then Moses sent to [1]spy out
[k]Jazer; and they took its villages and drove
out the Amorites who *were* there.

King Og Defeated

33 [l]And they turned and went up by the
way to [m]Bashan. So Og king of Bashan
went out against them, he and all his people, to battle [n]at Edrei. 34 Then the LORD
said to Moses, [o]"Do not fear him, for I have
[2]delivered him into your hand, with all his
people and his land; and [p]you shall do to
him as you did to Sihon king of the Amorites, who dwelt at Heshbon." 35 [q]So they
defeated him, his sons, and all his people,
until there was no survivor left him; and
they took possession of his land.

15 [q] Num. 21:28; Deut. 2:9, 18, 29
16 [r] Judg. 9:21
17 [s] Ex. 15:1
18 [t] Is. 33:22
20 [u] Num. 23:28 [6] Lit. *field* [7] Heb. *Jeshimon*
21 [v] Num. 32:33; Deut. 2:26-37; Judg. 11:19
22 [w] Num. 20:16, 17
23 [x] Deut. 29:7 [y] Deut. 2:32; Judg. 11:20 [8] *attacked*
24 [z] Deut. 2:33; Josh. 12:1; Neh. 9:22; Ps. 135:10; 136:19; Amos 2:9
25 [a] Amos 2:10
27 [9] *parables*
28 [b] Jer. 48:45, 46 [c] Deut. 2:9, 18; Is. 15:1 [d] Num. 22:41; 33:52
29 [e] Jer. 48:46 [f] Judg. 11:24; 1 Kin. 11:33; 2 Kin. 23:13 [g] Is. 15:2, 5 [h] Is. 16:2
30 [i] Num. 32:3, 34; Jer. 48:18, 22 [j] Is. 15:2
32 [k] Num. 32:1, 3, 35; Jer. 48:32 [1] *secretly search*
33 [l] Deut. 29:7 [m] Deut. 3:1 [n] Josh. 13:12
34 [o] Deut. 3:2 [p] Num. 21:24; Ps. 135:10; 136:20 [2] *given you victory over him*
35 [q] Deut. 3:3, 4; 29:7; Josh. 13:12

book of victory songs that was current at the time of Moses, possibly written by Moses or a contemporary. The work is cited here as evidence that the Arnon River was the northern boundary of Moab.

21:16 Beer. Lit. "well." Here God provided water for Israel. In response, Israel praised the Lord with a song which might have also come from "The Book of the Wars of the LORD" (vv. 17,18).

21:21-32 As with Edom (21:14-19), Israel requested passage through the land of Sihon, a king of the Amorites. Since there was no requirement from the Lord not to engage the Amorites in warfare as there had been for Edom, when Sihon brought out his army, he was attacked and defeated by Israel. Israel thus took the land bounded by the Arnon River on the S, the Dead Sea and Jordan River on the W, the Jabbok River on the N, and the land of the Ammonites on the E.

21:27 those who speak in proverbs say. These words came from the wise men, probably among the Amorites. The words of vv. 27-30 describe the Amorites' defeat of the Moabites N of the Arnon River. Ironically, as the Amorites had taken the Land from the Moabites, the Israelites had taken the Land from the Amorites. The purpose of these words cited by Moses was to substantiate Israel's right to this Land. According to God's commandments, the territory belonging to the Moabites was not to be taken by Israel because the Moabites were descendants of Lot (Deut. 2:9). However, what belonged to the Amorites had been promised to Israel and was theirs for the taking.

21:33-35 The land N of the Jabbok River was under the control of Og, another Amorite king. Og attacked Israel and suffered a devastating defeat. Thus, all of the land in the Transjordan from the Arnon River in the S to the heights of Bashan in the N came under Israelite control.

Balak Sends for Balaam

22 Then [a]the children of Israel moved, and camped in the plains of Moab on the side of the Jordan *across from* Jericho.

2 Now [b]Balak the son of Zippor saw all that Israel had done to the Amorites. 3 And [c]Moab was exceedingly afraid of the people because they *were* many, and Moab was sick with dread because of the children of Israel. 4 So Moab said to [d]the elders of Midian, "Now this company will [1]lick up everything around us, as an ox licks up the grass of the field." And Balak the son of Zippor *was* king of the Moabites at that time. 5 Then [e]he sent messengers to Balaam the son of Beor at [f]Pethor, which *is* near [2]the River in the land of [3]the sons of his people, to call him, saying: "Look, a people has come from Egypt. See, they cover the face of the earth, and are settling next to me! 6 [g]Therefore please come at once, [h]curse this people for me, for they *are* too mighty for me. Perhaps I shall be able to defeat them and drive them out of the land, for I know that he whom you bless *is* blessed, and he whom you curse is cursed."

7 So the elders of Moab and the elders of Midian departed with [i]the diviner's fee in their hand, and they came to Balaam and spoke to him the words of Balak. 8 And he said to them, [j]"Lodge here tonight, and I will bring back word to you, as the LORD speaks to me." So the princes of Moab stayed with Balaam.

9 [k]Then God came to Balaam and said, "Who *are* these men with you?"

10 So Balaam said to God, "Balak the son of Zippor, king of Moab, has sent to me, *saying,* 11 'Look, a people has come out of Egypt, and they cover the face of the earth. Come now, curse them for me; perhaps I shall be able to overpower them and drive them out.' "

12 And God said to Balaam, "You shall not go with them; you shall not curse the people, for [l]they *are* blessed."

13 So Balaam rose in the morning and said to the princes of Balak, "Go back to your land, for the LORD has refused to give me permission to go with you."

14 And the princes of Moab rose and went to Balak, and said, "Balaam refuses to come with us."

15 Then Balak again sent princes, more numerous and more [4]honorable than they. 16 And they came to Balaam and said to him, "Thus says Balak the son of Zippor: 'Please let nothing hinder you from coming to me; 17 for I will certainly [m]honor you greatly, and I will do whatever you say to me. [n]Therefore please come, curse this people for me.' "

18 Then Balaam answered and said to the servants of Balak, [o]"Though Balak were to give me his house full of silver and gold, [p]I could not go beyond the word of the LORD my God, to do less or more. 19 Now therefore, please, you also [q]stay here tonight, that I may know what more the LORD will say to me."

20 [r]And God came to Balaam at night and said to him, "If the men come to call you, rise *and* go with them; but [s]only the word which I speak to you—that you shall

CHAPTER 22
1 [a] Num. 33:48, 49
2 [b] Josh. 24:9; Judg. 11:25; Mic. 6:5; Rev. 2:14
3 [c] Ex. 15:15
4 [d] Num. 25:15-18; 31:1-3; Josh. 13:21 [1] *consume*
5 [e] Num. 31:8, 16; Deut. 23:4; Josh. 13:22; 24:9; Neh. 13:1, 2; Mic. 6:5; 2 Pet. 2:15; Jude 11; Rev. 2:14 [f] Deut. 23:4 [2] The Euphrates [3] Or *the people of Amau*
6 [g] Num. 22:17; 23:7, 8 [h] Num. 22:12; 24:9
7 [i] 1 Sam. 9:7, 8
8 [j] Num. 22:19
9 [k] Gen. 20:3
12 [l] Num. 23:20; [Rom. 11:28]
15 [4] *distinguished*
17 [m] Num. 24:11 [n] Num. 22:6
18 [o] Num. 22:38; 24:13 [p] 1 Kin. 22:14; 2 Chr. 18:13
19 [q] Num. 22:8
20 [r] Num. 22:9 [s] Num. 22:35; 23:5, 12, 16, 26; 24:13

22:1 With their control of Transjordan secured, Israel moved unimpeded to the plains of Moab in preparation for assault on Canaan.

22:2–24:25 The narrative changes to center on Balaam, a pagan prophet. His oracles reassert the faithfulness of the Lord to the Abrahamic Covenant and His purpose to bless Israel. In 22:2-40, the events leading to Balaam's words are recorded. This is followed in 22:41–24:24 with the words of his prophecies, and the conclusion is in 24:25.

22:3 Moab was exceedingly afraid. The Moabites were descendants of Lot (see Gen. 19:36,37). Balak, their king, had seen how the Israelites destroyed the Amorites. Not knowing that Israel was forbidden by God to attack Moab, he was terrified that the same end awaited him and his people (Deut. 2:9).

22:4 Midian. The Midianites were descendants of Abraham through Keturah (see Gen. 25:1-4), who lived S of Moab's border. When Moab communicated to the elders of Midian that they were in danger of being destroyed by Israel as well, they joined with Moab in an alliance to defeat Israel.

22:5 Balaam. Balaam was from Pethor, a city on the Euphrates River, perhaps near Mari, where the existence of a cult of prophets whose activities resembled those of Balaam have been found. Balaam practiced magic and divination (24:1) and eventually led Israel into apostasy (31:16). Later Scripture identifies Balaam as a false prophet (Deut. 23:3-6; Josh. 13:22; 24:9,10; Neh. 13:1-3; Mic. 6:5; 2 Pet. 2:15,16; Jude 11; Rev. 2:14).

22:6 curse this people. Knowing that Israel was too strong to defeat militarily, Balak called for Balaam to come and curse Israel. A curse was a spoken word that was believed to bring misfortune upon the one it was spoken against. Balak acknowledged that Balaam had the reputation of pronouncing curses that actually worked.

22:8 as the LORD speaks to me. Throughout these chapters Balaam himself used the name "LORD," i.e., Israel's God (22:13,18-19; 23:3,12; 24:13). In 22:18 he even called the Lord, "the LORD my God." In this verse it must be assumed that Balaam expected the God of Israel to speak to him. As a pagan prophet he would anticipate making contact with the gods of any people.

22:9 God came to Balaam. Israel's God did communicate to Balaam. However, rather than using the term "LORD," which indicates a covenant relationship, God consistently used the word "God" when He spoke to him (22:9,12,20). Though Balaam used the word "LORD," the biblical text makes it clear that he did not have a relationship with Israel's God.

22:12 they *are* blessed. Balaam could not curse Israel because the Lord had determined to give them blessing only.

22:20 only the word which I speak to you. Because of his great desire for the material wealth that would come to him, Balaam desired to go to Balak. He implored the Lord even after God had told him not to go. God acceded to Balaam's request to let him go, but told him that he could speak only the true Word from God.

do." 21 So Balaam rose in the morning, saddled his donkey, and went with the princes
of Moab.

Balaam, the Donkey, and the Angel

22 Then God's anger was aroused because he went, [t]and the Angel of the LORD
took His stand in the way as an adversary
against him. And he was riding on his donkey, and his two servants *were* with him.
23 Now [u]the donkey saw the Angel of the
LORD standing in the way with His drawn
sword in His hand, and the donkey turned
aside out of the way and went into the
field. So Balaam struck the donkey to turn
her back onto the road. 24 Then the Angel
of the LORD stood in a narrow path between the vineyards, *with* a wall on this
side and a wall on that side. 25 And when
the donkey saw the Angel of the LORD, she
pushed herself against the wall and
crushed Balaam's foot against the wall; so
he struck her again. 26 Then the Angel of
the LORD went further, and stood in a narrow place where there *was* no way to turn
either to the right hand or to the left.
27 And when the donkey saw the Angel of
the LORD, she lay down under Balaam; so
Balaam's anger was aroused, and he struck
the donkey with his staff.

28 Then the LORD [v]opened the mouth of
the donkey, and she said to Balaam, "What
have I done to you, that you have struck
me these three times?"

29 And Balaam said to the donkey, "Because you have [5]abused me. I wish there
were a sword in my hand, [w]for now I
would kill you!"

30 [x]So the donkey said to Balaam, "*Am* I
not your donkey on which you have ridden, ever since *I became* yours, to this day?
Was I ever [6]disposed to do this to you?"

And he said, "No."

31 Then the LORD [y]opened Balaam's
eyes, and he saw the Angel of the LORD
standing in the way with His drawn sword
in His hand; and he bowed his head and
fell flat on his face. 32 And the Angel of the
LORD said to him, "Why have you struck
your donkey these three times? Behold, I
have come out [7]to stand against you, because *your* way is [z]perverse[8] before Me.
33 The donkey saw Me and turned aside
from Me these three times. If she had not
turned aside from Me, surely I would also
have killed you by now, and let her live."
34 And Balaam said to the Angel of the
LORD, [a]"I have sinned, for I did not know
You stood in the way against me. Now
therefore, if it [9]displeases You, I will turn
back."

35 Then the Angel of the LORD said to
Balaam, "Go with the men, [b]but only the
word that I speak to you, that you shall
speak." So Balaam went with the princes
of Balak.

36 Now when Balak heard that Balaam
was coming, [c]he went out to meet him at
the city of Moab, [d]which *is* on the border at
the Arnon, the boundary of the territory.
37 Then Balak said to Balaam, "Did I not
earnestly send to you, calling for you?
Why did you not come to me? Am I not
able [e]to honor you?"

38 And Balaam said to Balak, "Look, I
have come to you! Now, have I any power
at all to say anything? [f]The word that God
puts in my mouth, that I must speak."
39 So Balaam went with Balak, and they
came to Kirjath Huzoth. 40 Then Balak offered oxen and sheep, and he sent *some* to
Balaam and to the princes who *were* with
him.

Balaam's First Prophecy

41 So it was, the next day, that Balak took
Balaam and brought him up to the [g]high
places of Baal, that from there he might observe [1]the extent of the people.

23 Then Balaam said to Balak, [a]"Build
seven altars for me here, and prepare for me here seven bulls and seven
rams."

2 And Balak did just as Balaam had spoken, and Balak and Balaam [b]offered a bull
and a ram on *each* altar. 3 Then Balaam said
to Balak, [c]"Stand by your burnt offering,
and I will go; perhaps the LORD will come
[d]to meet me, and whatever He shows me I
will tell you." So he went to a desolate

22 [t] Ex. 4:24
23 [u] Josh. 5:13; 2 Kin. 6:17; Dan. 10:7; Acts 22:9
28 [v] 2 Pet. 2:16
29 [w] [Prov. 12:10; Matt. 15:19] [5] *mocked*
30 [x] 2 Pet. 2:16 [6] *accustomed*
31 [y] Gen. 21:19; 2 Kin. 6:17; Luke 24:16, 31
32 [z] [2 Pet. 2:14, 15] [7] *as an adversary* [8] *contrary*
34 [a] 1 Sam. 15:24, 30; 26:21; 2 Sam. 12:13 [9] Lit. *is evil in your eyes*
35 [b] Num. 22:20
36 [c] Gen. 14:17 [d] Num. 21:13
37 [e] Num. 22:17; 24:11
38 [f] Num. 23:26; 24:13; 1 Kin. 22:14; 2 Chr. 18:13
41 [g] Num. 21:28; Deut. 12:2 [1] *the farthest extent*

CHAPTER 23

1 [a] Num. 23:29
2 [b] Num. 23:14, 30
3 [c] Num. 23:15 [d] Num. 23:4, 16

22:22 because he went. Even though God had given Balaam permission to go (v. 20), He knew that his motive was not right. Thus the anger of the Lord burned against Balaam because God knew that he was not yet submissive to what He required. The result of God's confrontation with Balaam was a reaffirmation of the word given in v. 20, repeated in v. 35, that he was to speak only the words that God wanted him to speak. That Balaam got the message is explicitly stated in v. 38. **the Angel of the LORD.** The Angel of the Lord was a manifestation of the presence of the Lord Himself. He was equated with deity (see Gen. 16:7; 18:1,2; Ex. 3:1-6). *See note on Ex. 3:2.*

22:28 the LORD opened the mouth of the donkey. Balaam's donkey was able to see the Angel of the Lord with his drawn sword (v. 27). Realizing the danger to herself, she sought to avoid the Angel. In doing this, she preserved Balaam as well. Miraculously, the donkey was able to communicate with Balaam.

22:31 the LORD opened Balaam's eyes. The Lord allowed Balaam to see things as they really were, especially those things that are not ordinarily visible to humans and to be submissive to His will as he went to Balak.

22:41–23:12 Balaam's first oracle emphatically stated that Israel could not be cursed (23:8). She was unlike all the other nations of the world (23:9). Balaam even wished to share in her blessing (23:10).

height. 4 [e]And God met Balaam, and he
said to Him, "I have prepared the seven altars, and I have offered on *each* altar a bull
and a ram."
5 Then the LORD [f]put a word in Balaam's
mouth, and said, "Return to Balak, and
thus you shall speak." 6 So he returned to
him, and there he was, standing by his
burnt offering, he and all the princes of
Moab.
7 And he [g]took up his [1]oracle and said:

"Balak the king of Moab has
brought me from Aram,
From the mountains of the east.
[h]'Come, curse Jacob for me,
And come, [i]denounce Israel!'

8 "How[j] shall I curse whom God has
not cursed?
And how shall I denounce *whom*
the LORD has not denounced?
9 For from the top of the rocks I see
him,
And from the hills I behold him;
There! [k]A people dwelling alone,
[l]Not reckoning itself among the
nations.

10 "Who[m] can count the [2]dust of Jacob,
Or number one-fourth of Israel?
Let me die [n]the death of the
righteous,
And let my end be like his!"

11 Then Balak said to Balaam, "What
have you done to me? [o]I took you to curse
my enemies, and look, you have blessed
them bountifully!"
12 So he answered and said, [p]"Must I not
take heed to speak what the LORD has put
in my mouth?"

Balaam's Second Prophecy

13 Then Balak said to him, "Please come
with me to another place from which you
may see them; you shall see only the outer
part of them, and shall not see them all;
curse them for me from there." 14 So he
brought him to the field of Zophim, to the
top of Pisgah, [q]and built seven altars, and
offered a bull and a ram on *each* altar.

15 And he said to Balak, "Stand here by
your burnt offering while I [3]meet *the* LORD
over there."
16 Then the LORD met Balaam, and [r]put a
word in his mouth, and said, "Go back to
Balak, and thus you shall speak." 17 So he
came to him, and there he was, standing by
his burnt offering, and the princes of Moab
were with him. And Balak said to him,
"What has the LORD spoken?"
18 Then he took up his oracle and said:

[s]"Rise up, Balak, and hear!
Listen to me, son of Zippor!

19 "God[t] *is* not a man, that He should
lie,
Nor a son of man, that He should
repent.
Has He [u]said, and will He not do?
Or has He spoken, and will He not
make it good?
20 Behold, I have received *a command*
to bless;
[v]He has blessed, and I cannot
reverse it.

21 "He[w] has not observed iniquity in
Jacob,
Nor has He seen [4]wickedness in
Israel.
The LORD his God *is* with him,
[x]And the shout of a King *is* among
them.
22 [y]God brings them out of Egypt;
He has [z]strength like a wild ox.

23 "For *there is* no [5]sorcery against
Jacob,
Nor any [6]divination against Israel.
It now must be said of Jacob
And of Israel, 'Oh, [a]what God has
done!'
24 Look, a people rises [b]like a lioness,
And lifts itself up like a lion;
[c]It shall not lie down until it
devours the prey,
And drinks the blood of the slain."

25 Then Balak said to Balaam, "Neither
curse them at all, nor bless them at all!"
26 So Balaam answered and said to

4 [e] Num. 23:16
5 [f] Num. 22:20, 35, 38; 23:16; Deut. 18:18; Jer. 1:9
7 [g] Deut. 23:4; Job 27:1; 29:1; Ps. 78:2 [h] Num. 22:6, 11, 17 [i] 1 Sam. 17:10 [1] *prophetic discourse*
8 [j] Num. 22:12
9 [k] Deut. 32:8; 33:28; Josh. 11:23 [l] Ex. 33:16; Ezra 9:2; [Eph. 2:14]
10 [m] Gen. 13:16; 22:17; 28:14; 2 Chr. 1:9 [n] Ps. 116:15 [2] Or *dust cloud*
11 [o] Num. 22:11
12 [p] Num. 22:38
14 [q] Num. 23:1, 2
15 [3] So with MT, Tg., Vg.; Syr. *call;* LXX *go and ask God*
16 [r] Num. 22:35; 23:5
18 [s] Judg. 3:20
19 [t] 1 Sam. 15:29; Mal. 3:6; James 1:17 [u] Num. 11:23; 1 Kin. 8:56
20 [v] Gen. 12:2; 22:17; Num. 22:12
21 [w] Ps. 32:2; [Rom. 4:7, 8] [x] Ps. 89:15-18 [4] *trouble*
22 [y] Num. 24:8 [z] Deut. 33:17; Job 39:10
23 [a] Ps. 31:19; 44:1 [5] *enchantment* [6] *fortune-telling*
24 [b] Gen. 49:9 [c] Gen. 49:27; Josh. 11:23

23:5 the LORD put a word in Balaam's mouth. Even though Balak and Balaam offered sacrifices on pagan altars, it was the Lord who gave Balaam his oracle.

23:7 he took up his oracle. This statement introduces each of Balaam's speeches (23:6,18; 24:3,20,21,23).

23:10 Who can count the dust of Jacob. Here is Oriental hyperbole signifying a very populous nation as Jacob's posterity was to be (cf. Gen 13:16; 28:14). **one-fourth of Israel.** The camp was divided into 4 parts, one on each side of the tabernacle. If one could not count the part, certainly no one could count the whole.

23:13-26 Balaam's second oracle reaffirmed the Lord's determination to bless Israel. The iniquity in Israel was mercifully set aside by the Lord (23:21) and therefore would not stop His plan. The God who supernaturally brought Israel out of Egypt (23:22) would give victory over all her enemies (23:24).

23:19 God *is* not a man. In contrast to the unreliability of man, so well seen in Balaam himself, God is reliable and immutable. He does not change; therefore, His Words always come to pass.

Balak, "Did I not tell you, saying, [d]'All that
the LORD speaks, that I must do'?"

Balaam's Third Prophecy

27 Then Balak said to Balaam, "Please
come, I will take you to another place; perhaps it will please God that you may curse
them for me from there." 28 So Balak took
Balaam to the top of Peor, that [e]overlooks
[7]the wasteland. 29 Then Balaam said to
Balak, "Build for me here seven altars, and
prepare for me here seven bulls and seven
rams." 30 And Balak did as Balaam had
said, and offered a bull and a ram on *every*
altar.

24 Now when Balaam saw that it
pleased the LORD to bless Israel, he
did not go as at [a]other times, to seek to use
[1]sorcery, but he set his face toward the
wilderness. 2 And Balaam raised his eyes,
and saw Israel [b]encamped according to
their tribes; and [c]the Spirit of God came
upon him.
3 [d]Then he took up his oracle and said:

"The utterance of Balaam the son of
Beor,
The utterance of the man whose
eyes are opened,
4 The utterance of him who hears
the words of God,
Who sees the vision of the
Almighty,
Who [e]falls down, with eyes wide
open:

5 "How lovely are your tents,
O Jacob!
Your dwellings, O Israel!
6 Like valleys that stretch out,
Like gardens by the riverside,
[f]Like aloes [g]planted by the LORD,
Like cedars beside the waters.
7 He shall pour water from his
buckets,
And his seed *shall be* [h]in many
waters.

"His king shall be higher than [i]Agag,
And his [j]kingdom shall be exalted.

8 "God[k] brings him out of Egypt;
He has strength like a wild ox;
He shall [l]consume the nations, his
enemies;
He shall [m]break their bones
And [n]pierce *them* with his arrows.
9 'He[o] bows down, he lies down as a
lion;
And as a lion, who shall rouse
him?'

[p]"Blessed *is* he who blesses you,
And cursed *is* he who curses you."

10 Then Balak's anger was aroused
against Balaam, and he [q]struck his hands
together; and Balak said to Balaam, [r]"I
called you to curse my enemies, and look,
you have bountifully blessed *them* these
three times! 11 Now therefore, flee to your
place. [s]I said I would greatly honor you,
but in fact, the LORD has kept you back
from honor."
12 So Balaam said to Balak, "Did I not
also speak to your messengers whom you
sent to me, saying, 13 'If Balak were to give
me his house full of silver and gold, I could
not go beyond the word of the LORD, to do
good or bad of my own will. What the
LORD says, that I must speak'? 14 And now,
indeed, I am going to my people. Come, [t]I
will advise you what this people will do to
your people in the [u]latter days."

Balaam's Fourth Prophecy

15 So he took up his oracle and said:

"The utterance of Balaam the son of
Beor,

26 [d] Num. 22:38
28 [e] Num. 21:20
[7] Heb. *Jeshimon*

CHAPTER 24

1 [a] Num. 23:3, 15
[1] *enchantments*
2 [b] Num. 2:2, 34
[c] Num. 11:25; 1 Sam. 10:10; 19:20, 23; 2 Chr. 15:1
3 [d] Num. 23:7, 18
4 [e] Ezek. 1:28
6 [f] Ps. 1:3; Jer. 17:8
[g] Ps. 104:16
7 [h] Jer. 51:13; Rev. 17:1, 15 [i] 1 Sam. 15:8, 9 [j] 2 Sam. 5:12; 1 Chr. 14:2
8 [k] Num. 23:22
[l] Num. 14:9; 23:24
[m] Ps. 2:9; Jer. 50:17
[n] Ps. 45:5
9 [o] Gen. 49:9; Num. 23:24 [p] Gen. 12:3; 27:29
10 [q] Ezek. 21:14, 17
[r] Num. 23:11; Neh. 13:2
11 [s] Num. 22:17, 37
14 [t] [Mic. 6:5] [u] Gen. 49:1; Deut. 4:30; Dan. 2:28

23:27–24:14 Balaam's third oracle focused on the ultimate King (the "Messiah"), who would bring the blessings of the Abrahamic Covenant both to Israel and the nations.

23:28 Peor. Also named Beth Peor (Deut. 3:29), it was the location of a temple to Baal (25:3).

24:2 the Spirit of God came upon him. This terminology was regularly used in the OT for those whom God uniquely prepared to do His work (see Judg. 3:10). Unlike the previous two oracles, Balaam does not involve himself in divination before giving this third oracle. He is empowered with the Holy Spirit to utter God's Word accurately.

24:3 whose eyes are opened. His inner eye of understanding had been opened by God's Spirit.

24:7 Agag. In 1 Sam. 15:32,33, an Amalekite king bore this name. The Amalekites were the first people to attack Israel after they left Egypt (see Ex. 17:8-15). "Agag" may be a proper name or a title of Amalekite rulers, like "Pharaoh" in Egypt.

24:8 God brings him out of Egypt. Because of the verbal similarities between 24:8 and 9, with 23:22 and 24, the "him" in this verse is usually interpreted to be Israel. However, since the "him" is sing. and the closest reference in v. 7 is to the coming king, it is better to see vv. 8 and 9 as referring to Israel's king. Numbers 24:9 is a direct quote from Gen. 49:9, which speaks of the ultimate King who will come from Judah, the Messiah.

24:9 Blessed *is* he who blesses you. These words refer to Gen. 12:3. The ultimate fulfillment of the Abrahamic Covenant centers around the coming Messiah. It is the one who blesses him who will ultimately reap God's blessing in the future.

24:14 in the latter days. Lit. "at the end of days." This term is rightfully used in the OT for the distant future. Balaam's fourth oracle takes the truth communicated in the third and applies it to Moab.

And the utterance of the man
whose eyes are opened;
16 The utterance of him who hears
the words of God,
And has the knowledge of the
Most High,
Who sees the vision of the
Almighty,
Who falls down, with eyes wide
open:

17 "I[v] see Him, but not now;
I behold Him, but not near;
[w]A Star shall come out of Jacob;
[x]A Scepter shall rise out of Israel,
And [2]batter the brow of Moab,
And destroy all the sons of [3]tumult.

18 " And [y]Edom shall be a possession;
Seir also, his enemies, shall be a
possession,
While Israel does [4]valiantly.
19 [z]Out of Jacob One [5]shall have
dominion,
And destroy the remains of the
city."

20 Then he looked on Amalek, and he
took up his oracle and said:

" Amalek *was* first among the nations,
But *shall be* last until he perishes."

21 Then he looked on the Kenites, and he
took up his oracle and said:

"Firm is your dwelling place,
And your nest is set in the rock;
22 Nevertheless Kain shall be burned.
How long until Asshur carries you
away captive?"

23 Then he took up his oracle and said:

" Alas! Who shall live when God
does this?

17 [v] Rev. 1:7; Matt. 1:2; Luke 3:34 [w] Matt. 2:2 [x] Gen. 49:10 [2] *shatter the forehead* [3] Heb. *Sheth*, Jer. 48:45
18 [y] 2 Sam. 8:14 [4] *mightily*
19 [z] Gen. 49:10; Amos 9:11, 12 [5] *shall rule*

24 [a] Gen. 10:4; Ezek. 27:6; Dan. 11:30 [b] Gen. 10:21, 25 [6] Heb. *Kittim* [7] Lit. *he* or *that one*
25 [c] Num. 22:5; 31:8

CHAPTER 25

1 [a] Num. 33:49; Josh. 2:1 [b] Rev. 2:14 [1] Heb. *Shittim*
2 [c] Josh. 22:17; Hos. 9:10 [d] Ex. 34:15; Deut. 32:38; 1 Cor. 10:20 [e] Ex. 20:5
3 [f] Ps. 106:28, 29
4 [g] Deut. 4:3 [h] Num. 25:11; Deut. 13:17
5 [i] Ex. 18:21 [j] Deut. 13:6, 9
6 [k] Joel 2:17
7 [l] Ps. 106:30 [m] Ex. 6:25
8 [n] Ps. 106:30 [o] Num. 16:46-48
9 [p] Deut. 4:3
11 [q] Ps. 106:30

24 But ships *shall come* from the coasts
of [a]Cyprus,[6]
And they shall afflict Asshur and
afflict [b]Eber,
And so shall [7]*Amalek*, until he
perishes."

25 So Balaam rose and departed and [c]re-
turned to his place; Balak also went his
way.

Israel's Harlotry in Moab

25 Now Israel remained in [a]Acacia
Grove,[1] and the [b]people began to
commit harlotry with the women of Moab.
2 [c]They invited the people to [d]the sacrifices
of their gods, and the people ate and
[e]bowed down to their gods. 3 So Israel was
joined to Baal of Peor, and [f]the anger of the
LORD was aroused against Israel.
4 Then the LORD said to Moses, [g]"Take
all the leaders of the people and hang the
offenders before the LORD, out in the sun,
[h]that the fierce anger of the LORD may turn
away from Israel."
5 So Moses said to [i]the judges of Israel,
[j]"Every one of you kill his men who were
joined to Baal of Peor."
6 And indeed, one of the children of Israel came and presented to his brethren a
Midianite woman in the sight of Moses
and in the sight of all the congregation of
the children of Israel, [k]who *were* weeping
at the door of the tabernacle of meeting.
7 Now [l]when Phinehas [m]the son of Eleazar, the son of Aaron the priest, saw *it*, he
rose from among the congregation and
took a javelin in his hand; 8 and he went
after the man of Israel into the tent and
thrust both of them through, the man of Israel, and the woman through her body. So
[n]the plague was [o]stopped among the children of Israel. 9 And [p]those who died in
the plague were twenty-four thousand.
10 Then the LORD spoke to Moses, saying: 11 [q]"Phinehas the son of Eleazar, the

24:15-19 Balaam's fourth oracle predicted the future coming of Israel's king, who would "shatter the forehead of Moab" (see marginal note, v. 17) and conquer Edom. He will have total dominion.

24:20-24 Balaam's final 3 oracles look at the future of the nations. First, Amalek will come to an end (24:20). Second, the Kenites, identical to or a part of the Midianites, will be carried away by Asshur, i.e., Assyria (24:21,22). Third, Assyria and Eber, probably Israel herself (Gen. 10:21), will be afflicted by Cyprus, (this name came to represent the Mediterranean region W of Palestine and in Dan. 11:30 refers to Rome), until Cyprus comes to ruin.

25:1-18 The final failure of Israel before the conquest of Canaan occurred in the plains of Moab. According to 31:16, the incident was brought about by the counsel of Balaam. Failing to be able to curse Israel, he gave the Moabites and Midianites direction in how to provoke the Lord's anger against His people.

25:1 Acacia Grove. The region across the Jordan River from Jericho where Israel invaded the land of Canaan (see Josh. 2:1).

25:3 joined to Baal of Peor. Israel engaged in acts of sexual immorality with the women of Moab. Since this was part of the pagan cult that was worshiped by the Moabites, the Israelites joined in these idolatrous practices. The Israelites yoked themselves to the false god of the Moabites and the Midianites, referred to as Baal of Peor. This was a violation of the first commandment.

25:6 Cf. vv. 14,15.

25:9 twenty-four thousand. This is to be differentiated from the plague over the golden calf where 23,000 died (cf. Ex. 32:1-14,28; 1 Cor. 10:8).

25:10-13 Because of Phinehas' zeal for God's holiness, the Lord made "a covenant of an everlasting priesthood" with him so that

son of Aaron the priest, has turned back My wrath from the children of Israel, because he was zealous with My zeal among them, so that I did not consume the children of Israel in [r]My zeal. 12 Therefore say, [s]'Behold, I give to him My [t]covenant of peace; 13 and it shall be to him and [u]his descendants after him a covenant of [v]an everlasting priesthood, because he was [w]zealous for his God, and [x]made [2]atonement for the children of Israel.' "

14 Now the name of the Israelite who was killed, who was killed with the Midianite woman, *was* Zimri the son of Salu, a leader of a father's house among the Simeonites. 15 And the name of the Midianite woman who was killed *was* Cozbi the daughter of [y]Zur; he *was* head of the people of a father's house in Midian.

16 Then the LORD spoke to Moses, saying: 17 [z]"Harass the Midianites, and [3]attack them; 18 for they harassed you with their [a]schemes[4] by which they seduced you in the matter of Peor and in the matter of Cozbi, the daughter of a leader of Midian, their sister, who was killed in the day of the plague because of Peor."

The Second Census of Israel

26 And it came to pass, after the [a]plague, that the LORD spoke to Moses and Eleazar the son of Aaron the priest, saying: 2 [b]"Take a census of all the congregation of the children of Israel [c]from twenty years old and above, by their fathers' houses, all who are able to go to war in Israel." 3 So Moses and Eleazar the priest spoke with them [d]in the plains of Moab by the Jordan, *across from* Jericho, saying: 4 "*Take a census of the people* from twenty years old and above, just as the LORD [e]commanded Moses and the children of Israel who came out of the land of Egypt."

5 [f]Reuben *was* the firstborn of Israel. The children of Reuben *were: of* Hanoch, the family of the Hanochites; *of* Pallu, the family of the Palluites; 6 *of* Hezron, the family of the Hezronites; *of* Carmi, the family of the Carmites. 7 These *are* the families of the Reubenites: those who were numbered of them were forty-three thousand seven hundred and thirty. 8 And the son of Pallu *was* Eliab. 9 The sons of Eliab *were* Nemuel, Dathan, and Abiram. These *are* the Dathan and Abiram, [g]representatives of the congregation, who contended against Moses and Aaron in the company of Korah, when they contended against the LORD; 10 [h]and the earth opened its mouth and swallowed them up together with Korah when that company died, when the fire devoured two hundred and fifty men; [i]and they became a sign. 11 Nevertheless [j]the children of Korah did not die.

12 The sons of Simeon according to their families *were: of* [1]Nemuel, the family of the Nemuelites; *of* Jamin, the family of the Jaminites; *of* [2]Jachin, the family of the Jachinites; 13 *of* [3]Zerah, the family of the Zarhites; *of* Shaul, the family of the Shaulites. 14 These *are* the families of the Simeonites: twenty-two thousand two hundred.

15 The sons of Gad according to their families *were: of* [4]Zephon, the family of the Zephonites; *of* Haggi, the family of the Haggites; *of* Shuni, the family of the Shunites; 16 *of* [5]Ozni, the family of the Oznites; *of* Eri, the family of the Erites; 17 *of* [6]Arod, the family of the Arodites; *of* Areli, the family of the Arelites. 18 These *are* the families

11 [r] [Ex. 20:5]; Deut. 32:16, 21; 1 Kin. 14:22; Ps. 78:58; Ezek. 16:38
12 [s] [Mal. 2:4, 5; 3:1] [t] Is. 54:10; Ezek. 34:25; 37:26; Mal. 2:5
13 [u] 1 Chr. 6:4-15 [v] Ex. 40:15 [w] Acts 22:3; Rom. 10:2 [x] [Heb. 2:17] [2] *Lit. covering*
15 [y] Num. 31:8; Josh. 13:21
17 [z] Num. 31:1-3 [3] *be hostile toward*
18 [a] Num. 31:16; Rev. 2:14 [4] *tricks*

CHAPTER 26

1 [a] Num. 25:9
2 [b] Ex. 30:12; 38:25, 26; Num. 1:2; 14:29 [c] Num. 1:3
3 [d] Num. 22:1; 31:12; 33:48; 35:1
4 [e] Num. 1:1
5 [f] Gen. 46:8; Ex. 6:14; 1 Chr. 5:1-3
9 [g] Num. 1:16; 16:1, 2
10 [h] Num. 16:32-35 [i] Num. 16:38-40; 1 Cor. 10:6; 2 Pet. 2:6
11 [j] Ex. 6:24; 1 Chr. 6:22, 23
12 [1] *Jemuel*, Gen. 46:10; Ex. 6:15 [2] *Jarib*, 1 Chr. 4:24
13 [3] *Zohar*, Gen. 46:10
15 [4] *Ziphion*, Gen. 46:16
16 [5] *Ezbon*, Gen. 46:16
17 [6] Sam., Syr. *Arodi* and Gen. 46:16

through his family line would come all future, legitimate High-Priests (cf. Ps. 106:30,31). This promise will extend even into the millennial kingdom (cf. Ezek. 40:46; 44:10,15; 48:11).

25:17 Harass the Midianites. Because the Midianites had attacked Israel by their schemes of sexual and idolatrous seduction, the Lord called Israel to attack them in return. This attack is recorded in 31:1-24.

26:1–36:13 The final major section of Numbers records the renewed obedience of Israel. God continued to speak (26:1,2,52; 27:6,12,18; 28:1; 31:1,25; 33:50; 34:1,16; 35:1,9), and the second generation of Israel obeyed. Most of the commandments in this section related to Israel's life after they entered the Land.

26:1–32:19 These chapters begin and end speaking of going to war (26:2; 32:20,29,32) and the ensuing inheritance of Canaan (26:52-56; 32:32). Israel was being prepared for the conquest of the Promised Land.

26:1-51 This second census, like the first taken over 38 years earlier (1:1-46), counted all the men 20 years of age and older, fit for military service.

26:5-51 The numbers for each tribe with the net gain or loss were as follows:

Reuben	43,730	(v. 7)	-2,770
Simeon	22,200	(v. 14)	-37,100
Gad	40,500	(v. 18)	-5,150
Judah	76,500	(v. 22)	+1,900
Issachar	64,300	(v. 25)	+9,900
Zebulun	60,500	(v. 27)	+3,100
Manasseh	52,700	(v. 34)	+20,500
Ephraim	32,500	(v. 37)	-8,000
Benjamin	45,600	(v. 41)	+10,200
Dan	64,400	(v. 43)	+1,700
Asher	53,400	(v. 47)	+11,900
Naphtali	45,400	(v. 50)	-8,000
Total	601,730	(v. 51)	-1,820

The great decline in the tribe of Simeon might be due to its participation in the sin of Baal of Peor (see 25:14).

26:9 Dathan and Abiram. These were singled out for special mention because of their part in the rebellion recorded in 16:1-40. Mention of them was a reminder of God's judgment against rebellion.

26:11 the children of Korah. These sons of Korah were spared

of the sons of Gad according to those who
were numbered of them: forty thousand
five hundred.
19 [k]The sons of Judah *were* Er and Onan;
and Er and Onan died in the land of
Canaan. 20 And [l]the sons of Judah according to their families were: *of* Shelah, the
family of the Shelanites; *of* Perez, the family of the Parzites; *of* Zerah, the family of
the Zarhites. 21 And the sons of Perez
were: *of* Hezron, the family of the Hezronites; *of* Hamul, the family of the Hamulites.
22 These *are* the families of Judah according
to those who were numbered of them: seventy-six thousand five hundred.
23 The sons of Issachar according to their
families *were: of* Tola, the family of the Tola-
ites; of [7]Puah, the family of the [8]Punites;
24 of [9]Jashub, the family of the Jashubites;
of Shimron, the family of the Shimronites.
25 These *are* the families of Issachar according to those who were numbered of them:
sixty-four thousand three hundred.
26 [m]The sons of Zebulun according to
their families *were:* of Sered, the family of
the Sardites; of Elon, the family of the Elon-
ites; of Jahleel, the family of the Jahleelites.
27 These *are* the families of the Zebulunites
according to those who were numbered of
them: sixty thousand five hundred.
28 [n]The sons of Joseph according to their
families, by Manasseh and Ephraim, *were:*
29 The sons of [o]Manasseh: of [p]Machir, the
family of the Machirites; and Machir begot
Gilead; of Gilead, the family of the Gileadites. 30 These *are* the sons of Gilead: *of* [1]Je-
ezer, the family of the Jeezerites; of Helek,
the family of the Helekites; 31 *of* Asriel, the
family of the Asrielites; *of* Shechem, the
family of the Shechemites; 32 *of* Shemida,
the family of the Shemidaites; *of* Hepher,
the family of the Hepherites. 33 Now [q]Ze-
lophehad the son of Hepher had no sons,
but daughters; and the names of the
daughters of Zelophehad *were* Mahlah,
Noah, Hoglah, Milcah, and Tirzah.
34 These *are* the families of Manasseh; and
those who were numbered of them *were*
fifty-two thousand seven hundred.
35 These *are* the sons of Ephraim according to their families: of Shuthelah, the family of the Shuthalhites; of [2]Becher, the family of the Bachrites; of Tahan, the family of
the Tahanites. 36 And these *are* the sons of
Shuthelah: of Eran, the family of the Eran-
ites. 37 These *are* the families of the sons of
Ephraim according to those who were
numbered of them: thirty-two thousand
five hundred.
These *are* the sons of Joseph according to
their families.
38 [r]The sons of Benjamin according to
their families were: of Bela, the family of
the Belaites; of Ashbel, the family of the
Ashbelites; of [s]Ahiram, the family of the
Ahiramites; 39 of [t]Shupham, [3]the family of
the Shuphamites; of [4]Hupham, the family
of the Huphamites. 40 And the sons of Bela
were [5]Ard and Naaman: [u]*of Ard,* the family of the Ardites; of Naaman, the family of
the Naamites. 41 These *are* the sons of Benjamin according to their families; and those
who were numbered of them *were* forty-
five thousand six hundred.
42 These *are* the sons of Dan according to
their families: of [6]Shuham, the family of
the Shuhamites. These *are* the families of
Dan according to their families. 43 All the
families of the Shuhamites, according to
those who were numbered of them, *were*
sixty-four thousand four hundred.
44 [v]The sons of Asher according to their
families *were:* of Jimna, the family of the
Jimnites; of Jesui, the family of the Jesuites;
of Beriah, the family of the Beriites. 45 Of
the sons of Beriah: of Heber, the family of
the Heberites; of Malchiel, the family of the
Malchielites. 46 And the name of the
daughter of Asher *was* Serah. 47 These *are*
the families of the sons of Asher according
to those who were numbered of them:
fifty-three thousand four hundred.
48 [w]The sons of Naphtali according to
their families *were:* of [7]Jahzeel, the family
of the Jahzeelites; of Guni, the family of the
Gunites; 49 of Jezer, the family of the Jezer-
ites; of [x]Shillem, the family of the Shillem-
ites. 50 These *are* the families of Naphtali
according to their families; and those who
were numbered of them *were* forty-five
thousand four hundred.
51 [y]These *are* those who were numbered
of the children of Israel: six hundred and
one thousand seven hundred and thirty.
52 Then the LORD spoke to Moses, say-
ing: 53 [z]"To these the land shall be [a]divided
as an inheritance, according to the number
of names. 54 [b]To a large *tribe* you shall give

19 [k]Gen. 38:2; 46:12
20 [l]1 Chr. 2:3
23 [7]So with Sam., LXX, Syr., Vg.; Heb. *Puvah,* Gen. 46:13; 1 Chr. 7:1 [8]Sam., LXX, Syr., Vg. *Puaites*
24 [9]*Job,* Gen. 46:13
26 [m]Gen. 46:14
28 [n]Gen. 46:20; Deut. 33:16
29 [o]Josh. 17:1 [p]1 Chr. 7:14, 15
30 [1]*Abiezer,* Josh. 17:2
33 [q]Num. 27:1; 36:11
35 [2]*Bered,* 1 Chr. 7:20
38 [r]Gen. 46:21; 1 Chr. 7:6 [s]Gen. 46:21; 1 Chr. 8:1, 2
39 [t]1 Chr. 7:12 [3]MT *Shephupham; Shephuphan,* 1 Chr. 8:5 [4]*Huppim,* Gen. 46:21
40 [u]1 Chr. 8:3 [5]*Addar,* 1 Chr. 8:3
42 [6]*Hushim,* Gen. 46:23
44 [v]Gen. 46:17; 1 Chr. 7:30
48 [w]Gen. 46:24; 1 Chr. 7:13 [7]*Jahziel,* 1 Chr. 7:13
49 [x]1 Chr. 7:13
51 [y]Ex. 12:37; 38:26; Num. 1:46; 11:21
53 [z]Josh. 11:23; 14:1 [a]Num. 33:54
54 [b]Num. 33:54

judgment because they separated themselves from their father's house (see 16:26).

26:19 Er and Onan. These two sons of Judah did not receive an inheritance in the Land because of their great evil (see Gen. 38:1-10).

26:33 Zelophehad. The mentioning of Zelophehad having no sons, but only daughters, laid the basis for the laws of inheritance stated in 27:1-11; 36:1-12.

26:52-56 These census numbers would be used to decide the size of each tribe's inheritance in the Land. The exact locations would be determined by lot (see Josh. 13:1-7; 14:1–19:51 for the outworking of these words).

a larger inheritance, and to a small *tribe*
you shall give a smaller inheritance. Each
shall be given its inheritance according to
those who were numbered of them. 55 But
the land shall be [c]divided by lot; they shall
inherit according to the names of the tribes
of their fathers. 56 According to the lot
their inheritance shall be divided between
the larger and the smaller."
57 [d]And these *are* those who were numbered of the Levites according to their families: of Gershon, the family of the Gershonites; of Kohath, the family of the
Kohathites; of Merari, the family of
the Merarites. 58 These *are* the families of
the Levites: the family of the Libnites, the
family of the Hebronites, the family of the
Mahlites, the family of the Mushites, and
the family of the Korathites. And Kohath
begot Amram. 59 The name of Amram's
wife *was* [e]Jochebed the daughter of Levi,
who was born to Levi in Egypt; and to
Amram she bore Aaron and Moses and
their sister Miriam. 60 [f]To Aaron were born
Nadab and Abihu, Eleazar and Ithamar.
61 And [g]Nadab and Abihu died when they
offered profane fire before the LORD.
62 [h]Now those who were numbered of
them were twenty-three thousand, every
male from a month old and above; [i]for
they were not numbered among the other
children of Israel, because there was [j]no
inheritance given to them among the children of Israel.
63 These *are* those who were numbered
by Moses and Eleazar the priest, who
numbered the children of Israel [k]in the
plains of Moab by the Jordan, *across from*
Jericho. 64 [l]But among these there was not
a man of those who were numbered by
Moses and Aaron the priest when they
numbered the children of Israel in the
[m]Wilderness of Sinai. 65 For the LORD had
said of them, "They [n]shall surely die in the
wilderness." So there was not left a man of
them, [o]except Caleb the son of Jephunneh
and Joshua the son of Nun.

Inheritance Laws

27 Then came the daughters of [a]Ze-
lophehad the son of Hepher, the son
of Gilead, the son of Machir, the son of Manasseh, from the families of Manasseh the
son of Joseph; and these *were* the names of
his daughters: Mahlah, Noah, Hoglah,
Milcah, and Tirzah. 2 And they stood before Moses, before Eleazar the priest, and
before the leaders and all the congregation,
by the doorway of the tabernacle of meeting, saying: 3 "Our father [b]died in the
wilderness; but he was not in the company
of those who gathered together against the
LORD, [c]in company with Korah, but he
died in his own sin; and he had no sons.
4 Why should the name of our father be
[d]removed[1] from among his family because
he had no son? [e]Give us a [2]possession
among our father's brothers."
5 So Moses [f]brought their case before the
LORD.
6 And the LORD spoke to Moses, saying:
7 "The daughters of Zelophehad speak
what is right; [g]you shall surely give them a
possession of inheritance among their father's brothers, and cause the inheritance
of their father to pass to them. 8 And you
shall speak to the children of Israel, saying:
'If a man dies and has no son, then you
shall cause his inheritance to pass to his
daughter. 9 If he has no daughter, then you
shall give his inheritance to his brothers.
10 If he has no brothers, then you shall give
his inheritance to his father's brothers.
11 And if his father has no brothers, then
you shall give his inheritance to the relative closest to him in his family, and he
shall possess it.' " And it shall be to the
children of Israel [h]a statute of judgment,
just as the LORD commanded Moses.

Joshua the Next Leader of Israel

12 Now the LORD said to Moses: [i]"Go up
into this Mount Abarim, and see the land
which I have given to the children of Israel.
13 And when you have seen it, you also
[j]shall [3]be gathered to your people, as Aaron
your brother was gathered. 14 For in the
Wilderness of Zin, during the strife of the
congregation, you [k]rebelled against My
command to hallow Me at the waters before
their eyes." (These *are* the [l]waters of Meribah, at Kadesh in the Wilderness of Zin.)

55 [c]Num. 33:54; 34:13; Josh. 11:23; 14:2
57 [d]Gen. 46:11; Ex. 6:16-19; Num. 3:15; 1 Chr. 6:1, 16
59 [e]Ex. 2:1, 2; 6:20
60 [f]Num. 3:2
61 [g]Lev. 10:1, 2; Num. 3:3, 4; 1 Chr. 24:2
62 [h]Num. 3:39 [i]Num. 1:49 [j]Num. 18:20, 23, 24
63 [k]Num. 26:3
64 [l]Num. 14:29-35; Deut. 2:14-16; Heb. 3:17 [m]Num. 1:1-46
65 [n]Num. 14:26-35; [1 Cor. 10:5, 6] [o]Num. 14:30

CHAPTER 27

1 [a]Num. 26:33; 36:1, 11; Josh. 17:3
3 [b]Num. 14:35; 26:64, 65 [c]Num. 16:1, 2
4 [d]Deut. 25:6 [e]Josh. 17:4 [1]*withdrawn* [2]*inheritance*
5 [f]Ex. 18:13-26
7 [g]Num. 36:2; Josh. 17:4
11 [h]Num. 35:29
12 [i]Num. 33:47; Deut. 3:23-27; 32:48-52; 34:1-4
13 [j]Num. 20:12, 24, 28; 31:2; Deut. 10:6; 34:5, 6 [3]Die and join your ancestors
14 [k]Num. 20:12, 24; Deut. 1:37; 32:51; Ps. 106:32, 33 [l]Ex. 17:7

26:57-65 As in the first census (3:14-39), the Levites were counted separately. The total number of Levites was 23,000 (v. 62), an increase of 1,000 over the previous census (see 3:39).

27:1-11 The coming distribution of the land of Canaan presented a dilemma for the family of Zelophehad since he had no sons. His 5 daughters boldly asked that they inherit their father's name and his inheritance (vv. 1-4). The Lord's decision that the daughters should receive his inheritance became the basis of a perpetual statute in Israel governing inheritances (vv. 5-11).

27:3 he died in his own sin. Zelophehad had not been involved in Korah's rebellion. Instead, he had died under God's judgment in the wilderness, like the rest of the faithless Exodus generation.

27:8-11 The following is the order of inheritance: son, daughter, brother, paternal uncle, and closest relative in the family. This same order (with the exception of the daughter) was followed in Lev. 25:48,49 dealing with the various cases of redemption of the Land in the Jubilee year.

27:12-14 God reaffirmed that Moses could not enter the land of Canaan, although he was able to see it from Mt. Nebo, across from Jericho (see Deut. 32:49).

15 Then Moses spoke to the LORD, saying: 16 "Let the LORD, [m]the God of the spirits of all flesh, set a man over the congregation, 17 [n]who may go out before them
and go in before them, who may lead them
out and bring them in, that the congregation of the LORD may not be [o]like sheep
which have no shepherd."
18 And the LORD said to Moses: "Take
Joshua the son of Nun with you, a man [p]in
whom *is* the Spirit, and [q]lay your hand on
him; 19 set him before Eleazar the priest
and before all the congregation, and [r]inau-
gurate[4] him in their sight. 20 And [s]you
shall give *some* of your authority to him,
that all the congregation of the children of
Israel [t]may be obedient. 21 [u]He shall stand
before Eleazar the priest, who shall inquire
before the LORD for him [v]by the judgment
of the Urim. [w]At his word they shall go
out, and at his word they shall come in, he
and all the children of Israel with him—all
the congregation."
22 So Moses did as the LORD commanded him. He took Joshua and set him before
Eleazar the priest and before all the congregation. 23 And he laid his hands on him
[x]and [5]inaugurated him, just as the LORD
commanded by the hand of Moses.

Daily Offerings

28 Now the LORD spoke to Moses, saying, 2 "Command the children of Israel, and say to them, 'My offering, [a]My
food for My offerings made by fire as a
sweet aroma to Me, you shall be careful to
offer to Me at their appointed time.'
3 "And you shall say to them, [b]'This *is*
the offering made by fire which you shall
offer to the LORD: two male lambs in their
first year without blemish, day by day, as a
regular burnt offering. 4 The one lamb you
shall offer in the morning, the other lamb
you shall offer in the evening, 5 and [c]one-
tenth of an ephah of fine flour as a [d]grain
offering mixed with one-fourth of a hin of
pressed oil. 6 *It is* [e]a regular burnt offering
which was ordained at Mount Sinai for a
sweet aroma, an offering made by fire to
the LORD. 7 And its drink offering *shall be*
one-fourth of a hin for each lamb; [f]in a
holy *place* you shall pour out the drink to
the LORD as an offering. 8 The other lamb
you shall offer in the evening; as the morning grain offering and its drink offering,
you shall offer *it* as an offering made by
fire, a [1]sweet aroma to the LORD.

Sabbath Offerings

9 'And on the Sabbath day two lambs in
their first year, without blemish, and two-
tenths *of an ephah* of fine flour as a grain offering, mixed with oil, with its drink offering— 10 *this is* [g]the burnt offering for every
Sabbath, besides the regular burnt offering
with its drink offering.

Monthly Offerings

11 [h]'At the beginnings of your months
you shall present a burnt offering to the
LORD: two young bulls, one ram, and seven
lambs in their first year, without blemish;
12 [i]three-tenths *of an ephah* of fine flour as a
grain offering, mixed with oil, for each
bull; two-tenths *of an ephah* of fine flour as
a grain offering, mixed with oil, for the one
ram; 13 and one-tenth *of an ephah* of fine
flour, mixed with oil, as a grain offering for
each lamb, as a burnt offering of sweet
aroma, an offering made by fire to the
LORD. 14 Their drink offering shall be half a
hin of wine for a bull, one-third of a hin for
a ram, and one-fourth of a hin for a lamb;
this *is* the burnt offering for each month
throughout the months of the year. 15 Also
[j]one kid of the goats as a sin offering to the
LORD shall be offered, besides the regular
burnt offering and its drink offering.

Offerings at Passover

16 [k]'On the fourteenth day of the first
month *is* the Passover of the LORD. 17 [l]And
on the fifteenth day of this month *is* the
feast; unleavened bread shall be eaten for
seven days. 18 On the [m]first day *you shall*
have a holy [2]convocation. You shall do no

16 [m] Num. 16:22; Heb. 12:9
17 [n] Deut. 31:2; 1 Sam. 8:20; 18:13; 2 Chr. 1:10 [o] 1 Kin. 22:17; Zech. 10:2; Matt. 9:36; Mark 6:34
18 [p] Gen. 41:38; Judg. 3:10; 1 Sam. 16:13, 18 [q] Deut. 34:9
19 [r] Deut. 3:28; 31:3, 7, 8, 23 [4] *commission*
20 [s] Num. 11:17 [t] Josh. 1:16-18
21 [u] Judg. 20:18, 23, 26; 1 Sam. 23:9; 30:7 [v] Ex. 28:30; 1 Sam. 28:6 [w] Josh. 9:14; 1 Sam. 22:10
23 [x] Deut. 3:28; 31:7, 8 [5] *commissioned*

CHAPTER 28

2 [a] Lev. 3:11; 21:6, 8; [Mal. 1:7, 12]
3 [b] Ex. 29:38-42
5 [c] Ex. 16:36; Num. 15:4 [d] Lev. 2:1
6 [e] Ex. 29:42; Amos 5:25
7 [f] Ex. 29:42
8 [1] *pleasing*
10 [g] Ezek. 46:4
11 [h] Num. 10:10; 1 Sam. 20:5; 1 Chr. 23:31; 2 Chr. 2:4; Ezra 3:5; Neh. 10:33; Is. 1:13, 14; Ezek. 45:17; 46:6, 7; Hos. 2:11; Col. 2:16
12 [i] Num. 15:4-12
15 [j] Num. 15:24; 28:3, 22
16 [k] Ex. 12:1-20; Lev. 23:5-8; Num. 9:2-5; Deut. 16:1-8; Ezek. 45:21
17 [l] Lev. 23:6
18 [m] Ex. 12:16; Lev. 23:7 [2] *assembly* or *gathering*

27:15-17 Moses' greatest concern was that Israel have a good leader who was like a shepherd. The Lord answered his request in the man Joshua.

27:18 lay your hand on him. Joshua already had the inner endowment for leadership. He was empowered by the Holy Spirit. This inner endowment was to be recognized by an external ceremony. Moses publicly laid his hands upon Joshua. This act signified the transfer of Moses' leadership to Joshua. The laying on of hands can accompany a dedication to an office (see Num. 8:10).

27:20 give *some* of your authority. Moses was to pass on some of the "honor" or "majesty" that he had to Joshua. See Josh. 3:7.

27:21 Eleazar...shall inquire before the LORD for him. Moses had been able to communicate directly with God (12:8), but Joshua would receive the Word from the Lord through the High-Priest. **Urim.** *See note on Exodus 28:30* for this part of the High-Priest's breastplate (Ex. 39:8-21) as a means of determining God's will (cf. Deut. 33:8; 1 Sam. 28:6).

28:1–29:40 Instructions concerning the regular celebrations in Israel's worship calendar had been given previously. Now, poised to enter the Land, Moses gave an orderly reiteration and summary of the regular offerings for each time of celebration, adding some additional offerings.

28:3-8 See Ex. 29:38-42.

28:9,10 These were newly revealed offerings for the Sabbath.

28:11-15 These were newly revealed offerings for the "beginning of the month."

[3]customary work. 19 And you shall present
an offering made by fire as a burnt offering
to the LORD: two young bulls, one ram, and
seven lambs in their first year. [n]Be sure
they are without blemish. 20 Their grain offering shall be of fine flour mixed with oil:
three-tenths *of an ephah* you shall offer for a
bull, and two-tenths for a ram; 21 you shall
offer one-tenth *of an ephah* for each of the
seven lambs; 22 also [o]one goat *as* a sin offering, to make [4]atonement for you. 23 You
shall offer these besides the burnt offering
of the morning, which *is* for a regular
burnt offering. 24 In this manner you shall
offer the food of the offering made by fire
daily for seven days, as a sweet aroma to
the LORD; it shall be offered besides the
regular burnt offering and its drink offering. 25 And [p]on the seventh day you shall
have a holy convocation. You shall do no
customary work.

Offerings at the Feast of Weeks

26 'Also [q]on the day of the firstfruits,
when you bring a new grain offering to the
LORD at your *Feast of* Weeks, you shall have
a holy convocation. You shall do no customary work. 27 You shall present a burnt
offering as a sweet aroma to the LORD: [r]two
young bulls, one ram, and seven lambs in
their first year, 28 with their grain offering
of fine flour mixed with oil: three-tenths *of
an ephah* for each bull, two-tenths for the
one ram, 29 and one-tenth for each of the
seven lambs; 30 *also* one kid of the goats, to
make [5]atonement for you. 31 [s]Be sure they
are without [6]blemish. You shall present
them with their drink offerings, besides the
regular burnt offering with its grain offering.

Offerings at the Feast of Trumpets

29 'And in the seventh month, on the
first *day* of the month, you shall
have a holy convocation. You shall do no
customary work. For you [a]it is a day of
blowing the trumpets. 2 You shall offer a
burnt offering as a sweet aroma to the
LORD: one young bull, one ram, *and* seven
lambs in their first year, without blemish.
3 Their grain offering *shall be* fine flour
mixed with oil: three-tenths *of an ephah* for
the bull, two-tenths for the ram, 4 and one-
tenth for each of the seven lambs; 5 also
one kid of the goats *as* a sin offering, to
make atonement for you; 6 besides [b]the
burnt offering with its grain offering for
the New Moon, [c]the regular burnt offering
with its grain offering, and their drink offerings, [d]according to their ordinance, as a
sweet aroma, an offering made by fire to
the LORD.

Offerings on the Day of Atonement

7 [e]'On the tenth *day* of this seventh
month you shall have a holy convocation.
You shall [f]afflict your souls; you shall not
do any work. 8 You shall present a burnt
offering to the LORD *as* a sweet aroma: one
young bull, one ram, *and* seven lambs in
their first year. [g]Be sure they are without
blemish. 9 Their grain offering *shall be of*
fine flour mixed with oil: three-tenths *of an
ephah* for the bull, two-tenths for the one
ram, 10 and one-tenth for each of the seven
lambs; 11 also one kid of the goats *as* a sin
offering, besides [h]the sin offering for
atonement, the regular burnt offering with
its grain offering, and their drink offerings.

Offerings at the Feast of Tabernacles

12 [i]'On the fifteenth day of the seventh
month you shall have a holy convocation.
You shall do no customary work, and you
shall keep a feast to the LORD seven days.
13 [j]You shall present a burnt offering, an
offering made by fire as a sweet aroma to
the LORD: thirteen young bulls, two rams,
and fourteen lambs in their first year. They
shall be without blemish. 14 Their grain offering *shall be of* fine flour mixed with oil:
three-tenths *of an ephah* for each of the thirteen bulls, two-tenths for each of the two
rams, 15 and one-tenth for each of the fourteen lambs; 16 also one kid of the goats *as* a
sin offering, besides the regular burnt offering, its grain offering, and its drink offering.

17 'On the [k]second day *present* twelve
young bulls, two rams, fourteen lambs in
their first year without blemish, 18 and
their grain offering and their drink offerings for the bulls, for the rams, and for the
lambs, by their number, [l]according to the
ordinance; 19 also one kid of the goats *as* a
sin offering, besides the regular burnt offering with its grain offering, and their
drink offerings.

20 'On the third day *present* eleven bulls,
two rams, fourteen lambs in their first year
without blemish, 21 and their grain offering and their drink offerings for the bulls,
for the rams, and for the lambs, by their
number, [m]according to the ordinance;
22 also one goat *as* a sin offering, besides

18 [3] *occupational*
19 [n] Lev. 22:20; Num. 28:31; 29:8; Deut. 15:21
22 [o] Num. 28:15 [4] Lit. *covering*
25 [p] Ex. 12:16; 13:6; Lev. 23:8
26 [q] Ex. 23:16; 34:22; Lev. 23:10-21; Deut. 16:9-12; Acts 2:1
27 [r] Lev. 23:18, 19
30 [5] Lit. *covering*
31 [s] Num. 28:3, 19 [6] *defect*

CHAPTER 29

1 [a] Ex. 23:16; 34:22; Lev. 23:23-25
6 [b] Num. 28:11-15 [c] Num. 28:3
[d] Num. 15:11, 12
7 [e] Lev. 16:29-34; 23:26-32 [f] Ps. 35:13; Is. 58:5
8 [g] Num. 28:19
11 [h] Lev. 16:3, 5
12 [i] Lev. 23:33-35; Deut. 16:13-15; Ezek. 45:25
13 [j] Ezra 3:4
17 [k] Lev. 23:36
18 [l] Num. 15:12; 28:7, 14; 29:3, 4, 9, 10
21 [m] Num. 29:18

28:16-25 See Lev. 23:5-8.
28:26-31 See Lev. 23:18.
29:1-6 See Lev. 23:23-25.
29:7-11 See Lev. 23:27-32.

the regular burnt offering, its grain offering, and its drink offering.
23 'On the fourth day *present* ten bulls,
two rams, *and* fourteen lambs in their first
year, without blemish, 24 and their grain
offering and their drink offerings for the
bulls, for the rams, and for the lambs, by
their number, according to the ordinance;
25 also one kid of the goats *as* a sin offering,
besides the regular burnt offering, its grain
offering, and its drink offering.
26 'On the fifth day *present* nine bulls,
two rams, *and* fourteen lambs in their first
year without blemish, 27 and their grain offering and their drink offerings for the
bulls, for the rams, and for the lambs, by
their number, according to the ordinance;
28 also one goat *as* a sin offering, besides
the regular burnt offering, its grain offering, and its drink offering.
29 'On the sixth day *present* eight bulls,
two rams, *and* fourteen lambs in their first
year without blemish, 30 and their grain offering and their drink offerings for the
bulls, for the rams, and for the lambs, by
their number, according to the ordinance;
31 also one goat *as* a sin offering, besides
the regular burnt offering, its grain offering, and its drink offering.
32 'On the seventh day *present* seven
bulls, two rams, *and* fourteen lambs in
their first year without blemish, 33 and
their grain offering and their drink offerings for the bulls, for the rams, and for the
lambs, by their number, according to the
ordinance; 34 also one goat *as* a sin offering, besides the regular burnt offering, its
grain offering, and its drink offering.
35 'On the eighth day you shall have a
[n]sacred[1] assembly. You shall do no customary work. 36 You shall present a burnt
offering, an offering made by fire as a
sweet aroma to the LORD: one bull, one
ram, seven lambs in their first year without
blemish, 37 and their grain offering and
their drink offerings for the bull, for the
ram, and for the lambs, by their number,
according to the ordinance; 38 also one
goat *as* a sin offering, besides the regular
burnt offering, its grain offering, and its
drink offering.
39 'These you shall present to the LORD at
your [o]appointed feasts (besides your
[p]vowed offerings and your freewill offerings) as your burnt offerings and your
grain offerings, as your drink offerings and
your peace offerings.' "
40 So Moses told the children of Israel
everything, just as the LORD commanded
Moses.

The Law Concerning Vows

30 Then Moses spoke to [a]the heads of
the tribes concerning the children of
Israel, saying, "This *is* the thing which the
LORD has commanded: 2 [b]If a man makes a
vow to the LORD, or [c]swears an oath to
bind himself by some agreement, he shall
not break his word; he shall [d]do according
to all that proceeds out of his mouth.
3 "Or if a woman makes a vow to the
LORD, and binds *herself* by some agreement
while in her father's house in her youth,
4 and her father hears her vow and the
agreement by which she has bound herself, and her father [1]holds his peace, then
all her vows shall stand, and every agreement with which she has bound herself
shall stand. 5 But if her father overrules her
on the day that he hears, then none of her
vows nor her agreements by which she has
bound herself shall stand; and the LORD
will release her, because her father overruled her.
6 "If indeed she takes a husband, while
bound by her vows or by a rash utterance
from her lips by which she bound herself,
7 and her husband hears *it,* and makes no
response to her on the day that he hears,
then her vows shall stand, and her agreements by which she bound herself shall
stand. 8 But if her husband [e]overrules her
on the day that he hears *it,* he shall make
void her vow which she took and what she
uttered with her lips, by which she bound
herself, and the LORD will release her.
9 "Also any vow of a widow or a divorced woman, by which she has bound
herself, shall stand against her.
10 "If she vowed in her husband's house,
or bound herself by an agreement with an
oath, 11 and her husband heard *it,* and
made no response to her *and* did not overrule her, then all her vows shall stand, and
every agreement by which she bound herself shall stand. 12 But if her husband truly
made them void on the day he heard *them,*
then whatever proceeded from her lips

35 [n]Lev. 23:36 [1]*solemn*
39 [o]Lev. 23:1-44; 1 Chr. 23:31; 2 Chr. 31:3; Ezra 3:5; Neh. 10:33; Is. 1:14 [p]Lev. 7:16; 22:18, 21, 23; 23:38

CHAPTER 30

1 [a]Num. 1:4, 16; 7:2
2 [b]Lev. 27:2; Deut. 23:21-23; Judg. 11:30, 31, 35; Eccl. 5:4 [c]Lev. 5:4; Matt. 14:9; Acts 23:14 [d]Job 22:27; Ps. 22:25; 50:14; 66:13, 14; Nah. 1:15
4 [1]*says nothing* to interfere
8 [e][Gen. 3:16]

29:12-38 See Lev. 23:33-43.

30:1-16 This chapter added clarification to the laws regarding vows given in Lev. 27:1-33. The basic principle for men is restated in v. 2. Then, it was asserted that a man was also responsible for the vows made by women in his household (vv. 3-16). A father or husband could overrule the vow of a daughter or wife, but a man's silence, if he knew of the vow, meant it must be accomplished.

30:2 a vow…some agreement. A promise to do something or a promise not to do something. Christ could have had this text in mind (Matt. 5:33).

30:9 a widow or a divorced woman. These were not viewed as being under a man's authority, so the word of the woman alone sufficed.

concerning her vows or concerning the
agreement binding her, it shall not stand;
her husband has made them [2]void, and the
LORD will release her. 13 Every vow and
every binding oath to afflict her soul, her
husband may confirm it, or her husband
may make it void. 14 Now if her husband
makes no response whatever to her from
day to day, then he confirms all her vows
or all the agreements that bind her; he confirms them, because he made no response
to her on the day that he heard *them.* 15 But
if he does make them void after he has
heard *them,* then he shall bear her guilt."
16 These *are* the statutes which the LORD
commanded Moses, between a man and
his wife, and between a father and his
daughter in her youth in her father's house.

Vengeance on the Midianites

31 And the LORD spoke to Moses, saying: 2 [a]"Take vengeance on the
Midianites for the children of Israel. Afterward you shall [b]be gathered to your people."
3 So Moses spoke to the people, saying,
"Arm some of yourselves for war, and let
them go against the Midianites to take
vengeance for the LORD on [c]Midian. 4 A
thousand from each tribe of all the tribes of
Israel you shall send to the war."
5 So there were recruited from the divisions of Israel one thousand from *each*
tribe, twelve thousand armed for war.
6 Then Moses sent them to the war, one
thousand from *each* tribe; he sent them to
the war with Phinehas the son of Eleazar
the priest, with the holy articles and [d]the
signal trumpets in his hand. 7 And they
warred against the Midianites, just as the
LORD commanded Moses, and [e]they killed
all the [f]males. 8 They killed the kings of
Midian with *the rest of* those who were
killed—[g]Evi, Rekem, [h]Zur, Hur, and Reba,
the five kings of Midian. [i]Balaam the son
of Beor they also killed with the sword.
9 And the children of Israel took the
women of Midian captive, with their little
ones, and took as spoil all their cattle, all
their flocks, and all their goods. 10 They
also burned with fire all the cities where
they dwelt, and all their forts. 11 And [j]they
took all the spoil and all the booty—of man
and beast.

Return from the War

12 Then they brought the captives, the
booty, and the spoil to Moses, to Eleazar
the priest, and to the congregation of the
children of Israel, to the camp in the plains
of Moab by the Jordan, *across from* Jericho.
13 And Moses, Eleazar the priest, and all
the leaders of the congregation, went to
meet them outside the camp. 14 But Moses
was angry with the officers of the army,
with the captains over thousands and captains over hundreds, who had come from
the battle.
15 And Moses said to them: "Have you
kept [k]all the women alive? 16 Look, [l]these
women caused the children of Israel,
through the [m]counsel of Balaam, to trespass against the LORD in the incident of
Peor, and [n]there was a plague among the
congregation of the LORD. 17 Now therefore, [o]kill every male among the little ones,
and kill every woman who has known a
man intimately. 18 But keep alive [p]for
yourselves all the young girls who have
not known a man intimately. 19 And as for
you, [q]remain outside the camp seven days;
whoever has killed any person, and [r]who-
ever has touched any slain, purify yourselves and your captives on the third day
and on the seventh day. 20 Purify every
garment, everything made of leather,
everything woven of goats' *hair,* and
everything made of wood."
21 Then Eleazar the priest said to the
men of war who had gone to the battle,
"This *is* the [1]ordinance of the law which
the LORD commanded Moses: 22 "Only the
gold, the silver, the bronze, the iron, the
tin, and the lead, 23 everything that can endure fire, you shall put through the fire,
and it shall be clean; and it shall be purified [s]with the water of purification. But all
that cannot endure fire you shall put
through water. 24 [t]And you shall wash
your clothes on the seventh day and be
clean, and afterward you may come into
the camp."

12 [2] *annulled* or *invalidated*

CHAPTER 31

2 [a] Num. 25:17 [b] Num. 27:12, 13
3 [c] Josh. 13:21
6 [d] Num. 10:9
7 [e] Deut. 20:13; Judg. 21:11; 1 Sam. 27:9; 1 Kin. 11:15, 16 [f] Gen. 34:25
8 [g] Josh. 13:21 [h] Num. 25:15 [i] Num. 31:16; Josh. 13:22
11 [j] Deut. 20:14
15 [k] Deut. 20:14
16 [l] Num. 25:2 [m] Num. 24:14; 2 Pet. 2:15; Rev. 2:14 [n] Num. 25:9
17 [o] Deut. 7:2; 20:16-18; Judg. 21:11
18 [p] Deut. 21:10-14
19 [q] Num. 5:2 [r] Num. 19:11-22
21 [1] *statute*
23 [s] Num. 19:9, 17
24 [t] Lev. 11:25

31:1-54 This chapter has many links with previous passages in Numbers: vengeance on Midian (vv. 2,3; 10:2-10); Zur the Midianite (v. 8; 25:15); Balaam (vv. 8,16; 22:2–24:25); Peor (v. 16; 25:1-9,14,15); purification after contact with the dead (vv. 19-24; 19:11-19); care for the priests and Levites (vv. 28-47; 18:8-32). This battle with the Midianites modeled God's requirements for holy war when Israel took vengeance on His enemies (see Deut. 20:1-18).

31:1-11 Israel was commanded by the Lord to take vengeance on Midian because they were responsible for corrupting Israel at Peor (25:1-18).

31:2 gathered to your people. A euphemism for death (see Gen. 25:8,17; 35:29).

31:12-24 All the Midianites, except the virgin women, were to be put to death. Both the soldiers and the spoil needed to be cleansed.

31:17 The execution of all male children and women of childbearing age insured the extermination of the Midianites and prevented them from ever again seducing Israel to sin. Reference to Midianites later (Judg. 6:1-6) was to a different clan. It was the Midianites living in Moab who were destroyed here.

Division of the Plunder

25 Now the LORD spoke to Moses, saying: 26 "Count up the plunder that was
[2]taken—of man and beast—you and Eleazar the priest and the chief fathers of the
congregation; 27 and [u]divide the plunder
into two parts, between those who took
part in the war, who went out to battle,
and all the congregation. 28 And levy a
[3]tribute for the LORD on the men of war
who went out to battle: [v]one of every five
hundred of the persons, the cattle, the
donkeys, and the sheep; 29 take *it* from
their half, and [w]give *it* to Eleazar the priest
as a heave offering to the LORD. 30 And
from the children of Israel's half you shall
take [x]one of every fifty, drawn from the
persons, the cattle, the donkeys, and the
sheep, from all the livestock, and give
them to the Levites [y]who [4]keep charge of
the tabernacle of the LORD." 31 So Moses
and Eleazar the priest did as the LORD
commanded Moses.
32 The booty remaining from the plunder, which the men of war had taken, was
six hundred and seventy-five thousand
sheep, 33 seventy-two thousand cattle,
34 sixty-one thousand donkeys, 35 and thirty-two thousand persons in all, of women
who had not known a man intimately.
36 And the half, the portion for those who
had gone out to war, was in number three
hundred and thirty-seven thousand five
hundred sheep; 37 and the LORD's [5]tribute
of the sheep was six hundred and seventy-
five. 38 The cattle *were* thirty-six thousand,
of which the LORD's tribute *was* seventy-
two. 39 The donkeys *were* thirty thousand
five hundred, of which the LORD's tribute
was sixty-one. 40 The persons *were* sixteen
thousand, of which the LORD's tribute *was*
thirty-two persons. 41 So Moses gave the
tribute *which was* the LORD's heave offering
to Eleazar the priest, [z]as the LORD commanded Moses.
42 And from the children of Israel's half,
which Moses separated from the men who
fought— 43 now the half belonging to the
congregation was three hundred and thirty-seven thousand five hundred sheep,
44 thirty-six thousand cattle, 45 thirty thousand five hundred donkeys, 46 and sixteen
thousand persons— 47 and [a]from the children of Israel's half Moses took one of
every fifty, drawn from man and beast,
and gave them to the Levites, who kept
charge of the tabernacle of the LORD, as the
LORD commanded Moses.
48 Then the officers who *were* over thousands of the army, the captains of thousands and captains of hundreds, came near
to Moses; 49 and they said to Moses, "Your
servants have taken a count of the men of
war who *are* under our command, and not
a man of us is missing. 50 Therefore we
have brought an offering for the LORD,
what every man found of ornaments of
gold: armlets and bracelets and signet
rings and earrings and necklaces, [b]to make
[6]atonement for ourselves before the
LORD." 51 So Moses and Eleazar the priest
received the gold from them, all the fashioned ornaments. 52 And all the gold of the
offering that they offered to the LORD, from
the captains of thousands and captains of
hundreds, was sixteen thousand seven
hundred and fifty shekels. 53 [c](The men of
war had taken spoil, every man for himself.) 54 And Moses and Eleazar the priest
received the gold from the captains of
thousands and of hundreds, and brought it
into the tabernacle of meeting [d]as a memorial for the children of Israel before the
LORD.

The Tribes Settling East of the Jordan

32 Now the children of Reuben and
the children of Gad had a very great
multitude of livestock; and when they saw
the land of [a]Jazer and the land of [b]Gilead,
that indeed the region *was* a place for livestock, 2 the children of Gad and the children of Reuben came and spoke to Moses,
to Eleazar the priest, and to the leaders of
the congregation, saying, 3 "Ataroth,
Dibon, Jazer, [c]Nimrah, [d]Heshbon, Elealeh,
[e]Shebam, Nebo, and [f]Beon, 4 the country
[g]which the LORD defeated before the congregation of Israel, *is* a land for livestock,
and your servants have livestock." 5 Therefore they said, "If we have found favor in
your sight, let this land be given to your
servants as a possession. Do not take us
over the Jordan."
6 And Moses said to the children of Gad
and to the children of Reuben: "Shall your
brethren go to war while you sit here?
7 Now why will you [h]discourage the heart
of the children of Israel from going over
into the land which the LORD has given

26 [2]*captured*
27 [u]Josh. 22:8; 1 Sam. 30:24
28 [v]Num. 31:30, 47 [3]*tax*
29 [w]Deut. 18:1-5
30 [x]Num. 31:42-47 [y]Num. 3:7, 8, 25, 31, 36; 18:3, 4 [4]*perform the service*
37 [5]*tax*
41 [z]Num. 5:9, 10; 18:8, 19
47 [a]Num. 31:30
50 [b]Ex. 30:12-16 [6]Lit. *covering*
53 [c]Num. 31:32; Deut. 20:14
54 [d]Ex. 30:16

CHAPTER 32

1 [a]Num. 21:32; Josh. 13:25; 2 Sam. 24:5 [b]Deut. 3:13
3 [c]Num. 32:36 [d]Josh. 13:17, 26 [e]Num. 32:38 [f]Num. 32:38
4 [g]Num. 21:24, 34, 35
7 [h]Num. 13:27-14:4

31:25-54 The plunder was divided equally between those who went and fought and those who stayed.

32:1-42 The tribes of Reuben and Gad desired to live in the land already conquered because they possessed much livestock and the land was good for grazing. Moses gave them, along with the half tribe of Manasseh, portions of the land only on the condition that they would fully participate in the conquest of Canaan.

32:3 Ataroth...Beon. The places mentioned here cannot be identified, but all lie between the Arnon River to the S and the Jabbok River to the N.

them? 8 Thus your fathers did [i]when I sent them away from Kadesh Barnea [j]to see the land. 9 For [k]when they went up to the Valley of Eshcol and saw the land, they discouraged the heart of the children of Israel, so that they did not go into the land which the LORD had given them. 10 [l]So the LORD's anger was aroused on that day, and He swore an oath, saying, 11 'Surely none of the men who came up from Egypt, [m]from twenty years old and above, shall see the land of which I swore to Abraham, Isaac, and Jacob, because [n]they have not wholly followed Me, 12 except Caleb the son of Jephunneh, the Kenizzite, and Joshua the son of Nun, [o]for they have wholly followed the LORD.' 13 So the LORD's anger was aroused against Israel, and He made them [p]wander in the wilderness forty years, until [q]all the generation that had done evil in the sight of the LORD was gone. 14 And look! You have risen in your fathers' place, a brood of sinful men, to increase still more the [r]fierce anger of the LORD against Israel. 15 For if you [s]turn away from following Him, He will once again leave them in the wilderness, and you will destroy all these people."

16 Then they came near to him and said: "We will build sheepfolds here for our livestock, and cities for our little ones, 17 but [t]we ourselves will be armed, ready *to go* before the children of Israel until we have brought them to their place; and our little ones will dwell in the fortified cities because of the inhabitants of the land. 18 [u]We will not return to our homes until every one of the children of Israel has [1]received his inheritance. 19 For we will not inherit with them on the other side of the Jordan and beyond, [v]because our inheritance has fallen to us on this eastern side of the Jordan."

20 Then [w]Moses said to them: "If you do this thing, if you arm yourselves before the LORD for the war, 21 and all your armed men cross over the Jordan before the LORD until He has driven out His enemies from before Him, 22 and [x]the land is subdued before the LORD, then afterward [y]you may return and be blameless before the LORD and before Israel; and [z]this land shall be your possession before the LORD. 23 But if you do not do so, then take note, you have sinned against the LORD; and be sure [a]your sin will find you out. 24 [b]Build cities for your little ones and folds for your sheep, and do [2]what has proceeded out of your mouth."

25 And the children of Gad and the children of Reuben spoke to Moses, saying: "Your servants will do as my lord commands. 26 [c]Our little ones, our wives, our flocks, and all our livestock will be there in the cities of Gilead; 27 [d]but your servants will cross over, every man armed for war, before the LORD to battle, just as my lord says."

28 So Moses gave command [e]concerning them to Eleazar the priest, to Joshua the son of Nun, and to the chief fathers of the tribes of the children of Israel. 29 And Moses said to them: "If the children of Gad and the children of Reuben cross over the Jordan with you, every man armed for battle before the LORD, and the land is subdued before you, then you shall give them the land of Gilead as a possession. 30 But if they do not cross over armed with you, they shall have possessions among you in the land of Canaan."

31 Then the children of Gad and the children of Reuben answered, saying: "As the LORD has said to your servants, so we will do. 32 We will cross over armed before the LORD into the land of Canaan, but the possession of our inheritance *shall remain* with us on this side of the Jordan."

33 So [f]Moses gave to the children of Gad, to the children of Reuben, and to half the tribe of Manasseh the son of Joseph, [g]the kingdom of Sihon king of the Amorites and the kingdom of Og king of Bashan, the land with its cities within the borders, the cities of the surrounding country. 34 And the children of Gad built [h]Dibon and Ataroth and [i]Aroer, 35 Atroth and Shophan and [j]Jazer and Jogbehah, 36 [k]Beth Nimrah and Beth Haran, [l]fortified cities, and folds for sheep. 37 And the children of Reuben built [m]Heshbon and Elealeh and Kirjathaim, 38 [n]Nebo and [o]Baal Meon [p](*their* names being changed) and Shibmah; and they gave *other* names to the cities which they built.

8 [i] Num. 13:3, 26 [j] Deut. 1:19-25
9 [k] Num. 13:24, 31; Deut. 1:24, 28
10 [l] Num. 14:11; Deut. 1:34-36
11 [m] Num. 14:28, 29; 26:63-65; Deut. 1:35 [n] Num. 14:24, 30
12 [o] Num. 14:6-9, 24, 30; Deut. 1:36; Josh. 14:8, 9
13 [p] Num. 14:33-35 [q] Num. 26:64, 65
14 [r] Num. 11:1; Deut. 1:34
15 [s] Deut. 30:17, 18; Josh. 22:16-18; 2 Chr. 7:19; 15:2
17 [t] Josh. 4:12, 13
18 [u] Josh. 22:1-4 [1] *possessed*
19 [v] Josh. 12:1; 13:8
20 [w] Deut. 3:18; Josh. 1:14
22 [x] Deut. 3:20; Josh. 11:23 [y] Josh. 22:4 [z] Deut. 3:12, 15, 16, 18; Josh. 1:15; 13:8, 32; 22:4, 9
23 [a] Gen. 4:7; 44:16; Josh. 7:1-26; Is. 59:12; [Gal. 6:7]
24 [b] Num. 32:16 [2] *what you said you would do*
26 [c] Josh. 1:14
27 [d] Josh. 4:12
28 [e] Josh. 1:13
33 [f] Deut. 3:8-17; 29:8; Josh. 12:1-6; 13:8-31; 22:4 [g] Num. 21:24, 33, 35
34 [h] Num. 33:45, 46 [i] Deut. 2:36
35 [j] Num. 32:1, 3
36 [k] Num. 32:3 [l] Num. 32:24
37 [m] Num. 21:27
38 [n] Is. 46:1 [o] Ezek. 25:9 [p] Ex. 23:13; Josh. 23:7

32:8 Thus your fathers did. Moses feared that if these two tribes were comfortably settled, they would not join with the other 10 tribes in conquering Canaan, and that could be the beginning of a general revolt against entering the Land. As the 10 spies had dissuaded the people at Kadesh nearly 40 years earlier from conquering the Land (vv. 9-13; 13:26–14:4), the refusal of these two tribes could cause the people to fail again (v. 15).

32:23 your sin will find you out. The two tribes committed themselves to provide their warriors for the conquest of the Land. This agreement satisfied Moses, although he added that non-participation would be sin and God would certainly find and judge the tribes for their sin.

32:33 half the tribe of Manasseh. Once the agreement was reached with Reuben and Gad concerning settlement on the E side of the Jordan, the half tribe of Manasseh, also rich with flocks, joined in seeking land in that territory. However, vv. 39-42 indicate that Manasseh conquered cities not yet taken and settled in the northern area of Gilead.

39 And the children of [q]Machir the son of
Manasseh went to Gilead and took it, and
[3]dispossessed the Amorites who *were* in it.
40 So Moses [r]gave Gilead to Machir the son
of Manasseh, and he dwelt in it. 41 Also
[s]Jair the son of Manasseh went and took its
small towns, and called them [t]Havoth
Jair.[4] 42 Then Nobah went and took Kenath
and its villages, and he called it Nobah,
after his own name.

Israel's Journey from Egypt Reviewed

33 These *are* the journeys of the children of Israel, who went out of the
land of Egypt by their armies under the
[a]hand of Moses and Aaron. 2 Now Moses
wrote down the starting points of their
journeys at the command of the LORD. And
these *are* their journeys according to their
starting points:
3 They [b]departed from Rameses in [c]the
first month, on the fifteenth day of the first
month; on the day after the Passover the
children of Israel went out [d]with boldness
in the sight of all the Egyptians. 4 For the
Egyptians were burying all *their* firstborn,
[e]whom the LORD had killed among them.
Also [f]on their gods the LORD had executed
judgments.
5 [g]Then the children of Israel moved
from Rameses and camped at Succoth.
6 They departed from [h]Succoth and
camped at Etham, which *is* on the edge of
the wilderness. 7 [i]They moved from Etham
and turned back to Pi Hahiroth, which *is*
east of Baal Zephon; and they camped near
Migdol. 8 They departed [1]from before Hahiroth and [j]passed through the midst of
the sea into the wilderness, went three
days' journey in the Wilderness of Etham,
and camped at Marah. 9 They moved from
Marah and [k]came to Elim. At Elim *were*
twelve springs of water and seventy palm
trees; so they camped there.
10 They moved from Elim and camped
by the Red Sea. 11 They moved from the
Red Sea and camped in the [l]Wilderness of
Sin. 12 They journeyed from the Wilderness of Sin and camped at Dophkah.
13 They departed from Dophkah and
camped at Alush. 14 They moved from
Alush and camped at [m]Rephidim, where
there was no water for the people to drink.
15 They departed from Rephidim and
camped in the [n]Wilderness of Sinai.
16 They moved from the Wilderness of Sinai and camped [o]at [2]Kibroth Hattaavah.
17 They departed from Kibroth Hattaavah
and [p]camped at Hazeroth. 18 They departed from Hazeroth and camped at
[q]Rithmah. 19 They departed from Rithmah
and camped at Rimmon Perez. 20 They departed from Rimmon Perez and camped at
Libnah. 21 They moved from Libnah and
camped at Rissah. 22 They journeyed from
Rissah and camped at Kehelathah. 23 They
went from Kehelathah and camped at
Mount Shepher. 24 They moved from
Mount Shepher and camped at Haradah.
25 They moved from Haradah and camped
at Makheloth. 26 They moved from Makheloth and camped at Tahath. 27 They departed from Tahath and camped at Terah.
28 They moved from Terah and camped at
Mithkah. 29 They went from Mithkah and
camped at Hashmonah. 30 They departed
from Hashmonah and [r]camped at Moseroth. 31 They departed from Moseroth
and camped at Bene Jaakan. 32 They
moved from [s]Bene Jaakan and [t]camped at
Hor Hagidgad. 33 They went from Hor Hagidgad and camped at Jotbathah. 34 They
moved from Jotbathah and camped at
Abronah. 35 They departed from Abronah

39 [q]Gen. 50:23; Num. 27:1; 36:1 [3]*drove out*
40 [r]Deut. 3:12, 13, 15; Josh. 13:31
41 [s]Deut. 3:14; Josh. 13:30 [t]Judg. 10:4; 1 Kin. 4:13 [4]Lit. *Towns of Jair*

CHAPTER 33

1 [a]Ps. 77:20
3 [b]Ex. 12:37 [c]Ex. 12:2; 13:4 [d]Ex. 14:8
4 [e]Ex. 12:29 [f][Ex. 12:12; 18:11]; Is. 19:1
5 [g]Ex. 12:37
6 [h]Ex. 13:20
7 [i]Ex. 14:1, 2, 9
8 [j]Ex. 14:22; 15:22, 23 [1]Many Heb. mss., Sam., Syr., Tg., Vg. *from Pi Hahiroth;* cf. Num. 33:7
9 [k]Ex. 15:27
11 [l]Ex. 16:1
14 [m]Ex. 17:1; 19:2
15 [n]Ex. 16:1; 19:1, 2
16 [o]Num. 11:34 [2]Lit. *Graves of Craving*
17 [p]Num. 11:35
18 [q]Num. 12:16
30 [r]Deut. 10:6
32 [s]Deut. 10:6 [t]Deut. 10:7

33:1-49 The Lord commanded Moses to write a list of Israel's encampments between Egypt and the plains of Moab. Significantly, 40 places were mentioned (not including Rameses and the plains of Moab), reflecting the 40 years spent in the wilderness. Some sites recorded earlier are not listed and other sites are only mentioned here. The God who would lead the Israelites in the conquest of Canaan (33:50-56) was the one who had led them through the wilderness.

From the Wilderness to the Jordan

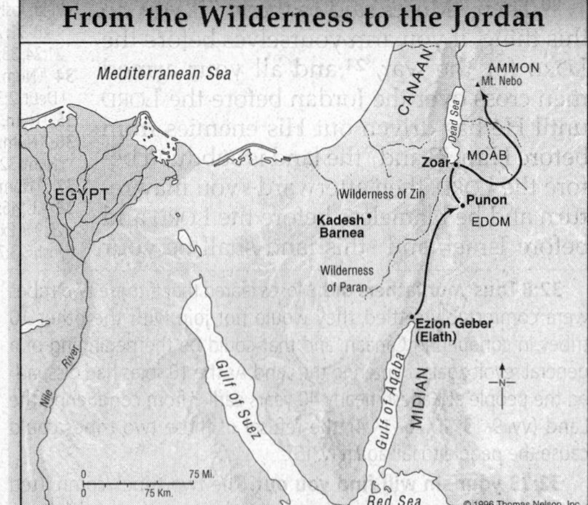

The last phase of Israel's wilderness wanderings placed them in the plains of Moab, looking across the Jordan to the Promised Land.

[u]and camped at Ezion Geber. 36 They
moved from Ezion Geber and camped in
the [v]Wilderness of Zin, which *is* Kadesh.
37 They moved from [w]Kadesh and camped
at Mount Hor, on the boundary of the land
of Edom.
38 Then [x]Aaron the priest went up to
Mount Hor at the command of the LORD,
and died there in the fortieth year after the
children of Israel had come out of the land
of Egypt, on the first *day* of the fifth month.
39 Aaron *was* one hundred and twenty-
three years old when he died on Mount
Hor.
40 Now [y]the king of Arad, the Canaanite, who dwelt in the South in the land of
Canaan, heard of the coming of the children of Israel.
41 So they departed from Mount Hor
and camped at Zalmonah. 42 They departed from Zalmonah and camped at Punon.
43 They departed from Punon and
[z]camped at Oboth. 44 [a]They departed from
Oboth and camped at Ije Abarim, at the
border of Moab. 45 They departed from
[3]Ijim and camped [b]at Dibon Gad. 46 They
moved from Dibon Gad and camped at
[c]Almon Diblathaim. 47 They moved from
Almon Diblathaim [d]and camped in the
mountains of Abarim, before Nebo.
48 They departed from the mountains of
Abarim and [e]camped in the plains of Moab
by the Jordan, *across from* Jericho. 49 They
camped by the Jordan, from Beth Jesimoth
as far as the [f]Abel Acacia Grove[4] in the
plains of Moab.

Instructions for the Conquest of Canaan

50 Now the LORD spoke to Moses in the
plains of Moab by the Jordan, *across from*
Jericho, saying, 51 "Speak to the children of
Israel, and say to them: [g]'When you have
crossed the Jordan into the land of Canaan,
52 [h]then you shall drive out all the inhabitants of the land from before you, destroy
all their engraved stones, destroy all their
molded images, and demolish all their
[5]high places; 53 you shall dispossess *the inhabitants of* the land and dwell in it, for I
have given you the land to [i]possess.
54 And [j]you shall divide the land by lot as
an inheritance among your families; to the
larger you shall give a larger inheritance,
and to the smaller you shall give a smaller
inheritance; there everyone's *inheritance*
shall be whatever falls to him by lot. You
shall inherit according to the tribes of your
fathers. 55 But if you do not drive out the
inhabitants of the land from before you,
then it shall be that those whom you let remain *shall be* [k]irritants in your eyes and
thorns in your sides, and they shall harass
you in the land where you dwell. 56 Moreover it shall be *that* I will do to you as I
thought to do to them.' "

The Appointed Boundaries of Canaan

34 Then the LORD spoke to Moses, saying, 2 "Command the children of Israel, and say to them: 'When you come
into [a]the land of Canaan, this *is* the land
that shall fall to you as an inheritance—the
land of Canaan to its boundaries. 3 [b]Your
southern border shall be from the Wilderness of Zin along the border of Edom; then
your southern border shall extend eastward to the end of [c]the Salt Sea; 4 your border shall turn from the southern side of
[d]the Ascent of Akrabbim, continue to Zin,
and be on the south of [e]Kadesh Barnea;
then it shall go on to [f]Hazar Addar, and
continue to Azmon; 5 the border shall turn
from Azmon [g]to the Brook of Egypt, and it
shall end at the Sea.
6 'As for the [h]western border, you shall
have the Great Sea for a border; this shall
be your western border.
7 'And this shall be your northern border: From the Great Sea you shall mark out
your *border* line to [i]Mount Hor; 8 from
Mount Hor you shall mark out *your border*
[j]to the entrance of Hamath; then the direction of the border shall be toward [k]Zedad;
9 the border shall proceed to Ziphron, and
it shall end at [l]Hazar Enan. This shall be
your northern border.
10 'You shall mark out your eastern border from Hazar Enan to Shepham; 11 the
border shall go down from Shepham [m]to
Riblah on the east side of Ain; the border
shall go down and reach to the eastern
[1]side of the Sea [n]of Chinnereth; 12 the border shall go down along the Jordan, and it
shall end at [o]the Salt Sea. This shall be your
land with its surrounding boundaries.' "
13 Then Moses commanded the children

35 [u] Deut. 2:8; 1 Kin. 9:26; 22:48
36 [v] Num. 20:1; 27:14
37 [w] Num. 20:22, 23; 21:4
38 [x] Num. 20:25, 28; Deut. 10:6; 32:50
40 [y] Num. 21:1
43 [z] Num. 21:10
44 [a] Num. 21:11
45 [b] Num. 32:34 [3] Same as *Ije Abarim*, v. 44
46 [c] Jer. 48:22; Ezek. 6:14
47 [d] Num. 21:20; Deut. 32:49
48 [e] Num. 22:1; 31:12; 35:1
49 [f] Num. 25:1; Josh. 2:1 [4] Heb. *Abel Shittim*
51 [g] Deut. 7:1, 2; 9:1; Josh. 3:17
52 [h] Ex. 23:24, 33; 34:13; Deut. 7:2, 5; 12:3; Judg. 2:2; Ps. 106:34-36 [5] Places for pagan worship
53 [i] Deut. 11:31; Josh. 21:43
54 [j] Num. 26:53-56
55 [k] Josh. 23:13; Judg. 2:3

CHAPTER 34

2 [a] Gen. 17:8; Deut. 1:7, 8; Ps. 78:54, 55; 105:11
3 [b] Josh. 15:1-3; Ezek. 47:13, 19 [c] Gen. 14:3; Josh. 15:2
4 [d] Josh. 15:3 [e] Num. 13:26; 32:8 [f] Josh. 15:3, 4
5 [g] Gen. 15:18; Josh. 15:4, 47; 1 Kin. 8:65; Is. 27:12
6 [h] Ex. 23:31; Josh. 15:12; Ezek. 47:20
7 [i] Num. 33:37
8 [j] Num. 13:21; Josh. 13:5; 2 Kin. 14:25 [k] Ezek. 47:15
9 [l] Ezek. 47:17
11 [m] 2 Kin. 23:33; Jer. 39:5, 6 [n] Deut. 3:17; Josh. 11:2; 12:3; 13:27; 19:35; Matt. 14:34; Luke 5:1 [1] Lit. *shoulder*
12 [o] Num. 34:3

33:50–36:13 The Promised Land had been Israel's goal from the beginning of Numbers. This last part of the book anticipated the settlement of Canaan.

33:50-56 God commanded that all of the Canaanites were to be exterminated, along with all their idolatrous symbols.

33:52 their high places. Hills on which Canaanite altars and shrines were placed.

33:56 I will do to you as I thought to do to them. If Israel failed to obey God, she would be the object of God's punishment in exactly the same way as the Canaanites were.

34:1-15 God gave precise instruction to Israel concerning the boundaries of the Land of Canaan. Sadly, the actual conquest of the Land fell far short of these boundaries.

of Israel, saying: [p]"This *is* the land which
you shall inherit by lot, which the LORD has
commanded to give to the nine tribes and
to the half-tribe. 14 [q]For the tribe of the
children of Reuben according to the house
of their fathers, and the tribe of the children of Gad according to the house of their
fathers, have received *their inheritance;* and
the half-tribe of Manasseh has received its
inheritance. 15 The two tribes and the half-
tribe have received their inheritance on
this side of the Jordan, *across from* Jericho
eastward, toward the sunrise."

The Leaders Appointed to Divide the Land

16 And the LORD spoke to Moses, saying,
17 "These *are* the names of the men who
shall divide the land among you as an inheritance: [r]Eleazar the priest and Joshua
the son of Nun. 18 And you shall take one
[s]leader of every tribe to divide the land for
the inheritance. 19 These *are* the names of
the men: from the tribe of Judah, Caleb the
son of Jephunneh; 20 from the tribe of the
children of Simeon, Shemuel the son of
Ammihud; 21 from the tribe of Benjamin,
Elidad the son of Chislon; 22 a leader from
the tribe of the children of Dan, Bukki the
son of Jogli; 23 from the sons of Joseph: a
leader from the tribe of the children of Manasseh, Hanniel the son of Ephod, 24 and a
leader from the tribe of the children of
Ephraim, Kemuel the son of Shiphtan; 25 a
leader from the tribe of the children of
Zebulun, Elizaphan the son of Parnach;
26 a leader from the tribe of the children of
Issachar, Paltiel the son of Azzan; 27 a
leader from the tribe of the children of
Asher, Ahihud the son of Shelomi; 28 and a
leader from the tribe of the children of
Naphtali, Pedahel the son of Ammihud."
29 These *are* the ones the LORD commanded to [2]divide the inheritance among
the children of Israel in the land of Canaan.

Cities for the Levites

35 And the LORD spoke to Moses in
[a]the plains of Moab by the Jordan
across from Jericho, saying: 2 [b]"Command
the children of Israel that they give the
Levites cities to dwell in from the inheritance of their possession, and you shall *also*
give the Levites [c]common-land around the
cities. 3 They shall have the cities to dwell
in; and their common-land shall be for their
cattle, for their herds, and for all their animals. 4 The common-land of the cities
which you will give the Levites *shall extend*
from the wall of the city outward a thousand cubits all around. 5 And you shall
measure outside the city on the east side
two thousand cubits, on the south side two
thousand cubits, on the west side two thousand cubits, and on the north side two
thousand cubits. The city *shall be* in the
middle. This shall belong to them as common-land for the cities.
6 "Now among the cities which you will
give to the Levites *you shall appoint* [d]six
cities of refuge, to which a manslayer may
flee. And to these you shall add forty-two
cities. 7 So all the cities you will give to the
Levites *shall be* [e]forty-eight; these *you shall
give* with their common-land. 8 And the
cities which you will give *shall be* [f]from the
possession of the children of Israel; [g]from
the larger *tribe* you shall give many, from
the smaller you shall give few. Each shall
give some of its cities to the Levites, in
proportion to the inheritance that each receives."

Cities of Refuge

9 Then the LORD spoke to Moses, saying,
10 "Speak to the children of Israel, and say
to them: [h]'When you cross the Jordan into
the land of Canaan, 11 then [i]you shall appoint cities to be cities of refuge for you,
that the manslayer who kills any person
accidentally may flee there. 12 [j]They shall
be cities of refuge for you from the
avenger, that the manslayer may not die
until he stands before the congregation in
judgment. 13 And of the cities which you
give, you shall have [k]six cities of refuge.
14 [l]You shall appoint three cities on this
side of the Jordan, and three cities you

13 [p] Gen. 15:18; Num. 26:52-56; Deut. 11:24; Josh. 14:1-5
14 [q] Num. 32:33
17 [r] Josh. 14:1, 2; 19:51
18 [s] Num. 1:4, 16
29 [2] *apportion*

CHAPTER 35

1 [a] Num. 33:50
2 [b] Josh. 14:3, 4; 21:2, 3; Ezek. 45:1; 48:10-20 [c] Lev. 25:32-34
6 [d] Deut. 4:41; Josh. 20:2, 7, 8; 21:3, 13
7 [e] Josh. 21:41
8 [f] Josh. 21:3 [g] Num. 26:54; 33:54
10 [h] Deut. 19:2; Josh. 20:1-9
11 [i] Ex. 21:13; Num. 35:22-25; Deut. 19:1-13
12 [j] Deut. 19:6; Josh. 20:3, 5, 6
13 [k] Num. 35:6
14 [l] Deut. 4:41; Josh. 20:8

34:13 give to the nine tribes and to the half-tribe. The land to be conquered was to be given to the 9½ tribes. The other 2½ tribes already had their inheritance in Transjordan (32:1-42).

34:16-29 The Lord appointed the men who were to assign the portions of the land of Canaan: Eleazar the priest (20:25,26), Joshua the commander (27:18-23), and the leaders of each of the 10 tribes which were to receive an inheritance. None of these men were sons of the leaders listed in 1:5-15.

35:1-8 Forty-eight cities throughout the Land were to be given to the Levites. The tribe of Levi did not receive a tribal allotment, but lived among the other tribes. Joshua 21:1-42 gave the list of these 48 cities.

35:2 from the inheritance of their possession. According to 18:23, the Levites were to have no land as inheritance in Canaan, so the Levites did not inherit these towns; they only lived in them. **common-land around the cities.** The Levites were also given grazing land around the cities given to them so that their animals might feed.

35:9-34 Six of the Levitical cities were to be established as "cities of refuge" (see Deut. 19:1-13). These cities were to be havens giving protection to any person who accidentally killed another person (manslaughter).

35:12 the avenger. The meaning of this term is "near of kin." It refers to the person chosen by a family to deal with a loss suffered in

shall appoint in the land of Canaan, *which*
will be cities of refuge. 15 These six cities
shall be for refuge for the children of Israel,
[m]for the stranger, and for the sojourner
among them, that anyone who kills a person accidentally may flee there.
16 [n]'But if he strikes him with an iron implement, so that he dies, he *is* a murderer;
the murderer shall surely be put to death.
17 And if he strikes him with a stone in the
hand, by which one could die, and he does
die, he *is* a murderer; the murderer shall
surely be put to death. 18 Or *if* he strikes
him with a wooden hand weapon, by
which one could die, and he does die, he *is*
a murderer; the murderer shall surely be
put to death. 19 [o]The [1] avenger of blood
himself shall put the murderer to death;
when he meets him, he shall put him to
death. 20 [p]If he pushes him out of hatred
or, [q]while lying in wait, hurls something at
him so that he dies, 21 or in enmity he
strikes him with his hand so that he dies,
the one who struck *him* shall surely be put
to death. He *is* a murderer. The avenger of
blood shall put the murderer to death
when he meets him.
22 'However, if he pushes him suddenly
[r]without enmity, or throws anything at
him without lying in wait, 23 or uses a
stone, by which a man could die, throwing
it at him without seeing *him,* so that he
dies, while he was not his enemy or seeking his harm, 24 then [s]the congregation
shall judge between the manslayer and the
avenger of blood according to these judgments. 25 So the congregation shall deliver
the manslayer from the hand of the
avenger of blood, and the congregation
shall return him to the city of refuge where
he had fled, and [t]he shall remain there
until the death of the high priest [u]who was
anointed with the holy oil. 26 But if the
manslayer at any time goes outside the
limits of the city of refuge where he fled,
27 and the avenger of blood finds him outside the limits of his city of refuge, and the
avenger of blood kills the manslayer, he
shall not be guilty of [2]blood, 28 because he
should have remained in his city of refuge
until the death of the high priest. But after
the death of the high priest the manslayer
may return to the land of his possession.
29 'And these *things* shall be [v]a statute of
judgment to you throughout your generations in all your dwellings. 30 Whoever
kills a person, the murderer shall be put to
death on the [w]testimony of witnesses; but
one witness is not *sufficient* testimony
against a person for the death *penalty.*
31 Moreover you shall take no ransom for
the life of a murderer who *is* guilty of
death, but he shall surely be put to death.
32 And you shall take no ransom for him
who has fled to his city of refuge, that he
may return to dwell in the land before the
death of the priest. 33 So you shall not pollute the land where you *are;* for blood [x]de-
files the land, and no [3]atonement can be
made for the land, for the blood that is
shed on it, except [y]by the blood of him
who shed it. 34 Therefore [z]do not defile the
land which you inhabit, in the midst of
which I dwell; for [a]I the LORD dwell among
the children of Israel.' "

Marriage of Female Heirs

36 Now the chief fathers of the families
of the [a]children of Gilead the son of
Machir, the son of Manasseh, of the families
of the sons of Joseph, came near and [b]spoke
before Moses and before the leaders, the
chief fathers of the children of Israel. 2 And
they said: [c]"The LORD commanded my lord
Moses to give the land as an inheritance by
lot to the children of Israel, and [d]my lord
was commanded by the LORD to give the
inheritance of our brother Zelophehad to
his daughters. 3 Now if they are married to
any of the sons of the *other* tribes of the children of Israel, then their inheritance will be
[e]taken from the inheritance of our fathers,
and it will be added to the inheritance of
the tribe into which they marry; so it will be
taken from the lot of our inheritance. 4 And
when [f]the Jubilee of the children of Israel
comes, then their inheritance will be added
to the inheritance of the tribe into which

15 [m] Num. 15:16
16 [n] Ex. 21:12, 14; Lev. 24:17; Deut. 19:11, 12
19 [o] Num. 35:21, 24, 27; Deut. 19:6, 12 [1] A family member who is to avenge the victim
20 [p] Gen. 4:8; 2 Sam. 3:27; 20:10; 1 Kin. 2:31, 32 [q] Ex. 21:14; Deut. 19:11, 12
22 [r] Ex. 21:13
24 [s] Num. 35:12; Josh. 20:6
25 [t] Josh. 20:6 [u] Ex. 29:7; Lev. 4:3; 21:10
27 [2] Murder
29 [v] Num. 27:11
30 [w] Deut. 17:6; 19:15; Matt. 18:16; John 7:51; 8:17, 18; 2 Cor. 13:1; Heb. 10:28
33 [x] Deut. 21:7, 8; Ps. 106:38 [y] Gen. 9:6 [3] Lit. *covering*
34 [z] Lev. 18:24, 25; Deut. 21:23 [a] Ex. 29:45, 46

CHAPTER 36

1 [a] Num. 26:29 [b] Num. 27:1-11
2 [c] Num. 26:55; 33:54; Josh. 17:4 [d] Num. 27:1, 5-7
3 [e] Num. 27:4
4 [f] Lev. 25:10

that family. Here the close relative of a homicide victim would seek to avenge his death, but not it until proper judgment was made.

35:19 Swift retribution according to the law of Gen. 9:5,6.

35:24 the congregation shall judge between the manslayer and the avenger. The congregation was called to decide the motive of the killer, whether it was with or without hostility. If there was evil intent, the killer was turned over to the avenger to be put to death. If, however, hostility could not be proven to exist between the killer and the victim, then the killer was allowed to remain in the city of refuge.

35:25 until the death of the high priest. The manslayer without evil intent was to remain in the city of refuge until the death of the High-Priest. The death of the High-Priest marked the end of an old era and the beginning of a new one for the manslayer.

35:30 witnesses. No one could be judged guilty of death on the testimony of only one witness. Two or more witnesses were required in all capital cases (cf. Deut. 17:6; 19:15).

35:33 blood defiles the land. Though murder and inadvertent killing polluted the land, murder was atoned for by the death of the murderer. Failure to observe these principles would make the Land unclean. If the whole Land became unclean, then the Lord would no longer be able to dwell in their midst.

36:1-13 The issue raised here stemmed from a decision regarding female inheritance in 27:1-11. Since a tribe would lose an allotted

they marry; so their inheritance will be
taken away from the inheritance of the
tribe of our fathers."
5 Then Moses commanded the children
of Israel according to the word of the LORD,
saying: [g]"What the tribe of the sons of Joseph speaks is right. 6 This *is* what the
LORD commands concerning the daughters
of Zelophehad, saying, 'Let them [1]marry
whom they think best, [h]but they may
marry only within the family of their father's tribe.' 7 So the inheritance of the
children of Israel shall not change hands
from tribe to tribe, for every one of the children of Israel shall [i]keep the inheritance of
the tribe of his fathers. 8 And [j]every
daughter who possesses an inheritance in
any tribe of the children of Israel shall be
the wife of one of the family of her father's
tribe, so that the children of Israel each
may possess the inheritance of his fathers.
9 Thus no inheritance shall change hands
from *one* tribe to another, but every tribe of
the children of Israel shall keep its own inheritance."
10 Just as the LORD commanded Moses,
so did the daughters of Zelophehad; 11 [k]for
Mahlah, Tirzah, Hoglah, Milcah, and
Noah, the daughters of Zelophehad, were
married to the sons of their father's brothers. 12 They were married into the families
of the children of Manasseh the son of Joseph, and their inheritance remained in the
tribe of their father's family.
13 These *are* the commandments and the
judgments which the LORD commanded
the children of Israel by the hand of Moses
[l]in the plains of Moab by the Jordan, *across
from* Jericho.

5 [g] Num. 27:7
6 [h] Num. 36:11, 12
[1] Lit. *be wives to*
7 [i] 1 Kin. 21:3
8 [j] 1 Chr. 23:22
11 [k] Num. 26:33; 27:1
13 [l] Num. 26:3; 33:50

inheritance in the year of Jubilee if an inheriting woman had married into another tribe, the woman of any tribe who inherited land must marry within her own tribe.

36:12 They were married into...Manasseh. The daughters of Zelophehad exemplified the obedience to God's commandments that should have been practiced by all of Israel. Their inheritance was a direct result of their obedience to the Lord—a basic lesson stressed throughout the whole book of Numbers.

The Fifth Book of Moses Called
DEUTERONOMY

Title

The English title "Deuteronomy" comes from the Greek Septuagint (LXX) mistranslation of "copy of this law" in 17:18 as "second law," which was rendered *Deuteronomium* in the Latin version (Vulgate). The Hebrew title of the book is translated "These are the words," from the first two Hebrew words of the book. The Hebrew title is a better description of the book since it is not a "second law," but rather the record of Moses' words of explanation concerning the law. Deuteronomy completes the five-part literary unit called the Pentateuch.

Author and Date

Moses has been traditionally recognized as the author of Deuteronomy, since the book itself testifies that Moses wrote it (1:1,5; 31:9,22,24). Both the OT (1 Kin. 2:3; 8:53; 2 Kin. 14:6; 18:12) and the NT (Acts 3:22,23; Rom. 10:19) support the claim of Mosaic authorship. While Deut. 32:48–34:12 was added after Moses' death (probably by Joshua), the rest of the book came from Moses' hand just before his death in 1405 B.C.

The majority of the book is comprised of farewell speeches that the 120-year-old Moses gave to Israel, beginning on the first day of the 11th month of the 40th year after the Exodus from Egypt (1:3). These speeches can be dated Jan.–Feb., 1405 B.C. In the last few weeks of Moses' life, he committed these speeches to writing and gave them to the priests and elders for the coming generations of Israel (31:9,24-26).

Background and Setting

Like Leviticus, Deuteronomy does not advance historically, but takes place entirely in one location over about one month of time (cf. Deut. 1:3 and 34:8 with Josh. 5:6-12). Israel was encamped in the central rift valley to the E of the Jordan River (Deut. 1:1). This location was referred to in Num. 36:13 as "the plains of Moab," an area N of the Arnon River across the Jordan River from Jericho. It had been almost 40 years since the Israelites had exited Egypt.

The book of Deuteronomy concentrates on events that took place in the final weeks of Moses' life. The major event was the verbal communication of divine revelation from Moses to the people of Israel (1:1–30:20; 31:30–32:47; 33:1-29). The only other events recorded were: 1) Moses' recording the law in a book and his commissioning of Joshua as the new leader (31:1-29); 2) Moses' viewing of the land of Canaan from Mt. Nebo (32:48-52; 34:1-4); and 3) his death (34:5-12).

The original recipients of Deuteronomy, both in its verbal and written presentations, were the second generation of the nation of Israel. All of that generation from 40 to 60 years of age (except Joshua and Caleb, who were older) had been born in Egypt and had participated as children or teens in the Exodus. Those under 40 had been born and reared in the wilderness. Together, they comprised the generation that was on the verge of conquering the land of Canaan under Joshua, 40 years after they had left Egypt (1:34-39).

Historical and Theological Themes

Like Leviticus, Deuteronomy contains much legal detail, but with an emphasis on the people rather than the priests. As Moses called the second generation of Israel to trust the Lord and be obedient to His covenant made at Horeb (Sinai), he illustrated his points with references to Israel's past history. He reminded Israel of her rebellion against the Lord at Horeb (9:7–10:11) and at Kadesh (1:26-46), which brought devastating consequences. He also reminded her of the Lord's faithfulness in giving victory over her enemies (2:24–3:11; 29:2,7,8). Most importantly, Moses called the people to take the land that God had promised by oath to their forefathers Abraham, Isaac, and Jacob (1:8; 6:10; 9:5; 29:13; 30:20; 34:4; cf. Gen. 15:18-21; 26:3-5; 35:12). Moses not only looked back, he also looked ahead and saw that Israel's future failure to obey God would lead to her being scattered among the nations before the fulfillment of His oath to the patriarchs would be completed (4:25-31; 29:22–30:10; 31:26-29).

The book of Deuteronomy, along with Psalms and Isaiah, reveals much about the attributes of God. Thus, it is directly quoted over 40 times in the NT (exceeded only by Psalms and Isaiah) with many more allusions to its content. Deuteronomy reveals that the Lord is the only God (4:39; 6:4), and that He is jealous (4:24), faithful (7:9), loving (7:13), merciful (4:31), yet angered by sin (6:15). This is the God who called Israel to Himself. Over 250 times, Moses repeated the phrase, "the LORD your God" to Israel. Israel was called to obey (28:2), fear (10:12), love (10:12), and serve (10:12) her God by walking in His ways and keeping His commandments (10:12,13). By obeying Him, the people of Israel would receive His blessings (28:1-14). Obedience and the pursuit of personal holiness is always based upon the character of God. Because of who He is, His people are to be holy (cf., 7:6-11; 8:6,11,18; 10:12,16,17; 11:13; 13:3,4; 14:1,2).

Interpretive Challenges

Three interpretive challenges face the reader of Deuteronomy. First, is the book a singular record, or is it only a part of the larger literary whole, the Pentateuch? The remainder of the Scripture always views the Pentateuch as a unit, and the ultimate meaning of Deuteronomy cannot be divorced from its context in the Pentateuch. The book also assumes the reader is already familiar with the 4 books that precede it; in fact, Deuteronomy brings into focus all that had been revealed in Genesis to Numbers, as well as its implications for the people as they entered the Land. However, every available Hebrew manuscript divides the Pentateuch in exactly the same way as the present text, indicating that the book is a well defined unit recounting the final speeches of Moses to Israel, so it may also be viewed as a singular record.

Second, is the structure of Deuteronomy based on the secular treaties of Moses' day? During the last 35 years, many evangelical scholars have supported the Mosaic authorship of Deuteronomy by appealing to the similarities between the structure of the book and the ancient Near Eastern treaty form of the mid-second millennium B.C. (the approximate time of Moses). These secular suzerainty treaties (i.e., a ruler dictating his will to his vassals) followed a set pattern not used in the mid-first millennium B.C. These treaties usually contained the following elements: 1) preamble—identifying the parties to the covenant; 2) historical prologue—a history of the king's dealing with his vassals; 3) general and specific stipulations; 4) witnesses; 5) blessings and curses; and 6) oaths and covenant ratification. Deuteronomy, it is believed, approximates this basic structure. While there is agreement that 1:1-5 is a preamble, 1:5–4:43 a historical prologue, and chaps. 27,28 feature blessings and cursings, there is no consensus as to how the rest of Deuteronomy fits this structure. While there might have been a covenant renewal on the plains of Moab, this is neither clearly explicit nor implicit in Deuteronomy. It is best to take the book for what it claims to be: the explanation of the law given by Moses for the new generation. The structure follows the speeches given by Moses. See Outline.

Third, what was the covenant made in the land of Moab (29:1)? The majority opinion posits this covenant as a renewal of the Sinaitic Covenant made nearly 40 years before with the first generation. Here, Moses supposedly updated and renewed this same covenant with the second generation of Israel. The second view sees this covenant as a Palestinian Covenant which guarantees the nation of Israel's right to the land, both at that time and in the future. A third position is that Moses in chaps. 29,30 anticipated the New Covenant, since he knew Israel would fail to keep the Sinaitic Covenant. The third view seems the best.

Outline

I. Introduction: The Historical Setting of Moses' Speeches (1:1-4)

II. The First Address by Moses: A Historical Prologue (1:5–4:43)
- A. A Historical Review of God's Gracious Acts from Horeb to Beth Peor (1:5–3:29)
- B. An Exhortation to Obey the Law (4:1-40)
- C. The Setting Apart of Three Cities of Refuge (4:41-43)

III. The Second Address by Moses: The Stipulations of the Sinaitic Covenant (4:44–28:68)
- A. Introduction (4:44-49)
- B. The Basic Elements of Israel's Relationship with the Lord (5:1–11:32)
  1. The Ten Commandments (5:1-33)
  2. The total commitment to the Lord (6:1-25)
  3. Separation from the gods of other nations (7:1-26)
  4. A warning against forgetting the Lord (8:1-20)
  5. Illustrations of Israel's rebellion in the past (9:1–10:11)
  6. An admonition to fear and love the Lord and obey His will (10:12–11:32)
- C. The Specific Stipulations for Life in the New Land (12:1–26:19)
  1. Instructions for the life of worship (12:1–16:17)
  2. Instructions for leadership (16:18–18:22)
  3. Instructions for societal order (19:1–23:14)
  4. Instructions from miscellaneous laws (23:15–25:19)
  5. The firstfruits and tithes in the land (26:1-15)
  6. The affirmation of obedience (26:16-19)
- D. The Blessings and Curses of the Covenant (27:1–28:68)

IV. The Third Address by Moses: Another Covenant (29:1–30:20)

V. The Concluding Events (31:1–34:12)
- A. The Change of Leadership (31:1-8)
- B. The Future Reading of the Law (31:9-13)
- C. The Song of Moses (31:14–32:47)
  1. The anticipation of Israel's failure (31:14-29)
  2. The witness of Moses' song (31:30–32:43)
  3. The communicating of Moses' song (32:44-47)
- D. The Final Events of Moses' Life (32:48–34:12)
  1. The directives for Moses' death (32:48-52)
  2. The blessing of Moses (33:1-29)
  3. The death of Moses (34:1-12)

The Previous Command to Enter Canaan

1 These *are* the words which Moses
spoke to all Israel [a]on this side of the
Jordan in the wilderness, in the [1]plain opposite [2]Suph, between Paran, Tophel,
Laban, Hazeroth, and Dizahab. 2 *It is*
eleven days' *journey* from Horeb by way of
Mount Seir [b]to Kadesh Barnea. 3 Now it
came to pass [c]in the fortieth year, in the
eleventh month, on the first *day* of the
month, *that* Moses spoke to the children of
Israel according to all that the LORD had
given him as commandments to them,
4 [d]after he had killed Sihon king of the
Amorites, who dwelt in Heshbon, and Og
king of Bashan, who dwelt at Ashtaroth
[e]in[3] Edrei.
5 On this side of the Jordan in the land of
Moab, Moses began to explain this law,
saying, 6 "The LORD our God spoke to us
[f]in Horeb, saying: 'You have dwelt long
[g]enough at this mountain. 7 Turn and take
your journey, and go to the mountains of
the Amorites, to all the neighboring *places*
in the [4]plain, in the mountains and in the
lowland, in the South and on the seacoast,
to the land of the Canaanites and to Lebanon, as far as the great river, the River Euphrates. 8 See, I have set the land before
you; go in and possess the land which the
LORD [5]swore to your fathers—to [h]Abra-
ham, Isaac, and Jacob—to give to them and
their descendants after them.'

Tribal Leaders Appointed

9 "And [i]I spoke to you at that time, saying: 'I [6]alone am not able to bear you.
10 The LORD your God has multiplied you,
[j]and here you *are* today, as the stars of
heaven in multitude. 11 [k]May the LORD
God of your fathers make you a thousand
times more numerous than you are, and
bless you [l]as He has promised you!
12 [m]How can I alone bear your problems
and your burdens and your complaints?
13 Choose wise, understanding, and
knowledgeable men from among your

CHAPTER 1
1 [a] Deut. 4:44-46; Josh. 9:1, 10 [1] Heb. *arabah* [2] One LXX ms., Tg., Vg. *Red Sea*
2 [b] Num. 13:26; 32:8; Deut. 9:23
3 [c] Num. 33:38
4 [d] Num. 21:23, 24, 33-35; Deut. 2:26-35; Josh. 13:10; Neh. 9:22 [e] Josh. 13:12 [3] LXX, Syr., Vg. *and;* cf. Josh. 12:4
6 [f] Ex. 3:1, 12 [g] Ex. 19:1, 2
7 [4] Heb. *arabah*
8 [h] Gen. 12:7; 15:5; 22:17; 26:3; 28:13; Ex. 33:1; Num. 14:23; 32:11 [5] *promised*
9 [i] Ex. 18:18, 24; Num. 11:14, 24 [6] *am not able to bear you by myself*
10 [j] Gen. 15:5; 22:17; Ex. 32:13; Deut. 7:7; 10:22; 26:5; 28:62
11 [k] 2 Sam. 24:3 [l] Gen. 15:5
12 [m] 1 Kin. 3:8, 9

1:1-4 This introduction gives the setting of Deuteronomy and its purpose.

1:1 The words which Moses spoke. Almost all of Deuteronomy consists of speeches given by Moses at the end of his life. According to v. 3, Moses acted upon the authority of God since his inspired words were in accordance with the commandments that God had given. **to all Israel.** This expression is used 12 times in this book and emphasizes the unity of Israel, and the universal applications of these words. **the plain opposite Suph.** Except for Jordan and the Arabah (see marginal note), the exact location of the places named in 1:1 is not known with certainty, although they may have been along Israel's route N from the Gulf of Aqabah (cf. Num. 33). The plain referred to is the large rift valley that extends from the Sea of Galilee in the N to the Gulf of Aqabah in the S. Israel was encamped to the E of the Jordan River in this valley.

1:2 eleven days' *journey*. The distance from Horeb to Kadesh Barnea was about 150 mi. Kadesh was on the southern border of the Promised Land. This trip took 11 days on foot, but for Israel lasted 38 more years. **Horeb.** The usual name in Deuteronomy for Mt. Sinai means "desolation," a fitting name since the area around Sinai is barren and uninviting. **Mount Seir.** South of the Dead Sea in Edom.

1:3 the fortieth year. The 40th year after the Exodus from Egypt. The years of divine judgment (Num. 14:33,34) were ending. **the eleventh month.** Jan.-Feb., 1405 B.C. Numbers 20–36 records the events of the 40th year.

1:4 Sihon…Og. The two kings of the Amorites which the Jews defeated in Transjordan (see 2:24–3:11; Num. 21:21-35).

1:5–4:43 These verses are mainly Moses' first speech. Moses introduced his explanation of the law with a call to enter the land of Canaan (vv. 6-8), which had been promised by the Abrahamic Covenant from God (cf. Gen. 15:18-21). Throughout this book, he refers to that covenant promise (1:35; 4:31; 6:10,18,23; 7:8,12; 8:1,18; 9:5; 10:11; 11:9,21; 13:17; 19:8; 26:3,15; 27:3; 28:11; 29:13; 30:20; 31:7,20-23; 34:4). He then gave a historical review of God's gracious acts (1:9–3:29) and a call to Israel for obedience to the covenant given to them by the Lord at Sinai (4:1-40). This introductory section ends with a brief narrative recounting the appointment of the 3 cities of refuge E of the Jordan (4:41-43).

1:5 explain. To make clear, distinct, or plain. The purpose of the book was to make the sense and purpose of the law clear to the people as they entered the Land. It was to be their guide to the law while living in the Land. Moses did not review what happened at Horeb (Sinai), which is recorded by him in Exodus, Leviticus, and Numbers (cf. Ex. 20:1–Num. 10:10), but rather gave Israel instruction in how to walk with God and how to fulfill God's will in the Land and be blessed.

1:7,8 the land. The Land which the Lord set before Israel to go in and possess was clearly described in v. 7. The mountains of the Amorites referred to the hill country to the W of the Dead Sea. The plain (Arabah) was the land in the rift valley from the Sea of Galilee in the N to the Dead Sea in the S. The mountains were the hills that run through the center of the Land N and S. These hills are to the W of the Sea of Galilee and the Jordan River. The lowland referred to the low rolling hills that sloped toward the Mediterranean coast (Shephelah). The S (Negev) described the dry wasteland stretching southward from Beersheba to the wilderness. The seacoast referred to the Land along the Mediterranean Sea. The boundaries of the Land of the Canaanites were given in Num. 34:1-15. Lebanon to the N marked the northwestern boundary on the coast. The NE boundary of the Land was the Euphrates River. Cf. Num. 34:1-12.

1:8 the LORD swore. God's command to take possession of this Land by conquest was based upon the promise of the Land that had been given in a covenant to Abraham (Gen 15:18-21) and reiterated to Isaac and Jacob (Gen. 26:3-5; 28:13-15; 35:12). These 3 patriarchs are mentioned 7 times in Deuteronomy (1:8; 6:10; 9:5,27; 29:13; 30:20; 34:4). The Lord sealed His promise to the patriarchs with an oath (swore) indicating that He would never change His plan (cf. Ps. 110:4).

1:9-18 *See notes on Ex. 18* for the background.

1:10 the stars of heaven. The Lord had promised Abraham that his descendants would be as numerous as the stars in the sky (see Gen. 15:5; 22:17). The nation's growth proved both God's intention and ability to fulfill His original promises to Abraham.

1:11 a thousand times. A Semitic way of saying "an infinitely large number."

1:13 Choose wise…men. The fulfillment of God's promise to give to Abraham such a large posterity created a problem for Moses.

tribes, and I will make them [7]heads over
you.' 14 And you answered me and said,
'The thing which you have told *us* to do *is*
good.' 15 So I took [n]the heads of your
tribes, wise and knowledgeable men, and
[8]made them heads over you, leaders of
thousands, leaders of hundreds, leaders of
fifties, leaders of tens, and officers for your
tribes.
16 "Then I commanded your judges at
that time, saying, 'Hear *the cases* between
your brethren, and [o]judge righteously between a man and his [p]brother or the
stranger who is with him. 17 [q]You shall
not show partiality in judgment; you shall
hear the small as well as the great; you
shall not be afraid in any man's presence,
for [r]the judgment *is* God's. The case that
is too hard for you, [s]bring to me, and I
will hear it.' 18 And I commanded you at
that time all the things which you should
do.

Israel's Refusal to Enter the Land

19 "So we departed from Horeb, [t]and
went through all that great and terrible
wilderness which you saw on the way to
the mountains of the Amorites, as the LORD
our God had commanded us. Then [u]we
came to Kadesh Barnea. 20 And I said to
you, 'You have come to the mountains of
the Amorites, which the LORD our God is
giving us. 21 Look, the LORD your God has
set the land before you; go up *and* possess
it, as the LORD God of your fathers has spoken to you; [v]do not fear or be discouraged.'
22 "And every one of you came near to
me and said, 'Let us send men before us,
and let them search out the land for us, and
bring back word to us of the way by which
we should go up, and of the cities into
which we shall come.'

13 [7] *rulers*
15 [n] Ex. 18:25 [8] *appointed*
16 [o] Deut. 16:18; John 7:24 [p] Lev. 24:22
17 [q] Lev. 19:15; Deut. 10:17; 16:19; 24:17; 1 Sam. 16:7; Prov. 24:23-26; Acts 10:34; James 2:1, 9 [r] 2 Chr. 19:6 [s] Ex. 18:22, 26
19 [t] Num. 10:12; Deut. 2:7; 8:15; 32:10; Jer. 2:6 [u] Num. 13:26
21 [v] Josh. 1:6, 9
23 [w] Num. 13:2, 3
24 [x] Num. 13:21-25
25 [y] Num. 13:27
26 [z] Num. 14:1-4; Ps. 106:24
27 [a] Ps. 106:25 [b] Deut. 9:28
28 [c] Num. 13:28, 31-33; Deut. 9:1, 2 [d] Num. 13:28 [9] Lit. *melted*
29 [e] Num. 14:9; Deut. 7:18
30 [f] Ex. 14:14; Deut. 3:22; 20:4; Neh. 4:20
31 [g] Deut. 32:10-12; Is. 46:3, 4; 63:9; Hos. 11:3
32 [h] Num. 14:11; 20:12; Ps. 106:24; Heb. 3:9, 10, 16-19; 4:1, 2; Jude 5
33 [i] Ex. 13:21; Num. 9:15-23; Neh. 9:12; Ps. 78:14 [j] Num. 10:33; Ezek. 20:6
34 [k] Deut. 2:14, 15
35 [l] Num. 14:22, 23; Ps. 95:10, 11

23 "The plan pleased me well; so [w]I took
twelve of your men, one man from *each*
tribe. 24 [x]And they departed and went up
into the mountains, and came to the Valley
of Eshcol, and spied it out. 25 They also
took *some* of the fruit of the land in their
hands and brought *it* down to us; and they
brought back word to us, saying, '*It is* a
[y]good land which the LORD our God is giving us.'
26 [z]"Nevertheless you would not go up,
but rebelled against the command of the
LORD your God; 27 and you [a]complained in
your tents, and said, 'Because the LORD
[b]hates us, He has brought us out of the
land of Egypt to deliver us into the hand of
the Amorites, to destroy us. 28 Where can
we go up? Our brethren have [9]discour-
aged our hearts, saying, [c]"The people *are*
greater and taller than we; the cities *are*
great and fortified up to heaven; moreover
we have seen the sons of the [d]Anakim
there." '
29 "Then I said to you, 'Do not be terrified, [e]or afraid of them. 30 [f]The LORD your
God, who goes before you, He will fight
for you, according to all He did for you in
Egypt before your eyes, 31 and in the
wilderness where you saw how the LORD
your God carried you, as a [g]man carries his
son, in all the way that you went until you
came to this place.' 32 Yet, for all that, [h]you
did not believe the LORD your God, 33 [i]who
went in the way before you [j]to search out a
place for you to pitch your tents, to show
you the way you should go, in the fire by
night and in the cloud by day.

The Penalty for Israel's Rebellion

34 "And the LORD heard the sound of
your words, and was angry, [k]and took an
oath, saying, 35 [l]'Surely not one of these
men of this evil generation shall see that

The nation had become too large for Moses to govern effectively. The solution was the appointment by Moses of men to help him lead the people (see Ex. 18:13-27). These men were to be 1) wise, i.e., men who knew how to apply their knowledge; 2) understanding, i.e., those who had discernment and so were able to judge; and 3) knowledgeable, i.e., experienced and respected. Cf. Ex. 18:21.

1:19-21 *See notes on Num. 10:11–12:16* for the background.

1:22-46 *See notes on Num. 13, 14* for the background.

1:22 Let us send men before us. When challenged by Moses to take the Land (vv. 20, 21), the people requested that spies be sent first. Moses, it seems, took their request to the Lord, who also approved their plan and commanded Moses to appoint the spies (Num. 13:1, 2). Thus, Moses selected 12 men who went to see what the Land was like (Num. 13:17-20).

1:26 but rebelled. Israel, at Kadesh Barnea, deliberately and defiantly refused to respond to God's command to take the Land (Num. 14:1-9).

1:27 you complained. Israel grumbled in their tents that the Lord hated them. They assumed the Lord brought them from Egypt to have them destroyed by the Amorites.

1:28 the Anakim. Lit. "sons of the Anakim" (i.e., the Anakites). The Anakites were early inhabitants of Canaan described as "giants" (2:10, 21; 9:2; Num. 13:32, 33). They were larger than the Israelites and were especially feared because of their military power.

1:32 you did not believe the LORD your God. The failure of the people to take the land at the beginning of their time in the wilderness was explained here in the same way as in Num. 14:11. Israel did not take the Lord at His Word and, therefore, did not obey His command. The Israelites' lack of obedience is explained as the outcome of their lack of faith in the Lord.

1:33 in the fire…and in the cloud. The cloud by day and the fire by night were the means of God's direction for Israel in the wilderness (Ex. 13:21; Num. 9:15-23). The Lord who guided Israel through the wandering journey was the same Lord who had already searched out a place for Israel in the Land. As He had directed them in the past, He would direct them also in the future.

good land of which I [1]swore to give to
your fathers, **36** [m]except Caleb the son of
Jephunneh; he shall see it, and to him and
his children I am giving the land on which
he walked, because [n]he [2]wholly followed
the LORD.' **37** [o]The LORD was also angry
with me for your sakes, saying, 'Even you
shall not go in there. **38** [p]Joshua the son of
Nun, [q]who stands before you, he shall go
in there. [r]Encourage him, for he shall cause
Israel to inherit it.
39 [s]'Moreover your little ones and your
children, who [t]you say will be victims,
who today [u]have no knowledge of good
and evil, they shall go in there; to them I
will give it, and they shall possess it.
40 [v]But *as for* you, turn and take your journey into the wilderness by the Way of the
Red Sea.'
41 "Then you answered and said to me,
[w]'We have sinned against the LORD; we will
go up and fight, just as the LORD our God
commanded us.' And when everyone of
you had girded on his weapons of war, you
were ready to go up into the mountain.
42 "And the LORD said to me, 'Tell them,
[x]"Do not go up nor fight, for I *am* not
among you; lest you be defeated before
your enemies."' **43** So I spoke to you; yet
you would not listen, but [y]rebelled against
the command of the LORD, and [z]presump-
tuously[3] went up into the mountain.
44 And the Amorites who dwelt in that
mountain came out against you and
chased you [a]as bees do, and drove you
back from Seir to Hormah. **45** Then you returned and wept before the LORD, but the
LORD would not listen to your voice nor
give ear to you.
46 [b]"So you remained in Kadesh many
days, according to the days that you spent
there.

The Desert Years

2 "Then we turned and [a]journeyed into
the wilderness of the Way of the Red
Sea, [b]as the LORD spoke to me, and we
[1]skirted Mount Seir for many days.
2 "And the LORD spoke to me, saying:
3 'You have skirted this mountain [c]long
enough; turn northward. **4** And command
the people, saying, [d]"You *are about to* pass
through the territory of [e]your brethren, the
descendants of Esau, who live in Seir; and
they will be afraid of you. Therefore watch
yourselves carefully. **5** Do not meddle with
them, for I will not give you *any* of their
land, no, not so much as one footstep, [f]be-
cause I have given Mount Seir to Esau *as* a
possession. **6** You shall buy food from
them with money, that you may eat; and
you shall also buy water from them with
money, that you may drink.
7 "For the LORD your God has blessed
you in all the work of your hand. He
knows your [2]trudging through this great
wilderness. [g]These forty years the LORD
your God *has been* with you; you have
lacked nothing."'
8 "And when we passed beyond our
brethren, the descendants of Esau who
dwell in Seir, away from the road of the

35 [1] *promised*
36 [m] Num. 14:24; [Josh. 14:9] [n] Num. 32:11, 12 [2] *fully*
37 [o] Num. 20:12; 27:14; Deut. 3:26; 4:21; 34:4; Ps. 106:32
38 [p] Num. 14:30 [q] Ex. 24:13; 33:11; 1 Sam. 16:22 [r] Num. 27:18, 19; Deut. 31:7, 23; Josh. 11:23
39 [s] Num. 14:31 [t] Num. 14:3 [u] Is. 7:15, 16
40 [v] Num. 14:25
41 [w] Num. 14:40
42 [x] Num. 14:41-43
43 [y] Num. 14:44 [z] Deut. 17:12, 13 [3] *willfully*
44 [a] Num. 14:45; Ps. 118:12
46 [b] Num. 13:25; 20:1, 22; Deut. 2:7, 14

CHAPTER 2

1 [a] Deut. 1:40 [b] Num. 14:25 [1] *circled around*
3 [c] Deut. 2:7, 14
4 [d] Num. 20:14-21 [e] Deut. 23:7
5 [f] Gen. 36:8; Josh. 24:4
7 [g] Deut. 8:2-4; [Matt. 6:8, 32] [2] Lit. *goings*

1:36-38 Caleb...Joshua. They were excluded from this judgment because of exemplary faith and obedience (cf. Num. 14:24; Josh. 14:8,9).

1:37 The LORD was also angry with me. Although his disobedience occurred almost 39 years after the failure of Israel at Kadesh (Num. 20:1-13), Moses included it here with Israel's disobedience to the Lord because his disobedience was of the same kind. Moses, like Israel, failed to honor the Word of the Lord and thus, in rebellion for self glory, disobeyed God's clear command and struck the rock rather than speaking to it. Thus, he suffered the same result of God's anger and, like Israel, was not allowed to go into the Land (Num. 20:12).

1:41-45 Israel's further defiance of the Lord's command was shown by their presumption in seeking to go into the Land after God said they should not. This time they rebelled by attempting to go in and conquer the Land, only to be chased back by the Amorites. The Lord showed His displeasure by not helping them or sympathizing with their defeat, and for that generation there was no escape from death in the desert during the next 38 years (cf. Num. 15–19).

1:46 you remained in Kadesh many days. These words suggest that Israel spent a large part of the 38 years in the wilderness around Kadesh Barnea.

2:1–3:11 *See notes on Num. 20:14–21:35* for the background.

2:1-23 This section deals with encounters with Israel's relatives, the Edomites (vv. 1-8), Moabites (vv. 9-18), and Ammonites (vv. 19-23).

2:1 the Way of the Red Sea. Cf. Num. 21:4. After spending a long time at Kadesh, the Israelites set out once again at the command of the Lord through Moses. They traveled away from their Promised Land in a southeasterly direction from Kadesh toward the Gulf of Aqabah on the road to the Red Sea. Thus began the wanderings that were about to end. **skirted Mount Seir.** Israel spent many days wandering in the vicinity of Mt. Seir, the mountain range of Edom, S of the Dead Sea and extending down the eastern flank of the Arabah.

2:3 turn northward. The departure from Kadesh had been in a southeasterly direction away from the Promised Land, until the Lord commanded Israel to turn again northward in the direction of the Promised Land.

2:4 your brethren, the descendants of Esau. Esau was the brother of Jacob (Gen. 25:25,26). The Edomites, the descendants of Esau, lived in Mt. Seir. According to Num. 20:14-21, the Edomites refused to allow Israel to pass through their land. Verse 8, reflecting this refusal, states that the Israelites went around the border of the descendants of Esau, i.e., to the E of their territory.

2:5 I will not give you *any* of their land. God had granted to the descendants of Esau an inheritance (Mt. Seir was their possession). In v. 9, the same is said about the Moabites and in v. 19, about the Ammonites.

2:8 from Elath and Ezion Geber. Two towns located just N of the Gulf of Aqabah. Israel passed to the E of Edom and to the E of Moab on their journey northward.

plain, away from [h]Elath and Ezion Geber,
we [i]turned and passed by way of the
Wilderness of Moab. **9** Then the LORD said
to me, 'Do not harass Moab, nor contend
with them in battle, for I will not give you
any of their land *as* a possession, because I
have given [j]Ar to [k]the descendants of Lot
as a possession.' "
10 [l](The Emim had dwelt there in times
past, a people as great and numerous and
tall as [m]the Anakim. **11** They were also regarded as [3]giants, like the Anakim, but the
Moabites call them Emim. **12** [n]The Horites
formerly dwelt in Seir, but the descendants
of Esau dispossessed them and destroyed
them from before them, and dwelt in their
[4]place, just as Israel did to the land of their
possession which the LORD gave them.)
13 " 'Now rise and cross over [o]the [5]Val-
ley of the Zered.' So we crossed over the
Valley of the Zered. **14** And the time we
took to come [p]from Kadesh Barnea until
we crossed over the Valley of the Zered *was*
thirty-eight years, [q]until all the generation
of the men of war [6]was consumed from the
midst of the camp, [r]just as the LORD had
sworn to them. **15** For indeed the hand of
the LORD was against them, to destroy
them from the midst of the camp until they
[7]were consumed.
16 "So it was, when all the men of war
had finally perished from among the people, **17** that the LORD spoke to me, saying:
18 'This day you are to cross over at Ar, the
boundary of Moab. **19** And *when* you come
near the people of Ammon, do not harass
them or meddle with them, for I will not
give you *any* of the land of the people of
Ammon *as* a possession, because I have
given it to [s]the descendants of Lot *as* a possession.' "
20 (That was also regarded as a land of
[8]giants; giants formerly dwelt there. But
the Ammonites call them [t]Zamzummim,
21 [u]a people as great and numerous and
tall as the Anakim. But the LORD destroyed
them before them, and they dispossessed
them and dwelt in their place, **22** just as He
had done for the descendants of Esau,
[v]who dwelt in Seir, when He destroyed
[w]the Horites from before them. They
dispossessed them and dwelt in their
place, even to this day. **23** And [x]the Avim,
who dwelt in villages as far as Gaza—[y]the
Caphtorim, who came from Caphtor, destroyed them and dwelt in their place.)
24 " 'Rise, take your journey, and [z]cross
over the River Arnon. Look, I have given
into your hand [a]Sihon the Amorite, king of
Heshbon, and his land. Begin [9]to possess
it, and engage him in battle. **25** [b]This day I
will begin to put the dread and fear of you
upon the nations [1]under the whole heav-
en, who shall hear the report of you, and
shall [c]tremble and be in anguish because of
you.'

King Sihon Defeated

26 "And I [d]sent messengers from the
Wilderness of Kedemoth to Sihon king of
Heshbon, [e]with words of peace, saying,
27 [f]'Let me pass through your land; I will
keep strictly to the road, and I will turn
neither to the right nor to the left. **28** You
shall sell me food for money, that I may
eat, and give me water for money, that I
may drink; [g]only let me pass through on
foot, **29** [h]just as the descendants of Esau

8 [h]Judg. 11:18; 1 Kin. 9:26 [i]Num. 21:4
9 [j]Num. 21:15, 28; Deut. 2:18, 29 [k]Gen. 19:36-38
10 [l]Gen. 14:5 [m]Num. 13:22, 33; Deut. 9:2
11 [3]Heb. *rephaim*
12 [n]Gen. 14:6; 36:20; Deut. 2:22 [4]*stead*
13 [o]Num. 21:12 [5]*Wadi* or *Brook*
14 [p]Num. 13:26 [q]Num. 14:33; 26:64; Deut. 1:34, 35 [r]Num. 14:35; Ezek. 20:15 [6]*perished*
15 [7]*perished*
19 [s]Gen. 19:38; Num. 21:24
20 [t]Gen. 14:5 [8]Heb. *rephaim*
21 [u]Deut. 2:10
22 [v]Gen. 36:8; Deut. 2:5 [w]Gen. 14:6; 36:20-30
23 [x]Josh. 13:3 [y]Gen. 10:14; 1 Chr. 1:12; Jer. 47:4; Amos 9:7
24 [z]Num. 21:13, 14; Judg. 11:18 [a]Deut. 1:4 [9]*to take possession*
25 [b]Ex. 23:27; Deut. 11:25; Josh. 2:9 [c]Ex. 15:14-16 [1]*everywhere under the heavens*
26 [d]Num. 21:21-32; Deut. 1:4; Judg. 11:19-21 [e]Deut. 20:10
27 [f]Num. 21:21, 22; Judg. 11:19
28 [g]Num. 20:19
29 [h]Num. 20:18; Deut. 23:3, 4; Judg. 11:17

2:10 The Emim. Apparently a Moabite term (see v. 11) meaning "terrible ones." This people, numerous and tall, were the pre-Moabite occupants of the land of Moab.

2:12 their possession which the LORD gave them. The Horites were Hurrians, a people who lived in various places in Syria and Palestine. Those living in the region of Seir had been displaced by the descendants of Esau. The displacement of the Horites by the Edomites was analogous to the Israelites' possession of their own land.

2:13 Zered. A brook that ran into the Dead Sea from the SE. It seems to have constituted the southern boundary of Moab. In contrast to the disobedience associated with Kadesh, the people obeyed the command to cross over the brook Zered. There was a new spirit of obedience toward the Lord among the people.

2:14 thirty-eight years. From 1444–1406 B.C. These were the years from the failure at Kadesh to the obedience at Zered. It was during this time that the rebellious generation, who had been denied access to the Promised Land by the oath of the Lord, had all died.

2:20 Zamzummim. Apparently an Ammonite term used to describe their precursors in their land. They were characterized as being as tall as the Anakim. But the Lord had destroyed them and given their land to the Ammonites. This was an encouragement to the Israelites that God could also defeat the Anakim in the land of Canaan and give that land to Israel.

2:23 the Avim. The ancient village dwellers of southwestern Palestine along the Mediterranean coast as far as the city of Gaza. **the Caphtorim.** Caphtor probably refers to Crete and may be a reference to an early Philistine group from that island who invaded the coast of Palestine, defeated the Avim, and then dwelt there. These Caphtorim were precursors to the later, greater Philistine invasion of ca. 1200 B.C.

2:24–3:29 Moses continues the historical survey detailing the defeat of two Amorite kings, Sihon and Og, and the takeover of their territory.

2:24 the River Arnon. The northern boundary of Moab. Israel was allowed to attack Sihon the Amorite because the Amorites were not relatives of Israel.

2:25 fear of you. As the conquest began, God put the fear of Israel into the hearts of their enemies.

2:26 the Wilderness of Kedemoth. Kedemoth means "eastern regions." It was probably a few mi. N of the Arnon River and near to the eastern border of the Amorite state.

2:27 Let me pass through. As with the Edomites previously (Num. 20:17), Moses asked to pass peacefully through the territory of Sihon.

who dwell in Seir and the Moabites who
dwell in Ar did for me, until I cross the Jordan to the land which the LORD our God is
giving us.'
30 [i]"But Sihon king of Heshbon would
not let us pass through, for [j]the LORD your
God [k]hardened his spirit and made his
heart obstinate, that He might deliver him
into your hand, as *it is* this day.
31 "And the LORD said to me, 'See, I have
begun to [l]give Sihon and his land over to
you. Begin to possess *it,* that you may inherit his land.' 32 [m]Then Sihon and all his
people came out against us to fight at
Jahaz. 33 And [n]the LORD our God delivered
him [2]over to us; so [o]we defeated him, his
sons, and all his people. 34 We took all his
cities at that time, and we [p]utterly destroyed the men, women, and little ones of
every city; we left none remaining. 35 We
took only the livestock as plunder for ourselves, with the spoil of the cities which we
took. 36 [q]From Aroer, which *is* on the bank
of the River Arnon, and *from* [r]the city that
is in the ravine, as far as Gilead, there was
not one city too strong for us; [s]the LORD
our God delivered all to us. 37 Only you
did not go near the land of the people of
Ammon—anywhere along the River [t]Jab-
bok, or to the cities of the mountains, or
[u]wherever the LORD our God had forbidden us.

King Og Defeated

3 "Then we turned and went up the road
to Bashan; and [a]Og king of Bashan
came out against us, he and all his people,
to battle [b]at Edrei. 2 And the LORD said to
me, 'Do not fear him, for I have delivered
him and all his people and his land into
your hand; you shall do to him as you did
to [c]Sihon king of the Amorites, who dwelt
at Heshbon.'
3 "So the LORD our God also delivered
into our hands Og king of Bashan, with all
his people, and we [1]attacked him until he
had no survivors remaining. 4 And we
took all his cities at that time; there was not
a city which we did not take from them:
sixty cities, [d]all the region of Argob, the
kingdom of Og in Bashan. 5 All these cities
were fortified with high walls, gates, and
bars, besides a great many rural towns.
6 And we utterly destroyed them, as we
did to Sihon king [e]of Heshbon, utterly destroying the men, women, and children of
every city. 7 But all the livestock and the
spoil of the cities we took as booty for ourselves.
8 "And at that time we took the [f]land
from the hand of the two kings of the Amorites who *were* on this side of the Jordan,
from the River Arnon to Mount [g]Hermon
9 (the Sidonians call [h]Hermon Sirion, and
the Amorites call it Senir), 10 [i]all the cities
of the plain, all Gilead, and [j]all Bashan, as
far as Salcah and Edrei, cities of the kingdom of Og in Bashan.
11 [k]"For only Og king of Bashan remained of the remnant of [l]the [2]giants. Indeed his bedstead *was* an iron bedstead. (*Is*
it not in [m]Rabbah of the people of Ammon?) Nine cubits *is* its length and four cubits its width, according to the standard
cubit.

The Land East of the Jordan Divided

12 "And this [n]land, *which* we possessed
at that time, [o]from Aroer, which *is* by the
River Arnon, and half the mountains of
Gilead and [p]its cities, I gave to the
Reubenites and the Gadites. 13 [q]The rest of
Gilead, and all Bashan, the kingdom of
Og, I gave to half the tribe of Manasseh.
(All the region of Argob, with all Bashan,
was called the land of the [3]giants. 14 [r]Jair
the son of Manasseh took all the region of
Argob, [s]as far as the border of the Geshu-
rites and the Maachathites, and [t]called
Bashan after his own name, [4]Havoth Jair,
to this day.)
15 "Also I gave [u]Gilead to Machir.
16 And to the Reubenites [v]and the Gadites
I gave from Gilead as far as the River
Arnon, the middle of the river as *the* border, as far as the River Jabbok, [w]the border

30 [i]Num. 21:23 [j]Josh. 11:20 [k]Ex. 4:21
31 [l]Deut. 1:3, 8
32 [m]Num. 21:23
33 [n]Ex. 23:31; Deut. 7:2 [o]Num. 21:24 [2]Lit. *before us*
34 [p]Lev. 27:28
36 [q]Deut. 3:12; 4:48; Josh. 13:9 [r]Josh. 13:9, 16 [s]Ps. 44:3
37 [t]Gen. 32:22; Num. 21:24; Deut. 3:16 [u]Deut. 2:5, 9, 19

CHAPTER 3

1 [a]Num. 21:33-35; Deut. 29:7 [b]Deut. 1:4
2 [c]Num. 21:34; Josh. 13:21
3 [1]*struck*
4 [d]Deut. 3:13, 14
6 [e]Deut. 2:24, 34, 35
8 [f]Num. 32:33; Josh. 12:6; 13:8-12 [g]Deut. 4:48; 1 Chr. 5:23
9 [h]1 Chr. 5:23
10 [i]Deut. 4:49 [j]Josh. 12:5; 13:11
11 [k]Amos 2:9 [l]Gen. 14:5; Deut. 2:11, 20 [m]2 Sam. 12:26; Jer. 49:2; Ezek. 21:20 [2]Heb. *rephaim*
12 [n]Num. 32:33; Josh. 12:6; 13:8-12 [o]Deut. 2:36; Josh. 12:2 [p]Num. 34:14
13 [q]Josh. 13:29-31; 17:1 [3]Heb. *rephaim*
14 [r]1 Chr. 2:22 [s]Josh. 13:13; 2 Sam. 3:3; 10:6 [t]Num. 32:41 [4]Lit. *Towns of Jair*
15 [u]Num. 32:39, 40
16 [v]2 Sam. 24:5 [w]Num. 21:24; Deut. 2:37; Josh. 12:2

2:30 hardened his spirit. Sihon, by his own conscious will, refused Israel's request to journey through his land. God confirmed what was already in Sihon's heart, namely arrogance against the Lord and His people Israel, so that He might defeat him in battle and give his land to Israel.

2:32 Jahaz. The place of battle between Sihon and the Israelites, probably a few mi. to the N of Kedemoth (v. 26).

3:1 Bashan. A fertile region located E of the Sea of Galilee and the Jordan River extending from Mt. Hermon in the N to the Yarmuk River in the S. Israel met King Og and his army in battle at Edrei, a city on the Yarmuk River. The Amorite king ruled over 60 cities (vv. 4-10; Josh. 13:30), which were taken by Israel; this kingdom was assigned to the Transjordanic tribes, especially the half tribe of Manasseh (v. 13).

3:8 this side of the Jordan. East of the Jordan River, Israel controlled the territory from the Arnon River to Mt. Hermon, a length of about 150 mi. Note that the perspective of the speaker was to the E of the Jordan; the W of the Jordan still needed to be conquered. This statement helps date these speeches as pre-conquest.

3:11 an iron bedstead. The bedstead may actually have been a coffin, which would have been large enough to also hold tomb objects. The size of the "bedstead," 13½ by 6 ft., emphasized the largeness of Og, who was a giant (the last of the Rephaim, a race of giants). As God had given Israel victory over the giant Og, so He would give them victory over the giants in the Land.

3:12-20 *See notes on Num. 32:1-42; 34:13-15* for background.

of the people of Ammon; 17 the plain also,
with the Jordan as *the* border, from Chinnereth [x]as far as the east side of the Sea of the
Arabah [y](the Salt Sea), below the slopes of
Pisgah.
18 "Then I commanded you at that time,
saying: 'The LORD your God has given you
this land to possess. [z]All you men of valor
shall cross over armed before your
brethren, the children of Israel. 19 But your
wives, your little ones, and your livestock
(I know that you have much livestock)
shall stay in your cities which I have given
you, 20 until the LORD has given [a]rest to
your brethren as to you, and they also possess the land which the LORD your God is
giving them beyond the Jordan. Then each
of you may [b]return to his possession which
I have given you.'
21 "And [c]I commanded Joshua at that
time, saying, 'Your eyes have seen all that
the LORD your God has done to these two
kings; so will the LORD do to all the kingdoms through which you pass. 22 You
must not fear them, for [d]the LORD your
God Himself fights for you.'

Moses Forbidden to Enter the Land

23 "Then [e]I pleaded with the LORD at
that time, saying: 24 'O Lord GOD, You
have begun to show Your servant [f]Your
greatness and Your [5]mighty hand, for
[g]what god *is there* in heaven or on earth
who can do *anything* like Your works and
Your mighty *deeds?* 25 I pray, let me cross
over and see [h]the good land beyond the
Jordan, those pleasant mountains, and
Lebanon.'
26 "But the LORD [i]was angry with me on
your account, and would not listen to me.
So the LORD said to me: 'Enough of that!
Speak no more to Me of this matter. 27 [j]Go
up to the top of Pisgah, and lift your eyes
toward the west, the north, the south, and
the east; behold *it* with your eyes, for you
shall not cross over this Jordan. 28 But
[k]command [6] Joshua, and encourage him
and strengthen him; for he shall go over
before this people, and he shall cause them
to inherit the land which you will see.'
29 "So we stayed in [l]the valley opposite
Beth Peor.

Moses Commands Obedience

4 "Now, O Israel, listen to [a]the statutes
and the judgments which I teach you to
observe, that you may live, and go in and
[1]possess the land which the LORD God of
your fathers is giving you. 2 [b]You shall not
add to the word which I command you, nor
take from it, that you may keep the commandments of the LORD your God which I
command you. 3 Your eyes have seen what
the LORD did at [c]Baal Peor; for the LORD
your God has destroyed from among you
all the men who followed Baal of Peor.
4 But you who held fast to the LORD your
God *are* alive today, every one of you.
5 "Surely I have taught you statutes and
judgments, just as the LORD my God commanded me, that you should act according
to them in the land which you go to possess. 6 Therefore be careful to observe *them;*
for this *is* [d]your wisdom and your understanding in the sight of the peoples who
will hear all these statutes, and say, 'Surely
this great nation *is* a wise and understanding people.'

17 [x] Num. 34:11, 12; Deut. 4:49; Josh. 12:3 [y] Gen. 14:3; Josh. 3:16
18 [z] Num. 32:20; Josh. 4:12, 13
20 [a] Deut. 12:9, 10 [b] Josh. 22:4
21 [c] [Num. 27:22, 23]; Josh. 11:23
22 [d] Ex. 14:14; Deut. 1:30; 20:4; Neh. 4:20
23 [e] [2 Cor. 12:8, 9]
24 [f] Deut. 5:24; 11:2 [g] Ex. 8:10; 15:11; 2 Sam. 7:22; Ps. 71:19; 86:8 [5] *strong*
25 [h] Ex. 3:8; Deut. 4:22
26 [i] Num. 20:12; 27:14; Deut. 1:37; 31:2; 32:51, 52; 34:4
27 [j] Num. 23:14; 27:12
28 [k] Num. 27:18, 23; Deut. 31:3, 7, 8, 23 [6] *charge*
29 [l] Deut. 4:46; 34:6

CHAPTER 4

1 [a] Lev. 19:37; 20:8; 22:31; Deut. 5:1; 8:1; Ezek. 20:11; [Rom. 10:5] [1] *take possession of*
2 [b] Deut. 12:32; [Josh. 1:7]; Prov. 30:6; [Rev. 22:18, 19]
3 [c] Num. 25:1-9; Josh. 22:17; Ps. 106:28
6 [d] Deut. 30:19, 20; 32:46, 47; Job 28:28; Ps. 19:7; 111:10; Prov. 1:7; [2 Tim. 3:15]

3:20 rest. A peaceful situation with the Land free from external threat and oppression. The eastern 2½ tribes had the responsibility to battle alongside their western brethren until the conquest was complete (cf. Josh. 22).

3:22 the LORD your God Himself fights for you. Moses commanded Joshua not to be afraid because the Lord Himself would provide supernatural power and give them the victory (cf. 1:30; 31:6-8; Josh. 1:9).

3:23 I pleaded with the LORD. With the victories over Sihon and Og, Moses made one final passionate plea to the Lord to be allowed to enter the Promised Land. However, the Lord would not allow Moses that privilege. He did, however, allow Moses to go to the top of Pisgah and see the Land (cf. Deut. 32:48-52; 34:1-4).

3:26 the LORD was angry. *See note on 1:37*; cf. 4:21-24.

3:29 Beth Peor. Located E of the Jordan River, probably opposite Jericho (*see notes on Num. 22–25* for the background).

4:1 O Israel, listen. Moses called the people to hear and obey the rules of conduct that God had given them to observe. Successful conquest and full enjoyment of life in the Land was based on submission to God's law. **the statutes and the judgments.** The first are permanent rules for conduct fixed by the reigning authority, while the second deal with judicial decisions which served as precedents for future guidance.

4:2 You shall not add...nor take from. The Word that God had given to Israel through Moses was complete and sufficient to direct the people. Thus, this law, the gift of God at Horeb, could not be supplemented or reduced. Anything that adulterated or contradicted God's law would not be tolerated (cf. 12:32; Prov. 30:6; Rev. 22:18, 19).

4:3,4 Moses used the incident at Baal Peor (Num. 25:1-9) to illustrate from the Israelites' own history that their very lives depended on obeying God's law. Only those who had held fast to the Lord by obeying His commands were alive that day to hear Moses.

4:6 the peoples. Israel's obedience to God's law would provide a testimony to the world that God was near to His people and that His laws were righteous. One purpose of the law was to make Israel morally and spiritually unique among all the nations and, therefore, draw those nations to the true and living God. They were from their beginnings to be a witness nation. Though they failed and have been temporarily set aside, the prophets revealed that in the future kingdom of Messiah they will be a nation of faithful witnesses (cf. Is. 45:14; Zech. 8:23). **a wise and understanding people.** The nations would see 3 things in Israel (vv. 6-8). First, the Israelites would know how to apply God's knowledge so as to have discernment and to be able to judge matters accurately. (*See following notes.*)

7 "For [e]what great nation *is there* that has
[f]God[2] *so* near to it, as the LORD our God *is*
to us, for whatever *reason* we may call
upon Him? 8 And what great nation *is there*
that has *such* statutes and righteous judgments as are in all this law which I set before you this day? 9 Only take heed to
yourself, and diligently [g]keep yourself, lest
you [h]forget the things your eyes have seen,
and lest they depart from your heart all the
days of your life. And [i]teach them to your
children and your grandchildren, 10 *especially concerning* [j]the day you stood before
the LORD your God in Horeb, when the
LORD said to me, 'Gather the people to Me,
and I will let them hear My words, that
they may learn to fear Me all the days they
live on the earth, and *that* they may teach
their children.'
11 "Then you came near and stood at the
foot of the mountain, and the mountain
burned with fire to the midst of heaven,
with darkness, cloud, and thick darkness.
12 [k]And the LORD spoke to you out of the
midst of the fire. You heard the sound of
the words, but saw no [3]form; [l]*you* only
heard a voice. 13 [m]So He declared to you
His covenant which He commanded you
to perform, [n]the Ten Commandments; and
[o]He wrote them on two tablets of stone.
14 And [p]the LORD commanded me at that
time to teach you statutes and judgments,
that you might [4]observe them in the land
which you cross over to possess.

Beware of Idolatry

15 [q]"Take careful heed to yourselves, for
you saw no [r]form when the LORD spoke to
you at Horeb out of the midst of the fire,
16 lest you [s]act corruptly and [t]make for
yourselves a carved image in the [5]form of
any figure: [u]the likeness of male or female,
17 the likeness of any animal that *is* on the
earth or the likeness of any winged bird
that flies in the air, 18 the likeness of anything that creeps on the ground or the likeness of any fish that *is* in the water beneath
the earth. 19 And *take heed,* lest you [v]lift
your eyes to heaven, and *when* you see the
sun, the moon, and the stars, [w]all the host
of heaven, you feel driven to [x]worship
them and serve them, which the LORD your
God has [6]given to all the peoples under the
whole heaven as a heritage. 20 But the
LORD has taken you and [y]brought you out
of the iron furnace, out of Egypt, to be [z]His
people, an inheritance, as you are this day.
21 Furthermore [a]the LORD was angry with
me for your sakes, and swore that [b]I would
not cross over the Jordan, and that I would
not enter the good land which the LORD
your God is giving you as an inheritance.
22 But [c]I must die in this land, [d]I must not
cross over the Jordan; but you shall cross
over and [7]possess [e]that good land. 23 Take
heed to yourselves, lest you forget the
covenant of the LORD your God which He
made with you, [f]and make for yourselves
a carved image in the form of anything
which the LORD your God has forbidden
you. 24 For [g]the LORD your God *is* a consuming fire, [h]a jealous God.
25 "When you beget children and
grandchildren and have grown old in the
land, and act corruptly and make a
carved image in the form of anything,
and [i]do evil in the sight of the LORD your
God to provoke Him to anger, 26 [j]I call

7 [e][Deut. 4:32-34; 2 Sam. 7:23] [f][Ps. 46:1; Is. 55:6] [2]Or *a god*
9 [g]Prov. 4:23 [h]Deut. 29:2-8 [i]Gen. 18:19; Deut. 4:10; 6:7, 20-25; Ps. 78:5, 6; Prov. 22:6; Eph. 6:4
10 [j]Ex. 19:9, 16, 17
12 [k]Deut. 5:4, 22 [l]Ex. 19:17-19; 20:22; 1 Kin. 19:11-18 [3]*similitude*
13 [m]Deut. 9:9, 11 [n]Ex. 34:28; Deut. 10:4 [o]Ex. 24:12
14 [p]Ex. 21:1 [4]*do* or *perform*
15 [q]Josh. 23:11 [r]Is. 40:18
16 [s]Ex. 32:7; Deut. 9:12; 31:29 [t]Ex. 20:4, 5 [u]Rom. 1:23 [5]*similitude*
19 [v]Deut. 17:3; Job 31:26-28 [w]2 Kin. 21:3 [x][Rom. 1:25] [6]*divided*
20 [y]1 Kin. 8:51; Jer. 11:4 [z]Deut. 7:6; 27:9; [Titus 2:14]
21 [a]Num. 20:12; Deut. 1:37; 3:26 [b]Num. 27:13, 14
22 [c]2 Pet. 1:13-15 [d]Deut. 3:27 [e]Deut. 3:25 [7]*take possession of*
23 [f]Ex. 20:4, 5; Deut. 4:16
24 [g]Ex. 24:17; Deut. 9:3; Is. 33:14; Heb. 12:29 [h]Ex. 20:5; 34:14
25 [i]2 Kin. 17:17
26 [j]Deut. 30:18, 19; 2 Chr. 36:14-20; Is. 1:2; Mic. 6:2

4:7 God *so* near to it. Second, faithfulness to the Lord would allow the nations to see that the Lord had established intimacy with Israel.

4:8 statutes and righteous judgments. Third, the nations would see that Israel's law was distinctive, for its source was the Lord indicating its character was righteous.

4:9-31 This section carries the most basic lesson for Israel to learn—to fear and reverence God.

4:9 teach them to your children. Deuteronomy stresses the responsibility of parents to pass on their experiences with God and the knowledge they have gained from Him to their children (cf. 6:7; 11:19).

4:10 *especially concerning* the day. One experience of Israel to be passed on from generation to generation was the great theophany (the self-revelation of God in physical form) which took place at Horeb (cf. Ex. 19:9–20:19).

4:12 no form. Israel was to remember that when God revealed Himself at Sinai, His presence came through His voice, i.e., the sound of His words. They did not see Him. God is Spirit (John 4:24), which rules out any idolatrous representation of God in any physical form (vv. 16-18) or any worship of the created order (v. 19).

4:13 the Ten Commandments. Lit. "ten statements," from which comes the term "Decalogue." These summarize and epitomize all the commandments the Lord gave to Israel through Moses. Though the phrase occurs only here, in 10:4, and in Ex. 34:28, there are 26 more references to it in Deuteronomy (*see notes on Matt. 19:16-23; 22:34-40; Mark 10:17-22; Rom. 13:8-10*).

4:15-19 This is a strong emphasis on commandments one and two (cf. Rom. 1:18-23).

4:20 the iron furnace. A fire was used to heat iron sufficiently to be hammered into different shapes or welded to other objects. The iron furnace here suggests that Israel's time in Egypt was a period of ordeal, testing, and purifying for the Hebrews, readying them for usefulness as God's witness nation.

4:24 a jealous God. God is zealous to protect what belongs to Him. He will not allow another to have the honor that is due to Him alone (cf. Is. 42:8; 48:11).

4:25-31 Cf. 8:18,19. In fact, this briefly outlined the future judgment of Israel, which culminated in the northern 10 tribes being exiled to Assyria (ca. 722 B.C.; 2 Kin. 17) and the southern two tribes being deported to Babylon (ca. 605–586 B.C.; 2 Kin. 24,25). Although the Jews returned in the days of Ezra and Nehemiah (ca. 538–445 B.C.), they never regained their autonomy or dominance. Thus, the days of promised restoration and return look forward to Messiah's return to set up the millennial kingdom.

heaven and earth to witness against you
this day, that you will soon utterly perish
from the land which you cross over the
Jordan to possess; you will not [8]prolong
your days in it, but will be utterly destroyed. 27 And the LORD [k]will scatter
you among the peoples, and you will be
left few in number among the nations
where the LORD will drive you. 28 And
[l]there you will serve gods, the work of
men's hands, wood and stone, [m]which
neither see nor hear nor eat nor smell.
29 [n]But from there you will seek the LORD
your God, and you will find *Him* if you
seek Him with all your heart and with all
your soul. 30 When you are in [9]distress,
and all these things come upon you in the
[o]latter days, when you [p]turn to the LORD
your God and obey His voice 31 (for the
LORD your God *is* a merciful God), He
will not forsake you nor [q]destroy you,
nor forget the covenant of your fathers
which He swore to them.

32 "For [r]ask now concerning the days
that are past, which were before you,
since the day that God created man on the
earth, and *ask* [s]from one end of heaven to
the other, whether *any* great *thing* like this
has happened, or *anything* like it has been
heard. 33 [t]Did *any* people *ever* hear the
voice of God speaking out of the midst of
the fire, as you have heard, and live? 34 Or
did God *ever* try to go *and* take for Himself
a nation from the midst of *another* nation,
[u]by trials, [v]by signs, by wonders, by war,
[w]by a mighty hand and [x]an outstretched
arm, [y]and by great [1]terrors, according to
all that the LORD your God did for you in
Egypt before your eyes? 35 To you it was
shown, that you might know that the
LORD Himself *is* God; [z]*there is* none other
besides Him. 36 [a]Out of heaven He let you
hear His voice, that He might instruct
you; on earth He showed you His great
fire, and you heard His words out of the
midst of the fire. 37 And because [b]He
loved your fathers, therefore He chose
their [2]descendants after them; and [c]He
brought you out of Egypt with His Presence, with His mighty power, 38 [d]driving
out from before you nations greater and
mightier than you, to bring you in, to give
you their land *as* an inheritance, as *it is*
this day. 39 Therefore know this day, and
consider *it* in your heart, that [e]the LORD
Himself *is* God in heaven above and on
the earth beneath; *there is* no other. 40 [f]You
shall therefore keep His statutes and His
commandments which I command you
today, that [3]it may go well with you and
with your children after you, and that you
may [4]prolong *your* days in the land which
the LORD your God is giving you for all
time."

Cities of Refuge East of the Jordan

41 Then Moses [g]set apart three cities on
this side of the Jordan, toward the rising of
the sun, 42 [h]that the manslayer might flee
there, who kills his neighbor unintentionally, without having hated him in
time past, and that by fleeing to one of
these cities he might live: 43 [i]Bezer in the
wilderness on the plateau for the Reubenites, Ramoth in Gilead for the Gadites, and
Golan in Bashan for the Manassites.

Introduction to God's Law

44 Now this *is* the law which Moses set
before the children of Israel. 45 These *are*

26 [8] *live long on it*
27 [k] Lev. 26:33; Deut. 28:62; Neh. 1:8
28 [l] Deut. 28:64; 1 Sam. 26:19; Jer. 16:13 [m] Ps. 115:4-7; 135:15-17; Is. 44:9; 46:7
29 [n] [Lev. 26:39-45; Deut. 30:1-3; 2 Chr. 15:4; Neh. 1:9]
30 [o] Gen. 49:1; Deut. 31:29; Jer. 23:20; Hos. 3:5 [p] Joel 2:12; Heb. 1:2 [9] *tribulation*
31 [q] Lev. 26:44; Jer. 30:11
32 [r] Deut. 32:7; Job 8:8 [s] Deut. 28:64; Matt. 24:31
33 [t] Ex. 20:22; 24:11; Deut. 5:24-26
34 [u] Deut. 7:19 [v] Ex. 7:3 [w] Ex. 13:3 [x] Ex. 6:6 [y] Deut. 26:8 [1] *calamities*
35 [z] Ex. 8:10; 9:14; [Deut. 4:39; 32:12, 39; 1 Sam. 2:2; Is. 43:10-12; 44:6-8; 45:5-7]; Mark 12:32
36 [a] Ex. 19:9, 19; 20:18, 22; Deut. 4:33; Neh. 9:13; Heb. 12:19, 25
37 [b] Deut. 7:7, 8; 10:15; 33:3 [c] Ex. 13:3, 9, 14 [2] Lit. *seed*
38 [d] Deut. 7:1
39 [e] Deut. 4:35; Josh. 2:11
40 [f] Lev. 22:31; Deut. 5:16; 32:46, 47 [3] *you may prosper* [4] *live long*
41 [g] Num. 35:6; Deut. 19:2-13; Josh. 20:7-9
42 [h] Deut. 19:4
43 [i] Josh. 20:8

4:27 the LORD will scatter you. Moses warned Israel that the judgment for idolatry would be their dispersion among the nations by the Lord (see 28:64-67).

4:30 the latter days. Lit. "the end of days." Moses saw in the distant future a time when repentant Israel would turn again to the Lord and obey Him. Throughout the Pentateuch, "the latter days" refers to the time when Messiah will establish His kingdom (see Gen. 49:1,8-12; Num. 24:14-24; Deut. 32:39-43).

4:31 the covenant of your fathers. God mercifully, not because they deserve it, will fulfill the covenant He made with Abraham, Isaac, and Jacob with repentant Israel in the future. God will not forget the Word that He has given to Abraham and his seed (cf. Rom. 11:25-27).

4:32-40 A historical apologetic, appealing for the nation's obedience to God's law.

4:32-39 since the day that God created man on the earth. In all of human history, no other nation has had the privilege that Israel had of hearing God speak, as He did in giving the law at Mt. Sinai, and surviving such an awesome experience. Nor had any other people been so blessed, chosen and delivered from bondage by such mighty miracles as Israel saw. God did this to reveal to them that He alone is God (vv. 35,39).

4:37 His Presence. Lit. "His face." God Himself had brought Israel out of Egypt. The Exodus resulted from the electing love that God had for the patriarchs and their descendants.

4:40 Such gracious privilege, as remembered in vv. 32-39, should elicit obedience, particularly in view of the unconditional promise that the Land will be theirs permanently ("for all time") as is detailed in chaps. 29,30.

4:41-43 These 3 verses are a narrative insertion at the end of Moses' speech. The setting aside of 3 cities on the E side of the Jordan by Moses showed that Moses willingly obeyed the commandments God gave him. He was an example of the type of obedience that God was calling for in 4:1-40 (cf. Num. 35:14; Josh. 20:18).

4:44–28:68 The heart of Deuteronomy is found in this long second speech of Moses. "And this is the law" (4:44) which Moses explained to Israel (cf. 1:5). After a brief introduction (4:44-49), Moses gave the people a clear understanding of what the law directed concerning their relationship with the Lord in the Land (5:1–26:19), then concluded by recounting the blessings or the curses which would come upon the nation as a consequence of their response to the stipulations of this law (27:1–28:68).

the testimonies, the statutes, and the judgments which Moses spoke to the children
of Israel after they came out of Egypt, 46 on
this side of the Jordan, [j]in the valley opposite Beth Peor, in the land of Sihon king of
the Amorites, who dwelt at Heshbon,
whom Moses and the children of Israel
[k]defeated[5] after they came out of Egypt.
47 And they took possession of his land
and the land [l]of Og king of Bashan, two
kings of the Amorites, who *were* on this
side of the Jordan, toward the [6]rising of the
sun, 48 [m]from Aroer, which *is* on the bank
of the River Arnon, even to Mount [7]Sion
(that is, [n]Hermon), 49 and all the plain on
the east side of the Jordan as far as the Sea
of the Arabah, below the [o]slopes of Pisgah.

The Ten Commandments Reviewed

5 And Moses called all Israel, and said to
them: "Hear, O Israel, the statutes and
judgments which I speak in your hearing
today, that you may learn them and be
careful to observe them. 2 [a]The LORD our
God made a covenant with us in Horeb.
3 The LORD [b]did not make this covenant
with our fathers, but with us, those who
are here today, all of us who *are* alive.
4 [c]The LORD talked with you face to face on
the mountain from the midst of the fire.
5 [d]I stood between the LORD and you at
that time, to declare to you the word of the
LORD; for [e]you were afraid because of the
fire, and you did not go up the mountain.
He said:
6 [f]'I *am* the LORD your God who
brought you out of the land of
Egypt, out of the house of [1]bond-
age.
7 [g]'You shall have no other gods [2]be-
fore Me.
8 [h]'You shall not make for yourself a
carved image—any likeness *of*
anything that *is* in heaven above,
or that *is* in the earth beneath, or
that *is* in the water under the
earth; 9 you shall not [i]bow[3] down
to them nor serve them. For I, the
LORD your God, *am* a jealous
God, [4]visiting the iniquity of the
fathers upon the children to the
third and fourth *generations* of
those who hate Me, 10 [j]but showing mercy to thousands, to those
who love Me and [5]keep My commandments.
11 [k]'You shall not take the name of the
LORD your God in vain, for the
LORD will not hold *him* [6]guiltless
who takes His name in vain.
12 [l]'Observe the Sabbath day, to [7]keep it
holy, as the LORD your God commanded you. 13 [m]Six days you
shall labor and do all your work,
14 but the seventh day *is* the [n]Sab-
bath of the LORD your God. *In it*
you shall do no work: you, nor
your son, nor your daughter, nor
your male servant, nor your female servant, nor your ox, nor
your donkey, nor any of your cattle, nor your stranger who *is*
within your gates, that your male

46 [j] Deut. 3:29 [k] Num. 21:24; Deut. 1:4 [5] *struck*
47 [l] Num. 21:33-35 [6] *east*
48 [m] Deut. 2:36; 3:12 [n] Deut. 3:9; Ps. 133:3 [7] Syr. *Sirion*
49 [o] Deut. 3:17

CHAPTER 5

2 [a] Ex. 19:5; Deut. 4:23; Mal. 4:4
3 [b] Jer. 31:32; Matt. 13:17; Heb. 8:9
4 [c] Ex. 19:9
5 [d] Ex. 20:21; Gal. 3:19 [e] Ex. 19:16
6 [f] Ex. 20:2-17; Lev. 26:1; Deut. 6:4; Ps. 81:10 [1] *slavery*
7 [g] Ex. 20:2, 3; 23:13; Hos. 13:4 [2] *besides*
8 [h] Ex. 20:4
9 [i] Ex. 34:7, 14-16; Num. 14:18; Deut. 7:10 [3] *worship them* [4] *punishing*
10 [j] Num. 14:18; Deut. 7:9; Jer. 32:18; Dan. 9:4 [5] *observe*
11 [k] Ex. 20:7; Lev. 19:12; Deut. 6:13; 10:20; Matt. 5:33 [6] *innocent*
12 [l] Ex. 20:8; Ezek. 20:12; Mark 2:27 [7] *sanctify it*
13 [m] Ex. 23:12; 35:2
14 [n] [Gen. 2:2]; Ex. 16:29; [Heb. 4:4]

4:45 testimonies...statutes...judgments. God's instruction to Israel was set forth in: 1) the testimonies, the basic covenant stipulations (5:6-21); 2) statutes, words that were inscribed and therefore fixed; and 3) judgments, the decisions made by a judge on the merits of the situation. This law was given to Israel when they came out of Egypt. Moses is not giving further law, he is now explaining that which has already been given.

4:48 Mount Sion. This reference to Mt. Hermon is not to be confused with Mt. Zion in Jerusalem.

4:49 Sea of the Arabah. The Dead Sea.

5:1–11:32 As Moses began his second address to the people of Israel, he reminded them of the events and the basic commands from God that were foundational to the Sinaitic Covenant (5:1-33; see Ex. 19:1–20:21). Then, in 6:1–11:32, Moses expounded and applied the first 3 of the Ten Commandments to the present experience of the people.

5:1 Hear, O Israel. The verb "hear" carried the sense "obey." A hearing that leads to obedience was demanded of all the people (cf: 6:4; 9:1; 20:3; 27:9).

5:2 a covenant with us in Horeb. The second generation of Israel, while children, received the covenant that God made with Israel at Sinai.

5:3 did not make this covenant with our fathers. The "fathers" were not the people's immediate fathers, who had died in the wilderness, but their more distant ancestors, the patriarchs (see 4:31,37; 7:8,12; 8:18). The Sinaitic or Mosaic Covenant was in addition to and distinct from the Abrahamic Covenant made with the patriarchs.

5:6-21 The first 5 commandments involve relationship with God, the last 5 deal with human relationships; together they were the foundation of Israel's life before God. Moses here reiterated them as given originally at Sinai. Slight variations from the Exodus text are accounted for by Moses' explanatory purpose in Deuteronomy. *See notes on Ex. 20:1-17* for an additional explanation of these commands.

5:7 no other gods. Cf. Ex. 20:3. "Other gods" were non-existent pagan gods, which were made in the form of idols and shaped by the minds of their worshipers. The Israelite was to be totally faithful to the God to whom he was bound by covenant. Cf. Matt. 16:24-27; Mark 8:34-38; Luke 9:23-26; 14:26-33.

5:8 a carved image. Cf. Ex. 20:4,5. Reducing the infinite God to any physical likeness was intolerable, as the people found out in their attempt to cast God as a golden calf (cf. Ex. 32).

5:9,10 third and fourth *generations*...thousands. *See note on Ex. 20:5,6* for an explanation of this often misunderstood text. **those who hate Me...love Me.** Disobedience is equal to hatred of God, as love is equal to obedience (cf. Matt. 22:34-40; Rom. 13:8-10).

5:11 take the name...in vain. Cf. Ex. 20:7. Attach God's name to emptiness. Cf. Ps. 111:9; Matt. 6:9; Luke 1:49; John 17:6,26.

5:12 as the LORD your God commanded you. Cf. Ex. 20:8-10. These words are missing from Ex. 20:8, but refer back to this commandment given to Israel at Sinai 40 years earlier.

servant and your female servant
may rest as well as you. 15 [o]And
remember that you were a slave
in the land of Egypt, and the
LORD your God brought you out
from there [p]by a mighty hand
and by an outstretched arm;
therefore the LORD your God
commanded you to keep the Sabbath day.

16 [q]'Honor your father and your mother, as the LORD your God has
commanded you, [r]that your days
may be long, and that it may be
well with [s]you in the land which
the LORD your God is giving you.

17 [t]'You shall not murder.

18 [u]'You shall not commit adultery.

19 [v]'You shall not steal.

20 [w]'You shall not bear false witness
against your neighbor.

21 [x]'You shall not covet your neighbor's
wife; and you shall not desire
your neighbor's house, his field,
his male servant, his female servant, his ox, his donkey, or anything that *is* your neighbor's.'

22 "These words the LORD spoke to all
your assembly, in the mountain from the
midst of the fire, the cloud, and the thick
darkness, with a loud voice; and He added
no more. And [y]He wrote them on two
tablets of stone and gave them to me.

The People Afraid of God's Presence

23 [z]"So it was, when you heard the voice
from the midst of the darkness, while the
mountain was burning with fire, that you
came near to me, all the heads of your
tribes and your elders. 24 And you said:
'Surely the LORD our God has shown us
His glory and His greatness, and [a]we have
heard His voice from the midst of the fire.
We have seen this day that God speaks
with man; yet he [b]*still* lives. 25 Now therefore, why should we die? For this great fire
will consume us; [c]if we hear the voice of
the LORD our God anymore, then we shall
die. 26 [d]For who *is there* of all flesh who has
heard the voice of the living God speaking
from the midst of the fire, as we *have,* and
lived? 27 You go near and hear all that the
LORD our God may say, and [e]tell us all that
the LORD our God says to you, and we will
hear and do *it.*'

28 "Then the LORD heard the voice of
your words when you spoke to me, and
the LORD said to me: 'I have heard the
voice of the words of this people which
they have spoken to you. [f]They are right *in*
all that they have spoken. 29 [g]Oh, that they
had such a heart in them that they would
fear Me and [h]always keep all My commandments, [i]that it might be well with
them and with their children forever! 30 Go
and say to them, "Return to your tents."
31 But as for you, stand here by Me, [j]and I
will speak to you all the commandments,
the statutes, and the judgments which you
shall teach them, that they may observe
them in the land which I am giving them to
possess.'

32 "Therefore you shall [8]be careful to do
as the LORD your God has commanded
you; [k]you shall not turn aside to the right
hand or to the left. 33 You shall walk in [l]all
the ways which the LORD your God has
commanded you, that you may live [m]and
that it may be well with you, and *that* you
may prolong *your* days in the land which
you shall possess.

15 [o]Deut. 15:15 [p]Deut. 4:34, 37
16 [q]Ex. 20:12; Lev. 19:3; Matt. 15:4; Eph. 6:2, 3; Col. 3:20 [r]Deut. 6:2 [s]Deut. 4:40
17 [t]Ex. 20:13; Matt. 5:21
18 [u]Ex. 20:14; Mark 10:19; Luke 18:20; [Rom. 13:9]; James 2:11
19 [v]Ex. 20:15; Lev. 19:11; [Rom. 13:9]
20 [w]Ex. 20:16; 23:1; Matt. 19:18
21 [x]Ex. 20:17; [Rom. 7:7; 13:9]
22 [y]Ex. 24:12; 31:18; Deut. 4:13
23 [z]Ex. 20:18, 19
24 [a]Ex. 19:19 [b]Deut. 4:33; Judg. 13:22
25 [c]Ex. 20:18, 19; Deut. 18:16
26 [d]Deut. 4:33
27 [e]Ex. 20:19; Heb. 12:19
28 [f]Deut. 18:17
29 [g]Deut. 32:29; Ps. 81:13; Is. 48:18 [h]Deut. 11:1 [i]Deut. 4:40
31 [j][Gal. 3:19]
32 [k]Deut. 17:20; 28:14; Josh. 1:7; 23:6; Prov. 4:27 [8]*observe*
33 [l]Deut. 10:12; Ps. 119:3; Jer. 7:23; Luke 1:6 [m]Deut. 4:40; Eph. 6:3

5:15 brought you out from there. Here an additional reason is given for God's rest after creation (i.e., for the observance of the Sabbath; see Ex. 20:11)—God's deliverance of the people from Egypt. While the Israelites had been slaves in Egypt, they were not allowed rest from their continual labor, so the Sabbath was also to function as a day of rest in which their deliverance from bondage would be remembered with thanksgiving as the sign of their redemption and continual sanctification (cf. Ex. 31:13-17; Ezek 20:12).

5:16-20 Cf. Matt. 19:18-19; Mark 10:19; Luke 18:20.

5:16 that your days may be long. Cf. Ex. 20:12; Matt. 15:4; Mark 7:10; Eph. 6:2,3. Paul indicated that this was the first commandment with a promise attached (Eph. 6:2). Jesus also had much to say about honoring parents (see Matt. 10:37; 19:29; Luke 2:49-51; John 19:26,27).

5:17 murder. Cf. Ex. 20:13; Matt. 5:21; James 2:11.

5:18 adultery. Cf. Ex. 20:14; Matt. 5:27.

5:19 steal. Cf. Ex. 20:15; Eph. 4:28.

5:20 bear false witness. Cf. Ex. 20:16; Col. 3:9.

5:21 covet...desire. Cf. Ex. 20:17. Both the lusting after a neighbor's wife and a strong desire for a neighbor's property were prohibited by the tenth commandment (cf. Rom. 7:7).

5:22 and He added no more. These Ten Commandments alone were identified as direct quotations by God. The rest of the stipulations of the covenant were given to Moses, who in turn gave them to the Israelites. These basic rules, which reflect God's character, continue to be a means by which God reveals the sinful deeds of the flesh (cf. Rom. 7:7-14; Gal. 3:19-24; 5:13-26). They are also a holy standard for conduct that the saved live by through the Spirit's power, with the exception of keeping the Sabbath (cf. Col. 2:16,17). **two tablets of stone.** The tablets were written on both sides (see Ex. 32:15).

5:22-27 The frightening circumstances of God's presence at Sinai caused the people to have enough fear to ask Moses to receive the words from God and communicate those words to them, after which they promised to obey all that God said (see v. 27).

5:28,29 God affirmed that the pledge to be obedient was the right response (v. 28), and then expressed His loving passion for them to fulfill their promise so they and their children would prosper.

5:30-33 They asked to be given all God's Word (v. 27), so God dismissed the people and told Moses He was going to give the law to him to teach the people (v. 31). At stake was life and prosperity in the Land of Promise.

The Greatest Commandment

6 "Now this *is* [a]the commandment, *and*
these are the statutes and judgments
which the LORD your God has commanded
to teach you, that you may observe *them* in
the land which you are crossing over to
possess, 2 [b]that you may fear the LORD
your God, to keep all His statutes and His
commandments which I command you,
you and your son and your grandson, all
the days of your life, [c]and that your days
may be prolonged. 3 Therefore hear, O Israel, and [1]be careful to observe *it,* that it
may be well with you, and that you may
[d]multiply greatly [e]as the LORD God of your
fathers has promised you—[f]'a land flowing with milk and honey.'
4 [g]"Hear, O Israel: [2]The LORD our God,
the LORD *is* one! 5 [h]You shall love the LORD
your God with all your heart, [i]with all
your soul, and with all your strength.
6 "And [j]these words which I command
you today shall be in your heart. 7 [k]You
shall teach them diligently to your children, and shall talk of them when you sit
in your house, when you walk by the way,
when you lie down, and when you rise up.
8 [l]You shall bind them as a sign on your
hand, and they shall be as frontlets between your eyes. 9 [m]You shall write them
on the doorposts of your house and on
your gates.

Caution Against Disobedience

10 "So it shall be, when the LORD your
God brings you into the land of which He
[3]swore to your fathers, to Abraham, Isaac,
and Jacob, to give you large and beautiful
cities [n]which you did not build, 11 houses
full of all good things, which you did not
fill, hewn-out wells which you did not dig,
vineyards and olive trees which you did
not plant—[o]when you have eaten and are
full— 12 *then* beware, lest you forget the
[p]LORD who brought you out of the land of
Egypt, from the house of bondage. 13 You
shall [q]fear the LORD your God and serve
Him, and [r]shall take oaths in His name.
14 You shall not go after other gods, [s]the
gods of the peoples who *are* all around you
15 (for [t]the LORD your God *is* a jealous God
[u]among you), lest the anger of the LORD
your God be aroused against you and destroy you from the face of the earth.
16 [v]"You shall not [4]tempt the LORD your
God [w]as you [5]tempted *Him* in Massah.
17 You shall [x]diligently keep the commandments of the LORD your God, His testimonies, and His statutes which He has
commanded you. 18 And you [y]shall do
what is right and good in the sight of the
LORD, that it may be well with you, and
that you may go in and possess the good
land of which the LORD swore to your fathers, 19 [z]to cast out all your enemies from
before you, as the LORD has spoken.
20 [a]"When your son asks you in time to
come, saying, 'What *is the meaning of* the
testimonies, the statutes, and the judgments which the LORD our God has commanded you?' 21 then you shall say to your

CHAPTER 6
1 [a] Deut. 12:1
2 [b] Ex. 20:20; Deut. 10:12, 13; [Ps. 111:10; 128:1; Eccl. 12:13] [c] Deut. 4:40
3 [d] Deut. 7:13 [e] Gen. 22:17 [f] Ex. 3:8, 17 [1] Lit. *observe to do*
4 [g] Deut. 4:35; Mark 12:29; John 17:3; [1 Cor. 8:4, 6] [2] Or *The LORD is our God, the LORD alone,* i.e., the only one
5 [h] Matt. 22:37; Mark 12:30; Luke 10:27 [i] 2 Kin. 23:25
6 [j] Deut. 11:18-20; Ps. 119:11, 98
7 [k] Deut. 4:9; 11:19; [Eph. 6:4]
8 [l] Ex. 12:14; 13:9, 16; Deut. 11:18; Prov. 3:3; 6:21; 7:3
9 [m] Deut. 11:20; Is. 57:8
10 [n] Deut. 9:1; 19:1; Josh. 24:13; Ps. 105:44 [3] *promised*
11 [o] Deut. 8:10; 11:15; 14:29
12 [p] Deut. 8:11-18
13 [q] Deut. 13:4; Matt. 4:10; Luke 4:8 [r] Deut. 5:11; [Is. 45:23; Jer. 4:2]
14 [s] Deut. 13:7
15 [t] Ex. 20:5; Deut. 4:24 [u] Ex. 33:3
16 [v] Matt. 4:7; Luke 4:12 [w] [1 Cor. 10:9] [4] *test* [5] *tested*
17 [x] Deut. 11:22; Ps. 119:4
18 [y] Ex. 15:26; Deut. 8:7-10
19 [z] Num. 33:52, 53
20 [a] Ex. 13:8, 14

6:1-3 days...prolonged. Moses' concern is that successive generations maintain the obedience to God's laws that insures life and prosperity.

6:3 a land flowing with milk and honey. A description that included the richness of the Land which the Israelites were soon to possess (see 11:9; 26:9,15; 27:3; 31:20).

6:4,5 Cf. Mark 12:29,30,32,33.

6:4 Hear, O Israel. See 5:1. Deuteronomy 6:4-9, known as the *Shema* (Heb. for "hear"), has become the Jewish confession of faith, recited twice daily by the devout, along with 11:13-21 and Num. 15:37-41. **The LORD...LORD *is* one.** The intent of these words was to give a clear statement of the truth of monotheism, that there is only one God. Thus, it has also been translated "the LORD is our God, the LORD alone." The word used for "one" in this passage does not mean "singleness," but "unity." The same word is used in Gen. 2:24, where the husband and wife were said to be "one flesh." Thus, while this verse was intended as a clear and concise statement of monotheism, it does not exclude the concept of the Trinity.

6:5-9 You shall love the LORD your God. First in the list of all that was essential for the Jew was unreserved, wholehearted commitment expressed in love to God. Since this relationship of love for God could not be represented in any material way as with idols, it had to be demonstrated in obedience to God's law in daily life. Cf. 11:16-21; Matt. 22:37; Luke 10:27.

6:6 these words...in your heart. The people were to think about these commandments and meditate on them so that obedience would not be a matter of formal legalism, but a response based upon understanding. The law written upon the heart would be an essential characteristic of the later New Covenant (see Jer. 31:33).

6:7 teach them diligently to your children. The commandments were to be the subject of conversation, both inside and outside the home, from the beginning of the day to its end.

6:8 hand...frontlets between your eyes. The Israelite was to continually meditate upon and be directed by the commandments that God had given to him. Later in Jewish history, this phrase was taken literally and the people tied phylacteries (boxes containing these verses) to their hands and foreheads with thongs of leather.

6:10,11 the LORD your God brings you into the land. God reiterated that He was going to give Israel the Land in fulfillment of the promises that He had made to Abraham, Isaac, and Jacob, both with title and prosperity.

6:13 take oaths in His name. An oath was a solemn pledge to affirm something said as absolutely true. The invoking of the Lord's name in the oath meant that one was bound under obligation before God to fulfill that word (cf. Matt. 4:10; Luke 4:8).

6:15 a jealous God. *See note on 4:24.*

6:16 Massah. This name actually means "testing" (cf. Ex. 17:1-7; Matt. 4:7; Luke 4:12).

6:20 When your son asks you in time to come. When a young son asked the meaning of the law, his father was to use the following pattern in explaining it to him. First, the Israelites were in bondage in

son: 'We were slaves of Pharaoh in Egypt,
and the LORD brought us out of Egypt
[b]with a mighty hand; 22 and the LORD
showed signs and wonders before our
eyes, great and severe, against Egypt, Pharaoh, and all his household. 23 Then He
brought us out from there, that He might
bring us in, to give us the land of which He
[6]swore to our fathers. 24 And the LORD
commanded us to [7]observe all these [8]stat-
utes, [c]to fear the LORD our God, [d]for our
good always, that [e]He might preserve us
alive, as *it is* [9]this day. 25 Then [f]it will be
righteousness for us, if we are careful to observe all these commandments before the
LORD our God, as He has commanded us.'

A Chosen People

7 "When the LORD your God brings you
into the land which you go to [a]possess,
and has cast out many [b]nations before you,
[c]the Hittites and the Girgashites and the
Amorites and the Canaanites and the
Perizzites and the Hivites and the Jebusites, seven nations greater and mightier
than you, 2 and when the LORD your God
delivers [d]them over to you, you shall conquer them *and* utterly destroy them. [e]You
shall make no covenant with them nor
show mercy to them. 3 [f]Nor shall you
make marriages with them. You shall not
give your daughter to their son, nor take
their daughter for your son. 4 For they will
turn your sons away from following Me, to
serve other gods; [g]so the anger of the LORD
will be aroused against you and destroy
you suddenly. 5 But thus you shall deal
with them: you shall [h]destroy their altars,
and break down their *sacred* pillars, and
cut down their [1]wooden images, and burn
their carved images with fire.
6 "For you *are* a [2]holy people to the LORD
your God; [i]the LORD your God has chosen
you to be a people for Himself, a special
treasure above all the peoples on the face of
the earth. 7 The LORD did not set His [j]love
on you nor choose you because you were
more in number than any other people, for
you were [k]the least of all peoples; 8 but [l]be-
cause the LORD loves you, and because He
would keep [m]the oath which He swore to
your fathers, [n]the LORD has brought you
out with a mighty hand, and redeemed you
from the house of [3]bondage, from the hand
of Pharaoh king of Egypt.
9 "Therefore know that the LORD your
God, He *is* God, [o]the faithful God [p]who
keeps covenant and mercy for a thousand
generations with those who love Him and
keep His commandments; 10 and He repays those who hate Him to their face, to
destroy them. He will not [4]be [q]slack with
him who hates Him; He will repay him to
his face. 11 Therefore you shall keep the
commandment, the statutes, and the judgments which I command you today, to observe them.

Blessings of Obedience

12 "Then it shall come to pass, because
you listen to these judgments, and keep
and do them, that the LORD your God will
keep with you the covenant and the mercy
which He swore to your fathers. 13 And He

21 [b] Ex. 13:3
23 [6] *promised*
24 [c] Deut. 6:2 [d] Deut. 10:12, 13; Job 35:7, 8; Jer. 32:39 [e] Deut. 4:1 [7] *do* [8] *ordinances* [9] *today*
25 [f] Deut. 24:13; [Rom. 10:3, 5]

CHAPTER 7

1 [a] Deut. 6:10 [b] Gen. 15:19-21 [c] Ex. 33:2
2 [d] Num. 31:17; Deut. 20:16-18 [e] Ex. 23:32, 33; Josh. 2:14
3 [f] Ex. 34:15, 16; Josh. 23:12; 1 Kin. 11:2; Ezra 9:2
4 [g] Deut. 6:15
5 [h] Ex. 23:24; 34:13; Deut. 12:3 [1] Heb. *Asherim,* Canaanite deities
6 [i] Ex. 19:5, 6; Amos 3:2; 1 Pet. 2:9 [2] *set-apart*
7 [j] Deut. 4:37 [k] Deut. 10:22
8 [l] Deut. 10:15 [m] Luke 1:55, 72, 73 [n] Ex. 13:3, 14 [3] *slavery*
9 [o] 1 Cor. 1:9; 2 Thess. 3:3; 2 Tim. 2:13 [p] Ex. 20:6; Deut. 5:10; Neh. 1:5; Dan. 9:4
10 [q] [2 Pet. 3:9, 10] [4] *delay*

Egypt (v. 21a). Second, God miraculously delivered the Israelites and judged the Egyptians (v. 21b). Third, this work was in accord with His promise to the patriarchs (v. 23). Fourth, God gave His law to Israel that His people might obey it (vv. 24,25).

6:25 righteousness for us. A true and personal relationship with God that would be manifest in the lives of the people of God. There was no place for legalism or concern about the external since the compelling motive for this righteousness was to be love for God (v. 5).

7:1-26 This section discusses how the Israelites should relate to the inhabitants of Canaan including their destruction, the forbidding of intermarriage, and the elimination of all altars and idols. It was God's time for judgment on that land.

7:1 seven nations. These 7 groups controlled areas of land usually centered around one or more fortified cities. Together they had greater population and military strength than Israel. Six of these 7 are mentioned elsewhere (see Ex. 3:8). The unique nation here is the Girgashites, who are referred to in Gen. 10:16; Josh. 3:10; 24:11; 1 Chr. 1:14, and in Ugaritic texts. They may have been tribal people living in the N of Palestine.

7:2 utterly destroy them. All the men, women and children were to be put to death. Even though this action seems extreme, the following needs to be kept in mind: 1) the Canaanites deserved to die for their sin (9:4,5; cf. Gen. 15:16); 2) the Canaanites persisted in their hatred of God (7:10); and 3) the Canaanites constituted a moral cancer that had the potential of introducing idolatry and immorality which would spread rapidly among the Israelites (20:17,18).

7:3 Nor...make marriages. Because of the intimate nature of marriage, the idolatrous spouse could lead her mate astray (see 1 Kin. 11:1-8 for the example of Solomon).

7:5 destroy their altars. This destructive action would remove any consequent temptation for the Israelites to follow the religious practices of the nations they were to displace from the Land.

7:6 a holy people to the LORD your God. The basis for the command to destroy the Canaanites is found in God's election of Israel. God had set apart Israel for His own special use and they were His treasured possession. As God's people, Israel needed to be separated from the moral pollution of the Canaanites.

7:8 loves you...keep the oath. The choosing of Israel as a holy nation set apart for God was grounded in God's love and His faithfulness to the promises He had made to the patriarchs, not in any merit or intrinsic goodness in Israel.

7:9 a thousand generations. *See note on Deut. 1:11.*

7:12-15 The Lord promised Israel particular blessings for their obedience, which are further enumerated in 28:1-14.

7:12 the LORD your God will keep with you the covenant. If Israel was obedient to the Lord, they would experience His covenantal mercy. However, the people could forfeit the blessings of the covenant through their own disobedience.

will [r]love you and bless you and [5]multiply
you; [s]He will also bless the fruit of your
womb and the fruit of your land, your
grain and your new wine and your oil, the
increase of your cattle and the offspring of
your flock, in the land of which He [6]swore
to your fathers to give you. 14 You shall be
blessed above all peoples; there shall not
be a male or female [t]barren among you or
among your livestock. 15 And the LORD
will take away from you all sickness, and
will afflict you with none of the [u]terrible
diseases of Egypt which you have known,
but will lay *them* on all those who hate you.
16 Also you shall [7]destroy all the peoples
whom the LORD your God delivers over to
you; your eye shall have no pity on them;
nor shall you serve their gods, for that *will*
[v]*be* a snare to you.
17 "If you should say in your heart, 'These
nations are greater than I; how can I dispossess them?'— 18 you shall not be afraid of
them, *but* you shall [w]remember well what
the LORD your God did to Pharaoh and to all
Egypt: 19 [x]the great trials which your eyes
saw, the signs and the wonders, the mighty
hand and the outstretched arm, by which
the LORD your God brought you out. So
shall the LORD your God do to all the peoples of whom you are afraid. 20 [y]Moreover
the LORD your God will send the hornet
among them until those who are left, who
hide themselves from you, are destroyed.
21 You shall not be terrified of them; for the
LORD your God, the great and awesome
God, *is* among you. 22 And the LORD your
God will drive out those nations before you
[z]little by little; you will be unable to [8]destroy
them at once, lest the beasts of the field become *too* numerous for you. 23 But the LORD
your God will deliver them over to you, and
will inflict defeat upon them until they are
destroyed. 24 And [a]He will deliver their
kings into your hand, and you will destroy
their name from under heaven; [b]no one shall
be able to stand [9]against you until you have
destroyed them. 25 You shall burn the
carved images of their gods with fire; you
shall not [c]covet[1] the silver or gold *that is* on
them, nor take *it* for yourselves, lest you be
snared by it; for it *is* an abomination to the
LORD your God. 26 Nor shall you bring an
abomination into your house, lest you be
doomed to destruction like it. You shall utterly detest it and utterly abhor it, [d]for it *is*
an [2]accursed thing.

Remember the LORD Your God

8 "Every commandment which I command you today [a]you must [1]be careful
to observe, that you may live and [b]multi-
ply,[2] and go in and possess the land of
which the LORD [3]swore to your fathers.
2 And you shall remember that the LORD
your God [c]led you all the way these forty
years in the wilderness, to humble you *and*
[d]test you, [e]to know what *was* in your heart,
whether you would keep His command-
ments or not. 3 So He humbled you, [f]al-
lowed you to hunger, and [g]fed you with
manna which you did not know nor did
your fathers know, that He might make
you know that man shall [h]not live by
bread alone; but man lives by every *word*
that proceeds from the mouth of the LORD.
4 [i]Your garments did not wear out on you,
nor did your foot swell these forty years.
5 [j]You should [4]know in your heart that as
a man chastens his son, *so* the LORD your
God chastens you.

13 [r]Ps. 146:8; Prov. 15:9; John 14:21 [s]Deut. 28:4 [5]*cause you to increase* [6]*promised*
14 [t]Ex. 23:26
15 [u]Ex. 9:14; 15:26; Deut. 28:27, 60
16 [v]Ex. 23:33; Judg. 8:27; Ps. 106:36 [7]*consume*
18 [w]Ps. 105:5
19 [x]Deut. 4:34; 29:3
20 [y]Ex. 23:28; Josh. 24:12
22 [z]Ex. 23:29, 30 [8]*consume*
24 [a]Josh. 10:24, 42; 12:1-24 [b]Josh. 23:9 [9]*before*
25 [c]Prov. 23:6 [1]*desire*
26 [d]Deut. 13:17 [2]*devoted* or *banned*

CHAPTER 8

1 [a]Deut. 4:1; 6:24 [b]Deut. 30:16 [1]*observe to do* [2]*increase in number* [3]*promised*
2 [c]Deut. 1:3; 2:7; 29:5; Ps. 136:16; Amos 2:10 [d]Ex. 16:4 [e][John 2:25]
3 [f]Ex. 16:2, 3 [g]Ex. 16:12, 14, 35 [h]Matt. 4:4; Luke 4:4
4 [i]Deut. 29:5; Neh. 9:21
5 [j]2 Sam. 7:14; Ps. 89:30-33; Prov. 3:11, 12; Heb. 12:5-11; Rev. 3:19 [4]*consider*

7:13 grain…new wine…oil. These were the 3 principal food products of Palestine. "Grain" included wheat and barley. "New wine" was the grape juice as it came from the presses. The "oil" was the olive oil used in cooking and in the lamps.

7:15 the terrible diseases of Egypt. Some virulent and malignant diseases such as elephantiasis, ophthalmia, and dysentery were common in Egypt.

7:20 God will send the hornet. The hornet or wasp was a large insect, common in Canaan, that may have had a potentially fatal sting. Here the reference was probably figurative in the sense of a great army sent into panic when the Lord would inflict His sting on them (see 11:25). *See notes on Ex. 23:28.*

7:22 little by little. Even though the Lord promised that the defeat of the people of the land would be quick (4:26; 9:3), the process of settlement would be more gradual to avoid the danger of the land returning to a primitive state of natural anarchy.

7:26 You shall utterly detest it and utterly abhor it. "Detest" and "abhor" were strong words of disapproval and rejection. Israel was to have the same attitude toward the idols of the Canaanites as did God Himself. **it *is* an accursed thing.** The images or idols were to be set aside for destruction.

8:2 remember. The people were to recall what God had done for them (cf. 5:15; 7:18; 8:18; 9:7; 15:15; 16:3,12; 24:9,18; 25:17), and not forget (cf. 4:9,23,31; 6:12; 8:11,14,19; 9:7; 25:19; 26:13). **to know what *was* in your heart.** Israel's 40 years in the wilderness was a time of God's affliction and testing so that the basic attitude of the people toward God and His commandments could be made known. God chose to sustain His hungry people in the wilderness by a means previously unknown to them. Through this miraculous provision, God both humbled the people and tested their obedience.

8:3 manna which you did not know. God sustained the people in the wilderness with a food previously unknown to them. See Ex. 16:15 for the beginning of the giving of the manna and Josh. 5:12 for its cessation. **man shall not live by bread alone.** Israel's food in the wilderness was decreed by the Word of God. They had manna because it came by God's command; therefore, ultimately it was not bread that kept them alive, but God's Word (cf. Matt. 4:4; Luke 4:4).

8:4 Your garments did not wear out. This miraculous provision is also mentioned in 29:5.

8:5 the LORD your God chastens you. Israel's sojourn in the wilderness was viewed as a time of God's discipline of His children. He was seeking to correct their wayward attitude so that they might be prepared to obediently go into the Land.

6 "Therefore you shall keep the commandments of the LORD your God, [k]to
walk in His ways and to fear Him. 7 For
the LORD your God is bringing you into a
good land, [l]a land of brooks of water, of
fountains and springs, that flow out of valleys and hills; 8 a land of wheat and barley,
of vines and fig trees and pomegranates, a
land of olive oil and honey; 9 a land in
which you will eat bread without scarcity,
in which you will lack nothing; a land
whose stones *are* iron and out of whose
hills you can dig copper. 10 [m]When you
have eaten and are full, then you shall
bless the LORD your God for the good land
which He has given you.
11 "Beware that you do not forget the
LORD your God by not keeping His commandments, His judgments, and His
statutes which I command you today,
12 [n]lest—*when* you have eaten and are
[5]full, and have built beautiful houses and
dwell *in them;* 13 and *when* your herds and
your flocks multiply, and your silver and
your gold are [6]multiplied, and all that you
have is multiplied; 14 [o]when your heart [7]is
lifted up, and you [p]forget the LORD your
God who brought you out of the land of
Egypt, from the house of bondage; 15 who
[q]led you through that great and terrible
wilderness, [r]*in which were* fiery serpents
and scorpions and thirsty land where there
was no water; [s]who brought water for you
out of the flinty rock; 16 who fed you in the
wilderness with [t]manna, which your fathers did not know, that He might humble
you and that He might test you, [u]to do you
good in the end— 17 then you say in your
heart, 'My power and the might of my
hand have gained me this wealth.'
18 "And you shall remember the LORD
your God, [v]for *it is* He who gives you
power to get wealth, [w]that He may [8]estab-
lish His covenant which He swore to your
fathers, as *it is* this day. 19 Then it shall be,
if you by any means forget the LORD your
God, and follow other gods, and serve
them and worship them, [x]I testify against
you this day that you shall surely perish.
20 As the nations which the LORD destroys
before you, [y]so you shall perish, because
you would not be obedient to the voice of
the LORD your God.

Israel's Rebellions Reviewed

9 "Hear, O Israel: You *are* to cross over
the Jordan today, and go in to dispossess nations greater and mightier than
yourself, cities great and fortified up to
heaven, 2 a people great and tall, the [a]de-
scendants of the Anakim, whom you
know, and *of whom* you heard *it said,* 'Who
can stand before the descendants of Anak?'
3 Therefore understand today that the
LORD your God *is* He who [b]goes over before you *as* a [c]consuming fire. [d]He will destroy them and bring them down before
you; [e]so you shall drive them out and destroy them quickly, as the LORD has said to
you.
4 [f]"Do not think in your heart, after the
LORD your God has cast them out before
you, saying, 'Because of my righteousness
the LORD has brought me in to possess this

6 [k][Deut. 5:33]
7 [l]Deut. 11:9-12; Jer. 2:7
10 [m]Deut. 6:11, 12
12 [n]Deut. 28:47; Prov. 30:9; Hos. 13:6 [5]*satisfied*
13 [6]*increased*
14 [o]1 Cor. 4:7 [p]Deut. 8:11; Ps. 106:21 [7]*becomes proud*
15 [q]Is. 63:12-14 [r]Num. 21:6 [s]Ex. 17:6; Num. 20:11
16 [t]Ex. 16:15 [u]Jer. 24:5, 6; [Heb. 12:11]
18 [v]Prov. 10:22; Hos. 2:8 [w]Deut. 7:8, 12 [8]*confirm*
19 [x]Deut. 4:26; 30:18
20 [y][Dan. 9:11, 12]

CHAPTER 9

2 [a]Num. 13:22, 28, 33; Josh. 11:21, 22
3 [b]Deut. 1:33; 31:3; Josh. 3:11; 5:14; John 10:4 [c]Deut. 4:24; Heb. 12:29 [d]Deut. 7:24 [e]Ex. 23:31
4 [f]Deut. 8:17; [Rom. 11:6, 20; 1 Cor. 4:4, 7]

8:6-10 An extensive description of God's abundant blessings for Israel in the Land (cf. 7:7-9).

8:7 a good land. In contrast to the desolation of the wilderness, vv. 7-9 describe the abundance of Israel's new land.

8:9 iron...copper. The mountains of southern Lebanon and the region E of the Sea of Galilee and S of the Dead Sea contained iron. Both copper and iron were found in the Rift Valley S of the Dead Sea.

8:11 do not forget the LORD your God. Sufficient food would lead to the satisfaction of Israel in the Land (vv. 10,12). This satisfaction and security could lead to Israel forgetting God. Forgetting God means no longer having Him in the daily thoughts of one's life. This forgetfulness would lead to a disobedience of His commandments. Whereas, in the wilderness, Israel had to depend on God for the necessities of life, in the rich land there would be a tempting sense of self-sufficiency.

8:14 when your heart is lifted up. Pride was viewed as the root of forgetfulness. In their prosperity, the people might claim that their power and strength had produced their wealth (v. 17).

8:15 water...out of the...rock. Cf. Num. 20:9-13.

8:16 to do you good in the end. God designed the test of the wilderness so that Israel might be disciplined to obey Him. Through her obedience, she received the blessing of the Land. Thus, God's design was to do good for Israel at the end of the process.

8:18,19 *See notes on Deut. 4:25-31.*

8:19 if you by any means forget. Forgetting God would lead to worshiping other gods, which in turn would result in certain destruction. As God destroyed the Canaanites for their idolatry, so also would He judge Israel.

9:1–10:1 This part of Moses' speech rehearses the sins of the Israelites at Horeb (cf. Ex. 32).

9:2 the Anakim. Moses remembered the people's shock when they heard the original report of the 12 spies concerning the size, strength, and number of the inhabitants of Canaan (Num. 13:26–14:6). Therefore, He emphasized that from a purely military and human point of view, their victory was impossible. The fear of the spies and the people focused on the Anakim, a tall, strong people who lived in the land of Canaan (*see note on 1:28*).

9:3 a consuming fire. The Lord was pictured as a fire which burned everything in its path. So the Lord would go over into Canaan and exterminate Canaanites. **destroy them quickly.** Israel was to be the human agent of the Lord's destruction of the Canaanites. The military strength of the Canaanites would be destroyed quickly (see Josh. 6:1–11:23), though the complete subjugation of the Land would take time (see 7:22; Josh. 13:1).

9:4 Because of my righteousness. Three times in vv. 4-6, Moses emphasized that the victory was not because of Israel's goodness, but was entirely the work of God. It was the wickedness of the Canaanites that led to their expulsion from the land (cf. Rom. 10:6).

land'; but *it is* [g]because of the wickedness
of these nations *that* the LORD is driving
them out from before you. **5** [h]*It is* not because of your righteousness or the uprightness of your heart *that* you go in to
possess their land, but because of the
wickedness of these nations *that* the LORD
your God drives them out from before
you, and that He may [1]fulfill the [i]word
which the LORD swore to your fathers, to
Abraham, Isaac, and Jacob. **6** Therefore
understand that the LORD your God is not
giving you this good land to possess because of your righteousness, for you *are* a
[j]stiff-necked[2] people.
7 "Remember! Do not forget how you
[k]provoked the LORD your God to wrath in
the wilderness. [l]From the day that you departed from the land of Egypt until you
came to this place, you have been rebellious against the LORD. **8** Also [m]in Horeb
you provoked the LORD to wrath, so that
the LORD was angry *enough* with you to
have destroyed you. **9** [n]When I went up
into the mountain to receive the tablets of
stone, the tablets of the covenant which
the LORD made with you, then I stayed on
the mountain forty days and [o]forty nights.
I neither ate bread nor drank water.
10 [p]Then the LORD delivered to me two
tablets of stone written with the finger of
God, and on them *were* all the words
which the LORD had spoken to you on the
mountain from the midst of the fire [q]in[3]
the day of the assembly. **11** And it came to
pass, at the end of forty days and forty
nights, *that* the LORD gave me the two
tablets of stone, the tablets of the
covenant.
12 "Then the LORD said to me, [r]'Arise, go
down quickly from here, for your people
whom you brought out of Egypt have
acted corruptly; they have [s]quickly turned
aside from the way which I commanded
them; they have made themselves a molded image.'
13 "Furthermore [t]the LORD spoke to me,
saying, 'I have seen this people, and indeed [u]they are a [4]stiff-necked people.
14 [v]Let Me alone, that I may destroy them
and [w]blot out their name from under heav-
en; [x]and I will make of you a nation mightier and greater than they.'
15 [y]"So I turned and came down from
the mountain, and [z]the mountain burned
with fire; and the two tablets of the
covenant *were* in my two hands. **16** And [a]I
looked, and behold, you had sinned
against the LORD your God—had made
for yourselves a molded calf! You had
turned aside quickly from the way which
the LORD had commanded you. **17** Then I
took the two tablets and threw them out
of my two hands and [b]broke them before
your eyes. **18** And I [c]fell[5] down before the
LORD, as at the first, forty days and forty
nights; I neither ate bread nor drank
water, because of all your sin which you
committed in doing wickedly in the sight
of the LORD, to provoke Him to anger.
19 [d]For I was afraid of the anger and hot
displeasure with which the LORD was
angry with you, to destroy you. [e]But the
LORD listened to me at that time also.
20 And the LORD was very angry with
Aaron *and* would have destroyed him; so
I prayed for Aaron also at the same time.
21 Then I took your sin, the calf which you
had made, and burned it with fire and
crushed it *and* ground *it* very small, until
it was as fine as dust; and I [f]threw its dust
into the brook that descended from the
mountain.
22 "Also at [g]Taberah and [h]Massah and
[i]Kibroth Hattaavah you [6]provoked the
LORD to wrath. **23** Likewise, [j]when the
LORD sent you from Kadesh Barnea, saying, 'Go up and possess the land which I
have given you,' then you rebelled against
the commandment of the LORD your God,
and [k]you did not believe Him nor obey His

4 [g]Gen. 15:16; Lev. 18:3, 24-30; Deut. 12:31; 18:9-14
5 [h][Titus 3:5] [i]Gen. 50:24 [1]*perform*
6 [j]Ex. 34:9; Deut. 31:27 [2]*stubborn* or *rebellious*
7 [k]Num. 14:22 [l]Ex. 14:11
8 [m]Ex. 32:1-8; Ps. 106:19
9 [n]Ex. 24:12, 15; Deut. 5:2-22 [o]Ex. 24:18
10 [p]Ex. 31:18; Deut. 4:13 [q]Ex. 19:17 [3]*when you were all gathered together*
12 [r]Ex. 32:7, 8 [s]Deut. 31:29
13 [t]Ex. 32:9 [u]Deut. 9:6 [4]*stubborn* or *rebellious*
14 [v]Ex. 32:10 [w]Deut. 29:20 [x]Num. 14:12
15 [y]Ex. 32:15-19 [z]Ex. 19:18
16 [a]Ex. 32:19
17 [b]Ex. 32:19
18 [c]Ex. 34:28; Ps. 106:23 [5]*prostrated myself*
19 [d]Ex. 32:10, 11; Heb. 12:21 [e]Ex. 32:14
21 [f]Ex. 32:20
22 [g]Num. 11:1, 3 [h]Ex. 17:7 [i]Num. 11:4, 34 [6]*caused the LORD to be angry*
23 [j]Num. 13:3 [k]Ps. 106:24, 25

9:6 a stiff-necked people. Lit. "hard of neck." A figurative expression for the stubborn, intractable, obdurate, and unbending attitude of Israel. In vv. 7-29, Moses illustrated Israel's rebellious attitude and actions toward the Lord.

9:7 Remember! Moses challenged Israel to call to mind the long history of their stubbornness and provocation of God which had extended from the time of the Exodus from Egypt for 40 years until the present moment on the Plains of Moab.

9:10 the finger of God. God Himself had written the Ten Commandments on the two tablets of stone at Mt. Sinai (see Ex. 31:18).

9:14 blot out their name from under heaven. God threatened to destroy the people of Israel so completely that He pictured it as an obliteration of all memory of them from the world of men. This threat was taken by Moses as an invitation to intercede for the children of Israel (Num. 14:11-19).

9:19 Cf. Heb. 12:21.

9:20 I prayed for Aaron. Moses interceded on behalf of Aaron, on whom the immediate responsibility for the Israelites' sin of the golden calf rested. Aaron had thus incurred the wrath of God, and his life was in danger (see Ex. 32:1-6). This is the only verse in the Pentateuch which specifically states that Moses prayed for Aaron.

9:22 Taberah...Massah...Kibroth Hattaavah. These 3 places were all associated with Israel's rebellion against the Lord. Taberah, "burning," was where the people had complained of their misfortunes (Num. 11:1-3). At Massah, "testing," they had found fault with everything and in presumption had put God to the test (Ex. 17:1-7). At Kibroth Hattaavah, "graves of craving," the people had again incurred God's anger by complaining about their food (Num. 11:31-35).

9:23 Kadesh Barnea. There they sinned by both lack of faith in God and disobedience (cf. Num. 13,14).

voice. 24 [l]You have been rebellious against
the LORD from the day that I knew you.
25 [m]"Thus I [7]prostrated myself before the
LORD; forty days and forty nights I kept
prostrating myself, because the LORD had
said He would destroy you. 26 Therefore I
prayed to the LORD, and said: 'O Lord GOD,
do not destroy Your people and [n]Your inheritance whom You have redeemed
through Your greatness, whom You have
brought out of Egypt with a mighty hand.
27 Remember Your servants, Abraham,
Isaac, and Jacob; do not look on the stubbornness of this people, or on their wickedness or their sin, 28 lest the land from which
You brought us should say, "Because the
LORD was not able to bring them to the land
which He promised them, and because He
hated them, He has brought them out to
kill them in the wilderness." 29 Yet they *are*
Your people and Your inheritance, whom
You brought out by Your mighty power
and by Your outstretched arm.'

The Second Pair of Tablets

10 "At that time the LORD said to me,
[1]'Hew for yourself two tablets of
stone like the first, and come up to Me on
the mountain and make yourself an [a]ark of
wood. 2 And I will write on the tablets the
words that were on the first tablets, which
you broke; and [b]you shall put them in the
ark.'
3 "So I made an ark of acacia wood,
hewed two tablets of stone like the first,
and went up the mountain, having the two
tablets in my hand. 4 And He wrote on the
tablets according to the first writing, the
Ten [2]Commandments, [c]which the LORD
had spoken to you in the mountain from
the midst of the fire in the day of the assembly; and the LORD gave them to me.
5 Then I turned and [d]came down from the
mountain, and [e]put the tablets in the ark
which I had made; [f]and there they are, just
as the LORD commanded me."
6 (Now the children of Israel journeyed
from the wells of Bene Jaakan to Moserah,
where Aaron [g]died, and where he was
buried; and Eleazar his son ministered as
priest in his [3]stead. 7 [h]From there they journeyed to Gudgodah, and from Gudgodah
to Jotbathah, a land of [4]rivers of water. 8 At
that time [i]the LORD [5]separated the tribe of
Levi [j]to bear the ark of the covenant of the
LORD, [k]to stand before the LORD to minister
to Him and [l]to bless in His name, to this
day. 9 [m]Therefore Levi has no portion nor
inheritance with his brethren; the LORD *is*
his inheritance, just as the LORD your God
promised him.)
10 "As at the first time, [n]I stayed in the
mountain forty days and forty nights; [o]the
LORD also heard me at that time, *and*
the LORD chose not to destroy you. 11 [p]Then
the LORD said to me, 'Arise, begin *your* journey before the people, that they may go in
and possess the land which I swore to their
fathers to give them.'

The Essence of the Law

12 "And now, Israel, [q]what does the
LORD your God require of you, but to fear
the LORD your God, to walk in all His ways
and to [r]love Him, to serve the LORD your
God with all your heart and with all your
soul, 13 *and* to keep the commandments of
the LORD and His statutes which I com-

24 [l]Deut. 9:7; 31:27
25 [m]Deut. 9:18 [7]*fell down*
26 [n]Deut. 32:9

CHAPTER 10

1 [a]Ex. 25:10 [1]*Cut out*
2 [b]Ex. 25:16, 21
4 [c]Ex. 20:1; 34:28 [2]Lit. *Words*
5 [d]Ex. 34:29 [e]Ex. 40:20 [f]1 Kin. 8:9
6 [g]Num. 20:25-28; 33:38 [3]*place*
7 [h]Num. 33:32-34 [4]*brooks*
8 [i]Num. 3:6 [j]Num. 4:5, 15; 10:21 [k]Deut. 18:5 [l]Num. 6:23 [5]*set apart*
9 [m]Num. 18:20, 24; Deut. 18:1, 2; Ezek. 44:28
10 [n]Ex. 34:28; Deut. 9:18 [o]Ex. 32:14
11 [p]Ex. 33:1
12 [q]Mic. 6:8 [r]Deut. 6:5; Matt. 22:37; 1 Tim. 1:5

9:24 You have been rebellious against the LORD. Moses concluded that his dealings with Israel as God's mediator had been one of continual rebellion on Israel's part, which led to his intercession (vv. 25-29).

9:28 the land from which You brought us. Moses' prayer of intercession to the Lord on behalf of Israel appealed to the Lord to forgive His people because the Egyptians could have interpreted God's destruction of Israel as His inability to fulfill His promise and His hate for His people.

10:1-3 two tablets of stone like the first. God had listened to Moses' intercession and dealt mercifully with the Israelites who had broken the covenant by rewriting the Ten Commandments on two tablets prepared for that purpose by Moses. The second tablets were made of the same material and were the same size as the first.

10:1 an ark of wood. This refers to the ark of the covenant. Moses telescoped the events in these verses. Later, at the construction of the ark of the covenant, Moses placed the two new stone tablets within that ark (see Ex. 37:1-9).

10:6-9 These verses show that the priesthood of Aaron and service of the Levites was restored after the incident of the golden calf.

10:6 Moserah, where Aaron died. Aaron was not killed at Sinai, but lived until the 40th year of the Exodus, which shows the effectiveness of Moses' intercession before the Lord (cf. Num. 20:22-29; 33:38,39). After Aaron's death, the priestly ministry continued in the appointment of Eleazar. Moserah is the district in which Mt. Hor stands, on which Aaron died (cf. Num. 20:27,28; 33:38).

10:8 At that time. This refers to the time that Israel was at Mt. Sinai.

10:9 no portion. The family of Levi received no inheritance in the land of Canaan (see Num. 18:20,24).

10:10,11 Because of Moses' intercession, not because of their righteousness, the Israelites were encamped on the banks of the Jordan, ready to enter the Promised Land.

10:12,13 what does the LORD your God require of you...? This rhetorical question led into Moses' statement of the 5 basic requirements that God expected of His people (cf. Mic. 6:8): 1) **to fear the LORD your God.** To hold God in awe and submit to Him; 2) **to walk in all His ways.** To conduct life in accordance with the will of God; 3) **to love Him.** To choose to set one's affections on the Lord and on Him alone; 4) **to serve the LORD your God.** To have the worship of the Lord as the central focus of life; 5) **to keep the commandments of the LORD.** To obey the requirements the Lord had imposed.

mand you today [s]for your [6]good? **14** Indeed heaven and the highest heavens belong to the [t]LORD your God, *also* the earth with all that *is* in it. **15** The LORD delighted only in your fathers, to love them; and He chose their [7]descendants after them, you above all peoples, as *it is* this day. **16** Therefore circumcise the foreskin of your [u]heart, and be [v]stiff-necked[8] no longer. **17** For the LORD your God *is* [w]God of gods and [x]Lord of lords, the great God, [y]mighty and awesome, who [z]shows no partiality nor takes a bribe. **18** [a]He administers justice for the fatherless and the widow, and loves the stranger, giving him food and clothing. **19** Therefore love the stranger, for you were strangers in the land of Egypt. **20** [b]You shall fear the LORD your God; you shall serve Him, and to Him you shall hold fast, and take oaths in His name. **21** He *is* your praise, and He *is* your God, who has done for you these great and awesome things which your eyes have seen. **22** Your fathers went down to Egypt with seventy persons, and now the LORD your God has made you as the stars of heaven in multitude.

Love and Obedience Rewarded

11 "Therefore you shall love the LORD your God, and keep His charge, His statutes, His judgments, and His commandments always. **2** Know today that *I do* not *speak* with your children, who have not known and who have not seen the [1]chastening of the LORD your God, His greatness and His mighty hand and His outstretched arm— **3** His signs and His acts which He did in the midst of Egypt, to Pharaoh king of Egypt, and to all his land; **4** what He did to the army of Egypt, to their horses and their chariots: [a]how He made the waters of the Red Sea overflow them as they pursued you, and *how* the LORD has destroyed them to this day; **5** what He did for you in the wilderness until you came to this place; **6** and [b]what He did to Dathan and Abiram the sons of Eliab, the son of Reuben: how the earth opened its mouth and swallowed them up, their households, their tents, and all the substance that *was* [2]in their possession, in the midst of all Israel— **7** but your eyes have [c]seen every great [3]act of the LORD which He did.

8 "Therefore you shall keep every commandment which I command you today, that you may [d]be strong, and go in and possess the land which you cross over to possess, **9** and [e]that you may prolong *your* days in the land [f]which the LORD [4]swore to give your fathers, to them and their descendants, [g]'a land flowing with milk and honey.' **10** For the land which you go to possess *is* not like the land of Egypt from which you have come, where you sowed your seed and watered *it* by foot, as a vegetable garden; **11** [h]but the land which you cross over to possess *is* a land of hills and valleys, which drinks water from the rain of heaven, **12** a land for which the LORD your God cares; [i]the eyes of the LORD your God *are* always on it, from the beginning of the year to the very end of the year.

13 'And it shall be that if you earnestly [5]obey My commandments which I command you today, to love the LORD your God and serve Him with all your heart and with all your soul, **14** then [j]I[6] will give *you* the rain for your land in its season, [k]the

13 [s]Deut. 6:24 [6]*benefit or welfare*
14 [t][Neh. 9:6; Ps. 68:33; 115:16]
15 [7]Lit. *seed*
16 [u]Lev. 26:41; Deut. 30:6; Jer. 4:4; Rom. 2:28, 29 [v]Deut. 9:6, 13 [8]*rebellious*
17 [w]Deut. 4:35, 39; Is. 44:8; 46:9; Dan. 2:47; 1 Cor. 8:5, 6 [x]Rev. 19:16 [y]Deut. 7:21 [z]Acts 10:34
18 [a]Ex. 22:22-24; Ps. 68:5; 146:9
20 [b]Matt. 4:10

CHAPTER 11

2 [1]*discipline*
4 [a]Ex. 14:28; Ps. 106:11
6 [b]Num. 16:1-35; Ps. 106:16-18 [2]*at their feet*
7 [c]Deut. 10:21; 29:2 [3]*work*
8 [d]Deut. 31:6, 7, 23; Josh. 1:6, 7
9 [e]Deut. 4:40; 5:16, 33; 6:2; Prov. 10:27 [f]Deut. 9:5 [g]Ex. 3:8 [4]*promised*
11 [h]Deut. 8:7
12 [i]1 Kin. 9:3
13 [5]Lit. *listen to*
14 [j]Lev. 26:4; Deut. 28:12 [k]Joel 2:23; James 5:7 [6]So with MT, Tg.; Sam., LXX, Vg. *He*

10:14,15 God, with the same sovereignty by which He controls all things, had chosen the patriarchs and the nation of Israel to be His special people.

10:16 Therefore circumcise...your heart. Moses called the Israelites to cut away all the sin in their hearts, as the circumcision surgery cut away the skin. This would leave them with a clean relationship to God (cf. 30:6; Lev. 26:40,41; Jer. 4:4; 9:25; Rom. 2:29). *See note on Jer. 4:4.*

10:18 He administers justice. The sovereign, authoritative God is also impartial (v. 17), as seen in His concern for the orphan, the widow, and the alien (cf. Lev. 19:9-18; James 1:27).

10:20 to Him you shall hold fast. The verb means "to stick to," "to cling to," or "to hold onto." As a husband is to be united to his wife (Gen. 2:24), so Israel was to cling intimately to her God.

10:22 seventy persons. See Ex. 1:5. One of the great and awesome things God had done for Israel was multiplying the 70 people who went to Egypt into a nation of over two million people.

11:2 your children. Moses distinguished between the adults and the children in his audience. The adults were those who had seen the Exodus from Egypt as children and had experienced the Lord's discipline in the wilderness. It was to these adults that Moses could say, "your eyes have seen every great act of the Lord which He did" (v. 7). It was that specially blessed generation of adults that were called to pass on the teaching of what they had learned to their children (v. 19).

11:6 Dathan and Abiram. These two sons of Eliab, of the tribe of Reuben, had rebelled against the authority of Moses, the Lord's chosen leader. The basis of their complaint was that Moses had brought Israel out of Egypt, a fertile and prosperous land, and not brought them into Canaan. Because of their rebellion against Moses, God had judged them by having the earth open and swallow them up (see Num. 16:12-14,25-27,31-33). God's judgment of their rebellion was spoken of here by Moses in the context of his contrast between the land of Egypt and the land of Canaan (vv. 10-12).

11:10,11 the land which you go to possess. The land of Canaan was different from Egypt. The land of Egypt depended upon the Nile River for its fertility. By contrast, the land of Canaan depended upon the rains that came from heaven for its fertility.

11:10 watered *it* by foot. Probably a reference to carrying water to each garden or the practice of indenting the ground with foot-dug channels through which irrigating water would flow.

11:13 Cf. 6:5.

11:14 I will give *you* the rain for your land. Since the land of Canaan was dependent upon the rainfall for its fertility, God promised in response to Israel's obedience to give them the rain necessary for

early rain and the latter rain, that you may gather in your grain, your new wine, and your oil. **15** [l]And I will send grass in your fields for your livestock, that you may [m]eat and be [7]filled.' **16** Take heed to yourselves, [n]lest your heart be deceived, and you turn aside and [o]serve other gods and worship them, **17** lest [p]the LORD's anger be aroused against you, and He [q]shut up the heavens so that there be no rain, and the land yield no produce, and [r]you perish quickly from the good land which the LORD is giving you.

18 "Therefore [s]you shall [8]lay up these words of mine in your heart and in your [t]soul, and [u]bind them as a sign on your hand, and they shall be as frontlets between your eyes. **19** [v]You shall teach them to your children, speaking of them when you sit in your house, when you walk by the way, when you lie down, and when you rise up. **20** [w]And you shall write them on the doorposts of your house and on your gates, **21** that [x]your days and the days of your children may be multiplied in the land of which the LORD swore to your fathers to give them, like [y]the days of the heavens above the earth.

22 "For if [z]you carefully keep all these commandments which I command you to do—to love the LORD your God, to walk in all His ways, and [a]to hold fast to Him— **23** then the LORD will [b]drive out all these nations from before you, and you will [c]dispossess greater and mightier nations than yourselves. **24** [d]Every place on which the sole of your foot treads shall be yours: [e]from the wilderness and Lebanon, from the river, the River Euphrates, even to the [9]Western Sea, shall be your territory. **25** No man shall be able to [f]stand [1]against you; the LORD your God will put the [g]dread of you and the fear of you upon all the land where you tread, just as He has said to you.

26 [h]"Behold, I set before you today a blessing and a curse: **27** [i]the blessing, if you obey the commandments of the LORD your God which I command you today; **28** and the [j]curse, if you do not obey the commandments of the LORD your God, but turn aside from the way which I command you today, to go after other gods which you have not known. **29** Now it shall be, when the LORD your God has brought you into the land which you go to possess, that you shall put the [k]blessing on Mount Gerizim and the [l]curse on Mount Ebal. **30** *Are* they not on the other side of the Jordan, toward the setting sun, in the land of the Canaanites who dwell in the plain opposite Gilgal, [m]beside the terebinth trees of Moreh? **31** For you will cross over the Jordan and go in to possess the land which the LORD your God is giving you, and you will possess it and dwell in it. **32** And you shall be careful to observe all the statutes and judgments which I set before you today.

A Prescribed Place of Worship

12 "These [a]*are* the statutes and judgments which you shall be careful to observe in the land which the LORD God of your fathers is giving you to possess, [b]all [1] the days that you live on the earth. **2** [c]You shall utterly destroy all the places where the nations which you shall dispossess served their gods, [d]on the high mountains and on the hills and under every green

15 [l]Ps. 104:14 [m]Deut. 6:11; Joel 2:19 [7]*satisfied*
16 [n]Deut. 29:18; Job 31:27 [o]Deut. 8:19
17 [p]Deut. 6:15; 9:19 [q]Deut. 28:24; 1 Kin. 8:35; 2 Chr. 6:26; 7:13 [r]Deut. 4:26; 2 Chr. 36:14-20
18 [s]Deut. 6:6-9 [t]Ps. 119:2, 34 [u]Deut. 6:8 [8]Lit. *put*
19 [v]Deut. 4:9, 10; 6:7; Prov. 22:6
20 [w]Deut. 6:9
21 [x]Deut. 4:40 [y]Ps. 72:5; 89:29; Prov. 3:2; 4:10; 9:11
22 [z]Deut. 11:1 [a]Deut. 10:20
23 [b]Deut. 4:38 [c]Deut. 9:1
24 [d]Josh. 1:3; 14:9 [e]Gen. 15:18; Ex. 23:31; Deut. 1:7, 8
[9]Mediterranean
25 [f]Deut. 7:24 [g]Ex. 23:27; Deut. 2:25; Josh. 2:9-11 [1]*before*
26 [h]Deut. 30:1, 15, 19
27 [i]Deut. 28:1-14
28 [j]Deut. 28:15-68
29 [k]Deut. 27:12, 13; Josh. 8:33 [l]Deut. 27:13-26
30 [m]Gen. 12:6

CHAPTER 12

1 [a]Deut. 6:1 [b]Deut. 4:9, 10; 1 Kin. 8:40 [1]As long as
2 [c]Ex. 34:13 [d]2 Kin. 16:4; 17:10, 11

that fertility (vv. 16,17). **the early rain and the latter rain.** The early rain was the autumn rain from Oct. to Jan. The latter rain was the spring rain which came through Mar./Apr.

11:18-21 For the children and all subsequent generations, God's great acts had not been seen "with their own eyes," as had been the case for that first generation. God's acts were to be "seen" for them in the Word of Scripture. It was to be in Moses' words that the acts of God would be put before the eyes of their children. The first priority, therefore, was given to Scripture as the means of teaching the law and grace of God (cf. Deut. 6:6-9).

11:24 Every place...your foot treads. In response to the obedience of Israel (vv. 22,23), the Lord promised to give to Israel all of the land they personally traversed to the extent of the boundaries that He had given. This same promise was repeated in Josh. 1:3-5. Had Israel obeyed God faithfully, her boundaries would have been enlarged to fulfill the promise made to Abraham (Gen. 15:18). But because of Israel's disobedience, the complete promise of the whole land still remains, to be fulfilled in the future kingdom of Messiah (cf. Ezek. 36:8-38).

11:26-32 As a final motive for driving home the importance of obedience and trust in God, Moses gave instruction for a ceremony which the people were to carry out when they entered the Land. They were to read the blessings and the curses of the covenant on Mt. Gerizim and Mt. Ebal (see 27:1-14) as they actually would do later (Josh. 8:30-35).

12:1–26:19 Having delineated the general principles of Israel's relationship with the Lord (5:1–11:32), Moses then explained specific laws that would help the people subordinate every area of their lives to the Lord. These instructions were given for Israel "to observe in the land" (12:1).

12:1–16:17 The first specific instructions that Moses gives deal with the public worship of the Lord by Israel as they come into the Land.

12:1-32 Moses begins by repeating his instructions concerning what to do with the false worship centers after Israel had taken possession of the land of the Canaanites (see 7:1-6). They were to destroy them completely.

12:2 the high mountains...hills...every green tree. The Canaanite sanctuaries to be destroyed were located in places believed to have particular religious significance. The mountain or hill was thought to be the home of a god and by ascending the mountain, the worshiper was in some symbolic sense closer to the deity. Certain trees were considered to be sacred and symbolized fertility, a dominant theme in Canaanite religion.

tree. 3 And [e]you shall destroy their altars,
break their *sacred* pillars, and burn their
[2]wooden images with fire; you shall cut
down the carved images of their gods and
destroy their names from that place. 4 You
shall not [f]worship the LORD your God *with*
such *things*.
5 "But you shall seek the [g]place where
the LORD your God chooses, out of all your
tribes, to put His name for His [h]dwelling[3]
place; and there you shall go. 6 [i]There you
shall take your burnt offerings, your sacrifices, your tithes, the heave offerings of
your hand, your vowed offerings, your
freewill offerings, and the [j]firstborn of
your herds and flocks. 7 And [k]there you
shall eat before the LORD your God, and
[l]you shall rejoice in [4]all to which you have
put your hand, you and your households,
in which the LORD your God has blessed
you.
8 "You shall not at all do as we are doing
here today—[m]every man doing whatever
is right in his own eyes— 9 for as yet you
have not come to the [n]rest[5] and the inheritance which the LORD your God is giving
you. 10 But *when* you cross over the Jordan
and dwell in the land which the LORD your
God is giving you to inherit, and He gives
you [o]rest from all your enemies round
about, so that you dwell in safety, 11 then
there will be the place where the LORD
your God chooses to make His name
abide. There you shall bring all that I command you: your burnt offerings, your sacrifices, your tithes, the heave offerings of
your hand, and all your choice offerings
which you vow to the LORD. 12 And [p]you
shall rejoice before the LORD your God, you
and your sons and your daughters, your
male and female servants, and the [q]Levite
who *is* within your gates, since he has no
portion nor inheritance with you. 13 Take
heed to yourself that you do not offer your
burnt offerings in every place that you see;
14 but in the place which the LORD chooses,
in one of your tribes, there you shall offer
your burnt offerings, and there you shall
do all that I command you.
15 "However, [r]you may slaughter and
eat meat within all your gates, whatever
your heart desires, according to the blessing of the LORD your God which He has
given you; [s]the unclean and the clean may
eat of it, [t]of the gazelle and the deer alike.
16 [u]Only you shall not eat the blood; you
shall pour it on the earth like water. 17 You
may not eat within your gates the tithe of
your grain or your new wine or your oil,
of the firstborn of your herd or your flock,
of any of your offerings which you vow, of
your freewill offerings, or of the [6]heave offering of your hand. 18 But you must eat
them before the LORD your God in the
place which the LORD your God chooses,
you and your son and your daughter, your
male servant and your female servant, and
the Levite who *is* within your gates; and
you shall rejoice before the LORD your God
in [7]all to which you put your hands.
19 [8]Take heed to yourself that you do not
forsake the Levite as long as you live in
your land.
20 "When the LORD your God [v]enlarges
your border as He has promised you, and
you say, 'Let me eat meat,' because you
long to eat meat, you may eat as much
meat as your heart desires. 21 If the place
where the LORD your God chooses to put
His name is too far from [w]you, then you
may slaughter from your herd and from
your flock which the LORD has given you,
just as I have commanded you, and you
may eat within your gates as much as your
heart desires. 22 Just as the gazelle and the
deer are eaten, so you may eat them; the

3 [e]Num. 33:52; Deut. 7:5; Judg. 2:2 [2]Heb. *Asherim*
4 [f]Deut. 12:31
5 [g]Ex. 20:24 [h]Ex. 15:13; 1 Sam. 2:29 [3]*home*
6 [i]Lev. 17:3, 4 [j]Deut. 14:23
7 [k]Deut. 14:26 [l]Deut. 12:12, 18 [4]*all that you undertake*
8 [m]Judg. 17:6; 21:25
9 [n]Deut. 3:20; 25:19; Ps. 95:11 [5]*Or place of rest*
10 [o]Josh. 11:23
12 [p]Deut. 12:18; 26:11 [q]Deut. 10:9; 14:29
15 [r]Deut. 12:21 [s]Deut. 12:22 [t]Deut. 14:5
16 [u]Gen. 9:4; Lev. 7:26; 17:10-12; 1 Sam. 14:33; Acts 15:20, 29
17 [6]*contribution*
18 [7]*all your undertakings*
19 [8]*Be careful*
20 [v]Gen. 15:18; Ex. 34:24; Deut. 11:24; 19:8
21 [w]Deut. 14:24

12:3 their altars,...pillars,...wooden images...carved images. These were elements of Canaanite worship, which included human sacrifice (v. 31). If they remained, the people might mix the worship of God with those places (v. 4).

12:5 the place where the LORD your God chooses. Cf. vv. 10,18,21. Various places of worship were chosen after the people settled in Canaan, such as Mt. Ebal (27:1-8; Josh. 8:30-35), Shechem (Josh. 24:1-28) and Shiloh (Josh. 18:1), which was the center of worship through the period of Judges (Judg. 21:19). The tabernacle, the Lord's dwelling place, was located in Canaan, where the Lord chose to dwell. The central importance of the tabernacle was in direct contrast to the multiple places (see v. 2) where the Canaanites practiced their worship of idols. Eventually, the tabernacle was brought to Jerusalem by David (cf. 2 Sam. 6:12-19).

12:6 *See notes on Lev. 1–7* for descriptions of these various ceremonies.

12:7 eat...rejoice. Some of the offerings were shared by the priests, Levites, and the worshipers (cf. Lev. 7:15-18). The worship of God was to be holy and reverent, yet full of joy.

12:8 every man doing whatever *is* right in his own eyes. There seems to have been some laxity in the offering of the sacrifices in the wilderness which was not to be allowed when Israel came into the Promised Land. This self-centered attitude became a major problem in the time of Judges (cf. Judg. 17:6; 21:25).

12:15 slaughter...within all your gates. While sacrificial offerings were brought to the appointed centers for worship as well as the central sanctuary, the killing and eating of meat for regular eating could be engaged in anywhere. The only restriction on eating nonsacrificial meat was the prohibition of the blood and the fat.

12:17-19 All sacrifices and offerings had to be brought to the place chosen by God.

12:21 If the place...is too far. Moses envisioned the enlarging of the borders of Israel according to God's promise. This meant that people would live further and further away from the central sanctuary. Except for sacrificial animals, all others could be slaughtered and eaten close to home.

unclean and the clean alike may eat them.
23 Only be sure that you do not eat the
blood, [x]for the blood *is* the life; you may
not eat the life with the meat. 24 You shall
not eat it; you shall pour it on the earth like
water. 25 You shall not eat it, [y]that it may
go well with you and your children after
you, [z]when you do *what is* right in the
sight of the LORD. 26 Only the [a]holy things
which you have, and your vowed offerings, you shall take and go to the place
which the LORD chooses. 27 And [b]you shall
offer your burnt offerings, the meat and
the blood, on the altar of the LORD your
God; and the blood of your sacrifices shall
be poured out on the altar of the LORD your
God, and you shall eat the meat. 28 Observe and obey all these words which I
command you, [c]that it may go well with
you and your children after you forever,
when you do *what is* good and right in the
sight of the LORD your God.

Beware of False Gods

29 "When [d]the LORD your God cuts off
from before you the nations which you go
to dispossess, and you displace them and
dwell in their land, 30 take heed to yourself
that you are not ensnared to follow them,
after they are destroyed from before you,
and that you do not inquire after their
gods, saying, 'How did these nations serve
their gods? I also will do likewise.' 31 [e]You
shall not worship the LORD your God in
that way; for every [9]abomination to the
LORD which He hates they have done to
their gods; for [f]they burn even their sons
and daughters in the fire to their gods.
32 "Whatever I command you, be careful
to observe it; [g]you shall not add to it nor
take away from it.

Punishment of Apostates

13 "If there arises among you a
prophet or a [a]dreamer of dreams,
[b]and he gives you a sign or a wonder,
2 and [c]the sign or the wonder comes to
pass, of which he spoke to you, saying, 'Let
us go after other gods'—which you have
not known—'and let us serve them,' 3 you
shall not listen to the words of that prophet
or that dreamer of dreams, for the LORD
your God [d]is testing you to know whether
you love the LORD your God with all your
heart and with all your soul. 4 You shall
[e]walk[1] after the LORD your God and fear
Him, and keep His commandments and
obey His voice; you shall serve Him and
[f]hold fast to Him. 5 But [g]that prophet or
that dreamer of dreams shall be put to
death, because he has spoken in order to
turn *you* away from the LORD your God,
who brought you out of the land of Egypt
and redeemed you from the house of
bondage, to entice you from the way in
which the LORD your God commanded
you to walk. [h]So you shall [2]put away the
evil from your midst.
6 [i]"If your brother, the son of your mother, your son or your daughter, [j]the wife [3]of
your bosom, or your friend [k]who is as your
own soul, secretly entices you, saying, 'Let
us go and serve other gods,' which you
have not known, neither you nor your fathers, 7 of the gods of the people which *are*
all around you, near to you or far off from
you, from *one* end of the earth to the *other*
end of the earth, 8 you shall [l]not [4]consent
to him or listen to him, nor shall your eye

23 [x]Gen. 9:4; Lev. 17:10-14; Deut. 12:16
25 [y]Deut. 4:40; 6:18; Is. 3:10 [z]Ex. 15:26; 1 Kin. 11:38
26 [a]Num. 5:9, 10; 18:19
27 [b]Lev. 1:5, 9, 13, 17
28 [c]Deut. 12:25
29 [d]Ex. 23:23; Deut. 19:1; Josh. 23:4
31 [e]Lev. 18:3, 26, 30; 20:1, 2 [f]Deut. 18:10; Ps. 106:37; Jer. 32:35
[9] *detestable action*
32 [g]Deut. 4:2; 13:18; Josh. 1:7; Prov. 30:6; Rev. 22:18, 19

CHAPTER 13

1 [a]Num. 12:6; Jer. 23:28; Zech. 10:2 [b]Matt. 24:24; Mark 13:22; 2 Thess. 2:9
2 [c]Deut. 18:22
3 [d]Ex. 20:20; Deut. 8:2, 16
4 [e]Deut. 10:12, 20; 2 Kin. 23:3 [f]Deut. 30:20 [1] *follow the* LORD
5 [g]Deut. 18:20; Jer. 14:15 [h]Deut. 17:5, 7; 1 Cor. 5:13
[2] *exterminate*
6 [i]Deut. 17:2 [j]Gen. 16:5 [k]1 Sam. 18:1, 3
[3] Whom you cherish
8 [l]Deut. 7:16; Prov. 1:10 [4] *yield*

12:23 the blood *is* the life. See Gen. 9:4-6 and Lev. 17:10-14. The blood symbolized life. By refraining from eating blood, the Israelite demonstrated respect for life and ultimately for the Creator of life. Blood, representing life, was the ransom price for sins. So blood was sacred and not to be consumed by the people. This relates to atonement in Lev. 16; Heb. 9:12-14; 1 Pet. 1:18,19; 1 John 1:7.

12:29,30 Cf. 2 Cor. 6:14–7:1, where Paul gives a similar exhortation.

12:31 they burn even their sons and daughters. One of the detestable practices of Canaanite worship was the burning of their sons and daughters in the fire as sacrifices to Molech (cf. Lev. 18:21; 20:2-5; 1 Kin. 11:7; 2 Kin. 23:10; Jer. 32:35).

12:32 you shall not add...nor take away. *See notes on 4:2.*

13:1-18 After the general prohibition of involvement in Canaanite worship (12:29-31), Moses discussed 3 ways in which the temptation to idolatry was likely to come to Israel: 1) through a false prophet (vv. 1-5); 2) through a family member (vv. 6-11); or 3) through apostates in some Canaanite city (vv. 12-18).

13:2 the sign or the wonder comes to pass. Miraculous signs alone were never meant to be a test of truth (cf. Pharaoh's magicians in Ex. 7–10). A prophet or a dreamer's prediction may come true, but if his message contradicted God's commands, the people were to trust God and His Word rather than such experience. **Let us go after other gods.** The explicit temptation was to renounce allegiance to the Lord and go after other gods. The result of this apostasy would be the serving of these false gods by worshiping them, which would be in direct contradiction to the first commandment (5:7).

13:3 the LORD your God is testing you. God, in His sovereignty, allowed the false prophets to entice the people to apostasy to test the true disposition of the hearts of the Israelites. And while the temptation was dangerous, the overcoming of that temptation would strengthen the people in their love for God and obedience to His commandments. Cf. 6:5.

13:5 put away the evil from your midst. The object of the severe penalty was not only the punishment of the evildoer, but also the preservation of the community. Paul must have had this text in mind when he gave a similar command to the Corinthian church (cf. 1 Cor. 5:13; also Deut. 17:7; 19:19; 21:21; 22:21; 24:7).

13:6 your brother...friend. The temptation to idolatry might also come from a member of the immediate family or from an intimate friend. While the temptation from the false prophet would be made openly based on a sign or wonder, this temptation would be made secretly and would be based upon the intimacy of relationship.

pity him, nor shall you spare him or conceal him; 9 but you shall surely kill him; your hand shall be first against him to put him to [m]death, and afterward the hand of all the people. 10 And you shall stone him with stones until he dies, because he sought to entice you away from the LORD your God, who brought you out of the land of Egypt, from the house of bondage.
11 So all Israel shall hear and [n]fear, and not again do such wickedness as this among you.

12 [o]"If you hear someone in one of your cities, which the LORD your God gives you to dwell in, saying, 13 [5]'Corrupt men have gone out from among you and enticed the inhabitants of their city, saying, "Let us go and serve other gods" '—which you have not known— 14 then you shall inquire, search out, and ask diligently. And *if it is* indeed true *and* certain *that* such an [6]abomination was committed among you,
15 you shall surely strike the inhabitants of that city with the edge of the sword, utterly destroying it, all that is in it and its livestock—with the edge of the sword.

9 [m] Lev. 24:14; Deut. 17:7
11 [n] Deut. 17:13
12 [o] Judg. 20:1-48
13 [5] Lit. *Sons of Belial*
14 [6] *detestable action*

16 [p] Josh. 6:24 [q] Josh. 8:28; Is. 17:1; 25:2; Jer. 49:2 [7] *Or as a whole-offering* [8] Lit. *mound or ruin*
17 [r] Josh. 6:18 [s] Josh. 7:26 [9] *increase*
18 [t] Deut. 12:25, 28, 32

CHAPTER 14

1 [a] [Rom. 8:16; Gal. 3:26] [b] Lev. 19:28; 21:1-5 [1] *make any baldness between your eyes*
2 [c] Lev. 20:26; Deut. 7:6; [Rom. 12:1]

16 And you shall gather all its plunder into the middle of the street, and [7]completely [p]burn with fire the city and all its plunder, for the LORD your God. It shall be [q]a [8]heap forever; it shall not be built again. 17 [r]So none of the accursed things shall remain in your hand, that the LORD may [s]turn from the fierceness of His anger and show you mercy, have compassion on you and [9]multiply you, just as He swore to your fathers, 18 because you have listened to the voice of the LORD your God, [t]to keep all His commandments which I command you today, to do *what is* right in the eyes of the LORD your God.

Improper Mourning

14 "You *are* [a]the children of the LORD your God; [b]you shall not cut yourselves nor [1]shave the front of your head for the dead. 2 [c]For you *are* a holy people to the LORD your God, and the LORD has chosen you to be a people for Himself, a special treasure above all the peoples who *are* on the face of the earth.

13:10 until he dies. The convicting witness cast the first stone. Love for family and friends must not take precedence over devotion to God (cf. Luke 14:26).

13:12 one of your cities. He has in mind an entire city of Canaan given by God to the Israelites, yet enticed to idolatry.

13:13 Corrupt men. Lit. "sons of Belial (worthlessness)." *Belial* is used of Satan in 2 Cor. 6:15. It is a way to describe evil, worthless, or wicked men (Judg. 19:22; 1 Sam. 2:12; 1 Kin. 21:10,13).

14:1 you shall not cut…nor shave. The two practices, lacerating the body and shaving the head, were associated with mourning customs of foreign religions. Though the actions could in themselves appear to be innocent, they were associated with practices and beliefs reprehensible to the Lord. Cf. Lev. 27,28; 21:5 1 Kin. 18:28; 1 Cor. 3:17.

14:2 you *are* a holy people to the LORD your God. Again comes the important reminder of their peculiar relation to God. Over 250 times, Moses emphasized to Israel, "the Lord *your* God."

The Death Penalty

Crime	Scripture Reference
1. Premeditated Murder	Genesis 9:6; Exodus 21:12-14,22,23
2. Kidnapping	Exodus 21:16; Deuteronomy 24:7
3. Striking or Cursing Parents	Exodus 21:15; Leviticus 20:9; Proverbs 20:20; Matthew 15:4; Mark 7:10
4. Magic and Divination	Exodus 22:18
5. Bestiality	Exodus 22:19; Leviticus 20:15,16
6. Sacrificing to False Gods	Exodus 22:20
7. Profaning the Sabbath	Exodus 35:2; Numbers 15:32-36
8. Offering Human Sacrifice	Leviticus 20:2
9. Adultery	Leviticus 20:10-21; Deuteronomy 22:22
10. Incest	Leviticus 20:11,12,14
11. Homosexuality	Leviticus 20:13
12. Blasphemy	Leviticus 24:11-14,16,23
13. False Prophecy	Deuteronomy 13:1-10
14. Incorrigible Rebelliousness	Deuteronomy 17:12; 21:18-21
15. Fornication	Deuteronomy 22:20,21
16. Rape of Betrothed Virgin	Deuteronomy 22:23-27

Clean and Unclean Meat

3 [d]"You shall not eat any [2]detestable
thing. 4 [e]These *are* the animals which you
may eat: the ox, the sheep, the goat, 5 the
deer, the gazelle, the roe deer, the wild
goat, the [3]mountain goat, the antelope,
and the mountain sheep. 6 And you may
eat every animal with cloven hooves, having the hoof split into two parts, *and that*
chews the cud, among the animals. 7 Nevertheless, of those that chew the cud or
have cloven hooves, you shall not eat, *such*
as these: the camel, the hare, and the rock
hyrax; for they chew the cud but do not
have cloven hooves; they *are* unclean for
you. 8 Also the swine is unclean for you,
because it has cloven hooves, yet *does* not
chew the cud; you shall not eat their flesh
[f]or touch their dead carcasses.
9 [g]"These you may eat of all that *are* in
the waters: you may eat all that have fins
and scales. 10 And whatever does not have
fins and scales you shall not eat; it *is* unclean for you.
11 "All clean birds you may eat. 12 [h]But
these you shall not eat: the eagle, the vulture, the buzzard, 13 the red kite, the falcon, and the kite after their kinds; 14 every
raven after its kind; 15 the ostrich, the
short-eared owl, the sea gull, and the hawk
after their kinds; 16 the little owl, the
screech owl, the white owl, 17 the jackdaw,
the carrion vulture, the fisher owl, 18 the
stork, the heron after its kind, and the
hoopoe and the bat.
19 "Also [i]every [4]creeping thing that flies
is unclean for you; [j]they shall not be eaten.
20 "You may eat all clean birds.
21 [k]"You shall not eat anything that dies
of itself; you may give it to the alien who *is*
within your gates, that he may eat it, or
you may sell it to a foreigner; [l]for you *are* a
holy people to the LORD your God.
[m]"You shall not boil a young goat in its
mother's milk.

Tithing Principles

22 [n]"You shall truly tithe all the increase
of your grain that the field produces year
by year. 23 [o]And you shall eat before the
LORD your God, in the place where He
chooses to make His name abide, the tithe
of your grain and your new wine and your
oil, of [p]the firstborn of your herds and your
flocks, that you may learn to fear the LORD
your God always. 24 But if the journey is
too long for you, so that you are not able to
carry *the tithe, or* [q]if the place where the
LORD your God chooses to put His name is
too far from you, when the LORD your God
has blessed you, 25 then you shall exchange
it for money, take the money in your hand,
and go to the place which the LORD your
God chooses. 26 And you shall spend that
money for whatever your heart desires: for
oxen or sheep, for wine or similar drink, for
whatever your heart desires; you shall eat
there before the LORD your God, and you
shall [r]rejoice, you and your household.
27 You shall not [5]forsake the [s]Levite who *is*
within your gates, for he has no part nor inheritance with you.
28 [t]"At the end of *every* third year you
shall bring out the [u]tithe of your produce
of that year and store *it* up within your
gates. 29 And the Levite, because he has no
portion nor inheritance with you, and the
stranger and the fatherless and the widow
who *are* within your gates, may come and
eat and be satisfied, that the LORD your
God may bless you in all the work of your
hand which you do.

3 [d]Ezek. 4:14 [2]*abominable*
4 [e]Lev. 11:2-45
5 [3]*Or addax*
8 [f]Lev. 11:26, 27
9 [g]Lev. 11:9
12 [h]Lev. 11:13
19 [i]Lev. 11:20 [j]Lev. 11:23 [4]*swarming*
21 [k]Lev. 17:15; 22:8; Ezek. 4:14; 44:31
[l]Deut. 14:2 [m]Ex. 23:19; 34:26
22 [n]Lev. 27:30; Deut. 12:6, 17; Neh. 10:37
23 [o]Deut. 12:5-7 [p]Deut. 15:19, 20
24 [q]Deut. 12:5, 21
26 [r]Deut. 12:7
27 [s]Deut. 12:12 [5]*neglect*
28 [t]Deut. 26:12; Amos 4:4 [u]Num. 18:21-24

14:3-21 This summary of clean and unclean animals is drawn from the list in Lev. 11:2-23. The ground for the allowances and prohibitions of the eating of certain animals was that Israel was to be holy to the Lord (vv. 2, 21). These special dietary laws were to separate them from social mixing with pagan idolatrous people, to prevent them from being lured into idolatry.

14:21 anything that dies *of itself*. Eating the meat of an animal that had died a natural death was prohibited because the animal had not been killed in the proper fashion and the blood drained out (*see note on 12:23*). The animal, however, could be eaten by "the alien who *is* within your gates." *See notes on Lev. 17:10-15.* **a young goat in its mother's milk.** This prohibition no doubt reflected a common practice in Canaanite religion which was superstitiously observed hoping that fertility and productivity would be increased (cf. Ex. 23:19; 34:26).

14:22 tithe. A tenth. The tithe specified in these verses was only that of the agricultural produce which the land would provide. This was a second tithe to be used for the celebration of convocations of worship at the sanctuary (vv. 23-26), in addition to the first tithe mentioned, known as the Levitical tithe which went to support the priests and Levites who served the people. Cf. Lev. 27:30-33 and Num. 18:21-32. A third welfare tithe was also offered every 3 years (*see notes on 14:28; 26:12*).

14:23 eat before the LORD. The tithe was to be taken to the central sanctuary where the worshipers were to eat a portion in fellowship with the Lord.

14:24 if the journey is too long. If certain Israelites lived too far from the sanctuary for it to be practical for them to carry their agricultural tithe there, then they could exchange the tithe locally for silver and subsequently convert the money back into substance at the sanctuary.

14:26 for wine or similar drink. *See notes on Prov. 20:1; 23:29-35; 31:4-7.*

14:28 At the end of *every* third year. In year 3 and year 6 of the 7 year sabbatical cycle, rather than taking this tithe to the central sanctuary, it was instead stored up within the individual cities in the Land. This tithe was used to feed the Levites, the orphan, the widow, and the stranger (i.e., foreigner) who lived with the Israelites. Cf. 26:12; Num. 18:26-32.

Debts Canceled Every Seven Years

15 "At the end of [a]*every* seven years you shall grant a [1]release *of debts.* 2 And this *is* the form of the release: Every creditor who has lent *anything* to his neighbor shall [2]release *it;* he shall not [3]require *it* of his neighbor or his brother, because it is called the LORD's release. 3 Of a foreigner you may require *it;* but you shall give up your claim to what is owed by your brother, 4 except when there may be no poor among you; for the LORD will greatly [b]bless you in the land which the LORD your God is giving you to possess *as* an inheritance— 5 only if you carefully obey the voice of the LORD your God, to observe with care all these commandments which I command you today. 6 For the LORD your God will bless you just as He promised you; [c]you shall lend to many nations, but you shall not borrow; you shall reign over many nations, but they shall not reign over you.

Generosity to the Poor

7 "If there is among you a poor man of your brethren, within any of the [4]gates in your land which the LORD your God is giving you, [d]you shall not harden your heart nor shut your hand from your poor brother, 8 but [e]you shall [5]open your hand wide to him and willingly lend him sufficient for his need, whatever he needs. 9 Beware lest there be a wicked thought in your heart, saying, 'The seventh year, the year of release, is at hand,' and your [f]eye be evil against your poor brother and you give him nothing, and [g]he cry out to the LORD against you, and [h]it become sin among you. 10 You shall surely give to him, and [i]your heart should not be grieved when you give to him, because [j]for this thing the LORD your God will bless you in all your works and in all to which you put your hand. 11 For [k]the poor will never cease from the land; therefore I command you, saying, 'You shall [6]open your hand wide to your brother, to your poor and your needy, in your land.'

The Law Concerning Bondservants

12 [l]"If your brother, a Hebrew man, or a Hebrew woman, is [m]sold to you and serves you six years, then in the seventh year you shall let him go free from you. 13 And when you [7]send him away free from you, you shall not let him go away empty-handed; 14 you shall supply him liberally from your flock, from your threshing floor, and from your winepress. *From what* the LORD has [n]blessed you with, you shall give to him. 15 [o]You shall remember that you were a slave in the land of Egypt, and the LORD your God redeemed you; therefore I command you this thing today. 16 And [p]if it happens that he says to you, 'I will not go away from you,' because he loves you and your house, since he prospers with you, 17 then you shall take an awl and thrust *it* through his ear to the door, and he shall be your servant forever. Also to your female servant you shall do likewise. 18 It shall not seem hard to you when you send him away free from you; for he has been worth [q]a double hired servant in serving you six years. Then the LORD your God will bless you in all that you do.

CHAPTER 15

1 [a] Ex. 21:2; 23:10, 11; Lev. 25:4; Jer. 34:14 [1] *remission*
2 [2] *cancel the debt* [3] *exact it*
4 [b] Deut. 7:13
6 [c] Deut. 28:12, 44
7 [d] Ex. 23:6; Lev. 25:35-37; Deut. 24:12-14; [1 John 3:17] [4] *towns*
8 [e] Matt. 5:42; Gal. 2:10 [5] *freely open*
9 [f] Deut. 28:54, 56 [g] Ex. 22:23; Deut. 24:15; Job 34:28; Ps. 12:5; James 5:4 [h] [Matt. 25:41, 42]
10 [i] 2 Cor. 9:5, 7 [j] Deut. 14:29; Ps. 41:1; Prov. 22:9
11 [k] Matt. 26:11; Mark 14:7; John 12:8 [6] *freely open*
12 [l] Ex. 21:2-6; Jer. 34:14 [m] Lev. 25:39-46
13 [7] *set him free*
14 [n] Prov. 10:22
15 [o] Deut. 5:15
16 [p] Ex. 21:5, 6
18 [q] Is. 16:14

15:1 At the end of *every* seven years...grant a release *of debts.* The sabbatical year was established and described in Ex. 23:10,11 and Lev. 25:1-7. However, while these texts stated that in the seventh year the land was to lie fallow without any crops being planted, only here did Moses prescribe a cancellation of debts. On the basis of vv. 9-11, the debt was canceled completely and permanently, not just a cancellation of payment during that year.

15:3 Of a foreigner you may require *it.* The provision for sabbatical release of debts was not intended for one who stayed only temporarily in the Land. That foreigner was still responsible to pay his debts.

15:4 except when there may be no poor. Idealistically, there was the possibility that poverty would be eradicated in the Land "for the Lord will greatly bless you in the land." The fullness of that blessing, however, would be contingent on the completeness of Israel's obedience. Thus, vv. 4-6 were an encouragement to strive for a reduction of poverty while at the same time they stressed the abundance of the provision God would make in the Promised Land.

15:8 willingly lend him sufficient for his need. The attitude of the Israelites toward the poor in their community was to be one of warmth and generosity. The poor were given whatever was necessary to meet their needs, even with the realization that such "loans" would never need to be paid back. *See note on 23:19,20.*

15:11 For the poor will never cease from the land. Realistically (in contrast to v. 4), the disobedience toward the Lord on Israel's part meant that there would always be poor people in the land of Israel. Jesus repeated this truism in Matt. 26:11.

15:12 If your brother...is sold. In the context of vv. 1-11, the reason for the sale would be default, an alternative repayment of a debt, and a period of servitude would substitute for that repayment. The Hebrew slave would serve his master 6 years following the sale with freedom being declared in the seventh year.

15:13 you shall not let him go away empty-handed. When a slave had completed his time of service, his former owner was to make ample provision for him so that he would not begin his state of new freedom in destitution.

15:15 remember. The Israelites, formerly enslaved in Egypt, were to treat their own slaves as God had treated them.

15:17 an awl...through his ear. In certain circumstances, a slave might prefer to remain with the family after the required 6 years of servitude. He would then be marked with a hole in his ear and become a servant forever (cf. Ex. 21:5,6).

15:18 worth a double hired servant. The slave was worth double to his owner because the owner not only had the service of the slave, but he also did not have to pay out anything for that service as he would have for a hired hand.

The Law Concerning Firstborn Animals

19 [r]"All the firstborn males that come from your herd and your flock you shall [8]sanctify to the LORD your God; you shall do no work with the firstborn of your herd, nor shear the firstborn of your flock. **20** [s]You and your household shall eat *it* before the LORD your God year by year in the place which the LORD chooses. **21** [t]But if there is a defect in it, *if it is* lame or blind *or has* any serious defect, you shall not sacrifice it to the LORD your God. **22** You may eat it within your gates; [u]the unclean and the clean *person* alike *may eat it,* as *if it were* a gazelle or a deer. **23** Only you shall not eat its blood; you shall pour it on the ground like water.

The Passover Reviewed

16 "Observe the [a]month of Abib, and keep the Passover to the LORD your God, for [b]in the month of Abib the LORD your God brought you out of Egypt by night. **2** Therefore you shall sacrifice the Passover to the LORD your God, from the flock and [c]the herd, in the [d]place where the LORD chooses to put His name. **3** You shall eat no leavened bread with it; [e]seven days you shall eat unleavened bread with it, *that is,* the bread of affliction (for you came out of the land of Egypt in haste), that you may [f]remember the day in which you came out of the land of Egypt all the days of your life. **4** [g]And no leaven shall be seen among you in all your territory for seven days, nor shall *any* of the meat which you sacrifice the first day at twilight remain overnight until [h]morning.

5 "You may not sacrifice the Passover within any of your gates which the LORD your God gives you; **6** but at the place where the LORD your God chooses to make His name abide, there you shall sacrifice the Passover [i]at twilight, at the going down of the sun, at the time you came out

19 [r]Ex. 13:2, 12 [8]*set apart* or *consecrate*
20 [s]Lev. 7:15-18; Deut. 12:5; 14:23
21 [t]Lev. 22:19-25; Deut. 17:1
22 [u]Deut. 12:15, 16, 22

CHAPTER 16

1 [a]Ex. 12:2 [b]Ex. 13:4
2 [c]Num. 28:19 [d]Deut. 12:5, 26; 15:20
3 [e]Num. 29:12 [f]Ex. 13:3; Deut. 4:9
4 [g]Ex. 13:7 [h]Num. 9:12
6 [i]Ex. 12:7-10

15:19 All the firstborn...sanctify. The firstborn was the first to be produced during the bearing life of an animal. It was to be consecrated to the Lord. The firstborn would be sacrificed annually and the offerers would participate in the sacrificial meal (see 14:23). **nor shear.** The firstborn ox or bull was not to be worked, nor the firstborn sheep or goat shorn in the time before their sacrifice to the Lord.

15:21 a defect. An imperfect firstborn animal was not acceptable as a sacrifice. It was to be treated like any other nonsacrificial animal (see 12:15,16) and eaten at home (cf. Mal. 1:6-14).

16:1-17 Moses discusses the feasts during which all the men over 20 years of age were to appear before the Lord at the central worship site. If possible, their families were to go as well (see vv. 11,14). Cf. Ex. 23; Lev. 23; Num. 28,29.

16:1 the month of Abib. Abib (which was later called Nisan) occurred in the spring (approximately Mar. or Apr.).

16:1-8 keep the Passover. The offering of Passover itself was to be only a lamb (Ex. 12:3-11). However, additional offerings were also to be made during the Passover and the subsequent 7 days of the Feast of Unleavened Bread (cf. Ex. 12:15-20; 13:3-10; Lev. 23:6-8; Num. 28:19-25). Therefore, sacrifices from both the flock and the herd were used in keeping the Passover.

16:3 remember. This was the key word at Passover time as it is for the Lord's Supper today (cf. Matt. 26:26-30; Luke 22:14-19; 1 Cor. 11:23-26).

16:5,6 at the place...God chooses. The Passover sacrifices could no longer be slain by every family in their house (see Ex. 12:46). From this point on, the Passover sacrifices must be killed at the central place of worship.

Israel's Calendar

Month	Of Year		
Pre-/Post-Exilic	**Sacred/Civil**	**Modern Equivalent**	**Characteristics**
Abib/Nisan	1/7	March/April	Latter Rains; Barley Harvest
Ziv/Iyyar	2/8	April/May	Dry Season Begins
Sivan	3/9	May/June	Wheat Harvest; Early Figs
Tammuz	4/10	June/July	Hot Season; Grape Harvest
Ab	5/11	July/August	Olive Harvest
Elul	8/12	August/September	Dates, Summer Figs
Ethanim/Tishri	7/1	September/October	Former Rains; Plowing Time
Bul/Heshvan	8/2	October/November	Rains; Wheat, Barley Sown
Chislev	9/3	November/December	Winter Begins
Tebeth	10/4	December/January	Rains
Shebat	11/5	January/February	Almond Trees Blossom
Adar	12/6	February/March	Latter Rains Begin; Citrus Harvest

of Egypt. 7 And you shall roast and eat *it*
[j]in the place which the LORD your God
chooses, and in the morning you shall turn
and go to your tents. 8 Six days you shall
eat unleavened bread, and [k]on the seventh
day there *shall be* a [1]sacred assembly to the
LORD your God. You shall do no work *on it.*

The Feast of Weeks Reviewed

9 "You shall count seven weeks for yourself; begin to count the seven weeks from
the time you begin *to put* the sickle to the
grain. 10 Then you shall keep the [l]Feast of
Weeks to the LORD your God with the tribute of a freewill offering from your hand,
which you shall give [m]as the LORD your
God blesses you. 11 [n]You shall rejoice before the LORD your God, you and your son
and your daughter, your male servant and
your female servant, the Levite who *is*
within your gates, the stranger and the fatherless and the widow who *are* among
you, at the place where the LORD your God
chooses to make His name abide. 12 [o]And
you shall remember that you were a slave
in Egypt, and you shall be careful to observe these statutes.

The Feast of Tabernacles Reviewed

13 [p]"You shall observe the Feast of
Tabernacles seven days, when you have
gathered from your threshing floor and
from your winepress. 14 And [q]you shall rejoice in your feast, you and your son and
your daughter, your male servant and
your female servant and the Levite, the
stranger and the fatherless and the widow,
who *are* within your [2]gates. 15 [r]Seven days
you shall keep a sacred feast to the LORD
your God in the place which the LORD
chooses, because the LORD your God will
bless you in all your produce and in all the
work of your hands, so that you surely
rejoice.

16 [s]"Three times a year all your males
shall appear before the LORD your God in
the place which He chooses: at the Feast of
Unleavened Bread, at the Feast of Weeks,
and at the Feast of Tabernacles; and [t]they
shall not appear before the LORD empty-
handed. 17 Every man *shall give* as he is
able, [u]according to the blessing of the LORD
your God which He has given you.

Justice Must Be Administered

18 "You shall appoint [v]judges and officers in all your [3]gates, which the LORD
your God gives you, according to your
tribes, and they shall judge the people with
just judgment. 19 [w]You shall not pervert
justice; [x]you shall not [4]show partiality,
[y]nor take a bribe, for a bribe blinds the
eyes of the wise and [5]twists the words of
the righteous. 20 You shall follow what is
altogether just, that you may [z]live and inherit the land which the LORD your God is
giving you.

21 [a]"You shall not plant for yourself any
tree, as a [6]wooden image, near the altar
which you build for yourself to the LORD
your God. 22 [b]You shall not set up a sacred
pillar, which the LORD your God hates.

17 "You [a]shall not sacrifice to the LORD
your God a bull or sheep which has
any [1]blemish *or* defect, for that *is* an
[2]abomination to the LORD your God.

2 [b]"If there is found among you, within
any of your [3]gates which the LORD your
God gives you, a man or a woman who has
been wicked in the sight of the LORD your
God, [c]in transgressing His covenant, 3 who
has gone and served other gods and wor-

7 [j] 2 Kin. 23:23
8 [k] Ex. 12:16; 13:6; Lev. 23:8, 36 [1] Lit. *restraint*
10 [l] Ex. 34:22; Lev. 23:15, 16; Num. 28:26 [m] 1 Cor. 16:2
11 [n] Deut. 16:14
12 [o] Deut. 15:15
13 [p] Ex. 23:16
14 [q] Neh. 8:9 [2] *towns*
15 [r] Lev. 23:39-41
16 [s] Ex. 23:14-17; 34:22-24 [t] Ex. 23:15
17 [u] Lev. 14:30, 31; Deut. 16:10
18 [v] Ex. 23:1-8; Deut. 1:16, 17; John 7:24 [3] *towns*
19 [w] Ex. 23:2, 6 [x] Deut. 1:17 [y] Ex. 23:8 [4] Lit. *regard faces* [5] *perverts*
20 [z] Ezek. 18:5-9
21 [a] Ex. 34:13 [6] Or *Asherah*
22 [b] Lev. 26:1

CHAPTER 17

1 [a] Deut. 15:21; Mal. 1:8, 13 [1] Lit. *evil thing* [2] *detestable thing*
2 [b] Deut. 13:6 [c] Josh. 7:11 [3] *towns*

16:7 in the morning...go to your tents. After the sacrifice of the Passover animal and the eating and the night vigil which followed, in the morning the people would return to their lodgings or tents where they were staying for the duration of the feast.

16:10-12 the Feast of Weeks. Seven weeks later this second feast was celebrated. It was also called the "Feast of Harvest" (Ex. 23:16) or the "day of firstfruits" (Lev. 23:9-22; Num. 28:26-31) and later came to be known as "Pentecost" (Acts 2:1). With the grain harvest completed, this one day festival was a time of rejoicing. The outpouring of the Holy Spirit, 50 days after the death of Christ at the Passover, was on Pentecost and gives special meaning to that day for Christians (cf. Joel 2:28-32; Acts 2:14-18).

16:13-15 the Feast of Tabernacles. This was also called the "Feast of Ingathering" and the "Feast of Booths" (cf. Ex. 23:16; 34:22; Lev. 23:33-43; Num. 29:12-39).

16:18–18:22 This section deals with the responsibilities of the officials who were to maintain pure worship within the Land and to administer justice impartially.

16:18 appoint judges and officers. Moses had appointed leaders at Sinai to help him in the administration of the people (1:13). Here he specified that such important leadership should continue in each city. "Judges" were those who adjudicated cases with the application of the law. "Officials" were subordinate leaders of various kinds.

16:19 a bribe blinds the eyes. Accepting a bribe was wrong since it perverted the ability of judges to act in fairness to the parties in litigation.

16:21,22 wooden image...sacred pillar. A reference to the wooden poles, images, or trees that represented the Canaanite goddess Asherah. A stone pillar symbolic of male fertility was also prevalent in the Canaanite religion. These were forbidden by the first two commandments (Ex. 20:3-6; Deut. 5:7-10).

17:1 any...defect. To bring a defective sacrifice to the Lord was to bring something into the sanctuary that was forbidden. Such a sacrifice was an abomination to the Lord. To offer less than the best to God was to despise His name (see Mal. 1:6-8). Offering a less than perfect sacrifice was, in effect, failing to acknowledge God as the ultimate provider of all that was best in life.

17:3-7 served other gods. The local judges were to see that false worshipers were executed, so that idolatry was dealt with severely.

shiped them, either [d]the sun or moon or
any of the host of heaven, [e]which I have
not commanded, 4 [f]and it is told you, and
you hear *of it,* then you shall inquire diligently. And if *it is* indeed true *and* certain
that such an [4]abomination has been committed in Israel, 5 then you shall bring out
to your gates that man or woman who has
committed that wicked thing, and [g]shall
stone [h]to death that man or woman with
stones. 6 Whoever is deserving of death
shall be put to death on the testimony of
two or three [i]witnesses; he shall not be put
to death on the testimony of one witness.
7 The hands of the witnesses shall be the
first against him to put him to death, and
afterward the hands of all the people. So
you shall put away the evil from among
[j]you.

8 [k]"If a matter arises which is too hard
for you to judge, between degrees of guilt
for bloodshed, between one judgment or
another, or between one punishment or
another, matters of controversy within
your gates, then you shall arise and go up
to the [l]place which the LORD your God
chooses. 9 And [m]you shall come to the
priests, the Levites, and [n]to the judge *there*
in those days, and inquire *of them;* [o]they
shall pronounce upon you the sentence of
judgment. 10 You shall do according to the
sentence which they pronounce upon you
in that place which the LORD chooses. And
you shall be careful to do according to all
that they order you. 11 According to the
sentence of the law in which they instruct
you, according to the judgment which
they tell you, you shall do; you shall not
turn aside *to* the right hand or *to* the left
from the sentence which they pronounce
upon you. 12 Now [p]the man who acts presumptuously and will not heed the priest
who stands to minister there before the
LORD your God, or the judge, that man
shall die. So you shall put away the evil
from Israel. 13 [q]And all the people shall
hear and fear, and no longer act presumptuously.

Principles Governing Kings

14 "When you come to the land which
the LORD your God is giving you, and possess it and dwell in it, and say, [r]'I will set a
king over me like all the nations that *are*
around me,' 15 you shall surely set a king
over you [s]whom the LORD your God
chooses; *one* [t]from among your brethren
you shall set as king over you; you may
not set a foreigner over you, who *is* not
your brother. 16 But he shall not multiply
[u]horses for himself, nor cause the people
[v]to return to Egypt to multiply horses, for
[w]the LORD has said to you, [x]'You shall not
return that way again.' 17 Neither shall he
multiply wives for himself, lest his heart
turn away; nor shall he greatly multiply
silver and [y]gold for himself.

18 "Also it shall be, when he sits on the
throne of his kingdom, that he shall write
for himself a copy of this law in a book,
from *the one* [z]before the priests, the Levites.
19 And [a]it shall be with him, and he shall
read it all the days of his life, that he may
learn to fear the LORD his God and be careful to observe all the words of this law and
these statutes, 20 that his heart may not [5]be
lifted above his brethren, that he [b]may not
turn aside from the commandment *to* the
right hand or *to* the left, and that he may
[6]prolong *his* days in his kingdom, he and
his children in the midst of Israel.

3 [d] Deut. 4:19 [e] Jer. 7:22
4 [f] Deut. 13:12, 14 [4] *detestable thing*
5 [g] Lev. 24:14-16; Josh. 7:25 [h] Deut. 13:6-18
6 [i] Num. 35:30; Deut. 19:15; Matt. 18:16; John 8:17; 2 Cor. 13:1; 1 Tim. 5:19; Heb. 10:28
7 [j] Deut. 13:5; 19:19; 1 Cor. 5:13
8 [k] Deut. 1:17; 2 Chr. 19:10 [l] Deut. 12:5; 16:2
9 [m] Jer. 18:18 [n] Deut. 19:17-19 [o] Ezek. 44:24
12 [p] Num. 15:30; Deut. 1:43
13 [q] Deut. 13:11
14 [r] 1 Sam. 8:5, 19, 20; 10:19
15 [s] 1 Sam. 9:15, 16; 10:24; 16:12, 13; 1 Chr. 22:8-10; Hos. 8:4 [t] Jer. 30:21
16 [u] 1 Kin. 4:26; 10:26-29; Ps. 20:7 [v] Is. 31:1; Ezek. 17:15 [w] Ex. 13:17, 18; Hos. 11:5 [x] Deut. 28:68
17 [y] 1 Kin. 10:14
18 [z] Deut. 31:24-26
19 [a] Ps. 119:97, 98
20 [b] Deut. 5:32; 1 Kin. 15:5 [5] *become proud* [6] *continue long in his kingdom*

17:6,7 two or three witnesses. The execution of the idolater could not take place on the basis of hearsay. There had to be at least two valid witnesses against the accused person in order for a case to be established. One witness was not sufficient in a case of this severity; this standard avoided false testimony. The way in which the execution was carried out emphasized the burden of responsibility for truthful testimony that rested on the witnesses in a case involving capital punishment. The witnesses, by casting the first stone, accepted responsibility for their testimony (cf. 19:15; 1 Cor. 5:13).

17:8-13 a matter...too hard for you to judge. If a judge thought a case was too difficult for him to decide, he could take it to a central tribunal, consisting of priests and an officiating chief judge, to be established at the future site of the central sanctuary. The decision of that tribunal would be final, and anyone refusing to abide by that court's decision was subject to the death penalty.

17:14 a king. The office of kingship was anticipated by Moses in the Pentateuch (see Gen. 17:16; 35:11; 49:9-12; Num. 24:7,17). He anticipated the time when the people would ask for a king and here gave explicit instruction concerning the qualifications of that future king.

17:15 from among your brethren. How the Lord would make that choice was not said, but the field was narrowed by the specification that he must be a brother Israelite.

17:16,17 multiply...multiply...multiply. Restrictions were placed on the king: 1) he must not acquire many horses; 2) he must not take multiple wives; and 3) he must not accumulate much silver and gold. The king was not to rely on military strength, political alliances, or wealth for his position and authority, but he was to look to the Lord. Solomon violated all of those prohibitions, while his father, David, violated the last two. Solomon's wives brought idolatry into Jerusalem, which resulted in the kingdom being divided (1 Kin. 11:1-43).

17:18 write...a copy of this law. The ideal set forth was that of the king who was obedient to the will of God, which he learned from reading the law. The result of his reading of the Pentateuch would be fear of the Lord and humility. The king was pictured as a scribe and scholar of Scripture. Josiah reinstituted this approach at a bleak time in Israel's history (cf. 2 Kin. 22).

17:20 his heart may not be lifted above his brethren. The king was not to be above God's law, any more than any other Israelite.

The Portion of the Priests and Levites

18 "The priests, the Levites—all the
tribe of Levi—shall have [1]no part
nor [a]inheritance with Israel; they shall eat
the offerings of the LORD made by fire, and
His portion. 2 Therefore they shall have no
inheritance among their brethren; the LORD
is their inheritance, as He said to them.
3 "And this shall be the priest's [b]due[2]
from the people, from those who offer a
sacrifice, whether *it is* bull or sheep: they
shall give to the priest the shoulder, the
cheeks, and the stomach. 4 [c]The firstfruits
of your grain and your new wine and your
oil, and the first of the fleece of your sheep,
you shall give him. 5 For [d]the LORD your
God has chosen him out of all your tribes
[e]to stand to minister in the name of the
LORD, him and his sons forever.
6 "So if a Levite comes from any of your
[3]gates, from where he [f]dwells among all
Israel, and comes with all the desire of his
mind [g]to the place which the LORD chooses, 7 then he may serve in the name of the
LORD his God [h]as all his brethren the
Levites *do,* who stand there before the
LORD. 8 They shall have equal [i]portions to
eat, besides what comes from the sale of
his inheritance.

Avoid Wicked Customs

9 "When you come into the land which
the LORD your God is giving you, [j]you
shall not learn to follow the [4]abominations
of those nations. 10 There shall not be
found among you *anyone* who makes his
son or his daughter [k]pass[5] through the fire,
[l]*or one* who practices witchcraft, *or* a soothsayer, or one who interprets omens, or a
sorcerer, 11 [m]or one who conjures spells, or
a medium, or a spiritist, or [n]one who calls
up the dead. 12 For all who do these things
are [6]an abomination to the LORD, and [o]be-
cause of these abominations the LORD your
God drives them out from before you.
13 You shall be [7]blameless before the LORD
your God. 14 For these nations which you
will dispossess listened to soothsayers and
diviners; but as for you, the LORD your
God has not [8]appointed such for you.

A New Prophet Like Moses

15 [p]"The LORD your God will raise up for
you a Prophet like me from your midst,
from your brethren. Him you shall hear,
16 according to all you desired of the LORD
your God in Horeb [q]in the day of the assembly, saying, [r]'Let me not hear again the
voice of the LORD my God, nor let me see
this great fire anymore, lest I die.'
17 "And the LORD said to me: [s]'What
they have spoken is good. 18 [t]I will raise
up for them a Prophet like you from
among their brethren, and [u]will put My
words in His mouth, [v]and He shall speak
to them all that I command Him. 19 [w]And
it shall be *that* whoever will not hear My
words, which He speaks in My name, I
will require *it* of him. 20 But [x]the prophet
who presumes to speak a word in My
name, which I have not commanded him
to speak, or [y]who speaks in the name of
other gods, that prophet shall die.' 21 And
if you say in your heart, 'How shall we
know the word which the LORD has not
spoken?'— 22 [z]when a prophet speaks in
the name of the LORD, [a]if the thing does not

CHAPTER 18

1 [a] Deut. 10:9; 1 Cor. 9:13 [1] *no portion*
3 [b] Lev. 7:32-34; Num. 18:11, 12; 1 Sam. 2:13-16, 29 [2] *right*
4 [c] Ex. 22:29
5 [d] Ex. 28:1 [e] Deut. 10:8
6 [f] Num. 35:2 [g] Deut. 12:5; 14:23 [3] *towns*
7 [h] Num. 1:50; 2 Chr. 31:2
8 [i] Lev. 27:30-33; Num. 18:21-24; 2 Chr. 31:4; Neh. 12:44
9 [j] Lev. 18:26, 27, 30; Deut. 12:29, 30; 20:16-18 [4] *detestable acts*
10 [k] Lev. 18:21; Deut. 12:31 [l] Ex. 22:18; Lev. 19:26, 31; 20:6, 27; Is. 8:19 [5] Be burned as an offering to an idol
11 [m] Lev. 20:27 [n] 1 Sam. 28:7
12 [o] Lev. 18:24; Deut. 9:4 [6] *detestable*
13 [7] Lit. *perfect*
14 [8] *allowed you to do so*
15 [p] Matt. 21:11; Luke 1:76; 2:25-34; 7:16; 24:19; Acts 3:22
16 [q] Deut. 5:23-27 [r] Ex. 20:18, 19; Heb. 12:19
17 [s] Deut. 5:28
18 [t] Deut. 34:10; John 1:45; Acts 3:22 [u] Num. 23:5; Is. 49:2; 51:16; John 17:8 [v] [John 4:25; 8:28]
19 [w] Acts 3:23; [Heb. 12:25]
20 [x] Deut. 13:5; Jer. 14:14, 15; Zech. 13:2-5 [y] Deut. 13:1-3; Jer. 2:8
22 [z] Jer. 28:9 [a] Deut. 13:2

18:1 all the tribe of Levi. Unlike the other 12 tribes, none of the tribe of Levi, including the priests, was given an allotment of land to settle and cultivate. The Levites lived in the cities assigned to them throughout the Land (Num. 35:1-8; Josh. 21) while the priests lived near the central sanctuary, where they went to officiate in their appropriate course (cf. 1 Chr. 6:57-60). Levites assisted the priests (Num. 3,4,8).

18:3-5 the priest's due. In place of a land inheritance and in recognition of their priestly duties, the priests had a right to specific portions of the animals offered for sacrifices.

18:6-8 a Levite. If a Levite wanted to go to the central sanctuary to minister there in the Lord's name, he was permitted to do so and to receive equal support along with other Levites.

18:9-12 the abominations of those nations. Moses gave a strict injunction not to copy, imitate, or do what the polytheistic Canaanites did. Nine detestable practices of the Canaanites were delineated in vv. 10,11, namely: 1) sacrificing children in the fire (see 12:31); 2) witchcraft, seeking to determine the will of the gods by examining and interpreting omens; 3) soothsaying, attempting to control the future through power given by evil spirits; 4) interpreting omens, telling the future based on signs; 5) sorcery, inducing magical effects by drugs or some other sort of potion; 6) conjuring spells, binding other people by magical muttering; 7) being a medium, one who supposedly communicates with the dead, but actually communicates with demons; 8) being a spiritist, one who has an intimate acquaintance with the demonic, spiritual world; and 9) calling up the dead, investigating and seeking information from the dead. These evil practices were the reason the Lord was going to drive the Canaanites out of the land.

18:15-19 a Prophet like me. The singular pronoun emphasizes the ultimate Prophet who was to come. Both the OT (34:10) and the NT (Acts 3:22,23; 7:37) interpret this passage as a reference to the coming Messiah, who like Moses would receive and preach divine revelation and lead His people (cf. John 1:21,25,43-45; 6:14; 7:40). In fact, Jesus was like Moses in several other ways: 1) He was spared death as a baby (Ex. 2; Matt. 2:13-23); 2) He renounced a royal court (Phil. 2:5-8; Heb. 11:24-27); 3) He had compassion on His people (Num. 27:17; Matt. 9:36); 4) He made intercession for the people (Deut. 9:18; Heb. 7:25); 5) He spoke with God face to face (Ex. 34:29,30; 2 Cor. 3:7); and 6) He was the mediator of a covenant (Deut. 29:1; Heb. 8:6,7).

18:20-22 who speaks in the name of other gods. In contrast to the true prophet, Moses predicted there would be false prophets who would come to Israel, speaking not in the name of the Lord, but in the name of false gods. How could the people tell if a prophet was authentically speaking for God? Moses said, "if the thing does not happen or come to pass, that *is* the thing which the LORD has not spoken; the prophet has spoken it [b]presumptuously; you shall not be afraid of him.

Three Cities of Refuge

19 "When the LORD your God [a]has cut off the nations whose land the LORD your God is giving you, and you dispossess them and dwell in their cities and in their houses, **2** [b]you shall separate three cities for yourself in the midst of your land which the LORD your God is giving you to possess. **3** You shall prepare roads for yourself, and divide into three parts the territory of your land which the LORD your God is giving you to inherit, that any manslayer may flee there.

4 "And [c]this *is* the case of the manslayer who flees there, that he may live: Whoever kills his neighbor [1]unintentionally, not having hated him in time past— **5** as when *a man* goes to the woods with his neighbor to cut timber, and his hand swings a stroke with the ax to cut down the tree, and the head slips from the handle and strikes his neighbor so that he dies—he shall flee to one of these cities and live; **6** [d]lest the avenger of blood, while his anger is hot, pursue the manslayer and overtake him, because the way is long, and kill him, though he *was* not deserving of death, since he had not hated the victim in time past. **7** Therefore I command you, saying, 'You shall separate three cities for yourself.'

8 "Now if the LORD your God [e]enlarges your territory, as He swore to [f]your fathers, and gives you the land which He promised to give to your fathers, **9** and if you keep all these commandments and do them, which I command you today, to love the LORD your God and to walk always in His ways, [g]then you shall add three more cities for yourself besides these three, **10** [h]lest innocent blood be shed in the midst of your land which the LORD your God is giving you *as* an inheritance, and *thus* guilt of bloodshed be upon you.

11 "But [i]if anyone hates his neighbor, lies in wait for him, rises against him and strikes him mortally, so that he dies, and he flees to one of these cities, **12** then the elders of his city shall send and bring him from there, and deliver him over to the hand of the avenger of blood, that he may die. **13** [j]Your eye shall not pity him, [k]but you shall [2]put away *the guilt of* innocent blood from Israel, that it may go well with you.

Property Boundaries

14 [l]"You shall not remove your neighbor's landmark, which the men of old have set, in your inheritance which you will inherit in the land that the LORD your God is giving you to possess.

The Law Concerning Witnesses

15 [m]"One witness shall not rise against a man concerning any iniquity or any sin that he commits; by the mouth of two or three witnesses the matter shall be established. **16** If a false witness [n]rises against any man to testify against him of wrongdoing, **17** then both men in the controversy shall stand before the LORD, [o]before the priests and the judges who serve in those days. **18** And the judges shall make careful inquiry, and indeed, *if* the witness *is* a false witness, who has testified falsely against his brother, **19** [p]then you shall do to him as he thought to have done to his brother; so [q]you shall put away the evil from among

22 [b]Deut. 18:20

CHAPTER 19

1 [a]Deut. 12:29
2 [b]Ex. 21:13; Num. 35:10-15; Deut. 4:41; Josh. 20:2
4 [c]Num. 35:9-34; Deut. 4:42 [1]*ignorantly*, lit. *without knowledge*
6 [d]Num. 35:12
8 [e]Deut. 12:20 [f]Gen. 15:18-21
9 [g]Josh. 20:7-9
10 [h]Num. 35:33; Deut. 21:1-9
11 [i]Num. 35:16, 24; Deut. 27:24; [1 John 3:15]
13 [j]Deut. 13:8 [k]Num. 35:33, 34; 1 Kin. 2:31 [2]*purge the blood of the innocent*
14 [l]Deut. 27:17; Job 24:2; Prov. 22:28; Hos. 5:10
15 [m]Num. 35:30; Deut. 17:6; Matt. 18:16; John 8:17; 2 Cor. 13:1; 1 Tim. 5:19; Heb. 10:28
16 [n]Ex. 23:1; Ps. 27:12; 35:11
17 [o]Deut. 17:8-11; 21:5
19 [p]Prov. 19:5; Dan. 6:24 [q]Deut. 13:5; 17:7; 21:21; 22:21

happen," it was not from God. The characteristic of false prophets is the failure of their predictions to always come true. Sometimes false prophets speak and it happens as they said, but they are representing false gods and trying to turn people from the true God—they must be rejected and executed (13:1-5). Other times, false prophets are more subtle and identify with the true God but speak lies. If ever a prophecy of such a prophet fails, he is shown to be false. Cf. Jer. 28:15-17; 29:30-32.

19:1–23:14 The statutes explained by Moses in this part of Deuteronomy deal broadly with social and community order. These laws focus on interpersonal relationships.

19:1-13 See Num. 35:9-34 for the purpose of the cities of refuge.

19:2 three cities. Three cities of refuge were to be set aside in Canaan after the conquest of the Land (see Josh. 20:7) for Israel's obedience to this command. These 3 cities to the W of the Jordan River were in addition to the 3 already established E of it (see 4:41-43 for the eastern cities of refuge).

19:9 add three more cities. If the Israelites had been faithful in following the Lord fully, then He would have enlarged their territory to the boundaries promised in the Abrahamic Covenant (Gen. 15:18-21). In that case, 3 more cities of refuge, for a total of 9, would have been needed.

19:14 your neighbor's landmark. These "landmarks" referred to stones bearing inscriptions which identified the owner of the property. Moving a neighbor's boundary stone was equivalent to stealing his property (cf. Prov. 22:28; 23:10).

19:15 by the mouth of two or three witnesses. More than one witness was necessary to convict a man of a crime. This principle was to act as a safeguard against the false witness who might bring an untruthful charge against a fellow Israelite. By requiring more than one witness, greater accuracy and objectivity was gained (cf. Deut. 17:6; Matt. 18:15-17; 2 Cor. 13:1).

19:16-19 a false witness. In some cases, there would only be one witness who brought a charge against someone. When such a case was taken to the central tribunal of priests and judges for trial, and upon investigation the testimony of the witness was found to be false, the accuser received the punishment appropriate for the alleged crime.

you. 20 [r]And those who remain shall hear
and fear, and hereafter they shall not again
commit such evil among you. 21 [s]Your eye
shall not pity: [t]life *shall be* for life, eye for
eye, tooth for tooth, hand for hand, foot for
foot.

Principles Governing Warfare

20 "When you go out to battle against
your enemies, and see [a]horses and
chariots *and* people more numerous than
you, do not be [b]afraid of them; for the
LORD your God *is* [c]with you, who brought
you up from the land of Egypt. 2 So it shall
be, when you are on the verge of battle,
that the priest shall approach and speak to
the people. 3 And he shall say to them,
'Hear, O Israel: Today you are on the verge
of battle with your enemies. Do not let
your heart faint, do not be afraid, and do
not tremble or be terrified because of them;
4 for the LORD your God *is* He who goes
with you, [d]to fight for you against your enemies, to save you.'
5 "Then the officers shall speak to the
people, saying: 'What man *is there* who
has built a new house and has not [e]dedi-
cated it? Let him go and return to his
house, lest he die in the battle and another man dedicate it. 6 Also what man *is
there* who has planted a vineyard and has
not eaten of it? Let him go and return to
his house, lest he die in the battle and another man eat of it. 7 [f]And what man *is
there* who is betrothed to a woman and
has not married her? Let him go and return to his house, lest he die in the battle
and another man marry her.'
8 "The officers shall speak further to the
people, and say, [g]'What man *is there who is*
fearful and fainthearted? Let him go and
return to his house, [1]lest the heart of his
brethren faint like his heart.' 9 And so it
shall be, when the officers have finished
speaking to the people, that they shall
make captains of the armies to lead the
people.
10 "When you go near a city to fight
against it, [h]then proclaim an offer of peace
to it. 11 And it shall be that if they accept
your offer of peace, and open to you, then
all the people *who are* found in it shall be
placed under tribute to you, and serve you.
12 Now if *the city* will not make peace with
you, but war against you, then you shall
besiege it. 13 And when the LORD your God
delivers it into your hands, [i]you shall
strike every male in it with the edge of the
sword. 14 But the women, the little ones,
[j]the livestock, and all that is in the city, all
its spoil, you shall plunder for yourself;
and [k]you shall eat the enemies' plunder
which the LORD your God gives you.
15 Thus you shall do to all the cities *which
are* very far from you, which *are* not of the
cities of these nations.
16 "But [l]of the cities of these peoples
which the LORD your God gives you *as* an
inheritance, you shall let nothing that
breathes remain alive, 17 but you shall utterly destroy them: the Hittite and the
Amorite and the Canaanite and the Perizzite and the Hivite and the Jebusite, just as
the LORD your God has commanded you,
18 lest [m]they teach you to do according to
all their [2]abominations which they have
done for their gods, and you [n]sin against
the LORD your God.
19 "When you besiege a city for a long
time, while making war against it to take it,

20 [r]Deut. 17:13; 21:21
21 [s]Deut. 19:13 [t]Ex. 21:23, 24; Lev. 24:20; Matt. 5:38, 39

CHAPTER 20

1 [a]Ps. 20:7; Is. 31:1 [b]Deut. 7:18 [c]Num. 23:21; Deut. 5:6; 31:6, 8; 2 Chr. 13:12; 32:7, 8; Ps. 23:4; Is. 41:10
4 [d]Deut. 1:30; 3:22; Josh. 23:10
5 [e]Neh. 12:27
7 [f]Deut. 24:5
8 [g]Judg. 7:3

[1] So with MT, Tg.; Sam., LXX, Syr., Vg. *lest he make his brother's heart faint*
10 [h]2 Sam. 10:19
13 [i]Num. 31:7
14 [j]Josh. 8:2 [k]1 Sam. 14:30
16 [l]Ex. 23:31-33; Num. 21:2, 3; Deut. 7:1-5; Josh. 11:14
18 [m]Ex. 34:12-16; Deut. 7:4; 12:30; 18:9 [n]Ex. 23:33; 2 Kin. 21:3-15; Ps. 106:34-41 [2] *detestable things*

19:20 hear and fear. When the fate of the false witness became known in Israel, it would serve as a deterrent against giving false testimony in Israel's courts.

19:21 eye for eye. This principle of legal justice (called *lex talionis,* "law of retaliation") was given to encourage appropriate punishment of a criminal in cases where there might be a tendency to be either too lenient or too strict (*see notes on Ex. 21:23-25; Lev. 24:17-22*). Jesus confronted the Jews of His day for taking this law out of the courts and using it for purposes of personal vengeance (cf. Matt. 5:38-42).

20:1-20 The humanitarian principles applicable in war under Mosaic law are in stark contrast to the brutality and cruelty of other nations.

20:1 do not be afraid. When Israelites went into battle, they were never to fear an enemy's horses or chariots because the outcome of a battle would never be determined by mere military strength. The command not to be afraid was based on God's power and faithfulness, which had already been proved to Israel in their deliverance from Egypt.

20:2-4 the priest shall...speak to the people. The role of the priest in battle was to encourage the soldiers by God's promise, presence, and power to be strong in faith. A lack of trust in God's ability to fight for them would affect the strength of their will so that they would become fainthearted. Victory was linked to their faith in God.

20:5-8 Let him go and return to his house. Four exemptions from service in Israel's volunteer army were cited to illustrate the principle that anyone whose heart was not in the fight should not be there. Those who had other matters on their minds or were afraid were allowed to leave the army and return to their homes, since they would be useless in battle and even influence others to lose courage (v. 8).

20:10-15 offer of peace. Cities outside of Canaan were not under the judgment of total destruction, so to them Israel was to offer a peace treaty. If the city agreed to become a vassal to Israel, then the people would become tributary subjects. However, if the offer of peace was rejected, Israel was to besiege and take the city, killing the men and taking possession of the rest of the people and animals as spoils of war. Note here the principle that the proclamation of peace preceded judgment (cf. Matt. 10:11-15).

20:16-18 utterly destroy. The Canaanite cities were to be totally destroyed, i.e., nothing was to be spared, in order to destroy their influence toward idolatry (cf. 7:22-26).

you shall not destroy its trees by wielding
an ax against them; if you can eat of them,
do not cut them down to use in the siege,
for the tree of the field *is* man's *food.* 20 Only
the trees which you know *are* not trees for
food you may destroy and cut down, to
build siegeworks against the city that
makes war with you, until it is subdued.

The Law Concerning Unsolved Murder

21 "If *anyone* is found slain, lying in the
field in the land which the LORD
your God is giving you to possess, *and* it is
not known who killed him, 2 then your elders and your judges shall go out and measure *the distance* from the slain man to the
surrounding cities. 3 And it shall be *that* the
elders of the city nearest to the slain man
will take a heifer which has not been
worked *and* which has not pulled with a
[a]yoke. 4 The elders of that city shall bring
the heifer down to a valley with flowing
water, which is neither plowed nor sown,
and they shall break the heifer's neck there
in the valley. 5 Then the priests, the sons of
Levi, shall come near, for [b]the LORD your
God has chosen them to minister to Him
and to bless in the name of the LORD; [c]by
their word every controversy and every
[1]assault shall be *settled.* 6 And all the elders
of that city nearest to the slain *man* [d]shall
wash their hands over the heifer whose
neck was broken in the valley. 7 Then they
shall answer and say, 'Our hands have not
shed this blood, nor have our eyes seen *it.*
8 Provide atonement, O LORD, for Your people Israel, whom You have redeemed, [e]and
do not lay innocent blood to the charge of
Your people Israel.' And atonement shall
be provided on their behalf for the blood.
9 So [f]you shall put away the *guilt of* innocent blood from among you when you do
what is right in the sight of the LORD.

Female Captives

10 "When you go out to war against your
enemies, and the LORD your God delivers
them into your hand, and you take them
captive, 11 and you see among the captives
a beautiful woman, and desire her and
would take her for your [g]wife, 12 then you
shall bring her home to your house, and
she shall [h]shave her head and trim her
nails. 13 She shall put off the clothes of her
captivity, remain in your house, and
[i]mourn her father and her mother a full
month; after that you may go in to her and
be her husband, and she shall be your wife.
14 And it shall be, if you have no delight in
her, then you shall set her free, but you certainly shall not sell her for money; you
shall not treat her brutally, because you
have [j]humbled her.

Firstborn Inheritance Rights

15 "If a man has two wives, one loved
[k]and the other unloved, and they have
borne him children, *both* the loved and the

CHAPTER 21

3 [a] Num. 19:2
5 [b] Deut. 10:8; 1 Chr. 23:13 [c] Deut. 17:8, 9 [1] Lit. *stroke*
6 [d] Ps. 19:12; 26:6; Matt. 27:24
8 [e] Deut. 19:10, 13; Jon. 1:14
9 [f] Deut. 19:13
11 [g] Num. 31:18
12 [h] Lev. 14:8, 9; Num. 6:9
13 [i] Ps. 45:10
14 [j] Gen. 34:2; Deut. 22:29; Judg. 19:24
15 [k] Gen. 29:33

20:19,20 you shall not destroy its trees. When besieging a city, armies in the ancient world would cut down the trees to build ramps and weapons, as well as facilities for the long siege. However, Israel was not to use fruit trees in the siege of a city so they could enjoy the fruit of the Land God had given to them (7:12,13).

21:1-9 it is not known who killed him. This law, which dealt with an unsolved homicide, was not given elsewhere in the Pentateuch. In the event that the guilty party was unknown, justice could not adequately be served. However, the people were still held responsible to deal with the crime. The elders of the city closest to the place where the body of a dead man was found were to accept responsibility for the crime. This precluded inter-city strife, in case relatives sought revenge. They would go to a valley (idol altars were always on high places, so this avoided association with idolatry) and there break the neck of a heifer, indicating that the crime deserved to be punished. But the handwashing of the elders (v. 6) would show that, although they accepted responsibility for what had happened, they were nevertheless free from the guilt attached to the crime.

21:5 This distinctly indicates that final judicial authority in the theocracy of Israel rested with the priests.

21:11-14 a beautiful woman. According to ancient war customs, a female captive became the servant of the victors. Moses was given instruction to deal in a kind way with such issues. In the event her conquerors were captivated by her beauty and contemplated marriage with her, one month was required to elapse, during which her troubled feelings might settle, her mind would be reconciled to the new conditions of conquest, and she could sorrow over the loss of her parents as she left home to marry a stranger. One month was the usual mourning period for Jews, and the features of this period, e.g., shaving the head, trimming the nails, and removing her lovely clothes (ladies on the eve of captivity dressed to be attractive to their captors), were typical signs of Jewish grief. This action was important to show kindness to the woman and to test the strength of the man's affection. After the 30 days, they could marry. If later he decided divorce was appropriate (based on the provisions of 24:1-4), he could not sell her as a slave. She was to be set completely free because "you have humbled her." This phrase clearly refers to sexual activity, in which the wife has fully submitted herself to her husband (cf. 22:23,24,28,29). It should be noted that divorce appears to have been common among the people, perhaps learned from their time in Egypt, and tolerated by Moses because of their "hard hearts" (*see notes on Deut. 24:1-4; Matt. 19:8*).

21:11,12 among the captives a beautiful woman. Such a woman would be from a non-Canaanite city that Israel had captured (see 20:14) since all the Canaanites were to be killed (v. 16). These discarded items were symbolic of the casting off of her former life and carried purification symbolism (cf. Lev. 14:18; Num. 8:7).

21:15-17 has two wives. In the original, the words are rendered "has had two wives," referring to events that have already taken place, evidently intimating that one wife is dead and another has taken her place. Moses, then, is not legislating on a polygamous case where a man has two wives at the same time, but on that of a man who has married twice in succession. The man may prefer the second wife and be exhorted by her to give his inheritance to one of her sons. The issue involves the principle of the inheritance of the firstborn (the right of primogenitor). The firstborn son of the man,

unloved, and *if* the firstborn son is of her
who is unloved, 16 then it shall be, [l]on the
day he bequeaths his possessions to his
sons, *that* he must not bestow firstborn status on the son of the loved wife in preference to the son of the unloved, the *true*
firstborn. 17 But he shall acknowledge the
son of the unloved wife *as* the firstborn
[m]by giving him a double portion of all that
he has, for he [n]*is* the beginning of his
strength; [o]the right of the firstborn *is* his.

The Rebellious Son

18 "If a man has a stubborn and rebellious son who will not obey the voice of his
father or the voice of his mother, and *who,*
when they have chastened him, will not
heed them, 19 then his father and his mother shall take hold of him and bring him out
to the elders of his city, to the gate of his
city. 20 And they shall say to the elders of
his city, 'This son of ours is stubborn and
rebellious; he will not obey our voice; he is
a glutton and a drunkard.' 21 Then all the
men of his city shall stone him to death
with stones; [p]so you shall put away the
evil from among you, [q]and all Israel shall
hear and fear.

Miscellaneous Laws

22 "If a man has committed a sin [r]de-
serving of death, and he is put to death,
and you hang him on a tree, 23 [s]his body
shall not remain overnight on the tree, but
you shall surely bury him that day, so that
[t]you do not defile the land which the
LORD your God is giving you *as* an inheritance; for [u]he who is hanged *is* accursed
of God.

16 [l] 1 Chr. 5:2; 26:10 **17** [m] 2 Kin. 2:9 [n] Gen. 49:3 [o] Gen. 25:31, 33 **21** [p] Deut. 13:5; 19:19, 20; 22:21, 24 [q] Deut. 13:11 **22** [r] Deut. 22:26; Matt. 26:66; Mark 14:64; Acts 23:29 **23** [s] Josh. 8:29; 10:26, 27; John 19:31 [t] Lev. 18:25; Num. 35:34 [u] Gal. 3:13

22 "You [a]shall not see your brother's
ox or his sheep going astray, and
[1]hide yourself from them; you shall certainly bring them back to your brother.
2 And if your brother *is* not near you, or if
you do not know him, then you shall bring
it to your own house, and it shall remain
with you until your brother seeks it; then
you shall restore it to him. 3 You shall do
the same with his donkey, and so shall you
do with his garment; with any lost thing of
your brother's, which he has lost and you
have found, you shall do likewise; you
[2]must not hide yourself.
4 [b]"You shall not see your brother's donkey or his ox fall down along the road, and
hide yourself from them; you shall surely
help him lift *them* up again.
5 "A woman shall not wear anything
that pertains to a man, nor shall a man put
on a woman's garment, for all who do so
are [3]an abomination to the LORD your God.
6 "If a bird's nest happens to be before
you along the way, in any tree or on the
ground, with young ones or eggs, with the
mother sitting on the young or on the eggs,
[c]you shall not take the mother with the
young; 7 you shall surely let the mother go,
and take the young for yourself, [d]that it
may be well with you and *that* you may
prolong *your* days.
8 "When you build a new house, then
you shall make a parapet for your roof,
that you may not bring guilt of bloodshed
on your household if anyone falls from it.
9 [e]"You shall not sow your vineyard
with different kinds of seed, lest the yield
of the seed which you have sown and the
fruit of your vineyard be defiled.

CHAPTER 22

1 [a] Ex. 23:4 [1] *ignore them* **3** [2] *may not avoid responsibility* **4** [b] Ex. 23:5 **5** [3] *detestable* **6** [c] Lev. 22:28 **7** [d] Deut. 4:40 **9** [e] Lev. 19:19

whether from the favorite wife or not, was to receive the double portion of the inheritance. The father did not have the authority to transfer this right to another son. This did not apply to sons of a concubine (Gen. 21:9-13) or in cases of misconduct (Gen. 49:3,4).

21:18-21 a stubborn and rebellious son. Cf. 27:16. The long-term pattern of rebellion and sin of a child who was incorrigibly disobedient is in view. No hope remained for such a person who flagrantly violated the fifth commandment (Ex. 20:12), so he was to be stoned to death.

21:22,23 hang him on a tree. After an execution, the body was permitted to hang on a tree for the rest of the day as a public display of the consequences of disobedience. However, the body was not to remain on the tree overnight, but was to be properly buried before sunset. Cf. Gal. 3:13, where Paul quotes this text in regard to the death of the Lord Jesus Christ.

22:1–26:19 While loving God was the first duty (cf. 6:5), loving one's neighbor came next (cf. Matt. 22:37-40). In this section, the law of loving one's neighbor is applied to domestic and social relationships.

22:1-4 hide yourself. The Israelite must not hide his eyes from such an obvious loss. It was his duty to pursue and bring back the lost property of his neighbor.

22:5 anything that pertains to a man…woman's garment. Found only here in the Pentateuch, this statute prohibited a man from wearing any item of feminine clothing or ornamentation, or a woman from wearing any item of masculine clothing or ornamentation. The same word translated "abomination" was used to describe God's view of homosexuality (Lev. 18:22; 20:13). This instance specifically outlawed transvestism. The creation order distinctions between male and female were to be maintained without exception (cf. Gen 1:27).

22:6 a bird's nest. Found only here in the Pentateuch, this law showed that God cared for the long-term provisions for His people. By letting the mother go, food could be acquired without killing the source of future food.

22:8 a parapet. Found only here in the Pentateuch, this refers to the roof of a home in ancient Israel, which was flat and usually reached by outside stairs. To prevent injury or death from falling, a fence was to be built around the roof. This, too, expressed love for those who might otherwise be injured or killed.

22:9 different kinds of seed. The aim of the legislation seems to be to maintain healthy crops by keeping the seeds separate from one another. *See note on Lev. 19:19.*

22:10 an ox and a donkey together. According to the dietary

10 [f]"You shall not plow with an ox and a
donkey together.
11 [g]"You shall not wear a garment of different sorts, *such as* wool and linen mixed
together.
12 "You shall make [h]tassels on the four
corners of the clothing with which you
cover *yourself*.

Laws of Sexual Morality

13 "If any man takes a wife, and goes in
to her, and [i]detests her, 14 and charges her
with shameful conduct, and brings a bad
name on her, and says, 'I took this woman,
and when I came to her I found she *was* not
a virgin,' 15 then the father and mother of
the young woman shall take and bring out
the evidence of the young woman's virginity
to the elders of the city at the gate. 16 And
the young woman's father shall say to the
elders, 'I gave my daughter to this man as
wife, and he detests her. 17 Now he has
charged her with shameful conduct, saying, "I found your daughter *was* not a virgin," and yet these *are the evidences of* my
daughter's virginity.' And they shall
spread the cloth before the elders of the
city. 18 Then the elders of that city shall
take that man and punish him; 19 and they
shall fine him one hundred *shekels* of silver
and give *them* to the father of the young
woman, because he has brought a bad
name on a virgin of Israel. And she shall be
his wife; he cannot divorce her all his days.
20 "But if the thing is true, *and evidences
of* virginity are not found for the young
woman, 21 then they shall bring out the
young woman to the door of her father's
house, and the men of her city shall stone
her to death with [j]stones, because she has
[k]done a disgraceful thing in Israel, to play
the harlot in her father's house. [l]So you
shall [4]put away the evil from among you.

10 [f][2 Cor. 6:14-16]
11 [g] Lev. 19:19
12 [h] Num. 15:37-41; Matt. 23:5
13 [i] Deut. 21:15; 24:3
21 [j] Deut. 21:21 [k] Gen. 34:7; Judg. 20:5-10; 2 Sam. 13:12, 13 [l] Deut. 13:5 [4] *purge the evil person*
22 [m] Lev. 20:10; Num. 5:22-27; Ezek. 16:38; [Matt. 5:27, 28]; John 8:5; [1 Cor. 6:9; Heb. 13:4]
23 [n] Lev. 19:20-22; Matt. 1:18, 19
24 [o] Deut. 21:14 [p] Deut. 22:21, 22; 1 Cor. 5:2, 13
28 [q] Ex. 22:16, 17
29 [r] Ex. 22:16, 17 [s] Deut. 22:24
30 [t] Lev. 18:8; 20:11; Deut. 27:20; 1 Cor. 5:1 [u] Ruth 3:9; Ezek. 16:8

CHAPTER 23

1 [a] Lev. 21:20; 22:24

22 [m]"If a man is found lying with a
woman married to a husband, then both of
them shall die—the man that lay with the
woman, and the woman; so you shall put
away the evil from Israel.
23 "If a young woman *who is* a virgin is
[n]betrothed to a husband, and a man finds
her in the city and lies with her, 24 then you
shall bring them both out to the gate of that
city, and you shall stone them to death
with stones, the young woman because
she did not cry out in the city, and the man
because he [o]humbled his neighbor's wife;
[p]so you shall put away the evil from
among you.
25 "But if a man finds a betrothed young
woman in the countryside, and the man
forces her and lies with her, then only the
man who lay with her shall die. 26 But you
shall do nothing to the young woman; *there
is* in the young woman no sin *deserving* of
death, for just as when a man rises against
his neighbor and kills him, even so *is* this
matter. 27 For he found her in the countryside, *and* the betrothed young woman
cried out, but *there was* no one to save her.
28 [q]"If a man finds a young woman *who
is* a virgin, who is not betrothed, and he
seizes her and lies with her, and they are
found out, 29 then the man who lay with
her shall give to the young woman's father
[r]fifty *shekels* of silver, and she shall be his
wife [s]because he has humbled her; he shall
not be permitted to divorce her all his
days.
30 [t]"A man shall not take his father's
wife, nor [u]uncover his father's bed.

Those Excluded from the Congregation

23 "He who is emasculated by crushing or mutilation shall [a]not enter
the assembly of the LORD.
2 "One of illegitimate birth shall not

laws prescribed earlier (14:1-8), the ox was a "clean" animal, but the donkey was "unclean." Even more compelling was the fact that these two different animals couldn't together plow a straight furrow. Their temperaments, natural instincts, and physical characteristics made it impossible. As with the seed (v. 9), God is protecting his people's food.

22:11 garment...wool and linen. *See note on Lev. 19:19.*

22:12 make tassels. See Num. 15:38-40 for the purpose of these tassels.

22:13-30 This section is on family life (cf. Lev. 18:1-30; 20:10-21).

22:13-21 An Israelite who doubted the virginity of his bride was to make a formal accusation to the "elders of the city." If her parents gave proof of virginity showing the accusation was false, the husband was to pay a penalty and was prohibited from divorcing the woman. However, if she was found not to be a virgin, then she was to be put to death.

22:15 *the evidence of* the young woman's virginity. Probably a blood-stained garment or a bed sheet from the wedding night.

22:19 *shekels.* This word is not in the Hebrew text, but the context suggests it. A shekel weighed .4 oz., so the total fine would be about 2.5 lbs. of silver.

22:22-29 Adultery was punished by death for the two found in the act. If the adulterous persons were a man with a woman who was pledged to be married to someone else, this consentual act led to the death of both parties (vv. 23,24). However, if the man forced (i.e., raped) the woman, then only the man's life was required (vv. 25-27). If the woman was a virgin not pledged in marriage, then the man had to pay a fine, marry the girl, and keep her as his wife as long as he lived (vv. 28,29).

22:30 A man shall not take his father's wife. In no case was a man to marry his father's wife or have sexual relations with her. This probably has relations with a stepmother in view, though incest was certainly forbidden (cf. Lev. 18:6-8).

23:1 the assembly of the LORD. From the sanctification of the home and marriage in the previous chapter, Moses proceeds to the sanctification of their union as a congregation and speaks of the right

enter the assembly of the LORD; even to the
tenth generation none of his *descendants*
shall enter the assembly of the LORD.
3 [b]"An Ammonite or Moabite shall not
enter the assembly of the LORD; even to
the tenth generation none of his *descendants* shall enter the assembly of the LORD
forever, 4 [c]because they did not meet you
with bread and water on the road when
you came out of Egypt, and [d]because they
hired against you Balaam the son of Beor
from Pethor of [1]Mesopotamia, to curse
you. 5 Nevertheless the LORD your God
would not listen to Balaam, but the LORD
your God turned the curse into a blessing
for you, because the LORD your God
[e]loves you. 6 [f]You shall not seek their
peace nor their prosperity all your days
forever.
7 "You shall not abhor an Edomite, [g]for
he *is* your brother. You shall not abhor an
Egyptian, because [h]you were an alien in
his land. 8 The children of the third generation born to them may enter the assembly
of the LORD.

Cleanliness of the Camp Site

9 "When the army goes out against your
enemies, then keep yourself from every
wicked thing. 10 [i]If there is any man
among you who becomes unclean by some
occurrence in the night, then he shall go
outside the camp; he shall not come inside
the camp. 11 But it shall be, when evening
comes, that [j]he shall wash with water; and
when the sun sets, he may come into the
camp.
12 "Also you shall have a place outside
the camp, where you may go out; 13 and
you shall have an implement among your
equipment, and when you sit down outside, you shall dig with it and turn and
cover your refuse. 14 For the LORD your
God [k]walks in the midst of your camp, to
deliver you and give your enemies over to
you; therefore your camp shall be holy,
that He may see no unclean thing among
you, and turn away from you.

Miscellaneous Laws

15 [l]"You shall not give back to his master
the slave who has escaped from his master
to you. 16 He may dwell with you in your
midst, in the place which he chooses within one of your gates, where it [2]seems best
to him; [m]you shall not oppress him.
17 "There shall be no *ritual* [3]harlot [n]of
the daughters of Israel, or a [o]perverted[4]
one of the sons of Israel. 18 You shall not
bring the wages of a harlot or the price of
a dog to the house of the LORD your God
for any vowed offering, for both of these
are [5]an abomination to the LORD your
God.
19 [p]"You shall not charge interest to
your brother—interest on money *or* food
or anything that is lent out at interest.
20 [q]To a foreigner you may charge interest,

3 [b] Neh. 13:1, 2
4 [c] Deut. 2:27-30 [d] Num. 22:5, 6; 23:7; Josh. 24:9; 2 Pet. 2:15; Jude 11 [1] Heb. *Aram Naharaim*
5 [e] Deut. 4:37
6 [f] Ezra 9:12
7 [g] Gen. 25:24-26; Deut. 2:4, 8; Amos 1:11; Obad. 10, 12 [h] Ex. 22:21; 23:9; Lev. 19:34; Deut. 10:19
10 [i] Lev. 15:16
11 [j] Lev. 15:5
14 [k] Lev. 26:12; Deut. 7:21
15 [l] 1 Sam. 30:15
16 [m] Ex. 22:21; Prov. 22:22 [2] *pleases him best*
17 [n] Lev. 19:29; Deut. 22:21 [o] Gen. 19:5; 2 Kin. 23:7 [3] Heb. *qedeshah*, fem. of *qadesh* (note 2) [4] Heb. *qadesh*, one practicing sodomy and prostitution in religious rituals
18 [5] *detestable*
19 [p] Ex. 22:25; Lev. 25:35-37; Neh. 5:2-7; Ps. 15:5
20 [q] Deut. 15:3

of citizenship, including being gathered before the presence of the Lord to worship Him. Most likely, this law did not exclude one from residence in the area where Israel was to live, but from public offices and honors, intermarriage, and participation in the religious rights at the tabernacle plus later at the temple. The emasculated (v. 1), the illegitimate (v. 2), and the Ammonites and Moabites (vv. 3-6) were not allowed to worship the Lord. The general rule was that strangers and foreigners, for fear of friendship or marriage connections which would lead Israel into idolatry, were not admissible until their conversion to God and the Jewish faith. This purge, however, describes some limitations to the general rule. Eunuchs, illegitimate children, and people from Ammon and Moab were excluded. Eunuchs were forbidden because such willful mutilation (lit. in Heb., by crushing, which was the way such an act was generally performed) violated God's creation of man, was associated with idolatrous practices and was done by pagan parents to their children so that they might serve as eunuchs in the homes of the great (cf. 25:11,12). The illegitimate were excluded so as to place an indelible stigma as a discouragement to shameful sexual misconduct. People from Ammon and Moab were excluded, not because they were born out of incest (cf. Gen 19:30ff.), but on account of their vicious hostility toward God and His people Israel. Many of the Israelites were settled E of the Jordan in the immediate neighborhood of these people, so God raised this wall to prevent the evils of idolatrous influence. Individuals from all 3 of these outcast groups are offered grace and acceptance by Isaiah upon personal faith in the true God (cf. Is. 56:1-8). Ruth the Moabitess serves as a most notable example (cf. Ruth 1:4,16).

23:2,3 to the tenth generation. The use of the word "forever" in vv. 3,6 seems to indicate that this phrase is an idiom denoting permanent exclusion from the worshiping community of Israel. In contrast, an Edomite or Egyptian might worship in Israel in the third generation (see vv. 7,8). Though these nations had also been enemies, Edom was a near relative, coming from Jacob's family, while individual Egyptians had shown kindness to the Israelites at the Exodus (cf. Ex. 12:36).

23:9-14 Because the camp of Israelite soldiers was a place of God's presence (v. 14), the camp was to be kept clean. Instruction was given concerning nocturnal emission (vv. 10,11) and defecation (vv. 12,13). Such instruction for external cleanness illustrated what God wanted in the heart.

23:15–25:19 Moses selected 21 sample laws to further illustrate the nature of the requirements of living under the Sinaitic Covenant.

23:15,16 A fugitive slave was not to be turned over to his master. Evidently this has in mind a slave from the Canaanites or other neighboring nations who was driven out by oppression or with a desire to know Israel's God.

23:17,18 Prostitution as a form of worship was forbidden. "Dog" was a reference to male prostitutes (cf. Rev. 22:15).

23:19,20 This prohibition of lending money at interest to a fellow Israelite is qualified by Ex. 22:25 and Lev. 25:35,36, which indicates that it restricts its application to the poor and prevents further impoverishment, but it was allowed for foreigners who were engaged in trade and commerce to enlarge their wealth. According to Deut. 15:1,2, it is also clear that money could be legitimately lent in the normal course of business, subject to forgiveness of all unpaid debt in the sabbatical year (cf. 24:10).

but to your brother you shall not charge
interest, [r]that the LORD your God may
bless you in all to which you set your hand
in the land which you are entering to possess.
21 [s]"When you make a vow to the LORD
your God, you shall not delay to pay it; for
the LORD your God will surely require it of
you, and it would be sin to you. 22 But if
you abstain from vowing, it shall not be sin
to you. 23 [t]That which has gone from your
lips you shall keep and perform, for you
voluntarily vowed to the LORD your God
what you have promised with your
mouth.
24 "When you come into your neighbor's vineyard, you may eat your fill of
grapes at your pleasure, but you shall not
put *any* in your container. 25 When you
come into your neighbor's standing grain,
[u]you may pluck the heads with your hand,
but you shall not use a sickle on your
neighbor's standing grain.

Law Concerning Divorce

24 "When a [a]man takes a wife and
marries her, and it happens that she
finds no favor in his eyes because he has
found some [1]uncleanness in her, and he
writes her a [b]certificate of divorce, puts *it*
in her hand, and sends her out of his
house, 2 when she has departed from his
house, and goes and becomes another
man's *wife,* 3 *if* the latter husband detests
her and writes her a certificate of divorce,
puts *it* in her hand, and sends her out of his
house, or if the latter husband dies who
took her as his wife, 4 [c]*then* her former husband who divorced her must not take her
back to be his wife after she has been defiled; for that *is* [2]an abomination before the
LORD, and you shall not bring sin on the
land which the LORD your God is giving
you *as* an inheritance.

Miscellaneous Laws

5 [d]"When a man has taken a new wife,
he shall not go out to war or be charged
with any business; he shall be free at home
one year, and [e]bring happiness to his wife
whom he has taken.
6 "No man shall take the lower or the
upper millstone in pledge, for he takes
[3]*one's* living in pledge.
7 "If a man is [f]found [4]kidnapping any of
his brethren of the children of Israel, and
mistreats him or sells him, then that kid-
napper shall die; [g]and you shall put away
the evil from among you.
8 "Take heed in [h]an outbreak of leprosy,
that you carefully observe and do according to all that the priests, the Levites, shall
teach you; just as I commanded them, *so*
you shall be careful to do. 9 [i]Remember
what the LORD your God did [j]to Miriam on
the way when you came out of Egypt!
10 "When you [k]lend your brother anything, you shall not go into his house to
get his pledge. 11 You shall stand outside,
and the man to whom you lend shall bring
the pledge out to you. 12 And if the man *is*
poor, you shall not [5]keep his pledge
overnight. 13 [l]You shall in any case return
the pledge to him again when the sun goes
down, that he may sleep in his own garment and [m]bless you; and [n]it shall be

20 [r] Deut. 15:10
21 [s] Num. 30:1, 2; Job 22:27; Ps. 61:8; Eccl. 5:4, 5; Matt. 5:33
23 [t] Num. 30:2; Ps. 66:13, 14
25 [u] Matt. 12:1; Mark 2:23; Luke 6:1

CHAPTER 24

1 [a] [Matt. 5:31; 19:7; Mark 10:4] [b] [Jer. 3:8] [1] *indecency,* lit. *nakedness of a thing*
4 [c] [Jer. 3:1]
[2] *a detestable thing*
5 [d] Deut. 20:7 [e] Prov. 5:18
6 [3] *life*
7 [f] Ex. 21:16 [g] Deut. 19:19 [4] Lit. *stealing*
8 [h] Lev. 13:2; 14:2
9 [i] [1 Cor. 10:6] [j] Num. 12:10
10 [k] Matt. 5:42
12 [5] Lit. *sleep with his pledge*
13 [l] Ex. 22:26; Ezek. 18:7 [m] Job 29:11; 2 Tim. 1:18 [n] Deut. 6:25; Ps. 106:31; Dan. 4:27

23:21-23 Though vows were made voluntarily, they were to be promptly kept once made. Cf. Num. 30:2.

23:24,25 Farmers were to share their produce with the people in the Land, but the people were not to profit from the farmers' generosity.

24:1-4 This passage does not command, commend, condone, or even suggest divorce. Rather, it recognizes that divorce occurs and permits it only on restricted grounds. The case presented here is designed to convey the fact that divorcing produced defilement. Notice the following sequence: 1) if a man finds an uncleanness (some impurity or something vile, cf. 23:14) in his wife, other than adultery, which was punished by execution (cf. 22:22); 2) if he legally divorces her (although God hates divorce, as Mal. 2:16 says; He has designed marriage for life, as Gen. 2:24 declares; and He allowed divorce because of hard hearts, as Matt. 19:8 reveals); 3) if she then marries another man; 4) if the new husband then dies or divorces her; then that woman could not return to her first husband (v. 4). This is so because she was "defiled" with such a defilement that is an abomination to the Lord and a sinful pollution of the Promised Land. What constitutes that defilement? Only one thing is possible—she was defiled in the remarriage because there was no ground for the divorce. So when she remarried, she became an adulteress (Matt. 5:31,32) and is thus defiled so that her former husband can't take her back. Illegitimate divorce proliferates adultery. *See notes on Matt. 5:31,32; 19:4-9.*

24:5 During the first year of marriage, a man was not held responsible for military service or any other duty. He was to devote that year of marriage to the enjoyment and establishment of his marriage.

24:6 Two millstones were needed to grind grain. Neither was to be taken in pledge because it was indispensable to one's daily subsistence.

24:7 The death penalty would be exacted on kidnappers who kidnaped a brother Israelite for involuntary servitude or as merchandise to sell.

24:8,9 Moses exhorted the people to follow the commands of the Lord regarding infectious skin diseases (*see notes on Lev. 13:1–14:57*).

24:10-13 his pledge. This would often be a cloak, an outer garment, which was given in pledge to guarantee the repayment of a loan. God's people were to act righteously in the lending of money. An example of a righteous lender was one who did not forcefully exact payment and who allowed a poor person to retain his pledge (cloak) overnight if it was necessary to keep him warm. Lending to the poor was permitted, but without 1) interest (23:19,20); 2) coercion to repay; and 3) extension of the loan beyond the sabbatical year (15:1,2).

righteousness to you before the LORD your
God.
14 "You shall not [o]oppress a hired servant *who is* poor and needy, *whether* one of
your brethren or one of the aliens who *is* in
your land within your gates. 15 Each day
[p]you shall give *him* his wages, and not let
the sun go down on it, for he *is* poor and
has set his heart on it; [q]lest he cry out
against you to the LORD, and it be sin to
you.
16 [r]"Fathers shall not be put to death for
their children, nor shall children be put to
death for *their* fathers; a person shall be put
to death for his own sin.
17 [s]"You shall not pervert justice due the
stranger or the fatherless, [t]nor take a
widow's garment as a pledge. 18 But [u]you
shall remember that you were a slave in
Egypt, and the LORD your God redeemed
you from there; therefore I command you
to do this thing.
19 [v]"When you reap your harvest in
your field, and forget a sheaf in the field,
you shall not go back to get it; it shall be for
the stranger, the fatherless, and the widow,
that the LORD your God may [w]bless you in
all the work of your hands. 20 When you
beat your olive trees, you shall not go over
the boughs again; it shall be for the stranger, the fatherless, and the widow. 21 When
you gather the grapes of your vineyard,
you shall not glean *it* afterward; it shall be
for the stranger, the fatherless, and the
widow. 22 And you shall remember that
you were a slave in the land of Egypt;
therefore I command you to do this thing.

25 "If there is a [a]dispute between men,
and they come to [1]court, that *the
judges* may judge them, and they [b]justify
the righteous and condemn the wicked,
2 then it shall be, if the wicked man [c]de-
serves to be beaten, that the judge will
cause him to lie down [d]and be beaten in
his presence, according to his guilt, with a
certain number of blows. 3 [e]Forty blows he
may give him *and* no more, lest he should
exceed this and beat him with many blows
above these, and your brother [f]be humiliated in your sight.
4 [g]"You shall not muzzle an ox while it
[2]treads out *the grain.*

Marriage Duty of the Surviving Brother

5 [h]"If brothers dwell together, and one of
them dies and has no son, the widow of
the dead man shall not be *married* to a
stranger outside *the family;* her husband's
brother shall go in to her, take her as his
wife, and perform the duty of a husband's
brother to her. 6 And it shall be *that* the
firstborn son which she bears [i]will succeed
to the name of his dead brother, that [j]his
name may not be blotted out of Israel.
7 But if the man does not want to take his
brother's wife, then let his brother's wife
go up to the [k]gate to the elders, and say,
'My husband's brother refuses to raise up
a name to his brother in Israel; he will not
perform the duty of my husband's brother.' 8 Then the elders of his city shall call
him and speak to him. But *if* he stands firm
and says, [l]'I do not want to take her,' 9 then
his brother's wife shall come to him in the
presence of the elders, [m]remove his sandal
from his foot, spit in his face, and answer
and say, 'So shall it be done to the man
who will not [n]build up his brother's
house.' 10 And his name shall be called in
Israel, 'The house of him who had his sandal removed.'

Miscellaneous Laws

11 "If *two* men fight together, and the

---

14 [o] Lev. 19:13; Deut. 15:7-18; [Prov. 14:31]; Amos 4:1; [Mal. 3:5; 1 Tim. 5:18]
15 [p] Lev. 19:13; Jer. 22:13 [q] Ex. 22:23; Deut. 15:9; Job 35:9; James 5:4
16 [r] 2 Kin. 14:6; 2 Chr. 25:4; Jer. 31:29, 30; Ezek. 18:20
17 [s] Ex. 23:6 [t] Ex. 22:26
18 [u] Deut. 24:22
19 [v] Lev. 19:9, 10 [w] Deut. 15:10; Ps. 41:1; Prov. 19:17

CHAPTER 25

1 [a] Deut. 17:8-13; 19:17; Ezek. 44:24 [b] Prov. 17:15 [1] Lit. *the judgment*
2 [c] Prov. 19:29; Luke 12:48
[d] Matt. 10:17
3 [e] 2 Cor. 11:24 [f] Job 18:3
4 [g] [Prov. 12:10; 1 Cor. 9:9; 1 Tim. 5:18] [2] *threshes*
5 [h] Matt. 22:24; Mark 12:19; Luke 20:28
6 [i] Gen. 38:9 [j] Ruth 4:5, 10
7 [k] Ruth 4:1, 2
8 [l] Ruth 4:6
9 [m] Ruth 4:7, 8 [n] Ruth 4:11

24:14,15 Day laborers were to be paid on the day they labored because they lived day to day on such wages (cf. Lev. 19:13; Matt. 20:1-16).

24:16 Punishment for a crime was to be born only by the offender. *See notes on Ezek. 18.* The death of Saul's 7 grandsons (2 Sam. 21:5-9) is a striking exception of national proportion grounded in God's sovereign wisdom, as was the death of David and Bathsheba's first son (2 Sam. 12:14).

24:17,18 The administration of law should be carried out with equity for all members of society, including those with the least power and influence, e.g., widows, orphans, and immigrants.

24:19-22 The practice of allowing the needy to glean in the field was grounded in the remembrance of Israel's hard service in Egypt (v. 18).

25:1-3 Corporal punishment for crimes committed was to be equitably carried out in the presence of the judges and was limited to 40 stripes.

25:4 A worker must be allowed to enjoy the fruit of his own labor (cf. 1 Cor. 9:9; 1 Tim. 5:18; 2 Tim. 2:6).

25:5-10 Levirate marriages (from Latin, *levir,* "husband's brother") provided that the brother of a dead man who died childless was to marry the widow in order to provide an heir. These were not compulsory marriages in Israel, but were applied as strong options to brothers who shared the same estate. Obviously, this required that the brother be unmarried and desired to keep the property in the family by passing it on to a son. Cf. Lev. 18:16; 20:21 where adultery with a living brother's wife is forbidden. Though not compulsory, this practice reflected fraternal affection, and if a single brother refused to conform to this practice, he was confronted with contempt and humiliation by the elders. The perpetuation of his name as a member of the covenant people witnessed to the dignity of the individual. Since Num. 27:4-8 gave daughters the right of inheritance when there were no sons in a family, it is reasonable to read "no child" rather than "no son" in v. 5. Cf. Tamar, Gen. 38:8-10, and the Boaz-Ruth marriage, Ruth 4:1-17.

25:5 Cf. Matt. 22:24; Mark 12:19; Luke 20:28.

25:11,12 The consequence of the immodest act was the only example of punishment by mutilation in the Pentateuch.

wife of one draws near to rescue her husband from the hand of the one attacking
him, and puts out her hand and seizes him
by the genitals, 12 then you shall cut off her
hand; [o]your eye shall not pity *her.*
13 [p]"You shall not have in your bag differing weights, a heavy and a light. 14 You
shall not have in your house differing measures, a large and a small. 15 You shall have
a perfect and just weight, a perfect and just
measure, [q]that your days may be length-
ened in the land which the LORD your God
is giving you. 16 For [r]all who do such
things, all who behave unrighteously, *are*
[3]an abomination to the LORD your God.

Destroy the Amalekites

17 [s]"Remember what Amalek did to you
on the way as you were coming out of
Egypt, 18 how he met you on the way and
attacked your rear ranks, all the stragglers
at your rear, when you *were* tired and
weary; and he [t]did not fear God. 19 Therefore it shall be, [u]when the LORD your God
has given you rest from your enemies all
around, in the land which the LORD your
God is giving you to possess *as* an inheritance, *that* you will [v]blot out the remembrance of Amalek from under heaven. You
shall not forget.

Offerings of Firstfruits and Tithes

26 "And it shall be, when you come
into the land which the LORD your
God is giving you *as* an inheritance, and
you possess it and dwell in it, 2 [a]that you
shall take some of the first of all the produce of the ground, which you shall bring
from your land that the LORD your God is
giving you, and put *it* in a basket and [b]go
to the place where the LORD your God
chooses to make His name abide. 3 And
you shall go to the one who is priest in
those days, and say to him, 'I declare today
to the LORD [1]your God that I have come to
the country which the LORD swore to our
fathers to give us.'
4 "Then the priest shall take the basket
out of your hand and set it down before
the altar of the LORD your God. 5 And you
shall answer and say before the LORD your
God: 'My father *was* [c]a [2]Syrian, [d]about to
perish, and [e]he went down to Egypt and
[3]dwelt there, [f]few in number; and there he
became a nation, [g]great, mighty, and populous. 6 But the [h]Egyptians mistreated us,
afflicted us, and laid hard bondage on us.
7 [i]Then we cried out to the LORD God of
our fathers, and the LORD heard our voice
and looked on our affliction and our labor
and our oppression. 8 So [j]the LORD brought
us out of Egypt with a mighty hand and
with an outstretched arm, [k]with great terror and with signs and wonders. 9 He has
brought us to this place and has given us
this land, [l]"a land flowing with milk and
honey"; 10 and now, behold, I have
brought the firstfruits of the land which
you, O LORD, have given me.'
"Then you shall set it before the LORD
your God, and worship before the LORD
your God. 11 So [m]you shall rejoice in every
good *thing* which the LORD your God has
given to you and your house, you and the
Levite and the stranger who *is* among you.
12 "When you have finished laying aside
all the [n]tithe of your increase in the third

12 [o]Deut. 7:2; 19:13
13 [p]Lev. 19:35-37; Prov. 11:1; 20:23; Ezek. 45:10; Mic. 6:11
15 [q]Ex. 20:12
16 [r]Prov. 11:1; [1 Thess. 4:6] [3]*detestable*
17 [s]Ex. 17:8-16; 1 Sam. 15:1-3
18 [t][Ps. 36:1]; Rom. 3:18
19 [u]1 Sam. 15:3 [v]Ex. 17:14

CHAPTER 26

2 [a]Ex. 22:29; 23:16, 19; Num. 18:13; Deut. 16:10; Prov. 3:9
[b]Deut. 12:5
3 [1]LXX *my*
5 [c]Gen. 25:20; Hos. 12:12 [d]Gen. 43:1, 2; 45:7, 11 [e]Gen. 46:1, 6; Acts 7:15 [f]Gen. 46:27; Deut. 10:22 [g]Deut. 1:10 [2]Or *Aramean* [3]As a resident alien
6 [h]Ex. 1:8-11, 14
7 [i]Ex. 2:23-25; 3:9; 4:31
8 [j]Ex. 12:37, 51; 13:3, 14, 16; Deut. 5:15 [k]Deut. 4:34; 34:11, 12
9 [l]Ex. 3:8, 17
11 [m]Deut. 12:7; 16:11; Eccl. 3:12, 13; 5:18-20
12 [n]Lev. 27:30; Num. 18:24

25:13-16 The weights and measures of trade were to be kept equitably so people were not cheated. Obedience meant prosperous years in the Land.

25:17-19 The admonition to remember the treachery of the Amalekites was repeated to the new generation (*see notes on Ex. 17:9-16*). For execution of the command, see 1 Sam. 15.

26:1-15 As the stipulation section of Deuteronomy came to an end (chaps. 5–25), Moses commanded the people to keep two rituals when they had conquered the Land and began to enjoy its produce. These two rituals were the initial firstfruits offering (26:1-11) and the first third-year special tithe (26:12-15). In both cases, there is an emphasis upon the prayer of confession to be given at the time of the rituals (26:5-10,13-15). These special offerings were given in order to celebrate Israel's transition from a nomadic existence to a settled agrarian community, made possible by the Lord's blessing.

26:2 the first of all the produce. Baskets of the firstfruits of the first harvest reaped by Israel once they were in the land of Canaan were to be taken to the tabernacle (cf. Ex. 23:19; 34:26; Num. 18:12-17). This is to be distinguished from the annual Feast of Firstfruits (cf. Lev. 23:9-14) celebrated in conjunction with the Passover and the Feast of Unleavened Bread.

26:5 you shall...say before the LORD your God. The offering of the firstfruits was to be accompanied by an elaborate confession of the Lord's faithfulness in preserving Israel and bringing the people into the Land. The essential aspects of the worshiper's coming to the sanctuary were the presentation of the firstfruits, bowing in worship, and rejoicing in the Lord's goodness. In this manner the visit to the sanctuary was a confession and acknowledgment of God. It was a time of praise and rejoicing because of God's goodness and mercy extended to former generations and evidence of divine sustaining grace at that time. **a Syrian, about to perish.** The word "perish" is better translated here "wandering." "A wandering Syrian" referred to Jacob, who was each Israelite's father or ancestor. When Jacob fled from his home in Beersheba he passed through Syria (Aram) to Mesopotamia (Aram-naharaim, Gen. 24:10) to live with Laban his uncle. Returning from there, Jacob was overtaken by Laban after he came through Syria at the Jabbok River, where he not only faced the wrath of Laban but also that of Esau his brother. Later, the famine in Canaan necessitated his migration to Egypt. When the Israelites became populous and powerful, they were oppressed by the Egyptians, but it was God who responded to their prayers and miraculously delivered them out of Egypt. It was God who enabled them to enter and conquer the Land from which the firstfruits were presented before the altar.

26:12 the tithe. I.e., the tithe collected every third year of Israel in the land of Canaan (see 14:28). Apparently this tithe was not taken to

year—[o]the year of tithing—and have given
it to the Levite, the stranger, the fatherless,
and the widow, so that they may eat within your gates and be filled, 13 then you
shall say before the LORD your God: 'I have
removed the [4]holy *tithe* from *my* house,
and also have given them to the Levite, the
stranger, the fatherless, and the widow, according to all Your commandments which
You have commanded me; I have not
transgressed Your commandments, [p]nor
have I forgotten *them.* 14 [q]I have not eaten
any of it [5]when in mourning, nor have I removed *any* of it [6]for an unclean *use,* nor
given *any* of it for the dead. I have obeyed
the voice of the LORD my God, and have
done according to all that You have commanded me. 15 [r]Look down from Your
holy [7]habitation, from heaven, and bless
Your people Israel and the land which You
have given us, just as You swore to our fathers, [s]"a land flowing with milk and
honey." '

A Special People of God

16 "This day the LORD your God commands you to observe these statutes and
judgments; therefore you shall be careful
to observe them with all your heart and
with all your soul. 17 Today you have [t]pro-
claimed the LORD to be your God, and that
you will walk in His ways and keep His
statutes, His commandments, and His
judgments, and that you will [u]obey His
voice. 18 Also today [v]the LORD has proclaimed you to be His special people, just
as He promised you, that *you* should keep
all His commandments, 19 and that He
will set you [w]high above all nations which
He has made, in praise, in name, and in
honor, and that you may be [x]a [8]holy people to the LORD your God, just as He has
spoken."

The Law Inscribed on Stones

27 Now Moses, with the elders of Israel, commanded the people, saying: "Keep all the commandments which I
command you today. 2 And it shall be, on
the day [a]when you cross over the Jordan to
the land which the LORD your God is giving you, that [b]you shall set up for yourselves large stones, and whitewash them
with lime. 3 You shall write on them all the
words of this law, when you have crossed
over, that you may enter the land which
the LORD your God is giving you, [c]'a land
flowing with milk and honey,' just as the
LORD God of your fathers promised you.
4 Therefore it shall be, when you have
crossed over the Jordan, *that* [d]on Mount
Ebal you shall set up these stones, which I
command you today, and you shall whitewash them with lime. 5 And there you
shall build an altar to the LORD your God,
an altar of stones; [e]you shall not use an

12 [o] Deut. 14:28, 29
13 [p] Ps. 119:141, 153, 176 [4] *hallowed things*
14 [q] Lev. 7:20; Jer. 16:7; Hos. 9:4 [5] Lit. *in my mourning* [6] Or *while I was unclean*
15 [r] Ps. 80:14; Is. 63:15; Zech. 2:13 [s] Ex. 3:8 [7] *home*
17 [t] Ex. 20:19 [u] Deut. 15:5
18 [v] Ex. 6:7; 19:5; Deut. 7:6; 14:2; 28:9; [Titus 2:14; 1 Pet. 2:9]
19 [w] Deut. 4:7, 8; 28:1 [x] Ex. 19:6; Deut. 7:6; 28:9; Is. 62:12; [1 Pet. 2:9] [8] *consecrated*

CHAPTER 27

2 [a] Josh. 4:1 [b] Josh. 8:32
3 [c] Ex. 3:8
4 [d] Deut. 11:29; Josh. 8:30, 31
5 [e] Ex. 20:25; Josh. 8:31

---

the central sanctuary, but distributed locally to Levites, immigrants, widows, and orphans. For the other regular annual tithes, *see note on 14:22.*

26:13,14 you shall say before the LORD your God. The confession to be made in connection with the offering of this first tithe consisted of a statement of obedience (vv. 13,14) and a prayer for God's blessing (v. 15). In this manner, the Israelite confessed his continual dependence on God and lived in obedient expectance of God's continued gracious blessing.

26:15 Look down from...heaven. This was the first reference to God's dwelling place being in heaven. From His abode in heaven, God had given the Israelites the Land flowing with milk and honey as He had promised to the patriarchs. His continued blessing on both the people and the Land was requested.

26:16-19 These 4 verses concluded Moses' explanation of the law's stipulations by calling for the total commitment by Israel to the Lord and His commands. These verses can be viewed as the formal ratification of the Sinaitic Covenant between the Lord and the second generation of Israel. In accepting the terms of this agreement, acknowledging that the Lord is their God, and promising wholehearted obedience plus a desire to listen to God's voice, the Israelites were assured that they were His people and the chosen over all other nations to receive His blessings and the calling to witness to His glory to all the world. See Ex. 19:5,6.

26:16 This day. I.e., the first day of the 11th month of the 40th year (1:3). Note also, "today" in vv. 17,18.

27:1–28:68 In these two chapters, Moses explained the curses and the blessings associated with the Sinaitic Covenant. He first called Israel to perform an elaborate ceremony to ratify the covenant when they entered the Land (27:1-26; carried out by Joshua in Josh. 8:30-35). This was to remind the people that it was essential to obey the covenant and its laws. Then, Moses further explained the blessings for obedience and the curses for disobedience (28:1-68).

27:2,4 whitewash them with lime. Upon arrival in the Land of Promise, under Joshua, large stone pillars were to be erected. Following the method used in Egypt, they were to be prepared for writing by whitewashing with plaster. When the law was written on the stones, the white background would make it clearly visible and easily read. These inscribed stones were to offer constant testimony to all people and coming generations of their relationship to God and His law (cf. 31:26; Josh. 24:26,27).

27:3,8 all the words of this law. Probably a reference to the whole book of Deuteronomy.

27:4 Mount Ebal. A mountain in the center of the Promised Land, just to the N of the city of Shechem. It was at Shechem that the Lord first appeared to Abraham in the land and where Abraham built his first altar to the Lord (Gen. 12:6,7). This mountain, where the stone pillars with the law and the altar (v. 5) were built, was the place where the curses were to be read (v. 13).

27:5-7 build an altar. In addition to setting up the stones, the Israelites were to build an altar of uncut stones. On this altar the offerings were to be brought to the Lord, and together the people would rejoice in God's presence. This is what was done when the covenantal relationship was established at Mt. Sinai (Ex. 24:1-8). The burnt offerings, completely consumed, represented complete devotion to God; the peace offerings expressed thanks to Him.

iron *tool* on them. 6 You shall build with
[1]whole stones the altar of the LORD your
God, and offer burnt offerings on it to the
LORD your God. 7 You shall offer peace offerings, and shall eat there, and [f]rejoice before the LORD your God. 8 And you shall
[g]write very plainly on the stones all the
words of this law."
9 Then Moses and the priests, the
Levites, spoke to all Israel, saying, "Take
heed and listen, O Israel: [h]This day you
have become the people of the LORD your
God. 10 Therefore you shall obey the voice
of the LORD your God, and observe His
commandments and His statutes which I
command you today."

Curses Pronounced from Mount Ebal

11 And Moses commanded the people
on the same day, saying, 12 "These shall
stand [i]on Mount Gerizim to bless the people, when you have crossed over the Jordan: Simeon, Levi, Judah, Issachar, Joseph,
and Benjamin; 13 and [j]these shall stand on
Mount Ebal to curse: Reuben, Gad, Asher,
Zebulun, Dan, and Naphtali.
14 "And [k]the Levites shall speak with a
loud voice and say to all the men of Israel:
15 [l]'Cursed *is* the one who makes a carved
or molded image, [2]an abomination to the
LORD, the work of the hands of the craftsman, and sets *it* up in secret.'
[m]"And all the people shall answer and
say, 'Amen!'
16 [n]'Cursed *is* the one who treats his father or his mother with contempt.'
"And all the people shall say, 'Amen!'
17 [o]'Cursed *is* the one who moves his
neighbor's landmark.'
"And all the people shall say, 'Amen!'
18 [p]'Cursed *is* the one who makes the
blind to wander off the road.'
"And all the people shall say, 'Amen!'
19 [q]'Cursed *is* the one who perverts the
justice due the stranger, the fatherless, and
widow.'
"And all the people shall say, 'Amen!'
20 [r]'Cursed *is* the one who lies with his
father's wife, because he has uncovered
his father's bed.'
"And all the people shall say, 'Amen!'
21 [s]'Cursed *is* the one who lies with any
kind of animal.'
"And all the people shall say, 'Amen!'
22 [t]'Cursed *is* the one who lies with his
sister, the daughter of his father or the
daughter of his mother.'
"And all the people shall say, 'Amen!'
23 [u]'Cursed *is* the one who lies with his
mother-in-law.'
"And all the people shall say, 'Amen!'
24 [v]'Cursed *is* the one who attacks his
neighbor secretly.'
"And all the people shall say, 'Amen!'
25 [w]'Cursed *is* the one who takes a bribe
to slay an innocent person.'
"And all the people shall say, 'Amen!'
26 [x]'Cursed *is* the one who does not confirm *all* the words of this law.'
"And all the people shall say, 'Amen!' "

6 [1] *uncut*
7 [f] Deut. 26:11
8 [g] Josh. 8:32
9 [h] Deut. 26:18
12 [i] Deut. 11:29; Josh. 8:33; Judg. 9:7
13 [j] Deut. 11:29; Josh. 8:33
14 [k] Deut. 33:10; Josh. 8:33; Dan. 9:11
15 [l] Ex. 20:4, 23; 34:17; Lev. 19:4; 26:1; Deut. 4:16, 23; Is. 44:9; Hos. 13:2 [m] Num. 5:22; Jer. 11:5; 1 Cor. 14:16 [2] *a detestable thing*
16 [n] Ex. 20:12; Lev. 19:3; 20:9; Deut. 5:16; 21:18-21; Ezek. 22:7
17 [o] Deut. 19:14; Prov. 22:28
18 [p] Lev. 19:14
19 [q] Ex. 22:21, 22; 23:9; Lev. 19:33; Deut. 10:18; 24:17
20 [r] Lev. 18:8; 20:11; Deut. 22:30; 1 Cor. 5:1
21 [s] Ex. 22:19; Lev. 18:23; 20:15, 16
22 [t] Lev. 18:9
23 [u] Lev. 18:17; 20:14
24 [v] Ex. 20:13; 21:12; Lev. 24:17; Num. 35:30, 31
25 [w] Ex. 23:7; Ps. 15:5; Ezek. 22:12
26 [x] Ps. 119:21; Jer. 11:3; Gal. 3:10

27:12,13 These...these. The 12 tribes were divided into two groups of 6 each. The tribe of Levi was to participate in the first group. The tribes of Manasseh and Ephraim were together as the tribe of Joseph.

27:12 Mount Gerizim. This was the mountain just to the S of Mt. Ebal with the city of Shechem in the valley between, from which the blessings were to be read. Perhaps the actual arrangement provided that the priests stood by the ark of the covenant, in the valley between the two mountains, with 6 tribes located northward toward Mt. Ebal and 6 southward toward Mt. Gerizim. The priests and Levites read the curses and blessings with the people responding with the "Amen" of affirmation. **to bless.** The blessings that were to be recited from Mt. Gerizim were not recorded in this passage, no doubt omitted here to stress that Israel did not prove themselves obedient to the covenant and, therefore, did not enjoy the blessings.

27:15-26 Twelve offenses serve as examples of the kind of iniquities that made one subject to the curse. These offenses might have been chosen because they are representative of sins that might escape detection and so remain secret (vv. 15,24).

27:15 one who makes a carved...image. The first curse concerned idolatry, the breaking of the first and second commandments (5:7-10). **Amen!** To each curse all the people responded, "Amen." The word means "so be it." The people thereby indicated their understanding and agreement with the statement made.

27:16 treats his father or his mother with contempt. The dishonoring of parents was the breaking of the fifth commandment (5:16).

27:17 landmark. *See note on 19:14.*

27:18 makes the blind to wander. This refers to abusing a blind man.

27:19 perverts the justice. The taking advantage of those members of society who could be easily abused.

27:20 lies with his father's wife. Incest. *See note on 22:30.*

27:21 lies with any kind of animal. Bestiality. See Ex. 22:19; Lev. 18:23; 20:15,16.

27:22 lies with his sister. The committing of incest with either a full sister or a half sister.

27:23 lies with his mother-in-law. See Lev. 18:17; 20:14.

27:24 attacks his neighbor secretly. A secret attempt to murder a neighbor.

27:25 takes a bribe. This relates to a paid assassin.

27:26 does not confirm *all* the words of this law. The final curse covered all the rest of God's commandments enunciated by Moses on the plains of Moab (cf. Gal. 3:10). Total obedience is demanded by the law and required by God. Only the Lord Jesus Christ accomplished this (2 Cor. 5:21). **Amen!** All the people agreed to be obedient (cf. Ex. 24:1-8), a promise they would soon violate.

Blessings on Obedience

28 "Now it shall come to pass, [a]if you
diligently obey the voice of the
LORD your God, to observe carefully all His
commandments which I command you
today, that the LORD your God [b]will set you
high above all nations of the earth. 2 And
all these blessings shall come upon you
and [c]overtake you, because you obey the
voice of the LORD your God:
3 [d]"Blessed *shall* you *be* in the city, and
blessed *shall* you *be* [e]in the country.
4 "Blessed *shall be* [f]the [1]fruit of your
body, the produce of your ground and the
increase of your herds, the increase of your
cattle and the offspring of your flocks.
5 "Blessed *shall be* your basket and your
kneading bowl.
6 [g]"Blessed *shall* you *be* when you come
in, and blessed *shall* you *be* when you go
out.
7 "The LORD [h]will cause your enemies
who rise against you to be defeated before
your face; they shall come out against you
one way and flee before you seven ways.
8 "The LORD will [i]command the blessing
on you in your storehouses and in all to
which you [j]set your hand, and He will
bless you in the land which the LORD your
God is giving you.
9 [k]"The LORD will establish you as a holy
people to Himself, just as He has sworn to
you, if you keep the commandments of the
LORD your God and walk in His ways.
10 Then all peoples of the earth shall see
that you are [l]called by the name of the
LORD, and they shall be [m]afraid of you.
11 And [n]the LORD will grant you plenty of
goods, in the fruit of your body, in the increase of your livestock, and in the produce of your ground, in the land of which
the LORD [2]swore to your fathers to give
you. 12 The LORD will open to you His
good [3]treasure, the heavens, [o]to give the
rain to your land in its season, and [p]to
bless all the work of your hand. [q]You shall
lend to many nations, but you shall not
borrow. 13 And the LORD will make [r]you
the head and not the tail; you shall be
above only, and not be beneath, if you
[4]heed the commandments of the LORD
your God, which I command you today,
and are careful to observe *them*. 14 [s]So you
shall not turn aside from any of the words
which I command you this day, *to* the right
or the left, to go after other gods to serve
them.

Curses on Disobedience

15 "But it shall come to pass, [t]if you do
not obey the voice of the LORD your God,
to observe carefully all His commandments and His statutes which I command
you today, that all these curses will come
upon you and overtake you:

CHAPTER 28
1 [a] Ex. 15:26; Lev. 26:3-13; Deut. 7:12-26; 11:13 [b] Deut. 26:19; 1 Chr. 14:2
2 [c] Deut. 28:15
3 [d] Ps. 128:1, 4 [e] Gen. 39:5
4 [f] Gen. 22:17 [1] *offspring*
6 [g] Ps. 121:8
7 [h] Lev. 26:7, 8
8 [i] Lev. 25:21 [j] Deut. 15:10
9 [k] Ex. 19:5, 6
10 [l] Num. 6:27; 2 Chr. 7:14; Is. 63:19; Dan. 9:18, 19 [m] Deut. 11:25
11 [n] Deut. 30:9 [2] *promised*
12 [o] Lev. 26:4; Deut. 11:14 [p] Deut. 14:29 [q] Deut. 15:6 [3] *storehouse*
13 [r] [Is. 9:14, 15] [4] *listen to*
14 [s] Deut. 5:32; Josh. 1:7
15 [t] Lev. 26:14-39; Josh. 23:15; Dan. 9:10-14; Mal. 2:2

28:1-68 In his responsibility as leader and mediator, Moses had previously told the people the promise of God's blessing and the warning that they should not turn to other gods when the covenant was given at Sinai (Ex. 23:20-33). After their rebellion against that covenant, Moses warned them (Lev. 26) of the divine judgment that would come if they disobeyed. Here, Moses gives an exhortation based upon the blessings and the curses of the covenant (see Lev. 26:1-45). The blessings and the curses in this chapter follow the same structure. First, Moses clearly explained that the quality of Israel's future experience would come on the basis of obedience or disobedience to God (28:1,2,15). Second, the actual blessings and curses were succinctly stated (28:3-6,16-19). Third, Moses gave a sermonic elaboration of the basic blessings and curses (28:7-14,20-68). Just as the curses were given more prominence in the ceremony of 27:11-26, so the curses incurred by disobedience to the covenant were much more fully developed here. The perspective of Moses was that Israel would not prove faithful to the covenant (31:16-18,27) and so would not enjoy the blessings of the covenant; therefore, the curses received much more attention.

28:1-14 See Josh. 21:45; 23:14,15; 1 Kin. 8:56 for blessing fulfillment.

28:1,2 diligently obey the voice of the LORD your God. "Diligently obey" stressed the need for complete obedience on the part of Israel. The people could not legally or personally merit God's goodness and blessing, but their constant desire to obey, worship and maintain a right relation to Him was evidence of their true faith in and love for Him (cf. 6:5). It was also evidence of God's gracious work in their hearts.

28:1 high above all nations. If Israel obeyed the Lord, ultimate blessing would be given in the form of preeminence above all the nations of the world (see 26:19). The indispensable condition for obtaining this blessing was salvation, resulting in obedience to the Lord, in the form of keeping His commandments. This blessing will ultimately come to pass in the millennial kingdom, particularly designed to exalt Israel's King, the Messiah, and His nation (see Zech. 13:1–14:21; Rom. 11:25-27).

28:3-6 Blessed. These beatitudes summarize the various spheres where the blessing of God would extend to Israel's life. God's favor is also intended to permeate all their endeavors as emphasized further in the expanded summary in 28:7-14, on the condition of obedience (vv. 1,2,9,13,14). They will know victory, prosperity, purity, respect, abundance, and dominance—comprehensive blessing.

28:6 come in...go out. An idiomatic way of referring to the normal everyday activities of life (see 31:2). This is a fitting conclusion to the "blessings and curses" (v. 19) since it sums up everything.

28:10 called by the name of the LORD. Israel's obedience and blessing would cause all the people of the earth to fear Israel because they were clearly the people of God. This was God's intention for them all along, to be a witness to the nations of the one true and living God and draw the Gentiles out of idol worship. They will be that witness nation in the last days (see Rev. 7:4-10; 14:1) and in the kingdom (see Zech. 8:1-12).

28:13 the head and not the tail. Israel was to be the leader over the other nations ("the head") and not to be in subjection to another nation ("the tail").

28:15-68 The curses are outlined as God warned His people of the price of the absence of love for Him and disobedience.

28:15 Cf. Josh. 23:15,16.

16 "Cursed *shall* you *be* in the city, and
cursed *shall* you *be* in the country.
17 "Cursed *shall be* your basket and your
kneading bowl.
18 "Cursed *shall be* the [5]fruit of your
body and the produce of your land, the increase of your cattle and the offspring of
your flocks.
19 "Cursed *shall* you *be* when you come
in, and cursed *shall* you *be* when you go out.
20 "The LORD will send on you [u]cursing,
[v]confusion, and [w]rebuke in all that you set
your hand to do, until you are destroyed
and until you perish quickly, because of
the wickedness of your doings in which
you have forsaken Me. 21 The LORD will
make the [6]plague cling to you until He has
consumed you from the land which you
are going to possess. 22 [x]The LORD will
strike you with consumption, with fever,
with inflammation, with severe burning
fever, with the sword, with [y]scorching,[7]
and with mildew; they shall pursue you
until you perish. 23 And [z]your heavens
which *are* over your head shall be bronze,
and the earth which is under you *shall be*
iron. 24 The LORD will change the rain of
your land to powder and dust; from the
heaven it shall come down on you until
you are destroyed.
25 [a]"The LORD will cause you to be defeated before your enemies; you shall go
out one way against them and flee seven
ways before them; and you shall become
[8]troublesome to all the kingdoms of the
earth. 26 [b]Your carcasses shall be food for
all the birds of the air and the beasts of the
earth, and no one shall frighten *them* away.
27 The LORD will strike you with [c]the boils
of Egypt, with [d]tumors, with the scab, and
with the itch, from which you cannot be
healed. 28 The LORD will strike you with
madness and blindness and [e]confusion of
heart. 29 And you shall [f]grope at noonday,
as a blind man gropes in darkness; you
shall not prosper in your ways; you shall
be only oppressed and plundered continually, and no one shall save *you.*
30 [g]"You shall betroth a wife, but another man shall lie with her; [h]you shall build
a house, but you shall not dwell in it; [i]you
shall plant a vineyard, but shall not gather
its grapes. 31 Your ox *shall be* slaughtered
before your eyes, but you shall not eat of it;
your donkey *shall be* violently taken away
from before you, and shall not be restored
to you; your sheep *shall be* given to your
enemies, and you shall have no one to rescue *them.* 32 Your sons and your daughters
shall be given to [j]another people, and your
eyes shall look and [k]fail *with longing* for
them all day long; and *there shall be* [9]no
strength in your [l]hand. 33 A nation whom
you have not known shall eat [m]the fruit of
your land and the produce of your labor,
and you shall be only oppressed and
crushed continually. 34 So you shall be
driven mad because of the sight which
your eyes see. 35 The LORD will strike you
in the knees and on the legs with severe
boils which cannot be healed, and from the
sole of your foot to the top of your head.
36 "The LORD will [n]bring you and the
king whom you set over you to a nation
which neither you nor your fathers have
known, and [o]there you shall serve other
gods—wood and stone. 37 And you shall
become [p]an[1] astonishment, a proverb,
[q]and a byword among all nations where
the LORD will drive you.
38 [r]"You shall carry much seed out to the
field but gather little in, for [s]the locust
shall [2]consume it. 39 You shall plant vineyards and tend *them,* but you shall neither

18 [5] *offspring* **20** [u] Mal. 2:2 [v] Is. 65:14 [w] Ps. 80:16; Is. 30:17 **21** [6] *pestilence* **22** [x] Lev. 26:16 [y] Amos 4:9 [7] *blight* **23** [z] Lev. 26:19 **25** [a] Deut. 32:30 [8] *a terror* **26** [b] 1 Sam. 17:44; Ps. 79:2 **27** [c] Ex. 15:26 [d] 1 Sam. 5:6

28 [e] Jer. 4:9 **29** [f] Job 5:14 **30** [g] 2 Sam. 12:11; Job 31:10; Jer. 8:10 [h] Amos 5:11; Zeph. 1:13 [i] Deut. 20:6; Job 31:8; Jer. 12:13; Mic. 6:15 **32** [j] 2 Chr. 29:9 [k] Ps. 119:82 [l] Neh. 5:5 [9] *nothing you can do* **33** [m] Lev. 26:16; Jer. 5:15, 17 **36** [n] 2 Kin. 17:4, 6; 24:12, 14; 25:7, 11; 2 Chr. 36:1-21; Jer. 39:1-9 [o] Deut. 4:28; Jer. 16:13 **37** [p] 1 Kin. 9:7, 8; Jer. 24:9; 25:9 [q] Ps. 44:14 [1] *a thing of horror* **38** [r] Mic. 6:15; Hag. 1:6 [s] Ex. 10:4; Joel 1:4 [2] *devour*

28:16-19 These are parallels to the blessings in vv. 3-6.

28:20 until you are destroyed. Moses was aware that the Israelites were apt to be unfaithful to God, so he portrays in extended warnings the disastrous results of the loss of their Land and their place of worship if they disobeyed God. Destruction was the ultimate calamity for Israel's sin (vv. 20,21,24,45,48,51,61,63).

28:21 Cf. Jer. 14:12; 21:6; Ezek. 5:12; 6:11.

28:22 Cf. Amos 4:9.

28:23 bronze...iron. The heavens would be as bright as bronze, but no rain would fall from them to water the ground. The earth would be as hard as iron, so any rain that would fall would run off and not penetrate (cf. Amos 4:7).

28:25 Cf. 2 Chr. 29:8; Neh. 1:8; Jer. 15:4.

28:26 Cf. Jer. 7:33; 16:4; 19:7; 34:20.

28:27 the boils of Egypt. The disease with which God afflicted the Egyptians prior to the Exodus (see Ex. 9:9; Amos 4:10).

28:30 These 3 curses were in contrast to the exemptions from military service granted in 20:5-7. The exemptions were possible because God would grant His people victory in battle. Disobedience to the Lord, however, would mean that God would no longer fight for His people. Those normally exempted from military service would be forced to fight and be killed. Consequently, the soldier's betrothed wife would be violated and his house and grapes taken by the foreign invader (cf. Jer. 8:10; Amos 5:11; Zeph. 1:13).

28:32 Cf. 2 Chr. 29:9.

28:35 sole of your foot...head. Diseases of the skin would afflict the people cursed by God. The disease mentioned here is like that from which Job suffered (see Job 2:7).

28:36 the king whom you set over you. Though they had no king at the time of entering the Land, Moses anticipated that Israel would have a king over them when this curse came—a future king of Israel who would be taken with them into exile. **to a nation which neither you nor your fathers have known.** The Israelites would be taken captive to a nation other than Egypt, where they had recently been in bondage. This future nation would be particularly steeped in idolatry (cf. 2 Kin. 17:41; Jer. 16:13).

28:37 Cf. 1 Kin. 9:8; 2 Chr. 29:8; Jer. 19:8; 25:9,18; 29:18.

drink *of* the [t]wine nor gather the *grapes;* for
the worms shall eat them. 40 You shall have
olive trees throughout all your territory,
but you shall not anoint *yourself* with the
oil; for your olives shall drop off. 41 You
shall beget sons and daughters, but they
shall not be yours; for [u]they shall go into
captivity. 42 Locusts shall [3]consume all
your trees and the produce of your land.

43 "The alien who *is* among you shall
rise higher and higher above you, and you
shall come down lower and lower. 44 He
shall lend to you, but you shall not lend to
him; he shall be the head, and you shall be
the tail.

45 "Moreover all these curses shall come
upon you and pursue and overtake you,
until you are destroyed, because you [4]did
not obey the voice of the LORD your God, to
keep His commandments and His statutes
which He commanded you. 46 And they
shall be upon [v]you for a sign and a wonder,
and on your descendants forever.

47 [w]"Because you did not serve the LORD
your God with joy and gladness of heart,
[x]for the abundance of everything, 48 therefore you shall serve your enemies, whom
the LORD will send against you, in [y]hunger,
in thirst, in nakedness, and in need of
everything; and He [z]will put a yoke of iron
on your neck until He has destroyed you.
49 [a]The LORD will bring a nation against
you from afar, from the end of the earth,
[b]*as swift* as the eagle flies, a nation whose
language you will not understand, 50 a nation of fierce countenance, [c]which does not
respect the elderly nor show favor to the
young. 51 And they shall eat the increase of
your livestock and the produce of your
land, until you are destroyed; they shall
not leave you grain or new wine or oil, *or*
the increase of your cattle or the offspring
of your flocks, until they have destroyed
you.

39 [t]Zeph. 1:13
41 [u]Lam. 1:5
42 [3]*possess*
45 [4]*did not listen to*
46 [v]Num. 26:10; Is. 8:18; Ezek. 14:8
47 [w]Deut. 12:7; Neh. 9:35-37 [x]Deut. 32:15
48 [y]Lam. 4:4-6 [z]Jer. 28:13, 14
49 [a]Is. 5:26-30; 7:18-20; Jer. 5:15 [b]Jer. 48:40; 49:22; Lam. 4:19; Hos. 8:1
50 [c]2 Chr. 36:17
52 [d]2 Kin. 25:1, 2, 4
53 [e]Lev. 26:29; 2 Kin. 6:28, 29; Jer. 19:9; Lam. 2:20; 4:10 [5]*offspring*
54 [f]Deut. 15:9 [g]Deut. 13:6 [6]Lit. *tender* [7]Lit. *his eye shall be evil toward*
56 [8]*sensitive* [9]*refined* [1]Lit. *her eye shall be evil toward*
57 [h]Gen. 49:10 [2]*afterbirth*
58 [i]Ex. 6:3
59 [j]Dan. 9:12
60 [k]Deut. 7:15

52 "They shall [d]besiege you at all your
gates until your high and fortified walls, in
which you trust, come down throughout
all your land; and they shall besiege you at
all your gates throughout all your land
which the LORD your God has given you.
53 [e]You shall eat the [5]fruit of your own
body, the flesh of your sons and your
daughters whom the LORD your God has
given you, in the siege and desperate
straits in which your enemy shall distress
you. 54 The [6]sensitive and very refined
man among you [f]will[7] be hostile toward
his brother, toward [g]the wife of his bosom,
and toward the rest of his children whom
he leaves behind, 55 so that he will not give
any of them the flesh of his children whom
he will eat, because he has nothing left in
the siege and desperate straits in which
your enemy shall distress you at all your
gates. 56 The [8]tender and [9]delicate woman
among you, who would not venture to set
the sole of her foot on the ground because
of her delicateness and sensitivity, [1]will
refuse to the husband of her bosom, and to
her son and her daughter, 57 her [2]placenta
which comes out [h]from between her feet
and her children whom she bears; for she
will eat them secretly for lack of everything in the siege and desperate straits in
which your enemy shall distress you at all
your gates.

58 "If you do not carefully observe all the
words of this law that are written in this
book, that you may fear [i]this glorious and
awesome name, THE LORD YOUR GOD,
59 then the LORD will bring upon you and
your descendants [j]extraordinary plagues—
great and prolonged plagues—and serious
and prolonged sicknesses. 60 Moreover He
will bring back on you all [k]the diseases of
Egypt, of which you were afraid, and they
shall cling to you. 61 Also every sickness
and every plague, which *is* not written in

28:38-40 Cf. Is. 5:10; Joel 1:4; Mic. 6:15.

28:46 Cf. 2 Chr. 29:8; Jer. 18:6; Ezek. 14:8.

28:49 a nation…from the end of the earth. God would raise up a nation to act as His own instrument of judgment against His ungrateful people. This foreign nation was described as coming from a far distance from Israel, a nation that would arise quickly and one that would completely devastate the Land. This was fulfilled first by Assyria (Is. 5:26; 7:18-20; 28:11; 37:18; Hos. 8:1) and second, by Babylon (Jer. 5:15; Lam. 4:19; Ezek. 17:3; Hab. 1:6-8).

28:50 Cf. 2 Chr. 36:17.

28:52-57 Ultimately, an invading nation would besiege all of the cities of Judah (*see note on 28:49*). In vv. 53-57, Moses gave a revolting description of the Israelites' response to those siege conditions. The unthinkable activity of cannibalism is introduced in v. 53 and then illustrated in the verses that follow (see 2 Kin. 6:28,29; Lam. 2:20; 4:10).

28:52 Cf. 2 Chr. 32:10; Jer. 10:17,18; Ezek. 5:2; Hos. 11:6.

28:53 Cf. Jer. 19:9.

28:58-63 this glorious and awesome name, THE LORD YOUR GOD. Israel's obedience to the law (i.e., the Sinaitic Covenant) would lead to fearing the Lord, whose "name" represents His presence and character. The title "LORD (Yahweh)" revealed the glory and greatness of God (see Ex. 3:15). Significantly, the phrase "the LORD your God" is used approximately 280 times in the book of Deuteronomy. The full measure of the divine curse would come on Israel when its disobedience had been hardened into disregard for the glorious and awesome character of God. In vv. 15,45 Moses described curses for disobedience; hence the worst of the curses come when disobedience is hardened into failure to fear God. Only God's grace would save a small remnant (v. 62), thus keeping Israel from being annihilated (cf. Mal. 2:2). In contrast to the promise made to Abraham in Gen. 15:5, the physical seed of Abraham under God's curse would be reduced; as God had multiplied the seed of the patriarchs in Egypt (see Ex. 1:7), He would decimate their numbers to make them as nothing until His restoration of the nation in a future day (see 30:5).

this Book of the Law, will the LORD bring
upon you until you are destroyed. 62 You
[l]shall be left few in number, whereas you
were [m]as the stars of heaven in multitude,
because you would not obey the voice of
the LORD your God. 63 And it shall be, *that*
just as the LORD [n]rejoiced over you to do
you good and multiply you, so the LORD
[o]will rejoice over you to destroy you and
bring you to nothing; and you shall be
[p]plucked[3] from off the land which you go
to possess.
64 "Then the LORD [q]will scatter you
among all peoples, from one end of the
earth to the other, and [r]there you shall
serve other gods, which neither you nor
your fathers have known—wood and
stone. 65 And [s]among those nations you
shall find no rest, nor shall the sole of your
foot have a resting place; [t]but there the
LORD will give you a [4]trembling heart, failing eyes, and [u]anguish of soul. 66 Your life
shall hang in doubt before you; you shall
fear day and night, and have no assurance
of life. 67 [v]In the morning you shall say,
'Oh, that it were evening!' And at evening
you shall say, 'Oh, that it were morning!'
because of the fear which terrifies your
heart, and [w]because of the sight which
your eyes see.
68 "And the LORD [x]will take you back to
Egypt in ships, by the way of which I said
to you, [y]'You shall never see it again.' And
there you shall be offered for sale to your
enemies as male and female slaves, but no
one will buy *you*."

The Covenant Renewed in Moab

29 These *are* the words of the covenant
which the LORD commanded Moses
to make with the children of Israel in the
land of Moab, besides the [a]covenant which
He made with them in Horeb.
2 Now Moses called all Israel and said to
them: [b]"You have seen all that the LORD
did before your eyes in the land of Egypt,
to Pharaoh and to all his servants and to all
his land— 3 [c]the great trials which your
eyes have seen, the signs, and those great
wonders. 4 Yet [d]the LORD has not given
you a heart to [1]perceive and eyes to see
and ears to hear, to this *very* day. 5 [e]And I
have led you forty years in the wilderness.
[f]Your clothes have not worn out on you,
and your sandals have not worn out on
your feet. 6 [g]You have not eaten bread, nor
have you drunk wine or *similar* drink, that
you may know that I *am* the LORD your
God. 7 And when you came to this place,
[h]Sihon king of Heshbon and Og king of

62 [l]Deut. 4:27 [m]Deut. 10:22; Neh. 9:23
63 [n]Deut. 30:9; Jer. 32:41 [o]Prov. 1:26; [Is. 1:24] [p]Jer. 12:14; 45:4 [3]*torn*
64 [q]Lev. 26:33; Deut. 4:27, 28; Neh. 1:8; Jer. 16:13; Amos 9:9 [r]Deut. 28:36
65 [s]Lam. 1:3; Amos 9:4 [t]Lev. 26:36 [u]Lev. 26:16 [4]*anxious*
67 [v]Job 7:4 [w]Deut. 28:34
68 [x]Jer. 43:7; Hos. 8:13 [y]Deut. 17:16

CHAPTER 29

1 [a]Lev. 26:46; Deut. 5:2, 3
2 [b]Ex. 19:4; Deut. 11:7
3 [c]Deut. 4:34; 7:19
4 [d][Is. 6:9, 10; Ezek. 12:2]; Matt. 13:14; [Acts 28:26, 27]; Rom. 11:8; [Eph. 4:18] [1]*understand or know*
5 [e]Deut. 1:3; 8:2 [f]Deut. 8:4
6 [g]Ex. 16:12; Deut. 8:3
7 [h]Num. 21:23, 24; Deut. 2:26–3:3

28:59-61 Cf. Amos 4:10.

28:61 this Book of the Law. A definite, particular written document was meant (see 31:9), referring not just to Deuteronomy (cf. 31:9), but to the Pentateuch, as far as it had been written. This is evident from vv. 60,61, which indicate that the diseases of Egypt were written in the book of the law, thus referring to Exodus, which records those plagues.

28:63 Cf. Jer. 12:14; 45:4.

28:64 the LORD will scatter you. The Jews remaining after the curses fall would be dispersed by the Lord ultimately to serve false gods, restlessly and fearfully throughout all the nations of the earth (cf. Neh. 1:8,9; Jer. 30:11; Ezek. 11:16). This dispersion began with the captivity of the northern kingdom, Israel (722 B.C.), then the southern kingdom , Judah (586 B.C.), and is still a reality today. In the future earthly kingdom of Messiah, Israel will experience its regathering in faith, salvation, and righteousness. See. Is. 59:19-21; Jer. 31:31-34; Ezek. 36:8–37:14; Zech. 12:10–14:21. The unbearable nature of Israel's present condition was emphasized since the people longed for another time (v. 67). Cf. Jer. 44:7; Hos. 8:13; 9:3; 11:4,5.

28:68 but no one will buy *you*. Israel would be so abandoned by God that she would not even be able to sell herself into slavery. The curse of God would bring Israel into a seemingly hopeless condition (cf. Hos. 8:13; 9:3). The specific mention of Egypt could be symbolic for any lands where the Jews have been taken into bondage or sold as slaves. But it is true that after the destruction of Jerusalem in A.D. 70, which was a judgment on the apostasy of Israel and their rejection and execution of the Messiah, this prophecy was actually fulfilled. The Roman general Titus, who conquered Jerusalem and Israel, sent 17,000 adult Jews to Egypt to perform hard labor there and had those who were under 17 years old publicly sold. Under the Roman emperor Hadrian, countless Jews were sold and suffered such bondage and cruelty.

29:1–30:20 These chapters contain the third address of Moses, which is a contrast between the covenant at Sinai and the covenant he envisioned for Israel in the future. Though the past had seen Israel's failure to keep the covenant and to trust in God, there was hope for the future. It was this hope that Moses emphasized in the content of these chapters focusing clearly on the themes of the New Covenant.

29:1 These *are* the words. The Heb. text numbers this verse as 28:69 rather than 29:1, seeing it as the conclusion to the second address of Moses. However, as in 1:1, these words introduce what follows, serving as the introduction to Moses' third address. **the covenant...in the land of Moab.** The majority of interpreters view the covenant stated here as a reference to the covenant made at Sinai. According to this view, the covenant that God made with Israel at Sinai (Horeb) was renewed in Moab. However, this verse clearly states that the covenant of which Moses now speaks was "besides," or "in addition to," the previous covenant. This was another covenant distinct from the one made at Sinai. This other covenant is viewed by some interpreters as the Palestinian Covenant, which gave Israel the title to the land (see 30:5). However, the emphasis of these two chapters is not on the Land, but on the change of Israel's heart (see the contrast between 29:4 and 30:6). It was exactly this change of heart which the later prophets would term "The New Covenant" (see Jer. 31:31-34; Ezek. 36:26,27). In response to Israel's certain failure under the provisions of the Sinaitic Covenant (29:23-28), Moses anticipated the New Covenant under which Israel would be obedient to the Lord and finally reap His blessings (30:1-10).

29:4 the LORD has not given you...eyes to see. In spite of all they had experienced (vv. 2,3), Israel was spiritually blind to the significance of what the Lord had done for them, lacking spiritual understanding, even as Moses was speaking. This spiritual blindness of Israel continues to the present day (Rom. 11:8), and it will not be reversed until Israel's future day of salvation (see Rom. 11:25-27). The

Bashan came out against us to battle, and
we conquered them. 8 We took their land
and [i]gave it as an inheritance to the Reubenites, to the Gadites, and to half the tribe
of Manasseh. 9 Therefore [j]keep the words
of this covenant, and do them, that you
may [k]prosper in all that you do.
10 "All of you stand today before the
LORD your God: your leaders and your
tribes and your elders and your officers, all
the men of Israel, 11 your little ones and
your wives—also the stranger who *is* in
your camp, from [l]the one who cuts your
wood to the one who draws your water—
12 that you may enter into covenant with
the LORD your God, and [m]into His oath,
which the LORD your God makes with you
today, 13 that He may [n]establish you today
as a people for Himself, and *that* He may
be God to you, [o]just as He has spoken to
you, and [p]just as He has sworn to your fathers, to Abraham, Isaac, and Jacob.
14 "I make this covenant and this oath,
[q]not with you alone, 15 but with *him* who
stands here with us today before the LORD
our God, [r]as well as with *him* who *is* not
here with us today 16 (for you know that
we dwelt in the land of Egypt and that we
came through the nations which you
passed by, 17 and you saw their [2]abomina-
tions and their idols which *were* among
them—wood and stone and silver and
gold); 18 so that there may not be among
you man or woman or family or tribe,
[s]whose heart turns away today from the
LORD our God, to go *and* serve the gods of
these nations, [t]and that there may not be
among you a root bearing [u]bitterness or
wormwood; 19 and so it may not happen,
when he hears the words of this curse, that
he blesses himself in his heart, saying, 'I
shall have peace, even though I [3]follow
the [v]dictates of my heart'—[w]as though the
drunkard could be included with the
sober.
20 [x]"The LORD would not spare him; for
then [y]the anger of the LORD and [z]His jealousy would burn against that man, and
every curse that is written in this book
would settle on him, and the LORD [a]would
blot out his name from under heaven.
21 And the LORD [b]would separate him
from all the tribes of Israel for adversity,
according to all the curses of the covenant
that are written in this Book of the [c]Law,
22 so that the coming generation of your
children who rise up after you, and the foreigner who comes from a far land, would
say, when they [d]see the plagues of that
land and the sicknesses which the LORD
has laid on it:
23 'The whole land *is* brimstone, [e]salt,
and burning; it is not sown, nor does it
bear, nor does any grass grow there, [f]like
the overthrow of Sodom and Gomorrah,
Admah, and Zeboiim, which the LORD
overthrew in His anger and His wrath.'
24 All nations would say, [g]'Why has the
LORD done so to this land? What does the
heat of this great anger mean?' 25 Then *people* would say: 'Because they have forsaken
the covenant of the LORD God of their fathers, which He made with them when He
brought them out of the land of Egypt;
26 for they went and served other gods and
worshiped them, gods that they did not

8 [i]Num. 32:33; Deut. 3:12, 13
9 [j]Deut. 4:6; 1 Kin. 2:3 [k]Josh. 1:7
11 [l]Josh. 9:21, 23, 27
12 [m]Neh. 10:29
13 [n]Deut. 28:9 [o]Ex. 6:7 [p]Gen. 17:7, 8
14 [q][Jer. 31:31; Heb. 8:7, 8]
15 [r]Acts 2:39
17 [2]*detestable things*
18 [s]Deut. 11:16 [t]Heb. 12:15 [u]Deut. 32:32; Acts 8:23
19 [v]Jer. 3:17; 7:24 [w]Is. 30:1 [3]*walk in the stubbornness* or *imagination*
20 [x]Ezek. 14:7 [y]Ps. 74:1 [z]Ps. 79:5; Ezek. 23:25 [a]Ex. 32:33; Deut. 9:14; 2 Kin. 14:27
21 [b][Matt. 24:51] [c]Deut. 30:10
22 [d]Jer. 19:8; 49:17; 50:13
23 [e]Jer. 17:6; Zeph. 2:9 [f]Gen. 19:24, 25; Is. 1:9; Jer. 20:16; Hos. 11:8
24 [g]1 Kin. 9:8; Jer. 22:8

Lord had not given them an understanding heart, simply because the people had not penitently sought it (cf. 2 Chr. 7:14).

29:9 keep the words of this covenant. The spiritual experience of God's faithfulness to Israel should have led to obedience to the stipulations of the Sinaitic Covenant in the future, but could not without a transformed heart (vv. 4,18) and the true knowledge of God (v. 6).

29:10,11 All of you stand today before the LORD your God. All the people were likely stationed in an orderly way before Moses, but this is not a call to outward order, but inward devotion, to make the covenant a matter of the heart and life.

29:12 enter into covenant...and...oath. "Enter into" expresses entire submission in faith and repentance before God, resulting in heart obedience. The people were to bind themselves in an oath to obey the stipulations of God's covenant (cf. Gen 26:28).

29:14,15 not with you alone. All of Israel, present and future, were to be bound by the stipulations of the covenant to obey God and be blessed. Thus they would be able to lead all nations to the blessedness of salvation (cf. John 17:20,21; Acts 2:39).

29:18 a root bearing bitterness or wormwood. The picture was of a root spreading poison and bitterness into the whole tree. The metaphor indicates permeation of idolatry throughout Israel because of the action of an individual family or tribe, precipitating God's curse and wrath.

29:19 as though the drunkard...included with the sober. This could be translated "to destroy the watered land along with the dry land." With either translation, the meaning is that the deceived individual rebel against the Lord follows only his wicked heart and could not hide within the total community. The idolater would stand out and bear the judgment for his idolatry.

29:20 blot out his name from under heaven. The idolater would have no place among God's people, because God would curse him and then kill him (cf. 25:19: Ex. 17:14). This very strong language reveals how God feels about idolatry, which is forbidden in the Decalogue (Ex. 20:2-7).

29:21 this Book of the Law. *See note on 31:9.*

29:22 the coming generation...and the foreigner. In a future day, both Israel and the nations would see the results of God's judgment upon the Land of Israel because of Israel's disobedience, as a witness to the holy standard God has established in His law. Cf. Lev. 26:31,32.

29:23 Sodom. The punishment the Lord would bring upon Israel in the future was likened to that of Sodom and her allies whom the Lord buried in fiery brimstone in the time of Abraham and Lot (see Gen. 19:24-29). It should be noted that Sodom and vicinity resembled paradise, the garden of God, before its destruction (cf. Gen. 13:10).

29:24 This question is answered in vv. 25-28.

know and that He had not given to them.
27 Then the anger of the LORD was aroused
against this land, [h]to bring on it every
curse that is written in this book. 28 And
the LORD [i]uprooted them from their land
in anger, in wrath, and in great indignation, and cast them into another land, as *it*
is this day.'
29 "The secret *things belong* to the LORD
our God, but those *things which are* revealed
belong to us and to our children forever, that
we may do all the words of this law.

The Blessing of Returning to God

30 "Now [a]it shall come to pass, when
[b]all these things come upon you,
the blessing and the [c]curse which I have
set before you, and [d]you [1]call *them* to mind
among all the nations where the LORD your
God drives you, 2 and you [e]return to the
LORD your God and obey His voice, according to all that I command you today,
you and your children, with all your heart
and with all your soul, 3 [f]that the LORD
your God will bring you back from captivity, and have compassion on you, and
[g]gather you again from all the nations
where the LORD your God has scattered
you. 4 [h]If *any* of you are driven out to the
farthest *parts* under heaven, from there the
LORD your God will gather you, and from
there He will bring you. 5 Then the LORD
your God will bring you to the land which
your fathers possessed, and you shall possess it. He will prosper you and multiply
you more than your fathers. 6 And [i]the
LORD your God will circumcise your heart
and the heart of your descendants, to love
the LORD your God with all your heart and
with all your soul, that you may live.
7 "Also the LORD your God will put all
these [j]curses on your enemies and on those
who hate you, who persecuted you. 8 And
you will [k]again obey the voice of the LORD
and do all His commandments which I
command you today. 9 [l]The LORD your
God will make you abound in all the work
of your hand, in the [2]fruit of your body, in
the increase of your livestock, and in the
produce of your land for good. For the
LORD will again [m]rejoice over you for good
as He rejoiced over your fathers, 10 if you
obey the voice of the LORD your God, to
keep His commandments and His statutes
which are written in this Book of the Law,
and if you turn to the LORD your God with
all your heart and with all your soul.

The Choice of Life or Death

11 "For this commandment which I command you today [n]*is* [3]not *too* mysterious for
you, nor *is* it far off. 12 [o]It *is* not in heaven,

27 [h] Dan. 9:11
28 [i] 1 Kin. 14:15; 2 Chr. 7:20; Ps. 52:5; Prov. 2:22

CHAPTER 30

1 [a] Lev. 26:40 [b] Deut. 28:2 [c] Deut. 28:15-45 [d] Deut. 4:29, 30 [1] Lit. *cause them to return to your heart*
2 [e] Deut. 4:29, 30; Neh. 1:9; Is. 55:7; Lam. 3:40; Joel 2:12
3 [f] Ps. 106:45; Jer. 29:14; Lam. 3:22, 32 [g] Ps. 147:2; Jer. 32:37; Ezek. 34:13
4 [h] Deut. 28:64; Neh. 1:9; Is. 62:11
6 [i] Deut. 10:16; Jer. 32:39; Ezek. 11:19
7 [j] Is. 54:15-17; Jer. 30:16, 20
8 [k] Zeph. 3:20
9 [l] Deut. 28:11 [m] Deut. 28:63; Jer. 32:41 [2] *offspring*
11 [n] Is. 45:19 [3] *not hidden from*
12 [o] Prov. 30:4; Rom. 10:6-8

29:29 The secret *things* . . . those *things which are* revealed. That which is revealed included the law with its promises and threats; consequently, that which is hidden only can refer to the specific way in which God will carry out His will in the future, which is revealed in His Word and completed in His great work of salvation, in spite of the apostasy of His people.

30:1-10 The rejection of God by Israel, and of Israel by God and the subsequent dispersion were not the end of the story of God's people. Having anticipated a time when Israel's disobedience would lead to her captivity in a foreign land, Moses looked beyond the destruction of that time of judgment to an even more distant time of restoration and redemption for Israel (cf. Lev. 26:40-45). This future restoration and blessing of Israel would take place under the New Covenant (*see notes on Jer. 31:31-34; 32:37-42; Ezek. 36:25-27*). For a comparison of the New Covenant with the Old Covenant, *see notes on 2 Cor. 3:6-18*.

30:1-3 you call *them* to mind. Moses moved to the future when curses would be over and blessings would come. At some future time, after disobedience to the Lord brought upon Israel the curses of the covenant, the people will remember that the circumstances in which they found themselves were the inevitable consequence of their disobedience, and in repentance they will return to the Lord. This repentance will lead to a wholehearted commitment of obedience to God's commandments (v. 8) and the consequent end of Israel's distress (v. 3). This is the ultimate salvation of Israel by faith in Christ, spoken of by Isaiah (54:4-8), Jeremiah (31:31-34; 32:37-42), Ezekiel (36:23-38), Hosea (14:1-9), Joel (3:16-21), Amos (9:11-15), Zephaniah (3:14-20), Zechariah (12:10–13:9), Malachi (3:16–4:4), and Paul (Rom. 11:25-27).

30:4,5 The gathering of Jews out of all the countries of the earth will follow Israel's final redemption. Restoration to the Land will be in fulfillment of the promise of the covenant given to Abraham (see Gen. 12:7; 13:15; 15:18-21; 17:8) and so often reiterated by Moses and the prophets.

30:6 the LORD...will circumcise your heart. Cf. 10:16. This work of God in the innermost being of the individual is the true salvation that grants a new will to obey Him in place of the former spiritual insensitivity and stubbornness (cf. Jer. 4:4; 9:25; Rom. 2:28,29). This new heart will allow the Israelite to love the Lord wholeheartedly, and is the essential feature of the New Covenant (see 29:4,18; 30:10,17; Jer. 31:31-34; 32:37-42; Ezek. 11:19; 36:26). *See note on Jer. 4:4.*

30:7 on your enemies. The curses that had fallen on Israel because of disobedience will in the future come upon the nations that have enslaved the Jews. The judgment of God would come upon those who cursed the physical seed of Abraham in fulfillment of Gen. 12:3.

30:8,9 you will again obey the voice of the LORD. With a new heart under the New Covenant, Israel would obey all the commandments of the Lord. This would result in the Lord's blessing, which would bring greater prosperity than Israel had ever previously experienced.

30:10 Here is a renewed enforcement of the indispensable fruit of salvation and another echo of the constant theme of this book.

30:11-14 After remembering the failures of the past and the prospects for the future, Moses earnestly admonished the people to make the right choice. The issue facing them was to enjoy salvation and blessing by loving God so wholeheartedly that they would willingly live in obedience to His Word. The choice was simple, yet profound. It was stated in simple terms so that they could understand and grasp what God expected of them (v. 11). Although God had spoken from heaven, He had spoken through Moses in words every person could understand (v. 12). Neither did they have to search at some

that you should say, 'Who will ascend into
heaven for us and bring it to us, that we
may hear it and do it?' 13 Nor *is* it beyond
the sea, that you should say, 'Who will go
over the sea for us and bring it to us, that
we may hear it and do it?' 14 But the word
is very near you, [p]in your mouth and in
your heart, that you may do it.

15 "See, [q]I have set before you today life
and good, death and evil, 16 in that I command you today to love the LORD your God,
to walk in His ways, and to keep His commandments, His statutes, and His judgments, that you may live and multiply; and
the LORD your God will bless you in the
land which you go to possess. 17 But if your
heart turns away so that you do not hear,
and are drawn away, and worship other
gods and serve them, 18 [r]I announce to you
today that you shall surely perish; you shall
not prolong *your* days in the land which
you cross over the Jordan to go in and possess. 19 [s]I call heaven and earth as witnesses
today against you, *that* [t]I have set before
you life and death, blessing and cursing;
therefore choose life, that both you and
your descendants may live; 20 that you may
love the LORD your God, that you may obey
His voice, and that you may cling to Him,
for He *is* your [u]life and the length of your
days; and that you may dwell in the land
which the LORD swore to your fathers, to
Abraham, Isaac, and Jacob, to give them."

14 [p] Rom. 10:8
15 [q] Deut. 30:1, 19
18 [r] Deut. 4:26; 8:19
19 [s] Deut. 4:26
[t] Deut. 30:15
20 [u] Ps. 27:1; [John 11:25; 14:6; Col. 3:4]

CHAPTER 31

2 [a] Ex. 7:7; Deut. 34:7 [b] Num. 27:17; 1 Kin. 3:7 [c] Num. 20:12
3 [d] Deut. 9:3; Josh. 11:23 [e] Num. 27:18 [f] Num. 27:21
4 [g] Deut. 3:21 [h] Num. 21:24, 33
5 [i] Deut. 7:2; 20:10-20
6 [j] Josh. 10:25; 1 Chr. 22:13 [k] Deut. 1:29 [l] Deut. 20:4 [m] Josh. 1:5; Heb. 13:5
7 [n] Num. 27:19; Deut. 31:23; Josh. 1:6
8 [o] Ex. 13:21 [p] Deut. 31:6; Josh. 1:5; 1 Chr. 28:20; Heb. 13:5

Joshua the New Leader of Israel

31 Then Moses went and spoke these
words to all Israel. 2 And he said to
them: "I [a]*am* one hundred and twenty years
old today. I can no longer [b]go out and come
in. Also the LORD has said to me, [c]'You shall
not cross over this Jordan.' 3 The LORD your
God [d]Himself crosses over before you; He
will destroy these nations from before you,
and you shall dispossess them. [e]Joshua
himself crosses over before you, just [f]as the
LORD has said. 4 [g]And the LORD will do to
them [h]as He did to Sihon and Og, the kings
of the Amorites and their land, when He destroyed them. 5 [i]The LORD will give them
over to you, that you may do to them according to every commandment which I
have commanded you. 6 [j]Be strong and of
good courage, [k]do not fear nor be afraid of
them; for the LORD your God, [l]He *is* the One
who goes with you. [m]He will not leave you
nor forsake you."

7 Then Moses called Joshua and said to
him in the sight of all Israel, [n]"Be strong
and of good courage, for you must go with
this people to the land which the LORD has
sworn to their fathers to give them, and
you shall cause them to inherit it. 8 And
the LORD, [o]He *is* the One who goes before
you. [p]He will be with you, He will not
leave you nor forsake you; do not fear nor
be dismayed."

---

point beyond the sea (v. 13). The truth was there, through Moses, now in their hearts and minds (v. 14). All the truth necessary for choosing to love and obey God and thus avoid disobedience and cursing, they had heard and known (v. 15). Paul quotes vv. 12-14 in Rom. 10:6-8.

30:15 Here Moses pinpoints the choice—to love and obey God is life and good, to reject God is death and evil. If they chose to love God and obey His Word, they would enjoy all God's blessings (v. 16). If they refused to love and obey Him, they would be severely and immediately punished (vv. 17,18). Paul, in speaking about salvation in the NT, makes use of this appeal made by Moses (Rom. 10:1-13). Like Moses, Paul is saying that the message of salvation is plain and understandable.

30:19 choose life. Moses forces the decision, exhorting Israel on the plains of Moab before God (heaven) and man (earth) to choose by believing in and loving God, the life available through the New Covenant (see v. 6). Sadly, Israel failed to respond to this call to the right choice (see 31:16-18,27-29). Choosing life or death was also emphasized by Jesus. The one who believed in Him had the promise of eternal life; while the one who refused to believe faced eternal death (cf. John 3:1-36). Every person faces this same choice.

31:1–34:12 Two themes dominate the last 4 chapters of Deuteronomy: 1) the death of Moses (31:1,2,14,16,26-29; 32:48-52; 33:1; 34:1-8,10-12) and 2) the succession of Joshua (31:1-8,14,23; 32:44; 34:9). These final chapters are centered around two more speeches by Moses: 1) the Song of Moses (32:1-43), and 2) the Blessings of Moses (33:1-29).

31:1 Moses went and spoke. Though some interpreters view this verse as the conclusion to the foregoing address in chaps. 29,30, it is better to see these words as an introduction to the words of Moses which follow, based upon the general pattern of Deuteronomy. Verses 2-6 are addressed to every Israelite.

31:2 one hundred and twenty years old. This was the age of Moses at his death. According to Acts 7:30, Moses spent 40 years in Midian tending sheep. Thus, the life of Moses is broken down into three 40-year periods. His first 40 years were spent in Egypt (Ex. 2:1-15). The second 40 years were spent in Midian (Ex. 2:15–4:19). His final 40 years were spent leading Israel out of Egypt and through the wilderness to the Promised Land. The life and ministry of Moses were completed, but God's work would go on (v. 3a). **go out and come in.** Here is an idiom for engaging in a normal day's work and activity. Though still strong for his age (cf. 34:7), Moses admitted that he no longer could provide the daily leadership necessary for Israel. Furthermore, God would not allow him to enter the Land over the Jordan because of his sin at the waters of Meribah (see 32:51).

31:3 God Himself...Joshua himself crosses over. Though Joshua was to be the new human leader over Israel (see 31:3-7,23), it was the Lord Himself who was the real leader and power. He would cross over ahead of them to enable them to destroy the nations.

31:4 Sihon and Og. Israel was assured that the nations of the Land would be destroyed by the Lord in the same way that He had recently defeated the Amorite kings, Sihon and Og, on the E side of the Jordan River (see 2:26–3:11). That was a preview of what was to come (v. 5).

31:6-8 Be strong and of good courage. The strength and courage of the warriors of Israel would come from their confidence that their God was with them and would not forsake them. In vv. 7,8, Moses repeated the substance of his exhortation, this time addressing it specifically to Joshua in the presence of the people to encour-

The Law to Be Read Every Seven Years

9 So Moses wrote this law [q]and delivered it to the priests, the sons of Levi, [r]who
bore the ark of the covenant of the LORD,
and to all the elders of Israel. 10 And Moses
commanded them, saying: "At the end of
every seven years, at the appointed time in
the [s]year of release, [t]at the Feast of Tabernacles, 11 when all Israel comes to [u]appear
before the LORD your God in the [v]place
which He chooses, [w]you shall read this law
before all Israel in their hearing. 12 [x]Gather
the people together, men and women and
little ones, and the stranger who *is* within
your gates, that they may hear and that
they may learn to fear the LORD your God
and carefully observe all the words of this
law, 13 and *that* their children, [y]who have
not known it, [z]may hear and learn to fear
the LORD your God as long as you live in
the land which you cross the Jordan to possess."

Prediction of Israel's Rebellion

14 Then the LORD said to Moses, [a]"Behold, the days approach when you must
die; call Joshua, and present yourselves in
the tabernacle of meeting, that [b]I may [1]in-
augurate him."
So Moses and Joshua went and presented themselves in the tabernacle of meeting.
15 Now [c]the LORD appeared at the tabernacle in a pillar of cloud, and the pillar of
cloud stood above the door of the tabernacle.
16 And the LORD said to Moses: "Behold,
you will [2]rest with your fathers; and this
people will [d]rise and [e]play the harlot with
the gods of the foreigners of the land,
where they go *to be* among them, and they
will [f]forsake Me and [g]break My covenant
which I have made with them. 17 Then My
anger shall be [h]aroused against them in
that day, and [i]I will forsake them, and I
will [j]hide My face from them, and they
shall be [3]devoured. And many evils and
troubles shall befall them, so that they will
say in that day, [k]'Have not these evils come
upon us because our God *is* [l]not among
us?' 18 And [m]I will surely hide My face in
that day because of all the evil which they
have done, in that they have turned to
other gods.
19 "Now therefore, write down this song
for yourselves, and teach it to the children
of Israel; put it in their mouths, that this
song may be [n]a witness for Me against the
children of Israel. 20 When I have brought
them to the land flowing with milk and
honey, of which I swore to their fathers,
and they have eaten and filled themselves
[o]and grown fat, [p]then they will turn to
other gods and serve them; and they will
provoke Me and break My covenant.
21 Then it shall be, [q]when many evils and
troubles have come upon them, that this
song will testify against them as a witness;
for it will not be forgotten in the mouths of
their descendants, for [r]I know the inclination [s]of their behavior today, even before I
have brought them to the land of which I
swore *to give them*."
22 Therefore Moses wrote this song the
same day, and taught it to the children of
Israel. 23 [t]Then He inaugurated Joshua the
son of Nun, and said, [u]"Be strong and of
good courage; for you shall bring the children of Israel into the land of which I
swore to them, and I will be with you."

9 [q] Deut. 17:18; 31:25, 26 [r] Num. 4:5, 6, 15; Deut. 10:8; 31:25, 26; Josh. 3:3
10 [s] Deut. 15:1, 2 [t] Lev. 23:34; Deut. 16:13
11 [u] Deut. 16:16 [v] Deut. 12:5 [w] Josh. 8:34; 2 Kin. 23:2
12 [x] Deut. 4:10
13 [y] Deut. 11:2 [z] Ps. 78:6, 7
14 [a] Num. 27:13 [b] Num. 27:19; Deut. 3:28 [1] *commission*
15 [c] Ex. 33:9
16 [d] Deut. 29:22 [e] Ex. 34:15; Deut. 4:25-28; Judg. 2:11, 12, 17 [2] *Die and join your ancestors* [f] Deut. 32:15 [g] Judg. 2:20
17 [h] Judg. 2:14; 6:13 [i] 2 Chr. 15:2 [j] Deut. 32:20 [k] Judg. 6:13 [l] Num. 14:42 [3] *consumed*
18 [m] Deut. 31:17; [Is. 1:15, 16]
19 [n] Deut. 31:22, 26
20 [o] Deut. 32:15-17 [p] Deut. 31:16
21 [q] Deut. 31:17 [r] Hos. 5:3 [s] Amos 5:25, 26
23 [t] Num. 27:23; Deut. 31:14 [u] Deut. 31:7

age him and to remind the people that Joshua's leadership was being assumed with the full approval of God. This principle for faith and confidence is repeated in 31:23; Josh. 1:5-7; 2 Sam. 10:12; 2 Kin. 2:2; 1 Chr. 22:11-13; 2 Chr. 32:1-8; Ps. 27:14. The writer of Hebrews quotes vv. 6,8 in 13:5.

31:9 Moses wrote this law. At the least, Moses, perhaps with the aid of some scribes or elders who assisted him in leading Israel, wrote down the law that he had explained in the first 32 chapters of Deuteronomy (cf. v. 24). However, since the law explained in Deuteronomy had been given in portions of Exodus through Numbers, it seems best to view this written law as all that is presently found in Scripture from Gen. 1 through Deut. 32:47. After Moses' death, Deut. 32:48–34:12 were added to complete the canonical Torah, perhaps by one of the elders who had served with Moses, even Joshua.

31:11 you shall read this law before all Israel. The law that Moses wrote down was given to the priests who were required to be its custodians and protectors and to read it in the hearing of all Israel at the Feast of Tabernacles during each sabbatical year. This reading of the law every 7 years was to remind the people to live in submission to their awe-inspiring God.

31:14 the tabernacle of meeting. The Lord told Moses to summon Joshua to the tent where He met Israel, and the presence of the Lord appeared in the pillar of cloud standing at the door of the Holy Place (v. 15). This signaled God's confirmation of Joshua, the former military captain (see Ex. 17:9-14) and spy (see Num. 13:16), as Israel's new leader. God's message to Joshua is summed up in vv. 16-22.

31:16-21 they will forsake Me and break My covenant. After Moses' death, the Lord Himself predicts that in spite of what He has commanded (30:11,20), the Israelites would forsake Him by turning to worship other gods and thereby break the Sinaitic Covenant. Having forsaken God, the people would then be forsaken by God with the inevitable result that disaster would fall upon them at every turn. This is one of the saddest texts in the OT. After all God had done, He knew they would forsake Him.

31:19,22 write down this song. The song that the Lord gave Moses to teach the Israelites would be a constant reminder of their disobedience to the Lord and the results of that disobedience. The song was written that same day and is recorded in 32:1-43.

31:23 I will be with you. Joshua was to assume his lonely role of leadership over Israel with an assurance of the companionship and strength of the Lord. God's presence with him was sufficient to enable him to meet boldly every obstacle that the future could bring (see Josh. 1:5; 3:7).

24 So it was, when Moses had completed
writing the words of this law in a book,
when they were finished, 25 that Moses
commanded the Levites, who bore the ark
of the covenant of the LORD, saying:
26 "Take this Book of the Law, [v]and put it
beside the ark of the covenant of the LORD
your God, that it may be there [w]as a witness against you; 27 [x]for I know your rebellion and your [y]stiff neck. *If* today, while
I am yet alive with you, you have been rebellious against the LORD, then how much
more after my death? 28 Gather to me all
the elders of your tribes, and your officers,
that I may speak these words in their hearing [z]and call heaven and earth to witness
against them. 29 For I know that after my
death you will [a]become utterly corrupt,
and turn aside from the way which I have
commanded you. And [b]evil will befall you
[c]in the latter days, because you will do evil
in the sight of the LORD, to provoke Him to
anger through the work of your hands."

The Song of Moses

30 Then Moses spoke in the hearing of all
the assembly of Israel the words of this
song until they were ended:

26 [v] 2 Kin. 22:8 [w] Deut. 31:19
27 [x] Deut. 9:7, 24 [y] Ex. 32:9; Deut. 9:6, 13
28 [z] Deut. 30:19
29 [a] Deut. 32:5; Judg. 2:19; [Acts 20:29, 30] [b] Deut. 28:15 [c] Gen. 49:1; Deut. 4:30

CHAPTER 32

1 [a] Deut. 4:26; Ps. 50:4; Is. 1:2 [b] Jer. 6:19
2 [c] Is. 55:10, 11 [d] Ps. 72:6 [1] *doctrine*
3 [e] Deut. 28:58 [f] 1 Chr. 29:11
4 [g] Deut. 32:15, 18, 30; Ps. 18:2 [h] 2 Sam. 22:31 [i] Deut. 7:9; Is. 65:16; Jer. 10:10 [j] Job 34:10
5 [k] Deut. 4:25; 31:29 [l] Phil. 2:15
6 [m] Ps. 116:12 [n] Ex. 4:22; Deut. 1:31; Is. 63:16 [o] Ps. 74:2 [p] Deut. 32:15 [2] *repay the*

32 "Give [a]ear, O heavens, and I will
speak;
And hear, O [b]earth, the words of
my mouth.
2 Let [c]my [1]teaching drop as the rain,
My speech distill as the dew,
[d]As raindrops on the tender herb,
And as showers on the grass.
3 For I proclaim the [e]name of the
LORD:
[f]Ascribe greatness to our God.
4 *He is* [g]the Rock, [h]His work *is*
perfect;
For all His ways *are* justice,
[i]A God of truth and [j]without
injustice;
Righteous and upright *is* He.

5 "They[k] have corrupted themselves;
They are not His children,
Because of their blemish:
A [l]perverse and crooked generation.
6 Do you thus [m]deal[2] with the LORD,
O foolish and unwise people?
Is He not [n]your Father, *who*
[o]bought you?
Has He not [p]made you and
established you?

31:24 in a book. The words that Moses had spoken were written down in a book that was placed beside the ark of the covenant (v. 26). Only the Ten Commandments were placed in the ark itself (Ex. 25:16; 31:18). The "Book of the Law" (v. 26) was one of the titles for the Pentateuch in the rest of Scripture (Josh. 1:8; 8:34).

31:27 your rebellion and your stiff neck. See 9:6,13; 10:16. Moses was well acquainted with Israel's obstinate ways even in the most gracious of divine provision.

31:29 you will become utterly corrupt. Dominated by the practice of idolatry (see 4:16,25; 9:12), the people would become wicked. **evil will befall you in the latter days.** "The latter days" (lit. "at the end of the days") referred to the far distant future. This was the time when the king would come from Judah (Gen. 49:8-12) to defeat Israel's enemies (Num. 24:17-19). Here it is revealed that it would also be a time when disaster would fall upon Israel because of evil done, thus bringing the Lord's wrath. The description of God's judgment on Israel and the nations in this song can't be limited to the immediate future of the people as they entered the Land, but extends to issues which are eschatological in time and global in extent, as the song indicates (32:1-43).

31:30–32:43 This prophetic, poetic song has as its central theme Israel's apostasy, which brings God's certain judgment. The song begins with a short introduction emphasizing the steadfast God and the fickle nation (vv. 1-6). The song describes God's election of Israel (vv. 8,9) and His care for them from the time of the wilderness wanderings (vv. 10-12) to their possession and initial enjoyment of the blessings in the Land (vv. 13,14). However, Israel's neglect of God's goodness and her apostasy (vv. 15-18) would bring God's future outpouring of wrath on His people (vv. 19-27) and Israel's continuing blindness in the face of God's wrath (vv. 28-33). Ultimately, God's vengeance would strip Israel of all power and turn the nation from idolatry (vv. 34-38). Then, God would bring His judgment upon the nations, both His enemies and Israel's (vv. 39-42). The song ends with a call to the nations to rejoice with Israel because God would punish His enemies and spiritually heal both Israel and her Land (v. 43). Ezekiel 16 should be studied as a comparison to this chapter. It recites similar matters in graphic and picturesque language.

32:1 Give ear, O heavens…And hear, O earth. All of creation was called to be an audience to hear the message to Israel as in 30:19 because the truth Moses was about to proclaim concerned the whole universe. It did so because it involved the honor of God the Creator so disregarded by sinners, the justification of God so righteous in all His ways, and the manifestation in heaven and earth of God's judgment and salvation (v. 43).

32:2 my teaching. Moses imparted instruction that if received would, like rain, dew, raindrops, and showers to the earth, bring benefit to the hearts and the minds of the hearers.

32:3 Ascribe greatness to our God. Cf. 3:24; 5:24; 9:26; 11:2; Ps. 150:2. This command refers to the greatness of God revealed in His acts of omnipotence.

32:4 the Rock. This word, representing the stability and permanence of God, was placed at the beginning of the verse for emphasis and was followed by a series of phrases which elaborated the attributes of God as the Rock of Israel. It is one of the principle themes in this song (see vv. 15,18,30,31), stressing the unchanging nature of God in contrast with the fickle nature of the people.

32:5 A perverse and crooked generation. Israel, in contrast to God, was warped and twisted. Jesus used this phrase in Matt. 17:17 of an unbelieving generation and Paul in Phil. 2:15 of the dark world of mankind in rebellion against God.

32:6 your Father. The foolishness and stupidity of Israel would be seen in the fact that they would rebel against God who as a Father had brought them forth and formed them into a nation. As Father, He was the progenitor and originator of the nation and the One who had matured and sustained it. This idea of God as Father of the nation is emphasized in the OT (cf. 1 Chr. 29:10; Is. 63:16; 64:8; Mal. 2:10) while the idea of God as Father of individual believers is developed in the NT (cf. Rom. 8:15; Gal. 4:6).

7 "Remember[q] the days of old,
Consider the years of many
generations.
[r]Ask your father, and he will show
you;
Your elders, and they will tell you:
8 When the Most High [s]divided
their inheritance to the
nations,
When He [t]separated the sons of
Adam,
He set the boundaries of the peoples
According to the number of the
[3]children of Israel.
9 For [u]the LORD's portion *is* His
people;
Jacob *is* the place of His inheritance.

10 "He found him [v]in a desert land
And in the wasteland, a howling
wilderness;
He encircled him, He instructed
him,
He [w]kept him as the [4]apple of His
eye.
11 [x]As an eagle stirs up its nest,
Hovers over its young,
Spreading out its wings, taking
them up,
Carrying them on its wings,
12 *So* the LORD alone led him,
And *there was* no foreign god with
him.

7 [q] Ps. 44:1 [r] Ex. 12:26; 13:14; Ps. 78:5-8
8 [s] Acts 17:26 [t] Gen. 11:8 [3] LXX, DSS *angels of God;* Symmachus, Lat. *sons of God*
9 [u] Ex. 19:5
10 [v] Jer. 2:6; Hos. 13:5 [w] Ps. 17:8; Prov. 7:2; Zech. 2:8 [4] *pupil*
11 [x] Is. 31:5

13 "He[y] made him ride in the heights
of the earth,
That he might eat the produce of
the fields;
He made him draw honey from the
rock,
And oil from the flinty rock;
14 Curds from the cattle, and milk of
the flock,
[z]With fat of lambs;
And rams of the breed of Bashan,
and goats,
With the choicest wheat;
And you drank wine, the [a]blood of
the grapes.

15 "But Jeshurun grew fat and kicked;
[b]You grew fat, you grew thick,
You are obese!
Then he [c]forsook God *who* [d]made
him,
And scornfully esteemed the [e]Rock
of his salvation.
16 [f]They provoked Him to jealousy
with foreign *gods;*
With [5]abominations they provoked
Him to anger.
17 [g]They sacrificed to demons, not to
God,
To gods they did not know,
To new *gods,* new arrivals
That your fathers did not fear.

13 [y] Is. 58:14
14 [z] Ps. 81:16 [a] Gen. 49:11
15 [b] Deut. 31:20 [c] Is. 1:4 [d] Is. 51:13 [e] Ps. 95:1
16 [f] Ps. 78:58; 1 Cor. 10:22 [5] *detestable acts*
17 [g] Rev. 9:20

32:7 Remember the days of old. A call to reflect on past history and to inquire about the lessons to be learned.

32:8,9 the Most High. This title for God emphasized His sovereignty and authority over all the nations (see Gen. 11:9; 10:32; 14:18; Num. 24:16) with the amazing revelation that in the whole plan for the world, God had as His goal the salvation of His chosen people. God ordained a plan where the number of nations (70 according to Gen. 10) corresponded to the number of the children of Israel (70 according to Gen. 46:27). Further, as God gave the nations their lands, He established their boundaries, leaving Israel enough land to sustain their expected population.

32:10-14 This whole description of what God did for Israel is figurative. Israel is like a man in the horrible desert in danger of death, without food or water, who is rescued by the Lord.

32:10 as the apple of His eye. Lit. "the little man of His eye," i.e., the pupil. Just as the pupil of the eye is essential for vision and, therefore, closely protected, especially in a howling wind, so God closely protected Israel. Cf. Ps. 17:8; Prov. 7:2.

32:11 Hovers over its young. The Lord exercised His loving care for Israel like an eagle caring for its young, especially as they were taught to fly. As they began to fly and had little strength, they would start to fall. At that point, an eagle would stop their fall by spreading its wings so they could land on them; so the Lord has carried Israel and not let the nation fall. He has been training Israel to fly on His wings of love and omnipotence.

32:12 no foreign god. Moses makes clear that God alone carried Israel through all its struggles and victories, thus depriving the people of any excuse for apostasy from the Lord by interest in false gods.

32:13 honey from the rock. A reference to honeycombs located in the fissures of the faces of a cliff is used because Canaan had many wild bees. **oil from the flinty rock.** Likely a reference to olive trees growing in rocky places otherwise bereft of fruit-growing trees. These metaphoric phrases regarding honey and oil point to the most valuable products coming out of the most unproductive places.

32:14 rams of...Bashan. *See note on 3:1.*

32:15 Jeshurun. The word means "righteous" (lit. "the upright one"), i.e., a name for Israel which sarcastically expresses the fact that Israel did not live up to God's law after entering the Land. God uses this name to remind Israel of His calling and to severely rebuke apostasy. **grew fat and kicked.** Like an ox which had become fat and intractable, Israel became affluent because of the bountiful provisions of God but, instead of being thankful and obedient, became rebellious against the Lord (cf. 6:10-15).

32:16 foreign *gods.* Israel turned to worship the gods of the people in the land. These were gods they had not before acknowledged (v. 17).

32:17 demons. Cf. Lev. 17:7; 2 Chr. 11:15; Ps. 106:37. The term describes those angels who fell with Satan and constitute the evil force that fights against God and His holy angels. Idol worship is a form of demon worship as demon spirits impersonate the idol and work their wicked strategies through the system of false religion tied to the false god.

32:18-33 For this foolish apostasy, the Lord will severely judge Israel. This visitation of anger is in the form of a divine resolution to punish Israelites whenever they pursue idols, including the next generation of sons and daughters (v. 19). In vv. 20-22, Moses quotes the Lord Himself.

18 [h]Of the Rock *who* begot you, you are
unmindful,
And have [i]forgotten the God who
fathered you.
19 "And[j] when the LORD saw *it*, He
spurned *them*,
Because of the provocation of His
sons and His daughters.
20 And He said: 'I will hide My face
from them,
I will see what their end *will be*,
For they *are* a perverse generation,
[k]Children in whom *is* no faith.
21 [l]They have provoked Me to
jealousy by *what* is not God;
They have moved Me to anger [m]by
their [6]foolish idols.
But [n]I will provoke them to jealousy
by *those who are* not a nation;
I will move them to anger by a
foolish nation.
22 For [o]a fire is kindled in My anger,
And shall burn to the [7]lowest [8]hell;
It shall consume the earth with her
increase,
And set on fire the foundations of
the mountains.

23 'I will [p]heap disasters on them;
[q]I will spend My arrows on them.
24 *They shall be* wasted with hunger,
Devoured by pestilence and bitter
destruction;
I will also send against them the
[r]teeth of beasts,
With the poison of serpents of the
dust.
25 The sword shall destroy outside;
There shall be terror within
For the young man and virgin,
The nursing child with the man of
gray hairs.
26 [s]I would have said, "I will dash
them in pieces,
I will make the memory of them to
cease from among men,"
27 Had I not feared the wrath of the
enemy,
Lest their adversaries should
misunderstand,
Lest they should say, [t]"Our hand *is*
high;
And it is not the LORD who has
done all this." '

28 "For they *are* a nation void of
counsel,
Nor *is there any* understanding in
them.
29 [u]Oh, that they were wise, *that* they
understood this,
That they would consider their
[v]latter end!
30 How could one chase a thousand,
And two put ten thousand to flight,
Unless their Rock [w]had sold them,
And the LORD had surrendered
them?
31 For their rock *is* not like our Rock,
[x]Even our enemies themselves *being*
judges.
32 For [y]their vine *is* of the vine of
Sodom
And of the fields of Gomorrah;
Their grapes *are* grapes of gall,
Their clusters *are* bitter.
33 Their wine *is* [z]the poison of
serpents,
And the cruel [a]venom of cobras.

34 '*Is* this not [b]laid up in store with Me,
Sealed up among My treasures?
35 [c]Vengeance is Mine, and
recompense;
Their foot shall slip in *due* time;
[d]For the day of their calamity *is* at
hand,
And the things to come hasten
upon them.'

18 [h]Is. 17:10 [i]Jer. 2:32 **19** [j]Judg. 2:14 **20** [k]Matt. 17:17 **21** [l]Ps. 78:58 [m]Ps. 31:6 [n]Rom. 10:19 [6]*foolishness*, lit. *vanities* **22** [o]Num. 16:33-35; Ps. 18:7, 8; Lam. 4:11 [7]*lowest part of* [8]Or *Sheol* **23** [p]Ex. 32:12; Deut. 29:21, 24 [q]Ps. 7:12, 13 **24** [r]Lev. 26:22 **26** [s]Ezek. 20:23

27 [t]Is. 10:12-15 **29** [u]Ps. 81:13; [Luke 19:42] [v]Deut. 31:29 **30** [w]Judg. 2:14; Ps. 44:12 **31** [x][1 Sam. 4:7, 8; Jer. 40:2, 3] **32** [y]Is. 1:8-10 **33** [z]Ps. 58:4 [a]Rom. 3:13 **34** [b][Jer. 2:22] **35** [c]Ps. 94:1; Rom. 12:19; Heb. 10:30 [d]2 Pet. 2:3

32:21 not a nation. As the Lord was provoked to jealousy by Israel's worship of that which was "not God," so He would provoke Israel to jealousy and anger by humiliation before a foolish, vile "no-nation." In Rom. 10:19, Paul applied the term "not a nation" to the Gentile nations generally. Jews who worship a "no-god" will be judged by a "no-people."

32:22 a fire is kindled…to the lowest hell. Cf. 29:20. Once the fire of God's anger was kindled, it knew no limits in its destructive force, reaching to even those in the grave, an indication of God's eternal judgment against those who oppose Him.

32:23 disasters…arrows. The disasters (lit. "evil") are described in v. 24. The arrows represent the enemies who would defeat Israel in war and are further described in vv. 25-27.

32:27 Our hand *is* high. Military arrogance. The only thing that would prevent the Lord from permitting the complete destruction of His people would be His concern that the Gentiles might claim for themselves the honor of victory over Israel.

32:31 rock…Rock. A contrast between the gods of the nations ("rock") and Israel's true God ("Rock"). Israel could smite its foes with very little difficulty because of the weakness of their gods, who are not like the Rock Jehovah.

32:32 the vine of Sodom. Employing the metaphor of a vineyard, its grapes and its wine, the wickedness of Israel's enemies was described as having its roots in Sodom and Gomorrah, the evil cities destroyed by God as recorded in Gen. 19:1-29.

32:34 Sealed up among My treasures. The wicked acts of Israel's enemies were known to God and are stored up in His storehouse. At the proper time, God will avenge. Paul uses this image in Rom. 2:4,5.

32:35 Vengeance is Mine, and recompense. The manner and timing of the repayment of man's wickedness is God's prerogative. This principle is reaffirmed in the NT in Rom. 12:19; Heb. 10:30.

36 "For[e] the LORD will judge His people
[f]And have compassion on His
servants,
When He sees that *their* power is
gone,
And [g]*there is* no one *remaining*,
bond or free.
37 He will say: [h]'Where *are* their gods,
The rock in which they sought
refuge?
38 Who ate the fat of their sacrifices,
And drank the wine of their drink
offering?
Let them rise and help you,
And be your refuge.

39 'Now see that [i]I, *even* I, *am* He,
And [j]*there is* no God besides Me;
[k]I kill and I make alive;
I wound and I heal;
Nor *is there any* who can deliver
from My hand.
40 For I raise My hand to heaven,
And say, "*As* I live forever,
41 [l]If I [9]whet My glittering sword,
And My hand takes hold on
judgment,
I will render vengeance to My
enemies,
And repay those who hate Me.
42 I will make My arrows drunk with
blood,
And My sword shall devour flesh,
With the blood of the slain and the
captives,
From the heads of the leaders of
the enemy." '

43 "Rejoice,[m] O Gentiles, *with* His
[1]people;
For He will [n]avenge the blood of
His servants,
And render vengeance to His
adversaries;
He [o]will provide atonement for His
land *and* His people."

44 So Moses came with [2]Joshua the son
of Nun and spoke all the words of this
song in the hearing of the people. 45 Moses
finished speaking all these words to all Israel, 46 and he said to them: [p]"Set your
hearts on all the words which I testify
among you today, which you shall command your [q]children to be careful to observe—all the words of this law. 47 For it *is*
not a [3]futile thing for you, because it *is*
your [r]life, and by this word you shall prolong *your* days in the land which you cross
over the Jordan to possess."

Moses to Die on Mount Nebo

48 Then the LORD spoke to Moses that
very same day, saying: 49 [s]"Go up this
mountain of the Abarim, Mount Nebo,
which *is* in the land of Moab, across from
Jericho; view the land of Canaan, which I
give to the children of Israel as a possession; 50 and die on the mountain which
you ascend, and be [4]gathered to your people, just as [t]Aaron your brother died on
Mount Hor and was gathered to his people; 51 because [u]you trespassed against Me
among the children of Israel at the waters
of [5]Meribah Kadesh, in the Wilderness of
Zin, because you [v]did not hallow Me in the
midst of the children of Israel. 52 [w]Yet you
shall see the land before *you*, though you
shall not go there, into the land which I am
giving to the children of Israel."

36 [e]Ps. 135:14; Heb. 10:30 [f]Ps. 106:45; Jer. 31:20 [g]2 Kin. 14:26 **37** [h]Judg. 10:14; Jer. 2:28 **39** [i]Is. 41:4; 43:10 [j]Deut. 32:12; Is. 45:5 [k]1 Sam. 2:6; Ps. 68:20 **41** [l]Is. 1:24; 66:16; Jer. 50:28-32 [9]*sharpen* **43** [m]Rom. 15:10 [1]DSS fragment adds *And let all the gods (angels) worship Him;* cf. LXX and Heb. 1:6 [n]2 Kin. 9:7; Rev. 6:10; 19:2 [o]Ps. 65:3; 79:9; 85:1 **44** [2]Heb. *Hoshea,* Num. 13:8, 16 **46** [p]Ezek. 40:4; 44:5 [q]Deut. 11:19 **47** [r]Deut. 8:3; 30:15-20 [3]*vain* **49** [s]Num. 27:12-14; Deut. 3:27 **50** [t]Num. 20:25, 28; 33:38 [4]Join your ancestors **51** [u]Num. 20:11-13 [v]Lev. 10:3 [5]Lit. *Contention at Kadesh* **52** [w]Num. 27:12; Deut. 34:1-5

32:36 This is the promise that the Lord will judge Israel as a nation, but that the nation is composed of righteous and wicked. God actually helps the righteous by destroying the wicked. "His servants" are the righteous, all who in the time of judgment are faithful to the Lord (cf. Mal. 3:16–4:3). The Lord has judged Israel, not to destroy the nation, but to punish the sinners and show the folly of their false gods (vv. 37,38). At the same time, the Lord has always shown compassion for those who have loved and obeyed Him.

32:39 I, *even* I, *am* He. After showing the worthlessness of false gods (vv. 37,38), this declaration of the nature of God was presented in contrast to show that the God of Israel is the living God, the only One who can offer help and protection to Israel. He has the power of life and death with regard to Israel (cf. 1 Sam. 2:6; 2 Kin. 5:7) and the power to wound and heal them (cf. Is. 30:26; 57:17,18; Jer. 17:14; Hos. 6:1).

32:40-42 I raise My hand. God takes an oath to bring vengeance on His enemies. Here (as in Ex. 6:8; Num. 14:28) the hand is used anthropomorphically of God, who can swear by no greater than His eternal Self (cf. Is. 45:23; Jer. 22:5; Heb. 6:17).

32:43 Rejoice, O Gentiles, *with* His people. As a result of the execution of God's vengeance, all nations will be called upon to praise with Israel the Lord who will have provided redemptively for them in Christ and also provided a new beginning in the Land. This atonement for the Land is the satisfaction of God's wrath by the sacrifice of His enemies in judgment. The atonement for the people is by the sacrifice of Jesus Christ on the cross (cf. Ps. 79:9). Paul quotes this passage in Rom. 15:10, as does the writer of Hebrews (1:6).

32:47 it *is* your life. Moses reiterated to Israel that obedience to the Lord's commands was to be the key to her living long in the land that God had prepared and called for this song to be a kind of national anthem which the leaders should see is frequently repeated to animate the people to love and obey God.

32:48–34:12 The anticipation of and record of Moses' death (32:48-52; 34:1-12) bracket the recording of Moses' blessing given to Israel before his death. This literary unit was composed and added to the text after the death of Moses.

32:49 Mount Nebo. A peak in the Abarim range of mountains to the E of the N end of the Dead Sea, from where Moses would be able to see across to the Promised Land, which he was not permitted to enter.

32:50 gathered to your people. An idiom for death. See Gen. 25:8,17; 35:29; 49:33; Num. 20:24,26; 31:2.

Moses' Final Blessing on Israel

33 Now this *is* [a]the blessing with which Moses [b]the man of God blessed the children of Israel before his death. 2 And he said:

[c]"The LORD came from Sinai,
And dawned on them from [d]Seir;
He shone forth from [e]Mount
Paran,
And He came with [f]ten thousands
of saints;
From His right hand
Came a fiery law for them.
3 Yes, [g]He loves the people;
[h]All His saints *are* in Your hand;
They [i]sit down at Your feet;
Everyone [j]receives Your words.
4 [k]Moses [1]commanded a law for us,
[l]A heritage of the congregation of
Jacob.
5 And He was [m]King in [n]Jeshurun,
When the leaders of the people
were gathered,
All the tribes of Israel together.

6 "Let [o]Reuben live, and not die,
Nor let his men be few."

7 And this he said of [p]Judah:

"Hear, LORD, the voice of Judah,
And bring him to his people;
[q]Let his hands be sufficient for
him,
And may You be [r]a help against
his enemies."

8 And of [s]Levi he said:

[t]"*Let* Your [2]Thummim and Your
Urim *be* with Your holy one,
[u]Whom You tested at Massah,
And with whom You contended at
the waters of Meribah,
9 [v]Who says of his father and mother,
'I have not [w]seen them';
[x]Nor did he acknowledge his
brothers,
Or know his own children;
For [y]they have observed Your word
And kept Your covenant.
10 [z]They shall teach Jacob Your
judgments,
And Israel Your law.
They shall put incense before You,
[a]And a whole burnt sacrifice on
Your altar.
11 Bless his substance, LORD,
And [b]accept the work of his hands;
Strike the loins of those who rise
against him,
And of those who hate him, that
they rise not again."

12 Of Benjamin he said:

"The beloved of the LORD shall
dwell in safety by Him,
Who shelters him all the day long;
And he shall dwell between His
shoulders."

13 And of Joseph he said:

[c]"Blessed of the LORD *is* his land,

CHAPTER 33
1 [a]Gen. 49:28 [b]Ps. 90
2 [c]Ex. 19:18, 20; Ps. 68:8, 17; Hab. 3:3 [d]Deut. 2:1, 4 [e]Num. 10:12 [f]Dan. 7:10; Acts 7:53; Rev. 5:11
3 [g]Ps. 47:4; Hos. 11:1 [h]1 Sam. 2:9 [i][Luke 10:39] [j]Prov. 2:1
4 [k]Deut. 4:2; John 1:17; 7:19 [l]Ps. 119:111 [1]*charged us with*
5 [m]Ex. 15:18 [n]Deut. 32:15
6 [o]Gen. 49:3, 4
7 [p]Gen. 49:8-12 [q]Gen. 49:8 [r]Ps. 146:5
8 [s]Gen. 49:5 [t]Ex. 28:30; Lev. 8:8 [u]Num. 20:2-13; Deut. 6:2, 3, 16; Ps. 81:7 [2]Lit. *Perfections and Your Lights*
9 [v][Num. 25:5-8; Matt. 10:37; 19:29] [w][Gen. 29:32] [x]Ex. 32:26-28 [y]Mal. 2:5, 6
10 [z]Lev. 10:11; Deut. 31:9-13; Mal. 2:7 [a]Lev. 1:9; Ps. 51:19
11 [b]2 Sam. 24:23; Ezek. 20:40
13 [c]Gen. 49:22-26

33:1-29 The final words of Moses to the people were a listing of the blessings of each of the tribes of Israel, Simeon excluded (vv. 6-25). These blessings were introduced and concluded with passages which praise God (vv. 2-5,26-29). That these blessings of Moses are presented in this chapter as recorded by someone other than Moses is clear because in v. 1, Moses was viewed as already being dead, and as the words of Moses were presented, the clause "he said" (vv. 2,7,8,12,13,18,20,22,23,24) was used.

33:1 the man of God. The first use of this phrase in Scripture. Subsequently, some 70 times in the OT, messengers of God (especially prophets) are called "a man of God" (1 Sam. 2:27; 9:6; 1 Kin. 13:1; 17:18; 2 Kin. 4:7). The NT uses this title for Timothy (1 Tim. 6:11; 2 Tim. 3:17). Moses was viewed among such prophets in this conclusion to the book (see 34:10).

33:2 Sinai…Seir…Paran. These are mountains associated with the giving of the law—Sinai on the S, Seir on the NE, and Paran on the N. These mountains provide a beautiful metaphor, borrowed from the dawn. God, like the morning sun, is the Light that rises to give His beams to all the Promised Land. **saints.** Lit. "holy ones." Probably a reference to the angels who assisted God when the law was mediated to Moses at Mt. Sinai (see Acts 7:53; Gal. 3:19; Heb. 2:2).

33:3 He loves the people. Notwithstanding the awe-inspiring symbols of majesty displayed at Sinai, the law was given in kindness and love to provide both temporal and eternal blessing to those with a heart to obey it. Cf. Rom. 13:8-10.

33:5 King in Jeshurun. *See note on 32:15.* Since Moses is nowhere else in Scripture referred to as king, most interpret this as a reference to the Lord as King over Israel. However, Moses is the closest antecedent of the pronoun "he" in this clause, and the most natural understanding is that Moses is being referred to as a king. Moses certainly exercised kingly authority over Israel and could be viewed as a prototype of the coming King. Thus, united in the figure of Moses, the coming prophet like unto Moses (18:15) would be the prophet-king.

33:6 Reuben. Here is the prayer that this tribe would survive in large numbers (cf. Num. 1:21; 2:11).

33:7 Judah. Moses prayed that this tribe would be powerful in leading the nation to be victorious in battle through the help of the Lord.

33:8-11 Levi. Moses prays for the Levites to fulfill their tasks, God granting to them protection from their enemies. Moses omitted Simeon, but that tribe did receive a number of allies in the southern territory of Judah (Josh. 19:2-9) and did not lose their identity (cf. 1 Chr. 4:34-38).

33:12 Benjamin. That this tribe would have security and peace because the Lord would shield them was Moses' request. They were given the land in the N of Judah near Jerusalem.

33:13-17 Joseph. This included both Ephraim and Manasseh (v. 17), who would enjoy material prosperity (vv. 13-16) and military

With the precious things of heaven,
with the [d]dew,
And the deep lying beneath,
14 With the precious fruits of the sun,
With the precious produce of the
months,
15 With the best things of [e]the ancient
mountains,
With the precious things [f]of the
everlasting hills,
16 With the precious things of the
earth and its fullness,
And the favor of [g]Him who dwelt
in the bush.
Let *the blessing* come [h]'on the head
of Joseph,
And on the crown of the head of
him *who was* separate from
his brothers.'
17 His glory *is like* a [i]firstborn bull,
And his horns *like* the [j]horns of the
wild ox;
Together with them
[k]He shall push the peoples
To the ends of the earth;
[l]They *are* the ten thousands of
Ephraim,
And they *are* the thousands of
Manasseh."

18 And of Zebulun he said:

[m]"Rejoice, Zebulun, in your going out,
And Issachar in your tents!
19 They shall [n]call the peoples *to* the
mountain;
There [o]they shall offer sacrifices of
righteousness;
For they shall partake *of* the
abundance of the seas
And *of* treasures hidden in the
sand."

20 And of Gad he said:

"Blessed *is* he who [p]enlarges Gad;
He dwells as a lion,
And tears the arm and the crown
of his head.
21 [q]He provided the first *part* for
himself,
Because a lawgiver's portion was
reserved there.
[r]He came *with* the heads of the
people;
He administered the justice of the
LORD,
And His judgments with Israel."

22 And of Dan he said:

"Dan *is* a lion's whelp;
[s]He shall leap from Bashan."

23 And of Naphtali he said:

"O Naphtali, [t]satisfied with favor,
And full of the blessing of the LORD,
[u]Possess the west and the south."

24 And of Asher he said:

[v]"Asher *is* most blessed of sons;
Let him be favored by his brothers,
And let him [w]dip his foot in oil.
25 Your sandals *shall be* [x]iron and
bronze;
As your days, *so shall* your strength
be.

26 "*There is* [y]no one like the God of
[z]Jeshurun,
[a]*Who* rides the heavens to help you,
And in His excellency on the clouds.
27 The eternal God *is your* [b]refuge,
And underneath *are* the everlasting
arms;
[c]He will thrust out the enemy from
before you,
And will say, 'Destroy!'
28 Then [d]Israel shall dwell in safety,
[e]The fountain of Jacob [f]alone,
In a land of grain and new wine;
His [g]heavens shall also drop dew.

13 [d]Gen. 27:28
15 [e]Gen. 49:26 [f]Hab. 3:6
16 [g]Ex. 3:2-4; Acts 7:30-35 [h]Gen. 49:26
17 [i]1 Chr. 5:1 [j]Num. 23:22 [k]1 Kin. 22:11; Ps. 44:5 [l]Gen. 48:19
18 [m]Gen. 49:13-15
19 [n]Ex. 15:17; Ps. 2:6; Is. 2:3 [o]Ps. 4:5; 51:19
20 [p]1 Chr. 12:8
21 [q]Num. 32:16, 17 [r]Josh. 4:12
22 [s]Gen. 49:16, 17; Josh. 19:47
23 [t]Gen. 49:21 [u]Josh. 19:32
24 [v]Gen. 49:20 [w]Job 29:6
25 [x]Deut. 8:9
26 [y]Ex. 15:11; Deut. 4:35; Ps. 86:8; Jer. 10:6 [z]Deut. 32:15 [a]Deut. 10:14; Ps. 68:3, 33, 34; 104:3
27 [b][Ps. 90:1; 91:2, 9] [c]Deut. 9:3-5
28 [d]Deut. 33:12; Jer. 23:6; 33:16 [e]Deut. 8:7, 8 [f]Num. 23:9 [g]Gen. 27:28

might (v. 17), which would compensate and reward them for the Egyptian slavery of their ancestor (see Gen. 49:26). Ephraim would have greater military success in the future than Manasseh as the outworking of Jacob's blessing of the younger over the older (see Gen. 48:20).

33:18 Zebulun...Issachar. Moses prayed that these two tribes from the fifth and sixth sons of Leah would receive God's blessing in their daily lives, particularly through the trade on the seas.

33:20 Gad. This tribe had large territory E of the Jordan and was a leader in gaining the victory in battles in Canaan.

33:22 Dan. Dan had the potential for great energy and strength and leaped from its southern settlement to establish a colony in the N. Cf. Gen. 49:17, 18, where Dan is compared to a serpent.

33:23 Naphtali. This tribe would enjoy the favor of God in the fullness of His blessing, having land in the W of Galilee and S of the northern Danites.

33:24 Asher. The request is that this tribe would experience abundant fertility and prosperity, depicted by reference to a foot-operated oil press. Shoes of hard metal suited both country people and soldiers.

33:26,27 the God of Jeshurun. Moses concluded his blessings with a reminder of the uniqueness of Israel's God. For "Jeshurun," *see note on 32:15.*

33:28,29 This pledge was only partially fulfilled after they entered the Land, but it awaits a complete fulfillment in the kingdom of Messiah.

33:28 The fountain of Jacob. This is a euphemism for Jacob's seed, referring to his posterity.

29 [h]Happy *are* you, O Israel!
[i]Who *is* like you, a people saved by
the LORD,
[j]The shield of your help
And the sword of your majesty!
Your enemies [k]shall submit to
you,
And [l]you shall tread down their
[3]high places."

Moses Dies on Mount Nebo

34 Then Moses went up from the
plains of Moab [a]to Mount Nebo, to
the top of Pisgah, which is across from Jericho. And the LORD showed him all the
land of Gilead as far as Dan, 2 all Naphtali
and the land of Ephraim and Manasseh, all
the land of Judah as far as the [1]Western
Sea, 3 the South, and the plain of the Valley
of Jericho, [b]the city of palm trees, as far as
Zoar. 4 Then the LORD said to him, [c]"This *is*
the land of which I swore to give Abraham,
Isaac, and Jacob, saying, 'I will give it to
your descendants.' [d]I have caused you to
see *it* with your eyes, but you shall not
cross over there."

29 [h] Ps. 144:15 [i] Deut. 4:32-34; 2 Sam. 7:23 [j] Gen. 15:1; Ps. 115:9 [k] Ps. 18:44; 66:3 [l] Num. 33:52 [3] Places for pagan worship

CHAPTER 34

1 [a] Num. 27:12; Deut. 32:49
2 [1] Mediterranean
3 [b] 2 Chr. 28:15
4 [c] Gen. 12:7 [d] Deut. 3:27
5 [e] Num. 20:12; Deut. 32:50; Josh. 1:1, 2
6 [f] Jude 9
7 [g] Deut. 31:2 [h] Gen. 27:1; 48:10 [2] *eyesight was not weakened* [3] *reduced*
8 [i] Gen. 50:3, 10
9 [j] Is. 11:2 [k] Num. 27:18, 23
10 [l] Deut. 18:15, 18 [m] Ex. 33:11; Num. 12:8; Deut. 5:4
11 [n] Deut. 7:19

5 [e]So Moses the servant of the LORD died
there in the land of Moab, according to the
word of the LORD. 6 And He buried him in
a valley in the land of Moab, opposite Beth
Peor; but [f]no one knows his grave to this
day. 7 [g]Moses *was* one hundred and twenty years old when he died. [h]His [2]eyes were
not dim nor his natural vigor [3]diminished.
8 And the children of Israel wept for Moses
in the plains of Moab [i]thirty days. So the
days of weeping *and* mourning for Moses
ended.
9 Now Joshua the son of Nun was full of
the [j]spirit of wisdom, for [k]Moses had laid
his hands on him; so the children of Israel
heeded him, and did as the LORD had commanded Moses.
10 But since then there [l]has not arisen in
Israel a prophet like Moses, [m]whom the
LORD knew face to face, 11 in all [n]the signs
and wonders which the LORD sent him to
do in the land of Egypt, before Pharaoh,
before all his servants, and in all his land,
12 and by all that mighty power and all the
great terror which Moses performed in the
sight of all Israel.

34:1-12 This concluding chapter was obviously written by someone other than Moses (probably the writer of Joshua) to bridge out of Deuteronomy into Joshua.

34:1 Pisgah. The range or ridge of which Mt. Nebo was the highest point.

34:1-4 the LORD showed him. From the top of the mountain, Moses was allowed to see the panorama of the Land the Lord had promised to give (the Land of Canaan) to the patriarchs and their seed in Gen. 12:7; 13:15; 15:18-21; 26:4; 28:13,14.

34:6 He buried him. The context indicates that the Lord is the one who buried Moses, and man did not have a part in it. Cf. Jude 9, which recounts Michael's and Satan's dispute over Moses' body.

34:7 not dim…diminished. Moses' physical vision and physical health were not impaired. It was not death by natural causes that kept Moses from leading Israel into the Promised Land; it was his unfaithfulness to the Lord at Meribah (see Num. 20:12).

34:8 thirty days. The mourning period for Moses conformed to that of Aaron (Num. 20:29).

34:9 spirit of wisdom…laid his hands. Joshua received 1) confirmation of the military and administrative ability necessary to the task the Lord had given him, as well as, 2) the spiritual wisdom to rely on and to be committed to the Lord through the laying on of Moses' hands.

34:10 a prophet like Moses. Moses was the greatest of all the OT prophets, one whom the Lord knew intimately. Not until John the Baptist was there another prophet greater than Moses (see Matt. 11:11). After John, the Prophet came of whom Moses wrote (cf. John 1:21,25; 6:14 with Deut. 18:15,18; Acts 3:22; 7:37). Moses next appeared on the Mt. of Transfiguration together with Elijah and Jesus Christ (Matt. 17:3; Mark 9:4; Luke 9:30,31).

The Book of JOSHUA

Title

This is the first of the 12 historical books, and it gained its name from the exploits of Joshua, the understudy whom Moses prayed for and commissioned as a leader in Israel (Num. 27:12-23). "Joshua" means "Jehovah saves," or "the LORD is salvation," and corresponds to the NT name "Jesus." God delivered Israel in Joshua's day when He was personally present as the saving Commander who fought on Israel's behalf (5:14–6:2; 10:42; 23:3,5; Acts 7:45).

Author and Date

Although the author is not named, the most probable candidate is Joshua, who was the key eyewitness to the events recorded (cf. 18:9; 24:26). An assistant whom Joshua groomed could have finished the book by attaching such comments as those concerning Joshua's death (24:29-33). Some have even suggested that this section was written by the High-Priest Eleazar, or his son, Phinehas. Rahab was still living at the time Josh. 6:25 was penned. The book was completed before David's reign (15:63; cf. 2 Sam. 5:5-9). The most likely writing period is ca. 1405–1385 B.C.

Joshua was born in Egyptian slavery, trained under Moses, and by God's choice rose to his key position of leading Israel into Canaan. Distinguishing features of his life include: 1) service (Ex. 17:10; 24:13; 33:11; Num. 11:28); 2) soldiering (Ex. 17:9-13); 3) scouting (Num. 13,14); 4) supplication by Moses (Num. 27:15-17); 5) the sovereignty of God (Num 27:18ff.); 6) the Spirit's presence (Num. 27:18; Deut. 34:9); 7) separation by Moses (Num. 27:18-23; Deut. 31:7,8,13-15); and 8) selflessness in wholly following the Lord (Num. 32:12).

Background and Setting

When Moses passed the baton of leadership on to Joshua before he died (Deut. 34), Israel was at the end of its 40 year wilderness wandering period ca. 1405 B.C. Joshua was approaching 90 years of age when he became Israel's leader. He later died at the age of 110 (24:29), having led Israel to drive out most of the Canaanites and having divided the Land among the 12 tribes. Poised on the plains of Moab, E of the Jordan River and the Land which God had promised (Gen. 12:7; 15:18-21), the Israelites awaited God's direction to conquer the Land. They faced peoples on the western side of the Jordan who had become so steeped in iniquity that God would cause the Land, so to speak, to spew out these inhabitants (Lev. 18:24,25). He would give Israel the Land by conquest, primarily to fulfill the covenant He had pledged to Abraham and his descendants, but also to pass just judgment on the sinful inhabitants (cf. Gen. 15:16). Long possession of different parts of the Land by various peoples had pre-dated even Abraham's day (Gen. 10:15-19; 12:6; 13:7). Its inhabitants had continued on a moral decline in the worship of many gods up to Joshua's time.

Historical and Theological Themes

A keynote feature is God's faithfulness to fulfill His promise of giving the Land to Abraham's descendants (Gen. 12:7; 15:18-21; 17:8). By His leading (cf. 5:14–6:2), they inhabited the territories E and W of the Jordan, and so the word "possess" appears nearly 20 times.

Related to this theme is Israel's failure to press their conquest to every part of the Land (13:1). Judges 1–2 later describes the tragic results from this sin. Key verses focus on: 1) God's promise of possession of the Land (1:3,6); 2) meditation on God's law, which was strategic for His people (1:8); and 3) Israel's actual possession of the Land in part (11:23; 21:45; 22:4).

Specific allotment of distinct portions in the Land was Joshua's task, as recorded in chaps. 13–22. Levites were placed strategically in 48 towns so that God's spiritual services through them would be reasonably within reach of the Israelites, wherever they lived.

God wanted His people to possess the Land: 1) to keep His promise (Gen. 12:7); 2) to set the stage for later developments in His kingdom plan (cf. Gen. 17:8; 49:8-12), e.g., positioning Israel for events in the periods of the kings and prophets; 3) to punish peoples that were an affront to Him because of extreme sinfulness (Lev. 18:25); and 4) to be a testimony to other peoples (Josh. 2:9-11), as God's covenant heart reached out to all nations (Gen. 12:1-3).

Interpretive Challenges

Miracles always challenge readers either to believe that the God who created heaven and earth (Gen. 1:1) can do other mighty works, too, or to explain them away. As in Moses' day, miracles in this book were a part of God's purpose, such as: 1) His holding back the Jordan's waters (Josh. 3:7-17); 2) the fall of Jericho's walls (Josh. 6:1-27); 3) the hailstones (Josh. 10:1-11); and 4) the long day (Josh. 10:12-15).

Other challenges include: 1) How did God's blessing on the harlot Rahab, who responded to Him in faith, relate to her telling a lie (Josh. 2)? 2) Why were Achan's family members executed with him (Josh. 7)? 3) Why was Ai, with fewer men than Israel, hard to conquer (Josh. 7–8)? 4) What does God's "sending the hornet" before Israel mean (Josh. 24:12)? These questions will be addressed in the notes.

Outline

I. Entering the Promised Land (1:1–5:15)

II. Conquering the Promised Land (6:1–12:24)
   - A. The Central Campaign (6:1–8:35)
   - B. The Southern Campaign (9:1–10:43)
   - C. The Northern Campaign (11:1-15)
   - D. The Summary of Conquests (11:16–12:24)

III. Distributing Portions in the Promised Land (13:1–22:34)
   - A. Summary of Instructions (13:1–33)
   - B. West of the Jordan (14:1–19:51)
   - C. Cities of Refuge (20:1-9)
   - D. Cities of the Levites (21:1–45)
   - E. East of the Jordan (22:1–34)

IV. Retaining the Promised Land (23:1–24:28)
   - A. The First Speech by Joshua (23:1-16)
   - B. The Second Speech by Joshua (24:1-28)

V. Postscript (24:29-33)

God's Commission to Joshua

1 After the death of Moses the servant of
the LORD, it came to pass that the LORD
spoke to Joshua the son of Nun, Moses'
[a]assistant, saying: 2 [b]"Moses My servant is
dead. Now therefore, arise, go over this
Jordan, you and all this people, to the land
which I am giving to them—the children of
Israel. 3 [c]Every place that the sole of your
foot will tread upon I have given you, as I
said to Moses. 4 [d]From the wilderness and
this Lebanon as far as the great river, the
River Euphrates, all the land of the Hittites, and to the Great Sea toward the going
down of the sun, shall be your territory.
5 [e]No man shall *be able to* stand before you
all the days of your life; [f]as I was with Moses, *so* [g]I will be with you. [h]I will not leave
you nor forsake you. 6 [i]Be strong and of
good courage, for to this people you shall
[1]divide as an inheritance the land which I
swore to their fathers to give them. 7 Only
be strong and very courageous, that you
may observe to do according to all the law
[j]which Moses My servant commanded
you; [k]do not turn from it to the right hand
or to the left, that you may [2]prosper wherever you go. 8 [l]This Book of the Law shall
not depart from your mouth, but [m]you[3]
shall meditate in it day and night, that you
may observe to do according to all that is
written in it. For then you will make your
way prosperous, and then you will have
good success. 9 [n]Have I not commanded
you? Be strong and of good courage; [o]do
not be afraid, nor be dismayed, for the
LORD your God *is* with you wherever you
go."

The Order to Cross the Jordan

10 Then Joshua commanded the officers
of the people, saying, 11 "Pass through the
camp and command the people, saying,
'Prepare provisions for yourselves, for
[p]within three days you will cross over this
Jordan, to go in to possess the land which
the LORD your God is giving you to possess.'"
12 And to the Reubenites, the Gadites,
and half the tribe of Manasseh Joshua
spoke, saying, 13 "Remember [q]the word
which Moses the servant of the LORD commanded you, saying, 'The LORD your God
is giving you rest and is giving you this

CHAPTER 1

1 [a] Ex. 24:13; Num. 13:16; 14:6, 29, 30, 37, 38; Deut. 1:38; Acts 7:45
2 [b] Num. 12:7; Deut. 34:5
3 [c] Deut. 11:24; Josh. 11:23
4 [d] Gen. 15:18; Ex. 23:31; Num. 34:3-12
5 [e] Deut. 7:24 [f] Ex. 3:12 [g] Deut. 31:8, 23 [h] Deut. 31:6, 7; Heb. 13:5
6 [i] Deut. 31:7, 23 [1] *give as a possession*
7 [j] Num. 27:23; Deut. 31:7; Josh. 11:15 [k] Deut. 5:32 [2] *have success or act wisely*
8 [l] Deut. 17:18, 19; 31:24, 26; Josh. 8:34 [m] Deut. 29:9; Ps. 1:1-3 [3] *you shall be constantly in*
9 [n] Deut. 31:7 [o] Ps. 27:1
11 [p] Deut. 9:1; Josh. 3:17
13 [q] Num. 32:20-28

1:2 the land which I am giving. This is the land God promised in His covenant with Abraham and often reaffirmed later (Gen. 12:7; 13:14-15; 15:18-21).

1:4 Borders of the Promised Land are: *west,* the Mediterranean seacoast; *east,* Euphrates River far to the east; *south,* the wilderness over to the Nile of Egypt; *north,* Lebanon.

1:5 The promise of divine power for Joshua's task.

1:6 I swore to their fathers. Cf. Gen. 12:7; 15:18-21; 17:8; 26:3; 28:13; 35:12 to Abraham, Isaac, and Jacob.

1:7 strong and very courageous. *See note on Deut. 31:6-8.*

1:8 This Book of the Law. A reference to Scripture, specifically Genesis through Deuteronomy, written by Moses (cf. Ex. 17:14; Deut. 31:9-11,24). **meditate in it.** To read with thoughtfulness, to linger over God's Word. The parts of Scripture they possessed have always been the main spiritual food of those who served Him, e.g., Job (Job 23:12); the psalmist (Ps. 1:1-3); Jeremiah (Jer. 15:16); and Jesus (John 4:34). **prosperous...good success.** The promise of God's blessing on the great responsibility God has given Joshua. The principle here is central to all spiritual effort and enterprise, namely the deep understanding and application of Scripture at all times.

1:9 LORD...*is* with you. This assurance has always been the staying sufficiency for His servants such as: Abraham (Gen. 15:1); Moses and his people (Ex. 14:13); Isaiah (Is. 41:10); Jeremiah (Jer. 1:7,8); and Christians through the centuries (Matt. 28:20; Heb. 13:5).

1:11 within three days. In some cases, events which took place before this announcement and these 3 days (cf. 3:2) are described later on, e.g., Joshua's sending two scouts to check out the Land (2:22).

1:12 half the tribe of Manasseh. In Gen. 48 Jacob blessed both sons of Joseph, Ephraim, and Manasseh, so that Joseph actually received a double blessing (Gen. 48:22). This allowed for 12 allotments of the Land, Levi being excluded because of priestly function.

Joshua's Preparation for Ministry

1. Ex. 17:9,10,13-14	Joshua led the victorious battle against the Amalekites.
2. Ex. 24:13	Joshua, the servant of Moses, accompanied the Jewish leader to the mountain of God (cf. 32:17).
3. Num. 11:28	Joshua was the attendant of Moses from his youth.
4. Num. 13:16	Moses changed his name from Hosea ("salvation") to Joshua ("the Lord saves").
5. Num. 14:6-10,30,38	Joshua, along with Caleb, spied out the land of Canaan with 10 others. Only Joshua and Caleb urged the nation to possess the land and, thus, only they of the 12 actually entered Canaan.
6. Num. 27:18	Joshua was indwelt by the Holy Spirit.
7. Num. 27:18-23	Joshua was commissioned for spiritual service the first time, to assist Moses.
8. Num. 32:12	Joshua followed the Lord fully.
9. Deut. 31:23	Joshua was commissioned a second time, to replace Moses.
10. Deut. 34:9	Joshua was filled with the spirit of wisdom.

land.' 14 Your wives, your little ones, and
your livestock shall remain in the land
which Moses gave you on this side of the
Jordan. But you shall [4]pass before your
brethren armed, all your mighty men of
valor, and help them, 15 until the LORD has
given your brethren rest, as He *gave* you,
and they also have taken possession of the
land which the LORD your God is giving
them. [r]Then you shall return to the land of
your possession and enjoy it, which Moses
the LORD's servant gave you on this side of
the Jordan toward the sunrise."
16 So they answered Joshua, saying, "All
that you command us we will do, and
wherever you send us we will go. 17 Just as
we heeded Moses in all things, so we will
heed you. Only the LORD your God [s]be
with you, as He was with Moses. 18 Whoever rebels against your command and
does not heed your words, in all that you
command him, shall be put to death. Only
be strong and of good courage."

Rahab Hides the Spies

2 Now Joshua the son of Nun sent out
two men [a]from [1]Acacia Grove to spy
secretly, saying, "Go, view the land, especially Jericho."
So they went, and [b]came to the house of
a harlot named [c]Rahab, and [2]lodged there.
2 And [d]it was told the king of Jericho, saying, "Behold, men have come here tonight
from the children of Israel to search out the
country."
3 So the king of Jericho sent to Rahab,
saying, "Bring out the men who have come
to you, who have entered your house, for
they have come to search out all the country."
4 [e]Then the woman took the two men
and hid them. So she said, "Yes, the men
came to me, but I did not know where they
were from. 5 And it happened as the gate
was being shut, when it was dark, that the
men went out. Where the men went I do
not know; pursue them quickly, for you
may overtake them." 6 (But [f]she had
brought them up to the roof and hidden
them with the stalks of flax, which she had
laid in order on the roof.) 7 Then the men
pursued them by the road to the Jordan, to
the fords. And as soon as those who pursued them had gone out, they shut the gate.
8 Now before they lay down, she came
up to them on the roof, 9 and said to the
men: [g]"I know that the LORD has given you
the land, that [h]the terror of you has fallen
on us, and that all the inhabitants of the
land [i]are fainthearted because of you.
10 For we have heard how the LORD [j]dried
up the water of the Red Sea for you when
you came out of Egypt, and [k]what you did
to the two kings of the Amorites who *were*
on the other side of the Jordan, Sihon and
Og, whom you [l]utterly destroyed. 11 And
as soon as we [m]heard *these things*, [n]our
hearts melted; neither did there remain
any more courage in anyone because of
you, for [o]the LORD your God, He *is* God in
heaven above and on earth beneath.
12 Now therefore, I beg you, [p]swear to me
by the LORD, since I have shown you kindness, that you also will show kindness to
[q]my father's house, and [r]give me [3]a true
token, 13 and [s]spare my father, my mother,
my brothers, my sisters, and all that they
have, and deliver our lives from death."
14 So the men answered her, "Our lives
for yours, if none of you tell this business
of ours. And it shall be, when the LORD has
given us the land, that [t]we will deal kindly and truly with you."
15 Then she [u]let them down by a rope

14 [4] *cross over ahead of*
15 [r] Josh. 22:1-4
17 [s] 1 Sam. 20:13; 1 Kin. 1:37

CHAPTER 2

1 [a] Num. 25:1; Josh. 3:1 [b] Heb. 11:31; James 2:25 [c] Matt. 1:5 [1] Heb. *Shittim* [2] Lit. *lay down*
2 [d] Josh. 2:22
4 [e] 2 Sam. 17:19, 20
6 [f] Ex. 1:17; 2 Sam. 17:19
9 [g] Deut. 1:8 [h] Gen. 35:5; Ex. 23:27; Deut. 2:25; 11:25; Josh. 9:9, 10 [i] Ex. 15:15; Josh. 5:1
10 [j] Ex. 14:21; Josh. 4:23 [k] Num. 21:21-35 [l] Deut. 20:17; Josh. 6:21
11 [m] Ex. 15:14, 15 [n] Josh. 5:1; 7:5; Ps. 22:14; Is. 13:7 [o] Deut. 4:39
12 [p] 1 Sam. 20:14, 15, 17 [q] 1 Tim. 5:8 [r] Ex. 12:13; Josh. 2:18 [3] *a pledge of truth*
13 [s] Josh. 6:23-25
14 [t] Gen. 47:29; Judg. 1:24; [Matt. 5:7]
15 [u] Acts 9:25

1:13-18 The LORD...is giving you this land. God gave them these lands directly across the Jordan River on the E. (cf. Num. 32). Yet, it was their duty to assist the other tribes of Israel to invade and conquer their allotted land to the W.

2:1 Acacia Grove...Jericho. The grove (cf. 3:1) was situated in foothills about 7 mi. E of the Jordan, and Jericho lay seven mi. W of the river. **two men...to spy.** These scouts would inform Joshua on various features of the topography, food, drinking water, and defenses to be overcome in the invasion. **house of a harlot.** Their purpose was not impure; rather, the spies sought a place where they would not be conspicuous. Resorting to such a house would be a good cover, from where they might learn something of Jericho. Also, a house on the city wall (v. 15) would allow a quick getaway. In spite of this precaution, their presence became known (vv. 2,3). God, in his sovereign providence, wanted them there for the salvation of the harlot. She would provide an example of His saving by faith a woman at the bottom of social strata, as He saved Abraham at the top (cf. James 2:18-25). Most importantly, by God's grace she was in the Messianic line (Matt. 1:15).

2:2 the king. He was not over a broad domain, but only the city-state. Kings over other city areas appear later during this conquest (cf. 8:23; 12:24).

2:4,5 Cf. vv. 9-11. Lying is sin to God (Ex. 20:16), for He cannot lie (Titus 1:2). God commended her faith (Heb. 11:31; James 2:25) as expressed in vv. 9-16, not her lie. He never condones any sin, yet none are without some sin (cf. Rom. 3:23), thus the need for forgiveness. But He also honors true faith, small as it is, and imparts saving grace (Ex. 34:7).

2:6 stalks of flax. These fibers, used for making linen, were stems about 3 feet long, left to sit in water, then piled in the sun or on a level roof to dry.

2:11 God in heaven above and on earth beneath. She confessed the realization that He is the sovereign Creator and Sustainer of all that exists (cf. Deut. 4:39; Acts 14:15; 17:23-28), thus the Supreme One.

2:15,16 Her home was on the city wall, with the Jordan (v. 7) to the E. The rugged mountains to the W provided many hiding places.

through the window, for her house *was* on the city wall; she dwelt on the wall. **16** And she said to them, "Get to the mountain, lest the pursuers meet you. Hide there three days, until the pursuers have returned. Afterward you may go your way."

17 So the men said to her: "We *will be* [v]blameless[4] of this oath of yours which you have made us swear, **18** [w]unless, *when* we come into the land, you bind this line of scarlet cord in the window through which you let us down, [x]and unless you [5]bring your father, your mother, your brothers, and all your father's household to your own home. **19** So it shall be *that* whoever goes outside the doors of your house into the street, his blood *shall be* on his own head, and we *will be* [6]guiltless. And whoever is with you in the house, [y]his [7]blood *shall be* on our head if a hand is laid on him. **20** And if you tell this business of ours, then we will be [8]free from your oath which you made us swear."

21 Then she said, "According to your words, so *be* it." And she sent them away, and they departed. And she bound the scarlet cord in the window.

22 They departed and went to the mountain, and stayed there three days until the pursuers returned. The pursuers sought *them* all along the way, but did not find *them.* **23** So the two men returned, descended from the mountain, and crossed over; and they came to Joshua the son of Nun, and told him all that had befallen them. **24** And they said to Joshua, "Truly [z]the LORD has delivered all the land into our hands, for indeed all the inhabitants of the country are fainthearted because of us."

Israel Crosses the Jordan

3 Then Joshua rose early in the morning; and they set out [a]from [1]Acacia Grove and came to the Jordan, he and all the children of Israel, and lodged there before they crossed over. **2** So it was, [b]after three days, that the officers went through the camp; **3** and they commanded the people, saying, [c]"When you see the ark of the covenant of the LORD your God, [d]and the priests, the Levites, [2]bearing it, then you shall set out from your place and go after it. **4** [e]Yet there shall be a space between you and it, about two thousand cubits by measure. Do not come near it, that you may know the way by which you must go, for you have not passed *this* way before."

5 And Joshua said to the people, [f]"Sanctify[3] yourselves, for tomorrow the LORD will do wonders among you." **6** Then Joshua spoke to the priests, saying, [g]"Take up the ark of the covenant and cross over before the people."

So they took up the ark of the covenant and went before the people.

7 And the LORD said to Joshua, "This day I will begin to [h]exalt[4] you in the sight of all Israel, that they may know that, [i]as I was with Moses, *so* I will be with you. **8** You shall command [j]the priests who bear the ark of the covenant, saying, 'When you have come to the edge of the water of the Jordan, [k]you shall stand in the Jordan.' "

9 So Joshua said to the children of Israel, "Come here, and hear the words of the LORD your God." **10** And Joshua said, "By this you shall know that [l]the living God *is* among you, and *that* He will without fail [m]drive out from before you the [n]Canaanites and the Hittites and the Hivites and the Perizzites and the Girgashites and the Amorites and the Jebusites: **11** Behold, the ark of the covenant of [o]the Lord of all the earth is crossing over before you into the Jordan. **12** Now therefore, [p]take for yourselves twelve men from the tribes of Israel, one man from every tribe. **13** And it shall come to pass, [q]as soon as the soles of the feet of the priests who bear the ark of the LORD, [r]the Lord of all the earth, shall rest in the waters of the Jordan, *that* the waters of the Jordan shall be cut off, the waters that come down from upstream, and they [s]shall stand as a heap."

14 So it was, when the people set out from their camp to cross over the Jordan, with the priests bearing the [t]ark of the covenant before the people, **15** and as those who bore the ark came to the Jordan, and [u]the feet of the priests who bore the ark

17 [v]Ex. 20:7 [4]*free from obligation to this oath*
18 [w]Josh. 2:12 [x]Josh. 6:23 [5]Lit. *gather*
19 [y]1 Kin. 2:32; Matt. 27:25 [6]*free from obligation* [7]*guilt of bloodshed*
20 [8]*free from obligation to*
24 [z]Ex. 23:31; Josh. 6:2; 21:44

CHAPTER 3

1 [a]Josh. 2:1 [1]Heb. *Shittim*
2 [b]Josh. 1:10, 11
3 [c]Num. 10:33 [d]Deut. 31:9, 25
[2]*carrying*
4 [e]Ex. 19:12
5 [f]Ex. 19:10, 14, 15; Lev. 20:7; Num. 11:18; Josh. 7:13; 1 Sam. 16:5; Job 1:5; Joel 2:16 [3]*Consecrate*
6 [g]Num. 4:15
7 [h]Josh. 4:14; 1 Chr. 29:25; 2 Chr. 1:1 [i]Josh. 1:5, 9 [4]*make you great*
8 [j]Josh. 3:3 [k]Josh. 3:17
10 [l]Deut. 5:26; Josh. 11:23; 1 Sam. 17:26; 2 Kin. 19:4; Hos. 1:10; Matt. 16:16; 1 Thess. 1:9 [m]Ex. 33:2; Deut. 7:1; 18:12; Ps. 44:2 [n]Acts 13:19
11 [o]Josh. 3:13; Job 41:11; Ps. 24:1; Mic. 4:13; Zech. 4:14; 6:5
12 [p]Josh. 4:2, 4
13 [q]Josh. 3:15, 16 [r]Josh. 3:11 [s]Ps. 78:13; 114:3
14 [t]Ps. 132:8; Acts 7:44, 45
15 [u]Josh. 3:13

2:18 cord. A different word from "rope" (v. 15). Scarlet, unlike drab green, brown, gray, etc., is better seen to mark the house for protection. The color also is fitting for these whose blood (v. 19) was under God's pledge of safety.

3:3 the ark. Symbolized God's presence going before His people. Kohathites customarily carried the ark (Num. 4:15; 7:9), but in this unusual case the Levitical priests transported it, as in Josh. 6:6 and 1 Kin. 8:3-6.

3:4 two thousand cubits. 1,000 yards.

3:8 stand in the Jordan. The priests were to stand there to permit time for God's words (v. 9) to stimulate reflection on the greatness of God's eminent action in giving the Land as He showed His presence (v. 10). Also, it was a preparation to allow the people following to get set for God's miracle which stopped the waters for a crossing (vv. 13-17).

3:10 Canaanite people to be killed or defeated were sinful to the point of extreme (cf. Gen. 15:16; Lev. 18:24,25). God, as moral judge, has the right to deal with all people, as at the end (Rev. 20:11-15) or any other time when He deems it appropriate for His purposes. The question is not why God chose to destroy these sinners, but why He had let them live so long, and why all sinners are not destroyed far sooner than they are. It is grace that allows any sinner to draw one more breath of life (cf. Gen. 2:17; Ezek. 18:20; Rom. 6:23).

dipped in the edge of the water (for the
[v]Jordan overflows all its banks [w]during the
whole time of harvest), 16 that the waters
which came down from upstream stood
still, and rose in a heap very far away [5]at
Adam, the city that *is* beside [x]Zaretan. So
the waters that went down [y]into the Sea of
the Arabah, [z]the Salt Sea, failed, *and* were
cut off; and the people crossed over opposite Jericho. 17 Then the priests who bore
the ark of the covenant of the LORD stood
firm on dry ground in the midst of the Jordan; [a]and all Israel crossed over on dry
ground, until all the people had crossed
completely over the Jordan.

15 [v] 1 Chr. 12:15; Jer. 12:5; 49:19 [w] Josh. 4:18; 5:10, 12
16 [x] 1 Kin. 4:12; 7:46 [y] Deut. 3:17 [z] Gen. 14:3; Num. 34:3 [5] Qr., many mss. and vss. *from Adam*
17 [a] Gen. 50:24; Ex. 3:8; 6:1-8; 14:21, 22, 29; 33:1; Deut. 6:10; Heb. 11:29

CHAPTER 4
1 [a] Deut. 27:2; Josh. 3:17
2 [b] Josh. 3:12
3 [c] Josh. 3:13 [d] Josh. 4:19, 20

The Memorial Stones

4 And it came to pass, when all the people had completely crossed [a]over the
Jordan, that the LORD spoke to Joshua, saying: 2 [b]"Take for yourselves twelve men
from the people, one man from every tribe,
3 and command them, saying, 'Take for
yourselves twelve stones from here, out of
the midst of the Jordan, from the place
where [c]the priests' feet stood firm. You
shall carry them over with you and leave
them in [d]the lodging place where you
lodge tonight.' "
4 Then Joshua called the twelve men
whom he had appointed from the children
of Israel, one man from every tribe; 5 and

3:16 rose in a heap. The God of all power, who created heaven, earth, and all else according to Gen. 1, worked miracles here. The waters were dammed up at Adam, a city 15 mi. N of the crossing, and also in tributary creeks. Once the miracle was completed, God permitted waters to flow again (4:18) after all the people had walked to the other side on dry ground (3:17). As the Exodus had begun (cf. Ex. 14), so it ended.

4:1-8 Twelve stones picked up from the riverbed became a memorial to God's faithfulness. They were set up at Gilgal (about 1¼ mi. from Jericho), which was Israel's first campsite in the invaded land (vv. 19,20). Placing 12 stones in the riverbed itself commemorated the place which God dried up, where His ark had been held, and where He showed by a miracle His mighty presence and worthiness of respect (vv. 9-11,21-24).

The Peoples Around the Promised Land

(cf. Ex. 34:10-17; Deut. 20:17; Josh. 3:10; 9:1; 24:11)

1. AMALEKITES	The descendants of Amalek, the firstborn of Esau (Gen. 36:12), who dwelt S of Palestine in the Negev.
2. AMMONITES	The descendants of Ammon, the grandson of Lot by his youngest daughter (Gen. 19:38), who lived E of the Jordan River and N of Moab.
3. AMORITES	A general term for the inhabitants of the Land, but especially for the descendants of Canaan who inhabited the hill country on both sides of the Jordan.
4. CANAANITES	Broadly speaking, these are the descendants of Canaan, son of Ham, son of Noah (cf. Gen. 10:15-18), and included many of the other groups named here.
5. EDOMITES	The descendants of Esau who settled SE of Palestine (cf. Gen. 25:30) in the land of Seir.
6. GEBALITES	People of the ancient seaport later known as Byblos, about 20 mi. N of modern Beirut (Josh. 13:5).
7. GESHURITES	The inhabitants of Geshur, E of the Jordan and to the S of Syria (Josh. 12:5).
8. GIBEONITES	The inhabitants of Gibeon and surrounding area (Josh. 9:17).
9. GIRGASHITES	A tribe descended from Canaan, which was included among the general population of the Land without specific geographical identity.
10. GIRZITES	An obscure group which lived in the NW part of the Negev, before they were destroyed by David (1 Sam. 27:8, 9).
11. HITTITES	Immigrants from the Hittite Empire (in the region of Syria) to the central region of the Land (cf. Gen. 23:10; 2 Sam. 11:3).
12. HIVITES	Descendants of Canaan who lived in the northern reaches of the Land.
13. HORITES	Ancient residents of Edom from an unknown origin who were destroyed by Esau's descendants (Deut. 2:22).
14. JEBUSITES	Descendants of Canaan who dwelt in the hill country around Jerusalem (cf. Gen. 15:21; Ex. 3:8).
15. KENITES	A Midianite tribe that originally dwelt in the Gulf of Aqabah region (1 Sam. 27:10).
16. MOABITES	The descendants of Moab, the grandson of Lot by his eldest daughter (Gen. 19:37), who lived E of the Dead Sea.
17. PERIZZITES	People included among the general population of the Land who do not trace their lineage to Canaan. Their exact identity is uncertain.

Joshua said to them: "Cross over before the
ark of the LORD your God into the midst of
the Jordan, and each one of you take up a
stone on his shoulder, according to the
number of the tribes of the children of Israel, 6 that this may be [e]a sign among you
[f]when your children ask in time to come,
saying, 'What do these stones *mean* to
you?' 7 Then you shall answer them that
[g]the waters of the Jordan were cut off before the ark of the covenant of the LORD;
when it crossed over the Jordan, the waters
of the Jordan were cut off. And these
stones shall be for [h]a memorial to the children of Israel forever."
8 And the children of Israel did so, just
as Joshua commanded, and took up twelve
stones from the midst of the Jordan, as the
LORD had spoken to Joshua, according to
the number of the tribes of the children of
Israel, and carried them over with them to
the place where they lodged, and laid
them down there. 9 Then Joshua set up
twelve stones in the midst of the Jordan, in
the place where the feet of the priests who
bore the ark of the covenant stood; and
they are there to this day.
10 So the priests who bore the ark stood
in the midst of the Jordan until everything
was finished that the LORD had commanded Joshua to speak to the people, according
to all that Moses had commanded Joshua;
and the people hurried and crossed over.
11 Then it came to pass, when all the people had completely crossed over, that the
[i]ark of the LORD and the priests crossed
over in the presence of the people. 12 And
[j]the men of Reuben, the men of Gad, and
half the tribe of Manasseh crossed over
armed before the children of Israel, as Moses had spoken to them. 13 About forty
thousand [1]prepared for war crossed over
before the LORD for battle, to the plains of
Jericho. 14 On that day the LORD [k]exalted[2]
Joshua in the sight of all Israel; and they
feared him, as they had feared Moses, all
the days of his life.
15 Then the LORD spoke to Joshua, saying, 16 "Command the priests who bear
[l]the ark of the Testimony to come up from
the Jordan." 17 Joshua therefore commanded the priests, saying, "Come up from the
Jordan." 18 And it came to pass, when the
priests who bore the ark of the covenant of
the LORD had come from the midst of the
Jordan, *and* the soles of the priests' feet
touched the dry land, that the waters of the
Jordan returned to their place [m]and overflowed all its banks as before.
19 Now the people came up from the Jordan on the tenth *day* of the first month, and
they camped [n]in Gilgal on the east border
of Jericho. 20 And [o]those twelve stones
which they took out of the Jordan, Joshua
set up in Gilgal. 21 Then he spoke to the
children of Israel, saying: [p]"When your
children ask their fathers in time to come,
saying, 'What *are* these stones?' 22 then you
shall let your children know, saying, [q]'Israel crossed over this Jordan on [r]dry land';
23 for the LORD your God dried up the waters of the Jordan before you until you had
crossed over, as the LORD your God did to
the Red Sea, [s]which He dried up before us
until we had crossed over, 24 [t]that all the
peoples of the earth may know the hand of
the LORD, that it *is* [u]mighty, that you may
[v]fear the LORD your God [3]forever."

The Second Generation Circumcised

5 So it was, when all the kings of the
Amorites who *were* on the west side of
the Jordan, and all the kings of the Canaanites [a]who *were* by the sea, [b]heard that the
LORD had dried up the waters of the Jordan
from before the children of Israel until [1]we
had crossed over, that [2]their heart melted;
[c]and there was no spirit in them any longer
because of the children of Israel.
2 At that time the LORD said to Joshua,
"Make [d]flint knives for yourself, and circumcise the sons of Israel again the second
time." 3 So Joshua made flint knives for
himself, and circumcised the sons of Israel
at [3]the hill of the foreskins. 4 And this *is* the
reason why Joshua circumcised them: [e]All
the people who came out of Egypt *who*
were males, all the men of war, had died in
the wilderness on the way, after they had
come out of Egypt. 5 For all the people
who came out had been circumcised, but
all the people born in the wilderness, on
the way as they came out of Egypt, had not
been circumcised. 6 For the children of Israel walked [f]forty years in the wilderness,
till all the people *who were* men of war, who

6 [e] Deut. 27:2; Ps. 103:2 [f] Ex. 12:26; 13:14; Deut. 6:20
7 [g] Josh. 3:13, 16 [h] Ex. 12:14; Num. 16:40
11 [i] Josh. 3:11; 6:11
12 [j] Num. 32:17, 20, 27, 28; Josh. 1:14
13 [1] *equipped*
14 [k] Josh. 3:7; 1 Chr. 29:25 [2] *made Joshua great*
16 [l] Ex. 25:16, 22
18 [m] Josh. 3:15; 1 Chr. 12:15
19 [n] Josh. 5:9
20 [o] Deut. 11:30; Josh. 4:3; 5:9, 10
21 [p] Josh. 4:6
22 [q] Ex. 12:26, 27; 13:8-14; Deut. 26:5-9 [r] Josh. 3:17
23 [s] Ex. 14:21
24 [t] 1 Kin. 8:42; 2 Kin. 19:19; Ps. 106:8 [u] Ex. 15:16; 1 Chr. 29:12; Ps. 89:13 [v] Ex. 14:31; Deut. 6:2; Ps. 76:7; Jer. 10:7 [3] Lit. *all days*

CHAPTER 5

1 [a] Num. 13:29 [b] Ex. 15:14, 15 [c] Josh. 2:10, 11; 9:9; 1 Kin. 10:5 [1] So with Kt.; Qr., some Heb. mss. and editions, LXX, Syr., Tg., Vg. *they* [2] *their courage failed*
2 [d] Ex. 4:25
3 [3] Heb. *Gibeath Haaraloth*
4 [e] Num. 14:29; 26:64, 65; Deut. 2:14-16
6 [f] Num. 14:33; Deut. 1:3; 29:5

4:19 tenth *day*...first month. March-April. Abib was the term used by pre-exilic Jews; Nisan later came to be used by post-exilic Israel.

5:1 heard. Reports of God's supernaturally opening a crossing struck fear into the Canaanites. The miracle was all the more incredible and shocking since God performed it when the Jordan was swollen to flood height (3:15). To the people in the Land, this miracle was a powerful demonstration proving that God is mighty (4:24). This came on top of reports about the Red Sea miracle (2:10).

5:2 circumcise. God commanded Joshua to see that this was done to all males under 40. These were sons of the generation who died in the wilderness, survivors (cf. vv. 6,7) from the new generation God spared in Num. 13,14. This surgical sign of a faith commitment to the Abrahamic Covenant (see Gen. 17:9-14) had been ignored during the wilderness trek. Now God wanted it reinstated, so the Israelites would start out right in the Land they were possessing. *See note on Jer. 4:4.*

came out of Egypt, were [4]consumed, because they did not obey the voice of the LORD—to whom the LORD swore that [g]He would not show them the land which the LORD had sworn to their fathers that He would give us, [h]"a land flowing with milk and honey." 7 Then Joshua circumcised [i]their sons *whom* He raised up in their place; for they were uncircumcised, because they had not been circumcised on the way.

8 So it was, when they had finished circumcising all the people, that they stayed in their places in the camp [j]till they were healed. 9 Then the LORD said to Joshua, "This day I have rolled away [k]the reproach of Egypt from you." Therefore the name of the place is called [l]Gilgal[5] to this day.

10 Now the children of Israel camped in Gilgal, and kept the Passover [m]on the fourteenth day of the month at twilight on the plains of Jericho. 11 And they ate of the produce of the land on the day after the Passover, unleavened bread and [6]parched grain, on the very same day. 12 Then [n]the manna ceased on the day after they had eaten the produce of the land; and the children of Israel no longer had manna, but they ate the food of the land of Canaan that year.

The Commander of the Army of the LORD

13 And it came to pass, when Joshua was by Jericho, that he lifted his eyes and looked, and behold, [o]a Man stood opposite him [p]with His sword drawn in His hand. And Joshua went to Him and said to Him, "*Are* You for us or for our adversaries?"

14 So He said, "No, but *as* Commander of the army of the LORD I have now come."

And Joshua [q]fell on his face to the earth and [r]worshiped, and said to Him, "What does my Lord say to His servant?"

15 Then the Commander of the LORD's army said to Joshua, [s]"Take your sandal off your foot, for the place where you stand *is* holy." And Joshua did so.

The Destruction of Jericho

6 Now [a]Jericho was securely shut up because of the children of Israel; none went out, and none came in. 2 And the LORD said to Joshua: "See! [b]I have given Jericho into your hand, its [c]king, *and* the mighty men of valor. 3 You shall march around the city, all *you* men of war; you shall go all around the city once. This you shall do six days. 4 And seven priests shall bear seven [d]trumpets of rams' horns before the ark. But the seventh day you shall march around the city [e]seven times, and [f]the priests shall blow the trumpets. 5 It shall come to pass, when they make a long *blast* with the ram's horn, *and* when you hear the sound of the trumpet, that all the people shall shout with a great shout; then the wall of the city will fall down flat. And the people shall go up every man straight before him."

6 Then Joshua the son of Nun called the priests and said to them, "Take up the ark of the covenant, and let seven priests bear seven trumpets of rams' horns before the ark of the LORD." 7 And he said to the people, "Proceed, and march around the city, and let him who is armed advance before the ark of the LORD."

8 So it was, when Joshua had spoken to the people, that the seven priests bearing the seven trumpets of rams' horns before the LORD advanced and blew the trumpets, and the ark of the covenant of the LORD followed them. 9 The armed men went before the priests who blew the trumpets, [g]and the rear guard came after the ark, while *the priests* continued blowing the trumpets. 10 Now Joshua had commanded the people, saying, "You shall not shout or make any noise with your voice, nor shall a word proceed out of your mouth, until the day I say to you, 'Shout!' Then you shall shout."

6 [g] Num. 14:23, 29-35; 26:23-65; Heb. 3:11 [h] Ex. 3:8 [4] *destroyed*
7 [i] Num. 14:31; Deut. 1:39
8 [j] Gen. 34:25
9 [k] Gen. 34:14 [l] Josh. 4:19 [5] Lit. *Rolling*
10 [m] Ex. 12:6; Num. 9:5
11 [6] *roasted*
12 [n] Ex. 16:35
13 [o] Gen. 18:1, 2; 32:24, 30; Ex. 23:23; Num. 22:31; Zech. 1:8; Acts 1:10 [p] Num. 22:23; 1 Chr. 21:16
14 [q] Gen. 17:3; Num. 20:6 [r] Ex. 34:8
15 [s] Ex. 3:5; Acts 7:33

CHAPTER 6
1 [a] Josh. 2:1
2 [b] Josh. 2:9, 24; 8:1 [c] Deut. 7:24
4 [d] Lev. 25:9; Judg. 7:16, 22 [e] 1 Kin. 18:43; 2 Kin. 4:35; 5:10 [f] Num. 10:8
9 [g] Num. 10:25

5:8 they were healed. This speaks of the time needed to recover from such a painful and potentially infected wound.

5:9 rolled away the reproach. By His miracle of bringing the people into the Land, God removed (rolled away) the ridicule which the Egyptians had heaped on them.

5:10 Passover. Commemorated God's deliverance from Egypt, recorded in Ex. 7–12. Such a remembrance was a strengthening preparation for trusting God to work in possessing the new land.

5:12 manna ceased. God had begun to provide this food from the time of Ex. 16 and did so for 40 years (Ex. 16:35). Since food was plentiful in the land of Canaan, they could provide for themselves with produce such as dates, barley, and olives.

5:13-15 Commander. The Lord Jesus Christ (6:2; cf. 5:15 with Ex. 3:2,5) in a pre-incarnate appearance (Christophany). He came as the Angel (Messenger) of the Lord, as if He were a man (cf. the one of 3 "angels," Gen. 18). Joshua fittingly was reverent in worship. The Commander, sword drawn, showed a posture indicating He was set to give Israel victory over the Canaanites (6:2; cf. 1:3).

6:1 Jericho. The city was fortified by a double ring of walls, the outer 6 ft. thick and the inner 12; timbers were laid across these, supporting houses on the walls. Since Jericho was built on a hill, it could be taken only by mounting a steep incline, which put the Israelites at a great disadvantage. Attackers of such a "fortress" often used a siege of several months to force surrender through starvation.

6:3-21 The bizarre military strategy of marching around Jericho gave occasion for the Israelites to take God at His promise (v. 2). They would also heighten the defenders' uneasiness. Seven is sometimes a number used to signify completeness (cf. 2 Kin. 5:10,14).

6:5 God assured Israel of an astounding miracle, just as He had done at the Jordan.

11 So he had [h]the ark of the LORD circle the
city, going around *it* once. Then they came
into the camp and [1]lodged in the camp.
12 And Joshua rose early in the morning,
[i]and the priests took up the ark of the
LORD. 13 Then seven priests bearing seven
trumpets of rams' horns before the ark of
the LORD went on continually and blew
with the trumpets. And the armed men
went before them. But the rear guard came
after the ark of the LORD, while *the priests*
continued blowing the trumpets. 14 And
the second day they marched around the
city once and returned to the camp. So they
did six days.
15 But it came to pass on the seventh day
that they rose early, about the dawning of
the day, and marched around the city
seven times in the same manner. On that
day only they marched around the city
seven times. 16 And the seventh time it
happened, when the priests blew the trumpets, that Joshua said to the people:
"Shout, for the LORD has given you the
city! 17 Now the city shall be [j]doomed by
the LORD to destruction, it and all who *are*
in it. Only [k]Rahab the harlot shall live, she
and all who *are* with her in the house, because [l]she hid the messengers that we sent.
18 And you, [m]by all means abstain from
the accursed things, lest you become accursed when you take of the accursed
things, and make the camp of Israel a
curse, [n]and trouble it. 19 But all the silver
and gold, and vessels of bronze and iron,
are [2]consecrated to the LORD; they [3]shall
come into the treasury of the LORD."
20 So the people shouted when *the priests*
blew the trumpets. And it happened when
the people heard the sound of the trumpet,
and the people shouted with a great shout,
that [o]the wall fell down flat. Then the people went up into the city, every man
straight before him, and they took the city.
21 And they [p]utterly destroyed all that *was*
in the city, both man and woman, young
and old, ox and sheep and donkey, with
the edge of the sword.
22 But Joshua had said to the two men
who had spied out the country, "Go into
the harlot's house, and from there bring out
the woman and all that she has, [q]as you
swore to her." 23 And the young men who
had been spies went in and brought out
Rahab, [r]her father, her mother, her brothers, and all that she had. So they brought
out all her relatives and left them outside
the camp of Israel. 24 But they burned the
city and all that *was* in it with fire. Only the
silver and gold, and the vessels of bronze
and iron, they put into the treasury of the
house of the LORD. 25 And Joshua spared
Rahab the harlot, her father's household,
and all that she had. So [s]she dwells in Israel
to this day, because she hid the messengers
whom Joshua sent to spy out Jericho.
26 Then Joshua [4]charged *them* at that
time, saying, [t]"Cursed *be* the man before
the LORD who rises up and builds this city
Jericho; he shall lay its foundation with his
firstborn, and with his youngest he shall
set up its gates."
27 So the LORD was with Joshua, and his
fame spread throughout all the country.

Defeat at Ai

7 But the children of Israel [1]committed a
[a]trespass regarding the [b]accursed[2]
things, for [c]Achan the son of Carmi, the
son of [3]Zabdi, the son of Zerah, of the tribe
of Judah, took of the accursed things; so
the anger of the LORD burned against the
children of Israel.
2 Now Joshua sent men from Jericho to
Ai, which *is* beside Beth Aven, on the east
side of Bethel, and spoke to them, saying,
"Go up and spy out the country." So the
men went up and spied out Ai. 3 And they
returned to Joshua and said to him, "Do
not let all the people go up, but let about
two or three thousand men go up and attack Ai. Do not weary all the people there,
for *the people of Ai are* few." 4 So about three
thousand men went up there from the people, [d]but they fled before the men of Ai.
5 And the men of Ai struck down about
thirty-six men, for they chased them *from*
before the gate as far as Shebarim, and
struck them down on the descent; therefore [e]the[4] hearts of the people melted and
became like water.

11 [h] Josh. 4:11 [1] *spent the night*
12 [i] Deut. 31:25
17 [j] Deut. 13:17; Josh. 7:1 [k] Josh. 2:1; Matt. 1:5 [l] Josh. 2:4, 6
18 [m] Deut. 7:26 [n] Josh. 7:1, 12, 25; 1 Kin. 18:17, 18; [Jon. 1:12]
19 [2] *set apart* [3] *shall go*
20 [o] Heb. 11:30
21 [p] Deut. 7:2; 20:16, 17
22 [q] Josh. 2:12-19; Heb. 11:31
23 [r] Josh. 2:13
25 [s] [Matt. 1:5]
26 [t] 1 Kin. 16:34 [4] *warned*

CHAPTER 7

1 [a] Josh. 7:20, 21 [b] Josh. 6:17-19 [c] Josh. 22:20 [1] *acted unfaithfully* [2] *devoted* [3] *Zimri,* 1 Chr. 2:6
4 [d] Lev. 26:17; Deut. 28:25
5 [e] Lev. 26:36; Josh. 2:9, 11 [4] *the people's courage failed*

6:16 The loud shout in unison expressed an expectation of God's action to fulfill His guaranteed promise (vv. 2,5,16).

6:17 doomed. The Heb. term means "utterly destroyed," as in v. 21; i.e., to ban or devote as spoil for a deity. Here it is stated to be retained for God's possession, a tribute belonging to Him for the purpose of destruction.

6:22-25 Joshua honored the promise of safety to the household of Rahab. The part of the wall securing this house must not have fallen, and all possessions in the dwelling were safe.

6:26 God put a curse on whoever would rebuild Jericho. While the area around it was later occupied to some extent (2 Sam. 10:5), in Ahab's reign Hiel rebuilt Jericho and experienced the curse by losing his eldest and youngest sons (1 Kin. 16:34).

6:27 God kept His pledge that He would be with Joshua (1:5-9).

7:1-5 Israel's defeat here is similar to an earlier setback against the Amalekites (Num. 14:39-45).

7:2 Ai. A town situated W of the Jordan, in the hills E of Bethel (cf. Gen. 12:8).

7:3 few. The "few" inhabitants of Ai are numbered at 12,000 in 8:25 (cf. 8:3).

6 Then Joshua [f]tore his clothes, and fell
to the earth on his face before the ark of the
LORD until evening, he and the elders of Israel; and they [g]put dust on their heads.
7 And Joshua said, "Alas, Lord [5]GOD,
[h]why have You brought this people over
the Jordan at all—to deliver us into the
hand of the Amorites, to destroy us? Oh,
that we had been content, and dwelt on the
other side of the Jordan! 8 O Lord, what
shall I say when Israel turns its [6]back before its enemies? 9 For the Canaanites and
all the inhabitants of the land will hear *it*,
and surround us, and [i]cut off our name
from the earth. Then [j]what will You do for
Your great name?"

The Sin of Achan

10 So the LORD said to Joshua: "Get up!
Why do you lie thus on your face? 11 Israel
has sinned, and they have also transgressed My covenant which I commanded
them. [k]For they have even taken some of
the [7]accursed things, and have both stolen
and [l]deceived; and they have also put *it*
among their own stuff. 12 [m]Therefore the
children of Israel could not stand before
their enemies, *but* turned *their* backs before
their enemies, because [n]they have become
doomed to destruction. Neither will I be
with you anymore, unless you destroy the
accursed from among you. 13 Get up,
[o]sanctify[8] the people, and say, [p]'Sanctify
yourselves for tomorrow, because thus
says the LORD God of Israel: *"There is* an accursed thing in your midst, O Israel; you
cannot stand before your enemies until
you take away the accursed thing from
among you." 14 In the morning therefore
you shall be brought according to your
tribes. And it shall be *that* the tribe which
[q]the LORD takes shall come according to
families; and the family which the LORD
takes shall come by households; and the
household which the LORD takes shall
come man by man. 15 [r]Then it shall be *that*
he who is taken with the accursed thing
shall be burned with fire, he and all that he
has, because he has [s]transgressed[9] the
covenant of the LORD, and because he [t]has
done a disgraceful thing in Israel.' "
16 So Joshua rose early in the morning
and brought Israel by their tribes, and the
tribe of Judah was taken. 17 He brought the
clan of Judah, and he took the family of the
Zarhites; and he brought the family of the
Zarhites man by man, and Zabdi was
taken. 18 Then he brought his household
man by man, and Achan the son of Carmi,
the son of Zabdi, the son of Zerah, of the
tribe of Judah, [u]was taken.
19 Now Joshua said to Achan, "My son, I
beg you, [v]give glory to the LORD God of Israel, [w]and make confession to Him, and
[x]tell me now what you have done; do not
hide *it* from me."
20 And Achan answered Joshua and
said, "Indeed [y]I have sinned against the
LORD God of Israel, and this is what I have
done: 21 When I saw among the spoils a
beautiful Babylonian garment, two hundred shekels of silver, and a wedge of gold
weighing fifty shekels, I [1]coveted them
and took them. And there they are, hidden
in the earth in the midst of my tent, with
the silver under it."
22 So Joshua sent messengers, and they
ran to the tent; and there it was, hidden in
his tent, with the silver under it. 23 And
they took them from the midst of the tent,
brought them to Joshua and to all the children of Israel, and laid them out before the
LORD. 24 Then Joshua, and all Israel with
him, took Achan the son of Zerah, the silver, the garment, the wedge of gold, his
sons, his daughters, his oxen, his donkeys,
his sheep, his tent, and [z]all that he had,
and they brought them to [a]the Valley of
Achor. 25 And Joshua said, [b]"Why have
you troubled us? The LORD will trouble
you this day." [c]So all Israel stoned him
with stones; and they burned them with
fire after they had stoned them with
stones.
26 Then they [d]raised over him a great
heap of stones, still there to this day. So
[e]the LORD turned from the fierceness of His
anger. Therefore the name of that place has
been called [f]the Valley of [2]Achor to this
day.

The Fall of Ai

8 Now the LORD said to Joshua: [a]"Do not
be afraid, nor be dismayed; take all the
people of war with you, and arise, go up to
Ai. See, [b]I have given into your hand the
king of Ai, his people, his city, and his
land. 2 And you shall do to Ai and its king

6 [f]Gen. 37:29, 34 [g]1 Sam. 4:12
7 [h]Ex. 17:3; Num. 21:5 [5]Heb. *YHWH*, LORD
8 [6]Lit. *neck*
9 [i]Deut. 32:26 [j]Ex. 32:12; Num. 14:13
11 [k]Josh. 6:17-19 [l]Acts 5:1, 2 [7]*devoted*
12 [m]Judg. 2:14 [n]Deut. 7:26; [Hag. 2:13, 14]
13 [o]Ex. 19:10 [p]Josh. 3:5 [8]*set apart*
14 [q][Prov. 16:33]
15 [r]1 Sam. 14:38, 39 [s]Josh. 7:11 [t]Gen. 34:7; Judg. 20:6 [9]*overstepped*
18 [u]1 Sam. 14:42
19 [v]1 Sam. 6:5; Jer. 13:16; John 9:24 [w]Num. 5:6, 7; 2 Chr. 30:22; Ezra 10:10, 11; Ps. 32:5; Prov. 28:13; Jer. 3:12, 13; Dan. 9:4 [x]1 Sam. 14:43
20 [y]Num. 22:34; 1 Sam. 15:24
21 [1]*desired*
24 [z]Num. 16:32, 33; Dan. 6:24 [a]Josh. 7:26; 15:7
25 [b]Josh. 6:18; 1 Chr. 2:7; [Gal. 5:12] [c]Deut. 17:5
26 [d]Josh. 8:29; 2 Sam. 18:17; Lam. 3:53 [e]Deut. 13:17 [f]Josh. 7:24; Is. 65:10; Hos. 2:15 [2]Lit. *Trouble*

CHAPTER 8

1 [a]Deut. 1:21; 7:18; 31:8; Josh. 1:9; 10:8 [b]Josh. 6:2

7:9 what will You do for Your great name? The main issue is the glory and honor of God (cf. Daniel's prayer in Dan. 9:16-19).

7:15,24,25 Achan's family faced execution with him. They were regarded as co-conspirators in what he did. They helped cover up his guilt and withheld information from others. Similarly, family members died in Korah's rebellion (Num. 16), Haman's fall (Esth. 9:13-14), and after Daniel's escape (Dan. 6:24).

7:21 I saw. There are 4 steps in the progress of Achan's sin: "I saw... I coveted... I took... I concealed." David's sin with Bathsheba followed the same path (2 Sam. 11; cf. James 1:14,15). **a beautiful Babylonian garment.** A costly, ornate robe of Shinar beautified by colored figures of men or animals, woven or done in needlework, and perhaps trimmed with jewels. The word is used for a king's robe in Jon. 3:6.

7:24 Achor. Lit. "trouble" (cf. Is. 65:10; Hos. 2:15).

as you did to [c]Jericho and its king. Only [d]its spoil and its cattle you shall take as booty for yourselves. Lay an ambush for the city behind it."

3 So Joshua arose, and all the people of war, to go up against Ai; and Joshua chose thirty thousand mighty men of valor and sent them away by night. 4 And he commanded them, saying: "Behold, [e]you shall lie in ambush against the city, behind the city. Do not go very far from the city, but all of you be ready. 5 Then I and all the people who *are* with me will approach the city; and it will come about, when they come out against us as at the first, that [f]we shall flee before them. 6 For they will come out after us till we have drawn them from the city, for they will say, '*They are* fleeing before us as at the first.' Therefore we will flee before them. 7 Then you shall rise from the ambush and seize the city, for the LORD your God will deliver it into your hand. 8 And it will be, when you have taken the city, *that* you shall set the city on fire. According to the commandment of the LORD you shall do. [g]See, I have commanded you."

9 Joshua therefore sent them out; and they went to lie in ambush, and stayed between Bethel and Ai, on the west side of Ai; but Joshua lodged that night among the people. 10 Then Joshua rose up early in the morning and mustered the people, and went up, he and the elders of Israel, before the people to Ai. 11 [h]And all the people of war who *were* with him went up and drew near; and they came before the city and camped on the north side of Ai. Now a valley *lay* between them and Ai. 12 So he took about five thousand men and set them in ambush between Bethel and Ai, on the west side of [1]the city. 13 And when they had set the people, all the army that *was* on the north of the city, and its rear guard on the west of the city, Joshua went that night into the midst of the valley.

14 Now it happened, when the king of Ai saw *it,* that the men of the city hurried and rose early and went out against Israel to battle, he and all his people, at an appointed place before the plain. But he [i]did not know that *there was* an ambush against him behind the city. 15 And Joshua and all Israel [j]made as if they were beaten before them, and fled by the way of the wilderness. 16 So all the people who *were* in Ai were called together to pursue them. And they pursued Joshua and were drawn away from the city. 17 There was not a man left in Ai or Bethel who did not go out after Israel. So they left the city open and pursued Israel.

18 Then the LORD said to Joshua, "Stretch out the spear that *is* in your hand toward Ai, for I will give it into your hand." And Joshua stretched out the spear that *was* in his hand toward the city. 19 So *those in* ambush arose quickly out of their place; they ran as soon as he had stretched out his hand, and they entered the city and took it, and hurried to set the city on fire. 20 And when the men of Ai looked behind them, they saw, and behold, the smoke of the city ascended to heaven. So they had no power to flee this way or that way, and the people who had fled to the wilderness turned back on the pursuers.

21 Now when Joshua and all Israel saw that the ambush had taken the city and that the smoke of the city ascended, they turned back and struck down the men of Ai. 22 Then the others came out of the city against them; so they were *caught* in the midst of Israel, some on this side and some on that side. And they struck them down, so that they [k]let none of them remain or escape. 23 But the king of Ai they took alive, and brought him to Joshua.

24 And it came to pass when Israel had made an end of slaying all the inhabitants of Ai in the field, in the wilderness where they pursued them, and when they all had fallen by the edge of the sword until they were consumed, that all the Israelites returned to Ai and struck it with the edge of the sword. 25 So it was *that* all who fell that day, both men and women, *were* twelve thousand—all the people of Ai. 26 For Joshua did not draw back his hand, with which he stretched out the spear, until he had [l]utterly destroyed all the inhabitants of Ai. 27 [m]Only the livestock and the spoil of that city Israel took as booty for themselves, according to the word of the LORD which He had [n]commanded Joshua. 28 So Joshua burned Ai and made it [o]a heap forever, a desolation to this day. 29 [p]And the

2 [c] Josh. 6:21 [d] Deut. 20:14; Josh. 8:27
4 [e] Judg. 20:29
5 [f] Josh. 7:5; Judg. 20:32
8 [g] 2 Sam. 13:28
11 [h] Josh. 8:5
12 [1] Ai
14 [i] Judg. 20:34; Eccl. 9:12
15 [j] Judg. 20:36
22 [k] Deut. 7:2
26 [l] Josh. 6:21
27 [m] Num. 31:22, 26 [n] Josh. 8:2
28 [o] Deut. 13:16
29 [p] Josh. 10:26

8:3 thirty thousand...men. Joshua's elite force was far superior to that of Ai, with a mere 12,000 total population (8:25). This time Joshua took no small force presumptuously (cf. 7:3,4), but had 30,000 to sack and burn Ai, a decoy group to lure defenders out (vv. 5,6), and a third detachment of about 5,000 to prevent Bethel from helping Ai (v. 12).

8:7 God will deliver it into your hand. God had sovereignly caused Israel's defeat earlier due to Achan's disobedience (7:1-5). Yet, this time, despite Israel's overwhelming numbers, God was still the sovereign power for this victory (8:7).

8:18 the spear. Joshua's hoisted javelin represented the go-ahead indicator to occupy Ai. Possibly the raising was even a signal of confidence in God: "for I will give it into your hand." Earlier, Moses' uplifted rod and arms probably signified trusting contact with God for victory over Amalek (Ex. 17:8-13).

king of Ai he hanged on a tree until
evening. [q]And as soon as the sun was
down, Joshua commanded that they
should take his corpse down from the tree,
cast it at the entrance of the gate of the city,
and [r]raise over it a great heap of stones *that*
remains to this day.

Joshua Renews the Covenant

30 Now Joshua built an altar to the LORD
God of Israel [s]in Mount Ebal, 31 as Moses
the servant of the LORD had commanded
the children of Israel, as it is written in the
Book of the Law of Moses: [t]"an altar of
whole stones over which no man has wielded an iron *tool*." And [u]they offered on it
burnt offerings to the LORD, and sacrificed
peace offerings. 32 And there, in the presence of the children of Israel, [v]he wrote on
the stones a copy of the law of Moses, which
he had written. 33 Then all Israel, with their
elders and officers and judges, stood on either side of the ark before the priests, the
Levites, [w]who bore the ark of the covenant
of the LORD, [x]the stranger as well as he who
was born among them. Half of them *were* in
front of Mount Gerizim and half of them in
front of Mount Ebal, [y]as Moses the servant
of the LORD had commanded before, that
they should bless the people of Israel.
34 And afterward [z]he read all the words of
the law, [a]the blessings and the cursings, according to all that is written in the [b]Book of
the Law. 35 There was not a word of all that
Moses had commanded which Joshua did
not read before all the assembly of Israel,
[c]with the women, the little ones, [d]and the
strangers who were living among them.

The Treaty with the Gibeonites

9 And it came to pass when [a]all the
kings who *were* on this side of the Jordan, in the hills and in the lowland and
in all the coasts of [b]the Great Sea toward
Lebanon—[c]the Hittite, the Amorite, the
Canaanite, the Perizzite, the Hivite, and
the Jebusite—heard *about it*, 2 that they
[d]gathered together to fight with Joshua
and Israel with one [1]accord.
3 But when the inhabitants of [e]Gibeon
[f]heard what Joshua had done to Jericho
and Ai, 4 they worked craftily, and went
and [2]pretended to be ambassadors. And
they took old sacks on their donkeys, old
wineskins torn and [3]mended, 5 old and
patched sandals on their feet, and old garments on themselves; and all the bread of
their provision was dry *and* moldy. 6 And
they went to Joshua, [g]to the camp at Gilgal, and said to him and to the men of Israel, "We have come from a far country;
now therefore, make a [4]covenant with us."
7 Then the men of Israel said to the
[h]Hivites, "Perhaps you dwell among us; so
[i]how can we make a covenant with you?"
8 But they said to Joshua, [j]"We *are* your
servants."
And Joshua said to them, "Who *are* you,
and where do you come from?"
9 So they said to him: [k]"From a very far
country your servants have come, because
of the name of the LORD your God; for we
have [l]heard of His fame, and all that He did
in Egypt, 10 and [m]all that He did to the two
kings of the Amorites who *were* beyond the
Jordan—to Sihon king of Heshbon, and Og
king of Bashan, who was at Ashtaroth.
11 Therefore our elders and all the inhabitants of our country spoke to us, saying,
'Take provisions with you for the journey,
and go to meet them, and say to them, "We
are your servants; now therefore, make a
covenant with us." ' 12 This bread of ours
we took hot *for* our provision from our
houses on the day we departed to come to
you. But now look, it is dry and moldy.
13 And these wineskins which we filled *were*
new, and see, they are torn; and these our
garments and our sandals have become old
because of the very long journey."
14 Then the men of Israel took some of
their provisions; [n]but they [5]did not ask
counsel of the LORD. 15 So Joshua [o]made
peace with them, and made a covenant
with them to let them live; and the rulers of
the congregation swore to them.
16 And it happened at the end of three
days, after they had made a covenant with
them, that they heard that they *were* their
neighbors who dwelt near them. 17 Then

29 [q] Deut. 21:22, 23; Josh. 10:27 [r] Josh. 7:26; 10:27
30 [s] Deut. 27:4-8
31 [t] Ex. 20:25; Deut. 27:5, 6 [u] Ex. 20:24
32 [v] Deut. 27:2, 3, 8
33 [w] Deut. 31:9, 25 [x] Deut. 31:12 [y] Deut. 11:29; 27:12
34 [z] Deut. 31:11; Neh. 8:3 [a] Deut. 28:2, 15, 45; 29:20, 21; 30:19 [b] Josh. 1:8
35 [c] Ex. 12:38; Deut. 31:12 [d] Josh. 8:33

CHAPTER 9

1 [a] Num. 13:29; Josh. 3:10 [b] Num. 34:6 [c] Ex. 3:17; 23:23
2 [d] Josh. 10:5; Ps. 83:3, 5 [1] Lit. *mouth*
3 [e] Josh. 9:17, 22; 10:2; 21:17; 2 Sam. 21:1, 2
[f] Josh. 6:27
4 [2] *acted as envoys* [3] Lit. *tied up*
6 [g] Josh. 5:10 [4] *treaty*
7 [h] Josh. 9:1; 11:19 [i] Ex. 23:32; Deut. 7:2
8 [j] Deut. 20:11; 2 Kin. 10:5
9 [k] Deut. 20:15 [l] Ex. 15:14; Josh. 2:9, 10; 5:1
10 [m] Num. 21:24, 33
14 [n] Num. 27:21; Is. 30:1 [5] Lit. *did not inquire at the mouth of*
15 [o] 2 Sam. 21:2

8:29 the king of Ai. The complete execution of Ai's populace included hanging even the king. This wise move prevented later efforts to muster a Canaanite army. Further, as a wicked king, he was worthy of punishment according to biblical standards (Deut. 21:22; Josh. 10:26,27). This carried out the vengeance of God on His enemies.

8:30-35 This ceremony took place in obedience to Deut. 27:1-26 at the conclusion of Joshua's central campaign (cf. 6:1–8:35).

8:30,31 Thanks is offered to God for giving victory. The altar, in obedience to the instruction of Ex. 20:24-26, was built of uncut stones, thus keeping worship simple and untainted by man's showmanship. Joshua gave God's Word a detailed and central place.

9:3 inhabitants. Gibeon of the Hivites (v. 7), or Horites (cf. Gen. 36:2,20), was NW of Jerusalem and about 7 mi. from the area of Ai. It was a strong city with capable fighting men (10:2). Three other towns were in league with it (9:17).

9:4-15 The Gibeonite plot to trick Israel worked. Israel's sinful failure occurred because they were not vigilant in prayer to assure that they acted by God's counsel (v. 14; cf. Prov. 3:5,6).

9:15 Israel precipitously made peace with the Gibeonites (11:19) who lived nearby, even though God had instructed them to eliminate the people of cities in the Land (Deut. 7:1,2). God permitted peace with cities outside (Deut. 20:11-15).

the children of Israel journeyed and came
to their cities on the third day. Now their
cities *were* [p]Gibeon, Chephirah, Beeroth,
and Kirjath Jearim. 18 But the children of
Israel did not [6]attack them, [q]because the
rulers of the congregation had sworn to
them by the LORD God of Israel. And all
the congregation complained against the
rulers.
19 Then all the rulers said to all the congregation, "We have sworn to them by the
LORD God of Israel; now therefore, we
may not touch them. 20 This we will do to
them: We will let them live, lest [r]wrath be
upon us because of the oath which we
swore to them." 21 And the rulers said to
them, "Let them live, but let them be
[s]woodcutters and water carriers for all the
congregation, as the rulers had [t]promised
them."
22 Then Joshua called for them, and he
spoke to them, saying, "Why have you deceived us, saying, [u]'We *are* very far from
you,' when [v]you dwell near us? 23 Now
therefore, you *are* [w]cursed, and none of
you shall be freed from being slaves—
woodcutters and water carriers for the
house of my God."
24 So they answered Joshua and said,
"Because your servants were clearly told
that the LORD your God [x]commanded His
servant Moses to give you all the land, and
to destroy all the inhabitants of the land
from before you; therefore [y]we were very
much afraid for our lives because of you,
and have done this thing. 25 And now, here
we are, [z]in your hands; do with us as it
seems good and right to do to us." 26 So he
did to them, and delivered them out of the
hand of the children of Israel, so that they
did not kill them. 27 And that day Joshua
made them [a]woodcutters and water carriers for the congregation and for the altar of
the LORD, [b]in the place which He would
choose, even to this day.

The Sun Stands Still

10 Now it came to pass when Adoni-
Zedek king of Jerusalem [a]heard
how Joshua had taken [b]Ai and had utterly
destroyed it—[c]as he had done to Jericho
and its king, so he had done to [d]Ai and its
king—and [e]how the inhabitants of Gibeon
had made peace with Israel and were
among them, 2 that they [f]feared greatly, because Gibeon *was* a great city, like one of
the royal cities, and because it *was* greater
than Ai, and all its men *were* mighty.
3 Therefore Adoni-Zedek king of Jerusalem sent to Hoham king of Hebron, Piram
king of Jarmuth, Japhia king of Lachish,
and Debir king of Eglon, saying, 4 "Come
up to me and help me, that we may attack
Gibeon, for [g]it has made peace with Joshua
and with the children of Israel." 5 Therefore the five kings of the [h]Amorites, the
king of Jerusalem, the king of Hebron, the
king of Jarmuth, the king of Lachish,
and the king of Eglon, [i]gathered together
and went up, they and all their armies, and
camped before Gibeon and made war
against it.
6 And the men of Gibeon sent to Joshua
at the camp [j]at Gilgal, saying, "Do not
forsake your servants; come up to us
quickly, save us and help us, for all the
kings of the Amorites who dwell in the
mountains have gathered together
against us."
7 So Joshua ascended from Gilgal, he
and [k]all the people of war with him, and
all the mighty men of valor. 8 And the
LORD said to Joshua, [l]"Do not fear them,
for I have delivered them into your hand;
[m]not a man of them shall [n]stand before
you." 9 Joshua therefore came upon them
suddenly, having marched all night from
Gilgal. 10 So the LORD [o]routed them before Israel, killed them with a great
slaughter at Gibeon, chased them along
the road that goes [p]to Beth Horon, and
struck them down as far as [q]Azekah and
Makkedah. 11 And it happened, as they
fled before Israel *and* were on the descent
of Beth Horon, [r]that the LORD cast down
large hailstones from heaven on them as
far as Azekah, and they died. *There were*
more who died from the hailstones than
the children of Israel killed with the
sword.
12 Then Joshua spoke to the LORD in the
day when the LORD delivered up the
Amorites before the children of Israel, and
he said in the sight of Israel:

17 [p]Josh. 18:25
18 [q]Ps. 15:4 [6]*strike*
20 [r]2 Sam. 21:1, 2, 6; Ezek. 17:13, 15
21 [s]Deut. 29:11 [t]Josh. 9:15
22 [u]Josh. 9:6, 9 [v]Josh. 9:16
23 [w]Gen. 9:25
24 [x]Ex. 23:31-33; Deut. 7:1, 2 [y]Ex. 15:14
25 [z]Gen. 16:6
27 [a]Josh. 9:21, 23 [b]Deut. 12:5

CHAPTER 10

1 [a]Josh. 9:1 [b]Josh. 8:1 [c]Josh. 6:21 [d]Josh. 8:22, 26, 28 [e]Josh. 9:15
2 [f]Ex. 15:14-16; Deut. 11:25; 1 Chr. 14:17
4 [g]Josh. 9:15; 10:1
5 [h]Num. 13:29 [i]Josh. 9:2
6 [j]Josh. 5:10; 9:6
7 [k]Josh. 8:1
8 [l]Josh. 11:6; Judg. 4:14 [m]Josh. 1:5, 9 [n]Josh. 21:44
10 [o]Judg. 4:15; 1 Sam. 7:10, 12; Is. 28:21 [p]Josh. 16:3, 5 [q]Josh. 15:35
11 [r]Is. 30:30; Rev. 16:21

9:21-23 While honoring the pledge of peace with the Gibeonites (v. 19), Joshua made them woodcutters and water carriers because of the deception. This curse extended the perpetual (v. 23) part of "cursed be Canaan" (Gen. 9:26). Gibeon became a part of Benjamin's land area (Josh. 18:25). Later, Joshua consigned Gibeon as one of the Levite towns (21:17). Nehemiah had help from some Gibeonites in rebuilding the walls of Jerusalem (Neh. 3:7).

10:1-11 Gibeon and 3 other towns (9:17) were attacked by a coalition of 5 cities. Israel came to the rescue, with God giving the victory (v. 10).

10:11 The hailstones were miraculous. Note their: 1) source, God; 2) size, large; 3) slaughter, more by stones than by sword; 4) selectivity, only on the enemy; 5) swath, "as far as Azekah"; 6) situation, during a trek down a slope and while God caused the sun to stand still; and 7) similarity to miraculous stones God will fling down during the future wrath (Rev. 16:21).

[s]"Sun, stand still over Gibeon;
And Moon, in the Valley of
[t]Aijalon."
13 So the sun stood still,
And the moon stopped,
Till the people had revenge
Upon their enemies.

[u]*Is* this not written in the Book of Jasher?
So the sun stood still in the midst of heav-
en, and did not hasten to go *down* for about
a whole day. 14 And there has been [v]no day
like that, before it or after it, that the LORD
heeded the voice of a man; for [w]the LORD
fought for Israel.
15 [x]Then Joshua returned, and all Israel
with him, to the camp at Gilgal.

The Amorite Kings Executed

16 But these five kings had fled and hidden themselves in a cave at Makkedah.
17 And it was told Joshua, saying, "The
five kings have been found hidden in the
cave at Makkedah."
18 So Joshua said, "Roll large stones
against the mouth of the cave, and set men
by it to guard them. 19 And do not stay
there yourselves, *but* pursue your enemies,
and attack their rear *guard.* Do not allow
them to enter their cities, for the LORD your
God has delivered them into your hand."
20 Then it happened, while Joshua and the
children of Israel made an end of slaying
them with a very great slaughter, till they
had finished, that those who escaped entered fortified cities. 21 And all the people
returned to the camp, to Joshua at Makkedah, in peace.
[y]No one [1]moved his tongue against any
of the children of Israel.
22 Then Joshua said, "Open the mouth of
the cave, and bring out those five kings to
me from the cave." 23 And they did so, and
brought out those five kings to him from
the cave: the king of Jerusalem, the king of
Hebron, the king of Jarmuth, the king of
Lachish, *and* the king of Eglon.
24 So it was, when they brought out
those kings to Joshua, that Joshua called
for all the men of Israel, and said to the
captains of the men of war who went with
him, "Come near, put your feet on the
necks of these kings." And they drew near
and [z]put their feet on their necks. 25 Then
Joshua said to [2]them, [a]"Do not be afraid,
nor be dismayed; be strong and of good
courage, for [b]thus the LORD will do to all
your enemies against whom you fight."
26 And afterward Joshua struck [3]them and
killed them, and hanged them on five
trees; and they [c]were hanging on the trees
until evening. 27 So it was at the time of the
going down of the sun *that* Joshua commanded, and they [d]took them down from

12 [s]Is. 28:21; Hab. 3:11 [t]Judg. 12:12
13 [u]2 Sam. 1:18
14 [v]Is. 38:7, 8 [w]Ex. 14:14; Deut. 1:30; 20:4; Josh. 10:42; 23:3
15 [x]Josh. 10:43
21 [y]Ex. 11:7 [1]*criticized,* lit. *sharpened his tongue*
24 [z]Ps. 107:40; Is. 26:5, 6; Mal. 4:3
25 [a]Deut. 31:6-8; Josh. 1:9 [b]Deut. 3:21; 7:19 [2]The captains
26 [c]Josh. 8:29; 2 Sam. 21:9 [d]Deut. 21:22, 23; Josh. 8:29 [3]The kings

10:12-14 sun stood still, And the moon stopped. Some say an eclipse hid the sun, keeping its heat from Joshua's worn soldiers and allowing coolness for battle. Others suppose a local (not universal) refraction of the sun's rays such as the local darkness in Egypt (Ex. 10:21-23). Another view has it as only language of observation; i.e., it only seemed to Joshua's men that the sun and moon stopped as God helped them do in one literal 24-hour day what would normally take longer. Others view it as lavish poetic description, not literal fact. However, such ideas fail to do justice to 10:12-14, and needlessly question God's power as Creator. This is best accepted as an outright, monumental miracle. Joshua, moved by the Lord's will, commanded the sun to delay (Heb., "be still, silent, leave off"). The earth actually stopped revolving or, more likely, the sun moved in the same way to keep perfect pace with the battlefield. The moon also ceased its orbiting. This permitted Joshua's troops time to finish the battle with complete victory (v. 11).

10:13-15 Book of Jasher. *Jasher* means "upright." It may be the same as the book called Wars of the Lord (Num. 21:14). The Book of Jasher is mentioned again in 2 Sam. 1:18 and a portion is recorded in 1:19-27. The book appears to have been a compilation of Hebrew songs in honor of Israel's leaders and exploits in battle.

10:24 feet on the necks. This gesture 1) symbolized victory and 2) promised assurance of future conquest (v. 25).

The first ten chapters of Joshua describe the invasion of the Land of Promise and the conquest of its central and southern regions.

The Central and Southern Campaigns

the trees, cast them into the cave where
they had been hidden, and laid large
stones against the cave's mouth, *which re-*
main until this very day.

Conquest of the Southland

28 On that day Joshua took Makkedah,
and struck it and its king with the edge of
the sword. He utterly [e]destroyed [4]them—
all the people who *were* in it. He let none remain. He also did to the king of Makkedah
[f]as he had done to the king of Jericho.
29 Then Joshua passed from Makkedah,
and all Israel with him, to [g]Libnah; and they
fought against Libnah. 30 And the LORD also
delivered it and its king into the hand of Israel; he struck it and all the people who *were*
in it with the edge of the sword. He let none
remain in it, but did to its king as he had
done to the king of Jericho.
31 Then Joshua passed from Libnah, and
all Israel with him, to Lachish; and they encamped against it and fought against it.
32 And the LORD delivered Lachish into the
hand of Israel, who took it on the second
day, and struck it and all the people who
were in it with the edge of the sword, according to all that he had done to Libnah.
33 Then Horam king of Gezer came up to
help Lachish; and Joshua struck him and
his people, until he left him none remaining.
34 From Lachish Joshua passed to Eglon,
and all Israel with him; and they encamped against it and fought against it.
35 They took it on that day and struck it
with the edge of the sword; all the people
who *were* in it he utterly destroyed that
day, according to all that he had done to
Lachish.
36 So Joshua went up from Eglon, and all
Israel with him, to [h]Hebron; and they
fought against it. 37 And they took it and
struck it with the edge of the sword—its
king, all its cities, and all the people who
were in it; he left none remaining, according to all that he had done to Eglon, but utterly destroyed it and all the people who
were in it.
38 Then Joshua returned, and all Israel
with him, to [i]Debir; and they fought
against it. 39 And he took it and its king
and all its cities; they struck them with the
edge of the sword and utterly destroyed all
the people who *were* in it. He left none remaining; as he had done to Hebron, so he
did to Debir and its king, as he had done
also to Libnah and its king.
40 So Joshua conquered all the land: the
[j]mountain country and the [5]South and the
lowland and the wilderness slopes, and
[k]all their kings; he left none remaining,
but [l]utterly destroyed all that breathed, as
the LORD God of Israel had commanded.
41 And Joshua conquered them from [m]Ka-
desh Barnea as far as [n]Gaza, [o]and all the
country of Goshen, even as far as Gibeon.
42 All these kings and their land Joshua
took at one time, [p]because the LORD God of
Israel fought for Israel. 43 Then Joshua returned, and all Israel with him, to the camp
at Gilgal.

The Northern Conquest

11 And it came to pass, when Jabin
king of Hazor heard *these things,*
that he [a]sent to Jobab king of Madon, to the
king [b]of Shimron, to the king of Achshaph,
2 and to the kings who *were* from the north,
in the mountains, in the plain south of
[c]Chinneroth, in the lowland, and in the
heights [d]of Dor on the west, 3 to the Canaanites in the east and in the west, the
[e]Amorite, the Hittite, the Perizzite, the
Jebusite in the mountains, [f]and the Hivite
below [g]Hermon [h]in the land of Mizpah.
4 So they went out, they and all their
armies with them, *as* many people [i]*as* the
sand that *is* on the seashore in multitude,
with very many horses and chariots. 5 And
when all these kings had [1]met together,
they came and camped together at the waters of Merom to fight against Israel.
6 But the LORD said to Joshua, [j]"Do not
be afraid because of them, for tomorrow
about this time I will deliver all of them
slain before Israel. You shall [k]hamstring
their horses and burn their chariots with
fire." 7 So Joshua and all the people of war
with him came against them suddenly by

28 [e]Deut. 7:2, 16 [f]Josh. 6:21 [4]So with MT and most authorities; many Heb. mss., some LXX mss., and some Tg. mss. *it*
29 [g]Josh. 15:42; 21:13; 2 Kin. 8:22; 19:8
36 [h]Num. 13:22; Josh. 14:13-15; 15:13; Judg. 1:10, 20; 2 Sam. 5:1, 3, 5, 13; 2 Chr. 11:10
38 [i]Josh. 15:15; Judg. 1:11; 1 Chr. 6:58
40 [j]Deut. 1:7 [k]Deut. 7:24 [l]Deut. 20:16, 17 [5]Heb. *Negev,* and so throughout the book
41 [m]Num. 13:26; Deut. 9:23 [n]Gen. 10:19; Josh. 11:22 [o]Josh. 11:16; 15:51
42 [p]Josh. 10:14

CHAPTER 11

1 [a]Josh. 10:3 [b]Josh. 19:15
2 [c]Num. 34:11 [d]Josh. 17:11; Judg. 1:27; 1 Kin. 4:11
3 [e]Josh. 9:1 [f]Deut. 7:1; Judg. 3:3, 5; 1 Kin. 9:20 [g]Josh. 11:17; 13:5, 11 [h]Gen. 31:49
4 [i]Gen. 22:17; 32:12; Judg. 7:12; 1 Sam. 13:5
5 [1]Lit. *assembled by appointment*
6 [j]Josh. 10:8 [k]2 Sam. 8:4

10:40-43 A summary of Joshua's southern campaign (cf. 9:1–10:43).

10:42 Tribute belongs to the Lord for all the victories, as "in everything give thanks" (1 Thess. 5:18).

11:1 Hazor. A city 5 mi. SW of Lake Huleh, 10 mi. N of the Sea of Galilee. King Jabin led a coalition of kings from several city-states in Galilee and to the W against Joshua, whose victory reports in the S had spread northward.

11:2 south…in the lowland. This refers to the deep rift of the Jordan River valley to the S of the Lake of Chinneroth (12:3), later called the Sea of Galilee. Chinneroth was probably a town not far N of the lake. The lowland or foothills are an area somewhat W of the Jordan, toward the Mediterranean Sea. Here also is the plain of Sharon and the heights of Dor, i.e., foothills extending to Mt. Carmel, nearer the Mediterranean coast and Dor, a seaport city.

11:5 Merom. These copious springs a few mi. SW of Lake Huleh, about 13 mi. N from the Lake of Chinneroth, which provided the northern armies a rendezvous point.

11:6 hamstring. They cut the large sinew or ligament at the back of the hock on the rear leg, which crippled the horses, making them useless.

the waters of Merom, and they attacked
them. 8 And the LORD delivered them into
the hand of Israel, who defeated them and
chased them to [2]Greater [l]Sidon, to the
[3]Brook [m]Misrephoth, and to the Valley of
Mizpah eastward; they attacked them until
they left none of them remaining. 9 So
Joshua did to them as the LORD had told
him: he hamstrung their horses and
burned their chariots with fire.

10 Joshua turned back at that time and
took Hazor, and struck its king with the
sword; for Hazor was formerly the head of
all those kingdoms. 11 And they struck all
the people who *were* in it with the edge of
the sword, [n]utterly destroying *them*. There
was none left [o]breathing. Then he burned
Hazor with fire.

12 So all the cities of those kings, and all
their kings, Joshua took and struck with
the edge of the sword. He utterly destroyed them, [p]as Moses the servant of the
LORD had commanded. 13 But *as for* the
cities that stood on their [4]mounds, Israel
burned none of them, except Hazor only,
which Joshua burned. 14 And all the [q]spoil
of these cities and the livestock, the children of Israel took as booty for themselves; but they struck every man with the
edge of the sword until they had destroyed them, and they left none breathing. 15 [r]As the LORD had commanded Moses his servant, so [s]Moses commanded
Joshua, and [t]so Joshua did. [5]He left nothing undone of all that the LORD had commanded Moses.

Summary of Joshua's Conquests

16 Thus Joshua took all this land: [u]the
mountain country, all the South, [v]all the
land of Goshen, the lowland, and the Jordan [6]plain—the mountains of Israel and its
lowlands, 17 [w]from [7]Mount Halak and the
ascent to Seir, even as far as Baal Gad in the
Valley of Lebanon below Mount Hermon.
He captured [x]all their kings, and struck
them down and killed them. 18 Joshua
made war a long time with all those kings.
19 There was not a city that made peace
with the children of Israel, except [y]the
Hivites, the inhabitants of Gibeon. All *the*
others they took in battle. 20 For [z]it was of
the LORD [8]to harden their hearts, that they
should come against Israel in battle, that
He might utterly destroy them, *and* that
they might receive no mercy, but that He
might destroy them, [a]as the LORD had
commanded Moses.

21 And at that time Joshua came and cut
off [b]the Anakim from the mountains: from
Hebron, from Debir, from Anab, from all
the mountains of Judah, and from all the
mountains of Israel; Joshua utterly destroyed them with their cities. 22 None of

8 [l]Gen. 49:13 [m]Josh. 13:6 [2]Heb. *Sidon Rabbah* [3]Heb. *Misrephoth Maim*, lit. *Burnings of Water* **11** [n]Deut. 20:16 [o]Josh. 10:40 **12** [p]Num. 33:50-56; Deut. 7:2; 20:16 **13** [4]Heb. *tel*, a heap of successive city ruins **14** [q]Deut. 20:14-18 **15** [r]Ex. 34:10-17 [s]Deut. 31:7, 8 [t]Josh. 1:7 [5]Lit. *He turned aside from nothing* **16** [u]Josh. 12:8 [v]Josh. 10:40, 41 [6]Heb. *arabah* **17** [w]Josh. 12:7 [x]Deut. 7:24 [7]Lit. *The Smooth* or *Bald Mountain* **19** [y]Josh. 9:3-7 **20** [z]Deut. 2:30 [a]Deut. 20:16, 17 [8]Lit. *to make strong* **21** [b]Num. 13:22, 33; Deut. 1:28; 9:2; Josh. 15:13, 14

11:8 Greater Sidon. A city on the Phoenician coast, N of Hazor. "Greater" may refer to surrounding areas along with the city itself. **Misrephoth.** This location lay W of Hazor and also on the Mediterranean.

11:12-15 A summary of Joshua's northern campaign (11:1-15).

11:16,17 Joshua took all this land. The sweeping conquest covered much of Palestine. **mountain country.** In the S, in Judah. **South.** South of the Dead Sea. **Goshen.** Probably the land between Gaza and Gibeon. **lowland.** Or foothills; refers to an area between the Mediterranean coastal plain and the hills of Judah. **Jordan plain.** The rift valley running S of the Dead Sea all the way to the Red Sea's Gulf of Aqabah. The hill country of Israel is distinct from that in 11:16, lying in the northern part of Palestine. The conquest reached from Mt. Halak, about 6 mi. S of the Dead Sea, to Mt. Hermon about 40 mi. NE from the Lake of Chinneroth.

11:18 war a long time. The conquest took approximately 7 years—ca. 1405–1398 B.C. (cf. 14:10). Only Gibeon submitted without a fight (v. 19).

11:20 it was of the LORD to harden their hearts. God turned the Canaanites' hearts to fight in order that Israel might be His judging instrument to destroy them. They were willfully guilty of rejecting the true God with consequent great wickedness, and were as unfit to remain in the Land as vomit spewed out of the mouth (Lev. 18:24,25).

11:21 Anakim. Enemies who dwelt in the southern area which Joshua had defeated. They descended from Anak ("long-necked"), and were related to the giants who made Israel's spies feel small as grasshoppers by comparison (Num. 13:28-33). Compare also Deut. 2:10,11,21. Their territory was later given to Caleb as a reward for his loyalty (14:6-15).

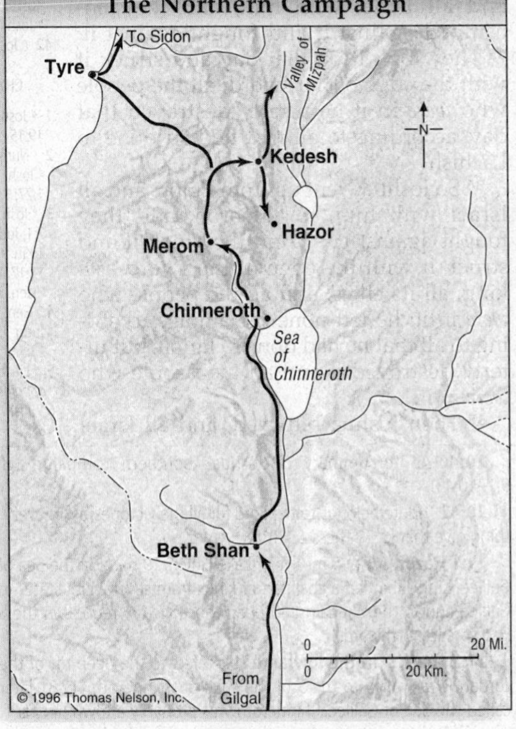

the Anakim were left in the land of the children of Israel; they remained only [c]in Gaza, in Gath, [d]and in Ashdod.

23 So Joshua took the whole land, [e]according to all that the LORD had said to Moses; and Joshua gave it as an inheritance to Israel [f]according to their divisions by their tribes. Then the land [g]rested from war.

The Kings Conquered by Moses

12 These *are* the kings of the land whom the children of Israel defeated, and whose land they possessed on the other side of the Jordan toward the rising of the sun, [a]from the River Arnon [b]to Mount Hermon, and all the eastern Jordan plain: 2 *One king was* [c]Sihon king of the Amorites, who dwelt in Heshbon *and* ruled half of Gilead, from Aroer, which is on the bank of the River Arnon, from the middle of that river, even as far as the River Jabbok, *which is* the border of the Ammonites, 3 and [d]the eastern Jordan plain from the [1]Sea of Chinneroth as far as the [2]Sea of the Arabah (the Salt Sea), [e]the road to Beth Jeshimoth, and [3]southward below [f]the[4] slopes of Pisgah. 4 [g]*The other king was* Og king of Bashan and his territory, *who was* of [h]the remnant of the giants, [i]who dwelt at Ashtaroth and at Edrei, 5 and reigned over [j]Mount Hermon, [k]over Salcah, over all Bashan, [l]as far as the border of the Geshurites and the Maachathites, and over half of Gilead *to* the border of Sihon king of Heshbon.

6 [m]These Moses the servant of the LORD and the children of Israel had conquered; and [n]Moses the servant of the LORD had given it *as* a possession to the Reubenites, the Gadites, and half the tribe of Manasseh.

The Kings Conquered by Joshua

7 And these *are* the kings of the country [o]which Joshua and the children of Israel conquered on this side of the Jordan, on the west, from Baal Gad in the Valley of Lebanon as far as [5]Mount Halak and the ascent to [p]Seir, which Joshua [q]gave to the tribes of Israel *as* a possession according to their divisions, 8 [r]in the mountain country, in the lowlands, in the *Jordan* plain, in the slopes, in the wilderness, and in the South—[s]the Hittites, the Amorites, the Canaanites, the Perizzites, the Hivites, and the Jebusites: 9 [t]the king of Jericho, one; [u]the king of Ai, which *is* beside Bethel, one; 10 [v]the king of Jerusalem, one; the king of Hebron, one; 11 the king of Jarmuth, one; the king of Lachish, one; 12 the king of Eglon, one; [w]the king of Gezer, one; 13 [x]the king of Debir, one; the king of Geder, one; 14 the king of Hormah, one; the king of Arad, one; 15 [y]the king of Libnah, one; the king of Adullam, one; 16 [z]the king of Makkedah, one; [a]the king of Bethel, one; 17 the king of Tappuah, one; [b]the king of Hepher, one; 18 the king of Aphek, one; the king of [6]Lasharon, one; 19 the king of Madon, one; [c]the king of Hazor, one; 20 the king of [d]Shimron Meron, one; the king of Achshaph, one; 21 the king of Taanach, one; the king of Megiddo, one; 22 [e]the king of Kedesh, one; the king of Jokneam in Carmel, one; 23 the king of Dor in the [f]heights of Dor, one; the king of [g]the people of Gilgal, one; 24 the king of Tirzah, one—[h]all the kings, thirty-one.

Remaining Land to Be Conquered

13 Now Joshua [a]was old, advanced in years. And the LORD said to him: "You are old, advanced in years, and there remains very much land yet to be possessed. 2 [b]This is the land that yet remains: [c]all the territory of the Philistines and all [d]*that of* the Geshurites, 3 [e]from Sihor,

22 [c]1 Sam. 17:4 [d]Josh. 15:46; 1 Sam. 5:1; Is. 20:1
23 [e]Ex. 33:2; Num. 34:2-15 [f]Num. 26:53; Josh. 14; 15 [g]Deut. 12:9, 10; 25:19; [Heb. 4:8]

CHAPTER 12
1 [a]Num. 21:24 [b]Deut. 3:8
2 [c]Num. 21:24; Deut. 2:24-27
3 [d]Deut. 3:17 [e]Josh. 13:20 [f]Deut. 3:17; 4:49 [1]Sea of Galilee [2]Lit. *Sea of the Plain,* the Dead Sea [3]Or *Teman* [4]Or *Ashdoth Pisgah*
4 [g]Num. 21:33; Deut. 3:4, 10 [h]Deut. 3:11; Josh. 13:12 [i]Deut. 1:4
5 [j]Deut. 3:8 [k]Deut. 3:10; Josh. 13:11; 1 Chr. 5:11 [l]Deut. 3:14; 1 Sam. 27:8
6 [m]Num. 21:24, 35 [n]Num. 32:29-33; Deut. 3:12; Josh. 13:8
7 [o]Josh. 11:17 [p]Gen. 14:6; 32:3; Deut. 2:1, 4 [q]Josh. 11:23 [5]Lit. *The Bald Mountain*
8 [r]Josh. 10:40; 11:16 [s]Ex. 3:8; 23:23; Josh. 9:1
9 [t]Josh. 6:2 [u]Josh. 8:29
10 [v]Josh. 10:23
12 [w]Josh. 10:33
13 [x]Josh. 10:38, 39
15 [y]Josh. 10:29, 30
16 [z]Josh. 10:28 [a]Josh. 8:17; Judg. 1:22
17 [b]1 Kin. 4:10
18 [6]Or *Sharon*
19 [c]Josh. 11:10
20 [d]Josh. 11:1; 19:15
22 [e]Josh. 19:37; 20:7; 21:32
23 [f]Josh. 11:2 [g]Gen. 14:1, 2; Is. 9:1
24 [h]Deut. 7:24

CHAPTER 13 1 [a]Josh. 14:10; 23:1, 2 2 [b]Judg. 3:1-3 [c]Joel 3:4 [d]Josh. 13:13; 2 Sam. 3:3 3 [e]1 Chr. 13:5; Jer. 2:18

11:22 Anakim...Gath. Some of them remained in Philistine territory, most notably Goliath (cf. 1 Sam. 17:4).

11:23 the whole land. Here is a key verse for the book which sums up 11:16-22. How does this relate to 13:1, where God tells Joshua that he did *not* take the whole land? It may mean that the major battles had been fought and supremacy demonstrated, even if further incidents would occur and not every last pocket of potential resistance had yet been rooted out.

12:1-24 the kings...defeated. The actual list of 31 kings conquered (v. 24) follows and fills out the summary of "the whole land" in 11:16,17,23. The roster shows the kings whom "Moses defeated" E of the Jordan earlier (vv. 1-6; cf. Num. 21; Deut. 2:24–3:17); then those whom Joshua conquered W of the Jordan—a summary (7,8); central kings (9); southern kings (10-16); and northern kings (17-24).

12:24 The conquest of all these kings, covering areas up and down the "whole land" (11:23), was due to the Lord's faithful help, which fulfilled His Word. God promised the Land in His covenant with Abraham (Gen. 12:7), and reaffirmed that He would give success in conquest (Josh. 1:3,6).

13:1 Joshua was old. By this time he was approaching 100, in comparison to Caleb's 85 years (14:10). In 23:1, he was 110 and near death (24:29).

13:1,2 very much land. Some land had not yet actually been occupied by the Israelites through the previous general victories. Pockets or areas in 13:2-6 still lay untouched by specific invasion and occupation (*see 11:23 and note*). When Joshua allotted areas to individuals and tribes, they bore the challenge to drive out lingering resisters; if not, they would disobey God's mandate to be resolute in conquest (Deut. 11:22,23). Failure to do this thoroughly is a sad theme in Judg. 1.

13:3 Sihor. Probably related to the Nile (Is. 23:3; Jer. 2:18), and possibly a name for that river or an eastern tributary of it. The name could

which *is* east of Egypt, as far as the border
of Ekron northward (*which* is counted as
Canaanite); the [f]five lords of the Philistines—the Gazites, the Ashdodites, the
Ashkelonites, the Gittites, and the Ekronites; also [g]the Avites; 4 from the south, all
the land of the Canaanites, and Mearah
that belongs to the Sidonians [h]as far as
Aphek, to the border of [i]the Amorites;
5 the land of [j]the [1]Gebalites, and all Lebanon, toward the sunrise, [k]from Baal Gad
below Mount Hermon as far as the entrance to Hamath; 6 all the inhabitants of
the mountains from Lebanon as far as [l]the
[2]Brook Misrephoth, *and* all the Sidonians—them [m]I will drive out from before
the children of Israel; only [n]divide[3] it by
lot to Israel as an inheritance, as I have
commanded you. 7 Now therefore, divide
this land as an inheritance to the nine
tribes and half the tribe of Manasseh."

The Land Divided East of the Jordan

8 With the other half-tribe the Reubenites and the Gadites received their inheritance, [o]which Moses had given them, [p]be-
yond the Jordan eastward, as Moses the
servant of the LORD had given them:
9 from Aroer which *is* on the bank of the
River Arnon, and the town that *is* in the
midst of the ravine, [q]and all the plain of
Medeba as far as Dibon; 10 [r]all the cities of
Sihon king of the Amorites, who reigned
in Heshbon, as far as the border of the
children of Ammon; 11 [s]Gilead, and the
border of the Geshurites and Maachathites, all Mount Hermon, and all Bashan
as far as Salcah; 12 all the kingdom of Og
in Bashan, who reigned in Ashtaroth and
Edrei, who remained of [t]the remnant of
the giants; [u]for Moses had [4]defeated and
[5]cast out these.

13 Nevertheless the children of Israel
[v]did not drive out the Geshurites or the
Maachathites, but the Geshurites and the
Maachathites dwell among the Israelites
until this day.

14 [w]Only to the tribe of Levi he had
given [6]no inheritance; the sacrifices of the
LORD God of Israel made by fire *are* their
inheritance, [x]as He said to them.

The Land of Reuben

15 [y]And Moses had given to the tribe of
the children of Reuben *an inheritance* according to their families. 16 Their territory
was [z]from Aroer, which *is* on the bank of
the River Arnon, [a]and the city that *is* in the
midst of the ravine, [b]and all the plain by
Medeba; 17 [c]Heshbon and all its cities that
are in the plain: Dibon, Bamoth Baal, Beth
Baal Meon, 18 [d]Jahaza, Kedemoth, Mephaath, 19 [e]Kirjathaim, [f]Sibmah, Zereth Shahar

3 [f]Judg. 3:3 [g]Deut. 2:23
4 [h]Josh. 12:18; 19:30; 1 Sam. 4:1; 1 Kin. 20:26, 30 [i]Judg. 1:34
5 [j]1 Kin. 5:18; Ezek. 27:9 [k]Josh. 12:7 [1]Or *Giblites*
6 [l]Josh. 11:8 [m]Josh. 23:13; Judg. 2:21, 23 [n]Josh. 14:1, 2 [2]Heb. *Misrephoth Maim*, lit. *Burnings of Water* [3]*apportion*
8 [o]Num. 32:33; Deut. 3:12, 13; Josh. 22:4 [p]Josh. 12:1-6
9 [q]Num. 21:30; Josh. 13:16
10 [r]Num. 21:24, 25
11 [s]Num. 32:1; Josh. 12:5
12 [t]Deut. 3:11; Josh. 12:4 [u]Num. 21:24, 34, 35 [4]Lit. *struck* [5]*dispossessed*
13 [v]Josh. 13:11
14 [w]Num. 18:20, 23, 24; Deut. 18:1; Josh. 14:3, 4 [x]Josh. 13:33 [6]*no land as a possession*
15 [y]Num. 34:14; Josh. 13:15-23
16 [z]Josh. 12:2 [a]Num. 21:28 [b]Num. 21:30; Josh. 13:9
17 [c]Num. 21:28, 30
18 [d]Num. 21:23; Judg. 11:20; Is. 15:4; Jer. 48:34
19 [e]Num. 32:37; Jer. 48:1, 23; Ezek. 25:9 [f]Num. 32:38

also refer to a seasonal rain trough which runs to the Mediterranean, the Wadi-el-Arish in the desert S of Palestine, NE of Egypt.

13:7 divide this land. God commanded Joshua to devise allotments within boundaries for inheritances as He had prepared for earlier (Num. 32–34). Joshua announced divisions made clear by lot to tribes E of the Jordan (13:8-33), tribes W of the Jordan (Josh. 14–19), Caleb (14:6-15; cf. 15:13-19), his own area (19:49-51), cities of refuge (20:1-9), and Levite towns (21).

In the second half of the Book of Joshua, the land conquered in the first half of the book is divided among the tribes of Israel.

Division of Land Among the Tribes

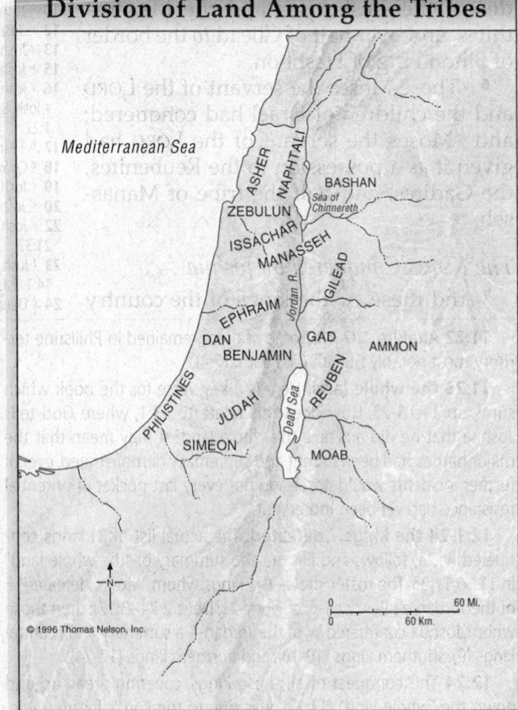

on the mountain of the valley, 20 Beth Peor,
[g]the slopes of Pisgah, and Beth Jeshimoth— 21 [h]all the cities of the plain and all
the kingdom of Sihon king of the Amorites, who reigned in Heshbon, [i]whom Moses had struck [j]with the princes of Midian:
Evi, Rekem, Zur, Hur, and Reba, who *were*
princes of Sihon dwelling in the country.
22 The children of Israel also killed with
the sword [k]Balaam the son of Beor, the
[7]soothsayer, among those who were killed
by them. 23 And the border of the children
of Reuben was the bank of the Jordan. This
was the inheritance of the children of Reuben according to their families, the cities
and their villages.

The Land of Gad

24 [l]Moses also had given *an inheritance* to
the tribe of Gad, to the children of Gad according to their families. 25 [m]Their territory was Jazer, and all the cities of Gilead,
[n]and half the land of the Ammonites as far
as Aroer, which *is* before [o]Rabbah, 26 and
from Heshbon to Ramath Mizpah and
Betonim, and from Mahanaim to the border of Debir, 27 and in the valley [p]Beth
Haram, Beth Nimrah, [q]Succoth, and Zaphon, the rest of the kingdom of Sihon
king of Heshbon, with the Jordan as *its*
border, as far as the edge [r]of the [8]Sea of
Chinnereth, on the other side of the Jordan
eastward. 28 This *is* the inheritance of the
children of Gad according to their families,
the cities and their villages.

Half the Tribe of Manasseh (East)

29 [s]Moses also had given *an inheritance* to
half the tribe of Manasseh; it was for half
the tribe of the children of Manasseh according to their families: 30 Their territory
was from Mahanaim, all Bashan, all the
kingdom of Og king of Bashan, and [t]all the
towns of Jair which are in Bashan, sixty
cities; 31 half of Gilead, and [u]Ashtaroth
and Edrei, cities of the kingdom of Og in
Bashan, *were* for the [v]children of Machir
the son of Manasseh, for half of the children of Machir according to their families.
32 These *are the areas* which Moses had
[9]distributed as an inheritance in the plains
of Moab on the other side of the Jordan, by
Jericho eastward. 33 [w]But to the tribe of
Levi Moses had given no inheritance; the
LORD God of Israel *was* their inheritance,
[x]as He had said to them.

The Land Divided West of the Jordan

14 These *are the areas* which the children of Israel inherited in the land
of Canaan, [a]which Eleazar the priest,
Joshua the son of Nun, and the heads of
the fathers of the tribes of the children of
Israel distributed as an inheritance to
them. 2 Their inheritance *was* [b]by lot, as the
LORD had commanded by the hand of Mo-
ses, for the nine tribes and the half-tribe.
3 [c]For Moses had given the inheritance of
the two tribes and the half-tribe on the
other side of the Jordan; but to the Levites
he had given no inheritance among them.
4 For [d]the children of Joseph were two
tribes: Manasseh and Ephraim. And they
gave no part to the Levites in the land, except [e]cities to dwell *in,* with their common-
lands for their livestock and their property.
5 [f]As the LORD had commanded Moses, so
the children of Israel did; and they divided
the land.

Caleb Inherits Hebron

6 Then the children of Judah came to
Joshua in Gilgal. And Caleb the son of Jephunneh the [g]Kenizzite said to him: "You
know [h]the word which the LORD said to
Moses the man of God concerning [i]you
and me in Kadesh Barnea. 7 I *was* forty
years old when Moses the servant of the
LORD [j]sent me from Kadesh Barnea to spy
out the land, and I brought back word to
him as *it was* in my heart. 8 Nevertheless
[k]my brethren who went up with me made
the [1]heart of the people melt, but I wholly
[l]followed the LORD my God. 9 So Moses
swore on that day, saying, [m]'Surely the
land [n]where your foot has trodden shall be
your inheritance and your children's forever, because you have wholly followed
the LORD my God.' 10 And now, behold,
the LORD has kept me [o]alive, [p]as He said,

20 [g] Deut. 3:17; Josh. 12:3
21 [h] Deut. 3:10 [i] Num. 21:24 [j] Num. 31:8
22 [k] Num. 22:5; 31:8 [7] *diviner*
24 [l] Num. 34:14; 1 Chr. 5:11
25 [m] Num. 32:1, 35 [n] Judg. 11:13, 15 [o] Deut. 3:11; 2 Sam. 11:1; 12:26
27 [p] Num. 32:36 [q] Gen. 33:17; 1 Kin. 7:46 [r] Num. 34:11; Deut. 3:17 [8] Sea of Galilee
29 [s] Num. 34:14; 1 Chr. 5:23
30 [t] Num. 32:41; 1 Chr. 2:23
31 [u] Josh. 9:10; 12:4; 13:12; 1 Chr. 6:71 [v] Num. 32:39, 40; Josh. 17:1
32 [9] *apportioned*
33 [w] Deut. 18:1; Josh. 13:14; 18:7 [x] Num. 18:20; Deut. 10:9; 18:1, 2

CHAPTER 14

1 [a] Num. 34:16-29
2 [b] Num. 26:55; 33:54; 34:13; Ps. 16:5
3 [c] Num. 32:33; Josh. 13:8, 32, 33
4 [d] Gen. 41:51; 46:20; 48:1, 5; Num. 26:28; 2 Chr. 30:1 [e] Num. 35:2-8; Josh. 21:1-42
5 [f] Num. 35:2; Josh. 21:2
6 [g] Num. 32:11, 12 [h] Num. 14:24, 30 [i] Num. 13:26
7 [j] Num. 13:6, 17; 14:6
8 [k] Num. 13:31, 32; Deut. 1:28 [l] Num. 14:24; Deut. 1:36 [1] *courage of the people fail*
9 [m] Num. 14:23, 24 [n] Num. 13:22; Deut. 1:36
10 [o] Num. 14:24, 30, 38 [p] Josh. 5:6; Neh. 9:21

13:22 Israel also killed…Balaam. This Israelite slaying of the infamous false prophet occurred at an unidentified point during the conquest (cf. Num. 21–25; 31:16; Josh. 24:9,10; 2 Pet. 2:15,16; Jude 11; Rev. 2:14).

13:33 to…Levi…no inheritance. God did not give this tribe a normal allotment of land. This suited His choice of Levites for the special ministry of the tabernacle service. Their inheritance consisted in this unique role to share His holy ministrations (18:7). God did assign them cities and adjacent lands (14:4; Num. 35:2,4,5), scattered at 48 places (21:41) throughout all the tribes. This made these religious servants accessible to all the people (cf. chap. 21).

14:1 the land of Canaan. The name for the land W of the Jordan.

14:5 so the children of Israel did. They obeyed in some things, but not in all (*see 13:1,2 and note*).

14:6-9 Caleb. This passage reviews what is also recounted in Num. 13,14. This includes a celebration of God's faithfulness (vv. 7-11), and Caleb's specific inheritance (vv. 12-15). Later, he conquered the area (15:13,14) and conferred blessing on Othniel and his daughter (15:15-19).

these forty-five years, ever since the LORD
spoke this word to Moses while Israel
[2]wandered in the wilderness; and now,
here I am this day, eighty-five years old.
11 [q]As yet I *am as* strong this day as on the
day that Moses sent me; just as my
strength *was* then, so now *is* my strength
for war, both [r]for going out and for coming
in. 12 Now therefore, give me this mountain of which the LORD spoke in that day;
for you heard in that day how [s]the Anakim
were there, and *that* the cities *were* great *and*
fortified. [t]It may be that the LORD *will be*
with me, and [u]I shall be able to drive them
out as the LORD said."
13 And Joshua [v]blessed him, [w]and gave
Hebron to Caleb the son of Jephunneh as
an inheritance. 14 [x]Hebron therefore became the inheritance of Caleb the son of Jephunneh the Kenizzite to this day, because
he [y]wholly followed the LORD God of Israel. 15 And [z]the name of Hebron formerly
was Kirjath Arba (*Arba was* the greatest
man among the Anakim).
[a]Then the land had rest from war.

The Land of Judah

15 So *this* was the [1]lot of the tribe of
the children of Judah according to
their families:
[a]The border of Edom at the [b]Wilderness
of Zin southward *was* the extreme southern boundary. 2 And their [c]southern border began at the shore of the Salt Sea, from
the bay that faces southward. 3 Then it
went out to the southern side of [d]the Ascent of Akrabbim, passed along to Zin, ascended on the south side of Kadesh Barnea, passed along to Hezron, went up to
Adar, and went around to Karkaa. 4 *From*
there it passed [e]toward Azmon and went
out to the Brook of Egypt; and the border
ended at the sea. This shall be your southern border.
5 The east border *was* the Salt Sea as far
as the mouth of the Jordan.
And the [f]border on the northern quarter
began at the bay of the sea at the mouth of
the Jordan. 6 The border went up to [g]Beth
Hoglah and passed north of Beth Arabah;
and the border went up [h]to the stone of
Bohan the son of Reuben. 7 Then the border went up toward [i]Debir from [j]the Valley of Achor, and it turned northward toward Gilgal, which *is* before the Ascent of
Adummim, which *is* on the south side of
the valley. The border continued toward
the waters of En Shemesh and ended at
[k]En Rogel. 8 And the border went up [l]by
the Valley of the Son of Hinnom to the
southern slope of the [m]Jebusite *city* (which
is Jerusalem). The border went up to the
top of the mountain that *lies* before the Valley of Hinnom westward, which *is* at the
end of the Valley [n]of [2]Rephaim northward.
9 Then the border went around from the
top of the hill to [o]the fountain of the water
of Nephtoah, and extended to the cities of
Mount Ephron. And the border went
around [p]to Baalah (which *is* [q]Kirjath Jearim). 10 Then the border [3]turned westward
from Baalah to Mount Seir, passed along to
the side of Mount Jearim on the north
(which *is* Chesalon), went down to Beth
Shemesh, and passed on to [r]Timnah.
11 And the border went out to the side of
[s]Ekron northward. Then the border went
around to Shicron, passed along to Mount
Baalah, and extended to Jabneel; and the
border ended at the sea.
12 The west border *was* [t]the coastline of
the Great Sea. This *is* the boundary of the
children of Judah all around according to
their families.

Caleb Occupies Hebron and Debir

13 [u]Now to Caleb the son of Jephunneh
he gave a share among the children of [v]Ju-
dah, according to the commandment of the
LORD to Joshua, *namely,* [w]Kirjath Arba,
which *is* Hebron (*Arba was* the father of
Anak). 14 Caleb drove out [x]the three sons
of Anak from there: [y]Sheshai, Ahiman, and
Talmai, the children of Anak. 15 Then [z]he
went up from there to the inhabitants of
Debir (formerly the name of Debir *was* Kirjath Sepher).
16 [a]And Caleb said, "He who [4]attacks
Kirjath Sepher and takes it, to him I will
give Achsah my daughter as wife." 17 So
[b]Othniel the [c]son of Kenaz, the brother of
Caleb, took it; and he gave him [d]Achsah
his daughter as wife. 18 [e]Now it was so,
when she came *to him,* that she persuaded

10 [2] Lit. *walked*
11 [q] Deut. 34:7 [r] Deut. 31:2
12 [s] Num. 13:28, 33 [t] Rom. 8:31 [u] Josh. 15:14; Judg. 1:20
13 [v] Josh. 22:6 [w] Josh. 10:37; 15:13
14 [x] Josh. 21:12 [y] Josh. 14:8, 9
15 [z] Gen. 23:2; Josh. 15:13 [a] Josh. 11:23

CHAPTER 15
1 [a] Num. 34:3 [b] Num. 33:36 [1] *allotment*
2 [c] Num. 34:3, 4
3 [d] Num. 34:4
4 [e] Num. 34:5
5 [f] Josh. 18:15-19
6 [g] Josh. 18:19, 21 [h] Josh. 18:17
7 [i] Josh. 13:26 [j] Josh. 7:26 [k] 2 Sam. 17:17; 1 Kin. 1:9
8 [l] Josh. 18:16; 2 Kin. 23:10; Jer. 19:2, 6 [m] Josh. 15:63; 18:28; Judg. 1:21; 19:10 [n] Josh. 18:16 [2] Lit. *Giants*
9 [o] Josh. 18:15 [p] 1 Chr. 13:6 [q] Judg. 18:12
10 [r] Gen. 38:13; Judg. 14:1 [3] *turned around*
11 [s] Josh. 19:43
12 [t] Num. 34:6, 7; Josh. 15:47
13 [u] Josh. 14:13 [v] Num. 13:6 [w] Josh. 14:15
14 [x] Judg. 1:10, 20 [y] Num. 13:22
15 [z] Josh. 10:38; Judg. 1:11
16 [a] Judg. 1:12 [4] Lit. *strikes*
17 [b] Judg. 1:13; 3:9 [c] Num. 32:12; Josh. 14:6 [d] Judg. 1:12
18 [e] Judg. 1:14

14:10 eighty-five years old. Given 1) that Caleb was 40 at Kadesh Barnea and 2) that the Israelites had wandered in the wilderness 38 years, then the conquering of the Land took 7 years (ca. 1405–1398 B.C.), Caleb was now 85 years old.

14:12-14 Based on His promise (v. 9), God granted Caleb's desire for Hebron because of his faithfulness to believe that God would give the Land to the Israelites as He promised.

14:15 Anakim. See 15:13; *see note on 11:21.*

15:1-12 the lot of…Judah. The tribe's southern boundary (v. 1) ran from the lower tip of the Salt or Dead Sea in a sweep through the desert over to the Wadi, the Brook of Egypt (*see 13:3 and note*), and along it to the Mediterranean. The eastern limit (v. 5) ran the length of the Salt Sea itself. On the N, it extended from the N end of the Salt Sea by various lines working to the Mediterranean (vv. 5-11). The Mediterranean coastline served as the western border (v. 12).

15:17 Othniel. A conqueror like Caleb, who was his father-in-law, he would later be a judge in Israel (Judg. 3:9-11).

him to ask her father for a field. So [f]she dismounted from *her* donkey, and Caleb said
to her, "What do you wish?" 19 She answered, "Give me a [g]blessing; since you
have given me land in the South, give me
also springs of water." So he gave her the
upper springs and the lower springs.

The Cities of Judah

20 This *was* the inheritance of the tribe of
the children of Judah according to their
families:
21 The cities at the limits of the tribe of
the children of Judah, toward the border of
Edom in the South, were Kabzeel, [h]Eder,
Jagur, 22 Kinah, Dimonah, Adadah,
23 Kedesh, Hazor, Ithnan, 24 [i]Ziph, Telem,
Bealoth, 25 Hazor, Hadattah, Kerioth,
Hezron (which *is* Hazor), 26 Amam,
Shema, Moladah, 27 Hazar Gaddah, Hesh-
mon, Beth Pelet, 28 Hazar Shual, [j]Beer-
sheba, Bizjothjah, 29 Baalah, Ijim, Ezem,
30 Eltolad, Chesil, [k]Hormah, 31 [l]Ziklag,
Madmannah, Sansannah, 32 Lebaoth, Shil-
him, Ain, and [m]Rimmon: all the cities *are*
twenty-nine, with their villages.
33 In the lowland: [n]Eshtaol, Zorah, Ashnah, 34 Zanoah, En Gannim, Tappuah,
Enam, 35 Jarmuth, [o]Adullam, Socoh, Azekah, 36 Sharaim, Adithaim, Gederah, and
Gederothaim: fourteen cities with their villages; 37 Zenan, Hadashah, Migdal Gad,
38 Dilean, Mizpah, [p]Joktheel, 39 [q]Lachish,
Bozkath, [r]Eglon, 40 Cabbon, [5]Lahmas,
Kithlish, 41 Gederoth, Beth Dagon, Naamah, and Makkedah: sixteen cities with
their villages; 42 [s]Libnah, Ether, Ashan,
43 Jiphtah, Ashnah, Nezib, 44 Keilah, Achzib, and Mareshah: nine cities with their
villages; 45 Ekron, with its towns and villages; 46 from Ekron to the sea, all that *lay*
near [t]Ashdod, with their villages; 47 Ashdod with its towns and villages, Gaza with
its towns and villages—as far as [u]the
Brook of Egypt and [v]the Great Sea with *its*
coastline.
48 And in the mountain country: Shamir,
Jattir, Sochoh, 49 Dannah, Kirjath Sannah
(which *is* Debir), 50 Anab, Eshtemoh,
Anim, 51 [w]Goshen, Holon, and Giloh:
eleven cities with their villages; 52 Arab,
Dumah, Eshean, 53 Janum, Beth Tappuah,
Aphekah, 54 Humtah, [x]Kirjath Arba
(which *is* Hebron), and Zior: nine cities
with their villages; 55 [y]Maon, Carmel,
Ziph, Juttah, 56 Jezreel, Jokdeam, Zanoah,
57 Kain, Gibeah, and Timnah: ten cities
with their villages; 58 Halhul, Beth Zur,
Gedor, 59 Maarath, Beth Anoth, and Elte-
kon: six cities with their villages; 60 [z]Kir-
jath Baal (which *is* Kirjath Jearim) and Rabbah: two cities with their villages.
61 In the wilderness: Beth Arabah, Mid-
din, Secacah, 62 Nibshan, the City of Salt,
and [a]En Gedi: six cities with their villages.
63 As for the Jebusites, the inhabitants of
Jerusalem, [b]the children of Judah could not
drive them out; [c]but the Jebusites dwell
with the children of Judah at Jerusalem to
this day.

Ephraim and West Manasseh

16 The lot [1]fell to the children of Joseph from the Jordan, by Jericho, to
the waters of Jericho on the east, to the
[a]wilderness that goes up from Jericho
through the mountains to [2]Bethel, 2 then
went out [3]from [b]Bethel to Luz, passed
along to the border of the Archites at Ataroth, 3 and went down westward to the
boundary of the Japhletites, [c]as far as the
boundary of Lower Beth Horon to [d]Gezer;
and [4]it ended at the sea.
4 [e]So the children of Joseph, Manasseh
and Ephraim, took their [5]inheritance.

The Land of Ephraim

5 [f]The border of the children of Ephraim,
according to their families, was *thus:* The
border of their inheritance on the east side
was [g]Ataroth Addar [h]as far as Upper Beth
Horon.
6 And the border went out toward the
sea on the north side of [i]Michmethath;
then the border went around eastward to
Taanath Shiloh, and passed by it on the
east of Janohah. 7 Then it went down from
Janohah to Ataroth and [6]Naarah, reached
to Jericho, and came out at the Jordan.
8 The border went out from [j]Tappuah

18 [f]Gen. 24:64; 1 Sam. 25:23
19 [g]Gen. 33:11
21 [h]Gen. 35:21
24 [i]1 Sam. 23:14
28 [j]Gen. 21:31; Josh. 19:2
30 [k]Josh. 19:4
31 [l]Josh. 19:5; 1 Sam. 27:6; 30:1
32 [m]Judg. 20:45, 47
33 [n]Judg. 13:25; 16:31
35 [o]1 Sam. 22:1
38 [p]2 Kin. 14:7
39 [q]2 Kin. 14:19 [r]Josh. 10:3
40 [5]Or *Lahmam*
42 [s]Josh. 21:13
46 [t]Josh. 11:22
47 [u]Josh. 15:4 [v]Num. 34:6
51 [w]Josh. 10:41; 11:16
54 [x]Josh. 14:15
55 [y]1 Sam. 23:24, 25
60 [z]Josh. 18:14; 1 Sam. 7:1, 2
62 [a]1 Sam. 23:29; Ezek. 47:10
63 [b]Judg. 1:8, 21; 2 Sam. 5:6; 1 Chr. 11:4 [c]Judg. 1:21

CHAPTER 16

1 [a]Josh. 8:15; 18:12 [1]Lit. *went out* [2]LXX *Bethel Luz*
2 [b]Josh. 18:13; Judg. 1:26 [3]LXX *to Bethel,*
3 [c]Josh. 18:13; 1 Kin. 9:17; 2 Chr. 8:5 [d]Josh. 21:21; 1 Kin. 9:15; 1 Chr. 7:28 [4]Lit. *the goings out of it were at the sea*
4 [e]Josh. 17:14 [5]*possession*
5 [f]Judg. 1:29; 1 Chr. 7:28, 29 [g]Josh. 18:13 [h]2 Chr. 8:5
6 [i]Josh. 17:7
7 [6]*Naaran,* 1 Chr. 7:28
8 [j]Josh. 17:8

15:18,19 Caleb's daughter sought blessing and exercised real faith for it—like father, like daughter.

15:20-62 The inheritance of...Judah. Judah's cities are grouped in 4 areas: S (vv. 20-32); lowland or foothills over near the Mediterranean (vv. 33-47); hilly central region (vv. 48-60); Judean wilderness dropping eastward down to the Dead Sea (vv. 61,62).

15:63 Jebusites. The inhabitants of Jerusalem were descendants from the third son of Canaan (Gen. 10:15,16; 15:21). Joshua killed their king who had joined a pact against Gibeon (Josh. 10). Israelites called the area "Jebus" until David ordered Joab and his soldiers to capture the city (2 Sam. 5:6,7) and made it his capital. Judges 1:8,21 show that the Israelites conquered Jebus and burned it, but the Jebusites later regained control until David's day. Melchizedek had been a very early king (Gen. 14), a believer in the true God, when the site was "Salem" (cf. Ps. 76:2, "Salem" is "Jerusalem").

16:1-4 children of Joseph. Joseph's territory was double as it was given to his sons Manasseh and Ephraim, who had inheritances stretching over a good portion of the central area in the Promised Land.

16:5-9 border of...Ephraim. The description is of the land N of Judah's territory, from the Jordan W to the Mediterranean Sea. There was the inclusion of some cities in the territory of Manasseh, since Ephraim's land was small compared to its population.

westward to the [k]Brook Kanah, and [7]it ended at the sea. This *was* the inheritance of the tribe of the children of Ephraim according to their families. 9 [l]The separate cities for the children of Ephraim *were* among the inheritance of the children of Manasseh, all the cities with their villages.

10 [m]And they did not drive out the Canaanites who dwelt in Gezer; but the Canaanites dwell among the Ephraimites to this day and have become forced laborers.

The Other Half-Tribe of Manasseh (West)

17 There was also a lot for the tribe of Manasseh, for he *was* the [a]firstborn of Joseph: *namely* for [b]Machir the firstborn of Manasseh, the father of Gilead, because he was a man of war; therefore he was given [c]Gilead and Bashan. 2 And there was *a lot* for [d]the rest of the children of Manasseh according to their families: [e]for the children of [1]Abiezer, the children of Helek, [f]the children of Asriel, the children of Shechem, [g]the children of Hepher, and the children of Shemida; these *were* the male children of Manasseh the son of Joseph according to their families.

3 But [h]Zelophehad the son of Hepher, the son of Gilead, the son of Machir, the son of Manasseh, had no sons, but only daughters. And these *are* the names of his daughters: Mahlah, Noah, Hoglah, Milcah, and Tirzah. 4 And they came near before [i]Eleazar the priest, before Joshua the son of Nun, and before the rulers, saying, [j]“The LORD commanded Moses to give us an [2]inheritance among our brothers.” Therefore, according to the commandment of the LORD, he gave them an inheritance among their father’s brothers. 5 Ten shares fell to [k]Manasseh, besides the land of Gilead and Bashan, which *were* on the other side of the Jordan, 6 because the daughters of Manasseh received an inheritance among his sons; and the rest of Manasseh’s sons had the land of Gilead.

7 And the territory of Manasseh was from Asher to [l]Michmethath, that *lies* east of Shechem; and the border went along south to the inhabitants of En Tappuah. 8 Manasseh had the land of Tappuah, but [m]Tappuah on the border of Manasseh *belonged* to the children of Ephraim. 9 And the [3]border descended to the [4]Brook Kanah, southward to the brook. [n]These cities of Ephraim *are* among the cities of Manasseh. The border of Manasseh *was* on the north side of the brook; and it ended at the sea.

10 Southward *it was* Ephraim’s, northward *it was* Manasseh’s, and the sea was its border. Manasseh’s territory was adjoining Asher on the north and Issachar on the east. 11 And in Issachar and in Asher, [o]Manasseh had [p]Beth Shean and its towns, Ibleam and its towns, the inhabitants of Dor and its towns, the inhabitants of En Dor and its towns, the inhabitants of Taanach and its towns, and the inhabitants of Megiddo and its towns—three hilly regions. 12 Yet [q]the children of Manasseh could not drive out *the inhabitants of* those cities, but the Canaanites were determined to dwell in that land. 13 And it happened, when the children of Israel grew strong, that they put the Canaanites to [r]forced labor, but did not utterly drive them out.

More Land for Ephraim and Manasseh

14 [s]Then the children of Joseph spoke to Joshua, saying, “Why have you given us *only* [t]one [5]lot and one share to inherit, since we *are* [u]a great people, inasmuch as the LORD has blessed us until now?”

15 So Joshua answered them, “If you *are* a great people, *then* go up to the forest *country* and clear a place for yourself there in the land of the Perizzites and the giants, since the mountains of Ephraim are too confined for you.”

16 But the children of Joseph said, “The mountain country is not enough for us; and all the Canaanites who dwell in the land of the valley have [v]chariots of iron, *both those* who *are* of Beth Shean and its towns and *those* who *are* [w]of the Valley of Jezreel.”

17 And Joshua spoke to the house of Joseph—to Ephraim and Manasseh—saying, “You *are* a great people and have great power; you shall not have *only* one [6]lot, 18 but the mountain country shall be yours. Although it *is* wooded, you shall cut it

8 [k]Josh. 17:9 [7]Lit. *the goings out of it were at the sea*
9 [l]Josh. 17:9
10 [m]Josh. 15:63; 17:12, 13; Judg. 1:29; 1 Kin. 9:16

CHAPTER 17

1 [a]Gen. 41:51; 46:20; 48:18 [b]Gen. 50:23; Judg. 5:14 [c]Deut. 3:15
2 [d]Num. 26:29-33 [e]1 Chr. 7:18 [f]Num. 26:31 [g]Num. 26:32 [1]*Jeezer,* Num. 26:30
3 [h]Num. 26:33; 27:1; 36:2
4 [i]Josh. 14:1 [j]Num. 27:2-11 [2]*possession*
5 [k]Josh. 22:7
7 [l]Josh. 16:6
8 [m]Josh. 16:8
9 [n]Josh. 16:9 [3]*boundary* [4]*Wadi*
11 [o]1 Chr. 7:29 [p]Judg. 1:27; 1 Sam. 31:10; 1 Kin. 4:12
12 [q]Judg. 1:19, 27, 28
13 [r]Josh. 16:10
14 [s]Josh. 16:4 [t]Gen. 48:22 [u]Gen. 48:19; Num. 26:34, 37 [5]*allotment*
16 [v]Josh. 17:18; Judg. 1:19; 4:3 [w]Josh. 19:18; 1 Kin. 4:12
17 [6]*allotment*

16:10 Ephraim did not drive the Canaanites from their area. This is the first mention of the fatal policy of neglecting to exterminate the idolaters (cf. Deut. 20:16).

17:1-18 Manasseh. The other half-tribe of Manasseh, distinct from the half in 16:4, received its portion of the split inheritance W of the Jordan to the N and E near the Lake of Chinneroth (Galilee).

17:3-6 Zelophehad. In Manasseh’s tribe, this man had no sons as heirs, but his 5 daughters received the inheritance. God led Moses to give this right to women (Num. 27:1-11, cited in v. 4).

17:12-18 children of Manasseh. Tribesmen of Manasseh complained that Joshua did not allot them land sufficient to their numbers and that the Canaanites were too tough for them to drive out altogether. He permitted them extra land in forested hills that they could clear. Joshua told them that they could drive out the Canaanites for God had promised to be with them in victory against chariots (Deut. 20:1).

down, and its [7]farthest extent shall be
yours; for you shall drive out the Canaanites, [x]though they have iron chariots *and*
are strong."

The Remainder of the Land Divided

18 Now the whole congregation of the
children of Israel assembled togeth-
er [a]at Shiloh, and [b]set up the tabernacle of
meeting there. And the land was subdued
before them. 2 But there remained among
the children of Israel seven tribes which
had not yet received their inheritance.
3 Then Joshua said to the children of Israel: [c]"How long will you neglect to go
and possess the land which the LORD God
of your fathers has given you? 4 Pick out
from among you three men for *each* tribe,
and I will send them; they shall rise and go
through the land, survey it according to
their inheritance, and come *back* to me.
5 And they shall divide it into seven parts.
[d]Judah shall remain in their territory on
the south, and the [e]house of Joseph shall
remain in their territory on the north. 6 You
shall therefore [1]survey the land in seven
parts and bring *the survey* here to me, [f]that
I may cast lots for you here before the LORD
our God. 7 [g]But the Levites have no part
among you, for the priesthood of the LORD
is their inheritance. [h]And Gad, Reuben,
and half the tribe of Manasseh have received their inheritance beyond the Jordan
on the east, which Moses the servant of the
LORD gave them."
8 Then the men arose to go away; and
Joshua charged those who went to [2]survey
the land, saying, "Go, walk [i]through the
land, survey it, and come back to me, that
I may cast lots for you here before the LORD
in Shiloh." 9 So the men went, passed
through the land, and [3]wrote the survey in
a book in seven parts by cities; and they
came to Joshua at the camp in Shiloh.
10 Then Joshua cast [j]lots for them in Shiloh
before the LORD, and there [k]Joshua divided
the land to the children of Israel according
to their [4]divisions.

The Land of Benjamin

11 [l]Now the lot of the tribe of the children of Benjamin came up according to
their families, and the territory of their lot
came out between the children of Judah
and the children of Joseph. 12 [m]Their border on the north side began at the Jordan,
and the border went up to the side of Jericho on the north, and went up through the
mountains westward; it ended at the
Wilderness of Beth Aven. 13 The border
went over from there toward Luz, to the
side of Luz [n](which *is* Bethel) southward;
and the border descended to Ataroth
Addar, near the hill that *lies* on the south
side [o]of Lower Beth Horon.
14 Then the border extended around the
west side to the south, from the hill that *lies*
before Beth Horon southward; and [5]it
ended at [p]Kirjath Baal (which *is* Kirjath
Jearim), a city of the children of Judah. This
was the west side.
15 The south side *began* at the end of Kirjath Jearim, and the border extended on
the west and went out to [q]the spring of the
waters of Nephtoah. 16 Then the border
came down to the end of the mountain that
lies before [r]the Valley of the Son of Hinnom, which *is* in the Valley of the [6]Repha-
im on the north, descended to the Valley of
Hinnom, to the side of the Jebusite *city* on
the south, and descended to [s]En Rogel.
17 And it went around from the north,
went out to En Shemesh, and extended toward Geliloth, which is before the Ascent
of Adummim, and descended to [t]the stone
of Bohan the son of Reuben. 18 Then it
passed along toward the north side of
[7]Arabah, and went down to Arabah.
19 And the border passed along to the
north side of Beth Hoglah; then [8]the border ended at the north bay at the [u]Salt Sea,
at the south end of the Jordan. This *was* the
southern boundary.
20 The Jordan was its border on the east
side. This *was* the inheritance of the children of Benjamin, according to its boundaries all around, according to their families.
21 Now the cities of the tribe of the children of Benjamin, according to their families, were Jericho, Beth Hoglah, Emek
Keziz, 22 Beth Arabah, Zemaraim, Bethel,
23 Avim, Parah, Ophrah, 24 Chephar Ha-
ammoni, Ophni, and Gaba: twelve cities
with their villages; 25 [v]Gibeon, [w]Ramah,
Beeroth, 26 Mizpah, Chephirah, Mozah,

18 [x]Deut. 20:1 [7]Lit. *goings out*

CHAPTER 18

1 [a]Josh. 19:51; 21:2; 22:9; Jer. 7:12 [b]Judg. 18:31; 1 Sam. 1:3, 24; 4:3, 4
3 [c]Judg. 18:9
5 [d]Josh. 15:1 [e]Josh. 16:1–17:18
6 [f]Josh. 14:2; 18:10 [1]*describe in writing*
7 [g]Num. 18:7, 20; Josh. 13:33 [h]Josh. 13:8
8 [i]Gen. 13:17 [2]*describe in writing*
9 [3]*described it in writing*
10 [j]Acts 13:19 [k]Num. 34:16-29; Josh. 19:51 [4]*portions*
11 [l]Judg. 1:21
12 [m]Josh. 16:1
13 [n]Gen. 28:19; Josh. 16:2; Judg. 1:23 [o]Josh. 16:3
14 [p]Josh. 15:9 [5]Lit. *its goings out were*
15 [q]Josh. 15:9
16 [r]Josh. 15:8 [s]Josh. 15:7 [6]Lit. *Giants*
17 [t]Josh. 15:6
18 [7]*Beth Arabah*, Josh. 15:6; 18:22
19 [u]Josh. 15:2, 5 [8]Lit. *the goings out of the border were*
25 [v]Josh. 11:19; 21:17; 1 Kin. 3:4, 5 [w]Jer. 31:15

18:1 Shiloh. Israel as a whole, having had their camp first at Gilgal (4:20; 5:9), converged to Shiloh for worship at the tabernacle. Shiloh, about 9 mi. N of Bethel and 20 mi. N of Jerusalem, remained the center of spiritual attention, as in Judg. 18:31 and 1 Sam. 1:3. Due to Israel's sin, God would later let the Philistines devastate Israel at Shiloh and capture the ark (1 Sam. 4:10,17), and He would later use Shiloh as an example of judgment (Jer. 7:12).

18:8,10. Seven tribes were yet to receive land (v. 2). Joshua obtained from their 21 surveyor scouts (vv. 2-4) descriptions of the 7 areas of land, then cast lots to decide the choices. The High-Priest Eleazar served him, seeking God's will by casting lots (19:51). This was not some act of mere chance, but a means God used to reveal His will (*see note on Prov. 16:33*).

18:11-28 the lot of...Benjamin. This inheritance lay between Judah's and Ephraim's, and embraced Jerusalem (v. 28).

27 Rekem, Irpeel, Taralah, 28 Zelah, Eleph, [x]Jebus (which *is* Jerusalem), Gibeath, *and* Kirjath: fourteen cities with their villages. This was the inheritance of the children of Benjamin according to their families.

Simeon's Inheritance with Judah

19 The [a]second lot came out for Simeon, for the tribe of the children of Simeon according to their families. [b]And their inheritance was within the inheritance of the children of Judah. 2 [c]They had in their inheritance Beersheba (Sheba), Moladah, 3 Hazar Shual, Balah, Ezem, 4 Eltolad, Bethul, Hormah, 5 Ziklag, Beth Marcaboth, Hazar Susah, 6 Beth Lebaoth, and Sharuhen: thirteen cities and their villages; 7 Ain, Rimmon, Ether, and Ashan: four cities and their villages; 8 and all the villages that *were* all around these cities as far as Baalath Beer, [d]Ramah of the South. This *was* the inheritance of the tribe of the children of Simeon according to their families.

9 The inheritance of the children of Simeon *was included* in the share of the children of Judah, for the share of the children of Judah was [1]too much for them. [e]Therefore the children of Simeon had *their* inheritance within the inheritance of [2]that people.

The Land of Zebulun

10 The third lot came out for the children of Zebulun according to their families, and the border of their inheritance was as far as Sarid. 11 [f]Their border went toward the west and to Maralah, went to Dabbasheth, and extended along the brook that is [g]east of Jokneam. 12 Then from Sarid it went eastward toward the sunrise along the border of Chisloth Tabor, and went out toward [h]Daberath, bypassing Japhia. 13 And from there it passed along on the east of [i]Gath Hepher, toward Eth Kazin, and extended to Rimmon, which borders on Neah. 14 Then the border went around it on the north side of Hannathon, and [3]it ended in the Valley of Jiphthah El. 15 Included were Kattath, Nahallal, Shimron, Idalah, and Bethlehem: twelve cities with their villages. 16 This *was* the inheritance of the children of Zebulun according to their families, these cities with their villages.

28 [x]Josh. 15:8, 63

CHAPTER 19

1 [a]Judg. 1:3 [b]Josh. 19:9
2 [c]1 Chr. 4:28
8 [d]1 Sam. 30:27
9 [e]Josh. 19:1 [1]*too large* [2]Lit. *them*
11 [f]Gen. 49:13 [g]Josh. 12:22
12 [h]1 Chr. 6:72
13 [i]2 Kin. 14:25
14 [3]Lit. *the goings out of it were*

The Land of Issachar

17 The fourth lot came out to Issachar, for the children of Issachar according to their families. 18 And their territory went to Jezreel, and *included* Chesulloth, Shunem, 19 Haphraim, Shion, Anaharath, 20 Rabbith, Kishion, Abez, 21 Remeth, En Gannim, En Haddah, and Beth Pazzez. 22 And the border reached to Tabor, Shahazimah, and [j]Beth Shemesh; their border ended at the Jordan: sixteen cities with their villages. 23 This *was* the inheritance of the tribe of the children of Issachar according to their families, the cities and their villages.

The Land of Asher

24 [k]The fifth lot came out for the tribe of the children of Asher according to their families. 25 And their territory included Helkath, Hali, Beten, Achshaph, 26 Alammelech, Amad, and Mishal; it reached to [l]Mount Carmel westward, along *the Brook* Shihor Libnath. 27 It turned toward the sunrise to Beth Dagon; and it reached to Zebulun and to the Valley of Jiphthah El, then northward beyond Beth Emek and Neiel, bypassing [m]Cabul *which was* on the left, 28 including [4]Ebron, Rehob, Hammon, and Kanah, [n]as far as Greater Sidon. 29 And the border turned to Ramah and to the fortified city of Tyre; then the border turned to Hosah, and ended at the sea by the region of [o]Achzib. 30 Also Ummah, Aphek, and Rehob *were included:* twenty-two cities with their villages. 31 This *was* the inheritance of the tribe of the children of Asher according to their families, these cities with their villages.

The Land of Naphtali

32 [p]The sixth lot came out to the children of Naphtali, for the children of Naphtali according to their families. 33 And their border began at Heleph, enclosing the ter-

22 [j]Josh. 15:10; Judg. 1:33
24 [k]Judg. 1:31, 32
26 [l]1 Sam. 15:12; 1 Kin. 18:20; Is. 33:9; 35:2; Jer. 46:18
27 [m]1 Kin. 9:13
28 [n]Gen. 10:19; Josh. 11:8; Judg. 1:31; Acts 27:3 [4]So with MT, Tg., Vg.; a few Heb. mss. *Abdon* (cf. 21:30 and 1 Chr. 6:74)
29 [o]Judg. 1:31
32 [p]Josh. 19:32-39; Judg. 1:33

19:1-9 Simeon. This area was a southern portion of Judah's territory, since that allotment was more than Judah needed (v. 9).

19:10-16 Zebulun. This allotment lay W of the Lake of Chinneroth (Sea of Galilee) and ran to the Mediterranean Sea.

19:17-23 Issachar. The area basically ran just below the Sea of Galilee from the Jordan W over to Mt. Tabor, circling SW almost to Megiddo, N of Manasseh's portion.

19:24-31 Asher. This territory was a long, broad strip flanking the Mediterranean on the W, then Naphtali's and Zebulun's claims on the E, running S to Manasseh's. It reached from Mt. Carmel in the S to the area of Tyre in the N.

19:32-39 Naphtali. This region took in a long stretch of land with a border at the northern edge of all the Israelite inheritances, a line on the W dividing it from Asher, southward to follow Zebulun's northern border. Then it struck eastward toward the Sea of Galilee with land to the W alongside that sea and down to Issachar's claim, over to the Jordan River. The eastern line ran northward, including the city of Hazor and also Dan, then swung N of Dan. Jesus' Galilean ministry would take place largely in this area (Is. 9:1,2; Matt. 4:13-17).

ritory from the terebinth tree in Zaa-
nannim, Adami Nekeb, and Jabneel, as far
as Lakkum; [5]it ended at the Jordan.
34 [q]From Heleph the border extended
westward to Aznoth Tabor, and went out
from there toward Hukkok; it adjoined
Zebulun on the south side and Asher on
the west side, and ended at Judah by the
Jordan toward the sunrise. 35 And the fortified cities *are* Ziddim, Zer, Hammath,
Rakkath, Chinnereth, 36 Adamah, Ramah,
Hazor, 37 [r]Kedesh, Edrei, En Hazor,
38 Iron, Migdal El, Horem, Beth Anath, and
Beth Shemesh: nineteen cities with their
villages. 39 This *was* the inheritance of the
tribe of the children of Naphtali according
to their families, the cities and their villages.

The Land of Dan

40 [s]The seventh lot came out for the tribe
of the children of Dan according to their
families. 41 And the territory of their inheritance was Zorah, [t]Eshtaol, Ir Shemesh,
42 [u]Shaalabbin, [v]Aijalon, Jethlah, 43 Elon,
Timnah, [w]Ekron, 44 Eltekeh, Gibbethon,
Baalath, 45 Jehud, Bene Berak, Gath Rimmon, 46 Me Jarkon, and Rakkon, with the
region [6]near [7]Joppa. 47 And the [x]border of
the children of Dan went beyond these, because the children of Dan went up to fight
against Leshem and took it; and they
struck it with the edge of the sword, took
possession of it, and dwelt in it. They
called Leshem, [y]Dan, after the name of
Dan their father. 48 This *is* the inheritance
of the tribe of the children of Dan according to their families, these cities with their
villages.

Joshua's Inheritance

49 When they had [8]made an end of dividing the land as an inheritance according
to their borders, the children of Israel gave
an inheritance among them to Joshua the
son of Nun. 50 According to the word of
the LORD they gave him the city which he
asked for, [z]Timnath [a]Serah in the mountains of Ephraim; and he built the city and
dwelt in it.

51 [b]These *were* the inheritances which Eleazar the priest, Joshua the son of Nun,
and the heads of the fathers of the tribes of
the children of Israel divided as an inheritance by lot [c]in Shiloh before the LORD, at
the door of the tabernacle of meeting. So
they made an end of dividing the country.

The Cities of Refuge

20 The LORD also spoke to Joshua, saying, 2 "Speak to the children of Israel, saying: [a]'Appoint[1] for yourselves
cities of refuge, of which I spoke to you
through Moses, 3 that the slayer who kills

33 [5] Lit. *its goings out were*
34 [q] Deut. 33:23
37 [r] Josh. 20:7
40 [s] Josh. 19:40-48; Judg. 1:34-36
41 [t] Josh. 15:33
42 [u] Judg. 1:35; 1 Kin. 4:9 [v] Josh. 10:12; 21:24
43 [w] Josh. 15:11; Judg. 1:18
46 [6] *over against* [7] Heb. *Japho*
47 [x] Judg. 18
[y] Judg. 18:29
49 [8] *finished*
50 [z] Josh. 24:30 [a] 1 Chr. 7:24
51 [b] Num. 34:17; Josh. 14:1 [c] Josh. 18:1, 10

CHAPTER 20

2 [a] Ex. 21:13; Num. 35:6-34; Deut. 19:2, 9 [1] *Designate*

19:33 terebinth tree. This was an oak tree (or an oak forest if taken in a collective sense, as the word possibly means in Gen. 12:6) near Kedesh and NW of the waters at Merom. According to Judg. 4:11, it was the site where Jael killed Sisera with a hammer and tent peg (4:21).

19:40-48 Dan. The tribal allotment was a narrow, roughly U-shaped strip just N of Judah's claim and S of Ephraim's. The Mediterranean coast lay on the western arm of the "U." Joppa was on the coast near the N end. Later the Danites, failing to possess their original claim (Judg. 1:34-36), migrated northeastward to a territory by Laish or Leshem (Josh. 19:47). They conquered this area N of the Sea of Galilee and Hazor, and renamed it Dan (Josh. 19:47,48; Judg. 18:27-29).

19:49,50 Joshua received his own inheritance from the children of Israel, an area he preferred in the hills of his tribe, Ephraim (Num. 13:8). He built a city, Timnath Serah, about 16 mi. SW of Shechem. His inheritance was an intrinsic part of God's promise to him, as was also Caleb's inheritance (Num. 14:30).

20:1-9 cities of refuge. Moses had spoken God's Word to name 6 cities in Israel as refuge centers. A person who inadvertently killed another could flee to the nearest of these for protection (cf. Num. 35:9-34). Three lay W of the Jordan, and 3 lay to the E, each reachable in a day for those in its area. The slayer could flee there to escape pursuit by a family member seeking to exact private justice. Authorities at the refuge guarded him and escorted him to a trial. If found innocent, he was guarded at the refuge until the death of the current High-Priest, a kind of statute of limitations (Josh. 20:6). He could then return home. If found guilty of murder, he suffered due punishment.

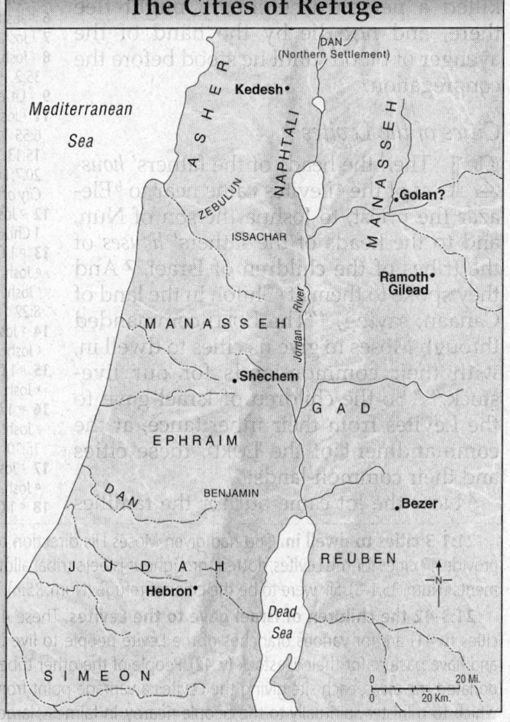

a person accidentally *or* unintentionally
may flee there; and they shall be your
refuge from the avenger of blood. **4** And
when he flees to one of those cities, and
stands at the entrance of the gate of the
city, and [2]declares his case in the hearing
of the elders of that city, they shall take him
into the city as one of them, and give him a
place, that he may dwell among them.
5 [b]Then if the avenger of blood pursues
him, they shall not deliver the slayer into
his hand, because he struck his neighbor
unintentionally, but did not hate him beforehand. **6** And he shall dwell in that city
[c]until he stands before the congregation
for judgment, *and* until the death of the one
who is high priest in those days. Then the
slayer may return and come to his own city
and his own house, to the city from which
he fled.' "
7 So they appointed [d]Kedesh in Galilee,
in the mountains of Naphtali, [e]Shechem in
the mountains of Ephraim, and [f]Kirjath
Arba (which *is* Hebron) in [g]the mountains
of Judah. **8** And on the other side of the Jordan, by Jericho eastward, they assigned
[h]Bezer in the wilderness on the plain, from
the tribe of Reuben, [i]Ramoth in Gilead,
from the tribe of Gad, and [j]Golan in
Bashan, from the tribe of Manasseh.
9 [k]These were the cities appointed for all
the children of Israel and for the stranger
who [3]dwelt among them, that whoever
killed a person accidentally might flee
there, and not die by the hand of the
avenger of blood [l]until he stood before the
congregation.

Cities of the Levites

21 Then the heads of the fathers' *houses* of the [a]Levites came near to [b]Ele-
azar the priest, to Joshua the son of Nun,
and to the heads of the fathers' *houses* of
the tribes of the children of Israel. **2** And
they spoke to them at [c]Shiloh in the land of
Canaan, saying, [d]"The LORD commanded
through Moses to give us cities to dwell in,
with their common-lands for our livestock." **3** So the children of Israel gave to
the Levites from their inheritance, at the
commandment of the LORD, these cities
and their common-lands:
4 Now the lot came out for the families
of the Kohathites. And [e]the children of
Aaron the priest, *who were* of the Levites,
[f]had thirteen cities by lot from the tribe of
Judah, from the tribe of Simeon, and from
the tribe of Benjamin. **5** [g]The rest of the
children of Kohath had ten cities by lot
from the families of the tribe of Ephraim,
from the tribe of Dan, and from the half-
tribe of Manasseh.
6 And [h]the children of Gershon had thirteen cities by lot from the families of the
tribe of Issachar, from the tribe of Asher,
from the tribe of Naphtali, and from the
half-tribe of Manasseh in Bashan.
7 [i]The children of Merari according to
their families had twelve cities from the
tribe of Reuben, from the tribe of Gad, and
from the tribe of Zebulun.
8 [j]And the children of Israel gave these
cities with their common-lands by lot to
the Levites, [k]as the LORD had commanded
by the hand of Moses.
9 So they gave from the tribe of the children of Judah and from the tribe of the
children of Simeon these cities which are
[1]designated by name, **10** which were for
the children of Aaron, one of the families of
the Kohathites, *who were* of the children of
Levi; for the lot was theirs first. **11** [l]And
they gave them [2]Kirjath Arba (*Arba was* the
father of [m]Anak), [n]which *is* Hebron, in the
mountains of Judah, with the common-
land surrounding it. **12** But [o]the fields of
the city and its villages they gave to Caleb
the son of Jephunneh as his possession.
13 Thus [p]to the children of Aaron the
priest they gave [q]Hebron with its common-land (a city of refuge for the slayer),
[r]Libnah with its common-land, **14** [s]Jattir
with its common-land, [t]Eshtemoa with its
common-land, **15** [u]Holon with its common-land, [v]Debir with its common-land,
16 [w]Ain with its common-land, [x]Juttah
with its common-land, and [y]Beth Shemesh
with its common-land: nine cities from
those two tribes; **17** and from the tribe of
Benjamin, [z]Gibeon with its common-land,
[a]Geba with its common-land, **18** Anathoth
with its common-land, and [b]Almon with
its common-land: four cities. **19** All the
cities of the children of Aaron, the priests,
were thirteen cities with their common-
lands.

4 [2] *states*
5 [b] Num. 35:12
6 [c] Num. 35:12, 24, 25
7 [d] Josh. 21:32; 1 Chr. 6:76 [e] Josh. 21:21; 2 Chr. 10:1 [f] Josh. 14:15; 21:11, 13 [g] Luke 1:39
8 [h] Deut. 4:43; Josh. 21:36; 1 Chr. 6:78 [i] Josh. 21:38; 1 Kin. 22:3 [j] Josh. 21:27
9 [k] Num. 35:15 [l] Josh. 20:6 [3] As a resident alien

CHAPTER 21

1 [a] Num. 35:1-8 [b] Num. 34:16-29; Josh. 14:1; 17:4
2 [c] Josh. 18:1 [d] Num. 35:2
4 [e] Josh. 21:8, 19 [f] Josh. 19:51
5 [g] Josh. 21:20
6 [h] Josh. 21:27
7 [i] Josh. 21:34
8 [j] Josh. 21:3 [k] Num. 35:2
9 [1] Lit. *called*
11 [l] Josh. 20:7; 1 Chr. 6:55 [m] Josh. 14:15; 15:13, 14 [n] Josh. 20:7; Luke 1:39 [2] Lit. *City of Arba*
12 [o] Josh. 14:14; 1 Chr. 6:56
13 [p] 1 Chr. 6:57 [q] Josh. 15:54; 20:2, 7 [r] Josh. 15:42; 2 Kin. 8:22
14 [s] Josh. 15:48 [t] Josh. 15:50
15 [u] 1 Chr. 6:58 [v] Josh. 15:49
16 [w] 1 Chr. 6:59 [x] Josh. 15:55 [y] Josh. 15:10
17 [z] Josh. 18:25 [a] Josh. 18:24
18 [b] 1 Chr. 6:60

21:1-3 cities to dwell in. God had given Moses His direction to provide 48 cities for the Levites, dotted throughout Israel's tribal allotments (Num. 35:1-8). Six were to be the cities of refuge (Num. 35:6).

21:3-42 the children of Israel gave to the Levites. These 48 cities (v. 41) are for various branches of the Levite people to live in and have pasture for their livestock (v. 42). People of the other tribes donated the areas, each site giving the Levites a vantage point from which to minister spiritually to the people nearby. In fairness, larger tribes devoted more land, smaller ones less (Num. 35:8). Only the Kohathites were priests, with other branches of Levites assisting in various roles of ritual worship and manual labors.

21:4 Kohathites. Under God's guiding wisdom, these received 13 city areas in the vicinity of Jerusalem or at a reasonable distance within allotments of Judah, Benjamin, and Simeon. This would give them access to carry out priestly functions where God would later have the ark moved and the temple situated (2 Sam. 6).

20 [c]And the families of the children of
Kohath, the Levites, the rest of the children
of Kohath, even they had the cities of their
[3]lot from the tribe of Ephraim. 21 For they
gave them [d]Shechem with its common-
land in the mountains of Ephraim (a city of
refuge for the slayer), [e]Gezer with its common-land, 22 Kibzaim with its common-
land, and Beth Horon with its common-
land: four cities; 23 and from the tribe of
Dan, Eltekeh with its common-land,
Gibbethon with its common-land, 24 [f]Aija-
lon with its common-land, *and* Gath Rimmon with its common-land: four cities;
25 and from the half-tribe of Manasseh,
Tanach with its common-land and Gath
Rimmon with its common-land: two cities.
26 All the ten cities with their common-
lands were for the rest of the families of the
children of Kohath.
27 [g]Also to the children of Gershon, of the
families of the Levites, from the *other* half-
tribe of Manasseh, *they gave* [h]Golan in
Bashan with its common-land (a city of
refuge for the slayer), and Be Eshterah with
its common-land: two cities; 28 and from the
tribe of Issachar, Kishion with its common-
land, Daberath with its common-land,
29 Jarmuth with its common-land, *and* En
Gannim with its common-land: four cities;
30 and from the tribe of Asher, Mishal with
its common-land, Abdon with its common-
land, 31 Helkath with its common-land, and
Rehob with its common-land: four cities;
32 and from the tribe of Naphtali, [i]Kedesh
in Galilee with its common-land (a city of
refuge for the slayer), Hammoth Dor with
its common-land, and Kartan with its common-land: three cities. 33 All the cities of the
Gershonites according to their families *were*
thirteen cities with their common-lands.
34 [j]And to the families of the children of
Merari, the rest of the Levites, from the
tribe of Zebulun, Jokneam with its common-land, Kartah with its common-land,
35 Dimnah with its common-land, *and* Na-
halal with its common-land: four cities;
36 [4]and from the tribe of Reuben, [k]Bezer
with its common-land, Jahaz with its common-land, 37 Kedemoth with its common-
land, and Mephaath with its common-
land: four cities; 38 and from the tribe of
Gad, [l]Ramoth in Gilead with its common-
land (a city of refuge for the slayer), Mahanaim with its common-land, 39 Heshbon
with its common-land, *and* Jazer with its
common-land: four cities in all. 40 So all the
cities for the children of Merari according
to their families, the rest of the families of
the Levites, were *by* their lot twelve cities.
41 [m]All the cities of the Levites within
the possession of the children of Israel *were*
forty-eight cities with their common-lands.
42 Every one of these cities had its common-land surrounding it; thus *were* all
these cities.

The Promise Fulfilled

43 So the LORD gave to Israel [n]all the land
of which He had sworn to give to their fathers, and they [o]took possession of it and
dwelt in it. 44 [p]The LORD gave them [q]rest
all around, according to all that He had
sworn to their fathers. And [r]not a man of
all their enemies stood against them; the
LORD delivered all their enemies into their
hand. 45 [s]Not a word failed of any good
thing which the LORD had spoken to the
house of Israel. All came to pass.

Eastern Tribes Return to Their Lands

22 Then Joshua called the Reubenites,
the Gadites, and half the tribe of
Manasseh, 2 and said to them: "You have
kept [a]all that Moses the servant of the
LORD commanded you, [b]and have obeyed
my voice in all that I commanded you.
3 You have not [1]left your brethren these
many days, up to this day, but have kept
the charge of the commandment of the
LORD your God. 4 And now the LORD your
God has given [c]rest to your brethren, as He
promised them; now therefore, return and
go to your tents *and* to the land of your
possession, [d]which Moses the servant of
the LORD gave you on the other side of the
Jordan. 5 But [e]take[2] careful heed to do the
commandment and the law which Moses
the servant of the LORD commanded you,
[f]to love the LORD your God, to walk in all
His ways, to keep His commandments, to
hold fast to Him, and to serve Him with all
your heart and with all your soul." 6 So
Joshua [g]blessed them and sent them away,
and they went to their tents.
7 Now to half the tribe of Manasseh

20 [c] 1 Chr. 6:66 [3] *allotment*
21 [d] Josh. 20:7 [e] Judg. 1:29
24 [f] Josh. 10:12
27 [g] Josh. 21:6; 1 Chr. 6:71 [h] Josh. 20:8
32 [i] Josh. 20:7
34 [j] Josh. 21:7; 1 Chr. 6:77-81
36 [k] Deut. 4:43; Josh. 20:8 [4] So with LXX, Vg. (cf. 1 Chr. 6:78, 79); MT, Bg., Tg. omit vv. 36, 37
38 [l] Josh. 20:8
41 [m] Num. 35:7
43 [n] Gen. 12:7; 26:3, 4; 28:4, 13, 14 [o] Num. 33:53; Josh. 1:11
44 [p] Deut. 7:23, 24; Josh. 11:23; 22:4 [q] Josh. 1:13, 15; 11:23 [r] Deut. 7:24
45 [s] [Num. 23:19]; Josh. 23:14; 1 Kin. 8:56

CHAPTER 22

2 [a] Num. 32:20-22; Deut. 3:18 [b] Josh. 1:12-18
3 [1] *forsaken*
4 [c] Josh. 21:44 [d] Num. 32:33
5 [e] Deut. 6:6, 17; 11:22; Jer. 12:16 [f] Deut. 10:12; 11:13, 22 [2] *be very careful to do*
6 [g] Gen. 47:7; Ex. 39:43; Josh. 14:13; 2 Sam. 6:18; Luke 24:50

21:43-45 So the LORD gave to Israel all the land. This sums up God's fulfillment of His covenant promise to give Abraham's people the Land (Gen. 12:7; Josh. 1:2,5-9). God also kept His Word in giving the people rest (Deut. 12:9,10). In a valid sense, the Canaanites were in check, under military conquest as God had pledged (Josh. 1:5), not posing an immediate threat. Not every enemy had been driven out, however, leaving some to stir up trouble later. But, God's people failed to exercise their responsibility and possess their land to the full degree in various areas.

22:1 Reubenites...Gadites...Manasseh. The tribes from E of the Jordan had helped their people conquer the land W of the river. Now they were ready to go back to their families to the E.

22:4 Moses...gave you. Clearance from Moses and Joshua for these tribes to possess land E of the Jordan was of God (v. 9; 24:8; Num. 32:30-33).

Moses had given a possession in Bashan,
[h]but to the *other* half of it Joshua gave *a pos-*
session among their brethren on this side of
the Jordan, westward. And indeed, when
Joshua sent them away to their tents, he
blessed them, **8** and spoke to them, saying,
"Return with much riches to your tents,
with very much livestock, with silver, with
gold, with bronze, with iron, and with very
much clothing. [i]Divide the [3]spoil of your
enemies with your brethren."
9 So the children of Reuben, the children
of Gad, and half the tribe of Manasseh returned, and departed from the children of
Israel at Shiloh, which *is* in the land of
Canaan, to go to [j]the country of Gilead, to
the land of their possession, which they
had obtained according to the word of the
LORD by the hand of Moses.

An Altar by the Jordan

10 And when they came to the region of
the Jordan which *is* in the land of Canaan,
the children of Reuben, the children of
Gad, and half the tribe of Manasseh built
an altar there by the Jordan—a great, impressive altar. **11** Now the children of Israel
[k]heard *someone* say, "Behold, the children
of Reuben, the children of Gad, and half
the tribe of Manasseh have built an altar on
the [4]frontier of the land of Canaan, in the
region of the Jordan—on the children of Israel's side." **12** And when the children of
Israel heard *of it,* [l]the whole congregation
of the children of Israel gathered together
at Shiloh to go to war against them.
13 Then the children of Israel [m]sent
[n]Phinehas the son of Eleazar the priest to
the children of Reuben, to the children of
Gad, and to half the tribe of Manasseh, into
the land of Gilead, **14** and with him ten
rulers, one ruler each from the chief house
of every tribe of Israel; and [o]each one *was*
the head of the house of his father among
the [5]divisions of Israel. **15** Then they came
to the children of Reuben, to the children
of Gad, and to half the tribe of Manasseh,
to the land of Gilead, and they spoke with
them, saying, **16** "Thus says the whole congregation of the LORD: 'What [p]treachery [6]*is*
this that you have committed against the
God of Israel, to turn away this day from
following the LORD, in that you have built
for yourselves an altar, [q]that you might
rebel this day against the LORD? **17** *Is* the iniquity [r]of Peor not enough for us, from
which we are not cleansed till this day, although there was a plague in the congregation of the LORD, **18** but that you must
turn away this day from following the
LORD? And it shall be, if you rebel today
against the LORD, that tomorrow [s]He will
be angry with the whole congregation of
Israel. **19** [7]Nevertheless, if the land of your
possession *is* unclean, *then* cross over to the
land of the possession of the LORD, [t]where
the LORD's tabernacle stands, and take possession among us; but do not rebel against
the LORD, nor rebel against us, by building
yourselves an altar besides the altar of the
LORD our God. **20** [u]Did not Achan the son
of Zerah [8]commit a trespass in the [9]ac-
cursed thing, and wrath fell on all the congregation of Israel? And that man did not
perish alone in his iniquity.' "
21 Then the children of Reuben, the children of Gad, and half the tribe of Manasseh answered and said to the heads of
the [1]divisions of Israel: **22** "The LORD [v]God
of gods, the LORD God of gods, He
[w]knows, and let Israel itself know—if *it is*
in rebellion, or if in treachery against the
LORD, do not save us this day. **23** If we have
built ourselves an altar to turn from following the LORD, or if to offer on it burnt
offerings or grain offerings, or if to offer
peace offerings on it, let the LORD Himself
[x]require *an account.* **24** But in fact we have
done it [2]for fear, for a reason, saying, 'In
time to come your descendants may speak
to our descendants, saying, "What have
you to do with the LORD God of Israel?
25 For the LORD has made the Jordan a border between you and us, *you* children of
Reuben and children of Gad. You have no
part in the LORD." So your descendants
would make our descendants cease fearing the LORD.' **26** Therefore we said, 'Let us
now prepare to build ourselves an altar,
not for burnt offering nor for sacrifice,
27 but *that* it *may be* [y]a [3]witness between
you and us and our generations after us,
that we may [z]perform the service of the
LORD before Him with our burnt offerings,
with our sacrifices, and with our peace offerings; that your descendants may not
say to our descendants in time to come,
"You have no part in the LORD." ' **28** Therefore we said that it will be, when they say
this to us or to our generations in time to
come, that we may say, 'Here is the replica
of the altar of the LORD which our fathers

7 [h]Josh. 17:1-13
8 [i]Num. 31:27; 1 Sam. 30:24 [3]*plunder*
9 [j]Num. 32:1, 26, 29
11 [k]Deut. 13:12-18; Judg. 20:12, 13 [4]*Lit. front*
12 [l]Josh. 18:1; Judg. 20:1
13 [m]Deut. 13:14; Judg. 20:12 [n]Ex. 6:25; Num. 25:7, 11-13
14 [o]Num. 1:4 [5]*Lit. thousands*
16 [p]Deut. 12:5-14 [q]Lev. 17:8, 9 [6]*unfaithful act*
17 [r]Num. 25:1-9; Deut. 4:3
18 [s]Num. 16:22
19 [t]Josh. 18:1 [7]*However*
20 [u]Josh. 7:1-26 [8]*act unfaithfully* [9]*devoted thing*
21 [1]*Lit. thousands*
22 [v]Deut. 4:35; 10:17; Is. 44:8; 45:5; 46:9; [1 Cor. 8:5, 6] [w][Job 10:7; 23:10; Jer. 12:3; 2 Cor. 11:11, 31]
23 [x]Deut. 18:19; 1 Sam. 20:16
24 [2]*Lit. from fear*
27 [y]Gen. 31:48; Josh. 22:34; 24:27 [z]Deut. 12:5, 14 [3]*testimony*

22:10-34 an altar...by the Jordan. The special altar built by the 2½ tribes near the river, though well-meant, aroused suspicions among western tribes. They feared rebellion against the Shiloh altar that served all the tribes in unity. When challenged, men of the eastern tribes explained their motives to follow the true God, be in unity with the rest of Israel, and not be regarded as outsiders. The explanation met with other Israelites' approval.

made, though not for burnt offerings nor
for sacrifices; but it *is* a witness between
you and us.' 29 Far be it from us that we
should rebel against the LORD, and turn
from following the LORD this day, [a]to build
an altar for burnt offerings, for grain offerings, or for sacrifices, besides the altar of
the LORD our God which *is* before His
tabernacle."
30 Now when Phinehas the priest and
the rulers of the congregation, the heads of
the [4]divisions of Israel who *were* with him,
heard the words that the children of Reuben, the children of Gad, and the children
of Manasseh spoke, it pleased them.
31 Then Phinehas the son of Eleazar the
priest said to the children of Reuben, the
children of Gad, and the children of Manasseh, "This day we perceive that the
LORD *is* [b]among us, because you have not
committed this treachery against the LORD.
Now you have delivered the children of Israel out of the hand of the LORD."
32 And Phinehas the son of Eleazar the
priest, and the rulers, returned from the
children of Reuben and the children of
Gad, from the land of Gilead to the land of
Canaan, to the children of Israel, and
brought back word to them. 33 So the thing
pleased the children of Israel, and the children of Israel [c]blessed God; they spoke no
more of going against them in battle, to destroy the land where the children of Reuben and Gad dwelt.
34 The children of Reuben and the children of [5]Gad called the altar, *Witness*, "For
it is a witness between us that the LORD *is*
God."

Joshua's Farewell Address

23 Now it came to pass, a long time
after the LORD [a]had given rest to Israel from all their enemies round about,
that Joshua [b]was old, advanced in age.
2 And Joshua [c]called for all Israel, for their
elders, for their heads, for their judges, and
for their officers, and said to them:
"I am old, advanced in age. 3 You have
seen all that the [d]LORD your God has done
to all these nations because of you, for the
[e]LORD your God *is* He who has fought for
you. 4 See, [f]I have divided to you by lot
these nations that remain, to be an inheritance for your tribes, from the Jordan, with
all the nations that I have cut off, as far as
the Great Sea westward. 5 And the LORD
your God [g]will expel them from before
you and drive them out of your sight. So
you shall possess their land, [h]as the LORD
your God promised you. 6 [i]Therefore be
very courageous to keep and to do all that
is written in the Book of the Law of Moses,
[j]lest you turn aside from it to the right
hand or to the left, 7 *and* lest you [k]go[1]
among these nations, these who remain
among you. You shall not [l]make mention
of the name of their gods, nor cause *anyone*
to [m]swear *by them;* you shall not [n]serve
them nor bow down to them, 8 but you
shall [o]hold fast to the LORD your God, as
you have done to this day. 9 [p]For the LORD
has [2]driven out from before you great and
strong nations; but *as for* you, no one has
been able to stand against you to this day.
10 [q]One man of you shall chase a thousand,
for the LORD your God *is* He who fights for
you, [r]as He promised you. 11 [s]Therefore
take careful heed to yourselves, that you
love the LORD your God. 12 Or else, if indeed you do [t]go back, and cling to the
remnant of these nations—these that remain among you—and [u]make marriages
with them, and go in to them and they to
you, 13 know for certain that [v]the LORD
your God will no longer drive out these
nations from before you. [w]But they shall be
snares and traps to you, and scourges on
your sides and thorns in your eyes, until
you perish from this good land which the
LORD your God has given you.
14 "Behold, this day [x]I[3] *am* going the
way of all the earth. And you know in all
your hearts and in all your souls that [y]not
one thing has failed of all the good things
which the LORD your God spoke concerning you. All have come to pass for you; not
one word of them has failed. 15 [z]Therefore
it shall come to pass, that as all the good
things have come upon you which the
LORD your God promised you, so the LORD
will bring upon you [a]all harmful things,
until He has destroyed you from this good
land which the LORD your God has given
you. 16 [4]When you have transgressed the
covenant of the LORD your God, which He
commanded you, and have gone and
served other gods, and bowed down to
them, then the [b]anger of the LORD will

29 [a] Deut. 12:13, 14
30 [4] Lit. *thousands*
31 [b] Ex. 25:8; Lev. 26:11, 12; 2 Chr. 15:2; Zech. 8:23
33 [c] 1 Chr. 29:20; Neh. 8:6; Dan. 2:19; Luke 2:28
34 [5] LXX adds *and half the tribe of Manasseh*

CHAPTER 23

1 [a] Josh. 21:44; 22:4 [b] Josh. 13:1; 24:29
2 [c] Deut. 31:28
3 [d] Ps. 44:3 [e] Ex. 14:14; Deut. 1:30; Josh. 10:14, 42
4 [f] Josh. 13:2, 6; 18:10
5 [g] Ex. 23:30; 33:2 [h] Num. 33:53
6 [i] Josh. 1:7 [j] Deut. 5:32
7 [k] Ex. 23:33; Deut. 7:2, 3; [Prov. 4:14; Eph. 5:11] [l] Ex. 23:13; Ps. 16:4; Jer. 5:7; Hos. 2:17 [m] Deut. 6:13; 10:20 [n] Ex. 20:5 [1] *associate with*
8 [o] Deut. 10:20
9 [p] Deut. 7:24; 11:23; Josh. 1:5 [2] *dispossessed*
10 [q] Lev. 26:8; Deut. 28:7; Is. 30:17 [r] Ex. 14:14
11 [s] Josh. 22:5
12 [t] [2 Pet. 2:20, 21] [u] Deut. 7:3, 4; Ezra 9:2; Neh. 13:25
13 [v] Judg. 2:3 [w] Ex. 23:33; 34:12; Deut. 7:16
14 [x] 1 Kin. 2:2 [y] Josh. 21:45; [Luke 21:33] [3] I am going to die.
15 [z] Deut. 28:63 [a] Lev. 26:14-39; Deut. 28:15-68
16 [b] Deut. 4:24-28 [4] Or *if ever*

23:1 Joshua was old. A long time had passed since he led the conquest ca. 1405–1398 B.C.; Joshua had grown very old, and was 110 when he died (24:29), ca. 1385–1383 B.C. (*see note on 13:1*).

23:5 the LORD...will expel them. God was ready to help His people drive the remaining Canaanites out so that they could possess their claims more fully. Such moves needed to be gradual (Deut. 7:22), but determined, in obedience to God.

23:7,8 The dangers from being incomplete about possessing all the Land included that of intermingling with the godless, as in marriages (v. 12), and committing to their gods, thus drifting from worshiping the true God. The Canaanites would become snares, traps, scourges, and thorns, causing Israelites to eventually lose the Land (vv. 13,15-16).

23:15,16 This actually occurred 800 years later, when Babylon exiled the Israelites ca. 605–586 B.C. (cf. 2 Kin. 24–25).

burn against you, and you shall perish
quickly from the good land which He has
given you."

The Covenant at Shechem

24

Then Joshua gathered all the tribes
of Israel to [a]Shechem and [b]called
for the elders of Israel, for their heads, for
their judges, and for their officers; and they
[c]presented themselves before God. 2 And
Joshua said to all the people, "Thus says
the LORD God of Israel: [d]'Your fathers, *including* Terah, the father of Abraham and
the father of Nahor, dwelt on the other side
of [1]the River in old times; and [e]they served
other gods. 3 [f]Then I took your father
Abraham from the other side of [2]the River,
led him throughout all the land of Canaan,
and multiplied his [3]descendants and
[g]gave him Isaac. 4 To Isaac I gave [h]Jacob
and Esau. To [i]Esau I gave the mountains of
Seir to possess, [j]but Jacob and his children
went down to Egypt. 5 [k]Also I sent Moses
and Aaron, and [l]I plagued Egypt, according to what I did among them. Afterward I
brought you out.

6 'Then I [m]brought your fathers out of
Egypt, and you came to the sea; and the
Egyptians pursued your fathers with chariots and horsemen to the Red Sea. 7 So they
cried out to the LORD; and He put [n]dark-
ness between you and the Egyptians,
brought the sea upon them, and covered
them. And [o]your eyes saw what I did in
Egypt. Then you dwelt in the wilderness
[p]a long time. 8 And I brought you into the
land of the Amorites, who dwelt on the
other side of the Jordan, [q]and they fought
with you. But I gave them into your hand,
that you might possess their land, and I destroyed them from before you. 9 Then
[r]Balak the son of Zippor, king of Moab,
arose to make war against Israel, and [s]sent
and called Balaam the son of Beor to curse
you. 10 [t]But I would not listen to Balaam;
[u]therefore he continued to bless you. So I
delivered you out of his hand. 11 Then
[v]you went over the Jordan and came to Jericho. And [w]the men of Jericho fought
against you—*also* the Amorites, the Perizzites, the Canaanites, the Hittites, the
Girgashites, the Hivites, and the Jebusites.
But I delivered them into your hand. 12 [x]I
sent the hornet before you which drove
them out from before you, *also* the two
kings of the Amorites, *but* [y]not with your
sword or with your bow. 13 I have given
you a land for which you did not labor,
and [z]cities which you did not build, and
you dwell in them; you eat of the vineyards and olive groves which you did not
plant.'

14 [a]"Now therefore, fear the LORD, serve
Him in [b]sincerity and in truth, and [c]put
away the gods which your fathers served
on the other side of [4]the River and [d]in
Egypt. Serve the LORD! 15 And if it seems
evil to you to serve the LORD, [e]choose for
yourselves this day whom you will serve,
whether [f]the gods which your fathers
served that *were* on the other side of [5]the
River, or [g]the gods of the Amorites, in
whose land you dwell. [h]But as for me and
my house, we will serve the LORD."

16 So the people answered and said: "Far
be it from us that we should forsake the
LORD to serve other gods; 17 for the LORD
our God *is* He who brought us and our fathers up out of the land of Egypt, from the
house of bondage, who did those great
signs in our sight, and preserved us in all
the way that we went and among all the
people through whom we passed. 18 And
the LORD drove out from before us all the
people, including the Amorites who dwelt
in the land. [i]We also will serve the LORD,
for He *is* our God."

19 But Joshua said to the people, [j]"You
cannot serve the LORD, for He *is* a [k]holy
God. He *is* [l]a jealous God; [m]He will not forgive your transgressions nor your sins.
20 [n]If you forsake the LORD and serve foreign gods, [o]then He will turn and do you
harm and consume you, after He has done
you good."

21 And the people said to Joshua, "No,
but we will serve the LORD!"

22 So Joshua said to the people, "You *are*

CHAPTER 24
1 [a]Gen. 35:4 [b]Josh. 23:2 [c]1 Sam. 10:19
2 [d]Gen. 11:7-32 [e]Josh. 24:14 [1]The Euphrates
3 [f]Gen. 12:1; Acts 7:2, 3 [g]Gen. 21:1-8; [Ps. 127:3] [2]The Euphrates [3]Lit. *seed*
4 [h]Gen. 25:24-26 [i]Gen. 36:8; Deut. 2:5 [j]Gen. 46:1, 3, 6
5 [k]Ex. 3:10 [l]Ex. 7–10
6 [m]Ex. 12:37, 51; 14:2-31
7 [n]Ex. 14:20 [o]Deut. 4:34 [p]Josh. 5:6
8 [q]Num. 21:21-35
9 [r]Judg. 11:25 [s]Num. 22:2-14
10 [t]Deut. 23:5 [u]Num. 23:11, 20; 24:10
11 [v]Josh. 3:14, 17 [w]Josh. 6:1; 10:1
12 [x]Ex. 23:28; Deut. 7:20 [y]Ps. 44:3
13 [z]Deut. 6:10, 11
14 [a]Deut. 10:12, 13; 1 Sam. 12:24 [b]2 Cor. 1:12 [c]Josh. 24:2, 23; Ezek. 20:18 [d]Ezek. 20:7, 8 [4]The Euphrates
15 [e]Ruth 1:15; 1 Kin. 18:21 [f]Josh. 24:2; Ezek. 20:39 [g]Ex. 23:24, 32 [h]Gen. 18:19; Ps. 101:2; [1 Tim. 3:4, 5] [5]The Euphrates
18 [i]Ps. 116:16
19 [j]Matt. 6:24 [k]Lev. 11:44, 45; 1 Sam. 6:20 [l]Ex. 20:5 [m]Ex. 23:21
20 [n]1 Chr. 28:9; Ezra 8:22; Is. 1:28; 63:10; 65:11, 12; Jer. 17:13 [o]Deut. 4:24-26; Josh. 23:15

24:1-25 It was time for worship and thanksgiving for all God had done leading up to and including the conquest of Canaan.

24:1-5 Joshua reviewed the history recorded in Gen. 11 to Ex. 15.

24:2 the River. The Euphrates, where Abraham's family had lived. It is clear here that God's calling of Abraham out to Himself was also a call out of idolatry, as He does with others (cf. 1 Thess. 1:9).

24:6-13 Joshua reviewed the history recorded in Ex. 12 to Josh. 22.

24:8,15 Amorites. Sometimes this is used as a general term for the entire pagan populace (cf. v. 11) in Canaan, as elsewhere (Gen. 15:16; Judg. 1:34,35). At other times, the name has a narrower reference to people of the hill country (Num. 13:29), distinct from others.

24:9,10 Balaam. *See the note on Josh. 13:22* about the unsavory nature of Balaam in Num. 21–25.

24:12 I sent the hornet before you. This description, as also in Ex. 23:28, is a picturesque figure (cf. also 23:13) portraying God's own fighting to assist Israel (23:3,5,10,18). This awesome force put the enemy to flight, as the feared hornets lit. can do (Deut. 7:20,21).

24:15 choose...this day whom you will serve. Joshua's fatherly model (reminiscent of Abraham's, Gen. 18:19) was for himself and his family to serve the Lord, not false gods. He called others in Israel to this, and they committed themselves to serve the Lord also (vv. 21,24).

24:18 The population joined Joshua in claiming total commitment to serve the Lord (cf. Ex. 19:8).

witnesses against yourselves that [p]you
have chosen the LORD for yourselves, to
serve Him."
And they said, "*We are* witnesses!"
23 "Now therefore," *he said*, [q]"put away
the foreign gods which *are* among you,
and [r]incline your heart to the LORD God of
Israel."
24 And the people [s]said to Joshua, "The
LORD our God we will serve, and His voice
we will obey!"
25 So Joshua [t]made[6] a covenant with the
people that day, and made for them a
statute and an ordinance [u]in Shechem.
26 Then Joshua [v]wrote these words in
the Book of the Law of God. And he took
[w]a large stone, and [x]set it up there [y]under
the oak that *was* by the sanctuary of the
LORD. 27 And Joshua said to all the people,
"Behold, this stone shall be [z]a witness to
us, for [a]it has heard all the words of the
LORD which He spoke to us. It shall therefore be a witness to you, lest you deny
your God." 28 So [b]Joshua let the people depart, each to his own inheritance.

22 [p] Ps. 119:173
23 [q] Gen. 35:2; Josh. 24:14; Judg. 10:15, 16; 1 Sam. 7:3 [r] 1 Kin. 8:57, 58; Ps. 119:36; 141:4
24 [s] Ex. 19:8; 24:3, 7; Deut. 5:24-27
25 [t] Ex. 15:25 [u] Josh. 24:1 [6] Lit. *cut a covenant*
26 [v] Deut. 31:24 [w] Judg. 9:6 [x] Gen. 28:18 [y] Gen. 35:4
27 [z] Gen. 31:48 [a] Deut. 32:1
28 [b] Judg. 2:6, 7
29 [c] Judg. 2:8
30 [d] Josh. 19:50; Judg. 2:9
31 [e] Judg. 2:7 [f] Deut. 11:2
32 [g] Gen. 50:25; Ex. 13:19; Heb. 11:22 [h] Gen. 33:19; John 4:5 [7] Heb. *qesitah*, an unknown ancient measure of weight
33 [i] Ex. 28:1; Num. 20:28; Josh. 14:1 [j] Ex. 6:25

Death of Joshua and Eleazar

29 [c]Now it came to pass after these things
that Joshua the son of Nun, the servant of
the LORD, died, *being* one hundred and ten
years old. 30 And they buried him within
the border of his inheritance at [d]Timnath
Serah, which *is* in the mountains of Ephraim, on the north side of Mount Gaash.
31 [e]Israel served the LORD all the days of
Joshua, and all the days of the elders who
outlived Joshua, who had [f]known all the
works of the LORD which He had done for
Israel.
32 [g]The bones of Joseph, which the children of Israel had brought up out of Egypt,
they buried at Shechem, in the plot of
ground [h]which Jacob had bought from the
sons of Hamor the father of Shechem for
one hundred [7]pieces of silver, and which
had become an inheritance of the children
of Joseph.
33 And [i]Eleazar the son of Aaron died.
They buried him in a hill *belonging to*
[j]Phinehas his son, which was given to him
in the mountains of Ephraim.

24:26 Book of the Law. Joshua expands the first 5 books of Moses, as the canon of revealed Scripture develops. **by the sanctuary.** God's tabernacle, the ark of the covenant, was at Shiloh (21:2). The stone of witness by the holy place (sanctuary) here was at Shechem (24:1). This holy place is not a formal tent or building, but a sacred place by a tree (cf. Gen. 12:6; 35:4), as other places had significance in the past for worship to God (Gen. 21:33).

24:29-33 Joshua…Eleazar. Three prominent leaders were buried as the conquering generation was passing on: Joseph, Joshua, and the High-Priest Eleazar.

24:29 one hundred and ten years old. This was ca. 1383 B.C. (cf. 14:7-10).

24:31 Faithfulness to God extended only one generation (cf. Judg. 2:6-13).

24:32 The bones of Joseph. These had been carried by the Israelites in the Exodus (Ex. 13:19) as Joseph had made them promise (Gen. 50:25). He wanted his remains to lie in the Land of covenant pledge. So now his people laid them to rest at Shechem, in the Land God had guaranteed (Gen. 12:7).

The Book of JUDGES

Title

The book bears the fitting name "Judges," which refers to unique leaders God gave to His people for preservation against their enemies (2:16-19). The Hebrew title means "deliverers" or "saviors," as well as judges (cf. Deut. 16:18; 17:9; 19:17). Twelve such judges arose before Samuel; then Eli and Samuel raised the count to 14. God Himself is the higher Judge (11:27). Judges spans about 350 years from Joshua's conquest (ca. 1398 B.C.) until Eli and Samuel judged prior to the establishment of the monarchy (ca. 1043 B.C.).

Author and Date

No author is named in the book, but the Jewish Talmud identifies Samuel, a key prophet who lived at the time these events took place and could have personally summed up the era (cf. 1 Sam. 10:25). The time was earlier than David's capture of Jerusalem ca. 1004 B.C. (2 Sam. 5:6,7) since Jebusites still controlled the site (Judg. 1:21). Also, the writer deals with a time before a king ruled (17:6; 18:1; 21:25). Since Saul began his reign ca. 1043 B.C., a time shortly after his rule began is probably when Judges was written.

Background and Setting

Judges is a tragic sequel to Joshua. In Joshua, the people were obedient to God in conquering the Land. In Judges, they were disobedient, idolatrous, and often defeated. Judges 1:1–3:6 focuses on the closing days of the book of Joshua. Judges 2:6-9 gives a review of Joshua's death (cf. Josh. 24:28-31). The account describes 7 distinct cycles of Israel's drifting away from the Lord starting even before Joshua's death, with a full departure into apostasy afterward. Five basic reasons are evident for these cycles of Israel's moral and spiritual decline: 1) disobedience in failing to drive the Canaanites out of the Land (Judg. 1:19,21,35); 2) idolatry (2:12); 3) intermarriage with wicked Canaanites (3:5,6); 4) not heeding judges (2:17); and 5) turning away from God after the death of the judges (2:19).

A four-part sequence repeatedly occurred in this phase of Israel's history: 1) Israel's departure from God; 2) God's chastisement in permitting military defeat and subjugation; 3) Israel's prayer pleading for deliverance; and 4) God raising up "judges," either civil or sometimes local military champions who led in shaking off the oppressors. Fourteen judges arose, six of them military judges (Othniel, Ehud, Deborah, Gideon, Jephthah, and Samson). Two men were of special significance for contrast in spiritual leadership: 1) Eli, judge and High-Priest (not a good example); and 2) Samuel, judge, priest, and prophet (a good example).

Historical and Theological Themes

Judges is thematic rather than chronological; foremost among its themes is God's power and covenant mercy in graciously delivering the Israelites from the consequences of their failures, which were suffered for sinful compromise (cf. 2:18,19; 21:25). In 7 periods of sin to salvation (cf. Introduction: Outline), God compassionately delivered His people throughout the different geographical areas of tribal inheritances which He had earlier given through Joshua (Josh. 13–22). The apostasy covered the whole land, as indicated by the fact that each area is specifically identified: southern (3:7-31); northern (4:1–5:31); central (6:1–10:5); eastern (10:6–12:15); and western (13:1–16:31). His power to faithfully rescue shines against the dark backdrop of pitiful human compromise and sometimes bizarre twists of sin, as in the final summary (Judg. 17–21). The last verse (21:25) sums up the account: "In those days *there was* no king in Israel; everyone did *what was* right in his own eyes."

Interpretive Challenges

The most stimulating challenges are: 1) how to view men's violent acts against enemies or fellow countrymen, whether with God's approval or without it; 2) God's use of leaders who at times do His will and at times follow their own sinful impulse (Gideon, Eli, Jephthah, Samson); 3) how to view Jephthah's vow and offering of his daughter (11:30-40); and 4) how to resolve God's sovereign will with His providential working in spite of human sin (cf. 14:4).

The chronology of the various judges in different sectors of the Land raises questions about how much time passed and how the time totals can fit into the entire time span from the Exodus (ca. 1445 B.C.) to Solomon's fourth year, ca. 967/966 B.C., which is said to be 480 years (1 Kin. 6:1; *see Judg. 11:26 and note*). A reasonable explanation is that the deliverances and years of rest under the judges in distinct parts of the Land included overlaps, so that some of them did not run consecutively but rather concurrently during the 480 years. Paul's estimate of "about 450" years in Acts 13:20 is an approximation.

Outline

- I. Introduction and Summary—The Disobedience of Israel (1:1–3:6)
  - A. Incomplete Conquest over the Canaanites (1:1-36)
  - B. The Decline and Judgment of Israel (2:1–3:6)
- II. A Selected History of the Judges—The Deliverance of Israel (3:7–16:31)
  - A. First Period: Othniel vs. Mesopotamians (3:7-11)
  - B. Second Period: Ehud and Shamgar vs. Moabites (3:12-31)
  - C. Third Period: Deborah vs. Canaanites (4:1–5:31)
  - D. Fourth Period: Gideon vs. Midianites (6:1–8:32)
  - E. Fifth Period : Tola and Jair vs. Abimelech's Effects (8:33–10:5)
  - F. Sixth Period: Jephthah, Ibzan, Elon, and Abdon vs. Philistines and Ammonites (10:6–12:15)
  - G. Seventh Period: Samson vs. Philistines (13:1–16:31)
- III. Epilogue—The Dereliction of Israel (17:1–21:25)
  - A. The Idolatry of Micah and the Danites (17:1–18:31)
  - B. The Crime at Gibeah and War Against Benjamin (19:1–21:25)

The Continuing Conquest of Canaan

1 Now after the [a]death of Joshua it came
to pass that the children of Israel
[b]asked the LORD, saying, "Who shall be
first to go up for us against the [c]Canaanites
to fight against them?"
2 And the LORD said, [d]"Judah shall go
up. Indeed I have delivered the land into
his hand."

3 So Judah said to [e]Simeon his brother,
"Come up with me to my allotted territory,
that we may fight against the Canaanites;
and [f]I will likewise go with you to your allotted territory." And Simeon went with
him. 4 Then Judah went up, and the LORD
delivered the Canaanites and the Perizzites into their hand; and they killed ten
thousand men at [g]Bezek. 5 And they found
Adoni-Bezek in Bezek, and fought against
him; and they defeated the Canaanites and
the Perizzites. 6 Then Adoni-Bezek fled,
and they pursued him and caught him and
cut off his thumbs and big toes. 7 And
Adoni-Bezek said, "Seventy kings with
their thumbs and big toes cut off used to
gather *scraps* under my table; [h]as I have
done, so God has repaid me." Then they
brought him to Jerusalem, and there he
died.

8 Now [i]the children of Judah fought
against Jerusalem and took it; they struck
it with the edge of the sword and set the
city on fire. 9 [j]And afterward the children
of Judah went down to fight against the
Canaanites who dwelt in the mountains, in
the [1]South, and in the lowland. 10 Then Judah [2]went against the Canaanites who
dwelt in [k]Hebron. (Now the name of Hebron *was* formerly [l]Kirjath Arba.) And they
killed Sheshai, Ahiman, and Talmai.

11 [m]From there they went against the
inhabitants of Debir. (The name of Debir
was formerly Kirjath Sepher.)

12 [n]Then Caleb said, "Whoever attacks
Kirjath Sepher and takes it, to him I will
give my daughter Achsah as wife." 13 And
Othniel the son of Kenaz, [o]Caleb's younger
brother, took it; so he gave him his daughter Achsah as wife. 14 [p]Now it happened,
when she came *to him,* that [3]she urged him
to ask her father for a field. And she dismounted from *her* donkey, and Caleb said
to her, "What do you wish?" 15 So she said
to him, [q]"Give me a blessing; since you
have given me land in the South, give me
also springs of water."

And Caleb gave her the upper springs
and the lower springs.

16 [r]Now the children of the Kenite, Moses' father-in-law, went up [s]from the City
of Palms with the children of Judah into
the Wilderness of Judah, which *lies* in the
South *near* [t]Arad; [u]and they went and
dwelt among the people. 17 [v]And Judah
went with his brother Simeon, and they attacked the Canaanites who inhabited
Zephath, and utterly destroyed it. So the
name of the city was called [w]Hormah.
18 Also Judah took [x]Gaza with its territory,
Ashkelon with its territory, and Ekron with
its territory. 19 So the LORD was with Judah.
And they drove out the mountaineers, but
they could not drive out the inhabitants of
the lowland, because they had [y]chariots of
iron. 20 [z]And they gave Hebron to Caleb,
as Moses had said. Then he [4]expelled from
there the [a]three sons of Anak. 21 [b]But the
children of Benjamin did not drive out the
Jebusites who inhabited Jerusalem; so the
Jebusites dwell with the children of Benjamin in Jerusalem to this day.

22 And the [5]house of Joseph also went
up against Bethel, [c]and the LORD *was* with

CHAPTER 1

1 [a] Josh. 24:29 [b] Num. 27:21; Judg. 20:18 [c] Josh. 17:12, 13
2 [d] Gen. 49:8, 9; Rev. 5:5
3 [e] Josh. 19:1 [f] Judg. 1:17
4 [g] 1 Sam. 11:8
7 [h] Lev. 24:19; 1 Sam. 15:33; [James 2:13]
8 [i] Josh. 15:63; Judg. 1:21
9 [j] Josh. 10:36; 11:21; 15:13 [1] Heb. *Negev,* and so throughout the book
10 [k] Josh. 15:13-19 [l] Josh. 14:15 [2] *attacked*
11 [m] Josh. 15:15
12 [n] Josh. 15:16, 17
13 [o] Judg. 3:9
14 [p] Josh. 15:18, 19 [3] LXX, Vg. *he urged her*
15 [q] Gen. 33:11
16 [r] Num. 10:29-32; Judg. 4:11, 17; 1 Sam. 15:6; 1 Chr. 2:55 [s] Deut. 34:3; Judg. 3:13 [t] Josh. 12:14 [u] 1 Sam. 15:6
17 [v] Judg. 1:3 [w] Num. 21:3; Josh. 19:4
18 [x] Josh. 11:22
19 [y] Josh. 17:16, 18; Judg. 4:3, 13
20 [z] Num. 14:24; Josh. 14:9, 14 [a] Josh. 15:14; Judg. 1:10 [4] *drove out from there*
21 [b] Josh. 15:63; Judg. 1:8
22 [c] Judg. 1:19 [5] *family*

1:1 after the death of Joshua. Ca. 1383 B.C. (cf. Josh. 14:7-10 with Josh. 24:29). Descriptions of the book's setting in Judg. 1,2 vary between times after Joshua's death and flashbacks summarizing conditions while he was alive (as 2:2-6). Compare Josh. 1:1, "After the death of Moses...."

1:2 Judah shall go up. This tribe received God's first go-ahead to push for a more thorough conquest of its territory. The reason probably lay in God's choice that Judah be the leader among the tribes (Gen. 49:8-12; 1 Chr. 5:1,2) and set the example for them in the other territories.

1:6,7 cut off his thumbs and big toes. Removing the king's thumbs hampered effective use of a weapon; taking off his big toes rendered footing unreliable in battle. The Lord Himself is nowhere said to endorse this tactic, but it was an act of retributive justice for what Adoni-Bezek had done to others. It appears from his confession that he was acknowledging he deserved it.

1:12-15 Caleb said. This repeats the account of Caleb and his family (*see note on Josh. 15:15-19*).

1:16 the City of Palms. Since Jericho was destroyed in the invasion, this refers to the area around Jericho, an oasis of springs and palms (Deut. 34:3).

1:19 they could not drive out. "They" of Judah could not. They had been promised by Joshua that they could conquer the lowland (Josh. 17:16,18) and should have remembered Josh. 11:4-9. This is a recurring failure among the tribes to rise to full trust and obedience for victory by God's power. Compromising for less than what God was able to give (Josh. 1:6-9) began even in Joshua's day (Judg. 2:2-6) and earlier (Num. 13,14). In another sense, God permitted enemies to hold out as a test to display whether His people would obey Him (2:20-23; 3:1,4). Another factor involved keeping the wild animal count from rising too fast (Deut. 7:22).

1:20 sons of Anak. Anak was an early inhabitant of central Canaan near Hebron from whom came an entire group of unusually tall people called the Anakim (Deut. 2:10). They frightened the 10 spies (Num. 13:33; Deut. 9:2), but were finally driven out of the Land by Caleb (Josh. 14:12-15; 15:13-14; 21:11) with the exception of some who resettled with the Philistines (Josh. 11:22). "The sons of Anak" was used as a term equivalent to "the Anakim."

them. 23 So the [6]house of Joseph [d]sent
men to spy out Bethel. (The name of the
city *was* formerly [e]Luz.) 24 And when the
spies saw a man coming out of the city,
they said to him, "Please show us the entrance to the city, and [f]we will show you
mercy." 25 So he showed them the entrance to the city, and they struck the city
with the edge of the sword; but they let
the man and all his family go. 26 And the
man went to the land of the Hittites, built
a city, and called its name Luz, which *is* its
name to this day.

Incomplete Conquest of the Land

27 [g]However, Manasseh did not drive
out *the inhabitants of* Beth Shean and its villages, or [h]Taanach and its villages, or the
inhabitants of [i]Dor and its villages, or the
inhabitants of Ibleam and its villages, or
the inhabitants of Megiddo and its villages; for the Canaanites were determined
to dwell in that land. 28 And it came to
pass, when Israel was strong, that they put
the Canaanites [7]under tribute, but did not
completely drive them out.
29 [j]Nor did Ephraim drive out the
Canaanites who dwelt in Gezer; so the
Canaanites dwelt in Gezer among them.
30 Nor did [k]Zebulun drive out the inhabitants of Kitron or the inhabitants of
Nahalol; so the Canaanites dwelt among
them, and [8]were put under tribute.
31 [l]Nor did Asher drive out the inhabitants of Acco or the inhabitants of Sidon, or
of Ahlab, Achzib, Helbah, Aphik, or
Rehob. 32 So the Asherites [m]dwelt among
the Canaanites, the inhabitants of the land;
for they did not drive them out.
33 [n]Nor did Naphtali drive out the inhabitants of Beth Shemesh or the inhabitants of Beth Anath; but they dwelt among
the Canaanites, the inhabitants of the land.
Nevertheless the inhabitants of Beth
Shemesh and Beth Anath were put under
tribute to them.
34 And the Amorites forced the children
of Dan into the mountains, for they would
not allow them to come down to the valley;
35 and the Amorites were determined to
dwell in Mount Heres, [o]in Aijalon, and in
[9]Shaalbim; yet when the strength of the
house of Joseph became greater, they
[1]were put under tribute.
36 Now the boundary of the Amorites
was [p]from the Ascent of Akrabbim, from
Sela, and upward.

Israel's Disobedience

2 Then the Angel of the LORD came up
from Gilgal to Bochim, and said: [a]"I
led you up from Egypt and [b]brought you
to the land of which I swore to your fathers; and [c]I said, 'I will never break My
covenant with you. 2 And [d]you shall make
no [1]covenant with the inhabitants of this
land; [e]you shall tear down their altars.'
[f]But you have not obeyed My voice. Why
have you done this? 3 Therefore I also said,
'I will not drive them out before you; but
they shall be [g]*thorns*[2] in your side, and
[h]their gods shall [3]be a [i]snare to you.'" 4 So
it was, when the Angel of the LORD spoke
these words to all the children of Israel,
that the people lifted up their voices and
wept.
5 Then they called the name of that place
[4]Bochim; and they sacrificed there to the
LORD. 6 And when [j]Joshua had dismissed
the people, the children of Israel went each
to his own inheritance to possess the land.

Death of Joshua

7 [k]So the people served the LORD all the
days of Joshua, and all the days of the elders who outlived Joshua, who had seen
all the great works of the LORD which He
had done for Israel. 8 Now [l]Joshua the son
of Nun, the servant of the LORD, died *when*
he was one hundred and ten years old.
9 [m]And they buried him within the border
of his inheritance at [n]Timnath Heres, in the
mountains of Ephraim, on the north side of
Mount Gaash. 10 When all that generation
had [5]been gathered to their fathers, another generation arose after them who [o]did
not know the LORD nor the work which He
had done for Israel.

Israel's Unfaithfulness

11 Then the children of Israel did [p]evil in
the sight of the LORD, and served the Baals;

23 [d] Josh. 2:1; 7:2 [e] Gen. 28:19 [6] *family*
24 [f] Josh. 2:12, 14
27 [g] Josh. 17:11-13 [h] Josh. 21:25 [i] Josh. 17:11
28 [7] *to forced labor*
29 [j] Josh. 16:10; 1 Kin. 9:16
30 [k] Josh. 19:10-16 [8] *became forced laborers*
31 [l] Josh. 19:24-31
32 [m] Ps. 106:34, 35
33 [n] Josh. 19:32-39
35 [o] Josh. 19:42 [9] *Shaalabbin*, Josh. 19:42 [1] *became forced laborers*
36 [p] Num. 34:4; Josh. 15:3

CHAPTER 2

1 [a] Ex. 20:2; Judg. 6:8, 9 [b] Deut. 1:8 [c] Gen. 17:7, 8; Lev. 26:42, 44; Deut. 7:9; Ps. 89:34
2 [d] Ex. 23:32; Deut. 7:2 [e] Ex. 34:12, 13; Deut. 12:3 [f] Ps. 106:34 [1] *treaty*
3 [g] Num. 33:55; Josh. 23:13 [h] Judg. 3:6 [i] Ex. 23:33; Deut. 7:16; Ps. 106:36 [2] LXX, Tg., Vg. *enemies to you* [3] *entrap you*
5 [4] Lit. *Weeping*
6 [j] Josh. 22:6; 24:28-31
7 [k] Josh. 24:31
8 [l] Josh. 24:29
9 [m] Josh. 24:30 [n] Josh. 19:49, 50
10 [o] Ex. 5:2; 1 Sam. 2:12; Gal. 4:8; [Titus 1:16] [5] Died and joined their ancestors
11 [p] Judg. 3:7, 12; 4:1; 6:1

1:34 Amorites forced...Dan. Like all other tribes, Dan had a territory given them, but they failed to claim the power of God to conquer that territory. Later they capitulated even more by accepting defeat and migrating to another territory in the N, becoming idolatrous (Judg. 18).

2:1 the Angel of the LORD. One of 3 pre-incarnate theophanies by the Lord Jesus Christ in Judges (cf. 6:11-18; 13:3-23). This same Divine Messenger had earlier led Israel out of Egypt (cf. Ex. 14:19). *See note on Ex. 3:2.* **I will never break My covenant with you.** God would be faithful until the end, but the people would forfeit blessing for trouble, due to their disobedience (cf. v. 3).

2:10 another generation...did not know. The first people in the Land had vivid recollections of all the miracles and judgments and were devoted to faith, duty, and purity. The new generation were ignorant of the experiences of their parents and yielded more easily to corruption. To a marked degree the people of this new generation were not true believers, and were not tuned to the God of miracles and victory. Still, many of the judges did genuinely know the Lord, and some who did not live by faith eventually threw themselves on God's mercy during oppressions.

12 and they [q]forsook the LORD God of their
fathers, who had brought them out of the
land of Egypt; and they followed [r]other
gods from *among* the gods of the people
who *were* all around them, and they
[s]bowed down to them; and they provoked
the LORD to anger. 13 They forsook the
LORD [t]and served [6]Baal and the [7]Ashto-
reths. 14 [u]And the anger of the LORD was
hot against Israel. So He [v]delivered them
into the hands of plunderers who de-
spoiled them; and [w]He sold them into the
hands of their enemies all around, so that
they [x]could no longer stand before their
enemies. 15 Wherever they went out, the
hand of the LORD was against them for
calamity, as the LORD had said, and as the
LORD had [y]sworn to them. And they were
greatly distressed.
16 Nevertheless, [z]the LORD raised up
judges who delivered them out of the hand
of those who plundered them. 17 Yet they
would not listen to their judges, but they
[a]played the harlot with other gods, and
bowed down to them. They turned quickly from the way in which their fathers
walked, in obeying the commandments of
the LORD; they did not do so. 18 And when
the LORD raised up judges for them, [b]the
LORD was with the judge and delivered
them out of the hand of their enemies all
the days of the judge; [c]for the LORD was
moved to pity by their groaning because of
those who oppressed them and harassed
them. 19 And it came to pass, [d]when the
judge was dead, that they reverted and behaved more corruptly than their fathers,
by following other gods, to serve them and
bow down to them. They did not cease
from their own doings nor from their stubborn way.
20 Then the anger of the LORD was hot
against Israel; and He said, "Because this
nation has [e]transgressed My covenant
which I commanded their fathers, and has
not heeded My voice, 21 I also will no

12 [q]Deut. 31:16; Judg. 8:33; 10:6 [r]Deut. 6:14 [s]Ex. 20:5
13 [t]Judg. 10:6; Ps. 106:36 [6]A Canaanite god [7]Canaanite goddesses
14 [u]Deut. 31:17; Judg. 3:8; Ps. 106:40-42 [v]2 Kin. 17:20 [w]Is. 50:1 [x]Lev. 26:37; Josh. 7:12, 13
15 [y]Lev. 26:14-26; Deut. 28:15-68
16 [z]Judg. 3:9, 10, 15; Ps. 106:43-45
17 [a]Ex. 34:15
18 [b]Josh. 1:5 [c]Gen. 6:6
19 [d]Judg. 3:12
20 [e][Josh. 23:16]
21 [f]Josh. 23:4, 5, 13
22 [g]Judg. 3:1, 4 [h]Deut. 8:2, 16; 13:3

CHAPTER 3

1 [a]Judg. 1:1; 2:21, 22 [1]*experienced*
3 [b]Josh. 13:3
4 [2]*find out*
5 [c]Ps. 106:35
6 [d]Ex. 34:15, 16; Deut. 7:3, 4; Josh. 23:12
7 [e]Judg. 2:11 [f]Deut. 32:18 [3]Name or symbol for Canaanite goddesses
8 [g]Deut. 32:30; Judg. 2:14 [h]Hab. 3:7
9 [i]Judg. 3:15 [j]Judg. 2:16

longer drive out before them any of the nations which Joshua [f]left when he died,
22 so [g]that through them I may [h]test Israel,
whether they will keep the ways of the
LORD, to walk in them as their fathers kept
them, or not." 23 Therefore the LORD left
those nations, without driving them out
immediately; nor did He deliver them into
the hand of Joshua.

The Nations Remaining in the Land

3 Now these *are* [a]the nations which the
LORD left, that He might test Israel by
them, *that is,* all who had not [1]known any
of the wars in Canaan 2 (*this was* only so
that the generations of the children of Israel
might be taught to know war, at least those
who had not formerly known it), 3 *namely,*
[b]five lords of the Philistines, all the
Canaanites, the Sidonians, and the Hivites
who dwelt in Mount Lebanon, from Mount
Baal Hermon to the entrance of Hamath.
4 And they were *left, that He might* test Israel by them, to [2]know whether they
would obey the commandments of the
LORD, which He had commanded their fathers by the hand of Moses.
5 [c]Thus the children of Israel dwelt
among the Canaanites, the Hittites, the
Amorites, the Perizzites, the Hivites, and
the Jebusites. 6 And [d]they took their
daughters to be their wives, and gave their
daughters to their sons; and they served
their gods.

Othniel

7 So the children of Israel did [e]evil in the
sight of the LORD. They [f]forgot the LORD
their God, and served the Baals and [3]Ashe-
rahs. 8 Therefore the anger of the LORD was
hot against Israel, and He [g]sold them into
the hand of [h]Cushan-Rishathaim king of
Mesopotamia; and the children of Israel
served Cushan-Rishathaim eight years.
9 When the children of Israel [i]cried out to
the LORD, the LORD [j]raised up a deliverer

2:12 they followed other gods. Idol worship, such as the golden calf in the wilderness (Ex. 32), flared up again. Spurious gods of Canaan were plentiful. El was the supreme Canaanite deity, a god of uncontrolled lust and a bloody tyrant, as shown in writings found at Ras Shamra in N Syria. His name means "strong, powerful." Baal, son and successor of El, was "lord of heaven," a farm god of rain and storm, his name meaning "lord, possessor." His cult at Phoenicia included animal sacrifices, ritual meals, and licentious dances. Chambers catered to sacred prostitution by men and women (cf. 1 Kin. 14:23,24; 2 Kin. 23:7). Anath, sister-wife of Baal, also called Ashtoreth (Astarte), patroness of sex and war, was called "virgin" and "holy" but was actually a "sacred prostitute." Many other gods besides these also attracted worship.

2:14 the anger of the LORD was hot. Calamities designed as chastisement brought discipline intended to lead the people to repentance.

2:16 the LORD raised up judges. A "judge" or deliverer was distinct from a judge in the English world today. Such a leader guided military expeditions against foes as here and arbitrated judicial matters (cf. 4:5). There was no succession or national rule. They were local deliverers, lifted up to leadership by God when the deplorable condition of Israel in the region around them prompted God to rescue the people.

3:1 nations…left. The purpose was to use them to test (cf. v. 4) and discipline the sinful Israelites, as well as to aid the young in learning the art of war.

3:5 *See notes on 1:1-20.*

3:6 *See note on 1:19.* The Israelites failed God's test, being enticed into 1) marriages with Canaanites and 2) worship of their gods. Disobedience was repeated frequently through the centuries, and led God to use the Assyrians (2 Kin. 17) and Babylonians (2 Kin. 24,25) to expel them from the land gained here.

The Judges of Israel

Judge and Tribe	Scripture References	Oppressors	Period of Oppression/Rest
(1) **Othniel** (Judah) Son of Kenaz, younger brother of Caleb	Judg. 1:11-15; 3:1-11; Josh. 15:16-19; 1 Chr. 4:13	Cushan-Rishathaim, king of Mesopotamia	8 years/40 years
(2) **Ehud** (Benjamin) Son of Gera	Judg. 3:12–4:1	Eglon, king of Moab; Ammonites; Amalekites	18 years/80 years
(3) **Shamgar** (Perhaps foreign) Son of Anath	Judg. 3:31; 5:6	Philistines	Not given/Not given
(4) **Deborah** (Ephraim), **Barak** (Naphtali) Son of Abinoam	Judg. 4:1–5:31 Heb. 11:32	Jabin, king of Canaan; Sisera commander of the army	20 years/40 years
(5) **Gideon** (Manasseh) Son of Joash the Abiezrite. Also called: Jerubbaal (6:32; 7:1); Jerubbesheth (2 Sam. 11:21)	Judg. 6:1–8:32 Heb. 11:32	Midianites; Amalekites; "People of the East"	7 years/40 years
(6) **Abimelech** (Manasseh) Son of Gideon by a concubine	Judg. 8:33–9:57; 2 Sam. 11:21	Civil war	Abimelech ruled over Israel 3 years
(7) **Tola** (Issachar) Son of Puah	Judg. 10:1, 2		Judged Israel 23 years
(8) **Jair** (Gilead-Manasseh)	Judg. 10:3-5		Judged Israel 22 years
(9) **Jephthah** (Gilead-Manasseh) Son of Gilead by a harlot	Judg. 10:6–12:7 Heb. 11:32	Philistines; Ammonites; Civil war with the Ephramites	18 years/ Judged Israel 6 years
(10) **Ibzan** (Judah or Zebulun) (Bethlehem-Zebulun; cf. Josh. 19:15)	Judg. 12:8-10		Judged Israel 7 years
(11) **Elon** (Zebulun)	Judg. 12:11, 12		Judged Israel 10 years
(12) **Abdon** (Ephraim) Son of Hillel	Judg. 12:13-15		Judged Israel 8 years
(13) **Samson** (Dan) Son of Manoah	Judg. 13:1–16:31 Heb. 11:32	Philistines	40 years/ Judged Israel 20 years

for the children of Israel, who delivered
them: [k]Othniel the son of Kenaz, Caleb's
younger brother. 10 [l]The Spirit of the LORD
came upon him, and he judged Israel. He
went out to war, and the LORD delivered
Cushan-Rishathaim king of Mesopotamia
into his hand; and his hand prevailed over
Cushan-Rishathaim. 11 So the land had
rest for forty years. Then Othniel the son of
Kenaz died.

Ehud

12 [m]And the children of Israel again did
evil in the sight of the LORD. So the LORD
strengthened [n]Eglon king of Moab against
Israel, because they had done evil in the
sight of the LORD. 13 Then he gathered to
himself the people of Ammon and [o]Ama-
lek, went and [4]defeated Israel, and took
possession of [p]the City of Palms. 14 So the
children of Israel [q]served Eglon king of
Moab eighteen years.
15 But when the children of Israel [r]cried
out to the LORD, the LORD raised up a deliverer for them: Ehud the son of Gera, the
Benjamite, a [s]left-handed man. By him the
children of Israel sent tribute to Eglon king
of Moab. 16 Now Ehud made himself a
dagger (it was double-edged and a cubit in
length) and fastened it under his clothes on
his right thigh. 17 So he brought the tribute
to Eglon king of Moab. (Now Eglon *was* a
very fat man.) 18 And when he had finished presenting the tribute, he sent away
the people who had carried the tribute.
19 But he himself turned back [t]from the
[5]stone images that *were* at Gilgal, and said,
"I have a secret message for you, O king."
He said, "Keep silence!" And all who attended him went out from him.
20 So Ehud came to him (now he was sitting upstairs in his cool private chamber).
Then Ehud said, "I have a message from
God for you." So he arose from *his* seat.
21 Then Ehud reached with his left hand,
took the dagger from his right thigh, and
thrust it into his belly. 22 Even the [6]hilt
went in after the blade, and the fat closed
over the blade, for he did not draw the
dagger out of his belly; and his entrails
came out. 23 Then Ehud went out through
the porch and shut the doors of the upper
room behind him and locked them.
24 When he had gone out, [7]*Eglon's* servants came to look, and *to their* surprise,
the doors of the upper room were locked.
So they said, "He is probably [u]attending[8]
to his needs in the cool chamber." 25 So
they waited till they were [v]embarrassed,
and still he had not opened the doors of
the upper room. Therefore they took the
key and opened *them.* And there was their
master, fallen dead on the floor.
26 But Ehud had escaped while they delayed, and passed beyond the [9]stone images and escaped to Seirah. 27 And it happened, when he arrived, that [w]he blew the
trumpet in the [x]mountains of Ephraim,
and the children of Israel went down with
him from the mountains; and [1]he led them.
28 Then he said to them, "Follow *me,* for
[y]the LORD has delivered your enemies the
Moabites into your hand." So they went
down after him, seized the [z]fords of the
Jordan leading to Moab, and did not allow
anyone to cross over. 29 And at that time
they killed about ten thousand men of
Moab, all stout men of valor; not a man escaped. 30 So Moab was subdued that day
under the hand of Israel. And [a]the land
had rest for eighty years.

Shamgar

31 After him was [b]Shamgar the son of
Anath, who killed six hundred men of the
Philistines [c]with an ox goad; [d]and he also
delivered [e]Israel.

Deborah

4 When Ehud was dead, [a]the children of
Israel again did [b]evil in the sight of the
LORD. 2 So the LORD [c]sold them into the
hand of Jabin king of Canaan, who reigned
in [d]Hazor. The commander of his army *was*
[e]Sisera, who dwelt in [f]Harosheth Hagoyim. 3 And the children of Israel cried
out to the LORD; for Jabin had nine hundred [g]chariots of iron, and for twenty
years [h]he had harshly oppressed the children of Israel.

9 [k]Judg. 1:13
10 [l]Num. 27:18; 1 Sam. 11:6; 2 Chr. 15:1
12 [m]Judg. 2:19 [n]1 Sam. 12:9
13 [o]Judg. 5:14 [p]Deut. 34:3; Judg. 1:16; 2 Chr. 28:15 [4]*struck*
14 [q]Deut. 28:48
15 [r]Ps. 78:34 [s]Judg. 20:16
19 [t]Josh. 4:20 [5]Tg. *quarries*
22 [6]*handle*
24 [u]1 Sam. 24:3 [7]Lit. *his* [8]Lit. *covering his feet*
25 [v]2 Kin. 2:17; 8:11
26 [9]Tg. *quarries*
27 [w]Judg. 6:34; 1 Sam. 13:3 [x]Josh. 17:15 [1]Lit. *he went before them*
28 [y]Judg. 7:9, 15; 1 Sam. 17:47 [z]Josh. 2:7; Judg. 12:5
30 [a]Judg. 3:11
31 [b]Judg. 5:6 [c]1 Sam. 17:47 [d]Judg. 2:16 [e]1 Sam. 4:1

CHAPTER 4

1 [a]Judg. 2:19 [b]Judg. 2:11
2 [c]Judg. 2:14 [d]Josh. 11:1, 10 [e]1 Sam. 12:9; Ps. 83:9 [f]Judg. 4:13, 16
3 [g]Deut. 20:1; Judg. 1:19 [h]Ps. 106:42

3:10 The Spirit of the LORD came. Certain judges were expressly said to have the Spirit of the Lord come upon them (6:34; 11:29; 13:25; 14:6,19; 15:14); others apparently also had this experience. This is a common OT expression signifying a unique act of God which conferred power and wisdom for victory. But this did not guarantee that the will of God would be done in absolutely all details, as is apparent in Gideon (8:24-27,30), Jephthah (11:34-40), and Samson (16:1).

3:20 "I have a message from God for you." Ehud claimed he came to do God's will in answer to prayer (v. 15). Calmly and confidently, Ehud acted and later credited the defeat of the wicked king to God (v. 28; cf. Ps. 75:6,7,10; Dan. 4:25), though it was by means of Ehud, as Jael used her way (4:21) and Israel's armies used the sword (4:16). By God's power, Ehud's army would slay a greater number (v. 29). Men's evil provokes God's judgment (Lev. 18:25).

3:24 "He is...attending to his needs...." The dead king's servants guessed he was indisposed in privacy, lit. "covering his feet," a euphemism for bathroom functions.

3:31 Shamgar. His extraordinary exploit causes one to think of Samson (15:16). **an ox goad.** This was a stout stick about 8-10 ft. long and 6 in. around, with a sharp metal tip to prod or turn oxen. The other end was a flat, curved blade for cleaning a plow.

4 Now Deborah, a prophetess, the wife of Lapidoth, was judging Israel at that time. 5 [i]And she would sit under the palm tree of Deborah between Ramah and Bethel in the mountains of Ephraim. And the children of Israel came up to her for judgment. 6 Then she sent and called for [j]Barak the son of Abinoam from [k]Kedesh in Naphtali, and said to him, "Has not the LORD God of Israel commanded, 'Go and [1]deploy *troops* at Mount [l]Tabor; take with you ten thousand men of the sons of Naphtali and of the sons of Zebulun; 7 and against you [m]I will deploy Sisera, the commander of Jabin's army, with his chariots and his multitude at the [n]River Kishon; and I will [2]deliver him into your hand'?"

8 And Barak said to her, "If you will go with me, then I will go; but if you will not go with me, I will not go!"

9 So she said, "I will surely go with you; nevertheless there will be no glory for you in the journey you are taking, for the LORD will [o]sell Sisera into the hand of a woman." Then Deborah arose and went with Barak to Kedesh. 10 And Barak called [p]Zebulun and Naphtali to Kedesh; he went up with ten thousand men [q]under[3] his command, and Deborah went up with him.

11 Now Heber [r]the Kenite, of the children of [s]Hobab the father-in-law of Moses, had separated himself from the Kenites and pitched his tent near the terebinth tree at Zaanaim, [t]which *is* beside Kedesh.

12 And they reported to Sisera that Barak the son of Abinoam had gone up to Mount Tabor. 13 So Sisera gathered together all his chariots, nine hundred chariots of iron, and all the people who *were* with him, from Harosheth Hagoyim to the River Kishon.

14 Then Deborah said to Barak, [4]"Up! For this *is* the day in which the LORD has delivered Sisera into your hand. [u]Has not the LORD gone out before you?" So Barak went down from Mount Tabor with ten thousand men following him. 15 And the LORD routed Sisera and all *his* chariots and all *his* army with the edge of the sword before Barak; and Sisera alighted from *his* chariot and fled away on foot. 16 But Barak pursued the chariots and the army as far as Harosheth Hagoyim, and all the army of Sisera fell by the edge of the sword; not a man was [v]left.

17 However, Sisera had fled away on foot to the tent of [w]Jael, the wife of Heber the Kenite; for *there was* peace between Jabin king of Hazor and the house of Heber the Kenite. 18 And Jael went out to meet Sisera, and said to him, "Turn aside, my lord, turn aside to me; do not fear." And when he had turned aside with her into the tent, she covered him with a [5]blanket.

19 Then he said to her, "Please give me a little water to drink, for I am thirsty." So she opened [x]a jug of milk, gave him a drink, and covered him. 20 And he said to her, "Stand at the door of the tent, and if any man comes and inquires of you, and says, 'Is there any man here?' you shall say, 'No.' "

21 Then Jael, Heber's wife, [y]took a tent peg and took a hammer in her hand, and went softly to him and drove the peg into his temple, and it went down into the ground; for he was fast asleep and weary. So he died. 22 And then, as Barak pursued Sisera, Jael came out to meet him, and said to him, "Come, I will show you the man whom you seek." And when he went into her *tent*, there lay Sisera, dead with the peg in his temple.

23 So on that day God subdued Jabin king of Canaan in the presence of the children of Israel. 24 And the hand of the children of Israel grew stronger and stronger against Jabin king of Canaan, until they had destroyed Jabin king of Canaan.

The Song of Deborah

5 Then Deborah and Barak the son of Abinoam [a]sang on that day, saying:

2 "When[1] leaders [b]lead in Israel,
[c]When the people [2]willingly offer
themselves,
Bless the LORD!

3 "Hear,[d] O kings! Give ear, O princes!
I, *even* [e]I, will sing to the LORD;
I will sing praise to the LORD God
of Israel.

5 [i] Gen. 35:8
6 [j] Heb. 11:32 [k] Josh. 19:37; 21:32 [l] Judg. 8:18 [1] *march*
7 [m] Ex. 14:4 [n] Judg. 5:21; 1 Kin. 18:40; Ps. 83:9, 10 [2] Lit. *draw*
9 [o] Judg. 2:14
10 [p] Judg. 5:18 [q] Ex. 11:8; 1 Kin. 20:10 [3] Lit. *at his feet*
11 [r] Judg. 1:16 [s] Num. 10:29 [t] Judg. 4:6
14 [u] Deut. 9:3; 31:3; 2 Sam. 5:24; Ps. 68:7; Is. 52:12 [4] *Arise!*
16 [v] Ex. 14:28; Ps. 83:9
17 [w] Judg. 5:6
18 [5] *rug*
19 [x] Judg. 5:24-27
21 [y] Judg. 5:24-27

CHAPTER 5

1 [a] Ex. 15:1; Judg. 4:4
2 [b] Ps. 18:47 [c] 2 Chr. 17:16 [1] Or *When locks are loosed* [2] *volunteer*
3 [d] Deut. 32:1, 3 [e] Ps. 27:6

4:4 Deborah, a prophetess. She was an unusual woman of wisdom and influence who did the tasks of a judge, except for military leadership. God can use women mightily for civil, religious, or other tasks, e.g., Huldah the prophetess (2 Kin. 22:14), Philip's daughters in prophesying (Acts 21:8,9), and Phoebe a deaconess (Rom. 16:1). Deborah's rise to such a role is the exception in the book because of Barak's failure to show the courage to lead courageously (vv. 8,14). God rebuked his cowardice by the pledge that a woman would slay Sisera (v. 9).

4:19,20 she…gave him a drink, and covered him. Usually, this was the strongest pledge of protection possible.

4:21 a tent peg and…a hammer. Jael's bold stroke in a tent rather than on a battlefield draws Deborah's and Barak's praise (5:24-27). Her strength and skill had no doubt been toughened by a common Bedouin duty of hammering down pegs to secure tents, or striking them loose to take down tents.

5:1 sang on that day. The song (vv. 1-31) was in tribute to God for victory in Judg. 4:13-25. Various songs praise God for His help, e.g., Moses' (Ex. 15), David's (2 Sam. 23:1-7), and the Lamb's (Rev. 15:3,4).

4 "LORD, [f]when You went out from
Seir,
When You marched from [g]the field
of Edom,
The earth trembled and the
heavens poured,
The clouds also poured water;
5 [h]The mountains [3]gushed before the
LORD,
[i]This Sinai, before the LORD God of
Israel.

6 "In the days of [j]Shamgar, son of
Anath,
In the days of [k]Jael,
[l]The highways were deserted,
And the travelers walked along the
byways.
7 Village life ceased, it ceased in
Israel,
Until I, Deborah, arose,
Arose a mother in Israel.
8 They chose [m]new gods;
Then *there was* war in the gates;
Not a shield or spear was seen
among forty thousand in
Israel.
9 My heart *is* with the rulers of Israel
Who offered themselves willingly
with the people.
Bless the LORD!

10 "Speak, you who ride on white
[n]donkeys,
Who sit in judges' attire,
And who walk along the road.
11 Far from the noise of the archers,
among the watering places,
There they shall recount the
righteous acts of the LORD,
The righteous acts *for* His villagers
in Israel;
Then the people of the LORD shall
go down to the gates.

12 "Awake,[o] awake, Deborah!
Awake, awake, sing a song!
Arise, Barak, and lead your
captives away,
O son of Abinoam!

4 [f]Deut. 33:2; Ps. 68:7 [g]Ps. 68:8
5 [h]Ps. 97:5 [i]Ex. 19:18 [3]*flowed*
6 [j]Judg. 3:31 [k]Judg. 4:17 [l]Is. 33:8
8 [m]Deut. 32:17
10 [n]Judg. 10:4; 12:14
12 [o]Ps. 57:8

13 "Then the survivors came down, the
people against the nobles;
The LORD came down for me
against the mighty.
14 From Ephraim *were* those whose
roots were in [p]Amalek.
After you, Benjamin, with your
peoples,
From Machir rulers came down,
And from Zebulun those who bear
the recruiter's staff.
15 And [4]the princes of Issachar *were*
with Deborah;
As Issachar, so *was* Barak
Sent into the valley [5]under his
command;
Among the divisions of Reuben
There were great resolves of heart.
16 Why did you sit among the
sheepfolds,
To hear the pipings for the flocks?
The divisions of Reuben have great
searchings of heart.
17 [q]Gilead stayed beyond the Jordan,
And why did Dan remain [6]on
ships?
[r]Asher continued at the seashore,
And stayed by his inlets.
18 [s]Zebulun *is* a people *who*
jeopardized their lives to the
point of death,
Naphtali also, on the heights of the
battlefield.

19 "The kings came *and* fought,
Then the kings of Canaan fought
In [t]Taanach, by the waters of
Megiddo;
They took no spoils of silver.
20 They fought from the heavens;
The stars from their courses fought
against Sisera.
21 [u]The torrent of Kishon swept them
away,
That ancient torrent, the torrent of
Kishon.
O my soul, march on in strength!
22 Then the horses' hooves pounded,
The galloping, galloping of his
steeds.

14 [p]Judg. 3:13
15 [4]So with LXX, Syr., Tg., Vg.; MT *And my princes in Issachar* [5]Lit. *at his feet*
17 [q]Josh. 22:9 [r]Josh. 19:29, 31 [6]Or *at ease*
18 [s]Judg. 4:6, 10
19 [t]Judg. 1:27
21 [u]Judg. 4:7

5:10 white donkeys. Because of this unusual color, they were a prize of kings and the rich.

5:11 Far from the noise of the archers, among the watering places. The wells were at a little distance from towns in the E, away from the battles and often places for pleasant reflection.

5:14 roots were in Amalek. Ephraim as a tribe took the central hill area, which the Amalekites had held with deep roots.

5:17 why did Dan remain on ships? Danites migrated from their territory to Laish N of the Lake of Chinneroth (Sea of Galilee) before the Israelite triumph of Judg. 4, though details of it are not given until Judg. 18. They became involved with Phoenicians of the NW in ship commerce (cf. Joppa as a coastal city, Josh. 19:46). As with some other tribes, they failed to make the trek to assist in the battle of Judg. 4.

5:20 stars...fought. A poetic way to say that God used these heavenly bodies to help Israel. They are bodies representing and synonymous with the heavens, the sky from which He sent a powerful storm and flood (cf. "torrent" of the Kishon River, v. 21) that swept Syrians from their chariots. God also hid the stars by clouds, increasing Syrian ineffectiveness.

23 'Curse Meroz,' said the [7]angel of
the LORD,
'Curse its inhabitants bitterly,
Because they did not come to the
help of the LORD,
To the help of the LORD against the
mighty.'

24 "Most blessed among women is
Jael,
The wife of Heber the Kenite;
[v]Blessed is she among women in
tents.
25 He asked for water, she gave milk;
She brought out cream in a lordly
bowl.
26 She stretched her hand to the tent
peg,
Her right hand to the workmen's
hammer;
She pounded Sisera, she pierced
his head,
She split and struck through his
temple.
27 At her feet he sank, he fell, he lay
still;
At her feet he sank, he fell;
Where he sank, there he fell [w]dead.

28 "The mother of Sisera looked
through the window,
And cried out through the lattice,
'Why is his chariot *so* long in
coming?
Why tarries the clatter of his
chariots?'
29 Her wisest [8]ladies answered her,
Yes, she [9]answered herself,
30 'Are they not finding and dividing
the spoil:
To every man a girl *or* two;
For Sisera, plunder of dyed
garments,
Plunder of garments embroidered
and dyed,
Two pieces of dyed embroidery for
the neck of the looter?'

31 "Thus let all Your enemies [x]perish,
O LORD!
But *let* those who love Him *be* [y]like
the [z]sun
When it comes out in full
[a]strength."

So the land had rest for forty years.

Midianites Oppress Israel

6 Then the children of Israel did [a]evil in
the sight of the LORD. So the LORD delivered them into the hand of [b]Midian for
seven years, 2 and the hand of Midian prevailed against Israel. Because of the Midianites, the children of Israel made for
themselves the dens, [c]the caves, and the
strongholds which *are* in the mountains.
3 So it was, whenever Israel had sown,
Midianites would come up; also Amalekites and the [d]people of the East would
come up against them. 4 Then they would
encamp against them and [e]destroy the produce of the earth as far as Gaza, and leave
no sustenance for Israel, neither sheep nor
ox nor [f]donkey. 5 For they would come up
with their livestock and their tents, coming
in as numerous as locusts; both they and
their camels were [1]without number; and
they would enter the land to destroy it.
6 So Israel was greatly impoverished because of the Midianites, and the children of
Israel [g]cried out to the LORD.
7 And it came to pass, when the children
of Israel cried out to the LORD because of
the Midianites, 8 that the LORD sent a
prophet to the children of Israel, who said
to them, "Thus says the LORD God of Israel:
'I brought you up from Egypt and brought
you out of the [h]house of [2]bondage; 9 and I
delivered you out of the hand of the Egyptians and out of the hand of all who oppressed you, and [i]drove them out before
you and gave you their land. 10 Also I said
to you, "I *am* the LORD your God; [j]do not
fear the gods of the Amorites, in whose
land you dwell." But you have not obeyed
My [k]voice.' "

Gideon

11 Now the Angel of the LORD came and
sat under the terebinth tree which *was* in
Ophrah, which *belonged* to Joash [l]the Abi-

23 [7] Or *Angel*
24 [v] [Luke 1:28]
27 [w] Judg. 4:18-21
29 [8] *princesses* [9] Lit. *repeats her words to herself*
31 [x] Ps. 92:9 [y] 2 Sam. 23:4 [z] Ps. 37:6; 89:36, 37 [a] Ps. 19:5

CHAPTER 6

1 [a] Judg. 2:11 [b] Num. 22:4; 31:1-3
2 [c] 1 Sam. 13:6; Heb. 11:38
3 [d] Judg. 7:12
4 [e] Lev. 26:16 [f] Deut. 28:31
5 [1] *innumerable*
6 [g] Ps. 50:15; Hos. 5:15
8 [h] Josh. 24:17 [2] *slavery*
9 [i] Ps. 44:2, 3
10 [j] 2 Kin. 17:35, 37, 38; Jer. 10:2 [k] Judg. 2:1, 2
11 [l] Josh. 17:2; Judg. 6:15

5:24-27 Though this act was murder and a breach of honor, likely motivated by her desire for favor with the conquering Israelites, and though it was without regard for God on her part, God's overruling providence caused great blessing to flow from it. Thus the words of vv. 24-27 in the victory song.

5:31 The intercessory prayer committed to God's will ends a song that has other aspects: blessing God (v. 2), praise (v. 3), affirming God's work in tribute (vv. 4,20), and voicing God's curse (v. 23).

6:1 Midian. These wandering herdsmen from E of the Red Sea had been dealt a severe blow in Moses' time (Num. 31:1-18) and still resented the Israelites. They became the worst scourge yet to afflict Israel.

6:8 the LORD sent a prophet. He used prophets in isolated cases before Samuel, the band of prophets Samuel probably founded (1 Sam. 10:5), and later such prophets as Elijah, Elisha, and the writing prophets—major and minor. Here the prophet is sent to bring the divine curse because of their infidelity (v. 10).

6:11 the Angel. This angel (lit. "messenger") of the Lord is identified as "the LORD" Himself (vv. 14,16,23,25,27). Cf. Gen. 16:7-14; 18:1; 32:24-30 for other appearances. *See note on Ex. 3:2.* **Gideon**

ezrite, while his son [m]Gideon threshed
wheat in the winepress, in order to hide *it*
from the Midianites. 12 And the [n]Angel of
the LORD appeared to him, and said to him,
"The LORD *is* [o]with you, you mighty man
of valor!"
13 Gideon said to Him, "O [3]my lord, if the
LORD is with us, why then has all this happened to us? And [p]where *are* all His miracles
[q]which our fathers told us about, saying,
'Did not the LORD bring us up from Egypt?'
But now the LORD has [r]forsaken us and delivered us into the hands of the Midianites."
14 Then the LORD turned to him and
said, [s]"Go in this might of yours, and you
shall save Israel from the hand of the Midianites. [t]Have I not sent you?"
15 So he said to Him, "O [4]my Lord, how
can I save Israel? Indeed [u]my clan *is* the
weakest in Manasseh, and I *am* the least in
my father's house."
16 And the LORD said to him, [v]"Surely I
will be with you, and you shall [5]defeat the
Midianites as one man."
17 Then he said to Him, "If now I have
found favor in Your sight, then [w]show me
a sign that it is You who talk with me.
18 [x]Do not depart from here, I pray, until I
come to You and bring out my offering and
set *it* before You."
And He said, "I will wait until you come
back."
19 [y]So Gideon went in and prepared a
young goat, and unleavened bread from
an ephah of flour. The meat he put in a basket, and he put the broth in a pot; and he
brought *them* out to Him under the terebinth tree and presented *them*. 20 The
Angel of God said to him, "Take the meat
and the unleavened bread and [z]lay *them* on
this rock, and [a]pour out the broth." And he
did so.
21 Then the Angel of the LORD put out
the end of the staff that *was* in His hand,
and touched the meat and the unleavened
bread; and [b]fire rose out of the rock and
consumed the meat and the unleavened
bread. And the Angel of the LORD departed
out of his sight.
22 Now Gideon [c]perceived that He *was*
the Angel of the LORD. So Gideon said,
"Alas, O Lord GOD! [d]For I have seen the
Angel of the LORD face to face."
23 Then the LORD said to him, [e]"Peace *be*
with you; do not fear, you shall not die."
24 So Gideon built an altar there to the LORD,
and called it [6]The-LORD-*Is*-Peace. To this
day it *is* still [f]in Ophrah of the Abiezrites.
25 Now it came to pass the same night that
the LORD said to him, "Take your father's
young bull, the second bull of seven years
old, and [g]tear down the altar of [h]Baal that
your father has, and [i]cut down the [7]wooden
image that *is* beside it; 26 and build an altar
to the LORD your God on top of this [8]rock in
the proper arrangement, and take the second bull and offer a burnt sacrifice with the
wood of the image which you shall cut
down." 27 So Gideon took ten men from
among his servants and did as the LORD had
said to him. But because he feared his father's household and the men of the city too
much to do *it* by day, he did *it* by night.

Gideon Destroys the Altar of Baal

28 And when the men of the city arose
early in the morning, there was the altar of
Baal, torn down; and the wooden image
that *was* beside it was cut down, and the
second bull was being offered on the altar
which had been built. 29 So they said to one
another, "Who has done this thing?" And
when they had inquired and asked, they
said, "Gideon the son of Joash has done
this thing." 30 Then the men of the city said
to Joash, "Bring out your son, that he may
die, because he has torn down the altar of
Baal, and because he has cut down the
wooden image that *was* beside it."
31 But Joash said to all who stood against
him, "Would you [9]plead for Baal? Would
you save him? Let the one who would
plead for him be put to death by morning!
If he *is* a god, let him plead for himself, because his altar has been torn down!"
32 Therefore on that day he called him [j]Jer-
ubbaal,[1] saying, "Let Baal plead against
him, because he has torn down his altar."

11 [m] Judg. 7:1; Heb. 11:32
12 [n] Judg. 13:3; Luke 1:11, 28 [o] Josh. 1:5
13 [p] [Is. 59:1] [q] Josh. 4:6, 21; Ps. 44:1 [r] Deut. 31:17; 2 Chr. 15:2; Ps. 44:9-16 [3] Heb. *adoni*, used of man
14 [s] 1 Sam. 12:11 [t] Josh. 1:9
15 [u] 1 Sam. 9:21 [4] Heb. *Adonai*, used of God
16 [v] Ex. 3:12; Josh. 1:5 [5] Lit. *strike*
17 [w] Judg. 6:36, 37; 2 Kin. 20:8; Ps. 86:17; Is. 7:11; 38:7, 8
18 [x] Gen. 18:3, 5
19 [y] Gen. 18:6-8
20 [z] Judg. 13:19 [a] 1 Kin. 18:33, 34
21 [b] Lev. 9:24
22 [c] Gen. 32:30; Ex. 33:20; Judg. 13:21, 22 [d] Gen. 16:13
23 [e] Dan. 10:19
24 [f] Judg. 8:32 [6] Heb. *YHWH Shalom*
25 [g] Judg. 2:2 [h] Judg. 3:7 [i] Ex. 34:13; Deut. 7:5 [7] Heb. *Asherah*, a Canaanite goddess
26 [8] *stronghold*
31 [9] *contend*
32 [j] Judg. 7:1; 1 Sam. 12:11; 2 Sam. 11:21 [1] Lit. *Let Baal Plead*

threshed wheat in the winepress…to hide *it*. This indicated a situation of serious distress; also it indicated a small amount of grain. This is clear because he is doing it rather than having cattle tread it. It is on bare ground or in the winepress rather than on a threshing floor made of wood, and is done remotely under a tree out of view. The fear of the Midianites caused this.

6:13 Gideon's language here indicates a weak theology. The very chastisements of God were proof of His care for and presence with Israel.

6:17 Like Moses (Ex. 33), Gideon desired a sign; in both incidents revelation was so rare and wickedness so prevalent that they desired full assurance. God graciously gave it.

6:18-23 In the realization of the presence of God, the sensitive sinner is conscious of great guilt. Fire from God further filled Gideon with awe and even the fear of death. When he saw the Lord, he knew the Lord had also seen him in his fallenness. Thus he feared the death that sinners should die before Holy God. But God graciously promised life (v. 23). For a similar reaction to the presence of God, see Manoah in 13:22,23 (cf. Ezek. 1:26-28; Is. 6:1-9; Rev. 1:17).

6:27 he feared. Very real human fear and wise precaution interplays with trust in an all-sufficient God.

6:32 Jerubaal (lit. "let Baal contend") became a fitting and honorable second name for Gideon (7:1; 8:29; 9:1,2). This was a bold rebuke to the non-existent deity, who was utterly unable to respond.

33 Then all [k]the Midianites and Amalekites, the people of the East, gathered together; and they crossed over and encamped in [l]the Valley of Jezreel. 34 But
[m]the Spirit of the LORD came upon Gideon;
then he [n]blew the trumpet, and the Abiezrites gathered behind him. 35 And he
sent messengers throughout all Manasseh,
who also gathered behind him. He also
sent messengers to [o]Asher, [p]Zebulun, and
Naphtali; and they came up to meet them.

The Sign of the Fleece

36 So Gideon said to God, "If You will
save Israel by my hand as You have said—
37 [q]look, I shall put a fleece of wool on the
threshing floor; if there is dew on the fleece
only, and *it is* dry on all the ground, then I
shall know that You will save Israel by my
hand, as You have said." 38 And it was so.
When he rose early the next morning and
squeezed the fleece together, he wrung the
dew out of the fleece, a bowlful of water.
39 Then Gideon said to God, [r]"Do not be
angry with me, but let me speak just once
more: Let me test, I pray, just once more
with the fleece; let it now be dry only on
the fleece, but on all the ground let there be
dew." 40 And God did so that night. It was
dry on the fleece only, but there was dew
on all the ground.

Gideon's Valiant Three Hundred

7 Then [a]Jerubbaal (that *is*, Gideon) and
all the people who *were* with him rose
early and encamped beside the well of
Harod, so that the camp of the Midianites
was on the north side of them by the hill of
Moreh in the valley.
2 And the LORD said to Gideon, "The
people who *are* with you *are* too many for
Me to give the Midianites into their hands,
lest Israel [b]claim glory for itself against
Me, saying, 'My own hand has saved me.'
3 Now therefore, proclaim in the hearing of
the people, saying, [c]'Whoever *is* fearful
and afraid, let him turn and depart at once
from Mount Gilead.'" And twenty-two
thousand of the people returned, and ten
thousand remained.
4 But the LORD said to Gideon, "The people *are* still *too* many; bring them down to
the water, and I will test them for you there.
Then it will be, *that* of whom I say to you,
'This one shall go with you,' the same shall
go with you; and of whomever I say to you,
'This one shall not go with you,' the same
shall not go." 5 So he brought the people
down to the water. And the LORD said to
Gideon, "Everyone who laps from the
water with his tongue, as a dog laps, you
shall set apart by himself; likewise everyone who gets down on his knees to drink."
6 And the number of those who lapped,
putting their hand to their mouth, was three
hundred men; but all the rest of the people
got down on their knees to drink water.
7 Then the LORD said to Gideon, [d]"By the
three hundred men who lapped I will save
you, and deliver the Midianites into your
hand. Let all the *other* people go, every man
to his [1]place." 8 So the people took provisions and their trumpets in their hands.
And he sent away all *the rest of* Israel, every
man to his tent, and retained those three
hundred men. Now the camp of Midian
was below him in the valley.
9 It happened on the same [e]night that
the LORD said to him, "Arise, go down
against the camp, for I have delivered it
into your hand. 10 But if you are afraid to
go down, go down to the camp with Purah
your servant, 11 and you shall [f]hear what
they say; and afterward [2]your hands shall
be strengthened to go down against the
camp." Then he went down with Purah his
servant to the outpost of the armed men
who *were* in the camp. 12 Now the Midianites and Amalekites, [g]all the people of the
East, were lying in the valley [h]as numerous
as locusts; and their camels *were* [3]without
number, as the sand by the seashore in
multitude.
13 And when Gideon had come, there
was a man telling a dream to his companion. He said, "I have had a dream: *To my*

33 [k]Judg. 6:3 [l]Josh. 17:16; Hos. 1:5
34 [m]Judg. 3:10; 1 Chr. 12:18; 2 Chr. 24:20 [n]Num. 10:3; Judg. 3:27
35 [o]Judg. 5:17; 7:23 [p]Judg. 4:6, 10; 5:18
37 [q][Ex. 4:3-7]
39 [r]Gen. 18:32

CHAPTER 7

1 [a]Judg. 6:32
2 [b]Deut. 8:17; Is. 10:13
3 [c]Deut. 20:8
7 [d]1 Sam. 14:6 [1]*home*
9 [e]Gen. 46:2, 3; Judg. 6:25
11 [f]Gen. 24:14; 1 Sam. 14:9, 10 [2]*you shall be encouraged*
12 [g]Judg. 6:3, 33; 8:10 [h]Judg. 6:5 [3]*innumerable*

6:36-40 Gideon's two requests for signs in the fleece should be viewed as weak faith; even Gideon recognized this when he said "do not be angry with me" (v. 9) since God had already specifically promised His presence and victory (vv. 12,14,16). But they were also legitimate requests for confirmation of victory against seemingly impossible odds (6:5; 7:2,12). God nowhere reprimanded Gideon, but was very compassionate in giving what his inadequacy requested. In 7:10-15, God volunteered a sign to boost Gideon's faith. He should have believed God's promise in 7:9 but needed bolstering, so God graciously gave it without chastisement.

7:2 The people...*are* too many. Those of faith, though inadequate by human weakness, gain victory only through God's power (cf. 2 Cor. 3:5; 4:7; 12:7-9). Three hundred men win against an incredible Midianite host (Judg. 7:7,16-25). God gains the glory by making the outcome conspicuously His act, and no sinful pride is cultivated.

7:5 Everyone who laps. Soldiers who lapped as a dog, scooping water with their hands as a dog uses its tongue, were chosen; while those who sank to their knees to drink were rejected. No reason for such distinction is given, so that it showed nothing about their ability as soldiers. It was merely a way to divide the crowd. Their abilities as soldiers had no bearing on the victory anyway since the enemy soldiers killed themselves and fled without engaging Gideon's men at all.

7:10 if you are afraid. God sensitively recognized Gideon's normal fear since he was the commander. God encouraged him to take his servant as protection. *See note on 6:36-40.*

surprise, a loaf of barley bread tumbled
into the camp of Midian; it came to a tent
and struck it so that it fell and overturned,
and the tent collapsed."
14 Then his companion answered and
said, "This *is* nothing else but the sword of
Gideon the son of Joash, a man of Israel!
Into his hand [i]God has delivered Midian
and the whole camp."
15 And so it was, when Gideon heard the
telling of the dream and its interpretation,
that he worshiped. He returned to the
camp of Israel, and said, "Arise, for the
LORD has delivered the camp of Midian
into your hand." 16 Then he divided the
three hundred men *into* three companies,
and he put a trumpet into every man's
hand, with empty pitchers, and torches inside the pitchers. 17 And he said to them,
"Look at me and do likewise; watch, and
when I come to the edge of the camp you
shall do as I do: 18 When I blow the trumpet, I and all who *are* with me, then you
also blow the trumpets on every side of the
whole camp, and say, '*The sword of* the
LORD and of Gideon!' "
19 So Gideon and the hundred men who
were with him came to the outpost of the
camp at the beginning of the middle
watch, just as they had posted the watch;
and they blew the trumpets and broke the
pitchers that *were* in their hands. 20 Then
the three companies blew the trumpets
and broke the pitchers—they held the
torches in their left hands and the trumpets
in their right hands for blowing—and they
cried, "The sword of the LORD and of Gideon!" 21 And [j]every man stood in his place
all around the camp; [k]and the whole army
ran and cried out and fled. 22 When the
three hundred [l]blew the trumpets, [m]the
LORD set [n]every man's sword against his
companion throughout the whole camp;
and the army fled to [4]Beth Acacia, toward
Zererah, as far as the border of [o]Abel Meholah, by Tabbath.
23 And the men of Israel gathered together from [p]Naphtali, Asher, and all Manasseh, and pursued the Midianites.
24 Then Gideon sent messengers
throughout all the [q]mountains of Ephraim,
saying, "Come down against the Midianites, and seize from them the watering
places as far as Beth Barah and the Jordan." Then all the men of Ephraim gathered together and [r]seized the watering
places as far as [s]Beth Barah and the Jordan.
25 And they captured [t]two princes of the
Midianites, [u]Oreb and Zeeb. They killed
Oreb at the rock of Oreb, and Zeeb they
killed at the winepress of Zeeb. They pursued Midian and brought the heads of
Oreb and Zeeb to Gideon on the [v]other
side of the Jordan.

Gideon Subdues the Midianites

8 Now [a]the men of Ephraim said to him,
"Why have you done this to us by not
calling us when you went to fight with the
Midianites?" And they reprimanded him
sharply.
2 So he said to them, "What have I done
now in comparison with you? *Is* not the
[1]gleaning *of the grapes* of Ephraim better
than [2]the vintage of [b]Abiezer? 3 [c]God has
delivered into your hands the princes of
Midian, Oreb and Zeeb. And what was I
able to do in comparison with you?" Then
their [d]anger toward him subsided when he
said that.
4 When Gideon came [e]to the Jordan, he
and [f]the three hundred men who *were* with
him crossed over, exhausted but still in
pursuit. 5 Then he said to the men of [g]Suc-
coth, "Please give loaves of bread to the
people who follow me, for they are exhausted, and I am pursuing Zebah and
Zalmunna, kings of Midian."
6 And the leaders of Succoth said, [h]"*Are*[3]
the hands of Zebah and Zalmunna now in
your hand, that [i]we should give bread to
your army?"
7 So Gideon said, "For this cause, when
the LORD has delivered Zebah and Zalmunna into my hand, [j]then I will tear your

14 [i]Judg. 6:14, 16
21 [j]Ex. 14:13, 14; 2 Chr. 20:17 [k]2 Kin. 7:7
22 [l]Josh. 6:4, 16, 20 [m]Ps. 83:9; Is. 9:4 [n]1 Sam. 14:20; 2 Chr. 20:23 [o]1 Kin. 4:12 [4]Heb. *Beth Shittah*
23 [p]Judg. 6:35
24 [q]Judg. 3:27 [r]Judg. 3:28 [s]John 1:28
25 [t]Judg. 8:3 [u]Ps. 83:11; Is. 10:26 [v]Judg. 8:4

CHAPTER 8

1 [a]Judg. 12:1; 2 Sam. 19:41
2 [b]Judg. 6:11 [1]Few grapes left after the harvest [2]The whole harvest
3 [c]Judg. 7:24, 25 [d]Prov. 15:1
4 [e]Judg. 7:25 [f]Judg. 7:6
5 [g]Gen. 33:17; Ps. 60:6
6 [h]1 Kin. 20:11; Judg. 8:15 [i]1 Sam. 25:11 [3]Lit. *Is the palm*
7 [j]Judg. 8:16

7:15 Arise. God said this in 7:9. Infused with courage, Gideon is in step with the Lord.

7:16 Trumpets and torches at first concealed within clay pitchers were suddenly displayed at the most startling moment. The impression caused by blaring noise, the always terrible shouts of Israel (cf. Num. 28:21), and sudden lights surrounding the sleeping hosts and shattering the stillness conveyed one idea: Each light could mean a legion behind it, so that they believed an incredible host had moved in to catch the awaking army in a death trap.

7:18 *The sword of* the LORD and of Gideon! Here was the power of God in harmony with the obedience of man. Such shouts reminded the enemies that the threat of the sword of Gideon and of God was for real. The impression was one of doom and terror.

7:19 beginning...middle watch. About 10 p.m.

7:22 every man's sword against his companion. Panic followed shock. Every soldier was on his own, in desperate retreat. In the darkness and crash of sounds the soldiers were unable to distinguish friend from enemy, and with their swords they slashed a path of escape through their own men.

8:2 gleaning *of the grapes* of Ephraim. Ephraim resented being slighted in the call to battle but was placated by Gideon's compliment. His figures of speech implied that Ephraimite capital punishment of the two fleeing Midianite leaders (7:25) was "the vintage of Ephraim," to use an image drawn from their grape horticulture. It played a more strategic role than taking part in "the vintage of Abiezer," the suicide of the enemy under Gideon's leadership (cf. v. 3).

flesh with the thorns of the wilderness and
with briers!" 8 Then he went up from there
[k]to Penuel and spoke to them in the same
way. And the men of Penuel answered him
as the men of Succoth had answered. 9 So
he also spoke to the men of Penuel, saying,
"When I [l]come back in peace, [m]I will tear
down this tower!"

10 Now Zebah and Zalmunna *were* at
Karkor, and their armies with them, about
fifteen thousand, all who were left of [n]all
the army of the people of the East; for [o]one
hundred and twenty thousand men who
drew the sword had fallen. 11 Then Gideon
went up by the road of those who dwell in
tents on the east of [p]Nobah and Jogbehah;
and he [4]attacked the army while the camp
felt [q]secure. 12 When Zebah and Zalmunna
fled, he pursued them; and he [r]took the
two kings of Midian, Zebah and Zalmunna, and routed the whole army.

13 Then Gideon the son of Joash returned from battle, from the Ascent of
Heres. 14 And he caught a young man of
the men of Succoth and interrogated him;
and he wrote down for him the leaders of
Succoth and its elders, seventy-seven men.
15 Then he came to the men of Succoth and
said, "Here are Zebah and Zalmunna,
about whom you [s]ridiculed me, saying,
'*Are* the hands of Zebah and Zalmunna
now in your hand, that we should give
bread to your weary men?' " 16 [t]And he
took the elders of the city, and thorns of the
wilderness and briers, and with them he
[5]taught the men of Succoth. 17 [u]Then he
tore down the tower of [v]Penuel and killed
the men of the city.

18 And he said to Zebah and Zalmunna,
"What kind of men *were they* whom you
killed at [w]Tabor?"

So they answered, "As you *are,* so *were*
they; each one resembled the son of a
king."

19 Then he said, "They *were* my brothers,
the sons of my mother. *As* the LORD lives, if
you had let them live, I would not kill

8 [k]Gen. 32:30, 31; 1 Kin. 12:25
9 [l]1 Kin. 22:27 [m]Judg. 8:17
10 [n]Judg. 7:12 [o]Judg. 6:5
11 [p]Num. 32:35, 42 [q]Judg. 18:27; [1 Thess. 5:3] [4]Lit. *struck*
12 [r]Ps. 83:11
15 [s]Judg. 8:6
16 [t]Judg. 8:7 [5]*disciplined*
17 [u]Judg. 8:9 [v]1 Kin. 12:25
18 [w]Judg. 4:6; Ps. 89:12

you." 20 And he said to Jether his firstborn,
"Rise, kill them!" But the youth would not
draw his sword; for he was afraid, because
he *was* still a youth.

21 So Zebah and Zalmunna said, "Rise
yourself, and kill us; for as a man *is, so is*
his strength." So Gideon arose and [x]killed
Zebah and Zalmunna, and took the crescent ornaments that *were* on their camels'
necks.

Gideon's Ephod

22 Then the men of Israel said to Gideon,
[y]"Rule over us, both you and your son,
and your grandson also; for you have [z]de-
livered us from the hand of Midian."

23 But Gideon said to them, "I will not
rule over you, nor shall my son rule over
you; [a]the LORD shall rule over you."
24 Then Gideon said to them, "I would like
to [6]make a request of you, that each of you
would give me the earrings from his plunder." For they had golden earrings, [b]be-
cause they *were* Ishmaelites.

25 So they answered, "We will gladly
give *them.*" And they spread out a garment, and each man threw into it the earrings from his plunder. 26 Now the weight
of the gold earrings that he requested was
one thousand seven hundred *shekels* of
gold, besides the crescent ornaments, pendants, and purple robes which *were* on the
kings of Midian, and besides the chains
that *were* around their camels' necks.
27 Then Gideon [c]made it into an ephod
and set it up in his city, [d]Ophrah. And all
Israel [e]played the harlot with it there. It
became [f]a snare to Gideon and to his
house.

28 Thus Midian was subdued before the
children of Israel, so that they lifted their
heads no more. [g]And the country was
quiet for forty years in the days of Gideon.

Death of Gideon

29 Then [h]Jerubbaal the son of Joash went
and dwelt in his own house. 30 Gideon had

21 [x]Ps. 83:11
22 [y][Judg. 9:8] [z]Judg. 3:9; 9:17
23 [a]1 Sam. 8:7; 10:19; 12:12; Ps. 10:16
24 [b]Gen. 37:25, 28 [6]Lit. *request a request*
27 [c]Judg. 17:5 [d]Judg. 6:11, 24 [e][Ps. 106:39] [f]Deut. 7:16
28 [g]Judg. 5:31
29 [h]Judg. 6:32; 7:1

8:7 thorns. Gideon's threatened discipline of Succoth's leaders for refusing to help their brothers came due. He had them dragged under heavy weights over thorns and briers, which painfully tore their bodies. This was a cruel torture to which ancient captives were often subjected. He did it on his return, not wanting to delay the pursuit (v. 16).

8:9 tower. They probably had defiantly boasted of their strength and defensibility because of the tower. He kept his promise and more (v. 17).

8:20 Jether...kill them. Gideon desired to place a great honor on his son by killing the enemies of Israel and of God.

8:21 killed Zebah and Zalmunna. The earlier Midianite scourge inflicted on Israel was the worst, so this victory lived long in their minds (cf. Ps. 83:11).

8:22,23 Rule over us. Israelites sinned by the misguided motive and request that Gideon reign as king. To his credit, the leader declined, insisting that God alone rule (cf. Ex. 19:5,6).

8:24 Ishmaelites. Synonymous with Midianites (cf. Gen. 37:25,28).

8:24-27 Gideon made...an ephod. This was certainly a sad end to Gideon's influence as he, perhaps in an expression of pride, sought to lift himself up in the eyes of the people. Gideon intended nothing more than to make a breastplate as David did (1 Chr. 15:27) to indicate civil, not priestly rule. It was never intended to set up idolatrous worship, but to be a symbol of civil power. That no evil was intended can be noted from the subduing of Midian (v. 28), quietness from wars (v. 28), and the fact that idolatry came after Gideon's death (v. 33) as well as the commendation of Gideon (v. 35).

8:26 the weight of the gold. The total was about 42 lbs.

[i]seventy sons who were his own offspring,
for he had many wives. 31 [j]And his concubine who *was* in Shechem also bore him a
son, whose name he called Abimelech.
32 Now Gideon the son of Joash died [k]at a
good old age, and was buried in the tomb
of Joash his father, [l]in Ophrah of the Abiezrites.
33 So it was, [m]as soon as Gideon was
dead, that the children of Israel again
[n]played the harlot with the Baals, [o]and
made Baal-Berith their god. 34 Thus the
children of Israel [p]did not remember the
LORD their God, who had delivered them
from the hands of all their enemies on
every side; 35 [q]nor did they show kindness
to the house of Jerubbaal (Gideon) in accordance with the good he had done for Israel.

Abimelech's Conspiracy

9 Then Abimelech the son of Jerubbaal
went to Shechem, to [a]his mother's
brothers, and spoke with them and with all
the family of the house of his mother's father, saying, 2 "Please speak in the hearing
of all the men of Shechem: 'Which is better
for you, that all [b]seventy of the sons of Jerubbaal reign over you, or that one reign
over you?' Remember that I *am* your own
flesh and [c]bone."
3 And his mother's brothers spoke all
these words concerning him in the hearing
of all the men of Shechem; and their heart
was inclined to follow Abimelech, for they
said, "He is our [d]brother." 4 So they gave
him seventy *shekels* of silver from the temple of [e]Baal-Berith, with which Abimelech
hired [f]worthless and reckless men; and
they followed him. 5 Then he went to his
father's house [g]at Ophrah and [h]killed his
brothers, the seventy sons of Jerubbaal, on
one stone. But Jotham the youngest son of
Jerubbaal was left, because he hid himself.
6 And all the men of Shechem gathered together, all of Beth Millo, and they went and
made Abimelech king beside the terebinth
tree at the pillar that *was* in Shechem.

The Parable of the Trees

7 Now when they told Jotham, he went
and stood on top of [i]Mount Gerizim, and
lifted his voice and cried out. And he said
to them:

"Listen to me, you men of Shechem,
That God may listen to you!

8 "The[j] trees once went forth to
anoint a king over them.
And they said to the olive tree,
[k]'Reign over us!'
9 But the olive tree said to them,
'Should I cease giving my oil,
[l]With which they honor God and
men,
And go to sway over trees?'
10 "Then the trees said to the fig tree,
'You come *and* reign over us!'
11 But the fig tree said to them,
'Should I cease my sweetness and
my good fruit,
And go to sway over trees?'
12 "Then the trees said to the vine,
'You come *and* reign over us!'
13 But the vine said to them,
'Should I cease my new wine,
[m]Which cheers *both* God and men,
And go to sway over trees?'
14 "Then all the trees said to the
bramble,
'You come *and* reign over us!'
15 And the bramble said to the trees,
'If in truth you anoint me as king
over you,
Then come *and* take shelter in my
[n]shade;
But if not, [o]let fire come out of the
bramble
And devour the [p]cedars of
Lebanon!'

16 "Now therefore, if you have acted in
truth and sincerity in making Abimelech
king, and if you have dealt well with Jerubbaal and his house, and have done to him
[q]as[1] he deserves— 17 for my [r]father fought
for you, risked his life, and [s]delivered you
out of the hand of Midian; 18 [t]but you have
risen up against my father's house this day,
and killed his seventy sons on one stone,
and made Abimelech, the son of his [u]fe-
male servant, king over the men of
Shechem, because he is your brother— 19 if
then you have acted in truth and sincerity

30 [i] Judg. 9:2, 5
31 [j] Judg. 9:1
32 [k] Gen. 25:8; Job 5:26 [l] Judg. 6:24; 8:27
33 [m] Judg. 2:19 [n] Judg. 2:17 [o] Judg. 9:4, 46
34 [p] Deut. 4:9; Judg. 3:7; Ps. 78:11, 42; 106:13, 21
35 [q] Judg. 9:16-18

CHAPTER 9

1 [a] Judg. 8:31, 35
2 [b] Judg. 8:30; 9:5, 18 [c] Gen. 29:14
3 [d] Gen. 29:15
4 [e] Judg. 8:33 [f] Judg. 11:3; 2 Chr. 13:7; Acts 17:5
5 [g] Judg. 6:24 [h] Judg. 8:30; 9:2, 18; 2 Kin. 11:1, 2
7 [i] Deut. 11:29; 27:12; Josh. 8:33; John 4:20
8 [j] 2 Kin. 14:9 [k] Judg. 8:22, 23
9 [l] [John 5:23]
13 [m] Ps. 104:15
15 [n] Is. 30:2; Dan. 4:12; Hos. 14:7 [o] Num. 21:28; Judg. 9:20; Ezek. 19:14 [p] 2 Kin. 14:9; Is. 2:13; Ezek. 31:3
16 [q] Judg. 8:35 [1] Lit. *according to the doing of his hands*
17 [r] Judg. 7 [s] Judg. 8:22
18 [t] Judg. 8:30, 35; 9:2, 5, 6 [u] Judg. 8:31

8:30,31 many wives. Gideon fell severely into the sin of polygamy, an iniquity tolerated by many but which never was God's blueprint for marriage (Gen. 2:24). Abimelech, a son by yet another illicit relationship, grew up to be the wretched king in Judg. 9. Polygamy always resulted in trouble.

9:5 killed...brothers. This atrocity, common in ancient times, eliminated the greatest threat in the revolution—all the legitimate competitors.

9:6 Beth Millo. Lit. "house of the fortress." This was a section of Shechem, probably involving the tower stronghold of v. 46.

9:14 You come *and* reign over us! In Jotham's parable of trees asking for a king (vv. 7-15), the olive, fig, and vine decline. They do not represent specific men who declined, rather they build the suspense and heighten the idea that the bramble (thornbush) is inferior and unsuitable. The bush represents Abimelech (vv. 6, 16).

with Jerubbaal and with his house this day,
then [v]rejoice in Abimelech, and let him also
rejoice in you. 20 But if not, [w]let fire come
from Abimelech and devour the men of
Shechem and Beth Millo; and let fire come
from the men of Shechem and from Beth
Millo and devour Abimelech!" 21 And
Jotham ran away and fled; and he went to
[x]Beer and dwelt there, for fear of Abimelech his brother.

Downfall of Abimelech

22 After Abimelech had reigned over Israel three years, 23 [y]God sent a [z]spirit of ill
will between Abimelech and the men of
Shechem; and the men of Shechem [a]dealt
treacherously with Abimelech, 24 [b]that the
crime *done* to the seventy sons of Jerubbaal
might be settled and their [c]blood be laid on
Abimelech their brother, who killed them,
and on the men of Shechem, who aided
him in the killing of his brothers. 25 And
the men of Shechem set [2]men in ambush
against him on the tops of the mountains,
and they robbed all who passed by them
along that way; and it was told Abimelech.
26 Now Gaal the son of Ebed came with
his brothers and went over to Shechem;
and the men of Shechem put their confidence in him. 27 So they went out into the
fields, and gathered *grapes* from their vineyards and trod *them,* and [3]made merry.
And they went into [d]the house of their
god, and ate and drank, and cursed
Abimelech. 28 Then Gaal the son of Ebed
said, [e]"Who *is* Abimelech, and who *is*
Shechem, that we should serve him? *Is he*
not the son of Jerubbaal, and *is not* Zebul
his officer? Serve the men of [f]Hamor the
father of Shechem; but why should we
serve him? 29 [g]If only this people were
under my [4]authority! Then I would remove Abimelech." So [5]he said to Abimelech, "Increase your army and come out!"
30 When Zebul, the ruler of the city,
heard the words of Gaal the son of Ebed,
his anger was aroused. 31 And he sent messengers to Abimelech secretly, saying,
"Take note! Gaal the son of Ebed and his
brothers have come to Shechem; and here
they are, fortifying the city against you.
32 Now therefore, get up by night, you and
the people who *are* with you, and [6]lie in
wait in the field. 33 And it shall be, as soon
as the sun is up in the morning, *that* you
shall rise early and rush upon the city; and
when he and the people who are with him
come out against you, you may then do to
them [7]as you find opportunity."
34 So Abimelech and all the people who
were with him rose by night, and [8]lay in
wait against Shechem in four companies.
35 When Gaal the son of Ebed went out
and stood in the entrance to the city gate,
Abimelech and the people who *were* with
him rose from lying in wait. 36 And when
Gaal saw the people, he said to Zebul,
"Look, people are coming down from the
tops of the mountains!"

But Zebul said to him, "You see the
shadows of the mountains as *if they were*
men."
37 So Gaal spoke again and said, "See,
people are coming down from the center of
the land, and another company is coming
from the [9]Diviners' Terebinth Tree."
38 Then Zebul said to him, "Where indeed *is* your mouth now, with which you
[h]said, 'Who is Abimelech, that we should
serve him?' *Are* not these the people whom
you despised? Go out, if you will, and fight
with them now."
39 So Gaal went out, leading the men of
Shechem, and fought with Abimelech.
40 And Abimelech chased him, and he fled
from him; and many fell wounded, to the
very entrance of the gate. 41 Then Abimelech dwelt at Arumah, and Zebul [1]drove
out Gaal and his brothers, so that they
would not dwell in Shechem.
42 And it came about on the next day
that the people went out into the field, and
they told Abimelech. 43 So he took his people, divided them into three companies,
and lay in wait in the field. And he looked,
and there were the people, coming out of
the city; and he rose against them and [2]at-
tacked them. 44 Then Abimelech and the
company that *was* with him rushed forward and stood at the entrance of the gate
of the city; and the *other* two companies
rushed upon all who *were* in the fields and
killed them. 45 So Abimelech fought
against the city all that day; [i]he took the
city and killed the people who *were* in it;
and he [j]demolished the city and sowed it
with salt.
46 Now when all the men of the tower of
Shechem had heard *that,* they entered the
[3]stronghold of the temple [k]of the god

19 [v] Is. 8:6; [Phil. 3:3]
20 [w] Judg. 9:15, 45, 56, 57
21 [x] Num. 21:16
23 [y] 1 Kin. 12:15; Is. 19:14 [z] 1 Sam. 16:14; 18:9, 10; 1 Kin. 22:22; 2 Chr. 18:22 [a] Is. 33:1
24 [b] 1 Kin. 2:32; Esth. 9:25; Matt. 23:35, 36 [c] Num. 35:33
25 [2] Lit. *liers-in-wait for*
27 [d] Judg. 9:4 [3] *rejoiced*
28 [e] 1 Sam. 25:10; 1 Kin. 12:16 [f] Gen. 34:2, 6; Josh. 24:32
29 [g] 2 Sam. 15:4 [4] Lit. *hand* [5] So with MT, Tg.; DSS *they;* LXX *I*
32 [6] Set up an ambush
33 [7] Lit. *as your hand can find*
34 [8] Set up an ambush
37 [9] Heb. *Meonenim*
38 [h] Judg. 9:28, 29
41 [1] *exiled*
43 [2] Lit. *struck*
45 [i] Judg. 9:20 [j] Deut. 29:23; 2 Kin. 3:25
46 [k] Judg. 8:33 [3] *fortified room*

9:23 God sent a spirit of ill will. In the course of God's providence, there appeared jealousy, distrust, and hate. God allowed it to work as punishment for the idolatry and mass murder.

9:26-45 A failed coup.

9:37 Diviners' Terebinth Tree. A tree regarded superstitiouly where mystical ceremonies and soothsaying were done.

9:45 sowed it with salt. An act polluting soil and water, as well as symbolizing a verdict of permanent barrenness (Deut. 29:23; Jer. 17:6). Abimelech's intent finally was nullified when Jeroboam I rebuilt the city as his capital (1 Kin. 12:25), ca. 930–910 B.C.

Berith. 47 And it was told Abimelech that
all the men of the tower of Shechem were
gathered together. 48 Then Abimelech
went up to Mount [l]Zalmon, he and all the
people who *were* with him. And Abimelech
took an ax in his hand and cut down a
bough from the trees, and took it and laid
it on his shoulder; then he said to the people who were with him, "What you have
seen me do, make haste *and* do as I *have*
done." 49 So each of the people likewise cut
down his own bough and followed Abimelech, put *them* against the [4]stronghold, and
set the stronghold on fire above them, so
that all the people of the tower of Shechem
died, about a thousand men and women.
50 Then Abimelech went to Thebez, and
he [5]encamped against Thebez and took it.
51 But there was a strong tower in the city,
and all the men and women—all the people of the city—fled there and shut themselves in; then they went up to the top of
the tower. 52 So Abimelech came as far as
the tower and fought against it; and he
drew near the door of the tower to burn it
with fire. 53 But a certain woman
[m]dropped an upper millstone on Abimelech's head and crushed his skull. 54 Then
[n]he called quickly to the young man, his
armorbearer, and said to him, "Draw your
sword and kill me, lest men say of me, 'A
woman killed him.' " So his young man
thrust him through, and he died. 55 And
when the men of Israel saw that Abimelech
was dead, they departed, every man to his
[6]place.
56 [o]Thus God repaid the wickedness of
Abimelech, which he had done to his father by killing his seventy brothers. 57 And
all the evil of the men of Shechem God returned on their own heads, and on them
came [p]the curse of Jotham the son of Jerubbaal.

Tola

10 After Abimelech there [a]arose to
save Israel Tola the son of Puah, the
son of Dodo, a man of Issachar; and he
dwelt in Shamir in the mountains of
Ephraim. 2 He judged Israel twenty-three
years; and he died and was buried in
Shamir.

Jair

3 After him arose Jair, a Gileadite; and he
judged Israel twenty-two years. 4 Now he
had thirty sons who [b]rode on thirty donkeys; they also had thirty towns, [c]which
are called [1]"Havoth Jair" to this day, which
are in the land of Gilead. 5 And Jair died
and was buried in Camon.

Israel Oppressed Again

6 Then [d]the children of Israel again did
evil in the sight of the LORD, and [e]served
the Baals and the Ashtoreths, [f]the gods of
Syria, the gods of [g]Sidon, the gods of
Moab, the gods of the people of Ammon,
and the gods of the Philistines; and they
forsook the LORD and did not serve Him.
7 So the anger of the LORD was hot against
Israel; and He [h]sold them into the hands of
the [i]Philistines and into the hands of the
people of [j]Ammon. 8 From that year they
[2]harassed and oppressed the children of
Israel for eighteen years—all the children
of Israel who *were* on the other side of the
Jordan in the [k]land of the Amorites, in
Gilead. 9 Moreover the people of Ammon
crossed over the Jordan to fight against Judah also, against Benjamin, and against the
house of Ephraim, so that Israel was severely distressed.
10 [l]And the children of Israel cried out to
the LORD, saying, "We have [m]sinned
against You, because we have both forsak-
en our God and served the Baals!"
11 So the LORD said to the children of Israel, "*Did I* not *deliver you* [n]from the Egyptians and [o]from the Amorites and [p]from
the people of Ammon and [q]from the Philistines? 12 Also [r]the Sidonians [s]and Amalekites and [3]Maonites [t]oppressed you; and
you cried out to Me, and I delivered you
from their hand. 13 [u]Yet you have forsaken
Me and served other gods. Therefore I will
deliver you no more. 14 Go and [v]cry out to
the gods which you have chosen; let them
deliver you in your time of distress."
15 And the children of Israel said to the
LORD, "We have sinned! [w]Do to us whatever seems best to You; only deliver us this
day, we pray." 16 [x]So they put away the
foreign gods from among them and served

48 [l] Ps. 68:14
49 [4] *fortified room*
50 [5] *besieged*
53 [m] 2 Sam. 11:21
54 [n] 1 Sam. 31:4
55 [6] *home*
56 [o] Judg. 9:24; Job 31:3; Prov. 5:22
57 [p] Judg. 9:20

CHAPTER 10

1 [a] Judg. 2:16
4 [b] Judg. 5:10; 12:14 [c] Deut. 3:14 [1] Lit. *Towns of Jair*, Num. 32:41; Deut. 3:14
6 [d] Judg. 2:11; 3:7; 6:1; 13:1 [e] Judg. 2:13 [f] Judg. 2:12 [g] 1 Kin. 11:33; Ps. 106:36
7 [h] Judg. 2:14; 4:2; 1 Sam. 12:9 [i] Judg. 13:1 [j] Judg. 3:13
8 [k] Num. 32:33 [2] Lit. *shattered*
10 [l] Judg. 6:6; 1 Sam. 12:10 [m] Deut. 1:41
11 [n] Ex. 14:30 [o] Num. 21:21, 24, 25 [p] Judg. 3:12, 13 [q] Judg. 3:31
12 [r] Judg. 1:31; 5:19 [s] Judg. 6:3; 7:12 [t] Ps. 106:42, 43 [3] LXX mss. *Midianites*
13 [u] [Deut. 32:15; Judg. 2:12; Jer. 2:13]
14 [v] Deut. 32:37, 38
15 [w] 1 Sam. 3:18; 2 Sam. 15:26
16 [x] 2 Chr. 7:14; Jer. 18:7, 8

9:57 That curse was pronounced in 9:20 for the pervasive idolatry.

10:3-5 Most likely, the judgeship of Jair was the time period of Ruth.

10:10 We have sinned. Confession is followed by true repentance (vv. 15,16).

10:13,14 Here is the form of God's wrath, by which He abandons persistent, willful sinners to the consequences of their sins. This aspect of divine judgment is referred to in the case of Samson (16:20), as well as the warnings of Prov. 1:20-31 and Rom. 1:24-28. It is a pattern of rejection seen throughout history (cf. Acts 14:15,16) even among the Jews (cf. Hos. 4:17; Matt. 15:14).

10:15 Do to us whatever seems best. Genuine repentance acknowledges God's right to chasten, so His punishment is seen as just and He is thereby glorified. It also seeks the remediation that chastening brings, because genuine contrition pursues holiness.

the LORD. And [y]His soul could no longer
endure the misery of Israel.
17 Then the people of Ammon gathered
together and encamped in Gilead. And the
children of Israel assembled together and
encamped in [z]Mizpah. 18 And the people,
the leaders of Gilead, said to one another,
"Who *is* the man who will begin the fight
against the people of Ammon? He shall [a]be
head over all the inhabitants of Gilead."

Jephthah

11 Now [a]Jephthah the Gileadite was [b]a
mighty man of valor, but he *was* the
son of a harlot; and Gilead begot Jephthah.
2 Gilead's wife bore sons; and when his
wife's sons grew up, they drove Jephthah
out, and said to him, "You shall have [c]no
inheritance in our father's house, for you
are the son of another woman." 3 Then
Jephthah fled from his brothers and dwelt
in the land of [d]Tob; and [e]worthless men
banded together with Jephthah and went
out *raiding* with him.
4 It came to pass after a time that the
[f]people of Ammon made war against Israel. 5 And so it was, when the people of
Ammon made war against Israel, that the
elders of Gilead went to get Jephthah from
the land of Tob. 6 Then they said to Jephthah, "Come and be our commander, that
we may fight against the people of
Ammon."
7 So Jephthah said to the elders of Gilead, [g]"Did you not hate me, and expel me
from my father's house? Why have you
come to me now when you are in [1]dis-
tress?"
8 [h]And the elders of Gilead said to Jephthah, "That is why we have [i]turned[2] again
to you now, that you may go with us and
fight against the people of Ammon, and be
[j]our head over all the inhabitants of Gilead."
9 So Jephthah said to the elders of Gilead, "If you take me back home to fight
against the people of Ammon, and the
LORD delivers them to me, shall I be your
head?"
10 And the elders of Gilead said to Jephthah, [k]"The LORD will be a witness between us, if we do not do according to
your words." 11 Then Jephthah went with
the elders of Gilead, and the people made
him [l]head and commander over them; and
Jephthah spoke all his words [m]before the
LORD in Mizpah.
12 Now Jephthah sent messengers to the
king of the people of Ammon, saying,
[n]"What do you have against me, that you
have come to fight against me in my
land?"
13 And the king of the people of Ammon
answered the messengers of Jephthah,
[o]"Because Israel took away my land when
they came up out of Egypt, from [p]the
Arnon as far as [q]the Jabbok, and to the Jordan. Now therefore, restore those *lands*
peaceably."
14 So Jephthah again sent messengers to
the king of the people of Ammon, 15 and
said to him, "Thus says Jephthah: [r]'Israel
did not take away the land of Moab, nor
the land of the people of Ammon; 16 for
when Israel came up from Egypt, they
walked through the wilderness as far as
the Red Sea and [s]came to Kadesh. 17 Then
[t]Israel sent messengers to the king of
Edom, saying, "Please let me pass through
your land." [u]But the king of Edom would
not heed. And in like manner they sent to
the [v]king of Moab, but he would not *consent*. So Israel [w]remained in Kadesh.
18 And they [x]went along through the
wilderness and [y]bypassed the land of
Edom and the land of Moab, came to the
east side of the land of Moab, and encamped on the other side of the Arnon. But
they did not enter the border of Moab, for
the Arnon *was* the border of Moab. 19 Then
[z]Israel sent messengers to Sihon king of
the Amorites, king of Heshbon; and Israel
said to him, "Please [a]let us pass through
your land into our place." 20 [b]But Sihon
did not trust Israel to pass through his territory. So Sihon gathered all his people together, encamped in Jahaz, and fought
against Israel. 21 And the LORD God of Israel [c]delivered Sihon and all his people
into the hand of Israel, and they [d]defeated[3]
them. Thus Israel gained possession of all

16 [y]Ps. 106:44, 45; Is. 63:9
17 [z]Gen. 31:49; Judg. 11:11, 29
18 [a]Judg. 11:8, 11

CHAPTER 11

1 [a]Heb. 11:32 [b]Judg. 6:12; 2 Kin. 5:1
2 [c]Gen. 21:10; Deut. 23:2
3 [d]2 Sam. 10:6, 8 [e]1 Sam. 22:2
4 [f]Judg. 10:9, 17
7 [g]Gen. 26:27 [1]trouble
8 [h]Judg. 10:18 [i][Luke 17:4] [j]Judg. 10:18 [2]returned
10 [k]Gen. 31:49, 50; Jer. 29:23; 42:5
11 [l]Judg. 11:8 [m]Judg. 10:17; 20:1; 1 Sam. 10:17
12 [n]2 Sam. 16:10
13 [o]Num. 21:24-26 [p]Josh. 13:9 [q]Gen. 32:22
15 [r]Deut. 2:9, 19
16 [s]Num. 13:26; 20:1
17 [t]Num. 20:14 [u]Num. 20:14-21 [v]Josh. 24:9 [w]Num. 20:1
18 [x]Deut. 2:9, 18, 19 [y]Num. 21:4
19 [z]Num. 21:21; Deut. 2:26-36 [a]Num. 21:22; Deut. 2:27
20 [b]Num. 21:23; Deut. 2:27
21 [c]Josh. 24:8 [d]Num. 21:24, 25 [3]Lit. *struck*

11:1 mighty man of valor. In a military situation, this means a strong, adept warrior, such as Gideon (6:12). In response to their repentance, God raised up Jephthah to lead the Israelites to freedom from the 18 years of oppression (v. 8).

11:3 *raiding.* Such attacks would be against the Ammonites and other pagan peoples and brought fame to Jephthah.

11:11 spoke...before the LORD. Refers to confirming the agreement in a solemn public meeting with prayer invoking God as witness (v. 10).

11:13 Israel took away my land. The Ammonite ruler was claiming rights to the lands occupied by the Israelites. Jephthah's answer was direct: 1) those lands were not in the possession of Ammonites when Israel took them, but were Amorite lands; 2) Israel had been there 300 years in undisputed possession; 3) God had chosen to give them the lands, and thus they were entitled to them, just as the Ammonites felt they received their lands from their god (cf. v. 24).

11:15 Israel did not take away the land. These people initiated the hostility, and being at fault, invited loss of possession (vv. 16-22). This fit perfectly the will of God, who has ultimate rights (cf. Gen. 1:1; Ps. 24:1) to give the land to Israel. God said, "The land *is* Mine" (Lev. 25:23; cf. Ezek. 36:5).

the land of the Amorites, who inhabited
that country. 22 They took possession of
[e]all the territory of the Amorites, from the
Arnon to the Jabbok and from the wilderness to the Jordan.
23 'And now the LORD God of Israel has
[4]dispossessed the Amorites from before
His people Israel; should you then possess
it? 24 Will you not possess whatever
[f]Chemosh your god gives you to possess?
So whatever [g]the LORD our God takes possession of before us, we will possess.
25 And now, *are* you any better than [h]Balak
the son of Zippor, king of Moab? Did he
ever strive against Israel? Did he ever fight
against them? 26 While Israel dwelt in
[i]Heshbon and its villages, in [j]Aroer and its
villages, and in all the cities along the
banks of the Arnon, for three hundred
years, why did you not recover *them* within that time? 27 Therefore I have not sinned
against you, but you wronged me by fighting against me. May the LORD, [k]the Judge,
[l]render judgment this day between the
children of Israel and the people of
Ammon.' " 28 However, the king of the
people of Ammon did not heed the words
which Jephthah sent him.

Jephthah's Vow and Victory

29 Then [m]the Spirit of the LORD came
upon Jephthah, and he passed through
Gilead and Manasseh, and passed
through Mizpah of Gilead; and from Mizpah of Gilead he advanced *toward* the
people of Ammon. 30 And Jephthah
[n]made a vow to the LORD, and said, "If
You will indeed deliver the people of
Ammon into my hands, 31 then it will be
that whatever comes out of the doors of
my house to meet me, when I return in
peace from the people of Ammon, [o]shall
surely be the LORD's, [p]and I will offer it up
as a burnt offering."
32 So Jephthah advanced toward the
people of Ammon to fight against them,
and the LORD delivered them into his
hands. 33 And he [5]defeated them from
Aroer as far as [q]Minnith—twenty cities—
and to [6]Abel Keramim, with a very great
slaughter. Thus the people of Ammon
were subdued before the children of Israel.

Jephthah's Daughter

34 When Jephthah came to his house at
[r]Mizpah, there was [s]his daughter, coming out to meet him with timbrels and
dancing; and she *was his* only child. Besides her he had neither son nor daughter. 35 And it came to pass, when he saw
her, that he [t]tore his clothes, and said,
"Alas, my daughter! You have brought
me very low! You are among those who
trouble me! For I [u]have [7]given my word
to the LORD, and [v]I cannot [8]go back on
it."
36 So she said to him, "My father, *if* you
have given your word to the LORD, [w]do to
me according to what has gone out of your
mouth, because [x]the LORD has avenged
you of your enemies, the people of
Ammon." 37 Then she said to her father,
"Let this thing be done for me: let me alone
for two months, that I may go and wander
on the mountains and [9]bewail my virginity, my [1]friends and I."
38 So he said, "Go." And he sent her
away *for* two months; and she went with
her friends, and bewailed her virginity on
the mountains. 39 And it was so at the
end of two months that she returned to
her father, and he [y]carried out his vow
with her which he had vowed. She [2]knew
no man.
And it became a custom in Israel 40 *that*
the daughters of Israel went four days each
year to [3]lament the daughter of Jephthah
the Gileadite.

22 [e]Deut. 2:36, 37 **23** [4]*driven out* **24** [f]Num. 21:29; 1 Kin. 11:7; Jer. 48:7 [g][Deut. 9:4, 5; Josh. 3:10] **25** [h]Num. 22:2; Josh. 24:9; Mic. 6:5 **26** [i]Num. 21:25, 26 [j]Deut. 2:36 **27** [k]Gen. 18:25 [l]Gen. 16:5; 31:53; [1 Sam. 24:12, 15] **29** [m]Judg. 3:10 **30** [n]Gen. 28:20; Num. 30:2; 1 Sam. 1:11 **31** [o]Lev. 27:2, 3, 28; 1 Sam. 1:11 [p]Ps. 66:13

33 [q]Ezek. 27:17 [5]Lit. *struck* [6]Lit. *Plain of Vineyards* **34** [r]Judg. 10:17; 11:11 [s]Ex. 15:20; 1 Sam. 18:6; Ps. 68:25; Jer. 31:4 **35** [t]Gen. 37:29, 34 [u]Eccl. 5:2, 4, 5 [v]Num. 30:2 [7]Lit. *opened my mouth* [8]Lit. *take it back* **36** [w]Num. 30:2 [x]2 Sam. 18:19, 31 **37** [9]*lament* [1]*companions* **39** [y]Judg. 11:31 [2]Remained a virgin **40** [3]*commemorate*

11:26 three hundred years. With an early Exodus from Egypt (ca. 1445 B.C.), one can approximate the 480 years covered in Judges to 1 Kin. 6:1, Solomon's fourth year 967/966 B.C.: 38 from the Exodus to Heshbon; 300 from Heshbon to Jephthah in 11:26; possibly 7 more years for Jephthah; 40 for Samson, 20 for Eli, 20 for Samuel, 15–16 beyond Samuel for Saul, 40 for David, and 4 for Solomon, which totals about 480 years. It is quite possible that 300 has been rounded off.

11:29 the Spirit...came upon Jephthah. That the Lord graciously empowered Jephthah for war on behalf of his people does not mean that all of the warrior's decisions were of God's wisdom. The rash vow (vv. 30,31) is an example.

11:30 made a vow to the LORD. This was a custom among generals to promise the god of their worship something of great value as a reward for that god's giving them victory.

11:31 I will offer it. Some interpreters reason that Jephthah offered his daughter as a living sacrifice in perpetual virginity. With this idea, v. 31 is made to mean "shall surely be the LORD's" or "I will offer it up as a burnt offering." The view sees only perpetual virginity in vv. 37-40, and rejects his offering a human sacrifice as being against God's revealed will (Deut. 12:31). On the other hand, since he was 1) beyond the Jordan, 2) far from the tabernacle, 3) a hypocrite in religious devotion, 4) familiar with human sacrifice among other nations, 5) influenced by such superstition, and 6) wanting victory badly, he likely meant a burnt offering. The translation in v. 31 is "and," not "or." His act came in an era of bizarre things, even inconsistency by leaders whom God otherwise empowered (cf. Gideon in 8:27).

11:34 his daughter, coming out to meet him. She was thus to be the sacrificed pledge.

11:35 Alas. Here is indicated the pain felt by her father in having to take the life of his only daughter to satisfy his pious, but unwise pledge.

Jephthah's Conflict with Ephraim

12 Then [a]the men of Ephraim [1]gath-
ered together, crossed over toward
Zaphon, and said to Jephthah, "Why did
you cross over to fight against the people
of Ammon, and did not call us to go with
you? We will burn your house down on
you with fire!"
2 And Jephthah said to them, "My people and I were in a great struggle with the
people of Ammon; and when I called you,
you did not deliver me out of their hands.
3 So when I saw that you would not deliver *me,* I [b]took my life in my hands and
crossed over against the people of
Ammon; and the LORD delivered them into
my hand. Why then have you come up to
me this day to fight against me?" 4 Now
Jephthah gathered together all the men of
Gilead and fought against Ephraim. And
the men of Gilead defeated Ephraim, because they said, "You Gileadites [c]*are* fugitives of Ephraim among the Ephraimites
and among the Manassites." 5 The Gileadites seized the [d]fords of the Jordan before
the Ephraimites *arrived.* And when *any*
Ephraimite who escaped said, "Let me
cross over," the men of Gilead would say
to him, "*Are* you an Ephraimite?" If he
said, "No," 6 then they would say to him,
"Then say, [e]'Shibboleth'!"[2] And he would
say, "Sibboleth," for he could not [3]pro-
nounce *it* right. Then they would take him
and kill him at the fords of the Jordan.
There fell at that time forty-two thousand
Ephraimites.
7 And Jephthah judged Israel six years.
Then Jephthah the Gileadite died and was
buried among the cities of Gilead.

Ibzan, Elon, and Abdon

8 After him, Ibzan of Bethlehem judged
Israel. 9 He had thirty sons. And he gave
away thirty daughters in marriage, and
brought in thirty daughters from elsewhere for his sons. He judged Israel seven
years. 10 Then Ibzan died and was buried
at Bethlehem.
11 After him, Elon the Zebulunite
judged Israel. He judged Israel ten years.
12 And Elon the Zebulunite died and was
buried at Aijalon in the country of Zebulun.
13 After him, Abdon the son of Hillel the
Pirathonite judged Israel. 14 He had forty
sons and thirty grandsons, who [f]rode on
seventy young donkeys. He judged Israel
eight years. 15 Then Abdon the son of Hillel the Pirathonite died and was buried in
Pirathon in the land of Ephraim, [g]in the
mountains of the Amalekites.

The Birth of Samson

13 Again the children of Israel [a]did
evil in the sight of the LORD, and the
LORD delivered them [b]into the hand of the
Philistines for forty years.
2 Now there was a certain man from
[c]Zorah, of the family of the Danites,
whose name *was* Manoah; and his wife
was barren and had no children. 3 And the
[d]Angel of the LORD appeared to the
woman and said to her, "Indeed now, you
are barren and have borne no children, but
you shall conceive and bear a son. 4 Now
therefore, please be careful [e]not to drink
wine or *similar* drink, and not to eat anything unclean. 5 For behold, you shall conceive and bear a son. And no [f]razor shall
come upon his head, for the child shall be
[g]a Nazirite to God from the womb; and he
shall [h]begin to deliver Israel out of the
hand of the Philistines."
6 So the woman came and told her husband, saying, [i]"A Man of God came to me,
and His [j]countenance[1] *was* like the countenance of the Angel of God, very awesome;
but I [k]did not ask Him where He *was* from,
and He did not tell me His name. 7 And He
said to me, 'Behold, you shall conceive and
bear a son. Now drink no wine or *similar*
drink, nor eat anything unclean, for the
child shall be a Nazirite to God from the
womb to the day of his death.' "
8 Then Manoah prayed to the LORD, and
said, "O my Lord, please let the Man of
God whom You sent come to us again and
teach us what we shall do for the child
who will be born."

CHAPTER 12

1 [a]Judg. 8:1 [1]*were summoned*
3 [b]1 Sam. 19:5; 28:21; Job 13:14
4 [c]1 Sam. 25:10
5 [d]Josh. 22:11
6 [e]Ps. 69:2, 15 [2]Lit. *a flowing stream;* used as a test of dialect [3]Lit. *speak so*
14 [f]Judg. 5:10; 10:4
15 [g]Judg. 3:13, 27; 5:14

CHAPTER 13

1 [a]Judg. 2:11 [b]Judg. 10:7; 1 Sam. 12:9
2 [c]Josh. 19:41; Judg. 16:31
3 [d]Judg. 6:12
4 [e]Num. 6:2, 3, 20; Judg. 13:4; Luke 1:15
5 [f]Num. 6:5; 1 Sam. 1:11 [g]Num. 6:2 [h]1 Sam. 7:13; 2 Sam. 8:1; 1 Chr. 18:1
6 [i]Gen. 32:24-30 [j]Matt. 28:3; Luke 9:29; Acts 6:15 [k]Judg. 13:17, 18 [1]*appearance*

12:1 Why did you…not call us…? Ephraim's newest threat (cf. 8:1) was their jealousy of Jephthah's success and possibly a lust to share in his spoils. The threat was not only to burn the house, but to burn him.

12:4 fugitives. Here was a mockery referring to the Gileadites as low lifes, the outcasts of Ephraim. They retaliated with battle.

12:6 Shibboleth. The method used for discovering an Ephraimite was the way in which they pronounced this word. If they mispronounced it by an "s" rather than "sh" sound, it gave them away, being a unique indicator of their dialect.

12:9,14 thirty sons. Very large families suggest the fathers' marriage to several wives, a part of life tolerated but never matching God's blueprint of one wife at a time (Gen. 2:24). To have many children had the lure of extending one's human power and influence.

13:3 the Angel of the LORD. In this case, it was a pre-incarnate appearance of the Lord Himself (vv. 6-22), as elsewhere (*see note on 6:11*). *See note on Ex. 3:2.*

13:5 Nazirite. The word is from the Heb. "to separate." For rigid Nazirite restrictions, such as here in Samson's case, *see notes on Num. 6:1-8.* God gave 3 restrictions: no wine (vv. 3,4), no razor cutting the hair (v. 5), no touching a dead body and being defiled (v. 6). Such outward actions indicated an inner dedication to God.

9 And God listened to the voice of Manoah, and the Angel of God came to the
woman again as she was sitting in the
field; but Manoah her husband *was* not
with her. 10 Then the woman ran in haste
and told her husband, and said to him,
"Look, the Man who came to me the *other*
day has just now appeared to me!"
11 So Manoah arose and followed his
wife. When he came to the Man, he said to
Him, "Are You the Man who spoke to this
woman?"
And He said, "I *am.*"
12 Manoah said, "Now let Your words
come *to pass!* What will be the boy's rule of
life, and his work?"
13 So the Angel of the LORD said to Manoah, "Of all that I said to the woman let
her be careful. 14 She may not eat anything
that comes from the vine, [l]nor may she
drink wine or *similar* drink, nor eat anything unclean. All that I commanded her
let her observe."
15 Then Manoah said to the Angel of the
LORD, "Please [m]let us detain You, and we
will prepare a young goat for You."
16 And the Angel of the LORD said to
Manoah, "Though you detain Me, I will
not eat your food. But if you offer a burnt
offering, you must offer it to the LORD."
(For Manoah did not know He *was* the
Angel of the LORD.)
17 Then Manoah said to the Angel of the
LORD, "What *is* Your name, that when Your
words come *to pass* we may honor You?"
18 And the Angel of the LORD said to
him, [n]"Why do you ask My name, seeing it
is wonderful?"
19 So Manoah took the young goat with
the grain offering, [o]and offered it upon the
rock to the LORD. And He did a wondrous
thing while Manoah and his wife looked
on— 20 it happened as the flame went up
toward heaven from the altar—the Angel
of the LORD ascended in the flame of the
altar! When Manoah and his wife saw *this,*
they [p]fell on their faces to the ground.
21 When the Angel of the LORD appeared
no more to Manoah and his wife, [q]then
Manoah knew that He *was* the Angel of the
LORD.
22 And Manoah said to his wife, [r]"We
shall surely die, because we have seen
God!"

14 [l] Num. 6:3, 4; Judg. 13:4
15 [m] Gen. 18:5; Judg. 6:18
18 [n] Gen. 32:29
19 [o] Judg. 6:19-21
20 [p] Lev. 9:24; 1 Chr. 21:16; Ezek. 1:28; Matt. 17:6
21 [q] Judg. 6:22
22 [r] Gen. 32:30; Ex. 33:20; Deut. 5:26; Judg. 6:22, 23

13:16 offer it to the LORD. Manoah needed this explanation because he was going to offer this to Him, not as the Lord Himself, or even an angel, but just a human messenger. The instruction is intended to emphasize that this visitor is indeed the Lord.

13:17 What *is* Your name? This secret name is again indicative that the Angel is the Lord.

13:18 Why do you ask My name…? That the Angel would not divulge his name reminds one of the Angel (God) whom Jacob encountered (Ex. 32:24-30), who likewise did not give His name.

13:20 flame went up toward heaven. This miraculous act points to divine acceptance of the offering.

13:22 We shall surely die. This reaction of the fear of death is familiar with those who come into God's presence. Many did die when facing God, as the OT records. It is the terror in the heart of the sinner when in the presence of holy God. Cf. Ezekiel (Ezek. 1:28), Isaiah (Is. 6:5), the 12 (Mark 4:35-41), Peter (Luke 5:8), and John (Rev. 1:17,18).

The Geography of the Judges

The Lord raised up judges in every region of the Land of Promise.

23 But his wife said to him, "If the LORD
had desired to kill us, He would not have
accepted a burnt offering and a grain offering from our hands, nor would He have
shown us all these *things*, nor would He
have told us *such things* as these at this
time."
24 So the woman bore a son and called
his name [s]Samson; and [t]the child grew,
and the LORD blessed him. 25 [u]And the
Spirit of the LORD began to move upon him
at [2]Mahaneh Dan [v]between Zorah and
[w]Eshtaol.

Samson's Philistine Wife

14 Now Samson went down [a]to Timnah, and [b]saw a woman in Timnah
of the daughters of the Philistines. 2 So he
went up and told his father and mother,
saying, "I have seen a woman in Timnah of
the daughters of the Philistines; now therefore, [c]get her for me as a wife."
3 Then his father and mother said to
him, "*Is there* no woman among the daughters of [d]your brethren, or among all my
people, that you must go and get a wife
from the [e]uncircumcised Philistines?"
And Samson said to his father, "Get her
for me, for [1]she pleases me well."
4 But his father and mother did not
know that it was [f]of the LORD—that He
was seeking an occasion to move against
the Philistines. For at that time [g]the Philistines had dominion over Israel.
5 So Samson went down to Timnah with
his father and mother, and came to the
vineyards of Timnah.
Now *to his* surprise, a young lion *came*
roaring against him. 6 And [h]the Spirit of
the LORD came mightily upon him, and he
tore the lion apart as one would have torn
apart a young goat, though *he had* nothing
in his hand. But he did not tell his father or
his mother what he had done.
7 Then he went down and talked with
the woman; and she pleased Samson well.
8 After some time, when he returned to get
her, he turned aside to see the carcass of
the lion. And behold, a swarm of bees and
honey *were* in the carcass of the lion. 9 He
took some of it in his hands and went
along, eating. When he came to his father
and mother, he gave *some* to them, and
they also ate. But he did not tell them that
he had taken the honey out of the [i]carcass
of the lion.
10 So his father went down to the
woman. And Samson gave a feast there,
for young men used to do so. 11 And it
happened, when they saw him, that they
brought thirty companions to be with him.
12 Then Samson said to them, "Let me
[j]pose a riddle to you. If you can correctly
solve and explain it to me [k]within the
seven days of the feast, then I will give you
thirty linen garments and thirty [l]changes
of clothing. 13 But if you cannot explain *it*
to me, then you shall give me thirty linen
garments and thirty changes of clothing."
And they said to him, [m]"Pose your riddle, that we may hear it."
14 So he said to them:

> "Out of the eater came something to
> eat,
> And out of the strong came
> something sweet."

Now for three days they could not explain
the riddle.
15 But it came to pass on the [2]seventh
day that they said to Samson's wife, [n]"Entice your husband, that he may explain the
riddle to us, [o]or else we will burn you and
your father's house with fire. Have you invited us in order to take what is ours? *Is
that* not *so*?"
16 Then Samson's wife wept on him, and
said, [p]"You only hate me! You do not love
me! You have posed a riddle to the sons of
my people, but you have not explained *it*
to me."
And he said to her, "Look, I have not explained *it* to my father or my mother; so
should I explain *it* to you?" 17 Now she
had wept on him the seven days while

24 [s]Heb. 11:32 [t]1 Sam. 3:19; Luke 1:80
25 [u]Judg. 3:10; 1 Sam. 11:6; Matt. 4:1 [v]Josh. 15:33; Judg. 18:11 [w]Judg. 16:31 [2]Lit. *Camp of Dan,* Judg. 18:12

CHAPTER 14

1 [a]Gen. 38:13; Josh. 15:10, 57 [b]Gen. 34:2
2 [c]Gen. 21:21
3 [d]Gen. 24:3, 4 [e]Gen. 34:14; Ex. 34:16; Deut. 7:3 [1]Lit. *she is right in my eyes*
4 [f]Josh. 11:20; 1 Kin. 12:15; 2 Kin. 6:33; 2 Chr. 10:15 [g]Deut. 28:48; Judg. 13:1
6 [h]Judg. 3:10
9 [i]Lev. 11:27
12 [j]1 Kin. 10:1; Ezek. 17:2 [k]Gen. 29:27 [l]Gen. 45:22; 2 Kin. 5:22
13 [m]Ezek. 17:2
15 [n]Judg. 16:5 [o]Judg. 15:6 [2]So with MT, Tg., Vg.; LXX, Syr. *fourth*
16 [p]Judg. 16:15

14:1-4 she pleases me well. The Philistines were not among the 7 nations of Canaan which Israel was specifically forbidden to marry. Nonetheless Samson's choice was seriously weak. Samson sins here, but God is sovereign and was able to turn the situation to please Him (14:4). He was not at a loss, but used the opportunity to work against the wicked Philistines and provided gracious help to His people. He achieved destruction of these people, not by an army, but by the miraculous power of one man.

14:7 talked. Such conversation was not acceptable in the E, unless a couple was betrothed.

14:8 to get her. Usually a year until the wedding.

14:9 He took some...in his hands. Some scholars suggest that Samson violated his Nazirite standard by coming in contact with a dead body (*see 13:5 and note*). Others reason that Num. 6 specifies the body of a person, not an animal. Whether or not he sinned here, the context does show instances of him sinning.

14:10 feast. The wedding feast usually lasted a week.

14:15 seventh. Some ancient authorities read "fourth." The number may be "fourth" (4 days starting after the 3 in v. 14), totaling 7 as in v. 17. Or v. 15 may mean "fourth," and v. 17 that the woman wept for the rest of the 7-day period of v. 12, after the 3 days of v. 14.

14:16-18 Samson's wife wept. She cheated and manipulated, working against Samson's expectations that the men must come up with the answer. The men also cheated and threatened, having murder in their hearts (v. 15) and putting pressure on the woman.

their feast lasted. And it happened on the
seventh day that he told her, because she
pressed him so much. Then she explained
the riddle to the sons of her people. **18** So
the men of the city said to him on the seventh day before the sun went down:

"What *is* sweeter than honey?
And what *is* stronger than a lion?"

And he said to them:

"If you had not plowed with my
heifer,
You would not have solved my
riddle!"

19 Then [q]the Spirit of the LORD came
upon him mightily, and he went down to
Ashkelon and killed thirty of their men,
took their apparel, and gave the changes *of
clothing* to those who had explained the
riddle. So his anger was aroused, and he
went back up to his father's house. **20** And
Samson's wife [r]was *given* to his companion, who had been [s]his best man.

Samson Defeats the Philistines

15 After a while, in the time of wheat
harvest, it happened that Samson
visited his wife with a [a]young goat. And
he said, "Let me go in to my wife, into *her*
room." But her father would not permit
him to go in.
2 Her father said, "I really thought that
you thoroughly [b]hated her; therefore I
gave her to your companion. *Is* not her
younger sister better than she? Please, take
her instead."
3 And Samson said to them, "This time I
shall be blameless regarding the Philistines
if I harm them!" **4** Then Samson went and
caught three hundred foxes; and he took
torches, turned *the foxes* tail to tail, and put
a torch between each pair of tails. **5** When
he had set the torches on fire, he let *the
foxes* go into the standing grain of the Philistines, and burned up both the shocks
and the standing grain, as well as the vineyards *and* olive groves.
6 Then the Philistines said, "Who has
done this?"
And they answered, "Samson, the son-
in-law of the Timnite, because he has taken
his wife and given her to his companion."
[c]So the Philistines came up and burned her
and her father with fire.
7 Samson said to them, "Since you
would do a thing like this, I will surely
take revenge on you, and after that I will
cease." **8** So he attacked them hip and thigh
with a great slaughter; then he went down
and dwelt in the cleft of the rock of [d]Etam.
9 Now the Philistines went up, encamped in Judah, and deployed themselves [e]against Lehi. **10** And the men of Judah said, "Why have you come up against
us?"
So they answered, "We have come up to
[1]arrest Samson, to do to him as he has
done to us."
11 Then three thousand men of Judah
went down to the cleft of the rock of Etam,
and said to Samson, "Do you not know
that the Philistines [f]rule over us? What *is*
this you have done to us?"
And he said to them, "As they did to me,
so I have done to them."
12 But they said to him, "We have come
down to arrest you, that we may deliver
you into the hand of the Philistines."
Then Samson said to them, "Swear to
me that you will not kill me yourselves."
13 So they spoke to him, saying, "No, but
we will tie you securely and deliver you
into their hand; but we will surely not kill
you." And they bound him with two [g]new
ropes and brought him up from the rock.
14 When he came to Lehi, the Philistines
came shouting against him. Then [h]the
Spirit of the LORD came mightily upon
him; and the ropes that *were* on his arms

19 [q]Judg. 3:10; 13:25
20 [r]Judg. 15:2 [s]John 3:29

CHAPTER 15

1 [a]Gen. 38:17
2 [b]Judg. 14:20
6 [c]Judg. 14:15
8 [d]2 Chr. 11:6
9 [e]Judg. 15:19
10 [1]Lit. *bind*
11 [f]Lev. 26:25; Deut. 28:43; Judg. 13:1; 14:4; Ps. 106:40-42
13 [g]Judg. 16:11, 12
14 [h]Judg. 3:10; 14:6

14:19 his anger. God blesses the one who had been wronged. Samson's anger may be legitimate—righteous indignation against deceit (cf. Mark 3:5). The battle with the men at Ashkelon, about 23 mi. away, was a part of the war between Israel and Philistia.

14:20 Samson's wife was *given*. Another act of treachery was done. The Philistine father had no reason to assume that Samson would not be back, nor had Samson given word about not returning. He, as a Philistine, did not want his daughter marrying the enemy.

15:1 wheat harvest. Samson tactfully made his move when wheat harvest kept men busy. This was probably around May. A token of reconciliation was offered as he brought a young goat, showing the father and the daughter that they had nothing to fear.

15:2 I...thought. This flimsy excuse by the father was an effort to escape the trap he was in. He feared the Philistines if he turned on the new husband, yet feared Samson, so he offered his second daughter as a way out. This was insulting and unlawful (cf. Lev. 18:18).

15:3 The cycle of retaliation began, and it ends in 16:30,31.

15:4 caught three hundred foxes. Samson, insulted and provoked to fleshly resentment, took vengeance on the Philistines. It must have taken a while to catch so many foxes or jackals and to keep them penned and fed until the number reached 300. Apparently he tied them in pairs with a slow-burning torch, sending the pairs down the hills into fields thrashing with fire, igniting all the standing grain so dry at harvest. This was a loss of great proportion to the Philistine farmers.

15:6 the Philistines...burned her and her father. The general principle of reaping what is sown is apropos here (cf. Gal. 6:7).

15:8 he attacked them hip and thigh. This is proverbial for a ruthless slaughter.

became like flax that is burned with fire,
and his bonds [2]broke loose from his hands.
15 He found a fresh jawbone of a donkey,
reached out his hand and took it, and
[i]killed a thousand men with it. 16 Then
Samson said:

> "With the jawbone of a donkey,
> Heaps upon heaps,
> With the jawbone of a donkey
> I have slain a thousand men!"

17 And so it was, when he had finished
speaking, that he threw the jawbone from
his hand, and called that place [3]Ramath
Lehi.
18 Then he became very thirsty; so he
cried out to the LORD and said, [j]"You have
given this great deliverance by the hand of
Your servant; and now shall I die of thirst
and fall into the hand of the uncircumcised?" 19 So God split the hollow place
that *is* in [4]Lehi, and water came out, and he
drank; and [k]his spirit returned, and he revived. Therefore he called its name [5]En
Hakkore, which is in Lehi to this day.
20 And [l]he judged Israel [m]twenty years [n]in
the days of the Philistines.

Samson and Delilah

16 Now Samson went to [a]Gaza and
saw a harlot there, and went in to
her. 2 *When* the Gazites *were told,* "Samson
has come here!" they [b]surrounded *the place*
and lay in wait for him all night at the gate
of the city. They were quiet all night, saying, "In the morning, when it is daylight,
we will kill him." 3 And Samson lay *low* till
midnight; then he arose at midnight, took
hold of the doors of the gate of the city and
the two gateposts, pulled them up, bar and
all, put *them* on his shoulders, and carried
them to the top of the hill that faces Hebron.
4 Afterward it happened that he loved a
woman in the Valley of Sorek, whose name
was Delilah. 5 And the [c]lords of the Philistines came up to her and said to her,
[d]"Entice him, and find out where his great
strength *lies,* and by what *means* we may
overpower him, that we may bind him to
afflict him; and every one of us will give
you eleven hundred *pieces* of silver."
6 So Delilah said to Samson, "Please tell
me where your great strength *lies,* and
with what you may be bound to afflict
you."
7 And Samson said to her, "If they bind
me with seven fresh bowstrings, not yet
dried, then I shall become weak, and be
like any *other* man."
8 So the lords of the Philistines brought
up to her seven fresh bowstrings, not yet
dried, and she bound him with them.
9 Now *men were* lying in wait, staying with
her in the room. And she said to him, "The
Philistines *are* upon you, Samson!" But he
broke the bowstrings as a strand of yarn
breaks when it touches fire. So the secret of
his strength was not known.
10 Then Delilah said to Samson, "Look,
you have mocked me and told me lies.
Now, please tell me what you may be
bound with."
11 So he said to her, "If they bind me securely with [e]new ropes [1]that have never
been used, then I shall become weak, and
be like any *other* man."
12 Therefore Delilah took new ropes and
bound him with them, and said to him,
"The Philistines *are* upon you, Samson!"
And *men were* lying in wait, staying in the
room. But he broke them off his arms like a
thread.
13 Delilah said to Samson, "Until now
you have mocked me and told me lies. Tell
me what you may be bound with."
And he said to her, "If you weave the
seven locks of my head into the web of the
loom"—
14 So she wove *it* tightly with the batten
of the loom, and said to him, "The Philistines *are* upon you, Samson!" But he
awoke from his sleep, and pulled out the
batten and the web from the loom.
15 Then she said to him, [f]"How can you
say, 'I love you,' when your heart *is* not
with me? You have mocked me these three

14 [2] Lit. *were melted*
15 [i] Lev. 26:8; Josh. 23:10; Judg. 3:31
17 [3] Lit. *Jawbone Height*
18 [j] Ps. 3:7
19 [k] Gen. 45:27; Is. 40:29 [4] Lit. *Jawbone,* Judg. 15:14 [5] Lit. *Spring of the Caller*
20 [l] Judg. 10:2; 12:7-14 [m] Judg. 16:31 [n] Judg. 13:1

CHAPTER 16

1 [a] Josh. 15:47
2 [b] 1 Sam. 23:26; Ps. 118:10-12
5 [c] Josh. 13:3 [d] Judg. 14:15
11 [e] Judg. 15:13 [1] Lit. *with which work has never been done*
15 [f] Judg. 14:16

15:15 killed a thousand men. Cf. 3:31. God gave miraculous power to Samson for destruction, but also to show fearful Israelites (v. 11) that He was with them, despite their lack of trust.

15:19 water came out. God worked a miracle of supplying a spring in response to Samson's prayerful cry in thirst. He called the place "the spring of him that called" (cf. Jer. 33:3).

16:1-3 God was merciful in allowing Samson to be delivered from this iniquity, but chastening was only postponed. Sin blinds and later grinds (v. 21).

16:3 hill that faces Hebron. This place was about 38 mi. from Gaza.

16:4 loved...Delilah. His weakness for women of low character and Philistine loyalty reappeared (cf. Prov. 6:27,28). He erred continually by going to her daily (v. 16), allowing himself to be entrapped in her deceptions.

16:5 eleven hundred *pieces* of silver. Since there were 5 rulers of the Philistines, each giving that amount, this was a large sum.

16:7 And Samson said. Samson played a lying game and gave away his manhood, here a little, there a little. He also played with giving away his secret—and finally gave it up, i.e., "told her all" (v. 17). He could be bought for a price, and Delilah paid it. Compare Esau selling his birthright (Gen. 25:29-33) and Judas denying Jesus (Matt. 26:14-16).

16:11 new ropes. Cf. 15:13.

times, and have not told me where your
great strength *lies*." 16 And it came to pass,
when she pestered him daily with her
words and pressed him, *so* that his soul
was [2]vexed to death, 17 that he [g]told her all
his heart, and said to her, [h]"No razor has
ever come upon my head, for I *have been* a
Nazirite to God from my mother's womb.
If I am shaven, then my strength will leave
me, and I shall become weak, and be like
any *other* man."
18 When Delilah saw that he had told
her all his heart, she sent and called for the
lords of the Philistines, saying, "Come up
once more, for he has told me all his
heart." So the lords of the Philistines came
up to her and brought the money in their
hand. 19 [i]Then she lulled him to sleep on
her knees, and called for a man and had
him shave off the seven locks of his head.
Then [3]she began to torment him, and his
strength left him. 20 And she said, "The
Philistines *are* upon you, Samson!" So he
awoke from his sleep, and said, "I will go
out as before, at other times, and shake
myself free!" But he did not know that the
LORD [j]had departed from him.
21 Then the Philistines took him and
[4]put out his [k]eyes, and brought him down
to Gaza. They bound him with bronze fetters, and he became a grinder in the
prison. 22 However, the hair of his head
began to grow again after it had been
shaven.

Samson Dies with the Philistines

23 Now the lords of the Philistines gathered together to offer a great sacrifice to
[l]Dagon their god, and to rejoice. And they
said:

"Our god has delivered into our
hands
Samson our enemy!"

24 When the people saw him, they
[m]praised their god; for they said:

"Our god has delivered into our
hands our enemy,
The destroyer of our land,
And the one who multiplied our
dead."

25 So it happened, when their hearts were
[n]merry, that they said, "Call for Samson,
that he may perform for us." So they called
for Samson from the prison, and he performed for them. And they stationed him
between the pillars. 26 Then Samson said
to the lad who held him by the hand, "Let
me feel the pillars which support the temple, so that I can lean on them." 27 Now the
temple was full of men and women. All the
lords of the Philistines *were* there—about
three thousand men and women on the
[o]roof watching while Samson performed.
28 Then Samson called to the LORD, saying, "O Lord GOD, [p]remember me, I pray!
Strengthen me, I pray, just this once, O
God, that I may with one *blow* take
vengeance on the Philistines for my two
eyes!" 29 And Samson took hold of the two
middle pillars which supported the temple, and he braced himself against them,
one on his right and the other on his left.
30 Then Samson said, "Let me die with the
Philistines!" And he pushed with *all his*
might, and the temple fell on the lords and
all the people who *were* in it. So the dead
that he killed at his death were more than
he had killed in his life.
31 And his brothers and all his father's
household came down and took him, and
brought *him* up and [q]buried him between
Zorah and Eshtaol in the tomb of his father
Manoah. He had judged Israel [r]twenty
years.

16 [2] Lit. *impatient to the point of*
17 [g] [Mic. 7:5] [h] Num. 6:5; Judg. 13:5
19 [i] Prov. 7:26, 27 [3] So with MT, Tg., Vg.; LXX *he began to be weak,*
20 [j] Num. 14:9, 42, 43; [Josh. 7:12]; 1 Sam. 16:14; 18:12; 28:15, 16; 2 Chr. 15:2
21 [k] 2 Kin. 25:7 [4] Lit. *bored out*
23 [l] 1 Sam. 5:2
24 [m] Dan. 5:4
25 [n] Judg. 9:27
27 [o] Deut. 22:8
28 [p] Jer. 15:15
31 [q] Judg. 13:25 [r] Judg. 15:20

16:17 If I am shaven. His strength came from his unique relation to God, based on his Nazirite pledge. His long hair was only a sign of it. When Delilah became more important to him than God, his strength was removed.

16:20 he did not know that the LORD had departed from him. Here was the tragedy of the wrath of abandonment. His sin had caused him to forfeit the power of God's presence. This principle is seen in Gen. 6:3; Prov. 1:24-31; Matt. 15:14; Rom. 1:24-32. *See note on Judg. 10:13,14.*

16:21 Gaza. The last town encountered in SW Palestine as a traveler went from Jerusalem toward Egypt, near the coast. It was nearly 40 mi. from Samson's birthplace, Zorah. There he was humiliated.

16:22 hair...began to grow. His hair grew with his repentance, and his strength with his hair.

16:23 Dagon. He was a sea-god, an idol with the head of a fish and the body of a man.

16:24 they praised their god. It is tragic when a person's sin contributes to the unsaved community giving praise to a false god, for God alone is worthy of praise.

16:28 remember me, I pray! A prayer of repentance and trust pours from Samson.

16:29,30 Some Philistine temples had roofs overlooking a courtyard, above wooden columns planted on stone foundations. The central pillars were set close to furnish extra support for the roof. Here the victory celebration and taunts flung at the prisoner below drew a big crowd. The full strength of Samson, renewed by God, enabled him to buckle the columns. As a result, the roof collapsed and the victory was Israel's, not Philistia's. He died for the cause of his country and his God. He was not committing suicide, but rather bringing God's judgment on His enemies and willing to leave his own life or death to God. He was the greatest champion of all Israel, yet a man of passion capable of severe sin. Still, he is in the list of the faithful (cf. Heb. 11:32).

Micah's Idolatry

17 Now there was a man from the
mountains of Ephraim, whose name
was [a]Micah. 2 And he said to his mother,
"The eleven hundred *shekels* of silver that
were taken from you, and on which you
[b]put a curse, even saying it in my ears—
here *is* the silver with me; I took it."
And his mother said, [c]"*May you be*
blessed by the LORD, my son!" 3 So when
he had returned the eleven hundred *shekels*
of silver to his mother, his mother said, "I
had wholly dedicated the silver from my
hand to the LORD for my son, to [d]make a
carved image and a molded image; now
therefore, I will return it to you." 4 Thus he
returned the silver to his mother. Then his
mother [e]took two hundred *shekels* of silver
and gave them to the silversmith, and he
made it into a carved image and a molded
image; and they were in the house of
Micah.
5 The man Micah had a [f]shrine, and
made an [g]ephod and [h]household[1] idols;
and he consecrated one of his sons, who
became his priest. 6 [i]In those days *there was*
no king in Israel; [j]everyone did *what was*
right in his own eyes.
7 Now there was a young man from
[k]Bethlehem in Judah, of the family of Judah; he *was* a Levite, and [l]was staying
there. 8 The man departed from the city of
Bethlehem in Judah to stay wherever he
could find *a place*. Then he came to the
mountains of Ephraim, to the house of
Micah, as he journeyed. 9 And Micah said
to him, "Where do you come from?"
So he said to him, "I *am* a Levite from
Bethlehem in Judah, and I am on my way
to find *a place* to stay."
10 Micah said to him, "Dwell with me,
[m]and be a [n]father and a priest to me, and I
will give you ten *shekels* of silver per year,
a suit of clothes, and your sustenance." So
the Levite went in. 11 Then the Levite was
content to dwell with the man; and the
young man became like one of his sons to
him. 12 So Micah [o]consecrated[2] the Levite,
and the young man [p]became his priest,
and lived in the house of Micah. 13 Then
Micah said, "Now I know that the LORD
will be good to me, since I have a Levite as
[q]priest!"

The Danites Adopt Micah's Idolatry

18 In [a]those days *there was* no king in
Israel. And in those days [b]the tribe
of the Danites was seeking an inheritance
for itself to dwell in; for until that day *their*
inheritance among the tribes of Israel had
not fallen to them. 2 So the children of Dan
sent five men of their family from their territory, men of valor from [c]Zorah and
Eshtaol, [d]to spy out the land and search it.
They said to them, "Go, search the land."
So they went to the mountains of Ephraim,
to the [e]house of Micah, and lodged there.
3 While they *were* at the house of Micah,
they recognized the voice of the young
Levite. They turned aside and said to him,
"Who brought you here? What are you
doing in this *place?* What do you have
here?"
4 He said to them, "Thus and so Micah
did for me. He has [f]hired me, and I have
become his priest."
5 So they said to him, "Please [g]inquire
[h]of God, that we may know whether the
journey on which we go will be prosperous."
6 And the priest said to them, [i]"Go in
peace. [1]The presence of the LORD *be* with
you on your way."
7 So the five men departed and went to
[j]Laish. They saw the people who *were*
there, [k]how they dwelt safely, in the manner of the Sidonians, quiet and secure.
There were no rulers in the land who might
put *them* to shame for anything. They *were*
far from the [l]Sidonians, and they had no
ties [2]with anyone.
8 Then *the spies* came back to their
brethren at [m]Zorah and Eshtaol, and their
brethren said to them, "What *is* your *re-*
port?"
9 So they said, [n]"Arise, let us go up
against them. For we have seen the land,
and indeed it *is* very good. *Would* you [o]*do*
nothing? Do not hesitate to go, *and* enter to

CHAPTER 17

1 [a] Judg. 18:2
2 [b] Lev. 5:1 [c] Gen. 14:19
3 [d] Ex. 20:4, 23; 34:17; Lev. 19:4
4 [e] Is. 46:6
5 [f] Judg. 18:24 [g] Judg. 8:27; 18:14 [h] Gen. 31:19, 30; Hos. 3:4 [1] Heb. *teraphim*
6 [i] Judg. 18:1; 19:1 [j] Deut. 12:8; Judg. 21:25
7 [k] Josh. 19:15; Judg. 19:1; Ruth 1:1, 2; Mic. 5:2; Matt. 2:1, 5, 6 [l] Deut. 18:6
10 [m] Judg. 18:19 [n] Gen. 45:8; Job 29:16
12 [o] Judg. 17:5 [p] Judg. 18:30 [2] Lit. *filled the hand of*
13 [q] Judg. 18:4

CHAPTER 18

1 [a] Judg. 17:6; 19:1; 21:25 [b] Josh. 19:40-48
2 [c] Judg. 13:25 [d] Num. 13:17; Josh. 2:1 [e] Judg. 17:1
4 [f] Judg. 17:10, 12
5 [g] 1 Kin. 22:5; [Is. 30:1]; Hos. 4:12 [h] Judg. 1:1; 17:5; 18:14
6 [i] 1 Kin. 22:6 [1] Lit. *The LORD is before the way in which you go*
7 [j] Josh. 19:47 [k] Judg. 18:27-29 [l] Judg. 10:12 [2] So with MT, Tg., Vg.; LXX *with Syria*
8 [m] Judg. 18:2
9 [n] Num. 13:30; Josh. 2:23, 24 [o] 1 Kin. 22:3

17:1 Chapters 17–21 give miscellaneous appendixes to illustrate the pervasively depraved conditions in the era of the judges.

17:5 Micah had a shrine. A counterfeit shrine and personal idols with a private priest is set up within the tribe of Ephraim (v. 1), whereas God's priests were of the tribe of Levi (cf. v. 13). The defection is one example of personal and family idolatry.

17:6 everyone did . . . own eyes. This is the general characterization of the time, and of sinful behavior in all times. This attitude had been mentioned much earlier in Israel's history (cf. Deut. 12:8; Judg. 21:25).

17:7-13 a Levite. He compromised in departing from one of the 48 cities God gave for Levite service to Israel (Josh. 21). Then he sinned grossly by prostituting himself as a priest in a private idolatry.

18:2 On the migration by the tribe of Dan to a new territory, *see note on 1:34*. Dan was an example of tribal idolatry.

18:5 Please inquire of God. The passage does not say if the Levite did in fact seek God's counsel before giving reassurance (v. 6); the Danites should have prayed to seek God's counsel before making this trip or consulting a disobedient priest as one would an oracle.

18:7 Laish. Known also as Leshem (cf. Josh. 19:47), this was a secluded, rich land.

possess the land. 10 When you go, you will
come to a [p]secure people and a large land.
For God has given it into your hands, [q]a
place where *there is* no lack of anything
that *is* on the earth."
11 And six hundred men of the family of
the Danites went from there, from Zorah
and Eshtaol, armed with weapons of war.
12 Then they went up and encamped in
[r]Kirjath Jearim in Judah. (Therefore they
call that place [s]Mahaneh Dan[3] to this day.
There *it is,* west of Kirjath Jearim.) 13 And
they passed from there to the mountains of
Ephraim, and came to [t]the house of Micah.
14 [u]Then the five men who had gone to
spy out the country of Laish answered and
said to their brethren, "Do you know that
[v]there are in these houses an ephod,
household idols, a carved image, and a
molded image? Now therefore, consider
what you should do." 15 So they turned
aside there, and came to the house of the
young Levite man—to the house of
Micah—and greeted him. 16 The [w]six hundred men armed with their weapons of
war, who *were* of the children of Dan, stood
by the entrance of the gate. 17 Then [x]the
five men who had gone to spy out the land
went up. Entering there, they took [y]the
carved image, the ephod, the household
idols, and the molded image. The priest
stood at the entrance of the gate with the
six hundred men *who were* armed with
weapons of war.
18 When these went into Micah's house
and took the carved image, the ephod, the
household idols, and the molded image,
the priest said to them, "What are you
doing?"
19 And they said to him, "Be quiet, [z]put
your hand over your mouth, and come
with us; [a]be a father and a priest to us. *Is it*
better for you to be a priest to the household of one man, or that you be a priest to
a tribe and a family in Israel?" 20 So the
priest's heart was glad; and he took the
ephod, the household idols, and the carved
image, and took his place among the people.
21 Then they turned and departed, and
put the little ones, the livestock, and the
goods in front of them. 22 When they were
a good way from the house of Micah, the
men who *were* in the houses near Micah's
house gathered together and overtook the
children of Dan. 23 And they called out to
the children of Dan. So they turned around
and said to Micah, [b]"What ails you, that
you have gathered such a company?"
24 So he said, "You have [c]taken away my
[4]gods which I made, and the priest, and
you have gone away. Now what more do I
have? How can you say to me, 'What ails
you?' "
25 And the children of Dan said to him,
"Do not let your voice be heard among us,
lest [5]angry men fall upon you, and you
lose your life, with the lives of your household!" 26 Then the children of Dan went
their way. And when Micah saw that they
were too strong for him, he turned and
went back to his house.

Danites Settle in Laish

27 So they took *the things* Micah had
made, and the priest who had belonged to
him, and went to Laish, to a people quiet
and secure; [d]and they struck them with the
edge of the sword and burned the city with
fire. 28 *There was* no deliverer, because it
was [e]far from Sidon, and they had no ties
with anyone. It was in the valley that belongs [f]to Beth Rehob. So they rebuilt the
city and dwelt there. 29 And [g]they called
the name of the city [h]Dan, after the name
of Dan their father, who was born to Israel.
However, the name of the city formerly
was Laish.
30 Then the children of Dan set up for
themselves the carved image; and Jonathan the son of Gershom, the son of [6]Ma-
nasseh, and his sons were priests to the
tribe of Dan [i]until the day of the captivity
of the land. 31 So they set up for themselves Micah's carved image which he
made, [j]all the time that the house of God
was in Shiloh.

The Levite's Concubine

19 And it came to pass in those days,
[a]when *there was* no king in Israel,
that there was a certain Levite staying in

10 [p] Judg. 18:7, 27 [q] Deut. 8:9
12 [r] Josh. 15:60 [s] Judg. 13:25 [3] Lit. *Camp of Dan*
13 [t] Judg. 18:2
14 [u] 1 Sam. 14:28 [v] Judg. 17:5
16 [w] Judg. 18:11
17 [x] Judg. 18:2, 14 [y] Judg. 17:4, 5
19 [z] Job 21:5; 29:9; 40:4; Mic. 7:16 [a] Judg. 17:10
23 [b] 2 Kin. 6:28
24 [c] Gen. 31:30; Judg. 17:5 [4] *idols*
25 [5] Lit. *bitter of soul*
27 [d] Josh. 19:47
28 [e] Judg. 18:7 [f] Num. 13:21; 2 Sam. 10:6
29 [g] Josh. 19:47 [h] Judg. 20:1; 1 Kin. 12:29, 30; 15:20
30 [i] 2 Kin. 15:29 [6] LXX, Vg. *Moses*
31 [j] Deut. 12:1-32; Josh. 18:1, 8; Judg. 19:18; 21:12

CHAPTER 19
1 [a] Judg. 17:6; 18:1; 21:25

18:14-26 The Danites sinfully seized the idols of Micah by force, probably because they believed those false idols were the source of power to give them the land they had spied. The apostate Levite who had served Micah as priest, named Jonathan, sold out again to be a priest for the Danites (vv. 18-20,30), who were not bothered by his defection, but rather believed in his spiritual power.

18:29 name of the city Dan. This was in the northernmost extremity of the land of Canaan, hence the origin of the phrase, "from Dan to Beersheba," as indicating the land from N to S (cf. 20:1).

18:30 the son of Manasseh. Some manuscripts say "son of Manasseh," others "son of Moses," which may be more probable as Gershom was a son of Moses (Ex. 2:22; 18:3). This idolatrous priestly service continued until the captivity. This is most likely 1) the captivity of Israel by Assyria in 722 B.C. (2 Kin. 15:29; 17:1-6), or possibly 2) the Philistine captivity of the ark from Shiloh (see Judg. 18:31) in 1 Sam. 4:11.

18:31 the house of God was in Shiloh. The ark of God was far away from them, so they justified their idolatry by their distance from the rest of Israel. This caused perpetual idolatry for many generations.

the remote mountains of Ephraim. He
took for himself a concubine from [b]Bethle-
hem in Judah. 2 But his concubine played
the harlot against him, and went away
from him to her father's house at Bethlehem in Judah, and was there four whole
months. 3 Then her husband arose and
went after her, to [c]speak [1]kindly to her *and*
bring her back, having his servant and a
couple of donkeys with him. So she
brought him into her father's house; and
when the father of the young woman saw
him, he was glad to meet him. 4 Now his
father-in-law, the young woman's father,
detained him; and he stayed with him
three days. So they ate and drank and
lodged there.
5 Then it came to pass on the fourth day
that they arose early in the morning, and
he stood to depart; but the young woman's
father said to his son-in-law, [d]"Refresh
your heart with a morsel of bread, and afterward go your way."
6 So they sat down, and the two of them
ate and drank together. Then the young
woman's father said to the man, "Please be
content to stay all night, and let your heart
be merry." 7 And when the man stood to
depart, his father-in-law urged him; so he
lodged there again. 8 Then he arose early
in the morning on the fifth day to depart,
but the young woman's father said,
"Please refresh your heart." So they delayed until afternoon; and both of them
ate.
9 And when the man stood to depart—
he and his concubine and his servant—his
father-in-law, the young woman's father,
said to him, "Look, the day is now drawing toward evening; please spend the
night. See, the day is coming to an end;
lodge here, that your heart may be merry.
Tomorrow go your way early, so that you
may get [2]home."
10 However, the man was not willing to
spend that night; so he rose and departed,
and came opposite [e]Jebus (that *is,* Jerusalem). With him were the two saddled donkeys; his concubine *was* also with him.
11 They *were* near Jebus, and the day was
far spent; and the servant said to his master, "Come, please, and let us turn aside
into this city [f]of the Jebusites and lodge
in it."
12 But his master said to him, "We will
not turn aside here into a city of foreigners,
who *are* not of the children of Israel; we
will go on [g]to Gibeah." 13 So he said to his
servant, "Come, let us draw near to one of
these places, and spend the night in Gibeah or in [h]Ramah." 14 And they passed by
and went their way; and the sun went
down on them near Gibeah, which belongs
to Benjamin. 15 They turned aside there to
go in to lodge in Gibeah. And when he
went in, he sat down in the open square of
the city, for no one would [i]take them into
his house to spend the night.
16 Just then an old man came in from [j]his
work in the field at evening, who also *was*
from the mountains of Ephraim; he was
staying in Gibeah, whereas the men of the
place *were* Benjamites. 17 And when he
raised his eyes, he saw the traveler in the
open square of the city; and the old man
said, "Where are you going, and where do
you come from?"
18 So he said to him, "We *are* passing
from Bethlehem in Judah toward the remote mountains of Ephraim; I *am* from
there. I went to Bethlehem in Judah; *now* I
am going to [k]the house of the LORD. But
there *is* no one who will take me into his
house, 19 although we have both straw and
fodder for our donkeys, and bread and
wine for myself, for your female servant,
and for the young man *who is* with your
servant; *there is* no lack of anything."
20 And the old man said, [l]"Peace *be* with
you! However, *let* all your needs *be* my responsibility; [m]only do not spend the night
in the open square." 21 [n]So he brought him
into his house, and gave fodder to the donkeys. [o]And they washed their feet, and ate
and drank.

Gibeah's Crime

22 As they were [p]enjoying themselves,

1 [b] Judg. 17:7; Ruth 1:1
3 [c] Gen. 34:3; 50:21
[1] Lit. *to her heart*
5 [d] Gen. 18:5; Judg. 19:8; Ps. 104:15
9 [2] Lit. *to your tent*
10 [e] Josh. 18:28; 1 Chr. 11:4, 5
11 [f] Josh. 15:8, 63; Judg. 1:21; 2 Sam. 5:6
12 [g] Josh. 18:28
13 [h] Josh. 18:25
15 [i] Matt. 25:43
16 [j] Ps. 104:23
18 [k] Josh. 18:1; Judg. 18:31; 20:18; 1 Sam. 1:3, 7
20 [l] Gen. 43:23; Judg. 6:23; 1 Sam. 25:6
[m] Gen. 19:2
21 [n] Gen. 24:32; 43:24
[o] Gen. 18:4; John 13:5
22 [p] Judg. 16:25; 19:6, 9

19:1-10 Here is an example of the kind of personal immorality that went on during this era.

19:1 concubine. Priests could marry (Lev. 21:7,13,14). Though a concubine wife (usually a slave) was culturally legal, the practice was not acceptable to God (Gen. 2:24).

19:2 played the harlot. She should have been killed as the law required and could have been if there was a devotion to holiness and obedience to Scripture (cf. Lev. 20:10). A priest was not allowed to marry a harlot (Lev. 21:14), so his ministry was greatly tainted. Yet, he made little of her sin and separation and sought her back sympathetically (v. 3).

19:10 Jebus. An early title for Jerusalem because of Jebusite control (Judg. 1:21) until David wrested it away to become his capital (2 Sam. 5:6-9). Another early name for the city was Salem (Gen. 14:18; cf. Ps. 76:2).

19:12 Gibeah. Jerusalem was still partially out of the control of Israelites. Gibeah was under Israelite control and safer.

19:15 People of the Benjamite town of Gibeah failed to extend the expected courtesy of a lodging. This opened the door to immorality.

19:18 going to the house of the LORD. He was headed for Shiloh to return to priestly duty.

19:20 night in the open square. The old man knew the danger of such a place at night.

suddenly [q]certain men of the city, [r]per-
verted[3] men, surrounded the house *and*
beat on the door. They spoke to the master
of the house, the old man, saying, [s]"Bring
out the man who came to your house, that
we may know him *carnally!*"
23 But [t]the man, the master of the house,
went out to them and said to them, "No,
my brethren! I beg you, do not act *so*
wickedly! Seeing this man has come into
my house, [u]do not commit this outrage.
24 [v]Look, *here is* my virgin daughter and
[4]*the man's* concubine; let me bring them
out now. [w]Humble them, and do with
them as you please; but to this man do not
do such a vile thing!" **25** But the men
would not heed him. So the man took his
concubine and brought *her* out to them.
And they [x]knew her and abused her all
night until morning; and when the day
began to break, they let her go.
26 Then the woman came as the day was
dawning, and fell down at the door of the
man's house where her master *was,* till it
was light.
27 When her master arose in the morning, and opened the doors of the house and
went out to go his way, there was his concubine, fallen *at* the door of the house with
her hands on the threshold. **28** And he said
to her, "Get up and let us be going." But
[y]there was no answer. So the man lifted
her onto the donkey; and the man got up
and went to his place.
29 When he entered his house he took a
knife, laid hold of his concubine, and [z]di-
vided her into twelve pieces, [5]limb by
limb, and sent her throughout all the territory of Israel. **30** And so it was that all who
saw it said, "No such deed has been done
or seen from the day that the children of Israel came up from the land of Egypt until
this day. Consider it, [a]confer, and speak
up!"

Israel's War with the Benjamites

20 So [a]all the children of Israel came
out, from [b]Dan to [c]Beersheba, as
well as from the land of Gilead, and the congregation gathered together as one man before the LORD [d]at Mizpah. **2** And the leaders
of all the people, all the tribes of Israel, presented themselves in the assembly of the
people of God, four hundred thousand foot
soldiers [e]who drew the sword. **3** (Now the
children of Benjamin heard that the children
of Israel had gone up to Mizpah.)
Then the children of Israel said, "Tell *us,*
how did this wicked deed happen?"
4 So the Levite, the husband of the
woman who was murdered, answered and
said, "My concubine and [f]I went into Gibeah, which belongs to Benjamin, to spend
the night. **5** [g]And the men of Gibeah rose
against me, and surrounded the house at
night because of me. They intended to kill
me, [h]but instead they ravished my concubine so that she died. **6** So [i]I took hold of
my concubine, cut her in pieces, and sent
her throughout all the territory of the inheritance of Israel, because they [j]commit-
ted lewdness and outrage in Israel. **7** Look!
All of you *are* children of Israel; [k]give your
advice and counsel here and now!"
8 So all the people arose as one man, saying, "None *of us* will go to his tent, nor will
any turn back to his house; **9** but now this
is the thing which we will do to Gibeah: *We
will go up* [l]against it by lot. **10** We will take
ten men out of *every* hundred throughout
all the tribes of Israel, a hundred out of
every thousand, and a thousand out of
every ten thousand, to make provisions for
the people, that when they come to Gibeah
in Benjamin, they may repay all the vileness that they have done in Israel." **11** So
all the men of Israel were gathered against
the city, united together as one man.
12 [m]Then the tribes of Israel sent men

22 [q]Gen. 19:4, 5; Judg. 20:5; Hos. 9:9; 10:9 [r]Deut. 13:13; 1 Sam. 2:12; 1 Kin. 21:10; [2 Cor. 6:15] [s]Gen. 19:5; [Rom. 1:26, 27] [3]Lit. *sons of Belial*
23 [t]Gen. 19:6, 7 [u]Gen. 34:7; Deut. 22:21; Judg. 20:6, 10; 2 Sam. 13:12
24 [v]Gen. 19:8 [w]Gen. 34:2; Deut. 21:14 [4]Lit. *his*
25 [x]Gen. 4:1
28 [y]Judg. 20:5
29 [z]Judg. 20:6; 1 Sam. 11:7 [5]Lit. *with her bones*
30 [a]Judg. 20:7; Prov. 13:10

CHAPTER 20

1 [a]Josh. 22:12; Judg. 20:11; 21:5 [b]Judg. 18:29; 1 Sam. 3:20; 2 Sam. 3:10; 24:2 [c]Josh. 19:2 [d]Judg. 10:17; 1 Sam. 7:5
2 [e]Judg. 8:10
4 [f]Judg. 19:15
5 [g]Judg. 19:22 [h]Judg. 19:25, 26
6 [i]Judg. 19:29 [j]Josh. 7:15
7 [k]Judg. 19:30
9 [l]Judg. 1:3
12 [m]Deut. 13:14; Josh. 22:13, 16

19:22 perverted men. Lit. "sons of Belial," i.e., worthless men, who desired to commit sodomy against the Levite. The phrase elsewhere is used for idolaters (Deut. 13:13), neglecters of the poor (Deut. 15:9), drunks (1 Sam. 1:16), immoral people (1 Sam. 2:12), and rebels against the civil authority (2 Sam. 20:1; Prov. 19:28). "Belial" can be traced to the false god Baal, and is also a term for yoke (they cast off the yoke of decency), and a term for entangling or injuring. It is used in the NT of Satan (2 Cor. 6:15).

19:24 let me bring them out. The host showed a disgraceful compromise in his exaggerated desire to extend hospitality to his male guest. He should have protected all in his house, and so should the Levite, even at the risk of their own lives in guarding the women. His sad estimate of women was demonstrated by his willingness to hand his daughter or the guest concubine over to indecent men. Lot's plunge from decency was similar (Gen. 19). Here, repeated rape and finally murder were the pitiful sequel.

19:25 the man took his concubine...to them. This is unthinkable weakness and cowardice for any man, especially a priest of God. Apparently he even slept through the night, or stayed in bed out of fear, since he didn't see her again until he awakened and prepared to leave (cf. v. 28).

19:29 divided her into twelve pieces. The Levite's bizarre butchery to divide the woman's body into 12 parts was his shocking summons for aroused Israelite redress. No doubt a message went with each part, and the fact that he "sent" assumes messengers (cf. 1 Sam. 11:7). As he calculated, many were incensed and desired to avenge the atrocity (v. 30; chap. 20). Nothing could have aroused universal indignation and horror more than this radical summons from the Levite.

20:1 all the children of Israel came out. As a result of this horrible tragedy, a national assembly was convened with people coming from the N (Dan) and the S (Beersheba). **as one man before the LORD.** This indicated a humble attitude and desire to seek help from God for the nation.

through all the tribe of Benjamin, saying,
"What *is* this wickedness that has occurred
among you? 13 Now therefore, deliver up
the men, [n]the [1]perverted men who *are* in
Gibeah, that we may put them to death
and [o]remove the evil from Israel!" But the
children of Benjamin would not listen to
the voice of their brethren, the children of
Israel. 14 Instead, the children of Benjamin
gathered together from their cities to Gibeah, to go to battle against the children of Israel. 15 And from their cities at that time
[p]the children of Benjamin numbered twenty-six thousand men who drew the sword,
besides the inhabitants of Gibeah, who
numbered seven hundred select men.
16 Among all this people *were* seven hundred select men *who were* [q]left-handed;
every one could sling a stone at a hair's
breadth and not miss. 17 Now besides Benjamin, the men of Israel numbered four
hundred thousand men who drew the
sword; all of these *were* men of war.

18 Then the children of Israel arose and
[r]went up to [2]the house of God to [s]inquire
of God. They said, "Which of us shall go
up first to battle against the children of
Benjamin?"

The LORD said, [t]"Judah first!"

19 So the children of Israel rose in the
morning and encamped against Gibeah.
20 And the men of Israel went out to battle
against Benjamin, and the men of Israel
put themselves in battle array to fight
against them at Gibeah. 21 Then [u]the children of Benjamin came out of Gibeah, and
on that day cut down to the ground twenty-two thousand men of the Israelites.
22 And the people, that is, the men of Israel, encouraged themselves and again
formed the battle line at the place where
they had put themselves in array on the
first day. 23 [v]Then the children of Israel
went up and wept before the LORD until
evening, and asked counsel of the LORD,
saying, "Shall I again draw near for battle
against the children of my brother Benjamin?"

And the LORD said, "Go up against
him."

24 So the children of Israel approached
the children of Benjamin on the second
day. 25 And [w]Benjamin went out against
them from Gibeah on the second day, and
cut down to the ground eighteen thousand
more of the children of Israel; all these
drew the sword.

26 Then all the children of Israel, that is,
all the people, [x]went up and came to [3]the
house of God and wept. They sat there before the LORD and fasted that day until
evening; and they offered burnt offerings
and peace offerings before the LORD. 27 So
the children of Israel inquired of the LORD
([y]the ark of the covenant of God *was* there
in those days, 28 [z]and Phinehas the son of
Eleazar, the son of Aaron, [a]stood before it
in those days), saying, "Shall I yet again go
out to battle against the children of my
brother Benjamin, or shall I cease?"

And the LORD said, "Go up, for tomorrow I will deliver them into your hand."

29 Then Israel [b]set men in ambush all
around Gibeah. 30 And the children of Israel went up against the children of Benjamin on the third day, and put themselves
in battle array against Gibeah as at the
other times. 31 So the children of Benjamin
went out against the people, *and* were
drawn away from the city. They began to
strike down *and* kill some of the people, as
at the other times, in the highways [c](one of
which goes up to Bethel and the other to
Gibeah) and in the field, about thirty men
of Israel. 32 And the children of Benjamin
said, "They *are* defeated before us, as at
first."

But the children of Israel said, "Let us
flee and draw them away from the city to
the highways." 33 So all the men of Israel
rose from their place and put themselves in
battle array at Baal Tamar. Then Israel's
men in ambush burst forth from their position in the plain of Geba. 34 And ten thousand select men from all Israel came
against Gibeah, and the battle was fierce.
[d]But [4]*the Benjamites* did not know that
disaster *was* upon them. 35 The LORD [5]de-
feated Benjamin before Israel. And the children of Israel destroyed that day twenty-
five thousand one hundred Benjamites; all
these drew the sword.

36 So the children of Benjamin saw that
they were defeated. [e]The men of Israel had

13 [n]Deut. 13:13; Judg. 19:22 [o]Deut. 17:12; 1 Cor. 5:13 [1]Lit. *sons of Belial*
15 [p]Num. 1:36, 37; 2:23; 26:41
16 [q]Judg. 3:15; 1 Chr. 12:2
18 [r]Judg. 20:23, 26 [s]Num. 27:21 [t]Judg. 1:1, 2 [2]Or *Bethel*
21 [u][Gen. 49:27]
23 [v]Judg. 20:26, 27
25 [w]Judg. 20:21
26 [x]Judg. 20:18, 23; 21:2 [3]Or *Bethel*
27 [y]Josh. 18:1; 1 Sam. 1:3; 3:3; 4:3, 4
28 [z]Num. 25:7, 13; Josh. 24:33 [a]Deut. 10:8; 18:5
29 [b]Josh. 8:4
31 [c]Judg. 21:19
34 [d]Josh. 8:14; Job 21:13; Is. 47:11 [4]Lit. *they*
35 [5]Lit. *struck*
36 [e]Josh. 8:15

20:13 the children of Benjamin would not listen. They hardened their hearts against the justice and decency of turning over the criminals. Even greatly outnumbered in war, they would not yield to what was right (cf. v. 15-17). So civil war resulted.

20:18 to inquire of God. The Lord gave His counsel from the location of the ark at Shiloh, probably through the Urim and Thummim (vv. 27,28). The tribe of Judah was responsible to lead in battle since God had chosen a leadership role for that tribe (Gen. 49:8-12; 1 Chr. 5:1,2). *See note on Ex. 28:30.*

20:22-25 The Lord twice allowed great defeat and death to Israel to bring them to their spiritual senses regarding the cost of tolerating apostasy. Also, while they sought counsel, they placed too much reliance on their own prowess and on satisfying their own outrage. Finally, when desperate enough, they fasted and offered sacrifices (v. 26). The Lord then gave victory with strategy similar to that at Ai (Josh. 8).

20:32 Here was a battle strategy that lured the Benjamite army into a disastrous ambush (cf. vv. 36-46).

given ground to the Benjamites, because
they relied on the men in ambush whom
they had set against Gibeah. 37 [f]And the
men in ambush quickly rushed upon
Gibeah; the men in ambush spread out
and struck the whole city with the edge of
the sword. 38 Now the appointed signal
between the men of Israel and the men in
ambush was that they would make a great
cloud of [g]smoke rise up from the city,
39 whereupon the men of Israel would
turn in battle. Now Benjamin had begun
[6]to strike *and* kill about thirty of the men
of Israel. For they said, "Surely they are
defeated before us, as *in* the first battle."
40 But when the cloud began to rise from
the city in a column of smoke, the Benjamites [h]looked behind them, and there was
the whole city going up *in smoke* to heav-
en. 41 And when the men of Israel turned
back, the men of Benjamin panicked, for
they saw that disaster had come upon
them. 42 Therefore they [7]turned *their backs*
before the men of Israel in the direction of
the wilderness; but the battle overtook
them, and whoever *came* out of the cities
they destroyed in their midst. 43 They surrounded the Benjamites, chased them, *and*
easily trampled them down as far as the
front of Gibeah toward the east. 44 And
eighteen thousand men of Benjamin fell;
all these *were* men of valor. 45 Then [8]they
turned and fled toward the wilderness to
the rock of [i]Rimmon; and they cut down
five thousand of them on the highways.
Then they pursued them relentlessly up to
Gidom, and killed two thousand of them.
46 So all who fell of Benjamin that day
were twenty-five thousand men who
drew the sword; all these *were* [9]men of
valor.
47 [j]But six hundred men turned and fled
toward the wilderness to the rock of Rimmon, and they stayed at the rock of Rimmon for four months. 48 And the men of
Israel turned back against the children of
Benjamin, and struck them down with the
edge of the sword—from *every* city, men
and beasts, all who were found. They also
set fire to all the cities they came to.

37 [f] Josh. 8:19
38 [g] Josh. 8:20
39 [6] Lit. *to strike the slain ones*
40 [h] Josh. 8:20
42 [7] *fled*
45 [i] Josh. 15:32; 1 Chr. 6:77; Zech. 14:10
[8] LXX *the rest*
46 [9] *valiant warriors*
47 [j] Judg. 21:13

Wives Provided for the Benjamites

21 Now [a]the men of Israel had sworn
an oath at Mizpah, saying, "None of
us shall give his daughter to Benjamin as a
wife." 2 Then the people came [b]to [1]the
house of God, and remained there before
God till evening. They lifted up their voices and wept bitterly, 3 and said, "O LORD
God of Israel, why has this come to pass in
Israel, that today there should be one tribe
missing in Israel?"
4 So it was, on the next morning, that the
people rose early and [c]built an altar there,
and offered burnt offerings and peace offerings. 5 The children of Israel said, "Who
is there among all the tribes of Israel who
did not come up with the assembly to the
LORD?" [d]For they had made a great oath
concerning anyone who had not come up
to the LORD at Mizpah, saying, "He shall
surely be put to death." 6 And the children
of Israel grieved for Benjamin their brother, and said, "One tribe is cut off from Israel today. 7 What shall we do for wives for
those who remain, seeing we have sworn
by the LORD that we will not give them our
daughters as wives?"
8 And they said, "What one *is there* from
the tribes of Israel who did not come up to
Mizpah to the LORD?" And, in fact, no one
had come to the camp from [e]Jabesh Gilead
to the assembly. 9 For when the people
were counted, indeed, not one of the inhabitants of Jabesh Gilead *was* there. 10 So
the congregation sent out there twelve
thousand of their most valiant men, and
commanded them, saying, [f]"Go and strike
the inhabitants of Jabesh Gilead with the
edge of the sword, including the women
and children. 11 And this *is* the thing that
you shall do: [g]You shall utterly destroy
every male, and every woman who has
known a man intimately." 12 So they found
among the inhabitants of Jabesh Gilead
four hundred young virgins who had not
known a man intimately; and they brought
them to the camp at [h]Shiloh, which is in
the land of Canaan.
13 Then the whole congregation sent
word to the children of Benjamin [i]who *were*

CHAPTER 21

1 [a] Judg. 20:1
2 [b] Judg. 20:18, 26
[1] Or *Bethel*
4 [c] Deut. 12:5; 2 Sam. 24:25
5 [d] Judg. 20:1-3
8 [e] 1 Sam. 11:1; 31:11
10 [f] Num. 31:17; Judg. 5:23; 1 Sam. 11:7
11 [g] Num. 31:17; Deut. 20:13, 14
12 [h] Josh. 18:1; Judg. 18:31
13 [i] Judg. 20:47

20:46 twenty-five thousand. A rounded number for the more exact 25,100 (cf. v. 35).

20:47 The number of Benjamites adds up to the 26,700 (v. 15) in a reasonable way: 18,000 killed (v. 44); 5,000 (v. 45); 2,000 (v. 45); 600 survived (v. 47); leaving an estimated 1,100 lost the first two days (v. 48).

21:1 an oath at Mizpah. The Israelites made an oath not to "give" their daughters to the 600 surviving Benjamites (20:47). But they realized that the latter would fade as a tribe unless they had wives (cf. 21:6,7), since the Benjamite women had died in the total sack of Gibeah (20:37). Cf. v. 9.

21:8 No one had come from Jabesh Gilead, so the Israelites conquered Jabesh Gilead, which did not help against the Benjamites, and gave 400 virgins from there to the tribe (vv. 12-14).

21:8-16 Jabesh Gilead. Israelites placed such a premium on the unity of their tribes that they saw this city's non-cooperation in battle as worthy of widespread death. The passage does not give God's approval to this destruction of men, women and children (vv. 10,11). It is another of the bizarre actions of men when they do what is right in their own eyes, which is the point that both begins and ends this dark final section (17:6; 21:25).

at the rock of Rimmon, and announced
peace to them. 14 So Benjamin came back at
that time, and they gave them the women
whom they had saved alive of the women
of Jabesh Gilead; and yet they had not
found enough for them.
15 And the people [j]grieved for Benjamin,
because the LORD had made a void in the
tribes of Israel.
16 Then the elders of the congregation
said, "What shall we do for wives for those
who remain, since the women of Benjamin
have been destroyed?" 17 And they said,
"*There must be* an inheritance for the survivors of Benjamin, that a tribe may not be
destroyed from Israel. 18 However, we cannot give them wives from our daughters,
[k]for the children of Israel have sworn an
oath, saying, 'Cursed *be* the one who gives
a wife to Benjamin.' " 19 Then they said, "In
fact, *there is* a yearly [l]feast of the LORD in
[m]Shiloh, which *is* north of Bethel, on the
east side of the [n]highway that goes up from
Bethel to Shechem, and south of Lebonah."
20 Therefore they instructed the children
of Benjamin, saying, "Go, lie in wait in the
vineyards, 21 and watch; and just when the
daughters of Shiloh come out [o]to perform
their dances, then come out from the vineyards, and every man catch a wife for himself from the daughters of Shiloh; then go
to the land of Benjamin. 22 Then it shall be,
when their fathers or their brothers come
to us to complain, that we will say to them,
'Be kind to them for our sakes, because we
did not take a wife for any of them in the
war; for *it is* not *as though* you have given
the *women* to them at this time, making
yourselves guilty of your oath.' "
23 And the children of Benjamin did so;
they took enough wives for their number
from those who danced, whom they
caught. Then they went and returned to
their inheritance, and they [p]rebuilt the
cities and dwelt in them. 24 So the children
of Israel departed from there at that time,
every man to his tribe and family; they
went out from there, every man to his inheritance.
25 [q]In those days *there was* no king in Israel; [r]everyone did *what was* right in his
own eyes.

15 [j] Judg. 21:6
18 [k] Judg. 11:35; 21:1
19 [l] Lev. 23:2 [m] Deut. 12:5; Josh. 18:1; Judg. 18:31; 1 Sam. 1:3 [n] Judg. 20:31
21 [o] Ex. 15:20; Judg. 11:34; 1 Sam. 18:6
23 [p] Judg. 20:48
25 [q] Judg. 17:6; 18:1; 19:1 [r] Deut. 12:8; Judg. 17:6

21:16 wives for those who remain. Having recognized that the 200 others needed wives (vv. 17,18), they decided to allow them to snatch brides on their own at a dance in Shiloh (vv. 16-22), not believing that this violated their oath of not directly "giving" their daughters.

21:25 Judges 17–21 vividly demonstrates how bizarre and deep sin can become when people throw off the authority of God as mediated through the king (cf. 17:6). This was the appropriate, but tragic, conclusion to a bleak period of Israelite history (cf. Deut. 12:8).

The Book of

RUTH

Title

Ancient versions and modern translations consistently entitle this book after Ruth the Moabitess heroine, who is mentioned by name 12 times (1:4 to 4:13). Only two OT books receive their names from women—Ruth and Esther. The OT does not again refer to Ruth, while the NT mentions her just once—in the context of Christ's genealogy (Matt. 1:5; cf. Ruth 4:18-22). "Ruth" most likely comes from a Moabite and/or Hebrew word meaning "friendship." Ruth arrived in Bethlehem as a foreigner (2:10), became a maidservant (2:13), married wealthy Boaz (4:13), and was included in the physical lineage of Christ (Matt. 1:5).

Author and Date

Jewish tradition credits Samuel as the author, which is plausible since he did not die (1 Sam. 25:1) until after he had anointed David as God's chosen king (1 Sam. 16:6-13). However, neither internal features nor external testimony conclusively identify the writer. This exquisite story most likely appeared shortly before or during David's reign in Israel (1011–971 B.C.), since David is mentioned (4:17,22) but not Solomon. Goethe reportedly labeled this piece of anonymous but unexcelled literature as "the loveliest, complete work on a small scale." What Venus is to statuary and the Mona Lisa is to paintings, Ruth is to literature.

Background and Setting

Aside from Bethlehem (1:1), Moab (the perennial enemy of Israel, which was E of the Dead Sea), stands as the only other mentioned geographic/national entity (1:1,2). This country originated when Lot fathered Moab by an incestuous union with his oldest daughter (Gen. 19:37). Centuries later the Jews encountered opposition from Balak, king of Moab, through the prophet Balaam (Num. 22–25). For 18 years Moab oppressed Israel during the time of the judges (3:12-30). Saul defeated the Moabites (1 Sam. 14:47) while David seemed to enjoy a peaceful relationship with them (1 Sam. 22:3,4). Later, Moab again troubled Israel (2 Kin. 3:5-27; Ezra 9:1). Because of Moab's idolatrous worship of Chemosh (1 Kin. 11:7,33; 2 Kin. 23:13) and its opposition to Israel, God cursed Moab (Is. 15,16; Jer. 48; Ezek. 25:8-11; Amos 2:1-3).

The story of Ruth occurred in the days "when the judges ruled" Israel (1:1), ca. 1370 to 1041 B.C. (Judg. 2:16-19), and thus bridges time from the judges to Israel's monarchy. God used "a famine in the land" of Judah (1:1) to set in motion this beautiful drama, although the famine does not receive mention in Judges, which causes difficulty in dating the events of Ruth. However, by working backward in time from the well known date of David's reign (1011–971 B.C.), the time period of Ruth would most likely be during the judgeship of Jair, ca. 1126–1105 B.C. (Judg. 10:3-5).

Moab to Bethlehem

Ruth covers about 11 or 12 years according to the following scenario: 1) 1:1-18, ten years in Moab (1:4); 2) 1:19–2:23, several months (mid-Apr. to mid-June) in Boaz's field (1:22; 2:23); 3) 3:1-18, one day in Bethlehem and one night at the threshing floor; and 4) 4:1-22, about one year in Bethlehem.

Historical and Theological Themes

All 85 verses of Ruth have been accepted as canonical by the Jews. Along with Song of Solomon, Esther, Ecclesiastes, and Lamentations, Ruth stands with the OT books of the Megilloth or "five scrolls." Rabbis read these books in the synagogue on 5 special occasions during the year—Ruth being read at Pentecost due to the harvest scenes of Ruth 2,3.

Genealogically, Ruth looks back almost 900 years to events in the time of Jacob (4:11) and forward about 100 years to the coming reign of David (4:17,22). While Joshua and Judges emphasize the legacy of the nation and their land of promise, Ruth focuses on the lineage of David back to the patriarchal era.

At least 7 major theological themes emerge in Ruth. First, Ruth the Moabitess illustrates that God's redemptive plan extended beyond the Jews to Gentiles (2:12). Second, Ruth demonstrates that women are co-heirs with men of God's salvation grace (cf. Gal. 3:28). Third, Ruth portrays the virtuous woman of Prov. 31:10 (cf. 3:11). Fourth, Ruth describes God's sovereign (1:6; 4:13) and providential care (2:3) of seemingly unimportant people at apparently insignificant times which later prove to be monumentally crucial to accomplishing God's will. Fifth, Ruth along with Tamar (Gen. 38), Rahab (Josh. 2), and Bathsheba (2 Sam. 11,12) stand in the genealogy of the messianic line (4:17,22; cf. Matt. 1:5). Sixth, Boaz, as a type of Christ, becomes Ruth's kinsman-redeemer (4:1-12). Finally, David's right (and thus Christ's right) to the throne of Israel is traced back to Judah (4:18-22; cf. Gen. 49:8-12).

Interpretive Challenges

Ruth should be understood as a true historical account. The reliable facts surrounding Ruth, in addition to its complete compatibility with Judges plus 1 and 2 Samuel, confirm Ruth's authenticity. However, some individual difficulties require careful attention. First, how could Ruth worship at the tabernacle then in Shiloh (1 Sam. 4:4), since Deuteronomy 23:3 expressly forbids Moabites from entering the assembly for 10 generations? Since the Jews entered the land ca. 1405 B.C. and Ruth was not born until ca. 1150 B.C., she then represented at least the 11th generation (probably later) if the time limitation ended at ten generations. If "ten generations" was an idiom meaning "forever" as Neh. 13:1 implies, then Ruth would be like the foreigner of Is. 56:1-8 who joined himself to the Lord (1:16), thus gaining entrance to the assembly.

Second, are there not immoral overtones to Boaz and Ruth spending the night together before marriage (3:3-18)? Ruth engaged in a common ancient Near Eastern custom by asking Boaz to take her for his wife, symbolically pictured by throwing a garment over the intended woman (3:9), just as Jehovah spread His garment over Israel (Ezek. 16:8). The text does not even hint at the slightest moral impropriety, noting that Ruth slept at his feet (3:14). Thus, Boaz became God's answer to his own earlier prayer for Ruth (2:12).

Third, would not the levirate principle of Deut. 25:5,6 lead to incest and/or polygamy if the nearest relative was already married? God would not design a good plan to involve the grossest of immoralities punishable by death. It is to be assumed that the implementation of Deut. 25:5,6 could involve only the nearest relative who was eligible for marriage as qualified by other stipulations of the law.

Fourth, was not marriage to a Moabitess strictly forbidden by the law? The nations or people to whom marriage was prohibited were those possessing the land that Israel would enter (Ex. 34:16; Deut. 7:1-3; Josh. 23:12) which did not include Moab (cf. Deut. 7:1). Further, Boaz married Ruth, a devout proselyte to Jehovah (1:16,17), not a pagan worshiper of Chemosh—Moab's chief deity (cf. later problems in Ezra 9:1,2 and Neh. 13:23-25).

Outline

I. Elimelech and Naomi's Ruin in Moab (1:1-5)
II. Naomi and Ruth Return to Bethlehem (1:6-22)
III. Boaz Receives Ruth in His Field (2:1-23)
IV. Ruth's Romance with Boaz (3:1-18)
V. Boaz Redeems Ruth (4:1-12)
VI. God Rewards Boaz and Ruth with a Son (4:13-17)
VII. David's Right to the Throne of Judah (4:18-22)

Elimelech's Family Goes to Moab

1 Now it came to pass, in the days when
[a]the judges [1]ruled, that there was [b]a
famine in the land. And a certain man of
[c]Bethlehem, Judah, went to [2]dwell in the
country of [d]Moab, he and his wife and his
two sons. 2 The name of the man *was*
Elimelech, the name of his wife *was* Naomi, and the names of his two sons *were*
Mahlon and Chilion—[e]Ephrathites of
Bethlehem, Judah. And they went [f]to the
country of Moab and remained there.
3 Then Elimelech, Naomi's husband, died;
and she was left, and her two sons. 4 Now
they took wives of the women of Moab: the
name of the one *was* Orpah, and the name
of the other Ruth. And they [3]dwelt there
about ten years. 5 Then both Mahlon and
Chilion also died; so the woman survived
her two sons and her husband.

Naomi Returns with Ruth

6 Then she arose with her daughters-in-
law that she might return from the country
of Moab, for she had heard in the country of
Moab that the LORD had [g]visited[4] His people by [h]giving them bread. 7 Therefore she
went out from the place where she was, and
her two daughters-in-law with her; and they
went on the way to return to the land of Judah. 8 And Naomi said to her two daughters-in-law, [i]"Go, return each to her mother's house. [j]The LORD deal kindly with you,
as you have dealt [k]with the dead and with
me. 9 The LORD grant that you may find
[l]rest, each in the house of her husband."
So she kissed them, and they lifted up
their voices and wept. 10 And they said to
her, "Surely we will return with you to
your people."
11 But Naomi said, "Turn back, my
daughters; why will you go with me? *Are*
there still sons in my womb, [m]that they
may be your husbands? 12 Turn back, my
daughters, go—for I am too old to have a
husband. If I should say I have hope, *if* I
should have a husband tonight and should
also bear sons, 13 would you wait for them
till they were grown? Would you restrain
yourselves from having husbands? No, my
daughters; for it grieves me very much for
your sakes that [n]the hand of the LORD has
gone out against me!"
14 Then they lifted up their voices and
wept again; and Orpah kissed her mother-
in-law, but Ruth [o]clung to her.
15 And she said, "Look, your sister-in-
law has gone back to [p]her people and to
her gods; [q]return after your sister-in-law."

CHAPTER 1

1 [a] Judg. 2:16-18 [b] Gen. 12:10; 26:1; 2 Kin. 8:1 [c] Judg. 17:8; Mic. 5:2 [d] Gen. 19:37 [1] Lit. *judged* [2] As a resident alien
2 [e] Gen. 35:19; 1 Sam. 1:1; 1 Kin. 11:26 [f] Judg. 3:30
4 [3] *lived*
6 [g] Ex. 3:16; 4:31; Jer. 29:10; Zeph. 2:7; Luke 1:68 [h] Ps. 132:15; Matt. 6:11 [4] *attended to*
8 [i] Josh. 24:15 [j] 2 Tim. 1:16-18 [k] Ruth 2:20
9 [l] Ruth 3:1
11 [m] Gen. 38:11; Deut. 25:5
13 [n] Judg. 2:15; Job 19:21; Ps. 32:4; 38:2
14 [o] [Prov. 17:17]
15 [p] Judg. 11:24 [q] Josh. 1:15

1:1-5 This introduction to Ruth sets in motion the following events, which culminate in Obed's birth and his relationship to the Davidic line of Christ. See Introduction: Background and Setting.

1:1 famine. This disaster sounds similar to the days of Abraham (Gen. 12), Isaac (Gen. 26), and Jacob (Gen. 46). The text does not specify whether or not this famine was God's judgment (cf. 1 Kin. 17,18, esp. 18:2). **Bethlehem, Judah.** Bethlehem ("house of bread") lies in the territory given to the tribe of Judah (Josh. 15) about 6 mi. S of Jerusalem. Rachel, the wife of Jacob, was buried nearby (Gen. 35:19; cf. 4:11). Bethlehem eventually received the title "city of David" (Luke 2:4,11). Later, Mary delivered Christ (Luke 2:4-7; cf. Mic. 5:2) and Herod slaughtered the infants here (Matt. 2:16). This title (Judg. 17:7,9; 19:1,2,18) serves to distinguish it from Bethlehem of Zebulun (Josh. 19:15). **dwell.** Elimelech intended to live temporarily in Moab as a resident alien until the famine passed. **Moab.** See Introduction: Background and Setting.

1:2 Elimelech. His name means "my God is king," signifying a devout commitment to the God of Israel. Most likely, he was a prominent man in the community whose brothers might have included the unnamed close relative and Boaz (cf. 4:3). **Naomi.** Her name means "pleasant." **Mahlon and Chilion.** Their names mean "sick" and "pining" respectively. **Ephrathites.** A title used of people who lived in the area anciently known as Ephrath (Gen. 35:16,19; 48:7) or Ephrathah (Ruth 4:11; Mic. 5:2), but later more prominently called Bethlehem (1:1). Jesse, father of David, is called "an Ephrathite of Bethlehem" (1 Sam. 17:12) and "Jesse the Bethlehemite" (1 Sam. 16:1,18; 17:58).

1:4 the women of Moab. See Introduction: Interpretive Challenges. **Orpah.** Her name means "stubborn." **Ruth.** Her name means "friendship." **about ten years.** This period would seem to include the entire time of Naomi's residency in Moab.

1:5 the woman survived. Naomi, a widow in Moab whose two sons had died also, believed that the Lord had afflicted her with bitter days until she would die (1:13,20,21). No reason for the death of these 3 men in her life is given. Ruth married Mahlon, and Orpah united with Chilion (cf. 4:10).

1:6-22 The death of Elimelech and his two sons (1:3,5) prepared the way for Naomi and Ruth to leave Orpah in Moab (1:6-14) and return together to Bethlehem (1:15-22).

1:6 the LORD had visited His people. Obviously the Lord had sent rain to break the famine. The sovereignty of Jehovah on behalf of Israel permeates the pages of Ruth in several ways: 1) actually for good (2:12; 4:12-14), 2) perceived by Naomi for bad (1:13,21), and 3) in the context of prayer/blessing (1:8,9,17; 2:4,12,20; 3:10,13; 4:11). The return of physical prosperity only shadowed the reality of a coming spiritual prosperity through the line of David in the person of Christ.

1:7 she went out. Naomi had friends (1:19), family (2:1), and prosperity (4:3) awaiting her in Bethlehem.

1:8-10 Naomi graciously encouraged her two daughters-in-law to return to their homes (1:8) and to remarry (1:9), but they emotionally insisted on going to Jerusalem (1:10).

1:11-13 Naomi selflessly reasoned a second time for their return, because she would be unable to provide them with new husbands (possibly in the spirit of a levirate marriage as described in Deut. 25:5,6). If Orpah and Ruth waited, they would most likely have become as old as Naomi was then before they could remarry (cf. Gen. 38:11).

1:12 I am too old. Naomi was probably over 50.

1:13 the hand of the LORD. A figure of speech which describes the Lord's work. The Lord is spirit (John 4:24) and therefore does not have a literal hand.

1:14,15 At the second plea to return, Orpah turned back. Naomi pleaded with Ruth a third time to return.

1:15 her gods. Refers to Chemosh the chief Moabite deity who required child sacrifice (2 Kin. 3:27) and other local deities.

16 But Ruth said:
[r]"Entreat[5] me not to leave you,
Or to turn back from following
after you;
For wherever you go, I will go;
And wherever you lodge, I will
lodge;
[s]Your people *shall be* my people,
And your God, my God.
17 Where you die, I will die,
And there will I be buried.
[t]The LORD do so to me, and more
also,
If *anything but* death parts you and
me."

18 [u]When she saw that she [6]was determined
to go with her, she stopped speaking to her.
19 Now the two of them went until they
came to Bethlehem. And it happened,
when they had come to Bethlehem, that
[v]all the city was excited because of them;
and the women said, [w]"*Is* this Naomi?"
20 But she said to them, "Do not call me
[7]Naomi; call me [8]Mara, for the Almighty
has dealt very bitterly with me. 21 I went
out full, [x]and the LORD has brought me
home again empty. Why do you call me
Naomi, since the LORD has testified against
me, and [9]the Almighty has afflicted me?"
22 So Naomi returned, and Ruth the
Moabitess her daughter-in-law with her,
who returned from the country of Moab.
Now they came to Bethlehem [y]at the beginning of barley harvest.

16 [r] 2 Kin. 2:2, 4, 6 [s] Ruth 2:11, 12 [5] *Urge me not*
17 [t] 1 Sam. 3:17; 2 Sam. 19:13; 2 Kin. 6:31
18 [u] Acts 21:14 [6] Lit. *made herself strong to go*
19 [v] Matt. 21:10 [w] Is. 23:7; Lam. 2:15
20 [7] Lit. *Pleasant* [8] Lit. *Bitter*
21 [x] Job 1:21 [9] Heb. *Shaddai*
22 [y] Ruth 2:23; 2 Sam. 21:9

CHAPTER 2

1 [a] Ruth 3:2, 12 [b] Ruth 1:2 [c] Ruth 4:21
2 [d] Lev. 19:9, 10; 23:22; Deut. 24:19
4 [e] Ruth 1:1 [f] Ps. 129:7, 8; Luke 1:28; 2 Thess. 3:16
6 [g] Ruth 1:22

Ruth Meets Boaz

2 There was a [a]relative of Naomi's husband, a man of great wealth, of the
family of [b]Elimelech. His name *was* [c]Boaz.
2 So Ruth the Moabitess said to Naomi,
"Please let me go to the [d]field, and glean
heads of grain after *him* in whose sight I
may find favor."
And she said to her, "Go, my daughter."
3 Then she left, and went and gleaned in
the field after the reapers. And she happened to come to the part of the field *belonging* to Boaz, who *was* of the family of
Elimelech.
4 Now behold, Boaz came from [e]Bethle-
hem, and said to the reapers, [f]"The LORD *be*
with you!"
And they answered him, "The LORD
bless you!"
5 Then Boaz said to his servant who was
in charge of the reapers, "Whose young
woman *is* this?"
6 So the servant who was in charge of the
reapers answered and said, "It *is* the young
Moabite woman [g]who came back with Naomi from the country of Moab. 7 And she
said, 'Please let me glean and gather after
the reapers among the sheaves.' So she came
and has continued from morning until now,
though she rested a little in the house."

1:16-18 Ruth recited her hallmark expression of loyalty to Naomi and commitment to the family she married into.

1:16 And your God, my God. This testimony evidenced Ruth's conversion from worshiping Chemosh to Jehovah of Israel (cf. 1 Thess. 1:9,10).

1:17 The LORD do so to me. Ruth's vow bore further testimony to her conversion. She followed the path first blazed by Abraham (Josh. 24:2).

1:19 they came to Bethlehem. A trip from Moab (at least 60–75 mi.) would have taken about 7–10 days. Having descended about 4,500 ft. from Moab into the Jordan Valley, they then ascended 3,750 ft. through the hills of Judea. **all the city.** Naomi had been well known in her prior residency (cf. Ephrathites of Bethlehem, 1:2). The question, "Is this Naomi?" most likely reflected the hard life of the last decade and the toll that it took on her appearance.

1:20,21 Naomi…Mara…full…empty. Naomi's outlook on life, although grounded in God's sovereignty, was not hopeful; thus she asked to be renamed "Mara," which means "bitter." Her experiences were not unlike Job's (Job 1,2), but her perspective resembled that of Job's wife (Job 2:10). In reality, Naomi had 1) a full harvest prospect, 2) Ruth plus Boaz, and 3) the hope of God's future blessing.

1:22 Ruth the Moabitess. This title also appears at 2:2,21; 4:5,10. Ruth stands out as a foretaste of future Gentile conversions (cf. Rom. 11). **at the beginning of barley harvest.** Normally the middle to the end of Apr.

2:1-23 Two widows, newly at home in Bethlehem after Naomi's 10 year absence, needed the basics of life. Ruth volunteered to go out and glean the fields for food (cf. James 1:27). In so doing, she unintentionally went to the field of Boaz, a close family relative, where she found great favor in his sight.

2:1 relative…of the family. Possibly as close as a brother of Elimelech (cf. 4:3), but if not, certainly within the tribe or clan. **a man of great wealth.** Lit. "a man of valor" (cf. Judg. 6:12; 11:1) who had unusual capacity to obtain and protect his property. **Boaz.** His name means "in him is strength." He had never married or was a widower (cf. 1 Chr. 2:11,12; Matt. 1:5; Luke 3:32).

2:2 glean. The Mosaic law commanded that the harvest should not be reaped to the corners nor the gleanings picked up (Lev. 19:9,10). Gleanings were stalks of grain left after the first cutting (cf. 2:3,7,8,15,17). These were dedicated to the needy, especially widows, orphans, and strangers (Lev. 23:22; Deut. 24:19-21).

2:3 she happened to come. Here was a classic example of God's providence at work. **part of the field.** Possibly a large community field in which Boaz had a plot.

2:4-17 Note throughout how Boaz manifested the spirit of the law in going beyond what the Mosaic legislation required by 1) feeding Ruth (2:14), 2) letting Ruth glean among the sheaves (2:15), and 3) leaving extra grain for her to glean (2:16).

2:4 The LORD *be* with you. This unusual labor practice speaks to the exceptional godliness of Boaz and his workers.

2:7 sheaves. Bundles of grain stalks tied together for transport to the threshing floor.

2:7,17 morning…evening. Ruth proved to be diligent in her care for Naomi.

2:7 the house. Most likely a temporary shelter built with branches by the side of the field (cf. 3:18).

8 Then Boaz said to Ruth, "You will listen, my daughter, will you not? Do not go
to glean in another field, nor go from here,
but stay close by my young women. 9 *Let*
your eyes *be* on the field which they reap,
and go after them. Have I not commanded
the young men not to touch you? And
when you are thirsty, go to the vessels and
drink from what the young men have
drawn."
10 So she [h]fell on her face, bowed down
to the ground, and said to him, "Why have
I found [i]favor in your eyes, that you
should take notice of me, since I *am* a foreigner?"
11 And Boaz answered and said to her,
"It has been fully reported to me, [j]all that
you have done for your mother-in-law
since the death of your husband, and *how*
you have left your father and your mother
and the land of your birth, and have come
to a people whom you did not know before. 12 [k]The LORD repay your work, and a
full reward be given you by the LORD God
of Israel, [l]under whose wings you have
come for refuge."
13 Then she said, [m]"Let me find favor in
your sight, my lord; for you have comforted me, and have spoken [1]kindly to your
maidservant, [n]though I am not like one of
your maidservants."
14 Now Boaz said to her at mealtime,
"Come here, and eat of the bread, and dip
your piece of bread in the vinegar." So she
sat beside the reapers, and he passed
parched *grain* to her; and she ate and [o]was
satisfied, and kept some back. 15 And
when she rose up to [2]glean, Boaz commanded his young men, saying, "Let her
glean even among the sheaves, and do not
[3]reproach her. 16 Also let *grain* from the
bundles fall purposely for her; leave *it* that
she may glean, and do not rebuke her."
17 So she gleaned in the field until
evening, and beat out what she had
gleaned, and it was about an ephah of
[p]barley. 18 Then she took *it* up and went
into the city, and her mother-in-law saw
what she had gleaned. So she brought out
and gave to her [q]what she had kept back
after she had been satisfied.
19 And her mother-in-law said to her,
"Where have you gleaned today? And
where did you work? Blessed be the one
who [r]took notice of you."
So she told her mother-in-law with
whom she had worked, and said, "The
man's name with whom I worked today *is*
Boaz."
20 Then Naomi said to her daughter-in-
law, [s]"Blessed *be* he of the LORD, who [t]has
not forsaken His kindness to the living and
the dead!" And Naomi said to her, "This
man *is* a relation of ours, [u]one of [4]our close
relatives."
21 Ruth the Moabitess said, "He also
said to me, 'You shall stay close by my
young men until they have finished all my
harvest.'"
22 And Naomi said to Ruth her daughter-in-law, "*It is* good, my daughter, that
you go out with his young women, and
that people do not [5]meet you in any other
field." 23 So she stayed close by the young

10 [h] 1 Sam. 25:23 [i] 1 Sam. 1:18
11 [j] Ruth 1:14-18
12 [k] 1 Sam. 24:19; Ps. 58:11 [l] Ruth 1:16; Ps. 17:8; 36:7; 57:1; 61:4; 63:7; 91:4
13 [m] Gen. 33:15; 1 Sam. 1:18 [n] 1 Sam. 25:41 [1] Lit. *to the heart of*
14 [o] Ruth 2:18
15 [2] Gather after the reapers [3] *rebuke*
17 [p] Ruth 1:22
18 [q] Ruth 2:14
19 [r] Ruth 2:10; [Ps. 41:1]
20 [s] Ruth 3:10; 2 Sam. 2:5 [t] Prov. 17:17 [u] Ruth 3:9; 4:4, 6 [4] *our redeemers*, Heb. *goalenu*
22 [5] *encounter*

2:8 my daughter. Boaz was about 45–55 years old and a contemporary of Elimelech and Naomi. He would naturally see Ruth as a daughter (3:10,11), much like Naomi did (cf. 2:2,22; 3:1,16,18). Boaz contrasted himself with younger men (3:10). **my young women.** The ones who tied up the sheaves.

2:9 young men. The ones who cut the grain with hand sickles (cf. 2:21).

2:10 a foreigner. Ruth remained ever mindful that she was an alien and, as such, must conduct herself humbly. Possibly she had knowledge of Deut. 23:3,4. She acknowledged the grace (lit. "favor") of Boaz.

2:11 fully reported to me. This speaks to both Naomi's quickness to speak kindly of Ruth and Boaz's network of influence in Bethlehem. Ruth remained true to her promise (1:16,17).

2:12 wings…refuge. Scripture pictures God as catching Israel up on His wings in the Exodus (Ex. 19:4; Deut. 32:11). God is here portrayed as a mother bird sheltering the young and fragile with her wings (cf. Pss. 17:8; 36:7; 57:1; 61:4; 63:7; 91:1,4). Boaz blessed Ruth in light of her newfound commitment to and dependence on the Lord. Later, he would become God's answer to this prayer (cf. 3:9).

2:14 vinegar. Sour wine, mixed with a little oil, used to quench thirst.

2:15 among the sheaves. Boaz granted her request (2:7) to go beyond the letter of the law.

2:17 ephah. Over one-half bushel, weighing about 30 to 40 lbs.

2:18 what she had kept back. Not the gleaned grain, but rather the lunch ration which Ruth did not eat (cf. 2:14).

2:20 His kindness. Naomi began to understand God's sovereign working, covenant loyalty, lovingkindness, and mercy toward her because Ruth, without human direction (2:3), found the near relative Boaz. **one of our close relatives.** The great kinsman-redeemer theme of Ruth begins here (cf. 3:9,12; 4:1,3,6,8,14). A close relative could redeem 1) a family member sold into slavery (Lev. 25:47-49), 2) land which needed to be sold under economic hardship (Lev. 25:23-28), and/or 3) the family name by virtue of a levirate marriage (Deut. 25:5-10). This earthly custom pictures the reality of God the Redeemer doing a greater work (Pss. 19:14; 78:35; Is. 41:14; 43:14) by reclaiming those who needed to be spiritually redeemed out of slavery to sin (Ps. 107:2; Is. 62:12). Thus, Boaz pictures Christ, who as a Brother (Heb. 2:17), redeemed those who 1) were slaves to sin (Rom. 6:15-18), 2) had lost all earthly possessions/privileges in the Fall (Gen. 3:17-19), and 3) had been alienated by sin from God (2 Cor. 5:18-21). Boaz stands in the direct line of Christ (Matt. 1:5; Luke 3:32). This turn of events marks the point where Naomi's human emptiness (1:21) begins to be refilled by the Lord. Her night of earthly doubt has been broken by the dawning of new hope (cf. Rom. 8:28-39).

2:22 do not meet you. Ruth the Moabitess would not be treated with such mercy and grace by strangers outside of the family.

women of Boaz, to glean until the end of
barley harvest and wheat harvest; and she
dwelt with her mother-in-law.

Ruth's Redemption Assured

3 Then Naomi her mother-in-law said to
her, "My daughter, [a]shall I not seek
[b]security[1] for you, that it may be well with
you? 2 Now Boaz, [c]whose young women
you were with, *is he* not our relative? In
fact, he is winnowing barley tonight at the
threshing floor. 3 Therefore wash yourself
and [d]anoint yourself, put on your *best* garment and go down to the threshing floor;
but do not make yourself known to the
man until he has finished eating and
drinking. 4 Then it shall be, when he lies
down, that you shall notice the place
where he lies; and you shall go in, uncover
his feet, and lie down; and he will tell you
what you should do."
5 And she said to her, "All that you say
to me I will do."
6 So she went down to the threshing
floor and did according to all that her
mother-in-law instructed her. 7 And after
Boaz had eaten and drunk, and [e]his heart
was cheerful, he went to lie down at the
end of the heap of grain; and she came
softly, uncovered his feet, and lay down.
8 Now it happened at midnight that the
man was startled, and turned himself; and
there, a woman was lying at his feet. 9 And
he said, "Who *are* you?"
So she answered, "I *am* Ruth, your
maidservant. [f]Take[2] your maidservant
under your wing, for you are [g]a [3]close relative."
10 Then he said, [h]"Blessed *are* you of the
LORD, my daughter! For you have shown
more kindness at the end than [i]at the beginning, in that you did not go after young
men, whether poor or rich. 11 And now,
my daughter, do not fear. I will do for you
all that you request, for all the people of
my town know that you *are* [j]a virtuous
woman. 12 Now it is true that I *am* a [k]close
relative; however, [l]there is a relative closer
than I. 13 Stay this night, and in the morning it shall be *that* if he will [m]perform the
duty of a close relative for you—good; let
him do it. But if he does not want to perform the duty for you, then I will perform
the duty for you, [n]*as* the LORD lives! Lie
down until morning."
14 So she lay at his feet until morning,
and she arose before one could recognize
another. Then he said, [o]"Do not let it be
known that the woman came to the threshing floor." 15 Also he said, "Bring the
[4]shawl that *is* on you and hold it." And
when she held it, he measured six *ephahs* of
barley, and laid *it* on her. Then [5]she went
into the city.

CHAPTER 3

1 [a] 1 Cor. 7:36; 1 Tim. 5:8 [b] Ruth 1:9 [1] Lit. *rest*
2 [c] Ruth 2:3, 8
3 [d] 2 Sam. 14:2
7 [e] Judg. 19:6, 9, 22; 2 Sam. 13:28; Esth. 1:10
9 [f] Ezek. 16:8 [g] Ruth 2:20; 3:12 [2] Or *Spread the corner of your garment over your maidservant* [3] *redeemer,* Heb. *goel*
10 [h] Ruth 2:20 [i] Ruth 1:8
11 [j] Prov. 12:4; 31:10-31
12 [k] Ruth 3:9 [l] Ruth 4:1
13 [m] Deut. 25:5-10; Ruth 4:5, 10; Matt. 22:24 [n] Judg. 8:19; Jer. 4:2; 12:16
14 [o] [Rom. 12:17; 14:16; 1 Cor. 10:32; 2 Cor. 8:21; 1 Thess. 5:22]
15 [4] *cloak* [5] Many Heb. mss., Syr., Vg. *she;* MT, LXX, Tg. *he*

2:23 the end of…harvest. Barley harvest usually began about mid-Apr. and wheat harvest extended to mid-June—a period of intense labor for about two months. This generally coincided with the 7 weeks between Passover and the Feast of Weeks, i.e., Pentecost (cf. Lev. 23:15,16; Deut. 16:9-12).

3:1-18 Encouraged by Ruth's day in Boaz's field, Naomi instructed Ruth in the way she should go to insure a brighter future. Ruth carefully followed Naomi's directions to solicit redemption by Boaz, while the Lord had prepared Boaz to redeem Ruth. Only one potential obstacle remained, a relative nearer than Boaz.

3:1 security. Naomi felt responsible, just as she did in 1:9, for Ruth's future husband and home.

3:2 tonight. Winnowing (tossing grain into the air to finish separating the grain from the chaff) normally occurred in late afternoon when the Mediterranean winds prevailed. Sifting and bagging the grain would have carried over past dark, and Boaz may have remained all night to guard the grain from theft. **threshing floor.** Usually a large, hard area of earth or stone on the downwind (E) side of the village where threshing took place (loosening the grain from the straw and winnowing).

3:3,4 Naomi instructed Ruth 1) to put on her best appearance and 2) to propose marriage to Boaz by utilizing an ancient Near Eastern custom. Since Boaz was a generation older than Ruth (2:8), this overture would indicate Ruth's desire to marry Boaz, which the older, gracious Boaz would not have initiated with a younger woman.

3:7 his heart was cheerful. Using the same language of 3:1 ("security"…"be well"), Boaz is described as having a sense of well being, which is most readily explained by the full harvest in contrast to previous years of famine (cf. Judg. 18:20; 1 Kin. 21:7).

3:9 Take your maidservant. Ruth righteously appealed to Boaz, using the language of Boaz's earlier prayer (2:12), to marry her according to the levirate custom (Deut. 25:5-10). See Introduction: Interpretive Challenges.

3:10 kindness. Ruth's loyalty to Naomi, the Lord, and even Boaz is commended by Boaz. **after young men.** Ruth demonstrated moral excellence in that 1) she did not engage in immorality, 2) she did not remarry outside the family, and 3) she had appealed for levirate redemption to an older, godly man.

3:11 virtuous. In all respects, Ruth personifies excellence (cf. Prov. 31:10). This same language has been used of Boaz ("a man of great wealth" or more likely "a man of valor" in 2:1), thus making them the perfectly matched couple for an exemplary marriage.

3:12 a relative closer than I. Boaz righteously deferred to someone else who was nearer in relationship to Elimelech. The nearer relative may have been Boaz's older brother (cf. 4:3) or Boaz may have been his cousin. The fact that the neighbor women said, "There is a son born to Naomi" at Obed's birth would suggest the brother or cousin relationship to Elimelech (4:17).

3:13 I will perform the duty. Boaz willingly accepted Ruth's proposal, if the nearer relative was unable or unwilling to exercise his levirate duty. ***as* the LORD lives.** The most solemn, binding oath an Israelite could vow.

3:14 lay at his feet. According to the text, no immorality occurred. Boaz even insisted on no appearance of evil.

3:15 six *ephahs*. The Hebrew text gives no standard of measurement; *ephah* has been inserted by the translators only as a possibility. However, 6 ephahs would weigh about 200 lbs., which was far too much for Ruth to carry home in her shawl. Therefore, deemed most reasonable is 6 seahs (60-80 lbs.), which would have been twice the amount Ruth had previously gleaned (see 2:17).

16 When she came to her mother-in-law,
she said, [6]"*Is* that you, my daughter?"
Then she told her all that the man had
done for her. **17** And she said, "These six
ephahs of barley he gave me; for he said to
me, 'Do not go empty-handed to your
mother-in-law.' "
18 Then she said, [p]"Sit still, my daughter,
until you know how the matter will turn
out; for the man will not rest until he has
concluded the matter this day."

Boaz Redeems Ruth

4 Now Boaz went up to the gate and sat
down there; and behold, [a]the close relative of whom Boaz had spoken came by.
So Boaz said, "Come aside, [1]friend, sit
down here." So he came aside and sat
down. **2** And he took ten men of [b]the elders of the city, and said, "Sit down here."
So they sat down. **3** Then he said to the
close relative, "Naomi, who has come back
from the country of Moab, sold the piece of
land [c]which *belonged* to our brother Elimelech. **4** And I thought to [2]inform you, saying, [d]'Buy *it* back [e]in the presence of the inhabitants and the elders of my people. If
you will redeem *it*, redeem *it;* but if [3]you
will not redeem *it, then* tell me, that I may
know; [f]for *there is* no one but you to redeem *it*, and I *am* next after you.' "
And he said, "I will redeem *it*."
5 Then Boaz said, "On the day you buy
the field from the hand of Naomi, you
must also buy *it* from Ruth the Moabitess,
the wife of the dead, [g]to [4]perpetuate the
name of the dead through his inheritance."
6 [h]And the close relative said, "I cannot
redeem *it* for myself, lest I ruin my own inheritance. You redeem my right of redemption for yourself, for I cannot redeem *it*."
7 [i]Now this *was the custom* in former
times in Israel concerning redeeming and
exchanging, to confirm anything: one man
took off his sandal and gave *it* to the other,
and this *was* a confirmation in Israel.
8 Therefore the close relative said to Boaz,
"Buy *it* for yourself." So he took off his sandal. **9** And Boaz said to the elders and all the
people, "You *are* witnesses this day that I
have bought all that was Elimelech's, and
all that *was* Chilion's and Mahlon's, from
the hand of Naomi. **10** Moreover, Ruth the
Moabitess, the widow of Mahlon, I have acquired as my wife, to perpetuate the name
of the dead through his inheritance, [j]that
the name of the dead may not be cut off
from among his brethren and from [5]his position at the gate. You *are* witnesses this
day."
11 And all the people who *were* at the
gate, and the elders, said, "*We are* witnesses. [k]The LORD make the woman who is
coming to your house like Rachel and
Leah, the two who [l]built the house of Israel; and may you prosper in [m]Ephrathah

16 [6] Or *How are you,*
18 [p] [Ps. 37:3, 5]

CHAPTER 4

1 [a] Ruth 3:12 [1] Heb. *peloni almoni*, lit. *so and so*
2 [b] 1 Kin. 21:8; Prov. 31:23
3 [c] Lev. 25:25
4 [d] Jer. 32:7, 8 [e] Gen. 23:18 [f] Lev. 25:25 [2] Lit. *uncover your ear* [3] So with many Heb. mss., LXX, Syr., Tg., Vg.; MT *he*
5 [g] Gen. 38:8; Deut. 25:5, 6; Ruth 3:13; Matt. 22:24 [4] Lit. *raise up*
6 [h] Ruth 3:12, 13; Job 19:14
7 [i] Deut. 25:7-10
10 [j] Deut. 25:6 [5] Probably his civic office
11 [k] Ps. 127:3; 128:3 [l] Gen. 29:25-30; Deut. 25:9 [m] Gen. 35:16-18

3:18 this day. Naomi knew that Boaz was a man of integrity and would fulfill his promise with a sense of urgency. They needed to wait on the Lord to work through Boaz.

4:1-22 God's divine plan fully blossomed as Boaz redeemed Naomi's land and Ruth's hand in marriage. Naomi, once empty (1:21), is full; Ruth, once a widow (1:5), is married; most importantly, the Lord has prepared Christ's line of descent in David, through Boaz and Obed, back to Judah (Gen. 49:10) to fulfill the proper messianic lineage.

4:1 went up. Apparently the threshing floor was below the level of the gate. Compare Ruth 3:3, "go down to the threshing floor." **the gate.** The normal public place to transact business in ancient times (cf. 2 Sam. 15:2; Job 29:7; Lam. 5:14). **friend.** The Heb. text is not clear whether Boaz called him directly by name (which is then not mentioned by the author) or addressed him indirectly.

4:2 ten men. This number apparently comprised a quorum to officially transact business, although only two or three witnesses were needed for judicial proceedings (cf. Deut. 17:6; 19:15).

4:3 Naomi...sold. This phrase could possibly be translated, "Naomi is about to sell..." (cf. Jer. 32:6-15). As a widow, she needed the money for living expenses, knowing that the land would ultimately be returned at Jubilee (Lev. 25:28). **our brother Elimelech.** Boaz and the unnamed relative were most likely either brothers or cousins.

4:4 Buy *it* back. As authorized by the Mosaic law (Lev. 25:23-28).

4:5 you must also buy. Both redeeming Ruth and the land would not have been required by the letter of the levirate law (Deut. 25:5,6). Perhaps this exemplified Boaz's desire to obey the spirit of the law (*see note on 2:4-17*) or maybe redemption of land and marriage had been combined by local tradition. The levirate principle appears first in Scripture at Gen. 38:8 (cf. Matt. 22:23-28).

4:6 lest I ruin my own inheritance. He was unwilling to have the family portfolio split between his existing children and the potential offspring of a union with Ruth. **You redeem.** The closer relative relinquished his legal right to the land and Ruth. This cleared the way for Boaz to redeem both.

4:7 took off his sandal. The Scripture writer explained to his own generation what had been a custom in former generations. This kind of tradition appears in Deut. 25:5-10 and apparently continued at least to the time of Amos (cf. 2:6; 8:6). The closer relative legally transferred his right to the property as symbolized by the sandal, most likely that of the nearer relative.

4:9 I have bought. Boaz exercised his legal option to redeem both the land and Ruth before appropriate witnesses.

4:10 the widow of Mahlon. Only here is Ruth's former husband identified (cf. 1:5 note). Therefore, it can also be assumed that Chilion married Orpah. **I have acquired as my wife.** Boaz exercised the spirit of the law and became Ruth's kinsman-redeemer (Deut. 25:5,6). **the name of the dead.** Perpetuation of the family name (1 Sam. 24:21) was an important feature that the levirate process provided (cf. Deut. 25:6).

4:11 *We are* witnesses. This affirmation signaled the strong approval of the city. **like Rachel and Leah.** Rachel, the most beloved wife of Jacob, was buried nearby (Gen. 35:19); Leah was the mother of Judah (by Jacob), their namesake descendant (Gen. 29:35). This remembrance went back almost 900 years to ca. 1915 B.C. **Ephrathah...Bethlehem.** The ancient name of Bethlehem (Gen. 35:19; 48:7). *See note on 1:2.* Micah later prophetically wrote that this city would be the birthplace of Messiah (5:2).

and be famous in [n]Bethlehem. 12 May your
house be like the house of [o]Perez, [p]whom
Tamar bore to Judah, because of [q]the offspring which the LORD will give you from
this young woman."

Descendants of Boaz and Ruth

13 So Boaz [r]took Ruth and she became
his wife; and when he went in to her, [s]the
LORD gave her conception, and she bore a
son. 14 Then [t]the women said to Naomi,
"Blessed *be* the LORD, who has not left you
this day without a [6]close relative; and
may his name be famous in Israel! 15 And
may he be to you a restorer of life and a
[7]nourisher of your old age; for your
daughter-in-law, who loves you, who is
[u]better to you than seven sons, has borne
him." 16 Then Naomi took the child and
laid him on her bosom, and became a
nurse to him. 17 [v]Also the neighbor wom-
en gave him a name, saying, "There is a
son born to Naomi." And they called his
name Obed. He *is* the father of Jesse, the
father of David.
18 [w]Now this *is* the genealogy of Perez:
[x]Perez begot Hezron; 19 Hezron begot
Ram, and Ram begot Amminadab; 20 Amminadab begot [y]Nahshon, and Nahshon
begot [z]Salmon;[8] 21 Salmon begot Boaz,
and Boaz begot Obed; 22 Obed begot Jesse,
and Jesse begot [a]David.

11 [n]1 Sam. 16:4-13; Mic. 5:2; Matt. 2:1-8
12 [o]1 Chr. 2:4; Matt. 1:3 [p]Gen. 38:6-29 [q]1 Sam. 2:20
13 [r]Ruth 3:11 [s]Gen. 29:31; 33:5; Matt. 1:5
14 [t]Luke 1:58; [Rom. 12:15] [6]*redeemer*, Heb. *goel*
15 [7]*sustainer* [u]1 Sam. 1:8
17 [v]Luke 1:58
18 [w]1 Chr. 2:4, 5; Matt. 1:1-7 [x]Num. 26:20, 21
20 [y]Num. 1:7 [z]Matt. 1:4 [8]Heb. *Salmah*
22 [a]1 Chr. 2:15; Matt. 1:6

4:12 Perez...Tamar...Judah. Read Gen. 38:1-30 for the background to these 3. Tamar, the widow of Judah's first son, Er, when denied a levirate marriage to Judah's remaining son, Shelah (38:14), took matters into her own hands and immorally consorted with her father-in-law Judah (38:18). Perez, the firstborn of twins by Tamar, became the main ancestor of the Ephrathites and Bethlehemites (1 Chr. 2:3-5,19,50,51; 4:4). *See note on 4:18.* **offspring.** The firstborn son would be considered the son of Mahlon. Additional sons would legally be the offspring of Boaz (Deut. 25:6).

4:13 he went in to her. OT euphemism for sexual intercourse. **the LORD gave her conception.** As with Rachel (Gen. 30:22) and Leah (Gen. 29:31), so also with Ruth (cf. Ps. 127:3).

4:14 the LORD...has not left you. In contrast to Naomi's worst moments of despair (1:20,21). **a close relative...his name.** Refers to Obed, not Boaz (cf. 4:11), who cared for Naomi in her latter years.

4:15 better...than seven sons. Seven represented the number of perfection and thus 7 sons would make the complete family (cf. 1 Sam. 2:5). However, Ruth exceeded this standard all by herself.

4:16 a nurse to him. This expresses the natural affection of a godly grandmother for her God-given grandson.

4:17 the neighbor women gave him a name. Here is the only place in the OT where a child was named by someone other than the immediate family. Obed means "servant." **a son born to Naomi.** Ruth vicariously bore the son that would restore the family name of Naomi's deceased son Mahlon (cf. 4:1). **Obed...Jesse...David.** This complete genealogy appears identically in 4 other biblical texts (Ruth 4:21,22; 1 Chr. 2:12-15; Matt. 1:5,6; Luke 3:31,32). Boaz and Ruth were the great-grandparents of David.

4:18-22 Perez...David. This representative genealogy, which spans 9 centuries from Perez (ca. 1885 B.C.) to David (ca. 1040 B.C.), specifically names 10 generations. The first 5 (Perez to Nashon) cover the patriarchal times to the Exodus and wilderness wanderings. Salmon to David covers Joshua's lifetime and the judges to the monarchy. This genealogical compression by omission does not signal faulty records, because in Jewish thinking, "son" could mean "descendant" (cf. Matt. 1:1). The purpose of a family record was not necessarily to include every generation, but rather to establish incontestable succession by way of the more notable ancestors.

4:18 Perez. *See note on v. 12.* Although this genealogy only goes back to Perez, it conclusively establishes that David's lineage extends further back through Judah (Gen. 49:8-12), Jacob (Gen. 28:10-17), and Isaac (Gen. 26:24) to Abraham (Gen. 12:1-3).

4:18,19 Hezron. Cf. Gen. 46:12.

4:19 Ram. Listed as Arni in some Gr. texts of Luke 3:33.

4:19,20 Amminadab. The father-in-law of Aaron (Ex. 6:23), who does not appear in 1 Chr. 2:10, but is cited in Matt. 1:4 and Luke 3:33. Some Heb. mss. also include Admin between Ram and Amminadab in Luke 3:33.

4:20 Nahshon. The leader of Judah in the Exodus (Num. 1:7; 2:3; 7:12,17; 10:14).

4:20,21 Salmon. The husband of Rahab the harlot (cf. Matt. 1:5).

4:21 Salmon begot Boaz. Since Matt. 1:5 lists Rahab the harlot, who lived ca. 1425–1350 B.C., as Salmon's wife, it thus indicates that some generations have been selectively omitted between Salmon and Boaz (ca. 1160–1090 B.C.).

4:22 David. Looking back at Ruth from a NT perspective, latent messianic implications become more apparent (cf. Matt. 1:1). The fruit which is promised later on in the Davidic Covenant (2 Sam. 7:1-17) finds its seedbed here. The hope of a messianic king and kingdom (2 Sam. 7:12-14) will be fulfilled in the Lord Jesus Christ (Rev. 19,20) through the lineage of David's grandfather Obed, who was born to Boaz and Ruth the Moabitess.

Ruth: The Proverbs 31 Wife

The "virtuous" wife of Proverbs 31:10 is personified by "virtuous" Ruth of whom the same Heb. word is used (3:11). With amazing parallel, they share at least 8 character traits (see below). One wonders (in concert with Jewish tradition) if King Lemuel's mother might not have been Bathsheba, who orally passed the family heritage of Ruth's spotless reputation along to David's son Solomon. Lemuel, which means "devoted to God," could have been a family name for Solomon (cf. Jedediah, 2 Sam. 12:25), who then could have penned Prov. 31:10-31 with Ruth in mind. Each woman was:

1. Devoted to her family (Ruth 1:15-18 // Prov. 31:10-12,23)
2. Delighting in her work (Ruth 2:2 // Prov. 31:13)
3. Diligent in her labor (Ruth 2:7,17,23 // Prov. 31:14-18,19-21,24,27)
4. Dedicated to godly speech (Ruth 2:10,13 // Prov. 13:26)
5. Dependent on God (Ruth 2:12 // Prov. 31:25b,30)
6. Dressed with care (Ruth 3:3 // Prov. 31:22,25a)
7. Discreet with men (Ruth 3:6-13 // Prov. 31:11,12,23)
8. Delivering blessings (Ruth 4:14,15 // Prov. 31:28, 29,31)

The First and Second Books of SAMUEL

Title

First and Second Samuel were considered as one book in the earliest Hebrew manuscript, and were later divided into the two books by the translators of the Greek version, the Septuagint (LXX), a division followed by the Latin Vulgate (Vg.), English translations, and modern Hebrew Bibles. The earliest Hebrew manuscripts entitled the one book "Samuel" after the man God used to establish the kingship in Israel. Later Hebrew texts and the English versions call the divided book "1 and 2 Samuel." The LXX designated them "The First and Second Books of Kingdoms" and the Vg., "First and Second Kings," with our 1 and 2 Kings being "Third and Fourth Kings."

Author and Date

Jewish tradition ascribed the writing of "Samuel" to Samuel himself or to Samuel, Nathan, and Gad (based on 1 Chr. 29:29). But Samuel cannot be the writer because his death is recorded in 1 Sam. 25:1, before the events associated with David's reign even took place. Further, Nathan and Gad were prophets of the Lord during David's lifetime and would not have been alive when the book of Samuel was written. Though the written records of these 3 prophets could have been used for information in the writing of 1 and 2 Samuel, the human author of these books is unknown. The work comes to the reader as an anonymous writing, i.e., the human author speaks for the Lord and gives the divine interpretation of the events narrated.

The books of Samuel contain no clear indication of the date of composition. That the author wrote after the division of the kingdom between Israel and Judah in 931 B.C. is clear, due to the many references to Israel and Judah as distinct entities (1 Sam. 11:8; 17:52; 18:16; 2 Sam. 5:5; 11:11; 12:8; 19:42-43; 24:1,9). Also, the statement concerning Ziklag's belonging "to the kings of Judah to this day" in 1 Sam. 27:6 gives clear evidence of a post-Solomonic date of writing. There is no such clarity concerning how late the date of writing could be. However, 1 and 2 Samuel are included in the Former Prophets in the Hebrew canon, along with Joshua, Judges, and 1 and 2 Kings. If the Former Prophets were composed as a unit, then Samuel would have been written during the Babylonian captivity (ca. 560–540 B.C.), since 2 Kings concludes during the exile (2 Kin. 25:27-30). However, since Samuel has a different literary style than Kings, it was most likely penned before the Exile during the period of the divided kingdom (ca. 931–722 B.C.) and later made an integral part of the Former Prophets.

Background and Setting

The majority of the action recorded in 1 and 2 Samuel took place in and around the central highlands in the land of Israel. The nation of Israel was largely concentrated in an area that ran about 90 mi. from the hill country of Ephraim in the N (1 Sam. 1:1; 9:4) to the hill country of Judah in the S (Josh. 20:7; 21:11) and between 15 to 35 mi. E to W. This central spine ranges in height from 1,500 ft. to 3,300 ft. above sea level. The major cities of 1 and 2 Samuel are to be found in these central highlands: Shiloh, the residence of Eli and the tabernacle; Ramah, the hometown of Samuel; Gibeah, the headquarters of Saul; Bethlehem, the birthplace of David; Hebron, David's capital when he ruled over Judah; and Jerusalem, the ultimate "city of David."

The events of 1 and 2 Samuel took place between the years ca. 1105 B.C., the birth of Samuel (1 Sam. 1:1-28), to ca. 971 B.C., the last words of David (2 Sam. 23:1-7). Thus, the books span about 135 years of history. During those years, Israel was transformed from a loosely knit group of tribes under "judges" to a united nation under the reign of a centralized monarchy. They look primarily at Samuel (ca. 1105–1030 B.C.), Saul who reigned ca. 1052–1011 B.C., and David who was king of the united monarchy ca. 1011–971 B.C.

Historical and Theological Themes

As 1 Samuel begins, Israel was at a low point spiritually. The priesthood was corrupt (1 Sam. 2:12-17,22-26), the ark of the covenant was not at the tabernacle (1 Sam. 4:3–7:2), idolatry was practiced (1 Sam. 7:3,4), and the judges were dishonest (1 Sam. 8:2,3). Through the influence of godly Samuel

(1 Sam. 12:23) and David (1 Sam. 13:14), these conditions were reversed. Second Samuel concludes with the anger of the Lord being withdrawn from Israel (2 Sam. 24:25).

During the years narrated in 1 and 2 Samuel, the great empires of the ancient world were in a state of weakness. Neither Egypt nor the Mesopotamian powers, Babylon and Assyria, were threats to Israel at that time. The two nations most hostile to the Israelites were the Philistines (1 Sam. 4; 7; 13,14; 17; 23; 31; 2 Sam. 5) to the W and the Ammonites (1 Sam. 11; 2 Sam. 10–12) to the E. The major contingent of the Philistines had migrated from the Aegean Islands and Asia Minor in the 12th century B.C. After being denied access to Egypt, they settled among other preexisting Philistines along the Mediterranean coast of Palestine. The Philistines controlled the use of iron, which gave them a decided military and economic advantage over Israel (1 Sam. 13:19-22). The Ammonites were descendants of Lot (Gen. 19:38) who lived on the Transjordan Plateau. David conquered the Philistines (2 Sam. 8:1) and the Ammonites (2 Sam. 12:29-31), along with other nations that surrounded Israel (2 Sam. 8:2-14).

There are four predominant theological themes in 1 and 2 Samuel. The first is the Davidic Covenant. The books are literarily framed by two references to the "anointed" king in the prayer of Hannah (1 Sam. 2:10) and the song of David (2 Sam. 22:51). This is a reference to the Messiah, the King who will triumph over the nations who are opposed to God (see Gen. 49:8-12; Num. 24:7-9,17-19). According to the Lord's promise, this Messiah will come through the line of David and establish David's throne forever (2 Sam. 7:12-16). The events of David's life recorded in Samuel foreshadow the actions of David's greater Son (i.e., Christ) in the future.

A second theme is the sovereignty of God, clearly seen in these books. One example is the birth of Samuel in response to Hannah's prayer (1 Sam. 9:17; 16:12,13). Also, in relation to David, it is particularly evident that nothing can frustrate God's plan to have him rule over Israel (1 Sam. 24:20).

Third, the work of the Holy Spirit in empowering men for divinely appointed tasks is evident. The Spirit of the Lord came upon both Saul and David after their anointing as king (1 Sam. 10:10; 16:13). The power of the Holy Spirit brought forth prophecy (1 Sam. 10:6) and victory in battle (1 Sam. 11:6).

Fourth, the books of Samuel demonstrate the personal and national effects of sin. The sins of Eli and his sons resulted in their deaths (1 Sam. 2:12-17,22-25; 3:10-14; 4:17,18). The lack of reverence for the ark of the covenant led to the death of a number of Israelites (1 Sam. 6:19; 2 Sam. 6:6,7). Saul's disobedience resulted in the Lord's judgment, and he was rejected as king over Israel (1 Sam. 13:9,13,14; 15:8,9,20-23). Although David was forgiven for his sin of adultery and murder after his confession (2 Sam. 12:13), he still suffered the inevitable and devastating consequences of his sin (2 Sam. 12:14).

Interpretive Challenges

The books of Samuel contain a number of interpretive issues that have been widely discussed: 1) Which of the ancient mss. is closest to the original autograph? The standard Hebrew (Masoretic) text has been relatively poorly preserved, and the LXX often differs from it. Thus, the exact reading of the original autograph of the text is in places hard to determine (see 1 Sam. 13:1). The NKJV uses the Masoretic text with significant variant readings in the marginal notes. The Masoretic text will be assumed to represent the original text unless there is a grammatical or contextual impossibility. This accounts for many of the numerical discrepancies. 2) Is Samuel ambivalent to the establishment of the human kingship in Israel? It is claimed that while 1 Sam. 9–11 presents a positive view of the kingship, 1 Sam. 8 and 12 are strongly anti-monarchial. It is preferable, however, to see the book as presenting a balanced perspective of the human kingship. While the desire of Israel for a king was acceptable (Deut. 17:15), their reason for wanting a king showed a lack of faith in the Lord (*see notes on 1 Sam. 8:5,20*). 3) How does one explain the bizarre behavior of the prophets? It is commonly held that 1 and 2 Samuel present the prophets as ecstatic speakers with bizarre behavior just like the pagan prophets of the other nations. But there is nothing in the text which is inconsistent with seeing the prophets as communicators of divine revelation, at times prophesying with musical accompaniment (*see notes on 1 Sam. 10:5; 19:23,24*). 4) How did the Holy Spirit minister before Pentecost? The ministry of the Holy Spirit in 1 Sam. 10:6,10; 11:16; 16:13,14; 19:20,23; 2 Sam. 23:2 was not describing salvation in the NT sense, but an empowering by the Lord for His service (see also Judg. 3:10; 6:34; 11:29; 13:25; 14:6,19; 15:14). 5) What was the identity of the "distressing spirit from the Lord"? Is it a personal being, i.e., a demon, or a spirit of discontent created by God in the heart (cf. Judg. 9:23)? Traditionally, it has been viewed as a demon (*see note on 1 Sam. 16:14*). 6) How did Samuel appear in 1 Sam. 28:3-5? It seems best to understand the appearance of Samuel as the Lord allowing the dead Samuel to speak with Saul. 7) What is the identity of David's seed in 2 Sam. 7:12-15? It is usually taken as Solomon. However, the NT refers the words to Jesus, God's Son in Heb. 1:5 (*see notes on 2 Sam. 7:12-15*).

Outline of 1 Samuel

I. Samuel: Prophet and Judge to Israel (1:1–7:17)
   A. Samuel the Prophet (1:1–4:1a)
      1. The birth of Samuel (1:1-28)
      2. The prayer of Hannah (2:1-10)
      3. The growth of Samuel (2:11-26)
      4. The oracle against Eli's house (2:27-36)
      5. The Word of the Lord through Samuel (3:1–4:1a)
   B. Samuel the Judge (4:1b–7:17)
      1. The saga of the ark (4:1b–7:1)
      2. Israel's victory over the Philistines and the judgeship of Samuel (7:2-17)

II. Saul: First King Over Israel (8:1–15:35)
   A. The Rise of Saul to the Kingship (8:1–12:25)
      1. The demand of Israel for a king (8:1-22)
      2. The process of Saul becoming king (9:1–11:13)
      3. The exhortation of Samuel to Israel concerning the king (11:14–12:25)
   B. The Decline of Saul in the Kingship (13:1–15:35)
      1. The rebuke of Saul (13:1-15)
      2. The wars of Saul (13:16–14:52)
      3. The rejection of Saul (15:1-35)

III. David and Saul: Transfer of the Kingship in Israel (16:1–31:13)
   A. The Introduction of David (16:1–17:58)
      1. The anointing of David (16:1-13)
      2. David in the court of Saul (16:14-23)
      3. David, the warrior of the Lord (17:1-58)
   B. David Driven from the Court of Saul (18:1–20:42)
      1. The anger and fear of Saul toward David (18:1-30)
      2. The defense of David by Jonathan and Michal (19:1–20:42)
   C. David's Flight from Saul's Pursuit (21:1–28:2)
      1. Saul's killing of the priests at Nob (21:1–22:23)
      2. Saul's life spared twice by David (23:1–26:25)
      3. David's despair and Philistine refuge (27:1–28:2)
   D. The Death of Saul (28:3–31:13)
      1. Saul's final night (28:3-25)
      2. David's dismissal by the Philistines (29:1-11)
      3. David's destruction of the Amalekites (30:1-31)
      4. Saul's final day (31:1-13)

The Family of Elkanah

1 Now there was a certain man of Ramathaim Zophim, of the [a]mountains
of Ephraim, and his name *was* [b]Elkanah
the son of Jeroham, the son of [1]Elihu, the
son of [2]Tohu, the son of Zuph, [c]an Ephraimite. **2** And he had [d]two wives: the name
of one *was* Hannah, and the name of the
other Peninnah. Peninnah had children,
but Hannah had no children. **3** This man
went up from his city [e]yearly [f]to worship
and sacrifice to the LORD of hosts in
[g]Shiloh. Also the two sons of Eli, Hophni
and Phinehas, the priests of the LORD,
were there. **4** And whenever the time came
for Elkanah to make an [h]offering, he
would give portions to Peninnah his wife
and to all her sons and daughters. **5** But to
Hannah he would give a double portion,
for he loved Hannah, [i]although the LORD
had closed her womb. **6** And her rival also
[j]provoked her severely, to make her miserable, because the LORD had closed her
womb. **7** So it was, year by year, when she
went up to the house of the LORD, that she
provoked her; therefore she wept and did
not eat.

CHAPTER 1

1 [a]Josh. 17:17, 18; 24:33 [b]1 Chr. 6:27, 33-38 [c]Ruth 1:2 [1]*Eliel,* 1 Chr. 6:34 [2]*Toah,* 1 Chr. 6:34
2 [d]Deut. 21:15-17
3 [e]Ex. 34:14, 23; Judg. 21:19; 1 Sam. 1:21; Luke 2:41 [f]Deut. 12:5-7; 16:16 [g]Josh. 18:1
4 [h]Deut. 12:17, 18
5 [i]Gen. 16:1; 30:1, 2
6 [j]Job 24:21
8 [k]Ruth 4:15
9 [l]1 Sam. 3:3 [3]*palace* or *temple,* Heb. *heykal*
10 [m]Job 7:11 [4]Lit. *wept greatly*
11 [n]Gen. 28:20; Num. 30:6-11 [o]Ps. 25:18 [p]Gen. 8:1 [q]Num. 6:5; Judg. 13:5

Hannah's Vow

8 Then Elkanah her husband said to her,
"Hannah, why do you weep? Why do you
not eat? And why is your heart grieved?
Am I not [k]better to you than ten sons?"
9 So Hannah arose after they had finished eating and drinking in Shiloh. Now
Eli the priest was sitting on the seat by the
doorpost of [l]the [3]tabernacle of the LORD.
10 [m]And she *was* in bitterness of soul, and
prayed to the LORD and [4]wept in anguish.
11 Then she [n]made a vow and said, "O
LORD of hosts, if You will indeed [o]look on
the affliction of Your maidservant and [p]re-
member me, and not forget Your maidservant, but will give Your maidservant a
male child, then I will give him to the LORD
all the days of his life, and [q]no razor shall
come upon his head."
12 And it happened, as she continued
praying before the LORD, that Eli watched
her mouth. **13** Now Hannah spoke in her
heart; only her lips moved, but her voice
was not heard. Therefore Eli thought she
was drunk. **14** So Eli said to her, "How long
will you be drunk? Put your wine away
from you!"

1:1–7:17 This first major division of the book begins and ends in Samuel's home town of Ramah (1:1; 7:17). The focus of these chapters is on the life and ministry of Samuel. First Samuel 1:1–4:1a concentrates on Samuel as a prophet of the Lord (see the concluding statement of 4:1a, "and the word of Samuel came to all Israel"). The text in 4:1b–7:17 emphasizes Samuel as judge (see 7:17, "there he judged Israel").

1:1 a certain man. This verse resembles the introduction to the birth of Samson in Judg. 13:2. The strong comparison highlights similarities between Samson and Samuel: Both men were judges over Israel, fighters of the Philistines, and lifelong Nazirites. **Ramathaim.** Possibly meaning "two heights," the name occurs only here in the OT. Elsewhere, the town is simply called Ramah. It was located about 5 mi. N of Jerusalem. **Elkanah.** Meaning "God has created," he was the father of Samuel. **of Zuph.** "Zuph" is both a place (9:5) and a personal name (1 Chr. 6:35), as here. **Ephraimite.** First Chronicles 6:27 identifies Elkanah as a member of the Kohathite branch of the tribe of Levi. The Levites lived among the other tribes (Josh. 21:20-22). Ephraim was the tribal area where this Levite lived.

1:2 two wives. Although polygamy was not God's intention for mankind (Gen. 2:24), it was tolerated, but never endorsed in Israel (see Deut. 21:15-17). Elkanah probably married Peninnah because Hannah was barren. **Hannah.** Meaning "grace," she was probably Elkanah's first wife. **Peninnah.** Meaning "ruby," she was Elkanah's second wife and the first bearer of his children.

1:3 This man went up...yearly. All Israelite men were required to attend 3 annual feasts at the central sanctuary (Deut. 16:1-17). Elkanah regularly attended these festivals with his wives. The festival referred to here was probably the Feast of Tabernacles (Sept./Oct.) because of the feasting mentioned in 1:9. **the LORD of hosts.** This is the first OT occurrence of "hosts" being added to the divine name. "Hosts" can refer to human armies (Ex. 7:4), celestial bodies (Deut. 4:19), or heavenly creatures (Josh. 5:14). This title emphasizes the Lord as sovereign over all of the powers in heaven and on earth, especially over the armies of Israel. **Shiloh.** Located about 20 mi. N of Jerusalem in Ephraim, the tabernacle and ark of the covenant resided here (Josh. 18:1; Judg. 18:31). **Eli.** Meaning "exalted is the LORD." He was the High-Priest at Shiloh. **Hophni and Phinehas.** Each of Eli's two priestly sons had an Egyptian name: Hophni ("tadpole") and Phinehas ("nubian").

1:4 an offering. A peace offering since the worshipers ate a portion of the offering (see Lev. 7:11-18).

1:5 the LORD had closed her womb. Hannah's barrenness was the result of divine providence like Sarah's (Gen. 16:2) and Rachel's (Gen. 30:2).

1:6 her rival. The other wife was an adversary. **provoked her.** Lit. "to thunder against" her; see 2:10 for the same word.

1:7 did not eat. Hannah fasted because of the provocation of Peninnah. She did not eat of the peace offerings.

1:8 your heart grieved. The idiom used reflects anger, not sadness (see Deut. 15:10 for the same idiom).

1:9 tabernacle. See marginal note. The mention of sleeping quarters (3:2,3) and doors (3:15) implies that at this time the tabernacle was part of a larger, more permanent building complex.

1:11 vow. Hannah pledged to give the Lord her son in return for God's favor in giving her that son. A married woman's vow could be confirmed or nullified by her husband according to Num. 30:6-15. **Your maidservant.** A humble, submissive way of referring to herself in the presence of her superior, sovereign God. **remember me.** Hannah requested special attention and care from the Lord. **all the days of his life.** A contrast to the normal Nazirite vow, which was only for a specified period of time (see Num. 6:4,5,8). **no razor.** Though not specified as such in this chapter, the Nazirite vow is certainly presupposed. The nonshaving of the hair on one's head is one of the 3 requirements of the vow (Num. 6:5). This expression was used elsewhere only of the Nazirite Samson (Judg. 13:5; 16:17).

1:13 drunk. Public prayer in Israel was usually audible. However, Hannah was praying silently, leaving Eli to surmise that she was drunk.

15 But Hannah answered and said, "No,
my lord, I *am* a woman of sorrowful spirit.
I have drunk neither wine nor intoxicating
drink, but have [r]poured out my soul before the LORD. 16 Do not consider your
maidservant a [s]wicked[5] woman, for out of
the abundance of my complaint and grief I
have spoken until now."
17 Then Eli answered and said, [t]"Go in
peace, and [u]the God of Israel grant your
petition which you have asked of Him."
18 And she said, [v]"Let your maidservant
find favor in your sight." So the woman
[w]went her way and ate, and her face was
no longer *sad*.

Samuel Is Born and Dedicated

19 Then they rose early in the morning
and worshiped before the LORD, and returned and came to their house at Ramah.
And Elkanah [x]knew Hannah his wife, and
the LORD [y]remembered her. 20 So it came to
pass in the process of time that Hannah
conceived and bore a son, and called his
name [6]Samuel, *saying,* "Because I have
asked for him from the LORD."
21 Now the man Elkanah and all his
house [z]went up to offer to the LORD the
yearly sacrifice and his vow. 22 But Hannah did not go up, for she said to her husband, "*Not* until the child is weaned; then
I will [a]take him, that he may appear before
the LORD and [b]remain there [c]forever."
23 So [d]Elkanah her husband said to her,
"Do what seems best to you; wait until you
have weaned him. Only let the LORD [7]es-
tablish [8]His word." Then the woman
stayed and nursed her son until she had
weaned him.

15 [r]Job 30:16; Ps. 42:4; 62:8; Lam. 2:19
16 [s]Deut. 13:13 [5]Lit. *daughter of Belial*
17 [t]Judg. 18:6; 1 Sam. 25:35; 2 Kin. 5:19; Mark 5:34; Luke 7:50 [u]Ps. 20:3-5
18 [v]Gen. 33:15; Ruth 2:13 [w]Prov. 15:13; Eccl. 9:7; Rom. 15:13
19 [x]Gen. 4:1 [y]Gen. 21:1; 30:22
20 [6]Lit. *Heard by God*
21 [z]Deut. 12:11; 1 Sam. 1:3
22 [a]Luke 2:22 [b]1 Sam. 1:11, 28 [c]Ex. 21:6
23 [d]Num. 30:7, 10, 11 [7]*confirm* [8]So with MT, Tg., Vg.; DSS, LXX, Syr. *your*
24 [e]Num. 15:9, 10; Deut. 12:5, 6 [f]Josh. 18:1; 1 Sam. 4:3, 4 [9]DSS, LXX, Syr. *a three-year-old bull*
25 [g]Luke 2:22
26 [h]2 Kin. 2:2, 4, 6; 4:30
27 [i][Matt. 7:7]
28 [j]Gen. 24:26, 52 [1]*granted*

24 Now when she had weaned him, she
[e]took him up with her, with [9]three bulls,
one ephah of flour, and a skin of wine,
and brought him to [f]the house of the LORD
in Shiloh. And the child *was* young.
25 Then they slaughtered a bull, and
[g]brought the child to Eli. 26 And she said,
"O my lord! [h]As your soul lives, my lord,
I *am* the woman who stood by you here,
praying to the LORD. 27 [i]For this child I
prayed, and the LORD has granted me my
petition which I asked of Him. 28 Therefore I also have lent him to the LORD; as
long as he lives he shall be [1]lent to the
LORD." So they [j]worshiped the LORD
there.

Hannah's Prayer

2 And Hannah [a]prayed and said:

[b]"My heart rejoices in the LORD;
[c]My [1]horn is exalted in the LORD.
[2]I smile at my enemies,
Because I [d]rejoice in Your
salvation.

2 "No[e] one is holy like the LORD,
For *there is* [f]none besides You,
Nor *is there* any [g]rock like our
God.

3 "Talk no more so very proudly;
[h]Let no arrogance come from your
mouth,
For the LORD *is* the God of
[i]knowledge;
And by Him actions are weighed.

CHAPTER 2
1 [a]Phil. 4:6 [b]1 Sam. 2:1-10; Ps. 97:11, 12; Luke 1:46-55 [c]Ps. 75:10; 89:17, 24; 92:10; 112:9 [d]Ps. 9:14; 13:5; 35:9; Is. 12:2, 3 [1]Strength [2]Lit. *My mouth is enlarged*
2 [e]Ex. 15:11; Ps. 86:8; Rev. 15:4 [f]Deut. 4:35 [g]Deut. 32:4, 30, 31; 2 Sam. 22:32; Ps. 18:2 3 [h]Ps. 94:4 [i]1 Sam. 16:7

1:16 wicked. See marginal note and cf. 2:12.

1:20 Samuel. The name lit. meant "name of God," but sounded like "heard by God." For Hannah the assonance was most important, because God had heard her prayer.

1:21 his vow. Elkanah supported and joined with his wife in her vow to the Lord. With the birth of Samuel he brought his votive offering to the Lord (Lev. 7:16).

1:22 weaned. As was customary in the ancient world, Samuel was probably breast fed for two to three years. Then he was left to serve the Lord at the tabernacle for the rest of his life.

1:23 His word. Probably an earlier word of the Lord not recorded in the text.

1:24 three bulls...ephah of flour...skin of wine. According to Num. 15:8-10, a bull, flour, and wine were to be sacrificed in fulfillment of a vow. Hannah brought all 3 in larger measure than required. An ephah was about .75 bu.

1:26 As your soul lives. Lit. "by the light of your soul," a common oath formula.

1:27,28 asked...lent. These terms are from the same Heb. root used 4 times in these two verses. Twice in v. 27 it has the usual meaning of "asked." Twice in v. 28 it bears the derived meaning "lent on request." The son Hannah requested God had given, and she gives her gift back to the Giver.

2:1-10 In contrast to the prayer that came from her bitterness (1:10), Hannah prayed from joy in these verses. The prominent idea in Hannah's prayer is that the Lord is a righteous judge. He had brought down the proud (Peninnah) and exalted the humble (Hannah). The prayer has four sections: 1) Hannah prays to the Lord for His salvation (vv. 1,2); 2) Hannah warned the proud of the Lord's humbling (vv. 3-8d); 3) Hannah affirmed the Lord's faithful care for His saints (vv. 8e-9b); 4) Hannah petitioned the Lord to judge the world and to prosper His anointed king (vv. 10d-e). This prayer has a number of striking verbal similarities with David's song of 2 Sam. 22:2-51: "horn" (2:1; 22:3), "rock" (2:2; 22:2,3), salvation/deliverance (2:1,2; 22:2,3), grave/Sheol (2:6; 22:6), "thunder" (2:10; 22:14), "king" (2:10; 22:51), and "anointed" (2:10; 22:51).

2:1 horn. A symbol of strength, power (see Deut. 33:17).

2:2 rock. A metaphor for God that emphasized His strength and the security of those who trust in Him (see Deut. 32:4; Ps. 18:1,2).

2:3 proudly...arrogance. The majestic and powerful God humbles all those who vaunt themselves against Him. The idea of God's humbling of the very proud is shown throughout 1, 2 Samuel, toward Peninnah, Eli's sons, the Philistines, Goliath, Saul, Nabal, Absalom, Shimei, Sheba, and even David.

4 "The[j] bows of the mighty men *are* broken,
And those who stumbled are girded with strength.
5 *Those who were* full have hired themselves out for bread,
And the hungry have ceased *to hunger.*
Even [k]the barren has borne seven,
And [l]she who has many children has become feeble.

6 "The[m] LORD kills and makes alive;
He brings down to the grave and brings up.
7 The LORD [n]makes poor and makes rich;
[o]He brings low and lifts up.
8 [p]He raises the poor from the dust
And lifts the beggar from the ash heap,
[q]To set *them* among princes
And make them inherit the throne of glory.

[r]"For the pillars of the earth *are* the LORD's,
And He has set the world upon them.
9 [s]He will guard the feet of His saints,
But the [t]wicked shall be silent in darkness.

"For by strength no man shall prevail.
10 The adversaries of the LORD shall be [u]broken in pieces;
[v]From heaven He will thunder against them.
[w]The LORD will judge the ends of the earth.

[x]"He will give [y]strength to His king,
And [z]exalt the [3]horn of His anointed."

11 Then Elkanah went to his house at
Ramah. But the child [4]ministered to the
LORD before Eli the priest.

The Wicked Sons of Eli

12 Now the sons of Eli *were* [a]corrupt;[5]
[b]they did not know the LORD. 13 And the
priests' custom with the people *was that*
when any man offered a sacrifice, the
priest's servant would come with a three-
pronged fleshhook in his hand while the
meat was boiling. 14 Then he would
thrust *it* into the pan, or kettle, or caldron,
or pot; and the priest would take for himself all that the fleshhook brought up. So
they did in [c]Shiloh to all the Israelites
who came there. 15 Also, before they
[d]burned the fat, the priest's servant
would come and say to the man who sacrificed, "Give meat for roasting to the
priest, for he will not take boiled meat
from you, but raw."
16 And *if* the man said to him, "They
should really burn the fat first; *then* you
may take *as much* as your heart desires," he
would then answer him, "*No,* but you
must give *it* now; and if not, I will take *it*
by force."
17 Therefore the sin of the young men
was very great [e]before the LORD, for men
[f]abhorred[6] the offering of the LORD.

4 [j] Ps. 37:15; 46:9
5 [k] Ps. 113:9 [l] Is. 54:1; Jer. 15:9
6 [m] Deut. 32:39; 2 Kin. 5:7; Job 5:18; [Rev. 1:18]
7 [n] Deut. 8:17, 18; Job 1:21 [o] Job 5:11; Ps. 75:7; James 4:10
8 [p] Job 42:10-12; Ps. 75:7; 113:7; Luke 1:52 [q] Job 36:7; Ps. 113:8 [r] Job 38:4-6; Ps. 75:3; 104:5
9 [s] Ps. 37:23, 24; 91:11, 12; 94:18; 121:3; Prov. 3:26; [1 Pet. 1:5] [t] [Rom. 3:19]
10 [u] Ex. 15:6; Ps. 2:9 [v] 1 Sam. 7:10; 2 Sam. 22:14, 15; Ps. 18:13, 14 [w] Ps. 96:13; 98:9; [Matt. 25:31, 32] [x] [Matt. 28:18] [y] Ps. 21:1, 7 [z] Ps. 89:24 [3] Strength
11 [4] *served*
12 [a] Deut. 13:13 [b] Judg. 2:10; [Rom. 1:28] [5] Lit. *sons of Belial*
14 [c] 1 Sam. 1:3
15 [d] Lev. 3:3-5, 16
17 [e] Gen. 6:11 [f] [Mal. 2:7-9] [6] *despised*

2:4-7 Seven contrasts are found in these 4 verses: 1) mighty and weak; 2) full and hungry; 3) barren and fertile; 4) dead and alive; 5) sick and well; 6) poor and rich; and 7) humbled and exalted.

2:5 has borne seven. This is not a personal testimony since Hannah bore only 6 children (2:21). "Seven" here is a general reference to women whom God blesses.

2:8 pillars of the earth. A figure of speech which pictures the earth's stability (cf. Pss. 75:3; 82:5; 104:5).

2:10 The LORD will judge the ends of the earth. The Lord will impose His righteous rule upon all the nations and peoples (see Is. 2:2-4). **His king.** Moses had already predicted the coming of a king who would exercise God's rule over all the nations of the earth (Gen. 49:8-12; Num. 24:7-9, 17-19). It was this future, victorious king whom Hannah anticipated and Saul and David prefigured. **His anointed.** Previously in the OT, both the tabernacle and its utensils along with the priests (Aaron and his sons) had been anointed with oil. This pictured their consecrated and holy status before the Lord (Ex. 30:26-30). In Samuel, first Saul (10:1), and then David (16:13; 2 Sam. 2:4; 5:3) were anointed as they were inaugurated for the kingship. From this point in the OT, it is usually the king who is referred as "the anointed (of the LORD)" (12:3; 24:6; 26:9, 11, 16; 2 Sam. 1:14, 16; 19:21). The kings of Israel, particularly David, foreshadowed the Lord's ultimate anointed king. The English word "Messiah" represents the Heb. word used here meaning "anointed." Thus, this ultimate King who would rule over the nations of the earth, came to be referred to as "the Messiah," as here and 2:35; cf. 2 Sam. 22:51.

2:11 ministered to the LORD. As a Levite, the boy Samuel performed services that assisted Eli, the High-Priest.

2:12 corrupt. "Sons of Belial" was a Heb. way of saying base, worthless, or wicked men. See 2 Cor. 6:15, where it is used as a name for Satan. Eli had falsely considered Hannah a wicked woman (1:16). Eli's sons were, in fact, wicked men. **they did not know the LORD.** Eli's sons had no personal experience of, nor fellowship with, the Lord. The boy Samuel came to "know the LORD" when the Lord revealed Himself to him (see 3:7).

2:13 the priests' custom. Not content with the specified portions of the sacrifices given to the priests (Deut. 18:3), Eli's sons would take for themselves whatever meat a 3-pronged fork would collect from a boiling pot.

2:15 before they burned the fat. The law mandated that the fat of the sacrificial animal was to be burned on the altar to the Lord (Lev. 7:31). In contrast, Eli's sons demanded raw meat, including the fat, from the worshipers.

Samuel's Childhood Ministry

18 [g]But Samuel ministered before the
LORD, *even as* a child, [h]wearing a linen
ephod. 19 Moreover his mother used to
make him a little robe, and bring *it* to him
year by year when she [i]came up with her
husband to offer the yearly sacrifice.
20 And Eli [j]would bless Elkanah and his
wife, and say, "The LORD give you descendants from this woman for the [7]loan that
was [k]given to the LORD." Then they would
go to their own home.
21 And the LORD [l]visited[8] Hannah, so
that she conceived and bore three sons and
two daughters. Meanwhile the child Samuel [m]grew before the LORD.

Prophecy Against Eli's Household

22 Now Eli was very old; and he heard
everything his sons did to all Israel, [9]and
how they lay with [n]the women who assembled at the door of the tabernacle of
meeting. 23 So he said to them, "Why do
you do such things? For I hear of your evil
dealings from all the people. 24 No, my
sons! For *it is* not a good report that I hear.
You make the LORD's people transgress.
25 If one man sins against another, [o]God[1]
will judge him. But if a man [p]sins against
the LORD, who will intercede for him?"
Nevertheless they did not heed the voice
of their father, [q]because the LORD desired
to kill them.
26 And the child Samuel [r]grew in
stature, and [s]in favor both with the LORD
and men.
27 Then a [t]man of God came to Eli and
said to him, "Thus says the LORD: [u]'Did I
not clearly reveal Myself to the house of
your father when they were in Egypt in
Pharaoh's house? 28 Did I not [v]choose him
out of all the tribes of Israel *to be* My priest,
to offer upon My altar, to burn incense,
and to wear an ephod before Me? And
[w]did I not give to the house of your father
all the offerings of the children of Israel
made by fire? 29 Why do you [x]kick at My
sacrifice and My offering which I have
commanded *in My* [y]dwelling place, and
honor your sons more than [z]Me, to make
yourselves fat with the best of all the offerings of Israel My people?' 30 Therefore the

18 [g] 1 Sam. 2:11; 3:1 [h] Ex. 28:4
19 [i] 1 Sam. 1:3, 21
20 [j] Gen. 14:19 [k] 1 Sam. 1:11, 27, 28 [7] *gift*
21 [l] Gen. 21:1 [m] Judg. 13:24; 1 Sam. 2:26; 3:19-21; Luke 1:80; 2:40 [8] *attended to*
22 [n] Ex. 38:8 [9] So with MT, Tg., Vg.; DSS, LXX omit rest of verse
25 [o] Deut. 1:17; 25:1, 2 [p] Num. 15:30 [q] Josh. 11:20 [1] Tg. *the Judge*
26 [r] 1 Sam. 2:21 [s] Prov. 3:4
27 [t] Deut. 33:1; Judg. 13:6; 1 Sam. 9:6; 1 Kin. 13:1 [u] Ex. 4:14-16; 12:1
28 [v] Ex. 28:1, 4; Num. 16:5 [w] Lev. 2:3, 10; 6:16; 7:7, 8, 34, 35; Num. 5:9
29 [x] Deut. 32:15 [y] Deut. 12:5; Ps. 26:8 [z] Matt. 10:37

2:18 But Samuel. The faithful ministry of Samuel before the Lord was in sharp contrast to the disobedience of Eli's sons. **linen ephod.** A close fitting, sleeveless outer vest extending to the hips and worn by priests, especially when officiating before the altar (Ex. 28:6-14).

2:19 little robe. A sleeveless garment reaching to the knees, worn under the ephod (Ex. 28:31).

2:20 the loan. The same word used in 1:27,28 translated "granted," "asked," "lent" there. Here it is a reminder of Hannah's faithfulness to her vow to the Lord. By providing Hannah with additional children, the Lord continued to be gracious to her.

2:22 lay with the women. Eli's sons included in their vile behavior having sexual relationships with the women who served at the tabernacle (see Ex. 38:8 for a notation concerning these women). Such religious prostitution was common among Israel's Canaanite neighbors.

2:25 God will judge. Eli's point to his sons was that if God would surely judge when one sinned against another man, how much more would He bring judgment against those who sinned against Him. **the LORD desired to kill them.** Because Eli's sons had persisted in their evil ways, God had already determined to judge them. This divine, judicial hardening, the result of defiant refusal to repent in the past, was the reason Hophni and Phinehas refused to heed Eli's warnings.

2:26 grew in stature, and in favor. In contrast to the apostate sons of Eli, Samuel was maturing both spiritually and socially (cf. Luke 2:52).

2:27 man of God. Usually used as a synonym for "prophet" (see 9:9,10). **house of your father…in Egypt.** Although Eli's genealogy was not recorded in the OT, he was a descendant of Aaron. The Lord had revealed Himself to Aaron in Egypt before the Exodus (see Ex. 4:4-16). Aaron had been divinely chosen to serve the Lord as the first in a long line of priests (Ex. 28:1-4).

2:28 *to be* My priest. The chief duties of the priests were: 1) to place the offerings upon the altar; 2) to burn the incense in the holy place; and 3) to wear the linen ephod (see v. 18).

2:29 My offering. In recognition of their service to God and His people, the priests were allocated specific parts of the offering which were brought to the sanctuary (see Lev. 2:3,10; 7:31-36).

2:29 honor. By condoning the sin of Hophni and Phinehas, Eli had shown preference for his sons above the Lord. Therefore, Eli was unworthy of the Lord's blessing.

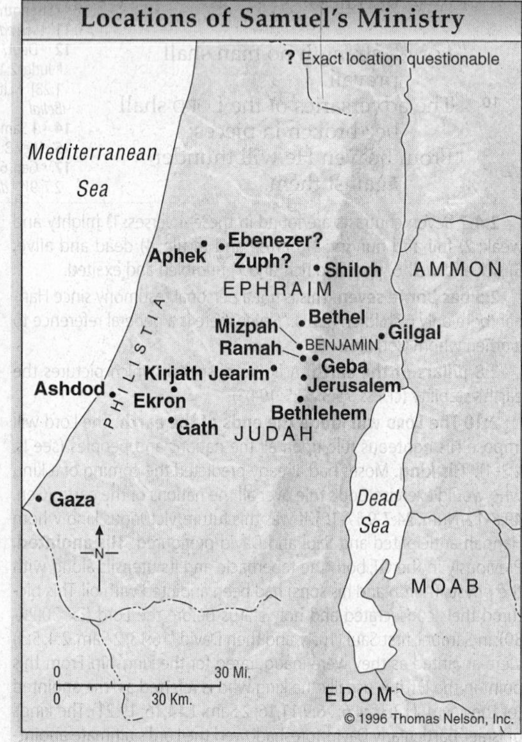

LORD God of Israel says: [a]'I said indeed
that your house and the house of your father would walk before Me forever.' But
now the LORD says: [b]'Far be it from Me; for
those who honor Me I will honor, and
[c]those who despise Me shall be lightly esteemed. 31 Behold, [d]the days are coming
that I will cut off your [2]arm and the arm of
your father's house, so that there will not
be an old man in your house. 32 And you
will see an enemy *in My* dwelling place, *de-*
spite all the good which God does for Israel. And there shall not be [e]an old man in
your house forever. 33 But any of your men
whom I do not cut off from My altar shall
consume your eyes and grieve your heart.
And all the descendants of your house
shall die in the flower of their age. 34 Now
this *shall be* [f]a sign to you that will come
upon your two sons, on Hophni and
Phinehas: [g]in one day they shall die, both
of them. 35 Then [h]I will raise up for Myself
a faithful priest *who* shall do according to
what *is* in My heart and in My mind. [i]I will
build him a sure house, and he shall walk
before [j]My anointed forever. 36 [k]And it
shall come to pass that everyone who is
left in your house will come *and* bow down
to him for a piece of silver and a morsel of
bread, and say, "Please, [3]put me in one of
the priestly positions, that I may eat a piece
of bread." ' "

Samuel's First Prophecy

3 Now [a]the boy Samuel ministered to
the LORD before Eli. And [b]the word of
the LORD was rare in those days; *there was*
no widespread revelation. 2 And it came to
pass at that time, while Eli *was* lying down
in his place, and when his eyes had begun
to grow [c]so dim that he could not see,
3 and before [d]the lamp of God went out in
the [1]tabernacle of the LORD where the ark
of God *was,* and while Samuel was lying
down, 4 that the LORD called Samuel. And
he answered, "Here I am!" 5 So he ran to
Eli and said, "Here I am, for you called
me."

And he said, "I did not call; lie down
again." And he went and lay down.

6 Then the LORD called yet again, "Samuel!"

So Samuel arose and went to Eli, and
said, "Here I am, for you called me." He
answered, "I did not call, my son; lie down
again." 7 (Now Samuel [e]did not yet know
the LORD, nor was the word of the LORD yet
revealed to him.)

8 And the LORD called Samuel again the
third time. So he arose and went to Eli,
and said, "Here I am, for you did call
me."

Then Eli perceived that the LORD had
called the boy. 9 Therefore Eli said to Samuel, "Go, lie down; and it shall be, if He
calls you, that you must say, [f]'Speak, LORD,
for Your servant hears.' " So Samuel went
and lay down in his place.

10 Now the LORD came and stood and
called as at other times, "Samuel! Samuel!"

And Samuel answered, "Speak, for Your
servant hears."

11 Then the LORD said to Samuel: "Behold, I will do something in Israel [g]at

30 [a] Ex. 29:9; Num. 25:13 [b] Jer. 18:9, 10 [c] Ps. 91:14; Mal. 2:9-12
31 [d] 1 Sam. 4:11-18; 22:18, 19; 1 Kin. 2:27, 35 [2] *strength*
32 [e] Zech. 8:4
34 [f] 1 Sam. 10:7-9; 1 Kin. 13:3 [g] 1 Sam. 4:11, 17
35 [h] 1 Kin. 2:35; Ezek. 44:15; [Heb. 2:17; 7:26-28] [i] 2 Sam. 7:11, 27; 1 Kin. 11:38 [j] Ps. 18:50
36 [k] 1 Kin. 2:27 [3] *assign*

CHAPTER 3

1 [a] 1 Sam. 2:11, 18 [b] Ps. 74:9; Ezek. 7:26; Amos 8:11, 12
2 [c] Gen. 27:1; 48:10; 1 Sam. 4:15
3 [d] Ex. 27:20, 21 [1] *palace* or *temple*
7 [e] 1 Sam. 2:12; Acts 19:2; 1 Cor. 13:11
9 [f] 1 Kin. 2:17
11 [g] 2 Kin. 21:12; Jer. 19:3

2:30 I said indeed. The Lord had promised that Aaron's descendants would always be priests (Ex. 29:9), and He had confirmed that promise by oath (Num. 25:13). Because of flagrant disobedience, the house of Eli would forfeit their priesthood. Although the Aaronic priesthood was perpetual, priests could forfeit their position by their sin.

2:31 will not be an old man in your house. The judgment of untimely death followed the descendants of Eli. Eli's sons died in the flower of their manhood (4:11). Later, Saul massacred the priests at Nob (22:16-19). Ultimately, Solomon removed Abiathar from the priesthood (1 Kin. 2:26,27) and the priestly line of Eleazar prevailed, as God promised (cf. Num. 25:18,19).

2:32 an enemy *in My* dwelling place. This probably referred to the desecration of the tabernacle, where the Lord dwelt, at Shiloh by the Philistines (see Jer. 7:12-14).

2:34 a sign to you. The death of Eli's two sons on the same day validated the prophecy (cf. 4:11,17).

2:35 I will raise up for Myself a faithful priest. Although some have identified this priest as Samuel and others Christ, it is better to view the prophecy as fulfilled in the accession of Zadok and his family to the priestly office in the time of Solomon (see 1 Kin. 1:7,8; 2:26,27, 35). This reestablished the office of High-Priest in the line of Eleazar and Phinehas (cf. Num. 25:10-13). **I will build him a sure house.** The sons of Zadok will also serve in the millennial temple (see Ezek. 44:15; 48:11). **My anointed.** This refers to the messiah who will defeat God's enemies and establish His rule in the Millennium (see v. 10).

2:36 a morsel of bread. The judgment corresponded to the sin. Those who had gorged themselves on the sacrifices (vv. 12-17) were reduced to begging for a morsel of food.

3:1 the boy Samuel. Samuel was no longer a child (2:21,26). While Jewish historian Josephus suggested he was 12 years of age, he was probably a teenager at this time. The same Heb. term translated here "boy" was used of David when he slew Goliath (17:33). **the word of the LORD was rare.** The time of the judges was a period of extremely limited prophetic activity. The few visions that God did give were not widely known. **revelation.** Lit. "vision." A divine revelation mediated through an auditory or visual encounter.

3:3 before the lamp of God went out. The golden lampstand, located in the Holy Place of the tabernacle, was filled with olive oil and lit at twilight (Ex. 30:8). The lamp was kept burning from evening until morning (Ex. 27:20,21). Just before dawn, while the golden lampstand was still burning, Samuel was called to his prophetic ministry. **ark of God.** See Ex. 25:10-22.

3:7 Samuel did not yet know the LORD. Samuel had not yet encountered the Lord in a personal way, nor had he received God's Word by divine revelation (see 2:12).

3:8 Then Eli perceived. Eli was slow to recognize that God was calling Samuel. This indicates that Eli's spiritual perception was not what it should have been as the priest and judge of Israel (see also 1:12-16).

3:10 hears. "To hear with interest," or "to hear so as to obey."

which both ears of everyone who hears it
will tingle. 12 In that day I will perform
against Eli [h]all that I have spoken concerning his house, from beginning to end.
13 [i]For I have told him that I will [j]judge his
house forever for the iniquity which he
knows, because [k]his sons made themselves
vile, and he [l]did not [2]restrain them. 14 And
therefore I have sworn to the house of Eli
that the iniquity of Eli's house [m]shall not
be atoned for by sacrifice or offering forever."
15 So Samuel lay down until [3]morning,
and opened the doors of the house of the
LORD. And Samuel was afraid to tell Eli the
vision. 16 Then Eli called Samuel and said,
"Samuel, my son!"
He answered, "Here I am."
17 And he said, "What *is* the word that
the LORD spoke to you? Please do not hide
it from me. [n]God do so to you, and more
also, if you hide anything from me of all
the things that He said to you." 18 Then
Samuel told him everything, and hid nothing from him. And he said, [o]"It *is* the LORD.
Let Him do what seems good to Him."
19 So Samuel [p]grew, and [q]the LORD was
with him [r]and let none of his words [4]fall to
the ground. 20 And all Israel [s]from Dan to
Beersheba knew that Samuel *had been* [5]es-
tablished as a prophet of the LORD. 21 Then
the LORD appeared again in Shiloh. For the
LORD revealed Himself to Samuel in Shiloh
by [t]the word of the LORD.

4 And the word of Samuel came to all
[1]Israel.

The Ark of God Captured

Now Israel went out to battle against the
Philistines, and encamped beside [a]Ebe-
nezer; and the Philistines encamped in

12 [h] 1 Sam. 2:27-36; Ezek. 12:25; Luke 21:33
13 [i] 1 Sam. 2:29-31 [j] 1 Sam. 2:22; Ezek. 7:3; 18:30 [k] 1 Sam. 2:12, 17, 22 [l] 1 Sam. 2:23, 25 [2] Lit. *rebuke*
14 [m] Num. 15:30, 31; Is. 22:14; Heb. 10:4, 26-31
15 [3] So with MT, Tg., Vg.; LXX adds *and he arose in the morning*
17 [n] Ruth 1:17
18 [o] Gen. 24:50; Ex. 34:5-7; Lev. 10:3; Is. 39:8; Acts 5:39
19 [p] 1 Sam. 2:21 [q] Gen. 21:22; 28:15; 39:2, 21, 23 [r] 1 Sam. 9:6 [4] *fail*
20 [s] Judg. 20:1 [5] *confirmed*
21 [t] 1 Sam. 3:1, 4

CHAPTER 4 1 [a] 1 Sam. 7:12 [1] So with MT, Tg.; LXX, Vg. add *And it came to pass in those days that the Philistines gathered themselves together to fight;* LXX adds further *against Israel*

3:11 ears...will tingle. A message of impending destruction, here of Eli's house (see 2 Kin. 21:12; Jer. 19:3).

3:12 all that I have spoken. See 2:27-36. The repetition of the oracle against Eli to Samuel confirmed the word spoken by the man of God.

3:13 made themselves vile. LXX reads "his sons blasphemed God." Cursing God was an offense worthy of death (see Lev. 24:11-16,23). **did not restrain them.** Eli was implicated in the sins of his sons because he did not intervene with judgment. If his sons were blaspheming God, they should have been stoned (see Lev. 24:15,16).

3:14 not be atoned for...forever. Eli's family was apparently guilty of presumptuous sin. For such defiant sin, there was no atonement and the death penalty could be immediately applied (see Num. 15:30,31).

3:15 the doors of the house of the LORD. The doors of the tabernacle compound (see 1:9).

3:17 God do so to you, and more also. This is an oath of imprecation. Eli called down God's judgment on Samuel if he refused to tell everything he knew.

3:18 Let Him do what seems good to Him. Eli resigned himself to divine sovereignty, without reluctance.

3:19 the LORD was with him. The Lord's presence was with Samuel, as it would be later with David (16:18; 18:12). The Lord's presence validated His choice of a man for His service. **let none of his words fall to the ground.** Everything Samuel said with divine authorization came true. This fulfillment of Samuel's word proved that he was a true prophet of God (see Deut. 18:21,22).

3:20 Dan to Beersheba. The traditional limits of the land of Israel from the N to the S. **prophet of the LORD.** Samuel's status as a spokesman of God's message was acknowledged by all throughout Israel.

4:1 the word of Samuel came to all Israel. The text of 1:1–3:21 climaxes with the establishment of Samuel as God's spokesman/representative. Observe that "the word of the Lord" (3:21) has become equivalent to "the word of Samuel." **Philistines.** From the period of the judges through the end of David's reign, the Philistines ("Sea Peoples") were an ever-present enemy of Israel. They were non-Semitic immigrants (see Gen. 10:14; 1 Chr. 1:12; Jer. 47:4,5; Amos 9:7) who settled along the coastal regions of southern Canaan, organizing their power in five chief cities: Ashdod, Ashkelon, Ekron, Gath, and Gaza (1 Sam. 6:17; Judg. 3:13). The introduction of the Philistines into the narrative provides a link between the judgeship of Samuel and the judgeship which Samson was not able to complete (Judg. 13–16). **Ebenezer.** The location of this site has not been specifically identified. Opposite Aphek in Israelite territory, it is possibly modern Izbet Sarteh on the road to Shiloh. When translated it means "stone of help," and its mention here (and 5:1) and again in 7:12 of another location mark this section as a literary unit. **Aphek.** This site is located near the source of the Yarkon River,

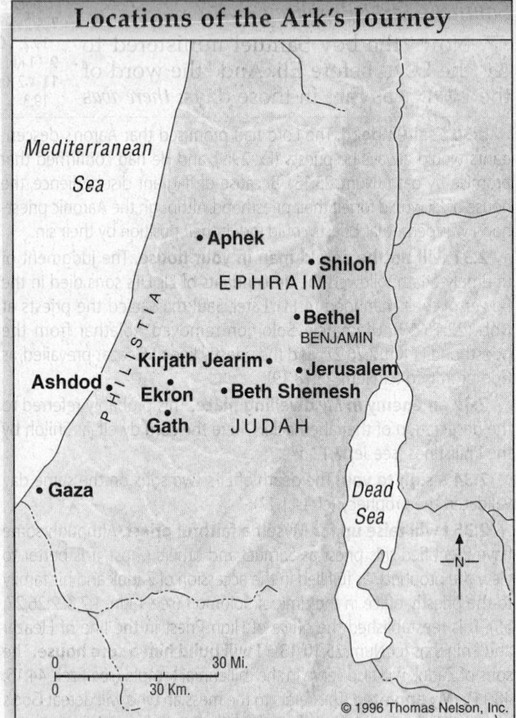

Aphek. **2** Then the [b]Philistines put themselves in battle array against Israel. And
when they joined battle, Israel was [2]de-
feated by the Philistines, who killed about
four thousand men of the army in the field.
3 And when the people had come into the
camp, the elders of Israel said, "Why has
the LORD defeated us today before the Philistines? [c]Let us bring the ark of the
covenant of the LORD from Shiloh to us,
that when it comes among us it may save
us from the hand of our enemies." **4** So the
people sent to Shiloh, that they might
bring from there the ark of the covenant of
the LORD of hosts, [d]who dwells *between*
[e]the cherubim. And the [f]two sons of Eli,
Hophni and Phinehas, *were* there with the
ark of the covenant of God.
5 And when the ark of the covenant of
the LORD came into the camp, all Israel
shouted so loudly that the earth shook.
6 Now when the Philistines heard the noise
of the shout, they said, "What *does* the
sound of this great shout in the camp of the
Hebrews *mean?*" Then they understood
that the ark of the LORD had come into the
camp. **7** So the Philistines were afraid, for
they said, "God has come into the camp!"
And they said, [g]"Woe to us! For such a
thing has never happened before. **8** Woe to
us! Who will deliver us from the hand of
these mighty gods? These *are* the gods who
struck the Egyptians with all the plagues
in the wilderness. **9** [h]Be strong and conduct
yourselves like men, you Philistines, that
you do not become servants of the Hebrews, [i]as they have been to you. [3]Con-
duct yourselves like men, and fight!"
10 So the Philistines fought, and [j]Israel
was [4]defeated, and every man fled to his
tent. There was a very great slaughter, and
there fell of Israel thirty thousand foot soldiers. **11** Also [k]the ark of God was captured; and [l]the two sons of Eli, Hophni and
Phinehas, died.

Death of Eli

12 Then a man of Benjamin ran from the
battle line the same day, and [m]came to
Shiloh with his clothes torn and [n]dirt on his
head. **13** Now when he came, there was Eli,
sitting on [o]a seat [5]by the wayside watching,
for his heart [6]trembled for the ark of God.
And when the man came into the city and
told *it,* all the city cried out. **14** When Eli
heard the noise of the outcry, he said,
"What *does* the sound of this tumult *mean?*"
And the man came quickly and told Eli.
15 Eli was ninety-eight years old, and [p]his
eyes were so [7]dim that he could not see.
16 Then the man said to Eli, "I *am* he who
came from the battle. And I fled today
from the battle line."
And he said, [q]"What happened, my son?"
17 So the messenger answered and said,
"Israel has fled before the Philistines, and
there has been a very great slaughter among the
people. Also your two sons, Hophni and

2 [b] 1 Sam. 12:9 [2] Lit. *struck*
3 [c] Num. 10:35; Josh. 6:6-21
4 [d] Ex. 25:18-21; 1 Sam. 6:2; Ps. 80:1 [e] Num. 7:89 [f] 1 Sam. 2:12
7 [g] Ex. 15:14
9 [h] 1 Cor. 16:13 [i] Judg. 13:1; 1 Sam. 14:21 [3] Lit. *Be men*
10 [j] Lev. 26:17; Deut. 28:15, 25; 1 Sam. 4:2; 2 Sam. 18:17; 19:8; 2 Kin. 14:12; 2 Chr. 25:22 [4] Lit. *struck down*
11 [k] 1 Sam. 2:32; Ps. 78:60, 61 [l] 1 Sam. 2:34; Ps. 78:64
12 [m] 2 Sam. 1:2 [n] Josh. 7:6; 2 Sam. 13:19; 15:32; Neh. 9:1; Job 2:12
13 [o] 1 Sam. 1:9; 4:18 [5] So with MT, Vg.; LXX *beside the gate watching the road* [6] *trembled with anxiety*
15 [p] 1 Sam. 3:2; 1 Kin. 14:4 [7] *fixed*
16 [q] 2 Sam. 1:4

at the southern end of the coastal plain of Sharon, approximately 5 mi. E of the Mediterranean. This city marked the northeastern edge of Philistine territory.

4:3 Why has the LORD defeated us. The question of the elders reflected their knowledge that the Lord both fought their battles (2:10; 17:47) and allowed their defeat. To be defeated clearly meant that God was not "with" them (Num. 14:42; Deut. 1:42). Instead of inquiring of the Lord for direction, they proceeded to take the matter into their own hands. **Let us bring the ark.** The ark symbolized the presence and power of the Lord. Yet, Israel treated it like a good-luck charm, which would ensure them victory over the Philistines. Knowing that victory or defeat depended upon the Lord's presence, they confused the symbol of His presence with His actual presence. In this way, their understanding of God resembled that of the Philistines (4:8).

4:4 dwells *between* the cherubim. A repeated phrase used to describe the Lord (see 2 Sam. 6:2; 2 Kin. 19:15; 1 Chr. 13:6; Ps. 80:1; 99:1; Is. 37:16). It spoke of His sovereign majesty. **Hophni and Phinehas.** These were the two wicked sons of Eli (2:12-17,27-37), of whom it was said that they "did not know the LORD" (2:12). The fact that they were mentioned together recalls the prophecy that they would die together (2:34).

4:6 Hebrews. In Gen. 14:13, the name "Hebrew" was applied to Abram. Consequently, the name came to refer to the physical descendants of Abraham. It was used to distinguish them as a class of people distinct from the foreigners around them. It means that Abram was a descendant of Eber in the line of Shem (cf. 10:25; 11:14-16).

4:7 God has come into the camp. The idol, to the Philistine, was thought to be the actual dwelling place of his deity. Hence, when Israel brought the ark into the camp, the Philistines concluded that God was present, an exclamation that reflected a knowledge of God's power.

4:8 the gods who struck the Egyptians. Evidently, the news of God's victory over the Egyptians was common knowledge to the Philistines.

4:9 servants...as they have been to you. Israel's failure to uproot all the inhabitants of Canaan (see Judg. 1:28) caused them to fall under the judgment of God. As a consequence of this judgment, Israel was enslaved to Philistine oppression (see Judg. 10,13-16). The Philistines feared was that they would become servants of the Hebrews.

4:11 the ark of God was captured. In spite of their hopes to manipulate God into giving them the victory, Israel was defeated and the ark fell into the hands of the Philistines. The view of having the ark of God being equivalent to having control of God, possessed both by Israel and then the Philistines, is to be contrasted with the power and providence of God in the remaining narrative. **Hophni and Phinehas, died.** In fulfillment of 2:34 and 3:12, Eli's sons died together.

4:12 his clothes torn and dirt on his head. The actions of the man of Benjamin were considered to be universal signs of both mourning for the dead and of national calamity (cf. 2 Sam. 15:32).

4:13 his heart trembled for the ark of God. Eli's concern for the ark stands in stark contrast to his earlier actions of honoring his two sons over honoring the Lord (2:29,30; cf. 4:17,18).

Phinehas, are dead; and the ark of God has
been captured."
18 Then it happened, when he made
mention of the ark of God, that Eli fell off
the seat backward by the side of the gate;
and his neck was broken and he died, for
the man was old and heavy. And he had
judged Israel forty years.

Ichabod

19 Now his daughter-in-law, Phinehas'
wife, was with child, *due* to be delivered;
and when she heard the news that the ark
of God was captured, and that her father-
in-law and her husband were dead, she
bowed herself and gave birth, for her labor
pains came upon her. 20 And about the
time of her death [r]the women who stood
by her said to her, "Do not fear, for you
have borne a son." But she did not answer,
nor did she [8]regard *it*. 21 Then she named
the child [s]Ichabod,[9] saying, [t]"The glory
has departed from Israel!" because the ark
of God had been captured and because of
her father-in-law and her husband. 22 And
she said, "The glory has departed from Israel, for the ark of God has been captured."

The Philistines and the Ark

5 Then the Philistines took the ark of
God and brought it [a]from Ebenezer to
Ashdod. 2 When the Philistines took the
ark of God, they brought it into the house
of [b]Dagon[1] and set it by Dagon. 3 And
when the people of Ashdod arose early in
the morning, there was Dagon, [c]fallen on
its face to the earth before the ark of the
LORD. So they took Dagon and [d]set it in its
place again. 4 And when they arose early
the next morning, there was Dagon, fallen
on its face to the ground before the ark of
the LORD. [e]The head of Dagon and both the
palms of its hands *were* broken off on the
threshold; only [2]Dagon's torso was left of
it. 5 Therefore neither the priests of Dagon
nor any who come into Dagon's house
[f]tread on the threshold of Dagon in Ashdod to this day.

20 [r]Gen. 35:16-19 [8]*pay any attention to*
21 [s]1 Sam. 14:3 [t]Ps. 26:8; 78:61; [Jer. 2:11] [9]Lit. *Inglorious*

CHAPTER 5

1 [a]1 Sam. 4:1; 7:12
2 [b]Judg. 16:23-30; 1 Chr. 10:8-10 [1]A Philistine idol
3 [c]Is. 19:1; 46:1, 2 [d]Is. 46:7
4 [e]Jer. 50:2; Ezek. 6:4, 6; Mic. 1:7 [2]So with LXX, Syr., Tg., Vg.; MT *Dagon*
5 [f]Zeph. 1:9

4:18 Eli…died. As was the case with Hophni and Phinehas, Eli died. Thus, in fulfillment of the word of the Lord, all of the priestly line through Eli had been wiped out (2:29-34). *See note on 2:31.* **he had judged Israel forty years.** Over that time Eli fulfilled the office of both priest and judge in Israel.

4:21 Ichabod…The glory has departed. Due primarily to the loss of the ark, the symbol of God's presence, Phinehas' wife names her child Ichabod, meaning either "Where is the glory?" or "no glory." To the Hebrew, "glory" was often used to refer to God's presence; hence, the text means "Where is God?" The word "departed" carries the idea of having gone into exile. Thus, to the people of Israel, the capturing of the ark was a symbol that God had gone into exile. Although this was the mindset of Israel, the text narrative will reveal that God was present, even when He disciplined His people. *See note on Ezek. 10:18, 19.*

5:1 Ashdod. One of the 5 chief Philistine cities, inland from the coast (3 mi.) and approximately 33 mi. W of Jerusalem.

5:2 Dagon. Ugaritic literature identifies this deity as a god of grain or vegetation, whose image had the lower body of a fish and upper body of a man. Dagon seems to have been the leader of the Philistine pantheon (Judg. 16:23) and is noted to be the father of Baal. The placing of the ark of God in the temple of Dagon was supposed to be a sign of Dagon's power and Yahweh's inferiority, a visual representation that the god of the Philistines was victorious over the God of the Hebrews. In addition, the textual connection of Dagon reinforces the affinity between the events written here and those in the life of Samson (cf. Judg. 13–16).

5:3 fallen on its face. Ironically, God Himself overturned the supposed supremacy of Dagon by having Dagon fallen over, as if paying homage to the Lord.

5:4 head…hands *were* broken off. The first display of God's authority over Dagon was not perceived. God's second display of authority, the cutting off of Dagon's head and hands, was a common sign that the enemy was dead (Judg. 7:25; 8:6; 1 Sam. 17:54; 31:9; 2 Sam. 4:12), and was to be understood as God's divine judgment on the false idol.

5:5 tread on the threshold. Because the head and hands of Dagon fell on the threshold, superstition developed that it was cursed; therefore, the Philistines would not tread on it. **to this day.** This phrase supports the claim that the writer was living at a time removed from the actual event itself (see Introduction: Author and Date). This phrase and phrases equivalent to it are found throughout 1, 2 Samuel (6:18; 26:6; 30:25; 2 Sam. 4:3; 6:8; 18:18).

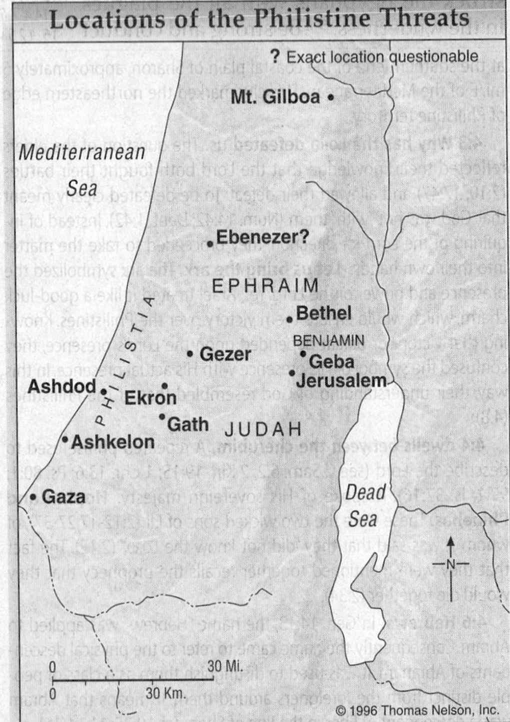

6 But the [g]hand of the LORD was heavy
on the people of Ashdod, and He [h]rav-
aged them and struck them with [i]tumors,[3]
both Ashdod and its [j]territory. 7 And when
the men of Ashdod saw how *it was,* they
said, "The ark of the [k]God of Israel must
not remain with us, for His hand is harsh
toward us and Dagon our god." 8 Therefore they sent and gathered to themselves
all the [l]lords of the Philistines, and said,
"What shall we do with the ark of the God
of Israel?"

And they answered, "Let the ark of the
God of Israel be carried away to [m]Gath."
So they carried the ark of the God of Israel
away. 9 So it was, after they had carried it
away, that [n]the hand of the LORD was
against the city with a very great destruction; and He struck the men of the city,
both small and great, [4]and tumors broke
out on them.

10 Therefore they sent the ark of God to
Ekron. So it was, as the ark of God came to
Ekron, that the Ekronites cried out, saying,
"They have brought the ark of the God of
Israel to us, to kill us and our people!"
11 So they sent and gathered together all
the lords of the Philistines, and said, "Send
away the ark of the God of Israel, and let it
go back to its own place, so that it does not
kill us and our people." For there was a
deadly destruction throughout all the city;
the hand of God was very heavy there.
12 And the men who did not die were
stricken with the tumors, and the [o]cry of
the city went up to heaven.

The Ark Returned to Israel

6 Now the ark of the LORD was in the
country of the Philistines seven
months. 2 And the Philistines [a]called for
the priests and the diviners, saying, "What
shall we do with the ark of the LORD? Tell
us how we should send it to its place."

3 So they said, "If you send away the ark
of the God of Israel, do not send it [b]empty;
but by all means return *it* to Him *with* [c]a
trespass offering. Then you will be healed,
and it will be known to you why His hand
is not removed from you."

4 Then they said, "What *is* the trespass
offering which we shall return to Him?"

They answered, [d]"Five golden tumors
and five golden rats, *according to* the number of the lords of the Philistines. For the
same plague *was* on all of [1]you and on
your lords. 5 Therefore you shall make images of your tumors and images of your
rats that [e]ravage the land, and you shall
[f]give glory to the God of Israel; perhaps He
will [g]lighten[2] His hand from you, from
[h]your gods, and from your land. 6 Why
then do you harden your hearts [i]as the
Egyptians and Pharaoh hardened their
hearts? When He did mighty things
among them, [j]did they not let the people
go, that they might depart? 7 Now therefore, make [k]a new cart, take two milk cows

6 [g] Ex. 9:3; Deut. 2:15; 1 Sam. 5:7; 7:13; Ps. 32:4; 145:20; 147:6 [h] 1 Sam. 6:5 [i] Deut. 28:27; Ps. 78:66 [j] Josh. 15:46, 47 [3] Probably bubonic plague. LXX, Vg. add *And in the midst of their land rats sprang up, and there was a great death panic in the city.*
7 [k] 1 Sam. 6:5
8 [l] 1 Sam. 6:4 [m] Josh. 11:22
9 [n] Deut. 2:15; 1 Sam. 5:11; 7:13; 12:15 [4] Vg. *and they had tumors in their secret parts*
12 [o] 1 Sam. 9:16; Jer. 14:2

CHAPTER 6

2 [a] Gen. 41:8; Ex. 7:11; Is. 2:6; 47:13; Dan. 2:2; 5:7
3 [b] Ex. 23:15; Deut. 16:16 [c] Lev. 5:15, 16
4 [d] 1 Sam. 5:6, 9, 12; 6:17 [1] Lit. *them*
5 [e] 1 Sam. 5:6 [f] Josh. 7:19; 1 Chr. 16:28, 29; Is. 42:12; Jer. 13:16; Mal. 2:2; Rev. 14:7 [g] 1 Sam. 5:6, 11; Ps. 39:10 [h] 1 Sam. 5:3, 4, 7 [2] *ease*
6 [i] Ex. 7:13; 8:15; 9:34; 14:17 [j] Ex. 12:31
7 [k] 2 Sam. 6:3

5:6 the hand of the LORD was heavy. In contrast to the hands of Dagon being cut off, symbolizing his helplessness against the power of Yahweh, the Lord was pictured to be actively involved in judging the Philistines. The imagery of God's hand is found throughout the ark narrative (4:8; 5:6,7,9,11; 6:3,5,9). **tumors.** It has been suggested that this word refers to the sores or boils caused by an epidemic of the bubonic plague carried by rats (6:4,5). The spread of the disease and its deadly effect (5:6,9,12; 6:11,17) make this a likely view.

5:8 lords of the Philistines. Refers to those men who ruled the chief Philistine cities as kings (*see note on 4:1*). **Gath.** Another main Philistine city, located about 12 mi. E of Ashdod (cf. 5:1).

5:10 Ekron. With judgment on Gath, the Philistines sent the ark away to the next main city to see if God was behind their calamity. Located about 6 mi. N of Gath, it was the closest major Philistine city to Israel's border. **the ark...to kill us.** The cry of the Ekronites was an admission that the Philistines had gotten the message that God was the source of their troubles. It is curious that the Philistines knew of God's power to smite the Egyptians (4:8), yet they proudly believed themselves stronger than Egypt. The severity of the plagues grew increasingly worse in vv. 6-12, corresponding with the failure of the Philistines to humble themselves before God. Their actions were very similar to those of the Egyptians (Ex. 5–14).

6:2 the priests and the diviners. These men of the Philistines, specifically identified in Scripture as having notable fame (Is. 2:6), were summoned to figure out how to appease God so that He would stop the plague. **send it to its place.** The Philistines understood that they had offended God. Their diviners decided to rightfully appease His wrath by sending the ark back to Israel.

6:3 trespass offering. The purpose behind this offering was to both acknowledge and compensate for their trespass of dishonoring the God of Israel. These pagans recognized their sin and the need for manifest repentance, which they did according to their religious tradition by means of votive trespass offerings.

6:4 Five golden tumors and five golden rats. It was their custom to make models of their sores (and the rats which brought the plague), in hopes that the deity would recognize that they knew why he was angry and remove the evil which had fallen upon them. The context of v. 17 suggests that the items were in the writer's presence at the time the account was recorded. The number 5 represents each of the Philistine cities and lords affected by God's judgment.

6:5 give glory to the God of Israel...He will lighten His hand. While sympathetic magic was the Philistine custom, this statement expressly affirms the intention behind the offerings: They were to halt the dishonor, confess their sin, and give glory to the God of Israel by acknowledging who it was that they had offended and who was the supreme Deity.

6:6 Why then do you harden your hearts. The diviners correlate the Philistines' actions of not recognizing God with those of Pharaoh and the Egyptians. This is the same word "harden" that was used in Ex. 7:14; 8:15,32. It is an interesting correlation, because the dominant purpose in Ex. 5–14 is that the Egyptians might "know that I am the LORD" (Ex. 7:5).

[l]which have never been yoked, and hitch
the cows to the cart; and take their calves
home, away from them. 8 Then take the
ark of the LORD and set it on the cart; and
put [m]the articles of gold which you are returning to Him *as* a trespass offering in a
chest by its side. Then send it away, and let
it go. 9 And watch: if it goes up the road to
its own territory, to [n]Beth Shemesh, *then*
He has done [3]us this great evil. But if not,
then [o]we shall know that *it is* not His hand
that struck us—it happened to us by
chance."
10 Then the men did so; they took two
milk cows and hitched them to the cart,
and shut up their calves at home. 11 And
they set the ark of the LORD on the cart, and
the chest with the gold rats and the images
of their tumors. 12 Then the cows headed
straight for the road to Beth Shemesh, *and*
went along the [p]highway, lowing as they
went, and did not turn aside to the right
hand or the left. And the lords of the Philistines went after them to the border of
Beth Shemesh.
13 Now *the people of* Beth Shemesh *were*
reaping their [q]wheat harvest in the valley;
and they lifted their eyes and saw the ark,
and rejoiced to see *it*. 14 Then the cart came
into the field of Joshua of Beth Shemesh,
and stood there; a large stone *was* there. So
they split the wood of the cart and offered
the cows as a burnt offering to the LORD.
15 The Levites took down the ark of the
LORD and the chest that *was* with it, in
which *were* the articles of gold, and put
them on the large stone. Then the men of
Beth Shemesh offered burnt offerings and
made sacrifices the same day to the LORD.
16 So when [r]the five lords of the Philistines
had seen *it*, they returned to Ekron the
same day.
17 [s]These *are* the golden tumors which
the Philistines returned *as* a trespass offering to the LORD: one for Ashdod, one for
Gaza, one for Ashkelon, one for [t]Gath, one
for Ekron; 18 and the golden rats, *according*
to the number of all the cities of the Philistines *belonging* to the five lords, *both* fortified cities and country villages, even as
far as the large *stone of* Abel on which they
set the ark of the LORD, *which stone remains*
to this day in the field of Joshua of Beth
Shemesh.
19 Then [u]He struck the men of Beth
Shemesh, because they had looked into the
ark of the LORD. [4]He [v]struck fifty thousand
and seventy men of the people, and the
people lamented because the LORD had
struck the people with a great slaughter.

The Ark at Kirjath Jearim

20 And the men of Beth Shemesh said,
[w]"Who is able to stand before this holy
LORD God? And to whom shall it go up
from us?" 21 So they sent messengers to the
inhabitants of [x]Kirjath Jearim, saying, "The
Philistines have brought back the ark of the
LORD; come down *and* take it up with you."
7 Then the men of [a]Kirjath Jearim came
and took the ark of the LORD, and
brought it into the house of [b]Abinadab on

7 [l] Num. 19:2; Deut. 21:3, 4
8 [m] 1 Sam. 6:4, 5
9 [n] Josh. 15:10; 21:16 [o] 1 Sam. 6:3 [3] *this calamity to us*
12 [p] Num. 20:19
13 [q] 1 Sam. 12:17
16 [r] Josh. 13:3; Judg. 3:3
17 [s] 1 Sam. 6:4 [t] 1 Sam. 5:8
19 [u] Ex. 19:21; Num. 4:5, 15, 16, 20 [v] 2 Sam. 6:7 [4] *Or He struck seventy men of the people and fifty oxen of a man*
20 [w] Lev. 11:44, 45; Ps. 24:3, 4; Mal. 3:2; Rev. 6:17
21 [x] Josh. 9:17; 15:9, 60; 18:14; Judg. 18:12; 1 Chr. 13:5, 6

CHAPTER 7

1 [a] 1 Sam. 6:21; Ps. 132:6 [b] 2 Sam. 6:3, 4

6:7 never been yoked. To know without a doubt that the God of Israel was behind all of their troubles, the diviners devised a plan that would reveal whether God was the One responsible. Using cows which had "never been yoked" meant using animals that were untrained to pull a cart and probably would not go anywhere. **take their calves...away from them.** The second element in their plan was to use nursing cows taken away from their calves. For the cows unnaturally to head off in the opposite direction from their calves would be a clear sign that the cause of their judgment was supernatural.

6:9 Beth Shemesh. Named "house of the sun" and located in the Sorek Valley, this was a Levitical city about 15 mi. W of Jerusalem. Originally designated for the descendants of Aaron (Josh. 21:16), it was chosen to be the destination of the cows pulling the cart.

6:12 lowing as they went. With the moaning from instinctive unwillingness to leave their calves behind, the cows went straight to Beth Shemesh, not turning to the right or left, leaving the inescapable conclusion that God had judged them.

6:13 reaping their wheat harvest. Sometime in June. These harvests were accomplished with the whole city participating.

6:14 Joshua of Beth Shemesh. The cows stopped in the field of Joshua, where there was a large stone which was verifiable to the writer at the time the account was written. **burnt offering.** Because the cows and cart were used for sacred purposes, they could not be used for normal everyday purposes. Therefore, the men of Beth Shemesh sacrificed the cows using the cart for the fire.

6:15 Levites. The men of Beth Shemesh, being Levites, were qualified to move the ark. **put *them* on the large stone.** The stone mentioned was used as a pedestal for both the items of gold and the ark. At the time the account was written, it stood as a witness that God had returned to the land.

6:16 five lords of the Philistines. The lords of the Philistines, upon seeing that the ark arrived safely, returned to Ekron.

6:19 looked into the ark. This action on the part of the men of Beth Shemesh constituted the sin of presumption. This is first addressed in Num. 4:20 and is mentioned again in 2 Sam. 6:6,7. **fifty thousand and seventy men.** Some debate whether this figure is too large. However, retaining the larger number is more consistent with the context of "a great slaughter," and the reference to 30,000 in 4:10 (cf. 11:8). However, a scribal error could have occurred, in which case the number would omit the 50,000 and likely be "seventy," as in the LXX and Josephus (see marginal note).

6:20 Who is able to stand. This question climaxes the narrative of the ark. No one is able to stand against God's judgment. This applied to the people outside the covenant as well as those under the covenant. Presumption before God is unacceptable. **to whom shall it go.** The expression was used to denote the desire to take the ark away from them.

6:21 Kirjath Jearim. A city located approximately 10 mi. NE of Beth Shemesh. It would remain the resting place of the ark until David brought it to Jerusalem (2 Sam. 6:1-19). This location had long been associated with Baal worship (cf. Josh. 15:9,60; 18:14).

the hill, and [c]consecrated Eleazar his son
to keep the ark of the LORD.

Samuel Judges Israel

2 So it was that the ark remained in Kirjath Jearim a long time; it was there twenty
years. And all the house of Israel lamented
after the LORD.
3 Then Samuel spoke to all the house of
Israel, saying, "If you [d]return to the LORD
with all your hearts, *then* [e]put away the
foreign gods and the [f]Ashtoreths[1] from
among you, and [g]prepare your hearts for
the LORD, and [h]serve Him only; and He
will deliver you from the hand of the Philistines." 4 So the children of Israel put
away the [i]Baals and the [2]Ashtoreths, and
served the LORD only.
5 And Samuel said, [j]"Gather all Israel to
Mizpah, and [k]I will pray to the LORD for
you." 6 So they gathered together at Mizpah, [l]drew water, and poured *it* out before
the LORD. And they [m]fasted that day, and
said there, [n]"We have sinned against the
LORD." And Samuel judged the children of
Israel at Mizpah.
7 Now when the Philistines heard that
the children of Israel had gathered together at Mizpah, the lords of the Philistines
went up against Israel. And when the children of Israel heard *of it,* they were afraid
of the Philistines. 8 So the children of Israel
said to Samuel, [o]"Do not cease to cry out to
the LORD our God for us, that He may save
us from the hand of the Philistines."
9 And Samuel took a [p]suckling lamb and
offered *it as* a whole burnt offering to the
LORD. Then [q]Samuel cried out to the LORD
for Israel, and the LORD answered him.
10 Now as Samuel was offering up the
burnt offering, the Philistines drew near to
battle against Israel. [r]But the LORD thundered with a loud thunder upon the Philistines that day, and so confused them that
they were overcome before Israel. 11 And
the men of Israel went out of Mizpah and
pursued the Philistines, and [3]drove them
back as far as below Beth Car. 12 Then Samuel [s]took a stone and set *it* up between
Mizpah and Shen, and called its name [4]Eb-
enezer, saying, "Thus far the LORD has
helped us."
13 [t]So the Philistines were subdued, and
they [u]did not come anymore into the territory of Israel. And the hand of the LORD
was against the Philistines all the days of
Samuel. 14 Then the cities which the Philistines had taken from Israel were restored
to Israel, from Ekron to Gath; and Israel
recovered its territory from the hands of
the Philistines. Also there was peace between Israel and the Amorites.
15 And Samuel [v]judged Israel all the
days of his life. 16 He went from year to
year on a circuit to Bethel, Gilgal, and Mizpah, and judged Israel in all those places.

1 [c] Lev. 21:8
3 [d] Deut. 30:2-10; 1 Kin. 8:48; Is. 55:7; Hos. 6:1; Joel 2:12-14 [e] Gen. 35:2; Josh. 24:14, 23; Judg. 10:16 [f] Judg. 2:13; 1 Sam. 31:10 [g] 2 Chr. 30:19; Job 11:13 [h] Deut. 6:13; 10:20; 13:4; Josh. 24:14; Matt. 4:10; Luke 4:8 [1] Images of Canaanite goddesses
4 [i] Judg. 2:11; 10:16 [2] Images of Canaanite goddesses
5 [j] Judg. 10:17; 20:1; 1 Sam. 10:17 [k] 1 Sam. 12:17-19
6 [l] 2 Sam. 14:14 [m] Judg. 20:26; Neh. 9:1, 2; Dan. 9:3-5; Joel 2:12 [n] Judg. 10:10; 1 Sam. 12:10; 1 Kin. 8:47; Ps. 106:6
8 [o] 1 Sam. 12:19-24; Is. 37:4
9 [p] Lev. 22:27 [q] 1 Sam. 12:18; Ps. 99:6; Jer. 15:1
10 [r] Josh. 10:10; 2 Sam. 22:14, 15; Ps. 18:13, 14
11 [3] *struck them down*
12 [s] Gen. 28:18; 35:14; Josh. 4:9; 24:26 [4] Lit. *Stone of Help*
13 [t] Judg. 13:1 [u] 1 Sam. 13:5
15 [v] 1 Sam. 12:11

7:2 twenty years. Coupled with v. 3, the 20 years designated the period Israel neglected God and chased after foreign gods. After those 20 years, Israel returned to the Lord.

7:3 prepare your hearts for the LORD...and He will deliver you. This statement recalls the cycle in the book of Judges: apostasy, oppression, repentance, and deliverance. It previews the contents of this chapter.

7:4 the Baals and the Ashtoreths. Most dominant of the Canaanite pantheon, these deities were the fertility gods which plagued Israel. "Baal" and "Ashtoreth" are plurals of majesty, which signify their supreme authority over other Canaanite deities. Ashtoreth represented the female goddess, while Baal represented the male sky god who fertilized the land.

7:5 Mizpah. This city was located 8 mi. NE of Kirjath Jearim in Benjamin. It became one of the cities of Samuel's circuit (v. 16). **I will pray.** Samuel was a man of prayer (7:8,9; 8:6; 12:19,23; 15:11).

7:6 drew water, and poured *it* out before the LORD. The pouring out of water before the Lord was a sign of repentance. This act is repeated in 2 Sam. 23:16. **We have sinned against the LORD.** The symbol of Samuel pouring out the water and the acknowledgment of the people reveal a situation where true repentance had taken place. The condition of the heart superseded the importance or righteous of the ritual. **Samuel judged.** At this point Samuel is introduced as the judge of Israel. His judgeship encompassed both domestic leadership and the conduct of war. The word links the text back to the last comment about Eli who judged 40 years (4:18). Samuel is shown to be the one taking over Eli's judgeship. He served as the last judge before the first king (cf. 1 Sam. 8:50).

7:7 Israel...afraid of the Philistines. When Israel heard that the Philistines had come up against them for war, they were afraid.

7:10 the LORD thundered...upon the Philistines. In a literal manner, the Lord did to His enemies what was said by Hannah in her prayer (2:10).

7:11 Beth Car. The location is unknown.

7:12 Ebenezer. A different location from the one mentioned in 4:1 and 5:1. The name functions as the literary knot for the two ends of this unit (*see note on 4:1*). **Thus far the LORD has helped us.** This expression means that the Lord was the one responsible for getting Israel to this point. He was Israel's Sovereign One in times of both faithfulness and rebellion. He fought the battles and provided the blessings.

7:13 did not come anymore into the territory of Israel. The Lord gave Israel the victory over the Philistines, discontinuing their threat for the immediate future during Samuel's judgeship. **all the days of Samuel.** As the section opened in 4:1 with Samuel pictured as God's agent, so here the section closed with the Lord working powerfully through all the days of Samuel.

7:14 Ekron to Gath. These two cities, mentioned earlier as chief Philistine cities (5:8,10), became the eastern border of the Philistines. The territory to the E of these cities was freed from Philistine control and returned to Israel. **Amorites.** Whereas the Philistines resided in the coastal plains, the Amorites resided in the hills W of Israel between the Jordan Valley and the coastal plain. As with the Philistines, Israel was at peace with the Amorites.

7:16 a circuit. The circuit was an annual trip made by Samuel; he would travel to Bethel, Gilgal, Mizpah, and return once again to Ramah, which allowed him to manage the affairs of the people.

17 But [w]he always returned to Ramah, for
his home *was* there. There he judged Israel,
and there he [x]built an altar to the LORD.

Israel Demands a King

8 Now it came to pass when Samuel was
[a]old that he [b]made his [c]sons judges
over Israel. 2 The name of his firstborn was
Joel, and the name of his second, Abijah;
they were judges in Beersheba. 3 But his
sons [d]did not walk in his ways; they
turned aside [e]after dishonest gain, [f]took
bribes, and perverted justice.
4 Then all the elders of Israel gathered
together and came to Samuel at Ramah,
5 and said to him, "Look, you are old, and
your sons do not walk in your ways. Now
[g]make us a king to judge us like all the nations."
6 But the thing [h]displeased Samuel
when they said, "Give us a king to judge
us." So Samuel [i]prayed to the LORD. 7 And
the LORD said to Samuel, "Heed the voice
of the people in all that they say to you; for
[j]they have not rejected you, but [k]they have
rejected Me, that I should not reign over
them. 8 According to all the works which
they have done since the day that I brought
them up out of Egypt, even to this day—
with which they have forsaken Me and
served other gods—so they are doing to
you also. 9 Now therefore, heed their
voice. However, you shall solemnly forewarn them, and [l]show them the behavior
of the king who will reign over them."
10 So Samuel told all the words of the
LORD to the people who asked him for a
king. 11 And he said, [m]"This will be the behavior of the king who will reign over you:
He will take your [n]sons and appoint *them*
for his own [o]chariots and *to be* his horsemen, and *some* will run before his chariots.
12 He will [p]appoint captains over his thousands and captains over his fifties, *will set*
some to plow his ground and reap his harvest, and *some* to make his weapons of war
and equipment for his chariots. 13 He will
take your daughters *to be* perfumers,
cooks, and bakers. 14 And [q]he will take the
best of your fields, your vineyards, and
your olive groves, and give *them* to his servants. 15 He will take a tenth of your grain
and your vintage, and give it to his officers
and servants. 16 And he will take your
male servants, your female servants, your
finest [1]young men, and your donkeys, and
put *them* to his work. 17 He will take a
tenth of your sheep. And you will be his
servants. 18 And you will cry out in that
day because of your king whom you have
chosen for yourselves, and the LORD [r]will
not hear you in that day."
19 Nevertheless the people [s]refused to
obey the voice of Samuel; and they said,
"No, but we will have a king over us,
20 that we also may be [t]like all the nations,

17 [w] 1 Sam. 8:4 [x] Judg. 21:4

CHAPTER 8

1 [a] 1 Sam. 12:2 [b] Deut. 16:18, 19; 2 Chr. 19:5 [c] Judg. 10:4
3 [d] Jer. 22:15-17 [e] Ex. 18:21 [f] Ex. 23:6-8; Deut. 16:19; 1 Sam. 12:3
5 [g] Deut. 17:14, 15; Hos. 13:10, 11; Acts 13:21
6 [h] 1 Sam. 12:17 [i] 1 Sam. 7:9
7 [j] Ex. 16:8 [k] 1 Sam. 10:19
9 [l] 1 Sam. 8:11-18
11 [m] Deut. 17:14-20 [n] 1 Sam. 14:52 [o] 2 Sam. 15:1
12 [p] 1 Sam. 22:7
14 [q] 1 Kin. 21:7; [Ezek. 46:18]
16 [1] LXX *cattle*
18 [r] Prov. 1:25-28; Is. 1:15; Mic. 3:4
19 [s] Is. 66:4; Jer. 44:16
20 [t] 1 Sam. 8:5

7:17 Ramah. The first major division of the book (1:1–7:17) ends with Samuel returning to Ramah to judge the people.

8:1–15:35 This division of the book concentrates on the interaction between Israel, Samuel, and Saul. These chapters begin with the elders of Israel coming to Samuel at Ramah (8:4) and conclude with Samuel's leaving Saul and returning to Ramah (15:34). Chapters 8:1–12:25 describe the establishment of the kingship over the nation of Israel and the advent of Saul as the first king. These chapters are linked by reference to Samuel's being old (8:1; 12:2) and "heeding the voice" of the people (8:7,9,19,22; 12:1,14,15). Chapters 13:1–15:35 recount the failures of Saul as king over Israel. The events of these chapters are bracketed by two interactions between Saul and Samuel that both take place in Gilgal (13:4,7,8,12,15; 15:12,21,33).

8:1 Samuel was old. Samuel was about 60 years of age (1043 B.C.). He appointed his two sons to serve as judges in Beersheba, a city about 57 mi. S of Ramah.

8:2 Joel. The name means "the LORD is God." **Abijah.** The name means "my Father is the LORD."

8:3 his sons did not walk in his ways. The perverted desire for riches led Samuel's sons to take bribes and thereby pervert justice. These actions were strictly forbidden for judges in Deut. 16:19. The sins of Samuel's sons became the pretext for Israel's demand for a king (vv. 4,5).

8:5 Now make us a king...like all the nations. When Israel entered the land, they encountered Canaanite city-states that were led by kings (see Josh. 12:7-24). Additionally, during the period of the judges, Israel was enslaved by nations that were led by kings (Judg. 3:8,12; 4:2; 8:5; 11:12). However, at the time of the judges there was no king in Israel (Judg. 17:6; 18:1; 19:1; 21:25). As Israel lived in the land surrounded by nations that had kings, the desire arose for a king in Israel also. According to Deut. 17:14, God knew this would be their desire and He would allow it to occur. However, v. 20 revealed a motive which was definitely counter to the Lord's will. *See note on 8:20.*

8:7 Heed the voice of the people. The Lord had predicted that there would be kings over Israel (Gen. 35:11; 36:31; 49:10; Num. 24:7-9,17; Deut. 17:14; 28:36). Here, the Lord told Samuel to obey the request of the people and give them a king. **they have not rejected you, but...Me.** The nature of this rejection of the Lord by Israel is explained in vv. 19,20.

8:9 you shall solemnly forewarn them. Samuel obeyed the Lord by describing the behavior of a human king in vv. 10-18. A king would: 1) draft young men and women for his service (vv. 11-13); 2) tax the people's crops and flocks (vv. 14,15,17a); 3) appropriate the best of their animals and servants (v. 16); and 4) place limitations on their personal freedom (v. 17b).

8:10 who asked him for a king. Just as Hannah asked for a son (1:20), Israel asked for a king. *See note on 9:2.*

8:18 you will cry out...because of your king whom you have chosen. Samuel warned the people that they would live to regret their decision for a king and would later cry out for freedom from his rule (1 Kin. 12:4). **the LORD will not hear you.** In contrast to the Lord's response to Israel during the period of the judges (Judg. 2:18), the Lord would not be moved to pity and therefore would refuse to deliver the people out of the hand of their king who oppressed them.

8:19 we will have a king over us. In spite of Samuel's warnings, the people demanded a king.

and that our king may judge us and go out
before us and fight our battles."
21 And Samuel heard all the words of
the people, and he repeated them in the
hearing of the LORD. 22 So the LORD said to
Samuel, [u]"Heed their voice, and make
them a king."
And Samuel said to the men of Israel,
"Every man go to his city."

Saul Chosen to Be King

9 There was a man of Benjamin whose
name *was* [a]Kish the son of Abiel, the
son of Zeror, the son of Bechorath, the son
of Aphiah, a Benjamite, a mighty man of
[1]power. 2 And he had a choice and handsome son whose name *was* Saul. *There was*
not a more handsome person than he
among the children of Israel. [b]From his
shoulders upward *he was* taller than any of
the people.
3 Now the donkeys of Kish, Saul's father,
were lost. And Kish said to his son Saul,
"Please take one of the servants with you,
and arise, go and look for the donkeys."
4 So he passed through the mountains of
Ephraim and through the land of [c]Shali-
sha, but they did not find *them*. Then they
passed through the land of Shaalim, and
they were not *there*. Then he passed through
the land of the Benjamites, but they did not
find *them*.
5 When they had come to the land of
[d]Zuph, Saul said to his servant who *was*
with him, "Come, let [e]us return, lest my father cease *caring* about the donkeys and
become worried about us."
6 And he said to him, "Look now, *there is*
in this city [f]a man of God, and *he is* an honorable man; [g]all that he says surely comes

22 [u] 1 Sam. 8:7; Hos. 13:11

CHAPTER 9

1 [a] 1 Sam. 14:51; 1 Chr. 8:33; 9:36-39 [1] *wealth*
2 [b] 1 Sam. 10:23
4 [c] 2 Kin. 4:42
5 [d] 1 Sam. 1:1 [e] 1 Sam. 10:2
6 [f] Deut. 33:1; 1 Kin. 13:1; 2 Kin. 5:8 [g] 1 Sam. 3:19
7 [h] Judg. 6:18; 13:17; 1 Kin. 14:3; 2 Kin. 4:42; 8:8
9 [i] Gen. 25:22 [j] 2 Sam. 24:11; 2 Kin. 17:13; 1 Chr. 26:28; 29:29; 2 Chr. 16:7, 10; Is. 30:10; Amos 7:12 [2] Lit. *to seek God*
10 [3] Lit. *Your word is good*
11 [k] Gen. 24:11, 15; 29:8, 9; Ex. 2:16
12 [l] Gen. 31:54; 1 Sam. 16:2 [m] 1 Sam. 7:17; 10:5; 1 Kin. 3:2
15 [n] 1 Sam. 15:1

to pass. So let us go there; perhaps he can
show us the way that we should go."
7 Then Saul said to his servant, "But
look, *if* we go, [h]what shall we bring the
man? For the bread in our vessels is all
gone, and *there is* no present to bring to the
man of God. What do we have?"
8 And the servant answered Saul again
and said, "Look, I have here at hand one-
fourth of a shekel of silver. I will give *that*
to the man of God, to tell us our way."
9 (Formerly in Israel, when a man [i]went
[2]to inquire of God, he spoke thus: "Come,
let us go to the seer"; for *he who is* now
called a prophet was formerly called [j]a
seer.)
10 Then Saul said to his servant, [3]"Well
said; come, let us go." So they went to the
city where the man of God *was*.
11 As they went up the hill to the city,
[k]they met some young women going out
to draw water, and said to them, "Is the
seer here?"
12 And they answered them and said,
"Yes, there he is, just ahead of you. Hurry
now; for today he came to this city, because
[l]there is a sacrifice of the people today [m]on
the high place. 13 As soon as you come into
the city, you will surely find him before he
goes up to the high place to eat. For the
people will not eat until he comes, because
he must bless the sacrifice; afterward those
who are invited will eat. Now therefore, go
up, for about this time you will find him."
14 So they went up to the city. As they were
coming into the city, there was Samuel,
coming out toward them on his way up to
the high place.
15 [n]Now the LORD had told Samuel in his
ear the day before Saul came, saying,

8:20 fight our battles. Up until this point, the Lord Himself had fought the battles for Israel and given continual victory (Josh. 10:14; 1 Sam. 7:10). Israel no longer wanted the Lord to be their warrior; replacing Him with a human king was their desire. It was in this way that Israel rejected the Lord (see v. 7). The problem was not in having a king; but, rather the reason the people wanted a king, i.e., to be like other nations. They also foolishly assumed there would be some greater power in a king leading them in battle.

9:1 a mighty man of power. I.e., "a man of wealth," confirmed by the reference to donkeys and servants in v. 3 (cf. Boaz in Ruth 2:1).

9:2 a choice and handsome son. Emphasis was placed on the external appearance of leaders (cf. David in 16:18). **Saul.** Son of Kish, a Benjamite, he was Israel's first king. The Heb. root for "Saul" means "asked (of God)." In 8:10, the people "asked…for a king." Although God appointed Saul, he was really the people's choice, given by the Lord in answer to their request. The Lord's choice would be from the tribe of Judah (cf. Gen. 49:10).

9:3 the donkeys…were lost. "Lost donkeys" meant "lost wealth." Kish had servants who could have gone looking, but Saul was chosen to oversee this important task.

9:4 Shalisha…Shaalim. The locations are geographically unknown.

9:6 a man of God. A description of the prophet and judge, Samuel. "Man of God" referred to a prophet (see 2:27). *See note on Deut. 33:1.*

9:7 no present to bring. A gift expressed gratitude and thankfulness for the service of the "man of God." Gifts were offered to prophets in 1 Kin. 14:3; 2 Kin. 4:42; 5:15,16; 8:8,9.

9:8 one-fourth of a shekel. About one-tenth of an ounce.

9:9 a prophet was formerly called a seer. Due to the God-given ability to know or "see" the future, the "seer" was so named in close relationship with what he did. The person called a prophet, by the time this book was written, had been termed a seer in the earlier time of Saul.

9:12 high place. This is essentially Canaanite in background (cf. Deut. 12:2-5). Before the temple was built, the high place was used for worship and sacrifice because it provided the best vantage point for the participation of the people in worship and allowed them to visually see the sacrifice being made for them.

9:13 he must bless the sacrifice. The sacrifice was offered to the Lord as an act of worship by the "man of God."

16 "Tomorrow about this time [o]I will send
you a man from the land of Benjamin, [p]and
you shall anoint him [4]commander over
My people Israel, that he may save My
people from the hand of the Philistines; for
I have [q]looked upon My people, because
their cry has come to Me."
17 So when Samuel saw Saul, the LORD
said to him, [r]"There he is, the man of
whom I spoke to you. This one shall reign
over My people." 18 Then Saul drew near
to Samuel in the gate, and said, "Please tell
me, where *is* the seer's house?"
19 Samuel answered Saul and said, "I *am*
the seer. Go up before me to the high place,
for you shall eat with me today; and tomorrow I will let you go and will tell you
all that *is* in your heart. 20 But as for [s]your
donkeys that were lost three days ago, do
not be anxious about them, for they have
been found. And [5]on whom [t]*is* all the desire of Israel? *Is it* not on you and on all
your father's house?"
21 And Saul answered and said, [u]"*Am* I
not a Benjamite, of the [v]smallest of the
tribes of Israel, and [w]my family the least of
all the families of the [6]tribe of Benjamin?
Why then do you speak like this to me?"
22 Now Samuel took Saul and his servant and brought them into the hall, and
had them sit in the place of honor among
those who were invited; there *were* about
thirty persons. 23 And Samuel said to the
cook, "Bring the portion which I gave you,
of which I said to you, 'Set it apart.'" 24 So
the cook took up [x]the thigh with its upper
part and set *it* before Saul. And *Samuel*
said, "Here it is, what was kept back. *It*
was set apart for you. Eat; for until this
time it has been kept for you, since I said I
invited the people." So Saul ate with Samuel that day.

25 When they had come down from the
high place into the city, [7]*Samuel* spoke
with Saul on [y]the top of the house. 26 They
arose early; and it was about the dawning
of the day that Samuel called to Saul on
the top of the house, saying, "Get up, that
I may send you on your way." And Saul
arose, and both of them went outside, he
and Samuel.

Saul Anointed King

27 As they were going down to the outskirts of the city, Samuel said to Saul, "Tell
the servant to go on ahead of us." And he
went on. "But you stand here [8]awhile, that
I may announce to you the word of God."
10 Then [a]Samuel took a flask of oil
and poured *it* on his head, [b]and
kissed him and said: "*Is it* not because
[c]the LORD has anointed you commander
over [d]His [1]inheritance? 2 When you have
departed from me today, you will find
two men by [e]Rachel's tomb in the territory of Benjamin [f]at Zelzah; and they will
say to you, 'The donkeys which you went
to look for have been found. And now
your father has ceased caring about the
donkeys and is worrying about [g]you, saying, "What shall I do about my son?"'
3 Then you shall go on forward from there
and come to the terebinth tree of Tabor.
There three men going up [h]to God at
Bethel will meet you, one carrying three
young goats, another carrying three
loaves of bread, and another carrying a
skin of wine. 4 And they will [2]greet you
and give you two *loaves* of bread, which
you shall receive from their hands. 5 After
that you shall come to the hill of God

16 [o] Deut. 17:15 [p] 1 Sam. 10:1 [q] Ex. 2:23-25; 3:7, 9 [4] *prince* or *ruler*
17 [r] 1 Sam. 16:12; Hos. 13:11
20 [s] 1 Sam. 9:3 [t] 1 Sam. 8:5, 19; 12:13 [5] *for whom*
21 [u] 1 Sam. 15:17 [v] Judg. 20:46-48; Ps. 68:27 [w] Judg. 6:15 [6] Lit. *tribes*
24 [x] Ex. 29:22, 27; Lev. 7:32, 33; Num. 18:18; Ezek. 24:4
25 [y] Deut. 22:8; 2 Sam. 11:2; Luke 5:19; Acts 10:9 [7] So with MT, Tg.; LXX omits *He spoke with Saul on the top of the house*; LXX, Vg. afterward add *And he prepared a bed for Saul on the top of the house, and he slept.*
27 [8] *now*

CHAPTER 10

1 [a] Ex. 30:23-33; 1 Sam. 9:16; 16:13; 2 Kin. 9:3, 6 [b] Ps. 2:12 [c] 2 Sam. 5:2; Acts 13:21 [d] Ex. 34:9; Deut. 32:9; Ps. 78:71 [1] So with MT, Tg., Vg.; LXX *people Israel; and you shall rule the people of the Lord;* LXX, Vg. add *And you shall deliver His people from the hands of their enemies all around them. And this shall be a sign to you, that God has anointed you to be a prince.* **2** [e] Gen. 35:16-20; 48:7 [f] Josh. 18:28 [g] 1 Sam. 9:3-5 **3** [h] Gen. 28:22; 35:1, 3, 7 **4** [2] *ask you about your welfare*

9:16 anoint him. This represents a setting apart for service to the Lord, which occurs in 10:1. *See note on 2:10.* **commander.** Lit. "one given prominence, one placed in front." The title referred to "one designated to rule" (cf. 1 Kin. 1:35; 2 Chr. 11:22). **their cry has come to Me.** The people had been crying out for deliverance from the Philistines, their longstanding rivals, just as they did for liberation from Egypt (cf. Ex. 2:25; 3:9).

9:17 This one shall reign over My people. God identified Saul to Samuel, assuring there was no mistaking whom God was choosing to be king.

9:18 where *is* the seer's house? A reference to Samuel's house.

9:20 all the desire of Israel. Saul was to become the focus of Israel's hope for military victories over her enemies (cf. 8:19, 20).

9:21 a Benjamite...the least of all the families. Saul's humility and timidity was expressed by his proper assessment of his tribe and a humble estimation of his family.

9:22 the hall. The place where those who were invited ate with Samuel after the offering of the sacrifice on the high place (cf. vv. 12, 13).

9:24 the thigh...set apart for you. Samuel was following Lev. 7:28-36. Samuel received the thigh, the portion of the sacrifice reserved for the priest. Samuel's giving of this choice piece of meat to Saul was a distinct honor and reflected Saul's new status as the designated king.

9:25 the top of the house. The roof of Samuel's house provided a place for Saul and his servant to sleep for the night.

9:27 the word of God. Special revelation from God, given to Samuel and intended for Saul. *See note on 3:1.*

10:1 the LORD has anointed you commander. The Lord chose Saul to be the leader of Israel and communicated His choice through the private anointing by Samuel, signifying a setting aside for God's service (see 2:10). **His inheritance.** The inheritance was God's nation, Israel, in the sense that she uniquely belonged to Him (Deut. 4:20; 9:26).

10:2 Zelzah. Only mentioned here. Probably near Ramah, located between Bethel and Bethlehem, where Rachel died (Gen. 35:19; 48:7).

10:3 Tabor. This is not the far-distant Mt. Tabor, but a location unknown, probably near Bethel.

[i]where the Philistine garrison *is.* And it
will happen, when you have come there
to the city, that you will meet a group of
prophets coming down [j]from the high
place with a stringed instrument, a tambourine, a flute, and a harp before them;
[k]and they will be prophesying. 6 Then
[l]the Spirit of the LORD will come upon
you, and [m]you will prophesy with them
and be turned into another man. 7 And let
it be, when these [n]signs come to you, *that*
you do as the occasion demands; for [o]God
is with you. 8 You shall go down before
me [p]to Gilgal; and surely I will come
down to you to offer burnt offerings *and*
make sacrifices of peace offerings. [q]Seven
days you shall wait, till I come to you and
show you what you should do."
9 So it was, when he had turned his back
to go from Samuel, that God [3]gave him another heart; and all those signs came to
pass that day. 10 [r]When they came there to
the hill, there was [s]a group of prophets to
meet him; then the Spirit of God came
upon him, and he prophesied among
them. 11 And it happened, when all who
knew him formerly saw that he indeed
prophesied among the prophets, that the
people said to one another, "What *is* this
that has come upon the son of Kish? [t]*Is*
Saul also among the prophets?" 12 Then a
man from there answered and said, "But
[u]who *is* their father?" Therefore it became
a proverb: "*Is* Saul also among the
prophets?" 13 And when he had finished
prophesying, he went to the high place.
14 Then Saul's [v]uncle said to him and his
servant, "Where did you go?"
So he said, "To look for the donkeys.
When we saw that *they were* nowhere *to be*
found, we went to Samuel."
15 And Saul's uncle said, "Tell me,
please, what Samuel said to you."
16 So Saul said to his uncle, "He told us
plainly that the donkeys had been
[w]found." But about the matter of the kingdom, he did not tell him what Samuel had
said.

Saul Proclaimed King

17 Then Samuel called the people together [x]to the LORD [y]at Mizpah, 18 and said to
the children of Israel, [z]"Thus says the LORD
God of Israel: 'I brought up Israel out of
Egypt, and delivered you from the hand of
the Egyptians *and* from the hand of all
kingdoms and from those who oppressed
you.' 19 [a]But you have today rejected your
God, who Himself saved you from all your
adversities and your tribulations; and you
have said to Him, 'No, set a king over us!'
Now therefore, present yourselves before
the LORD by your tribes and by your
[4]clans."
20 And when Samuel had [b]caused all the
tribes of Israel to come near, the tribe of
Benjamin was chosen. 21 When he had
caused the tribe of Benjamin to come near
by their families, the family of Matri was
chosen. And Saul the son of Kish was chosen. But when they sought him, he could
not be found. 22 Therefore they [c]inquired
of the LORD further, "Has the man come
here yet?"
And the LORD answered, "There he is,
hidden among the equipment."
23 So they ran and brought him from
there; and when he stood among the

5 [i] 1 Sam. 13:2, 3 [j] 1 Sam. 19:12, 20; 2 Kin. 2:3, 5, 15 [k] Ex. 15:20, 21; 2 Kin. 3:15; 1 Chr. 25:1-6; 1 Cor. 14:1
6 [l] Num. 11:25, 29; Judg. 14:6; 1 Sam. 16:13 [m] 1 Sam. 10:10; 19:23, 24
7 [n] Ex. 4:8; Luke 2:12 [o] Josh. 1:5; Judg. 6:12; 1 Sam. 3:19; [Heb. 13:5]
8 [p] 1 Sam. 11:14, 15; 13:8 [q] 1 Sam. 13:8-10
9 [3] *changed his heart*
10 [r] 1 Sam. 10:5 [s] 1 Sam. 19:20
11 [t] 1 Sam. 19:24; Amos 7:14, 15; Matt. 13:54-57; John 7:15; Acts 4:13
12 [u] John 5:30, 36
14 [v] 1 Sam. 14:50
16 [w] 1 Sam. 9:20
17 [x] Judg. 20:1 [y] 1 Sam. 7:5, 6
18 [z] Judg. 6:8, 9; 1 Sam. 8:8; 12:6, 8
19 [a] 1 Sam. 8:7, 19; 12:12 [4] Lit. *thousands*
20 [b] Acts 1:24, 26
22 [c] 1 Sam. 23:2, 4, 10, 11

10:5 the Philistine garrison. Most likely the garrison in Geba in Benjamin, about 5 mi. N of Jerusalem. **a group of prophets.** Lit. "sons of the prophets." They were young men being trained by Samuel for the prophetic ministry (see 19:18-20). **prophesying.** The prophet, as God's messenger, declared the Word of the Lord (2 Sam. 7:5; 12:1), sometimes accompanied by music (1 Chr. 25:1). Here, "prophesying" connotes praising God and instructing the people with musical accompaniment.

10:6 the Spirit of the LORD will come upon you. The Holy Spirit would enable Saul to declare the Word of the Lord with the prophets. **turned into another man.** With this empowerment by the Holy Spirit, Saul would emerge another man (cf. 10:9), equipped in the manner of Gideon and Jepthah for deeds of valor (cf. v. 9; Judg. 6:34; 11:29).

10:7 signs. The 3 signs of vv. 2-6: 1) the report of the found donkeys; 2) the encounter of the 3 men going to Bethel; and 3) the encounter with the prophets. **do as the occasion demands.** Saul was to do what his hand found to do (Eccl. 9:10).

10:8 Gilgal. The town where Saul eventually would be declared king by Samuel (11:14,15), offer sacrifice before the Lord without the prophet Samuel (13:12), and where Samuel slew king Agag (15:33). Gilgal was to the E of Jericho, but W of the Jordan River. **burnt offerings *and*...peace offerings.** *See notes on Lev. 1:3-17; 3:1-17.* **Seven days.** The appointed time Saul was to wait for Samuel to come and tell him what to do (see 13:8).

10:9 God gave him another heart. Lit. "God changed him for another heart," i.e., God prepared Saul for the kingship by having the Holy Spirit come upon him (cf. v. 6).

10:12 who *is* their father? A question asked to find out the identity of the leader of the prophetic band that now included Saul. **a proverb.** A saying of common occurrence.

10:16 the matter of the kingdom. The information Samuel gave Saul about becoming king he did not tell his uncle. This might reflect Saul's humility (cf. v. 22).

10:17 Samuel called the people. The Lord's choice of Saul was made public at Mizpah, the place of the spiritual revival before Israel's victory over the Philistines (7:5-8).

10:18,19 the LORD God of Israel...delivered you. Despite the past faithfulness of God to His people, they still desired a human king to deliver them from the hands of their enemies.

10:20,21 chosen. Probably Saul was selected by the casting of lots (cf. Lev. 16:8-10; Josh. 7:15-18). *See note on Prov. 16:33.*

10:22 hidden among the equipment. Overwhelmed, Saul had hidden himself in the military supplies.

people, [d]he was taller than any of the people from his shoulders upward. **24** And
Samuel said to all the people, "Do you see
him [e]whom the LORD has chosen, that *there*
is no one like him among all the people?"
So all the people shouted and said,
[f]"Long[5] live the king!"
25 Then Samuel explained to the people
[g]the behavior of royalty, and wrote *it* in a
book and laid *it* up before the LORD. And
Samuel sent all the people away, every
man to his house. **26** And Saul also went
home [h]to Gibeah; and valiant *men* went
with him, whose hearts God had touched.
27 [i]But some [j]rebels said, "How can this
man save us?" So they despised him, [k]and
brought him no presents. But he [6]held his
peace.

Saul Saves Jabesh Gilead

11 Then [a]Nahash the Ammonite came
up and [1]encamped against [b]Jabesh
Gilead; and all the men of Jabesh said to
Nahash, [c]"Make a covenant with us, and
we will serve you."
2 And Nahash the Ammonite answered
them, "On this *condition* I will make *a*
covenant with you, that I may put out all
your right eyes, and bring [d]reproach on all
Israel."
3 Then the elders of Jabesh said to him,
"Hold off for seven days, that we may
send messengers to all the territory of Israel. And then, if *there is* no one to [2]save us,
we will come out to you."
4 So the messengers came [e]to Gibeah of
Saul and told the news in the hearing of
the people. And [f]all the people lifted up
their voices and wept. **5** Now there was
Saul, coming behind the herd from the
field; and Saul said, "What *troubles* the
people, that they weep?" And they told
him the words of the men of Jabesh.
6 [g]Then the Spirit of God came upon Saul
when he heard this news, and his anger
was greatly aroused. **7** So he took a yoke of
oxen and [h]cut them in pieces, and sent
them throughout all the territory of Israel
by the hands of messengers, saying,
[i]"Whoever does not go out with Saul and
Samuel to battle, so it shall be done to his
oxen."
And the fear of the LORD fell on the people, and they came out [3]with one consent.
8 When he numbered them in [j]Bezek, the
children [k]of Israel were three hundred
thousand, and the men of Judah thirty
thousand. **9** And they said to the messengers who came, "Thus you shall say to the
men of Jabesh Gilead: 'Tomorrow, by *the*
time the sun is hot, you shall have help.'"
Then the messengers came and reported *it*
to the men of Jabesh, and they were glad.
10 Therefore the men of Jabesh said, "Tomorrow we will come out to you, and you
may do with us whatever seems good to
you."
11 So it was, on the next day, that [l]Saul
put the people [m]in three companies; and
they came into the midst of the camp in the
morning watch, and killed Ammonites
until the heat of the day. And it happened
that those who survived were scattered, so
that no two of them were left together.
12 Then the people said to Samuel,
[n]"Who *is* he who said, 'Shall Saul reign
over us?' [o]Bring the men, that we may put
them to death."

23 [d]1 Sam. 9:2
24 [e]Deut. 17:15; 1 Sam. 9:16; 2 Sam. 21:6 [f]1 Kin. 1:25, 39 [5]Lit. *May the king live*
25 [g]Deut. 17:14-20; 1 Sam. 8:11-18
26 [h]Judg. 20:14
27 [i]1 Sam. 11:12 [j]Deut. 13:13; 1 Sam. 25:17 [k]2 Sam. 8:2; 1 Kin. 4:21; 10:25; 2 Chr. 17:5; Matt. 2:11 [6]*kept silent*

CHAPTER 11

1 [a]1 Sam. 12:12 [b]Judg. 21:8; 1 Sam. 31:11 [c]Gen. 26:28; 1 Kin. 20:34; Job 41:4; Ezek. 17:13 [1]*besieged*
2 [d]Gen. 34:14; 1 Sam. 17:26; Ps. 44:13
3 [2]*deliver*
4 [e]1 Sam. 10:26; 15:34; 2 Sam. 21:6 [f]Gen. 27:38; Judg. 2:4; 20:23, 26; 21:2; 1 Sam. 30:4
6 [g]Judg. 3:10; 6:34; 11:29; 13:25; 14:6; 1 Sam. 10:10; 16:13
7 [h]Judg. 19:29 [i]Judg. 21:5, 8, 10 [3]Lit. *as one man*
8 [j]Judg. 1:5 [k]2 Sam. 24:9
11 [l]1 Sam. 31:11 [m]Judg. 7:16, 20
12 [n]1 Sam. 10:27 [o]Luke 19:27

10:23 taller...from his shoulders upward. Saul's physical stature was impressive; being head and shoulders above the rest gave Saul a kingly presence.

10:25 the behavior of royalty. Samuel reminded the people of the regulations governing the conduct of kings according to Deut. 17:14-20.

10:26 whose hearts God had touched. Valiant men who were eager to affirm God's choice of Saul and, in response to a divine impulse, joined him.

10:27 rebels. Lit. "sons of Belial" (*see note on 2:12*). Those who did not recognize Saul with the respect befitting a king.

11:1 Nahash the Ammonite. Nahash, meaning "snake," was king of the Ammonites, the descendants of Lot (cf. Gen. 19:36-38) who lived E of the Jordan. **Jabesh Gilead.** A town E of the Jordan River, about 22 mi. S of the Sea of Galilee, in the tribal territory of Manasseh (cf. Judg. 21:8-14).

11:2 put out all your right eyes. This barbarous mutilation was a common punishment of usurpers in the ancient Near East which would disable the warriors' depth-perception and peripheral vision, rendering them useless in battle.

11:3 seven days. The elders at Jabesh were hoping for deliverance from the Israelites W of the Jordan.

11:4 Gibeah of Saul. Saul's home and the first capital city of the monarchy, about 3 mi. N of Jerusalem (cf. 10:26).

11:5 from the field. Saul continued to work as a farmer while waiting for the time to answer Israel's expectations of him as the king.

11:6 the Spirit of God came upon Saul. To fill him with divine indignation and to empower him to deliver the citizens of Jabesh Gilead (cf. 10:6).

11:7 cut them in pieces. Saul divided the oxen in sections to be taken throughout Israel to rouse the people for battle (see a similar action in Judg. 19:29; 20:6).

11:8 Bezek. A city 13 mi. N of Shechem and 17 mi. W of Jabesh Gilead. **children of Israel...men of Judah.** This distinction made between Israel and Judah before the kingdom was divided indicates the book was written after 931 B.C. when the kingdom had been divided. See Introduction: Author and Date.

11:11 three companies. A military strategy of dividing up forces, it lessened the possibility of losing everyone to a sneak attack while giving greater military options. **in the morning watch.** The last of the 3 watches (2:00–6:00 a.m.), this surprise attack was before dawn, before the Ammonites were prepared for battle.

13 But Saul said, [p]"Not a man shall be
put to death this day, for today [q]the LORD
has accomplished salvation in Israel."
14 Then Samuel said to the people,
"Come, let us go [r]to Gilgal and renew the
kingdom there." 15 So all the people went
to Gilgal, and there they made Saul king
[s]before the LORD in Gilgal. [t]There they
made sacrifices of peace offerings before
the LORD, and there Saul and all the men of
Israel rejoiced greatly.

Samuel's Address at Saul's Coronation

12 Now Samuel said to all Israel: "Indeed I have [1]heeded [a]your voice in
all that you said to me, and [b]have made a
king over you. 2 And now here is the king,
[c]walking before you; [d]and I am old and
grayheaded, and look, my sons *are* with
you. I have walked before you from my
childhood to this day. 3 Here I am. Witness
against me before the LORD and before [e]His
anointed: [f]Whose ox have I taken, or
whose donkey have I taken, or whom have
I cheated? Whom have I oppressed, or
from whose hand have I received *any*
[g]bribe with which to [h]blind my eyes? I will
restore *it* to you."
4 And they said, [i]"You have not cheated
us or oppressed us, nor have you taken
anything from any man's hand."
5 Then he said to them, "The LORD *is* witness against you, and His anointed *is* witness this day, [j]that you have not found
anything [k]in my hand."
And they answered, "*He is* witness."
6 Then Samuel said to the people, [l]"*It is*
the LORD who raised up Moses and Aaron,
and who brought your fathers up from the
land of Egypt. 7 Now therefore, stand still,

13 [p] 1 Sam. 10:27; 2 Sam. 19:22 [q] Ex. 14:13, 30; 1 Sam. 19:5
14 [r] 1 Sam. 7:16; 10:8
15 [s] 1 Sam. 10:17 [t] Josh. 8:31; 1 Sam. 10:8

CHAPTER 12

1 [a] 1 Sam. 8:5, 7, 9, 20, 22 [b] 1 Sam. 10:24; 11:14, 15 [1] *listened to*
2 [c] Num. 27:17; 1 Sam. 8:20 [d] 1 Sam. 8:1, 5
3 [e] 1 Sam. 10:1; 24:6; 2 Sam. 1:14, 16 [f] Num. 16:15; Acts 20:33; 1 Thess. 2:5 [g] Ex. 23:8 [h] Deut. 16:19
4 [i] Lev. 19:13
5 [j] John 18:38; Acts 23:9; 24:20 [k] Ex. 22:4
6 [l] Ex. 6:26; Mic. 6:4
7 [m] Is. 1:18; Ezek. 20:35; Mic. 6:1-5 [n] Judg. 5:11; Ps. 103:6
8 [o] Gen. 46:5, 6; Ps. 105:23 [p] Ex. 2:23-25 [q] Ex. 3:10; 4:14-16 [2] So with MT, Tg., Vg.; LXX adds *and the Egyptians afflicted them*
9 [r] Deut. 32:18; Judg. 3:7 [s] Judg. 4:2 [t] Judg. 3:31; 10:7; 13:1 [u] Judg. 3:12-30
10 [v] Judg. 10:10 [w] Judg. 2:13; 3:7 [3] Images of Canaanite goddesses
11 [x] Judg. 11:1 [y] 1 Sam. 7:13 [4] Gideon, cf. Judg. 6:25-32; Syr. *Deborah;* Tg. *Gideon* [5] LXX, Syr. *Barak;* Tg. *Simson* [6] Syr. *Simson*
12 [z] 1 Sam. 11:1, 2 [a] 1 Sam. 8:5, 19, 20 [b] Judg. 8:23; 1 Sam. 8:7; Ps. 59:13

that I may [m]reason with you before the
LORD concerning all the [n]righteous acts of
the LORD which He did to you and your fathers: 8 [o]When Jacob had gone into [2]Egypt,
and your fathers [p]cried out to the LORD,
then the LORD [q]sent Moses and Aaron, who
brought your fathers out of Egypt and
made them dwell in this place. 9 And when
they [r]forgot the LORD their God, He sold
them into the hand of [s]Sisera, commander
of the army of Hazor, into the hand of the
[t]Philistines, and into the hand of the king of
[u]Moab; and they fought against them.
10 Then they cried out to the LORD, and said,
[v]'We have sinned, because we have forsak-
en the LORD [w]and served the Baals and
[3]Ashtoreths; but now deliver us from the
hand of our enemies, and we will serve
You.' 11 And the LORD sent [4]Jerubbaal,
[5]Bedan, [x]Jephthah, and [y]Samuel,[6] and delivered you out of the hand of your enemies
on every side; and you dwelt in safety.
12 And when you saw that [z]Nahash king of
the Ammonites came against you, [a]you said
to me, 'No, but a king shall reign over us,'
when [b]the LORD your God *was* your king.
13 "Now therefore, [c]here is the king
[d]whom you have chosen *and* whom you
have desired. And take note, [e]the LORD has
set a king over you. 14 If you [f]fear the LORD
and serve Him and obey His voice, and do
not rebel against the commandment of the
LORD, then both you and the king who
reigns over you will continue following
the LORD your God. 15 However, if you do
[g]not obey the voice of the LORD, but [h]rebel
against the commandment of the LORD,

13 [c] 1 Sam. 10:24 [d] 1 Sam. 8:5; 12:17, 19 [e] Hos. 13:11 14 [f] Josh. 24:14 15 [g] Deut. 28:15 [h] Lev. 26:14, 15; Josh. 24:20; Is. 1:20

11:13 the LORD has accomplished salvation in Israel. Saul recognized the deliverance of the Lord and refused to kill those who had rebelled against his kingship (10:27).

11:14 Gilgal. *See note on 10:8.* **renew the kingdom.** The reaffirmation of Saul's kingship by public acclamation.

11:15 they made Saul king before the LORD. All the people came to crown Saul king that day. The process of entering the kingship was the same for both Saul and David: 1) commissioned by the Lord (9:1–10:16; 16:1-13); 2) confirmed by military victory (10:17–11:11; 16:14–2 Sam. 1:27); and 3) crowned (11:12-15; 2 Sam. 2:4; 5:3). **peace offerings.** Sacrifices of thanksgiving (cf. Lev. 7:13). **rejoiced greatly.** Along with the victory over the Ammonites, there was a great celebration over the nation being united.

12:1 I have heeded your voice. Samuel had obeyed the will of the Lord and the people and set the king of God's choice over them, though he had personal reservations concerning the monarchy.

12:3 Here I am. These familiar words for Samuel throughout his entire life (cf. 3:4,5,6,8,16) emphasized his availability to God and the people. **Witness.** Samuel requested the people to "testify against" any covenant stipulations that he had violated.

12:7 I may reason with you before the LORD. Despite the nation being unified under the new king, Samuel still wanted to rebuke the nation for ignoring and rejecting what God had done without a king.

12:11 the LORD sent...and delivered you. It was the Lord who delivered them through the hands of the judges, not themselves.

12:12 when you saw that Nahash king of the Ammonites came against you. According to the DSS and Josephus, Nahash was campaigning over a large area. It was that Ammonite threat that seemingly provoked Israel to demand a human king (8:1-20). **the LORD your God *was* your king.** The clearest indictment of Israel for choosing a mere man to fight for her instead of the Lord God (cf. 8:20).

12:13 the king whom you have chosen...desired. The Lord gave them their request (cf. Ps. 106:15).

12:14 fear the LORD. A reminder of Josh. 24:14. Israel was to stand in awe of the Lord and submit to Him (cf. Deut. 10:12). **you and the king...following the LORD your God.** Both the people and the king were given the same command. The standard was the same, obedience to God's commands.

12:15 rebel. "Disobey, not heed, forsake." Echoing the promises of Deut. 28, there would be blessings for obeying and curses for disobeying the commands of the Lord.

then the hand of the LORD will be against
you, as *it was* against your fathers.
16 "Now therefore, [i]stand and see this
great thing which the LORD will do before
your eyes: 17 *Is* today not the [j]wheat harvest? [k]I will call to the LORD, and He will
send thunder and [l]rain, that you may perceive and see that [m]your wickedness *is*
great, which you have done in the sight of
the LORD, in asking a king for yourselves."
18 So Samuel called to the LORD, and the
LORD sent thunder and rain that day; and
[n]all the people greatly feared the LORD and
Samuel.
19 And all the people said to Samuel,
[o]"Pray for your servants to the LORD your
God, that we may not die; for we have
added to all our sins the evil of asking a
king for ourselves."
20 Then Samuel said to the people, "Do
not fear. You have done all this wickedness; [p]yet do not turn aside from following the LORD, but serve the LORD with all
your heart. 21 And [q]do not turn aside; [r]for
then you would go after empty things which
cannot profit or deliver, for they *are* nothing. 22 For [s]the LORD will not forsake [t]His
people, [u]for His great name's sake, because [v]it has pleased the LORD to make
you His people. 23 Moreover, as for me, far
be it from me that I should sin against the
LORD [w]in ceasing to pray for you; but [x]I
will teach you the [y]good and the right
way. 24 [z]Only fear the LORD, and serve
Him in truth with all your heart; for [a]con-
sider what [b]great things He has done for
you. 25 But if you still do wickedly, [c]you
shall be swept away, [d]both you and your
king."

Saul's Unlawful Sacrifice

13 Saul [1]reigned one year; and when
he had reigned two years over Israel, 2 Saul chose for himself three thousand *men* of Israel. Two thousand were
with Saul in [a]Michmash and in the mountains of Bethel, and a thousand were with
[b]Jonathan in [c]Gibeah of Benjamin. The rest
of the people he sent away, every man to
his tent.
3 And Jonathan attacked [d]the garrison of
the Philistines that *was* in [e]Geba, and the
Philistines heard *of it.* Then Saul blew the
trumpet throughout all the land, saying,
"Let the Hebrews hear!" 4 Now all Israel
heard it said *that* Saul had attacked a garrison of the Philistines, and *that* Israel had
also become [2]an abomination to the Philistines. And the people were called together to Saul at Gilgal.
5 Then the Philistines gathered together to fight with Israel, [3]thirty thousand
chariots and six thousand horsemen, and
people [f]as the sand which *is* on the
seashore in multitude. And they came up
and encamped in Michmash, to the east
of [g]Beth Aven. 6 When the men of Israel
saw that they were in danger (for the people were distressed), then the people [h]hid
in caves, in thickets, in rocks, in holes,
and in pits. 7 And *some of* the Hebrews
crossed over the Jordan to the [i]land of
Gad and Gilead.
As for Saul, he *was* still in Gilgal, and all
the people followed him trembling.
8 [j]Then he waited seven days, according to
the time set by Samuel. But Samuel did not
come to Gilgal; and the people were scattered from him. 9 So Saul said, "Bring a

16 [i] Ex. 14:13, 31
17 [j] Gen. 30:14 [k] Josh. 10:12; 1 Sam. 7:9, 10; [James 5:16-18] [l] Ezra 10:9 [m] 1 Sam. 8:7
18 [n] Ex. 14:31
19 [o] Ex. 9:28; 1 Sam. 7:8; [James 5:15; 1 John 5:16]
20 [p] Deut. 11:16
21 [q] 2 Chr. 25:15 [r] Is. 41:29; Jer. 16:19; Hab. 2:18; 1 Cor. 8:4
22 [s] Deut. 31:6; 1 Kin. 6:13 [t] Is. 43:21 [u] Ex. 32:12; Num. 14:13; Josh. 7:9; Ps. 106:8; Jer. 14:21 [v] Deut. 7:6-11; 1 Pet. 2:9
23 [w] Acts 12:5; Rom. 1:9; Col. 1:9; 2 Tim. 1:3 [x] Ps. 34:11; Prov. 4:11 [y] 1 Kin. 8:36
24 [z] Eccl. 12:13 [a] Is. 5:12 [b] Deut. 10:21
25 [c] Josh. 24:20 [d] Deut. 28:36

CHAPTER 13
1 [1] Heb. is difficult; cf. 2 Sam. 5:4; 2 Kin. 14:2; see also 2 Sam. 2:10; Acts 13:21
2 [a] 1 Sam. 14:5, 31 [b] 1 Sam. 14:1 [c] 1 Sam. 10:26
3 [d] 1 Sam. 10:5 [e] 2 Sam. 5:25
4 [2] *odious*
5 [f] Judg. 7:12 [g] Josh. 7:2; 1 Sam. 14:23 [3] So with MT, LXX, Tg., Vg.; Syr. and some mss. of LXX *three thousand*
6 [h] Judg. 6:2; 1 Sam. 14:11
7 [i] Num. 32:1-42
8 [j] 1 Sam. 10:8

12:16 this great thing. Though rain during the wheat harvest (late May to early June) was unusual, the Lord sent the rain and thunder to authenticate Samuel's words to the people.

12:19 Pray for your servants. The people's response to the power of God was their recognition of their sinful motives in asking for a king. They needed Samuel's prayers to intercede for them.

12:20 serve the LORD with all your heart. An often-expressed covenant requirement (Deut. 10:12,13; 11:13,14).

12:21 empty things. "Futile things," i.e., idols.

13:1 one year...two years. The original numbers have not been preserved in this text. It lit. reads, "Saul was one year old when he became king and ruled two years over Israel." Acts 13:21 states that Saul ruled Israel 40 years. His age at his accession is recorded nowhere in Scripture. Probably the best reconstruction of vv. 1,2 is "Saul was one and (perhaps) thirty years old when he began to reign, and when he had reigned two years over Israel, then Saul chose for himself three thousand men of Israel..."

13:2 Michmash. This area was located about 7 mi. NE of Jerusalem. **Jonathan.** "The LORD has given." Saul's firstborn son and heir apparent to the throne was evidently old enough to serve as a commander in Israel's army at this time, much like David when he slew Goliath (1 Sam. 17:32-37). **Gibeah of Benjamin.** This city was located 3 mi. N of Jerusalem. It was called Gibeah of Saul in 11:4.

13:3 Geba. This outpost was located about 5 mi. NNE of Jerusalem, 1 ½ mi. SW of Michmash. **blew the trumpet.** Saul used the trumpet to summon additional troops for battle.

13:4 an abomination. Israel could expect retaliation from the Philistines for Jonathan's raid. **Gilgal.** This is the town of Saul's confirmation as king by Samuel and the people (11:14,15). Saul chose Gilgal because of Samuel's word in 10:8.

13:5 thirty thousand chariots. This is probably a scribal error, since the number is too large for the corresponding horsemen. Three thousand is more reasonable and is found in some OT manuscripts. **Michmash.** *See note on 13:2.* **Beth Aven.** Lit. "house of nothingness." It was less than one mi. SW of Michmash.

13:7 Gad and Gilead. Areas E of the Jordan River. **all the people followed him trembling.** The people were in fear over probable Philistine retaliation.

13:8 seven days...the time set by Samuel. This is a direct reference to Samuel's word in 10:8. Saul was commanded to wait 7 days to meet Samuel in Gilgal. **the people were scattered.** Saul's men were deserting him because of anxiety and fear over the coming battle.

burnt offering and peace offerings here to
me." And he offered the burnt offering.
10 Now it happened, as soon as he had finished presenting the burnt offering, that
Samuel came; and Saul went out to meet
him, that he might [4]greet him.
11 And Samuel said, "What have you
done?"
Saul said, "When I saw that the people
were scattered from me, and *that* you did
not come within the days appointed, and
that the Philistines gathered together at
Michmash, 12 then I said, 'The Philistines
will now come down on me at Gilgal, and
I have not made supplication to the LORD.'
Therefore I felt compelled, and offered a
burnt offering."
13 And Samuel said to Saul, [k]"You have
done foolishly. [l]You have not kept the commandment of the LORD your God, which He
commanded you. For now the LORD would
have established your kingdom over Israel
forever. 14 [m]But now your kingdom shall
not continue. [n]The LORD has sought for
Himself a man [o]after His own heart, and the
LORD has commanded him *to be* commander over His people, because you have [p]not
kept what the LORD commanded you."

10 [4] Lit. *bless him*
13 [k] 2 Chr. 16:9 [l] 1 Sam. 15:11, 22, 28
14 [m] 1 Sam. 15:28; 31:6 [n] 1 Sam. 16:1 [o] Ps. 89:20; Acts 7:46; 13:22 [p] 1 Sam. 15:11, 19
15 [q] 1 Sam. 13:2, 6, 7; 14:2 [5] So with MT, Tg.; LXX, Vg. add *And the rest of the people went up after Saul to meet the people who fought against them, going from Gilgal to Gibeah in the hill of Benjamin.*
16 [6] Heb. *Geba*
17 [r] Josh. 18:23
18 [s] Josh. 16:3; 18:13, 14 [t] Gen. 14:2; Neh. 11:34
19 [u] Judg. 5:8; 2 Kin. 24:14; Jer. 24:1; 29:2
21 [7] About two-thirds shekel weight

15 Then Samuel arose and went up from
Gilgal to Gibeah of [5]Benjamin. And Saul
numbered the people present with him,
[q]about six hundred men.

No Weapons for the Army

16 Saul, Jonathan his son, and the people
present with them remained in [6]Gibeah of
Benjamin. But the Philistines encamped in
Michmash. 17 Then raiders came out of the
camp of the Philistines in three companies.
One company turned onto the road to
[r]Ophrah, to the land of Shual, 18 another
company turned to the road *to* [s]Beth
Horon, and another company turned *to* the
road of the border that overlooks the Valley of [t]Zeboim toward the wilderness.
19 Now [u]there was no blacksmith to be
found throughout all the land of Israel, for
the Philistines said, "Lest the Hebrews
make swords or spears." 20 But all the Israelites would go down to the Philistines to
sharpen each man's plowshare, his mattock, his ax, and his sickle; 21 and the
charge for a sharpening was a [7]pim for the
plowshares, the mattocks, the forks, and
the axes, and to set the points of the goads.
22 So it came about, on the day of battle,

13:9 he offered the burnt offering. Saul's sin was not specifically that he made a sacrifice (cf. 2 Sam. 24:25; 1 Kin. 8:62-64), but that he did not wait for priestly assistance from Samuel. See 10:8. He wished to rule as an autocrat, who possessed absolute power in civil and sacred matters. Samuel had wanted the 7 days as a test of Saul's character and obedience to God, but Saul failed it by invading the priestly office himself.

13:11 When I saw. Saul reacted disobediently based upon what he saw and not by faith. He feared losing his men and did not properly consider what God would have him do.

13:13 You have not kept the commandment. Saul's disobedience was a direct violation of the command from Samuel in 10:8. **your kingdom...forever.** How could this be in light of God's promise to Judah (Gen. 49:10)? This only recognized the Saul was not of Judah as evidenced by his abysmal disobedience.

13:14 a man after His own heart. Instead of Saul, God was going to choose one whose heart was like his own, i.e., one who had a will to obey God. Paul quotes this passage in Acts 13:22 of David (cf. 16:7). **commander.** Someone else, namely David, had already been chosen to be God's leader over His people.

13:15 from Gilgal to Gibeah. This was about a 10 mi. trip westward. Samuel left Saul, realizing that Saul's kingship was doomed. **six hundred men.** This indicates the mass departure of the Israelites (v. 6) and gives a perspective on what Saul saw (v. 5).

13:17 raiders...in three companies. Lit. these were "destroyers" in the Philistine army, divided into 3 groups.

13:19 no blacksmith. The Philistines had superior iron and metal-working craftsmen until David's time (cf. 1 Chr. 22:3), accounting for their formidable military force.

13:20 mattock. A pickax to work the ground by hand.

13:21 The Philistines charged a high price to sharpen instruments potentially that could be used against them.

Locations of Saul's Military Campaigns

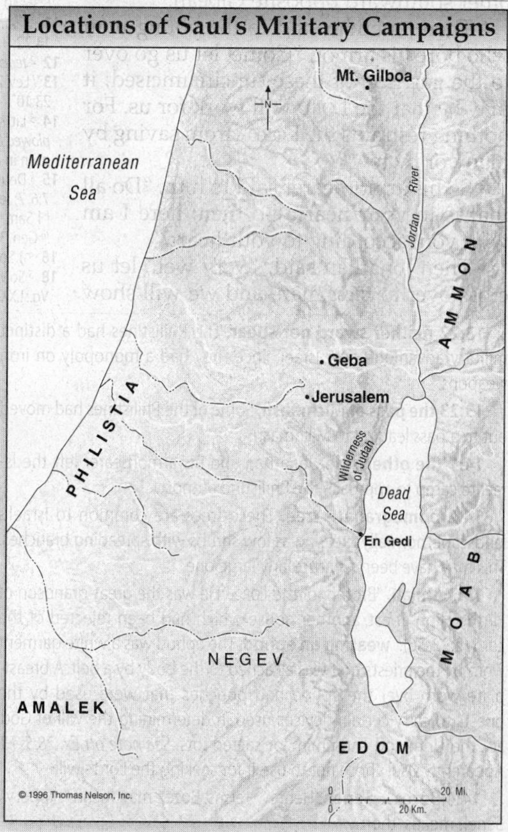

that [v]there was neither sword nor spear
found in the hand of any of the people who
were with Saul and Jonathan. But they were
found with Saul and Jonathan his son.
23 [w]And the garrison of the Philistines
went out to the pass of Michmash.

Jonathan Defeats the Philistines

14 Now it happened one day that Jonathan the son of Saul said to the young
man who [1]bore his armor, "Come, let us go
over to the Philistines' garrison that *is* on the
other side." But he did not tell his father.
2 And Saul was sitting in the outskirts of
[a]Gibeah under a pomegranate tree which *is*
in Migron. The people who *were* with him
were about six hundred men. 3 [b]Ahijah the
son of Ahitub, [c]Ichabod's brother, the son of
Phinehas, the son of Eli, the LORD's priest in
Shiloh, was [d]wearing an ephod. But the people did not know that Jonathan had gone.
4 Between the passes, by which Jonathan
sought to go over [e]to the Philistines' garrison, *there was* a sharp rock on one side and
a sharp rock on the other side. And the
name of one *was* Bozez, and the name of
the other Seneh. 5 The front of one faced
northward opposite Michmash, and the
other southward opposite Gibeah.
6 Then Jonathan said to the young man
who bore his armor, "Come, let us go over
to the garrison of these [f]uncircumcised; it
may be that the LORD will work for us. For
nothing restrains the LORD [g]from saving by
many or by few."
7 So his armorbearer said to him, "Do all
that is in your heart. Go then; here I am
with you, according to your heart."
8 Then Jonathan said, "Very well, let us
cross over to *these* men, and we will show
ourselves to them. 9 If they say thus to us,
'Wait until we come to you,' then we will
stand still in our place and not go up to
them. 10 But if they say thus, 'Come up to
us,' then we will go up. For the LORD has
delivered them into our hand, and [h]this
will be a sign to us."
11 So both of them showed themselves to
the garrison of the Philistines. And the Philistines said, "Look, the Hebrews are coming out of the holes where they have [i]hid-
den." 12 Then the men of the garrison
called to Jonathan and his armorbearer,
and said, "Come up to us, and we will
[2]show you something."
Jonathan said to his armorbearer, "Come
up after me, for the LORD has delivered
them into the hand of Israel." 13 And Jonathan climbed up on his hands and knees
with his armorbearer after him; and they
[j]fell before Jonathan. And as he came after
him, his armorbearer killed them. 14 That
first slaughter which Jonathan and his armorbearer made was about twenty men
within about [3]half an acre of land.
15 And [k]there was [4]trembling in the
camp, in the field, and among all the people. The garrison and [l]the raiders also trembled; and the earth quaked, so that it was [m]a
very great trembling. 16 Now the watchmen
of Saul in Gibeah of Benjamin looked, and
there was the multitude, melting away; and
they [n]went here and there. 17 Then Saul
said to the people who *were* with him,
"Now call the roll and see who has gone
from us." And when they had called the
roll, surprisingly, Jonathan and his armorbearer *were* not *there*. 18 And Saul said to
Ahijah, "Bring the [5]ark of God here" (for at
that time the [5]ark of God was with the chil-

22 [v]Judg. 5:8
23 [w]1 Sam. 14:1, 4

CHAPTER 14

1 [1]*carried*
2 [a]1 Sam. 13:15, 16
3 [b]1 Sam. 22:9, 11, 20 [c]1 Sam. 4:21 [d]1 Sam. 2:28
4 [e]1 Sam. 13:23
6 [f]1 Sam. 17:26, 36; Jer. 9:25, 26 [g]Judg. 7:4, 7; 1 Sam. 17:46, 47; 2 Chr. 14:11; [Ps. 115:3; 135:6; Zech. 4:6; Matt. 19:26; Rom. 8:31]
10 [h]Gen. 24:14; Judg. 6:36-40
11 [i]1 Sam. 13:6; 14:22
12 [2]*teach*
13 [j]Lev. 26:8; Josh. 23:10
14 [3]Lit. *half the area plowed by a yoke of oxen in a day*
15 [k]Deut. 28:7; 2 Kin. 7:6, 7; Job 18:11 [l]1 Sam. 13:17 [m]Gen. 35:5 [4]*terror*
16 [n]1 Sam. 14:20
18 [5]So with MT, Tg., Vg.; LXX *ephod*

13:22 neither sword nor spear. The Philistines had a distinct military advantage over Israel since they had a monopoly on iron weapons.

13:23 the pass of Michmash. Some of the Philistines had moved out to a pass leading to Michmash.

14:1 the other side. Jonathan and his armorbearer left the Israelite camp to approach the Philistine outpost.

14:2 pomegranate tree. These trees are common to Israel's landscape, normally growing as low shrubs with spreading branches. This may have been a particularly large one.

14:3 Ahijah. "Brother of the LORD." He was the great-grandson of Eli the High-Priest, another house which had been rejected of the Lord (2:22-36). **wearing an ephod.** The ephod was a white garment worn by the priests that was attached to the body by a belt. A breastplate worn over the ephod had pouches that were used by the priests to carry certain devices used in determining the will of God, i.e., the Urim and Thummim, or sacred lots. *See note on Ex. 28:5-13.* Apparently, Saul chose not to use it for seeking the Lord's will.

14:4 Bozez...Seneh. Hebrew terms. Bozez may mean "slippery." Seneh means "thorny."

14:6 uncircumcised. This was a derogatory term used by the Israelites to describe the Philistines. **by many or by few.** Jonathan demonstrated the great faith that should have been demonstrated by the king (cf. 13:11).

14:10 a sign to us. This was an unusual manner for determining the will of the Lord, but not without similar precedent, e.g., Gideon's fleece (Judg. 6:36-46). Jonathan was allowed to determine the will of God by the reaction of his enemies.

14:11 Hebrews. The oldest term used by Gentile nations to refer to the people of Israel. **the holes where they have hidden.** Many of the Israelites were hiding in fear over the battle. Apparently they thought Jonathan and his armorbearer were Israelite deserters coming to the Philistine side.

14:15 the earth quaked. The earthquake affirms the fact that divine intervention aided Jonathan and his armorbearer in their raid. The earthquake caused a panic among the Philistines. God would have intervened on Saul's behalf in such a manner had he chosen to be faithfully patient (cf. 13:9).

14:18 ark of God. The LXX reads "ephod" instead of "ark," and this seems more likely since the ark was at Kirjath Jearim and the language of 14:19 better fits the ephod (v. 3) than the ark. See marginal note.

dren of Israel). 19 Now it happened, while
Saul [o]talked to the priest, that the noise
which *was* in the camp of the Philistines
continued to increase; so Saul said to the
priest, "Withdraw your hand." 20 Then Saul
and all the people who *were* with him assembled, and they went to the battle; and
indeed [p]every man's sword was against his
neighbor, *and there was* very great confusion.
21 Moreover the Hebrews *who* were with
the Philistines before that time, who went
up with them into the camp *from the* surrounding *country,* they also joined the Israelites who *were* with Saul and Jonathan.
22 Likewise all the men of Israel who [q]had
hidden in the mountains of Ephraim, *when*
they heard that the Philistines fled, they
also followed hard after them in the battle.
23 [r]So the LORD saved Israel that day, and
the battle shifted [s]to Beth Aven.

Saul's Rash Oath

24 And the men of Israel were distressed
that day, for Saul had [t]placed the people
under oath, saying, "Cursed *is* the man
who eats *any* food until evening, before I
have taken vengeance on my enemies." So
none of the people tasted food. 25 [u]Now all
the people of the land came to a forest; and
there was [v]honey on the ground. 26 And
when the people had come into the woods,
there was the honey, dripping; but no one
put his hand to his mouth, for the people
feared the oath. 27 But Jonathan had not
heard his father charge the people with the
oath; therefore he stretched out the end of
the rod that *was* in his hand and dipped it
in a honeycomb, and put his hand to his
mouth; and his [6]countenance brightened.
28 Then one of the people said, "Your father strictly charged the people with an
oath, saying, 'Cursed *is* the man who eats
food this day.' " And the people were faint.
29 But Jonathan said, "My father has
troubled the land. Look now, how my
countenance has brightened because I tasted a little of this honey. 30 How much better if the people had eaten freely today of
the spoil of their enemies which they
found! For now would there not have been
a much greater slaughter among the Philistines?"
31 Now they had [7]driven back the Philistines that day from Michmash to Aijalon. So the people were very faint. 32 And
the people rushed on the [8]spoil, and took
sheep, oxen, and calves, and slaughtered
them on the ground; and the people ate
them [w]with the blood. 33 Then they told
Saul, saying, "Look, the people are sinning
against the LORD by eating with the
blood!"
So he said, "You have dealt treacherously; roll a large stone to me this day."
34 Then Saul said, "Disperse yourselves
among the people, and say to them, 'Bring
me here every man's ox and every man's
sheep, slaughter *them* here, and eat; and do
not sin against the LORD by eating with the
blood.' " So every one of the people
brought his ox with him that night, and
slaughtered *it* there. 35 Then Saul [x]built an
altar to the LORD. This was the first altar
that he built to the LORD.
36 Now Saul said, "Let us go down after
the Philistines by night, and plunder them
until the morning light; and let us not
leave a man of them."
And they said, "Do whatever seems
good to you."
Then the priest said, "Let us draw near
to God here."
37 So Saul [y]asked counsel of God, "Shall I
go down after the Philistines? Will You deliver them into the hand of Israel?" But [z]He
did not answer him that day. 38 And Saul

19 [o] Num. 27:21
20 [p] Judg. 7:22; 2 Chr. 20:23
22 [q] 1 Sam. 13:6
23 [r] Ex. 14:30; 2 Chr. 32:22; Hos. 1:7 [s] 1 Sam. 13:5
24 [t] Josh. 6:26
25 [u] Deut. 9:28; Matt. 3:5 [v] Ex. 3:8; Num. 13:27; Matt. 3:4
27 [6] Lit. *eyes*
31 [7] Lit. *struck*
32 [w] Gen. 9:4; Lev. 3:17; 17:10-14; 19:26; Deut. 12:16, 23, 24; Acts 15:20 [8] *plunder*
35 [x] 1 Sam. 7:12, 17; 2 Sam. 24:25
37 [y] Judg. 20:18 [z] 1 Sam. 28:6

14:19 Withdraw your hand. Saul, in a hurry, ordered the priest to stop the inquiry into the will of the Lord.

14:21 Hebrews. This is a reference to Israelite deserters or mercenaries.

14:22 the mountains of Ephraim. A large and partially wooded area N and W of Michmash.

14:23 So the LORD saved Israel. The writer uses similar language to that of the Exodus. In spite of their disobedient king, God was faithful to deliver Israel from her enemies. **Beth Aven.** *See note on 13:5.*

14:24 were distressed. Saul's inept leadership failed to provide for the physical needs of his men, leaving them weak and fatigued. **Cursed.** Saul's first foolish oath pronounced a curse upon anyone tasting food until the battle was over. The scene fits chronologically after Jonathan's departure.

14:25 honey on the ground. This was a reference to honeycombs found in the forest (v. 27).

14:27 Jonathan had not heard. Jonathan apparently had departed before Saul made his oath.

14:29 My father has troubled the land. Jonathan saw the foolishness of Saul's oath and how it actually hurt Israel's cause instead of helping it.

14:31 Aijalon. This area is located 15 mi. W of Michmash. This would have been a normal path back to the land of the Philistines.

14:32 ate *them* with the blood. The people were so severely hungry because of the oath (v. 24) that they disobeyed the law by eating the meat raw and not draining the blood (cf. Lev. 17:10-14).

14:35 the first altar. The first and only altar built by Saul mentioned in Scripture.

14:36 Let us draw near to God. Ahijah the priest requested that they first seek the Lord regarding their course of action.

14:37 Saul asked counsel of God. At the request of Ahijah, Saul inquired of the Lord regarding his battle plan. **He did not answer him.** Because of the sin that Saul had caused in his army, God did not answer his inquiry. This would not be the last time that the Lord would refuse to respond to sinful Saul (cf. 28:6).

said, [a]"Come over here, all you chiefs of the people, and know and see what this sin was today. 39 For [b]*as* the LORD lives, who saves Israel, though it be in Jonathan my son, he shall surely die." But not a man among all the people answered him. 40 Then he said to all Israel, "You be on one side, and my son Jonathan and I will be on the other side."

And the people said to Saul, "Do what seems good to you."

41 Therefore Saul said to the LORD God of Israel, [c]"Give[9] a perfect *lot*." [d]So Saul and Jonathan were taken, but the people escaped. 42 And Saul said, "Cast *lots* between my son Jonathan and me." So Jonathan was taken. 43 Then Saul said to Jonathan, [e]"Tell me what you have done."

And Jonathan told him, and said, [f]"I only tasted a little honey with the end of the rod that *was* in my hand. So now I must die!"

44 Saul answered, [g]"God do so and more also; [h]for you shall surely die, Jonathan."

45 But the people said to Saul, "Shall Jonathan die, who has accomplished this great deliverance in Israel? Certainly not! [i]*As* the LORD lives, not one hair of his head shall fall to the ground, for he has worked [j]with God this day." So the people rescued Jonathan, and he did not die.

46 Then Saul returned from pursuing the Philistines, and the Philistines went to their own place.

Saul's Continuing Wars

47 So Saul established his sovereignty over Israel, and fought against all his enemies on every side, against Moab, against the people of [k]Ammon, against Edom, against the kings of [l]Zobah, and against the Philistines. Wherever he turned, he [1]harassed *them.* 48 And he gathered an army and [m]attacked[2] the Amalekites, and delivered Israel from the hands of those who plundered them.

49 [n]The sons of Saul were Jonathan, [3]Jishui, and Malchishua. And the names of his two daughters *were these:* the name of the firstborn Merab, and the name of the younger [o]Michal. 50 The name of Saul's wife *was* Ahinoam the daughter of Ahimaaz. And the name of the commander of his army *was* Abner the son of Ner, Saul's [p]uncle. 51 [q]Kish *was* the father of Saul, and Ner the father of Abner *was* the son of Abiel.

52 Now there was fierce war with the Philistines all the days of Saul. And when Saul saw any strong man or any valiant man, [r]he took him for himself.

Saul Spares King Agag

15 Samuel also said to Saul, [a]"The LORD sent me to anoint you king over His people, over Israel. Now therefore, heed the voice of the words of the LORD. 2 Thus says the LORD of hosts: 'I will punish Amalek *for* what he did to Israel, [b]how he ambushed him on the way when he came up from Egypt. 3 Now go and [c]attack[1] Amalek, and [d]utterly destroy all that they have, and do not spare them. But kill both man and woman, infant and nursing child, ox and sheep, camel and donkey.' "

4 So Saul gathered the people together and numbered them in Telaim, two hundred thousand foot soldiers and ten thousand men of Judah. 5 And Saul came to a city of Amalek, and lay in wait in the valley.

6 Then Saul said to [e]the Kenites, [f]"Go, depart, get down from among the Amalekites, lest I destroy you with them. For

38 [a] Josh. 7:14; 1 Sam. 10:19
39 [b] 1 Sam. 14:24, 44; 2 Sam. 12:5
41 [c] Prov. 16:33; Acts 1:24-26 [d] Josh. 7:16; 1 Sam. 10:20, 21 [9] So with MT, Tg.; LXX, Vg. *Why do You not answer Your servant today? If the injustice is with me or Jonathan my son, O* LORD *God of Israel, give proof; and if You say it is with Your people Israel, give holiness.*
43 [e] Josh. 7:19 [f] 1 Sam. 14:27
44 [g] Ruth 1:17; 1 Sam. 25:22 [h] 1 Sam. 14:39
45 [i] 2 Sam. 14:11; 1 Kin. 1:52; Luke 21:18; Acts 27:34 [j] [2 Cor. 6:1; Phil. 2:12, 13]
47 [k] 1 Sam. 11:1-13 [l] 2 Sam. 10:6 [1] LXX, Vg. *prospered*
48 [m] Ex. 17:16; 1 Sam. 15:3-7 [2] Lit. *struck*
49 [n] 1 Sam. 31:2; 1 Chr. 8:33 [o] 1 Sam. 18:17-20, 27; 19:12 [3] *Abinadab,* 1 Chr. 8:33; 9:39
50 [p] 1 Sam. 10:14
51 [q] 1 Sam. 9:1, 21
52 [r] 1 Sam. 8:11

CHAPTER 15

1 [a] 1 Sam. 9:16; 10:1
2 [b] Ex. 17:8, 14; Num. 24:20; Deut. 25:17-19
3 [c] Deut. 25:19 [d] Lev. 27:28, 29; Num. 24:20; Deut. 20:16-18; Josh. 6:17-21 [1] Lit. *strike*
6 [e] Num. 24:21; Judg. 1:16; 4:11-22; 1 Chr. 2:55 [f] Gen. 18:25; 19:12, 14; Rev. 18:4

14:39 *as* the LORD lives. As an encore to his previous oath, Saul followed with another foolish oath, unknowingly jeopardizing his own son's life.

14:41 taken. The practice of casting lots was used to distinguish one person or group from another. Jonathan was indicated as the guilty party, though he acted innocently (v. 27).

14:44 God do so and more also. Saul, proud and concerned with his own authority and honor, was intent on fulfilling his vow.

14:45 worked with God this day. Jonathan, in stark contrast to his father the king, understood the sufficiency of God for the task and obediently relied on Him for the victory.

14:46 the Philistines went to their own place. The Philistines were left to continue their retreat unhindered.

14:47,48 Saul's military accomplishments were significant and expanded Israel's borders in all directions: to the S (Edom), E (Ammon and Moab), N (Zobah), and W (Philistia). The defeat of the Amalekites is recorded in chap. 15.

14:49-51 Saul's children, Jonathan and Michal, would both play significant roles in the life of the next king, David. Nothing further is known of Saul's wife or other children mentioned here.

14:50 Abner. A cousin of Saul who commanded his army (cf. 1 Sam. 17:55, 59; 20:25; 26:14, 15).

14:52 fierce war. The Philistines' opposition to Israel was persistent and continual to the very last day of Saul's life (1 Sam. 31:1-3). **strong…valiant man.** Saul looked for the good warriors and attached them to his personal force. David was one such man, who would also continue this practice under his rule (2 Sam. 23:8-39).

15:2 Amalek. The Amalekites, a nomadic people of the desert and descendants of Esau (Gen. 36:12), became a marked people when they attacked Israel in the wilderness after leaving Egypt (*see notes on Ex. 17:8-16*; cf. Num. 24:20; Deut. 25:17-19; Judg. 6:3-5).

15:3 utterly destroy. God gave Saul an opportunity to redeem himself with obedience. The judgment was to be a complete and total annihilation of anything that breathed. God's judgment was severe on those who would destroy His people. It was equally severe to those who disobeyed (cf. Achan in Josh. 7:10-26).

15:4 Telaim. The precise location of this area is unknown, but it may be a reference to Telem found in Josh. 15:24.

15:5 a city of Amalek. This was possibly modern-day Tel Masos located about 7 mi. ESE of Beersheba.

15:6 the Kenites. Moses' father-in-law was a Kenite (cf. Judg. 1:16), a people friendly to the Israelites.

[g]you showed kindness to all the children
of Israel when they came up out of Egypt."
So the Kenites departed from among the
Amalekites. 7 [h]And Saul attacked the
Amalekites, from [i]Havilah all the way to
[j]Shur, which is east of Egypt. 8 [k]He also
took Agag king of the Amalekites alive,
and [l]utterly destroyed all the people with
the edge of the sword. 9 But Saul and the
people [m]spared Agag and the best of the
sheep, the oxen, the fatlings, the lambs,
and all *that was* good, and were unwilling
to utterly destroy them. But everything despised and worthless, that they utterly destroyed.

Saul Rejected as King

10 Now the word of the LORD came to
Samuel, saying, 11 [n]"I greatly regret that I
have set up Saul *as* king, for he has [o]turned
back from following Me, [p]and has not performed My commandments." And it
[q]grieved Samuel, and he cried out to the
LORD all night. 12 So when Samuel rose
early in the morning to meet Saul, it was
told Samuel, saying, "Saul went to
[r]Carmel, and indeed, he set up a monument for himself; and he has gone on
around, passed by, and gone down to Gilgal." 13 Then Samuel went to Saul, and
Saul said to him, [s]"Blessed *are* you of the
LORD! I have performed the commandment of the LORD."
14 But Samuel said, "What then *is* this
bleating of the sheep in my ears, and the
lowing of the oxen which I hear?"
15 And Saul said, "They have brought
them from the Amalekites; [t]for the people
spared the best of the sheep and the oxen,
to sacrifice to the LORD your God; and the
rest we have utterly destroyed."
16 Then Samuel said to Saul, "Be quiet!
And I will tell you what the LORD said to
me last night."
And he said to him, "Speak on."
17 So Samuel said, [u]"When you *were* little in your own eyes, *were* you not head of
the tribes of Israel? And did not the LORD
anoint you king over Israel? 18 Now the
LORD sent you on a mission, and said, 'Go,
and utterly destroy the sinners, the Amalekites, and fight against them until they
are [2]consumed.' 19 Why then did you not
obey the voice of the LORD? Why did you
swoop down on the [3]spoil, and do evil in
the sight of the LORD?"
20 And Saul said to Samuel, [v]"But I have
obeyed the voice of the LORD, and gone on
the mission on which the LORD sent me,
and brought back Agag king of Amalek; I
have utterly destroyed the Amalekites.
21 [w]But the people took of the plunder,
sheep and oxen, the best of the things
which should have been utterly destroyed, to sacrifice to the LORD your God
in Gilgal."
22 So Samuel said:

[x]"Has the LORD *as great* delight in
burnt offerings and sacrifices,
As in obeying the voice of the
LORD?
Behold, [y]to obey is better than
sacrifice,
And to heed than the fat of rams.

6 [g]Ex. 18:10, 19; Num. 10:29, 32
7 [h]1 Sam. 14:48 [i]Gen. 2:11; 25:17, 18 [j]Gen. 16:7; Ex. 15:22; 1 Sam. 27:8
8 [k]1 Sam. 15:32, 33 [l]1 Sam. 27:8, 9
9 [m]1 Sam. 15:3, 15, 19
11 [n]Gen. 6:6, 7; 1 Sam. 15:35; 2 Sam. 24:16 [o]Josh. 22:16; 1 Kin. 9:6 [p]1 Sam. 13:13; 15:3, 9 [q]1 Sam. 15:35; 16:1
12 [r]Josh. 15:55; 1 Sam. 25:2
13 [s]Gen. 14:19; Judg. 17:2; Ruth 3:10; 2 Sam. 2:5
15 [t][Gen. 3:12, 13; Ex. 32:22, 23]; 1 Sam. 15:9, 21; [Prov. 28:13]
17 [u]1 Sam. 9:21; 10:22
18 [2]*exterminated*
19 [3]*plunder*
20 [v]1 Sam. 15:13; [Prov. 28:13]
21 [w]1 Sam. 15:15
22 [x]Ps. 50:8, 9; 51:16, 17; [Prov. 21:3; Is. 1:11-17; Jer. 7:22, 23; Mic. 6:6-8; Heb. 10:4-10] [y][Eccl. 5:1; Hos. 6:6; Matt. 5:24; 9:13; 12:7; Mark 12:33]

15:7 from Havilah…to Shur. Saul's victory was extensive, covering much of the Amalekite territory. However, the Amalekites were not completely destroyed (cf. 27:8; 30:1).

15:8 Agag. Another example of Saul's incomplete obedience, in the case of Agag, is recorded because it had such far-reaching implications. Over 5 centuries later an Agagite named Haman attempted to exterminate the Jewish race from his power base in Persia (cf. Esth. 3:1ff.). **all the people.** The Israelites killed everyone they came across, except for the king.

15:9 Saul and the people spared. Motivated by covetousness, both Saul and the people greedily spared the choice spoil of the land, disobeying God's Word and demonstrating their faithlessness.

15:11 grieved Samuel. Samuel's role as priest over the people gave him great concern over the poor performance of the king, who was like the kings of other nations (1 Sam. 6:19,20) i.e., self-centered, self-willed, and utterly disobedient to the things of God.

15:12 Carmel. This is not Mt. Carmel of Elijah fame (1 Kin. 18:20ff.), but a Carmel located 7 mi. S of Hebron. **monument for himself.** Saul, apparently taking credit for the victory, established a monument to himself (cf. Absalom in 2 Sam. 18:18). This foolish act of contemptible pride was Saul's expression of self-worship rather than true worship of God and another evidence of his spiritual weakness. **Gilgal.** The site of Samuel's first confrontation with Saul (13:7b-15) became the site of this pronouncement of judgment.

15:13 I have performed the commandment of the LORD. Saul, either ignorantly or deceitfully, maintained that he did what was commanded (15:20).

15:15 the people spared the best…to sacrifice. Saul began to place blame on others, making room for his own excuses just as he had done earlier (cf. 13:11,12). Then he tried to justify his sin by saying that the animals would be used to sacrifice to the God of Samuel. Saul's blatant disobedience at least pained his conscience so that he could not claim God as his God.

15:17 little in your own eyes. Saul's status before he became king was as a humble and lowly Benjamite (cf. 9:21).

15:19 swoop down on the spoil. Saul and the people greedily took the spoil like a bird of prey diving on its victim.

15:20,21 I have obeyed the voice of the LORD. Instead of confessing his sin and repenting, Saul continued to justify himself.

15:22 to obey is better than sacrifice. This is an essential OT truth. Samuel stated that God desires heart obedience over the ritual sacrifice of animals (cf. Ps. 51:16,17; Is. 1:10-17). The sacrificial system was never intended to function in place of living an obedient life, but was rather to be an expression of it (cf. Hos. 6:6; Amos 5:21-27; Mic. 6:6-8).

23 For rebellion *is as* the sin of
[4]witchcraft,
And stubbornness *is as* iniquity
and idolatry.
Because you have rejected the
word of the LORD,
[z]He also has rejected you from *being*
king."

24 [a]Then Saul said to Samuel, "I have
sinned, for I have transgressed the commandment of the LORD and your words,
because I [b]feared the people and obeyed
their voice. 25 Now therefore, please pardon my sin, and return with me, that I may
worship the LORD."
26 But Samuel said to Saul, "I will not return with you, [c]for you have rejected the
word of the LORD, and the LORD has rejected you from being king over Israel."
27 And as Samuel turned around to go
away, [d]*Saul* seized the edge of his robe, and
it tore. 28 So Samuel said to him, [e]"The
LORD has torn the kingdom of Israel from
you today, and has given it to a neighbor of
yours, *who is* better than you. 29 And also
the Strength of Israel [f]will not lie nor relent.
For He *is* not a man, that He should relent."
30 Then he said, "I have sinned; *yet*
[g]honor me now, please, before the elders of
my people and before Israel, and return
with me, that I may worship the LORD your
God." 31 So Samuel turned back after Saul,
and Saul worshiped the LORD.
32 Then Samuel said, "Bring Agag king
of the Amalekites here to me." So Agag
came to him cautiously.
And Agag said, "Surely the bitterness of
death is past."
33 But Samuel said, [h]"As your sword has
made women childless, so shall your
mother be childless among women." And
Samuel hacked Agag in pieces before the
LORD in Gilgal.
34 Then Samuel went to [i]Ramah, and
Saul went up to his house at [j]Gibeah of
Saul. 35 And [k]Samuel went no more to
see Saul until the day of his death. Nevertheless Samuel mourned for Saul, and the
LORD regretted that He had made Saul
king over Israel.

David Anointed King

16 Now the LORD said to Samuel,
[a]"How long will you mourn for
Saul, seeing I have rejected him from reigning over Israel? [b]Fill your horn with oil,
and go; I am sending you to [c]Jesse the
Bethlehemite. For [d]I have [1]provided Myself a king among his sons."
2 And Samuel said, "How can I go? If
Saul hears *it*, he will kill me."
But the LORD said, "Take a heifer with
you, and say, [e]'I have come to sacrifice to

23 [z]1 Sam. 13:14; 16:1 [4]*divination*
24 [a]Num. 22:34; Josh. 7:20; 1 Sam. 26:21; 2 Sam. 12:13; Ps. 51:4 [b][Ex. 23:2; Prov. 29:25; Is. 51:12, 13]
26 [c]1 Sam. 2:30
27 [d]1 Kin. 11:30, 31
28 [e]1 Sam. 28:17, 18; 1 Kin. 11:31
29 [f]Num. 23:19; Ezek. 24:14; 2 Tim. 2:13; Titus 1:2
30 [g][John 5:44; 12:43]
33 [h][Gen. 9:6]; Num. 14:45; Judg. 1:7; [Matt. 7:2]
34 [i]1 Sam. 7:17 [j]1 Sam. 11:4
35 [k]1 Sam. 19:24

CHAPTER 16

1 [a]1 Sam. 15:23, 35 [b]1 Sam. 9:16; 10:1; 2 Kin. 9:1 [c]Ruth 4:18-22 [d]Ps. 78:70, 71; Acts 13:22 [1]Lit. *seen*
2 [e]1 Sam. 9:12

15:23 rebellion...stubbornness. Saul needed to see that his real worship was indicated by his behavior and not by his sacrifices. He demonstrated himself to be an idolater whose idol was himself. He had failed the conditions (12:13-15) which would have brought blessing on the nation. His disobedience here was on the same level as witchcraft and idolatry, sins worthy of death. **Because you have rejected...He also has rejected.** A universal principle is given here that those who continually reject God will one day be rejected by Him. The sins of Saul caused God to immediately depose Saul and his descendants forever from the throne of Israel.

15:24 I have sinned. This overdue confession appears to be generated more by a concern over consequences (regret) than by sorrow over having offended holy God (repentance). He bypasses his personal responsibility by shifting blame to the people.

15:25 return with me. Saul was concerned about having Samuel's visible presence as a show of support in front of the people (cf. 15:30).

15:28 torn the kingdom. Saul's judgment was a settled matter on the day of his disobedience with the Amalekites. Samuel used the illustration as it vividly portrayed how God would take the kingdom from Saul as he had just torn Samuel's robe. **a neighbor of yours.** This was a reference to David (cf. 28:17).

15:29 the Strength of Israel. This was a unique title of God. It could also be translated "the glory of Israel" (cf. Mic. 1:15). **will not lie nor relent.** Samuel emphasized God's attribute of immutability in regard to the judgment upon Saul.

15:30 honor me. Saul was still thinking of himself and how he could best salvage the situation for self-gain.

15:31 Samuel turned back. Samuel agreed to follow Saul, perhaps seeing this as the wisest course of action for the nation at that time.

15:33 hacked Agag in pieces. This was an act of divine judgment to show the holy wrath of God against wanton sin. Sadly, the Israelites did not exterminate the wicked Amalekites, so they came back later to raid the southern territory and take women and children captive, including David's family (see 1 Sam. 30).

15:35 Samuel went no more...mourned. Samuel never went to visit the rejected King Saul again in his life (cf. 1 Sam. 28:11-19). On at least one further occasion, Saul sought Samuel (cf. 19:24).

16:1–31:13 The third major division of Samuel recounts the steady demise of Saul and the selection and preparation of David for the kingship. Chapter 16 begins with Samuel mourning for Saul as one would mourn for the dead. The death of Saul (31:1-13) concludes this last division of the book.

16:1 Jesse the Bethlehemite. God's new king of Israel (and ultimately the Messiah; Gen. 3:15; Num. 24:17; 1 Sam. 2:10; Ps. 2) would come from the tribe of Judah (Jesse; cf. Ruth 4:12,22; Gen. 49:10) and from Bethlehem of Judah (cf. Mic. 5:2; Matt. 2:2-6). **I have provided Myself.** The king was chosen and provided by God (Deut. 17:15), who orders all things according to the counsel of His own will (Is. 40:14), not according to human desires (8:5,6; 2 Sam. 2:8,9).

16:2 Saul...will kill me. Saul's unbalanced emotional state was already known in Israel. It is ironic that Samuel's initial reaction to the word of the Lord was fear of Saul instead of rejoicing at God's provision to Israel (and ultimately to all the nations; e.g., 1 Kin. 8:41-43). The route from Ramah to Bethlehem would take Samuel through Gibeah of Saul (cf. 10:26; 11:14). **I have come to sacrifice.** The place of sacrifice could be in any town until the establishment of the house of God in Jerusalem (Deut. 12:11).

the LORD.' 3 Then invite Jesse to the sacrifice, and I will show you what you shall
do; you shall anoint for Me the one I name
to you."
4 So Samuel did what the LORD said, and
went to Bethlehem. And the elders of the
town [f]trembled at his coming, and said,
[g]"Do you come peaceably?"
5 And he said, "Peaceably; I have come
to sacrifice to the LORD. [h]Sanctify[2] yourselves, and come with me to the sacrifice."
Then he consecrated Jesse and his sons,
and invited them to the sacrifice.
6 So it was, when they came, that he
looked at [i]Eliab and [j]said, "Surely the
LORD's anointed *is* before Him!"
7 But the LORD said to Samuel, [k]"Do not
look at his appearance or at his physical
stature, because I have [3]refused him. [l]For[4]
the LORD does not *see* as man sees; for man
[m]looks at the outward appearance, but the
LORD looks at the [n]heart."
8 So Jesse called Abinadab, and made
him pass before Samuel. And he said,
"Neither has the LORD chosen this one."
9 Then Jesse made Shammah pass by. And
he said, "Neither has the LORD chosen this
one." 10 Thus Jesse made seven of his sons
pass before Samuel. And Samuel said to
Jesse, "The LORD has not chosen these."
11 And Samuel said to Jesse, "Are all the
young men here?" Then he said, "There remains yet the youngest, and there he is,
keeping the [o]sheep."
And Samuel said to Jesse, "Send and
bring him. For we will not [5]sit down till he
comes here." 12 So he sent and brought
him in. Now he *was* [p]ruddy, [q]with [6]bright
eyes, and good-looking. [r]And the LORD
said, "Arise, anoint him; for this *is* the
one!" 13 Then Samuel took the horn of oil
and anointed him in the midst of his brothers; and [s]the Spirit of the LORD came upon
David from that day forward. So Samuel
arose and went to Ramah.

A Distressing Spirit Troubles Saul

14 [t]But the Spirit of the LORD departed
from Saul, and [u]a distressing spirit from
the LORD troubled him. 15 And Saul's servants said to him, "Surely, a distressing
spirit from God is troubling you. 16 Let our
master now command your servants, *who
are* before you, to seek out a man *who is* a

4 [f] 1 Sam. 21:1 [g] 1 Kin. 2:13; 2 Kin. 9:22
5 [h] Gen. 35:2; Ex. 19:10 [2] *Consecrate*
6 [i] 1 Sam. 17:13, 28 [j] 1 Kin. 12:26
7 [k] Ps. 147:10 [l] Is. 55:8, 9 [m] 2 Cor. 10:7 [n] 1 Kin. 8:39 [3] *rejected* [4] LXX *For God does not see as man sees;* Tg. *It is not by the appearance of a man;* Vg. *Nor do I judge according to the looks of a man*
11 [o] 2 Sam. 7:8; Ps. 78:70-72 [5] So with LXX, Vg.; MT *turn around;* Tg., Syr. *turn away*
12 [p] 1 Sam. 17:42 [q] Gen. 39:6; Ex. 2:2; Acts 7:20 [r] 1 Sam. 9:17 [6] Lit. *beautiful*
13 [s] Num. 27:18; 1 Sam. 10:6, 9, 10
14 [t] Judg. 16:20; 1 Sam. 11:6; 18:12; 28:15 [u] Judg. 9:23; 1 Sam. 16:15, 16; 18:10; 19:9; 1 Kin. 22:19-22

16:3 anoint. David's first anointing was performed by Samuel, symbolizing God's recognition/ordination (cf. 2:10). The following two anointings (2 Sam. 2:7; 5:3) were to establish David as king publicly for the benefit of Judah and Israel respectively.

16:4 the elders of the town trembled. The elders, and no doubt all Israel, had heard of Samuel's execution of Agag (15:33). Israel still closely associated the "seer," or prophet, with the not-so-distant past office of "judge."

16:5 Sanctify yourselves. Worship of Yahweh was always preceded by cleansing or washing, both of the outward garments and the inner man (Ex. 19:10,14; 1 John 1:9).

16:6 Eliab. Lit. "My God is Father." Since Eliab was the first of Jesse's sons to catch Samuel's eye, he must have been an impressive young man by outward appearance.

16:7 his appearance...physical stature. Samuel needed to be reminded that God's anointed was not chosen because of physical attributes. This was initially a difficult concept for Samuel as he was accustomed to a king whose only positive attributes were physical. **the LORD looks at the heart.** The Hebrew concept of "heart" embodies emotions, will, intellect, and desires. The life of the man will reflect his heart (cf. Matt. 12:34,35).

16:8 Abinadab. Lit. "My Father is noble." Samuel, now more sensitive to the leading of God's Spirit, quickly discerned that Abinadab was not God's anointed.

16:9 Shammah. Lit. "Yahweh hears (or heard)." See 16:8.

16:10 seven...sons. With David, Jesse had 8 sons. The fact that 1 Chr. 2:13 indicates 7 sons must mean that one of the 8 died afterward and this is not considered in the Chronicles account.

16:11 the youngest...keeping the sheep. God's favor/choice often fell on the younger and the least (cf. Jacob, Joseph, Gideon). David, although the youngest, was the firstborn over Israel (Ps. 89:27), whose humble beginnings as a shepherd, and later rule as king, typify Jesus: the ultimate Shepherd and King of Israel.

16:12 ruddy...bright eyes...good-looking. God's chosen king was handsome to look at, although that was not the reason for his selection by God. His appearance was perhaps enhanced by a genuine faith and joy in Yahweh. See also 17:42.

16:13 anointed him in the midst of his brothers. David's first anointing is before his family/house. His second anointing would be before the assembly of his tribe, Judah; and his third anointing would be before the nation Israel. (*See note on 16:3.*) **the Spirit of the LORD came upon David.** This familiar OT expression relates to empowerment for some God-given task (cf. 10:6,11; 11:6; 19:20,23; 2 Sam. 23:2; 2 Chr. 20:14; Is. 11:2; 61:1; Ezek. 11:5; 37:1). David's anointing was an external symbol of an inward work of God. The operation of the Holy Spirit in this case was not for regeneration, but for empowerment to perform his (David's) role in God's program for Israel (cf. Saul, 10:6). After David sinned with Bathsheba (2 Sam. 11,12), he prayed, "...Do not take Your Holy Spirit from me" (Ps. 51:11).

16:14 the Spirit of the LORD departed from Saul. When David's ascent to the throne began, Saul's slow and painful descent began also (cf. 18:12). Without God's empowering Holy Spirit, Saul was effectively no longer king over Israel (15:28), although his physical removal from the throne, and his death, happened many years later. **a distressing spirit.** God, in His sovereignty, allowed an evil spirit to torment Saul (cf. Judg. 9:23; 1 Kin. 22:19-23; Job 1:6-12) for His purpose of establishing the throne of David. This spirit, a messenger from Satan, is to be distinguished from a troubled emotional state brought on by indwelling sin, or the harmful consequences of the sinful acts of others (e.g., spirit of jealousy, Num. 5:14). This demon spirit attacked Saul from without, for there is no evidence that the demon indwelt Saul. **troubled him.** Saul, whose inward constitution was already prone to questionable judgment and the fear of men, began to experience God's judgment in the form of severe bouts of depression, anger, and delusion, initiated and aggravated by the evil spirit assigned to him. There are several NT occasions where God turned people over to demons or Satan for judgment (see Acts 5:1-3; 1 Cor. 5:1-7; 1 Tim. 1:18-20). He also used Satan or demons for the strengthening of the saints. See Job 1:1–2:6; Matt. 4:1ff.; Luke 22:31,32; 2 Cor. 12:7-10.

skillful player on the harp. And it shall be
that he will [v]play it with his hand when
the [7]distressing spirit from God is upon
you, and you shall be well."
17 So Saul said to his servants, [8]"Provide
me now a man who can play well, and
bring *him* to me."
18 Then one of the servants answered
and said, "Look, I have seen a son of Jesse
the Bethlehemite, *who is* skillful in playing,
a mighty man of valor, a man of war, prudent in speech, and a handsome person;
and [w]the LORD *is* with him."
19 Therefore Saul sent messengers to
Jesse, and said, "Send me your son David,
who *is* with the sheep." 20 And Jesse [x]took
a donkey *loaded with* bread, a skin of wine,
and a young goat, and sent *them* by his son
David to Saul. 21 So David came to Saul
and [y]stood before him. And he loved him
greatly, and he became his armorbearer.
22 Then Saul sent to Jesse, saying, "Please
let David stand before me, for he has found
favor in my sight." 23 And so it was, whenever the spirit from God was upon Saul,
that David would take a harp and play *it*
with his hand. Then Saul would become
refreshed and well, and the distressing
spirit would depart from him.

David and Goliath

17 Now the Philistines gathered their
armies together to battle, and were
gathered at [a]Sochoh, which *belongs* to Judah; they encamped between Sochoh and
Azekah, in Ephes Dammim. 2 And Saul
and the men of Israel were gathered together, and they encamped in the Valley of
Elah, and drew up in battle array against
the Philistines. 3 The Philistines stood on a
mountain on one side, and Israel stood on
a mountain on the other side, with a valley
between them.
4 And a champion went out from the
camp of the Philistines, named [b]Goliath,
from [c]Gath, whose height *was* six cubits
and a span. 5 *He had* a bronze helmet on his
head, and he *was* [1]armed with a coat of
mail, and the weight of the coat *was* five
thousand shekels of bronze. 6 And *he had*
bronze armor on his legs and a bronze
javelin between his shoulders. 7 Now the
staff of his spear *was* like a weaver's beam,
and his iron spearhead *weighed* six hundred shekels; and a shield-bearer went before him. 8 Then he stood and cried out to
the armies of Israel, and said to them,
"Why have you come out to line up for
battle? *Am* I not a Philistine, and you the
[d]servants of Saul? Choose a man for yourselves, and let him come down to me. 9 If
he is able to fight with me and kill me, then
we will be your servants. But if I prevail
against him and kill him, then you shall be
our servants and [e]serve us." 10 And the
Philistine said, "I [f]defy the armies of Israel
this day; give me a man, that we may fight
together." 11 When Saul and all Israel
heard these words of the Philistine, they
were dismayed and greatly afraid.
12 Now David *was* [g]the son of that
[h]Ephrathite of Bethlehem Judah, whose

16 [v] 1 Sam. 18:10; 19:9; 2 Kin. 3:15 [7] Lit. *evil*
17 [8] Lit. *Look now for a man for me*
18 [w] 1 Sam. 3:19; 18:12, 14
20 [x] 1 Sam. 10:4, 27; Prov. 18:16
21 [y] Gen. 41:46; Prov. 22:29

CHAPTER 17
1 [a] Josh. 15:35; 2 Chr. 28:18
4 [b] 2 Sam. 21:19 [c] Josh. 11:21, 22
5 [1] *clothed with scaled body armor*
8 [d] 1 Sam. 8:17
9 [e] 1 Sam. 11:1
10 [f] 1 Sam. 17:26, 36, 45; 2 Sam. 21:21
12 [g] Ruth 4:22; 1 Sam. 16:1, 18; 17:58 [h] Gen. 35:19

16:16 he will play...you shall be well. God used the evil which had befallen Saul to introduce David into the court of the king and to the watching eyes of Israel.

16:18 skillful in playing...a handsome person. The writer of Samuel introduces David the sweet psalmist of Israel (2 Sam. 23:1) before introducing David the warrior. Later proven so skillful in the art of war and killing, David was also a tender musician of exceptional skill and reputation. **the LORD *is* with him.** The saints of God, OT and NT, are recognized by their fruit (2:26; Luke 2:40). God's approval of David was already recognized by certain people in Israel.

16:19 Send me your son David. Verbal link with 16:1, "I have provided myself a king among his (Jesse's) sons." David's lineage was of importance to Saul in the near future when he arranged a marriage between Michal, his daughter, and David. **with the sheep.** David's lowly, humble occupation is emphasized. He gave evidence of that humility and patience as he returned faithfully to his duty following Samuel's anointing.

16:21 he loved him greatly. Saul loved David for his abilities, but later grew to jealously hate him because he knew he was blessed by the Lord (cf. 18:29). **his armorbearer.** David was most likely one of many such young men assigned to Saul's barracks.

17:1 Sochoh...Azekah...Ephes Dammim. Following the anointing of David and his installation into the court of the king, there is this update on the situation of Israel in regards to Israel's enemies. Sochoh and Azekah were towns of Judah (Josh. 15:20,35; Jer. 34:7) approximately 15 mi. W and 17 mi. NW (respectively) of Bethlehem. Ephes Dammim (1 Chr. 11:12,13; cf., 2 Sam. 23:9), the camp of the Philistines, probably lay one mi. to the S of Azekah.

17:2 Valley of Elah. Where the camp of Israel was, approximately 3 mi. E of Ephes Dammin.

17:4-7 On human terms alone, Goliath was invincible. However, David counted on the Lord being with him and making the difference (17:34-37).

17:4 champion. Lit. "the man between two." An appropriate appellation as Goliath stood between the two armies of the Philistines and Israel, and offered his challenge to a "duel" of hand-to-hand combat, the outcome of which would settle the battle for both sides. **Gath.** One of the 5 chief, Philistine cities, located 5 mi. W of Azekah. **six cubits and a span.** One cubit measures approximately 18 in. and one span about 9 in., making Goliath about 9 ft. 9 in. in height (cf. "Egyptian," 1 Chr. 11:23, and "Og of Bashan," Deut. 3:11).

17:5 five thousand shekels. 125 lbs.

17:7 six hundred shekels. 15 lbs.

17:11 Saul...dismayed and greatly afraid. Saul and Israel had proven themselves to be greatly concerned with outward appearances (10:23,24; 15:30) and able to be influenced by the fear of men (12:12; 15:24). It is only natural that Goliath would be their worst nightmare come true.

17:12 Ephrathite. Ephrath(ah), another name for the Bethlehem in Judah (cf. Ruth 4:11; Mic. 5:2).

name *was* Jesse, and who had [i]eight sons.
And the man was old, advanced *in years,* in
the days of Saul. 13 The three oldest sons of
Jesse had gone to follow Saul to the battle.
The [j]names of his three sons who went to
the battle *were* Eliab the firstborn, next to
him Abinadab, and the third Shammah.
14 David *was* the youngest. And the three
oldest followed Saul. 15 But David occasionally went and returned from Saul [k]to
feed his father's sheep at Bethlehem.
16 And the Philistine drew near and presented himself forty days, morning and
evening.
17 Then Jesse said to his son David,
"Take now for your brothers an ephah of
this dried *grain* and these ten loaves, and
run to your brothers at the camp. 18 And
carry these ten cheeses to the captain of
their thousand, and [l]see how your brothers
fare, and bring back news of them."
19 Now Saul and they and all the men of Israel *were* in the Valley of Elah, fighting
with the Philistines.
20 So David rose early in the morning,
left the sheep with a keeper, and took *the
things* and went as Jesse had commanded
him. And he came to the camp as the army
was going out to the fight and shouting
for the battle. 21 For Israel and the Philistines had drawn up in battle array, army
against army. 22 And David left his supplies in the hand of the supply keeper, ran
to the army, and came and greeted his
brothers. 23 Then as he talked with them,
there was the champion, the Philistine of
Gath, Goliath by name, coming up from
the armies of the Philistines; and he spoke
[m]according to the same words. So David
heard *them.* 24 And all the men of Israel,
when they saw the man, fled from him
and were dreadfully afraid. 25 So the men
of Israel said, "Have you seen this man
who has come up? Surely he has come up
to defy Israel; and it shall be *that* the man
who kills him the king will enrich with
great riches, [n]will give him his daughter,
and give his father's house exemption
from taxes in Israel."
26 Then David spoke to the men who
stood by him, saying, "What shall be done
for the man who kills this Philistine and
takes away [o]the reproach from Israel? For
who *is* this [p]uncircumcised Philistine, that
he should [q]defy the armies of [r]the living
God?"
27 And the people answered him in this
manner, saying, [s]"So shall it be done for
the man who kills him."
28 Now Eliab his oldest brother heard
when he spoke to the men; and Eliab's [t]an-
ger was aroused against David, and he
said, "Why did you come down here? And
with whom have you left those few sheep
in the wilderness? I know your pride and
the insolence of your heart, for you have
come down to see the battle."
29 And David said, "What have I done
now? [u]*Is*[2] *there* not a cause?" 30 Then he
turned from him toward another and [v]said
the same thing; and these people answered
him as the first ones *did.*
31 Now when the words which David
spoke were heard, they reported *them* to
Saul; and he sent for him. 32 Then David
said to Saul, [w]"Let no man's heart fail because of him; [x]your servant will go and
fight with this Philistine."
33 And Saul said to David, [y]"You are not
able to go against this Philistine to fight
with him; for you *are* a youth, and he a
man of war from his youth."
34 But David said to Saul, "Your servant
used to keep his father's sheep, and when
a [z]lion or a bear came and took a lamb out
of the flock, 35 I went out after it and
struck it, and delivered *the lamb* from its
mouth; and when it arose against me, I
caught *it* by its beard, and struck and
killed it. 36 Your servant has killed both
lion and bear; and this uncircumcised Philistine will be like one of them, seeing he

12 [i] 1 Sam. 16:10, 11; 1 Chr. 2:13-15
13 [j] 1 Sam. 16:6, 8, 9; 1 Chr. 2:13
15 [k] 1 Sam. 16:11, 19; 2 Sam. 7:8
18 [l] Gen. 37:13, 14
23 [m] 1 Sam. 17:8-10
25 [n] Josh. 15:16
26 [o] 1 Sam. 11:2 [p] 1 Sam. 14:6; 17:36; Jer. 9:25, 26 [q] 1 Sam. 17:10 [r] Deut. 5:26; 2 Kin. 19:4; Jer. 10:10
27 [s] 1 Sam. 17:25
28 [t] Gen. 37:4, 8-36; [Prov. 18:19; Matt. 10:36]
29 [u] 1 Sam. 17:17 [2] Lit. *Is it not a word?* or *matter?*
30 [v] 1 Sam. 17:26, 27
32 [w] Deut. 20:1-4 [x] 1 Sam. 16:18
33 [y] Num. 13:31; Deut. 9:2
34 [z] Judg. 14:5

17:15 David occasionally went and returned from Saul. David's duties were divided between his billet with Saul as one of many armorbearers (16:21), and tending his father's sheep in Bethlehem. Doubtless, David learned important lessons regarding the weight of responsibility during this time, lessons that were later put to use in ruling over Israel.

17:17 ephah. About .75 of a bu.

17:23 the same words. Goliath continued to offer the challenge of 17:10, as he had been doing for 40 mornings and evenings (17:16).

17:25 great riches…his daughter. The reward of a daughter in marriage for a great victory over an enemy of Israel was not unusual (cf. Josh. 15:13-17).

17:26 the reproach from Israel. David knew that although Goliath's challenge had been issued to (any) individual of the camp of Israel, Goliath's defiant attitude was a reproach to all Israel.

17:28 Eliab's anger. Eliab, perhaps still feeling the sting/rejection of having his "little" brother chosen over him by God/Samuel (16:6,7), expressed his jealousy in anger (cf. Gen. 37:4,5,8,11).

17:32 Let no man's heart fail. Joshua and Caleb exhorted Israel in the same fashion regarding the giant Anakim 400 years prior (cf. Num. 13:30; 14:8,9). The heathens' hearts fail at the name of the Lord God of Israel (cf. Rahab, Josh. 2:11).

17:33 You are not able. David's faith, like that of Joshua and Caleb, was met with disbelief on the part of Saul. By all outward appearances, Saul was absolutely correct in his assessment, but he failed to consider the Lord's presence in David's life.

17:36 lion and bear. Just as David tended his flock of sheep and protected them from the lion and bear, his new responsibility as shepherd over Israel required him to eliminate the threat of Goliath.

has defied the armies of the living God."
37 Moreover David said, [a]"The LORD, who
delivered me from the paw of the lion and
from the paw of the bear, He will deliver
me from the hand of this Philistine."
And Saul said to David, [b]"Go, and the
LORD be with you!"
38 So Saul clothed David with his [3]ar-
mor, and he put a bronze helmet on his
head; he also clothed him with a coat of
mail. 39 David fastened his sword to his
armor and tried to walk, for he had not
tested *them.* And David said to Saul, "I cannot walk with these, for I have not tested
them." So David took them off.
40 Then he took his staff in his hand; and
he chose for himself five smooth stones
from the brook, and put them in a shepherd's bag, in a pouch which he had, and
his sling was in his hand. And he drew
near to the Philistine. 41 So the Philistine
came, and began drawing near to David,
and the man who bore the shield *went* before him. 42 And when the Philistine
looked about and saw David, he [c]dis-
dained[4] him; for he was *only* a youth,
[d]ruddy and good-looking. 43 So the Philistine [e]said to David, "*Am* I a dog, that
you come to me with sticks?" And the Philistine cursed David by his gods. 44 And
the Philistine [f]said to David, "Come to me,
and I will give your flesh to the birds of the
air and the beasts of the field!"
45 Then David said to the Philistine,
"You come to me with a sword, with a
spear, and with a javelin. [g]But I come to
you in the name of the LORD of hosts, the
God of the armies of Israel, whom you
have [h]defied. 46 This day the LORD will deliver you into my hand, and I will strike
you and take your head from you. And
this day I will give [i]the carcasses of the
camp of the Philistines to the birds of the
air and the wild beasts of the earth, [j]that
all the earth may know that there is a God
in Israel. 47 Then all this assembly shall
know that the LORD [k]does not save with
sword and spear; for [l]the battle *is* the
LORD's, and He will give you into our
hands."
48 So it was, when the Philistine arose
and came and drew near to meet David,
that David hurried and [m]ran toward the
army to meet the Philistine. 49 Then David
put his hand in his bag and took out a
stone; and he slung *it* and struck the Philistine in his forehead, so that the stone
sank into his forehead, and he fell on his

37 [a][2 Cor. 1:10; 2 Tim. 4:17, 18] [b]1 Sam. 20:13; 1 Chr. 22:11, 16
38 [3]Lit. *clothes*
42 [c][Ps. 123:4; Prov. 16:18; 1 Cor. 1:27, 28] [d]1 Sam. 16:12 [4]*belittled*
43 [e]1 Sam. 24:14; 2 Sam. 3:8; 9:8; 16:9; 2 Kin. 8:13
44 [f]1 Sam. 17:46; 1 Kin. 20:10, 11
45 [g]2 Sam. 22:33, 35; 2 Chr. 32:8; Ps. 124:8; [2 Cor. 10:4]; Heb. 11:33, 34 [h]1 Sam. 17:10
46 [i]Deut. 28:26 [j]Josh. 4:24; 1 Kin. 8:43; 18:36; 2 Kin. 19:19; Is. 52:10
47 [k]1 Sam. 14:6; 2 Chr. 14:11; 20:15; Ps. 44:6; Hos. 1:7; Zech. 4:6 [l]2 Chr. 20:15
48 [m]Ps. 27:3

17:37 The LORD...He will deliver me. Just as Jonathan believed earlier (14:6). David had a wholehearted faith in the God of Israel. **the LORD be with you.** One of the first explicit indications in the text that Saul knew that the Lord was with David (cf. 15:28).

17:40 staff...stones...sling. The tools of the shepherd proved to be appropriate weapons also for Israel's shepherd. One of David's honorable and chief men of battle, Benaiah, the son of Jehoiada, slew a formidable Egyptian warrior (2 Sam. 23:20,21) with a staff like the one David carried toward Goliath.

17:43 dog. Goliath uttered a statement of ironic truth about himself of which even he was unaware. As a wild dog can be a threat to the flock and must be chased away or killed, so must Goliath.

17:45 in the name of the LORD of Hosts. Goliath came out to battle in his own name; David came to battle in the name of the Lord of all the hosts (armies). Cf. Deut. 20:1-5.

17:46 all the earth may know. David fought in the name of the Lord and for the glory of the Lord, whose name and glory will extend to the uttermost parts of the earth, to all nations (cf. Josh. 4:24; 2 Sam. 22:50; Ps. 2).

17:47 the battle *is* the LORD's. Cf. Deut. 31:6; Judg. 7:18. David fully understood the chief issue, i.e., the Philistines were in effect challenging the Lord by confronting the Lord's people.

17:48 David...ran. David, unencumbered by armor or fear and emboldened by faith in God, ran to meet Goliath.

Before David Became King

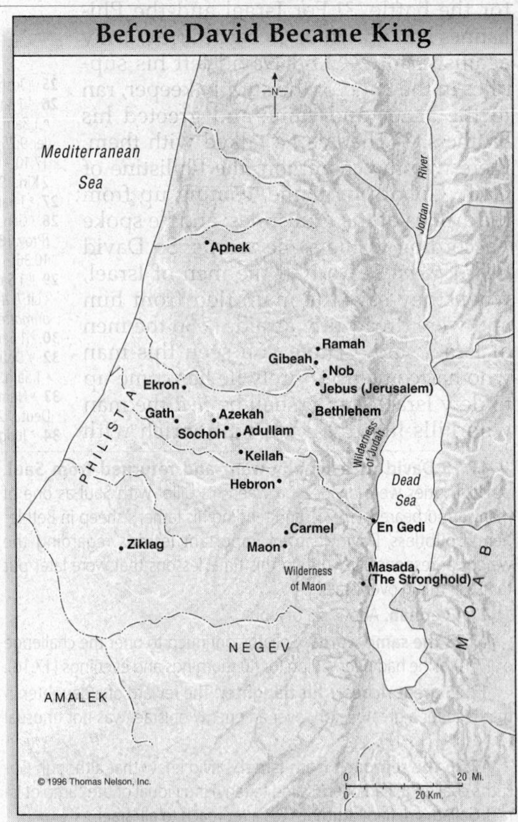

This map represents the geography of the Promised Land during Saul's reign before David's rule.

face to the earth. 50 So David prevailed
over the Philistine with a [n]sling and a
stone, and struck the Philistine and killed
him. But *there was* no sword in the hand of
David. 51 Therefore David ran and stood
over the Philistine, took his [o]sword and
drew it out of its sheath and killed him,
and cut off his head with it.

And when the Philistines saw that their
champion was dead, [p]they fled. 52 Now
the men of Israel and Judah arose and
shouted, and pursued the Philistines as
far as the entrance of [5]the valley and to
the gates of Ekron. And the wounded of
the Philistines fell along the road to [q]Sha-
araim, even as far as Gath and Ekron.
53 Then the children of Israel returned
from chasing the Philistines, and they
plundered their tents. 54 And David took
the head of the Philistine and brought it to
Jerusalem, but he put his armor in his
tent.

55 When Saul saw David going out
against the Philistine, he said to [r]Abner,
the commander of the army, "Abner,
[s]whose son *is* this youth?"

And Abner said, "As your soul lives, O
king, I do not know."

56 So the king said, "Inquire whose son
this young man *is*."

57 Then, as David returned from the
slaughter of the Philistine, Abner took him
and brought him before Saul [t]with the
head of the Philistine in his hand. 58 And
Saul said to him, "Whose son *are* you,
young man?"

So David answered, [u]"*I am* the son of
your servant Jesse the Bethlehemite."

Saul Resents David

18 Now when he had finished speaking to Saul, [a]the [1]soul of Jonathan
was knit to the soul of David, [b]and Jonathan loved him as his own soul. 2 Saul took
him that day, [c]and would not let him go
home to his father's house anymore. 3 Then
Jonathan and David made a [d]covenant, because he loved him as his own soul. 4 And
Jonathan took off the robe that *was* on him
and gave it to David, with his armor, even
to his sword and his bow and his belt.

5 So David went out wherever Saul sent
him, *and* [2]behaved wisely. And Saul set
him over the men of war, and he was accepted in the sight of all the people and
also in the sight of Saul's servants. 6 Now it
had happened as they were coming *home*,
when David was returning from the
slaughter of the [3]Philistine, that [e]the
women had come out of all the cities of Israel, singing and dancing, to meet King
Saul, with tambourines, with joy, and with
musical instruments. 7 So the women [f]sang
as they danced, and said:

> [g]"Saul has slain his thousands,
> And David his ten thousands."

8 Then Saul was very angry, and the saying
[h]displeased him; and he said, "They have
ascribed to David ten thousands, and to
me they have ascribed *only* thousands.
Now *what* more can he have but [i]the kingdom?" 9 So Saul [4]eyed David from that
day forward.

10 And it happened on the next day that
[j]the distressing spirit from God came upon
Saul, [k]and he prophesied inside the house.

50 [n]Judg. 3:31; 15:15; 20:16
51 [o]1 Sam. 21:9; 2 Sam. 23:21 [p]Heb. 11:34
52 [q]Josh. 15:36 [5]So with MT, Syr., Tg., Vg.; LXX *Gath*
55 [r]1 Sam. 14:50 [s]1 Sam. 16:21, 22
57 [t]1 Sam. 17:54
58 [u]1 Sam. 17:12

CHAPTER 18

1 [a]Gen. 44:30 [b]Deut. 13:6; 1 Sam. 20:17; 2 Sam. 1:26 [1]*life of Jonathan was bound up with the life of*
2 [c]1 Sam. 17:15
3 [d]1 Sam. 20:8-17
5 [2]Or *prospered*
6 [e]Ex. 15:20, 21; Judg. 11:34; Ps. 68:25; 149:3 [3]*Philistines*
7 [f]Ex. 15:21 [g]1 Sam. 21:11; 29:5
8 [h]Eccl. 4:4 [i]1 Sam. 15:28
9 [4]Viewed with suspicion
10 [j]1 Sam. 16:14 [k]1 Sam. 19:24; 1 Kin. 18:29; Acts 16:16

17:50 no sword. Iron weapons were scarce in Israel (13:9).

17:51 cut off his head. David completed his promise given to Goliath in v. 46a. The Philistines would later do the same with Saul's head (1 Sam. 31:9). **fled.** David's exclamation that there is a God in Israel (v. 46) was proven before the Philistines, who were no strangers to the wrath of Yahweh (1 Sam. 5–7). They wisely fled in terror, but did not honor the terms of Goliath if he lost (17:6-9).

17:54 to Jerusalem. The Jebusites, who were the inhabitants of Jerusalem, were a stubborn, resistant people (cf. Josh. 15:63; Judg. 1:21; 19:10,11), particularly to the tribe of Judah. They doubtless began to feel some anxiety concerning the victory of this Bethlehemite. The head of Goliath was a constant warning to them over the ensuing days as to their future (cf. 2 Sam. 5:6-10).

17:55 Abner. *See note on 14:50.* **whose son.** David's lineage was of the utmost importance to Saul at this point, since the victor over Goliath would marry into his family (cf. 17:25; 18:18).

18:1 Jonathan loved him. Jonathan loved David with a loyalty and devotion indicative of covenantal love (18:3). Hiram of Tyre had much the same covenantal love for David (cf. 2 Sam. 5:11; 1 Kin. 5:1; 9:11). David's later reign from Jerusalem is marked by loyalty to his covenant with Jonathan (2 Sam. 9:1).

18:2 would not let him go home. Saul's interest in keeping David in his household was more self-serving than a token of generous hospitality. Saul was aware of his promise of wife and wealth (17:25), and, no doubt, the stirrings of anxiety/fear were in his heart toward David, who appeared as a threat. Saul preferred to have him in the court to keep a watchful eye on the young upstart.

18:3 covenant. See v. 1. Further mention of this honorable relationship is made in: 19:1; 20:8,13-17,42; 22:8; 23:18.

18:4 robe...belt. Jonathan willingly and subserviently relinquished the outer garments and instruments that signified his position as prince of Israel and heir to the throne. Jonathan, a godly worshiper of Yahweh, quickly discerned that David was God's anointed and, without reservation, offered the robe of succession to the true king of Israel.

18:7 David his ten thousands. This is a song that Saul grew to hate (cf. 21:11; 28:5) because it exalted David over him.

18:8 the kingdom. Saul's jealousy and malice toward David were now explicit. By his own statement, Saul acknowledged that David was the rightful heir to the throne and the one of whom Samuel spoke in Gilgal (15:28).

18:10 the distressing spirit. The painful descent and eventual demise of Saul was marked by the persistent vexing of this spirit. See 16:14. **prophesied.** This means to speak before people, not predict

So David [l]played *music* with his hand, as at
other times; [m]but *there was* a spear in Saul's
hand. 11 And Saul [n]cast the spear, for he
said, "I will pin David to the wall!" But David escaped his presence twice.
12 Now Saul was [o]afraid of David, because [p]the LORD was with him, but had
[q]departed from Saul. 13 Therefore Saul removed him from [5]his presence, and made
him his captain over a thousand; and [r]he
went out and came in before the people.
14 And David behaved wisely in all his
ways, and [s]the LORD *was* with him.
15 Therefore, when Saul saw that he behaved very wisely, he was afraid of him.
16 But [t]all Israel and Judah loved David,
because he went out and came in before
them.

David Marries Michal

17 Then Saul said to David, "Here is my
older daughter Merab; [u]I will give her to
you as a wife. Only be valiant for me, and
fight [v]the LORD's battles." For Saul
thought, [w]"Let my hand not be against
him, but let the hand of the Philistines be
against him."
18 So David said to Saul, [x]"Who *am* I,
and what *is* my life *or* my father's family in
Israel, that I should be son-in-law to the
king?" 19 But it happened at the time when
Merab, Saul's daughter, should have been
given to David, that she was given to
[y]Adriel the [z]Meholathite as a wife.
20 [a]Now Michal, Saul's daughter, loved
David. And they told Saul, and the thing
pleased him. 21 So Saul said, "I will give
her to him, that she may [6]be a snare to him,
and that [b]the hand of the Philistines may
be against him." Therefore Saul said to David a second time, [c]"You shall be my son-
in-law today."
22 And Saul commanded his servants,
"Communicate with David secretly, and
say, 'Look, the king has delight in you, and
all his servants love you. Now therefore,
become the king's son-in-law.' "
23 So Saul's servants spoke those words
in the hearing of David. And David said,
"Does it seem to you *a* light *thing* to be a
king's son-in-law, seeing I *am* a poor and
lightly esteemed man?" 24 And the servants of Saul told him, saying, [7]"In this
manner David spoke."
25 Then Saul said, "Thus you shall say to
David: 'The king does not desire any
[d]dowry but one hundred foreskins of the
Philistines, to take [e]vengeance on the
king's enemies.' " But Saul [f]thought to
make David fall by the hand of the Philistines. 26 So when his servants told David
these words, it pleased David well to become the king's son-in-law. Now [g]the days
had not expired; 27 therefore David arose
and went, he and [h]his men, and killed two
hundred men of the Philistines. And [i]Da-
vid brought their foreskins, and they gave
them in full count to the king, that he
might become the king's son-in-law. Then
Saul gave him Michal his daughter as a
wife.
28 Thus Saul saw and knew that the
LORD *was* with David, and *that* Michal,
Saul's daughter, loved him; 29 and Saul

10 [l]1 Sam. 16:23 [m]1 Sam. 19:9, 10
11 [n]1 Sam. 19:10; 20:33
12 [o]1 Sam. 18:15, 29 [p]1 Sam. 16:13, 18 [q]1 Sam. 16:14; 28:15
13 [r]Num. 27:17; 1 Sam. 18:16; 29:6; 2 Sam. 5:2 [5]Lit. *himself*
14 [s]Gen. 39:2, 3, 23; Josh. 6:27; 1 Sam. 16:18
16 [t]Num. 27:16, 17; 1 Sam. 18:5; 2 Sam. 5:2; 1 Kin. 3:7
17 [u]1 Sam. 14:49; 17:25 [v]Num. 32:20, 27, 29; 1 Sam. 25:28 [w]1 Sam. 18:21, 25; 2 Sam. 12:9
18 [x]1 Sam. 9:21; 18:23; 2 Sam. 7:18
19 [y]2 Sam. 21:8 [z]Judg. 7:22; 2 Sam. 21:8; 1 Kin. 19:16
20 [a]1 Sam. 18:28
21 [b]1 Sam. 18:17 [c]1 Sam. 18:26 [6]*be bait for*
24 [7]Lit. *According to these words*
25 [d]Gen. 34:12; Ex. 22:17 [e]1 Sam. 14:24 [f]1 Sam. 18:17
26 [g]1 Sam. 18:21
27 [h]1 Sam. 18:13 [i]2 Sam. 3:14

the future. Saul's speeches in the midst of the house were the ravings of one troubled by an evil spirit like other false prophets (cf. 1 Kin. 22:19-23).

18:11 David escaped…twice. As Saul's behavior was becoming increasingly violent, he made more than one attempt on David's life with the javelin. It was evident that God was with David, as it would be no small feat to dodge a javelin cast by such an experienced warrior as Saul.

18:12 Saul was afraid of David. Saul, faced with the same conclusion reached by Jonathan in vv. 1-4, reacted with fear. Saul, a man who viewed life from a human perspective rather than a divine one, could view David only as a personal threat, rather than a blessing to Israel.

18:13 captain over a thousand. Saul gave David a military commission, intended as kind of an honorable exile. But this duty only served to give David opportunity to display his remarkable quality of character and strengthen his hold on the people's affections.

18:16 loved David. The writer of Samuel, inspired by the Holy Spirit, offers an editorial comment full of truth.

18:17 Merab. Lit. "compensation" or "substitute" (cf. 14:49). Saul's later retraction of the betrothal to Merab (v. 19) was similar to Laban's trickery with Jacob and Rachel (Gen. 29:25). **fight the LORD's battles.** A phrase Saul knew would appeal to David. Saul made the offer out of a treacherous heart, desiring evil and calamity for David. Notice the similarity between Saul's treachery and that of David with Uriah (2 Sam. 11:15).

18:18 son-in-law. The familial lineage was crucial when marrying into the king's family. David asked, "Who am I…or my father's family in Israel, that I should be son-in-law to the king?" Saul had asked of David's lineage 3 times previously (17:55,56,58).

18:19 Adriel the Meholathite. Merab married this man and bore children, 5 of whom were sons later executed by David as punishment for Saul's disregard of Joshua's covenant with the Gibeonites (2 Sam. 21:8; cf. Josh. 9:20).

18:20 Michal. Lit. "Who is like God?" Michal sincerely loved David and perhaps was aware, as Jonathan, of his certain ascent (and right) to the throne. Ironically, Saul offered her to David, not from a benevolent heart, but as a "snare" (v. 21).

18:25 dowry. Lit. "price." Saul resorted to the same treachery in his offer of betrothal to Merab, plotting to eliminate David by placing him in jeopardy with the Philistines. David, already having proved himself wise in many things (16:18), was aware, to some extent, of Saul's intent and acted obediently, valiantly, and wisely.

18:25,27 foreskins. Such mutilations of the bodies of slain enemies were commonly practiced in ancient warfare. The number indicated the extent of the victory. Saul's intent was to expose David to deadly danger by engaging in such an extensive and hazardous task.

18:27 his men. Cf. 22:2; 25:12,13; 2 Sam. 23:8-39.

was still more afraid of David. So Saul became David's enemy [g]continually. 30 Then
the princes of the Philistines [j]went out *to*
war. And so it was, whenever they went
out, *that* David [k]behaved more wisely than
all the servants of Saul, so that his name
became highly esteemed.

Saul Persecutes David

19 Now Saul spoke to Jonathan his son
and to all his servants, that they
should kill [a]David; but Jonathan, Saul's son,
[b]delighted greatly in David. 2 So Jonathan
told David, saying, "My father Saul seeks to
kill you. Therefore please be on your guard
until morning, and stay in a secret *place* and
hide. 3 And I will go out and stand beside
my father in the field where you *are,* and I
will speak with my father about you. Then
what I observe, I will tell [c]you."
4 Thus Jonathan [d]spoke well of David to
Saul his father, and said to him, "Let not
the king [e]sin against his servant, against
David, because he has not sinned against
you, and because his works *have been* very
good toward you. 5 For he took his [f]life in
his hands and [g]killed the Philistine, and
[h]the LORD brought about a great deliverance for all Israel. You saw *it* and rejoiced.
[i]Why then will you [j]sin against innocent
blood, to kill David without a cause?"
6 So Saul heeded the voice of Jonathan,
and Saul swore, "*As* the LORD lives, he shall
not be killed." 7 Then Jonathan called David, and Jonathan told him all these things.
So Jonathan brought David to Saul, and he
was in his presence [k]as in times past.
8 And there was war again; and David

29 [g] *all the days*
30 [j] 2 Sam. 11:1
[k] 1 Sam. 18:5

CHAPTER 19

1 [a] 1 Sam. 8:8, 9
[b] 1 Sam. 18:1
3 [c] 1 Sam. 20:8-13
4 [d] 1 Sam. 20:32; [Prov. 31:8, 9] [e] Gen. 42:22; [Prov. 17:13]; Jer. 18:20
5 [f] Judg. 9:17; 12:3
[g] 1 Sam. 17:49, 50
[h] 1 Sam. 11:13; 1 Chr. 11:14 [i] 1 Sam. 20:32
[j] [Deut. 19:10-13]
7 [k] 1 Sam. 16:21; 18:2, 10, 13
8 [l] 1 Sam. 18:27; 23:5
9 [m] 1 Sam. 16:14; 18:10, 11
11 [n] Judg. 16:2; Ps. 59:title
12 [o] Josh. 2:15; Acts 9:25; 2 Cor. 11:33
13 [1] *household idols,* Heb. *teraphim*
17 [p] 2 Sam. 2:22
18 [q] 1 Sam. 16:13
[r] 1 Sam. 7:17

went out and fought with the Philistines,
[l]and struck them with a mighty blow, and
they fled from him.
9 Now [m]the distressing spirit from the
LORD came upon Saul as he sat in his house
with his spear in his hand. And David was
playing *music* with *his* hand. 10 Then Saul
sought to pin David to the wall with the
spear, but he slipped away from Saul's
presence; and he drove the spear into the
wall. So David fled and escaped that night.
11 [n]Saul also sent messengers to David's
house to watch him and to kill him in the
morning. And Michal, David's wife, told
him, saying, "If you do not save your life
tonight, tomorrow you will be killed."
12 So Michal [o]let David down through a
window. And he went and fled and escaped. 13 And Michal took [1]an image and
laid *it* in the bed, put a cover of goats' *hair*
for his head, and covered *it* with clothes.
14 So when Saul sent messengers to take
David, she said, "He *is* sick."
15 Then Saul sent the messengers *back* to
see David, saying, "Bring him up to me in
the bed, that I may kill him." 16 And when
the messengers had come in, there was the
image in the bed, with a cover of goats' *hair*
for his head. 17 Then Saul said to Michal,
"Why have you deceived me like this, and
sent my enemy away, so that he has escaped?"
And Michal answered Saul, "He said to
me, 'Let me go! [p]Why should I kill you?' "
18 So David fled and escaped, and went
to [q]Samuel at [r]Ramah, and told him all
that Saul had done to him. And he and
Samuel went and stayed in Naioth. 19 Now

18:29 Saul became David's enemy. All of Saul's plans came to naught. Saul asked for 100 Philistine foreskins; David brought 200. Saul offered Michal as a "snare"; Michal loved David as did Saul's own son, Jonathan. There remained nothing else for Saul to contrive except open hatred toward David.

19:1 kill David. Saul no longer tried to disguise or cover his evil intent toward David, but ironically made known his intent to those who held David in the highest esteem (cf. 16:18; 18:1-4). God, in his mercy, made sure that David had sympathetic ears within Saul's court to inform him of Saul's evil plans (e.g., 19:7; 20:2).

19:4 Jonathan spoke well of David. Jonathan attempted to persuade his father with calm reason. Jonathan's reason was tempered by a godly attitude centered on a remembrance of the Torah (14:6, cf. Num. 11:23; 14:9) and a covenantal loyalty toward and faithfulness for David.

19:4,5 he has not sinned. Jonathan reminded Saul that David had done nothing to deserve death; in fact, he was worthy of honor for his good works toward the king and Israel. Jonathan knew that the spilling of innocent blood would affect all Israel, not just the house of Saul (Deut. 21:8,9).

19:6 he shall not be killed. Saul temporarily responded to reason and conviction in his heart. His mental capacity was so unbalanced, however, that this response would not last for long.

19:9 the distressing spirit. Jealousy, rage, and anger once again dominated Saul, who was enraged by David's success against the Philistines. See 6:14; 18:10.

19:10 pin David...with the spear. Saul's already diminished capacity for reason was once again completely clouded by anger, and he responded toward David with murderous intent (cf. 18:10,11).

19:11 Michal...told him. Michal, far from being a "snare" (18:21) to David, was instrumental in saving his life. Michal, at this time in her relationship with David, displayed a covenantal love and faithfulness similar to that of Jonathan. See the title of Ps. 59.

19:13 an image. Heb. *teraphim.* The writer of Samuel draws a parallel between David/Michal/Saul and Jacob/Rachel/Laban (*see note on 18:17*), in that both Rachel and Michal employed the use of household gods ("teraphim") in trickery and out of loyalty for their husbands rather than their fathers (cf. Gen. 31:30-35).

19:17 He said to me. Michal lied in telling Saul the exact opposite of what she said to David (v. 11).

19:18 Ramah. With the mention of Samuel's birthplace, the author establishes a verbal link with 1:1, and also reminds the reader of Saul's first encounter with Samuel the seer in Zuph (Ramathaim Zophim). **Naioth.** Perhaps dwellings or quarters within the town limits of Ramah, where Samuel and his company of prophet-disciples met for training, prayer, and fellowship (cf. Elisha at Gilgal, 2 Kin. 6:1,2).

it was told Saul, saying, "Take note, David
is at Naioth in Ramah!" 20 Then [s]Saul sent
messengers to take David. [t]And when they
saw the group of prophets prophesying,
and Samuel standing *as* leader over them,
the Spirit of God came upon the messengers of Saul, and they also [u]prophesied.
21 And when Saul was told, he sent other
messengers, and they prophesied likewise.
Then Saul sent messengers again the third
time, and they prophesied also. 22 Then he
also went to Ramah, and came to the great
well that *is* at Sechu. So he asked, and said,
"Where *are* Samuel and David?"
And *someone* said, "Indeed *they are* at
Naioth in Ramah." 23 So he went there to
Naioth in Ramah. Then [v]the Spirit of God
was upon him also, and he went on and
prophesied until he came to Naioth in
Ramah. 24 [w]And he also stripped off his
clothes and prophesied before Samuel in
like manner, and lay down [x]naked all that
day and all that night. Therefore they say,
[y]"*Is* Saul also among the prophets?"

Jonathan's Loyalty to David

20 Then David fled from Naioth in
Ramah, and went and said to Jonathan, "What have I done? What *is* my iniquity, and what *is* my sin before your father,
that he seeks my life?"
2 So Jonathan said to him, "By no means!
You shall not die! Indeed, my father will
do nothing either great or small without
first telling me. And why should my father
hide this thing from me? It *is* not *so!*"
3 Then David took an oath again, and
said, "Your father certainly knows that I
have found favor in your eyes, and he has
said, 'Do not let Jonathan know this, lest he
be grieved.' But [a]truly, *as* the LORD lives
and *as* your soul lives, *there is* but a step between me and death."
4 So Jonathan said to David, "Whatever
you yourself desire, I will do *it* for you."
5 And David said to Jonathan, "Indeed
tomorrow *is* the [b]New Moon, and I should
not fail to sit with the king to eat. But let
me go, that I may [c]hide in the field until
the third *day* at evening. 6 If your father
misses me at all, then say, 'David earnestly
asked *permission* of me that he might run
over [d]to Bethlehem, his city, for *there is* a
yearly sacrifice there for all the family.' 7 [e]If
he says thus: '*It is* well,' your servant will
be safe. But if he is very angry, be sure that
[f]evil is determined by him. 8 Therefore you
shall [g]deal kindly with your servant, for
[h]you have brought your servant into a
covenant of the LORD with you. Nevertheless, [i]if there is iniquity in me, kill me yourself, for why should you bring me to your
father?"
9 But Jonathan said, "Far be it from you!
For if I knew certainly that evil was determined by my father to come upon you,
then would I not tell you?"
10 Then David said to Jonathan, "Who
will tell me, or what *if* your father answers
you roughly?"
11 And Jonathan said to David, "Come,
let us go out into the field." So both of
them went out into the field. 12 Then Jonathan said to David: "The LORD God of Israel *is witness!* When I have [1]sounded out
my father sometime tomorrow, *or* the third
day, and indeed *there is* good toward David, and I do not send to you and tell you,
13 may [j]the LORD do so and much more to
Jonathan. But if it pleases my father *to do*
you evil, then I will report it to you and
send you away, that you may go in safety.

20 [s]1 Sam. 19:11, 14; John 7:32 [t]1 Sam. 10:5, 6, 10; [1 Cor. 14:3, 24, 25] [u]Num. 11:25; Joel 2:28
23 [v]1 Sam. 10:10
24 [w]Is. 20:2 [x]Mic. 1:8 [y]1 Sam. 10:10-12

CHAPTER 20

3 [a]1 Sam. 27:1; 2 Kin. 2:6
5 [b]Num. 10:10; 28:11-15 [c]1 Sam. 19:2, 3
6 [d]1 Sam. 16:4; 17:12; John 7:42
7 [e]Deut. 1:23; 2 Sam. 17:4 [f]1 Sam. 25:17; Esth. 7:7
8 [g]Josh. 2:14 [h]1 Sam. 18:3; 20:16; 23:18 [i]2 Sam. 14:32
12 [1]*searched out*
13 [j]Ruth 1:17; 1 Sam. 3:17

19:20 group of prophets prophesying. These prophets were declaring the Word of God, probably with musical accompaniment. Saul's messengers could not fulfill their task of taking David captive because they were irresistibly led to join the prophets and speak for and praise God.

19:22 great well...at Sechu. The exact location is unknown; the probable location was approximately two mi. N of Ramah.

19:23 the Spirit of God was upon him. This was the last time the Spirit of the Lord would rest on Saul. God turned Saul's heart to prophesy and not harm David. *See note on 16:13.*

19:24 stripped off his clothes. Saul removed his armor and royal garments (cf. Jonathan, 18:4), prompted by the Spirit of God, thus signifying God's rejection of Saul as king over Israel. **lay down naked.** Without the royal garments, Saul was figuratively "naked," perhaps so overwhelmed by the Spirit of God as to be in a deep sleep. Other than Saul's utter despair and pitiful state at the home of the witch at Endor (28:20) and his end at Mt. Gilboa (31:4-6), this episode represents one of the severest humblings in Saul's life. ***Is* Saul also among the prophets?** This is a final editorial comment tying together the Spirit of God's presence at Saul's inauguration (10:10,11), and the final departure of the same at his rejection (19:24).

20:1 Naioth in Ramah. *See note on 19:18.*

20:2 my father hide this thing from me. Although Jonathan expressed his certainty that Saul was not seeking David's life, he may have been unaware of the most recent attempts on David's life (19:9-24) and was trusting in his father's oath not to harm David (19:6). Jonathan expected to be informed by Saul of any change in his plans.

20:5 the New Moon. The first day of the month, referred to as "the New Moon," was celebrated with a sacrificial meal (cf. 2 Kin. 4:23; Is. 1:13; Amos 8:5) and served both as a religious and civil festival (Num. 10:10; 28:11-15). **hide in the field.** As in 19:2,3, David hid from Saul in a secret place.

20:6 a yearly sacrifice. Apparently, David's family held an annual family reunion that coincided with one of the monthly New Moon celebrations (cf. vv. 28,29).

20:8 covenant. Cf. 18:1,3. Jonathan and David had solemnly pledged their friendship and loyalty to each other before the Lord. Their covenant is further amplified in vv. 13-17,42; 23:17,18. **kill me yourself.** As his covenant friend, David asked Jonathan to kill him, if he was deserving of death because of his possible sin.

And [k]the LORD be with you as He has
[l]been with my father. 14 And you shall not
only show me the kindness of the LORD
while I still live, that I may not die; 15 but
[m]you shall not [2]cut off your kindness from
my [3]house forever, no, not when the LORD
has cut off every one of the enemies of David from the face of the earth." 16 So Jonathan made *a covenant* with the [4]house of
David, *saying,* [n]"Let the LORD require *it* at
the hand of David's enemies."
17 Now Jonathan again caused David to
vow, because he loved him; [o]for he loved
him as he loved his own soul. 18 Then Jonathan said to David, [p]"Tomorrow *is* the
New Moon; and you will be missed, because your seat will be empty. 19 And *when*
you have stayed three days, go down
quickly and come to [q]the place where you
hid on the day of the deed; and remain by
the stone Ezel. 20 Then I will shoot three arrows to the side, as though I shot at a target; 21 and there I will send a lad, *saying,*
'Go, find the arrows.' If I expressly say to
the lad, 'Look, the arrows *are* on this side of
you; get them and come'—then, [r]as the
LORD lives, *there is* safety for you and no
harm. 22 But if I say thus to the young man,
'Look, the arrows *are* beyond you'—go
your way, for the LORD has sent you away.
23 And as for [s]the matter which you and I
have spoken of, indeed the LORD *be* between you and me forever."
24 Then David hid in the field. And
when the New Moon had come, the king
sat down to eat the feast. 25 Now the king
sat on his seat, as at other times, on a seat
by the wall. And [5]Jonathan arose, and
Abner sat by Saul's side, but David's place
was empty. 26 Nevertheless Saul did not
say anything that day, for he thought,
"Something has happened to him; he *is* unclean, surely he *is* [t]unclean." 27 And it happened the next day, the second *day* of the
month, that David's place was empty. And
Saul said to Jonathan his son, "Why has
the son of Jesse not come to eat, either yesterday or today?"
28 So Jonathan [u]answered Saul, "David
earnestly asked *permission* of me *to go* to
Bethlehem. 29 And he said, 'Please let me
go, for our family has a sacrifice in the city,
and my brother has commanded me *to be
there.* And now, if I have found favor in
your eyes, please let me get away and see
my brothers.' Therefore he has not come to
the king's table."
30 Then Saul's anger was aroused
against Jonathan, and he said to him, "You
son of a perverse, rebellious *woman!* Do I
not know that you have chosen the son of
Jesse to your own shame and to the shame
of your mother's nakedness? 31 For as long
as the son of Jesse lives on the earth, you
shall not be established, nor your kingdom. Now therefore, send and bring him
to me, for he [6]shall surely die."
32 And Jonathan answered Saul his father, and said to him, [v]"Why should he be
killed? What has he done?" 33 Then Saul
[w]cast a spear at him to [7]kill him, [x]by which
Jonathan knew that it was determined by
his father to kill David.
34 So Jonathan arose from the table in
fierce anger, and ate no food the second
day of the month, for he was grieved for
David, because his father had treated him
shamefully.
35 And so it was, in the morning, that
Jonathan went out into the field at the time
appointed with David, and a little lad *was*
with him. 36 Then he said to his lad, "Now
run, find the arrows which I shoot." As the
lad ran, he shot an arrow beyond him.
37 When the lad had come to the place
where the arrow was which Jonathan had
shot, Jonathan cried out after the lad and
said, *"Is* not the arrow beyond you?"
38 And Jonathan cried out after the lad,
"Make haste, hurry, do not delay!" So Jonathan's lad gathered up the arrows and
came back to his master. 39 But the lad did
not know anything. Only Jonathan and

13 [k] Josh. 1:5; 1 Sam. 17:37; 18:12; 1 Chr. 22:11, 16 [l] 1 Sam. 10:7
15 [m] 1 Sam. 24:21; 2 Sam. 9:1, 3, 7; 21:7 [2] *stop being kind* [3] *family*
16 [n] Deut. 23:21; 1 Sam. 25:22; 31:2; 2 Sam. 4:7; 21:8 [4] *family*
17 [o] 1 Sam. 18:1
18 [p] 1 Sam. 20:5, 24
19 [q] 1 Sam. 19:2
21 [r] Jer. 4:2
23 [s] 1 Sam. 20:14, 15
25 [5] So with MT, Syr., Tg., Vg.; LXX *he sat across from Jonathan*
26 [t] Lev. 7:20, 21; 15:5
28 [u] 1 Sam. 20:6
31 [6] Lit. *is a son of death*
32 [v] Gen. 31:36; 1 Sam. 19:5; [Prov. 31:9]; Matt. 27:23; Luke 23:22
33 [w] 1 Sam. 18:11; 19:10 [x] 1 Sam. 20:7 [7] *strike him down*

20:14 the kindness of the LORD. Jonathan acknowledged that David would one day be Israel's king. With that in mind, Jonathan requested protection for him and his family when David took the throne.

20:16 the house of David. This covenant was not only binding on Jonathan and David, but also upon the descendants of each. See 2 Sam. 9:1-8 for the account of David's kindness to a descendant of Jonathan in fulfillment of this covenant. **David's enemies.** Jonathan perceived that among David's adversaries who would be cut off when he became king was his own father, Saul (cf. 18:29; 19:17).

20:17 vow. In response to Jonathan's words, David solemnly pledged to fulfill the covenant between himself and Jonathan. **loved him as...his own soul.** A deep concern and affection was the basis of the covenantal relationship between Jonathan and David. This is the affection commanded by God when He said "Love your neighbor as yourself" (Lev. 19:18; Matt. 22:39).

20:19 stone Ezel. Ezel may mean "departure stone." The location of this stone is unknown, but it was a well known landmark in the field where David was hiding.

20:25 Abner. Saul's cousin and commander of his army (*see note on 14:50*).

20:26 unclean. At first, Saul did not question David's absence at the feast, assuming that he was ritually unclean and thus could not participate in the meal (cf. Lev. 7:20,21; 15:16).

20:30 son of a perverse, rebellious *woman!* With a vile epithet, Saul was cursing Jonathan, not Jonathan's mother, for having sided with David to his own shame and the shame of the mother who birthed him.

David knew of the matter. 40 Then Jonathan gave his [8]weapons to his lad, and said
to him, "Go, carry *them* to the city."
41 As soon as the lad had gone, David
arose from *a place* toward the south, fell on
his face to the ground, and bowed down
three times. And they kissed one another;
and they wept together, but David more
so. 42 Then Jonathan said to David, [y]"Go in
peace, since we have both sworn in the
name of the LORD, saying, 'May the LORD
be between you and me, and between your
descendants and my descendants, forever.' " So he arose and departed, and Jonathan went into the city.

David and the Holy Bread

21 Now David came to Nob, to Ahimelech the priest. And [a]Ahimelech
was [b]afraid when he met David, and said
to him, "Why *are* you alone, and no one is
with you?"
2 So David said to Ahimelech the priest,
"The king has ordered me on some business, and said to me, 'Do not let anyone
know anything about the business on
which I send you, or what I have commanded you.' And I have directed *my*
young men to such and such a place.
3 Now therefore, what have you on hand?
Give *me* five *loaves of* bread in my hand, or
whatever can be found."
4 And the priest answered David and
said, "*There is* no [1]common bread on hand;
but there is [c]holy[2] bread, [d]if the young
men have at least kept themselves from
women."
5 Then David answered the priest, and
said to him, "Truly, women *have been* kept
from us about three days since I came out.
And [3]the [e]vessels of the young men are
holy, and *the bread is* in effect common,
even though it was consecrated [f]in the vessel this day."
6 So the priest [g]gave him holy *bread;* for
there was no bread there but the showbread [h]which had been taken from before
the LORD, in order to put hot bread *in its*
place on the day when it was taken away.
7 Now a certain man of the servants of
Saul *was* there that day, detained before the
LORD. And his name *was* [i]Doeg, an Edomite, the chief of the herdsmen who *belonged*
to Saul.
8 And David said to Ahimelech, "Is
there not here on hand a spear or a sword?
For I have brought neither my sword nor
my weapons with me, because the king's
business required haste."
9 So the priest said, "The sword of Goliath
the Philistine, whom you killed in [j]the Valley of Elah, [k]there it is, wrapped in a cloth
behind the ephod. If you will take that, take
it. For *there is* no other except that one here."
And David said, "*There is* none like it;
give it to me."

David Flees to Gath

10 Then David arose and fled that day
from before Saul, and went to Achish the
king of Gath. 11 And [l]the servants of
Achish said to him, "*Is* this not David the
king of the land? Did they not sing of him
to one another in dances, saying:

40 [8] *equipment* **42** [y] 1 Sam. 1:17

CHAPTER 21

1 [a] 1 Sam. 14:3; Mark 2:26 [b] 1 Sam. 16:4 **4** [c] Ex. 25:30; Lev. 24:5-9; Matt. 12:4 [d] Ex. 19:15 [1] *ordinary* [2] *consecrated*

5 [e] Ex. 19:14, 15; 1 Thess. 4:4 [f] Lev. 8:26 [3] The young men are ceremonially undefiled **6** [g] Matt. 12:3, 4; Mark 2:25, 26; Luke 6:3, 4 [h] Lev. 24:8, 9 **7** [i] 1 Sam. 14:47; 22:9; Ps. 52:title **9** [j] 1 Sam. 17:2, 50 [k] 1 Sam. 31:10 **11** [l] Ps. 56:title

20:41 bowed down three times. David's bowing down more than once acknowledged Jonathan as the prince, and expressed humble affection for him.

20:42 sworn. *See note on 20:17.* **the city.** I.e., Gibeah, the home of Saul. From this point until Saul's death, David was an outcast from the royal court.

21:1 Nob. "The city of the priests" (22:19). The priests dwelt on Mt. Scopus, about one mi. NE of Jerusalem. David went there for necessary supplies and for comfort and counsel. **Ahimelech.** A great grandson of Eli (1:9), who is possibly the brother of Ahijah (14:3; 22:11), or Abimelech may be another name for Ahijah. Not only is there a rejected king on the throne (15:26-29) but also a disqualified priest (2:30-36). *See note on Mark 2:26.*

21:2 The king has ordered me. David, fearing someone might tell Saul where he was, deceived Ahimelech the priest into thinking that he was on official business for the king. He supposed, as many do, that it is excusable to lie for the purpose of saving one's life. But what is essentially sinful can never, because of circumstances, change its immoral character (cf. Ps. 119:29). David's lying led tragically to the deaths of the priests (22:9-18).

21:4 holy bread. Consecrated bread was set apart for use in the tabernacle to be eaten only by the priests (Ex. 25:30; Lev. 24:5-9). Ahimelech sought the Lord and received approval (22:10) when he recognized that his spiritual obligation to preserve David's life superseded the ceremonial regulation concerning who could eat the consecrated bread (see Matt. 12:3,4; Mark 2:25,26). **kept themselves from women.** Though this was not a spiritual mission or religious journey, David and his men were ceremonially clean (see Ex. 19:15).

21:5 the vessels. A euphemism for the bodies of the young men, as in 1 Thess. 4:4.

21:5,6 *bread*...common. Since that bread was no longer on the Lord's table, having been replaced by hot bread, it was to be eaten by the priests and in these exigencies, by David under the law of necessity and mercy. *See note on 21:4.* The removal of the old bread and the replacing with new was done on the Sabbath (Lev. 24:8).

21:7 Doeg, an Edomite. The head shepherd of Saul's herd, who witnessed the encounter between David and Ahimelech and told Saul (cf. 22:9,10), had embraced the Hebrew religion and was at the tabernacle, perhaps detained because it was the Sabbath and he could not travel.

21:9 The sword of Goliath. The sword which David had used to behead Goliath in the valley of Elah (17:51) was kept in the place for storing the sacred vestments ("the ephod") deposited there as a memorial to divine goodness in the deliverance of Israel. **the ephod.** *See note on 2:28.*

21:10 Achish the king of Gath. One of the kings or lords of the Philistines. *See notes on 4:1; 5:8* for Gath. This seemed to be a dangerous place to go, since David was their greatest enemy and carried Goliath's sword into the giant's hometown.

[m]'Saul has slain his thousands,
And David his ten thousands'?"

12 Now David [n]took these words [4]to
heart, and was very much afraid of Achish
the king of Gath. 13 So [o]he changed his behavior before them, pretended [5]madness
in their hands, [6]scratched on the doors of
the gate, and let his saliva fall down on his
beard. 14 Then Achish said to his servants,
"Look, you see the man is insane. Why
have you brought him to me? 15 Have I
need of madmen, that you have brought
this *fellow* to play the madman in my presence? Shall this *fellow* come into my
house?"

David's Four Hundred Men

22 David therefore departed from
there and [a]escaped [b]to the cave of
Adullam. So when his brothers and all his
father's house heard *it*, they went down
there to him. 2 [c]And everyone *who was* in
distress, everyone who *was* in debt, and
everyone *who was* [1]discontented gathered
to him. So he became captain over them.
And there were about [d]four hundred men
with him.
3 Then David went from there to Mizpah
of [e]Moab; and he said to the king of Moab,
"Please let my father and mother come
here with you, till I know what God will
do for me." 4 So he brought them before
the king of Moab, and they dwelt with him
all the time that David was in the stronghold.
5 Now the prophet [f]Gad said to David,
"Do not stay in the stronghold; depart, and
go to the land of Judah." So David departed and went into the forest of Hereth.

11 [m] 1 Sam. 18:6-8; 29:5
12 [n] Luke 2:19 [4] Lit. *in his heart*
13 [o] Ps. 34:title [5] *insanity* [6] *scribbled*

CHAPTER 22

1 [a] Ps. 57:title; 142:title [b] Josh. 12:15; 15:35; 2 Sam. 23:13
2 [c] Judg. 11:3 [d] 1 Sam. 25:13 [1] Lit. *bitter of soul*
3 [e] 2 Sam. 8:2
5 [f] 2 Sam. 24:11; 1 Chr. 21:9; 29:29; 2 Chr. 29:25

6 [g] 1 Sam. 15:34
7 [h] 1 Sam. 8:14
8 [i] 1 Sam. 18:3; 20:16, 30
9 [j] 1 Sam. 21:7; 22:22; Ps. 52:title [k] 1 Sam. 21:1 [l] 1 Sam. 14:3
10 [m] Num. 27:21; 1 Sam. 10:22 [n] 1 Sam. 21:6, 9

Saul Murders the Priests

6 When Saul heard that David and the
men who *were* with him had been discovered—now Saul was staying in [g]Gibeah
under a tamarisk tree in Ramah, with his
spear in his hand, and all his servants
standing about him— 7 then Saul said to
his servants who stood about him, "Hear
now, you Benjamites! Will the son of Jesse
[h]give every one of you fields and vineyards, *and* make you all captains of thousands and captains of hundreds? 8 All of
you have conspired against me, and *there is*
no one who reveals to me that [i]my son has
made a covenant with the son of Jesse; and
there is not one of you who is sorry for me
or reveals to me that my son has stirred up
my servant against me, to lie in wait, as *it*
is this day."
9 Then answered [j]Doeg the Edomite,
who was set over the servants of Saul, and
said, "I saw the son of Jesse going to Nob,
to [k]Ahimelech the son of [l]Ahitub. 10 [m]And
he inquired of the LORD for him, [n]gave him
provisions, and gave him the sword of Goliath the Philistine."
11 So the king sent to call Ahimelech the
priest, the son of Ahitub, and all his father's house, the priests who *were* in Nob.
And they all came to the king. 12 And Saul
said, "Hear now, son of Ahitub!"
He answered, "Here I am, my lord."
13 Then Saul said to him, "Why have
you conspired against me, you and the son
of Jesse, in that you have given him bread
and a sword, and have inquired of God for
him, that he should rise against me, to lie
in wait, as it is this day?"
14 So Ahimelech answered the king and
said, "And who among all your servants *is*

21:13 changed his behavior. David feared for his life, lacked trust in God to deliver him, and feigned insanity to persuade Achish to send him away. See the titles of Pss. 34,56. Drooling in one's beard was considered in the East an intolerable indignity, as was spitting in another's beard.

22:1 cave of Adullam. A cave near Adullum was David's refuge. Adullum, which may mean "refuge," was located in the western foothills of Judah (Josh. 15:33), about 17 mi. SW of Jerusalem and 10 mi. SE of Gath. See titles of Pss. 57,142, which could possibly refer to 1 Sam. 24:3. **brothers and all his father's house.** David's family members went down from Bethlehem to join David in Adullam, a journey of about 12 mi..

22:2 captain over…four hundred men. David became the leader of a formidable force of men united by adverse circumstances. This personal army would soon grow to 600 (23:13).

22:3 Mizpah of Moab. Mizpah means "watch tower," or "place that overlooks." Located on one of the heights of the tableland E of the Dead Sea, this site cannot be exactly identified. **king of Moab.** This ruler was probably a mutual enemy of King Saul. David had Moabite blood from his great-grandmother Ruth, and thus sought refuge for his father and mother in Moab (see Ruth 1:4-18; 4:13-22).

22:4 the stronghold. Transliterated *mesudah*, this may refer to Masada, the mountain fortress above the shores of the Dead Sea, or some unknown location.

22:5 prophet Gad. As the prophet Samuel had helped and advised Saul, so now Gad performed the same functions for David (cf. 2 Sam 24:11, where Gad is called "David's seer"). **forest of Hereth.** Location in Judah unknown.

22:6 tamarisk tree. Possibly located on a hill outside Gibeah which had been given over to pagan worship (cf. Ezek. 16:24,25, 31,39). A reminder of the threat that Saul was to friend and foe alike (cf. 18:10,11; 19:9,10; 20:3).

22:7 Benjamites. Saul asked those of his own tribe whether associating themselves with David would provide for them more possessions and privileges than they already had from Saul.

22:8 my son has made a covenant. *See notes on 20:8,23.*

22:8-13 to lie in wait. Saul insinuated that David was plotting his death. This was not true, as David would later spare Saul's life (vv. 24,26).

22:9,10 Doeg the Edomite. *See note on 21:7* and the title of Ps. 52.

22:13 conspired against me. Saul insisted falsely that Ahimelech was in league with his enemy David.

as [o]faithful as David, who is the king's son-
in-law, who goes at your bidding, and is
honorable in your house? 15 Did I then
begin to inquire of God for him? Far be it
from me! Let not the king impute anything
to his servant, *or* to any in the house of my
father. For your servant knew nothing of
all this, little or much."
16 And the king said, "You shall surely
die, Ahimelech, you and all [p]your father's
house!" 17 Then the king said to the guards
who stood about him, "Turn and kill the
priests of the LORD, because their hand also
is with David, and because they knew
when he fled and did not tell it to me." But
the servants of the king [q]would not lift
their hands to strike the priests of the LORD.
18 And the king said to Doeg, "You turn
and kill the priests!" So Doeg the Edomite
turned and [2]struck the priests, and [r]killed
on that day eighty-five men who wore a
linen ephod. 19 [s]Also Nob, the city of the
priests, he struck with the edge of the
sword, both men and women, children and
nursing infants, oxen and donkeys and
sheep—with the edge of the sword.
20 [t]Now one of the sons of Ahimelech the
son of Ahitub, named Abiathar, [u]escaped
and fled after David. 21 And Abiathar told
David that Saul had killed the LORD's
priests. 22 So David said to Abiathar, "I
knew that day, when Doeg the Edomite *was*
there, that he would surely tell Saul. I have
caused *the death* of all the persons of your
father's [3]house. 23 Stay with me; do not
fear. [v]For he who seeks my life seeks your
life, but with me you *shall be* safe."

David Saves the City of Keilah

23 Then they told David, saying,
"Look, the Philistines are fighting
against [a]Keilah, and they are robbing the
threshing floors."

14 [o] 1 Sam. 19:4, 5; 20:32; 24:11
16 [p] Deut. 24:16
17 [q] Ex. 1:17
18 [r] 1 Sam. 2:31 [2] *attacked*
19 [s] Josh. 21:1-45; 1 Sam. 22:9, 11
20 [t] 1 Sam. 23:6, 9; 30:7; 1 Kin. 2:26, 27 [u] 1 Sam. 2:33
22 [3] *family*
23 [v] 1 Kin. 2:26

CHAPTER 23

1 [a] Josh. 15:44; Neh. 3:17, 18

2 [b] 1 Sam. 22:10; 23:4, 6, 9; 28:6; 30:8; 2 Sam. 5:19, 23 [1] Lit. *strike*
5 [c] 1 Sam. 19:8; 2 Sam. 5:20
6 [d] 1 Sam. 22:20
9 [e] Num. 27:21; 1 Sam. 23:6; 30:7
10 [f] 1 Sam. 22:19
12 [2] Lit. *shut up*

2 Therefore David [b]inquired of the LORD,
saying, "Shall I go and [1]attack these Philistines?"
And the LORD said to David, "Go and attack the Philistines, and save Keilah."
3 But David's men said to him, "Look,
we are afraid here in Judah. How much
more then if we go to Keilah against the
armies of the Philistines?" 4 Then David
inquired of the LORD once again.
And the LORD answered him and said,
"Arise, go down to Keilah. For I will deliver the Philistines into your hand." 5 And
David and his men went to Keilah and
[c]fought with the Philistines, struck them
with a mighty blow, and took away their
livestock. So David saved the inhabitants
of Keilah.
6 Now it happened, when Abiathar the
son of Ahimelech [d]fled to David at Keilah,
that he went down *with* an ephod in his
hand.
7 And Saul was told that David had
gone to Keilah. So Saul said, "God has delivered him into my hand, for he has shut
himself in by entering a town that has
gates and bars." 8 Then Saul called all the
people together for war, to go down to Keilah to besiege David and his men.
9 When David knew that Saul plotted
evil against him, [e]he said to Abiathar the
priest, "Bring the ephod here." 10 Then David said, "O LORD God of Israel, Your servant has certainly heard that Saul seeks to
come to Keilah [f]to destroy the city for my
sake. 11 Will the men of Keilah deliver me
into his hand? Will Saul come down, as
Your servant has heard? O LORD God of Israel, I pray, tell Your servant."
And the LORD said, "He will come down."
12 Then David said, "Will the men of Keilah [2]deliver me and my men into the hand
of Saul?"

22:14 your bidding. Ahimelech responded to Saul by defending David's character as loyal to Saul.

22:16-19 This fulfills the curse on Eli's house (*see note on 1 Sam. 2:31*), with the exception of Abiathar, who was later dismissed from the priesthood by Solomon (1 Kin. 2:26-29).

22:17 would not...strike the priests. Although Saul condemned Ahimelech and the priests to death, his servants knew better than to raise their weapons against the priests of the Lord.

22:18 linen ephod. *See note on 2:18.*

22:19 Nob, the city of the priests. *See note on 21:1.* What Saul failed to do righteously to the Amalekites (15:3,8,9), he unrighteously did to the citizens of Nob.

22:20 Abiathar. Lit. "The father is excellent." A son of Ahimelech (cf. 21:1) who escaped the slaughter and joined David's company, he performed priestly functions for David for the rest of David's life (cf. 23:6,9; 30:7; 2 Sam. 8:17). *See note on 22:16-19.*

22:22 I have caused. David recognized his responsibility for causing the deaths of the priests' families and animals, acknowledging the devastating consequences of his lie to Ahimelech (cf. 21:1,2).

23:1 Keilah. A city located in the western foothills of Judah (see Josh. 15:44), about 18 mi. SW of Jerusalem and 3 mi. SE of Abdulam.

23:2 inquired of the LORD. Such inquiries were made using the sacred lots, the Urim and Thummim, stored in the priestly ephod which Abiathar had brought to David (v. 6). *See note on Ex. 28:30.*

23:7 gates and bars. Lit. "two doors and a bar." Keilah perhaps had only one gateway in its wall. Its two reinforced wooden doors had hinged posts at the sides of the entrance, meeting in the center and secured with a heavy bar spanning the entrance horizontally. Since there was only this one way in and out of the city, Saul believed he had David trapped.

23:11 deliver me. David inquired of the Lord again, using the ephod with the Urim and Thummim by which God revealed His will. David wanted to know whether the men of Keilah would be disloyal and surrender him into the hands of Saul. The Lord answered in the affirmative in v. 12.

And the LORD said, "They will deliver
you."
13 So David and his men, [g]about six
hundred, arose and departed from Keilah
and went wherever they could go. Then it
was told Saul that David had escaped from
Keilah; so he halted the expedition.

David in Wilderness Strongholds

14 And David stayed in strongholds in
the wilderness, and remained in [h]the
mountains in the Wilderness of [i]Ziph. Saul
[j]sought him every day, but God did not deliver him into his hand. 15 So David saw
that Saul had come out to seek his life. And
David *was* in the Wilderness of Ziph [3]in a
forest. 16 Then Jonathan, Saul's son, arose
and went to David in the woods and
[4]strengthened his hand in God. 17 And he
said to him, [k]"Do not fear, for the hand of
Saul my father shall not find you. You shall
be king over Israel, and I shall be next to
you. [l]Even my father Saul knows that."
18 So the two of them [m]made a covenant
before the LORD. And David stayed in the
woods, and Jonathan went to his own
house.
19 Then the Ziphites [n]came up to Saul
at Gibeah, saying, "Is David not hiding
with us in strongholds in the woods, in
the hill of Hachilah, which *is* on the south
of Jeshimon? 20 Now therefore, O king,
come down according to all the desire of
your soul to come down; and [o]our part
shall be to deliver him into the king's
hand."
21 And Saul said, "Blessed *are* you of
the LORD, for you have compassion on
me. 22 Please go and find out for sure,
and see the place where his hideout is,
and who has seen him there. For I am told

13 [g] 1 Sam. 22:2; 25:13
14 [h] Ps. 11:1 [i] Josh. 15:55; 2 Chr. 11:8 [j] Ps. 32:7; 54:3, 4
15 [3] Or *in Horesh*
16 [4] *encouraged him*
17 [k] [Ps. 27:1-3; Heb. 13:6] [l] 1 Sam. 20:31; 24:20
18 [m] 1 Sam. 18:3; 20:12-17, 42; 2 Sam. 9:1; 21:7
19 [n] 1 Sam. 26:1; Ps. 54:title
20 [o] Ps. 54:3
23 [5] Lit. *thousands*
24 [p] Josh. 15:55; 1 Sam. 25:2
25 [6] Or *from the rock*
26 [q] Ps. 31:22 [r] Ps. 17:9
27 [s] 2 Kin. 19:9
28 [7] Heb. *Sela Hammahlekoth*
29 [t] Josh. 15:62; 2 Chr. 20:2

CHAPTER 24

1 [a] 1 Sam. 23:19, 28, 29
2 [b] 1 Sam. 26:2; Ps. 38:12

he is very crafty. 23 See therefore, and
take knowledge of all the lurking places
where he hides; and come back to me
with certainty, and I will go with you.
And it shall be, if he is in the land, that I
will search for him throughout all the
[5]clans of Judah."
24 So they arose and went to Ziph before
Saul. But David and his men *were* in the
Wilderness [p]of Maon, in the plain on the
south of Jeshimon. 25 When Saul and his
men went to seek *him*, they told David.
Therefore he went down [6]to the rock, and
stayed in the Wilderness of Maon. And
when Saul heard *that*, he pursued David
in the Wilderness of Maon. 26 Then Saul
went on one side of the mountain, and David and his men on the other side of the
mountain. [q]So David made haste to get
away from Saul, for Saul and his men
[r]were encircling David and his men to
take them.
27 [s]But a messenger came to Saul, saying, "Hurry and come, for the Philistines
have invaded the land!" 28 Therefore Saul
returned from pursuing David, and went
against the Philistines; so they called that
place [7]the Rock of Escape. 29 Then David
went up from there and dwelt in strongholds at [t]En Gedi.

David Spares Saul

24 Now it happened, [a]when Saul had
returned from following the Philistines, that it was told him, saying,
"Take note! David *is* in the Wilderness of
En Gedi." 2 Then Saul took three thousand chosen men from all Israel, and
[b]went to seek David and his men on the
Rocks of the Wild Goats. 3 So he came to
the sheepfolds by the road, where there

23:13 men, about six hundred. *See note on 22:2* when David had only 400 men.

23:14 strongholds in the wilderness. The wilderness of Judah is the barren desert area between the hill country and the Dead Sea. Many ravines and caves are found in this rugged region which David used as a place of refuge from Saul. The title of Ps. 63 may refer to this incident or to 2 Sam. 15:23-28. **Wilderness of Ziph.** The wilderness surrounding Ziph, 4 mi. S of Hebron. **God did not deliver him.** God sovereignly protected David from Saul for the fulfilling of His own divine purposes (cf. Is. 46:9-11).

23:16,17 strengthened his hand in God. Jonathan encouraged David by reminding him of the Lord's promise to him and concern for him, by emphatically assuring him that the Lord would make him the next king over Israel, as Saul well knew (see 20:30,31).

23:18 covenant. *See notes on 18:3; 20:8,23.*

23:19 hill of Hachilah. Location unknown, somewhere between Ziph and the Dead Sea. See the title of Ps. 54. **Jeshimon.** Another name for the wilderness of Judea.

23:24 Wilderness of Maon. The barren territory in the vicinity of Maon (see Josh. 15:48,55), about 5 mi. S of Ziph.

23:25 the rock. A landmark in the wilderness of Maon, soon to be given a name (v. 28).

23:26 encircling David. Saul probably divided his forces into two groups and so surrounded David.

23:27 Philistines have invaded the land. Providentially, a messenger came to Saul telling him that the Philistines were invading the land so that he had no choice but to withdraw and postpone his pursuit of David.

23:28 the Rock of Escape. The timely retreat of Saul's men from David's men led to this name.

23:29 En Gedi. An oasis on the western shore of the Dead Sea 14 mi. E of Ziph, where there is a fresh water spring and lush vineyards (Song 1:14), standing in stark contrast to the surrounding wilderness. The limestone that dominates this region is permeated with caves, which provided good hiding places for David.

24:2 three thousand chosen men. See 26:2. These were the most skilled soldiers. **Rocks of the Wild Goats.** The location of this cave is unknown, although "wild goats" stresses the inaccessibility of the cave (cf. Job 39:1). See the titles of Pss. 57,142, which could also possibly refer to 1 Sam. 22:1.

was a cave; and [c]Saul went in to [d]attend to
his needs. ([e]David and his men were staying in the recesses of the cave.) **4** [f]Then the
men of David said to him, "This is the day
of which the LORD said to you, 'Behold, I
will deliver your enemy into your hand,
that you may do to him as it seems good
to you.' " And David arose and secretly
cut off a corner of Saul's robe. **5** Now it
happened afterward that [g]David's heart
troubled him because he had cut Saul's
robe. **6** And he said to his men, [h]"The LORD
forbid that I should do this thing to my
master, the LORD's anointed, to stretch out
my hand against him, seeing he *is* the
anointed of the LORD." **7** So David [i]re-
strained his servants with *these* words,
and did not allow them to rise against
Saul. And Saul got up from the cave and
went on *his* way.

8 David also arose afterward, went out
of the cave, and called out to Saul, saying,
"My lord the king!" And when Saul
looked behind him, David stooped with
his face to the earth, and bowed down.
9 And David said to Saul: [j]"Why do you
listen to the words of men who say, 'Indeed David seeks your harm'? **10** Look,
this day your eyes have seen that the
LORD delivered you today into my hand
in the cave, and *someone* urged *me* to kill
you. But *my eye* spared you, and I said, 'I
will not stretch out my hand against my
lord, for he *is* the LORD's anointed.'
11 Moreover, my father, see! Yes, see the
corner of your robe in my hand! For in
that I cut off the corner of your robe, and
did not kill you, know and see that *there is*
[k]neither evil nor rebellion in my hand,
and I have not sinned against you. Yet
you [l]hunt my life to take it. **12** [m]Let the
LORD judge between you and me, and let
the LORD avenge me on you. But my hand
shall not be against you. **13** As the proverb
of the ancients says, [n]'Wickedness proceeds from the wicked.' But my hand
shall not be against you. **14** After whom
has the king of Israel come out? Whom do
you pursue? [o]A dead dog? [p]A flea?
15 [q]Therefore let the LORD be judge, and
judge between you and me, and [r]see and
[s]plead my case, and deliver me out of
your hand."

16 So it was, when David had finished
speaking these words to Saul, that Saul
said, [t]"*Is* this your voice, my son David?"
And Saul lifted up his voice and wept.
17 [u]Then he said to David: "You *are* [v]more
righteous than I; for [w]you have rewarded
me with good, whereas I have rewarded
you with evil. **18** And you have shown this
day how you have dealt well with me; for
when [x]the LORD delivered me into your
hand, you did not kill me. **19** For if a man
finds his enemy, will he let him get away
safely? Therefore may the LORD reward
you with good for what you have done to
me this day. **20** And now [y]I know indeed
that you shall surely be king, and that the
kingdom of Israel shall be established in
your hand. **21** [z]Therefore swear now to me
by the LORD [a]that you will not cut off my
descendants after me, and that you will
not destroy my name from my father's
house."

22 So David swore to Saul. And Saul
went home, but David and his men went
up to [b]the stronghold.

3 [c] 1 Sam. 24:10 [d] Judg. 3:24 [e] Ps. 57:title; 142:title
4 [f] 1 Sam. 26:8-11
5 [g] 2 Sam. 24:10
6 [h] 1 Sam. 26:11
7 [i] Ps. 7:4; [Matt. 5:44; Rom. 12:17, 19]
9 [j] Ps. 141:6; [Prov. 16:28; 17:9]
11 [k] Judg. 11:27; Ps. 7:3; 35:7
[l] 1 Sam. 26:20
12 [m] Gen. 16:5; Judg. 11:27; 1 Sam. 26:10-23; Job 5:8
13 [n] [Matt. 7:16-20]
14 [o] 1 Sam. 17:43; 2 Sam. 9:8 [p] 1 Sam. 26:20
15 [q] 1 Sam. 24:12 [r] 2 Chr. 24:22 [s] Ps. 35:1; 43:1; 119:154; Mic. 7:9
16 [t] 1 Sam. 26:17
17 [u] 1 Sam. 26:21 [v] Gen. 38:26 [w] [Matt. 5:44]
18 [x] 1 Sam. 26:23
20 [y] 1 Sam. 23:17
21 [z] Gen. 21:23; 1 Sam. 20:14-17 [a] 2 Sam. 21:6-8
22 [b] 1 Sam. 23:29

24:3 attend to his needs. Lit. "to cover his feet." This is a euphemism for having a bowel movement, as the person would crouch with his inner garment dropped to his feet.

24:4 the day of which the LORD said to you. David's men perhaps believed that God had providentially placed Saul in the same cave where they were hiding so David could kill the king. However, nothing revelatory had previously been said by the Lord that indicated He wanted David to lift a hand against Saul.

24:5 David's heart troubled him. David was able to cut off a piece of Saul's robe undetected. However, touching Saul's clothing was tantamount to touching his person, and David's conscience troubled him on this account.

24:6 LORD's anointed. David recognized that the Lord Himself had placed Saul into the kingship. Thus the judgment and removal of Saul had to be left to the Lord.

24:11 neither evil nor rebellion. If David were a wicked rebel against the rule of Saul, as Saul had said (22:8,13), he would have killed Saul when given this opportunity. The corner of the robe was proof to Saul that David was not his enemy.

24:12 Let the LORD judge. David called for the Lord Himself, the only fair and impartial Judge (cf. Judg. 11:27), to decide the fate of David and Saul (also v. 15).

24:13 proverb. A traditional pithy statement that evil deeds are perpetrated only by evil men. A similar point is made by Jesus in Matt. 7:16,20.

24:14 A dead dog? A flea? David hereby expresses his lowliness and entire committal of his cause to God, who alone is the Judge and to whom alone belongs vengeance.

24:17 You *are* more righteous than I. Upon hearing David's testimony, Saul was moved with emotion and acknowledged that David was more righteous than he was. His testimony to David's righteousness recognized David's right to the kingship.

24:20 you shall surely be king. Saul emphatically acknowledged that David would be the ruler over the kingdom of Israel. Saul had already been told by Samuel that God would take the kingdom away from him and give it to a man after his own heart (13:14; 15:28). Jonathan had testified that Saul already knew that David would be king (23:17). However, this recognition did not mean that Saul was ready to give up the kingdom.

24:22 David swore to Saul. By solemn oath, David agreed to preserve Saul's family and family name. While most of Saul's family was later slain (2 Sam. 21:8,9), this pledge was fulfilled in the life of Mephibosheth (*see note on 2 Sam. 21:7*).

Death of Samuel

25 Then [a]Samuel died; and the Israelites gathered together and [b]la-
mented for him, and buried him at his
home in Ramah. And David arose and
went down [c]to the Wilderness of [1]Paran.

David and the Wife of Nabal

2 Now *there was* a man [d]in Maon whose
business *was* in [e]Carmel, and the man *was*
very rich. He had three thousand sheep
and a thousand goats. And he was shearing his sheep in Carmel. 3 The name of the
man *was* Nabal, and the name of his wife
Abigail. And *she was* a woman of good understanding and beautiful appearance; but
the man *was* harsh and evil in *his* doings.
He *was of the house of* [f]Caleb.
4 When David heard in the wilderness
that Nabal was [g]shearing his sheep, 5 David sent ten young men; and David said to
the young men, "Go up to Carmel, go to
Nabal, and greet him in my name. 6 And
thus you shall say to him who lives *in pros-*
perity: [h]'Peace *be* to you, peace to your
house, and peace to all that you have!
7 Now I have heard that you have shearers.
Your shepherds were with us, and we did
not hurt them, [i]nor was there anything
missing from them all the while they were
in Carmel. 8 Ask your young men, and
they will tell you. Therefore [2]let *my* young
men find favor in your eyes, for we come
on [j]a feast day. Please give whatever
comes to your hand to your servants and
to your son David.' "
9 So when David's young men came,
they spoke to Nabal according to all these
words in the name of David, and waited.
10 Then Nabal answered David's servants, and said, [k]"Who *is* David, and who
is the son of Jesse? There are many servants
nowadays who break away each one from
his master. 11 [l]Shall I then take my bread
and my water and my [3]meat that I have
killed for my shearers, and give *it* to men
when I do not know where they *are* from?"
12 So David's young men turned on their
heels and went back; and they came and
told him all these words. 13 Then David
said to his men, "Every man gird on his
sword." So every man girded on his sword,
and David also girded on his sword. And
about four hundred men went with David,
and two hundred [m]stayed with the supplies.
14 Now one of the young men told Abigail, Nabal's wife, saying, "Look, David
sent messengers from the wilderness to
greet our master; and he [4]reviled them.
15 But the men *were* very good to us, and
[n]we were not hurt, nor did we miss anything as long as we accompanied them,
when we were in the fields. 16 They were
[o]a wall to us both by night and day, all the
time we were with them keeping the
sheep. 17 Now therefore, know and consider what you will do, for [p]harm is determined against our master and against all
his household. For he *is such* a [q]scoundrel[5]
that *one* cannot speak to him."
18 Then Abigail made haste and [r]took
two hundred *loaves* of bread, two skins of
wine, five sheep already dressed, five
seahs of roasted *grain*, one hundred clusters of raisins, and two hundred cakes of
figs, and loaded *them* on donkeys. 19 And
she said to her servants, [s]"Go on before
me; see, I am coming after you." But she
did not tell her husband Nabal.

CHAPTER 25

1 [a] 1 Sam. 28:3 [b] Num. 20:29; Deut. 34:8 [c] Gen. 21:21; Num. 10:12; 13:3 [1] So with MT, Syr., Tg., Vg.; LXX *Maon*
2 [d] 1 Sam. 23:24 [e] Josh. 15:55
3 [f] Josh. 15:13; 1 Sam. 30:14
4 [g] Gen. 38:13; 2 Sam. 13:23
6 [h] Judg. 19:20; 1 Chr. 12:18; Ps. 122:7; Luke 10:5
7 [i] 1 Sam. 25:15, 21
8 [j] Neh. 8:10-12; Esth. 8:17; 9:19, 22 [2] *be gracious to the young men*
10 [k] Judg. 9:28
11 [l] Judg. 8:6, 15 [3] Lit. *slaughter*
13 [m] 1 Sam. 30:24
14 [4] *scolded or scorned at*
15 [n] 1 Sam. 25:7, 21
16 [o] Ex. 14:22; Job 1:10
17 [p] 1 Sam. 20:7 [q] Deut. 13:13; Judg. 19:22 [5] Lit. *son of Belial*
18 [r] Gen. 32:13; [Prov. 18:16; 21:14]
19 [s] Gen. 32:16, 20

25:1 the Israelites…lamented for him. The death of Samuel, the last of the judges, brought Israel to the end of an era. So widespread was Samuel's influence among the people that all Israel gathered to lament his death. **Wilderness of Paran.** A desert area in the NE region of the Sinai Peninsula.

25:2 Carmel. "Vineyard land," "garden spot." About 7 mi. S of Hebron and one mi. N of Maon. This was the same spot where Saul erected a monument in his own honor (15:12).

25:3 Nabal. "Fool." An appropriate name in view of his foolish behavior (v. 25). **Abigail.** "My father is joy." The wife of Nabal who was intelligent and beautiful in contrast to her evil husband. ***the house of* Caleb.** Nabal was a descendant of Caleb and lived in Caleb's tribal holdings (Josh. 14:13; 15:13), but did not possess the spiritual qualities of his illustrious forefather.

25:4,5 shearing his sheep. While hiding out in the wilderness, David and his men took the job of protecting the flocks of Nabal (vv. 7,15,16). Upon hearing that Nabal was shearing his sheep, David sent 10 of his men to collect their rightful compensation for the good they had done (v. 8).

25:8 a feast day. A special day of rejoicing over the abundance of sheared wool from the sheep (cf. v. 11).

25:10,11 This pretended ignorance of David was surely a sham. The knowledge of the young king-elect was widespread. Nabal pretended not to know to excuse his unwillingness to do what was right.

25:14 reviled. David sent his messengers to "greet" (lit. "bless") Nabal, but David's men were viciously rebuffed by Nabal. This term emphasized the wickedness of Nabal's action.

25:15,16 The testimony of one of Nabal's men affirmed the value of David's protection. It was like a fortress "wall" enclosing a city, providing total security.

25:17 *one* cannot speak to him. Nabal was a "son of Belial," a worthless fellow (*see note on 2:12*). Nabal's situation was the product of his own wickedness. His unwillingness to seek the counsel of others ultimately led to his demise.

25:18 five seahs. Slightly more than one bu.

25:19 did not tell her husband. Abigail knew that Nabal would disagree with her actions, but knowing the Lord's choice of David (v. 28), she recognized the consequences involved in Nabal's cursing of David. By her actions, she chose to obey God rather than man (see Acts 5:29), as a wife may sometimes need to do.

20 So it was, *as* she rode on the donkey,
that she went down under cover of the hill;
and there were David and his men, coming
down toward her, and she met them.
21 Now David had said, "Surely in vain I
have protected all that this *fellow* has in the
wilderness, so that nothing was missed of
all that *belongs* to him. And he has [t]repaid
me evil for good. 22 [u]May God do so, and
more also, to the enemies of David, if I
[v]leave [w]one male of all who *belong* to him
by morning light."
23 Now when Abigail saw David, she
[x]dismounted quickly from the donkey, fell
on her face before David, and bowed down
to the ground. 24 So she fell at his feet and
said: "On me, my lord, *on* me *let* this iniquity *be!* And please let your maidservant
[6]speak in your ears, and hear the words of
your maidservant. 25 Please, let not my
lord [7]regard this scoundrel Nabal. For as
his name *is,* so *is* he: [8]Nabal *is* his name,
and folly *is* with him! But I, your maidservant, did not see the young men of my lord
whom you sent. 26 Now therefore, my
lord, [y]*as* the LORD lives and *as* your soul
lives, since the LORD has [z]held you back
from coming to bloodshed and from
[a]avenging[9] yourself with your own hand,
now then, [b]let your enemies and those
who seek harm for my lord be as Nabal.
27 And now [c]this present which your
maidservant has brought to my lord, let it
be given to the young men who follow my
lord. 28 Please forgive the trespass of your
maidservant. For [d]the LORD will certainly
make for my lord an enduring house, because my lord [e]fights the battles of the
LORD, [f]and evil is not found in you
throughout your days. 29 Yet a man has
risen to pursue you and seek your life, but
the life of my lord shall be [g]bound in the
bundle of the living with the LORD your
God; and the lives of your enemies He
shall [h]sling out, *as from* the pocket of a
sling. 30 And it shall come to pass, when
the LORD has done for my lord according to
all the good that He has spoken concerning
you, and has appointed you [i]ruler over Israel, 31 that this will be no grief to you, nor
offense of heart to my lord, either that you
have shed blood without cause, or that my
lord has avenged himself. But when the
LORD has dealt well with my lord, then remember your maidservant."
32 Then David said to Abigail: [j]"Blessed
is the LORD God of Israel, who sent you this
day to meet me! 33 And blessed *is* your advice and blessed *are* you, because you have
[k]kept me this day from coming to bloodshed and from avenging myself with my
own hand. 34 For indeed, *as* the LORD God
of Israel lives, who has [l]kept me back from
hurting you, unless you had hurried and
come to meet me, surely [m]by morning light
no males would have been left to Nabal!"
35 So David received from her hand what
she had brought him, and said to her, [n]"Go
up in peace to your house. See, I have
heeded your voice and [o]respected your
person."
36 Now Abigail went to Nabal, and there
he was, [p]holding a feast in his house, like
the feast of a king. And Nabal's heart *was*
merry within him, for he *was* very drunk;
therefore she told him nothing, little or
much, until morning light. 37 So it was, in
the morning, when the wine had gone
from Nabal, and his wife had told him
these things, that his heart died within
him, and he became *like* a stone. 38 Then it
happened, *after* about ten days, that the
LORD [q]struck Nabal, and he died.
39 So when David heard that Nabal was
dead, he said, [r]"Blessed *be* the LORD, who
has [s]pleaded the cause of my reproach
from the hand of Nabal, and has [t]kept His
servant from evil! For the LORD has [u]re-
turned the wickedness of Nabal on his
own head."
And David sent and proposed to Abigail, to take her as his wife. 40 When the
servants of David had come to Abigail at
Carmel, they spoke to her saying, "David
sent us to you, to ask you to become his
wife."

21 [t] 1 Sam. 24:17; Ps. 109:5; [Prov. 17:13]
22 [u] Ruth 1:17; 1 Sam. 3:17; 20:13, 16 [v] 1 Sam. 25:34 [w] 1 Kin. 14:10; 21:21; 2 Kin. 9:8
23 [x] Josh. 15:18; Judg. 1:14
24 [6] *speak to you*
25 [7] *pay attention to* [8] Lit. *Fool*
26 [y] 2 Kin. 2:2 [z] Gen. 20:6; 1 Sam. 25:33 [a] [Rom. 12:19] [b] 2 Sam. 18:32 [9] Lit. *saving yourself*
27 [c] Gen. 33:11; 1 Sam. 30:26; 2 Kin. 5:15
28 [d] 2 Sam. 7:11-16, 27; 1 Kin. 9:5; 1 Chr. 17:10, 25 [e] 1 Sam. 18:17 [f] 1 Sam. 24:11; Ps. 7:3
29 [g] [Ps. 66:9; Col. 3:3] [h] Jer. 10:18
30 [i] 1 Sam. 13:14; 15:28
32 [j] Gen. 24:27; Ex. 18:10; 1 Kin. 1:48; Ps. 41:13; 72:18; 106:48; Luke 1:68
33 [k] 1 Sam. 25:26
34 [l] 1 Sam. 25:26 [m] 1 Sam. 25:22
35 [n] 1 Sam. 20:42; 2 Sam. 15:9; 2 Kin. 5:19; Luke 7:50; 8:48 [o] Gen. 19:21
36 [p] 2 Sam. 13:28; Prov. 20:1; Is. 5:11; Dan. 5:1; [Hos. 4:11]
38 [q] 1 Sam. 26:10; 2 Sam. 6:7; Ps. 104:29
39 [r] 1 Sam. 25:32 [s] 1 Sam. 24:15; Prov. 22:23 [t] 1 Sam. 25:26, 34 [u] 1 Kin. 2:44

25:22 May God do so. A strong oath of self-imprecation. David swore that he would kill every male in Nabal's household by daybreak.

25:25 this scoundrel. I.e., "troublemaker." **as his name *is,* so *is* he.** A name was not simply a label of distinguishing one thing from another, but a profound insight into the character of the one named. "Fool" has the connotation of one who is "morally deficient."

25:28 an enduring house. Abigail's perceptive insight fit an essential feature of the Davidic Covenant (see 2 Sam. 7:11-16). **fights the battles of the LORD.** Unlike the king previously desired by the people (8:20), David was a man who fought the Lord's battles. He was truly God's king.

25:29 bound in the bundle of the living. A metaphor that reflects the custom of binding valuables in a bundle to protect them from injury. The point here was that God cared for His own as a man would his valuable treasure. David, she said, enjoyed the protection of divine providence which destined him for great things. On the other hand, God would fling his enemies away like a stone in a slingshot.

25:30 ruler over Israel. Abigail was certain that David would exercise effective rule over Israel after Saul's death. In the meantime, however, she did not want him to do anything to jeopardize his future, endanger his throne, or violate God's will by seeking personal vengeance in anger (vv. 33,34).

25:37,38 heart died...became *like* a stone. Intoxicated, Nabal apparently suffered a stroke and became paralyzed until he died.

41 Then she arose, bowed her face to the
earth, and said, "Here is your maidservant,
a servant to [v]wash the feet of the servants
of my lord." 42 So Abigail rose in haste and
rode on a donkey, [1]attended by five of her
maidens; and she followed the messengers
of David, and became his wife. 43 David
also took Ahinoam [w]of Jezreel, [x]and so
both of them were his wives.
44 But Saul had given [y]Michal his
daughter, David's wife, to [2]Palti the son of
Laish, who *was* from [z]Gallim.

David Spares Saul a Second Time

26 Now the Ziphites came to Saul at
Gibeah, saying, [a]"Is David not hiding in the hill of Hachilah, opposite Jeshimon?" 2 Then Saul arose and went
down to the Wilderness of Ziph, having
[b]three thousand chosen men of Israel with
him, to seek David in the Wilderness of
Ziph. 3 And Saul encamped in the hill of
Hachilah, which *is* opposite Jeshimon, by
the road. But David stayed in the wilderness, and he saw that Saul came after him
into the wilderness. 4 David therefore sent
out spies, and understood that Saul had indeed come.
5 So David arose and came to the place
where Saul had encamped. And David
saw the place where Saul lay, and [c]Abner
the son of Ner, the commander of his army.
Now Saul lay within the camp, with the
people encamped all around him. 6 Then
David answered, and said to Ahimelech
the Hittite and to Abishai [d]the son of Zeruiah, brother of [e]Joab, saying, "Who will
[f]go down with me to Saul in the camp?"
And [g]Abishai said, "I will go down with
you."
7 So David and Abishai came to the people by night; and there Saul lay sleeping
within the camp, with his spear stuck in the
ground by his head. And Abner and the
people lay all around him. 8 Then Abishai
said to David, [h]"God has delivered your
enemy into your hand this day. Now therefore, please, let me strike him [1]at once with
the spear, right to the earth; and I will not
have to strike him a second time!"
9 But David said to Abishai, "Do not destroy him; [i]for who can stretch out his
hand against the LORD's anointed, and be
guiltless?" 10 David said furthermore, "*As*
the LORD lives, [j]the LORD shall strike him,
or [k]his day shall come to die, or he shall
[l]go out to battle and perish. 11 [m]The LORD
forbid that I should stretch out my hand
against the LORD's anointed. But please,
take now the spear and the jug of water
that *are* by his head, and let us go." 12 So
David took the spear and the jug of water
by Saul's head, and they got away; and no
man saw or knew *it* or awoke. For they
were all asleep, because [n]a deep sleep from
the LORD had fallen on them.
13 Now David went over to the other
side, and stood on the top of a hill afar off,
a great distance *being* between them.
14 And David called out to the people and
to Abner the son of Ner, saying, "Do you
not answer, Abner?"
Then Abner answered and said, "Who
are you, calling out to the king?"
15 So David said to Abner, "*Are* you not
a man? And who *is* like you in Israel? Why
then have you not guarded your lord the
king? For one of the people came in to destroy your lord the king. 16 This thing that
you have done *is* not good. *As* the LORD
lives, you deserve to die, because you have
not guarded your master, the LORD's
anointed. And now see where the king's
spear *is*, and the jug of water that *was* by
his head."
17 Then Saul knew David's voice, and
said, [o]"*Is* that your voice, my son David?"
David said, "*It is* my voice, my lord, O
king." 18 And he said, [p]"Why does my lord
thus pursue his servant? For what have I
done, or what evil *is* in my hand? 19 Now
therefore, please, let my lord the king hear
the words of his servant: If the LORD has
[q]stirred you up against me, let Him accept
an offering. But if *it is* the children of men,
may they *be* cursed before the LORD, [r]for

41 [v][Prov. 15:33]; Luke 7:38, 44
42 [1]Lit. *with five of her maidens at her feet*
43 [w]Josh. 15:56 [x]1 Sam. 27:3; 30:5
44 [y]1 Sam. 18:20; 2 Sam. 3:14 [z]Is. 10:30 [2]*Paltiel,* 2 Sam. 3:15

CHAPTER 26

1 [a]1 Sam. 23:19; Ps. 54:title
2 [b]1 Sam. 13:2; 24:2
5 [c]1 Sam. 14:50, 51; 17:55
6 [d]1 Chr. 2:16 [e]2 Sam. 2:13 [f]Judg. 7:10, 11 [g]2 Sam. 2:18, 24
8 [h]1 Sam. 24:4 [1]Or *one time*
9 [i]1 Sam. 24:6, 7; 2 Sam. 1:14, 16
10 [j][Deut. 32:35]; 1 Sam. 25:26, 38; [Luke 18:7; Rom. 12:19; Heb. 10:30] [k]Gen. 47:29; Deut. 31:14; [Job 7:1; 14:5]; Ps. 37:13 [l]1 Sam. 31:6
11 [m]1 Sam. 24:6-12; [Rom. 12:17, 19]
12 [n]Gen. 2:21; 15:12; Is. 29:10
17 [o]1 Sam. 24:16
18 [p]1 Sam. 24:9, 11-14
19 [q]2 Sam. 16:11; 24:1 [r]Deut. 4:27, 28

25:43 Ahinoam of Jezreel. David's third wife, joining Michal and Abigail. For Jezreel, *see notes on 29:1*.

25:44 Palti...from Gallim. Palti means "my deliverance." The location of Gallim is unknown, but was probably a few mi. N of Jerusalem. See 2 Sam. 3:13-16 for Michal's return to David.

26:1 hill of Hachilah...Jeshimon. *See notes on 23:19.*

26:2 three thousand chosen men. See 24:2.

26:5 Saul lay. Saul was sleeping in an apparently invulnerable place. He had his commander beside him, inside the camp, surrounded by his entire army. **Abner.** *See note on 14:50.*

26:6 Ahimelech the Hittite. Mentioned only here, he was one of the many mercenaries who formed a part of David's army. **Abishai the son of Zeruiah, brother of Joab.** *See note on 2 Sam. 2:18.* He joined with Ahimelech in going down with David into the camp of Saul.

26:9 the LORD's anointed. *See note on 24:6.*

26:10 *As* the LORD lives. An oath usually associated with life-or-death matters. The sovereign God would decide when, where, and how Saul would perish, not David.

26:12 spear and the jug. Like the corner of Saul's robe (24:4), these were taken as proof that David had Saul's life in his hand (cf. v. 16). **a deep sleep from the LORD.** As with Adam in Gen. 2:21 and Abraham in Gen. 15:12, the Lord caused Saul to be unaware of what was taking place around him.

26:19 If the LORD...the children of men. David set forth two possibilities for why Saul was pursuing him. First, David had sinned

they have driven me out this day from
sharing in the [s]inheritance of the LORD,
saying, 'Go, serve other gods.' 20 So now,
do not let my blood fall to the earth before
the face of the LORD. For the king of Israel
has come out to seek [t]a flea, as when one
hunts a partridge in the mountains."
21 Then Saul said, [u]"I have sinned. Return, my son David. For I will harm you no
more, because my life was precious in your
eyes this day. Indeed I have played the fool
and erred exceedingly."
22 And David answered and said, "Here
is the king's spear. Let one of the young
men come over and get it. 23 [v]May the LORD
[w]repay every man *for* his righteousness and
his faithfulness; for the LORD delivered you
into *my* hand today, but I would not stretch
out my hand against the LORD's anointed.
24 And indeed, as your life was valued
much this day in my eyes, so let my life be
valued much in the eyes of the LORD, and let
Him deliver me out of all tribulation."
25 Then Saul said to David, "*May* you *be*
blessed, my son David! You shall both do
great things and also still [x]prevail."
So David went on his way, and Saul returned to his place.

David Allied with the Philistines

27 And David said in his heart, "Now I
shall perish someday by the hand of
Saul. *There is* nothing better for me than that
I should speedily escape to the land of the
Philistines; and Saul will [1]despair of me, to
seek me anymore in any part of Israel. So I
shall escape out of his hand." 2 Then David
arose [a]and went over with the six hundred
men who *were* with him [b]to Achish the son
of Maoch, king of Gath. 3 So David dwelt
with Achish at Gath, he and his men, each
man with his household, *and* David [c]with
his two wives, Ahinoam the Jezreelitess,
and Abigail the Carmelitess, Nabal's
widow. 4 And it was told Saul that David
had fled to Gath; so he sought him no more.
5 Then David said to Achish, "If I have
now found favor in your eyes, let them
give me a place in some town in the country, that I may dwell there. For why should
your servant dwell in the royal city with
you?" 6 So Achish gave him Ziklag that
day. Therefore [d]Ziklag has belonged to the
kings of Judah to this day. 7 Now [2]the time
that David [e]dwelt in the country of the Philistines was one full year and four months.
8 And David and his men went up and
raided [f]the Geshurites, [g]the [3]Girzites, and
the [h]Amalekites. For those nations were
the inhabitants of the land from [4]of old, [i]as
you go to Shur, even as far as the land of
Egypt. 9 Whenever David [5]attacked the
land, he left neither man nor woman alive,
but took away the sheep, the oxen, the
donkeys, the camels, and the apparel, and
returned and came to Achish. 10 Then
Achish would say, "Where have you made
a raid today?" And David would say,
"Against the southern *area* of Judah, or
against the southern *area* of [j]the Jerahmeelites, or against the southern *area* of [k]the
Kenites." 11 David would save neither man

19 [s]2 Sam. 14:16; 20:19
20 [t]1 Sam. 24:14
21 [u]Ex. 9:27; 1 Sam. 15:24, 30; 24:17; 2 Sam. 12:13
23 [v]1 Sam. 24:19; Ps. 7:8; 18:20; 62:12 [w]2 Sam. 22:21
25 [x]Gen. 32:28; 1 Sam. 24:20

CHAPTER 27

1 [1]*despair of searching for*
2 [a]1 Sam. 25:13 [b]1 Sam. 21:10; 1 Kin. 2:39
3 [c]1 Sam. 25:42, 43
6 [d]Josh. 15:31; 19:5; 1 Chr. 12:1; Neh. 11:28
7 [e]1 Sam. 29:3 [2]Lit. *the number of days*
8 [f]Josh. 13:2, 13 [g]Josh. 16:10; Judg. 1:29 [h]Ex. 17:8, 16; 1 Sam. 15:7, 8 [i]Gen. 25:18; Ex. 15:22 [3]Or *Gezrites* [4]*ancient times*
9 [5]Lit. *struck*
10 [j]1 Chr. 2:9, 25 [k]Judg. 1:16

against the Lord. If that was the case, he was willing to offer a sacrifice for atonement. Second, evil men had caused Saul's hostility toward David. If that were the case, these men should be judged. **the inheritance of the LORD.** I.e., the land of Israel (cf. 2 Sam. 20:19; 21:3). **Go, serve other gods.** David's exile from the land was virtually equivalent to forcing him to abandon the worship of the Lord, for there were no sanctuaries to the Lord outside of Israelite territory.

26:20 flea...partridge. The flea represents something that was worthless and the partridge something that was impossible to catch. Saul was wasting his time with his pursuit of David.

26:21 I have sinned. As in 24:17, Saul confessed his sin and wrongdoing. Although Saul may have been sincere, he could not be trusted and David wisely did not accept his invitation to return with him. **I have played the fool.** Saul had been foolish in his actions toward David, as had Nabal.

26:25 still prevail. Saul recognized the certain success of David's future as Israel's king (cf. 24:20).

27:1 by the hand of Saul. In direct contrast to Saul's word that David would prevail (26:25), David thought that Saul would ultimately kill him. This anxious thinking and the fear that fell upon him explain David's actions in this chapter. God had told him to stay in Judah (22:5), but he was afraid and sought protection again among the Philistine enemies of Israel (cf. 21:10-15).

27:3 two wives. His third wife, Michal, had been temporarily given to another man by Saul (cf. 25:44).

27:4 sought him no more. Saul was no longer able to pursue David since he was out of the land of Israel.

27:5 the royal city. I.e., Gath. David requested a city of his own in the country so that he could be free from the constant surveillance to which he was exposed in Gath, and so that he could avoid the pagan influence of that Philistine city.

27:6 Ziklag. This was a city located about 13 mi. NW of Beersheba that had been an Israelite possession (Josh. 15:31; 19:5), but was then under Philistine control. **to this day.** Ziklag became a part of Judah and was still so at the time of the writing of Samuel, which is clearly in the post-Solomonic, divided kingdom era. See Introduction: Author and Date.

27:7 one full year and four months. For 16 months David was able to deceive Achish concerning his actions. He remained there until after Saul's death when he moved to Hebron (2 Sam. 1:1; 2:1,2).

27:8 Geshurites...Girzites...Amalekites. These peoples lived in southern Canaan and northern Sinai. **Shur...Egypt.** *See note on 15:7.*

27:9 he left neither man nor woman alive. David left no survivors from his raids in order that Achish might not learn the true nature of his desert exploits (see v. 11).

27:10 Judah...Jerahmeelites...Kenites. The regions S of the hill country centering around Beersheba. This region was far enough away from Gath so that Achish would be ignorant of David's movements. David implied to Achish that the hostility of Judah toward

nor woman alive, to bring *news* to Gath,
saying, "Lest they should inform on us,
saying, 'Thus David did.' " And thus *was*
his behavior all the time he dwelt in the
country of the Philistines. 12 So Achish believed David, saying, "He has made his
people Israel utterly abhor him; therefore
he will be my servant forever."

28 Now [a]it happened in those days
that the Philistines gathered their
armies together for war, to fight with Israel. And Achish said to David, "You assuredly know that you will go out with me
to battle, you and your men."
2 So David said to Achish, "Surely you
know what your servant can do."
And Achish said to David, "Therefore I
will make you one of my chief guardians
forever."

Saul Consults a Medium

3 Now [b]Samuel had died, and all Israel
had lamented for him and buried him in
[c]Ramah, in his own city. And Saul had put
[d]the mediums and the spiritists out of the
land.
4 Then the Philistines gathered together,
and came and encamped at [e]Shunem. So
Saul gathered all Israel together, and they
encamped at [f]Gilboa. 5 When Saul saw the
army of the Philistines, he was [g]afraid, and
his heart trembled greatly. 6 And when
Saul inquired of the LORD, [h]the LORD did
not answer him, either by [i]dreams or [j]by
Urim or by the prophets.
7 Then Saul said to his servants, "Find
me a woman who is a medium, [k]that I may
go to her and inquire of her."
And his servants said to him, "In fact,
there is a woman who is a medium at En
Dor."
8 So Saul disguised himself and put on
other clothes, and he went, and two men
with him; and they came to the woman by
night. And [l]he said, "Please conduct a
séance for me, and bring up for me the one
I shall name to you."
9 Then the woman said to him, "Look,
you know what Saul has done, how he has
[m]cut off the mediums and the spiritists
from the land. Why then do you lay a snare
for my life, to cause me to die?"
10 And Saul swore to her by the LORD,

CHAPTER 28
1 [a] 1 Sam. 29:1, 2
3 [b] 1 Sam. 25:1 [c] 1 Sam. 1:19 [d] Ex. 22:18; Lev. 19:31; 20:27; Deut. 18:10, 11; 1 Sam. 15:23; 28:9
4 [e] Josh. 19:18; 1 Sam. 28:4; 1 Kin. 1:3; 2 Kin. 4:8 [f] 1 Sam. 31:1
5 [g] Job 18:11; [Is. 57:20]
6 [h] 1 Sam. 14:37; Prov. 1:28; Lam. 2:9 [i] Num. 12:6; Joel 2:28 [j] Ex. 28:30; Num. 27:21; Deut. 33:8
7 [k] 1 Chr. 10:13
8 [l] Deut. 18:10, 11; 1 Chr. 10:13; Is. 8:19
9 [m] 1 Sam. 28:3

David was increasing, while in fact he was gaining the appreciation and loyalty of Judah toward himself by raiding their wilderness neighbors. Achish thought David was more securely his servant as his own people turned against him (v. 24), but just the opposite was true.

28:1 You assuredly know. The kindness showed to David and his men by Achish in Gath was not without expectation of reciprocation. This phrase seems to presuppose an understanding of this expectation.

28:2 what your servant can do. Being a man of honor, David would not fail to help those who had shown him kindness. David was drawing attention to the fact that he had proven himself as a valiant and successful warrior and was assuring Achish of his fidelity and ability. **chief guardians.** In light of David's victory over Goliath (17:49-54) and imagined bad reputation among the Israelites, Achish was expressing considerable trust in David's loyalty and ability, for "chief guardian" lit. means "keeper of my head."

28:3-13 Having deprived himself of every legitimate means of spiritual input as a result of his own disobedience and rebellion, Saul walked in foolishness again by seeking out the very resource (a medium) he had previously removed from the land. Saul swore to the medium an oath of safety by the very God that he was disobeying even then. Yet the inexorable curiosity of Saul to consult Samuel, in spite of Samuel's death, was satisfied by the medium's willingness to "bring up" Samuel.

28:3 mediums and the spiritists. By divine law, they were banned from Israel (Deut. 18:11), and Israel was not to be defiled by them (Lev. 19:31). Turning to them was tantamount to playing the harlot and would result in God setting His face against the person and cutting him off from among His people (Lev. 20:6). Mediums and spiritists were to be put to death by stoning (Lev. 20:27). Even Saul understood this and had previously dealt with the issue (see v. 9).

28:4 Shunem. Situated SW of the hill of Moreh and 16 mi. SW of the Sea of Galilee; the Philistines designated it as their camp site. **Gilboa.** The mountain range beginning 5 mi. S of Shunem and extending southward along the eastern edge of the plain of Jezreel. *See note on 31:1.*

28:5 his heart trembled greatly. Saul had hid himself when he was chosen by lot to be king (10:22). When the Spirit of the Lord came upon him, he was changed (10:6), but after the Spirit had departed (16:14), he was afraid and dismayed by Goliath (17:11, 24). He feared at Gilgal when faced by the overwhelming size of the Philistine army (13:11, 12). Saul was also afraid of David because he knew that the Lord was with David (18:12, 29). But, Saul was to fear God (12:24), not people.

28:6 dreams...Urim...prophets. These were the 3 basic ways through which God revealed His Word and His will. Dreams and visions were the common manner through which the Lord revealed Himself and His will during the time of Moses (Num. 12:6). The Urim was used by the priest as a means of inquiring of the Lord (Num. 27:21). It was originally put in the breastpiece of judgment with the Thummim and worn over Aaron's heart when he went in before the Lord (*see note on Ex. 28:30*). Somehow, unknown to us, God revealed His will by it. Prophets were formerly called seers (9:9) and were used as a reference for inquiring of the Lord. God also used prophets to declare His Word when people were not interested in it (Amos 7:12, 13). Since Saul had rejected the Lord, God had rejected him (15:23). Saul appears to have had no court prophet in the manner that Gad and Nathan were to David (22:5; 2 Sam. 12); and, by this time, the ephod with the Urim was in David's possession by virtue of Abiathar the priest (23:6).

28:7 Find me...a medium. In Saul's desperation, he sought the very source that he had formerly removed from the land (28:3). In spite of the ban, Saul's servant knew exactly where to find a medium. **En Dor.** Located about 3.5 mi. NW of Shunem between Mt. Tabor and the Hill of Moreh. Saul risked his life by venturing into the Philistine-held territory to seek out the counsel of the medium; thus he went in disguise by night (v. 8).

28:10 swore to her by the LORD. Though blatantly walking in disobedience to God, it is ironic that Saul would swear by the very existence of the Lord as a means of assuring his credibility to the medium. Even more, Saul swore that no punishment would come upon her when the Levitical law required her to be stoned to death (Lev. 20:27).

saying, "*As* the LORD lives, no punishment
shall come upon you for this thing."
11 Then the woman said, "Whom shall I
bring up for you?"
And he said, "Bring up Samuel for me."
12 When the woman saw Samuel, she
cried out with a loud voice. And the
woman spoke to Saul, saying, "Why have
you deceived me? For you *are* Saul!"
13 And the king said to her, "Do not be
afraid. What did you see?"
And the woman said to Saul, "I saw [n]a [1]
spirit ascending out of the earth."
14 So he said to her, "What *is* his form?"
And she said, "An old man is coming
up, and he *is* covered with [o]a mantle." And
Saul perceived that it *was* Samuel, and he
stooped with *his* face to the ground and
bowed down.
15 Now Samuel said to Saul, "Why have
you [p]disturbed me by bringing me up?"
And Saul answered, "I am deeply distressed; for the Philistines make war
against me, and [q]God has departed from
me and [r]does not answer me anymore, neither by prophets nor by dreams. Therefore
I have called you, that you may reveal to
me what I should do."
16 Then Samuel said: "So why do you
ask me, seeing the LORD has departed from
you and has become your enemy? 17 And
the LORD has done for [2]Himself [s]as He
spoke by me. For the LORD has torn the
kingdom out of your hand and given it to
your neighbor, David. 18 [t]Because you did
not obey the voice of the LORD nor execute
His fierce wrath upon [u]Amalek, therefore
the LORD has done this thing to you this
day. 19 Moreover the LORD will also deliver
Israel with you into the hand of the Philistines. And tomorrow you and your sons
will be with [v]me. The LORD will also deliver the army of Israel into the hand of the
Philistines."
20 Immediately Saul fell full length on
the ground, and was dreadfully afraid because of the words of Samuel. And there
was no strength in him, for he had eaten no
food all day or all night.
21 And the woman came to Saul and saw
that he was severely troubled, and said to
him, "Look, your maidservant has obeyed
your voice, and I have [w]put my life in my
hands and heeded the words which you
spoke to me. 22 Now therefore, please,
heed also the voice of your maidservant,
and let me set a piece of bread before you;
and eat, that you may have strength when
you go on *your* way."
23 But he refused and said, "I will not
eat."
So his servants, together with the
woman, urged him; and he heeded their
voice. Then he arose from the ground and
sat on the bed. 24 Now the woman had a
fatted calf in the house, and she hastened
to kill it. And she took flour and kneaded
it, and baked unleavened bread from it.
25 So she brought *it* before Saul and his servants, and they ate. Then they rose and
went away that night.

The Philistines Reject David

29 Then [a]the Philistines gathered together all their armies [b]at Aphek,
and the Israelites encamped by a fountain
which *is* in Jezreel. 2 And the [c]lords of the
Philistines [1]passed in review by hundreds

13 [n]Ex. 22:28; Ps. 138:1 [1]Heb. *elohim*
14 [o]1 Sam. 15:27; 2 Kin. 2:8, 13
15 [p]Is. 14:9 [q]1 Sam. 16:14; 18:12 [r]1 Sam. 28:6
17 [s]1 Sam. 15:28 [2]Or *him*, i.e., David
18 [t]1 Sam. 13:9-13; 15:1-26; 1 Kin. 20:42; 1 Chr. 10:13; Jer. 48:10 [u]1 Sam. 15:3-9
19 [v]1 Sam. 31:1-6; Job 3:17-19
21 [w]Judg. 12:3; 1 Sam. 19:5; Job 13:14

CHAPTER 29
1 [a]1 Sam. 28:1 [b]Josh. 12:18; 19:30; 1 Sam. 4:1; 1 Kin. 20:30
2 [c]1 Sam. 6:4; 7:7 [1]*passed on in the rear*

28:12 the woman saw Samuel. Though questions have arisen as to the nature of Samuel's appearance, the text clearly indicates that Samuel, not an apparition, was evident to the eyes of the medium. God miraculously permitted the actual spirit of Samuel to speak (vv. 16-19). Because she understood her inability to raise the dead in this manner, she immediately knew 1) that it must have been by the power of God and 2) that her disguised inquirer must be Saul.

28:13 a spirit ascending out of the earth. The word translated "spirit" is actually the Heb. word meaning "God, gods, angel, ruler, or judge." It can also be used to designate a likeness to one of these. From the medium's perspective, Samuel appeared to be "like a spirit" ascending out of the earth. There is no other such miracle as this in all of Scripture.

28:14 old man…with a mantle. Obviously age and clothing do not exist in the realm of the spirits of those who have died, but God miraculously gave such appearances so that Saul was able to perceive that the spirit was Samuel. The question arises whether all believers will remain in the form they were in when they died. Samuel may have been as such simply for the benefit of Saul, or he might be in this state until he receives his resurrection body. Since Scripture teaches that the resurrection of OT saints is yet future (see Dan. 12:1,2), Samuel must have temporarily been in this condition solely for the benefit of Saul.

28:15 disturbed me. Samuel's comment expresses agitation caused by Saul's efforts to contact him since living humanity was not allowed to seek out discussions with the dead (Deut. 18:11; Lev. 20:6). Witchcraft puts the seeker in contact with demons impersonating those who are being sought, since the dead person cannot ordinarily be contacted, except in this unique case.

28:16,18 your enemy. See 15:26-35.

28:19 *will be* with me. This could mean with him in "the abode of the righteous." There is no doubt that Samuel meant this to serve as a premonition of Saul's soon death.

28:20 no strength in him. Already afraid with a heart that "trembled greatly" because of the Philistines (v. 5), Saul's fear was so heightened by the words of Samuel that he was completely deprived of strength and vigor, which was reinforced by a lack of nourishment. The woman met his physical needs, and he returned to his camp to await his doom (vv. 21-25).

29:1 gathered…encamped. The Philistines were assembling for battle while the Israelites were still camping by the spring. This picks up the story line originally started in 28:1, but which was sidelined to communicate Saul's encounter with the medium. **Aphek.** Located about 24 mi. N of Gath (cf. 4:1). **Jezreel.** Only a few mi. S of Shunem, and 40 mi. NE of Aphek, Jezreel was N of Mt. Gilboa.

and by thousands, but [d]David and his
men passed in review at the rear with
Achish. 3 Then the princes of the Philistines said, "What *are* these Hebrews *doing here?*"

And Achish said to the princes of the
Philistines, "*Is* this not David, the servant
of Saul king of Israel, who has been with
me [e]these days, or these years? And to this
day I have [f]found no fault in him since he
defected *to me.*"

4 But the princes of the Philistines were
angry with him; so the princes of the Philistines said to him, [g]"Make this fellow return, that he may go back to the place
which you have appointed for him, and
do not let him go down with us to [h]battle,
lest [i]in the battle he become our adversary. For with what could he reconcile
himself to his master, if not with the heads
of these [j]men? 5 *Is* this not David, [k]of
whom they sang to one another in dances,
saying:

> [l]"Saul has slain his thousands,
> And David his ten thousands'?"

6 Then Achish called David and said to
him, "Surely, *as* the LORD lives, you have
been upright, and [m]your going out and
your coming in with me in the army *is*
good in my sight. For to this day [n]I have
not found evil in you since the day of your
coming to me. Nevertheless the lords do
not favor you. 7 Therefore return now, and
go in peace, that you may not displease the
lords of the Philistines."

8 So David said to Achish, "But what
have I done? And to this day what have

2 [d] 1 Sam. 28:1, 2
3 [e] 1 Sam. 27:7
[f] 1 Sam. 27:1-6; 1 Chr. 12:19, 20; Dan. 6:5
4 [g] 1 Sam. 27:6
[h] 1 Sam. 14:21
[i] 1 Sam. 29:9 [j] 1 Chr. 12:19, 20
5 [k] 1 Sam. 21:11
[l] 1 Sam. 18:7
6 [m] 2 Sam. 3:25; 2 Kin. 19:27 [n] 1 Sam. 29:3

9 [o] 2 Sam. 14:17, 20; 19:27 [p] 1 Sam. 29:4
10 [q] 1 Chr. 12:19, 22
[2] So with MT, Tg., Vg.; LXX adds *and go to the place which I have selected for you there; and set no bothersome word in your heart, for you are good before me. And rise on your way*
11 [r] 2 Sam. 4:4

CHAPTER 30

1 [a] 1 Sam. 27:6
[b] 1 Sam. 15:7; 27:8
2 [c] 1 Sam. 27:2, 3
5 [d] 1 Sam. 25:42, 43

you found in your servant as long as I
have been with you, that I may not go and
fight against the enemies of my lord the
king?"

9 Then Achish answered and said to David, "I know that you *are* as good in my
sight [o]as an angel of God; nevertheless
[p]the princes of the Philistines have said,
'He shall not go up with us to the battle.'
10 Now therefore, rise early in the morning
with your master's servants [q]who have
come with [2]you. And as soon as you are up
early in the morning and have light, depart."

11 So David and his men rose early to depart in the morning, to return to the land of
the Philistines. [r]And the Philistines went
up to Jezreel.

David's Conflict with the Amalekites

30 Now it happened, when David
and his men came to [a]Ziklag, on
the third day, that the [b]Amalekites had invaded the South and Ziklag, attacked Ziklag and burned it with fire, 2 and had
taken captive the [c]women and those who
were there, from small to great; they did
not kill anyone, but carried *them* away
and went their way. 3 So David and his
men came to the city, and there it was,
burned with fire; and their wives, their
sons, and their daughters had been taken
captive. 4 Then David and the people who
were with him lifted up their voices and
wept, until they had no more power to
weep. 5 And David's two [d]wives, Ahinoam the Jezreelitess, and Abigail the
widow of Nabal the Carmelite, had been
taken captive. 6 Now David was greatly

29:3 no fault. David had proven himself as an honorable and righteous man before Achish, who knew that he could trust David.

29:4 he become our adversary. The Philistine lords were not as willing as Achish to give favor and trust to David. Being very shrewd in their estimation of potential hazards, they realized that he might be feigning loyalty to the Philistines in order to seize a strategic moment in the battle when he could betray and fight against them.

29:5 David, of whom they sang. The fame of David had spread throughout the land. The Philistine lords were no stranger to the skill and the victories that God had given to mighty David.

29:6 *as* the LORD lives. When seeking the highest standard by which to assure David of his credibility, Achish swore by the existence of David's God. It is evident that the pagan world knows of God, but the irony is that their knowledge does not necessarily lead to repentance.

29:8 the enemies of my lord the king. David's fidelity to Achish seemed to be at its climax in this expression of loyalty. David appears to have been fully prepared to do battle on behalf of Achish against his enemies, namely Israel. In light of David's former refusal to stretch out his hand against the Lord's anointed (24:6,10; 26:9,11,21), David might to have been capitulating and compromising. He did not inquire of the Lord before going to live with Achish, nor did he inquire of the Lord as to whether he should go out to battle with Achish. On the other hand, it could be that while David gave the appearance of loyalty, he actually believed the Philistines would not let him go out to battle, just as it actually happened (cf. 27:8-12). The providence of God kept David from fighting against the Lord's anointed and his own countrymen.

29:9 an angel of God. The degree to which Achish praised David has led some to believe that his eulogy was merely a formal attempt at flattery.

29:11 Jezreel. This was used to designate both a city about 56 mi. N of Jerusalem as well as the plain of Jezreel, which served as a major battlefield for many nations. The city was situated in the territory of Issachar (Josh. 19:18). It was bounded on the N and S by Megiddo and Beth Shean (1 Kin. 4:12) and on the W and E by Mt. Carmel and Mt. Gilboa.

30:1 Ziklag. Serving as a temporary place of residence for David and his 600 men, Ziklag was located in the Negev and given to David by Achish the king of Gath (27:6). David used it as the base from which he would make raids on the neighboring tribes (27:8-11). **Amalekites.** Reaping the consequences of Saul's failure to utterly destroy the Amalekites (1 Sam. 15) and David's raids against them (27:8), David and his men were the victims of a successful raid in which the Amalekites took all of their wives and livestock captive before burning Ziklag, their city.

distressed, for [e]the people spoke of stoning him, because the soul of all the people
was [1]grieved, every man for his sons and
his daughters. [f]But David strengthened
himself in the LORD his God.
7 [g]Then David said to Abiathar the
priest, Ahimelech's son, "Please bring the
ephod here to me." And [h]Abiathar brought
the ephod to David. 8 [i]So David inquired
of the LORD, saying, "Shall I pursue this
troop? Shall I overtake them?"

And He answered him, "Pursue, for you
shall surely overtake *them* and without fail
recover *all*."
9 So David went, he and the six hundred
men who *were* with him, and came to the
Brook Besor, where those stayed who were
left behind. 10 But David pursued, he and
four hundred men; [j]for two hundred
stayed *behind*, who were so weary that they
could not cross the Brook Besor.
11 Then they found an Egyptian in the
field, and brought him to David; and they
gave him bread and he ate, and they let
him drink water. 12 And they gave him a
piece of [k]a cake of figs and two clusters of
raisins. So [l]when he had eaten, his strength
came back to him; for he had eaten no
bread nor drunk water for three days and
three nights. 13 Then David said to him,
"To whom do you *belong*, and where *are*
you from?"

And he said, "I *am* a young man from
Egypt, servant of an Amalekite; and my
master left me behind, because three days
ago I fell sick. 14 We made an invasion of
the southern *area* of [m]the Cherethites, in
the *territory* which *belongs* to Judah, and of
the southern *area* [n]of Caleb; and we burned
Ziklag with fire."
15 And David said to him, "Can you take
me down to this troop?"

So he said, "Swear to me by God that
you will neither kill me nor deliver me into
the hands of my [o]master, and I will take
you down to this troop."
16 And when he had brought him down,
there they were, spread out over all the
land, [p]eating and drinking and dancing,
because of all the great spoil which they
had taken from the land of the Philistines
and from the land of Judah. 17 Then David
attacked them from twilight until the
evening of the next day. Not a man of
them escaped, except four hundred young
men who rode on camels and fled. 18 So
David recovered all that the Amalekites
had carried away, and David rescued his
two wives. 19 And nothing of theirs was
lacking, either small or great, sons or
daughters, spoil or anything which they
had taken from them; [q]David recovered
all. 20 Then David took all the flocks and
herds they had driven before those *other*
livestock, and said, "This *is* David's spoil."
21 Now David came to the [r]two hundred men who had been so weary that
they could not follow David, whom they
also had made to stay at the Brook Besor.
So they went out to meet David and to
meet the people who *were* with him. And
when David came near the people, he

6 [e] Ex. 17:4; John 8:59 [f] 1 Sam. 23:16; Is. 25:4; Hab. 3:17-19 [1] Lit. *bitter*
7 [g] 1 Sam. 23:2-9 [h] 1 Sam. 23:6
8 [i] 1 Sam. 23:2, 4; Ps. 50:15; 91:15
10 [j] 1 Sam. 30:9, 21
12 [k] 1 Sam. 25:18; 1 Kin. 20:7 [l] Judg. 15:19; 1 Sam. 14:27
14 [m] 2 Sam. 8:18; 1 Kin. 1:38, 44; Ezek. 25:16; Zeph. 2:5 [n] Josh. 14:13; 15:13
15 [o] Deut. 23:15
16 [p] 1 Thess. 5:3
19 [q] 1 Sam. 30:8
21 [r] 1 Sam. 30:10

30:6 distressed...grieved. Arriving home to the reality of their great tragedy caused David immense distress and provoked the wickedness of his men to entertain the treasonous idea of stoning him. Having not inquired of the Lord before his departure to support Achish in battle, David was in need of God's getting his attention. **strengthened himself in the LORD his God.** This was the key to David being a man after God's heart (cf. 1 Sam. 13:14; Acts 13:22).

30:7 Abiathar brought the ephod. Serving as a source through which one could make direct and specific inquiry into the will of God, the High-Priest's ephod, which contained the Urim and Thummim was sought by David. The distress of the moment drew his focus away from the treasonous thoughts of his men and back to God in his desperation to know what God would have him do.

30:9,10 Brook Besor. David most likely encountered the brook about 13 mi. S of Ziklag. It consisted of seasonal rivers from the area of Beersheba which ran NW and emptied into the Mediterranean. Likely, this was during the latter rains (Jan.-Apr.) and the brook was filled with a rampaging runoff that would account for the soldiers who were unable to cross over.

30:14 southern *area* of the Cherethites. Benaiah the son of Jehoiada was over the Cherethites and the Pelethites (2 Sam. 8:18), who are almost always mentioned together. They fled Jerusalem as allies with David (2 Sam. 15:8), and pursued Sheba the son of Bichri with Joab (2 Sam. 20:7). They were hand-picked by David to be present at Solomon's anointing as king. The Cherethites appear to have come from Crete, and to have been a part of the king's bodyguard (2 Sam. 23:20,23). **southern *area* of Caleb.** Caleb, the son of Jephunneh, was one of 12 spies chosen to check out the Land, and one of only 2 spies who gave a favorable report (Num. 13:6; 13:30). This was the land assigned to his family (Josh. 14:13,14).

30:16 all the great spoil. The Amalekites had not only what they took from Ziklag, but much more plunder from all their raids. After David conquered the Amalekites (vv. 17,18) he returned what belonged to Ziklag (vv. 19,26) and spread the rest all over Judah (vv. 26-31).

30:17 four hundred young men. It is obvious from Moses' encounter (Ex. 17:8-16), Saul's failure (1 Sam. 15), and Mordecai's opposition (Esth. 3:1,10-13) that the Amalekites were wicked people who hated God's people and died hard.

30:19 nothing...was lacking. In spite of David's previous failures, God showed Himself to be more than gracious and abundant in His stewardship of the wives, children, livestock, and possessions of David and his men.

30:22 worthless men. From the beginning of David's flight from Saul, he became captain of those who were in distress, discontent, and in debt (22:2), the least likely to exercise kindness and grace to others. This same expression was used of the sons of Eli (2:12), of those who doubted Saul's ability as king (10:27), of Nabal the fool by his servant (25:17), of Nabal the fool by his wife (25:25), of David when he was cursed by Shimei (2 Sam. 16:7), of Sheba the son of Bichri who led a revolt against David (2 Sam. 20:1), and of those who would be thrust away like thorns by David (2 Sam. 23:6).

[2]greeted them. 22 Then all the wicked and
[s]worthless[3] men of those who went with
David answered and said, "Because they
did not go with us, we will not give them
any of the spoil that we have recovered,
except for every man's wife and children,
that they may lead *them* away and depart."
23 But David said, "My brethren, you
shall not do so with what the LORD has
given us, who has preserved us and delivered into our hand the troop that came
against us. 24 For who will heed you in this
matter? But [t]as his part *is* who goes down
to the battle, so *shall* his part *be* who stays
by the supplies; they shall share alike."
25 So it was, from that day forward; he
made it a statute and an ordinance for Israel to this day.
26 Now when David came to Ziklag, he
sent *some* of the [4]spoil to the elders of Judah, to his friends, saying, "Here is a present for you from the spoil of the enemies of
the LORD"— 27 to *those* who *were* in Bethel,
those who *were* in [u]Ramoth of the South,
those who *were* in [v]Jattir, 28 *those* who *were*
in [w]Aroer, *those* who *were* in [x]Siphmoth,
those who *were* in [y]Eshtemoa, 29 *those* who
were in Rachal, *those* who *were* in the cities
of [z]the Jerahmeelites, *those* who *were* in the
cities of the [a]Kenites, 30 *those* who *were* in
[b]Hormah, *those* who *were* in [5]Chorashan,
those who *were* in Athach, 31 *those* who *were*
in [c]Hebron, and to all the places where David himself and his men were accustomed
to [d]rove.

21 [2] *asked them concerning their welfare*
22 [s] Deut. 13:13; Judg. 19:22 [3] Lit. *men of Belial*
24 [t] Num. 31:27; Josh. 22:8
26 [4] *booty*
27 [u] Josh. 19:8 [v] Josh. 15:48; 21:14
28 [w] Josh. 13:16 [x] 1 Chr. 27:27 [y] Josh. 15:50
29 [z] 1 Sam. 27:10 [a] Judg. 1:16; 1 Sam. 15:6; 27:10
30 [b] Num. 14:45; 21:3; Josh. 12:14; 15:30; 19:4; Judg. 1:17 [5] Or *Borashan*
31 [c] Num. 13:22; Josh. 14:13-15; 21:11-13; 2 Sam. 2:1 [d] 1 Sam. 23:22

CHAPTER 31

1 [a] 1 Chr. 10:1-12 [b] 1 Sam. 28:4
2 [c] 1 Sam. 14:49; 1 Chr. 8:33
3 [d] 2 Sam. 1:6 [1] Lit. *found him*
4 [e] Judg. 9:54; 1 Chr. 10:4 [f] Judg. 14:3; 1 Sam. 14:6; 17:26, 36 [g] 2 Sam. 1:14 [h] 2 Sam. 1:6, 10 [2] *torture*
9 [i] Judg. 16:23, 24; 2 Sam. 1:20

The Tragic End of Saul and His Sons

31 Now [a]the Philistines fought against
Israel; and the men of Israel fled
from before the Philistines, and fell slain
on Mount [b]Gilboa. 2 Then the Philistines
followed hard after Saul and his sons. And
the Philistines killed [c]Jonathan, Abinadab,
and Malchishua, Saul's sons. 3 [d]The battle
became fierce against Saul. The archers
[1]hit him, and he was severely wounded by
the archers.
4 [e]Then Saul said to his armorbearer,
"Draw your sword, and thrust me through
with it, lest [f]these uncircumcised men come
and thrust me through and [2]abuse me."
But his armorbearer would not, [g]for he
was greatly afraid. Therefore Saul took a
sword and [h]fell on it. 5 And when his armorbearer saw that Saul was dead, he also
fell on his sword, and died with him. 6 So
Saul, his three sons, his armorbearer, and
all his men died together that same day.
7 And when the men of Israel who *were*
on the other side of the valley, and *those*
who *were* on the other side of the Jordan,
saw that the men of Israel had fled and that
Saul and his sons were dead, they forsook
the cities and fled; and the Philistines came
and dwelt in them. 8 So it happened the
next day, when the Philistines came to strip
the slain, that they found Saul and his
three sons fallen on Mount Gilboa. 9 And
they cut off his head and stripped off his
armor, and sent *word* throughout the land
of the Philistines, to [i]proclaim *it in* the tem-

30:25 a statute and an ordinance. In spite of the opposition David received from the worthless men among him, he legislated his practice of kindness and equity into law for the people.

30:26-31 Being no stranger to adversity and a life lived on the run, David realized the important role that so many others had played in his safety and welfare. Being the recipient of such kindness, David missed no opportunity to reciprocate kindness and generosity. It would be presumptuous to think that David was merely paying off debts or buying support; rather he was giving back as he had received, expressing his debt of gratitude for the kindness and support shown him. *See note on 30:16.*

31:1-13 See 2 Sam. 1:4-12; 1 Chr. 10:1-12.

31:1 Mount Gilboa. Formerly the site of the Israeli camp, it was turned into the sight of the Israeli massacre. Saul and his sons lost their lives on Mt. Gilboa. *See note on 28:4.*

31:2 Jonathan, Abinadab, and Malchishua. Three of the 4 sons of Saul were killed the same day in battle. The fourth son, Eshbaal, would later be referred to as Ish-bosheth, meaning "man of shame," an appropriate designation in light of his apparent absence from the battlefield (cf. 2 Sam. 2:8ff.). Jonathan, Ishvi, and Malchishua were named as Saul's sons in 14:49, but Jonathan, Abinadab, and Malchishua are named here; Ishvi and Abinadab are thus one and the same. First Chronicles 8:33 and 9:39 are the only verses naming all 4 sons.

31:4 uncircumcised men. A common term of derision used among Israelites to designate non-Israelites. Circumcision was given as the sign of the Abrahamic Covenant in Gen. 17:10-14. *See note on 14:6.* **abuse.** Having engaged in several battles against the Philistines, Saul had succeeded in provoking their hatred and resentment. As the king, Saul had certainly received especially cruel treatment from the hands of his enemies, who would have likely made sport of him and tortured him before his death. **Saul took a sword and fell on it.** Though Saul's suicide is considered by some to be an act of heroism, Saul should have found his strength and courage in God as David did in 23:16 and 30:6 to fight to the end or to surrender. Saul's suicide is the ultimate expression of his faithlessness towards God at this moment in his life.

31:6 all his men. The question is whether "all" was used in a qualified sense or in an absolute sense. In consideration of the context, the meaning was most likely intended to be qualified, not absolute. It is not necessary to conclude that every single one of Saul's 3,000 men died that day and that none escaped. Where such a meaning is intended, the text usually provides more reinforcement, as in Josh. 8:22 where the author specifically states, "and they slew them until no one was left of those who survived or escaped." In fact, Abner the general of Saul's army survived (2 Sam. 2:8). "All" here means those who were personally assigned to Saul's special guard (cf. 31:7).

31:9 cut off his head. There is a parallelism between the death of Saul and the death of Goliath. The giant champion of the Philistines had his head cut off by David and the Philistines fled (17:51). The Philistines had taken revenge and done likewise to the giant champion of Israel, King Saul, who was "taller than any of the people from his shoulders upward" (30:23).

ple of their idols and among the people.
10 [j]Then they put his armor in the temple
of the [k]Ashtoreths, and [l]they fastened his
body to the wall of [m]Beth[3] Shan.
11 [n]Now when the inhabitants of Jabesh
Gilead heard what the Philistines had
done to Saul, 12 [o]all the valiant men arose
and traveled all night, and took the body
of Saul and the bodies of his sons from the
wall of Beth Shan; and they came to Jabesh
and [p]burned them there. 13 Then they took
their bones and [q]buried *them* under the
tamarisk tree at Jabesh, [r]and fasted seven
days.

10 [j] 1 Sam. 21:9 [k] Judg. 2:13; 1 Sam. 7:3 [l] 2 Sam. 21:12 [m] Judg. 1:27 [3] *Beth Shean*, Josh. 17:11
11 [n] 1 Sam. 11:1-13
12 [o] 1 Sam. 11:1-11; 2 Sam. 2:4-7 [p] 2 Chr. 16:14; Jer. 34:5; Amos 6:10
13 [q] 2 Sam. 2:4, 5; 21:12-14 [r] Gen. 50:10

31:10 the Ashtoreths. These were the fertility goddesses of the Canaanites, to whom the Philistines gave homage by placing the weapons of their defeated foe in the temple of the Ashtoreths. As the sword of Goliath was put in the house of the Lord behind the ephod (1 Sam. 21:9), so the weapons of Saul were taken by the Philistines and put in the temple of the Ashtoreths. Military victory was attributed to the gods, since the belief was that military encounters were battles between the deities of rival nations. **Beth Shan.** Located in the Jordan Valley about 16 mi. S of the Sea of Galilee.

31:11 Jabesh Gilead. Located E of the Jordan, its people stayed out of the war against Benjamin and suffered severe consequences as a result (Judg. 21). The men of Jabesh Gilead showed kindness and respect to Saul, a Benjamite, by rescuing his body from the wall of Beth Shan because Saul and his sons had saved Jabesh Gilead from the Ammonites (11:9-12) just after he had been chosen as king of Israel. By this act, they honored Saul for his faithfulness to them.

31:12 bodies…burned. In light of Saul's head having been cut off and the mutilation that had taken place, it is thought that the citizens of Jabesh Gilead burned his body to hide the damage.

31:13 bones…buried. It was considered disrespectful not to bury the dead. Abraham went to great lengths to bury Sarah (Gen. 23:4-15), and Jacob made Joseph swear that he would not bury him in Egypt (Gen. 47:29,30). **fasted seven days.** In relation to death, fasting was often associated with mourning in the Hebrew culture. It was a sign of respect, seriousness, and grief. First Samuel began with the ark of the covenant being captured by the Philistines (1 Sam. 4:11) and in the end Israel's king had been killed by them. Second Samuel will recount how God vindicated His honor by David's defeating the Philistines (2 Sam. 5:17-25), establishing an uncontested kingdom (1 Kin. 2:12), and safely bringing the ark to Jerusalem, the city of God (2 Sam. 6:16-19).

The Second Book of SAMUEL

Introduction

See 1 Samuel for the Introductory Discussion.

Outline

I. The Reign of David as King over Israel (1:1–20:26)
  A. David's Accession to Kingship over Judah (1:1–3:5)
    1. The deaths of Saul and Jonathan (1:1-27)
    2. David anointed by Judah (2:1-7)
    3. David's victories over the house of Saul (2:8–3:1)
    4. David's wives/sons in Hebron (3:2-5)
  B. David's Accession to Kingship over Israel (3:6–5:16)
    1. The deaths of Abner and Ishbosheth (3:6–4:12)
    2. David anointed by all Israel (5:1-5)
    3. David's conquest of Jerusalem (5:6-12)
    4. David's wives/sons in Jerusalem (5:13-16)
  C. David's Triumphal Reign (5:17–8:18)
    1. David's victories over the Philistines (5:17-25)
    2. David's spiritual victories (6:1–7:29)
    3. David's victories over the Philistines, Moabites, Arameans, and Edomites (8:1-18)
  D. David's Troubled Reign (9:1–20:26)
    1. David's kindness to Mephibosheth (9:1-13)
    2. David's sins of adultery and murder (10:1–12:31)
    3. David's family troubles (13:1–14:33)
      a. The rape of Tamar (13:1-22)
      b. The murder of Amnon (13:23-39)
      c. The recall and return of Absalom (14:1-33)
    4. The rebellions against David (15:1–20:26)
      a. The rebellion of Absalom (15:1–19:43)
      b. The rebellion of Sheba (20:1-26)

II. Epilogue (21:1–24:25)
  A. The Lord's Judgment against Israel (21:1-14)
  B. David's Heroes (21:15-22)
  C. David's Song of Praise (22:1-51)
  D. David's Last Words (23:1-7)
  E. David's Mighty Men (23:8-39)
  F. The Lord's Judgment against David (24:1-25)

The Report of Saul's Death

1 Now it came to pass after the [a]death of
Saul, when David had returned from
[b]the slaughter of the Amalekites, and David had stayed two days in Ziklag, 2 on the
third day, behold, it happened that [c]a man
came from Saul's camp [d]with his clothes
[1]torn and dust on his head. So it was,
when he came to David, that he [e]fell to the
ground and prostrated himself.
3 And David said to him, "Where have
you come from?"
So he said to him, "I have escaped from
the camp of Israel."
4 Then David said to him, [f]"How did the
matter go? Please tell me."
And he answered, "The people have fled
from the battle, many of the people are fall-
en and dead, and Saul and [g]Jonathan his
son are dead also."
5 So David said to the young man who
told him, "How do you know that Saul
and Jonathan his son are dead?"
6 Then the young man who told him
said, "As I happened by chance *to be* on
[h]Mount Gilboa, there was [i]Saul, leaning on
his spear; and indeed the chariots and
horsemen followed hard after him. 7 Now
when he looked behind him, he saw me
and called to me. And I answered, 'Here I
am.' 8 And he said to me, 'Who *are* you?' So
I answered him, 'I *am* an Amalekite.' 9 He
said to me again, 'Please stand over me and
kill me, for [2]anguish has come upon me,
but my life still *remains* in me.' 10 So I stood
over him and [j]killed him, because I was
sure that he could not live after he had fall-
en. And I took the crown that *was* on his
head and the bracelet that *was* on his arm,
and have brought them here to my lord."
11 Therefore David took hold of his own
clothes and [k]tore them, and *so did* all the
men who *were* with him. 12 And they
[l]mourned and wept and [m]fasted until
evening for Saul and for Jonathan his son,
for the [n]people of the LORD and for the
house of Israel, because they had fallen by
the sword.
13 Then David said to the young man
who told him, "Where *are* you from?"
And he answered, "I *am* the son of an
alien, an Amalekite."
14 So David said to him, "How [o]was it
you were not [p]afraid to [q]put forth your
hand to destroy the LORD's anointed?"
15 Then [r]David called one of the young
men and said, "Go near, *and* execute him!"
And he struck him so that he died. 16 So
David said to him, [s]"Your blood *is* on your
own head, for [t]your own mouth has testified against you, saying, 'I have killed the
LORD's anointed.' "

The Song of the Bow

17 Then David lamented with this
lamentation over Saul and over Jonathan
his son, 18 [u]and he told *them* to teach the
children of Judah *the Song of* the Bow; indeed *it is* written [v]in the Book [3]of Jasher:

CHAPTER 1

1 [a] 1 Sam. 31:6 [b] 1 Sam. 30:1, 17, 26
2 [c] 2 Sam. 4:10 [d] 1 Sam. 4:12 [e] 1 Sam. 25:23 [1] To show grief
4 [f] 1 Sam. 4:16; 31:3 [g] 1 Sam. 31:2
6 [h] 1 Sam. 31:1 [i] 1 Sam. 31:2-4
9 [2] *agony*
10 [j] Judg. 9:54; 2 Kin. 11:12
11 [k] 2 Sam. 3:31; 13:31
12 [l] 2 Sam. 3:31 [m] 1 Sam. 31:13 [n] 2 Sam. 6:21
14 [o] Num. 12:8 [p] 1 Sam. 31:4 [q] 1 Sam. 24:6; 26:9
15 [r] 2 Sam. 4:10, 12
16 [s] 1 Sam. 26:9; 2 Sam. 3:28; 1 Kin. 2:32-37 [t] 2 Sam. 1:10; Luke 19:22
18 [u] 1 Sam. 31:3 [v] Josh. 10:13 [3] Lit. *of the Upright*

1:1-35 David ascends to the kingship of Judah.

1:1 the death of Saul. Second Samuel 1:1-14 begins where 1 Sam. 31:1-13 ends, with the death of Saul (cf. 1 Chr. 10:1-12). **Amalekites.** The mention of these people serves as a reminder of David's obedience to the Lord (1 Sam. 30:1-31) and Saul's disobedience (1 Sam. 15:1-33). *See note on Ex. 17:8-16.* **Ziklag.** *See notes on 1 Sam. 27:6; 30:1.* This town was not so completely sacked and destroyed that David and his 600 men with their families could not stay there.

1:2 clothes torn and dust on his head. This was a common cultural sign of anguish and mourning over a death. Cf. 15:32; 1 Sam. 4:12.

1:4-12 See 1 Sam. 31:1-13; 1 Chr. 10:1-12.

1:6 chariots and horsemen. Chariots and horsemen were a symbol of power and strength (cf. Ex. 14:9; 1 Sam. 8:11; 13:5; 2 Sam. 8:4; 1 Kin. 4:26; 9:19; 10:26; 1 Chr. 19:6; 2 Chr. 1:14; 9:25; 12:3; 16:8; Dan. 11:40). The Philistines were in pursuit of Saul with an abundant number of warriors, making Saul's escape hopeless.

1:8 Amalekite. The man claiming to have killed Saul was from among the people whom David recently slaughtered (v. 1), whom God wanted eliminated (Ex. 17:14; 1 Sam. 15:3), and who would plague Israel for generations (Ex. 17:16) due to Saul's disobedience (1 Sam. 15:9-11).

1:10 killed him. The Amalekite claimed responsibility for Saul's death, saying that Saul was still alive when he found him. However, 1 Sam. 31:3-6 makes it clear that Saul died by falling on his own sword, not by the hand of the Amalekite. Thus, this man, who may have witnessed Saul's suicide, claimed to have killed Saul when in reality he had only reached his body before the Philistines and had fabricated the story to ingratiate himself with the new king by killing his enemy and by bringing Saul's crown and bracelet to David. The crown and bracelet in the hands of the Amalekite show that he was the first to pass by the body of Saul.

1:12 mourned and wept and fasted. David demonstrates genuine, heartfelt grief for the death of Saul and Jonathan by mourning and weeping, as well as fasting, which were common ways to demonstrate grief (cf. Esth. 4:3; Joel 2:12).

1:14 the LORD's anointed. Despite Saul's many attempts on David's life, David would not allow himself to see Saul as just a mere man or human monarch; he remained "the LORD's anointed," who occupied a sacred role before God (cf. 1 Sam. 24:1-15; 26:1-20).

1:15 execute him! This most certainly came as a great surprise to the Amalekite, for he intended to win the favor of David by saying he had killed Saul. This story is very similar to that of the men who later killed Ishbosheth, thinking they would be able to endear themselves to David (4:5-12).

1:16 Your blood *is* on your own head. David executed the Amalekite on the basis of his own testimony, not on the basis of the truthfulness of his story.

1:17 lamentation. David chose to have both Saul and his noble son Jonathan remembered through this lamentation, which would be taught to all Israel as a national war song.

1:18 *the Song of* the Bow. This was the title of the poem in which the word "Bow" may have been chosen with reference to Jonathan, whose bow is mentioned in v. 22. **Book of Jasher.** A poetic collection

19 "The beauty of Israel is slain on
your high places!
[w]How the mighty have fallen!
20 [x]Tell *it* not in Gath,
Proclaim *it* not in the streets of
[y]Ashkelon—
Lest [z]the daughters of the
Philistines rejoice,
Lest the daughters of [a]the
uncircumcised triumph.

21 "O [b]mountains of Gilboa,
[c]*Let there be* no dew nor rain upon
you,
Nor fields of offerings.
For the shield of the mighty is [4]cast
away there!
The shield of Saul, not [d]anointed
with oil.
22 From the blood of the slain,
From the fat of the mighty,
[e]The bow of Jonathan did not turn
back,
And the sword of Saul did not
return empty.

23 "Saul and Jonathan *were* beloved
and pleasant in their lives,
And in their [f]death they were not
divided;
They were swifter than eagles,
They were [g]stronger than lions.

19 [w] 2 Sam. 1:27
20 [x] 1 Sam. 27:2; 31:8-13; Mic. 1:10 [y] 1 Sam. 6:17; Jer. 25:20 [z] Ex. 15:20; Judg. 11:34; 1 Sam. 18:6 [a] 1 Sam. 31:4
21 [b] 1 Sam. 31:1 [c] Ezek. 31:15 [d] 1 Sam. 10:1 [4] Lit. *defiled*
22 [e] Deut. 32:42; 1 Sam. 18:4
23 [f] 1 Sam. 31:2-4 [g] Judg. 14:18
26 [h] 1 Sam. 18:1-4; 19:2; 20:17
27 [i] 2 Sam. 1:19, 25

CHAPTER 2

1 [a] Judg. 1:1; 1 Sam. 23:2, 4, 9; 30:7, 8 [b] 1 Sam. 30:31; 2 Sam. 2:11; 5:1-3; 1 Kin. 2:11
2 [c] 1 Sam. 25:42, 43; 30:5
3 [d] 1 Sam. 27:2, 3; 30:1; 1 Chr. 12:1

24 "O daughters of Israel, weep over
Saul,
Who clothed you in scarlet, with
luxury;
Who put ornaments of gold on
your apparel.

25 "How the mighty have fallen in the
midst of the battle!
Jonathan *was* slain in your high
places.
26 I am distressed for you, my brother
Jonathan;
You have been very pleasant to me;
[h]Your love to me was wonderful,
Surpassing the love of women.

27 "How [i]the mighty have fallen,
And the weapons of war
perished!"

David Anointed King of Judah

2 It happened after this that David [a]in-
quired of the LORD, saying, "Shall I go
up to any of the cities of Judah?"
And the LORD said to him, "Go up."
David said, "Where shall I go up?"
And He said, "To [b]Hebron."
2 So David went up there, and his [c]two
wives also, Ahinoam the Jezreelitess, and
Abigail the widow of Nabal the Carmelite.
3 And David brought up [d]the men who

of Israel's wars in which Israel's events and great men were commemorated (cf. Josh. 10:13).

1:19 The beauty of Israel. Lit. the gazelle or antelope of Israel, the chosen symbol of youthful elegance and symmetry, most likely referring to Jonathan. Thus, the song began and ended with Saul's noble son (vv. 25,26). **high places.** These were open-air worship sites generally established at high elevations. In this case the high place was Mt. Gilboa, where Saul had died. **How the mighty have fallen!** They were not only Israel's slain "beauty," but Saul and Jonathan were mighty men who had fallen in battle. This phrase is repeated as a refrain in vv. 25 and 27.

1:20 Gath...Ashkelon. Two chief cities which together could represent all of the Philistine territory. Gath was situated in the eastern part of the Philistine territory, while Ashkelon was in the W by the sea. David did not want the Philistines to rejoice at the calamities of Israel as Israel had rejoiced at the defeat of the Philistines (1 Sam. 18:7).

1:21 no dew nor rain. David spoke a curse, seeking the absence of dew or rain upon the mountain where Saul and Jonathan died. **not anointed with oil.** It was necessary in those times to anoint a shield with oil (cf. Is. 21:5) to prevent the leather from being hard and cracked. But there on Mt. Gilboa lay the shield of Saul dried out, a symbol of defeat and death.

1:22 bow...sword. These two weapons were used by Saul and Jonathan with much power, accuracy, and effectiveness. It was also with the bow that Jonathan helped David escape Saul's wrath (1 Sam. 20:35-42).

1:23 beloved. This generous commendation, including Saul who was seeking to kill David, showed David's gracious, forgiving attitude—a model of gracious love (cf. Matt. 5:43-48).

1:26 Surpassing the love of women. The bond between David and Jonathan was strong. However, this does not mean that their friendship was necessarily superior to the bond of love between a man and a woman. The commitment shared between the two of them was a noble, loyal, and selfless devotion (cf. 1 Sam. 18:3), which neither of them had ever felt for a woman. Unlike love between a man and a woman in which a sexual element is part of the strong attraction, this love between these two men had no such sexual feature, yet was compellingly strong.

1:27 weapons of war. A figurative expression referring to Saul and Jonathan.

2:1 David inquired of the LORD. After the death of Saul, David could move about the land freely as the Lord directed him. A contrast can be seen between Saul, who had inquired of the Lord and the Lord would not answer (cf. 1 Sam. 28:6) and David, who also inquired of the Lord and the Lord gave him direction. **cities of Judah.** David sought guidance from the Lord as to where to start his reign. David first asked if he should begin in the southern area of Judah. The Lord responded affirmatively and thus David sought for a more precise destination. The nucleus of David's future government would come from the cities of Judah. **Hebron.** With the highest elevation of any town in Judah, the city was strategically chosen to be the initial location of David's rule over Israel. Hebron is located 20 mi. SSW of Jerusalem. Abraham had located there long before (Gen. 13:18), and later Hebron had been given to Caleb (Josh. 14:13,14; Judg. 1:20) when Israel occupied the land after the wilderness wanderings.

2:2 Ahinoam...Abigail. Abigail became David's wife after the death of Nabal (cf. 1 Sam. 25:40-44).

were with him, every man with his household. So they dwelt in the cities of Hebron.
4 [e]Then the men of Judah came, and
there they [f]anointed David king over the
house of Judah. And they told David, saying, [g]"The men of Jabesh Gilead *were the*
ones who buried Saul." 5 So David sent
messengers to the men of Jabesh Gilead,
and said to them, [h]"You *are* blessed of the
LORD, for you have shown this kindness to
your lord, to Saul, and have buried him.
6 And now may [i]the LORD show kindness
and truth to you. I also will repay you this
kindness, because you have done this
thing. 7 Now therefore, let your hands be
strengthened, and be valiant; for your master Saul is dead, and also the house of Judah has anointed me king over them."

Ishbosheth Made King of Israel

8 But [j]Abner the son of Ner, commander
of Saul's army, took [1]Ishbosheth the son of
Saul and brought him over to [k]Mahanaim;
9 and he made him king over [l]Gilead, over
the [m]Ashurites, over [n]Jezreel, over Ephraim, over Benjamin, and over all Israel.
10 Ishbosheth, Saul's son, *was* forty years
old when he began to reign over Israel, and
he reigned two years. Only the house of Judah followed David. 11 And [o]the [2]time
that David was king in Hebron over the
house of Judah was seven years and six
months.

Israel and Judah at War

12 Now Abner the son of Ner, and the
servants of Ishbosheth the son of Saul,
went out from Mahanaim to [p]Gibeon.
13 And [q]Joab the son of Zeruiah, and the
servants of David, went out and met them
by [r]the pool of Gibeon. So they sat down,
one on one side of the pool and the other
on the other side of the pool. 14 Then
Abner said to Joab, "Let the young men
now arise and compete before us."
And Joab said, "Let them arise."
15 So they arose and went over by number, twelve from Benjamin, *followers* of Ishbosheth the son of Saul, and twelve from
the servants of David. 16 And each one
grasped his opponent by the head and
thrust his sword in his opponent's side; so
they fell down together. Therefore that
place was called [3]the Field of Sharp
Swords, which *is* in Gibeon. 17 So there
was a very fierce battle that day, and Abner
and the men of Israel were beaten before
the servants of David.
18 Now the [s]three sons of Zeruiah were
there: Joab and Abishai and Asahel. And
Asahel *was* [t]as fleet of foot [u]as a wild
gazelle. 19 So Asahel pursued Abner, and
in going he did not turn to the right hand
or to the left from following Abner.
20 Then Abner looked behind him and
said, "*Are* you Asahel?"
He answered, "I *am*."
21 And Abner said to him, "Turn aside to
your right hand or to your left, and lay

4 [e] 1 Sam. 30:26; 2 Sam. 2:11; 5:5; 19:14, 41-43 [f] 1 Sam. 16:13; 2 Sam. 5:3 [g] 1 Sam. 31:11-13
5 [h] Ruth 2:20; 3:10
6 [i] Ex. 34:6; 2 Tim. 1:16, 18
8 [j] 1 Sam. 14:50; 2 Sam. 3:6 [k] Gen. 32:2; Josh. 21:38; 2 Sam. 17:24 [1] *Esh-Baal*, 1 Chr. 8:33; 9:39
9 [l] Josh. 22:9 [m] Judg. 1:32 [n] 1 Sam. 29:1
11 [o] 2 Sam. 5:5; 1 Kin. 2:11 [2] Lit. *number of days*
12 [p] Josh. 10:2-12; 18:25
13 [q] 1 Sam. 26:6; 2 Sam. 8:16; 1 Chr. 2:16; 11:6 [r] Jer. 41:12
16 [3] Heb. *Helkath Hazzurim*
18 [s] 1 Chr. 2:16 [t] 1 Chr. 12:8; Hab. 3:19 [u] Ps. 18:33

2:4 anointed David king. David had already been privately anointed king by Samuel (cf. 1 Sam. 16:3). This anointing recognized his rule in the southern area of Judah. Later he would be anointed as king over all Israel (cf. 2 Sam. 5:3). **men of Jabesh Gilead.** Jabesh, a city of Israel E of the Jordan, demonstrated its loyalty to Saul by giving him a proper burial (cf. 1 Sam. 31:11-13).

2:7 your master Saul is dead. David referred to Saul as "your master" so as not to antagonize the men of Jabesh Gilead. He sought to win Israel over to his side, not force them into submission.

2:8 Abner. Abner, cousin of Saul and general of his army (1 Sam. 14:50,51), did not desire to follow the Lord's new anointed king, but placed Ishbosheth on the throne, causing tension between Judah and the rest of the tribes in Israel. **Ishbosheth.** His name means "man of shame." Saul's only surviving son was placed as king over the northern tribes of Israel and the eastern ones across the Jordan. **Mahanaim.** A town in Gilead to the E of the Jordan River. Ishbosheth established himself there and reigned for two years in this city. This was the same city where Jacob saw the angels while on his way to Penuel (Gen. 32:2). It was appointed to be a Levitical city from the territory of Gad (Josh. 21:28; 1 Chr. 6:80). It later became the haven for David while fleeing from Absalom (17:24,27; 19:32; 1 Kin. 2:8), because likely it was well fortified (cf. 18:24).

2:9 king over Gilead...all Israel. Ishbosheth's power seemed more solidified in the land of Gilead (E of the Jordan) than in the rest of Israel.

2:10 the house of Judah. A natural opposition arose between the tribe of Judah and the rest of Israel since Judah was under the reign of David, while the rest of Israel recognized the reign of Ishbosheth.

2:11 seven years and six months. Several years passed before Ishbosheth assumed the throne of Israel, so that Ishbosheth's two year reign came at the end of David's 7 year and 6 month reign over Judah. It must have taken Ishbosheth about 5 years to regain the northern territory from the Philistines.

2:12 Gibeon. During the time of Joshua, Gibeon was a very important city (Josh. 10:2). Its people probably had sided with David because Saul had broken a treaty with the Gibeonites and acted treacherously towards them (21:1).

2:13 Joab the son of Zeruiah. Joab was the leader of David's army and thus led the men against Abner. Although Ishbosheth and David sat on the thrones of their respective territories, Joab and Abner truly had wielded the power and control by leading the military forces. Zeruiah was the sister of David (cf. 1 Chr. 2:16).

2:14 the young men...compete. Rather than all-out war, Abner proposed a representative contest between champions on behalf of the opposing armies. Because all 24 of the contestants lay fallen and dying in combat (vv. 15,16), the contest settled nothing, but excited passions so that a battle between the two armies ensued (v. 17).

2:18 Abishai. Brother of Joab, he was an aide to David throughout his rise to power. Abishai was with David in the camp of Saul when David had opportunity to kill Saul and encouraged the murder of Saul, which David would not allow (cf. 1 Sam. 26:6-9). **Asahel.** Another brother of Joab, Asahel was single-minded with dogged determination; though he was extremely fleet-footed, his determination would prove to be fatal (v. 23).

hold on one of the young men and take his
armor for yourself." But Asahel would not
turn aside from following him. 22 So Abner
said again to Asahel, "Turn aside from following me. Why should I strike you to the
ground? How then could I face your brother Joab?" 23 However, he refused to turn
aside. Therefore Abner struck him [v]in the
stomach with the blunt end of the spear, so
that the spear came out of his back; and he
fell down there and died on the spot. So it
was *that* as many as came to the place
where Asahel fell down and died, stood
[w]still.

24 Joab and Abishai also pursued Abner.
And the sun was going down when they
came to the hill of Ammah, which *is* before
Giah by the road to the Wilderness of Gibeon. 25 Now the children of Benjamin gathered together behind Abner and became [4]a
unit, and took their stand on top of a hill.
26 Then Abner called to Joab and said,
"Shall the sword devour forever? Do you
not know that it will be bitter in the latter
end? How long will it be then until you tell
the people to return from pursuing their
brethren?"

27 And Joab said, "*As* God lives, [5]unless
[x]you had spoken, surely then by morning
all the people would have given up pursuing their brethren." 28 So Joab blew a trumpet; and all the people stood still and did
not pursue Israel anymore, nor did they
fight anymore. 29 Then Abner and his men
went on all that night through the plain,
crossed over the Jordan, and went through
all Bithron; and they came to Mahanaim.

30 So Joab returned from pursuing
Abner. And when he had gathered all the
people together, there were missing of David's servants nineteen men and Asahel.
31 But the servants of David had struck
down, of Benjamin and Abner's men, three
hundred and sixty men who died. 32 Then
they took up Asahel and buried him in his
father's tomb, which *was in* [y]Bethlehem.
And Joab and his men went all night, and
they came to Hebron at daybreak.

3 Now there was a long [a]war between
the house of Saul and the house of David. But David grew stronger and stronger,
and the house of Saul grew weaker and
weaker.

Sons of David

2 Sons were born [b]to David in Hebron:
His firstborn was Amnon [c]by Ahinoam
the Jezreelitess; 3 his second, [1]Chileab, by
Abigail the widow of Nabal the Carmelite;
the third, [d]Absalom the son of Maacah,
the daughter of Talmai, king [e]of Geshur;
4 the fourth, [f]Adonijah the son of Haggith;
the fifth, Shephatiah the son of Abital;
5 and the sixth, Ithream, by David's wife
Eglah. These were born to David in Hebron.

Abner Joins Forces with David

6 Now it was so, while there was war between the house of Saul and the house of

23 [v]2 Sam. 3:27; 4:6; 20:10 [w]2 Sam. 20:12
25 [4]*one band*
27 [x]2 Sam. 2:14 [5]*if you had not spoken*
32 [y]1 Sam. 20:6

CHAPTER 3
1 [a]1 Kin. 14:30; [Ps. 46:9]
2 [b]1 Chr. 3:1-4 [c]1 Sam. 25:42, 43
3 [d]2 Sam. 15:1-10 [e]Josh. 13:13; 1 Sam. 27:8; 2 Sam. 13:37; 14:32; 15:8 [1]*Daniel,* 1 Chr. 3:1
4 [f]1 Kin. 1:5

2:21 take his armor. To gain the armor of the enemy general, Abner, who was fleeing the defeat, would be to possess the greatest trophy. Asahel was ambitious to get it, while Abner kept warning him and suggested he take the armor of some other soldier for his trophy, since he was not able to defeat Abner.

2:22 How then could I face your brother Joab? Abner sought to spare Asahel so as to avoid unnecessary vengeance from Joab or David. Abner tried to give Asahel reasons to stop his pursuit, but Asahel was determined. Abner did not wish to strike down Asahel, but Asahel refused to listen, so he was forced to stop his effort with a fatal back stab by the blunt end of his spear.

2:26 Shall the sword devour forever? As Abner had earlier proposed that the hostilities begin, he now proposed that they cease.

2:29 Bithron. After the death of Asahel, Abner moved through this gorge as he approached Mahanaim (*see note on 2:8*).

3:1 a long war. The conflict between Ishbosheth and David did not end in quick victory. There was a gradual transfer of power from the house of Saul to the house of David (v. 10) that lasted at least through the two-year reign of Ishbosheth and maybe longer.

3:2-5 See 1 Chr. 3:1-4.

3:2 Amnon. He raped and defiled his half-sister Tamar and later, by the command of Absalom, was killed for his crime (13:1-39).

3:3 Chileab. He apparently died before he was able to enter into position to contend for the throne, for nothing more is said about him. This child was born to David by the wife whom David had taken upon the death of Nabal (see 1 Sam. 25:3). **Absalom.** Lit. "My Divine Father Is Peace" or "Divine Father of Peace." Absalom was the son of Maacah who was a Geshurite princess from a region in Syria, not Israel. David may have married her as part of a diplomatic agreement made with Talmai, the Geshurite king, to give David an ally N of Ishbosheth. Later Absalom, in fear of his life, fled to Geshur (13:37,38).

3:4 Adonijah. He was a prominent figure in the contention for David's throne at the end of his reign (1 Kin. 1,2), but was assassinated, allowing the throne to be given to Solomon (1 Kin. 2:25). Haggith was probably married to David after his accession to the throne. **Shephatiah...Abital.** Shephatiah means "The Lord Judges." Abital means "My Divine Father is Dew" or "My Divine Father of Dew."

3:5 Eglah. Eglah is called the "wife of David." This may be because she is the last of the list and serves to draw emphasis to David's polygamy. The inclusion of these sons indicates all who would have been in contention for the throne. **born to David.** More children were born to David when he moved to Jerusalem (5:14).

3:6–5:16 David assumed the kingdom of all Israel by a similar progression of events as those which led to his assuming the throne of Judah. In both cases, a man comes seeking David's favor (Amalekite, 1:1-13; Abner, 3:6-21). Both of these men are executed for their deeds (Amalekite, 1:14-16; Abner, 3:22-32). In both cases, this is followed by a lament of David (1:17-27; 3:33-39). Close to the middle of both accounts is a brief look at the anointing of David as king (over Judah, 2:1-7; over Israel, 5:1-5). After this, David and his men are successful in defeating their enemies (2:8–3:1; 5:6-12). Each section concludes with a list of the children born to David (Hebron, 3:2-5; Jerusalem, 5:13-16).

David, that Abner was strengthening *his*
hold on the house of Saul.
7 And Saul had a concubine, whose
name *was* [g]Rizpah, the daughter of Aiah.
So *Ishbosheth* said to Abner, "Why have
you [h]gone in to my father's concubine?"
8 Then Abner became very angry at the
words of Ishbosheth, and said, "*Am* I [i]a
dog's head that belongs to Judah? Today I
show loyalty to the house of Saul your father, to his brothers, and to his friends, and
have not delivered you into the hand of
David; and you charge me today with a
fault concerning this woman? 9 [j]May God
do so to Abner, and more also, if I do not
do for David [k]as the LORD has sworn to
him— 10 to transfer the kingdom from the
[2]house of Saul, and set up the throne of
David over Israel and over Judah, [l]from
Dan to Beersheba." 11 And he could not
answer Abner another word, because he
feared him.
12 Then Abner sent messengers on his
behalf to David, saying, "Whose *is* the
land?" saying *also*, "Make your covenant
with me, and indeed my hand *shall be* with
you to bring all Israel to you."
13 And *David* said, "Good, I will make a
covenant with you. But one thing I require
of you: [m]you shall not see my face unless
you first bring [n]Michal, Saul's daughter,
when you come to see my face." 14 So David sent messengers to [o]Ishbosheth, Saul's
son, saying, "Give *me* my wife Michal,
whom I betrothed to myself [p]for a hundred
foreskins of the Philistines." 15 And Ishbosheth sent and took her from *her* husband, from [3]Paltiel the son of Laish.
16 Then her husband went along with her
to [q]Bahurim, [4]weeping behind her. So
Abner said to him, "Go, return!" And he
returned.
17 Now Abner had communicated with
the elders of Israel, saying, "In time past
you were seeking for David *to be* king over
you. 18 Now then, do *it!* [r]For the LORD has
spoken of David, saying, 'By the hand of
My servant David, [5]I will save My people
Israel from the hand of the Philistines and
the hand of all their enemies.' " 19 And
Abner also spoke in the hearing of [s]Benja-
min. Then Abner also went to speak in the
hearing of David in Hebron all that
seemed good to Israel and the whole house
of Benjamin.
20 So Abner and twenty men with him
came to David at Hebron. And David
made a feast for Abner and the men who
were with him. 21 Then Abner said to David, "I will arise and go, and [t]gather all Israel to my lord the king, that they may
make a covenant with you, and that you

7 [g] 2 Sam. 21:8-11 [h] 2 Sam. 16:21
8 [i] Deut. 23:18; 1 Sam. 24:14; 2 Sam. 9:8; 16:9
9 [j] Ruth 1:17; 1 Kin. 19:2 [k] 1 Sam. 15:28; 16:1, 12; 28:17; 1 Chr. 12:23
10 [l] Judg. 20:1; 1 Sam. 3:20; 2 Sam. 17:11; 1 Kin. 4:25 [2] *family*
13 [m] Gen. 43:3 [n] 1 Sam. 18:20; 19:11; 25:44; 2 Sam. 6:16
14 [o] 2 Sam. 2:10 [p] 1 Sam. 18:25-27
15 [3] *Palti*, 1 Sam. 25:44
16 [q] 2 Sam. 16:5; 19:16 [4] Lit. *going and weeping*
18 [r] 2 Sam. 3:9 [5] So with many Heb. mss., LXX, Syr., Tg.; MT *he*
19 [s] 1 Sam. 10:20, 21; 1 Chr. 12:29
21 [t] 2 Sam. 3:10, 12

3:6 Abner was strengthening *his hold*. Abner was the military leader of the country and the one who had put Ishbosheth on the throne and whose power held him there. As time passed, Abner began to make his own move to take the throne.

3:7 Rizpah. By taking Rizpah, the concubine of Saul, Abner made a clear statement to the people that he would take the place of Saul as king over Israel. Going in to the king's concubine was a statement of power and rightful claim to the throne (cf. 16:21,22 in regard to Absalom). Ishbosheth reacted strongly against Abner, so Abner resented his reaction as an indignity and, compelled by revenge, determined to transfer all the weight of his influence and power to David's side (vv. 9,10).

3:8 dog's head. This was another way to ask, "Am I a contemptible traitor allied with Judah?" This was a common expression to show disdain (1 Sam. 17:43). Abner used this opportunity to condemn Ishbosheth by reminding him that he would not have been in power had Abner himself not placed him there.

3:9 as the LORD has sworn to him. Abner seemed to demonstrate the knowledge that David was to be the next king of Israel as God had sworn to David (1 Sam. 13:14; 15:28; 24:20).

3:10 transfer the kingdom. Part of Saul's kingdom had already been transferred to David, namely Judah; however, Abner vowed to complete the process by helping David obtain the rest of the kingdom. **Dan to Beersheba.** This was an expression meaning the whole country (cf. Judg. 20:1), i.e., from Dan in the N to Beersheba in the S.

3:12 Whose *is* the land? Though Abner's language (vv. 9,10) implied the conviction that in supporting Ishbosheth he had been going against God's purpose of conferring the sovereignty of the kingdom on David, this acknowledgment was no justification of his motives. He selfishly wanted to be on the winning side and to be honored as the one who brought all the people under David's rule.

3:13 Michal, Saul's daughter. David requested Michal for two reasons. One, it would right the wrong Saul had committed toward David by having given Michal, who was David's wife and who loved him (1 Sam. 18:20,28), to another man (1 Sam. 25:44). Two, it would serve to strengthen David's claim to the throne of all Israel by inclining some of Saul's house to be favorable to his cause.

3:14 a hundred foreskins of the Philistines. David reminded Ishbosheth that he had not only paid the dowry to Saul for his daughter, 100 foreskins of the Philistines, but had delivered double the asking price (1 Sam. 18:25-27). Thus, Michal rightfully belonged to David.

3:16 Bahurim. Located just E of Jerusalem, it became the final location where Paltiel (cf. 1 Sam. 25:44) would see Michal. This was also the town of Shimei, the man who cursed David during his flight from Jerusalem before Absalom (16:5). David's soldiers also found refuge in a well at Bahurim while being pursued by Absalom's men (19:16).

3:17 elders of Israel. These men were the recognized leaders of the people serving as Ishbosheth's advisers who would have been consulted when important decisions needed to be made (cf. 19:7).

3:18 My servant David. David is called "the LORD's servant" more than 30 times in the OT. Abner's words to the elders of Israel clearly recognized David as the servant of the Lord, thus having the right to the throne according to God's sovereign will.

3:19 Benjamin. Abner gave special attention to the tribe of Benjamin, for they were Saul's and Ishbosheth's kinsmen (see 1 Sam. 9:1,2).

3:21 covenant with you. This covenant moved beyond the personal agreement made between Abner and David and was operative

may [u]reign over all that your heart desires." So David sent Abner away, and he
went in peace.

Joab Murders Abner

22 At that moment the servants of David
and Joab came from a raid and brought
much [6]spoil with them. But Abner *was* not
with David in Hebron, for he had sent him
away, and he had gone in peace. 23 When
Joab and all the troops that *were* with him
had come, they told Joab, saying, "Abner the
son of Ner came to the king, and he sent him
away, and he has gone in peace." 24 Then
Joab came to the king and said, "What have
you done? Look, Abner came to you; why *is*
it *that* you sent him away, and he has already
gone? 25 Surely you realize that Abner the
son of Ner came to deceive you, to know
[v]your going out and your coming in, and to
know all that you are doing."
26 And when Joab had gone from David's presence, he sent messengers after
Abner, who brought him back from the
well of Sirah. But David did not know *it*.
27 Now when Abner had returned to Hebron, Joab [w]took him aside in the gate to
speak with him privately, and there
[7]stabbed him [x]in the stomach, so that he
died for the blood of [y]Asahel his brother.
28 Afterward, when David heard *it*, he
said, "My kingdom and I *are* [8]guiltless before the LORD forever of the blood of Abner
the son of Ner. 29 [z]Let it rest on the head of
Joab and on all his father's house; and let
there never fail to be in the [9]house of Joab
one [a]who has a discharge or is a leper, who
leans on a staff or falls by the sword, or who
lacks bread." 30 So Joab and Abishai his
brother killed Abner, because he had killed
their brother [b]Asahel at Gibeon in the battle.

21 [u] 1 Kin. 11:37
22 [6] *booty*
25 [v] Deut. 28:6; 1 Sam. 29:6; Is. 37:28
27 [w] 2 Sam. 20:9, 10; 1 Kin. 2:5 [x] 2 Sam. 4:6 [y] 2 Sam. 2:23 [7] Lit. *struck*
28 [8] *innocent*
29 [z] Deut. 21:6-9; 1 Kin. 2:32, 33 [a] Lev. 15:2 [9] *family*
30 [b] 2 Sam. 2:23

David's Mourning for Abner

31 Then David said to Joab and to all the
people who were with him, [c]"Tear your
clothes, [d]gird yourselves with sackcloth,
and mourn for Abner." And King David
followed the coffin. 32 So they buried
Abner in Hebron; and the king lifted up his
voice and wept at the grave of Abner, and
all the people wept. 33 And the king sang *a
lament* over Abner and said:

"Should Abner die as a [e]fool dies?
34 Your hands were not bound
Nor your feet put into fetters;
As a man falls before wicked men,
so you fell."

Then all the people wept over him again.
35 And when all the people came [f]to persuade David to eat food while it was still
day, David took an oath, saying, [g]"God do
so to me, and more also, if I taste bread or
anything else [h]till the sun goes down!"
36 Now all the people took note *of it*, and it
pleased them, since whatever the king did
pleased all the people. 37 For all the people
and all Israel understood that day that it
had not been the king's *intent* to kill Abner
the son of Ner. 38 Then the king said to his
servants, "Do you not know that a prince
and a great man has fallen this day in Israel?
39 And I *am* weak today, though anointed
king; and these men, the sons of Zeruiah,
[i]*are* too harsh for me. [j]The LORD shall repay
the evildoer according to his wickedness."

31 [c] Josh. 7:6; 2 Sam. 1:2, 11 [d] Gen. 37:34
33 [e] 2 Sam. 13:12, 13
35 [f] 2 Sam. 12:17; Jer. 16:7, 8 [g] Ruth 1:17 [h] Judg. 20:26; 2 Sam. 1:12
39 [i] 2 Sam. 19:5-7 [j] 1 Kin. 2:5, 6, 32-34; 2 Tim. 4:14

Ishbosheth Is Murdered

4 When Saul's [1]son heard that Abner
had died in Hebron, [a]he [2] lost heart,
and all Israel was [b]troubled. 2 Now Saul's
son *had* two men *who were* captains of

CHAPTER 4

1 [a] Ezra 4:4; Is. 13:7 [b] Matt. 2:3 [1] Ishbosheth [2] Lit. *his hands dropped*

on the national level, uniting both N and S. **in peace.** The repetition of this phrase in vv. 22,23 serves to emphasize the fact that David sought to ensure peace with Abner. This also accentuates the fact that David was not involved in Abner's death (vv. 26-30).

3:25 Abner...came to deceive you. It is ironic that Joab accused Abner of deception in spying on David in v. 25 when in v. 26 he deceived David by not telling him of his request to have Abner returned to Hebron. Joab used this deception to slay Abner out of personal vengeance for the death of his brother Asahel (v. 27; see 2:19-23).

3:26 well of Sirah. The only mention of this location is found here. The town was located about 2.5 mi. NW of Hebron.

3:27 in the stomach. Abner died in a similar manner to Joab's brother Asahel, the man he had killed (2:23). However, Abner struck Asahel during battle (cf. 2:18-23) in self-defense, while, Joab murdered Abner to avenge the death of Asahel.

3:28 the blood of Abner. Since life is in the blood (cf. Gen. 9:4; Lev. 17:11,14; Deut. 12:23), this expression refers to the life of Abner. David made it clear he had nothing to do with the murder of Abner, and David sought the Lord's help to punish Joab for his evil deed (v. 39).

3:31 mourn. Joab was instructed to mourn for the death of Abner, as was the custom for commemorating the death of an individual. To further demonstrate David's condemnation of the killing of Abner, he instructed "all the people" to mourn the death of Abner, including Joab and his men (vv. 32-34).

3:35-39 David's feelings and conduct in response to Abner's death tended not only to remove all suspicion of guilt from him, but even turned the tide of public opinion in his favor and paved the way for his reigning over all the tribes much more honorably than by the negotiations of Abner (3:17-19).

3:39 weak...harsh. David had not yet solidified his power enough to exact his own judgment without jeopardizing his command. He was still "weak" and needed time to consolidate his authority. Once that was accomplished, he no longer needed to fear the strength of Joab and Abishai, who were Zeruiah's sons (2:18).

4:1 lost heart...troubled. Lit. "his hands became weak or limp" (cf. 17:2; 2 Chr. 15:7). Ishbosheth and all of Israel realized that Abner had been the source of strength and stability for Israel. With Abner dead, Israel was troubled because Ishbosheth no longer had a leader for the army which secured him in power.

troops. The name of one *was* Baanah and
the name of the other Rechab, the sons of
Rimmon the Beerothite, of the children of
Benjamin. (For [c]Beeroth also was [3]*part*
of Benjamin, **3** because the Beerothites fled
to [d]Gittaim and have been sojourners there
until this day.)
4 [e]Jonathan, Saul's son, had a son *who*
was lame in *his* feet. He was five years old
when the news about Saul and Jonathan
came [f]from Jezreel; and his nurse took him
up and fled. And it happened, as she made
haste to flee, that he fell and became lame.
His name *was* [g]Mephibosheth.[4]
5 Then the sons of Rimmon the Beerothite, Rechab and Baanah, set out and came
at about the heat of the day to the [h]house
of Ishbosheth, who was lying on his bed at
noon. **6** And they came there, all the way
into the house, *as though* to get wheat, and
they [5]stabbed him [i]in the stomach. Then
Rechab and Baanah his brother escaped.
7 For when they came into the house, he
was lying on his bed in his bedroom; then
they struck him and killed him, beheaded
him and took his head, and were all night
escaping through the plain. **8** And they
brought the head of Ishbosheth to David at
Hebron, and said to the king, "Here is the
head of Ishbosheth, the son of Saul your
enemy, [j]who sought your life; and the
LORD has avenged my lord the king this
day of Saul and his descendants."
9 But David answered Rechab and Baanah his brother, the sons of Rimmon the
Beerothite, and said to them, "*As* the LORD
lives, [k]who has redeemed my life from all
adversity, **10** when [l]someone told me, saying, 'Look, Saul is dead,' thinking to have
brought good news, I arrested him and
had him executed in Ziklag—the one who
thought I would give him a reward for *his*
news. **11** How much more, when wicked
men have killed a righteous person in his
own house on his bed? Therefore, shall I
not now [m]require his [6]blood at your hand
and [7]remove you from the earth?" **12** So
David [n]commanded his young men, and
they executed them, cut off their hands
and feet, and hanged *them* by the pool in
Hebron. But they took the head of Ishbosheth and buried *it* in the [o]tomb of
Abner in Hebron.

David Reigns over All Israel

5 Then all the tribes of Israel [a]came to
David at Hebron and spoke, saying,
"Indeed [b]we *are* your bone and your flesh.
2 Also, in time past, when Saul was king
over us, [c]you were the one who led Israel
out and brought them in; and the LORD
said to you, [d]'You shall shepherd My people Israel, and be ruler over Israel.' "
3 [e]Therefore all the elders of Israel came to
the king at Hebron, [f]and King David made
a covenant with them at Hebron [g]before
the LORD. And they anointed David king
over Israel. **4** David *was* [h]thirty years old
when he began to reign, *and* [i]he reigned
forty years. **5** In Hebron he reigned over
Judah [j]seven years and six months, and in
Jerusalem he reigned thirty-three years
over all Israel and Judah.

2 [c] Josh. 18:25 [3] *considered part of*
3 [d] Neh. 11:33
4 [e] 2 Sam. 9:3 [f] 1 Sam. 29:1, 11 [g] 2 Sam. 9:6 [4] *Merib-Baal,* 1 Chr. 8:34; 9:40
5 [h] 2 Sam. 2:8, 9
6 [i] 2 Sam. 2:23; 20:10 [5] Lit. *struck*
8 [j] 1 Sam. 19:2, 10, 11; 23:15; 25:29
9 [k] Gen. 48:16; 1 Kin. 1:29; Ps. 31:7
10 [l] 2 Sam. 1:2-16
11 [m] [Gen. 9:5, 6; Ps. 9:12] [6] Or *bloodshed* [7] Lit. *consume you*
12 [n] 2 Sam. 1:15 [o] 2 Sam. 3:32

CHAPTER 5

1 [a] 1 Chr. 11:1-3 [b] Gen. 29:14; Judg. 9:2; 2 Sam. 19:12, 13
2 [c] 1 Sam. 18:5, 13, 16 [d] 1 Sam. 16:1
3 [e] 2 Sam. 3:17; 1 Chr. 11:3 [f] 2 Sam. 2:4; 3:21; 2 Kin. 11:17 [g] Judg. 11:11; 1 Sam. 23:18
4 [h] Gen. 41:46; Num. 4:3; Luke 3:23 [i] 1 Kin. 2:11; 1 Chr. 26:31; 29:27
5 [j] 2 Sam. 2:11; 1 Chr. 3:4; 29:27

4:2 children of Benjamin. It is stressed that these men were of the tribe of Benjamin (vv. 2,3), perhaps to show the friction within the house of Saul and his son Ishbosheth, and how the grab for power began once Abner was gone.

4:2,3 Beeroth…Gittaim. Beeroth was a Canaanite town belonging to the tribe of Benjamin. Gittaim was also a village of the tribe of Benjamin.

4:4 Mephibosheth. He may be introduced here to demonstrate that his youth and physical handicap disqualified him from being considered for ruling Israel. He would have been only 12 years old at the time of Ishbosheth's death. For the history of this man, see 9:6-13; 16:1-4; 19:24-30; 21:7.

4:5,6 It was the custom to secure wheat for the soldiers under their command (v. 2) along with some pay. Under the pretense of that normal routine, they came and killed the king.

4:7 the plain. To avoid easy detection, the men traveled by way of the Arabah (cf. 2:29), i.e., the Jordan Valley. This plain extended about 30 mi. from Mahanaim to Hebron.

4:8 the LORD has avenged. The murderers of Ishbosheth came to David and proclaimed, "the LORD has avenged" David. However, as happened earlier to the Amalekite (1:2-15), the men were very surprised at the response of David. David did not see their deed as the Lord's vengeance, but as murder of an innocent man.

4:9 the LORD…has redeemed my life from all adversity. A striking contrast is shown between David and the two murderers who claimed they were performing the Lord's work by killing Ishbosheth. However, David praised the Lord for His providential work through Ishbosheth's life and proclaimed the Lord's deliverance; thus, David condemned the murderers of Ishbosheth and had them executed as he had done to the man who claimed to kill Saul (1:15,16).

5:1-3 See 1 Chr. 11:1-3.

5:1,2 all the tribes of Israel. The term "all" is used 3 times (vv. 1,3,5) to emphasize that the kingdom established under King David was truly a united monarchy. The "elders" of Israel (v. 3), representing the "tribes" (v. 1), came to David at Hebron with the express purpose of submitting to his rule. Three reasons were given by the Israelites for wanting to make David king: 1) he was an Israelite brother (cf. Deut. 17:15); 2) he was Israel's best warrior and commander; and 3) he had been chosen by the Lord to be the king of Israel.

5:3 King David made a covenant. David bound himself formally to certain obligations toward the Israelites, including their rights and responsibilities to one another and to the Lord (cf. 2 Kin. 11:17). As good as this covenant was, it did not end the underlying sense of separate identity felt by Israel and Judah as the revolt of Sheba (20:1) and the dissolution of the united kingdom under Rehoboam (1 Kin. 12:16) would later demonstrate. **they anointed David.** David's third anointing (2:4; 1 Sam. 16:13) resulted in the unification of the 12 tribes under his kingship.

5:5 Israel and Judah. The united kingdom was still known by its two component parts.

The Conquest of Jerusalem

6 [k]And the king and his men went to Jerusalem against [l]the Jebusites, the inhabitants of the land, who spoke to David, saying, "You shall not come in here; but the
blind and the lame will repel you," thinking, "David cannot come in here." 7 Nevertheless David took the stronghold of Zion
[m](that *is,* the City of David).
8 Now David said on that day, "Whoever climbs up by way of the water shaft
and defeats the Jebusites (the lame and the
blind, *who are* hated by David's soul), [n]*he*
shall be chief and captain." Therefore they
say, "The blind and the lame shall not
come into the house."
9 Then David dwelt in the stronghold,
and called it [o]the City of David. And David
built all around from [1]the Millo and inward. 10 So David went on and became
great, and [p]the LORD God of hosts *was* with
[q]him.
11 Then [r]Hiram [s]king of Tyre sent messengers to David, and cedar trees, and
carpenters and masons. And they built
David a house. 12 So David knew that the

6 [k]Judg. 1:21 [l]Josh. 15:63; Judg. 1:8; 19:11, 12
7 [m]2 Sam. 6:12, 16; 1 Kin. 2:10; 8:1; 9:24
8 [n]1 Chr. 11:6-9
9 [o]2 Sam. 5:7; 1 Kin. 9:15, 24 [1]Lit. *The Landfill*
10 [p]1 Sam. 17:45 [q]1 Sam. 18:12, 28
11 [r]1 Kin. 5:1-18 [s]1 Chr. 14:1

5:6-10 See 1 Chr. 11:4-9.

5:6 Jerusalem. This city is mentioned in the Bible more than any other (from Gen. 14:18 to Rev. 21:10). The city was located in the territory of Benjamin, near the northern border of Judah and was excellently fortified because of its elevation and the surrounding deep valleys, which made it naturally defensible on 3 sides. In addition, it had a good water supply, the Gihon spring, and was close to travel routes for trade. The city had earlier been conquered by Judah (Judg. 1:8), but neither Judah nor Benjamin had been successful in permanently dislodging the Jebusite inhabitants (Josh. 15:33; Judg. 1:21). By taking Jerusalem, David was able to eliminate the foreign wedge between the northern and southern tribes and to establish his capital. **Jebusites.** A people of Canaanite descent (Gen. 10:16-18). Since the earlier inhabitants of Jerusalem were Amorites (Josh. 10:5), it seems that the Jebusites took control of Jerusalem after the time of the Israelite conquest. **the blind and the lame.** The Jebusites taunted the Israelites and mocked the power of David by boasting that the blind and the lame could defend Jerusalem against him.

5:7 stronghold of Zion. This is the first occurrence of "Zion" in the Bible and the only one in 1 and 2 Samuel. Referring here to the Jebusite citadel on the southeastern hill, the name was also later used of the temple mount (Is. 10:12) and of the entire city of Jerusalem (Is. 28:16). **City of David.** Both Bethlehem, David's birthplace (Luke 2:4), and Jerusalem, David's place of reign, were called by this title.

5:8 water shaft. A tunnel that channeled the city's water supply from the Gihon spring outside the city walls on the E side into the citadel.

5:9 Millo. Lit. "filling." Stone-filled terraces were built to serve as part of Jerusalem's northern defenses, since the city was most open to attack from that direction.

5:11-16 See 1 Chr. 14:1-7.

5:11 Hiram king of Tyre. Tyre was a Phoenician port city about 35 mi. N of Mt. Carmel and 25 mi. S of Sidon. During the latter part of David's reign and much of Solomon's, the friendly Hiram traded building materials for agricultural products. He also provided craftsmen to build David's palace, indicating how the long war had brought the nation to a low place where there were few good artisans. Psalm 30 could possibly refer to the dedication of this house or to the temporary shelter for the ark in Jerusalem (6:17).

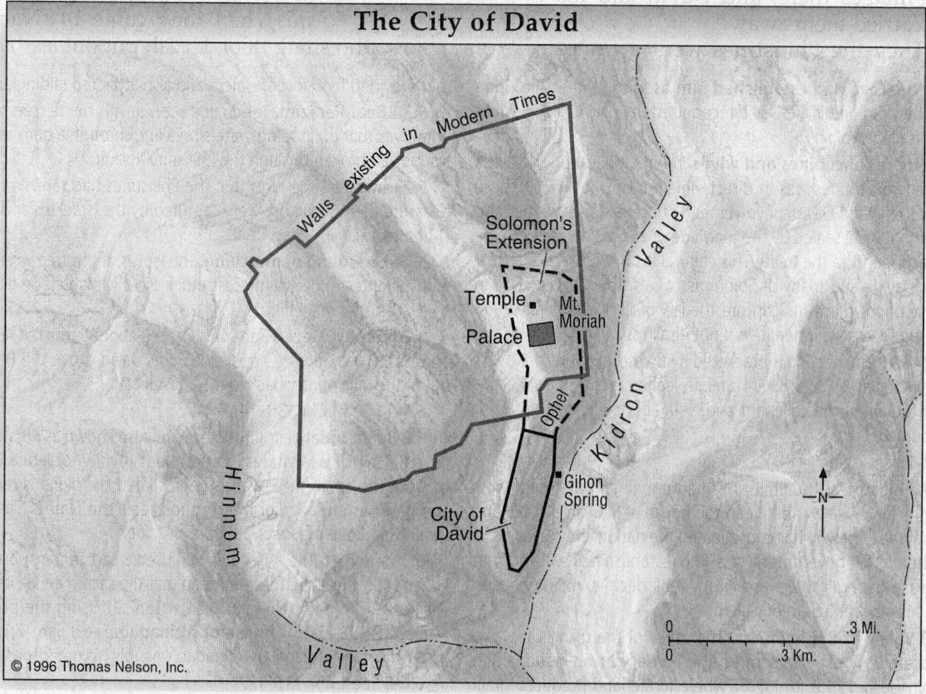

LORD had established him as king over Israel, and that He had [t]exalted His kingdom [u]for the sake of His people Israel.
13 And [v]David took more concubines
and wives from Jerusalem, after he had
come from Hebron. Also more sons and
daughters were born to David. 14 Now
[w]these *are* the names of those who were
born to him in Jerusalem: [2]Shammua,
Shobab, Nathan, [x]Solomon, 15 Ibhar, [3]Eli-
shua, Nepheg, Japhia, 16 Elishama, Eliada,
and Eliphelet.

The Philistines Defeated

17 [y]Now when the Philistines heard that
they had anointed David king over Israel,
all the Philistines went up to search for David. And David heard *of it* [z]and went
down to the stronghold. 18 The Philistines
also went and deployed themselves in [a]the
Valley of Rephaim. 19 So David [b]inquired
of the LORD, saying, "Shall I go up against
the Philistines? Will You deliver them into
my hand?"
And the LORD said to David, "Go up, for
I will doubtless deliver the Philistines into
your hand."
20 So David went to [c]Baal Perazim, and
David defeated them there; and he said,
"The LORD has broken through my enemies before me, like a breakthrough of
water." Therefore he called the name of
that place [4]Baal Perazim. 21 And they left
their [5]images there, and David and his
men [d]carried them away.
22 [e]Then the Philistines went up once
again and deployed themselves in the Valley of Rephaim. 23 Therefore [f]David inquired of the LORD, and He said, "You shall
not go up; circle around behind them, and
come upon them in front of the mulberry
trees. 24 And it shall be, when you [g]hear
the sound of marching in the tops of the
mulberry trees, then you shall advance
quickly. For then [h]the LORD will go out before you to strike the camp of the Philistines." 25 And David did so, as the LORD
commanded him; and he drove back the
Philistines from [i]Geba[6] as far as [j]Gezer.

The Ark Brought to Jerusalem

6 Again David gathered all *the* choice
men of Israel, thirty thousand. 2 And
[a]David arose and went with all the people
who *were* with him from [1]Baale Judah to
bring up from there the ark of God, whose
name is called [2]by the Name, the LORD of
Hosts, [b]who dwells *between* the cherubim.
3 So they set the ark of God on a new cart,
and brought it out of the house of Abinadab, which *was* on [c]the hill; and Uzzah and
Ahio, the sons of Abinadab, drove the new
[3]cart. 4 And they brought it out of [d]the
house of Abinadab, which *was* on the hill,
accompanying the ark of God; and Ahio
went before the ark. 5 Then David and all
the house of Israel [e]played *music* before the
LORD on all kinds of *instruments of* fir wood,
on harps, on stringed instruments, on tambourines, on sistrums, and on cymbals.
6 And when they came to [f]Nachon's
threshing floor, Uzzah put out *his* [g]*hand* to

12 [t]Num. 24:7 [u]Is. 45:4
13 [v][Deut. 17:17]; 1 Chr. 3:9
14 [w]1 Chr. 3:5-8 [x]2 Sam. 12:24 [2]*Shimea,* 1 Chr. 3:5
15 [3]*Elishama,* 1 Chr. 3:6
17 [y]1 Chr. 11:16 [z]2 Sam. 23:14
18 [a]Gen. 14:5; Josh. 15:8; 1 Chr. 11:15; Is. 17:5
19 [b]1 Sam. 23:2; 2 Sam. 2:1
20 [c]1 Chr. 14:11; Is. 28:21 [4]Lit. *Master of Breakthroughs*
21 [d]Deut. 7:5, 25 [5]*idols*
22 [e]1 Chr. 14:13
23 [f]2 Sam. 5:19
24 [g]2 Kin. 7:6; 1 Chr. 14:15 [h]Judg. 4:14
25 [i]1 Chr. 14:16 [j]Josh. 16:10 [6]So with MT, Tg., Vg.; LXX *Gibeon*

CHAPTER 6

2 [a]1 Chr. 13:5, 6 [b]Ex. 25:22; 1 Sam. 4:4; Ps. 80:1 [1]*Baalah, Kirjath Jearim,* Josh. 15:9; 1 Chr. 13:6 [2]LXX, Tg., Vg. omit *by the Name;* many Heb. mss., Syr. *there*
3 [c]1 Sam. 26:1 [3]LXX adds *with the ark*
4 [d]1 Sam. 7:1; 1 Chr. 13:7
5 [e]1 Sam. 18:6, 7
6 [f]1 Chr. 13:9 [g]Num. 4:15, 19, 20

5:12 the LORD had established him as king. Witnessing God's evident blessing on his life, David recognized the Lord's role in establishing his kingship.

5:13 more concubines and wives. The multiplication of David's wives and concubines was in direct violation of Deut. 17:17. These marriages reflected David's involvement in international treaties and alliances that were sealed by the marriage of a king's daughter to the other participants in the treaty. This cultural institution accounted for some of David's and many of Solomon's wives (see 1 Kin. 11:1-3). In each case of polygamy in Scripture, the law of God was violated and the consequences were negative, if not disastrous.

5:17–8:18 This section is bracketed by the descriptions of David's military victories (5:17-25; 8:1-14). In between (6:1–7:29), David's concern for the ark of the covenant and a suitable building to house it are recounted.

5:17-23 See 1 Chr. 14:8-17.

5:17 Philistines. The Philistines had remained quiet neighbors during the long civil war between the house of Saul and David, but, jealous of the king who has consolidated the nation, they resolved to attack before his government was fully established. Realizing that David was no longer their vassal, they took decisive military action against his new capital of Jerusalem.

5:18 Valley of Rephaim. Lit. "the valley of the giants." It was a plain located SW of Jerusalem on the border between Judah and Benjamin (Josh. 15:1,8; 18:11,16), where fertile land produced grain that provided food for Jerusalem and also attracted raiding armies.

5:20 Baal Perazim. The image seen in this name (see marginal note) was that of flooding waters breaking through a dam as David's troops had broken through the Philistine assault.

5:21 images. The idols that the Philistines had taken into battle to assure them of victory were captured by the Israelites and burned (1 Chr. 14:12).

5:24 the sound of marching. The leaves of this tree would rustle at the slightest movement of air, much of which would be generated by a large army marching.

5:25 Geba...Gezer. Geba was located about 5 mi. N of Jerusalem and Gezer was about 20 mi. W of Geba. David drove the Philistines out of the hill country back to the coastal plain.

6:1-11 See 1 Chr. 13:1-14.

6:2 Baale Judah. Lit. "lords of Judah." Also known as Kirjath Jearim (1 Sam. 7:1,2), this town was located about 10 mi. W of Jerusalem. **ark of God.** The ark of the covenant represented the glorious reputation and gracious presence of the Lord to Israel. **the Name.** *See note on Deut. 12:5.* **LORD of Hosts.** *See note on 1 Sam. 1:3.*

6:3 new cart. The Philistines had used a cart to transport the ark (1 Sam. 6:7). But the OT law required that the sacred ark be carried by the sons of Kohath (Num. 3:30,31; 4:15; 7:9), using the poles prescribed (Ex. 25:12-15). **house of Abinadab.** See 1 Sam. 7:1. **Uzzah and Ahio.** Descendants of Abinadab, possibly his grandsons.

6:6-8 See 1 Chr. 13:9-12.

the ark of God and [4]took hold of it, for the
oxen stumbled. 7 Then the anger of the
LORD was aroused against Uzzah, and God
struck him there for *his* [5]error; and he died
there by the ark of God. 8 And David became angry because of the LORD's outbreak
against Uzzah; and he called the name of
the place [6]Perez Uzzah to this day.
9 [h]David was afraid of the LORD that
day; and he said, "How can the ark of the
LORD come to me?" 10 So David would not
move the ark of the LORD with him into the
[i]City of David; but David took it aside into
the house of Obed-Edom the [j]Gittite.
11 [k]The ark of the LORD remained in the
house of Obed-Edom the Gittite three
months. And the LORD [l]blessed Obed-
Edom and all his household.
12 Now it was told King David, saying,
"The LORD has blessed the house of Obed-
Edom and all that *belongs* to him, because of
the ark of God." [m]So David went and
brought up the ark of God from the house of
Obed-Edom to the City of David with gladness. 13 And so it was, when [n]those bearing
the ark of the LORD had gone six paces, that
he sacrificed [o]oxen and fatted sheep. 14 Then
David [p]danced[7] before the LORD with all *his*
might; and David *was* wearing [q]a linen
ephod. 15 [r]So David and all the house of Israel brought up the ark of the LORD with
shouting and with the sound of the trumpet.
16 Now as the ark of the LORD came into
the City of David, [s]Michal, Saul's daughter, looked through a window and saw
King David leaping and whirling before
the LORD; and she despised him in her
heart. 17 So [t]they brought the ark of the
LORD, and set it in [u]its place in the midst of
the tabernacle that David had erected for
it. Then David [v]offered burnt offerings and
peace offerings before the LORD. 18 And
when David had finished offering burnt
offerings and peace offerings, [w]he blessed
the people in the name of the LORD of
hosts. 19 [x]Then he distributed among all
the people, among the whole multitude of
Israel, both the women and the men, to
everyone a loaf of bread, a piece *of meat,*
and a cake of raisins. So all the people departed, everyone to his house.
20 [y]Then David returned to bless his
household. And Michal the daughter of
Saul came out to meet David, and said,
"How glorious was the king of Israel today,
[z]uncovering himself today in the eyes of the
maids of his servants, as one of the [a]base
fellows [8]shamelessly uncovers himself!"
21 So David said to Michal, "*It was* before
the LORD, [b]who chose me instead of your
father and all his house, to appoint me
ruler over the [c]people of the LORD, over Israel. Therefore I will play *music* before the
LORD. 22 And I will be even more undignified than this, and will be humble in my
own sight. But as for the maidservants of
whom you have spoken, by them I will be
held in honor."
23 Therefore Michal the daughter of Saul
had no children [d]to the day of her death.

6 [4] *held it*
7 [5] Or *irreverence*
8 [6] Lit. *Outburst Against Uzzah*
9 [h] Deut. 9:19; Ps. 119:120; Luke 5:8
10 [i] 2 Sam. 5:7 [j] 1 Chr. 13:13; 26:4-8
11 [k] 1 Chr. 13:14 [l] Gen. 30:27; 39:5
12 [m] 1 Chr. 15:25–16:3
13 [n] Num. 4:15; Josh. 3:3; 1 Sam. 6:15; 2 Sam. 15:24; 1 Chr. 15:2, 15 [o] 1 Kin. 8:5
14 [p] Ps. 30:11; 149:3 [q] 1 Sam. 2:18, 28 [7] *whirled about*
15 [r] 1 Chr. 15:28
16 [s] 2 Sam. 3:14
17 [t] 1 Chr. 16:1 [u] 1 Chr. 15:1; 2 Chr. 1:4 [v] 1 Kin. 8:5, 62, 63
18 [w] 1 Kin. 8:14, 15, 55
19 [x] 1 Chr. 16:3
20 [y] Ps. 30:title [z] 2 Sam. 6:14, 16 [a] Judg. 9:4 [8] *openly*
21 [b] 1 Sam. 13:14; 15:28 [c] 2 Kin. 11:17
23 [d] 1 Sam. 15:35; Is. 22:14

6:7 for *his* error. No matter how innocently it was done, touching the ark was in direct violation of God's law and was to result in death (see Num. 4:15). This was a means of preserving the sense of God's holiness and the fear of drawing near to Him without appropriate preparation.

6:8 David became angry. Probably anger directed at himself because the calamity resulted from David's own carelessness. He was confused as to whether to carry on the transportation of the ark to Jerusalem (v. 9) and would not move it, fearing more death and calamity might come on him or the people (v. 10). It is likely that he waited to see the wrath of God subside before moving the ark.

6:10 Obed-Edom the Gittite. Lit. "servant of Edom." The term "Gittite" can refer to someone from the Philistine city of Gath, but here it is better to see the term related to Gath Rimmon, one of the Levitical cities (cf. Josh. 21:24,25). Obed-Edom is referred to as a Levite in Chronicles (1 Chr. 15:17-25; 16:5,38; 26:4,5,8,15; 2 Chr. 25:24).

6:12-19 See 1 Chr. 15:25–16:3.

6:12 blessed...because of the ark. During the 3 months when the ark remained with Obed-Edom, the Lord blessed his family. In the same way God had blessed Obed-Edom, David was confident that with the presence of the ark, the Lord would bless his house in ways that would last forever (7:29).

6:13 bearing the ark. In David's second attempt to bring the ark to Jerusalem, it was transported in the manner prescribed by OT law. *See note on v. 3.* **six paces.** I.e., after the first 6 steps, not after every 6 steps.

6:14 David danced before the LORD. Cf. Ps. 150:4. The Hebrews, like other ancient and modern people, had their physical expressions of religious joys as they praised God. **linen ephod.** See 1 Sam. 2:18.

6:16 Michal...despised him. Michal's contempt for David is explained by her sarcastic remark in v. 20. She considered David's unbridled, joyful dancing as conduct unbefitting for the dignity and gravity of a king because it exposed him in some ways.

6:17 tabernacle. David had made a tent for the ark of the covenant until a permanent building for it could be built. Psalm 30 could refer possibly to this tent or to David's own home (5:11,12).

6:20 bless his household. David desired the same inevitable success from the Lord as experienced in the household of Obed-Edom (see v. 11). The attitude of Michal aborted the blessing at that time, but the Lord would bless David's house in the future (7:29). **uncovering.** A derogatory reference to the priestly attire that David wore (v. 14) in place of his royal garments.

6:21 before the LORD. David's actions were for the delight of the Lord, not for the maidens.

6:22 humble in my own sight. David viewed himself with humility. It is the humble whom the Lord will exalt (cf. 1 Sam. 7:7,8).

6:23 Michal...had no children. Whether David ceased to have marital relations with Michal or the Lord disciplined Michal for her contempt of David, Michal bore no children. In OT times, it was a reproach to be childless (1 Sam. 1:5,6). Michal's childlessness prevented her from providing a successor to David's throne from the family of Saul (cf. 1 Sam. 15:22-28).

God's Covenant with David

7 Now it came to pass [a]when the king
was dwelling in his house, and the
LORD had given him rest from all his enemies all around, 2 that the king said to Nathan the prophet, "See now, I dwell in [b]a
house of cedar, [c]but the ark of God dwells
inside tent [d]curtains."
3 Then Nathan said to the king, "Go, do
all that *is* in your [e]heart, for the LORD *is*
with you."
4 But it happened that night that the
word of the LORD came to Nathan, saying,
5 "Go and tell My servant David, 'Thus
says the LORD: [f]"Would you build a house
for Me to dwell in? 6 For I have not dwelt
in a house [g]since the time that I brought
the children of Israel up from Egypt, even
to this day, but have moved about in [h]a
tent and in a tabernacle. 7 Wherever I have
[i]moved about with all the children of Israel, have I ever spoken a word to anyone
from the tribes of Israel, whom I commanded [j]to shepherd My people Israel,
saying, 'Why have you not built Me a
house of cedar?' " ' 8 Now therefore, thus
shall you say to My servant David, 'Thus
says the LORD of hosts: [k]"I took you from
the sheepfold, from following the sheep, to
be ruler over My people, over Israel. 9 And
[l]I have been with you wherever you have
gone, [m]and have [1]cut off all your enemies
from before you, and have made you a
great name, like the name of the great men
who *are* on the earth. 10 Moreover I will appoint a place for My people Israel, and will
[n]plant them, that they may dwell in a place
of their own and move no more; [o]nor shall
the sons of wickedness oppress them anymore, as previously, 11 [p]since the time that
I commanded judges *to be* over My people
Israel, and have caused you to rest from all
your enemies. Also the LORD [2]tells you
[q]that He will make you a [3]house.
12 [r]"When your days are fulfilled and
you [s]rest with your fathers, [t]I will set up
your seed after you, who will come from
your body, and I will establish his kingdom. 13 [u]He shall build a house for My
name, and I will [v]establish the throne of
his kingdom forever. 14 [w]I will be his Father, and he shall be [x]My son. If he commits iniquity, I will chasten him with the
rod of men and with the [4]blows of the sons

CHAPTER 7

1 [a] 1 Chr. 17:1-27
2 [b] 2 Sam. 5:11 [c] Acts 7:46 [d] Ex. 26:1
3 [e] 1 Kin. 8:17, 18; 1 Chr. 22:7
5 [f] 1 Kin. 5:3, 4; 8:19; 1 Chr. 22:8
6 [g] Josh. 18:1; 1 Kin. 8:16 [h] Ex. 40:18, 34
7 [i] Lev. 26:11, 12 [j] 2 Sam. 5:2; [Acts 20:28]
8 [k] 1 Sam. 16:11, 12; Ps. 78:70, 71
9 [l] 1 Sam. 18:14; 2 Sam. 5:10 [m] 1 Sam. 31:6 [1] *destroyed*
10 [n] Ex. 15:17; Ps. 44:2; 80:8; Jer. 24:6 [o] Ps. 89:22, 23; Is. 60:18
11 [p] Judg. 2:14-16 [q] Ex. 1:21; 1 Sam. 25:28; 2 Sam. 7:27 [2] *declares to you* [3] Royal dynasty
12 [r] 1 Kin. 2:1 [s] Deut. 31:16; Acts 13:36 [t] 1 Kin. 8:20; Ps. 132:11; Matt. 1:6; Luke 3:31
13 [u] 1 Kin. 5:5; 8:19; 2 Chr. 6:2 [v] 2 Sam. 7:16; [Is. 9:7; 49:8]
14 [w] [Heb. 1:5] [x] [Ps. 2:7; 89:26, 27, 30]; Matt. 3:17 [4] *strokes*

7:1-17 See 1 Chr. 17:1-15. These verses record the establishment of the Davidic Covenant, God's unconditional promise to David and his posterity. While not called a covenant here, it is later (23:5). This promise is an important key to understanding God's irrevocable pledge of a king from the line of David to rule forever (v. 16). It has been estimated that over 40 individual biblical passages are directly related to these verses (cf. Pss. 89; 110; 132); thus, this text is a major highlight in the OT. The ultimate fulfillment comes at Christ's second advent when He sets up His millennial kingdom on earth (cf. Ezek. 37; Zech. 14; Rev. 19). This is the fourth of 5 irrevocable, unconditional covenants made by God. The first 3 include: 1) the Noahic Covenant (Gen. 9:8-17); 2) the Abrahamic Covenant (Gen. 15:12-21); and 3) the Levitic or Priestly Covenant (Num. 3:1-18; 18:1-20; 25; 10–13). The New Covenant, which actually provided redemption, was revealed later through Jeremiah (Jer. 31:31-34) and accomplished by the death and resurrection of Jesus Christ. *See note on Matt. 26:28.*

7:1 dwelling in his house. See 5:11. David's palace was built with help from Hiram of Tyre. Since Hiram did not become king of Tyre until around 980 B.C., the events narrated in this chapter occurred in the last decade of David's reign. **rest from all his enemies.** David had conquered all the nations that were around Israel. See 8:1-14 for the details which occur prior to 2 Sam. 7.

7:2 Nathan. Mentioned here for the first time, Nathan played a significant role in chap. 12 (confronting David's sin with Bathsheba) and 1 Kin. 1 (upsetting Adonijah's plot to usurp the throne from Solomon). **inside tent curtains.** *See note on 6:17.*

7:3 Go, do. Nathan the prophet encouraged David to pursue the noble project he had in mind and assured him of the Lord's blessing. However, neither David nor Nathan had consulted the Lord.

7:4-16 The Lord revealed His will to Nathan in this matter, to redirect the best human thoughts of the king.

7:5 Would you build a house. Verses 5-7 are framed by two questions asked by the Lord, both of which pertain to building a temple for Him. The first question, asking if David was the one who should build the temple, expected a negative answer (see 1 Chr. 17:4). According to 1 Chr. 22:8; 28:3, David was not chosen by God to build the temple because he was a warrior who had shed much blood.

7:7 Why have you not built Me a house? The second question, asking if the Lord had ever commanded any leader to build a temple for His ark, also expected a negative answer. So, contrary to Nathan's and David's intentions and assumptions, God did not want a house at that time and did not want David to build one.

7:8-16 a great name. These verses state the promises the Lord gave to David. Verses 8-11a give the promises to be realized during David's lifetime. Verses 11b-16 state the promises that would be fulfilled after David's death. During David's lifetime, the Lord: 1) gave David "a great name" (*see note on Gen. 12:2*); 2) appointed a place for Israel; and 3) gave David "rest" from all his enemies. After David's death, the Lord gave David: 1) a son to sit on his national throne, whom the Lord would oversee as a father with necessary chastening, discipline, and mercy (Solomon); and 2) a Son who would rule a kingdom that will be established forever (Messiah). This prophecy referred in its immediacy to Solomon and to the temporal kingdom of David's family in the land. But in a larger and more sublime sense, it refers to David's greater Son of another nature, Jesus Christ (cf. Heb. 1:8).

7:11 the LORD...will make you a house. Although David desired to build the Lord a "house," i.e., a temple, instead it would be the Lord who would build David a "house," i.e., a dynasty.

7:12 your seed. According to the rest of Scripture, it was the coming Messiah who would establish David's kingdom forever (see Is. 9:6,7; Luke 1:32,33).

7:14 his Father...My son. These words are directly related to Jesus the Messiah in Heb. 1:5. In Semitic thought, since the son had the full character of the father, the future seed of David would have the same essence of God. That Jesus Christ was God incarnate is the central theme of John's gospel (see Introduction to John). **If he commits iniquity.** As a human father disciplines his sons, so the Lord would discipline the seed, if he committed iniquity. This has reference

of men. 15 But My mercy shall not depart
from him, [y]as I took *it* from Saul, whom I
removed from before you. 16 And [z]your
house and your kingdom shall be established forever before [5]you. Your throne
shall be established forever." ' "
17 According to all these words and according to all this vision, so Nathan spoke
to David.

David's Thanksgiving to God

18 Then King David went in and sat before the LORD; and he said: [a]"Who *am* I, O
Lord GOD? And what is my house, that You
have brought me this far? 19 And yet this
was a small thing in Your sight, O Lord
GOD; and You have also spoken of Your
servant's house for a great while to come.
[b]*Is* this the manner of man, O Lord GOD?
20 Now what more can David say to You?
For You, Lord GOD, [c]know Your servant.
21 For Your word's sake, and according to
Your own heart, You have done all these
great things, to make Your servant know
them. 22 Therefore [d]You are great, [6]O Lord
GOD. For [e]*there is* none like You, nor *is there*
any God besides You, according to all that
we have heard with our [f]ears. 23 And who
is like Your people, like Israel, [g]the one nation on the earth whom God went to redeem for Himself as a people, to make for
Himself a name—and to do for Yourself
great and awesome deeds for Your land—

15 [y] 1 Sam. 15:23, 28; 16:14
16 [z] 2 Sam. 7:13; Ps. 89:36, 37; Matt. 25:31; John 12:34 [5] LXX *Me*
18 [a] Gen. 32:10; Ex. 3:11; 1 Sam. 18:18
19 [b] [Is. 55:8, 9]
20 [c] [1 Sam. 16:7]; Ps. 139:1; John 21:17
22 [d] Deut. 10:17; 1 Chr. 16:25; 2 Chr. 2:5; Ps. 86:10; Jer. 10:6 [e] Ex. 15:11; Deut. 3:24; 4:35; 32:39 [f] Ex. 10:2; Ps. 44:1 [6] Tg., Syr. *O LORD God*
23 [g] Ps. 147:20
[h] Deut. 9:26; 33:29
24 [i] Gen. 17:7, 8; Ex. 6:7; [Deut. 26:18] [j] Ps. 48:14
28 [k] Ex. 34:6; Josh. 21:45; John 17:17
29 [l] 2 Sam. 22:51

CHAPTER 8

1 [1] Lit. *struck* [2] Lit. *The Bridle of the Mother City*
2 [a] Num. 24:17

before [h]Your people whom You redeemed
for Yourself from Egypt, the nations, and
their gods? 24 For [i]You have made Your
people Israel Your very own people forever; [j]and You, LORD, have become their God.
25 "Now, O LORD God, the word which
You have spoken concerning Your servant
and concerning his house, establish *it* forever and do as You have said. 26 So let Your
name be magnified forever, saying, 'The
LORD of hosts *is* the God over Israel.' And
let the house of Your servant David be established before You. 27 For You, O LORD of
hosts, God of Israel, have revealed *this* to
Your servant, saying, 'I will build you a
house.' Therefore Your servant has found it
in his heart to pray this prayer to You.
28 "And now, O Lord GOD, You are God,
and [k]Your words are true, and You have
promised this goodness to Your servant.
29 Now therefore, let it please You to bless
the house of Your servant, that it may continue before You forever; for You, O Lord
GOD, have spoken *it,* and with Your blessing let the house of Your servant be blessed
[l]forever."

David's Further Conquests

8 After this it came to pass that David
[1]attacked the Philistines and subdued
them. And David took [2]Metheg Ammah
from the hand of the Philistines.
2 Then [a]he defeated Moab. Forcing them

to the intermediary seed until Messiah's arrival (any king of David's line from Solomon on). However, the ultimate Seed of David will not be a sinner like David and his descendants were, as recorded in Samuel and Kings (see 2 Cor. 5:21). Significantly, Chronicles, focusing more directly on the Messiah, does not include this statement in its record of Nathan's words (1 Chr. 17:13).

7:15 This is an expression of the unconditional character of the Davidic Covenant. The Messiah will come to His glorious, eternal Kingdom and that promise will not change.

7:16 your house...your kingdom...Your throne. Luke 1:32b, 33 indicates that these 3 terms are fulfilled in Jesus, "...and the Lord God will give Him the *throne* of His father David. And He will reign over the *house* of Jacob forever, and of His *kingdom* there will be no end." **forever.** This word conveys the idea of 1) an indeterminately long time or 2) into eternity future. It does not mean that there cannot be interruptions, but rather that the outcome is guaranteed. Christ's Davidic reign will conclude human history.

7:18-29 See 1 Chr. 17:16-27. David prayed with awe and thanksgiving over God's sovereign claim to bestow the divine blessing on his seed and nation.

7:18 sat before the LORD. I.e., before the ark of the covenant in the temporary tent. **Who *am* I.** David was overwhelmed by the Lord's promise that He would bring His kingdom through David's seed. In vv. 18-29, David referred to himself 10 times as "your servant" (vv. 19,20,21,25,26,27,28,29), acknowledging his God-given title, "My servant David" (v. 4).

7:19 a great while to come. David recognized that the Lord had spoken about the distant future, not only about his immediate descendant, Solomon. **the manner of man.** Lit. "and this is the law of man." This statement is better taken as a declaration rather than a question, with the idea being that God's covenant promise is for an eternal kingdom, whereby the whole world of man shall be blessed, through the coming seed of David. The Davidic Covenant is thus a grant, conferring powers, rights, and privileges to David and his seed for the benefit of mankind, a promise that left David speechless (vv. 20-22).

7:23 Your people...Your land. David is remembering aspects of the Abrahamic Covenant (cf. Gen. 12,15,17). **Israel.** In vv. 18-21, David praised the Lord for His favor to himself. In vv. 22-24, David praised the Lord for the favor shown to the nation of Israel (cf. Deut. 7:6-11).

7:25 the word...You have spoken. In vv. 25-29, David prayed for the fulfillment of the divine promise spoken to him.

7:26-29 Your words are true. David's prayer indicated that he fully accepted by faith the extraordinary, irrevocable promises God made to David as king and to Israel as a nation.

8:1-14 These verses outline the expansion of David's kingdom under the hand of the Lord (vv. 6,14). Israel's major enemies were all defeated as David's kingdom extended N, S, E, and W. See 1 Chr. 18:1-13. This conquering occurred before the event of chap. 7 (see 7:1).

8:1 Philistines...subdued. David's first priority was to deal with the Philistines to the W, whom he quickly defeated and subjugated (see 5:25). **Metheg Ammah.** Note the marginal reference. Probably a reference to the "chief city" of the Philistines, Gath (cf. 1 Chr. 18:1). He defeated his enemies to the W.

8:2 Moab. David also defeated the Moabites who dwelt in Transjordan, E of the Dead Sea. This represented a change from the good

down to the ground, he measured them off
with a line. With two lines he measured off
those to be put to death, and with one full
line those to be kept alive. So the Moabites
became David's [b]servants, *and* [c]brought
tribute.
3 David also defeated Hadadezer the
son of Rehob, king of [d]Zobah, as he went
to recover [e]his territory at the River Euphrates. 4 David took from him one thousand *chariots,* [3]seven hundred horsemen,
and twenty thousand foot soldiers. Also
David [f]hamstrung all the chariot horses,
except that he spared *enough* of them for
one hundred chariots.
5 [g]When the Syrians of Damascus came
to help Hadadezer king of Zobah, David
killed twenty-two thousand of the Syrians.
6 Then David put garrisons in Syria of Damascus; and the Syrians became David's
servants, *and* brought tribute. So [h]the LORD
preserved David wherever he went. 7 And
David took [i]the shields of gold that had
belonged to the servants of Hadadezer,
and brought them to Jerusalem. 8 Also
from [4]Betah and from [j]Berothai,[5] cities of
Hadadezer, King David took a large
amount of bronze.
9 When [6]Toi king of [k]Hamath heard that
David had defeated all the army of Hadadezer, 10 then Toi sent [7]Joram his son to
King David, to [8]greet him and bless him,
because he had fought against Hadadezer
and defeated him (for Hadadezer had been
at war with Toi); and *Joram* brought with
him articles of silver, articles of gold, and
articles of bronze. 11 King David also [l]ded-
icated these to the LORD, along with the silver and gold that he had dedicated from
all the nations which he had subdued—
12 from [9]Syria, from Moab, from the people of Ammon, from the [m]Philistines, from
Amalek, and from the spoil of Hadadezer
the son of Rehob, king of Zobah.
13 And David made *himself* a [n]name
when he returned from killing [o]eighteen
thousand [1]Syrians in [p]the Valley of Salt.
14 He also put garrisons in Edom; throughout all Edom he put garrisons, and [q]all the
Edomites became David's servants. And
the LORD preserved David wherever he
went.

David's Administration

15 So David reigned over all Israel; and
David administered judgment and justice
to all his people. 16 [r]Joab the son of Zeruiah
was over the army; [s]Jehoshaphat the son of
Ahilud *was* recorder; 17 [t]Zadok the son of
Ahitub and Ahimelech the son of Abiathar
were the priests; [2]Seraiah *was* the [3]scribe;

2 [b]2 Sam. 12:31 [c]1 Sam. 10:27; 1 Kin. 4:21
3 [d]1 Sam. 14:47; 2 Sam. 10:16, 19 [e]Gen. 15:18; 2 Sam. 10:15-19
4 [f]Josh. 11:6, 9 [3]*seven thousand,* 1 Chr. 18:4
5 [g]1 Kin. 11:23-25
6 [h]2 Sam. 7:9; 8:14
7 [i]1 Kin. 10:16
8 [j]Ezek. 47:16 [4]*Tibhath,* 1 Chr. 18:8 [5]*Chun,* 1 Chr. 18:8
9 [k]1 Kin. 8:65; 2 Kin. 14:28; 2 Chr. 8:4 [6]*Tou,* 1 Chr. 18:9
10 [7]*Hadoram,* 1 Chr. 18:10 [8]Lit. *ask him of his welfare*
11 [l]1 Kin. 7:51
12 [m]2 Sam. 5:17-25 [9]LXX, Syr., Heb. mss. *Edom*
13 [n]2 Sam. 7:9 [o]2 Kin. 14:7 [p]1 Chr. 18:12; Ps. 60:title [1]LXX, Syr., Heb. mss. *Edomites* and 1 Chr. 18:12
14 [q]Gen. 27:29, 37-40; Num. 24:18; 1 Kin. 11:15
16 [r]2 Sam. 19:13; 20:23; 1 Chr. 11:6 [s]1 Kin. 4:3
17 [t]1 Chr. 6:4-8; 24:3 [2]*Shavsha,* 1 Chr. 18:16 [3]*secretary*

relationship David once enjoyed with the Moabite royalty (cf. 1 Sam. 22:3,4). He defeated his enemies to the E. **he measured off.** This could mean that David spared the young Moabites (whose height was approximately one cord) and executed the adults (whose height was two cords) or that one out of 3 rows of soldiers was arbitrarily chosen to be spared from execution. Such was a common practice of eastern kings in dealing with deadly enemies.

8:3-8 He defeated his enemies to the N. David had already defeated the Amalekites to the S (1 Sam. 30:16,17).

8:3 Hadadezer. Lit. "Hadad (the personal name of the Canaanite storm god) is my help." Psalm 60 was written to commemorate this battle. **Zobah.** An Aramaean kingdom N of Damascus (cf. 1 Sam. 14:47). **River Euphrates.** I.e., the most southwesterly point of the Euphrates River around the city of Tiphsah.

8:4 seven hundred. The reading of "7,000" in 1 Chr. 18:4 is preferable, as per marginal note. *See note on 1 Chr. 18:4.* **hamstrung all the chariot horses.** Hamstringing the horses disabled them from military action by cutting the back sinews of the hind legs (Josh. 11:6).

8:5 Syrians. I.e., Aramaeans, who were peoples located around the city of Damascus as well as in the area of Zobah.

8:7 shields of gold. Ceremonial or decorative insignias that were not used in battle, but for decoration.

8:8 bronze. First Chronicles 18:8 notes 3 towns belonging to Hadadezer which yielded bronze that was later used in the construction of the temple.

8:9 Toi king of Hamath. Hamath was another Aramaean territory located about 100 mi. N of Damascus. The king, Toi, was thankful to see his enemy Zobah crushed and desired to establish good relations with David. So he gave David gifts to indicate that he voluntarily submitted to him as his vassal.

8:12 Syria. See marginal reading of "Edom," which is preferred. These were David's enemies to the S.

8:13 a name. The Lord began to fulfill His promise of giving David a great name (see 7:9). **Syrians.** There is an alternate ms. reading that makes this a reference to David's defeat of the Edomites, not the Syrians. This reading is supported by Ps. 60 and 1 Chr. 18:12. **Valley of Salt.** An area S of the Dead Sea.

8:15-18 See 1 Chr. 18:14-17. This is the record of the cabinet under David's rule.

8:15 judgment and justice. David ruled his kingdom in a righteous manner, and in the future the "Messiah" will rule in a similar fashion (Is. 9:7; Jer. 23:5; 33:15).

8:16 Joab. David's general (2:13; 1 Sam. 26:6). **Jehoshaphat... recorder.** The keeper of state records, and possibly the royal herald (1 Kin. 4:3).

8:17 Zadok the son of Ahitub. Zadok, meaning "righteous," was a Levitical priest descended from Aaron through Eleazar (1 Chr. 6:3-8,50-53), who, along with his house, were the fulfillment of the oracle by the man of God in 1 Sam. 2:35. Future sons of Zadok will be priests in the millennial kingdom of Messiah (Ezek. 44:15). Later, he became the only High-Priest in Solomon's reign, fulfilling God's promise to Phinehas (cf. Num. 25:10-13). **Ahimelech the son of Abiathar.** See 1 Sam. 22:20, which indicates that Abiathar is the son of Ahimelech. This is best accounted for by a scribal copying error (cf. 1 Chr. 18:16; 24:3,6,31). Abiathar was David's priest along with Zadok (15:24,35; 19:11). Abiathar traced his lineage through Eli (1 Kin. 2:27) to Ithamar (1 Chr. 24:3). With Abiathar's removal (1 Kin. 2:26,27), God's curse on Eli was completed (1 Sam. 2:33), and God's promise to Phinehas of Eleazar's line was fulfilled (cf. Num. 25:10-13; 1 Sam. 2:35). **Seraiah *was* the scribe.** His name means "The LORD prevails," and he served as the official secretary of David.

18 [u]Benaiah the son of Jehoiada *was over*
both the [v]Cherethites and the Pelethites;
and David's sons were [4]chief ministers.

David's Kindness to Mephibosheth

9 Now David said, "Is there still anyone
who is left of the house of Saul, that I
may [a]show him [1]kindness for Jonathan's
sake?"
2 And *there was* a servant of the house of
Saul whose name *was* [b]Ziba. So when they
had called him to David, the king said to
him, "*Are* you Ziba?"
He said, "At your service!"
3 Then the king said, "*Is* there not still
someone of the house of Saul, to whom I
may show [c]the kindness of God?"
And Ziba said to the king, "There is still
a son of Jonathan *who is* [d]lame in *his* feet."
4 So the king said to him, "Where *is* he?"
And Ziba said to the king, "Indeed he *is*
in the house of [e]Machir the son of Ammiel,
in Lo Debar."
5 Then King David sent and brought
him out of the house of Machir the son of
Ammiel, from Lo Debar.
6 Now when [f]Mephibosheth[2] the son of
Jonathan, the son of Saul, had come to David, he fell on his face and prostrated himself. Then David said, "Mephibosheth?"
And he answered, "Here is your servant!"
7 So David said to him, "Do not fear, for
I will surely show you kindness for Jonathan your father's sake, and will restore to
you all the land of Saul your grandfather;
and you shall eat bread at my table continually."
8 Then he bowed himself, and said,
"What *is* your servant, that you should
look upon such [g]a dead dog as I?"
9 And the king called to Ziba, Saul's servant, and said to him, [h]"I have given to
your master's son all that belonged to Saul
and to all his house. 10 You therefore, and
your sons and your servants, shall work
the land for him, and you shall bring in *the
harvest*, that your master's son may have
food to eat. But Mephibosheth your master's son [i]shall eat bread at my table always." Now Ziba had [j]fifteen sons and
twenty servants.
11 Then Ziba said to the king, "According to all that my lord the king has commanded his servant, so will your servant
do."
"As for Mephibosheth," *said the king*, "he
shall eat at [3]my table like one of the king's
sons." 12 Mephibosheth had a young son
[k]whose name *was* Micha. And all who
dwelt in the house of Ziba *were* servants of
Mephibosheth. 13 So Mephibosheth dwelt
in Jerusalem, [l]for he ate continually at the
king's table. And he [m]was lame in both his
feet.

The Ammonites and Syrians Defeated

10 It happened after this that the [a]king
of the people of Ammon died, and
Hanun his son reigned in his place. 2 Then
David said, "I will show [b]kindness to
Hanun the son of [c]Nahash, as his father
showed kindness to me."
So David sent by the hand of his servants to comfort him concerning his father.
And David's servants came into the land
of the people of Ammon. 3 And the princes
of the people of Ammon said to Hanun

18 [u]1 Kin. 1:8; 1 Chr. 18:17 [v]1 Sam. 30:14; 1 Kin. 1:38 [4]Lit. *priests*

CHAPTER 9

1 [a]1 Sam. 18:3; 20:14-16; 2 Sam. 21:7; [Prov. 27:10] [1]*covenant faithfulness*
2 [b]2 Sam. 16:1-4; 19:17, 29
3 [c]1 Sam. 20:14 [d]2 Sam. 4:4
4 [e]2 Sam. 17:27-29
6 [f]2 Sam. 16:4; 19:24-30 [2]Or *Merib-Baal*
8 [g]2 Sam. 16:9
9 [h]2 Sam. 16:4; 19:29
10 [i]2 Sam. 9:7, 11, 13; 19:28 [j]2 Sam. 19:17
11 [3]LXX *David's table*
12 [k]1 Chr. 8:34
13 [l]2 Sam. 9:7, 10, 11; 1 Kin. 2:7; 2 Kin. 25:29 [m]2 Sam. 9:3

CHAPTER 10

1 [a]2 Sam. 11:1; 1 Chr. 19:1
2 [b]2 Sam. 9:1; 1 Kin. 2:7 [c]1 Sam. 11:1

8:18 Benaiah. His name means "The LORD builds," and he served as the commander of David's personal bodyguard. He later became the commander-in-chief of Solomon's army (1 Kin. 2:34,35; 4:4), after he killed Joab, David's general (cf. 1 Kin. 2:28-35). **Cherethites and the Pelethites.** *See note on 1 Sam. 30:14.* **chief ministers.** Though the Heb. text referred to the sons of David as priests, the LXX referred to them as "princes of the court." The latter reading is supported by 1 Chr. 18:17, which refers to David's sons as "chief ministers at the king's side."

9:1–20:26 These chapters begin with "the house of Saul" (9:1) and end with "Sheba…a Benjamite" (20:1). As with Saul, David is shown to be a failed king, albeit a repentant failure. It was only the grace and mercy of the Lord and His irrevocable covenant that kept David from being removed from the kingship, as Saul had been (cf. 7:15). The emphasis in this section is upon the troubles of David, troubles brought on by his own sin.

9:1 show him kindness for Jonathan's sake. David continued to display loving loyalty toward Jonathan (1 Sam. 20:42) by ministering to the physical needs of his crippled son, Mephibosheth (cf. 4:4).

9:2 Ziba. A former servant of Saul, who is first mentioned here.

9:4 Machir the son of Ammiel. A man of wealth (see 17:27-29). **Lo Debar.** A city located in Gilead, E of the Jordan, about 10 mi. S of the Sea of Galilee.

9:6 Mephibosheth. *See note on 4:4.*

9:7 restore…the land of Saul your grandfather. The estate belonging to Saul was probably quite substantial. **eat bread at my table.** David desired to honor Mephibosheth by bringing him into the royal palace and providing for his daily needs (see 2 Kin. 25:29).

9:8 dead dog. A "dead dog" was considered contemptible and useless. Mephibosheth saw himself as such in that he knew that he had not merited David's kindness and that there was no way for him to repay it. David's offer was an extraordinary expression of grace and beauty to his covenant with Jonathan (cf. 1 Sam. 18:3; 20:15,42).

9:10 fifteen sons and twenty servants. This number shows the power and influence of Ziba. It also shows that the land given by David was substantial.

9:12 Micha. The descendants of Micha, the son of Mephibosheth, are listed in 1 Chr. 8:35-38; 9:41-44.

10:1-19 See 1 Chr. 19:1-19.

10:1 king…of Ammon. I.e., Nahash (*see note on 1 Sam. 11:1*).

10:2 show kindness to Hanun. Since Nahash was an enemy of Saul, he was viewed as a friend and supporter of David. It was implied that David and Nahash had entered into a covenant relationship, on the basis of which David desired to communicate his continuing loyalty to Nahash's son, Hanun.

their lord, "Do you think that David really
honors your father because he has sent
comforters to you? Has David not *rather*
sent his servants to you to search the city,
to spy it out, and to overthrow it?"
4 Therefore Hanun took David's servants, shaved off half of their beards, cut
off their garments in the middle, [d]at their
buttocks, and sent them away. 5 When they
told David, he sent to meet them, because
the men were greatly [1]ashamed. And the
king said, "Wait at Jericho until your
beards have grown, and *then* return."
6 When the people of Ammon saw that
they [e]had made themselves repulsive to
David, the people of Ammon sent and
hired [f]the Syrians of [g]Beth Rehob and the
Syrians of Zoba, twenty thousand foot soldiers; and from the king of [h]Maacah one
thousand men, and from [i]Ish-Tob twelve
thousand men. 7 Now when David heard
of it, he sent Joab and all the army of [j]the
mighty men. 8 Then the people of Ammon
came out and put themselves in battle
array at the entrance of the gate. And [k]the
Syrians of Zoba, Beth Rehob, Ish-Tob, and
Maacah *were* by themselves in the field.

4 [d] Is. 20:4; 47:2
5 [1] *humiliated*
6 [e] Gen. 34:30; Ex. 5:21 [f] 2 Sam. 8:3, 5 [g] Judg. 18:28 [h] Deut. 3:14; Josh. 13:11, 13 [i] Judg. 11:3, 5
7 [j] 2 Sam. 23:8
8 [k] 2 Sam. 10:6
10 [l] 1 Sam. 26:6; 2 Sam. 3:30
12 [m] Deut. 31:6; Josh. 1:6, 7, 9; Neh. 4:14 [n] 1 Sam. 4:9; 1 Cor. 16:13 [o] 1 Sam. 3:18
14 [p] 2 Sam. 11:1
16 [2] Heb. *Hadarezer* [3] The Euphrates

9 When Joab saw that the battle line was
against him before and behind, he chose
some of Israel's best and put *them* in battle
array against the Syrians. 10 And the rest of
the people he put under the command of
[l]Abishai his brother, that he might set *them*
in battle array against the people of
Ammon. 11 Then he said, "If the Syrians
are too strong for me, then you shall help
me; but if the people of Ammon are too
strong for you, then I will come and help
you. 12 [m]Be of good courage, and let us [n]be
strong for our people and for the cities of
our God. And may [o]the LORD do *what is*
good in His sight."
13 So Joab and the people who *were* with
him drew near for the battle against the Syrians, and they fled before him. 14 When the
people of Ammon saw that the Syrians were
fleeing, they also fled before Abishai, and
entered the city. So Joab returned from the
people of Ammon and went to [p]Jerusalem.
15 When the Syrians saw that they had
been defeated by Israel, they gathered together. 16 Then [2]Hadadezer sent and
brought out the Syrians who *were* beyond
[3]the River, and they came to Helam. And

The Kingdom of David

© 1996 Thomas Nelson, Inc.

The vast extent of David's ancient kingdom

10:3 the city. I.e., Rabbah (*see note on 11:1*).

10:4 shaved off half of their beards. Forced shaving was considered an insult and a sign of submission (cf. Is. 7:20). **cut off their garments…at their buttocks.** To those who wore long garments in that time, exposure of the buttocks was a shameful practice inflicted on prisoners of war (cf. Is. 20:4). Perhaps this was partly the concern of Michal in regard to David's dancing (see 6:14,20).

10:5 Jericho. The first place W of the Jordan River that would have been reached by the servants of David as they returned from Rabbah.

10:6 Beth Rehob. An Aramaean district located SW of Zobah (cf. Num. 13:21; Judg. 18:28). **Zoba.** *See note on "Zobah" on 8:3.* **Maacah.** The region N of Lake Huleh N of Galilee (Deut. 3:14; Josh. 13:11-13). **Ish-Tob.** A city E of the Jordan River, located 45 mi. NE of Rabbah (Judg. 11:3,5).

10:6-11 The Ammonite army was in the city ready for defense, while the Syrian mercenaries were at some distance, encamped in the fields around the city. Joab divided his forces to deal with both. *See note on 1 Sam. 11:1.*

10:12 Be of good courage…may the LORD do *what is* good in His sight. Finding himself fighting on two fronts, Joab urged the army to "be strong" and recognize that the outcome of the battle depended ultimately upon the Lord (cf. 15:26). It was a just and necessary war forced on Israel, so they could hope for God's blessing—and they received it (vv. 13,14).

10:14 So Joab returned. He did not attempt to siege and capture the city of Rabbah at this time because the time was unseasonable (*see note on 11:1*). Cf. 12:26-29.

10:16 Hadadezer. *See note on 8:3.* **Helam.** The place of battle, about 7 mi. N of Tob.

[4]Shobach the commander of Hadadezer's
army *went* before them. 17 When it was
told David, he gathered all Israel, crossed
over the Jordan, and came to Helam. And
the Syrians set themselves in battle array
against David and fought with him.
18 Then the Syrians fled before Israel; and
David killed seven hundred charioteers
and forty thousand [q]horsemen of the Syrians, and struck Shobach the commander
of their army, who died there. 19 And when
all the kings *who were* servants to [5]Had-
adezer saw that they were defeated by Israel, they made peace with Israel and
[r]served them. So the Syrians were afraid to
help the people of Ammon anymore.

David, Bathsheba, and Uriah

11 It happened in the spring of the
year, at the [a]time when kings go out
to battle, that [b]David sent Joab and his servants with him, and all Israel; and they destroyed the people of Ammon and besieged [c]Rabbah. But David remained at
Jerusalem.
2 Then it happened one evening that David arose from his bed [d]and walked on the
roof of the king's house. And from the roof
he [e]saw a woman bathing, and the woman
was very beautiful to behold. 3 So David
sent and inquired about the woman. And
someone said, "*Is* this not [1]Bathsheba, the
daughter of [2]Eliam, the wife [f]of Uriah the
[g]Hittite?" 4 Then David sent messengers,
and took her; and she came to him, and [h]he
lay with her, for she was [i]cleansed from
her impurity; and she returned to her
house. 5 And the woman conceived; so she
sent and told David, and said, "I *am* with
child."
6 Then David sent to Joab, *saying,* "Send
me Uriah the Hittite." And Joab sent Uriah
to David. 7 When Uriah had come to him,
David asked how Joab was doing, and
how the people were doing, and how the
war prospered. 8 And David said to Uriah,
"Go down to your house and [j]wash your
feet." So Uriah departed from the king's
house, and a gift *of food* from the king followed him. 9 But Uriah slept at the [k]door
of the king's house with all the servants of
his lord, and did not go down to his house.
10 So when they told David, saying, "Uriah
did not go down to his house," David said
to Uriah, "Did you not come from a journey? Why did you not go down to your
house?"
11 And Uriah said to David, [l]"The ark
and Israel and Judah are dwelling in tents,
and [m]my lord Joab and the servants of my
lord are encamped in the open fields. Shall
I then go to my house to eat and drink, and

16 [4]*Shophach,* 1 Chr. 19:16
18 [q]1 Chr. 19:18
19 [r]2 Sam. 8:6 [5]Heb. *Hadarezer*

CHAPTER 11

1 [a]1 Kin. 20:22-26 [b]1 Chr. 20:1 [c]2 Sam. 12:26; Jer. 49:2, 3; Amos 1:14
2 [d]Deut. 22:8; 1 Sam. 9:25; Matt. 24:17; Acts 10:9 [e]Gen. 34:2; [Ex. 20:17]; Job 31:1; [Matt. 5:28]
3 [f]2 Sam. 23:39 [g]1 Sam. 26:6 [1]*Bathshua,* 1 Chr. 3:5 [2]*Ammiel,* 1 Chr. 3:5
4 [h][Lev. 20:10; Deut. 22:22]; Ps. 51:title; [James 1:14, 15] [i]Lev. 15:19, 28
8 [j]Gen. 18:4; 19:2
9 [k]1 Kin. 14:27, 28
11 [l]2 Sam. 7:2, 6 [m]2 Sam. 20:6-22

10:18 seven hundred...horsemen. *See note on 1 Chr. 19:18.*

10:19 made peace with Israel. All the petty kingdoms of Syria became subject to Israel and feared to aid Ammon against Israel.

11:1 the spring...when kings go out *to battle.* In the Near East, kings normally went out to battle in the spring of the year because of the good weather and the abundance of food available along the way. *See note on 10:14.* **David sent Joab.** David dispatched Joab, his army commander, with his mercenary soldiers and the army of Israel to continue the battle against Ammon begun the previous year (10:14). **Rabbah.** The capital of the Ammonites, about 24 mi. E of the Jordan River opposite Jericho. The previous year, Abishai had defeated the Ammonite army in the open country, after which the remaining Ammonites fled behind the walls of the city of Rabbah for protection (10:14). Joab returned the next year to besiege the city. **But David remained at Jerusalem.** Staying home in such situations was not David's usual practice (5:2; 8:1-14; 10:17; but cf. 18:3; 21:17); this explicit remark implies criticism of David for remaining behind, as well as setting the stage for his devastating iniquity.

11:2 walked on the roof. The higher elevation of the palace roof allowed David to see into the courtyard of the nearby house. That same roof would later become the scene of other sinful immoralities (see 16:22).

11:3 Bathsheba. Not until 12:24 is her name used again. Rather, to intensify the sin of adultery, it is emphasized that she was the wife of Uriah (vv. 3, 26; 12:10, 15). Even the NT says "her of Uriah" (Matt. 1:6). Cf. Ex. 20:17. **Eliam.** The father of Bathsheba was one of David's mighty men (23:34). Since Eliam was the son of Ahithophel, Bathsheba was Ahithophel's granddaughter (cf. 15:12; 16:15). This could explain why Ahithophel, one of David's counselors (15:12), later gave his allegiance to Absalom in his revolt against David. **Uriah.** Also one of David's mighty men (23:39). Although a Hittite (cf. Gen. 15:20; Ex. 3:8, 17, 23), Uriah bore a Heb. name meaning "the LORD is my light," indicating he was a worshiper of the one true God.

11:4 she came...he lay. These terms are euphemistic references to sexual intercourse (cf. Gen. 19:34), indicating that both Bathsheba and David were guilty of adultery. **her impurity.** Her recent days had involved menstruation and the required ceremonial purification (Lev. 15:19-30). They were followed by adulterous intercourse. The fact that she had just experienced menstruation makes it plain that Bathsheba was not pregnant by Uriah when she came to lie with David.

11:5 I *am* with child. The only words of Bathsheba recorded concerning this incident acknowledge the resultant condition of her sin, which became evident by her pregnancy and was punishable by death (Lev. 20:10; Deut. 22:22).

11:6,7 This inane conversation was a ploy to get Uriah to come home and sleep with his wife, so it would appear that he had fathered the child, thus sparing David the public shame and Bathsheba possible death.

11:8 wash your feet. Since this washing was done before going to bed, the idiom means to go home and go to bed. To a soldier coming from the battlefield, it said boldly, "enjoy your wife sexually." Hopefully, David's tryst with Bathsheba would be masked by Uriah's union. **gift *of food.*** This was designed to help Uriah and Bathsheba enjoy their evening together.

11:9 Uriah slept. Wanting to be a loyal example to his soldiers who were still in the field, Uriah did not take advantage of the king's less-than-honorable offer (v. 11).

11:11 The ark. The ark of the covenant was residing in either the tent in Jerusalem (6:17) or in a tent with the army of Israel on the battlefield (1 Sam. 4:6; 14:18).

to lie with my wife? *As* you live, and *as*
your soul lives, I will not do this thing."
12 Then David said to Uriah, "Wait here
today also, and tomorrow I will let you depart." So Uriah remained in Jerusalem that
day and the next. 13 Now when David
called him, he ate and drank before him;
and he made him [n]drunk. And at evening
he went out to lie on his bed [o]with the servants of his lord, but he did not go down to
his house.
14 In the morning it happened that David [p]wrote a letter to Joab and sent *it* by the
hand of Uriah. 15 And he wrote in the letter, saying, "Set Uriah in the forefront of
the [3]hottest battle, and retreat from him,
that he may [q]be struck down and die."
16 So it was, while Joab besieged the city,
that he assigned Uriah to a place where he
knew there *were* valiant men. 17 Then the
men of the city came out and fought with
Joab. And *some* of the people of the servants of David fell; and Uriah the Hittite
died also.
18 Then Joab sent and told David all the
things concerning the war, 19 and charged
the messenger, saying, "When you have
finished telling the matters of the war to
the king, 20 if it happens that the king's
wrath rises, and he says to you: 'Why did
you approach so near to the city when you
fought? Did you not know that they would
shoot from the wall? 21 Who struck [r]Abim-
elech the son of [4]Jerubbesheth? Was it not
a woman who cast a piece of a millstone on
him from the wall, so that he died in Thebez? Why did you go near the wall?'—then
you shall say, 'Your servant Uriah the Hittite is dead also.' "
22 So the messenger went, and came and
told David all that Joab had sent by him.
23 And the messenger said to David,
"Surely the men prevailed against us and

13 [n]Gen. 19:33,35 [o]2 Sam. 11:9
14 [p]1 Kin. 21:8,9
15 [q]2 Sam. 12:9 [3]*fiercest*
21 [r]Judg. 9:50-54 [4]*Jerubbaal* (Gideon), Judg. 6:32ff.

25 [5]Lit. *be evil in your sight*
27 [s]2 Sam. 12:9 [t]1 Chr. 21:7; [Heb. 13:4] [6]Lit. *was evil in the eyes of*

CHAPTER 12

1 [a]Ps. 51:title [b]1 Kin. 20:35-41
5 [1]*deserves to die*, lit. *is a son of death*

came out to us in the field; then we drove
them back as far as the entrance of the gate.
24 The archers shot from the wall at your
servants; and *some* of the king's servants
are dead, and your servant Uriah the Hittite is dead also."
25 Then David said to the messenger,
"Thus you shall say to Joab: 'Do not let this
thing [5]displease you, for the sword devours one as well as another. Strengthen
your attack against the city, and overthrow
it.' So encourage him."
26 When the wife of Uriah heard that Uriah her husband was dead, she mourned for
her husband. 27 And when her mourning
was over, David sent and brought her to his
house, and she [s]became his wife and bore
him a son. But the thing that David had
done [t]displeased[6] the LORD.

Nathan's Parable and David's Confession

12 Then the LORD sent Nathan to David. And [a]he came to him, and [b]said
to him: "There were two men in one city,
one rich and the other poor. 2 The rich *man*
had exceedingly many flocks and herds.
3 But the poor *man* had nothing, except one
little ewe lamb which he had bought and
nourished; and it grew up together with
him and with his children. It ate of his own
food and drank from his own cup and lay
in his bosom; and it was like a daughter to
him. 4 And a traveler came to the rich man,
who refused to take from his own flock
and from his own herd to prepare one for
the wayfaring man who had come to him;
but he took the poor man's lamb and prepared it for the man who had come to
him."
5 So David's anger was greatly aroused
against the man, and he said to Nathan,
"*As* the LORD lives, the man who has done
this [1]shall surely die! 6 And he shall restore

11:13 made him drunk. Failing in his first attempt to cover up his sin, David tried unsuccessfully to make Uriah drunk so he would lose his resolve and self-discipline and return to his home and his wife's bed.

11:15 he may...die. Failing twice to cover up his sin with Bathsheba, the frustrated and panicked David plotted the murder of Uriah by taking advantage of Uriah's unswerving loyalty to him as king, even having Uriah deliver his own death warrant. Thus David engaged in another crime deserving of capital punishment (Lev. 24:17). This is graphic proof of the extremities people go to in pursuit of sin and in the absence of restraining grace.

11:18-24 Joab sent...Uriah...dead. He sent a messenger with a veiled message to tell David his wish had been carried out. Joab must have known the reason behind this otherwise stupid military deployment.

11:25 So encourage him. David hypocritically expressed indifference to those who died, and he consoled Joab, authorizing him to continue the attack against Rabbah.

11:26,27 her mourning was over. The customary period of mourning was probably 7 days (Gen. 50:10; 1 Sam. 31:13). Significantly, the text makes no mention of mourning by David.

11:27 displeased the LORD. Lit. "was evil in the eyes of the LORD," and would bring forth evil consequences.

12:1-14 Psalm 51 records David's words of repentance after being confronted by Nathan over his sin with Bathsheba (cf. Ps. 32, where David expresses his agony after Nathan's confrontation).

12:1 the LORD sent Nathan. The word "LORD" is conspicuously absent from the narrative of chap. 11 until v. 27, but then the Lord became actively involved by confronting David with his sin. As Joab had sent a messenger to David (11:18,19), so the Lord now sent His messenger to David.

12:1-4 two men...rich...poor. To understand this parable, it is necessary only to recognize that the rich man represented David, the poor man, Uriah, and the ewe lamb, Bathsheba.

12:5 shall surely die. According to Ex. 22:1, the penalty for stealing and slaughtering an ox or a sheep was not death, but restitution.

[c]fourfold for the lamb, because he did this
thing and because he had no pity."
[7] Then Nathan said to David, "You *are*
the man! Thus says the LORD God of Israel:
'I [d]anointed you king over Israel, and I delivered you from the hand of Saul. [8] I gave
you your master's house and your master's wives into your keeping, and gave
you the house of Israel and Judah. And if
that had been too little, I also would have
given you much more! [9] [e]Why have you
[f]despised the commandment of the LORD,
to do evil in His sight? [g]You have killed
Uriah the Hittite with the sword; you have
taken his wife *to be* your wife, and have
killed him with the sword of the people of
Ammon. [10] Now therefore, [h]the sword
shall never depart from your house, because you have despised Me, and have
taken the wife of Uriah the Hittite to be
your wife.' [11] Thus says the LORD: 'Behold,
I will raise up adversity against you from
your own house; and I will [i]take your
wives before your eyes and give *them* to
your neighbor, and he shall lie with your
wives in the sight of this sun. [12] For you
did *it* secretly, [j]but I will do this thing before all Israel, before the sun.' "
[13] [k]So David said to Nathan, [l]"I have
sinned against the LORD."
And Nathan said to David, "The LORD
also has [m]put away your sin; you shall not
die. [14] However, because by this deed you
have given great occasion to the enemies of
the LORD [n]to blaspheme, the child also *who*
is born to you shall surely die." [15] Then
Nathan departed to his house.

The Death of David's Son

And the [o]LORD struck the child that Uriah's wife bore to David, and it became ill.
[16] David therefore pleaded with God for
the child, and David fasted and went in
and [p]lay all night on the ground. [17] So the
elders of his house arose *and went* to him,
to raise him up from the ground. But he
would not, nor did he eat food with them.
[18] Then on the seventh day it came to pass
that the child died. And the servants of David were afraid to tell him that the child
was dead. For they said, "Indeed, while
the child was alive, we spoke to him, and
he would not heed our voice. How can we
tell him that the child is dead? He may do
some harm!"
[19] When David saw that his servants
were whispering, David perceived that the
child was dead. Therefore David said to
his servants, "Is the child dead?"
And they said, "He is dead."
[20] So David arose from the ground,
washed and [q]anointed himself, and
changed his clothes; and he went into the
house of the LORD and [r]worshiped. Then
he went to his own house; and when he requested, they set food before him, and he
ate. [21] Then his servants said to him,
"What *is* this that you have done? You fasted and wept for the child *while he was* alive,
but when the child died, you arose and ate
food."

6 [c][Ex. 22:1]; Luke 19:8
7 [d]1 Sam. 16:13; 2 Sam. 5:3
9 [e]1 Sam. 15:19 [f]Num. 15:31 [g]2 Sam. 11:14-17, 27
10 [h]2 Sam. 13:28; 18:14; 1 Kin. 2:25; [Amos 7:9]
11 [i]Deut. 28:30; 2 Sam. 16:21, 22
12 [j]2 Sam. 16:22
13 [k]1 Sam. 15:24 [l]2 Sam. 24:10; Job 7:20; Ps. 51; Luke 18:13 [m]2 Sam. 24:10; Job 7:21; [Ps. 32:1-5; Prov. 28:13; Mic. 7:18]; Zech. 3:4
14 [n]Is. 52:5; [Ezek. 36:20, 23]; Rom. 2:24
15 [o]1 Sam. 25:38
16 [p]2 Sam. 13:31
20 [q]Ruth 3:3; Matt. 6:17 [r]Job 1:20

However, in the parable, the stealing and slaughtering of the lamb represented the adultery with Bathsheba and the murder of Uriah by David. According to the Mosaic law, both adultery (Lev. 20:10) and murder (Lev. 24:17) required punishment by death. In pronouncing this judgment on the rich man in the story, David unwittingly condemned himself to death.

12:6 fourfold. Exodus 22:1 demanded a 4-fold restitution for the stealing of sheep. There is an allusion here to the subsequent death of 4 of David's sons: Bathsheba's first son (v. 18), Amnon (13:28,29), Absalom (16:14,15), and Adonijah (1 Kin. 2:25).

12:7 anointed. Earlier, the prophet Samuel's confrontation with the sinful Saul emphasized the same point (1 Sam. 15:17).

12:8 your master's wives. This phraseology means nothing more than that God in His providence had given David, as king, everything that was Saul's. There is no evidence that he ever married any of Saul's wives, though the harem of eastern kings passed to their successors. Ahinoam, the wife of David (2:2; 3:2; 1 Sam. 25:43; 27:3; 30:5), is always referred to as the Jezreelitess, whereas Ahinoam, the wife of Saul, is distinguished clearly from her by being called "the daughter of Ahimaaz" (1 Sam. 14:50).

12:9 despised. To despise the word of the Lord was to break His commands and thus incur punishment (cf. Num. 15:31). In summarizing David's violations, his guilt is divinely affirmed.

12:10 the sword shall never depart from your house. David's tragic punishment was a lingering one. Since Uriah was killed by violence, the house of David would be continually plagued by violence. These words anticipated the violent deaths of Amnon (13:28,29), Absalom (18:14,15), and Adonijah (1 Kin. 2:24,25).

12:11 adversity…from your own house. David had done evil to another man's family (11:27). Therefore, he would receive evil in his own family, such as Amnon's rape of Tamar (13:1-14), Absalom's murder of Amnon (13:28,29), and Absalom's rebellion against David (15:1-12). **lie with your wives in the sight of this sun.** This prediction was fulfilled by Absalom's public appropriation of David's royal concubines during his rebellion (16:21,22).

12:13 I have sinned against the LORD. David did not attempt to rationalize or justify his sin. When confronted with the facts, David's confession was immediate. The fuller confessions of David are found in Pss. 32 and 51. **The LORD also has put away your sin.** The Lord graciously forgave David's sin, but the inevitable temporal consequences of sin were experienced by him. Forgiveness does not always remove the consequences of sin in this life, only in the life to come. **you shall not die.** Although the sins of David legally demanded his death (see v. 5), the Lord graciously released David from the required death penalty. There are events in the OT record where God required death and others where He showed grace and spared the sinner. This is consistent with justice and grace. Those who perished are illustrations of what all sinners deserve. Those who were spared are proofs and examples of God's grace.

12:14 the enemies of the LORD. Because of God's reputation among those who opposed Him, David's sin had to be judged. The judgment would begin with the death of Bathsheba's baby son.

22 And he said, "While the child was
alive, I fasted and wept; [s]for I said, 'Who
can tell *whether* [2]the LORD will be gracious
to me, that the child may live?' 23 But now
he is dead; why should I fast? Can I bring
him back again? I shall go [t]to him, but [u]he
shall not return to me."

Solomon Is Born

24 Then David comforted Bathsheba his
wife, and went in to her and lay with her.
So [v]she bore a son, and [w]he[3] called his
name Solomon. Now the LORD loved him,
25 and He sent *word* by the hand of Nathan
the prophet: So [4]he called his name [5]Jedi-
diah, because of the LORD.

Rabbah Is Captured

26 Now [x]Joab fought against [y]Rabbah of
the people of Ammon, and took the royal
city. 27 And Joab sent messengers to David, and said, "I have fought against Rabbah, and I have taken the city's water *supply.* 28 Now therefore, gather the rest of the
people together and encamp against the
city and take it, lest I take the city and it be
called after my name." 29 So David gathered all the people together and went to
Rabbah, fought against it, and took it.
30 [z]Then he took their king's crown from
his head. Its weight *was* a talent of gold,
with precious stones. And it was *set* on
David's head. Also he brought out the
[6]spoil of the city in great abundance.
31 And he brought out the people who
were in it, and put *them to work* with saws
and iron picks and iron axes, and made
them cross over to the brick works. So he
did to all the cities of the people of
Ammon. Then David and all the people
returned to Jerusalem.

22 [s]Is. 38:1-5; Joel 2:14; Jon. 3:9 [2]Heb. mss., Syr. *God*
23 [t]Gen. 37:35 [u]Job 7:8-10
24 [v]Matt. 1:6 [w]1 Chr. 22:9 [3]So with Kt., LXX, Vg.; Qr., a few Heb. mss., Syr., Tg. *she*
25 [4]Qr., some Heb. mss., Syr., Tg. *she* [5]Lit. *Beloved of the LORD*
26 [x]1 Chr. 20:1 [y]Deut. 3:11; 2 Sam. 11:1
30 [z]1 Chr. 20:2 [6]*plunder*

Amnon and Tamar

13 After this [a]Absalom the son of David had a lovely sister, whose name
was [b]Tamar; and [c]Amnon the son of David
loved her. 2 Amnon was so distressed over
his sister Tamar that he became sick; for
she *was* a virgin. And it was improper for
Amnon to do anything to her. 3 But
Amnon had a friend whose name *was*
Jonadab [d]the son of Shimeah, David's
brother. Now Jonadab *was* a very crafty
man. 4 And he said to him, "Why *are* you,
the king's son, becoming thinner day after
day? Will you not tell me?"

Amnon said to him, "I love Tamar, my
brother Absalom's sister."

5 So Jonadab said to him, "Lie down on
your bed and pretend to be ill. And when
your father comes to see you, say to him,
'Please let my sister Tamar come and give
me food, and prepare the food in my sight,
that I may see *it* and eat it from her
hand.' " 6 Then Amnon lay down and pretended to be ill; and when the king came to
see him, Amnon said to the king, "Please
let Tamar my sister come and [e]make a couple of cakes for me in my sight, that I may
eat from her hand."

7 And David sent home to Tamar, saying, "Now go to your brother Amnon's
house, and prepare food for him." 8 So
Tamar went to her brother Amnon's house;
and he was lying down. Then she took
flour and kneaded *it,* made cakes in his
sight, and baked the cakes. 9 And she took
the pan and placed *them* out before him,
but he refused to eat. Then Amnon said,
[f]"Have everyone go out from me." And
they all went out from him. 10 Then
Amnon said to Tamar, "Bring the food into
the bedroom, that I may eat from your
hand." And Tamar took the cakes which
she had made, and brought *them* to Amnon

CHAPTER 13
1 [a]2 Sam. 3:2, 3; 1 Chr. 3:2 [b]1 Chr. 3:9 [c]2 Sam. 3:2
3 [d]1 Sam. 16:9
6 [e]Gen. 18:6
9 [f]Gen. 45:1

12:23 I shall go to him. I.e., David would someday join his son after his own death (cf. 1 Sam. 28:19). Here is the confidence that there is a future reunion after death, which includes infants who have died being reunited with saints who die (*see note on Matt. 15:14;* cf. Mark 10:13-16).

12:24 Solomon. Either "(God is) peace" or "His replacement." Both were true of this child.

12:25 Jedidiah. "Beloved of the LORD" was Nathan's name for Solomon, who was loved in the sense of being chosen by the Lord to be the successor to David's throne, a remarkable instance of God's goodness and grace considering the sinful nature of the marriage.

12:29-31 See 1 Chr. 20:1-3.

12:29 David…took it. David completed what Joab had begun by capturing the city of Rabbah.

12:30 a talent of gold. About 75 lbs.

12:31 put *them to work.* The NKJV indicates here and in 1 Chr. 20:3 that David imposed hard labor on the Ammonites. But these verses can also be translated with the sense that the Ammonites were cut with saws, indicating that David imposed cruel death on the captives in accordance with Ammonite ways (cf. 1 Sam. 11:2; Amos 1:13).

13:1,2 Tamar. "Palm tree." She was David's daughter by Maacah, the daughter of Talmai, King of Geshur (3:3), Absalom's (David's third son) full sister and half-sister of Amnon, David's first son by Ahinoam (3:2). Amnon's love for her was not filial, but lustful, as became clear in the story. Unmarried daughters were kept in seclusion from men, so that none could see them alone. Amnon had seen Tamar because of their family relationship and had conceived a violent passion for her. This was forbidden by God (see Lev. 18:11), yet with the example of Abraham (Gen. 20:12) and the common practice among the surrounding nations of marrying half-sisters, he felt justified and wanted his passion fulfilled with Tamar.

13:3 Jonadab. The son of David's brother, called Shammah in 1 Sam. 16:9; 17:3 and Shimea in 1 Chr. 2:13. Jonadab was Amnon's cousin and counselor who gave Amnon the plan by which he was able to rape Tamar.

her brother in the bedroom. 11 Now when
she had brought *them* to him to eat, [g]he
took hold of her and said to her, "Come, lie
with me, my sister."
12 But she answered him, "No, my
brother, do not [1]force me, for [h]no such
thing should be done in Israel. Do not do
this [i]disgraceful thing! 13 And I, where
could I take my shame? And as for you,
you would be like one of the fools in Israel.
Now therefore, please speak to the king;
[j]for he will not withhold me from you."
14 However, he would not heed her voice;
and being stronger than she, he [k]forced her
and lay with her.
15 Then Amnon hated her [2]exceedingly,
so that the hatred with which he hated her
was greater than the love with which he
had loved her. And Amnon said to her,
"Arise, be gone!"
16 So she said to him, "No, indeed! This
evil of sending me away *is* worse than the
other that you did to me."
But he would not listen to her. 17 Then
he called his servant who attended him,
and said, "Here! Put this *woman* out, away
from me, and bolt the door behind her."
18 Now she had on [l]a robe of many colors,
for the king's virgin daughters wore such
apparel. And his servant put her out and
bolted the door behind her.

11 [g] Gen. 39:12; [Deut. 27:22]; Ezek. 22:11
12 [h] [Lev. 18:9-11; 20:17] [i] Gen. 34:7; Judg. 19:23; 20:6 [1] Lit. *humble me*
13 [j] Gen. 20:12
14 [k] Lev. 18:9; [Deut. 22:25; 27:22]; 2 Sam. 12:11
15 [2] *with a very great hatred*
18 [l] Gen. 37:3; Judg. 5:30; Ps. 45:13, 14
19 [m] Josh. 7:6; 2 Sam. 1:2; Job 2:12; 42:6 [n] Jer. 2:37
22 [o] Gen. 24:50; 31:24 [p] [Lev. 19:17, 18; 1 John 2:9, 11; 3:10, 12, 15]
23 [q] Gen. 38:12, 13; 1 Sam. 25:4

19 Then Tamar put [m]ashes on her head,
and tore her robe of many colors that *was*
on her, and [n]laid her hand on her head and
went away crying bitterly. 20 And Absalom
her brother said to her, "Has Amnon your
brother been with you? But now hold your
peace, my sister. He *is* your brother; do not
take this thing to heart." So Tamar remained desolate in her brother Absalom's
house.
21 But when King David heard of all
these things, he was very angry. 22 And
Absalom spoke to his brother Amnon [o]nei-
ther good nor bad. For Absalom [p]hated
Amnon, because he had forced his sister
Tamar.

Absalom Murders Amnon

23 And it came to pass, after two full
years, that Absalom [q]had sheepshearers in
Baal Hazor, which *is* near Ephraim; so
Absalom invited all the king's sons.
24 Then Absalom came to the king and
said, "Kindly note, your servant has
sheepshearers; please, let the king and his
servants go with your servant."
25 But the king said to Absalom, "No,
my son, let us not all go now, lest we be a
burden to you." Then he urged him, but he
would not go; and he blessed him.

13:12,13 this disgraceful thing. Lit. "a wicked thing." Tamar appealed to Amnon with 4 reasons that he should not rape her. First, it was an utterly deplored act in Israel because it violated the law of God (see Lev. 18:11) and Tamar knew that such action could bring disharmony and bloodshed to the king's family, as it did. **my shame.** Second, as a fornicator, Tamar would be scorned as an object of reproach. Even though resistant to the evil crime perpetuated against her, Tamar would bear the stigma of one defiled. **like one of the fools in Israel.** Third, Amnon would be regarded by the people as a wicked fool, a God-rejecting man without principles who offended ordinary standards of morality, thereby jeopardizing Amnon's right to the throne. **the king...will not withhold me from you.** Fourth, Tamar appealed to Amnon to fulfill his physical desire for her through marriage. She surely knew that such a marriage between half siblings was not allowed by the Mosaic law (Lev. 18:9,11; 20:17; Deut. 27:22), but in the desperation of the moment, Tamar was seeking to escape the immediate situation.

13:14 forced. A euphemism for "raped."

13:15 hated her. Amnon's "love" (v. 1) was nothing but sensual desire that, once gratified, turned to hatred. His sudden revulsion was the result of her unwilling resistance, the atrocity of what he had done, feelings of remorse, and dread of exposure and punishment. All of these rendered her intolerably undesirable to him.

13:15-17 Amnon's sending Tamar away was a greater wrong than the rape itself because it would inevitably have been supposed that she had been guilty of some shameful conduct, i.e., that the seduction had come from her.

13:18 robe of many colors. See Gen. 37:33. A garment which identified the wearer's special position. For Tamar, the robe identifying her as a virgin daughter of the king. The tearing of this robe symbolized her loss of this special position (v. 19).

13:19 put ashes...tore her robe...laid her hand...went away crying bitterly. The ashes were a sign of mourning. The torn robe symbolized the ruin of her life. The hand on the head was emblematic of exile and banishment. The crying showed that she viewed herself as good as dead.

13:20 do not take this thing to heart. Absalom told his sister not to pay undue attention or worry about the consequences of the rape. Absalom minimized the significance of what had taken place only for the moment, while already beginning to plot his revenge in using this crime as reason to do what he wanted to do anyway—remove Amnon from the line of succession to the throne (note also v. 32, where Jonadab knew of Absalom's plans). **desolate.** She remained unmarried and childless. Her full brother was her natural protector and the children of polygamists lived by themselves in different family units.

13:21 David...was very angry. Fury and indignation were David's reactions to the report of the rape (Gen. 34:7). Because he did not punish Amnon for his crime, he abdicated his responsibility both as king and as father. The lack of justice in the land would come back to haunt David in a future day (15:4).

13:22 Absalom hated Amnon. As Amnon hated Tamar (v. 15), Absalom loathed his half-brother, Amnon.

13:23-27 Baal Hazor. The Benjamite village of Hazor (Neh. 11:33), located about 12 mi. NE of Jerusalem, was the place for a sheep-shearing feast put on by Absalom, to which he invited all his brothers and half-brothers, as well as King David and his royal court (v. 24). David declined, but encouraged Absalom to hold the feast for "the king's sons" as a means to unity and harmony (vv. 25-27). With David's denial of the invitation, Absalom requested that Amnon go as his representative. Although David had reservations concerning Absalom's intent, he allowed all his sons to go.

26 Then Absalom said, "If not, please let
my brother Amnon go with us."
And the king said to him, "Why should
he go with you?" 27 But Absalom urged
him; so he let Amnon and all the king's
sons go with him.
28 Now Absalom had commanded his
servants, saying, "Watch now, when
Amnon's [r]heart is merry with wine, and
when I say to you, 'Strike Amnon!' then
kill him. Do not be afraid. Have I not commanded you? Be courageous and [3]val-
iant." 29 So the servants of Absalom [s]did to
Amnon as Absalom had commanded.
Then all the king's sons arose, and each
one got on [t]his mule and fled.
30 And it came to pass, while they were
on the way, that news came to David, saying, "Absalom has killed all the king's
sons, and not one of them is left!" 31 So
the king arose and [u]tore his garments and
[v]lay on the ground, and all his servants
stood by with their clothes torn. 32 Then
[w]Jonadab the son of Shimeah, David's
brother, answered and said, "Let not my
lord suppose they have killed all the
young men, the king's sons, for only
Amnon is dead. For by the command of
Absalom this has been determined from
the day that he forced his sister Tamar.
33 Now therefore, [x]let not my lord the
king take the thing to his heart, to think
that all the king's sons are dead. For only
Amnon is dead."

Absalom Flees to Geshur

34 [y]Then Absalom fled. And the young
man who was keeping watch lifted his
eyes and looked, and there, many people
were coming from the road on the hillside
behind [4]him. 35 And Jonadab said to the
king, "Look, the king's sons are coming; as
your servant said, so it is." 36 So it was, as
soon as he had finished speaking, that the
king's sons indeed came, and they lifted
up their voice and wept. Also the king and
all his servants wept very bitterly.
37 But Absalom fled and went to [z]Talmai
the son of Ammihud, king of Geshur. And
David mourned for his son every day. 38 So
Absalom fled and went to [a]Geshur, and
was there three years. 39 And [5]King David
[6]longed to go to Absalom. For he had been
[b]comforted concerning Amnon, because he
was dead.

Absalom Returns to Jerusalem

14 So Joab the son of Zeruiah perceived that the king's heart *was*
concerned [a]about Absalom. 2 And Joab
sent to [b]Tekoa and brought from there a
wise woman, and said to her, "Please pretend to be a mourner, [c]and put on mourning apparel; do not anoint yourself with
oil, but act like a woman who has been
mourning a long time for the dead. 3 Go
to the king and speak to him in this manner." So Joab [d]put the words in her
mouth.
4 And when the woman of Tekoa [1]spoke
to the king, she [e]fell on her face to the
ground and prostrated herself, and said,
[f]"Help, O king!"
5 Then the king said to her, "What troubles you?"
And she answered, [g]"Indeed I *am* a
widow, my husband is dead. 6 Now your
maidservant had two sons; and the two
fought with each other in the field, and
there was no one to part them, but the one
struck the other and killed him. 7 And
now the whole family has risen up against
your maidservant, and they said, 'Deliver
him who struck his brother, that we may
execute him [h]for the life of his brother
whom he killed; and we will destroy the
heir also.' So they would extinguish my
ember that is left, and leave to my husband *neither* name nor remnant on the
earth."

28 [r]Judg. 19:6, 9, 22; Ruth 3:7; 1 Sam. 25:36; Esth. 1:10 [3]Lit. *sons of valor*
29 [s]2 Sam. 12:10 [t]2 Sam. 18:9; 1 Kin. 1:33, 38
31 [u]2 Sam. 1:11 [v]2 Sam. 12:16
32 [w]2 Sam. 13:3-5
33 [x]2 Sam. 19:19
34 [y]2 Sam. 13:37, 38 [4]LXX adds *And the watchman went and told the king, and said, "I see men from the way of Horonaim, from the regions of the mountains."*
37 [z]2 Sam. 3:3; 1 Chr. 3:2
38 [a]2 Sam. 14:23, 32; 15:8
39 [b]Gen. 38:12; 2 Sam. 12:19, 23 [5]So with MT, Syr., Vg.; LXX *the spirit of the king;* Tg. *the soul of King David* [6]So with MT, Tg.; LXX, Vg. *ceased to pursue after*

CHAPTER 14

1 [a]2 Sam. 13:39
2 [b]2 Sam. 23:26; 2 Chr. 11:6; Amos 1:1 [c]Ruth 3:3
3 [d]Ex. 4:15; 2 Sam. 14:19
4 [e]1 Sam. 20:41; 25:23; 2 Sam. 1:2 [f]2 Kin. 6:26, 28 [1]Many Heb. mss., LXX, Syr., Vg. *came*
5 [g][Zech. 7:10]
7 [h]Num. 35:19; Deut. 19:12, 13

13:28,29 kill him. Absalom murdered Amnon through his servants (cf. 11:15-17), just as David had killed Uriah through others (11:14-17). Though rape was punishable by death, personal vengeance such as this was unacceptable to God. Due course of law was to be carried out.

13:29 his mule. Mules were ridden by the royal family in David's kingdom (18:9; 1 Kin. 1:33,38,44).

13:30 all the king's sons. This exaggeration plunged everyone into grief (v. 31) until it was corrected (v. 32).

13:32 Jonadab…answered. Jonadab knew of Absalom's plot to kill Amnon (see v. 20) for the rape of Tamar. Death was prescribed in Lev. 18:11,29 ("cut off" means to execute). *See note on vv. 28,29.*

13:34,37 Absalom fled. The law regarding premeditated murder, as most would view Absalom's act, gave him no hope of returning (see Num 35:21). The cities of refuge would afford him no sanctuary, so he left his father's kingdom to live in Geshur, E of the Sea of Galilee, under the protection of the king who was the grandfather of both Tamar and Absalom (*see notes on 13:1,2*).

13:39 longed to go. David gradually accepted the fact of Amnon's death and desired to see Absalom again, but took no action to bring him back.

14:1 David was strongly attached to Absalom, and, having gotten over the death of Amnon, he desired the fellowship of his exiled son, 3 years absent. But the fear of public opinion made him hesitant to pardon his son. Joab, perceiving this struggle between parental affection and royal duty, devised a plan involving a wise country woman and a story told to the king.

14:2 Tekoa. A town about 10 mi. S of Jerusalem (cf. Amos 1:1).

14:2,3 Joab put the words in her mouth. Joab used a story, as Nathan had (12:1-12), to show David the error of his ways and to encourage him to call Absalom back to Jerusalem.

8 Then the king said to the woman, "Go
to your house, and I will give orders concerning you."
9 And the woman of Tekoa said to the
king, "My lord, O king, *let* [i]the [2]iniquity *be*
on me and on my father's house, [j]and the
king and his throne *be* guiltless."
10 So the king said, "Whoever says *any-*
thing to you, bring him to me, and he shall
not touch you anymore."
11 Then she said, "Please let the king remember the LORD your God, and do not
permit [k]the avenger of blood to destroy
anymore, lest they destroy my son."
And he said, [l]"*As* the LORD lives, not one
hair of your son shall fall to the ground."
12 Therefore the woman said, "Please, let
your maidservant speak *another* word to
my lord the king."
And he said, "Say on."
13 So the woman said: "Why then have
you schemed such a thing against [m]the
people of God? For the king speaks this
thing as one who is guilty, *in that* the king
does not bring [n]his banished one home
again. 14 For we [o]will surely die and *be-*
come like water spilled on the ground,
which cannot be gathered up again. Yet
God does not [p]take away a life; but He
[q]devises means, so that His banished ones
are not [3]expelled from Him. 15 Now therefore, I have come to speak of this thing to
my lord the king because the people have
made me afraid. And your maidservant
said, 'I will now speak to the king; it may
be that the king will perform the request
of his maidservant. 16 For the king will
hear and deliver his maidservant from the
hand of the man *who would* destroy me
and my son together from the [r]inheritance
of God.' 17 Your maidservant said, 'The
word of my lord the king will now be
comforting; for [s]as the angel of God, so *is*
my lord the king in [t]discerning good and
evil. And may the LORD your God be with
you.' "
18 Then the king answered and said to
the woman, "Please do not hide from me
anything that I ask you."
And the woman said, "Please, let my
lord the king speak."
19 So the king said, "*Is* the hand of Joab
with you in all this?" And the woman answered and said, "*As* you live, my lord the
king, no one can turn to the right hand or
to the left from anything that my lord the
king has spoken. For your servant Joab
commanded me, and [u]he put all these
words in the mouth of your maidservant.
20 To bring about this change of affairs
your servant Joab has done this thing; but
my lord *is* wise, [v]according to the wisdom
of the angel of God, to know everything
that *is* in the earth."
21 And the king said to Joab, "All right, I
have granted this thing. Go therefore,
bring back the young man Absalom."
22 Then Joab fell to the ground on his face
and bowed himself, and [4]thanked the king.
And Joab said, "Today your servant knows
that I have found favor in your sight, my
lord, O king, in that the king has fulfilled
the request of his servant." 23 So Joab arose
[w]and went to Geshur, and brought Absalom to Jerusalem. 24 And the king said, "Let
him return to his own house, but [x]do not let
him see my face." So Absalom returned to
his own house, but did not see the king's
face.

David Forgives Absalom

25 Now in all Israel there was no one
who was praised as much as Absalom for
his good looks. [y]From the sole of his foot to

9 [i]Gen. 27:13; 43:9; 1 Sam. 25:24; Matt. 27:25 [j]2 Sam. 3:28, 29; 1 Kin. 2:33 [2]*guilt*
11 [k]Num. 35:19, 21; [Deut. 19:4-10] [l]1 Sam. 14:45; 1 Kin. 1:52; Matt. 10:30; Acts 27:34
13 [m]Judg. 20:2 [n]2 Sam. 13:37, 38
14 [o]Job 30:23; 34:15; [Heb. 9:27] [p]Job 34:19; Matt. 22:16; Acts 10:34; Rom. 2:11 [q]Num. 35:15 [3]*cast out*
16 [r]Deut. 32:9; 1 Sam. 26:19; 2 Sam. 20:19
17 [s]1 Sam. 29:9; 2 Sam. 19:27 [t]1 Kin. 3:9
19 [u]2 Sam. 14:3
20 [v]2 Sam. 14:17; 19:27
22 [4]Lit. *blessed*
23 [w]2 Sam. 13:37, 38
24 [x]Gen. 43:3; 2 Sam. 3:13
25 [y]Deut. 28:35; Job 2:7; Is. 1:6

14:7 leave to my husband *neither* name nor remnant. The story the woman told involved one brother killing another (v. 6). If the death penalty for murder was invoked (cf. Ex. 21:12; Lev. 24:17), there would be no living heir in the family, leaving that family with no future, a situation the law sought to avoid (Deut. 25:5-10). This would extinguish the last "ember" of hope for a future for her line. Cf. 21:17; Ps. 132:17, where the lamp refers to posterity.

14:9 *let* the iniquity *be* on me. The woman was willing to receive whatever blame might arise from the sparing of her guilty son.

14:11 avenger of blood. This is a specific term identifying the nearest relative of the deceased who would seek to put to death the murderer (Num. 35:6-28; Deut. 19:1-13; Matt. 27:25). **not one hair.** This is an expression meaning not any harm will come to the son of the widow in the story.

14:13 against the people of God. The woman asserted that by allowing Absalom to remain in exile, David had jeopardized the future welfare of Israel. If he would be so generous to a son he did not know in a family he did not know, would he not forgive his own son?

14:14 like water spilled on the ground. I.e., death is irreversible. **God does not take away a life.** The woman stated that since God acts according to the dictates of mercy, as in David's own experience (12:13), David was obligated to do likewise.

14:15,16 the people...the man *who would* destroy me. Those who were seeking to kill the son of the woman were like the people David feared who resented what Absalom had done and would have stood against a pardon for him.

14:18-20 David gets the intent of the story and discerns the source as Joab.

14:22 Joab's motives were selfish, in that he sought to ingratiate himself further with David for greater influence and power.

14:23 Geshur. *See note on 13:34,37.*

14:24 do not let him see my face. Absalom returned to Jerusalem, but the estrangement with his father continued.

14:25 his good looks. As with Saul before him (1 Sam. 9:1,2), Absalom looked like a king. His extraordinary popularity arose from his appearance.

the crown of his head there was no blemish
in him. 26 And when he cut the hair of his
head—at the end of every year he cut *it* because it was heavy on him—when he cut it,
he weighed the hair of his head at two
hundred shekels according to the king's
standard. 27 [z]To Absalom were born three
sons, and one daughter whose name *was*
Tamar. She was a woman of beautiful appearance.
28 And Absalom dwelt two full years in
Jerusalem, [a]but did not see the king's face.
29 Therefore Absalom sent for Joab, to send
him to the king, but he would not come to
him. And when he sent again the second
time, he would not come. 30 So he said to
his servants, "See, Joab's field is near mine,
and he has barley there; go and set it on
fire." And Absalom's servants set the field
on fire.
31 Then Joab arose and came to Absalom's house, and said to him, "Why have
your servants set my field on fire?"
32 And Absalom answered Joab, "Look, I
sent to you, saying, 'Come here, so that I
may send you to the king, to say, "Why
have I come from Geshur? *It would be* better for me *to be* there still."' Now therefore,
let me see the king's face; but [b]if there is iniquity in me, let him execute me."
33 So Joab went to the king and told him.
And when he had called for Absalom, he
came to the king and bowed himself on his
face to the ground before the king. Then
the king [c]kissed Absalom.

27 [z] 2 Sam. 13:1; 18:18
28 [a] 2 Sam. 14:24
32 [b] 1 Sam. 20:8; [Prov. 28:13]
33 [c] Gen. 33:4; 45:15; Luke 15:20

CHAPTER 15

1 [a] 2 Sam. 12:11 [b] 1 Kin. 1:5
2 [c] Deut. 19:17 [1] Lit. *controversy*
3 [2] Lit. *words* [3] Lit. *listener*
4 [d] Judg. 9:29
5 [e] 2 Sam. 14:33; 20:9
6 [f] [Rom. 16:18]
7 [g] [Deut. 23:21] [h] 2 Sam. 3:2, 3 [4] LXX mss., Syr., Josephus *four*
8 [i] 1 Sam. 16:2 [j] Gen. 28:20, 21 [k] 2 Sam. 13:38

Absalom's Treason

15 After this [a]it happened that Absalom [b]provided himself with chariots and horses, and fifty men to run before
him. 2 Now Absalom would rise early and
stand beside the way to the gate. *So* it was,
whenever anyone who had a [c]lawsuit[1]
came to the king for a decision, that Absalom would call to him and say, "What city
are you from?" And he would say, "Your
servant *is* from such and such a tribe of Israel." 3 Then Absalom would say to him,
"Look, your [2]case *is* good and right; but
there is no [3]deputy of the king to hear you."
4 Moreover Absalom would say, [d]"Oh, that
I were made judge in the land, and everyone who has any suit or cause would come
to me; then I would give him justice."
5 And *so* it was, whenever anyone came
near to bow down to him, that he would
put out his hand and take him and [e]kiss
him. 6 In this manner Absalom acted toward all Israel who came to the king for
judgment. [f]So Absalom stole the hearts of
the men of Israel.
7 Now it came to pass [g]after [4]forty years
that Absalom said to the king, "Please, let
me go to [h]Hebron and pay the vow which
I made to the LORD. 8 [i]For your servant
[j]took a vow [k]while I dwelt at Geshur in
Syria, saying, 'If the LORD indeed brings
me back to Jerusalem, then I will serve the
LORD.'"
9 And the king said to him, "Go in
peace." So he arose and went to Hebron.
10 Then Absalom sent spies throughout

14:26 hair of his head. At his annual haircut, it was determined that Absalom's head produced approximately 5 lbs. of hair that had to be cut off.

14:27 three sons. *See note on 18:18.* **daughter...Tamar.** Absalom named his daughter after his sister Tamar.

14:28 two full years. Whatever were David's errors in recalling Absalom, he displayed great restraint in wanting to stay apart from Absalom to lead his son through a time of repentance and a real restoration. Rather than produce repentance, however, Absalom's non-access to the royal court and all its amenities frustrated him so that he sent for Joab to intercede (v. 29).

14:30-32 set the field on fire. This was an act of aggression by Absalom to force Joab to act in his behalf with David, his father. Such a crime was serious, as it destroyed the livelihood of the owner and workers. It reveals that Absalom's heart was not repentant and submissive, but manipulative. He wanted an ultimatum delivered to David: Accept me or kill me!

14:33 the king kissed Absalom. The kiss signified David's forgiveness and Absalom's reconciliation with the family.

15:1 chariots and horses, and fifty men. After the reconciliation, Absalom possessed the symbols of royalty (see 1 Sam. 8:11).

15:1-6 stole the hearts. Public hearings were always conducted early in the morning in a court held outside by the city gates. Absalom positioned himself there to win favor. Because King David was busy with other matters or with wars, and was also aging, many matters were left unresolved, building a deep feeling of resentment among the people. Absalom used that situation to undermine his father, by gratifying all he could with a favorable settlement and showing them all warm cordiality. Thus, he won the people to himself, without them knowing his wicked ambition.

15:7 forty years. See the marginal reference. The better reading is "four" because the number "forty" could refer neither to the age of Absalom since he was born at Hebron after David had begun to rule (3:2-5), nor the time of David's reign, since he ruled only 40 years total (5:4,5). The 4-year period began either with Absalom's return from Geshur (14:23) or with his reconciliation with David (14:33).

15:7-9 Hebron. The city of Absalom's birth (3:2,3), and the place where David was first anointed king over Judah (2:4) and over all Israel (5:3). Absalom said he had made a vow while in Geshur (*see note on 13:34,37*) that if he was restored to Jerusalem, he would offer a sacrifice of thanksgiving in Hebron, where sacrifices were often made before the temple was built. David, who always encouraged such religious devotion, gave his consent.

15:10-12 Absalom formed a conspiracy, which included taking some of the leading men to create the impression that the king supported this action, and was in his old age sharing the kingdom. All of this was a subtle disguise so Absalom could have freedom to plan his revolution. Absalom was able to do this against his father not merely because of his cleverness, but also because of the laxness of his father (see 1 Kin. 1:6).

all the tribes of Israel, saying, "As soon as
you hear the sound of the trumpet, then
you shall say, 'Absalom [l]reigns in Hebron!' " 11 And with Absalom went two
hundred men [m]invited from Jerusalem,
and they [n]went along innocently and did
not know anything. 12 Then Absalom sent
for Ahithophel the Gilonite, [o]David's counselor, from his city—from [p]Giloh—while he
offered sacrifices. And the conspiracy grew
strong, for the people with Absalom [q]con-
tinually increased in number.

David Escapes from Jerusalem

13 Now a messenger came to David, saying, [r]"The hearts of the men of Israel are
[5]with Absalom."
14 So David said to all his servants who
were with him at Jerusalem, "Arise, and let
us [s]flee, or we shall not escape from Absalom. Make haste to depart, lest he overtake
us suddenly and bring disaster upon us,
and strike the city with the edge of the
sword."
15 And the king's servants said to the
king, "We *are* your servants, *ready to do*
whatever my lord the king commands."
16 Then [t]the king went out with all his
household after him. But the king left [u]ten
women, concubines, to keep the house.
17 And the king went out with all the people after him, and stopped at the outskirts.
18 Then all his servants passed [6]before
him; [v]and all the Cherethites, all the
Pelethites, and all the Gittites, [w]six hundred men who had followed him from
Gath, passed before the king.
19 Then the king said to [x]Ittai the Gittite,
"Why are you also going with us? Return
and remain with the king. For you *are* a
foreigner and also an exile from your own
place. 20 In fact, you came *only* yesterday.
Should I make you wander up and down
with us today, since I go [y]I know not
where? Return, and take your brethren
back. Mercy and truth *be* with you."
21 But Ittai answered the king and said,
[z]"*As* the LORD lives, and *as* my lord the
king lives, surely in whatever place my
lord the king shall be, whether in death or
life, even there also your servant will be."
22 So David said to Ittai, "Go, and cross
over." Then Ittai the Gittite and all his men
and all the little ones who *were* with him
crossed over. 23 And all the country wept
with a loud voice, and all the people
crossed over. The king himself also crossed
over the Brook Kidron, and all the people
crossed over toward the way of the [a]wil-
derness.
24 There was [b]Zadok also, and all the
Levites with him, bearing the [c]ark of the
covenant of God. And they set down
the ark of God, and [d]Abiathar went up
until all the people had finished crossing
over from the city. 25 Then the king said to
Zadok, "Carry the ark of God back into the
city. If I find favor in the eyes of the LORD,
He [e]will bring me back and show me *both*
it and [f]His dwelling place. 26 But if He says
thus: 'I have no [g]delight in you,' here I am,
[h]let Him do to me as seems good to Him."
27 The king also said to Zadok the priest,
"*Are* you *not* a [i]seer?[7] Return to the city in
peace, and [j]your two sons with you,
Ahimaaz your son, and Jonathan the son
of Abiathar. 28 See, [k]I will wait in the plains
of the wilderness until word comes from
you to inform me." 29 Therefore Zadok
and Abiathar carried the ark of God back
to Jerusalem. And they remained there.
30 So David went up by the Ascent of the
Mount of Olives, and wept as he went up;
and he [l]had his head covered and went
[m]barefoot. And all the people who *were*
with him [n]covered their heads and went

10 [l] 1 Kin. 1:34; 2 Kin. 9:13
11 [m] 1 Sam. 16:3, 5 [n] Gen. 20:5
12 [o] 2 Sam. 16:15; 1 Chr. 27:33; Ps. 41:9; 55:12-14 [p] Josh. 15:51 [q] Ps. 3:1
13 [r] Judg. 9:3; 2 Sam. 15:6 [5] Lit. *after*
14 [s] 2 Sam. 12:11; Ps. 3:title
16 [t] Ps. 3:title [u] 2 Sam. 12:11; 16:21, 22
18 [v] 2 Sam. 8:18 [w] 1 Sam. 23:13; 25:13; 30:1, 9 [6] Lit. *by his hand*
19 [x] 2 Sam. 18:2
20 [y] 1 Sam. 23:13
21 [z] Ruth 1:16, 17; [Prov. 17:17]
23 [a] 2 Sam. 15:28; 16:2
24 [b] 2 Sam. 8:17 [c] Num. 4:15; 1 Sam. 4:4 [d] 1 Sam. 22:20
25 [e] [Ps. 43:3] [f] Ex. 15:13; Jer. 25:30
26 [g] Num. 14:8; 2 Sam. 22:20; 1 Kin. 10:9; 2 Chr. 9:8; Is. 62:4 [h] 1 Sam. 3:18
27 [i] 1 Sam. 9:6-9 [j] 2 Sam. 17:17-20 [7] *prophet*
28 [k] Josh. 5:10; 2 Sam. 17:16
30 [l] 2 Sam. 19:4; Esth. 6:12; Ezek. 24:17, 23 [m] Is. 20:2-4 [n] Jer. 14:3, 4

15:12 Ahithophel. A counselor of David whose advice was so accurate that it was regarded as if it were the very "oracle of God" (16:23). This man was the father of Eliam (23:34) and the grandfather of Bathsheba (11:3; 23:24-39), who may have been looking for revenge on David. **Giloh.** A town in the hill country of Judah (Josh. 15:48,51), probably located a few mi. S of Hebron.

15:13-17 David's escape from Absalom is remembered in Ps. 3. Because he wanted to preserve the city he had beautified, and not have a war there, and since he felt that he could find greater support in the country, David left the city with all his household and personal guards.

15:18 Cherethites...Pelethites. Foreign mercenary soldiers of King David. *See note on 1 Sam. 30:14.* **Gittites.** Mercenary soldiers from Gath, i.e., Philistines.

15:19-22 Ittai. The commander of the Gittites, who had only recently joined David. In spite of David's words, he displayed his loyalty by going into exile with him. Ittai's later appointment as commander of one-third of the army (18:2,5,12) was David's way of expressing appreciation for his loyalty.

15:23-28 Psalm 63 has this occasion in view or possibly 1 Sam. 23:14.

15:23 Brook Kidron. This familiar valley, running N/S along the eastern side of Jerusalem, separates the city from the Mt. of Olives.

15:24-29 Zadok...Abiathar. *See notes on 8:17.* They brought the ark to comfort David with assurance of God's blessing, but he saw that as placing more confidence in the symbol than in God and sent it back. David knew the possession of the ark did not guarantee God's blessing (cf. 1 Sam. 4:3).

15:28 plains of the wilderness. Probably the region along the western bank of the Jordan River (see 17:16; Josh. 5:10).

15:30 *Mount of* Olives. The hill to the E of the city of Jerusalem was the location for David's contrition and remorse over his sins and their results. This was the location from which Jesus ascended to heaven (Acts 1:9-12).

up, [o]weeping as they went up. 31 Then
someone told David, saying, [p]"Ahithophel
is among the conspirators with Absalom."
And David said, "O LORD, I pray, [q]turn the
counsel of Ahithophel into foolishness!"
32 Now it happened when David had
come to the top *of the mountain,* where he
worshiped God—there was Hushai the
[r]Archite coming to meet him [s]with his
robe torn and dust on his head. 33 David
said to him, "If you go on with me, then
you will become [t]a burden to me. 34 But if
you return to the city, and say to Absalom,
[u]'I will be your servant, O king; *as* I *was*
your father's servant previously, so I *will*
now also *be* your servant,' then you may
defeat the counsel of Ahithophel for me.
35 And *do* you not *have* Zadok and Abiathar the priests with you there? Therefore
it will be *that* whatever you hear from the
king's house, you shall tell to [v]Zadok and
Abiathar the priests. 36 Indeed *they have*
there [w]with them their two sons, Ahimaaz,
Zadok's *son,* and Jonathan, Abiathar's *son;*
and by them you shall send me everything
you hear."
37 So Hushai, [x]David's friend, went into
the city. [y]And Absalom came into Jerusalem.

Mephibosheth's Servant

16 When[a] David was a little past the
top *of the mountain,* there was [b]Ziba
the servant of Mephibosheth, who met him
with a couple of saddled donkeys, and on
them two hundred *loaves* of bread, one
hundred clusters of raisins, one hundred
summer fruits, and a skin of wine. 2 And
the king said to Ziba, "What do you mean
to do with these?"
So Ziba said, "The donkeys *are* for the
king's household to ride on, the bread and
summer fruit for the young men to eat, and
the wine for [c]those who are faint in the
wilderness to drink."
3 Then the king said, "And where *is* your
[d]master's son?"
[e]And Ziba said to the king, "Indeed he is
staying in Jerusalem, for he said, 'Today
the house of Israel will restore the kingdom of my father to me.' "
4 So the king said to Ziba, "Here, all that
belongs to Mephibosheth *is* yours."
And Ziba said, "I humbly bow before
you, *that* I may find favor in your sight, my
lord, O king!"

Shimei Curses David

5 Now when King David came to [f]Ba-
hurim, there was a man from the family of
the house of Saul, whose name *was*
[g]Shimei the son of Gera, coming from
there. He came out, cursing continuously
as he came. 6 And he threw stones at David
and at all the servants of King David. And
all the people and all the mighty men *were*
on his right hand and on his left. 7 Also
Shimei said thus when he cursed: "Come
out! Come out! You [1]bloodthirsty man,
[h]you [2]rogue! 8 The LORD has [i]brought
upon you all [j]the blood of the house of
Saul, in whose place you have reigned; and
the LORD has delivered the kingdom into
the hand of Absalom your son. So now you
are caught in your own evil, because you
are a [3]bloodthirsty man!"
9 Then Abishai the son of Zeruiah said to
the king, "Why should this [k]dead dog
[l]curse my lord the king? Please, let me go
over and take off his head!"
10 But the king said, [m]"What have I to do
with you, you sons of Zeruiah? So let him

30 [o][Ps. 126:6]
31 [p]Ps. 3:1, 2; 55:12 [q]2 Sam. 16:23; 17:14, 23
32 [r]Josh. 16:2 [s]2 Sam. 1:2
33 [t]2 Sam. 19:35
34 [u]2 Sam. 16:19
35 [v]2 Sam. 17:15, 16
36 [w]2 Sam. 15:27
37 [x]2 Sam. 16:16; 1 Chr. 27:33 [y]2 Sam. 16:15

CHAPTER 16

1 [a]2 Sam. 15:30, 32 [b]2 Sam. 9:2; 19:17, 29
2 [c]2 Sam. 15:23; 17:29
3 [d]2 Sam. 9:9, 10 [e]2 Sam. 19:27
5 [f]2 Sam. 3:16 [g]2 Sam. 19:21; 1 Kin. 2:8, 9, 44-46
7 [h]Deut. 13:13 [1]Lit. *man of bloodshed* [2]*worthless man*
8 [i]Judg. 9:24, 56, 57; 1 Kin. 2:32, 33 [j]2 Sam. 1:16; 3:28, 29; 4:11, 12 [3]Lit. *man of bloodshed*
9 [k]1 Sam. 24:14; 2 Sam. 9:8 [l]Ex. 22:28
10 [m]2 Sam. 3:39; 19:22; [1 Pet. 2:23]

15:32 top *of the mountain.* This was the place from which David could look toward the city and the temple to the W. **Hushai the Archite.** Hushai was of the clan of the Archites who lived in Ephraim on the border with Manasseh (Josh. 16:2) and served as an official counselor to David (v. 37; 1 Chr. 27,33). David persuaded Hushai to return to Jerusalem and attach himself to Absalom as a counselor. His mission was to contradict the advice of Ahithophel (17:5-14) and to communicate Absalom's plans to David (17:21; 18:19).

16:1 Ziba. *See note on 9:2.* **Mephibosheth.** Saul's grandson by Jonathan (*see note on 4:4*).

16:3 where *is* your master's son? According to 9:9,10, Ziba was able to garner such food and drink. His master had been Saul before his death and was then Mephibosheth. **restore the kingdom of my father.** Ziba, evidently trying to commend himself in the eyes of David by bringing these gifts, accused his master of disloyalty to the king and participation in Absalom's conspiracy for the purpose of bringing down the whole Davidic house. Thus the house of Saul would re-take the throne, and he would be king. This was a false accusation (see 19:24,25), but it was convincing to David, who believed the story and made a severe and rash decision that inflicted injury on a true friend, Mephibosheth.

16:5 Bahurim. *See note on 3:16.*

16:5-8 Shimei. Shimei was a distant relative of Saul, from the tribe of Benjamin, who cursed David as "a man of bloodshed" (vv. 7,8) and "a man of Belial" (*see note on 1 Sam. 2:12*). He could possibly be the Cush of Ps. 7. Shimei declared that the loss of David's throne was God's retribution on his past sins (v. 8), and David accepted his curse as from the Lord (v. 11). It could be that Shimei was accusing David of the murders of Abner (3:27-39), Ishbosheth (4:1-12), and Uriah (11:15-27).

16:9 Abishai. *See note on 2:18.* **dead dog.** I.e., worthless and despised (cf. 9:8).

16:10-14 The patience and restraint of David on this occasion was amazingly different than his violent reaction to the slanderous words of Nabal (1 Sam. 25:2ff.). On that occasion, he was eager to kill the man until placated by the wisdom of Abigail. He was a broken man at this later time and knew that while the rancor of Shimei was uncalled for, his accusations were true. He was penitent.

curse, because [n]the LORD has said to him,
'Curse David.' [o]Who then shall say, 'Why
have you done so?' "
11 And David said to Abishai and all his
servants, "See how [p]my son who [q]came
from my own body seeks my life. How
much more now *may this* Benjamite? Let
him alone, and let him curse; for so the
LORD has ordered him. 12 It may be that the
LORD will look on [4]my affliction, and that
the LORD will [r]repay me with [s]good for his
cursing this day." 13 And as David and his
men went along the road, Shimei went
along the hillside opposite him and cursed
as he went, threw stones at him and
[5]kicked up dust. 14 Now the king and all
the people who *were* with him became
weary; so they refreshed themselves there.

The Advice of Ahithophel

15 Meanwhile [t]Absalom and all the people, the men of Israel, came to Jerusalem;
and Ahithophel *was* with him. 16 And so it
was, when Hushai the Archite, [u]David's
friend, came to Absalom, that [v]Hushai said
to Absalom, "*Long* live the king! *Long* live
the king!"
17 So Absalom said to Hushai, "*Is* this
your loyalty to your friend? [w]Why did you
not go with your friend?"
18 And Hushai said to Absalom, "No,
but whom the LORD and this people and all
the men of Israel choose, his I will be, and
with him I will remain. 19 "Furthermore,
[x]whom should I serve? *Should I* not *serve* in
the presence of his son? As I have served in
your father's presence, so will I be in your
presence."
20 Then Absalom said to [y]Ahithophel,
"Give advice as to what we should do."
21 And Ahithophel said to Absalom, "Go
in to your father's [z]concubines, whom he
has left to keep the house; and all Israel
will hear that you [a]are abhorred by your
father. Then [b]the hands of all who are with
you will be strong." 22 So they pitched a
tent for Absalom on the top of the house,
and Absalom went in to his father's concubines [c]in the sight of all Israel.
23 Now the advice of Ahithophel, which
he gave in those days, *was* as if one had inquired at the oracle of God. So *was* all the
advice of Ahithophel [d]both with David
and with Absalom.

17 Moreover Ahithophel said to Absalom, "Now let me choose twelve
thousand men, and I will arise and pursue
David tonight. 2 I will come upon him
while he *is* [a]weary and weak, and make
him [1]afraid. And all the people who *are*
with him will flee, and I will [b]strike only
the king. 3 Then I will bring back all the
people to you. When all return except the
man whom you seek, all the people will be
at peace." 4 And the saying pleased Absalom and all the [c]elders of Israel.

The Advice of Hushai

5 Then Absalom said, "Now call Hushai
the Archite also, and let us hear what he
[d]says too." 6 And when Hushai came to
Absalom, Absalom spoke to him, saying,
"Ahithophel has spoken in this manner.
Shall we do as he says? If not, speak up."
7 So Hushai said to Absalom: "The advice that Ahithophel has given *is* not good
at this time. 8 For," said Hushai, "you
know your father and his men, that they
are mighty men, and they *are* enraged in
their minds, like [e]a bear robbed of her cubs
in the field; and your father *is* a man of
war, and will not camp with the people.
9 Surely by now he is hidden in some pit,
or in some *other* place. And it will be, when
some of them are overthrown at the first,
that whoever hears *it* will say, 'There is a
slaughter among the people who follow
Absalom.' 10 And even he *who is* valiant,
whose heart *is* like the heart of a lion, will
[f]melt completely. For all Israel knows that
your father *is* a mighty man, and *those* who
are with him *are* valiant men. 11 Therefore I
advise that all Israel be fully gathered to
you, [g]from Dan to Beersheba, [h]like the
sand that *is* by the sea for multitude, and

10 [n]2 Kin. 18:25; [Lam. 3:38] [o][Rom. 9:20]
11 [p]2 Sam. 12:11 [q]Gen. 15:4
12 [r]Deut. 23:5; Neh. 13:2; Prov. 20:22 [s]Deut. 23:5; [Rom. 8:28; Heb. 12:10, 11] [4]So with Kt., LXX, Syr., Vg.; Qr. *my eyes;* Tg. *tears of my eyes*
13 [5]Lit. *dusted him with dust*
15 [t]2 Sam. 15:12, 37
16 [u]2 Sam. 15:37 [v]2 Sam. 15:34
17 [w]2 Sam. 19:25; [Prov. 17:17]
19 [x]2 Sam. 15:34
20 [y]2 Sam. 15:12
21 [z]2 Sam. 15:16; 20:3 [a]Gen. 34:30; 1 Sam. 13:4 [b]2 Sam. 2:7; Zech. 8:13
22 [c]2 Sam. 12:11, 12
23 [d]2 Sam. 15:12

CHAPTER 17

2 [a]Deut. 25:18; 2 Sam. 16:14 [b]Zech. 13:7 [1]*tremble with fear*
4 [c]2 Sam. 5:3; 19:11
5 [d]2 Sam. 15:32-34
8 [e]Hos. 13:8
10 [f]Josh. 2:11
11 [g]Judg. 20:1; 2 Sam. 3:10 [h]Gen. 22:17; Josh. 11:4; 1 Kin. 20:10

16:15 Ahithophel. *See note on 15:12.*

16:15-23 Absalom set up his royal court in Jerusalem.

16:16 Hushai. *See note on 15:32.*

16:21,22 your father's concubines. David had left behind in Jerusalem 10 concubines to take care of the palace (15:16). In the Near East, possession of the harem came with the throne. Ahithophel advised Absalom to have sexual relations with David's concubines and thereby assert his right to his father's throne. On the roof of the palace in the most public place (cf. 11:2), a tent was set up for this scandalous event, thereby fulfilling the judgment announced by Nathan in 12:11,12.

17:1-4 Ahithophel's second piece of advice to Absalom was that he immediately pursue and kill David to remove any possibility of his reclaiming the throne, which would incline David's followers to return and submit to Absalom.

17:4 all the elders of Israel. The same prominent tribal leaders who had accepted David's kingship in 5:3 had been won over as participants in Absalom's rebellion.

17:7-13 Providentially, the Lord took control of the situation through the counsel of Hushai (*see note on 15:32*) who advised Absalom in such a way as to give David time to prepare for war with Absalom. Hushai's plan seemed best to the elders. It had two features: 1) the need for an army larger than 12,000 (v. 1), so that Absalom would not lose, and 2) the king leading the army into battle (an appeal to Absalom's arrogance).

17:11 Dan to Beersheba. *See note on 3:10.*

that you go to battle in person. 12 So we
will come upon him in some place where
he may be found, and we will fall on him
as the dew falls on the ground. And of him
and all the men who *are* with him there
shall not be left so much as one. 13 Moreover, if he has withdrawn into a city, then
all Israel shall bring ropes to that city; and
we will [i]pull it into the river, until there is
not one small stone found there."
14 So Absalom and all the men of Israel
said, "The advice of Hushai the Archite *is*
better than the advice of Ahithophel." For
[j]the LORD had purposed to defeat the good
advice of Ahithophel, to the intent that the
LORD might bring disaster on Absalom.

Hushai Warns David to Escape

15 [k]Then Hushai said to Zadok and Abiathar the priests, "Thus and so Ahithophel
advised Absalom and the elders of Israel,
and thus and so I have advised. 16 Now
therefore, send quickly and tell David, saying, 'Do not spend this night [l]in the plains
of the wilderness, but speedily cross over,
lest the king and all the people who *are*
with him be swallowed up.' " 17 [m]Now
Jonathan and Ahimaaz [n]stayed at [o]En
Rogel, for they dared not be seen coming
into the city; so a female servant would
come and tell them, and they would go
and tell King David. 18 Nevertheless a lad
saw them, and told Absalom. But both of
them went away quickly and came to a
man's house [p]in Bahurim, who had a well
in his court; and they went down into it.
19 [q]Then the woman took and spread a
covering over the well's mouth, and
spread ground grain on it; and the thing
was not known. 20 And when Absalom's
servants came to the woman at the house,
they said, "Where *are* Ahimaaz and Jonathan?"
So [r]the woman said to them, "They have
gone over the water brook."
And when they had searched and could
not find *them,* they returned to Jerusalem.
21 Now it came to pass, after they had departed, that they came up out of the well
and went and told King David, and said to
David, [s]"Arise and cross over the water
quickly. For thus has Ahithophel advised
against you." 22 So David and all the people who *were* with him arose and crossed
over the Jordan. By morning light not one
of them was left who had not gone over
the Jordan.
23 Now when Ahithophel saw that his
advice was not followed, he saddled a
donkey, and arose and went home to [t]his
house, to his city. Then he [2]put his [u]house-
hold in order, and [v]hanged himself, and
died; and he was buried in his father's
tomb.
24 Then David went to [w]Mahanaim. And
Absalom crossed over the Jordan, he and
all the men of Israel with him. 25 And
Absalom made [x]Amasa captain of the
army instead of Joab. This Amasa *was* the
son of a man whose name *was* [3]Jithra, an
[4]Israelite, who had gone in to [y]Abigail the
daughter of Nahash, sister of Zeruiah,
Joab's mother. 26 So Israel and Absalom
encamped in the land of Gilead.
27 Now it happened, when David had
come to Mahanaim, that [z]Shobi the son of
Nahash from Rabbah of the people of
Ammon, [a]Machir the son of Ammiel from
Lo Debar, and [b]Barzillai the Gileadite from
Rogelim, 28 brought beds and basins,
earthen vessels and wheat, barley and
flour, parched *grain* and beans, lentils and

13 [i] Mic. 1:6
14 [j] 2 Sam. 15:31, 34
15 [k] 2 Sam. 15:35, 36
16 [l] 2 Sam. 15:28
17 [m] 2 Sam. 15:27, 36; 1 Kin. 1:42, 43 [n] Josh. 2:4-6 [o] Josh. 15:7; 18:16
18 [p] 2 Sam. 3:16; 16:5
19 [q] Josh. 2:4-6
20 [r] Ex. 1:19; [Lev. 19:11]; Josh. 2:3-5
21 [s] 2 Sam. 17:15, 16
23 [t] 2 Sam. 15:12 [u] 2 Kin. 20:1 [v] Matt. 27:5 [2] Lit. *gave charge concerning his house*
24 [w] Gen. 32:2; Josh. 13:26; 2 Sam. 2:8; 19:32
25 [x] 2 Sam. 19:13; 20:9-12; 1 Kin. 2:5, 32 [y] 1 Chr. 2:16 [3] *Jether,* 1 Chr. 2:17 [4] So with MT, some LXX mss., Tg.; some LXX mss. *Ishmaelite* (cf. 1 Chr. 2:17); Vg. *of Jezrael*
27 [z] 1 Sam. 11:1; 2 Sam. 10:1; 12:29 [a] 2 Sam. 9:4 [b] 2 Sam. 19:31, 32; 1 Kin. 2:7

17:13 ropes. In besieging the town, hooks attached to ropes were cast over the protective wall and, with a large number of men pulling, the walls were pulled down.

17:14 the LORD had purposed. The text notes that Ahithophel's advice was rejected by Absalom because the Lord had determined to defeat the rebellion of Absalom, as prayed for by David (15:31). God's providence was controlling all the intrigues among the usurper's counselors.

17:16 cross over. Crossing over from the W side to the E side of the Jordan River was the means of protecting David and his people from the immediate onslaught if Ahithophel's plan was followed.

17:17 Jonathan and Ahimaaz. Jonathan was the son of the priest Abiathar and Ahimaaz the son of the priest Zadok (15:27). They were designated to take information from Hushai in Jerusalem to David by the Jordan River. **En Rogel.** A spring in the Kidron Valley on the border between Benjamin and Judah (Josh. 15:1,7; 18:11,16) less than a mi. SE of Jerusalem.

17:18 Bahurim. *See note on 3:16.*

17:19 well's mouth. Using an empty cistern as a place for a covering of dry grain was a common practice.

17:23 hanged himself. When Ahithophel saw that his counsel to Absalom had not been followed, he took his own life. He probably foresaw Absalom's defeat and knew that he would then be accountable to David for his disloyalty.

17:24 Mahanaim. *See note on 2:8.*

17:25 Amasa. Absalom appointed Amasa as commander of the army of Israel, replacing Joab who had accompanied David on his flight from Jerusalem. Amasa was the son of Abigail, either David's sister or his half-sister (1 Chr. 2:17), making him David's nephew. His mother was also the sister of Zeruiah, the mother of Joab. Therefore, Amasa was a cousin of Absalom, Joab, and Abishai. Under his lead, the armies crossed the Jordan (v. 24) into Gilead, the high-eastern area. Sufficient time had passed for building the large army Hushai suggested, and so David had readied himself for the war (*see note on 17:7-13*).

17:27 Shobi. A son of Nahash and brother of Hanun, kings of the Ammonites (10:1,2). **Machir.** *See note on 9:4.* **Barzillai.** An aged, wealthy benefactor of David from Gilead, on the east side of the Jordan (see 19:31-39; 1 Kin. 2:7).

parched *seeds*, 29 honey and curds, sheep and cheese of the herd, for David and the people who *were* with him to eat. For they said, "The people are hungry and weary and thirsty [c]in the wilderness."

Absalom's Defeat and Death

18 And David [1]numbered the people
who *were* with him, and [a]set captains of thousands and captains of hundreds over them. 2 Then David sent out
one third of the people under the hand of
Joab, [b]one third under the hand of Abishai
the son of Zeruiah, Joab's brother, and one
third under the hand of [c]Ittai the Gittite.
And the king said to the people, "I also
will surely go out with you myself."
3 [d]But the people answered, "You shall
not go out! For if we flee away, they will
not care about us; nor if half of us die, will
they care about us. But *you are* worth ten
thousand of us now. For you are now more
help to us in the city."
4 Then the king said to them, "Whatever
seems best to you I will do." So the king
stood beside the gate, and all the people
went out by hundreds and by thousands.
5 Now the king had commanded Joab,
Abishai, and Ittai, saying, "*Deal* gently for
my sake with the young man Absalom."
[e]And all the people heard when the king
gave all the captains orders concerning
Absalom.
6 So the people went out into the field of
battle against Israel. And the battle was in
the [f]woods of Ephraim. 7 The people of Israel were overthrown there before the servants of David, and a great slaughter of
twenty thousand took place there that day.
8 For the battle there was scattered over the
face of the whole countryside, and the
woods devoured more people that day
than the sword devoured.
9 Then Absalom met the servants of David. Absalom rode on a mule. The mule
went under the thick boughs of a great
terebinth tree, and [g]his head caught in the
terebinth; so he was left hanging between
heaven and earth. And the mule which *was*
under him went on. 10 Now a certain man
saw *it* and told Joab, and said, "I just saw
Absalom hanging in a terebinth tree!"
11 So Joab said to the man who told him,
"You just saw *him!* And why did you not
strike him there to the ground? I would
have given you ten *shekels* of silver and a
belt."
12 But the man said to Joab, "Though I
were to receive a thousand *shekels* of silver
in my hand, I would not raise my hand
against the king's son. [h]For in our hearing
the king commanded you and Abishai and
Ittai, saying, [2]'Beware lest anyone *touch* the
young man Absalom!' 13 Otherwise I
would have dealt falsely against my own
life. For there is nothing hidden from the
king, and you yourself would have set
yourself against *me*."
14 Then Joab said, "I cannot linger with
you." And he took three spears in his hand
and thrust them through Absalom's heart,
while he was *still* alive in the midst of the
terebinth tree. 15 And ten young men who
bore Joab's armor surrounded Absalom,
and struck and killed him.
16 So Joab blew the trumpet, and the
people returned from pursuing Israel. For
Joab held back the people. 17 And they
took Absalom and cast him into a large pit
in the woods, and [i]laid a very large heap of
stones over him. Then all Israel [j]fled,
everyone to his tent.
18 Now Absalom in his lifetime had

29 [c] 2 Sam. 16:2, 14

CHAPTER 18

1 [a] Ex. 18:25; Num. 31:14; 1 Sam. 22:7 [1] Lit. *attended to*
2 [b] Judg. 7:16; 1 Sam. 11:11 [c] 2 Sam. 15:19-22
3 [d] 2 Sam. 21:17
5 [e] 2 Sam. 18:12
6 [f] Josh. 17:15, 18; 2 Sam. 17:26
9 [g] 2 Sam. 14:26
12 [h] 2 Sam. 18:5 [2] Vss. *'Protect the young man Absalom for me!'*
17 [i] Deut. 21:20, 21; Josh. 7:26; 8:29 [j] 2 Sam. 19:8; 20:1, 22

18:2 A 3-pronged attack was a customary military strategy (see Judg. 7:16; 1 Sam. 11:11; 13:17).

18:3 You shall not go out. David desired to lead his men into the battle; however, the people recognized that the death of David would mean sure defeat and Absalom would then be secure in the kingship. The people's words echo what Ahithophel had earlier pointed out to Absalom (17:2,3). So David was persuaded to remain at Mahanaim.

18:5 *Deal* gently. David ordered his 3 commanders not to harm Absalom. The 4 uses of "the young man Absalom" (vv. 5,12,29,32) imply that David sentimentally viewed Absalom as a youthful rebel who could be forgiven.

18:6 the woods of Ephraim. A dense forest existed E of the Jordan River and N of the Jabbok River in Gilead, where the battle was waged.

18:8 the woods devoured more. Amazingly, because of the density of the trees and the rugged nature of the terrain, the pursuit through the forest resulted in more deaths than the actual combat (see v. 9).

18:9 mule. *See note on 13:29.* **his head caught in the terebinth.** Either Absalom's neck was caught in a fork formed by two of the branches growing out from a large oak tree or his hair was caught in a tangle of thick branches. The terminology and context (cf. 14:26) favor the latter view.

18:10 a certain man. One of David's soldiers, who refused to disobey the order of the king recorded in v. 5 to treat Absalom "gently," had done nothing for the suspended prince.

18:11,12 ten...thousand. Four ounces and 25 pounds respectively.

18:14 alive. The spears of Joab killed Absalom while Joab's armor bearers struck him to make sure that he was dead (v. 15). In this action, Joab disobeyed the explicit order of David (v. 5).

18:16 blew the trumpet. Joab recalled his soldiers from the battle (cf. 2:28).

18:17 a very large heap of stones. Absalom was buried in a deep pit that was covered over with stones, perhaps symbolic of stoning, which was the legal penalty due to a rebel son (Deut. 21:20, 21). A heap of stones often showed that the one buried was a criminal or enemy (Josh. 7:26; 8:29).

taken and set up a [3]pillar for himself,
which *is* in [k]the King's Valley. For he said,
[l]"I have no son to keep my name in remembrance." He called the pillar after his
own name. And to this day it is called
Absalom's Monument.

David Hears of Absalom's Death

19 Then [m]Ahimaaz the son of Zadok
said, "Let me run now and take the news
to the king, how the LORD has [4]avenged
him of his enemies."
20 And Joab said to him, "You shall not
take the news this day, for you shall take
the news another day. But today you shall
take no news, because the king's son is
dead." 21 Then Joab said to the Cushite,
"Go, tell the king what you have seen." So
the Cushite bowed himself to Joab and ran.
22 And Ahimaaz the son of Zadok said
again to Joab, "But [5]whatever happens,
please let me also run after the Cushite."
So Joab said, "Why will you run, my
son, since you have no news ready?"
23 "But whatever happens," *he said,* "let
me run."
So he said to him, "Run." Then Ahimaaz
ran by way of the plain, and outran the
Cushite.
24 Now David was sitting between the
[n]two gates. And the watchman went up to
the roof over the gate, to the wall, lifted his
eyes and looked, and there was a man,
running alone. 25 Then the watchman cried
out and told the king. And the king said,
"If he *is* alone, *there is* news in his mouth."
And he came rapidly and drew near.
26 Then the watchman saw *another* man
running, and the watchman called to the
gatekeeper and said, "There is *another*
man, running alone!"
And the king said, "He also brings news."
27 So the watchman said, [6]"I think the
running of the first is like the running of
Ahimaaz the son of Zadok."
And the king said, "He *is* a good man,
and comes with [o]good news."

28 So Ahimaaz called out and said to the
king, [7]"All is well!" Then he bowed down
with his face to the earth before the king,
and said, [p]"Blessed *be* the LORD your God,
who has delivered up the men who raised
their hand against my lord the king!"
29 The king said, "Is the young man
Absalom safe?"
Ahimaaz answered, "When Joab sent
the king's servant and *me* your servant, I
saw a great tumult, but I did not know
what *it was about.*"
30 And the king said, "Turn aside *and*
stand here." So he turned aside and stood
still.
31 Just then the Cushite came, and the
Cushite said, "There is good news, my lord
the king! For the LORD has avenged you
this day of all those who rose against you."
32 And the king said to the Cushite, "Is
the young man Absalom safe?"
So the Cushite answered, "May the enemies of my lord the king, and all who rise
against you to do harm, be like *that* young
man!"

David's Mourning for Absalom

33 Then the king was deeply moved, and
went up to the chamber over the gate, and
wept. And as he went, he said thus: [q]"O
my son Absalom—my son, my son Absalom—if only I had died in your place! O
Absalom my son, [r]my son!"

19 And Joab was told, "Behold, the king
is weeping and [a]mourning for Absalom." 2 So the victory that day was *turned*
into [b]mourning for all the people. For the
people heard it said that day, "The king is
grieved for his son." 3 And the people [1]stole
back [c]into the city that day, as people who
are ashamed steal away when they flee in
battle. 4 But the king [d]covered his face, and
the king cried out with a loud voice, [e]"O my
son Absalom! O Absalom, my son, my son!"
5 Then [f]Joab came into the house to the
king, and said, "Today you have disgraced
all your servants who today have saved

18 [k]Gen. 14:17 [l]2 Sam. 14:27 [3]*monument*
19 [m]2 Sam. 15:36; 17:17 [4]*vindicated*
22 [5]Lit. *be what may*
24 [n]Judg. 5:11; 2 Sam. 13:34; 2 Kin. 9:17
27 [o]1 Kin. 1:42 [6]Lit. *I see the running*
28 [p]2 Sam. 16:12 [7]*Peace be to you*
33 [q]2 Sam. 12:10 [r]2 Sam. 19:4

CHAPTER 19

1 [a]Jer. 14:2
2 [b]Esth. 4:3
3 [c]2 Sam. 17:24, 27; 19:32 [1]*went by stealth*
4 [d]2 Sam. 15:30 [e]2 Sam. 18:33
5 [f]2 Sam. 18:14

18:18 pillar for himself. Absalom had memorialized himself by erecting a monument in his own honor (cf. Saul's action in 1 Sam. 15:12). There is today a monument, a tomb in that area, called Absalom's tomb (perhaps on the same site) on which orthodox Jews spit when passing by. **King's Valley.** Traditionally, the Kidron Valley immediately E of the city of Jerusalem. **no son.** According to 14:27, Absalom had 3 sons, unnamed in the text, all of whom had died before him.

18:19 Ahimaaz. *See note on 17:17.*

18:21 Cushite. Cush was the area S of Egypt.

18:27 good man…good news. David believed that the choice of the messenger was indicative of the content of the message.

18:29 I did not know. Ahimaaz concealed his knowledge of Absalom's death as Joab requested (v. 20).

18:32 like *that* young man. The Cushite's reply was not so much indirect as culturally phrased (cf. 1 Sam. 25:26).

18:33 my son. Repeated 5 times in this verse, David lamented the death of Absalom, his son (cf. 19:5). In spite of all the harm that Absalom had caused, David was preoccupied with his personal loss in a melancholy way that seems to be consistent with his weakness as a father. It was an unwarranted zeal for such a worthless son, and a warning about the pitiful results of sin.

19:3 the people stole back. Because of David's excessive grief, his soldiers returned from battle not as rejoicing victors, but as if they had been humiliated by defeat.

19:5 disgraced all your servants. Joab sternly rebuked David for being so absorbed in his personal trauma and failing to appreciate the victory that his men had won for him.

your life, the lives of your sons and daughters, the lives of your wives and the lives of
your concubines, **6** in that you love your
enemies and hate your friends. For you
have declared today that you [2]regard neither princes nor servants; for today I perceive that if Absalom had lived and all of
us had died today, then it would have
pleased you well. **7** Now therefore, arise,
go out and speak [3]comfort to your servants. For I swear by the LORD, if you do
not go out, not one will stay with you this
night. And that will be worse for you than
all the evil that has befallen you from your
youth until now." **8** Then the king arose
and sat in the [g]gate. And they told all the
people, saying, "There is the king, sitting
in the gate." So all the people came before
the king.

For everyone of Israel had [h]fled to his
tent.

David Returns to Jerusalem

9 Now all the people were in a dispute
throughout all the tribes of Israel, saying,
"The king saved us from the hand of our
[i]enemies, he delivered us from the hand of
the [j]Philistines, and now he has [k]fled from
the land because of Absalom. **10** But Absalom, whom we anointed over us, has died
in battle. Now therefore, why do you say
nothing about bringing back the king?"

11 So King David sent to [l]Zadok and
Abiathar the priests, saying, "Speak to the
elders of Judah, saying, 'Why are you the
last to bring the king back to his house,
since the words of all Israel have come to
the king, to his *very* house? **12** You *are* my
brethren, you *are* [m]my bone and my flesh.
Why then are you the last to bring back the
king?' **13** [n]And say to Amasa, '*Are* you not
my bone and my flesh? [o]God do so to me,
and more also, if you are not commander
of the army before me [4]continually in place
of Joab.' " **14** So he swayed the hearts of all
the men of Judah, [p]just as *the heart of* one
man, so that they sent *this word* to the king:
"Return, you and all your servants!"

15 Then the king returned and came to
the Jordan. And Judah came to [q]Gilgal, to
go to meet the king, to escort the king
[r]across the Jordan. **16** And [s]Shimei the son
of Gera, a Benjamite, who *was* from Bahurim, hurried and came down with the
men of Judah to meet King David. **17** *There
were* a thousand men of [t]Benjamin with
him, and [u]Ziba the servant of the house of
Saul, and his fifteen sons and his twenty
servants with him; and they went over the
Jordan before the king. **18** Then a ferryboat
went across to carry over the king's household, and to do what he thought good.

David's Mercy to Shimei

Now Shimei the son of Gera fell down
before the king when he had crossed the
Jordan. **19** Then he said to the king, [v]"Do
not let my lord [5]impute iniquity to me, or
remember what [w]wrong your servant did
on the day that my lord the king left Jerusalem, that the king should [x]take *it* to
heart. **20** For I, your servant, know that I
have sinned. Therefore here I am, the first
to come today of all [y]the house of Joseph to
go down to meet my lord the king."

21 But Abishai the son of Zeruiah answered and said, "Shall not Shimei be put
to death for this, [z]because he [a]cursed the
LORD's anointed?"

22 And David said, [b]"What have I to do
with you, you sons of Zeruiah, that you
should be adversaries to me today? [c]Shall
any man be put to death today in Israel?
For do I not know that today I *am* king

6 [2] *have no respect for*
7 [3] Lit. *to the heart of*
8 [g] 2 Sam. 15:2; 18:24 [h] 2 Sam. 18:17
9 [i] 2 Sam. 8:1-14 [j] 2 Sam. 3:18 [k] 2 Sam. 15:14
11 [l] 2 Sam. 15:24
12 [m] 2 Sam. 5:1; 1 Chr. 11:1
13 [n] 2 Sam. 17:25; 1 Chr. 2:17 [o] Ruth 1:17

[4] *permanently*
14 [p] Judg. 20:1
15 [q] Josh. 5:9; 1 Sam. 11:14, 15 [r] 2 Sam. 17:22
16 [s] 2 Sam. 16:5; 1 Kin. 2:8
17 [t] 2 Sam. 3:19; 1 Kin. 12:21 [u] 2 Sam. 9:2, 10; 16:1, 2
19 [v] 1 Sam. 22:15 [w] 2 Sam. 16:5, 6 [x] 2 Sam. 13:33 [5] *charge me with iniquity*
20 [y] Judg. 1:22; 1 Kin. 11:28
21 [z] [Ex. 22:28] [a] [1 Sam. 26:9]
22 [b] 2 Sam. 3:39; 16:10 [c] 1 Sam. 11:13

19:7 not one will stay with you. Joab, who was the esteemed general of the army, was a dangerous person because of that power. He was also dangerous to David because he had disobeyed his command to spare Absalom, and killed him with no remorse. When he warned David that he would be in deep trouble if he did not immediately express appreciation to his men for their victory, David knew he could be in serious danger.

19:8 sat in the gate. It was at the gate of Mahanaim that David had reviewed his troops as they had marched out to battle (18:4). David's sitting in the gate represented a return to his exercise of kingly authority.

19:9 a dispute. An argument arose in Israel concerning whether David should be returned to the kingship. David's past military victories over the Philistines and the failure of Absalom argued for David's return. Therefore, David's supporters insisted on knowing why their fellow Israelites remained quiet about returning David to his rightful place on the throne in Jerusalem.

19:11 elders of Judah. Through the priests who had stayed in Jerusalem during the rebellion, David appealed to the leaders of his own tribe to take the initiative in restoring him to the throne in Jerusalem (see 2:4; 1 Sam. 30:26). Though this appeal produced the desired result, it also led to tribal jealousies (vv. 40-43).

19:13 Amasa. *See note on 17:25.* **commander of the army… in place of Joab.** David appointed Amasa commander of his army, hoping to secure the allegiance of those who had followed Amasa when he led Absalom's forces, especially those of Judah. This appointment did persuade the tribe of Judah to support David's return to the kingship (v. 14) and secured the animosity of Joab against Amasa for taking his position (cf. 20:8-10).

19:15 Gilgal. *See note on 1 Sam. 10:8.*

19:16 Shimei. *See note on 16:5.* Shimei confessed his sin of cursing David and his life was spared, temporarily, for on his deathbed David ordered that Shimei be punished for his crime (1 Kin. 2:8,9,36-46).

19:20 house of Joseph. A reference to Ephraim, the descendant of Joseph, a large tribe of Israel which was representative of the 10 northern tribes. Here, even Shimei's tribe Benjamin was included.

over Israel?" 23 Therefore [d]the king said to
Shimei, "You shall not die." And the king
swore to him.

David and Mephibosheth Meet

24 Now [e]Mephibosheth the son of Saul
came down to meet the king. And he had
not cared for his feet, nor trimmed his
mustache, nor washed his clothes, from
the day the king departed until the day he
returned in peace. 25 So it was, when he
had come to Jerusalem to meet the king,
that the king said to him, [f]"Why did you
not go with me, Mephibosheth?"

26 And he answered, "My lord, O king,
my servant deceived me. For your servant
said, 'I will saddle a donkey for myself,
that I may ride on it and go to the king,' because your servant *is* lame. 27 And [g]he has
slandered your servant to my lord the
king, [h]but my lord the king *is* like the angel
of God. Therefore do *what is* good in your
eyes. 28 For all my father's house were but
dead men before my lord the king. [i]Yet
you set your servant among those who eat
at your own table. Therefore what right
have I still to [6]cry out anymore to the
king?"

29 So the king said to him, "Why do you
speak anymore of your matters? I have
said, 'You and Ziba divide the land.' "

30 Then Mephibosheth said to the king,
"Rather, let him take it all, inasmuch as my
lord the king has come back in peace to his
own house."

David's Kindness to Barzillai

31 And [j]Barzillai the Gileadite came
down from Rogelim and went across the
Jordan with the king, to escort him across
the Jordan. 32 Now Barzillai was a very
aged man, eighty years old. And [k]he had
provided the king with supplies while he
stayed at Mahanaim, for he *was* a very rich
man. 33 And the king said to Barzillai,
"Come across with me, and I will provide
for you while you are with me in Jerusalem."

34 But Barzillai said to the king, "How
long have I to live, that I should go up with
the king to Jerusalem? 35 I *am* today [l]eighty
years old. Can I discern between the good
and bad? Can your servant taste what I eat
or what I drink? Can I hear any longer the
voice of singing men and singing women?
Why then should your servant be a further
burden to my lord the king? 36 Your servant will go a little way across the Jordan
with the king. And why should the king
repay me *with* such a reward? 37 Please let
your servant turn back again, that I may
die in my own city, near the grave of my father and mother. But here is your servant
[m]Chimham; let him cross over with my
lord the king, and do for him what seems
good to you."

38 And the king answered, "Chimham
shall cross over with me, and I will do for
him what seems good to you. Now whatever you request of me, I will do for you."
39 Then all the people went over the Jordan. And when the king had crossed over,
the king [n]kissed Barzillai and blessed him,
and he returned to his own place.

The Quarrel About the King

40 Now the king went on to Gilgal, and
[7]Chimham went on with him. And all the
people of Judah escorted the king, and also
half the people of Israel. 41 Just then all the
men of Israel came to the king, and said to
the king, "Why have our brethren, the men
of Judah, stolen you away and [o]brought
the king, his household, and all David's
men with him across the Jordan?"

42 So all the men of Judah answered the
men of Israel, "Because the king *is* [p]a close
relative of ours. Why then are you angry
over this matter? Have we ever eaten at the
king's *expense*? Or has he given us any
gift?"

43 And the men of Israel answered the

23 [d] 1 Kin. 2:8, 9, 37, 46
24 [e] 2 Sam. 9:6; 21:7
25 [f] 2 Sam. 16:17
27 [g] 2 Sam. 16:3, 4 [h] 2 Sam. 14:17, 20
28 [i] 2 Sam. 9:7-13 [6] *complain*
31 [j] 2 Sam. 17:27-29; 1 Kin. 2:7
32 [k] 2 Sam. 17:27-29
35 [l] Ps. 90:10
37 [m] 2 Sam. 19:40; Jer. 41:17
39 [n] Gen. 31:55; Ruth 1:14; 2 Sam. 14:33
40 [7] MT *Chimhan*
41 [o] 2 Sam. 19:15
42 [p] 2 Sam. 19:12

19:24-30 Mephibosheth. *See note on 4:4.* Mephibosheth also met David, exhibiting the traditional marks of mourning, and explained that he had not followed David into exile because he had been deceived by his servant Ziba (see 16:1-4). He came to David with great humility, generosity of spirit, and gratitude, recognizing all the good the king had done for him before the evil deception (v. 28).

19:29 divide the land. David had previously given the estate of Saul to Mephibosheth to be farmed under him by Ziba (9:9,10). Then when David was deceived, he gave it all to Ziba (16:4). Now David decided to divide Saul's estate between Ziba and Mephibosheth since he was either uncertain of the truth of Mephibosheth's story or who was guilty of what, and was too distracted to inquire fully into the matter. It was, in any case, a poor decision to divide the estate between the noble-hearted son of Jonathan and a lying deceiver. Mephibosheth was unselfish and suggested that his disloyal servant take it all—it was enough for him that David was back.

19:31-39 Barzillai. *See note on 17:27.* David offered to let Barzillai live in Jerusalem as his guest, but Barzillai preferred to live out his last years in his own house.

19:37 Chimham. Probably a son of Barzillai (see 1 Kin. 2:7). It is probable that David gave a part of his personal estate in Bethlehem to this man and his seed (see Jer. 41:17).

19:41 stolen you away. Because only the troops of Judah had escorted David as he crossed over the Jordan River, the 10 northern tribes complained to David that the men of Judah had "kidnapped" him from them.

19:42 a close relative. The men of Judah answered the men of Israel by stating that David was a member of their tribe. Nor had they taken advantage of their relationship to the king, as had some from the northern tribes.

men of Judah, and said, "We have [q]ten
shares in the king; therefore we also have
more *right* to David than you. Why then do
you despise us—were we not the first to
advise bringing back our king?"
Yet [r]the words of the men of Judah
were [8]fiercer than the words of the men of
Israel.

The Rebellion of Sheba

20 And there happened to be there a
[1]rebel, whose name *was* Sheba the
son of Bichri, a Benjamite. And he blew a
trumpet, and said:

[a]"We have no share in David,
Nor do we have inheritance in the
son of Jesse;
[b]Every man to his tents, O Israel!"

2 So every man of Israel deserted David,
and followed Sheba the son of Bichri. But
the [c]men of Judah, from the Jordan as far
as Jerusalem, remained loyal to their king.
3 Now David came to his house at Jerusalem. And the king took the ten women,
[d]his concubines whom he had left to keep
the house, and put them in seclusion and
supported them, but did not go in to them.
So they were shut up to the day of their
death, living in widowhood.
4 And the king said to Amasa, [e]"Assemble the men of Judah for me within three
days, and be present here yourself." 5 So

43 [q] 1 Kin. 11:30, 31 [r] Judg. 8:1; 12:1 [8] *harsher*

CHAPTER 20

1 [a] 2 Sam. 19:43; 1 Kin. 12:16 [b] 1 Sam. 13:2; 2 Sam. 18:17; 2 Chr. 10:16 [1] Lit. *man of Belial*
2 [c] 2 Sam. 19:14
3 [d] 2 Sam. 15:16; 16:21, 22
4 [e] 2 Sam. 17:25; 19:13
6 [f] 2 Sam. 21:17 [g] 2 Sam. 11:11; 1 Kin. 1:33
7 [h] 2 Sam. 8:18; 1 Kin. 1:38, 44 [i] 2 Sam. 15:18
9 [j] Matt. 26:49; Luke 22:47
10 [k] 2 Sam. 3:27; 1 Kin. 2:5 [l] 2 Sam. 2:23

Amasa went to assemble *the men of* Judah.
But he delayed longer than the set time
which David had appointed him. 6 And
David said to [f]Abishai, "Now Sheba the
son of Bichri will do us more harm than
Absalom. Take [g]your lord's servants and
pursue him, lest he find for himself fortified cities, and escape us." 7 So Joab's men,
with the [h]Cherethites, the Pelethites, and
[i]all the mighty men, went out after him.
And they went out of Jerusalem to pursue
Sheba the son of Bichri. 8 When they *were*
at the large stone which *is* in Gibeon,
Amasa came before them. Now Joab was
dressed in battle armor; on it was a belt
with a sword fastened in its sheath at his
hips; and as he was going forward, it fell
out. 9 Then Joab said to Amasa, "*Are* you in
health, my brother?" [j]And Joab took Amasa by the beard with his right hand to kiss
him. 10 But Amasa did not notice the
sword that *was* in Joab's hand. And [k]he
struck him with it [l]in the stomach, and his
entrails poured out on the ground; and he
did not *strike* him again. Thus he died.
Then Joab and Abishai his brother pursued Sheba the son of Bichri. 11 Meanwhile
one of Joab's men stood near Amasa, and
said, "Whoever favors Joab and whoever *is*
for David—follow Joab!" 12 But Amasa
wallowed in *his* blood in the middle of the
highway. And when the man saw that all
the people stood still, he moved Amasa
from the highway to the field and threw a

19:43 ten shares. The men of Israel replied to the men of Judah that they had a greater right to David, since there were 10 northern tribes in contrast to the one tribe of Judah. Contrast the "ten shares" here with the "no share" in 20:1. **you despise us.** The Israel-Judah hostility evidenced here led to the rebellion of Sheba (20:1-22) and eventually to the division of the united kingdom (1 Kin. 12:1-24).

20:1 rebel. See marginal reference and *note on 1 Sam. 2:12.* **Sheba.** Though nothing is known of this man, he must have been a person of considerable power and influence to raise so sudden and extensive a sedition. He belonged to Saul's tribe, where adherents of Saul's dynasty were still many, and he could see the disgust of the 10 tribes for Judah's presumption in the restoration. He sought to overturn David's authority in Israel. **no share...inheritance.** Sheba's declaration that the northern tribes had no part in David's realm was similar to words later used in 1 Kin. 12:16 when Israel seceded from the united kingdom under Jeroboam.

20:2 Israel deserted David. Once the 10 tribes withdrew, Judah was left alone to escort the king to Jerusalem. It seems that the disloyalty of the N continued as long as Sheba lived.

20:3 his concubines. When David returned to Jerusalem, he confined his concubines to a life of abstinence because of their sexual relations with Absalom (16:21,22).

20:4 Amasa. Amasa was Absalom's general (*see note on 17:25*), whom David promised would be commander of his army after Absalom's death (*see note on 19:13*). Amasa was installed publicly because David thought it would be seen favorably by the 10 tribes. He was told to assemble an army in 3 days to end the insurrection started by Sheba, but could not in such a brief time.

20:6 Abishai. *See note on 2:18.* When Amasa failed to follow David's orders, David did not reinstate Joab, his former general who had Absalom killed against David's orders (see 18:5-15), but appointed Joab's brother Abishai as commander of his forces. **your lord's servants.** Called "Joab's men" in v. 7. Abishai was to take the army of Joab to pursue the rebel leader. Joab went also, determined to take vengeance on his rival Amasa.

20:7 the Cherethites, the Pelethites. *See note on 1 Sam. 30:14.* **mighty men.** Those men are listed in 23:8-39.

20:8 Gibeon. *See note on 2:13.* **Amasa came before them.** Having collected some forces, he marched rapidly and came first to Gibeon, thus assuming the role of commander. It is possible that Joab purposely let the sword fall from its sheath as he approached Amasa, in order that stooping as if to pick up the accidentally fallen weapon, he might salute the new general with his sword already in hand, without generating any suspicion of his intent. He used this ploy to gain the position to stab the new commander, whom he considered as usurping his post.

20:9 my brother. *See note on 17:25.* **by the beard.** Joab, present with his men, seized Amasa by his beard with his right hand apparently to give the kiss of greeting. Instead, with his left hand, he thrust his sword into Amasa's stomach (cf. 3:27).

20:11 one of Joab's men. Joab was reinstated as commander of David's army by his troops. It is a striking illustration of Joab's influence over the army that he could murder the commander whom David had chosen, a killing right before their eyes, and they would follow him unanimously as their leader in pursuit of Sheba.

garment over him, when he saw that
everyone who came upon him halted.
13 When he was removed from the highway, all the people went on after Joab to
pursue Sheba the son of Bichri.
14 And he went through all the tribes of
Israel to [m]Abel and Beth Maachah and all
the Berites. So they were gathered together and also went after [2]*Sheba.* 15 Then they
came and besieged him in Abel of Beth
Maachah; and they [n]cast up a siege
mound against the city, and it stood by
the rampart. And all the people who *were*
with Joab battered the wall to throw it
down.
16 Then a wise woman cried out from
the city, "Hear, hear! Please say to Joab,
'Come nearby, that I may speak with
you.' " 17 When he had come near to her,
the woman said, "*Are* you Joab?"
He answered, "I *am.*"
Then she said to him, "Hear the words
of your maidservant."
And he answered, "I am listening."
18 So she spoke, saying, "They used to
talk in former times, saying, 'They shall
surely seek *guidance* at Abel,' and so they
would end *disputes.* 19 I *am among the*
peaceable *and* faithful in Israel. You seek to
destroy a city and a mother in Israel. Why
would you swallow up [o]the inheritance of
the LORD?"
20 And Joab answered and said, "Far be
it, far be it from me, that I should swallow
up or destroy! 21 That *is* not so. But a man
from the mountains of Ephraim, Sheba
the son of Bichri by name, has raised his
hand against the king, against David. Deliver him only, and I will depart from the
city."
So the woman said to Joab, "Watch, his
head will be thrown to you over the
wall." 22 Then the woman [p]in her wisdom
went to all the people. And they cut off
the head of Sheba the son of Bichri, and
threw *it* out to Joab. Then he blew a trumpet, and they withdrew from the city,
every man to his tent. So Joab returned to
the king at Jerusalem.

David's Government Officers

23 And [q]Joab *was* over all the army of Israel; Benaiah the son of Jehoiada *was* over
the Cherethites and the Pelethites; 24 Adoram *was* [r]in charge of revenue; [s]Jehosha-
phat the son of Ahilud *was* recorder;
25 Sheva *was* scribe; [t]Zadok and Abiathar
were the priests; 26 [u]and Ira the Jairite was
[3]a chief minister under David.

David Avenges the Gibeonites

21 Now there was a famine in the days
of David for three years, year after
year; and David [a]inquired of the LORD.
And the LORD answered, "*It is* because of
Saul and *his* [1]bloodthirsty house, because
he killed the Gibeonites." 2 So the king
called the Gibeonites and spoke to them.
Now the Gibeonites *were* not of the children of Israel, but [b]of the remnant of the

14 [m] 1 Kin. 15:20; 2 Kin. 15:29; 2 Chr. 16:4 [2] Lit. *him*
15 [n] 2 Kin. 19:32; Ezek. 4:2
19 [o] 1 Sam. 26:19; 2 Sam. 14:16; 21:3
22 [p] 2 Sam. 20:16; [Eccl. 9:13-16]
23 [q] 2 Sam. 8:16-18; 1 Kin. 4:3-6
24 [r] 1 Kin. 4:6 [s] 2 Sam. 8:16; 1 Kin. 4:3
25 [t] 2 Sam. 8:17; 1 Kin. 4:4
26 [u] 2 Sam. 8:18 [3] Or *David's priest*

CHAPTER 21

1 [a] Num. 27:21; 2 Sam. 5:19 [1] Lit. *house of bloodshed*
2 [b] Josh. 9:3, 15-20

20:14 Abel and Beth Maachah. I.e., Abel Beth-Maacha. About 25 mi. N of the Sea of Galilee, 4 mi. W of the city of Dan.

20:16-19 This woman (probably a prominent judge in the city) was making an appeal based on the laws of warfare in Deut. 20:10 that required the assaulting army to offer peace before making war. She pleaded for Joab to ask the city if they wanted peace and thus avert war (v. 18).

20:19 a mother in Israel. This is a reference to a specially honored city or a recognized capital of the region. **the inheritance of the LORD.** This refers to the land of Israel (see 1 Sam. 10:1).

20:20,21 The ruthless general was a patriot at heart, who on taking the leader of the insurrection, was ready to end further bloodshed. The woman eagerly responded with the promise of Sheba's head.

20:21 mountains of Ephraim. A large, partially forested plateau that extended into the tribal territory of Benjamin from the N.

20:22 David could not get rid of Joab, though he hated him. He had to ignore the murder of Amasa and recognize Joab as army commander.

20:23-26 Cf. a similar list in 8:15-18.

20:24 Adoram. Rendered "Adoniram" in 1 Kin. 4:6,28. He was in charge of the "revenue," a term used to describe the hard labor imposed on subjugated peoples (Ex. 1:11; Josh. 16:10; Judg. 1:28). Adoram oversaw the forced labor on such projects as the building of highways, temples, and houses.

20:25 Sheva. He replaced Seraiah (8:17) as David's secretary.

20:26 Ira. He was David's royal adviser.

21:1–24:25 This is the final division of First Samuel. Like the book of Judges (Judg. 17:1–21:25), it concludes with this epilogue that contains material, not necessarily chronological, that further describes David's reign. There is a striking literary arrangement of the sections in this division of the book. The first and last sections (21:1-14; 24:1-25) are narratives that describe two occurrences of the Lord's anger against Israel. The second and fifth sections (21:15-22; 23:8-39) are accounts of David's warriors. The third and fourth sections (22:1-51; 23:1-7) record two of David's songs.

21:1-14 This event occurred after the display of David's kindness to Mephibosheth (v. 7; cf. 9:1-13) and before Shimei's cursing of David (cf. 16:7,8).

21:1 a famine. When Israel experienced 3 years of famine, David recognized it as divine discipline (cf. Deut. 28:47,48) and sought God for the reason.

21:1,2 Saul and *his* bloodthirsty house. By divine revelation David learned that the famine was a result of sin committed by Saul; namely that he had slain the Gibeonites. There is no further reference to this event. Saul was probably trying to do as God commanded and rid the land of the remnant of heathen in order that Israel might prosper (v. 2). But in his zeal he had committed a serious sin; he had broken a covenant that had been made 400 years before between Joshua and the Gibeonites, who were in the land when Israel took possession of it. They deceived Joshua into making the covenant, but it was, nevertheless, a covenant (see Josh. 9:3-27). Covenant keeping was no small matter to God (see Josh. 9:20).

Amorites; the children of Israel had sworn
protection to them, but Saul had sought to
kill them [c]in his zeal for the children of Israel and Judah.
3 Therefore David said to the Gibeonites,
"What shall I do for you? And with what
shall I make atonement, that you may bless
[d]the inheritance of the LORD?"
4 And the Gibeonites said to him, "We
will have no silver or gold from Saul or
from his house, nor shall you kill any man
in Israel for us."
So he said, "Whatever you say, I will do
for you."
5 Then they answered the king, "As for
the man who consumed us and plotted
against us, *that* we should be destroyed
from remaining in any of the territories of
Israel, **6** let seven men of his descendants
be delivered [e]to us, and we will hang them
before the LORD [f]in Gibeah of Saul, [g]*whom*
the LORD chose."
And the king said, "I will give *them*."
7 But the king spared [h]Mephibosheth
the son of Jonathan, the son of Saul, because of [i]the LORD's oath that *was* between
them, between David and Jonathan the son
of Saul. **8** So the king took Armoni and Mephibosheth, the two sons of [j]Rizpah the
daughter of Aiah, whom she bore to Saul,
and the five sons of [2]Michal the daughter
of Saul, whom she [3]brought up for Adriel
the son of Barzillai the Meholathite; **9** and
he delivered them into the hands of the
Gibeonites, and they hanged them on the
hill [k]before the LORD. So they fell, *all* seven
together, and were put to death in the days
of harvest, in the first *days*, in the beginning of barley harvest.
10 Now [l]Rizpah the daughter of Aiah
took sackcloth and spread it for herself on
the rock, [m]from the beginning of harvest
until the late rains poured on them from
heaven. And she did not allow the birds of
the air to rest on them by day nor the
beasts of the field by night.
11 And David was told what Rizpah the
daughter of Aiah, the concubine of Saul,
had done. **12** Then David went and took
the bones of Saul, and the bones of Jonathan his son, from the men of [n]Jabesh Gilead who had stolen them from the street of
[4]Beth Shan, where the [o]Philistines had
hung them up, after the Philistines had
struck down Saul in Gilboa. **13** So he
brought up the bones of Saul and the
bones of Jonathan his son from there; and
they gathered the bones of those who had
been hanged. **14** They buried the bones of
Saul and Jonathan his son in the country of
Benjamin in [p]Zelah, in the tomb of Kish his
father. So they performed all that the king
commanded. And after that [q]God heeded
the prayer for the land.

Philistine Giants Destroyed

15 When the Philistines were at war
again with Israel, David and his servants
with him went down and fought against
the Philistines; and David grew faint.
16 Then Ishbi-Benob, who *was* one of the
sons of [5]the [r]giant, the weight of whose

2 [c][Ex. 34:11-16]
3 [d]1 Sam. 26:19; 2 Sam. 20:19
6 [e]Num. 25:4 [f]1 Sam. 10:26 [g]1 Sam. 10:24; [Hos. 13:11]
7 [h]2 Sam. 4:4; 9:10 [i]1 Sam. 18:3; 20:12-17; 23:18; 2 Sam. 9:1-7
8 [j]2 Sam. 3:7 [2]*Merab,* 1 Sam. 18:19; 25:44; 2 Sam. 3:14; 6:23 [3]Lit. *bore to Adriel*
9 [k]2 Sam. 6:17
10 [l]2 Sam. 3:7; 21:8 [m]Deut. 21:23
12 [n]1 Sam. 31:11-13 [o]1 Sam. 31:8 [4]*Beth Shean,* Josh. 17:11
14 [p]Josh. 18:28 [q]Josh. 7:26; 2 Sam. 24:25
16 [r]Num. 13:22, 28; Josh. 15:14; 2 Sam. 21:18-22 [5]Or *Rapha*

21:2 Amorites. One of the names sometimes used to designate all the pre-Israelite inhabitants of Canaan (Gen. 15:16; Josh. 24:18; Judg. 6:10). More precisely, the Gibeonites were called Hivites (Josh. 9:7; 11:19).

21:3 the inheritance of the LORD. *See note on 20:19.*

21:6 seven...descendants. "Seven" symbolized completeness, not necessarily the number of Gibeonites slain by Saul. "Descendants" could be either sons or grandsons. **Gibeah of Saul.** *See note on 1 Sam. 11:4.*

21:7 the LORD's oath...between David and Jonathan. Because Mephibosheth was the son of Jonathan, he was spared in accordance with the covenant between David and Jonathan (1 Sam. 20:14,15) and also between David and Saul (*see note on 1 Sam. 24:22*).

21:8 Mephibosheth. A son of Saul, different from the son of Jonathan with the same name. **Rizpah.** Saul's concubine (see 3:7). **Michal.** Since Michal was childless (6:23), Merab was the actual birth mother of these 5 sons. She was the wife of Adriel (1 Sam. 18:19). Michal must have adopted them and brought them up under her care. **Barzillai the Meholathite.** A different man than Barzillai the Gileadite (17:27; 19:31).

21:9 before the LORD. These pagans were not bound by the law of Deut. 21:22,23, which forbade leaving a dead body hanging over night. Their intention was to let the bodies hang until God signaled He was satisfied and sent rain to end the famine. Such a heathen practice, designed to propitiate their gods, was a superstition of these Gibeonites. God, in His providence, allowed this memorable retaliation as a lesson about keeping covenants and promises. **the beginning of barley harvest.** April (see Ruth 1:22).

21:10 sackcloth...spread. Rizpah erected a tent nearby to keep watch over the bodies, to scare away birds and beasts. It was considered a disgrace for the bodies of the slain to become food for the birds and beasts (cf. Deut. 28:26; 1 Sam. 17:44,46; Rev. 19:17,18). **the late rains.** An unseasonably late spring or early summer shower. Possibly, the rain that ended the drought.

21:11-14 Finally, after the rain had come, David, encouraged by the example of the woman's devotion to her dead family members, ordered the remains of Saul and Jonathan transferred from their obscure grave in Jabesh Gilead (cf. 1 Sam. 31:11,12), along with the 7 sons' bones, to the honorable family grave in Zelah (cf. Josh. 18:28; 1 Sam. 10:2, "Zelzah"). This location is unknown.

21:14 God heeded the prayer. The famine ended and God restored the land to prosperity.

21:15-22 This section describes the defeat of 4 Philistine giants at the hands of David and his men. Though these events cannot be located chronologically with any certainty, the narratives of victory provide a fitting preface to David's song of praise, which magnifies God's deliverance (22:1-51). See 1 Chr. 20:4-8.

21:16 the giant. The Heb. term used in vv. 16,18,20,22 is "rapha" (see side reference). This was not the name of an individual, but a term used collectively for the "Rephaim" who inhabited the land of Canaan and were noted for their inordinate size (cf. Gen. 15:19-21; Num. 13:33; Deut. 2:11; 3:11,13). The term "Rephaim" was used of the

bronze spear *was* three hundred *shekels,*
who was bearing a new *sword,* thought he
could kill David. 17 But [s]Abishai the son of
Zeruiah came to his aid, and struck the
Philistine and killed him. Then the men of
David swore to him, saying, [t]"You shall go
out no more with us to battle, lest you
quench the [u]lamp of Israel."
18 [v]Now it happened afterward that
there was again a battle with the Philistines at Gob. Then [w]Sibbechai the
Hushathite killed [6]Saph, who *was* one of
the sons of [7]the giant. 19 Again there was
war at Gob with the Philistines, where [x]El-
hanan the son of [8]Jaare-Oregim the Bethlehemite killed [y]*the brother of* Goliath the Gittite, the shaft of whose spear *was* like a
weaver's beam.
20 Yet again [z]there was war at Gath,
where there was a man of *great* stature,
who had six fingers on each hand and six
toes on each foot, twenty-four in number;
and he also was born to [9]the giant. 21 So
when he [a]defied Israel, Jonathan the son of
[1]Shimea, David's brother, killed him.
22 [b]These four were born to [2]the giant in
Gath, and fell by the hand of David and by
the hand of his servants.

17 [s] 2 Sam. 20:6-10 [t] 2 Sam. 18:3 [u] 2 Sam. 22:29; 1 Kin. 11:36
18 [v] 1 Chr. 20:4-8 [w] 1 Chr. 11:29; 27:11 [6] *Sippai,* 1 Chr. 20:4 [7] Or *Rapha*
19 [x] 2 Sam. 23:24 [y] 1 Sam. 17:4; 1 Chr. 20:5 [8] *Jair,* 1 Chr. 20:5
20 [z] 1 Chr. 20:6 [9] Or *Rapha*
21 [a] 1 Sam. 17:10 [1] *Shammah,* 1 Sam. 16:9 and elsewhere
22 [b] 1 Chr. 20:8 [2] Or *Rapha*

CHAPTER 22
1 [a] Ex. 15:1; Deut. 31:30; Judg. 5:1 [b] Ps. 18:title; 34:19
2 [c] Ps. 18 [d] Deut. 32:4; 1 Sam. 2:2 [e] Ps. 91:2
3 [f] Ps. 7:1; Heb. 2:13 [g] Gen. 15:1; Deut. 33:29; Ps. 84:11 [h] Luke 1:69 [i] Prov. 18:10 [j] Ps. 9:9; 46:1, 7, 11; Jer. 16:19 [1] Strength
5 [2] Or *overwhelmed*
6 [k] Ps. 116:3
7 [l] Ps. 116:4; 120:1

Praise for God's Deliverance

22 Then David [a]spoke to the LORD the
words of this song, on the day when
the LORD had [b]delivered him from the
hand of all his enemies, and from the hand
of Saul. 2 And he [c]said:

[d]"The LORD *is* my rock and my
[e]fortress and my deliverer;
3 The God of my strength, [f]in whom
I will trust;
My [g]shield and the [h]horn[1] of my
salvation,
My [i]stronghold and my [j]refuge;
My Savior, You save me from
violence.
4 I will call upon the LORD, *who is
worthy* to be praised;
So shall I be saved from my enemies.

5 "When the waves of death
surrounded me,
The floods of ungodliness [2]made
me afraid.
6 The [k]sorrows of Sheol surrounded
me;
The snares of death confronted me.
7 In my distress [l]I called upon the
LORD,

people called the "Anakim" (Deut. 2:10,11,20,21), distinguished for their size and strength. According to Josh. 11:21,22 the "Anakim" were driven from the hill country of Israel and Judah, but remained in the Philistine cities of Gaza, Gath, and Ashdod. Though the Philistines had succumbed to the power of Israel's army, the appearance of some great champion revived their courage and invited their hope for victory against the Israelite invaders. **three hundred *shekels.*** Approximately 7.5 lbs. **a new *sword.*** Lit. "a new thing." The weapon was not specified.

21:17 Abishai. *See note on 2:18.* **lamp of Israel.** David, who with God's help brought the light of prosperity and well being to the whole land of Israel, was the symbol of Israel's hope and promise of security. Continued blessing resided in David and his house.

21:18 Gob. Near Gezer (cf. 1 Chr. 20:4), about 22 mi. W of Jerusalem.

21:19 Elhanan…killed *the brother of* Goliath. The minor scribal omission of "the brother of" (in the Heb.) belongs in this verse, based on 1 Chr. 20:5 which includes them, and because clearly the Scripture says that David killed Goliath as recorded in 1 Sam. 17:50. The NKJV gives the most likely solution, that there has been a scribal error in the text which should read, "Elhanan…killed *the brother of* Goliath." A second possible solution is that Elhanan and David may be different names for the same person, just as Solomon had another name (cf. 12:24,25). A third solution is, perhaps that there were two giants named Goliath.

21:20 Gath. About 12 mi. S of Geza and 26 mi. SW of Jerusalem.

21:21 Jonathan. David's nephew, the son of Shimeah, also called Shammah in 1 Sam. 16:9, different from the son of Saul.

22:1-51 David's song of praise here is almost identical to Ps. 18. This song also has many verbal links to Hannah's prayer (*see note on 1 Sam. 2:1-10*) and together with it forms the framework for the books of Samuel. This song focuses on the Lord's deliverance of David from all his enemies, in response to which David praised the Lord, his deliverer (vv. 2-4). The major part of the song (vv. 5-46) states the reason for this praise of the Lord. David first describes how the Lord had delivered him from his enemies (vv. 5-20), then declares why the Lord had delivered him from his enemies (vv. 21-28), then states the extent of the Lord's deliverance from his enemies (vv. 29-46). The song concludes with David's resolve to praise his delivering Lord, even among the Gentiles (vv. 47-51). *See notes on Ps. 18:1-50* for a more detailed explanation.

22:1 all his enemies. Cf. 7:1,9,11. David composed this song toward the end of his life when the Lord had given him a settled kingdom and the promise of the Messianic seed embodied in the Davidic Covenant.

22:2-4 This introduction contains the sum and substance of the whole psalm, as David extols God as his defense, refuge, and deliverer in the many experiences of his agitated life.

22:2 rock. *See notes on 1 Sam. 2:2; Deut. 32:4.* **fortress.** This term had previously been used to describe the citadel of Jerusalem (5:9) and the cave of Adullam (1 Sam. 22:1).

22:3 shield. See Gen. 15:1; Deut. 33:29. **horn.** *See note on 1 Sam. 2:1.* **stronghold.** A secure, lofty retreat that the enemy finds inaccessible. As such, the Lord is the refuge of His chosen one, secure from all hostile attacks.

22:5-7 David described how he cried to the Lord in the midst of his distress.

22:5,6 death. Pictured as violent floods of water like waves ready to break over him and traps set by a hunter to snare him, David faced the reality of imminent death in his personal experience, most frequently when pursued by Saul, but also in Absalom's conspiracy and in certain wars (see 21:16).

22:7 distress. The particular trouble David was referring to was the potential of his imminent death (vv. 5,6). **His temple.** God's heavenly dwelling place (cf. Ps. 11:4; 29:9).

And cried out to my God;
He [m]heard my voice from His
temple,
And my cry *entered* His ears.

8 "Then [n]the earth shook and
trembled;
[o]The foundations of [3]heaven
quaked and were shaken,
Because He was angry.
9 Smoke went up from His nostrils,
And devouring [p]fire from His
mouth;
Coals were kindled by it.
10 He [q]bowed the heavens also, and
came down
With [r]darkness under His feet.
11 He rode upon a cherub, and flew;
And He [4]was seen [s]upon the
wings of the wind.
12 He made [t]darkness canopies
around Him,
Dark waters *and* thick clouds of the
skies.
13 From the brightness before Him
Coals of fire were kindled.

14 "The LORD [u]thundered from heaven,
And the Most High uttered His
voice.
15 He sent out [v]arrows and scattered
them;
Lightning bolts, and He
vanquished them.
16 Then the channels of the sea [w]were
seen,
The foundations of the world were
uncovered,
At the [x]rebuke of the LORD,
At the blast of the breath of His
nostrils.

17 "He[y] sent from above, He took me,
He drew me out of many waters.
18 He delivered me from my strong
enemy,
From those who hated me;
For they were too strong for me.

19 They confronted me in the day of
my calamity,
But the LORD was my [z]support.
20 [a]He also brought me out into a
broad place;
He delivered me because He
[b]delighted in me.

21 "The[c] LORD rewarded me according
to my righteousness;
According to the [d]cleanness of my
hands
He has recompensed me.
22 For I have [e]kept the ways of the
LORD,
And have not wickedly departed
from my God.
23 For all His [f]judgments *were* before
me;
And *as for* His statutes, I did not
depart from them.
24 I was also [g]blameless before Him,
And I kept myself from my
iniquity.
25 Therefore [h]the LORD has
[5]recompensed me according
to my righteousness,
According to [6]my cleanness in His
eyes.

26 "With [i]the merciful You will show
Yourself merciful;
With a blameless man You will
show Yourself blameless;
27 With the pure You will show
Yourself pure;
And [j]with the devious You will
show Yourself shrewd.
28 You will save the [k]humble[7] people;
But Your eyes *are* on [l]the haughty,
that You may bring *them*
down.

29 "For You *are* my [m]lamp, O LORD;
The LORD shall enlighten my
darkness.
30 For by You I can run against a
troop;
By my God I can leap over a [n]wall.

7 [m] Ex. 3:7; Ps. 34:6, 15
8 [n] Judg. 5:4; Ps. 77:18; 97:4 [o] Job 26:11 [3] So with MT, LXX, Tg.; Syr., Vg. *hills* (cf. Ps. 18:7)
9 [p] Deut. 32:22; Ps. 97:3, 4; Heb. 12:29
10 [q] Ex. 19:16-20; Is. 64:1 [r] Ex. 20:21
11 [s] Ps. 104:3 [4] So with MT, LXX; many Heb. mss., Syr., Vg. *flew* (cf. Ps. 18:10); Tg. *spoke with power*
12 [t] Job 36:29; Ps. 97:2
14 [u] 1 Sam. 2:10; Job 37:2-5; Ps. 29:3
15 [v] Deut. 32:23; Josh. 10:10; 1 Sam. 7:10; Ps. 7:13
16 [w] Nah. 1:4 [x] Ex. 15:8
17 [y] Ps. 144:7; Is. 43:2
19 [z] Is. 10:20
20 [a] Ps. 31:8; 118:5 [b] 2 Sam. 15:26
21 [c] 1 Sam. 26:23; [Ps. 7:8] [d] [Job 17:9]; Ps. 24:4
22 [e] Gen. 18:19; 2 Chr. 34:33; Ps. 119:3
23 [f] [Deut. 6:6-9; 7:12]; Ps. 119:30, 102
24 [g] Gen. 6:9; 7:1; Job 1:1; [Eph. 1:4; Col. 1:21, 22]
25 [h] 2 Sam. 22:21 [5] *rewarded* [6] LXX, Syr., Vg. *the cleanness of my hands in His sight* (cf. Ps. 18:24); Tg. *my cleanness before His word*
26 [i] [Matt. 5:7]
27 [j] [Lev. 26:23, 24; Rom. 1:28]
28 [k] Ps. 72:12 [l] Job 40:11 [7] *afflicted*
29 [m] Ps. 119:105; 132:17
30 [n] 2 Sam. 5:6-8

22:8-16 In reaffirming the great majesty of God, David described His coming in power from heaven to earth (cf. Ex. 19:16-20; Ezek. 1:4-28; Hab. 3:3-15).

22:14 The LORD thundered. *See note on 1 Sam. 7:10.*

22:17-20 In personalizing what he just said in vv. 8-16, David explained how God reached down from heaven to save him on the earth.

22:20 He delighted in me. This expression that the Lord was "pleased" with David (cf. 15:26) provided a transition to vv. 21-28, where David described the basis of God's saving deliverance.

22:21-25 David was not claiming to be righteous or sinless in any absolute sense. Rather, David believed God, was considered righteous by faith, and desired to please the Lord and be obedient to His commands. Thus he was blameless when compared with his enemies.

22:26-28 David stated the basic principles that the Lord follows in delivering or judging people.

22:28 humble...haughty. For the idea that the Lord saves the humble, but brings low the proud, see also 1 Sam. 2:4-7.

22:29-46 Empowered by God (vv. 29-37), David was able to gain total victory over his enemies (vv. 38-43), both in Israel and throughout the nations (vv. 44-46).

22:29 my lamp. David as the "lamp" of Israel (*see note on 21:17*) reflected the light of the glory of God, who was the "Lamp" of David himself.

31 *As for* God, [o]His way *is* perfect;
[p]The word of the LORD *is* proven;
He *is* a shield to all who trust in
Him.

32 "For [q]who *is* God, except the LORD?
And who *is* a rock, except our God?
33 [8]God *is* my [r]strength *and* power,
And He [s]makes [9]my way [t]perfect.
34 He makes [1]my feet [u]like the *feet* of
deer,
And [v]sets me on my high places.
35 He teaches my hands [2]to make war,
So that my arms can bend a bow of
bronze.

36 "You have also given me the shield
of Your salvation;
Your gentleness has made me
great.
37 You [w]enlarged my path under me;
So my feet did not slip.

38 "I have pursued my enemies and
destroyed them;
Neither did I turn back again till
they were destroyed.
39 And I have destroyed them and
wounded them,
So that they could not rise;
They have fallen [x]under my feet.
40 For You have [y]armed me with
strength for the battle;
You have [3]subdued under me
[z]those who rose against me.
41 You have also [4]given me the
[a]necks of my enemies,
So that I destroyed those who
hated me.
42 They looked, but *there was* none to
save;
Even [b]to the LORD, but He did not
answer them.
43 Then I beat them as fine [c]as the
dust of the earth;
I trod them [d]like dirt in the streets,
And I [5]spread them out.

44 "You[e] have also delivered me from
the [6]strivings of my people;
You have kept me as the [f]head of
the nations.
[g]A people I have not known shall
serve me.
45 The foreigners submit to me;
As soon as they hear, they obey me.
46 The foreigners fade away,
And [7]come frightened [h]from their
hideouts.

47 "The LORD lives!
Blessed *be* my Rock!
Let God be exalted,
The [i]Rock of my salvation!
48 *It is* God who avenges me,
And [j]subdues the peoples under
me;
49 He delivers me from my enemies.
You also lift me up above those
who rise against me;
You have delivered me from the
[k]violent man.
50 Therefore I will give thanks to You,
O LORD, among [l]the Gentiles,
And sing praises to Your [m]name.

51 "*He*[n] *is* the tower of salvation to His
king,
And shows mercy to His [o]anointed,
To David and [p]his descendants
forevermore."

David's Last Words

23 Now these *are* the last words of
David.

Thus says David the son of Jesse;
Thus says [a]the man raised up on
high,
[b]The anointed of the God of Jacob,
And the sweet psalmist of Israel:

2 "The[c] Spirit of the LORD spoke by
me,
And His word *was* on my tongue.
3 The God of Israel said,
[d]The Rock of Israel spoke to me:
'He who rules over men *must be*
just,
Ruling [e]in the fear of God.

31 [o] [Deut. 32:4]; Dan. 4:37; [Matt. 5:48] [p] Ps. 12:6; [Prov. 30:5] **32** [q] Is. 45:5, 6 **33** [r] Ps. 27:1 [s] [Heb. 13:21] [t] Ps. 101:2, 6 [8] DSS, LXX, Syr., Vg. *It is God who arms me with strength* (cf. Ps. 18:32); Tg. *It is God who sustains me with strength* [9] So with Qr., LXX, Syr., Tg., Vg. (cf. Ps. 18:32); Kt. *His* **34** [u] 2 Sam. 2:18; Hab. 3:19 [v] Is. 33:16 [1] So with Qr., LXX, Syr., Tg., Vg. (cf. Ps. 18:33); Kt. *His* **35** [2] Lit. *for the war* **37** [w] 2 Sam. 22:20; Prov. 4:12 **39** [x] Mal. 4:3 **40** [y] [Ps. 18:32] [z] [Ps. 44:5] [3] Lit. *caused to bow down* **41** [a] Gen. 49:8; Josh. 10:24 [4] *given me victory over* **42** [b] 1 Sam. 28:6; Prov. 1:28; Is. 1:15 **43** [c] 2 Kin. 13:7; Ps. 18:42 [d] Is. 10:6 [5] *scattered* **44** [e] 2 Sam. 3:1 [6] *contentions*

[f] Deut. 28:13 [g] [Is. 55:5] **46** [h] 1 Sam. 14:11; [Mic. 7:17] [7] So with LXX, Tg., Vg. (cf. Ps. 18:45); MT *gird themselves* **47** [i] [2 Sam. 22:3]; Ps. 89:26 **48** [j] 1 Sam. 24:12; Ps. 144:2 **49** [k] Ps. 140:1, 4, 11 **50** [l] 2 Sam. 8:1-14 [m] Ps. 57:7; Rom. 15:9 **51** [n] Ps. 144:10 [o] Ps. 89:20 [p] 2 Sam. 7:12-16; Ps. 89:29

CHAPTER 23

1 [a] 2 Sam. 7:8, 9; Ps. 78:70, 71 [b] 1 Sam. 16:12, 13; Ps. 89:20 **2** [c] Matt. 22:43; [2 Pet. 1:21] **3** [d] [Deut. 32:4] [e] Ex. 18:21; [Is. 11:1-5]

22:50 Paul quotes this in Rom. 15:9.

22:51 His king…His anointed. These terms are singular and thus do not seem to refer to David and his descendants. Rather they refer to the promised "seed," the Messiah of 7:12. The deliverance and ultimate triumph of David foreshadow that of the coming Messiah. At the end of his life, David looked back in faith at God's promises and forward in hope to their fulfillment in the coming of a future "king," the "anointed one" (*see note on 1 Sam. 2:10*).

23:1-7 last words. This is David's final literary legacy to Israel, not his final oral speech (see 1 Kin. 2:1-10).

23:1 says. "Declares as an oracle" (cf. Num. 24:3,15; 1 Sam. 2:30; Prov. 30:1). David realized that the psalms he wrote, as directed by the Holy Spirit, were the very Word of God.

23:2 Spirit. God's Holy Spirit is the divine instrument of revelation and inspiration (cf. Zech. 7:12; 2 Tim. 3:16,17; 2 Pet. 1:19-21).

23:3,4 He who rules. These words begin the record of direct speech from God, whose ideal king must exercise His authority with justice, in complete submission to divine sovereignty. Such a king is like the helpful rays of sun at dawn and the life-giving showers which nourish the earth. This ideal king was identified in the OT as the coming Messiah (cf. Is. 9:6,7).

4 And [f]he *shall be* like the light of the
morning *when* the sun rises,
A morning without clouds,
Like the tender grass *springing* out
of the earth,
By clear shining after rain.'

5 "Although my house *is* not so with
God,
[g]Yet He has made with me an
everlasting covenant,
Ordered in all *things* and secure.
For *this is* all my salvation and all
my desire;
Will He not make *it* increase?
6 But *the sons* of rebellion *shall* all *be*
as thorns thrust away,
Because they cannot be taken with
hands.
7 But the man *who* touches them
Must be [1]armed with iron and the
shaft of a spear,
And they shall be utterly burned
with fire in *their* place."

David's Mighty Men

8 These *are* the names of the mighty men
whom David had: [2]Josheb-Basshebeth the
Tachmonite, chief among [3]the captains. He
was called Adino the Eznite, because he
had killed eight hundred men at one time.
9 And after him *was* [h]Eleazar the son of
[4]Dodo, the Ahohite, *one* of the three
mighty men with David when they defied
the Philistines *who* were gathered there for
battle, and the men of Israel had retreated.
10 He arose and attacked the Philistines
until his hand was [i]weary, and his hand
stuck to the sword. The LORD brought
about a great victory that day; and the people returned after him only to [j]plunder.
11 And after him *was* [k]Shammah the son of
Agee the Hararite. [l]The Philistines had
gathered together into a troop where there
was a piece of ground full of lentils. So the
people fled from the Philistines. 12 But he
stationed himself in the middle of the field,
defended it, and killed the Philistines. So
the LORD brought about a great victory.
13 Then [m]three of the thirty chief men
went down at harvest time and came to
David at [n]the cave of Adullam. And the
troop of Philistines encamped in [o]the Valley of Rephaim. 14 David *was* then in [p]the
stronghold, and the garrison of the Philistines *was* then *in* Bethlehem. 15 And David said with longing, "Oh, that someone
would give me a drink of the water from
the well of Bethlehem, which *is* by the
gate!" 16 So the three mighty men broke
through the camp of the Philistines, drew
water from the well of Bethlehem that *was*
by the gate, and took it and brought *it* to
David. Nevertheless he would not drink it,
but poured it out to the LORD. 17 And he
said, "Far be it from me, O LORD, that I
should do this! Is *this not* [q]the blood of the
men who went in *jeopardy of* their lives?"
Therefore he would not drink it.

These things were done by the three
mighty men.

18 Now [r]Abishai the brother of Joab, the
son of Zeruiah, was chief of [5]*another* three.
He lifted his spear against three hundred
men, killed *them,* and won a name among
these three. 19 Was he not the most honored
of three? Therefore he became their captain. However, he did not attain to the *first*
three.

20 Benaiah *was* the son of Jehoiada, the
son of a valiant man from [s]Kabzeel, [6]who
had done many deeds. [t]He had killed two

4 [f]Ps. 89:36; Is. 60:1
5 [g]2 Sam. 7:12; Ps. 89:29; Is. 55:3
7 [1]Lit. *filled*
8 [2]Lit. *One Who Sits in the Seat* (1 Chr. 11:11) [3]So with MT, Tg.; LXX, Vg. *the three*
9 [h]1 Chr. 11:12; 27:4 [4]*Dodai,* 1 Chr. 27:4
10 [i]Judg. 8:4 [j]1 Sam. 30:24, 25
11 [k]1 Chr. 11:27 [l]1 Chr. 11:13, 14
13 [m]1 Chr. 11:15 [n]1 Sam. 22:1 [o]2 Sam. 5:18
14 [p]1 Sam. 22:4, 5
17 [q][Lev. 17:10]
18 [r]2 Sam. 21:17; 1 Chr. 11:20 [5]So with MT, LXX, Vg.; some Heb. mss., Syr. *thirty;* Tg. *the mighty men*
20 [s]Josh. 15:21 [t]Ex. 15:15 [6]Lit. *great of acts*

23:5 my house *is* not so with God. In response to God's standard for His ideal king, David confessed that his house had not always ruled over God's people in righteousness and in the fear of God, and thus were not the fulfillment of 7:12-16. Further, none of the kings of David's line (according to 1 and 2 Kings) met God's standard of righteous obedience. **everlasting covenant.** The promise given by the Lord to David recorded in 7:12-16 is here referred to as a "covenant," a binding agreement from the Lord that He will fulfill. In spite of the fact that David and his own household had failed (chaps. 9–20), David rightly believed that the Lord would not fail, but would be faithful to His promise of hope for the future in the seed of David, the Eternal King, the anointed one (*see note on 7:12*), who would establish a kingdom of righteousness and peace forever.

23:6 *sons* of rebellion. Lit. "Belial" (*see note on 1 Sam. 2:12*). The wicked enemies of God will be cast aside in judgment when the Messiah, the fulfillment of the Davidic Covenant, establishes His rule upon the earth (cf. Is. 63:1-6).

23:8-39 This fifth inset recalls David's mighty men. See 1 Chr. 11:10-41.

23:8 the mighty men. David's bravest warriors and most outstanding soldiers are memorialized. This list appears in 1 Chr. 11:11-41, with slight variations. According to 1 Chr. 11:10, these men helped David to become king. The listing of these men is presented in 3 sets: first, "the three" (vv. 8-12); second, two more honored other than "the thirty," but not attaining to "the three" (vv. 18-23); third, "the thirty" which is actually 32 (vv. 24-39). This list is expanded by 16 names in 1 Chr. 11:41-47. **eight hundred.** Probably a textual error. 1 Chr. 11:11 has "three hundred," the likely number.

23:13-17 three of the thirty. Three of the soldiers mentioned in vv. 34-39.

23:13 cave of Adullam. *See note on 1 Sam. 22:1.* **Valley of Rephaim.** *See note on 5:18.*

23:14 stronghold. *See note on 1 Sam. 22:4.*

23:16 poured it out to the LORD. Because David's men brought him water from Bethlehem's well at the risk of their own lives, he considered it as "blood" and refused to drink it. Instead, he poured it out on the ground as a sacrifice to the Lord (cf. Gen. 35:14; Ex. 30:9; Lev. 23:13,18,37).

23:18 Abishai. *See note on 2:18.*

23:20 Benaiah. *See note on 8:18.*

lion-like heroes of Moab. He also had gone
down and killed a lion in the midst of a pit
on a snowy day. 21 And he killed an Egyptian, [7]a spectacular man. The Egyptian *had*
a spear in his hand; so he went down to
him with a staff, wrested the spear out of
the Egyptian's hand, and killed him with
his own spear. 22 These *things* Benaiah the
son of Jehoiada did, and won a name
among three mighty men. 23 He was more
honored than the thirty, but he did not attain to the *first* three. And David appointed
him [u]over his guard.
24 [v]Asahel the brother of Joab *was* one of
the thirty; Elhanan the son of Dodo of
Bethlehem, 25 [w]Shammah the Harodite,
Elika the Harodite, 26 Helez the Paltite, Ira
the son of Ikkesh the Tekoite, 27 Abiezer
the Anathothite, Mebunnai the Hushathite, 28 Zalmon the Ahohite, Maharai the
Netophathite, 29 Heleb the son of Baanah
(the Netophathite), Ittai the son of Ribai
from Gibeah of the children of Benjamin,
30 Benaiah a Pirathonite, Hiddai from the
brooks of [x]Gaash, 31 Abi-Albon the Arbathite, Azmaveth the Barhumite, 32 Eliahba
the Shaalbonite (of the sons of Jashen), Jonathan, 33 [y]Shammah the [8]Hararite, Ahiam
the son of Sharar the Hararite, 34 Eliphelet
the son of Ahasbai, the son of the Maachathite, Eliam the son of [z]Ahithophel the
Gilonite, 35 [9]Hezrai the Carmelite, Paarai
the Arbite, 36 Igal the son of Nathan of
[a]Zobah, Bani the Gadite, 37 Zelek the Ammonite, Naharai the Beerothite (armorbearer of Joab the son of Zeruiah), 38 [b]Ira
the Ithrite, Gareb the Ithrite, 39 *and* [c]Uriah
the Hittite: thirty-seven in all.

21 [7] Lit. *a man of appearance*
23 [u] 2 Sam. 8:18; 20:23
24 [v] 2 Sam. 2:18; 1 Chr. 27:7
25 [w] 1 Chr. 11:27
30 [x] Judg. 2:9
33 [y] 2 Sam. 23:11 [8] *Or Ararite*
34 [z] 2 Sam. 15:12
35 [9] *Hezro*, 1 Chr. 11:37
36 [a] 2 Sam. 8:3
38 [b] 1 Chr. 2:53
39 [c] 2 Sam. 11:3, 6

CHAPTER 24

1 [a] 2 Sam. 21:1, 2 [b] Num. 26:2; 1 Chr. 27:23, 24 [1] *take a census of*
2 [c] Judg. 20:1; 2 Sam. 3:10 [d] [Jer. 17:5]
3 [e] Deut. 1:11
4 [2] *overruled*
5 [f] Deut. 2:36; Josh. 13:9, 16 [g] Num. 32:1, 3
6 [h] Josh. 19:47; Judg. 18:29 [i] Josh. 19:28; Judg. 18:28
7 [j] Josh. 19:29 [k] Josh. 11:3; Judg. 3:3
9 [l] 1 Chr. 21:5

David's Census of Israel and Judah

24 Again [a]the anger of the LORD was
aroused against Israel, and He
moved David against them to say, [b]"Go,
[1]number Israel and Judah."
2 So the king said to Joab the commander of the army who *was* with him, "Now go
throughout all the tribes of Israel, [c]from
Dan to Beersheba, and count the people,
that [d]I may know the number of the people."
3 And Joab said to the king, "Now may
the LORD your God [e]add to the people a
hundred times more than there are, and may
the eyes of my lord the king see *it*. But why
does my lord the king desire this thing?"
4 Nevertheless the king's word [2]prevailed
against Joab and against the captains of the
army. Therefore Joab and the captains of the
army went out from the presence of the king
to count the people of Israel.
5 And they crossed over the Jordan and
camped in [f]Aroer, on the right side of the
town which *is* in the midst of the ravine of
Gad, and toward [g]Jazer. 6 Then they came
to Gilead and to the land of Tahtim Hod-
shi; they came to [h]Dan Jaan and around to
[i]Sidon; 7 and they came to the stronghold
of [j]Tyre and to all the cities of the [k]Hivites
and the Canaanites. Then they went out to
South Judah *as far as* Beersheba. 8 So when
they had gone through all the land, they
came to Jerusalem at the end of nine
months and twenty days. 9 Then Joab gave
the sum of the number of the people to the
king. [l]And there were in Israel eight hundred thousand valiant men who drew the

23:24 Asahel. *See note on 2:18.*

23:24-39 thirty. A technical term for a small military contingent, named "the thirty" since it usually consisted of around 30 men, whereas 32 men are listed here, counting Joab.

23:39 Uriah. Here is inserted a mention of one of David's great soldiers, a reminder of David's great sin (11:1-27), and a preparation for David's further failure recorded in 24:1-10. **thirty-seven.** The 3 (vv. 8-12) with Abishai (vv. 18-19) and Benaiah (vv. 20-23) plus the 32 men of "the thirty" (vv. 24-39).

24:1-17 *See notes on 1 Chr. 21:1-17.*

24:1 Again. A second outbreak of the divine wrath occurred after the 3-year famine recorded in 21:1. **against Israel.** The inciting of David to conduct a census was a punishment on Israel from the Lord for some unspecified sins. Perhaps sins of pride and ambition had led him to increase the size of his army unnecessarily and place heavy burdens of support on the people. Whatever the sin, it is clear God was dissatisfied with David's motives, goals, and actions and brought judgment. **He moved David.** Satan incited David to take this census, and the Lord sovereignly and permissively used Satan to accomplish His will. *See note on 1 Chr. 21:1.* **number Israel and Judah.** A census was usually for military purposes, which seems to be the case here (see v. 9). Numbering the potential army of Israel had been done in the past (Num. 1:1,2; 26:1-4). However, this census of Israel's potential army did not have the sanction of the Lord and proceeded from wrong motives. David either wanted to glory in the size of his fighting force or take more territory than what the Lord had granted him. He shifted his trust from God to military power (this is a constant theme in the Psalms; cf. 20:7; 25:2; 44:6).

24:2 from Dan to Beersheba. A proverbial statement for all the land of Israel from N to S.

24:3 But why. Although Joab protested the plan, he was overruled by David with no reason for the census being stated by David.

24:5 Aroer. The census began about 14 mi. E of the Dead Sea on the northern bank of the Arnon River, in the southeastern corner of Israel, and continued in a counterclockwise direction through the land. **Jazer.** A town in the territory of Gad about 6 mi. W of Rabbah. Jazer was close to the border of the Ammonite territory.

24:6 Gilead. The Transjordan territory N of Gad. **Dan Jaan.** Either a village near the town of Dan or a fuller name for Dan itself. Dan is 25 mi. N of the Sea of Galilee.

24:7 Tyre. The census takers seem to have gone N from Dan and then W towards Sidon before turning S toward Tyre, a city on the coast of the Mediterranean Sea ruled by David's friend Hiram (*see note on 5:11*), but remaining in Israelite territory. **Beersheba.** A major settlement in the S of the land of Israel located about 45 mi. SW of Jerusalem.

24:9 Israel eight hundred thousand...Judah...five hundred

sword, and the men of Judah were five hundred thousand men.

The Judgment on David's Sin

10 And [m]David's heart condemned him after he had numbered the people. So [n]David said to the LORD, [o]"I have sinned greatly in what I have done; but now, I pray, O LORD, take away the iniquity of Your servant, for I have [p]done very foolishly."

11 Now when David arose in the morning, the word of the LORD came to the prophet [q]Gad, David's [r]seer, saying, **12** "Go and tell David, 'Thus says the LORD: "I offer you three *things;* choose one of them for yourself, that I may do *it* to you." ' " **13** So Gad came to David and told him; and he said to him, "Shall [s]seven[3] years of famine come to you in your land? Or shall you flee three months before your enemies, while they pursue you? Or shall there be three days' plague in your land? Now consider and see what answer I should take back to Him who sent me."

14 And David said to Gad, "I am in great distress. Please let us fall into the hand of the LORD, [t]for His mercies *are* great; but [u]do not let me fall into the hand of man."

15 So [v]the LORD sent a plague upon Israel from the morning till the appointed time. From Dan to Beersheba seventy thousand men of the people died. **16** [w]And when the [4]angel stretched out His hand over Jerusalem to destroy it, [x]the LORD relented from the destruction, and said to the [4]angel who was destroying the people, "It is enough; now restrain your hand." And the [4]angel of the LORD was by the threshing floor of [5]Araunah the Jebusite.

17 Then David spoke to the LORD when he saw the angel who was striking the people, and said, "Surely [y]I have sinned, and I have done wickedly; but these sheep, what have they done? Let Your hand, I pray, be against me and against my father's house."

The Altar on the Threshing Floor

18 And Gad came that day to David and said to him, [z]"Go up, erect an altar to the LORD on the threshing floor of Araunah the Jebusite." **19** So David, according to the word of Gad, went up as the LORD commanded. **20** Now Araunah looked, and saw the king and his servants coming toward him. So Araunah went out and bowed before the king with his face to the ground.

21 Then Araunah said, "Why has my lord the king come to his servant?"

[a]And David said, "To buy the threshing floor from you, to build an altar to the LORD, that [b]the plague may be withdrawn from the people."

22 Now Araunah said to David, "Let my lord the king take and offer up whatever *seems* good to him. [c]Look, *here are* oxen for burnt sacrifice, and threshing implements and the yokes of the oxen for wood. **23** All these, O king, Araunah has given to the king."

And Araunah said to the king, "May the LORD your God [d]accept you."

24 Then the king said to Araunah, "No,

10 [m] 1 Sam. 24:5 [n] 2 Sam. 23:1 [o] 2 Sam. 12:13 [p] 1 Sam. 13:13; [2 Chr. 16:9]
11 [q] 1 Sam. 22:5 [r] 1 Sam. 9:9; 1 Chr. 29:29
13 [s] Ezek. 14:21 [3] So with MT, Syr., Tg., Vg.; LXX *three* (cf. 1 Chr. 21:12)
14 [t] [Ps. 51:1; 103:8, 13, 14; 119:156; 130:4, 7] [u] [Is. 47:6; Zech. 1:15]
15 [v] 1 Chr. 21:14
16 [w] Ex. 12:23; 2 Kin. 19:35; Acts 12:23 [x] Gen. 6:6; 1 Sam. 15:11 [4] Or *Angel*
[5] *Ornan,* 1 Chr. 21:15
17 [y] 2 Sam. 7:8; 1 Chr. 21:17; Ps. 74:1
18 [z] 1 Chr. 21:18
21 [a] Gen. 23:8-16 [b] Num. 16:48, 50
22 [c] 1 Sam. 6:14; 1 Kin. 19:21
23 [d] [Ezek. 20:40, 41]

thousand. First Chronicles 21:5 has "one million one hundred thousand" and "four hundred and seventy thousand," respectively. A solution can be found in seeing the 1 Chronicles figure including all the available men of military age, whether battle seasoned or not. But the 2 Samuel figure could be 800,000 battle-seasoned soldiers with the additional 300,000 being of military age who were in reserve but never fought, or it could be the 288,000 in the standing army (1 Chr. 27:1-15) rounded off to 300,000. Either of these two contingents would make up the 1.1 million number of 1 Chr. 21. As far as Judah was concerned, the number in 2 Samuel is 30,000 more than the 1 Chronicles figure. First Chronicles makes it clear that the numbering was not completed by Joab, because he didn't get to the census regarding Benjamin (or Levi) before David came under conviction about completing it all. Joab was glad to stop when he saw the king's changed heart. Because of the procedure selected (*see note on 24:5*) the numbering of Benjamin would have been last, so their number was not included. In the record of 2 Samuel the figure for Judah included the already-known number of 30,000 troops from Benjamin, hence the total of 500,000. The Benjamites remained loyal to David and Judah.

24:10 David's heart condemned him. Although God's prohibition is not clear in the text, it was clear to David. **sinned greatly...done very foolishly.** David recognized the enormity of his willful rebellion against God. David's insight saw the seriousness of his error in relying on numerical strength instead of on the Lord, who can deliver by many or few (see 1 Sam. 14:6).

24:11 Gad. *See note on 1 Sam. 22:5.*

24:13 famine...enemies...plague. David was given a choice of 3 possible punishments for his sin of numbering the people: 1) 3 years of famine in Israel (see marginal note and *note on 1 Chr. 21:12*); 2) 3 months of fleeing from his enemies; or 3) 3 days of pestilence in the land. Implicit in the threat of pursuit by "enemies" was death by the sword. Famine, sword, and plague were OT punishments of the Lord against His sinful people (Lev. 26:23-26; Deut. 28:21-26; Jer. 14:12).

24:14 fall into the hand of the LORD. David knew that the Lord would be more merciful than his enemies, so he took the third option.

24:16 relented. Or "repented, grieved," an expression of God's deep sorrow concerning man's sin and evil (see 1 Sam. 15:11,29). **Araunah the Jebusite.** Araunah (or Ornan) was a pre-Israelite inhabitant of Jerusalem. He owned a threshing floor N of the citadel of Jerusalem and outside its fortified area.

24:17 Let Your hand...be against me. Rather than witness the further destruction of his people, David called down the wrath upon himself and his own family (cf. Ex. 32:32).

24:18-25 See 1 Chr. 21:18-27.

24:18 altar. At this time, the altar associated with the tabernacle of Moses was located at Gibeon (1 Chr. 21:29; 2 Chr. 1:2-6). David was instructed by Gad to build another altar to the Lord at the place

but I will surely buy *it* from you for a price;
nor will I offer burnt offerings to the LORD
my God with that which costs me nothing." So [e]David bought the threshing floor
and the oxen for fifty shekels of silver.

24 [e] 1 Chr. 21:24, 25
25 [f] 2 Sam. 21:14 [g] 2 Sam. 24:21

25 And David built there an altar to the
LORD, and offered burnt offerings and
peace offerings. [f]So the LORD heeded the
prayers for the land, and [g]the plague was
withdrawn from Israel.

where the plague had stopped. This indicated where the Lord's choice was for the building of His temple.

24:24 costs me nothing. Sacrifice is an essential part of worship and service to God (see Mal. 1:6-10; 2 Cor. 8:1-5).

24:24 fifty shekels. A little more than a pound of silver. First Chronicles 21:25 says David paid 600 shekels of gold. How is this discrepancy resolved? In the initial transaction, David either bought or leased the small threshing floor (usually 30 or 40 ft. square) and purchased the oxen. Fifty shekels of silver was appropriate. After that, 1 Chr. 21:25 says he bought "the place," costing 180 times as much, and referring to the entire area of Mt. Moriah.

24:25 the plague was withdrawn. This indicates that judgment is not the final action of the Lord toward either Israel or the house of David. God will fulfill the Abrahamic and Davidic Covenants (cf. Ezek. 37).

The First and Second Books of the
KINGS

Title

First and Second Kings were originally one book, called in the Hebrew text, "Kings," from the first word in 1:1. The Greek translation of the OT, the Septuagint (LXX), divided the book in two, and this was followed by the Latin Vulgate (Vg.) version and English translations. The division was for the convenience of copying this lengthy book on scrolls and codexes and was not based on features of content. Modern Hebrew Bibles title the books "Kings A" and "Kings B." The LXX and Vg. connected Kings with the books of Samuel, so that the titles in the LXX are "The Third and Fourth Books of Kingdoms" and in the Vg. "Third and Fourth Kings." The books of 1 and 2 Samuel and 1 and 2 Kings combined are a chronicle of the entire history of Judah's and Israel's kingship from Saul to Zedekiah. First and Second Chronicles provides only the history of Judah's monarchy.

Author and Date

Jewish tradition proposed that Jeremiah wrote Kings, though this is unlikely because the final event recorded in the book (see 2 Kin. 25:27-30) occurred in Babylon in 561 B.C. Jeremiah never went to Babylon, but to Egypt (Jer. 43:1-7), and would have been at least 86 years old by 561 B.C. Actually, the identity of the unnamed author remains unknown. Since the ministry of prophets is emphasized in Kings, it seems that the author was most likely an unnamed prophet of the Lord who lived in exile with Israel in Babylon.

Kings was written between 561–538 B.C. Since the last narrated event (2 Kin. 25:27-30) sets the earliest possible date of completion and because there is no record of the end of the Babylonian captivity in Kings, the release from exile (538 B.C.) identifies the latest possible writing date. This date is sometimes challenged on the basis of "to this day" statements in 1 Kin. 8:8; 9:13,20,21; 10:12; 12:19; 2 Kin. 2:22; 8:22; 10:27; 14:7; 16:6; 17:23,34,41; 21:15. However, it is best to understand these statements as those of the sources used by the author, rather than statements of the author himself.

It is clear that the author used a variety of sources in compiling this book, including "the book of the acts of Solomon" (1 Kin. 11:41), "the chronicles of the kings of Israel" (1 Kin. 14:19; 15:31; 16:5,14,20,27; 22:39; 2 Kin. 1:18; 10:34; 13:8,12; 14:15,28; 15:11,15,21,26,31), and "the chronicles of the kings of Judah" (1 Kin. 14:29; 15:7,23; 22:45; 2 Kin. 8:23; 12:19; 14:18; 15:6,36; 16:19; 20:20; 21:17,25; 23:28; 24:5). Further, Is. 36:1–39:8 provided information used in 2 Kin. 18:9–20:19, and Jer. 52:31-34 seems to be the source for 2 Kin. 25:27-29. This explanation posits a single inspired author, living in Babylon during the Exile, using these pre-Exilic source materials at his disposal.

Background and Setting

A distinction must be made between the setting of the books' sources and that of the books' author. The source material was written by participants in and eyewitnesses of the events. It was reliable information, which was historically accurate concerning the sons of Israel, from the death of David and the accession of Solomon (971 B.C.) to the destruction of the temple and Jerusalem by the Babylonians (586 B.C.). Thus, Kings traces the histories of two sets of kings and two nations of disobedient people, Israel and Judah, both of whom were growing indifferent to God's law and His prophets and were headed for captivity.

The book of Kings is not only accurate history, but interpreted history. The author, an exile in Babylon, wished to communicate the lessons of Israel's history to the exiles. Specifically, he taught the exilic community why the Lord's judgment of exile had come. The writer established early in his narrative that the Lord required obedience by the kings to the Mosaic law, if their kingdom was to receive His blessing; disobedience would bring exile (1 Kin. 9:3-9). The sad reality that history revealed was that all the kings of Israel and the majority of the kings of Judah "did evil in the sight of the LORD." These evil kings were apostates, who led their people to sin by not confronting idolatry, but sanctioning it. Because of the kings' failure, the Lord sent His prophets to confront both the monarchs and the people with their sin and their need to return to Him. Because the message of the prophets was rejected, the prophets foretold that the nation(s) would be carried into exile (2 Kin. 17:13-23; 21:10-15). Like every prophecy uttered by the prophets in Kings, this word from the Lord came to pass (2 Kin. 17:5,6; 25:1-11). Therefore, Kings interpreted the people's experience of exile and helped them to see why they had suffered God's punishment for idolatry. It also explained that just as God had shown mercy to Ahab (1 Kin. 22:27-29) and Jehoiachin (2 Kin. 25:27-30), so He was willing to show them mercy.

The predominant geographical setting of Kings is the whole Land of Israel, from Dan to Beersheba (1 Kin. 4:25), including Transjordan. Four invading nations played a dominant role in the affairs of Israel and Judah from 971 to 561 B.C. In the tenth century B.C., Egypt impacted Israel's history during the reigns of Solomon and Rehoboam (1 Kin. 3:1; 1:14-22,40; 12:2; 14:25-27). Syria (Aram) posed a great threat to Israel's security during the ninth century B.C., ca. 890–800 B.C. (1 Kin. 15:9-22; 20:1-34; 22:1-4,29-40; 2 Kin. 6:8–7:20; 8:7-15; 10:32,33; 12:17-18; 13:22-25). The years from ca. 800-750 B.C. were a half-century of peace and prosperity for Israel and Judah, because Assyria neutralized Syria and did not threaten to the south. This changed during the kingship of Tiglath-Pileser III (2 Kin. 15:19,20,29). From the mid-eighth century to the late seventh century B.C., Assyria terrorized Palestine, finally conquering and destroying Israel (the northern kingdom) in 722 B.C. (2 Kin. 17:4-6) and besieging Jerusalem in 701 B.C. (2 Kin. 18:17–19:37). From 612 to 539 B.C., Babylon was the dominant power in the ancient world. Babylon invaded Judah (the southern kingdom) 3 times, with the destruction of Jerusalem and the temple occurring in 586 B.C. during that third assault (2 Kin. 24:1–25:21).

Historical and Theological Themes

Kings concentrates, then, on the history of the sons of Israel from 971 to 561 B.C. First Kings 1:1–11:43 deals with Solomon's accession and reign (971–931 B.C.). The two divided kingdoms of Israel and Judah (931–722 B.C.) are covered in 1 Kin. 12:1; 2 Kin. 17:41. The author arranged the material in a distinctive way in that the narration follows the kings in both the N and the S. For each reign described, there is the following literary framework. Every king is introduced with: 1) his name and relation to his predecessor; 2) his date of accession in relationship to the year of the contemporary ruler in the other kingdom; 3) his age on coming to the throne (for kings of Judah only); 4) his length of reign; 5) his place of reign; 6) his mother's name (for Judah only); and 7) spiritual appraisal of his reign. This introduction is followed by a narration of the events that occurred during the reign of each king. The details of this narration vary widely. Each reign is concluded with: 1) a citation of sources; 2) additional historical notes; 3) notice of death; 4) notice of burial; 5) the name of the successor; and 6) in a few instances, an added postscript (i.e., 1 Kin. 15:32; 2 Kin. 10:36). Second Kings 18:1–25:21 deals with the time when Judah survived alone (722–586 B.C.). Two concluding paragraphs speak of events after the Babylonian exile (2 Kin. 25:22-26,27-30).

Three theological themes are stressed in Kings. First, the Lord judged Israel and Judah because of their disobedience to His law (2 Kin 17:7-23). This unfaithfulness on the part of the people was furthered by the apostasy of the evil kings who led them into idolatry (2 Kin. 17:21,22; 21:11), so the Lord exercised His righteous wrath against His rebellious people. Second, the word of the true prophets came to pass (1 Kin. 13:2,3; 22:15-28; 2 Kin. 23:16; 24:2). This confirmed that the Lord did keep His Word, even His warnings of judgment. Third, the Lord remembered His promise to David (1 Kin. 11:12-13,34-36; 15:4; 2 Kin. 8:19). Even though the kings of the Davidic line proved themselves to be disobedient to the Lord, He did not bring David's family to an end as He did the families of Jeroboam I, Omri, and Jehu in Israel. Even as the book closes, the line of David still exists (2 Kin. 25:27-30), so there is hope for the coming "seed" of David (see 2 Sam. 7:12-16). The Lord is thus seen as faithful, and His Word is trustworthy.

Interpretive Challenges

The major interpretive challenge in Kings concerns the chronology of the kings of Israel and Judah. Though abundant chronological data is presented in the book of Kings, this data is difficult to interpret for two reasons. First, there seems to be internal inconsistency in the information given. For instance, 1 Kin. 16:23 states that Omri, king of Israel, began to reign in the 31st year of Asa, king of Judah, and that he reigned 12 years. But according to 1 Kin. 16:29, Omri was succeeded by his son Ahab in the 38th year of Asa, giving Omri a reign of only 7 years, not 12 (for resolution, *see note on 1 Kin. 16:23*). Second, from extrabiblical sources (Greek, Assyrian, and Babylonian), correlated with astronomical data, a reliable series of dates can be calculated from 892 to 566 B.C. Since Ahab and Jehu, kings of Israel, are believed to be mentioned in Assyrian records, 853 B.C. can be fixed as the year of Ahab's death and 841 B.C. as the year Jehu began to reign. With these fixed dates, it is possible to work backward and forward to determine that the date of the division of Israel from Judah was ca. 931 B.C., the fall of Samaria 722 B.C., and the fall of Jerusalem 586 B.C. But when the total years of royal reigns in Kings are added, the number for Israel is 241 years (not the 210 years of 931 to 722 B.C.) and Judah 393 years (not the 346 years of 931 to 586 B.C.). It is recognized that in both kingdoms there were some co-regencies, i.e., a period of rulership when two kings, usually father and son, ruled at the same time, so the overlapping years were counted twice in the total for both kings. Further, different methods of reckoning the years of a king's rule and even different calendars were used at differing times in the two kingdoms, resulting in the seeming internal inconsistencies. The general accuracy of the chronology in Kings can be demonstrated and confirmed.

A second major interpretive challenge deals with Solomon's relationship to the Abrahamic and Davidic Covenants. First Kings 4:20,21 has been interpreted by some as the fulfillment of the promises given to Abraham (cf. Gen. 15:18-21; 22:17). However, according to Num. 34:6, the western border of the Land promised to Abraham was the Mediterranean Sea. In 1 Kin. 5:1ff., Hiram is seen as the independent king of Tyre (along the Mediterranean), dealing with Solomon as an equal. Solomon's empire was not the fulfillment of the Land promise given to Abraham by the Lord, although a great portion of that land was under Solomon's control. Further, the statements of Solomon in 1 Kin. 5:5 and 8:20 are his claims to be the promised seed of the Davidic Covenant (cf. 2 Sam. 7:12-16). The author of Kings holds out the possibility that Solomon's temple was the fulfillment of the Lord's promise to David. However, while the conditions for the fulfillment of the promise to David are reiterated to Solomon (1 Kin. 6:12), it is clear that Solomon did not meet these conditions (1 Kin. 11:9-13). In fact, none of the historical kings in the house of David met the condition of complete obedience that was to be the sign of the Promised One. According to Kings, the fulfillment of the Abrahamic and Davidic Covenants did not take place in Israel's past, thus laying the foundation for the latter prophets (Isaiah, Jeremiah, Ezekiel, and the Twelve) who would point Israel to a future hope under Messiah when the Covenants would be fulfilled (see Is. 9:6,7).

Outline

Since the division of 1 and 2 Kings arbitrarily takes place in the middle of the narrative concerning King Ahaziah in Israel, the following outline is for both 1 and 2 Kings.

Outline

I. The United Kingdom: The Reign of Solomon (1 Kin. 1:1–11:43)
  A. The Rise of Solomon (1 Kin. 1:1–2:46)
  B. The Beginning of Solomon's Wisdom and Wealth (1 Kin. 3:1–4:34)
  C. The Preparations for the Building of the Temple (1 Kin. 5:1-18)
  D. The Building of the Temple and Solomon's House (1 Kin. 6:1–9:9)
  E. The Further Building Projects of Solomon (1 Kin. 9:10-28)
  F. The Culmination of Solomon's Wisdom and Wealth (1 Kin. 10:1-29)
  G. The Decline of Solomon (1 Kin. 11:1-43)

II. The Divided Kingdom: The Kings of Israel and Judah (1 Kin. 12:1–2 Kin. 17:41)
  A. The Rise of Idolatry: Jeroboam of Israel/Rehoboam of Judah (1 Kin. 12:1–14:31)
  B. Kings of Judah/Israel (1 Kin. 15:1–16:22)
  C. The Dynasty of Omri and Its Influence: The Rise and Fall of Baal Worship in Israel and Judah (1 Kin. 16:23–2 Kin. 13:25)
    1. The introduction of Baal worship (1 Kin. 16:23-34)
    2. The opposition of Elijah to Baal worship (1 Kin. 17:1–2 Kin. 1:18)
    3. The influence of Elisha concerning the true God (2 Kin. 2:1–9:13)
    4. The overthrow of Baal worship in Israel (2 Kin. 9:14–10:36)
    5. The overthrow of Baal worship in Judah (2 Kin. 11:1–12:21)
    6. The death of Elisha (2 Kin. 13:1-25)
  D. Kings of Judah/Israel (2 Kin. 14:1–15:38)
  E. The Defeat and Exile of Israel by Assyria (2 Kin. 16:1–17:41)

III. The Surviving Kingdom: The Kings of Judah (2 Kin. 18:1–25:21)
  A. Hezekiah's Righteous Reign (2 Kin. 18:1–20:21)
  B. Manasseh's and Amon's Wicked Reigns (2 Kin. 21:1-26)
  C. Josiah's Righteous Reign (2 Kin. 22:1–23:30)
  D. The Defeat and Exile of Judah by Babylon (2 Kin. 23:31–25:21)

IV. Epilogue: The People's Continued Rebellion and the Lord's Continued Mercy (2 Kin. 25:22-30)

The Kings of Israel and Judah

KING	SCRIPTURE
United Kingdom	
Saul	1 Samuel 9:1–31:13; 1 Chronicles 10:1-14
David	2 Samuel; 1 Kings 1:1–2:9; 1 Chronicles 11:1–29:30
Solomon	1 Kings 2:10–11:43; 2 Chronicles 1:1–9:31
Northern Kingdom (Israel)	
Jeroboam I	1 Kings 12:25–14:20
Nadab	1 Kings 15:25-31
Baasha	1 Kings 15:32–16:7
Elah	1 Kings 16:8-14
Zimri	1 Kings 16:15-20
Tibni	1 Kings 16:21,22
Omri	1 Kings 16:21-28
Ahab	1 Kings 16:29–22:40
Ahaziah	1 Kings 22:51-53; 2 Kings 1:1-18
Jehoram (Joram)	2 Kings 2:1–8:15
Jehu	2 Kings 9:1–10:36
Jehoahaz	2 Kings 13:1-9
Jehoash (Joash)	2 Kings 13:10-25
Jeroboam II	2 Kings 14:23-29
Zechariah	2 Kings 15:8-12
Shallum	2 Kings 15:13-15
Menahem	2 Kings 15:16-22
Pekahiah	2 Kings 15:23-26
Pekah	2 Kings 15:27-31
Hoshea	2 Kings 17:1-41
Southern Kingdom (Judah)	
Rehoboam	1 Kings 12:1–14:31; 2 Chronicles 10:1–12:16
Abijam (Abijah)	1 Kings 15:1-8; 2 Chronicles 13:1-22
Asa	1 Kings 15:9-24; 2 Chronicles 14:1–16:14
Jehoshaphat	1 Kings 22:41-50; 2 Chronicles 17:1–20:37
Joram (Jehoram)	2 Kings 8:16-24; 2 Chronicles 21:1-20
Ahaziah	2 Kings 8:25-29; 2 Chronicles 22:1-9
Athaliah (queen)	2 Kings 11:1-16; 2 Chronicles 22:1–23:21
Joash (Jehoash)	2 Kings 11:17–12:21; 2 Chronicles 23:16–24:27
Amaziah	2 Kings 14:1-22; 2 Chronicles 25:1-28
Uzziah (Azariah)	2 Kings 15:1-7; 2 Chronicles 26:1-23
Jotham	2 Kings 15:32-38; 2 Chronicles 27:1-9
Ahaz	2 Kings 16:1-20; 2 Chronicles 28:1-27
Hezekiah	2 Kings 18:1–20:21; 2 Chronicles 29:1–32:33
Manasseh	2 Kings 21:1-18; 2 Chronicles 33:1-20
Amon	2 Kings 21:19-26; 2 Chronicles 33:21-25
Josiah	2 Kings 22:1–23:30; 2 Chronicles 34:1–35:27
Jehoahaz	2 Kings 23:31-33; 2 Chronicles 36:1-4
Jehoiakim	2 Kings 23:34–24:7; 2 Chronicles 36:5-8
Jehoiachin	2 Kings 24:8-16; 2 Chronicles 36:9,10
Zedekiah	2 Kings 24:18–25:21; 2 Chronicles 36:11-21

The First Book of the

KINGS

Adonijah Presumes to Be King

1 Now King David was [a]old, [1]advanced in years; and they put covers on him, but he could not get warm. 2 Therefore his servants said to him, "Let a young woman, a virgin, be sought for our lord the king, and let her [2]stand before the king, and let her care for him; and let her lie in your bosom, that our lord the king may be warm." 3 So they sought for a lovely young woman throughout all the territory of Israel, and found [b]Abishag the [c]Shunammite, and brought her to the king. 4 The young woman *was* very lovely; and she cared for the king, and served him; but the king did not know her.

5 Then [d]Adonijah the [3]son of Haggith exalted himself, saying, "I will [4]be king"; and [e]he prepared for himself chariots and horsemen, and fifty men to run before him. 6 (And his father had not [5]rebuked him at any time by saying, "Why have you done so?" He *was* also very good-looking. [f]*His mother* had borne him after Absalom.) 7 Then he conferred with [g]Joab the son of Zeruiah and with [h]Abiathar the priest, and [i]they followed and helped Adonijah. 8 But [j]Zadok the priest, [k]Benaiah the son of Jehoiada, [l]Nathan the prophet, [m]Shimei, Rei, and [n]the mighty men who *belonged* to David were not with Adonijah.

9 And Adonijah sacrificed sheep and oxen and fattened cattle by the stone of [6]Zoheleth, which *is* by [o]En Rogel;[7] he also invited all his brothers, the king's sons, and all the men of Judah, the king's servants. 10 But he did not invite Nathan the prophet, Benaiah, the mighty men, or [p]Solomon his brother.

11 So Nathan spoke to Bathsheba the

CHAPTER 1

1 [a] 1 Chr. 23:1 [1] Seventy years
2 [2] Or *serve*
3 [b] 1 Kin. 2:17 [c] Josh. 19:18; 1 Sam. 28:4
5 [d] 2 Sam. 3:4 [e] 2 Sam. 15:1 [3] The fourth son [4] Lit. *reign*
6 [f] 2 Sam. 3:3,4; 1 Chr. 3:2 [5] Lit. *pained*
7 [g] 1 Chr. 11:6 [h] 2 Sam. 20:25 [i] 1 Kin. 2:22,28
8 [j] 1 Kin. 2:35 [k] 1 Kin. 2:25; 2 Sam. 8:18 [l] 2 Sam. 12:1 [m] 1 Kin. 4:18 [n] 2 Sam. 23:8
9 [o] Josh. 15:7; 18:16; 2 Sam. 17:17 [6] Lit. *Serpent* [7] A spring south of Jerusalem in the Kidron Valley
10 [p] 2 Sam. 12:24

1:1–11:43 The first division of Kings chronicles the reign of Solomon. The literary structure is centered around the building activities of Solomon (6:1–9:9) and climaxes with the failure of Solomon to follow the Lord wholeheartedly (11:1-43).

1:1 advanced in years. David was 70 years old (cf. 2 Sam. 5:4,5).

1:2 the king may be warm. In his old age, circulatory problems plagued King David so he had trouble keeping warm. The royal staff proposed a solution that a young virgin nurse watch over him and, at night, warm him with her body heat. This was in harmony with the medical customs of that day; both the Jewish historian Josephus (first century A.D.) and the Greek physician Galen (second century A.D.) record such a practice.

1:3 Abishag the Shunammite. Abishag was a very beautiful teenager from the town of Shunem, in the territory of Issachar located 3 mi. N of Jezreel (Josh. 19:18; 1 Sam. 28:4; 2 Kin. 4:8). Though from the same town, she is not to be identified with the Shulamite in the Song of Solomon (6:13).

1:4 the king did not know her. Although apparently joining David's harem (cf. 2:17,22-24), Abishag remained a virgin.

1:5 Adonijah. Adonijah was the fourth son of David (2 Sam. 3:4) and probably the oldest living son, since Amnon (2 Sam. 13:28,29) and Absalom (2 Sam. 18:14,15) had been killed, and Chileab apparently died in his youth, since there is no mention of him beyond his birth. As David's oldest surviving heir, Adonijah attempted to claim the kingship. **chariots and horsemen.** Like Absalom (2 Sam. 15:1), Adonijah sought to confirm and support his claim to kingship by raising a small army.

1:7 Joab. David's nephew (1 Chr. 2:16), the commander of the army of Israel (2 Sam. 8:16) and a faithful supporter of David's kingship (2 Sam. 18:2; 20:22). He was guilty of the illegal killings of Abner and Amasa (2:5; cf. 2 Sam. 3:39; 20:10). Adonijah wanted his support in his bid for the throne. **Abiathar.** One of the two High-Priests serving concurrently during David's reign (2 Sam. 8:17), whose influence Adonijah sought.

1:8 Zadok. The other High-Priest serving during David's reign (2 Sam. 8:17), whose ancestors will serve the millennial temple (see Ezek. 44:15). He had been High-Priest in the tabernacle at Gibeon under Saul (1 Chr. 16:39). **Benaiah.** The commander of the Cherethites and Pelethites (v. 44), David's official guards distinguished for bravery (see 1 Sam. 23:20). *See note on 1 Sam. 30:14.* He was regarded by Joab as a rival. **Nathan.** The most influential prophet during David's reign (2 Sam. 7:1-17; 12:1-15,25). **Shimei.** Cf. 4:18. A different individual than the Shimei referred to in 2 Sam. 16:5-8; 1 Kin. 2:8,36-46. **the mighty men.** See 2 Sam. 23:8-39.

1:9 Zoheleth. Or "Serpent Stone," a standard landmark identified with a previous Jebusite snake worship location. **En Rogel.** Lit. "the spring of the fuller." Typically identified as being located at the N/W confluence of the Kidron and Hinnom Valleys. See marginal note for location. Here Adonijah held a political event to court popularity and secure his claim to the throne.

1:11-27 The revolt of Adonijah was defeated by Nathan, who knew the Lord's will (see 2 Sam. 7:12; 1 Chr. 22:9) and acted quickly, by having Bathsheba go to David first to report what was happening, after which he would follow (v. 23).

1:11 Bathsheba the mother of Solomon. The mothers of the kings of the Davidic line are continually noted (2:13,19; 14:21; 15:2;

mother of Solomon, saying, "Have you not
heard that Adonijah the son of [q]Haggith
has become king, and David our lord does
not know *it?* 12 Come, please, let me now
give you advice, that you may save your
own life and the life of your son Solomon.
13 Go immediately to King David and say
to him, 'Did you not, my lord, O king,
swear to your maidservant, saying, [r]"Assuredly your son Solomon shall reign after
me, and he shall sit on my throne"? Why
then has Adonijah become king?' 14 Then,
while you are still talking there with the
king, I also will come in after you and confirm your words."
15 So Bathsheba went into the chamber
to the king. (Now the king was very old,
and Abishag the Shunammite was serving
the king.) 16 And Bathsheba bowed and
did homage to the king. Then the king
said, "What is your wish?"
17 Then she said to him, "My lord, [s]you
swore by the LORD your God to your
maidservant, *saying,* 'Assuredly Solomon
your son shall reign after me, and he shall
sit on my throne.' 18 So now, look! Adonijah has become king; and now, my lord
the king, you do not know about *it.* 19 [t]He
has sacrificed oxen and fattened cattle and
sheep in abundance, and has invited all the
sons of the king, Abiathar the priest, and
Joab the commander of the army; but Solomon your servant he has not invited.
20 And as for you, my lord, O king, the
eyes of all Israel *are* on you, that you
should tell them who will sit on the throne
of my lord the king after him. 21 Otherwise
it will happen, when my lord the king
[u]rests with his fathers, that I and my son
Solomon will be counted as offenders."
22 And just then, while she was still talking with the king, Nathan the prophet also
came in. 23 So they told the king, saying,
"Here is Nathan the prophet." And when
he came in before the king, he bowed
down before the king with his face to the
ground. 24 And Nathan said, "My lord, O
king, have you said, 'Adonijah shall reign
after me, and he shall sit on my throne'?
25 [v]For he has gone down today, and has
sacrificed oxen and fattened cattle and
sheep in abundance, and has invited all the
king's sons, and the commanders of the
army, and Abiathar the priest; and look!
They are eating and drinking before him;
and they say, [w]'*Long*[8] live King Adonijah!'
26 But he has not invited me—me your servant—nor Zadok the priest, nor Benaiah
the son of Jehoiada, nor your servant Solomon. 27 Has this thing been done by my
lord the king, and you have not told your
servant who should sit on the throne of my
lord the king after him?"

David Proclaims Solomon King

28 Then King David answered and said,
"Call Bathsheba to me." So she came into
the king's presence and stood before the
king. 29 And the king took an oath and
said, [x]"*As* the LORD lives, who has redeemed my life from every distress,
30 [y]just as I swore to you by the LORD God
of Israel, saying, 'Assuredly Solomon your
son shall be king after me, and he shall sit
on my throne in my place,' so I certainly
will do this day."
31 Then Bathsheba bowed with *her* face
to the earth, and paid homage to the king,
and said, [z]"Let my lord King David live
forever!"
32 And King David said, "Call to me
Zadok the priest, Nathan the prophet, and
Benaiah the son of Jehoiada." So they came
before the king. 33 The king also said to
them, [a]"Take with you the servants of your
lord, and have Solomon my son ride on my
own [b]mule, and take him down to
[c]Gihon.[9] 34 There let Zadok the priest and
Nathan the prophet [d]anoint him king over
Israel; and [e]blow the horn, and say, [1]'*Long*

11 [q] 2 Sam. 3:4
13 [r] 1 Kin. 1:30; 1 Chr. 22:9-13
17 [s] 1 Kin. 1:13, 30
19 [t] 1 Kin. 1:7-9, 25
21 [u] Deut. 31:16; 2 Sam. 7:12; 1 Kin. 2:10
25 [v] 1 Kin. 1:9, 19 [w] 1 Sam. 10:24 [8] Lit. *Let King Adonijah live*
29 [x] 2 Sam. 4:9; 12:5
30 [y] 1 Kin. 1:13, 17
31 [z] Neh. 2:3; Dan. 2:4; 3:9
33 [a] 2 Sam. 20:6 [b] Esth. 6:8 [c] 2 Chr. 32:30; 33:14 [9] A spring east of Jerusalem in the Kidron Valley
34 [d] 1 Sam. 10:1; 16:3, 12; 2 Sam. 2:4; 5:3; 1 Kin. 19:16; 2 Kin. 9:3; 11:12; 1 Chr. 29:22 [e] 2 Sam. 15:10; 2 Kin. 9:13; 11:14 [1] Lit. *Let King Solomon live*

2 Kin. 8:26; 12:1; 14:2; 15:2,33; 18:2; 21:1,19; 22:1; 23:31,36; 24:8). The queen mother held an influential position in the royal court. For the story of how David sinfully took her, see 2 Sam. 11.

1:12 save…the life of your son. If Adonijah had become king, the lives of Bathsheba and Solomon would have been in jeopardy, because often in the ancient Near East potential claimants to the throne and their families were put to death (cf. 15:29; 16:11; 2 Kin. 10:11).

1:13 Did you not…swear. This oath was given privately (unrecorded in Scripture) by David, perhaps to both Nathan and Bathsheba. Solomon's choice by the Lord was implicit in his name Jedediah, meaning "loved by the Lord" (2 Sam. 12:24,25) and explicit in David's declaration to Solomon (1 Chr. 22:6-13). Cf. vv. 17,20,35.

1:28-53 See 1 Chr. 29:21-25.

1:29 the king took an oath. David swore another oath to carry out his earlier oath to make Solomon king, and he made good on it that very day.

1:33 my own mule. The riding of David's royal mule showed Israel that Solomon was David's chosen successor (see 2 Sam. 13:29). **Gihon.** This spring, which was Jerusalem's main water supply (see marginal note), was located about one-half mi. N of En Rogel (v. 9) and hidden from it by an intervening hill. Thus, the sound of Solomon's anointing ceremony could have been heard without being seen by Adonijah's party.

1:34 anoint him king. Saul and David had been anointed by Samuel, the Lord's priest and prophet (1 Sam. 10:1; 16:13); Solomon was also to be recognized by priest and prophet. The participation of the prophet Nathan gave Solomon's coronation evidence of the Lord's blessing. Throughout the book of Kings, God identified His chosen kings through prophets (11:37; 15:28,29; 16:12; 2 Kin. 9:3). **blow the horn.** The blowing of the trumpet signaled a public assembly where the people corporately recognized Solomon's new status as co-regent with and successor to David (vv. 39,40).

live King Solomon!' 35 Then you shall
come up after him, and he shall come and
sit on my throne, and he shall be king in
my place. For I have appointed him to be
ruler over Israel and Judah."
36 Benaiah the son of Jehoiada answered
the king and said, [f]"Amen! May the LORD
God of my lord the king say so *too.* 37 [g]As
the LORD has been with my lord the king,
even so may He be with Solomon, and
[h]make his throne greater than the throne of
my lord King David."
38 So Zadok the priest, Nathan the
prophet, [i]Benaiah the son of Jehoiada, the
[j]Cherethites, and the Pelethites went down
and had Solomon ride on King David's
mule, and took him to Gihon. 39 Then
Zadok the priest took a horn of [k]oil from
the tabernacle and [l]anointed Solomon.
And they blew the horn, [m]and all the people said, [2]"*Long* live King Solomon!"
40 And all the people went up after him;
and the people played the flutes and rejoiced with great joy, so that the earth
seemed to split with their sound.
41 Now Adonijah and all the guests who
were with him heard *it* as they finished eating. And when Joab heard the sound of the
horn, he said, "Why *is* the city in such a
noisy uproar?" 42 While he was still speaking, there came [n]Jonathan, the son of Abiathar the priest. And Adonijah said to him,
"Come in, for [o]you *are* a prominent man,
and bring good news."
43 Then Jonathan answered and said to
Adonijah, "No! Our lord King David has
made Solomon king. 44 The king has sent
with him Zadok the priest, Nathan the
prophet, Benaiah the son of Jehoiada, the
Cherethites, and the Pelethites; and they
have made him ride on the king's mule.
45 So Zadok the priest and Nathan the
prophet have anointed him king at Gihon;
and they have gone up from there rejoicing, so that the city is in an uproar. This *is*
the noise that you have heard. 46 Also Solomon [p]sits on the throne of the kingdom.
47 And moreover the king's servants have
gone to bless our lord King David, saying,
[q]'May God make the name of Solomon better than your name, and may He make his
throne greater than your throne.' [r]Then the
king bowed himself on the bed. 48 Also the
king said thus, 'Blessed *be* the LORD God of
Israel, who has [s]given *one* to sit on my
throne this day, while my eyes see [t]*it!*' "
49 So all the guests who were with Adonijah were afraid, and arose, and each one
went his way.
50 Now Adonijah was afraid of Solomon;
so he arose, and went and [u]took hold of the
horns of the altar. 51 And it was told Solomon, saying, "Indeed Adonijah is afraid of
King Solomon; for look, he has taken hold
of the horns of the altar, saying, 'Let King
Solomon swear to me today that he will not
put his servant to death with the sword.' "
52 Then Solomon said, "If he proves
himself a worthy man, [v]not one hair of him
shall fall to the earth; but if wickedness is
found in him, he shall die." 53 So King Solomon sent them to bring him down from
the altar. And he came and fell down before King Solomon; and Solomon said to
him, "Go to your house."

David's Instructions to Solomon

2 Now [a]the days of David drew near
that he should die, and he [1]charged
Solomon his son, saying: 2 [b]"I go the way
of all the earth; [c]be strong, therefore, and
prove yourself a man. 3 And keep the
charge of the LORD your God: to walk in
His ways, to keep His statutes, His commandments, His judgments, and His testimonies, as it is written in the Law of Moses, that you may [d]prosper in all that you
do and wherever you turn; 4 that the LORD
may [e]fulfill His word which He spoke concerning me, saying, [f]'If your sons take

36 [f] Jer. 28:6
37 [g] Josh. 1:5, 17; 1 Sam. 20:13 [h] 1 Kin. 1:47
38 [i] 2 Sam. 8:18; 23:20-23 [j] 2 Sam. 20:7; 1 Chr. 18:17
39 [k] Ex. 30:23, 25, 32; Ps. 89:20 [l] 1 Chr. 29:22 [m] 1 Sam. 10:24 [2] Lit. *Let King Solomon live*
42 [n] 2 Sam. 17:17, 20 [o] 2 Sam. 18:27
46 [p] 1 Kin. 2:12; 1 Chr. 29:23
47 [q] 1 Kin. 1:37 [r] Gen. 47:31
48 [s] 1 Kin. 3:6; [Ps. 132:11, 12] [t] 2 Sam. 7:12
50 [u] Ex. 27:2; 30:10; 1 Kin. 2:28
52 [v] 1 Sam. 14:45; 2 Sam. 14:11; Acts 27:34

CHAPTER 2

1 [a] Gen. 47:29; Deut. 31:14 [1] *commanded*
2 [b] Josh. 23:14 [c] Deut. 31:7, 23; 1 Chr. 22:13
3 [d] [Deut. 29:9; Josh. 1:7]; 1 Chr. 22:12, 13
4 [e] 2 Sam. 7:25 [f] [Ps. 132:12]

1:35 Israel and Judah. The two major geographical components of David's and Solomon's kingdoms. Even while still unified these two separate entities, that would later divide (12:20), were clearly identifiable.

1:39 tabernacle. This was the tent David set up in Jerusalem (2 Sam. 6:17; 1 Chr. 15:1) to house the ark of the covenant, not the tabernacle of Moses (see 3:4).

1:41-49 Adonijah...heard *it*. The loud shouts hailing Solomon as king reached the ears of those at Adonijah's feast at En Rogel nearby. A messenger came with the full report of the coronation of Solomon, so that the cause of Adonijah was lost and the party ended with the people leaving in fear.

1:42 Jonathan. The son of Abiathar the priest was an experienced messenger (2 Sam. 15:36; 17:17).

1:50 horns of the altar. Cf. 2:28. The "horns" were corner projections on the altar of burnt offering on which the priests smeared the blood of the sacrifices (Ex. 27:2; 29:12). By taking hold of the horns, Adonijah sought to place himself under the protection of God (see Ex. 21:13,14).

2:1 he charged Solomon. Leaders typically exhorted their successors, i.e., Moses (Deut. 31:7,8), Joshua (Josh. 23:1-6), and Samuel (1 Sam. 12:1-25). So also David gave Solomon a final exhortation.

2:2 the way of all the earth. An expression for death (Josh. 23:14; cf. Gen 3:19). **be strong...prove yourself a man.** An expression of encouragement (Deut. 31:7,23; Josh. 1:6,7,9,18; 1 Sam. 4:9) with which David sought to prepare Solomon for the difficult tasks and the battles in his future.

2:3 keep the charge of the LORD your God. David admonished Solomon to obey the Mosaic law so he could have a successful kingship (cf. Deut. 17:18-20).

2:4 His word. The unconditional Davidic Covenant was made by God with David in 2 Sam. 7:4-17 and confirmed to Solomon in

heed to their way, to [g]walk before Me in
truth with all their heart and with all their
soul,' He said, [h]'you shall not lack a man
on the throne of Israel.'
5 "Moreover you know also what Joab
the son of Zeruiah [i]did to me, *and* what he
did to the two commanders of the armies of
Israel, to [j]Abner the son of Ner and [k]Amasa
the son of Jether, whom he killed. And he
shed the blood of war in peacetime, and
put the blood of war on his belt that *was*
around his waist, and on his sandals that
were on his feet. 6 Therefore do [l]according
to your wisdom, and do not let his gray
hair go down to the grave in peace.
7 "But show kindness to the sons of
[m]Barzillai the Gileadite, and let them be
among those who [n]eat at your table, for so
[o]they came to me when I fled from Absalom your brother.
8 "And see, *you have* with you [p]Shimei
the son of Gera, a Benjamite from Bahurim,
who cursed me with a malicious curse in
the day when I went to Mahanaim. But [q]he
came down to meet me at the Jordan, and [r]I
swore to him by the LORD, saying, 'I will
not put you to death with the sword.'
9 Now therefore, [s]do not hold him guiltless,
for you *are* a wise man and know what you
ought to do to him; but [t]bring his gray hair
down to the grave with blood."

Death of David

10 So [u]David [2]rested with his fathers,
and was buried in [v]the City of David.
11 The period that David [w]reigned over Israel *was* forty years; seven years he reigned
in Hebron, and in Jerusalem he reigned
thirty-three years. 12 [x]Then Solomon sat on
the throne of his father David; and his
kingdom was [y]firmly established.

Solomon Executes Adonijah

13 Now Adonijah the son of Haggith
came to Bathsheba the mother of Solomon.
So she said, [z]"Do you come peaceably?"
And he said, "Peaceably." 14 Moreover
he said, "I have something *to say* to you."
And she said, "Say it."
15 Then he said, "You know that the
kingdom was [a]mine, and all Israel had set
their expectations on me, that I should
reign. However, the kingdom has been
turned over, and has become my brother's;
for [b]it was his from the LORD. 16 Now I ask
one petition of you; do not [3]deny me."
And she said to him, "Say it."
17 Then he said, "Please speak to King
Solomon, for he will not refuse you, that he
may give me [c]Abishag the Shunammite as
wife."
18 So Bathsheba said, "Very well, I will
speak for you to the king."
19 Bathsheba therefore went to King Solomon, to speak to him for Adonijah. And
the king rose up to meet her and [d]bowed
down to her, and sat down on his throne
and had a throne set for the king's mother;
[e]so she sat at his right hand. 20 Then she
said, "I desire one small petition of you; do
not [4]refuse me."
And the king said to her, "Ask it, my
mother, for I will not refuse you."
21 So she said, "Let Abishag the
Shunammite be given to Adonijah your
brother as wife."
22 And King Solomon answered and
said to his mother, "Now why do you ask
Abishag the Shunammite for Adonijah?
Ask for him the kingdom also—for he *is*
my [f]older brother—for him, and for [g]Abia-
thar the priest, and for Joab the son of Zeruiah." 23 Then King Solomon swore by

4 [g]2 Kin. 20:3 [h]2 Sam. 7:12, 13; 1 Kin. 8:25
5 [i]2 Sam. 3:39; 18:5, 12, 14 [j]2 Sam. 3:27; 1 Kin. 2:32 [k]2 Sam. 20:10
6 [l]1 Kin. 2:9; Prov. 20:26
7 [m]2 Sam. 19:31-39 [n]2 Sam. 9:7, 10; 19:28 [o]2 Sam. 17:17-29
8 [p]2 Sam. 16:5-13 [q]2 Sam. 19:18 [r]2 Sam. 19:23
9 [s]Ex. 20:7; Job 9:28 [t]Gen. 42:38; 44:31
10 [u]1 Kin. 1:21; Acts 2:29; 13:36 [v]2 Sam. 5:7; 1 Kin. 3:1 [2]Died and joined his ancestors
11 [w]2 Sam. 5:4, 5; 1 Chr. 3:4; 29:26, 27
12 [x]1 Kin. 1:46; 1 Chr. 29:23 [y]1 Kin. 2:46; 2 Chr. 1:1
13 [z]1 Sam. 16:4, 5
15 [a]1 Kin. 1:11, 18 [b]1 Chr. 22:9, 10; 28:5-7; [Dan. 2:21]
16 [3]Lit. *turn away the face*
17 [c]1 Kin. 1:3, 4
19 [d][Ex. 20:12] [e]Ps. 45:9
20 [4]Lit. *turn away the face*
22 [f]1 Kin. 1:6; 2:15; 1 Chr. 3:2, 5 [g]1 Kin. 1:7

1 Kin. 9:5, promising the perpetuation of the Davidic dynasty over Israel. **If your sons take heed to their way.** David declared that the king's obedience to the law of Moses was a necessary condition for the fulfillment of divine promise. The book of Kings demonstrates that none of the descendants of David remained faithful to God's law; none of them met the conditions for the fulfillment of the divine promise. Rather, David's words provided a basis for explaining the Exile. Thus, the ultimate and final King of Israel would appear at a later, undesignated time.

2:5 Abner...Amasa. These were victims of Joab's jealousy and vengeance, who were killed after warfare had ceased (2 Sam. 3:27; 20:10), thus bringing Joab's punishment as a murderer (Deut. 19:11-13).

2:7 sons of Barzillai. David told Solomon to repay Barzillai's kindness to David (2 Sam. 17:27-29) by showing similar kindness to Barzillai's sons. **eat at your table.** A position of honor that could include a royal stipend (2 Sam. 9:7; 1 Kin. 18:19; 2 Kin. 25:29).

2:8 Shimei. He had angrily stoned and vehemently cursed David when David was escaping from Absalom (2 Sam. 16:5-13). Shimei's actions were worthy of death (Ex. 22:28), and David counseled Solomon through subtle means to arrange for his just punishment (vv. 36-46).

2:10-12 See 2 Sam. 5:5; 1 Chr. 29:26-28.

2:10 the City of David. I.e., Jerusalem (cf. 8:1).

2:11 forty years. David ruled from ca. 1011–971 B.C., probably with Solomon as co-regent during his final year (cf. 11:41).

2:12 firmly established. Solomon's succession enjoyed the Lord's approval, and Solomon exercised unchallenged authority, prosperity, and renown (v. 46).

2:15 all Israel had set their expectations on me. A reference to Adonijah's perceived right to the kingship as the oldest surviving son according to ancient Near East custom.

2:17 give me Abishag. In the ancient Near East, possession of the royal harem was a sign of kingship (cf. 2 Sam. 3:8; 12:8; 16:20-22). Adonijah's request for Abishag was an attempt to support his claim to the kingship and perhaps generate a revolt to usurp the throne. Bathsheba didn't see the treachery (vv. 18-21).

2:22 Ask for...the kingdom also. Solomon recognized Adonijah's request as the prelude to his usurping of the throne. Because Adonijah's request violated the terms of loyalty Solomon had previ-

the LORD, saying, [h]"May God do so to me,
and more also, if Adonijah has not spoken
this word against his own life! 24 Now
therefore, *as* the LORD lives, who has confirmed me and set me on the throne of David my father, and who has established a
[5]house for me, as He [i]promised, Adonijah
shall be put to death today!"
25 So King Solomon sent by the hand of
[j]Benaiah the son of Jehoiada; and he struck
him down, and he died.

Abiathar Exiled, Joab Executed

26 And to Abiathar the priest the king
said, "Go to [k]Anathoth, to your own fields,
for [6]you *are* deserving of death; but I will
not put you to death at this time, [l]because
you carried the ark of the Lord GOD before
my father David, and because you were afflicted every time my father was afflicted."
27 So Solomon removed Abiathar from
being priest to the LORD, that he might
[m]fulfill the word of the LORD which He
spoke concerning the house of Eli at Shiloh.
28 Then news came to Joab, for Joab
[n]had defected to Adonijah, though he had
not defected to Absalom. So Joab fled to
the tabernacle of the LORD, and [o]took hold
of the horns of the altar. 29 And King Solomon was told, "Joab has fled to the tabernacle of the LORD; there *he is*, by the altar."
Then Solomon sent Benaiah the son of Jehoiada, saying, "Go, [p]strike him down."
30 So Benaiah went to the tabernacle of the
LORD, and said to him, "Thus says the king,
[q]'Come out!' "
And he said, "No, but I will die here."
And Benaiah brought back word to the
king, saying, "Thus said Joab, and thus he
answered me."
31 Then the king said to him, [r]"Do as he
has said, and strike him down and bury
him, [s]that you may take away from me
and from the house of my father the innocent blood which Joab shed. 32 So the LORD
[t]will return his [7]blood on his head, because he struck down two men more righteous [u]and better than he, and killed them
with the sword—[v]Abner the son of Ner,
the commander of the army of Israel, and
[w]Amasa the son of Jether, the commander
of the army of Judah—though my father
David did not know *it*. 33 Their blood shall
therefore return upon the head of Joab and
[x]upon the head of his descendants forever.
[y]But upon David and his descendants,
upon his house and his throne, there shall
be peace forever from the LORD."
34 So Benaiah the son of Jehoiada went
up and struck and killed him; and he was
buried in his own house in the wilderness.
35 The king put Benaiah the son of Jehoiada
in his place over the army, and the king put
[z]Zadok the priest in the place of [a]Abiathar.

Shimei Executed

36 Then the king sent and called for
[b]Shimei, and said to him, "Build yourself a
house in Jerusalem and dwell there, and
do not go out from there anywhere. 37 For
it shall be, on the day you go out and cross
[c]the Brook Kidron, know for certain you
shall surely die; [d]your [8]blood shall be on
your own head."
38 And Shimei said to the king, "The
saying *is* good. As my lord the king has
said, so your servant will do." So Shimei
dwelt in Jerusalem many days.
39 Now it happened at the end of three
years, that two slaves of Shimei ran away
to [e]Achish the son of Maachah, king of
Gath. And they told Shimei, saying, "Look,
your slaves *are* in Gath!" 40 So Shimei
arose, saddled his donkey, and went to
Achish at Gath to seek his slaves. And
Shimei went and brought his slaves from
Gath. 41 And Solomon was told that
Shimei had gone from Jerusalem to Gath
and had come back. 42 Then the king sent
and called for Shimei, and said to him,

23 [h] Ruth 1:17
24 [i] 2 Sam. 7:11, 13; 1 Chr. 22:10 [5] Royal dynasty
25 [j] 2 Sam. 8:18; 1 Kin. 4:4
26 [k] Josh. 21:18; Jer. 1:1 [l] 1 Sam. 22:23; 23:6; 2 Sam. 15:14, 29 [6] Lit. *you are a man of death*
27 [m] 1 Sam. 2:31-35
28 [n] 1 Kin. 1:7 [o] 1 Kin. 1:50
29 [p] 1 Kin. 2:5, 6
30 [q] [Ex. 21:14]
31 [r] [Ex. 21:14] [s] [Num. 35:33; Deut. 19:13; 21:8, 9]
32 [t] [Gen. 9:6]; Judg. 9:24, 57 [u] 2 Chr. 21:13, 14 [v] 2 Sam. 3:27 [w] 2 Sam. 20:9, 10 [7] Or *bloodshed*
33 [x] 2 Sam. 3:29 [y] [Prov. 25:5]
35 [z] 1 Sam. 2:35; 1 Kin. 4:4; 1 Chr. 6:53; 24:3; 29:22 [a] 1 Kin. 2:27
36 [b] 2 Sam. 16:5-13; 1 Kin. 2:8
37 [c] 2 Sam. 15:23; 2 Kin. 23:6; John 18:1 [d] Lev. 20:9; Josh. 2:19; 2 Sam. 1:16; Ezek. 18:13 [8] Or *bloodshed*
39 [e] 1 Sam. 27:2

ously specified (1:52), he pronounced a formal, legal death sentence on Adonijah (vv. 23,24).

2:24 as He promised. Solomon viewed himself as the fulfillment of the Lord's promise to David in 2 Sam. 7:12-16 (see also 5:5; 8:18-21). The ultimate fulfillment will be the Messiah, Jesus, who will return to Israel and set up His kingdom (see Is. 9:6,7).

2:26 Anathoth. A priestly town, 3 mi. NE of Jerusalem (cf. Jer. 1:1). There Abiathar, the disloyal High-Priest (1:7), lived in banishment.

2:27 fulfill the word of the LORD. Solomon's removal of Abiathar from the office of priest fulfilled God's prophecy that Eli's line of priests would be cut off (1 Sam. 2:30-35). This reestablished the line of Eleazar/Phinehas in Zadok (2:35), as promised by God (cf. Num. 25:10-13).

2:28 Joab fled to the tabernacle. Cf. 1:50. He knew he would have been killed already if he had not been so popular with the army. The altar provided no real sanctuary to the rebel and murderer (cf. Ex. 21:14).

2:31 strike him down. Like Adonijah (1:50), Joab sought asylum at the altar (2:28). The protection of the Lord at the altar applied only to accidental crimes, not premeditated murder (Ex. 21:14), so Solomon ordered Benaiah to administer the violent death sought by David (2:6).

2:33 peace forever. This pledge is ultimately to be fulfilled in the Messiah's kingdom (see Is. 2:2-4; 9:6,7).

2:34 wilderness. The tomb of Joab's father was near Bethlehem (2 Sam. 2:32). Joab's house was probably on the edge of the Judean wilderness, E of Bethlehem.

2:36 do not go out. Shimei had not provoked Solomon directly as Adonijah had. Therefore, Solomon determined to keep Shimei under close watch by confining him to Jerusalem.

2:39 Gath. A major Philistine city about 30 mi. SW of Jerusalem.

"Did I not make you swear by the LORD,
and warn you, saying, 'Know for certain
that on the day you go out and travel anywhere, you shall surely die'? And you said
to me, 'The word I have heard *is* good.'
43 Why then have you not kept the oath of
the LORD and the commandment that I
gave you?" 44 The king said moreover to
Shimei, "You know, as your heart acknowledges, [f]all the wickedness that you did to
my father David; therefore the LORD will
[g]return your wickedness on your own
head. 45 But King Solomon *shall be* blessed,
and [h]the throne of David shall be established before the LORD forever."
46 So the king commanded Benaiah the
son of Jehoiada; and he went out and
struck him down, and he died. Thus the
[i]kingdom was established in the hand of
Solomon.

Solomon Requests Wisdom

3 Now [a]Solomon made [1]a treaty with
Pharaoh king of Egypt, and married
Pharaoh's daughter; then he brought her
[b]to the City of David until he had finished
building his [c]own house, and [d]the house of
the LORD, and [e]the wall all around Jerusalem. 2 [f]Meanwhile the people sacrificed at
the high places, because there was no
house built for the name of the LORD until
those days. 3 And Solomon [g]loved the
LORD, [h]walking in the statutes of his father
David, except that he sacrificed and
burned incense at the high places.
4 Now [i]the king went to Gibeon to sacrifice there, [j]for that *was* the great high place:
Solomon offered a thousand burnt offerings
on that altar. 5 [k]At Gibeon the LORD appeared to Solomon [l]in a dream by night; and
God said, "Ask! What shall I give you?"
6 [m]And Solomon said: "You have shown
great mercy to Your servant David my father, because he [n]walked before You in
truth, in righteousness, and in uprightness
of heart with You; You have continued this
great kindness for him, and You [o]have
given him a son to sit on his throne, as *it is*
this day. 7 Now, O LORD my God, You have
made Your servant king instead of my father David, but I *am* a [p]little child; I do not
know *how* [q]to go out or come in. 8 And
Your servant *is* in the midst of Your people
whom You [r]have chosen, a great people,
[s]too numerous to be numbered or counted.
9 [t]Therefore give to Your servant an [2]un-
derstanding heart [u]to judge Your people,
that I may [v]discern between good and evil.
For who is able to judge this great people
of Yours?"
10 The speech pleased the LORD, that Solomon had asked this thing. 11 Then God
said to him: "Because you have asked this
thing, and have [w]not asked long life for
yourself, nor have asked riches for yourself, nor have asked the life of your enemies, but have asked for yourself understanding to discern justice, 12 [x]behold, I
have done according to your words; [y]see, I
have given you a wise and understanding
heart, so that there has not been anyone
like you before you, nor shall any like you

44 [f]2 Sam. 16:5-13 [g]1 Sam. 25:39; 2 Kin. 11:1, 12-16; Ps. 7:16; Ezek. 17:19
45 [h]2 Sam. 7:13; [Prov. 25:5]
46 [i]1 Kin. 2:12; 2 Chr. 1:1

CHAPTER 3

1 [a]1 Kin. 7:8; 9:24 [b]2 Sam. 5:7 [c]1 Kin. 7:1 [d]1 Kin. 6 [e]1 Kin. 9:15, 19 [1]*an alliance*
2 [f][Deut. 12:2-5, 13, 14]; 1 Kin. 11:7; 22:43
3 [g][Rom. 8:28] [h][1 Kin. 3:6, 14]
4 [i]1 Kin. 9:2; 2 Chr. 1:3 [j]1 Chr. 16:39; 21:29
5 [k]1 Kin. 9:2; 11:9; 2 Chr. 1:7 [l]Num. 12:6; Matt. 1:20; 2:13
6 [m]2 Chr. 1:8 [n]1 Kin. 2:4; 9:4; 2 Kin. 20:3 [o]2 Sam. 7:8-17; 1 Kin. 1:48
7 [p]1 Chr. 22:5; Jer. 1:6, 7 [q]Num. 27:17; 2 Sam. 5:2
8 [r][Ex. 19:6; Deut. 7:6] [s]Gen. 13:6; 15:5; 22:17
9 [t]2 Chr. 1:10; [James 1:5] [u]Ps. 72:1, 2 [v]2 Sam. 14:17; Is. 7:15; [Heb. 5:14] [2]*Lit. hearing*
11 [w][James 4:3]
12 [x][1 John 5:14, 15] [y]1 Kin. 4:29-31; 5:12; 10:24; Eccl. 1:16

2:45 throne of David. In contrast to Shimei's curse (2 Sam. 16:5-8), the Lord's blessing was to come through the ruler of David's, not Saul's, line (cf. 2 Sam. 7:12,13,16).

2:46 With the death of Shimei, all the rival factions were eliminated.

3:1 a treaty with Pharaoh. The Pharaoh was probably Siamun, the next-to-last ruler of the weak 21st dynasty. Solomon's treaty with Pharaoh signified that he held a high standing in the world of his day. Pharaoh's daughter was the most politically significant of Solomon's 700 wives (cf: 7:8; 9:16; 11:1).

3:2 the high places. The open-air, hilltop worship centers which the Israelites inherited from the Canaanites had been rededicated to the Lord; the use of pagan altars had been forbidden (Num. 33:52; Deut. 7:5; 12:3). After the building of the temple, worship at the high places was condemned (11:7,8; 12:31; 2 Kin. 16:17-20; 21:3; 23:26). **no house...for the name of the LORD.** "Name" represented the character and presence of the Lord (cf. Ex. 3:13,14). He had promised to choose one place "to put His name for His dwelling place" (Deut. 12:5). The temple at Jerusalem was to be that place (cf. 5:3,5; 8:16,17, 18,19,20,29,43,44,48; 9:3,7). In the ancient Near East, to identify a temple with a god's name meant that the god owned the place and dwelt there.

3:3 except. Solomon's failure in completely following the Lord was exhibited in his continual worship at the high places.

3:4-15 See 2 Chr. 1:7-13.

3:4 Gibeon. A town about 7 mi. NW of Jerusalem, where the tabernacle of Moses and the original bronze altar were located (1 Chr. 21:29; 2 Chr. 1:2-6).

3:5 dream. God often gave revelation in dreams (Gen. 26:24; 28:12; 46:2; Dan. 2:7; 7:1; Matt. 1:20; 2:12,19,22). However, this dream was unique, a two-way conversation between the Lord and Solomon.

3:6 great mercy...great kindness. These terms imply covenant faithfulness. Solomon viewed his succession to David as evidence of the Lord's faithfulness to His promises to David.

3:7 little child. Since Solomon was probably only about 20 years of age, he readily admitted his lack of qualification and experience to be king (cf. 1 Chr. 22:5; 29:1). *See note on Num. 27:15-17.*

3:8 a great people. Based on the census, which recorded 800,000 men of fighting age in Israel and 500,000 in Judah (2 Sam. 24:9), the total population was over 4 million, approximately double what it had been at the time of the Conquest (see Num. 26:1-65).

3:9 an understanding heart. Humbly admitting his need, Solomon sought "a listening heart" to govern God's people with wisdom.

3:10 pleased the LORD. The Lord was delighted that Solomon had not asked for personal benefits, e.g., long life, wealth, or the death of his enemies.

3:12 anyone like you. Solomon was one of a kind in judicial insight, as illustrated in vv. 16-27.

arise after you. 13 And I have also [z]given
you what you have not asked: both [a]riches
and honor, so that there shall not be anyone like you among the kings all your
days. 14 So [b]if you walk in My ways, to
keep My statutes and My commandments,
[c]as your father David walked, then I will
[d]lengthen[3] your days."
15 Then Solomon [e]awoke; and indeed it
had been a dream. And he came to Jerusalem and stood before the ark of the
covenant of the LORD, offered up burnt offerings, offered peace offerings, and [f]made
a feast for all his servants.

Solomon's Wise Judgment

16 Now two women *who were* harlots
came to the king, and [g]stood before him.
17 And one woman said, "O my lord, this
woman and I dwell in the same house; and
I gave birth while she *was* in the house.
18 Then it happened, the third day after I
had given birth, that this woman also gave
birth. And we *were* together; [4]no one *was*
with us in the house, except the two of us
in the house. 19 And this woman's son died
in the night, because she lay on him. 20 So
she arose in the middle of the night and
took my son from my side, while your
maidservant slept, and laid him in her
bosom, and laid her dead child in my
bosom. 21 And when I rose in the morning
to nurse my son, there he was, dead. But
when I had examined him in the morning,
indeed, he was not my son whom I had
borne."
22 Then the other woman said, "No! But
the living one *is* my son, and the dead one
is your son."
And the first woman said, "No! But the
dead one *is* your son, and the living one *is*
my son."

13 [z][Matt. 6:33; Eph. 3:20] [a]1 Kin. 4:21, 24; 10:23; 1 Chr. 29:12
14 [b][1 Kin. 6:12] [c]1 Kin. 15:5 [d]Ps. 91:16; Prov. 3:2 [3]*prolong*
15 [e]Gen. 41:7 [f]Gen. 40:20; 1 Kin. 8:65; Esth. 1:3; Dan. 5:1; Mark 6:21
16 [g]Num. 27:2
18 [4]Lit. *no stranger*
26 [h]Gen. 43:30; Is. 49:15; Jer. 31:20; Hos. 11:8
28 [i]1 Kin. 3:9, 11, 12; 2 Chr. 1:12; Dan. 1:17; [Col. 2:2, 3]

CHAPTER 4

3 [a]2 Sam. 8:16; 20:24 [1]*secretaries*
4 [b]1 Kin. 2:35 [c]1 Kin. 2:27
5 [d]1 Kin. 4:7 [e]2 Sam. 8:18; 20:26 [f]2 Sam. 15:37; 16:16; 1 Chr. 27:33
6 [g]1 Kin. 5:14

Thus they spoke before the king.
23 And the king said, "The one says,
'This *is* my son, who lives, and your son *is*
the dead one'; and the other says, 'No! But
your son *is* the dead one, and my son *is* the
living one.' " 24 Then the king said, "Bring
me a sword." So they brought a sword before the king. 25 And the king said, "Divide
the living child in two, and give half to
one, and half to the other."
26 Then the woman whose son *was* living spoke to the king, for [h]she yearned
with compassion for her son; and she said,
"O my lord, give her the living child, and
by no means kill him!"
But the other said, "Let him be neither
mine nor yours, *but* divide *him*."
27 So the king answered and said, "Give
the first woman the living child, and by no
means kill him; she *is* his mother."
28 And all Israel heard of the judgment
which the king had rendered; and they
feared the king, for they saw that the [i]wis-
dom of God *was* in him to administer justice.

Solomon's Administration

4 So King Solomon was king over all Israel. 2 And these *were* his officials: Azariah the son of Zadok, the priest; 3 Eli-
horeph and Ahijah, the sons of Shisha,
[1]scribes; [a]Jehoshaphat the son of Ahilud,
the recorder; 4 [b]Benaiah the son of Jehoiada, over the army; Zadok and [c]Abiathar,
the priests; 5 Azariah the son of Nathan,
over [d]the officers; Zabud the son of Nathan, [e]a priest *and* [f]the king's friend; 6 Ahi-
shar, over the household; and [g]Adoniram
the son of Abda, over the labor force.
7 And Solomon had twelve governors
over all Israel, who provided food for the
king and his household; each one made

3:14 lengthen your days. In contrast to riches and honor that were already his, a long life was dependent on Solomon's future obedience to the Lord's commands. Because of his disobedience, Solomon died before reaching 70 years of age (cf. Ps. 90:10).

3:16-27 harlots came to the king. Here is an illustration of how wisely Solomon ruled. In Israel, the king was the ultimate "judge" of the land, and any citizen, even the basest prostitute, could petition him for a verdict (2 Sam. 14:2-21; 15:1-4; 2 Kin. 8:1-6).

3:25 half...half. In ordering his servants to cut the child in two, he knew the liar would not object, but out of maternal compassion the real mother would (cf. Ex. 21:35).

3:28 feared the king. Israel was in awe of and willing to submit to the rule of Solomon because of his wisdom from God.

4:1 all Israel. Solomon was in firm control of all of the people. Israel's squabbling factions had fallen in line behind the king.

4:2 Azariah...the son of. Actually, he was the son of Ahimaaz and the grandson of Zadok, as "son of" can mean "descendant of" (cf. 1 Chr. 6:8,9). In David's roster of officials, the army commander came first (2 Sam. 8:16; 20:23). Under Solomon, the priest and other officials preceded the military leader.

4:3 scribes. Probably they prepared royal edicts and kept official records. **recorder.** Likely, he maintained the records of all important daily affairs in the kingdom.

4:4 priests. Zadok and Abiathar had served together as High-Priests under David (2 Sam. 8:17; 20:25). Although Abiathar had been removed from priestly service and exiled (2:26-27,35), he maintained his priestly title until his death.

4:5 Nathan. Whether this is the prophet Nathan (*see note on 1:8*) or another person by that name is uncertain, but it could be that Solomon was honoring the sons of the prophet.

4:6 over the household. One who managed Solomon's properties, both lands and buildings (cf. 16:9; 18:3; 2 Kin. 18:18,37; 19:2). **over the labor force.** One who oversaw the conscripted workers of Solomon (cf. 5:13-18).

4:7 twelve governors. Solomon divided the land into 12 geographical districts (different from the tribal boundaries), each supervised by a governor. Each month a different governor collected provisions in his district to supply the king and his staff.

provision for one month of the year.
8 These *are* their names: [2]Ben-Hur, in the
mountains of Ephraim; 9 [3]Ben-Deker, in
Makaz, Shaalbim, Beth Shemesh, and Elon
Beth Hanan; 10 [4]Ben-Hesed, in Arubboth;
to him *belonged* Sochoh and all the land of
Hepher; 11 [5]Ben-Abinadab, *in* all the regions of Dor; he had Taphath the daughter
of Solomon as wife; 12 Baana the son of
Ahilud, *in* Taanach, Megiddo, and all Beth
Shean, which *is* beside Zaretan below
Jezreel, from Beth Shean to Abel Meholah,
as far as the other side of Jokneam;
13 [6]Ben-Geber, in Ramoth Gilead; to him
belonged [h]the towns of Jair the son of Manasseh, in Gilead; to him *also belonged* [i]the
region of Argob in Bashan—sixty large
cities with walls and bronze gate-bars;
14 Ahinadab the son of Iddo, *in* Mahanaim; 15 [j]Ahimaaz, in Naphtali; he also
took Basemath the daughter of Solomon
as wife; 16 Baanah the son of [k]Hushai, in
Asher and Aloth; 17 Jehoshaphat the son
of Paruah, in Issachar; 18 [l]Shimei the son
of Elah, in Benjamin; 19 Geber the son of
Uri, in the land of Gilead, *in* [m]the country
of Sihon king of the Amorites, and of Og
king of Bashan. *He was* the only governor
who *was* in the land.

Prosperity and Wisdom of Solomon's Reign

20 Judah and Israel *were* as numerous [n]as
the sand by the sea in multitude, [o]eating
and drinking and rejoicing. 21 So [p]Solomon
reigned over all kingdoms from [q]the[7]
River *to* the land of the Philistines, as far as
the border of Egypt. [r]*They* brought tribute
and served Solomon all the days of his life.
22 [s]Now Solomon's [8]provision for one
day was thirty [9]kors of fine flour, sixty
kors of meal, 23 ten fatted oxen, twenty
oxen from the pastures, and one hundred
sheep, besides deer, gazelles, roebucks,
and fatted fowl.
24 For he had dominion over all *the region* on this side of [1]the River from Tiphsah
even to Gaza, namely over [t]all the kings on
this side of the River; and [u]he had peace on

8 [2] Lit. *Son of Hur*
9 [3] Lit. *Son of Deker*
10 [4] Lit. *Son of Hesed*
11 [5] Lit. *Son of Abinadab*
13 [h] Num. 32:41; 1 Chr. 2:22 [i] Deut. 3:4 [6] Lit. *Son of Geber*
15 [j] 2 Sam. 15:27
16 [k] 2 Sam. 15:32; 1 Chr. 27:33
18 [l] 1 Kin. 1:8
19 [m] Deut. 3:8-10
20 [n] Gen. 22:17; 32:12; 1 Kin. 3:8; [Prov. 14:28] [o] Ps. 72:3, 7; Mic. 4:4
21 [p] Ex. 34:24; 2 Chr. 9:26; Ps. 72:8 [q] Gen. 15:18; Josh. 1:4 [r] Ps. 68:29 [7] The Euphrates
22 [s] Neh. 5:18 [8] Lit. *bread* [9] *Each about 5 bushels*
24 [t] Ps. 72:11 [u] 1 Kin. 5:4; 1 Chr. 22:9 [1] The Euphrates

4:20 numerous as the sand by the sea. A clear allusion to the Lord's promise to Abraham in Gen. 22:17. The early years of Solomon's reign, characterized by population growth, peace, and prosperity, were a foreshadowing of the blessings that will prevail in Israel when the Abrahamic Covenant is fulfilled.

4:21 all kingdoms. The borders of the kingdoms which Solomon influenced echoed the Lord's promise to Abram in Gen. 15:18. However, Solomon's reign was not the fulfillment of the Abrahamic Covenant for 3 reasons: 1) Israel still only lived in the land "from Dan as far as Beersheba" (v. 25). Abraham's seed did not inhabit all the land promised to Abraham. 2) The non-Israelite kingdoms did not lose their identity and independence, but rather recognized Solomon's authority and brought him tribute without surrendering title to their lands. 3) According to Num. 34:6, the Mediterranean Sea is to be the western border of the Land of Promise, indicating that Tyre was to be a part of the Promised Land. However, Hiram king of Tyre was a sovereign who entered into a bilateral or parity treaty (between equals) with Solomon (5:1-12).

4:22 provision. I.e., the daily provisions for Solomon's palace.

4:24 Tiphsah...Gaza. Tiphsah was located on the W bank of the Euphrates and Gaza on the southwestern Mediterranean coast. These towns represented the NE and SW points of Solomon's influence.

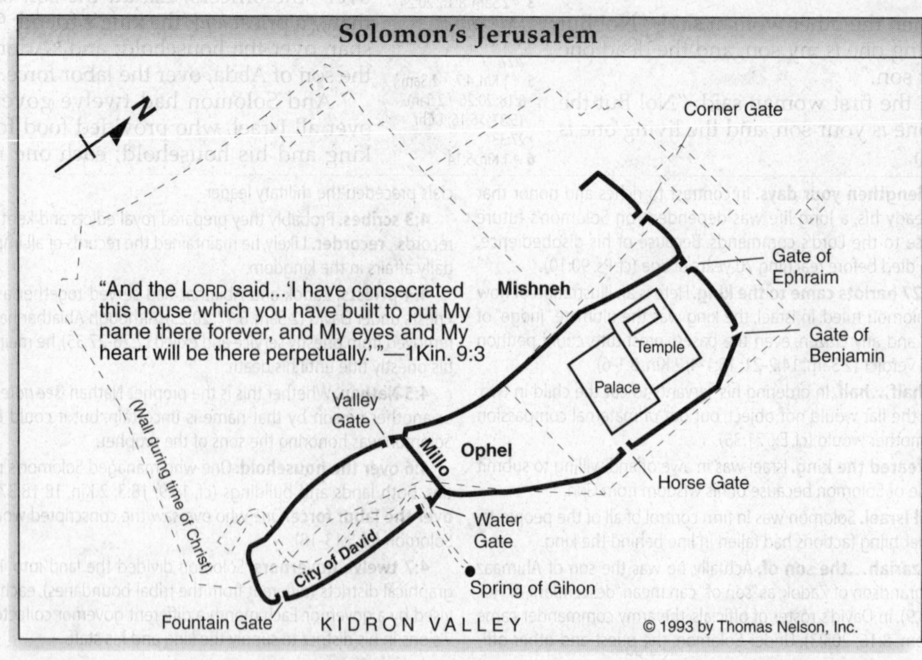

every side all around him. 25 And Judah
and Israel [v]dwelt[2] safely, [w]each man under
his vine and his fig tree, [x]from Dan as far
as Beersheba, all the days of Solomon.
26 [y]Solomon had [3]forty thousand stalls
of [z]horses for his chariots, and twelve
thousand horsemen. 27 And [a]these governors, each man in his month, provided
food for King Solomon and for all who
came to King Solomon's table. There was
no lack in their supply. 28 They also
brought barley and straw to the proper
place, for the horses and steeds, each man
according to his charge.
29 And [b]God gave Solomon wisdom and
exceedingly great understanding, and
largeness of heart like the sand on the
seashore. 30 Thus Solomon's wisdom excelled the wisdom of all the men [c]of the East
and all [d]the wisdom of Egypt. 31 For he was
[e]wiser than all men—[f]than Ethan the Ezrahite, [g]and Heman, Chalcol, and Darda, the
sons of Mahol; and his fame was in all the
surrounding nations. 32 [h]He spoke three
thousand proverbs, and his [i]songs were one
thousand and five. 33 Also he spoke of trees,
from the cedar tree of Lebanon even to the
hyssop that springs out of the wall; he
spoke also of animals, of birds, of creeping
things, and of fish. 34 And men of all nations, from all the kings of the earth who
had heard of his wisdom, [j]came to hear the
wisdom of Solomon.

Solomon Prepares to Build the Temple

5 Now [a]Hiram king of Tyre sent his servants to Solomon, because he heard
that they had anointed him king in place of
his father, [b]for Hiram had always loved David. 2 Then [c]Solomon sent to Hiram, saying:

3 [d]You know how my father David
could not build a house for the
name of the LORD his God [e]because
of the wars which were fought
against him on every side, until the
LORD put [1]*his foes* under the soles
of his feet.
4 But now the LORD my God has
given me [f]rest[2] on every side; *there
is* neither adversary nor [3]evil
occurrence.
5 [g]And behold, [4]I propose to build a
house for the name of the LORD my
God, [h]as the LORD spoke to my
father David, saying, "Your son,
whom I will set on your throne in
your place, he shall build the
house for My name."
6 Now therefore, command that they
cut down [i]cedars for me from Lebanon; and my servants will be with
your servants, and I will pay you
wages for your servants according
to whatever you say. For you know
there is none among us who has skill
to cut timber like the Sidonians.

7 So it was, when Hiram heard the words
of Solomon, that he rejoiced greatly and
said,

Blessed *be* the LORD this day, for He
has given David a wise son over
this great people!

25 [v][Jer. 23:6] [w][Mic. 4:4; Zech. 3:10] [x]Judg. 20:1 [2]*lived in safety*
26 [y]1 Kin. 10:26; 2 Chr. 1:14 [z][Deut. 17:16] [3]So with MT, most other authorities; some LXX mss. *four thousand;* cf. 2 Chr. 9:25
27 [a]1 Kin. 4:7
29 [b]1 Kin. 3:12
30 [c]Gen. 25:6 [d]Is. 19:11, 12; Acts 7:22
31 [e]1 Kin. 3:12 [f]1 Chr. 15:19; Ps. 89:title [g]1 Chr. 2:6; Ps. 88:title
32 [h]Prov. 1:1; 10:1; 25:1; Eccl. 12:9 [i]Song 1:1
34 [j]1 Kin. 10:1; 2 Chr. 9:1, 23

CHAPTER 5

1 [a]1 Kin. 5:10, 18; 2 Chr. 2:3 [b]2 Sam. 5:11; 1 Chr. 14:1
2 [c]2 Chr. 2:3
3 [d]1 Chr. 28:2, 3 [e]1 Chr. 22:8; 28:3 [1]Lit. *them*
4 [f]1 Kin. 4:24; 1 Chr. 22:9 [2]*peace* [3]*misfortune*
5 [g]2 Chr. 2:4 [h]2 Sam. 7:12, 13; 1 Kin. 6:38; 1 Chr. 17:12; 22:10; 28:6; 2 Chr. 6:2 [4]Lit. *I am saying*
6 [i]2 Chr. 2:8, 10

4:26 forty thousand stalls. Though the Heb. text reads 40,000, this was probably a copyist's error in transcribing the text, and it should read 4,000 as in 2 Chr. 9:25.

4:30 the East...Egypt. The men to the East of Israel in Mesopotamia and Arabia (cf. Job 1:3) and in Egypt were known for their wisdom. Egypt had been renowned for learning and science, as well as culture. Solomon's wisdom was superior to all at home or abroad (v. 31).

4:31 sons of Mahol. This probably meant "singers," a guild of musicians who created sacred songs.

4:32 proverbs...songs. Hundreds of Solomon's proverbs have been preserved in the book of Proverbs (see Introduction to Proverbs). One of his songs is the Song of Solomon.

4:33 trees...animals...birds. Solomon described and taught about all kinds of plant and animal life e.g., Prov. 6:6-8; 28:15; 30:19.

4:34 men of all nations. Solomon acquired an international reputation for his wisdom. Many important visitors came from faraway places to learn from Solomon's wisdom (cf. 10:1-13).

5:1-16 See 2 Chr. 2:1-18.

5:1 Hiram king of Tyre. Tyre was an important port city on the Mediterranean Sea N of Israel. Two towering mountain ranges ran within Lebanon's borders, and on their slopes grew thick forests of cedars. Hiram I ruled there ca. 978–944 B.C. He had earlier provided building materials and workers for David to build his palace (2 Sam. 5:11). Solomon maintained the friendly relations with Hiram established by David. They were beneficial to both as Israel exchanged wheat and oil for timber (see vv. 9-11).

5:4 rest. The guarantee of peace with the peoples surrounding Israel allowed Solomon to build the temple (cf. 4:24).

5:5 the name. "Name" represents the character and nature of the person indicated. *See note on 3:2.* **Your son.** Solomon claimed to be the promised offspring of David, the fulfillment of the Lord's promise to David in 2 Sam. 7:12,13. However, Solomon's later disobedience proved that he was not the ultimate, promised offspring (11:9-13).

5:6 cedars...from Lebanon. The cedars of Lebanon symbolized majesty and might (Ps. 92:12; Ezek. 31:3). Because it was durable, resistant to rot and worms, closely-grained, and could be polished to a fine shine, its wood was regarded as the best timber for building. The logs were tied together and floated down the Mediterranean to Joppa (see v. 9; 2 Chr. 2:16), from where they could be transported to Jerusalem, 35 mi. inland. **Sidonians.** These are the inhabitants of the city of Sidon, located on the Mediterranean Sea about 22 mi. N of Tyre. Here, the term probably referred, in a general sense, to the Phoenicians, who were skilled craftsmen.

5:7 Blessed *be* the LORD. Perhaps Hiram was a worshiper of the true God, but it is equally possible that he was only acknowledging Jehovah as the God of the Hebrews (cf. 2 Chr. 2:16). **a wise son.** Hiram recognized Solomon's wisdom in seeking to honor his father David's desires.

8 Then Hiram sent to Solomon, saying:

I have considered *the message*
which you sent me, *and* I will do
all you desire concerning the cedar
and cypress logs.
9 My servants shall bring *them* down
[j]from Lebanon to the sea; I will
float them in rafts by sea to the
place you indicate to me, and will
have them broken apart there; then
you can take *them* away. And you
shall fulfill my desire [k]by giving
food for my household.

10 Then Hiram gave Solomon cedar and
cypress logs *according to* all his desire.
11 [l]And Solomon gave Hiram twenty thousand [5]kors of wheat *as* food for his household, and [6]twenty kors of pressed oil. Thus
Solomon gave to Hiram year by year.
12 So the LORD gave Solomon wisdom,
[m]as He had promised him; and there was
peace between Hiram and Solomon, and
the two of them made a treaty together.
13 Then King Solomon raised up a labor
force out of all Israel; and the labor force
was thirty thousand men. 14 And he sent
them to Lebanon, ten thousand a month in
shifts: they were one month in Lebanon *and*
two months at home; [n]Adoniram *was* in
charge of the labor force. 15 [o]Solomon had
seventy thousand who carried burdens,
and eighty thousand who quarried *stone* in
the mountains, 16 besides three thousand
[7]three hundred from the [p]chiefs of Solomon's deputies, who supervised the people who labored in the work. 17 And the
king commanded them to quarry large
stones, costly stones, *and* [q]hewn stones, to
lay the foundation of the [8]temple. 18 So Solomon's builders, Hiram's builders, and the
Gebalites quarried *them;* and they prepared
timber and stones to build the [9]temple.

9 [j]Ezra 3:7 [k]Ezek. 27:17; Acts 12:20
11 [l]2 Chr. 2:10 [5]Each about 5 bushels [6]So with MT, Tg., Vg.; LXX, Syr. *twenty thousand kors*
12 [m]1 Kin. 3:12
14 [n]1 Kin. 12:18
15 [o]1 Kin. 9:20-22; 2 Chr. 2:17, 18
16 [p]1 Kin. 9:23 [7]So with MT, Tg., Vg.; LXX *six hundred*
17 [q]1 Kin. 6:7; 1 Chr. 22:2 [8]Lit. *house*
18 [9]Lit. *house*

CHAPTER 6

1 [a]2 Chr. 3:1, 2 [b]Acts 7:47 [1]So with MT, Tg., Vg.; LXX *fortieth* [2]*Or Ayyar,* April or May
2 [c]Ezek. 41:1
3 [3]Heb. *heykal;* here the main room of the temple; elsewhere called the holy place, Ex. 26:33; Ezek. 41:1 [4]About 30 feet [5]Lit. *it* [6]About 15 feet
4 [d]Ezek. 40:16; 41:16
5 [e]Ezek. 41:6 [f]1 Kin. 6:16, 19-21, 31 [7]Lit. *house* [8]Heb. *debir;* here the inner room of the temple; elsewhere called the Most Holy Place, v. 16
6 [9]Lit. *house*
7 [g]Ex. 20:25; Deut. 27:5, 6

Solomon Builds the Temple

6 And [a]it came to pass in the four hundred and [1]eightieth year after the children of Israel had come out of the land of
Egypt, in the fourth year of Solomon's
reign over Israel, in the month of [2]Ziv,
which *is* the second month, [b]that he began
to build the house of the LORD. 2 Now [c]the
house which King Solomon built for the
LORD, its length *was* sixty cubits, its width
twenty, and its height thirty cubits. 3 The
vestibule in front of the [3]sanctuary of the
house *was* [4]twenty cubits long across the
width of the house, *and* the width of [5]*the*
vestibule extended [6]ten cubits from the front
of the house. 4 And he made for the house
[d]windows with beveled frames.
5 Against the wall of the [7]temple he built
[e]chambers all around, *against* the walls of
the temple, all around the sanctuary [f]and
the [8]inner sanctuary. Thus he made side
chambers all around it. 6 The lowest chamber *was* five cubits wide, the middle *was* six
cubits wide, and the third *was* seven cubits
wide; for he made narrow ledges around
the outside of the temple, so that *the sup-*
port beams would not be fastened into the
walls of the [9]temple. 7 And [g]the temple,
when it was being built, was built with

5:9 food for my household. Tyre's rocky terrain grew great trees, but little good food. Hiram asked Solomon for food for his court in exchange for his lumber.

5:13 a labor force out of all Israel. Lit. "conscripted labor." These 30,000 men who labored in Lebanon were Israelites of the land. They were sent to Lebanon, 10,000 a month in rotation. For every month they worked, they were off two months, which meant they worked only 4 months per year. These Israelite laborers must be distinguished from the Canaanite remnant who were made into permanent slaves. *See note on 9:21,22.* The 30,000 Israelites were free and performed the task of felling trees.

5:16 three thousand three hundred. *See note on 2 Chr. 2:2.* **people who labored.** According to 2 Chr. 2:17,18, these 150,000 laborers (5:15) and their supervisors were non-Israelite inhabitants of the land.

5:18 Gebalites. Inhabitants of Gebal, a town located about 60 mi. N of Tyre.

6:1-38 See 2 Chr. 3:1-17; 7:15-22.

6:1 four hundred and eightieth year. Solomon began to build the temple by laying its foundation (v. 37) 480 years after the Exodus from Egypt. The 480 years are to be taken as the actual years between the Exodus and the building of the temple, because references to numbers of years in the book of Kings are consistently taken in a literal fashion. Also, the literal interpretation correlates with Jephthah's statement recorded in Judg. 11:26. **fourth year.** I.e., 966 B.C. Thus, the Exodus is to be dated 1445 B.C.

6:2 cubits. Normally the cubit was about 18 in. This would make the temple structure proper 90 ft. long, 30 ft. wide, and 45 ft. high. However, 2 Chr. 3:3 may indicate that the longer royal cubit of approximately 21 in. was used in the construction of the temple. On this measurement, the temple structure proper would have been 105 ft. long, 35 ft. wide and 52 ½ ft. high. The dimensions of the temple seem to be double those of the tabernacle (see Ex. 26:15-30; 36:20-34).

6:3 vestibule. A porch about 15 ft. long in front of the temple building proper.

6:4 windows. Placed high on the inner side of the temple wall, these openings had lattices or shutters capable of being opened, shut, or partially opened. They served to let out the vapors of the lamps and the smoke of incense, as well as to give light.

6:5 chambers. Another attached structure surrounded the main building, excluding the vestibule. It provided rooms off of the main hall to house temple personnel and to store equipment and treasure (cf. 7:51).

6:6 lowest...middle...third. This attached structure to the temple was 3 stories high. Each upper story was one cubit wider than the one below it. Instead of being inserted into the temple walls, beams supporting the stories rested on recessed ledges in the temple walls themselves.

stone finished at the quarry, so that no
hammer or chisel *or* any iron tool was
heard in the temple while it was being
built. **8** The doorway for the [1]middle story
was on the right side of the temple. They
went up by stairs to the middle *story,* and
from the middle to the third.
9 [h]So he built the [2]temple and finished
it, and he paneled the temple with beams
and boards of cedar. **10** And he built side
chambers against the entire temple, each
five cubits high; they were attached to the
temple with cedar beams.
11 Then the word of the LORD came to
Solomon, saying: **12** "*Concerning* this [3]tem-
ple which you are building, [i]if you walk in
My statutes, execute My judgments, keep
all My commandments, and walk in them,
then I will perform My [4]word with you,
[j]which I spoke to your father David. **13** And
[k]I will dwell among the children of Israel,
and will not [l]forsake My people Israel."
14 So Solomon built the temple and finished it. **15** And he built the inside walls of
the temple with cedar boards; from the
floor of the temple to the ceiling he paneled the inside with wood; and he covered
the floor of the temple with planks of cypress. **16** Then he built the twenty-cubit
room at the rear of the temple, from floor
to ceiling, with cedar boards; he built *it* inside as the inner sanctuary, as the [m]Most
Holy *Place.* **17** And in front of it the temple
sanctuary was forty cubits *long.* **18** The inside of the temple was cedar, carved with

8 [1] So with MT, Vg.; LXX *upper story;* Tg. *ground story*
9 [h] 1 Kin. 6:14, 38 [2] Lit. *house*
12 [i] 1 Kin. 2:4; 9:4 [3] Lit. *house*
[j] [2 Sam. 7:13; 1 Chr. 22:10] [4] *promise*
13 [k] Ex. 25:8; Lev. 26:11; [2 Cor. 6:16; Rev. 21:3] [l] [Deut. 31:6]
16 [m] Ex. 26:33; Lev. 16:2; 1 Kin. 8:6; 2 Chr. 3:8; Ezek. 45:3; Heb. 9:3

6:7 stone finished at the quarry. The erection of the temple went much faster by utilizing pre-cut and pre-fitted materials moved on rollers to the temple site. In addition, the relative quiet would be consistent with the sacredness of the undertaking.

6:8 doorway…stairs. The entrance to the side rooms was on the S side, probably in the middle. Access to the second and third stories was by means of a spiral staircase that led through the middle story to the third floor.

6:11-13 During the construction of the temple, the Lord spoke to Solomon, probably through a prophet, and reiterated that the fulfillment of His Word to David through his son was contingent on Solomon's obedience to His commands (cf. 2:3,4; 3:14; 9:4-8). The use of the same words, "I will dwell among the children of Israel," in v. 13 as in Ex. 29:45, implied that Solomon's temple was the legitimate successor to the tabernacle. The Lord forewarned Solomon and Israel that the temple was no guarantee of His presence; only their continued obedience would assure that.

6:16 the Most Holy *Place.* This inner sanctuary, partitioned off from the main hall by cedar planks, was a perfect cube about 30 ft. on a side (v. 20) and was the most sacred area of the temple. The Most Holy Place is further described in vv. 19-28. The tabernacle also had "a Most Holy Place" (Ex. 26:33,34).

6:17 the temple sanctuary. This was the Holy Place, just outside the Most Holy Place, 60 ft. long, 30 ft. wide and 45 ft. high, that housed the altar of incense, the golden tables of the showbread, and the golden lampstands (7:48,49).

Solomon's Temple

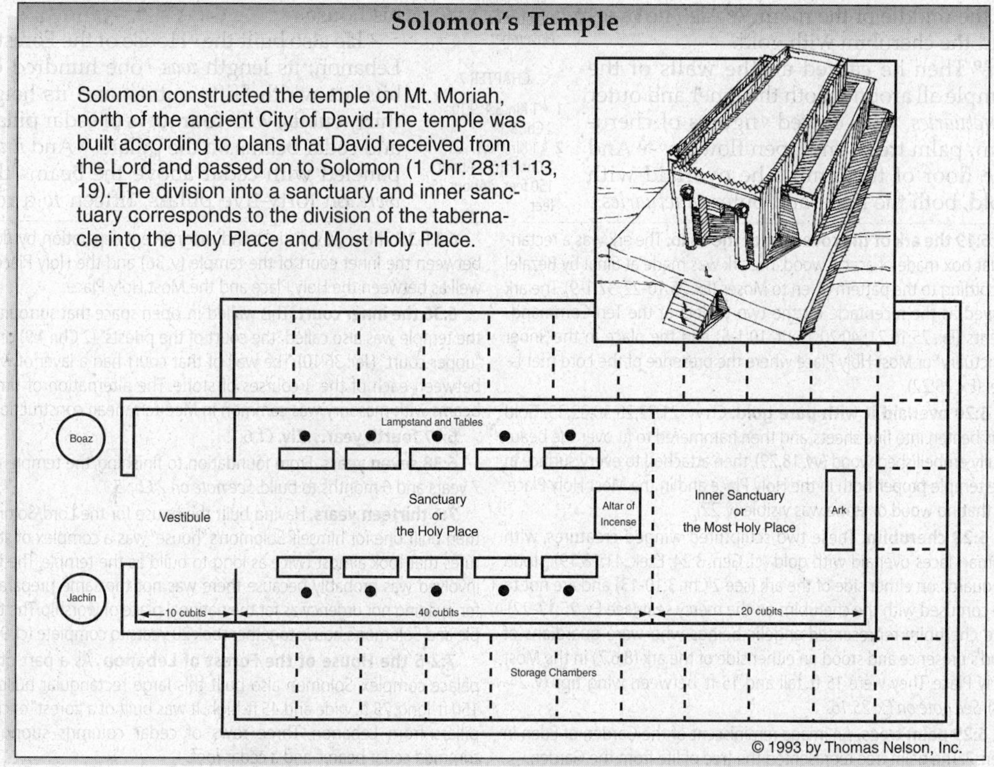

Solomon constructed the temple on Mt. Moriah, north of the ancient City of David. The temple was built according to plans that David received from the Lord and passed on to Solomon (1 Chr. 28:11-13, 19). The division into a sanctuary and inner sanctuary corresponds to the division of the tabernacle into the Holy Place and Most Holy Place.

ornamental buds and open flowers. All
was cedar; there was no stone *to be* seen.
19 And he prepared the [5]inner sanctuary
inside the temple, to set the ark of the
covenant of the LORD there. 20 The inner
sanctuary *was* twenty cubits long, twenty
cubits wide, and twenty cubits high. He
overlaid it with pure gold, and overlaid
the altar of cedar. 21 So Solomon overlaid
the inside of the temple with pure gold. He
stretched gold chains across the front of
the inner sanctuary, and overlaid it with
gold. 22 The whole temple he overlaid with
gold, until he had finished all the temple;
also he overlaid with gold [n]the entire altar
that *was* by the inner sanctuary.
23 Inside the inner sanctuary [o]he made
two cherubim *of* olive wood, *each* ten cubits
high. 24 One wing of the cherub *was* five cubits, and the other wing of the cherub five
cubits: ten cubits from the tip of one wing
to the tip of the other. 25 And the other
cherub *was* ten cubits; both cherubim *were*
of the same size and shape. 26 The height of
one cherub *was* ten cubits, and so *was* the
other cherub. 27 Then he set the cherubim
inside the inner [6]room; and [p]they stretched
out the wings of the cherubim so that the
wing of the one touched *one* wall, and the
wing of the other cherub touched the other
wall. And their wings touched each other
in the middle of the room. 28 Also he overlaid the cherubim with gold.
29 Then he carved all the walls of the
temple all around, both the inner and outer
sanctuaries, with carved [q]figures of cherubim, palm trees, and open flowers. 30 And
the floor of the temple he overlaid with
gold, both the inner and outer *sanctuaries.*
31 For the entrance of the inner sanctuary he made doors *of* olive wood; the lintel
and doorposts *were* [7]one-fifth *of the wall.*
32 The two doors *were of* olive wood; and
he carved on them figures of cherubim,
palm trees, and open flowers, and overlaid
them with gold; and he spread gold on the
cherubim and on the palm trees. 33 So for
the door of the [8]sanctuary he also made
doorposts *of* olive wood, [9]one-fourth *of the*
wall. 34 And the two doors *were of* cypress
wood; [r]two panels *comprised* one folding
door, and two panels *comprised* the other
folding door. 35 Then he carved cherubim,
palm trees, and open flowers *on them,* and
overlaid *them* with gold applied evenly on
the carved work.
36 And he built the [s]inner court with
three rows of hewn stone and a row of
cedar beams.
37 [t]In the fourth year the foundation of
the house of the LORD was laid, in the
month of [1]Ziv. 38 And in the eleventh year,
in the month of [2]Bul, which is the eighth
month, the house was finished in all its details and according to all its plans. So he
was [u]seven years in building it.

Solomon's Other Buildings

7 But Solomon took [a]thirteen years to
build his own house; so he finished all
his house.
2 He also built the [b]House of the Forest of
Lebanon; its length *was* [1]one hundred cubits, its width [2]fifty cubits, and its height
thirty cubits, with four rows of cedar pillars,
and cedar beams on the pillars. 3 And *it was*
paneled with cedar above the beams that
were on forty-five pillars, fifteen *to* a row.

19 [5]The Most Holy Place
22 [n]Ex. 30:1, 3, 6
23 [o]Ex. 37:7-9; 2 Chr. 3:10-12
27 [p]Ex. 25:20; 37:9; 1 Kin. 8:7; 2 Chr. 5:8 [6]Lit. *house*
29 [q]Ex. 36:8, 35
31 [7]Or *five-sided*
33 [8]*temple* [9]Or *four-sided*
34 [r]Ezek. 41:23-25
36 [s]1 Kin. 7:12; Jer. 36:10
37 [t]1 Kin. 6:1 [1]Or *Ayyar,* April or May
38 [u]2 Sam. 7:13; 1 Kin. 5:5; 6:1; 8:19 [2]Or *Heshvan,* October or November

CHAPTER 7

1 [a]1 Kin. 3:1; 9:10; 2 Chr. 8:1
2 [b]1 Kin. 10:17, 21; 2 Chr. 9:16 [1]About 150 feet [2]About 75 feet

6:19 the ark of the covenant of the LORD. The ark was a rectangular box made of acacia wood. The ark was made at Sinai by Bezalel according to the pattern given to Moses (Ex. 25:10-22; 37:1-9). The ark served as the receptacle for the two tablets of the Ten Commandments (Ex. 25:16, 21; 40:20; Deut. 10:1-5) and the place in the "inner sanctuary" or Most Holy Place where the presence of the Lord met Israel (Ex. 25:22).

6:20 overlaid it with pure gold. Cf. vv. 21, 22, 28, 30, 32, 35. Gold was beaten into fine sheets, and then hammered to fit over the beautifully embellished wood (vv. 18, 29), then attached to every surface in the temple proper, both in the Holy Place and in the Most Holy Place, so that no wood or stone was visible (v. 22).

6:23 cherubim. These two sculptured winged creatures, with human faces overlaid with gold (cf. Gen. 3:24; Ezek. 41:18, 19), stood as guards on either side of the ark (see 2 Chr. 3:10-13) and are not to be confused with the cherubim on the mercy seat (see Ex. 25:17-22). The cherubim represented angelic beings who were guardians of God's presence and stood on either side of the ark (8:6, 7) in the Most Holy Place. They were 15 ft. tall and 15 ft. between wing tips (v. 24-26). *See note on Ex. 25:16.*

6:29 palm trees. An image reminiscent of the Garden of Eden in Gen. 2. The palm tree represented the tree of life from the Garden.

6:31-35 There was distinct and magnificent separation by doors between the inner court of the temple (v. 36) and the Holy Place, as well as between the Holy Place and the Most Holy Place.

6:36 the inner court. This walled-in, open space that surrounded the temple was also called "the court of the priests" (2 Chr. 4:9) or the "upper court" (Jer. 36:10). The wall of that court had a layer of wood between each of the 3 courses of stone. The alternation of timber beams with masonry was common in Mediterranean construction.

6:37 fourth year...Ziv. Cf. 6:1.

6:38 seven years. From foundation to finishing, the temple took 7 years and 6 months to build. *See note on 2 Chr. 5:1.*

7:1 thirteen years. Having built the house for the Lord, Solomon then built one for himself. Solomon's "house" was a complex of structures that took almost twice as long to build as the temple. The time involved was probably because there was not the same preparation for building nor urgency as for the national place of worship. The temple and Solomon's house together took 20 years to complete (cf. 9:10).

7:2-5 the House of the Forest of Lebanon. As a part of the palace complex, Solomon also built this large rectangular building, 150 ft. long, 75 ft. wide and 45 ft. high. It was built of a "forest" of cedar pillars from Lebanon. Three rows of cedar columns supported trimmed cedar beams and a cedar roof.

4 *There were* windows *with beveled frames in*
three rows, and window *was* opposite window *in* three tiers. 5 And all the doorways
and doorposts *had* rectangular frames; and
window *was* opposite window *in* three tiers.
6 He also made the Hall of Pillars: its
length *was* fifty cubits, and its width thirty
cubits; and in front of them *was* a portico
with pillars, and a canopy *was* in front of
them.
7 Then he made a hall for the throne, the
Hall of Judgment, where he might judge;
and *it was* paneled with cedar from floor to
[3]ceiling.
8 And the house where he dwelt *had* another court inside the hall, of like workmanship. Solomon also made a house like
this hall for Pharaoh's daughter, [c]whom he
had taken *as wife.*
9 All these *were of* costly stones cut to
size, trimmed with saws, inside and out,
from the foundation to the eaves, and also
on the outside to the great court. 10 The
foundation *was of* costly stones, large
stones, some ten cubits and some eight cubits. 11 And above *were* costly stones, hewn
to size, and cedar wood. 12 The great court
was enclosed with three rows of hewn
stones and a row of cedar beams. So were
the [d]inner court of the house of the LORD
[e]and the vestibule of the temple.

Hiram the Craftsman

13 Now King Solomon sent and brought
[4]Huram from Tyre. 14 [f]He *was* the son of a
widow from the tribe of Naphtali, and [g]his
father *was* a man of Tyre, a bronze worker;
[h]he was filled with wisdom and understanding and skill in working with all
kinds of bronze work. So he came to King
Solomon and did all his work.

The Bronze Pillars for the Temple

15 And he [5]cast [i]two pillars of bronze,
each one eighteen cubits high, and a line of
twelve cubits measured the circumference
of each. 16 Then he made two capitals *of* cast
bronze, to set on the tops of the pillars. The
height of one capital *was* five cubits, and the
height of the other capital *was* five cubits.
17 *He made* a lattice network, with wreaths
of chainwork, for the capitals which *were* on
top of the pillars: seven chains for one capital and seven for the other capital. 18 So he
made the pillars, and two rows of pomegranates above the network all around to
cover the capitals that *were* on top; and thus
he did for the other capital.
19 The capitals which *were* on top of the
pillars in the hall *were* in the shape of lilies,
four cubits. 20 The capitals on the two pillars
also *had pomegranates* above, by the convex
surface which *was* next to the network; and
there *were* [j]two hundred such pomegranates
in rows on each of the capitals all around.
21 [k]Then he set up the pillars by the
vestibule of the temple; he set up the pillar
on the right and called its name [6]Jachin,
and he set up the pillar on the left and
called its name [7]Boaz. 22 The tops of the
pillars were in the shape of lilies. So the
work of the pillars was finished.

The Sea and the Oxen

23 And he made [l]the Sea of cast bronze,
ten cubits from one brim to the other; *it was*

7 [3] Lit. *floor* of the upper level
8 [c] 1 Kin. 3:1; 9:24; 11:1; 2 Chr. 8:11
12 [d] 1 Kin. 6:36 [e] John 10:23; Acts 3:11
13 [4] Heb. *Hiram;* cf. 2 Chr. 2:13, 14
14 [f] 2 Chr. 2:14 [g] 2 Chr. 4:16 [h] Ex. 31:3; 36:1
15 [i] 2 Kin. 25:17; 2 Chr. 3:15; 4:12; Jer. 52:21 [5] *fashioned*
20 [j] 2 Chr. 3:16; 4:13; Jer. 52:23
21 [k] 2 Chr. 3:17 [6] Lit. *He Shall Establish* [7] Lit. *In It Is Strength*
23 [l] 2 Kin. 25:13; 2 Chr. 4:2; Jer. 52:17

7:6 the Hall of Pillars. This colonnade was probably an entry hall or waiting area for the Hall of Judgment, which was probably used for the transaction of public business.

7:7 the Hall of Judgment. The place where Solomon would publicly hear petitions from Israelites and render judgments was added to the grand palace site.

7:8 house...court...house. Behind the Hall of Judgment was an open court. Within this court, Solomon built his own personal residence, a palace for his harem, and royal apartments for the Egyptian princess he had married.

7:9-12 A fortune was spent on building, adjacent to the temple, the whole palace with its 3 parts: 1) the king's home, 2) the courtyard in the middle, and 3) the house of the women on the other side.

7:13 Huram. See marginal note. Although having the same Heb. name, this individual was distinct from the King of Tyre (5:1). Huram had a Tyrian father, but his mother was of the tribe of Naphtali. Second Chronicles 2:14 states that Huram's mother came from the tribe of Dan. Probably one verse refers to her place of birth and the other to her place of residence. Or, if his parents were originally from the two tribes, then he could legitimately claim either. The description of Huram's skills in v. 14 is exactly the same as that of Bezalel who made the tabernacle (Ex. 31:3; 36:1). Huram made the pillars (vv. 14-22). *See note on 2 Chr. 2:13,14.*

7:15 two pillars. One bronze pillar was on each side of the temple's entrance (v. 21). Each pillar was 27 ft. high and 18 ft. around. *See note on 2 Chr. 3:15.*

7:16 capitals. These distinctively treated upper ends of the bronze pillars, which added 7.5 ft. to the height of each pillar.

7:18 pomegranates. One of the fruits of the Promised Land (Num. 13:23; Deut. 8:8), these were popular decorative motifs used on the hem of Aaron's priestly garment (Ex. 28:33,34).

7:21 Jachin...Boaz. See marginal note for the meanings. It is likely that each name recalls promises given to the Davidic house, and that they perpetually reminded the worshipers of God's grace in providing the Davidic monarchy as well as each king's need to depend on God for his success. *See note on 2 Chr. 3:17.* They were also symbolic of the strength and stability of God's promise of a kingdom forever, even though the temple would come down (see Jer. 52:17).

7:23 the Sea. A huge circular bronze basin corresponding to the laver of the tabernacle. According to v. 26, this great basin's capacity was about 12,000 gal. (*see note on 2 Chr. 4:5*). The Sea stood in the courtyard on the temple's SE side and provided the priests water to wash themselves and their sacrifices (2 Chr. 4:6). It probably also supplied water for the 10 movable basins (vv. 38,39). *See note on 2 Chr. 4:2.*

completely round. Its height *was* five cubits, and a line of thirty cubits measured its
circumference.
24 Below its brim *were* ornamental buds
encircling it all around, ten to a cubit, [m]all
the way around the Sea. The ornamental
buds *were* cast in two rows when it was
cast. 25 It stood on [n]twelve oxen: three
looking toward the north, three looking toward the west, three looking toward the
south, and three looking toward the east;
the Sea *was set* upon them, and all their
back parts *pointed* inward. 26 It *was* a handbreadth thick; and its brim was shaped like
the brim of a cup, *like* a lily blossom. It contained [8]two thousand baths.

The Carts and the Lavers

27 He also made ten [9]carts of bronze;
four cubits *was* the length of each cart, four
cubits its width, and three cubits its height.
28 And this *was* the design of the carts:
They had panels, and the panels *were* between frames; 29 on the panels that *were* between the frames *were* lions, oxen, and
cherubim. And on the frames *was* a
pedestal on top. Below the lions and oxen
were wreaths of plaited work. 30 Every cart
had four bronze wheels and axles of
bronze, and its four feet had supports.
Under the laver *were* supports of cast
bronze beside each wreath. 31 Its opening
inside the crown at the top *was* one cubit in
diameter; and the opening *was* round,
shaped *like* a pedestal, one and a half cubits in outside diameter; and also on the
opening *were* engravings, but the panels
were square, not round. 32 Under the panels *were* the four wheels, and the axles of
the wheels *were joined* to the cart. The
height of a wheel *was* one and a half cubits.
33 The workmanship of the wheels *was* like
the workmanship of a chariot wheel; their
axle pins, their rims, their spokes, and their
hubs *were* all of cast *bronze*. 34 And *there*
were four supports at the four corners of
each cart; its supports *were* part of the cart
itself. 35 On the top of the cart, at the height
of half a cubit, *it was* perfectly round. And
on the top of the cart, its flanges and its
panels *were* of the same casting. 36 On the
plates of its flanges and on its panels he engraved cherubim, lions, and palm trees,
wherever there was a clear space on each,
with wreaths all around. 37 Thus he made
the ten carts. All of them were of [1]the same
mold, one measure, *and* one shape.
38 Then [o]he made ten lavers of bronze;
each laver contained [2]forty baths, *and* each
laver *was* four cubits. On each of the ten
carts *was* a laver. 39 And he put five carts
on the right side of the house, and five on
the left side of the house. He set the Sea on
the right side of the house, toward the
southeast.

Furnishings of the Temple

40 [p]Huram[3] made the lavers and the
shovels and the bowls. So Huram finished
doing all the work that he was to do for
King Solomon *for* the house of the LORD:
41 the two pillars, the *two* bowl-shaped capitals that *were* on top of the two pillars; the
two [q]networks covering the two bowl-
shaped capitals which *were* on top of the pillars; 42 [r]four hundred pomegranates for the
two networks (two rows of pomegranates
for each network, to cover the two bowl-
shaped capitals that *were* on top of the pillars); 43 the ten carts, and ten lavers on the
carts; 44 one Sea, and twelve oxen under the
Sea; 45 [s]the pots, the shovels, and the bowls.
All these articles which [4]Huram made
for King Solomon *for* the house of the LORD
were of burnished bronze. 46 [t]In the plain of
Jordan the king had them cast in clay
molds, between [u]Succoth and [v]Zaretan.
47 And Solomon did not weigh all the articles, because *there were* so many; the
weight of the bronze was not [w]determined.
48 Thus Solomon had all the furnishings
made for the house of the LORD: [x]the altar of
gold, and [y]the table of gold on which *was*
[z]the showbread; 49 the lampstands of pure

24 [m] 2 Chr. 4:3
25 [n] 2 Chr. 4:4, 5; Jer. 52:20
26 [8] About 12,000 gallons; *three thousand,* 2 Chr. 4:5
27 [9] Or *stands*
37 [1] *one*
38 [o] Ex. 30:18; 2 Chr. 4:6 [2] About 240 gallons
40 [p] 2 Chr. 4:11–5:1 [3] Heb. *Hiram;* cf. 2 Chr. 2:13, 14
41 [q] 1 Kin. 7:17, 18
42 [r] 1 Kin. 7:20
45 [s] Ex. 27:3; 2 Chr. 4:16 [4] Heb. *Hiram;* cf. 2 Chr. 2:13, 14
46 [t] 2 Chr. 4:17 [u] Gen. 33:17; Josh. 13:27 [v] Josh. 3:16
47 [w] 1 Chr. 22:3, 14
48 [x] Ex. 37:25, 26; 2 Chr. 4:8 [y] Ex. 37:10, 11 [z] Lev. 24:5-8

7:25 twelve oxen. Huram arranged 3 oxen facing in each of the 4 directions of the compass to support the Sea. *See note on 2 Chr. 4:4.*

7:26 two thousand baths. *See note on 2 Chr. 4:5.*

7:27-37 carts. Huram made 10 movable stands of bronze 6 ft. square and 4.5 ft. high. Each consisted of 4 upright corner poles joined together by square panels. For mobility, the stands rode on 4 wheels of bronze (v. 30).

7:38 lavers. Huram made 10 bronze basins as water containers for the stands. Each measured 6 ft. across and held about 240 gal. of water.

7:40 the shovels and the bowls. Shovels were used to scoop up the ashes that were then emptied into the bowls for disposal. The same tools served the same purpose in the tabernacle (Ex. 27:3).

7:45 burnished bronze. I.e., bronze polished to a high shine.

7:46 between Succoth and Zaretan. Succoth was located on the E side of the Jordan River just N of the Jabbok River (Gen. 33:17; Josh. 13:27; Judg. 8:4,5). Zaretan was nearby. This location was conducive to good metallurgy, because it abounded in clay suitable for molds and lay close to a source of charcoal for heat, namely the forests across the Jordan.

7:48 the altar of gold. The altar of incense stood in front of the Most Holy Place (cf. Ex. 30:1-4). **the table of gold.** The table was made on which the showbread was placed, which the Law required to be continually in God's presence (Ex. 25:30).

7:49 lampstands. Ten golden lampstands standing directly in front of the Most Holy Place, 5 on either side of the doors, provided a corridor of light.

gold, five on the right *side* and five on the left
in front of the inner sanctuary, with the flowers and the lamps and the wick-trimmers of
gold; 50 the basins, the trimmers, the bowls,
the ladles, and the [5]censers of pure gold;
and the hinges of gold, *both* for the doors of
the inner room (the Most Holy *Place*) *and* for
the doors of the main hall of the temple.
51 So all the work that King Solomon
had done for the house of the LORD was
finished; and Solomon brought in the
things [a]which his father David had dedicated: the silver and the gold and the furnishings. He put them in the treasuries of
the house of the LORD.

The Ark Brought into the Temple

8 Now [a]Solomon assembled the elders
of Israel and all the heads of the tribes,
the chief fathers of the children of Israel, to
King Solomon in Jerusalem, [b]that they
might bring [c]up the ark of the covenant of
the LORD from the City of David, which *is*
Zion. 2 Therefore all the men of Israel assembled with King Solomon at the [d]feast
in the month of [1]Ethanim, which *is* the seventh month. 3 So all the elders of Israel
came, [e]and the priests took up the ark.
4 Then they brought up the ark of the
LORD, [f]the [2]tabernacle of meeting, and all
the holy furnishings that *were* in the tabernacle. The priests and the Levites brought
them up. 5 Also King Solomon, and all the
congregation of Israel who were assembled with him, *were* with him before the
ark, [g]sacrificing sheep and oxen that could
not be counted or numbered for multitude.
6 Then the priests [h]brought in the ark of
the covenant of the LORD to [i]its place, into
the inner sanctuary of the temple, to the
Most Holy *Place,* [j]under the wings of the
cherubim. 7 For the cherubim spread *their*
two wings over the place of the ark, and
the cherubim overshadowed the ark and
its poles. 8 The poles [k]extended so that the
[3]ends of the poles could be seen from the
holy *place,* in front of the inner sanctuary;
but they could not be seen from outside.
And they are there to this day. 9 [l]Nothing
was in the ark [m]except the two tablets of
stone which Moses [n]put there at Horeb,
[o]when the LORD made *a covenant* with the
children of Israel, when they came out of
the land of Egypt.
10 And it came to pass, when the priests
came out of the holy *place,* that the cloud
[p]filled the house of the LORD, 11 so that the
priests could not continue ministering because of the cloud; for the [q]glory of the
LORD filled the house of the LORD.
12 [r]Then Solomon spoke:

"The LORD said He would dwell [s]in
the dark cloud.
13 [t]I have surely built You an exalted
house,
[u]And a place for You to dwell in
forever."

Solomon's Speech at Completion of the Work

14 Then the king turned around and
[v]blessed the whole assembly of Israel,

50 [5] *firepans*
51 [a] 2 Sam. 8:11; 1 Chr. 18:11; 2 Chr. 5:1

CHAPTER 8

1 [a] Num. 1:4; 7:2; 2 Chr. 5:2-14 [b] 2 Sam. 6:12-17; 1 Chr. 15:25-29 [c] 2 Sam. 5:7; 6:12, 16
2 [d] Lev. 23:34; 1 Kin. 8:65; 2 Chr. 7:8-10 [1] Or *Tishri,* September or October
3 [e] Num. 4:15; 7:9; Deut. 31:9; Josh. 3:3, 6
4 [f] 1 Kin. 3:4; 2 Chr. 1:3 [2] *tent*
5 [g] 2 Sam. 6:13; 2 Chr. 1:6
6 [h] 2 Sam. 6:17 [i] Ex. 26:33, 34; 1 Kin. 6:19 [j] 1 Kin. 6:27
8 [k] Ex. 25:13-15; 37:4, 5 [3] *heads*
9 [l] Ex. 25:21; Deut. 10:2 [m] Ex. 25:16; Deut. 10:5; Heb. 9:4 [n] Ex. 24:7, 8; 40:20; Deut. 4:13 [o] Ex. 34:27, 28
10 [p] Ex. 40:34, 35; 2 Chr. 7:1, 2
11 [q] 2 Chr. 7:1, 2
12 [r] 2 Chr. 6:1 [s] Lev. 16:2; Ps. 18:11; 97:2
13 [t] 2 Sam. 7:13 [u] [Ex. 15:17]; Ps. 132:14
14 [v] 2 Sam. 6:18; 1 Kin. 8:55

7:51 David had dedicated. Solomon deposited that which David had dedicated to the Lord (2 Sam. 8:7-12) in the side rooms of the temple.

8:1-21 See 2 Chr. 5:2–6:11.

8:1 elders...heads. The "elders" of Israel were respected men who were in charge of local government and justice throughout Israel (Ex. 18:13-26; Num. 11:16-30; 1 Sam. 8:1-9). They advised the king on important matters of state (1 Sam. 15:30; 2 Sam. 17:5; 1 Kin. 12:6-11). The "heads" of the tribes or "chief fathers" were the oldest living males within each extended family unit. They were the ones responsible for learning the law and leading their families to obey it.

8:2 seventh month. Solomon finished building the temple in the eighth month of the previous year (6:38; see 2 Chr. 5:1); all its detail signifying the magnificence and beauty of God's nature and His transcendent, uncommon glory. The celebration, then, did not take place until 11 months later. Apparently Solomon intentionally scheduled the dedication of the temple to coincide with the Feast of Tabernacles held in the seventh month, when there would be a general assembly of the people in Jerusalem. That was also a Jubilee year, so it was especially appropriate (Lev. 23:33-36,39-43; Deut. 16:13-15).

8:4-6 brought up the ark. The ark of the covenant was transported by the priests and the Levites from the tent that David had made for it in Jerusalem (2 Sam. 6:17). They also brought to the temple the tabernacle and all its furnishings which had been located at Gibeon (2 Chr. 1:2-6). The ark was placed into the Most Holy Place (v. 6).

8:7,8 poles. God had originally commanded that poles be used to carry the ark (Ex. 25:13-15). They were left protruding to serve as a guide so the High-Priest could be guided by them when he entered the dark inner sanctuary.

8:8 to this day. The phrase is used from the perspective of one who lived and wrote before the destruction of the temple in 586 B.C. The writer of 1 Kings incorporated such sources into his book (cf. 9:13,21; 10:12; 12:19).

8:9 two tablets of stone. At this time the ark of the covenant contained only the two tablets inscribed with the Ten Commandments. The pot of manna (Ex. 16:33) and Aaron's rod that budded (Num. 17:10) were no longer in the ark. See Heb. 9:4.

8:10 the cloud. The cloud was "the glory of the LORD," the visible symbol of God's presence. It signaled the Lord's approval of this new temple. A similar manifestation took place when the tabernacle was dedicated (Ex. 40:34,35). *See note on Lev. 9:23.*

8:12-21 See 2 Chr. 6:1-11.

8:12,13 Solomon's solemn declaration was addressed to the Lord. Solomon recognized the thick darkness as the manifestation of the Lord's gracious presence among His people (cf. Ex. 19:9; 20:21; Lev. 16:2) and affirmed that he had built the temple so that the Lord could dwell there in the glory of thick darkness.

8:14-21 Solomon turned around from addressing the Lord and spoke to the assembly of Israel gathered at the temple. Solomon, in vv. 15-19 rehearsed the story of 2 Sam. 7:12-16 and claimed that he,

while all the assembly of Israel was standing. 15 And he said: [w]"Blessed *be* the LORD
God of Israel, who [x]spoke with His mouth
to my father David, and with His hand has
fulfilled *it,* saying, 16 'Since the day that I
brought My people Israel out of Egypt, I
have chosen no city from any tribe of Israel
in which to build a house, that [y]My name
might be there; but I chose [z]David to be
over My people Israel.' 17 Now [a]it was in
the heart of my father David to build a
[4]temple for the name of the LORD God of
Israel. 18 [b]But the LORD said to my father
David, 'Whereas it was in your heart to
build a temple for My name, you did well
that it was in your heart. 19 Nevertheless
[c]you shall not build the temple, but your
son who will come from your body, he
shall build the temple for My name.' 20 So
the LORD has fulfilled His word which He
spoke; and I have [5]filled the position of my
father David, and sit on the throne of Israel, [d]as the LORD promised; and I have
built a temple for the name of the LORD
God of Israel. 21 And there I have made a
place for the ark, in which *is* [e]the covenant
of the LORD which He made with our fathers, when He brought them out of the
land of Egypt."

Solomon's Prayer of Dedication

22 Then Solomon stood before [f]the altar
of the LORD in the presence of all the assembly of Israel, and [g]spread out his hands
toward heaven; 23 and he said: "LORD God
of Israel, [h]*there is* no God in heaven above
or on earth below like You, [i]who keep *Your*
covenant and mercy with Your servants
who [j]walk before You with all their hearts.
24 You have kept what You promised Your
servant David my father; You have both
spoken with Your mouth and fulfilled *it*
with Your hand, as *it is* this day. 25 Therefore, LORD God of Israel, now keep what
You promised Your servant David my father, saying, [k]'You shall not fail to have a
man sit before Me on the throne of Israel,
only if your sons take heed to their way,
that they walk before Me as you have
walked before Me.' 26 [l]And now I pray, O
God of Israel, let Your word come true,
which You have spoken to Your servant
David my father.
27 "But [m]will God indeed dwell on the
earth? Behold, heaven and the [n]heaven of
heavens cannot contain You. How much
less this temple which I have built! 28 Yet regard the prayer of Your servant and his supplication, O LORD my God, and listen to the
cry and the prayer which Your servant is
praying before You today: 29 that Your eyes
may be open toward this [6]temple night and
day, toward the place of which You said,
[o]'My name shall be [p]there,' that You may
hear the prayer which Your servant makes
[q]toward this place. 30 [r]And may You hear
the supplication of Your servant and of Your
people Israel, when they pray toward this
place. Hear in heaven Your dwelling place;
and when You hear, forgive.
31 "When anyone sins against his neighbor, and is forced to take [s]an oath, and
comes *and* takes an oath before Your altar
in this temple, 32 then hear in heaven, and
act, and judge Your servants, [t]condemning
the wicked, bringing his way on his head,
and justifying the righteous by giving him
according to his righteousness.
33 [u]"When Your people Israel are defeated before an enemy because they have
sinned against You, and [v]when they turn
back to You and confess Your name, and
pray and make supplication to You in this
temple, 34 then hear in heaven, and forgive
the sin of Your people Israel, and bring
them back to the land which You gave to
their [w]fathers.
35 [x]"When the heavens are shut up and
there is no rain because they have sinned
against You, when they pray toward this
place and confess Your name, and turn
from their sin because You afflict them,
36 then hear in heaven, and forgive the sin
of Your servants, Your people Israel, that
You may [y]teach them [z]the good way in
which they should walk; and send rain on

15 [w] 1 Chr. 29:10, 20; Neh. 9:5; Luke 1:68 [x] 2 Sam. 7:2, 12, 13, 25; 1 Chr. 22:10
16 [y] Deut. 12:5; 1 Kin. 8:29 [z] 1 Sam. 16:1; 2 Sam. 7:8; 1 Chr. 28:4
17 [a] 2 Sam. 7:2, 3; 1 Chr. 17:1, 2 [4] Lit. *house,* and so in vv. 18-20
18 [b] 2 Chr. 6:8, 9
19 [c] 2 Sam. 7:5, 12, 13; 1 Kin. 5:3, 5; 6:38; 1 Chr. 17:11, 12; 22:8-10; 2 Chr. 6:2
20 [d] 1 Chr. 28:5, 6 [5] *risen in the place of*
21 [e] Deut. 31:26; 1 Kin. 8:9
22 [f] 1 Kin. 8:54; 2 Chr. 6:12 [g] Ex. 9:33; Ezra 9:5
23 [h] Ex. 15:11; 2 Sam. 7:22 [i] [Deut. 7:9; Neh. 1:5; Dan. 9:4] [j] [Gen. 17:1; 1 Kin. 3:6]; 2 Kin. 20:3
25 [k] 2 Sam. 7:12, 16; 1 Kin. 2:4; 9:5
26 [l] 2 Sam. 7:25
27 [m] [2 Chr. 2:6; Is. 66:1; Acts 7:49; 17:24] [n] 2 Cor. 12:2
29 [o] Deut. 12:11 [p] 1 Kin. 9:3; 2 Chr. 7:15 [q] Dan. 6:10 [6] Lit. *house*
30 [r] Neh. 1:6
31 [s] Ex. 22:8-11
32 [t] Deut. 25:1
33 [u] Lev. 26:17; Deut. 28:25 [v] Lev. 26:39, 40
34 [w] [Lev. 26:40-42; Deut. 30:1-3]
35 [x] Lev. 26:19; Deut. 28:23
36 [y] Ps. 25:4; 27:11; 94:12 [z] 1 Sam. 12:23

having built the temple, had become the fulfillment of God's promise to his father David (vv. 20,21). However, Solomon's claim was premature because the Lord later appeared to him declaring the necessity of obedience for the establishment of Solomon's throne (9:4-9), an obedience which would be lacking in Solomon (11:6,9,10).

8:22-53 *See notes on 2 Chr. 6:12-40.* Solomon then moved to the altar of burnt offering to offer a lengthy prayer of consecration to the Lord. First, he affirmed that no god could compare to Israel's God, the Lord (vv. 23,24). Second, he asked the Lord for His continued presence and protection (vv. 25-30). Third, he listed 7 typical Israelite prayers that would require the Lord's response (vv. 31-54). These supplications recalled the detailed list of curses that Deut. 28:15-68 ascribed for the breaking of the law. Specifically, Solomon prayed that the Lord would judge between the wicked and the righteous (vv. 31,32); the Lord would forgive the sins that had caused defeat in battle (vv. 33,34); the Lord would forgive the sins had brought on drought (vv. 35,36); the Lord would forgive the sins that had resulted in national calamities (vv. 37-40); the Lord would show mercy to God-fearing foreigners (vv. 41-43); the Lord would give victory in battle (vv. 44,45); and the Lord would bring restoration after captivity (vv. 46-54).

8:22 spread out his hands. The spreading of open hands toward heaven was a normal posture of individual prayer (Ex. 9:29; Is. 1:15).

8:27 heaven...cannot contain You. Solomon confessed that even though the Lord had chosen to dwell among His people in the cloud at the temple, He far transcended containment by anything in all creation.

Your land which You have given to Your
people as an inheritance.
37 [a]"When there is famine in the land,
pestilence *or* blight *or* mildew, locusts *or*
grasshoppers; when their enemy besieges
them in the land of their [7]cities; whatever
plague or whatever sickness *there is;*
38 whatever prayer, whatever supplication
is made by anyone, *or* by all Your people
Israel, when each one knows the plague of
his own heart, and spreads out his hands
toward this temple: 39 then hear in heaven
Your dwelling place, and forgive, and act,
and give to everyone according to all his
ways, whose heart You know (for You
alone [b]know the hearts of all the sons of
men), 40 [c]that they may fear You all the
days that they live in the land which You
gave to our fathers.
41 "Moreover, concerning a foreigner,
who *is* not of Your people Israel, but has
come from a far country for Your name's
sake 42 (for they will hear of Your great
name and Your [d]strong hand and Your outstretched arm), when he comes and prays
toward this temple, 43 hear in heaven Your
dwelling place, and do according to all for
which the foreigner calls to You, [e]that all
peoples of the earth may know Your name
and [f]fear You, as *do* Your people Israel, and
that they may know that this temple which
I have built is called by Your name.
44 "When Your people go out to battle
against their enemy, wherever You send
them, and when they pray to the LORD toward the city which You have chosen and
the temple which I have built for Your
name, 45 then hear in heaven their prayer
and their supplication, and maintain their
[8]cause.
46 "When they sin against You [g](for *there*
is no one who does not sin), and You become angry with them and deliver them to
the enemy, and they take them captive [h]to
the land of the enemy, far or near; 47 [i]*yet*
when they [9]come to themselves in the land
where they were carried captive, and repent, and make supplication to You in the
land of those who took them captive, [j]say-
ing, 'We have sinned and done wrong, we
have committed wickedness'; 48 and *when*
they [k]return to You with all their heart and
with all their soul in the land of their enemies who led them away captive, and
[l]pray to You toward their land which You
gave to their fathers, the city which You
have chosen and the temple which I have
built for Your name: 49 then hear in heaven
Your dwelling place their prayer and their
supplication, and maintain their [1]cause,
50 and forgive Your people who have
sinned against You, and all their transgressions which they have transgressed
against You; and [m]grant them compassion
before those who took them captive, that
they may have compassion on them 51 (for
[n]they *are* Your people and Your inheritance, whom You brought out of Egypt,
[o]out of the iron furnace), 52 [p]that Your eyes
may be open to the supplication of Your
servant and the supplication of Your people Israel, to listen to them whenever they
call to You. 53 For You separated them from
among all the peoples of the earth *to be*
Your inheritance, [q]as You spoke by Your
servant Moses, when You brought our fathers out of Egypt, O Lord GOD."

Solomon Blesses the Assembly

54 [r]And so it was, when Solomon had
finished praying all this prayer and supplication to the LORD, that he arose from before the altar of the LORD, from kneeling on
his knees with his hands spread up to
heaven. 55 Then he stood [s]and blessed all
the assembly of Israel with a loud voice,
saying: 56 "Blessed *be* the LORD, who has
given [t]rest[2] to His people Israel, according
to all that He promised. [u]There has not
failed one word of all His good promise,
which He promised through His servant
Moses. 57 May the LORD our God be with
us, as He was with our fathers. [v]May He
not leave us nor forsake us, 58 that He may
[w]incline our hearts to Himself, to walk in
all His ways, and to keep His commandments and His statutes and His judgments,
which He commanded our fathers. 59 And
may these words of mine, with which I
have made supplication before the LORD,
be near the LORD our God day and night,
that He may maintain the cause of His servant and the cause of His people Israel, as
each day may require, 60 [x]that all the peoples of the earth may know that [y]the LORD
is God; *there is* no other. 61 Let your [z]heart
therefore be [3]loyal to the LORD our God, to
walk in His statutes and keep His commandments, as at this day."

Solomon Dedicates the Temple

62 Then [a]the king and all Israel with him
offered sacrifices before the LORD. 63 And
Solomon offered a sacrifice of peace offer-

37 [a] Lev. 26:16, 25, 26; Deut. 28:21, 22, 27, 38, 42, 52 [7] Lit. *gates*
39 [b] [1 Sam. 16:7; 1 Chr. 28:9; Jer. 17:10]; Acts 1:24
40 [c] [Ps. 130:4]
42 [d] Ex. 13:3; Deut. 3:24
43 [e] [Ex. 9:16; 1 Sam. 17:46; 2 Kin. 19:19] [f] Ps. 102:15
45 [8] *justice*
46 [g] 2 Chr. 6:36; Ps. 130:3; Prov. 20:9; Eccl. 7:20; [Rom. 3:23; 1 John 1:8, 10] [h] Lev. 26:34, 44; Deut. 28:36, 64; 2 Kin. 17:6, 18; 25:21
47 [i] [Lev. 26:40-42]; Neh. 9:2 [j] Ezra 9:6, 7; Neh. 1:6; Ps. 106:6; Dan. 9:5 [9] Lit. *bring back to their heart*
48 [k] Jer. 29:12-14 [l] Dan. 6:10; Jon. 2:4
49 [1] *justice*
50 [m] [2 Chr. 30:9]; Ezra 7:6; Ps. 106:46; Acts 7:10
51 [n] Ex. 32:11, 12; Deut. 9:26-29; Neh. 1:10; [Rom. 11:28, 29] [o] Deut. 4:20; Jer. 11:4
52 [p] 1 Kin. 8:29
53 [q] Ex. 19:5, 6
54 [r] 2 Chr. 7:1
55 [s] Num. 6:23-26; 2 Sam. 6:18; 1 Kin. 8:14
56 [t] 1 Chr. 22:18 [u] Deut. 12:10; Josh. 21:45; 23:14 [2] *peace*
57 [v] Deut. 31:6; Josh. 1:5; 1 Sam. 12:22; [Rom. 8:31-37]; Heb. 13:5
58 [w] Ps. 119:36; Jer. 31:33
60 [x] Josh. 4:24; 1 Sam. 17:46; 1 Kin. 8:43; 2 Kin. 19:19 [y] Deut. 4:35, 39; 1 Kin. 18:39; [Jer. 10:10-12]
61 [z] Deut. 18:13; 1 Kin. 11:4; 15:3, 14; 2 Kin. 20:3 [3] Lit. *at peace with*
62 [a] 2 Chr. 7:4-10

8:54-61 Solomon arose to pronounce a benediction on the people. His words were substantially a brief recapitulation of the preceding prayer in which he affirmed the faithfulness of the Lord to Israel (v. 56) and exhorted Israel to faithfulness to the Lord (vv. 57-61).

8:62-66 See 2 Chr. 7:1-10.

8:62 offered sacrifices. To complete the temple's dedication,

ings, which he offered to the LORD, twenty-
two thousand bulls and one hundred and
twenty thousand sheep. So the king and all
the children of Israel dedicated the house
of the LORD. 64 On [b]the same day the king
consecrated the middle of the court that
was in front of the house of the LORD; for
there he offered burnt offerings, grain offerings, and the fat of the peace offerings,
because the [c]bronze altar that *was* before
the LORD *was* too small to receive the burnt
offerings, the grain offerings, and the fat of
the peace offerings.
65 At that time Solomon held [d]a feast,
and all Israel with him, a great assembly
from [e]the entrance of Hamath to [f]the Brook
of Egypt, before the LORD our God, [g]seven
days and seven *more* days—fourteen days.
66 [h]On the eighth day he sent the people
away; and they [4]blessed the king, and went
to their tents joyful and glad of heart for all
the good that the LORD had done for His
servant David, and for Israel His people.

God's Second Appearance to Solomon

9 And [a]it came to pass, when Solomon
had finished building the house of the
LORD [b]and the king's house, and [c]all Solomon's desire which he wanted to do,
2 that the LORD appeared to Solomon the
second time, [d]as He had appeared to him
at Gibeon. 3 And the LORD said to him: [e]"I
have heard your prayer and your supplication that you have made before Me; I
have consecrated this house which you
have built [f]to put My name there forever,
[g]and My eyes and My heart will be there
perpetually. 4 Now if you [h]walk before Me
[i]as your father David walked, in integrity
of heart and in uprightness, to do according to all that I have commanded you, *and*
if you [j]keep My statutes and My judgments, 5 then I will establish the throne of
your kingdom over Israel forever, [k]as I
promised David your father, saying, 'You
shall not fail to have a man on the throne of
Israel.' 6 [l]*But* if you or your sons at all
[1]turn from following Me, and do not keep
My commandments *and* My statutes which
I have set before you, but go and serve
other gods and worship them, 7 [m]then I
will [2]cut off Israel from the land which I
have given them; and this house which
I have consecrated [n]for My name I will cast
out of My sight. [o]Israel will be a proverb
and a byword among all peoples. 8 And *as
for* [p]this house, *which* is exalted, everyone
who passes by it will be astonished and
will hiss, and say, [q]'Why has the LORD
done thus to this land and to this house?'
9 Then they will answer, 'Because they forsook the LORD their God, who brought
their fathers out of the land of Egypt, and
have embraced other gods, and worshiped
them and served them; therefore the LORD
has brought all this [r]calamity on them.' "

Solomon and Hiram Exchange Gifts

10 Now [s]it happened at the end of twenty years, when Solomon had built the two
houses, the house of the LORD and the
king's house 11 [t](Hiram the king of Tyre

64 [b] 2 Chr. 7:7 [c] 2 Chr. 4:1
65 [d] Lev. 23:34; 1 Kin. 8:2 [e] Num. 34:8; Josh. 13:5; Judg. 3:3; 2 Kin. 14:25 [f] Gen. 15:18; Ex. 23:31; Num. 34:5 [g] 2 Chr. 7:8
66 [h] 2 Chr. 7:9 [4] *thanked*

CHAPTER 9

1 [a] 2 Chr. 7:11 [b] 1 Kin. 7:1 [c] 2 Chr. 8:6
2 [d] 1 Kin. 3:5; 11:9; 2 Chr. 1:7
3 [e] 2 Kin. 20:5; Ps. 10:17 [f] 1 Kin. 8:29 [g] Deut. 11:12
4 [h] Gen. 17:1 [i] 1 Kin. 11:4, 6; 15:5 [j] 1 Kin. 8:61
5 [k] 2 Sam. 7:12, 16; 1 Kin. 2:4; 6:12; 8:25; 1 Chr. 22:10; Matt. 1:6; 25:31
6 [l] 2 Sam. 7:14-16; 2 Chr. 7:19, 20; Ps. 89:30 [1] *turn back*
7 [m] [Lev. 18:24-29]; Deut. 4:26; 2 Kin. 17:23; 25:21 [n] [Jer. 7:4-14] [o] Deut. 28:37; Ps. 44:14; Jer. 24:9 [2] *destroy*
8 [p] 2 Chr. 7:21 [q] [Deut. 29:24-26]; Jer. 22:8, 9
9 [r] [Deut. 29:25-28]
10 [s] 1 Kin. 6:37, 38; 7:1; 2 Chr. 8:1
11 [t] 1 Kin. 5:1

Solomon led the people in offering peace offerings to the Lord (cf. Lev. 3:1-17; 7:11-21), in which they consumed 22,000 bulls and 120,000 sheep and goats (v. 63). Although the number of sacrifices offered seems high, it was in keeping with the magnitude of this event. Obviously, the single bronze altar could not accommodate such an enormous number of sacrifices. Solomon first had to consecrate the entire middle courtyard, the one directly in front of the temple (v. 64). After consecrating the court, Solomon probably had a series of auxiliary altars set up in the court to accommodate all the peace offerings.

8:65 the entrance of Hamath to the Brook of Egypt. "The entrance of Hamath" was located about 20 mi. S of Kadesh on the Orontes River and was the northern boundary of the land promised to Israel (Num. 34:7-9; Josh. 13:5). "The Brook of Egypt" is be equated with Wadi El-Armish in the northeastern Sinai, the southern boundary of the land promised to Israel. These locations show that people from all over Israel attended the dedication of the temple.

9:1-9 See 2 Chr. 7:11-22.

9:1,2 finished...the king's house. According to 6:1, Solomon began building the temple in Apr./May 966 B.C. The temple was completed in Oct./Nov. 959 B.C. (6:38). The temple dedication and Solomon's prayer to the Lord occurred 11 months after the completion of the temple in Sep./Oct. 958 B.C. The Lord did not appear to Solomon this second time (cf. 3:5-14) until Solomon had completed the building of his own palace in 946 B.C. (cf. 7:1). Thus, the Lord's response came approximately 12 years after Solomon's prayer and supplication to the Lord recorded in 8:22-53.

9:3 consecrated. The Lord made the temple holy by being present in the cloud (cf. 8:10). As proof of the temple's consecration, the Lord told Solomon that He had put His name there (cf. 3:2). **forever.** God was not saying He will dwell in that building forever, since in less than 400 years it was destroyed by the Babylonians (cf. vv. 7-9). He was saying that Jerusalem and the temple mount are to be His earthly throne as long as the earth remains, through the millennial kingdom (see Is. 2:1-4; Zech. 14:16). Even during the New Heaven and New Earth, the eternal state, there will be the heavenly Jerusalem, where God will eternally dwell (see Rev. 21:1,2). **eyes...heart.** These symbolized, respectively, the Lord's constant attention toward and deep affection for Israel. By implication, He promised them access to His presence and answers to their prayers.

9:4-9 See 2 Chr. 7:17-22.

9:4 if you walk. The Lord reiterated to Solomon the importance of obedience to the Mosaic statutes in order to experience the blessings of the Davidic Covenant (cf. 2:3,4).

9:6 if you...turn. If Israel ("you" is pl.) abandoned the Lord to worship other gods, God would expel Israel from the Land and destroy the temple (v. 7).

9:9 this calamity. The destruction of Jerusalem and exile from the Land (v. 8) were predicted by Moses in Deut. 29:24-28. The devastation of the temple, which came in 586 B.C., graphically demonstrated the Lord's anger against Israel's sin, particularly the sin of idolatry.

9:10-28 See 2 Chr. 8:1-18.

9:10 at the end of twenty years. The completion of the building

had supplied Solomon with cedar and cypress and gold, as much as he desired), *that*
King Solomon then gave Hiram twenty
cities in the land of Galilee. 12 Then Hiram
went from Tyre to see the cities which Solomon had given him, but they did not
please him. 13 So he said, "What *kind of*
cities *are* these which you have given me,
my brother?" [u]And he called them the
land of [3]Cabul, as they are to this day.
14 Then Hiram sent the king one hundred
and twenty talents of gold.

Solomon's Additional Achievements

15 And this *is* the reason for [v]the labor
force which King Solomon raised: to build
the house of the LORD, his own house, [4]the
[w]Millo, the wall of Jerusalem, [x]Hazor,
[y]Megiddo, and [z]Gezer. 16 (Pharaoh king of
Egypt had gone up and taken Gezer and
burned it with fire, [a]had killed the Canaanites who dwelt in the city, and had given it
as a dowry to his daughter, Solomon's
wife.) 17 And Solomon built Gezer, Lower
[b]Beth Horon, 18 [c]Baalath, and Tadmor in
the wilderness, in the land *of Judah*, 19 all
the storage cities that Solomon had, cities
for [d]his chariots and cities for his [e]cavalry,
and whatever Solomon [f]desired to build in
Jerusalem, in Lebanon, and in all the land
of his dominion.
20 [g]All the people *who were* left of the
Amorites, Hittites, Perizzites, Hivites, and
Jebusites, who *were* not of the children of
Israel— 21 that is, their descendants [h]who
were left in the land after them, [i]whom the

13 [u]Josh. 19:27 [3]Lit. *Good for Nothing*
15 [v]1 Kin. 5:13 [w]2 Sam. 5:9; 1 Kin. 9:24 [x]Josh. 11:1; 19:36 [y]Josh. 17:11 [z]Josh. 16:10 [4]Lit. *The Landfill*
16 [a]Josh. 16:10; Judg. 1:29
17 [b]Josh. 10:10; 16:3; 21:22; 2 Chr. 8:5
18 [c]Josh. 19:44; 2 Chr. 8:4
19 [d]1 Kin. 10:26; 2 Chr. 1:14 [e]1 Kin. 4:26 [f]1 Kin. 9:1
20 [g]2 Chr. 8:7
21 [h]Judg. 1:21-36; 3:1 [i]Josh. 15:63; 17:12, 13
[j]Judg. 1:28, 35 [k]Ezra 2:55, 58; Neh. 7:57
22 [l][Lev. 25:39]
23 [m]2 Chr. 8:10
24 [n]1 Kin. 3:1 [o]1 Kin. 7:8 [p]2 Sam. 5:9; 1 Kin. 11:27; 2 Chr. 32:5 [5]Lit. *he*; cf. 2 Chr. 8:11
25 [q]Ex. 23:14-17; Deut. 16:16; 2 Chr. 8:12, 13
26 [r]2 Chr. 8:17, 18 [s]Num. 33:35; Deut. 2:8; 1 Kin. 22:48 [6]Heb. *Eloth*
27 [t]1 Kin. 5:6, 9; 10:11
28 [u]Job 22:24

CHAPTER 10
1 [a]2 Chr. 9:1; Matt. 12:42; Luke 11:31

children of Israel had not been able to destroy completely—[j]from these Solomon
raised [k]forced labor, as it is to this day.
22 But of the children of Israel Solomon
[l]made no forced laborers, because they
were men of war and his servants: his officers, his captains, commanders of his chariots, and his cavalry.
23 Others *were* chiefs of the officials who
were over Solomon's work: [m]five hundred
and fifty, who ruled over the people who
did the work.
24 But [n]Pharaoh's daughter came up
from the City of David to [o]her house which
[5]*Solomon* had built for her. [p]Then he built
the Millo.
25 [q]Now three times a year Solomon offered burnt offerings and peace offerings
on the altar which he had built for the
LORD, and he burned incense with them *on
the altar* that *was* before the LORD. So he finished the temple.
26 [r]King Solomon also built a fleet of
ships at [s]Ezion Geber, which *is* near [6]Elath
on the shore of the Red Sea, in the land of
Edom. 27 [t]Then Hiram sent his servants
with the fleet, seamen who knew the sea, to
work with the servants of Solomon. 28 And
they went to [u]Ophir, and acquired four
hundred and twenty talents of gold from
there, and brought *it* to King Solomon.

The Queen of Sheba's Praise of Solomon

10 Now when the [a]queen of Sheba
heard of the fame of Solomon con-

of the temple (7 years) and the building of Solomon's palace (13 years) would be ca. 946 B.C. (*see note on 9:1*).

9:11 Solomon then gave Hiram twenty cities. Solomon sold these 20 cities in Galilee to Hiram in exchange for the gold (about 4.5 tons) mentioned in v. 14. Probably these cities lay along the border between Tyre and Israel, just outside the territory of Asher. Later, Hiram gave the towns back to Solomon. *See note on 2 Chr. 8:2.*

9:13 to this day. *See note on 8:8.*

9:15 the Millo. A landfill in the depression between the city of David and the temple and palace complex to the N (see 2 Sam. 5:9). **Hazor.** Ten mi. N of the Sea of Galilee, Hazor protected Israel's northeastern entrance from Syria and Mesopotamia. **Megiddo.** Megiddo guarded a crucial pass in the Carmel mountains, which linked the valley of Jezreel and the international coastal highway to Egypt. **Gezer.** Twenty mi. W of Jerusalem, Gezer lay in the coastal plain at the intersection of the coastal highway and the main road to Jerusalem.

9:17 Lower Beth Horon. About 12 mi. NW of Jerusalem along a road connecting Gibeon with the western lowlands and providing a western approach to Jerusalem. *See note on 2 Chr. 8:5.*

9:18 Baalath. The designation of several cities in Canaan. *See note on 2 Chr. 8:6.* **Tadmor.** Probably the same as Tamar, 16 mi. SW of the Dead Sea on the southeastern boundary of the Land (cf. Ezek. 47:19; 48:28). Another Tadmor existed 150 mi. NE of Damascus, which is possibly the reference of 2 Chr. 8:4.

9:19 storage cities. Cities whose primary purpose was to store food (2 Chr. 17:12; 32:28). **cities for his chariots.** Solomon built military outposts for his chariots and horses. To defend his kingdom, these garrisons were probably located along key roads throughout the nation. All the cities listed in vv. 15-19 met this requirement.

9:20-23 See 2 Chr. 8:7-10.

9:21,22 forced labor. I.e., "conscripted slave labor." *See note on 5:13.* Only resident aliens permanently became part of this force since the law did not allow Israelites to make fellow-Israelites slaves against their will (Ex. 21:2-11; Lev. 25:44-46; Deut. 15:12-18). Additionally, v. 22 adds that he did not move someone from an established post, even for a specific project.

9:21 to this day. *See note on 8:8.*

9:25 Solomon offered. Once the temple had been built, Solomon's practice of sacrificing to God at the various high places ceased (cf. 3:2-4). He kept Israel's 3 great annual feasts, Unleavened Bread, Pentecost, and Tabernacles (Deut. 16:1-17), at the temple in Jerusalem.

9:26 Ezion Geber. Solomon's port located on the modern Gulf of Aqabah.

9:28 Ophir. The location of Ophir is unknown. It has been suggested it was located on the southwestern Arabian peninsula. First Kings 10:11,12 possibly suggests that Ophir was close to or a part of the kingdom of Sheba. **four hundred and twenty talents.** This was about 16 tons of gold. Second Chronicles 8:18 has 450 talents (*see note on 2 Chr. 8:18*).

10:1-29 See 2 Chr. 9:1-28.

cerning the name of the LORD, she came [b]to
test him with hard questions. 2 She came to
Jerusalem with a very great [1]retinue, with
camels that bore spices, very much gold,
and precious stones; and when she came to
Solomon, she spoke with him about all
that was in her heart. 3 So Solomon answered all her questions; there was nothing [2]so difficult for the king that he could
not explain *it* to her. 4 And when the queen
of Sheba had seen all the wisdom of Solomon, the house that he had built, 5 the
food on his table, the seating of his servants, the service of his waiters and their
apparel, his cupbearers, [c]and his entryway
by which he went up to the house of the
LORD, there was no more spirit in her.
6 Then she said to the king: "It was a true
report which I heard in my own land about
your words and your wisdom. 7 However
I did not believe the words until I came
and saw with my own eyes; and indeed
the half was not told me. Your wisdom and
prosperity exceed the fame of which I
heard. 8 [d]Happy *are* your men and happy
are these your servants, who stand continually before you *and* hear your wisdom!
9 [e]Blessed be the LORD your God, who [f]de-
lighted in you, setting you on the throne of
Israel! Because the LORD has loved Israel
forever, therefore He made you king, [g]to
do justice and righteousness."
10 Then she [h]gave the king one hundred
and twenty talents of gold, spices in great
quantity, and precious stones. There never
again came such abundance of spices as
the queen of Sheba gave to King Solomon.
11 [i]Also, the ships of Hiram, which
brought gold from Ophir, brought great
quantities of [3]almug wood and precious
stones from Ophir. 12 [j]And the king made
[4]steps of the almug wood for the house of
the LORD and for the king's house, also
harps and stringed instruments for
singers. There never again came such [k]al-
mug wood, nor has the like been seen to
this day.
13 Now King Solomon gave the queen of
Sheba all she desired, whatever she asked,
besides what Solomon had given her according to the royal generosity. So she
turned and went to her own country, she
and her servants.

Solomon's Great Wealth

14 The weight of gold that came to Solomon yearly was six hundred and sixty-six
talents of gold, 15 besides *that* from the
[l]traveling merchants, from the income of
traders, [m]from all the kings of Arabia, and
from the governors of the country.
16 And King Solomon made two hundred
large shields *of* hammered gold; six hundred *shekels* of gold went into each shield.
17 He also *made* [n]three hundred shields *of*
hammered gold; three minas of gold went
into each shield. The king put them in the
[o]House of the Forest of Lebanon.
18 [p]Moreover the king made a great
throne of ivory, and overlaid it with pure
gold. 19 The throne had six steps, and the
top of the throne *was* round at the back;
there were armrests on either side of the
place of the seat, and two lions stood beside the armrests. 20 Twelve lions stood
there, one on each side of the six steps;
nothing like *this* had been made for any
other kingdom.
21 [q]All King Solomon's drinking vessels
were gold, and all the vessels of the House
of the Forest of Lebanon *were* pure gold.
Not *one was* silver, for this was accounted
as nothing in the days of Solomon. 22 For
the king had [r]merchant[5] ships at sea with
the fleet of Hiram. Once every three years
the merchant [s]ships came bringing gold,
silver, ivory, apes, and [6]monkeys. 23 So
[t]King Solomon surpassed all the kings of
the earth in riches and wisdom.
24 Now all the earth sought the presence

1 [b] Judg. 14:12; Ps. 49:4; Prov. 1:6
2 [1] *company*
3 [2] *too*
5 [c] 1 Chr. 26:16; 2 Chr. 9:4
8 [d] Prov. 8:34
9 [e] 1 Kin. 5:7 [f] 2 Sam. 22:20 [g] 2 Sam. 8:15; Ps. 72:2; [Prov. 8:15]
10 [h] Ps. 72:10, 15
11 [i] 1 Kin. 9:27, 28; Job 22:24 [3] *algum,* 2 Chr. 9:10, 11
12 [j] 2 Chr. 9:11 [k] 2 Chr. 9:10 [4] Or *supports*
15 [l] 2 Chr. 1:16 [m] 2 Chr. 9:24; Ps. 72:10
17 [n] 1 Kin. 14:26 [o] 1 Kin. 7:2
18 [p] 1 Kin. 10:22; 2 Chr. 9:17; Ps. 45:8
21 [q] 2 Chr. 9:20
22 [r] Gen. 10:4; 2 Chr. 20:36 [s] 1 Kin. 9:26–28; 22:48; Ps. 72:10 [5] Lit. *ships of Tarshish,* deep-sea vessels [6] Or *peacocks*
23 [t] 1 Kin. 3:12, 13; 4:30; 2 Chr. 1:12

10:1 Sheba. Sheba was located in southwestern Arabia, about 1,200 mi. from Jerusalem. **concerning the name of the LORD.** The primary motive for the queen's visit was to verify Solomon's reputation for wisdom and devotion to the Lord. **hard questions.** Riddles designed to stump the hearer (cf. Judg. 14:12).

10:5 no more spirit in her. Lit. the experience "left her breathless."

10:9 the LORD your God. The queen was willing to credit Solomon's God with giving him wisdom that resulted in just and righteous decisions. Though she recognized the Lord as Israel's national God, there was no confession that Solomon's God had become her God to the exclusion of all others. There is no record that she made any offerings to God at the temple.

10:10 one hundred and twenty talents. About 4.5 tons (cf. 9:28).

10:11 almug wood. Probably the strong, long-lasting sandalwood, which is black on the outside and ruby red inside.

10:12 to this day. *See note on 8:8.*

10:14 six hundred and sixty-six talents. About 25 tons of gold.

10:15 Gold also came to Solomon from tolls and tariffs from traders, revenues from loyal administrators, and taxes from Arabian kings who used caravan routes under Solomon's control.

10:16,17 shields. From his gold revenues, Solomon made 200 large shields, containing about 7.5 pounds of gold each, and 300 small shields, having 3.75 pounds of gold each, that were ornamental in design and restricted to ceremonial use.

10:21 silver. To show the wealth of Solomon's kingdom, the writer explains that gold was so plentiful that the value of silver dropped to nothing. *For note on the "House of the forest of Lebanon," see 7:2.*

10:22 merchant ships. These "ships of Tarshish" were large, all-weather cargo vessels designed to make long ocean voyages.

of Solomon to hear his wisdom, which
God had put in his heart. 25 Each man
brought his present: articles of silver and
gold, garments, armor, spices, horses, and
mules, at a set rate year by year.
26 [u]And Solomon [v]gathered chariots and
horsemen; he had one thousand four hundred chariots and twelve thousand horsemen, whom he [7]stationed in the chariot
cities and with the king at Jerusalem. 27 [w]The
king made silver *as common* in Jerusalem as
stones, and he made cedar trees as abundant
as the sycamores which *are* in the lowland.
28 [x]Also Solomon had horses imported
from Egypt and Keveh; the king's merchants bought them in Keveh at the *current*
price. 29 Now a chariot that was imported
from Egypt cost six hundred *shekels* of silver, and a horse one hundred and fifty;
[y]and [8]thus, through their agents, they exported *them* to all the kings of the Hittites
and the kings of Syria.

Solomon's Heart Turns from the LORD

11 But [a]King Solomon loved [b]many
foreign women, as well as the
daughter of Pharaoh: women of the Moabites, Ammonites, Edomites, Sidonians, *and*
Hittites— 2 from the nations of whom the
LORD had said to the children of Israel,
[c]"You shall not intermarry with them, nor
they with you. Surely they will turn away
your hearts after their gods." Solomon
clung to these in love. 3 And he had seven
hundred wives, princesses, and three hundred concubines; and his wives turned
away his heart. 4 For it was so, when Solomon was old, [d]that his wives turned his
heart after other gods; and his [e]heart was
not [1]loyal to the LORD his God, [f]as *was* the
heart of his father David. 5 For Solomon
went after [g]Ashtoreth the goddess of the
Sidonians, and after [h]Milcom[2] the
abomination of the [i]Ammonites. 6 Solomon did evil in the sight of the LORD, and
did not fully follow the LORD, as *did* his father David. 7 [j]Then Solomon built a [3]high
place for [k]Chemosh the abomination of
Moab, on [l]the hill that *is* east of Jerusalem,
and for Molech the abomination of the
people of Ammon. 8 And he did likewise

26 [u] 1 Kin. 4:26; 2 Chr. 1:14; 9:25 [v] [Deut. 17:16]; 1 Kin. 9:19 [7] So with LXX, Syr., Tg., Vg. (cf. 2 Chr. 9:25); MT *led*
27 [w] [Deut. 17:17]; 2 Chr. 1:15-17
28 [x] [Deut. 17:16]; 2 Chr. 1:16; 9:28
29 [y] Josh. 1:4; 2 Kin. 7:6, 7 [8] Lit. *by their hands*

CHAPTER 11

1 [a] [Neh. 13:26] [b] [Deut. 17:17]; 1 Kin. 3:1
2 [c] Ex. 34:16; [Deut. 7:3, 4]
4 [d] [Deut. 17:17; Neh. 13:26] [e] 1 Kin. 8:61 [f] 1 Kin. 9:4 [1] Lit. *at peace with*
5 [g] Judg. 2:13; 1 Kin. 11:33 [h] [Lev. 20:2-5] [i] 2 Kin. 23:13 [2] Or *Molech*
7 [j] Num. 33:52 [k] Num. 21:29; Judg. 11:24 [l] 2 Kin. 23:13 [3] A place for pagan worship

10:25 silver and gold…horses. The wisdom God had given to Solomon (v. 24) caused many rulers, like the queen of Sheba (vv. 1-13), to bring presents to Solomon as they sought to buy his wisdom to be applied in their own nations. These gifts led Solomon to multiply for himself both horses, as well as silver and gold, precisely that which God's king was warned against in Deut. 17:16,17. Solomon became ensnared by the blessings of his own wisdom and disobeyed God's commands.

10:28 Keveh. Keveh was in Cilicia, an area S of the Taurus Mountains in Asia Minor. In antiquity, Cilicia was fabled for breeding and selling the best horses.

10:29 six hundred *shekels*. About 15 lbs. of silver. **one hundred and fifty.** About 3.75 lbs. of silver. **Hittites.** The majority of Hittites lived in Anatolia (Asia Minor). From ca. 1720–1200 B.C. a unified kingdom ruled over the Hittites. These kings spread the influence of the Hittites throughout the ancient Near East; the Hittite empire reached the peak of its power ca. 1380–1350 B.C. When the Hittite empire collapsed, ca. 1200 B.C., many Hittite city-states developed, each with its own king. These rulers were called "the kings of the Hittites" and were scattered in Solomon's day throughout Anatolia and northern Aram (Syria). **Syria.** This familiar geographical area within the bounds set by the Taurus Mountains in the N, the western bend of the Euphrates River and the edge of the desert in the E, the Litani River to the S and the Mediterranean Sea to the W, had as its major city, Damascus. "Syria" is actually a later Gr. term; the land was known in OT times as Aram.

11:1-6 loved many foreign women. Many of Solomon's marriages were for the purpose of ratifying treaties with other nations, a common practice in the ancient Near East. The practice of multiplying royal wives, prohibited in Deut. 17:17 because the practice would turn the king's heart away from the Lord, proved to be accurate in the experience of Solomon. His love for his wives (vv. 1,2) led him to abandon his loyalty to the Lord and worship other gods (vv. 3-6). No sadder picture can be imagined than the ugly apostasy of his later years (over 50), which can be traced back to his sins with foreign wives. Polygamy was tolerated among the ancient Hebrews, though most in the East had only one wife. A number of wives was seen as a sign of wealth and importance. The king desired to have a larger harem than any of his subjects, and Solomon resorted to this form of state magnificence. But it was a sin directly violating God's law, and the very result which that law was designed to prevent happened.

11:1 Moabites. Descendants of Lot (Gen. 19:37) who lived in the land E of the Dead Sea between the Arnon River to the N and the Zered Brook to the S. **Ammonites.** Descendants of Lot (Gen. 19:38) who were located in the area of the Transjordan beginning about 25 mi. E of the Jordan River. **Edomites.** Descendants of Esau (Gen. 36:1) who were located in the area S of Moab, to the SE of the Dead Sea. **Sidonians.** *See note on 5:6.* **Hittites.** *See note on 10:29.*

11:4 as…David. Cf. v. 6. David is consistently presented in Kings as the standard by which other kings were to act and be judged (3:14; 9:4; 14:8; 15:3; 2 Kin. 8:19; 22:2). This was not because David had not sinned (cf. 2 Sam. 11,12), but rather because he repented appropriately from his sin (Pss. 32, 51), and because sin did not continue as the pattern of his life.

11:5 Ashtoreh. A deliberate distortion of the Canaanite "ashtart," re-vocalized based on the Heb. word for "shame." She was the goddess of love and fertility, especially worshiped at Tyre and Sidon. **Milcom.** Another name for Molech (v. 7), the national god of the Ammonites. His name seems to mean "the one who rules." The worship of Molech was associated with the sacrifice of children in the fire (Lev. 18:21; 20:2,3,4,5; Jer. 32:35).

11:6 evil in the sight of the LORD. The particular evil of Solomon was his tolerance of and personal practice of idolatry. These same words were used throughout the book of Kings to describe the rulers who promoted and practiced idolatry (15:26,34; 16:19,25,30; 22:52; 2 Kin. 3:2; 8:18,27; 13:2,11; 14:24; 15:9,18,24,28; 17:2; 21:2,20; 23:32,37; 24:9,19). Solomon became an open idolater, worshiping images of wood and stone in the sight of the temple which, in his early years, he had erected to the one true God.

11:7 Chemosh. The god of the Moabites, to whom the sacrifice of children as a burnt offering was customary (2 Kin. 3:27). **hill…east of Jerusalem.** Probably, the Mt. of Olives. This is the area called Tophet in Jer. 7:30-34 and the Mt. of Corruption in 2 Kin. 23:13.

for all his foreign wives, who burned incense and sacrificed to their gods.
9 So the LORD became angry with Solomon, because his heart had turned from
the LORD God of Israel, [m]who had appeared
to him twice, 10 and [n]had commanded him
concerning this thing, that he should not go
after other gods; but he did not keep what
the LORD had commanded. 11 Therefore the
LORD said to Solomon, "Because you have
done this, and have not kept My covenant
and My statutes, which I have commanded
you, [o]I will surely tear the kingdom away
from you and give it to your [p]servant.
12 Nevertheless I will not do it in your days,
for the sake of your father David; I will tear
it out of the hand of your son. 13 [q]However
I will not tear away the whole kingdom; I
will give [r]one tribe to your son [s]for the sake
of my servant David, and for the sake of Jerusalem [t]which I have chosen."

Adversaries of Solomon

14 Now the LORD [u]raised up an adversary against Solomon, Hadad the Edomite;
he *was* a descendant of the king in Edom.
15 [v]For it happened, when David was in
Edom, and Joab the commander of the
army had gone up to bury the slain, [w]after
he had killed every male in Edom 16 (because for six months Joab remained there
with all Israel, until he had cut down every
male in Edom), 17 that Hadad fled to go to
Egypt, he and certain Edomites of his father's servants with him. Hadad *was* still a
little child. 18 Then they arose from Midian
and came to Paran; and they took men
with them from Paran and came to Egypt,
to Pharaoh king of Egypt, who gave him a
house, apportioned food for him, and gave
him land. 19 And Hadad found great favor
in the sight of Pharaoh, so that he gave him
as wife the sister of his own wife, that is,
the sister of Queen Tahpenes. 20 Then the
sister of Tahpenes bore him Genubath his
son, whom Tahpenes weaned in Pharaoh's
house. And Genubath was in Pharaoh's
household among the sons of Pharaoh.
21 [x]So when Hadad heard in Egypt that
David [4]rested with his fathers, and that
Joab the commander of the army was
dead, Hadad said to Pharaoh, [5]"Let me
depart, that I may go to my own country."
22 Then Pharaoh said to him, "But what
have you lacked with me, that suddenly
you seek to go to your own country?"
So he answered, "Nothing, but do let me
go anyway."
23 And God raised up *another* adversary
against him, Rezon the son of Eliadah, who
had fled from his lord, [y]Hadadezer king of
Zobah. 24 So he gathered men to him and
became captain over a band *of raiders*,
[z]when David killed those *of Zobah*. And
they went to Damascus and dwelt there,
and reigned in Damascus. 25 He was an adversary of Israel all the days of Solomon
(besides the trouble that Hadad *caused*); and
he abhorred Israel, and reigned over Syria.

Jeroboam's Rebellion

26 Then Solomon's servant, [a]Jeroboam
the son of Nebat, an Ephraimite from Zere-
da, whose mother's name *was* Zeruah, a
widow, [b]also [c]rebelled against the king.
27 And this *is* what caused him to rebel

9 [m] 1 Kin. 3:5; 9:2
10 [n] 1 Kin. 6:12; 9:6, 7
11 [o] 1 Kin. 11:31; 12:15, 16 [p] 1 Kin. 11:31, 37
13 [q] 2 Sam. 7:15; 1 Chr. 17:13; Ps. 89:33 [r] 1 Kin. 12:20 [s] 2 Sam. 7:15, 16 [t] Deut. 12:11; 1 Kin. 9:3; 14:21
14 [u] 1 Chr. 5:26
15 [v] 2 Sam. 8:14; 1 Chr. 18:12, 13 [w] Num. 24:18, 19; [Deut. 20:13]
21 [x] 1 Kin. 2:10, 34 [4] Died and joined his ancestors [5] Lit. *Send me away*
23 [y] 2 Sam. 8:3; 10:16
24 [z] 2 Sam. 8:3; 10:8, 18
26 [a] 1 Kin. 12:2 [b] 1 Kin. 11:11; 2 Chr. 13:6 [c] 2 Sam. 20:21

11:9,10 appeared to him twice. Once was at Gibean (3:5), the next at Jerusalem (9:2). On both occasions, God had warned Solomon, so he had no excuses.

11:11 not kept My covenant. Solomon failed to obey the commandments to honor God (Ex. 20:3-6), which were part of the Mosaic Covenant. Obedience to that Covenant was necessary for receiving the blessings of the Davidic Covenant (see 2:3,4). **tear the kingdom away from you.** The Lord's tearing of the kingdom from Solomon was announced in Ahijah's symbolic action of tearing his garment in vv. 29-39. The tearing of the robe, picturing the loss of the kingdom, recalls the interaction between Samuel and Saul (1 Sam. 15:27,28), when the Lord took the kingdom away from Saul because of his disobedience. The great gifts to Solomon followed by his great abuse warranted such a judgment.

11:12 not do it in your days. The Lord's great love for David caused Him to temper His judgment with mercy by not disrupting the kingdom in Solomon's lifetime (cf. v. 34). This showed that Solomon's disobedience did not annul the Davidic Covenant; the Lord's commitment to fulfill His Word to David remained firm (cf. 2 Sam. 7:12-16).

11:13 one tribe. The one tribe that remained loyal to the Davidic dynasty was Judah (cf. 12:20). **for the sake of Jerusalem.** The Lord had chosen Jerusalem as the place where His name would dwell forever (9:3). Therefore, Jerusalem and the temple would remain so that the divine promise might stand.

11:14-18 Hadad the Edomite. Even though Hadad belonged to the royal family that ruled Edom, he escaped death at the hands of David's army when he was a child, and he fled to Egypt (cf. 2 Sam. 8:13,14; 1 Chr. 18:12,13).

11:18 Midian. The land directly E of Edom, to which Hadad first fled on his way to Egypt. **Paran.** A wilderness SE of Kadesh in the central area of the Sinai Peninsula (cf. Num. 12:16; 13:3).

11:21 Let me depart. Like Moses (Ex. 2:10), Hadad's son grew up in Pharaoh's household. As did Moses (Ex. 5:1), Hadad requested that Pharaoh allow him to leave Egypt. Hearing of the deaths of David and Joab, he renounced his easy position and possessions in Egypt to return to Edom in order to regain his throne. His activities gave great trouble to Israel (v. 25).

11:23-25 Rezon. After David conquered Zobar (2 Sam. 8:3-8), Rezon and his men took Damascus and established the strong dynasty of Syrian kings that severely troubled Israel in the ninth century B.C. (cf. 15:18; 20:1).

11:26 Jeroboam the son of Nebat. In contrast to Hadad and Rezon, who were external adversaries of Solomon, God raised up Jeroboam from a town in Ephraim as an internal adversary. Jeroboam was from Ephraim, the leading tribe of Israel's northern 10 tribes. He

against the king: [d]Solomon had built the
Millo *and* [6]repaired the damages to the
City of David his father. 28 The man Jeroboam *was* a mighty man of valor; and Solomon, seeing that the young man was [e]in-
dustrious, made him the officer over all the
labor force of the house of Joseph.

29 Now it happened at that time, when
Jeroboam went out of Jerusalem, that the
prophet [f]Ahijah the Shilonite met him on
the way; and he had clothed himself with a
new garment, and the two *were* alone in the
field. 30 Then Ahijah took hold of the new
garment that *was* on him, and [g]tore it *into*
twelve pieces. 31 And he said to Jeroboam,
"Take for yourself ten pieces, for [h]thus says
the LORD, the God of Israel: 'Behold, I will
tear the kingdom out of the hand of Solomon and will give ten tribes to you 32 (but
he shall have one tribe for the sake of My
servant David, and for the sake of Jerusalem, the city which I have chosen out of all
the tribes of Israel), 33 [i]because [7]they have
forsaken Me, and worshiped Ashtoreth the
goddess of the Sidonians, Chemosh the
god of the Moabites, and Milcom the god of
the people of Ammon, and have not
walked in My ways to do *what is* right in
My eyes and *keep* My statutes and My judgments, as *did* his father David. 34 However
I will not take the whole kingdom out of his
hand, because I have made him ruler all the
days of his life for the sake of My servant
David, whom I chose because he kept My
commandments and My statutes. 35 But [j]I
will take the kingdom out of his son's hand
and give it to you—ten tribes. 36 And to his
son I will give one tribe, that [k]My servant
David may always have a lamp before Me
in Jerusalem, the city which I have chosen
for Myself, to put My name there. 37 So I
will take you, and you shall reign over all
your heart desires, and you shall be king
over Israel. 38 Then it shall be, if you heed
all that I command you, walk in My ways,
and do *what is* right in My sight, to keep My
statutes and My commandments, as My
servant David did, then [l]I will be with you
and [m]build for you an enduring house, as I
built for David, and will give Israel to you.
39 And I will afflict the descendants of David because of this, but not forever.' "

40 Solomon therefore sought to kill Jeroboam. But Jeroboam arose and fled to
Egypt, to [n]Shishak king of Egypt, and was
in Egypt until the death of Solomon.

Death of Solomon

41 Now [o]the rest of the acts of Solomon,
all that he did, and his wisdom, *are* they
not written in the book of the acts of Solomon? 42 [p]And the period that Solomon
reigned in Jerusalem over all Israel *was*
forty years. 43 [q]Then Solomon [8]rested with
his fathers, and was buried in the City of
David his father. And Rehoboam his son
reigned in his [r]place.

The Revolt Against Rehoboam

12 And [a]Rehoboam went to [b]Shechem,
for all Israel had gone to Shechem
to make him king. 2 So it happened, when
[c]Jeroboam the son of Nebat heard *it* (he

27 [d] 1 Kin. 9:15, 24 [6] Lit. *closed up the breaches*
28 [e] [Prov. 22:29]
29 [f] 1 Kin. 12:15; 14:2; 2 Chr. 9:29
30 [g] 1 Sam. 15:27, 28; 24:5
31 [h] 1 Kin. 11:11, 13
33 [i] 1 Sam. 7:3; 1 Kin. 11:5-8 [7] So with MT, Tg.; LXX, Syr., Vg. *he has*
35 [j] 1 Kin. 12:16, 17
36 [k] [1 Kin. 15:4; 2 Kin. 8:19]
38 [l] Deut. 31:8; Josh. 1:5 [m] 2 Sam. 7:11, 27
40 [n] 1 Kin. 11:17; 14:25; 2 Chr. 12:2-9
41 [o] 2 Chr. 9:29
42 [p] 2 Chr. 9:30
43 [q] 1 Kin. 2:10; 2 Chr. 9:31 [r] 1 Kin. 14:21; 2 Chr. 10:1 [8] Died and joined his ancestors

CHAPTER 12

1 [a] 2 Chr. 10:1 [b] Judg. 9:6
2 [c] 1 Kin. 11:26

was a young man of talent and energy who, having been appointed by Solomon as leader over the building works around Jerusalem, rose to public notice.

11:28 labor force. *See note on 5:13.*

11:29 Ahijah the Shilonite. Ahijah was a prophet of the Lord who lived in Shiloh, a town in Ephraim about 20 mi. N of Jerusalem. *See note on 1 Sam. 1:3.*

11:30-32 Here is a monumental prophecy that because of Solomon's sins the kingdom would be divided and Jeroboam would rule in the northern area (cf. vv. 35-37).

11:33 *See notes on 11:5,7.*

11:36 a lamp before Me. A lighted lamp represented the life of an individual (Job 18:6; Ps. 132:17). God promised that from the tribe of Judah David would continue to have descendants ruling in Jerusalem (cf. 2 Sam. 21:17; 1 Kin. 15:4; 2 Kin. 8:19).

11:38 if you heed all that I command you. The Lord gave to Jeroboam the same promise that He had made to David—an enduring royal dynasty over Israel, the 10 northern tribes, if he obeyed God's law. The Lord imposed on Jeroboam the same conditions for his kingship that He had imposed on David (2:3,4; 3:14).

11:39 but not forever. This statement implied that the kingdom's division was not to be permanent and that David's house would ultimately rule all the tribes of Israel again (cf. Ezek. 37:15-28).

11:40 kill Jeroboam. Though the prophecy was private (v. 29), the king heard about it and Jeroboam became a marked man, guilty in Solomon's eyes of rebellion and worthy of the death penalty. **Shishak.** Shishak was the founder of the 22nd dynasty in Egypt. He reigned ca. 945–924 B.C. He invaded Judah during the reign of Rehoboam (14:25,26).

11:42 forty years. 971–931 B.C.

12:1–2 Kin. 17:41 The division of Solomon's kingdom had been predicted by the Lord to Solomon (11:11-13) and through Ahijah to Jeroboam (11:29-37). This section of the books of Kings shows how the Word of the Lord through the prophet was fulfilled and narrates the history of the divided kingdom, Israel (the northern kingdom) and Judah (the southern kingdom), from 931–722 B.C.

12:1–14:31 This section describes the disruption of the Kingdom (12:1-24) plus the establishment and royal sanctioning of idolatry in Israel (12:25–14:20) and Judah (14:21-31). The reigns of Solomon's son, Rehoboam, in the S (ca. 931–913 B.C.) and Solomon's servant, Jeroboam, in the N (ca. 931–910 B.C.) are discussed. See 2 Chr. 10:1–12:16.

12:1 Shechem. A city located in the hill country of northern Ephraim, 30 mi. N of Jerusalem. Shechem had a long and important history as a political and religious center (cf. Gen. 12:6; Josh. 8:30-35; 24:1-28,32). **all Israel.** The representatives of the 10 northern tribes assembled to accept Rehoboam as king (cf. 2 Sam. 5:3).

12:2 heard *it*. Jeroboam, in Egypt (11:40), learned about the death of Solomon (11:43).

was still in [d]Egypt, for he had fled from the
presence of King Solomon and had been
dwelling in Egypt), 3 that they sent and
called him. Then Jeroboam and the whole
assembly of Israel came and spoke to Rehoboam, saying, 4 "Your father made our
[e]yoke [1]heavy; now therefore, lighten the
burdensome service of your father, and his
heavy yoke which he put on us, and we
will serve you."
5 So he said to them, "Depart *for* three
days, then come back to me." And the people departed.
6 Then King Rehoboam consulted the elders who stood before his father Solomon
while he still lived, and he said, "How do
you advise *me* to answer these people?"
7 And they spoke to him, saying, [f]"If
you will be a servant to these people today,
and serve them, and answer them, and
speak good words to them, then they will
be your servants forever."
8 But he rejected the advice which the elders had given him, and consulted the
young men who had grown up with him,
who stood before him. 9 And he said to
them, "What advice do you give? How
should we answer this people who have
spoken to me, saying, 'Lighten the yoke
which your father put on us'?"
10 Then the young men who had grown
up with him spoke to him, saying, "Thus
you should speak to this people who have
spoken to you, saying, 'Your father made
our yoke heavy, but you make *it* lighter on
us'—thus you shall say to them: 'My little
finger shall be thicker than my father's
waist! 11 And now, whereas my father put
a heavy yoke on you, I will add to your
yoke; my father chastised you with whips,
but I will chastise you with [2]scourges!'"
12 So Jeroboam and all the people came
to Rehoboam the third day, as the king had
directed, saying, "Come back to me the
third day." 13 Then the king answered the
people [3]roughly, and rejected the advice
which the elders had given him; 14 and he
spoke to them according to the advice of
the young men, saying, "My father made
your yoke heavy, but I will add to your
yoke; my father chastised you with whips,
but I will chastise you with [4]scourges!"
15 So the king did not listen to the people;
for [g]the turn *of events* was from the LORD,
that He might fulfill His word, which the

2 [d] 1 Kin. 11:40
4 [e] 1 Sam. 8:11-18; 1 Kin. 4:7; 5:13-15
[1] *hard*
7 [f] 2 Chr. 10:7; [Prov. 15:1]
11 [2] Scourges with points or barbs, lit. *scorpions*
13 [3] *harshly*
14 [4] Lit. *scorpions*
15 [g] Deut. 2:30; Judg. 14:4; 1 Kin. 12:24; 2 Chr. 10:15

The Land of the Divided Kingdom

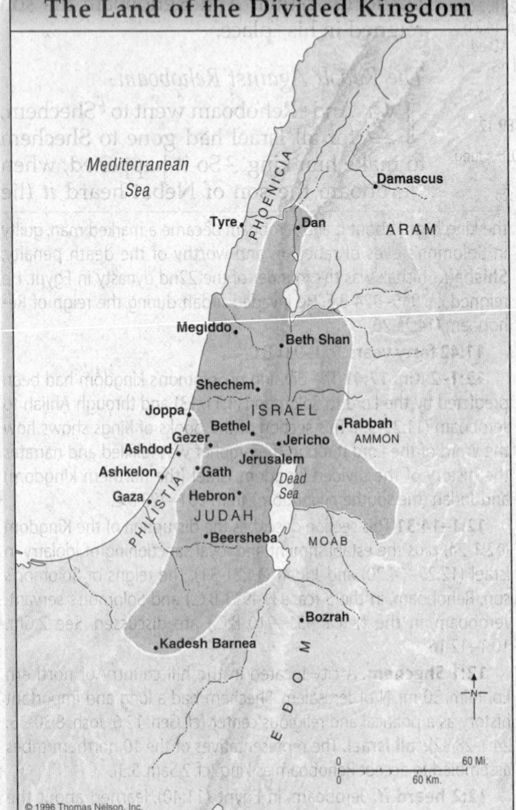

Because of Solomon's idolatry, the Lord divided the kingdom (11:9-13).

12:3 Jeroboam...spoke. The 10 northern tribes summoned Jeroboam from Egypt to become their representative and spokesman in their dealings with Rehoboam.

12:4 yoke. The hardships that resulted from Solomon's policy of compulsory labor service (cf. 5:13; 9:22; 11:28) and excessive taxes (cf. 4:7) came because the splendor of his courts, the magnitude of his wealth, and the profits of his enterprises were not enough to sustain his demands.

12:6,7 the elders. These were older, experienced counselors and administrators who had served Solomon. They counseled Rehoboam to give concessions to the 10 tribes.

12:8-10 the young men. The contemporaries of Rehoboam, about forty years of age (cf. 14:21), who were acquainted only with the royal court life of Solomon, recommended that Rehoboam be even harsher on the 10 tribes than was Solomon.

12:10 My little *finger*...my father's waist. A proverbial manner of saying he was going to come at them with greater force than Solomon had exhibited (vv. 11-14).

12:15 from the LORD. God sovereignly used the foolishness of Rehoboam to fulfill Ahijah's prophecy (11:29-39).

LORD had [h]spoken by Ahijah the Shilonite
to Jeroboam the son of Nebat.
16 Now when all Israel saw that the king
did not listen to them, the people answered the king, saying:

[i]"What share have we in David?
We have no inheritance in the son
of Jesse.
To your tents, O Israel!
Now, see to your own house,
O David!"

So Israel departed to their tents. 17 But
Rehoboam reigned over [j]the children of Israel who dwelt in the cities of Judah.
18 Then King Rehoboam [k]sent Adoram,
who *was* in charge of the revenue; but all
Israel stoned him with stones, and he died.
Therefore King Rehoboam mounted his
chariot in haste to flee to Jerusalem. 19 So
[l]Israel has been in rebellion against the
house of David to this day.
20 Now it came to pass when all Israel
heard that Jeroboam had come back, they
sent for him and called him to the congregation, and made him king over all [m]Israel.
There was none who followed the house of
David, but the tribe of Judah [n]only.
21 And when [o]Rehoboam came to Jerusalem, he assembled all the house of Judah
with the tribe of [p]Benjamin, one hundred
and eighty thousand chosen *men* who were
warriors, to fight against the house of Israel,
that he might restore the kingdom to Rehoboam the son of Solomon. 22 But [q]the word
of God came to Shemaiah the man of God,
saying, 23 "Speak to Rehoboam the son of
Solomon, king of Judah, to all the house of
Judah and Benjamin, and to the rest of the
people, saying, 24 'Thus says the LORD: "You
shall not go up nor fight against your
brethren the children of Israel. Let every
man return to his house, [r]for this thing is
from Me." ' " Therefore they obeyed the
word of the LORD, and turned back, according to the word of the LORD.

Jeroboam's Gold Calves

25 Then Jeroboam [s]built[5] Shechem in the
mountains of Ephraim, and dwelt there.
Also he went out from there and built [t]Pe-
nuel. 26 And Jeroboam said in his heart,
"Now the kingdom may return to the
house of David: 27 If these people [u]go up
to offer sacrifices in the house of the LORD
at Jerusalem, then the heart of this people
will turn back to their lord, Rehoboam
king of Judah, and they will kill me and go
back to Rehoboam king of Judah."
28 Therefore the king asked advice,
[v]made two calves of gold, and said to the
people, "It is too much for you to go up to
Jerusalem. [w]Here are your gods, O Israel,
which brought you up from the land of
Egypt!" 29 And he set up one in [x]Bethel,

15 [h] 1 Kin. 11:11, 29, 31
16 [i] 2 Sam. 20:1
17 [j] 1 Kin. 11:13, 36; 2 Chr. 11:14-17
18 [k] 1 Kin. 4:6; 5:14
19 [l] 2 Kin. 17:21
20 [m] 2 Kin. 17:21 [n] 1 Kin. 11:13, 32, 36
21 [o] 2 Chr. 11:1-4 [p] 2 Sam. 19:17
22 [q] 2 Chr. 11:2; 12:5-7
24 [r] 1 Kin. 12:15
25 [s] Gen. 12:6; Judg. 9:45-49; 1 Kin. 12:1 [t] Gen. 32:30, 31; Judg. 8:8, 17 [5] *fortified*
27 [u] [Deut. 12:5-7, 14]
28 [v] 2 Kin. 10:29; 17:16; [Hos. 8:4-7] [w] Ex. 32:4, 8
29 [x] Gen. 28:19

12:16 David. These words of Israel (v. 16) expressed deliberate, willful rebellion against the dynasty of David (cf. v. 19). Defiantly, the Israelites quoted the rallying cry used in Sheba's failed rebellion against David (2 Sam. 20:1). The northern tribes declared that they had no legal tie with David and went their way.

12:17 the children of Israel. People from the northern tribes who had migrated S and settled in Judah.

12:18 Adoram. Sending the chief of taxation and forced labor (Adoniram in 4:6; 5:14) to negotiate with the northern tribes was foolish (cf. v. 4).

12:19 to this day. *See note on 8:8.*

12:20-24 The kingdom was divided at that point. Israel (the northern 10 tribes) had its own king.

12:21 the tribe of Benjamin. The tribe of Benjamin had split loyalty and land during the divided-kingdom era. According to v. 20, only the tribe of Judah remained completely loyal to the house of David, but in vv. 21,23 it is said that Benjamin was associated with "all the house of Judah," the emphasis being on the tribe of Judah. Certain towns of northern Benjamin, most notably Bethel (v. 29), were included in the northern kingdom. Simeon, the tribe originally given land in the southern section of Judah's territory (Josh. 19:1-9), had apparently migrated N and was counted with the 10 northern tribes (cf. 1 Chr. 12:23-25; 2 Chr. 15:9; 34:6). Thus, the 10 northern tribes were Reuben, Simeon, Zebulun, Issachar, Dan, Gad, Asher, Naphtali, Manasseh, and Ephraim. The southern kingdom was the tribe of Judah only. The 12th tribe, Benjamin, was split between the two kingdoms. The tribe of Levi, originally scattered throughout both kingdoms (Josh. 21:1-42), resided in Judah during the divided kingdom (see 2 Chr. 11:13-16).

12:22 the man of God. Cf. 17:24. A common OT expression designating a man with a message from God who would speak authoritatively on the Lord's behalf (cf. Deut 33:1; 2 Tim. 3:17). *See note on Deut. 33:1.*

12:24 this thing is from Me. Through the prophet Shenaiah, the Lord commanded Rehoboam and his army not to invade Israel. God, in judgment, had ordained the N-S split (v. 15; 11:29-39), so to attack Israel was to oppose God Himself.

12:25 Shechem. Cf. v. 1. Jeroboam fortified the city of Shechem and made it into his royal residence. Cf. Judg. 9:1-47. **Penuel.** Jeroboam also fortified Penuel, a city about 10 mi. E of the Jordan River on the River Jabbok, asserting his sovereignty over the Israelites E of the Jordan.

12:26 return to the house of David. The Lord had ordained a political, not a religious, division of Solomon's kingdom. The Lord had promised Jeroboam political control of the 10 northern tribes (11:31,35,37). However, Jeroboam was to religiously follow the Mosaic law, which demanded that he follow the Lord's sacrificial system at the temple in Jerusalem (11:38). Having received the kingdom from God, he should have relied on divine protection, but he did not. Seeking to keep his subjects from being influenced by Rehoboam when they went to Jerusalem to worship, he set up worship in the north (vv. 27,28).

12:28 two calves of gold. These two calves, probably made of wood overlaid with gold, were presented to Israel as pedestals on which the Lord supposedly sat or stood. He publicly presented them with the very words with which idolatrous Israel had welcomed Aaron's golden calf. He repeated Aaron's destructive sin of trying to make an earthly image of God. *See note on Ex. 32:4.*

12:29 Bethel...Dan. Bethel was located about 11 mi. N of

and the other he put in [y]Dan. 30 Now this
thing became [z]a sin, for the people went *to*
worship before the one as far as Dan. 31 He
made [6]shrines on the high places, [a]and
made priests from every class of people,
who were not of the sons of Levi.
32 Jeroboam [7]ordained a feast on the fifteenth day of the eighth month, like [b]the
feast that *was* in Judah, and offered sacrifices on the altar. So he did at Bethel, sacrificing to the calves that he had made. [c]And
at Bethel he installed the priests of the high
places which he had made. 33 So he made
offerings on the altar which he had made
at Bethel on the fifteenth day of the eighth
month, in the month which he had [d]de-
vised in his own heart. And he [8]ordained a
feast for the children of Israel, and offered
sacrifices on the altar and [e]burned incense.

29 [y] Judg. 18:26-31 **30** [z] 1 Kin. 13:34; 2 Kin. 17:21 **31** [a] [Num. 3:10; 17:1-11]; Judg. 17:5; 1 Kin. 13:33; 2 Kin. 17:32; 2 Chr. 11:14, 15 [6] Lit. *a house*; cf. 1 Kin. 13:32, lit. *houses* **32** [b] Lev. 23:33, 34; Num. 29:12; 1 Kin. 8:2, 5 [c] Amos 7:10-13 [7] *instituted* **33** [d] Num. 15:39 [e] 1 Kin. 13:1 [8] *instituted*

Jerusalem within the territory of Benjamin (Josh. 18:11-13,22). It lay at the southern end of Jeroboam's kingdom on the main N-S road to Jerusalem. Israel had long revered Bethel as a sacred place because Jacob had worshiped there (Gen. 28:10-22; 35:1-15). Dan was located in the northernmost part of Jeroboam's kingdom, about 25 mi. N of the Sea of Galilee. A paganized worship of the Lord was practiced at Dan during the period of the judges (Judg. 18:30,31).

12:30 this thing became a sin. Jeroboam's policy promoted gross and flagrant violation of the second commandment (Ex. 20:4-6) and led to violation of the first commandment (Ex. 20:3).

12:31 the high places. Jeroboam built minor sanctuaries on high places throughout the land of Israel. Over the centuries these high places became the breeding ground of Israel's idolatrous apostasy (cf. Hos. 5:1). *See note on 3:2.* **priests.** Jeroboam appointed priests to run his sanctuaries from all his tribes. His action blatantly violated the stipulation that only Aaron's descendants were to hold that office in Israel (Num. 3:10).

12:32 ordained a feast. Jeroboam instituted a religious festival to compete with the Feast of the Tabernacles held at the temple in Jerusalem and scheduled it for the 15th day of the 8th month (Oct./Nov.), exactly one month after its divinely ordained Judean counterpart (Ex. 34:22,23; Lev. 23:33-36,39,40).

The Kings of the Divided Kingdom

Judah		Israel	
Rehoboam	931–913	Jeroboam I	931–910
Abijah (Abijam)	913–911		
Asa	911–870	Nadab	910–909
		Baasha	909–886
		Elah	886–885
		Zimri	885
		Tibni	885–880
Jehoshaphat	873–848	Omri	885–874
		Ahab	874–853
		Ahaziah	853–852
Jehoram (Joram)	853–841	Joram (Jehoram)	852–841
Ahaziah	841	Jehu	841–814
Athaliah (queen)	841–835		
Joash (Jehoash)	835-796		
		Jehoahaz	814–798
Amaziah	796–767	Jehoash (Joash)	798–782
Azariah (Uzziah)	790–739	Jeroboam II	793–753
Jotham	750–731	Zechariah	753
		Shallum	752
Ahaz	735–715	Menahem	752–742
		Pekahiah	742–740
Hezekiah	715–686	Pekah	752–732
		Hoshea	732–722
Manasseh	695–642		
Amon	642–640		
Josiah	640–609		
Jehoahaz	609		
Jehoiakim	609–597		
Jehoiachin	597		
Zedekiah	597–586		

The Message of the Man of God

13 And behold, [a]a man of God went
from Judah to Bethel [1]by the word
of the LORD, [b]and Jeroboam stood by the
altar to burn incense. 2 Then he cried out
against the altar [2]by the word of the LORD,
and said, "O altar, altar! Thus says the
LORD: 'Behold, a child, [c]Josiah by name,
shall be born to the house of David; and on
you he shall sacrifice the priests of the high
places who burn incense on you, and
men's bones shall be [d]burned on you.' "
3 And he gave [e]a sign the same day, saying,
"This *is* the sign which the LORD has spoken: Surely the altar shall split apart, and
the ashes on it shall be poured out."
4 So it came to pass when King Jeroboam
heard the saying of the man of God, who
cried out against the altar in Bethel, that he
stretched out his hand from the altar, saying, "Arrest him!" Then his hand, which he
stretched out toward him, withered, so
that he could not pull it back to himself.
5 The altar also was split apart, and the
ashes poured out from the altar, according
to the sign which the man of God had
given by the word of the LORD. 6 Then the
king answered and said to the man of God,
"Please [f]entreat the favor of the LORD your
God, and pray for me, that my hand may
be restored to me."
So the man of God entreated the LORD,
and the king's hand was restored to him,
and became as before. 7 Then the king said
to the man of God, "Come home with me
and refresh yourself, and [g]I will give you a
reward."
8 But the man of God said to the king,
[h]"If you were to give me half your house, I
would not go in with you; nor would I eat
bread nor drink water in this place. 9 For
so it was commanded me by the word of
the LORD, saying, [i]'You shall not eat bread,
nor drink water, nor return by the same
way you came.' " 10 So he went another
way and did not return by the way he
came to Bethel.

Death of the Man of God

11 Now an [j]old prophet dwelt in Bethel,
and his [3]sons came and told him all the
works that the man of God had done that
day in Bethel; they also told their father the
words which he had spoken to the king.
12 And their father said to them, "Which
way did he go?" For his sons [4]had seen
which way the man of God went who
came from Judah. 13 Then he said to his
sons, "Saddle the donkey for me." So they
saddled the donkey for him; and he rode
on it, 14 and went after the man of God,
and found him sitting under an oak. Then
he said to him, "*Are* you the man of God
who came from Judah?"
And he said, "I *am*."
15 Then he said to him, "Come home
with me and eat bread."
16 And he said, [k]"I cannot return with
you nor go in with you; neither can I eat
bread nor drink water with you in this
place. 17 For [5]I have been told [l]by the word
of the LORD, 'You shall not eat bread nor
drink water there, nor return by going the
way you came.' "
18 He said to him, "I too *am* a prophet as
you *are*, and an angel spoke to me by the
word of the LORD, saying, 'Bring him back
with you to your house, that he may eat
bread and drink water.' " (He was lying to
him.)
19 So he went back with him, and ate
bread in his house, and drank water.
20 Now it happened, as they sat at the
table, that the word of the LORD came to
the prophet who had brought him back;
21 and he cried out to the man of God who

CHAPTER 13

1 [a] 2 Kin. 23:17 [b] 1 Kin. 12:32, 33 [1] *at the LORD's command*
2 [c] 2 Kin. 23:15, 16 [d] [Lev. 26:30] [2] *at the LORD's command*
3 [e] Ex. 4:1-5; Judg. 6:17; Is. 7:14; 38:7; John 2:18; 1 Cor. 1:22
6 [f] Ex. 8:8; 9:28; 10:17; Num. 21:7; Jer. 37:3; Acts 8:24; [James 5:16]
7 [g] 1 Sam. 9:7; 2 Kin. 5:15
8 [h] Num. 22:18; 24:13; 1 Kin. 13:16, 17
9 [i] [1 Cor. 5:11]
11 [j] 1 Kin. 13:25 [3] Lit. *son*
12 [4] LXX, Syr., Tg., Vg. *showed him*
16 [k] 1 Kin. 13:8, 9
17 [l] 1 Kin. 20:35; 1 Thess. 4:15 [5] Lit. *a command came to me by*

13:1 man of God. *See note on 12:22.*

13:2 Josiah. He ruled Judah about 300 years later ca. 640–609 B.C. (cf. 2 Kin. 22:1–23:30). **sacrifice the priests of the high places.** The prophet predicted that Josiah would slaughter the illegitimate priests of the high places of his day who made offerings on the altar at Bethel. This prophecy was realized in 2 Kin. 23:15-20, executing the divine judgment on the non-Levitical priesthood established by Jeroboam (12:31,32).

13:3 sign. An immediate "wonder" that served to authenticate the reliability of the long-term prediction (cf. Deut. 18:21,22), this sign came to pass in v. 5. **the ashes on it shall be poured out.** Proper ritual required the disposal of sacrificial ashes in a special "clean" place (Lev. 4:12; 6:10,11). Contact with the ground would render the ashes "unclean" and nullify the procedure.

13:9 commanded me by the word of the LORD. The prophet's divine commission expressly forbade receiving any hospitality at Bethel. It even required him to return home by a different route from the one by which he came, lest he should be recognized. The prophet's own conduct was to symbolize the Lord's total rejection of Israel's false worship and the recognition that all the people had become apostates.

13:11 an old prophet. Here was a spokesman for the Lord who had compromised his ministry by his willingness to live at the very center of the false system of worship without speaking out against it.

13:18 He was lying to him. Why the old prophet deceived the man of God the text does not state. It may be that his own son's were worshipers at Bethel or perhaps priests, and this man wanted to gain favor with the king by showing up the man of God as an imposter who acted contrary to his own claim to have heard from God. Accustomed to receiving direct revelations, the Judean prophet should have regarded the supposed angelic message with suspicion and sought divine verification of this revised order.

13:20 the word of the LORD. The lie arose from his own imagination (cf. Jer. 23:16; Ezek. 13:2,7), but the true prophecy came from the Lord (cf. Ex. 4:16; Deut. 18:18; Jer. 1:9).

came from Judah, saying, "Thus says the
LORD: 'Because you have disobeyed the
word of the LORD, and have not kept the
commandment which the LORD your God
commanded you, 22 but you came back,
ate bread, and drank water in the [m]place of
which *the LORD* said to you, "Eat no bread
and drink no water," your corpse shall not
come to the tomb of your fathers.' "
23 So it was, after he had eaten bread and
after he had drunk, that he saddled the
donkey for him, the prophet whom he had
brought back. 24 When he was gone, [n]a
lion met him on the road and killed him.
And his corpse was thrown on the road,
and the donkey stood by it. The lion also
stood by the corpse. 25 And there, men
passed by and saw the corpse thrown on
the road, and the lion standing by the
corpse. Then they went and told *it* in the
city where the old prophet dwelt.
26 Now when the prophet who had
brought him back from the way heard *it*,
he said, "It *is* the man of God who was
disobedient to the word of the LORD.
Therefore the LORD has delivered him to
the lion, which has torn him and killed
him, according to the word of the LORD
which He spoke to him." 27 And he spoke
to his sons, saying, "Saddle the donkey for
me." So they saddled *it*. 28 Then he went
and found his corpse thrown on the road,
and the donkey and the lion standing by
the corpse. The lion had not eaten the
corpse nor torn the donkey. 29 And the
prophet took up the corpse of the man of
God, laid it on the donkey, and brought it
back. So the old prophet came to the city to
mourn, and to bury him. 30 Then he laid
the corpse in his own tomb; and they
mourned over him, *saying*, [o]"Alas, my
brother!" 31 So it was, after he had buried
him, that he spoke to his sons, saying,
"When I am dead, then bury me in the
tomb where the man of God *is* buried; [p]lay
my bones beside his bones. 32 [q]For the
[6]saying which he cried out by the word of
the LORD against the altar in Bethel, and
against all the [7]shrines on the high places
which *are* in the cities of [r]Samaria, will
surely come to pass."
33 [s]After this event Jeroboam did not
turn from his evil way, but again he made
priests from every class of people for the
high places; whoever wished, he consecrated him, and he became *one* of the
priests of the high places. 34 [t]And this
thing was the sin of the house of Jeroboam,
so as [u]to exterminate and destroy *it* from
the face of the earth.

Judgment on the House of Jeroboam

14 At that time Abijah the son of Jeroboam became sick. 2 And Jeroboam
said to his wife, "Please arise, and disguise
yourself, that they may not recognize you
as the wife of Jeroboam, and go to Shiloh.
Indeed, Ahijah the prophet *is* there, who
told me that [a]*I would be* king over this people. 3 [b]Also take [1]with you ten loaves, *some*
cakes, and a jar of honey, and go to him; he
will tell you what will become of the
child." 4 And Jeroboam's wife did so; she
arose [c]and went to Shiloh, and came to the
house of Ahijah. But Ahijah could not see,
for his eyes were [2]glazed by reason of his
age.
5 Now the LORD had said to Ahijah,
"Here is the wife of Jeroboam, coming to
ask you something about her son, for he *is*
sick. Thus and thus you shall say to her; for
it will be, when she comes in, that she will
pretend *to be* another *woman*."
6 And so it was, when Ahijah heard the
sound of her footsteps as she came
through the door, he said, "Come in, wife
of Jeroboam. Why do you pretend *to be* another *person*? For I *have been* sent to you
with bad *news*. 7 Go, tell Jeroboam, 'Thus
says the LORD God of Israel: [d]"Because I

22 [m] 1 Kin. 13:9
24 [n] 1 Kin. 20:36
30 [o] Jer. 22:18
31 [p] Ruth 1:17; 2 Kin. 23:17, 18
32 [q] 1 Kin. 13:2; 2 Kin. 23:16, 19 [r] 1 Kin. 16:24; John 4:5; Acts 8:14 [6] Lit. *word* [7] Lit. *houses*
33 [s] 1 Kin. 12:31, 32; 2 Chr. 11:15; 13:9
34 [t] 1 Kin. 12:30; 2 Kin. 17:21 [u] [1 Kin. 14:10; 15:29, 30]

CHAPTER 14

2 [a] 1 Kin. 11:29-31
3 [b] 1 Sam. 9:7, 8; 1 Kin. 13:7; 2 Kin. 4:42 [1] Lit. *in your hand*
4 [c] 1 Kin. 11:29 [2] Lit. *set*
7 [d] 2 Sam. 12:7, 8; 1 Kin. 16:2

13:22 your corpse shall not come to the tomb of your fathers. Israelites buried their dead with the bones of ancestors in a common grave (Judg. 8:32; 2 Sam. 2:32). The lack of such a burial was considered in Israel a severe punishment and disgrace. *See note on Eccl. 6:3.*

13:24 donkey…lion. Both the donkey and the lion acted unnaturally: The donkey did not run and the lion did not attack the donkey or disturb the man's body. Unlike the disobedient prophet, the beasts bent their wills to God's sovereignty.

13:32 will surely come to pass. The old prophet instructed his sons to bury him beside the Judean prophet (v. 31). The old prophet was finally willing to identify himself with the message that the man of God from Judah had given against worship at Bethel.

13:33 again he made priests. Unlike the old prophet, Jeroboam did not change his evil ways, but continued appointing priests outside the tribe of Levi to serve the high places (12:30-32).

14:1 At that time. Probably indicating a time shortly after the incident recorded in chap. 13. **Abijah.** Meaning "my father is the Lord," Jeroboam's son's name implies that his father desired to be regarded as a worshiper of the Lord at the time of his son's birth. Abijah was referred to as a "child" (vv. 3,12,17), a term which can be used from childhood through young adulthood. Of all of Jeroboam's family, Abijah was the most responsive to the Lord (v. 13). Jeroboam's son, Abijah, should not be confused with Rehoboam's son of the same name (*see note on 15:1*).

14:2 disguise yourself. Probably for the avoidance of recognition by the people. Jeroboam did not want his subjects to know that he was consulting a prophet of the Lord. **Shiloh.** *See note on 11:29.*

14:3 take…ten loaves. A simple ordinary food gift added to the disguise (cf. 1 Sam. 9:7,8; 2 Kin. 8:8). Ten loaves of bread, some cakes, and a jar of honey reflected the means of a common person, not royalty.

exalted you from among the people, and made you ruler over My people Israel, **8** and [e]tore the kingdom away from the house of David, and gave it to you; and *yet* you have not been as My servant David, [f]who kept My commandments and who followed Me with all his heart, to do only *what was* right in My eyes; **9** but you have done more evil than all who were before you, [g]for you have gone and made for yourself other gods and molded images to provoke Me to anger, and [h]have cast Me behind your back— **10** therefore behold! [i]I will bring disaster on the house of Jeroboam, and [j]will cut off from Jeroboam every male in Israel, [k]bond and free; I will take away the remnant of the house of Jeroboam, as one takes away refuse until it is all gone. **11** The dogs shall eat [l]whoever belongs to Jeroboam and dies in the city, and the birds of the air shall eat whoever dies in the field; for the LORD has spoken!"' **12** Arise therefore, go to your own house. [m]When your feet enter the city, the child shall die. **13** And all Israel shall mourn for him and bury him, for he is the only one of Jeroboam who shall [3]come to the grave, because in him [n]there is found something good toward the LORD God of Israel in the house of Jeroboam.

14 [o]"Moreover the LORD will raise up for Himself a king over Israel who shall cut off the house of Jeroboam; [4]this is the day. What? Even now! **15** For the LORD will strike Israel, as a reed is shaken in the water. He will [p]uproot Israel from this [q]good land which He gave to their fathers, and will scatter them [r]beyond [5]the River, [s]because they have made their [6]wooden images, provoking the LORD to anger. **16** And He will give Israel up because of the sins of Jeroboam, [t]who sinned and who made Israel sin."

17 Then Jeroboam's wife arose and departed, and came to [u]Tirzah. [v]When she came to the threshold of the house, the child died. **18** And they buried him; and all Israel mourned for him, [w]according to the word of the LORD which He spoke through His servant Ahijah the prophet.

Death of Jeroboam

19 Now the rest of the acts of Jeroboam, how he [x]made war and how he reigned, indeed they *are* written in the book of the chronicles of the kings of Israel. **20** The period that Jeroboam reigned *was* twenty-two years. So he rested with his fathers. Then [y]Nadab his son reigned in his place.

Rehoboam Reigns in Judah

21 And Rehoboam the son of Solomon reigned in Judah. [z]Rehoboam *was* forty-one years old when he became king. He reigned seventeen years in Jerusalem, the city [a]which the LORD had chosen out of all the tribes of Israel, to put His name there. [b]His mother's name *was* Naamah, an Ammonitess. **22** [c]Now Judah did evil in the sight of the LORD, and they [d]provoked Him to jealousy with their sins which they committed, more than all that their fathers had done. **23** For they also built for themselves [e]high[7] places, [f]*sacred* pillars, and [g]wooden images on every high hill and [h]under every green tree. **24** [i]And there were also [8]perverted persons in the land. They did according to all the [j]abominations of the nations which the LORD had cast out before the children of [k]Israel.

25 [l]It happened in the fifth year of King Rehoboam *that* Shishak king of Egypt came up against Jerusalem. **26** [m]And he took away the treasures of the house of the LORD and the treasures of the king's house; he took away everything. He also took away all the gold shields [n]which Solomon had made. **27** Then King Rehoboam made bronze shields in their place, and [9]committed *them* to the hands of the captains of the [1]guard, who guarded the doorway of the king's house. **28** And whenever the king

8 [e] 1 Kin. 11:31 [f] 1 Kin. 11:33, 38; 15:5
9 [g] 1 Kin. 12:28; 2 Chr. 11:15 [h] 2 Chr. 29:6; Neh. 9:26; Ps. 50:17
10 [i] 1 Kin. 15:29 [j] 1 Kin. 21:21; 2 Kin. 9:8 [k] Deut. 32:36; 2 Kin. 14:26
11 [l] 1 Kin. 16:4; 21:24
12 [m] 1 Kin. 14:17
13 [n] 2 Chr. 12:12; 19:3 [3] Be buried
14 [o] 1 Kin. 15:27-29 [4] Or *this day and from now on*
15 [p] Deut. 29:28; 2 Kin. 17:6; Ps. 52:5 [q] [Josh. 23:15, 16] [r] 2 Kin. 15:29 [s] [Ex. 34:13, 14; Deut. 12:3] [5] The Euphrates [6] Heb. *Asherim*, Canaanite deities
16 [t] 1 Kin. 12:30; 13:34; 15:30, 34; 16:2
17 [u] 1 Kin. 15:21, 33; 16:6, 8, 15, 23; Song 6:4 [v] 1 Kin. 14:12
18 [w] 1 Kin. 14:13
19 [x] 1 Kin. 14:30; 2 Chr. 13:2-20
20 [y] 1 Kin. 15:25
21 [z] 2 Chr. 12:13 [a] 1 Kin. 11:32, 36 [b] 1 Kin. 14:31
22 [c] 2 Chr. 12:1, 14 [d] Deut. 32:21; Ps. 78:58; 1 Cor. 10:22
23 [e] Deut. 12:2; Ezek. 16:24, 25 [f] [Deut. 16:22] [g] [2 Kin. 17:9, 10] [h] Is. 57:5; Jer. 2:20 [7] Places for pagan worship
24 [i] Gen. 19:5; Deut. 23:17; 1 Kin. 15:12; 22:46; 2 Kin. 23:7 [j] Deut. 20:18 [k] [Deut. 9:4, 5] [8] Heb. *qadesh*, one practicing sodomy and prostitution in religious rituals
25 [l] 1 Kin. 11:40; 2 Chr. 12:2
26 [m] 1 Kin. 15:18; 2 Chr. 12:9-11 [n] 1 Kin. 10:17
27 [9] *entrusted* [1] Lit. *runners*

14:9 more evil. Jeroboam had not only failed to live up to the standard of David, but his wickedness had surpassed even that of Saul and Solomon. He had installed a paganized system of worship for the entire population of the northern kingdom (cf. 16:25,30; 2 Kin. 21:11).

14:11 dogs...birds. The covenant curse of Deut. 28:26 was applied to Jeroboam's male descendants.

14:13 the grave. *See note on 13:22.*

14:14 a king. I.e., Daasha (15:27-30).

14:15 Ahijah announced God's stern judgment on Israel for joining Jeroboam's apostasy. Struck by the Lord, Israel would sway like a reed in a rushing river, a biblical metaphor for political instability (cf. Matt. 11:7; Luke 7:24). One day, the Lord would uproot Israel from Palestinian soil and scatter it in exile E of the Euphrates. The fulfillment of this prophecy is recorded in 2 Kin. 17:23.

14:17 Tirzah. Jeroboam had apparently moved his capital from Shechem to Tirzah (cf. 12:25), located in the tribal region of Manasseh, about 7 mi. NE of Shechem and 35 mi. N of Jerusalem. Tirzah was famous for its beauty (Song 6:4).

14:20 twenty-two years. 931–910 B.C.

14:21 seventeen years. 931–913 B.C.

14:22-24 Judah outdid her ancestors in evil, provoking the Lord to jealous anger (v. 22). Signs of idolatrous practice were everywhere (vv. 23,24). She even practiced sacred prostitution to promote fertility (v. 24). Judah had begun the downward slide toward doom that Israel was in.

14:25 fifth year. 927/926 B.C. **Shishak.** *See note on 11:40.*

14:27 bronze shields. These bronze shields replaced Solomon's gold shields, which were used as a ransom paid to Shishak. The bronze shields illustrate the sharp decline from the reign of Solomon to Rehoboam.

entered the house of the LORD, the guards
carried them, then brought them back into
the guardroom.
29 [o]Now the rest of the acts of Rehoboam, and all that he did, *are* they not written in the book of the chronicles of the
kings of Judah? 30 And there was [p]war between Rehoboam and Jeroboam all *their*
days. 31 [q]So Rehoboam [2]rested with his fathers, and was buried with his fathers in
the City of David. [r]His mother's name *was*
Naamah, an Ammonitess. Then [s]Abijam[3]
his son reigned in his place.

Abijam Reigns in Judah

15 In[a] the eighteenth year of King Jeroboam the son of Nebat, Abijam became king over Judah. 2 He reigned three
years in Jerusalem. [b]His mother's name
was [c]Maachah the granddaughter of
[d]Abishalom. 3 And he walked in all the
sins of his father, which he had done before
him; [e]his heart was not [1]loyal to the LORD
his God, as was the heart of his father David. 4 Nevertheless [f]for David's sake the
LORD his God gave him a lamp in Jerusalem, by setting up his son after him and by
establishing Jerusalem; 5 because David
[g]did *what was* right in the eyes of the LORD,
and had not turned aside from anything
that He commanded him all the days of his
life, [h]except in the matter of Uriah the Hittite. 6 [i]And there was war between [2]Reho-
boam and Jeroboam all the days of his life.
7 [j]Now the rest of the acts of Abijam, and
all that he did, *are* they not written in the
book of the chronicles of the kings of Judah? And there was war between Abijam
and Jeroboam.
8 [k]So Abijam [3]rested with his fathers,
and they buried him in the City of David.
Then Asa his son reigned in his place.

Asa Reigns in Judah

9 In the twentieth year of Jeroboam king
of Israel, Asa became king over Judah.
10 And he reigned forty-one years in Jerusalem. His grandmother's name *was* Maachah the granddaughter of Abishalom.
11 [l]Asa did *what was* right in the eyes of the
LORD, as *did* his father David. 12 [m]And he
banished the [4]perverted persons from the
land, and removed all the idols that his fathers had made. 13 Also he removed [n]Maa-
chah his grandmother from *being* queen
mother, because she had made an obscene
image of [5]Asherah. And Asa cut down her
obscene image and [o]burned *it* by the Brook
Kidron. 14 [p]But the [6]high places were not
removed. Nevertheless Asa's [q]heart was
loyal to the LORD all his days. 15 He also
brought into the house of the LORD the
things which his father [r]had dedicated,
and the things which he himself had dedicated: silver and gold and utensils.
16 Now there was war between Asa and
Baasha king of Israel all their days. 17 And
[s]Baasha king of Israel came up against Judah, and built [t]Ramah, [u]that he might let
none go out or come in to Asa king of Judah. 18 Then Asa took all the silver and
gold *that was* left in the treasuries of the

29 [o] 2 Chr. 12:15, 16 **30** [p] 1 Kin. 12:21-24; 15:6 **31** [q] 2 Chr. 12:16 [r] 1 Kin. 14:21 [s] 2 Chr. 12:16 [2] Died and joined his ancestors [3] *Abijah,* 2 Chr. 12:16

CHAPTER 15

1 [a] 2 Chr. 13:1 **2** [b] 2 Chr. 11:20-22 [c] 2 Chr. 13:2 [d] 2 Chr. 11:21 **3** [e] 1 Kin. 11:4; Ps. 119:80 [1] Lit. *at peace with* **4** [f] 2 Sam. 21:17; 1 Kin. 11:32, 36; 2 Chr. 21:7 **5** [g] 1 Kin. 9:4; 14:8; Luke 1:6 [h] 2 Sam. 11:3, 15-17; 12:9, 10 **6** [i] 1 Kin. 14:30; 2 Chr. 12:15–13:20 [2] So with MT, LXX, Tg., Vg.; some Heb. mss., Syr. *Abijam* **7** [j] 2 Chr. 13:2-22

8 [k] 2 Chr. 14:1 [3] Died and joined his ancestors **11** [l] 2 Chr. 14:2 **12** [m] Deut. 23:17; 1 Kin. 14:24; 22:46 [4] Heb. *qedeshim,* those practicing sodomy and prostitution in religious rituals **13** [n] 2 Chr. 15:16-18 [o] Ex. 32:20 [5] A Canaanite goddess

14 [p] 1 Kin. 3:2; 22:43; 2 Kin. 12:3; 2 Chr. 15:17, 18 [q] [1 Sam. 16:7]; 1 Kin. 8:61; 15:3 [6] Places for pagan worship **15** [r] 1 Kin. 7:51 **17** [s] 2 Chr. 16:1-6 [t] Josh. 18:25; 1 Kin. 15:21, 22 [u] 1 Kin. 12:26-29

14:30 war...all *their* days. Many border skirmishes erupted as the armies in the N/S maneuvered for tactical advantage and control of territory (14:19; 15:6). A major battle ultimately erupted during the reign of Abijam (cf. 2 Chr. 13:1-20).

15:1–16:22 Having documented the establishment of idolatry in both Israel and Judah (12:1–14:31), the text moves to a quick survey of the kings of Judah and Israel from 913 to 885 B.C. The author notes that the high places remained in Judah (15:14), and the sins of Jeroboam continued in Israel (15:26,34; 16:13,19).

15:1-8 Abijam. He was at first called Abijah in 2 Chr. 13:1,2. Since Abijam means "father of the sea," and Abijah, "my father is the LORD," he may have had his name changed because of his sin. *See notes on 2 Chr. 13:1-22.*

15:2 three years. 913–911 B.C. Parts of years were considered as whole years in this reckoning (cf. v. 9).

15:3 his heart was not loyal. Cf. 11:4, where the same statement was made concerning Solomon. Cf. v. 14.

15:4 a lamp. *See note on 11:36.*

15:5 *what was* right in the eyes of the LORD. This commendation is frequently used in speaking of kings of Judah and means only that they did or did not do what was generally acceptable to God, i.e., v. 11.

15:7 war. See 14:30; 2 Chr. 13:1-20.

15:9-24 Asa. He was the first of the religiously good kings of Judah (cf. v. 11). *See notes on 2 Chr. 14:1–16:14.*

15:10 forty-one years. 911–870 B.C.

15:11-15 Asa did 4 good things: 1) he removed the "sacred" prostitutes (v. 12); 2) he rid the land of all the idols made by his predecessors (v. 12); 3) he removed the corrupt queen mother and burned the idol she had made; and 4) he placed "holy things," items that he and his father had dedicated to the Lord, back in the temple (v. 15). Though he never engaged in idolatry, Asa's failure was his toleration of "the high places" (v. 14).

15:13 obscene image. This term is derived from the verb "to shudder" (Job 9:6). "Horrible, repulsive thing" suggests a shocking, perhaps even a sexually explicit, idol. Asa removed his grandmother, Maacah, the official queen mother, because of her association with this idol. **Brook Kidron.** A seasonal river that ran through the Kidron Valley that marks the eastern boundary of Jerusalem.

15:16 Baasha. Asa, who ruled Israel (ca. 909–886 B.C.), enjoyed 10 years of peace after Jeroboam's defeat by Abijam (2 Chr. 13:19,20) until this king began attacking. *See notes on 15:27–16:7; 2 Chr. 16:1-6.*

15:17 Ramah. A strategic town in Benjamin, located about 5 mi. N of Jerusalem along the main N-S highway, built by Baasha, king of Israel, to effectively blockade the city of Jerusalem.

house of the LORD and the treasuries of the
king's house, and delivered them into the
hand of his servants. And King Asa sent
them to [v]Ben-Hadad the son of Tabrimmon, the son of Hezion, king of Syria,
who dwelt in [w]Damascus, saying, 19 "*Let
there be* a treaty between you and me, as
there was between my father and your father. See, I have sent you a present of silver
and gold. Come and break your treaty
with Baasha king of Israel, so that he will
withdraw from me."
20 So Ben-Hadad heeded King Asa, and
[x]sent the captains of his armies against the
cities of Israel. He attacked [y]Ijon, [z]Dan,
[a]Abel Beth Maachah, and all Chinneroth,
with all the land of Naphtali. 21 Now it
happened, when Baasha heard *it,* that he
stopped building Ramah, and remained in
[b]Tirzah.
22 [c]Then King Asa made a proclamation
throughout all Judah; none *was* exempted.
And they took away the stones and timber
of Ramah, which Baasha had used for
building; and with them King Asa built
[d]Geba of Benjamin, and [e]Mizpah.
23 The rest of all the acts of Asa, all his
might, all that he did, and the cities which
he built, *are* they not written in the book of
the chronicles of the kings of Judah? But
[f]in the time of his old age he was diseased
in his feet. 24 So Asa [7]rested with his fathers, and was buried with his fathers in
the City of David his father. [g]Then [h]Je-
hoshaphat his son reigned in his place.

Nadab Reigns in Israel

25 Now [i]Nadab the son of Jeroboam became king over Israel in the second year of
Asa king of Judah, and he reigned over Israel two years. 26 And he did evil in the
sight of the LORD, and walked in the way
of his father, and in [j]his sin by which he
had made Israel sin.
27 [k]Then Baasha the son of Ahijah, of the
house of Issachar, conspired against him.
And Baasha killed him at [l]Gibbethon,
which *belonged* to the Philistines, while
Nadab and all Israel laid siege to Gibbethon. 28 Baasha killed him in the third year
of Asa king of Judah, and reigned in his
place. 29 And it was so, when he became
king, *that* he killed all the house of Jeroboam. He did not leave to Jeroboam anyone that breathed, until he had destroyed
him, according to [m]the word of the LORD
which He had spoken by His servant Ahijah the Shilonite, 30 [n]because of the sins of
Jeroboam, which he had sinned and by
which he had made Israel sin, because of
his provocation with which he had provoked the LORD God of Israel to anger.
31 Now the rest of the acts of Nadab, and
all that he did, *are* they not written in the
book of the chronicles of the kings of Israel? 32 [o]And there was war between Asa
and Baasha king of Israel all their days.

Baasha Reigns in Israel

33 In the third year of Asa king of Judah,
Baasha the son of Ahijah became king over
all Israel in Tirzah, and *reigned* twenty-four
years. 34 He did evil in the sight of the
LORD, and walked in [p]the way of Jeroboam, and in his sin by which he had made
Israel sin.

16 Then the word of the LORD came to
[a]Jehu the son of [b]Hanani, against
[c]Baasha, saying: 2 [d]"Inasmuch as I lifted
you out of the dust and made you ruler

18 [v]2 Kin. 12:17, 18; 2 Chr. 16:2 [w]Gen. 14:15; 1 Kin. 11:23, 24
20 [x]1 Kin. 20:1 [y]2 Kin. 15:29 [z]Judg. 18:29; 1 Kin. 12:29 [a]2 Sam. 20:14, 15
21 [b]1 Kin. 14:17; 16:15-18
22 [c]2 Chr. 16:6 [d]Josh. 21:17 [e]Josh. 18:26
23 [f]2 Chr. 16:11-14
24 [g]2 Chr. 17:1 [h]1 Kin. 22:41-44; Matt. 1:8 [7]Died and joined his ancestors
25 [i]1 Kin. 14:20
26 [j]1 Kin. 12:28-33; 14:16
27 [k]1 Kin. 14:14 [l]Josh. 19:44; 21:23; 1 Kin. 16:15
29 [m]1 Kin. 14:10-14
30 [n]1 Kin. 14:9, 16
32 [o]1 Kin. 15:16
34 [p]1 Kin. 13:33; 14:16

CHAPTER 16

1 [a]1 Kin. 16:7; 2 Chr. 19:2; 20:34 [b]2 Chr. 16:7-10 [c]1 Kin. 15:27
2 [d]1 Sam. 2:8; 1 Kin. 14:7

15:18 Ben-Hadad. Ben-Hadad I, the grandson of Hezion (probably Rezon; *see note on 11:23*, ca. 940–915 B.C.) and the son of Tabrimmon (ca. 912–890 B.C.). He was the powerful ruler of the Syrian kingdom (Aramea; *see note on 10:29*), centered in Damascus. The majority of historians think that Ben-Hadad reigned ca. 900–860 B.C. and was succeeded by a son or grandson, Ben-Hadad II, who ruled ca. 860–841 B.C. (cf. 20:34). Asa sent a sizable gift to influence Ben-Hadad I to break his treaty with Israel, enter instead a treaty with Judah, and invade Israel from the N.

15:20 Ijon...Naphtali. The army of Ben-Hadad I invaded Israel and took cities in the land N of the Sea of Galilee, a conquest giving Syria control of the trade routes to the Mediterranean coast and Israel's fertile Jezreel Valley, and also making Syria a great military threat to Israel. Baasha gave up fortifying Ramah and went to live in Tirzah, the capital of the northern kingdom.

15:22 Geba...Mizpah. With the threat to Judah from Israel removed, Asa conscripted a Judean labor force to fortify Geba, about 6 mi. NE of Jerusalem, and Mizpah, about 7 mi. N of Jerusalem, using the very building material for those fortifications that Baasha had used at Ramah.

15:25 Nadab...two years. 910–909 B.C.

15:27–16:7 Baasha. *See note on 15:16.*

15:27 Gibbethon. This city, located about 32 mi. W of Jerusalem, within the territory of Dan, was given to the Levites (Josh. 19:44) but controlled by the Philistines, on whose border it lay.

15:29 he killed all the house of Jeroboam. Baasha, the northern king, in a vicious practice too common in the ancient Near East, annihilated all of Jeroboam's family. This act fulfilled Ahijah's prophecy against Jeroboam (cf. 14:9-11). However, Baasha went beyond the words of the prophecy, since 14:10 specified judgment only on every male, while Baasha killed all men, women, and children.

15:30 This epitaph for wicked Jeroboam of Israel follows through the history of the northern kingdom relentlessly as the standard of sin by which judgment fell on the successive kings (see 15:34; 16:2,19,31; 22:52; 2 Kin. 3:3; 10:29,31; 13:2,11; 14:24; 15:9,18,24,28).

15:33 twenty-four years. 909–886 B.C.

16:1 Jehu the son of Hanani. Cf. v. 7 This Hanani may have been the prophet who warned Judah's King Asa (2 Chr. 16:7-9). Jehu, like Ahijah before him (14:7-16), delivered the Lord's message of judgment to the king of Israel. The pattern emerges in the book of Kings that the Lord used His prophets as a legitimate means by which to confront the sin of Israel's kings.

over My people Israel, and [e]you have
walked in the way of Jeroboam, and have
made My people Israel sin, to provoke Me
to anger with their sins, 3 surely I will
[f]take[1] away the posterity of Baasha and
the posterity of his house, and I will make
your house like [g]the house of Jeroboam the
son of Nebat. 4 The dogs shall eat [h]who-
ever belongs to Baasha and dies in the city,
and the birds of the air shall eat whoever
dies in the fields."
5 Now the rest of the acts of Baasha,
what he did, and his might, [i]*are* they not
written in the book of the chronicles of the
kings of Israel? 6 So Baasha [2]rested with
his fathers and was buried in [j]Tirzah. Then
Elah his son reigned in his place.
7 And also the word of the LORD came by
the prophet [k]Jehu the son of Hanani
against Baasha and his house, because of
all the evil that he did in the sight of the
LORD in provoking Him to anger with the
work of his hands, in being like the house
of Jeroboam, and because [l]he killed them.

Elah Reigns in Israel

8 In the twenty-sixth year of Asa king of
Judah, Elah the son of Baasha became king
over Israel, *and reigned* two years in Tirzah.
9 [m]Now his servant Zimri, commander of
half *his* chariots, conspired against him as
he was in Tirzah drinking himself drunk in
the house of Arza, [n]steward[3] of *his* house
in Tirzah. 10 And Zimri went in and struck
him and killed him in the twenty-seventh
year of Asa king of Judah, and reigned in
his place.
11 Then it came to pass, when he began
to reign, as soon as he was seated on his
throne, *that* he killed all the household of
Baasha; he [o]did not leave him one male,
neither of his relatives nor of his friends.
12 Thus Zimri destroyed all the household
of Baasha, [p]according to the word of the
LORD, which He spoke against Baasha by
Jehu the prophet, 13 for all the sins of Baasha and the sins of Elah his son, by which
they had sinned and by which they had
made Israel sin, in provoking the LORD
God of Israel to anger [q]with their [4]idols.
14 Now the rest of the acts of Elah, and
all that he did, *are* they not written in the
book of the chronicles of the kings of Israel?

Zimri Reigns in Israel

15 In the twenty-seventh year of Asa
king of Judah, Zimri had reigned in Tirzah
seven days. And the people *were* encamped [r]against Gibbethon, which *be-*
longed to the Philistines. 16 Now the people
who were encamped heard it said, "Zimri
has conspired and also has killed the
king." So all Israel made Omri, the commander of the army, king over Israel that
day in the camp. 17 Then Omri and all Israel with him went up from Gibbethon,
and they besieged Tirzah. 18 And it happened, when Zimri saw that the city was
[5]taken, that he went into the citadel of the
king's house and burned the king's house
[6]down upon himself with fire, and died,
19 because of the sins which he had committed in doing evil in the sight of the
LORD, [s]in walking in the [t]way of Jeroboam,
and in his sin which he had committed to
make Israel sin.
20 Now the rest of the acts of Zimri, and
the treason he committed, *are* they not
written in the book of the chronicles of the
kings of Israel?

Omri Reigns in Israel

21 Then the people of Israel were divided into two parts: half of the people followed Tibni the son of Ginath, to make
him king, and half followed Omri. 22 But
the people who followed Omri prevailed
over the people who followed Tibni the
son of Ginath. So Tibni died and Omri
reigned. 23 In the thirty-first year of Asa
king of Judah, Omri became king over Is-

2 [e] 1 Kin. 12:25-33; 15:34
3 [f] 1 Kin. 16:11; 21:21 [g] 1 Kin. 14:10; 15:29 [1] *consume*
4 [h] 1 Kin. 14:11; 21:24
5 [i] 2 Chr. 16:11
6 [j] 1 Kin. 14:17; 15:21 [2] Died and joined his ancestors
7 [k] 1 Kin. 16:1 [l] 1 Kin. 15:27, 29
9 [m] 2 Kin. 9:30-33 [n] Gen. 24:2; 39:4; 1 Kin. 18:3 [3] Lit. *who was over the house*
11 [o] 1 Sam. 25:22
12 [p] 1 Kin. 16:3
13 [q] Deut. 32:21; 1 Sam. 12:21; [Is. 41:29; Jon. 2:8; 1 Cor. 8:4; 10:19] [4] Lit. *vanities*
15 [r] 1 Kin. 15:27
18 [5] *captured* [6] Lit. *over him*
19 [s] 1 Kin. 15:26, 34 [t] 1 Kin. 12:25-33

16:2-4 Baasha had angered the Lord by following the sinful paths of Jeroboam. Appropriately, he faced the same humiliating judgment Jeroboam had (14:10,11). Though he waded through slaughter to his throne, he owed it to the permission of God, by whom all kings reign. His judgment was that no long line of heirs would succeed him; instead, his family would be totally annihilated and their corpses shamefully scavenged by hungry dogs and birds.

16:8-14 Elah...two years. Ca. 886–885 B.C.

16:11 friends. I.e., "relatives able to redeem." Cf. Ruth 2:1. Zimri not only killed Elah and his immediate sons, but all of the extended relatives of Baasha who could help his family.

16:15 seven days. Zimri's reign (885 B.C.) was the shortest of any king of Israel. **Gibbethon.** *See note on 15:27.*

16:16 Omri. When the soldiers of Israel in the field heard of Elah's death, they immediately acclaimed Omri, the commander of Israel's army, as the new king.

16:21 Tibni. The death of Zimri (vv. 17,18) automatically placed the kingdom in Omri's hands. Half of the population including the army, sided with Omri, but the other half backed Tibni. Nothing further is known of Tibni, but he was strong enough to rival Omri for about 4 years (cf. v. 15 with v. 23).

16:21-28 Omri. Ruled the northern kingdom ca. 885–874 B.C.

16:23–2 Kin. 13:25 This section is strategic in the book(s) of Kings and contains over one third of the total narrative of the book(s). The coming of the dynasty of Omri to the kingship of Israel brought with it the introduction of Baal worship with official sanction in Israel (16:31,32). Through intermarriage with the house of Omri, Baal worship penetrated into Judah and corrupted the line of David (2 Kin. 8:18,27), initiating a gigantic struggle before Baalism was officially eradicated in both Israel and Judah (2 Kin. 19:14–12:21).

rael, *and reigned* twelve years. Six years he
reigned in [u]Tirzah. 24 And he bought the
hill of Samaria from Shemer for two talents
of silver; then he built on the hill, and
called the name of the city which he built,
[v]Samaria,[7] after the name of Shemer,
owner of the hill. 25 [w]Omri did evil in the
eyes of the LORD, and did worse than all
who *were* before him. 26 For he [x]walked in
all the ways of Jeroboam the son of Nebat,
and in his sin by which he had made Israel
sin, provoking the LORD God of Israel to
anger with their [y]idols.[8]
27 Now the rest of the acts of Omri
which he did, and the might that he
showed, *are* they not written in the book of
the chronicles of the kings of Israel?
28 So Omri rested with his fathers and
was buried in Samaria. Then Ahab his son
reigned in his place.

Ahab Reigns in Israel

29 In the thirty-eighth year of Asa king of
Judah, Ahab the son of Omri became king
over Israel; and Ahab the son of Omri
reigned over Israel in Samaria twenty-two
years. 30 Now Ahab the son of Omri did
evil in the sight of the LORD, more than all
who *were* before him. 31 And it came to
pass, as though it had been a trivial thing
for him to walk in the sins of Jeroboam the
son of Nebat, [z]that he took as wife Jezebel
the daughter of Ethbaal, king of the [a]Si-
donians; [b]and he went and served Baal
and worshiped him. 32 Then he set up an
altar for Baal in [c]the temple of Baal, which
he had built in Samaria. 33 [d]And Ahab
made a [9]wooden image. Ahab [e]did more
to provoke the LORD God of Israel to anger
than all the kings of Israel who were before
him. 34 In his days Hiel of Bethel built Jericho. He laid its foundation [1]with Abiram
his firstborn, and with his youngest *son*
Segub he set up its gates, [f]according to the
word of the LORD, which He had spoken
through Joshua the son of Nun.

Elijah Proclaims a Drought

17 And Elijah the Tishbite, of the [a]in-
habitants of Gilead, said to Ahab,
[b]"*As* the LORD God of Israel lives, [c]before
whom I stand, [d]there shall not be dew nor
rain [e]these years, except at my word."
2 Then the word of the LORD came to him,
saying, 3 "Get away from here and turn eastward, and hide by the Brook Cherith, which
flows into the Jordan. 4 And it will be *that*
you shall drink from the brook, and I have
commanded the [f]ravens to feed you there."
5 So he went and did according to the
word of the LORD, for he went and stayed
by the Brook Cherith, which flows into the
Jordan. 6 The ravens brought him bread
and meat in the morning, and bread and
meat in the evening; and he drank from the
brook. 7 And it happened after a while that
the brook dried up, because there had been
no rain in the land.

23 [u] 1 Kin. 15:21; 2 Kin. 15:14
24 [v] 1 Kin. 13:32; 2 Kin. 17:24; John 4:4 [7] Heb. *Shomeron*
25 [w] Mic. 6:16
26 [x] 1 Kin. 16:19 [y] 1 Kin. 16:13 [8] Lit. *vanities*
31 [z] Deut. 7:3 [a] Judg. 18:7; 1 Kin. 11:1-5 [b] 1 Kin. 21:25, 26; 2 Kin. 10:18; 17:16
32 [c] 2 Kin. 10:21, 26, 27
33 [d] 2 Kin. 13:6 [e] 1 Kin. 14:9; 16:29, 30; 21:25 [9] Heb. *Asherah*, a Canaanite goddess
34 [f] Josh. 6:26 [1] At the cost of the life of

CHAPTER 17

1 [a] Judg. 12:4 [b] 1 Kin. 18:10; 22:14; 2 Kin. 3:14; 5:20 [c] Deut. 10:8 [d] 1 Kin. 18:1; James 5:17 [e] Luke 4:25
4 [f] Job 38:41

16:23 twelve years. Omri ruled 12 years (ca. 885-874 B.C.), from Asa's 27th year (16:15) to Asa's 38th year (v. 29). This notice of his beginning to reign in Asa's 31st year must be a reference to his sole rule.

16:24 Samaria. The hill of Samaria, named after its owner, Shemer, was located 7 mi. NW of Shechem and stood 300 ft. high. Though ringed by other mountains, it stood by itself so that attackers had to charge uphill from every side. This new capital amounted to the northern equivalent of Jerusalem. Its central location gave Israelites easy access to it.

16:29–22:40 Ahab...twenty-two years. Ca. 874–853 B.C.; *see notes on 2 Chr. 18:1-34.*

16:30 evil...more than all who *were* before him. With Ahab, Israel's spiritual decay reached its lowest point. He was even worse than his father, Omri, who was more wicked than all before him (v. 25). Ahab's evil consisted of perpetuating all the sins of Jeroboam and promoting the worship of Baal in Israel (vv. 31,32). Of all Israel's kings, Ahab outraged the Lord most (v. 33).

16:31 Jezebel. The wretched wife of Ahab became symbolic of the evil of false religion (cf. Rev. 2:20). **Ethbaal.** His name meant "Baal is alive." The father of Jezebel was the king of Phoenicia (including Tyre and Sidon) who had murdered his predecessor and, according to Josephus, was a priest of the gods Melqart and Astarte.

16:31,32 Baal. Meaning "lord, husband, owner," Baal was the predominant god in Canaanite religion. He was the storm god who provided the rain necessary for the fertility of the land. The worship of Baal was widespread among the Canaanites with many local manifestations under various other titles, the Tyrians calling him Baal Melqart. The worship of Baal had infiltrated Israel long before the time of Ahab (Judg. 2:11,13; 3:7; 10:6,10; 1 Sam. 12:10). However, Ahab gave it official sanction in Samaria through building a temple for Baal (see 2 Kin. 3:2). As David had captured Jerusalem and his son Solomon had built a temple for the Lord there, so Omri established Samaria and his son Ahab built a temple for Baal there.

16:34 Hiel of Bethel built Jericho. The re-fortification of Jericho was forbidden by God, who had supernaturally destroyed it. But Joshua predicted that a man and his sons would violate God's restriction (*see note on Josh. 6:26*). Two of Hiel's sons died when they sought to assist him to fortify the city (see marginal note).

17:1 Elijah. His name means "the LORD is God." The prophet Elijah's ministry corresponded to his name: He was sent by God to confront Baalism and to declare to Israel that the Lord was God and there was no other. **Tishbite.** Elijah lived in a town called Tishbe, E of the Jordan River in the vicinity of the Jabbok River. **not be dew nor rain.** The autumn and spring rains and summer dew were necessities for the crops of Israel. The Lord had threatened to withhold these from the Land if His people turned from Him to serve other gods (Lev. 26:18,19; Deut. 11:16,17; 28:23,24). Elijah had prayed for the drought (cf. James 5:17) and God answered. It lasted 3 years and 6 months according to James (5:17). The drought proved that Baal, the god of the rains and fertility, was impotent before the Lord.

17:3 Brook Cherith. Probably this was a seasonal brook that flowed during the rainy season but dried up when the weather turned hot. It was located E of the Jordan River.

17:6 ravens brought. God's supernatural provision, much like the manna and quail during Israel's wilderness wanderings (Ex. 16:13-36).

Elijah and the Widow

8 Then the word of the LORD came to him,
saying, 9 "Arise, go to [g]Zarephath, which
belongs to [h]Sidon, and dwell there. See, I
have commanded a widow there to provide
for you." 10 So he arose and went to Zarephath. And when he came to the gate of the
city, indeed a widow *was* there gathering
sticks. And he called to her and said,
"Please bring me a little water in a cup, that
I may drink." 11 And as she was going to
get *it*, he called to her and said, "Please
bring me a morsel of bread in your hand."
12 So she said, "As the LORD your God
lives, I do not have bread, only a handful
of flour in a bin, and a little oil in a [1]jar; and
see, I *am* gathering a couple of sticks that I
may go in and prepare it for myself and
my son, that we may eat it, and [i]die."
13 And Elijah said to her, "Do not fear;
go *and* do as you have said, but make me a
small cake from it first, and bring *it* to me;
and afterward make *some* for yourself and
your son. 14 For thus says the LORD God of
Israel: 'The bin of flour shall not be used
up, nor shall the jar of oil run dry, until the
day the LORD sends rain on the earth.' "
15 So she went away and did according
to the word of Elijah; and she and he and
her household ate for *many* days. 16 The
bin of flour was not used up, nor did the
jar of oil run dry, according to the word of
the LORD which He spoke by Elijah.

Elijah Revives the Widow's Son

17 Now it happened after these things
that the son of the woman who owned the
house became sick. And his sickness was
so [2]serious that [3]there was no breath left in
him. 18 So she said to Elijah, [j]"What have I
to do with you, O man of God? Have you
come to me to bring my sin to remembrance, and to kill my son?"
19 And he said to her, "Give me your
son." So he took him out of her arms and
carried him to the upper room where he
was staying, and laid him on his own bed.
20 Then he cried out to the LORD and said,
"O LORD my God, have You also brought
tragedy on the widow with whom I lodge,
by killing her son?" 21 [k]And he stretched
himself out on the child three times, and
cried out to the LORD and said, "O LORD
my God, I pray, let this child's soul come
back to him." 22 Then the LORD heard the
voice of Elijah; and the soul of the child
came back to him, and he [l]revived.
23 And Elijah took the child and brought
him down from the upper room into the
house, and gave him to his mother. And
Elijah said, "See, your son lives!"
24 Then the woman said to Elijah, "Now
by this [m]I know that you *are* a man of God,
and that the word of the LORD in your
mouth *is* the truth."

Elijah's Message to Ahab

18 And it came to pass *after* [a]many
days that the word of the LORD
came to Elijah, in the third year, saying,
"Go, present yourself to Ahab, and [b]I will
send rain on the earth."
2 So Elijah went to present himself to
Ahab; and *there was* a severe famine in Samaria. 3 And Ahab had called Obadiah,

9 [g] Obad. 20; Luke 4:25, 26 [h] 2 Sam. 24:6
12 [i] Deut. 28:23, 24 [1] Lit. *pitcher* or *water jar*
17 [2] *severe* [3] *He died.*
18 [j] Luke 5:8
21 [k] 2 Kin. 4:34, 35; Acts 20:10
22 [l] Luke 7:14, 15; Heb. 11:35
24 [m] John 2:11; 3:2; 16:30

CHAPTER 18

1 [a] 1 Kin. 17:1; Luke 4:25; James 5:17 [b] Deut. 28:12

17:9 Zarephath. A town on the Mediterranean coast about 7 mi. S of Sidon. Elijah was sent to live there, in a territory controlled by Ahab's father-in-law, Ethbaal. In this way, he showed the power of God in the very area where the impotent Baal was worshiped, as He provided miraculously for the widow in the famine (vv. 10-16).

17:23 your son lives. Canaanite myths claimed that Baal could revive the dead, but here it was the Lord, not Baal, who gave back the boy's life. This conclusively demonstrated that the Lord was the only true God and Elijah was His prophet (v. 24).

17:24 a man of God. *See note on 12:22.* A man of God has a true word from God.

18:1 third year. Cf. James 5:17.

18:2 famine. This was to give Ahab opportunity to repent. He was the cause of national judgment in the famine. If he repented, rain would come.

18:3 Obadiah. His name means "servant of the LORD." He was the manager of Ahab's royal palace and a devout worshiper of the Lord, who had demonstrated his devotion to the Lord by protecting 100 of

Resuscitations From the Dead

1.	Widow of Zarephath's son, raised by Elijah	1 Kin. 17:22
2.	Shunammite woman's son, raised by Elisha	2 Kin. 4:34,35
3.	Man raised when he came into contact with the bones of Elisha	2 Kin. 13:20,21
4.	Widow of Nain's son, raised by Jesus	Luke 7:14,15
5.	Jairus' daughter, raised by Jesus	Luke 8:52-56
6.	Lazarus of Bethany, brother of Mary and Martha, raised by Jesus	John 11
7.	Dorcas, raised by Peter	Acts 9:40
8.	Eutychus, raised by Paul	Acts 20:9-12

who *was* [1]in charge of *his* house. (Now
Obadiah feared the LORD greatly. 4 For so it
was, while Jezebel [2]massacred the
prophets of the LORD, that Obadiah had
taken one hundred prophets and hidden
them, fifty to a cave, and had fed them
with bread and water.) 5 And Ahab had
said to Obadiah, "Go into the land to all
the springs of water and to all the brooks;
perhaps we may find grass to keep the
horses and mules alive, so that we will not
have to kill any livestock." 6 So they divided the land between them to explore it;
Ahab went one way by himself, and Obadiah went another way by himself.
7 Now as Obadiah was on his way, suddenly Elijah met him; and he [c]recognized
him, and fell on his face, and said, "*Is* that
you, my lord Elijah?"
8 And he answered him, "*It is* I. Go, tell
your master, 'Elijah *is here.*' "
9 So he said, "How have I sinned, that
you are delivering your servant into the
hand of Ahab, to kill me? 10 *As* the LORD
your God lives, there is no nation or kingdom where my master has not sent someone to hunt for you; and when they said,
'*He is* not *here,*' he took an oath from the
kingdom or nation that they could not find
you. 11 And now you say, 'Go, tell your
master, "Elijah *is here*" '! 12 And it shall
come to pass, *as soon as* I am gone from
you, that [d]the Spirit of the LORD will carry
you to a place I do not know; so when I go
and tell Ahab, and he cannot find you, he
will kill me. But I your servant have feared
the LORD from my youth. 13 Was it not reported to my lord what I did when Jezebel
killed the prophets of the LORD, how I hid
one hundred men of the LORD's prophets,
fifty to a cave, and fed them with bread
and water? 14 And now you say, 'Go, tell
your master, "Elijah *is here.*" ' He will kill
me!"

15 Then Elijah said, "*As* the LORD of hosts
lives, before whom I stand, I will surely
present myself to him today."
16 So Obadiah went to meet Ahab, and
told him; and Ahab went to meet Elijah.
17 Then it happened, when Ahab saw
Elijah, that Ahab said to him, [e]"*Is that* you,
O [f]troubler of Israel?"
18 And he answered, "I have not troubled Israel, but you and your father's
house *have,* [g]in that you have forsaken the
commandments of the LORD and have followed the Baals. 19 Now therefore, send
and gather all Israel to me on [h]Mount
Carmel, the four hundred and fifty
prophets of Baal, [i]and the four hundred
prophets of [3]Asherah, who [4]eat at Jezebel's table."

Elijah's Mount Carmel Victory

20 So Ahab sent for all the children of Israel, and [j]gathered the prophets together
on Mount Carmel. 21 And Elijah came to
all the people, and said, [k]"How long will
you falter between two opinions? If the
LORD *is* God, follow Him; but if Baal, [l]fol-
low him." But the people answered him
not a word. 22 Then Elijah said to the people, [m]"I alone am left a prophet of the
LORD; [n]but Baal's prophets *are* four hundred and fifty men. 23 Therefore let them
give us two bulls; and let them choose one
bull for themselves, cut it in pieces, and lay
it on the wood, but put no fire *under it;* and
I will prepare the other bull, and lay *it* on
the wood, but put no fire *under it.* 24 Then
you call on the name of your gods, and I
will call on the name of the LORD; and the
God who [o]answers by fire, He is God."
So all the people answered and said, [5]"It
is well spoken."
25 Now Elijah said to the prophets of
Baal, "Choose one bull for yourselves and
prepare *it* first, for you *are* many; and call

3 [1] Lit. *over the house*
4 [2] Lit. *cut off*
7 [c] 2 Kin. 1:6-8
12 [d] 2 Kin. 2:16; Ezek. 3:12, 14; Matt. 4:1; Acts 8:39
17 [e] 1 Kin. 21:20 [f] Josh. 7:25; Acts 16:20
18 [g] 1 Kin. 16:30-33; [2 Chr. 15:2]
19 [h] Josh. 19:26; 2 Kin. 2:25 [i] 1 Kin. 16:33 [3] A Canaanite goddess [4] Are provided for by Jezebel
20 [j] 1 Kin. 22:6
21 [k] 2 Kin. 17:41; [Matt. 6:24] [l] Josh. 24:15
22 [m] 1 Kin. 19:10, 14 [n] 1 Kin. 18:19
24 [o] 1 Kin. 18:38; 1 Chr. 21:26 [5] Lit. *The word is good*

---

the Lord's prophets from death by Jezebel (vv. 4,13) which had put him on tenuous ground with Ahab.

18:12 the Spirit of the LORD will carry you. The servant had been asked to tell Ahab Elijah was present to speak with him (vv. 7,18), but he was afraid because Ahab was seeking Elijah so intensely. Since Elijah had disappeared from sight earlier (17:5), Obadiah was afraid that the Holy Spirit would carry Elijah away again (cf. 2 Kin. 2:16) and the irrational Ahab would kill him for the false report of Elijah's presence.

18:17 troubler. Such was one who brought misfortune on a community by breaking an oath or by making a foolish one (Josh. 6:18; 7:25).

18:18 Baals. These were the local idols of Baal (cf. Judg. 2:11). The prophet boldly told Ahab that the calamity of drought and famine was traceable directly to his and his family's patronage and practice of idolatry.

18:19 Mount Carmel. The Carmel range of mountains, rising to 1,800 ft. at its highest point, extends about 30 mi. to the SE from the shores of the Mediterranean Sea into the S of the Jezreel Valley. A series of rounded peaks and valleys, it became a symbol of beauty and fruitfulness because of its lush tree cover (Song 7:5; Is. 35:2). It is not known at exactly what point along this ridge the contest between Elijah and the prophets of Baal took place. The queen cared for 850 false prophets who were associated with her.

18:21 falter between two opinions. Lit. "limp along on or between two twigs." Israel had not totally rejected the Lord, but was seeking to combine worship of Him with the worship of Baal. The issue posed by Elijah was that Israel had to choose who was God, the Lord or Baal, and then serve God wholeheartedly. Rather than decide by his message, Elijah sought a visible sign from heaven.

18:24 the God who answers by fire. Since Baal's followers believed that he controlled the thunder, lightning, and storms, and the Lord's followers declared the same (Ps. 18:14; 29:3-9; 104:3), this would prove to be a fair test to show who was God.

on the name of your god, but put no fire
under it."
26 So they took the bull which was given
them, and they prepared *it,* and called on
the name of Baal from morning even till
noon, saying, "O Baal, [6]hear us!" But *there*
was [p]no voice; no one answered. Then they
[7]leaped about the altar which they had
made.
27 And so it was, at noon, that Elijah
mocked them and said, "Cry [8]aloud, for he
is a god; either he is meditating, or he is
busy, or he is on a journey, *or* perhaps he is
sleeping and must be awakened." 28 So
they cried aloud, and [q]cut themselves, as
was their custom, with [9]knives and lances,
until the blood gushed out on them. 29 And
when midday was past, [r]they prophesied
until the *time* of the offering of the *evening*
sacrifice. But *there was* [s]no voice; no one answered, no one paid attention.
30 Then Elijah said to all the people,
"Come near to me." So all the people came
near to him. [t]And he repaired the altar of
the LORD *that was* broken down. 31 And Elijah took twelve stones, according to the
number of the tribes of the sons of Jacob, to
whom the word of the LORD had come,
saying, [u]"Israel shall be your name."
32 Then with the stones he built an altar [v]in
the name of the LORD; and he made a
trench around the altar large enough to
hold two seahs of seed. 33 And he [w]put the
wood in order, cut the bull in pieces, and
laid *it* on the wood, and said, "Fill four
waterpots with water, and [x]pour *it* on the
burnt sacrifice and on the wood." 34 Then
he said, "Do *it* a second time," and they
did *it* a second time; and he said, "Do *it* a
third time," and they did *it* a third time.
35 So the water ran all around the altar; and
he also filled [y]the trench with water.
36 And it came to pass, at *the time of* the offering of the *evening* sacrifice, that Elijah the
prophet came near and said, "LORD [z]God of
Abraham, Isaac, and Israel, [a]let it be known
this day that You *are* God in Israel and I *am*
Your servant, and *that* [b]I have done all these
things at Your word. 37 Hear me, O LORD,
hear me, that this people may know that
You *are* the LORD God, and *that* You have
turned their hearts back *to You* again."
38 Then [c]the fire of the LORD fell and consumed the burnt sacrifice, and the wood

26 [p] Ps. 115:5; Jer. 10:5; [1 Cor. 8:4] [6] *answer* [7] *Lit. limped about, leaped in dancing around*
27 [8] *with a loud voice*
28 [q] [Lev. 19:28; Deut. 14:1] [9] *swords*
29 [r] Ex. 29:39, 41 [s] 1 Kin. 18:26
30 [t] 1 Kin. 19:10, 14; 2 Chr. 33:16
31 [u] Gen. 32:28; 35:10; 2 Kin. 17:34
32 [v] [Ex. 20:25; Col. 3:17]
33 [w] Gen. 22:9; Lev. 1:6-8 [x] Judg. 6:20
35 [y] 1 Kin. 18:32, 38
36 [z] Gen. 28:13; Ex. 3:6; 4:5; [Matt. 22:32] [a] 1 Kin. 8:43; 2 Kin. 19:19 [b] Num. 16:28
38 [c] Gen. 15:17; Lev. 9:24; 10:1, 2; Judg. 6:21; 2 Kin. 1:12; 1 Chr. 21:26; 2 Chr. 7:1; Job 1:16

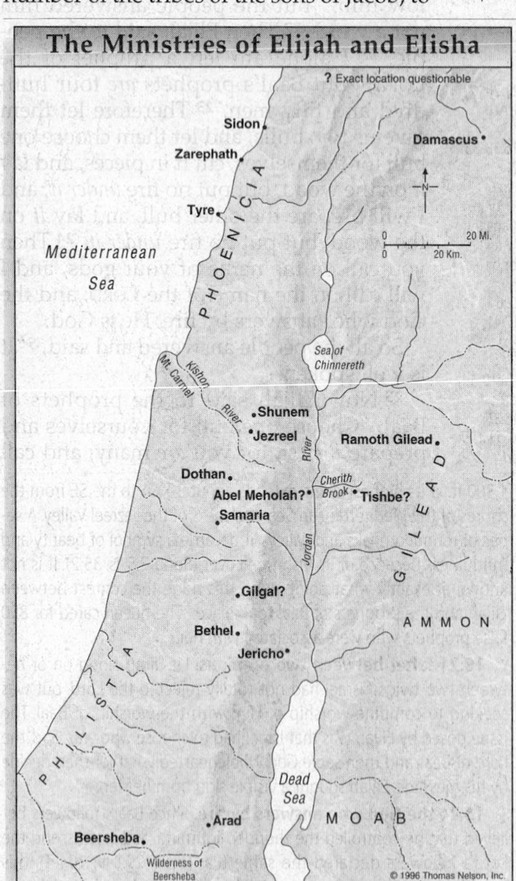

This map locates the chief geographical points of ministry for these two pre-Exilic prophets.

18:27 mocked. The myths surrounding Baal portrayed him as musing on actions to take, fighting a war, traveling, and even dying and coming back to life. Elijah's sarcastic advice to the prophets of Baal played on these beliefs.

18:28 the blood gushed out. Self-laceration was practiced to rouse a god's pity and response in the ancient world, but was prohibited by the OT law (Lev. 19:28; Deut. 14:1).

18:29 no...no...no. This 3-fold declaration emphasized the complete lack of response on the part of Baal. The fact that there was no response indicated Baal's impotence and non-existence (Jer. 10:5).

18:31 twelve stones. The 12 stones represented the 12 tribes, since this contest had significance for both Judah and Israel. Although the tribes had been divided into two nations, they were still one people in the Lord's plans, with the same covenants and a single destiny.

18:32 two seahs. This was about 4 gal. or a third of a bu. of seed.

18:36 the *evening* sacrifice. This sacrifice was offered around 3:00 p.m. (Ex. 29:38-41; Num. 28:3-8).

and the stones and the dust, and it licked
up the water that *was* in the trench. 39 Now
when all the people saw *it*, they fell on
their faces; and they said, [d]"The LORD, He
is God! The LORD, He *is* God!"
40 And Elijah said to them, [e]"Seize the
prophets of Baal! Do not let one of them escape!" So they seized them; and Elijah
brought them down to the Brook [f]Kishon
and [g]executed them there.

The Drought Ends

41 Then Elijah said to Ahab, "Go up, eat
and drink; for *there is* the sound of abundance of rain." 42 So Ahab went up to eat
and drink. And Elijah went up to the top of
Carmel; [h]then he bowed down on the
ground, and put his face between his
knees, 43 and said to his servant, "Go up
now, look toward the sea."
So he went up and looked, and said,
"*There is* nothing." And seven times he
said, "Go again."
44 Then it came to pass the seventh *time*,
that he said, "There is a cloud, as small as
a man's hand, rising out of the sea!" So he
said, "Go up, say to Ahab, [1]'Prepare *your*
chariot, and go down before the rain stops
you.'"
45 Now it happened in the meantime
that the sky became black with clouds and
wind, and there was a heavy rain. So Ahab
rode away and went to Jezreel. 46 Then the
[i]hand of the LORD came upon Elijah; and
he [j]girded[2] up his loins and ran ahead of
Ahab to the entrance of Jezreel.

Elijah Escapes from Jezebel

19 And Ahab told Jezebel all that Elijah had done, also how he had [a]ex-
ecuted all the prophets with the sword.
2 Then Jezebel sent a messenger to Elijah,
saying, [b]"So let the gods do *to me,* and
more also, if I do not make your life as the
life of one of them by tomorrow about this
time." 3 And when he saw *that*, he arose
and ran for his life, and went to Beersheba,
which *belongs* to Judah, and left his servant
there.
4 But he himself went a day's journey
into the wilderness, and came and sat
down under a [1]broom tree. And he
[c]prayed that he might die, and said, "It is
enough! Now, LORD, take my life, for I *am*
no better than my fathers!"
5 Then as he lay and slept under a broom
tree, suddenly an [2]angel touched him, and
said to him, "Arise *and* eat." 6 Then he
looked, and there by his head *was* a cake
baked on [3]coals, and a jar of water. So he
ate and drank, and lay down again. 7 And
the [4]angel of the LORD came back the second time, and touched him, and said,
"Arise *and* eat, because the journey *is* too
great for you." 8 So he arose, and ate and
drank; and he went in the strength of that
food forty days and [d]forty nights as far as
[e]Horeb, the mountain of God.
9 And there he went into a cave, and

39 [d] 1 Kin. 18:21, 24
40 [e] 2 Kin. 10:25 [f] Judg. 4:7; 5:21 [g] [Deut. 13:5; 18:20]
42 [h] James 5:17, 18
44 [1] Lit. *Bind* or *Harness*
46 [i] 2 Kin. 3:15; Is. 8:11; Ezek. 3:14 [j] 2 Kin. 4:29; 9:1; Jer. 1:17; 1 Pet. 1:13 [2] Tucked the skirts of his robe in his belt in preparation for quick travel

CHAPTER 19

1 [a] 1 Kin. 18:40
2 [b] Ruth 1:17; 1 Kin. 20:10; 2 Kin. 6:31
4 [c] Num. 11:15; Jer. 20:14-18; Jon. 4:3, 8 [1] *juniper*
5 [2] Or *Angel*
6 [3] *hot stones*
7 [4] Or *Angel*
8 [d] Ex. 24:18; 34:28; Deut. 9:9-11, 18; Matt. 4:2 [e] Ex. 3:1; 4:27

18:40 Seize the prophets. Taking advantage of the excited feelings of the people over the manifestation of Jehovah as the true God, Elijah called on them to seize the priestly imposters and fill the river with their blood, the river that was dried up by their idolatry. **Brook Kishon.** This river, which drains the Jezreel Valley from E to the NW, was in the valley N of Mt. Carmel. **executed them.** The killing of the 450 prophets of Baal (18:19) fulfilled the law's demands that false prophets be executed (Deut. 13:1-5) and that those embracing idolatry or inciting others to practice it were worthy of death (Deut. 13:13-18; 17:2-7). Further, these deaths were just retribution for Jezebel's killing of the Lord's prophets (vv. 4,13).

18:41 eat and drink. Elijah instructed Ahab to celebrate the end of the drought.

18:42 bowed down. Elijah's actions expressed his and Israel's humble submission to God. Elijah prayed for rain this time (cf. 17:1; James 5:17) and God again answered (cf. James 5:18). Since the Lord's curse was lifted, the rains would be coming.

18:45 Jezreel. A town located in the tribal allotment of Issachar at the eastern end of the Jezreel Valley, N of Mt. Gilboa, about 55 mi. N of Jerusalem. Jezreel was Ahab's winter capital (see 21:1), situated between 15 to 25 mi. E of the Carmel Range.

18:46 ran ahead. It was customary in the ancient Near East for kings to have runners before their chariots. The prophet showed Ahab his loyalty by rendering to him that service. Empowered by God, Elijah ran on foot ahead of Ahab's chariot the 15 to 25 mi. from Mt. Carmel to Jezreel.

19:3 he saw. His hope shattered, Elijah fled as a prophet, broken by Jezebel's threats (v. 2), her unrepentant Baalism, and her continuing power over Israel. Elijah expected Jezebel to surrender; when she did not capitulate, he became a discouraged man (vv. 4,10,14). **Beersheba.** A city located 100 mi. S of Jezreel (18:45,46) in the Negev, it marked the southern boundary of the population of Judah.

19:4 broom tree. A desert bush that grew to a height of 10 ft. It had slender branches featuring small leaves and fragrant blossoms. **take my life.** Since Israelites believed that suicide was an affront to the Lord, it was not an option, whatever the distress. So Elijah asked the Lord for death (cf. Jon. 4:3,8) because he viewed the situation as hopeless. Job (Job 6:8,9), Moses (Num. 11:10-15), and Jeremiah (Jer. 20:14-18) had also reacted in similar fashion during their ministries.

19:6 cake...and...water. As at Cherith and Zarephath (17:6,19), God provided food and drink for Elijah in the midst of his distress and the surrounding famine.

19:8 forty days. Elijah's trip took over double the time it should have taken. Therefore, the period had symbolic meaning as well as showing literal time. As the people of Israel had a notable spiritual failure and so wandered 40 years in the wilderness (Num. 14:26-35), so a discouraged Elijah was to spend 40 days in the desert. As Moses had spent 40 days on the mountain without bread and water, sustained only by God as he awaited a new phase of service (Ex. 34:28), so Elijah was to spend 40 days depending on God's enablement as he prepared for a new commission from the Lord. As Moses had seen the presence of God (Ex. 33:12-23), so Elijah experienced a manifestation of God. **Horeb.** An alternate name for Mt. Sinai, located about 200 mi. S of Beersheba.

spent the night in that place; and behold,
the word of the LORD *came* to him, and He
said to him, "What are you doing here, Elijah?"
10 So he said, [f]"I have been very [g]zeal-
ous for the LORD God of hosts; for the children of Israel have forsaken Your
covenant, torn down Your altars, and
[h]killed Your prophets with the sword. [i]I
alone am left; and they seek to take my
life."

God's Revelation to Elijah

11 Then He said, "Go out, and stand [j]on
the mountain before the LORD." And behold, the LORD [k]passed by, and [l]a great and
strong wind tore into the mountains and
broke the rocks in pieces before the LORD,
but the LORD *was* not in the wind; and after
the wind an earthquake, *but* the LORD *was*
not in the earthquake; 12 and after the
earthquake a fire, *but* the LORD *was* not in
the fire; and after the fire [5]a still small
voice.
13 So it was, when Elijah heard *it*, that
[m]he wrapped his face in his mantle and
went out and stood in the entrance of the
cave. [n]Suddenly a voice *came* to him, and
said, "What are you doing here, Elijah?"
14 [o]And he said, "I have been very zealous for the LORD God of hosts; because the
children of Israel have forsaken Your
covenant, torn down Your altars, and
killed Your prophets with the sword. I
alone am left; and they seek to take my
life."
15 Then the LORD said to him: "Go, return on your way to the Wilderness of Damascus; [p]and when you arrive, anoint
Hazael *as* king over Syria. 16 Also you shall
anoint [q]Jehu the son of Nimshi *as* king
over Israel. And [r]Elisha the son of Shaphat
of Abel Meholah you shall anoint *as*
prophet in your place. 17 [s]It shall be *that*
whoever escapes the sword of Hazael,
Jehu will [t]kill; and whoever escapes the
sword of Jehu, [u]Elisha will kill. 18 [v]Yet I
have reserved seven thousand in Israel, all
whose knees have not bowed to Baal, [w]and
every mouth that has not kissed him."

Elisha Follows Elijah

19 So he departed from there, and found
Elisha the son of Shaphat, who *was* plowing *with* twelve yoke *of oxen* before him,
and he was with the twelfth. Then Elijah
passed by him and threw his [x]mantle on
him. 20 And he left the oxen and ran after
Elijah, and said, [y]"Please let me kiss my father and my mother, and *then* I will follow
you."
And he said to him, "Go back again, for
what have I done to you?"
21 So *Elisha* turned back from him, and
took a yoke of oxen and slaughtered them
and [z]boiled their flesh, using the oxen's
equipment, and gave it to the people, and
they ate. Then he arose and followed Elijah, and became his servant.

Ahab Defeats the Syrians

20 Now [a]Ben-Hadad the king of Syria
gathered all his forces together;
thirty-two kings *were* with him, with horses and chariots. And he went up and besieged [b]Samaria, and made war against it.

10 [f]Rom. 11:3 [g]Num. 25:11, 13; Ps. 69:9 [h]1 Kin. 18:4 [i]1 Kin. 18:22; Rom. 11:3
11 [j]Ex. 19:20; 24:12, 18 [k]Ex. 33:21, 22 [l]Ezek. 1:4; 37:7
12 [5]*a delicate whispering voice*
13 [m]Ex. 3:6; Is. 6:2 [n]1 Kin. 19:9
14 [o]1 Kin. 19:10
15 [p]2 Kin. 8:8-15
16 [q]2 Kin. 9:1-10 [r]1 Kin. 19:19-21; 2 Kin. 2:9-15
17 [s]2 Kin. 8:12; 13:3, 22 [t]2 Kin. 9:14–10:28 [u][Hos. 6:5]
18 [v]Rom. 11:4 [w]Hos. 13:2
19 [x]1 Sam. 28:14; 2 Kin. 2:8, 13, 14
20 [y][Matt. 8:21, 22; Luke 9:61, 62]; Acts 20:37
21 [z]2 Sam. 24:22

CHAPTER 20

1 [a]1 Kin. 15:18, 20; 2 Kin. 6:24 [b]1 Kin. 16:24; 2 Kin. 6:24

19:10,14 Elijah viewed the Israelites as rebels against the Mosaic Covenant, a rebellion that his ministry had been unable to arrest (see v. 3). Paul used this incident as an illustration in Rom. 11:3.

19:11 the LORD passed by. The 3 phenomena, wind, earthquake, and fire, announced the imminent arrival of the Lord (cf. Ex. 19:16-19; Ps. 18:7-15; Hab. 3:3-6). The Lord's self-revelation to Elijah came in a faint, whispering voice (v. 12). The lesson for Elijah was that Almighty God was quietly, sometimes imperceptibly, doing His work in Israel (v. 18).

19:15 the Wilderness of Damascus. The Syrian Desert S and E of the city of Damascus, the city located to the NE of Israel.

19:15-17 The Lord instructed Elijah to anoint Hazael of Syria (see 2 Kin. 8:8), Jehu (see 2 Kin. 9:2), and Elisha (v. 19) for the purpose of commissioning them to destroy Baal worship in Israel. Through these 3 men, the Lord completed the execution of Baal worshipers that Elijah had begun. Actually, Elijah commissioned only the last of these 3 men directly—the other two were indirectly commissioned through Elisha. Elisha was involved in Hazael's becoming Syria's king (2 Kin. 8:7-14), and one of Elisha's associates anointed Jehu (2 Kin. 9:1-3). By the time the last of these men died (2 Kin. 13:24), Baalism had been officially barred from Israel.

19:16 Abel Melohah. The hometown of Elisha was located in the Jordan Valley, 10 mi. S of Beth-Shanon, in the tribal allotment of Manasseh.

19:18 Paul used God's response to Elijah as an illustration in Rom. 11:4. **kissed him.** Kissing the image or symbol of Baal was apparently a common act in worship (cf. Hos. 13:2).

19:19 Elisha. This name means "my God is salvation" and belonged to Elisha, the successor to Elijah (see 2 Kin. 2:9-15). **Shaphat.** Elisha's father, whose name meant "he judges." **twelve yoke *of oxen*.** It was a common practice for several teams of oxen, each with his own plow and driver, to work together in a row. After letting the others pass, Elijah threw his mantle around the last man, Elisha, thus designating him as his successor.

19:20 Go back again. Elijah instructed Elisha to go, but to keep in mind the solemn call of God and not to allow any earthly affection to detain his obedience.

19:21 slaughtered. The slaughter of the oxen was a farewell feast for family and friends, indicating that Elisha was making a decisive break. He followed Elijah and became his servant (lit. "aide," the same term used for Joshua's relationship with Moses in Ex. 24:13; 33:11). Just as Elijah resembled Moses, so Elisha resembled Joshua.

20:1 Ben-Hadad. This was likely Ben-Hadad II of Syria (*see note on 15:18-20*), who marched on the capital of Israel and demanded surrender by Ahab (vv. 2-6) **thirty-two kings.** These were probably rulers of client city-states in the land of Syria (*see notes on 10:29*).

2 Then he sent messengers into the city to
Ahab king of Israel, and said to him, "Thus
says Ben-Hadad: 3 'Your silver and your
gold *are* mine; your loveliest wives and
children are mine.' "
4 And the king of Israel answered and
said, "My lord, O king, just as you say, I
and all that I have *are* yours."
5 Then the messengers came back and
said, "Thus speaks Ben-Hadad, saying, 'Indeed I have sent to you, saying, "You shall
deliver to me your silver and your gold,
your wives and your children"; 6 but I will
send my servants to you tomorrow about
this time, and they shall search your house
and the houses of your servants. And it
shall be, *that* whatever is [1]pleasant in your
eyes, they will put *it* in their hands and
take *it*.' "
7 So the king of Israel called all the elders of the land, and said, "Notice, please,
and see how this *man* seeks trouble, for he
sent to me for my wives, my children, my
silver, and my gold; and I did not deny
him."
8 And all the elders and all the people
said to him, "Do not listen or consent."
9 Therefore he said to the messengers of
Ben-Hadad, "Tell my lord the king, 'All
that you sent for to your servant the first
time I will do, but this thing I cannot do.' "
And the messengers departed and
brought back word to him.
10 Then Ben-Hadad sent to him and
said, [c]"The gods do so to me, and more
also, if enough dust is left of Samaria for a
handful for each of the people [2]who follow
me."
11 So the king of Israel answered and
said, "Tell *him*, 'Let not the one who puts
on *his armor* [d]boast like the one who takes
it off.' "
12 And it happened when *Ben-Hadad*
heard this message, as he and the kings
were [e]drinking at the [3]command post, that
he said to his servants, "Get ready." And
they got ready to attack the city.
13 Suddenly a prophet approached Ahab
king of Israel, saying, "Thus says the LORD:
'Have you seen all this great multitude?
Behold, [f]I will deliver it into your hand
today, and you shall know that I *am* the
LORD.' "
14 So Ahab said, "By whom?"
And he said, "Thus says the LORD: 'By
the young leaders of the provinces.' "
Then he said, "Who will set the battle in
order?"
And he answered, "You."
15 Then he mustered the young leaders
of the provinces, and there were two hundred and thirty-two; and after them he
mustered all the people, all the children of
Israel—seven thousand.
16 So they went out at noon. Meanwhile
Ben-Hadad and the thirty-two kings helping him were [g]getting drunk at the command post. 17 The young leaders of the
provinces went out first. And Ben-Hadad
sent out *a patrol*, and they told him, saying,
"Men are coming out of Samaria!" 18 So he
said, "If they have come out for peace, take
them alive; and if they have come out for
war, take them alive."
19 Then these young leaders of the
provinces went out of the city with the
army which followed them. 20 And each
one killed his man; so the Syrians fled, and
Israel pursued them; and Ben-Hadad the
king of Syria escaped on a horse with the
cavalry. 21 Then the king of Israel went out
and attacked the horses and chariots, and
killed the Syrians with a great slaughter.
22 And the prophet came to the king of
Israel and said to him, "Go, strengthen
yourself; take note, and see what you
should do, [h]for [4]in the spring of the year
the king of Syria will come up against
you."

The Syrians Again Defeated

23 Then the servants of the king of Syria
said to him, "Their gods *are* gods of the
hills. Therefore they were stronger than

6 [1] *pleasing*
10 [c] 1 Kin. 19:2; 2 Kin. 6:31 [2] Lit. *at my feet*
11 [d] Prov. 27:1; [Eccl. 7:8]
12 [e] 1 Kin. 20:16 [3] Lit. *booths* or *shelters*
13 [f] 1 Kin. 20:28
16 [g] 1 Kin. 16:9; 20:12; [Prov. 20:1]
22 [h] 2 Sam. 11:1; 1 Kin. 20:26 [4] Lit. *at the return*

20:9 I will do...I cannot do. Ahab was willing to give tribute to Ben-Hadad as his vassal (vv. 2-4), but he refused to allow the Syrian king to plunder his palace (vv. 5-8).

20:10,11 Ben-Hadad boasted that his army would level the hill of Samaria to dust (v. 10). Ahab replied that Ben-Hadad should not boast of the outcome of the battle before it began (v. 11).

20:13 I will deliver it into your hand today. These were the words of assurance given before battles when the Lord was about to fight on Israel's side (Josh. 6:2,16; 8:1,18; Judg. 7:2; 18:10; 1 Sam. 23:4; 24:4). Further, the victory would show Ahab that the Lord was in every respect the mighty God He claimed to be. Though the people and king of Israel had dishonored God, He would not utterly cast them off (vv. 14,15).

20:17-21 The battle strategy was to send out the young leaders who could perhaps draw near to the Syrians without arousing too much alarm and then, at a given signal, initiate a charge joined by Ahab's main striking force that would catch the drunken Syrians off guard and throw them into confusion. The glorious victory, won so easily and with such a small force, was granted so that Ahab and the people would know that God was sovereign.

20:22 the spring of the year. Spring was the usual time for battles in the ancient Near East (*see note on 2 Sam. 11:1*), and a prophet warned Ahab that Ben-Hadad would retaliate in the following year.

20:23 gods of the hills. The advisors of Ben-Hadad believed that Israel had won the previous battle because it occurred in mountainous terrain, the area they believed was ruled by Israel's "gods." They counseled Ben-Hadad to strengthen his army and fight Israel again,

we; but if we fight against them in the
plain, surely we will be stronger than they.
24 So do this thing: Dismiss the kings, each
from his position, and put captains in their
[5]places; 25 and you shall muster an army
like the army [6]that you have lost, horse for
horse and chariot for chariot. Then we will
fight against them in the plain; surely we
will be stronger than they."
And he listened to their voice and did so.
26 So it was, in the spring of the year, that
Ben-Hadad mustered the Syrians and went
up to [i]Aphek to fight against Israel. 27 And
the children of Israel were mustered and
given provisions, and they went against
them. Now the children of Israel encamped
before them like two little flocks of goats,
while the Syrians filled the [j]countryside.
28 Then a [k]man of God came and spoke
to the king of Israel, and said, "Thus says
the LORD: 'Because the Syrians have said,
"The LORD *is* God of the hills, but He *is* not
God of the valleys," therefore [l]I will deliver all this great multitude into your hand,
and you shall know that I *am* the LORD.' "
29 And they encamped opposite each other
for seven days. So it was that on the seventh day the battle was joined; and the
children of Israel killed one hundred thousand foot soldiers *of* the Syrians in one day.
30 But the rest fled to Aphek, into the city;
then a wall fell on twenty-seven thousand
of the men *who were* left.
And Ben-Hadad fled and went into the
city, into an inner chamber.

Ahab's Treaty with Ben-Hadad

31 Then his servants said to him, "Look
now, we have heard that the kings of the
house of Israel *are* merciful kings. Please,
let us [m]put sackcloth around our waists
and ropes around our heads, and go out to
the king of Israel; perhaps he will spare
your life." 32 So they wore sackcloth
around their waists and *put* ropes around
their heads, and came to the king of Israel
and said, "Your servant Ben-Hadad says,
'Please let me live.' "
And he said, "*Is* he still alive? He *is* my
brother."
33 Now the men were watching closely
to see whether *any sign of mercy would come*
from him; and they quickly grasped *at this
word* and said, "Your brother Ben-Hadad."
So he said, "Go, bring him." Then Ben-
Hadad came out to him; and he had him
come up into the chariot.
34 So *Ben-Hadad* said to him, [n]"The cities
which my father took from your father I
will restore; and you may set up marketplaces for yourself in Damascus, as my father did in Samaria."
Then *Ahab said,* "I will send you away
with this treaty." So he made a treaty with
him and sent him away.

Ahab Condemned

35 Now a certain man of [o]the sons of the
prophets said to his neighbor [p]by the word
of the LORD, "Strike me, please." And the
man refused to strike him. 36 Then he said
to him, "Because you have not obeyed the
voice of the LORD, surely, as soon as you
depart from me, a lion shall kill you." And
as soon as he left him, [q]a lion found him
and killed him.
37 And he found another man, and said,
"Strike me, please." So the man struck him,
inflicting a wound. 38 Then the prophet departed and waited for the king by the road,
and disguised himself with a bandage over
his eyes. 39 Now [r]as the king passed by, he
cried out to the king and said, "Your servant went out into the midst of the battle;
and there, a man came over and brought a
man to me, and said, 'Guard this man; if by
any means he is missing, [s]your life shall be
for his life, or else you shall [7]pay a talent of

24 [5]*positions*
25 [6]Lit. *that fell from you*
26 [i]Josh. 13:4; 2 Kin. 13:17
27 [j]Judg. 6:3-5; 1 Sam. 13:5-8
28 [k]1 Kin. 17:18 [l]1 Kin. 20:13
31 [m]Gen. 37:34; 2 Sam. 3:31
34 [n]1 Kin. 15:20
35 [o]2 Kin. 2:3, 5, 7, 15 [p]1 Kin. 13:17, 18
36 [q]1 Kin. 13:24
39 [r]2 Sam. 12:1 [s]2 Kin. 10:24 [7]Lit. *weigh*

only on level ground (v. 25). Obviously, this attitude insulted Israel's God, the Lord, who is sovereign over the whole earth (cf. 2 Kin. 19:16-19). That blasphemous depreciation of the Lord's power meant certain defeat for the Syrians (v. 28).

20:26 Aphek. Though several towns in Israel bore the name Aphek, the one mentioned here probably lay about 3 mi. E of the Sea of Galilee, N of the Yarmuk River.

20:27 like two little flocks of goats. Compared to the massive herd of Arameans covering the land, Israel looked like two little goat flocks. Goats were never seen in large flocks or scattered like sheep; hence the description of the two compact, small divisions.

20:28 man of God. *See note on 12:22.*

20:30 inner chamber. Lit. "a room in a room," a safe, well-hidden place.

20:31 sackcloth...and ropes. Sackcloth traditionally symbolized mourning and penitence. Ropes around the heads were symbols of surrender.

20:34 marketplaces. Lit. "streets, outside places." Bazaars were set up in a foreign land (cf. Neh. 13:16), a lucrative market for Israelite goods.

20:35 sons of the prophets. An association of prophets that met and possibly lived together for study, encouragement, and service (*see note on 1 Sam. 10:5*).

20:35,36 The prophet needed to be wounded as if in battle to carry out the drama. The refusal to do as the prophet said was wrong, as it was a withholding of necessary aid to a prophet of God in the discharge of his duty. It was severely punished as a warning to others (cf. 13:2-24).

20:39-43 The prophet illustrated that, just as a soldier pays dearly for losing a prisoner in war, Ahab will pay for letting Ben-Hadad, the idolatrous enemy of God, live.

20:39 a talent of silver. This was about 75 lbs. of silver, more than a common soldier could afford and for which debt he would face death.

silver.' 40 While your servant was busy
here and there, he was gone."
Then the king of Israel said to him, "So
shall your judgment *be;* you yourself have
decided *it.*"
41 And he hastened to take the bandage
away from his eyes; and the king of Israel
recognized him as one of the prophets.
42 Then he said to him, "Thus says the
LORD: [t]'Because you have let slip out of
your hand a man whom I appointed to
utter destruction, therefore your life shall
go for his life, and your people for his people.' "
43 So the king of Israel [u]went to his
house sullen and displeased, and came to
Samaria.

Naboth Is Murdered for His Vineyard

21 And it came to pass after these
things *that* Naboth the Jezreelite
had a vineyard which *was* in [a]Jezreel, next
to the palace of Ahab king of Samaria. 2 So
Ahab spoke to Naboth, saying, "Give me
your [b]vineyard, that I may have it for a
vegetable garden, because it *is* near, next to
my house; and for it I will give you a vineyard better than it. *Or,* if it seems good to
you, I will give you its worth in money."
3 But Naboth said to Ahab, "The LORD
forbid [c]that I should give the inheritance of
my fathers to you!"
4 So Ahab went into his house sullen and
displeased because of the word which
Naboth the Jezreelite had spoken to him;
for he had said, "I will not give you the inheritance of my fathers." And he lay down
on his bed, and turned away his face, and
would eat no food. 5 But [d]Jezebel his wife
came to him, and said to him, "Why is
your spirit so sullen that you eat no food?"
6 He said to her, "Because I spoke to
Naboth the Jezreelite, and said to him,
'Give me your vineyard for money; or else,
if it pleases you, I will give you *another*
vineyard for it.' And he answered, 'I will
not give you my vineyard.' "
7 Then Jezebel his wife said to him, "You
now exercise authority over Israel! Arise,
eat food, and let your heart be cheerful; I
will give you the vineyard of Naboth the
Jezreelite."
8 And she wrote letters in Ahab's name,
sealed *them* with his seal, and sent the letters to the elders and the nobles who *were*
dwelling in the city with Naboth. 9 She
wrote in the letters, saying,

> Proclaim a fast, and seat Naboth
> [1]with high honor among the
> people; 10 and seat two men,
> scoundrels, before him to bear
> witness against him, saying, You
> have [e]blasphemed God and the
> king. *Then* take him out, and [f]stone
> him, that he may die.

11 So the men of his city, the elders and
nobles who were inhabitants of his city,
did as Jezebel had sent to them, as it *was*
written in the letters which she had sent to
them. 12 [g]They proclaimed a fast, and seated Naboth with high honor among the
people. 13 And two men, scoundrels, came
in and sat before him; and the scoundrels
[h]witnessed against him, against Naboth, in
the presence of the people, saying,
"Naboth has blasphemed God and the

42 [t] 1 Kin. 22:31-37
43 [u] 1 Kin. 21:4

CHAPTER 21

1 [a] Judg. 6:33; 1 Kin. 18:45, 46
2 [b] 1 Sam. 8:14
3 [c] [Lev. 25:23; Num. 36:7; Ezek. 46:18]
5 [d] 1 Kin. 19:1, 2

9 [1] Lit. *at the head*
10 [e] [Ex. 22:28; Lev. 24:15, 16]; Acts 6:11 [f] [Lev. 24:14]
12 [g] Is. 58:4
13 [h] [Ex. 20:16; 23:1, 7]

20:40 your judgment. This "judicial parable" was designed to trap Ahab into announcing the punishment for his own crime (see 2 Sam. 12:1-12). Unknowingly, Ahab declared his own judgment (v. 42).

20:42 utter destruction. By declaring the battles to be holy war (vv. 13,22,28), the Lord had put Ben-Hadad and the Syrians under the ban, a reference to something belonging to the Lord and destined to be destroyed (Deut. 7:2; 20:16). By freeing Ben-Hadad, Ahab had disobeyed the law and would suffer the ban in place of Ben-Hadad.

20:43 sullen and displeased. Ahab was resentful and angry because of the Lord's reaction to his actions (cf. 21:4).

21:1 Jezreel. *See note on 18:45.* Ahab had built a second palace in Jezreel, where he lived when not in the capital at Samaria.

21:2 Give me your vineyard. In Canaanite culture, since land was simply a commodity to be traded and sold for profit, Ahab's offer to Naboth of an exchange of property or offer of purchase were common transactions in the Near East.

21:3 The LORD forbid. Naboth's words implied that trading or selling his property would be a disregard of the law and thus displeasing in God's eyes (cf. 1 Sam. 24:6; 26:11; 2 Sam. 23:17). The reason was that the vineyard was his ancestral property. The Lord, the owner of all of the land of Israel, had forbidden Israelite families to surrender ownership of family lands permanently (Lev. 25:23-28; Num. 36:7-9). Out of loyalty to God, Naboth declined Ahab's offer.

21:7 You now exercise authority over Israel! This statement can be taken as an exclamation or a question. Either way, Jezebel was sarcastically rebuking Ahab for not exercising absolute royal power in the matter.

21:8 she wrote letters. Written by the royal scribe, ancient letters were mainly in the form of a scroll sealed in clay or wax with the sender's personal sign. The seal made the contents of the letters a royal mandate and implied that disobedience would certainly lead to some kind of punishment.

21:9 Proclaim a fast. To call an assembly for solemn fasting implied that a disaster threatened the people that could be averted only if they would humble themselves before the Lord and remove any person whose sin had brought God's judgment upon them (cf. Judg. 20:26; 1 Sam. 7:5,6; 2 Chr. 20:2-4).

21:10 two men. The Mosaic law required two witnesses in capital cases (Num. 35:30; Deut. 17:6; 19:5). **scoundrels.** Lit. "sons of Belial." These were utterly wicked men. *See note on 1 Sam. 2:12.* **blasphemed God and the king.** The penalty for cursing God and the king was death (Ex. 22:28).

king!" [i]Then they took him outside the city
and stoned him with stones, so that he
died. 14 Then they sent to Jezebel, saying,
"Naboth has been stoned and is dead."
15 And it came to pass, when Jezebel
heard that Naboth had been stoned and
was dead, that Jezebel said to Ahab,
"Arise, take possession of the vineyard of
Naboth the Jezreelite, which he refused to
give you for money; for Naboth is not
alive, but dead." 16 So it was, when Ahab
heard that Naboth was dead, that Ahab got
up and went down to take possession of
the vineyard of Naboth the Jezreelite.

The LORD Condemns Ahab

17 [j]Then the word of the LORD came to
[k]Elijah the Tishbite, saying, 18 "Arise, go
down to meet Ahab king of Israel, [l]who
lives in Samaria. There *he is,* in the vineyard
of Naboth, where he has gone down to
take possession of it. 19 You shall speak to
him, saying, 'Thus says the LORD: "Have
you murdered and also taken possession?"' And you shall speak to him, saying, 'Thus says the LORD: [m]"In the place
where dogs licked the blood of Naboth,
dogs shall lick your blood, even yours."'"
20 So Ahab said to Elijah, [n]"Have you
found me, O my enemy?"

And he answered, "I have found *you,* because [o]you have sold yourself to do evil in
the sight of the LORD: 21 'Behold, [p]I will
bring calamity on you. I will take away
your [q]posterity, and will cut off from Ahab
[r]every male in Israel, both [s]bond and free.
22 I will make your house like the house of
[t]Jeroboam the son of Nebat, and like the
house of [u]Baasha the son of Ahijah, because of the provocation with which you
have provoked *Me* to anger, and made Israel sin.' 23 And [v]concerning Jezebel the
LORD also spoke, saying, 'The dogs shall
eat Jezebel by the [2]wall of Jezreel.' 24 The
dogs shall eat [w]whoever belongs to Ahab
and dies in the city, and the birds of the air
shall eat whoever dies in the field."
25 But [x]there was no one like Ahab who
sold himself to do wickedness in the sight
of the LORD, [y]because Jezebel his wife
[3]stirred him up. 26 And he behaved very
abominably in following idols, according
to all [z]*that* the Amorites had done, whom
the LORD had cast out before the children
of Israel.
27 So it was, when Ahab heard those
words, that he tore his clothes and [a]put
sackcloth on his body, and fasted and lay
in sackcloth, and went about mourning.
28 And the word of the LORD came to Elijah the Tishbite, saying, 29 "See how Ahab
has humbled himself before Me? Because
he [b]has humbled himself before Me, I will
not bring the calamity in his days. [c]In the
days of his son I will bring the calamity on
his house."

Micaiah Warns Ahab

22 Now three years passed without
war between Syria and Israel.
2 Then it came to pass, in the third year,
that [a]Jehoshaphat the king of Judah went
down to *visit* the king of Israel.
3 And the king of Israel said to his servants, "Do you know that [b]Ramoth in
Gilead *is* ours, but we hesitate to take it out
of the hand of the king of Syria?" 4 So he
said to Jehoshaphat, "Will you go with me
to fight at Ramoth Gilead?"
Jehoshaphat said to the king of Israel, [c]"I

13 [i]2 Kin. 9:26; 2 Chr. 24:21; Acts 7:58, 59; Heb. 11:37
17 [j][Ps. 9:12] [k]1 Kin. 19:1
18 [l]1 Kin. 13:32; 2 Chr. 22:9
19 [m]1 Kin. 22:38; 2 Kin. 9:26
20 [n]1 Kin. 18:17 [o]1 Kin. 21:25; 2 Kin. 17:17; [Rom. 7:14]
21 [p]1 Kin. 14:10; 2 Kin. 9:8 [q]2 Kin. 10:10 [r]1 Sam. 25:22 [s]1 Kin. 14:10
22 [t]1 Kin. 15:29 [u]1 Kin. 16:3, 11
23 [v]2 Kin. 9:10, 30-37 [2]So with MT, LXX; some Heb. mss., Syr., Tg., Vg. *plot of ground* instead of *wall* (cf. 2 Kin. 9:36)
24 [w]1 Kin. 14:11; 16:4
25 [x]1 Kin. 16:30-33; 21:20 [y]1 Kin. 16:31 [3]*incited him*
26 [z]Gen. 15:16; [Lev. 18:25-30]; 2 Kin. 21:11
27 [a]Gen. 37:34; 2 Sam. 3:31; 2 Kin. 6:30
29 [b][2 Kin. 22:19] [c]2 Kin. 9:25; 10:11, 17

CHAPTER 22

2 [a]1 Kin. 15:24; 2 Chr. 18:2
3 [b]Deut. 4:43; Josh. 21:38; 1 Kin. 4:13
4 [c]2 Kin. 3:7

21:13 outside the city. They hypocritically climaxed their violent murder by killing the innocent Naboth in a place that was in accordance with the Mosaic law (Lev. 24:14; Num. 15:35,36). He was stoned to death in the open fields and his sons were killed with him (2 Kin. 9:26), eliminating all possible heirs.

21:19 Elijah's first announcement of judgment applied to Ahab personally. He said that the dogs would lick Ahab's blood in the same place that Naboth died, outside the city of Jezreel. This prophecy was not fulfilled because of his repentance (vv. 27-29), but was partially fulfilled in the licking of Ahab's blood by dogs at the pool in Samaria (22:37,38).

21:21-24 Elijah's second announcement of judgment applied to Ahab and his house. The judgment was virtually identical with one made to Jeroboam (14:10,11) and similar to the one made to Baasha (16:3,4).

21:23 concerning Jezebel. Jezebel was singled out for judgment because of her initiative in driving Ahab in the promotion of Baalism (v. 25). Elijah's prophecy concerning her was literally fulfilled in 2 Kin. 9:10,30-37.

21:27 tore his clothes. The tearing of garments was a common expression of grief, terror, or repentance in the face of great personal or national calamity (Num. 14:6; Josh. 7:6; Judg. 11:35; 2 Sam. 1:2; 3:31).

21:29 days of his son. Since Ahab had truly humbled himself before the Lord, he did not see the disaster forecast for him (v. 19). Instead, God postponed it until the reign of his son, Joram, ca. 852–841 B.C. (2 Kin. 9:25,26). Joram died in the field of Naboth (cf. v. 19).

22:1 three years. Israel had peace for 3 years following the two years of war with Syria described in 20:1-34. During this peace, Ben-Hadad, Ahab, and 10 other kings formed a coalition to repel an Assyrian invasion. Assyrian records described the major battle fought at Qarqar on the Orontes River in 853 B.C. Though Assyria claimed victory, later events show that they were stopped from further advance southward at that time. With the Assyrian threat neutralized, Ahab turned his attention to the unfinished conflict with Syria.

22:2 Jehoshaphat. The king of Judah , ca. 873–848, whose reign is described in vv. 41-50. *See notes on 2 Chr. 17:1–21:3.*

22:3 Ramoth in Gilead. Ramoth was a Levitical city E of the Jordan River in Gilead, on the N border of Gad the home of Jephthah (Judg. 11:34) and a key administrative center in Solomon's kingdom (4:13). It seems to have been one of the cities that Ben-Hadad should have returned to Israel (20:34).

am as you *are,* my people as your people,
my horses as your horses." 5 Also Jehoshaphat said to the king of Israel, [d]"Please inquire for the word of the LORD today."
6 Then the king of Israel [e]gathered [1]the
prophets together, about four hundred
men, and said to them, "Shall I go against
Ramoth Gilead to fight, or shall I refrain?"
So they said, "Go up, for the Lord will
deliver *it* into the hand of the king."
7 And [f]Jehoshaphat said, "*Is there* not
still a prophet of the LORD here, that we
may inquire of [2]Him?"
8 So the king of Israel said to Jehoshaphat, "*There is* still one man, Micaiah the son
of Imlah, by whom we may inquire of the
LORD; but I hate him, because he does not
prophesy good concerning me, but evil."
And Jehoshaphat said, "Let not the king
say such things!"
9 Then the king of Israel called an officer
and said, "Bring Micaiah the son of Imlah
quickly!"
10 The king of Israel and Jehoshaphat the
king of Judah, having put on *their* robes,
sat each on his throne, at a threshing floor
at the entrance of the gate of Samaria; and
all the prophets prophesied before them.
11 Now Zedekiah the son of Chenaanah
had made [g]horns of iron for himself; and
he said, "Thus says the LORD: 'With these
you shall [h]gore the Syrians until they are
destroyed.' " 12 And all the prophets
prophesied so, saying, "Go up to Ramoth
Gilead and prosper, for the LORD will deliver *it* into the king's hand."
13 Then the messenger who had gone to
call Micaiah spoke to him, saying, "Now
listen, the words of the prophets with one
accord encourage the king. Please, let your
word be like the word of one of them, and
speak encouragement."
14 And Micaiah said, "*As* the LORD lives,
[i]whatever the LORD says to me, that I will
speak."
15 Then he came to the king; and the king
said to him, "Micaiah, shall we go to war
against Ramoth Gilead, or shall we refrain?"
And he answered him, "Go and prosper,
for the LORD will deliver *it* into the hand of
the king!"
16 So the king said to him, "How many
times shall I make you swear that you tell
me nothing but the truth in the name of the
LORD?"
17 Then he said, "I saw all Israel [j]scat-
tered on the mountains, as sheep that have
no shepherd. And the LORD said, 'These
have no master. Let each return to his
house in peace.' "
18 And the king of Israel said to Jehoshaphat, "Did I not tell you he would not
prophesy good concerning me, but evil?"
19 Then *Micaiah* said, "Therefore hear the
word of the LORD: [k]I saw the LORD sitting
on His throne, [l]and all the host of heaven
standing by, on His right hand and on His
left. 20 And the LORD said, 'Who will persuade Ahab to go up, that he may fall at
Ramoth Gilead?' So one spoke in this manner, and another spoke in that manner.
21 Then a spirit came forward and stood
before the LORD, and said, 'I will persuade
him.' 22 The LORD said to him, 'In what
way?' So he said, 'I will go out and be a
lying spirit in the mouth of all his
prophets.' And the LORD said, [m]'You shall
persuade *him,* and also prevail. Go out and
do so.' 23 [n]Therefore look! The LORD has
put a lying spirit in the mouth of all these
prophets of yours, and the LORD has declared disaster against you."
24 Now Zedekiah the son of Chenaanah
went near and [o]struck Micaiah on the cheek,

5 [d] 2 Kin. 3:11
6 [e] 1 Kin. 18:19 [1] The false prophets
7 [f] 2 Kin. 3:11 [2] Or *him*
11 [g] Zech. 1:18-21 [h] Deut. 33:17
14 [i] Num. 22:38; 24:13
17 [j] Num. 27:17; 1 Kin. 22:34-36; 2 Chr. 18:16; Matt. 9:36; Mark 6:34
19 [k] Is. 6:1; Ezek. 1:26-28; Dan. 7:9 [l] Job 1:6; 2:1; Ps. 103:20; Dan. 7:10; Zech. 1:10; [Matt. 18:10; Heb. 1:7, 14]
22 [m] Judg. 9:23; 1 Sam. 16:14; 18:10; 19:9; Job 12:16; [Ezek. 14:9; 2 Thess. 2:11]
23 [n] [Ezek. 14:9]
24 [o] Jer. 20:2

22:5 inquire for the word of the LORD. Jehoshaphat was willing to help Ahab fight Syria (v. 4), but reminded Ahab of the need to seek the will of the Lord before going into battle (cf. 1 Sam. 23:1-5,9-13; 2 Sam. 2:1; 5:19-25; 2 Kin. 3:11-20).

22:6 prophets. These 400 prophets of Ahab were not true prophets of the Lord. They worshiped at Bethel in the golden-calf center set up by Jeroboam (12:28,29) and were supported by Ahab, whose religious policy also permitted Baal worship. Their words were designed to please Ahab (v. 8), so they refused to begin with the authoritative "thus says the LORD" and did not use the covenant name for Israel's God, "LORD."

22:7 a prophet of the LORD. Jehoshaphat recognized that the 400 prophets were not true prophets of the Lord, and wished to hear from a true prophet.

22:8 Micaiah. His name means "Who is like the LORD?"

22:10 throne. A portable, high-backed chair made of wood with arm rests and separate foot stool.

22:11 Zedekiah. He was the spokesman for the false prophets. In contrast to v. 6, he used the introductory formula and God's covenant name.

22:15 Go and prosper. Micaiah sarcastically repeated the message of the false prophets as he had been encouraged to do (v. 13). Ahab clearly sensed the sarcasm and demanded that Micaiah tell him the truth (v. 16).

22:17 sheep that have no shepherd. The image of the king as a shepherd and his people as the sheep was a familiar one (Num. 27:16,17; Zech. 13:7). Micaiah's point was that Israel's shepherd, King Ahab, would be killed and his army scattered.

22:22 a lying spirit. This must be Satan, whom the Lord allowed to speak through 400 demons who indwelt the 400 false prophets.

22:24 struck...on the cheek. This was a rebuke by the leader of the false prophets (v. 6) for the perceived insolence of Micaiah and his claim to truly speak for God. It was followed by a sarcastic question asking if the prophet could tell which direction the spirit in Zedekiah had gone.

and said, [p]"Which way did the spirit from
the LORD go from me to speak to you?"
25 And Micaiah said, "Indeed, you shall
see on that day when you go into an [q]inner
chamber to hide!"
26 So the king of Israel said, "Take Micaiah, and return him to Amon the governor of the city and to Joash the king's son;
27 and say, 'Thus says the king: "Put this
fellow in [r]prison, and feed him with bread
of affliction and water of affliction, until I
come in peace." ' "
28 But Micaiah said, "If you ever return
in peace, [s]the LORD has not spoken by me."
And he said, "Take heed, all you people!"

Ahab Dies in Battle

29 So the king of Israel and Jehoshaphat
the king of Judah went up to Ramoth Gilead. 30 And the king of Israel said to Jehoshaphat, "I will disguise myself and go
into battle; but you put on your robes." So
the king of Israel [t]disguised himself and
went into battle.
31 Now the [u]king of Syria had commanded the thirty-two [v]captains of his
chariots, saying, "Fight with no one small
or great, but only with the king of Israel."
32 So it was, when the captains of the chariots saw Jehoshaphat, that they said, "Surely it *is* the king of Israel!" Therefore they
turned aside to fight against him, and Jehoshaphat [w]cried out. 33 And it happened,
when the captains of the chariots saw that
it *was* not the king of Israel, that they
turned back from pursuing him. 34 Now a
certain man drew a bow at random, and
struck the king of Israel between the joints
of his armor. So he said to the driver of his
chariot, "Turn around and take me out of
the battle, for I am wounded."
35 The battle increased that day; and the
king was propped up in his chariot, facing
the Syrians, and died at evening. The
blood ran out from the wound onto the
floor of the chariot. 36 Then, as the sun was
going down, a shout went throughout the
army, saying, "Every man to his city, and
every man to his own country!"
37 So the king died, and was brought to
Samaria. And they buried the king in Samaria. 38 Then *someone* washed the chariot
at a pool in Samaria, and the dogs licked
up his blood while [3]the harlots bathed, according [x]to the word of the LORD which He
had spoken.
39 Now the rest of the acts of Ahab, and
all that he did, [y]the ivory house which he
built and all the cities that he built, *are* they
not written in the book of the chronicles of
the kings of Israel? 40 So Ahab [4]rested with
his fathers. Then [z]Ahaziah his son reigned
in his place.

Jehoshaphat Reigns in Judah

41 [a]Jehoshaphat the son of Asa had become king over Judah in the fourth year of
Ahab king of Israel. 42 Jehoshaphat *was*
thirty-five years old when he became king,
and he reigned twenty-five years in Jerusalem. His mother's name *was* Azubah the
daughter of Shilhi. 43 And [b]he walked in
all the ways of his father Asa. He did not
turn aside from them, doing *what was* right
in the eyes of the LORD. Nevertheless [c]the
high places were not taken away, *for* the
people offered sacrifices and burned incense on the high places. 44 Also [d]Jehosha-
phat made [e]peace with the king of Israel.
45 Now the rest of the acts of Jehoshaphat, the might that he showed, and how
he made war, *are* they not written [f]in the
book of the chronicles of the kings of Judah? 46 [g]And the rest of the [5]perverted
persons, who remained in the days of his
father Asa, he banished from the land.

24 [p]2 Chr. 18:23
25 [q]1 Kin. 20:30
27 [r]2 Chr. 16:10; 18:25-27
28 [s]Num. 16:29; Deut. 18:20-22
30 [t]2 Chr. 35:22
31 [u]1 Kin. 20:1 [v]1 Kin. 20:24; 2 Chr. 18:30
32 [w]2 Chr. 18:31
38 [x]1 Kin. 21:19 [3]Tg., Syr. *they washed his armor*
39 [y]Ps. 45:8; Amos 3:15
40 [z]2 Kin. 1:2, 18 [4]Died and joined his ancestors
41 [a]2 Chr. 20:31
43 [b]2 Chr. 17:3; 20:32, 33 [c]1 Kin. 14:23; 15:14; 2 Kin. 12:3
44 [d]2 Chr. 19:2 [e]2 Chr. 18:1
45 [f]2 Chr. 20:34
46 [g]Gen. 19:5; Deut. 23:17; 1 Kin. 14:24; 15:12; 2 Kin. 23:7; Jude 7 [5]Heb. *qadesh*, one practicing sodomy and prostitution in religious rituals

22:28 If you ever return. In accordance with Deut. 18:21,22, Micaiah declared to Ahab that if he lived to return from the battle, then he had uttered a false prophecy.

22:30 disguise myself. Rejecting the prophecy, but fearing it also, Ahab decided not to wear his official robe, but the clothes of an ordinary soldier.

22:31 only with the king of Israel. The very Syrian king, Ben-Hadad, whose life Ahab had spared (20:34), ungratefully singled him out for death.

22:32 Jehoshaphat cried out. According to 2 Chr. 18:31, this was a prayer for the Lord's deliverance. Jehoshaphat's cry showed the Syrians that he was not Ahab.

22:34 at random. The Syrian bowman shot at an Israelite soldier, not knowing that it was the disguised Ahab. The arrow found a small groove between the breastplate and the flexible scale armor that covered the lower abdomen and thighs. Instantly, Ahab slumped in his chariot, mortally wounded in the stomach and bleeding to death.

22:38 while the harlots bathed. The Heb. text may read "where" or "while." In either case, the point is the same: Ahab, the spiritual harlot (i.e., idolater), was associated with the physical harlots at his death. **according to the word of the LORD.** Ahab's death fulfilled the prophecies spoken by Elijah (21:19) and Micaiah (v. 17).

22:39 the ivory house. Ahab's palace at Samaria had internal walled panels that were made of inlaid ivory, indicative of his kingdom's economic prosperity. **cities that he built.** Archeological excavations show that Ahab strengthened the fortifications of Samaria, Megiddo, and Hazor.

22:41 fourth year. A reference to the beginning of Jehoshaphat's reign, after being co-regent with his father Asa, in 870 B.C.

22:42 twenty-five years. 873–848 B.C.

22:43 doing *what was* right. Jehoshaphat faithfully followed in his father Asa's footsteps, doing what pleased the Lord. His only fault, like that of his father, was his failure to close down the high places.

22:44 made peace. In 2 Chr. 19:2, Jehu the prophet rebuked Jehoshaphat for this alliance.

22:45 made war. See 2 Kin. 3:7-27; 2 Chr. 17:11; 20:1-30.

47 [h]*There was* then no king in Edom, only a deputy of the king.

48 [i]Jehoshaphat [j]made [6]merchant ships to go to [k]Ophir for gold; [l]but they never sailed, for the ships were wrecked at [m]Ezion Geber. 49 Then Ahaziah the son of Ahab said to Jehoshaphat, "Let my servants go with your servants in the ships." But Jehoshaphat would not.

50 And [n]Jehoshaphat [7]rested with his fathers, and was buried with his fathers in the City of David his father. Then Jehoram his son reigned in his place.

47 [h] 2 Sam. 8:14; 2 Kin. 3:9; 8:20
48 [i] 2 Chr. 20:35-37 [j] 1 Kin. 10:22 [k] 1 Kin. 9:28 [l] 2 Chr. 20:37 [m] 1 Kin. 9:26 [6] Or *ships of Tarshish*
50 [n] 2 Chr. 21:1 [7] Died and joined his ancestors
51 [o] 1 Kin. 22:40
52 [p] 1 Kin. 15:26; 21:25
53 [q] Judg. 2:11 [r] 1 Kin. 16:30-32 [8] In the same way that

Ahaziah Reigns in Israel

51 [o]Ahaziah the son of Ahab became king over Israel in Samaria in the seventeenth year of Jehoshaphat king of Judah, and reigned two years over Israel. 52 He did evil in the sight of the LORD, and [p]walked in the way of his father and in the way of his mother and in the way of Jeroboam the son of Nebat, who had made Israel sin; 53 for [q]he served Baal and worshiped him, and provoked the LORD God of Israel to anger, [r]according [8] to all that his father had done.

22:47-49 Jehoshaphat controlled Edom, which gave him access to Ezion Geber. He sought to emulate Solomon's fleet and wealth (9:26-28), but was unsuccessful. According to 2 Chr. 20:36, 37, the Lord destroyed his fleet because of Jehoshaphat's alliance to build it with Ahaziah, king of Israel. First Kings 22: 49 apparently refers to a subsequent attempt by Ahaziah to continue the joint venture after the disaster.

22:51–2 Kin. 1:18 Ahaziah…two years. 853–852 B.C.

22:53 he served Baal. Ahaziah continued the official promotion of Baal worship (cf. 16:31,32). First Kings ends at this point in the middle of Ahaziah's reign which is picked up in 2 Kin. 1:1-18. The explanation for this unusual break is found in Introduction: Title.

The Second Book of the KINGS[1]

God Judges Ahaziah

1 Moab [a]rebelled against Israel[b] after the
death of Ahab.
2 Now [c]Ahaziah fell through the lattice
of his upper room in Samaria, and was injured; so he sent messengers and said to
them, "Go, inquire of [d]Baal-Zebub,[1] the
god of [e]Ekron, whether I shall recover
from this injury." 3 But the [2]angel of the
LORD said to Elijah the Tishbite, "Arise, go
up to meet the messengers of the king of
Samaria, and say to them, '*Is it* because
there is no God in Israel *that* you are going
to inquire of Baal-Zebub, the god of
Ekron?' 4 Now therefore, thus says the
LORD: 'You shall not come down from the
bed to which you have gone up, but you
shall surely die.' " So Elijah departed.
5 And when the messengers returned to
[3]him, he said to them, "Why have you
come back?"
6 So they said to him, "A man came up to
meet us, and said to us, 'Go, return to the
king who sent you, and say to him, "Thus
says the LORD: '*Is it* because *there is* no God
in Israel *that* you are sending to inquire of
Baal-Zebub, the god of Ekron? Therefore
you shall not come down from the bed to
which you have gone up, but you shall
surely die.' " ' "
7 Then he said to them, "What kind of
man *was it* who came up to meet you and
told you these words?"
8 So they answered him, [f]"A hairy man
wearing a leather belt around his waist."
And he said, [g]"It *is* Elijah the Tishbite."
9 Then the king sent to him a captain of
fifty with his fifty men. So he went up to
him; and there he was, sitting on the top of
a hill. And he spoke to him: "Man of God,
the king has said, 'Come down!' "
10 So Elijah answered and said to the
captain of fifty, "If I *am* a man of God,
then [h]let fire come down from heaven
and consume you and your fifty men."
And fire came down from heaven and
consumed him and his fifty. 11 Then he
sent to him another captain of fifty with
his fifty men.
And he answered and said to him: "Man
of God, thus has the king said, 'Come
down quickly!' "

Title [1] See 1 Kings for the Introductory Discussion and Outline.

CHAPTER 1

1 [a] 2 Sam. 8:2 [b] 2 Kin. 3:5
2 [c] 1 Kin. 22:40 [d] 2 Kin. 1:3, 6, 16; Matt. 10:25; Mark 3:22 [e] 1 Sam. 5:10 [1] Lit. *Lord of Flies*
3 [2] Or *Angel*
5 [3] Ahaziah
8 [f] Zech. 13:4; Matt. 3:4; Mark 1:6 [g] 1 Kin. 18:7
10 [h] 1 Kin. 18:36-38; Luke 9:54

1:1 Moab rebelled. *See notes on Gen. 19:37,38;* Introduction to Ruth: Background and Setting; cf. 3:4-27.

1:2 Ahaziah. This king of the northern kingdom of Israel is not to be confused with Ahaziah of Judah (8:25–9:29). **lattice of his upper room.** Ahaziah's rooftop room was enclosed with crossbars of interwoven reed or wood strips, which shut out direct sunlight while letting in cool breezes. It was not sturdy enough to keep Ahaziah from falling to the ground below (for unexplained reasons). This took place ca. 852 B.C. **Baal-Zebub.** This was a local expression of the Baal cult at Ekron (*see note on 1 Kin. 16:31,32*). Baal-Zebub meant "lord of the flies," suggesting that he was the storm god who controlled diseases brought by flies. On the other hand, the name may have been the sarcastic Israelite parody of Baal-Zebul, meaning "prince Baal" or "exalted lord," a common title for Baal in extrabiblical Canaanite texts. The NT preserved the name in the form Beelzebul, a name for Satan, the prince of the demons (Matt. 10:25; 12:24; Mark 3:22; Luke 11:15). **Ekron.** The northernmost of the major Philistine cities, located about 22 mi. W of Jerusalem (*see note on 1 Sam. 5:10*).

1:3 the angel of the LORD. Although some interpret this as a reference to the pre-incarnate Christ (e.g., Gen. 16:7-14; Judg. 2:1-4; *see note on Ex. 3:2*), probably here the reference is to an angelic messenger, like the one sent earlier by the Lord to Elijah (cf. 19:35; 1 Kin. 19:7). The Lord's messenger was in contrast to the messengers of the wicked king (vv. 2,3,5). **Elijah.** The record of this unusual prophet to Israel begins in 1 Kin. 17:1 and extends to 2 Kin. 2:11 (*see note on 1 Kin. 17:1*).

1:4 you shall surely die. The Lord's punishment on Ahaziah for consulting a false god instead of the true God was that he would fail to recover from his injuries. This was a merciful application of the Mosaic Law (cf. Ex. 22:20), which demanded death. Cf. vv. 16,17.

1:8 A hairy man. Lit. "possessor of hair." This has been interpreted in two ways: 1) Elijah was physically hairy; or 2) Elijah wore a garment made of hair. The language supports the second viewpoint that Elijah wore a coarse wool garment girded at the waist with a leather belt. Zechariah 13:4 describes such a garment as belonging to prophets (cf. Matt. 7:15). Further, the NT describes John the Baptist, who came in the spirit and likeness of Elijah, as clothed in camel's hair (Matt. 3:4).

1:9 Man of God. A technical title for a man who spoke for God. *See notes on Deut. 33:1; 1 Kin. 12:22; 1 Tim. 6:11.*

1:10-12 fire came down from heaven. This was the proof that Elijah was a prophet of the Lord and entitled to respect. Additionally, it was an indication that Elijah was like Moses, who also was validated as the Lord's prophet by fire from heaven (Num. 16:35).

12 So Elijah answered and said to them,
"If I *am* a man of God, let fire come down
from heaven and consume you and your
fifty men." And the fire of God came down
from heaven and consumed him and his
fifty.
13 Again, he sent a third captain of fifty
with his fifty men. And the third captain of
fifty went up, and came and [4]fell on his
knees before Elijah, and pleaded with him,
and said to him: "Man of God, please let
my life and the life of these fifty servants of
yours [i]be precious in your sight. 14 Look,
fire has come down from heaven and
burned up the first two captains of fifties
with their fifties. But let my life now be
precious in your sight."
15 And the [5]angel of the LORD said to Elijah, "Go down with him; do not be afraid
of him." So he arose and went down with
him to the king. 16 Then he said to him,
"Thus says the LORD: 'Because you have
sent messengers to inquire of Baal-Zebub,
the god of Ekron, *is it* because *there is* no
God in Israel to inquire of His word?
Therefore you shall not come down from
the bed to which you have gone up, but
you shall surely die.' "
17 So *Ahaziah* died according to the word
of the LORD which Elijah had spoken. Because he had no son, [j]Jehoram[6] became
king in his place, in the second year of Jehoram the son of Jehoshaphat, king of Judah.
18 Now the rest of the acts of Ahaziah
which he did, *are* they not written in the
book of the chronicles of the kings of Israel?

13 [i] 1 Sam. 26:21; Ps. 72:14 [4] Lit. *bowed down*
15 [5] Or *Angel*
17 [j] 1 Kin. 22:50; 2 Kin. 8:16; Matt. 1:8 [6] The son of Ahab king of Israel, 2 Kin. 3:1

CHAPTER 2

1 [a] Gen. 5:24; [Heb. 11:5] [b] 1 Kin. 19:16-21
2 [c] Ruth 1:15, 16 [d] 1 Sam. 1:26; 2 Kin. 2:4, 6; 4:30
3 [e] 1 Kin. 20:35; 2 Kin. 2:5, 7, 15; 4:1, 38; 9:1 [1] Lit. *from your head*
8 [f] Ex. 14:21, 22; Josh. 3:16; 2 Kin. 2:14

Elijah Ascends to Heaven

2 And it came to pass, when the LORD
was about to [a]take up Elijah into heav-
en by a whirlwind, that Elijah went with
[b]Elisha from Gilgal. 2 Then Elijah said to
Elisha, [c]"Stay here, please, for the LORD
has sent me on to Bethel."
But Elisha said, "*As* the LORD lives, and
[d]*as* your soul lives, I will not leave you!" So
they went down to Bethel.
3 Now [e]the sons of the prophets who
were at Bethel came out to Elisha, and said
to him, "Do you know that the LORD will
take away your master [1]from over you
today?"
And he said, "Yes, I know; keep silent!"
4 Then Elijah said to him, "Elisha, stay
here, please, for the LORD has sent me on to
Jericho."
But he said, "*As* the LORD lives, and *as*
your soul lives, I will not leave you!" So
they came to Jericho.
5 Now the sons of the prophets who *were*
at Jericho came to Elisha and said to him,
"Do you know that the LORD will take
away your master from over you today?"
So he answered, "Yes, I know; keep
silent!"
6 Then Elijah said to him, "Stay here,
please, for the LORD has sent me on to the
Jordan."
But he said, "*As* the LORD lives, and *as*
your soul lives, I will not leave you!" So
the two of them went on. 7 And fifty men
of the sons of the prophets went and stood
facing *them* at a distance, while the two of
them stood by the Jordan. 8 Now Elijah
took his mantle, rolled *it* up, and struck the
water; and [f]it was divided this way and

1:15 angel of the LORD. *See note on 1:3.*

1:16 Baal-Zebub. *See note on 1:2.*

1:17 Jehoram...Jehoram. The first Jehoram mentioned here was, like Ahaziah (1 Kin. 22:51), a son of Ahab (3:1), who ruled over the northern kingdom of Israel for 12 years, ca. 852–841 B.C. (*see note on 3:1*). The second Jehoram mentioned was the son and successor to Jehoshaphat, who ruled in the southern kingdom of Judah, ca. 853–841 B.C. (cf. 8:16-24). **second year.** Ca. 852 B.C. This was the second year of Jehoram of Judah's co-regency with Jehoshaphat his father (*see notes on 3:1; 8:17; 2 Chr. 21:4-20*).

2:1 by a whirlwind. Lit. "in the whirlwind." This was a reference to the specific storm with lightning and thunder in which Elijah was taken to heaven (v. 11). The Lord's presence was connected with a whirlwind in Job 38:1; 40:6; Jer. 23:19; 25:32; 30:23; Zech. 9:14. **Elisha.** The record of this prophet, who was the successor to Elijah, begins in 1 Kin. 19:16 and extends to his death in 2 Kin. 13:20 (*see note on 1 Kin. 19:16*). **Gilgal.** Although some take this to be the Gilgal located W of the Jordan River near Jericho (cf. Josh. 4:19; 5:9), the close affinity to Bethel (v. 2) and its distance from Jericho (v. 4) seem to indicate that the Gilgal mentioned here was located in the hill country of Ephraim about 7 mi. N of Bethel.

2:2 Bethel. A town in Benjamin about 8 mi. N of Jerusalem, where one of Israel's false worship centers was located (*see note on 1 Kin. 12:29*).

2:3 the sons of the prophets. *See note on 1 Kin. 20:35.* **take away.** The same term was used of Enoch's translation to heaven in Gen. 5:24. The question from the sons of the prophets implied that the Lord had revealed Elijah's imminent departure to them. Elisha's response that he didn't need to hear about it ("keep silent") explicitly stated that Elijah's departure had been revealed by the Lord to him also (cf. v. 5). **from over you.** I.e., from supervising you, an allusion to the habit of students sitting beneath the feet of their master, elevated on a platform. Elisha would soon change from being Elijah's assistant to serving as the leader among the prophets.

2:4 Jericho. A city about 14 mi. SE of Bethel in the Jordan River Valley (cf. Josh. 2:1; 6:1), to which Elisha accompanied Elijah (cf. v. 6).

2:8 water...was divided. Elijah rolled up his cloak into a kind of rod and struck the water of the Jordan River. Immediately, the water parted, leaving a dry path through the river bed for the two prophets to cross. Elijah's act recalled Moses' parting of the Red Sea with his rod (Ex. 14:21,22) and the parting of the Jordan when Israel crossed over into the Land (Josh. 3:14-17). The crossing put Elijah on the Jordan's E bank, the area where Moses' life came to an end (Deut. 34:1-6).

that, so that the two of them crossed over
on dry [g]ground.
9 And so it was, when they had crossed
over, that Elijah said to Elisha, "Ask! What
may I do for you, before I am taken away
from you?"
Elisha said, "Please let a double portion
of your spirit be upon me."
10 So he said, "You have asked a hard
thing. *Nevertheless,* if you see me *when I am*
taken from you, it shall be so for you; but if
not, it shall not be *so.*" 11 Then it happened,
as they continued on and talked, that suddenly [h]a chariot of fire *appeared* with horses of fire, and separated the two of them;
and Elijah [i]went up by a whirlwind into
heaven.
12 And Elisha saw *it,* and he cried out,
[j]"My father, my father, the chariot of Israel
and its horsemen!" So he saw him no
more. And he took hold of his own clothes
and tore them into two pieces. 13 He also
took up the mantle of Elijah that had fallen
from him, and went back and stood by the
bank of the Jordan. 14 Then he took the
mantle of Elijah that had fallen from him,
and struck the water, and said, "Where *is*
the LORD God of Elijah?" And when he also
had struck the water, [k]it was divided this
way and that; and Elisha crossed over.
15 Now when the sons of the prophets
who *were* [l]from[2] Jericho saw him, they
said, "The spirit of Elijah rests on Elisha."
And they came to meet him, and bowed to
the ground before him. 16 Then they said
to him, "Look now, there are fifty strong
men with your servants. Please let them go
and search for your master, [m]lest perhaps
the Spirit of the LORD has taken him up and
cast him upon some mountain or into
some valley."
And he said, "You shall not send anyone."
17 But when they urged him till he was
[n]ashamed, he said, "Send *them!*" Therefore
they sent fifty men, and they searched for
three days but did not find him. 18 And
when they came back to him, for he had
stayed in Jericho, he said to them, "Did I
not say to you, 'Do not go'?"

Elisha Performs Miracles

19 Then the men of the city said to Elisha, "Please notice, the situation of this
city *is* pleasant, as my lord sees; but the
water *is* bad, and the ground barren."
20 And he said, "Bring me a new bowl,
and put salt in it." So they brought *it* to
him. 21 Then he went out to the source of
the water, and [o]cast in the salt there, and
said, "Thus says the LORD: 'I have [3]healed
this water; from it there shall be no more
death or barrenness.' " 22 So the water remains [p]healed to this day, according to the
word of Elisha which he spoke.
23 Then he went up from there to Bethel;
and as he was going up the road, some
youths came from the city and mocked

8 [g] Josh. 3:17
11 [h] 2 Kin. 6:17; Ps. 104:4 [i] Gen. 5:24; Heb. 11:5
12 [j] 2 Kin. 13:14
14 [k] 2 Kin. 2:8
15 [l] 2 Kin. 2:7 [2] *Or at Jericho opposite him saw*
16 [m] 1 Kin. 18:12; Ezek. 8:3; Acts 8:39
17 [n] 2 Kin. 8:11
21 [o] Ex. 15:25, 26; 2 Kin. 4:41; 6:6; John 9:6 [3] *purified*
22 [p] Ezek. 47:8, 9

2:9 a double portion. In Israel, the firstborn son inherited a double share of his father's possessions and with it the right of succession (Deut. 21:17). "A double portion of your spirit" was not merely Elisha's request to succeed Elijah in his prophetic ministry, since the Lord had already revealed this succession in 1 Kin. 19:16-21. Nor was it Elisha's desire for ministry superior to Elijah's, though Elisha did, in fact, do twice as many recorded miracles as Elijah. Apparently, Elisha was asking to succeed Elijah in the prophetic office, as God had promised, with spiritual power beyond his own capabilities to meet the responsibilities of his position as Elijah's successor. He desired that Elijah's mighty power might continue to live through him.

2:10 a hard thing. Since only God can give spiritual power, Elijah did not have the ability to grant Elisha's request. Elijah told Elisha that if Elisha saw his departure, it would be the sign that God Himself would grant Elisha's request.

2:11 chariot of fire...with horses of fire. The horse-drawn chariot was the fastest means of transport and the mightiest means of warfare in that day. Thus, the chariot and horses symbolized God's powerful protection, which was the true safety of Israel (v. 12). As earthly kingdoms are dependent for their defense on such military force as represented by horses and chariots, one single prophet had done more by God's power to preserve his nation than all their military preparations.

2:12 My father. The sons of the prophet recognized the leader of their company as their spiritual father. This title of respect for a person of authority (Gen. 45:8; Judg. 17:10) was later used for Elisha (6:21; 13:14).

2:13 the mantle of Elijah. Elijah's cloak (*see note on 1:8*), picked up by Elisha, authenticated him as Elijah's legitimate spiritual successor.

2:14 water...was divided. Elisha repeated the action of Elijah (v. 8) in using the cloak to immediately part the waters of the Jordan River, allowing Elisha to recross on dry land. This confirmed that Elisha had received from God the same great power as his master, Elijah.

2:15 bowed to the ground. This action symbolized the submission of the prophets to the preeminence of Elisha as the prophet in Israel.

2:16 They knew that when souls went into God's presence at death, bodies remained on earth. Out of sensitivity to the body of Elijah, they wanted to retrieve it for appropriate care. Elisha knew Elijah's body would not be left behind, because he had seen his bodily ascension (v. 11) while the others had not, so he said, "No."

2:17 ashamed. In 8:11 and Judg. 3:25, this term was used for the feeling of embarrassment under the unrelenting pressure of their request. But with shame for his own failure to believe what he had seen, Elisha was also embarrassed for the prophets, knowing the futile outcome of their search (v. 18). Cf. 1 Kin. 18:12.

2:20,21 bowl...salt. Salt purifies water, but the small amount used there could not clean the whole water supply. Rather, the use of salt from a new bowl symbolized the cleansing of the waters that God would miraculously do. The healing of Jericho's water, through Elisha, freed the city from Joshua's curse, making it habitable for humans once again (cf. Josh. 6:26; 1 Kin. 16:34).

2:23 youths. These were not children, but infidels and idolatrous young men in their late teens or twenties (cf. Gen. 22:12; 37:2; 1 Kin

him, and said to him, "Go up, you baldhead! Go up, you baldhead!"
24 So he turned around and looked at
them, and [q]pronounced a curse on them in
the name of the LORD. And two female
bears came out of the woods and mauled
forty-two of the youths.
25 Then he went from there to [r]Mount
Carmel, and from there he returned to Samaria.

Moab Rebels Against Israel

3 Now [a]Jehoram the son of Ahab became king over Israel at Samaria in the
eighteenth year of Jehoshaphat king of Judah, and reigned twelve years. 2 And he
did evil in the sight of the LORD, but not
like his father and mother; for he put away
the *sacred* pillar of Baal [b]that his father had
made. 3 Nevertheless he persisted in [c]the
sins of Jeroboam the son of Nebat, who
had made Israel sin; he did not depart
from them.
4 Now Mesha king of Moab was a sheepbreeder, and he [d]regularly paid the king of
Israel one hundred thousand [e]lambs and the
wool of one hundred thousand rams. 5 But it
happened, when [f]Ahab died, that the king
of Moab rebelled against the king of Israel.
6 So King Jehoram went out of Samaria
at that time and mustered all Israel. 7 Then
he went and sent to Jehoshaphat king of
Judah, saying, "The king of Moab has rebelled against me. Will you go with me to
fight against Moab?"
And he said, "I will go up; [g]I *am* as you
are, my people as your people, my horses
as your horses." 8 Then he said, "Which
way shall we go up?"
And he answered, "By way of the
Wilderness of Edom."
9 So the king of Israel went with the king
of Judah and the king of Edom, and they
marched on that roundabout route seven
days; and there was no water for the army,
nor for the animals that followed them.
10 And the king of Israel said, "Alas! For the
LORD has called these three kings together
to deliver them into the hand of Moab."
11 But [h]Jehoshaphat said, "*Is there* no
prophet of the LORD here, that we may inquire of the LORD by him?"
So one of the servants of the king of Israel answered and said, "Elisha the son of
Shaphat *is* here, who [i]poured[1] water on
the hands of Elijah."
12 And Jehoshaphat said, "The word of
the LORD is with him." So the king of Israel
and Jehoshaphat and the king of Edom
[j]went down to him.
13 Then Elisha said to the king of Israel,
[k]"What have I to do with you? [l]Go to [m]the

24 [q] Deut. 27:13-26
25 [r] 1 Kin. 18:19, 20; 2 Kin. 4:25

CHAPTER 3

1 [a] 2 Kin. 1:17
2 [b] 1 Kin. 16:31, 32
3 [c] 1 Kin. 12:28-32
4 [d] 2 Sam. 8:2 [e] Is. 16:1, 2
5 [f] 2 Kin. 1:1
7 [g] 1 Kin. 22:4
11 [h] 1 Kin. 22:7 [i] 1 Kin. 19:21; [John 13:4, 5, 13, 14] [1] Was the personal servant of
12 [j] 2 Kin. 2:25
13 [k] [Ezek. 14:3] [l] Judg. 10:14; Ruth 1:15 [m] 1 Kin. 22:6-11

20:14,15). **baldhead.** Baldness was regarded as a disgrace (cf. Is. 3:17,24). The baldness of Elisha referred to here may be: 1) natural loss of hair; 2) a shaved head denoting his separation to the prophetic office; or more likely, 3) an epithet of scorn and contempt, Elijah not being literally bald. These youths were sarcastically taunting and insulting the Lord's prophet by telling him to repeat Elijah's translation ("go up").

2:24 pronounced a curse. Because these young people of about 20 years of age or older (the same term is used of Solomon in 1 Kin. 3:7) so despised the prophet of the Lord, Elisha called upon the Lord to deal with the rebels as He saw fit. The Lord's punishment was the mauling of 42 youths by two female bears. The penalty was clearly justified, for to ridicule Elisha was to ridicule the Lord Himself. The gravity of the penalty mirrored the gravity of the crime. The appalling judgment was God's warning to any and all who attempted to interfere with the newly invested prophet's ministry.

2:25 Mount Carmel. For the location, *see note on 1 Kin. 18:19.* Elisha associated his prophetic ministry with Elijah's stand against Baalism. **Samaria.** The capital city of the northern kingdom, located in central Palestine (cf. 1 Kin. 16:24).

3:1 Jehoram. *See note on 1:17.* He was Ahaziah's brother (1 Kin. 22:51). **eighteenth year.** Ca. 852 B.C. This was Jehoshaphat of Judah's 18th year of rule after the death of his father Asa in 870 B.C. Jehoshaphat was co-regent with Asa from 873–870 B.C. Jehoshaphat's son Jehoram was co-regent with his father from 853–848 B.C. (*see notes on 1:17; 8:17*). **twelve years.** 852–841 B.C.

3:2 pillar of Baal. This was probably an image of the god Baal that King Ahab had made and placed in the temple he built to Baal (1 Kin. 16:32,33). This image was only put in storage, not permanently destroyed, because it reappeared at the end of Jehoram's reign (10:26,27).

3:3 Jeroboam. Ca. 931–910 B.C. *See notes on 1 Kin. 11:26–14:20; 2 Chr. 9:29–13:20.*

3:4 Mesha king of Moab. According to the Moabite Stone (discovered at Dihon, Moab, in A.D. 1868 and dated to ca. 840–820 B.C.), Moab, which is located E of the Dead Sea between the Arnon River and the Brook Zered, had been Israel's vassal since Omri (ca. 880 B.C.). Moab's king, Mesha, was a sheep breeder (cf. Amos 1:1) who supplied the king of Israel with lambs and wool. This was Moab's annual tribute to the Israelite king.

3:5 Moab rebelled. Mesha used Ahab's death as an opportunity to cast off the political domination of Israel with its heavy economic burden. Moab's rebellion took place in 853 B.C. during the reign of Ahaziah (1:1). Jehoram determined to put down Moab's rebellion upon his accession to Israel's throne in 852 B.C. He mobilized Israel for war (v. 6) and asked Jehoshaphat of Judah to join him in the battle (v. 7).

3:8 the Wilderness of Edom. This was the long and circuitous route by the lower bend of the Dead Sea, the arid land in the great depression S of the sea known as the Arabah, or an area of marshes on Edom's western side. According to the Moabite Stone (*see note on 3:4*), Mesha's army firmly controlled the northern approach into Moab. Therefore, an attack from the S had a much better chance of success. It was the most defenseless position and Mesha could enlist help from the forces of Edom (v. 9).

3:11 poured water on the hands. Probably derived from the custom of washing hands before and after meals. The idiom meant that Elisha had personally served Elijah. Jehoshaphat recognized that Elisha was a true prophet of the Lord (v. 12).

3:13 What have I to do with you? A Heb. idiom that expressed the completely different perspective of two individuals (cf. 2 Sam. 16:10). Elisha sarcastically ordered Jehoram to consult the prophets of

prophets of your father and the [n]prophets
of your mother."
But the king of Israel said to him, "No,
for the LORD has called these three kings *to-*
gether to deliver them into the hand of
Moab."
14 And Elisha said, [o]"*As* the LORD of
hosts lives, before whom I stand, surely
were it not that I regard the presence of Jehoshaphat king of Judah, I would not look
at you, nor see you. 15 But now bring me [p]a
musician."
Then it happened, when the musician
[q]played, that [r]the hand of the LORD came
upon him. 16 And he said, "Thus says the
LORD: [s]'Make this valley full of [2]ditches.'
17 For thus says the LORD: 'You shall not
see wind, nor shall you see rain; yet that
valley shall be filled with water, so that
you, your cattle, and your animals may
drink.' 18 And this is a simple matter in the
sight of the LORD; He will also deliver the
Moabites into your hand. 19 Also you shall
attack every fortified city and every choice
city, and shall cut down every good tree,
and stop up every spring of water, and
ruin every good piece of land with stones."
20 Now it happened in the morning,
when [t]the grain offering was offered, that
suddenly water came by way of Edom,
and the land was filled with water.
21 And when all the Moabites heard that
the kings had come up to fight against
them, all who were able to bear arms and
older were [3]gathered; and they stood at
the border. 22 Then they rose up early in
the morning, and the sun was shining on
the water; and the Moabites saw the water
on the other side *as* red as blood. 23 And
they said, "This is blood; the kings have
surely struck swords and have killed one
another; now therefore, Moab, to the
spoil!"
24 So when they came to the camp of Israel, Israel rose up and attacked the Moabites, so that they fled before them; and they
entered *their* land, killing the Moabites.
25 Then they destroyed the cities, and each
man threw a stone on every good piece of
land and filled it; and they stopped up all
the springs of water and cut down all the
good trees. But they left the stones of [u]Kir
Haraseth *intact*. However the slingers surrounded and attacked it.
26 And when the king of Moab saw that
the battle was too fierce for him, he took
with him seven hundred men who drew
swords, to break through to the king of
Edom, but they could not. 27 Then [v]he took
his eldest son who would have reigned in
his place, and offered him *as* a burnt offering upon the wall; and there was great [4]in-
dignation against Israel. [w]So they departed
from him and returned to *their own* land.

Elisha and the Widow's Oil

4 A certain woman of the wives of [a]the
sons of the prophets cried out to Elisha, saying, "Your servant my husband is
dead, and you know that your servant
feared the LORD. And the creditor is coming [b]to take my two sons to be his slaves."
2 So Elisha said to her, "What shall I do
for you? Tell me, what do you have in the
house?" And she said, "Your maidservant
has nothing in the house but a jar of oil."

13 [n]1 Kin. 18:19
14 [o]1 Kin. 17:1; 2 Kin. 5:16
15 [p]1 Sam. 10:5 [q]1 Sam. 16:16, 23; 1 Chr. 25:1 [r]Ezek. 1:3; 3:14, 22; 8:1
16 [s]Jer. 14:3 [2]*water canals*
20 [t]Ex. 29:39, 40
21 [3]*summoned*
25 [u]Is. 16:7, 11; Jer. 48:31, 36
27 [v][Deut. 18:10; Amos 2:1; Mic. 6:7] [w]2 Kin. 8:20 [4]*wrath*

CHAPTER 4

1 [a]1 Kin. 20:35; 2 Kin. 2:3 [b][Lev. 25:39-41, 48]; 1 Sam. 22:2; Neh. 5:2-5; Matt. 18:25

his father Ahab, prophets of the northern kingdom's deviant religion (1 Kin. 22:6,10-12), and the prophets of his mother Jezebel, the prophets of Baal and Asherah (1 Kin. 18:19).

3:14 regard the presence. Elisha agreed to seek word from the Lord because of his great respect for Jehoshaphat, the king of Judah, who did what was right in the eyes of the Lord (1 Kin. 22:43).

3:15 a musician. The music was used to accompany praise and prayer, which calmed the mind of the prophet that he might clearly hear the word of the Lord. Music often accompanied prophecies in the OT (cf. 1 Chr. 25:1).

3:16 this valley. Probably the NE area of the Arabah, W of the highlands of Moab and SE of the Dead Sea (see v. 8).

3:20 the grain offering. This was offered daily (see Ex. 29:38-41). **water came by way of Edom.** Divinely created flash floods from the mountains of Edom caused water to flow in the direction of the Dead Sea. This water was caught in the canals that had been built in the valley (v. 16).

3:22 water...red as blood. As the Moabites looked down at the unfamiliar water in the ditches dug in the valley below them, the combination of the sun's rays and the red sandstone terrain gave the water a reddish color, like pools of blood. Unaccustomed to water being in those places and having heard no storm (see v. 17), the Moabites thought that the coalition of kings had slaughtered each other (v. 23) and so went after the spoils. The coalition army led by Israel defeated the Moabites, who had been delivered into their hands by the Lord (see vv. 18,24).

3:25 Kir Haraseth. The coalition army invaded Moab and besieged its capital city, Kir Haraseth, located about 11 mi. E of the Dead Sea and about 20 mi. NE of the Arabah.

3:27 his eldest son...offered him. In desperate hope for intervention by his idol god, Mesha sacrificed his oldest son to the Moabite god Chemosh. This was done in plain view of everyone inside and outside the city in an attempt to induce Chemosh to deliver the Moabites from disastrous defeat. **great indignation against Israel.** It seems best to understand that the king's sacrifice inspired the Moabites to hate Israel more and fight more intensely. This fierceness perhaps led Israel to believe that Chemosh was fighting for the Moabites. Thus, the indignation or fury came from the Moabites.

4:1 the sons of the prophets. *See note on 1 Kin. 20:35.* **my two sons to be his slaves.** According to the Mosaic law, creditors could enslave debtors and their children to work off a debt when they could not pay (Ex. 21:2-4; Deut. 15:12-18). The period of servitude could last until the next year of Jubilee (Lev. 25:39,40). Rich people and creditors, however, were not to take advantage of the destitute (see Deut. 15:1-18).

4:2 jar of oil. A flask of oil used to anoint the body.

3 Then he said, "Go, borrow vessels
from everywhere, from all your neighbors—empty vessels; [c]do not gather just a
few. 4 And when you have come in, you
shall shut the door behind you and your
sons; then pour it into all those vessels, and
set aside the full ones."
5 So she went from him and shut the
door behind her and her sons, who
brought *the vessels* to her; and she poured *it*
out. 6 Now it came to pass, when the vessels were full, that she said to her son,
"Bring me another vessel."
And he said to her, "*There is* not another
vessel." So the oil ceased. 7 Then she came
and told the man of God. And he said,
"Go, sell the oil and pay your debt; and
you *and* your sons live on the rest."

Elisha Raises the Shunammite's Son

8 Now it happened one day that Elisha
went to [d]Shunem, where there *was* a [1]no-
table woman, and she [2]persuaded him to
eat some food. So it was, as often as he
passed by, he would turn in there to eat
some food. 9 And she said to her husband,
"Look now, I know that this *is* a holy man
of God, who passes by us regularly.
10 Please, let us make [3]a small upper room
on the wall; and let us put a bed for him
there, and a table and a chair and a lampstand; so it will be, whenever he comes to
us, he can turn in there."
11 And it happened one day that he
came there, and he turned in to the upper
room and lay down there. 12 Then he said
to [e]Gehazi his servant, "Call this Shunammite woman." When he had called her, she
stood before him. 13 And he said to him,
"Say now to her, 'Look, you have been concerned for us with all this care. What *can I*
do for you? Do you want me to speak on
your behalf to the king or to the commander of the army?' "
She answered, "I dwell among my own
people."
14 So he said, "What then *is* to be done
for her?"
And Gehazi answered, "Actually, she
has no son, and her husband is old."
15 So he said, "Call her." When he had
called her, she stood in the doorway.
16 Then he said, [4]"About this time next
year you shall embrace a son."
And she said, "No, my lord. Man of
God, [f]do not lie to your maidservant!"
17 But the woman conceived, and bore a
son when the appointed time had come, of
which Elisha had told her.
18 And the child grew. Now it happened
one day that he went out to his father, to
the reapers. 19 And he said to his father,
"My head, my head!"
So he said to a servant, "Carry him to his
mother." 20 When he had taken him and
brought him to his mother, he sat on her
knees till noon, and *then* died. 21 And she
went up and laid him on the bed of the man
of God, shut *the door* upon him, and went
out. 22 Then she called to her husband, and
said, "Please send me one of the young
men and one of the donkeys, that I may run
to the man of God and come back."
23 So he said, "Why are you going to him
today? *It is* neither the [g]New Moon nor the
Sabbath."

3 [c] 2 Kin. 3:16
8 [d] Josh. 19:18 [1] Lit. *great* [2] Lit. *laid hold on him*
10 [3] *Or a small walled upper chamber*
12 [e] 2 Kin. 4:29-31; 5:20-27; 8:4, 5
16 [f] 2 Kin. 4:28 [4] Lit. *About this season, as the time of life*
23 [g] Num. 10:10; 28:11; 1 Chr. 23:31

4:4 shut the door behind you. Since the widow's need was private, the provision was to be private also. Further, the absence of Elisha demonstrated that the miracle happened only by God's power. God's power multiplied "little" into "much," filling all the vessels to meet the widow's need (cf. 1 Kin. 17:7-16).

4:8 Shunem. A town in the territory of Issachar near Jezreel (Josh. 19:18), on the slopes of Mt. Moreh, overlooking the eastern end of the Jezreel Valley (*see note on 1 Kin. 1:3*). **a notable woman.** The woman was "great" in wealth and in social prominence.

4:9 man of God. *See note on 1:9.* The woman recognized Elisha as a prophet uniquely separated unto God. Elisha's holiness prompted the woman to ask her husband that a separate, small, walled upper room be provided for the prophet (v. 10). The woman must have feared the "holy" Elisha coming into contact with their "profane" room (cf. Lev. 10:10).

4:12 Gehazi. Elisha's personal servant who was prominent here and in 5:20-27. Probably Gehazi is the unnamed servant in v. 43; the term "servant" used there was used in 1 Kin. 19:21 of Elisha's relationship to Elijah. Throughout this narrative, Elisha contacted the Shunammite woman through Gehazi (vv. 11-13,15,25,29). Gehazi was involved in this ministry so that he might have opportunity to mature in his service to the Lord.

4:13 "I dwell among my own people." This reply expressed her contentment, since she wanted nothing.

4:14 no son, and her husband is old. This remark implied two things: 1) she suffered the shame of being a barren woman (cf. Gen. 16:1; 18:10-15; 25:21; 30:1,2; 1 Sam. 1:6); and 2) her husband might die without an heir to carry on his name (Deut. 25:5-10).

4:16 No, my lord. In response to Elisha's announcement that she would have a son, the woman asked Elisha not to build up her hopes if she would be disappointed later. Her reply indicated that she felt having a son was impossible. **Man of God.** *See note on 1:9.*

4:17 conceived...bore. This was like Abraham and Sarah (Gen. 21:1,2).

4:19 My head, my head! The child probably suffered sunstroke. The cries of the boy, the part affected, and the season of the year ("reapers") lead to that conclusion. Sunstroke could be fatal, as in this case (v. 20).

4:23 neither the New Moon nor the Sabbath. The first day of the month and the seventh day of the week were both marked with special religious observances and rest from work (cf. Num. 28:9-15). The husband implied that only on such dates would a person visit a prophet. She apparently concealed the death of the child from him ("*It is* well") to spare him unnecessary grief, in light of the power of the man of God whom she believed might do a miracle for the boy.

And she said, [5]"*It is* well." 24 Then she
saddled a donkey, and said to her servant,
"Drive, and go forward; do not slacken the
pace for me unless I tell you." 25 And so
she departed, and went to the man of God
[h]at Mount Carmel.
So it was, when the man of God saw her
afar off, that he said to his servant Gehazi,
"Look, the Shunammite woman! 26 Please
run now to meet her, and say to her, '*Is it*
well with you? *Is it* well with your husband? *Is it* well with the child?' "
And she answered, "*It is* well." 27 Now
when she came to the man of God at the
hill, she caught him by the feet, but Gehazi
came near to push her away. But the man
of God said, "Let her alone; for her soul *is*
in deep distress, and the LORD has hidden
it from me, and has not told me."
28 So she said, "Did I ask a son of my
lord? [i]Did I not say, 'Do not deceive me'?"
29 Then he said to Gehazi, [j]"Get[6] yourself ready, and take my staff in your hand,
and be on your way. If you meet anyone,
[k]do not greet him; and if anyone greets
you, do not answer him; but [l]lay my staff
on the face of the child."
30 And the mother of the child said,
[m]"*As* the LORD lives, and *as* your soul lives,
I will not [n]leave you." So he arose and followed her. 31 Now Gehazi went on ahead
of them, and laid the staff on the face of the
child; but *there was* neither voice nor hearing. Therefore he went back to meet him,
and told him, saying, "The child has [o]not
awakened."
32 When Elisha came into the house,
there was the child, lying dead on his bed.
33 He [p]went in therefore, shut the door behind the two of them, [q]and prayed to the
LORD. 34 And he went up and lay on the
child, and put his mouth on his mouth, his
eyes on his eyes, and his hands on his
hands; and [r]he stretched himself out on
the child, and the flesh of the child became
warm. 35 He returned and walked back
and forth in the house, and again went up
[s]and stretched himself out on him; then
[t]the child sneezed seven times, and the
child opened his eyes. 36 And he called Gehazi and said, "Call this Shunammite
woman." So he called her. And when she
came in to him, he said, "Pick up your
son." 37 So she went in, fell at his feet, and
bowed to the ground; then she [u]picked up
her son and went out.

Elisha Purifies the Pot of Stew

38 And Elisha returned to [v]Gilgal, and
there was a [w]famine in the land. Now the
sons of the prophets *were* [x]sitting before
him; and he said to his servant, "Put on the
large pot, and boil stew for the sons of the
prophets." 39 So one went out into the field
to gather herbs, and found a wild vine, and
gathered from it a lapful of wild gourds,
and came and sliced *them* into the pot of
stew, though they did not know *what they*
were. 40 Then they served it to the men to
eat. Now it happened, as they were eating
the stew, that they cried out and said,
"Man of God, *there is* [y]death in the pot!"
And they could not eat *it*.
41 So he said, "Then bring some flour."
And [z]he put *it* into the pot, and said,
"Serve *it* to the people, that they may eat."
And there was nothing harmful in the pot.

Elisha Feeds One Hundred Men

42 Then a man came from [a]Baal Shalisha,
[b]and brought the man of God bread of the
firstfruits, twenty loaves of barley bread,
and newly ripened grain in his knapsack.
And he said, "Give *it* to the people, that
they may eat."
43 But his servant said, [c]"What? Shall I
set this before one hundred men?"
He said again, "Give it to the people,
that they may eat; for thus says the LORD:
[d]'They shall eat and have *some* left over.' "

23 [5] Or *It will be well*
25 [h] 2 Kin. 2:25
28 [i] 2 Kin. 4:16
29 [j] 1 Kin. 18:46; 2 Kin. 9:1 [k] Luke 10:4 [l] Ex. 7:19; 14:16; 2 Kin. 2:8, 14; Acts 19:12 [6] Lit. *Gird up your loins.* The skirt of the robe was wrapped around the legs and tucked in the belt to gain freedom of movement.
30 [m] 2 Kin. 2:2 [n] 2 Kin. 2:4
31 [o] John 11:11
33 [p] 2 Kin. 4:4; [Matt. 6:6]; Luke 8:51 [q] 1 Kin. 17:20
34 [r] 1 Kin. 17:21-23; Acts 20:10
35 [s] 1 Kin. 17:21 [t] 2 Kin. 8:1, 5
37 [u] 1 Kin. 17:23; [Heb. 11:35]
38 [v] 2 Kin. 2:1 [w] 2 Kin. 8:1 [x] Luke 10:39; Acts 22:3
40 [y] Ex. 10:17
41 [z] Ex. 15:25; 2 Kin. 2:21
42 [a] 1 Sam. 9:4 [b] 1 Sam. 9:7; [1 Cor. 9:11; Gal. 6:6]
43 [c] Luke 9:13; John 6:9 [d] Luke 9:17; John 6:11

4:25 Mount Carmel. *See note on 1 Kin. 18:19.* The distance from Shunem was about 15 to 25 mi.

4:26 *It is* well. She withheld the real sorrow of her son's death, waiting to tell the prophet Elisha directly.

4:27 by the feet. The grasping of the feet was a sign of humiliation and veneration.

4:28 See v. 16.

4:29 lay my staff on the face of the child. Elisha sent Gehazi ahead because he was younger and, therefore, faster. He may have expected the Lord to restore the child's life when his staff was placed upon him, viewing that staff as representative of his own presence and a symbol of divine power (cf. 2:8).

4:34 stretched himself out on the child. Like Elijah (*see notes on 1 Kin. 17:17-24*), Elisha demonstrated the Lord's power over death by raising their son from the dead. Also like Elijah, part of the restoration process involved lying on top of the boy's body.

4:38 Gilgal. *See note on 2:1.* This was about 40 mi. S of Shunem. **sons of the prophets.** *See note on 1 Kin. 20:35.*

4:39 wild gourds. Probably a kind of wild cucumber that can be fatally poisonous if eaten in large quantities.

4:41 flour. The flour itself did not make the noxious stew edible, but a miraculous cure was accomplished through the flour. Like Elijah (cf. 1 Kin. 17:14-16), Elisha used flour to demonstrate the concern of God for man.

4:42 Baal Shalisha. The exact location is uncertain. **bread of the firstfruits.** Normally, the firstfruits were reserved for God (Lev. 23:20) and the Levitical priests (Num. 18:13; Deut. 18:4,5). Though the religion in the northern kingdom was apostate, the man who brought the loaves to Elisha was a representative of godly religion in Israel.

4:43,44 The multiplication of the loaves in accordance with the Word of the Lord through his prophet anticipated the messianic ministry of Jesus Himself (cf. Matt. 14:16-20; 15:36,37; John 6:11-13).

44 So he set *it* before them; and they ate
[e]and had *some* left over, according to the
word of the LORD.

Naaman's Leprosy Healed

5 Now [a]Naaman, commander of the
army of the king of Syria, was [b]a great
and honorable man in the eyes of his master, because by him the LORD had given
victory to Syria. He was also a mighty man
of valor, *but* a leper. 2 And the Syrians had
gone out [c]on[1] raids, and had brought back
captive a young girl from the land of Israel.
She [2]waited on Naaman's wife. 3 Then she
said to her mistress, "If only my master
were with the prophet who *is* in Samaria!
For he would heal him of his leprosy."
4 And *Naaman* went in and told his master,
saying, "Thus and thus said the girl who *is*
from the land of Israel."
5 Then the king of Syria said, "Go now,
and I will send a letter to the king of Israel."
So he departed and [d]took with him ten
talents of silver, six thousand *shekels* of
gold, and ten changes of clothing. 6 Then
he brought the letter to the king of Israel,
which said,

> Now be advised, when this letter comes to you, that I have sent Naaman my servant to you, that you may heal him of his leprosy.

7 And it happened, when the king of Israel
read the letter, that he tore his clothes and
said, "*Am* I [e]God, to kill and make alive,
that this man sends a man to me to heal him
of his leprosy? Therefore please consider,
and see how he seeks a quarrel with me."
8 So it was, when Elisha the man of God
heard that the king of Israel had torn his
clothes, that he sent to the king, saying,
"Why have you torn your clothes? Please
let him come to me, and he shall know that
there is a prophet in Israel."
9 Then Naaman went with his horses and
chariot, and he stood at the door of Elisha's
house. 10 And Elisha sent a messenger to
him, saying, "Go and [f]wash in the Jordan
seven times, and your flesh shall be restored
to you, and *you shall* be clean." 11 But Naaman became furious, and went away and
said, "Indeed, I said to myself, 'He will
surely come out *to me,* and stand and call on
the name of the LORD his God, and wave his
hand over the place, and heal the leprosy.'
12 *Are* not the [3]Abanah and the Pharpar, the
rivers of Damascus, better than all the waters of Israel? Could I not wash in them and
be clean?" So he turned and went away in a
rage. 13 And his [g]servants came near and
spoke to him, and said, "My father, *if* the
prophet had told you *to do* something great,
would you not have done *it?* How much
more then, when he says to you, 'Wash, and
be clean'?" 14 So he went down and dipped
seven times in the Jordan, according to the
saying of the man of God; and his [h]flesh
was restored like the flesh of a little child,
and [i]he was clean.

44 [e]Matt. 14:20; 15:37; John 6:13

CHAPTER 5

1 [a]Luke 4:27 [b]Ex. 11:3
2 [c]2 Kin. 6:23; 13:20 [1]Or *in bands* [2]Served, lit. *was before*
5 [d]1 Sam. 9:8; 2 Kin. 8:8, 9
7 [e][Gen. 30:2; Deut. 32:39; 1 Sam. 2:6]
10 [f]2 Kin. 4:41; John 9:7
12 [3]So with Kt., LXX, Vg.; Qr., Syr., Tg. *Amanah*
13 [g]1 Sam. 28:23
14 [h]2 Kin. 5:10; Job 33:25 [i]Luke 4:27; 5:13

5:1 Naaman. A common name in ancient Syria, meaning "gracious, fair." Four phrases describe the importance of Naaman: 1) he was the supreme commander of the army of Syria as indicated by the term "commander," used of an army's highest ranking officer (Gen. 21:22; 1 Sam. 12:9; 1 Chr. 27:34); 2) he was "a great man," a man of high social standing and prominence; 3) he was "an honorable man in the eyes of his master," a man highly regarded by the king of Syria because of the military victories he had won; and 4) he was "a mighty man of valor," a term used in the OT for both a man of great wealth (Ruth 2:1) and a courageous warrior (Judg. 6:12; 11:1). Severely mitigating against all of this was the fact that he suffered from leprosy, a serious skin disease (cf. v. 27; *see notes on Lev. 13,14*). **king of Syria.** Either Ben-Hadad I or, more likely, Ben-Hadad II. *See note on 1 Kin. 15:18.* **by him the LORD had given victory to Syria.** Naaman's military success was attributable to the God of Israel, who is sovereign over all the nations (cf. Is. 10:13; Amos 9:7).

5:2 raids. Naaman led the Syrian army in quick penetrations across Israel's border (cf. 1 Sam. 30:8,15). On one of his raids, he captured a young Israelite girl used as a servant, who ultimately told him of Elisha.

5:3 the prophet...in Samaria. Elisha maintained a residence in the city of Samaria (6:32).

5:5 king of Israel. Jehoram. *See note on 1:17.* **ten talents of silver, six thousand *shekels* of gold.** About 750 lbs. of silver and 150 lbs. of gold.

5:7 tore his clothes. This action was a sign of distress and grief (cf. 1 Kin. 21:27). Jehoram thought that Ben-Hadad expected him to cure Naaman's leprosy. Since Jehoram knew that this was impossible, he thought he was doomed to have a major battle with the Syrians. When Elisha heard of Jehoram's distress, he told the king to send Naaman to him for healing (v. 8).

5:11 surely come out *to me.* Because of his personal greatness (v. 1), his huge gift (v. 5), and diplomatic letter (v. 6), Naaman expected personal attention to his need. However, Elisha did not even go out to meet him. Instead, he sent his instructions for healing through a messenger (v. 10). Naaman was angry because he anticipated a personal cleansing ceremony from the prophet himself.

5:12 Abanah...Pharpar. The Abanah River (modern Barada) began in the Lebanon mountains and flowed to Damascus, its clear water producing orchards and gardens. The Pharpar River flowed E from Mt. Hermon to the S of Damascus. If Naaman needed to wash in a river, those two rivers were superior to the muddy Jordan. However, it was obedience to God's Word that was the issue, not the quality of the water.

5:13 My father. The title "father" was not usually employed by servants to their masters. The use of the term here may indicate something of the warmness that the servants felt for Naaman (cf. 2:12). His servants pointed out to Naaman that he had been willing to do anything, no matter how hard, to be cured. He should be even more willing, therefore, to do something as easy as washing in a muddy river.

5:14 flesh of a little child. This description indicates that ancient leprosy was a disease of the skin, distinct from modern leprosy, a disease primarily of the nerves.

15 And he returned to the man of God,
he and all his aides, and came and stood
before him; and he said, "Indeed, now I
know that *there is* [j]no God in all the earth,
except in Israel; now therefore, please take
[k]a gift from your servant."
16 But he said, [l]"*As* the LORD lives, before whom I stand, [m]I will receive nothing." And he urged him to take *it*, but he
refused.
17 So Naaman said, "Then, if not, please
let your servant be given two mule-loads
of earth; for your servant will no longer
offer either burnt offering or sacrifice to
other gods, but to the LORD. 18 Yet in this
thing may the LORD pardon your servant:
when my master goes into the temple of
Rimmon to worship there, and [n]he leans
on my hand, and I bow down in the temple of Rimmon—when I bow down in the
temple of Rimmon, may the LORD please
pardon your servant in this thing."
19 Then he said to him, "Go in peace." So
he departed from him a short distance.

Gehazi's Greed

20 But [o]Gehazi, the servant of Elisha the
man of God, said, "Look, my master has
spared Naaman this Syrian, while not receiving from his hands what he brought;
but *as* the LORD lives, I will run after him
and take something from him." 21 So Gehazi pursued Naaman. When Naaman
saw *him* running after him, he got down
from the chariot to meet him, and said, "*Is*
all well?"
22 And he said, "All *is* [p]well. My master
has sent me, saying, 'Indeed, just now two
young men of the sons of the prophets
have come to me from the mountains of
Ephraim. Please give them a talent of silver
and two changes of garments.' "
23 So Naaman said, "Please, take two talents." And he urged him, and bound two
talents of silver in two bags, with two
changes of garments, and handed *them* to
two of his servants; and they carried *them*
on ahead of him. 24 When he came to [4]the
citadel, he took *them* from their hand, and
stored *them* away in the house; then he let
the men go, and they departed. 25 Now he
went in and stood before his master. Elisha
said to him, "Where *did you go,* Gehazi?"
And he said, "Your servant did not go
anywhere."
26 Then he said to him, "Did not my
heart go *with you* when the man turned
back from his chariot to meet you? *Is it*
[q]time to receive money and to receive
clothing, olive groves and vineyards,
sheep and oxen, male and female servants?
27 Therefore the leprosy of Naaman [r]shall
cling to you and your descendants forever." And he went out from his presence
[s]leprous, *as white* as snow.

The Floating Ax Head

6 And [a]the sons of the prophets said to
Elisha, "See now, the place where we
dwell with you is too small for us. 2 Please,
let us go to the Jordan, and let every man
take a beam from there, and let us make
there a place where we may dwell."
So he answered, "Go.

15 [j] Dan. 2:47; 3:29; 6:26, 27 [k] Gen. 33:11
16 [l] 2 Kin. 3:14 [m] Gen. 14:22, 23; 2 Kin. 5:20, 26; [Matt. 10:8]; Acts 8:18, 20
18 [n] 2 Kin. 7:2, 17
20 [o] 2 Kin. 4:12; 8:4, 5
22 [p] 2 Kin. 4:26
24 [4] Lit. *the hill*
26 [q] [Eccl. 3:1, 6]
27 [r] [1 Tim. 6:10] [s] Ex. 4:6; Num. 12:10; 2 Kin. 15:5

CHAPTER 6
1 [a] 2 Kin. 4:38

5:15 *there is* no God...except in Israel. Upon his healing, Naaman returned from the Jordan River to Elisha's house in Samaria (about 25 mi.) to give confession of his new belief. Naaman confessed that there was only one God, Israel's God, the Lord. In saying this, Naaman put to shame the Israelites who continued to blasphemously believe that both the Lord and Baal were gods (cf. 1 Kin. 18:21).

5:16 he refused. To show that he was not driven by the mercenary motives of pagan priests and prophets, Elisha, though accepting gifts on other occasions (cf. 4:42), declined them here so the Syrians would see the honor of God only.

5:17 two mule-loads of earth. In the ancient Near East it was thought that a god could be worshiped only on the soil of the nation to which he was bound. Therefore, Naaman wanted a load of Israelite soil on which to make burnt offerings and sacrifices to the Lord when he returned to Damascus. This request confirmed how Naaman had changed—whereas he had previously disparaged Israel's river, now he wanted to take a pile of Israel's soil to Damascus.

5:18 Rimmon. The Heb. term "Rimmon" (lit. "pomegranate") is a parody of the Syrian deity, Hadad, whom the Assyrians named "Rananu" (lit. "the thunderer"). Hadad was the storm god, usually identified with the Canaanite god, Baal. As an aide to Syria's king, Naaman's duty demanded that he accompany the king to religious services at the temple of Rimmon in Damascus. Naaman requested that the Lord forgive this outward compromise of his true faith in and commitment to the Lord.

5:22 My master has sent me. A lie for selfish gain revealed the sad state of Gehazi's character. Another lie followed to cover up (v. 25).

5:23 two talents of silver. About 150 lbs. of silver.

5:26 Did not my heart go *with you.* Elisha knew Gehazi lied. Though his body did not move, Elisha's mind had seen all that had transpired between Gehazi and Naaman.

5:27 leprosy...shall cling to you. Gehazi's greed had cast a shadow over the integrity of Elisha's prophetic office. This made him no better in the people's thinking than Israel's false prophets, who prophesied for material gain, the very thing he wanted to avoid (vv. 15,16). Gehazi's act betrayed a lack of faith in the Lord's ability to provide. As a result, Elisha condemned Gehazi and his descendants to suffer Naaman's skin disease forever. The punishment was a twist for Gehazi, who had gone to "take something" from Naaman (v. 20), but what he received was Naaman's disease.

6:1 place where we dwell. Some have understood the term "dwell" in the sense of "live." This leads to the conclusion that the sons of the prophets, those specially instructed by Elisha, lived together in a communal setting. However, the term "dwell" can also be understood as "sit before." The term is used this way of David sitting before the Lord in worship (2 Sam. 7:18) and the elders sitting before Ezekiel to hear his advice (Ezek. 8:1; 14:1). Thus, the "place" here refers to a dormitory where Elisha also instructed the sons of the prophets. The growing number of men who wished to be taught led to the need for a larger building.

3 Then one said, [b]"Please consent to go
with your servants."
And he answered, "I will go." 4 So he
went with them. And when they came to
the Jordan, they cut down trees. 5 But as
one was cutting down a tree, the iron *ax
head* fell into the water; and he cried out
and said, "Alas, master! For it was [c]bor-
rowed."
6 So the man of God said, "Where did it
fall?" And he showed him the place. So [d]he
cut off a stick, and threw *it* in there; and he
made the iron float. 7 Therefore he said,
"Pick *it* up for yourself." So he reached out
his hand and took it.

The Blinded Syrians Captured

8 Now the [e]king of Syria was making
war against Israel; and he consulted with
his servants, saying, "My camp *will be* in
such and such a place." 9 And the man of
God sent to the king of Israel, saying, "Beware that you do not pass this place, for
the Syrians are coming down there."
10 Then the king of Israel sent *someone* to
the place of which the man of God had told
him. Thus he warned him, and he was
watchful there, not just once or twice.
11 Therefore the heart of the king of
Syria was greatly troubled by this thing;
and he called his servants and said to
them, "Will you not show me which of us
is for the king of Israel?"
12 And one of his servants said, "None,
my lord, O king; but Elisha, the prophet
who *is* in Israel, tells the king of Israel the
words that you speak in your bedroom."
13 So he said, "Go and see where he *is*,
that I may send and get him."
And it was told him, saying, "Surely *he
is* in [f]Dothan."
14 Therefore he sent horses and chariots
and a great army there, and they came by
night and surrounded the city. 15 And
when the servant of the man of God arose
early and went out, there was an army, surrounding the city with horses and chariots.
And his servant said to him, "Alas, my
master! What shall we do?"
16 So he answered, [g]"Do not fear, for
[h]those who *are* with us *are* more than those
who *are* with them." 17 And Elisha prayed,
and said, "LORD, I pray, open his eyes that he
may see." Then the LORD [i]opened the eyes of
the young man, and he saw. And behold, the
mountain *was* full of [j]horses and chariots of
fire all around Elisha. 18 So when *the Syrians*
came down to him, Elisha prayed to the
LORD, and said, "Strike this people, I pray,
with blindness." And [k]He struck them with
blindness according to the word of Elisha.
19 Now Elisha said to them, "This *is* not
the way, nor *is* this the city. Follow me, and
I will bring you to the man whom you
seek." But he led them to Samaria.
20 So it was, when they had come to Samaria, that Elisha said, "LORD, open the
eyes of these *men*, that they may see." And
the LORD opened their eyes, and they saw;
and there *they were*, inside Samaria!

3 [b] 2 Kin. 5:23
5 [c] [Ex. 22:14]
6 [d] Ex. 15:25; 2 Kin. 2:21; 4:41
8 [e] 2 Kin. 8:28, 29
13 [f] Gen. 37:17
16 [g] Ex. 14:13; 1 Kin. 17:13 [h] 2 Chr. 32:7; Ps. 55:18; [Rom. 8:31]
17 [i] Num. 22:31; Luke 24:31 [j] 2 Kin. 2:11; Ps. 34:7; 68:17; Zech. 1:8; 6:1-7
18 [k] Gen. 19:11; Acts 13:11

6:4 Jordan…trees. The Jordan Valley had mostly smaller kinds of trees, e.g., willow, tamarisk, and acacia that did not give heavy lumber. The resulting structure would be a humble, simple building.

6:5 iron…borrowed. Iron was expensive and relatively rare in Israel at that time and the student-prophet was very poor. The ax head was loaned to the prophet since he could not have afforded it on his own and would have had no means to reimburse the owner for it.

6:6 made the iron float. Elisha threw a stick in the river at the exact spot where the ax head entered, and the stick caused the heavy iron object to float to the surface. Through this miracle, the Lord again provided for one who was faithful to Him.

6:8 king of Syria. Either Ben-Hadad I or, more likely, Ben-Hadad II (v. 24). *See note on 1 Kin. 15:18.* **making war.** The Syrian king was probably sending raiding parties (v. 23) to pillage and plunder Israelite towns.

6:9 the man of God. I.e., Elisha (v. 12). *See note on Deut. 33:1.* **king of Israel.** I.e., Jehoram. *See note on 1:17.*

6:9,10 do not pass this place. Elisha, receiving supernatural revelation, continually identified to Jehoram the Israelite towns which the king of Syria planned to attack. Jehoram then took the proper precautions and appropriately fortified those towns so as to frustrate the Syrian plan.

6:11 which of us. The Syrian king was sure someone in his household was revealing his plans to Israel.

6:13 Dothan. A town in the hill country of Manasseh located about 10 mi. N of Samaria and 12 mi. S of Jezreel. Dothan commanded a key mountain pass along a main road that connected Damascus and Egypt (cf. Gen. 37:17). **get him.** The king of Syria's plan was to capture Elisha, who knew all his secrets (v. 12), so that no matter how great Elisha's knowledge might be, he would not be free to inform Israel's king.

6:14 a great army. In contrast to the smaller raiding parties (vv. 8,23), the king of Syria sent a sizable force, including horses and chariots, to take Elisha prisoner. Arriving at Dothan, the army encircled the town.

6:16 those who *are* with us. Elisha was referring to God's heavenly army or "host" (cf. Josh. 5:13-15; 2 Chr. 32:7,8; Dan 10:20; 12:1).

6:17 open his eyes. Elisha asked the Lord to enable his servant to see this heavenly host. The Lord gave his servant the ability to see the normally unseen world of God's heavenly armies, here waiting to do battle with the Syrians (cf. Gen. 32:1,2).

6:18 blindness. This word occurs only here and in Gen. 19:11. The term is related to "light" and seems to mean "a dazzling from bright light" (note the "chariots of fire" in v. 17). Both biblical uses of the term involve a miraculous act with angelic presence and both are used in the context of deliverance from danger.

6:19 Follow me…to the man whom you seek. By going to Samaria himself, Elisha did not lie, but did truly lead the Syrian army to where he ultimately would be found.

6:20 inside Samaria. God delivered a sizable portion of the Syrian army into the hands of the king of Israel without bloodshed. The Syrians discovered they were surrounded and captives of Israel.

21 Now when the king of Israel saw
them, he said to Elisha, "My [l]father, shall I
kill *them?* Shall I kill *them?*"
22 But he answered, "You shall not kill
them. Would you kill those whom you have
taken captive with your sword and your
bow? [m]Set food and water before them,
that they may eat and drink and go to their
master." 23 Then he prepared a great feast
for them; and after they ate and drank, he
sent them away and they went to their
master. So [n]the bands of Syrian *raiders*
came no more into the land of Israel.

Syria Besieges Samaria in Famine

24 And it happened after this that [o]Ben-
Hadad king of Syria gathered all his army,
and went up and besieged Samaria. 25 And
there was a great [p]famine in Samaria; and
indeed they besieged it until a donkey's
head was *sold* for eighty *shekels* of silver,
and one-fourth of a [1]kab of dove droppings for five *shekels* of silver.
26 Then, as the king of Israel was passing
by on the wall, a woman cried out to him,
saying, "Help, my lord, O king!"
27 And he said, "If the LORD does not
help you, where can I find help for you?
From the threshing floor or from the winepress?" 28 Then the king said to her, "What
is troubling you?"

And she answered, "This woman said to
me, 'Give your son, that we may eat him
today, and we will eat my son tomorrow.'
29 So [q]we boiled my son, and ate him. And
I said to her on the next day, 'Give your
son, that we may eat him'; but she has hidden her son."
30 Now it happened, when the king
heard the words of the woman, that he
[r]tore his clothes; and as he passed by on
the wall, the people looked, and there underneath *he had* sackcloth on his body.
31 Then he said, [s]"God do so to me and
more also, if the head of Elisha the son of
Shaphat remains on him today!"
32 But Elisha was sitting in his house,
and [t]the elders were sitting with him. And
the king sent a man ahead of him, but before the messenger came to him, he said to
the elders, [u]"Do you see how this son of [v]a
murderer has sent someone to take away
my head? Look, when the messenger
comes, shut the door, and hold him fast at
the door. *Is* not the sound of his master's
feet behind him?" 33 And while he was still
talking with them, there was the messenger, coming down to him; and then *the king*
said, "Surely this calamity *is* from the
LORD; [w]why should I wait for the LORD any
longer?"

21 [l] 2 Kin. 2:12; 5:13; 8:9
22 [m] [Rom. 12:20]
23 [n] 2 Kin. 5:2; 6:8, 9
24 [o] 1 Kin. 20:1
25 [p] 2 Kin. 4:38; 8:1
[1] Approximately 1 pint

29 [q] Lev. 26:27-29; Deut. 28:52-57; Lam. 4:10
30 [r] 1 Kin. 21:27
31 [s] Ruth 1:17; 1 Kin. 19:2
32 [t] Ezek. 8:1; 14:1; 20:1 [u] Luke 13:32 [v] 1 Kin. 18:4, 13, 14; 21:10, 13
33 [w] Job 2:9

6:21 My father. *See note on 5:13.* By using this expression, which conveyed the respect a child had for his father, King Jehoram of Israel acknowledged the authority of Elisha.

6:22 You shall not kill *them.* Elisha, bearing divinely delegated authority, prohibited the execution of the captives. It was uncommon and unusually cruel to put war captives to death in cold blood, even when taken by the point of a sword, but especially by the miraculous power of God. Kindness would testify to the goodness of God and likely stall future opposition from the Syrian raiders. These kind deeds gained a moral conquest (v. 23).

6:23 a great feast. In the ancient Near East, a common meal could signify the making of a covenant between two parties (cf. Lev. 7:15-18).

6:24 Ben-Hadad. *See note on 1 Kin. 15:18.* This same Ben-Hadad had laid siege to Samaria earlier (1 Kin. 20:1), which was the result of Ahab's foolish and misplaced kindness (1 Kin. 20:42). **all his army.** In contrast to the smaller raiding parties (vv. 8,23) and the larger force seeking Elisha's capture (v. 14), Ben-Hadad gathered his entire army, marched to Samaria, and besieged the capital.

6:25 a donkey's head...eighty *shekels* of silver. The siege resulted in a terrible famine gripping the city of Samaria. This ignominious body part of an unclean animal (Lev. 11:2-7; Deut. 14:4-8) sold at an overvalued price of about two lbs. of silver. **dove droppings... five *shekels* of silver.** "Dove droppings" was either a nickname for some small pea or root, or literal dung to be used as fuel or food in the desperate situation. Approximately one pt. cost about two oz. of silver.

6:26 Help, my lord, O king! The woman asked King Jehoram to render a legal decision in her dispute with another woman (*see note on 1 Kin. 3:16*).

6:28,29 Give your son, that we may eat him. The curses of the Mosaic Covenant, especially for the sin of apostasy, predicted this sort of pagan cannibalism (Lev. 26:29; Deut. 28:52-57). The way in which the woman presented her case without feeling added to the horror of it.

6:30 tore his clothes. A sign of distress and grief (*see note on 1 Kin. 21:27*). **sackcloth on his body.** A coarse cloth, made from goat's hair, worn as a sign of mourning (cf. Gen. 37:34). He was not truly humbled for his sins and the nation's or he would not have called for vengeance on Elisha.

6:31 the head of Elisha. Jehoram swore an oath to have Elisha killed. The reason Jehoram desired the death of Elisha could have been: 1) the king viewed the siege as the work of the Lord (v. 33), so he assumed that the Lord's representative, the prophet, with whom the kings of Israel were in conflict, was involved as well; or 2) the king remembered when Elijah had ended a famine (1 Kin. 18:41-46); or 3) Jehoram thought that Elisha's clemency to the Syrian army (v. 22) had somehow led to and added intensity to the present siege; or 4) because Elisha had miracle power, he should have ended the famine. But, most likely, the reason he wanted Elisha dead was because he expected that his mourning, perhaps counseled by the prophet as an act of true repentance (which it was not; *see note on v. 30*), would result in the end of the siege. When it did not, he sought the prophet's head.

6:32 the elders were sitting with him. The elders were the leading citizens of Samaria, whose gathering indicated the high regard in which Elisha was held by the prominent of Samarian society. **son of a murderer.** This phrase can mean both that: 1) Jehoram was the son of Ahab, who was guilty of murder (1 Kin. 21:1-16); and that 2) he had the character of a murderer.

6:33 why should I wait for the LORD any longer? Jehoram rightly viewed the Lord as the instigator of the siege and famine in

7 Then Elisha said, "Hear the word of
the LORD. Thus says the LORD: [a]'Tomorrow about this time a [1]seah of fine
flour *shall be sold* for a shekel, and two
seahs of barley for a shekel, at the gate of
Samaria.' "
2 [b]So an officer on whose hand the king
leaned answered the man of God and said,
"Look, [c]*if* the LORD would make windows
in heaven, could this thing be?"
And he said, "In fact, you shall see *it*
with your eyes, but you shall not eat of it."

The Syrians Flee

3 Now there were four leprous men [d]at
the entrance of the gate; and they said to
one another, "Why are we sitting here until
we die? 4 If we say, 'We will enter the city,'
the famine *is* in the city, and we shall die
there. And if we sit here, we die also. Now
therefore, come, let us surrender to the
[e]army of the Syrians. If they keep us alive,
we shall live; and if they kill us, we shall
only die." 5 And they rose at twilight to go
to the camp of the Syrians; and when they
had come to the outskirts of the Syrian
camp, to their surprise no one *was* there.
6 For the LORD had caused the army of the
Syrians [f]to hear the noise of chariots and
the noise of horses—the noise of a great
army; so they said to one another, "Look,
the king of Israel has hired against us [g]the
kings of the Hittites and the kings of the
Egyptians to attack us!" 7 Therefore they
[h]arose and fled at twilight, and left the
camp intact—their tents, their horses, and
their donkeys—and they fled for their
lives. 8 And when these lepers came to the
outskirts of the camp, they went into one
tent and ate and drank, and carried from it
silver and gold and clothing, and went and
hid *them;* then they came back and entered
another tent, and carried *some* from there
also, and went and hid *it.*
9 Then they said to one another, "We are
not doing right. This day *is* a day of good
news, and we remain silent. If we wait until
morning light, some [2]punishment will
come upon us. Now therefore, come, let us
go and tell the king's household." 10 So
they went and called to the gatekeepers of
the city, and told them, saying, "We went to
the Syrian camp, and surprisingly no one
was there, not a human sound—only horses and donkeys tied, and the tents intact."
11 And the gatekeepers called out, and they
told *it* to the king's household inside.
12 So the king arose in the night and said
to his servants, "Let me now tell you what
the Syrians have done to us. They know
that we *are* [i]hungry; therefore they have
gone out of the camp to [3]hide themselves
in the field, saying, 'When they come out
of the city, we shall catch them alive, and
get into the city.' "
13 And one of his servants answered and
said, "Please, let several *men* take five of
the remaining horses which are left in the
city. Look, they *may either become* like all the
multitude of Israel that are left in it; or indeed, *I say,* they *may become* like all the
multitude of Israel left from those who are
consumed; so let us send them and see."
14 Therefore they took two chariots with
horses; and the king sent them in the direction of the Syrian army, saying, "Go and
see." 15 And they went after them to the
Jordan; and indeed all the road *was* full of
garments and weapons which the Syrians

CHAPTER 7

1 [a]2 Kin. 7:18, 19 [1]A third of an ephah, or about 8 gallons
2 [b]2 Kin. 5:18; 7:17, 19, 20 [c]Gen. 7:11; Mal. 3:10
3 [d][Lev. 13:45, 46; Num. 5:2-4; 12:10-14]
4 [e]2 Kin. 6:24
6 [f]2 Sam. 5:24; 2 Kin. 19:7; Job 15:21 [g]1 Kin. 10:29
7 [h]Ps. 48:4-6; [Prov. 28:1]
9 [2]Calamity
12 [i]2 Kin. 6:24-29 [3]Hide themselves in ambush

Samaria and declared that he saw no hope that the Lord would reverse this situation.

7:1 a seah...for a shekel. About 7 quarts of flour (not 8 gal., as in marginal note) would sell for about two-fifths of an ounce of silver. **two seahs...for a shekel.** About 13-14 quarts of barley would also sell for about two-fifths of an ounce of silver. These prices, when compared to those in 6:25, indicated that the next day the famine in Samaria would end. **at the gate.** In ancient Israel, the city gate was the marketplace where business was transacted (cf. Ruth 4:1; 2 Sam. 15:1-5). Normal trade at the city gate of Samaria implied that the siege would be lifted.

7:2 an officer on whose hand the king leaned. For "officer" *see note on 9:25.* The king depended upon this officer as his chief adviser. **you shall see...but...not eat.** The royal official questioned the Lord's ability to provide food within the day. For that offense against God, Elisha predicted that the officer would witness the promised miracle, but he would not eat any of it. How this prophecy was fulfilled is described in vv. 16,17.

7:3 leprous men. The account of these lepers is used to tell of the siege's end and the provisions for Samaria (vv. 3-11). **at the entrance of the gate.** In the area immediately outside the city gate, 4 lepers lived, shut out of Samaria because of their disease (Lev. 13:46; Num. 5:3). The lepers knew that living in Samaria, whether just outside or inside the gate, offered them nothing but death.

7:5 the outskirts of the Syrian camp. Lit. "the edge of the camp." The normal meaning of this phrase would refer to the back edge of the army camp, the farthest point from the wall of Samaria.

7:6 the Hittites and...Egyptians. Sometime before the arrival of the lepers, the Lord had made the Syrians hear the terrifying sound of a huge army approaching. They thought the Israelite king had hired two massive foreign armies to attack them. The Hittites were descendants of the once-great Hittite empire who lived in small groups across northern Syria (*see note on 1 Kin. 10:29*). Egypt was in decline at this time, but its army would still have represented a great danger to the Syrians.

7:9 punishment. The lepers did not fear that the Syrians would return, but that the Lord would punish them for their sin of not telling the Israelite king of their discovery.

7:12 what the Syrians have done to us. Jehoram greeted the report from the lepers with great suspicion. He thought that the Syrians were feigning the pull back to appear defeated, in order to lure the Israelites out of Samaria for a surprise attack on them to gain entrance into the city. However, vv. 13-15 describe how the leper's report was confirmed.

had thrown away in their haste. So the
messengers returned and told the king.
16 Then the people went out and plundered the tents of the Syrians. So a seah of
fine flour was *sold* for a shekel, and two
seahs of barley for a shekel, [j]according to
the word of the LORD.
17 Now the king had appointed the officer on whose hand he leaned to have
charge of the gate. But the people trampled
him in the gate, and he died, just [k]as the
man of God had said, who spoke when the
king came down to him. 18 So it happened
just as the man of God had spoken to the
king, saying, [l]"Two seahs of barley for a
shekel, and a seah of fine flour for a shekel,
shall be *sold* tomorrow about this time in
the gate of Samaria."
19 Then that officer had answered the
man of God, and said, "Now look, *if* the
LORD would make windows in heaven,
could such a thing be?"
And he had said, "In fact, you shall see
it with your eyes, but you shall not eat of
it." 20 And so it happened to him, for the
people trampled him in the gate, and he
died.

16 [j] 2 Kin. 7:1
17 [k] 2 Kin. 6:32; 7:2
18 [l] 2 Kin. 7:1

The King Restores the Shunammite's Land

8 Then Elisha spoke to the woman
[a]whose son he had restored to life, saying, "Arise and go, you and your household, and stay wherever you can; for the
LORD [b]has called for a [c]famine, and furthermore, it will come upon the land for
seven years." 2 So the woman arose and
did according to the saying of the man of
God, and she went with her household
and dwelt in the land of the Philistines
seven years.
3 It came to pass, at the end of seven
years, that the woman returned from the
land of the Philistines; and she went to
make an appeal to the king for her house
and for her land. 4 Then the king talked
with [d]Gehazi, the servant of the man of
God, saying, "Tell me, please, all the great
things Elisha has done." 5 Now it happened, as he was telling the king how he
had restored the dead to life, that there was
the woman whose son he had [e]restored to
life, appealing to the king for her house
and for her land. And Gehazi said, "My
lord, O king, this *is* the woman, and this *is*
her son whom Elisha restored to life."
6 And when the king asked the woman,
she told him.
So the king appointed a certain officer
for her, saying, "Restore all that *was* hers,
and all the proceeds of the field from the
day that she left the land until now."

Death of Ben-Hadad

7 Then Elisha went to Damascus, and
[f]Ben-Hadad king of Syria was sick; and it
was told him, saying, "The man of God
has come here." 8 And the king said to
[g]Hazael, [h]"Take a present in your hand,
and go to meet the man of God, and [i]in-
quire of the LORD by him, saying, 'Shall I
recover from this disease?' " 9 So [j]Hazael

CHAPTER 8
1 [a] 2 Kin. 4:18, 31-35 [b] Ps. 105:16; Hag. 1:11 [c] 2 Sam. 21:1; 1 Kin. 18:2; 2 Kin. 4:38; 6:25
4 [d] 2 Kin. 4:12; 5:20-27
5 [e] 2 Kin. 4:35
7 [f] 2 Kin. 6:24
8 [g] 1 Kin. 19:15 [h] 1 Sam. 9:7; 1 Kin. 14:3; 2 Kin. 5:5 [i] 2 Kin. 1:2
9 [j] 1 Kin. 19:15

7:16-20 By repeating words from vv. 1,2 and by explicit statements ("according to the word of the LORD," v. 16; "just as the man of God had said/spoken," vv. 17,18), the text emphasizes that Elisha's prophecy in 7:2 literally came to pass.

8:1-6 The chronological question of when the events recounted in these verses took place in Elisha's ministry has been much debated. Interpreters hold to one of 3 positions: 1) The encounter between the Shunammite woman, the king of Israel, and Gehazi took place toward the end of the reign of Jehoram in Israel. However, this would mean Gehazi was in the presence of the king (vv. 4,5) although afflicted with leprosy (5:27) and King Jehoram was asking what great things Elisha had done after personally witnessing the events recorded in 6:8–7:19. 2) Because the king of Israel did not know Elisha's exploits, some interpreters place the final encounter during the early reign of Jehu. However, there are still the issues of Gehazi's leprosy and Jehu's being well acquainted with the prophecy of Elijah (9:36,37; 10:17) that predicted Elisha's ministry (1 Kin. 19:15-18). 3) The best explanation is that the record is out of chronological sequence, being thematically tied to the subject of famine in 6:24–7:20, but having occurred earlier in the reign of King Jehoram of Israel, before the events recorded in 5:1–7:20.

8:1 a famine...for seven years. Seven-year famines were known in the ancient Near East (cf. Gen. 41:29-32). Since the Shunammite woman would have been only a resident alien in a foreign land, her return within 7 years may have aided her legal claim to her property (cf. Ex. 21:2; 23:10,11; Lev. 25:1-7; Deut. 15:1-6).

8:2 land of the Philistines. The area located SW of Israel along the Mediterranean Sea coastal plain between the Jarkon River in the N and the Besor Brook in the S. The fact that the famine was localized in Israel demonstrated that this was a curse, a punishment for apostasy (cf. Deut. 28:38-40), because of Israel's disobedience of the Mosaic Covenant.

8:3 an appeal to the king. The Shunammite woman made a legal appeal to the king to support her ownership claim. In Israel, the king was the final arbiter of such disputes (*see note on 1 Kin. 3:16-28*). Providentially, the widow arrived just as Gehazi was describing how Elisha had raised her son from the dead (v. 5).

8:6 Restore all...and all the proceeds. The king's judgment was to return to the woman everything she owned, including the land's earnings during her absence.

8:7 Elisha went to Damascus. It was unusual for a prophet to visit foreign capitals, but not unknown (cf. Jon. 3:3). Elisha went to Damascus, the capital of Syria, to carry out one of the 3 commands God had given to Elijah at Horeb (1 Kin. 19:15,16). **Ben-Hadad.** *See note on 1 Kin. 15:18.* Ben-Hadad died ca. 841 B.C., the same year as Jehoram of Israel (3:1), Jehoram of Judah (8:17), and Ahaziah of Judah (8:25,26). **man of God.** *See note on Deut. 33:1.*

8:8 Hazael. His name means "God sees" or "whom God beholds." Hazael was a servant of Ben-Hadad and not a member of the royal family. Assyrian records called Hazael the "son of a nobody" and his lineage was not recorded because he was a commoner.

went to meet him and took a present with
him, of every good thing of Damascus,
forty camel-loads; and he came and stood
before him, and said, "Your son Ben-
Hadad king of Syria has sent me to you,
saying, 'Shall I recover from this
disease?' "
10 And Elisha said to him, "Go, say to
him, 'You shall certainly recover.' However the LORD has shown me that [k]he will really die." 11 Then he [1]set his countenance
in a stare until he was ashamed; and the
man of God [l]wept. 12 And Hazael said,
"Why is my lord weeping?"

He answered, "Because I know [m]the evil
that you will do to the children of Israel:
Their strongholds you will set on fire, and
their young men you will kill with the
sword; and you [n]will dash their children,
and rip open their women with child."
13 So Hazael said, "But what [o]*is* your
servant—a dog, that he should do this
gross thing?"

And Elisha answered, [p]"The LORD has
shown me that you *will become* king over
Syria."
14 Then he departed from Elisha, and
came to his master, who said to him,
"What did Elisha say to you?" And he answered, "He told me you would surely recover." 15 But it happened on the next day
that he took a thick cloth and dipped *it* in
water, and spread *it* over his face so that he
died; and Hazael reigned in his place.

Jehoram Reigns in Judah

16 Now [q]in the fifth year of Joram the
son of Ahab, king of Israel, Jehoshaphat
having been king of Judah, [r]Jehoram the son
of Jehoshaphat began to reign as [2]king of
Judah. 17 He was [s]thirty-two years old
when he became king, and he reigned
eight years in Jerusalem. 18 And he walked
in the way of the kings of Israel, just as the
house of Ahab had done, for [t]the daughter
of Ahab was his wife; and he did evil in the
sight of the LORD. 19 Yet the LORD would
not destroy Judah, for the sake of his servant David, [u]as He promised him to give a
lamp to him *and* his sons forever.
20 In his days [v]Edom revolted against
Judah's authority, [w]and made a king over
themselves. 21 So [3]Joram went to Zair, and
all his chariots with him. Then he rose by
night and attacked the Edomites who had
surrounded him and the captains of the
chariots; and the troops fled to their tents.
22 Thus Edom has been in revolt against
Judah's authority to this day. [x]And Libnah
revolted at that time.
23 Now the rest of the acts of Joram,
and all that he did, *are* they not written in

10 [k]2 Kin. 8:15
11 [l]Luke 19:41 [1]*fixed his gaze*
12 [m]2 Kin. 10:32; 12:17; 13:3,7; Amos 1:3,4 [n]2 Kin. 15:16; Hos. 13:16; Amos 1:13; Nah. 3:10
13 [o]1 Sam. 17:43; 2 Sam. 9:8 [p]1 Kin. 19:15
16 [q]2 Kin. 1:17; 3:1 [r]2 Chr. 21:3 [2]*Co-regent with his father*
17 [s]2 Chr. 21:5-10
18 [t]2 Kin. 8:26, 27
19 [u]2 Sam. 7:13; 1 Kin. 11:36; 15:4; 2 Chr. 21:7
20 [v]Gen. 27:40; 2 Chr. 21:8-10 [w]1 Kin. 22:47
21 [3]*Jehoram*, v. 16
22 [x]Josh. 21:13; 2 Kin. 19:8; 2 Chr. 21:10

8:9 every good thing of Damascus. The city of Damascus was a trade center between Egypt, Asia Minor, and Mesopotamia. It had within it the finest merchandise of the ancient Near East. Ben-Hadad evidently thought that an impressive gift would influence Elisha's prediction. **Your son.** Ben-Hadad approached Elisha with the humble respect of a son for his father (cf. 5:13; 6:21).

8:10 recover...die. Ben-Hadad wanted to know whether or not he would recover from his present illness. In response, Elisha affirmed two interrelated things: 1) Ben-Hadad would be restored to health; his present sickness would not be the means of his death. 2) Ben-Hadad would surely die by some other means.

8:11 he was ashamed. With a fixed gaze, Elisha stared at Hazael because it had been revealed to him what Hazael would do, including the murder of Ben-Hadad (v. 15). Hazael was embarrassed, knowing that Elisha knew of his plan to assassinate the Syrian king.

8:12 the evil. Elisha mourned, knowing the atrocities that Hazael would bring on Israel. The harsh actions mentioned here were common in ancient wars (Ps. 137:9; Is. 13:16; Hos. 10:14; 13:16; Amos 1:13; Nah. 3:10). Hazael did prove to be a constant foe of Israel (9:14-16; 10:32; 12:17,18; 13:3,22).

8:13 your servant—a dog. To call oneself a dog was an expression of humility (*see note on 2 Sam. 9:8*). Hazael sought to deny that he would ever have the power to commit such atrocities. He was trying to convince Elisha that he had no plan to take over the kingship of Syria. **you *will become* king over Syria.** In response to Hazael's feigned self-deprecation, Elisha affirmed that the Lord willed that Hazael be king over Syria (cf. 1 Kin. 19:15).

8:15 he died. Hazael took a bed furnishing, soaked it, and killed Ben-Hadad by suffocation. **Hazael reigned.** Upon Ben-Hadad's death, Hazael took the kingship of Syria and ruled ca. 841–801 B.C., during the reigns of Jehoram, Jehu, and Jehoahaz in Israel and Ahaziah, Athaliah, and Joash in Judah.

8:16 fifth year. Ca. 848 B.C., the year Jehoshaphat of Judah died. **Joram.** An alternate name for the king referred to as Jehoram previously (1:17; 3:1,6). *See notes on 2 Chr. 21:4-20.*

8:17 eight years. 848–841 B.C. *See notes on 2 Chr. 21:4-20.* Jehoram of Judah served as co-regent with his father Jehoshaphat for the final 4 years of his reign, 853–848 B.C. Joram (Jehoram) became king of Israel during the second year of this co-regency, 852 B.C. (*see note on 1:17; 3:1*). Jehoram of Judah ruled alone for 8 years after his father's death, until 841 B.C. (cf. 2 Chr. 21:15). Most likely, Obadiah prophesied during his reign.

8:18 as the house of Ahab. Jehoram officially sanctioned Baal worship in Judah as Ahab had in Israel (1 Kin. 16:31-33). **the daughter of Ahab.** Jehoram was married to Athaliah, the daughter of Ahab and Jezebel (v. 26). Just as Jezebel incited Ahab to do evil in the sight of the Lord (1 Kin. 21:25), so Athaliah influenced Jehoram. Athaliah's wicked actions are recorded in 11:1-16; 2 Chr. 22:10–23:15.

8:19 a lamp...forever. *See note on 1 Kin. 11:36.*

8:20 Edom revolted. Edom had been a vassal of the united kingdom, and of the southern kingdom of Judah since David's reign (2 Sam. 8:13,14).

8:21 Zair. The exact location is unknown.

8:22 Edom has been in revolt...to this day. During the reign of Jehoram, Edom defeated the Judean army, took some border lands, and became independent of Judah's rule. The continuing sovereignty of Edom proved that none of the future kings of Judah recorded in 2 Kings was the anticipated Messiah because He would possess Edom (cf. Num. 24:18). **Libnah.** A town located in the Shephelah on the border with Philistia, about 20 mi. SW of Jerusalem (Josh. 15:42; 21:13). The revolt of Libnah was probably connected with that of the Philistines and Arabians recounted in 2 Chr. 21:16,17.

the book of the chronicles of the kings of
Judah? 24 So Joram [4]rested with his fathers, and was buried with his fathers in
the City of David. Then [y]Ahaziah[5] his
son reigned in his place.

Ahaziah Reigns in Judah

25 In the twelfth year of Joram the son of
Ahab, king of Israel, Ahaziah the son of
Jehoram, king of Judah, began to reign.
26 Ahaziah *was* [z]twenty-two years old
when he became king, and he reigned one
year in Jerusalem. His mother's name *was*
Athaliah the granddaughter of Omri, king
of Israel. 27 [a]And he walked in the way of
the house of Ahab, and did evil in the
sight of the LORD, like the house of Ahab,
for he *was* the son-in-law of the house of
Ahab.
28 Now he went [b]with Joram the son of
Ahab to war against Hazael king of Syria
at [c]Ramoth Gilead; and the Syrians
wounded Joram. 29 Then [d]King Joram
went back to Jezreel to recover from the
wounds which the Syrians had inflicted on
him at [6]Ramah, when he fought against
Hazael king of Syria. [e]And Ahaziah the
son of Jehoram, king of Judah, went down
to see Joram the son of Ahab in Jezreel, because he was sick.

Jehu Anointed King of Israel

9 And Elisha the prophet called one of
[a]the sons of the prophets, and said to
him, [b]"Get[1] yourself ready, take this flask
of oil in your hand, [c]and go to Ramoth
Gilead. 2 Now when you arrive at that
place, look there for Jehu the son of Jehoshaphat, the son of Nimshi, and go in
and make him rise up from among [d]his associates, and take him to an inner room.
3 Then [e]take the flask of oil, and pour *it* on
his head, and say, 'Thus says the LORD: "I
have anointed you king over Israel." '
Then open the door and flee, and do not
delay."
4 So the young man, the servant of the
prophet, went to Ramoth Gilead. 5 And
when he arrived, there *were* the captains of
the army sitting; and he said, "I have a
message for you, Commander."
Jehu said, "For which *one* of us?"
And he said, "For you, Commander."
6 Then he arose and went into the house.
And he poured the oil on his head, and
said to him, [f]"Thus says the LORD God of
Israel: 'I have anointed you king over the
people of the LORD, over Israel. 7 You shall
strike down the house of Ahab your master, that I may [g]avenge the blood of My servants the prophets, and the blood of all the
servants of the LORD, [h]at the hand of Jezebel. 8 For the whole house of Ahab shall
perish; and [i]I will cut off from Ahab all [j]the
males in Israel, both [k]bond and free. 9 So I
will make the house of Ahab like the house
of [l]Jeroboam the son of Nebat, and like the
house of [m]Baasha the son of Ahijah.
10 [n]The dogs shall eat Jezebel on the plot *of
ground* at Jezreel, and *there shall be* none to
bury *her*.' " And he opened the door and
fled.
11 Then Jehu came out to the servants of
his master, and *one* said to him, "*Is* all well?
Why did [o]this madman come to you?"

24 [y]2 Chr. 22:1, 7 [4]Died and joined his ancestors [5]Or *Azariah* or *Jehoahaz*
26 [z]2 Chr. 22:2
27 [a]2 Chr. 22:3, 4
28 [b]2 Chr. 22:5 [c]1 Kin. 22:3, 29
29 [d]2 Kin. 9:15 [e]2 Kin. 9:16; 2 Chr. 22:6, 7 [6]*Ramoth*, v. 28

CHAPTER 9

1 [a]1 Kin. 20:35 [b]2 Kin. 4:29; Jer. 1:17 [c]2 Kin. 8:28, 29 [1]Lit. *Gird up your loins*
2 [d]2 Kin. 9:5, 11
3 [e]1 Kin. 19:16
6 [f]1 Sam. 2:7, 8; 1 Kin. 19:16; 2 Kin. 9:3; 2 Chr. 22:7
7 [g][Deut. 32:35, 41] [h]1 Kin. 18:4; 21:15
8 [i]1 Kin. 14:10; 21:21; 2 Kin. 10:17 [j]1 Sam. 25:22 [k]Deut. 32:36; 2 Kin. 14:26
9 [l]1 Kin. 14:10; 15:29; 21:22 [m]1 Kin. 16:3, 11
10 [n]1 Kin. 21:23; 2 Kin. 9:35, 36
11 [o]Jer. 29:26; Hos. 9:7; Mark 3:21; John 10:20; Acts 26:24; [1 Cor. 4:10]

8:25-29 The reign of Ahaziah (ca. 841 B.C.) is not to be confused with that of Judah's King Ahaziah (1 Kin. 22:51–2 Kin. 1:8). *See notes on 2 Kin. 9:27-29; 2 Chr. 22:1-9.*

8:26 twenty-two. This reading is preferred over the "forty-two" of 2 Chr. 22:2 (*see note there*). **Athaliah.** *See note on v. 18.*

8:27 like the house of Ahab. Like his father, Jehoram, Ahaziah continued the official sanctioning of Baal worship in Judah (*see note on v. 18*).

8:28 Ramoth Gilead. *See note on 1 Kin. 22:3.*

8:29 went down to see Joram. Ahaziah's travel to visit the recuperating Joram (also called Jehoram) king of Israel placed him in Jezreel (W of the Jordan, SW of the Sea of Galilee) during Jehu's purge of the house of Omri (see 9:21-29).

9:2 Jehu. The Lord had previously told Elijah that Jehu would become king over Israel and kill those involved in the worship of Baal (*see notes on 1 Kin. 19:16,17*). The fulfillment of the prophecy is recorded from 9:1–10:31. **inner room.** A private room that could be closed off to the public. Elisha commissioned one of the younger prophets to anoint Jehu alone behind closed doors. The rite was to be a secret affair without Elisha present so that Jehoram would not suspect that a coup was coming.

9:3 anointed you king over Israel. The anointing with olive oil by a prophet of the Lord confirmed that God Himself had earlier chosen that man to be king (cf. 1 Sam. 10:1; 16:13). This action of anointing by a commissioned prophet indicated divine investiture with God's sovereign power to Jehu. **flee, and do not delay.** The need for haste by the young prophet underscored the danger of the assignment. A prophet in the midst of Israel's army camp would alert the pro-Jehoram elements to the possibility of the coup.

9:7 avenge the blood. Jehu was to be the Lord's avenger (cf. Num. 35:12) for the murders of the Lord's prophets (1 Kin. 18:4) and of people like Naboth who served the Lord (1 Kin. 21:1-16).

9:9 like the house of Jeroboam…Baasha. God would thoroughly annihilate Ahab's line in the same way as Jeroboam's dynasty and Baasha's dynasty had previously ended violently (1 Kin. 15:27-30; 16:8-13).

9:10 dogs shall eat. Dogs were considered scavengers in the ancient Near East and they would devour the corpse of Jezebel. **Jezreel.** Formerly the area of Naboth's vineyard (1 Kin. 21:1-16). **none to bury *her*.** In Israel, the failure to be buried indicated disgrace (*see note on 1 Kin. 13:22*).

9:11 this madman. The soldier demonstrated his disdain for Elisha's servant (vv. 1,4) by referring to him as crazy or demented. In Jer. 29:26 and Hos. 9:7 this same term was used as a derogatory term for prophets whose messages were considered crazy. Jehu's response referred to the prophet's "babble," not his behavior.

And he said to them, "You know the
man and his babble."
12 And they said, "A lie! Tell us now."
So he said, "Thus and thus he spoke to
me, saying, 'Thus says the LORD: "I have
anointed you king over Israel." ' "
13 Then each man hastened [p]to take his
garment and put *it* [2]under him on the top
of the steps; and they blew trumpets, saying, "Jehu is king!"

Joram of Israel Killed

14 So Jehu the son of Jehoshaphat, the
son of Nimshi, conspired against [q]Joram.
(Now Joram had been defending Ramoth
Gilead, he and all Israel, against Hazael
king of Syria. 15 But [r]King [3]Joram had returned to Jezreel to recover from the
wounds which the Syrians had inflicted on
him when he fought with Hazael king of
Syria.) And Jehu said, "If you are so minded, let no one leave *or* escape from the city
to go and tell *it* in Jezreel." 16 So Jehu rode
in a chariot and went to Jezreel, for Joram
was laid up there; [s]and Ahaziah king of Judah had come down to see Joram.
17 Now a watchman stood on the tower
in Jezreel, and he saw the company of Jehu
as he came, and said, "I see a company of
men."
And Joram said, "Get a horseman and
send him to meet them, and let him say,
[4]'*Is it* peace?' "
18 So the horseman went to meet him,
and said, "Thus says the king: '*Is it*
peace?' "
And Jehu said, "What have you to do
with peace? [5]Turn around and follow me."
So the watchman reported, saying, "The
messenger went to them, but is not coming
back."
19 Then he sent out a second horseman
who came to them, and said, "Thus says
the king: '*Is it* peace?' "
And Jehu answered, "What have you to
do with peace? Turn around and follow
me."
20 So the watchman reported, saying,
"He went up to them and is not coming
back; and the driving *is* like the driving of
Jehu the son of Nimshi, for he drives furiously!"
21 Then Joram said, [6]"Make ready." And
his chariot was made ready. Then [t]Joram
king of Israel and Ahaziah king of Judah
went out, each in his chariot; and they
went out to meet Jehu, and [7]met him [u]on
the property of Naboth the Jezreelite.
22 Now it happened, when Joram saw
Jehu, that he said, "*Is it* peace, Jehu?"
So he answered, "What peace, as long as
the harlotries of your mother Jezebel and
her witchcraft *are so* many?"
23 Then Joram turned around and fled,
and said to Ahaziah, "Treachery, Ahaziah!"
24 Now Jehu [8]drew his bow with full
strength and shot Jehoram between his
arms; and the arrow came out at his heart,
and he sank down in his chariot. 25 Then
Jehu said to Bidkar his captain, "Pick *him*
up, *and* throw him into the tract of the field
of Naboth the Jezreelite; for remember,
when you and I were riding together behind Ahab his father, that [v]the LORD laid
this [w]burden upon him: 26 'Surely I saw
yesterday the blood of Naboth and the
blood of his sons,' says the LORD, [x]'and I
will repay you [9]in this plot,' says the LORD.
Now therefore, take *and* throw him on the
plot *of ground*, according to the word of the
LORD."

13 [p] Matt. 21:7, 8; Mark 11:7, 8 [2] Lit. *under his feet*
14 [q] 2 Kin. 8:28
15 [r] 2 Kin. 8:29 [3] *Jehoram*, v. 24
16 [s] 2 Kin. 8:29
17 [4] Are you peaceful?
18 [5] Lit. *Turn behind me*
21 [t] 1 Kin. 19:17; 2 Chr. 22:7 [u] 1 Kin. 21:1-14 [6] *Harness up* [7] Lit. *found*
24 [8] Lit. *filled his hand*
25 [v] 1 Kin. 21:19, 24-29 [w] Is. 13:1
26 [x] 1 Kin. 21:13, 19 [9] *on this property*

9:12 Thus and thus. This refers to the repeating of the prophecy in vv. 4-10.

9:13 they blew trumpets. Having laid their cloaks under Jehu's feet with the steps of the house serving as a makeshift throne, the officers blew trumpets acclaiming Jehu as king. A trumpet often heralded such a public proclamation and assembly, including the appointment of a king (cf. 11:14; 2 Sam. 15:10; 1 Kin. 1:34).

9:15 let no one...go and tell *it* in Jezreel. For Jehu to succeed in his revolt and to avoid a civil conflict, it was important to take Joram totally by surprise. Therefore, Jehu ordered the city of Ramoth Gilead where he had been anointed (vv. 2,3) to be sealed lest someone loyal to Joram escape and notify the king.

9:16 to Jezreel. From Ramoth Gilead, Jezreel was straight W across the Jordan, N of Mt. Gilboa.

9:21 Naboth the Jezreelite. Providentially, the kings of Israel and Judah met Jehu at the very place where Ahab and Jezebel had Naboth killed (1 Kin. 21:1-16). The alarmed king, aware by then of impending disaster, summoned his forces and, accompanied by Ahaziah, met Jehu as Jehu's men ascended the slope up to the city from the northern side.

9:22 What peace. Joram wished to know if Jehu's coming meant peace, apparently unsure of Jehu's rebellious plans. Jehu replied that there could be no true peace in Israel because of Jezebel's influence. "Harlotries," a common biblical metaphor for idolatry, and "witchcraft," i.e., seeking information from demonic forces, described the nature of Jezebel's influence. Idolatry had lured Israel into demonic practices.

9:25 Bidkar his captain. "Captain" originally referred to the third man in a chariot, besides the driver and a warrior; it was his task to hold the shield and arms of the warrior. The term was eventually applied to a high-ranking official (cf. 7:2). Jehu and Bidkar either rode together in one chariot as part of the chariot team or were in different chariots behind Ahab when Elijah gave his prediction to Ahab recorded in 1 Kin. 21:17-24. **the LORD laid this burden upon him.** The term "burden" referred to a prophetic oracle, the prophetic utterance of Elijah recorded in 1 Kin. 21:19,20-24. Jehu viewed himself as God's avenging agent fulfilling Elijah's prediction.

9:26 Naboth...sons. Although their deaths are not expressly mentioned in the record concerning Naboth, they are plainly implied in the confiscation of his property (see 1 Kin. 21:16).

Ahaziah of Judah Killed

27 But when Ahaziah king of Judah saw *this,* he fled by the road to [1]Beth Haggan. So Jehu pursued him, and said, [2]"Shoot him also in the chariot." *And they shot him* at the Ascent of Gur, which is by Ibleam. Then he fled to [y]Megiddo, and died there. 28 And his servants carried him in the chariot to Jerusalem, and buried him in his tomb with his fathers in the City of David. 29 In the eleventh year of Joram the son of Ahab, Ahaziah had become king over Judah.

Jezebel's Violent Death

30 Now when Jehu had come to Jezreel, Jezebel heard *of it;* [z]and she put paint on her eyes and adorned her head, and looked through a window. 31 Then, as Jehu entered at the gate, she said, [a]"*Is it* peace, Zimri, murderer of your master?"

32 And he looked up at the window, and said, "Who *is* on my side? Who?" So two *or* three eunuchs looked out at him. 33 Then he said, "Throw her down." So they threw her down, and *some* of her blood spattered on the wall and on the horses; and he trampled her underfoot. 34 And when he had gone in, he ate and drank. Then he said, "Go now, see to this accursed *woman,* and bury her, for [b]she was a king's daughter." 35 So they went to bury her, but they found no more of her than the skull and the feet and the palms of *her* hands. 36 Therefore they came back and told him. And he said, "This *is* the word of the LORD, which He spoke by His servant Elijah the Tishbite, saying, [c]'On the plot *of ground* at Jezreel dogs shall eat the flesh of Jezebel; 37 and the corpse of Jezebel shall be [d]as refuse on the surface of the field, in the plot at Jezreel, so that they shall not say, "Here *lies* Jezebel." ' "

Ahab's Seventy Sons Killed

10 Now Ahab had seventy sons in Samaria. And Jehu wrote and sent letters to Samaria, to the rulers of [1]Jezreel, to the elders, and to [2]those who reared Ahab's *sons,* saying:

2 Now as soon as this letter comes
to you, since your master's sons
are with you, and you have
chariots and horses, a fortified city
also, and weapons, 3 choose the
[3]best qualified of your master's
sons, set *him* on his father's
throne, and fight for your master's
house.

4 But they were exceedingly afraid, and said, "Look, [a]two kings could not [4]stand up to him; how then can we stand?" 5 And he who *was* in charge of the house, and he who *was* in charge of the city, the elders also, and those who reared *the sons,* sent to Jehu, saying, "We *are* your servants, we will do all you tell us; but we will not make anyone king. Do *what is* good in your sight." 6 Then he wrote a second letter to them, saying:

27 [y] 2 Chr. 22:7, 9 [1] Lit. *The Garden House* [2] Lit. *Strike*
30 [z] [Jer. 4:30]; Ezek. 23:40
31 [a] 1 Kin. 16:9-20; 2 Kin. 9:18-22
34 [b] [Ex. 22:28]; 1 Kin. 16:31
36 [c] 1 Kin. 21:23
37 [d] Ps. 83:10

CHAPTER 10

1 [1] So with MT, Syr., Tg.; LXX *Samaria;* Vg. *city* [2] *the guardians of*
3 [3] *most upright*
4 [a] 2 Kin. 9:24, 27 [4] Lit. *stand before*

9:27 Ahaziah king of Judah...died. Ahaziah fled by way of the road to Beth Haggan, a town 7 mi. SW of Jezreel. Jehu and his men pursued Ahaziah and wounded him at the Ascent of Gur by Ibleam which was just S of Beth Haggan. According to 2 Chr. 22:9, Ahaziah reached Samaria, about 8 mi. S of Beth Haggan, where he hid for awhile. Ahaziah then fled N to Megiddo, about 12 mi. N of Samaria, where he died.

9:29 eleventh year. Ca. 841 B.C. Cf. 8:25, "twelfth year." In 8:25, the non-accession-year system of dating was used, so that Joram's accession year was counted as the first year of his reign (*see note on 12:6*). Here, the accession-year dating system was used, where Joram's accension year and his second year were counted as the first year of his reign.

9:30 paint on her eyes. The painting of the eyelids with a black powder mixed with oil and applied with a brush, darkened them to give an enlarged effect. Jezebel's appearance at the window gave the air of a royal audience to awe Jehu.

9:31 Zimri. In referring to Jehu by that name, Jezebel sarcastically alluded to the previous purge of Zimri (1 Kin. 16:9-15). Since Zimri died 7 days after beginning to reign, Jezebel was implying that the same fate awaited Jehu.

9:32 eunuchs. Some of Jezebel's own officials threw her out of a second-story window, after which Jehu drove his horses and chariots over her body.

9:34 a king's daughter. Jehu recognized Jezebel's royalty, while denying that she deserved to be the queen of Israel.

9:36 This *is* the word of the LORD. Where and how Jezebel died fulfilled Elijah's prophetic oracle (1 Kin. 21:23).

10:1 seventy sons. These were the male descendants of Ahab, both sons and grandsons. Ahab had a number of wives (1 Kin. 20:5) and therefore many descendants. Since these living relatives could avenge a dead kinsman by killing the person responsible for his death (cf. Num. 35:12), Jehu's life was in jeopardy while Ahab's male descendants survived. **Samaria.** Ahab's surviving family members were living in the capital city of the northern kingdom, located about 25 mi. S of Jezreel. **rulers...elders...those who reared.** Jehu sent the same message (vv. 2,3) in a number of letters to: 1) the royal officials, who had probably fled from Jezreel to Samaria; 2) the leaders of the tribes of Israel; and 3) those appointed as the custodians and educators of the royal children.

10:3 fight for your master's house. Realizing potential conflict existed between himself and Ahab's family, Jehu was demanding that Ahab's appointed officials either fight to continue the royal line of Ahab or select a new king from Ahab's descendants who would fight Jehu in battle to decide which family would rule Israel (cf. 1 Sam. 17:8,9; 2 Sam. 2:9).

10:5 he who *was* in charge of the house...city. These two officials were the palace administrator and the city governor, probably the commander of the city's fighting force. **We *are* your servants.** These officials and leaders transferred their allegiance from the house of Omri to Jehu.

If you *are* for me and will obey my
voice, take the heads of the men,
your master's sons, and come to me
at Jezreel by this time tomorrow.

Now the king's sons, seventy persons, *were* with the great men of the city, *who* were rearing them. 7 So it was, when the letter came to them, that they took the king's sons and [b]slaughtered seventy persons, put their heads in baskets and sent *them* to him at Jezreel.

8 Then a messenger came and told him, saying, "They have brought the heads of the king's sons."

And he said, "Lay them in two heaps at the entrance of the gate until morning."

9 So it was, in the morning, that he went out and stood, and said to all the people, "You *are* righteous. Indeed [c]I conspired against my master and killed him; but who killed all these? 10 Know now that nothing shall [d]fall to the earth of the word of the LORD which the LORD spoke concerning the house of Ahab; for the LORD has done what He spoke [e]by His servant Elijah." 11 So Jehu killed all who remained of the house of Ahab in Jezreel, and all his great men and his close acquaintances and his priests, until he left him none remaining.

Ahaziah's Forty-two Brothers Killed

12 And he arose and departed and went to Samaria. On the way, at [5]Beth Eked of the Shepherds, 13 [f]Jehu met with the brothers of Ahaziah king of Judah, and said, "Who *are* you?"

So they answered, "We *are* the brothers of Ahaziah; we have come down to greet the sons of the king and the sons of the queen mother."

14 And he said, "Take them alive!" So they took them alive, and [g]killed them at the well of [6]Beth Eked, forty-two men; and he left none of them.

The Rest of Ahab's Family Killed

15 Now when he departed from there, he [7]met [h]Jehonadab the son of [i]Rechab, *coming* to meet him; and he greeted him and said to him, "Is your heart right, as my heart *is* toward your heart?"

And Jehonadab answered, "It is."

Jehu said, "If it is, [j]give *me* your hand." So he gave *him* his hand, and he took him up to him into the chariot. 16 Then he said, "Come with me, and see my [k]zeal for the LORD." So they had him ride in his chariot. 17 And when he came to Samaria, [l]he killed all who remained to Ahab in Samaria, till he had destroyed them, according to the word of the LORD [m]which He spoke to Elijah.

Worshipers of Baal Killed

18 Then Jehu gathered all the people together, and said to them, [n]"Ahab served Baal a little, Jehu will serve him much. 19 Now therefore, call to me all the [o]prophets of Baal, all his servants, and all his priests. Let no one be missing, for I have a great sacrifice for Baal. Whoever is missing shall not live." But Jehu acted deceptively, with the intent of destroying the worshipers of Baal. 20 And Jehu said, [8]"Proclaim a solemn assembly for Baal." So they proclaimed *it*. 21 Then Jehu sent throughout all Israel; and all the worshipers of Baal came, so that there was not a man left who did not come. So they came into the [9]temple of Baal, and the [p]temple of Baal was full from one end to the other.

7 [b] Judg. 9:5; 1 Kin. 21:21; 2 Kin. 11:1
9 [c] 2 Kin. 9:14-24
10 [d] 1 Sam. 3:19; 1 Kin. 8:56; Jer. 44:28 [e] 1 Kin. 21:17-24, 29
12 [5] Or *The Shearing House*
13 [f] 2 Chr. 22:8
14 [g] 2 Chr. 22:8 [6] Or *The Shearing House*
15 [h] Jer. 35:6 [i] 1 Chr. 2:55 [j] Ezra 10:19; Ezek. 17:18 [7] Lit. *found*
16 [k] 1 Kin. 19:10
17 [l] 2 Kin. 9:8; 2 Chr. 22:8 [m] 1 Kin. 21:21, 29
18 [n] 1 Kin. 16:31, 32
19 [o] 1 Kin. 18:19; 22:6
20 [8] *Consecrate*
21 [p] 1 Kin. 16:32; 2 Kin. 11:18 [9] Lit. *house*

10:6 the heads of the men. As a tangible sign of their surrender, Jehu required the officials to decapitate all of Ahab's male descendants and bring their heads to Jehu at Jezreel by the next day.

10:7 heads in baskets. Out of fear, the officials obeyed Jehu by decapitating Ahab's male descendants. However, they did not personally go to Jehu in Jezreel, probably fearing that a similar fate would await them.

10:8 two heaps. The practice of piling the heads of conquered subjects at the city gate was common in the ancient Near East, especially by the Assyrians. The practice was designed to dissuade rebellion.

10:9 I conspired…killed. Jehu is referring to his murder of Joram (9:14-24).

10:10 word of the LORD. God had prophesied through Elijah the destruction of Ahab's house (1 Kin. 21:17-24).

10:11 Jehu killed all. Jehu went beyond God's mandate and executed all of Ahab's officials, a deed for which God later judged Jehu's house (cf. Hos. 1:4).

10:13 brothers of Ahaziah. Since the brothers of Ahaziah, the slain king of Judah (9:27-29), had been previously killed by the Philistines (2 Chr. 21:17), these must have been relatives of Ahaziah in a broader sense, like nephews and cousins.

10:14 This slaughter by Jehu was because these people might have stimulated and strengthened those who were still loyal to the family of Ahab.

10:15 Jenonadab the son of Rechab. This man was a faithful follower of the Lord and a strict observer of the Mosaic law, leading a life of austerity and abstinence. According to Jer. 35:1-16, the Rechabites did not plant fields or drink wine. They shook hands, indicating a pledge of support for Jehu from this influential man.

10:18,19 Ahab served Baal a little, Jehu will serve him much. Though it was in fact a ruse (v. 19), Jehu promised to outdo Ahab's devotion to Baal. The people of Samaria might have thought that Jehu was seeking a military, not a religious, reformation. If so, Jehu was seeking Baal's blessing on his reign as king (v. 20).

10:21 temple of Baal. The idolatrous worship center that Ahab had built in Samaria (1 Kin. 16:32). All the worshipers could fit into that one edifice because the number of Baal devotees had been reduced by the influence of Elijah and Elisha and by the neglect and discontinuance of Baal worship under Joram.

22 And he said to the one in charge of the
wardrobe, "Bring out vestments for all the
worshipers of Baal." So he brought out
vestments for them. 23 Then Jehu and Jehonadab the son of Rechab went into the
temple of Baal, and said to the worshipers
of Baal, "Search and see that no servants of
the LORD are here with you, but only the
worshipers of Baal." 24 So they went in to
offer sacrifices and burnt offerings. Now
Jehu had appointed for himself eighty men
on the outside, and had said, "*If* any of the
men whom I have brought into your hands
escapes, *whoever lets him escape, it shall be*
[q]his life for the life of the other."
25 Now it happened, as soon as he had
made an end of offering the burnt offering,
that Jehu said to the guard and to the captains, "Go in *and* kill them; let no one come
out!" And they killed them with the edge
of the sword; then the guards and the officers threw *them* out, and went into the [1]in-
ner room of the temple of Baal. 26 And they
brought the [r]*sacred* pillars out of the temple of Baal and burned them. 27 Then they
broke down the *sacred* pillar of Baal, and
tore down the [2]temple of Baal and [s]made
it a refuse dump to this day. 28 Thus Jehu
destroyed Baal from Israel.
29 However Jehu did not turn away from
the sins of Jeroboam the son of Nebat, who
had made Israel sin, *that is,* from [t]the golden
calves that *were* at Bethel and Dan. 30 And
the LORD [u]said to Jehu, "Because you have
done well in doing *what is* right in My sight,
and have done to the house of Ahab all that
was in My heart, [v]your sons shall sit on the
throne of Israel to the fourth *generation.*"
31 But Jehu [3]took no heed to walk in the law

24 [q] 1 Kin. 20:39
25 [1] Lit. *city*
26 [r] [Deut. 7:5, 25]; 1 Kin. 14:23; 2 Kin. 3:2
27 [s] Ezra 6:11; Dan. 2:5; 3:29 [2] Lit. *house*
29 [t] 1 Kin. 12:28-30; 13:33, 34
30 [u] 2 Kin. 9:6, 7 [v] 2 Kin. 13:1, 10; 14:23; 15:8, 12
31 [3] *was not careful*

of the LORD God of Israel with all his heart;
for he did not depart from [w]the sins of Jeroboam, who had made Israel sin.

Death of Jehu

32 In those days the LORD began to cut
off *parts* of Israel; and [x]Hazael conquered
them in all the territory of Israel 33 from
the Jordan eastward: all the land of Gilead—Gad, Reuben, and Manasseh—from
[y]Aroer, which *is* by the River Arnon, including [z]Gilead and Bashan.
34 Now the rest of the acts of Jehu, all that
he did, and all his might, *are* they not written in the book of the chronicles of the kings
of Israel? 35 So Jehu [4]rested with his fathers,
and they buried him in Samaria. Then [a]Je-
hoahaz his son reigned in his place. 36 And
the period that Jehu reigned over Israel in
Samaria *was* twenty-eight years.

Athaliah Reigns in Judah

11 When [a]Athaliah [b]the mother of
Ahaziah saw that her son was
[c]dead, she arose and destroyed all the royal
heirs. 2 But [1]Jehosheba, the daughter of
King Joram, sister of [d]Ahaziah, took [2]Joash
the son of Ahaziah, and stole him away
from among the king's sons *who were* being
murdered; and they hid him and his nurse
in the bedroom, from Athaliah, so that he
was not killed. 3 So he was hidden with her
in the house of the LORD for six years, while
Athaliah reigned over the land.

Joash Crowned King of Judah

4 In [e]the seventh year Jehoiada sent and
brought the captains of hundreds—of the
bodyguards and the [3]escorts—and brought

[w] 1 Kin. 14:16
32 [x] 1 Kin. 19:17; 2 Kin. 8:12; 13:22
33 [y] Deut. 2:36 [z] Amos 1:3-5
35 [a] 2 Kin. 13:1 [4] Died and joined his ancestors

CHAPTER 11

1 [a] 2 Chr. 22:10 [b] 2 Kin. 8:26 [c] 2 Kin. 9:27
2 [d] 2 Kin. 8:25 [1] *Jehoshabeath,* 2 Chr. 22:11 [2] Or *Jehoash*
4 [e] 2 Kin. 12:2; 2 Chr. 23:1 [3] *guards*

10:26 *sacred* pillars. These were wooden idols distinct from the main image "pillar" of Baal (v. 27).

10:27 a refuse dump. Lit. "place of dung." This desecration of the site discouraged any rebuilding of the temple of Baal.

10:28 destroyed Baal from Israel. Jehu rid the northern kingdom of royally sanctioned Baal worship. It was done, however, not from spiritual and godly motives, but because Jehu believed that Baalism was inextricably bound to the dynasty and influence of Ahab. By its extermination, he thought he would kill all the last vestiges of Ahab loyalists and incur the support of those in the land who worshiped the true God. Jonadab didn't know of that motive, so he concurred with what Jehu did.

10:29 the sins of Jeroboam. However, Jehu did continue to officially sanction other idolatry introduced into the northern kingdom by Jeroboam I (cf. 1 Kin. 12:28-33).

10:33 from the Jordan eastward. Because Jehu failed to keep the Lord's law wholeheartedly (v. 31), the Lord punished him by giving Israel's land E of the Jordan River to Syria. This lost region was the homeland of the tribes of Gad, Reuben, and half of Manasseh (Num. 32:1-42).

10:36 twenty-eight years. 841–814 B.C.

11:1 Athaliah. A granddaughter of Omri (8:26) and daughter of Ahab and Jezebel. She was zealous to rule after the death of her son, Ahaziah (9:27) and was dedicated to seeing the worship of Baal officially sanctioned in Judah (*see note on 8:18*). She reigned for 6 years (v. 3) ca. 841–835 B.C. *See notes on 2 Chr. 22:10–23:21.* **destroyed all the royal heirs.** The previous deaths of Jehoram's brothers (2 Chr. 21:4) and Ahaziah's brothers and relatives (10:12-14; 2 Chr. 21:17) left only her grandchildren for Athaliah to put to death to destroy the Davidic line. Though the Lord had promised that the house of David would rule over Israel and Judah forever (2 Sam. 7:16), Athaliah's purge brought the house of David to the brink of extinction.

11:2 Jehosheba. She was probably the daughter of Jehoram by a wife other than Athaliah, and so a half-sister of Ahaziah, who was married to the High-Priest, Jehoida (2 Chr. 22:11). **Joash.** The grandson of Athaliah who escaped her purge. **bedroom.** Lit. "the room of the beds." It was either the palace storeroom where servants kept the bedding or a room in the living quarters of the temple priests.

11:3 in the house of the LORD. The temple in Jerusalem. **six years.** 841–835 B.C.

11:4 seventh year. The beginning of Athaliah's 7th year of reign, 835 B.C. **Jehoiada.** The High-Priest during Athaliah's reign (*see note on 2 Chr. 24:15, 16*). He was the husband of Jehosheba (v. 2; 2 Chr. 22:11). **captains of hundreds.** These were the commanders of

them into the house of the LORD to him.
And he made a covenant with them and
took an oath from them in the house of the
LORD, and showed them the king's son.
5 Then he commanded them, saying, "This
is what you shall do: One-third of you who
[4]come on duty [f]on the Sabbath shall be
keeping watch over the king's house, 6 one-
third *shall be* at the gate of Sur, and one-
third at the gate behind the escorts. You
shall keep the watch of the house, lest it be
broken down. 7 The two [5]contingents of
you who go off duty on the Sabbath shall
keep the watch of the house of the LORD for
the king. 8 But you shall surround the king
on all sides, every man with his weapons in
his hand; and whoever comes within
range, let him be put to death. You are to be
with the king as he goes out and as he
comes in."
9 [g]So the captains of the hundreds did
according to all that Jehoiada the priest
commanded. Each of them took his men
who were to be on duty on the Sabbath,
with those who were going off duty on the
Sabbath, and came to Jehoiada the priest.
10 And the priest gave the captains of hundreds the spears and shields which *had belonged* to King David, [h]that were in the
temple of the LORD. 11 Then the escorts
stood, every man with his weapons in his
hand, all around the king, from the right
[6]side of the temple to the left side of the
temple, by the altar and the house. 12 And
he brought out the king's son, put the
crown on him, and *gave him* the [i]Testi-
mony;[7] they made him king and anointed
him, and they clapped their hands and
said, [j]"Long live the king!"

Death of Athaliah

13 [k]Now when Athaliah heard the noise
of the escorts *and* the people, she came to
the people *in* the temple of the LORD.
14 When she looked, there was the king
standing by [l]a pillar according to custom;
and the leaders and the trumpeters were
by the king. All the people of the land were
rejoicing and blowing trumpets. So Athaliah tore her clothes and cried out, "Treason! Treason!"
15 And Jehoiada the priest commanded
the captains of the hundreds, the officers of
the army, and said to them, "Take her outside [8]under guard, and slay with the
sword whoever follows her." For the priest
had said, "Do not let her be killed in the
house of the LORD." 16 So they seized her;
and she went by way of the horses' entrance *into* the king's house, and there she
was killed.
17 [m]Then Jehoiada [n]made a covenant between the LORD, the king, and the people,
that they should be the LORD's people, and
also [o]between the king and the people.
18 And all the people of the land went to
the [p]temple of Baal, and tore it down. They
thoroughly [q]broke in pieces its altars and
[9]images, and [r]killed Mattan the priest of
Baal before the altars. And [s]the priest

5 [f] 1 Chr. 9:25 [4] Lit. *enter in*
7 [5] *companies*
9 [g] 2 Chr. 23:8
10 [h] 2 Sam. 8:7; 1 Chr. 18:7
11 [6] Lit. *shoulder*
12 [i] Ex. 25:16; 31:18 [j] 1 Sam. 10:24 [7] Law, Ex. 25:16, 21; Deut. 31:9
13 [k] 2 Kin. 8:26; 2 Chr. 23:12
14 [l] 2 Kin. 23:3; 2 Chr. 34:31
15 [8] Lit. *between ranks*
17 [m] 2 Chr. 23:16 [n] Josh. 24:24, 25; 2 Chr. 15:12-15 [o] 2 Sam. 5:3
18 [p] 2 Kin. 10:26, 27 [q] [Deut. 12:3] [r] 1 Kin. 18:40; 2 Kin. 10:11 [s] 2 Chr. 23:18 [9] Idols

each 100 soldier unit; 2 Chr. 23:1,2 names 5 of these commanders. The bodyguards were "Carites" associated with the Pelethites (2 Sam. 20:23), who were mercenary soldiers serving as royal bodyguards. The escorts, lit. "runners," were probably another unit of royal bodyguards who provided palace security (see 1 Kin. 14:27). Jehoiada received an agreement of support from the royal guards, sealed with an oath of allegiance, and then presented Joash to them. The military leaders supported the plan to dispose of Athaliah and make Joash king.

11:5-8 Jehoiada outlined his plan to crown Joash as the king. On a selected Sabbath, the royal guards coming on duty, including priests and Levites (2 Chr. 23:4), would guard the palace as usual. They would especially make sure that no word concerning the coup in the temple courtyard reached Athaliah and those loyal to her. The companies going off duty would not return to their quarters as usual, but would instead report to the temple to form a tight security ring around the young potential king. The successful accomplishment of Jehoiada's plan is recorded in vv. 9-12.

11:6 gate of Sur. The exact location of this gate is unknown. Verse 19 implies that this gate connected the temple with the palace.

11:10 spears and shields. These were probably part of the plunder David captured from King Hadadezer of Zobah (2 Sam. 8:3-12). Dedicated to David by the Lord (2 Sam. 8:7,11), these articles were stored in the temple. Since the soldiers were already armed, these additional ancient weapons symbolically reassured the soldiers that the temple authorities approved of their actions.

11:12 the Testimony. This was a copy of the whole law (Ps. 119:88). According to Deut. 17:18-20, a copy of the law was to be kept with the king always so that it became his guide for life. **anointed.** A priest or prophet customarily anointed kings, as here (1 Sam. 10:1; 16:13; 1 Kin. 1:39; 2 Kin. 9:6).

11:14 pillar. Either one of the two pillars, Jachin or Boaz, on the temple's front porch (1 Kin. 7:21), or a raised platform in the court of the temple (cf. 2 Chr. 6:13). **people of the land.** Probably Jehoiada chose to stage his coup on the Sabbath during one of the major religious festivals, when those from Judah who were loyal to the Lord would be in Jerusalem.

11:16 king's house...she was killed. Execution was not appropriate in the temple area since it was a place of worship (cf. 2 Chr. 24:20-22). Thus, the soldiers seized Athaliah and put her to death at one of the entrances to the palace grounds.

11:17 a covenant. The renewal of the agreement between the people and the Lord and between the house of David and the people was appropriate because of the disruption under Athaliah. A similar ceremony was held later, during the reign of Josiah (23:1-3). *See notes on Ex. 24:3-8.*

11:18 the temple of Baal. A temple that had been built in Jerusalem and used by Athaliah to promote the worship of Baal in Judah. As Jezebel had promoted Baalism in Israel, her daughter Athaliah had sought its sanction in Judah. During Athaliah's reign as queen, Baalism gained its strongest foothold in Judah. This purge of Baalism in Judah paralleled the earlier purge of Baalism led by Jehu in the northern kingdom (10:18-29).

appointed [1]officers over the house of the
LORD. **19** Then he took the captains of hundreds, the bodyguards, the escorts, and all
the people of the land; and they brought
the king down from the house of the LORD,
and went by way of the gate of the escorts
to the king's house. Then he sat on the
throne of the kings. **20** So all the people of
the land rejoiced; and the city was quiet,
for they had slain Athaliah with the sword
in the king's house. **21** Jehoash *was* [t]seven
years old when he became king.

Jehoash Repairs the Temple

12 In the seventh year of Jehu, [a]Je-
hoash[1] became king, and he
reigned forty years in Jerusalem. His mother's name *was* Zibiah of Beersheba. **2** Jehoash did *what was* right in the sight of the
LORD all the days in which [b]Jehoiada the
priest instructed him. **3** But [c]the [2]high
places were not taken away; the people
still sacrificed and burned incense on the
high places.
4 And Jehoash said to the priests, [d]"All
the money of the dedicated gifts that are
brought into the house of the LORD—each
man's [e]census[3] money, each man's [f]assess-
ment money—*and* all the money that [4]a
man [g]purposes in his heart to bring into
the house of the LORD, **5** let the priests take
it themselves, each from his constituency;
and let them repair the [5]damages of the
temple, wherever any dilapidation is
found."
6 Now it was so, by the twenty-third
year of King Jehoash, [h]*that* the priests had
not repaired the damages of the temple.
7 [i]So King Jehoash called Jehoiada the
priest and the *other* priests, and said to
them, "Why have you not repaired the
damages of the temple? Now therefore, do
not take *more* money from your constituency, but deliver it for repairing the damages
of the temple." **8** And the priests agreed
that they would neither receive *more*
money from the people, nor repair the
damages of the temple.
9 Then Jehoiada the priest took [j]a chest,
bored a hole in its lid, and set it beside the
altar, on the right side as one comes into
the house of the LORD; and the priests who
[6]kept the door put [k]there all the money
brought into the house of the LORD. **10** So it
was, whenever they saw that *there was*
much money in the chest, that the king's
[l]scribe[7] and the high priest came up and
[8]put it in bags, and counted the money
that was found in the house of the LORD.
11 Then they gave the money, which had
been apportioned, into the hands of those
who did the work, who had the oversight
of the house of the LORD; and they [9]paid it
out to the carpenters and builders who
worked on the house of the LORD, **12** and to
masons and stonecutters, and for buying
timber and hewn stone, to [m]repair the

18 [1] Lit. *offices*
21 [t] 2 Chr. 24:1-14

CHAPTER 12

1 [a] 2 Chr. 24:1 [1] *Joash,* 2 Kin. 11:2ff.
2 [b] 2 Kin. 11:4
3 [c] 1 Kin. 15:14; 22:43; 2 Kin. 14:4; 15:35 [2] *Places for pagan worship*
4 [d] 2 Kin. 22:4 [e] Ex. 30:13-16 [f] Lev. 27:2-28 [g] Ex. 35:5; 1 Chr. 29:3-9 [3] Lit. *the money coming over* [4] *any man's heart prompts him to bring*
5 [5] Lit. *breaches*
6 [h] 2 Chr. 24:5
7 [i] 2 Chr. 24:6
9 [j] 2 Chr. 23:1; 24:8 [k] Mark 12:41; Luke 21:1 [6] *guarded at the door*
10 [l] 2 Sam. 8:17; 2 Kin. 19:2; 22:3, 4, 12 [7] *secretary* [8] *tied it up*
11 [9] Lit. *weighed*
12 [m] 2 Kin. 22:5, 6

11:21 Jehoash. Jehoash and Joash are variants of the same name, meaning "The LORD gave." *See notes on 2 Chr. 24:1-27.*

12:1 seventh year. 835 B.C. Jehu of Israel began his reign in 841 B.C. (*see notes on 9:29; 10:36*). **forty years.** 835–796 B.C.

12:2 all the days…Jehoiada…instructed him. Joash did what pleased the Lord while Jehoida served as his parental guardian and tutor. After Jehoida died, Joash turned away from the Lord (*see note on 2 Chr. 24:17,18a*).

12:3 the high places. *See note on 1 Kin. 3:2.* As with most kings of Judah, Joash failed to remove these places of worship where, contrary to the Mosaic law, the people sacrificed and burned incense to the Lord (cf. Deut. 12:2-7,13,14).

12:4-16 *See notes on 2 Chr. 24:5-14.*

12:4 the dedicated gifts. Lit. "holy gifts." These offerings were given to the priests and used to support the temple. These 3 main offerings were the half a shekel assessed from every male 20 years old and above whenever a census was taken (Ex. 30:11-16), the payments of personal vows (Lev. 27:1-8), and voluntary offerings (Lev. 22:18-23; Deut. 16:10).

12:5 his constituency. This person would be a friend of the priest who either gave offerings or collected the offerings for the priest. Such friends of the priest would make up his "constituency." However, some interpret the Heb. term to mean "treasurer." This understanding views the individual as a member of the temple personnel who assisted the priests with the valuation of sacrifices and offerings brought to the temple. **repair the damages of the temple.** During the reign of Athaliah, the temple had suffered major damages and temple articles had been taken for use in the temple of Baal (2 Chr. 24:7). Joash ordered the priests to channel the temple offerings to fund the needed repairs. This was to be in addition to the normal temple expenses.

12:6 twenty-third year. Ca. 813 B.C. Judah seems to have used the non-accession-year system during the reigns of Athaliah and Joash (*see note on 13:1*), which did not count the first year of the reign but began with the second. This is how we count ages today, starting with the beginning of the second year as one. Joash was 29 years of age.

12:7,8 The plan of Joash did not work. Either the revenue from these sources was inadequate to support the priests and Levites and also to pay for the temple repairs, or the priests for some unknown reason would not fund the temple repairs. Therefore, the priests no longer received the offerings from the people, nor did they fund the temple repairs from the income they had already received.

12:9-16 Joash instituted a new plan. First, a single collection box was to receive all incoming offerings. When the chest was full, only the royal secretary and High-Priest would be authorized to empty it. Second, from the funds thus generated, men were hired to supervise and pay the carpenters, builders, masons, and stonecutters who worked on the temple repairs. The men involved were so trustworthy that no accounting was taken of them (v. 15).

12:9 priests who kept the door. These were priests who normally screened the people to keep unclean worshipers from entering the temple (25:18; Jer. 52:24). These priests took the offerings from the worshipers, who then personally watched the priests drop them into the chest.

damage of the house of the LORD, and for
all that was paid out to repair the temple.
13 However [n]there were not made for the
house of the LORD basins of silver, trimmers, sprinkling-bowls, trumpets, any articles of gold or articles of silver, from the
money brought into the house of the LORD.
14 But they gave that to the workmen, and
they repaired the house of the LORD with it.
15 Moreover [o]they did not require an account from the men into whose hand they
delivered the money to be paid to workmen, for they dealt faithfully. 16 [p]The
money from the trespass offerings and the
money from the sin offerings was not
brought into the house of the LORD. [q]It belonged to the priests.

Hazael Threatens Jerusalem

17 [r]Hazael king of Syria went up and
fought against Gath, and took it; then
[s]Hazael set his face to [1]go up to Jerusalem. 18 And Jehoash king of Judah [t]took
all the sacred things that his fathers, Jehoshaphat and Jehoram and Ahaziah,
kings of Judah, had dedicated, and his
own sacred things, and all the gold found
in the treasuries of the house of the LORD
and in the king's house, and sent *them* to
Hazael king of Syria. Then he went away
from Jerusalem.

Death of Joash

19 Now the rest of the acts of [2]Joash,
and all that he did, *are* they not written in
the book of the chronicles of the kings of
Judah?
20 And [u]his servants arose and formed a
conspiracy, and killed Joash in the house of
[3]the Millo, which goes down to Silla. 21 For
[4]Jozachar the son of Shimeath and Jehozabad the son of [5]Shomer, his servants,
struck him. So he died, and they buried
him with his fathers in the City of David.
Then [v]Amaziah his son reigned in his
place.

Jehoahaz Reigns in Israel

13 In the twenty-third year of [a]Joash[1]
the son of Ahaziah, king of Judah,
[b]Jehoahaz the son of Jehu became king
over Israel in Samaria, *and reigned* seventeen years. 2 And he did evil in the sight of
the LORD, and followed the [c]sins of Jeroboam the son of Nebat, who had made Israel sin. He did not [2]depart from them.
3 Then [d]the anger of the LORD was
aroused against Israel, and He delivered
them into the hand of [e]Hazael king of
Syria, and into the hand of [f]Ben-Hadad
the son of Hazael, all *their* days. 4 So Jehoahaz [g]pleaded with the LORD, and the
LORD listened to him; for [h]He saw the oppression of Israel, because the king of
Syria oppressed them. 5 [i]Then the LORD
gave Israel a deliverer, so that they escaped from under the hand of the Syrians;
and the children of Israel dwelt in their
tents as before. 6 Nevertheless they did
not depart from the sins of the house of

13 [n]2 Chr. 24:14
15 [o]2 Kin. 22:7; [1 Cor. 4:2]; 2 Cor. 8:20
16 [p][Lev. 5:15, 18] [q][Lev. 7:7; Num. 18:9]
17 [r]2 Kin. 8:12 [s]2 Chr. 24:23 [1]Advance upon
18 [t]1 Kin. 15:18; 2 Kin. 16:8; 18:15, 16
19 [2]*Jehoash*, vv. 1-18
20 [u]2 Kin. 14:5; 2 Chr. 24:25 [3]Lit. *The Landfill*
21 [v]2 Chr. 24:27 [4]*Zabad*, 2 Chr. 24:26 [5]*Shimrith*, 2 Chr. 24:26

CHAPTER 13

1 [a]2 Kin. 12:1 [b]2 Kin. 10:35 [1]*Jehoash*, 2 Kin. 12:1-18
2 [c]1 Kin. 12:26-33 [2]Lit. *turn*
3 [d]Judg. 2:14 [e]2 Kin. 8:12 [f]Amos 1:4
4 [g][Ps. 78:34] [h][Ex. 3:7, 9; Judg. 2:18]; 2 Kin. 14:26
5 [i]2 Kin. 13:25; 14:25, 27; Neh. 9:27

12:16 money from the trespass offerings and...sin offerings. The income from these offerings was distinct from the income mentioned in v. 4 and so was not used in the repair of the temple, but remained the property of the priests (see Lev. 4:1–6:7). The temple repairs did not deprive the priests of their income (Lev. 7:7).

12:17 Hazael. *See notes on 8:8-15.* **Gath.** One of the 5 major Philistine cities (1 Sam. 5:8), located about 25 mi. SW of Jerusalem. Gath had previously belonged to Judah (2 Chr. 11:8).

12:18 all the sacred things. When Joash's army was defeated by Hazael and his leading men killed (2 Chr. 24:23,24), he averted further attacks against Jerusalem by sending tribute to the king of Syria. This tribute included gifts donated to the temple in Jerusalem by kings of Judah (cf. 1 Kin. 15:15,18).

12:19 acts of Joash. A more complete account of the reign of Joash is found in 2 Chr. 22:10–24:27.

12:20 a conspiracy. Some of the officials of Joash conspired against him because he had killed the High-Priest Zechariah, the son of the priest Jehoiada (2 Chr. 24:20-22). **house of the Millo.** Probably a house built on a landfill N of David's city of Jerusalem and S of the temple mount. Cf. 2 Chr. 24:25. **Silla.** Possibly a ramp that descended from the landfill to the Kidron Valley.

12:21 Amaziah. See 14:1-22 for the reign of Amaziah.

13:1 twenty-third year. 814 B.C. Joash of Judah began his reign in 835 B.C. (*see notes on 12:1*) and Jehu of Israel died in 814 B.C. (*see note on 10:36*). Thus the 23rd year of Joash of Judah was calculated according to the non-accession-year system (*see notes on 12:6; 13:10*). **seventeen years.** 814–798 B.C., i.e., part of 17 calendar years, with the actual reign counted as 16 years.

13:2 Jeroboam. For his sins, *see notes on 1 Kin. 12:25-33.* This description of Jeroboam as one who "made Israel sin" occurs in 13:6,11; 1 Kin. 14:16; 15:30; 16:31; 2 Kin. 3:3; 10:29,31; 14:24; 15:9,18,24,28; 17:21,22.

13:2-7 The record of the reign of Jehoahaz, the king of Israel, has literary and verbal similarities to the book of Judges: 1) Jehoahaz did evil in the sight of the Lord (v. 2; cf. Judg. 2:11-13; 3:7); 2) the anger of the Lord was aroused against Israel and He delivered them over to their enemies (v. 3; cf. Judg. 2:14,15; 3:8); 3) Jehoahaz cried out to the Lord who saw their oppression (v. 4; cf. Judg. 2:18; 3:9); 4) the Lord raised up a deliverer for Israel who rescued them out of the hand of their enemies (v. 5; cf. Judg. 2:16,18; 3:9); and 5) Israel continued in her evil ways with the result of further oppression (vv. 6,7; cf. Judg. 2:19; 3:12-14).

13:3 Hazael. *See notes on 8:8-15.* **Ben-Hadad.** Either Ben-Hadad II or, more likely, III (*see note on 1 Kin. 15:18*). His reign as king of Syria began ca. 801 B.C. The length of his rule is unknown.

13:5 a deliverer. The deliverer was not specifically named. This deliverer was: 1) the Assyrian king Adad-Nirari III (ca. 810–783 B.C.), whose attack on the Syrians enabled the Israelites to break Syria's control over Israelite territory (see v. 25; 14:25); or 2) Elisha, who as the leader of Israel's military successes (see v. 14; cf. 6:13,16-23) commissioned Joash to defeat the Syrians (vv. 15-19); or 3) Jeroboam II (ca. 793–753 B.C.), who was able to extend Israel's boundaries back into Syrian territory (14:25-27).

Jeroboam, who had made Israel sin, *but*
walked in them; [j]and the [3]wooden image
also remained in Samaria. 7 For He left of
the army of Jehoahaz only fifty horsemen,
ten chariots, and ten thousand foot soldiers; for the king of Syria had destroyed
them [k]and made them [l]like the dust at
threshing.
8 Now the rest of the acts of Jehoahaz, all
that he did, and his might, *are* they not written in the book of the chronicles of the kings
of Israel? 9 So Jehoahaz [4]rested with his fathers, and they buried him in Samaria. Then
[5]Joash his son reigned in his place.

Jehoash Reigns in Israel

10 In the thirty-seventh year of Joash
king of Judah, [6]Jehoash the son of Jehoahaz became king over Israel in Samaria,
and reigned sixteen years. 11 And he did
evil in the sight of the LORD. He did not depart from all the sins of Jeroboam the son
of Nebat, who made Israel sin, *but* walked
in them.
12 [m]Now the rest of the acts of Joash, [n]all
that he did, and [o]his might with which he
fought against Amaziah king of Judah, *are*
they not written in the book of the chronicles of the kings of Israel? 13 So Joash [p]rest-
ed[7] with his fathers. Then Jeroboam sat on
his throne. And Joash was buried in Samaria with the kings of Israel.

Death of Elisha

14 Elisha had become sick with the illness of which he would die. Then Joash the
king of Israel came down to him, and wept
over his face, and said, "O my father, my
father, [q]the chariots of Israel and their
horsemen!"
15 And Elisha said to him, "Take a bow
and some arrows." So he took himself a
bow and some arrows. 16 Then he said to
the king of Israel, "Put your hand on the
bow." So he put his hand *on it,* and Elisha
put his hands on the king's hands. 17 And
he said, "Open the east window"; and he
opened *it.* Then Elisha said, "Shoot"; and
he shot. And he said, "The arrow of the
LORD's deliverance and the arrow of deliverance from Syria; for you must strike the
Syrians at [r]Aphek till you have destroyed
them." 18 Then he said, "Take the arrows";
so he took *them.* And he said to the king of
Israel, "Strike the ground"; so he struck
three times, and stopped. 19 And the man
of God was angry with him, and said,
"You should have struck five or six times;
then you would have struck Syria till you
had destroyed *it!* [s]But now you will strike
Syria *only* three times."
20 Then Elisha [8]died, and they buried
him. And the [t]*raiding* bands from Moab invaded the land in the spring of the year.
21 So it was, as they were burying a man,
that suddenly they spied a band *of raiders;*
and they put the man in the tomb of Elisha;
and when the man was let down and
touched the bones of Elisha, he revived
and stood on his feet.

6 [j] 1 Kin. 16:33 [3] Heb. *Asherah,* a Canaanite goddess
7 [k] 2 Kin. 10:32 [l] [Amos 1:3]
9 [4] Died and joined his ancestors [5] Or *Jehoash*
10 [6] *Joash,* v. 9
12 [m] 2 Kin. 14:8-15 [n] 2 Kin. 13:14-19, 25 [o] 2 Kin. 14:9; 2 Chr. 25:17-25
13 [p] 2 Kin. 14:16 [7] Died and joined his ancestors
14 [q] 2 Kin. 2:12
17 [r] 1 Kin. 20:26
19 [s] 2 Kin. 13:25
20 [t] 2 Kin. 3:5; 24:2 [8] Having prophesied at least 55 years

13:6 sins...of Jeroboam. *See note on v. 2.* **wooden image.** This idol representing Asherah, a Canaanite goddess and a consort of Baal, had been set up by Ahab (1 Kin. 16:33) and had escaped destruction by Jehu when he purged Baal worship from Samaria (10:27,28). Along with the other idolatrous religion of Jeroboam II, there were still remnants of Baal worship in the northern kingdom.

13:7 the army. Syria was able to dominate Israel militarily because the Lord had left Jehoahaz only a small army with very few chariots. **dust at threshing.** The army of Israel was so inconsequential, particularly when compared to the armies of Syria and Assyria, that it was likened to the dust left over after grain had been winnowed at a threshing floor.

13:10 thirty-seventh year. Ca. 798 B.C. Joash of Judah began his reign in 835 B.C. (*see note on 12:1*). There is a change here to the accession-year system of dating for the reign of Joash of Judah (*see note on 13:1*). This explains how Jehoahaz of Israel could reign 16 years with only a 15 year advance on Joash of Judah's regnal years (cf. v. 1). **Jehoash.** This king of Israel had the same name as his contemporary, the king of Judah (*see note on 11:21*). **sixteen years.** 798–782 B.C.

13:12 fought against Amaziah. *See notes on 14:8-16.*

13:14 Elisha. The last previous reference to Elisha the prophet was in 9:1 when Jehu was anointed king of Israel. Since Jehu and Jehoahaz reigned from 841–798 B.C. (*see notes on 10:36; 13:1*), nothing was recorded for over 40 years of Elisha's life. Elisha began ministering with Elijah during the kingship of Ahab ca. 874–853 B.C. (1 Kin. 19:19-21) and so must have been over 70 years of age when these final events of his life took place. **my father.** Jehoash humbly voiced his great respect for Elisha and his dependence upon his counsel (*see note on 2:12*). **the chariots of Israel and their horsemen.** Jehoash acknowledged through this metaphor that the Lord, through Elisha, was the real strength and power of Israel against all her adversaries (*see note on 2:11*).

13:15,16 Elisha put his hands on the king's hands. This symbolic act indicated that Jehoash would exert power against the Syrians that came from the Lord through His prophet.

13:17 east window. This window opened toward the E to the Transjordan region controlled by Syria (10:32,33). **The arrow of the LORD's deliverance.** When Jehoash obeyed Elisha by shooting an arrow out the window, the prophet interpreted the meaning of the action. The shot symbolized the Lord's deliverance for Israel through the defeat of the Syrian army by Jehoash (cf. v. 5). **Aphek.** *See note on 1 Kin. 20:26.*

13:19 three times. Further, Elisha commanded Jehoash to shoot the remaining arrows into the ground (v. 18). Jehoash shot only 3 arrows into the ground instead of emptying the entire quiver. Because of his lack of faith, Jehoash would win only 3 victories over the Syrians instead of completely destroying them. The account of these victories is given in v. 25.

13:20 spring. The prophet, who was Israel's defense (v. 14), was dead and it was the season for war campaigns to begin after the rains of winter.

13:21 he revived. A dead man returned to life after touching Elisha's bones. This miracle was a sign that God's power continued to

Israel Recaptures Cities from Syria

22 And [u]Hazael king of Syria oppressed
Israel all the days of Jehoahaz. 23 But the
LORD was [v]gracious to them, had compassion on them, and [w]regarded them, [x]be-
cause of His covenant with Abraham,
Isaac, and Jacob, and would not yet destroy them or cast them from His presence.
24 Now Hazael king of Syria died. Then
Ben-Hadad his son reigned in his place.
25 And [9]Jehoash the son of Jehoahaz recaptured from the hand of Ben-Hadad, the son
of Hazael, the cities which he had taken
out of the hand of Jehoahaz his father by
war. [y]Three times Joash defeated him and
recaptured the cities of Israel.

Amaziah Reigns in Judah

14 In [a]the second year of Joash the son
of Jehoahaz, king of Israel, [b]Ama-
ziah the son of Joash, king of Judah, became king. 2 He was twenty-five years old
when he became king, and he reigned
twenty-nine years in Jerusalem. His mother's name was Jehoaddan of Jerusalem.
3 And he did *what was* right in the sight of
the LORD, yet not like his father David; he
did everything [c]as his father Joash had
done. 4 [d]However the [1]high places were
not taken away, and the people still sacrificed and burned incense on the high
places.
5 Now it happened, as soon as the kingdom was established in his hand, that he
executed his servants [e]who had murdered
his father the king. 6 But the children of the
murderers he did not execute, according to
what is written in the Book of the Law of
Moses, in which the LORD commanded,
saying, [f]"Fathers shall not be put to death
for their children, nor shall children be put
to death for their fathers; but a person shall
be put to death for his own sin."
7 [g]He killed ten thousand Edomites in
[h]the Valley of Salt, and took [2]Sela by war,
[i]and called its name Joktheel to this day.
8 [j]Then Amaziah sent messengers to [3]Je-
hoash the son of Jehoahaz, the son of Jehu,
king of Israel, saying, "Come, let us face
one another *in battle*." 9 And Jehoash king
of Israel sent to Amaziah king of Judah,
saying, [k]"The thistle that *was* in Lebanon
sent to the [l]cedar that *was* in Lebanon, saying, 'Give your daughter to my son as
wife'; and a wild beast that *was* in Lebanon
passed by and trampled the thistle. 10 You
have indeed defeated Edom, and [m]your
heart has [4]lifted you up. Glory *in that*, and

22 [u] 2 Kin. 8:12, 13
23 [v] 2 Kin. 14:27 [w] [Ex. 2:24, 25] [x] Gen. 13:16, 17; 17:2-7; Ex. 32:13
25 [y] 2 Kin. 13:18, 19 [9] *Joash*, vv. 12-14, 25

CHAPTER 14
1 [a] 2 Kin. 13:10 [b] 2 Chr. 25:1, 2
3 [c] 2 Kin. 12:2
4 [d] 2 Kin. 12:3 [1] Places for pagan worship
5 [e] 2 Kin. 12:20
6 [f] Deut. 24:16; [Jer. 31:30; Ezek. 18:4, 20]
7 [g] 2 Chr. 25:5-16 [h] 2 Sam. 8:13; 1 Chr. 18:12; Ps. 60:title [i] Josh. 15:38 [2] Lit. *The Rock;* the city of Petra
8 [j] 2 Chr. 25:17, 18 [3] *Joash*, 2 Kin. 13:9, 12-14, 25; 2 Chr. 25:17ff.
9 [k] Judg. 9:8-15 [l] 1 Kin. 4:33
10 [m] Deut. 8:14; 2 Chr. 32:25; [Ezek. 28:2, 5, 17; Hab. 2:4] [4] Made you proud

work in relationship to Elisha even after his death. What God had promised to Jehoash through Elisha when he was alive would surely come to pass after the prophet's death (cf. vv. 19,25) in the defeat of the enemy, the recovery of the cities that had been taken, and their restoration to the kingdom of Israel (vv. 22-25).

13:22 *See note on 8:12.*

13:23 His covenant with Abraham, Isaac, and Jacob. During the wicked reign of Jehoahaz (vv. 2-7), the Lord was very patient and did not bring the ultimate military defeat that would lead to exile for Israel. This was because of His agreement with the patriarchs to give their descendants the land (Gen. 15:18-21; 26:2-5; 28:13-15). It was God's promise, not the Israelites' goodness, that motivated God to be merciful and compassionate toward Israel.

14:1–15:38 This section quickly surveys the kings and selected events of the northern and southern kingdoms from 796 to 735 B.C. In contrast to the previous 19 chapters (1 Kin. 17:1–2 Kin. 13:25), which narrated 90 years of history (885–796 B.C.) with a concentration on the ministries of Elijah and Elisha during the final 65 years of that period (860–796 B.C.), 62 years are covered in these two chapters. The previous section concluded with a shadow of hope: officially sanctioned Baal worship had been eradicated in both Israel (10:18-28) and Judah (11:17,18); the temple of the Lord in Jerusalem had been repaired (12:9-15); and the Syrian threat to Israel had been overcome (13:25). However, this section emphasizes that the fundamental problems still remained: the false religion established by Jeroboam I continued in Israel even with the change of royal families (14:24–15:9,18,24,28), and the high places were not removed in Judah even though there were only good kings there during those years (14:4; 15:4,35).

14:1 second year. 796 B.C. **Amaziah.** *See notes on 2 Chr. 25:1-28.*

14:2 twenty-nine years. 796–767 B.C.

14:3 not like…David. David set a high standard of unswerving devotion to the Lord for the kings of Judah who were his descendants to follow (cf. 1 Kin. 11:4,6; 15:3). Amaziah did not follow the Lord completely ,as David had, because he, like his father Joash, did not remove the high places (v. 4) where, in disregard for Mosaic law, the people worshiped the Lord (Deut. 12:2-7,13,14). Further, according to 2 Chr. 25:14-16, Amaziah embraced the false gods of the Edomites.

14:5,6 When firmly in control of the kingdom, Amaziah took revenge on Jozachar and Jehozabad, the officials who assassinated his father Joash (12:20,21). However, he spared the lives of their sons, in obedience to the Mosaic law that children were not to die for their fathers' sins (Deut. 24:16; cf. Ezek. 18:1-20).

14:7 For an elaboration of Amaziah's war with Edom, *see the notes on 2 Chr. 25:5-16.* Edom had revolted in Joram's reign (see 8:20) so the king wanted them subjugated again. **the Valley of Salt.** Probably a marshy plain at the S end of the Dead Sea (*see note on 2 Sam. 8:13*). **Sela…Joktheel.** Sela (meaning "rock" in Heb.) is best identified as Petra (meaning "rock" in Gr.), a city carved out of sheer mountain walls located about 50 mi. S of the Dead Sea, though some prefer to place it in northern Edom near Bozra on the King's Highway (Judg. 1:36). Renaming a captured city, as Amaziah did with the name Joktheel, implied his control over it.

14:8 Jehoash…of Israel. *See notes on 13:10-25.* **face one another.** Amaziah's challenge to Jehoash constituted a declaration of war. Amaziah, emboldened by his victory over Edom (v. 10), thought he could defeat the stronger army of Israel (cf. 13:25). He was probably also upset by the refusal of Jehoash to establish a marriage alliance with him (v. 9).

14:9 thistle…cedar. In this parable (cf. Judg. 9:8-15) the thistle (Amaziah), an irritating and worthless plant, sought to become the equal of the majestic cedar (Jehoash), but a wild animal crushed the thistle. Jehoash counseled Amaziah that he was overestimating his power and prominence and should not to go war with Israel lest he be crushed (v. 10).

stay at home; for why should you meddle
with trouble so that you fall—you and Judah with you?"
11 But Amaziah would not heed. Therefore Jehoash king of Israel went out; so he
and Amaziah king of Judah faced one another at [n]Beth Shemesh, which *belongs* to
Judah. 12 And Judah was defeated by Israel, and every man fled to his tent.
13 Then Jehoash king of Israel captured
Amaziah king of Judah, the son of Jehoash,
the son of Ahaziah, at Beth Shemesh; and
he went to Jerusalem, and broke down the
wall of Jerusalem from [o]the Gate of Ephraim to [p]the Corner Gate—[5]four hundred
cubits. 14 And he took all [q]the gold and silver, all the articles that were found in the
house of the LORD and in the treasuries of
the king's house, and hostages, and returned to Samaria.
15 [r]Now the rest of the acts of Jehoash
which he did—his might, and how he
fought with Amaziah king of Judah—*are*
they not written in the book of the chronicles of the kings of Israel? 16 So Jehoash
[6]rested with his fathers, and was buried in
Samaria with the kings of Israel. Then Jeroboam his son reigned in his place.
17 [s]Amaziah the son of Joash, king of Judah, lived fifteen years after the death of
Jehoash the son of Jehoahaz, king of Israel.
18 Now the rest of the acts of Amaziah, *are*
they not written in the book of the chronicles of the kings of Judah? 19 And [t]they
formed a conspiracy against him in Jerusalem, and he fled to [u]Lachish; but they sent
after him to Lachish and killed him there.
20 Then they brought him on horses, and
he was buried at Jerusalem with his fathers
in the City of David.
21 And all the people of Judah took [v]Aza-
riah,[7] who *was* sixteen years old, and made
him king instead of his father Amaziah.
22 He built [w]Elath[8] and restored it to Judah,
after [9]the king rested with his fathers.

Jeroboam II Reigns in Israel

23 In the fifteenth year of Amaziah the son
of Joash, king of Judah, Jeroboam the son of
Joash, king of Israel, became king in Samaria, *and reigned* forty-one years. 24 And he
did evil in the sight of the LORD; he did not
depart from all the [x]sins of Jeroboam the son
of Nebat, who had made Israel sin. 25 He
[y]restored the [1]territory of Israel [z]from the
entrance of Hamath to [a]the[2] Sea of the Arabah, according to the word of the LORD God
of Israel, which He had spoken through His
servant [b]Jonah the son of Amittai, the
prophet who *was* from [c]Gath Hepher. 26 For

11 [n] Josh. 19:38; 21:16
13 [o] Neh. 8:16; 12:39 [p] Jer. 31:38; Zech. 14:10 [5] About 600 feet
14 [q] 1 Kin. 7:51; 2 Kin. 12:18; 16:8
15 [r] 2 Kin. 13:12, 13
16 [6] Died and joined his ancestors
17 [s] 2 Chr. 25:25-28
19 [t] 2 Chr. 25:27 [u] Josh. 10:31
21 [v] 2 Kin. 15:13; 2 Chr. 26:1 [7] *Uzziah,* 2 Chr. 26:1ff.; Is. 6:1; etc.
22 [w] 1 Kin. 9:26; 2 Kin. 16:6; 2 Chr. 8:17 [8] Heb. *Eloth* [9] Amaziah died and joined his ancestors.
24 [x] 1 Kin. 12:26-33
25 [y] 2 Kin. 10:32; 13:5, 25 [z] Num. 13:21; 34:8; 1 Kin. 8:65 [a] Deut. 3:17 [b] Jon. 1:1; Matt. 12:39, 40 [c] Josh. 19:13 [1] *border* [2] The Dead Sea

14:11 Beth Shemesh. A town about 15 mi. W of Jerusalem, where the armies of Israel and Judah faced each other in battle.

14:13 Jehoash...captured Amaziah. Winning the battle, Jehoash also captured Amaziah. Jehoash probably took Amaziah back to Samaria as a hostage (v. 14). The king of Judah was forced to stay in Samaria until the death of Jehoash in 782 B.C. (v. 17). **Gate of Ephraim...Corner Gate.** The Corner Gate (cf. Jer. 31:38; Zech. 14:10) was at the NW corner of the wall around Jerusalem. The Ephraim Gate was in Jerusalem's northern wall facing Ephraim, 600 ft. E of the Corner Gate. This northwestern section of the wall of Jerusalem, torn down by Jehoash, was the point where Jerusalem was most vulnerable.

14:14 he took. Jehoash plundered both the temple at Jerusalem and the palace of Amaziah. The value of the plundered articles was probably not great, because Jehoash of Judah had previously sent the temple and palace treasures to pay tribute to Hazael of Damascus (12:17,18). Jehoash probably took hostages from Jerusalem to Samaria to secure additional payments of tribute in view of the small war booty.

14:17 fifteen years. 782–767 B.C.

14:18 the acts of Amaziah. His apostasy (2 Chr. 25:27), his disastrous war with Israel, the ruinous condition of Jerusalem, the plunder of the temple, and the loss of hostages lost him the respect of his people who rebelled and killed him.

14:19 Lachish. A town about 25 mi. SW of Jerusalem to which Amaziah fled seeking to escape death.

14:21 sixteen years old. Azariah, a.k.a. Uzziah (*see note on 15:1*) had actually begun to reign at the age of 16 in 790 B.C. when his father Amaziah was taken prisoner to Samaria (v. 13). When Amaziah returned to Judah, Azariah ruled with him as co-regent from 782–767 B.C. (v. 17). In 767 B.C. when Amaziah was killed (v. 19), Azariah began his sole rule (15:1). *See notes on 2 Chr. 26:1-23.*

14:22 Elath. Elath was located on the northern coast of the Gulf of Aqabah and was closely associated with Ezion Geber, a seaport of Solomon (1 Kin. 9:26). Azariah's restoration of Elath to Judah marked the first significant act of his sole rule; his further successes are summarized in 2 Chr. 26:6-15.

14:23 fifteenth year. Ca. 782 B.C. This marked the beginning of the sole reign of Jeroboam II. Since his son Zechariah succeeded him in 753 B.C. (see 15:8), Jeroboam II must have had a co-regency with his father Jehoash for 11 years, making a total reign of 41 years (793–753 B.C.), longer than any other king in the northern kingdom. **Jeroboam.** This was Jeroboam II, who like the other kings of Israel, followed the false religion of Jeroboam I. During the reign of Jeroboam II, the prophets Hosea (Hos. 1:1) and Amos (Amos 1:1) ministered to the northern kingdom. These prophets showed that Jeroboam II's reign was a time of great prosperity and greater spiritual apostasy in Israel.

14:25 restored the territory of Israel. Jeroboam II's greatest accomplishment was the restoration of Israel's boundaries to approximately their extent in Solomon's time, excluding the territory belonging to Judah. The northern boundary was the entrance of Hamath, the same as Solomon's (cf. 1 Kin. 8:65) and the southern boundary was the Sea of the Arabah, the Dead Sea (Josh. 3:16; 12:3). Jeroboam II took Hamath, a major city located on the Orontes River, about 160 mi. N of the Sea of Galilee. He also controlled Damascus, indicating that the Transjordan territory S to Moab was also under his authority. These victories of Jeroboam II were accomplished because the Syrians had been weakened by attacks from the Assyrians, while Assyria herself was weak at this time, suffering from threats on her northern border, internal dissension, and a series of weak kings. **Jonah.** The territorial extension of Jeroboam II was in accordance with the will of the Lord as revealed through the prophet Jonah. This was the same Jonah who traveled to Nineveh with God's message of repentance for the Assyrians (see Introduction to Jonah). **Gath Hepher.** A town located in the tribal area of Zebulun, about 14 mi. W of the Sea of Galilee (Josh. 19:13).

the LORD [d]saw *that* the affliction of Israel *was*
very bitter; and whether bond or free, [e]there
was no helper for Israel. 27 [f]And the LORD
did not say that He would blot out the name
of Israel from under heaven; but He saved
them by the hand of Jeroboam the son of
Joash.
28 Now the rest of the acts of Jeroboam,
and all that he did—his might, how he
made war, and how he recaptured for Israel, from [g]Damascus and Hamath, [h]*what*
had belonged to Judah—*are* they not written
in the book of the chronicles of the kings of
Israel? 29 So Jeroboam [3]rested with his fathers, the kings of Israel. Then [i]Zechariah
his son reigned in his place.

Azariah Reigns in Judah

15 In the twenty-seventh year of Jeroboam king of Israel, [a]Azariah the
son of Amaziah, king of Judah, [b]became
king. 2 He was sixteen years old when he
became king, and he reigned fifty-two
years in Jerusalem. His mother's name *was*
Jecholiah of Jerusalem. 3 And he did *what*
was right in the sight of the LORD, according to all that his father Amaziah had
done, 4 [c]except that the [1]high places were
not removed; the people still sacrificed and
burned incense on the high places. 5 Then
the LORD [d]struck the king, so that he was a
leper until the day of his [e]death; so he
[f]dwelt in an isolated house. And Jotham
the king's son *was* over the *royal* house,
judging the people of the land.
6 Now the rest of the acts of Azariah, and
all that he did, *are* they not written in the
book of the chronicles of the kings of Judah? 7 So Azariah [2]rested with his fathers,
and [g]they buried him with his fathers in
the City of David. Then Jotham his son
reigned in his place.

Zechariah Reigns in Israel

8 In the thirty-eighth year of Azariah
king of Judah, [h]Zechariah the son of Jeroboam reigned over Israel in Samaria six
months. 9 And he did evil in the sight of
the LORD, [i]as his fathers had done; he did
not depart from the sins of Jeroboam the
son of Nebat, who had made Israel sin.
10 Then Shallum the son of Jabesh conspired against him, and [j]struck and killed
him in front of the people; and he reigned
in his place.
11 Now the rest of the acts of Zechariah,
indeed they *are* written in the book of the
chronicles of the kings of Israel.
12 This *was* the word of the LORD which
He spoke to Jehu, saying, [k]"Your sons shall
sit on the throne of Israel to the fourth *gen-*
eration." And so it was.

Shallum Reigns in Israel

13 Shallum the son of Jabesh became
king in the thirty-ninth year of [3]Uzziah
king of Judah; and he reigned a full month
in Samaria. 14 For Menahem the son of
Gadi went up from [l]Tirzah, came to Samaria, and struck Shallum the son of
Jabesh in Samaria and killed him; and he
reigned in his place.
15 Now the rest of the acts of Shallum,
and the conspiracy which he [4]led, indeed

26 [d] Ex. 3:7; 2 Kin. 13:4; Ps. 106:44 [e] Deut. 32:36
27 [f] [2 Kin. 13:5, 23]
28 [g] 1 Kin. 11:24 [h] 2 Sam. 8:6; 1 Kin. 11:24; 2 Chr. 8:3
29 [i] 2 Kin. 15:8 [3] Died and joined his ancestors

CHAPTER 15

1 [a] 2 Kin. 15:13, 30 [b] 2 Kin. 14:21; 2 Chr. 26:1, 3, 4
4 [c] 2 Kin. 12:3; 14:4; 15:35 [1] Places for pagan worship
5 [d] 2 Chr. 26:19-23; Ps. 78:31 [e] Is. 6:1 [f] [Lev. 13:46]; Num. 12:14
7 [g] 2 Chr. 26:23 [2] Died and joined his ancestors
8 [h] 2 Kin. 14:29
9 [i] 2 Kin. 14:24
10 [j] Amos 7:9
12 [k] 2 Kin. 10:30
13 [3] *Azariah*, 2 Kin. 14:21ff.; 15:1ff.
14 [l] 1 Kin. 14:17; Song 6:4
15 [4] Lit. *conspired*

14:25,26 The explanation for Jonah's prophecy is given here. The Lord Himself had personally witnessed the heavy, bitter affliction borne by all in Israel with no human help available (v. 26). Further, the Lord had not decreed Israel's final doom (v. 27). To "blot out the name of Israel from under heaven" meant to annihilate Israel totally, leaving no trace or memory of her (Deut. 9:14; 29:20). Thus, moved with compassion, the Lord Himself used Jeroboam II's reign to rescue His suffering people. However, as the books of Hosea and Amos show, Israel did not respond to God's grace with repentance.

14:28 Without devotion to the Lord, Jeroboam, by might and clever leadership, brought Israel more prosperity than the country had known since Solomon. The people rested in their prosperity rather than God's power. Material blessing was no sign of God's blessing, since they had no commitment to Him.

15:1 twenty-seventh year. 767 B.C. This included the 11 years of Jeroboam II's co-regency with Jehoash (*see note on 14:23*). **Azariah.** The name means "The LORD has helped" (14:21; 15:6,7,8,17,23,27; 1 Chr. 3:12). He was also called Uzziah, meaning "The LORD is my strength" (15:13,30,32,34; 2 Chr. 26:1-23; Is. 1:1; 6:1; Hos. 1:1; Amos 1:1; Zech. 14:5). Isaiah the prophet began his public ministry during Azariah's reign (Is. 1:1).

15:2 fifty-two years. 790–739 B.C. Azariah was 16 when he began his co-regency with his father Amaziah. Azariah's sole rule began in 767 B.C. (*see note on v. 8*).

15:4 Cf. 12:3; 14:4.

15:5 leper. Azariah suffered from leprosy as punishment for usurping the priestly function of burning incense on the altar in the temple (*see notes on 2 Chr. 26:16-18,19,20*). The disease eventually killed him (*see note on Is. 6:1*). **isolated house.** Lit. "in a house of freedom." Azariah was relieved of all royal responsibilities. His son Jotham served as co-regent until Azariah's death (750–739 B.C.; *see notes on 15:2,32*). As co-regent, Jotham specifically supervised the palace and governed the nation.

15:8 thirty-eighth year. 753 B.C., making Azariah's co-reign with his father Amaziah (*see notes on 14:21; 15:2*) begin in 792–791 B.C. (accession year) or 790 B.C. (non-accession year). **Zechariah.** Zechariah was the fourth and final generation of the dynasty of Jehu (ca. 753/752 B.C.). His death fulfilled the prophecy given by the Lord (cf. 15:12; 10:30).

15:10 Shallum. Shallum killed Zechariah and replaced him as king of Israel. Assyrian records call Shallum "the son of nobody," indicating that he was not from the royal family.

15:13 thirty-ninth year. 752 B.C. Zechariah's reign spanned the last months of Azariah's 38th year (v. 8) and the first months of the following year.

15:14 Menahem. Menahem had probably been a military commander under Zechariah. **Tirzah.** The former capital of the northern kingdom (1 Kin. 14:17; 15:21,33), located about 9 mi. E of Samaria. Menahem was probably stationed with his troops at Tirzah.

they *are* written in the book of the chronicles of the kings of Israel. 16 Then from
Tirzah, Menahem attacked [m]Tiphsah, all
who *were* there, and its territory. Because
they did not surrender, therefore he attacked *it.* All [n]the women there who were
with child he ripped open.

Menahem Reigns in Israel

17 In the thirty-ninth year of Azariah
king of Judah, Menahem the son of Gadi
became king over Israel, *and reigned* ten
years in Samaria. 18 And he did evil in the
sight of the LORD; he did not depart all his
days from the sins of Jeroboam the son of
Nebat, who had made Israel sin. 19 [o]Pul[5]
king of Assyria came against the land; and
Menahem gave Pul a thousand talents of
silver, that his [6]hand might be with him to
[p]strengthen the kingdom under his control. 20 And Menahem [q]exacted[7] the
money from Israel, from all the very
wealthy, from each man fifty shekels of silver, to give to the king of Assyria. So the
king of Assyria turned back, and did not
stay there in the land.

21 Now the rest of the acts of Menahem,
and all that he did, *are* they not written in the
book of the chronicles of the kings of Israel?
22 So Menahem [8]rested with his fathers.
Then Pekahiah his son reigned in his place.

16 [m] 1 Kin. 4:24 [n] 2 Kin. 8:12; Hos. 13:16
19 [o] 1 Chr. 5:26; Is. 66:19; Hos. 8:9 [p] 2 Kin. 14:5 [5] Tiglath-Pileser III, v. 29 [6] Support
20 [q] 2 Kin. 23:35 [7] *took*
22 [8] Died and joined his ancestors

Pekahiah Reigns in Israel

23 In the fiftieth year of Azariah king of Judah, Pekahiah the son of Menahem became
king over Israel in Samaria, *and reigned* two
years. 24 And he did evil in the sight of the
LORD; he did not depart from the sins of Jeroboam the son of Nebat, who had made Israel sin. 25 Then Pekah the son of Remaliah,
an officer of his, conspired against him and
[9]killed him in Samaria, in the [r]citadel of the
king's house, along with Argob and Arieh;
and with him were fifty men of Gilead. He
killed him and reigned in his place.

26 Now the rest of the acts of Pekahiah,
and all that he did, indeed they *are* written
in the book of the chronicles of the kings of
Israel.

Pekah Reigns in Israel

27 In the fifty-second year of Azariah
king of Judah, [s]Pekah the son of Remaliah
became king over Israel in Samaria, *and
reigned* twenty years. 28 And he did evil in
the sight of the LORD; he did not depart
from the sins of Jeroboam the son of Nebat,
who had made Israel sin. 29 In the days of
Pekah king of Israel, [1]Tiglath-Pileser king
of Assyria [t]came and took [u]Ijon, Abel Beth
Maachah, Janoah, Kedesh, Hazor, Gilead,
and Galilee, all the land of Naphtali; and

25 [r] 1 Kin. 16:18 [9] Lit. *struck*
27 [s] 2 Chr. 28:6; Is. 7:1
29 [t] 2 Kin. 16:7, 10; 1 Chr. 5:26 [u] 1 Kin. 15:20 [1] A later name of *Pul,* v. 19

15:16 Tiphsah. Since Tiphsah was located on the Euphrates River about 325 mi. N of Samaria (1 Kin. 4:24), a majority of interpreters translate this term "Tappuah," a town 14 mi. SW of Tirzah (Josh. 17:8). **ripped open.** The ripping open of pregnant women was a barbarous practice and elsewhere associated only with foreign armies (8:12; Hos. 13:16; Amos 1:13). Menahem probably did this as a visible reminder of the city's failure to "open up" to his demands.

15:17 thirty-ninth year. 752 B.C. **ten years.** 752–742 B.C. With Menahem, the northern kingdom changed from the non-accession to the accession-year system of computing reigns.

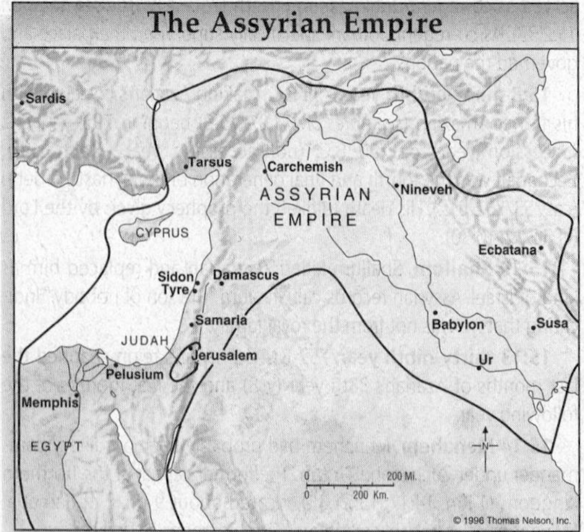

15:19 Pul. Assyrian kings frequently had two names, a throne name for Assyria and another for Babylon. Pul was the Babylonian throne name of the Assyrian king Tiglath-Pileser III (cf. 1 Chr. 5:26) who reigned ca. 745–727 B.C.

15:19,20 Tiglath-Pileser III invaded Israel in 743 B.C. Menahem paid tribute of 1,000 talents of silver (ca. 37 tons) raised from the wealthy men of Israel. Each of 60,000 men paid 20 oz. of silver to raise the required 37 tons of silver. For his tribute, Tiglath-Pileser III supported Menahem's claim to the throne of Israel and withdrew his army. By this action, Menahem became a vassal of the Assyrian king.

15:23 fiftieth year. 742 B.C. **two years.** 742–740 B.C.

15:24 sins of Jeroboam. *See notes on 13:2; 2 Kin. 12:25-32.*

15:25 Pekah. *See note on 15:27.* Pekah was one of Pekahiah's military officers, probably commanding Gilead, since 50 Gileadites accompanied him when he assassinated Pekahiah. Argob and Arieh were either Pekahiah's sons or loyal military officers. Pekah probably represented the anti-Assyrian faction in Israel (cf. 16:5).

15:27 fifty-second year. 740 B.C. **twenty years.** On the basis of Assyrian records, it can be determined that Tiglath-Pileser III deposed Pekah as king of Israel in 732 B.C., evidently using Hoshea as his instrument. Therefore, Pekah reigned ca. 752–732 B.C., using the accession-year system of dating (that is, counting the first year as one). For an explanation of this dating system see 1 Kings Introduction: Interpretive Challenges. This included the years 752–740 B.C., when Pekah ruled in Gilead while Menahem (vv. 17-22) and Pekahiah (vv. 23-26) reigned in Samaria (the Jordan River being the boundary of the split kingdom). Verse 25 seems to indicate that Pekah had an alliance with Menahem and Pekahiah, ruling Gilead for them.

15:29 Ijon...Naphtali. The areas of Galilee and Gilead are described here. When Pekah and Rezin, the king of Syria, sought to have Judah join their anti-Assyrian alliance, another invasion by Assyria

he [v]carried them captive to Assyria.
30 Then Hoshea the son of Elah led a conspiracy against Pekah the son of Remaliah,
and struck and killed him; so he [w]reigned
in his place in the twentieth year of Jotham
the son of Uzziah.
31 Now the rest of the acts of Pekah, and
all that he did, indeed they *are* written in the
book of the chronicles of the kings of Israel.

Jotham Reigns in Judah

32 In the second year of Pekah the son of
Remaliah, king of Israel, [x]Jotham the son
of Uzziah, king of Judah, began to reign.
33 He was twenty-five years old when he
became king, and he reigned sixteen years
in Jerusalem. His mother's name *was* [2]Je-
rusha the daughter of Zadok. 34 And he
did *what was* right in the sight of the LORD;
he did [y]according to all that his father Uzziah had done. 35 [z]However the [3]high
places were not removed; the people still
sacrificed and burned incense on the high
places. [a]He built the Upper Gate of the
house of the LORD.
36 Now the rest of the acts of Jotham, and
all that he did, *are* they not written in the
book of the chronicles of the kings of Judah?
37 In those days the LORD began to send
[b]Rezin king of Syria and [c]Pekah the son of
Remaliah against Judah. 38 So Jotham [4]rest-
ed with his fathers, and was buried with his
fathers in the City of David his father. Then
Ahaz his son reigned in his place.

Ahaz Reigns in Judah

16 In the seventeenth year of Pekah the
son of Remaliah, Ahaz the son of
Jotham, king of Judah, began to reign.
2 Ahaz *was* twenty years old when he became king, and he reigned sixteen years in
Jerusalem; and he did not do *what was*
right in the sight of the LORD his God, as
his father David *had done.* 3 But he walked
in the way of the kings of Israel; indeed [a]he
made his son pass through the fire, according to the [b]abominations of the nations
whom the LORD had cast out from before
the children of Israel. 4 And he sacrificed
and burned incense on the [c]high places,
[d]on the hills, and under every green tree.
5 [e]Then Rezin king of Syria and Pekah the
son of Remaliah, king of Israel, came up to
Jerusalem to *make* war; and they besieged

29 [v] 2 Kin. 17:6
30 [w] 2 Kin. 17:1; [Hos. 10:3, 7, 15]
32 [x] 2 Chr. 27:1
33 [2] *Jerushah,* 2 Chr. 27:1
34 [y] 2 Kin. 15:3, 4; 2 Chr. 26:4, 5
35 [z] 2 Kin. 15:4 [a] 2 Chr. 23:20; 27:3 [3] Places for pagan worship
37 [b] 2 Kin. 16:5-9; Is. 7:1-17 [c] 2 Kin. 15:26, 27
38 [4] Died and joined his ancestors

CHAPTER 16

3 [a] [Lev. 18:21]; 2 Kin. 17:17; 2 Chr. 28:3; Ps. 106:37, 38; Is. 1:1 [b] [Deut. 12:31]; 2 Kin. 21:2, 11
4 [c] 2 Kin. 15:34, 35 [d] [Deut. 12:2]; 1 Kin. 14:23
5 [e] 2 Kin. 15:37; Is. 7:1, 4

was provoked (cf. 16:5-9) in 733/732 B.C. Tiglath-Pileser III took Galilee and Gilead and converted them into 3 Assyrian provinces governed by royal appointees. He also was involved in replacing Pekah with Hoshea as king over the remaining area of Israel (*see note on 15:27*).

15:30 twentieth year. Jotham of Judah began his reign in 750 B.C. (*see note on 15:32*). His 20th year was 732 B.C., according to the non-accession-year system. Assyrian records confirm that Hoshea began to rule Israel in 732 B.C. (*see notes on v. 27; 2 Chr. 27:1-9*).

15:32 second year. 750 B.C., the year of Pekah's second year of rule in Gilead, according to the accession-year system (*see note on 15:27*).

15:33 sixteen years. 750-735 B.C. According to v. 30, Jotham reigned until 731 B.C. Jotham was probably replaced as a functioning king of Judah by a pro-Assyrian faction who established Ahaz as ruler (*see notes on 15:1,2*) while leaving Jotham as a powerless co-regent. Isaiah (Is. 1:1) and Micah (Mic. 1:1) the prophets ministered to Judah during Jotham's reign.

15:35 the Upper Gate. Probably the Upper Benjamin Gate, which stood along the N side of the temple complex facing the territory of Benjamin (cf. Jer. 20:2; Ezek. 9:2; Zech. 14:10). Other accomplishments of Jotham are noted in 2 Chr. 27:3-6.

15:37 Rezin...Pekah. *See notes on 16:5-9.*

16:1–17:41 At this point the narrative turns to the defeat and exile of Israel by Assyria. In 17:7-23, the prophetic writer states the reasons why Israel was punished by the Lord. A major reason was the sinful religion established by Jeroboam I (17:21-23), which was followed by every king in Israel. Ominously, the section begins with the narrative concerning Ahaz of Judah who "walked in the way of the kings of Israel" (16:3). The kind of punishment that came upon Israel would come later upon Judah for the same reason (17:19,20).

16:1 seventeenth year. 735 B.C., since Pekah's reign began in 752 B.C. (*see note on 15:27*). Although Jotham, the father of Ahaz, was still alive (*see note on 15:30*), Ahaz exercised the sovereign authority in Judah from 735 B.C. to Jotham's death in ca. 731 B.C. Isaiah (Is. 1:1–7:1) and Micah (Mic. 1:1) the prophets continued to minister to Judah during the reign of Ahaz. *See notes on 2 Chr. 28:1-27.*

16:2 sixteen years. 731–715 B.C. The principle of "dual dating" was followed here. See 1 Kings Introduction: Interpretive Challenges for an explanation of this principle. In 16:1 and 17:1, Ahaz was recognized as king in the year he came to the throne as a co-regent, but the year of his official accession was determined as the year when he began to reign alone. Ahaz shared royal power with Azariah (to 739 B.C.) and Jotham from 744 to 735 B.C. (*see note on 17:1*); he exercised total authority as co-regent with Jotham from 735–731 B.C. (*see note on 16:1*); he was sole king from 731 to 729 B.C. and was co-regent with his son Hezekiah from 729 to 715 B.C. (*see note on 18:1*).

16:3 walked in the way of the kings of Israel. This does not necessarily mean that Ahaz participated in the calf worship introduced by Jeroboam I at Bethel and Dan, but that he increasingly brought pagan, idolatrous practices into the worship of the Lord in Jerusalem. These are specified in vv. 10-16 and parallel those of Jeroboam I in the northern kingdom. This included idols to Baal (2 Chr. 28:2). **made his son pass through the fire.** As a part of the ritual worship of Molech, the god of the Moabites, children were sacrificed by fire (cf. 3:27). This horrific practice was continually condemned in the OT (Lev. 18:21; 20:2-5; Deut. 18:10; Jer. 7:31; 19:5; 32:35). **the abominations of the nations.** *See note on Deut. 18:9-12.*

16:4 the high places. Ahaz was the first king in the line of David since Solomon who was said to have personally worshiped at the high places. While all the other kings of Judah had tolerated the high places, Ahaz actively participated in the immoral Canaanite practices that were performed at the "high places" on hilltops under large trees (cf. Hos. 4:13).

16:5 Rezin...Pekah. The kings of Syria and Israel wanted to overthrow Ahaz in order to force Judah into their anti-Assyrian coalition. The two kings with their armies besieged Jerusalem, seeking to replace Ahaz with their own king (cf. Is. 7:1-6). The Lord delivered Judah and Ahaz from this threat because of His promise to David (cf. Is. 7:7-16).

Ahaz but could not overcome *him.* 6 At
that time Rezin king of Syria [f]captured
[1]Elath for Syria, and drove the men of Judah from Elath. Then the [2]Edomites went
to Elath, and dwell there to this day.
7 So Ahaz sent messengers to [g]Tiglath-
Pileser[3] king of Assyria, saying, "I *am*
your servant and your son. Come up and
save me from the hand of the king of Syria
and from the hand of the king of Israel,
who rise up against me." 8 And Ahaz
[h]took the silver and gold that was found
in the house of the LORD, and in the treasuries of the king's house, and sent *it as* a
present to the king of Assyria. 9 So the
king of Assyria heeded him; for the king of
Assyria went up against [i]Damascus and
[j]took it, carried *its people* captive to [k]Kir,
and killed Rezin.
10 Now King Ahaz went to Damascus
to meet Tiglath-Pileser king of Assyria,
and saw an altar that *was* at Damascus;
and King Ahaz sent to Urijah the priest
the design of the altar and its pattern, according to all its workmanship. 11 Then
[l]Urijah the priest built an altar according
to all that King Ahaz had sent from Damascus. So Urijah the priest made *it* before King Ahaz came back from Damascus. 12 And when the king came back
from Damascus, the king saw the altar;
and [m]the king approached the altar and
made offerings on it. 13 So he burned his
burnt offering and his grain offering; and
he poured his drink offering and sprinkled the blood of his peace offerings on
the altar. 14 He also brought [n]the bronze
altar which *was* before the LORD, from the
front of the [4]temple—from between the
new altar and the house of the LORD—and
put it on the north side of the *new* altar.
15 Then King Ahaz commanded Urijah
the priest, saying, "On the great *new* altar
burn [o]the morning burnt offering, the
evening grain offering, the king's burnt
sacrifice, and his grain offering, with the
burnt offering of all the people of the
land, their grain offering, and their drink
offerings; and sprinkle on it all the blood
of the burnt offering and all the blood of
the sacrifice. And the bronze altar shall be
for me to inquire *by.*" 16 Thus did Urijah
the priest, according to all that King Ahaz
commanded.
17 [p]And King Ahaz cut off [q]the panels of
the carts, and removed the lavers from
them; and he took down [r]the Sea from the
bronze oxen that *were* under it, and put it
on a pavement of stones. 18 Also he removed the Sabbath pavilion which they
had built in the temple, and he removed
the king's outer entrance from the house of
the LORD, on account of the king of Assyria.
19 Now the rest of the acts of Ahaz
which he did, *are* they not written in the
book of the chronicles of the kings of Judah? 20 So Ahaz rested with his fathers,
and [s]was buried with his fathers in the
City of David. Then Hezekiah his son
reigned in his place.

6 [f]2 Kin. 14:22; 2 Chr. 26:2 [1]Lit. *Large Tree;* sing. of *Eloth* [2]A few ancient mss. *Syrians*
7 [g]2 Kin. 15:29; 1 Chr. 5:26; 2 Chr. 28:20 [3]A later name of *Pul,* 2 Kin. 15:19
8 [h]2 Kin. 12:17, 18; 2 Chr. 28:21
9 [i]2 Kin. 14:28 [j]Amos 1:5 [k]Is. 22:6; Amos 9:7
11 [l]Is. 8:2
12 [m]2 Chr. 26:16, 19
14 [n]Ex. 27:1, 2; 40:6, 29; 2 Chr. 4:1 [4]Lit. *house*
15 [o]Ex. 29:39-41
17 [p]2 Chr. 28:24 [q]1 Kin. 7:27-29 [r]1 Kin. 7:23-25
20 [s]2 Chr. 28:27

16:6 Elath. The Syrians did displace Judah from Elath (*see note on 14:22*). Later this important port town on the Gulf of Aqabah was captured by the Edomites.

16:7 Tiglath-Pileser. *See notes on 15:19,29.* **your servant and your son.** Ahaz willingly became a vassal of the Assyrian king in exchange for his military intervention. This was a pledge that Judah would serve Assyria from this point on. In support of his pledge, Ahaz sent Tiglath-Pileser III silver and gold from the temple and from the palace treasuries (v. 8). Evidently the prosperous reigns of Azariah and Jotham had replenished the treasures plundered by Jehoash of Israel 50 years earlier during Amaziah's reign (14:14).

16:9 the king of Assyria heeded him. According to Assyrian records, in 733 B.C. Tiglath-Pileser III's army marched against Damascus, the Syrian capital, laid siege for two years, and captured it. The victorious Assyrian king executed Rezin and deported his subjects to Kir, whose location is unknown.

16:10 the altar. When Ahaz traveled to Damascus to meet Tiglath-Pileser III, he saw a large altar (v. 15) which was most likely Assyrian. Ahaz sent a sketch of this altar to Uriah the High-Priest in Jerusalem and Uriah built an altar just like it. The serious iniquity in this was meddling with and changing, according to personal taste, the furnishings of the temple, the design for which had been given by God (Ex. 25:40; 26:30; 27:1-8; 1 Chr. 28:19). This was like building an idol in the temple, done to please the pagan Assyrian king, whom Ahaz served instead of God.

16:12,13 offerings. As did Solomon and Jeroboam before him (1 Kin. 8:63; 12:32), Ahaz dedicated the new altar by offering sacrifices.

16:14-16 bronze altar. Feeling confident about his alterations in the temple, Ahaz moved the old bronze altar dedicated by Solomon (1 Kin. 8:22,54,64), which stood in front of the temple between the new altar and the temple itself (v. 14). Ahaz had the bronze altar moved to a spot N of the new altar, thereby relegating it to a place of secondary importance. All offerings from then on were to be given on the altar dedicated by Ahaz, while Ahaz reserved the bronze altar for his personal use in seeking guidance (v. 15). The term "inquire" probably referred here to pagan divination through religious rituals. Deut. 18:9-14 expressly forbade such divination in Israel.

16:17,18 Ahaz made further changes in the temple at Jerusalem. First, he removed the side panels and basins from the portable stands (cf. 1 Kin. 7:27-29,38,39). Second, he removed the large ornate reservoir called "the Sea" from atop the 12 bronze bulls to a new stone base (cf. 1 Kin. 7:23-26). Third, he removed the "Sabbath pavilion," probably some sort of canopy used by the king on the Sabbath. Fourth, he removed "the king's outer entrance," probably a special entrance to the temple used by the king on Sabbaths and feast days (cf. 1 Kin. 10:5).

16:18 on account of the king of Assyria. Both items mentioned here were moved into the temple in hope that if the king of Assyria laid siege to Jerusalem, Ahaz could secure the entrance of the temple from him.

16:20 Hezekiah. For his reign, see 18:1–20:21.

Hoshea Reigns in Israel

17 In the twelfth year of Ahaz king of
Judah, [a]Hoshea the son of Elah became king of Israel in Samaria, *and he*
reigned nine years. 2 And he did evil in the
sight of the LORD, but not as the kings of Israel who were before him. 3 [b]Shalmaneser
king of Assyria came up against him; and
Hoshea [c]became his vassal, and paid him
tribute money. 4 And the king of Assyria
uncovered a conspiracy by Hoshea; for he
had sent messengers to So, king of Egypt,
and brought no tribute to the king of Assyria, as *he had done* year by year. Therefore
the king of Assyria shut him up, and
bound him in prison.

Israel Carried Captive to Assyria

5 Now [d]the king of Assyria went
throughout all the land, and went up to Samaria and besieged it for three years. 6 [e]In
the ninth year of Hoshea, the king of Assyria took Samaria and [f]carried Israel
away to Assyria, [g]and placed them in
Halah and by the Habor, the River of
Gozan, and in the cities of the Medes.
7 For [h]so it was that the children of Israel
had sinned against the LORD their God,
who had brought them up out of the land
of Egypt, from under the hand of Pharaoh
king of Egypt; and they had [i]feared other
gods, 8 and [j]had walked in the statutes of
the nations whom the LORD had cast out
from before the children of Israel, and of
the kings of Israel, which they had made.
9 Also the children of Israel secretly did
against the LORD their God things that *were*
not right, and they built for themselves
[1]high places in all their cities, [k]from watchtower to fortified city. 10 [l]They set up for
themselves *sacred* pillars and [m]wooden images[2] [n]on every high hill and under every
green tree. 11 There they burned incense on
all the high places, like the nations whom

CHAPTER 17
1 [a] 2 Kin. 15:30
3 [b] 2 Kin. 18:9-12 [c] 2 Kin. 24:1
5 [d] 2 Kin. 18:9; Hos. 13:16
6 [e] 2 Kin. 18:10, 11; Is. 7:7-9; Hos. 1:4; 13:16; Amos 4:2 [f] Lev. 26:32, 33; [Deut. 28:36, 64; 29:27, 28] [g] 1 Chr. 5:26
7 [h] [Josh. 23:16] [i] Judg. 6:10
8 [j] [Lev. 18:3; Deut. 18:9]; 2 Kin. 16:3
9 [k] 2 Kin. 18:8 [1] Places for pagan worship
10 [l] 1 Kin. 14:23; Is. 57:5 [m] [Ex. 34:12-14; Deut. 16:21]; Mic. 5:14 [n] [Deut. 12:2]; 2 Kin. 16:4 [2] Heb. *Asherim,* Canaanite deities

17:1 twelfth year. 732 B.C. This date for the accession of Hoshea as king of Israel is well established according to biblical and extra-biblical data (*see note on 15:27*). Therefore, Ahaz of Judah must have become co-regent with his father Jotham, who was himself co-regent with his father, Azariah, at that time (*see notes on 15:30,33*), in 744 B.C. (*see note on 16:2*). **nine years.** 732-722 B.C. according to the accession-year system. Hoshea was imprisoned (v. 4) during the siege of Samaria by Assyria in 724–722 B.C. (v. 5).

17:2 he did evil. Though Hoshea was characterized as a wicked king, it is not stated that he promoted the religious practices of Jeroboam I. In this way, he was some improvement on the kings of Israel who had gone before him. However, this slight improvement did not offset the centuries of sin by Israel's kings nor divert her inevitable doom.

17:3 Shalmaneser. Shalmaneser V succeeded his father Tiglath-Pileser III as king of Assyria and reigned from 727–722 B.C. During the siege of Samaria, when the Assyrians began the destruction and captivity of the northern kingdom, Shalmaneser V died and was succeeded by Sargon II (see Is. 20:1), who completed the siege, captured the city, destroyed the nation of Israel, and exiled the inhabitants (v. 6). Sargon II reigned as king from 722–705 B.C. *See note on Hosea 10:14.*

17:4 So, king of Egypt. Instead of paying his yearly tribute owed as a vassal of Assyria, Hoshea tried to make a treaty with Osorkon IV (ca. 727-716 B.C.), king of Egypt. This was foolish because Assyria was powerful. It was also against God's will, which forbade such alliances with pagan rulers (cf. Deut. 7:2). This rebellion led to Israel's destruction (vv. 5,6).

17:5 Samaria…besieged. In 724 B.C., Shalmaneser V invaded Israel and quickly conquered the land and captured Hoshea. However, the capital city of Samaria resisted the Assyrian invaders until 722 B.C. Like all major cities, Samaria had an internal water supply and plenty of stored food that allowed her to endure the siege for 3 years.

17:6 king of Assyria. Sargon II (*see note on 17:3*). **carried Israel away.** The capture of Samaria marked the end of the northern kingdom. According to Assyrian records, the Assyrians deported 27,290 inhabitants of Israel to distant locations. The relocation of populations was characteristic of Assyrian policy during that era. The Israelites were resettled in the upper Tigris-Euphrates Valley and never returned to the Promised Land. "Halah" was a city NE of Nineveh. The "Habor" River was a northern tributary of the Euphrates. The "cities of the Medes" were NE of Nineveh. Samaria was resettled with foreigners (v. 24). God did what He said He would do in Deut. 28. The Jews were carried as far E as Susa, where the book of Esther later took place.

17:7-23 In these verses, the writer departs from quoting his written sources and gives his own explanation for the captivity of Israel. Judah is included, though her captivity did not occur until 605/604–586 B.C. at the hands of the Babylonians. Her sins were the same. Here is a very full and impressive vindication of God's action in punishing His privileged but rebellious and apostate people. In v. 7, he begins by stating that the Israelites had sinned against the Lord who had redeemed them from Egypt. Gross perversion of the worship of God and national propensity to idolatry finally exhausted divine patience. The idolatry of Israel is described in vv. 7-12. In response to Israel's actions, the Lord sent His prophets to Israel and Judah with a message of repentance (v. 13). However, the people failed to respond to the prophets' messages, because, like their fathers, they did not have faith in the Lord (v. 14). Their lack of faith resulted in disobedience to the Lord's commands and the further pursuit of idolatry (vv. 15-17). The idolatry of Israel (and Judah) brought forth the anger of the Lord, which resulted in exile (v. 18). The "great sin" of both Israel and Judah was their continual following of the sinful pattern of Jeroboam I, departing from the Lord and practicing idolatry, thus bringing down the judgment of captivity predicted by the prophets (vv. 19-23).

17:7 feared other gods. The primary cause of Israel's exile was the worship of other gods. The fear of the Lord led to listening to His Word and obeying His ordinances and statutes (Deut. 4:10; 5:29; 6:24), but the fear of the gods of Canaan led Israel to obey the laws of the Canaanite gods (v. 8). The result of this obedience to false gods is recorded in vv. 9-12,16,17.

17:8 walked in the statutes of the nations. This was expressly forbidden in Lev. 18:3; 20:23.

17:9 built…high places. In addition to their private sins ("secret"), judgment came for public wickedness and idolatry. These were not the high places utilized by Israel for worshiping God before the building of the temple (*see note on 1 Kin. 3:2*). In direct disobedience to Deut. 12:1-4, the Israelites built new raised altars in the Canaanite pattern after the temple was constructed. These high places were in all the habitations of Israel, from small fortified structures to large garrison cities, i.e., from the smallest to largest towns. The "high place" altars were on wooded hills with images representing the false gods (v. 10; cf. Deut. 16:21,22).

the LORD had carried away before them;
and they did wicked things to provoke the
LORD to anger, 12 for they served idols, [o]of
which the LORD had said to them, [p]"You
shall not do this thing."
13 Yet the LORD testified against Israel
and against Judah, by all of His [q]prophets,
[r]every seer, saying, [s]"Turn from your evil
ways, and keep My commandments *and*
My statutes, according to all the law which
I commanded your fathers, and which I
sent to you by My servants the prophets."
14 Nevertheless they would not hear, but
[t]stiffened their necks, like the necks of
their fathers, who [u]did not believe in the
LORD their God. 15 And they [v]rejected His
statutes [w]and His covenant that He had
made with their fathers, and His testimonies which He had testified against
them; they followed [x]idols, [y]became idolaters, and *went* after the nations who *were*
all around them, *concerning* whom the
LORD had charged them that they should
[z]not do like them. 16 So they left all the
commandments of the LORD their God,
[a]made for themselves a molded image *and*
two calves, [b]made a wooden image and
worshiped all the [c]host of heaven, [d]and
served Baal. 17 [e]And they caused their sons
and daughters to pass through the fire,
[f]practiced witchcraft and soothsaying, and
[g]sold themselves to do evil in the sight of
the LORD, to provoke Him to anger.
18 Therefore the LORD was very angry with
Israel, and removed them from His sight;
there was none left [h]but the tribe of Judah
alone.
19 Also [i]Judah did not keep the commandments of the LORD their God, but
walked in the statutes of Israel which they

12 [o][Ex. 20:3-5; Lev. 26:1; Deut. 5:7, 8] [p][Deut. 4:19]
13 [q]Neh. 9:29, 30 [r]1 Sam. 9:9 [s][Jer. 18:11; 25:5; 35:15; Ezek. 18:31]
14 [t]Ex. 32:9; 33:3; Deut. 31:27; [Prov. 29:1; Acts 7:51] [u]Deut. 9:23; Ps. 78:22
15 [v]Jer. 44:3 [w]Ex. 24:6-8; Deut. 29:25 [x]Deut. 32:21; 1 Kin. 16:31; [1 Cor. 8:4] [y]2 Chr. 13:7; Jer. 2:5; [Rom. 1:21-23] [z][Deut. 12:30, 31]
16 [a]Ex. 32:8; 1 Kin. 12:28 [b][1 Kin. 14:15] [c][Deut. 4:19] [d]1 Kin. 16:31; 22:53
17 [e][Lev. 18:21]; 2 Kin. 16:3; Ezek. 23:37 [f][Lev. 19:26; Deut. 18:10-12] [g]1 Kin. 21:20
18 [h]1 Kin. 11:13, 32
19 [i]Jer. 3:8
20 [j]Judg. 2:14; 2 Kin. 13:3; 15:29 [k]2 Kin. 24:20
21 [l]1 Kin. 11:11, 31 [m]1 Kin. 12:20, 28
23 [n]1 Kin. 14:16; Is. 8:4 [o]2 Kin. 17:6
24 [p]Ezra 4:2, 10 [q]2 Kin. 18:34

made. 20 And the LORD rejected all the descendants of Israel, afflicted them, and [j]de-
livered them into the hand of plunderers,
until He had cast them from His [k]sight.
21 For [l]He tore Israel from the house of David, and [m]they made Jeroboam the son of
Nebat king. Then Jeroboam drove Israel
from following the LORD, and made them
commit a great sin. 22 For the children of
Israel walked in all the sins of Jeroboam
which he did; they did not depart from
them, 23 until the LORD removed Israel out
of His sight, [n]as He had said by all His servants the prophets. [o]So Israel was carried
away from their own land to Assyria, *as it
is* to this day.

Assyria Resettles Samaria

24 [p]Then the king of Assyria brought *people* from Babylon, Cuthah, [q]Ava, Hamath,
and from Sepharvaim, and placed *them* in
the cities of Samaria instead of the children
of Israel; and they took possession of Samaria and dwelt in its cities. 25 And it was
so, at the beginning of their dwelling there,
that they did not fear the LORD; therefore
the LORD sent lions among them, which
killed *some* of them. 26 So they spoke to the
king of Assyria, saying, "The nations
whom you have removed and placed in the
cities of Samaria do not know the rituals of
the God of the land; therefore He has sent
lions among them, and indeed, they are
killing them because they do not know the
rituals of the God of the land." 27 Then the
king of Assyria commanded, saying, "Send
there one of the priests whom you brought
from there; let him go and dwell there, and
let him teach them the rituals of the God of
the land." 28 Then one of the priests whom

17:13 Turn from your evil ways. The prophets continually called the people to repentance (cf. Jer. 7:3,5; 18:11; Ezek. 33:11).

17:14 stiffened their necks. A stubborn refusal to respond (*see note on Deut. 9:6*; cf. Ex. 32:9; 33:3,5; 34:9; Acts 7:51).

17:16 a molded image *and* two calves. The text should be translated "molded images even two calves." Worship of them was instituted by Jeroboam (see 1 Kin. 12:25-33). **wooden image.** Built by Rehoboam (see 1 Kin. 14:15,23). **the host of heaven.** In the ancient Near East, the sun, moon, and stars were deified and worshiped. This astral worship entered Israel and Judah (21:5; 23:4,5; Ezek. 8:15,16; Amos 5:26). The worship of the heavenly bodies was prohibited by the Mosaic law (Deut. 4:19; 17:3).

17:17 pass through the fire. *See notes on 3:27; 16:3.* **witchcraft and soothsaying.** *See note on Deut. 18:9-14.* Isaiah prophesied of the devastation these practices would produce (8:19-22).

17:19 Judah followed Israel into sin and judgment.

17:21 He tore Israel. *See notes on 1 Kin. 11:11-13,29-39.*

17:22 the sins of Jeroboam. *See notes on 1 Kin. 12:25-33.* The sins of that king put in motion an unbroken pattern of idolatrous iniquity. *See note on 13:2.*

17:23 *as it is* to this day. The exiles of Israel never returned en masse as did Judah (*see note on 1 Chr. 9:1*).

17:24 Samaria. After its conquest by the Assyrians, the central hill and coastal plain region of the former northern kingdom of Israel became an Assyrian province, all of which was called "Samaria" after the ancient capital city (cf. vv. 28,29). The Assyrian king, Sargon II, settled alien people, who came from widely scattered areas also conquered by Assyria, into the abandoned Israelite towns. Babylon and Cuthah were located in southern Mesopotamia. Hamath was a town on the Orontes River in Syria. The exact location of Ava and Sepharvaim are unknown. These people, who intermarried with the Jews who escaped exile, became the Samaritans—a mixed Jew and Gentile people, later hated by NT Jews (cf. Matt. 10:5; John 4:9; *see notes on Luke 10:29-37*).

17:25 lions among them. Lions were employed occasionally as instruments of punishment by God (cf. 1 Kin. 13:24; 20:36).

17:26 the rituals of the God. The newcomers interpreted the lions as a punishment from the God of Israel, whom they viewed as a deity who needed to be placated. Since they did not know how to appease Him, they appealed for help to Sargon II.

17:27,28 one of the priests. In response, the Assyrian king ordered an Israelite priest back to Samaria from exile to teach the people what the God of the land required in worship.

they had carried away from Samaria came
and dwelt in Bethel, and taught them how
they should fear the LORD.
29 However every nation continued to
make gods of its own, and put *them* [r]in the
shrines on the high places which the Samaritans had made, *every* nation in the
cities where they dwelt. 30 The men of
[s]Babylon made Succoth Benoth, the men of
Cuth made Nergal, the men of Hamath
made Ashima, 31 [t]and the Avites made
Nibhaz and Tartak; and the Sepharvites
[u]burned their children in fire to Adrammelech and Anammelech, the gods of Sepharvaim. 32 So they feared the LORD, [v]and
from every class they appointed for themselves priests of the [3]high places, who sacrificed for them in the shrines of the high
places. 33 [w]They feared the LORD, yet
served their own gods—according to the
rituals of the nations from among whom
they were carried away.
34 To this day they continue practicing
the former rituals; they do not fear the
LORD, nor do they follow their statutes or
their ordinances, or the law and commandment which the LORD had commanded the children of Jacob, [x]whom He named
Israel, 35 with whom the LORD had made a
covenant and charged them, saying: [y]"You
shall not fear other gods, nor [z]bow down
to them nor serve them nor sacrifice to
them; 36 but the LORD, who [a]brought you
up from the land of Egypt with great
power and [b]an outstretched arm, [c]Him
you shall fear, Him you shall worship, and
to Him you shall offer sacrifice. 37 And the
statutes, the ordinances, the law, and the
commandment which He wrote for you,
[d]you shall be careful to observe forever;
you shall not fear other gods. 38 And the
covenant that I have made with you, [e]you
shall not forget, nor shall you fear other
gods. 39 But the LORD your God you shall
fear; and He will deliver you from the
hand of all your enemies." 40 However
they did not obey, but they followed their
former rituals. 41 [f]So these nations feared
the LORD, yet served their carved images;
also their children and their children's children have continued doing as their fathers
did, even to this day.

Hezekiah Reigns in Judah

18 Now it came to pass in the third
year of [a]Hoshea the son of Elah,
king of Israel, *that* [b]Hezekiah the son of
Ahaz, king of Judah, began to reign. 2 He
was twenty-five years old when he became
king, and he reigned twenty-nine years in
Jerusalem. His mother's name *was* [c]Abi[1]
the daughter of Zechariah. 3 And he did
what was right in the sight of the LORD, according to all that his father David had
done.
4 [d]He removed the [2]high places and
broke the *sacred* pillars, cut down the
[3]wooden image and broke in pieces the

29 [r]1 Kin. 12:31; 13:32
30 [s]2 Kin. 17:24
31 [t]Ezra 4:9 [u][Lev. 18:21; Deut. 12:31]
32 [v]1 Kin. 12:31; 13:33 [3]Places for pagan worship
33 [w]Zeph. 1:5
34 [x]Gen. 32:28; 35:10
35 [y]Judg. 6:10 [z][Ex. 20:5]
36 [a]Ex. 14:15-30 [b]Ex. 6:6; 9:15 [c][Deut. 10:20]
37 [d]Deut. 5:32
38 [e]Deut. 4:23; 6:12
41 [f]2 Kin. 17:32, 33

CHAPTER 18

1 [a]2 Kin. 17:1 [b]2 Chr. 28:27; 29:1
2 [c]Is. 38:5 [1]*Abijah*, 2 Chr. 29:ff.
4 [d]2 Chr. 31:1 [2]Places for pagan worship [3]Heb. *Asherah*, a Canaanite goddess

17:29-32 Though they had been taught the proper way to worship God, these people all placed God alongside their other gods in an eclectic kind of worship that was blasphemy to the one true and living God.

17:30 Succoth Benoth. Lit. "tents of the daughters," probably indicating some deity worshiped by sexual orgies. **Nergal.** Perhaps the Assyrian god of war. **Ashima.** An idol in the form of a bald he-goat.

17:31 Nibhaz. A dog-like idol. **Tartak.** Either a donkey or a celestial body, Saturn. **Adrammelech.** Perhaps the same as Molech, worshiped in the form of the sun, a mule or a peacock. **Anammelech.** A rabbit or a goat idol.

17:33 served their own gods. The religion of the Samaritans was syncretistic; it combined elements of the worship of the Lord with the worship practices of the gods which the Assyrian settlers had brought with them (*see note on v. 24*).

17:34-41 Having shown how the Samaritan people and their religion came into being (vv. 24-33), the writer of Kings shows how the syncretistic worship of the Samaritans continued for generations, even to his own day (cf. v. 41; during the Babylonian exile). The religion of the Samaritans was, at its foundation, no different from Jeroboam I's deviant religion.

18:1–25:21 With the fall of Samaria, the northern kingdom of Israel came to an end (17:5,6; 18:9-12). This last major division of the books of Kings narrate the events in the surviving southern kingdom of Judah from 722 B.C. to its captivity and destruction in 586 B.C. These chapters are dominated by the accounts of two good kings, Hezekiah (18:1–20:21) and Josiah (22:1–23:30). However, the reforms of these two godly kings did not reverse the effects of the two worst kings of Judah, Ahaz (16:1-20) and Manasseh (21:1-18). The result of Judah's apostasy was exile, just like it was for Israel (23:31–25:21). The books of Kings begin with the building of the temple (1 Kin. 5:1–6:38) and end with its destruction (25:8,9,13-17), chronicling the sad journey from the establishment of true worship to the destruction of apostasy.

18:1 third year. Ca. 729 B.C. Hoshea began to reign in 732 B.C. (*see notes on 15:27; 17:1*). Hezekiah was co-regent with Ahaz to 715 B.C. (*see note on 16:2*). *See notes on 2 Chr. 29:1–32:33.* With this verse, the writer returned from his digression summarizing the causes of captivity to the historical record of the kings of the southern kingdom, Judah.

18:2 twenty-nine years. 715–686 B.C. He reigned by himself for 20 years (715–695 B.C.), and with his son, Manasseh, for 9 years (695–686 B.C.). The 29 years given here indicate only those years after his co-regency with Ahaz was over, when he was the actual sovereign. During Hezekiah's reign, the prophets Isaiah (19:2; Is. 1:1; 37:21) and Micah (Mic. 1:1) continued to minister in Judah.

18:4 removed the high places. Hezekiah was the first king of Judah to totally eradicate the high places, i.e., the worship centers built contrary to the Mosaic law (cf. Deut. 12:2-7,13,14). ***sacred* pillars...wooden image.** Hezekiah destroyed the idols used in the worship of Baal and Asherah. **the bronze serpent.** Hezekiah broke the Nehushtan into pieces, i.e., the bronze snake made by Moses in the wilderness (*see notes on Num. 21:4-9*), because Judah had come to worship it as an idol, perhaps influenced by Canaanite religion, which regarded snakes as fertility symbols.

[e]bronze serpent that Moses had made; for
until those days the children of Israel
burned incense to it, and called it [4]Ne-
hushtan. 5 He [f]trusted in the LORD God of
Israel, [g]so that after him was none like him
among all the kings of Judah, nor who
were before him. 6 For he [h]held fast to the
LORD; he did not depart from following
Him, but kept His commandments, which
the LORD had commanded Moses. 7 The
LORD [i]was with him; he [j]prospered wherever he went. And he [k]rebelled against the
king of Assyria and did not serve him.
8 [l]He [5]subdued the Philistines, as far as
Gaza and its territory, [m]from watchtower
to fortified city.

9 Now [n]it came to pass in the fourth year
of King Hezekiah, which *was* the seventh
year of Hoshea the son of Elah, king of Israel, *that* Shalmaneser king of Assyria came
up against Samaria and besieged it. 10 And
at the end of three years they took it. In the
sixth year of Hezekiah, that *is,* [o]the ninth
year of Hoshea king of Israel, Samaria was
taken. 11 [p]Then the king of Assyria carried
Israel away captive to Assyria, and put
them [q]in Halah and by the Habor, the River
of Gozan, and in the cities of the Medes,
12 because they [r]did not obey the voice of
the LORD their God, but transgressed His
covenant *and* all that Moses the servant of
the LORD had commanded; and they would
neither hear nor do *them.*

13 And [s]in the fourteenth year of King
Hezekiah, Sennacherib king of Assyria
came up against all the fortified cities of Judah and took them. 14 Then Hezekiah king
of Judah sent to the king of Assyria at
Lachish, saying, "I have done wrong; turn
away from me; whatever you impose on
me I will pay." And the king of Assyria assessed Hezekiah king of Judah three hundred talents of silver and thirty talents of
gold. 15 So Hezekiah [t]gave *him* all the silver that was found in the house of the
LORD and in the treasuries of the king's
house. 16 At that time Hezekiah stripped
the gold from the doors of the temple of the
LORD, and *from* the pillars which Hezekiah
king of Judah had overlaid, and gave [6]it to
the king of Assyria.

Sennacherib Boasts Against the LORD

17 Then the king of Assyria sent *the* [7]Tar-
tan, *the* [8]Rabsaris, *and the* [9]Rabshakeh from
Lachish, with a great army against Jerusalem, to King Hezekiah. And they went up
and came to Jerusalem. When they had
come up, they went and stood by the [u]aq-
ueduct from the upper pool, [v]which *was* on
the highway to the Fuller's Field. 18 And
when they had called to the king, [w]Eliakim
the son of Hilkiah, who *was* over the
household, Shebna the [1]scribe, and Joah
the son of Asaph, the recorder, came out to
them. 19 Then *the* Rabshakeh said to them,

4 [e] Num. 21:5-9 [4] Lit. *Bronze Thing,* also similar to Heb. *nahash, serpent*
5 [f] 2 Kin. 19:10; [Job 13:15; Ps. 13:5] [g] 2 Kin. 23:25
6 [h] Deut. 10:20; Josh. 23:8
7 [i] [2 Chr. 15:2] [j] Gen. 39:2, 3; 1 Sam. 18:5, 14; Ps. 60:12 [k] 2 Kin. 16:7
8 [l] 1 Chr. 4:41; 2 Chr. 28:18; Is. 14:29 [m] 2 Kin. 17:9 [5] Lit. *struck*
9 [n] 2 Kin. 17:3
10 [o] 2 Kin. 17:6
11 [p] 2 Kin. 17:6; Hos. 1:4; Amos 4:2 [q] 1 Chr. 5:26
12 [r] 2 Kin. 17:7-18
13 [s] 2 Chr. 32:1; Is. 36:1–39:8
15 [t] 1 Kin. 15:18, 19; 2 Kin. 12:18; 16:8
16 [6] Lit. *them*
17 [u] 2 Kin. 20:20 [v] Is. 7:3 [7] A title, probably *Commander in Chief* [8] A title, probably *Chief Officer* [9] A title, probably *Chief of Staff* or *Governor*
18 [w] 2 Kin. 19:2; Is. 22:20 [1] *secretary*

18:5 He trusted in the LORD God of Israel. The most noble quality of Hezekiah (in dramatic contrast to his father, Ahaz) was that he relied on the Lord as his exclusive hope in every situation. What distinguished him from all other kings of Judah (after the division of the kingdom) was his firm trust in the Lord during a severe national crisis (18:17–19:34). Despite troublesome events, Hezekiah clung tightly to the Lord, faithfully following Him and obeying His commands (v. 6). As a result, the Lord was with him and gave him success (v. 7).

18:7 He rebelled against...Assyria. Before he became king, his father had submitted to Assyria. Courageously, Hezekiah broke that control by Assyria and asserted independence (cf. Deut. 7:2).

18:8 Gaza. The southernmost city of the Philistines, located about 55 mi. SW of Jerusalem. Since Assyria had controlled Philistia, Hezekiah's invasion defied Assyrian rule and brought the threat of retaliation.

18:9-12 These verses flash back to the time just before Israel's destruction and captivity to give a summary of the fall of Samaria (more fully narrated in 17:5-23) as a graphic reminder of the Assyrian power and the threat they still were to Judah. This review sets the scene for the siege of Jerusalem with its reminder of Israel's apostasy against which Hezekiah's faith in the Lord was a bright contrast.

18:13–20:19 This narrative, with a few omissions and additions, is found in Is. 36:1–39:8. *See Isaiah notes* for amplification.

18:13 fourteenth year. 701 B.C. Hezekiah began his sole rule in 715 B.C. (*see notes on 18:1,2*). This date for the siege of Jerusalem is confirmed in Assyrian sources. **Sennacherib.** He succeeded Sargon II as king of Assyria in 705 B.C. and ruled until 681 B.C. Hezekiah had rebelled against him (v. 7) , probably by withholding tribute when he invaded Philistia. **fortified cities.** *See note on Is. 36:1.*

18:14-16 Hezekiah sought to rectify the situation with Sennacherib by admitting his error in rebelling and paying the tribute the Assyrian king demanded. Sennacherib asked for about 11 tons of silver and one ton of gold. To pay, Hezekiah emptied the temple and palace treasuries and stripped the layers of gold off the doors and doorposts of the temple.

18:17-24 The tribute did not satisfy Sennacherib, who sent messengers to demand Hezekiah's complete surrender.

18:17 Tartan. General of the Assyrian army (cf. Is. 20:1). **Rabsaris.** A high official in the palace. **Rabshakeh.** The word is not a proper noun, but means "commander." He was the spokesman for Sennacherib, who represented the king against Jerusalem on this occasion. **Lachish.** *See note on 14:19.* Sennacherib's conquest of this city was in its closing phase when he sent the messengers. **great army.** This was a token force of the main army (19:35) with which Sennacherib hoped to bluff Judah into submitting. **aqueduct from the upper pool.** Isaiah had met Ahaz at the same spot to try, unsuccessfully, to dissuade him from trusting in foreign powers (Is 7:3). It was probably located on the higher ground NW of Jerusalem on the main N-S highway between Judah and Samaria. **Fuller's.** The word means "launderer" and indicates the field where such activity was done, being near the water supply.

18:18 Eliakim...Shebna. Eliakim was the palace administrator and Shebna, the secretary. *See notes on Is. 22:19-22.* **Joah...the recorder.** The position was that of an intermediary between the king and the people (cf. 2 Sam. 8:16).

18:19-25 The Rabshakeh's logic was twofold: 1) Egypt would be unable to deliver Jerusalem (vv. 20,21,23,24); and 2) the Lord had called on the Assyrians to destroy Judah (vv. 22,25).

"Say now to Hezekiah, 'Thus says the
great king, the king of Assyria: [x]"What
confidence *is* this in which you trust?
20 You speak of *having* plans and power for
war; but *they are* [2]mere words. And in
whom do you trust, that you rebel against
me? 21 [y]Now look! You are trusting in the
staff of this broken reed, Egypt, on which if
a man leans, it will go into his hand and
pierce it. So *is* Pharaoh king of Egypt to all
who trust in him. 22 But if you say to me,
'We trust in the LORD our God,' *is* it not He
[z]whose [3]high places and whose altars
Hezekiah has taken away, and said to Judah and Jerusalem, 'You shall worship before this altar in Jerusalem'?"' 23 Now
therefore, I urge you, give a pledge to my
master the king of Assyria, and I will give
you two thousand horses—if you are able
on your part to put riders on them! 24 How
then will you repel one captain of the least
of my master's servants, and put your
trust in Egypt for chariots and horsemen?
25 Have I now come up without the LORD
against this place to destroy it? The LORD
said to me, 'Go up against this land, and
destroy it.' "
26 [a]Then Eliakim the son of Hilkiah,
Shebna, and Joah said to *the* Rabshakeh,
"Please speak to your servants in [b]Aramaic, for we understand *it;* and do not
speak to us in [4]Hebrew in the hearing of
the people who *are* on the wall."
27 But *the* Rabshakeh said to them, "Has
my master sent me to your master and to
you to speak these words, and not to the
men who sit on the wall, who will eat and
drink their own waste with you?"
28 Then *the* Rabshakeh stood and called
out with a loud voice in [5]Hebrew, and
spoke, saying, "Hear the word of the great
king, the king of Assyria! 29 Thus says the
king: [c]'Do not let Hezekiah deceive you,
for he shall not be able to deliver you from
his hand; 30 nor let Hezekiah make you
trust in the LORD, saying, "The LORD will

19 [x] 2 Chr. 32:10; [Ps. 118:8, 9]
20 [2] Lit. *a word of the lips*
21 [y] Is. 30:2-7; Ezek. 29:6, 7
22 [z] 2 Kin. 18:4; 2 Chr. 31:1; 32:12 [3] Places for pagan worship
26 [a] Is. 36:11–39:8 [b] Ezra 4:7; Dan. 2:4 [4] Lit. *Judean*
28 [5] Lit. *Judean*
29 [c] 2 Chr. 32:15

18:19 great king. Cf. v. 28. The self-appropriated title of Assyrian kings. In contrast, Rabshakeh rudely omitted any title for Hezekiah (vv. 19,22,29,30,31,32).

18:20 mere words. *See note on Is. 36:5.* **whom do you trust?** The implication was that Assyria was so strong, there was none stronger.

18:21 broken reed, Egypt. The Assyrian's advice strongly resembled that of Isaiah (Is. 19:14-16; 30:7; 31:3). Egypt was not strong and could not be counted on for help.

18:22 He whose high places and whose altars. The Rabshakeh mistakenly thought Hezekiah's reforms in removing idols from all over the land and reestablishing central worship in Jerusalem (18:4; 2 Chr. 31:1) had removed opportunities to worship the Lord, and thus cut back on honoring Judah's God, thereby displeasing Him and forfeiting His help in war. **this altar.** That all worship should center in Solomon's temple was utterly foreign to the polytheistic Assyrians.

18:23,24 *See note on Is. 36:8,9.*

18:25 The LORD said. *See note on Is. 36:10.*

18:26 Aramaic...Hebrew. *See note on Is. 36:11.*

18:27 men...on the wall. *See note on Is. 36:12.*

18:28-32 The Rabshakeh spoke longer and louder in Heb. suggesting that Hezekiah could not save the city, but the great king, of Assyria, would fill the people with abundance if they would promise to surrender to his sovereign control, give tribute to him and be willing to go into a rich and beneficial exile (vv. 31,32).

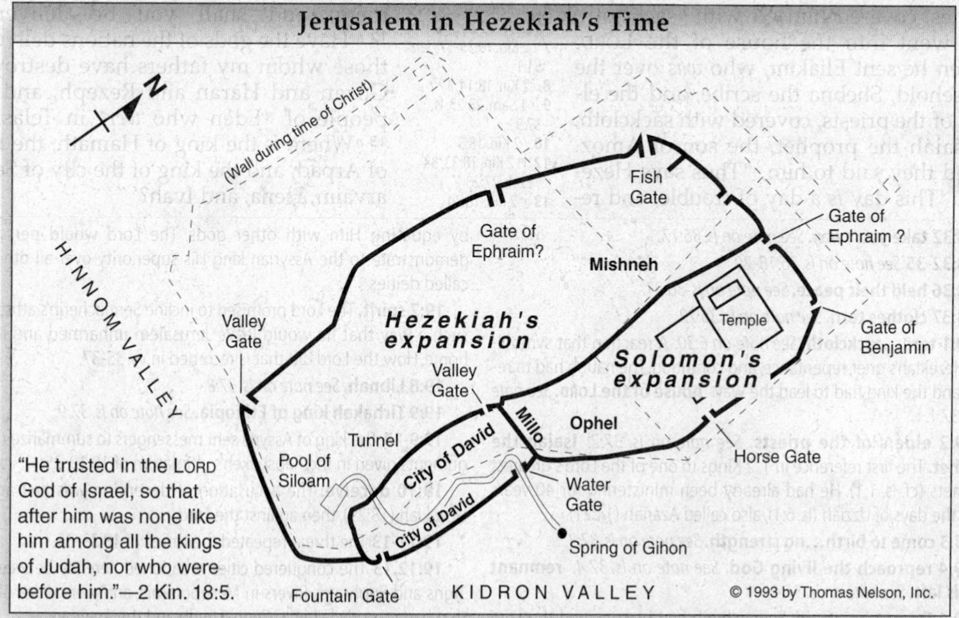

surely deliver us; this city shall not be
given into the hand of the king of Assyria." ' 31 Do not listen to Hezekiah; for
thus says the king of Assyria: 'Make *peace*
with me [6]by a present and come out to me;
and every one of you eat from his own
[d]vine and every one from his own fig tree,
and every one of you drink the waters of
his own cistern; 32 until I come and take
you away to a land like your own land, [e]a
land of grain and new wine, a land of
bread and vineyards, a land of olive groves
and honey, that you may live and not die.
But do not listen to Hezekiah, lest he persuade you, saying, "The LORD will deliver
us." 33 [f]Has any of the gods of the nations
at all delivered its land from the hand of
the king of Assyria? 34 Where *are* the gods
of [g]Hamath and Arpad? Where *are* the
gods of Sepharvaim and Hena and [h]Ivah?
Indeed, have they delivered Samaria from
my hand? 35 Who among all the gods of
the lands have delivered their countries
from my hand, [i]that the LORD should deliver Jerusalem from my hand?' "
36 But the people held their peace and
answered him not a word; for the king's
commandment was, "Do not answer him."
37 Then Eliakim the son of Hilkiah, who
was over the household, Shebna the scribe,
and Joah the son of Asaph, the recorder,
came to Hezekiah [j]with *their* clothes torn,
and told him the words of *the* Rabshakeh.

Isaiah Assures Deliverance

19 And [a]so it was, when King Hezekiah heard *it*, that he tore his
clothes, covered himself with [b]sackcloth,
and went into the house of the LORD.
2 Then he sent Eliakim, who *was* over the
household, Shebna the scribe, and the elders of the priests, covered with sackcloth,
to Isaiah the prophet, the son of Amoz.
3 And they said to him, "Thus says Hezekiah: 'This day *is* a day of trouble, and rebuke, and blasphemy; for the children
have come to birth, but *there is* no strength
to [1]bring them forth. 4 [c]It may be that the
LORD your God will hear all the words of
the Rabshakeh, whom his master the king
of Assyria has sent to [d]reproach the living
God, and will [e]rebuke the words which the
LORD your God has heard. Therefore lift up
your prayer for the remnant that is left.' "
5 So the servants of King Hezekiah came
to Isaiah. 6 [f]And Isaiah said to them, "Thus
you shall say to your master, 'Thus says
the LORD: "Do not be [g]afraid of the words
which you have heard, with which the
[h]servants of the king of Assyria have blasphemed Me. 7 Surely I will send [i]a spirit
upon him, and he shall hear a rumor and
return to his own land; and I will cause
him to fall by the sword in his own
land." ' "

Sennacherib's Threat and Hezekiah's Prayer

8 Then *the* Rabshakeh returned and
found the king of Assyria warring against
Libnah, for he heard that he had departed
[j]from Lachish. 9 And [k]the king heard concerning Tirhakah king of Ethiopia, "Look,
he has come out to make war with you."
So he again sent messengers to Hezekiah,
saying, 10 "Thus you shall speak to Hezekiah king of Judah, saying: 'Do not let your
God [l]in whom you trust deceive you, saying, "Jerusalem shall not be given into the
hand of the king of Assyria." 11 Look! You
have heard what the kings of Assyria have
done to all lands by utterly destroying
them; and shall you be delivered?
12 [m]Have the gods of the nations delivered
those whom my fathers have destroyed,
Gozan and Haran and Rezeph, and the
people of [n]Eden who *were* in Telassar?
13 [o]Where *is* the king of Hamath, the king
of Arpad, and the king of the city of Sepharvaim, Hena, and Ivah?' "

31 [d]1 Kin. 4:20, 25 [6]By paying tribute
32 [e]Deut. 8:7-9; 11:12
33 [f]2 Kin. 19:12; Is. 10:10, 11
34 [g]2 Kin. 19:13 [h]2 Kin. 17:24
35 [i]Dan. 3:15
37 [j]Is. 33:7

CHAPTER 19

1 [a]2 Kin. 18:13; 2 Chr. 32:20-22; Is. 37:1 [b]Ps. 69:11
3 [1]*give birth*
4 [c]2 Sam. 16:12 [d]2 Kin. 18:35 [e]Ps. 50:21
6 [f]Is. 37:6 [g][Ps. 112:7] [h]2 Kin. 18:17
7 [i]2 Kin. 19:35-37; Jer. 51:1
8 [j]2 Kin. 18:14, 17
9 [k]1 Sam. 23:27; Is. 37:9
10 [l]2 Kin. 18:5
12 [m]2 Kin. 18:33, 34 [n]Ezek. 27:23
13 [o]2 Kin. 18:34

18:32 take you away. *See note on Is. 36:17.*

18:32-35 *See note on Is. 36:18-20.*

18:36 held their peace. *See note on Is. 36:21.*

18:37 clothes torn. *See note on Is. 36:22.*

19:1 tore...sackcloth. *See note on 6:30.* A reaction that symbolized Hezekiah's grief, repentance, and contrition. The nation had to repent and the king had to lead the way. **house of the LORD.** *See note on Is. 37:1.*

19:2 elders of the priests. *See note on Is. 37:2.* **Isaiah the prophet.** The first reference in 1, 2 Kings to one of the Lord's greatest prophets (cf. Is. 1:1). He had already been ministering for 40 years since the days of Uzziah (Is. 6:1), also called Azariah (14:21).

19:3 come to birth...no strength. *See note on Is. 37:3.*

19:4 reproach the living God. *See note on Is. 37:4.* **remnant that is left.** *See note on Is. 37:4.*

19:6 Do not be afraid. Sennacherib had blasphemed the Lord by equating Him with other gods. The Lord would personally demonstrate to the Assyrian king His superiority over all other so-called deities.

19:7 spirit. The Lord promised to incline Sennacherib's attitude in such a way that he would leave Jerusalem unharmed and return home. How the Lord did that is recorded in vv. 35-37.

19:8 Libnah. *See note on Is. 37:8.*

19:9 Tirhakah king of Ethiopia. *See note on Is. 37:9.*

19:9-13 The king of Assyria sent messengers to summarize the arguments given in the Rabshakeh's ultimatum of 18:19-25.

19:10 deceive. The accusation of deception was first against Hezekiah (18:29), then against the Lord.

19:11-13 The threat repeated the thrust of 18:33-35.

19:12,13 The conquered cities mentioned here lay between the Tigris and Euphrates Rivers in Mesopotamia, and were cities of Syria that had recently fallen to Sennacherib and the Assyrians.

14 [p]And Hezekiah received the letter
from the hand of the messengers, and read
it; and Hezekiah went up to the house of
the LORD, and spread it before the LORD.
15 Then Hezekiah prayed before the LORD,
and said: "O LORD God of Israel, *the One*
[q]who dwells *between* the cherubim, [r]You
are God, You alone, of all the kingdoms of
the earth. You have made heaven and
earth. 16 [s]Incline Your ear, O LORD, and
hear; [t]open Your eyes, O LORD, and see;
and hear the words of Sennacherib, [u]which
he has sent to reproach the living God.
17 Truly, LORD, the kings of Assyria have
laid waste the nations and their lands,
18 and have cast their gods into the fire; for
they *were* [v]not gods, but [w]the work of
men's hands—wood and stone. Therefore
they destroyed them. 19 Now therefore, O
LORD our God, I pray, save us from his
hand, [x]that all the kingdoms of the earth
may [y]know that You *are* the LORD God, You
alone."

The Word of the LORD Concerning Sennacherib

20 Then Isaiah the son of Amoz sent to
Hezekiah, saying, "Thus says the LORD
God of Israel: [z]'Because you have prayed
to Me against Sennacherib king of Assyria,
[a]I have heard.' 21 This *is* the word which
the LORD has spoken concerning him:

'The virgin, [b]the daughter of Zion,
Has despised you, laughed you to scorn;
The daughter of Jerusalem
[c]Has shaken *her* head behind your back!

22 'Whom have you reproached and blasphemed?
Against whom have you raised *your* voice,
And lifted up your eyes on high?
Against [d]the Holy *One* of Israel.
23 [e]By your messengers you have reproached the Lord,
And said: [f]"By the multitude of my chariots
I have come up to the height of the mountains,
To the limits of Lebanon;
I will cut down its tall cedars
And its choice cypress trees;
I will enter the extremity of its borders,
To its fruitful forest.
24 I have dug and drunk strange water,
And with the soles of my feet I have [g]dried up
All the brooks of defense."

25 'Did you not hear long ago
How [h]I made it,
From ancient times that I formed it?
Now I have brought it to pass,
That [i]you should be
For crushing fortified cities *into* heaps of ruins.
26 Therefore their inhabitants had little power;
They were dismayed and confounded;
They were *as* the grass of the field
And the green herb,
As [j]the grass on the housetops
And *grain* blighted before it is grown.

27 'But [k]I know your dwelling place,
Your going out and your coming in,
And your rage against Me.
28 Because your rage against Me and your tumult
Have come up to My ears,
Therefore [l]I will put My hook in your nose
And My bridle in your lips,
And I will turn you back
[m]By the way which you came.

29 'This *shall be* a [n]sign to you:

You shall eat this year such as grows [2]of itself,
And in the second year what springs from the same;

14 [p] Is. 37:14
15 [q] Ex. 25:22; Ps. 80:1; Is. 37:16 [r] [Is. 44:6]
16 [s] Ps. 31:2; Is. 37:17 [t] 1 Kin. 8:29; 2 Chr. 6:40 [u] 2 Kin. 19:4
18 [v] [Is. 44:9-20; Jer. 10:3-5] [w] Ps. 115:4; Jer. 10:3; [Acts 17:29]
19 [x] Ps. 83:18 [y] 1 Kin. 8:42, 43
20 [z] Is. 37:21 [a] 2 Kin. 20:5; Ps. 65:2
21 [b] Jer. 14:17; Lam. 2:13 [c] Ps. 22:7, 8
22 [d] Jer. 51:5
23 [e] 2 Kin. 18:17 [f] Ps. 20:7
24 [g] Is. 19:6
25 [h] [Is. 45:7] [i] Is. 10:5, 6
26 [j] Ps. 129:6
27 [k] Ps. 139:1-3; Is. 37:28
28 [l] Job 41:2; Ezek. 29:4; 38:4; Amos 4:2 [m] 2 Kin. 19:33, 36
29 [n] Ex. 3:12; 1 Sam. 2:34; 2 Kin. 20:8, 9; Is. 7:11-14; Luke 2:12 [2] Without cultivation

19:14 house of the LORD. Godly Hezekiah returned to the house of the Lord (cf. v. 1) as he should have, in contrast to Ahaz who in a similar crisis refused even to ask a sign from the Lord (Is. 7:11,12).

19:15 *the One* who dwells…heaven and earth. *See note on Is. 37:16.*

19:16 hear…see…hear. *See note on Is. 37:17.*

19:17,18 *See note on Is. 37:18,19.*

19:19 You alone. *See note on Is. 37:20.*

19:20 Isaiah the son of Amoz. *See note on Is. 37:21.*

19:21 laughed you to scorn. *See note on Is. 37:22.*

19:22 you reproached and blasphemed? The Lord had heard Sennacherib's reproach against Him (v. 16).

19:23,24 *See note on Is. 37:24,25.*

19:25-28 I have brought it to pass. *See notes on Is. 37:26-29.*

19:29 sign. The two years in which they were sustained by the growth of the crops were the two in which Sennacherib ravaged them. He left immediately after the deliverance (v. 36), so in the third year the people remaining could plant again.

Also in the third year sow and
reap,
Plant vineyards and eat the fruit of
them.
30 [o]And the remnant who have
escaped of the house of Judah
Shall again take root downward,
And bear fruit upward.
31 For out of Jerusalem shall go a
remnant,
And those who escape from Mount
Zion.
[p]The zeal of the LORD [3]of hosts will
do this.'

32 "Therefore thus says the LORD concerning the king of Assyria:

'He shall [q]not come into this city,
Nor shoot an arrow there,
Nor come before it with shield,
Nor build a siege mound against it.
33 By the way that he came,
By the same shall he return;
And he shall not come into this
city,'
Says the LORD.
34 'For [r]I will [s]defend this city, to save
it
For My own sake and [t]for My
servant David's sake.' "

Sennacherib's Defeat and Death

35 And [u]it came to pass on a certain
night that the [4]angel of the LORD went out,
and killed in the camp of the Assyrians one
hundred and eighty-five thousand; and
when *people* arose early in the morning,
there were the corpses—all dead. 36 So
Sennacherib king of Assyria departed and
went away, returned *home,* and remained
at [v]Nineveh. 37 Now it came to pass, as he
was worshiping in the temple of Nisroch
his god, that his sons [w]Adrammelech and
Sharezer [x]struck him down with the
sword; and they escaped into the land of
Ararat. Then [y]Esarhaddon his son reigned
in his place.

Hezekiah's Life Extended

20 In [a]those days Hezekiah was sick
and near death. And Isaiah the
prophet, the son of Amoz, went to him and
said to him, "Thus says the LORD: 'Set your
house in order, for you shall die, and not
live.' "

2 Then he turned his face toward the
wall, and prayed to the LORD, saying,
3 [b]"Remember now, O LORD, I pray, how I
have walked before You in truth and with
a loyal heart, and have done *what was* good
in Your sight." And Hezekiah wept bitterly.

4 And it happened, before Isaiah had
gone out into the middle court, that the
word of the LORD came to him, saying,
5 "Return and tell Hezekiah [c]the leader of
My people, 'Thus says the LORD, the God
of David your father: [d]"I have heard your
prayer, I have seen [e]your tears; surely I will
heal you. On the third day you shall go up
to the house of the LORD. 6 And I will add
to your days fifteen years. I will deliver
you and this city from the hand of the king
of Assyria; and [f]I will defend this city for
My own sake, and for the sake of My servant David." ' "

7 Then [g]Isaiah said, "Take a lump of

30 [o] 2 Kin. 19:4; 2 Chr. 32:22, 23
31 [p] 2 Kin. 25:26; Is. 9:7 [3] So with many Heb. mss. and ancient vss. (cf. Is. 37:32); MT omits *of hosts*
32 [q] Is. 8:7-10
34 [r] 2 Kin. 20:6; 2 Chr. 32:21 [s] Is. 31:5 [t] 1 Kin. 11:12, 13
35 [u] Ex. 12:29; Is. 10:12-19; 37:36; Hos. 1:7 [4] Or *Angel*
36 [v] Gen. 10:11
37 [w] 2 Kin. 17:31 [x] 2 Kin. 19:7; 2 Chr. 32:21 [y] Ezra 4:2

CHAPTER 20

1 [a] 2 Kin. 18:13; 2 Chr. 32:24; Is. 38:1-22
3 [b] 2 Kin. 18:3-6; Neh. 13:22
5 [c] 1 Sam. 9:16; 10:1 [d] 2 Kin. 19:20; Ps. 65:2 [e] Ps. 39:12; 56:8
6 [f] 2 Kin. 19:34; 2 Chr. 32:21
7 [g] Is. 38:21

19:30,31 remnant...remnant. From the remnant of survivors in Jerusalem came descendants who covered the land once again (cf. Is. 1:9,27; 3:10; 4:3; 6:13; 8:16,17; 10:20,22; 11:12,16; 26:1-4,8; 27:12; 28:5; 37:4).

19:31 zeal of the LORD of hosts. The same confirmation of God's promise in 19:7 assured the future establishment of the messianic kingdom. Deliverance from Sennacherib in Hezekiah's day was a down payment on the literal, final restoration of Israel at Christ's second coming.

19:32 shall not come...build a siege mound. *See note on Is. 37:33.*

19:33 shall he return. *See note on Is. 37:34.*

19:34 For My own sake. Since Sennacherib had directly challenged the Lord's faithfulness to His Word (v. 10), the faithfulness of God was at stake in this contest with the Assyrians (cf. Ezek. 36:22,23). **for My servant David's sake.** God pledged to perpetuate David's line on his throne (2 Sam. 7:16; cf. Is. 9:6,7; 11:1; 55:3).

19:35 the angel of the LORD. For identification, *see note on Ex. 3:2.* For the angel as an agent of destruction, see Gen. 19:15; 2 Sam. 24:16.

19:35-37 killed. *See notes on Is. 37:36-38.*

20:1 In those days...sick. The date of Hezekiah's sickness poses 3 reasonable possibilities: 1) since Hezekiah would be given 15 years of life and delivered from the Assyrians (v. 6), the sickness occurred ca. 701 B.C.; 2) since Berodach-Baladan (v. 12) died in 703 B.C., the sickness occurred shortly before and was followed by the embassy from Babylon that saw the temple treasures (vv. 12-19); or 3) since Berodach-Baladan's greatest power was ca. 721–710 B.C., Hezekiah's sickness occurred during those years. The first or second possibility is most likely. **Set your house in order.** An instruction telling Hezekiah to make his final will known to his family (cf. 2 Sam. 17:23). **you shall die, and not live.** The prediction sounded final, but Hezekiah knew God was willing to hear his appeal (cf. Ex. 32:7-14).

20:2,3 prayed...wept bitterly. Hezekiah reminded the Lord in prayer of his piety and devotion to God. He did not specifically ask to be healed. Based on the interpretation of the date from v. 1, Hezekiah wept because: 1) he thought his death would give Sennacherib cause for boasting; or 2) his son Manasseh was too young to become king.

20:3 loyal heart. *See note on Is. 38:3.*

20:6 fifteen years. The Lord's immediate (v. 4) response granted the king's request. Having to reverse a prophecy so quickly did not alarm Isaiah as it did Jonah later on (Jon. 4:2,3). Isaiah resembled Nathan in this respect (2 Sam. 7:3-6). **I will deliver...this city.** *See note on Is. 38:6.*

figs." So they took and laid *it* on the boil,
and he recovered.
8 And Hezekiah said to Isaiah, [h]"What *is*
the sign that the LORD will heal me, and
that I shall go up to the house of the LORD
the third day?"
9 Then Isaiah said, [i]"This is the sign to
you from the LORD, that the LORD will do
the thing which He has spoken: *shall* the
shadow go forward ten degrees or go
backward ten degrees?"
10 And Hezekiah answered, "It is an
easy thing for the shadow to go down ten
[1]degrees; no, but let the shadow go backward ten degrees."
11 So Isaiah the prophet cried out to the
LORD, and [j]He brought the shadow ten
[2]degrees backward, by which it had gone
down on the sundial of Ahaz.

The Babylonian Envoys

12 [k]At that time [3]Berodach-Baladan the
son of Baladan, king of Babylon, sent letters and a present to Hezekiah, for he
heard that Hezekiah had been sick. 13 And
[l]Hezekiah was attentive to them, and
showed them all the house of his treasures—the silver and gold, the spices and
precious ointment, and [4]all [5]his armory—
all that was found among his treasures.
There was nothing in his house or in all his
dominion that Hezekiah did not show
them.
14 Then Isaiah the prophet went to King
Hezekiah, and said to him, "What did
these men say, and from where did they
come to you?"
So Hezekiah said, "They came from a far
country, from Babylon."
15 And he said, "What have they seen in
your house?"
So Hezekiah answered, [m]"They have
seen all that *is* in my house; there is nothing among my treasures that I have not
shown them."
16 Then Isaiah said to Hezekiah, "Hear
the word of the LORD: 17 'Behold, the days
are coming when all that *is* in your house,
and what your fathers have accumulated
until this day, [n]shall be carried to Babylon;
nothing shall be left,' says the LORD.
18 'And [o]they shall take away some of your
sons who will [6]descend from you, whom
you will beget; [p]and they shall be [q]eu-
nuchs in the palace of the king of Babylon.' "
19 So Hezekiah said to Isaiah, [r]"The
word of the LORD which you have spoken
is good!" For he said, "Will there not be
peace and truth at least in my days?"

Death of Hezekiah

20 [s]Now the rest of the acts of Hezekiah—all his might, and how he [t]made a
[u]pool and a [7]tunnel and [v]brought water
into the city—*are* they not written in the
book of the chronicles of the kings of Judah? 21 So [w]Hezekiah [8]rested with his fathers. Then Manasseh his son reigned in
his place.

8 [h]Judg. 6:17, 37, 39; Is. 7:11, 14; 38:22
9 [i]Num. 23:19; Is. 38:7, 8
10 [1]Lit. *steps*
11 [j]Josh. 10:12-14; Is. 38:8 [2]Lit. *steps*
12 [k]2 Kin. 8:8, 9; 2 Chr. 32:31; Is. 39:1-8 [3]*Merodach-Baladan,* Is. 39:1
13 [l]2 Kin. 16:9; 2 Chr. 32:27, 31 [4]So with many Heb. mss., Syr., Tg.; MT omits *all* [5]Lit. *the house of his armor*
15 [m]2 Kin. 20:13
17 [n]2 Kin. 24:13; 25:13-15; 2 Chr. 36:10; Jer. 27:21, 22; 52:17
18 [o]2 Kin. 24:12; 2 Chr. 33:11 [p]Dan. 1:3-7 [q]Dan. 1:11, 18 [6]*be born from*
19 [r]1 Sam. 3:18
20 [s]2 Chr. 32:32 [t]Neh. 3:16 [u]2 Kin. 18:17; Is. 7:3 [v]2 Chr. 32:3, 30 [7]*aqueduct*
21 [w]2 Kin. 16:20; 2 Chr. 32:33 [8]Died and joined his ancestors

20:8-11 sign…ten degrees backward. Here is the first biblical mention of any means of marking time. Hezekiah requested this sign to confirm the Lord's promise of healing.

20:12 At that time. Just after Hezekiah's sickness and recovery. **Berodach-Baladan.** Berodach-Baladan (see marginal note), ruler of the city of Babylon, defied Assyria repeatedly between 721 and 710 B.C. He apparently approached Hezekiah (ca. 703 B.C.) for help against Sargon, king of Assyria, though interest in the reversal of the sundial (2 Chr. 32:31) and Hezekiah's recovery may have been part of his motivation.

20:13 Hezekiah was attentive. The text does not say whether it was because of flattery or out of a desire for help against the Assyrian threat. Cf. "pleased" in Is. 39:2.

20:13,14 treasures…treasures. *See notes on Is. 39:2,3.*

20:16,17 word of the LORD…carried to Babylon. Isaiah predicted the Babylonian captivity that would come over a century later (586 B.C.), another prophecy historically fulfilled in all of its expected detail.

20:17 nothing shall be left. Hezekiah's sin of parading his wealth before the visitors backfired, though this sin was only symptomatic of the ultimate reason for the captivity. The major cause was the corrupt leadership of Manasseh, Hezekiah's son (21:11-15).

20:18 sons who will descend from you. Hezekiah's sons had to go into captivity. See 24:12-16; 2 Chr. 33:11; Dan. 1:3,4,6 for the prophecy's fulfillment.

20:19 word of the LORD…good. A surprising response to the negative prophecy of vv. 16-18. It acknowledged Isaiah as God's faithful messenger, and God's goodness in not destroying Jerusalem during Hezekiah's lifetime. **peace and truth…in my days.** Hezekiah might have reacted selfishly, or perhaps he looked for a bright spot to lighten the gloomy fate of his descendants.

20:20 tunnel. *See note on 2 Chr. 32:30.*

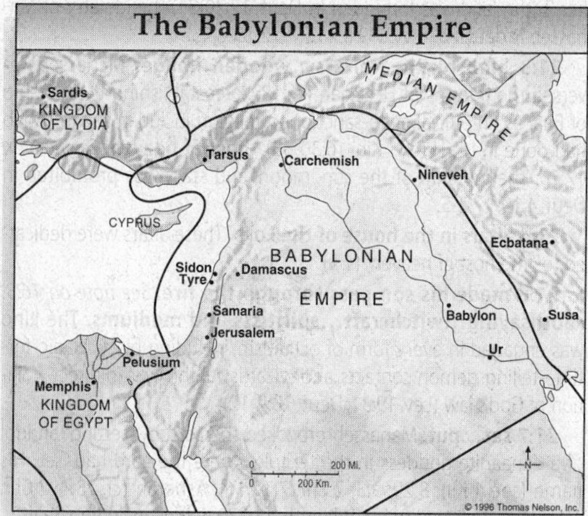

Manasseh Reigns in Judah

21 Manasseh [a]*was* twelve years old when he became king, and he reigned fifty-five years in Jerusalem. His mother's name *was* Hephzibah. **2** And he did evil in the sight of the LORD, [b]according to the abominations of the nations whom the LORD had cast out before the children of Israel. **3** For he rebuilt the [1]high places [c]which Hezekiah his father had destroyed; he raised up altars for Baal, and made a [2]wooden image, [d]as Ahab king of Israel had done; and he [e]worshiped all [3]the host of heaven and served them. **4** [f]He also built altars in the house of the LORD, of which the LORD had said, [g]"In Jerusalem I will put My name." **5** And he built altars for all the host of heaven in the [h]two courts of the house of the LORD. **6** [i]Also he made his son pass through the fire, practiced [j]soothsaying, used witchcraft, and consulted spiritists and mediums. He did much evil in the sight of the LORD, to provoke *Him* to anger. **7** He even set a carved image of [4]Asherah that he had made, in the [5]house of which the LORD had said to David and to Solomon his son, [k]"In this house and in Jerusalem, which I have chosen out of all the tribes of Israel, I will put My name forever; **8** [l]and I will not make the feet of Israel wander anymore from the land which I gave their fathers—only if they are careful to do according to all that I have commanded them, and according to all the law that My servant Moses commanded them." **9** But they paid no attention, and Manasseh [m]seduced them to do more evil than the nations whom the LORD had destroyed before the children of Israel.

10 And the LORD spoke [n]by His servants the prophets, saying, **11** [o]"Because Manasseh king of Judah has done these abominations ([p]he has acted more wickedly than all the [q]Amorites who *were* before him, and [r]has also made Judah sin with his idols), **12** therefore thus says the LORD God of Israel: 'Behold, *I* am bringing *such* calamity upon Jerusalem and Judah, that whoever hears of it, both [s]his ears will tingle. **13** And I will stretch over Jerusalem [t]the measuring line of Samaria and the plummet of the house of Ahab; [u]I will wipe Jerusalem as *one* wipes a dish, wiping *it* and turning *it* upside down. **14** So I will forsake the [v]remnant of My inheritance and deliver them into the hand of their enemies; and they shall become victims of plunder to all their enemies, **15** because they have done evil in My sight, and have provoked Me to anger since the day their fathers came out of Egypt, even to this day.' "

16 [w]Moreover Manasseh shed very

CHAPTER 21

1 [a]2 Chr. 33:1-9
2 [b]2 Kin. 16:3
3 [c]2 Kin. 18:4, 22 [d]1 Kin. 16:31-33 [e][Deut. 4:19; 17:2-5]; 2 Kin. 17:16; 23:5 [1]Places for pagan worship [2]Heb. *Asherah*, a Canaanite goddess [3]The gods of the Assyrians
4 [f]Jer. 7:30; 32:34 [g]1 Kin. 11:13
5 [h]1 Kin. 6:36; 7:12; 2 Kin. 23:12
6 [i][Lev. 18:21; 20:2]; 2 Kin. 16:3; 17:17 [j]Lev. 19:26, 31; [Deut. 18:10-14]; 2 Kin. 17:17
7 [k]2 Sam. 7:13; 1 Kin. 8:29; 9:3; 2 Kin. 23:27; 2 Chr. 7:12, 16; Jer. 32:34 [4]A Canaanite goddess [5]Temple
8 [l]2 Sam. 7:10; [2 Kin. 18:11, 12]
9 [m][Prov. 29:12]
10 [n]2 Kin. 17:13
11 [o]2 Kin. 23:26, 27; 24:3, 4 [p]1 Kin. 21:26 [q]Gen. 15:16 [r]2 Kin. 21:9
12 [s]1 Sam. 3:11; Jer. 19:3
13 [t]Lam. 2:8; Amos 7:7, 8 [u]2 Kin. 22:16-19; 25:4-11
14 [v]Jer. 6:9
16 [w]2 Kin. 24:4

21:1 twelve years old. Manasseh began to reign as co-regent alongside his father, Hezekiah, in 695 B.C. Since the years of the subsequent royal reigns in Judah total 10 years longer than the actual historical period and the dates of the later kings synchronize well with history, it is best to assume a 10 year co-regency in Manasseh's long reign. Hezekiah groomed his son as a youth to succeed him as king; however, Manasseh turned out to be the worst king in Judah's history. **fifty-five years.** 695–642 B.C. *See notes on 2 Chr. 33:1-20.*

21:2 the abominations of the nations. The detestable practices of the Canaanites were enumerated in Deut. 18:9-12. Israel's reproduction of these abominable practices of the nations that preceded her in the land was forbidden in Deut. 12:29-31. The idolatry of Manasseh is detailed in vv. 3-9 (cf. 17:7-12, 15-17).

21:3 high places...altars...wooden image. Manasseh reversed the reforms of Hezekiah (cf. 18:4), reestablishing the worship of Baal as an official state-sanctioned religion in Judah, just as Ahab had done in Israel (cf. 1 Kin. 16:30-33). **host of heaven.** *See note on 17:16.* The worship of the sun, moon, and stars was prohibited in Deut. 4:19; 17:2-5.

21:4 altars in the house of the LORD. These altars were dedicated to "the host of heaven" (v. 5).

21:6 made his son pass through the fire. *See note on 16:3.* **soothsaying...witchcraft...spiritists and mediums.** The king was engaged in every form of occultism, including black magic, fortune-telling, demon contacts, and wizards. All this was in direct violation of God's law (Lev. 19:31; Deut. 18:9-12).

21:7 set...put. Manasseh provoked the Lord by "setting" an idol of a Canaanite goddess in the temple where the Lord had "set" His name (see 1 Kin. 8:29; 9:3; 2 Chr. 7:12, 16). Asherah (cf. 23:4; 2 Chr. 15:16) was believed to be the mother of 70 deities, including Baal.

21:8,9 This alludes to the promise of 2 Sam. 7:10. From the very start of their time in Canaan, the people were called to this obedience, but because the people of Judah did not follow carefully the stipulations of the Mosaic law, they were again led into idolatry by Manasseh. Their idolatry even exceeded the idolatry of the Canaanites from whom they took the land.

21:10 the prophets. Through his spokesman, the Lord announced Judah's judgment. In vv. 11-15, the prophetic message to Judah is summarized.

21:11 Amorites. A general designation of the original inhabitants of Canaan (cf. Gen. 15:16; Josh. 24:8).

21:13 the plummet. These were weighted lines dropped from walls to see whether they were structurally straight (cf. Is. 28:17; Amos 7:7, 8). Walls out of line were torn down. The Lord had measured Jerusalem by the standard of His Word and had determined that the fate of Samaria (Israel) was also to befall Jerusalem. **wipe Jerusalem.** As one would wipe food off a dish, the Lord would wipe Jerusalem clean off the earth, i.e., obliterate her, and leave her turned upside down, empty, and useless.

21:14 forsake. The Lord was going to abandon His people into the hands of enemies who would plunder them (cf. Jer. 12:7). **remnant.** Judah, the only remaining group of the chosen people.

21:15 provoked Me to anger. The history of God's people Israel was a history of disobedience toward the Lord. With the reign of Manasseh, the sin of God's people climaxed, God's patience was withdrawn, and the judgment of exile became inevitable (cf. 24:1-4).

21:16 very much innocent blood. The reference here is ambiguous and several interpretations have been offered: 1) child sacrifice (cf. v. 6); 2) oppression and persecution of the weak (Jer. 7:6;

much innocent blood, till he had filled Jerusalem from one end to another, besides
his sin by which he made Judah sin, in
doing evil in the sight of the LORD.
17 Now [x]the rest of the acts of [y]Ma-
nasseh—all that he did, and the sin that he
committed—*are* they not written in the
book of the chronicles of the kings of Judah? 18 So [z]Manasseh [6]rested with his fathers, and was buried in the garden of his
own house, in the garden of Uzza. Then his
son Amon reigned in his place.

Amon's Reign and Death

19 [a]Amon *was* twenty-two years old
when he became king, and he reigned two
years in Jerusalem. His mother's name *was*
Meshullemeth the daughter of Haruz of
Jotbah. 20 And he did evil in the sight of
the LORD, [b]as his father Manasseh had
done. 21 So he walked in all the ways that
his father had walked; and he served the
idols that his father had served, and worshiped them. 22 He [c]forsook the LORD God
of his fathers, and did not walk in the way
of the LORD.
23 [d]Then the servants of Amon [e]con-
spired against him, and killed the king in
his own house. 24 But the people of the
land [f]executed all those who had conspired against King Amon. Then the people of the land made his son Josiah king in
his place.
25 Now the rest of the acts of Amon
which he did, *are* they not written in the
book of the chronicles of the kings of Judah? 26 And he was buried in his tomb in
the garden of Uzza. Then Josiah his son
reigned in his place.

17 [x] 2 Chr. 33:11-19 [y] 2 Kin. 20:21
18 [z] 2 Chr. 33:20 [6] Died and joined his ancestors
19 [a] 2 Chr. 33:21-23
20 [b] 2 Kin. 21:2-6, 11, 16
22 [c] Judg. 2:12, 13; 1 Kin. 11:33; 1 Chr. 28:9
23 [d] 1 Chr. 3:14; 2 Chr. 33:24, 25; Matt. 1:10 [e] 2 Kin. 12:20; 14:19
24 [f] 2 Kin. 14:5

CHAPTER 22
1 [a] 1 Kin. 13:2; 2 Chr. 34:1 [b] Josh. 15:39
2 [c] Deut. 5:32; Josh. 1:7
3 [d] 2 Chr. 34:8
4 [e] 2 Kin. 12:4 [f] 2 Kin. 12:9, 10
5 [g] 2 Kin. 12:11-14
7 [h] 2 Kin. 12:15; [1 Cor. 4:2]
8 [i] Deut. 31:24-26; 2 Chr. 34:14
9 [1] Lit. *poured out*

Josiah Reigns in Judah

22 Josiah [a]*was* eight years old when he
became king, and he reigned thirty-
one years in Jerusalem. His mother's name
was Jedidah the daughter of Adaiah of
[b]Bozkath. 2 And he did *what was* right in
the sight of the LORD, and walked in all the
ways of his father David; he [c]did not turn
aside to the right hand or to the left.

Hilkiah Finds the Book of the Law

3 [d]Now it came to pass, in the eighteenth
year of King Josiah, *that* the king sent
Shaphan the scribe, the son of Azaliah, the
son of Meshullam, to the house of the
LORD, saying: 4 "Go up to Hilkiah the high
priest, that he may count the money which
has been [e]brought into the house of the
LORD, which [f]the doorkeepers have gathered from the people. 5 And let them [g]de-
liver it into the hand of those doing the
work, who are the overseers in the house
of the LORD; let them give it to those who
are in the house of the LORD doing the
work, to repair the damages of the house—
6 to carpenters and builders and masons—
and to buy timber and hewn stone to repair the house. 7 However [h]there need be
no accounting made with them of the
money delivered into their hand, because
they deal faithfully."
8 Then Hilkiah the high priest said to
Shaphan the scribe, [i]"I have found the
Book of the Law in the house of the LORD."
And Hilkiah gave the book to Shaphan,
and he read it. 9 So Shaphan the scribe
went to the king, bringing the king word,
saying, "Your servants have [1]gathered the
money that was found in the house, and
have delivered it into the hand of those

22:3,17; Ezek. 22:6-31); or 3) the martyrdom of God's prophets (cf. v. 10). A combination of all 3 is most likely. Jewish and Christian tradition alike report that Manasseh had Isaiah sawn in two inside a hollow log (cf. Heb. 11:37).

21:19 two years. 642–640 B.C. Amon continued the idolatrous practices of his father, abandoning the Lord completely (vv. 20-22). *See notes on 2 Chr. 33:21-25.*

21:24 the people of the land. Probably a group of Judah's national leaders who killed the assassins of Amon and installed his son Josiah on the throne. Apparently, they desired to maintain the Davidic dynasty (cf. 2 Kin. 11:14-18).

22:1 thirty-one years. 640–609 B.C. During Josiah's reign, power in the ancient Near East passed from Assyria to Babylon. Nineveh, the capital of Assyria, was destroyed by the Babylonians in 612 B.C. and the whole Assyrian empire fell in 609 B.C. Josiah was the last good king of the Davidic line prior to the Babylonian exile. Jeremiah (Jer. 1:2), possibly Habakkuk, and Zephaniah (Zeph. 1:1) were prophets to Judah during the reign of Josiah. *See notes on 2 Chr. 34:1–35:27.*

22:2 did not turn aside. Josiah had complete devotion to God's approved course of conduct for his life (cf. 23:25). He obeyed the Mosaic stipulations as he came to know them, following the example of David, who set the pattern for the rulers of God's people (Deut. 17:11,20; Josh. 1:7).

22:3 eighteenth year. 622 B.C., when Josiah was 26 years of age.

22:4 Hilkiah. The High-Priest was the father of Azariah and the grandfather of Seraiah, the High-Priest who would be executed at the time of the exile by the Babylonians (cf. 25:8-20).

22:4-7 the doorkeepers. *See note on 12:9.* Josiah used the same procedure as King Joash had for collecting funds to repair the temple after its abuse in the days of Manasseh and Amon.

22:8 the Book of the Law. A scroll containing the Torah (the Pentateuch), the revelation of God through Moses to Israel (*see notes on 23:2; Deut. 28:61*). Manasseh may have destroyed all the copies of God's law that were not hidden. This could have been the official copy laid beside the ark of the covenant in the Most Holy Place (Deut. 31:25,26). It may have been removed from its place under Ahaz, Manasseh, or Amon (cf. 2 Chr. 35:3), but was found during repair work.

22:9,10 Some believe that Shaphan must have read Deut. 28–30, in which is recorded a renewal of the national covenant and a listing of the terrible threats and curses against all who violate the law of God.

who do the work, who oversee the house
of the LORD." 10 Then Shaphan the scribe
showed the king, saying, "Hilkiah the
priest has given me a book." And Shaphan
read it before the king.
11 Now it happened, when the king
heard the words of the Book of the Law,
that he tore his clothes. 12 Then the king
commanded Hilkiah the priest, [j]Ahikam
the son of Shaphan, [2]Achbor the son of
Michaiah, Shaphan the scribe, and Asaiah
a servant of the king, saying, 13 "Go, inquire of the LORD for me, for the people
and for all Judah, concerning the words of
this book that has been found; for great *is*
[k]the wrath of the LORD that is aroused
against us, because our fathers have not
obeyed the words of this book, to do according to all that is written concerning
us."
14 So Hilkiah the priest, Ahikam, Achbor, Shaphan, and Asaiah went to Huldah
the prophetess, the wife of Shallum the
son of [l]Tikvah, the son of Harhas, keeper
of the wardrobe. (She dwelt in Jerusalem
in the Second Quarter.) And they spoke
with her. 15 Then she said to them, "Thus
says the LORD God of Israel, 'Tell the man
who sent you to Me, 16 "Thus says the
LORD: 'Behold, [m]I will bring calamity on
this place and on its inhabitants—all the
words of the book which the king of Judah
has read— 17 [n]because they have forsaken
Me and burned incense to other gods, that
they might provoke Me to anger with all
the works of their hands. Therefore My
wrath shall be aroused against this place
and shall not be quenched.' " ' 18 But as
for [o]the king of Judah, who sent you to inquire of the LORD, in this manner you shall

12 [j] 2 Kin. 25:22; Jer. 26:24 [2] *Abdon the son of Micah,* 2 Chr. 34:20
13 [k] [Deut. 29:23-28; 31:17, 18]
14 [l] 2 Chr. 34:22
16 [m] Deut. 29:27; [Dan. 9:11-14]
17 [n] Deut. 29:25-27; 2 Kin. 21:22
18 [o] 2 Chr. 34:26

19 [p] 1 Sam. 24:5; [Ps. 51:17; Is. 57:15] [q] Ex. 10:3; 1 Kin. 21:29; [2 Chr. 7:14] [r] Lev. 26:31, 32 [s] Jer. 26:6; 44:22
20 [t] 2 Kin. 23:30; [Ps. 37:37; Is. 57:1, 2] [3] Cause you to join your ancestors in death [4] Die a natural death

CHAPTER 23

1 [a] 2 Sam. 19:11; 2 Chr. 34:29, 30
2 [b] Deut. 31:10-13 [c] 2 Kin. 22:8
3 [d] 2 Kin. 11:14 [e] 2 Kin. 11:17
4 [f] 2 Kin. 25:18; Jer. 52:24 [g] 2 Kin. 21:3-7

speak to him, 'Thus says the LORD God of
Israel: "*Concerning* the words which you
have heard— 19 because your [p]heart was
tender, and you [q]humbled yourself before
the LORD when you heard what I spoke
against this place and against its inhabitants, that they would become [r]a desolation and [s]a curse, and you tore your
clothes and wept before Me, I also have
heard *you*," says the LORD. 20 Surely, therefore, I will [3]gather you to your fathers,
and you [t]shall [4]be gathered to your grave
in peace; and your eyes shall not see all
the calamity which I will bring on this
place." ' " So they brought back word to
the king.

Josiah Restores True Worship

23 Now [a]the king sent them to gather
all the elders of Judah and Jerusalem to him. 2 The king went up to the
house of the LORD with all the men of Judah, and with him all the inhabitants of Jerusalem—the priests and the prophets and
all the people, both small and great. And
he [b]read in their hearing all the words of
the Book of the Covenant [c]which had been
found in the house of the LORD.
3 Then the king [d]stood by a pillar and
made a [e]covenant before the LORD, to follow the LORD and to keep His commandments and His testimonies and His
statutes, with all *his* heart and all *his* soul,
to perform the words of this covenant that
were written in this book. And all the people took a stand for the covenant. 4 And
the king commanded Hilkiah the high
priest, the [f]priests of the second order, and
the doorkeepers, to bring [g]out of the temple of the LORD all the articles that were

22:11 tore his clothes. Josiah's reaction at the reading of the law was one of immediate contrition, expressed by the common sign of lamentation and grief (see 18:37; 19:1). Josiah's grief sprang from Judah's guilt and God's punishment (v. 13).

22:14 Huldah. This prophetess is otherwise unknown in the OT. She was held in some regard for her prophetic gift, though why she was consulted and not another prophet like Jeremiah or Zephaniah (*see note on 22:1*) is unexplained. Rarely did God speak to the nation through a woman (cf. Miriam, Ex. 15; Deborah, Judg. 5) and never did a woman have an ongoing prophetic ministry identified in Scripture. No woman was inspired to author any of Scripture's 66 books. **the wardrobe.** Likely, these were the royal garments or those used by the priests. **the Second Quarter.** This district of Jerusalem was called "second" because it comprised the city's first major expansion. It was probably located on the western hill of Jerusalem, an area enclosed by the city wall and built during the reign of Hezekiah. The expansion of the city during Hezekiah's reign was perhaps to accommodate Jewish refugees who had escaped from the Assyrian invasion of Israel.

22:15-20 Huldah gave God's message to Josiah through his messengers. First, the Lord confirmed to Josiah that He was surely going to bring His judgment upon Jerusalem because of her idolatry (vv. 15-17). Second, the Lord's personal word to Josiah was that he would die "in peace" (v. 20), meaning that he would escape the horrors in store for Jerusalem. This promise was based on Josiah's response of tenderness and humility before the Lord when he heard the scroll describing Judah's future devastation (vv. 18,19).

22:20 in peace. His heart was at peace with God and he never lived to see Jerusalem destroyed, but he did die in battle (2 Chr. 35:23).

23:2 Book of the Covenant. Although this designation was used in Ex. 24:7 with reference to the contents of Ex. 20:22–23:33, it seems here to refer to a larger writing. Since the larger part of the Pentateuch focused on the Mosaic Covenant, these 5 books came to be called thusly. Since all the men of Judah and all the inhabitants of Jerusalem were assembled together by Josiah, it seems best to view this as the reading of the whole written law found in Gen. 1 through Deut. 34 (*see notes on Deut. 31:9,11*).

23:3 pillar. *See note on 11:14.* **a covenant...this covenant.** Josiah made a public, binding agreement to completely obey the Lord by doing all that was commanded in the Book of the Covenant that the people had just heard read to them. Following Josiah's example, all the people promised to keep the stipulations of the Mosaic Covenant. *See notes on 11:17; Ex. 24:3-8.*

made for Baal, for [1]Asherah, and for all
[2]the host of heaven; and he burned them
outside Jerusalem in the fields of Kidron,
and carried their ashes to Bethel. **5** Then he
removed the idolatrous priests whom the
kings of Judah had ordained to burn incense on the high places in the cities of Judah and in the places all around Jerusalem,
and those who burned incense to Baal, to
the sun, to the moon, to the [3]constellations,
and to [h]all the host of heaven. **6** And he
brought out the [i]wooden[4] image from the
house of the LORD, to the Brook Kidron
outside Jerusalem, burned it at the Brook
Kidron and ground *it* to [j]ashes, and threw
its ashes on [k]the graves of the common
people. **7** Then he tore down the *ritual*
[5]booths [l]of the [6]perverted persons that
were in the house of the LORD, [m]where the
[n]women wove hangings for the wooden
image. **8** And he brought all the priests
from the cities of Judah, and defiled the
high places where the priests had burned
incense, from [o]Geba to Beersheba; also he
broke down the high places at the gates
which *were* at the entrance of the Gate of
Joshua the governor of the city, which *were*
to the left of the city gate. **9** [p]Nevertheless
the priests of the high places did not come
up to the altar of the LORD in Jerusalem,
[q]but they ate unleavened bread among
their brethren.

10 And he defiled [r]Topheth, which *is* in
[s]the Valley of the [7]Son of Hinnom, [t]that no
man might make his son or his daughter
[u]pass through the fire to Molech. **11** Then
he removed the horses that the kings of Judah had [8]dedicated to the sun, at the entrance to the house of the LORD, by the
chamber of Nathan-Melech, the officer
who *was* in the court; and he burned the
chariots of the sun with fire. **12** The altars
that *were* [v]on the roof, the upper chamber
of Ahaz, which the kings of Judah had
made, and the altars which [w]Manasseh
had made in the two courts of the house of
the LORD, the king broke down and pul-
verized there, and threw their dust into the
Brook Kidron. **13** Then the king defiled the
[9]high places that *were* east of Jerusalem,
which *were* on the [1]south of [2]the Mount of
Corruption, which [x]Solomon king of Israel
had built for Ashtoreth the abomination of
the Sidonians, for Chemosh the abomination of the Moabites, and for Milcom the
abomination of the people of Ammon.
14 And he [y]broke in pieces the *sacred* pillars
and cut down the wooden images, and
filled their places with the bones of men.

15 Moreover the altar that *was* at Bethel,
and the [3]high place [z]which Jeroboam the
son of Nebat, who made Israel sin, had
made, both that altar and the high place he
broke down; and he burned the high place
and crushed *it* to powder, and burned the
wooden image. **16** As Josiah turned, he saw
the tombs that *were* there on the mountain.
And he sent and took the bones out of the
tombs and burned *them* on the altar, and
defiled it according to the [a]word of the
LORD which the man of God proclaimed,

4 [1] A Canaanite goddess [2] The gods of the Assyrians
5 [h] 2 Kin. 21:3 [3] Of the Zodiac
6 [i] 2 Kin. 21:7 [j] Ex. 32:20 [k] 2 Chr. 34:4 [4] Heb. *Asherah*, a Canaanite goddess
7 [l] 1 Kin. 14:24; 15:12 [m] Ex. 35:25, 26; Ezek. 16:16 [n] Ex. 38:8 [5] Lit. *houses* [6] Heb. *qedeshim*, those practicing sodomy and prostitution in religious rituals
8 [o] Josh. 21:17; 1 Kin. 15:22
9 [p] [Ezek. 44:10-14] [q] 1 Sam. 2:36
10 [r] Is. 30:33; Jer. 7:31, 32 [s] Josh. 15:8 [t] [Lev. 18:21; Deut. 18:10]; Ezek. 23:37-39 [u] 2 Kin. 21:6 [7] Kt. *Sons*
11 [8] *given*
12 [v] Jer. 19:13; Zeph. 1:5 [w] 2 Kin. 21:5; 2 Chr. 33:5
13 [x] 1 Kin. 11:5-7 [9] Places for pagan worship [1] Lit. *right of* [2] The Mount of Olives
14 [y] [Ex. 23:24; Deut. 7:5-25]
15 [z] 1 Kin. 12:28-33 [3] A place for pagan worship
16 [a] 1 Kin. 13:2

23:4 Asherah. *See note on 21:7.* **the fields of Kidron.** Josiah burned everything in the temple that was devoted to idolatry. This was done in the lower portion of the Kidron Valley, E of the city of Jerusalem (cf. v. 6). **ashes to Bethel.** Located about 10 mi. N of Jerusalem, Bethel was one of the two original places where Jeroboam I established an apostate worship center (1 Kin. 12:28-33). Bethel was located just N of the border of Judah in the former northern kingdom, which was then the Assyrian province of Samaria. With a decline in Assyrian power, Josiah was able to exert his religious influence in the N. He used the ashes of the burned articles of idolatry to desecrate Jeroboam's religious center (cf. vv. 15-20).

23:5 constellations. Cf. 21:3. The astrologers were also removed. See Is. 47:13.

23:6 wooden image. The idol of Asherah (*see note on 21:7*). **graves of the common people.** The Kidron Valley contained a burial ground for the common people (cf. Jer. 26:23). Scattering ashes from the object of idolatry is said in 2 Chr. 34:4 to have been on the graves of those who sacrificed to that idol. The "common people" had followed their leaders to apostasy, defilement, and damnation—all symbolized by the act of scattering the ashes.

23:7 booths. Tents (called "Succoth Benoth" in 17:30) used by women who were devoted to Asherah, in which they made hangings and committed sexual sins.

23:8 Geba to Beersheba. Geba was located about 7 mi. NE of Jerusalem at the far N of Judah and Beersheba was located ca. 45 mi. S of Jerusalem at the southern end of Judah. Thus, this phrase was an idiomatic way of saying "throughout all of Judah."

23:10 Topheth. Meaning "a drum" and identifying the area in the Valley of Hinnom where child sacrifice occurred (cf. Is. 30:33; Jer. 7:31,32; 19:5,6). Perhaps called "drum" because drums were beaten to drown out the cries of the children being sacrificed.

23:11 horses...dedicated to the sun. The horses and the chariots of the sun were probably thought to symbolize the sun blazing a trail across the sky and were a part of worshiping the sun. Recently, a religious shrine with horse figurines has been found in Jerusalem (cf. Ezek. 8:16).

23:12 on the roof. Altars were erected on the flat roofs of houses so people could worship the "host of heaven" by burning incense (Zeph. 1:5; Jer. 19:13).

23:13 Solomon...had built. Solomon had built high places E of Jerusalem on the Mt. of Olives, renamed after the desecration, to be used in worship of foreign gods, e.g., the fertility goddess Ashtoreth from Sidon, the Moabite god Chemosh, and the Ammonite god Molech (1 Kin. 11:7). These altars existed for over 300 years before Josiah finally destroyed them. The placing of human bones defiled them and, thus, rendered these sites unclean and unsuitable as places of worship.

23:15 the altar...at Bethel. Josiah reduced the altar that Jeroboam I had built at Bethel to dust and ashes (see 1 Kin. 12:28-33).

23:16 tombs. Seeing tombs nearby, perhaps where idolatrous priests were buried, Josiah had their bones removed and burned on the altar at Bethel to defile it. This action fulfilled a prophecy given about the altar approximately 300 years before (1 Kin. 13:2).

who proclaimed these words. 17 Then he
said, "What gravestone *is* this that I see?"
So the men of the city told him, "*It is* [b]the
tomb of the man of God who came from
Judah and proclaimed these things which
you have done against the altar of Bethel."
18 And he said, "Let him alone; let no
one move his bones." So they let his bones
alone, with the bones of [c]the prophet who
came from Samaria.
19 Now Josiah also took away all the
[4]shrines of the [5]high places that *were* [d]in
the cities of Samaria, which the kings of Israel had made to provoke [6]the LORD to
anger; and he did to them according to all
the deeds he had done in Bethel. 20 [e]He
[f]executed all the priests of the [7]high places
who *were* there, on the altars, and [g]burned
men's bones on them; and he returned to
Jerusalem.
21 Then the king commanded all the
people, saying, [h]"Keep the Passover to the
LORD your God, [i]as *it is* written in this
Book of the Covenant." 22 [j]Such a Passover
surely had never been held since the days
of the judges who judged Israel, nor in all
the days of the kings of Israel and the kings
of Judah. 23 But in the eighteenth year of
King Josiah this Passover was held before
the LORD in Jerusalem. 24 Moreover Josiah
put away those who consulted mediums
and spiritists, the household gods and
idols, all the abominations that were seen
in the land of Judah and in Jerusalem, that
he might perform the words of [k]the law
which were written in the book [l]that Hilkiah the priest found in the house of the
LORD. 25 [m]Now before him there was no
king like him, who turned to the LORD with
all his heart, with all his soul, and with all
his might, according to all the Law of Moses; nor after him did *any* arise like him.

Impending Judgment on Judah

26 Nevertheless the LORD did not turn
from the fierceness of His great wrath,
with which His anger was aroused
against Judah, [n]because of all the provocations with which Manasseh had provoked Him. 27 And the LORD said, "I will
also remove Judah from My sight, as [o]I
have removed Israel, and will cast off this
city Jerusalem which I have chosen, and
the house of which I said, [p]'My name
shall be there.' "

Josiah Dies in Battle

28 Now the rest of the acts of Josiah, and
all that he did, *are* they not written in the
book of the chronicles of the kings of Judah? 29 [q]In his days Pharaoh Necho king
of Egypt went [8]to the aid of the king of Assyria, to the River Euphrates; and King Josiah went against him. And *Pharaoh Necho*
killed him at [r]Megiddo when he [s]con-
fronted him. 30 [t]Then his servants moved
his body in a chariot from Megiddo,
brought him to Jerusalem, and buried him
in his own tomb. And [u]the people of the
land took Jehoahaz the son of Josiah,
anointed him, and made him king in his father's place.

The Reign and Captivity of Jehoahaz

31 [v]Jehoahaz *was* twenty-three years old
when he became king, and he reigned
three months in Jerusalem. His mother's
name *was* [w]Hamutal the daughter of Jeremiah of Libnah. 32 And he did evil in the
sight of the LORD, according to all that his
fathers had done. 33 Now Pharaoh Necho

17 [b] 1 Kin. 13:1, 30, 31
18 [c] 1 Kin. 13:11, 31
19 [d] 2 Chr. 34:6, 7 [4] Lit. *houses* [5] Places for pagan worship [6] So with LXX, Syr., Vg.; MT, Tg. omit *the LORD*
20 [e] 1 Kin. 13:2 [f] [Ex. 22:20]; 1 Kin. 18:40; 2 Kin. 10:25; 11:18 [g] 2 Chr. 34:5 [7] Places for pagan worship
21 [h] Num. 9:5; Josh. 5:10; 2 Chr. 35:1 [i] Ex. 12:3; Lev. 23:5; Num. 9:2; Deut. 16:2-8
22 [j] 2 Chr. 35:18, 19
24 [k] [Lev. 19:31; 20:27]; Deut. 18:11 [l] 2 Kin. 22:8
25 [m] 2 Kin. 18:5
26 [n] 2 Kin. 21:11, 12; 24:3, 4; Jer. 15:4
27 [o] 2 Kin. 17:18, 20; 18:11; 21:13 [p] 1 Kin. 8:29; 9:3; 2 Kin. 21:4, 7
29 [q] 2 Chr. 35:20; Jer. 2:16; 46:2 [r] Judg. 5:19; Zech. 12:11 [s] 2 Kin. 14:8 [8] Or *to attack*, Heb. *al* can mean *together with* or *against*
30 [t] 2 Chr. 35:24; 2 Kin. 22:20 [u] 2 Chr. 36:1-4
31 [v] 1 Chr. 3:15; Jer. 22:11 [w] 2 Kin. 24:18

23:17,18 See 1 Kin. 13:1-32, especially vv. 31,32.

23:18 Samaria. The former northern kingdom of Israel had become known as Samaria, so named as an Assyrian province (*see note on 17:24*).

23:19 cities of Samaria. The desecration of the high place at Bethel was only the beginning of Josiah's desecration of all the high places in the Assyrian province of Samaria.

23:20 executed all the priests. These non-Levitical priests, who led apostate worship in the former northern kingdom, were idolaters who seduced God's people into idolatry. They were put to death in accordance with the statutes of Deut. 13:6-18; 17:2-7, and their graves were doubly defiled with burned bones.

23:21,22 Such a Passover. Judah's celebration of this Passover (see Deut. 16:2-8) more closely conformed to the instructions given in the Mosaic law than any in the previous 400 years of Israel's history. Though the Passover was observed by Hezekiah (2 Chr. 30), no observance had been in exact conformity to God's law since the judges. Further details of this Passover observance are found in 2 Chr. 35:1-19.

23:23 eighteenth year. Ca. 622 B.C. All the reforms of Josiah described took place in the same year (cf. 22:3).

23:24 the book...found. See 22:8.

23:25 no king like him. Of all the kings in David's line, including David himself, no king more closely approximated the royal ideal of Deut. 17:14-20 than Josiah (cf. Matt. 22:37). Yet, even Josiah fell short of complete obedience because he had multiple wives (cf. vv. 31,36; *see note on Gen. 2:24*). However, even this righteous king could not turn away the Lord's wrath because of Manasseh's sin (vv. 26,27). See chaps. 17,18.

23:29 Necho. Pharaoh Necho II (609-594 B.C.) was an ally of Assyria against the growing power of Babylon. For some unstated reason, Josiah was determined to stop Necho and his army from joining the Assyrian army at the Euphrates River to fight Babylon. **Megiddo.** The well-fortified stronghold overlooking the Jezreel Valley about 65 mi. N of Jerusalem. Megiddo guarded a strategic pass on the route between Egypt and Mesopotamia. Josiah's death is explained in more detail in 2 Chr. 35:20-27.

23:31 three months. Jehoahaz reigned during 609 B.C., became a prisoner of Pharaoh Necho II, and ultimately died in Egypt. *See notes on 2 Chr. 36:1-4.*

put him in prison [x]at Riblah in the land of
Hamath, that he might not reign in Jerusalem; and he imposed on the land a tribute
of one hundred talents of silver and a talent of gold. 34 Then [y]Pharaoh Necho made
Eliakim the son of Josiah king in place of
his father Josiah, and [z]changed his name to
[a]Jehoiakim. And *Pharaoh* took Jehoahaz
[b]and went to Egypt, and [9]he died there.

Jehoiakim Reigns in Judah

35 So Jehoiakim gave [c]the silver and
gold to Pharaoh; but he taxed the land to
give money according to the command of
Pharaoh; he exacted the silver and gold
from the people of the land, from every
one according to his assessment, to give *it*
to Pharaoh Necho. 36 [d]Jehoiakim *was* twenty-five years old when he became king,
and he reigned eleven years in Jerusalem.
His mother's name *was* Zebudah the
daughter of Pedaiah of Rumah. 37 And he
did evil in the sight of the LORD, according
to all that his fathers had done.

Judah Overrun by Enemies

24 In [a]his days Nebuchadnezzar king
of [b]Babylon came up, and Jehoiakim became his vassal *for* three years.
Then he turned and rebelled against him.
2 [c]And the LORD sent against him *raiding*
[1]bands of Chaldeans, bands of Syrians,
bands of Moabites, and bands of the people of Ammon; He sent them against Judah to destroy it, [d]according to the word
of the LORD which He had spoken by His
servants the prophets. 3 Surely at the commandment of the LORD *this* came upon
Judah, to remove *them* from His sight [e]be-
cause of the sins of Manasseh, according
to all that he had done, 4 [f]and also because
of the innocent blood that he had shed; for
he had filled Jerusalem with innocent
blood, which the LORD would not pardon.
5 Now the rest of the acts of Jehoiakim,
and all that he did, *are* they not written in
the book of the chronicles of the kings of
Judah? 6 [g]So Jehoiakim rested with his fathers. Then Jehoiachin his son reigned in
his place.
7 And [h]the king of Egypt did not come
out of his land anymore, for [i]the king of
Babylon had taken all that belonged to the
king of Egypt from the Brook of Egypt to
the River Euphrates.

The Reign and Captivity of Jehoiachin

8 [j]Jehoiachin[2] *was* eighteen years old
when he became king, and he reigned in
Jerusalem three months. His mother's
name *was* Nehushta the daughter of Elnathan of Jerusalem. 9 And he did evil in
the sight of the LORD, according to all that
his father had done.
10 [k]At that time the servants of Nebuchadnezzar king of Babylon came up
against Jerusalem, and the city [3]was besieged. 11 And Nebuchadnezzar king of

33 [x] 2 Kin. 25:6; Jer. 52:27
34 [y] 2 Chr. 36:4 [z] 2 Kin. 24:17; Dan. 1:7 [a] Matt. 1:11 [b] Jer. 22:11, 12; Ezek. 19:3, 4 [9] Jehoahaz
35 [c] 2 Kin. 23:33
36 [d] 2 Chr. 36:5; Jer. 22:18, 19; 26:1

CHAPTER 24

1 [a] 2 Chr. 36:6; Jer. 25:1, 9; Dan. 1:1 [b] 2 Kin. 20:14
2 [c] Jer. 25:9; 32:28; 35:11; Ezek. 19:8 [1] *troops* [d] 2 Kin. 20:17; 21:12-14; 23:27
3 [e] 2 Kin. 21:2, 11; 23:26
4 [f] 2 Kin. 21:16
6 [g] 2 Chr. 36:6, 8; Jer. 22:18, 19
7 [h] Jer. 37:5-7 [i] Jer. 46:2
8 [j] 1 Chr. 3:16; 2 Chr. 36:9 [2] *Jeconiah,* 1 Chr. 3:16; Jer. 24:1; or *Coniah,* Jer. 22:24, 28
10 [k] Dan. 1:1 [3] *Lit. came into siege*

23:33 Riblah in the land of Hamath. Jehoahaz was in prison at Pharaoh Necho II's military headquarters located on the Orontes River in the N Lebanon Valley (*see note on 25:6*). **silver...gold.** The tax imposed on Judah, whose king was imprisoned, was 750 lbs. of silver and 7.5 lbs. of gold.

23:34 Eliakim...Jehoiakim. In 609 B.C., Pharaoh Necho II placed Jehoahaz's older brother on the throne of Judah. Necho changed his name from Eliakim, meaning "God has established," to Jehoiakim, "the Lord has established." The naming of a person was regarded in the ancient Near East as sign of authority; so by naming Jehoiakim, Necho demonstrated that he was the lord who controlled Judah. As a vassal of Egypt, Judah risked attack by Egypt's enemy Babylon. *See notes on 2 Chr. 36:5-8.*

23:35 Jehoiakim taxed his people severely to pay tribute to Egypt, though he still had enough to build a magnificent palace for himself (see Jer. 22:13,14).

23:36 eleven years. 609–597 B.C.

24:1 Nebuchadnezzar. Nebuchadnezzar II was the son of Nabopolassar, king of Babylon from 626–605 B.C. As crown prince, Nebuchadnezzar had led his father's army against Pharaoh Necho and the Egyptians at Carchemish on the Euphrates River in northern Syria (605 B.C.). By defeating the Egyptians, Babylon was established as the strongest nation in the ancient Near East. Egypt and its vassals, including Judah, became vassals of Babylon with this victory. Nebuchadnezzar followed up his victory at Carchemish by invading the land of Judah. Later, in 605 B.C., Nebuchadnezzar took some captives to Babylon, including Daniel and his friends (cf. Dan. 1:1-3). Toward the end of 605 B.C., Nabopolassar died and Nebuchadnezzar succeeded him as king of Babylon, 3 years after Jehoiakim had taken the throne in Judah (Jer. 25:1). Nebuchadnezzar reigned from 605–562 B.C. **three years.** Nebuchadnezzar returned to the W in 604 B.C. and took tribute from all of the kings of the W, including Jehoiakim of Judah. Jehoiakim submitted to Babylonian rule from 604–602 B.C. In 602 B.C., Jehoiakim rebelled against Babylon, disregarding the advice of the prophet Jeremiah (Jer. 27:9-11).

24:2 the LORD sent...*raiding* bands. As punishment for Jehoiakim's disobedience of the Lord's Word through His prophet Jeremiah, the Lord sent Babylonian troops, along with the troops of other loyal nations, to inflict military defeats upon Judah.

24:4 innocent blood. *See note on 21:16.*

24:7 king of Egypt. In 601 B.C., Nebuchadnezzar again marched W against Egypt and was turned back by strong Egyptian resistance. However Egypt, though able to defend its own land, was not able to be aggressive and recover its conquered lands or provide any help for its allies, including Judah.

24:8 eighteen. This reading is preferred over the "eight" of 2 Chr. 36:9 (*see note*). **three months.** Having regrouped, Nebuchadnezzar invaded Judah for a second time in the spring of 597 B.C. Before he could enter Jerusalem, Jehoiakim died and was succeeded as king of Judah by his son, Jehoiachin. Jehoiachin ruled for a short time in 597 B.C. *See notes on 2 Chr. 36:9,10.*

24:10-12 The Babylonian siege of Jerusalem was begun by the troops of Nebuchadnezzar. Later, Nebuchadnezzar himself went to Jerusalem and it was to the king himself that Jehoiachin surrendered (v. 12).

Babylon came against the city, as his servants were besieging it. 12 [l]Then Jehoiachin king of Judah, his mother, his servants, his princes, and his officers went out
to the king of Babylon; and the king of
Babylon, [m]in the eighth year of his reign,
took him prisoner.

The Captivity of Jerusalem

13 [n]And he carried out from there all the
treasures of the house of the LORD and the
treasures of the king's house, and he [o]cut in
pieces all the articles of gold which Solomon king of Israel had made in the temple
of the LORD, [p]as the LORD had said. 14 Also
[q]he carried into captivity all Jerusalem: all
the captains and all the mighty men of
valor, [r]ten thousand captives, and [s]all the
craftsmen and smiths. None remained except [t]the poorest people of the land. 15 And
[u]he carried Jehoiachin captive to Babylon.
The king's mother, the king's wives, his officers, and the mighty of the land he carried
into captivity from Jerusalem to Babylon.
16 [v]All the valiant men, seven thousand,
and craftsmen and smiths, one thousand,
all *who were* strong *and* fit for war, these the
king of Babylon brought captive to Babylon.

Zedekiah Reigns in Judah

17 Then [w]the king of Babylon made Mattaniah, [x]*Jehoiachin's*[4] uncle, king in his
place, and [y]changed his name to Zedekiah.
18 [z]Zedekiah *was* twenty-one years old
when he became king, and he reigned
eleven years in Jerusalem. His mother's
name *was* [a]Hamutal the daughter of Jeremiah of Libnah. 19 [b]He also did evil in the
sight of the LORD, according to all that Jehoiakim had done. 20 For because of the
anger of the LORD *this* happened in Jerusalem and Judah, that He finally cast them
out from His presence. [c]Then Zedekiah rebelled against the king of Babylon.

The Fall and Captivity of Judah

25 Now it came to pass [a]in the ninth
year of his reign, in the tenth
month, on the tenth *day* of the month, *that*
Nebuchadnezzar king of Babylon and all
his army came against Jerusalem and encamped against it; and they built a siege
wall against it all around. 2 So the city was
besieged until the eleventh year of King
Zedekiah. 3 By the ninth *day* of the [b]*fourth*

12 [l]Jer. 22:24-30; 24:1; 29:1, 2; Ezek. 17:12 [m]2 Chr. 36:10
13 [n]2 Kin. 20:17; Is. 39:6 [o]Dan. 5:2, 3 [p]Jer. 20:5
14 [q]Is. 3:2, 3; Jer. 24:1 [r]2 Kin. 24:16; Jer. 52:28 [s]1 Sam. 13:19 [t]2 Kin. 25:12
15 [u]2 Chr. 36:10; Esth. 2:6; Jer. 22:24-28; Ezek. 17:12
16 [v]Jer. 52:28
17 [w]Jer. 37:1 [x]1 Chr. 3:15; 2 Chr. 36:10 [y]2 Chr. 36:4 [4]Lit. *his*
18 [z]2 Chr. 36:11; Jer. 52:1 [a]2 Kin. 23:31
19 [b]2 Chr. 36:12
20 [c]2 Chr. 36:13; Ezek. 17:15

CHAPTER 25

1 [a]2 Chr. 36:17; Jer. 6:6; 34:2; Ezek. 4:2; 24:1, 2; Hab. 1:6
3 [b]2 Kin. 6:24, 25; Is. 3:1; Jer. 39:2; Lam. 4:9, 10

24:12 eighth year. 597 B.C. For the first time, the books of Kings dated an event in Israelite history by a non-Israelite king. This indicated that Judah's exile was imminent and the land would be in the hands of Gentiles.

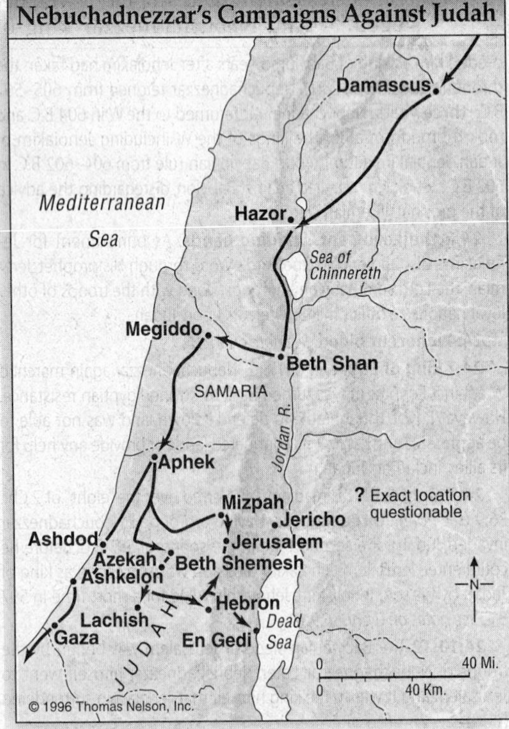

24:13 Nebuchadnezzar plundered the treasures of the temple and king's palace, just as the Lord had said he would (cf. 20:16-18).

24:14-16 In 597 B.C., Nebuchadnezzar took an additional 10,000 Judeans as captives to Babylon, in particular the leaders of the nation. This included the leaders of the military and those whose skills would support the military. Included in this deportation was the prophet Ezekiel (*see notes on Ezek. 1:1-3*). Only the lower classes remained behind in Jerusalem. The Babylonian policy of captivity was different from that of the Assyrians, who took most of the people into exile and resettled the land of Israel with foreigners (17:24). The Babylonians took only the leaders and the strong, while leaving the weak and poor, elevating those left to leadership and thereby earning their loyalty. Those taken to Babylon were allowed to work and live in the mainstream of society. This kept the captive Jews together, so it would be possible for them to return, as recorded in Ezra.

24:17 Mattaniah...Zedekiah. Mattaniah was a son of Josiah and an uncle of Jehoiachin (cf. 1 Chr. 3:15; Jer. 1:3). Mattaniah's name, meaning "gift of the LORD," was changed to Zedekiah, "righteousness of the LORD." Nebuchadnezzar's changing of Zedekiah's name demonstrated his authority as lord over him (*see note on 23:34*). *See notes on 2 Chr. 36:11-21.*

24:18 eleven years. Zedekiah ruled in Jerusalem, under Babylonian sovereignty, from 597–586 B.C.

24:20 Zedekiah rebelled. In 588 B.C., Apries (also called Hophra), the grandson of Necho, became Pharaoh over Egypt. He appears to have influenced Zedekiah to revolt against Babylon (cf. Ezek. 17:15-18).

25:1 ninth year. Responding to Zedekiah's rebellion (24:20), Nebuchadnezzar sent his whole army to lay siege against the city of Jerusalem. The siege began in the ninth year of Zedekiah's reign, Jan., 588 B.C. The "siege wall" was comprised of either wood towers higher than the walls of the city or a dirt rampart encircling the city.

25:2 eleventh year. Jerusalem withstood the siege until the 11th year of Zedekiah, July, 586 B.C. Hezekiah's tunnel guaranteed the city an uninterrupted supply of fresh water (20:20) and an Egyptian foray

month the famine had become so severe in
the city that there was no food for the people of the land.
4 Then [c]the city wall was broken
through, and all the men of war *fled* at
night by way of the gate between two
walls, which was by the king's garden,
even though the Chaldeans *were* still encamped all around against the city. And
[d]*the king*[1] went by way of the [2]plain. 5 But
the army of the Chaldeans pursued the
king, and they overtook him in the plains
of Jericho. All his army was scattered from
him. 6 So they took the king and brought
him up to the king of Babylon [e]at Riblah,
and they pronounced judgment on him.
7 Then they killed the sons of Zedekiah before his eyes, [f]put[3] out the eyes of Zedekiah, bound him with bronze fetters, and
took him to Babylon.
8 And in the fifth month, [g]on the seventh
day of the month (which *was* [h]the nineteenth year of King Nebuchadnezzar king
of Babylon), [i]Nebuzaradan the captain of
the guard, a servant of the king of Babylon,
came to Jerusalem. 9 [j]He burned the house
of the LORD [k]and the king's house; all the
houses of Jerusalem, that is, all the houses
of the great, [l]he burned with fire. 10 And
all the army of the Chaldeans who *were*
with the captain of the guard [m]broke down
the walls of Jerusalem all around.
11 Then Nebuzaradan the captain of the
guard carried away captive [n]the rest of the
people *who* remained in the city and the
defectors who had deserted to the king of
Babylon, with the rest of the multitude.
12 But the captain of the guard [o]left *some* of
the poor of the land as vinedressers and
farmers. 13 [p]The bronze [q]pillars that *were* in
the house of the LORD, and [r]the carts and
[s]the bronze Sea that *were* in the house of
the LORD, the Chaldeans broke in pieces,
and [t]carried their bronze to Babylon.
14 They also took away [u]the pots, the shovels, the trimmers, the spoons, and all the
bronze utensils with which the priests
ministered. 15 The firepans and the basins,
the things of solid gold and solid silver, the
captain of the guard took away. 16 The two
pillars, one Sea, and the carts, which Solomon had made for the house of the LORD,
[v]the bronze of all these articles was beyond
measure. 17 [w]The height of one pillar *was*
[4]eighteen cubits, and the capital on it *was*
of bronze. The height of the capital was
three cubits, and the network and pomegranates all around the capital were all of
bronze. The second pillar was the same,
with a network.
18 [x]And the captain of the guard took
[y]Seraiah the chief priest, [z]Zephaniah the
second priest, and the three doorkeepers.
19 He also took out of the city an officer
who had charge of the men of war, [a]five
men of [5]the king's close associates who
were found in the city, the chief recruiting
officer of the army, who mustered the people of the land, and sixty men of the people
of the land *who were* found in the city. 20 So
Nebuzaradan, captain of the guard, took
these and brought them to the king of
Babylon at Riblah. 21 Then the king of
Babylon struck them and put them to

4 [c] Jer. 39:2 [d] Jer. 39:4-7; Ezek. 12:12 [1] Lit. *he* [2] Or *Arabah*, the Jordan Valley
6 [e] 2 Kin. 23:33; Jer. 52:9
7 [f] Jer. 39:7; Ezek. 17:16 [3] *blinded*
8 [g] Jer. 52:12 [h] 2 Kin. 24:12 [i] Jer. 39:9
9 [j] 2 Kin. 25:13; 2 Chr. 36:19; Ps. 79:1; Jer. 7:14 [k] Jer. 39:8 [l] Jer. 17:27
10 [m] 2 Kin. 14:13; Neh. 1:3
11 [n] Is. 1:9; Jer. 5:19; 39:9
12 [o] 2 Kin. 24:14; Jer. 39:10; 40:7; 52:16
13 [p] Jer. 52:17 [q] 1 Kin. 7:15 [r] 1 Kin. 7:27 [s] 1 Kin. 7:23 [t] 2 Kin. 20:17; Jer. 27:19-22
14 [u] Ex. 27:3; 1 Kin. 7:45
16 [v] 1 Kin. 7:47
17 [w] 1 Kin. 7:15-22; Jer. 52:21 [4] About 27 feet
18 [x] Jer. 39:9-13; 52:12-16, 24 [y] 1 Chr. 6:14; Ezra 7:1 [z] Jer. 21:1; 29:25, 29
19 [a] Esth. 1:14; Jer. 52:25 [5] Lit. *those seeing the king's face*

into Judah gave the city a temporary reprieve from the siege (Jer. 37:5).

25:3 famine. After a siege of 2½ years, the food supply in Jerusalem ran out (Jer. 38:2,3).

25:4 the city wall was broken. The two walls near the king's garden were probably located at the extreme SE corner of the city, giving direct access to the Kidron Valley. This gave Zedekiah and his soldiers an opportunity to flee for their lives to the E.

25:5 plains of Jericho. Zedekiah fled toward the Jordan Rift Valley. Babylonian pursuers caught him in the Jordan Valley S of Jericho, about 20 mi. E of Jerusalem.

25:6 Riblah. Located on the Orontes River about 180 mi. N of Jerusalem, Riblah was Nebuchadnezzar's military headquarters for his invasion of Judah. This location was ideally situated as a field headquarters for military forces because ample provisions could be found nearby (cf. 23:33). The captured traitor Zedekiah was brought to Nebuchadnezzar at Riblah, where he was blinded after witnessing the death of his sons. The execution of the royal heirs ensured the impossibility of a future claim to the throne or rebellion from his descendants. The blinding made his own future rebellion or retaliation impossible. Jeremiah had warned Zedekiah that he would see Nebuchadnezzar (*see notes on Jer. 32:4; 34:3*), while Ezekiel had said he would not see Babylon (*see note on Ezek 12:13*). Both prophecies were accurately fulfilled.

25:8 seventh *day*. *See note on Jer. 52:12.* This was Aug., 586 B.C., one month after the Babylonian breakthrough of Jerusalem's walls (vv. 2-4). **Nebuzaradan.** He was the commander of Nebuchadnezzar's own imperial guard, sent by the king to oversee the destruction of Jerusalem. The dismantling and destruction of Jerusalem was accomplished by the Babylonians in an orderly progression.

25:9 First, Jerusalem's most important buildings were burned.

25:10 Second, the Babylonian army tore down Jerusalem's outer walls, the city's main defense.

25:11,12 Third, Nebuzaradan organized and led a forced march of remaining Judeans into exile in Babylon. The exiles included survivors from Jerusalem and those who had surrendered to the Babylonians before the capture of the city. Only poor, unskilled laborers were left behind to tend the vineyards and farm the fields.

25:13-17 Fourth, the items made with precious metals in the temple were carried away to Babylon. *See the notes on 1 Kin. 7:15-50* for a description of these temple items.

25:17 three cubits. *See note on Jer. 52:22.*

25:18-21 Fifth, Nebuzaradan took Jerusalem's remaining leaders to Riblah, where Nebuchadnezzar had them executed. This insured that they would never lead another rebellion against Babylon.

25:18 Seraiah. Seraiah was the grandson of Hilkiah (22:4,8; 1 Chr. 6:13,14) and an ancestor of Ezra (Ezra 7:1). Even though Seraiah was executed, his sons were deported (1 Chr. 6:15).

death at Riblah in the land of Hamath.
[b]Thus Judah was carried away captive
from its own land.

Gedaliah Made Governor of Judah

22 Then he made Gedaliah the son of
[c]Ahikam, the son of Shaphan, governor
over [d]the people who remained in the land
of Judah, whom Nebuchadnezzar king of
Babylon had left. 23 Now when all the
[e]captains of the armies, they and *their* men,
heard that the king of Babylon had made
Gedaliah governor, they came to Gedaliah
at Mizpah—Ishmael the son of Nethaniah,
Johanan the son of Careah, Seraiah the son
of Tanhumeth the Netophathite, and [6]Jaaz-
aniah the son of a Maachathite, they and
their men. 24 And Gedaliah took an oath
before them and their men, and said to
them, "Do not be afraid of the servants of
the Chaldeans. Dwell in the land and serve
the king of Babylon, and it shall be well
with you."

25 But [f]it happened in the seventh month
that Ishmael the son of Nethaniah, the son
of Elishama, of the royal family, came with
ten men and struck and killed Gedaliah,
the Jews, as well as the Chaldeans who
were with him at Mizpah. 26 And all the
people, small and great, and the captains
of the armies, arose [g]and went to Egypt;
for they were afraid of the Chaldeans.

Jehoiachin Released from Prison

27 [h]Now it came to pass in the thirty-seventh year of the captivity of Jehoiachin
king of Judah, in the twelfth month, on the
twenty-seventh *day* of the month, *that*
[7]Evil-Merodach king of Babylon, in the
year that he began to reign, [i]released Jehoiachin king of Judah from prison. 28 He
spoke kindly to him, and gave him a more
prominent seat than those of the kings who
were with him in Babylon. 29 So Jehoiachin
changed from his prison garments, and he
[j]ate [8]bread regularly before the king all the
days of his life. 30 And as for his [9]provi-
sions, *there was* a [1]regular ration given him
by the king, a portion for each day, all the
days of his life.

21 [b]Lev. 26:33; Deut. 28:36, 64; 2 Kin. 23:27
22 [c]2 Kin. 22:12 [d]Is. 1:9; Jer. 40:5
23 [e]Jer. 40:7-9 [6]*Jezaniah*, Jer. 40:8
25 [f]Jer. 41:1-3
26 [g]2 Kin. 19:31; Jer. 43:4-7
27 [h]2 Kin. 24:12, 15; Jer. 52:31-34 [i]Gen. 40:13, 20 [7]Lit. *Man of Marduk*
29 [j]2 Sam. 9:7 [8]Food
30 [9]Lit. *allowance* [1]Lit. *allowance*

25:21 Judah...carried away captive. Exile was the ultimate curse brought upon Judah because of her disobedience to the Mosaic Covenant (cf. Lev. 26:33; Deut. 28:36,64). The book of Lamentations records the sorrow of Jeremiah over this destruction of Jerusalem.

25:22-30 The books of Kings conclude with this brief epilogue. Despite the punishment of the Lord experienced by Israel and Judah, the people were still rebellious (vv. 22-26). However, due to the Lord's mercy, the house of David endured (vv. 27-30). The books of Kings end with a note of hope.

25:22 Gedaliah. In an attempt to maintain political stability, Nebuchadnezzar appointed a governor from an important Judean family. A more detailed account of Gedaliah's activities is found in Jer. 40:7–41:18. Gedaliah's grandfather, Shaphan, was Josiah's secretary, who had implemented that king's reforms (22:3). His father, Ahikam, was part of Josiah's delegation sent to Huldah (22:14) and a supporter of the prophet Jeremiah (Jer. 26:24).

25:23 Mizpah. Located about 8 mi. N of Jerusalem, Mizpah became the new center of Judah. Mizpah might have been one of the few towns left standing after the Babylonian invasion.

25:24 oath. As governor, Gedaliah pledged to the remaining people that loyalty to the Babylonians would ensure their safety.

25:25 seventh month. October, 586 B.C., two months after the destruction of Jerusalem (cf. v. 8). **Ishmael.** Elishama, Ishmael's grandfather, was a secretary under Jehoiakim (Jer. 36:12; 41:1). Ishmael probably assassinated Gedaliah because he wished to reestablish the kingship in Judah with himself as king, since he was of royal blood (cf. Jer. 41:1).

25:26 went to Egypt. Fearing reprisals from the Babylonians, the people fled to Egypt.

25:27 thirty-seventh year. March, 561 B.C. Jehoiachin was about 55 years old (cf. 24:8). **Evil-Merodach.** The son and successor of Nebuchadnezzar, he ruled as king of Babylon from 562–560 B.C. To gain favor with the Jews, the king released Jehoiachin from his imprisonment and gave him special privileges.

25:28-30 spoke kindly to him. This good word from the king of Babylon to the surviving representative of the house of David served as a concluding reminder of God's good Word to David. Through the curse of exile, the dynasty of David had survived. There was still hope that God's good Word to David concerning the seed who will build God's temple and establish God's eternal kingdom would be fulfilled (cf. 2 Sam. 7:12-16). The book of 2 Kings opened with Elijah being carried away to heaven, the destination of all those faithful to God. The book ends with Israel, and then Judah, being carried away to pagan lands as a result of failing to be faithful to God.

The First and Second Books of the

CHRONICLES

Title

The original title in the Hebrew Bible read "The annals (i.e., events or happenings) of the days." First and Second Chronicles were comprised of one book until later divided into separate books in the Greek OT translation, the Septuagint (LXX), ca. 200 B.C. The title also changed at that time to the inaccurate title, "the things omitted," i.e., reflecting material not in 1, 2 Samuel and 1, 2 Kings. The English title "Chronicles" originated with Jerome's Latin Vulgate translation (ca. 400 A.D.), which used the fuller title "The Chronicles of the Entire Sacred History."

Author and Date

Neither 1 nor 2 Chronicles contains direct statements regarding the human author, though Jewish tradition strongly favors Ezra the priest (cf. Ezra 7:1-6) as "the chronicler." These records were most likely recorded ca. 450–430 B.C. The genealogical record in 1 Chr. 1–9 supports a date after 450 B.C. for the writing. The NT does not directly quote either 1 or 2 Chronicles.

Background and Setting

The immediate historical backdrop encompassed the Jews' three-phase return to the Promised Land from the Babylonian exile: 1) Zerubbabel in Ezra 1–6 (ca. 538 B.C.); 2) Ezra in Ezra 7–10 (ca. 458 B.C.); and 3) Nehemiah in Neh. 1–13 (ca. 445 B.C.). Previous history looks back to the Babylonian deportation/Exile (ca. 605–538 B.C.) as predicted/reported by 2 Kings, Esther, Jeremiah, Ezekiel, Daniel, and Habakkuk. The prophets of this restoration era were Haggai, Zechariah, and Malachi.

The Jews had returned from their 70 years of captivity (ca. 538 B.C.) to a land that was markedly different from the one once ruled by King David (ca. 1011–971 B.C.) and King Solomon (971–931 B.C.): 1) there was no Hebrew king, but rather a Persian governor (Ezra 5:3; 6:6); 2) there was no security for Jerusalem, so Nehemiah had to rebuild the wall (Neh. 1–7); 3) there was no temple, so Zerubbabel had to reconstruct a pitiful semblance of the Solomonic temple's former glory (Ezra 3); 4) the Jews no longer dominated the region, but rather were on the defensive (Ezra 4; Neh. 4); 5) they enjoyed few divine blessings beyond the fact of their return; 6) they possessed little of the kingdom's former wealth; and 7) God's divine presence no longer resided in Jerusalem, having departed ca. 597–591 B.C. (Ezek. 8–11).

To put it mildly, their future looked bleak compared to their majestic past, especially the time of David and Solomon. The return could best be described as bittersweet, i.e., bitter because their present poverty brought hurtful memories about what was forfeited by God's judgment on their ancestors' sin, but sweet because at least they were back in the Land God had given Abraham 17 centuries earlier (Gen. 12:1-3). The chronicler's selective genealogy and history of Israel, stretching from Adam (1 Chr. 1:1) to the return from Babylon (2 Chr 26:23), was intended to remind the Jews of God's promises and intentions about: 1) the Land; 2) the nation; 3) the Davidic king; 4) the Levitical priests; 5) the temple; and 6) true worship, none of which had been abrogated because of the Babylonian captivity. All of this was to remind them of their spiritual heritage during the difficult times they faced, and to encourage them to be faithful to God.

Historical and Theological Themes

First and Second Chronicles, as named by Jerome, recreate an OT history in miniature, with particular emphases on the Davidic Covenant and temple worship. In terms of literary parallel, 1 Chronicles is the partner of 2 Samuel, in that both detail the reign of King David. First Chronicles opens with Adam (1:1) and closes with the death of David (29:26-30) in 971 B.C. Second Chronicles begins with Solomon (1:1) and covers the same historical period as 1 and 2 Kings, while focusing exclusively on the kings of the southern kingdom of Judah, thus excluding the history of the northern 10 tribes and their rulers, because of their complete wickedness and false worship. It ranges from the reign of Solomon (1:1) in 971 B.C. to the return from Babylon in 538 B.C. (36:23). Over 55 percent of the material in Chronicles is unique, i.e., not found in 2 Samuel or 1 and 2 Kings. The "chronicler" tended to omit what was negative or in opposition to the Davidic kingship; on the other hand, he tended to make unique contributions in validating temple worship and the line of David. Whereas 2 Kings 25 ends dismally with the deportation of Judah to Babylon, 2 Chronicles 36:22-23 concludes hopefully with the Jews' release from Persia and return to Jerusalem.

These two books were written to the repatriated Jewish exiles as a chronicle of God's intention of future blessing, in spite of the nation's past moral/spiritual failure for which the people paid dearly under God's wrath. First and Second Chronicles could be briefly summarized as follows:

I. A Selected Genealogical History of Israel (1 Chr. 1–9)
II. Israel's United Kingdom Under Saul (1 Chr. 10), David (1 Chr. 11–29), and Solomon (2 Chr. 1–9)
III. Judah's Monarchy in the Divided Kingdom (2 Chr. 10–36:21)
IV. Judah's Release From Their Seventy Year Captivity (2 Chr. 36:22,23).

The historical themes are inextricably linked with the theological in that God's divine purposes for Israel have been and will be played out on the stage of human history. These two books are designed to assure the returning Jews that, in spite of their checkered past and present plight, God will be true to His covenant promises. They have been returned by God to the Land first given to Abraham as a race of people whose ethnic identity (Jewish) was not obliterated by the deportation and whose national identity (Israel) has been preserved (Gen. 12:1-3; 15:5), although they are still under God's judgment as prescribed by the Mosaic legislation (Deut. 28:15-68). The priestly line of Eleazar's son Phinehas and the Levitical line were still intact so that temple worship could continue in the hopes that God's presence would one day return (Num. 25:10-13; Mal. 3:1). The Davidic promise of a king was still valid, although future in its fulfillment (2 Sam. 7:8-17; 1 Chr. 17:7-15). Their individual hope of eternal life and restoration of God's blessings forever rested in the New Covenant (Jer. 31:31-34).

Two basic principles enumerated in these two books prevail throughout the OT, namely, obedience brings blessing, disobedience brings judgment. In the Chronicles, when the king obeyed and trusted the Lord, God blessed and protected. But when the king disobeyed and/or put his trust in something or someone other than the Lord, God withdrew His blessing and protection. Three basic failures by the kings of Judah brought God's wrath: 1) personal sin; 2) false worship/idolatry; and/or 3) trust in man rather than God.

Interpretive Challenges

First and Second Chronicles present a combination of selective genealogical and historical records and no insurmountable challenges within the two books are encountered. A few issues arise, such as: 1) Who wrote 1 and 2 Chronicles? Does the overlap of 2 Chr. 36:22-23 with Ezra 1:1-3 point to Ezra as author? 2) Does the use of multiple sources taint the inerrancy doctrine of Scripture? 3) How does one explain the variations in the genealogies of 1 Chr. 1–9 from other OT genealogies? 4) Are the curses of Deut. 28 still in force, even though the 70 year captivity has concluded? 5) How does one explain the few variations in numbers when comparing Chronicles with parallel passages in Samuel and Kings? These will be dealt with in the notes at the appropriate places.

Outline

I. Selective Genealogy (1:1–9:34)
   - A. Adam to Before David (1:1–2:55)
   - B. David to the Captivity (3:1-24)
   - C. Twelve Tribes (4:1–9:2)
   - D. Jerusalem Dwellers (9:3-34)

II. David's Ascent (9:35–12:40)
   - A. Saul's Heritage and Death (9:35–10:14)
   - B. David's Anointing (11:1-3)
   - C. Jerusalem's Conquest (11:4-9)
   - D. David's Men (11:10–12:40)

III. David's Reign (13:1–29:30)
   - A. The Ark of the Covenant (13:1–16:43)
   - B. The Davidic Covenant (17:1–17:27)
   - C. Selected Military History (18:1–21:30)
   - D. Temple-Building Preparations (22:1–29:20)
   - E. Transition to Solomon (29:21–29:30)

The Family of Adam—Seth to Abraham

1 Adam,[a] [b]Seth, Enosh, 2 Cainan, Ma-
halalel, Jared, 3 Enoch, Methuselah,
Lamech, 4 [c]Noah,[1] Shem, Ham, and
Japheth.
5 [d]The sons of Japheth *were* Gomer,
Magog, Madai, Javan, Tubal, Meshech, and
Tiras. 6 The sons of Gomer *were* Ashkenaz,
[2]Diphath, and Togarmah. 7 The sons of
Javan *were* Elishah, [3]Tarshishah, Kittim,
and [4]Rodanim.
8 [e]The sons of Ham *were* Cush, Mizraim,
Put, and Canaan. 9 The sons of Cush *were*
Seba, Havilah, [5]Sabta, [6]Raama, and Sabte-
cha. The sons of Raama *were* Sheba and
Dedan. 10 Cush [f]begot Nimrod; he began
to be a mighty one on the earth. 11 Mizraim begot Ludim, Anamim, Lehabim,
Naphtuhim, 12 Pathrusim, Casluhim (from
whom came the Philistines and the
[g]Caphtorim). 13 [h]Canaan begot Sidon, his
firstborn, and Heth; 14 the Jebusite, the
Amorite, and the Girgashite; 15 the Hivite,
the Arkite, and the Sinite; 16 the Arvadite,
the Zemarite, and the Hamathite.
17 The sons of [i]Shem *were* Elam, Asshur,
[j]Arphaxad, Lud, Aram, Uz, Hul, Gether,
and [7]Meshech. 18 Arphaxad begot Shelah,
and Shelah begot Eber. 19 To Eber were
born two sons: the name of one *was* [8]Peleg,
for in his days the [9]earth was divided; and
his brother's name *was* Joktan. 20 [k]Joktan
begot Almodad, Sheleph, Hazarmaveth,
Jerah, 21 Hadoram, Uzal, Diklah, 22 [1]Ebal,
Abimael, Sheba, 23 Ophir, Havilah, and
Jobab. All these *were* the sons of Joktan.
24 [l]Shem, Arphaxad, Shelah, 25 [m]Eber,
Peleg, Reu, 26 Serug, Nahor, Terah, 27 and
[n]Abram, who *is* Abraham. 28 [o]The sons of
Abraham *were* [p]Isaac and [q]Ishmael.

The Family of Ishmael

29 These *are* their genealogies: The [r]first-
born of Ishmael *was* Nebajoth; then Kedar,
Adbeel, Mibsam, 30 Mishma, Dumah,
Massa, [2]Hadad, Tema, 31 Jetur, Naphish,
and Kedemah. These *were* the sons of
Ishmael.

The Family of Keturah

32 Now [s]the sons born to Keturah, Abraham's concubine, *were* Zimran, Jokshan,
Medan, Midian, Ishbak, and Shuah. The
sons of Jokshan *were* Sheba and Dedan.
33 The sons of Midian *were* Ephah, Epher,
Hanoch, Abida, and Eldaah. All these were
the children of Keturah.

The Family of Isaac

34 And [t]Abraham begot Isaac. [u]The sons
of Isaac *were* Esau and Israel. 35 The sons of
[v]Esau *were* Eliphaz, Reuel, Jeush, Jaalam,
and Korah. 36 And the sons of Eliphaz *were*
Teman, Omar, [3]Zephi, Gatam, *and* Kenaz;
and *by* [w]Timna, Amalek. 37 The sons of
Reuel *were* Nahath, Zerah, Shammah, and
Mizzah.

The Family of Seir

38 [x]The sons of Seir *were* Lotan, Shobal,
Zibeon, Anah, Dishon, Ezer, and Dishan.
39 And the sons of Lotan *were* Hori and
[4]Homam; Lotan's sister *was* Timna. 40 The
sons of Shobal *were* [5]Alian, Manahath,
Ebal, [6]Shephi, and Onam. The sons of
Zibeon *were* Ajah and Anah. 41 The son of
Anah *was* [y]Dishon. The sons of Dishon
were [7]Hamran, Eshban, Ithran, and Cheran. 42 The sons of Ezer *were* Bilhan, Zaa-
van, *and* [8]Jaakan. The sons of Dishan *were*
Uz and Aran.

The Kings of Edom

43 Now these *were* the [z]kings who
reigned in the land of Edom before a king
reigned over the children of Israel: Bela the
son of Beor, and the name of his city was
Dinhabah. 44 And when Bela died, Jobab
the son of Zerah of Bozrah reigned in his
place. 45 When Jobab died, Husham of the
land of the Temanites reigned in his place.
46 And when Husham died, Hadad the son
of Bedad, who [9]attacked Midian in the
field of Moab, reigned in his place. The
name of his city *was* Avith. 47 When Hadad
died, Samlah of Masrekah reigned in his
place. 48 [a]And when Samlah died, Saul of
Rehoboth-by-the-River reigned in his
place. 49 When Saul died, Baal-Hanan the
son of Achbor reigned in his place. 50 And
when Baal-Hanan died, [1]Hadad reigned in
his place; and the name of his city was
[2]Pai. His wife's name was Mehetabel the
daughter of Matred, the daughter of Meza-

CHAPTER 1

1 [a] Gen. 1:27; 2:7; 5:1, 2, 5 [b] Gen. 4:25, 26; 5:3-9
4 [c] Gen. 5:28–10:1 [1] So with MT, Vg.; LXX adds *the sons of Noah*
5 [d] Gen. 10:2-4
6 [2] *Riphath*, Gen. 10:3
7 [3] *Tarshish*, Gen. 10:4 [4] *Dodanim*, Gen. 10:4
8 [e] Gen. 10:6
9 [5] *Sabtah*, Gen. 10:7 [6] *Raamah*, Gen. 10:7
10 [f] Gen. 10:8-10, 13
12 [g] Deut. 2:23
13 [h] Gen. 9:18, 25-27; 10:15
17 [i] Gen. 10:22-29; 11:10 [j] Luke 3:36 [7] *Mash*, Gen. 10:23
19 [8] Lit. *Division*, Gen. 10:25 [9] Or *land*
20 [k] Gen. 10:26
22 [1] *Obal*, Gen. 10:28
24 [l] Gen. 11:10-26; Luke 3:34-36
25 [m] Gen. 11:15
27 [n] Gen. 17:5
28 [o] Gen. 21:2, 3 [p] Gen. 21:2 [q] Gen. 16:11, 15
29 [r] Gen. 25:13-16
30 [2] *Hadar*, Gen. 25:15
32 [s] Gen. 25:1-4
34 [t] Gen. 21:2 [u] Gen. 25:9, 25, 26, 29; 32:28
35 [v] Gen. 36:10-19
36 [w] Gen. 36:12 [3] *Zepho*, Gen. 36:11
38 [x] Gen. 36:20-28
39 [4] *Hemam* or *Heman*, Gen. 36:22
40 [5] *Alvan*, Gen. 36:23 [6] *Shepho*, Gen. 36:23
41 [y] Gen. 36:25 [7] *Hemdan*, Gen. 36:26
42 [8] *Akan*, Gen. 36:27
43 [z] Gen. 36:31-43
46 [9] Lit. *struck*
48 [a] Gen. 36:37
50 [1] *Hadar*, Gen. 36:39 [2] *Pau*, Gen. 36:39

1:1–9:44 This abbreviated genealogy summarizes the divinely selected course of redemptive history: 1) from Adam to Noah (1:1-4; Gen. 1–6); 2) from Noah's son Shem to Abraham (1:4-27; Gen. 7–11); 3) from Abraham to Jacob (1:28; Gen. 12–25); 4) from Jacob to the 12 tribes (1:28–2:1,2; Gen. 25–50); and 5) from the 12 tribes to those who had returned to Jerusalem after the 70-year captivity (2:3–9:44; Ex. 1:1–2 Chr. 36:23). This genealogical listing is unique to the purposes of "the chronicler" and is not intended to necessarily be an exact duplication of any other list(s) in Scripture.

1:19 days...divided. Peleg, which means "divided," apparently lived when the Lord divided, or scattered, the human race because of Babel (cf. Gen. 11:1-9).

1:28-31 These 12 sons of Ishmael developed 12 tribes and settled the great northern desert of Arabia and became Arab peoples.

1:43 kings...Edom. Esau's children settled in Edom, E and S of Israel, and are included among the Arab nations.

hab. 51 Hadad died also. And the chiefs of
Edom were Chief Timnah, Chief [3]Aliah,
Chief Jetheth, 52 Chief Aholibamah, Chief
Elah, Chief Pinon, 53 Chief Kenaz, Chief
Teman, Chief Mibzar, 54 Chief Magdiel,
and Chief Iram. These *were* the chiefs of
Edom.

The Family of Israel

2 These *were* the [a]sons of [1]Israel: [b]Reu-
ben, Simeon, Levi, Judah, Issachar,
Zebulun, 2 Dan, Joseph, Benjamin,
Naphtali, Gad, and Asher.

From Judah to David

3 The sons of [c]Judah *were* Er, Onan, and
Shelah. *These* three were born to him by the
daughter of [d]Shua, the Canaanitess. [e]Er,
the firstborn of Judah, was wicked in the
sight of the LORD; so He killed him. 4 And
[f]Tamar, his daughter-in-law, [g]bore him
Perez and Zerah. All the sons of Judah *were*
five.
5 The sons of [h]Perez *were* Hezron and
Hamul. 6 The sons of Zerah *were* [2]Zimri,
[i]Ethan, Heman, Calcol, and [3]Dara—five of
them in all.
7 The son of [j]Carmi *was* [4]Achar, the troubler of Israel, who transgressed in the [k]ac-
cursed[5] thing.
8 The son of Ethan *was* Azariah.
9 Also the sons of Hezron who were
born to him *were* Jerahmeel, [6]Ram, and
[7]Chelubai. 10 Ram [l]begot Amminadab,
and Amminadab begot Nahshon, [m]leader
of the children of Judah; 11 Nahshon
begot [8]Salma, and Salma begot Boaz;
12 Boaz begot Obed, and Obed begot
Jesse; 13 [n]Jesse begot Eliab his firstborn,
Abinadab the second, [9]Shimea the third,
14 Nethanel the fourth, Raddai the fifth,
15 Ozem the sixth, *and* David the [o]sev-
enth.
16 Now their sisters *were* Zeruiah and
Abigail. [p]And the sons of Zeruiah *were*
Abishai, Joab, and Asahel—three. 17 Abigail bore Amasa; and the father of Amasa
was [1]Jether the Ishmaelite.

The Family of Hezron

18 Caleb the son of Hezron had children
by Azubah, *his* wife, and by Jerioth. Now
these were her sons: Jesher, Shobab, and
Ardon. 19 When Azubah died, Caleb [2]took
[q]Ephrath[3] as his wife, who bore him Hur.
20 And Hur begot Uri, and Uri begot
[r]Bezalel.
21 Now afterward Hezron went in to the
daughter of [s]Machir the father of Gilead,
whom he married when he *was* sixty years
old; and she bore him Segub. 22 Segub
begot [t]Jair,[4] who had twenty-three cities in
the land of Gilead. 23 [u](Geshur and Syria
took from them the towns of Jair, with Kenath and its towns—sixty towns.) All these
belonged to the sons of Machir the father of
Gilead. 24 After Hezron died in Caleb
Ephrathah, Hezron's wife Abijah bore him
[v]Ashhur the father of Tekoa.

51 [3] *Alvah,* Gen. 36:40

CHAPTER 2

1 [a] Gen. 29:32-35; 35:23, 26; 46:8-27 [b] Gen. 29:32; 35:22 [1] *Jacob,* Gen. 32:28
3 [c] Gen. 38:3-5; 46:12; Num. 26:19 [d] Gen. 38:2 [e] Gen. 38:7
4 [f] Gen. 38:6 [g] Matt. 1:3
5 [h] Gen. 46:12; Ruth 4:18
6 [i] 1 Kin. 4:31 [2] *Zabdi,* Josh. 7:1 [3] *Darda,* 1 Kin. 4:31
7 [j] 1 Chr. 4:1 [k] Josh. 6:18 [4] *Achan,* Josh. 7:1 [5] *banned or devoted*
9 [6] *Aram,* Matt. 1:3, 4 [7] *Caleb,* vv. 18, 42
10 [l] Ruth 4:19-22; Matt. 1:4 [m] Num. 1:7; 2:3
11 [8] *Salmon,* Ruth 4:21; Luke 3:32
13 [n] 1 Sam. 16:6 [9] *Shammah,* 1 Sam. 16:9
15 [o] 1 Sam. 16:10, 11; 17:12
16 [p] 2 Sam. 2:18
17 [1] *Jithra the Israelite,* 2 Sam. 17:25
19 [q] 1 Chr. 2:50 [2] Lit. *took to himself* [3] Or *Ephrathah*
20 [r] Ex. 31:2; 38:22
21 [s] Num. 27:1; Judg. 5:14; 1 Chr. 7:14
22 [t] Judg. 10:3 [4] Reckoned to Manasseh through the daughter of Machir, Num. 32:41; Deut. 3:14; 25:5, 6; 1 Kin. 4:13; 1 Chr. 7:14
23 [u] Num. 32:41; Deut. 3:14; Josh. 13:30 **24** [v] 1 Chr. 4:5

2:1–7:40 These genealogies reflect the lineage of Jacob/Israel through his 12 sons. The tribe of Judah leads the list, indicating its importance, no doubt because of the Davidic heritage. After Judah, Levi receives the most attention, indicating the importance of their priestly role. Joseph (2:2) is later enumerated in terms of his sons Manasseh and Ephraim. Dan and Zebulun are not mentioned here, although they both are identified in the millennial distribution of land (cf. Ezek. 48:1,2,26,27). The exact reason for these omissions is unknown. Benjamin is given additional attention in 8:1-40. The tribes are mentioned as follows: 1) Judah (2:3–4:23); 2) Simeon (4:24-43); 3) Reuben (5:1-10); 4) Gad (5:11-22); 5) Manasseh-East (5:23-26); 6) Levi (6:1-81); 7) Issachar (7:1-5); 8) Benjamin (7:6-12); 9) Naphtali (7:13); 10) Manasseh-West (7:14-19); 11) Ephraim (7:20-29); and 12) Asher (7:30-40).

2:7 Achar. This is a variant spelling of Achan, who in Josh. 7:1-26 disobeyed the Lord by taking goods from under God's Jericho ban.

A Short Harmony of Samuel, Kings, and Chronicles

1.	Selected Genealogies	———	1 Chr. 1–9
2.	Samuel's Judgeship	1 Sam. 1–8	———
3.	Saul's Reign	1 Sam. 9–31	1 Chr. 10
4.	David's Reign	2 Sam. 1–24	1 Chr. 11–29
5.	Solomon's Reign	1 Kin. 1–11	2 Chr. 1–9
6.	Divided Kingdom Pt. 1 (to the Assyrian exile)	1 Kin. 12–2 Kin. 17	2 Chr. 10–27
7.	Divided Kingdom Pt. 2 (to the Babylonian exile)	2 Kin. 18–25	2 Chr. 28–36:21
8.	Return from Babylon	———	2 Chr. 36:22,23

The Family of Jerahmeel

25 The sons of Jerahmeel, the firstborn of
Hezron, *were* Ram, the firstborn, and
Bunah, Oren, Ozem, *and* Ahijah. 26 Jerahmeel had another wife, whose name
was Atarah; she was the mother of Onam.
27 The sons of Ram, the firstborn of Jerahmeel, were Maaz, Jamin, and Eker.
28 The sons of Onam were Shammai and
Jada. The sons of Shammai *were* Nadab
and Abishur.
29 And the name of the wife of Abishur
was Abihail, and she bore him Ahban and
Molid. 30 The sons of Nadab *were* Seled
and Appaim; Seled died without children.
31 The son of Appaim *was* Ishi, the son of
Ishi *was* Sheshan, and [w]Sheshan's son *was*
Ahlai. 32 The sons of Jada, the brother of
Shammai, *were* Jether and Jonathan; Jether
died without children. 33 The sons of Jonathan *were* Peleth and Zaza. These were the
sons of Jerahmeel.
34 Now Sheshan had no sons, only
daughters. And Sheshan had an Egyptian
servant whose name *was* Jarha. 35 Sheshan
gave his daughter to Jarha his servant as
wife, and she bore him Attai. 36 Attai begot
Nathan, and Nathan begot [x]Zabad;
37 Zabad begot Ephlal, and Ephlal begot
[y]Obed; 38 Obed begot Jehu, and Jehu begot
Azariah; 39 Azariah begot Helez, and
Helez begot Eleasah; 40 Eleasah begot Sismai, and Sismai begot Shallum; 41 Shallum
begot Jekamiah, and Jekamiah begot
Elishama.

The Family of Caleb

42 The descendants of Caleb the brother
of Jerahmeel *were* Mesha, his firstborn,
who was the father of Ziph, and the sons of
Mareshah the father of Hebron. 43 The sons
of Hebron *were* Korah, Tappuah, Rekem,
and Shema. 44 Shema begot Raham the father of Jorkoam, and Rekem begot Shammai. 45 And the son of Shammai *was* Maon,
and Maon *was* the father of Beth Zur.
46 Ephah, Caleb's concubine, bore
Haran, Moza, and Gazez; and Haran begot
Gazez. 47 And the sons of Jahdai *were*
Regem, Jotham, Geshan, Pelet, Ephah, and
Shaaph.
48 Maachah, Caleb's concubine, bore
Sheber and Tirhanah. 49 She also bore
Shaaph the father of Madmannah, Sheva
the father of Machbenah and the father of
Gibea. And the daughter of Caleb *was*
[z]Achsah.[5]
50 These were the descendants of Caleb:
The sons of [a]Hur, the firstborn of [6]Ephra-
thah, *were* Shobal the father of [b]Kirjath Jearim, 51 Salma the father of Bethlehem, *and*
Hareph the father of Beth Gader.
52 And Shobal the father of Kirjath Jearim had descendants: [7]Haroeh, *and* half of
the [8]*families of* Manuhoth. 53 The families
of Kirjath Jearim *were* the Ithrites, the
Puthites, the Shumathites, and the Mishra-
ites. From these came the Zorathites and
the Eshtaolites.
54 The sons of Salma *were* Bethlehem, the
Netophathites, [9]Atroth Beth Joab, half of
the Manahethites, and the Zorites.
55 And the families of the scribes who
dwelt at Jabez *were* the Tirathites, the
Shimeathites, *and* the Suchathites. These
were the [c]Kenites who came from Hammath, the father of the house of [d]Rechab.

The Family of David

3 Now these were the sons of David who
were born to him in Hebron: The firstborn *was* [a]Amnon, by [b]Ahinoam the
[c]Jezreelitess; the second, [1]Daniel, by [d]Abi-
gail the Carmelitess; 2 the third, [e]Absalom
the son of Maacah, the daughter of Talmai,
king of Geshur; the fourth, [f]Adonijah the
son of Haggith; 3 the fifth, Shephatiah, by
Abital; the sixth, Ithream, by his wife
[g]Eglah.
4 *These* six were born to him in Hebron.
[h]There he reigned seven years and six
months, and [i]in Jerusalem he reigned thirty-three years. 5 [j]And these were born to
him in Jerusalem: [2]Shimea, Shobab, Nathan, and [k]Solomon—four by [3]Bathshua
the daughter of [4]Ammiel. 6 Also *there* were
Ibhar, [5]Elishama, [6]Eliphelet, 7 Nogah,
Nepheg, Japhia, 8 Elishama, [7]Eliada, and
Eliphelet—[l]nine *in all.* 9 *These were* all the
sons of David, besides the sons of the concubines, and [m]Tamar their sister.

The Family of Solomon

10 Solomon's son *was* [n]Rehoboam; [8]Abi-
jah *was* his son, Asa his son, Jehoshaphat his
son, 11 [9]Joram his son, [1]Ahaziah his son,
[2]Joash his son, 12 Amaziah his son, [3]Aza-
riah his son, Jotham his son, 13 Ahaz his
son, Hezekiah his son, Manasseh his son,
14 Amon his son, *and* Josiah his son. 15 The
sons of Josiah *were* Johanan the firstborn,

31 [w] 1 Chr. 2:34, 35
36 [x] 1 Chr. 11:41
37 [y] 2 Chr. 23:1
49 [z] Josh. 15:17 [5] Or *Achsa*
50 [a] 1 Chr. 4:4 [b] Josh. 9:17; 18:14 [6] *Ephrath*, v. 19
52 [7] *Reaiah*, 1 Chr. 4:2 [8] Or *Manuhothites*, same as *Manahethites*, v. 54
54 [9] Or *Ataroth of the house of Joab*
55 [c] Judg. 1:16 [d] 2 Kin. 10:15; Jer. 35:2

CHAPTER 3

1 [a] 2 Sam. 3:2-5 [b] 1 Sam. 25:43 [c] Josh. 15:56 [d] 1 Sam. 25:39-42 [1] *Chileab*, 2 Sam. 3:3
2 [e] 2 Sam. 13:37; 15:1 [f] 1 Kin. 1:5
3 [g] 2 Sam. 3:5
4 [h] 2 Sam. 2:11 [i] 2 Sam. 5:5
5 [j] 1 Chr. 14:4-7 [k] 2 Sam. 12:24, 25 [2] *Shammua*, 1 Chr. 14:4; 2 Sam. 5:14 [3] *Bathsheba*, 2 Sam. 11:3 [4] *Eliam*, 2 Sam. 11:3
6 [5] *Elishua*, 1 Chr. 14:5; 2 Sam. 5:15 [6] *Elpelet*, 1 Chr. 14:5
8 [l] 2 Sam. 5:14-16 [7] *Beeliada*, 1 Chr. 14:7
9 [m] 2 Sam. 13:1
10 [n] 1 Kin. 11:43; Matt. 1:7-10 [8] *Abijam*, 1 Kin. 15:1
11 [9] *Jehoram*, 2 Kin. 1:17; 8:16 [1] Or *Azariah* or *Jehoahaz* [2] *Jehoash*, 2 Kin. 12:1
12 [3] *Uzziah*, Is. 6:1

3:1-4 See 2 Sam. 3:2-5.

3:1 David. The chief reason for such detailed genealogies is that they affirm the line of Christ from Adam (Luke 3:38) through Abraham and David (Matt. 1:1), thus emphasizing the kingdom intentions of God in Christ.

3:5-8 See 2 Sam. 5:14-16 and 2 Chr. 14:4-7.

3:10-16 Rehoboam…Zedekiah. The reigns of these sons of David are delineated in 2 Chr. 10:1–36:21.

the second [4]Jehoiakim, the third Zedekiah,
and the fourth [5]Shallum. 16 The sons of [o]Je-
hoiakim *were* [6]Jeconiah his son *and* [7]Zede-
kiah his son.

The Family of Jeconiah

17 And the sons of [8]Jeconiah [9]*were* Assir,
Shealtiel [p]his son, 18 *and* Malchiram, Pedaiah, Shenazzar, Jecamiah, Hoshama, and
Nedabiah. 19 The sons of Pedaiah *were* Zerubbabel and Shimei. The sons of Zerubbabel *were* Meshullam, Hananiah, Shelomith
their sister, 20 and Hashubah, Ohel, Berechiah, Hasadiah, and Jushab-Hesed—five
in all.
21 The sons of Hananiah *were* Pelatiah
and Jeshaiah, the sons of Rephaiah, the
sons of Arnan, the sons of Obadiah, and
the sons of Shechaniah. 22 The son of
Shechaniah was Shemaiah. The sons of
Shemaiah *were* [q]Hattush, Igal, Bariah, Neariah, and Shaphat—six *in all.* 23 The sons of
Neariah *were* Elioenai, Hezekiah, and Azrikam—three *in all.* 24 The sons of Elioenai
were Hodaviah, Eliashib, Pelaiah, Akkub,
Johanan, Delaiah, and Anani—seven *in all.*

The Family of Judah

4 The sons of Judah *were* [a]Perez, Hezron,
[1]Carmi, Hur, and Shobal. 2 And [2]Re-
aiah the son of Shobal begot Jahath, and Jahath begot Ahumai and Lahad. These *were*
the families of the Zorathites. 3 These *were*
the sons *of the father* of Etam: Jezreel,
Ishma, and Idbash; and the name of their
sister *was* Hazelelponi; 4 and Penuel *was*
the father of Gedor, and Ezer *was the* father
of Hushah.
These *were* the sons of [b]Hur, the firstborn
of Ephrathah the father of Bethlehem.
5 And [c]Ashhur the father of Tekoa had
two wives, Helah and Naarah. 6 Naarah
bore him Ahuzzam, Hepher, Temeni, and
Haahashtari. These *were* the sons of Naarah. 7 The sons of Helah *were* Zereth,
Zohar, and Ethnan; 8 and Koz begot Anub,
Zobebah, and the families of Aharhel the
son of Harum.
9 Now Jabez was [d]more honorable than
his brothers, and his mother called his
name [3]Jabez, saying, "Because I bore *him*
in pain." 10 And Jabez called on the God of
Israel saying, "Oh, that You would bless
me indeed, and enlarge my [4]territory, that
Your hand would be with me, and that You
would keep *me* from evil, that I may not
cause pain!" So God granted him what he
requested.
11 Chelub the brother of [e]Shuhah begot
Mehir, who *was* the father of Eshton.
12 And Eshton begot Beth-Rapha, Paseah,
and Tehinnah the father of [5]Ir-Nahash.
These *were* the men of Rechah.
13 The sons of Kenaz *were* [f]Othniel and
Seraiah. The sons of Othniel *were*
[6]Hathath, 14 and Meonothai *who* begot
Ophrah. Seraiah begot Joab the father of
[g]Ge Harashim,[7] for they were craftsmen.
15 The sons of [h]Caleb the son of Jephunneh
were Iru, Elah, and Naam. The son of Elah
was [8]Kenaz. 16 The sons of Jehallelel *were*
Ziph, Ziphah, Tiria, and Asarel. 17 The
sons of Ezrah *were* Jether, Mered, Epher,
and Jalon. And [9]*Mered's wife bore* Miriam,
Shammai, and Ishbah the father of Eshtemoa. 18 ([1]His wife Jehudijah bore Jered the
father of Gedor, Heber the father of Sochoh, and Jekuthiel the father of Zanoah.)
And these were the sons of Bithiah the
daughter of Pharaoh, whom Mered took.
19 The sons of Hodiah's wife, the sister
of Naham, *were* the fathers of Keilah the
Garmite and of Eshtemoa the [i]Maacha-
thite. 20 And the sons of Shimon *were*
Amnon, Rinnah, Ben-Hanan, and Tilon.
And the sons of Ishi *were* Zoheth and Ben-
Zoheth.
21 The sons of [j]Shelah [k]the son of Judah
were Er the father of Lecah, Laadah the father of Mareshah, and the families of the
house of the linen workers of the house of
Ashbea; 22 also Jokim, the men of Chozeba,
and Joash; Saraph, who ruled in Moab, and
Jashubi-Lehem. Now the [2]records are ancient. 23 These *were* the potters and those
who dwell at [3]Netaim and [4]Gederah; there
they dwelt with the king for his work.

The Family of Simeon

24 The [l]sons of Simeon *were* [5]Nemuel,
Jamin, [6]Jarib, [7]Zerah, *and* Shaul, 25 Shallum his son, Mibsam his son, and Mishma
his son. 26 And the sons of Mishma *were*
Hamuel his son, Zacchur his son, and
Shimei his son. 27 Shimei had sixteen sons
and six daughters; but his brothers did not
have many children, [m]nor did any of their
families multiply as much as the children
of Judah.
28 They dwelt at Beersheba, Moladah,

15 [4] *Eliakim,* 2 Kin. 23:34 [5] *Jehoahaz,* 2 Kin. 23:31
16 [o] Matt. 1:11 [6] *Jehoiachin,* 2 Kin. 24:8, or *Coniah,* Jer. 22:24 [7] *Mattaniah,* 2 Kin. 24:17
17 [p] Matt. 1:12 [8] *Jehoiachin,* 2 Kin. 24:8, or *Coniah,* Jer. 22:24 [9] *Or the captive were Shealtiel*
22 [q] Ezra 8:2

CHAPTER 4

1 [a] Gen. 38:29; 46:12 [1] *Chelubai,* 1 Chr. 2:9 or *Caleb,* 1 Chr. 2:18
2 [2] *Haroeh,* 1 Chr. 2:52
4 [b] Ex. 31:2; 1 Chr. 2:50
5 [c] 1 Chr. 2:24
9 [d] Gen. 34:19 [3] Lit. *He Will Cause Pain*
10 [4] *border*
11 [e] Job 8:1
12 [5] Lit. *City of Nahash*
13 [f] Josh. 15:17; Judg. 3:9, 11 [6] LXX, Vg. add *and Meonothai*
14 [g] Neh. 11:35 [7] Lit. *Valley of Craftsmen*
15 [h] Josh. 14:6, 14; 15:13, 17; 1 Chr. 6:56 [8] Or *Uknaz*
17 [9] Lit. *she*
18 [1] Or *His Judean wife*
19 [i] 2 Kin. 25:23
21 [j] Gen. 38:11, 14 [k] Gen. 38:1-5; 46:12
22 [2] Lit. *words*
23 [3] Lit. *Plants* [4] Lit. *Hedges*
24 [l] Num. 26:12-14 [5] *Jemuel,* Gen. 46:10; Ex. 6:15; Num. 26:12 [6] *Jachin,* Gen. 46:10; Num. 26:12 [7] *Zohar,* Gen. 46:10; Ex. 6:15
27 [m] Num. 2:9

3:16 Jeconiah. God's curse resulting in no royal descendants from the line of Jeconiah (a.k.a. Jehoiakin), as given by Jeremiah (Jer. 22:30), was enforced by God. Even though Jeconiah was in the line of Christ, the Messiah was not a physical child of that line, thus affirming the curse, yet sustaining the legality of His kingship through Joseph, who was in David's line. His blood birthright came through Mary, who traced her line to David through his son Nathan, not Solomon (cf. Luke 3:31).

3:22 six *in all.* Only 5 sons are named, so the number includes their father Shemaiah.

Hazar Shual, **29** [8]Bilhah, Ezem, [9]Tolad,
30 Bethuel, Hormah, Ziklag, **31** Beth Marcaboth, [1]Hazar Susim, Beth Biri, and at Sha-
araim. These *were* their cities until the reign
of David. **32** And their villages *were* [2]Etam,
Ain, Rimmon, Tochen, and Ashan—five
cities— **33** and all the villages that *were*
around these cities as far as [3]Baal. These
were their dwelling places, and they maintained their genealogy: **34** Meshobab, Jam-
lech, and Joshah the son of Amaziah;
35 Joel, and Jehu the son of Joshibiah, the
son of Seraiah, the son of Asiel; **36** Elioenai,
Jaakobah, Jeshohaiah, Asaiah, Adiel, Je-
simiel, and Benaiah; **37** Ziza the son of
Shiphi, the son of Allon, the son of Jedaiah,
the son of Shimri, the son of Shemaiah—
38 these mentioned by name *were* leaders
in their families, and their father's house
increased greatly.
39 So they went to the entrance of Gedor,
as far as the east side of the valley, to seek
pasture for their flocks. **40** And they found
rich, good pasture, and the land *was* broad,
quiet, and peaceful; for some Hamites formerly lived there.
41 These recorded by name came in the
days of Hezekiah king of Judah; and they
[n]attacked[4] their tents and the Meunites
who were found there, and [o]utterly destroyed them, as it is to this day. So they
dwelt in their place, because *there was* pasture for their flocks there. **42** Now *some* of
them, five hundred men of the sons of
Simeon, went to Mount Seir, having as
their captains Pelatiah, Neariah, Rephaiah,
and Uzziel, the sons of Ishi. **43** And they
[5]defeated [p]the rest of the Amalekites who
had escaped. They have dwelt there to this
day.

The Family of Reuben

5 Now the sons of Reuben the firstborn
of Israel—[a]he *was* indeed the firstborn,
but because he [b]defiled his father's bed,
[c]his birthright was given to the sons of Joseph, the son of Israel, so that the genealogy is not listed according to the birthright;
2 yet [d]Judah prevailed over his brothers,
and from him *came* a [e]ruler, although [1]the
birthright was Joseph's— **3** the sons of
[f]Reuben the firstborn of Israel were
Hanoch, Pallu, Hezron, and Carmi.
4 The sons of Joel *were* Shemaiah his son,
Gog his son, Shimei his son, **5** Micah his
son, Reaiah his son, Baal his son, **6** and Be-
erah his son, whom [2]Tiglath-Pileser king
of Assyria [g]carried into captivity. He *was*
leader of the Reubenites. **7** And his
brethren by their families, [h]when the genealogy of their generations was registered: the chief, Jeiel, and Zechariah, **8** and
Bela the son of Azaz, the son of Shema, the
son of Joel, who dwelt in [i]Aroer, as far as
Nebo and Baal Meon. **9** Eastward they settled as far as the [3]entrance of the wilderness this side of the River Euphrates, because their cattle had [4]multiplied [j]in the
land of Gilead.
10 Now in the days of Saul they made
war [k]with the Hagrites, who fell by their
hand; and they dwelt in their tents
throughout the entire *area* east of Gilead.

The Family of Gad

11 And the [l]children of Gad dwelt next
to them in the land of [m]Bashan as far as
[n]Salcah: **12** Joel *was* the chief, Shapham the
next, then Jaanai and Shaphat in Bashan,
13 and their brethren of their father's
house: Michael, Meshullam, Sheba, Jorai,
Jachan, Zia, and Eber—seven *in all.*
14 These *were* the children of Abihail the
son of Huri, the son of Jaroah, the son of
Gilead, the son of Michael, the son of Je-
shishai, the son of Jahdo, the son of Buz;
15 Ahi the son of Abdiel, the son of Guni,
was chief of their father's house. **16** And *the
Gadites* dwelt in Gilead, in Bashan and in
its villages, and in all the [5]common-lands
of [o]Sharon within their borders. **17** All
these were registered by genealogies in the
days of [p]Jotham king of Judah, and in the
days of [q]Jeroboam king of Israel.
18 The sons of Reuben, the Gadites, and
half the tribe of Manasseh *had* forty-four
thousand seven hundred and sixty valiant
men, men able to bear shield and sword, to
shoot with the bow, and skillful in war,
who went to war. **19** They made war with
the Hagrites, [r]Jetur, Naphish, and Nodab.
20 And [s]they were helped against them,
and the Hagrites were delivered into their
hand, and all who *were* with them, for they
[t]cried out to God in the battle. He [6]heeded
their prayer, because they [u]put their trust
in Him. **21** Then they took away their livestock—fifty thousand of their camels, two

29 [8] *Balah,* Josh. 19:3 [9] *Eltolad,* Josh. 19:4
31 [1] *Hazar Susah,* Josh. 19:5
32 [2] *Ether,* Josh. 19:7
33 [3] *Baalath Beer,* Josh. 19:8
41 [n] 2 Kin. 18:8 [o] 2 Kin. 19:11 [4] *Lit. struck*
43 [p] Ex. 17:14; 1 Sam. 15:8; 30:17 [5] *Lit. struck*

CHAPTER 5

1 [a] Gen. 29:32; 49:3 [b] Gen. 35:22; 49:4 [c] Gen. 48:15, 22
2 [d] Gen. 49:8, 10; Ps. 60:7; 108:8 [e] Mic. 5:2; Matt. 2:6 [1] *the right of the firstborn*
3 [f] Gen. 46:9; Ex. 6:14; Num. 26:5
6 [g] 2 Kin. 18:11 [2] *Heb. Tilgath-Pilneser*
7 [h] 1 Chr. 5:17
8 [i] Num. 32:34; Josh. 12:2; 13:15, 16
9 [j] Josh. 22:8, 9 [3] *beginning* [4] *increased*
10 [k] Gen. 25:12
11 [l] Num. 26:15-18 [m] Josh. 13:11, 24-28 [n] Deut. 3:10
16 [o] 1 Chr. 27:29; Song 2:1; Is. 35:2; 65:10 [5] *open lands*
17 [p] 2 Kin. 15:5, 32 [q] 2 Kin. 14:16, 28
19 [r] Gen. 25:15; 1 Chr. 1:31
20 [s] [1 Chr. 5:22] [t] 2 Chr. 14:11-13 [u] Ps. 9:10; 20:7, 8; 22:4, 5 [6] *Lit. was entreated for them*

4:41 Hezekiah. He ruled Judah ca. 715–686 B.C.

4:43 Amalekites. Longstanding enemies of Israel whom God purposed to exterminate. Another branch of the Amalekite family tree had appeared in Persia, represented by Haman, who attempted to exterminate the Jews (Esth. 3:1ff.).

5:2 Judah prevailed. In accordance with Jacob's blessing (Gen. 49:10), the king of Israel is to come from Judah. This prophecy had historical reference to the Davidic Covenant (cf. 2 Sam. 7; 1 Chr. 17) with full messianic implications.

5:6 Tiglath-Pileser. The king of Assyria (ca. 745–727 B.C.) who threatened Judah and made Ahaz pay a tribute (cf. 2 Kin. 16:7-20; 2 Chr. 28:16-21).

hundred and fifty thousand of their sheep,
and two thousand of their donkeys—also
one hundred thousand of their men; 22 for
many fell dead, because the war [v]*was*
God's. And they dwelt in their place until
[w]the captivity.

The Family of Manasseh (East)

23 So the children of the half-tribe of Manasseh dwelt in the land. Their *numbers* increased from Bashan to Baal Hermon, that
is, to [x]Senir, or Mount Hermon. 24 These
were the heads of their fathers' houses:
Epher, Ishi, Eliel, Azriel, Jeremiah, Hodaviah, and Jahdiel. They were mighty men
of valor, famous men, *and* heads of their fathers' houses.
25 And they were unfaithful to the God
of their fathers, and [y]played the harlot
after the gods of the peoples of the land,
whom God had destroyed before them.
26 So the God of Israel stirred up the spirit
of [z]Pul king of Assyria, that is, [a]Tiglath-Pi-
leser[7] king of Assyria. He carried the
Reubenites, the Gadites, and the half-tribe
of Manasseh into captivity. He took them
to [b]Halah, Habor, Hara, and the river of
Gozan to this day.

The Family of Levi

6 The sons of Levi *were* [a]Gershon,[1] Kohath, and Merari. 2 The sons of Kohath
were Amram, [b]Izhar, Hebron, and Uzziel.
3 The children of Amram *were* Aaron, Moses, and Miriam. And the sons of Aaron
were [c]Nadab, Abihu, Eleazar, and Ithamar.
4 Eleazar begot Phinehas, *and* Phinehas
begot Abishua; 5 Abishua begot Bukki, and
Bukki begot Uzzi; 6 Uzzi begot Zerahiah,
and Zerahiah begot Meraioth; 7 Meraioth
begot Amariah, and Amariah begot Ahitub;
8 [d]Ahitub begot [e]Zadok, and Zadok begot
Ahimaaz; 9 Ahimaaz begot Azariah, and
Azariah begot Johanan; 10 Johanan begot
Azariah (it was he [f]who ministered as
priest in the [g]temple[2] that Solomon built in
Jerusalem); 11 [h]Azariah begot [i]Amariah,
and Amariah begot Ahitub; 12 Ahitub
begot Zadok, and Zadok begot [3]Shallum;
13 Shallum begot Hilkiah, and Hilkiah
begot Azariah; 14 Azariah begot [j]Seraiah,
and Seraiah begot Jehozadak. 15 Jehozadak
went *into captivity* [k]when the LORD carried
Judah and Jerusalem into captivity by the
hand of Nebuchadnezzar.
16 The sons of Levi *were* [l]Gershon,[4] Kohath, and Merari. 17 These are the names of
the sons of Gershon: Libni and Shimei.
18 The sons of Kohath *were* Amram, Izhar,
Hebron, and Uzziel. 19 The sons of Merari
were Mahli and Mushi. Now these *are* the
families of the Levites according to their
fathers: 20 Of Gershon *were* Libni his son,
Jahath his son, [m]Zimmah his son, 21 [5]Joah
his son, [6]Iddo his son, Zerah his son, *and*
[7]Jeatherai his son. 22 The sons of Kohath
were [8]Amminadab his son, [n]Korah his son,
Assir his son, 23 Elkanah his son, Ebiasaph
his son, Assir his son, 24 Tahath his son,
Uriel his son, Uzziah his son, and Shaul his
son. 25 The sons of Elkanah *were* [o]Amasai
and Ahimoth. 26 *As for* Elkanah, the sons of
Elkanah *were* [9]Zophai his son, [1]Nahath his
son, 27 [2]Eliab his son, Jeroham his son, *and*
Elkanah his son. 28 The sons of Samuel
were [3]*Joel* the firstborn, and Abijah [4]the second. 29 The sons of Merari *were* Mahli,
Libni his son, Shimei his son, Uzzah his
son, 30 Shimea his son, Haggiah his son,
and Asaiah his son.

Musicians in the House of the LORD

31 Now these are [p]the men whom David
appointed over the service of song in the
house of the LORD, after the [q]ark came to
rest. 32 They were ministering with music
before the dwelling place of the tabernacle
of meeting, until Solomon had built the
house of the LORD in Jerusalem, and they
served in their office according to their
order.
33 And these *are* the ones who [5]minis-
tered with their sons: Of the sons of the
[r]Kohathites *were* Heman the singer, the son
of Joel, the son of Samuel, 34 the son of Elkanah, the son of Jeroham, the son of [6]Eliel,

22 [v][Josh. 23:10; 2 Chr. 32:8; Rom. 8:31] [w]2 Kin. 15:29; 17:6
23 [x]Deut. 3:9
25 [y]2 Kin. 17:7
26 [z]2 Kin. 15:19 [a]2 Kin. 15:29 [b]2 Kin. 17:6; 18:11 [7]Heb. *Tilgath-Pilneser*

CHAPTER 6

1 [a]Gen. 46:11; Ex. 6:16; Num. 26:57; 1 Chr. 23:6 [1]Or *Gershom*, v. 16
2 [b]1 Chr. 6:18, 22
3 [c]Lev. 10:1, 2
8 [d]2 Sam. 8:17 [e]2 Sam. 15:27
10 [f]2 Chr. 26:17, 18 [g]1 Kin. 6:1; 2 Chr. 3:1 [2]Lit. *house*
11 [h]Ezra 7:3 [i]2 Chr. 19:11
12 [3]*Meshullam*, 1 Chr. 9:11
14 [j]2 Kin. 25:18-21; Neh. 11:11
15 [k]2 Kin. 25:21
16 [l]Gen. 46:11; Ex. 6:16 [4]Heb. *Gershom*, an alternate spelling for *Gershon*, vv. 1, 17, 20, 43, 62, 71
20 [m]1 Chr. 6:42
21 [5]*Ethan*, v. 42 [6]*Adaiah*, v. 41 [7]*Ethni*, v. 41
22 [n]Num. 16:1 [8]*Izhar*, vv. 2, 18
25 [o]1 Chr. 6:35, 36
26 [9]*Zuph*, v. 35; 1 Sam. 1:1 [1]*Toah*, v. 34
27 [2]*Eliel*, v. 34
28 [3]So with LXX, Syr., Arab.; cf. v. 33 and 1 Sam. 8:2 [4]Heb. *Vasheni*
31 [p]1 Chr. 15:16-22, 27; 16:4-6 [q]2 Sam. 6:17; 1 Kin. 8:4; 1 Chr. 15:25–16:1
33 [r]Num. 26:57 [5]Lit. *stood with*
34 [6]*Elihu*, 1 Sam. 1:1

5:22 the captivity. The Assyrian deportation of 722 B.C. is meant (cf. 5:26).

6:1-15 This section lists the High-Priestly lineage from Levi (6:1) through Aaron (6:3), through Eleazar (6:3,4), and through Phinehas (6:4), with whom God covenanted for a perpetual priesthood (Num. 25:11-13).

6:8 Zadok. By the time of David's reign, the High-Priestly line had wrongly been shifted to the sons of Ithamar as represented by Abiathar. When Abiathar sided with Adonijah rather than Solomon, Zadok became the ruling High-Priest (1 Kin. 2:26,27) and restored the high-priesthood to the Levitical line through Phinehas (cf. Num. 25:10-13).

6:13 Hilkiah. The High-Priest who rediscovered the law in Josiah's reign ca. 622 B.C. (2 Kin. 22:8-13; 2 Chr. 34:14-21).

6:14 Seraiah. The High-Priest who was executed by the Babylonians after their occupation of Jerusalem ca. 586 B.C. (2 Kin. 25:18-21). **Jehozadak.** (A.k.a. Jozadak.) The father of Jeshua, the first High-Priest in the return (cf. Ezra 3:2; 5:2).

6:16-30 The temple duties of the sons of Levi (6:16-19) and their families (6:20-30) are given here.

6:27,28 Samuel's name in this Levitical lineage validates his acceptance into the priesthood (cf. 1 Sam. 1:24-28; 2:24–3:1). The fact that Elkanah was from Ephraim (1 Sam. 1:1) indicates where he lived, not his family history (Num. 35:6-8).

6:31-48 The Levitical musicians are listed as they relate to: 1) Kohath and Heman (6:33-38); 2) Gershon and Asaph (6:39-43); and 3) Merari and Ethan (6:44-47).

the son of [7]Toah, **35** the son of Zuph, the
son of Elkanah, the son of Mahath, the son
of Amasai, **36** the son of Elkanah, the son of
Joel, the son of Azariah, the son of Zephaniah, **37** the son of Tahath, the son of Assir,
the son of [s]Ebiasaph, the son of Korah,
38 the son of Izhar, the son of Kohath, the
son of Levi, the son of Israel. **39** And his
brother [t]Asaph, who stood at his right
hand, *was* Asaph the son of Berachiah, the
son of Shimea, **40** the son of Michael, the
son of Baaseiah, the son of Malchijah,
41 the son of [u]Ethni, the son of Zerah, the
son of Adaiah, **42** the son of Ethan, the son
of Zimmah, the son of Shimei, **43** the son of
Jahath, the son of Gershon, the son of Levi.
44 Their brethren, the sons of Merari, on
the left hand, *were* [8]Ethan the son of [9]Kishi,
the son of Abdi, the son of Malluch, **45** the
son of Hashabiah, the son of Amaziah, the
son of Hilkiah, **46** the son of Amzi, the son
of Bani, the son of Shamer, **47** the son of
Mahli, the son of Mushi, the son of Merari,
the son of Levi.
48 And their brethren, the Levites, *were*
appointed to every [v]kind of service of the
tabernacle of the house of God.

The Family of Aaron

49 [w]But Aaron and his sons offered sacrifices [x]on the altar of burnt offering and [y]on
the altar of incense, for all the work of the
Most Holy *Place*, and to make atonement
for Israel, according to all that Moses the
servant of God had commanded. **50** Now
these *are* the [z]sons of Aaron: Eleazar his
son, Phinehas his son, Abishua his son,
51 Bukki his son, Uzzi his son, Zerahiah his
son, **52** Meraioth his son, Amariah his son,
Ahitub his son, **53** Zadok his son, *and*
Ahimaaz his son.

Dwelling Places of the Levites

54 [a]Now these *are* their dwelling places
throughout their settlements in their territory, for they were *given* by lot to the sons
of Aaron, of the family of the Kohathites:
55 [b]They gave them Hebron in the land of
Judah, with its surrounding [1]common-
lands. **56** [c]But the fields of the city and its
villages they gave to Caleb the son of Jephunneh. **57** And [d]to the sons of Aaron
they gave *one of* the cities of refuge, Hebron; also Libnah with its common-lands,
Jattir, Eshtemoa with its common-lands,
58 [2]Hilen with its common-lands, Debir
with its common-lands, **59** [3]Ashan with its
common-lands, and Beth Shemesh with its
common-lands. **60** And from the tribe of
Benjamin: Geba with its common-lands,
[4]Alemeth with its common-lands, and
Anathoth with its common-lands. All their
cities among their families *were* thirteen.
61 [e]To the rest of the family of the tribe of
the Kohathites *they gave* [f]by lot ten cities
from half the tribe of Manasseh. **62** And to
the sons of Gershon, throughout their families, *they gave* thirteen cities from the tribe
of Issachar, from the tribe of Asher, from
the tribe of Naphtali, and from the tribe of
Manasseh in Bashan. **63** To the sons of Merari, throughout their families, *they gave*
[g]twelve cities from the tribe of Reuben,
from the tribe of Gad, and from the tribe of
Zebulun. **64** So the children of Israel gave
these cities with their [5]common-lands to
the Levites. **65** And they gave by lot from
the tribe of the children of Judah, from the
tribe of the children of Simeon, and from
the tribe of the children of Benjamin these
cities which are called by *their* names.
66 Now [h]some of the families of the sons
of Kohath *were given* cities as their territory
from the tribe of Ephraim. **67** [i]And they
gave them *one of* the cities of refuge,
Shechem with its common-lands, in the
mountains of Ephraim, also Gezer with its
common-lands, **68** [j]Jokmeam with its common-lands, Beth Horon with its common-
lands, **69** Aijalon with its common-lands,
and Gath Rimmon with its common-lands.
70 And from the half-tribe of Manasseh:
Aner with its common-lands and Bileam
with its common-lands, for the rest of the
family of the sons of Kohath.
71 From the family of the half-tribe of Manasseh the sons of Gershon *were given* Golan
in Bashan with its common-lands and
[6]Ashtaroth with its common-lands. **72** And
from the tribe of Issachar: [7]Kedesh with its
common-lands, Daberath with its common-
lands, **73** Ramoth with its common-lands,
and Anem with its common-lands. **74** And
from the tribe of Asher: Mashal with its
common-lands, Abdon with its common-
lands, **75** Hukok with its common-lands,
and Rehob with its common-lands. **76** And
from the tribe of Naphtali: Kedesh in Galilee with its common-lands, Hammon with
its common-lands, and Kirjathaim with its
common-lands.
77 From the tribe of Zebulun the rest of
the children of Merari *were given* [8]Rimmon

34 [7] *Tohu*, 1 Sam. 1:1
37 [s] Ex. 6:24
39 [t] 2 Chr. 5:12
41 [u] 1 Chr. 6:21
44 [8] *Jeduthun*, 1 Chr. 9:16; 25:1, 3, 6; 2 Chr. 35:15; Ps. 62:title [9] Or *Kushaiah*
48 [v] 1 Chr. 9:14-34
49 [w] Ex. 28:1; [Num. 18:1-8] [x] Lev. 1:8, 9 [y] Ex. 30:7
50 [z] 1 Chr. 6:4-8; Ezra 7:5
54 [a] Josh. 21
55 [b] Josh. 14:13; 21:11, 12 [1] *open lands*
56 [c] Josh. 14:13; 15:13
57 [d] Josh. 21:13, 19
58 [2] *Holon*, Josh. 21:15
59 [3] *Ain*, Josh. 21:16
60 [4] *Almon*, Josh. 21:18
61 [e] 1 Chr. 6:66-70 [f] Josh. 21:5
63 [g] Josh. 21:7, 34-40
64 [5] *open lands*
66 [h] 1 Chr. 6:61
67 [i] Josh. 21:21
68 [j] Josh. 21:22
71 [6] *Beeshterah*, Josh. 21:27
72 [7] *Kishon*, Josh. 21:28
77 [8] Heb. *Rimmono*, an alternate spelling of *Rimmon*, 1 Chr. 4:32

6:49-53 This is a repeat of the High-Priestly line enumerated in 6:4-8 through Zadok. This repeated genealogy could possibly point to the Zadokian high-priesthood for the temple in the Millennium (cf. Ezek. 40:46; 43:19; 44:15; 48:11).

6:54-81 This section rehearses the 48 cities given to the Levites instead of a section of land (cf. Num. 35:1-8; Josh. 21:1-42) which signals God's intention for the Jewish nation to have a priesthood and future in the land first given to Abraham (cf. Gen. 12:1-3).

with its common-lands and Tabor with its common-lands. 78 And on the other side of the Jordan, across from Jericho, on the east side of the Jordan, *they were given* from the tribe of Reuben: Bezer in the wilderness with its common-lands, Jahzah with its common-lands, 79 Kedemoth with its common-lands, and Mephaath with its common-lands. 80 And from the tribe of Gad: Ramoth in Gilead with its common-lands, Mahanaim with its common-lands, 81 Heshbon with its common-lands, and Jazer with its common-lands.

The Family of Issachar

7 The sons of Issachar *were* [a]Tola, [1]Puah, [2]Jashub, and Shimron—four *in all.* 2 The sons of Tola *were* Uzzi, Rephaiah, Jeriel, Jahmai, Jibsam, and Shemuel, heads of their father's house. *The sons* of Tola *were* mighty men of valor in their generations; [b]their number in the days of David *was* twenty-two thousand six hundred. 3 The son of Uzzi *was* Izrahiah, and the sons of Izrahiah *were* Michael, Obadiah, Joel, and Ishiah. All five of them *were* chief men. 4 And with them, by their generations, according to their fathers' houses, *were* thirty-six thousand troops ready for war; for they had many wives and sons.

5 Now their brethren among all the families of Issachar *were* mighty men of valor, listed by their genealogies, eighty-seven thousand in all.

The Family of Benjamin

6 *The sons* of [c]Benjamin *were* Bela, Becher, and Jediael—three *in all.* 7 The sons of Bela were Ezbon, Uzzi, Uzziel, Jerimoth, and Iri—five *in all.* They *were* heads of *their* fathers' houses, and they were listed by their genealogies, twenty-two thousand and thirty-four mighty men of valor.

8 The sons of Becher *were* Zemirah, Joash, Eliezer, Elioenai, Omri, Jerimoth, Abijah, Anathoth, and Alemeth. All these *are* the sons of Becher. 9 And they were recorded by genealogy according to their generations, heads of their fathers' houses, twenty thousand two hundred mighty men of valor. 10 The son of Jediael *was* Bilhan, and the sons of Bilhan *were* Jeush, Benjamin, Ehud, Chenaanah, Zethan, Tharshish, and Ahishahar.

11 All these sons of Jediael *were* heads of their fathers' houses; *there were* seventeen thousand two hundred mighty men of valor fit to go out for war *and* battle. 12 [3]Shuppim and [4]Huppim *were* the sons of [5]Ir, *and* Hushim *was* the son of [6]Aher.

The Family of Naphtali

13 The [d]sons of Naphtali *were* [7]Jahziel, Guni, Jezer, and [8]Shallum, the sons of Bilhah.

The Family of Manasseh (West)

14 The [e]descendants of Manasseh: his Syrian concubine bore him [f]Machir the father of Gilead, the father of Asriel. 15 Machir took as his wife *the sister* of [9]Huppim and [1]Shuppim, whose name *was* Maachah. The name of *Gilead's* [2]grandson *was* [g]Zelophehad, but Zelophehad begot only daughters. 16 (Maachah the wife of Machir bore a son, and she called his name Peresh. The name of his brother *was* Sheresh, and his sons *were* Ulam and Rakem. 17 The son of Ulam *was* [h]Bedan.) These *were* the descendants of Gilead the son of Machir, the son of Manasseh.

18 His sister Hammoleketh bore Ishhod, [3]Abiezer, and Mahlah.

19 And the sons of Shemida were Ahian, Shechem, Likhi, and Aniam.

The Family of Ephraim

20 [i]The sons of Ephraim *were* Shuthelah, Bered his son, Tahath his son, Eladah his son, Tahath his son, 21 Zabad his son, Shuthelah his son, and Ezer and Elead. The men of Gath who were born in *that* land killed *them* because they came down to take away their cattle. 22 Then Ephraim their father mourned many days, and his brethren came to comfort him.

23 And when he went in to his wife, she conceived and bore a son; and he called his name [4]Beriah, because tragedy had come upon his house. 24 Now his daughter *was* Sheerah, who built Lower and Upper [j]Beth Horon and Uzzen Sheerah; 25 and Rephah *was* his son, *as well* as Resheph, and Telah his son, Tahan his son, 26 Laadan his son, Ammihud his son, [k]Elishama his son, 27 [5]Nun his son, and [l]Joshua his son.

28 Now their [m]possessions and dwelling places *were* Bethel and its towns: to the east [6]Naaran, to the west Gezer and its towns, and Shechem and its towns, as far as [7]Ayyah and its towns; 29 and by the borders of the children of [n]Manasseh *were* Beth Shean and its towns, Taanach and its towns, [o]Megiddo and its towns, Dor and its towns. In these dwelt the children of Joseph, the son of Israel.

The Family of Asher

30 [p]The sons of Asher *were* Imnah, Ishvah, Ishvi, Beriah, and their sister Serah. 31 The sons of Beriah *were* Heber and

CHAPTER 7

1 [a] Num. 26:23-25 [1] *Puvah,* Gen. 46:13 [2] *Job,* Gen. 46:13
2 [b] 2 Sam. 24:1-9; 1 Chr. 27:1
6 [c] Gen. 46:21; Num. 26:38-41; 1 Chr. 8:1
12 [3] *Shupham,* Num. 26:39 [4] *Hupham,* Num. 26:39 [5] *Iri,* v. 7 [6] *Ahiram,* Num. 26:38
13 [d] Num. 26:48-50 [7] *Jahzeel,* Gen. 46:24 [8] *Shillem,* Gen. 46:24
14 [e] Num. 26:29-34 [f] 1 Chr. 2:21
15 [g] Num. 26:30-33; 27:1 [9] *Hupham,* v. 12; Num. 26:39 [1] *Shupham,* v. 12; Num. 26:39 [2] Lit. *the second*
17 [h] 1 Sam. 12:11
18 [3] *Jeezer,* Num. 26:30
20 [i] Num. 26:35-37
23 [4] Lit. *In Tragedy*
24 [j] Josh. 16:3, 5; 2 Chr. 8:5
26 [k] Num. 10:22
27 [l] Ex. 17:9, 14; 24:13; 33:11 [5] Heb. *Non*
28 [m] Josh. 16:1-10 [6] *Naarath,* Josh. 16:7 [7] Many Heb. mss., Bg., LXX, Tg., Vg. *Gazza*
29 [n] Gen. 41:51; Josh. 17:7 [o] Josh. 17:11
30 [p] Gen. 46:17; Num. 26:44-47

Malchiel, who was the father of [8]Birzaith.
32 And Heber begot Japhlet, [9]Shomer,
[1]Hotham, and their sister Shua. 33 The
sons of Japhlet *were* Pasach, Bimhal, and
Ashvath. These *were* the children of
Japhlet. 34 The sons of [q]Shemer *were* Ahi,
Rohgah, Jehubbah, and Aram. 35 And the
sons of his brother Helem *were* Zophah,
Imna, Shelesh, and Amal. 36 The sons of
Zophah *were* Suah, Harnepher, Shual, Beri,
Imrah, 37 Bezer, Hod, Shamma, Shilshah,
[2]Jithran, and Beera. 38 The sons of Jether
were Jephunneh, Pispah, and Ara. 39 The
sons of Ulla *were* Arah, Haniel, and Rizia.
40 All these *were* the children of Asher,
heads of *their* fathers' houses, choice men,
mighty men of valor, chief leaders. And
they were recorded by genealogies among
the army fit for battle; their number *was*
twenty-six thousand.

The Family Tree of King Saul of Benjamin

8 Now Benjamin begot [a]Bela his firstborn, Ashbel the second, [1]Aharah the
third, 2 Nohah the fourth, and Rapha the
fifth. 3 The sons of Bela *were* [2]Addar, Gera,
Abihud, 4 Abishua, Naaman, Ahoah,
5 Gera, [3]Shephuphan, and Huram.
6 These *are* the sons of Ehud, who were
the heads of the fathers' *houses* of the inhabitants of [b]Geba, and who forced them
to move to [c]Manahath: 7 Naaman, Ahijah,
and Gera who forced them to move. He
begot Uzza and Ahihud.
8 Also Shaharaim had children in the
country of Moab, after he had sent away
Hushim and Baara his wives. 9 By Hodesh
his wife he begot Jobab, Zibia, Mesha, Malcam, 10 Jeuz, Sachiah, and Mirmah. These
were his sons, heads of their fathers' *houses*.
11 And by Hushim he begot Abitub and
Elpaal. 12 The sons of Elpaal *were* Eber,
Misham, and Shemed, who built Ono and
Lod with its towns; 13 and Beriah and
[d]Shema, who *were* heads of their fathers'
houses of the inhabitants of Aijalon, who
drove out the inhabitants of Gath. 14 Ahio,
Shashak, Jeremoth, 15 Zebadiah, Arad,
Eder, 16 Michael, Ispah, and Joha *were* the
sons of Beriah. 17 Zebadiah, Meshullam,
Hizki, Heber, 18 Ishmerai, Jizliah, and
Jobab *were* the sons of Elpaal. 19 Jakim,
Zichri, Zabdi, 20 Elienai, Zillethai, Eliel,
21 Adaiah, Beraiah, and Shimrath *were* the
sons of [4]Shimei. 22 Ishpan, Eber, Eliel,
23 Abdon, Zichri, Hanan, 24 Hananiah,
Elam, Antothijah, 25 Iphdeiah, and Penuel
were the sons of Shashak. 26 Shamsherai,
Shehariah, Athaliah, 27 Jaareshiah, Elijah,
and Zichri *were* the sons of Jeroham.
28 These *were* heads of the fathers' *houses*
by their generations, chief men. These
dwelt in Jerusalem.
29 Now [5]the father of Gibeon, whose
[e]wife's name *was* Maacah, dwelt at Gibeon.
30 And his firstborn son *was* Abdon, then
Zur, Kish, Baal, Nadab, 31 Gedor, Ahio,
[6]Zecher, 32 and Mikloth, *who* begot
[7]Shimeah. They also dwelt [8]alongside
their [9]relatives in Jerusalem, with their
brethren. 33 [f]Ner[1] begot Kish, Kish begot
Saul, and Saul begot Jonathan, Malchishua, [2]Abinadab, and [3]Esh-Baal. 34 The
son of Jonathan *was* [4]Merib-Baal, and
Merib-Baal begot [g]Micah. 35 The sons of
Micah *were* Pithon, Melech, [5]Tarea, and
Ahaz. 36 And Ahaz begot [6]Jehoaddah; Jehoaddah begot Alemeth, Azmaveth, and
Zimri; and Zimri begot Moza. 37 Moza
begot Binea, [7]Raphah his son, Eleasah his
son, *and* Azel his son.
38 Azel had six sons whose names *were*
these: Azrikam, Bocheru, Ishmael, Sheariah, Obadiah, and Hanan. All these *were*
the sons of Azel. 39 And the sons of Eshek
his brother *were* Ulam his firstborn, Jeush
the second, and Eliphelet the third.
40 The sons of Ulam were mighty men of
valor—archers. *They* had many sons and
grandsons, one hundred and fifty *in all*.
These *were* all sons of Benjamin.

9 So [a]all Israel was [1]recorded by genealogies, and indeed, they *were* inscribed in the book of the kings of Israel.
But Judah was carried away captive to
Babylon because of their unfaithfulness.
2 [b]And the first inhabitants who *dwelt* in
their possessions in their cities *were* Israelites, priests, Levites, and [c]the Nethinim.

Dwellers in Jerusalem

3 Now in [d]Jerusalem the children of Judah dwelt, and some of the children of
Benjamin, and of the children of Ephraim
and Manasseh: 4 Uthai the son of Ammihud, the son of Omri, the son of Imri,
the son of Bani, of the descendants of
Perez, the son of Judah. 5 Of the Shilonites:

31 [8] Or *Birzavith* or *Birzoth*
32 [9] *Shemer*, 1 Chr. 7:34 [1] *Helem*, 1 Chr. 7:35
34 [q] 1 Chr. 7:32
37 [2] *Jether*, v. 38

CHAPTER 8

1 [a] Gen. 46:21; Num. 26:38; 1 Chr. 7:6 [1] *Ahiram*, Num. 26:38
3 [2] *Ard*, Num. 26:40
5 [3] *Shupham*, Num. 26:39, or *Shuppim*, 1 Chr. 7:12
6 [b] 1 Chr. 6:60 [c] 1 Chr. 2:52
13 [d] 1 Chr. 8:21
21 [4] *Shema*, 1 Chr. 7:13
29 [e] 1 Chr. 9:35-38 [5] *Jeiel*, 1 Chr. 9:35
31 [6] *Zechariah*, 1 Chr. 9:37
32 [7] *Shimeam*, 1 Chr. 9:38 [8] Lit. *opposite* [9] *brethren*
33 [f] 1 Sam. 14:51 [1] Also the son of Gibeon, 1 Chr. 9:36, 39 [2] *Jishui*, 1 Sam. 14:49 [3] *Ishbosheth*, 2 Sam. 2:8
34 [g] 2 Sam. 9:12 [4] *Mephibosheth*, 2 Sam. 4:4
35 [5] *Tahrea*, 1 Chr. 9:41
36 [6] *Jarah*, 1 Chr. 9:42
37 [7] *Raphaiah*, 1 Chr. 9:43

CHAPTER 9

1 [a] Ezra 2:59 [1] *enrolled*
2 [b] Ezra 2:70; Neh. 7:73 [c] Ezra 2:43; 8:20
3 [d] Neh. 11:1, 2

8:1-40 This section enlarges on the genealogy of Benjamin in 7:6-12, most likely because of that tribe's important relationship with Judah in the southern kingdom. Thus these two tribes taken in captivity together and the Levites make up the returning remnant in 538 B.C.

9:1 all Israel. Even though the northern kingdom of Israel never returned from dispersion in 722 B.C., many from the 10 tribes which made up that kingdom migrated S after the division in 931 B.C. The result was that Judah, the southern kingdom, had people from all tribes, so that when returning from captivity "all Israel" was truly represented.

9:2 first inhabitants. This chapter has genealogies of returning 1) Israelites (9:3-9); 2) priests (9:10-13); and 3) Levites (19:14-34). **Nethinim.** These were the temple servants (Ezra 8:20), possibly descendants of the Gibeonites (cf. Josh. 9:3,4,23).

Asaiah the firstborn and his sons. 6 Of the
sons of Zerah: Jeuel, and their brethren—
six hundred and ninety. 7 Of the sons of
Benjamin: Sallu the son of Meshullam, the
son of Hodaviah, the son of Hassenuah;
8 Ibneiah the son of Jeroham; Elah the son
of Uzzi, the son of Michri; Meshullam the
son of Shephatiah, the son of Reuel, the son
of Ibnijah; 9 and their brethren, according
to their generations—nine hundred and
fifty-six. All these men *were* heads of a father's *house* in their fathers' houses.

The Priests at Jerusalem

10 [e]Of the priests: Jedaiah, Jehoiarib, and
Jachin; 11 [2]Azariah the son of Hilkiah, the
son of Meshullam, the son of Zadok, the
son of Meraioth, the son of Ahitub, the [f]officer over the house of God; 12 Adaiah the
son of Jeroham, the son of Pashur, the son
of Malchijah; Maasai the son of Adiel, the
son of Jahzerah, the son of Meshullam, the
son of Meshillemith, the son of Immer;
13 and their brethren, heads of their fathers'
houses—one thousand seven hundred and
sixty. *They were* [3]very able men for the work
of the service of the house of God.

10 [e] Neh. 11:10-14
11 [f] 2 Chr. 31:13; Jer. 20:1 [2] *Seraiah*, Neh. 11:11
13 [3] Lit. *mighty men of strength*
15 [g] Neh. 11:17
16 [h] Neh. 11:17 [i] Neh. 11:17
19 [4] Lit. *thresholds*
20 [j] Num. 25:6-13; 31:6

The Levites at Jerusalem

14 Of the Levites: Shemaiah the son of
Hasshub, the son of Azrikam, the son of
Hashabiah, of the sons of Merari; 15 Bakbakkar, Heresh, Galal, and Mattaniah the
son of Micah, the son of [g]Zichri, the son of
Asaph; 16 [h]Obadiah the son of [i]Shemaiah,
the son of Galal, the son of Jeduthun; and
Berechiah the son of Asa, the son of Elkanah, who lived in the villages of the Netophathites.

The Levite Gatekeepers

17 And the gatekeepers *were* Shallum,
Akkub, Talmon, Ahiman, and their
brethren. Shallum *was* the chief. 18 Until
then *they had been* gatekeepers for the
camps of the children of Levi at the King's
Gate on the east.

19 Shallum the son of Kore, the son of
Ebiasaph, the son of Korah, and his
brethren, from his father's house, the
Korahites, *were* in charge of the work of the
service, [4]gatekeepers of the tabernacle.
Their fathers had been keepers of the entrance to the camp of the LORD. 20 And
[j]Phinehas the son of Eleazar had been the

The Chronicles' Sources

The inspiration of Scripture (2 Tim. 3:16) was sometimes accomplished through direct revelation from God without a human writer, e.g., the Mosaic law. At other times, God used human sources, as mentioned in Luke 1:1-4. Such was the experience of the chronicler as evidenced by the many contributing sources. Whether the material came through direct revelation or by existing resources, God's inspiration through the Holy Spirit prevented the original human authors of Scripture from any error (2 Pet. 1:19-21). Although relatively few scribal errors have been made in copying Scripture, they can be identified and corrected. Thus, the original, inerrant content of the Bible has been preserved.

1. Book of the Kings of Israel/Judah (1 Chr. 9:1; 2 Chr. 16:11; 20:34; 25:26; 27:7; 28:26; 32:32; 35:27; 36:8)
2. The Chronicles of David (1 Chr. 27:24)
3. Book of Samuel (1 Chr. 29:29)
4. Book of Nathan (1 Chr. 29:29; 2 Chr. 9:29)
5. Book of Gad (1 Chr. 29:29).
6. Prophecy of Ahijah the Shilonite (2 Chr. 9:29)
7. Visions of Iddo (2 Chr. 9:29)
8. Records of Shemaiah (2 Chr. 12:15)
9. Records of Iddo (2 Chr. 12:15)
10. Annals of Iddo (2 Chr. 13:22)
11. Annals of Jehu (2 Chr. 20:34)
12. Commentary on the Book of the Kings (2 Chr. 24:27)
13. Acts of Uzziah by Isaiah (2 Chr. 26:22)
14. Letters/Message of Sennacherib (2 Chr. 32:10-17)
15. Vision of Isaiah (2 Chr. 32:32)
16. Words of the Seers (2 Chr 33:18)
17. Sayings of Hozai (2 Chr. 33:19)
18. Written instructions of David and Solomon (2 Chr. 35:4)
19. The Laments (2 Chr. 35:25).

officer over them in time past; the LORD
was with him. 21 [k]Zechariah the son of Meshelemiah *was* [5]keeper of the door of the
tabernacle of meeting.

22 All those chosen as gatekeepers *were*
two hundred and twelve. [l]They were
recorded by their genealogy, in their villages. David and Samuel [m]the seer had
appointed them to their trusted office.
23 So they and their children *were* in
charge of the gates of the house of the
LORD, the house of the tabernacle, by assignment. 24 The gatekeepers were assigned to the four directions: the east,
west, north, and south. 25 And their
brethren in their villages *had* to come with
them from time to time [n]for seven days.
26 For in this trusted office *were* four chief
gatekeepers; they were Levites. And they
had charge over the chambers and treasuries of the house of God. 27 And they
lodged *all* around the house of God because [6]they *had* the [o]responsibility, and
they *were* in charge of opening *it* every
morning.

Other Levite Responsibilities

28 Now *some* of them were in charge of
the serving vessels, for they brought
them in and took them out by count.
29 *Some* of them *were* appointed over the
furnishings and over all the implements
of the sanctuary, and over the [p]fine flour
and the wine and the oil and the incense
and the spices. 30 And *some* of the sons of
the priests made [q]the ointment of the
spices.

31 Mattithiah of the Levites, the firstborn
of Shallum the Korahite, had the trusted
office [r]over the things that were baked in
the pans. 32 And some of their brethren of
the sons of the Kohathites [s]*were* in charge
of preparing the showbread for every Sabbath.

33 These are [t]the singers, heads of the fathers' *houses* of the Levites, *who lodged* in
the chambers, *and were* free *from other duties;* for they were employed in *that* work
day and night. 34 These heads of the fathers' *houses* of the Levites *were* heads
throughout their generations. They dwelt
at Jerusalem.

The Family of King Saul

35 Jeiel the father of Gibeon, whose
wife's name *was* [u]Maacah, dwelt at Gibeon. 36 His firstborn son *was* Abdon, then
Zur, Kish, Baal, Ner, Nadab, 37 Gedor,
Ahio, [7]Zechariah, and Mikloth. 38 And
Mikloth begot [8]Shimeam. They also dwelt
alongside their relatives in Jerusalem, with
their brethren. 39 [v]Ner begot Kish, Kish
begot Saul, and Saul begot Jonathan, Malchishua, Abinadab, and Esh-Baal. 40 The
son of Jonathan *was* Merib-Baal, and
Merib-Baal begot Micah. 41 The sons of
Micah *were* Pithon, Melech, [9]Tahrea, [w]*and*[1]
Ahaz. 42 And Ahaz begot [2]Jarah; Jarah
begot Alemeth, Azmaveth, and Zimri; and
Zimri begot Moza; 43 Moza begot Binea,
[3]Rephaiah his son, Eleasah his son, and
Azel his son.

44 And Azel had six sons whose names
were these: Azrikam, Bocheru, Ishmael,
Sheariah, Obadiah, and Hanan; these *were*
the sons of Azel.

Tragic End of Saul and His Sons

10 Now [a]the Philistines fought against
Israel; and the men of Israel fled
from before the Philistines, and fell slain
on Mount Gilboa. 2 Then the Philistines
followed hard after Saul and his sons. And
the Philistines killed Jonathan, [1]Abinadab,
and Malchishua, Saul's sons. 3 The battle
became fierce against Saul. The archers hit
him, and he was wounded by the archers.
4 Then Saul said to his armorbearer, "Draw
your sword, and thrust me through with it,
lest these uncircumcised men come and
abuse me." But his armorbearer would not,
for he was greatly afraid. Therefore Saul
took a sword and fell on it. 5 And when his
armorbearer saw that Saul was dead, he
also fell on his sword and died. 6 So Saul
and his three sons died, and all his house
died together. 7 And when all the men of
Israel who *were* in the valley saw that they
had fled and that Saul and his sons were
dead, they forsook their cities and fled;
then the Philistines came and dwelt in
them.

8 So it happened the next day, when the
Philistines came to [2]strip the slain, that
they found Saul and his sons fallen on
Mount Gilboa. 9 And they stripped him
and took his head and his armor, and sent
word *throughout* the land of the Philistines
to proclaim the news *in the temple* of their
idols and among the people. 10 [b]Then they
put his armor in the [3]temple of their gods,
and fastened his head in the temple of
Dagon.

11 And when all Jabesh Gilead heard all
that the Philistines had done to Saul, 12 all
the [c]valiant men arose and took the body

21 [k] 1 Chr. 26:2, 14 [5] *gatekeeper*
22 [l] 1 Chr. 26:1, 2 [m] 1 Sam. 9:9
25 [n] 2 Kin. 11:4-7; 2 Chr. 23:8
27 [o] 1 Chr. 23:30-32 [6] *the watch was committed to them*
29 [p] 1 Chr. 23:29
30 [q] Ex. 30:22-25
31 [r] Lev. 2:5; 6:21
32 [s] Lev. 24:5-8
33 [t] 1 Chr. 6:31; 25:1
35 [u] 1 Chr. 8:29-32
37 [7] *Zecher,* 1 Chr. 8:31
38 [8] *Shimeah,* 1 Chr. 8:32
39 [v] 1 Chr. 8:33-38
41 [w] 1 Chr. 8:35 [9] *Tarea,* 1 Chr. 8:35 [1] So with Arab., Syr., Tg., Vg. (cf. 8:35); MT, LXX omit *and Ahaz*
42 [2] *Jehoaddah,* 1 Chr. 8:36
43 [3] *Raphah,* 1 Chr. 8:37

CHAPTER 10
1 [a] 1 Sam. 31:1, 2
2 [1] *Jishui,* 1 Sam. 14:49
8 [2] *plunder*
10 [b] 1 Sam. 31:10 [3] Lit. *house*
12 [c] 1 Sam. 14:52

9:35-44 This section records Saul's lineage as a transition to the main theme of the rest of the book, which is the kingship of David (ca. 1011 B.C.).

10:1-12 *See notes on 1 Sam. 31:1-13* (cf. 2 Sam. 1:4-12).

of Saul and the bodies of his sons; and they
brought them to [d]Jabesh, and buried their
bones under the tamarisk tree at Jabesh,
and fasted seven days.
13 So Saul died for his unfaithfulness
which he had [4]committed against the
LORD, [e]because he did not keep the word of
the LORD, and also because [f]he consulted a
medium for guidance. 14 But *he* did not inquire of the LORD; therefore He killed him,
and [g]turned the kingdom over to David
the son of Jesse.

David Made King over All Israel

11 Then [a]all Israel came together to
David at Hebron, saying, "Indeed
we *are* your bone and your flesh. 2 Also, in
time past, even when Saul was king, you
were the one who led Israel out and
brought them in; and the LORD your [b]God
said to you, 'You shall [c]shepherd My people Israel, and be ruler over My people Israel.' " 3 Therefore all the elders of Israel
came to the king at Hebron, and David
made a covenant with them at Hebron before the LORD. And [d]they anointed David
king over Israel, according to the word of
the LORD [1]by [e]Samuel.

The City of David

4 And David and all Israel [f]went to Jerusalem, which is Jebus, [g]where the Jebusites
were, the inhabitants of the land. 5 But the
inhabitants of Jebus said to David, "You
shall not come in here!" Nevertheless David took the stronghold of Zion (that is, the
City of David). 6 Now David said, "Whoever attacks the Jebusites first shall be
[2]chief and captain." And Joab the son of
Zeruiah went up first, and became chief.
7 Then David dwelt in the stronghold;
therefore they called it [3]the City of David.
8 And he built the city around it, from [4]the
Millo to the surrounding area. Joab [5]re-
paired the rest of the city. 9 So David [h]went
on and became great, and the LORD of
hosts *was* with [i]him.

The Mighty Men of David

10 Now [j]these *were* the heads of the
mighty men whom David had, who
strengthened themselves with him in his
kingdom, with all Israel, to make him king,
according to [k]the word of the LORD concerning Israel.
11 And this *is* the number of the mighty
men whom David had: [l]Jashobeam the son
of a Hachmonite, [m]chief of [6]the captains;
he had lifted up his spear against three
hundred, killed *by him* at one time.
12 After him *was* Eleazar the son of
[n]Dodo, the Ahohite, who *was one* of the
three mighty men. 13 He was with David at
[7]Pasdammim. Now there the Philistines
were gathered for battle, and there was a
piece of ground full of barley. So the people fled from the Philistines. 14 But they
[8]stationed themselves in the middle of *that*
field, defended it, and killed the Philistines. So the LORD brought about a great
victory.
15 Now three of the thirty chief men
[o]went down to the rock to David, into the
cave of Adullam; and the army of the Philistines encamped [p]in the Valley of
[9]Rephaim. 16 David *was* then in the stronghold, and the garrison of the Philistines
was then in Bethlehem. 17 And David said
with longing, "Oh, that someone would
give me a drink of water from the well of
Bethlehem, which is by the gate!" 18 So the
three broke through the camp of the Philistines, drew water from the well of Bethlehem that *was* by the gate, and took *it* and
brought *it* to David. Nevertheless David
would not drink it, but poured it out to the
LORD. 19 And he said, "Far be it from me, O
my God, that I should do this! Shall I drink
the blood of these men *who have put* their
lives *in jeopardy?* For at the risk of their
lives they brought it." Therefore he would
not drink it. These things were done by the
three mighty men.
20 [q]Abishai the brother of Joab was chief
of *another* [1]three. He had lifted up his spear
against three hundred *men,* killed *them,*
and won a name among *these* three. 21 [r]Of
the three he was more honored than the
other two men. Therefore he became their
captain. However he did not attain to the
first three.
22 Benaiah was the son of Jehoiada, the

12 [d]2 Sam. 21:12
13 [e]1 Sam. 13:13, 14; 15:22-26 [f][Lev. 19:31; 20:6]; 1 Sam. 28:7 [4]Lit. *transgressed*
14 [g]1 Sam. 15:28; 2 Sam. 3:9, 10; 5:3; 1 Chr. 12:23

CHAPTER 11

1 [a]2 Sam. 5:1
2 [b]1 Sam. 16:1-3; Ps. 78:70-72 [c]2 Sam. 7:7
3 [d]2 Sam. 5:3 [e]1 Sam. 16:1, 4, 12, 13 [1]Lit. *by the hand of Samuel*
4 [f]2 Sam. 5:6 [g]Josh. 15:8, 63; Judg. 1:21; 19:10, 11
6 [2]Lit. *head*
7 [3]*Zion,* 2 Sam. 5:7
8 [4]Lit. *The Landfill* [5]Lit. *revived*
9 [h]2 Sam. 3:1 [i]1 Sam. 16:18
10 [j]2 Sam. 23:8 [k]1 Sam. 16:1, 12
11 [l]1 Chr. 27:2 [m]1 Chr. 12:18 [6]So with Qr.; Kt., LXX, Vg. *the thirty* (cf. 2 Sam. 23:8)
12 [n]1 Chr. 27:4
13 [7]*Ephes Dammim,* 1 Sam. 17:1
14 [8]Lit. *took their stand*
15 [o]2 Sam. 23:13 [p]2 Sam. 5:18; 1 Chr. 14:9 [9]Lit. *Giants*
20 [q]2 Sam. 23:18; 1 Chr. 18:12 [1]So with MT, LXX, Vg.; Syr. *thirty*
21 [r]2 Sam. 23:19

10:13,14 This summary is unique to 1 Chr. and provides the proper transition from Saul's kingship to David's reign.

10:14 He killed him. Though Saul killed himself (v. 4), God took responsibility for Saul's death, which was fully deserved for consulting a medium, an activity punishable by death (cf. Deut. 17:1-6). This demonstrates that human behavior is under the ultimate control of God, who achieves His purpose through the actions of people.

11:1–29:30 This section selectively recounts the reign of David with a heavy emphasis on the placement of the ark in Jerusalem and preparation to build the temple.

11:1-3 *See notes on 2 Sam. 5:1-3.*

11:4-9 *See notes on 2 Sam. 5:6-10.*

11:10-41 *See notes on 2 Sam. 23:8-39.*

11:11 Jashobeam...Hachmonite. In 27:2, he is called the son of Zabdiel, so Hachmon may be, strictly speaking, his grandfather (27:32). For a variation in name and number (300), *see note on 2 Sam. 23:8.* A copyist's error would best account for 800 being reported in 2 Sam. 23:8.

son of a valiant man from Kabzeel, who
[2]had done many deeds. [s]He had killed two
lion-like heroes of Moab. He also had gone
down and killed a lion in the midst of a pit
on a snowy day. **23** And he killed an Egyptian, a man of *great* height, [3]five cubits tall.
In the Egyptian's hand *there was* a spear
like a weaver's beam; and he went down
to him with a staff, wrested the spear out
of the Egyptian's hand, and killed him
with his own spear. **24** These *things* Benaiah the son of Jehoiada did, and won a
name among three mighty men. **25** Indeed
he was more honored than the thirty, but
he did not attain to the *first* three. And David appointed him over his guard.
26 Also the mighty warriors *were* [t]Asahel
the brother of Joab, Elhanan the son of
Dodo of Bethlehem, **27** [4]Shammoth the
Harorite, [u]Helez the [5]Pelonite, **28** [v]Ira the
son of Ikkesh the Tekoite, [w]Abiezer the
Anathothite, **29** [6]Sibbechai the Hushathite,
[7]Ilai the Ahohite, **30** [x]Maharai the Netophathite, [8]Heled the son of Baanah the
Netophathite, **31** [9]Ithai the son of Ribai of
Gibeah, of the sons of Benjamin, [y]Benaiah
the Pirathonite, **32** [1]Hurai of the brooks of
Gaash, [2]Abiel the Arbathite, **33** Azmaveth
the [3]Baharumite, Eliahba the Shaalbonite,
34 the sons of [4]Hashem the Gizonite, Jonathan the son of Shageh the Hararite,
35 Ahiam the son of [5]Sacar the Hararite,
[6]Eliphal the son of [7]Ur, **36** Hepher the Me-
cherathite, Ahijah the Pelonite, **37** [8]Hezro
the Carmelite, [9]Naarai the son of Ezbai,
38 Joel the brother of Nathan, Mibhar the
son of Hagri, **39** Zelek the Ammonite,
Naharai the [1]Berothite (the armorbearer of
Joab the son of Zeruiah), **40** Ira the Ithrite,
Gareb the Ithrite, **41** [z]Uriah the Hittite,
[2]Zabad the son of Ahlai, **42** Adina the son
of Shiza the Reubenite (a chief of the
Reubenites) and thirty with him, **43** Hanan
the son of Maachah, Joshaphat the Mith-
nite, **44** Uzzia the Ashterathite, Shama and
Jeiel the sons of Hotham the Aroerite, **45** Jediael the son of Shimri, and Joha his brother, the Tizite, **46** Eliel the Mahavite, Jeribai
and Joshaviah the sons of Elnaam, Ithmah
the Moabite, **47** Eliel, Obed, and Jaasiel the
Mezobaite.

22 [s]2 Sam. 23:20 [2]*was great in deeds*
23 [3]About 7½ feet
26 [t]2 Sam. 23:24
27 [u]2 Sam. 23:26; 1 Chr. 27:10 [4]*Shammah the Harodite,* 2 Sam. 23:25 [5]*Paltite,* 2 Sam. 23:26
28 [v]1 Chr. 27:9 [w]1 Chr. 27:12
29 [6]*Mebunnai,* 2 Sam. 23:27 [7]*Zalmon,* 2 Sam. 23:28
30 [x]1 Chr. 27:13 [8]*Heleb,* 2 Sam. 23:29, or *Heldai,* 1 Chr. 27:15
31 [y]1 Chr. 27:14 [9]*Ittai,* 2 Sam. 23:29
32 [1]*Hiddai,* 2 Sam. 23:30 [2]*Abi-Albon,* 2 Sam. 23:31
33 [3]*Barhumite,* 2 Sam. 23:31
34 [4]*Jashen,* 2 Sam. 23:32
35 [5]*Sharar,* 2 Sam. 23:33 [6]*Eliphelet,* 2 Sam. 23:34 [7]*Ahasbai,* 2 Sam. 23:34
37 [8]*Hezrai,* 2 Sam. 23:38 [9]*Paarai the Arbite,* 2 Sam. 23:35
39 [1]*Beerothite,* 2 Sam. 23:37
41 [z]2 Sam. 11 [2]The last sixteen are not added in 2 Sam. 23.

CHAPTER 12

1 [a]1 Sam. 27:2 [b]1 Sam. 27:6
2 [c]Judg. 3:15; 20:16
3 [1]Or *Hasmaah*
8 [d]2 Sam. 2:18 [2]Lit. *separated themselves to*
14 [e]1 Sam. 18:13
15 [f]Josh. 3:15; 4:18, 19
17 [3]Lit. *before them* [4]Lit. *violence*
18 [g]2 Sam. 17:25 [5]Lit. *clothed*

The Growth of David's Army

12 Now [a]these *were* the men who came
to David at [b]Ziklag while he was still
a fugitive from Saul the son of Kish; and
they *were* among the mighty men, helpers in
the war, **2** armed with bows, using both the
right hand and [c]the left in *hurling* stones
and *shooting* arrows with the bow. *They were*
of Benjamin, Saul's brethren.
3 The chief *was* Ahiezer, then Joash, the
sons of [1]Shemaah the Gibeathite; Jeziel
and Pelet the sons of Azmaveth; Berachah,
and Jehu the Anathothite; **4** Ishmaiah the
Gibeonite, a mighty man among the thirty,
and over the thirty; Jeremiah, Jahaziel, Johanan, and Jozabad the Gederathite; **5** Elu-
zai, Jerimoth, Bealiah, Shemariah, and
Shephatiah the Haruphite; **6** Elkanah, Jis-
shiah, Azarel, Joezer, and Jashobeam, the
Korahites; **7** and Joelah and Zebadiah the
sons of Jeroham of Gedor.
8 *Some* Gadites [2]joined David at the
stronghold in the wilderness, mighty men
of valor, men trained for battle, who could
handle shield and spear, whose faces *were
like* the faces of lions, and *were* [d]as swift as
gazelles on the mountains: **9** Ezer the first,
Obadiah the second, Eliab the third,
10 Mishmannah the fourth, Jeremiah the
fifth, **11** Attai the sixth, Eliel the seventh,
12 Johanan the eighth, Elzabad the ninth,
13 Jeremiah the tenth, and Machbanai the
eleventh. **14** These *were* from the sons of
Gad, captains of the army; the least was
over a hundred, and the greatest was over
a [e]thousand. **15** These *are* the ones who
crossed the Jordan in the first month, when
it had overflowed all its [f]banks; and they
put to flight all *those* in the valleys, to the
east and to the west.
16 Then some of the sons of Benjamin
and Judah came to David at the stronghold. **17** And David went out [3]to meet
them, and answered and said to them, "If
you have come peaceably to me to help
me, my heart will be united with you; but
if to betray me to my enemies, since *there is*
no [4]wrong in my hands, may the God of
our fathers look and bring judgment."
18 Then the Spirit [5]came upon [g]Amasai,
chief of the captains, *and he said:*

11:41-47 This adds new material to 2 Sam. 23.

12:1-40 These events predate those of 11:1-47. They are divided between David's time at Ziklag (12:1-22) and Hebron (12:23-40). They summarize the narrative covered in 1 Sam. 27–2 Sam. 5.

12:1 Ziklag. Located in the S near the Edomite border. The territory was ruled by the Philistines, who made David a ruler over it during the latter period of Saul's reign when he was pursuing David (1 Sam. 27:6,7). This was prior to David's taking the rule over all Israel (cf. v. 38).

12:1-14 Men from Benjamin (12:2,3,16-18), Gad (12:8-15), Judah (12:16-18), and Manasseh (12:19-22) came to help David conquer enemies on both sides of the Jordan (v. 15).

12:15 first month. Mar./Apr. when the Jordan River was at flood stage due to melting snow in the N. The Gadites would be crossing from E to W.

12:18 the Spirit. A temporary empowerment by the Holy Spirit to assure David that the Benjamites and Judahites were loyal to him and that the cause was blessed by God.

"*We are* yours, O David;
We *are* on your side, O son of Jesse!
Peace, peace to you,
And peace to your helpers!
For your God helps you."

So David received them, and made them captains of the troop.

19 And *some* from Manasseh defected to David [h]when he was going with the Philistines to battle against Saul; but they did not help them, for the lords of the Philistines sent him away by agreement, saying, [i]"He may defect to his master Saul *and endanger* our heads." 20 When he went to Ziklag, those of Manasseh who defected to him were Adnah, Jozabad, Jediael, Michael, Jozabad, Elihu, and Zillethai, captains of the thousands who *were* from Manasseh. 21 And they helped David against [j]the bands *of raiders,* for they *were* all mighty men of valor, and they were captains in the army. 22 For at *that* time they came to David day by day to help him, until *it was* a great army, [k]like the army of God.

David's Army at Hebron

23 Now these *were* the numbers of the [6]divisions *that were* equipped for war, *and* [l]came to David at [m]Hebron to [n]turn *over* the kingdom of Saul to him, [o]according to the word of the LORD: 24 of the sons of Judah bearing shield and spear, six thousand eight hundred [7]armed for war; 25 of the sons of Simeon, mighty men of valor fit for war, seven thousand one hundred; 26 of the sons of Levi four thousand six hundred; 27 Jehoiada, the leader of the Aaronites, and with him three thousand seven hundred; 28 [p]Zadok, a young man, a valiant warrior, and from his father's house twenty-two captains; 29 of the sons of Benjamin, relatives of Saul, three thousand (until then [q]the greatest part of them had remained loyal to the house of Saul); 30 of the sons of Ephraim twenty thousand eight hundred, mighty men of valor, [8]famous men throughout their father's house; 31 of the half-tribe of Manasseh eighteen thousand, who were designated by name to come and make David king; 32 of the sons of Issachar [r]who had understanding of the times, to know what Israel ought to do, their chiefs were two hundred; and all their brethren were at their command; 33 of Zebulun there were fifty thousand who went out to battle, expert in war with all weapons of war, [s]stouthearted men who could keep ranks; 34 of Naphtali one thousand captains, and with them thirty-seven thousand with shield and spear; 35 of the Danites who could keep battle formation, twenty-eight thousand six hundred; 36 of Asher, those who could go out to war, able to keep battle formation, forty thousand; 37 of the Reubenites and the Gadites and the half-tribe of Manasseh, from the other side of the Jordan, one hundred and twenty thousand armed for battle with every *kind* of weapon of war.

38 All these men of war, who could keep ranks, came to Hebron with a loyal heart, to make David king over all Israel; and all the rest of Israel *were* of [t]one mind to make David king. 39 And they were there with David three days, eating and drinking, for their brethren had prepared for them. 40 Moreover those who were near to them, from as far away as Issachar and Zebulun and Naphtali, were bringing food on donkeys and camels, on mules and oxen—provisions of flour and cakes of figs and cakes of raisins, wine and oil and oxen and sheep abundantly, for *there was* joy in Israel.

The Ark Brought from Kirjath Jearim

13 Then David consulted with the [a]captains of thousands and hundreds, *and* with every leader. 2 And David said to all the assembly of Israel, "If *it seems* good to you, and if it is of the LORD our God, let us send out to our brethren everywhere *who are* [b]left in all the land of Israel, and with them to the priests and Levites *who are* in their cities *and* their common-lands, that they may gather together to us; 3 and let us bring the ark of our God back to us, [c]for we have not inquired at it since the days of Saul." 4 Then all the assembly said that they would do so, for the thing was right in the eyes of all the people.

5 So [d]David gathered all Israel together,

19 [h] 1 Sam. 29:2 [i] 1 Sam. 29:4
21 [j] 1 Sam. 30:1, 9, 10
22 [k] Gen. 32:2; Josh. 5:13-15
23 [l] 2 Sam. 2:1-4 [m] 1 Chr. 11:1 [n] 1 Chr. 10:14 [o] 1 Sam. 16:1-4 [6] Lit. *heads of those*
24 [7] *equipped*
28 [p] 2 Sam. 8:17; 1 Chr. 6:8, 53
29 [q] 2 Sam. 2:8, 9
30 [8] Lit. *men of names*
32 [r] Esth. 1:13
33 [s] Ps. 12:2; [James 1:8]
38 [t] 2 Chr. 30:12

CHAPTER 13

1 [a] 1 Chr. 11:15; 12:34
2 [b] 1 Sam. 31:1; Is. 37:4
3 [c] 1 Sam. 7:1, 2
5 [d] 1 Sam. 7:5

12:19,20 First Samuel 29 provides the background.

12:21,22 First Samuel 30 provides the background.

12:23-37 This recounts the period of David's 7 year, 6 month reign in Hebron until he was crowned king of the entire nation and was ready to relocate in Jerusalem (2 Sam. 2–5). This narrative comes full circle back to 1 Chr. 11:1ff.

12:38-40 This feast was associated with the king's coronation in 2 Sam. 5.

13:1–16:43 This section recounts the ark of the covenant being brought from Kirjath-Jearim (v. 5) to Jerusalem.

13:1-14 *See notes on 2 Sam. 6:1-11.* First Chronicles 13:1-6 adds new material to the narrative.

13:3 the ark of our God. Not only had the ark been stolen and profaned by the Philistines (1 Sam. 5–6), but when it was returned, Saul neglected to seek God's instruction for it. Scripture records only one occasion when Saul sought God's ark after its return (cf. 1 Sam. 14:18).

from [e]Shihor in Egypt to as far as the entrance of Hamath, to bring the ark of God
[f]from Kirjath Jearim. 6 And David and all
Israel went up to [g]Baalah,[1] to Kirjath Jearim, which belonged to Judah, to bring up
from there the ark of God the LORD, [h]who
dwells *between* the cherubim, where *His*
name is proclaimed. 7 So they [2]carried the
ark of God [i]on a new cart [j]from the house
of Abinadab, and Uzza and Ahio drove the
cart. 8 Then [k]David and all Israel played
music before God with all *their* might, with
[3]singing, on harps, on stringed instruments, on tambourines, on cymbals, and
with trumpets.
9 And when they came to [4]Chidon's
threshing floor, Uzza put out his hand to
hold the ark, for the oxen [5]stumbled.
10 Then the anger of the LORD was aroused
against Uzza, and He struck him [l]because
he put his hand to the ark; and he [m]died
there before God. 11 And David became
angry because of the LORD's outbreak
against Uzza; therefore that place is called
[6]Perez Uzza to this day. 12 David was
afraid of God that day, saying, "How can I
bring the ark of God to me?"
13 So David would not move the ark
with him into the City of David, but took it
aside into the house of Obed-Edom the
Gittite. 14 [n]The ark of God remained with
the family of Obed-Edom in his house
three months. And the LORD blessed [o]the
house of Obed-Edom and all that he had.

David Established at Jerusalem

14 Now [a]Hiram king of Tyre sent messengers to David, and cedar trees,
with masons and carpenters, to build him
a house. 2 So David knew that the LORD
had established him as king over Israel, for
his kingdom was [b]highly exalted for the
sake of His people Israel.
3 Then David took more wives in Jerusalem, and David begot more sons and
daughters. 4 And [c]these are the names of
his children whom he had in Jerusalem:
[1]Shammua, Shobab, Nathan, Solomon,
5 Ibhar, [2]Elishua, [3]Elpelet, 6 Nogah,
Nepheg, Japhia, 7 Elishama, [4]Beeliada, and
Eliphelet.

The Philistines Defeated

8 Now when the Philistines heard that
[d]David had been anointed king over all Israel, all the Philistines went up to search
for David. And David heard *of it* and went
out against them. 9 Then the Philistines
went and made a raid [e]on the Valley of
[5]Rephaim. 10 And David [f]inquired of God,
saying, "Shall I go up against the Philistines? Will You deliver them into my
hand?"
The LORD said to him, "Go up, for I will
deliver them into your hand."
11 So they went up to Baal Perazim, and
David defeated them there. Then David
said, "God has broken through my enemies by my hand like a breakthrough of
water." Therefore they called the name of
that place [6]Baal Perazim. 12 And when
they left their gods there, David gave a
commandment, and they were burned
with fire.
13 [g]Then the Philistines once again made
a raid on the valley. 14 Therefore David inquired again of God, and God said to him,
"You shall not go up after them; circle
around them, [h]and come upon them in
front of the mulberry trees. 15 And it shall
be, when you hear a sound of marching in
the tops of the mulberry trees, then you
shall go out to battle, for God has gone out
before you to strike the camp of the Philistines." 16 So David did as God commanded him, and they drove back the
army of the Philistines from [7]Gibeon as far
as Gezer. 17 Then [i]the fame of David went
out into all lands, and the LORD [j]brought
the fear of him upon all nations.

The Ark Brought to Jerusalem

15 *David* built houses for himself in the
City of David; and he prepared a
place for the ark of God, [a]and pitched a
tent for it. 2 Then David said, "No one may

---

5 [e] Josh. 13:3 [f] 1 Sam. 6:21; 7:1, 2
6 [g] Josh. 15:9, 60 [h] Ex. 25:22; 1 Sam. 4:4; 2 Kin. 19:15 [1] *Baale Judah*, 2 Sam. 6:2
7 [i] Num. 4:15; 1 Sam. 6:7 [j] 1 Sam. 7:1 [2] Lit. *caused the ark of God to ride*
8 [k] 2 Sam. 6:5 [3] *songs*
9 [4] *Nachon*, 2 Sam. 6:6 [5] Or *let it go off*
10 [l] [Num. 4:15]; 1 Chr. 15:13, 15 [m] Lev. 10:2
11 [6] Lit. *Outburst Against Uzza*
14 [n] 2 Sam. 6:11 [o] [Gen. 30:27]; 1 Chr. 26:4-8

CHAPTER 14

1 [a] 2 Sam. 5:11; 1 Kin. 5:1
2 [b] Num. 24:7
4 [c] 1 Chr. 3:5-8 [1] *Shimea*, 1 Chr. 3:5
5 [2] *Elishama*, 1 Chr. 3:6 [3] *Eliphelet*, 1 Chr. 3:6
7 [4] *Eliada*, 2 Sam. 5:6; 1 Chr. 3:8
8 [d] 2 Sam. 5:17-21
9 [e] Josh. 17:15; 18:16; 1 Chr. 11:15; 14:13 [5] Lit. *Giants*
10 [f] 1 Sam. 23:2, 4; 30:8; 2 Sam. 2:1; 5:19, 23; 21:1
11 [6] Lit. *Master of Breakthroughs*
13 [g] 2 Sam. 5:22-25
14 [h] 2 Sam. 5:23
16 [7] *Geba*, 2 Sam. 5:25
17 [i] Josh. 6:27; 2 Chr. 26:8 [j] [Ex. 15:14-16; Deut. 2:25; 11:25]; 2 Chr. 20:29

CHAPTER 15

1 [a] 1 Chr. 16:1

13:5 Shihor. The "river of Egypt" was a small stream flowing into the Mediterranean, which forms the southern boundary of Israel (cf. Josh. 13:3). It is also called the "Brook of Egypt" (Josh. 15:4,47; Num. 34:5; 2 Chr. 7:8). **Hamath.** On the northern boundary of Israel's territory. **Kirjath Jearim.** A location approximately 10 mi. W of Jerusalem that the Canaanites called Baalah (cf. 13:6). The ark of God had resided here for the previous 20 years (cf. 1 Sam. 7:1,2).

13:7-14 *See notes on 2 Sam. 6:1-11.* The violation of divine directives (Num. 4:1-49) for moving the ark proved fatal to Uzza(h) (vv. 7-10).

14:1-7 *See notes on 2 Sam. 5:11-16.* The events of this chapter took place before those of 1 Chr. 13.

14:3-7 This is a repeat of 1 Chr. 3:5-9.

14:8-17 The Philistines desired to ruin David before the throne was consolidated. Their plan was to kill David, but God gave him victory over the Philistines (unlike Saul) and thus declared both to the Philistines and Israel His support of Israel's new king. For details, *see notes on 2 Sam. 5:17-23.*

14:12 gods...burned. Second Samuel 5:21 reports that the idols were carried away, presenting an apparent contradiction. Most likely the idols were first carried away and then burned later, according to the Mosaic law (cf. Deut. 7:5,25).

15:1-29 The chronicler picks up the narrative concerning the ark where it left off at 1 Chr. 13:14, as David brings the ark from Obed-Edom.

15:1 ***David* built houses for himself.** He was able by the alliance and help of Hiram (18:1) to build a palace for himself and separate

carry the [b]ark of God but the Levites, for
[c]the LORD has chosen them to carry the ark
of God and to minister before Him forever." 3 And David [d]gathered all Israel together at Jerusalem, to bring up the ark of
the LORD to its place, which he had prepared for it. 4 Then David assembled the
children of Aaron and the Levites: 5 of the
sons of Kohath, Uriel the chief, and one
hundred and twenty of his [1]brethren; 6 of
the sons of Merari, Asaiah the chief, and
two hundred and twenty of his brethren;
7 of the sons of Gershom, Joel the chief,
and one hundred and thirty of his
brethren; 8 of the sons of [e]Elizaphan, Shemaiah the chief, and two hundred of his
brethren; 9 of the sons of [f]Hebron, Eliel the
chief, and eighty of his brethren; 10 of the
sons of Uzziel, Amminadab the chief, and
one hundred and twelve of his brethren.

11 And David called for [g]Zadok and
[h]Abiathar the priests, and for the Levites:
for Uriel, Asaiah, Joel, Shemaiah, Eliel, and
Amminadab. 12 He said to them, "You *are*
the heads of the fathers' *houses* of the
Levites; [2]sanctify yourselves, you and
your brethren, that you may bring up the
ark of the LORD God of Israel to *the place* I
have prepared for it. 13 For [i]because you
did not *do it* the first *time,* [j]the LORD our
God broke out against us, because we did
not consult Him [3]about the proper order."

14 So the priests and the Levites [4]sancti-
fied themselves to bring up the ark of the
LORD God of Israel. 15 And the children of
the Levites bore the ark of God on their
shoulders, by its poles, as [k]Moses had
commanded according to the word of the
LORD.

16 Then David spoke to the leaders of the
Levites to appoint their brethren *to be* the
singers accompanied by instruments of
music, stringed instruments, harps, and
cymbals, by raising the voice with resounding joy. 17 So the Levites appointed
[l]Heman the son of Joel; and of his brethren,
[m]Asaph the son of Berechiah; and of their

2 [b][Num. 4:15]; 2 Sam. 6:1-11 [c]Num. 4:2-15; Deut. 10:8; 31:9
3 [d]Ex. 40:20, 21; 2 Sam. 6:12; 1 Kin. 8:1; 1 Chr. 13:5
5 [1]*kinsmen*
8 [e]Ex. 6:22
9 [f]Ex. 6:18
11 [g]2 Sam. 8:17; 15:24-29, 35, 36; 18:19, 22, 27; 19:11; 20:25; 1 Chr. 12:28 [h]1 Sam. 22:20-23; 23:6; 30:7; 1 Kin. 2:22, 26, 27; Mark 2:6
12 [2]*consecrate*
13 [i]2 Sam. 6:3 [j]1 Chr. 13:7-11 [3]*regarding the ordinance*
14 [4]*consecrated*
15 [k]Ex. 25:14; Num. 4:15; 7:9
17 [l]1 Chr. 6:33; 25:1 [m]1 Chr. 6:39

[n]1 Chr. 6:44
18 [5]So with MT, Vg.; LXX omits *Ben*
20 [o]Ps. 46:title [6]*Jaaziel,* v. 18
21 [p]Ps. 6:title
24 [q][Num. 10:8]; Ps. 81:3 [r]1 Chr. 13:13, 14
25 [s]2 Sam. 6:12, 13; 1 Kin. 8:1
27 [t]1 Sam. 2:18, 28
28 [u]Num. 23:21; Josh. 6:20; 1 Chr. 13:8; Zech. 4:7; 1 Thess. 4:16
29 [v]1 Sam. 18:20, 27; 19:11-17; 2 Sam. 3:13, 14; 6:16, 20-23

brethren, the sons of Merari, [n]Ethan the
son of Kushaiah; 18 and with them their
brethren of the second *rank:* Zechariah,
[5]Ben, Jaaziel, Shemiramoth, Jehiel, Unni,
Eliab, Benaiah, Maaseiah, Mattithiah,
Elipheleh, Mikneiah, Obed-Edom, and Jeiel, the gatekeepers; 19 the singers, Heman,
Asaph, and Ethan, *were* to sound the cymbals of bronze; 20 Zechariah, [6]Aziel, Shemiramoth, Jehiel, Unni, Eliab, Maaseiah,
and Benaiah, with strings according to
[o]Alamoth; 21 Mattithiah, Elipheleh, Mikneiah, Obed-Edom, Jeiel, and Azaziah, to
direct with harps on the [p]Sheminith;
22 Chenaniah, leader of the Levites, was instructor *in charge of* the music, because he
was skillful; 23 Berechiah and Elkanah *were*
doorkeepers for the ark; 24 Shebaniah,
Joshaphat, Nethanel, Amasai, Zechariah,
Benaiah, and Eliezer, the priests, [q]were to
blow the trumpets before the ark of God;
and [r]Obed-Edom and Jehiah, doorkeepers
for the ark.

25 So [s]David, the elders of Israel, and the
captains over thousands went to bring up
the ark of the covenant of the LORD from
the house of Obed-Edom with joy. 26 And
so it was, when God helped the Levites
who bore the ark of the covenant of the
LORD, that they offered seven bulls and
seven rams. 27 David was clothed with a
robe of fine [t]linen, as were all the Levites
who bore the ark, the singers, and Chenaniah the music master *with* the singers. David also wore a linen ephod. 28 [u]Thus all
Israel brought up the ark of the covenant
of the LORD with shouting and with the
sound of the horn, with trumpets and with
cymbals, making music with stringed instruments and harps.

29 And it happened, [v]*as* the ark of the
covenant of the LORD came to the City of
David, that Michal, Saul's daughter,
looked through a window and saw King
David whirling and playing music; and
she despised him in her heart.

houses for his wives and their children. While the ark remained near Jerusalem at the home of Obed-Edom for 3 months (13:13-14), David constructed a new tabernacle in Jerusalem to fulfill God's Word in Deut. 12:5-7 of a permanent residency.

15:2 carry the ark. After a lapse of 3 months (13:14), David followed the Mosaic directives for moving the ark (cf. Num. 4:1-49; Deut. 10:8; 18:5). These directions had been violated when the ark was moved from Kirjath-Jearim to Obed-Edom, and it cost Uzza(h) his life (cf. 13:6-11).

15:4-7 Kohath...Merari...Gershom. David conducted the ark's relocation with the same families as had Moses (cf. Num. 4). In the restoration from Babylon, these identical 3 divisions of Levi participated (cf. 1 Chr. 6:1-48).

15:11 Zadok...Abiathar. These two High-Priests, children of Aaron, heads of the two priestly houses of Eleazar and Ithamar, were colleagues in the high-priesthood (2 Sam. 20:25). They served the Lord simultaneously in David's reign. Zadok attended the tabernacle in Gibeon (1 Chr. 16:39), while Abiathar served the temporary place of the ark in Jerusalem. Ultimately, Zadok prevailed (cf. 1 Kin. 2:26,27).

15:12 sanctify yourselves. This was a special sanctification required on all special occasions, demanding complete cleanliness.

15:13 broke out. God's anger "broke out" when the ark had been improperly handled and transported by Uzza(h) (2 Sam. 6:6-8; 1 Chr. 13:9-12).

15:16-24 Eminent Levites were instructed to train the musicians and singers for the solemn procession.

15:25–16:3 *See notes on 2 Sam. 6:12-19.*

The Ark Placed in the Tabernacle

16 So [a]they brought the ark of God,
and set it in the midst of the tabernacle that David had erected for it. Then
they offered burnt offerings and peace offerings before God. 2 And when David had
finished offering the burnt offerings and
the peace offerings, [b]he blessed the people
in the name of the LORD. 3 Then he distributed to everyone of Israel, both man and
woman, to everyone a loaf of bread, a piece
of meat, and a cake of raisins.
4 And he appointed some of the Levites
to minister before the ark of the LORD, to
[c]commemorate, to thank, and to praise the
LORD God of Israel: 5 Asaph the chief, and
next to him Zechariah, *then* [d]Jeiel, Shemiramoth, Jehiel, Mattithiah, Eliab, Benaiah,
and Obed-Edom: Jeiel with stringed instruments and harps, but Asaph made
music with cymbals; 6 Benaiah and Jahaziel the priests regularly *blew* the trumpets
before the ark of the covenant of God.

David's Song of Thanksgiving

7 On that day [e]David [f]first delivered *this*
psalm into the hand of Asaph and his
brethren, to thank the LORD:

8 [g]Oh, give thanks to the LORD!
Call upon His name;
Make known His deeds among the
peoples!
9 Sing to Him, sing psalms to Him;
Talk of all His wondrous works!
10 Glory in His holy name;
Let the hearts of those rejoice who
seek the LORD!
11 Seek the LORD and His strength;
Seek His face evermore!
12 Remember His marvelous works
which He has done,
His wonders, and the judgments of
His mouth,
13 O seed of Israel His servant,
You children of Jacob, His chosen
ones!

14 He *is* the LORD our God;
His [h]judgments *are* in all the earth.
15 Remember His covenant forever,
The word which He commanded,
for a thousand generations,
16 *The* [i]*covenant which* He made with
Abraham,
And His oath to Isaac,
17 And [j]confirmed it to [k]Jacob for a
statute,
To Israel *for* an everlasting
covenant,
18 Saying, "To you I will give the land
of Canaan
As the allotment of your
inheritance,"
19 When you were [l]few in number,
Indeed very few, and strangers
in it.

20 When they went from one nation
to another,
And from *one* kingdom to another
people,
21 He permitted no man to do them
wrong;
Yes, He [m]rebuked kings for their
sakes,
22 *Saying,* [n]"Do not touch My
anointed ones,
And do My prophets no harm."

23 [o]Sing to the LORD, all the earth;
Proclaim the good news of His
salvation from day to day.
24 Declare His glory among the
nations,
His wonders among all peoples.

25 For the LORD *is* great and greatly to
be praised;
He *is* also to be feared above all
gods.
26 For all the gods [p]of the peoples *are*
[1]idols,
But the LORD made the heavens.
27 Honor and majesty *are* before Him;
Strength and gladness are in His
place.

28 Give to the LORD, O families of the
peoples,
Give to the LORD glory and
strength.
29 Give to the LORD the glory *due* His
name;
Bring an offering, and come before
Him.
Oh, worship the LORD in the
beauty of holiness!
30 Tremble before Him, all the earth.
The world also is firmly
established,
It shall not be moved.

31 Let the heavens rejoice, and let the
earth be glad;

CHAPTER 16
1 [a] 2 Sam. 6:17; 1 Chr. 15:1
2 [b] 1 Kin. 8:14
4 [c] Ps. 38:title; 70:title
5 [d] 1 Chr. 15:18
7 [e] 2 Sam. 22:1; 23:1 [f] Ps. 105:1-15
8 [g] 1 Chr. 17:19, 20; Ps. 105:1-15
14 [h] Ps. 48:10; [Is. 26:9]
16 [i] Gen. 17:2; 26:3; 28:13; 35:11
17 [j] Gen. 35:11, 12 [k] Gen. 28:10-15
19 [l] Gen. 34:30; Deut. 7:7
21 [m] Gen. 12:17; 20:3; Ex. 7:15-18
22 [n] Gen. 20:7; Ps. 105:15
23 [o] Ps. 96:1-13
26 [p] Lev. 19:4; [1 Cor. 8:5, 6] [1] *worthless things*

16:4-6 Levites...minister. As soon as the ark was placed into its tent, the Levites began their duties.

16:7-22 *See notes on Ps. 105:1-15.*

16:23-33 *See notes on Ps. 96:1-13.*

And let them say among the
nations, "The LORD reigns."
32 Let the sea roar, and all its fullness;
Let the field rejoice, and all that *is*
in it.
33 Then the [q]trees of the woods shall
rejoice before the LORD,
For He is [r]coming to judge the
earth.

34 [s]Oh, give thanks to the LORD, for *He*
is good!
For His mercy *endures* forever.
35 [t]And say, "Save us, O God of our
salvation;
Gather us together, and deliver us
from the Gentiles,
To give thanks to Your holy name,
To triumph in Your praise."

36 [u]Blessed *be* the LORD God of Israel
From everlasting to everlasting!

And all [v]the people said, "Amen!" and
praised the LORD.

Regular Worship Maintained

37 So he left [w]Asaph and his brothers
there before the ark of the covenant of the
LORD to minister before the ark regularly,
as every day's work [x]required; 38 and
[y]Obed-Edom with his sixty-eight
brethren, including Obed-Edom the son
of Jeduthun, and Hosah, *to be* gatekeepers; 39 and Zadok the priest and his
brethren the priests, [z]before the tabernacle of the LORD [a]at the [2]high place that
was at Gibeon, 40 to offer burnt offerings
to the LORD on the altar of burnt offering
regularly [b]morning and evening, and *to*
do according to all that is written in the
Law of the LORD which He commanded
Israel; 41 and with them Heman and Jeduthun and the rest who were chosen,
who were designated by name, to give
thanks to the LORD, [c]because His mercy
endures forever; 42 and with them Heman
and Jeduthun, to sound aloud with trumpets and cymbals and the musical instruments of God. Now the sons of Jeduthun
were gatekeepers.
43 [d]Then all the people departed, every
man to his house; and David returned to
bless his house.

33 [q] Is. 55:12, 13 [r] [Joel 3:1-14]; Zech. 14:1-14; [Matt. 25:31-46]
34 [s] 2 Chr. 5:13; 7:3; Ezra 3:11; Ps. 106:1; 107:1; 118:1; 136:1; Jer. 33:11
35 [t] Ps. 106:47, 48
36 [u] 1 Kin. 8:15, 56; Ps. 72:18 [v] Deut. 27:15; Neh. 8:6
37 [w] 1 Chr. 16:4, 5 [x] 2 Chr. 8:14; Ezra 3:4
38 [y] 1 Chr. 13:14
39 [z] 1 Chr. 21:29; 2 Chr. 1:3 [a] 1 Kin. 3:4 [2] Place for pagan worship
40 [b] [Ex. 29:38-42; Num. 28:3, 4]
41 [c] 1 Chr. 25:1-6; 2 Chr. 5:13; 7:3; Ezra 3:11; Jer. 33:11
43 [d] 2 Sam. 6:18-20

CHAPTER 17

1 [a] 2 Sam. 7:1; 1 Chr. 14:1
4 [b] [1 Chr. 28:2, 3]
7 [c] 1 Sam. 16:11-13 [1] *leader*
8 [2] *given you prestige*
9 [d] [Deut. 30:1-9; Jer. 16:14-16; 23:5-8; 24:6; Ezek. 37:21-27]; Amos 9:14
10 [3] Royal dynasty
11 [e] 1 Kin. 2:10; 1 Chr. 29:28 [f] 1 Kin. 5:5; 6:12; 8:19-21; [1 Chr. 22:9-13; 28:20]; Matt. 1:6; Luke 3:31 [4] Die and join your ancestors
12 [g] 1 Kin. 6:38; 2 Chr. 6:2; [Ps. 89:20-37]
13 [h] 2 Sam. 7:14, 15; Matt. 3:17; Mark 1:11; Luke 3:22; 2 Cor. 6:18; Heb. 1:5 [i] [1 Sam. 15:23-28]; 1 Chr. 10:14
14 [j] Ps. 89:3, 4; Matt. 19:28; 25:31; [Luke 1:31-33]

God's Covenant with David

17 Now [a]it came to pass, when David
was dwelling in his house, that David said to Nathan the prophet, "See now,
I dwell in a house of cedar, but the ark of
the covenant of the LORD *is* under tent curtains."
2 Then Nathan said to David, "Do all
that *is* in your heart, for God *is* with you."
3 But it happened that night that the
word of God came to Nathan, saying,
4 "Go and tell My servant David, 'Thus
says the LORD: "You shall [b]not build Me a
house to dwell in. 5 For I have not dwelt in
a house since the time that I brought up Israel, even to this day, but have gone from
tent to tent, and from *one* tabernacle *to an-*
other. 6 Wherever I have moved about with
all Israel, have I ever spoken a word to any
of the judges of Israel, whom I commanded to shepherd My people, saying, 'Why
have you not built Me a house of
cedar?' " ' 7 Now therefore, thus shall you
say to My servant David, 'Thus says the
LORD of hosts: "I took you [c]from the sheepfold, from following the sheep, to be [1]ruler
over My people Israel. 8 And I have been
with you wherever you have gone, and
have cut off all your enemies from before
you, and have [2]made you a name like the
name of the great men who *are* on the
earth. 9 Moreover I will appoint a place for
My people Israel, and will [d]plant them,
that they may dwell in a place of their own
and move no more; nor shall the sons of
wickedness oppress them anymore, as previously, 10 since the time that I commanded judges *to be* over My people Israel. Also
I will subdue all your enemies. Furthermore I tell you that the LORD will build you
a [3]house. 11 And it shall be, when your
days are [e]fulfilled, when you must [4]go *to*
be with your fathers, that I will set up your
[f]seed after you, who will be of your sons;
and I will establish his kingdom. 12 [g]He
shall build Me a house, and I will establish
his throne forever. 13 [h]I will be his Father,
and he shall be My son; and I will not take
My mercy away from him, [i]as I took *it*
from *him* who was before you. 14 And [j]I
will establish him in My house and in My
kingdom forever; and his throne shall be
established forever." ' "
15 According to all these words and ac-

16:34-36 *See notes on Ps. 106:1,47,48.*

16:37-42 regularly…every day's work. The ministry was established with continuity.

16:39 Gibeon. Located 6 mi. NW of Jerusalem.

17:1-27 This section recounts God's bestowing the Davidic Covenant. For a full explanation, *see notes on 2 Sam. 7.*

17:1,10 Second Samuel 7:1,11 adds that God had and would give David rest from all of his enemies.

17:5 Second Samuel 7:14-17 adds new material.

cording to all this vision, so Nathan spoke
to David.
16 [k]Then King David went in and sat before the LORD; and he said: "Who *am* I, O
LORD God? And what is my house, that
You have brought me this far? 17 And *yet*
this was a small thing in Your sight, O
God; and You have *also* spoken of Your servant's house for a great while to come, and
have regarded me according to the rank of
a man of high degree, O LORD God.
18 What more can David *say* to You for the
honor of Your servant? For You know Your
servant. 19 O LORD, for Your servant's sake,
and according to Your own heart, You have
done all this greatness, in making known
all these great things. 20 O LORD, *there is*
none like You, nor *is there any* God besides
You, according to all that we have heard
with our ears. 21 [l]And who *is* like Your
people Israel, the one nation on the earth
whom God went to redeem for Himself *as*
a people—to make for Yourself a name by
great and awesome deeds, by driving out
nations from before Your people whom
You redeemed from Egypt? 22 For You
have made Your people Israel Your very
own people forever; and You, LORD, have
become their God.
23 "And now, O LORD, the word which
You have spoken concerning Your servant
and concerning his house, *let it* be established forever, and do as You have said.
24 So let it be established, that Your name
may be magnified forever, saying, 'The
LORD of hosts, the God of Israel, *is* Israel's
God.' And let the house of Your servant
David be established before You. 25 For
You, O my God, [5]have revealed to Your
servant that You will build him a house.
Therefore Your servant has found it *in his*
heart to pray before You. 26 And now, LORD,
[6]You are God, and have promised this
goodness to Your servant. 27 Now You
have been pleased to bless the house of
Your servant, that it may continue before
You forever; for You have blessed it, O
LORD, and *it shall be* blessed forever."

16 [k] 2 Sam. 7:18
21 [l] [Deut. 4:6-8, 33-38]; Ps. 147:20
25 [5] Lit. *have uncovered the ear of*
26 [6] Or *You alone are*

CHAPTER 18

1 [a] 2 Sam. 8:1-18 [1] Lit. *struck*
2 [b] 2 Sam. 8:2; Zeph. 2:9 [c] Ps. 60:8 [2] Lit. *struck*
3 [d] 2 Sam. 8:3 [3] Lit. *struck* [4] Heb. *Hadarezer*
4 [5] *seven hundred,* 2 Sam. 8:4 [6] *crippled*
5 [e] 2 Sam. 8:5, 6; 1 Kin. 11:23-25
8 [f] 2 Sam. 8:8 [g] 1 Kin. 7:15, 23; 2 Chr. 4:12, 15, 16 [7] *Betah,* 2 Sam. 8:8 [8] *Berothai,* 2 Sam. 8:8 [9] Heb. *Hadarezer* [1] *Great laver or basin*
9 [2] *Toi,* 2 Sam. 8:9, 10 [3] Lit. *struck*
10 [h] 2 Sam. 8:10-12 [4] *Joram,* 2 Sam. 8:10 [5] Lit. *struck*
11 [i] 2 Sam. 10:14 [j] 2 Sam. 5:17-25 [k] 2 Sam. 1:1
12 [l] 2 Sam. 23:18; 1 Chr. 2:16 [m] 2 Sam. 8:13 [6] *Syrians,* 2 Sam. 8:13

David's Further Conquests

18 After this [a]it came to pass that David [1]attacked the Philistines, subdued them, and took Gath and its towns
from the hand of the Philistines. 2 Then he
[2]defeated [b]Moab, and the Moabites became David's [c]servants, *and* brought tribute.
3 And [d]David [3]defeated [4]Hadadezer
king of Zobah *as far as* Hamath, as he went
to establish his power by the River Euphrates. 4 David took from him one thousand chariots, [5]seven thousand horsemen,
and twenty thousand foot soldiers. Also
David [6]hamstrung all the chariot *horses*,
except that he spared enough of them for
one hundred chariots.
5 When the [e]Syrians of Damascus came
to help Hadadezer king of Zobah, David
killed twenty-two thousand of the Syrians.
6 Then David put *garrisons* in Syria of Damascus; and the Syrians became David's
servants, *and* brought tribute. So the LORD
preserved David wherever he went. 7 And
David took the shields of gold that were on
the servants of Hadadezer, and brought
them to Jerusalem. 8 Also from [7]Tibhath
and from [8]Chun, cities of [9]Hadadezer, David brought a large amount of [f]bronze,
with which [g]Solomon made the bronze
[1]Sea, the pillars, and the articles of bronze.
9 Now when [2]Tou king of Hamath heard
that David had [3]defeated all the army of
Hadadezer king of Zobah, 10 he sent [4]Ha-
doram his son to King David, to greet him
and bless him, because he had fought
against Hadadezer and [5]defeated him (for
Hadadezer had been at war with Tou); and
Hadoram brought with him all kinds of [h]arti-
cles of gold, silver, and bronze. 11 King David also dedicated these to the LORD, along
with the silver and gold that he had
brought from all *these* nations—from
Edom, from Moab, from the [i]people of
Ammon, from the [j]Philistines, and from
[k]Amalek.
12 Moreover [l]Abishai the son of Zeruiah
killed [m]eighteen thousand [6]Edomites in

18:1–21:30 This section selectively recounts David's military exploits.

18:1-11 *See notes on 2 Sam. 8:1-12.*

18:2 Second Samuel 8:2 adds details to the judgment of Moab.

18:4 The numbers here are correct; the number in 2 Sam. 8:4 for the horsemen is 700, which would not seem as consistent with the other numbers, so the 700 probably resulted from a copyist's error.

18:11 Second Samuel 8:12 adds new material.

18:12 Second Samuel 8:13 adds that David was involved.

For an exposition of the details and significance of the Davidic Covenant, see the notes on 2 Samuel 7.

The Davidic Covenant in Chronicles

1.	1 Chr. 17:7-27	God to Nathan to David
2.	1 Chr. 22:6-16	David to Solomon
3.	1 Chr. 28:6,7	David to Solomon
4.	2 Chr. 6:8,9,16,17	Solomon to the nation
5.	2 Chr. 7:17,18	God to Solomon
6.	2 Chr. 13:4,5	Abijah to Jeroboam
7.	2 Chr. 21:7	Chronicle's commentary

the Valley of Salt. 13 [n]He also put garrisons in Edom, and all the Edomites became David's servants. And the LORD preserved David wherever he went.

David's Administration

14 So David reigned over all Israel, and administered judgment and justice to all his people. 15 Joab the son of Zeruiah *was* over the army; Jehoshaphat the son of Ahilud *was* recorder; 16 Zadok the son of Ahitub and [7]Abimelech the son of Abiathar *were* the priests; [8]Shavsha *was* the scribe; 17 [o]Benaiah the son of Jehoiada *was* over the Cherethites and the Pelethites; and David's sons *were* [9]chief ministers at the king's side.

The Ammonites and Syrians Defeated

19 It[a] happened after this that Nahash the king of the people of Ammon died, and his son reigned in his place. 2 Then David said, "I will show kindness to Hanun the son of Nahash, because his father showed kindness to me." So David sent messengers to comfort him concerning his father. And David's servants came to Hanun in the land of the people of Ammon to comfort him.

3 And the princes of the people of Ammon said to Hanun, [1]"Do you think that David really honors your father because he has sent comforters to you? Did his servants not come to you to search and to overthrow and to spy out the land?" 4 Therefore Hanun took David's servants, shaved them, and cut off their garments [2]in the middle, at their [b]buttocks, and sent them away. 5 Then *some* went and told David about the men; and he sent to meet them, because the men were greatly ashamed. And the king said, "Wait at Jericho until your beards have grown, and *then* return."

6 When the people of Ammon saw that they had made themselves repulsive to David, Hanun and the people of Ammon sent a thousand talents of silver to hire for themselves chariots and horsemen from [3]Mesopotamia, from Syrian Maacah, [c]and from [4]Zobah. 7 So they hired for themselves thirty-two thousand chariots, with the king of Maacah and his people, who came and encamped before Medeba. Also the people of Ammon gathered together from their cities, and came to battle.

8 Now when David heard *of it,* he sent Joab and all the army of the mighty men. 9 Then the people of Ammon came out and put themselves in battle array before the gate of the city, and the kings who had come *were* by themselves in the field.

10 When Joab saw that the battle line was against him before and behind, he chose some of Israel's best, and put *them* in battle array against the Syrians. 11 And the rest of the people he put under the command of Abishai his brother, and they set *themselves* in battle array against the people of Ammon. 12 Then he said, "If the Syrians are too strong for me, then you shall help me; but if the people of Ammon are too strong for you, then I will help you. 13 Be of good courage, and let us be strong for our people and for the cities of our God. And may the LORD do *what is* good in His sight."

14 So Joab and the people who *were* with him drew near for the battle against the Syrians, and they fled before him. 15 When the people of Ammon saw that the Syrians were fleeing, they also fled before Abishai his brother, and entered the city. So Joab went to Jerusalem.

16 Now when the Syrians saw that they had been defeated by Israel, they sent messengers and brought the Syrians who were beyond [5]the River, and [6]Shophach the commander of Hadadezer's army *went* before them. 17 When it was told David, he gathered all Israel, crossed over the Jordan and came upon them, and set up in battle array against them. So when David had set up in *battle* array against the Syrians, they fought with him. 18 Then the Syrians fled before Israel; and David killed [7]seven thousand charioteers and forty thousand [8]foot soldiers of the Syrians, and killed Shophach the commander of the army. 19 And when the servants of Hadadezer saw that they were defeated by Israel, they made peace with David and became his servants. So the Syrians were not willing to help the people of Ammon anymore.

Rabbah Is Conquered

20 It[a] happened [1]in the spring of the year, at the time kings go out *to battle,* that Joab led out the armed forces and ravaged the country of the people of Ammon, and came and besieged Rabbah.

13 [n]Gen. 27:29-40; Num. 24:18; 2 Sam. 8:14
16 [7]*Ahimelech,* 2 Sam. 8:17 [8]*Seraiah,* 2 Sam. 8:17, or *Shisha,* 1 Kin. 4:3
17 [o]2 Sam. 8:18 [9]Lit. *at the hand of the king*

CHAPTER 19

1 [a]1 Sam. 11:1; 2 Sam. 10:1-19
3 [1]Lit. *In your eyes is David honoring your father because*
4 [b]Is. 20:4 [2]*in half*
6 [c]1 Chr. 18:5, 9 [3]Heb. *Aram Naharaim* [4]*Zoba,* 2 Sam. 10:6
16 [5]The Euphrates [6]*Zoba,* 2 Sam. 10:6, or *Shobach,* 2 Sam. 10:16
18 [7]*seven hundred,* 2 Sam. 10:18 [8]*horsemen,* 2 Sam. 10:18

CHAPTER 20

1 [a]2 Sam. 11:1 [1]Lit. *at the return of the year*

18:13 *See notes on 2 Sam. 8:14.*

18:14-17 *See notes on 2 Sam. 8:15-18.*

19:1-19 *See notes on 2 Sam. 10:1-19.*

19:18 seven thousand. Second Samuel 10:18 erroneously has 700; this is apparently a discrepancy due to copyist error. **foot soldiers.** This is likely more correct than "horsemen" in 2 Sam. 10:18.

20:1-3 *See notes on 2 Sam. 11:1; 12:29-31.* The chronicler was not inspired by God to mention David's sin with Bathsheba and subsequent sins recorded in 2 Sam. 11:2–12:23. The adultery and murder occurred at this time, while David stayed in Jerusalem instead of going to battle. The story was likely omitted because the book was written to focus on God's permanent interest in His people, Israel, and the perpetuity of David's kingdom.

But [b]David stayed at Jerusalem. And [c]Joab
defeated Rabbah and overthrew it. 2 Then
David [d]took their king's crown from his
head, and found it to weigh a talent of
gold, and *there were* precious stones in it.
And it was set on David's head. Also he
brought out the [2]spoil of the city in great
abundance. 3 And he brought out the people who *were* in it, and [3]put *them* to work
with saws, with iron picks, and with axes.
So David did to all the cities of the people
of Ammon. Then David and all the people
returned *to* Jerusalem.

Philistine Giants Destroyed

4 Now it happened afterward [e]that war
broke out at [4]Gezer with the Philistines, at
which time [f]Sibbechai the Hushathite
killed [5]Sippai, *who was one* of the sons of
[6]the giant. And they were subdued.
5 Again there was war with the Philistines, and Elhanan the son of [7]Jair killed
Lahmi the brother of Goliath the Gittite,
the shaft of whose spear *was* like a
weaver's [g]beam.
6 Yet again [h]there was war at Gath,
where there was a man of *great* stature,
with twenty-four fingers and toes, six *on
each hand* and six *on each foot;* and he also
was born to [8]the giant. 7 So when he defied
Israel, Jonathan the son of [9]Shimea, David's brother, killed him.
8 These were born to the giant in Gath,
and they fell by the hand of David and by
the hand of his servants.

The Census of Israel and Judah

21 Now [a]Satan stood up against Israel,
and moved David to [1]number Israel. 2 So David said to Joab and to the
leaders of the people, "Go, number Israel
from Beersheba to Dan, [b]and bring the
number of them to me that I may know *it.*"
3 And Joab answered, "May the LORD
make His people a hundred times more
than they are. But, my lord the king, *are*
they not all my lord's servants? Why then
does my lord require this thing? Why
should he be a cause of guilt in Israel?"
4 Nevertheless the king's word prevailed against Joab. Therefore Joab departed and went throughout all Israel and
came to Jerusalem. 5 Then Joab gave the
sum of the number of the people to David.
All Israel *had* one million one hundred
thousand men who drew the sword, and
Judah *had* four hundred and seventy thousand men who drew the sword. 6 [c]But he
did not count Levi and Benjamin among
them, for the king's [2]word was abominable to Joab.
7 And [3]God was displeased with this
thing; therefore He struck Israel. 8 So David said to God, [d]"I have sinned greatly,
because I have done this thing; [e]but now, I
pray, take away the iniquity of Your servant, for I have done very foolishly."
9 Then the LORD spoke to Gad, David's
[f]seer, saying, 10 "Go and tell David, [g]say-
ing, 'Thus says the LORD: "I offer you three
things; choose one of them for yourself,
that I may do *it* to you." ' "
11 So Gad came to David and said to
him, "Thus says the LORD: 'Choose for
yourself, 12 [h]either [4]three years of famine,
or three months to be defeated by your
foes with the sword of your enemies
overtaking *you,* or else for three days the
sword of the LORD—the plague in the land,
with the [5]angel of the LORD destroying

1 [b] 2 Sam. 11:2–12:25 [c] 2 Sam. 12:26
2 [d] 2 Sam. 12:30, 31 [2] *plunder*
3 [3] LXX *cut them with*
4 [e] 2 Sam. 21:18 [f] 1 Chr. 11:29 [4] *Gob,* 2 Sam. 21:18 [5] *Saph,* 2 Sam. 21:18 [6] Or *Raphah*
5 [g] 1 Sam. 17:7; 1 Chr. 11:23 [7] *Jaare-Oregim,* 2 Sam. 21:19
6 [h] 1 Sam. 5:8; 2 Sam. 21:20 [8] Or *Raphah*
7 [9] *Shammah,* 1 Sam. 16:9 or *Shimeah,* 2 Sam. 21:21

CHAPTER 21

1 [a] 2 Sam. 24:1-25; Job 1:6 [1] *take a census of*
2 [b] 1 Chr. 27:23, 24
6 [c] 1 Chr. 27:24 [2] *command*
7 [3] Lit. *it was evil in the eyes of God*
8 [d] 2 Sam. 24:10 [e] 2 Sam. 12:13
9 [f] 1 Sam. 9:9; 2 Kin. 17:13; 1 Chr. 29:29; 2 Chr. 16:7, 10; Is. 30:9, 10; Amos 7:12, 13
10 [g] 2 Sam. 24:12-14
12 [h] 2 Sam. 24:13 [4] *seven,* 2 Sam. 24:13 [5] Or *Angel,* and so throughout the chapter

---

20:4-8 *See notes on 2 Sam. 21:15-22.* The chronicler chose not to write of some of the darker days in David's reign, especially the revolt of David's son Absalom, for the same reason the iniquity of the king with Bathsheba was left out.

21:1 There is approximately a 20-year gap between 20:8 and 21:1, ca. 995–975 B.C.

21:1-27 For the explanation of this section, *see notes on 2 Sam. 24:1-25.*

21:1 Satan…moved. Second Samuel 24:1 reports that it was God who "moved" David. This apparent discrepancy is resolved by understanding that God sovereignly and permissively uses Satan to achieve His purposes. God uses Satan to judge sinners (cf. Mark 4:15; 2 Cor. 4:4), to refine saints (cf. Job 1:8–2:10; Luke 22:31,32), to discipline those in the church (cf. 1 Cor. 5:1-5; 1 Tim. 1:20), and to further purify obedient believers (cf. 2 Cor. 12:7-10). Neither God nor Satan forced David to sin (cf. James 1:13-15), but God allowed Satan to tempt David and he chose to sin. The sin surfaced his proud heart and God dealt with him for it. **number Israel.** David's census brought tragedy because, unlike the census in Moses' time (Num. 1, 2) which God had commanded, this census by David was to gratify his pride in the great strength of his army and consequent military power. He was also putting more trust in his forces than in his God. He was taking credit for his victories by the building of his great army. This angered God, who moved Satan to bring the sin to a head.

21:3,4 a cause of guilt in Israel. Joab knew David was operating on a sinful motive, but the king's arrogance led him to ignore the warning.

21:5 one million one hundred thousand. Second Samuel 24:9 reports 800,000 and 500,000 respectively. For the resolution of this discrepancy, *see notes on 2 Sam. 24:9.*

21:6 he did not count Levi and Benjamin. Levites were not soldiers (v. 5) and were not numbered in the Mosaic census (Num. 1:47-55). Benjamin had already been numbered (7:6-11) and the register preserved in the archives of that tribe. From the course followed in the census (2 Sam. 24:4-8), it appears Judah and Benjamin were last to be visited. Before the census could be finished in Judah and begin in Benjamin, David recognized his sin and called for it to stop (cf. 27:24).

21:7 He struck Israel. David's sin dramatically affected the entire kingdom in experiencing God's wrath.

21:12 "Three years" here is correct; "7 years" in 2 Sam. 24:13 is most likely a copyist's error, since it seems 3 years, 3 months, 3 days is the intent.

throughout all the territory of Israel.' Now
consider what answer I should take back
to Him who sent me."
13 And David said to Gad, "I am in great
distress. Please let me fall into the hand of
the LORD, for His [i]mercies *are* very great;
but do not let me fall into the hand of
man."
14 So the LORD sent a [j]plague upon Israel,
and seventy thousand men of Israel fell.
15 And God sent [6]an [k]angel to Jerusalem to
destroy it. As [7]he was destroying, the LORD
looked and [l]relented of the disaster, and
said to the angel who was destroying, "It is
enough; now restrain [8]your hand." And
the angel of the LORD stood by the [m]thresh-
ing floor of [9]Ornan the Jebusite.
16 Then David lifted his eyes and [n]saw
the angel of the LORD standing between
earth and heaven, having in his hand a
drawn sword stretched out over Jerusalem. So David and the elders, clothed in
sackcloth, fell on their faces. 17 And David
said to God, "Was it not I who commanded the people to be numbered? I am the
one who has sinned and done evil indeed;
but these [o]sheep, what have they done?
Let Your hand, I pray, O LORD my God, be
against me and my father's house, but not
against Your people that they should be
plagued."
18 Therefore, the [p]angel of the LORD
commanded Gad to say to David that David should go and erect an altar to the
LORD on the threshing floor of Ornan the
Jebusite. 19 So David went up at the word
of Gad, which he had spoken in the name
of the LORD. 20 Now Ornan turned and saw
the angel; and his four sons *who were* with
him hid themselves, but Ornan continued
threshing wheat. 21 So David came to
Ornan, and Ornan looked and saw David.
And he went out from the threshing floor,
and bowed before David with *his* face to
the ground. 22 Then David said to Ornan,
[1]"Grant me the place of *this* threshing
floor, that I may build an altar on it to the
LORD. You shall grant it to me at the full
price, that the plague may be withdrawn
from the people."
23 But Ornan said to David, "Take *it* to
yourself, and let my lord the king do *what*
is good in his eyes. Look, I *also* give *you* the
oxen for burnt offerings, the threshing implements for wood, and the wheat for the
grain offering; I give *it* all."
24 Then King David said to Ornan, "No,
but I will surely buy *it* for the full price, for
I will not take what is yours for the LORD,
nor offer burnt offerings with *that which*
costs *me* nothing." 25 So [q]David gave
Ornan six hundred shekels of gold by
weight for the place. 26 And David built
there an altar to the LORD, and offered
burnt offerings and peace offerings, and
called on the LORD; and [r]He answered him
from heaven by fire on the altar of burnt
offering.
27 So the LORD commanded the angel,
and he returned his sword to its sheath.
28 At that time, when David saw that the
LORD had answered him on the threshing
floor of Ornan the Jebusite, he sacrificed
there. 29 [s]For the tabernacle of the LORD
and the altar of the burnt offering, which
Moses had made in the wilderness, *were* at
that time at the high place in [t]Gibeon.
30 But David could not go before it to inquire of God, for he was afraid of the
sword of the angel of the LORD.

David Prepares to Build the Temple

22 Then David said, [a]"This *is* the
house of the LORD God, and this *is*

13 [i]Ps. 51:1; 130:4,7 **14** [j]1 Chr. 27:24 **15** [k]2 Sam. 24:16 [l]Gen. 6:6 [m]2 Chr. 3:1 [6]Or *the Angel* [7]Or *He* [8]Or *Your* [9]*Araunah*, 2 Sam. 24:16, 18-24 **16** [n]Josh. 5:13; 2 Chr. 3:1 **17** [o]2 Sam. 7:8; Ps. 74:1 **18** [p]1 Chr. 21:11, 12; 2 Chr. 3:1

22 [1]Lit. *Give* **25** [q]2 Sam. 24:24 **26** [r]Lev. 9:24; Judg. 6:21; 1 Kin. 18:36-38; 2 Chr. 3:1; 7:1 **29** [s]1 Kin. 3:4; 2 Chr. 1:3 [t]1 Chr. 16:39

CHAPTER 22

1 [a]Deut. 12:5; 2 Sam. 24:18; 1 Chr. 21:18, 19, 26, 28; 2 Chr. 3:1

21:15 Ornan. This is a Heb. name. He is called Araunah in 2 Sam. 24:18, a Jebusite or Canaanite equivalent. He had been converted to worship the true God.

21:16 This additional detail does not appear in the Heb. of 2 Sam. 24. The "angel of the LORD" was the executioner poised to destroy Jerusalem, whose menacing destruction was halted (v. 27) because David and the leaders repented as indicated by the "sackcloth" and falling "on their faces."

21:20,21 This additional detail does not appear in the Heb. of 2 Sam. 24. "Threshing wheat" was done by spreading the grain out on a high level area and driving back and forth over it with a heavy sled and rollers pulled by oxen. One would drive the oxen while others raked the chaff away from the kernels.

21:25 six hundred shekels. The 50 shekels reported in 2 Sam. 24:24 was for the instruments and oxen alone, while the price here includes the whole property, Mt. Moriah, on which the future temple stood. The threshing floor of Ornan is today believed to be the very flat rock under the Moslem mosque, the Dome of the Rock, inside the temple ground in Jerusalem.

21:28-30 This also is new data not included in 2 Sam. 24.

21:29 high place…Gibeon. The ark of the covenant resided at Jerusalem in a tent (1 Chr. 15) awaiting the building of the temple on Ornan's threshing floor, while the Mosaic tabernacle and altar remained in Gibeon until the temple was completed (cf. 1 Kin. 8:4).

21:30 the sword. Cf. 21:12,16,27. David continued to remain at the threshing floor and offer sacrifices because the Lord had appeared to him there (2 Chr. 3:1) and thus hallowed the place, and because he feared a menacing angel at Gibeon, the center of worship.

22:1–29:20 This section recounts David's preparations for Solomon to build the temple. General preparation and various charges are discussed in 22:1-19. The division of labor unfolds in 23:1–27:33. Solomon's final commission comes in 28:1–29:20.

22:1-19 David gives 3 charges to: 1) the workman (vv. 2-5); 2) Solomon (vv. 6-16); and 3) the leaders (vv. 17-19).

22:1 house. The land David had just purchased (21:22-30), he dedicated for the Jerusalem temple to be built by Solomon (v. 6; 28:9,10).

the altar of burnt offering for Israel.” 2 So
David commanded to gather the [b]aliens
who *were* in the land of Israel; and he appointed masons to [c]cut hewn stones to
build the house of God. 3 And David prepared iron in abundance for the nails of the
doors of the gates and for the joints, and
bronze in abundance [d]beyond measure,
4 and cedar trees in abundance; for the [e]Si-
donians and those from Tyre brought
much cedar wood to David.
5 Now David said, [f]“Solomon my son *is*
young and inexperienced, and the house to
be built for the LORD *must be* exceedingly
magnificent, famous and glorious throughout all countries. I will now make preparation for it.” So David made abundant
preparations before his death.
6 Then he called for his son Solomon,
and [1]charged him to build a house for the
LORD God of Israel. 7 And David said to
Solomon: “My son, as for me, [g]it was in
my mind to build a house [h]to the name of
the LORD my God; 8 but the word of the
LORD came to me, saying, [i]‘You have shed
much blood and have made great wars;
you shall not build a house for My name,
because you have shed much blood on the
earth in My sight. 9 [j]Behold, a son shall be
born to you, who shall be a man of rest;
and I will give him [k]rest from all his enemies all around. His name shall be [2]Sol-
omon, for I will give peace and quietness
to Israel in his days. 10 [l]He shall build a
house for My name, and [m]he shall be My
son, and I *will be* his Father; and I will establish the throne of his kingdom over Israel forever.’ 11 Now, my son, may [n]the
LORD be with you; and may you prosper,
and build the house of the LORD your
God, as He has said to you. 12 Only may
the LORD [o]give you wisdom and understanding, and give you charge concerning
Israel, that you may keep the law of the
LORD your God. 13 [p]Then you will prosper, if you take care to fulfill the statutes
and judgments with which the LORD
[3]charged Moses concerning Israel. [q]Be
strong and of good courage; do not fear
nor be dismayed. 14 Indeed I have taken
much trouble to prepare for the house of
the LORD one hundred thousand talents of
gold and one million talents of silver, and
bronze and iron [r]beyond measure, for it is
so abundant. I have prepared timber and
stone also, and you may add to them.
15 Moreover *there are* workmen with you
in abundance: woodsmen and stonecutters, and all types of skillful men for every
kind of work. 16 Of gold and silver and
bronze and iron *there is* no limit. Arise and
begin working, and [s]the LORD be with
you.”
17 David also commanded all the [t]lead-
ers of Israel to help Solomon his son, *saying*, 18 “*Is* not the LORD your God with
you? [u]And has He *not* given you rest on
every side? For He has given the inhabitants of the land into my hand, and the
land is subdued before the LORD and before His people. 19 Now set your heart and
your soul to seek the LORD your God.
Therefore arise and build the sanctuary of
the LORD God, to [v]bring the ark of the
covenant of the LORD and the holy articles
of God into the house that is to be built
[w]for the name of the LORD.”

2 [b] 1 Kin. 9:20, 21; 2 Chr. 2:17, 18 [c] 1 Kin. 5:17, 18
3 [d] 1 Kin. 7:47; 1 Chr. 22:14
4 [e] 1 Kin. 5:6-10
5 [f] 1 Kin. 3:7; 1 Chr. 29:1, 2
6 [1] *commanded*
7 [g] 2 Sam. 7:1, 2; 1 Kin. 8:17; 1 Chr. 17:1; 28:2 [h] Deut. 12:5, 11
8 [i] 2 Sam. 7:5-13; 1 Kin. 5:3; 1 Chr. 28:3
9 [j] 1 Chr. 28:5 [k] 1 Kin. 4:20, 25; 5:4 [2] Lit. *Peaceful*
10 [l] 2 Sam. 7:13; 1 Kin. 5:5; 6:38; 1 Chr. 17:12, 13; 28:6; 2 Chr. 6:2 [m] Heb. 1:5
11 [n] 1 Chr. 22:16
12 [o] 1 Kin. 3:9-12; 2 Chr. 1:10
13 [p] [Josh. 1:7, 8]; 1 Chr. 28:7 [q] [Deut. 31:7, 8; Josh. 1:6, 7, 9; 1 Chr. 28:20] [3] *commanded*
14 [r] 1 Chr. 22:3
16 [s] 1 Chr. 22:11
17 [t] 1 Chr. 28:1-6
18 [u] Deut. 12:10; Josh. 22:4; 2 Sam. 7:1; [1 Kin. 5:4; 8:56]
19 [v] 1 Kin. 8:1-11; 2 Chr. 5:2-14 [w] 1 Kin. 5:3

22:2 aliens. These were non-Israelite artisans made up of descendants of the Canaanites (2 Chr. 8:7-10) and war captives (2 Chr. 2:7), for whom the Mosaic legislation provided compassion and protection (cf. Ex. 22:21; 23:9; Lev. 19:33; Deut. 24:14,15) and from whom service was exacted. Only here were the laborers called "aliens" (cf. 1 Kin. 5:13-18).

22:3 iron...bronze. David would have acquired the iron technology from the Philistines (1 Sam. 13:19-21) and the bronze would have come from spoils of war (cf. 18:8).

22:4 cedar. This came from Lebanon, the heavily wooded and mountainous country N of Israel, and was provided by the residents of Sidon and Tyre, most likely under the leadership of David's friend, King Hiram (cf. 14:1; 1 Kin. 5:1).

22:5 young. Solomon was born early in David's reign (ca. 1000–990 B.C.) and was at this time 20 to 30 years of age. The magnificent and complex challenge of building such a monumental edifice with all its elements required an experienced leader for preparation. **magnificent.** David understood that the temple needed to reflect on earth something of God's heavenly majesty, so he devoted himself to the collection of the plans and materials, tapping the vast amount of spoils from people he had conquered and cities he had sacked (vv. 14-16).

22:6-16 Here is David's careful instruction to Solomon for the building which David could not do because he had killed so many in his battles (v. 8). Cf. 1 Kin. 5:3.

22:8-10 David reflects on the covenant God had made with him (cf. 2 Sam. 7; 1 Chr. 17), which included 1) the divine mandate that Solomon build the temple and 2) overtones of the messianic reign.

22:11-13 David's spiritual charge to Solomon resembles the Lord's exhortation to Joshua (cf. Josh. 1:6-9). Solomon asked God for and received the very "wisdom and understanding" his father, David, desired for him (cf. 2 Chr. 1:7-12; 1 Kin. 3:3-14). He learned the value of such spiritual counsel and passed it on in Eccl. 12:1,13.

22:14 one hundred thousand...gold. Assuming a talent weighed about 75 lbs., this would be approximately 750 tons, a staggering amount of gold. **one million.** This would be approximately 37,500 tons of silver.

22:17-19 Knowing that Solomon was young and inexperienced (22:5) and that he could not undertake this colossal project alone, David wisely enlisted the loyalty and help of his leaders to transfer their allegiance to Solomon who would carry out the divine will and the last wishes of his father. The Lord undertook to make Solomon the wisest man on earth (cf. 1 Kin. 3:3-14).

The Divisions of the Levites

23 So when David was old and full of
days, he made his son [a]Solomon
king over Israel.
2 And he gathered together all the leaders of Israel, with the priests and the
Levites. 3 Now the Levites were numbered
from the age of [b]thirty years and above;
and the number of individual males was
thirty-eight thousand. 4 Of these, twenty-
four thousand *were* to [c]look after the work
of the house of the LORD, six thousand *were*
[d]officers and judges, 5 four thousand *were*
gatekeepers, and four thousand [e]praised
the LORD with *musical* instruments,
[f]"which I made," *said David,* "for giving
praise."

CHAPTER 23

1 [a]1 Kin. 1:33-40; 1 Chr. 28:4, 5
3 [b]Num. 4:1-3
4 [c]2 Chr. 2:2, 18; Ezra 3:8, 9 [d]Deut. 16:18-20
5 [e]1 Chr. 15:16 [f]2 Chr. 29:25-27
6 [g]Ex. 6:16; Num. 26:57; 2 Chr. 8:14 [1]*groups*
7 [h]1 Chr. 26:21 [2]*Libni,* Ex. 6:17
10 [3]LXX, Vg. *Zizah* and v. 11
12 [i]Ex. 6:18

6 Also [g]David separated them into [1]divi-
sions among the sons of Levi: Gershon,
Kohath, and Merari.
7 Of the [h]Gershonites: [2]Laadan and
Shimei. 8 The sons of Laadan: the first Jehiel, then Zetham and Joel—three *in all.*
9 The sons of Shimei: Shelomith, Haziel,
and Haran—three *in all.* These were the
heads of the fathers' *houses* of Laadan.
10 And the sons of Shimei: Jahath, [3]Zina,
Jeush, and Beriah. These *were* the four sons
of Shimei. 11 Jahath was the first and Zizah
the second. But Jeush and Beriah did not
have many sons; therefore they were assigned as one father's house.
12 [i]The sons of Kohath: Amram, Izhar,
Hebron, and Uzziel—four *in all.* 13 The

23:1–27:34 This labor-intensive project needed more than building materials. David marshaled his human resources and announced their division of labor as follows: 1) the Levites (23:1-32); 2) the priests (24:1-31); 3) the singers (25:1-31); 4) the gatekeepers (26:1-19); 5) the administrators (26:20-32); 6) the army (27:1-24); and 7) the leaders (27:25-34). Remember, the original readers of Chronicles were the Jews, who returned from exile in Babylon and were rebuilding the destroyed temple. This would remind them of what their fathers' sin forfeited, and how inferior their new temple was.

23:1 he made. For fuller narrative of Solomon's coronation and the attempts to seize his throne, *see 1 Kin. 1:1–2:9; 1 Chr. 28,29.*

23:3 thirty years and above. Numbers 4:3 establishes the age of recognized priests from 30 to 50 years of age. A 5 year apprenticeship began at 25 (cf. Num. 8:24), and in some cases 20 (1 Chr. 23:24,27). This number, 38,000, is 4 times greater than the early census in Moses' time (cf. Num. 4,26).

23:4 look after. The duties of these Levites are discussed in 1 Chr. 24. **officers and judges.** This particular function is covered in 1 Chr. 26:20-32.

23:5 gatekeepers. First Chronicles 26:1-19 gives information on them. **praised.** First Chronicles 25 identifies and describes these musicians. **which I made.** David, a gifted musician, was not only the maker, but the inventor of musical instruments (cf. Amos 6:5).

23:6 divisions. The Levites were divided among the 3 groups with distinct duties, just as they were in Moses' day (Num. 3:14-37) and in Ezra's day (1 Chr. 6:16-30). The family of Gershon (23:7-11), Kohath (27:12-20), and Merari (27:21-23) are each discussed.

Temple Duties

Administrative Duties	Supervisors	1 Chronicles 23:4,5
	Baliffs	1 Chronicles 23:4,5
	Judges	1 Chronicles 23:4,5
	Public administrators	1 Chronicles 26:29,30
Ministerial Duties	Priests	1 Chronicles 24:1,2
	Prophets	1 Chronicles 25:1
	Assistants for sacrifices	1 Chronicles 23:29-31
	Assistants for purification ceremonies	1 Chronicles 23:27,28
Service Duties	Bakers of the Bread of the Presence	1 Chronicles 23:29
	Those who checked the weights and measures	1 Chronicles 23:29
	Custodians	1 Chronicles 23:28
Financial Duties	Those who cared for the treasury	1 Chronicles 26:20
	Those who cared for dedicated items	1 Chronicles 26:26-28
Artistic Duties	Musicians	1 Chronicles 25:6
	Singers	1 Chronicles 25:7
Protective Duties	Temple guards	1 Chronicles 23:5
	Guards for the gates and storehouses	1 Chronicles 26:12-18
Individual Assignments	Recording secretary	1 Chronicles 24:6
	Chaplain to the king	1 Chronicles 25:4
	Private prophet to the king	1 Chronicles 25:2
	Captain of the guard	1 Chronicles 26:1
	Chief officer of the treasury	1 Chronicles 26:23,24

sons of [j]Amram: Aaron and Moses; and
[k]Aaron was set apart, he and his sons forever, that he should [4]sanctify the most
holy things, [l]to burn incense before the
LORD, [m]to minister to Him, and [n]to give
the blessing in His name forever. 14 Now
[o]the sons of Moses the man of God were
reckoned to the tribe of Levi. 15 [p]The sons
of Moses *were* [5]Gershon and Eliezer. 16 Of
the sons of Gershon, [q]Shebuel[6] *was* the
first. 17 Of the descendants of Eliezer, [r]Re-
habiah was the first. And Eliezer had no
other sons, but the sons of Rehabiah were
very many. 18 Of the sons of Izhar, [s]She-
lomith *was* the first. 19 [t]Of the sons of Hebron, Jeriah *was* the first, Amariah the second, Jahaziel the third, and Jekameam the
fourth. 20 Of the sons of Uzziel, Michah
was the first and Jesshiah the second.

21 [u]The sons of Merari *were* Mahli and
Mushi. The sons of Mahli *were* Eleazar and
[v]Kish. 22 And Eleazar died, and [w]had no
sons, but only daughters; and their [7]breth-
ren, the sons of Kish, [x]took them *as wives.*
23 [y]The sons of Mushi *were* Mahli, Eder,
and Jeremoth—three *in all.*

24 These *were* the sons of [z]Levi by their
fathers' houses—the heads of the fathers'
houses as they were counted individually
by the number of their names, who did the
work for the service of the house of the
LORD, from the age of [a]twenty years and
above.

25 For David said, "The LORD God of Israel [b]has given rest to His people, that they
may dwell in Jerusalem forever"; 26 and
also to the Levites, "They shall no longer
[c]carry the tabernacle, or any of the articles
for its service." 27 For by the [d]last words of
David the Levites *were* numbered from
twenty years old and above; 28 because
their duty *was* to help the sons of Aaron in
the service of the house of the LORD, in the
courts and in the chambers, in the purifying of all holy things and the work of the
service of the house of God, 29 both with
[e]the showbread and [f]the fine flour for the
grain offering, with [g]the unleavened cakes
and [h]*what is baked in* the pan, with what is
mixed and with all kinds of [i]measures and
sizes; 30 to stand every morning to thank
and praise the LORD, and likewise at
evening; 31 and at every presentation of a
burnt offering to the LORD [j]on the Sabbaths
and on the New Moons and on the [k]set[8]
feasts, by number according to the ordinance governing them, regularly before
the LORD; 32 and that they should [l]attend
to the [m]needs of the tabernacle of meeting,
the needs of the holy *place,* and the [n]needs
of the sons of Aaron their brethren in the
work of the house of the LORD.

The Divisions of the Priests

24 Now *these are* the divisions of the
sons of Aaron. [a]The sons of Aaron
were Nadab, Abihu, Eleazar, and Ithamar.
2 And [b]Nadab and Abihu died before their
father, and had no children; therefore Eleazar and Ithamar ministered as priests.
3 Then David with Zadok of the sons of Eleazar, and [c]Ahimelech of the sons of Ithamar, divided them according to the schedule of their service.

4 There were more leaders found of the
sons of Eleazar than of the sons of Ithamar,
and *thus* they were divided. Among the
sons of Eleazar *were* sixteen heads of *their*
fathers' houses, and eight heads of their fathers' houses among the sons of Ithamar.
5 Thus they were divided by lot, one group
as another, for there were officials of the
sanctuary and officials *of the house* of God,
from the sons of Eleazar and from the sons
of Ithamar. 6 And the scribe, Shemaiah the
son of Nethanel, *one of* the Levites, wrote

13 [j]Ex. 6:20 [k]Ex. 28:1; Heb. 5:4 [l]Ex. 30:7; 1 Sam. 2:28 [m][Deut. 21:5] [n]Num. 6:23 [4]*consecrate*
14 [o]1 Chr. 26:20-24
15 [p]Ex. 18:3, 4 [5]Heb. *Gershom,* 1 Chr. 6:16
16 [q]1 Chr. 26:24 [6]*Shubael,* 1 Chr. 24:20
17 [r]1 Chr. 26:25
18 [s]1 Chr. 24:22
19 [t]1 Chr. 24:23
21 [u]1 Chr. 24:26 [v]1 Chr. 24:29
22 [w]1 Chr. 24:28 [x]Num. 36:6 [7]*kinsmen*
23 [y]1 Chr. 24:30
24 [z]Num. 10:17, 21 [a]Num. 1:3; Ezra 3:8
25 [b]1 Chr. 22:18
26 [c]Num. 4:5, 15; 7:9; Deut. 10:8
27 [d]2 Sam. 23:1
29 [e]Ex. 25:30 [f]Lev. 6:20 [g]Lev. 2:1, 4 [h]Lev. 2:5, 7 [i]Lev. 19:35
31 [j]Num. 10:10 [k]Lev. 23:2-4 [8]*appointed feasts*
32 [l]2 Chr. 13:10, 11 [m][Num. 1:53]; 1 Chr. 9:27 [n]Num. 3:6-9, 38

CHAPTER 24

1 [a]Lev. 10:1-6; Num. 26:60, 61; 1 Chr. 6:3
2 [b]Num. 3:1-4; 26:61
3 [c]1 Chr. 18:16

23:24,27 twenty years. *See note on 23:3.*

23:25-32 The duties of the non-priestly Levites are enumerated in their duties to provide the temple service in support of the priests who descended from Levi, through Kohath, through Aaron, through Eleazar and Ithamar (cf. 1 Chr. 6:1-3). The original duties of the 3 families are given specifically in Num. 3:25,31,36,37.

24:1-31 The divisions and duties of the priests are outlined. Temple worship was carefully structured, without hindering the Holy Spirit or true worship (cf. 1 Cor. 14:40).

24:1 Nadab, Abihu. Consult Lev. 10:1-3 for their disgrace and demise. **Eleazar.** The line of the High-Priest would be through Eleazar's offspring in accord with the priestly covenant made by God with Phinehas (Num. 25:11-13).

24:3 Zadok. *See notes on 1 Chr. 6:8,49-53.* **Ahimelech.** This was the son of Abiathar whom Solomon released from his duties for siding with Adonijah (cf. 1 Kin. 1,2) and the grandson of another Ahimelech, who was a priest killed by Saul (1 Sam. 22:11-18). Second Samuel 8:17 confirms the Zadok and Ahimelech high-priestly combination, one at Jerusalem where the ark was kept and the other at Gibeon serving the tabernacle. *See notes on 1 Chr. 15:11.*

24:4-19 Priesthood duties were divided up in David's day into 24 divisions, 16 of Eleazar and 8 of Ithamar. The reasons Eleazar's family had twice as many divisions were that: 1) he had received the birthright since his older brothers, Nadab and Abihu, had been killed (Lev. 10); 2) he had more descendants; and 3) his descendants had more leadership ability. These divisions each served for either 1) two week periods annually or, more likely, 2) a one month period every two years (cf. 27:1-15). These divisions appear again in Neh. 10:2-8; 12:1-7; 12:12-21. These divisions extended even into the time of Christ (cf. Luke 1:5-9). The rest of the time they ministered to people in their own hometowns.

24:5 divided by lot. The ancient method of discerning God's will (cf. Prov. 16:33; Acts. 1:26) was used to sort out all the duties, so that all cause for pride or jealousy was mitigated (cf. v. 31; 26:13).

them down before the king, the leaders,
Zadok the priest, Ahimelech the son of
Abiathar, and the heads of the fathers'
houses of the priests and Levites, one father's house taken for Eleazar and *one* for
Ithamar.
7 Now the first lot fell to Jehoiarib, the second to Jedaiah, 8 the third to Harim, the
fourth to Seorim, 9 the fifth to Malchijah, the
sixth to Mijamin, 10 the seventh to Hakkoz,
the eighth to [d]Abijah, 11 the ninth to Jeshua,
the tenth to Shecaniah, 12 the eleventh to
Eliashib, the twelfth to Jakim, 13 the thirteenth to Huppah, the fourteenth to Jeshebe-
ab, 14 the fifteenth to Bilgah, the sixteenth to
Immer, 15 the seventeenth to Hezir, the eighteenth to [1]Happizzez, 16 the nineteenth to
Pethahiah, the twentieth to [2]Jehezekel,
17 the twenty-first to Jachin, the twenty-second to Gamul, 18 the twenty-third to Delaiah, the twenty-fourth to Maaziah.
19 This *was* the schedule of their service
[e]for coming into the house of the LORD according to their ordinance by the hand of
Aaron their father, as the LORD God of Israel had commanded him.

Other Levites

20 And the rest of the sons of Levi: of the
sons of Amram, [3]Shubael; of the sons of
Shubael, Jehdeiah. 21 Concerning [f]Reha-
biah, of the sons of Rehabiah, the first *was*
Isshiah. 22 Of the Izharites, [4]Shelomoth; of
the sons of Shelomoth, Jahath. 23 Of the
sons [5]*of* [g]*Hebron*, Jeriah [5]*was the first*, Amariah the second, Jahaziel the third, *and* Jekameam the fourth. 24 *Of* the sons of Uzziel,
Michah; of the sons of Michah, Shamir.
25 The brother of Michah, Isshiah; of the
sons of Isshiah, Zechariah. 26 [h]The sons of
Merari *were* Mahli and Mushi; the son of
Jaaziah, Beno. 27 The sons of Merari by Jaaziah *were* Beno, Shoham, Zaccur, and Ibri.
28 Of Mahli: Eleazar, [i]who had no sons.
29 Of Kish: the son of Kish, Jerahmeel.
30 Also [j]the sons of Mushi *were* Mahli,
Eder, and Jerimoth. These *were* the sons of
the Levites according to their fathers'
houses.
31 These also cast lots just as their brothers the sons of Aaron did, in the presence
of King David, Zadok, Ahimelech, and the
heads of the fathers' *houses* of the priests
and Levites. The chief fathers *did* just as
their younger brethren.

The Musicians

25 Moreover David and the captains of
the army separated for the service
some of the sons of [a]Asaph, of Heman, and
of Jeduthun, who *should* prophesy with
harps, stringed instruments, and cymbals.
And the number of the skilled men performing their service was: 2 Of the sons of
Asaph: Zaccur, Joseph, Nethaniah, and
[1]Asharelah; the sons of Asaph *were* [2]under
the direction of Asaph, who prophesied according to the order of the king. 3 Of [b]Je-
duthun, the sons of Jeduthun: Gedaliah,
[3]Zeri, Jeshaiah, [4]Shimei, Hashabiah, and
Mattithiah, [5]six, under the direction of
their father Jeduthun, who prophesied
with a harp to give thanks and to praise
the LORD. 4 Of Heman, the sons of Heman:
Bukkiah, Mattaniah, [6]Uzziel, [7]Shebuel,
[8]Jerimoth, Hananiah, Hanani, Eliathah,
Giddalti, Romamti-Ezer, Joshbekashah,
Mallothi, Hothir, *and* Mahazioth. 5 All
these *were* the sons of Heman the king's
seer in the words of God, to [9]exalt his
[c]horn. For God gave Heman fourteen sons
and three daughters.
6 All these *were* under the direction of
their father for the music *in* the house of
the LORD, with cymbals, stringed instruments, and [d]harps, for the service of the
house of God. Asaph, Jeduthun, and
Heman *were* [e]under the authority of the
king. 7 So the [f]number of them, with their
brethren who were instructed in the songs
of the LORD, all who were skillful, *was* two
hundred and eighty-eight.
8 And they cast lots for their duty, the
small as well as the great, [g]the teacher with
the student.
9 Now the first lot for Asaph came out
for Joseph; the second for Gedaliah, him
with his brethren and sons, twelve; 10 the
third for Zaccur, his sons and his brethren,
twelve; 11 the fourth for [1]Jizri, his sons and
his brethren, twelve; 12 the fifth for Nethaniah, his sons and his brethren, twelve;

10 [d] Neh. 12:4, 17; Luke 1:5
15 [1] LXX, Vg. *Aphses*
16 [2] MT *Jehezkel*
19 [e] 1 Chr. 9:25
20 [3] *Shebuel*, 1 Chr. 23:16
21 [f] 1 Chr. 23:17
22 [4] *Shelomith*, 1 Chr. 23:18
23 [g] 1 Chr. 23:19; 26:31 [5] Supplied from 23:19 (following some Heb. mss. and LXX mss.)
26 [h] Ex. 6:19; 1 Chr. 23:21
28 [i] 1 Chr. 23:22
30 [j] 1 Chr. 23:23

CHAPTER 25

1 [a] 1 Chr. 6:30, 33, 39, 44; 2 Chr. 5:12
2 [1] *Jesharelah*, v. 14 [2] Lit. *at the hands of*
3 [b] 1 Chr. 16:41, 42 [3] *Jizri*, v. 11 [4] So with one Heb. ms., LXX mss. [5] Shimei is the sixth, v. 17
4 [6] *Azarel*, v. 18 [7] *Shubael*, v. 20 [8] *Jeremoth*, v. 22
5 [c] 1 Chr. 16:42 [9] Increase his power or influence
6 [d] 1 Chr. 15:16 [e] 1 Chr. 15:19; 25:2
7 [f] 1 Chr. 23:5
8 [g] 2 Chr. 23:13
11 [1] *Zeri*, v. 3

24:10 Abijah. The division of Zacharias, John the Baptist's father (cf. Luke 1:5).

25:1-31 David, the sweet psalmist of Israel (2 Sam. 23:1), established music as a central feature in the worship of God.

25:1 the captains of the army. David relied on his mighty men for help (cf. 11:10). **Asaph...Heman...Jeduthun.** David's 3 chief ministers of music (cf. 6:31-48). **prophesy.** This is not necessarily to be taken in a revelatory sense, but rather in the sense of proclamation and exhortation through the lyrics of their music (cf. 25:2,3). Prophesying is not necessarily predicting the future or even speaking direct revelation. It is proclaiming truth (v. 5) to people (cf. 1 Cor. 14:3), and music is a vehicle for such proclamation in praise (v. 3). David and the leaders selected those most capable (v. 7) of leading the people to worship God through their music.

25:5 seer. A term used to describe a prophet in that he knew and understood the ways and will of God.

25:9-31 The musicians were divided up into 24 divisions (corresponding to that of the priests [24:4-18]) of 12 musicians each, for a total of 288. These would give leadership to the 4,000 instrumentalists (23:5).

13 the sixth for Bukkiah, his sons and his
brethren, twelve; 14 the seventh for [2]Jesha-
relah, his sons and his brethren, twelve;
15 the eighth for Jeshaiah, his sons and his
brethren, twelve; 16 the ninth for Mattaniah, his sons and his brethren, twelve;
17 the tenth for Shimei, his sons and his
brethren, twelve; 18 the eleventh for [3]Aza-
rel, his sons and his brethren, twelve; 19 the
twelfth for Hashabiah, his sons and his
brethren, twelve; 20 the thirteenth for
[4]Shubael, his sons and his brethren,
twelve; 21 the fourteenth for Mattithiah, his
sons and his brethren, twelve; 22 the fifteenth for [5]Jeremoth, his sons and his
brethren, twelve; 23 the sixteenth for Hananiah, his sons and his brethren, twelve;
24 the seventeenth for Joshbekashah, his
sons and his brethren, twelve; 25 the eighteenth for Hanani, his sons and his
brethren, twelve; 26 the nineteenth for Mallothi, his sons and his brethren, twelve;
27 the twentieth for Eliathah, his sons and
his brethren, twelve; 28 the twenty-first for
Hothir, his sons and his brethren, twelve;
29 the twenty-second for Giddalti, his sons
and his brethren, twelve; 30 the twenty-
third for Mahazioth, his sons and his
brethren, twelve; 31 the twenty-fourth for
Romamti-Ezer, his sons and his brethren,
twelve.

The Gatekeepers

26 Concerning the divisions of the
gatekeepers: of the Korahites, [1]Me-
shelemiah the son of [a]Kore, of the sons of
[2]Asaph. 2 And the sons of Meshelemiah
were [b]Zechariah the firstborn, Jediael the
second, Zebadiah the third, Jathniel the
fourth, 3 Elam the fifth, Jehohanan the
sixth, Eliehoenai the seventh.
4 Moreover the sons of [c]Obed-Edom
were Shemaiah the firstborn, Jehozabad the
second, Joah the third, Sacar the fourth,
Nethanel the fifth, 5 Ammiel the sixth,
Issachar the seventh, Peulthai the eighth;
for God blessed him.
6 Also to Shemaiah his son were sons
born who governed their fathers' houses,
because they *were* men of great ability. 7 The
sons of Shemaiah *were* Othni, Rephael,
Obed, and Elzabad, whose brothers Elihu
and Semachiah *were* able men.
8 All these *were* of the sons of Obed-
Edom, they and their sons and their
brethren, [d]able men with strength for the
work: sixty-two of Obed-Edom.
9 And Meshelemiah had sons and
brethren, eighteen able men.
10 Also [e]Hosah, of the children of Merari, had sons: Shimri the first (for *though*
he was not the firstborn, his father made
him the first), 11 Hilkiah the second, Teba-
liah the third, Zechariah the fourth; all the
sons and brethren of Hosah *were* thirteen.
12 Among these *were* the divisions of the
gatekeepers, among the chief men, *having*
duties just like their brethren, to serve in
the house of the LORD. 13 And they [f]cast
lots for each gate, the small as well as the
great, according to their father's house.
14 The lot for the East *Gate* fell to [3]Shele-
miah. Then they cast lots *for* his son Zechariah, a wise counselor, and his lot came
out for the North Gate; 15 to Obed-Edom
the South Gate, and to his sons the [4]store-
house. 16 To Shuppim and Hosah *the lot
came out* for the West Gate, with the Shallecheth Gate on the [g]ascending highway—
watchman opposite watchman. 17 On the
east were *six* Levites, on the north four
each day, on the south four each day, and
for the [5]storehouse two by two. 18 As for
the [6]Parbar on the west, *there were* four on
the highway *and* two at the Parbar.
19 These were the divisions of the gatekeepers among the sons of Korah and
among the sons of Merari.

The Treasuries and Other Duties

20 Of the Levites, Ahijah *was* [h]over the
treasuries of the house of God and over the
treasuries of the [i]dedicated[7] things. 21 The
sons of [8]Laadan, the descendants of the
Gershonites of Laadan, heads of their fathers' *houses*, of Laadan the Gershonite: [9]Je-
hieli. 22 The sons of Jehieli, Zetham and Joel
his brother, *were* over the treasuries of the
house of the LORD. 23 Of the [j]Amramites,
the Izharites, the Hebronites, and the Uzzielites: 24 [k]Shebuel the son of Gershom, the
son of Moses, *was* overseer of the treasuries.

14 [2] *Asharelah*, v. 2
18 [3] *Uzziel*, v. 4
20 [4] *Shebuel*, v. 4
22 [5] *Jerimoth*, v. 4

CHAPTER 26

1 [a] Ps. 42:title [1] *Shelemiah*, v. 14 [2] *Ebiasaph*, 1 Chr. 6:37; 9:19
2 [b] 1 Chr. 9:21
4 [c] 1 Chr. 15:18, 21
8 [d] 1 Chr. 9:13
10 [e] 1 Chr. 16:38
13 [f] 1 Chr. 24:5, 31; 25:8
14 [3] *Meshelemiah*, v. 1
15 [4] Heb. *asuppim*
16 [g] 1 Kin. 10:5; 2 Chr. 9:4
17 [5] Heb. *asuppim*
18 [6] Probably a court or colonnade extending west of the temple
20 [h] 1 Chr. 9:26 [i] 2 Sam. 8:11; 1 Chr. 26:22, 24, 26; 28:12; Ezra 2:69 [7] *holy things*
21 [8] *Libni*, 1 Chr. 6:17 [9] *Jehiel*, 1 Chr. 23:8; 29:8
23 [j] Ex. 6:18; Num. 3:19
24 [k] 1 Chr. 23:16

26:1-19 Cf. 1 Chr. 9:17-27 for another discussion of the temple gatekeepers or guards as we would call them. They had other duties, such as checking out equipment and utensils; storing, ordering and maintaining food for the priests and sacrifices; caring for the temple furniture; mixing the incense daily burned; and accounting for gifts brought. Their "duties" (v. 12) are given in 1 Chr. 9:17-27.

26:14 East *Gate*. The gate assignments were based on 4 geographical points. Cf. also N (26:14), S (26:15), and W (26:16).

26:16 Shallecheth Gate. A gate assumed to be on the west side, but other details are unknown.

26:18 Parbar. Probably a courtyard, extending westward. Verses 17,18 indicate a total of 24 guards posted at all points of entrance and exit.

26:20-32 This section lists miscellaneous administrative posts handled by the Levites, by those in Jerusalem (26:20-28), and by those outside (26:29-32).

26:20 treasuries. The Levites watched over the store of valuables given to the Lord. This is a general reference to all the precious things committed to their trust, including contributions from David and the people, as well as war spoils given by triumphant soldiers (vv. 26,27).

25 And his brethren by Eliezer *were* Rehabiah his son, Jeshaiah his son, Joram his son,
Zichri his son, and [l]Shelomith his son.
26 This Shelomith and his brethren *were*
over all the treasuries of the dedicated
things [m]which King David and the heads
of fathers' *houses,* the captains over thousands and hundreds, and the captains of
the army, had dedicated. 27 Some of the
[1]spoils won in battles they dedicated to
maintain the house of the LORD. 28 And all
that Samuel [n]the seer, Saul the son of Kish,
Abner the son of Ner, and Joab the son of
Zeruiah had dedicated, every dedicated
thing, was under the hand of Shelomith
and his brethren.
29 Of the Izharites, Chenaniah and his
sons [o]*performed* duties as [p]officials and
judges over Israel outside Jerusalem.
30 Of the Hebronites, [q]Hashabiah and
his brethren, one thousand seven hundred
able men, had the oversight of Israel on the
west side of the Jordan for all the business
of the LORD, and in the service of the king.
31 Among the Hebronites, [r]Jerijah *was*
head of the Hebronites according to his genealogy of the fathers. In the fortieth year
of the reign of David they were sought,
and there were found among them capable
men [s]at Jazer of Gilead. 32 And his
brethren *were* two thousand seven hundred able men, heads of fathers' *houses,*
whom King David made officials over the
Reubenites, the Gadites, and the half-tribe
of Manasseh, for every matter pertaining
to God and the [t]affairs of the king.

The Military Divisions

27 And the children of Israel, according to their number, the heads of fathers' *houses,* the captains of thousands
and hundreds and their officers, served the
king in every matter of the *military* divisions. *These divisions* came in and went out
month by month throughout all the
months of the year, each division *having*
twenty-four thousand.
2 Over the first division for the first
month *was* [a]Jashobeam the son of Zabdiel,
and in his division *were* twenty-four thousand; 3 *he was* of the children of Perez, and
the chief of all the captains of the army for
the first month. 4 Over the division of the
second month *was* [1]Dodai an Ahohite, and
of his division Mikloth also *was* the leader;
in his division *were* twenty-four thousand.
5 The third captain of the army for the
third month *was* [b]Benaiah, the son of Jehoiada the priest, who was chief; in his
division *were* twenty-four thousand. 6 This
was the Benaiah *who was* [c]mighty *among*
the thirty, and was over the thirty; in his
division *was* Ammizabad his son. 7 The
fourth *captain* for the fourth month *was*
[d]Asahel the brother of Joab, and Zebadiah
his son after him; in his division *were* twenty-four thousand. 8 The fifth *captain* for the
fifth month *was* [2]Shamhuth the Izrahite; in
his division were twenty-four thousand.
9 The sixth *captain* for the sixth month *was*
[e]Ira the son of Ikkesh the Tekoite; in his
division *were* twenty-four thousand. 10 The
seventh *captain* for the seventh month *was*
[f]Helez the Pelonite, of the children of
Ephraim; in his division *were* twenty-four
thousand. 11 The eighth *captain* for the
eighth month *was* [g]Sibbechai the Hushathite, of the Zarhites; in his division *were*
twenty-four thousand. 12 The ninth *captain*
for the ninth month *was* [h]Abiezer the Anathothite, of the Benjamites; in his division
were twenty-four thousand. 13 The tenth
captain for the tenth month *was* [i]Maharai
the Netophathite, of the Zarhites; in his
division *were* twenty-four thousand. 14 The
eleventh *captain* for the eleventh month
was [j]Benaiah the Pirathonite, of the children of Ephraim; in his division *were* twenty-four thousand. 15 The twelfth *captain* for
the twelfth month *was* [3]Heldai the Netophathite, of Othniel; in his division *were*
twenty-four thousand.

Leaders of Tribes

16 Furthermore, over the tribes of Israel:
the officer over the Reubenites *was* Eliezer
the son of Zichri; over the Simeonites,
Shephatiah the son of Maachah; 17 *over* the
Levites, [k]Hashabiah the son of Kemuel;
over the Aaronites, Zadok; 18 *over* Judah,
[l]Elihu, *one* of David's brothers; *over* Issachar, Omri the son of Michael; 19 *over*
Zebulun, Ishmaiah the son of Obadiah;
over Naphtali, Jerimoth the son of Azriel;
20 *over* the children of Ephraim, Hoshea the
son of Azaziah; *over* the half-tribe of Manasseh, Joel the son of Pedaiah; 21 *over* the
half-*tribe* of Manasseh in Gilead, Iddo the

25 [l] 1 Chr. 23:18
26 [m] 2 Sam. 8:11
27 [1] *plunder*
28 [n] 1 Sam. 9:9
29 [o] Neh. 11:16
[p] 1 Chr. 23:4
30 [q] 1 Chr. 27:17
31 [r] 1 Chr. 23:19
[s] Josh. 21:39
32 [t] 2 Chr. 19:11

CHAPTER 27

2 [a] 1 Chr. 11:11
4 [1] Heb. *Dodai,* usually spelled *Dodo,* 2 Sam. 23:9
5 [b] 1 Chr. 18:17
6 [c] 2 Sam. 23:20-23
7 [d] 2 Sam. 23:24; 1 Chr. 11:26
8 [2] *Shammah,* 2 Sam. 23:11, or *Shammoth,* 1 Chr. 11:27
9 [e] 1 Chr. 11:28
10 [f] 1 Chr. 11:27
11 [g] 2 Sam. 21:18; 1 Chr. 11:29; 20:4
12 [h] 1 Chr. 11:28
13 [i] 2 Sam. 23:28; 1 Chr. 11:30
14 [j] 1 Chr. 11:31
15 [3] *Heleb,* 2 Sam. 23:29, or *Heled,* 1 Chr. 11:30
17 [k] 1 Chr. 26:30
18 [l] 1 Sam. 16:6

26:29-32 officials and judges. There were 6,000 magistrates exercising judicial functions throughout the Land.

26:31 fortieth year. The last year of David's reign (ca. 971 B.C.).

27:1-34 First Chronicles 23–26 discusses spiritual leadership, while here the chronicler focuses on the civil aspects of David's kingdom.

27:1-15 This section enumerates the standing army of Israel (288,000 men), which had responsibility to guard the nation and temple. They were divided into 12 divisions each of which served for one month during the year. When full war occurred, a larger force could be called into action (cf. 21:5).

27:16-22 While 12 officers are named, the tribes of Asher and Gad are not mentioned for unknown reasons.

son of Zechariah; *over* Benjamin, Jaasiel the
son of Abner; 22 *over* Dan, Azarel the son of
Jeroham. These *were* the leaders of the
tribes of Israel.

23 But David did not take the number of
those twenty years old and under, because
[m]the LORD had said He would multiply Israel like the [n]stars of the heavens. 24 Joab
the son of Zeruiah began a census, but he
did not finish, for [o]wrath came upon Israel
because of this census; nor was the number
recorded in the account of the chronicles of
King David.

Other State Officials

25 And Azmaveth the son of Adiel *was*
over the king's treasuries; and Jehonathan
the son of Uzziah was over the storehouses
in the field, in the cities, in the villages, and
in the fortresses. 26 Ezri the son of Chelub
was over those who did the work of the field
for tilling the ground. 27 And Shimei the
Ramathite *was* over the vineyards, and
Zabdi the Shiphmite was over the produce
of the vineyards for the supply of wine.
28 Baal-Hanan the Gederite was over the
olive trees and the sycamore trees that *were*
in the lowlands, and Joash *was* over the store
of oil. 29 And Shitrai the Sharonite *was* over
the herds that fed in Sharon, and Shaphat
the son of Adlai was over the herds *that were*
in the valleys. 30 Obil the Ishmaelite *was*
over the camels, Jehdeiah the Meronothite
was over the donkeys, 31 and Jaziz the
[p]Hagrite *was* over the flocks. All these *were*
the officials over King David's property.

32 Also Jehonathan, David's uncle, *was* a
counselor, a wise man, and a [4]scribe; and
Jehiel the [5]son of Hachmoni *was* with the
king's sons. 33 [q]Ahithophel *was* the king's
counselor, and [r]Hushai the Archite *was* the
king's companion. 34 After Ahithophel *was*
Jehoiada the son of Benaiah, then [s]Abia-
thar. And the general of the king's army
was [t]Joab.

23 [m][Deut. 6:3] [n]Gen. 15:5; 22:17; 26:4; Ex. 32:13; Deut. 1:10
24 [o]2 Sam. 24:12-15; 1 Chr. 21:1-7
31 [p]1 Chr. 5:10
32 [4]*secretary* [5]Or *Hachmonite*
33 [q]2 Sam. 15:12 [r]2 Sam. 15:32-37
34 [s]1 Kin. 1:7 [t]1 Chr. 11:6

CHAPTER 28

1 [a]1 Chr. 27:16 [b]1 Chr. 27:1, 2 [c]1 Chr. 27:25 [d]2 Sam. 23:8-39; 1 Chr. 11:10-47 [1]Or *livestock*
2 [e]2 Sam. 7:2 [f]Ps. 99:5; 132:7; [Is. 66:1]
3 [g]2 Sam. 7:5, 13; 1 Kin. 5:3 [h][1 Chr. 17:4; 22:8]
4 [i]1 Sam. 16:6-13 [j]Gen. 49:8-10; 1 Chr. 5:2; Ps. 60:7 [k]1 Sam. 16:1 [l]1 Sam. 13:14; 16:12, 13; Acts 13:22
5 [m]1 Chr. 3:1-9; 14:3-7; 23:1 [n]1 Chr. 22:9; 29:1
6 [o]2 Sam. 7:13, 14; 1 Kin. 6:38; 1 Chr. 22:9, 10; 2 Chr. 1:9; 6:2
7 [p]1 Chr. 22:13
9 [q][1 Sam. 12:24]; Jer. 9:24; Hos. 4:1; [John 17:3]

Solomon Instructed to Build the Temple

28 Now David assembled at Jerusalem
all [a]the leaders of Israel: the officers
of the tribes and [b]the captains of the divisions who served the king, the captains
over thousands and captains over hundreds, and [c]the stewards over all the substance and [1]possessions of the king and of
his sons, with the officials, the valiant men,
and all [d]the mighty men of valor.

2 Then King David rose to his feet and
said, "Hear me, my brethren and my people: [e]I *had* it in my heart to build a house of
rest for the ark of the covenant of the LORD,
and for [f]the footstool of our God, and had
made preparations to build it. 3 But God
said to me, [g]'You shall not build a house
for My name, because you *have been* a man
of war and have shed [h]blood.' 4 However
the LORD God of Israel [i]chose me above all
the house of my father to be king over Israel forever, for He has chosen [j]Judah *to be*
the ruler. And of the house of Judah, [k]the
house of my father, and [l]among the sons of
my father, He was pleased with me to
make *me* king over all Israel. 5 [m]And of all
my sons (for the LORD has given me many
sons) [n]He has chosen my son Solomon to
sit on the throne of the kingdom of the
LORD over Israel. 6 Now He said to me, 'It
is [o]your son Solomon *who* shall build My
house and My courts; for I have chosen
him *to be* My son, and I will be his Father.
7 Moreover I will establish his kingdom
forever, [p]if he is steadfast to observe My
commandments and My judgments, as it is
this day.' 8 Now therefore, in the sight of
all Israel, the assembly of the LORD, and in
the hearing of our God, be careful to seek
out all the commandments of the LORD
your God, that you may possess this good
land, and leave *it* as an inheritance for
your children after you forever.

9 "As for you, my son Solomon, [q]know
the God of your father, and serve Him

27:23,24 Here is further comment on the sinful census detailed in 1 Chr. 21:1-30. He didn't try to number all Israelites because they were too many (cf. Gen. 28:14). Nor did he finish the census, being interrupted by guilt and judgment.

27:24 the chronicles of King David. Daily records were kept of the king's reign. None was kept of this calamity because the record was too painful.

27:25-31 A summary of officials who looked over David's various agricultural assets.

27:32-34 A summary of those whose duties kept them in close contact with the king (cf. 18:14-17), perhaps like a cabinet. When David's son, Absalom, rebelled against him, Ahithophel betrayed David and joined the revolution. Hushan pretended loyalty to Absalom, and his advice caused Absalom's death (cf. 2 Sam. 15:31–17:23).

28:1–29:20 A record is given of David's last assembly in which the king charged Solomon and the people to build the temple for God's glory. These final chapters present the transition from David to Solomon. The chronicler does not mention Adonijah's conspiracy (1 Kin. 1:5-9) or David's weakness (1 Kin. 1:1-4), but looks at the positive contribution of the Davidic kingdom.

28:2-8 For the assembly's sake, David testified to the Davidic Covenant originally given by God to him in 2 Sam. 7 (cf. 17:7-27; 22:6-16). David makes it clear that Solomon was God's choice (v. 5) as had been frequently intimated (cf. 2 Sam. 12:24,25; 1 Kin. 1:13), just as the coming Christ will be God's chosen Son to ultimately fulfill kingdom promise.

28:8 Cf. Deut. 5:29,33; 6:1-3.

28:9-21 David turns his words to Solomon with 4 perspectives: 1) spiritual devotion (28:9,10); 2) architectural execution (28:11-19); 3) divine intervention (28:20); and 4) human participation (28:21).

28:9,10 Cf. note on 22:11-13,18,19.

[r]with a loyal heart and with a willing mind; for [s]the LORD searches all hearts and understands all the intent of the thoughts. [t]If you seek Him, He will be found by you; but if you forsake Him, He will [u]cast you off forever. 10 Consider now, [v]for the LORD has chosen you to build a house for the sanctuary; be strong, and do it."

11 Then David gave his son Solomon [w]the plans for the vestibule, its houses, its treasuries, its upper chambers, its inner chambers, and the place of the mercy seat; 12 and the [x]plans for all that he had by the Spirit, of the courts of the house of the LORD, of all the chambers all around, [y]of the treasuries of the house of God, and of the treasuries for the dedicated things; 13 also for the division of the priests and the [z]Levites, for all the work of the service of the house of the LORD, and for all the articles of service in the house of the LORD. 14 *He gave* gold by weight for *things* of gold, for all articles used in every kind of service; also *silver* for all articles of silver by weight, for all articles used in every kind of service; 15 the weight for the [a]lampstands of gold, and their lamps of gold, by weight for each lampstand and its lamps; for the lampstands of silver by weight, for the lampstand and its lamps, according to the use of each lampstand. 16 And by weight *he gave* gold for the tables of the showbread, for each [b]table, and silver for the tables of silver; 17 also pure gold for the forks, the basins, the pitchers of pure gold, and the golden bowls—*he gave gold* by weight for every bowl; and for the silver bowls, *silver* by weight for every bowl; 18 and refined gold by weight for the [c]altar of incense, and for the construction of the chariot, that is, the gold [d]cherubim that spread *their wings* and overshadowed the ark of the covenant of the LORD. 19 "All *this*," *said David*, [e]"the LORD made me understand in writing, by *His* hand upon me, all the [2]works of these plans."

20 And David said to his son Solomon, [f]"Be strong and of good courage, and do *it;* do not fear nor be dismayed, for the LORD God—my God—*will be* with you. [g]He will not leave you nor forsake you, until you have finished all the work for the service of the house of the LORD. 21 *Here are* [h]the divisions of the priests and the Levites for all the service of the house of God; and [i]every willing craftsman *will be* with you for all manner of workmanship, for every kind of service; also the leaders and all the people *will be* completely at your command."

Offerings for Building the Temple

29 Furthermore King David said to all the assembly: "My son Solomon, whom alone God has [a]chosen, *is* [b]young and inexperienced; and the work *is* great, because the [1]temple *is* not for man but for the LORD God. 2 Now for the house of my God I have prepared with all my might: gold for *things to be made of* gold, silver for *things of* silver, bronze for *things of* bronze, iron for *things of* iron, wood for *things of* wood, [c]onyx stones, *stones* to be set, glistening stones of various colors, all kinds of precious stones, and marble slabs in abundance. 3 Moreover, because I have set my affection on the house of my God, I have given to the house of my God, over and above all that I have prepared for the holy house, my own special treasure of gold and silver: 4 three thousand talents of gold, of the gold of [d]Ophir, and seven thousand talents of refined silver, to overlay the walls of the houses; 5 the gold for *things of* gold and the silver for *things of* silver, and for all kinds of work *to be done* by the hands of craftsmen. Who *then* is [e]willing to [2]consecrate himself this day to the LORD?"

6 Then [f]the leaders of the fathers' *houses*, leaders of the tribes of Israel, the captains of thousands and of hundreds, with [g]the officers over the king's work, [h]offered willingly. 7 They gave for the work of the

9 [r] 2 Kin. 20:3 [s] [1 Sam. 16:7; 1 Kin. 8:39; 1 Chr. 29:17]; Jer. 11:20; 17:10; 20:12; Rev. 2:23 [t] 2 Chr. 15:2; [Jer. 29:13] [u] Deut. 31:17
10 [v] 1 Chr. 22:13; 28:6
11 [w] 1 Kin. 6:3; 1 Chr. 28:19
12 [x] Ex. 25:40; Heb. 8:5 [y] 1 Chr. 26:20, 28
13 [z] 1 Chr. 23:6
15 [a] Ex. 25:31-39; 1 Kin. 7:49
16 [b] 1 Kin. 7:48
18 [c] Ex. 30:1-10 [d] Ex. 25:18-22; 1 Sam. 4:4; 1 Kin. 6:23
19 [e] Ex. 25:40; 1 Chr. 28:11, 12 [2] *details*
20 [f] Deut. 31:6, 7; [Josh. 1:6-9]; 1 Chr. 22:13 [g] Josh. 1:5; Heb. 13:5
21 [h] 1 Chr. 24–26 [i] Ex. 35:25-35; 36:1, 2; 2 Chr. 2:13, 14

CHAPTER 29

1 [a] 1 Chr. 28:5 [b] 1 Kin. 3:7; 1 Chr. 22:5; Prov. 4:3 [1] Lit. *palace*
2 [c] Is. 54:11, 12; Rev. 21:18
4 [d] 1 Kin. 9:28
5 [e] 2 Chr. 29:31; [2 Cor. 8:5, 12] [2] Lit. *fill his hand*
6 [f] 1 Chr. 27:1; 28:1 [g] 1 Chr. 27:25-31 [h] Ex. 35:21-35

28:18 the chariot. Using the imagery of Ps. 18:10, the cherubim are depicted as the vehicle in which God moves.

28:19 in writing. David wrote down the plans under the Holy Spirit's divine inspiration (non-canonical, written revelation). This divine privilege was much like that of Moses for the tabernacle (Ex. 25:9,40; 27:8; Heb. 8:5).

28:20,21 Solomon's associates in the building project were God, the owner and general contractor (28:20), plus the human work force (28:21).

29:1-5 David called for consecrated giving to the project (cf. 28:1), based on the example of his generosity (vv. 3,4). David gave his personal fortune to the temple building, a fortune almost immeasurable.

29:1 young and inexperienced. *See notes on 1 Chr. 22:5.*

29:4 three thousand talents. Assuming a talent weighed about 75 lbs., this amounts to almost 112 tons of gold, plus the 7,000 talents of silver which would be 260 tons. The total worth of such precious metals has been estimated in the billions of dollars. **gold of Ophir.** This was held to be the purest and finest in the world (cf. Job 22:24; 28:16; Is. 13:12).

29:6-9 willingly. Here is the key to all freewill giving, i.e., giving what one desires to give. Tithes were required for taxation, to fund the theocracy, similar to taxation today. The law required that to be paid. This, however, is the voluntary giving from the heart to the Lord. The NT speaks of this (cf. Luke 6:38; 2 Cor. 9:1-8) and never demands that a tithe be given to God, but that taxes be paid to one's government (cf. Rom. 13:6,7). Paying taxes and giving God whatever one is willing to give, based on devotion to Him and His glory, is biblical giving.

house of God five thousand talents and ten
thousand darics of gold, ten thousand talents of silver, eighteen thousand talents of
bronze, and one hundred thousand talents
of iron. **8** And whoever had *precious* stones
gave *them* to the treasury of the house of
the LORD, into the hand of [i]Jehiel[3] the
Gershonite. **9** Then the people rejoiced, for
they had offered willingly, because with a
loyal heart they had [j]offered willingly to
the LORD; and King David also rejoiced
greatly.

David's Praise to God

10 Therefore David blessed the LORD before all the assembly; and David said:

"Blessed are You, LORD God of
 Israel, our Father, forever and
 ever.
11 [k]Yours, O LORD, *is* the greatness,
The power and the glory,
The victory and the majesty;
For all *that is* in heaven and in
 earth *is Yours;*
Yours *is* the kingdom, O LORD,
And You are exalted as head over
 all.
12 [l]Both riches and honor *come* from
 You,
And You reign over all.
In Your hand *is* power and might;
In Your hand *it is* to make great
And to give strength to all.

13 "Now therefore, our God,
We thank You
And praise Your glorious name.
14 But who *am* I, and who *are* my
 people,
That we should be able to offer so
 willingly as this?
For all things *come* from You,
And [4]of Your own we have given
 You.

15 For [m]we *are* [5]aliens and [6]pilgrims
 before You,
As *were* all our fathers;
[n]Our days on earth *are* as a shadow,
And without hope.

16 "O LORD our God, all this abundance
that we have prepared to build You a
house for Your holy name is from Your
hand, and *is* all Your own. **17** I know also,
my God, that You [o]test the heart and [p]have
pleasure in uprightness. As for me, in the
uprightness of my heart I have willingly
offered all these *things;* and now with joy I
have seen Your people, who are present
here to offer willingly to You. **18** O LORD
God of Abraham, Isaac, and Israel, our fathers, keep this forever in the intent of the
thoughts of the heart of Your people, and
fix their heart toward You. **19** And [q]give
my son Solomon a loyal heart to keep Your
commandments and Your testimonies and
Your statutes, to do all *these things,* and to
build the [7]temple for which [r]I have made
provision."

20 Then David said to all the assembly,
"Now bless the LORD your God." So all the
assembly blessed the LORD God of their fathers, and bowed their heads and prostrated themselves before the LORD and the
king.

Solomon Anointed King

21 And they made sacrifices to the LORD
and offered burnt offerings to the LORD on
the next day: a thousand bulls, a thousand
rams, a thousand lambs, with their drink
offerings, and [s]sacrifices in abundance for
all Israel. **22** So they ate and drank before
the LORD with great gladness on that day.
And they made Solomon the son of David
king the second time, and [t]anointed *him* before the LORD *to be* the leader, and Zadok *to
be* priest. **23** Then Solomon sat on the throne
of the LORD as king instead of David his father, and prospered; and all Israel obeyed

8 [i] 1 Chr. 23:8 [3] Possibly the same as *Jehieli,* 1 Chr. 26:21, 22
9 [j] Ex. 25:2; 1 Kin. 8:61; 2 Cor. 9:7
11 [k] Matt. 6:13; 1 Tim. 1:17; Rev. 5:13
12 [l] Rom. 11:36
14 [4] Lit. *of Your hand*
15 [m] Lev. 25:23; Ps. 39:12; Heb. 11:13, 14; 1 Pet. 2:11 [n] Job 14:2; Ps. 90:9 [5] *sojourners,* temporary residents [6] *transients,* temporary residents in an even more temporary sense
17 [o] [1 Sam. 16:7; 1 Chr. 28:9] [p] Prov. 11:20
19 [q] [1 Chr. 28:9]; Ps. 72:1 [r] 1 Chr. 29:1, 2 [7] Lit. *palace*
21 [s] 1 Kin. 8:62, 63
22 [t] 1 Kin. 1:32-35, 39; 1 Chr. 23:1

29:7 five thousand talents. Assuming a talent weighed about 75 lbs., this amounts to 187 tons of gold. **darics.** A Persian coin, familiar to Jews from the captivity, possibly named after Darius I (cf. Ezra 8:27). The readers of this material in Ezra's day would know it as a contemporary measurement. **ten thousand talents.** This amounts to 375 tons of silver. **eighteen thousand talents.** This amounts to almost 675 tons of bronze. **one hundred thousand talents.** This amounts to 3,750 tons of iron. The sum of all this is staggering, and has been estimated into the billions of dollars.

29:10-15 David responds to the phenomenal offering expressing amazing sacrifices of wealth with praise in which he acknowledges that all things belong to and come from God. He concludes that God is everything and that man is nothing, much like Ps. 8. This magnificent prayer of thanks gives God all credit, even for the people's generosity (v. 14).

29:16-20 David leads in a prayer of commitment.

29:17 test the heart. Opportunities for giving to God are tests of the character of a believer's devotion to the Lord. The king acknowledges that the attitude of one's heart is significantly more important than the amount of offering in one's hand.

29:20 bowed...prostrated. The ultimate physical expression of an inward submission to God in all things.

29:21-30 The chronicler records in selective fashion the final days of David and the enthronement of Solomon. For a more complete treatment see 1 Kin. 1:1-53.

29:22 the second time. This most likely refers to a public ceremony subsequent to the private one of 1 Kin. 1:35-39 in response to Adonijah's conspiracy. David's High-Priest Zadok had been loyal to both father and son (1 Kin. 1:32-40; 2:27-29), so he continued on as High-Priest during Solomon's reign.

him. 24 All the leaders and the mighty men,
and also all the sons of King David, [u]sub-
mitted[8] themselves to King Solomon. 25 So
the LORD exalted Solomon exceedingly in
the sight of all Israel, and [v]bestowed on
him *such* royal majesty as had not been on
any king before him in Israel.

The Close of David's Reign

26 Thus David the son of Jesse reigned
over all Israel. 27 [w]And the period that he
reigned over Israel *was* forty years; [x]seven
years he reigned in Hebron, and thirty-
three *years* he reigned in Jerusalem. 28 So
he [y]died in a good old age, [z]full of days
and riches and honor; and Solomon his son
reigned in his place. 29 Now the acts of
King David, first and last, indeed they *are*
written in the [9]book of Samuel the seer, in
the book of Nathan the prophet, and in the
book of Gad the seer, 30 with all his reign
and his might, [a]and the events that happened to him, to Israel, and to all the kingdoms of the lands.

24 [u] Eccl. 8:2 [8] Lit. *gave the hand* **25** [v] 1 Kin. 3:13; 2 Chr. 1:12; Eccl. 2:9 **27** [w] 2 Sam. 5:4; 1 Kin. 2:11 [x] 2 Sam. 5:5 **28** [y] Gen. 25:8 [z] 1 Chr. 23:1 **29** [9] Lit. *words* **30** [a] Dan. 2:21; 4:23, 25

29:26-28 Cf. 1 Kin. 2:10-12.

29:27 forty years. Ca. 1011–971 B.C.

29:29 Samuel. This most likely refers to the canonical book of 1 and 2 Samuel. **seer…prophet…seer.** All 3 are different, but synonymous, Heb. terms referring to the prophetic office from the perspectives of: 1) to understand; 2) to proclaim; and 3) to understand respectively. **Nathan…Gad.** These are non-canonical, but reliable, historical records that the chronicler utilized. God's Spirit protected the record from error in the original writing (2 Tim. 3:16,17; 2 Pet. 1:20,21).

The Second Book of the CHRONICLES

Introduction

See 1 Chronicles for the Introductory Discussion.

Outline

I. The Reign of Solomon (1:1–9:31)
  - A. Coronation and Beginnings (1:1-17)
  - B. Temple Building (2:1–7:22)
  - C. Wealth/Achievements (8:1–9:28)
  - D. Death (9:29-31)

II. The Reign of the Kings of Judah (10:1–36:21)
  - A. Rehoboam (10:1–12:16)
  - B. Abijah (13:1-22)
  - C. Asa (14:1–16:14)
  - D. Jehoshaphat (17:1–21:3)
  - E. Jehoram (21:4-20)
  - F. Ahaziah (22:1-9)
  - G. Athaliah (22:10–23:21)
  - H. Joash (24:1-27)
  - I. Amaziah (25:1-28)
  - J. Uzziah (26:1-23)
  - K. Jotham (27:1-9)
  - L. Ahaz (28:1-27)
  - M. Hezekiah (29:1–32:33)
  - N. Manasseh (33:1-20)
  - O. Amon (33:21-25)
  - P. Josiah (34:1–35:27)
  - Q. Jehoahaz (36:1-4)
  - R. Jehoiakim (36:5-8)
  - S. Jehoiachin (36:9,10)
  - T. Zedekiah (36:11-21)

III. The Return Proclamation of Cyrus (36:22,23)

Solomon Requests Wisdom

1 Now [a]Solomon the son of David was
strengthened in his kingdom, and [b]the
LORD his God *was* with him and [c]exalted
him exceedingly.
2 And Solomon spoke to all Israel, to
[d]the captains of thousands and of hundreds, to the judges, and to every leader in
all Israel, the heads of the fathers' *houses.*
3 Then Solomon, and all the assembly with
him, went to [1]the high place that *was* at
[e]Gibeon; for the tabernacle of meeting with
God was there, which Moses the servant of
the LORD had [f]made in the wilderness.
4 [g]But David had brought up the ark of
God from Kirjath Jearim to *the place* David
had prepared for it, for he had pitched a
tent for it at Jerusalem. 5 Now [h]the bronze
altar that [i]Bezalel the son of Uri, the son of
Hur, had made, [2]he put before the tabernacle of the LORD; Solomon and the assembly sought Him *there.* 6 And Solomon went
up there to the bronze altar before the
LORD, which *was* at the tabernacle of meeting, and [j]offered a thousand burnt offerings on it.
7 [k]On that night God appeared to Solomon, and said to him, "Ask! What shall I
give you?"
8 And Solomon said to God: "You have
shown great [l]mercy to David my father,
and have made me [m]king in his place.
9 Now, O LORD God, let Your promise to
David my father be established, [n]for You
have made me king over a people like the
[o]dust of the earth in multitude. 10 [p]Now
give me wisdom and knowledge, that I
may [q]go out and come in before this people; for who can judge this great people of
Yours?"
11 [r]Then God said to Solomon: "Because
this was in your heart, and you have not
asked riches or wealth or honor or the life

CHAPTER 1

1 [a] 1 Kin. 2:46 [b] Gen. 39:2 [c] 1 Chr. 29:25
2 [d] 1 Chr. 27:1-34
3 [e] 1 Kin. 3:4; 1 Chr. 16:39; 21:29 [f] Ex. 25–27; 35:4–36:38 [1] Place for worship
4 [g] Ex. 25:10-22; 2 Sam. 6:2-17; 1 Chr. 15:25–16:1
5 [h] Ex. 27:1, 2; 38:1, 2 [i] Ex. 31:2 [2] Some authorities *it was there*
6 [j] 1 Kin. 3:4
7 [k] 1 Kin. 3:5-14; 9:2
8 [l] Ps. 18:50 [m] 1 Chr. 28:5
9 [n] 2 Sam. 7:8-16; 1 Kin. 3:7, 8 [o] Gen. 13:16; Num. 23:10
10 [p] 1 Kin. 3:9 [q] Num. 27:17; Deut. 31:2
11 [r] 1 Kin. 3:11-13

1:1–9:31 This section continues from 1 Chronicles and covers the rule of Solomon (ca. 971–931 B.C.; cf. 1 Kin. 3–11). The major theme is Solomon's building God's temple in Jerusalem for the purpose of centralizing and unifying the nation in the worship of God.

1:3 Gibeon. *See notes on 1 Chr. 16:39 and 21:29.* The tabernacle remained at Gibeon while the ark resided in Jerusalem, waiting for the temple to be built. **tabernacle.** Built in the days of Moses, this tent was where God met with the people (cf. Ex. 25:22; 29:42,43; 40:34-38). The center of worship was there until the temple was built (cf. v. 6).

1:4 Kirjath Jearim. *See note on 1 Chr. 13:5.*

1:5 Bezalel. The Spirit-enabled craftsman who built the bronze altar for the tabernacle (cf. Ex. 31:1-11; 38:1,2).

1:7-13 The account is paralleled in 1 Kin. 3:5-15. Every king of Israel needed to heed God's instructions recorded in Deut. 17:14-20.

1:9 Your promise. A reference to the Davidic Covenant in 2 Sam. 7; 1 Chr. 17.

1:10 Solomon had agreed with his father (cf. 1 Chr. 22:5 and 29:1) on his need for wisdom, and that is what he sought from God (cf. 1 Kin. 3:3-15; Prov. 3:15; James 1:5).

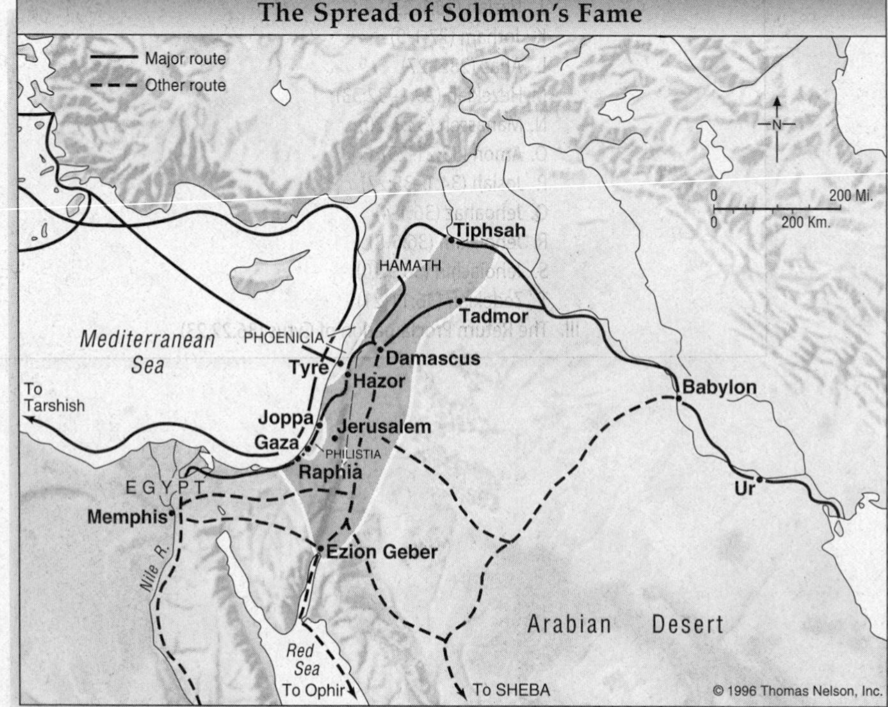

Solomon's influence in economic and political affairs was enhanced by the transporatation and trade routes that intersected his kingdom.

of your enemies, nor have you asked long
life—but have asked wisdom and knowledge for yourself, that you may judge My
people over whom I have made you
king— 12 wisdom and knowledge *are*
granted to you; and I will give you riches
and wealth and honor, such as [s]none of the
kings have had who *were* before you, nor
shall any after you have the like."

Solomon's Military and Economic Power

13 So Solomon came to Jerusalem from
[3]the high place that *was* at Gibeon, from
before the tabernacle of meeting, and
reigned over Israel. 14 [t]And Solomon gathered chariots and horsemen; he had one
thousand four hundred chariots and
twelve thousand horsemen, whom he stationed in the chariot cities and with the
king in Jerusalem. 15 [u]Also the king made
silver and gold as common in Jerusalem as
stones, and he made cedars as abundant as
the sycamores which *are* in the lowland.
16 [v]And Solomon had horses imported
from Egypt and Keveh; the king's merchants bought them in Keveh at the *current*
price. 17 They also acquired and imported
from Egypt a chariot for six hundred
shekels of silver, and a horse for one hundred and fifty; thus, [4]through their agents,
they exported them to all the kings of the
Hittites and the kings of Syria.

Solomon Prepares to Build the Temple

2 Then Solomon [a]determined to build a
temple for the name of the LORD, and a
royal house for himself. 2 [b]Solomon selected seventy thousand men to bear burdens,
eighty thousand to quarry *stone* in the
mountains, and three thousand six hundred to oversee them.
3 Then Solomon sent to [1]Hiram king of
Tyre, saying:

12 [s] 1 Kin. 10:23; 1 Chr. 29:25; 2 Chr. 9:22; Eccl. 2:9
13 [3] Place for worship
14 [t] 1 Kin. 10:26; 2 Chr. 9:25
15 [u] 1 Kin. 10:27; 2 Chr. 9:27; Job 22:24
16 [v] 1 Kin. 10:28; 22:36; 2 Chr. 9:28
17 [4] Lit. *by their hands*

CHAPTER 2

1 [a] 1 Kin. 5:5
2 [b] 1 Kin. 5:15, 16; 2 Chr. 2:18
3 [1] Heb. *Huram;* cf. 1 Kin. 5:1

[c] 1 Chr. 14:1
4 [d] 2 Chr. 2:1 [e] Ex. 30:7 [f] Ex. 25:30; Lev. 24:8 [g] Ex. 29:38-42 [h] Num. 28:3, 9-11 [2] Lit. *incense of spices* [3] *appointed*
5 [i] Ps. 135:5; [1 Cor. 8:5, 6]
6 [j] 1 Kin. 8:27; 2 Chr. 6:18; Is. 66:1
7 [k] 1 Chr. 22:15
8 [l] 1 Kin. 5:6
9 [4] Lit. *house*
10 [m] 1 Kin. 5:11

[c]As you have dealt with David my
father, and sent him cedars to build
himself a house to dwell in, *so deal
with me.* 4 Behold, [d]I am building a
temple for the name of the LORD
my God, to dedicate *it* to Him, [e]to
burn before Him [2]sweet incense,
for [f]the continual showbread, for
[g]the burnt offerings morning and
evening, on the [h]Sabbaths, on the
New Moons, and on the [3]set feasts
of the LORD our God. This *is an
ordinance* forever to Israel.

5 And the temple which I build *will
be* great, for [i]our God is greater
than all gods. 6 [j]But who is able to
build Him a temple, since heaven
and the heaven of heavens cannot
contain Him? Who *am* I then, that I
should build Him a temple, except
to burn sacrifice before Him?

7 Therefore send me at once a man
skillful to work in gold and silver,
in bronze and iron, in purple and
crimson and blue, who has skill to
engrave with the skillful men who
are with me in Judah and Jerusalem, [k]whom David my father
provided. 8 [l]Also send me cedar
and cypress and algum logs from
Lebanon, for I know that your
servants have skill to cut timber in
Lebanon; and indeed my servants
will be with your servants, 9 to
prepare timber for me in
abundance, for the [4]temple which I
am about to build *shall be* great and
wonderful.

10 [m]And indeed I will give to your
servants, the woodsmen who cut

1:14-17 1 Kin. 10:14-29 and 2 Chr. 9:13-28 also extol Solomon's wealth.

1:14 chariot cities. Gezer, Hazor, and Megiddo were among the chief cities.

1:16 Keveh. Possibly Cilicia.

1:17 six hundred *shekels*. Assuming a shekel weighs .4 oz., this represents 15 lbs. of silver for one chariot. **one hundred and fifty.** Assuming the weight is in shekels, this would be about 3.75 lbs. of silver. Deuteronomy 17:16 warned against the king's amassing horses. **the Hittites.** People, once expelled from Palestine, who lived N of Israel and NW of Syria.

2:1-18 This section reports how Solomon selected men to gather building materials for the temple. This was in addition to the massive supplies stockpiled by David (cf. 1 Chr. 22,29). This section parallels 1 Kin. 5:1-16.

2:1 temple for the name of the LORD. God's covenant name, Yahweh or Jehovah (cf. Ex. 3:14), is in mind. David wanted to do this, but was not allowed to do any more than plan and prepare (1 Chr. 23–26; 28:11-13), purchase the land (2 Sam. 24:18-25; 1 Chr. 22), and gather the materials (1 Chr. 22:14-16). **royal house.** See 1 Kin. 7:1-12 for details (cf. 2 Chr. 7:11; 8:1).

2:2 These numbers are repeated in 2:17,18. First Kings 5:16 records 3,300 overseers, compared to 3,600 in 2:18. If, however, the additional supervisors (250 in 2 Chr. 8:10, but 550 in 1 Kin. 9:23) are added, then both 1 Kings and 2 Chronicles agree that a total of 3,850 men worked. David had done similarly at an earlier date (1 Chr. 22:2).

2:3-10 Compare with the contents of 1 Kin. 5:3-6. The differences can be accounted for in much the same way as in the Gospels, by combining the narratives of 1 Kin. 5:3-6 and 2 Chr. 2:3-10 to complete the entire correspondence.

2:7 send me…a man…skillful. The Israelites were familiar with agriculture, but not metal working. They needed experts for that.

2:8 algum. A coniferous tree native to Lebanon. Some identify it as sandalwood, a smooth, expensive red wood that could be polished to a high gloss.

timber, twenty thousand kors of
ground wheat, twenty thousand
kors of barley, twenty thousand
baths of wine, and twenty
thousand baths of oil.

11 Then Hiram king of Tyre answered in
writing, which he sent to Solomon:

[n]Because the LORD loves His
people, He has made you king
over them.

12 [5]Hiram also said:

[o]Blessed *be* the LORD God of Israel,
[p]who made heaven and earth, for
He has given King David a wise
son, endowed with prudence and
understanding, who will build a
temple for the LORD and a royal
house for himself!

13 And now I have sent a skillful
man, endowed with
understanding, [6]Huram my [7]mas-
ter *craftsman* 14 [q](the son of a
woman of the daughters of Dan,
and his father was a man of Tyre),
skilled to work in gold and silver,
bronze and iron, stone and wood,
purple and blue, fine linen and
crimson, and to make any
engraving and to accomplish any
plan which may be given to him,
with your skillful men and with
the skillful men of my lord David
your father.

15 Now therefore, the wheat, the
barley, the oil, and the wine which
[r]my lord has spoken of, let him
send to his servants. 16 [s]And we
will cut wood from Lebanon, as
much as you need; we will bring it
to you in rafts by sea to [8]Joppa,
and you will carry it up to Jerusalem.

17 [t]Then Solomon numbered all the
aliens who *were* in the land of Israel, after
the census in which [u]David his father
had numbered them; and there were
found to be one hundred and fifty-three
thousand six hundred. 18 And he made
[v]seventy thousand of them bearers of
burdens, eighty thousand stonecutters in
the mountain, and three thousand six
hundred overseers to make the people
work.

Solomon Builds the Temple

3 Now [a]Solomon began to build the
house of the LORD at [b]Jerusalem on
Mount Moriah, where [1]*the LORD* had appeared to his father David, at the place
that David had prepared on the threshing
floor of [c]Ornan[2] the Jebusite. 2 And he
began to build on the second *day* of the
second month in the fourth year of his
reign.
3 This is the foundation [d]which Solomon
laid for building the house of God: The
length *was* sixty cubits (by cubits according
to the former measure) and the width
twenty cubits. 4 And the [e]vestibule that
was in front of [3]*the sanctuary* was twenty
cubits long across the width of the house,
and the height *was* [4]one hundred and
twenty. He overlaid the inside with pure
gold. 5 [f]The larger [5]room he [g]paneled with
cypress which he overlaid with fine gold,
and he carved palm trees and chainwork
on it. 6 And he decorated the house with
precious stones for beauty, and the gold
was gold from Parvaim. 7 He also overlaid
the house—the beams and doorposts, its
walls and doors—with gold; and he carved
cherubim on the walls.
8 And he made the [h]Most Holy Place. Its

11 [n]1 Kin. 10:9; 2 Chr. 9:8
12 [o]1 Kin. 5:7 [p]Gen. 1; 2; Acts 4:24; 14:15; Rev. 10:6 [5]Heb. *Huram;* cf. 1 Kin. 5:1
13 [6]*Hiram,* 1 Kin. 7:13 [7]Lit. *father,* 1 Kin. 7:13, 14
14 [q]1 Kin. 7:13, 14
15 [r]2 Chr. 2:10
16 [s]1 Kin. 5:8, 9 [8]Heb. *Japho*
17 [t]1 Kin. 5:13; 2 Chr. 8:7, 8 [u]1 Chr. 22:2
18 [v]2 Chr. 2:2

CHAPTER 3

1 [a]1 Kin. 6:1 [b]Gen. 22:2-14 [c]1 Chr. 21:18; 22:1 [1]Lit. *He,* following MT, Vg.; LXX *the LORD;* Tg. *the Angel of the LORD* [2]*Araunah,* 2 Sam. 24:16
3 [d]1 Kin. 6:2; 1 Chr. 28:11-19
4 [e]1 Kin. 6:3; 1 Chr. 28:11 [3]The holy place, the main room of the temple, 1 Kin. 6:3 [4]So with MT, LXX, Vg.; Arab., some LXX mss., Syr. *twenty*
5 [f]1 Kin. 6:17 [g]1 Kin. 6:15; Jer. 22:14 [5]Lit. *house*
8 [h]Ex. 26:33; 1 Kin. 6:16

2:10 This listing of goods is more complete than that of 1 Kin. 5:11. Lebanon traded with Israel regularly for food. **twenty thousand kors.** A kor is the same as a homer and could have measured as much as 7.5 bu., making this amount about 150,000 bu. **twenty thousand baths.** A bath measured about 6 gal. This would be about 120,000 gal. The 20 kors of "pressed oil" in 1 Kin. 5:11 is most likely not a scribal error but rather a finer grade of oil.

2:11-16 Compare with the context of 1 Kin. 5:7-9.

2:12 God...who made heaven and earth. This was the common identification of the true God when pagans spoke of or were told of Him (cf. 2 Chr. 36:23; Ezra 1:2; 5:11,12; 6:10; 7:12,21,23; Jer. 10:11,12; Acts 4:24; 14:15; 17:24-26; Col. 1:16,17; Rev. 11:1,6).

2:13,14 Huram. First Kings 7:14 states that his mother was of the tribe of Naphtali, not Dan, as reported here. This is resolved if she was of Naphtali by birth, but living in the territory of Dan. Or, if his parents were originally from the two tribes, then he could legitimately claim either. He was the parallel to Bezalel, who constructed the tabernacle. *See notes on 2 Chr. 1:5.*

2:16 Joppa. A major coastal port of Israel. Later, Jonah would sail from Joppa (Jon. 1:3), and much later Peter would be there to receive God's call in a vision (Acts 10:5ff.).

2:17,18 *See note on 2 Chr. 2:2.*

3:1-17 Cf. 1 Kin. 6:1-38; 7:15-22 for amplification and additional material on the building of the temple.

3:1 threshing floor. *See notes on Gen. 22:1-19; 2 Sam. 24:18-25; 1 Chr. 21:18-30.*

3:2 second month...fourth year. Ca. Apr.–May, 966 B.C. (cf. 1 Kin. 6:1). The project took 7 years, 6 months to complete ca. Oct.–Nov. 959 B.C. (cf. 1 Kin. 6:37,38).

3:3 cubits...former measure. About 18 in. or possibly the royal cubit of 21 in. (cf. Ezek. 40:5).

3:6 Parvaim. An unknown location.

length was according to the width of the
house, twenty cubits, and its width twenty cubits. He overlaid it with six hundred
talents of fine gold. 9 The weight of the
nails *was* fifty shekels of gold; and he overlaid the upper [i]area with gold. 10 [j]In the
Most Holy Place he made two cherubim,
fashioned by carving, and overlaid them
with gold. 11 The wings of the cherubim
were twenty cubits in *overall* length: one
wing *of the one cherub was* five cubits,
touching the wall of the room, and the
other wing *was* five cubits, touching the
wing of the other cherub; 12 *one* wing of
the other cherub *was* five cubits, touching
the wall of the room, and the other wing
also was five cubits, touching the wing of
the other cherub. 13 The wings of these
cherubim spanned twenty cubits overall.
They stood on their feet, and they faced inward. 14 And he made the [k]veil of blue,
purple, crimson, and fine linen, and wove
cherubim into it.
15 Also he made in front of the [6]temple
[l]two pillars [7]thirty-five cubits [8]high, and
the capital that *was* on the top of each of
them was five cubits. 16 He made wreaths of
chainwork, as in the inner sanctuary, and
put *them* on top of the pillars; and he made
[m]one hundred pomegranates, and put *them*
on the wreaths of chainwork. 17 Then he
[n]set up the pillars before the temple, one on
the right hand and the other on the left; he
called the name of the one on the right
hand [9]Jachin, and the name of the one on
the left [1]Boaz.

9 [i] 1 Chr. 28:11
10 [j] Ex. 25:18-20; 1 Kin. 6:23-28
14 [k] Ex. 26:31; Matt. 27:51; Heb. 9:3
15 [l] 1 Kin. 7:15-20; Jer. 52:21 [6] Lit. *house* [7] *eighteen,* 1 Kin. 7:15; 2 Kin. 25:17; Jer. 52:21 [8] Lit. *long*
16 [m] 1 Kin. 7:20
17 [n] 1 Kin. 7:21 [9] Lit. *He Shall Establish* [1] Lit. *In It Is Strength*

CHAPTER 4

1 [a] Ex. 27:1, 2; 2 Kin. 16:14; Ezek. 43:13, 16
2 [b] Ex. 30:17-21; 1 Kin. 7:23-26 [1] Great laver or basin
3 [c] 1 Kin. 7:24-26
4 [d] 1 Kin. 7:25
5 [2] About 8,000 gallons; *two thousand,* 1 Kin. 7:26
6 [e] 1 Kin. 7:38, 40 [f] Ex. 30:19-21 [3] Great basin
7 [g] 1 Kin. 7:49 [h] Ex. 25:31; 1 Chr. 28:12, 19
8 [i] 1 Kin. 7:48 [j] 1 Chr. 28:17
9 [k] 1 Kin. 6:36 [l] 2 Kin. 21:5

Furnishings of the Temple

4 Moreover he made [a]a bronze altar:
twenty cubits was its length, twenty
cubits its width, and ten cubits its height.
2 [b]Then he made the [1]Sea of cast *bronze,*
ten cubits from one brim to the other; *it was*
completely round. Its height *was* five cubits, and a line of thirty cubits measured its
circumference. 3 [c]And under it *was* the
likeness of oxen encircling it all around,
ten to a cubit, all the way around the Sea.
The oxen *were* cast in two rows, when it
was cast. 4 It stood on twelve [d]oxen: three
looking toward the north, three looking toward the west, three looking toward the
south, and three looking toward the east;
the Sea *was set* upon them, and all their
back parts *pointed* inward. 5 It *was* a handbreadth thick; and its brim was shaped like
the brim of a cup, *like* a lily blossom. It contained [2]three thousand baths.
6 He also made [e]ten lavers, and put five
on the right side and five on the left, to
wash in them; such things as they offered
for the burnt offering they would wash in
them, but the [3]Sea *was* for the [f]priests to
wash in. 7 [g]And he made ten lampstands
of gold [h]according to their design, and set
them in the temple, five on the right side
and five on the left. 8 [i]He also made ten tables, and placed *them* in the temple, five on
the right side and five on the left. And he
made one hundred [j]bowls of gold.
9 Furthermore [k]he made the court of the
priests, and the [l]great court and doors for
the court; and he overlaid these doors with

3:8 six hundred talents. Equal to almost 23 tons of gold.

3:9 fifty shekels. Equal to 1.25 lbs. Most likely, this small amount gilded only the spike heads.

3:10-13 two cherubim. *See notes on 1 Kin. 6:23-28.* This freestanding set of cherubim was in addition to the more diminutive set on the ark itself.

3:14 veil. Cf. Ex. 26:31-35 on the veil of the tabernacle. The veil separated the Holy Place from the Most Holy Place (the Holy of Holies), which was entered once annually by the High-Priest on the Day of Atonement (cf. Lev. 16). This highly-limited access to the presence of God was eliminated by the death of Christ, when the veil in Herod's temple was torn in two from top to bottom (Matt. 27:51). It signified that believers had immediate, full access to God's presence through their Mediator and High-Priest Jesus Christ, who was the perfect, once-for-all sacrifice (cf. Heb. 3:14-16; 9:19-22).

3:15 thirty-five cubits. First Kings 7:15, 2 Kin. 25:17, and Jer. 52:21 uniformly describe these cast-bronze pillars as 18 cubits high (about 27 ft.). Most likely this is accounted for because the chronicler gave the combined height of both as they were lying in their molds (cf. v. 17).

3:17 Jachin…Boaz. Most likely these were so named because of the names' meaning rather than in honor of particular people. Jachin means "He shall establish" and Boaz means "In it is strength" (cf. 1 Kin. 7:21).

4:1–5:1 See 1 Kin. 7:23-51 for amplification and additional details.

4:1 bronze altar. This is the main altar on which sacrifices were offered (cf. the millennial temple altar, Ezek. 43:13-17). For comparison to the tabernacle's altar, see Ex. 27:1-8; 38:1-7. If the cubit of 18 in. was used rather than the royal cubit of 21 in., it would make the altar 30 ft. by 30 ft. by 15 ft. high.

4:2 the Sea. This large laver was used for ritual cleansing (cf. Ex. 30:17-21 as it relates to the tabernacle). In Ezekiel's millennial temple, the laver will apparently be replaced by the waters that flow through the temple (Ezek. 47:1-12).

4:3 oxen. First Kings 7:24 reports "buds," which is the more likely translation. These were also around the laver, which was set on top of the 12 oxen.

4:4 twelve oxen. Very likely the 12 oxen represent the 12 tribes who were similarly arrayed around the tabernacle as they set out on their journey in the wilderness (cf. Num. 2:1-34).

4:5 three thousand baths. A bath equaled almost 6 gal. First Kings 7:26 reads 2,000 baths. This discrepancy has been reconciled by accounting here not only for the water the basin held, but also the water source that was necessary to keep it flowing as a fountain.

4:6 ten lavers. There were no such corresponding lavers in the tabernacle.

4:7,8 ten lampstands…ten tables. The tabernacle had one of each. Everything was large because of the crowds of thousands that came on a daily basis and for special occasions.

bronze. 10 [m]He set the Sea on the right side,
toward the southeast.
11 Then [n]Huram made the pots and the
shovels and the bowls. So Huram finished
doing the work that he was to do for King
Solomon for the house of God: 12 the two
pillars and [o]the bowl-shaped capitals *that*
were on top of the two pillars; the two networks covering the two bowl-shaped capitals which *were* on top of the pillars;
13 [p]four hundred pomegranates for the
two networks (two rows of pomegranates
for each network, to cover the two bowl-
shaped capitals that *were* on the pillars);
14 he also made [q]carts and the lavers on the
carts; 15 one Sea and twelve oxen under it;
16 also the pots, the shovels, the forks—
and all their articles [r]Huram his [4]master
craftsman made of burnished bronze for
King Solomon for the house of the LORD.
17 In the plain of Jordan the king had
them cast in clay molds, between Succoth
and [5]Zeredah. 18 [s]And Solomon had all
these articles made in such great abundance that the weight of the bronze was
not determined.
19 Thus [t]Solomon had all the furnishings
made for the house of God: the altar of
gold and the tables on which *was* [u]the
showbread; 20 the lampstands with their
lamps of pure gold, to burn [v]in the prescribed manner in front of the inner sanctuary, 21 with [w]the flowers and the lamps
and the wick-trimmers of gold, of purest
gold; 22 the trimmers, the bowls, the ladles,
and the censers of pure gold. As for the
entry of the [6]sanctuary, its inner doors to
the Most Holy *Place,* and the doors of the
main hall of the temple, *were* gold.
5 So [a]all the work that Solomon had
done for the house of the LORD was finished; and Solomon brought in the things
which his father David had dedicated: the
silver and the gold and all the furnishings.
And he put *them* in the treasuries of the
house of God.

The Ark Brought into the Temple

2 [b]Now Solomon assembled the elders
of Israel and all the heads of the tribes, the
chief fathers of the children of Israel, in Jerusalem, that they might bring the ark of
the covenant of the LORD up [c]from the City
of David, which *is* Zion. 3 [d]Therefore all
the men of Israel assembled with the king
[e]at the feast, which *was* in the seventh
month. 4 So all the elders of Israel came,
and the [f]Levites took up the ark. 5 Then
they brought up the ark, the tabernacle of
meeting, and all the holy furnishings that
were in the tabernacle. The priests and the
Levites brought them up. 6 Also King Solomon, and all the congregation of Israel
who were assembled with him before the
ark, were sacrificing sheep and oxen that
could not be counted or numbered for
multitude. 7 Then the priests brought in
the ark of the covenant of the LORD to its
place, into the [g]inner sanctuary of the
[1]temple, to the Most Holy *Place,* under the
wings of the cherubim. 8 For the cherubim
spread *their* wings over the place of the
ark, and the cherubim overshadowed the
ark and its poles. 9 The poles extended so
that the ends of the [h]poles of the ark could
be seen from *the holy place,* in front of the
inner sanctuary; but they could not be seen
from outside. And [2]they are there to this
day. 10 Nothing was in the ark except the
two tablets which Moses [i]put *there* at
Horeb, [3]when the LORD made *a covenant*
with the children of Israel, when they had
come out of Egypt.
11 And it came to pass when the priests
came out of the *Most* Holy *Place* (for all the
priests who *were* present had [4]sanctified
themselves, without keeping to their [j]divi-
sions), 12 [k]and the Levites *who were* the
singers, all those of Asaph and Heman
and Jeduthun, with their sons and their
brethren, stood at the east end of the altar,
clothed in white linen, having cymbals,
stringed instruments and harps, [l]and with
them one hundred and twenty priests
sounding with trumpets— 13 indeed it

10 [m] 1 Kin. 7:39
11 [n] 1 Kin. 7:40-51
12 [o] 1 Kin. 7:41
13 [p] 1 Kin. 7:20
14 [q] 1 Kin. 7:27, 43
16 [r] 1 Kin. 7:45; 2 Chr. 2:13 [4] Lit. *father*
17 [5] *Zaretan,* 1 Kin. 7:46
18 [s] 1 Kin. 7:47
19 [t] 1 Kin. 7:48-50 [u] Ex. 25:30
20 [v] Ex. 27:20, 21
21 [w] Ex. 25:31
22 [6] Lit. *house*

CHAPTER 5

1 [a] 1 Kin. 7:51
2 [b] 1 Kin. 8:1-9; Ps. 47:9 [c] 2 Sam. 6:12
3 [d] 1 Kin. 8:2 [e] Lev. 23:34; 2 Chr. 7:8-10
4 [f] 1 Chr. 15:2, 15
7 [g] 2 Chr. 4:20 [1] Lit. *house*
9 [h] Ex. 25:13-15 [2] Lit. *it is*
10 [i] Ex. 25:16; Deut. 10:2, 5; 2 Chr. 6:11; Heb. 9:4 [3] Or *where*
11 [j] 1 Chr. 24:1-5 [4] *consecrated*
12 [k] Ex. 32:26; 1 Chr. 25:1-7 [l] 1 Chr. 13:8; 15:16, 24

4:11–5:1 *See notes on 1 Kin. 7:40-51.* All these details emphasize the great care and concern for worship, and served as a manual for the new temple being built by Zerubbabel after the Jews returned from Babylon.

4:11 Huram. *See note on 2 Chr. 2:13.* He led the actual work which Solomon directed.

5:1 The temple took 7 years, 6 months to build and was completed in Solomon's 11th year (959 B.C.) in the eighth month (cf. 1 Kin. 6:38). Since it was dedicated in the seventh month (5:3), its dedication occurred 11 months later to coincide with the Feast of Tabernacles. *See note on 1 Kin. 8:2.* Why is there so much emphasis in the OT on the temple? 1) It was the center of worship that called people to correct belief through the generations. 2) It was the symbol of God's presence with His people. 3) It was the symbol of forgiveness and grace, reminding the people of the seriousness of sin and the availability of mercy. 4) It prepared the people for the true Lamb of God, Jesus Christ, who would take away sin. 5) It was a place of prayer. Cf. 7:12-17.

5:2-10 *See notes on 1 Kin. 8:1-9.*

5:2 The ark was in Jerusalem in a temporary tent (2 Sam. 6:17), not the original tabernacle, which was still at Gibeon (1 Chr. 16:39).

5:11 *Most* Holy *Place.* This was to be the last time anyone but the High-Priest went in, and then only once a year. It took several priests to place the ark in its new home.

5:12 Asaph...Heman...Jeduthun. *See notes on 1 Chr. 25.*

came to pass, when the trumpeters and
singers *were* as one, to make one sound to
be heard in praising and thanking the
LORD, and when they lifted up their voice
with the trumpets and cymbals and instruments of music, and praised the LORD,
saying:

[m]"*For He is* good,
For His mercy *endures* forever,"

that the house, the house of the LORD, was
filled with a cloud, 14 so that the priests
could not [5]continue ministering because of
the cloud; [n]for the glory of the LORD filled
the house of God.

6 Then [a]Solomon spoke:

"The LORD said He would dwell in
the [b]dark cloud.
2 I have surely built You an exalted
house,
And [c]a place for You to dwell in
forever."

Solomon's Speech upon Completion of the Work

3 Then the king turned around and
[d]blessed the whole assembly of Israel,
while all the assembly of Israel was standing. 4 And he said: "Blessed *be* the LORD
God of Israel, who has fulfilled with His
hands *what* He spoke with His mouth to
my father David, [e]saying, 5 'Since the day
that I brought My people out of the land of
Egypt, I have chosen no city from any tribe
of Israel *in which* to build a house, that My
name might be there, nor did I choose any
man to be a ruler over My people Israel.
6 [f]Yet I have chosen Jerusalem, that My
name may be there, and I [g]have chosen
David to be over My people Israel.' 7 Now
[h]it was in the heart of my father David to
build a [1]temple for the name of the LORD
God of Israel. 8 But the LORD said to my father David, 'Whereas it was in your heart
to build a temple for My name, you did
well in that it was in your heart. 9 Nevertheless you shall not build the temple, but
your son who will come from your body,
he shall build the temple for My [i]name.'
10 So the LORD has fulfilled His word
which He spoke, and I have filled the position of my father David, and [j]sit on the
throne of Israel, as the LORD promised; and
I have built the temple for the name of the
LORD God of Israel. 11 And there I have put
the ark, [k]in which *is* the covenant of the
LORD which He made with the children of
Israel."

Solomon's Prayer of Dedication

12 [l]Then [2]*Solomon* stood before the altar
of the LORD in the presence of all the assembly of Israel, and spread out his hands
13 (for Solomon had made a bronze platform five cubits long, five cubits wide, and
three cubits high, and had set it in the
midst of the court; and he stood on it,
knelt down on his knees before all the assembly of Israel, and spread out his hands
toward heaven); 14 and he said: "LORD
God of Israel, [m]*there is* no God in heaven
or on earth like You, who keep *Your*
[n]covenant and mercy with Your servants
who walk before You with all their hearts.
15 [o]You have kept what You promised
Your servant David my father; You have
both spoken with Your mouth and fulfilled *it* with Your hand, as *it is* this day.
16 Therefore, LORD God of Israel, now
keep what You promised Your servant David my father, saying, [p]'You shall not fail
to have a man sit before Me on the throne
of Israel, [q]only if your sons take heed to
their way, that they walk in My law as you
have walked before Me.' 17 And now, O
LORD God of Israel, let Your word come
true, which You have spoken to Your servant David.

18 "But will God indeed dwell with men
on the earth? [r]Behold, heaven and the
heaven of heavens cannot contain You.
How much less this [3]temple which I have
built! 19 Yet regard the prayer of Your servant and his supplication, O LORD my God,
and listen to the cry and the prayer which
Your servant is praying before You: 20 that
Your eyes may be [s]open toward this temple day and night, toward the place where
You said *You would* put Your name, that
You may hear the prayer which Your servant makes [t]toward this place. 21 And may
You hear the supplications of Your servant

13 [m] 1 Chr. 16:34, 41; 2 Chr. 7:3; Ezra 3:11; Ps. 100:5; 106:1; 136; Jer. 33:11
14 [n] Ex. 40:35; 1 Kin. 8:11; 2 Chr. 7:2; Ezek. 43:5 [5] Lit. *stand to minister*

CHAPTER 6

1 [a] Ex. 19:9; 20:21; 1 Kin. 8:12-21 [b] [Lev. 16:2]; Ps. 97:2
2 [c] 2 Sam. 7:13; 1 Chr. 17:12; 2 Chr. 7:12
3 [d] 2 Sam. 6:18
4 [e] 1 Chr. 17:5
6 [f] Deut. 12:5-7; 2 Chr. 12:13; Zech. 2:12 [g] 1 Sam. 16:7-13; 1 Chr. 28:4
7 [h] 2 Sam. 7:2; 1 Chr. 17:1; 28:2; Ps. 132:1-5 [1] Lit. *house,* and so in vv. 8-10
9 [i] 1 Chr. 28:3-6
10 [j] 1 Kin. 2:12; 10:9
11 [k] 2 Chr. 5:7-10
12 [l] 1 Kin. 8:22; 2 Chr. 7:7-9 [2] Lit. *he*
14 [m] [Ex. 15:11; Deut. 4:39] [n] [Deut. 7:9]
15 [o] 1 Chr. 22:9, 10
16 [p] 2 Sam. 7:12, 16; 1 Kin. 2:4; 6:12; 2 Chr. 7:18 [q] Ps. 132:12
18 [r] [2 Chr. 2:6; Is. 66:1; Acts 7:49] [3] Lit. *house*
20 [s] 2 Chr. 7:15 [t] Ps. 5:7; Dan. 6:10

5:13,14 the glory of the LORD. The Lord's presence indwelt the temple and the first service of worship was held. In the same manner He descended on the tabernacle (Ex. 40:34-38). He will do likewise on the millennial temple (Ezek. 43:1-5). His glory is representative of His person (cf. Ex. 33), and entering the temple signified His presence.

6:1-11 *See notes on 1 Kin. 8:12-21.*

6:11 the covenant of the LORD. The Mosaic law written on tablets of stone (cf. 5:10).

6:12-40 *See notes on 1 Kin. 8:22-50.* As Solomon led his people in prayer, he asked God to help them in many situations: 1) crime (vv. 22,23); 2) enemy attacks (vv. 24,25); 3) drought (vv. 26,27); 4) famine (vv. 28-31); 5) foreigners (vv. 32,33); 6) war (vv. 34,35); and 7) sin (vv. 36-39).

6:13 knelt. Solomon, in an unusually humbling act for a king, acknowledged God's sovereignty.

6:18 Solomon marveled that God would condescend to live there. Cf. John 1:14; Col. 2:9.

and of Your people Israel, when they pray toward this place. Hear from heaven Your dwelling place, and when You hear, [u]forgive.

22 "If anyone sins against his neighbor, and is forced to take an [v]oath, and comes *and* takes an oath before Your altar in this temple, 23 then hear from heaven, and act, and judge Your servants, bringing retribution on the wicked by bringing his way on his own head, and justifying the righteous by giving him according to his [w]righteousness.

24 "Or if Your people Israel are defeated before an [x]enemy because they have sinned against You, and return and confess Your name, and pray and make supplication before You in this temple, 25 then hear from heaven and forgive the sin of Your people Israel, and bring them back to the land which You gave to them and their fathers.

26 "When the [y]heavens are shut up and there is no rain because they have sinned against You, when they pray toward this place and confess Your name, and turn from their sin because You afflict them, 27 then hear *in* heaven, and forgive the sin of Your servants, Your people Israel, that You may teach them the good way in which they should walk; and send rain on Your land which You have given to Your people as an inheritance.

28 "When there [z]is famine in the land, pestilence or blight or mildew, locusts or grasshoppers; when their enemies besiege them in the land of their cities; whatever plague or whatever [a]sickness *there is;* 29 whatever prayer, whatever supplication is *made* by anyone, or by all Your people Israel, when each one knows his own burden and his own grief, and spreads out his hands to this temple: 30 then hear from heaven Your dwelling place, and forgive, and give to everyone according to all his ways, whose heart You know (for You alone [b]know the [c]hearts of the sons of men), 31 that they may fear You, to walk in Your ways as long as they live in the land which You gave to our fathers.

32 "Moreover, concerning a foreigner, [d]who is not of Your people Israel, but has come from a far country for the sake of Your great name and Your mighty hand and Your outstretched arm, when they come and pray in this temple; 33 then hear from heaven Your dwelling place, and do according to all for which the foreigner calls to You, that all peoples of the earth may know Your name and fear You, as *do* Your people Israel, and that they may know that [4]this temple which I have built is called by Your name.

34 "When Your people go out to battle against their enemies, wherever You send them, and when they pray to You toward this city which You have chosen and the temple which I have built for Your name, 35 then hear from heaven their prayer and their supplication, and maintain their cause.

36 "When they sin against You (for *there is* [e]no one who does not sin), and You become angry with them and deliver them to the enemy, and they take them [f]captive to a land far or near; 37 *yet* when they [5]come to themselves in the land where they were carried captive, and repent, and make supplication to You in the land of their captivity, saying, 'We have sinned, we have done wrong, and have committed wickedness'; 38 and *when* they return to You with all their heart and with all their soul in the land of their captivity, where they have been carried captive, and pray toward their land which You gave to their fathers, the [g]city which You have chosen, and toward the temple which I have built for Your name: 39 then hear from heaven Your dwelling place their prayer and their supplications, and maintain their cause, and forgive Your people who have sinned against You. 40 Now, my God, I pray, let Your eyes be [h]open and *let* Your ears *be* attentive to the prayer *made* in this place.

41 "Now[i] therefore,
Arise, O LORD God, to Your
[j]resting place,
You and the ark of Your strength.
Let Your priests, O LORD God, be
clothed with salvation,
And let Your saints [k]rejoice in
goodness.

42 "O LORD God, do not turn away the
face of Your Anointed;
[l]Remember the mercies of Your
servant David."

Solomon Dedicates the Temple

7 When [a]Solomon had finished praying, [b]fire came down from heaven and consumed the burnt offering and the sacrifices; and [c]the glory of the LORD filled the [1]temple. 2 [d]And the priests could not enter the house of the LORD, because the glory of

21 [u][Is. 43:25; 44:22; Mic. 7:18]
22 [v]Ex. 22:8-11
23 [w][Job 34:11]
24 [x]2 Kin. 21:14, 15
26 [y]Deut. 28:23, 24; 1 Kin. 17:1
28 [z]2 Chr. 20:9 [a][Mic. 6:13]
30 [b][1 Chr. 28:9; Prov. 21:2; 24:12] [c][1 Sam. 16:7]
32 [d]John 12:20; Acts 8:27
33 [4]Lit. *Your name is called upon this house*
36 [e]Prov. 20:9; Eccl. 7:20; [Rom. 3:9, 19; 5:12; Gal. 3:10]; James 3:2; 1 John 1:8 [f]Deut. 28:63-68
37 [5]Lit. *bring back to their hearts*
38 [g]Dan. 6:10
40 [h]2 Chr. 6:20
41 [i]Ps. 132:8-10, 16 [j]1 Chr. 28:2 [k]Neh. 9:25
42 [l]2 Sam. 7:15; Ps. 89:49; 132:1, 8-10; Is. 55:3

CHAPTER 7
1 [a]1 Kin. 8:54 [b]Lev. 9:24; Judg. 6:21; 1 Kin. 18:38; 1 Chr. 21:26 [c]1 Kin. 8:10, 11 [1]Lit. *house*
2 [d]2 Chr. 5:14

6:41-42 *See notes on Ps. 132:8-10; 1 Kin. 8:51-61.*

7:1-3 fire came down. This also occurred when the tabernacle was dedicated (Lev. 9:23,24). This was the genuine dedication, because only God can truly sanctify.

the LORD had filled the LORD's house.
3 When all the children of Israel saw how
the fire came down, and the glory of the
LORD on the temple, they bowed their faces
to the ground on the pavement, and worshiped and praised the LORD, *saying:*

[e]"For *He is* good,
[f]For His mercy *endures* forever."

4 [g]Then the king and all the people offered sacrifices before the LORD. **5** King Solomon offered a sacrifice of twenty-two
thousand bulls and one hundred and
twenty thousand sheep. So the king and all
the people dedicated the house of God.
6 [h]And the priests attended to their services; the Levites also with instruments of
the music of the LORD, which King David
had made to praise the LORD, saying, "For
His mercy *endures* forever," whenever David offered praise by their [2]ministry. [i]The
priests sounded trumpets opposite them,
while all Israel stood.
7 Furthermore [j]Solomon consecrated the
middle of the court that *was* in front of the
house of the LORD; for there he offered
burnt offerings and the fat of the peace offerings, because the bronze altar which
Solomon had made was not able to receive
the burnt offerings, the grain offerings, and
the fat.
8 [k]At that time Solomon kept the feast
seven days, and all Israel with him, a very
great assembly [l]from the entrance of
Hamath to [m]the[3] Brook of Egypt. **9** And on
the eighth day they held a [n]sacred assembly, for they observed the dedication of the
altar seven days, and the feast seven days.
10 [o]On the twenty-third day of the seventh
month he sent the people away to their
tents, joyful and glad of heart for the good
that the LORD had done for David, for Solomon, and for His people Israel. **11** Thus
[p]Solomon finished the house of the LORD
and the king's house; and Solomon successfully accomplished all that came into
his heart to make in the house of the LORD
and in his own house.

3 [e] 2 Chr. 5:13; Ps. 106:1; 136:1 [f] 1 Chr. 16:41; 2 Chr. 20:21
4 [g] 1 Kin. 8:62, 63
6 [h] 1 Chr. 15:16 [i] 2 Chr. 5:12 [2] Lit. *hand*
7 [j] 1 Kin. 8:64-66; 9:3
8 [k] 1 Kin. 8:65 [l] 1 Kin. 4:21, 24; 2 Kin. 14:25 [m] Josh. 13:3 [3] The Shihor, 1 Chr. 13:5
9 [n] Lev. 23:36
10 [o] 1 Kin. 8:66
11 [p] 1 Kin. 9:1

God's Second Appearance to Solomon

12 Then the LORD [q]appeared to Solomon by night, and said to him: "I have
heard your prayer, [r]and have chosen this
[s]place for Myself as a house of sacrifice.
13 [t]When I shut up heaven and there is no
rain, or command the locusts to devour
the land, or send pestilence among My
people, **14** if My people who are [u]called
by My name will [v]humble themselves,
and pray and seek My face, and turn
from their wicked ways, [w]then I will hear
from heaven, and will forgive their sin
and heal their land. **15** Now [x]My eyes will
be open and My ears attentive to prayer
made in this place. **16** For now [y]I have chosen and [4]sanctified this house, that My
name may be there forever; and [5]My eyes
and [6]My heart will be there perpetually.
17 [z]As for you, if you walk before Me as
your father David walked, and do according to all that I have commanded
you, and if you keep My statutes and My
judgments, **18** then I will establish the
throne of your kingdom, as I covenanted
with David your father, saying, [a]'You
shall not fail *to have* a man as ruler in Israel.'
19 [b]"But if you turn away and forsake
My statutes and My commandments
which I have set before you, and go and
serve other gods, and worship them,
20 [c]then I will uproot them from My land
which I have given them; and this house
which I have [7]sanctified for My name I
will cast out of My sight, and will make it
a proverb and a [d]byword among all peoples.
21 "And *as for* [e]this [8]house, which [9]is
exalted, everyone who passes by it will be
[f]astonished and say, [g]'Why has the LORD
done thus to this land and this house?'
22 Then they will answer, 'Because they
forsook the LORD God of their fathers,
who brought them out of the land of
Egypt, and embraced other gods, and
worshiped them and served them; therefore He has brought all this calamity on
them.' "

12 [q] 1 Kin. 3:5; 11:9 [r] Deut. 12:5, 11 [s] 2 Chr. 6:20
13 [t] Deut. 28:23, 24; 1 Kin. 17:1; 2 Chr. 6:26-28
14 [u] Deut. 28:10; [Is. 43:7] [v] 2 Chr. 12:6, 7; [James 4:10] [w] 2 Chr. 6:27, 30
15 [x] 2 Chr. 6:20, 40
16 [y] 1 Kin. 9:3; 2 Chr. 6:6 [4] *set apart* [5] My attention [6] My concern
17 [z] 1 Kin. 9:4
18 [a] 2 Sam. 7:12-16; 1 Kin. 2:4; 2 Chr. 6:16
19 [b] Lev. 26:14, 33; [Deut. 28:15, 36]
20 [c] Deut. 28:63-68; 2 Kin. 25:1-7 [d] Ps. 44:14 [7] *set apart*
21 [e] 2 Kin. 25:9 [f] 2 Chr. 29:8 [g] [Deut. 29:24, 25; Jer. 22:8, 9] [8] Temple [9] Or *was*

7:4,5 *See notes on 1 Kin. 8:62,63.*

7:8-10 Solomon's celebration included the special assembly to dedicate the altar on the 8th–14th of the 7th month (Sept.–Oct.) which included the Day of Atonement. It was immediately followed by the Feast of Tabernacles (15th–21st) and a special assembly on the 8th day, i.e., 22nd day of the month.

7:8 Hamath...Brook of Egypt. Lit. from the northern boundary to the southern boundary.

7:11,12 *See notes on 1 Kin. 9:1,2.* Perhaps years had passed since the dedication of the temple in chap. 6 during which he had also built "the King's house" (cf. 8:1). After all that time, God confirmed that He had heard Solomon's prayer (v. 12).

7:13-16 This section is almost all unique to 2 Chronicles. (cf. 1 Kin. 9:3), and features the conditions for national forgiveness of Israel's sins: 1) humility; 2) prayer; 3) longing for God; and 4) repentance.

7:17-22. *See notes on 1 Kin. 9:4-9.*

7:17,18 if...then. If there was obedience on the part of the nation, the kingdom would be established and they would have "a man as ruler." Their disobedience was legendary and so was the destruction of their kingdom and their dispersion. When Israel is saved (cf. Rom. 11:25-27; Zech. 12:14), then their King Messiah will set up this glorious kingdom (Rev. 20:1ff.).

Solomon's Additional Achievements

8 It [a]came to pass at the end of [b]twenty
years, when Solomon had built the
house of the LORD and his own house,
2 that the cities which [1]Hiram had given
to Solomon, Solomon built them; and he
settled the children of Israel there. **3** And
Solomon went to Hamath Zobah and
seized it. **4** [c]He also built Tadmor in the
wilderness, and all the storage cities
which he built in [d]Hamath. **5** He built
Upper Beth Horon and [e]Lower Beth
Horon, fortified cities *with* walls, gates,
and bars, **6** also Baalath and all the storage
cities that Solomon had, and all the chariot cities and the cities of the cavalry, and
all that Solomon [f]desired to build in Jerusalem, in Lebanon, and in all the land of
his dominion.

7 [g]All the people *who were* left of the Hittites, Amorites, Perizzites, Hivites, and
Jebusites, who *were* not of Israel— **8** that is,
their descendants who were left in the land
after them, whom the children of Israel did
not destroy—from these Solomon raised
forced labor, as it is to this day. **9** But Solomon did not make the children of Israel
[2]servants for his work. Some *were* men of
war, captains of his officers, captains of his
chariots, and his cavalry. **10** And others
were chiefs of the officials of King Solomon:
[h]two hundred and fifty, who ruled over the
people.

11 Now Solomon [i]brought the daughter
of Pharaoh up from the City of David to
the house he had built for her, for he said,
"My wife shall not dwell in the house of
David king of Israel, because *the places* to
which the ark of the LORD has come are
holy."

12 Then Solomon offered burnt offerings
to the LORD on the altar of the LORD which
he had built before the vestibule, **13** according to the [j]daily rate, offering according to
the commandment of Moses, for the Sabbaths, the New Moons, and the [k]three appointed yearly [l]feasts—the Feast of Unleavened Bread, the Feast of Weeks, and
the Feast of Tabernacles. **14** And, according
to the [3]order of David his father, he appointed the [m]divisions of the priests for
their service, [n]the Levites for their duties
(to praise and serve before the priests) as
the duty of each day required, and the
[o]gatekeepers by their divisions at each
gate; for so David the man of God had
commanded. **15** They did not depart from
the command of the king to the priests and
Levites concerning any matter or concerning the [p]treasuries.

16 Now all the work of Solomon was
well-ordered [4]from the day of the foundation of the house of the LORD until it was
finished. So the house of the LORD was
completed.

17 Then Solomon went to [q]Ezion Geber
and [5]Elath on the seacoast, in the land of
Edom. **18** [r]And Hiram sent him ships by
the hand of his servants, and servants
who knew the sea. They went with the
servants of Solomon to [s]Ophir, and acquired four hundred and fifty talents of
gold from there, and brought it to King
Solomon.

CHAPTER 8
1 [a] 1 Kin. 9:10-14 [b] 1 Kin. 6:38–7:1
2 [1] Heb. *Huram*, 2 Chr. 2:3
4 [c] 1 Kin. 9:17, 18 [d] 1 Chr. 18:3, 9
5 [e] 1 Chr. 7:24
6 [f] 2 Chr. 7:11
7 [g] Gen. 15:18-21; 1 Kin. 9:20
9 [2] *slaves*
10 [h] 1 Kin. 9:23
11 [i] 1 Kin. 3:1; 7:8; 9:24; 11:1
13 [j] Ex. 29:38-42; Num. 28:3, 9, 11, 26; 29:1 [k] Ex. 23:14-17; 34:22, 23; Deut. 16:16 [l] Lev. 23:1-44
14 [m] 1 Chr. 24:3 [n] 1 Chr. 25:1 [o] 1 Chr. 9:17; 26:1 [3] *ordinance*
15 [p] 1 Chr. 26:20-28
16 [4] So with LXX, Syr., Vg.; MT *as far as*
17 [q] 1 Kin. 9:26; 2 Chr. 20:36 [5] Heb. *Eloth*, 2 Kin. 14:22
18 [r] 1 Kin. 9:27; 2 Chr. 9:10, 13 [s] 1 Chr. 29:4

8:1 twenty years. Ca. 946 B.C., 24 years after Solomon's reign began.

8:2 Cf. 1 Kin. 9:10-14. Though these cities were within the boundaries of the Promised Land, they had never been conquered, so Solomon gave Hiram the right to settle them. Hiram, however, returned the Galilean cities which Solomon had given him because they were unacceptably poor. Solomon apparently then improved them and settled Israelites there.

8:3-6 Here are additional military campaigns and building projects not mentioned in 1 Kin. 9. He was building storage places for his commercial enterprises and fortifying his borders to secure his kingdom from invasion.

8:3 Hamath Zobah. A city located in Syria, N of Damascus and in close proximity to but S of Hamath.

8:4 Tadmor. A city 150 mi. NE of Damascus. **Hamath.** A city N of Damascus.

8:5 Beth Horon. Two cities NW of Jerusalem. Upper Beth Horon is at 2,022 ft., 11 mi. NW of Jerusalem. Lower Beth Horon is at 1,210 ft., 13 mi. NW of Jerusalem. They were both on a strategic road that connected Jerusalem with Joppa on the coast.

8:6 Baalath. A city originally in Danite territory (Josh. 19:44) ca. 30 mi. W of Jerusalem.

8:7-10 *See notes on 1 Kin. 9:20-23.*

8:10 two hundred and fifty. *See notes on 2 Chr. 2:2.*

8:11 the daughter of Pharaoh. Cf. 1 Kin. 9:24. First Kings 3:1 mentions the marriage and the fact that Solomon brought her to Jerusalem until he could build a house for her. Until that palace was built, Solomon lived in David's palace, but did not allow her to do so, because she was a heathen and because the ark of God had once been in David's house. He surely knew his marriage to this pagan did not please God (cf. Deut. 7:3,4). Eventually his pagan wives caused tragic consequences (1 Kin. 11:1-11).

8:12-15 This section expands on 1 Kin. 9:25, and indicates that Solomon was, in spite of his disobedience in marriage, still faithful to the religions practices required in the temple.

8:13 three...feasts. These were prescribed in the Mosaic legislation: 1) Unleavened Bread/Passover; 2) Pentecost; and 3) Tabernacles (cf. Ex. 23:14-17; Deut. 16:1-17).

8:17,18 *See notes on 1 Kin. 9:26-28.* These two ports where Solomon had received ships were located on the eastern gulf of the Red Sea, called Aqabah. Solomon was cultivating peace and commerce plus using Hiram's sailors to teach his people how to sail.

8:18 four hundred and fifty talents. First Kings 9:28 reports 420 talents, probably accounted for by a scribal error in transmission. This was about 17 tons of gold.

The Queen of Sheba's Praise of Solomon

9 Now [a]when the queen of Sheba heard of the fame of Solomon, she came to Jerusalem to test Solomon with hard questions, *having* a very great retinue, camels that bore spices, gold in abundance, and precious stones; and when she came to Solomon, she spoke with him about all that was in her heart. 2 So Solomon answered all her questions; there was nothing so difficult for Solomon that he could not explain it to her. 3 And when the queen of Sheba had seen the wisdom of Solomon, the house that he had built, 4 the food on his table, the seating of his servants, the service of his waiters and their apparel, his [b]cupbearers and their apparel, and his entryway by which he went up to the house of the LORD, there was no more spirit in her.

5 Then she said to the king: "*It was* a true report which I heard in my own land about your words and your wisdom. 6 However I did not believe their words until I came and saw with my own eyes; and indeed the half of the greatness of your wisdom was not told me. You exceed the fame of which I heard. 7 Happy *are* your men and happy *are* these your servants, who stand continually before you and hear your wisdom! 8 Blessed be the LORD your God, who delighted in you, setting you on His throne *to be* king for the LORD your God! Because your God has [c]loved Israel, to establish them forever, therefore He made you king over them, to do justice and righteousness."

9 And she gave the king one hundred and twenty talents of gold, spices in great abundance, and precious stones; there never were any spices such as those the queen of Sheba gave to King Solomon.

10 Also, the servants of Hiram and the servants of Solomon, [d]who brought gold from Ophir, brought [1]algum wood and precious stones. 11 And the king made walkways *of* the [2]algum wood for the house of the LORD and for the king's house, also harps and stringed instruments for singers; and there were none such *as these* seen before in the land of Judah.

12 Now King Solomon gave to the queen of Sheba all she desired, whatever she asked, *much more* than she had brought to the king. So she turned and went to her own country, she and her servants.

Solomon's Great Wealth

13 [e]The weight of gold that came to Solomon yearly was six hundred and sixty-six talents of gold, 14 besides *what* the traveling merchants and traders brought. And all the kings of Arabia and governors of the country brought gold and silver to Solomon. 15 And King Solomon made two hundred large shields of hammered gold; six hundred *shekels* of hammered gold went into each shield. 16 *He* also *made* three hundred shields of hammered gold; [3]three hundred *shekels* of gold went into each shield. The king put them in the [f]House of the Forest of Lebanon.

17 Moreover the king made a great throne of ivory, and overlaid it with pure gold. 18 The throne *had* six steps, with a footstool of gold, *which were* fastened to the throne; there were [4]armrests on either side of the place of the seat, and two lions stood beside the armrests. 19 Twelve lions stood there, one on each side of the six steps; nothing like *this* had been made for any *other* kingdom.

20 All King Solomon's drinking vessels *were* gold, and all the vessels of the House of the Forest of Lebanon *were* pure gold. Not *one was* silver, for this was accounted as nothing in the days of Solomon. 21 For the king's ships went to [g]Tarshish with the servants of [5]Hiram. Once every three years the [6]merchant ships came, bringing gold, silver, ivory, apes, and [7]monkeys.

22 So King Solomon surpassed all the kings of the earth in riches and wisdom. 23 And all the kings of the earth sought the presence of Solomon to hear his wisdom, which God had put in his heart. 24 Each man brought his present: articles of silver and gold, garments, [h]armor, spices, horses, and mules, at a set rate year by year.

25 Solomon [i]had four thousand stalls for horses and chariots, and twelve thousand horsemen whom he stationed in the chariot cities and with the king at Jerusalem.

26 [j]So he reigned over all the kings [k]from [8]the River to the land of the Philistines, as far as the border of Egypt. 27 [l]The king made silver *as common* in Jerusalem as

9:1-28 *See notes on 1 Kin. 10:1-29.*

9:8 His throne. The thought that Solomon sat on God's throne is not included in the queen of Sheba's words in 1 Kin. 10:9. The blessing of God on Israel and on Solomon was to last as long as he followed the Lord as David had (2 Chr. 7:17-21).

9:16 *shekels.* "Bekah," not *shekel* or "mina" (cf. margin), is the correct unit of weight. Since one mina equals 50 shekels and one shekel equals two bekahs, then the 3 minas in 1 Kin. 10:17 equals the 300 bekahs here and both texts agree. This would represent a little less than 4 lbs.

9:18 footstool of gold. The chronicler adds this detail, which is absent in 1 Kin. 10:19.

9:25 four thousand. This reading is preferable to "40,000" in 1 Kin. 4:26 (cf. margin).

CHAPTER 9

1 [a] 1 Kin. 10:1; Ps. 72:10; [Matt. 12:42; Luke 11:31]
4 [b] Neh. 1:11
8 [c] Deut. 7:8; 2 Chr. 2:11; [Ps. 44:3]
10 [d] 2 Chr. 8:18 [1] *almug,* 1 Kin. 10:11, 12
11 [2] *almug,* 1 Kin. 10:11, 12
13 [e] 1 Kin. 10:14-29
16 [f] 1 Kin. 7:2 [3] *three minas,* 1 Kin. 10:17
18 [4] Lit. *hands*
21 [g] 2 Chr. 20:36, 37; Ps. 72:10 [5] Heb. *Huram;* cf. 1 Kin. 10:22 [6] Lit. *ships of Tarshish,* deep-sea vessels [7] Or *peacocks*
24 [h] 1 Kin. 20:11
25 [i] Deut. 17:16; 1 Kin. 4:26; 10:26; 2 Chr. 1:14; Is. 2:7
26 [j] 1 Kin. 4:21 [k] Gen. 15:18; Ps. 72:8 [8] The Euphrates
27 [l] 1 Kin. 10:27

stones, and he made cedar trees [m]as abundant as the sycamores which *are* in the lowland. 28 [n]And they brought horses to Solomon from Egypt and from all lands.

Death of Solomon

29 [o]Now the rest of the acts of Solomon,
first and last, *are* they not written in the
book of Nathan the prophet, in the prophecy of [p]Ahijah the Shilonite, and in the visions of [q]Iddo the seer concerning Jeroboam
the son of Nebat? 30 [r]Solomon reigned in Jerusalem over all Israel forty years. 31 Then
Solomon [9]rested with his fathers, and was
buried in the City of David his father. And
Rehoboam his son reigned in his place.

The Revolt Against Rehoboam

10 And [a]Rehoboam went to Shechem,
for all Israel had gone to Shechem to
make him king. 2 So it happened, when Jeroboam the son of Nebat heard *it* (he was in
Egypt, [b]where he had fled from the presence of King Solomon), that Jeroboam returned from Egypt. 3 Then they sent for him
and called him. And Jeroboam and all Israel
came and spoke to Rehoboam, saying,
4 "Your father made our yoke heavy; now
therefore, lighten the burdensome service of
your father and his heavy yoke which he
put on us, and we will serve you."
5 So he said to them, "Come back to me
after three days." And the people departed.
6 Then King Rehoboam consulted the elders who stood before his father Solomon
while he still lived, saying, "How do you
advise *me* to answer these people?"
7 And they spoke to him, saying, "If you
are kind to these people, and please them,
and speak good words to them, they will
be your servants forever."
8 [c]But he rejected the advice which the
elders had given him, and consulted the
young men who had grown up with him,
who stood before him. 9 And he said to
them, "What advice do you give? How
should we answer this people who have
spoken to me, saying, 'Lighten the yoke
which your father put on us'?"
10 Then the young men who had grown
up with him spoke to him, saying, "Thus
you should speak to the people who have
spoken to you, saying, 'Your father made
our yoke heavy, but you make *it* lighter on
us'—thus you shall say to them: 'My little
finger shall be thicker than my father's
waist! 11 And now, whereas my father put
a heavy yoke on you, I will add to your
yoke; my father chastised you with whips,
but I *will chastise you* with [1]scourges!' "
12 So [d]Jeroboam and all the people came
to Rehoboam on the third day, as the king
had directed, saying, "Come back to me the
third day." 13 Then the king answered them
roughly. King Rehoboam rejected the advice of the elders, 14 and he spoke to them
according to the advice of the young men,
saying, [2]"My father made your yoke heavy,
but I will add to it; my father chastised you
with whips, but I *will chastise you* with
[3]scourges!" 15 So the king did not listen to
the people; [e]for the turn *of events* was from
God, that the LORD might fulfill His [f]word,
which He had spoken by the hand of Ahijah
the Shilonite to Jeroboam the son of Nebat.
16 Now when all Israel *saw* that the king
did not listen to them, the people answered the king, saying:

"What share have we in David?
We have no inheritance in the son
of Jesse.
Every man to your tents, O Israel!
Now see to your own house,
O David!"

So all Israel departed to their tents.
17 But Rehoboam reigned over the children
of Israel who dwelt in the cities of Judah.
18 Then King Rehoboam sent Hadoram,

27 [m]2 Chr. 1:15-17
28 [n]1 Kin. 10:28; 2 Chr. 1:16
29 [o]1 Kin. 11:41 [p]1 Kin. 11:29 [q]2 Chr. 12:15; 13:22
30 [r]1 Kin. 4:21; 11:42, 43; 1 Chr. 29:28
31 [9]Died and joined his ancestors

CHAPTER 10

1 [a]1 Kin. 12:1-20
2 [b]1 Kin. 11:40
8 [c]1 Kin. 12:8-11

11 [1]Scourges with points or barbs, lit. *scorpions*
12 [d]1 Kin. 12:12-14
14 [2]So with many Heb. mss., LXX, Syr., Vg. (cf. v. 10; 1 Kin. 12:14); MT / [3]Lit. *scorpions*
15 [e]Judg. 14:4; 1 Chr. 5:22; 2 Chr. 11:4; 22:7 [f]1 Kin. 11:29-39

9:29-31 *See notes on 1 Kin. 11:41-43.*

9:29 First Kings 11:41 reports that Solomon's deeds were written in "the book of the acts of Solomon." For the rest of the record of Solomon's life, read 1 Kin. 10:26–11:43. In later years, he turned away from God and, due to the influence of his wives, he led the nation into idolatry. This split the kingdom and sowed the seeds that led to its defeat and dispersion. The Chronicles do not record this sad end to Solomon's life because the focus is on encouraging the returning Jews from Babylon with God's pledge to them for a glorious future in the Davidic Covenant.

10:1–36:21 This section records all 20 of the Judean rulers in the divided kingdom from Solomon's son Rehoboam (ca. 931 B.C.) to Zedekiah (ca. 586 B.C.) when the people were taken captive to Babylon. The righteous kings and the revivals under them are presented, as well as the wicked kings and their disastrous influence. The northern kingdom is absent since Chronicles focuses on the Davidic line.

10:1–12:16 The reign of Rehoboam (ca. 931–913 B.C.). Cf. 1 Kin. 12–14.

10:1–11:4 For details on this chapter, *see notes on 1 Kin. 12:1-24.* Rehoboam followed foolish and bad advice from novices rather than the good counsel of wise, seasoned men. The result was the division of the nation. Amazingly, with all the strength of Solomon's reign, unity was fragile and one fool in the place of leadership ended it. Rehoboam tried to unite the people by force, but was not allowed to by God (11:1-4).

10:2 Jeroboam. He became the first king of the northern kingdom of Israel (ca. 931–910 B.C.). His story leading to his return from Egypt is told in 1 Kin. 11:26-40.

10:16-19 Here is recorded the beginning of the divided kingdom. Ten tribes followed Jeroboam and were called Israel. The other two tribes, Benjamin and Judah, stayed loyal to David's line, accepted Rehoboam's rule, and were called Judah. However, Benjamin at times demonstrated split loyalties (*see note on 1 Kin. 12:21*).

who *was* in charge of revenue; but the children of Israel stoned him with stones, and
he died. Therefore King Rehoboam mounted *his* chariot in haste to flee to Jerusalem.
19 [g]So Israel has been in rebellion against
the house of David to this day.

11 Now [a]when Rehoboam came to Jerusalem, he assembled from the
house of Judah and Benjamin one hundred
and eighty thousand chosen *men* who were
warriors, to fight against Israel, that he
might restore the kingdom to Rehoboam.
2 But the word of the LORD came [b]to Shemaiah the man of God, saying, 3 "Speak to
Rehoboam the son of Solomon, king of Judah, and to all Israel in Judah and Benjamin, saying, 4 'Thus says the LORD: "You
shall not go up or fight against your
brethren! Let every man return to his
house, for this thing is from Me." ' " Therefore they obeyed the words of the LORD,
and turned back from attacking Jeroboam.

Rehoboam Fortifies the Cities

5 So Rehoboam dwelt in Jerusalem, and
built cities for defense in Judah. 6 And he
built Bethlehem, Etam, Tekoa, 7 Beth Zur,
Sochoh, Adullam, 8 Gath, Mareshah, Ziph,
9 Adoraim, Lachish, Azekah, 10 Zorah,
Aijalon, and Hebron, which are in Judah
and Benjamin, fortified cities. 11 And he
fortified the strongholds, and put captains
in them, and stores of food, oil, and wine.
12 Also in every city *he put* shields and
spears, and made them very strong, having Judah and Benjamin on his side.

Priests and Levites Move to Judah

13 And from all their territories the
priests and the Levites who *were* in all Israel took their stand with him. 14 For the
Levites left [c]their common-lands and their
possessions and came to Judah and Jerusalem, for [d]Jeroboam and his sons had rejected them from serving as priests to the
LORD. 15 [e]Then he appointed for himself

priests for the [1]high places, for [f]the
demons, and [g]the calf idols which he had
made. 16 [h]And [2]after *the Levites left,* those
from all the tribes of Israel, such as set their
heart to seek the LORD God of Israel, [i]came
to Jerusalem to sacrifice to the LORD God of
their fathers. 17 So they [j]strengthened the
kingdom of Judah, and made Rehoboam
the son of Solomon strong for three years,
because they walked in the way of David
and Solomon for three years.

The Family of Rehoboam

18 Then Rehoboam took for himself as
wife Mahalath the daughter of Jerimoth
the son of David, *and of* Abihail the daughter of [k]Eliah the son of Jesse. 19 And she
bore him children: Jeush, Shamariah, and
Zaham. 20 After her he took [l]Maachah the
[3]granddaughter of [m]Absalom; and she
bore him [n]Abijah, Attai, Ziza, and Shelomith. 21 Now Rehoboam loved Maachah
the granddaughter of Absalom more than
all his [o]wives and his concubines; for he
took eighteen wives and sixty concubines,
and begot twenty-eight sons and sixty
daughters. 22 And Rehoboam [p]appointed
[q]Abijah the son of Maachah as chief, *to be*
leader among his brothers; for he *intended*
to make him king. 23 He dealt wisely, and
[4]dispersed some of his sons throughout all
the territories of Judah and Benjamin, to
every [r]fortified city; and he gave them
provisions in abundance. He also sought
many wives *for them.*

Egypt Attacks Judah

12 Now [a]it came to pass, when Rehoboam had established the kingdom
and had strengthened himself, that [b]he forsook the law of the LORD, and all Israel
along with him. 2 [c]And it happened in the
fifth year of King Rehoboam *that* Shishak
king of Egypt came up against Jerusalem,
because they had transgressed against the
LORD, 3 with twelve hundred chariots, sixty

19 [g] 1 Kin. 12:19

CHAPTER 11

1 [a] 1 Kin. 12:21-24
2 [b] 1 Chr. 12:5; 2 Chr. 12:15
14 [c] Num. 35:2-5 [d] 1 Kin. 12:28-33; 2 Chr. 13:9
15 [e] 1 Kin. 12:31; 13:33; 14:9; [Hos. 13:2]
[f] [Lev. 17:7; 1 Cor. 10:20] [g] 1 Kin. 12:28 [1] Places for pagan worship
16 [h] 2 Chr. 14:7 [i] 2 Chr. 15:9, 10; 30:11, 18 [2] Lit. *after them*
17 [j] 2 Chr. 12:1, 13
18 [k] 1 Sam. 16:6
20 [l] 2 Chr. 13:2 [m] 1 Kin. 15:2 [n] 1 Kin. 14:31 [3] Lit. *daughter,* but in the broader sense of granddaughter
21 [o] Deut. 17:17
22 [p] Deut. 21:15-17 [q] 2 Chr. 13:1
23 [r] 2 Chr. 11:5 [4] *distributed*

CHAPTER 12

1 [a] 2 Chr. 11:17 [b] 1 Kin. 14:22-24
2 [c] 1 Kin. 11:40; 14:25

11:6 built. To be understood as built further/strengthened/fortified (cf. 11:11,12).

11:13,14 The priests and Levites from all the northern 10 tribes were rejected by Israel's king, Jeroboam (ca. 931–910 B.C.), who saw them as a threat because of their loyalty to Jerusalem and the temple. He appointed his own idol priests and all true priests moved S and found refuge in Judah with Rehoboam.

11:15 he appointed. This is in reference to Jeroboam (cf. 1 Kin. 12:25-33), who established idolatry in the N. "Demons" is another term for idols (cf. Lev. 17:7).

11:16,17 God's blessing rested on Rehoboam for 3 years because the people's commitment to the ways of God was patterned after David and Solomon.

11:18-23 A summary of Rehoboam's life is given with special emphasis on succession to the throne. This is not a commendation of polygamy or concubinage, which violated God's law for marriage (cf. Gen. 2:24,25) and resulted in severe trouble and disaffection toward God. Never is polygamy commended in Scripture, and usually its tragic results are recorded.

11:21 The chronicler did not include the similar summary of Solomon's wives (cf. 1 Kin. 11:3), but clearly Rehoboam learned this disastrous marital style from his father Solomon. Even David was a polygamist. Polygamy was often practiced by the kings to secure alliances with nearby nations.

12:1,2 fifth year. Ca. 926 B.C. Presumably, Rehoboam's 3 years of blessing preceded a fourth year of spiritual rebellion, which God judged in his fifth year with judgment at the hand of the Egyptians.

12:2-5 Shishak. He ruled over Egypt ca. 945–924 B.C. An Egyptian record of this invasion written on stone has been found, recording that Shishak's army penetrated all the way N to the Sea of Galilee. He

thousand horsemen, and people without
number who came with him out of Egypt—
[d]the Lubim and the Sukkiim and the Ethiopians. 4 And he took the fortified cities of
Judah and came to Jerusalem.
5 Then [e]Shemaiah the prophet came to
Rehoboam and the leaders of Judah, who
were gathered together in Jerusalem because of Shishak, and said to them, "Thus
says the LORD: 'You have forsaken Me, and
therefore I also have left you in the hand of
Shishak.' "
6 So the leaders of Israel and the king
[f]humbled themselves; and they said,
[g]"The LORD *is* righteous."
7 Now when the LORD saw that they
humbled themselves, [h]the word of the
LORD came to Shemaiah, saying, "They
have humbled themselves; *therefore* I will
not destroy them, but I will grant them
some deliverance. My wrath shall not be
poured out on Jerusalem by the hand of
Shishak. 8 Nevertheless [i]they will be his
servants, that they may distinguish [j]My
service from the service of the kingdoms of
the nations."
9 [k]So Shishak king of Egypt came up
against Jerusalem, and took away the treasures of the house of the LORD and the treasures of the king's house; he took everything. He also carried away the gold
shields which Solomon had [l]made. 10 Then
King Rehoboam made bronze shields in
their place, and committed *them* [m]to the
hands of the captains of the guard, who
guarded the doorway of the king's house.
11 And whenever the king entered the
house of the LORD, the guard would go and
bring them out; then they would take them
back into the guardroom. 12 When he humbled himself, the wrath of the LORD turned
from him, so as not to destroy *him* completely; and things also went well in Judah.

The End of Rehoboam's Reign

13 Thus King Rehoboam strengthened
himself in Jerusalem and reigned. Now
[n]Rehoboam *was* forty-one years old when
he became king; and he reigned seventeen
years in Jerusalem, [o]the city which the
LORD had chosen out of all the tribes of Israel, to put His name there. His mother's
name *was* Naamah, an [p]Ammonitess.
14 And he did evil, because he did not prepare his heart to seek the LORD.
15 The acts of Rehoboam, first and last, *are*
they not written in the book of Shemaiah
the prophet, [q]and of Iddo the seer concerning genealogies? [r]And *there were* wars between Rehoboam and Jeroboam all their
days. 16 So Rehoboam [1]rested with his fathers, and was buried in the City of David.
Then [s]Abijah[2] his son reigned in his place.

Abijah Reigns in Judah

13 In [a]the eighteenth year of King Jeroboam, Abijah became king over
[b]Judah. 2 He reigned three years in Jerusalem. His mother's name *was* [1]Michaiah the
daughter of Uriel of Gibeah.
And there was war between Abijah and
Jeroboam. 3 Abijah set the battle in order
with an army of valiant warriors, four hundred thousand choice men. Jeroboam also
drew up in battle formation against him
with eight hundred thousand choice men,
mighty men of valor.
4 Then Abijah stood on Mount [c]Zema-
raim, which *is* in the mountains of Ephraim,
and said, "Hear me, Jeroboam and all Israel:

3 [d]2 Chr. 16:8; Nah. 3:9
5 [e]2 Chr. 11:2
6 [f][James 4:10] [g]Ex. 9:27; [Dan. 9:14]
7 [h]1 Kin. 21:28, 29
8 [i]Is. 26:13 [j][Deut. 28:47, 48]
9 [k]1 Kin. 14:25, 26 [l]1 Kin. 10:16, 17; 2 Chr. 9:15, 16
10 [m]1 Kin. 14:27
13 [n]1 Kin. 14:21 [o]2 Chr. 6:6 [p]1 Kin. 11:1, 5
15 [q]2 Chr. 9:29; 13:22 [r]1 Kin. 14:30
16 [s]2 Chr. 11:20-22 [1]Died and joined his ancestors [2]*Abijam,* 1 Kin. 14:31

CHAPTER 13

1 [a]1 Kin. 15:1 [b]1 Kin. 12:17
2 [1]*Maachah,* 1 Kin. 15:2; 2 Chr. 11:20, 21
4 [c]Josh. 18:22

wanted to restore Egypt's once-great power, but was unable to conquer both Israel and Judah. However, he was able to destroy cities in Judah and gain some control of trade routes. Judah came under Egyptian control.

12:6,7 humbled themselves. In the face of the Egyptian conqueror, the leaders responded to the Word of God through the prophet (v. 5) and repented, so that God would end His wrath worked through Shishak.

12:8 Nevertheless. A fitting punishment arose to remind the Jews of their heritage in relationship to Egypt. This was the first major military encounter with Egypt since the Exodus had ended hundreds of years of slavery there. A taste of being enslaved again to a people from whom God had given liberation was bitter. The message was crystal clear—if the Jews would forsake the true worship of God, they would also lose His protective hand of blessing. It was much better to serve God than to have to serve "kingdoms of the nations."

12:9 against Jerusalem. After the parenthetical section (vv. 5-8) describing the state of the beleaguered court, the historian returns to discuss the attack on Jerusalem and the pillage of the temple and palace.

12:9-16 *See notes on 1 Kin. 14:25-31.*

12:10,11 bronze. The pure gold was replaced by bronze, which was carefully guarded.

12:12 Cf. 12:7. God preserved Judah because of her repentance.

12:13 Ca. 931–913 B.C. By the general revival of true worship, Rehoboam's reign acquired new life and continued many years after the departure of Shishak. Sadly he faltered (v. 14), probably due largely to his heathen mother (v. 13).

12:16 Abijah. Cf. 11:20,22. In 1 Kin. 15:3, he is called a great sinner. But consistent with his pattern, the writer of the Chronicles highlights the little good he did to indicate that he was still in line with God's covenant promise to David.

13:1-22 In the succession of Judah's kings, the reign of Abijah/Abijam is next (ca. 913–911 B.C.; cf. 1 Kin. 15:1-8). The disobedient nature of Abijah's reign is mentioned in 1 Kin. 15:3, as is his faithless treaty with Syria (2 Chr. 16:3).

13:1,2 *See notes on 1 Kin. 15:1-8.* These numbers are large, but not surprising, given the immense number of capable men who could fight, as counted in David's census (cf. 1 Chr. 21:5). Both armies were set for civil war.

13:4 Mount Zemaraim. The exact location is unknown, but it is likely near Bethel (Josh. 18:22) inside Israel's territory.

5 Should you not know that the LORD God of
Israel [d]gave the dominion over Israel to David forever, to him and his sons, [e]by a
covenant of salt? 6 Yet Jeroboam the son of
Nebat, the servant of Solomon the son of David, rose up and [f]rebelled against his lord.
7 Then [g]worthless rogues gathered to him,
and strengthened themselves against Rehoboam the son of Solomon, when Rehoboam
was [h]young and inexperienced and could
not withstand them. 8 And now you think to
withstand the kingdom of the LORD, which
is in the hand of the sons of David; and you
are a great multitude, and with you are the
gold calves which Jeroboam [i]made for you
as gods. 9 [j]Have you not cast out the priests
of the LORD, the sons of Aaron, and the
Levites, and made for yourselves priests,
like the peoples of *other* lands, [k]so that whoever comes to consecrate himself with a
young bull and seven rams may be a priest
of [l]*things that are* not gods? 10 But as for us,
the LORD *is* our [m]God, and we have not forsaken Him; and the priests who minister to
the LORD *are* the sons of Aaron, and the
Levites *attend* to *their* duties. 11 [n]And they
burn to the LORD every morning and every
evening burnt sacrifices and sweet incense;
they also *set* the [o]showbread *in order on* the
pure *gold* table, and the lampstand of gold
with its lamps [p]to burn every evening; for
we keep the command of the LORD our God,
but you have forsaken Him. 12 Now look,
God Himself is with us as *our* [q]head, [r]and
His priests with sounding trumpets to
sound the alarm against you. O children of
Israel, do not fight against the LORD God of
your fathers, for you shall not prosper!"
13 But Jeroboam caused an ambush to go
around behind them; so they were in front
of Judah, and the ambush *was* behind
them. 14 And when Judah looked around,
to their surprise the battle line *was* at both
front and rear; and they [s]cried out to the
LORD, and the priests sounded the trumpets. 15 Then the men of Judah gave a
shout; and as the men of Judah shouted, it
happened that God [t]struck Jeroboam and
all Israel before Abijah and Judah. 16 And
the children of Israel fled before Judah,
and God delivered them into their hand.
17 Then Abijah and his people struck them
with a great slaughter; so five hundred
thousand choice men of Israel fell slain.
18 Thus the children of Israel were subdued at that time; and the children of Judah prevailed, [u]because they relied on the
LORD God of their fathers.
19 And Abijah pursued Jeroboam and
took cities from him: Bethel with its villages,
Jeshanah with its villages, and [v]Ephrain[2]
with its villages. 20 So Jeroboam did not recover strength again in the days of Abijah;
and the LORD [w]struck him, and [x]he died.
21 But Abijah grew mighty, married fourteen wives, and begot twenty-two sons and
sixteen daughters. 22 Now the rest of the
acts of Abijah, his ways, and his sayings *are*
written in [y]the [3]annals of the prophet Iddo.

14 So Abijah rested with his fathers,
and they buried him in the City of
David. Then [a]Asa his son reigned in his
place. In his days the land was quiet for ten
years.

Asa Reigns in Judah

2 Asa did *what was* good and right in the
eyes of the LORD his God, 3 for he removed

5 [d]2 Sam. 7:8-16 [e]Lev. 2:13; Num. 18:19
6 [f]1 Kin. 11:28; 12:20
7 [g]Judg. 9:4 [h]2 Chr. 12:13
8 [i]1 Kin. 12:28; 14:9; 2 Chr. 11:15; [Hos. 8:4-6]
9 [j]2 Chr. 11:13-15 [k]Ex. 29:29-33 [l]Jer. 2:11; 5:7
10 [m]Josh. 24:15
11 [n]Ex. 29:38; 2 Chr. 2:4 [o]Ex. 25:30; Lev. 24:5-9 [p]Ex. 27:20, 21; Lev. 24:2, 3
12 [q]Josh. 5:13-15; [Heb. 2:10] [r][Num. 10:8-10]
14 [s]Josh. 24:7; 2 Chr. 6:34, 35; 14:11
15 [t]1 Kin. 14:14; 2 Chr. 14:12
18 [u]1 Chr. 5:20; 2 Chr. 14:11; [Ps. 22:5]
19 [v]Josh. 15:9 [2]Or *Ephron*
20 [w]1 Sam. 2:6; 25:38; Acts 12:23 [x]1 Kin. 14:20
22 [y]2 Chr. 9:29 [3]Or *commentary*, Heb. *midrash*

CHAPTER 14
1 [a]1 Kin. 15:8

13:5 covenant of salt. Salt is associated elsewhere with the Mosaic Covenant sacrifices (Lev. 2:13), the Priestly Covenant (Num. 18:19), and the New Covenant symbolic sacrifices in the millennial kingdom (Ezek. 43:24). The preservative quality of salt represents the fidelity or loyalty intended in keeping the covenant. Here it would refer to God's irrevocable pledge and intended loyalty in fulfilling the Davidic Covenant and God's desire for the loyalty of David's lineage to Him if the people are to enjoy the blessings of the covenant.

13:6 For the story of Jeroboam, read 1 Kin. 11:26-40 and 2 Chr. 10. He was the first king of the northern kingdom called Israel.

13:7 young. He was 41 (cf. 2 Chr. 12:13).

13:8 kingdom of the LORD. Abijah reminds all that the Davidic Covenant is God's expressed will concerning who would rule on His behalf in the earthly kingdom. Thus Judah is God's nation, since the king is in the line of David. **gold calves.** Cf. 1 Kin. 12:25-33; 2 Chr. 11:15. Israel was full of idols and false priests, having driven out all the Levitical priests and, with them, the true worship of God.

13:10-12 Abijah confessed a national commitment to pure worship and thus confidence in God's favor in battle.

13:15 God struck Jeroboam and all Israel. At the time of certain defeat, with 400,000 troops behind and the same number in front, Judah was saved by divine intervention. What God did is unknown, but the army of Israel began to flee (v. 16), and the soldiers of Judah massacred 500,000 of them in an unimaginable blood bath (v. 17).

13:17 Before the battle, Jeroboam outnumbered Abijah two to one (13:3). After the fray, in which the Lord intervened on behalf of Judah, Abijah outnumbered Jeroboam 4 to 3.

13:19 Bethel. Located 12 mi. N of Jerusalem. Although their exact locations are unknown, Jeshanah and Ephron are believed to be in the vicinity of Bethel.

13:20 he died. Again God acted, in a manner not described, to end the life of this wicked ruler (ca. 910 B.C.).

13:22–14:1 *See notes on 1 Kin. 15:6-8.*

14:1–16:14 The reign of Asa (ca. 911–870 B.C.). Cf. 1 Kin. 15:9-24.

14:1,2 First Kings 15:11 says that Asa did as his forefather David had done—honoring God while building the kingdom (vv. 6-8). Times of peace were used for strengthening.

14:3-5 He removed elements of false worship that had accumulated over the years of Solomon, Rehoboam, and Abijah (cf. 1 Kin. 15:12,13). Apparently, he did not remove all the high places or, once removed, they reappeared (cf. 1 Kin. 15:14; 1 Chr. 15:6). His son Jehoshaphat later had to remove them (cf. 2 Chr. 17:6), although not completely (cf. 1 Chr. 20:33). This was done in an effort to comply with Deut. 12:2,3.

the altars of the foreign *gods* and [b]the [1]high places, and [c]broke down the *sacred* pillars [d]and cut down the wooden images. 4 He commanded Judah to [e]seek the LORD God of their fathers, and to observe the law and the commandment. 5 He also removed the [2]high places and the incense altars from all the cities of Judah, and the kingdom was quiet under him. 6 And he built fortified cities in Judah, for the land had rest; he had no war in those years, because the LORD had given him [f]rest. 7 Therefore he said to Judah, "Let us build these cities and make walls around *them,* and towers, gates, and bars, *while* the land *is* yet before us, because we have sought the LORD our God; we have sought *Him,* and He has given us rest on every side." So they built and prospered. 8 And Asa had an army of three hundred thousand from Judah who carried [3]shields and spears, and from Benjamin two hundred and eighty thousand men who carried shields and drew [g]bows; all these *were* mighty men of [h]valor.

9 [i]Then Zerah the Ethiopian came out against them with an army of a million men and three hundred chariots, and he came to [j]Mareshah. 10 So Asa went out against him, and they set the troops in battle array in the Valley of Zephathah at Mareshah. 11 And Asa [k]cried out to the LORD his God, and said, "LORD, *it is* [l]nothing for You to help, whether with many or with those who have no power; help us, O LORD our God, for we rest on You, and [m]in Your name we go against this multitude. O LORD, You *are* our God; do not let man prevail against You!"

12 So the LORD [n]struck the Ethiopians before Asa and Judah, and the Ethiopians fled. 13 And Asa and the people who *were* with him pursued them to [o]Gerar. So the Ethiopians were overthrown, and they could not recover, for they were broken before the LORD and His army. And they carried away very much [4]spoil. 14 Then they defeated all the cities around Gerar, for [p]the fear of the LORD came upon them; and they plundered all the cities, for there was exceedingly much [5]spoil in them. 15 They also [6]attacked the livestock enclosures, and carried off sheep and camels in abundance, and returned to Jerusalem.

The Reforms of Asa

15 Now [a]the Spirit of God came upon Azariah the son of Oded. 2 And he went out [1]to meet Asa, and said to him: "Hear me, Asa, and all Judah and Benjamin. [b]The LORD *is* with you while you are with Him. [c]If you seek Him, He will be found by you; but [d]if you forsake Him, He will forsake you. 3 [e]For a long time Israel *has been* without the true God, without a [f]teaching priest, and without [g]law; 4 but [h]when in their trouble they turned to the LORD God of Israel, and sought Him, He was found by them. 5 And in those times *there was* no peace to the one who went out, nor to the one who came in, but great turmoil *was* on all the inhabitants of the lands. 6 [i]So nation was [2]destroyed by nation, and city by city, for God troubled them with every adversity. 7 But you, be strong and do not let your hands be weak, for your work shall be rewarded!"

8 And when Asa heard these words and the prophecy of [3]Oded the prophet, he took courage, and removed the abominable idols from all the land of Judah and Benjamin and from the cities [j]which he had taken in the mountains of Ephraim; and he restored the altar of the LORD that *was* before the vestibule of the LORD. 9 Then he gathered all Judah and Benjamin, and [k]those who dwelt with them from Ephraim, Manasseh, and

3 [b] 1 Kin. 15:14; 2 Chr. 15:17 [c] [Ex. 34:13] [d] 1 Kin. 11:7 [1] Places for pagan worship
4 [e] [2 Chr. 7:14]
5 [2] Places for pagan worship
6 [f] 2 Chr. 15:15
8 [g] 1 Chr. 12:2 [h] 2 Chr. 13:3 [3] *large shields*
9 [i] 2 Chr. 12:2, 3; 16:8 [j] Josh. 15:44
11 [k] Ex. 14:10; 2 Chr. 13:14; [Ps. 22:5] [l] [1 Sam. 14:6] [m] 1 Sam. 17:45; [Prov. 18:10]
12 [n] 2 Chr. 13:15
13 [o] Gen. 10:19; 20:1 [4] *plunder*
14 [p] Gen. 35:5; Deut. 11:25; Josh. 2:9; 2 Chr. 17:10 [5] *plunder*
15 [6] Lit. *struck*

CHAPTER 15

1 [a] Num. 24:2; Judg. 3:10; 2 Chr. 20:14; 24:20
2 [b] [James 4:8] [c] [1 Chr. 28:9]; 2 Chr. 14:4; 33:12, 13; [Jer. 29:13; Matt. 7:7] [d] 2 Chr. 24:20 [1] Lit. *before*
3 [e] Hos. 3:4 [f] 2 Kin. 12:2 [g] Lev. 10:11; 2 Chr. 17:8, 9
4 [h] [Deut. 4:29]
6 [i] Matt. 24:7 [2] Lit. *beaten in pieces*
8 [j] 2 Chr. 13:19 [3] So with MT, LXX; Syr., Vg. *Azariah the son of Oded* (cf. v. 1)
9 [k] 2 Chr. 11:16

14:8 Asa had an army of 580,000 compared to Abijah's 400,000 (2 Chr. 13:3).

14:9-15 A major threat developed from Zerah, the Ethiopian, probably on behalf of the Egyptian Pharaoh, who was attempting to regain control as Shishak had during the days of Rehoboam (cf. 2 Chr. 12:7,8), ca. 901–900 B.C.

14:9 Mareshah. Located about 8 mi. SE of Gath and 25 mi. SW of Jerusalem. Rehoboam had earlier reinforced this city (2 Chr. 11:8).

14:11 Asa's appeal to God centered on God's omnipotence and reputation.

14:13-15 spoil. It appears that this great horde was a nomadic people who moved with all their possessions and had set up their camp near Gerar. The spoils of Judah's victory were immense.

14:13 Gerar. Approximately 8 mi. S of Gaza on the Mediterranean coast. Egypt does not appear on the scene again for over 150 years (cf. 2 Kin. 17:4).

15:1 Spirit of God. An act of the Holy Spirit, common in the OT enabling servants of God to speak or act uniquely for Him. **Azariah.** This man was a prophet mentioned only here, who met Asa as he returned from the victory and spoke to him before all his army.

15:2 The spiritual truth here is basic, namely that God is present and powerful in defense of His obedient people. Cf. Deut. 20:1; 1 Chr. 28:9; Is. 55:6,7; Jer. 29:12-14; James 4:8. While good Asa ruled for 41 years, 8 wicked kings ruled in Israel, including Jeroboam, who along with the others, was a negative illustration of this truth (cf. 12:1ff.).

15:8 the prophecy of Oded. Verse 1 says "Azariah the son of Oded." The marginal reading here is preferred, "Azariah the son of Oded," which corresponds with v. 1. **vestibule.** This refers to the area outside the Holy Place, where the altar of the burnt offering was located.

15:9 Ephraim, Manasseh, and Simeon. This indicates that not all the people in the 10 tribes which constituted the apostate northern kingdom of Israel had abandoned God. Many migrated S into Judah, so that all tribes were represented in the mix of Jews in Judah.

Simeon, for they came over to him in great
numbers from Israel when they saw that the
LORD his God was with him.
10 So they gathered together at Jerusalem in the third month, in the fifteenth
year of the reign of Asa. 11 [l]And they offered to the LORD [4]at that time seven hundred bulls and seven thousand sheep from
the [5]spoil they had brought. 12 Then they
[m]entered into a covenant to seek the LORD
God of their fathers with all their heart and
with all their soul; 13 [n]and whoever would
not seek the LORD God of Israel [o]was to be
put to death, whether small or great,
whether man or woman. 14 Then they took
an oath before the LORD with a loud voice,
with shouting and trumpets and rams'
horns. 15 And all Judah rejoiced at the
oath, for they had sworn with all their
heart and [p]sought Him with all their soul;
and He was found by them, and the LORD
gave them [q]rest all around.
16 Also he removed [r]Maachah, the
[6]mother of Asa the king, from *being* queen
mother, because she had made an obscene
image of [7]Asherah; and Asa cut down her
obscene image, then crushed and burned *it*
by the Brook Kidron. 17 But [s]the [8]high
places were not removed from Israel. Nevertheless the heart of Asa was loyal all his
days.
18 He also brought into the house of God
the things that his father had dedicated
and that he himself had dedicated: silver
and gold and utensils. 19 And there was no
war until the thirty-fifth year of the reign
of Asa.

11 [l] 2 Chr. 14:13-15 [4] Lit. *in that day* [5] *plunder*
12 [m] 2 Kin. 23:3; 2 Chr. 23:16; 34:31; Neh. 10:29
13 [n] Ex. 22:20 [o] Deut. 13:5-15
15 [p] 2 Chr. 15:2 [q] 2 Chr. 14:7
16 [r] 1 Kin. 15:2, 10, 13 [6] Or *grandmother* [7] A Canaanite deity
17 [s] 1 Kin. 15:14; 2 Chr. 14:3, 5 [8] Places for pagan worship

CHAPTER 16

1 [a] 1 Kin. 15:17-22 [b] 2 Chr. 15:9
7 [c] 1 Kin. 16:1; 2 Chr. 19:2 [d] 2 Chr. 32:8-10; Ps. 118:9; [Is. 31:1; Jer. 17:5]
8 [e] 2 Chr. 14:9 [f] 2 Chr. 12:3 [g] 2 Chr. 13:16, 18
9 [h] Job 34:21; [Prov. 5:21; 15:3; Jer. 16:17; 32:19]; Zech. 4:10

Asa's Treaty with Syria

16 In the thirty-sixth year of the reign
of Asa, [a]Baasha king of Israel came
up against Judah and built Ramah, [b]that he
might let none go out or come in to Asa
king of Judah. 2 Then Asa brought silver
and gold from the treasuries of the house
of the LORD and of the king's house, and
sent to Ben-Hadad king of Syria, who
dwelt in Damascus, saying, 3 "*Let there be* a
treaty between you and me, as there was
between my father and your father. See, I
have sent you silver and gold; come, break
your treaty with Baasha king of Israel, so
that he will withdraw from me."
4 So Ben-Hadad heeded King Asa, and
sent the captains of his armies against the
cities of Israel. They attacked Ijon, Dan,
Abel Maim, and all the storage cities of
Naphtali. 5 Now it happened, when Baasha heard *it*, that he stopped building
Ramah and ceased his work. 6 Then King
Asa took all Judah, and they carried away
the stones and timber of Ramah, which
Baasha had used for building; and with
them he built Geba and Mizpah.

Hanani's Message to Asa

7 And at that time [c]Hanani the seer came
to Asa king of Judah, and said to him:
[d]"Because you have relied on the king of
Syria, and have not relied on the LORD
your God, therefore the army of the king of
Syria has escaped from your hand. 8 Were
[e]the Ethiopians and [f]the Lubim not a huge
army with very many chariots and horsemen? Yet, because you relied on the LORD,
He delivered them into your [g]hand. 9 [h]For

15:10 fifteenth year. Ca. 897 B.C. in May/June. The Feast of Weeks would have been the occasion.

15:11-15 The assembled worshipers entered into a renewed promise to obey (cf. Ex. 24:1ff.) and to rigorously enforce the laws which made idolatry punishable by death (cf. Deut. 17:2-5). This was inaugurated with the sacrifices of animals taken in spoil from the Ethiopians (14:15).

15:16-18 *See notes on 1 Kin. 15:13-15.*

15:19 thirty-fifth year. Ca. 875 B.C.

16:1 thirty-sixth year. Since Baasha (ca. 909–886 B.C.) died in the 26th year of Asa's reign (cf. 1 Kin. 15:33), this could not mean that they were at war 10 years later. However, if the time reference was to the 35th year since the kingdom was divided, then the year is ca. 896 B.C. in the 14th year of Baasha's reign and the 16th of Asa's reign. This manner of reckoning was generally followed in the book of the record of the kings of Judah and Israel, the public annuals of that time, from which the inspired writer drew his account (cf. v. 11). This could be a cause for the defections of people from Israel to Judah as described in 2 Chr. 15:9. Cf. 1 Kin. 15:16,17. **Ramah.** This frontier town was on the high road about 6 mi. N of Jerusalem. Because of the topography and fortification of that city, this would effectively block all traffic into Jerusalem from the N. Cf. 1 Kin. 15:16-22.

16:2-6 Asa sinfully resorted to trusting in a pagan king, Ben-Hadad, for protection against the king of Israel in contrast to 1) Abijah (2 Chr. 13:2-20) and 2) even earlier to his own battle against Egypt (2 Chr. 14:9-15), when they both trusted wholly in the Lord. *See note on 1 Kin. 15:18.*

16:3 my father...your father. A previously unmentioned treaty between Abijah (ca. 913–911 B.C.) and Tabrimmon (ca. 912–890 B.C.).

16:4 Ijon. Along with the other cities mentioned, these were located N and E of the Sea of Galilee.

16:6 Geba...Mizpah. Located two mi. NNE and two miles E of Ramah respectively.

16:7 Hanani. God used this prophet to rebuke Asa 1) for his wicked appropriation of temple treasures devoted to God to purchase power, and 2) for his faithless dependence on a pagan king instead of the Lord, in contrast to before when opposed by Egypt (2 Chr. 14:9-15). **army of the king of Syria has escaped.** Asa forfeited by this sin the opportunity of gaining victory not only over Israel, but also Syria. This could have been a greater victory than over the Ethiopians, which would have deprived Syria of any future successful attacks on Judah. Though God had delivered them when they were outnumbered (13:3ff.; 14:9ff.), the king showed his own spiritual decline both in lack of trust and in his treatment of the prophet of God who spoke truth (v. 10).

the eyes of the LORD run to and fro
throughout the whole earth, to show Himself strong on behalf of *those* whose heart *is*
loyal to Him. In this [i]you have done foolishly; therefore from now on [j]you shall
have wars." **10** Then Asa was angry with
the seer, and [k]put him in prison, for *he was*
enraged at him because of this. And Asa
oppressed *some* of the people at that time.

Illness and Death of Asa

11 [l]Note that the acts of Asa, first and
last, are indeed written in the book of the
kings of Judah and Israel. **12** And in the
thirty-ninth year of his reign, Asa became
diseased in his feet, and his malady was
severe; yet in his disease he [m]did not seek
the LORD, but the physicians.
13 [n]So Asa [1]rested with his fathers; he
died in the forty-first year of his reign.
14 They buried him in his own tomb,
which he had [2]made for himself in the City
of David; and they laid him in the bed
which was filled [o]with spices and various
ingredients prepared in a mixture of ointments. They made [p]a very great burning
for him.

Jehoshaphat Reigns in Judah

17 Then [a]Jehoshaphat his son reigned
in his place, and strengthened himself against Israel. **2** And he placed troops
in all the fortified cities of Judah, and set
garrisons in the land of [b]Judah and in the
cities of Ephraim [c]which Asa his father
had taken. **3** Now the LORD was with Jehoshaphat, because he walked in the former ways of his father David; he did not
seek the Baals, **4** but sought [1]the God of his
father, and walked in His commandments
and not according to [d]the acts of Israel.
5 Therefore the LORD established the kingdom in his hand; and all Judah [e]gave presents to Jehoshaphat, [f]and he had riches
and honor in abundance. **6** And his heart
took delight in the ways of the LORD; moreover [g]he removed the [2]high places and
wooden images from Judah.
7 Also in the third year of his reign he
sent his leaders, Ben-Hail, Obadiah, Zechariah, Nethanel, and Michaiah, [h]to teach in
the cities of Judah. **8** And with them *he sent*
Levites: Shemaiah, Nethaniah, Zebadiah,
Asahel, Shemiramoth, Jehonathan, Adonijah, Tobijah, and Tobadonijah—the
Levites; and with them Elishama and Jehoram, the priests. **9** [i]So they taught in Judah, and *had* the Book of the Law of the
LORD with them; they went throughout all
the cities of Judah and taught the people.
10 And [j]the fear of the LORD fell on all
the kingdoms of the lands that *were* around
Judah, so that they did not make war
against Jehoshaphat. **11** Also *some* of the
Philistines [k]brought Jehoshaphat presents
and silver as tribute; and the Arabians
brought him flocks, seven thousand seven
hundred rams and seven thousand seven
hundred male goats.
12 So Jehoshaphat became increasingly
powerful, and he built fortresses and storage cities in Judah. **13** He had much property in the cities of Judah; and the men of
war, mighty men of valor, *were* in Jerusalem.
14 These *are* their numbers, according to
their fathers' houses. Of Judah, the captains of thousands: Adnah the captain, and
with him three hundred thousand mighty
men of valor; **15** and next to him *was* Jehohanan the captain, and with him two hundred and eighty thousand; **16** and next to
him *was* Amasiah the son of Zichri, [l]who
willingly offered himself to the LORD, and
with him two hundred thousand mighty
men of valor. **17** Of Benjamin: Eliada a
mighty man of valor, and with him two
hundred thousand men armed with bow
and shield; **18** and next to him *was* Jehozabad, and with him one hundred and eighty

9 [i] 1 Sam. 13:13 [j] 1 Kin. 15:32
10 [k] 2 Chr. 18:26; Jer. 20:2; Matt. 14:3
11 [l] 1 Kin. 15:23, 24; 2 Chr. 14:2
12 [m] [Jer. 17:5]
13 [n] 1 Kin. 15:24 [1] Died and joined his ancestors
14 [o] Gen. 50:2; Mark 16:1; John 19:39, 40 [p] 2 Chr. 21:19; Jer. 34:5 [2] Lit. *dug*

CHAPTER 17

1 [a] 1 Kin. 15:24; 2 Chr. 20:31
2 [b] 2 Chr. 11:5 [c] 2 Chr. 15:8
4 [d] 1 Kin. 12:28 [1] LXX *the LORD God*
5 [e] 1 Sam. 10:27; 1 Kin. 10:25 [f] 2 Chr. 18:1
6 [g] 1 Kin. 22:43; 2 Chr. 15:17; 19:3; 20:33 [2] Places for pagan worship
7 [h] 2 Chr. 15:3; 35:3
9 [i] Deut. 6:4-9; 2 Chr. 35:3; Neh. 8:3, 7
10 [j] Gen. 35:5; 2 Chr. 14:14
11 [k] 2 Sam. 8:2; 2 Chr. 9:14; 26:8
16 [l] Judg. 5:2, 9; 1 Chr. 29:9

16:9 show Himself strong...loyal to Him. *See note on 15:2.* **you shall have wars.** Divine judgment on the king's faithlessness.

16:10-12 During Asa's last 6 years, he uncharacteristically exhibited the ungodly behavior of: 1) anger at truth (v. 10); 2) oppression of God's prophet and people (v. 10); and 3) seeking man not God (v. 12).

16:12 thirty-ninth year. Ca. 872 B.C. He died as a result of what may have been severe gangrene.

16:13 forty-first year. Ca. 870 B.C.

16:14 great burning. Due to the longevity of his reign and his notable accomplishments, Asa was honored by the people in their memorial of his death. Cremation was rarely used by the Hebrews (cf. 21:19; 1 Sam. 31:13; Amos 6:10). Later, Jehoram was not honored by fire (21:19) because of his shameful reign.

17:1–21:3 The reign of Jehoshaphat (ca. 873–848 B.C.) Cf. 1 Kin. 15:24; 22:1-50.

17:1,2 Jehoshaphat prepared the nation militarily for any aggression, particularly from the northern kingdom of Israel.

17:3 the Baals. This is a general term used for idols. Cf. Judg. 2:11-13.

17:3-9 Jehoshaphat made three strategic moves, spiritually speaking: 1) he obeyed the Lord (17:3-6); 2) he removed false worship from the land (17:6); and 3) he sent out teachers who taught the people the law of the Lord (17:7-9).

17:10,11 Jehoshaphat's spiritual strategy accomplished its intended purpose, i.e., invoking God's blessing and protection, much like it did with Abijah (13:2-20) and Asa (14:9-15). It should be noted that the Jews needed animals for extensive sacrificial uses, as much as for food and clothing.

17:12,13 These verses indicate the massive wealth that developed under divine blessing (cf. 18:1), as well as formidable military power (vv. 14-19).

thousand prepared for war. 19 These served the king, besides [m]those the king put in the fortified cities throughout all Judah.

Micaiah Warns Ahab

18 Jehoshaphat [a]had riches and honor in abundance; and by marriage he [b]allied himself with [c]Ahab. 2 [d]After some years he went down to *visit* Ahab in Samaria; and Ahab killed sheep and oxen in abundance for him and the people who were with him, and persuaded him to go up *with him* to Ramoth Gilead. 3 So Ahab king of Israel said to Jehoshaphat king of Judah, "Will you go with me *against* Ramoth Gilead?"

And he answered him, "I *am* as you *are,* and my people as your people; *we will be* with you in the war."

4 Also Jehoshaphat said to the king of Israel, [e]"Please inquire for the word of the LORD today."

5 Then the king of Israel gathered the prophets together, four hundred men, and said to them, "Shall we go to war against Ramoth Gilead, or shall I refrain?"

So they said, "Go up, for God will deliver it into the king's hand."

6 But Jehoshaphat said, "*Is there* not still a prophet of the LORD here, that we may inquire of [f]Him?"[1]

7 So the king of Israel said to Jehoshaphat, "*There is* still one man by whom we may inquire of the LORD; but I hate him, because he never prophesies good concerning me, but always evil. He *is* Micaiah the son of Imla."

And Jehoshaphat said, "Let not the king say such things!"

8 Then the king of Israel called one *of his* officers and said, "Bring Micaiah the son of Imla quickly!"

9 The king of Israel and Jehoshaphat king of Judah, clothed in *their* robes, sat each on his throne; and they sat at a threshing floor at the entrance of the gate of Samaria; and all the prophets prophesied before them. 10 Now Zedekiah the son of Chenaanah had made [g]horns of iron for himself; and he said, "Thus says the LORD: 'With these you shall gore the Syrians until they are destroyed.' "

11 And all the prophets prophesied so, saying, "Go up to Ramoth Gilead and prosper, for the LORD will deliver *it* into the king's hand."

12 Then the messenger who had gone to call Micaiah spoke to him, saying, "Now listen, the words of the prophets with one accord encourage the king. Therefore please let your word be like *the word of* one of them, and speak encouragement."

13 And Micaiah said, "*As* the LORD lives, [h]whatever my God says, that I will speak."

14 Then he came to the king; and the king said to him, "Micaiah, shall we go to war against Ramoth Gilead, or shall I refrain?"

And he said, "Go and prosper, and they shall be delivered into your hand!"

15 So the king said to him, "How many times shall I make you swear that you tell me nothing but the truth in the name of the LORD?"

16 Then he said, "I saw all Israel [i]scattered on the mountains, as sheep that have no [j]shepherd. And the LORD said, 'These have no master. Let each return to his house in peace.' "

17 And the king of Israel said to Jehoshaphat, "Did I not tell you he would not prophesy good concerning me, but evil?"

18 Then *Micaiah* said, "Therefore hear the word of the LORD: I saw the LORD sitting on His [k]throne, and all the host of heaven standing on His right hand and His left. 19 And the LORD said, 'Who will persuade Ahab king of Israel to go up, that he may fall at Ramoth Gilead?' So one spoke in this manner, and another spoke in that manner. 20 Then a [l]spirit came forward and stood before the LORD, and said, 'I will persuade him.' The LORD said to him, 'In what way?' 21 So he said, 'I will go out and be a lying spirit in the mouth of all his prophets.' And *the LORD* said, 'You shall persuade *him* and also prevail; go out and do so.' 22 Therefore look! [m]The LORD has put a lying spirit in the mouth of these prophets of yours, and the LORD has declared disaster against you."

23 Then Zedekiah the son of Chenaanah went near and [n]struck Micaiah on the cheek, and said, "Which way did the spirit from the LORD go from me to speak to you?"

24 And Micaiah said, "Indeed you shall

19 [m] 2 Chr. 17:2

CHAPTER 18

1 [a] 2 Chr. 17:5 [b] 1 Kin. 22:44; 2 Kin. 8:18 [c] 1 Kin. 22:40
2 [d] [Ex. 23:2]; 1 Kin. 22:2
4 [e] 1 Sam. 23:2, 4, 9; 2 Sam. 2:1
6 [f] 2 Kin. 3:11 [1] Or *him*
10 [g] Zech. 1:18-21
13 [h] Num. 22:18-20, 35; 23:12, 26; 1 Kin. 22:14
16 [i] [Jer. 23:1-8; 31:10] [j] Num. 27:17; 1 Kin. 22:17; [Ezek. 34:5-8]; Matt. 9:36; Mark 6:34
18 [k] Is. 6:1-5; Dan. 7:9, 10
20 [l] Job 1:6; 2 Thess. 2:9
22 [m] Job 12:16, 17; Is. 19:12-14; Ezek. 14:9
23 [n] Jer. 20:2; Mark 14:65; Acts 23:2

18:1-34 *See notes on 1 Kin. 22:1-37.* Ahab was king in Israel. Jehoshaphat arranged for his son (cf. 21:6) to marry Athaliah, daughter of wicked Ahab, then made a military alliance with him. This folly had tragic results: 1) Jehoshaphat drew God's wrath (19:2); 2) After Jehoshaphat died and Athaliah became queen, she seized the throne and almost killed all of David's descendants (22:10ff.); and 3) She brought the wicked idols of Israel into Judah, which eventually led to the nation's destruction and captivity in Babylon. Jehoshaphat had a tendency to rely on other kings as evidenced by this unique report of a marriage alliance with Ahab (v. 1). See also 2 Chr. 20:35-37 concerning an alliance with Ahaziah (ca. 853–852 B.C.).

18:5 Evil kings had false prophets who told them what they wanted to hear (cf. Is. 30:10,11; Jer. 14:13-16; 23:16,21,30-36). The true prophet spoke God's Word and was arrested (v. 26).

see on that day when you go into an inner chamber to hide!"

25 Then the king of Israel said, "Take Micaiah, and return him to Amon the governor of the city and to Joash the king's son; 26 and say, 'Thus says the king: [o]"Put this *fellow* in prison, and feed him with bread of affliction and water of affliction, until I return in peace." ' "

27 But Micaiah said, "If you ever return in peace, the LORD has not spoken by [p]me." And he said, "Take heed, all you people!"

Ahab Dies in Battle

28 So the king of Israel and Jehoshaphat the king of Judah went up to Ramoth Gilead. 29 And the king of Israel said to Jehoshaphat, "I will [q]disguise myself and go into battle; but you put on your robes." So the king of Israel disguised himself, and they went into battle.

30 Now the king of Syria had commanded the captains of the chariots who *were* with him, saying, "Fight with no one small or great, but only with the king of Israel."

31 So it was, when the captains of the chariots saw Jehoshaphat, that they said, "It *is* the king of Israel!" Therefore they surrounded him to attack; but Jehoshaphat [r]cried out, and the LORD helped him, and God diverted them from him. 32 For so it was, when the captains of the chariots saw that it was not the king of Israel, that they turned back from pursuing him. 33 Now a certain man drew a bow at random, and struck the king of Israel between the [2]joints of his armor. So he said to the driver of his chariot, "Turn around and take me out of the battle, for I am wounded." 34 The battle increased that day, and the king of Israel propped *himself* up in *his* chariot facing the Syrians until evening; and about the time of sunset he died.

19 Then Jehoshaphat the king of Judah returned safely to his house in Jerusalem. 2 And Jehu the son of Hanani [a]the seer went out to meet him, and said to King Jehoshaphat, "Should you help the wicked and [b]love those who hate the LORD? Therefore the [c]wrath of the LORD *is* upon you. 3 Nevertheless [d]good things are found in you, in that you have removed the [1]wooden images from the land, and have [e]prepared your heart to seek God."

The Reforms of Jehoshaphat

4 So Jehoshaphat dwelt at Jerusalem; and he went out again among the people from Beersheba to the mountains of Ephraim, and brought them back to the LORD God of their [f]fathers. 5 Then he set [g]judges in the land throughout all the fortified cities of Judah, city by city, 6 and said to the judges, "Take heed to what you are doing, for [h]you do not judge for man but for the LORD, [i]who *is* with you [2]in the judgment. 7 Now therefore, let the fear of the LORD be upon you; take care and do *it,* for [j]*there is* no iniquity with the LORD our God, no [k]partiality, nor taking of bribes."

8 Moreover in Jerusalem, for the judgment of the LORD and for controversies, Jehoshaphat [l]appointed some of the Levites and priests, and some of the chief fathers of Israel, [3]when they returned to Jerusalem. 9 And he commanded them, saying, "Thus you shall act [m]in the fear of the LORD, faithfully and with a loyal heart: 10 [n]Whatever case comes to you from your brethren who dwell in their cities, whether of bloodshed or offenses against law or commandment, against statutes or ordinances, you shall warn them, lest they trespass against the LORD and [o]wrath come upon [p]you and your brethren. Do this, and you will not be guilty. 11 And take notice: [q]Amariah the chief priest *is* over you [r]in all matters of the LORD; and Zebadiah the son of Ishmael, the ruler of the house of Judah, for all the king's matters; also the Levites *will be* officials before you. Behave courageously, and the LORD will be [s]with the good."

Ammon, Moab, and Mount Seir Defeated

20 It happened after this *that* the people of [a]Moab with the people of [b]Ammon, and *others* with them besides the [c]Ammonites,[1] came to battle against Jehoshaphat. 2 Then some came and told Jehoshaphat, saying, "A great multitude is coming against you from beyond the sea,

26 [o] 2 Chr. 16:10
27 [p] Deut. 18:22
29 [q] 2 Chr. 35:22
31 [r] 2 Chr. 13:14, 15
33 [2] *Or scale armor and the breastplate*

CHAPTER 19

2 [a] 1 Sam. 9:9; 1 Kin. 16:1; 2 Chr. 20:34 [b] Ps. 139:21 [c] 2 Chr. 32:25
3 [d] 2 Chr. 17:4, 6 [e] 2 Chr. 30:19 [1] Or *Asherim,* Heb. *Asheroth*
4 [f] 2 Chr. 15:8-13
5 [g] [Deut. 16:18-20]
6 [h] [Lev. 19:15; Deut. 1:17]; Ps. 58:1 [i] Ps. 82:1; [Eccl. 5:8] [2] Lit. *in the matter of the judgment*
7 [j] [Gen. 18:25; Deut. 32:4]; Rom. 9:17 [k] [Deut. 10:17, 18; Job 34:19]; Acts 10:34; Rom. 2:11; Gal. 2:6; [Eph. 6:9; Col. 3:25]
8 [l] Deut. 16:18; 2 Chr. 17:8 [3] LXX, Vg. *for the inhabitants of Jerusalem*
9 [m] [2 Sam. 23:3]
10 [n] Deut. 17:8 [o] Num. 16:46 [p] [Ezek. 3:18]
11 [q] Ezra 7:3 [r] 1 Chr. 26:30 [s] [2 Chr. 15:2; 20:17]

CHAPTER 20

1 [a] 1 Chr. 18:2 [b] 1 Chr. 19:15 [c] 2 Chr. 26:7 [1] So with MT, Vg.; LXX *Meunites* (cf. 2 Chr. 26:7)

19:1-3 Having faced possible death that was diverted by God (18:31), Jehoshaphat was rebuked because of his alliances. The prophet condemned the king's alliance with God's enemy, Ahab (1 Kin. 22:2), yet there was mercy mingled with wrath because of the king's concern personally and nationally for the true worship of God.

19:2 Hanani. This same prophet had earlier given Jehoshaphat's father, Asa, a similar warning (2 Chr. 16:7-9).

19:4-11 Jehoshaphat put God's kingdom in greater spiritual order than at any time since Solomon. To insure this order, he set "judges" (v. 5) in place and gave them principles to rule by: 1) accountability to God (v. 6); 2) integrity and honesty (v. 7); 3) loyalty to God (v. 9); 4) concern for righteousness (v. 10); and 5) courage (v. 11). All are essentials to spiritual leadership.

20:1,2 The offspring of Lot, i.e., Moab and Ammon, located E of the Jordan, and those from Edom to the S (the offspring of Esau), had intentions of dethroning Jehoshaphat. They had come around the S end of the Dead Sea as far N as En-Gedi, at the middle of the western shore. This was a common route for enemies since they were invisible to the people on the other side of the mountains to the W.

from [2]Syria; and they are [d]in Hazazon
Tamar" (which *is* [e]En Gedi). 3 And Jehoshaphat feared, and set [3]himself to [f]seek
the LORD, and [g]proclaimed a fast throughout all Judah. 4 So Judah gathered together
to ask [h]*help* from the LORD; and from all the
cities of Judah they came to seek the LORD.
5 Then Jehoshaphat stood in the assembly of Judah and Jerusalem, in the house of
the LORD, before the new court, 6 and said:
"O LORD God of our fathers, *are* You not
[i]God in heaven, and [j]do You *not* rule over
all the kingdoms of the nations, and [k]in
Your hand *is there not* power and might, so
that no one is able to withstand You? 7 *Are*
You not [l]our God, *who* [m]drove out the inhabitants of this land before Your people
Israel, and gave it to the descendants of
Abraham [n]Your friend forever? 8 And they
dwell in it, and have built You a sanctuary
in it for Your name, saying, 9 [o]'If disaster
comes upon us—sword, judgment, pestilence, or famine—we will stand before this
temple and in Your presence (for Your
[p]name *is* in this temple), and cry out to You
in our affliction, and You will hear and
save.' 10 And now, here are the people of
Ammon, Moab, and Mount Seir—whom
You [q]would not let Israel invade when
they came out of the land of Egypt, but
[r]they turned from them and did not destroy them— 11 here they are, rewarding
us [s]by coming to throw us out of Your possession which You have given us to inherit. 12 O our God, will You not [t]judge them?
For we have no power against this great
multitude that is coming against us; nor do
we know what to do, but [u]our eyes *are*
upon You."

13 Now all Judah, with their little ones,
their wives, and their children, stood before the LORD.

14 Then [v]the Spirit of the LORD came
upon Jahaziel the son of Zechariah, the son
of Benaiah, the son of Jeiel, the son of Mattaniah, a Levite of the sons of Asaph, in the
midst of the assembly. 15 And he said, "Listen, all you of Judah and you inhabitants of
Jerusalem, and you, King Jehoshaphat!
Thus says the LORD to you: [w]'Do not be
afraid nor dismayed because of this great
multitude, [x]for the battle *is* not yours, but
God's. 16 Tomorrow go down against
them. They will surely come up by the Ascent of Ziz, and you will find them at the
end of the [4]brook before the Wilderness of
Jeruel. 17 [y]You will not *need* to fight in this
battle. Position yourselves, stand still and
see the salvation of the LORD, who is with
you, O Judah and Jerusalem!' Do not fear
or be dismayed; tomorrow go out against
them, [z]for the LORD *is* with you."

18 And Jehoshaphat [a]bowed his head
with *his* face to the ground, and all Judah
and the inhabitants of Jerusalem bowed
before the LORD, worshiping the LORD.
19 Then the Levites of the children of the
Kohathites and of the children of the Korahites stood up to praise the LORD God of Israel with voices loud and high.

20 So they rose early in the morning and
went out into the Wilderness of Tekoa; and
as they went out, Jehoshaphat stood and
said, "Hear me, O Judah and you inhabitants of Jerusalem: [b]Believe in the LORD
your God, and you shall be established; believe His prophets, and you shall prosper."
21 And when he had consulted with the
people, he appointed those who should
sing to the LORD, [c]and who should praise
the beauty of holiness, as they went out before the army and were saying:

[d]"Praise the LORD,
[e]For His mercy *endures* forever."

22 Now when they began to sing and to
praise, [f]the LORD set ambushes against the
people of Ammon, Moab, and Mount Seir,
who had come against Judah; and they

2 [d]Gen. 14:7 [e]Josh. 15:62 [2]So with MT, LXX, Vg.; Heb. mss., Old Lat. *Edom*
3 [f]2 Chr. 19:3 [g]1 Sam. 7:6; Ezra 8:21; Jer. 36:9; Jon. 3:5 [3]Lit. *his face*
4 [h]2 Chr. 14:11
6 [i]Deut. 4:39; Josh. 2:11; [1 Kin. 8:23]; Matt. 6:9 [j]Ps. 22:28; 47:2, 8; Dan. 4:17, 25, 32 [k]1 Chr. 29:12; 2 Chr. 25:8; Ps. 62:11; Matt. 6:13
7 [l]Gen. 13:14-17; 17:7; Ex. 6:7 [m]Ps. 44:2 [n]Is. 41:8; James 2:23
9 [o]1 Kin. 8:33, 37; 2 Chr. 6:28-30 [p]2 Chr. 6:20
10 [q]Deut. 2:4, 9, 19 [r]Num. 20:21
11 [s]Ps. 83:1-18
12 [t]Judg. 11:27; [1 Sam. 3:13] [u]Ps. 25:15; 121:1, 2; 123:1, 2; 141:8
14 [v]Num. 11:25, 26; 24:2; 2 Chr. 15:1; 24:20
15 [w]Ex. 14:13, 14; [Deut. 1:29, 30; 31:6, 8]; 2 Chr. 32:7 [x]1 Sam. 17:47; Zech. 14:3
16 [4]*streambed* or *wadi*
17 [y]Ex. 14:13, 14 [z]Num. 14:9; [2 Chr. 15:2; 32:8]
18 [a]Ex. 4:31; 2 Chr. 7:3; 29:28
20 [b]Is. 7:9
21 [c]1 Chr. 16:29; Ps. 29:2; 90:17; 96:9; 110:3 [d]1 Chr. 16:34; Ps. 106:1; 136:1 [e]1 Chr. 16:41; 2 Chr. 5:13
22 [f]Judg. 7:22; 1 Sam. 14:20

20:3,4 Jehoshaphat made the appropriate spiritual response, i.e., the king and the nation appealed to God in prayer and fasting. The fast was national, including even the children (v. 13). Cf. Joel 2:12-17; Jon. 3:7.

20:5-12 Jehoshaphat stood in the redecorated center court praying for the nation, appealing to the promises, the glory, and the reputation of God which were at stake since He was identified with Judah. In his prayer he acknowledged God's sovereignty (v. 6), God's covenant (v. 7), God's presence (vv. 8,9), God's goodness (v. 10), God's possession (v. 11), and their utter dependence on Him (v. 12).

20:10 Mount Seir. A prominent landmark in Edom.

20:14-17 The Lord responded immediately, sending a message of confidence through the prophet Jahaziel.

20:16 Ascent of Ziz...Wilderness of Jeruel. These areas lie between En-Gedi on the Dead Sea and Tekoa, which is 10 mi. S of Jerusalem and 17 mi. NW of En-Gedi. This is the pass that leads from the valley of the Dead Sea toward Jerusalem.

20:18-21 Here was the praise of faith. They were confident enough in God's promise of victory to begin the praise before the battle was won. So great was their trust that the choir marched in front of the army, singing psalms.

20:21 the beauty of holiness. The Lord is beautiful in holiness (cf. Ex. 15:11; Ps. 27:4), but the text here would better be translated "in holy attire," which was referring to the manner in which the Levite singers were clothed in symbolic sacred clothing (cf. 1 Chr. 16:29) in honor of the Lord's holiness.

20:22-24 Similar to God's intervention in Gideon's day (Judg. 7:15-23), God caused confusion among the enemy, who mistakenly turned upon themselves and slaughtered each other. Some think this may have been done by angels who appeared and set off this uncontrolled and deadly panic. The destruction was complete before Jehoshaphat and his army ever met the enemy (v. 24).

were defeated. 23 For the people of
Ammon and Moab stood up against the
inhabitants of Mount Seir to utterly kill
and destroy *them.* And when they [5]had
made an end of the inhabitants of Seir,
[g]they helped to destroy one another.
24 So when Judah came to a place overlooking the wilderness, they looked toward the multitude; and there *were* their
dead bodies, fallen on the earth. No one
had escaped.
25 When Jehoshaphat and his people
came to take away their spoil, they found
among them an abundance of valuables on
the [6]dead bodies, and precious jewelry,
which they stripped off for themselves,
more than they could carry away; and they
were three days gathering the spoil because
there was so much. 26 And on the fourth
day they assembled in the Valley of [7]Bera-
chah, for there they blessed the LORD; therefore the name of that place was called The
Valley of Berachah until this day. 27 Then
they returned, every man of Judah and Jerusalem, with Jehoshaphat in front of them,
to go back to Jerusalem with joy, for the
LORD had [h]made them rejoice over their enemies. 28 So they came to Jerusalem, with
stringed instruments and harps and trumpets, to the house of the LORD. 29 And [i]the
fear of God was on all the kingdoms of
those countries when they heard that the
LORD had fought against the enemies of Israel. 30 Then the realm of Jehoshaphat was
quiet, for his [j]God gave him rest all around.

The End of Jehoshaphat's Reign

31 [k]So Jehoshaphat was king over Judah.
He was thirty-five years old when he became king, and he reigned twenty-five
years in Jerusalem. His mother's name *was*
Azubah the daughter of Shilhi. 32 And he
walked in the way of his father [l]Asa, and
did not turn aside from it, doing *what was*
right in the sight of the LORD. 33 Nevertheless [m]the [8]high places were not taken away,
for as yet the people had not [n]directed their
hearts to the God of their fathers.
34 Now the rest of the acts of Jehoshaphat, first and last, indeed they *are* written
in the book of Jehu the son of Hanani,
[o]which *is* mentioned in the book of the
kings of Israel.
35 After this [p]Jehoshaphat king of Judah
allied himself with Ahaziah king of Israel,
[q]who acted very [r]wickedly. 36 And he allied
himself with him [s]to make ships to go to
Tarshish, and they made the ships in Ezion
Geber. 37 But Eliezer the son of Dodavah of
Mareshah prophesied against Jehoshaphat,
saying, "Because you have allied yourself
with Ahaziah, the LORD has destroyed your
works." [t]Then the ships were wrecked, so
that they were not able to go [u]to Tarshish.

Jehoram Reigns in Judah

21 And [a]Jehoshaphat [1]rested with his
fathers, and was buried with his fathers in the City of David. Then Jehoram
his son reigned in his place. 2 He had
brothers, the sons of Jehoshaphat: Azariah,
Jehiel, Zechariah, Azaryahu, Michael, and
Shephatiah; all these *were* the sons of Jehoshaphat king of Israel. 3 Their father
gave them great gifts of silver and gold
and precious things, with fortified cities in
Judah; but he gave the kingdom to Jehoram, because he *was* the firstborn.
4 Now when Jehoram [2]was established
over the kingdom of his father, he
strengthened himself and killed all his
brothers with the sword, and also *others* of
the princes of Israel.
5 [b]Jehoram *was* thirty-two years old
when he became king, and he reigned eight
years in Jerusalem. 6 And he walked in the
way of the kings of Israel, just as the house
of Ahab had done, for he had the daughter
of [c]Ahab as a wife; and he did evil in the
sight of the LORD. 7 Yet the LORD would not
destroy the house of David, because of the
[d]covenant that He had made with David,
and since He had promised to give a lamp
to him and to his [e]sons forever.
8 [f]In his days Edom revolted against Judah's authority, and made a king over
themselves. 9 So Jehoram went out with his
officers, and all his chariots with him. And
he rose by night and attacked the Edomites
who had surrounded him and the captains
of the chariots. 10 Thus Edom has been in
revolt against Judah's authority to this day.
At that time Libnah revolted against his
rule, because he had forsaken the LORD
God of his fathers. 11 Moreover he made
[3]high places in the mountains of Judah,
and caused the inhabitants of Jerusalem to
[g]commit harlotry, and led Judah astray.

23 [g]Judg. 7:22; 1 Sam. 14:20 [5]*had finished*
25 [6]A few Heb. mss., Old Lat., Vg. *garments;* LXX *armor*
26 [7]Lit. *Blessing*
27 [h]Neh. 12:43
29 [i]2 Chr. 14:14; 17:10
30 [j]1 Kin. 22:41-43; 2 Chr. 14:6, 7; 15:15; Job 34:29
31 [k][1 Kin. 22:41-43]
32 [l]2 Chr. 14:2
33 [m]2 Chr. 15:17; 17:6 [n]2 Chr. 12:14; 19:3 [8]Places for pagan worship
34 [o]1 Kin. 16:1, 7
35 [p]2 Chr. 18:1 [q]1 Kin. 22:48-53 [r][2 Chr. 19:2]
36 [s]1 Kin. 9:26; 10:22
37 [t]1 Kin. 22:48 [u]2 Chr. 9:21

CHAPTER 21

1 [a]1 Kin. 22:50 [1]Died and joined his ancestors
4 [2]Lit. *arose*
5 [b]2 Kin. 8:17-22
6 [c]2 Chr. 18:1
7 [d]2 Sam. 7:8-17 [e]1 Kin. 11:36; 2 Kin. 8:19; Ps. 132:11
8 [f]2 Kin. 8:20; 14:7, 10; 2 Chr. 25:14, 19
11 [g][Lev. 20:5] [3]Places for pagan worship

20:25-28 They went back just as they had gone out—with music (cf. vv. 21, 22).

20:29 This is the second time in Jehoshaphat's reign that fear came on the nations (cf. 2 Chr. 17:10), which was similar to that when Israel came out of Egypt (Ex. 23:27; Num. 22:3; Josh. 2:9-11; 9:9, 10).

20:31–21:3 *See notes on 1 Kin. 22:41-50.*

21:2-5 When the co-regency with his father ended at his father's death, Jehoram killed all who might have threatened his throne.

21:4-20 The reign of Jehoram (ca. 853–841 B.C.). Cf. 2 Kin. 8:16-24. Most likely, Obadiah prophesied during his reign.

21:4-10 *See notes on 2 Kin. 8:16-22.*

21:11 led Judah astray. Undoubtedly he was influenced by his

12 And a letter came to him from Elijah the prophet, saying,

Thus says the LORD God of your
father David:
Because you have not walked in
the ways of Jehoshaphat your
father, or in the ways of Asa king
of Judah, 13 but have walked in the
way of the kings of Israel, and
have [h]made Judah and the
inhabitants of Jerusalem to [i]play
the harlot like the [j]harlotry of the
house of Ahab, and also have
[k]killed your brothers, those of your
father's household, *who were* better
than yourself, 14 behold, the LORD
will strike your people with a
serious affliction—your children,
your wives, and all your
possessions; 15 and you *will become*
very sick with a [l]disease of your
intestines, until your intestines
come out by reason of the sickness,
day by day.

16 Moreover the [m]LORD [n]stirred up
against Jehoram the spirit of the Philistines
and the [o]Arabians who *were* near the Ethiopians. 17 And they came up into Judah
and invaded it, and carried away all the
possessions that were found in the king's
house, and also [p]his sons and his wives, so
that there was not a son left to him except
[4]Jehoahaz, the youngest of his sons.
18 After all this the LORD struck him [q]in
his intestines with an incurable disease.
19 Then it happened in the course of time,
after the end of two years, that his intestines came out because of his sickness;
so he died in severe pain. And his people
made no [5]burning for him, like [r]the burning for his fathers.
20 He was thirty-two years old when he
became king. He reigned in Jerusalem
eight years and, to no one's sorrow, de-
parted. However they buried him in the City of David, but not in the tombs of the kings.

Ahaziah Reigns in Judah

22 Then the inhabitants of Jerusalem
made [a]Ahaziah his youngest son
king in his place, for the raiders who came
with the [b]Arabians into the camp had
killed all the [c]older *sons*. So Ahaziah the
son of Jehoram, king of Judah, reigned.
2 Ahaziah *was* [1]forty-two years old when
he became king, and he reigned one year in
Jerusalem. His mother's name *was* [d]Atha-
liah the [2]granddaughter of Omri. 3 He also
walked in the ways of the house of Ahab,
for his mother advised him to do wickedly.
4 Therefore he did evil in the sight of the
LORD, like the house of Ahab; for they were
his counselors after the death of his father,
to his destruction. 5 He also followed their
advice, and went with [3]Jehoram the son of
Ahab king of Israel to war against Hazael
king of Syria at Ramoth Gilead; and the
Syrians wounded Joram. 6 [e]Then he returned to Jezreel to recover from the
wounds which he had received at Ramah,
when he fought against Hazael king of
Syria. And [4]Azariah the son of Jehoram,
king of Judah, went down to see Jehoram
the son of Ahab in Jezreel, because he was
sick.
7 His going to Joram [f]was God's occasion for Ahaziah's [5]downfall; for when he
arrived, [g]he went out with [6]Jehoram
against Jehu the son of Nimshi, [h]whom the
LORD had anointed to [7]cut off the house of
Ahab. 8 And it happened, when Jehu was
[i]executing judgment on the house of Ahab,
and [j]found the princes of Judah and the
sons of Ahaziah's brothers who served
Ahaziah, that he killed them. 9 [k]Then he
searched for Ahaziah; and they caught him
(he was hiding in Samaria), and brought
him to Jehu. When they had killed him,
they buried him, "because," they said, "he

13 [h]2 Chr. 21:11 [i][Ex. 34:15]; Deut. 31:16 [j]1 Kin. 16:31-33; 2 Kin. 9:22 [k]1 Kin. 2:32; 2 Chr. 21:4
15 [l]2 Chr. 21:18, 19
16 [m]2 Chr. 33:11; [Jer. 51:11] [n]1 Kin. 11:14, 23 [o]2 Chr. 17:11
17 [p]2 Chr. 24:7 [4]*Ahaziah* or *Azariah*, 2 Chr. 22:1
18 [q]2 Chr. 13:20; 21:15; Acts 12:23
19 [r]2 Chr. 16:14 [5]Burning of spices

CHAPTER 22
1 [a]2 Chr. 21:17; 22:6 [b]2 Chr. 21:16 [c]2 Chr. 21:17
2 [d]2 Chr. 21:6 [1]*twenty-two*, 2 Kin. 8:26 [2]Lit. *daughter*
5 [3]*Joram*, v. 7; 2 Kin. 8:28
6 [e]2 Kin. 9:15 [4]Heb. mss., LXX, Syr., Vg. *Ahaziah* and 2 Kin. 8:29
7 [f]Judg. 14:4; 1 Kin. 12:15; 2 Chr. 10:15 [g]2 Kin. 9:21-24 [h]2 Kin. 9:6, 7 [5]Lit. *crushing* [6]*Joram*, vv. 5, 7; 2 Kin. 8:28 [7]*destroy*
8 [i]2 Kin. 9:22-24 [j]2 Kin. 10:10-14; Hos. 1:4
9 [k][2 Kin. 9:27]

marriage to Ahab's daughter (cf. v. 6) and was influenced in the alliance just like his father (2 Chr. 18:1). They had not learned from Solomon's sinful example (cf. 1 Kin. 11:3,4). His wicked wife, Athaliah, later became ruler over Judah and tried to wipe out David's royal line (2 Chr. 22:10).

21:12-15 Elijah, best known for his confrontations with Israel's Ahab and Jezebel (1 Kin. 17–2 Kin. 2:11), confronted prophetically Jehoram's sins of idolatry and murder (21:13). The consequences from God's judgment extended beyond himself to his family and the nation (21:14,15). This event undoubtedly occurred in the early years of Jehoram's co-regency with his father Jehoshaphat and shortly before Elijah's departure to heaven, ca. 848 B.C. (cf. 2 Kin. 2:11,12).

21:16-20 The consequences of his sin were far-reaching. He suffered military losses, his country was ravaged, his capital taken, his palace plundered, his wives taken, all his children killed but the youngest, he died with a painful disease, and was buried without honor (21:16–22:1).

21:20 eight years. These were the years of his exclusive reign, not including his co-regency with his father.

22:1-9 The reign of Ahaziah (ca. 841 B.C.). Cf. 2 Kin. 8:25-29; 9:21-29.

22:1-6 *See notes on 2 Kin. 8:25-29.*

22:2 forty-two. This is a copyist's error, easily made due to the small stroke that differentiates two Heb. letters. The reading from 2 Kin. 8:26 of "twenty-two" should be followed.

22:3 his mother advised...wickedly. Athaliah and the rest of Ahab's house who were in the young king's life taught him wickedness and led him to moral corruption, idolatry, and folly in being induced to war with the Syrians (vv. 5,6).

22:7-9 *See notes on 2 Kin. 8:28–9:29.*

is the son of [l]Jehoshaphat, who [m]sought
the LORD with all his heart."
So the house of Ahaziah had no one to
assume power over the kingdom.

Athaliah Reigns in Judah

10 [n]Now when Athaliah the mother of
Ahaziah saw that her son was dead, she
arose and destroyed all the royal heirs of
the house of Judah. 11 But [8]Jehoshabeath,
the daughter of the king, took [o]Joash the
son of Ahaziah, and stole him away from
among the king's sons who were being
murdered, and put him and his nurse in a
bedroom. So Jehoshabeath, the daughter of
King Jehoram, the wife of Jehoiada the
priest (for she was the sister of Ahaziah),
hid him from Athaliah so that she did not
kill him. 12 And he was hidden with them
in the house of God for six years, while
Athaliah reigned over the land.

Joash Crowned King of Judah

23 In [a]the seventh year [b]Jehoiada
strengthened himself, *and made a*
covenant with the captains of hundreds:
Azariah the son of Jeroham, Ishmael the
son of Jehohanan, Azariah the son of
[c]Obed, Maaseiah the son of Adaiah, and
Elishaphat the son of Zichri. 2 And they
went throughout Judah and gathered the
Levites from all the cities of Judah, and the
[d]chief fathers of Israel, and they came to Jerusalem.
3 Then all the assembly made a covenant
with the king in the house of God. And he
said to them, "Behold, the king's son shall
reign, as the LORD has [e]said of the sons of
David. 4 This *is* what you shall do: One-
third of you [f]entering on the Sabbath, of
the priests and the Levites, *shall be* keeping
watch over the doors; 5 one-third *shall be* at
the king's house; and one-third at the Gate
of the Foundation. All the people *shall be* in
the courts of the house of the LORD. 6 But
let no one come into the house of the LORD
except the priests and [g]those of the Levites
who serve. They may go in, for they *are*
holy; but all the people shall keep the
watch of the LORD. 7 And the Levites shall
surround the king on all sides, every man
with his weapons in his hand; and whoever comes into the house, let him be put to
death. You are to be with the king when he
comes in and when he goes out."
8 So the Levites and all Judah did according to all that Jehoiada the priest commanded. And each man took his men who
were to be on duty on the Sabbath, with
those who were going *off duty* on the Sabbath; for Jehoiada the priest had not dismissed [h]the divisions. 9 And Jehoiada the
priest gave to the captains of hundreds the
spears and the large and small [i]shields
which *had belonged* to King David, that *were*
in the temple of God. 10 Then he set all the
people, every man with his weapon in his
hand, from the right side of the temple to
the left side of the temple, along by the
altar and by the temple, all around the
king. 11 And they brought out the king's
son, put the crown on him, [j]*gave him* the
[1]Testimony, and made him king. Then Jehoiada and his sons anointed him, and
said, "*Long* live the king!"

Death of Athaliah

12 Now when [k]Athaliah heard the noise
of the people running and praising the
king, she came to the people *in* the temple
of the LORD. 13 *When* she looked, there was
the king standing by his pillar at the entrance; and the leaders and the trumpeters
were by the king. All the people of the land
were rejoicing and blowing trumpets, also
the singers with musical instruments, and
[l]those who led in praise. So Athaliah tore
her clothes and said, [m]"Treason! Treason!"
14 And Jehoiada the priest brought out
the captains of hundreds who were set
over the army, and said to them, "Take her
outside under guard, and slay with the
sword whoever follows her." For the priest
had said, "Do not kill her in the house of
the LORD."
15 So they seized her; and she went by
way of the entrance [n]of the Horse Gate *into*
the king's house, and they killed her there.
16 Then Jehoiada made a [o]covenant between himself, the people, and the king,
that they should be the LORD's people.
17 And all the people went to the [2]temple
of Baal, and tore it down. They broke in
pieces its altars and images, and [p]killed
Mattan the priest of Baal before the altars.
18 Also Jehoiada appointed the oversight
of the house of the LORD to the hand of the
priests, the Levites, whom David had [q]as-

9 [l]1 Kin. 15:24 [m]2 Chr. 17:4; 20:3, 4
10 [n]2 Kin. 11:1-3
11 [o]2 Kin. 12:18 [8]*Jehosheba,* 2 Kin. 11:2

CHAPTER 23

1 [a]2 Kin. 11:4 [b]2 Kin. 12:2 [c]1 Chr. 2:37, 38
2 [d]Ezra 1:5
3 [e]2 Sam. 7:12; 1 Kin. 2:4; 9:5; 2 Chr. 6:16; 7:18; 21:7
4 [f]1 Chr. 9:25
6 [g]1 Chr. 23:28-32
8 [h]1 Chr. 24:1-31
9 [i]2 Sam. 8:7
11 [j]Deut. 17:18 [1]Law, Ex. 25:16, 21; 31:18
12 [k]2 Chr. 22:10
13 [l]1 Chr. 25:6-8 [m]2 Kin. 9:23
15 [n]Neh. 3:28; Jer. 31:40
16 [o]Josh. 24:24, 25; 2 Chr. 15:12-15
17 [p]Deut. 13:6-9; 1 Kin. 18:40 [2]Lit. *house*
18 [q]1 Chr. 23:6, 30, 31; 24:1

22:10–23:21 The reign of Athaliah (ca. 841–835 B.C.). Cf. 2 Kin. 11:1-20.

23:3 as the LORD...said. This is one of the most dramatic moments in messianic history. The human offspring of David have been reduced to one—Joash. If he had died, there would have been no human heir to the Davidic throne, and it would have meant the destruction of the line of the Messiah. However, God remedied the situation by providentially protecting Joash (2 Chr. 22:10-12) and eliminating Athaliah (1 Chr. 23:12-21).

23:11 Testimony. The usual meaning is a copy of the law (cf. Deut. 17:18; Job 31:35,36).

signed in the house of the LORD, to offer the
burnt offerings of the LORD, as *it is* written
in the [r]Law of Moses, with rejoicing and
with singing, *as it was established* by David.
19 And he set the [s]gatekeepers at the gates
of the house of the LORD, so that no one
who was in any way unclean should enter.
20 [t]Then he took the captains of hundreds, the nobles, the governors of the people, and all the people of the land, and
brought the king down from the house of
the LORD; and they went through the
Upper Gate to the king's house, and set the
king on the throne of the kingdom. 21 So all
the people of the land rejoiced; and the city
was quiet, for they had slain Athaliah with
the sword.

Joash Repairs the Temple

24 Joash [a]*was* seven years old when he
became king, and he reigned forty
years in Jerusalem. His mother's name *was*
Zibiah of Beersheba. 2 Joash [b]did *what was*
right in the sight of the LORD all the days of
Jehoiada the priest. 3 And Jehoiada took
two wives for him, and he had sons and
daughters.
4 Now it happened after this *that* Joash
set his heart on repairing the house of the
LORD. 5 Then he gathered the priests and
the Levites, and said to them, "Go out to
the cities of Judah, and [c]gather from all Israel money to repair the house of your God
from year to year, and see that you do it
quickly."
However the Levites did not do it
quickly. 6 [d]So the king called Jehoiada the
chief *priest,* and said to him, "Why have
you not required the Levites to bring in
from Judah and from Jerusalem the collection, *according to the commandment* of [e]Mo-
ses the servant of the LORD and of the assembly of Israel, for the [f]tabernacle of
witness?" 7 For [g]the sons of Athaliah, that
wicked woman, had broken into the house
of God, and had also presented all the
[h]dedicated things of the house of the LORD
to the Baals.
8 Then at the king's command [i]they
made a chest, and set it outside at the
gate of the house of the LORD. 9 And they
made a proclamation throughout Judah
and Jerusalem to bring to the LORD [j]the
collection *that* Moses the servant of God
had imposed on Israel in the wilderness.
10 Then all the leaders and all the people
rejoiced, brought their contributions, and
put *them* into the chest until all had given.
11 So it was, at that time, when the chest
was brought to the king's official by the
hand of the Levites, and [k]when they saw
that *there was* much money, that the
king's scribe and the high priest's officer
came and emptied the chest, and took it
and returned it to its place. Thus they did
day by day, and gathered money in abundance.
12 The king and Jehoiada gave it to
those who did the work of the service of
the house of the LORD; and they hired masons and carpenters to [l]repair the house of
the LORD, and also those who worked in
iron and bronze to restore the house of the
LORD. 13 So the workmen labored, and the
work was completed by them; they restored the house of God to its original condition and reinforced it. 14 When they had
finished, they brought the rest of the
money before the king and Jehoiada;
[m]they made from it articles for the house
of the LORD, articles for serving and offering, spoons and vessels of gold and silver.
And they offered burnt offerings in the
house of the LORD continually all the days
of Jehoiada.

Apostasy of Joash

15 But Jehoiada grew old and was full of
days, and he died; *he was* one hundred and
thirty years old when he died. 16 And they
buried him in the City of David among the
kings, because he had done good in Israel,
both toward God and His house.
17 Now after the death of Jehoiada the
leaders of Judah came and bowed down to
the king. And the king listened to them.
18 Therefore they left the house of the
LORD God of their fathers, and served
[n]wooden images and idols; and [o]wrath
came upon Judah and Jerusalem because
of their trespass. 19 Yet He [p]sent prophets
to them, to bring them back to the LORD;
and they testified against them, but they
would not listen.

18 [r] Num. 28:2
19 [s] 1 Chr. 26:1-19
20 [t] 1 Kin. 9:22; 2 Kin. 11:19

CHAPTER 24

1 [a] 2 Kin. 11:21; 12:1-15
2 [b] 2 Chr. 26:4, 5
5 [c] 2 Kin. 12:4
6 [d] 2 Kin. 12:7 [e] Ex. 30:12-16 [f] Num. 1:50; Acts 7:44
7 [g] 2 Chr. 21:17 [h] 2 Kin. 12:4
8 [i] 2 Kin. 12:9
9 [j] 2 Chr. 24:6
11 [k] 2 Kin. 12:10
12 [l] 2 Chr. 30:12
14 [m] 2 Kin. 12:13
18 [n] 1 Kin. 14:23 [o] [Ex. 34:12-14]; Judg. 5:8; 2 Chr. 19:2; 28:13; 29:8; 32:25
19 [p] 2 Kin. 17:13; 21:10-15; 2 Chr. 36:15, 16; Jer. 7:25, 26; 25:4

24:1-27 The reign of Joash (ca. 835–796 B.C.). Cf. 2 Kin. 11:17–12:21. Most likely, Joel prophesied during his reign, and his prophecy provides much helpful background to the time.

24:1-14 *See notes on 2 Kin. 11:17–12:16.*

24:15,16 Jehoiada. This man was the High-Priest of Athaliah's and Joash's reigns (cf. 2 Chr. 23:1–24:16), who championed God's cause of righteousness during days of evil by: 1) leading the fight against idols ; 2) permitting the coup against Athaliah; and 3) granting the throne to Joash to bring about the subsequent revival.

24:17,18a After Jehoiada's death, the leaders of Judah convinced King Joash that they needed to return to idolatry. With the death of the old priest came the turning point in the reign of Joash. He "listened" means Joash gave consent for the idol worship and thus it began.

24:18b,19 God's righteousness judged the evil of Judah, while at the same time His mercy sent prophets to preach the truth of repentance.

20 Then the Spirit of God [1]came upon
[q]Zechariah the son of Jehoiada the priest,
who stood above the people, and said to
them, "Thus says God: [r]'Why do you
transgress the commandments of the LORD,
so that you cannot prosper? [s]Because you
have forsaken the LORD, He also has forsaken you.' " 21 So they conspired against
him, and at the command of the king they
[t]stoned him with stones in the court of the
house of the LORD. 22 Thus Joash the king
did not remember the kindness which Jehoiada his [2]father had done to him, but
killed his son; and as he died, he said, "The
LORD look on *it*, and [u]repay!"

Death of Joash

23 So it happened in the spring of the
year *that* [v]the army of Syria came up
against him; and they came to Judah and
Jerusalem, and destroyed all the leaders of
the people from among the people, and
sent all their [3]spoil to the king of Damascus. 24 For the army of the Syrians [w]came
with a small company of men; but the
LORD [x]delivered a very great army into
their hand, because they had forsaken the
LORD God of their fathers. So they [y]exe-
cuted judgment against Joash. 25 And
when they had withdrawn from him (for
they left him severely wounded), [z]his own
servants conspired against him because of
the blood of the [4]sons of Jehoiada the
priest, and killed him on his bed. So he
died. And they buried him in the City of
David, but they did not bury him in the
tombs of the kings.
26 These are the ones who conspired
against him: [5]Zabad the son of Shimeath
the Ammonitess, and Jehozabad the son of
[6]Shimrith the Moabitess. 27 Now *concern-*
ing his sons, and [a]the many oracles about
him, and the repairing of the house of God,
indeed they *are* written in the [7]annals of
the book of the kings. [b]Then Amaziah his
son reigned in his place.

Amaziah Reigns in Judah

25 Amaziah [a]*was* twenty-five years old
when he became king, and he reigned
twenty-nine years in Jerusalem. His mother's name *was* Jehoaddan of Jerusalem.
2 And he did *what was* right in the sight of
the LORD, [b]but not with a loyal heart.
3 [c]Now it happened, as soon as the kingdom was established for him, that he executed his servants who had murdered his father the king. 4 However he did not execute
their children, but *did* as *it is* written in the
Law in the Book of Moses, where the LORD
commanded, saying, [d]"The fathers shall not
be put to death for their children, nor shall
the children be put to death for their fathers;
but a person shall die for his own sin."

The War Against Edom

5 Moreover Amaziah gathered Judah together and set over them captains of thousands and captains of hundreds, according
to *their* fathers' houses, throughout all Judah and Benjamin; and he numbered them
[e]from twenty years old and above, and
found them to be three hundred thousand
choice *men, able* to go to war, who could
handle spear and shield. 6 He also hired
one hundred thousand mighty men of
valor from Israel for one hundred talents
of silver. 7 But a [f]man of God came to him,
saying, "O king, do not let the army of Israel go with you, for the LORD *is* not with
Israel—*not with* any of the children of
Ephraim. 8 But if you go, be gone! Be

20 [q] Judg. 6:34; Matt. 23:35 [r] Num. 14:41; [Prov. 28:13] [s] [2 Chr. 15:2] [1] Lit. *clothed*
21 [t] [Neh. 9:26]; Matt. 23:35; Acts 7:58, 59
22 [u] [Gen. 9:5] [2] Foster father
23 [v] 2 Kin. 12:17; Is. 7:2 [3] *plunder*
24 [w] Lev. 26:8; [Deut. 32:30]; Is. 30:17 [x] Lev. 26:25; [Deut. 28:25] [y] 2 Chr. 22:8; Is. 10:5
25 [z] 2 Kin. 12:20, 21; 2 Chr. 25:3 [4] LXX, Vg. *son* and vv. 20-22
26 [5] *Jozachar*, 2 Kin. 12:21 [6] *Shomer*, 2 Kin. 12:21
27 [a] 2 Kin. 12:18 [b] 2 Kin. 12:21 [7] Or *commentary*, Heb. *midrash*

CHAPTER 25

1 [a] 2 Kin. 14:1-6
2 [b] 2 Kin. 14:4; 2 Chr. 25:14
3 [c] 2 Kin. 14:5; 2 Chr. 24:25
4 [d] Deut. 24:16; 2 Kin. 14:6; Jer. 31:30; [Ezek. 18:20]
5 [e] Num. 1:3
7 [f] 2 Chr. 11:2

24:20-22 The specific example of Zechariah, son of Jehoiada (not to be confused with Zechariah, son of Berechiah [Zech. 1:1; Matt. 23:35]) is alluded to by NT writers in such texts as Acts 7:51,52; Heb. 11:37. This priest told the people that faithfulness to the Lord is the condition for blessing (cf. 12:5; 15:2). The conspiracy against this man who spoke the truth was with the king's full authority, and he bore the greatest guilt for the murder (v. 22). *See note on Matt. 23:35.*

24:22 did not remember. Cf. 2 Chr. 23:11, where Jehoiada's wife preserved Joash from certain death as an infant, or 2 Chr. 23:1–24:1, where Jehoiada devised a plan to dethrone Athaliah and crown Joash king, or 2 Chr. 24:2, where Jehoiada is acknowledged as the voice of righteousness for Joash. Yet, Joash willfully ignored all that. Zechariah died pronouncing the just doom that would eventually come.

24:23-25 As Zechariah had prayed (24:22), so God repaid Joash's apostasy with defeat by Syria and death at the hands of his own people.

24:24 small company. As the Lord had previously given victory to Judah's smaller army because of their faithfulness (2 Chr. 13:2-20; 14:9-15), He gave Judah defeat at the hands of a lesser force because of their wickedness.

24:25 Unlike righteous Asa (2 Chr. 16:13,14), but like unrighteous Jehoram (2 Chr. 21:18-20), Joash died an ignominious death and received burial without honor.

24:26,27 *See notes on 2 Kin. 12:19-21.*

25:1-28 The reign of Amaziah (ca. 796–767 B.C.). Cf. 2 Kin. 14:1-20.

25:1-4 *See notes on 2 Kin. 14:1-6.*

25:4 Cf. Ezek. 18.

25:5-16 This section is an elaboration of 2 Kin. 14:7.

25:5-13 Amaziah gathered his army, which was small compared to the army of Jehoshaphat, which was over 1,000,000 (cf. 17:14-19). This shows how the northern kingdom had declined in 80 years.

25:6 one hundred talents. If a talent weighs 75 lbs., this represents almost 4 tons of silver. This wealth was paid to the king of Israel, Jehoahaz, who ordered the mercenaries of Israel to aid Amaziah against Edom.

25:7 man of God. This is a technical term used about 70 times in the OT, always referring to one who spoke for God. He warned Amaziah not to make idolatrous Israel his ally because the Lord was not with Ephraim, i.e., Israel, the capital of idolatry. *See note on Deut. 33:1.*

strong in battle! *Even so,* God shall make
you fall before the enemy; for God has
[g]power to help and to overthrow."
9 Then Amaziah said to the man of God,
"But what *shall we* do about the hundred
talents which I have given to the troops of
Israel?"
And the man of God answered, [h]"The
LORD is able to give you much more than
this." 10 So Amaziah discharged the troops
that had come to him from Ephraim, to go
back home. Therefore their anger was
greatly aroused against Judah, and they returned home in great anger.
11 Then Amaziah strengthened himself,
and leading his people, he went to [i]the Valley of Salt and killed ten thousand of the
people of Seir. 12 Also the children of Judah took captive ten thousand alive,
brought them to the top of the rock, and
cast them down from the top of the rock, so
that they all were dashed in pieces.
13 But as for the soldiers of the army
which Amaziah had discharged, so that
they would not go with him to battle, they
raided the cities of Judah from Samaria to
Beth Horon, killed three thousand in them,
and took much [1]spoil.
14 Now it was so, after Amaziah came
from the slaughter of the Edomites, that
[j]he brought the gods of the people of Seir,
set them up *to be* [k]his gods, and bowed
down before them and burned incense to
them. 15 Therefore the anger of the LORD
was aroused against Amaziah, and He sent
him a prophet who said to him, "Why
have you sought [l]the gods of the people,
which [m]could not rescue their own people
from your hand?"
16 So it was, as he talked with him, that
the king said to him, "Have we made you
the king's counselor? Cease! Why should
you be killed?"
Then the prophet ceased, and said, "I
know that God has [n]determined to destroy
you, because you have done this and have
not heeded my advice."

Israel Defeats Judah

17 Now [o]Amaziah king of Judah asked
advice and sent to [2]Joash the son of Jehoahaz, the son of Jehu, king of Israel, saying,
"Come, let us face one another *in battle.*"
18 And Joash king of Israel sent to Amaziah king of Judah, saying, "The thistle
that *was* in Lebanon sent to the cedar that
was in Lebanon, saying, 'Give your daughter to my son as wife'; and a wild beast that
was in Lebanon passed by and trampled
the thistle. 19 Indeed you say that you have
defeated the Edomites, and your heart is
lifted up to [p]boast. Stay at home now; why
should you meddle with trouble, that you
should fall—you and Judah with you?"
20 But Amaziah would not heed, for [q]it
came from God, that He might give them
into the hand *of their enemies,* because they
[r]sought the gods of Edom. 21 So Joash king
of Israel went out; and he and Amaziah
king of Judah faced one another at [s]Beth
Shemesh, which *belongs* to Judah. 22 And
Judah was defeated by Israel, and every
man fled to his tent. 23 Then Joash the king
of Israel captured Amaziah king of Judah,
the son of Joash, the son of [t]Jehoahaz, at
Beth Shemesh; and he brought him to Jerusalem, and broke down the wall of Jerusalem from the Gate of Ephraim to the Corner Gate—four hundred cubits. 24 And *he
took* all the gold and silver, all the articles
that were found in the house of God with
[u]Obed-Edom, the treasures of the king's
house, and hostages, and returned to Samaria.

Death of Amaziah

25 [v]Amaziah the son of Joash, king of Judah, lived fifteen years after the death of
Joash the son of Jehoahaz, king of Israel.
26 Now the rest of the acts of Amaziah,
from first to last, indeed *are* they not written in the book of the kings of Judah and Israel? 27 After the time that Amaziah turned
away from following the LORD, they made
a conspiracy against him in Jerusalem, and
he fled to Lachish; but they sent after him
to Lachish and killed him there. 28 Then
they brought him on horses and buried
him with his fathers in [3]the City of Judah.

8 [g] 2 Chr. 14:11; 20:6
9 [h] [Deut. 8:18]; Prov. 10:22
11 [i] 2 Kin. 14:7
13 [1] *plunder*
14 [j] 2 Chr. 28:23 [k] [Ex. 20:3, 5]
15 [l] [Ps. 96:5] [m] 2 Chr. 25:11
16 [n] [1 Sam. 2:25]
17 [o] 2 Kin. 14:8-14
[2] *Jehoash,* 2 Kin. 14:8ff.
19 [p] 2 Chr. 26:16; 32:25; [Prov. 16:18]
20 [q] 1 Kin. 12:15; 2 Chr. 22:7 [r] 2 Chr. 25:14
21 [s] Josh. 19:38
23 [t] 2 Chr. 21:17; 22:1, 6
24 [u] 1 Chr. 26:15
25 [v] 2 Kin. 14:17-22
28 [3] The City of David

25:8 God has power. *See note on 2 Chr. 24:24.* The man of God reminded the king sarcastically that he would need to be strong, since God wouldn't help.

25:9,10 The man of God told Amaziah to cut his losses and trust the Lord. The king obeyed and sent the Israelite mercenaries home in anger.

25:11 Valley of Salt. Most likely this is located at the southern end of the Dead Sea, where David had several centuries before been victorious (cf. 1 Chr. 18:12,13). **Seir.** Another name for Edom.

25:12 rock. This mode of execution was common among pagan nations (cf. Ps. 137:9).

25:13 Samaria. This was the well-known town of Israel from which they launched their attacks. **Beth Horon.** *See note on 2 Chr. 8:5.*

25:14-16 Amaziah did the unthinkable from both a biblical and political perspective—he embraced the false gods of the people whom he had just defeated. Perhaps he did this because he was seduced by the wicked pleasures of idolatry and because he thought it would help him in assuring no future threat from Edom. However, it only brought destruction to the king, who just wanted to silence the voice of God.

25:17-28 *See notes on 2 Kin. 14:8-20.*

Uzziah Reigns in Judah

26 Now all the people of Judah took
[1]Uzziah, who *was* sixteen years old,
and made him king instead of his father
Amaziah. 2 He built [2]Elath and restored it
to Judah, after the king rested with his fathers.
3 Uzziah *was* sixteen years old when he
became king, and he reigned fifty-two
years in Jerusalem. His mother's name was
Jecholiah of Jerusalem. 4 And he did *what*
was [a]right in the sight of the LORD, according to all that his father Amaziah had
done. 5 [b]He sought God in the days of
Zechariah, who [c]had understanding in the
[3]visions of God; and as long as he sought
the LORD, God made him [d]prosper.
6 Now he went out and [e]made war
against the Philistines, and broke down the
wall of Gath, the wall of Jabneh, and the
wall of Ashdod; and he built cities *around*
Ashdod and among the Philistines. 7 God
helped him against [f]the Philistines, against
the Arabians who lived in Gur Baal, and
against the Meunites. 8 Also the Ammonites [g]brought tribute to Uzziah. His fame
spread as far as the entrance of Egypt, for
he became exceedingly strong.
9 And Uzziah built towers in Jerusalem
at the [h]Corner Gate, at the Valley Gate, and
at the corner buttress of the wall; then he
fortified them. 10 Also he built towers in
the desert. He dug many wells, for he had
much livestock, both in the lowlands and
in the plains; *he also had* farmers and vinedressers in the mountains and in [4]Carmel,
for he loved the soil.
11 Moreover Uzziah had an army of
fighting men who went out to war by
companies, according to the number on
their roll as prepared by Jeiel the scribe
and Maaseiah the officer, under the hand
of Hananiah, *one* of the king's captains.
12 The total number of [5]chief officers of
the mighty men of valor *was* two thousand
six hundred. 13 And under their authority
was an army of three hundred and seven
thousand five hundred, that made war
with mighty power, to help the king
against the enemy. 14 Then Uzziah prepared for them, for the entire army,
shields, spears, helmets, body armor,
bows, and slings *to cast* stones. 15 And he
made devices in Jerusalem, invented by
[i]skillful men, to be on the towers and the
corners, to shoot arrows and large stones.
So his fame spread far and wide, for he
was marvelously helped till he became
strong.

The Penalty for Uzziah's Pride

16 But [j]when he was strong his heart was
[k]lifted up, to *his* destruction, for he transgressed against the LORD his God [l]by entering the temple of the LORD to burn incense on the altar of incense. 17 So
[m]Azariah the priest went in after him, and
with him were eighty priests of the LORD—
valiant men. 18 And they withstood King
Uzziah, and said to him, "*It* [n]*is* not for you,
Uzziah, to burn incense to the LORD, but
for the [o]priests, the sons of Aaron, who are
consecrated to burn incense. Get out of the
sanctuary, for you have trespassed! You
shall have no honor from the LORD God."
19 Then Uzziah became furious; and he
had a censer in his hand to burn incense.
And while he was angry with the priests,
[p]leprosy broke out on his forehead, before
the priests in the house of the LORD, beside
the incense altar. 20 And Azariah the chief
priest and all the priests looked at him, and
there, on his forehead, he *was* leprous; so
they thrust him out of that place. Indeed he

CHAPTER 26

1 [1] *Azariah*, 2 Kin. 14:21ff.
2 [2] Heb. *Eloth*
4 [a] 2 Chr. 24:2
5 [b] 2 Chr. 24:2 [c] Gen. 41:15; Dan. 1:17; 10:1 [d] [2 Chr. 15:2; 20:20; 31:21] [3] Heb. mss., LXX, Syr., Tg., Arab. *fear*
6 [e] Is. 14:29
7 [f] 2 Chr. 21:16
8 [g] 2 Sam. 8:2; 2 Chr. 17:11
9 [h] 2 Kin. 14:13; 2 Chr. 25:23; Neh. 3:13, 19, 32; Zech. 14:10
10 [4] Or *the fertile fields*
12 [5] Lit. *chief fathers*
15 [i] Ex. 39:3, 8
16 [j] [Deut. 32:15] [k] Deut. 8:14; 2 Chr. 25:19 [l] 1 Kin. 13:1-4; 2 Kin. 16:12, 13
17 [m] 1 Chr. 6:10
18 [n] [Num. 3:10; 16:39, 40; 18:7] [o] Ex. 30:7, 8; Heb. 7:14
19 [p] Lev. 13:42; Num. 12:10; 2 Kin. 5:25-27

26:1-23 The reign of Uzziah, a.k.a. Azariah (ca. 790–739 B.C.). Cf. 2 Kin. 14:21,22; 15:1-7. Hosea (Hos. 1:1), Amos (Amos 1:1), Jonah, and Isaiah (Is. 6) ministered during his reign.

26:1-4 *See notes on 2 Kin. 14:21,22; 15:1-3.*

26:5 Zechariah. An otherwise unknown prophet during Uzziah's reign, not the priestly spokesman of 24:20, nor the prophet Zechariah who wrote the prophetic book to Judah ca. 520 B.C. **sought…prosper.** This summarizes a major theme in 2 Chronicles.

26:6-15 A summary of Uzziah's prosperity in the realm of: 1) conquering the Philistines (26:6-8); 2) domestic affairs (26:9,10); and 3) military might (26:11-15).

26:6-8 A description of Judah's military success to the W, E, and S. Israel to the N is not mentioned.

26:6 Gath…Jabneh…Ashdod. Key Philistine cities to the SW of Jerusalem.

26:7 Arabians…Gur Baal. Most likely a nomadic group who lived in an area whose location is unknown. **Meunites.** A nomadic people living in Edom (cf. 2 Chr. 20:1).

26:8 Ammonites. Offspring of Lot who lived E of the Jordan.

26:9 Corner Gate. Located in the NW section of Jerusalem. **Valley Gate.** Located in the SW section of Jerusalem. **corner buttress.** Located in the E section of Jerusalem.

26:10 Carmel. Though there was a mountain range called Carmel, it was not in the territory under Uzziah, so most likely this should not be taken as a proper name, but rather translated as "fertile field," which also fits the rest of the general references in the verse.

26:11-15 With 375,000 in the army and the development of new weapons, he posed a threat to would-be assailants and thus secured the nation in peace.

26:16-18 Uzziah attempted to usurp the role of the priest which is forbidden in the Levitical code (cf. Num. 3:10; 18:7). Proverbs 16:18 indicates that pride precipitates a fall, and it did in his case. Even the king could not live above God's law.

26:19,20 God judged the king's refusal to heed the law but was merciful in that He did not kill Uzziah. With leprosy, Uzziah had to submit to the priests in a new way according to the laws of leprosy (cf. Lev. 13,14), and endure isolation the rest of his life from the temple as well.

also [q]hurried to get out, because the LORD had struck him.

21 [r]King Uzziah was a leper until the day of his death. He dwelt in an [s]isolated house, because he was a leper; for he was cut off from the house of the LORD. Then Jotham his son *was* over the king's house, judging the people of the land.

22 Now the rest of the acts of Uzziah, from first to last, the prophet [t]Isaiah the son of Amoz wrote. 23 [u]So Uzziah [6]rested with his fathers, and they buried him with his fathers in the field of burial which *belonged* to the kings, for they said, "He is a leper." Then Jotham his son reigned in his place.

Jotham Reigns in Judah

27 Jotham [a]*was* twenty-five years old when he became king, and he reigned sixteen years in Jerusalem. His mother's name *was* [1]Jerushah the daughter of Zadok. 2 And he did *what was* right in the sight of the LORD, according to all that his father Uzziah had done (although he did not enter the temple of the LORD). But still [b]the people acted corruptly.

3 He built the Upper Gate of the house of the LORD, and he built extensively on the wall of [c]Ophel. 4 Moreover he built cities in the mountains of Judah, and in the forests he built fortresses and towers. 5 He also fought with the king of the [d]Ammonites and defeated them. And the people of Ammon gave him in that year one hundred talents of silver, ten thousand kors of wheat, and ten thousand of barley. The people of Ammon paid this to him in the second and third years also. 6 So Jotham became mighty, [e]because he prepared his ways before the LORD his God.

7 Now the rest of the acts of Jotham, and all his wars and his ways, indeed they *are* written in the book of the kings of Israel and Judah. 8 He was twenty-five years old when he became king, and he reigned sixteen years in Jerusalem. 9 [f]So Jotham [2]rested with his fathers, and they buried him in the City of David. Then [g]Ahaz his son reigned in his place.

Ahaz Reigns in Judah

28 Ahaz [a]*was* twenty years old when he became king, and he reigned sixteen years in Jerusalem; and he did not do *what was* right in the sight of the LORD, as his father David *had done.* 2 For he walked in the ways of the kings of Israel, and made [b]molded images for [c]the Baals. 3 He burned incense in [d]the Valley of the Son of Hinnom, and burned [e]his children in the [f]fire, according to the abominations of the nations whom the LORD had [g]cast out before the children of Israel. 4 And he sacrificed and burned incense on the [1]high places, on the hills, and under every green tree.

Syria and Israel Defeat Judah

5 Therefore [h]the LORD his God delivered him into the hand of the king of Syria. They [i]defeated him, and carried away a great multitude of them as captives, and brought *them* to Damascus. Then he was also delivered into the hand of the king of Israel, who defeated him with a great slaughter. 6 For [j]Pekah the son of Remaliah killed one hundred and twenty thousand in Judah in one day, all valiant men, [k]because they had forsaken the LORD God of their fathers. 7 Zichri, a mighty man of Ephraim, killed Maaseiah the king's son, Azrikam the officer over the house, and Elkanah *who was* second to the king. 8 And the children of Israel carried away captive of their [l]brethren two hundred thousand women, sons, and daughters; and they also took away much [2]spoil from them, and brought the spoil to Samaria.

20 [q] Esth. 6:12
21 [r] 2 Kin. 15:5 [s] [Lev. 13:46; Num. 5:2]
22 [t] 2 Kin. 20:1; 2 Chr. 32:20, 32; Is. 1:1
23 [u] 2 Kin. 15:7; 2 Chr. 21:20; 28:27; Is. 6:1 [6] *Died and joined his ancestors*

CHAPTER 27

1 [a] 2 Kin. 15:32-35 [1] *Jerusha*, 2 Kin. 15:33
2 [b] 2 Kin. 15:35; Ezek. 20:44; 30:13
3 [c] 2 Chr. 33:14; Neh. 3:26
5 [d] 2 Chr. 26:8
6 [e] 2 Chr. 26:5
9 [f] 2 Kin. 15:38 [g] Is. 1:1; Hos. 1:1; Mic. 1:1 [2] Died and joined his ancestors

CHAPTER 28

1 [a] 2 Kin. 16:2-4
2 [b] Ex. 34:17; Lev. 19:4 [c] Judg. 2:11
3 [d] Josh. 15:8 [e] 2 Kin. 23:10 [f] [Lev. 18:21]; 2 Kin. 16:3; 2 Chr. 33:6 [g] [Lev. 18:24-30]
4 [1] Places for pagan worship
5 [h] [Is. 10:5] [i] 2 Kin. 16:5, 6; [2 Chr. 24:24]; Is. 7:1, 17
6 [j] 2 Kin. 15:27 [k] [2 Chr. 29:8]
8 [l] Deut. 28:25, 41; 2 Chr. 11:4 [2] *plunder*

26:21-23 *See notes on 2 Kin. 15:5-7.*

26:22 Not the canonical book of Isaiah, but rather a reference to some other volume that the prophet wrote.

26:23 It was in that very year that Isaiah had his vision of God's glory (cf. Is. 6:1ff.).

27:1-9 The reign of Jotham (ca. 750–731 B.C.). Cf. 2 Kin. 15:32-38. Isaiah (Is. 1:11) and Hosea (Hos. 1:1) continued to minister during his reign, plus Micah (Mic. 1:1) prophesied during that time also.

27:1-4,7-9 *See notes on 2 Kin. 15:33-38.*

27:3 wall of Ophel. Located on the S side of Jerusalem.

27:5 Ammonites. *See note on 2 Chr. 26:8.* Jotham repelled the invasion, pursuing the enemy into their own land and imposing a yearly tribute, which they paid for two years until Rezin, king of Syria and Pekah, King of Israel revolted and attacked. Jotham was too distracted to bother with the Ammonites (cf. 2 Kin. 15:37). **one hundred talents.** If a talent is about 75 lbs., this represents almost 4 tons of silver. **ten thousand kors.** If a kor is 7.5 bu., this represents 75,000 bu.

27:6 His one failure was in not removing the idolatrous high places and stopping idol worship by the people (cf. v. 2; 2 Kin. 15:35).

28:1-27 The reign of Ahaz (cf. 735–715 B.C.). Cf. 2 Kin. 16:1-20. Isaiah (Is. 1:1), Hosea (Hos. 1:1), and Micah (Mic. 1:1) all continued to minister during his reign. Second Kings 17:1-9 reports that it was after the 12th year of Ahaz, when Hosea was king in Israel, that the Assyrians took Israel into captivity (722 B.C.).

28:1-5a *See notes on 2 Kin. 16:1-6.*

28:2 Baals. *See note on 17:3.*

28:5b-8 Ahaz's gross disobedience earned him God's wrath, by which both Syria and Israel defeated his army, as they had in Jotham's day (cf. 2 Kin. 15:37). This was likely a continuation of the same campaign against Judah begun earlier.

28:5,6 Damascus. The capital city of Syria, NE of Judah. **Pekah.** King of Israel (ca. 752–732 B.C.).

28:8 Samaria. The capital city of the northern kingdom of Israel.

Israel Returns the Captives

9 But a [m]prophet of the LORD was there,
whose name *was* Oded; and he went out
before the army that came to Samaria, and
said to them: "Look, [n]because the LORD
God of your fathers was angry with Judah,
He has delivered them into your hand; but
you have killed them in a rage *that* [o]reach-
es up to heaven. 10 And now you propose
to force the children of Judah and Jerusalem to be your [p]male and female slaves;
but are you not also guilty before the LORD
your God? 11 Now hear me, therefore, and
return the captives, whom you have taken
captive from your brethren, [q]for the fierce
wrath of the LORD *is* upon you."
12 Then some of the heads of the children of Ephraim, Azariah the son of Johanan, Berechiah the son of Meshillemoth,
Jehizkiah the son of Shallum, and Amasa
the son of Hadlai, stood up against those
who came from the war, 13 and said to
them, "You shall not bring the captives
here, for we *already* have offended the
LORD. You intend to add to our sins and to
our guilt; for our guilt is great, and *there is*
fierce wrath against Israel." 14 So the
armed men left the captives and the [3]spoil
before the leaders and all the assembly.
15 Then the men [r]who were designated by
name rose up and took the captives, and
from the [4]spoil they clothed all who were
naked among them, dressed them and
gave them sandals, [s]gave them food and
drink, and anointed them; and they let all
the feeble ones ride on donkeys. So they
brought them to their brethren at Jericho,
[t]the city of palm trees. Then they returned
to Samaria.

Assyria Refuses to Help Judah

16 [u]At the same time King Ahaz sent to
the [5]kings of Assyria to help him. 17 For
again the [v]Edomites had come, attacked
Judah, and carried away captives. 18 [w]The
Philistines also had invaded the cities of
the lowland and of the South of Judah, and
had taken Beth Shemesh, Aijalon, Gederoth, Sochoh with its villages, Timnah
with its villages, and Gimzo with its villages; and they dwelt there. 19 For the
LORD [6]brought Judah low because of Ahaz
king of [x]Israel, for he had [y]encouraged
moral decline in Judah and had been continually unfaithful to the LORD. 20 Also
[z]Tiglath-Pileser[7] king of Assyria came to
him and distressed him, and did not assist
him. 21 For Ahaz took part *of the treasures*
from the house of the LORD, from the house
of the king, and from the leaders, and he
gave *it* to the king of Assyria; but he did
not help him.

Apostasy and Death of Ahaz

22 Now in the time of his distress King
Ahaz became increasingly unfaithful to the
LORD. This *is that* King Ahaz. 23 For [a]he sacrificed to the gods of Damascus which had
defeated him, saying, "Because the gods of
the kings of Syria help them, I will sacrifice
to them [b]that they may help me." But they
were the ruin of him and of all Israel. 24 So
Ahaz gathered the articles of the house of
God, cut in pieces the articles of the house
of God, [c]shut up the doors of the house of
the LORD, and made for himself altars in
every corner of Jerusalem. 25 And in every
single city of Judah he made [8]high places to
burn incense to other gods, and provoked
to anger the LORD God of his fathers.
26 [d]Now the rest of his acts and all his
ways, from first to last, indeed they *are*
written in the book of the kings of Judah
and Israel. 27 So Ahaz [9]rested with his fathers, and they buried him in the city, in Jerusalem; but they [e]did not bring him into
the tombs of the kings of Israel. Then Hezekiah his son reigned in his place.

Hezekiah Reigns in Judah

29 Hezekiah [a]became king *when he was*
twenty-five years old, and he
reigned twenty-nine years in Jerusalem.
His mother's name *was* [1]Abijah the daughter of Zechariah. 2 And he did *what was*
right in the sight of the LORD, according to
all that his father David had done.

9 [m] 2 Chr. 25:15 [n] Ps. 69:26; [Is. 10:5; 47:6]; Ezek. 25:12, 15; 26:2; Obad. 10; [Zech. 1:15] [o] Ezra 9:6; Rev. 18:5
10 [p] [Lev. 25:39, 42, 43, 46]
11 [q] Ps. 78:49; James 2:13
14 [3] *plunder*
15 [r] 2 Chr. 28:12 [s] [Prov. 25:21, 22; Luke 6:27; Rom. 12:20] [t] Deut. 34:3; Judg. 1:16 [4] *plunder*
16 [u] 2 Kin. 16:7 [5] LXX, Syr., Vg. *king* (cf. v. 20)
17 [v] 2 Chr. 21:10; Obad. 10-14
18 [w] 2 Chr. 21:16, 17; Ezek. 16:27, 57
19 [x] 2 Kin. 16:2; 2 Chr. 21:2 [y] Ex. 32:25 [6] *humbled Judah*
20 [z] 2 Kin. 15:29; 16:7-9; 1 Chr. 5:26 [7] Heb. *Tilgath-Pilneser*
23 [a] 2 Chr. 25:14 [b] Jer. 44:17, 18
24 [c] 2 Chr. 29:3, 7
25 [8] Places for pagan worship
26 [d] 2 Kin. 16:19, 20
27 [e] 2 Chr. 21:20; 24:25 [9] Died and joined his ancestors

CHAPTER 29

1 [a] 2 Kin. 18:1; 2 Chr. 32:22, 33 [1] *Abi,* 2 Kin. 18:2

28:9 Oded. An otherwise unknown prophet, with the same name as an earlier Oded (cf. 15:1,8). The prophet said that Israel had won the victory because God was judging Judah. But he protested the viciousness of the killing and the effort to enslave them (v. 10) and warned them of God's wrath for such action (v. 11). Amazingly the apostate and hostile Israelites complied with the prophet's warning (vv. 12-15).

28:16 kings of Assyria. Most likely sing. "king," as per marginal note, who was Tiglath-Pileser (ca. 745–727 B.C.).

28:18 cities…lowland. To the SW of Jerusalem.

28:20,21 Tiglath-Pileser. *See note on 2 Chr. 28:16.* In spite of temporary relief by the conquest of Damascus and slaughter of Rezin (2 Kin. 16:9), little benefit came from this king to Ahaz because he allied with Assyria.

28:22-27 Ahaz surrendered himself to idolatry with the ignorance of a wicked pagan and a ruthless defiance of God that ruined him and his nation. He was justly dishonored in his burial (v. 27).

29:1–32:33 The reign of Hezekiah (ca. 715–686 B.C.). Cf. 2 Kin. 18:1–20:21; Is. 36–39. Second Kings 18:5 notes that Hezekiah's trust in the Lord had not been equaled by any king who preceded him nor by any who followed (cf. 2 Chr. 31:21). Isaiah (Is. 1:1), Hosea (Hos. 1:1), and Micah (Mic. 1:1) prophesied during his reign.

29:1,2 *See notes on 2 Kin. 18:1-3.*

Hezekiah Cleanses the Temple

3 In the first year of his reign, in the first
month, he [b]opened the doors of the house
of the LORD and repaired them. 4 Then he
brought in the priests and the Levites, and
gathered them in the East Square, 5 and
said to them: "Hear me, Levites! Now
[2]sanctify yourselves, [c]sanctify the house of
the LORD God of your fathers, and carry
out the rubbish from the holy *place*. 6 For
our fathers have trespassed and done evil
in the eyes of the LORD our God; they have
forsaken Him, have [d]turned their faces
away from the [3]dwelling place of the
LORD, and turned *their* backs *on Him*.
7 [e]They have also shut up the doors of the
vestibule, put out the lamps, and have not
burned incense or offered burnt offerings
in the holy *place* to the God of Israel.
8 Therefore the [f]wrath of the LORD fell
upon Judah and Jerusalem, and He has
[g]given them up to trouble, to desolation,
and to [h]jeering, as you see with your [i]eyes.
9 For indeed, because of this [j]our fathers
have fallen by the sword; and our sons, our
daughters, and our wives *are* in captivity.
10 "Now *it is* in my heart to make [k]a
covenant with the LORD God of Israel, that
His fierce wrath may turn away from us.
11 My sons, do not be negligent now, for
the LORD has [l]chosen you to stand before
Him, to serve Him, and that you should
minister to Him and burn incense."
12 Then these Levites arose: [m]Mahath the
son of Amasai and Joel the son of Azariah,
of the sons of the [n]Kohathites; of the sons of
Merari, Kish the son of Abdi and Azariah
the son of Jehallelel; of the Gershonites,
Joah the son of Zimmah and Eden the son
of Joah; 13 of the sons of Elizaphan, Shimri
and Jeiel; of the sons of Asaph, Zechariah
and Mattaniah; 14 of the sons of Heman, Jehiel and Shimei; and of the sons of Jeduthun, Shemaiah and Uzziel.
15 And they gathered their brethren,
[o]sanctified[4] themselves, and went according to the commandment of the king, at the
words of the LORD, [p]to cleanse the house of
the LORD. 16 Then the priests went into the
inner part of the house of the LORD to
cleanse *it*, and brought out all the debris
that they found in the temple of the LORD
to the court of the house of the LORD. And
the Levites took *it* out and carried *it* to the
Brook [q]Kidron.
17 Now they began to [5]sanctify on the
first *day* of the first month, and on the
eighth day of the month they came to
the vestibule of the LORD. So they sanctified the house of the LORD in eight days,
and on the sixteenth day of the first month
they finished.
18 Then they went in to King Hezekiah
and said, "We have cleansed all the house
of the LORD, the altar of burnt offerings
with all its articles, and the table of the
showbread with all its articles. 19 Moreover all the articles which King Ahaz in his
reign had [r]cast aside in his transgression
we have prepared and [6]sanctified; and
there they *are*, before the altar of the LORD."

Hezekiah Restores Temple Worship

20 Then King Hezekiah rose early, gathered the rulers of the city, and went up to
the house of the LORD. 21 And they brought
seven bulls, seven rams, seven lambs, and
seven male goats for a [s]sin offering for the
kingdom, for the sanctuary, and for Judah.
Then he commanded the priests, the sons
of Aaron, to offer *them* on the altar of the
LORD. 22 So they killed the bulls, and the
priests received the blood and [t]sprinkled *it*
on the altar. Likewise they killed the rams
and sprinkled the blood on the altar. They
also killed the lambs and sprinkled the
blood on the altar. 23 Then they brought
out the male goats *for* the sin offering before the king and the assembly, and they
laid their [u]hands on them. 24 And the
priests killed them; and they presented
their blood on the altar as a sin offering [v]to
make an atonement for all Israel, for the
king commanded *that* the burnt offering
and the sin offering *be made* for all Israel.
25 [w]And he stationed the Levites in the
house of the LORD with cymbals, with
stringed instruments, and with harps, [x]ac-
cording to the commandment of David, of

3 [b] 2 Chr. 28:24; 29:7
5 [c] 1 Chr. 15:12; 2 Chr. 29:15, 34; 35:6 [2] *consecrate*
6 [d] [Is. 1:4]; Jer. 2:27; Ezek. 8:16 [3] *Temple*
7 [e] 2 Chr. 28:24
8 [f] 2 Chr. 24:18 [g] 2 Chr. 28:5 [h] 1 Kin. 9:8; Jer. 18:16; 19:8; 25:9, 18; 29:18 [i] Deut. 28:32
9 [j] Deut. 28:25; 2 Chr. 28:5-8, 17
10 [k] 2 Chr. 15:12; 23:16
11 [l] Num. 3:6; 8:14; 18:2, 6; 2 Chr. 30:16, 17
12 [m] 2 Chr. 31:13 [n] Num. 3:19, 20
15 [o] 2 Chr. 29:5 [p] 1 Chr. 23:28 [4] *consecrated*
16 [q] 2 Chr. 15:16; 30:14
17 [5] *consecrate*
19 [r] 2 Chr. 28:24 [6] *consecrated*
21 [s] Lev. 4:3-14
22 [t] Lev. 8:14, 15, 19, 24; Heb. 9:21
23 [u] Lev. 4:15, 24; 8:14
24 [v] Lev. 14:20
25 [w] 1 Chr. 16:4; 25:6 [x] 1 Chr. 23:5; 25:1; 2 Chr. 8:14

29:3 first year…first month. Hezekiah addressed the spiritual problems first, which reflected his life priorities. Hezekiah correctly diagnosed Judah's ills—she had abandoned the true worship of God. So the king stepped in to reverse the policy of his father (28:22-25) and to repair the temple and return proper temple worship as God had prescribed in His Word (vv. 3-7). He knew such a revival of devotion to God would turn God's wrath away from Judah (v. 10).

29:12-14 Fourteen leaders undertook to collect and prepare for the cleansing of the temple.

29:12 Kohathites…Merari…Gershonites. The 3 familiar lines of Levi (cf. 1 Chr. 6:1).

29:13 Elizaphan. An important leader among the Kohathites (cf. Num. 3:30; 1 Chr. 15:8). **Asaph…Heman…Jeduthun.** The 3 lines of Levitical musicians (cf. 1 Chr. 25:1).

29:15-19 to cleanse. Beginning with the outer courts and working for 8 days, they then went inside. But as the Levites were not allowed within the walls of the holy places, the priests had to bring out all the debris to be carted off. This took 8 more days.

29:16 Brook Kidron. To the E of Jerusalem, between the temple and the Mt. of Olives.

29:20-36 Hezekiah restored true temple worship as practiced in the time of David and Solomon, producing great joy (v. 36).

[y]Gad the king's seer, and of Nathan the prophet; [z]for thus *was* the commandment of the LORD by his prophets. **26** The Levites stood with the instruments [a]of David, and the priests with [b]the trumpets. **27** Then Hezekiah commanded *them* to offer the burnt offering on the altar. And when the burnt offering began, [c]the song of the LORD *also* began, with the trumpets and with the instruments of David king of Israel. **28** So all the assembly worshiped, the singers sang, and the trumpeters sounded; all *this continued* until the burnt offering was finished. **29** And when they had finished offering, [d]the king and all who were present with him bowed and worshiped. **30** Moreover King Hezekiah and the leaders commanded the Levites to sing praise to the LORD with the words of David and of Asaph the seer. So they sang praises with gladness, and they bowed their heads and worshiped.

31 Then Hezekiah answered and said, "Now *that* you have consecrated yourselves to the LORD, come near, and bring sacrifices and [e]thank offerings into the house of the LORD." So the assembly brought in sacrifices and thank offerings, and as many as were of a [f]willing heart *brought* burnt offerings. **32** And the number of the burnt offerings which the assembly brought was seventy bulls, one hundred rams, *and* two hundred lambs; all these *were* for a burnt offering to the LORD. **33** The consecrated things *were* six hundred bulls and three thousand sheep. **34** But the priests were too few, so that they could not skin all the burnt offerings; therefore [g]their brethren the Levites helped them until the work was ended and until the *other* priests had [7]sanctified themselves, [h]for the Levites were [i]more diligent in [j]sanctifying themselves than the priests. **35** Also the burnt offerings *were* in abundance, with [k]the fat of the peace offerings and *with* [l]the drink offerings for *every* burnt offering.

So the service of the house of the LORD was set in order. **36** Then Hezekiah and all the people rejoiced that God had prepared the people, since the events took place so suddenly.

25 [y] 2 Sam. 24:11 [z] 2 Chr. 30:12
26 [a] 1 Chr. 23:5; Amos 6:5 [b] Num. 10:8, 10; 1 Chr. 15:24; 16:6; 2 Chr. 5:12
27 [c] 2 Chr. 23:18
29 [d] 2 Chr. 20:18
31 [e] Lev. 7:12 [f] Ex. 35:5, 22
34 [g] 2 Chr. 35:11 [h] 2 Chr. 30:3 [i] Ps. 7:10 [j] 2 Chr. 29:5 [7] *consecrated*
35 [k] Lev. 3:15, 16 [l] Num. 15:5-10

CHAPTER 30

2 [a] Num. 9:10, 11; 2 Chr. 30:13, 15
3 [b] Ex. 12:6, 18 [c] 2 Chr. 29:17, 34 [1] The first month, Lev. 23:5; lit. *that time*
5 [2] *established a decree to*
6 [d] Esth. 8:14; Job 9:25; Jer. 51:31 [e] [Jer. 4:1; Joel 2:13] [f] 2 Kin. 15:19, 29 [g] 2 Chr. 28:20
7 [h] Ezek. 20:18 [i] Is. 1:9 [j] 2 Chr. 29:8
8 [k] Ex. 32:9; Deut. 10:16; Acts 7:51 [3] Rebellious

Hezekiah Keeps the Passover

30 And Hezekiah sent to all Israel and Judah, and also wrote letters to Ephraim and Manasseh, that they should come to the house of the LORD at Jerusalem, to keep the Passover to the LORD God of Israel. **2** For the king and his leaders and all the assembly in Jerusalem had agreed to keep the Passover in the second [a]month. **3** For they could not keep it [b]at [1]the regular time, [c]because a sufficient number of priests had not consecrated themselves, nor had the people gathered together at Jerusalem. **4** And the matter pleased the king and all the assembly. **5** So they [2]resolved to make a proclamation throughout all Israel, from Beersheba to Dan, that they should come to keep the Passover to the LORD God of Israel at Jerusalem, since they had not done *it* for a long *time* in the *prescribed* manner.

6 Then the [d]runners went throughout all Israel and Judah with the letters from the king and his leaders, and spoke according to the command of the king: "Children of Israel, [e]return to the LORD God of Abraham, Isaac, and Israel; then He will return to the remnant of you who have escaped from the hand of [f]the kings of [g]Assyria. **7** And do not be [h]like your fathers and your brethren, who trespassed against the LORD God of their fathers, so that He [i]gave them up to [j]desolation, as you see. **8** Now do not be [k]stiff-necked, [3] as your fathers *were, but* yield yourselves to the LORD; and enter His sanctuary, which He has sanctified forever, and serve the LORD your God,

29:26 instruments of David. The instruments David had made for the temple (cf. 1 Chr. 23:5).

29:34 Levites were more diligent…than the priests. Perhaps the priests had become used to participating in all the idol sacrifices they had instituted (cf. 28:25).

30:1-27 Hezekiah reached back to restore the Feast of Unleavened Bread and the Passover (Ex. 12:1-20; Lev. 23:1-8) which apparently had not been properly and regularly observed in some time, perhaps since the division of the kingdom 215 years earlier (v. 5). The Passover would later be revived again by Josiah (2 Chr. 35:1-9) and Zerubbabel (Ezra 6:19-22). It celebrated God's forgiveness and redemption of His believing people.

30:1 Israel. These would be the remnant of the northern 10 tribes (vv. 6, 25) left in the land or escaped from the enemy after the northern kingdom was taken captive following the invasion by Assyria in 722 B.C. (2 Kin. 17:1-9). Ephraim and Manasseh were the leading tribes.

30:2 second month. This call to Passover was to unite the nation again in worship. Normally the Passover would be in the first month (Mar./Apr.). The rule of exception for individuals who were unclean or absent (Num. 9:9-11) was applied to the whole nation.

30:5 Beersheba to Dan. These two cities were at the extreme ends of the country, so this expression was a way of saying, "from S to N."

30:6 return. The nation was required by law to annually celebrate 3 feasts in Jerusalem: 1) Passover; 2) Pentecost; and 3) Tabernacles (cf. Ex. 23; Lev. 23; Num. 28, 29; Deut. 16). God would have returned to bless the people of the northern apostate and idolatrous kingdom of Israel if they had returned to Him. Cf. 15:2; 20:20; 26:5; 31:21, where this recurring theme is affirmed.

30:8 stiff-necked. This is the same kind of language used by Stephen in Acts 7:51-53, which in effect says, "Don't be obstinate."

[l]that the fierceness of His wrath may turn
away from you. 9 For if you return to the
LORD, your brethren and your children *will*
be treated with [m]compassion by those who
lead them captive, so that they may come
back to this land; for the LORD your God *is*
[n]gracious and merciful, and will not turn
His face from you if you [o]return to Him."
10 So the runners passed from city to city
through the country of Ephraim and Manasseh, as far as Zebulun; but [p]they
laughed at them and mocked them.
11 Nevertheless [q]some from Asher, Manasseh, and Zebulun humbled themselves
and came to Jerusalem. 12 Also [r]the hand
of God was on Judah to give them singleness of heart to obey the command of the
king and the leaders, [s]at the word of the
LORD.
13 Now many people, a very great assembly, gathered at Jerusalem to keep the
Feast of [t]Unleavened Bread in the second
month. 14 They arose and took away the
[u]altars that *were* in Jerusalem, and they
took away all the incense altars and cast
them into the Brook [v]Kidron. 15 Then they
slaughtered the Passover *lambs* on the
fourteenth *day* of the second month. The
priests and the Levites [4]were [w]ashamed,
and [5]sanctified themselves, and brought
the burnt offerings to the house of the
LORD. 16 They stood in their [x]place [6]ac-
cording to their custom, according to the
Law of Moses the man of God; the priests
sprinkled the blood *received* from the hand
of the Levites. 17 For *there were* many in the
assembly who had not [7]sanctified themselves; [y]therefore the Levites had charge of
the slaughter of the Passover *lambs* for
everyone *who was* not clean, to sanctify
them to the LORD. 18 For a multitude of the
people, [z]many from Ephraim, Manasseh,
Issachar, and Zebulun, had not cleansed
themselves, [a]yet they ate the Passover contrary to what was written. But Hezekiah
prayed for them, saying, "May the good
LORD provide atonement for everyone
19 *who* [b]prepares his heart to seek God, the
LORD God of his fathers, though *he is* not
cleansed according to the purification of the
sanctuary." 20 And the LORD listened to
Hezekiah and healed the people.
21 So the children of Israel who were
present at Jerusalem kept [c]the Feast of Unleavened Bread seven days with great
gladness; and the Levites and the priests
praised the LORD day by day, *singing* to the
LORD, accompanied by loud instruments.
22 And Hezekiah gave encouragement to
all the Levites [d]who taught the good
knowledge of the LORD; and they ate
throughout the feast seven days, offering
peace offerings and [e]making confession to
the LORD God of their fathers.
23 Then the whole assembly agreed to
keep *the feast* [f]another seven days, and they
kept it *another* seven days with gladness.
24 For Hezekiah king of Judah [g]gave to the
assembly a thousand bulls and seven thousand sheep, and the leaders gave to the assembly a thousand bulls and ten thousand
sheep; and a great number of priests [h]sanc-
tified[8] themselves. 25 The whole assembly of
Judah rejoiced, also the priests and Levites,
all the assembly that came from Israel, the
sojourners [i]who came from the land of Israel, and those who dwelt in Judah. 26 So
there was great joy in Jerusalem, for since
the time of [j]Solomon the son of David, king
of Israel, *there had* been nothing like this in
Jerusalem. 27 Then the priests, the Levites,
arose and [k]blessed the people, and their
voice was heard; and their prayer came *up* to
[l]His holy dwelling place, to heaven.

The Reforms of Hezekiah

31 Now when all this was finished, all
Israel who were present went out to
the cities of Judah and [a]broke the sacred
pillars in pieces, cut down the wooden images, and threw down the [1]high places and
the altars—from all Judah, Benjamin,

8 [l]2 Chr. 29:10
9 [m]Ps. 106:46 [n][Ex. 34:6; Mic. 7:18] [o][Is. 55:7]
10 [p]2 Chr. 36:16
11 [q]2 Chr. 11:16; 30:18, 21
12 [r][2 Cor. 3:5; Phil. 2:13; Heb. 13:20, 21] [s]2 Chr. 29:25
13 [t]Lev. 23:6; Num. 9:11
14 [u]2 Chr. 28:24 [v]2 Chr. 29:16
15 [w]2 Chr. 29:34 [4]*humbled themselves* [5]*set themselves apart*
16 [x]2 Chr. 35:10, 15 [6]*Or in their proper order*
17 [y]2 Chr. 29:34 [7]*consecrated*
18 [z]2 Chr. 30:1, 11, 25 [a]Ex. 12:43-49; [Num. 9:10]
19 [b]2 Chr. 19:3
21 [c]Ex. 12:15; 13:6; 1 Kin. 8:65
22 [d][Deut. 33:10]; 2 Chr. 17:9; 35:3 [e]Ezra 10:11
23 [f]1 Kin. 8:65; 2 Chr. 35:17, 18
24 [g]2 Chr. 35:7, 8 [h]2 Chr. 29:34 [8]*consecrated*
25 [i]2 Chr. 30:11, 18
26 [j]2 Chr. 7:8-10
27 [k]Num. 6:23 [l]Deut. 26:15; Ps. 68:5

CHAPTER 31

1 [a]2 Kin. 18:4 [1]Places for pagan worship

30:9 Not all the people of Israel had been taken captive in the invasion of the Assyrians during Hezekiah's reign (cf. 2 Kin. 17:5-23; 18:9-12).

30:10 Scorn was the response of these tribes, showing their wickedness even after judgment on them had begun. Note v. 18 for the additional brazen sin of these tribes.

30:13 second month. Normally, Passover and the Feast of Unleavened Bread were held in the first month; however, at this special time it was better to be one month late, than not at all.

30:14 These altars had been erected to idols by Ahaz. *See notes on 2 Chr. 28:25; 29:16.* Hezekiah was able to cleanse the city of idols and altars, something his predecessors failed to do.

30:18-20 The attitude of the heart was to prevail over their outward activity (cf. 1 Sam. 15:22; Jer. 7:22,23; Hos. 6:6). Hezekiah reminded them that God forgives even the most heinous sins, and He did (v. 20).

30:23 This speaks to the authenticity of revival in that the people knew how sinful they had been and how desperately in need of cleansing they actually were. They doubled the time for the feast which pointed to God's salvation and deliverance of the faithful.

30:26 nothing like this. A telling statement about the spiritual degeneracy of the divided kingdom since the time of Solomon over 215 years earlier.

31:1 Judah, Benjamin, Ephraim, and Manasseh. The first two referred to the southern kingdom; the last two represented the northern kingdom. The Passover had been a real revival and they carried the conviction of it back to their homes to "utterly destroy" all the idolatry. So the reign of idolatry ended, and the worship of God was restored. The people went home in hope of divine blessing and a future of peace and prosperity.

Ephraim, and Manasseh—until they had
utterly destroyed them all. Then all the
children of Israel returned to their own
cities, every man to his possession.
2 And Hezekiah appointed [b]the divisions of the priests and the Levites according to their divisions, each man according
to his service, the priests and Levites [c]for
burnt offerings and peace offerings, to
serve, to give thanks, and to praise in the
gates of the [2]camp of the LORD. 3 The king
also *appointed* a [3]portion of his [d]posses-
sions[4] for the burnt offerings: for the
morning and evening burnt offerings, the
burnt offerings for the Sabbaths and the
New Moons and the set feasts, as *it is* written in the [e]Law of the LORD.
4 Moreover he commanded the people
who dwelt in Jerusalem to contribute [f]sup-
port[5] for the priests and the Levites, that
they might devote themselves to [g]the Law
of the LORD.
5 As soon as the commandment was circulated, the children of Israel brought in
abundance [h]the firstfruits of grain and
wine, oil and honey, and of all the produce
of the field; and they brought in abundantly the [i]tithe of everything. 6 And the children of Israel and Judah, who dwelt in the
cities of Judah, brought the tithe of oxen
and sheep; also the [j]tithe of holy things
which were consecrated to the LORD their
God they laid in heaps.
7 In the third month they began laying
them in heaps, and they finished in the
seventh month. 8 And when Hezekiah and
the leaders came and saw the heaps, they
blessed the LORD and His people Israel.
9 Then Hezekiah questioned the priests
and the Levites concerning the heaps.
10 And Azariah the chief priest, from the
[k]house of Zadok, answered him and said,
[l]"Since *the people* began to bring the offerings into the house of the LORD, we have
had enough to eat and have plenty left, for
the LORD has blessed His people; and what
is left *is* this great [m]abundance."
11 Now Hezekiah commanded *them* to
prepare [n]rooms[6] in the house of the LORD,
and they prepared them. 12 Then they
faithfully brought in the offerings, the
tithes, and the dedicated things; [o]Cono-
niah the Levite had charge of them, and
Shimei his brother *was* the next. 13 Jehiel,
Azaziah, Nahath, Asahel, Jerimoth, Jozabad, Eliel, Ismachiah, Mahath, and Benaiah *were* overseers under the hand of Cono-
niah and Shimei his brother, at the
commandment of Hezekiah the king and
Azariah the [p]ruler of the house of God.
14 Kore the son of Imnah the Levite, the
keeper of the East Gate, *was* over the [q]free-
will offerings to God, to distribute the offerings of the LORD and the most holy
things. 15 And under him *were* [r]Eden,
Miniamin, Jeshua, Shemaiah, Amariah,
and Shecaniah, *his* faithful assistants in
[s]the cities of the priests, to distribute [t]allot-
ments to their brethren by divisions, to the
great as well as the small.
16 Besides those males from three years
old and up who were written in the genealogy, they distributed to everyone who
entered the house of the LORD his daily
portion for the work of his service, by his
division, 17 and to the priests who were
written in the genealogy according to their
father's house, and to the Levites [u]from
twenty years old and up according to their
work, by their divisions, 18 and to all who
were written in the genealogy—their little
ones and their wives, their sons and
daughters, the whole company of them—
for in their faithfulness they [7]sanctified
themselves in holiness.
19 Also for the sons of Aaron the priests,
who were in [v]the fields of the common-
lands of their cities, in every single city,
there were men who were [w]designated by
name to distribute portions to all the males

2 [b]1 Chr. 23:6; 24:1 [c]1 Chr. 23:30, 31 [2]*Temple*
3 [d]2 Chr. 35:7 [e]Num. 28:1–29:40 [3]*share* [4]*property*
4 [f]Num. 18:8; 2 Kin. 12:16; Neh. 13:10; Ezek. 44:29 [g]Mal. 2:7 [5]*the portion due*
5 [h]Ex. 22:29; Neh. 13:12 [i][Lev. 27:30]; Deut. 14:28; 26:12, 13
6 [j][Lev. 27:30]; Deut. 14:28
10 [k]1 Chr. 6:8, 9 [l][Mal. 3:10]
[m]Ex. 36:5
11 [n]1 Kin. 6:5-8 [6]*storerooms*
12 [o]2 Chr. 35:9; Neh. 13:13
13 [p]1 Chr. 9:11; Jer. 20:1
14 [q]Deut. 23:23; 2 Chr. 35:8
15 [r]2 Chr. 29:12 [s]Josh. 21:1-3, 9 [t]1 Chr. 9:26
17 [u]1 Chr. 23:24, 27
18 [7]*consecrated*
19 [v]Lev. 25:34; Num. 35:1-4 [w]2 Chr. 31:12-15

31:2-19 divisions of the priests and the Levites. The priestly service had not been supported by the government during the reign of the wicked kings, so Hezekiah restored that support as God originally ordained it (cf. 1 Chr. 24:1ff.; 2 Chr. 8:12-14).

31:6 tithe. Since the priests and Levites served the nation, they were to be supported by the people through the taxation of the tithe. According to Lev. 27:30-33 and Num. 18:21,24, the people were to give the tenth (tithe) to supply all the needs of the Levites. Malachi 3:8 says they were robbing God when they did not give the tithe. Deuteronomy 12:6,7 called for a second tithe that was to support the nation's devotion to the temple by being used for the national festivals at the temple in Jerusalem. This was called the festival tithe. Deuteronomy 14:28,29 called for a third tithe every 3 years for the poor. The sum of this tax plan totaled about 23 percent annually.

31:7 third...seventh month. From the time of the Feast of First Fruits or Pentecost in May/June until the Feast of Tabernacles in Sept./Oct.

31:11 rooms. These were stone houses, granaries, and cellars to replace the old decayed ones. In these places the Levites stored the tithes (v. 12).

31:16 three years old. Possibly, this refers to children of the priests who accompanied their fathers and received their portions in the temple. Under 3 they were probably still being nursed, so needed no food. The families of the priests were cared for (v. 18).

31:17 twenty years old. *See notes on 1 Chr. 23:3.* Cf. Num. 4:3; 28:24.

31:19 common-lands. This refers to the 48 Levitical cities (cf. Josh. 21:1-42). The tithes-taxes collected from everyone were used not only for festivals at the temple, but also for regular daily support of the priests living and leading throughout the Land (*see note on v. 6*).

among the priests and to all who were listed by genealogies among the Levites.
20 Thus Hezekiah did throughout all Judah, and he [x]did what *was* good and right
and true before the LORD his God. 21 And
in every work that he began in the service
of the house of God, in the law and in the
commandment, to seek his God, he did *it*
with all his heart. So he [y]prospered.

Sennacherib Boasts Against the LORD

32 After [a]these deeds of faithfulness,
Sennacherib king of Assyria came
and entered Judah; he encamped against
the fortified cities, thinking to win them
over to himself. 2 And when Hezekiah saw
that Sennacherib had come, and that his
purpose was to make war against Jerusalem, 3 he consulted with his leaders and
[1]commanders to stop the water from the
springs which *were* outside the city; and
they helped him. 4 Thus many people
gathered together who stopped all the
[b]springs and the brook that ran through
the land, saying, "Why should the [2]kings
of Assyria come and find much water?"
5 And [c]he strengthened himself, [d]built up
all the wall that was broken, raised *it* up to
the towers, and *built* another wall outside;
also he repaired [3]the [e]Millo *in* the City of
David, and made [4]weapons and shields in
abundance. 6 Then he set military captains
over the people, gathered them together to
him in the open square of the city gate, and
[f]gave them encouragement, saying, 7 [g]"Be
strong and courageous; [h]do not be afraid
nor dismayed before the king of Assyria,
nor before all the multitude that *is* with
him; for [i]*there are* more with us than with
him. 8 With him *is* an [j]arm of flesh; but
[k]with us *is* the LORD our God, to help us
and to fight our battles." And the people
were strengthened by the words of Hezekiah king of Judah.
9 [l]After this Sennacherib king of Assyria
sent his servants to Jerusalem (but he and
all the forces with him *laid siege* against
Lachish), to Hezekiah king of Judah, and
to all Judah who *were* in Jerusalem, saying,
10 [m]"Thus says Sennacherib king of Assyria: 'In what do you trust, that you remain under siege in Jerusalem? 11 Does not
Hezekiah persuade you to give yourselves
over to die by famine and by thirst, saying,
[n]"The LORD our God will deliver us from
the hand of the king of Assyria"? 12 [o]Has
not the same Hezekiah taken away His
high places and His altars, and commanded Judah and Jerusalem, saying, "You shall
worship before one altar and burn incense
on [p]it"? 13 Do you not know what I and my
fathers have done to all the peoples of *other*
lands? [q]Were the gods of the nations of
those lands in any way able to deliver their
lands out of my hand? 14 Who *was there*
among all the gods of those nations that
my fathers utterly destroyed that could deliver his people from my hand, that your
God should be able to deliver you from my
[r]hand? 15 Now therefore, [s]do not let Hezekiah deceive you or persuade you like this,
and do not believe him; for no god of any
nation or kingdom was able to deliver his
people from my hand or the hand of my fathers. How much less will your God deliver you from my hand?' "
16 Furthermore, his servants spoke
against the LORD God and against His servant Hezekiah.
17 He also wrote letters to revile the LORD
God of Israel, and to speak against Him,
saying, [t]"As the gods of the nations of *other*
lands have not delivered their people from
my hand, so the God of Hezekiah will not
deliver His people from my [u]hand."
18 [v]Then they called out with a loud voice
in [5]Hebrew to the people of Jerusalem who
were on the wall, to frighten them and trouble them, that they might take the city.
19 And they spoke against the God of Jerusalem, as against the gods of the people of
the earth—[w]the work of men's hands.

Sennacherib's Defeat and Death

20 [x]Now because of this King Hezekiah
and [y]the prophet Isaiah, the son of Amoz,
prayed and cried out to heaven. 21 [z]Then
the LORD sent an angel who cut down
every mighty man of valor, leader, and
captain in the camp of the king of Assyria.
So he returned [a]shamefaced to his own
land. And when he had gone into the temple of his god, some of his own offspring
struck him down with the sword there.
22 Thus the LORD saved Hezekiah and the
inhabitants of Jerusalem from the hand of
Sennacherib the king of Assyria, and from
the hand of all *others,* and [6]guided them on
every side. 23 And many brought gifts to the
LORD at Jerusalem, and [b]presents[7] to Hezekiah king of Judah, so that he was [c]exalted
in the sight of all nations thereafter.

20 [x] 2 Kin. 20:3; 22:2
21 [y] 2 Chr. 26:5; 32:30; Ps. 1:3

CHAPTER 32

1 [a] 2 Kin. 18:13–19:37; Is. 36:1–37:38
3 [1] Lit. *mighty men*
4 [b] 2 Kin. 20:20 [2] So with MT, Vg.; Arab., LXX, Syr. *king*
5 [c] Is. 22:9, 10 [d] 2 Kin. 25:4; 2 Chr. 25:23 [e] 2 Sam. 5:9; 1 Kin. 9:15, 24; 11:27; 2 Kin. 12:20; 1 Chr. 11:8 [3] Lit. *The Landfill* [4] *javelins*
6 [f] 2 Chr. 30:22; Is. 40:2
7 [g] [Deut. 31:6] [h] 2 Chr. 20:15 [i] 2 Kin. 6:16; [Rom. 8:31]
8 [j] [Jer. 17:5; 1 John 4:4] [k] Ex. 14:13; [1 Sam. 17:45-47]; 2 Chr. 13:12; 20:17; [Rom. 8:31]
9 [l] 2 Kin. 18:17
10 [m] 2 Kin. 18:19
11 [n] 2 Kin. 18:30
12 [o] 2 Kin. 18:22
[p] 2 Chr. 31:1, 2
13 [q] 2 Kin. 18:33-35
14 [r] [Is. 10:5-12]
15 [s] 2 Kin. 18:29
17 [t] 2 Kin. 19:9; [1 Cor. 8:5, 6] [u] 2 Kin. 19:12; Dan. 3:15
18 [v] 2 Kin. 18:28; Ps. 59:6 [5] Lit. *Judean*
19 [w] 2 Kin. 19:18; [Ps. 96:5; 115:4-8]
20 [x] 2 Kin. 19:15 [y] 2 Kin. 19:2
21 [z] 2 Kin. 19:35; Is. 10:12-19; Zech. 14:3 [a] Ps. 44:7
22 [6] LXX *gave them rest;* Vg. *gave them treasures*
23 [b] 2 Sam. 8:10; 2 Chr. 17:5; 26:8; Ps. 45:12 [c] 2 Chr. 1:1 [7] Lit. *precious things*

31:20,21 *See notes on 2 Kin. 18:5-7.*

32:1-23 Hezekiah's dealings with Sennacherib, king of Assyria (ca. 705–681 B.C.). *See notes on 2 Kin. 18:13–19:37; Is. 36,37.* The Assyrian king came because Hezekiah, determined to recover the independence of his nation, refused to pay the tribute his father had bound him to pay to Assyria. Sennacherib retaliated, and Hezekiah fortified the city (v. 5) and trusted God (vv. 8,11), who delivered them (vv. 21,22) and was glorified (v. 23).

Hezekiah Humbles Himself

24 [d]In those days Hezekiah was sick and
near death, and he prayed to the LORD; and
He spoke to him and gave him a sign. 25 But
Hezekiah [e]did not repay according to the
favor *shown* him, for [f]his heart was lifted
up; [g]therefore wrath was looming over him
and over Judah and Jerusalem. 26 [h]Then
Hezekiah humbled himself for the pride of
his heart, he and the inhabitants of Jerusalem, so that the wrath of the LORD did not
come upon them [i]in the days of Hezekiah.

Hezekiah's Wealth and Honor

27 Hezekiah had very great riches and
honor. And he made himself treasuries for
silver, for gold, for precious stones, for
spices, for shields, and for all kinds of desirable items; 28 storehouses for the harvest
of grain, wine, and oil; and stalls for all
kinds of livestock, and [8]folds for flocks.
29 Moreover he provided cities for himself,
and possessions of flocks and herds in
abundance; for [j]God had given him very
much property. 30 [k]This same Hezekiah
also stopped the water outlet of Upper
Gihon, and [9]brought the water by tunnel
to the west side of the City of David. Hezekiah [l]prospered in all his works.
31 However, *regarding* the ambassadors
of the princes of Babylon, whom they
[m]sent to him to inquire about the wonder
that was *done* in the land, God withdrew
from him, in order to [n]test him, that He
might know all *that was* in his heart.

Death of Hezekiah

32 Now the rest of the acts of Hezekiah,
and his goodness, indeed they *are* written
in [o]the vision of Isaiah the prophet, the son
of Amoz, *and* in the [p]book of the kings of
Judah and Israel. 33 [q]So Hezekiah [1]rested
with his fathers, and they buried him in
the upper tombs of the sons of David; and
all Judah and the inhabitants of Jerusalem
[r]honored him at his death. Then Manasseh
his son reigned in his place.

24 [d] 2 Kin. 20:1-11; Is. 38:1-8
25 [e] Ps. 116:12 [f] 2 Chr. 26:16; [Hab. 2:4] [g] 2 Chr. 24:18
26 [h] Jer. 26:18, 19 [i] 2 Kin. 20:19
28 [8] So with LXX, Vg.; Arab., Syr. omit *folds for flocks;* MT *flocks for sheepfolds*
29 [j] 1 Chr. 29:12
30 [k] Is. 22:9-11 [l] 2 Chr. 31:21 [9] Lit. *brought it straight to* (cf. 2 Kin. 20:20)
31 [m] 2 Kin. 20:12; Is. 39:1 [n] [Deut. 8:2, 16]
32 [o] Is. 36–39 [p] 2 Kin. 18–20
33 [q] 1 Kin. 1:21; 2 Kin. 20:21 [r] Ps. 112:6; Prov. 10:7 [1] Died and joined his ancestors

CHAPTER 33

1 [a] 2 Kin. 21:1-9
2 [b] [Deut. 18:9-12]; 2 Chr. 28:3; [Jer. 15:4]
3 [c] 2 Kin. 18:4; 2 Chr. 30:14; 31:1 [d] Deut. 16:21; 2 Kin. 23:5, 6 [e] Deut. 17:3 [1] Places for pagan worship [2] The gods of the Assyrians
4 [f] Deut. 12:11; 1 Kin. 8:29; 9:3; 2 Chr. 6:6; 7:16
5 [g] 2 Chr. 4:9
6 [h] [Lev. 18:21]; Deut. 18:10; 2 Kin. 23:10; 2 Chr. 28:3; Ezek. 23:37, 39 [i] Deut. 18:11; 2 Kin. 17:17 [j] [Lev. 19:31; 20:27]; 2 Kin. 21:6
7 [k] 2 Kin. 21:7; 2 Chr. 25:14 [l] Ps. 132:14 [3] Temple
8 [m] 2 Sam. 7:10
10 [4] *obey*
11 [n] Deut. 28:36 [o] 2 Chr. 36:6; Job 36:8; Ps. 107:10, 11 [5] Nose hooks, 2 Kin. 19:28 [6] *chains*

Manasseh Reigns in Judah

33 Manasseh [a]*was* twelve years old
when he became king, and he
reigned fifty-five years in Jerusalem. 2 But
he did evil in the sight of the LORD, according to the [b]abominations of the nations
whom the LORD had cast out before the
children of Israel. 3 For he rebuilt the [1]high
places which Hezekiah his father had [c]bro-
ken down; he raised up altars for the Baals,
and [d]made wooden images; and he worshiped [e]all [2]the host of heaven and served
them. 4 He also built altars in the house of
the LORD, of which the LORD had said, [f]"In
Jerusalem shall My name be forever."
5 And he built altars for all the host of heav-
en [g]in the two courts of the house of the
LORD. 6 [h]Also he caused his sons to pass
through the fire in the Valley of the Son of
Hinnom; he practiced [i]soothsaying, used
witchcraft and sorcery, and [j]consulted
mediums and spiritists. He did much evil
in the sight of the LORD, to provoke Him to
anger. 7 [k]He even set a carved image, the
idol which he had made, in the [3]house of
God, of which God had said to David and
to Solomon his son, [l]"In this house and in
Jerusalem, which I have chosen out of all
the tribes of Israel, I will put My name forever; 8 [m]and I will not again remove the
foot of Israel from the land which I have
appointed for your fathers—only if they
are careful to do all that I have commanded
them, according to the whole law and the
statutes and the ordinances by the hand of
Moses." 9 So Manasseh seduced Judah and
the inhabitants of Jerusalem to do more evil
than the nations whom the LORD had destroyed before the children of Israel.

Manasseh Restored After Repentance

10 And the LORD spoke to Manasseh and
his people, but they would not [4]listen.
11 [n]Therefore the LORD brought upon them
the captains of the army of the king of Assyria, who took Manasseh with [5]hooks,
[o]bound him with [6]bronze *fetters,* and car-

32:24-26 *See notes on 2 Kin. 20:1-11 and Is. 38.*

32:27-31 *See notes on 2 Kin. 20:12-20 and Is. 39.*

32:30 A 1,700 ft. long tunnel cut through solid rock (below Jerusalem) redirected water from the spring Gihon outside of Jerusalem (to the E) toward the S of Jerusalem into the pool of Siloam within the city to provide water in time of siege. The tunnel was a remarkable feat of engineering and boring skill, often 60 ft. below the ground and large enough to walk through. It was discovered in 1838, but not until 1909 was it cleared of the debris left by the destruction of Jerusalem back in 586 B.C. This may not have been the first water shaft, since David may have entered Jerusalem 300 years earlier through a water shaft (cf. 2 Sam. 5:6-8).

32:31 Babylon. This empire was gradually gaining power as Assyria declined due to internal strife and weak kings. Assyria was crushed in 612 B.C. and Babylon, under Nebuchadnezzar, became the world ruler (cf. 2 Kin. 20:14).

32:32 Isaiah. Cf. Is. 1:1.

33:1-20 The reign of Manasseh (ca. 695–642 B.C.). Cf. 2 Kin. 21:1-18.

33:1-10 *See notes on 2 Kin. 21:1-10.*

33:6 Hinnom. This valley to the S and E of the temple was where the worship of Molech involved burning children to death (Ps. 106:37). This was forbidden in Lev. 18:21; 20:2-5; Deut 18:10. Such horrible practices appeared in Israel from the time of Ahaz (cf. 28:3).

33:11-17 God's retribution was swift. Manasseh apparently repented, but the spiritual damage was not easily reversed.

33:11 king of Assyria. Most likely Ashurbanipal (ca. 669–633 B.C.). Between 652 and 648 B.C., Babylon rebelled against Assyria. The

ried him off to Babylon. 12 Now when he
was in affliction, he implored the LORD his
God, and [p]humbled himself greatly before
the God of his fathers, 13 and prayed to
Him; and He [q]received his entreaty, heard
his supplication, and brought him back to
Jerusalem into his kingdom. Then Manasseh [r]knew that the LORD *was* God.
14 After this he built a wall outside the
City of David on the west side of [s]Gihon,
in the valley, as far as the entrance of the
Fish Gate; and *it* [t]enclosed Ophel, and he
raised it to a very great height. Then he
put military captains in all the fortified
cities of Judah. 15 He took away [u]the foreign gods and the idol from the house of
the LORD, and all the altars that he had
built in the mount of the house of the LORD
and in Jerusalem; and he cast *them* out of
the city. 16 He also repaired the altar of the
LORD, sacrificed peace offerings and
[v]thank offerings on it, and commanded
Judah to serve the LORD God of Israel.
17 [w]Nevertheless the people still sacrificed
on the [7]high places, *but* only to the LORD
their God.

Death of Manasseh

18 Now the rest of the acts of Manasseh,
his prayer to his God, and the words of
[x]the seers who spoke to him in the name of
the LORD God of Israel, indeed they *are
written* in the [8]book of the kings of Israel.
19 Also his prayer and *how God* received his
entreaty, and all his sin and trespass, and
the sites where he built [9]high places and
set up wooden images and carved images,
before he was humbled, indeed they *are*
written among the sayings of [1]Hozai.
20 [y]So Manasseh rested with his fathers,
and they buried him in his own house.
Then his son Amon reigned in his place.

Amon's Reign and Death

21 [z]Amon *was* twenty-two years old
when he became king, and he reigned two
years in Jerusalem. 22 But he did evil in
the sight of the LORD, as his father Manasseh had done; for Amon sacrificed to
all the carved images which his father
Manasseh had made, and served them.
23 And he did not humble himself before
the LORD, [a]as his father Manasseh had
humbled himself; but Amon trespassed
more and more.
24 [b]Then his servants conspired against
him, and [c]killed him in his own house.
25 But the people of the land executed all
those who had conspired against King
Amon. Then the people of the land made
his son Josiah king in his place.

Josiah Reigns in Judah

34 Josiah [a]*was* eight years old when he
became king, and he reigned thirty-
one years in Jerusalem. 2 And he did *what
was* right in the sight of the LORD, and
walked in the ways of his father David; *he*
did *not* turn aside to the right hand or to
the left.
3 For in the eighth year of his reign,
while he was still [b]young, he began to
[c]seek the God of his father David; and in
the twelfth year he began [d]to purge Judah
and Jerusalem [e]of the [1]high places, the
wooden images, the carved images, and
the molded images. 4 [f]They broke down
the altars of the Baals in his presence, and
the incense altars which *were* above them
he cut down; and the wooden images, the
carved images, and the molded images he
broke in pieces, and made dust of them
[g]and scattered *it* on the graves of those
who had sacrificed to them. 5 He also
[h]burned the bones of the priests on their
[i]altars, and cleansed Judah and Jerusalem.
6 And *so he did* in the cities of Manasseh,
Ephraim, and Simeon, as far as Naphtali
and all around, with [2]axes. 7 When he had
broken down the altars and the wooden
images, had [j]beaten the carved images into
powder, and cut down all the incense altars throughout all the land of Israel, he returned to Jerusalem.

12 [p] 2 Chr. 7:14; 32:26; [1 Pet. 5:6]
13 [q] 1 Chr. 5:20; Ezra 8:23 [r] 1 Kin. 20:13; Ps. 9:16; Dan. 4:25
14 [s] 1 Kin. 1:33 [t] 2 Chr. 27:3
15 [u] 2 Chr. 33:3, 5, 7
16 [v] Lev. 7:12
17 [w] 2 Chr. 32:12 [7] Places for pagan worship
18 [x] 1 Sam. 9:9 [8] Lit. *words*
19 [9] Places for pagan worship [1] LXX *the seers*
20 [y] 1 Kin. 1:21; 2 Kin. 21:18
21 [z] 2 Kin. 21:19-24; 1 Chr. 3:14
23 [a] 2 Chr. 33:12, 19
24 [b] 2 Kin. 21:23, 24; 2 Chr. 24:25 [c] 2 Chr. 25:27

CHAPTER 34

1 [a] 2 Kin. 22:1, 2; Jer. 1:2; 3:6
3 [b] Eccl. 12:1 [c] 2 Chr. 15:2; [Prov. 8:17] [d] 1 Kin. 13:2 [e] 2 Chr. 33:17-19, 22 [1] Places for pagan worship
4 [f] Lev. 26:30; 2 Kin. 23:4 [g] 2 Kin. 23:6
5 [h] 1 Kin. 13:2 [i] 2 Kin. 23:20
6 [2] Lit. *swords*
7 [j] Deut. 9:21

city of Babylon was defeated temporarily, but Assyria may have felt Manasseh supported Babylon's rebellion, so he was taken to trial in Babylon.

33:12,13 Manasseh. This king was very wicked and idolatrous, a murderer of his children, and a desecrater of the temple. God graciously forgave this "chief of sinners" (cf. 1 Tim. 1:15) when he repented. He did what he could to reverse the effect of his life (vv. 15-17). Although the people worshiped God and not idols, they were doing it in the wrong place and wrong way. God had commanded them to offer sacrifices only in certain places (Deut. 12:13,14) to keep them from corrupting the prescribed forms and to protect them from pagan religious influence. Disobedience to God's requirements in this matter surely contributed to the decline under the next king, Amon (vv. 21-23), whose corruption his successor, Josiah, had to eliminate (34:3-7).

33:14 A wall running from S of the temple and Ophel (W of the Kidron Valley) SE/NW reaching to the Fish Gate, NW of the temple.

33:18-20 *See notes on 2 Kin. 21:17,18.*

33:21-25 The reign of Amon (ca. 642–640 B.C.). Cf. 2 Kin. 21:19-26. *See notes on 2 Kin. 21:19-26.*

34:1–35:27 The reign of Josiah (ca. 640–609 B.C.). Cf. 2 Kin. 22:1–23:30. Jeremiah prophesied during this reign (2 Chr. 35:24; Jer. 1:2) as did Habakkuk, Zephaniah (Zeph. 1:1), and Nahum.

34:1,2 *See notes on 2 Kin. 22:1,2.* At the age of 16, Josiah began to cultivate a love for God in his heart, and by age 20 his character was strong enough in devotion to Him that he went into action to purge his nation.

34:3-7 *See notes on 2 Kin. 23:4-20.*

Hilkiah Finds the Book of the Law

8 [k]In the eighteenth year of his reign,
when he had purged the land and the
[3]temple, he sent [l]Shaphan the son of Azaliah, Maaseiah the [m]governor of the city,
and Joah the son of Joahaz the recorder, to
repair the house of the LORD his God.
9 When they came to Hilkiah the high
priest, they delivered [n]the money that was
brought into the house of God, which the
Levites who kept the doors had gathered
from the hand of Manasseh and Ephraim,
from all the [o]remnant of Israel, from all Judah and Benjamin, and *which* they had
brought back to Jerusalem. 10 Then they
put *it* in the hand of the foremen who had
the oversight of the house of the LORD; and
they gave it to the workmen who worked
in the house of the LORD, to repair and restore the house. 11 They gave *it* to the
craftsmen and builders to buy hewn stone
and timber for beams, and to floor the
houses which the kings of Judah had destroyed. 12 And the men did the work
faithfully. Their overseers *were* Jahath and
Obadiah the Levites, of the sons of Merari,
and Zechariah and Meshullam, of the sons
of the Kohathites, to supervise. *Others of*
the Levites, all of whom were skillful with
instruments of music, 13 *were* [p]over the
burden bearers and *were* overseers of all
who did work in any kind of service. [q]And
some of the Levites *were* scribes, officers,
and gatekeepers.

14 Now when they brought out the
money that was brought into the house of
the LORD, Hilkiah the priest [r]found the
Book of the Law of the LORD *given* by Moses. 15 Then Hilkiah answered and said to
Shaphan the scribe, "I have found the Book
of the Law in the house of the LORD." And
Hilkiah gave the [s]book to Shaphan. 16 So
Shaphan carried the book to the king,
bringing the king word, saying, "All that
was committed to your servants they are
doing. 17 And they have [4]gathered the
money that was found in the house of the
LORD, and have delivered it into the hand
of the overseers and the workmen."
18 Then Shaphan the scribe told the king,
saying, "Hilkiah the priest has given me a
book." And Shaphan read it before the
king.

19 Thus it happened, when the king
heard the words of the Law, that he tore his
clothes. 20 Then the king commanded Hilkiah, [t]Ahikam the son of Shaphan, [5]Abdon
the son of Micah, Shaphan the scribe, and
Asaiah a servant of the king, saying,
21 "Go, inquire of the LORD for me, and for
those who are left in Israel and Judah, concerning the words of the book that is
found; for great *is* the wrath of the LORD
that is poured out on us, because our fathers have not [u]kept the word of the LORD,
to do according to all that is written in this
book."

22 So Hilkiah and those the king *had appointed* went to Huldah the prophetess, the
wife of Shallum the son of [6]Tokhath, the
son of [7]Hasrah, keeper of the wardrobe.
(She dwelt in Jerusalem in the Second
Quarter.) And they spoke to her to that *effect*.

23 Then she answered them, "Thus says
the LORD God of Israel, 'Tell the man who
sent you to Me, 24 "Thus says the LORD:
'Behold, I will [v]bring calamity on this place
and on its inhabitants, all the curses that
are written in the [w]book which they have
read before the king of Judah, 25 because
they have forsaken Me and burned incense
to other gods, that they might provoke Me
to anger with all the works of their hands.
Therefore My wrath will be poured out on
this place, and not be quenched.' " ' 26 But
as for the king of Judah, who sent you to
inquire of the LORD, in this manner you
shall speak to him, 'Thus says the LORD
God of Israel: "*Concerning* the words
which you have heard— 27 because your
heart was tender, and you humbled yourself before God when you heard His words
against this place and against its inhabitants, and you humbled yourself before
Me, and you tore your clothes and wept
before Me, I also have heard *you*," says the
[x]LORD. 28 "Surely I will gather you to your
fathers, and you shall be gathered to your
grave in peace; and your eyes shall not see
all the calamity which I will bring on this
place and its inhabitants." ' " So they
brought back word to the king.

Josiah Restores True Worship

29 [y]Then the king sent and gathered all
the elders of Judah and Jerusalem. 30 The
king went up to the house of the LORD,
with all the men of Judah and the inhabitants of Jerusalem—the priests and the
Levites, and all the people, great and
small. And he [z]read in their hearing all the
words of the Book of the Covenant which
had been found in the house of the LORD.

8 [k]2 Kin. 22:3-20 [l]2 Kin. 25:22 [m]2 Chr. 18:25 [3]Lit. *house*
9 [n]2 Kin. 12:4 [o]2 Chr. 30:6
13 [p]2 Chr. 8:10 [q]1 Chr. 23:4, 5
14 [r]2 Kin. 22:8
15 [s]Deut. 31:24, 26
17 [4]Lit. *poured out*
20 [t]Jer. 26:24 [5]*Achbor the son of Michaiah*, 2 Kin. 22:12
21 [u]2 Kin. 17:15-19
22 [6]*Tikvah*, 2 Kin. 22:14 [7]*Harhas*, 2 Kin. 22:14
24 [v]2 Chr. 36:14-20 [w]Deut. 28:15-68
27 [x]2 Kin. 22:19; 2 Chr. 12:7; 30:6; 33:12, 13
29 [y]2 Kin. 23:1-3
30 [z]Neh. 8:1-3

34:8 repair the house of the LORD. During the 55-year reign of Manasseh (33:1) and the two year reign of Amon (33:21), the work of Hezekiah on the temple restoration was undone, which called for another extensive enterprise to "repair and restore" it (vv. 9-13).

34:8-13 *See notes on 2 Kin. 22:3-7.*

34:8-33 *See notes on 2 Kin. 22:8–23:20.*

31 Then the king [a]stood in [b]his place and
made a [c]covenant before the LORD, to follow the LORD, and to keep His commandments and His testimonies and His
statutes with all his heart and all his soul,
to perform the words of the covenant that
were written in this book. 32 And he made
all who were present in Jerusalem and
Benjamin take a stand. So the inhabitants
of Jerusalem did according to the covenant
of God, the God of their fathers. 33 Thus Josiah removed all the [d]abominations from
all the country that *belonged* to the children
of Israel, and made all who were present in
Israel [8]diligently serve the LORD their God.
[e]All his days they did not depart from following the LORD God of their fathers.

Josiah Keeps the Passover

35 Now [a]Josiah kept a Passover to the
LORD in Jerusalem, and they slaughtered the Passover *lambs* on the [b]fourteenth
day of the first month. 2 And he set the
priests in their [c]duties and [d]encouraged
them for the service of the house of the
LORD. 3 Then he said to the Levites [e]who
taught all Israel, who were holy to the
LORD: [f]"Put the holy ark [g]in the house
which Solomon the son of David, king of
Israel, built. [h]*It shall* no longer *be* a burden
on *your* shoulders. Now serve the LORD
your God and His people Israel. 4 Prepare
yourselves [i]according to your fathers'
[1]houses, according to your divisions, following the [j]written instruction of David
king of Israel and the [k]written instruction
of Solomon his son. 5 And [l]stand in the
holy *place* according to the divisions of the
fathers' houses of your brethren the *lay*
people, and *according to* the division of the
father's house of the Levites. 6 So slaughter
the Passover *offerings*, [m]consecrate yourselves, and prepare *them* for your brethren,
that *they* may do according to the word of
the LORD by the hand of Moses."
7 Then Josiah [n]gave the *lay* people lambs
and young goats from the flock, all for
Passover *offerings* for all who were present,
to the number of thirty thousand, as well
as three thousand cattle; these *were* from
the king's [o]possessions. 8 And his [p]leaders
gave willingly to the people, to the priests,
and to the Levites. Hilkiah, Zechariah, and
Jehiel, rulers of the house of God, gave to
the priests for the Passover *offerings* two
thousand six hundred *from the flock*, and
three hundred cattle. 9 Also [q]Conaniah, his
brothers Shemaiah and Nethanel, and
Hashabiah and Jeiel and Jozabad, chief of
the Levites, gave to the Levites for
Passover *offerings* five thousand *from the
flock* and five hundred cattle.
10 So the service was prepared, and the
priests [r]stood in their places, and the
[s]Levites in their divisions, according to
the king's command. 11 And they slaughtered the Passover *offerings*; and the priests
[t]sprinkled *the blood* with their hands, while
the Levites [u]skinned *the animals*. 12 Then
they removed the burnt offerings that *they*
might give them to the divisions of the fathers' houses of the *lay* people, to offer to
the LORD, as *it is* written [v]in the Book of
Moses. And so *they did* with the cattle.
13 Also they [w]roasted the Passover *offerings*
with fire according to the ordinance; but
the *other* holy *offerings* they [x]boiled in pots,
in caldrons, and in pans, and divided *them*
quickly among all the *lay* people. 14 Then
afterward they prepared portions for
themselves and for the priests, because the
priests, the sons of Aaron, *were busy* in offering burnt offerings and fat until night;
therefore the Levites prepared portions for
themselves and for the priests, the sons of
Aaron. 15 And the singers, the sons of
Asaph, *were* in their places, according to
the [y]command of David, Asaph, Heman,
and Jeduthun the king's seer. Also the
gatekeepers [z]were at each gate; they did
not have to leave their position, because
their brethren the Levites prepared portions for them.
16 So all the service of the LORD was prepared the same day, to keep the Passover
and to offer burnt offerings on the altar of
the LORD, according to the command of
King Josiah. 17 And the children of Israel

31 [a] 2 Chr. 6:13 [b] 2 Kin. 11:14; 23:3; 2 Chr. 30:16 [c] 2 Chr. 23:16; 29:10
33 [d] 1 Kin. 11:5; 2 Chr. 33:2 [e] Jer. 3:10 [8] Lit. *serve to serve*

CHAPTER 35

1 [a] 2 Kin. 23:21, 22 [b] Ex. 12:6; Num. 9:3; Ezra 6:19
2 [c] 2 Chr. 23:18; Ezra 6:18 [d] 2 Chr. 29:5-15
3 [e] Deut. 33:10; 2 Chr. 17:8, 9; Neh. 8:7 [f] 2 Chr. 34:14 [g] Ex. 40:21; 2 Chr. 5:7 [h] 1 Chr. 23:26
4 [i] 1 Chr. 9:10-13 [j] 1 Chr. 23–26 [k] 2 Chr. 8:14 [1] *households*
5 [l] Ps. 134:1
6 [m] 2 Chr. 29:5, 15
7 [n] 2 Chr. 30:24
[o] 2 Chr. 31:3
8 [p] Num. 7:2
9 [q] 2 Chr. 31:12
10 [r] Ezra 6:18; Heb. 9:6 [s] 2 Chr. 5:12; 7:6; 8:14, 15; 13:10; 29:25-34
11 [t] Ex. 12:22; 2 Chr. 29:22 [u] 2 Chr. 29:34
12 [v] Lev. 3:3; Ezra 6:18
13 [w] Ex. 12:8, 9; Deut. 16:7 [x] 1 Sam. 2:13-15
15 [y] 1 Chr. 25:1-6 [z] 1 Chr. 9:17, 18

34:33 All his days. This noble king had a life-long influence by the power of his godly life and firm devotion to God and His Word. The strength of his character held the nation together serving the Lord. It started because as a young man he "began to seek God" (cf. v. 3).

35:1-19 The chronicler, probably Ezra, gave much more attention to this Passover celebration than does 2 Kin. 23:21-23.

35:1,2 Obviously, the temple's contents had been disturbed and the sacrifices/festivals interrupted by lack of attention, idolatrous practices, and foreign intervention. As Hezekiah had restored the Passover in his time (30:1ff.), so did Josiah. This was the central feast in devotion to the Lord (Ex. 12,13).

35:3 the holy ark. The ark of the covenant which was to remain in the Most Holy Place had been removed, probably by Manasseh who set a carved image in its place (cf. 33:7). The law for the carrying of the ark during the tabernacle days, when it was portable, called for poles to be place through rings on the sides, and Levites (Kohathites) to carry it by the poles without touching it (cf. Ex. 25:14,15). Uzza(h) died for touching the ark while he was improperly transporting the ark on a cart (1 Chr. 13:6-10). Now that the temple was built and the ark had a permanent place, it no longer needed to be transported in the old way.

35:4 David...Solomon. *See notes on 1 Chr. 15,23-29; 2 Chr. 6–10.*

35:6 Moses. *See notes on Ex. 12,13.* The prescribed pattern for the Passover in the temple was followed (vv. 7-17).

who were present kept the Passover at that
time, and the Feast of [a]Unleavened Bread
for seven days. 18 [b]There had been no
Passover kept in Israel like that since the
days of Samuel the prophet; and none of
the kings of Israel had kept such a
Passover as Josiah kept, with the priests
and the Levites, all Judah and Israel who
were present, and the inhabitants of Jerusalem. 19 In the eighteenth year of the reign
of Josiah this Passover was kept.

Josiah Dies in Battle

20 [c]After all this, when Josiah had prepared the temple, Necho king of Egypt
came up to fight against [d]Carchemish by
the Euphrates; and Josiah went out against
him. 21 But he sent messengers to him, saying, "What have I to do with you, king of
Judah? *I have* not *come* against you this day,
but against the house with which I have
war; for God commanded me to make
haste. Refrain *from meddling with* God, who
is with me, lest He destroy you." 22 Nevertheless Josiah would not turn his face from
him, but [e]disguised himself so that he
might fight with him, and did not heed the
words of Necho from the mouth of God. So
he came to fight in the Valley of Megiddo.
23 And the archers shot King Josiah; and
the king said to his servants, "Take me
away, for I am severely wounded." 24 [f]His
servants therefore took him out of that
chariot and put him in the second chariot
that he had, and they brought him to Jerusalem. So he died, and was buried in *one of*
the tombs of his fathers. And [g]all Judah
and Jerusalem mourned for Josiah.
25 Jeremiah also [h]lamented for [i]Josiah.
And to this day [j]all the singing men and
the singing women speak of Josiah in their
lamentations. [k]They made it a custom in
Israel; and indeed they *are* written in the
Laments.
26 Now the rest of the acts of Josiah and
his goodness, according to *what was* written in the Law of the LORD, 27 and his
deeds from first to last, indeed they *are*
written in the book of the kings of Israel
and Judah.

The Reign and Captivity of Jehoahaz

36 Then [a]the people of the land took
Jehoahaz the son of Josiah, and
made him king in his father's place in Jerusalem. 2 [1]Jehoahaz *was* twenty-three years
old when he became king, and he reigned
three months in Jerusalem. 3 Now the king
of Egypt deposed him at Jerusalem; and he
imposed on the land a tribute of one hundred talents of silver and a talent of gold.
4 Then the king of Egypt made [2]*Jehoahaz's*
brother Eliakim king over Judah and Jerusalem, and changed his name to Jehoiakim.
And Necho took [3]Jehoahaz his brother and
carried him off to Egypt.

The Reign and Captivity of Jehoiakim

5 [b]Jehoiakim *was* twenty-five years old
when he became king, and he reigned
eleven years in Jerusalem. And he did [c]evil
in the sight of the LORD his God. 6 [d]Nebu-
chadnezzar king of Babylon came up
against him, and bound him in [4]bronze *fetters* to [e]carry him off to Babylon. 7 [f]Nebu-
chadnezzar also carried off *some* of the articles from the house of the LORD to
Babylon, and put them in his temple at
Babylon. 8 Now the rest of the acts of Jehoiakim, the abominations which he did,
and what was found against him, indeed
they *are* written in the book of the kings of

17 [a]Ex. 12:15; 13:6; 2 Chr. 30:21
18 [b]2 Kin. 23:22, 23
20 [c]2 Kin. 23:29 [d]Is. 10:9; Jer. 46:2
22 [e]1 Kin. 22:30; 2 Chr. 18:29
24 [f]2 Kin. 23:30 [g]1 Kin. 14:18; Zech. 12:11
25 [h]Lam. 4:20 [i]Jer. 22:10, 11 [j]Matt. 9:23
[k]Jer. 22:20

CHAPTER 36

1 [a]2 Kin. 23:30-34
2 [1]MT *Joahaz*
4 [2]Lit. *his* [3]MT *Joahaz*
5 [b]2 Kin. 23:36, 37; 1 Chr. 3:15 [c][Jer. 22:13-19]
6 [d]2 Kin. 24:1; Hab. 1:6 [e][Deut. 29:22-29]; 2 Chr. 33:11; Jer. 36:30 [4]*chains*
7 [f]2 Kin. 24:13; Dan. 1:1, 2

35:18 no Passover. Hezekiah's Passover (cf. 2 Chr. 30) differed. It was not celebrated strictly according to Mosaic law in that: 1) it was celebrated in the second month (2 Chr. 30:2); 2) not all the people were purified (2 Chr. 30:18); and 3) not all of the people came (2 Chr. 30:10).

35:18,19 since...Samuel. Ca. 1100–1015 B.C. It had been over 400 years, since before all the kings of Israel and Judah.

35:20-27 The details of Josiah's tragic death are given. When compared with the account in 2 Kin. 23:28-30, the events become clearer. Toward the end of Josiah's reign, the Egyptian Pharaoh Necho (ca. 609–594 B.C.) set out on a military expedition to aid the king of Assyria in a war at Carchemish, Assyria's latest capital, 250 mi. NE of Damascus on the bank of the Euphrates River. Fearing such an alliance would present future danger to Israel, Josiah decided to intercept Pharaoh Necho's army and fight to protect his nation. Coming from Egypt, likely by ship to Acco, a northern seaport in Israel, and by land up the coastal plain of Israel, the Egyptian army had landed and proceeded E to the Valley of Megiddo (v. 22), i.e., Jezreel on the plain of Esdraelon. This was the most direct way to Carchemish. There Josiah met him for battle and was wounded by an arrow. He made it back to Jerusalem (60 mi. S), where he died.

35:21 God commanded me. He is referring to the true God; whether he had a true revelation or not is unknown. Josiah had no way to know either, and it is apparent he did not believe that Necho spoke the Word of God. There is no reason to assume his death was punishment for refusing to believe. He probably thought Necho was lying and, once victorious with Assyria over Babylon, they would together be back to assault Israel.

35:25 There is no record of Jeremiah's elegy. The people continued to mourn the loss of Josiah up to the writing of the Chronicles in 450–430 B.C., nearly 200 years after the event. In fact, the location of the battle, the town of Hadad-rimmon in the valley of Megiddo, was part of a proverb lamenting Josiah's death even in Zechariah's day (Zech. 12:11), 90 years later.

36:1-4 The reign of Joahaz (ca. 609 B.C.). Cf. 2 Kin. 23:31-33. Jeremiah continued to prophesy during this reign (Jer. 1:3).

36:5-8 The reign of Jehoiakim, a.k.a. Eliakim (ca. 609–597 B.C.; cf. 2 Kin. 23:34–24:7). *See notes on 2 Kin. 23:34–24:7.* Daniel was taken captive to Babylon in 605 B.C. Jeremiah prophesied during this reign (Jer. 1:3), and Habakkuk likely appeared on the scene at this time of kingly abominations.

Israel and Judah. Then [5]Jehoiachin his son
reigned in his place.

The Reign and Captivity of Jehoiachin

9 [g]Jehoiachin *was* [6]eight years old when
he became king, and he reigned in Jerusalem three months and ten days. And he did
evil in the sight of the LORD. 10 At the turn
of the year [h]King Nebuchadnezzar summoned *him* and took him to Babylon, [i]with
the costly articles from the house of the
LORD, and made [j]Zedekiah,[7] [8]*Jehoiakim's*
brother, king over Judah and Jerusalem.

Zedekiah Reigns in Judah

11 [k]Zedekiah *was* twenty-one years old
when he became king, and he reigned
eleven years in Jerusalem. 12 He did evil in
the sight of the LORD his God, *and* [l]did not
humble himself before Jeremiah the
prophet, *who spoke* from the mouth of the
LORD. 13 And he also [m]rebelled against
King Nebuchadnezzar, who had made him
swear *an oath* by God; but he [n]stiffened his
neck and hardened his heart against turning to the LORD God of Israel. 14 Moreover
all the leaders of the priests and the people
transgressed more and more, *according* to
all the abominations of the nations, and defiled the house of the LORD which He had
consecrated in Jerusalem.

The Fall of Jerusalem

15 [o]And the LORD God of their fathers
sent *warnings* to them by His messengers,
rising up early and sending *them,* because
He had compassion on His people and on
His dwelling place. 16 But [p]they mocked
the messengers of God, [q]despised His
words, and [r]scoffed at His prophets, until
the [s]wrath of the LORD arose against His
people, till *there was* no remedy.

8 [5] Or *Jeconiah*
9 [g] 2 Kin. 24:8-17 [6] Heb. mss., LXX, Syr. *eighteen* and 2 Kin. 24:8
10 [h] 2 Kin. 24:10-17 [i] Dan. 1:1, 2 [j] Jer. 37:1 [7] Or *Mattaniah* [8] Lit. *his brother,* 2 Kin. 24:17
11 [k] 2 Kin. 24:18-20; Jer. 52:1
12 [l] Jer. 21:3-7; 44:10
13 [m] Jer. 52:3; Ezek. 17:15 [n] 2 Kin. 17:14; [2 Chr. 30:8]
15 [o] Jer. 7:13; 25:3, 4
16 [p] 2 Chr. 30:10; Jer. 5:12, 13 [q] [Prov. 1:24-32] [r] Jer. 38:6; Matt. 23:34 [s] 2 Chr. 34:25; Ps. 79:5
17 [t] Num. 33:56; Deut. 4:26; 28:49; 2 Kin. 25:1; Ezra 9:7; Is. 3:8 [u] Ps. 74:20
18 [v] 2 Kin. 25:13-15; 2 Chr. 36:7, 10
19 [w] 2 Kin. 25:9; Ps. 79:1, 7; Is. 1:7, 8; Jer. 52:13
20 [x] 2 Kin. 25:11; Jer. 5:19; Mic. 4:10 [y] Jer. 17:4; 27:7
21 [z] Jer. 25:9-12; 27:6-8; 29:10 [a] Lev. 26:34-43; Dan. 9:2 [b] Lev. 25:4, 5
22 [c] Ezra 1:1-3 [d] Jer. 29:10 [e] Is. 44:28; 45:1
23 [f] Ezra 1:2, 3 [9] Temple

17 [t]Therefore He brought against them
the king of the Chaldeans, who [u]killed
their young men with the sword in the
house of their sanctuary, and had no compassion on young man or virgin, on the
aged or the weak; He gave *them* all into his
hand. 18 [v]And all the articles from the
house of God, great and small, the treasures of the house of the LORD, and the
treasures of the king and of his leaders, all
these he took to Babylon. 19 [w]Then they
burned the house of God, broke down the
wall of Jerusalem, burned all its palaces
with fire, and destroyed all its precious
possessions. 20 And [x]those who escaped
from the sword he carried away to Babylon, [y]where they became servants to him
and his sons until the rule of the kingdom
of Persia, 21 to fulfill the word of the LORD
by the mouth of [z]Jeremiah, until the land
[a]had enjoyed her Sabbaths. As long as she
lay desolate [b]she kept Sabbath, to fulfill
seventy years.

The Proclamation of Cyrus

22 [c]Now in the first year of Cyrus king of
Persia, that the word of the LORD by the
mouth of [d]Jeremiah might be fulfilled, the
LORD stirred up the spirit of [e]Cyrus king of
Persia, so that he made a proclamation
throughout all his kingdom, and also *put it*
in writing, saying,

23 [f]Thus says Cyrus king of Persia:
All the kingdoms of the earth the
LORD God of heaven has given me.
And He has commanded me to
build Him a [9]house at Jerusalem
which is in Judah. Who *is* among
you of all His people? May the
LORD his God *be* with him, and let
him go up!

36:9,10 The reign of Jehoiachin (ca. 597 B.C.). Cf. 2 Kin. 24:8-16. *See notes on 2 Kin. 24:8-16; Jer. 52:1-3.* Ezekiel was taken captive to Babylon in 597 B.C. Jeremiah prophesied during this reign.

36:9 eight years old. Eighteen years old is preferable, as stated in 2 Kin. 24:8, because of the full development of his wickedness (see Ezekiel's description of him in 19:5-9). See marginal note.

36:11-21 The reign of Zedekiah, a.k.a. Mattaniah (ca. 597–586 B.C.). Cf. 2 Kin. 24:17–25:21; Jer. 52:4-27. Jeremiah prophesied during this reign (Jer. 1:3) and wrote Lamentations to mourn the destruction of Jerusalem and the temple in 586 B.C. Ezekiel received his commission during this reign (Ezek. 1:1) and prophesied from 592 B.C. to his death in 560 B.C.

36:11-20 *See notes on 2 Kin. 24:17–25:21.*

36:20 *See notes on 2 Kin. 25:22-30* for the fate of those who remained behind in Jerusalem.

36:21 Sabbaths. This suggests that the every seventh year Sabbath which God required for the land (Lev. 25:1-7) had not been kept for 490 years dating back to the days of Eli, ca. 1107–1067 B.C. (cf. 1 Sam. 1–4). Leviticus 26:27-46 warns of God's judgment in general if this law were to be violated. Jeremiah 25:1-11 applied this judgment to Judah from 605 B.C. at the time of the first Babylonian deportation until 536 B.C. when the first Jews returned to Jerusalem and started to rebuild the temple (cf. Ezra 3:8).

36:22,23 *See notes on Ezra 1:1-3.* The chronicler ended with a ray of hope because the 70 years were completed (cf. Dan. 9:1,2) and Abraham's offspring were returning to the Land to rebuild the temple.

The Book of EZRA

Title

Even though Ezra's name does not enter the account of Judah's post-Exilic return to Jerusalem until 7:1, the book bears his name ("Jehovah helps") as a title. This is because both Jewish and Christian tradition attribute authorship to this famous scribe-priest. New Testament writers do not quote the book of Ezra.

Author and Date

Ezra is most likely the author of both Ezra and Nehemiah, which might have originally been one book. Ezra 4:8–6:18 and 7:12-26 are written in Aramaic. Although Ezra never states his authorship, internal arguments favor him strongly. After his arrival in Jerusalem (ca. 458 B.C.), he changed from writing in the third person to writing in the first person. In the earlier section it is likely that he had used the third person because he was quoting his memoirs. Ezra is believed to possibly be the author of the books of the Chronicles. It would have been natural for the same author to continue the OT narrative by showing how God fulfilled His promise by returning His people to the Land after 70 years of captivity. There is also a strong priestly tone in Chronicles, and Ezra was a priestly descendant of Aaron (cf. 7:1-5). The concluding verses of 2 Chronicles (36:22,23) are virtually identical to the beginning verses of Ezra (1:1-3a), affirming his authorship of both.

Ezra was a scribe who had access to the myriad of administrative documents found in Ezra and Nehemiah, especially those in the book of Ezra. Very few people would have been allowed access to the royal archives of the Persian Empire, but Ezra proved to be the exception (cf. Ezra 1:2-4; 4:9-22; 5:7-17; 6:3-12). His role as a scribe of the law is spelled out in 7:10: "For Ezra had prepared his heart to seek the Law of the LORD, and to do *it,* and to teach statutes and ordinances in Israel." He was a strong and godly man who lived at the time of Nehemiah (cf. Neh. 8:1-9; 12:36). Tradition says he was founder of the Great Synagogue, where the complete OT canon was first formally recognized.

Ezra led the second return from Persia (ca. 458 B.C.), so the completed book was written sometime in the next several decades (ca. 457–444 B.C.).

Background and Setting

God had originally brought Israel out of the slave markets of Egypt in the Exodus (ca. 1445 B.C.). Hundreds of years later, before the events of Ezra, God told His people that if they chose to break their covenant with Him, He would again allow other nations to take them into slavery (Jer. 2:14-25). In spite of God's repeated warnings from the mouths of His prophets, Israel and Judah chose to reject their Lord and to participate in the worship of foreign gods, in addition to committing the abominable practices which accompanied idolatry (cf. 2 Kin. 17:7-18; Jer. 2:7-13). True to His promise, God brought the Assyrians and Babylonians to issue His chastisement upon wayward Israel and Judah.

In 722 B.C. the Assyrians deported the 10 northern tribes and scattered them all over their empire (cf. 2 Kin. 17:24-41; Is. 7:8). Several centuries later, in 605–586 B.C., God used the Babylonians to sack and nearly depopulate Jerusalem. Because Judah persisted in her unfaithfulness to the covenant, God chastened His people with 70 years of captivity (Jer. 25:11), from which they returned to Jerusalem as reported by Ezra and Nehemiah. Cyrus, the Persian, overthrew Babylon in 539 B.C., and the book of Ezra begins with the decree of Cyrus one year later for the Jews to return to Jerusalem (ca. 538 B.C.), and it chronicles the reestablishment of Judah's national calendar of feasts and sacrifices, including the rebuilding of the second temple (begun in 536 B.C. and completed in 516 B.C.).

As there had been 3 waves of deportation from Israel into Babylon (605 B.C., 597 B.C., and 586 B.C.), so there were actually 3 returns to Jerusalem over a 9-decade span. Zerubbabel first returned in 538 B.C. He was followed by Ezra, who led the second return in 458 B.C. Nehemiah did likewise 13 years later, in 445 B.C. Complete uncontested political autonomy, however, never returned. The prophets Haggai and Zechariah preached during Zerubbabel's time, about 520 B.C. and following.

Historical and Theological Themes

The Jews' return from the Babylonian captivity seemed like a second Exodus, sovereignly patterned in some ways after Israel's first redemption from Egyptian bondage. The return trip from Babylon involved activities similar to those of the original Exodus: 1) the rebuilding of the temple and the city walls; 2) the reinstitution of the law, which made Zerubbabel, Ezra, and Nehemiah collectively seem like a second Moses; 3) the challenge of the local enemies; and 4) the temptation to intermarry with non-Jews, resulting in idolatry. Other parallels between the original Exodus and the return from Babylon must have seemed to the returnees like they were given a fresh start by God.

In his account of the return, Ezra drew upon a collection of Persian administrative documents to which he had access as a scribe. The presence of actual royal administrative documents carries a powerful message when accompanied by the resounding line "the hand of the LORD my God *was* upon him/me"(7:6,28). The decrees, proclamations, letters, lists, genealogies, and memoranda, many of them written by the Persian administration, attest to the sovereign hand of God in Israel's restoration. The primary message of the book is that God orchestrated the past grim situation (captivity) and would continue to work through a pagan king and his successors to give Judah hope for the future (return). God's administration overrides that of any of the kings of this world, and thus the book of Ezra is a message of God's continuing covenant grace to Israel.

Another prominent theme which surfaces in Ezra is opposition from the local Samaritan residents whose ancestors had been imported from Assyria (4:2; cf. John 4:4-42). For reasons of spiritual sabotage, Israel's enemies requested to participate in rebuilding the temple (4:1,2). After being shunned, the enemies hired counselors against the Jews (cf. 4:4,5). But the Lord, through the preaching of Haggai and Zechariah, rekindled the spirit of the people and their leaders to build, with the words "...be strong...and work; for I *am* with you" (Hag. 2:4; cf. Ezra 4:24–5:2). The reconstruction resumed (ca. 520 B.C.) and the temple was soon finished, dedicated, and back in service to God (ca. 516 B.C.).

Interpretive Challenges

First, how do the post-Exilic historical books of 1 and 2 Chronicles, Ezra, Nehemiah, and Esther relate to the post-Exilic prophets Haggai, Zechariah, and Malachi? For the chronology of Ezra, Nehemiah, and Esther, *see the notes on Ezra 6:22–7:1.* The two books of Chronicles were written by Ezra as a reminder of the promised Davidic kingship, the Aaronic priesthood, and appropriate temple worship. Haggai and Zechariah prophesied in the period of Ezra 4–6 when temple construction was resumed. Malachi wrote during Nehemiah's revisit to Persia (cf. Neh. 13:6).

Second, what purpose does the book serve? Ezra historically reports the first two of three post-Exilic returns to Jerusalem from the Babylonian captivity. The first return (chaps. 1–6) was under Zerubbabel (ca. 538 B.C.) and the second (chaps. 7–10) was led by Ezra himself (ca. 458 B.C.). Spiritually, Ezra reestablished the importance of the Aaronic priesthood by tracing his ancestry to Eleazar, Phinehas, and Zadok (cf. Ezra 7:1-5). He reported on the rebuilding of the second temple (chaps. 3–6). How he dealt with the gross sin of intermarriage with foreigners is presented in chaps. 9,10. Most importantly, he reports how the sovereign hand of God moved kings and overcame varied opposition to reestablish Israel as Abraham's seed, nationally and individually, in the land promised to Abraham, David, and Jeremiah.

Third, the temple was built during the reign of Cyrus. Mention of Ahasuerus (4:6) and Artaxerxes (4:7-23) might lead one to conclude that the temple could also have been built during their reigns. Such a conclusion, however, violates history. Ezra was not writing about the construction accomplishments of Ahasuerus or Artaxerxes, but rather he continued to chronicle their oppositions after the temple was built, which continued even to Ezra's day. It is apparent, then, that Ezra 4:1-5 and 4:24–5:2 deal with rebuilding the temple under Zerubbabel, while 4:6-23 is a parenthesis recounting the history of opposition in the times of Ezra and Nehemiah.

Fourth, the interpreter must decide where Esther fits in to the time of Ezra. A careful examination indicates it took place between the events of chaps. 6 and 7. *See notes on Esther.*

Fifth, how does divorce in Ezra 10 correlate with the fact that God hates divorce (Mal. 2:16)? Ezra does not establish the norm, but rather deals with a special case in history. It seems to have been decided (Ezra 10:3) on the principle that the lesser wrong (divorce) would be preferable to the greater wrong of the Jewish race being polluted by intermarriage, so that the nation and the messianic line of David would not be ended by being mingled with Gentiles. To solve the problem this way magnifies the mercy of God in that the only other solution would have been to kill all of those involved (husband, wives, and children) by stoning, as was done during the first Exodus at Shittim (Num. 25:1-9).

Outline

- I. The First Return under Zerubbabel (1:1–6:22)
  - A. Cyrus' Decree to Return (1:1-4)
  - B. Treasures to Rebuild the Temple (1:5-11)
  - C. Those Who Returned (2:1-70)
  - D. Construction of the Second Temple (3:1–6:22)
    1. Building begins (3:1-13)
    2. Opposition surfaces (4:1-5)
    3. Excursus on future opposition (4:6-23)
    4. Construction renewed (4:24–5:2)
    5. Opposition renewed (5:3–6:12)
    6. Temple completed and dedicated (6:13-22)
- II. The Second Return under Ezra (7:1–10:44)
  - A. Ezra Arrives (7:1–8:36)
  - B. Ezra Leads Revival (9:1–10:44)

End of the Babylonian Captivity

1 Now in the first year of Cyrus king of
Persia, that the word of the LORD [a]by
the mouth of Jeremiah might be fulfilled,
the LORD stirred up the spirit of Cyrus king
of Persia, [b]so that he made a proclamation
throughout all his kingdom, and also *put it*
in writing, saying,

2 Thus says Cyrus king of Persia:
All the kingdoms of the earth the
LORD God of heaven has given me.
And He has [c]commanded me to
build Him a [1]house at Jerusalem
which *is* in Judah. 3 Who *is* among
you of all His people? May his God
be with him, and let him go up to
Jerusalem which *is* in Judah, and
build the house of the LORD God of
Israel [d](He *is* God), which *is* in Jerusalem. 4 And whoever is left in
any place where he dwells, let the
men of his place help him with
silver and gold, with goods and
livestock, besides the freewill
offerings for the house of God
which *is* in Jerusalem.

5 Then the heads of the fathers' *houses* of
Judah and Benjamin, and the priests and
the Levites, with all whose spirits [e]God
[2]had moved, arose to go up and build the
house of the LORD which *is* in Jerusalem.
6 And all those who *were* around them [3]en-
couraged them with articles of silver and
gold, with goods and livestock, and with
precious things, besides all *that* was [f]will-
ingly offered.
7 [g]King Cyrus also brought out the articles of the house of the LORD, [h]which Nebuchadnezzar had taken from Jerusalem
and put in the [4]temple of his gods; 8 and

CHAPTER 1

1 [a] 2 Chr. 36:22, 23; Jer. 25:12; 29:10 [b] Ezra 5:13, 14; Is. 44:28–45:13
2 [c] Is. 44:28; 45:1, 13 [1] Temple
3 [d] 1 Kin. 8:23; 18:39; Is. 37:16; Dan. 6:26
5 [e] [Phil. 2:13] [2] *stirred up*
6 [f] Ezra 2:68 [3] Lit. *strengthened their hands*
7 [g] Ezra 5:14; 6:5; Dan. 1:2; 5:2, 3 [h] 2 Kin. 24:13; 2 Chr. 36:7, 18 [4] Lit. *house*

1:1-3a These verses are almost identical to 2 Chr. 36:22,23. The pre-Exilic history of 1 and 2 Chronicles gave the post-Exilic returnees direction regarding the Davidic kingship, the Aaronic priesthood, and temple worship. This book continues the story.

1:1 first year. Ca. 538 B.C. **Cyrus king of Persia.** Ca. 550–530 B.C. The Lord had prophesied through Isaiah, who said of Cyrus, *"He is* My shepherd,...saying to Jerusalem, 'You shall be built,' and to the temple, 'Your foundation shall be laid' " (Is. 44:28). The historian Josephus records an account of the day when Daniel read Isaiah's prophesy to Cyrus, and in response he was moved to declare the proclamation of 1:2-4 (538 B.C.). **by the mouth of Jeremiah.** Jeremiah had prophesied the return of the exiles after a 70-year captivity in Babylon (Jer. 25:11; 29:10-14; cf. Dan. 9:2). This was no isolated event, but rather an outworking of the covenant promises made to Abraham in Gen. 12:1-3. **the LORD stirred up.** A strong expression of the fact that God sovereignly works in the lives of kings to effect His purposes (Prov. 21:1; Dan. 2:21; 4:17). **made a proclamation.** This was the most common form of spoken, public communication, usually from the central administration. The king would dispatch a herald, perhaps with a written document, into the city. In order to address the people, he would either go to the city gate, where people often congregated for social discourse, or gather the people together in a square, occasionally by the blowing of a horn. The herald would then make the proclamation to the people. A document called the Cyrus Cylinder, recovered in reasonably good condition by archeologists, commissions people from many lands to return to their cities to rebuild the temples to their gods, apparently as some sort of general policy of Cyrus. Whether or not this document was an extension of the proclamation made to the exiles in this passage must remain a matter of speculation (cf. 6:2-5). ***put it* in writing.** Proclamations were oral statements, usually made by a herald, which were often written down for recordkeeping.

1:2-4 It is possible that Daniel played a part in the Jews' receiving such favorable treatment (cf. Dan. 6:25-28). According to the Jewish historian Josephus, he was Cyrus' prime minister who shared Isaiah's prophecies with Cyrus (Is. 44:28; 46:1-4). The existence of such documents, written over a century before Cyrus was born, led him to acknowledge that all his power came from the God of Israel and prompted him to fulfill the prophecy.

1:2 LORD God of heaven. The God of Israel was recognized as the utmost divine authority (cf. 5:12; 6:9,10; 7:12,21,23), who sovereignly dispenses authority to human monarchs. **a house.** This refers to the second temple, which would be built after the return to the Land by Zerubbabel.

1:5 whose spirits God had moved. The primary underlying message of Ezra and Nehemiah is that the sovereign hand of God is at work in perfect keeping with His plan at His appointed times. The 70 years of captivity were complete, so God stirred up not only the spirit of Cyrus to make the decree, but His own people to go and build up Jerusalem and the temple (cf. 1:1).

1:6 all those who *were* around them. A basic similarity to the Exodus is seen throughout Ezra and Nehemiah. One can hear faint echoes of the Egyptians supplying treasures in order to provide splendor for the tabernacle (cf. Ex. 11:2; 12:35,36). Here other nations around Israel are called to contribute. They were assisted by some of their captive countrymen, who had been born in Babylon and chose to remain, and perhaps by some Babylonians and Assyrians who were favorably disposed to Cyrus and/or the Jews.

1:7 the articles of the house of the LORD. Cf. Ezra 6:5. These were the vessels which Nebuchadnezzar removed when he sacked the temple (ca. 605–586 B.C.; Dan. 1:2; 2 Kin. 24:13; 2 Kin. 25:14,15). God had preserved them (2 Chr. 36:7) with the Babylonians (cf. Dan. 5:1-4) for the return as prophesied by Jeremiah (Jer. 27:22).

Post-Exilic Returns to Jerusalem

Sequence	Date	Scripture	Jewish Leader	Persian Ruler
First	538 B.C.	Ezra 1–6	Zerubbabel, Joshua	Cyrus
Second	458 B.C.	Ezra 7–10	Ezra	Artaxerxes
Third	445 B.C.	Nehemiah 1–13	Nehemiah	Artaxerxes

Cyrus king of Persia brought them out by
the hand of Mithredath the treasurer, and
counted them out to [i]Sheshbazzar the prince
of Judah. 9 This *is* the number of them: thirty gold platters, one thousand silver platters, twenty-nine knives, 10 thirty gold
basins, four hundred and ten silver basins of
a similar *kind, and* one thousand other articles. 11 All the articles of gold and silver *were*
five thousand four hundred. All *these* Sheshbazzar took with the captives who were
brought from Babylon to Jerusalem.

The Captives Who Returned to Jerusalem

2 Now [a]these *are* the people of the
province who came back from the captivity, of those who had been carried away,
[b]whom Nebuchadnezzar the king of Babylon had carried away to Babylon, and
who returned to Jerusalem and Judah,
everyone to his *own* city.
2 *Those* who came with Zerubbabel *were*
Jeshua, Nehemiah, [1]Seraiah, [2]Reelaiah,
Mordecai, Bilshan, [3]Mispar, Bigvai,
[4]Rehum, *and* Baanah. The number of the
men of the people of Israel: 3 the people of
Parosh, two thousand one hundred and
seventy-two; 4 the people of Shephatiah,
three hundred and seventy-two; 5 the people of Arah, [c]seven hundred and seventy-
five; 6 the people of [d]Pahath-Moab, of the
people of Jeshua *and* Joab, two thousand
eight hundred and twelve; 7 the people of
Elam, one thousand two hundred and
fifty-four; 8 the people of Zattu, nine hundred and forty-five; 9 the people of Zaccai,
seven hundred and sixty; 10 the people of
[5]Bani, six hundred and forty-two; 11 the
people of Bebai, six hundred and twenty-
three; 12 the people of Azgad, one thousand two hundred and twenty-two; 13 the
people of Adonikam, six hundred and
sixty-six; 14 the people of Bigvai, two thousand and fifty-six; 15 the people of Adin,
four hundred and fifty-four; 16 the people
of Ater of Hezekiah, ninety-eight; 17 the
people of Bezai, three hundred and twenty-three; 18 the people of [6]Jorah, one hundred and twelve; 19 the people of Hashum,
two hundred and twenty-three; 20 the people of [7]Gibbar, ninety-five; 21 the people of
Bethlehem, one hundred and twenty-
three; 22 the men of Netophah, fifty-six;
23 the men of Anathoth, one hundred and
twenty-eight; 24 the people of [8]Azmaveth,
forty-two; 25 the people of [9]Kirjath Arim,
Chephirah, and Beeroth, seven hundred
and forty-three; 26 the people of Ramah
and Geba, six hundred and twenty-one;
27 the men of Michmas, one hundred and
twenty-two; 28 the men of Bethel and Ai,
two hundred and twenty-three; 29 the people of Nebo, fifty-two; 30 the people of
Magbish, one hundred and fifty-six; 31 the
people of the other [e]Elam, one thousand
two hundred and fifty-four; 32 the people
of Harim, three hundred and twenty;
33 the people of Lod, Hadid, and Ono,
seven hundred and twenty-five; 34 the
people of Jericho, three hundred and forty-
five; 35 the people of Senaah, three thousand six hundred and thirty.
36 The priests: the sons of [f]Jedaiah, of the
house of Jeshua, nine hundred and seventy-three; 37 the sons of [g]Immer, one thousand and fifty-two; 38 the sons of [h]Pashhur,
one thousand two hundred and forty-
seven; 39 the sons of [i]Harim, one thousand
and seventeen.
40 The Levites: the sons of Jeshua and
Kadmiel, of the sons of [1]Hodaviah, seventy-four.
41 The singers: the sons of Asaph, one
hundred and twenty-eight.

8 [i] Ezra 5:14, 16

CHAPTER 2

1 [a] Neh. 7:6-73; Jer. 32:15; 50:5; Ezek. 14:22 [b] 2 Kin. 24:14-16; 25:11; 2 Chr. 36:20
2 [1] *Azariah,* Neh. 7:7 [2] *Raamiah,* Neh. 7:7 [3] *Mispereth,* Neh. 7:7 [4] *Nehum,* Neh. 7:7
5 [c] Neh. 7:10
6 [d] Neh. 7:11
10 [5] *Binnui,* Neh. 7:15
18 [6] *Hariph,* Neh. 7:24
20 [7] *Gibeon,* Neh. 7:25
24 [8] *Beth Azmaveth,* Neh. 7:28
25 [9] *Kirjath Jearim,* Neh. 7:29
31 [e] Ezra 2:7
36 [f] 1 Chr. 24:7-18
37 [g] 1 Chr. 24:14
38 [h] 1 Chr. 9:12
39 [i] 1 Chr. 24:8
40 [1] *Judah,* Ezra 3:9, or *Hodevah,* Neh. 7:43

1:8 Sheshbazzar the prince of Judah. Cf. 1:11; 5:14,16. Nothing is said about this man biblically except in Ezra. Most likely, he was a political appointee of Cyrus to oversee Judah. He is not to be confused with Zerubbabel, who was the leader recognized by the Jews (cf. 2:2; 3:2,8; 4:2,3; 5:2) and by God (cf. Hag. 1–2; Zech. 4). While Zerubbabel did not serve as king, he was in the Davidic line of Messiah (cf. Hag. 2:23; Matt. 1:12).

1:9-11 The 2,499 articles counted in 1:9,10 are only representative of the total of 5,400 mentioned in 1:11.

1:11 captives. Those whom Nebuchadnezzar had taken into Babylonian captivity from Jerusalem, whose return probably occurred early in the reign of Cyrus (ca. 538/537 B.C.). **Babylon to Jerusalem.** A journey taking 3–5 months (cf. Ezra 7:8,9).

2:1-70 This list is given almost identically in Neh. 7:6-73 (*see notes there*).

2:1 the province. This refers to Judah, reduced from an illustrious, independent, and powerful kingdom to an obscure, servile province of the Persian Empire. The returning Jews were still considered subjects of Cyrus living in a Persian province.

2:2 Zerubbabel. This man was the rightful leader of Judah in that he was of the lineage of David through Jehoiakin (cf. 1 Chr. 3:17). He did not serve as king (cf. the curse on Jehoiakin's line, Jer. 22:24-30), but was still in the messianic line because the curse was bypassed (cf. Matt. 1:12; Luke 3:27) through a levirate marriage (*see note on Ruth 2:20*) of his mother to Pedaiah (1 Chr. 3:19). The curse of the messianic line for Christ was bypassed through this means, as it was also by the virgin birth. His name means "offspring of Babylon," indicating his place of birth. He, rather than Cyrus' political appointee Sheshbazzar (cf. 1:11), led Judah according to God's will. **Jeshua.** The High-Priest of the first return whose name means "Jehovah saves." He is called Joshua in Hag. 1:1 and Zech. 3:1. His father Jozadak (Ezra 3:2) had been exiled (cf. 1 Chr. 6:15). He came from the lineage of Levi, Aaron, Eleazar, and Phinehas; thus he was legitimately in the line of the High-Priest (cf. Num. 25:10-13). **Nehemiah...Mordecai.** These are not the same men in Nehemiah or Esther.

2:3-20 Various Jewish families are listed.

2:21-35 These were people from various Judean cities.

2:36-42 Priests and Levites. See Neh. 12:1-9 for additional details.

42 The sons of the gatekeepers: the sons
of Shallum, the sons of Ater, the sons of
Talmon, the sons of Akkub, the sons of Hatita, and the sons of Shobai, one hundred
and thirty-nine *in* all.
43 [j]The Nethinim: the sons of Ziha, the
sons of Hasupha, the sons of Tabbaoth,
44 the sons of Keros, the sons of [2]Siaha, the
sons of Padon, 45 the sons of Lebanah, the
sons of Hagabah, the sons of Akkub,
46 the sons of Hagab, the sons of Shalmai,
the sons of Hanan, 47 the sons of Giddel,
the sons of Gahar, the sons of Reaiah, 48 the
sons of Rezin, the sons of Nekoda, the sons
of Gazzam, 49 the sons of Uzza, the sons
of Paseah, the sons of Besai, 50 the sons of
Asnah, the sons of Meunim, the sons of
[3]Nephusim, 51 the sons of Bakbuk, the
sons of Hakupha, the sons of Harhur,
52 the sons of [4]Bazluth, the sons of Mehida,
the sons of Harsha, 53 the sons of Barkos,
the sons of Sisera, the sons of Tamah, 54 the
sons of Neziah, and the sons of Hatipha.
55 The sons of [k]Solomon's servants: the
sons of Sotai, the sons of [l]Sophereth,
the sons of [5]Peruda, 56 the sons of Jaala,
the sons of Darkon, the sons of Giddel,
57 the sons of Shephatiah, the sons of Hattil, the sons of Pochereth of Zebaim, and
the sons of [6]Ami. 58 All the [m]Nethinim and
the children of [n]Solomon's servants were
three hundred and ninety-two.
59 And these *were* the ones who came up
from Tel Melah, Tel Harsha, Cherub,
[7]Addan, and Immer; but they could not
[8]identify their father's house or their [9]ge-
nealogy, whether they *were* of Israel: 60 the
sons of Delaiah, the sons of Tobiah, and the
sons of Nekoda, six hundred and fifty-two;
61 and of the sons of the priests: the sons of
[o]Habaiah, the sons of [1]Koz, and the sons of
[p]Barzillai, who took a wife of the daughters of Barzillai the Gileadite, and was
called by their name. 62 These sought their
listing *among* those who were registered by
genealogy, but they were not found;
[q]therefore they *were excluded* from the
priesthood as defiled. 63 And the [2]gover-
nor said to them that they [r]should not eat
of the most holy things till a priest could
consult with the [s]Urim and Thummim.
64 [t]The whole assembly together *was*
forty-two thousand three hundred *and*
sixty, 65 besides their male and female servants, of whom *there were* seven thousand
three hundred and thirty-seven; and they
had two hundred men and women
singers. 66 Their horses *were* seven hundred and thirty-six, their mules two hundred and forty-five, 67 their camels four
hundred and thirty-five, and *their* donkeys
six thousand seven hundred and twenty.
68 [u]*Some* of the heads of the fathers' *hous-*
es, when they came to the house of the LORD
which *is* in Jerusalem, offered freely for the
house of God, to erect it in its place: 69 According to their ability, they gave to the
[v]treasury for the work sixty-one thousand
gold drachmas, five thousand minas of silver, and one hundred priestly garments.
70 [w]So the priests and the Levites, *some*
of the people, the singers, the gatekeepers,
and the Nethinim, dwelt in their cities, and
all Israel in their cities.

43 [j] 1 Chr. 9:2; Ezra 7:7
44 [2] *Sia,* Neh. 7:47
50 [3] *Nephishesim,* Neh. 7:52
52 [4] *Bazlith,* Neh. 7:54
55 [k] 1 Kin. 9:21 [l] Neh. 7:57-60 [5] *Perida,* Neh. 7:57
57 [6] *Amon,* Neh. 7:59
58 [m] Josh. 9:21, 27; 1 Chr. 9:2 [n] 1 Kin. 9:21
59 [7] Or *Addon,* Neh. 7:61 [8] Lit. *tell* [9] Lit. *seed*
61 [o] Neh. 7:63 [p] 2 Sam. 17:27; 1 Kin. 2:7 [1] Or *Hakkoz*
62 [q] Num. 3:10
63 [r] Lev. 22:2, 10, 15, 16 [s] Ex. 28:30; Num. 27:21 [2] Heb. *Tirshatha*
64 [t] Neh. 7:66; Is. 10:22
68 [u] Ezra 1:6; 3:5; Neh. 7:70
69 [v] 1 Chr. 26:20; Ezra 8:25-35
70 [w] Ezra 6:16, 17; Neh. 7:73

2:43-54 Nethinim. These were temple servants, descendants of the Gibeonites who performed servile duties at the temple.

2:55-58 Here are descendants of Solomon's servants.

2:59-62 Those whose genealogical information could not be verified.

2:63 Urim and Thummim. *See note on Ex. 28:30.* These objects, kept in the breastplate of the High-Priest, were used to determine God's will.

2:64,65 This gross amount is 12,000 more than the particular numbers given in the catalogue, when added together. Reckoning up the smaller numbers, we will find they amount to 29,818 in this chapter, and to 31,089 in the parallel chapter of Nehemiah. Ezra also mentions 494 persons omitted by Nehemiah, and Nehemiah mentions 1,765 not noticed by Ezra. If, therefore, Ezra's surplus is added to the sum in Nehemiah, and Nehemiah's surplus to the number in Ezra, they will both become 31,583. Subtracting this from 42,360, there is a deficiency of 10,777. These are omitted, because they did not belong to Judah and Benjamin, or to the priests, but to the other tribes. The servants and singers, male and female, are reckoned separately (v. 65), so that putting all these items together, the number of all who went with Zerubbabel amounted to 50,000 with 8,000 beasts of burden.

2:69 drachmas...minas. "Drachma" probably refers to a Persian coin, the daric, named after Darius I. This would have amounted to approximately 1,100 lbs. of gold. A mina weighed about 1.2 lbs., so this would represent 3 tons of silver (cf. 1 Chr. 29:7).

2:70 Nethinim. *See note on 2:43-54.*

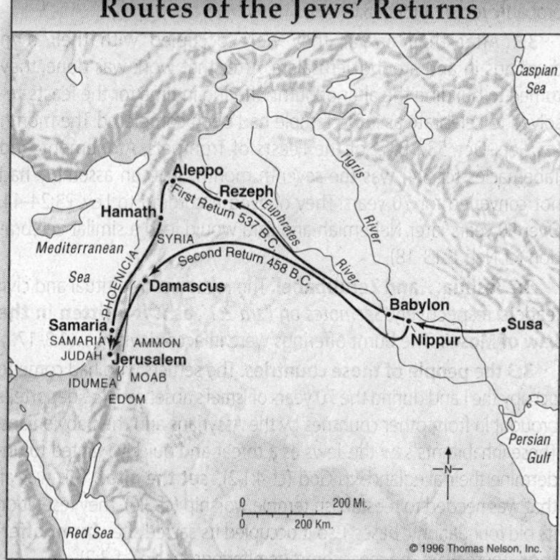

Worship Restored at Jerusalem

3 And when the [a]seventh month had
come, and the children of Israel *were* in
the cities, the people gathered together as
one man to Jerusalem. 2 Then [1]Jeshua the
son of [b]Jozadak[2] and his brethren the
priests, [c]and Zerubbabel the son of [d]She-
altiel and his brethren, arose and built the
altar of the God of Israel, to offer burnt offerings on it, as *it is* [e]written in the Law of
Moses the man of God. 3 Though fear *had*
come upon them because of the people of
those countries, they set the altar on its
[3]bases; and they offered [f]burnt offerings on
it to the LORD, *both* the morning and
evening burnt offerings. 4 [g]They also kept
the Feast of Tabernacles, [h]as *it is* written,
and [i]*offered* the daily burnt offerings in the
number required by ordinance for each
day. 5 Afterwards *they offered* the [j]regular
burnt offering, and *those* for New Moons
and for all the appointed feasts of the LORD
that were consecrated, and *those* of everyone who willingly offered a freewill offering to the LORD. 6 From the first day of the
seventh month they began to offer burnt offerings to the LORD, although the foundation of the temple of the LORD had not been
laid. 7 They also gave money to the masons
and the carpenters, and [k]food, drink, and
oil to the people of Sidon and Tyre to bring
cedar logs from Lebanon to the sea, to
[l]Joppa, [m]according to the permission
which they had from Cyrus king of Persia.

Restoration of the Temple Begins

8 Now in the second month of the second year of their coming to the house of
God at Jerusalem, [n]Zerubbabel the son of
Shealtiel, Jeshua the son of [4]Jozadak, and
the rest of their brethren the priests and the
Levites, and all those who had come out of
the captivity to Jerusalem, began *work* [o]and
appointed the Levites from twenty years
old and above to oversee the work of the
house of the LORD. 9 Then Jeshua *with* his
sons and brothers, Kadmiel *with* his sons,
and the sons of [5]Judah, arose as one to
oversee those working on the house of
God: the sons of Henadad *with* their sons
and their brethren the Levites.
10 When the builders laid the foundation
of the temple of the LORD, [p]the[6] priests
stood in their apparel with trumpets, and
the Levites, the sons of Asaph, with cymbals, to praise the LORD, according to the
[q]ordinance[7] of David king of Israel.
11 [r]And they sang responsively, praising
and giving thanks to the LORD:

> [s]"For *He is* good,
> [t]For His mercy *endures* forever
> toward Israel."

Then all the people shouted with a great
shout, when they praised the LORD, because the foundation of the house of the
LORD was laid.
12 But many of the priests and Levites
and [u]heads of the fathers' *houses,* old men
who had seen the first temple, wept with a
loud voice when the foundation of this
temple was laid before their eyes. Yet many
shouted aloud for joy, 13 so that the people
could not discern the noise of the shout of
joy from the noise of the weeping of the
people, for the people shouted with a loud
shout, and the sound was heard afar off.

CHAPTER 3

1 [a] Neh. 7:73; 8:1, 2
2 [b] 1 Chr. 6:14, 15; Ezra 4:3; Neh. 12:1, 8; Hag. 1:1; 2:2 [c] Ezra 2:2; 4:2, 3; 5:2 [d] 1 Chr. 3:17 [e] Deut. 12:5, 6 [1] Or *Joshua* [2] *Jehozadak,* 1 Chr. 6:14
3 [f] Num. 28:3 [3] *foundations*
4 [g] Lev. 23:33-43; Neh. 8:14-18; Zech. 14:16 [h] Ex. 23:16 [i] Num. 29:12, 13
5 [j] Ex. 29:38; Num. 28:3, 11, 19, 26; Ezra 1:4; 2:68; 7:15, 16; 8:28
7 [k] 1 Kin. 5:6, 9; 2 Chr. 2:10; Acts 12:20 [l] 2 Chr. 2:16; Acts 9:36 [m] Ezra 1:2; 6:3
8 [n] Ezra 3:2; 4:3 [o] 1 Chr. 23:4, 24 [4] *Jehozadak,* 1 Chr. 6:14
9 [5] *Hodaviah,* Ezra 2:40
10 [p] 1 Chr. 16:5, 6 [q] 1 Chr. 6:31; 16:4; 25:1 [6] So with LXX, Syr., Vg.; MT *they stationed the priests* [7] Lit. *hands*
11 [r] Ex. 15:21; 2 Chr. 7:3; Neh. 12:24 [s] 1 Chr. 16:34; Ps. 136:1 [t] 1 Chr. 16:41; Jer. 33:11
12 [u] Ezra 2:68

3:1-13 The worship and regular calendar resumed. The altar was probably rebuilt in 537 B.C.

3:1 After their arrival, they were occupied with their own dwellings in and around Jerusalem. After that work was done, they turned to building the altar of burnt offering in time for the feasts, resolved to celebrate as if the temple had been completed. The month (ca. Sep.-Oct. 537 B.C.) of the Feasts of Trumpets, Atonement, and Tabernacles (cf. 3:4) was the seventh month. Such an assembly had not convened for 70 years. They obeyed according to Lev. 23:24-44. Over 90 years later, Nehemiah and Ezra would lead a similar celebration (cf. Neh. 8:13-18).

3:2 Jeshua...and Zerubbabel. The recognized spiritual and civil leaders, respectively. *See notes on Ezra 2:1.* **as *it is* written in the Law of Moses.** The burnt offerings were in accord with Lev. 1:3-17.

3:3 the people of those countries. The settlers who had come to occupy the Land during the 70 years of Israel's absence were deportees brought in from other countries by the Assyrians and the Babylonians. These inhabitants saw the Jews as a threat and quickly wanted to undermine their allegiance to God (cf. 4:1,2). **set the altar.** This was all that was needed to reestablish temple worship (cf. 3:6). They reset it on its old foundation ("bases"), so it occupied its sacred site. **burnt offerings.** These were the most common offerings for sin (cf. 3:2).

3:4 number required by ordinance. According to Num. 29:12-38.

3:7 masons...carpenters...cedar logs. The process of rebuilding the temple sounds similar to the original construction under Solomon (1 Kin. 5,6; 1 Chr. 22; 2 Chr. 2). **Sidon and Tyre...Joppa.** The materials were shipped from the Phoenician ports of Sidon and Tyre S to Joppa, the main seaport, about 35 mi. from Jerusalem. **permission which they had from Cyrus.** Cf. 1:2-4.

3:8 second month...second year. Ca. Apr./May 536 B.C. This officially ended the 70 year captivity that began in 605 B.C.

3:11 they sang responsively. Their song of praise is similar to Ps. 136:1.

3:12 the first temple. The temple built by Solomon (cf. 1 Kin. 5–7). **wept with a loud voice.** The first temple had been destroyed 50 years earlier. The old men, who would have been about 60 years or older, knew that this second temple did not begin to match the splendor of Solomon's temple nor did the presence of God reside within it (cf. Hag. 2:1-4; Zech. 4:9,10). The nation was small and weak, the temple smaller and less beautiful by far. There were no riches as in David and Solomon's days. The ark was gone. But most disappointing was the absence of God's Shekinah glory. Thus the weeping. **shouted...for joy.** For those who did not have a point of comparison, this

Resistance to Rebuilding the Temple

4 Now when [a]the [1]adversaries of Judah
and Benjamin heard that the descendants of the captivity were building the
temple of the LORD God of Israel, 2 they
came to Zerubbabel and the heads of the fathers' *houses,* and said to them, "Let us build
with you, for we seek your God as you *do;*
and we have sacrificed to Him [b]since the
days of Esarhaddon king of Assyria, who
brought us here." 3 But Zerubbabel and
Jeshua and the rest of the heads of the fathers' *houses* of Israel said to them, [c]"You
may do nothing with us to build a [2]house
for our God; but we alone will build to the
LORD God of Israel, as [d]King Cyrus the king
of Persia has commanded us." 4 Then [e]the
people of the land tried to discourage the
people of Judah. They troubled them in
building, 5 and hired counselors against
them to frustrate their purpose all the days
of Cyrus king of Persia, even until the reign
of [f]Darius king of Persia.

Rebuilding of Jerusalem Opposed

6 In the reign of Ahasuerus, in the beginning of his reign, they wrote an accusation
against the inhabitants of Judah and Jerusalem.
7 In the days of [g]Artaxerxes also, [3]Bish-
lam, Mithredath, Tabel, and the rest of their
companions wrote to Artaxerxes king of
Persia; and the letter *was* written in [h]Ara-
maic script, and translated into the Aramaic
language. 8 [4]Rehum the commander and
Shimshai the scribe wrote a letter against Jerusalem to King Artaxerxes in this fashion:

9 [5]From Rehum the commander,
Shimshai the scribe, and the rest of
their companions—*representatives*
of [i]the Dinaites, the Apharsath-
chites, the Tarpelites, the people of
Persia and Erech and Babylon and
[6]Shushan, the Dehavites, the Elamites, 10 [j]and the rest of the nations
whom the great and noble Osnapper took captive and settled in
the cities of Samaria and the
remainder beyond [7]the River—
[k]and [8] so forth.

11 (This *is* a copy of the letter that they
sent him)

To King Artaxerxes from your
servants, the men *of the region*
beyond the River, [9]and so forth:

12 Let it be known to the king that the
Jews who came up from you have
come to us at Jerusalem, and are

CHAPTER 4
1 [a] Ezra 4:7-9 [1] *enemies*
2 [b] 2 Kin. 17:24; 19:37; Ezra 4:10
3 [c] Neh. 2:20 [d] Ezra 1:1-4 [2] *Temple*
4 [e] Ezra 3:3
5 [f] Ezra 5:5; 6:1
7 [g] Ezra 7:1, 7, 21 [3] *Or in peace*
[h] 2 Kin. 18:26
8 [4] The original language of Ezra 4:8 through 6:18 is Aramaic.
9 [i] 2 Kin. 17:30, 31 [5] *Lit. Then* [6] *Or Susa*
10 [j] 2 Kin. 17:24; Ezra 4:1 [k] Ezra 4:11, 17; 7:12 [7] *The Euphrates* [8] *Lit. and now*
11 [9] *Lit. and now*

was a great moment. Possibly Ps. 126 was written and sung for this occasion.

4:1 the adversaries. Cf. 5:3-17. These were Israel's enemies in the region, who resisted their reestablishment.

4:2 we have sacrificed to Him. This false claim represented the syncretistic worship of the Samaritans, whose ancestry came from intermarriage with foreign immigrants in Samaria after 722 B.C. (cf. 4:10). In the British Museum is a large cylinder and inscribed on it are the annals of Esarhaddon, an Assyrian king (ca. 681–669 B.C.), who deported a large population of Israelites from Palestine. A consequent settlement of Babylonian colonists took their place and intermarried with remaining Jewish women and their descendants. The result was the mongrel race called Samaritans. They had developed a superstitious form of worshiping God (cf. 2 Kin. 17:26-34).

4:3 we alone. Idolatry had been the chief cause for Judah's deportation to Babylon, and they wanted to avoid it altogether. While they still had their spiritual problems (Ezra 9,10), they rejected any form of mixed religion, particularly this offer of cooperation which had sabotage as its goal (cf. vv. 4,5). **King Cyrus...commanded us.** Cf. Ezra 1:2-4 (ca. 538 B.C.). This note gave authority to their refusal.

4:5 frustrate. This caused a 16-year delay (ca. 536–520 B.C.). As a result, the people took more interest in their personal affairs than spiritual matters (cf. Hag. 1:2-6). **Darius.** Darius ruled Persia ca. 521–486 B.C.

4:6-23 This section represents later opposition which Ezra chose to put here as a parenthetical continuation of the theme "opposition to resettling and rebuilding Judah" (see Introduction: Interpretative Challenges). He first referred to the opposition from Israel's enemies under King Ahasuerus (a regal title) or Xerxes (ca. 486–464 B.C.), who ruled at the time of Esther (4:6). Ezra 4:7-23 then recounts opposition in Nehemiah's day under Artaxerxes I (ca. 464–423 B.C.) expressed in a detailed letter of accusation against the Jews (vv. 7-16). It was successful in stopping the work, as the king's reply indicates (vv. 17-23). Most likely, this opposition is that also spoken of in Neh. 1:3. All this was the ongoing occurrence of severe animosity between the Israelites and Samaritans, which was later aggravated when the Samaritans built a rival temple on Mt. Gerizim (cf. John 4:9). The opposition to Zerubbabel picks up again at 4:24–5:2 during the reign of Darius I, who actually reigned before either Ahasuerus or Artaxerxes.

4:6 they wrote an accusation. The word translated "accusation" means "a complaint." Satan, meaning "legal adversary" or "opponent," is a related term.

4:7,8 letter...letter. Two different words are used here. The first is an official document as opposed to a simple letter. The second is the generic term for letter. The context verifies the choices of two different terms, since two different letters are indicated.

4:8–6:18 Since this section contains predominantly correspondence, it is written in Aramaic (also 7:12-26) rather than Hebrew, generally reflecting the diplomatic language of the day (cf. 2 Kin 18:26; Is. 36:11).

4:10 Osnapper. Most likely another name for the Assyrian king Ashurbanipal, ca. 669–633 B.C. **settled...cities of Samaria.** The race of Samaritans resulted from the intermarriage of these immigrants with the poor people who were not taken captive to Nineveh (*see note on 4:2* and 2 Kin. 17:24-41).

4:11 Artaxerxes. *See note on 4:6-23.* **beyond the River.** West of the Euphrates River.

4:12 Jews. This name was generally used after the Captivity because the exiles who returned were mainly of Judah. Most of the people of the 10 northern tribes were dispersed and the largest number of returnees came from the two southern tribes.

building the [l]rebellious and evil
city, and are finishing *its* [m]walls and
repairing the foundations. 13 Let it
now be known to the king that, if
this city is built and the walls
completed, they will not pay [n]tax,
tribute, or custom, and the king's
treasury will be diminished. 14 Now
because we receive support from
the palace, it was not proper for us
to see the king's dishonor; therefore
we have sent and informed the
king, 15 that search may be made in
the book of the records of your
fathers. And you will find in the
book of the records and know that
this city *is* a rebellious city, harmful
to kings and provinces, and that
they have incited sedition within
the city in former times, for which
cause this city was destroyed.

16 We inform the king that if this city is
rebuilt and its walls are completed,
the result will be that you will have
no dominion beyond the River.

17 The king sent an answer:

To Rehum the commander, *to*
Shimshai the scribe, *to* the rest of
their companions who dwell in Samaria,
and *to* the remainder
beyond the River:

Peace, [1]and so forth.

18 The letter which you sent to us has
been clearly read before me. 19 And
[2]I gave the command, and a search
has been made, and it was found
that this city in former times has
revolted against kings, and
rebellion and sedition have been
fostered in it. 20 There have also
been mighty kings over Jerusalem,
who have [o]ruled over all *the region*
[p]beyond the River; and tax, tribute,
and custom were paid to them.
21 Now [3]give the command to
make these men cease, that this
city may not be built until the
command is given by me.

22 Take heed now that you do not fail
to do this. Why should damage
increase to the hurt of the kings?

23 Now when the copy of King Artaxerxes'
letter *was* read before Rehum,
Shimshai the scribe, and their companions,
they went up in haste to Jerusalem against
the Jews, and by force of arms made them
cease. 24 Thus the work of the house of
God which *is* at Jerusalem ceased, and it
was discontinued until the second year of
the reign of Darius king of Persia.

Restoration of the Temple Resumed

5 Then the prophet [a]Haggai and [b]Zechariah
the son of Iddo, prophets, prophesied
to the Jews who *were* in Judah and Jerusalem,
in the name of the God of Israel,
who was over them. 2 So [c]Zerubbabel the
son of Shealtiel and Jeshua the son of
[1]Jozadak rose up and began to build the
house of God which *is* in Jerusalem; and
[d]the prophets of God *were* with them, helping
them.
3 At the same time [e]Tattenai the governor
of *the region* beyond [2]the River and
Shethar-Boznai and their companions
came to them and spoke thus to them:
[f]"Who has commanded you to build this

12 [l] 2 Chr. 36:13 [m] Ezra 5:3, 9
13 [n] Ezra 4:20; 7:24
17 [1] Lit. *and now*
19 [2] Lit. *by me a decree has been put forth*
20 [o] 1 Kin. 4:21; 1 Chr. 18:3; Ps. 72:8 [p] Gen. 15:18; Josh. 1:4
21 [3] *put forth a decree*

CHAPTER 5

1 [a] Hag. 1:1 [b] Zech. 1:1
2 [c] Ezra 3:2; Hag. 1:12 [d] Ezra 6:14; Hag. 2:4 [1] *Jehozadak*, 1 Chr. 6:14
3 [e] Ezra 5:6; 6:6 [f] Ezra 1:3; 5:9 [2] The Euphrates

4:13,14 This accusation is full of hypocrisy. They did not relish paying taxes either, but they did hate the Jews.

4:15 the book of the records. An administrative document called a "memorandum" kept on file in the royal archives. **city was destroyed.** A reference to Jerusalem's destruction by the Babylonian king Nebuchadnezzar (ca. 586 B.C.).

4:19 And I gave the command. The line might better be translated "I established a decree." In other words, this was no simple routine order given to one person, but rather a major edict to a large group of people.

4:21 Now give the command. No small order for one or two workers, but rather the efforts of 50,000 were called to a halt. The king was commissioning a decree of great significance. The original language calls for the difference. This decree would not lose its authority until the king established a new decree.

4:23 letter. Another official document, as opposed to a generic letter, came from Artaxerxes' transferring authority to the regional leaders to establish the decree. Without the king's official administrative correspondence, the decree could not be established.

4:24 ceased...discontinued. For 16 years, from 536 B.C. to 520 B.C., work on rebuilding was halted.

5:1 Haggai and Zechariah. The book of Haggai is styled as a "royal administrative correspondence" (cf. Hag. 1:13) sent from the Sovereign King of the Universe through the "messenger of the LORD," Haggai (Hag. 1:13). Part of its message is addressed specifically to Zerubbabel, the political leader, and Joshua, the religious leader, telling them to "take courage and work" on the temple because God was with them (Hag. 2:4). These two prophets gave severe reproaches and threats if the people did not return to the building and promised national prosperity if they did. Not long after the exiles heard this message, the temple work began afresh after a 16-year hiatus. *See notes on Haggai and Zechariah.*

5:2 prophets of God. These would be in addition to Haggai and Zechariah.

5:3 Tattenai. Most likely a Persian official. **Who has commanded you.** In other words, "Who issued you a royal decree to build?" Cf. Ezra 5:9.

[3]temple and finish this wall?” 4 [g]Then, accordingly, we told them the names of the
men who were constructing this building.
5 But [h]the eye of their God was upon the
elders of the Jews, so that they could not
make them cease till a report could go to
Darius. Then a [i]written answer was returned concerning this *matter.* 6 This is a
copy of the letter that Tattenai sent:

> The governor of *the region* beyond
> the River, and Shethar-Boznai, [j]and
> his companions, the Persians who
> *were in the region* beyond the River,
> to Darius the king.

7 (They sent a letter to him, in which was
written thus)

> To Darius the king:
>
> All peace.

8 Let it be known to the king that we
went into the province of Judea, to
the [4]temple of the great God,
which is being built with [5]heavy
stones, and timber is being laid in
the walls; and this work goes on
diligently and prospers in their
hands.

9 Then we asked those elders, *and*
spoke thus to them: [k]“Who
commanded you to build this
temple and to finish these walls?”
10 We also asked them their names
to inform you, that we might write
the names of the men who *were*
chief among them.

11 And thus they returned us an
answer, saying: “We are the
servants of the God of heaven and
earth, and we are rebuilding the
[6]temple that was built many years

3 [3] Lit. *house*
4 [g] Ezra 5:10
5 [h] 2 Chr. 16:9; Ezra 7:6, 28; Ps. 33:18 [i] Ezra 6:6
6 [j] Ezra 4:7-10
8 [4] Lit. *house* [5] Lit. *stones of rolling,* stones too heavy to be carried
9 [k] Ezra 5:3, 4
11 [6] Lit. *house*
[l] 1 Kin. 6:1, 38
12 [m] 2 Chr. 34:25; 36:16, 17 [n] 2 Kin. 24:2; 25:8-11; 2 Chr. 36:17; Jer. 52:12-15 [o] Jer. 13:19
13 [p] Ezra 1:1 [7] Temple
14 [q] Ezra 1:7, 8; 6:5; Dan. 5:2 [r] Hag. 1:14; 2:2, 21
16 [s] Ezra 3:8-10; Hag. 2:18 [t] Ezra 6:15
17 [u] Ezra 6:1, 2

CHAPTER 6

1 [a] Ezra 5:17 [1] Lit. *house of the scrolls*

ago, which a great king of Israel
built [l]and completed. 12 But [m]be-
cause our fathers provoked the
God of heaven to wrath, He gave
them into the hand of [n]Nebuchad-
nezzar king of Babylon, the Chaldean, *who* destroyed this temple
and [o]carried the people away to
Babylon. 13 However, in the first
year of [p]Cyrus king of Babylon,
King Cyrus issued a decree to build
this [7]house of God. 14 Also, [q]the
gold and silver articles of the house
of God, which Nebuchadnezzar
had taken from the temple that *was*
in Jerusalem and carried into the
temple of Babylon—those King
Cyrus took from the temple of
Babylon, and they were given to
[r]one named Sheshbazzar, whom he
had made governor. 15 And he said
to him, ‘Take these articles; go,
carry them to the temple *site* that *is*
in Jerusalem, and let the house of
God be rebuilt on its former site.’
16 Then the same Sheshbazzar came
and [s]laid the foundation of the
house of God which *is* in Jerusalem;
but from that time even until now
it has been under construction, and
[t]it is not finished.”

17 Now therefore, if *it seems* good to
the king, [u]let a search be made in
the king’s treasure house, which *is*
there in Babylon, whether it is *so*
that a decree was issued by King
Cyrus to build this house of God at
Jerusalem, and let the king send us
his pleasure concerning this *matter.*

The Decree of Darius

6 Then King Darius issued a decree,
[a]and a search was made in the [1]ar-
chives, where the treasures were stored in

5:5 But the eye of their God was upon the elders. God’s hand of protection which led this endeavor allowed the work to continue while official communication was going on with Darius, the Persian king *(see note on 4:5).*

5:8 heavy stones, and timber. This technique of using beams and stone blocks was a well known form of wall construction. The reason for mentioning it here was it seemed to be a preparation for conflict, or battle. Including this piece of information served as a threat to the Persian official who wanted no such conflict.

5:11 they returned us an answer. They sent back a report (official document for the archives). **a great king of Israel.** Solomon built the first temple (ca. 966–960; 1 Kin. 5–7).

5:12 gave them into the hand of Nebuchadnezzar. The expression is used commonly in royal administrative correspondence when a more powerful administrator, such as a king, relinquishes some of his authority to an underling and yet keeps the lower administrative official completely under his command. The point here is that God, as king of the universe, satisfied His wrath by relinquishing the authority for this administrative action to Nebuchadnezzar. The greatest king the ancient Near East has ever known was merely a petty official in the administration of the sovereign Lord.

5:13 Cyrus...decree. Cf. Ezra 1:2-4.

5:14,16 Sheshbazzar...laid the foundation. This seems to contradict the statement in Ezra 3:8-10 that Zerubbabel, Jeshua, and the Jewish workmen laid the foundation, but it actually does not, since Sheshbazzar was the political appointee of the Persian king over the Jews and thus is given official credit for work actually done by them. *See note on Ezra 1:11.*

6:1 King Darius issued a decree. Rather than a public edict, this was a simple order issued to a small group of officials.

Babylon. 2 And at [2]Achmetha, in the palace that *is* in the province of [b]Media, a scroll was found, and in it a record *was* written thus:

3 In the first year of King Cyrus,
King Cyrus issued a [c]decree *concerning* the house of God at Jerusalem: "Let the house be rebuilt, the place where they offered sacrifices; and let the foundations of it be firmly laid, its height sixty cubits *and* its width sixty cubits, 4 [d]*with* three rows of heavy stones and one row of new timber. Let the [e]expenses be paid from the king's treasury. 5 Also let [f]the gold and silver articles of the house of God, which Nebuchadnezzar took from the temple which *is* in Jerusalem and brought to Babylon, be restored and taken back to the temple which *is* in Jerusalem, *each* to its place; and deposit *them* in the house of God"—

6 [g]Now *therefore,* Tattenai, governor of *the region* beyond the River, and Shethar-Boznai, and your companions the Persians who *are* beyond the River, keep yourselves far from there. 7 Let the work of this house of God alone; let the governor of the Jews and the elders of the Jews build this house of God on its site.

8 Moreover I issue a decree *as to* what you shall do for the elders of these Jews, for the building of this [3]house of God: Let the cost be paid at the king's expense from taxes *on* *the region* beyond the River; this is to be given immediately to these men, so that they are not hindered. 9 And whatever they need—young bulls, rams, and lambs for the burnt offerings of the God of heaven, wheat, salt, wine, and oil, according to the request of the priests who *are* in Jerusalem—let it be given them day by day without fail, 10 [h]that they may offer sacrifices of sweet aroma to the God of heaven, and pray for the life of the king and his sons.

11 Also I issue a decree that whoever alters this edict, let a timber be pulled from his house and erected, and let him be hanged on it; [i]and let his house be made a refuse heap because of this. 12 And may the God who causes His [j]name to dwell there destroy any king or people who put their hand to alter it, or to destroy this [4]house of God which is in Jerusalem. I Darius issue a decree; let it be done diligently.

The Temple Completed and Dedicated

13 Then Tattenai, governor of *the region* beyond the River, Shethar-Boznai, and their companions diligently did according to what King Darius had sent. 14 [k]So the elders of the Jews built, and they prospered through the prophesying of Haggai the prophet and Zechariah the son of Iddo. And they built and finished *it,* according to the commandment of the God of Israel, and according to the [5]command of [l]Cyrus, [m]Darius, and [n]Artaxerxes king of Persia. 15 Now the temple was finished on the third day of

2 [b] 2 Kin. 17:6 [2] Probably *Ecbatana,* the ancient capital of Media
3 [c] Ezra 1:1; 5:13
4 [d] 1 Kin. 6:36 [e] Ezra 3:7
5 [f] Ezra 1:7, 8; 5:14
6 [g] Ezra 5:3, 6
8 [3] Temple
10 [h] Ezra 7:23; [Jer. 29:7; 1 Tim. 2:1, 2]
11 [i] Dan. 2:5; 3:29
12 [j] Deut. 12:5, 11; 1 Kin. 9:3 [4] Temple
14 [k] Ezra 5:1, 2 [l] Ezra 1:1; 5:13; 6:3 [m] Ezra 4:24; 6:12 [n] Ezra 7:1, 11; Neh. 2:1 [5] *decree*

6:1,2 Babylon…Achmetha. Achmetha is another name for the Persian capital of Ecbatana, 300 mi. NE of Babylon in the foothills, where Cyrus and others had their summer homes.

6:2 a record *was* written. A particular kind of document called a memorandum (Ezra 4:15; Mal. 3:16). Administrative officials often kept these documents of administrative decisions made, or issues remaining to be settled, to retain the details of administrative action for future reference.

6:3 first year. Ca. 538 B.C. (cf. Ezra 1:2-4). **sixty cubits…sixty cubits.** These dimensions exceed those of Solomon's temple (cf. 1 Kin. 6:2).

6:5 Nebuchadnezzar took. *See notes on Ezra 1:7.*

6:6,7 God so favored the Jews (cf. 5:5) that, through Darius, He forbade the officials from interfering with the building project.

6:8-10 Not only could the officials not hinder the building, but they also had to help finance it by giving the Jews some of their portion of taxes collected for the Persian king. The Jews could draw from the provincial treasury.

6:10 pray for the life of the king and his sons. This was essentially the same self-serving motive that prompted Cyrus to decree that all captured peoples should return to their countries, rebuild the temples that Nebuchadnezzar and others had destroyed, and placate the offended deities. He wanted all the gods on his side, including Israel's God.

6:11 pulled…erected…hanged…made a refuse heap. Typical punishment for a serious infraction (cf. Rev. 22:18,19). This was specifically directed at the hostile Samaritans.

6:14 prospered. Cf. Hag. 1:7-11. **the commandment of the God of Israel…the command of Cyrus.** This is not the normal term for commandment, but it is the same word translated "decree" or "administrative order" throughout the book. The message here is powerful. It was the decree from God, the Sovereign of the universe, which gave administrative authority to rebuild the temple. The decrees (same word) of 3 of the greatest monarchs in the history of the ancient Near East were only a secondary issue. God rules the universe and He raises up kings, then pulls them from their thrones when they have served His administration. **Artaxerxes.** Although he did not contribute to the project under Zerubbabel, he did under Ezra (cf. 7:11-26).

the month of Adar, which was in the sixth
year of the reign of King Darius. 16 Then the
children of Israel, the priests and the Levites
and the rest of the descendants of the captivity, celebrated [o]the dedication of this
[6]house of God with joy. 17 And they [p]offered
sacrifices at the dedication of this house of
God, one hundred bulls, two hundred rams,
four hundred lambs, and as a sin offering for
all Israel twelve male goats, according to the
number of the tribes of Israel. 18 They assigned the priests to their [q]divisions and the
Levites to their [r]divisions, over the service
of God in Jerusalem, [s]as it is written in the
Book of Moses.

The Passover Celebrated

19 [7]And the descendants of the captivity
kept the Passover [t]on the fourteenth *day* of
the first month. 20 For the priests and the
Levites had [u]purified themselves; all of
them *were ritually* clean. And they [v]slaugh-
tered the Passover *lambs* for all the descendants of the captivity, for their brethren the
priests, and for themselves. 21 Then the children of Israel who had returned from the
captivity ate together with all who had separated themselves from the [w]filth[8] of the
nations of the land in order to seek the LORD
God of Israel. 22 And they kept the [x]Feast of
Unleavened Bread seven days with joy; for
the LORD made them joyful, and [y]turned the
heart [z]of the king of Assyria toward them,
to strengthen their hands in the work of the
house of God, the God of Israel.

16 [o]1 Kin. 8:63; 2 Chr. 7:5 [6]Temple
17 [p]Ezra 8:35
18 [q]1 Chr. 24:1; 2 Chr. 35:5 [r]1 Chr. 23:6 [s]Num. 3:6; 8:9
19 [t]Ex. 12:6 [7]The Hebrew language resumes in Ezra 6:19 and continues through 7:11.
20 [u]2 Chr. 29:34; 30:15 [v]2 Chr. 35:11
21 [w]Ezra 9:11 [8]uncleanness
22 [x]Ex. 12:15; 13:6, 7; 2 Chr. 30:21; 35:17 [y]Ezra 7:27; [Prov. 21:1] [z]2 Kin. 23:29; 2 Chr. 33:11; Ezra 1:1; 6:1

CHAPTER 7

1 [a]Neh. 2:1 [b]1 Chr. 6:14 [c]Jer. 52:24 [d]2 Chr. 35:8
6 [e]Ezra 7:11, 12, 21 [f]Ezra 7:9, 28; 8:22
7 [g]Ezra 8:1-14 [h]Ezra 8:15 [i]Ezra 2:43; 8:20
9 [j]Ezra 7:6; Neh. 2:8, 18
10 [k]Ps. 119:45 [l]Deut. 33:10; Ezra 7:6, 25; Neh. 8:1-8; [Mal. 2:7] [1]Study

The Arrival of Ezra

7 Now after these things, in the reign of
[a]Artaxerxes king of Persia, Ezra the
[b]son of Seraiah, [c]the son of Azariah, the
son of [d]Hilkiah, 2 the son of Shallum, the
son of Zadok, the son of Ahitub, 3 the son
of Amariah, the son of Azariah, the son of
Meraioth, 4 the son of Zerahiah, the son of
Uzzi, the son of Bukki, 5 the son of Abishua, the son of Phinehas, the son of Eleazar, the son of Aaron the chief priest—
6 this Ezra came up from Babylon; and he
was [e]a skilled scribe in the Law of Moses,
which the LORD God of Israel had given.
The king granted him all his request, [f]ac-
cording to the hand of the LORD his God
upon him. 7 [g]*Some* of the children of Israel,
the priests, [h]the Levites, the singers, the
gatekeepers, and [i]the Nethinim came up to
Jerusalem in the seventh year of King Artaxerxes. 8 And Ezra came to Jerusalem in
the fifth month, which *was* in the seventh
year of the king. 9 On the first *day* of the
first month he began *his* journey from
Babylon, and on the first *day* of the fifth
month he came to Jerusalem, [j]according to
the good hand of his God upon him. 10 For
Ezra had prepared his heart to [k]seek[1] the
Law of the LORD, and to do *it*, and to [l]teach
statutes and ordinances in Israel.

The Letter of Artaxerxes to Ezra

11 This *is* a copy of the letter that King
Artaxerxes gave Ezra the priest, the scribe,

6:15 Adar…sixth year. The 12th month (Feb./Mar.) in 516 B.C.

6:18 divisions. Cf. 1 Chr. 24, where the priestly divisions are delineated. Although David arranged the priests and Levites in order according to families, it was Moses who assigned their rights, privileges, and duties (*see notes on Num. 3,4*). **the Book of Moses.** I.e., the Pentateuch.

6:19 Passover. Cf. Lev. 23:4-8. Other notable Passovers include Hezekiah's (2 Chr. 30:1-22) and Josiah's (2 Chr. 35:1-19). **first month.** Mar./Apr.

6:21 the filth of the nations. These were proselytes to Judaism, who had confessed their spiritual uncleanness before the Lord, been circumcised, and renounced idolatry to keep the Passover (v. 22).

6:22 turned the heart of the king of Assyria toward them. By turning the heart of the king in their favor in allowing them to complete the rebuilding, God encouraged His people. They understood the verse, "The king's heart *is* in the hand of the LORD" (Prov. 21:1) better through this ordeal. The title "King of Assyria" was held by every king who succeeded the great Neo-Assyrian Empire regardless of what country they may have come from.

6:22–7:1 The book of Esther fits in this 59-year gap between the completion of the temple (ca. 516 B.C.) under Zerubbabel (Ezra 1–6) and the second return (ca. 458 B.C.) under Ezra (Ezra 7–10). Ezra 4:6 provides a glimpse into this period also.

7:1–10:44 This section covers the return of the second group to Judah, led by Ezra (ca. 458 B.C.).

7:1 Artaxerxes. King of Persia from 464–423 B.C. **Ezra.** See Introduction: Author and Date. **the son of.** Ezra traced his lineage back through such notable High-Priests as Zadok (1 Kin. 2:35), Phinehas (Num. 25:10-13), and Eleazar (Num. 3:4).

7:6 a skilled scribe. Ezra's role as a scribe was critical to reinstate the nation since the leaders had to go back to the law and interpret it. This was no small task because many aspects of life had changed in the intervening 1,000 years since the law was first given. Tradition says Ezra had the law memorized and could write it from recall. **the hand of the LORD his God upon him.** This refrain occurs throughout the books of Ezra and Nehemiah. Its resounding presence assures the reader that it was not by the shrewd leadership skills of a few men that Judah, with its temple and walls, was rebuilt in the midst of a powerful Medo-Persian Empire. Rather it was the sovereign hand of the wise and powerful king of the universe that allowed this to happen.

7:7 Nethinim. *See notes on Ezra 2:43-54.* **seventh year.** Ca. 458 B.C.

7:8,9 The 4-month journey from Babylon to Jerusalem, covering almost 1,000 mi., started in Mar./Apr. and ended in Jul./Aug.

7:10 seek…do…teach. The pattern of Ezra's preparation is exemplary. He studied before he attempted to live a life of obedience, and he studied and practiced the law in his own life before he opened his mouth to teach that law. But the success of Ezra's leadership did not come from his strength alone, but most significantly because "the good hand of his God was upon him" (7:9).

7:11 copy of the letter. The original was usually kept for a record. The letter was addressed to Ezra because the decree recorded therein was the critical administrative document. Decrees were commonly

expert in the words of the commandments of the LORD, and of His statutes to Israel:

12 [2]Artaxerxes, [m]king of kings,

To Ezra the priest, a scribe of the Law of the God of heaven:

Perfect *peace,* [n]and [3]so forth.

13 I issue a decree that all those of the
people of Israel and the priests and
Levites in my realm, who
volunteer to go up to Jerusalem,
may go with you. 14 And whereas
you are being sent [4]by the king
and his [o]seven counselors to
inquire concerning Judah and Jerusalem, with regard to the Law of
your God which *is* in your hand;
15 and *whereas you are* to carry the
silver and gold which the king and
his counselors have freely offered
to the God of Israel, [p]whose
dwelling *is* in Jerusalem; 16 [q]and
whereas all the silver and gold that
you may find in all the province of
Babylon, along with the freewill
offering of the people and the
priests, *are to be* [r]freely offered for
the [5]house of their God in Jerusalem— 17 now therefore, be careful
to buy with this money bulls, rams,
and lambs, with their [s]grain
offerings and their drink offerings,
and [t]offer them on the altar of the
house of your God in Jerusalem.

18 And whatever seems good to you
and your brethren to do with the
rest of the silver and the gold, do it
according to the will of your God.
19 Also the articles that are given to
you for the service of the house of
your God, deliver in full before the
God of Jerusalem. 20 And whatever
more may be needed for the house
of your God, which you may have
occasion to provide, pay *for it* from
the king's treasury.

21 And I, *even* I, Artaxerxes the king,
issue a decree to all the treasurers
who *are in the region* beyond the
River, that whatever Ezra the
priest, the scribe of the Law of the
God of heaven, may require of
you, let it be done diligently, 22 up
to one hundred talents of silver,
one hundred kors of wheat, one
hundred baths of wine, one
hundred baths of oil, and salt
without prescribed limit. 23 Whatever [6]is commanded by the God of
heaven, let it diligently be done for
the [7]house of the God of heaven.
For why should there be wrath
against the realm of the king and
his sons?

24 Also we inform you that it shall
not be lawful to impose tax,
tribute, or custom *on* any of the
priests, Levites, singers,
gatekeepers, Nethinim, or servants
of this house of God. 25 And you,
Ezra, according to your God-given
wisdom, [u]set magistrates and
judges who may judge all the
people who *are in the region* beyond

12 [m]Ezek. 26:7; Dan. 2:37 [n]Ezra 4:10 [2]The original language of Ezra 7:12-26 is Aramaic. [3]Lit. *and now*
14 [o]Esth. 1:14 [4]*from before*
15 [p]2 Chr. 6:2; Ezra 6:12; Ps. 135:21
16 [q]Ezra 8:25 [r]1 Chr. 29:6, 9 [5]Temple
17 [s]Num. 15:4-13 [t]Deut. 12:5-11
23 [6]Lit. *is from the decree* [7]Temple
25 [u]Ex. 18:21, 22; Deut. 16:18

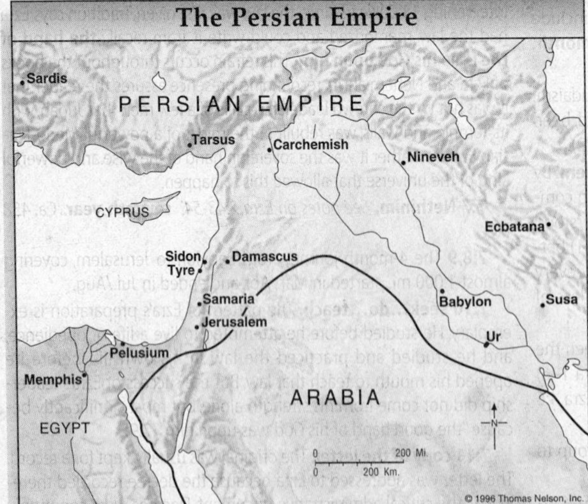

embedded in letters. The letter in essence authorized the document into Ezra's hands so that he could carry it and read it to its intended audience.

7:12-26 This is a remarkable decree that evidences God's sovereign rule over earthly kings and His intent to keep the Abrahamic, Davidic, and New Covenants with Israel. This section is in Aramaic, as was 4:8–6:18.

7:12 king of kings. Though it was true that Artaxerxes ruled over other kings, Jesus Christ is the ultimate King of Kings (cf. Rev. 19:16), who alone can genuinely make that claim since He will rule over all kings in His coming kingdom (cf. Rev. 11:15).

7:14 seven counselors. This number was according to the Persian tradition (cf. Esth. 1:14).

7:17 now therefore. The royal decree protocol recorded in the opening words of 7:13-16 leads up to the section introduced by these words.

7:22 one hundred talents. Approaching 4 tons in weight. **one hundred kors.** Approximately 750 bushels. **one hundred baths.** Six hundred gallons.

7:25 And you, Ezra. The letter in which the decree was

the River, all such as know the
laws of your God; and [v]teach those
who do not know *them.* 26 Whoever will not observe the law of
your God and the law of the king,
let judgment be executed speedily
on him, whether *it be* death, or
[8]banishment, or confiscation of
goods, or imprisonment.

27 [w]Blessed[9] *be* the LORD God of our fathers, [x]who has put *such a thing* as this in
the king's heart, to beautify the house of
the LORD which *is* in Jerusalem, 28 and [y]has
extended mercy to me before the king and
his counselors, and before all the king's
mighty princes.
So I was encouraged, as [z]the hand of the
LORD my God *was* upon me; and I gathered
leading men of Israel to go up with me.

Heads of Families Who Returned with Ezra

8 These *are* the heads of their fathers'
houses, and *this is* the genealogy of
those who went up with me from Babylon,
in the reign of King Artaxerxes: 2 of the
sons of Phinehas, Gershom; of the sons of
Ithamar, Daniel; of the sons of David,
[a]Hattush; 3 of the sons of Shecaniah, of the
sons of [b]Parosh, Zechariah; and registered
with him *were* one hundred and fifty
males; 4 of the sons of [c]Pahath-Moab, Eliehoenai the son of Zerahiah, and with him
two hundred males; 5 of [1]the sons of
Shechaniah, Ben-Jahaziel, and with him
three hundred males; 6 of the sons of Adin,
Ebed the son of Jonathan, and with him
fifty males; 7 of the sons of Elam, Jeshaiah
the son of Athaliah, and with him seventy
males; 8 of the sons of Shephatiah, Zebadiah the son of Michael, and with him
eighty males; 9 of the sons of Joab, Obadiah the son of Jehiel, and with him two
hundred and eighteen males; 10 of [2]the
sons of Shelomith, Ben-Josiphiah, and with
him one hundred and sixty males; 11 of the
sons of [d]Bebai, Zechariah the son of Bebai,
and with him twenty-eight males; 12 of the
sons of Azgad, Johanan [3]the son of Hakka-
tan, and with him one hundred and ten
males; 13 of the last sons of Adonikam,
whose names *are* these—Eliphelet, Jeiel,
and Shemaiah—and with them sixty
males; 14 also of the sons of Bigvai, Uthai
and [4]Zabbud, and with them seventy
males.

Servants for the Temple

15 Now I gathered them by the river that
flows to Ahava, and we camped there
three days. And I looked among the people
and the priests, and found none of the
[e]sons of Levi there. 16 Then I sent for Eliezer, Ariel, Shemaiah, Elnathan, Jarib, Elnathan, Nathan, Zechariah, and [f]Me-
shullam, leaders; also for Joiarib and
Elnathan, men of understanding. 17 And I
gave them a command for Iddo the chief
man at the place Casiphia, and [5]I told them
what they should say [6]to Iddo *and* his
brethren the Nethinim at the place Casiphia—that they should bring us servants
for the house of our God. 18 Then, by the
good hand of our God upon us, they
[g]brought us a man of understanding, of
the sons of Mahli the son of Levi, the son of
Israel, namely Sherebiah, with his sons and
brothers, eighteen men; 19 and [h]Hasha-
biah, and with him Jeshaiah of the sons of
Merari, his brothers and their sons, twenty
men; 20 [i]also of the Nethinim, whom David and the leaders had appointed for the
service of the Levites, two hundred and
twenty Nethinim. All of them were designated by name.

Fasting and Prayer for Protection

21 Then I [j]proclaimed a fast there at the
river of Ahava, that we might [k]humble
ourselves before our God, to seek from
Him the [l]right way for us and our little
ones and all our possessions. 22 For [m]I was
ashamed to request of the king an escort of

25 [v] 2 Chr. 17:7; Ezra 7:10; [Mal. 2:7; Col. 1:28]
26 [8] Lit. *rooting out*
27 [w] 1 Chr. 29:10 [x] Ezra 6:22; [Prov. 21:1] [9] The Hebrew language resumes in Ezra 7:27.
28 [y] Ezra 9:9 [z] Ezra 5:5; 7:6, 9; 8:18

CHAPTER 8

2 [a] 1 Chr. 3:22; Ezra 2:68
3 [b] Ezra 2:3
4 [c] Ezra 10:30
5 [1] So with MT, Vg.; LXX *the sons of Zatho, Shechaniah*
10 [2] So with MT, Vg.; LXX *the sons of Banni, Shelomith*
11 [d] Ezra 10:28
12 [3] Or *the youngest son,*
14 [4] Or *Zakkur*
15 [e] Ezra 7:7; 8:2
16 [f] Ezra 10:15
17 [5] Lit. *I put words in their mouths to say* [6] So with Vg.; MT *to Iddo his brother;* LXX *to their brethren*
18 [g] 2 Chr. 30:22; Neh. 8:7
19 [h] Neh. 12:24
20 [i] Ezra 2:43; 7:7
21 [j] 1 Sam. 7:6; 2 Chr. 20:3 [k] Lev. 16:29; 23:29; Is. 58:3, 5 [l] Ps. 5:8
22 [m] 1 Cor. 9:15

embedded was written to Ezra. The king turned to him in a demonstration of administrative trust and granted him permission to appoint magistrates and judges for the region. The effect of this decision would be to offer a measure of local autonomy to the Jews.

8:1-14 from Babylon. The list that follows no doubt includes those who lived in the surrounding areas. The total number of males in this section is 1,496 plus the men named, so with the addition of the women and children the number easily approaches 7–8,000. Just as these had not gone with the first group of returnees, so many Jews remained in Babylon after this group had departed. During the 70 years, many of the exiles had settled into a comfortable lifestyle. No small conflict arose between those who returned and those who stayed in Babylon.

8:15 river...Ahava. An unknown location where a canal/river flowed into the Euphrates. This was in Babylon and chosen for the place where the returning Jews would render vows for several days in preparation to leave. **none...of Levi.** There were no Levites who chose to return so Ezra pursued such needed men by sending a command to Iddo, who was chief of the Nethinim. Iddo's influence brought 38 Levites and 220 Nethinim (vv. 16-20).

8:17 Nethinim. *See note on 2:43-54.*

8:21-23 I proclaimed a fast. They would soon begin the long journey. Such travel was dangerous, for the roads were frequented by thieves who robbed for survival. Even messengers traveled with caravans to ensure their safety. Ezra and the people did not want to confuse the king regarding their trust in God's protection so they entreated Him for safety with a prayerful fast. God honored their prayer of faith with His protection.

soldiers and horsemen to help us against the enemy on the road, because we had spoken to the king, saying, [n]"The hand of our God *is* upon all those for [o]good who seek Him, but His power and His wrath *are* [p]against all those who [q]forsake Him." **23** So we fasted and entreated our God for this, and He [r]answered our prayer.

Gifts for the Temple

24 And I separated twelve of the leaders of the priests—Sherebiah, Hashabiah, and ten of their brethren with them— **25** and weighed out to them [s]the silver, the gold, and the articles, the offering for the house of our God which the king and his counselors and his princes, and all Israel *who were* present, had offered. **26** I weighed into their hand six hundred and fifty talents of silver, silver articles *weighing* one hundred talents, one hundred talents of gold, **27** twenty gold basins *worth* a thousand drachmas, and two vessels of fine polished bronze, precious as gold. **28** And I said to them, "You *are* [t]holy[7] to the LORD; the articles *are* [u]holy also; and the silver and the gold *are* a freewill offering to the LORD God of your fathers. **29** Watch and keep *them* until you weigh *them* before the leaders of the priests and the Levites and [v]heads of the fathers' *houses* of Israel in Jerusalem, *in* the chambers of the house of the LORD." **30** So the priests and the Levites received the silver and the gold and the articles by weight, to bring *them* to Jerusalem to the house of our God.

The Return to Jerusalem

31 Then we departed from the river of Ahava on the twelfth *day* of the first month, to go to Jerusalem. And [w]the hand of our God was upon us, and He delivered us from the hand of the enemy and from ambush along the road. **32** So we [x]came to Jerusalem, and stayed there three days.

33 Now on the fourth day the silver and the gold and the articles were [y]weighed in the house of our God by the hand of Meremoth the son of Uriah the priest, and with him *was* Eleazar the son of Phinehas; with them *were* the Levites, [z]Jozabad the son of Jeshua and Noadiah the son of Binnui, **34** with the number *and* weight of everything. All the weight was written down at that time.

35 The children of those who had been [a]carried away captive, who had come from the captivity, [b]offered burnt offerings to the God of Israel: twelve bulls for all Israel, ninety-six rams, seventy-seven lambs, and twelve male goats *as* a sin offering. All *this was* a burnt offering to the LORD.

36 And they delivered the king's [c]orders to the king's satraps and the governors *in the region* beyond [8]the River. So they gave support to the people and the [9]house of God.

Intermarriage with Pagans

9 When these things were done, the leaders came to me, saying, "The people of Israel and the priests and the Levites have not [a]separated themselves from the peoples of the lands, [b]with respect to the abominations of the Canaanites, the Hittites, the Perizzites, the Jebusites, the Ammonites, the Moabites, the Egyptians, and the Amorites. **2** For they have [c]taken some of their daughters *as wives* for themselves and their sons, so that the [d]holy seed is [e]mixed with the peoples of *those* lands. Indeed, the hand of the leaders and rulers has been foremost in this [1]trespass." **3** So when I heard this thing, [f]I tore my garment

22 [n] Ezra 7:6, 9, 28 [o] [Ps. 33:18, 19; 34:15, 22; Rom. 8:28] [p] [Ps. 34:16] [q] [2 Chr. 15:2]
23 [r] [1 Chr. 5:20]; 2 Chr. 33:13; Is. 19:22
25 [s] Ezra 7:15, 16
28 [t] Lev. 21:6-9; Deut. 33:8 [u] Lev. 22:2, 3; Num. 4:4, 15, 19, 20 [7] *consecrated*
29 [v] Ezra 4:3
31 [w] Ezra 7:6, 9, 28
32 [x] Neh. 2:11
33 [y] Ezra 8:26, 30 [z] Neh. 11:16
35 [a] Ezra 2:1 [b] Ezra 6:17
36 [c] Ezra 7:21-24 [8] The Euphrates [9] Temple

CHAPTER 9

1 [a] Ezra 6:21; Neh. 9:2 [b] Deut. 12:30, 31
2 [c] Ex. 34:16; [Deut. 7:3]; Ezra 10:2; Neh. 13:23 [d] Ex. 22:31; [Deut. 7:6] [e] [2 Cor. 6:14] [1] *unfaithfulness*
3 [f] Job 1:20

8:26 six hundred and fifty talents. Over 25 tons. **one hundred talents.** Almost 4 tons.

8:27 a thousand drachmas. About 20 lbs. *See note on 2:69.*

8:31 Ahava. *See note on v. 15.* **first month.** *See note on 7:8,9.* The 12-day delay occurred because of a 3-day delay searching for more Levites (8:15) and the fast which sought God's protection (8:21).

8:36 they delivered the king's orders. The plural "orders" may account for a change of terminology. This would include the decrees plus other orders in the official correspondence Artaxerxes gave to Ezra to deliver, to support the Jews and their building of the temple.

9:1 When these things were done. This refers to the implementation of the different trusts and duties committed to him. **priests...Levites.** As was the case before the Assyrian and Babylonian deportations, the spiritual leadership defaulted along with the people (cf. Is. 24:2; Jer. 5:30,31; 6:13-15; Hos. 3:9; Mal. 2:1-9; 2 Tim. 4:2-4). **abominations.** The reason for this exclusiveness was to keep the people pure. In the first settlement, Israel was warned not to make covenants with the nations, which would result in intermarriages and inevitably the worship of foreign gods (Ex. 34:10-17; Deut. 7:1-5). To a great extent, the continual violation of this precipitated the 70-year exile from which they had just returned. Ezra found out it had happened again and called for immediate repentance. Nehemiah (Neh. 13:23-27) and Malachi (Mal. 2:14-16) later encountered the same sin. It is unthinkable that the Jews would so quickly go down the same disastrous path of idolatry. Neither wrath from God in the exile to Babylon, nor grace from God in the return was enough to keep them from defecting again. **Canaanites...Amorites.** *See notes on Joshua 3:10.*

9:2 holy seed. The seed of Abraham that God had set apart (cf. Gen. 13:15,16; 17:4-14). It was not to be mixed with other nations; and if so, it violated God's covenant (cf. Deut. 7:2,3). This marriage with Gentile women would bring idolatry into the next generation for certain, so Ezra reacted strongly.

9:3 tore...plucked...sat. An outward expression of a grieving, disturbed spirit over sin (cf. 2 Chr. 34:27) characterized Ezra as he saw the people returning to their old ways which would bring judgment again.

and my robe, and plucked out some of the
hair of my head and beard, and sat down
[g]astonished. 4 Then everyone who [h]trem-
bled at the words of the God of Israel assembled to me, because of the transgression of those who had been carried away
captive, and I sat astonished until the [i]eve-
ning sacrifice.

5 At the evening sacrifice I arose from
my fasting; and having torn my garment
and my robe, I fell on my knees and
[j]spread out my hands to the LORD my God.
6 And I said: "O my God, I am too
[k]ashamed and humiliated to lift up my
face to You, my God; for [l]our iniquities
have risen higher than *our* heads, and our
guilt has [m]grown up to the heavens.
7 Since the days of our fathers to this day
[n]we *have been* very guilty, and for our iniquities [o]we, our kings, *and* our priests have
been delivered into the hand of the kings
of the lands, to the [p]sword, to captivity, to
plunder, and to [q]humiliation,[2] as *it is* this
day. 8 And now for a little while grace has
been *shown* from the LORD our God, to
leave us a remnant to escape, and to give
us a peg in His holy place, that our God
may [r]enlighten our eyes and give us a
measure of revival in our bondage. 9 [s]For
we *were* slaves. [t]Yet our God did not forsake us in our bondage; but [u]He extended
mercy to us in the sight of the kings of Persia, to revive us, to repair the house of our
God, to rebuild its ruins, and to give us [v]a
wall in Judah and Jerusalem. 10 And now,
O our God, what shall we say after this?
For we have forsaken Your commandments, 11 which You commanded by Your
servants the prophets, saying, 'The land
which you are entering to possess is an unclean land, with the [w]uncleanness of the
peoples of the lands, with their abominations which have filled it from one end to
another with their impurity. 12 Now therefore, [x]do not give your daughters as wives
for their sons, nor take their daughters to
your sons; and [y]never seek their peace or
prosperity, that you may be strong and eat
the good of the land, and [z]leave *it* as an inheritance to your children forever.' 13 And
after all that has come upon us for our evil
deeds and for our great guilt, since You our
God [a]have punished us less than our iniquities *deserve,* and have given us *such* deliverance as this, 14 should we [b]again break
Your commandments, and [c]join in marriage with the people *committing* these
abominations? Would You not be [d]angry
with us until You had [3]consumed *us,* so
that *there would be* no remnant or survivor?
15 O LORD God of Israel, [e]You *are* righteous,
for we are left as a remnant, as *it is* this day.
[f]Here we *are* before You, [g]in our guilt,
though no one can stand before You because of this!"

Confession of Improper Marriages

10 Now [a]while Ezra was praying, and
while he was confessing, weeping,
and bowing down [b]before the house of
God, a very large assembly of men,
women, and children gathered to him
from Israel; for the people wept very [c]bit-
terly. 2 And Shechaniah the son of Jehiel,
one of the sons of Elam, spoke up and said
to Ezra, "We have [d]trespassed[1] against
our God, and have taken pagan wives
from the peoples of the land; yet now

3 [g]Ps. 143:4
4 [h]Ezra 10:3; Is. 66:2 [i]Ex. 29:39
5 [j]Ex. 9:29
6 [k]Dan. 9:7, 8 [l]Ps. 38:4 [m]2 Chr. 28:9; [Ezra 9:13, 15]; Rev. 18:5
7 [n]2 Chr. 36:14-17; Ps. 106:6; Dan. 9:5, 6 [o]Deut. 28:36; Neh. 9:30 [p]Deut. 32:25 [q]Dan. 9:7, 8 [2]Lit. *shame of faces*
8 [r]Ps. 34:5
9 [s]Neh. 9:36; Esth. 7:4 [t]Neh. 9:17; Ps. 136:23 [u]Ezra 7:28 [v]Is. 5:2
11 [w]Ezra 6:21
12 [x][Ex. 23:32; 34:15, 16; Deut. 7:3, 4]; Ezra 9:2 [y]Deut. 23:6 [z][Prov. 13:22; 20:7]
13 [a][Ps. 103:10]
14 [b][John 5:14; 2 Pet. 2:20] [c]Neh. 13:23 [d]Deut. 9:8 [3]*destroyed*
15 [e]Neh. 9:33; Dan. 9:14 [f][Rom. 3:19] [g]1 Cor. 15:17

CHAPTER 10

1 [a]Dan. 9:4, 20 [b]2 Chr. 20:9 [c]Neh. 8:1-9
2 [d]Ezra 10:10, 13, 14, 17, 18; Neh. 13:23-27 [1]*been unfaithful to*

9:4 trembled at the words. In contrast to those who participated in the intermarriage, there were those who saw it as an abomination. They greatly feared the Lord's judgment on them again (cf. Is. 66:2,5) and sat with Ezra until the gathering of the people for the evening sacrifice, when there was surely public prayer and confession as Ezra fasted, lamented, and prayed (v. 5) in an effort to lead the leaders and people to repent.

9:5-15 Ezra's priestly prayer of intercession and confession is like Daniel's (Dan. 9:1-20) and Nehemiah's (Neh. 1:4-11), in that he used plural pronouns that identified himself with the people's sin, even though he did not participate in it. The use of "we," "our" and "us" demonstrates Ezra's understanding that the sin of the few is sufficient to contaminate the many.

9:8 a peg in His holy place. A figure of speech that indicated permanence and prominence.

9:8,9 grace...mercy. God had been true to His character and His covenant (cf. Lam. 3:22-23) in restoring Israel, Jerusalem, and the temple.

9:9 a wall. As a people scattered all over the Fertile Crescent, the Jews were vulnerable to the nations. Together in Judah, with God as protector, they were safe. The wall does not exclude the walls of Jerusalem yet to be built, but it speaks more broadly of God's provision for protection.

9:10-12 Your commandments. This is not a quotation of any single text of Scripture, but rather a summation of God's commands on the subject (cf. Ex. 34:15-17; Deut. 7:1-6).

9:13,14 Cf. a similar situation in the first Exodus, when the Israelites engaged in idolatry and immorality led by Aaron, who was then confronted by Moses (Ex. 32:1-35).

9:14 no remnant. Ezra feared that this sin would provoke the ultimate judgment of God and the abrogation of God's unconditional covenants. While God would judge sin, the coming of Messiah and Paul's insights on God's continued faithfulness in His promise to the Jews (Rom. 9–11) assures that God's calling of Israel as a beloved people and nation is irrevocable (Rom. 11:25-29).

9:15 no one can stand before You. All were reckoned guilty and had no right to stand in God's presence, yet they came penitently seeking the grace of forgiveness.

10:1 praying...confessing, weeping, and bowing down. Ezra's contrite spirit before the people was evident and they joined him. These extreme expressions of contrition demonstrate the seriousness of the sin and the genuineness of their repentance.

10:2 Shechaniah. This leader, not involved in the mixed marriages since his name does not appear in the list in vv. 18-44 (though his father and 5 paternal uncles do appear in v. 26), was bold and

there is hope in Israel in spite of this.
3 Now therefore, let us make [e]a covenant
with our God to put away all these wives
and those who have been born to them,
according to the advice of my master and
of those who [f]tremble at [g]the commandment of our God; and let it be done according to the [h]law. 4 Arise, for *this* matter
is your *responsibility.* We also *are* with you.
[i]Be of good courage, and do *it.*"
5 Then Ezra arose, and made the leaders
of the priests, the Levites, and all Israel
[j]swear an oath that they would do according to this word. So they swore an oath.
6 Then Ezra rose up from before the house
of God, and went into the chamber of Jehohanan the son of Eliashib; and *when* he
came there, he [k]ate no bread and drank no
water, for he mourned because of the guilt
of those from the captivity.
7 And they issued a proclamation
throughout Judah and Jerusalem to all the
descendants of the captivity, that they
must gather at Jerusalem, 8 and that whoever would not come within three days, according to the instructions of the leaders
and elders, all his property would be confiscated, and he himself would be separated from the assembly of those from the
captivity.
9 So all the men of Judah and Benjamin
gathered at Jerusalem within three days. It
was the ninth month, on the twentieth of
the month; and [l]all the people sat in the
open square of the house of God, trembling because of *this* matter and because of
heavy rain. 10 Then Ezra the priest stood
up and said to them, "You have [2]trans-
gressed and [3]have taken pagan wives,
adding to the guilt of Israel. 11 Now therefore, [m]make confession to the LORD God of
your fathers, and do His will; [n]separate
yourselves from the peoples of the land,
and from the pagan wives."
12 Then all the assembly answered and
said with a loud voice, "Yes! As you have
said, so we must do. 13 But *there are* many
people; *it is* the season for heavy rain, and
we are not able to stand outside. Nor *is this*
the work of one or two days, for *there are*
many of us who have transgressed in this
matter. 14 Please, let the leaders of our entire assembly stand; and let all those in our
cities who have taken pagan wives come at
appointed times, together with the elders
and judges of their cities, until [o]the fierce
wrath of our God is turned away from us
in this matter." 15 Only Jonathan the son of
Asahel and Jahaziah the son of Tikvah opposed this, and [p]Meshullam and Shabbethai the Levite gave them support.
16 Then the descendants of the captivity
did so. And Ezra the priest, *with* certain
[q]heads of the fathers' *households,* were set
apart by the fathers' *households,* each of
them by name; and they sat down on the
first day of the tenth month to examine the
matter. 17 By the first day of the first month
they finished *questioning* all the men who
had taken pagan wives.

Pagan Wives Put Away

18 And among the sons of the priests
who had taken pagan wives *the following*

3 [e]2 Chr. 34:31 [f]Ezra 9:4 [g]Deut. 7:2, 3 [h]Deut. 24:1, 2
4 [i]1 Chr. 28:10
5 [j]Ezra 10:12, 19; Neh. 5:12; 13:25
6 [k]Deut. 9:18
9 [l]1 Sam. 12:18; Ezra 9:4; 10:3
10 [2]acted unfaithfully [3]Heb. *have caused to dwell* or *have brought back*
11 [m][Lev. 26:40-42]; Josh. 7:19; [Prov. 28:13] [n]Ezra 10:3
14 [o]2 Kin. 23:26; 2 Chr. 28:11-13; 29:10; 30:8
15 [p]Ezra 8:16; Neh. 3:4
16 [q]Ezra 4:3

chose to obey God rather than please his relatives. **hope in Israel in spite of this.** This hope is centered in God's covenant love and forgiveness of truly repentant sinners.

10:3 make a covenant. Shechaniah calls for the people and leaders to accomplish the specific action of divorcing the wives and children and acknowledges that Ezra has counseled a course of action consistent with Scripture (cf. 2 Chr. 29:10). **those who tremble.** Cf. Is. 66:2,5. This refers to those who take the Word of God seriously, especially His judgment on their sin. **according to the law.** They wanted to get in line with God's law as revealed in Deut. 7:2,3.

10:4 your *responsibility.* Ezra is acknowledged as the chief spiritual leader with appropriate divine authority and human responsibility to take on the execution of this formidable task of dealing with divorces for so many (cf. vv. 18-44).

10:5 swear an oath. The oath in relation to the covenant specified in 10:3. Cf. Neh. 10:28-39 for the content of a later oath under similar conditions.

10:7 they issued a proclamation. A proclamation was delivered orally by a herald. It often had the force of law as did this one. Not participating in the assembly, as some might have been tempted to do, meant not just losing your property, but being ostracized from Israel.

10:8 three days. The message had to go out, and the people were required to respond within 72 hours. Since only the territories of Judah and Benjamin were involved, the greatest distance would have been no more than 40–50 mi.

10:9 all the men. Serious consequences highlighted the gravity of the situation, and thus everyone came. **ninth month.** Dec./Jan., the time of the heaviest rains and coldest weather, especially in Jerusalem, which is over 2,500 ft. in elevation.

10:11 confession...separate. Here are the two essential elements of repentance—agreeing with God and taking righteous action to separate from sin.

10:12-14 all...many people. This demonstrates how widespread this sin was among the people. With the heavy rain and the large number of people to be processed, the whole operation could go long, so the people made an administrative suggestion for dealing with the magnitude of the problem. For each unlawful marriage, a questioning or court session could be locally conducted. All of these details had to be treated with great care; thus, delegating the court process was a suggestion much like Jethro's back in the wilderness (cf. Ex. 18).

10:15 opposed this. It is unclear whether these 4 opposed the delay in dealing with the situation or whether they opposed dealing with the sin at all. It was, however, a good plan and brought about a reasonably fast resolution.

10:16,17 tenth month...first month. It took 3 months to rectify the situation in all cases, after which the people were prepared to celebrate Passover with a clear conscience.

were found of the sons of [r]Jeshua the son
of [4]Jozadak, and his brothers: Maaseiah,
Eliezer, Jarib, and Gedaliah. **19** And they
[s]gave their promise that they would put
away their wives; and *being* [t]guilty, *they*
presented a ram of the flock as their [u]tres-
pass offering.

20 Also of the sons of Immer: Hanani
and Zebadiah; **21** of the sons of Harim: Maaseiah, Elijah, Shemaiah, Jehiel, and Uzziah; **22** of the sons of Pashhur: Elioenai,
Maaseiah, Ishmael, Nethanel, Jozabad, and
Elasah.

23 Also of the Levites: Jozabad, Shimei,
Kelaiah (the same *is* Kelita), Pethahiah, Judah, and Eliezer.

24 Also of the singers: Eliashib; and of
the gatekeepers: Shallum, Telem, and Uri.

25 And others of Israel: of the [v]sons of
Parosh: Ramiah, Jeziah, Malchiah, Mijamin,
Eleazar, Malchijah, and Benaiah; **26** of the
sons of Elam: Mattaniah, Zechariah, Jehiel,
Abdi, Jeremoth, and Eliah; **27** of the sons of
Zattu: Elioenai, Eliashib, Mattaniah, Jere-
moth, Zabad, and Aziza; **28** of the [w]sons of
Bebai: Jehohanan, Hananiah, Zabbai, *and*
Athlai; **29** of the sons of Bani: Meshullam,
Malluch, Adaiah, Jashub, Sheal, *and*
[5]Ramoth; **30** of the [x]sons of Pahath-Moab:
Adna, Chelal, Benaiah, Maaseiah, Matta-
niah, Bezalel, Binnui, and Manasseh; **31** *of*
the sons of Harim: Eliezer, Ishijah, Malchijah, Shemaiah, Shimeon, **32** Benjamin,
Malluch, *and* Shemariah; **33** of the sons of
Hashum: Mattenai, Mattattah, Zabad,
Eliphelet, Jeremai, Manasseh, *and* Shimei;
34 of the sons of Bani: Maadai, Amram, Uel,
35 Benaiah, Bedeiah, [6]Cheluh, **36** Vaniah,
Meremoth, Eliashib, **37** Mattaniah, Mattenai,
[7]Jaasai, **38** Bani, Binnui, Shimei, **39** Shelemiah, Nathan, Adaiah, **40** Machnadebai,
Shashai, Sharai, **41** Azarel, Shelemiah, Shemariah, **42** Shallum, Amariah, *and* Joseph; **43** of
the sons of Nebo: Jeiel, Mattithiah, Zabad,
Zebina, [8]Jaddai, Joel, *and* Benaiah.

44 All these had taken pagan wives, and
some of them had wives *by whom* they had
children.

18 [r] Ezra 5:2; Hag. 1:1, 12; 2:4; Zech. 3:1; 6:11 [4] *Jehozadak,* 1 Chr. 6:14
19 [s] 2 Kin. 10:15 [t] Lev. 6:4, 6 [u] Lev. 5:6, 15
25 [v] Ezra 2:3; 8:3; Neh. 7:8
28 [w] Ezra 8:11
29 [5] Or *Jeremoth*
30 [x] Ezra 8:4
35 [6] Or *Cheluhi* or *Cheluhu*
37 [7] Or *Jaasu*
43 [8] Or *Jaddu*

10:18 the sons of Jeshua the son of Jozadak, and his brothers. At the head of the list of those who had intermarried were the descendants and other relatives of the High-Priest who first returned with Zerubbabel and led in the temple reconstruction. They set the example for all the people in giving the appropriate trespass offering (v. 19).

10:18-44 Given the fact that it took 3 months to resolve the situation, this list of 113 men could represent only those in leadership (cf. "many people," 10:13). There were apparently more violators among the people. Even though the problem was dealt with directly, it would eventually reappear (cf. Neh. 9–10; 13).

10:44 An appropriate provision was doubtlessly made for the divorced wives and the children.

The Book of NEHEMIAH

Title

Nehemiah ("Jehovah comforts") is a famous cupbearer, who never appears in Scripture outside of this book. As with the books of Ezra and Esther, named after his contemporaries (see Introductions to Ezra and Esther), the book recounts selected events of his leadership and was titled after him. Both the Greek Septuagint (LXX) and the Latin Vulgate named this book "Second Ezra." Even though the two books of Ezra and Nehemiah are separate in most English Bibles, they may have once been joined together in a single unit as currently in the Hebrew texts. New Testament writers do not quote Nehemiah.

Author and Date

Though much of this book was clearly drawn from Nehemiah's personal diaries and written from his first person perspective (1:1–7:5; 12:27-43; 13:4-31), both Jewish and Christian traditions recognize Ezra as the author. This is based on external evidence that Ezra and Nehemiah were originally one book as reflected in the LXX and Vulgate; it is also based on internal evidence such as the recurrent "hand of the LORD" theme which dominates both Ezra and Nehemiah and the author's role as a priest-scribe. As a scribe, he had access to the royal archives of Persia, which accounts for the myriad of administrative documents found recorded in the two books, especially in the book of Ezra. Very few people would have been allowed access to the royal archives of the Persian Empire, but Ezra proved to be the exception (cf. Ezra 1:2-4; 4:9-22; 5:7-17; 6:3-12).

The events in Nehemiah 1 commence late in the year 446 B.C., the 20th year of the Persian king, Artaxerxes (464–423 B.C.). The book follows chronologically from Nehemiah's first term as governor of Jerusalem ca. 445–433 B.C. (Neh. 1–12) to his second term, possibly beginning ca. 424 B.C. (Neh. 13). Nehemiah was written by Ezra sometime during or after Nehemiah's second term, but no later than 400 B.C.

Background and Setting

True to God's promise of judgment, He brought the Assyrians and Babylonians to deliver His chastisement upon wayward Judah and Israel. In 722 B.C. the Assyrians deported the 10 northern tribes and scattered them all over the then known world (2 Kin. 17). Several centuries later, ca. 605–586 B.C., God used the Babylonians to sack, destroy, and nearly depopulate Jerusalem (2 Kin. 25) because Judah had persisted in her unfaithfulness to the covenant. God chastened His people with 70 years of captivity in Babylon (Jer. 25:11).

During the Jews' captivity, world empire leadership changed hands from the Babylonians to the Persians (ca. 539 B.C.; Dan. 5), after which Daniel received most of his prophetic revelation (cf. Dan. 6,9-12). The book of Ezra begins with the decree of Cyrus, a Persian king, to return God's people to Jerusalem to rebuild God's house (ca. 539 B.C.), and chronicles the reestablishment of Judah's national calendar of feasts and sacrifices. Zerubbabel and Joshua led the first return (Ezra 1–6) and rebuilt the temple. Esther gives a glimpse of the Jews left in Persia (ca. 483–473 B.C.) when Haman attempted to eliminate the Jewish race. Ezra 7–10 recounts the second return led by Ezra in 458 B.C. Nehemiah chronicles the third return to rebuild the wall around Jerusalem (ca. 445 B.C.).

At that time in Judah's history, the Persian Empire dominated the entire Near Eastern world. Its administration of Judah, although done with a loose hand, was mindful of disruptions or any signs of rebellion from its vassals. Rebuilding the walls of conquered cities posed the most glaring threat to the Persian central administration. Only a close confidant of the king himself could be trusted for such an operation. At the most critical juncture in Judah's revitalization, God raised up Nehemiah to exercise one of the most trusted roles in the empire, the King's cupbearer and confidant. Life under the Persian king Artaxerxes (ca. 464–423 B.C.) had its advantages for Nehemiah. Much like Joseph, Esther, and Daniel, he had attained a significant role in the palace which then ruled the ancient world, a position from which God could use him to lead the rebuilding of Jerusalem's walls in spite of its implications for Persian control of that city.

Several other historical notes are of interest. First, Esther was Artaxerxes' stepmother (*see note on*

Esth. 1:9) and could have easily influenced him to look favorably upon the Jews, especially Nehemiah. Second, Daniel's prophetic 70 weeks began with the decree to rebuild the city issued by Artaxerxes in 445 B.C. (cf. chaps. 1,2; *see notes on Dan. 9:24-26*). Third, the Elephantine papyri (Egyptian documents), dated to the late 5th century B.C., support the account of Nehemiah by mentioning Sanballat the governor of Samaria (2:19), Jehohanan (6:18; 12:23), and Nehemiah's being replaced as governor of Jerusalem by Bigvai (ca. 410 B.C; Neh. 10:16). Finally, Nehemiah and Malachi represent the last of the OT canonical writings, both in terms of the time the events occurred (Mal. 1–4; Neh. 13) and the time when they were recorded by Ezra. Thus the next messages from God for Israel do not come until over 400 years of silence had passed, after which the births of John the Baptist and Jesus Christ were announced (Matt. 1; Luke 1,2).

With the full OT revelation of Israel's history prior to Christ's incarnation being completed, the Jews had not yet experienced the fullness of God's various covenants and promises to them. While there was a Jewish remnant, as promised to Abraham (cf. Gen. 15:5), it does not appear to be even as large as at the time of the Exodus (Num. 1:46). The Jews neither possessed the Land (Gen. 15:7) nor did they rule as a sovereign nation (Gen. 12:2). The Davidic throne was unoccupied (cf. 2 Sam. 7:16), although the High-Priest was of the line of Eleazar and Phinehas (cf. Num. 25:10-13). God's promise to consummate the New Covenant of redemption awaited the birth, crucifixion, and resurrection of Messiah (cf. Heb. 7–10).

Historical and Theological Themes

Careful attention to the reading of God's Word in order to perform His will is a constant theme. The spiritual revival came in response to Ezra's reading of "the Book of the Law of Moses" (8:1). After the reading, Ezra and some of the priests carefully explained its meaning to the people in attendance (8:8). The next day, Ezra met with some of the fathers of the households, the priests, and Levites, "in order to understand the words of the Law" (8:13). The sacrificial system was carried on with careful attention to perform it "as *it is* written in the Law" (10:34,36). So deep was their concern to abide by God's revealed will that they took "a curse and an oath to walk in God's Law…" (10:29). When the marriage reforms were carried out, they acted in accordance with that which "they read from the Book of Moses" (13:1).

A second major theme, the obedience of Nehemiah, is explicitly referred to throughout the book due to the fact that the book is based on the memoirs or first person accounts of Nehemiah. God worked through the obedience of Nehemiah; however, He also worked through the wrongly-motivated, wicked hearts of His enemies. Nehemiah's enemies failed, not so much as a result of the success of Nehemiah's strategies, but because "God had brought their plot to nothing" (4:15). God used the opposition of Judah's enemies to drive His people to their knees in the same way that He used the favor of Cyrus to return His people to the Land, to fund their building project, and to even protect the reconstruction of Jerusalem's walls. Not surprisingly, Nehemiah acknowledged the true motive of his strategy to repopulate Jerusalem: "my God put it into my heart" (7:5). It was He who accomplished it.

Another theme in Nehemiah, as in Ezra, is opposition. Judah's enemies started rumors that God's people had revolted against Persia. The goal was to intimidate Judah into forestalling reconstruction of the walls. In spite of opposition from without and heartbreaking corruption and dissension from within, Judah completed the walls of Jerusalem in only 52 days (6:15), experienced revival after the reading of the law by Ezra (8:1ff.), and celebrated the Feast of Tabernacles (8:14ff.; ca. 445 B.C.).

The book's detailed insight into the personal thoughts, motives, and disappointments of Nehemiah makes it easy for the reader to primarily identify with him, rather than "the sovereign hand of God" theme and the primary message of His control and intervention into the affairs of His people and their enemies. But the exemplary behavior of the famous cupbearer is eclipsed by God who orchestrated the reconstruction of the walls in spite of much opposition and many setbacks; the "good hand of God" theme carries through the book of Nehemiah (1:10; 2:8,18).

Interpretive Challenges

First, since much of Nehemiah is explained in relationship to Jerusalem's gates (cf. Neh. 2, 3, 8, 12), one needs to see the map "Jerusalem in Nehemiah's Day" for an orientation. Second, the reader must recognize that the time line of chapters 1–12 encompassed about one year (445 B.C.), followed by a long gap of time (over 20 years) after Neh. 12 and before Neh. 13 (*see "Time Line of Nehemiah"*). Finally, it must be recognized that Nehemiah actually served two governorships in Jerusalem, the first from 445–433 B.C. (cf. Neh. 5:14; 13:6) and the second beginning possibly in 424 B.C. and extending to no longer than 410 B.C.

Esth. 1:9) and could have easily influenced him to look favorably upon the Jews, especially Nehemiah. Second, Daniel's prophetic 70 weeks began with the decree to rebuild the city issued by Artaxerxes in 445 B.C. (cf. chaps. 1:2; see notes on Dan. 9:24–26). Third, the Elephantine papyri (Egyptian documents), dated to the [illegible] the gover- nor of Sam[illegible] of Jerusalem by Bigvai (ca. [illegible] the OT canoni- cal writings [illegible] when they were recorde[illegible] 00 years of silence had p[illegible] nounced (Matt. 1; Luke 1:2).

With the full [illegible] being completed, the Jews had not yet [illegible] While there was a Jewish re[illegible] large as at the time of the [illegible] they rule as a sovereign n[illegible] although the High- Priest was [illegible] consummate the New Cove[illegible] (cf. Heb. 7–10).

Outline

I. Nehemiah's First Term as Governor (1:1–12:47)
   A. Nehemiah's Return and Reconstruction (1:1–7:73a)
      1. Nehemiah goes to Jerusalem (1:1–2:20)
      2. Nehemiah and the people rebuild the walls (3:1–7:3)
      3. Nehemiah recalls the first return under Zerubbabel (7:4-73a)
   B. Ezra's Revival and Renewal (7:73b–10:39)
      1. Ezra expounds the law (7:73b–8:12)
      2. The people worship and repent (8:13–9:37)
      3. Ezra and the priests renew the covenant (9:38–10:39)
   C. Nehemiah's Resettlement and Rejoicing (11:1–12:47)
      1. Jerusalem is resettled (11:1–12:26)
      2. The people dedicate the walls (12:27-47)
II. Nehemiah's Second Term as Governor (13:1-31)

Historical and Theological Themes

Careful [illegible] theme. The spiritual r[illegible] (8:1). After the reading, Ezra and some of the priests carefully explained its meaning to the people in attendance (8:8). The next day, Ezra met with some of the fathers of the households, the priests, and Levites, "in order to understand the words of the Law" (8:13). The sacrificial system was carried on with careful attention to perform it "as it is written in the Law" (10:34,36). So deep was their concern to abide by God's revealed will that they took "a curse and an oath to walk in God's Law..." (10:29). When the marriage reforms were carried out, they acted in accordance with that which "they read from the Book of Moses" (13:1).

A second major theme, the obedience of Nehemiah, is explicitly referred to throughout the book due to the fact that the book is based on the memoirs or first person accounts of Nehemiah. God worked through the obedience of Nehemiah; however, He also worked through the wrongly-motivated, wicked hearts of His enemies. Nehemiah's enemies failed, not so much as a result of the success of Nehemiah's strategies, but because "God had brought their plot to nothing" (4:15). God used the opposition of Judah's enemies to drive His people to their knees in the same way that He used the favor of Cyrus to return His people to the Land, to fund their building project, and to even protect the reconstruction of Jerusalem's walls. Not surprisingly, Nehemiah acknowledged the true motive of his strategy to repopulate Jerusalem: "my God put it into my heart" (7:5). It was He who accomplished it.

Another theme in Nehemiah, as in Ezra, is opposition. Judah's enemies started rumors that God's people had revolted against Persia. The goal was to intimidate Judah into forestalling reconstruction of the walls. In spite of opposition from without and heartbreaking corruption and dissension from within, Judah completed the walls of Jerusalem in only 52 days (6:15), experienced revival after the reading of the law by Ezra (8:1ff.), and celebrated the Feast of Tabernacles (8:14ff.; ca. 445 B.C.).

The book's detailed insight into the personal thoughts, motives, and disappointments of Nehemiah makes it easy for the reader to primarily identify with him, rather than "the sovereign hand of God" theme and the primary message of His control and intervention into the affairs of His people and their enemies. But the exemplary behavior of the famous cupbearer is eclipsed by God who orchestrated the reconstruction of the walls in spite of much opposition and many setbacks; the "good hand of God" theme carries through the book of Nehemiah (1:10; 2:8,18).

Interpretive Challenges

First, since much of Nehemiah is explained in relationship to Jerusalem's gates (cf. Neh. 2, 3, 8, 12), one needs to see the map "Jerusalem in Nehemiah's Day" for an orientation. Second, the reader must recognize that the time line of chapters 1–12 encompassed about one year (445 B.C.), followed by a long gap of time (over 20 years) after Neh. 12 and before Neh. 13 (see "*Time Line of Nehemiah*"). Finally, it must be recognized that Nehemiah actually served two governorships in Jerusalem, the first from 445–433 B.C. (cf. Neh. 5:14; 13:6) and the second beginning possibly in 424 B.C. and extending to no longer than 410 B.C.

Nehemiah Prays for His People

1 The words of [a]Nehemiah the son of
Hachaliah.
It came to pass in the month of Chislev,
in the [b]twentieth year, as I was in [c]Shu-
shan[1] the [2]citadel, 2 that [d]Hanani one of
my brethren came with men from Judah;
and I asked them concerning the Jews who
had escaped, who had survived the captivity, and concerning Jerusalem. 3 And they
said to me, "The survivors who are left
from the captivity in the [e]province *are*
there in great distress and [f]reproach. [g]The
wall of Jerusalem [h]*is* also broken down,
and its gates *are* burned with fire."
4 So it was, when I heard these words,
that I sat down and wept, and mourned *for*
many days; I was fasting and praying before the God of heaven.
5 And I said: "I pray, [i]LORD God of heav-
en, O great and [j]awesome God, [k]*You* who
keep *Your* covenant and mercy with those
who love [3]You and observe [4]Your commandments, 6 please let Your ear be attentive and [l]Your eyes open, that You may
hear the prayer of Your servant which I
pray before You now, day and night, for
the children of Israel Your servants, and
[m]confess the sins of the children of Israel
which we have sinned against You. Both
my father's house and I have sinned. 7 [n]We
have acted very corruptly against You, and
have [o]not kept the commandments, the
statutes, nor the ordinances which You

CHAPTER 1

1 [a] Neh. 10:1 [b] Neh. 2:1 [c] Esth. 1:1, 2, 5; Dan. 8:2 [1] Or *Susa* [2] Or *fortified palace,* and so elsewhere in the book
2 [d] Neh. 7:2
3 [e] Neh. 7:6 [f] Neh. 2:17 [g] Neh. 2:17 [h] 2 Kin. 25:10
5 [i] Dan. 9:4 [j] Neh. 4:14 [k] [Ex. 20:6; 34:6, 7]; Ps. 89:2, 3 [3] Lit. *Him* [4] Lit. *His*
6 [l] 1 Kin. 8:28, 29; 2 Chr. 6:40; Dan. 9:17, 18 [m] Ezra 10:1; Neh. 9:2; Dan. 9:20
7 [n] Ps. 106:6; Dan. 9:5 [o] Deut. 28:15

1:1–7:73a Nehemiah returns to Jerusalem and successfully leads a 52 day "rebuilding of the wall" project (cf. 6:15).

1:1–2:20 This section details how Nehemiah became the governor of Judah (cf. 5:14; 8:9; 10:1; 12:26).

1:1 The words of Nehemiah. The personal records of this famous royal cupbearer, whose name means "Jehovah comforts," (cf. 3:16; 7:7; 8:9; 10:1; 12:26,47) contribute greatly to this book. Unlike Esther and Mordecai, named after Mesopotamian deities Ishtar and Marduk, Nehemiah was given a Heb. name. **Hachaliah.** Nehemiah's father is mentioned again in Neh. 10:1, but nowhere else in the OT. **Chislev.** This is in Nov./Dec. 446 B.C., 4 months before Nisan (Mar./Apr.), when Nehemiah came before the king to get permission to go to Jerusalem (2:1). **twentieth year.** The 20th year (ca. 446/445 B.C.) in the reign of Persian king Artaxerxes (ca. 464–423 B.C.; cf. 2:1). **Shushan.** Also known as Susa, this city was situated E of Babylon, about 150 mi. N of the Persian Gulf. Shushan was one of the Medo-Persian strongholds, a wintering city for many officials, and the setting of Esther.

1:2 Hanani. Apparently a sibling of Nehemiah (cf. 7:2), he had gone to Jerusalem in the second return under Ezra's leadership (ca. 458 B.C.). **Jews...Jerusalem.** Nehemiah was deeply concerned about the people and the city, especially during the previous 13 years, since the second return under Ezra (458 B.C.).

1:3 wall of Jerusalem...gates. The opposition had successfully thwarted the Jews' attempts to reestablish Jerusalem as a distinctively Jewish city capable of withstanding its enemies' assaults, which could possibly lead to another destruction of the newly rebuilt temple (ca. 516 B.C.; cf. Ezra 4:7-23).

1:4 sat down and wept, and mourned *for many* days. Although Nehemiah was neither a prophet nor a priest, he had a deep sense of Jerusalem's significance to God and was greatly distressed that affairs there had not advanced the cause and glory of God.

1:5-11 This prayer represents one of the Scripture's most moving confessions and intercessions before God (cf. Dan. 9:4-19; Ezra 9:6-15).

1:5 keep *Your* covenant and mercy with those who love You. After 70 years of captivity in Babylon, God kept His promise to restore His people to the Promised Land. The promise appeared to be failing, and Nehemiah appealed to God's character and covenant as the basis by which He must intervene and accomplish His pledges to His people.

1:6 we have sinned against You. Nehemiah may have believed that the sins of the returnees (cf. Ezra 9,10) had prompted God to change His mind and withhold His favor from the Jews.

1:7 commandments...statutes...ordinances. Those which are recorded in Exodus, Leviticus, Numbers, and Deuteronomy.

Time Line of Nehemiah

Reference	Date		Event
1:1,4	Nov./Dec.	446 B.C. (Kislev)	Nehemiah hears of problems and prays.
2:1,5	Mar./Apr.	445 B.C. (Nisan)	Nehemiah is dispatched to Jerusalem.
3:1; 6:15	July/Aug.	445 B.C. (Ab)	Nehemiah starts the wall.
6:15	Aug./Sept.	445 B.C. (Elul)	Nehemiah completes the wall.
7:73b	Sept./Oct.	445 B.C. (Tishri)	Day of Trumpets celebrated (implied).
8:13-15	Sept./Oct.	445 B.C. (Tishri)	Feast of Tabernacles celebrated.
9:1	Sept./Oct.	445 B.C. (Tishri)	Time of confession.
12:27	Sept./Oct.	445 B.C. (Tishri)	Wall dedicated.
13:6		445-433 B.C.	Nehemiah's first term as governor (Neh. 1-12).
13:6		433-424 B.C. (?)	Nehemiah returns to Persia.
No ref.		433-? B.C.	Malachi prophesies in Jerusalem during Nehemiah's absence.
13:1,4,7		424-? B.C.	Nehemiah returns and serves a second term as governor (Neh. 13).

commanded Your servant Moses. 8 Remember, I pray, the word that You commanded Your servant Moses, saying, [p]'If
you [5]are unfaithful, I will scatter you
among the nations; 9 [q]but *if* you return to
Me, and keep My commandments and do
them, [r]though some of you were cast out to
the farthest part of the heavens, *yet* I will
gather them from there, and bring them to
the place which I have chosen as a dwelling
for My name.' 10 [s]Now these *are* Your servants and Your people, whom You have redeemed by Your great power, and by Your
strong hand. 11 O Lord, I pray, please [t]let
Your ear be attentive to the prayer of Your
servant, and to the prayer of Your servants
who [u]desire to fear Your name; and let Your
servant prosper this day, I pray, and grant
him mercy in the sight of this man."
For I was the king's [v]cupbearer.

Nehemiah Sent to Judah

2 And it came to pass in the month of
Nisan, in the twentieth year of [a]King
[1]Artaxerxes, *when* wine *was* before him,
that [b]I took the wine and gave it to the
king. Now I had never been sad in his
presence before. 2 Therefore the king said
to me, "Why *is* your face sad, since you *are*
not sick? This *is* nothing but [c]sorrow of
heart."
So I became [2]dreadfully afraid, 3 and
said to the king, [d]"May the king live forever! Why should my face not be sad, when
[e]the city, the place of my fathers' tombs,
lies waste, and its gates are burned with
[f]fire?"
4 Then the king said to me, "What do
you request?"
So I [g]prayed to the God of heaven. 5 And
I said to the king, "If it pleases the king,
and if your servant has found favor in
your sight, I ask that you send me to Judah, to the city of my fathers' tombs, that I
may rebuild it."
6 Then the king said to me (the queen
also sitting beside him), "How long will
your journey be? And when will you return?" So it pleased the king to send me;
and I set him [h]a time.
7 Furthermore I said to the king, "If it
pleases the king, let letters be given to me

8 [p] Lev. 26:33; Deut. 4:25-27; 28:63-67 [5] *act treacherously*
9 [q] Lev. 26:39; [Deut. 4:29-31; 30:2-5] [r] Deut. 30:4
10 [s] Ex. 32:11; Deut. 9:29; Dan. 9:15
11 [t] Neh. 1:6 [u] Is. 26:8; [Heb. 13:18] [v] Gen. 40:21; Neh. 2:1

CHAPTER 2

1 [a] Ezra 7:1 [b] Neh. 1:11 [1] Artaxerxes Longimanus
2 [c] Prov. 15:13 [2] Lit. *very much*
3 [d] 1 Kin. 1:31; Dan. 2:4; 5:10; 6:6, 21 [e] 2 Kin. 25:8-10; 2 Chr. 36:19; Jer. 52:12-14 [f] 2 Kin. 24:10; Neh. 1:3
4 [g] Neh. 1:4
6 [h] Neh. 5:14; 13:6

1:8 Remember. Not a reminder to God as if He had forgotten, but a plea to activate His Word.

1:8,9 the word...Moses. This represents a summary of various Mosaic writings. On "scattering" (v. 8) see Deut. 4:25-28; 28:63-65. On "regathering" see Deut. 4:29-31; 30:1-5.

1:10 redeemed by Your great power, and by Your strong hand. His allusion to the Exodus redemption recalled the faithful and strong hand of God which had brought Israel out of bondage once before and grounded his confidence in God's power as the basis of his appeal for a second deliverance that will be as successful as the first.

1:11 who desire to fear Your name. Nehemiah alluded to the fact that Israel was the place which God had chosen for His name to dwell (1:9); the people desired to fear His name and, thus, were praying for God's intervention. **in the sight of this man.** The reference to King Artaxerxes anticipated the discussion in 2:1ff. **the king's cupbearer.** As an escort of the monarch at meals, the cupbearer had a unique advantage to petition the king. Not only did the king owe him his life since the cupbearer tested all the king's beverages for possible poison, thus putting his own life at risk, but he also became a close confidant. God sovereignly used this relationship between a Gentile and Jew to deliver His people, such as He did with Joseph, Daniel, Esther, and Mordecai.

2:1 Nisan. Mar./Apr. 545 B.C. **twentieth year.** *See note on 1:1.* ***when* wine *was* before him.** Since the act of tasting wine to ensure it was not dangerous to the king strengthened the trust between king and cupbearer, this was the appropriate time for Nehemiah to win Artaxerxes' attention and approval. Not surprisingly, kings often developed so much trust in their cupbearers that the latter became counselors to the kings. **Now I had never been sad.** Sadness was a dangerous emotion to express in the king's presence. The king wanted his subjects to be happy, since this reflected the well-being brought about by his administrative prowess.

2:2 dreadfully afraid. He feared that either his countenance, his explanation, or his request would anger the king and thus lead to his death (cf. Esth. 4:11 with 5:1-3).

2:3 tombs...gates. Nehemiah's deep concern and sadness over the condition of Jerusalem and his people was expressed in his reference to tombs and gates. A tomb was a place to show respect for dead community members who birthed the living generation and passed on their spiritual values to them. Tombs were also the place where the present generation hoped to be honored by burial at death. Gates were emblematic of the life of the city, since the people gathered for judicial procedure or basic social interaction near the gates. The burned gates represented the death of social life, i.e., the end of a community of people.

2:4 What do you request? The king rightly interpreted Nehemiah's sad countenance as a desire to take action on behalf of his people and homeland. His immediate response to the king's question illustrates how continual his prayer life was (cf. 1:6). **God of heaven.** *See note on Ezra 1:2.*

2:5 that I may rebuild it. The request undeniably referred to the city walls, for there could be no permanence without walls, but it also may have included political and administrative rebuilding as well.

2:6 the queen. Since Esther was the queen of the previous king Ahasuerus (Xerxes) ca. 486–464 B.C. and the stepmother of Artaxerxes, it could be that she had previously influenced the present king and queen to be favorably disposed to the Jews. **return.** This presupposes that Nehemiah was being dispatched on his desired mission and upon its completion would return to Persia (cf. Neh. 13:6).

2:7 let letters be given to me. Official letters transferred a portion of the king's authority to Nehemiah. In this context, he needed to pass through the lands of Judah's enemies who could harm him or prevent him from rebuilding Jerusalem. The roads upon which messengers, ambassadors, and envoys of all sorts traveled had stations where such letters could be inspected for passage. Three months of travel from Susa to Jerusalem was long, dangerous, and ridden with protocol where letters were required for passage. The danger associated with the passage, but particularly the administrative authority which Nehemiah carried in the letters, led Artaxerxes to send captains of the army and horsemen with Nehemiah for protection (2:9). *See notes on Ezra 1:11; 7:8,9.*

for the [i]governors *of the region* beyond [3]the
River, that they must permit me to pass
through till I come to Judah, **8** and a letter
to Asaph the keeper of the king's forest,
that he must give me timber to make
beams for the gates of the [4]citadel which
pertains [j]to the [5]temple, for the city wall,
and for the house that I will occupy." And
the king granted *them* to me [k]according to
the good hand of my God upon me.

9 Then I went to the governors *in the region* beyond the River, and gave them the
king's letters. Now the king had sent captains of the army and horsemen with me.
10 When [l]Sanballat the Horonite and Tobiah
the Ammonite [6]official heard *of it*, they were
deeply disturbed that a man had come to
seek the well-being of the children of Israel.

Nehemiah Views the Wall of Jerusalem

11 So I [m]came to Jerusalem and was
there three days. **12** Then I arose in the
night, I and a few men with me; I told no
one what my God had put in my heart to
do at Jerusalem; nor was there any animal
with me, except the one on which I rode.
13 And I went out by night [n]through the
Valley Gate to the Serpent Well and the
[7]Refuse Gate, and [8]viewed the walls of Jerusalem which were [o]broken down and its
gates which were burned with fire. **14** Then
I went on to the [p]Fountain Gate and to the
[q]King's Pool, but *there was* no room for the
animal under me to pass. **15** So I went up in
the night by the [r]valley,[9] and [1]viewed the
wall; then I turned back and entered by the
Valley Gate, and so returned. **16** And the
officials did not know where I had gone or
what I had done; I had not yet told the
Jews, the priests, the nobles, the officials,
or the others who did the work.

17 Then I said to them, "You see the distress that we *are* in, how Jerusalem *lies*
[2]waste, and its gates are burned with fire.
Come and let us build the wall of Jerusalem,
that we may no longer be [s]a reproach."
18 And I told them of [t]the hand of my God
which had been good upon me, and also of
the king's words that he had spoken to me.

So they said, "Let us rise up and build."
Then they [u]set[3] their hands to *this* good
work.

19 But when Sanballat the Horonite, Tobiah the Ammonite official, and Geshem
the Arab heard *of it*, they laughed at us and
despised us, and said, "What *is* this thing
that you are doing? [v]Will you rebel against
the king?"

20 So I answered them, and said to them,
"The God of heaven Himself will prosper

7 [i]Ezra 7:21; 8:36 [3]The Euphrates
8 [j]Neh. 3:7 [k]Ezra 5:5; 7:6, 9, 28; Neh. 2:18 [4]*palace* [5]Lit. *house*
10 [l]Neh. 2:19; 4:1 [6]Lit. *servant*
11 [m]Ezra 8:32
13 [n]2 Chr. 26:9; Neh. 3:13 [o]Neh. 1:3; 2:17 [7]*Dung* [8]*examined*
14 [p]Neh. 3:15 [q]2 Kin. 20:20
15 [r]2 Sam. 15:23; Jer. 31:40 [9]*torrent valley, wadi* [1]*examined*
17 [s]Neh. 1:3; Ps. 44:13; 79:4; Jer. 24:9; Ezek. 5:14, 15; 22:4 [2]*desolate*
18 [t]Neh. 2:8 [u]2 Sam. 2:7 [3]Lit. *strengthened*
19 [v]Neh. 6:6

2:8 and a letter to Asaph the keeper of the king's forest. Lumber was a very precious commodity. This is illustrated in a document from one ancient city in Mesopotamia in which a forest official is taken to court for cutting down a tree. Forests were carefully guarded, and written permission from the king would assure Nehemiah of the lumber he would need to build the citadel, wall reinforcements, and his own residence from which he would administrate the reconstruction. **citadel.** This edifice located next to the temple on the NW side was a fortified building for the purpose of guarding the temple. It was subsequently rebuilt by Herod and named Antonia. **the good hand of my God upon me.** This refrain is common to both Ezra and Nehemiah. It is a frequent reminder in these inspired books that God works through His servants to accomplish His will (cf. Ezra 1:5; 7:6).

2:9–3:1 The journey from Persia to Jerusalem and the preparation period was to be 3–4 months (cf. 2:1 with 6:15).

2:9 I went to the governors. Nehemiah's encroachment upon their provincial control posed a tremendous threat to these officials. If handled improperly, disregard for the other local officials would have put Nehemiah's life and the lives of those in Jerusalem in jeopardy. To prevent such a reaction, God had moved the Persian king to dispatch royal army captains and horsemen to accompany Nehemiah and to guard against such attacks.

2:10 Sanballat...Tobiah. These men were probably also behind the opposition described in Ezra 4:7-23 which stopped the work in Jerusalem. Sanballat served as governor of Samaria (Horonaim being a town in Moab, he was probably a Moabite) and Tobiah of the region E of the Jordan. These district magistrates were leaders of Samaritan factions (see chap. 6) to the N and E. They had lost any recourse to prevent Judah from rebuilding since God's people were authorized to fortify their settlement against attack from enemies such as these two officials. To overtly attack or oppose the Jews would be to oppose the Persian king.

2:11-16 Nehemiah spent 3 days discerning what course to follow before informing anyone of his plan; then, he wisely viewed the terrain in secret and surveyed the southern end of the city, noting the broken and burnt conditions of the walls and gates.

2:13,15 Valley Gate. Nehemiah began and ended his trip at the same spot (cf. 3:13) on the W side.

2:13 Serpent Well. The exact location is unknown, although it is somewhere in the southern section of Jerusalem. **Refuse Gate.** A.k.a. Dung Gate. At the southern tip of the city (cf. 3:13; 12:31) a common sewer ran to the Kidron Brook into the Valley of Hinnom.

2:14 Fountain Gate. The exact location is unknown, although it was somewhere in the southern section of Jerusalem, probably on the E side. **King's Pool.** Possibly the pool of Siloam (cf. 3:15).

2:15 the valley. The Kidron Valley, running N and S to the E of the temple mount.

2:17 we may no longer be a reproach. The destruction of the city by Nebuchadnezzar brought great reproach upon Israel, but particularly upon their God. Nehemiah assured the Jews (v. 20) that because God would prosper them in this endeavor for His glory, they should move ahead.

2:18 The sight of Nehemiah's credentials and his motivating message revived their drooping spirits to begin the building despite the bitter taunts of influential men (vv. 19,20).

2:19 Sanballat...Tobiah. *See note on 2:10.* **Geshem the Arab.** This ruler most likely officiated to the S of Jerusalem.

2:20 God of heaven. Cf. Neh. 1:5 and *see note on Ezra 1:2.* Not only did Nehemiah have the king's permission and was not rebelling, but he had God's protection. Those enemies who tried to intimidate against the work had neither, since they were not commissioned by God or the king.

us; therefore we His servants will arise and build, [w]but you have no heritage or right or memorial in Jerusalem."

Rebuilding the Wall

3 Then [a]Eliashib the high priest rose up with his brethren the priests [b]and built the Sheep Gate; they consecrated it and hung its doors. They built [c]as far as the Tower of [1]the Hundred, *and* consecrated it, then as far as the Tower of [d]Hananel.
2 [2]Next to *Eliashib* [e]the men of Jericho built. And next to them Zaccur the son of Imri built.
3 Also the sons of Hassenaah built [f]the Fish Gate; they laid its beams and [g]hung its doors with its bolts and bars. 4 And next to them [h]Meremoth the son of Urijah, the son of [3]Koz, made repairs. Next to them [i]Meshullam the son of Berechiah, the son of Meshezabel, made repairs. Next to them Zadok the son of Baana made repairs.
5 Next to them the Tekoites made repairs; but their nobles did not put their [4]shoulders to [j]the work of their Lord.
6 Moreover Jehoiada the son of Paseah and Meshullam the son of Besodeiah repaired [k]the Old Gate; they laid its beams and hung its doors, with its bolts and bars.
7 And next to them Melatiah the Gibeonite,

20 [w] Ezra 4:3; Neh. 6:16

CHAPTER 3

1 [a] Neh. 3:20; 12:10; 13:4, 7, 28 [b] John 5:2 [c] Neh. 12:39 [d] Jer. 31:38; Zech. 14:10 [1] Heb. *Hammeah*
2 [e] Ezra 2:34; Neh. 7:36 [2] Lit. *On his hand*
3 [f] 2 Chr. 33:14; Neh. 12:39; Zeph. 1:10 [g] Neh. 6:1; 7:1
4 [h] Ezra 8:33 [i] Ezra 10:15 [3] Or *Hakkoz*
5 [j] [Judg. 5:23] [4] Lit. *necks*
6 [k] Neh. 12:39

3:1–7:3 A detailed account of rebuilding the wall is given.

3:1 Eliashib the high priest. The grandson of Jeshua the High-Priest in Zerubbabel's era (cf. Neh. 12:10). **built.** On the fourth of Ab, (Jul./Aug.) 445 B.C. (cf. 6:15). **Sheep Gate.** This is located in the NE section of Jerusalem (cf. 3:32; 12:39). The narrative moves around the perimeter of Jerusalem in a counterclockwise direction. **Tower of the Hundred...Tower of Hananel.** This northern section of Jerusalem opened up to the central Benjamin plateau where enemy forces could attack most easily from the N. The rest of the perimeter of the city was protected by the natural valley topography.

3:3 Fish Gate. So named because merchants sold fish on the northern side of Jerusalem. Men of Tyre and other seacoast towns routinely brought fish to sell (cf. 12:39; 13:16).

3:5 nobles did not put their shoulders to the work of their Lord. One explanation, beyond just the laziness of the rich, is that these nobles had been pledged to Tobiah for personal gain (6:17-19).

3:6 the Old Gate. Believed to be in the NW corner of Jerusalem (cf. 12:39).

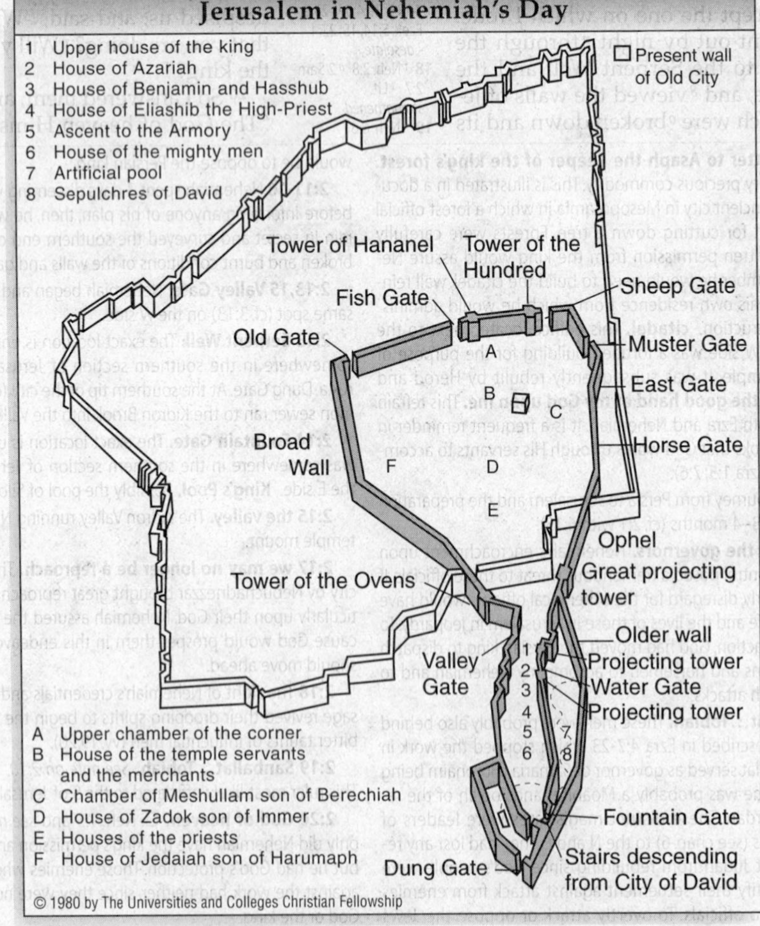

Jadon the Meronothite, the [l]men of Gibeon
and Mizpah, repaired the [m]residence[5] of
the governor *of the region* [6]beyond the
River. 8 Next to him Uzziel the son of Har-
haiah, one of the goldsmiths, made repairs.
Also next to him Hananiah, [7]one of the
perfumers, made repairs; and they [8]forti-
fied Jerusalem as far as the [n]Broad Wall.
9 And next to them Rephaiah the son of
Hur, leader of half the district of Jerusalem,
made repairs. 10 Next to them Jedaiah the
son of Harumaph made repairs in front of
his house. And next to him Hattush the son
of Hashabniah made repairs.

11 Malchijah the son of Harim and
Hashub the son of Pahath-Moab repaired
another section, [o]as well as the Tower of
the Ovens. 12 And next to him was Shallum the son of Hallohesh, leader of half the
district of Jerusalem; he and his daughters
made repairs.

13 Hanun and the inhabitants of Zanoah
repaired [p]the Valley Gate. They built it,
hung its doors with its bolts and bars, and
repaired a thousand cubits of the wall as far
as [q]the Refuse Gate.

14 Malchijah the son of Rechab, leader of
the district of [r]Beth Haccerem, repaired the
Refuse Gate; he built it and hung its doors
with its bolts and bars.

15 Shallun the son of Col-Hozeh, leader
of the district of Mizpah, repaired [s]the
Fountain Gate; he built it, covered it, hung
its doors with its bolts and bars, and repaired the wall of the Pool of [t]Shelah[9] by
the [u]King's Garden, as far as the stairs that
go down from the City of David. 16 After
him Nehemiah the son of Azbuk, leader of
half the district of Beth Zur, made repairs
as far as *the place* in front of the [1]tombs of
David, to the [v]man-made pool, and as far
as the House of the Mighty.

17 After him the Levites, *under* Rehum the
son of Bani, made repairs. Next to him
Hashabiah, leader of half the district of Keilah, made repairs for his district. 18 After
him their brethren, *under* [2]Bavai the son of
Henadad, leader of the *other* half of the district of Keilah, made repairs. 19 And next to
him Ezer the son of Jeshua, the leader of
Mizpah, repaired another section in front of
the Ascent to the Armory at the [w]buttress.[3]
20 After him Baruch the son of [4]Zabbai carefully repaired the other section, from the
[5]buttress to the door of the house of Eliashib
the high priest. 21 After him Meremoth the
son of Urijah, the son of [6]Koz, repaired another section, from the door of the house of
Eliashib to the end of the house of Eliashib.

22 And after him the priests, the men of
the plain, made repairs. 23 After him Benjamin and Hasshub made repairs opposite
their house. After them Azariah the son of
Maaseiah, the son of Ananiah, made repairs by his house. 24 After him [x]Binnui
the son of Henadad repaired another section, from the house of Azariah to [y]the
[7]buttress, even as far as the corner. 25 Palal
the son of Uzai *made repairs* opposite the
[8]buttress, and on the tower which projects
from the king's upper house that *was* by
the [z]court of the prison. After him Pedaiah
the son of Parosh *made repairs.*

26 Moreover [a]the Nethinim who dwelt
in [b]Ophel *made repairs* as far as *the place* in
front of [c]the Water Gate toward the east,
and on the projecting tower. 27 After them
the Tekoites repaired another section, next
to the great projecting tower, and as far as
the wall of Ophel.

28 Beyond the [d]Horse Gate the priests
made repairs, each in front of his *own* house.
29 After them Zadok the son of Immer made
repairs in front of his *own* house. After him
Shemaiah the son of Shechaniah, the keeper
of the East Gate, made repairs. 30 After him
Hananiah the son of Shelemiah, and Hanun,
the sixth son of Zalaph, repaired another
section. After him Meshullam the son of Berechiah made repairs in front of his [9]dwell-
ing. 31 After him Malchijah, [1]one of the
goldsmiths, made repairs as far as the house
of the Nethinim and of the merchants, in
front of the [2]Miphkad Gate, and as far as the
upper room at the corner. 32 And between
the upper room at the corner, as far as the
[e]Sheep Gate, the goldsmiths and the merchants made repairs.

7 [l] Neh. 7:25 [m] Ezra 8:36; Neh. 2:7-9 [5] Lit. *throne* [6] West of the Euphrates
8 [n] Neh. 12:38 [7] Lit. *the son* [8] *restored*
11 [o] Neh. 12:38
13 [p] Neh. 2:13, 15 [q] Neh. 2:13
14 [r] Jer. 6:1
15 [s] Neh. 2:14 [t] Is. 8:6; John 9:7 [u] 2 Kin. 25:4 [9] Or *Shiloah*
16 [v] 2 Kin. 20:20; Is. 7:3; 22:11 [1] LXX, Syr., Vg. *tomb*
18 [2] So with MT, Vg.; some Heb. mss., LXX, Syr. *Binnui* (cf. v. 24)
19 [w] 2 Chr. 26:9 [3] Lit. *turning*
20 [4] A few Heb. mss., Syr., Vg. *Zaccai* [5] Lit. *turning*
21 [6] Or *Hakkoz*
24 [x] Ezra 8:33 [y] Neh. 3:19 [7] Lit. *turning*
25 [z] Jer. 32:2; 33:1; 37:21 [8] Lit. *turning*
26 [a] Ezra 2:43; Neh. 11:21 [b] 2 Chr. 27:3 [c] Neh. 8:1, 3; 12:37
28 [d] 2 Kin. 11:16; 2 Chr. 23:15; Jer. 31:40
30 [9] Lit. *room*
31 [1] Lit. *a son of the goldsmiths* [2] Lit. *Inspection* or *Recruiting*
32 [e] Neh. 3:1; 12:39

3:8 the Broad Wall. On the western side of the northern sector (cf. 12:38).

3:11 Tower of the Ovens. On the western side of Jerusalem (cf. 12:38).

3:13 the Valley Gate. *See note on 2:13,15.* **the Refuse Gate.** *See note on 2:13.*

3:15 Pool of Shelah. *See note on 2:14.* **the King's Garden.** In the SE sector.

3:16 tombs of David. Cf. 2:5. Presumably in the SE sector. **House of the Mighty.** This location is probably associated with David's mighty men (cf. 2 Sam. 23:8-39).

3:19 the Armory. Located on the eastern side of Jerusalem.

3:26 Ophel. An area S of the temple mount, near the Water Gate, where the Nethinim lived (cf. 2 Chr. 27:3; 33:14; Neh. 11:21). **the Water Gate.** Near the Gihon Spring on the E side of Jerusalem (cf. 8:16; 12:37).

3:28 the Horse Gate. In the NE sector.

3:29 the East Gate. Possibly located to the E of the temple mount.

3:31 the Miphkad Gate. In the NE sector.

3:32 the Sheep Gate. Having traveled around Jerusalem in a counterclockwise direction, the narrative ends where it began (cf. 3:1; 12:39).

The Wall Defended Against Enemies

4 But it so happened, [a]when Sanballat
heard that we were rebuilding the wall,
that he was furious and very indignant, and
mocked the Jews. 2 And he spoke before his
brethren and the army of Samaria, and said,
"What are these feeble Jews doing? Will
they fortify themselves? Will they offer sacrifices? Will they complete it in a day? Will
they revive the stones from the heaps of
rubbish—*stones* that are burned?"
3 Now [b]Tobiah the Ammonite *was* beside him, and he said, "Whatever they
build, if even a fox goes up *on it,* he will
break down their stone wall."
4 [c]Hear, O our God, for we are despised;
[d]turn their reproach on their own heads,
and give them as plunder to a land of captivity! 5 [e]Do not cover their iniquity, and
do not let their sin be blotted out from before You; for they have provoked *You* to
anger before the builders.
6 So we built the wall, and the entire
wall was joined together up to half its
height, for the people had a mind to work.
7 Now it happened, [f]when Sanballat, Tobiah, [g]the Arabs, the Ammonites, and the
Ashdodites heard that the walls of Jerusalem were being restored and the [1]gaps were
beginning to be closed, that they became
very angry, 8 and all of them [h]conspired together to come *and* attack Jerusalem and
create confusion. 9 Nevertheless [i]we made
our prayer to our God, and because of them
we set a watch against them day and night.
10 Then Judah said, "The strength of the
laborers is failing, and *there is* so much rubbish that we are not able to build the wall."
11 And our adversaries said, "They will
neither know nor see anything, till we
come into their midst and kill them and
cause the work to cease."
12 So it was, when the Jews who dwelt
near them came, that they told us ten
times, "From whatever place you turn, *they
will be* upon us."
13 Therefore I positioned *men* behind the
lower parts of the wall, at the openings;
and I set the people according to their families, with their swords, their spears, and
their bows. 14 And I looked, and arose and
said to the nobles, to the leaders, and to the
rest of the people, [j]"Do not be afraid of
them. Remember the Lord, [k]great and
awesome, and [l]fight for your brethren,
your sons, your daughters, your wives,
and your houses."
15 And it happened, when our enemies
heard that it was known to us, and [m]*that*
God had brought their plot to nothing, that
all of us returned to the wall, everyone to
his work. 16 So it was, from that time on,
that half of my servants worked at construction, while the other half held the

CHAPTER 4
1 [a] Neh. 2:10, 19
3 [b] Neh. 2:10, 19
4 [c] Ps. 123:3, 4 [d] Ps. 79:12; Prov. 3:34
5 [e] Ps. 69:27, 28; 109:14, 15; Jer. 18:23
7 [f] Neh. 4:1 [g] Neh. 2:19 [1] Lit. *breaks*
8 [h] Ps. 83:3-5
9 [i] [Ps. 50:15]
14 [j] [Num. 14:9]; Deut. 1:29 [k] [Deut. 10:17] [l] 2 Sam. 10:12
15 [m] Job 5:12

4:1-23 This section describes the intimidation and opposition to the project.

4:2 the army of Samaria. While it is a possibility that his intentions were to provoke the military force to action, since that would have brought the Persian overlord down on Samaria swiftly, harassment and mockery (v. 3) became the primary strategy to prevent the reconstruction of the walls.

4:4,5 Nehemiah's dependence on his sovereign God is never more evident than in his prayer (cf. 1:5-11; 2:4).

4:7,8 the Ashdodites. Added to the list of enemies already given are the dwellers of Ashdod, one of the former Philistine cities to the W of Jerusalem. Apparently they came to the point where they were at least contemplating a full-scale attack on Jerusalem because of the rapid progress of the wall.

4:9 The Jews exhibited a balance between faith in God and readiness, employing some of the wall builders as guards.

4:10 so much rubbish. Lit. "dust," the term refers to the rubble or ruins of the prior destruction (586 B.C.), which they had to clear away before they could make significant progress on the rebuilding of the walls.

4:11,12 Part of the strategy of the enemy coalition was to frighten and intimidate the Jews by making them think their army would soon surprise them with a massive force that would quickly engulf them.

4:13-15 positioned *men*. Nehemiah and the others had received word that Sanballat had mustered the army of Samaria (4:2). In fact, God made sure the strategy was known by letting the nearby Jews know, so they would report it to Judah's leaders. Though vigilant, armed, and ready, Nehemiah and those he led consistently gave God the glory for their victories and construction successes.

4:16-18a The threats cut the work force in half, and even those who worked carried weapons in case of attack (cf. v. 21).

Seven Attempts to Stop Nehemiah's Work

1. 2:19	Sanballat, Tobiah, and Geshem mocked Nehemiah.
2. 4:1-3	Sanballat and Tobiah mocked Nehemiah.
3. 4:7-23	The enemy threatened a military attack.
4. 6:1-4	Sanballat and Geshem attempted to lure Nehemiah outside of Jerusalem to Ono.
5. 6:5-9	Sanballat threatened Nehemiah with false charges.
6. 6:10-14	Shemaiah, Noadiah, and others were paid to prophesy falsely and discredit Nehemiah.
7. 6:17-19	Tobiah had spies in Jerusalem and wrote Nehemiah letters in order to frighten him.

spears, the shields, the bows, and *wore*
armor; and the leaders [2]*were* behind all the
house of Judah. 17 Those who built on the
wall, and those who carried burdens,
loaded themselves so that with one hand
they worked at construction, and with the
other held a weapon. 18 Every one of the
builders had his sword girded at his side
as he built. And the one who sounded the
trumpet *was* beside me.
19 Then I said to the nobles, the rulers, and
the rest of the people, "The work *is* great and
extensive, and we are separated far from
one another on the wall. 20 Wherever you
hear the sound of the trumpet, rally to us
there. [n]Our God will fight for us."
21 So we labored in the work, and half of
[3]*the men* held the spears from daybreak
until the stars appeared. 22 At the same
time I also said to the people, "Let each
man and his servant stay at night in Jerusalem, that they may be our guard by night
and a working party by day." 23 So neither
I, my brethren, my servants, nor the men of
the guard who followed me took off our
clothes, *except* that everyone took them off
for washing.

Nehemiah Deals with Oppression

5 And there was a great [a]outcry of the
people and their wives against their
[b]Jewish brethren. 2 For there were those
who said, "We, our sons, and our daughters *are* many; therefore let us get grain,
that we may eat and live."
3 There were also *some* who said, "We
have mortgaged our lands and vineyards
and houses, that we might buy grain because of the famine."
4 There were also those who said, "We
have borrowed money for the king's tax *on*
our lands and vineyards. 5 Yet now [c]our
flesh *is* as the flesh of our brethren, our
children as their children; and indeed we
[d]are forcing our sons and our daughters to
be slaves, and *some* of our daughters have
been brought into slavery. *It is* not in our
power *to redeem them,* for other men have
our lands and vineyards."
6 And I became very angry when I heard
their outcry and these words. 7 After serious thought, I rebuked the nobles and
rulers, and said to them, [e]"Each of you is
[1]exacting usury from his brother." So I
[2]called a great assembly against them.
8 And I said to them, "According to our
ability we have [f]redeemed our Jewish
brethren who were sold to the nations.
Now indeed, will you even sell your
brethren? Or should they be sold to us?"
Then they were silenced and found nothing *to say.* 9 Then I said, "What you are doing
is not good. Should you not walk [g]in the fear
of our God [h]because of the reproach of the
nations, our enemies? 10 I also, *with* my
brethren and my servants, am lending them
money and grain. Please, let us stop this
[3]usury! 11 Restore now to them, even this
day, their lands, their vineyards, their olive
groves, and their houses, also a hundredth
of the money and the grain, the new wine
and the oil, that you have charged them."

16 [2] Supported
20 [n] Ex. 14:14,25; Deut. 1:30; 3:22; 20:4; Josh. 23:10; 2 Chr. 20:29
21 [3] Lit. *them*

CHAPTER 5

1 [a] Lev. 25:35-37; Neh. 5:7,8 [b] Deut. 15:7
5 [c] Is. 58:7 [d] Ex. 21:7; [Lev. 25:39]
7 [e] [Ex. 22:25; Lev. 25:36; Deut. 23:19, 20]; Ezek. 22:12 [1] *charging interest* [2] Lit. *held*
8 [f] Lev. 25:48
9 [g] Lev. 25:36 [h] 2 Sam. 12:14; Rom. 2:24; [1 Pet. 2:12]
10 [3] *interest*

4:18b-20 trumpet. Among other functions, trumpets were used to sound an alarm in the event of danger or to summon soldiers to battle. Nehemiah kept a trumpeter at his side always, so that the alarm could be sounded immediately. His plan also included perpetual diligence (vv. 22,23).

5:1-13 Enemy opposition and difficult times in general had precipitated economic conditions which had a devastating effect on Judah's fragile life. The effect of this extortion on the morale of the returnees was worse than the enemy opposition.

5:1-5 Jewish brethren. Perhaps this refers again to the nobles who would not work and had alliances with the enemies (*see note on 3:5*). The people were fatigued with hard labor, drained by the relentless harassment of enemies, poor and lacking the necessities of life, lacking tax money and borrowing for it, and working on the wall in the city rather than getting food from the country. On top of this came complaints against the terrible exploitation and extortion by the rich Jews who would not help, but forced people to sell their homes and children, while having no ability to redeem them back. Under normal conditions, the law offered the hope of releasing these young people through the remission of debts which occurred every 7 years or in the 50th year of Jubilee (Lev. 25). The custom of redemption made it possible to "buy back" the enslaved individual at almost any time, but the desperate financial situation of those times made that appear impossible.

5:7 I rebuked the nobles and rulers. The commitment of the nobles and rulers to the reconstruction project was negligible (cf. 3:5), while their loyalty to Tobiah and others in opposition added to their opportunistic attitudes, placing them close to the status of opposition. They had become the enemy from within. **exacting usury.** Usury can refer to normal interest or it can signify excessive interest. According to Mosaic law, the Jews were forbidden to take interest from their brothers on the loan of money, food, or anything else. If the person was destitute, they should consider it a gift. If they could pay it back later, it was to be without interest (see Lev. 25:36,37; Deut. 23:19,20). Such generosity marked the godly (see Ps. 15:5; Jer. 15:10; cf. Prov. 28:8). Interest could be taken from foreigners (v. 20). Interest loans were known to exceed 50 percent at times in ancient nations. Such usury took advantage of people's desperation and was virtually impossible to repay, consuming their entire family assets and reducing the debtors to permanent slavery. *See notes on Deut. 28:19,20; 24:10-13.*

5:8 we have redeemed. Nehemiah denounced with just severity the evil conduct of selling a brother by means of usury. He contrasted it with his own action of redeeming with his own money some of the Jewish exiles, who through debt had lost their freedom in Babylon.

5:10 I also. Nehemiah set the example again by making loans, but not in exacting usury.

5:11 Restore now to them. To remedy the evil that they had brought, those guilty of usury were to return the property they had confiscated from those who couldn't pay the loans back, as well as returning the interest they had charged (*see notes on Luke 19:1-10*).

12 So they said, "We will restore *it*, and
will require nothing from them; we will do
as you say."
Then I called the priests, [i]and required
an oath from them that they would do according to this promise. **13** Then [j]I shook
out [4]the fold of my garment and said, "So
may God shake out each man from his
house, and from his property, who does
not perform this promise. Even thus may
he be shaken out and emptied."
And all the assembly said, "Amen!" and
praised the LORD. [k]Then the people did according to this promise.

The Generosity of Nehemiah

14 Moreover, from the time that I was appointed to be their governor in the land of
Judah, from the twentieth year [l]until the
thirty-second year of King Artaxerxes,
twelve years, neither I nor my brothers
[m]ate the governor's provisions. **15** But the
former governors who *were* before me laid
burdens on the people, and took from
them bread and wine, besides forty shekels
of silver. Yes, even their servants bore rule
over the people, but [n]I did not do so, because of the [o]fear of God. **16** Indeed, I also
continued the [p]work on this wall, and [5]we
did not buy any land. All my servants *were*
gathered there for the work.
17 And [q]at my table *were* one hundred
and fifty Jews and rulers, besides those
who came to us from the nations around
us. **18** Now *that* [r]which was prepared
daily *was* one ox *and* six choice sheep.
Also fowl were prepared for me, and
once every ten days an abundance of all
kinds of wine. Yet in spite of this [s]I did
not demand the governor's provisions,
because the bondage was heavy on this
people.
19 [t]Remember me, my God, for good, *according to* all that I have done for this people.

Conspiracy Against Nehemiah

6 Now it happened [a]when Sanballat, Tobiah, [1]Geshem the Arab, and the rest of
our enemies heard that I had rebuilt the
wall, and *that* there were no breaks left in it
[b](though at that time I had not hung the
doors in the gates), **2** that Sanballat and
[2]Geshem [c]sent to me, saying, "Come, let
us meet together [3]among the villages in
the plain of [d]Ono." But they [e]thought to do
me harm.
3 So I sent messengers to them, saying,
"I *am* doing a great work, so that I cannot
come down. Why should the work cease
while I leave it and go down to you?"
4 But they sent me this message four
times, and I answered them in the same
manner.
5 Then Sanballat sent his servant to me
as before, the fifth time, with an open letter
in his hand. **6** In it *was* written:

It is reported among the nations,
and [4]Geshem says, *that* you and

12 [i] Ezra 10:5; Jer. 34:8,9
13 [j] Matt. 10:14; Acts 13:51; 18:6 [k] 2 Kin. 23:3 [4] Lit. *my lap*
14 [l] Neh. 2:1; 13:6 [m] [1 Cor. 9:4-15]
15 [n] 2 Cor. 11:9; 12:13 [o] Neh. 5:9
16 [p] Neh. 4:1; 6:1 [5] So with MT; LXX, Syr., Vg. *I*
17 [q] 2 Sam. 9:7; 1 Kin. 18:19
18 [r] 1 Kin. 4:22
[s] Neh. 5:14,15
19 [t] 2 Kin. 20:3; Neh. 13:14,22,31

CHAPTER 6

1 [a] Neh. 2:10,19; 4:1,7; 13:28 [b] Neh. 3:1,3 [1] Or *Gashmu*
2 [c] Prov. 26:24,25 [d] 1 Chr. 8:12; Neh. 11:35 [e] Ps. 37:12,32 [2] Or *Gashmu* [3] Or in *Kephirim*, exact location unknown
6 [4] Heb. *Gashmu*

5:12 an oath. The consciences of the guilty were struck by Nehemiah's words, so that their fear, shame, and contrition caused them to pledge the release of their loans and restore property and interest, including setting slaves free. This cancellation of debt had a profoundly unifying effect on both sides of the indebtedness. The proceedings were formally consummated with the people binding themselves by a solemn oath from the priests (with them as administrators) that they would be faithful to the pledge.

5:13 shook out the fold. This curse rite from the governor, Nehemiah, called down God's wrath upon anyone who would not follow through with his commitment to release debts. The people agreed and did as they had promised.

5:14 twentieth year. *See notes on 1:1; 2:1.* **thirty-second year.** The year Nehemiah returned to Artaxerxes in Persia (ca. 433 B.C.; cf. 13:6). **ate the governor's provisions.** This refers to the provisions from the Persian administration, but from which he had chosen not to partake because it would have to come from taxing his poverty-stricken people (v. 15). The statement is testimony to the wealth of Nehemiah gained as the king's cupbearer in Persia. Verses 17,18 record that he supported 150 men with abundant provisions who ruled with him (and their families), indicating the personal wealth he had brought from Babylon.

5:15 forty shekels. Approximately one lb. of silver. **because of the fear of God.** Nehemiah would not exact usury from his fellow countrymen as his predecessors had, because he viewed it as an act of disobedience toward God.

5:16 we did not buy any land. Even though the time to purchase property from those forced to sell couldn't have been better, Nehemiah maintained a consistent personal policy not to take advantage of another's distress. He worked on the wall rather than spending his time building personal wealth.

5:18 governor's provisions. *See note on 5:14.* In the ancient Near East, it was customary to calculate the expense of a king's establishment, not by the quantity of money, but by the quantity of his provisions (cf. 1 Kin. 4:22; 18:19; Eccl. 5:11).

5:19 Remember me. The first of 4 such prayers (cf. 13:14,22,31).

6:1 Sanballat, Tobiah, Geshem. *See notes on 2:10,19.*

6:2 sent to me. This suggests either a letter or an oral message delivered by messenger to Nehemiah. Satisfied that they could not prevent Nehemiah's project from succeeding by open military engagement (*see note on 4:13-15*), they decided to overcome him by deception. **plain of Ono.** Located S of Joppa on the western extremity of Judah along the seacoast.

6:3 So I sent messengers. Because he knew they were luring him into a trap, he sent representatives, who themselves might have been killed or imprisoned for ransom.

6:5 open letter. Official letters were typically rolled up and sealed with an official signet by the letter's sender or one of his assisting officials. An open or unsealed letter was not only a sign of disrespect and open criticism, but also suggested the information therein was public knowledge. The goal of this document was to intimidate Nehemiah into stopping the work.

6:6 It is reported among the nations. The letter suggested that Nehemiah's intent to revolt was common knowledge which would

the Jews plan to rebel; therefore,
according to these rumors, you are
rebuilding the wall, [f]that you may
be their king. 7 And you have also
appointed prophets to proclaim
concerning you at Jerusalem,
saying, "*There is* a king in Judah!"
Now these matters will be reported
to the king. So come, therefore, and
let us consult together.

8 Then I sent to him, saying, "No such
things as you say are being done, but you
invent them in your own heart."
9 For they all *were trying to* make us
afraid, saying, "Their hands will be weakened in the work, and it will not be done."
Now therefore, O *God,* strengthen my
hands.
10 Afterward I came to the house of Shemaiah the son of Delaiah, the son of Mehetabel, who *was* a secret informer; and he
said, "Let us meet together in the house of
God, within the [5]temple, and let us close
the doors of the temple, for they are coming to kill you; indeed, at night they will
come to kill you."
11 And I said, "Should such a man as I
flee? And who *is there* such as I who would
go into the temple to save his life? I will
not go in!" 12 Then I perceived that God
had not sent him at all, but that [g]he pronounced *this* prophecy against me because
Tobiah and Sanballat had hired him. 13 For
this reason he *was* hired, that I should be
afraid and act that way and sin, so *that*
they might have *cause* for an evil report,
that they might reproach me.
14 [h]My God, remember Tobiah and Sanballat, according to these their works, and
the [i]prophetess Noadiah and the rest of
the prophets who would have made me
afraid.

The Wall Completed

15 So the wall was finished on the twenty-fifth *day* of Elul, in fifty-two days. 16 And
it happened, [j]when all our enemies heard *of*
it, and all the nations around us saw *these*
things, that they were very disheartened in
their own eyes; for [k]they perceived that this
work was done by our God.
17 Also in those days the nobles of Judah
sent many letters to Tobiah, and *the letters*
of Tobiah came to them. 18 For many in Judah were pledged to him, because he was
the [l]son-in-law of Shechaniah the son of
Arah, and his son Jehohanan had married
the daughter of [m]Meshullam the son of
Berechiah. 19 Also they reported his good
deeds before me, and reported my [6]words
to him. Tobiah sent letters to frighten me.

7 Then it was, when the wall was built
and I had [a]hung the doors, when the
gatekeepers, the singers, and the Levites
had been appointed, 2 that I gave the
charge of Jerusalem to my brother [b]Hanani,
and Hananiah the leader [c]of the [1]citadel,

6 [f] Neh. 2:19
10 [5] Lit. *house*
12 [g] Ezek. 13:22
14 [h] Neh. 13:29 [i] Ezek. 13:17
16 [j] Neh. 2:10, 20; 4:1, 7; 6:1 [k] Ps. 126:2
18 [l] Neh. 13:4, 28 [m] Ezra 10:15; Neh. 3:4
19 [6] Or *affairs*

CHAPTER 7

1 [a] Neh. 6:1, 15
2 [b] Neh. 1:2 [c] Neh. 2:8; 10:23 [1] *palace*

get back to the king of Persia if he didn't come to the requested conference. **you and the Jews plan to rebel.** This information would have brought Persian troops against the Jews had it been true. Even though Judah had a reputation for breaking its allegiances with its overlord kings, on this occasion that was not the case. **rebuilding the wall, that you may be their king.** Artaxerxes had commissioned the rebuilding of the wall based on his relationship of trust with Nehemiah. Once the project was accomplished, the king expected Nehemiah to return to Susa. Allegations that Nehemiah was fortifying the city so that he might be made king would seriously violate the Persian king's trust, if not create a war. The plot was an attempt to intimidate Nehemiah with the idea that a wedge was to be driven between Nehemiah and Artaxerxes so that Nehemiah would come to the meeting with those enemies—a meeting that would have featured his death.

6:7 appointed prophets to proclaim. If there were such prophets, Sanballat actually hired them to feed incorrect information generating the false rumor (cf. 6:10-14). By dispatching such prophets to make public proclamations that Nehemiah had made himself king, the Persian imperial rule would have appeared to be supplanted.

6:10 secret informer. When the open letter failed to intimidate Nehemiah into stopping the work and coming to a meeting, his enemies decided to try intimidation from within. They hired a false prophet (v. 12), Shemaiah, to lure Nehemiah into the Holy Place in the temple for refuge from a murder plot. To enter and shut himself in the Holy Place would have been a desecration of the house of God and would have caused people to question his reverence for God. Shemaiah was the son of a priest who was an intimate friend of Nehemiah. This plan would give them grounds to raise an evil report against Nehemiah, who was not a priest and had no right to go into the Holy Place (cf. 6:13). It could also make the people question his courage (v. 11). Other disloyal Jews included: 1) the nobles (3:5; 6:17); 2) Jews who lived near Sanballat (4:12); 3) Noadiah (6:14); 4) Meshullam (6:17-19); 5) Eliashib (13:4,7); and 6) the High-Priest's grandson (13:28). **the house of God.** This is a frequently used name for the temple (cf. 8:16; 10:32-39; 11:11,16,22; 12:40; 13:4,7,9,11,14).

6:15 Elul. Aug./Sept., 445 B.C. Knowing that the project lasted 52 days, it commenced on the fourth of Ab (Jul./Aug.) 445 B.C.

6:16 this work was done by our God. While modern readers might be tempted to exalt the leadership qualities which brought the work to completion, Nehemiah's conclusion was seen through the eyes of his enemies, i.e., God works through faithful people, but it is God who works. This is a change from the attitudes indicated in 4:1 and 5:9.

6:17-19 the nobles of Judah sent many letters to Tobiah. Nehemiah added a footnote that in the days of building the wall, the nobles of Judah who refused to work (3:5) were in alliance and correspondence with Tobiah because, although his ancestors were Ammonites (2:19), he had married into a respectable Jewish family. Shemaiah was from the family of Arah (Ezra 2:5); his son Jehohanan was the son-in-law of Meshullam who shared in the work of building (3:4,30). According to 13:4, the High-Priest, Eliashib, was related to Tobiah (which is a Jewish name). The meddling of these nobles, by trying to play both sides through reports to Tobiah and to Nehemiah (v. 19), only widened the breach as Tobiah escalated efforts to frighten the governor.

7:2 Hanani. Cf. 1:2. **the citadel.** *See note on 2:8.*

for he *was* a faithful man and [d]feared God
more than many.
3 And I said to them, "Do not let the
gates of Jerusalem be opened until the sun
is hot; and while they stand *guard*, let them
shut and bar the doors; and appoint
guards from among the inhabitants of Jerusalem, one at his watch station and another in front of his own house."

The Captives Who Returned to Jerusalem

4 Now the city *was* large and spacious,
but the people in it *were* [e]few, and the
houses *were* not rebuilt. 5 Then my God put
it into my heart to gather the nobles, the
rulers, and the people, that they might be
registered by genealogy. And I found a register of the genealogy of those who had
come up in the first *return*, and found written in it:

6 [f]These *are* the people of the
province who came back from the
captivity, of those who had been
carried away, whom Nebuchadnezzar the king of Babylon had
carried away, and who returned to
Jerusalem and Judah, everyone to
his city.

7 Those who came with [g]Zerubbabel
were Jeshua, Nehemiah, [2]Azariah,
Raamiah, Nahamani, Mordecai,
Bilshan, [3]Mispereth, Bigvai,
Nehum, and Baanah.

The number of the men of the
people of Israel: 8 the sons of
Parosh, two thousand one hundred
and seventy-two;
9 the sons of Shephatiah, three
hundred and seventy-two;
10 the sons of Arah, six hundred
and fifty-two;
11 the sons of Pahath-Moab, of the
sons of Jeshua and Joab, two
thousand eight hundred and
eighteen;
12 the sons of Elam, one thousand
two hundred and fifty-four;
13 the sons of Zattu, eight hundred
and forty-five;
14 the sons of Zaccai, seven
hundred and sixty;
15 the sons of [4]Binnui, six hundred
and forty-eight;
16 the sons of Bebai, six hundred
and twenty-eight;
17 the sons of Azgad, two thousand
three hundred and twenty-two;
18 the sons of Adonikam, six
hundred and sixty-seven;
19 the sons of Bigvai, two thousand
and sixty-seven;
20 the sons of Adin, six hundred
and fifty-five;
21 the sons of Ater of Hezekiah,
ninety-eight;
22 the sons of Hashum, three
hundred and twenty-eight;
23 the sons of Bezai, three hundred
and twenty-four;
24 the sons of [5]Hariph, one
hundred and twelve;
25 the sons of [6]Gibeon, ninety-five;
26 the men of Bethlehem and Netophah, one hundred and eighty-
eight;
27 the men of Anathoth, one
hundred and twenty-eight;
28 the men of [7]Beth Azmaveth,
forty-two;
29 the men of [8]Kirjath Jearim, Chephirah, and Beeroth, seven
hundred and forty-three;
30 the men of Ramah and Geba, six
hundred and twenty-one;
31 the men of Michmas, one
hundred and twenty-two;
32 the men of Bethel and Ai, one
hundred and twenty-three;
33 the men of the other Nebo, fifty-
two;
34 the sons of the other [h]Elam, one
thousand two hundred and fifty-
four;
35 the sons of Harim, three
hundred and twenty;
36 the sons of Jericho, three
hundred and forty-five;
37 the sons of Lod, Hadid, and Ono,
seven hundred and twenty-one;
38 the sons of Senaah, three
thousand nine hundred and thirty.

39 The priests: the sons of [i]Jedaiah, of
the house of Jeshua, nine hundred
and seventy-three;

2 [d]Ex. 18:21
4 [e]Deut. 4:27
6 [f]Ezra 2:1-70
7 [g]Ezra 5:2; Neh. 12:1, 47; Matt. 1:12, 13
[2]*Seraiah*, Ezra 2:2
[3]*Mispar*, Ezra 2:2

15 [4]*Bani*, Ezra 2:10
24 [5]*Jorah*, Ezra 2:18
25 [6]*Gibbar*, Ezra 2:20
28 [7]*Azmaveth*, Ezra 2:24
29 [8]*Kirjath Arim*, Ezra 2:25
34 [h]Neh. 7:12
39 [i]1 Chr. 24:7

7:3 In the ancient Near East, it was customary to open the city gates at sunrise and close them at sunset. Nehemiah recommended that this not be done, because of the hostility of the enemies. Rather the gates were to be kept shut until well into the heat of the morning when everyone was up and active. When the gates were shut, they were to be guarded by sentinels at watch stations and in front of their own vulnerable homes (v. 4).

7:5a my God put it into my heart. Throughout the book, Nehemiah claimed the hand of God was at work in all circumstances (cf. 2:8,18; 6:16; 7:5).

7:5b,6 I found a register. Nehemiah discovered a register of the people made by Ezra in Babylon before the first group returned, a listing of the people who had come with Zerubbabel.

7:6-73a Nehemiah gave the list of those in the first return from

40 the sons of [j]Immer, one
thousand and fifty-two;
41 the sons of [k]Pashhur, one
thousand two hundred and forty-
seven;
42 the sons of [l]Harim, one
thousand and seventeen.

43 The Levites: the sons of Jeshua, of
Kadmiel,
and of the sons of [9]Hodevah,
seventy-four.

44 The singers: the sons of Asaph, one
hundred and forty-eight.

45 The gatekeepers: the sons of
Shallum,
the sons of Ater,
the sons of Talmon,
the sons of Akkub,
the sons of Hatita,
the sons of Shobai, one hundred
and thirty-eight.

46 The Nethinim: the sons of Ziha,
the sons of Hasupha,
the sons of Tabbaoth,
47 the sons of Keros,
the sons of [1]Sia,
the sons of Padon,
48 the sons of [2]Lebana,
the sons of [3]Hagaba,
the sons of [4]Salmai,
49 the sons of Hanan,
the sons of Giddel,
the sons of Gahar,
50 the sons of Reaiah,
the sons of Rezin,
the sons of Nekoda,
51 the sons of Gazzam,
the sons of Uzza,
the sons of Paseah,
52 the sons of Besai,
the sons of Meunim,
the sons of [5]Nephishesim,
53 the sons of Bakbuk,
the sons of Hakupha,
the sons of Harhur,
54 the sons of [6]Bazlith,
the sons of Mehida,
the sons of Harsha,
55 the sons of Barkos,
the sons of Sisera,
the sons of Tamah,
56 the sons of Neziah,
and the sons of Hatipha.

57 The sons of Solomon's servants:
the sons of Sotai,
the sons of Sophereth,
the sons of [7]Perida,
58 the sons of Jaala,
the sons of Darkon,
the sons of Giddel,
59 the sons of Shephatiah,
the sons of Hattil,
the sons of Pochereth of Zebaim,
and the children of [8]Amon.
60 All the Nethinim, and the sons
of Solomon's servants, *were* three
hundred and ninety-two.

61 And these *were* the ones who came
up from Tel Melah, Tel Harsha,
Cherub, [9]Addon, and Immer, but
they could not identify their
father's house nor their lineage,
whether they *were* of Israel: 62 the
sons of Delaiah,
the sons of Tobiah,
the sons of Nekoda, six hundred
and forty-two;
63 and of the priests: the sons of
Habaiah,
the sons of [1]Koz,
the sons of Barzillai, who took a
wife of the daughters of Barzillai
the Gileadite, and was called by
their name.
64 These sought their listing *among*
those who were registered by
genealogy, but it was not found;
therefore they were excluded from
the priesthood as defiled. 65 And
the [2]governor said to them that
they should not eat of the most holy
things till a priest could consult
with the Urim and Thummim.

66 Altogether the whole assembly *was*
forty-two thousand three hundred
and sixty, 67 besides their male and
female servants, of whom *there*
were seven thousand three hundred
and thirty-seven; and they had two
hundred and forty-five men and
women singers. 68 Their horses
were seven hundred and thirty-six,
their mules two hundred and
forty-five, 69 *their* camels four
hundred and thirty-five, *and*

40 [j] 1 Chr. 9:12
41 [k] Ezra 2:38; 10:22
42 [l] 1 Chr. 24:8
43 [9] *Hodaviah,* Ezra 2:40; or *Judah,* Ezra 3:9
47 [1] *Siaha,* Ezra 2:44
48 [2] MT *Lebanah* [3] MT *Hogabah* [4] *Shalmai,* Ezra 2:46; or *Shamlai*
52 [5] *Nephusim,* Ezra 2:50
54 [6] *Bazluth,* Ezra 2:52
57 [7] *Peruda,* Ezra 2:55
59 [8] *Ami,* Ezra 2:57
61 [9] *Addan,* Ezra 2:59
63 [1] Or *Hakkoz*
65 [2] Heb. *Tirshatha*

Persia to Jerusalem under Zerubbabel in 538 B.C. *See notes on Ezra 2:1-70.* Minor discrepancies are possibly due to Ezra listing those who intended to depart, while Nehemiah listed those who actually arrived; or some other unknown reason.

7:65 consult with the Urim and Thummim. One of the methods used to discern the will of God on a specific matter. *See note on Ex. 28:30.*

donkeys six thousand seven
hundred and twenty.

70 And some of the heads of the
fathers' houses gave to the work.
[m]The [3]governor gave to the
treasury one thousand gold
drachmas, fifty basins, and five
hundred and thirty priestly
garments. 71 Some of the heads of
the fathers' *houses* gave to the
treasury of the work [n]twenty
thousand gold drachmas, and two
thousand two hundred silver
minas. 72 And that which the rest
of the people gave *was* twenty
thousand gold drachmas, two
thousand silver minas, and sixty-
seven priestly garments.

73 So the priests, the Levites, the gatekeepers, the singers, *some* of the people, the
Nethinim, and all Israel dwelt in their
cities.

Ezra Reads the Law

[o]When the seventh month came, the
children of Israel *were* in their cities.
8 Now all [a]the people gathered together
as one man in the open square that
was [b]in front of the Water Gate; and they
told Ezra the [c]scribe to bring the Book of
the Law of Moses, which the LORD had
commanded Israel. 2 So Ezra the priest
brought [d]the Law before the assembly of
men and women and all who *could* hear
with understanding [e]on the first day of the
seventh month. 3 Then he [f]read from it in
the open square that *was* in front of the
Water Gate [1]from morning until midday,
before the men and women and those who
could understand; and the ears of all the
people *were attentive* to the Book of the
Law.
4 So Ezra the scribe stood on a platform
of wood which they had made for the purpose; and beside him, at his right hand,
stood Mattithiah, Shema, Anaiah, Urijah,
Hilkiah, and Maaseiah; and at his left hand
Pedaiah, Mishael, Malchijah, Hashum,
Hashbadana, Zechariah, *and* Meshullam.
5 And Ezra opened the book in the sight of
all the people, for he was *standing* above all
the people; and when he opened it, all the
people [g]stood up. 6 And Ezra blessed the
LORD, the great God.
Then all the people [h]answered, "Amen,
Amen!" while [i]lifting up their hands. And
they [j]bowed their heads and worshiped
the LORD with *their* faces to the ground.
7 Also Jeshua, Bani, Sherebiah, Jamin,
Akkub, Shabbethai, Hodijah, Maaseiah,
Kelita, Azariah, Jozabad, Hanan, Pelaiah,
and the Levites, [k]helped the people to understand the Law; and the people [l]*stood* in
their place. 8 So they read distinctly from
the book, in the Law of God; and they gave
the sense, and helped *them* to understand
the reading.
9 [m]And Nehemiah, who *was* the [2]gover-
nor, Ezra the priest *and* scribe, and the
Levites who taught the people said to all
the people, [n]"This day *is* holy to the LORD
your God; [o]do not mourn nor weep." For
all the people wept, when they heard the
words of the Law.

70 [m] Neh. 8:9 [3] Heb. *Tirshatha*
71 [n] Ezra 2:69
73 [o] Ezra 3:1

CHAPTER 8

1 [a] Ezra 3:1 [b] Neh. 3:26 [c] Ezra 7:6
2 [d] [Deut. 31:11, 12]; Neh. 8:9 [e] Lev. 23:24; Num. 29:1-6
3 [f] Deut. 31:9-11; 2 Kin. 23:2

[1] Lit. *from the light*
5 [g] Judg. 3:20; 1 Kin. 8:12-14
6 [h] Neh. 5:13; [1 Cor. 14:16] [i] Ps. 28:2; Lam. 3:41; 1 Tim. 2:8 [j] Ex. 4:31; 12:27; 2 Chr. 20:18
7 [k] Lev. 10:11; Deut. 33:10; 2 Chr. 17:7; [Mal. 2:7] [l] Neh. 9:3
9 [m] Ezra 2:63; Neh. 7:65, 70; 10:1 [n] Lev. 23:24; Num. 29:1 [o] Deut. 16:14; Eccl. 3:4 [2] Heb. *Tirshatha*

7:73b–10:39 God gave revival under Ezra's spiritual leadership.

7:73b–8:12 The revival began with an exposition of God's Word.

7:73b seventh month. The month of Tishri (Sept./Oct.), 445 B.C., less than one week after completing the walls (cf. 6:15). The Feast of Tabernacles usually began on the fifteenth day (cf. 6:14 with Lev. 23:33-44), but here it began on the second (cf. 8:13), and it was a feast to which the whole nation was called. Usually the Feast of Trumpets occurred on the first day (cf. Lev 23:23-25).

8:1,2 the Book…the Law. In response to the people's request, Ezra brought the law of the Lord, which he had set his heart to study, practice, and teach to the people (cf. Ezra 7:10). At this time, the law was a scroll, as opposed to a text consisting of bound pages. Such a reading was required every 7 years at the Feast of Tabernacles (cf. Deut. 31:10-13), even though it had been neglected since the Babylonian captivity until this occasion.

8:1 the Water Gate. *See note on 3:26.* **Ezra.** This is the first mention of Ezra in the book of Nehemiah, though he had been ministering in Jerusalem since 458 B.C. (cf. Ezra 7:1–13:44).

8:3 read…understand. Here is the general summary of the event of reading and explaining the Scripture from daybreak to noon, a period of at least 6 hours (more detail is added in vv. 4-8).

8:4 platform…beside him. The platform was big enough to hold 14 people for the long hours of reading and explaining (v. 8). The men, probably priests, stood with Nehemiah to show agreement.

8:5 stood up. In respect at the reading of God's Word, as though they were in the presence of God Himself, the people stood for all the hours of the exposition.

8:6 blessed the LORD. A praise befitting the reading. In a synagogue, the reading is preceded by a benediction. The response of "Amen, Amen" was an affirmation of what Ezra prayed.

8:7,8 Some of the Levites assisted Ezra with the people's understanding of the Scripture by reading and explaining it.

8:8 gave the sense. This may have involved translation for people who were only Aramaic speakers in exile, but more likely it means "to break down" the text into its parts so that the people could understand it. This was an exposition or explanation of the meaning and not just translation. **helped *them* to understand the reading.** In this act of instruction, Ezra's personal commitment to study the law, practice it in his own life, and then teach it (Ezra 7:10) were reflected.

8:9 governor. *See note on 5:14.* **Ezra the priest.** Cf. Ezra 7:11, 12,21; 10:10,16. **wept, when they heard the words of the Law.** When they heard and understood God's law, they understood their violations of it. Not tears of joy, but penitent sorrow (8:10) came forth as they were grieved by conviction (8:11) over the distressing manifestations of sin in transgressing the Lord's commands and the consequent punishments they had suffered in their captivity.

10 Then he said to them, "Go your way,
eat the fat, drink the sweet, [p]and send portions to those for whom nothing is prepared; for *this* day *is* holy to our Lord. Do
not sorrow, for the joy of the LORD is your
strength."
11 So the Levites quieted all the people,
saying, "Be still, for the day *is* holy; do not
be grieved." 12 And all the people went
their way to eat and drink, to [q]send portions and rejoice greatly, because they [r]un-
derstood the words that were declared to
them.

The Feast of Tabernacles

13 Now on the second day the heads of
the fathers' *houses* of all the people, with
the priests and Levites, were gathered to
Ezra the scribe, in order to understand the
words of the Law. 14 And they found written in the Law, which the LORD had commanded by Moses, that the children of Israel should dwell in [s]booths[3] during the
feast of the seventh month, 15 and [t]that
they should announce and proclaim in all
their cities and [u]in Jerusalem, saying, "Go
out to the mountain, and [v]bring olive
branches, branches of oil trees, myrtle
branches, palm branches, and branches of
leafy trees, to make booths, as *it is* written."
16 Then the people went out and
brought *them* and made themselves
booths, each one on the [w]roof of his house,
or in their courtyards or the courts of the
house of God, and in the open square of
the [x]Water Gate [y]and in the open square of
the Gate of Ephraim. 17 So the whole assembly of those who had returned from
the captivity made [4]booths and sat under
the booths; for since the days of Joshua the
son of Nun until that day the children of Israel had not done so. And there was very
[z]great gladness. 18 Also [a]day by day, from
the first day until the last day, he read from
the Book of the Law of God. And they kept
the feast [b]seven days; and on the [c]eighth
day *there was* a sacred assembly, according
to the *prescribed* manner.

The People Confess Their Sins

9 Now on the twenty-fourth day of [a]this
month the children of Israel were assembled with fasting, in sackcloth, [b]and
with [1]dust on their heads. 2 Then [c]those of
Israelite lineage separated themselves
from all foreigners; and they stood and
[d]confessed their sins and the iniquities of
their fathers. 3 And they stood up in their
place and [e]read from the Book of the Law
of the LORD their God *for one*-fourth of the
day; and *for another* fourth they confessed
and worshiped the LORD their God.
4 Then Jeshua, Bani, Kadmiel, Shebaniah, Bunni, Sherebiah, Bani, *and* Chenani
stood on the [2]stairs of the Levites and cried

10 [p][Deut. 26:11-13]; Esth. 9:19, 22; Rev. 11:10
12 [q]Neh. 8:10 [r]Neh. 8:7, 8
14 [s]Lev. 23:34, 40, 42; Deut. 16:13
[3] Temporary shelters
15 [t]Lev. 23:4 [u]Deut. 16:16 [v]Lev. 23:40
16 [w]Deut. 22:8 [x]Neh. 12:37 [y]2 Kin. 14:13; Neh. 12:39
17 [z]2 Chr. 30:21
[4] Temporary shelters
18 [a]Deut. 31:11 [b]Lev. 23:36 [c]Num. 29:35

CHAPTER 9

1 [a]Neh. 8:2 [b]Josh. 7:6; 1 Sam. 4:12; 2 Sam. 1:2; Job 2:12
[1] Lit. *earth on them*
2 [c]Ezra 10:11; Neh. 13:3, 30 [d]Neh. 1:6
3 [e]Neh. 8:7, 8
4 [2] Lit. *ascent*

8:10-12 the joy of the LORD is your strength. The event called for a holy day of worship to prepare them for the hard days ahead (cf. 12:43), so they were encouraged to rejoice. The words they had heard did remind them that God punishes sin, but also that God blesses obedience. That was reason to celebrate. They had not been utterly destroyed as a nation, in spite of their sin, and were, by God's grace, on the brink of a new beginning. That called for celebration.

8:13–9:37 The Jews celebrated the Feast of Tabernacles and confessed their history of sins.

8:13 in order to understand the words of the Law. The smaller group that gathered to Ezra consisted of those who had teaching responsibilities: the heads of the father's houses to their families, and the priests and Levites to the general population in the community (Mal. 2:6,7).

8:14 Cf. Ex. 23:16; Lev. 23:33-44; Num. 29:12-38; Deut. 16:13-17 for details on the Feast of Tabernacles.

8:15,16 they should announce and proclaim. Proclamations such as this carried the authority of the administration represented by leaders such as Nehemiah, who was the governor, and Ezra, the priest and scribe (8:9) who had been used to reestablish the city, its worship, and its social life. The people responded to their directive.

8:16 Water Gate. *See notes on 3:26; 12:37.* **Gate of Ephraim.** This is believed to have been near the Old Gate (cf. 3:6; 12:39).

8:17 since the days of Joshua...very great gladness. Tabernacles had been celebrated since Joshua (2 Chr. 7:8-10; Ezra 3:4), but not with such joy.

8:18 This was more than was required and arose from the exuberant zeal of the people.

9:1 this month. Tishri (Sept./Oct.), 445 B.C. (cf. 7:73b; 8:2). **with fasting, in sackcloth, and with dust.** The outward demonstration of deep mourning and heaviness of heart for their iniquity seems to have been done in the spirit of the Day of Atonement which was normally observed on the tenth day of the seventh month (cf. Lev. 16:1-34; 23:26-32).

9:2 separated themselves from all foreigners. This call for divorcing all lawful wives taken from among the heathen was needed, since the last time, prompted 13 years before by Ezra (*see notes on Ezra 10*) had only been partially successful. Many had escaped the required action of divorce and kept their pagan wives. Perhaps new defaulters had appeared also, and were confronted for the first time with this necessary action of divorce. Nehemiah's efforts were successful in removing this evil mixture.

9:3 they stood...read...confessed and worshiped. The succession of events helped to reestablish the essential commitment of Israel to God and His law. They read for 3 hours about the sins of their fathers and for 3 more hours confessed that they had been partakers of similar evil deeds. In response to all of this, they worshiped.

9:4-37 This long confession of sin in the context of the recitation of God's mighty redemptive acts on Israel's behalf are expressions of worship (v. 3) that recall some of the psalms in their theme and worshipful purpose. This season of national humiliation centered on adoring God for His great mercy in the forgiveness of their multiplied iniquities, in delivering them from judgment, protecting them, and blessing them graciously. Apparently, this great prayer of worship offered to God was recited by a group of Levites (vv. 4,5) indicating it had been prepared and adopted beforehand, probably by Ezra. This prayer initiated the 3 hours of confession and worship (v. 3), which led to a national promise of obedience to God in the future (v. 38).

out with a loud voice to the LORD their
God. 5 And the Levites, Jeshua, Kadmiel,
Bani, Hashabniah, Sherebiah, Hodijah,
Shebaniah, *and* Pethahiah, said:

"Stand up *and* bless the LORD your
God
Forever and ever!

"Blessed be [f]Your glorious name,
Which is exalted above all blessing
and praise!
6 [g]You alone *are* the LORD;
[h]You have made heaven,
[i]The heaven of heavens, with [j]all
their host,
The earth and everything on it,
The seas and all that is in them,
And You [k]preserve them all.
The host of heaven worships You.

7 "You *are* the LORD God,
Who chose [l]Abram,
And brought him out of Ur of the
Chaldeans,
And gave him the name
[m]Abraham;
8 You found his heart [n]faithful
before You,
And made a [o]covenant with him
To give the land of the Canaanites,
The Hittites, the Amorites,
The Perizzites, the Jebusites,
And the Girgashites—
To give *it* to his descendants.
You [p]have performed Your words,
For You *are* righteous.

9 "You[q] saw the affliction of our
fathers in Egypt,
And [r]heard their cry by the Red
Sea.
10 You [s]showed signs and wonders
against Pharaoh,
Against all his servants,
And against all the people of his
land.
For You knew that they [t]acted
[3]proudly against them.
So You [u]made a name for Yourself,
as *it is* this day.
11 [v]And You divided the sea before
them,
So that they went through the
midst of the sea on the dry
land;
And their persecutors You threw
into the deep,
[w]As a stone into the mighty waters.
12 Moreover You [x]led them by day
with a cloudy pillar,
And by night with a pillar of fire,
To give them light on the road
Which they should travel.

13 "You[y] came down also on Mount
Sinai,
And spoke with them from
heaven,
And gave them [z]just ordinances
and true laws,
Good statutes and commandments.
14 You made known to them Your
[a]holy Sabbath,
And commanded them precepts,
statutes and laws,
By the hand of Moses Your servant.
15 You [b]gave them bread from heaven
for their hunger,
And [c]brought them water out of
the rock for their thirst,
And told them to [d]go in to possess
the land
Which You had [4]sworn to give
them.

16 "But[e] they and our fathers acted
[5]proudly,
[f]Hardened [6] their necks,
And did not heed Your
commandments.
17 They refused to obey,
And [g]they were not mindful of
Your wonders
That You did among them.
But they hardened their necks,
And [7]in their rebellion
They appointed [h]a leader

5 [f] 1 Chr. 29:13
6 [g] Deut. 6:4; 2 Kin. 19:15, 19; [Ps. 86:10]; Is. 37:16, 20 [h] Gen. 1:1; Ex. 20:11; Rev. 14:7 [i] [Deut. 10:14]; 1 Kin. 8:27 [j] Gen. 2:1 [k] [Ps. 36:6]
7 [l] Gen. 11:31 [m] Gen. 17:5
8 [n] Gen. 15:6; 22:1-3; [James 2:21-23] [o] Gen. 15:18 [p] Josh. 23:14
9 [q] Ex. 2:25; 3:7 [r] Ex. 14:10
10 [s] Ex. 7–14 [t] Ex. 18:11
[3] *presumptuously* or *insolently*
[u] Jer. 32:20
11 [v] Ex. 14:20-28 [w] Ex. 15:1, 5
12 [x] Ex. 13:21, 22
13 [y] Ex. 20:1-18 [z] [Rom. 7:12]
14 [a] Gen. 2:3; Ex. 16:23; 20:8; 23:12
15 [b] Ex. 16:14-17; John 6:31 [c] Ex. 17:6; Num. 20:8; [1 Cor. 10:4] [d] Deut. 1:8
[4] Lit. *raised Your hand to*
16 [e] Ps. 106:6 [f] Deut. 1:26-33; 31:27; Neh. 9:29
[5] *presumptuously*
[6] *Stiffened their necks,* became stubborn
17 [g] Ps. 78:11, 42-45 [h] Num. 14:4; Acts 7:39 [7] So with MT, Vg.; LXX *in Egypt*

9:6 have made heaven. The recitation was ordered historically, although themes of promise and judgment are traced through Israel's history with God. The first feature is the celebration of God's greatness as Creator (cf. Gen. 1, 2). **The host of heaven worships You.** The praise which Israel offered on earth was also echoed in the heavens by angelic hosts.

9:8 found his heart faithful before You. The Abrahamic Covenant (Gen. 12:1-3; 15:4-7; 17:1-9) was based on God's faithfulness to His Word and given to a man who was faithful to Him. *See notes on Gen. 15:6 and Rom. 4,* where the faithful heart of Abraham is discussed. **a covenant with him to give the land.** The covenant was a covenant of salvation, but also involved the Promised Land. The people, having just returned from captivity, understandably emphasized that feature of the covenant, since God had returned them to the Land.

9:9-12 This section of the prayer of praise and confession recounts the Exodus (see Ex. 2–15).

9:10 made a name for Yourself. God established His righteous reputation over the powers of Egypt by the miracles of immense power performed in Egypt.

9:13-19 The months at Sinai are remembered (see Ex. 19–40).

9:17 They appointed a leader. The Heb. of this statement is almost a repeat of Num. 14:4, which records the discontent of the people with God's plan and Moses' leadership.

To return to their bondage.
But You *are* God,
Ready to pardon,
[i]Gracious and merciful,
Slow to anger,
Abundant in kindness,
And did not forsake them.

18 "Even [j]when they made a molded calf for themselves,
And said, 'This *is* your god
That brought you up out of Egypt,'
And worked great provocations,

19 Yet in Your [k]manifold mercies
You did not forsake them in the wilderness.
The [l]pillar of the cloud did not depart from them by day,
To lead them on the road;
Nor the pillar of fire by night,
To show them light,
And the way they should go.

20 You also gave Your [m]good Spirit to instruct them,
And did not withhold Your [n]manna from their mouth,
And gave them [o]water for their thirst.

21 [p]Forty years You sustained them in the wilderness;
They lacked nothing;
Their [q]clothes did not wear out
And their feet did not swell.

22 "Moreover You gave them kingdoms and nations,
And divided them into [8]districts.
So they took possession of the land of [r]Sihon,
[9]The land of the king of Heshbon,
And the land of Og king of Bashan.

23 You also multiplied [s]their children as the stars of heaven,
And brought them into the land
Which You had told their fathers
To go in and possess.

24 So [t]the [1]people went in
And possessed the land;
[u]You subdued before them the inhabitants of the land,
The Canaanites,
And gave them into their hands,
With their kings
And the people of the land,
That they might do with them as they wished.

25 And they took strong cities and a [v]rich land,
And possessed [w]houses full of all goods,
Cisterns *already* dug, vineyards, olive groves,
And [2]fruit trees in abundance.
So they ate and were filled and [x]grew fat,
And delighted themselves in Your great [y]goodness.

26 "Nevertheless they [z]were disobedient
And rebelled against You,
[a]Cast Your law behind their backs
And killed Your [b]prophets, who [3]testified against them
To turn them to Yourself;
And they worked great provocations.

27 [c]Therefore You delivered them into the hand of their enemies,
Who oppressed them;
And in the time of their trouble,
When they cried to You,
You [d]heard from heaven;
And according to Your abundant mercies
[e]You gave them deliverers who saved them
From the hand of their enemies.

28 "But after they had rest,
[f]They again did evil before You.
Therefore You left them in the hand of their enemies,
So that they had dominion over them;

17 [i] Joel 2:13
18 [j] Ex. 32:4-8, 31
19 [k] Ps. 106:45 [l] Ex. 13:20-22; 1 Cor. 10:1
20 [m] Num. 11:17 [n] Ex. 16:14-16 [o] Ex. 17:6
21 [p] Deut. 2:7 [q] Deut. 8:4; 29:5
22 [r] Num. 21:21-35 [8] Lit. *corners* [9] So with MT, Vg.; LXX omits *The land of*
23 [s] Gen. 15:5; 22:17; Heb. 11:12
24 [t] Josh. 1:2-4 [1] Lit. *sons* [u] Josh. 18:1; [Ps. 44:2, 3]
25 [v] Num. 13:27 [w] Deut. 6:11; Josh. 24:13 [x] [Deut. 32:15] [y] Hos. 3:5 [2] Lit. *trees for eating*
26 [z] Judg. 2:11 [a] 1 Kin. 14:9; Ps. 50:17 [b] 1 Kin. 18:4; 19:10; Matt. 23:37; Acts 7:52 [3] *admonished* or *warned them*
27 [c] Judg. 2:14; Ps. 106:41 [d] Ps. 106:44 [e] Judg. 2:18
28 [f] Judg. 3:12

9:19-21 This section remembers the 38 years of wandering in the wilderness (cf. Num. 9–19).

9:21 They lacked nothing. The same word is used in Ps. 23:1, "I shall not *want.*" Even during the long season of chastisement, God miraculously cared for their every need.

9:22-25 These verses encompass the period of possessing the Promised Land, as recorded in Num. 20–Josh. 24.

9:22 gave them kingdoms and nations. Canaan was comprised of a number of politically semi-autonomous groups all loosely connected under the waning authority of Egypt. The Lord divided Canaan into tribal districts, thus apportioning the Land for Israel's possession.

9:23 multiplied their children. A nation of offspring was another aspect of the promise made to Abraham (Gen. 12:1-3). God told Abraham that his seed would be like the stars of heaven (Gen. 15:5) and Ex. 1:1-3 reminded Israel that their multiplication in Egypt was nothing short of miraculous.

9:24 subdued before them. Moses said in Ex. 15:3, "The LORD *is* a man of war." As Israel's military leader and king, He led them into battle to defeat their enemies and take the Land.

9:26-31 This section summarizes the period from the judges to the Assyrian deportation (722 B.C.) and Babylonian exile (586 B.C.). See 2 Kin. 17–25.

9:26 who testified against them. God's prophets brought them to God's court to be judged by His law. This theme is repeated throughout the message (vv. 29,30,34).

Yet when they returned and cried
out to You,
You heard from heaven;
And [g]many times You delivered
them according to Your
mercies,
29 And [4]testified against them,
That You might bring them back to
Your law.
Yet they acted [5]proudly,
And did not heed Your
commandments,
But sinned against Your
judgments,
[h]'Which if a man does, he shall live
by them.'
And they shrugged their
shoulders,
[6]Stiffened their necks,
And would not hear.
30 Yet for many years You had
patience with them,
And [7]testified [i]against them by
Your Spirit [j]in Your prophets.
Yet they would not listen;
[k]Therefore You gave them into the
hand of the peoples of the
lands.
31 Nevertheless in Your great mercy
[l]You did not utterly consume them
nor forsake them;
For You *are* God, gracious and
merciful.
32 "Now therefore, our God,
The great, the [m]mighty, and
awesome God,
Who keeps covenant and mercy:
Do not let all the [8]trouble seem
small before You
That has come upon us,
Our kings and our princes,
Our priests and our prophets,
Our fathers and on all Your people,
[n]From the days of the kings of
Assyria until this day.
33 However [o]You *are* just in all that
has befallen us;
For You have dealt faithfully,
But [p]we have done wickedly.
34 Neither our kings nor our princes,
Our priests nor our fathers,
Have kept Your law,
Nor heeded Your commandments
and Your testimonies,
With which You testified against
them.
35 For they have [q]not served You in
their kingdom,
Or in the many good *things* that
You gave them,
Or in the large and rich land which
You set before them;
Nor did they turn from their
wicked works.

36 "Here [r]we *are*, servants today!
And the land that You gave to our
fathers,
To eat its fruit and its bounty,
Here we *are*, servants in it!
37 And [s]it yields much increase to the
kings
You have set over us,
Because of our sins;
Also they have [t]dominion over our
bodies and our cattle
At their pleasure;
And we *are* in great distress.
38 "And because of all this,
We [u]make a sure *covenant* and
write *it;*
Our leaders, our Levites, *and* our
priests [v]seal *it.*"

28 [g] Ps. 106:43
29 [h] Lev. 18:5; Rom. 10:5; [Gal. 3:12] [4] *admonished them* [5] *presumptuously* [6] Became stubborn
30 [i] 2 Kin. 17:13-18; 2 Chr. 36:11-20; Jer. 7:25 [j] [Acts 7:51]; 1 Pet. 1:11 [k] Is. 5:5 [7] *admonished* or *warned them*
31 [l] Jer. 4:27; [Rom. 11:2-5]
32 [m] [Ex. 34:6, 7] [n] 2 Kin. 15:19; 17:3-6; Ezra 4:2, 10 [8] *hardship*
33 [o] Ps. 119:137; [Dan. 9:14] [p] Ps. 106:6; [Dan. 9:5, 6, 8]
35 [q] Deut. 28:47
36 [r] Deut. 28:48; Ezra 9:9
37 [s] Deut. 28:33, 51 [t] Deut. 28:48
38 [u] 2 Kin. 23:3; 2 Chr. 29:10; Ezra 10:3 [v] Neh. 10:1

The People Who Sealed the Covenant

10

Now those who placed *their* seal on *the document were:*

1 Nehemiah the [1]governor, [a]the son of Hacaliah, and Zedekiah, 2 [b]Seraiah, Azariah, Jeremiah, 3 Pashhur, Amariah, Malchijah, 4 Hattush, Shebaniah, Malluch, 5 Harim, Meremoth, Obadiah, 6 Daniel,

CHAPTER 10
1 [a] Neh. 1:1 [1] Heb. *Tirshatha*
2 [b] Neh. 12:1-21

9:32 Now therefore. Having reviewed the faithfulness of God to the Abrahamic Covenant (vv. 7,8) throughout Israel's national history, the prayer picks up with the present time confessing their unfaithfulness to (vv. 33-35) and renewed commitment to the Mosaic Covenant (vv. 36-38). **kings of Assyria...this day.** This statement sweeps across a summary of Assyrian, Babylonian, and Persian domination of the nation for almost 4 centuries up to that time.

9:36,37 in it...over us. The praise prayer rejoices that the Jews have been returned to the Land, but grieves that Gentiles still rule over them.

9:37 much increase to the kings. Because God's people continued in widespread sin, enemy kings enjoyed the bounty that would have been Israel's.

9:38 because of all this. The history of God's faithfulness, in spite of Israel's unfaithfulness, is the ground of a pledge and promise which the people make to obey God and not repeat the sins of their fathers.

9:38–10:39 The nation makes a new covenant with God to keep the Mosaic law. Though well intended, as they had been in Ex. 24:1-8, their failure was forthcoming (*see note on 13:10-13*).

9:38 We make a sure *covenant* and write *it*. A covenant was a binding agreement between two parties. In short, it was a formalized relationship with commitments to loyalty. In this case, the nation initiated this covenant with God.

10:1-27 The list of sealed signatures on the covenant were from the leaders. Surprisingly, Ezra's name is not listed.

Ginnethon, Baruch, 7 Meshullam,
Abijah, Mijamin, 8 Maaziah, Bilgai,
and Shemaiah. These *were* the
priests.
9 The Levites: Jeshua the son of
Azaniah, Binnui of the sons of
Henadad, *and* Kadmiel.
10 Their brethren: Shebaniah, Hodijah, Kelita, Pelaiah, Hanan,
11 Micha, Rehob, Hashabiah,
12 Zaccur, Sherebiah, Shebaniah,
13 Hodijah, Bani, *and* Beninu.
14 The leaders of the people:
[c]Parosh, Pahath-Moab, Elam,
Zattu, Bani, 15 Bunni, Azgad,
Bebai, 16 Adonijah, Bigvai, Adin,
17 Ater, Hezekiah, Azzur, 18 Hodijah, Hashum, Bezai, 19 Hariph,
Anathoth, Nebai, 20 Magpiash, Meshullam, Hezir, 21 Meshezabel,
Zadok, Jaddua, 22 Pelatiah, Hanan,
Anaiah, 23 Hoshea, Hananiah,
Hasshub, 24 Hallohesh, Pilha,
Shobek, 25 Rehum, Hashabnah,
Maaseiah, 26 Ahijah, Hanan, Anan,
27 Malluch, Harim, *and* Baanah.

The Covenant That Was Sealed

28 [d]Now the rest of the people—the
priests, the Levites, the gatekeepers, the
singers, the Nethinim, [e]and all those who
had separated themselves from the peoples of the lands to the Law of God, their
wives, their sons, and their daughters,
everyone who had knowledge and understanding— 29 these joined with their
brethren, their nobles, [f]and entered into a
curse and an oath [g]to walk in God's Law,
which was given by Moses the servant of
God, and to observe and do all the commandments of the LORD our Lord, and His
ordinances and His statutes: 30 We would
not give [h]our daughters as wives to the
peoples of the land, nor take their daughters for our sons; 31 [i]*if* the peoples of the
land brought [2]wares or any grain to sell on
the Sabbath day, we would not buy it from
them on the Sabbath, or on a holy day; and
we would forego the [j]seventh year's *produce* and the [k]exacting[3] of every debt.
32 Also we made ordinances for ourselves, to exact from ourselves yearly [l]one-
third of a shekel for the service of the
house of our God: 33 for [m]the showbread,
for the regular grain offering, for the [n]reg-
ular burnt offering of the Sabbaths, the
New Moons, and the set feasts; for the holy
things, for the sin offerings to make atonement for Israel, and all the work of the
house of our God. 34 We cast lots among
the priests, the Levites, and the people,
[o]for *bringing* the wood offering into the
house of our God, according to our fathers'
houses, at the appointed times year by
year, to burn on the altar of the LORD our
God [p]as *it is* written in the Law.
35 And *we made ordinances* [q]to bring the
firstfruits of our ground and the firstfruits
of all fruit of all trees, year by year, to the
house of the LORD; 36 to bring the [r]firstborn
of our sons and our cattle, as *it is* written in
the Law, and the firstborn of our herds and
our flocks, to the house of our God, to the
priests who minister in the house of our
God; 37 [s]to bring the firstfruits of our
dough, our offerings, the fruit from all
kinds of trees, *the* new wine and oil, to the
priests, to the storerooms of the [4]house of
our God; and to bring [t]the tithes of our
land to the Levites, for the Levites should
receive the tithes in all our farming communities. 38 And the priest, the descendant

14 [c] Ezra 2:3
28 [d] Ezra 2:36-43 [e] Ezra 9:1; Neh. 13:3
29 [f] Deut. 29:12; Neh. 5:12; Ps. 119:106 [g] 2 Kin. 23:3; 2 Chr. 34:31
30 [h] Ex. 34:16; Deut. 7:3; [Ezra 9:12]
31 [i] Ex. 20:10; Lev. 23:3; Deut. 5:12 [j] Ex. 23:10, 11; Lev. 25:4; Jer. 34:14 [k] [Deut. 15:1, 2]; Neh. 5:12 [2] *merchandise* [3] *collection*
32 [l] Ex. 30:11-16; 38:25, 26; 2 Chr. 24:6, 9; Matt. 17:24
33 [m] Lev. 24:5; 2 Chr. 2:4 [n] Num. 28; 29
34 [o] Neh. 13:31; [Is. 40:16] [p] Lev. 6:12
35 [q] Ex. 23:19; 34:26; Lev. 19:23; Num. 18:12; Deut. 26:1, 2
36 [r] Ex. 13:2, 12, 13; Lev. 27:26, 27; Num. 18:15, 16
37 [s] Lev. 23:17; Num. 15:19; 18:12; Deut. 18:4; 26:2 [t] Lev. 27:30; Num. 18:21; Mal. 3:10 [4] *Temple*

10:28 Nethinim. *See note on Ezra 2:43-54.* **who had separated themselves.** These are those who 1) had followed the demand of Ezra and Nehemiah to divorce pagan spouses or 2) had been left in the Land but never joined themselves to any heathen, thus remaining separate. Intermarriage with the nations had previously precipitated an influence in Israel which had culminated in Babylonian slavery, thus playing a major role in Israel's unfaithfulness to the covenant.

10:29 a curse and an oath. Covenants characteristically were ratified by an oath ceremony in which the parties swore to the terms of the covenant. A curse rite was often included wherein the slaughtering of an animal indicated similar consequences for the covenant breaker. Israel's pledged adherence to the law was thus solemnly affirmed.

10:30 not give our daughters…nor take their daughters. Parents controlled marriages, so this part of the covenant came from them. Again, it stressed the serious matter of marrying a heathen from an idolatrous people (see Ezra 10).

10:32-39 The remainder of the conditions the people made in their covenant involved matters of the temple.

10:32,33 we made ordinances. What the people were committing themselves to do by covenant turned into law requiring a one-third shekel temple tax. The Mosaic ordinance required one-half of a shekel (see Ex. 30:11-16), but the severe economic straits of the time led to the reduced amount. By the time of Christ, the people had returned to the Mosaic stipulation of one-half of a shekel. *See note on Matt. 17:24.*

10:34 The carrying of the wood for the constantly burning altar (Lev. 6:12 ff.) had formerly been the duty of the Nethinim, but few of them had returned from Babylon (7:60) so more people were chosen to assist in this task.

10:35-39 Laws for all the offerings and titles were reinstated so as not to "neglect the house of our God" (v. 39).

10:35-37 firstfruits…firstborn…firstborn. These laws required the firstfruits of the ground (see Ex. 23:19; 34:26; Deut. 26:2), the firstfruits of the trees (see Lev. 19:24; Num. 18:13), the firstborn sons redeemed by the estimated price of the priest (see Num. 18:15), and the firstborn of the herds and flocks (see Ex. 13:12; Num. 18:15, 17). All of this was kept at the storehouses near the temple and distributed for the support of the priests and Levites. The Levites then gave a tenth of what they received to the priests (cf. Num. 18:26).

of Aaron, shall be with the Levites [u]when
the Levites receive tithes; and the Levites
shall bring up a tenth of the tithes to the
house of our God, to [v]the rooms of the
storehouse.
39 For the children of Israel and the children of Levi [w]shall bring the offering of the
grain, of the new wine and the oil, to the
storerooms where the articles of the sanctuary *are, where* the priests who minister and
the gatekeepers [x]and the singers *are;* and
we will not [y]neglect the house of our God.

The People Dwelling in Jerusalem

11 Now the leaders of the people
dwelt at Jerusalem; the rest of the
people cast lots to bring one out of ten to
dwell in Jerusalem, [a]the holy city, and
nine-tenths *were to dwell* in *other* cities.
2 And the people blessed all the men who
[b]willingly offered themselves to dwell at
Jerusalem.
3 [c]These *are* the heads of the province
who dwelt in Jerusalem. (But in the cities
of Judah everyone dwelt in his own possession in their cities—Israelites, priests,
Levites, [d]Nethinim, and [e]descendants of
Solomon's servants.) 4 Also [f]in Jerusalem
dwelt *some* of the children of Judah and of
the children of Benjamin.
The children of Judah: Athaiah the son
of Uzziah, the son of Zechariah, the son of
Amariah, the son of Shephatiah, the son of
Mahalalel, of the children of [g]Perez; 5 and
Maaseiah the son of Baruch, the son of Col-
Hozeh, the son of Hazaiah, the son of Adaiah, the son of Joiarib, the son of Zechariah,
the son of Shiloni. 6 All the sons of Perez
who dwelt at Jerusalem *were* four hundred
and sixty-eight valiant men.
7 And these are the sons of Benjamin:
Sallu the son of Meshullam, the son of
Joed, the son of Pedaiah, the son of Kolaiah, the son of Maaseiah, the son of Ithiel,
the son of Jeshaiah; 8 and after him Gabbai
and Sallai, nine hundred and twenty-eight.
9 Joel the son of Zichri *was* their overseer,
and Judah the son of [1]Senuah *was* second
over the city.
10 [h]Of the priests: Jedaiah the son of Joiarib, and Jachin; 11 Seraiah the son of Hilkiah, the son of Meshullam, the son of
Zadok, the son of Meraioth, the son of Ahitub, *was* the leader of the house of God.
12 Their brethren who did the work of the
house *were* eight hundred and twenty-two;
and Adaiah the son of Jeroham, the son of
Pelaliah, the son of Amzi, the son of Zechariah, the son of Pashhur, the son of Malchijah, 13 and his brethren, heads of the fathers' *houses, were* two hundred and
forty-two; and Amashai the son of Azarel,
the son of Ahzai, the son of Meshillemoth,
the son of Immer, 14 and their brethren,
mighty men of valor, *were* one hundred
and twenty-eight. Their overseer *was*
Zabdiel [2]the son of *one of* the great men.
15 Also of the Levites: Shemaiah the son
of Hasshub, the son of Azrikam, the son of
Hashabiah, the son of Bunni; 16 [i]Shabbe-
thai and [j]Jozabad, of the heads of the
Levites, *had* the oversight of [k]the business
outside of the [3]house of God; 17 Mattaniah
the son of [4]Micha, the son of Zabdi, the son
of Asaph, the leader *who* began the
thanksgiving with prayer; Bakbukiah, the
second among his brethren; and Abda the
son of Shammua, the son of Galal, the son
of Jeduthun. 18 All the Levites in [l]the holy
city *were* two hundred and eighty-four.
19 Moreover the gatekeepers, Akkub,
Talmon, and their brethren who kept the
gates, *were* one hundred and seventy-two.
20 And the rest of Israel, of the priests
and Levites, *were* in all the cities of Judah,
everyone in his inheritance. 21 [m]But the
Nethinim dwelt in Ophel. And Ziha and
Gishpa *were* over the Nethinim.
22 Also the overseer of the Levites at Jerusalem *was* Uzzi the son of Bani, the son
of Hashabiah, the son of Mattaniah, the
son of Micha, of the sons of Asaph, the
singers in charge of the [5]service of the
[6]house of God. 23 For [n]*it was* the king's
command concerning them that a [7]certain
portion should be for the singers, a quota
day by day. 24 Pethahiah the son of Meshezabel, of the children of [o]Zerah the son
of Judah, *was* [p]the [8] king's deputy in all
matters concerning the people.

The People Dwelling Outside Jerusalem

25 And as for the villages with their
fields, *some* of the children of Judah dwelt
in [q]Kirjath Arba and its villages, Dibon and
its villages, Jekabzeel and its villages; 26 in
Jeshua, Moladah, Beth Pelet, 27 Hazar
Shual, and Beersheba and its villages; 28 in

38 [u]Num. 18:26 [v]1 Chr. 9:26; 2 Chr. 31:11
39 [w]Deut. 12:6, 11; 2 Chr. 31:12; Neh. 13:12 [x]Neh. 13:10, 11 [y][Heb. 10:25]

CHAPTER 11

1 [a]Neh. 10:18; Matt. 4:5; 5:35; 27:53
2 [b]Judg. 5:9; 2 Chr. 17:16
3 [c]1 Chr. 9:2, 3 [d]Ezra 2:43 [e]Ezra 2:55
4 [f]1 Chr. 9:3 [g]Gen. 38:29
9 [1]Or *Hassenuah*
10 [h]1 Chr. 9:10
14 [2]Or *the son of Haggedolim*
16 [i]Ezra 10:15 [j]Ezra 8:33 [k]1 Chr. 26:29 [3]Temple
17 [4]Or *Michah*
18 [l]Neh. 11:1
21 [m]2 Chr. 27:3; Neh. 3:26
22 [5]*work* [6]Temple
23 [n]Ezra 6:8, 9; 7:20 [7]*fixed share*
24 [o]Gen. 38:30 [p]1 Chr. 18:17 [8]Lit. *at the king's hand*
25 [q]Josh. 14:15

11:1–13:31 Details of Nehemiah exercising his governorship are given in this section.

11:1–12:26 Jerusalem and Judah are resettled.

11:1 cast lots. A method of decision making which God honored (Prov. 16:33). Nehemiah redistributed the population so that one out of every 10 Jews lived in Jerusalem. The other 9 were free to reestablish their family heritage in the Land.

11:3-24 The people who dwelt in Jerusalem are identified.

11:21 Ophel. *See note on 3:26.*

11:25-36 These are the places where 90 percent of the people dwelt outside of Jerusalem (cf. Ezra 2:21-23,27,34).

Ziklag and Meconah and its villages; 29 in
En Rimmon, Zorah, Jarmuth, 30 Zanoah,
Adullam, and their villages; in Lachish
and its fields; in Azekah and its villages.
They dwelt from Beersheba to the Valley of
Hinnom.
31 Also the children of Benjamin from
Geba *dwelt* in Michmash, Aija, and Bethel,
and their villages; 32 in Anathoth, Nob,
Ananiah; 33 in Hazor, Ramah, Gittaim;
34 in Hadid, Zeboim, Neballat; 35 in Lod,
Ono, *and* [r]the Valley of Craftsmen. 36 Some
of the Judean divisions of Levites *were* in
Benjamin.

The Priests and Levites

12 Now these *are* the [a]priests and the
Levites who came up with [b]Ze-
rubbabel the son of Shealtiel, and Jeshua:
[c]Seraiah, Jeremiah, Ezra, 2 Amariah, [1]Mal-
luch, Hattush, 3 [2]Shechaniah, [3]Rehum,
[4]Meremoth, 4 Iddo, [5]Ginnethoi, [d]Abijah,
5 [6]Mijamin, [7]Maadiah, Bilgah, 6 Shemaiah,
Joiarib, Jedaiah, 7 [8]Sallu, Amok, Hilkiah,
and Jedaiah.
These *were* the heads of the priests and
their brethren in the days of [e]Jeshua.
8 Moreover the Levites *were* Jeshua,
Binnui, Kadmiel, Sherebiah, Judah, *and*
Mattaniah [f]*who led* the thanksgiving
psalms, he and his brethren. 9 Also Bakbukiah and Unni, their brethren, *stood* across
from them in *their* duties.
10 Jeshua begot Joiakim, Joiakim begot
Eliashib, Eliashib begot Joiada, 11 Joiada
begot Jonathan, and Jonathan begot Jaddua.
12 Now in the days of Joiakim, the
priests, the [g]heads of the fathers' *houses*
were: of Seraiah, Meraiah; of Jeremiah,
Hananiah; 13 of Ezra, Meshullam; of Amariah, Jehohanan; 14 of [9]Melichu, Jonathan;
of [1]Shebaniah, Joseph; 15 of [2]Harim, Adna;
of [3]Meraioth, Helkai; 16 of Iddo, Zechariah; of Ginnethon, Meshullam; 17 of Abijah, Zichri; *the son* of [4]Minjamin; of [5]Moa-
diah, Piltai; 18 of Bilgah, Shammua; of Shemaiah, Jehonathan; 19 of Joiarib, Mattenai;
of Jedaiah, Uzzi; 20 of [6]Sallai, Kallai; of
Amok, Eber; 21 of Hilkiah, Hashabiah; *and*
of Jedaiah, Nethanel.
22 During the reign of Darius the Persian, a record *was also kept* of the Levites
and priests *who had been* [h]heads of their fathers' *houses* in the days of Eliashib, Joiada,
Johanan, and Jaddua. 23 The sons of Levi,
the heads of the fathers' *houses* until the
days of Johanan the son of Eliashib, *were*
written in the book of the [i]chronicles.
24 And the heads of the Levites *were*
Hashabiah, Sherebiah, and Jeshua the son
of Kadmiel, with their brothers across from
them, to [j]praise *and* give thanks, [k]group[7] al-
ternating with group, [l]according to the
command of David the man of God. 25 Mattaniah, Bakbukiah, Obadiah, Meshullam,
Talmon, and Akkub *were* gatekeepers keeping the watch at the storerooms of the gates.
26 These *lived* in the days of Joiakim the son
of Jeshua, the son of [8]Jozadak, and in the
days of Nehemiah [m]the governor, and of
Ezra the priest, [n]the scribe.

Nehemiah Dedicates the Wall

27 Now at [o]the dedication of the wall of
Jerusalem they sought out the Levites in all
their places, to bring them to Jerusalem to
celebrate the dedication with gladness,
[p]both with thanksgivings and singing, *with*
cymbals and stringed instruments and
harps. 28 And the sons of the singers gathered together from the countryside around
Jerusalem, from the [q]villages of the Netophathites, 29 from the house of Gilgal, and
from the fields of Geba and Azmaveth; for
the singers had built themselves villages all
around Jerusalem. 30 Then the priests and
Levites [r]purified themselves, and purified
the people, the gates, and the wall.

35 [r] 1 Chr. 4:14

CHAPTER 12

1 [a] Ezra 2:1, 2; 7:7 [b] Neh. 7:7; Matt. 1:12, 13 [c] Neh. 10:2-8
2 [1] *Melichu,* v. 14
3 [2] *Shebaniah,* v. 14 [3] *Harim,* v. 15 [4] *Meraioth,* v. 15
4 [d] Luke 1:5 [5] *Ginnethon,* v. 16
5 [6] *Minjamin,* v. 17 [7] *Moadiah,* v. 17
7 [e] Ezra 3:2; Hag. 1:1; Zech. 3:1 [8] *Sallai,* v. 20
8 [f] Neh. 11:17
12 [g] Neh. 7:70, 71; 8:13; 11:13
14 [9] *Malluch,* v. 2 [1] *Shechaniah,* v. 3
15 [2] *Rehum,* v. 3 [3] *Meremoth,* v. 3
17 [4] *Mijamin,* v. 5 [5] *Maadiah,* v. 5
20 [6] *Sallu,* v. 7
22 [h] 1 Chr. 24:6
23 [i] 1 Chr. 9:14-22
24 [j] Neh. 11:17 [k] Ezra 3:11 [l] 1 Chr. 23–26 [7] Lit. *watch by watch*
26 [m] Neh. 8:9 [n] Ezra 7:6, 11 [8] *Jehozadak,* 1 Chr. 6:14
27 [o] Deut. 20:5; Neh. 7:1; Ps. 30:title [p] 1 Chr. 25:6; 2 Chr. 5:13; 7:6
28 [q] 1 Chr. 9:16
30 [r] Ezra 6:20; Neh. 13:22, 30

12:1-26 Originally there were 24 courses of priests, each course serving in the temple for a period of two weeks per year or for one month biannually (see 1 Chr. 24:1-20). Only four of those houses returned from Babylon (see 7:39-42; Ezra 2:36-39) but these were divided into 24 courses of which 22 are listed here. Perhaps two are omitted because their families had become extinct, because no sons were born since the time Zerubbabel originally named them. This then is a selective rather than exhaustive listing of priests and Levites from the time of Zerubbabel and Jeshua, recording the key priests and Levites through 3 generations of High-Priests: 1) Jeshua who came in the initial return with Zerubbabel ca. 538 B.C. (vv. 1-11); 2) Joiakim, the son of Jeshua (vv. 12-21); 3) Eliashib (cf. 3:1) the son of Joiakim (vv. 22,23); 4) a miscellaneous group who served in the days of Joiakim (vv. 24-26).

12:1 Zerubbabel. *See note on Ezra 2:1.* **Jeshua.** *See note on Ezra 2:2.*

12:10,11 This record lists 6 generations of High-Priests beginning with Jeshua. The Jonathan of v. 11 is the Johanan of v. 22.

12:12-21 Each of the 22 families in vv. 1-7 is repeated, except one (cf. Hattush; v. 2). Perhaps by the time of Joiakim's High-Priesthood, this family had become extinct, the fathers having no male offspring.

12:22 Darius the Persian. This refers to Darius II, ca. 423–404 B.C.

12:23 book of the chronicles. Lit. "were written on the scroll of the matters of the days." This involved precise genealogical records kept in the administrative archives of Judah.

12:27–13:3 The walls were dedicated.

12:27-43 the dedication of the wall. In the same manner marking the dedications of the temple in Solomon's day (2 Chr. 5–7) and the rebuilt temple several decades earlier (Ezra 6:16-18), the rebuilt walls were dedicated with the music of thanksgiving (most likely shortly after the events of Neh. 9).

12:30 purified. See Lev. 16:30 for the sense of moral purity in this symbolic act.

31 So I brought the leaders of Judah up
on the wall, and appointed two large
thanksgiving choirs. [s]*One* went to the right
hand on the wall [t]toward the Refuse Gate.
32 After them went Hoshaiah and half of
the leaders of Judah, 33 and Azariah, Ezra,
Meshullam, 34 Judah, Benjamin, Shemaiah,
Jeremiah, 35 and some of the priests' sons
[u]with trumpets—Zechariah the son of Jonathan, the son of Shemaiah, the son of Mattaniah, the son of Michaiah, the son of Zaccur, the son of Asaph, 36 and his brethren,
Shemaiah, Azarel, Milalai, Gilalai, Maai,
Nethanel, Judah, *and* Hanani, with [v]the
musical [w]instruments of David the man of
God. And Ezra the scribe *went* before them.
37 [x]By the Fountain Gate, in front of them,
they went up [y]the stairs of the [z]City of David, on the stairway of the wall, beyond
the house of David, as far as [a]the Water
Gate eastward.

38 [b]The other thanksgiving choir went
the opposite *way*, and I *was* behind them
with half of the people on the wall, going
past the [c]Tower of the Ovens as far as [d]the
Broad Wall, 39 [e]and above the Gate of
Ephraim, above [f]the Old Gate, above [g]the
Fish Gate, [h]the Tower of Hananel, the
Tower of [9]the Hundred, as far as [i]the
Sheep Gate; and they stopped by [j]the Gate
of the Prison.

40 So the two thanksgiving choirs stood
in the house of God, likewise I and the half
of the rulers with me; 41 and the priests,
Eliakim, Maaseiah, [1]Minjamin, Michaiah,
Elioenai, Zechariah, *and* Hananiah, with
trumpets; 42 also Maaseiah, Shemaiah, Eleazar, Uzzi, Jehohanan, Malchijah, Elam,

31 [s] Neh. 12:38 [t] Neh. 2:13; 3:13
35 [u] Num. 10:2, 8
36 [v] 1 Chr. 23:5 [w] 2 Chr. 29:26, 27
37 [x] Neh. 2:14; 3:15 [y] Neh. 3:15 [z] 2 Sam. 5:7-9 [a] Neh. 3:26; 8:1, 3, 16
38 [b] Neh. 12:31 [c] Neh. 3:11 [d] Neh. 3:8
39 [e] 2 Kin. 14:13; Neh. 8:16 [f] Neh. 3:6 [g] Neh. 3:3 [h] Neh. 3:1 [i] Neh. 3:32 [j] Jer. 32:2 [9] Heb. *Hammeah*
41 [1] Or *Mijamin*, v. 5
42 [2] Lit. *made their voice to be heard*
43 [k] Ezra 3:13
44 [l] 2 Chr. 31:11, 12; Neh. 13:5, 12, 13 [m] Neh. 10:37-39 [3] Lit. *stood*
45 [n] 1 Chr. 25; 26
46 [o] 1 Chr. 25:1; 2 Chr. 29:30
47 [p] Neh. 11:23 [q] Num. 18:21, 24 [r] Num. 18:26 [4] *set apart*

CHAPTER 13

1 [a] [Deut. 31:11, 12]; 2 Kin. 23:2; Neh. 8:3, 8; 9:3; Is. 34:16 [b] Deut. 23:3, 4
2 [c] Num. 22:5; Josh. 24:9, 10

and Ezer. The singers [2]sang loudly with
Jezrahiah the director.
43 Also that day they offered great sacrifices, and rejoiced, for God had made them
rejoice with great joy; the women and the
children also rejoiced, so that the joy of Jerusalem was heard [k]afar off.

Temple Responsibilities

44 [l]And at the same time some were appointed over the rooms of the storehouse
for the offerings, the firstfruits, and the
[m]tithes, to gather into them from the fields
of the cities the portions specified by the
Law for the priests and Levites; for Judah
rejoiced over the priests and Levites who
[3]ministered. 45 Both the singers and the
gatekeepers kept the charge of their God
and the charge of the purification, [n]accord-
ing to the command of David *and* Solomon
his son. 46 For in the days of David [o]and
Asaph of old *there were* chiefs of the
singers, and songs of praise and thanksgiving to God. 47 In the days of Zerubbabel
and in the days of Nehemiah all Israel gave
the portions for the singers and the gatekeepers, a portion for [p]each day. [q]They
also [4]consecrated *holy things* for the
Levites, [r]and the Levites consecrated *them*
for the children of Aaron.

Principles of Separation

13 On that day [a]they read from the
Book of Moses in the hearing of the
people, and in it was found written [b]that
no Ammonite or Moabite should ever
come into the assembly of God, 2 because
they had not met the children of Israel with
bread and water, but [c]hired Balaam

12:31-40 They probably assembled at the Valley Gate on the W. One of the choirs was led by Ezra (v. 36), the other accompanied by Nehemiah (v. 38). Moving in different directions (v. 38), they assembled together in the temple area (v. 40).

12:31 Refuse Gate. *See notes on 2:13; 3:13.*

12:36 the musical instruments of David. This phrase could refer to the same kind of instruments David's musicians used or the actual instruments constructed in David's time, now being used centuries later. Cf. 1 Chr. 15:16; 23:5; 2 Chr. 29:26; Ezra 3:10. **the man of God.** *See note on Deut. 33:1*; cf. Acts 13:22.

12:37 the Fountain Gate. *See note on 2:14.* **the Water Gate.** *See notes on 3:26; 8:16.*

12:38 opposite *way*. This second choir marched clockwise to the N (cf. 12:31). **Tower of the Ovens.** *See note on 3:11.*

12:39 the Gate of Ephraim. *See note on 8:16.* **the Old Gate.** *See note on 3:6.* **the Fish Gate.** *See note on 3:3.* **the Tower of Hananel.** *See note on 3:1.* **the Tower of the Hundred.** *See note on 3:1.* **the Sheep Gate.** *See notes on 3:1,32.* **the Gate of the Prison.** Located in the NE section of Jerusalem.

12:43 for God had made them rejoice. The God of all joy (cf. 1 Chr. 12:40; Neh. 8:10; Pss. 16:11; 33:1; 43:4; Gal. 5:22) activated their inner joy which brought corporate celebration. Though these may have been few and far between, moments like this characterized the life of obedience and blessing which God had set before Israel.

12:44-47 A listing of miscellaneous temple activities is given.

12:44 specified by the Law. Cf. Lev. 7:34-36; Deut. 18:1-5.

12:45 the command of David...Solomon. Cf. 1 Chr. 25, 26.

12:47 the children of Aaron. The priests.

13:1-31 Nehemiah left Jerusalem in the 32nd year of Artaxerxes ca. 433 B.C. (cf. 5:14; 13:6) and returned to Persia as he promised (cf. 2:6). During his absence, the people returned to their former ways, led by the High-Priest Eliashib (vv. 4,5). Such a defection called for the needed reforms of vv. 1-3,10-30. It was during Nehemiah's absence that Malachi also wrote his prophetic book indicting both priests and people for their sinful defection. Possibly having heard of Eliashib's evil, Nehemiah returned (vv. 4-7). Nehemiah 13 was the last portion of the OT to be written.

13:1,2 On that day they read from the Book of Moses. Not surprisingly, as they read on the regular calendar cycle, they were confronted with areas in which their thinking and practice had wavered from the Scriptures, specifically with regard to the requirements of Deut. 23:3-6.

13:2 Balaam. See Num. 22–24.

against them to curse them. [d]However, our
God turned the curse into a blessing. 3 So it
was, when they had heard the Law, [e]that
they separated all the mixed multitude
from Israel.

The Reforms of Nehemiah

4 Now before this, [f]Eliashib the priest,
having authority over the storerooms of
the house of our God, *was* allied with [g]To-
biah. 5 And he had prepared for him a
large room, [h]where previously they had
stored the grain offerings, the frankincense, the articles, the tithes of grain, the
new wine and oil, [i]which were commanded *to be given* to the Levites and singers and
gatekeepers, and the offerings for the
priests. 6 But during all this I was not in Jerusalem, [j]for in the thirty-second year of
Artaxerxes king of Babylon I had returned
to the king. Then after certain days I obtained leave from the king, 7 and I came to
Jerusalem and discovered the evil that
Eliashib had done for Tobiah, in [k]prepar-
ing a room for him in the courts of the
[1]house of God. 8 And it grieved me bitterly; therefore I threw all the household
goods of Tobiah out of the room. 9 Then I
commanded them to [l]cleanse the rooms;
and I brought back into them the articles of
the house of God, with the grain offering
and the frankincense.

10 I also realized that the portions for the
Levites had [m]not been given *them;* for each
of the Levites and the singers who did the
work had gone back to [n]his field. 11 So [o]I
contended with the rulers, and said,
[p]"Why is the house of God forsaken?" And
I gathered them together and set them in
their place. 12 [q]Then all Judah brought the
tithe of the grain and the new wine and the
oil to the storehouse. 13 [r]And I appointed
as treasurers over the storehouse Shelemiah the priest and Zadok the scribe, and
of the Levites, Pedaiah; and next to them
was Hanan the son of Zaccur, the son of
Mattaniah; for they were considered [s]faith-
ful, and their task *was* to distribute to their
brethren.

14 [t]Remember me, O my God, concerning this, and do not wipe out my good
deeds that I have done for the house of my
God, and for its services!

15 In those days I saw *people* in Judah
treading wine presses [u]on the Sabbath,
and bringing in sheaves, and loading donkeys with wine, grapes, figs, and all *kinds
of* burdens, [v]which they brought into Jerusalem on the Sabbath day. And I warned
them about the day on which they were
selling provisions. 16 Men of Tyre dwelt
there also, who brought in fish and all
kinds of goods, and sold *them* on the Sabbath to the children of Judah, and in Jerusalem.

17 Then I contended with the nobles of
Judah, and said to them, "What evil thing
is this that you do, by which you profane
the Sabbath day? 18 [w]Did not your fathers
do thus, and did not our God bring all this
disaster on us and on this city? Yet you
bring added wrath on Israel by profaning
the Sabbath."

19 So it was, at the gates of Jerusalem, as
it [x]began to be dark before the Sabbath,
that I commanded the gates to be shut, and
charged that they must not be opened till
after the Sabbath. [y]Then I posted *some* of
my servants at the gates, *so that* no burdens
would be brought in on the Sabbath day.
20 Now the merchants and sellers of all
kinds of [2]wares [3]lodged outside Jerusalem
once or twice.

21 Then I warned them, and said to
them, "Why do you spend the night
[4]around the wall? If you do *so* again, I will
lay hands on you!" From that time on they
came no *more* on the Sabbath. 22 And I

2 [d] Num. 23:1; 24:10; Deut. 23:5
3 [e] Neh. 9:2; 10:28
4 [f] Neh. 12:10 [g] Neh. 2:10; 4:3; 6:1
5 [h] Neh. 12:44 [i] Num. 18:21, 24
6 [j] Neh. 5:14-16
7 [k] Neh. 13:1, 5 [1] Temple
9 [l] 2 Chr. 29:5, 15, 16
10 [m] Neh. 10:37; Mal. 3:8 [n] Num. 35:2
11 [o] Neh. 13:17, 25 [p] Neh. 10:39
12 [q] Neh. 10:38; 12:44
13 [r] 2 Chr. 31:12 [s] 1 Cor. 4:2
14 [t] Neh. 5:19; 13:22, 31
15 [u] [Ex. 20:10] [v] Neh. 10:31; [Jer. 17:21]
18 [w] Ezra 9:13; [Jer. 17:21]
19 [x] Lev. 23:32 [y] Jer. 17:21, 22
20 [2] *merchandise* [3] *spent the night*
21 [4] Lit. *before*

13:3 This was done in compliance with their recent pledge (cf. 10:26-29) before Nehemiah left for Persia.

13:4 Tobiah. *See note on 2:10.* Eliashib had allied with Israel's enemy for some personal gain and taken it to such an extreme as to desecrate the house of God.

13:6 I had returned to the king. Nehemiah returned to Persia as he promised (cf. 2:6) ca. 433 B.C., in the 32nd year of Artaxerxes (cf. 5:14). It is unknown exactly how long Nehemiah remained in Persia, perhaps until ca. 424 B.C., but in that interval the disobedience developed.

13:7-9 Nehemiah's response to the desecration of the temple was similar to Christ's almost 5 centuries later (cf. Matt. 21:12,13; John 2:13-17).

13:9 articles of the house of God. In order to accommodate Tobiah, they had moved the articles of the house of God from their rightful place and put idols in the temple courts.

13:10-13 In Nehemiah's absence, the Jews violated their previous covenant with God regarding offerings (cf. 10:35-40) as reported by Mal. 1:6-14 and 3:8-12. In his presence, it was immediately restored (*see notes on 9:38–10:39*).

13:10 gone back to his field. By neglecting the tithe, the people failed to support the Levites. Consequently, they had to abandon their responsibilities in the house of God and perform field labor in order to survive.

13:14 Remember me. This refrain is used 3 times here, once after each rebuke (cf. 13:22,31).

13:15-17 They went against their previous covenant by violating the Sabbath (cf. 10:31).

13:16 Tyre. A Phoenician coastal town 20 mi. S of Sidon.

13:18 Jeremiah had rebuked their fathers for the same things (see Jer. 17:21ff.). By such acts their fathers had brought the misery of exile and oppression, and they were doing the same—increasing God's wrath against them.

13:19-22 Nehemiah had to force compliance with threats.

commanded the Levites that [z]they should
cleanse themselves, and that they should
go and guard the gates, to sanctify the Sabbath day.
Remember me, O my God, *concerning*
this also, and spare me according to the
greatness of Your mercy!
23 In those days I also saw Jews *who* [a]had
married women of [b]Ashdod, Ammon, *and*
Moab. 24 And half of their children spoke
the language of Ashdod, and could not
speak the language of Judah, but spoke according to the language of one or the other
people.
25 So I [c]contended with them and
[5]cursed them, struck some of them and
pulled out their hair, and made them
[d]swear by God, *saying*, "You shall not give
your daughters as wives to their sons, nor
take their daughters for your sons or yourselves. 26 [e]Did not Solomon king of Israel
sin by these things? Yet among many nations there was no king like him, [f]who was
beloved of his God; and God made him
king over all Israel. [g]Nevertheless pagan
women caused even him to sin. 27 Should
we then hear of your doing all this great
evil, [h]transgressing against our God by
marrying pagan women?"
28 And *one* of the sons [i]of Joiada, the son
of Eliashib the high priest, *was* a son-in-law
of [j]Sanballat the Horonite; therefore I
drove him from me.
29 [k]Remember them, O my God, because
they have defiled the priesthood and [l]the
covenant of the priesthood and the Levites.
30 [m]Thus I cleansed them of everything
pagan. I also [n]assigned duties to the priests
and the Levites, each to his service, 31 and
to bringing [o]the wood offering and the firstfruits at appointed times.
[p]Remember me, O my God, for good!

22 [z] 1 Chr. 15:12; Neh. 12:30
23 [a] [Ex. 34:16; Deut. 7:3,4]; Ezra 9:2; Neh. 10:30 [b] Neh. 4:7
25 [c] Prov. 28:4 [d] Ezra 10:5; Neh. 10:29,30
[5] *pronounced them cursed*
26 [e] 1 Kin. 11:1,2
[f] 2 Sam. 12:24,25
[g] 1 Kin. 11:4-8
27 [h] [Ezra 10:2]; Neh. 13:23
28 [i] Neh. 12:10,12 [j] Neh. 4:1,7; 6:1,2
29 [k] Neh. 6:14 [l] Mal. 2:4,11,12
30 [m] Neh. 10:30 [n] Neh. 12:1
31 [o] Neh. 10:34 [p] Neh. 13:14,22

13:23-29 Both the priests and the people had married pagans of the land in violation of the Mosaic law (cf. Ex. 34:15,16; Deut. 7:3), the earlier reforms of Ezra (cf. Ezra 9,10), and their own covenant (cf. 10:30). Malachi spoke against this sin (Mal. 2:10-16).

13:23 Ashdod. *See note on 4:7.* **Ammon, *and* Moab.** Neighboring countries E of the Jordan whose beginnings were by Lot's incestuous relationship with his two daughters (cf. Gen. 19:30-38).

13:28 Even the grandson of the High-Priest (cf. 12:10) sinfully married a daughter of Sanballat (*see note on 2:10*).

13:29,30 Malachi 2:1-8 recognizes the uncleanness within the priesthood.

13:31 Remember me. Nehemiah prayed this for the third time (cf. 13:14,22), desiring God's blessing on his obedient efforts.

The Book of ESTHER

Title

"Esther" serves as the title without variation through the ages. This book and the book of Ruth are the only OT books named after women. Like Song of Solomon, Obadiah, and Nahum, the NT does not quote or allude to Esther.

"Hadassah" (2:7), meaning "myrtle," was the Heb. name of Esther, which came either from the Persian word "star" or possibly from the name of the Babylonian love goddess, Ishtar. As the orphaned daughter of her father Abihail, Esther grew up in Persia with her older cousin, Mordecai, who raised her as if she were his own daughter (2:7,15).

Author and Date

The author remains unknown, although Mordecai, Ezra, and Nehemiah have been suggested. Whoever penned Esther possessed a detailed knowledge of Persian customs, etiquette, and history, plus particular familiarity with the palace at Shushan (1:5-7). He also exhibited intimate knowledge of the Hebrew calendar and customs, while additionally showing a strong sense of Jewish nationalism. Possibly a Persian Jew, who later moved back to Israel, wrote Esther.

Esther appears as the 17th book in the literary chronology of the OT and closes the OT historical section. Only Ezra 7–10, Nehemiah, and Malachi report later OT history than Esther. The account in Esther ends in 473 B.C. before Ahasuerus died by assassination (ca. 465 B.C.). Esther 10:2 speaks as though Ahasuerus' reign has been completed, so the earliest possible writing date would be after his reign around mid-fifth century B.C. The latest reasonable date would be prior to 331 B.C. when Greece conquered Persia.

Background and Setting

Esther occurred during the Persian period of world history, ca. 539 B.C. (Dan. 5:30,31) to ca. 331 B.C. (Dan. 8:1-27). Ahasuerus ruled from ca. 486 to 465 B.C.; Esther covers the 483–473 B.C. portion of his reign. The name Ahasuerus represents the Heb. transliteration of the Persian name "Khshayarsha," while "Xerxes" represents his Gr. name.

The events of Esther occurred during the wider time span between the first return of the Jews after the 70 year captivity in Babylon (Dan. 9:1-19) under Zerubbabel ca. 538 B.C. (Ezra 1–6) and the second return led by Ezra ca. 458 B.C. (Ezra 7–10). Nehemiah's journey (the third return) from Susa to Jerusalem (Neh. 1–2) occurred later (ca. 445 B.C.).

Esther and Exodus both chronicle how vigorously foreign powers tried to eliminate the Jewish race and how God sovereignly preserved His people in accordance with His covenant promise to Abraham ca. 2100–2075 B.C. (Gen. 12:1-3; 17:1-8). As a result of God's prevailing, Esther 9,10 records the beginning of Purim—a new annual festival in the 12th month (Feb.-Mar.) to celebrate the nation's survival. Purim became one of two festivals given outside of the Mosaic legislation to still be celebrated in Israel (Hanukkah, or the Festival of Lights, is the other, cf. John 10:22).

Historical and Theological Themes

All 167 verses of Esther have ultimately been accepted as canonical, although the absence of God's name anywhere has caused some to unnecessarily doubt its authenticity. The Greek Septuagint (LXX) added an extra 107 apocryphal verses which supposedly compensated for this lack. Along with Song of Solomon, Ruth, Ecclesiastes, and Lamentations, Esther stands with the OT books of the Megilloth, or "5 scrolls." Rabbis read these books in the synagogue on 5 special occasions during the year—Esther being read at Purim (cf. 9:20-32).

The historical genesis for the drama played out between Mordecai (a Benjamite descendant of Saul—2:5) and Haman (an Agagite—3:1,10; 8:3,5; 9:24) goes back almost 1,000 years when the Jews exited from Egypt (ca. 1445 B.C.) and were attacked by the Amalekites (Ex. 17:8-16), whose lineage began with Amalek, son of Esau (Gen. 36:12). God pronounced His curse on the Amalekites, which resulted in their total elimination as a people (Ex. 17:14; Deut. 25:17-19). Although Saul (ca. 1030 B.C.) received orders to kill all the Amalekites, including their king Agag (1 Sam. 15:2,3), he disobeyed (1 Sam. 15:7-9) and incurred God's displeasure (1 Sam. 15:11,26; 28:18). Samuel finally hacked Agag into pieces (1 Sam. 15:32,33). Because of his lineage from Agag, Haman carried deep hostility toward the Jews.

The time of Esther arrived 550 years after the death of Agag, but in spite of such passage of time, neither Haman the Agagite nor Mordecai the Benjamite had forgotten the tribal feud that still smoldered in their souls. This explains why Mordecai refused to bow down to Haman (3:2,3) and why Haman so viciously attempted to exterminate the Jewish race (3:5,6,13). As expected, God's prophecy to extinguish the Amalekites (Ex. 17:14; Deut. 25:17-19) and God's promise to preserve the Jews (Gen. 17:1-8) prevailed.

Because of God's faithfulness to save His people, the festival of Purim (named after the Akkadian word for "lot"—3:7; 9:26), an annual, two day holiday of feasting, rejoicing, sending food to one another, and giving gifts to the poor (9:21,22), was decreed to be celebrated in every generation, by every family, in every province and city (9:27,28). Esther later added a new feature of fasting with lamentation (9:31). Purim is not biblically mentioned again, although it has been celebrated throughout the centuries in Israel.

Esther could be compared to a chess game. God and Satan (as invisible players) moved real kings, queens, and nobles. When Satan put Haman into place, it was as if he announced "Check." God then positioned Esther and Mordecai in order to put Satan into "Checkmate!" Ever since the fall of man (Gen. 3:1-19), Satan has attempted to spiritually sever God's relationship with His human creation and disrupt God's covenant promises with Israel. For example, Christ's line through the tribe of Judah had been murderously reduced to Joash alone, who was rescued and preserved (2 Chr. 22:10-12). Later, Herod slaughtered the infants of Bethlehem, thinking Christ was among them (Matt. 2:16). Satan tempted Christ to denounce God and worship him (Matt. 4:9). Peter, at Satan's insistence, tried to block Christ's journey to Calvary (Matt. 16:22). Finally, Satan entered into Judas who then betrayed Christ to the Jews and Romans (Luke 22:3-6). While God was not mentioned in Esther, He was everywhere apparent as the One who opposed and foiled Satan's diabolical schemes by providential intervention.

In Esther, all of God's unconditional covenant promises to Abraham (Gen. 17:1-8) and to David (2 Sam. 7:8-16) were jeopardized. However, God's love for Israel is nowhere more apparent than in this dramatic rescue of His people from pending elimination. "Behold, He who keeps Israel shall neither slumber nor sleep" (Ps. 121:4).

Interpretive Challenges

The most obvious question raised by Esther comes from the fact that God is nowhere mentioned, as in Song of Solomon. Nor does the writer or any participant refer to the law of God, the Levitical sacrifices, worship, or prayer. The skeptic might ask, "Why would God never be mentioned when the Persian king receives over 175 references? Since God's sovereignty prevailed to save the Jews, why does He then not receive appropriate recognition?"

It seems satisfying to respond that if God desired to be mentioned, He could just as sovereignly have moved the author to write of Him as He acted to save Israel. This situation seems to be more of a problem at the human level than the divine, because Esther is the classic illustration of God's providence as He, the unseen power, controls everything for His purpose. There are no miracles in Esther, but the preservation of Israel through providential control of every event and person reveals the omniscience and omnipotence of Jehovah. Whether He is named is not the issue. He is clearly the main character in the drama.

Second, "Why were Mordecai and Esther so secular in their lifestyles?" Esther (2:6-20) does not seem to have the zeal for holiness like Daniel (Dan. 1:8-20). Mordecai kept his and Esther's Jewish heritage secret, unlike Daniel (Dan. 6:5). The law of God was absent in contrast to Ezra (Ezra 7:10). Nehemiah had a heart for Jerusalem that seemingly eluded the affections of Esther and Mordecai (Neh. 1:1–2:5).

The following observations help to shed some light on these issues. First, this short book does not record everything. Perhaps Mordecai and Esther actually possessed a deeper faith than becomes apparent here (cf. 4:16). Second, even godly Nehemiah did not mention his God when talking to King Artaxerxes (Neh. 2:1-8). Third, the Jewish festivals which provided structure for worship had been lost long before Esther, e.g., Passover (2 Kin. 23:22) and Pentecost (Neh. 8:17). Fourth, possibly the anti-Jewish letter written by the Samaritans to Ahasuerus several years earlier had frightened them (ca. 486 B.C.; Ezra 4:6). Fifth, the evil intentions of Haman did not just first surface when Mordecai refused to bow down (3:1,2). Most likely they were long before shared by others which would have intimidated the Jewish population. Sixth, Esther did identify with her Jewish heritage at a most appropriate time (7:3,4). And yet, the nagging question of why Esther and Mordecai did not seem to have the same kind of open devotion to God as did Daniel remains. Further, Nehemiah's prayer (Neh. 1:5-11, esp. v. 7) seems to indicate a spiritual lethargy among the Jewish exiles in Susa. So this issue must ultimately be resolved by God since He alone knows human hearts.

Outline

I. Esther Replaces Vashti (1:1–2:18)

- A. Vashti's Insubordination (1:1-22)
- B. Esther's Coronation (2:1-18)

II. Mordecai Overcomes Haman (2:19–7:10)

- A. Mordecai's Loyalty (2:19-23)
- B. Haman's Promotion and Decree (3:1-15)
- C. Esther's Intervention (4:1–5:14)
- D. Mordecai's Recognition (6:1-13)
- E. Haman's Fall (6:14–7:10)

III. Israel Survives Haman's Genocide Attempt (8:1–10:3)

- A. Esther and Mordecai's Advocacy (8:1-17)
- B. The Jews' Victory (9:1-19)
- C. Purim's Beginning (9:20-23)
- D. Mordecai's Fame (10:1-3)

The King Dethrones Queen Vashti

1 Now it came to pass in the days of
[a]Ahasuerus[1] (this *was* the Ahasuerus
who reigned [b]over one hundred and twenty-seven provinces, [c]from India to Ethiopia), 2 in those days when King Ahasuerus
[d]sat on the throne of his kingdom, which
was in [e]Shushan[2] the [3]citadel, 3 *that* in the
third year of his reign he [f]made a feast for
all his officials and servants—the powers
of Persia and Media, the nobles, and the
princes of the provinces *being* before him—
4 when he showed the riches of his glorious kingdom and the splendor of his excellent majesty for many days, one hundred and eighty days *in all.*
5 And when these days were completed,
the king made a feast lasting seven days
for all the people who were present in
[4]Shushan the [5]citadel, from great to small,
in the court of the garden of the king's
palace. 6 *There were* white and blue linen
curtains fastened with cords of fine linen
and purple on silver rods and marble pillars; *and the* [g]couches *were* of gold and silver on a *mosaic* pavement of alabaster,
turquoise, and white and black marble.
7 And they served drinks in golden vessels, each vessel being different from the
other, with royal wine in abundance, [h]ac-
cording to the [6]generosity of the king. 8 In
accordance with the law, the drinking was
not compulsory; for so the king had ordered all the officers of his household, that
they should do according to each man's
pleasure.
9 Queen Vashti also made a feast for the
women *in* the royal palace which *belonged*
to King Ahasuerus.
10 On the seventh day, when the heart of
the king was merry with wine, he commanded Mehuman, Biztha, [i]Harbona,
Bigtha, Abagtha, Zethar, and Carcas, seven
eunuchs who served in the presence of
King Ahasuerus, 11 to bring Queen Vashti
before the king, *wearing* her royal crown, in
order to show her beauty to the people and
the officials, for she *was* beautiful to behold. 12 But Queen Vashti refused to come
at the king's command *brought* by *his* eunuchs; therefore the king was furious, and
his anger burned within him.
13 Then the king said to the [j]wise men
[k]who understood the times (for this *was*
the king's manner toward all who knew
law and justice, 14 those closest to him *be-*
ing Carshena, Shethar, Admatha, Tarshish,
Meres, Marsena, and Memucan, the [l]seven
princes of Persia and Media, [m]who had access to the king's presence, *and* who
[7]ranked highest in the kingdom): 15 "What
shall we do to Queen Vashti, according to
law, because she did not obey the command of King Ahasuerus *brought to her* by
the eunuchs?"
16 And Memucan answered before the
king and the princes: "Queen Vashti has
not only wronged the king, but also all the
princes, and all the people who *are* in all
the provinces of King Ahasuerus. 17 For
the queen's behavior will become known
to all women, so that they will [n]despise
their husbands in their eyes, when they report, 'King Ahasuerus commanded Queen
Vashti to be brought in before him, but she
did not come.' 18 This very day the *noble*
ladies of Persia and Media will say to all
the king's officials that they have heard of
the behavior of the queen. Thus *there will be*
excessive contempt and wrath. 19 If it
pleases the king, let a royal [8]decree go out
from him, and let it be recorded in the laws
of the Persians and the Medes, so that it
will [o]not [9]be altered, that Vashti shall come
no more before King Ahasuerus; and let
the king give her royal position to another
who is better than she. 20 When the king's
decree which he will make is proclaimed
throughout all his empire (for it is great),
all wives will [p]honor their husbands, both
great and small."
21 And the reply pleased the king and the

CHAPTER 1

1 [a] Ezra 4:6; Dan. 9:1 [b] Esth. 8:9 [c] Dan. 6:1 [1] Generally identified with Xerxes I (485–464 B.C.)
2 [d] 1 Kin. 1:46 [e] Neh. 1:1; Dan. 8:2 [2] Or *Susa* [3] Or *fortified palace*, and so elsewhere in the book
3 [f] Gen. 40:20; Esth. 2:18
5 [4] Or *Susa* [5] *palace*
6 [g] Esth. 7:8; Ezek. 23:41; Amos 2:8; 6:4
7 [h] Esth. 2:18 [6] Lit. *hand*
10 [i] Esth. 7:9
13 [j] Jer. 10:7; Dan. 2:12; Matt. 2:1 [k] 1 Chr. 12:32
14 [l] Ezra 7:14 [m] 2 Kin. 25:19; [Matt. 18:10] [7] Lit. *sat in first place*
17 [n] [Eph. 5:33]
19 [o] Esth. 8:8; Dan. 6:8 [8] Lit. *word* [9] *pass away*
20 [p] [Eph. 5:33; Col. 3:18; 1 Pet. 3:1]

1:1 one hundred and twenty-seven provinces. The kingdom comprised 20 regions (3:12; 8:9; 9:3) which were further divided into provinces ruled over by governors (3:12). **India to Ethiopia.** Ethiopia, not Asia Minor, is mentioned as representing the western edge of the kingdom to avoid any remembrance of the king's previous defeat by the Greeks ca. 481–479 B.C. (cf. 8:9). This description also avoided any confusion with the Ahasuerus of Dan. 9:1. **Ahasuerus.** See Introduction: Background and Setting.

1:2 Shushan the citadel. Shushan (the Heb. rendering of the Gr. Susa), the winter residence, was one of 4 capital cities; the other 3 included Babylon, Ecbatana (Ezra 6:2), and Persepolis. The citadel refers to the fortified palace complex built above the city for protection.

1:3 the third year. Ca. 483 B.C. This probably included the planning phase for Ahasuerus' later campaign against Greece in which the king suffered a humiliating defeat (ca. 481–479 B.C.). **Persia and Media.** Cyrus the Persian inherited Media and thus the name Media became just as prominent as Persia (ca. 550 B.C.).

1:9 Queen Vashti. Greek literature records her name as Amestris. She gave birth (ca. 483 B.C.) to Ahasuerus' third son, Artaxerxes, who later succeeded his father Ahasuerus on the throne (Ezra 7:1).

1:12 Vashti refused. Her reason is not recorded, although suggestions have included that 1) her appearance would have involved lewd behavior before drunken men, or 2) that she was still pregnant with Artaxerxes.

1:14 the seven princes. These highest ranking officials (cf. Ezra 7:14) were perhaps equivalent to the magi of Dan. 1:20.

1:19 will not be altered. The irrevocable nature of Persian law (cf. Dan. 6:8,12,15) played an important role in how the rest of Esther concluded (cf. 8:8).

princes, and the king did according to the
word of Memucan. 22 Then he sent letters to
all the king's provinces, [q]to each province in
its own script, and to every people in their
own language, that each man should [r]be
master in his own house, and speak in the
language of his own people.

Esther Becomes Queen

2 After these things, when the wrath of
King Ahasuerus subsided, he remembered Vashti, [a]what she had done, and what
had been decreed against her. 2 Then the
king's servants who attended him said: "Let
beautiful young virgins be sought for the
king; 3 and let the king appoint officers in
all the provinces of his kingdom, that they
may gather all the beautiful young virgins
to [1]Shushan the [2]citadel, into the women's
quarters, under the custody of [3]Hegai the
king's eunuch, custodian of the women.
And let beauty preparations be given *them.*
4 Then let the young woman who pleases
the king be queen instead of Vashti."
This thing pleased the king, and he did
so.
5 In [4]Shushan the [5]citadel there was a
certain Jew whose name *was* Mordecai the
son of Jair, the son of Shimei, the son of
[b]Kish, a Benjamite. 6 [c]*Kish*[6] had been carried away from Jerusalem with the captives
who had been captured with [7]Jeconiah
king of Judah, whom Nebuchadnezzar the
king of Babylon had carried away. 7 And
Mordecai had brought up Hadassah, that *is,*
Esther, [d]his uncle's daughter, for she had
neither father nor mother. The young
woman *was* lovely and beautiful. When her
father and mother died, Mordecai took her
as his own daughter.
8 So it was, when the king's command
and decree were heard, and when many
young women were [e]gathered at [8]Shushan
the [9]citadel, *under* the custody of Hegai,
that Esther also was taken to the king's
palace, into the care of Hegai the custodian
of the women. 9 Now the young woman
pleased him, and she obtained his favor; so
he readily gave [f]beauty preparations to
her, besides [1]her allowance. Then seven
choice maidservants were provided for her
from the king's palace, and he moved her
and her maidservants to the best *place* in
the house of the women.
10 [g]Esther had not [2]revealed her people
or family, for Mordecai had charged her
not to reveal *it.* 11 And every day Mordecai
paced in front of the court of the women's
quarters, to learn of Esther's welfare and
what was happening to her.

22 [q] Esth. 3:12; 8:9 [r] [Eph. 5:22-24; 1 Tim. 2:12]

CHAPTER 2

1 [a] Esth. 1:19, 20
3 [1] Or *Susa* [2] *palace* [3] Heb. *Hege*
5 [4] Or *Susa* [5] *palace* [b] 1 Sam. 9:1
6 [c] 2 Kin. 24:14, 15; 2 Chr. 36:10, 20; Jer. 24:1 [6] Lit. *Who* [7] *Jehoiachin,* 2 Kin. 24:6
7 [d] Esth. 2:15
8 [e] Esth. 2:3 [8] Or *Susa* [9] *palace*
9 [f] Esth. 2:3, 12 [1] Lit. *her portions*
10 [g] Esth. 2:20 [2] Revealed the identity of

1:22 letters. The efficient Persian communication network (a rapid relay by horses) played an important role in speedily publishing kingdom edicts (cf. 3:12-14; 8:9,10,14; 9:20,30).

2:1 After these things. Most likely during the latter portion of the king's ill-fated war with Greece (ca. 481–479 B.C.). **he remembered Vashti.** The king was legally unable to restore Vashti (cf. 1:19-22), so the counselors proposed a new plan with promise.

2:5 Mordecai. See Introduction: Historical and Theological Themes. He was among the fourth generation of deported Jews. **Kish.** Mordecai's great grandfather who actually experienced the Babylonian deportation. After Babylon fell to Medo-Persia (ca. 539 B.C.), Jews were moved to other parts of the new kingdom. Kish represents a Benjamite family name that could be traced back (ca. 1100 B.C.) to Saul's father (1 Sam. 9:1).

2:6 Jeconiah. Former king of Judah (also known as Jehoiachin and Coniah) who was deported ca. 597 B.C. (cf. 2 Kin. 24:14,15; 2 Chr. 36:9,10). Due to his disobedience, the Lord removed his descendants from the line of David to Christ (Jer. 22:24-30). The family of Mordecai and Esther were part of the good figs in Jer. 24:1-7.

2:7 Esther. See Introduction: Title.

2:8 Esther also was taken. It is impossible to tell if Esther went voluntarily or against her will.

2:9 pleased him. That she pleased Hegai points to God's providential control.

2:10 not to reveal *it.* Possibly because of the hostile letter mentioned in Ezra 4:6 or the anti-Semitic sentiments of Haman and other like-minded people.

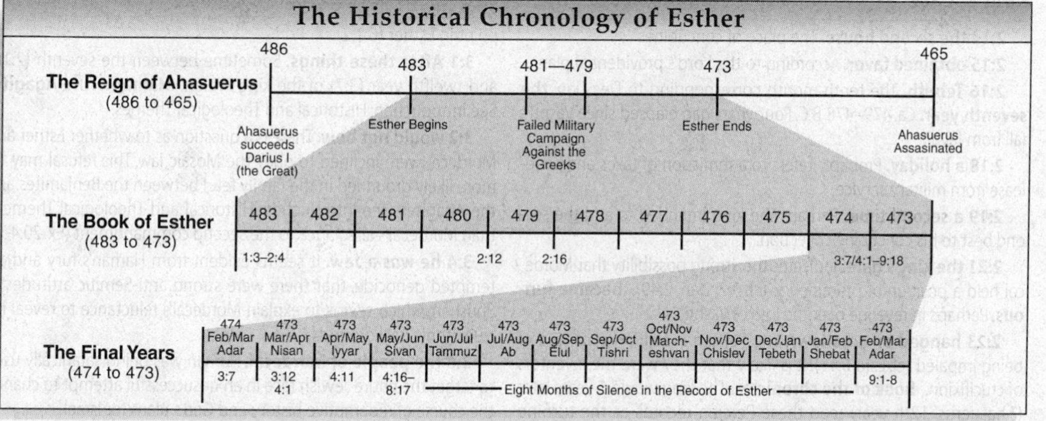

12 Each young woman's turn came to go
in to King Ahasuerus after she had completed twelve months' preparation, according to the regulations for the women,
for thus were the days of their preparation
apportioned: six months with oil of myrrh,
and six months with perfumes and preparations for beautifying women. 13 Thus
prepared, each young woman went to the
king, and she was given whatever she desired to take with her from the women's
quarters to the king's palace. 14 In the
evening she went, and in the morning she
returned to the second house of the
women, to the custody of Shaashgaz, the
king's eunuch who kept the concubines.
She would not go in to the king again unless the king delighted in her and called for
her by name.
15 Now when the turn came for Esther
[h]the daughter of Abihail the uncle of
Mordecai, who had taken her as his
daughter, to go in to the king, she requested nothing but what Hegai the king's eunuch, the custodian of the women, advised. And Esther [i]obtained favor in the
sight of all who saw her. 16 So Esther was
taken to King Ahasuerus, into his royal
palace, in the tenth month, which *is* the
month of Tebeth, in the seventh year of his
reign. 17 The king loved Esther more than
all the *other* women, and she obtained
grace and favor in his sight more than all
the virgins; so he set the royal [j]crown upon
her head and made her queen instead of
Vashti. 18 Then the king [k]made a great
feast, the Feast of Esther, for all his officials
and servants; and he proclaimed a holiday
in the provinces and gave gifts according
to the [3]generosity of a king.

Mordecai Discovers a Plot

19 When virgins were gathered together
a second time, Mordecai sat within the
king's gate. 20 [l]*Now* Esther had not revealed her family and her people, just as
Mordecai had charged her, for Esther
obeyed the command of Mordecai as when
she was brought up by him.
21 In those days, while Mordecai sat
within the king's gate, two of the king's
eunuchs, [4]Bigthan and Teresh, doorkeepers, became furious and sought to lay
hands on King Ahasuerus. 22 So the matter became known to Mordecai, [m]who
told Queen Esther, and Esther informed
the king in Mordecai's name. 23 And
when an inquiry was made into the matter, it was confirmed, and both were
hanged on a gallows; and it was written
in [n]the book of the chronicles in the presence of the king.

Haman's Conspiracy Against the Jews

3 After these things King Ahasuerus
promoted Haman, the son of Hammedatha the [a]Agagite, and [b]advanced him
and set his seat above all the princes who
were with him. 2 And all the king's servants who *were* [c]within the king's gate
bowed and paid homage to Haman, for so
the king had commanded concerning him.
But Mordecai [d]would not bow or pay
homage. 3 Then the king's servants who
were within the king's gate said to Mordecai, "Why do you transgress the [e]king's
command?" 4 Now it happened, when
they spoke to him daily and he would not
listen to them, that they told *it* to Haman,
to see whether Mordecai's words would
stand; for *Mordecai* had told them that he
was a Jew. 5 When Haman saw that
Mordecai [f]did not bow or pay him
homage, Haman was [g]filled with wrath.
6 But he disdained to lay hands on Mordecai alone, for they had told him of the people of Mordecai. Instead, Haman [h]sought
to destroy all the Jews who *were* throughout the whole kingdom of Ahasuerus—the
people of Mordecai.

15 [h]Esth. 2:7; 9:29 [i]Esth. 5:2, 8
17 [j]Esth. 1:11
18 [k]Esth. 1:3 [3]Lit. *hand*
20 [l]Esth. 2:10; [Prov. 22:6]
21 [4]*Bigthana,* Esth. 6:2
22 [m]Esth. 6:1, 2
23 [n]Esth. 6:1

CHAPTER 3

1 [a]Num. 24:7; 1 Sam. 15:8 [b]Esth. 5:11
2 [c]Esth. 2:19, 21; 5:9 [d]Esth. 3:5; Ps. 15:4
3 [e]Esth. 3:2
5 [f]Esth. 3:2; 5:9 [g]Dan. 3:19
6 [h]Ps. 83:4; [Rev. 12:1-17]

2:14 the second house. The place of concubines.

2:15 obtained favor. According to the Lord's providential plan.

2:16 Tebeth. The tenth month corresponding to Dec./Jan. **the seventh year.** Ca. 479–478 B.C. Four years had elapsed since Vashti's fall from favor.

2:18 a holiday. Probably refers to a remission of taxes and/or release from military service.

2:19 a second time. Perhaps the king intended to add the second best to his concubine collection.

2:21 the king's gate. Indicates the strong possibility that Mordecai held a position of prominence (cf. 3:2; Dan. 2:49). **became furious.** Perhaps in revenge over the loss of Vashti.

2:23 hanged on a gallows. The Persian execution consisted of being impaled (cf. Ezra 6:11). It is likely that they were the inventors of crucifixion. **book of the chronicles.** The king would 5 years later (Ahasuerus' 12th year) read these Persian records as the turning point in Esther (6:1,2).

3:1 After these things. Sometime between the seventh (2:16) and twelfth year (3:7) of the king's reign. **Haman...the Agagite.** See Introduction: Historical and Theological Themes.

3:2 would not bow. There is a question as to whether Esther and Mordecai were inclined to obey the Mosaic law. This refusal may be more likely grounded in the family feud between the Benjamites and the Agagites (see Introduction: Historical and Theological Themes), than Mordecai's allegiance to the second commandment (Ex. 20:4-6).

3:4 he *was* a Jew. It seems evident from Haman's fury and attempted genocide, that there were strong anti-Semitic attitudes in Shushan, which seems to explain Mordecai's reluctance to reveal his true ethnic background.

3:6 the people of Mordecai. Haman was being satanically used to target the entire Jewish race in an unsuccessful attempt to change the course of redemptive history and God's plans for Israel.

7 In the first month, which is the month
of Nisan, in the twelfth year of King Ahasuerus, [i]they cast Pur (that *is,* the lot), before
Haman [1]to determine the day and the
[2]month, [3]until *it fell on the* twelfth *month,*
which *is* the month of Adar.
8 Then Haman said to King Ahasuerus,
"There is a certain people scattered and
dispersed among the people in all the
provinces of your kingdom; [j]their laws *are*
different from all *other* people's, and they
do not keep the king's laws. Therefore it *is*
not fitting for the king to let them remain.
9 If it pleases the king, let *a decree* be written that they be destroyed, and I will pay
ten thousand talents of silver into the
hands of those who do the work, to bring
it into the king's treasuries."
10 So the king [k]took [l]his signet ring from
his hand and gave it to Haman, the son of
Hammedatha the Agagite, the [m]enemy of
the Jews. 11 And the king said to Haman,
"The money and the people *are* given to
you, to do with them as seems good to
you."
12 [n]Then the king's scribes were called
on the thirteenth day of the first month,
and *a decree* was written according to all
that Haman commanded—to the king's
satraps, to the governors who *were* over
each province, to the officials of all people,
to every province [o]according to its script,
and to every people in their language. [p]In
the name of King Ahasuerus it was written,
and sealed with the king's signet ring.
13 And the letters were [q]sent by couriers
into all the king's provinces, to destroy, to
kill, and to annihilate all the Jews, both
young and old, little children and women,
[r]in one day, on the thirteenth *day* of the
twelfth *month,* which *is* the month of Adar,
and [s]to plunder their [4]possessions. 14 [t]A
copy of the document was to be issued as
law in every province, being published for
all people, that they should be ready for
that day. 15 The couriers went out, hastened
by the king's command; and the decree was
proclaimed in [5]Shushan the [6]citadel. So the
king and Haman sat down to drink, but
[u]the city of Shushan was [7]perplexed.

Esther Agrees to Help the Jews

4 When Mordecai learned all that had
happened, [1]he [a]tore his clothes and
put on sackcloth [b]and ashes, and went out
into the midst of the city. He [c]cried out
with a loud and bitter cry. 2 He went as far
as the front of the king's gate, for no one
might enter the king's gate clothed with
sackcloth. 3 And in every province where
the king's command and decree arrived,
there was great mourning among the Jews,
with fasting, weeping, and wailing; and
many lay in sackcloth and ashes.
4 So Esther's maids and eunuchs came
and told her, and the queen was deeply distressed. Then she sent garments to clothe
Mordecai and take his sackcloth away from
him, but he would not accept *them.* 5 Then
Esther called Hathach, *one* of the king's eunuchs whom he had appointed to attend
her, and she gave him a command concerning Mordecai, to learn what and why this
was. 6 So Hathach went out to Mordecai in
the city square that *was* in front of the
king's gate. 7 And Mordecai told him all
that had happened to him, and [d]the sum of
money that Haman had promised to pay
into the king's treasuries to destroy the
Jews. 8 He also gave him [e]a copy of the
written decree for their destruction, which
was given at [2]Shushan, that he might show

7 [i] Esth. 9:24-26 [1] Lit. *from day to day and month to month* [2] LXX adds *to destroy the people of Mordecai in one day;* Vg. adds *the nation of the Jews should be destroyed* [3] So with MT, Vg.; LXX *and the lot fell on the fourteenth of the month*
8 [j] Ezra 4:12-15; Acts 16:20, 21
10 [k] Gen. 41:42 [l] Esth. 8:2, 8 [m] Esth. 7:6
12 [n] Esth. 8:9 [o] Esth. 1:22 [p] 1 Kin. 21:8; Esth. 8:8-10
13 [q] 2 Chr. 30:6; Esth. 8:10, 14 [r] Esth. 8:12
[s] Esth. 8:11; 9:10 [4] LXX adds the text of the letter here
14 [t] Esth. 8:13, 14
15 [u] Esth. 8:15; [Prov. 29:2] [5] Or *Susa* [6] *palace* [7] *in confusion*

CHAPTER 4

1 [a] 2 Sam. 1:11; Esth. 3:8-10; Jon. 3:5, 6 [b] Josh. 7:6; Ezek. 27:30 [c] Gen. 27:34 [1] Lit. *Mordecai*
7 [d] Esth. 3:9
8 [e] Esth. 3:14, 15 [2] Or *Susa*

3:7 Nisan. The time period Mar./Apr. Ironically, the Jews should have been celebrating the Passover to remind them of a former deliverance. **twelfth year.** Ca. 474 B.C. **they cast.** Haman's court of advisers who made decisions superstitiously based on astrology and casting of lots. **Pur...lot.** A lot would be like modern dice which were cast to determine future decisions (cf. the Hebrew lot, 1 Chr. 26:14; Neh. 10:34; Jonah 1:7). Proverbs 16:33 states that God providentially controlled the outcome of the lot. **Adar.** Feb./Mar. There would have been an 11 month interval between Haman's decree and its expected fulfillment.

3:8 a certain people. Haman never divulged their identity.

3:9 ten thousand talents. The exact dollar amount is uncertain, but reportedly it would have weighed 375 tons and equaled almost 70 percent of the king's annual revenue. Since this sum would have been derived from the plunder of the Jews, it indicates that they had grown prosperous.

3:10,11 The king would have easily been eager to eliminate any rebellion against his authority (cf. 3:8), although he did not seem to be interested in the money.

3:10 the enemy of the Jews. Cf. 7:6; 8:1; 9:10,24.

3:12 sealed...king's signet ring. This would be equivalent to the king's signature. The date has been calculated by historians to be Apr. 7, 474 B.C.

3:13 to destroy. An ambitious plot to annihilate the Jews in just one day. Historians have calculated the date to be Mar. 7, 473 B.C. The king had unwittingly approved this provision which would kill his own queen.

3:14 as law. It would be irrevocable (cf. 1:19; 8:5-8).

3:15 perplexed. No specific reason is stated. Most likely even this pagan population was puzzled at the extreme and deadly racism of the king and Haman.

4:1 sackcloth and ashes. An outward sign of inward distress and humiliation (cf. Jer. 6:26; Dan. 9:3; Matt. 11:21). Mordecai realized that he had prompted this genocidal retaliation by Haman.

4:4 she sent garments. Mordecai could then enter the king's gate (cf. 4:2) and talk with Esther directly (cf. Neh. 2:2).

4:5 Hathach. A trusted eunuch who knew of Esther's Jewish background.

4:7,8 That Mordecai possessed this specific knowledge and a copy of the edict further evidences his prominent position in Persia.

it to Esther and explain it to her, and that he
might command her to go in to the king to
make supplication to him and plead before
him for her people. 9 So Hathach returned
and told Esther the words of Mordecai.
10 Then Esther spoke to Hathach, and
gave him a command for Mordecai: 11 "All
the king's servants and the people of the
king's provinces know that any man or
woman who goes into [f]the inner court to
the king, who has not been called, [g]*he has*
but one law: put *all* to death, except the one
[h]to whom the king holds out the golden
scepter, that he may live. Yet I myself have
not been [i]called to go in to the king these
thirty days." 12 So they told Mordecai Esther's words.
13 And Mordecai told *them* to answer Esther: "Do not think in your heart that you
will escape in the king's palace any more
than all the other Jews. 14 For if you remain
completely silent at this time, relief and deliverance will arise for the Jews from another place, but you and your father's
house will perish. Yet who knows whether
you have come to the kingdom for *such* a
time as this?"
15 Then Esther told *them* to reply to
Mordecai: 16 "Go, gather all the Jews who
are present in [3]Shushan, and fast for me;
neither eat nor drink for [j]three days, night
or day. My maids and I will fast likewise.
And so I will go to the king, which *is*
against the law; [k]and if I perish, I perish!"
17 So Mordecai went his way and did according to all that Esther commanded [4]him.

Esther's Banquet

5 Now it happened [a]on the third day
that Esther put on *her* royal *robes* and
stood in [b]the inner court of the king's
palace, across from the king's house, while
the king sat on his royal throne in the royal
house, facing the entrance of the [1]house.
2 So it was, when the king saw Queen Esther standing in the court, *that* [c]she found
favor in his sight, and [d]the king held out to
Esther the golden scepter that *was* in his
hand. Then Esther went near and touched
the top of the scepter.
3 And the king said to her, "What do you
wish, Queen Esther? What *is* your request?
[e]It shall be given to you—up to half the
kingdom!"
4 So Esther answered, "If it pleases the
king, let the king and Haman come today
to the banquet that I have prepared for
him."
5 Then the king said, "Bring Haman
quickly, that he may do as Esther has said."
So the king and Haman went to the banquet that Esther had prepared.
6 At the banquet of wine [f]the king said
to Esther, [g]"What *is* your petition? It shall
be granted you. What *is* your request, up
to half the kingdom? It shall be done!"
7 Then Esther answered and said, "My
petition and request *is this:* 8 If I have
found favor in the sight of the king, and if
it pleases the king to grant my petition and
[2]fulfill my request, then let the king and
Haman come to the [h]banquet which I will
prepare for them, and tomorrow I will do
as the king has said."

Haman's Plot Against Mordecai

9 So Haman went out that day [i]joyful
and with a glad heart; but when Haman
saw Mordecai in the king's gate, and [j]that
he did not stand or tremble before him, he
was filled with indignation against Mordecai. 10 Nevertheless Haman [k]restrained
himself and went home, and he sent and
called for his friends and his wife Zeresh.
11 Then Haman told them of his great riches, [l]the multitude of his children, everything in which the king had promoted him,
and how he had [m]advanced him above the
officials and servants of the king.
12 Moreover Haman said, "Besides,
Queen Esther invited no one but me to
come in with the king to the banquet that
she prepared; and tomorrow I am again invited by her, along with the king. 13 Yet all

11 [f]Esth. 5:1; 6:4 [g]Dan. 2:9 [h]Esth. 5:2; 8:4 [i]Esth. 2:14
16 [j]Esth. 5:1 [k]Gen. 43:14 [3]Or *Susa*
17 [4]LXX adds a prayer of Mordecai here

CHAPTER 5

1 [a]Esth. 4:16 [b]Esth. 4:11; 6:4 [1]LXX adds many extra details in vv. 1, 2
2 [c][Prov. 21:1] [d]Esth. 4:11; 8:4
3 [e]Esth. 7:2; Mark 6:23
6 [f]Esth. 7:2 [g]Esth. 9:12
8 [h]Esth. 6:14 [2]Lit. *to do*
9 [i][Job 20:5; Luke 6:25] [j]Esth. 3:5
10 [k]2 Sam. 13:22
11 [l]Esth. 9:7-10 [m]Esth. 3:1

4:11 golden scepter. In order to protect the king's life from would-be assassins, this practice prevailed. Seemingly, the king would extend the scepter (a sign of kingly authority) only to those whom he knew and from whom he welcomed a visit (cf. 5:2; 8:4). **these thirty days.** Perhaps Esther feared she had lost favor with the king since he had not summoned her recently.

4:14 relief and deliverance. Mordecai exhibited a healthy faith in God's sovereign power to preserve His people. He may have remembered the Lord's promise to Abraham (cf. Gen. 12:3; 17:1-8). **you...will perish.** Mordecai indicated that Esther would not escape the sentence or be overlooked because of her prominence (cf. 4:13). ***such* a time as this.** Mordecai indirectly appealed to God's providential timing.

4:16 fast. The text does not mention prayer being included such as was Daniel's practice (Dan. 9:3), though it surely was. **perish.** Esther's heroic willingness to die for the sake of her fellow Jews is commendable.

5:2 she found favor. This actually means that Esther first found favor with the God of Israel (cf. Prov. 21:1).

5:3 What *is* your request? Esther deferred her real wish until 7:2,3.

5:3,6 up to half the kingdom. Royal hyperbole that was not intended to be taken at face value (cf. Mark 6:22,23).

5:4 the banquet. The first of two (cf. 5:4-8; 6:14–7:1) that Esther prepared. God would providentially intervene between the two (6:1,2).

5:11 the multitude of his children. At least 10 sons were fathered by Haman (cf. 9:13), who personified sinful pride (cf. Prov. 16:18; 1 Cor. 10:12; Gal. 6:3).

this avails me nothing, so long as I see
Mordecai the Jew sitting at the king's gate."
14 Then his wife Zeresh and all his
friends said to him, "Let a [n]gallows[3] be
made, [4]fifty cubits high, and in the morning [o]suggest to the king that Mordecai be
hanged on it; then go merrily with the king
to the banquet."
And the thing pleased Haman; so he had
[p]the gallows made.

The King Honors Mordecai

6 That night [1]the king could not sleep.
So one was commanded to bring [a]the
book of the records of the chronicles; and
they were read before the king. 2 And it
was found written that Mordecai had told
of [2]Bigthana and Teresh, two of the king's
eunuchs, the doorkeepers who had sought
to lay hands on King Ahasuerus. 3 Then
the king said, "What honor or dignity has
been bestowed on Mordecai for this?"
And the king's servants who attended
him said, "Nothing has been done for him."
4 So the king said, "Who *is* in the court?"
Now Haman had *just* entered [b]the outer
court of the king's palace [c]to suggest that
the king hang Mordecai on the gallows
that he had prepared for him.
5 The king's servants said to him,
"Haman is there, standing in the court."
And the king said, "Let him come in."
6 So Haman came in, and the king asked
him, "What shall be done for the man
whom the king delights to honor?"
Now Haman thought in his heart,
"Whom would the king delight to honor
more than [d]me?" 7 And Haman answered
the king, "*For* the man whom the king delights to honor, 8 let a royal robe be brought
which the king has worn, and [e]a horse on
which the king has ridden, which has a
royal [3]crest placed on its head. 9 Then let
this robe and horse be delivered to the hand
of one of the king's most noble princes, that
he may array the man whom the king delights to honor. Then [4]parade him on horseback through the city square, [f]and proclaim
before him: 'Thus shall it be done to the
man whom the king delights to honor!' "
10 Then the king said to Haman, "Hurry,
take the robe and the horse, as you have
suggested, and do so for Mordecai the Jew
who sits within the king's gate! Leave nothing undone of all that you have spoken."
11 So Haman took the robe and the
horse, arrayed Mordecai and led him on
horseback through the city square, and
proclaimed before him, "Thus shall it be
done to the man whom the king delights to
honor!"
12 Afterward Mordecai went back to the
king's gate. But Haman [g]hurried to his
house, mourning [h]and with his head covered. 13 When Haman told his wife Zeresh
and all his friends everything that had happened to him, his wise men and his wife
Zeresh said to him, "If Mordecai, before
whom you have begun to fall, is of Jewish
descent, you will not prevail against [i]him
but will surely fall before him."
14 While they *were* still talking with him,
the king's eunuchs came, and hastened to
bring Haman to [j]the banquet which Esther
had prepared.

Haman Hanged Instead of Mordecai

7 So the king and Haman went to dine
with Queen Esther. 2 And on the second day, [a]at the banquet of wine, the king
again said to Esther, "What *is* your petition, Queen Esther? It shall be granted you.
And what *is* your request, up to half the
kingdom? It shall be done!"

14 [n]Esth. 7:9 [o]Esth. 6:4 [p]Esth. 7:10 [3]Lit. *tree or wood* [4]About 75 feet

CHAPTER 6

1 [a]Esth. 2:23; 10:2 [1]Lit. *the king's sleep fled away*
2 [2]*Bigthan,* Esth. 2:21
4 [b]Esth. 5:1 [c]Esth. 5:14
6 [d][Prov. 16:18; 18:12]
8 [e]1 Kin. 1:33
[3]*crown*
9 [f]Gen. 41:43 [4]Lit. *cause him to ride*
12 [g]2 Chr. 26:20 [h]2 Sam. 15:30; Jer. 14:3, 4
13 [i][Gen. 12:3]; Zech. 2:8
14 [j]Esth. 5:8

CHAPTER 7

2 [a]Esth. 5:6

5:13 avails me nothing. Haman expressed raging fixation on killing Mordecai.

5:14 gallows. A stake on which a human would be impaled to death and/or displayed after death (cf. 2:23). **fifty cubits.** Approximately 75 ft. or almost 8 stories high. Perhaps the gallows involved displaying a shorter stake atop a building or wall to attain this height.

6:1 the book. Five years (cf. 2:16 with 3:7) had intervened since Mordecai's loyal, but as yet unrewarded, act (cf. 2:23). At exactly the proper moment, God providentially intervened so that the king suffered insomnia, called for the book of records, read of Mordecai's unrewarded deeds 5 years past, and then desired to reward him (cf. Dan. 6:18).

6:4 Who *is* in the court? The drama intensified as Haman arrived at just the wrong time and for just the wrong reason.

6:6,7 Haman ironically defined the honor to be given to Mordecai at Haman's expense. To his potential wealth from the Jewish plunder, he thought public acclaim would be added.

6:8 royal robe…royal crest. An honor which involved being treated as though the recipient were the king himself (cf. 8:15). This is reminiscent of Joseph in Egypt (Gen. 41:39-45). History affirms that horses were adorned with the royal crown.

6:9 the city square. Whereas Mordecai had been there the day before in sackcloth and ashes (4:6), he arrived with royal honor.

6:10 Mordecai the Jew. Cf. 8:7; 9:29,31; 10:3. Why the king did not remember Haman's edict against the Jews remains unknown.

6:12 mourning. Deservedly, Haman has inherited Mordecai's distress (cf. 4:1,2). What a difference a day makes! His imagined honors had quickly turned to unimaginable humiliation. **his head covered.** An extreme sign of shame (cf. 2 Sam. 15:30; Jer. 14:3,4).

6:13 you have begun to fall. Neither divine prophecy (Ex. 17:14) nor biblical history (1 Sam. 15:8,9) stood in Haman's favor. Haman's entourage seemed to have some knowledge of this biblical history.

6:14 Haman to the banquet. Like a lamb led to slaughter, Haman was escorted off to his just due.

7:2 second day. The first day reference point included the first banquet. This refers to the second banquet on the second day (cf. 5:8). **what *is* your request?** This was the third time that the king inquired (cf. 5:3,6).

³ Then Queen Esther answered and said,
"If I have found favor in your sight, O king,
and if it pleases the king, let my life be
given me at my petition, and my people at
my request. ⁴ For we have been [b]sold, my
people and I, to be destroyed, to be killed,
and to be annihilated. Had we been sold as
[c]male and female slaves, I would have held
my tongue, although the enemy could
never compensate for the king's loss."
⁵ So King Ahasuerus answered and said
to Queen Esther, "Who is he, and where is
he, who would dare presume in his heart
to do such a thing?"
⁶ And Esther said, "The adversary and
[d]enemy *is* this wicked Haman!"
So Haman was terrified before the king
and queen.
⁷ Then the king arose in his wrath from
the banquet of wine *and went* into the
palace garden; but Haman stood before
Queen Esther, pleading for his life, for he
saw that evil was determined against him
by the king. ⁸ When the king returned
from the palace garden to the place of the
banquet of wine, Haman had fallen across
[e]the couch where Esther *was.* Then the king
said, "Will he also assault the queen while
I *am* in the house?"
As the word left the king's mouth, they
[f]covered Haman's face. ⁹ Now [g]Harbonah,
one of the eunuchs, said to the king,
"Look! [h]The [1]gallows, fifty cubits high,
which Haman made for Mordecai, who
spoke [i]good on the king's behalf, is standing at the house of Haman."
Then the king said, "Hang him on it!"
¹⁰ So [j]they [k]hanged Haman on the gallows that he had prepared for Mordecai.
Then the king's wrath subsided.

Esther Saves the Jews

8 On that day King Ahasuerus gave
Queen Esther the house of Haman, the
[a]enemy of the Jews. And Mordecai came
before the king, for Esther had told [b]how
he *was related* to her. ² So the king took off
[c]his signet ring, which he had taken from
Haman, and gave it to Mordecai; and Esther appointed Mordecai over the house of
Haman.
³ Now Esther spoke again to the king,
fell down at his feet, and implored him
with tears to counteract the evil of Haman
the Agagite, and the scheme which he had
devised against the Jews. ⁴ And [d]the king
held out the golden scepter toward Esther.
So Esther arose and stood before the king,
⁵ and said, "If it pleases the king, and if I
have found favor in his sight and the thing
seems right to the king and I am pleasing in
his eyes, let it be written to revoke the [e]let-
ters devised by Haman, the son of Hammedatha the Agagite, which he wrote to
annihilate the Jews who *are* in all the king's
provinces. ⁶ For how can I endure to see
[f]the evil that will come to my people? Or
how can I endure to see the destruction of
my countrymen?"
⁷ Then King Ahasuerus said to Queen
Esther and Mordecai the Jew, "Indeed, [g]I
have given Esther the house of Haman,
and they have hanged him on the gallows
because he *tried to* lay his hand on the Jews.
⁸ You yourselves write *a decree* concerning
the Jews, [1]as you please, in the king's
name, and seal *it* with the king's signet
ring; for whatever is written in the king's
name and sealed with the king's signet
ring [h]no one can revoke."
⁹ [i]So the king's scribes were called at that
time, in the third month, which *is* the month
of Sivan, on the twenty-third *day;* and it was
written, according to all that Mordecai commanded, to the Jews, the satraps, the governors, and the princes of the provinces [j]from
India to Ethiopia, one hundred and twenty-
seven provinces *in all,* to every province [k]in
its own script, to every people in their own
language, and to the Jews in their own

4 [b] Esth. 3:9; 4:7 [c] Deut. 28:68
6 [d] Esth. 3:10
8 [e] Esth. 1:6 [f] Job 9:24
9 [g] Esth. 1:10 [h] Esth. 5:14; [Ps. 7:16; Prov. 11:5, 6] [i] Esth. 6:2 [1] Lit. *tree* or *wood*
10 [j] [Ps. 7:16; 94:23; Prov. 11:5, 6] [k] Ps. 37:35, 36; Dan. 6:24

CHAPTER 8

1 [a] Esth. 7:6 [b] Esth. 2:7, 15
2 [c] Esth. 3:10
4 [d] Esth. 4:11; 5:2
5 [e] Esth. 3:13
6 [f] Neh. 2:3; Esth. 7:4; 9:1
7 [g] Esth. 8:1; Prov. 13:22
8 [h] Esth. 1:19; Dan. 6:8, 12, 15 [1] Lit. *as is good in your eyes*
9 [i] Esth. 3:12 [j] Esth. 1:1 [k] Esth. 1:22; 3:12

7:3 my people. This plea paralleled God's message through Moses to Pharaoh, "Let my people go," almost 1,000 years earlier (Ex. 7:16).

7:4 sold. Refers back to Haman's bribe (cf. 3:9; 4:7). **destroyed...killed...annihilated.** Esther recounted the exact language of Haman's decree (cf. 3:13).

7:6 this wicked Haman. Similar to Nathan's famous accusation against King David, "You are the man" (2 Sam. 12:7). Haman's honor had quickly turned to humiliation, and then to horror.

7:8 assault the queen. Blinded by anger, Ahasuerus interpreted Haman's plea to be an act of violence against Esther rather than a plea for mercy.

7:9 Harbonah. Cf. 1:10. **Look!** Because the place prepared by Haman for Mordecai's execution towered above the city, it became the obvious spot for Haman's death. **Mordecai, who spoke good.** Haman heard the third capital offense charged against him. One, he manipulated the king in planning to kill the queen's people. Two, he was perceived to accost the queen. Three, he planned to execute a man whom the king had just greatly honored for extreme loyalty to the kingdom.

7:10 they hanged Haman. The ultimate expression of justice (cf. Ps. 9:15, 16).

8:1 the house of Haman. Property of a traitor by Persian custom returned to the king. In this case, he gave it to his queen, Esther, who put Mordecai over it (8:2). The outcome for Haman's wife Zerek and his wise men is unknown (5:14; 6:12, 13). Haman's 10 sons later died (9:7-10).

8:5 to revoke. This proved to be impossible in light of the inflexible nature of the king's edicts (1:19). However, a counter-decree was possible (cf. 8:8, 11, 12).

8:9 Sivan. Refers to the period May/June. It had been two months and 10 days since Haman's decree (cf. 3:12); 8 months and 20 days remained until both decrees became simultaneously effective (cf. 3:13).

script and language. 10 [l]And he wrote in the
name of King Ahasuerus, sealed *it* with the
king's signet ring, and sent letters by couriers on horseback, riding on royal horses
[2]bred from swift steeds.
11 By these letters the king permitted the
Jews who *were* in every city to [m]gather together and protect their lives—to [n]destroy,
kill, and annihilate all the forces of any
people or province that would assault
them, *both* little children and women, and
to plunder their possessions, 12 [o]on one
day in all the provinces of King Ahasuerus,
on the thirteenth *day* of the twelfth month,
which *is* the month of [3]Adar. 13 [p]A copy of
the document was to be issued as a decree
in every province and published for all
people, so that the Jews would be ready on
that day to avenge themselves on their enemies. 14 The couriers who rode on royal
horses went out, hastened and pressed on
by the king's command. And the decree
was issued in [4]Shushan the [5]citadel.
15 So Mordecai went out from the presence of the king in royal apparel of [6]blue
and white, with a great crown of gold and
a garment of fine linen and purple; and
[q]the city of [7]Shushan rejoiced and was
glad. 16 The Jews had [r]light and gladness,
joy and honor. 17 And in every province
and city, wherever the king's command
and decree came, the Jews had joy and
gladness, a feast [s]and a holiday. Then many
of the people of the land [t]became Jews, because [u]fear of the Jews fell upon them.

The Jews Destroy Their Tormentors

9 Now [a]in the twelfth month, that *is,* the
month of Adar, on the thirteenth day,
[b]*the time* came for the king's command and
his decree to be executed. On the day that
the enemies of the Jews had hoped to overpower them, the opposite occurred, in that
the Jews themselves [c]overpowered those
who hated them. 2 The Jews [d]gathered together in their cities throughout all the
provinces of King Ahasuerus to lay hands
on those who [e]sought their harm. And no
one could withstand them, [f]because fear of
them fell upon all people. 3 And all the officials of the provinces, the satraps, the
governors, and all those doing the king's
work, helped the Jews, because the fear of
Mordecai fell upon them. 4 For Mordecai
was great in the king's palace, and his fame
spread throughout all the provinces; for
this man Mordecai [g]became increasingly
prominent. 5 Thus the Jews defeated all
their enemies with the stroke of the sword,
with slaughter and destruction, and did
what they pleased with those who hated
them.
6 And in [h]Shushan[1] the [2]citadel the Jews
killed and destroyed five hundred men.
7 Also Parshandatha, Dalphon, Aspatha,
8 Poratha, Adalia, Aridatha, 9 Parmashta,
Arisai, Aridai, and Vajezatha— 10 [i]the ten
sons of Haman the son of Hammedatha,
the enemy of the Jews—they killed; [j]but
they did not lay a hand on the [3]plunder.
11 On that day the number of those who
were killed in [4]Shushan the [5]citadel [6]was
brought to the king. 12 And the king said to
Queen Esther, "The Jews have killed and
destroyed five hundred men in Shushan
the citadel, and the ten sons of Haman.
What have they done in the rest of the
king's provinces? Now [k]what *is* your petition? It shall be granted to you. Or what *is*
your further request? It shall be done."
13 Then Esther said, "If it pleases the
king, let it be granted to the Jews who *are*
in Shushan to do again tomorrow [l]accord-
ing to today's decree, and let Haman's ten
sons [m]be hanged on the gallows."
14 So the king commanded this to be
done; the decree was issued in Shushan,
and they hanged Haman's ten sons.
15 And the Jews who *were* in [7]Shushan
[n]gathered together again on the fourteenth

10 [l] 1 Kin. 21:8; Esth. 3:12, 13 [2] Lit. *sons of the swift horses*
11 [m] Esth. 9:2 [n] Esth. 9:10, 15, 16
12 [o] Esth. 3:13; 9:1 [3] LXX adds the text of the letter here
13 [p] Esth. 3:14, 15
14 [4] Or *Susa* [5] *palace*
15 [q] Esth. 3:15; Prov. 29:2 [6] *violet* [7] Or *Susa*
16 [r] Ps. 97:11; 112:4
17 [s] 1 Sam. 25:8; Esth. 9:19 [t] Ps. 18:43 [u] Gen. 35:5; Ex. 15:16; Deut. 2:25; 11:25; 1 Chr. 14:17; Esth. 9:2

CHAPTER 9

1 [a] Esth. 8:12 [b] Esth. 3:13 [c] 2 Sam. 22:41
2 [d] Esth. 8:11; 9:15-18 [e] Ps. 71:13, 14 [f] Esth. 8:17
4 [g] 2 Sam. 3:1; 1 Chr. 11:9; [Prov. 4:18]
6 [h] Esth. 1:2; 3:15; 4:16 [1] Or *Susa* [2] *palace*
10 [i] Esth. 5:11; 9:7-10; Job 18:19; 27:13-15; Ps. 21:10 [j] Esth. 8:11 [3] *spoil*
11 [4] Or *Susa* [5] *palace* [6] Lit. *came*
12 [k] Esth. 5:6; 7:2
13 [l] Esth. 8:11; 9:15 [m] 2 Sam. 21:6, 9
15 [n] Esth. 8:11; 9:2 [7] Or *Susa*

8:11 the king permitted. Just as the king had permitted Haman, so he permitted the Jews to defend themselves and to plunder their spoil (cf. vv. 10,15,16).

8:15 Mordecai went out. This second reward exceeded the first (cf. 6:6-9). Blue and white were the royal colors of the Persian Empire.

8:17 many…people…Jews. The population realized that the God of the Jews greatly exceeded anything that the pantheon of Persian deities could offer (cf. Ex. 15:14-16; Ps. 105:38; Acts 5:11), especially in contrast to their recent defeat by the Greeks.

9:1 twelfth month. During the period Feb.-Mar. Here is a powerful statement with regard to God's providential preservation of the Jewish race in harmony with God's unconditional promise to Abraham (Gen. 17:1-8). This providential deliverance stands in contrast to God's miraculous deliverance of the Jews from Egypt; yet in both cases the same end had been accomplished by the supernatural power of God.

9:3 the fear of Mordecai. Pragmatically, the nation had a change of heart toward the Jews, knowing that the king, the queen, and Mordecai were the ranking royal officials of the land. To be pro-Jewish would put one in favor with the king and his court and put one on the side of God, the ultimate King (cf. Rev. 19:16).

9:6,7 Five hundred men died in Shushan.

9:10 did not lay a hand. Unlike Saul, who did take the plunder (cf. 1 Sam. 15:3 with 15:9), the Jews focused only on the mission at hand, i.e., to preserve the Jewish race (cf. vv. 15,16), even though the king's edict permitted this (8:11).

9:12 further request? Even this pagan king served the cause of utterly blotting out the Amalekites in accord with God's original decree (Ex. 17:14) by allowing for a second day of killing in Shushan to eliminate all Jewish enemies.

9:13 be hanged. I.e., be publicly displayed.

9:15,16 Over 1,500 years earlier God had promised to curse those who curse Abraham's descendants (Gen. 12:3).

day of the month of Adar and killed three
hundred men at Shushan; [o]but they did
not lay a hand on the plunder.
16 The remainder of the Jews in the
king's provinces [p]gathered together and
protected their lives, had rest from their
enemies, and killed seventy-five thousand
of their enemies; [q]but they did not lay a
hand on the plunder. 17 *This was* on the
thirteenth day of the month of Adar. And
on the fourteenth of [8]*the month* they rested
and made it a day of feasting and gladness.

The Feast of Purim

18 But the Jews who *were* at [9]Shushan assembled together [r]on the thirteenth *day*, as
well as on the fourteenth; and on the fifteenth of [1]*the month* they rested, and made
it a day of feasting and gladness. 19 Therefore the Jews of the villages who dwelt in
the unwalled towns celebrated the fourteenth day of the month of Adar [s]*with*
gladness and feasting, [t]as a holiday, and
for [u]sending presents to one another.
20 And Mordecai wrote these things and
sent letters to all the Jews, near and far, who
were in all the provinces of King Ahasuerus,
21 to establish among them that they should
celebrate yearly the fourteenth and fifteenth
days of the month of Adar, 22 as the days on
which the Jews had rest from their enemies,
as the month which was turned from sorrow to joy for them, and from mourning to
a holiday; that they should make them days
of feasting and joy, of [v]sending presents to
one another and gifts to the [w]poor. 23 So the
Jews accepted the custom which they had
begun, as Mordecai had written to them,
24 because Haman, the son of Hammedatha
the Agagite, the enemy of all the Jews, [x]had
plotted against the Jews to annihilate them,
and had cast Pur (that *is,* the lot), to consume them and destroy them; 25 but [y]when
[2]*Esther* came before the king, he commanded by letter that [3]this wicked plot which
Haman had devised against the Jews should
[z]return on his own head, and that he and
his sons should be hanged on the gallows.
26 So they called these days Purim, after
the name [4]Pur. Therefore, because of all
the words of [a]this letter, what they had
seen concerning this matter, and what had
happened to them, 27 the Jews established
and imposed it upon themselves and their
descendants and all who would [b]join
them, that without fail they should celebrate these two days every year, according
to the written *instructions* and according to
the *prescribed* time, 28 *that* these days *should*
be remembered and kept throughout every
generation, every family, every province,
and every city, that these days of Purim
should not fail *to be observed* among the
Jews, and *that* the memory of them should
not perish among their descendants.
29 Then Queen Esther, [c]the daughter of
Abihail, with Mordecai the Jew, wrote with
full authority to confirm this [d]second letter
about Purim. 30 And *Mordecai* sent letters
to all the Jews, to [e]the one hundred and
twenty-seven provinces of the kingdom of
Ahasuerus, *with* words of peace and truth,
31 to confirm these days of Purim at their
appointed time, as Mordecai the Jew and
Queen Esther had prescribed for them, and
as they had decreed for themselves and
their descendants concerning matters of
their [f]fasting and lamenting. 32 So the decree of Esther confirmed these matters of
Purim, and it was written in the book.

Mordecai's Advancement

10 And King Ahasuerus imposed tribute on the land and *on* [a]the islands
of the sea. 2 Now all the acts of his power
and his might, and the account of the
greatness of Mordecai, [b]to which the king
[1]advanced him, *are* they not written in the
book of the [c]chronicles of the kings of
Media and Persia? 3 For Mordecai the Jew
was [d]second to King Ahasuerus, and was
great among the Jews and well received by
the multitude of his brethren, [e]seeking the
good of his people and speaking peace to
all his [2]countrymen.

15 [o]Esth. 9:10
16 [p]Esth. 9:2 [q]Esth. 8:11
17 [8]Lit. *it*
18 [r]Esth. 9:11, 15 [9]Or *Susa* [1]Lit. *it*
19 [s]Deut. 16:11, 14 [t]Esth. 8:16, 17 [u]Neh. 8:10, 12; Esth. 9:22
22 [v]Neh. 8:10; Esth. 9:19 [w][Deut. 15:7-11]; Job 29:16
24 [x]Esth. 3:6, 7; 9:26
25 [y]Esth. 7:4-10; 8:3; 9:13, 14 [z]Esth. 7:10 [2]Lit. *she* or *it* [3]Lit. *his*
26 [a]Esth. 9:20 [4]Lit. *Lot*
27 [b]Esth. 8:17; [Is. 56:3, 6]; Zech. 2:11
29 [c]Esth. 2:15 [d]Esth. 8:10; 9:20, 21
30 [e]Esth. 1:1
31 [f]Esth. 4:3, 16

CHAPTER 10

1 [a]Gen. 10:5; Ps. 72:10; Is. 11:11; 24:15
2 [b]Esth. 8:15; 9:4 [c]Esth. 6:1 [1]Lit. *made him great*
3 [d]Gen. 41:40, 43, 44; 2 Chr. 28:7 [e]Neh. 2:10; Ps. 122:8, 9 [2]Lit. *seed.* LXX, Vg. add a dream of Mordecai here; Vg. adds six more chapters

---

9:15 fourteenth day. Another 300 men died the second day of killing in Shushan, bringing the total dead in Shushan to 810.

9:16 killed. Outside of Shushan, only one day of killing occurred in which 75,000 enemies died.

9:18,19 This section recounted why Purim would be celebrated for two days rather than one.

9:20-25 A brief summary of God's providential intervention on behalf of the Jews.

9:26 Purim. The first and last biblically revealed, non-Mosaic festival with perpetual significance.

9:29 second letter. An additional letter (cf. v. 20 for the first letter), which added "fasting and lamenting" to the prescribed activity of Purim.

9:32 written in the book. This could be the chronicle referred to in 10:3, or another archival type document. It certainly does not hint that Esther wrote this canonical book.

10:1-3 Apparently a postscript.

10:3 Mordecai...*was* second. Mordecai joined the top echelon of Jewish international statesmen like Joseph, who ranked second in the Egyptian dynasty (Gen. 41:37-45), and Daniel, who succeeded in both the Babylonian (Dan. 2:46-49; 5:29) and Medo-Persian Empires (Dan. 6:28). **speaking peace.** Less than 10 years later (ca. 465 B.C.), Ahasuerus was assassinated. There are no further details concerning Esther and Mordecai. What Mordecai did for less than a decade on behalf of Israel, Jesus Christ will do for all eternity as the Prince of Peace (Is. 9:6,7; Zech. 9:9,10).

The Book of JOB

Title

As with other books of the Bible, Job bears the name of the narrative's primary character. This name might have been derived from the Hebrew word for "persecution," thus meaning "persecuted one," or from an Arabic word meaning "repent," thus bearing the name "repentant one." The author recounts an era in the life of Job, in which he was tested and the character of God was revealed. New Testament writers directly quote Job two times (Rom. 11:35; 1 Cor. 3:19), plus Ezekiel 14:14,20 and James 5:11 show Job was a real person.

Author and Date

The book does not name its author. Job is an unlikely candidate because the book's message rests on Job's ignorance of the events that occurred in heaven as they related to his ordeal. One Talmudic tradition suggests Moses as author since the land of Uz (1:1) was adjacent to Midian where Moses lived for 40 years, and he could have obtained a record of the story there. Solomon is also a good possibility due to the similarity of content with parts of the book of Ecclesiastes, as well as the fact that Solomon wrote the other Wisdom books (except Psalms, and he did author Pss. 72; 127). Though he lived long after Job, Solomon could have written about events that occurred long before his own time, in much the same manner as Moses was inspired to write about Adam and Eve. Elihu, Isaiah, Hezekiah, Jeremiah, and Ezra have also been suggested as possible authors, but without support.

The date of the book's writing may be much later than the events recorded therein. This conclusion is based on: 1) Job's age (42:16); 2) his life span of nearly 200 years (42:16) which fits the patriarchal period (Abraham lived 175 years; Gen. 25:7); 3) the social unit being the patriarchal family; 4) the Chaldeans who murdered Job's servants (1:17) were nomads and had not yet become city dwellers; 5) Job's wealth being measured in livestock rather than gold and silver (1:3; 42:12); 6) Job's priestly functions within his family (1:4,5); and 7) a basic silence on matters such as the covenant of Abraham, Israel, the Exodus, and the law of Moses. The events of Job's odyssey appear to be patriarchal. Job, on the other hand, seemed to know about Adam (31:33) and the Noahic flood (12:15). These cultural/historical features found in the book appear to place the events chronologically at a time probably after Babel (Gen. 11:1-9) but before or contemporaneous with Abraham (Gen. 11:27ff.).

Background and Setting

This book begins with a scene in heaven that explains everything to the reader (1:6–2:10). Job was suffering because God was contesting with Satan. Job never knew that, nor did any of his friends, so they all struggled to explain suffering from the perspective of their ignorance, until finally Job rested in nothing but faith in God's goodness and the hope of His redemption. That God vindicated his trust is the culminating message of the book. When there are no rational, or even theological, explanations for disaster and pain, trust God.

Historical and Theological Themes

The occasion and events that follow Job's sufferings present significant questions for the faith of believers in all ages. Why does Job serve God? Job is heralded for his righteousness, being compared with Noah and Daniel (Ezek. 14:14-20), and for his spiritual endurance (James 5:11). Several other questions are alluded to throughout Job's ordeal, for instance, "Why do the righteous suffer?" Though an answer to that question may seem important, the book does not set forth such an answer. Job never knew the reasons for his suffering and neither did his friends. The righteous sufferer does not appear to learn about any of the heavenly court debates between God and Satan that precipitated his pain. In fact, when finally confronted by the Lord of the universe, Job put his hand over his mouth and said nothing. Job's silent response in no way trivialized the intense pain and loss he had endured. It merely underscored the importance of trusting God's purposes in the midst of suffering because suffering, like all other human experiences, is directed by perfect divine wisdom. In the end, the lesson learned was that one may never know the specific reason for his suffering; but one must trust in Sovereign God. That is the real answer to suffering.

The book treats two major themes and many other minor ones, both in the narrative framework of the prologue (chaps. 1,2) and epilogue (42:7-17), and in the poetic account of Job's torment that lies in between (3:1–42:6). A key to understanding the first theme of the book is to notice the debate between God and Satan in heaven and how it connects with the 3 cycles of earthly debates between Job and his friends. God wanted to prove the character of believers to Satan and to all demons, angels, and people. The accusations are by Satan, who indicted God's claims of Job's righteousness as being untested, if not questionable. Satan accused the righteous of being faithful to God only for what they could get. Since Job did not serve God with pure motives, according to Satan, the whole relationship between him and God was a sham. Satan's confidence that he could turn Job against God came, no doubt, from the fact that he had led the holy angels to rebel with him (*see note on Rev. 12:3,4*). Satan thought he could destroy Job's faith in God by inflicting suffering on him, thus showing in principle that saving faith could be shattered. God released Satan to make his point if he could, but he failed, as true faith in God proved unbreakable. Even Job's wife told him to curse God (2:9), but he refused; his faith in God never failed (see 13:15). Satan tried to do the same to Peter (see Luke 22:31-34) and was unsuccessful in destroying Peter's faith (see John 21:15-19). When Satan has unleashed all that he can do to destroy saving faith, it stands firm (cf. Rom. 8:31-39). In the end, God proved His point with Satan that saving faith can't be destroyed no matter how much trouble a saint suffers, or how incomprehensible and undeserved it seems.

A second and related theme concerns proving the character of God to men. Does this sort of ordeal, in which God and His opponent Satan square off, with righteous Job as the test case, suggest that God is lacking in compassion and mercy toward Job? Not at all. As James says, "You have heard of the perseverance of Job and have seen the end *intended* by the Lord—that the Lord is very compassionate and merciful" (James 5:11). It was to prove the very opposite (42:10-17). Job says, "Shall we indeed accept good from God, and shall we not accept adversity?" (2:10). God's servant does not deny that he has suffered. He does deny that his suffering is a result of sin. Nor does he understand why he suffers. Job simply commits his ordeal with a devout heart of worship and humility (42:5,6) to a sovereign and perfectly wise Creator—and that was what God wanted him to learn in this conflict with Satan. In the end, God flooded Job with more blessings than he had ever known.

The major reality of the book is the inscrutable mystery of innocent suffering. God ordains that His children walk in sorrow and pain, sometimes because of sin (cf. Num. 12:10-12), sometimes for chastening (cf. Heb. 12:5-12), sometimes for strengthening (cf. 2 Cor. 12:7-10; 1 Pet. 5:10), and sometimes to give opportunity to reveal His comfort and grace (2 Cor. 1:3-7). But there are times when the compelling issue in the suffering of the saints is unknowable because it is for a heavenly purpose that those on earth can't discern (cf. Ex. 4:11; John 9:1-3).

Job and his friends wanted to analyze the suffering and look for causes and solutions. Using all of their sound theology and insight into the situation, they searched for answers, but found only useless and wrong ideas, for which God rebuked them in the end (42:7). They couldn't know why Job suffered because what happened in heaven between God and Satan was unknown to them. They thought they knew all the answers, but they only intensified the dilemma by their insistent ignorance.

By spreading out some of the elements of this great theme, we can see the following truths in Job's experience:

1) There are matters going on in heaven with God that believers know nothing about; yet, they affect their lives;
2) Even the best effort at explaining the issues of life can be useless;
3) God's people do suffer. Bad things happen all the time to good people, so one cannot judge a person's spirituality by his painful circumstances or successes;
4) Even though God seems far away, perseverance in faith is a most noble virtue since God is good and one can safely leave his life in His hands;
5) The believer in the midst of suffering should not abandon God, but draw near to Him, so out of the fellowship can come the comfort—without the explanation; and
6) Suffering may be intense, but it will ultimately end for the righteous and God will bless abundantly.

Interpretive Challenges

The most critical interpretive challenge involves the book's primary message. Although often thought to be the pressing issue of the book, the question of why Job suffers is never revealed to Job, though the reader knows that it involves God's proving a point to Satan—a matter which completely transcends Job's ability to understand. James' commentary on Job's case (5:11) draws the conclusion that it was to show God's compassion and mercy, but without apology, offers no explanation for Job's specific ordeal. Readers find themselves, putting their proverbial hands over their mouths, with no right to question or accuse the all-wise and all-powerful Creator, who will do as He pleases, and in so doing, both proves His points in the spiritual realm to angels and demons and defines His compassion and mercy. Engaging in "theodicy," i.e., man's attempt to defend God's involvement in calamity and suffering, is shown to be appropriate in these circumstances, though in the end, it is apparent that God does not need nor want a human advocate. The book of Job poignantly illustrates Deut. 29:29, "The secret *things belong* to the LORD our God…"

The nature of Job's guilt and innocence raises perplexing questions. God declared Job perfect, upright, fearing God, and shunning evil (Job 1:1). But Job's comforters raised a critical question based on Job's ordeal: Had not Job sinned? On several occasions Job readily admitted to having sinned (7:21; 13:26). But Job questioned the extent of his sin as compared to the severity of his suffering. God rebuked Job in the end for his demands to be vindicated of the comforters' accusations (Job 38–41). But He also declared that what Job said was correct and what the comforters said was wrong (42:7).

Another challenge comes in keeping separate the pre-understandings that Job and his comforters brought to Job's ordeal. At the outset, all agreed that God punishes evil, rewards obedience, and no exceptions are possible. Job, due to his suffering innocently, was forced to conclude that exceptions are possible in that the righteous also suffer. He also observed that the wicked prosper. These are more than small exceptions to the rule, thus forcing Job to rethink his simple understanding about God's sovereign interaction with His people. The type of wisdom Job comes to embrace was not dependent merely on the promise of reward or punishment. The long, peevish, disputes between Job and his accusers were attempts to reconcile the perceived inequities of God's retribution in Job's experiences. Such an empirical method is dangerous. In the end, God offered no explanation to Job, but rather called all parties to a deeper level of trust in the Creator, who rules over a sin-confused world with power and authority directed by perfect wisdom and mercy. *See notes on Ps. 73.*

Understanding this book requires 1) understanding the nature of wisdom, particularly the difference between man's wisdom and God's, and 2) admitting that Job and his friends lacked the divine wisdom to interpret Job's circumstances accurately, though his friends kept trying while Job learned to be content in God's sovereignty and mercy. The turning point or resolution for this matter is found in Job 28 where the character of divine wisdom is explained: divine wisdom is rare and priceless; man cannot hope to purchase it; and God possesses it all. We may not know what is going on in heaven or what God's purposes are, but we must trust Him. Because of this, the matter of believers suffering takes a back seat to the matter of divine wisdom.

Outline

- I. The Dilemma (1:1–2:13)
  - A. Introduction of Job (1:1-5)
  - B. Divine Debates with Satan (1:6–2:10)
  - C. Arrival of Friends (2:11-13)
- II. The Debates (3:1–37:24)
  - A. The First Cycle (3:1–14:22)
    1. Job's first speech expresses despair (3:1-26)
    2. Eliphaz's first speech kindly protests and urges humility and repentance (4:1–5:27)
    3. Job's reply to Eliphaz expresses anguish and questions the trials, asking for sympathy in his pain (6:1–7:21)
    4. Bildad's first speech accuses Job of impugning God (8:1-22)
    5. Job's response to Bildad admits he is not perfect, but may protest what seems unfair (9:1–10:22)
    6. Zophar's first speech tells Job to get right with God (11:1-20)
    7. Job's response to Zophar tells his friends they are wrong and only God knows and will, hopefully, speak to him (12:1–14:22)
  - B. The Second Cycle (15:1–21:34)
    1. Eliphaz's second speech accuses Job of presumption and disregarding the wisdom of the ancients (15:1-35)

2. Job's response to Eliphaz appeals to God against his unjust accusers (16:1–17:16)
3. Bildad's second speech tells Job he is suffering just what he deserves (18:1-21)
4. Job's response to Bildad cries out to God for pity (19:1-29)
5. Zophar's second speech accuses Job of rejecting God by questioning His justice (20:1-29)
6. Job's response to Zophar says he is out of touch with reality (21:1-34)

C. The Third Cycle (22:1–26:14)

1. Eliphaz's third speech denounces Job's criticism of God's justice (22:1-30)
2. Job's response to Eliphaz is that God knows he is without guilt, and yet in His providence and refining purpose He permits temporary success for the wicked (23:1–24:25)
3. Bildad's third speech scoffs at Job's direct appeal to God (25:1-6)
4. Job's response to Bildad that God is indeed perfectly wise and absolutely sovereign, but not simplistic as they thought (26:1-14)

D. The Final Defense of Job (27:1–31:40)

1. Job's first monologue affirms his righteousness and that man can't discover God's wisdom (27:1–28:28)
2. Job's second monologue remembers his past, describes his present, defends his innocence, and asks for God to defend him (29:1–31:40)

E. The Speeches of Elihu (32:1–37:24)

1. Elihu enters into the debate to break the impasse (32:1-22)
2. Elihu charges Job with presumption in criticizing God, not recognizing that God may have a loving purpose, even in allowing Job to suffer (33:1-33)
3. Elihu declares that Job has impugned God's integrity by claiming that it does not pay to lead a godly life (34:1-37)
4. Elihu urges Job to wait patiently for the Lord (35:1-16)
5. Elihu believes that God is disciplining Job (36:1-21)
6. Elihu argues that human observers can hardly expect to understand adequately God's dealings in administering justice and mercy (36:22–37:24)

III. The Deliverance (38:1–42:17)

A. God Interrogates Job (38:1–41:34)

1. God's first response to Job (38:1–40:2)
2. Job's answer to God (40:3-5)
3. God's second response to Job (40:6–41:34)

B. Job Confesses, Worships, and Is Vindicated (42:1-17)

1. Job passes judgment upon himself (42:1-6)
2. God rebukes Eliphaz, Bildad, and Zophar (42:7-9)
3. God restores Job's family, wealth, and long life (42:10-17)

Job and His Family in Uz

1 There was a man [a]in the land of Uz,
whose name *was* [b]Job; and that man
was [c]blameless and upright, and one who
[d]feared God and [1]shunned evil. 2 And
seven sons and three daughters were born
to him. 3 Also, his possessions were seven
thousand sheep, three thousand camels,
five hundred yoke of oxen, five hundred
female donkeys, and a very large household, so that this man was the greatest of
all the [2]people of the East.
4 And his sons would go and feast *in*
their houses, each on his *appointed* day,
and would send and invite their three sisters to eat and drink with them. 5 So it
was, when the days of feasting had run
their course, that Job would send and
[3]sanctify them, and he would rise early in
the morning [e]and offer burnt offerings *ac-*
cording to the number of them all. For Job
said, "It may be that my sons have sinned
and [f]cursed[4] God in their hearts." Thus
Job did regularly.

Satan Attacks Job's Character

6 Now [g]there was a day when the sons
of God came to present themselves before
the LORD, and [5]Satan also came among
them. 7 And the LORD said to [6]Satan,
"From where do you come?"
So Satan answered the LORD and said,
"From [h]going to and fro on the earth, and
from walking back and forth on it."
8 Then the LORD said to Satan, "Have
you [7]considered My servant Job, that *there*
is none like him on the earth, a blameless
and upright man, one who fears God and
[8]shuns evil?"
9 So Satan answered the LORD and said,
"Does Job fear God for nothing? 10 [i]Have
You not [9]made a hedge around him,
around his household, and around all that
he has on every side? [j]You have blessed
the work of his hands, and his possessions
have increased in the land. 11 [k]But now,
stretch out Your hand and touch all that he
has, and he will surely [l]curse[1] You to Your
face!"

CHAPTER 1

1 [a] 1 Chr. 1:17 [b] Ezek. 14:14, 20; James 5:11 [c] Gen. 6:9; 17:1; [Deut. 18:13] [d] [Prov. 16:6] [1] Lit. *turned away from*
3 [2] Lit. *sons*
5 [e] Gen. 8:20; [Job 42:8] [f] 1 Kin. 21:10, 13 [3] *consecrate* [4] Lit. *blessed,* but in an evil sense; cf. Job 1:11; 2:5, 9
6 [g] Job 2:1 [5] Lit. *the Adversary*
7 [h] [1 Pet. 5:8] [6] Lit. *the Adversary*
8 [7] Lit. *set your heart on* [8] Lit. *turns away from*
10 [i] Job 29:2–6; Ps. 34:7; Is. 5:2 [j] [Ps. 128:1, 2; Prov. 10:22] [9] Protected him
11 [k] Job 2:5; 19:21 [l] Is. 8:21; Mal. 3:13, 14 [1] Lit. *bless,* but in an evil sense; cf. Job 1:5

1:1–2:13 This section identifies the main persons and sets the stage for the drama to follow. **Uz.** Job's home was a walled city with gates (29:7,8), where he held a position of great respect. The city was in the land of Uz in northern Arabia, adjacent to Midian, where Moses lived for 40 years (Ex. 2:15). **Job.** The story begins on earth with Job as the central figure. He was a rich man with 7 sons and 3 daughters, in his middle years with a grown family, but still young enough to father 10 more children (see 42:13). He was good, a family man, rich, and widely known. **blameless...upright...feared God...shunned evil.** Cf. 1:8. Job was not perfect or without sin (cf. 6:24; 7:21; 9:20); however, it appears from the language that he had put his trust in God for redemption and faithfully lived a God-honoring, sincere life of integrity and consistency personally, maritally (2:10), and parentally (1:4,5).

1:3 sheep...camels...oxen...female donkeys. As typically in the ancient Near East, Job's wealth was not measured in money or land holdings, but in his numerous livestock, like the patriarchs (cf. Gen. 13:1-7). **greatest...of the East.** A major claim by any standard. Solomon held a similar reputation, "...Solomon's wisdom excelled the wisdom of all the men of the East..." (1 Kin. 4:30). The "east" denotes those living E of Palestine, as the people of the northern Arabian desert did (cf. Judg. 6:3; Ezek. 25:4).

1:4 on his *appointed* day. Of the week (7 sons). This reference to the main meal of each day of the week, which moved from house to house, implies the love and harmony of the family members. The sisters are especially noted to show these were cared for with love.

1:5 send and sanctify. At the end of every week, Job would offer up as many burnt offerings as he had sons (see Lev. 1:4), officiating as family priest weekly ("regularly") in a time before the Aaronic priesthood was established. These offerings were to cover any sin that his children may have committed that week, indicating the depth of his spiritual devotion. This record is included to demonstrate the righteousness and virtue of Job and his family, which made his suffering all the more amazing. **burnt offerings.** This kind of offering was known as early as Noah (Gen. 8:20).

1:6 sons of God. Job's life is about to be caught up in heavenly strategies as the scene moves from earth to heaven where God is holding council with His heavenly court. Neither Job nor his friends ever knew about this. The angelic host (cf. 38:7; Pss. 29:1; 89:7; Dan. 3:25) came to God's throne to render account of their ministry throughout the earth and heaven (cf. 1 Kin. 22:19-22). Like a Judas among the apostles, Satan was with the angels. **Satan.** Emboldened by the success he had with the unfallen Adam in paradise (Gen. 3:6-12,17-19), he was confident that the fear of God in Job, one of a fallen race, would not stand his tests. And he had fallen himself (see Is. 14:12). As opposed to a personal name, Satan as a title means "adversary," in either a personal or judicial sense. This demon is the ultimate spiritual adversary of all time and has been accusing the righteous throughout the ages (see Rev. 12:10). In a courtroom setting, the adversary usually stood to the right of the accused. This location is reported when Satan in heaven accused Joshua the High-Priest (Zech. 3:1). That he is still unsuccessful is the thesis of Rom. 8:31-39.

1:7 And the LORD said. Lest there be any question about God's role in this ordeal, it was He who initiated the dialogue. The adversary was not presiding. If anything, Satan raised the penetrating question that might well be asked by anyone, perhaps even Job himself: Does Job serve God with pure motives, or is he in it only as long as the blessings flow?

1:7,8 to and fro on the earth. The picture is of haste. No angel, fallen or holy, is an omnipresent creature, but they move rapidly. In Satan's case, as prince of this world (John 12:31; 14:30; 16:11) and ruler of demons (Matt. 9:34; 12:24), the earth is his domain where he prowls like a "roaring lion, seeking whom he may devour" (1 Pet. 5:8). God gave him Job to test.

1:9-11 Satan asserted that true believers are only faithful as long as they prosper. Take away their prosperity, he claims, and they will reject God. He wanted to prove that salvation is not permanent, that saving faith can be broken and those who were God's could become his. That is the first of the two great themes of this book (see Introduction: Historical and Theological Themes). Satan repeated this affront with Jesus (see Matt. 4), Peter (see Luke 22:31), and Paul (see 2 Cor. 12:7). The OT has many promises from God in which He pledges to sustain the faith of His children. Cf. Pss. 37:23,28; 97:10; 121:4-7. For NT texts, cf. Luke 22:31,32; Jude 24.

12 And the LORD said to Satan, "Behold,
all that he has *is* in your [2]power; only do
not lay a hand on his *person*."
So Satan went out from the presence of
the LORD.

Job Loses His Property and Children

13 Now there was a day [m]when his sons
and daughters *were* eating and drinking
wine in their oldest brother's house; 14 and
a messenger came to Job and said, "The
oxen were plowing and the donkeys feeding beside them, 15 when the [3]Sabeans
[4]raided *them* and took them away—indeed
they have killed the servants with the edge
of the sword; and I alone have escaped to
tell you!"
16 While he *was* still speaking, another
also came and said, "The fire of God fell
from heaven and burned up the sheep and
the servants, and [5]consumed them; and I
alone have escaped to tell you!"
17 While he *was* still speaking, another
also came and said, "The Chaldeans
formed three bands, raided the camels and
took them away, yes, and killed the servants with the edge of the sword; and I
alone have escaped to tell you!"
18 While he *was* still speaking, another
also came and said, [n]"Your sons and
daughters *were* eating and drinking wine
in their oldest brother's house, 19 and suddenly a great wind came from [6]across the
wilderness and struck the four corners of
the house, and it fell on the young people,
and they are dead; and I alone have escaped to tell you!"
20 Then Job arose, [o]tore his robe, and
shaved his head; and he [p]fell to the ground
and worshiped. 21 And he said:

[q]"Naked I came from my mother's
womb,
And naked shall I return there.
The LORD [r]gave, and the LORD has
[s]taken away;
[t]Blessed be the name of the LORD."

22 [u]In all this Job did not sin nor charge
God with wrong.

Satan Attacks Job's Health

2 Again [a]there was a day when the sons
of God came to present themselves before the LORD, and Satan came also among
them to present himself before the LORD.
2 And the LORD said to Satan, "From where
do you come?"
[b]Satan answered the LORD and said,
"From going to and fro on the earth, and
from walking back and forth on it."
3 Then the LORD said to Satan, "Have
you considered My servant Job, that *there is*
none like him on the earth, [c]a blameless
and upright man, one who fears God and
shuns evil? And still he [d]holds fast to his
integrity, although you incited Me against
him, [e]to [1]destroy him without cause."

12 [2]Lit. *hand*
13 [m][Eccl. 9:12]
15 [3]Lit. *Sheba;* cf. Job 6:19 [4]Lit. *fell upon*
16 [5]*destroyed*
18 [n]Job 1:4, 13
19 [6]LXX omits *across*
20 [o]Gen. 37:29, 34; Josh. 7:6; Ezra 9:3 [p][1 Pet. 5:6]
21 [q][Ps. 49:17; Eccl. 5:15]; 1 Tim. 6:7 [r]Eccl. 5:19; [James 1:17] [s]Gen. 31:16; [1 Sam. 2:6] [t]Eph. 5:20; [1 Thess. 5:18]
22 [u]Job 2:10

CHAPTER 2

1 [a]Job 1:6-8
2 [b]Job 1:7
3 [c]Job 1:1, 8 [d]Job 27:5, 6 [e]Job 9:17 [1]Lit. *consume*

1:12 power. God allowed Satan to test Job's faith by attacking "all that he has." With God's sovereign permission, Satan was allowed to move on Job, except that he could not attack Job physically.

1:13-19 With 4 rapid-fire disasters, Satan destroyed or removed Job's livestock, servants, and children. Only the 4 messengers survived.

1:15 Sabeans. Lit. "Sheba," part of Arabia. These people were terrorizing robbers, who had descended from Abraham and Keturah (Gen. 25:1-3).

1:16 fire of God...heaven. This probably refers to severe lightning.

Biographical Sketch of Job

1. A spiritually mature man (1:1, 8; 2:3)
2. Father of many children (1:2; 42:13)
3. Owner of many herds (1:3; 42:12)
4. A wealthy and influential man (1:3b)
5. A priest to his family (1:5)
6. A loving, wise husband (2:9)
7. A man of prominence in community affairs (29:7-11)
8. A man of benevolence (29:12-17; 31:32)
9. A wise leader (29:21-24)
10. Grower of crops (31:38-40)

1:17 Chaldeans. A semi-nomadic people of the Arabian desert, experienced in marauding and war (cf. Hab. 1:6-8).

1:19 great wind. Most likely a tornado-type wind. Cf. Is. 21:1; Hos. 13:15.

1:20,21 worshiped. He heard the other messages calmly, but on hearing about the death of his children, he expressed all the symbols of grief (cf. Gen. 37:34; Jer. 41:5; Mic. 1:16), but also worshiped God in the expression of v. 21. Instead of cursing, he blessed the name of Jehovah. Job's submissive response disproved the adversary's accusations (1:9-11). So far, Job was what God claimed him to be, a true believer with faith that cannot be broken (v. 8).

1:22 did not sin nor charge God with wrong. Better, "sin by charging God with wrong." Hasty words against God in the midst of grief are foolish and wicked. Christians are to submit to trials and still worship God, not because they see the reasons for them, but because God wills them and has His own reasons which believers are to trust.

2:1-3a The scene changes again to the heavenly court, where the angels came before the Lord and Satan was also present, having been again searching the earth for victims to assault. *See note on 1:6-8.*

2:3 he holds fast to his integrity. God affirmed that Job had won round one. **without cause.** God uses the same expression the adversary used in Job 1 "for nothing (1:9)...without cause (2:3)." The message behind God's turn of words is that the adversary is the guilty party in this case, not Job who had suffered all the disaster without any personal cause. He had done nothing to incur the pain and loss, though it was massive. The issue was purely a matter of conflict between God and Satan. This is a crucial statement, because when Job's friends tried to explain why all the disasters had befallen him, they al-

4 So Satan answered the LORD and said,
"Skin for skin! Yes, all that a man has he
will give for his life. 5 [f]But stretch out Your
hand now, and touch his [g]bone and his
flesh, and he will surely [2]curse You to Your
face!"
6 [h]And the LORD said to Satan, "Behold,
he *is* in your hand, but spare his life."
7 So Satan went out from the presence of
the LORD, and struck Job with painful boils
[i]from the sole of his foot to the crown of his
head. 8 And he took for himself a potsherd
with which to scrape himself [j]while he sat
in the midst of the ashes.
9 Then his wife said to him, "Do you still
hold fast to your integrity? [3]Curse God
and die!"
10 But he said to her, "You speak as one
of the foolish women speaks. [k]Shall we indeed accept good from God, and shall we
not accept adversity?" [l]In all this Job did
not [m]sin with his lips.

Job's Three Friends

11 Now when Job's three friends heard of
all this adversity that had come upon him,
each one came from his own place—Eliphaz the [n]Temanite, Bildad the [o]Shuhite,
and Zophar the Naamathite. For they had
made an appointment together to come
[p]and mourn with him, and to comfort him.
12 And when they raised their eyes from
afar, and did not recognize him, they lifted
their voices and wept; and each one tore his
robe and [q]sprinkled dust on his head toward heaven. 13 So they sat down with him
on the ground [r]seven days and seven
nights, and no one spoke a word to him, for
they saw that *his* grief was very great.

Job Deplores His Birth

3 After this Job opened his mouth and
cursed the day of his *birth.* 2 And Job
[1]spoke, and said:

3 "May[a] the day perish on which I
was born,
And the night *in which* it was said,
'A male child is conceived.'
4 May that day be darkness;

5 [f] Job 1:11 [g] Job 19:20 [2] Lit. *bless,* but in an evil sense; cf. Job 1:5
6 [h] Job 1:12
7 [i] Is. 1:6
8 [j] Job 42:6; Jer. 6:26; Ezek. 27:30; Jon. 3:6; Matt. 11:21
9 [3] Lit. *Bless,* but in an evil sense; cf. Job 1:5
10 [k] Job 1:21, 22; [Heb. 12:6; James 5:10, 11] [l] Job 1:22; [James 1:12] [m] Ps. 39:1

11 [n] Gen. 36:11; 1 Chr. 1:36; Job 6:19; Jer. 49:7; Obad. 9 [o] Gen. 25:2; 1 Chr. 1:32 [p] Job 42:11; Rom. 12:15
12 [q] Josh. 7:6; Neh. 9:1; Lam. 2:10; Ezek. 27:30
13 [r] Gen. 50:10; Ezek. 3:15

CHAPTER 3

2 [1] Lit. *answered*
3 [a] Job 10:18, 19; Jer. 20:14-18

ways put the blame on Job. Grasping this assessment from God—that Job had not been punished for something, but suffered for nothing related to him personally—is a crucial key to the story. Sometimes suffering is caused by divine purposes unknowable to us (see Introduction: Historical and Theological Themes).

2:4,5 Skin for skin. Satan contended that what he had done to Job so far was just touching the skin, scratching the surface. Job endured the loss of all that he had, even the lives of his children, but would not endure the loss of his own well-being. If God allowed Satan to make the disaster a personal matter of his own physical body, the Adversary contended, Job's faith would fail.

2:6 spare his life. The Lord sovereignly limited the Adversary, although death seemed preferable. Job believed that to be the case (cf. 7:15), as did his wife (2:9).

2:7 Satan...struck Job. This appears to be an exceptional case with no other exact parallel in Scripture. In the gospels, demons caused physical problems when they dwelled within people (cf. 13:11,16), but that is not the case here. God's permissive will operated for purposes Job can't know; God was hidden from him along with the reasons for his suffering. **painful boils.** Although the nature of Job's affliction cannot be diagnosed exactly, it produced extreme physical trauma (cf. 2:13; 3:24; 7:5,14; 13:28; 16:8; 19:17; 30:17,30; 33:21). One cannot fully understand Job's conversations throughout the book without considering the extraordinary physical distress he endured in a day without medicine or pain relief. His boils would have been similar to those of the Egyptians (Ex. 9:8-11) and Hezekiah (2 Kin. 20:7).

2:8 potsherd...ashes. Suffering terribly, Job took himself to where the lepers go: the ash heap outside the city where he scraped at his sores with a piece of broken pottery, perhaps breaking them open to release the infection.

2:9 your integrity. Through all this, Job's faith remained strong in the confusion, so that his wife could not accuse him of insincerity as Satan had. Her argument in effect was "let go of your piety and curse God; then He will end your life for blaspheming," (i.e., death under these conditions would be preferable to living). She added temptation to affliction because she advised him to sin.

2:10 foolish. Not meaning silly or ridiculous, but acting as one who rejects God or God's revealed will. The word is used of the unwise in the Psalms (14:1; 53:1) and in Proverbs (30:22). She is not seen nor heard of again in this book, except indirectly in 42:13-15. **accept.** Job lived out and explained the text of Deut. 29:29. His words and deeds demonstrated his confidence in God and vindicated God's confidence in him.

2:11-13 Here is one of the most moving scenes in the whole story, as Job's friends came to comfort and commiserate with him in his pain. They expressed all the traditional gestures of grief.

2:11 Temanite. Most likely Teman was a city of Edom (cf. Gen. 36:4,11; Jer. 49:7,20; Ezek. 25:13; Amos 1:12; Obad. 8,9). **Shuhite.** The Shuhites were descendants of Abraham through Keturah (Gen. 25:2,6). **Naamathite.** A resident of an unknown location probably in Edom or Arabia, although some have suggested Naamah on the Edomite border (cf. Josh. 15:41).

2:13 *his* grief was very great. The expression actually meant that his disease produced pain that was still increasing. The agony was so great, his friends were speechless for a week.

3:1–42:6 This whole section is poetry—a dramatic poem of speeches attempting to understand Job's suffering.

3:1–14:22 The first cycle of speeches given by Job and his 3 friends begins. Job was the first to break the week-long silence with a lament (3:1-26).

3:1-10 Job began his first speech by cursing the day of his birth, which should have been a day of great rejoicing, and welcomed the day he would finally die. In short, Job says "I wish I'd never been born." See Job 3:6,7; 9,10; 12–14; 16,17; 19; 21; 23,24; 26–31; 40:3-5; 42:1-6 for Job's speeches.

3:1 cursed the day of his *birth.* Job was in deep pain and despair. What God was allowing hurt desperately, but while Job did not curse God (cf. 2:8), he did curse his birth (vv. 10,11). He wished he had never been conceived (v. 3) or born because the joys of his life were not worth all the pain. He felt it would have been better to have never lived than to suffer like that; better to have never had wealth than to lose it; better to have never had children than to have them all killed. He never wanted his birthday remembered, and wished it had been obliterated from the calendar (vv. 4-7).

May God above not seek it,
Nor the light shine upon it.
5 May darkness and [b]the shadow of death claim it;
May a cloud settle on it;
May the blackness of the day terrify it.
6 *As for* that night, may darkness seize it;
May it not [2]rejoice among the days of the year,
May it not come into the number of the months.
7 Oh, may that night be barren!
May no joyful shout come into it!
8 May those curse it who curse the day,
Those [c]who are ready to arouse Leviathan.
9 May the stars of its morning be dark;
May it look for light, but *have* none,
And not see the [3]dawning of the day;
10 Because it did not shut up the doors of my *mother's* womb,
Nor hide sorrow from my eyes.

11 "Why[d] did I not die at birth?
Why did I *not* [4]perish when I came from the womb?
12 [e]Why did the knees receive me?
Or why the breasts, that I should nurse?
13 For now I would have lain still and been quiet,
I would have been asleep;
Then I would have been at rest
14 With kings and counselors of the earth,
Who [f]built ruins for themselves,
15 Or with princes who had gold,
Who filled their houses *with* silver;

5 [b] Job 10:21, 22; Jer. 13:16; Amos 5:8
6 [2] LXX, Syr., Tg., Vg. *be joined*
8 [c] Jer. 9:17
9 [3] *eyelids of the dawn*
11 [d] Job 10:18, 19 [4] *expire*
12 [e] Gen. 30:3
14 [f] Job 15:28; Is. 58:12
16 [g] Ps. 58:8
17 [h] Job 17:16 [5] Lit. *weary of strength*
18 [i] Job 39:7 [6] *are at ease*
20 [j] Jer. 20:18 [k] 2 Kin. 4:27
21 [l] Rev. 9:6 [m] Prov. 2:4 [7] Lit. *wait*
22 [n] Job 7:15, 16
23 [o] Job 19:8; Ps. 88:8; Lam. 3:7
24 [8] Lit. *my bread*
25 [p] [Job 9:28; 30:15]

16 Or *why* was I not hidden [g]like a stillborn child,
Like infants who never saw light?
17 There the wicked cease *from* troubling,
And there the [5]weary are at [h]rest.
18 *There* the prisoners [6]rest together;
[i]They do not hear the voice of the oppressor.
19 The small and great are there,
And the servant *is* free from his master.

20 "Why[j] is light given to him who is in misery,
And life to the [k]bitter of soul,
21 Who [l]long[7] for death, but it does not *come,*
And search for it more than [m]hidden treasures;
22 Who rejoice exceedingly,
And are glad when they can find the [n]grave?
23 *Why is light given* to a man whose way is hidden,
[o]And whom God has hedged in?
24 For my sighing comes before [8]I eat,
And my groanings pour out like water.
25 For the thing I greatly [p]feared has come upon me,
And what I dreaded has happened to me.
26 I am not at ease, nor am I quiet;
I have no rest, for trouble comes."

Eliphaz: Job Has Sinned

4 Then Eliphaz the Temanite answered and said:

2 "*If* one attempts a word with you, will you become weary?

3:8 who curse...Leviathan. Those who pronounce the most powerful curses, even to arousing the destructive sea monster (*see note on 41:1*; cf. Pss. 74:14; 104:26; Is. 27:1).

3:11-26 Job left the matter of never having been born (vv. 1-10) and moved to a desire to have been stillborn (vv. 11-19), then to a desire for the "light" of life to be extinguished in death (vv. 20-23). There is no hint that Job wanted to take his own life, for there was nothing stopping him. Job still trusted God for His sovereign hand in the matter of death, but he did consider the many ways in which death would be a perceived improvement to the present situation, because of the pain.

3:23 hedged in. Satan spoke of a hedge of protection and blessing (1:10), whereas Job spoke of this hedge as a prison of living death.

3:24 sighing...groanings. These destroyed any appetite he might have had.

3:25,26 the thing I greatly feared. Not a particular thing but a generic classification of suffering. The very worst fear that anyone could have was coming to pass in Job's life, and he is experiencing severe anxiety, fearing more.

4:1-37:24 This section covers the cycles of speeches between Job and his well meaning friends, including Elihu (chaps. 32-37).

4:1-5:27 Eliphaz. Eliphaz's first speech. See chaps. 15 and 22 for

The Script

1.	Job	Job 3; 6–7; 9–10; 12–14; 16–17; 19; 21; 23–24; 26–31; 40:3–5; 42:1–6
2.	Eliphaz	Job 4–5; 15; 22
3.	Bildad	Job 8; 18; 25
4.	Zophar	Job 11; 20
5.	Elihu	Job 32–37
6.	God	Job 38:1–40:2; 40:6–41:34

But who can withhold himself from speaking?
3 Surely you have instructed many,
And you [a]have strengthened weak hands.
4 Your words have upheld him who was stumbling,
And you [b]have strengthened the [1]feeble knees;
5 But now it comes upon you, and you are weary;
It touches you, and you are troubled.
6 *Is* not [c]your reverence [d]your confidence?
And the integrity of your ways your hope?

7 "Remember now, [e]who *ever* perished being innocent?
Or where were the upright *ever* cut off?
8 Even as I have seen,
[f]Those who plow iniquity
And sow trouble reap the same.
9 By the blast of God they perish,
And by the breath of His anger they are consumed.
10 The roaring of the lion,
The voice of the fierce lion,
And [g]the teeth of the young lions are broken.
11 [h]The old lion perishes for lack of prey,
And the cubs of the lioness are scattered.

12 "Now a word was secretly brought to me,
And my ear received a whisper of it.
13 [i]In disquieting thoughts from the visions of the night,
When deep sleep falls on men,
14 Fear came upon me, and [j]trembling,
Which made all my bones shake.
15 Then a spirit passed before my face;
The hair on my body stood up.
16 It stood still,
But I could not discern its appearance.
A form *was* before my eyes;
There was silence;
Then I heard a voice *saying:*
17 'Can a mortal be more righteous than God?
Can a man be more pure than his Maker?
18 If He [k]puts no trust in His servants,
If He charges His angels with error,
19 How much more those who dwell in houses of clay,
Whose foundation is in the dust,
Who are crushed before a moth?
20 [l]They are broken in pieces from morning till evening;
They perish forever, with no one regarding.
21 Does not their own excellence go away?
They die, even without wisdom.'

Eliphaz: Job Is Chastened by God

5 "Call out now;
Is there anyone who will answer you?
And to which of the holy ones will you turn?
2 For wrath kills a foolish man,
And envy slays a simple one.

CHAPTER 4
3 [a] Is. 35:3
4 [b] Is. 35:3 [1] Lit. *bending*
6 [c] Job 1:1 [d] Prov. 3:26
7 [e] [Job 8:20; 36:6, 7; Ps. 37:25]
8 [f] [Job 15:31, 35; Prov. 22:8; Hos. 10:13; Gal. 6:7]
10 [g] Job 5:15; Ps. 58:6
11 [h] Job 29:17; Ps. 34:10
13 [i] Job 33:15
14 [j] Hab. 3:16
18 [k] Job 15:15
20 [l] Ps. 90:5, 6

Eliphaz's other speeches. He spoke profoundly and gently, but knew nothing of the scene in heaven that had produced the suffering of Job.

4:2-6 Job's friend finally spoke after 7 days of silence and began kindly by acknowledging that Job was recognized for being a wise man. Unfortunately, with the opening of their mouths for the first speech, all the wisdom of their silence departed.

4:7 who *ever* perished being innocent? Eliphaz, recognizing Job's "reverence" and "integrity" (v. 6), was likely encouraging Job at the outset by saying he wouldn't die because he was innocent of any deadly iniquity, but must be guilty of some serious sin because he was reaping such anger from God. This was a moral universe and moral order was at work, he thought. He had oversimplified God's pattern of retribution. This simple axiom, "the righteous will prosper and the wicked will suffer," does not always hold up in human experience. It is true that plowing and sowing iniquity reaps judgment, so Eliphaz was partially right (cf. Gal. 6:7-9; 1 Pet. 3:12), but not everything we reap in life is the result of something we have sown (*see note on 2 Cor. 12:7-10*). Eliphaz was replacing theology with simplistic logic. To say that wherever there is suffering, it is the result of sowing sin is wrong (cf. Ex. 4:11; John 9:1-3).

4:10,11 Wanting to demonstrate that wicked men experience calamities in spite of their strength and resources, Eliphaz illustrated his point by the destruction that comes on lions in spite of their prowess. Five Heb. words were used here for lion, emphasizing the various characters of wicked people, all of whom can be broken and perish.

4:12-16 a word was secretly brought to me. Eliphaz spoke of a mysterious messenger in a vision, eerie fantasy, or a dream. He claimed to have had divine revelation to bolster his viewpoint.

4:17 Here is the conclusion of Eliphaz's revelation—that Job suffered because he was not holy enough, not righteous enough.

4:17-21 This is the content of the message which is, in effect, that God judges sin and sinners among men (described in v. 19 as "houses of clay") as He did among angels (v. 18; cf. Rev. 12:3,4).

5:1 holy ones. Angelic beings (cf. 4:18) are in view. Job was told that not even the angels could help him. He must recognize his mortality and sin if he would be healed.

3 [a]I have seen the foolish taking root,
But suddenly I cursed his dwelling
place.
4 His sons are [b]far from safety,
They are crushed in the gate,
And [c]*there is* no deliverer.
5 Because the hungry eat up his
harvest,
[1]Taking it even from the thorns,
[2]And a snare snatches their
[3]substance.
6 For affliction does not come from
the dust,
Nor does trouble spring from the
ground;
7 Yet man is [d]born to [4]trouble,
As the sparks fly upward.
8 "But as for me, I would seek God,
And to God I would commit my
cause—
9 Who does great things, and
unsearchable,
Marvelous things without number.
10 [e]He gives rain on the earth,
And sends waters on the fields.
11 [f]He sets on high those who are
lowly,
And those who mourn are lifted to
safety.
12 [g]He frustrates the devices of the
crafty,
So that their hands cannot carry
out their plans.
13 He catches the [h]wise in their own
craftiness,
And the counsel of the cunning
comes quickly upon them.
14 They meet with darkness in the
daytime,
And grope at noontime as in the
night.
15 But [i]He saves the needy from the
sword,
From the mouth of the mighty,
And from their hand.
16 [j]So the poor have hope,
And injustice shuts her mouth.

17 "Behold,[k] happy *is* the man whom
God corrects;
Therefore do not despise the
chastening of the Almighty.
18 [l]For He bruises, but He binds up;
He wounds, but His hands make
whole.
19 [m]He shall deliver you in six troubles,
Yes, in seven [n]no evil shall touch
you.
20 [o]In famine He shall redeem you
from death,
And in war from the [5]power of the
sword.
21 [p]You shall be hidden from the
scourge of the tongue,
And you shall not be afraid of
destruction when it comes.
22 You shall laugh at destruction and
famine,
And [q]you shall not be afraid of the
[r]beasts of the earth.
23 [s]For you shall have a covenant with
the stones of the field,
And the beasts of the field shall be
at peace with you.
24 You shall know that your tent *is* in
peace;
You shall visit your dwelling and
find nothing amiss.
25 You shall also know that [t]your
descendants *shall be* many,
And your offspring [u]like the grass
of the earth.
26 [v]You shall come to the grave at a
full age,
As a sheaf of grain ripens in its
season.
27 Behold, this we have [w]searched
out;
It *is* true.
Hear it, and know for yourself."

Job: My Complaint Is Just

6 Then Job answered and said:

2 "Oh, that my grief were fully
weighed,

CHAPTER 5

3 [a] [Ps. 37:35, 36]; Jer. 12:1-3
4 [b] Ps. 119:155 [c] Ps. 109:12
5 [1] LXX *They shall not be taken from evil men*; Vg. *And the armed man shall take him by violence* [2] LXX *The might shall draw them off*; Vg. *And the thirsty shall drink up their riches* [3] *wealth*
7 [d] Job 14:1 [4] *labor*
10 [e] [Job 36:27-29; 37:6-11; 38:26]
11 [f] Ps. 113:7
12 [g] Neh. 4:15
13 [h] [Job 37:24; 1 Cor. 3:19]
15 [i] Job 4:10, 11; Ps. 35:10
16 [j] 1 Sam. 2:8; Ps. 107:41, 42
17 [k] Ps. 94:12; [Prov. 3:11, 12; Heb. 12:5, 6; Rev. 3:19]
18 [l] [Deut. 32:39; 1 Sam. 2:6, 7]; Is. 30:26; Hos. 6:1
19 [m] Ps. 34:19; 91:3; [1 Cor. 10:13] [n] Ps. 91:10; [Prov. 24:16]
20 [o] Ps. 33:19, 20; 37:19 [5] Lit. *hand*
21 [p] Job 5:15; Ps. 31:20
22 [q] Ps. 91:13; Is. 11:9; 35:9; 65:25; Ezek. 34:25 [r] Hos. 2:18
23 [s] Ps. 91:12
25 [t] Ps. 112:2 [u] Ps. 72:16
26 [v] [Prov. 9:11; 10:27]
27 [w] Ps. 111:2

5:2-6 Job was told not to be a fool or simpleton, but to recognize that sin is judged, wrath kills, envy slays, foolishness is cursed (vv. 2-5), and this wasn't merely a physical matter (v. 6), but came from man's sin. Sin is inevitable in man; so is trouble (v. 7).

5:7 sparks. Lit. "the sons of Resheph," an expression which describes all sorts of fire-like movement (cf. Deut. 32:24; Ps. 78:48; Song 8:6).

5:8 Job's solution was to go to God and repent, his friend thought.

5:9-16 The whole of Eliphaz's argument is based on the moral perfection of God, so he extolled God's greatness and goodness.

5:13 Paul used this line from Eliphaz in 1 Cor. 3:19 to prove the foolishness of man's wisdom before God.

5:17 happy *is* the man whom God corrects. Eliphaz put a positive spin on his advice by telling Job that enviable or desirable is the situation of the one God cares enough to chasten. "If only Job admitted his sin, he could be happy again" was the advice.

5:18-27 The language of this section promising blessing for penitence was strongly reminiscent of Lev. 26, which elaborated the blessing of a faithful covenant relationship with God. If Job confessed, he would have prosperity, security, a family, and a rich life.

5:23 covenant...peace. Even the created order will be in harmony with the man whose relationship with God is corrected through God's disciplinary process.

6:1–7:21 Job's response to Eliphaz was recorded. On top of his physical misery and his tempting wife, he had to respond to ignorance and insensitivity from his friend, by expressing his frustration.

And my calamity laid with it on
the scales!
3 For then it would be heavier than
the sand of the sea—
Therefore my words have been
rash.
4 [a]For the arrows of the Almighty *are*
within me;
My spirit drinks in their poison;
[b]The terrors of God are arrayed
[c]against me.
5 Does the [d]wild donkey bray when
it has grass,
Or does the ox low over its fodder?
6 Can flavorless food be eaten
without salt?
Or is there *any* taste in the white of
an egg?
7 My soul refuses to touch them;
They *are* as loathsome food to me.

8 "Oh, that I might have my request,
That God would grant *me* the thing
that I long for!
9 That it would please God to crush
me,
That He would loose His hand and
[e]cut me off!
10 Then I would still have comfort;
Though in anguish I would exult,
He will not spare;
For [f]I have not concealed the
words of [g]the Holy One.

11 "What strength do I have, that I
should hope?
And what *is* my end, that I should
prolong my life?
12 *Is* my strength the strength of
stones?
Or is my flesh bronze?
13 *Is* my help not within me?
And is success driven from me?

14 "To [h]him who is [1]afflicted, kindness
should be shown by his friend,
Even though he forsakes the fear of
the Almighty.
15 [i]My brothers have dealt deceitfully
like a brook,
[j]Like the streams of the brooks that
pass away,
16 Which are dark because of the ice,
And into which the snow vanishes.
17 When it is warm, they cease to
flow;
When it is hot, they vanish from
their place.
18 The paths of their way turn aside,
They go nowhere and perish.
19 The caravans of [k]Tema look,
The travelers of [l]Sheba hope for
them.
20 They are [m]disappointed[2] because
they were confident;
They come there and are confused.
21 For now [n]you are nothing,
You see terror and [o]are afraid.
22 Did I ever say, 'Bring *something* to
me'?
Or, 'Offer a bribe for me from your
wealth'?
23 Or, 'Deliver me from the enemy's
hand'?
Or, 'Redeem me from the hand of
oppressors'?

24 "Teach me, and I will hold my
tongue;
Cause me to understand wherein I
have erred.
25 How forceful are right words!
But what does your arguing prove?
26 Do you intend to rebuke *my* words,
And the speeches of a desperate
one, *which are* as wind?
27 Yes, you overwhelm the fatherless,

CHAPTER 6
4 [a] Job 16:13; Ps. 38:2 [b] Ps. 88:15, 16 [c] Job 30:15
5 [d] Job 39:5-8
9 [e] Num. 11:15; 1 Kin. 19:4; Job 7:16; 9:21; 10:1
10 [f] Acts 20:20 [g] [Lev. 19:2; Is. 57:15]
14 [h] [Prov. 17:17] [1] Or *despairing*
15 [i] Ps. 38:11 [j] Jer. 15:18
19 [k] Gen. 25:15; Is. 21:14; Jer. 25:23 [l] 1 Kin. 10:1; Ps. 72:10; Ezek. 27:22, 23
20 [m] Jer. 14:3 [2] Lit. *ashamed*
21 [n] Job 13:4 [o] Ps. 38:11

6:2,3 The heaviness of his burden caused the rashness of his words.

6:4 the arrows of the Almighty...terrors of God. Here are figures of speech picturing the trials as coming from God, indicating that Job believed these were God's judgments.

6:5-7 These are all illustrations of the fact that Job complained because he had reason. Even animals expect palatable food.

6:8,9 my request. Job's request was that God would finish whatever process He began. Death was desirable for no other reason than it would be relief from the inevitable course of events (see chap. 3).

6:9 cut me off. This is a metaphor from a weaver, who cuts off the excess thread on the loom (cf. Is. 38:12).

6:10 the words of the Holy One. Job had not been avoiding the revelation of God that he had received. The commands of the Holy One were precious to him and he had lived by them. This was confusing to him, as he couldn't find any sinful source for his suffering. He would rejoice in his pain if he knew it would soon lead to death, but he couldn't see any hope for death or deliverance in himself (vv. 11-13).

6:14 kindness...Even though. Job rebuked his friends with sage words. Even if a man has forsaken God (which he hadn't), should not his friends still show kindness to him? How can Eliphaz be so unkind as to continually indict him?

6:15-23 Job described his friends as being about as useful with their counsel as a dry river bed in summer. "You are no help," he said (v. 21), "although all I asked for was a little sympathy, not some great gift or deliverance" (vv. 22,23).

6:19 Tema...Sheba. Tema in the N, named for the son of Ishmael (Gen. 25:15; Is. 21:14), and Sheba in the S (Jer. 6:20) were part of the Arabian desert, where water was precious.

6:24-30 Teach me...Cause me to understand wherein I have erred. Job was not admitting to having sinned. Rather he said to his accusers, "If I've sinned, show me where." The sufferer indicted his friends for their insensitivity, and while not claiming sinlessness, he was convinced there was no sin in his life that led directly to such suffering.

And you [p]undermine your friend.
28 Now therefore, be pleased to look at me;
For I would never lie to your face.
29 [q]Yield now, let there be no injustice!
Yes, concede, my [r]righteousness [3]still stands!
30 Is there injustice on my tongue?
Cannot my [4]taste discern the unsavory?

Job: My Suffering Is Comfortless

7 "*Is there* not [a]a time of hard service for man on earth?
Are not his days also like the days of a hired man?
2 Like a servant who [1]earnestly desires the shade,
And like a hired man who eagerly looks for his wages,
3 So I have been allotted [b]months of futility,
And wearisome nights have been appointed to me.
4 [c]When I lie down, I say, 'When shall I arise,
And the night be ended?'
For I have had my fill of tossing till dawn.
5 My flesh is [d]caked with worms and dust,
My skin is cracked and breaks out afresh.
6 "My[e] days are swifter than a weaver's shuttle,
And are spent without hope.
7 Oh, remember that [f]my life *is* a breath!
My eye will never again see good.
8 [g]The eye of him who sees me will see me no *more;*
While your *eyes* are upon me, I shall no longer *be.*
9 *As* the cloud disappears and vanishes away,
So [h]he who goes down to the grave does not come up.
10 He shall never return to his house,
[i]Nor shall his place know him anymore.

11 "Therefore I will [j]not restrain my mouth;
I will speak in the anguish of my spirit;
I will [k]complain in the bitterness of my soul.
12 *Am* I a sea, or a sea serpent,
That You set a guard over me?
13 [l]When I say, 'My bed will comfort me,
My couch will ease my complaint,'
14 Then You scare me with dreams
And terrify me with visions,
15 So that my soul chooses strangling
And death rather than [2]my body.
16 [m]I loathe *my life;*
I would not live forever.
[n]Let me alone,
For [o]my days *are but* [3]a breath.

27 [p]Ps. 57:6
29 [q]Job 17:10 [r]Job 27:5, 6; 34:5 [3]Lit. *is in it*
30 [4]*palate*

CHAPTER 7

1 [a][Job 14:5, 13, 14]; Ps. 39:4
2 [1]Lit. *pants for*
3 [b][Job 15:31]
4 [c]Deut. 28:67; Job 7:13, 14
5 [d]Is. 14:11
6 [e]Job 9:25; 16:22; 17:11; Is. 38:12; [James 4:14]
7 [f]Job 7:16; Ps. 78:39; 89:47
8 [g]Job 8:18; 20:9
9 [h]2 Sam. 12:23
10 [i]Ps. 103:16
11 [j]Ps. 39:1, 9 [k]1 Sam. 1:10
13 [l]Job 9:27
15 [2]Lit. *my bones*
16 [m]Job 10:1 [n]Job 14:6 [o]Ps. 62:9 [3]Without substance, futile

7:1-21 After having directed his words at his friends in chap. 6, Job then directed them at God. Throughout this section he used words and arguments that sounded much like Solomon in Ecclesiastes, i.e., "labor, vanity, trouble, and breath."

7:1-10 a time of hard service. He felt like a slave under tyranny of his master, longing for relief and reward (vv. 1,2); he was sleepless (v. 3,4); he was loathsome because of worms and scabs, dried filth and new running sores (v. 5); he was like a weaver's shuttle, tossed back and forth (v. 6); he was like a breath or cloud that comes and goes on it way to death (vv. 7-10). In this discourse, Job attempted to reconcile in his own mind what God was doing.

7:11 Therefore. On the basis of all he had said in vv. 1-10, he felt he had a right to express his complaint.

7:12 sea, or a sea serpent. The sea and the whale are two threatening forces that must be watched or curbed due to their destructive force. Job was not like that.

7:13,14 Even when he slept, he had terrifying dreams so that he longed for death (vv. 15,16).

Job's Living Death

1. Painful boils from head to toe (2:7, 13; 30:17)
2. Severe itching/irritation (2:7,8)
3. Great grief (2:13)
4. Lost appetite (3:24; 6:6, 7)
5. Agonizing discomfort (3:24)
6. Insomnia (7:4)
7. Worm and dust infested flesh (7:5)
8. Continual oozing of boils (7:5)
9. Hallucinations (7:14)
10. Decaying skin (13:28)
11. Shriveled up (16:8; 17:7; 19:20)
12. Severe halitosis (19:17)
13. Teeth fell out (19:20)
14. Relentless pain (30:17)
15. Skin turned black (30:30)
16. Raging fever (30:30)
17. Dramatic weight loss (33:21)

Job's intense physical suffering is mentioned throughout the book.

17 "What[p] *is* man, that You should
exalt him,
That You should set Your heart on
him,
18 That You should [4]visit him every
morning,
And test him every moment?
19 How long?
Will You not look away from me,
And let me alone till I swallow my
saliva?
20 Have I sinned?
What have I done to You, [q]O
watcher of men?
Why [r]have You set me as Your
target,
So that I am a burden [5]to myself?
21 Why then do You not pardon my
transgression,
And take away my iniquity?
For now I will lie down in the dust,
And You will seek me diligently,
But I *will* no longer *be*."

Bildad: Job Should Repent

8 Then Bildad the Shuhite answered and
said:

2 "How long will you speak these
things,
And the words of your mouth *be
like* a strong wind?
3 [a]Does God subvert judgment?
Or does the Almighty pervert
justice?
4 If [b]your sons have sinned against
Him,
He has cast them away [1]for their
transgression.
5 [c]If you would earnestly seek God
And make your supplication to the
Almighty,
6 If you *were* pure and upright,
Surely now He would [2]awake for
you,
And prosper your rightful
dwelling place.
7 Though your beginning was small,
Yet your latter end would [d]increase
abundantly.

8 "For[e] inquire, please, of the former
age,
And consider the things discovered
by their fathers;
9 For [f]we *were born* yesterday, and
know [3]nothing,
Because our days on earth *are* a
shadow.
10 Will they not teach you and tell
you,
And utter words from their heart?

11 "Can the papyrus grow up without
a marsh?
Can the reeds flourish without
water?
12 [g]While it *is* yet green *and* not cut
down,
It withers before any *other* plant.
13 So *are* the paths of all who [h]forget
God;
And the hope of the [i]hypocrite
shall perish,
14 Whose confidence shall be cut off,
And whose trust *is* [4]a spider's
web.
15 [j]He leans on his house, but it does
not stand.
He holds it fast, but it does not
endure.
16 He grows green in the sun,
And his branches spread out in his
garden.
17 His roots wrap around the rock
heap,

17 [p] Job 22:2; Ps. 8:4; 144:3; Heb. 2:6
18 [4] *attend to*
20 [q] Ps. 36:6 [r] Ps. 21:12 [5] So with MT, Tg., Vg.; LXX, Jewish tradition *to You*

CHAPTER 8

3 [a] Gen. 18:25; [Deut. 32:4; 2 Chr. 19:7; Job 34:10, 12; 36:23; 37:23]; Rom. 3:5
4 [b] Job 1:5, 18, 19 [1] Lit. *into the hand of their transgression*
5 [c] [Job 5:17-27; 11:13]
6 [2] *arise*
7 [d] Job 42:12
8 [e] Deut. 4:32; 32:7; Job 15:18; 20:4
9 [f] Gen. 47:9; [1 Chr. 29:15]; Job 7:6; [Ps. 39:5; 102:11; 144:4] [3] Lit. *not*
12 [g] Ps. 129:6
13 [h] Ps. 9:17 [i] Job 11:20; 18:14; 27:8; Ps. 112:10; [Prov. 10:28]
14 [4] Lit. *a spider's house*
15 [j] Job 8:22; 27:18; Ps. 49:11

7:17,18 Why is he so important, Job wonders, that God would spend all this attention on him? Why did God cause all this misery to one so insignificant as he?

7:19 till I swallow my saliva. This strange statement was an Arabic proverb, indicating a brief moment. Job was asking for a moment "to catch his breath," or in the case of the proverb, "swallow his saliva."

7:21 not pardon my transgression. Job conceded the argument of Eliphaz that he must have sinned, not because he was convinced, but because he seemed to find no other explanation (cf. 6:24).

8:1-22 The second friendly accuser, Bildad, now offered his wisdom to Job. Bildad, also absolutely certain that Job had sinned and should repent, was ruthless in the charges he raised against God's servant. See Job 18; 25 for Bildad's other speeches.

8:2-7 Bildad accused Job of defending his innocence with a lot of hot air and reasoned that Job's circumstances were God's judgment on his sins and those of his family. Again, this is logical, based on the principle that God punishes sin, but it failed to account for the mystery of the heavenly debate between God and Satan (see chaps. 1,2). He was sure something was wrong in Job's relationship with God, thus his call for repentance, with the confidence that when Job repented he would be blessed (vv. 6,7).

8:3 Almighty pervert justice. Bildad took Job's claims for innocence and applied them to his simplistic notion of retribution. He concluded that Job was accusing God of injustice when God must be meting out justice to Job. Job tried to avoid outright accusations of this sort, but the evidence led Bildad to this conclusion because he had no knowledge of the heavenly facts.

8:7 In fact, this was Job's outcome (cf. 42:10-17), not because Job repented of some specific sin, but because he humbled himself before the sovereign, inscrutable will of God.

8:8-10 Here Bildad appealed to past authorities, godly ancestors who taught the same principle—that where there is suffering, there must be sin. So he had history as a witness to his misjudgment.

8:11-19 He further supported his simple logic of cause and effect by illustrations from nature. Again he accused Job of sin, but surely he had forgotten God as well (v. 13).

And look for a place in the stones.
18 [k]If he is destroyed from his place,
Then *it* will deny him, *saying,* 'I have not seen you.'

19 "Behold, this is the joy of His way,
And [l]out of the earth others will grow.
20 Behold, [m]God will not [5]cast away the blameless,
Nor will He uphold the evildoers.
21 He will yet fill your mouth with laughing,
And your lips with [6]rejoicing.
22 Those who hate you will be [n]clothed with shame,
And the dwelling place of the wicked [7]will come to nothing."

Job: There Is No Mediator

9 Then Job answered and said:

2 "Truly I know *it is* so,
But how can a [a]man be [b]righteous before God?
3 If one wished to [1]contend with Him,
He could not answer Him one time out of a thousand.
4 [c]*God is* wise in heart and mighty in strength.
Who has hardened *himself* against Him and prospered?
5 He removes the mountains, and they do not know
When He overturns them in His anger;
6 He [d]shakes the earth out of its place,
And its [e]pillars tremble;
7 He commands the sun, and it does not rise;
He seals off the stars;
8 [f]He alone spreads out the heavens,
And [2]treads on the [3]waves of the sea;
9 [g]He made [4]the Bear, Orion, and the Pleiades,
And the chambers of the south;
10 [h]He does great things past finding out,
Yes, wonders without number.
11 [i]If He goes by me, I do not see *Him;*
If He moves past, I do not perceive Him;
12 [j]If He takes away, [5]who can hinder Him?
Who can say to Him, 'What are You doing?'
13 God will not withdraw His anger,
[k]The allies of [6]the proud lie prostrate beneath Him.

14 "How then can I answer Him,
And choose my words *to reason* with Him?
15 [l]For though I were righteous, I could not answer Him;
I would beg mercy of my Judge.
16 If I called and He answered me,
I would not believe that He was listening to my voice.
17 For He crushes me with a tempest,
And multiplies my wounds [m]without cause.
18 He will not allow me to catch my breath,
But fills me with bitterness.
19 If *it is a matter* of strength, indeed *He is* strong;
And if of justice, who will appoint my day *in court?*

18 [k]Job 7:10
19 [l]Ps. 113:7
20 [m]Job 4:7 [5]*reject*
21 [6]Lit. *shouts of joy*
22 [n]Ps. 35:26; 109:29 [7]Lit. *will not be*

CHAPTER 9

2 [a][Job 4:17; 15:14-16; Ps. 143:2; Rom. 3:20] [b][Hab. 2:4; Rom. 1:17; Gal. 3:11; Heb. 10:38]
3 [1]*argue*
4 [c]Job 36:5
6 [d]Is. 2:19, 21; Hag. 2:6; Heb. 12:26 [e]Job 26:11
8 [f]Gen. 1:6; Job 37:18; Ps. 104:2, 3; Is. 40:22 [2]*walks* [3]Lit. *heights*
9 [g]Gen. 1:16; Job 38:31; Amos 5:8 [4]Heb. *Ash, Kesil,* and *Kimah*
10 [h]Job 5:9
11 [i][Job 23:8, 9; 35:14]
12 [j][Is. 45:9; Dan. 4:35; Rom. 9:20] [5]Lit. *who can turn Him back?*
13 [k]Job 26:12 [6]Heb. *rahab*
15 [l]Job 10:15; 23:1-7
17 [m]Job 2:3

8:20 God will not cast away the blameless. This comment contains a veiled offer of hope. Job could laugh again but he must take steps to become blameless. But Bildad, like Job, was unaware of the dialogue between the Sovereign Judge and the Accuser in the opening chapters of the book and unaware that God had already pronounced Job "blameless" twice to heavenly beings (1:8; 2:3), as had the writer (1:1). Cf. Pss. 1:6; 126:2; 132:18.

9:1–10:22 Job, in a mood of deep despair, responded to Bildad's accusations with arguments surrounding God's nature, also raised by Bildad, and started to rationalize something about which he would later admit he knew dangerously little. Job concluded that God is holy, wise, and strong (vv. 4-10); but he wondered if He is fair (v. 22) and why He wouldn't make Himself known to him. Before the mighty God, Job felt only despair. If God is not fair, all is hopeless, he thought.

9:3 contend with Him. Job referred to disputing one's innocence or guilt before God as a useless endeavor. Psalm 130:3 illustrates the point, "If You…should mark iniquities (keep records of sin),…who could stand (innocently in judgment)?"

9:6 pillars tremble. In the figurative language of the day, this phrase described the supporting power that secured the position of the earth in the universe.

9:9 Bear, Orion…Pleiades. Three stellar constellations (cf. Job 38:31,32). **the chambers of the south.** These were other constellations in the southern hemisphere, unseen by those who could see and name the 3 in the northern skies.

9:13 the proud. Lit. "Rahab." This is symbolic of the ancient mythological sea monster (cf. 3:8; 7:12). God smiting the proud was a poetic way of saying that if the mythical monster of the sea (a metaphor for powerful, evil, chaotic forces) could not stand before God's anger, how could Job hope to? In a battle in God's court, he would lose. God is too strong (vv. 14-19).

9:15,20 though I were righteous. He means here, not sinless, but having spiritual integrity, i.e., a pure heart to love, serve, and obey God. He was affirming again that his suffering was not due to sins he was not willing to confess. Even at that, God found something to condemn him for, he felt, making it hopeless, then, to contend with God.

20 Though I were righteous, my own
mouth would condemn me;
Though I *were* blameless, it would
prove me perverse.

21 "I am blameless, yet I do not know
myself;
I despise my life.

22 It *is* all one *thing;*
Therefore I say, [n]'He destroys the
blameless and the wicked.'

23 If the scourge slays suddenly,
He laughs at the plight of the
innocent.

24 The earth is given into the hand of
the wicked.
He covers the faces of its judges.
If it is not *He,* who else could it be?

25 "Now [o]my days are swifter than a
runner;
They flee away, they see no good.

26 They pass by like [7]swift ships,
[p]Like an eagle swooping on its prey.

27 [q]If I say, 'I will forget my complaint,
I will put off my sad face and wear
a smile,'

28 [r]I am afraid of all my sufferings;
I know that You [s]will not hold me
innocent.

29 *If* I am condemned,
Why then do I labor in vain?

30 [t]If I wash myself with snow water,
And cleanse my hands with [8]soap,

31 Yet You will plunge me into the pit,
And my own clothes will [9]abhor
me.

32 "For [u]*He is* not a man, as I *am,*
That I may answer Him,
And that we should go to court
together.

33 [v]Nor is there any mediator between
us,
Who may lay his hand on us both.

34 [w]Let Him take His rod away from
me,
And do not let dread of Him
terrify me.

35 *Then* I would speak and not fear
Him,
But it is not so with me.

22 [n] [Eccl. 9:2, 3]; Ezek. 21:3
25 [o] Job 7:6, 7
26 [p] Job 39:29; Hab. 1:8 [7] Lit. *ships of reeds*
27 [q] Job 7:13
28 [r] Ps. 119:120 [s] Ex. 20:7
30 [t] [Jer. 2:22] [8] *lye*
31 [9] *loathe*
32 [u] Eccl. 6:10; [Is. 45:9; Jer. 49:19; Rom. 9:20]
33 [v] [1 Sam. 2:25]; Job 9:19; Is. 1:18
34 [w] Job 13:20, 21; Ps. 39:10

CHAPTER 10

1 [a] 1 Kin. 19:4; Job 7:16; Jon. 4:3 [b] Job 7:11 [1] Lit. *leave on myself*
4 [c] [1 Sam. 16:7; Job 28:24; 34:21]

Job: I Would Plead with God

10 "My [a]soul loathes my life;
I will [1]give free course to my
complaint,
[b]I will speak in the bitterness of my
soul.

2 I will say to God, 'Do not condemn
me;
Show me why You contend with
me.

3 *Does it* seem good to You that You
should oppress,
That You should despise the work
of Your hands,
And smile on the counsel of the
wicked?

4 Do You have eyes of flesh?
Or [c]do You see as man sees?

5 *Are* Your days like the days of a
mortal man?
Are Your years like the days of a
mighty man,

6 That You should seek for my
iniquity
And search out my sin,

7 Although You know that I am not
wicked,

9:24 covers the faces of its judges. Job here indicted God for the inequities of His world. He accused God of treating all the same way, unfairly (vv. 21-23), and of even covering the eyes of earthly judges so that they would not see injustice. These are the charges that bring about God's rebuke of Job (chaps. 38–41) and for which he eventually repented (42:1-6).

9:25,26 Couriers running with messages, ships cutting swiftly, and eagles swooping rapidly convey the blur of painful, meaningless days of despair that move by.

9:27,28 Job said if he promised to change to a happy mood, he would break that promise and God would add that to His list of accusations.

9:29,30 "God seems to have found me guilty," Job concluded, "so why struggle? Even if I make every effort to clean every aspect of my life, you will still punish me." This was deep despair and hopelessness.

9:32 *that* we should go to court together. Job acknowledged that, as a mere man, he had no right to call on God to declare his innocence or to contend with God over his innocence. Job was not arguing that he was sinless, but he didn't believe he had sinned to the extent that he deserved his severe suffering. Job held on to the same simplistic system of retribution as that of his accusers, which said that suffering was always caused by sin. And he knew he was not sinless, but he couldn't identify any unconfessed or unrepented sins. "Where is mercy?" he wondered.

9:33-35 any mediator between us. A court official who sees both sides clearly, as well as the source of disagreement, so as to bring resolution was not found. Where was an advocate, an arbitrator, an umpire, or a referee? Was there no one to remove God's rod and call for justice?

10:2 condemn me. Not the condemnation of Job's soul, but Job's physical suffering as a punishment. He held nothing back in his misery (v. 1), but asked God to show him why all this had happened.

10:3 the work of Your hands. This is a biblical expression identifying what someone produces, in this case man, as created by God (cf. 14:15; Ps. 102:25; Heb. 1:10).

10:4-7 see as man sees. Because he believed he was innocent, Job facetiously, somewhat sarcastically, asked if God was as limited in His ability to discern Job's spiritual condition as were Job's friends. He concluded by affirming that God did know he was innocent and that there was no higher court of appeal (v. 7).

And *there is* no one who can
deliver from Your hand?

8 'Your[d] hands have made me and
fashioned me,
An intricate unity;
Yet You would [e]destroy me.
9 Remember, I pray, [f]that You have
made me like clay.
And will You turn me into dust
again?
10 [g]Did You not pour me out like milk,
And curdle me like cheese,
11 Clothe me with skin and flesh,
And knit me together with bones
and sinews?
12 You have granted me life and favor,
And Your care has preserved my
spirit.

13 'And these *things* You have hidden
in Your heart;
I know that this *was* with You:
14 If I sin, then [h]You mark me,
And will not acquit me of my
iniquity.
15 If I am wicked, [i]woe to me;
[j]Even *if* I am righteous, I [2]cannot
lift up my head.
I am full of disgrace;
[k]See my misery!
16 If *my head* is exalted,
[l]You hunt me like a fierce lion,
And again You show Yourself
awesome against me.
17 You renew Your witnesses against
me,
And increase Your indignation
toward me;
Changes and war are *ever* with me.

18 'Why[m] then have You brought me
out of the womb?
Oh, that I had perished and no eye
had seen me!
19 I would have been as though I had
not been.
I would have been carried from the
womb to the grave.
20 [n]Are not my days few?
Cease! [o]Leave me alone, that I may
take a little comfort,
21 Before I go *to the place from which* I
shall not return,
[p]To the land of darkness [q]and the
shadow of death,
22 A land as dark as darkness *itself*,
As the shadow of death, without
any order,
Where even the light *is* like
darkness.' "

Zophar Urges Job to Repent

11 Then Zophar the Naamathite answered and said:

2 "Should not the multitude of words
be answered?
And should [1]a man full of talk be
vindicated?
3 Should your empty talk make men
[2]hold their peace?
And when you mock, should no
one rebuke you?
4 For you have said,
[a]'My doctrine *is* pure,
And I am clean in your eyes.'
5 But oh, that God would speak,
And open His lips against you,
6 That He would show you the
secrets of wisdom!

8 [d] Job 10:3; Ps. 119:73 [e] [Job 9:22] **9** [f] Gen. 2:7; Job 33:6 **10** [g] [Ps. 139:14-16] **14** [h] Job 7:20; Ps. 139:1 **15** [i] Job 10:7; Is. 3:11 [j] [Job 9:12, 15] [k] Ps. 25:18 [2] Lit. *will not* **16** [l] Is. 38:13; Lam. 3:10; Hos. 13:7 **18** [m] Job 3:11-13 **20** [n] Ps. 39:5 [o] Job 7:16, 19 **21** [p] Ps. 88:12 [q] Ps. 23:4

CHAPTER 11

2 [1] Lit. *a man of lips* **3** [2] *be silent* **4** [a] Job 6:30

10:8-12 Again he returned to the question "Why was I born?" The answer that God had created him is given in magnificent language, indicating that life begins at conception.

10:13-16 Job wondered if God had planned in His divine purpose not to be merciful to him.

10:17 renew Your witnesses. Job said God seemed to be sending people to accuse him. With each witness came another wave of condemnation and increased suffering.

10:18 brought me out of the womb. Job returned to the question of why God allowed him to be born. This time he was not just lamenting the day of his birth, but he was asking God for the reason He allowed it to occur.

10:20-22 "Since I was destined to these ills from my birth, at least give me a little breathing room during the brief days left to me, before I die," he said. Death was gloomily described as "darkness."

11:1-20 Zophar the Naamathite now stepped in to interrogate Job. He was quite close to his friends and chose to pound Job with the same law of retaliation. Job must repent, he said, not understanding the reality. He was indignant at Job's protests of innocence. See Job 20 for Zophar's other speech.

11:2,3 a man full of talk be vindicated. The allegations against Job moved to a new level. Not only was Job guilty and unrepentant, he was also an empty talker. In fact, Job's long-winded defense of his innocence and God's apparent injustice was sin worthy of rebuke, in Zophar's mind.

11:4 clean in your eyes. Job never claimed sinlessness; in fact, he acknowledged that he had sinned (Job 7:21; 13:26). But he still maintained his innocence of any great transgression or attitude of unrepentance, affirming his sincerity and integrity as a man of faith and obedience to God. This claim infuriated Zophar, and he wished God Himself would confirm the accusations of Job's friends (v. 5).

11:6 secrets of wisdom. Job would have been much wiser if he had only known the unknowable secrets of God; in this case the scene in heaven between God and Satan would have clarified everything. But Job couldn't know the secret wisdom of God (vv. 7-9). Zophar should have applied his point to himself. If God's wisdom was so deep, high, long, and broad, how was it that he could understand it and have all the answers? Like his friends, Zophar thought he understood God and reverted to the same law of retaliation, the sowing and reaping principle, to again indict Job. He implied that Job was wicked (vv. 10,11) and thought he was wise, though actually he was out of control as if he were a "wild donkey man"! (v. 12).

For *they would* double *your*
prudence.
Know therefore that [b]God [3]exacts
from you
Less than your iniquity *deserves.*

7 "Can[c] you search out the deep
things of God?
Can you find out the limits of the
Almighty?
8 *They are* higher than heaven—
what can you do?
Deeper than [4]Sheol— what can
you know?
9 Their measure *is* longer than the
earth
And broader than the sea.

10 "If[d] He passes by, imprisons, and
gathers *to judgment,*
Then who can [5]hinder Him?
11 For [e]He knows deceitful men;
He sees wickedness also.
Will He not then consider *it?*
12 For an [f]empty-headed man will be
wise,
When a wild donkey's colt is born
a man.

13 "If you would [g]prepare your heart,
And [h]stretch out your hands
toward Him;
14 If iniquity *were* in your hand, *and
you* put it far away,
And [i]would not let wickedness
dwell in your tents;
15 [j]Then surely you could lift up your
face without spot;
Yes, you could be steadfast, and
not fear;
16 Because you would [k]forget *your*
misery,
And remember *it* as waters *that
have* passed away,
17 And *your* life [l]would be brighter
than noonday.
Though you were dark, you would
be like the morning.
18 And you would be secure, because
there is hope;
Yes, you would dig *around you, and*
[m]take your rest in safety.
19 You would also lie down, and no
one would make *you* afraid;
Yes, many would court your favor.
20 But [n]the eyes of the wicked will
fail,
And they shall not escape,
And [o]their hope—[6]loss of life!"

Job Answers His Critics

12 Then Job answered and said:

2 "No doubt you *are* the people,
And wisdom will die with you!
3 But I have [1]understanding as well
as you;
I *am* not [a]inferior to you.
Indeed, who does not *know* such
things as these?

4 "I[b] am one mocked by his friends,
Who [c]called on God, and He
answered him,
The just and blameless *who is*
ridiculed.
5 A [2]lamp is despised in the thought
of one who is at ease;
It is made ready for [d]those whose
feet slip.
6 [e]The tents of robbers prosper,
And those who provoke God are
secure—
In what God provides by His hand.

7 "But now ask the beasts, and they
will teach you;

6 [b] [Ezra 9:13] [3] Lit. *forgets some of your iniquity for you*
7 [c] Job 33:12, 13; 36:26; [Eccl. 3:11; Rom. 11:33]
8 [4] The abode of the dead
10 [d] Job 9:12; [Rev. 3:7] [5] *restrain*
11 [e] [Ps. 10:14]
12 [f] [Ps. 39:5]; Rom. 1:22
13 [g] [1 Sam. 7:3] [h] Ps. 88:9
14 [i] Ps. 101:3
15 [j] Job 22:26; Ps. 119:6; [1 John 3:21]
16 [k] Is. 65:16
17 [l] Ps. 37:6; Prov. 4:18; Is. 58:8, 10
18 [m] Lev. 26:5, 6; Ps. 3:5; Prov. 3:24
20 [n] Lev. 26:16; Deut. 28:65; Job 17:5 [o] Job 18:14; [Prov. 11:7] [6] Lit. *the breathing out of life*

CHAPTER 12

3 [a] Job 13:2 [1] Lit. *a heart*
4 [b] Job 21:3 [c] Ps. 91:15
5 [d] Prov. 14:2 [2] Or *disaster*
6 [e] [Job 9:24; 21:6-16; Ps. 73:12; Jer. 12:1; Mal. 3:15]

11:13,14 Zophar set out 4 steps of Job's repentance: 1) devote your heart to God; 2) stretch your hands to Him in prayer for forgiveness; 3) put your sin far away; and 4) don't allow any sin in your tent. If Job did these things, he would be blessed (vv. 15-19). If Job didn't repent, he would die (v. 20). Zophar was right that the life of faith in God is based on penitence and obedience. He was right that God blesses His people with hope, security, and peace. But, like his friends, he was wrong in not understanding that God allows unpredictable and seemingly unfair suffering for reasons not known to us. He was wrong in presuming that the answer for Job was repentance.

11:13-20 Zophar started out this section speaking directly to Job, "If you would…" and concluded speaking proverbially, "But the eyes of the wicked…." In so doing Zophar avoided directly calling Job wicked, but succeeded with even greater force by being indirect. In the end, he told Job that his sin would bring about his death.

12:1–14:22 Job responded in his defense with strong words, completing the first cycle of speeches.

12:2-4 you *are* the people, and wisdom will die with you. Job responded with cutting sarcasm directed at his know-it-all friends (v. 2) and then reminded them that he understood the principles of which they had spoken (v. 3), but they were irrelevant to his situation. On top of that, he despaired at the pain of becoming a derision to his friends, though he was innocent (v. 4).

12:4 The just and blameless. If this sounds like presumption, one only need to recall that this was God's pronouncement on Job (1:8; 2:3).

12:5 A lamp. As a torch is to a wanderer, so Job was to his friends. When all was at ease with them, they didn't need him, and even mocked him.

12:6 God provides. Job refuted the simplistic idea that the righteous always prosper and the wicked always suffer, by reminding them that God allows thieves and sinners to be prosperous and secure. So, why not believe He may also allow the righteous to suffer?

12:7-10 All these elements (animals, birds, plants, and fish) of

And the birds of the air, and they will tell you;
8 Or speak to the earth, and it will teach you;
And the fish of the sea will explain to you.
9 Who among all these does not know
That the hand of the LORD has done this,
10 [f]In whose hand *is* the [3]life of every living thing,
And the [g]breath of [4]all mankind?
11 Does not the ear test words
And the [5]mouth taste its food?
12 Wisdom *is* with aged men,
And with [6]length of days, understanding.

13 "With Him *are* [h]wisdom and strength,
He has counsel and understanding.
14 If [i]He breaks *a thing* down, it cannot be rebuilt;
If He imprisons a man, there can be no release.
15 If He [j]withholds the waters, they dry up;
If He [k]sends them out, they overwhelm the earth.
16 With Him *are* strength and prudence.
The deceived and the deceiver *are* His.
17 He leads counselors away plundered,
And makes fools of the judges.
18 He loosens the bonds of kings,
And binds their waist with a belt.
19 He leads [7]princes away plundered,
And overthrows the mighty.
20 [l]He deprives the trusted ones of speech,
And takes away the discernment of the elders.
21 [m]He pours contempt on princes,
And [8]disarms the mighty.
22 He [n]uncovers deep things out of darkness,
And brings the shadow of death to light.
23 [o]He makes nations great, and destroys them;
He [9]enlarges nations, and guides them.
24 He takes away the [1]understanding of the chiefs of the people of the earth,
And [p]makes them wander in a pathless wilderness.
25 [q]They grope in the dark without light,
And He makes them [r]stagger like a drunken *man*.

13 "Behold, my eye has seen all *this*,
My ear has heard and understood it.
2 [a]What you know, I also know;
I *am* not inferior to you.
3 [b]But I would speak to the Almighty,
And I desire to reason with God.
4 But you forgers of lies,
[c]You *are* all worthless physicians.
5 Oh, that you would be silent,
And [d]it would be your wisdom!
6 Now hear my reasoning,
And heed the pleadings of my lips.
7 [e]Will you speak [1]wickedly for God,
And talk deceitfully for Him?
8 Will you show partiality for Him?
Will you contend for God?
9 Will it be well when He searches you out?
Or can you mock Him as one mocks a man?
10 He will surely rebuke you
If you secretly show partiality.
11 Will not His [2]excellence make you afraid,
And the dread of Him fall upon you?
12 Your platitudes *are* proverbs of ashes,
Your defenses are defenses of clay.

10 [f][Acts 17:28] [g]Job 27:3; 33:4 [3]Or *soul* [4]Lit. *all flesh of men*
11 [5]*palate*
12 [6]Long life
13 [h]Job 9:4; 36:5
14 [i]Job 11:10; Is. 25:2
15 [j]Deut. 11:17; [1 Kin. 8:35, 36] [k]Gen. 7:11-24
19 [7]Lit. *priests*, but not in a technical sense
20 [l]Job 32:9
21 [m][Job 34:19]; Ps. 107:40; [Dan. 2:21] [8]*loosens the belt of*
22 [n]Dan. 2:22; [1 Cor. 4:5]
23 [o]Is. 9:3; 26:15 [9]Lit. *spreads out*
24 [p]Ps. 107:4 [1]Lit. *heart*
25 [q]Job 5:14; 15:30; 18:18 [r]Ps. 107:27

CHAPTER 13
2 [a]Job 12:3
3 [b]Job 23:3; 31:35
4 [c]Job 6:21; [Jer. 23:32]
5 [d]Job 13:13; 21:5; Prov. 17:28
7 [e]Job 27:4; 36:4 [1]*unrighteously*
11 [2]Lit. *exaltation*

creation are called as an illustration that the violent prosper and live securely (v. 6). God made it so that the more vicious survive.

12:12 Wisdom *is* with aged men. The questioning force of the preceding verse may carry over to make this a question also. "Shouldn't aged men be wise?" If this is true, then v. 12 is stinging sarcasm against Job's aged friends who gave unwise advice (cf. 15:10), and heard and spoke only what suited them (v. 11).

12:13–13:3 This section gives vivid definition to the wisdom, power, and sovereignty of God (v. 13). Job, despite his questions about his suffering, affirms that God's power is visible in nature, human society, religious matters, and national and international affairs. Job, however, expressed this in terms of fatalistic despair. Job knew all this and it didn't help (13:1,2); so he didn't want to argue with them anymore—he wanted to take his case before God (v. 3).

13:4-19 Job addressed his ineffective counselors.

13:4,5 Job couldn't hold back from a blistering denunciation of his useless counselors, telling them that their silence would be true wisdom (cf. v. 13).

13:7 wickedly for God,...deceitfully for Him. He accused them of using lies and fallacies to vindicate God, when they asserted that Job was a sinner because he was a sufferer.

13:8 Will you contend for God? "Are you wise enough to argue in God's defense?" he asked. To think that is very brash and really mocks God by misrepresenting Him (v. 9) and should lead to fear of chastening (vv. 10,11).

13:12 ashes...clay. Ineffective and worthless.

13 "Hold[3] your peace with me, and let me speak,
Then let come on me what *may!*
14 Why [f]do I take my flesh in my teeth,
And put my life in my hands?
15 [g]Though He slay me, yet will I trust Him.
[h]Even so, I will defend my own ways before Him.
16 He also *shall* be my salvation,
For a [i]hypocrite could not come before Him.
17 Listen carefully to my speech,
And to my declaration with your ears.
18 See now, I have prepared *my* case,
I know that I shall be [j]vindicated.
19 [k]Who *is* he *who* will contend with me?
If now I hold my tongue, I perish.

Job's Despondent Prayer

20 "Only[l] two *things* do not do to me,
Then I will not hide myself from You:
21 [m]Withdraw Your hand far from me,
And let not the dread of You make me afraid.
22 Then call, and I will [n]answer;
Or let me speak, then You respond to me.
23 How many *are* my iniquities and sins?
Make me know my transgression and my sin.
24 [o]Why do You hide Your face,
And [p]regard me as Your enemy?
25 [q]Will You frighten a leaf driven to and fro?
And will You pursue dry stubble?
26 For You write bitter things against me,
And [r]make me inherit the iniquities of my youth.
27 [s]You put my feet in the stocks,
And watch closely all my paths.
You [4]set a limit for the [5]soles of my feet.

28 "*Man*[6] decays like a rotten thing,
Like a garment that is moth-eaten.

14 "Man *who is* born of woman
Is of few days and [a]full of [1]trouble.
2 [b]He comes forth like a flower and fades away;
He flees like a shadow and does not continue.
3 And [c]do You open Your eyes on such a one,
And [d]bring [2]me to judgment with Yourself?
4 Who [e]can bring a clean *thing* out of an unclean?
No one!
5 [f]Since his days *are* determined,
The number of his months *is* with You;
You have appointed his limits, so that he cannot pass.
6 [g]Look away from him that he may [3]rest,
Till [h]like a hired man he finishes his day.
7 "For there is hope for a tree,
If it is cut down, that it will sprout again,
And that its tender shoots will not cease.

13 [3] *Be silent*
14 [f] Job 18:4
15 [g] Ps. 23:4; [Prov. 14:32] [h] Job 27:5
16 [i] Job 8:13
18 [j] [Rom. 8:34]
19 [k] Job 7:21; 10:8; Is. 50:8
20 [l] Job 9:34
21 [m] Job 9:34; Ps. 39:10
22 [n] Job 9:16; 14:15
24 [o] [Deut. 32:20]; Ps. 13:1 [p] Lam. 2:5
25 [q] Is. 42:3
26 [r] Job 20:11
27 [s] Job 33:11 [4] Lit. *inscribe a print* [5] Lit. *roots*
28 [6] Lit. *He*

CHAPTER 14

1 [a] Job 5:7; Eccl. 2:23 [1] *turmoil*
2 [b] Job 8:9; Ps. 90:5, 6, 9; 102:11; 103:15; 144:4; Is. 40:6; James 1:10, 11; 1 Pet. 1:24
3 [c] Ps. 8:4; 144:3 [d] [Ps. 143:2] [2] LXX, Syr., Vg. *him*
4 [e] [Job 15:14; 25:4; Ps. 51:2, 5, 10; John 3:6; Rom. 5:12; Eph. 2:3]
5 [f] Job 7:1; 21:21; Heb. 9:27
6 [g] Job 7:16, 19; Ps. 39:13 [h] Job 7:1 [3] Lit. *cease*

13:14 A proverb meaning "Why should I anxiously desire to save my life?" Like an animal who holds its prey in its mouth to preserve it or a man who holds in his hand what he wants to secure, Job could try to preserve his life, but that was not his motive.

13:15 Though He slay me, yet will I trust Him. Job assured his accusers that his convictions were not self-serving, because he was ready to die trusting God. But still he would defend his innocence before God, and was confident that he was truly saved and not a hypocrite (v. 16).

13:17-19 declaration...case...vindicated...contend. The language of a courtroom came out strongly. He could not just be silent and die (v. 19). He finished strongly before turning to God in prayer (13:20–14:22).

13:20–14:22 Job turned to reason with God (v. 3) and pleaded his case.

13:20-22 Job asked God to end his pain and stop frightening him with such terrors (cf. v. 24), then speak to him. He was concerned with his misery, but even more with his relation to the God he loved and worshiped.

13:23 How many *are* my iniquities and sins? Job wanted to know how many so that he could determine if his measure of suffering matched the severity of his sin, and he could then repent for sins he was unaware of.

13:26 write bitter things against me. This a judicial phrase referencing the writing down of a sentence against a criminal, used figuratively for the extreme suffering as if it were a divine sentence as just punishment for extreme sin. Job felt God may be punishing him for sins committed years earlier in his youth.

13:27 watch closely all my paths. In another context these words would speak of protection, but here, Job questioned whether or not God had not held him on too tight a leash. The comment amounts to saying, that God is being overly-rigorous toward Job's sin, as compared to others.

13:28 This general comment on the plight of man should not be separated from 14:1ff., which it introduces.

14:1-12 Job embraced the fact of God's control over the issues of this life, but challenged their meaning. Life is short (vv. 1,2), all are sinners (v. 4), and days are limited (v. 5), then comes death (vv. 7-12). In light of this, Job asked God for a little grace instead of such intense judgment (v. 3), and a little rest from all the pain (v. 6), and suggested that a tree has more hope than he did (v. 7).

8 Though its root may grow old in the earth,
And its stump may die in the ground,
9 *Yet* at the scent of water it will bud
And bring forth branches like a plant.
10 But man dies and [4]is laid away;
Indeed he [5]breathes his last
And where *is* [i]he?
11 *As* water disappears from the sea,
And a river becomes parched and dries up,
12 So man lies down and does not rise.
[j]Till the heavens *are* no more,
They will not awake
Nor be roused from their sleep.

13 "Oh, that You would hide me in the grave,
That You would conceal me until Your wrath is past,
That You would appoint me a set time, and remember me!
14 If a man dies, shall he live *again?*
All the days of my hard service [k]I will wait,
Till my change comes.
15 [l]You shall call, and I will answer You;
You shall desire the work of Your hands.
16 For now [m]You number my steps,
But do not watch over my sin.
17 [n]My transgression *is* sealed up in a bag,
And You [6]cover my iniquity.

18 "But *as* a mountain falls *and* crumbles away,
And *as* a rock is moved from its place;
19 *As* water wears away stones,
And as torrents wash away the soil of the earth;
So You destroy the hope of man.
20 You prevail forever against him, and he passes on;
You change his countenance and send him away.
21 His sons come to honor, and [o]he does not know *it;*
They are brought low, and he does not perceive *it.*
22 But his flesh will be in pain over it,
And his soul will mourn over it."

Eliphaz Accuses Job of Folly

15 Then [a]Eliphaz the Temanite answered and said:

2 "Should a wise man answer with empty knowledge,
And fill [1]himself with the east wind?
3 Should he reason with unprofitable talk,
Or by speeches with which he can do no good?
4 Yes, you cast off fear,
And restrain [2]prayer before God.
5 For your iniquity teaches your mouth,
And you choose the tongue of the crafty.
6 [b]Your own mouth condemns you, and not I;
Yes, your own lips testify against you.

7 "*Are* you the first man *who* was born?
[c]Or were you made before the hills?
8 [d]Have you heard the counsel of God?
Do you limit wisdom to yourself?
9 [e]What do you know that we do not know?
What do you understand that *is* not in us?
10 [f]Both the gray-haired and the aged *are* among us,
Much older than your father.
11 *Are* the consolations of God too small for you,
And the word *spoken* [3]gently with you?
12 Why does your heart carry you away,
And [4]what do your eyes wink at,

10 [i] Job 10:21, 22 [4] *lies prostrate* [5] *expires*
12 [j] Ps. 102:25, 26; [Is. 51:6; 65:17; 66:22]; Acts 3:21; [2 Pet. 3:7, 10, 11; Rev. 20:11; 21:1]
14 [k] Job 13:15
15 [l] Job 13:22
16 [m] Job 10:6, 14; 13:27; 31:4; 34:21; Ps. 56:8; 139:1-3; Prov. 5:21; [Jer. 32:19]
17 [n] Deut. 32:32-34 [6] Lit. *plaster over*
21 [o] Eccl. 9:5; Is. 63:16

CHAPTER 15

1 [a] Job 4:1
2 [1] Lit. *his belly*
4 [2] *meditation* or *complaint*
6 [b] Job 9:20; [Luke 19:22]
7 [c] Job 38:4, 21; Ps. 90:2; Prov. 8:25
8 [d] Job 29:4; Rom. 11:34; [1 Cor. 2:11]
9 [e] Job 12:3; 13:2
10 [f] Job 8:8-10; 12:12; 32:6, 7
11 [3] Or *a secret thing*
12 [4] Or *why do your eyes flash*

14:13-17 Job asked to die and remain in the grave until God's anger was over, then be raised to life again when God called him back (vv. 13-15). If he were dead, God wouldn't be watching every step, counting every sin (v. 16); it would all be hidden (v. 17). Here was the hope of resurrection for those who trusted God. Job had hope that if he died, he would live again (v. 14).

14:18-22 Job returned to his complaint before God, and reverted to a hopeless mood, speaking about death as inevitable (vv. 18-20), and causing separation (v. 21). He was painfully sad to think of it (v. 22).

15:1–21:34 The second cycle of speeches given by Job and his 3 friends. Job's resistance to their viewpoint and his appeals energized them to greater intensity in their confrontation.

15:1-35 Eliphaz returns for his second session (See Job 4,5).

15:1-6 He began by accusing Job of sinning by attacking God with his complaints. He felt Job was guilty of empty words and had not exhibited godly fear and righteous prayer (v. 4), but rather was sinning in his prayer (vv. 5,6).

15:7-13 Eliphaz condemned Job for rejecting the conventional wisdom, as if he had more insight than other men (vv. 7-9) and could reject the wisdom of the aged (v. 10) and the kindness of God (v. 11).

13 That you turn your spirit against God,
And let *such* words go out of your mouth?

14 "What[g] *is* man, that he could be pure?
And *he who is* born of a woman, that he could be righteous?
15 [h]If *God* puts no trust in His saints,
And the heavens are not pure in His sight,
16 [i]How much less man, *who is* abominable and filthy,
[j]Who drinks iniquity like water!

17 "I will tell you, hear me;
What I have seen I will declare,
18 What wise men have told,
Not hiding *anything received* [k]from their fathers,
19 To whom alone the [5]land was given,
And [l]no alien passed among them:
20 The wicked man writhes with pain all *his* days,
[m]And the number of years is hidden from the oppressor.
21 [6]Dreadful sounds *are* in his ears;
[n]In prosperity the destroyer comes upon him.
22 He does not believe that he will [o]return from darkness,
For a sword is waiting for him.
23 He [p]wanders about for bread, *saying*, 'Where *is it?*'
He knows [q]that a day of darkness is ready at his hand.
24 Trouble and anguish make him afraid;
They overpower him, like a king ready for [7]battle.
25 For he stretches out his hand against God,
And acts defiantly against the Almighty,
26 Running stubbornly against Him
With his strong, embossed shield.

27 "Though [r]he has covered his face with his fatness,
And made *his* waist heavy with fat,
28 He dwells in desolate cities,
In houses which no one inhabits,
Which are destined to become ruins.
29 He will not be rich,
Nor will his wealth [s]continue,
Nor will his possessions overspread the earth.
30 He will not depart from darkness;
The flame will dry out his branches,
And [t]by the breath of His mouth he will go away.
31 Let him not [u]trust in futile *things*, deceiving himself,
For futility will be his reward.
32 It will be accomplished [v]before his time,
And his branch will not be green.
33 He will shake off his unripe grape like a vine,
And cast off his blossom like an olive tree.
34 For the company of hypocrites *will be* barren,
And fire will consume the tents of bribery.
35 [w]They conceive trouble and bring forth futility;
Their womb prepares deceit."

Job Reproaches His Pitiless Friends

16 Then Job answered and said:

2 "I have heard many such things;
[a]Miserable [1] comforters *are* you all!
3 Shall [2]words of wind have an end?
Or what provokes you that you answer?
4 I also could speak as you *do*,
If your soul were in my soul's place.
I could heap up words against you,
And [b]shake my head at you;

14 [g] Job 14:4; Prov. 20:9; [Eccl. 7:20; 1 John 1:8, 10]
15 [h] Job 4:18; 25:5
16 [i] Job 4:19; Ps. 14:3; 53:3 [j] Job 34:7; Prov. 19:28
18 [k] Job 8:8; 20:4
19 [l] Joel 3:17 [5] Or *earth*
20 [m] Ps. 90:12
21 [n] Job 20:21; 1 Thess. 5:3 [6] *Terrifying*
22 [o] Job 14:10-12
23 [p] Ps. 59:15; 109:10 [q] Job 18:12
24 [7] *attack*
27 [r] Ps. 17:10; 73:7; 119:70
29 [s] Job 20:28; 27:16, 17
30 [t] Job 4:9
31 [u] Job 35:13; Is. 59:4
32 [v] Job 22:16; Ps. 55:23; Eccl. 7:17
35 [w] Ps. 7:14; Is. 59:4; [Hos. 10:13]

CHAPTER 16

2 [a] Job 13:4; 21:34 [1] *Troublesome*
3 [2] *Empty words*
4 [b] Ps. 22:7; 109:25; Lam. 2:15; Zeph. 2:15; Matt. 27:39

15:14-16 A strong statement with regard to the sinfulness of man (cf. Rom. 3:23), that attacked Job's claim to righteousness. Verse 15 refers to holy angels who fell and brought impurity into the heavens (cf. Rev. 12:1-4). The truth is accurate, that all men are sinners—but irrelevant in Job's case, because his suffering was not due to any sin.

15:17-35 Eliphaz once again returned to the same perspective and indicted Job for sin because Job was suffering. To support his relentless point, he launched into a lengthy monologue about the wicked and their outcomes in life, including many parallels to the sufferings of Job. He had pain, and didn't know when his life would end (v. 20). He suffered from fear, every sound alarmed him, and he thought his destroyer was near (vv. 21,22). He worried about having food (v. 23). His suffering made him question God (vv. 24-26). Once well-nourished, housed, and rich (vv. 27-29), he would lose it all (vv. 30-33). Eliphaz concluded by calling Job a hypocrite (vv. 34,35), saying that this was the reason things were going so badly.

16:1–17:16 Job responded with his second rebuttal.

16:2-5 Miserable comforters *are* you all! Job's friends had come to comfort him. In spite of 7 blissful days of silence at the outset, their mission had failed miserably, and their comfort had turned into more torment for Job. What started out as Eliphaz's sincere efforts to help Job understand his dilemma had turned into rancor and sarcasm. In the end, their haranguing had heightened the frustrations of all parties involved. If the matter were reversed and Job was comforter to his friends, he would never treat them as they have treated him. He would have strengthened and comforted them.

5 *But* I would strengthen you with my mouth,
And the comfort of my lips would relieve *your grief.*
6 "Though I speak, my grief is not relieved;
And *if* I remain silent, how am I eased?
7 But now He has [c]worn me out;
You [d]have made desolate all my company.
8 You have shriveled me up,
And it is a [e]witness *against me;*
My leanness rises up against me
And bears witness to my face.
9 [f]He tears *me* in His wrath, and hates me;
He gnashes at me with His teeth;
[g]My adversary sharpens His gaze on me.
10 They [h]gape at me with their mouth,
They [i]strike me reproachfully on the cheek,
They gather together against me.
11 God [j]has delivered me to the ungodly,
And turned me over to the hands of the wicked.
12 I was at ease, but He has [k]shattered me;
He also has taken *me* by my neck, and shaken me to pieces;
He has [l]set me up for His target,
13 His archers surround me.
He pierces my [3]heart and does not pity;
He pours out my gall on the ground.
14 He breaks me with wound upon wound;
He runs at me like a [4]warrior.

15 "I have sewn sackcloth over my skin,
And [m]laid my [5]head in the dust.
16 My face is [6]flushed from weeping,
And on my eyelids *is* the shadow of death;
17 Although no violence *is* in my hands,
And my prayer *is* pure.

18 "O earth, do not cover my blood,
And [n]let my cry have no *resting* place!
19 Surely even now [o]my witness *is* in heaven,
And my evidence *is* on high.
20 My friends scorn me;
My eyes pour out *tears* to God.
21 [p]Oh, that one might plead for a man with God,
As a man *pleads* for his [7]neighbor!
22 For when a few years are finished,
I shall [q]go the way of no return.

Job Prays for Relief

17 "My spirit is broken,
My days are extinguished,
[a]The grave *is ready* for me.
2 *Are* not mockers with me?
And does not my eye [1]dwell on their [b]provocation?

3 "Now put down a pledge for me with Yourself.
Who *is* he *who* [c]will shake hands with me?
4 For You have hidden their heart from [d]understanding;
Therefore You will not exalt *them.*
5 He who speaks flattery to *his* friends,
Even the eyes of his children will [e]fail.

6 "But He has made me [f]a byword of the people,
And I have become one in whose face men spit.
7 [g]My eye has also grown dim because of sorrow,

7 [c]Job 7:3 [d]Job 16:20; 19:13-15
8 [e]Job 10:17
9 [f]Job 10:16, 17; 19:11; Hos. 6:1 [g]Job 13:24; 33:10
10 [h]Ps. 22:13; 35:21 [i]Is. 50:6; Lam. 3:30; Mic. 5:1; Matt. 26:67; Mark 14:65; Luke 22:63; Acts 23:2
11 [j]Job 1:15, 17
12 [k]Job 9:17 [l]Job 7:20; Lam. 3:12
13 [3]Lit. *kidneys*
14 [4]Vg. *giant*
15 [m]Job 30:19; Ps. 7:5 [5]Lit. *horn*
16 [6]Lit. *red*
18 [n]Job 27:9; [Ps. 66:18]
19 [o]Gen. 31:50; Rom. 1:9; Phil. 1:8; 1 Thess. 2:5
21 [p]Job 31:35; Eccl. 6:10; [Is. 45:9; Rom. 9:20] [7]*friend*
22 [q]Job 10:21; Eccl. 12:5

CHAPTER 17

1 [a]Ps. 88:3, 4
2 [b]1 Sam. 1:6; Job 12:4; 17:6; 30:1, 9; 34:7 [1]Lit. *lodge*
3 [c]Prov. 6:1; 17:18; 22:26
4 [d]Job 12:20; 32:9
5 [e]Job 11:20
6 [f]Job 30:9
7 [g]Ps. 6:7; 31:9

16:6-9,12-14 These poignant thoughts from Job lamented his suffering as severe judgment from God, who had worn him out, withered his strength, and chewed him up by severe scrutiny ("sharpens His gaze"). Job refers to God as "my Adversary," who had shattered, shaken, shot at, and sliced him (vv. 12-14).

16:15-20 He had no one to turn to in his sorrow, except God (v. 19), who was silent and had not vindicated him.

16:21 plead for a man with God. The pleading would be for a verdict of innocent on behalf of a friend or neighbor in a court setting before the judge/king. God anticipated the need of an advocate, and He has provided One in the person of the Lord Jesus Christ (cf. 1 Tim. 2:5; 1 John 2:1,2).

17:2 mockers. The would-be counselors had become actual enemies and the provocation for Job's tears (cf. 16:20).

17:3 pledge. He called on God to promise (by a symbolic handshake) that his case would be heard in the heavenly court.

17:4 not exalt *them.* The blindness of Job's friends toward his innocence came from God, so Job asked that God would not let them succeed in their efforts against him.

17:5 speaks flattery. This Heb. term came to mean "a prey," so that Job was referring to someone who delivers up a friend as prey to some enemy.

17:6 a byword. This refers to shame, reproach, and a reputation that is extremely bad (cf. Deut. 28:37; Ps. 69:11). **spit.** The most disdainful act a person could commit to heap scorn and shame on someone as a wicked and unworthy person. Job's friends were aiding him in getting such a reputation (vv. 7,8).

And all my members *are* like
shadows.
8 Upright *men* are astonished at this,
And the innocent stirs himself up
against the hypocrite.
9 Yet the righteous will hold to his
[h]way,
And he who has [i]clean hands will
be stronger and stronger.

10 "But please, [j]come back again, [2]all
of you,
For I shall not find *one* wise *man*
among you.
11 [k]My days are past,
My purposes are broken off,
Even the [3]thoughts of my heart.
12 They change the night into day;
'The light *is* near,' *they say,* in the
face of darkness.
13 If I wait *for* the grave *as* my house,
If I make my bed in the darkness,
14 If I say to corruption, 'You *are* my
father,'
And to the worm, 'You *are* my
mother and my sister,'
15 Where then *is* my [l]hope?
As for my hope, who can see it?
16 *Will* they go down [m]to the gates of
[4]Sheol?
Shall *we have* [n]rest together in the
dust?"

Bildad: The Wicked Are Punished

18 Then [a]Bildad the Shuhite answered
and said:

2 "How long *till* you put an end to
words?
Gain understanding, and afterward
we will speak.
3 Why are we counted [b]as beasts,
And regarded as stupid in your
sight?
4 [c]You [1] who tear yourself in anger,
Shall the earth be forsaken for you?
Or shall the rock be removed from
its place?

5 "The [d] light of the wicked indeed
goes out,
And the flame of his fire does not
shine.
6 The light is dark in his tent,
[e]And his lamp beside him is put
out.
7 The steps of his strength are
shortened,
And [f]his own counsel casts him
down.
8 For [g]he is cast into a net by his
own feet,
And he walks into a snare.
9 The net takes *him* by the heel,
And [h]a snare lays hold of him.
10 A noose *is* hidden for him on the
ground,
And a trap for him in the road.
11 [i]Terrors frighten him on every side,
And drive him to his feet.
12 His strength is starved,
And [j]destruction *is* ready at his
side.
13 It devours patches of his skin;
The firstborn of death devours his
[2]limbs.
14 He is uprooted from [k]the shelter of
his tent,
And they parade him before the
king of terrors.
15 They dwell in his tent *who are* none
of his;
Brimstone is scattered on his
dwelling.
16 [l]His roots are dried out below,
And his branch withers above.
17 [m]The memory of him perishes from
the earth,
And he has no name [3]among the
renowned.
18 [4]He is driven from light into
darkness,
And chased out of the world.
19 [n]He has neither son nor posterity
among his people,
Nor any remaining in his
dwellings.
20 Those [5]in the west are astonished
[o]at his day,
As those [6]in the east are
frightened.

9 [h] Prov. 4:18 [i] Ps. 24:4
10 [j] Job 6:29 [2] So with some Heb. mss., LXX, Syr., Vg.; MT, Tg. *all of them*
11 [k] Job 7:6 [3] *desires*
15 [l] Job 7:6; 13:15; 14:19; 19:10
16 [m] Jon. 2:6 [n] Job 3:17-19; 21:33 [4] The abode of the dead

CHAPTER 18
1 [a] Job 8:1
3 [b] Ps. 73:22
4 [c] Job 13:14 [1] Lit. *one who tears his soul*
5 [d] Job 21:17; Prov. 13:9; 20:20; 24:20
6 [e] Job 21:17; Ps. 18:28
7 [f] Job 5:12, 13; 15:6
8 [g] Job 22:10; Ps. 9:15; 35:8; Is. 24:17, 18
9 [h] Job 5:5
11 [i] Job 20:25; Jer. 6:25
12 [j] Job 15:23
13 [2] *parts*
14 [k] Job 11:20
16 [l] Job 29:19
17 [m] Job 24:20; [Ps. 34:16]; Prov. 10:7 [3] Lit. *before the outside,* i.e., the distinguished or famous
18 [4] Or *They drive him*
19 [n] Job 27:14, 15; Is. 14:22
20 [o] Ps. 37:13; Jer. 50:27; Obad. 12 [5] Lit. *who came after* [6] Lit. *who have gone before*

17:9 Yet the righteous will hold to his way. Job, and other righteous people who find themselves in a similar situation, must remain righteous. If they do, Job knew, the suffering would produce strength (cf. 2 Cor. 12:7-10).

17:10 Job was not unteachable. He invited his friends to speak again if they had something wise to say, for a change, but not to talk about his restoration because he was done (vv. 11-16).

17:15 Where then *is* my hope? Job's hope was in God alone.

17:16 gates of Sheol. A reference to death, also used by our Lord in Matt. 16:18.

18:1-21 Bildad, like his predecessor, ruthlessly attacked Job in his second speech (cf. chap. 8) by telling Job to stop complaining and to become sensible (v. 2). Next he turned to scorn (vv. 3,4). Then he turned to another long tale of the bad outcomes the wicked experience (vv. 5-21).

18:13 The firstborn of death. A poetical expression meaning the most deadly disease death ever produced.

18:14 the king of terrors. Death, with all its terrors to the ungodly, personified.

21 Surely such *are* the dwellings of the wicked,
And this *is* the place *of him who* [p]does not know God."

Job Trusts in His Redeemer

19 Then Job answered and said:
2 "How long will you torment my soul,
And break me in pieces with words?
3 These ten times you have [1]reproached me;
You are not ashamed *that* you [2]have wronged me.
4 And if indeed I have erred,
My error remains with me.
5 If indeed you [a]exalt *yourselves* against me,
And plead my disgrace against me,
6 Know then that [b]God has wronged me,
And has surrounded me with His net.

7 "If I cry out concerning [3]wrong, I am not heard.
If I cry aloud, *there is* no justice.
8 [c]He has [4]fenced up my way, so that I cannot pass;
And He has set darkness in my paths.
9 [d]He has stripped me of my glory,
And taken the crown *from* my head.
10 He breaks me down on every side,
And I am gone;
My [e]hope He has uprooted like a tree.
11 He has also kindled His wrath against me,
And [f]He counts me as *one of* His enemies.
12 His troops come together
And build up their road against me;
They encamp all around my tent.

13 "He[g] has removed my brothers far from me,
And my acquaintances are completely estranged from me.
14 My relatives have failed,
And my close friends have forgotten me.
15 Those who dwell in my house, and my maidservants,
Count me as a stranger;
I am an alien in their sight.
16 I call my servant, but he gives no answer;
I beg him with my mouth.
17 My breath is offensive to my wife,
And I am [5]repulsive to the children of my own body.
18 Even [h]young children despise me;
I arise, and they speak against me.
19 [i]All my close friends abhor me,
And those whom I love have turned against me.
20 [j]My bone clings to my skin and to my flesh,
And I have escaped by the skin of my teeth.

21 "Have pity on me, have pity on me,
O you my friends,
For the hand of God has struck me!
22 Why do you [k]persecute me as God *does*,
And are not satisfied with my flesh?

23 "Oh, that my words were written!
Oh, that they were inscribed in a book!
24 That they were engraved on a rock
With an iron pen and lead, forever!

21 [p]Jer. 9:3; 1 Thess. 4:5

CHAPTER 19

3 [1]*shamed or disgraced* [2]A Jewish tradition *make yourselves strange to me*
5 [a]Ps. 35:26; 38:16; 55:12, 13
6 [b]Job 16:11
7 [3]*violence*
8 [c]Job 3:23; Ps. 88:8; Lam. 3:7, 9 [4]*walled off my way*
9 [d]Job 12:17, 19; Ps. 89:44
10 [e]Job 17:14-16
11 [f]Job 13:24; 33:10
13 [g]Job 16:20; Ps. 31:11; 38:11; 69:8; 88:8, 18
17 [5]Lit. *strange*
18 [h]2 Kin. 2:23; Job 17:6
19 [i]Ps. 38:11; 55:12, 13
20 [j]Job 16:8; 33:21; Ps. 102:5; Lam. 4:8
22 [k]Job 13:24, 25; 16:11; 19:6; Ps. 69:26

18:21 *who* does not know God. This describes "know" in a redemptive sense and is here applied to an unbeliever.

19:1-29 Job's response to Bildad's second speech was desperate.

19:1-5 He began with the anguished cry that his friends have become recalcitrant and relentless for mentors (vv. 2,3), and they have had no effect on his dealing with the sin they imagine is present (v. 4).

19:5-7 Job confessed that if God sent him friends like Bildad, who needs enemies? He feared there was no justice.

19:8-21 Job rehearsed his suffering. God had closed him in, stripped him, broken him, and turned against him (vv. 8-12). His family and friends had failed him (vv. 15-19), so that he was to be pitied because God had caused this to occur (vv. 21,22).

19:12 build up their road against me. In the ancient world conquering armies often had their own road crews level out the rough places so that their military forces could attack.

19:20 skin of my teeth. This was the origin of a common slang phrase, referring to skin that is thin and fragile. The idea is that he had escaped death by a very slim margin. The loss of all his family, as well as the abuse of his friends was added to the terror of God-forsakeness which had gripped him.

19:23-29 At the point of Job's greatest despair, his faith appeared at its highest as he confidently affirmed that God was his Redeemer. He wanted that confidence in the record for all to know (vv. 23,24). Job wished that the activities of his life were put into words and "inscribed in granite," so all would know that he had not sinned to the magnitude of his suffering. God granted his prayer. God was his Redeemer (cf. Ex. 6:6, Ps. 19:14; 72:14; Is. 43:14; 47:4; 49:26; Jer. 50:34), who would vindicate him in that last day of judgment on the earth when justice was finally done (cf. Jer. 12:1-3; John 5:25,29; Rev. 20:11-15).

25 For I know *that* my Redeemer lives,
And He shall stand at last on the earth;
26 And after my skin is [6]destroyed, this *I know,*
That [l]in my flesh I shall see God,
27 Whom I shall see for myself,
And my eyes shall behold, and not another.
How my [7]heart yearns within me!
28 If you should say, 'How shall we persecute him?'—
Since the root of the matter is found in me,
29 Be afraid of the sword for yourselves;
For wrath *brings* the punishment of the sword,
That you may know *there is* a judgment."

Zophar's Sermon on the Wicked Man

20 Then [a]Zophar the Naamathite answered and said:

2 "Therefore my anxious thoughts make me answer,
Because of the turmoil within me.
3 I have heard the rebuke [1]that reproaches me,
And the spirit of my understanding causes me to answer.

4 "Do you *not* know this of [b]old,
Since man was placed on earth,
5 [c]That the triumphing of the wicked is short,
And the joy of the hypocrite is *but* for a [d]moment?
6 [e]Though his haughtiness mounts up to the heavens,
And his head reaches to the clouds,
7 *Yet* he will perish forever like his own refuse;
Those who have seen him will say, 'Where is he?'
8 He will fly away [f]like a dream, and not be found;
Yes, he [g]will be chased away like a vision of the night.
9 The eye *that* saw him will *see him* no more,
Nor will his place behold him anymore.
10 His children will seek the favor of the poor,
And his hands will restore his wealth.
11 His bones are full of [h]his youthful vigor,
[i]But it will lie down with him in the dust.

12 "Though evil is sweet in his mouth,
And he hides it under his tongue,
13 *Though* he spares it and does not forsake it,
But still keeps it in his [2]mouth,
14 *Yet* his food in his stomach turns sour;
It becomes cobra venom within him.
15 He swallows down riches
And vomits them up again;
God casts them out of his belly.
16 He will suck the poison of cobras;
The viper's tongue will slay him.
17 He will not see [j]the streams,
The rivers flowing with honey and cream.
18 He will restore that for which he labored,
And will not swallow *it* down;
From the proceeds of business
He will get no enjoyment.
19 For he has [3]oppressed *and* forsaken the poor,
He has violently seized a house which he did not build.

20 "Because[k] he knows no quietness in his [4]heart,
He will not save anything he desires.
21 Nothing is left for him to eat;
Therefore his well-being will not last.
22 In his self-sufficiency he will be in distress;
Every hand of [5]misery will come against him.

26 [l][Ps. 17:15]; Matt. 5:8; 1 Cor. 13:12; [1 John 3:2] [6]Lit. *struck off*
27 [7]Lit. *kidneys*

CHAPTER 20

1 [a]Job 11:1
3 [1]Lit. *of my insulting correction*
4 [b]Job 8:8; 15:10
5 [c]Ps. 37:35, 36 [d][Job 8:13; 13:16; 15:34; 27:8]
6 [e]Is. 14:13, 14
8 [f]Ps. 73:20; 90:5 [g]Job 18:18; 27:21-23
11 [h]Job 13:26 [i]Job 21:26
13 [2]Lit. *palate*
17 [j]Ps. 36:8; Jer. 17:8
19 [3]*crushed*
20 [k]Eccl. 5:13-15 [4]Lit. *belly*
22 [5]Or *the wretched or sufferer*

19:26,27 Job had no hope left for this life, but was confident that "after" he was dead, his Redeemer would vindicate him in the glory of a physical ("in my flesh") resurrection in which he would enjoy perfect fellowship with the Redeemer. That Jesus Christ is that Redeemer is the clear message of the gospel. See Luke 2:38; Rom. 3:24; Gal. 3:13; Eph. 1:7; Heb. 9:12.

19:28,29 Job warned his friends that their misjudgment of him and violence against him could bring punishment on them.

20:1-29 Zophar spoiled it all again for Job with his second and last speech (cf. 11:1-20), in which he admonished Job again to consider the fate of the wicked.

20:5,6 wicked…hypocrite…haughtiness. The application of Zophar's words about this wicked, hypocritical, proud person were aimed at Job. He would, like others so wicked, suffer the consequences of his sins (vv. 7-29).

20:11 The wicked die young.

20:12-22 Evil in a life takes away all the enjoyment, implying that Job had no joy because of sin, such as that in v. 19.

23 *When* he is about to fill his
stomach,
God will cast on him the fury of
His wrath,
And will rain *it* on him while he is
eating.
24 [l]He will flee from the iron weapon;
A bronze bow will pierce him
through.
25 It is drawn, and comes out of the
body;
Yes, [m]the glittering *point comes* out
of his [6]gall.
[n]Terrors *come* upon him;
26 Total darkness *is* reserved for his
treasures.
[o]An unfanned fire will consume
him;
It shall go ill with him who is left
in his tent.
27 The heavens will reveal his
iniquity,
And the earth will rise up against
him.
28 The increase of his house will
depart,
And his goods will flow away in the
day of His [p]wrath.
29 [q]This *is* the portion from God for a
wicked man,
The heritage appointed to him by
God."

Job's Discourse on the Wicked

21 Then Job answered and said:

2 "Listen carefully to my speech,
And let this be your [1]consolation.
3 Bear with me that I may speak,
And after I have spoken, keep
[a]mocking.

4 "As for me, *is* my complaint against
man?
And if *it were,* why should I not be
impatient?
5 Look at me and be astonished;
[b]Put *your* hand over *your* mouth.
6 Even when I remember I am
terrified,
And trembling takes hold of my
flesh.
7 [c]Why do the wicked live *and*
become old,
Yes, become mighty in power?
8 Their descendants are established
with them in their sight,
And their offspring before their
eyes.
9 Their houses *are* safe from fear,
[d]Neither *is* [2]the rod of God upon
them.
10 Their bull breeds without failure;
Their cow calves [e]without
miscarriage.
11 They send forth their little ones
like a flock,
And their children dance.
12 They sing to the tambourine and
harp,
And rejoice to the sound of the
flute.
13 They [f]spend their days in wealth,
And [3]in a moment go down to the
[4]grave.
14 [g]Yet they say to God, 'Depart from
us,
For we do not desire the
knowledge of Your ways.
15 [h]Who *is* the Almighty, that we
should serve Him?
And [i]what profit do we have if we
pray to Him?'
16 Indeed [5]their prosperity *is* not in
their hand;
[j]The counsel of the wicked is far
from me.

17 "How often is the lamp of the
wicked put out?
How often does their destruction
come upon them,
The sorrows *God* [k]distributes in
His anger?
18 [l]They are like straw before the
wind,
And like chaff that a storm [6]carries
away.
19 *They say,* 'God [7]lays up [8]one's
iniquity [m]for his children';
Let Him recompense him, that he
may know *it.*
20 Let his eyes see his destruction,

24 [l] Is. 24:18; Amos 5:19
25 [m] Job 16:13 [n] Job 18:11, 14 [6] Gallbladder
26 [o] Ps. 21:9
28 [p] Job 20:15; 21:30
29 [q] Job 27:13; 31:2, 3

CHAPTER 21

2 [1] *comfort*
3 [a] Job 16:10
5 [b] Judg. 18:19; Job 13:5; 29:9; 40:4
7 [c] Job 12:6; Ps. 17:10, 14; 73:3, 12; [Jer. 12:1]; Hab. 1:13, 16
9 [d] Ps. 73:5 [2] The rod of God's chastisement
10 [e] Ex. 23:26
13 [f] Job 21:23; 36:11 [3] Without lingering [4] Or *Sheol*
14 [g] Job 22:17
15 [h] Ex. 5:2; Job 22:17; 34:9 [i] Job 35:3; Mal. 3:14
16 [j] Job 22:18; Ps. 1:1; Prov. 1:10 [5] Lit. *their goal*
17 [k] [Job 31:2, 3; Luke 12:46]
18 [l] Ps. 1:4; 35:5; Is. 17:13; Hos. 13:3 [6] *steals away*
19 [m] [Ex. 20:5]; Jer. 31:29; Ezek. 18:2 [7] *stores up* [8] Lit. *his*

20:23-29 Zophar concluded that more than just losing the enjoyment of life by sin, the wicked fall under the fury of God determined for such wickedness.

21:1-34 Job's reply to Zophar's last speech, ending the second cycle of speeches, refuted the simplistic set of laws by which the mockers lived. He showed that the wicked prosper, and since it is clear that they do (they had argued that the wicked *only* suffer), then by inference, perhaps the righteous suffer. This presented serious problems for their supposed open and shut case against Job.

21:1-16 Job called for his friends to be quiet and to listen to some amazing and terrifying truth (vv. 1-6), namely that the wicked do prosper (vv. 7-13) though they deny God (vv. 14,15), and they prosper not by their doing, but God's (v. 16).

21:17-22 Playing off Bildad's sentiment (see 18:5,6,18,19), this whole section repeats the assertions of Job's friends regarding the judgment of sinners. To refute that perspective, Job suggested that his friends were guilty of telling God how He must deal with people (v. 22).

And [n]let him drink of the wrath of the Almighty.
21 For what does he care about his household after him,
When the number of his months is cut in half?

22 "Can[o] *anyone* teach God knowledge,
Since He judges those on high?
23 One dies in his full strength,
Being wholly at ease and secure;
24 His [9]pails are full of milk,
And the marrow of his bones is moist.
25 Another man dies in the bitterness of his soul,
Never having eaten with pleasure.
26 They [p]lie down alike in the dust,
And worms cover them.

27 "Look, I know your thoughts,
And the schemes *with which* you would wrong me.
28 For you say,
'Where *is* the house of the prince?
And where *is* [1]the tent,
The dwelling place of the wicked?'
29 Have you not asked those who travel the road?
And do you not know their signs?
30 [q]For the wicked are reserved for the day of doom;
They shall be brought out on the day of wrath.
31 Who condemns his way to his face?
And who repays him *for what* he has done?
32 Yet he shall be brought to the grave,
And a vigil kept over the tomb.
33 The clods of the valley shall be sweet to him;
[r]Everyone shall follow him,
As countless *have gone* before him.
34 How then can you comfort me with empty words,
Since [2]falsehood remains in your answers?"

20 [n] Ps. 75:8; Is. 51:17; Jer. 25:15; Rev. 14:10; 19:15
22 [o] Job 35:11; 36:22; [Is. 40:13; 45:9; Rom. 11:34; 1 Cor. 2:16]
24 [9] LXX, Vg. *bowels*; Syr. *sides*; Tg. *breasts*
26 [p] Job 3:13; 20:11; Eccl. 9:2
28 [1] Vg. omits *the tent*
30 [q] Job 20:29; [Prov. 16:4; 2 Pet. 2:9]
33 [r] Heb. 9:27
34 [2] *faithlessness*

CHAPTER 22

1 [a] Job 4:1; 15:1; 42:9
2 [b] Job 35:7; [Ps. 16:2; Luke 17:10]
6 [c] [Ex. 22:26, 27]; Deut. 24:6, 10, 17; Job 24:3, 9; Ezek. 18:16
7 [d] Deut. 15:7; Job 31:17; Is. 58:7; Ezek. 18:7; Matt. 25:42
8 [1] Lit. *man of arm*
9 [2] Lit. *arms*
11 [e] Job 38:34; Ps. 69:1, 2; 124:5; Lam. 3:54
13 [f] Ps. 73:11
14 [g] Ps. 139:11, 12

Eliphaz Accuses Job of Wickedness

22 Then [a]Eliphaz the Temanite answered and said:

2 "Can[b] a man be profitable to God,
Though he who is wise may be profitable to himself?
3 *Is it* any pleasure to the Almighty that you are righteous?
Or *is it* gain *to Him* that you make your ways blameless?

4 "Is it because of your fear of Him that He corrects you,
And enters into judgment with you?
5 *Is* not your wickedness great,
And your iniquity without end?
6 For you have [c]taken pledges from your brother for no reason,
And stripped the naked of their clothing.
7 You have not given the weary water to drink,
And you [d]have withheld bread from the hungry.
8 But the [1]mighty man possessed the land,
And the honorable man dwelt in it.
9 You have sent widows away empty,
And the [2]strength of the fatherless was crushed.
10 Therefore snares *are* all around you,
And sudden fear troubles you,
11 Or darkness *so that* you cannot see;
And an abundance of [e]water covers you.

12 "Is not God in the height of heaven?
And see the highest stars, how lofty they are!
13 And you say, [f]'What does God know?
Can He judge through the deep darkness?
14 [g]Thick clouds cover Him, so that He cannot see,

21:23-26 Some of the wicked live and die in prosperity, some don't, canceling the absolutist nature of his counselors' argument.

21:27,28 Again Job referred to the statements of his friends, Zophar in this case (see 20:7), who were trying to prove their "sin equals suffering" idea.

21:29-33 Job knew they would not listen to him, so he suggested they ask travelers, any of whom would tell them that wicked people prosper sometimes in this life, but there will be a day of doom for them when they die.

21:34 The boastful words of the counselors were contradicted by facts.

22:1–31:40 The third cycle of speeches is given by Job and his friends, with Zophar abstaining.

22:1-30 Eliphaz's last speech got nasty with Job, as his frustration rose.

22:2-4,12-14 This counselor repeated the emphasis on the almighty nature of God, saying that God was so lofty and transcendent that He had no direct concern at all with Job. God didn't care personally about his complaints and claims to righteousness. God was not involved in the trivia of his life.

22:5-11 This miserable comforter accused Job of wickedness that was great, naming various sins against humanity as the reasons for Job's trouble (vv. 10,11).

And He walks above the circle of heaven.'
15 Will you keep to the old way
Which wicked men have trod,
16 Who [h]were cut down before their time,
Whose foundations were swept away by a flood?
17 [i]They said to God, 'Depart from us!
What can the Almighty do to [3]them?'
18 Yet He filled their houses with good *things;*
But the counsel of the wicked is far from me.

19 "The[j] righteous see *it* and are glad,
And the innocent laugh at them:
20 'Surely our [4]adversaries are cut down,
And the fire consumes their remnant.'

21 "Now acquaint yourself with Him, and [k]be at peace;
Thereby good will come to you.
22 Receive, please, [l]instruction from His mouth,
And [m]lay up His words in your heart.
23 If you return to the Almighty, you will be built up;
You will remove iniquity far from your tents.
24 Then you will [n]lay your gold in the dust,
And the *gold* of Ophir among the stones of the brooks.
25 Yes, the Almighty will be your [5]gold
And your precious silver;
26 For then you will have your [o]delight in the Almighty,
And lift up your face to God.
27 [p]You will make your prayer to Him,
He will hear you,
And you will pay your vows.
28 You will also declare a thing,
And it will be established for you;
So light will shine on your ways.
29 When they cast *you* down, and you say, 'Exaltation *will come!'*
Then [q]He will save the humble *person.*
30 He will *even* deliver one who is not innocent;
Yes, he will be delivered by the purity of your hands."

Job Proclaims God's Righteous Judgments

23 Then Job answered and said:

2 "Even today my [a]complaint is bitter;
[1]My hand is listless because of my groaning.
3 [b]Oh, that I knew where I might find Him,
That I might come to His seat!
4 I would present *my* case before Him,
And fill my mouth with arguments.
5 I would know the words *which* He would answer me,
And understand what He would say to me.
6 [c]Would He contend with me in His great power?
No! But He would take *note* of me.
7 There the upright could reason with Him,
And I would be delivered forever from my Judge.

8 "Look,[d] I go forward, but He is not *there,*
And backward, but I cannot perceive Him;
9 When He works on the left hand, I cannot behold *Him;*
When He turns to the right hand, I cannot see *Him.*
10 But [e]He knows the way that I take;

16 [h] Job 14:19; 15:32; Ps. 90:5; Is. 28:2; Matt. 7:26, 27
17 [i] Job 21:14, 15 [3] LXX, Syr. *us*
19 [j] Ps. 52:6; 58:10; 107:42
20 [4] LXX *substance is*
21 [k] [Ps. 34:10]; Is. 27:5
22 [l] Job 6:10; 23:12; Prov. 2:6 [m] [Ps. 119:11]
24 [n] 2 Chr. 1:15
25 [5] Ancient vss. suggest *defense;* MT *gold,* as in v. 24
26 [o] Job 27:10; Ps. 37:4; Is. 58:14
27 [p] Job 11:13; 33:26; [Is. 58:9-11]
29 [q] Job 5:11; [Matt. 23:12; James 4:6; 1 Pet. 5:5]

CHAPTER 23

2 [a] Job 7:11 [1] So with MT, Tg., Vg.; LXX, Syr. *His*
3 [b] Job 13:3, 18; 16:21; 31:35
6 [c] Is. 57:16
8 [d] Job 9:11; 35:14
10 [e] [Ps. 1:6; 139:1-3]

22:15-19 Again, the fate of the wicked was expressed in the simplistic idea that all suffering comes from sin. Contrary to what Job had argued, the wicked characteristically die prematurely, and Job's claim that God prospered them (v. 18a) was counsel that Eliphaz rejected (vv. 18b-20).

22:21-30 Eliphaz painted a picture of the life of blessing in store for Job if only he would return to God and repent of his sin (v. 23), emphasizing again that he did not believe Job was innocent (v. 30). "Stop all the speeches and complaints, repent, and everything will be fine," he thought.

22:24 Ophir. A land with high quality gold, whose location is uncertain (cf. Gen. 10:29; Job 28:16).

23:1–24:25 Job's reply to Eliphaz's third speech was not a rebuttal, but expressed Job's longing for fellowship with God, so he could experience God's love and goodness and hear from Him the meaning of all his suffering.

23:3 His seat. A place of judgment.

23:4 *my* case. Job's claim to innocence.

23:6,7 contend. Engage in court debate over evidence, witnesses, etc. Job knew God was not going to enter a contest with him to determine, as in a court case, who was right. But he wanted God to at least listen to him, so confident was he that he could make his case, and be delivered by his Just Judge (cf. 1:8; 2:3).

23:8-12 Even though Job couldn't sense God's presence, he believed He was present and affirmed his commitment to God's purpose in this test (v. 10) and his continued obedience to God's Word, which were the most important issues in his life (vv. 11,12).

When [f]He has tested me, I shall
come forth as gold.
11 [g]My foot has held fast to His steps;
I have kept His way and not
turned aside.
12 I have not departed from the
[h]commandment of His lips;
[i]I have treasured the words of His
mouth
More than my [2]necessary *food.*

13 "But He *is* unique, and who can
make Him change?
And *whatever* [j]His soul desires, *that*
He does.
14 For He performs *what is*
[k]appointed for me,
And many such *things are* with
Him.
15 Therefore I am terrified at His
presence;
When I consider *this,* I am afraid of
Him.
16 For God [l]made my heart weak,
And the Almighty terrifies me;
17 Because I was not [m]cut off [3]from
the presence of darkness,
And He did *not* hide deep
darkness from my face.

10 [f][Ps. 17:3; 66:10; James 1:12]
11 [g]Job 31:7; Ps. 17:5
12 [h]Job 6:10; 22:22 [i]Ps. 44:18 [2]Lit. *appointed portion*
13 [j][Ps. 115:3]
14 [k][1 Thess. 3:2-4]
16 [l]Ps. 22:14
17 [m]Job 10:18, 19 [3]Or *by* or *before*

Job Complains of Violence on the Earth

24 "*Since* [a]times are not hidden from
the Almighty,
Why do those who know Him see
not His [b]days?

2 "*Some* remove [c]landmarks;
They seize flocks violently and
feed *on them;*
3 They drive away the donkey of the
fatherless;
They [d]take the widow's ox as a
pledge.
4 They push the needy off the road;
All the [e]poor of the land are forced
to hide.
5 Indeed, *like* wild donkeys in the
desert,
They go out to their work,
searching for food.
The wilderness *yields* food for them
and for *their* children.
6 They gather their fodder in the
field
And glean in the vineyard of the
wicked.
7 They [f]spend the night naked,
without clothing,
And have no covering in the cold.
8 They are wet with the showers of
the mountains,
And [g]huddle around the rock for
want of shelter.

9 "*Some* snatch the fatherless from the
breast,
And take a pledge from the poor.
10 They cause *the poor* to go naked,
without [h]clothing;
And they take away the sheaves
from the hungry.
11 They press out oil within their
walls,
And tread winepresses, yet suffer
thirst.
12 The dying groan in the city,
And the souls of the wounded cry
out;
Yet God does not charge *them* with
wrong.

13 "There are those who rebel against
the light;
They do not know its ways
Nor abide in its paths.
14 [i]The murderer rises with the light;
He kills the poor and needy;
And in the night he is like a thief.
15 [j]The eye of the adulterer waits for
the twilight,
[k]Saying, 'No eye will see me';
And he [1]disguises *his* face.
16 In the dark they break into houses

CHAPTER 24

1 [a][Acts 1:7] [b][Is. 2:12]; Jer. 46:10; [Obad. 15]; Zeph. 1:7
2 [c][Deut. 19:14; 27:17]; Prov. 22:28; 23:10; Hos. 5:10
3 [d][Deut. 24:6, 10, 12, 17]; Job 22:6, 9
4 [e]Job 29:16; Prov. 28:28
7 [f]Ex. 22:26, 27; [Deut. 24:12, 13]; Job 22:6; [James 2:15, 16]
8 [g]Lam. 4:5
10 [h]Job 31:19
14 [i]Ps. 10:8
15 [j]Prov. 7:7-10 [k]Ps. 10:11 [1]Lit. *puts a covering on his face*

23:14 He performs *what is* appointed for me. Job's resignation to God's sovereignty faltered at times in practice, but he returned to it repeatedly. It is the great lesson of the book: Trust sovereign God when you can't understand why things go badly in life.

24:1-25 Job had made the point that the unrighteous prosper in spite of their sin (chap. 21). Extending that theme, he listed the kinds of severe sins which go on in the world and God doesn't seem to do anything to stop them (vv. 2-17), so that the wicked, in general, prosper and live long lives, seemingly unabated. These sins—oppressing the orphans, widows, and poor as well as committing murder, thievery, and adultery—are the very ones forbidden in other parts of the OT.

24:1 times are not hidden. Job believed that God knew the appointed times for all activities under the sun (Eccl. 3:1-8), but he bemoaned the fact that God did not inform man about them.

24:2 remove landmarks. This ancient practice is addressed in Deut. 19:14; Prov. 22:28; 23:10, "Do not move the ancient landmark." Corrupt landowners often did this to increase their holdings, particularly where the land was owned by bereaved widows. Taking advantage of widows will be treated by the ultimate court in heaven.

24:7 spend the night. It was common practice to take an outer garment as a pledge for money owed. But OT law forbade keeping the garment at night since its owner could get cold and sick (cf. 24:10).

24:12 Yet God does not charge *them* with wrong. This is a stinging accusation from Job. Human courts prosecuted offenders for most of these social crimes. Job, in essence, was saying "If human courts punish the wicked, then why doesn't God?"

Which they marked for themselves
in the daytime;
[l]They do not know the light.
17 For the morning is the same to
them as the shadow of death;
If *someone* recognizes *them*,
They are in the terrors of the
shadow of death.

18 "They *should be* swift on the face of
the waters,
Their portion *should be* cursed in
the earth,
So that no *one would* turn into the
way of their vineyards.
19 As drought and heat [2]consume the
snow waters,
So [3]the grave *consumes those who*
have sinned.
20 The womb *should* forget him,
The worm *should* feed sweetly on
him;
[m]He *should* be remembered no more,
And wickedness *should* be broken
like a tree.
21 For he [4]preys on the barren *who* do
not bear,
And does no good for the widow.

22 "But *God* draws the mighty away
with His power;
He rises up, but no *man* is sure of
life.
23 He gives them security, and they
rely *on it;*
Yet [n]His eyes *are* on their ways.
24 They are exalted for a little while,
Then they are gone.
They are brought low;
They are [5]taken out of the way like
all *others;*
They dry out like the heads of
grain.

25 "Now if *it is* not *so,* who will prove
me a liar,
And make my speech worth
nothing?"

16 [l] [John 3:20]
19 [2] Lit. *seize* [3] Or *Sheol*
20 [m] Job 18:17; Ps. 34:16; Prov. 10:7
21 [4] Lit. *feeds on*
23 [n] Ps. 11:4; [Prov. 15:3]
24 [5] Lit. *gathered up*

Bildad: How Can Man Be Righteous?

25 Then [a]Bildad the Shuhite answered
and said:

2 "Dominion and fear *belong* to Him;
He makes peace in His high places.
3 [1]Is there any number to His armies?
Upon whom does [b]His light not
rise?
4 [c]How then can man be righteous
before God?
Or how can he be [d]pure *who is*
born of a woman?
5 If even the moon does not shine,
And the stars are not pure in His
[e]sight,
6 How much less man, *who is* [f]a
maggot,
And a son of man, *who is* a worm?"

CHAPTER 25

1 [a] Job 8:1; 18:1
3 [b] James 1:17 [1] Can His armies be counted?
4 [c] Job 4:17; 15:14; Ps. 130:3; 143:2 [d] [Job 14:4]
5 [e] Job 15:15
6 [f] Ps. 22:6

Job: Man's Frailty and God's Majesty

26 But Job answered and said:

2 "How have you helped *him who is*
without power?
How have you saved the arm *that*
has no strength?
3 How have you counseled *one who*
has no wisdom?
And *how* have you declared sound
advice to many?
4 To whom have you uttered words?
And whose spirit came from you?

5 "The dead tremble,
Those under the waters and those
inhabiting them.
6 [a]Sheol *is* naked before Him,
And Destruction has no covering.
7 [b]He stretches out the north over
empty space;
He hangs the earth on nothing.
8 [c]He binds up the water in His thick
clouds,
Yet the clouds [1]are not broken
under it.
9 He covers the face of *His* throne,
And spreads His cloud over it.

CHAPTER 26

6 [a] [Ps. 139:8]; Prov. 15:11; [Heb. 4:13]
7 [b] Job 9:8; Ps. 24:2; 104:2
8 [c] Job 37:11; Prov. 30:4 [1] *do not break*

24:18-21 Again Job referred to the opinions of his counselors, saying that, if their view were correct, all the wicked should be experiencing punishment. But it is obvious they were not.

24:22-25 Job's view was that their punishment would come eventually ("exalted for a little while"). Retribution needed the timing of God's wisdom, when He determined wrongs would be made right. Job was totally confident that his point could not be refuted.

25:1-6 Bildad made his third speech (the last speech for the three friends), and restated the same theory—that God was majestic and exalted (vv. 2,3) and man was sinful, especially Job (vv. 4-6).

26:1–31:40 Job made his last speech in rebuttal to Eliphaz, Bildad, and Zophar.

26:1-4 Job responded to Bildad's lack of concern for him, showing that all his friends, theological and rational words missed the point of Job's need altogether and had been no help.

26:5-14 As before, in chaps. 9 and 12, Job showed that he was not inferior to his friends in describing God's greatness. He understood that as well as they did. He described it as manifested in the realm of the dead called Sheol and Destruction (vv. 5,6), the earth and sky (v. 7), the waters above (vv. 8-10) and below (v. 12), and the stars (v. 13).

26:7 hangs the earth on nothing. A statement that is accurate, given in ancient time, before scientific verification. This indicates the divine authorship of Scripture.

10 [d]He drew a circular horizon on the face of the waters,
At the boundary of light and darkness.
11 The pillars of heaven tremble,
And are [2]astonished at His rebuke.
12 [e]He stirs up the sea with His power,
And by His understanding He breaks up [3]the storm.
13 [f]By His Spirit He adorned the heavens;
His hand pierced [g]the fleeing serpent.
14 Indeed these *are* the mere edges of His ways,
And how small a whisper we hear of Him!
But the thunder of His power who can understand?"

Job Maintains His Integrity

27 Moreover Job continued his discourse, and said:

2 "*As* God lives, [a]*who* has taken away my justice,
And the Almighty, *who* has made my soul bitter,
3 As long as my breath *is* in me,
And the breath of God in my nostrils,
4 My lips will not speak wickedness,
Nor my tongue utter deceit.
5 Far be it from me
That I should say you are right;
Till I die [b]I will not put away my integrity from me.
6 My righteousness I [c]hold fast, and will not let it go;
[d]My heart shall not [1]reproach *me* as long as I live.

7 "May my enemy be like the wicked,
And he who rises up against me like the unrighteous.
8 [e]For what is the hope of the hypocrite,
Though he may gain *much*,
If God takes away his life?
9 [f]Will God hear his cry
When trouble comes upon him?
10 [g]Will he delight himself in the Almighty?
Will he always call on God?

11 "I will teach you [2]about the hand of God;
What *is* with the Almighty I will not conceal.
12 Surely all of you have seen *it;*
Why then do you behave with complete nonsense?

13 "This[h] is the portion of a wicked man with God,
And the heritage of oppressors, received from the Almighty:
14 [i]If his children are multiplied, *it is* for the sword;
And his offspring shall not be satisfied with bread.
15 Those who survive him shall be buried in death,
And [j]their[3] widows shall not weep,
16 Though he heaps up silver like dust,
And piles up clothing like clay—

10 [d][Job 38:1-11]; Ps. 33:7; 104:9; Prov. 8:29; Jer. 5:22
11 [2]*amazed*
12 [e]Ex. 14:21; Job 9:13; Is. 51:15; [Jer. 31:35] [3]Heb. *rahab*
13 [f][Job 9:8]; Ps. 33:6 [g]Is. 27:1

CHAPTER 27
2 [a]Job 34:5
5 [b]Job 2:9; 13:15
6 [c]Job 2:3; 33:9 [d]Acts 24:16 [1]*reprove*
8 [e]Matt. 16:26; Luke 12:20
9 [f]Job 35:12, 13; Ps. 18:41; Prov. 1:28; 28:9; [Is. 1:15]; Jer. 14:12; Ezek. 8:18; [Mic. 3:4; John 9:31; James 4:3]
10 [g]Job 22:26, 27; [Ps. 37:4; Is. 58:14]
11 [2]Or *by*
13 [h]Job 20:29
14 [i]Deut. 28:41; Esth. 9:10; Hos. 9:13
15 [j]Ps. 78:64 [3]Lit. *his*

26:10 a circular horizon. This describes the earth as a circular globe, another scientifically accurate statement at a time when many thought the world was flat.

26:11 pillars of heaven. A figure of speech for the mountains that seem to hold up the sky (cf. Ps. 104:32).

26:12 breaks up the storm. Lit. "Rahab," cf. 7:12; 9:13; 26:13. This term seems to be widely used to describe various things that wreak havoc.

26:13 His Spirit. Cf. Job 33:4. The Holy Spirit worked mightily in creation (cf. Gen. 1:2). **the fleeing serpent.** This is figurative language for the idea that God brought all constellations into subjection under His authority (cf. 26:12). "Serpent" could be translated "crooked" and refer to any wayward stars or planets being brought under control by His mighty power.

26:14 Indeed these *are* the mere edges of His ways. Poetic language reminding his counselors that all that could be said and understood by man was only a glimpse of God's powerful hand.

27:1-12 Job turned from speaking about God (26:5-14) to defending his righteousness.

27:2 *who* has taken away my justice. God did not speak to declare Job innocent. Cf. the treatment of Christ in Is. 53:8 and Acts 8:33.

27:3-6 Job affirmed his true and steadfast devotion to righteous living, no matter what happens. He refused to live with a guilty conscience (v. 6b). This was no brash claim, because God had recognized Job's virtue (1:8; 2:3).

27:7 He could have been calling for God to judge his accusers as He judges the wicked.

27:8-10 Job reminded the friends that he would never be hypocritical because he understood the consequences.

27:11 I will teach you about the hand of God. Job had pinpointed the issue between him and his friends. They disagreed on the outworking of God's retribution. They agreed that God was powerful, wise, and sovereign. But because Job knew there was no cherished sin in his life that would bring upon him such intense suffering, Job was forced to conclude that the simplistic notion that all suffering comes from sin and all righteousness is rewarded, was wrong. At the outset, Job himself probably believed as the comforters still did, but he had seen that his friends' limitation of God's action was drastically in need of revision; in fact, it was nonsense. Job's comments here introduced his exposition on wisdom which follow in Job 28.

27:13-23 Job wanted it made clear he was not denying that the wicked are punished with severe distress, so he agreed that they suffer greatly and affirmed so in this section.

17 He may pile *it* up, but [k]the just will wear *it,*
And the innocent will divide the silver.
18 He builds his house like a [4]moth,
[l]Like a [5]booth *which* a watchman makes.
19 The rich man will lie down,
[6]But not be gathered *up;*
He opens his eyes,
And he *is* [m]no more.
20 [n]Terrors overtake him like a flood;
A tempest steals him away in the night.
21 The east wind carries him away, and he is gone;
It sweeps him out of his place.
22 It hurls against him and does not [o]spare;
He flees desperately from its [7]power.
23 *Men* shall clap their hands at him,
And shall hiss him out of his place.

Job's Discourse on Wisdom

28 "Surely there is a mine for silver,
And a place *where* gold is refined.
2 Iron is taken from the [1]earth,
And copper *is* smelted *from* ore.
3 *Man* puts an end to darkness,
And searches every recess
For ore in the darkness and the shadow of death.
4 He breaks open a shaft away from people;
In places forgotten by feet
They hang far away from men;
They swing to and fro.
5 *As for* the earth, from it comes bread,
But underneath it is turned up as by fire;
6 Its stones *are* the source of sapphires,
And it contains gold dust.
7 *That* path no bird knows,
Nor has the falcon's eye seen it.
8 The [2]proud lions have not trodden it,
Nor has the fierce lion passed over it.
9 He puts his hand on the flint;
He overturns the mountains [3]at the roots.
10 He cuts out channels in the rocks,
And his eye sees every precious thing.
11 He dams up the streams from trickling;
What is hidden he brings forth to light.

12 "But[a] where can wisdom be found?
And where *is* the place of understanding?
13 Man does not know its [b]value,
Nor is it found in the land of the living.
14 [c]The deep says, '*It is* not in me';
And the sea says, '*It is* not with me.'
15 It [d]cannot be purchased for gold,
Nor can silver be weighed *for* its price.
16 It cannot be valued in the gold of Ophir,
In precious onyx or sapphire.
17 Neither [e]gold nor crystal can equal it,
Nor can it be exchanged for [4]jewelry of fine gold.
18 No mention shall be made of [5]coral or quartz,
For the price of wisdom *is* above [f]rubies.
19 The topaz of Ethiopia cannot equal it,
Nor can it be valued in pure [g]gold.

20 "From[h] where then does wisdom come?
And where *is* the place of understanding?
21 It is hidden from the eyes of all living,
And concealed from the birds of the [6]air.
22 [i]Destruction[7] and Death say,
'We have heard a report about it with our ears.'
23 God understands its way,
And He knows its place.

17 [k] Prov. 28:8; [Eccl. 2:26] **18** [l] Is. 1:8; Lam. 2:6 [4] So with MT, Vg.; LXX, Syr. *spider* (cf. 8:14); Tg. *decay* [5] Temporary shelter **19** [m] Job 7:8, 21; 20:7 [6] So with MT, Tg.; LXX, Syr. *But shall not add* (i.e., do it again); Vg. *But take away nothing* **20** [n] Job 18:11 **22** [o] Jer. 13:14; Ezek. 5:11; 24:14 [7] Lit. *hand*

CHAPTER 28

2 [1] Lit. *dust* **8** [2] Lit. *sons of pride,* figurative of the great lions

9 [3] At the base **12** [a] Eccl. 7:24 **13** [b] Prov. 3:15 **14** [c] Job 28:22 **15** [d] Prov. 3:13-15; 8:10, 11, 19 **17** [e] Prov. 8:10; 16:16 [4] *vessels* **18** [f] Prov. 3:15; 8:11 [5] Heb. *ramoth* **19** [g] Prov. 8:19 **20** [h] Job 28:12; [Ps. 111:10; Prov. 1:7; 9:10] **21** [6] *heaven* **22** [i] Job 28:14 [7] Heb. *Abaddon*

27:18 house like a moth, like a booth. These are temporary dwellings which illustrate that the wicked will not live long.

27:23 clap their hands. A gesture of mocking.

28:1-28 Though Job had agreed that the wicked suffer (27:13-23), that explained nothing in his case, since he was righteous. So Job called on his friends to consider that maybe God's wisdom was beyond their comprehension. That is the theme of this chapter. The wisdom of God is not gained by natural or theoretical knowledge. What God does not reveal, we can't know.

28:1-11 References to mining silver, gold, iron, flint, and sapphires, as well as smelting copper. Tremendous effort is made by men who seek these precious things. Cf. Prov. 2:1-9.

28:12,20 These verses sum up the message of the chapter with the point that no amount of effort, even as vigorous and demanding as mining, will yield God's wisdom. It can't be valued or found in the world (vv. 13,14). It can't be bought for any price (vv. 15-19). The living can't find it (v. 21), and neither can the dead (v. 22; cf. 26:6).

28:16 Ophir. *See note on 22:24.*

28:23 God understands its way, and He knows its place. These are perhaps the most important thoughts in the chapter for

24 For He looks to the ends of the earth,
And [j]sees under the whole heavens,
25 [k]To establish a weight for the wind,
And apportion the waters by measure.
26 When He [l]made a law for the rain,
And a path for the thunderbolt,
27 Then He saw [8]*wisdom* and declared it;
He prepared it, indeed, He searched it out.
28 And to man He said,
'Behold, [m]the fear of the Lord, that *is* wisdom,
And to depart from evil *is* understanding.' "

24 [j] [Ps. 11:4; 33:13, 14; 66:7; Prov. 15:3]
25 [k] Ps. 135:7
26 [l] Job 37:3; 38:25
27 [8] Lit. *it*
28 [m] [Deut. 4:6; Ps. 111:10; Prov. 1:7; 9:10; Eccl. 12:13]

Job's Summary Defense

29 Job further continued his discourse, and said:

2 "Oh, that I were as *in* months [a]past,
As *in* the days *when* God [b]watched over me;
3 [c]When His lamp shone upon my head,
And when by His light I walked *through* darkness;
4 Just as I was in the days of my prime,
When [d]the friendly counsel of God *was* over my tent;
5 When the Almighty *was* yet with me,
When my children *were* around me;
6 When [e]my steps were bathed with [1]cream,
And [f]the rock poured out rivers of oil for me!
7 "When I went out to the gate by the city,
When I took my seat in the open square,
8 The young men saw me and hid,
And the aged arose *and* stood;
9 The princes refrained from talking,
And [g]put *their* hand on their mouth;
10 The voice of nobles was hushed,
And their [h]tongue stuck to the roof of their mouth.
11 When the ear heard, then it blessed me,
And when the eye saw, then it approved me;
12 Because [i]I delivered the poor who cried out,
The fatherless and *the one who* had no helper.
13 The blessing of a perishing *man* came upon me,
And I caused the widow's heart to sing for joy.
14 [j]I put on righteousness, and it clothed me;
My justice *was* like a robe and a turban.
15 I *was* [k]eyes to the blind,
And I *was* feet to the lame.
16 I *was* a father to the poor,
And [l]I searched out the case *that* I did not know.
17 I broke [m]the fangs of the wicked,
And plucked the victim from his teeth.

CHAPTER 29
2 [a] Job 1:1-5 [b] Job 1:10
3 [c] Job 18:6
4 [d] Job 15:8; [Ps. 25:14; Prov. 3:32]
6 [e] Gen. 49:11; Deut. 32:14; Job 20:17 [1] So with ancient vss. and a few Heb. mss. (cf. Job 20:17); MT *wrath* [f] Deut. 32:13; Ps. 81:16
9 [g] Job 21:5
10 [h] Ps. 137:6
12 [i] Job 31:16-23; [Ps. 72:12; Prov. 21:13; 24:11]
14 [j] Deut. 24:13; Job 27:5, 6; Ps. 132:9; [Is. 59:17; 61:10; Eph. 6:14]
15 [k] Num. 10:31
16 [l] Prov. 29:7
17 [m] Ps. 58:6; Prov. 30:14

the debates. Job and his friends have probed God's wisdom for 3 court rounds and basically have arrived nowhere near the truth. Finally, Job made the point clearly that the divine wisdom necessary to explain his suffering was inaccessible to man. Only God knew all about it, because he knows everything (v. 24). True wisdom belongs to the One who is the Almighty Creator (vv. 25,26). One can only know it if He declares it to him (cf. Deut. 29:29).

28:28 Behold, the fear of the Lord, that *is* wisdom. Job had made the connection that the others would not. While the specific features of God's wisdom may not be revealed to us, the alpha and omega of wisdom is to revere God and avoid sin(cf. Ps. 111:10; Prov. 1:7; 9:10; Eccl. 12:13,14), leaving the unanswered questions to Him in trusting submission. All we can do is trust and obey (cf. Eccl. 12:13) and that is enough wisdom (this is the wisdom of Prov. 1:7–2:9). One may never know the reasons for life's sufferings.

29:1-25 Job did not change his mind about his sin, but continued to deny that he had earned this pain with his iniquity. The realities of his own words in chap. 28 had not yet fully taken over his mind, so he swung back to despair and rehearsed his life before the events of Job 1,2, when he was so fulfilled because God was with him (v. 5). God still was with him, but it seemed as if He were gone.

29:5 When the Almighty *was* yet with me. Job felt abandoned by God. But God would demonstrate to Job, by addressing his criticisms, that God was with him all throughout this ordeal.

29:6 cream...oil. He had the richest milk and best olive oil in abundance.

29:7 gate...my seat. This was a place in society reserved for city leaders. Job had been one because he was a very wealthy and powerful man.

29:12,13 poor...fatherless...perishing *man*...widow's. All over the ancient Near Eastern world, a man's virtue was measured by his treatment of the weakest and most vulnerable members of society. If he protected and provided for this group, he was respected as being a noble man. These things, which Job had done, his accusers said he must not have done or he wouldn't be suffering (see 22:1-11).

29:15,16 blind...lame...poor. Contrary to the accusations of the 3 friends, Job went beyond the standards of the day to care for the widow, the orphan, the poor, the disabled, and the abused.

29:16 searched out the case. Much oppression occurred in unjust courts, and there Job protected the weak.

18 "Then I said, [n]'I shall die in my
nest,
And multiply *my* days as the sand.
19 [o]My root *is* spread out [p]to the
waters,
And the dew lies all night on my
branch.
20 My glory *is* fresh within me,
And my [q]bow is renewed in my
hand.'

21 "*Men* listened to me and waited,
And kept silence for my counsel.
22 After my words they did not speak
again,
And my speech settled on them *as*
dew.
23 They waited for me *as* for the rain,
And they opened their mouth wide
as for [r]the spring rain.
24 *If* I mocked at them, they did not
believe *it,*
And the light of my countenance
they did not cast down.
25 I chose the way for them, and sat
as chief;
So I dwelt as a king in the army,
As one *who* comforts mourners.

30 "But now they mock at me, *men*
[1]younger than I,
Whose fathers I disdained to put
with the dogs of my flock.
2 Indeed, what *profit* is the strength
of their hands to me?
Their vigor has perished.
3 *They are* gaunt from want and
famine,
Fleeing late to the wilderness,
desolate and waste,
4 Who pluck [2]mallow by the bushes,
And broom tree roots *for* their food.
5 They were driven out from among
men,
They shouted at them as *at* a thief.
6 *They had* to live in the clefts of the
[3]valleys,
In [4]caves of the earth and the
rocks.

18 [n] Ps. 30:6
19 [o] Job 18:16 [p] Ps. 1:3; [Jer. 17:7, 8]
20 [q] Gen. 49:24; Ps. 18:34
23 [r] [Zech. 10:1]

CHAPTER 30

1 [1] Lit. *of fewer days*
4 [2] A plant of the salty marshes
6 [3] *wadis* [4] Lit. *holes*

9 [a] Job 17:6; Ps. 69:12; Lam. 3:14, 63
10 [b] Num. 12:14; Deut. 25:9; Job 17:6; Is. 50:6; Matt. 26:67; 27:30
11 [c] Job 12:18 [5] So with MT, Syr., Tg.; LXX, Vg. *His*
12 [d] Job 19:12
16 [e] Ps. 42:4 [f] Ps. 22:14; Is. 53:12

7 Among the bushes they brayed,
Under the nettles they nestled.
8 *They were* sons of fools,
Yes, sons of vile men;
They were scourged from the land.

9 "And[a] now I am their taunting
song;
Yes, I am their byword.
10 They abhor me, they keep far from
me;
They do not hesitate [b]to spit in my
face.
11 Because [c]He has loosed [5]my
bowstring and afflicted me,
They have cast off restraint before
me.
12 At *my* right *hand* the rabble arises;
They push away my feet,
And [d]they raise against me their
ways of destruction.
13 They break up my path,
They promote my calamity;
They have no helper.
14 They come as broad breakers;
Under the ruinous storm they roll
along.
15 Terrors are turned upon me;
They pursue my honor as the
wind,
And my prosperity has passed like
a cloud.

16 "And[e] now my soul is [f]poured out
because of my *plight;*
The days of affliction take hold of
me.
17 My bones are pierced in me at
night,
And my gnawing pains take no
rest.
18 By great force my garment is
disfigured;
It binds me about as the collar of
my coat.
19 He has cast me into the mire,
And I have become like dust and
ashes.

29:18-20 Job had vigorous health like a widely rooted tree enjoying fresh dew, and he had expected to live a long life with his family ("nest").

29:21-25 Job reminded his friends that there had been a day when no one rejected his insights. He was the one sought for counsel.

29:24 mocked. This is likely a reference to saying something facetiously or jokingly. Job's word was so respected that they didn't believe his humor was humor, but took it seriously.

29:25 as a king. Job was not a king but some sort of high local official such as a mayor. Mayors, called "hazannu" in Job's day, performed all of the activities Job claimed in the previous section.

30:1-31 Job moved from the recollection of good days in the past (chap. 29) to lament his present losses.

30:2-8 Job described these mockers as dissipated vagabonds who, because of their uselessness and wickedness, were not welcome in society, so were driven out of the land. These base men had made Job the object of their sordid entertainment (vv. 9-15).

30:9 I am their taunting song. Job was the object of their jeering, whereas in former days he would not hire their fathers to tend his animals like sheepdogs (30:1).

30:16-19 Job's life ebbed away, suffering gripped him, his bones ached, gnawing pain never relented, his skin ("garment") was changed (v. 30), and he was reduced to mud, dirt, and ashes.

20 "I [g]cry out to You, but You do not
answer me;
I stand up, and You regard me.
21 *But* You have become cruel to me;
With the strength of Your hand You
[h]oppose me.
22 You lift me up to the wind and
cause me to ride *on it;*
You spoil my success.
23 For I know *that* You will bring me
to death,
And *to* the house [i]appointed for all
living.

24 "Surely He would not stretch out *His*
hand against a heap of ruins,
If they cry out when He destroys *it.*
25 [j]Have I not wept for him who was
in trouble?
Has *not* my soul grieved for the
poor?
26 [k]But when I looked for good, evil
came *to me;*
And when I waited for light, then
came darkness.
27 [6]My heart is in turmoil and cannot
rest;
Days of affliction confront me.
28 [l]I go about mourning, but not in the
sun;
I stand up in the assembly *and* cry
out for help.
29 [m]I am a brother of jackals,
And a companion of ostriches.
30 [n]My skin grows black and falls from
me;
[o]My bones burn with fever.
31 My harp is *turned* to mourning,
And my flute to the voice of those
who weep.

CHAPTER 31

31 "I have made a covenant with my
eyes;
Why then should I [1]look upon a
[a]young woman?
2 For what *is* the [b]allotment of God
from above,
And the inheritance of the
Almighty from on high?
3 *Is* it not destruction for the wicked,
And disaster for the workers of
iniquity?
4 [c]Does He not see my ways,
And count all my steps?

5 "If I have walked with falsehood,
Or if my foot has hastened to
deceit,
6 [2]Let me be weighed on honest
scales,
That God may know my [d]integrity.
7 If my step has turned from the
way,
Or [e]my heart walked after my
eyes,
Or if any spot adheres to my
hands,
8 *Then* [f]let me sow, and another eat;
Yes, let my harvest be [3]rooted out.

9 "If my heart has been enticed by a
woman,
Or *if* I have lurked at my
neighbor's door,
10 *Then* let my wife grind for
[g]another,
And let others bow down over her.
11 For that *would be* wickedness;
Yes, [h]it *would be* iniquity *deserving*
of judgment.
12 For that *would be* a fire *that*
consumes to destruction,
And would root out all my
increase.

13 "If I have [i]despised the cause of my
male or female servant
When they complained against me,
14 What then shall I do when [j]God
rises up?
When He punishes, how shall I
answer Him?
15 [k]Did not He who made me in the
womb make them?

---

20 [g] Job 19:7
21 [h] Job 10:3; 16:9, 14; 19:6, 22
23 [i] [Heb. 9:27]
25 [j] Ps. 35:13, 14; Rom. 12:15
26 [k] Job 3:25, 26; Jer. 8:15
27 [6] *I seethe inside*
28 [l] Job 30:31; Ps. 38:6; 42:9; 43:2
29 [m] Ps. 44:19; 102:6; Mic. 1:8
30 [n] Ps. 119:83; Lam. 4:8; 5:10 [o] Ps. 102:3

CHAPTER 31

1 [a] [Matt. 5:28] [1] *look intently* or *gaze*
2 [b] Job 20:29
4 [c] [2 Chr. 16:9]; Job 24:23; 28:24; 34:21; 36:7; [Prov. 5:21; 15:3; Jer. 32:19]
6 [d] Job 23:10; 27:5, 6 [2] Lit. *Let Him weigh me*
7 [e] Num. 15:39; [Eccl. 11:9]; Ezek. 6:9; [Matt. 5:29]
8 [f] Lev. 26:16; Deut. 28:30, 38; Job 20:18; Mic. 6:15 [3] *uprooted*
10 [g] Deut. 28:30; 2 Sam. 12:11; Jer. 8:10
11 [h] Gen. 38:24; [Lev. 20:10; Deut. 22:22]; Job 31:28
13 [i] [Deut. 24:14, 15]
14 [j] [Ps. 44:21]
15 [k] Job 34:19; Prov. 14:31; 22:2; [Mal. 2:10]

30:20 This caused the most suffering of all—what seemed to be the cruel silence of God (v. 21).

30:23 the house appointed. The grave.

30:24-26 This seems to be saying that God must have some sympathy, if Job has (v. 25), so as not to destroy altogether what is already ruined. Job thought that and reached out for help in his misery and received only evil (v. 26).

30:30 My skin...My bones. Job was describing the effect of his disease (see 2:7).

31:1-40 As Job became more forceful in his pursuit of being cleared of false accusations, he intensified the claim that he was innocent, comparatively speaking, and demanded justice. In situations where an individual was innocent, he would attest to it by taking an oath before the king or a deity. This procedure found among Job's neighboring nations was often protocol for court procedures. The repeated "If...then" statements amount to the terms of the oath: "If" tells what Job might have done wrong; "then" describes a curse which could result. He accepted the curses (the "then" statements through the chapter) if he deserved them. This represented Job's last attempt to defend himself before both God and man. In terms of purity (v. 1), sin in general (v. 2,3), truth (v. 5), covetousness (v. 7), marital faithfulness (v. 9), equity (v. 13), compassion (vv. 16-21), materialism (vv. 24,25), false religion (vv. 26,27), love for enemies and strangers (vv. 29-32), secret sin (vv. 33,34), and business relations (vv. 38-40) Job had no pattern of sin. He asked God to answer him (v. 35), and to explain why he suffered.

31:1 made a covenant with my eyes. He spoke here of purity toward women (cf. Prov. 6:25; Matt. 5:28).

Did not the same One fashion us in the womb?

16 "If I have kept the poor from *their* desire,
Or caused the eyes of the widow to [l]fail,
17 Or eaten my morsel by myself,
So that the fatherless could not eat of it
18 (But from my youth I reared him as a father,
And from my mother's womb I guided [4]*the widow*);
19 If I have seen anyone perish for lack of clothing,
Or any poor *man* without covering;
20 If his [5]heart has not [m]blessed me,
And *if* he was *not* warmed with the fleece of my sheep;
21 If I have raised my hand [n]against the fatherless,
When I saw I had help in the gate;
22 *Then* let my arm fall from my shoulder,
Let my arm be torn from the socket.
23 For [o]destruction *from* God *is* a terror to me,
And because of His magnificence I cannot endure.

24 "If[p] I have made gold my hope,
Or said to fine gold, '*You are* my confidence';
25 [q]If I have rejoiced because my wealth *was* great,
And because my hand had gained much;
26 [r]If I have observed the [6]sun when it shines,
Or the moon moving *in* brightness,
27 So that my heart has been secretly enticed,
And my mouth has kissed my hand;
28 This also *would be* an iniquity *deserving of* judgment,
For I would have denied God *who is* above.

29 "If[s] I have rejoiced at the destruction of him who hated me,
Or lifted myself up when evil found him
30 [t](Indeed I have not allowed my mouth to sin
By asking for a curse on his [7]soul);
31 If the men of my tent have not said,
'Who is there that has not been satisfied with his meat?'
32 [u](*But* no sojourner had to lodge in the street,
For I have opened my doors to the [8]traveler);
33 If I have covered my transgressions [v]as[9] Adam,
By hiding my iniquity in my bosom,
34 Because I feared the great [w]multitude,
And dreaded the contempt of families,
So that I kept silence
And did not go out of the door—
35 [x]Oh, that I had one to hear me!
Here is my mark.
Oh, [y]*that* the Almighty would answer me,
That my [1]Prosecutor had written a book!
36 Surely I would carry it on my shoulder,
And bind it on me *like* a crown;
37 I would declare to Him the number of my steps;
Like a prince I would approach Him.

38 "If my land cries out against me,
And its furrows weep together;
39 If [z]I have eaten its [2]fruit without money,
Or [a]caused its owners to lose their lives;
40 *Then* let [b]thistles grow instead of wheat,
And weeds instead of barley."

The words of Job are ended.

Elihu Contradicts Job's Friends

32 So these three men ceased answering Job, because he *was* [a]righteous in his own eyes. 2 Then the wrath of Elihu,

16 [l]Job 29:12
18 [4]Lit. *her*
20 [m][Deut. 24:13] [5]Lit. *loins*
21 [n]Job 22:9
23 [o]Is. 13:6
24 [p][Matt. 6:19, 20; Mark 10:23-25]
25 [q]Job 1:3, 10; Ps. 62:10
26 [r][Deut. 4:19; 17:3]; Ezek. 8:16 [6]Lit. *light*
29 [s][Prov. 17:5; 24:17]; Obad. 12
30 [t][Matt. 5:44] [7]Or *life*
32 [u]Gen. 19:2, 3 [8]So with LXX, Syr., Tg., Vg.; MT *road*
33 [v]Gen. 3:10; [Prov. 28:13] [9]Or *as men do*
34 [w]Ex. 23:2
35 [x]Job 19:7; 30:20, 24, 28 [y]Job 13:22, 24; 33:10 [1]Lit. *Accuser*
39 [z]Job 24:6, 10-12; [James 5:4] [a]1 Kin. 21:19 [2]Lit. *strength*
40 [b]Gen. 3:18

CHAPTER 32
1 [a]Job 6:29; 31:6; 33:9

31:33 as Adam. Perhaps best taken "as mankind" (cf. Hos. 6:7).

31:35 my Prosecutor had written a book. Job wished that God, the perfect Prosecutor who knows the allegations perfectly, had written a book that would have revealed God's will and wisdom and the reasons for Job's pain. This would have cleared him of all charges by his friends.

31:40 The words of Job are ended. The 3 cycles of speeches which began in Job 3:1 were finished and Job had the first and last word among his friends.

32:1–37:24 A new participant who had been there with the other 3 (vv. 3-5), entered the debate over Job's condition—the younger Elihu, who took a new approach to the issue of Job's suffering. Angry with the other 3, he had some new thoughts, but was very hard on Job. Elihu was angry, full of self-importance and verbose, but

the son of Barachel the [b]Buzite, of the family of Ram, was aroused against Job; his
wrath was aroused because he [c]justified
himself rather than God. 3 Also against his
three friends his wrath was aroused, because they had found no answer, and *yet*
had condemned Job.
4 Now because they *were* years older
than he, Elihu had waited [1]to speak to Job.
5 When Elihu saw that *there was* no answer
in the mouth of these three men, his wrath
was aroused.
6 So Elihu, the son of Barachel the
Buzite, answered and said:

"I *am* [d]young in years, and you *are*
very old;
Therefore I was afraid,
And dared not declare my opinion
to you.
7 I said, [2]'Age should speak,
And multitude of years should
teach wisdom.'
8 But *there is* a spirit in man,
And [e]the breath of the Almighty
gives him understanding.
9 [f]Great[3] men are not *always* wise,
Nor do the aged *always* understand
justice.

10 "Therefore I say, 'Listen to me,
I also will declare my opinion.'
11 Indeed I waited for your words,
I listened to your reasonings,
while you searched out what
to say.
12 I paid close attention to you;
And surely not one of you
convinced Job,
Or answered his words—
13 [g]Lest you say,
'We have found wisdom';
God will vanquish him, not man.
14 Now he has not [4]directed *his*
words against me;
So I will not answer him with your
words.

15 "They are dismayed and answer no
more;
Words escape them.
16 And I have waited, because they
did not speak,
Because they stood still *and*
answered no more.
17 I also will answer my part,
I too will declare my opinion.
18 For I am full of words;
The spirit within me compels me.
19 Indeed my [5]belly *is* like wine *that*
has no [6]vent;
It is ready to burst like new
wineskins.
20 I will speak, that I may find relief;
I must open my lips and answer.
21 Let me not, I pray, show partiality
to anyone;
Nor let me flatter any man.
22 For I do not know how to flatter,
Else my Maker would soon take
me [h]away.

Elihu Contradicts Job

33 "But please, Job, hear my speech,
And listen to all my words.
2 Now, I open my mouth;
My tongue speaks in my mouth.
3 My words *come* from my upright
heart;
My lips utter pure knowledge.
4 [a]The Spirit of God has made me,
And the breath of the Almighty
gives me life.
5 If you can answer me,
Set *your words* in order before me;
Take your stand.
6 [b]Truly I *am* [1]as your spokesman
before God;
I also have been formed out of clay.
7 [c]Surely no fear of me will terrify
you,
Nor will my hand be heavy on
you.

8 "Surely you have spoken [2]in my
hearing,
And I have heard the sound of
your words, *saying,*
9 'I[d] *am* pure, without transgression;
I *am* innocent, and *there is* no
iniquity in me.
10 Yet He finds occasions against me,
[e]He counts me as His enemy;
11 [f]He puts my feet in the stocks,
He watches all my paths.'

12 "Look, *in* this you are not righteous.
I will answer you,
For God is greater than man.

2 [b] Gen. 22:21 [c] Job 27:5, 6
4 [1] Vg. *till Job had spoken*
6 [d] Lev. 19:32
7 [2] Lit. *Days*, i.e., years
8 [e] 1 Kin. 3:12; 4:29; [Job 35:11; 38:36; Prov. 2:6; Eccl. 2:26; Dan. 1:17; 2:21; Matt. 11:25; James 1:5]
9 [f] [1 Cor. 1:26] [3] Or *Men of many years*
13 [g] [Jer. 9:23; 1 Cor. 1:29]
14 [4] *ordered*
19 [5] *bosom* [6] *opening*
22 [h] Job 27:8

CHAPTER 33

4 [a] [Gen. 2:7]; Job 32:8
6 [b] Job 4:19 [1] Lit. *as your mouth*
7 [c] Job 9:34
8 [2] Lit. *in my ears*
9 [d] Job 10:7
10 [e] Job 13:24; 16:9
11 [f] Job 13:27; 19:8

his approach was refreshing after listening repetitiously to the others, though not really helpful to Job. Why was it necessary to record and read those 4 blustering speeches by this man? Because they happened as part of the story, while Job was still waiting for God to disclose Himself (chaps. 38–41).

32:2 Buzite. Elihu's ancestry was traced to the Arabian tribe of Buz (cf. Jer. 25:23). The "family of Ram" is unknown.

32:6-8 He may have called it "opinion" (vv. 6, 10, 17), but he claimed it had come by inspiration from God (v. 8; cf. 33:6, 33).

33:1-33 The first of Elihu's challenges to Job began with proud claims (vv. 1-7), followed by references to Job's questions/complaints (vv. 8-11). Then came Elihu's answers (vv. 12-33).

13 Why do you [g]contend with Him?
For He does not give an accounting
of any of His words.
14 [h]For God may speak in one way, or
in another,
Yet man does not perceive it.
15 [i]In a dream, in a vision of the night,
When deep sleep falls upon men,
While slumbering on their beds,
16 [j]Then He opens the ears of men,
And seals their instruction.
17 In order to turn man *from his* deed,
And conceal pride from man,
18 He keeps back his soul from the
Pit,
And his life from [3]perishing by the
sword.

19 "*Man* is also chastened with pain on
his [k]bed,
And with strong *pain* in many of
his bones,
20 [l]So that his life abhors [m]bread,
And his soul [4]succulent food.
21 His flesh wastes away from sight,
And his bones stick out *which once*
were not seen.
22 Yes, his soul draws near the Pit,
And his life to the executioners.

23 "If there is a messenger for him,
A mediator, one among a
thousand,
To show man His uprightness,
24 Then He is gracious to him, and
says,
'Deliver him from going down to
the Pit;
I have found [5]a ransom';
25 His flesh shall be young like a
child's,
He shall return to the days of his
youth.
26 He shall pray to God, and He will
delight in him,
He shall see His face with joy,
For He restores to man His
righteousness.
27 Then he looks at men and [n]says,
'I have sinned, and perverted *what*
was right,
And it [o]did not profit me.'
28 He will [p]redeem [6]his soul from
going down to the Pit,
And [6]his life shall see the light.

29 "Behold, God works all these *things*,
Twice, *in fact*, three *times* with a
man,
30 [q]To bring back his soul from the Pit,
That he may be enlightened with
the light of life.

31 "Give ear, Job, listen to me;
Hold your peace, and I will speak.
32 If you have anything to say,
answer me;
Speak, for I desire to justify you.
33 If not, [r]listen to me;
[7]Hold your peace, and I will teach
you wisdom."

Elihu Proclaims God's Justice

34 Elihu further answered and said:

2 "Hear my words, you wise *men;*
Give ear to me, you who have
knowledge.
3 [a]For the ear tests words
As the palate tastes food.
4 Let us choose justice for ourselves;
Let us know among ourselves
what *is* good.

5 "For Job has said, [b]'I am righteous,
But [c]God has taken away my
justice;
6 [d]Should I lie concerning my right?
My [1]wound *is* incurable, *though I*
am without transgression.'
7 What man *is* like Job,
[e]*Who* drinks [2]scorn like water,

13 [g] Job 40:2; [Is. 45:9] **14** [h] Job 33:29; 40:5; Ps. 62:11 **15** [i] [Num. 12:6] **16** [j] [Job 36:10, 15] **18** [3] Lit. *passing* **19** [k] Job 30:17 **20** [l] Ps. 107:18 [m] Job 3:24; 6:7 [4] *desirable* **24** [5] *an atonement*

27 [n] [2 Sam. 12:13; Prov. 28:13; Luke 15:21; 1 John 1:9] [o] [Rom. 6:21] **28** [p] Is. 38:17 [6] Kt. *my* **30** [q] Ps. 56:13 **33** [r] Ps. 34:11 [7] *Keep silent*

CHAPTER 34

3 [a] Job 6:30; 12:11 **5** [b] Job 13:18; 33:9 [c] Job 27:2 **6** [d] Job 6:4; 9:17 [1] Lit. *arrow* **7** [e] Job 15:16 [2] *derision*

33:13 Job had complained that God did not speak to him. Elihu reminded Job that God didn't have to defend His will and actions to anyone.

33:14-18 God does speak, he contended, in many ways such as dreams and visions to protect people from evil and deadly ways (vv. 17,18).

33:18 the Pit. A reference to the realm of the dead (cf. vv. 21,24,30).

33:19-28 Job has lamented that his suffering was not deserved. Elihu answered that complaint by saying he was God's messenger, a mediator to Job to show him that God doesn't act in a whimsical way, but allows suffering as chastening to bring a person to submit to Him as upright (v. 23) and to repent (v. 27) that his life may be spared (vv. 24,28,30). God allows suffering for spiritual benefit.

33:32 I desire to justify you. Elihu expressed he was on Job's side and wanted to see him vindicated in his claims to righteousness, so he gave opportunity for Job to dialogue with him as he spoke (v. 33).

34:1-37 Elihu addressed Job and his accusers. His approach was to quote Job directly (vv. 5-9), then respond to his complaints, but at times he misinterpreted Job's remarks, and at other times he put the words of the accusers in Job's mouth. The most obvious example of the latter wrongdoing was in saying that Job claimed to be sinlessly perfect (v. 6). Job never claimed that; in fact, Job acknowledged his sin (7:21; 13:26). Elihu didn't know it, but God had pronounced Job innocent (1:8; 2:3). In answer to Job's complaints that God seemed unjust, Elihu reminded Job that God was too holy to do anything wrong (v. 10), fair in dealing with people (vv. 11,12), powerful (vv. 13,14), just (vv. 17,18), impartial (vv. 19,20), omniscient (vv. 21,22), the Judge of all (v. 23), and the Sovereign who does what He wills to prevent evil (vv. 24-30).

8 Who goes in company with the
workers of iniquity,
And walks with wicked men?
9 For [f]he has said, 'It profits a man
nothing
That he should delight in God.'

10 "Therefore listen to me, you [3]men of
understanding:
[g]Far be it from God *to do*
wickedness,
And *from* the Almighty to *commit*
iniquity.
11 [h]For He repays man *according to* his
work,
And makes man to find a reward
according to *his* way.
12 Surely God will never do wickedly,
Nor will the Almighty [i]pervert
justice.
13 Who gave Him charge over the
earth?
Or who appointed *Him over* the
whole world?
14 If He should set His heart on it,
If He should [j]gather to Himself His
Spirit and His breath,
15 [k]All flesh would perish together,
And man would return to dust.

16 "If *you have* understanding, hear
this;
Listen to the sound of my words:
17 [l]Should one who hates justice
govern?
Will you [m]condemn *Him who is*
most just?
18 [n]*Is it fitting* to say to a king, *'You are*
worthless,'
And to nobles, *'You are* wicked'?
19 Yet He [o]is not partial to princes,
Nor does He regard the rich more
than the poor;
For [p]they *are* all the work of His
hands.
20 In a moment they die, [q]in the
middle of the night;
The people are shaken and pass
away;
The mighty are taken away
without a hand.

21 "For [r] His eyes *are* on the ways of
man,
And He sees all his steps.
22 [s]There is no darkness nor shadow
of death
Where the workers of iniquity may
hide themselves.
23 For He need not further consider a
man,
That he should go before God in
judgment.
24 [t]He breaks in pieces mighty men
without inquiry,
And sets others in their place.
25 Therefore He knows their works;
He overthrows *them* in the night,
And they are crushed.
26 He strikes them as wicked *men*
In the open sight of others,
27 Because they [u]turned back from
Him,
And [v]would not consider any of
His ways,
28 So that they [w]caused the cry of the
poor to come to Him;
For He [x]hears the cry of the
afflicted.
29 When He gives quietness, who
then can make trouble?
And when He hides *His* face, who
then can see Him,
Whether *it is* against a nation or a
man alone?—
30 That the hypocrite should not
reign,
Lest the people be ensnared.

31 "For has *anyone* said to God,
I have borne *chastening;*
I will offend no more;
32 Teach me *what* I do not see;
If I have done iniquity, I will do no
more'?
33 Should He repay *it* according to
your *terms,*
Just because you disavow it?
You must choose, and not I;
Therefore speak what you know.

34 "Men of understanding say to me,
Wise men who listen to me:
35 'Job[y] speaks without knowledge,
His words *are* without wisdom.'
36 Oh, that Job were tried to the
utmost,

9 [f]Mal. 3:14
10 [g][Gen. 18:25; Deut. 32:4; 2 Chr. 19:7]; Job 8:3; 36:23; Ps. 92:15; Rom. 9:14 [3]*men of heart*
11 [h]Job 34:25; Ps. 62:12; [Prov. 24:12; Jer. 32:19]; Ezek. 33:20; [Matt. 16:27]; Rom. 2:6; [2 Cor. 5:10; Rev. 22:12]
12 [i]Job 8:3
14 [j]Job 12:10; Ps. 104:29; [Eccl. 12:7]
15 [k][Gen. 3:19]; Job 10:9; [Eccl. 12:7]
17 [l]2 Sam. 23:3; Job 34:30 [m]Job 40:8
18 [n]Ex. 22:28
19 [o][Deut. 10:17; Acts 10:34; Rom. 2:11, 12] [p]Job 31:15
20 [q]Ex. 12:29; Job 34:25; 36:20
21 [r][2 Chr. 16:9]; Job 31:4; Ps. 34:15; [Prov. 5:21; 15:3; Jer. 16:17; 32:19]
22 [s][Ps. 139:11, 12; Amos 9:2, 3]
24 [t]Job 12:19; [Dan. 2:21]
27 [u]1 Sam. 15:11 [v]Ps. 28:5; Is. 5:12
28 [w]Job 35:9; James 5:4 [x][Ex. 22:23]; Job 22:27
35 [y]Job 35:16; 38:2

34:9 For he has said. Elihu was incorrect. He was putting words into Job's mouth that Job did not utter.

34:23 go before God in judgment. These words do not refer to the judgment of the last days, but rather to the general accountability toward God that man experiences on a daily basis. The point Elihu made was that God did not need to go through all of the trappings of the court to get to the sentence. God "knows their works" (34:25).

34:31-33 God will not be regulated in His dealings by what men may think. He does not consult men. If He chooses to chasten He will decide when it is enough.

34:34-37 Apparently, Elihu was convinced Job hadn't had enough chastening because of how he answered his prosecutors. He continued to defend his innocence and speak to God.

Because *his* answers *are like* those
of wicked men!
37 For he adds [z]rebellion to his sin;
He claps *his hands* among us,
And multiplies his words against
God."

Elihu Condemns Self-Righteousness

35 Moreover Elihu answered and said:
2 "Do you think this is right?
Do you say,
'My righteousness is more than
God's'?
3 For [a]you say,
'What advantage will it be to You?
What profit shall I have, more than
if I had sinned?'

4 "I will answer you,
And [b]your companions with you.
5 [c]Look to the heavens and see;
And behold the clouds—
They are higher than you.
6 If you sin, what do you accomplish
[d]against Him?
Or, *if* your transgressions are
multiplied, what do you do to
Him?
7 [e]If you are righteous, what do you
give Him?
Or what does He receive from your
hand?
8 Your wickedness affects a man
such as you,
And your righteousness a son of
man.

9 "Because[f] of the multitude of
oppressions they cry out;
They cry out for help because of
the arm of the mighty.
10 But no one says, [g]'Where *is* God
my Maker,
[h]Who gives songs in the night,
11 Who [i]teaches us more than the
beasts of the earth,
And makes us wiser than the birds
of heaven?'
12 [j]There they cry out, but He does
not answer,
Because of the pride of evil men.
13 [k]Surely God will not listen to empty
talk,
Nor will the Almighty regard it.
14 [l]Although you say you do not see
Him,
Yet justice *is* before Him, and [m]you
must wait for Him.
15 And now, because He has not
[n]punished in His anger,
Nor taken much notice of folly,
16 [o]Therefore Job opens his mouth in
vain;
He multiplies words without
knowledge."

Elihu Proclaims God's Goodness

36 Elihu also proceeded and said:
2 "Bear with me a little, and I will
show you
That *there are* yet words to speak
on God's behalf.
3 I will fetch my knowledge from
afar;
I will ascribe righteousness to my
Maker.
4 For truly my words *are* not false;
One who is perfect in knowledge *is*
with you.

5 "Behold, God *is* mighty, but
despises *no one;*
[a]*He is* mighty in strength [1]of
understanding.
6 He does not preserve the life of the
wicked,
But gives justice to the [b]oppressed.
7 [c]He does not withdraw His eyes
from the righteous;

37 [z] Job 7:11; 10:1

CHAPTER 35

3 [a] Job 21:15; 34:9
4 [b] Job 34:8
5 [c] Gen. 15:5; [Job 22:12; Ps. 8:3]
6 [d] Job 7:20; [Prov. 8:36; Jer. 7:19]
7 [e] Job 22:2; Ps. 16:2; Prov. 9:12; [Luke 17:10]; Rom. 11:35
9 [f] Job 34:28
10 [g] Is. 51:13 [h] Job 8:21; Ps. 42:8; 77:6; 149:5; Acts 16:25
11 [i] Job 36:22; Ps. 94:12; [Is. 48:17]; Jer. 32:33; [1 Cor. 2:13]
12 [j] Prov. 1:28
13 [k] Job 27:9; [Prov. 15:29; Is. 1:15]; Jer. 11:11; [Mic. 3:4]
14 [l] Job 9:11 [m] [Ps. 37:5, 6]
15 [n] Ps. 89:32
16 [o] Job 34:35; 38:2

CHAPTER 36

5 [a] Job 12:13, 16; 37:23; [Ps. 99:2-5] [1] *of heart*
6 [b] Job 5:15
7 [c] [Ps. 33:18; 34:15]

35:1-16 Elihu again referred to Job's complaints, first of all his thinking that there appeared to be no advantage to being righteous (v. 3), which Job had said, as recorded in 21:15 and 34:9. The first part of his answer is that Job gained nothing by sinning or not sinning because God was so high that nothing men do affects Him (vv. 5-7). It only affects other men (v. 8). Job had also complained that God did not answer his prayers when he cried under this oppression (see 24:12; 30:20). Elihu coldly gave 3 reasons why Job's prayers had not been heard: pride (vv. 10,12), wrong motives (v. 13), and lack of patient trust (v. 14). Again, all this theoretical talk missed Job's predicament completely because he was righteous. Elihu was no more help than the other counselors.

35:15,16 Elihu suggested that although Job had suffered, his suffering was not the fullness of God's anger or He would have punished Job more for the sinfulness of his speeches. He thought God had actually overlooked the folly of Job in his useless words.

36:1–37:24 Elihu had agreed with his 3 co-counselors that Job had sinned, if nowhere else, in the way he questioned God (33:12), by seeing his suffering as indicating God is unjust (34:34-37) and by feeling that righteousness had no reward (35). In this final answer to Job, he turned to focus mostly on God rather than the sufferer (v. 2).

36:4 One who is perfect in knowledge. Elihu made what appeared to be an outrageous claim in order to give credibility to his remarks.

36:5-12 Elihu began by repeating the thought that though God sends trouble, He is just and merciful (v. 6); He watches over the righteous (v. 7); He convicts them of sin (vv. 8,9); He teaches them to turn from it (v. 10) and rewards their obedience (v. 11) or punishes their rebellion (v. 12-14).

But [d]*they are* on the throne with
kings,
For He has seated them forever,
And they are exalted.
8 And [e]if *they are* bound in [2]fetters,
Held in the cords of affliction,
9 Then He tells them their work and
their transgressions—
That they have acted [3]defiantly.
10 [f]He also opens their ear to
[4]instruction,
And commands that they turn
from iniquity.
11 If they obey and serve *Him*,
They shall [g]spend their days in
prosperity,
And their years in pleasures.
12 But if they do not obey,
They shall perish by the sword,
And they shall die [5]without
[h]knowledge.

13 "But the hypocrites in heart [i]store
up wrath;
They do not cry for help when He
binds them.
14 [j]They [6] die in youth,
And their life *ends* among the
[7]perverted persons.
15 He delivers the poor in their
affliction,
And opens their ears in
oppression.

16 "Indeed He would have brought
you out of dire distress,
[k]*Into* a broad place where *there is* no
restraint;
And [l]what is set on your table
would be full of [m]richness.
17 But you are filled with the
judgment due the [n]wicked;
Judgment and justice take hold *of*
you.
18 Because *there is* wrath, *beware* lest
He take you away with *one*
blow;
For [o]a large ransom would not
help you avoid *it*.
19 [p]Will your riches,
Or all the mighty forces,
Keep you from distress?
20 Do not desire the night,

7 [d] Job 5:11; Ps. 113:8
8 [e] Ps. 107:10 [2] *chains*
9 [3] *proudly*
10 [f] Job 33:16; 36:15 [4] *discipline*
11 [g] Job 21:13; [Is. 1:19, 20]
12 [h] Job 4:21 [5] MT *as one without knowledge*
13 [i] [Rom. 2:5]
14 [j] Ps. 55:23 [6] Lit. *Their soul dies* [7] Heb. *qedeshim*, those practicing sodomy or prostitution in religious rituals
16 [k] Ps. 18:19; 31:8; 118:5 [l] Ps. 23:5 [m] Ps. 36:8
17 [n] Job 22:5, 10, 11
18 [o] Ps. 49:7
19 [p] [Prov. 11:4]

21 [q] Job 36:10; [Ps. 31:6; 66:18] [r] Job 36:8, 15; [Heb. 11:25]
23 [s] Job 34:13; [Is. 40:13, 14] [t] [Deut. 32:4]; Job 8:3
24 [u] [Ps. 92:5; Rev. 15:3]
26 [v] Job 11:7-9; 37:23; [1 Cor. 13:12] [w] Job 10:5; [Ps. 90:2; 102:24, 27]; Heb. 1:12
27 [x] Job 5:10; 37:6, 11; 38:28; Ps. 147:8
28 [y] [Prov. 3:20]
30 [z] Job 37:3
31 [a] [Acts 14:17] [b] Gen. 9:3; Ps. 104:14, 15
32 [c] Ps. 147:8 [8] *strike the mark*
33 [d] 1 Kin. 18:41; Job 37:2 [9] Lit. *what is rising*

CHAPTER 37

3 [1] Or *light*

When people are cut off in their
place.
21 Take heed, [q]do not turn to iniquity,
For [r]you have chosen this rather
than affliction.

22 "Behold, God is exalted by His
power;
Who teaches like Him?
23 [s]Who has assigned Him His way,
Or who has said, 'You have done
[t]wrong'?

Elihu Proclaims God's Majesty

24 "Remember to [u]magnify His work,
Of which men have sung.
25 Everyone has seen it;
Man looks on *it* from afar.

26 "Behold, God *is* great, and we [v]do
not know *Him;*
[w]Nor can the number of His years *be*
discovered.
27 For He [x]draws up drops of water,
Which distill as rain from the mist,
28 [y]Which the clouds drop down
And pour abundantly on man.
29 Indeed, can *anyone* understand the
spreading of clouds,
The thunder from His canopy?
30 Look, He [z]scatters His light upon it,
And covers the depths of the sea.
31 For [a]by these He judges the
peoples;
He [b]gives food in abundance.
32 [c]He covers *His* hands with
lightning,
And commands it to [8]strike.
33 [d]His thunder declares it,
The cattle also, concerning [9]the
rising *storm.*

37 "At this also my heart trembles,
And leaps from its place.
2 Hear attentively the thunder of His
voice,
And the rumbling *that* comes from
His mouth.
3 He sends it forth under the whole
heaven,
His [1]lightning to the ends of the
earth.

36:15 opens their ears in oppression. This was a new insight and perhaps the most helpful thing Elihu said. He went beyond all that had been said about God's using suffering to chasten and bring repentance. He was saying that God used suffering to open men's ears, to draw them to Himself. But as long as Job kept complaining, he was turning to iniquity rather than drawing near to God in his suffering (vv. 16-21).

36:22–37:24 Instead of complaining and questioning God, as Job had been doing, which was sin (as Job will later confess in 42:6), he needed to see God in his suffering and worship Him (33:24).

36:26 we do not know *Him.* Though one may have a personal knowledge of God in salvation, the fullness of His glory is beyond human comprehension.

36:27–37:4 Elihu gave a picture of God's power in the rain storm.

36:31 judges...gives food. The rain storm can be a disaster of punishment from God or a source of abundant crops.

4 After it [a]a voice roars;
He thunders with His majestic voice,
And He does not restrain them when His voice is heard.
5 God thunders marvelously with His voice;
[b]He does great things which we cannot comprehend.
6 For [c]He says to the snow, 'Fall *on* the earth';
Likewise to the [2]gentle rain and the heavy rain of His strength.
7 He seals the hand of every man,
[d]That [e]all men may know His work.
8 The beasts [f]go into dens,
And remain in their lairs.
9 From the chamber *of the south* comes the whirlwind,
And cold from the scattering winds *of the north.*
10 [g]By the breath of God ice is given,
And the broad waters are frozen.
11 Also with moisture He saturates the thick clouds;
He scatters His [3]bright clouds.
12 And they swirl about, being turned by His guidance,
That they may [h]do whatever He commands them
On the face of [4]the whole earth.
13 [i]He causes it to come,
Whether for [5]correction,
Or [j]for His land,
Or [k]for mercy.

14 "Listen to this, O Job;
Stand still and [l]consider the wondrous works of God.
15 Do you know when God [6]dispatches them,
And causes the light of His cloud to shine?
16 [m]Do you know how the clouds are balanced,
Those wondrous works of [n]Him who is perfect in knowledge?
17 Why *are* your garments hot,
When He quiets the earth by the south *wind?*
18 With Him, have you [o]spread out the [p]skies,
Strong as a cast metal mirror?

19 "Teach us what we should say to Him,
For we can prepare nothing because of the darkness.
20 Should He be told that I *wish to* speak?
If a man were to speak, surely he would be swallowed up.
21 Even now *men* cannot look at the light *when it is* bright in the skies,
When the wind has passed and cleared them.
22 He comes from the north *as* golden *splendor;*
With God *is* awesome majesty.
23 *As for* the Almighty, [q]we cannot find Him;
[r]*He is* excellent in power,
In judgment and abundant justice;
He does not oppress.
24 Therefore men [s]fear Him;
He shows no partiality to any *who are* [t]wise of heart."

The LORD *Reveals His Omnipotence to Job*

38 Then the LORD answered Job [a]out of the whirlwind, and said:
2 "Who[b] *is* this who darkens counsel

4 [a]Ps. 29:3
5 [b]Job 5:9; 9:10; 36:26; Rev. 15:3
6 [c]Ps. 147:16, 17 [2]Lit. *shower of rain*
7 [d]Ps. 109:27 [e]Ps. 19:3, 4
8 [f]Job 38:40; Ps. 104:21, 22
10 [g]Job 38:29, 30; Ps. 147:17, 18
11 [3]*clouds of light*
12 [h]Job 36:32; Ps. 148:8 [4]Lit. *the world of the earth*
13 [i]Ex. 9:18, 23; 1 Sam. 12:18, 19 [j]Job 38:26, 27 [k]1 Kin. 18:41-46 [5]Lit. *a rod*
14 [l]Ps. 111:2
15 [6]*places them*
16 [m]Job 36:29 [n]Job 36:4
18 [o]Gen. 1:6; [Is. 44:24] [p]Job 9:8; Ps. 104:2; [Is. 45:12; Jer. 10:12; Zech. 12:1]
23 [q][Job 11:7, 8; Rom. 11:33, 34; 1 Tim. 6:16] [r][Job 9:4; 36:5]
24 [s][Matt. 10:28] [t][Job 5:13; Matt. 11:25]; 1 Cor. 1:26

CHAPTER 38
1 [a]Ex. 19:16; Job 40:6
2 [b]Job 34:35; 42:3

37:5-13 He described God's power expressed in the cold winter. The storms and the hard winters remind us of the world in which harsh things occur, but for God's good purposes of either "correction" or "mercy" (37:13).

37:14-18 These words picture the scene in the sky when the storms and winters have passed, the sunlight breaks through, the warm wind blows, and the sky clears.

37:19,20 In this passage Elihu reminded Job that since man can't explain the wonders of God's power and purpose, he ought to be silent and not contend with God. What a man has to say against God's plans is not worthy to utter and could bring judgment.

37:21-23 Elihu illustrated the folly of telling God what to do by describing staring into the golden sun on a brilliant day (vv. 21,22). We can't confront God in His great glory; we are not even able to look at the sun He created (v. 23).

37:24 shows no partiality. God is the Righteous Judge who will not take a bribe or perform favors in judgment. Thus, in his concluding speech, Elihu had pointed both Job and the reader up to God, who was ready, at last, to speak (38:1).

38:1–40:2 God appeared and engaged in His first interrogation of Job, who had raised some accusations against Him. God had His day in court with Job.

38:1 the LORD. Yahweh, the covenant LORD, was the name used for God in the book's prologue, where the reader was introduced to Job and his relationship with God. However, in chaps. 3–37, the name Yahweh is not used. God is called El Shaddai, God the Almighty. In this book that change becomes a way of illustrating that God has been detached and distant. The relationship is restored in rich terms as God reveals Himself to Job using His covenant name. **out of the whirlwind.** Job had repeatedly called God to court in order to verify his innocence. God finally came to interrogate Job on some of the comments he had made to his own accusers. God was about to be Job's vindicator, but He first brought Job to a right understanding of Himself.

38:2 Job's words had only further confused matters already confused by useless counselors.

By [c]words without knowledge?
3 [d]Now [1]prepare yourself like a man;
I will question you, and you shall
answer Me.

4 "Where[e] were you when I laid the
foundations of the earth?
Tell *Me,* if you have understanding.
5 Who determined its
measurements?
Surely you know!
Or who stretched the [2]line upon it?
6 To what were its foundations
fastened?
Or who laid its cornerstone,
7 When the morning stars sang
together,
And all [f]the sons of God shouted
for joy?

8 "Or[g] *who* shut in the sea with doors,
When it burst forth *and* issued
from the womb;
9 When I made the clouds its
garment,
And thick darkness its swaddling
band;
10 When [h]I fixed My limit for it,
And set bars and doors;
11 When I said,
'This far you may come, but no
farther,
And here your proud waves [i]must
stop!'

12 "Have you [j]commanded the
morning since your days
began,
And caused the dawn to know its
place,
13 That it might take hold of the ends
of the earth,
And [k]the wicked be shaken out of
it?
14 It takes on form like clay *under* a
seal,
And stands out like a garment.
15 From the wicked their [l]light is
withheld,
And [m]the [3]upraised arm is broken.

16 "Have you [n]entered the springs of
the sea?
Or have you walked in search of
the depths?
17 Have [o]the gates of death been
[4]revealed to you?
Or have you seen the doors of the
shadow of death?
18 Have you comprehended the
breadth of the earth?
Tell *Me,* if you know all this.

19 "Where *is* the way *to* the dwelling of
light?
And darkness, where *is* its place,
20 That you may take it to its
territory,
That you may know the paths *to* its
home?
21 Do you know *it,* because you were
born then,
Or *because* the number of your
days *is* great?

22 "Have you entered [p]the treasury of
snow,
Or have you seen the treasury of
hail,
23 [q]Which I have reserved for the time
of trouble,
For the day of battle and war?
24 By what way is light [5]diffused,
Or the east wind scattered over the
earth?

25 "Who [r]has divided a channel for the
overflowing *water,*

2 [c] 1 Tim. 1:7
3 [d] Job 40:7 [1] Lit. *gird up your loins like*
4 [e] Job 15:7; Ps. 104:5
5 [2] *measuring line*
7 [f] Job 1:6
8 [g] Gen. 1:9; Ps. 33:7; 104:9; Prov. 8:29; [Jer. 5:22]
10 [h] Job 26:10
11 [i] [Ps. 89:9; 93:4]
12 [j] [Ps. 74:16; 148:5]
13 [k] Job 34:25; Ps. 104:35
15 [l] Job 18:5; [Prov. 13:9] [m] [Num. 15:30]; Ps. 10:15; 37:17 [3] Lit. *high*
16 [n] [Ps. 77:19]; Prov. 8:24
17 [o] Ps. 9:13 [4] Lit. *opened*
22 [p] Ps. 135:7
23 [q] Ex. 9:18; Josh. 10:11; Is. 30:30; Ezek. 13:11, 13; Rev. 16:21
24 [5] Lit. *divided*
25 [r] Job 28:26

38:3 I will question you. God silenced Job's presumption in constantly wanting to ask the questions of God, by becoming Job's questioner. It must be noted that God never told Job about the reason for his pain, about the conflict between Himself and Satan, which was the reason for Job's suffering. He never gave Job any explanation at all about the circumstances of his trouble. He did one thing in all He said. He asked Job if he was as eternal, great, powerful, wise, and perfect as God. If not, Job would have been better off to be quiet and trust Him.

38:4-38 God asked Job if he participated in creation as He did. That was a crushing, humbling query with an obvious "no" answer.

38:4-7 Creation is spoken of using the language of building construction.

38:7 morning stars…sons of God. The angelic realm, God's ministering spirits.

38:8-11 God's power over the sea by raising the continents is described, along with the thick clouds that draw up its water to carry rain to the land.

38:12,13 The dawn rises, and as it spreads light over the earth, it exposes the wicked, like shaking the corners of a cloth exposes dirt.

38:14 clay *under* a seal. Documents written on clay tablets were signed using personal engraved seals upon which was written the bearer's name. The Heb. for "takes on form" is "turned." It conveys the idea that the earth is turned or rotated like a cylindrical seal rolled over the soft clay. Such rolling cylinder seals were found in Babylon. This speaks of the earth, rotating on its axis, an amazing statement that only God could reveal in ancient days. The dawn rolls across the earth as it rotates.

38:15 their light. The light of the wicked is darkness, because that is when they do their works. The dawn takes away their opportunity to do their deeds and stops their arm lifted and ready to harm. Was Job around when God created light? (v. 21).

38:22 treasury. The storehouse of these elements is the clouds.

Or a path for the thunderbolt,
26 To cause it to rain on a land *where there is* no one,
A wilderness in which *there is* no man;
27 [s]To satisfy the desolate waste,
And cause to spring forth the growth of tender grass?
28 [t]Has the rain a father?
Or who has begotten the drops of dew?
29 From whose womb comes the ice?
And the [u]frost of heaven, who gives it birth?
30 The waters harden like stone,
And the surface of the deep is [v]frozen.[6]

31 "Can you bind the cluster of the [w]Pleiades,[7]
Or loose the belt of Orion?
32 Can you bring out [8]Mazzaroth in its season?
Or can you guide [9]the Great Bear with its cubs?
33 Do you know [x]the ordinances of the heavens?
Can you set their dominion over the earth?

34 "Can you lift up your voice to the clouds,
That an abundance of water may cover you?
35 Can you send out lightnings, that they may go,
And say to you, 'Here we *are!*'?
36 [y]Who has put wisdom in [1]the mind?
Or who has given understanding to the heart?
37 Who can number the clouds by wisdom?
Or who can pour out the bottles of heaven,
38 When the dust hardens in clumps,
And the clods cling together?

39 "Can[z] you hunt the prey for the lion,
Or satisfy the appetite of the young lions,
40 When they crouch in *their* dens,
Or lurk in their lairs to lie in wait?
41 [a]Who provides food for the raven,
When its young ones cry to God,
And wander about for lack of food?

39 "Do you know the time when the wild [a]mountain goats bear young?
Or can you mark when [b]the deer gives birth?
2 Can you number the months *that* they fulfill?
Or do you know the time when they bear young?
3 They bow down,
They bring forth their young,
They deliver their [1]offspring.
4 Their young ones are healthy,
They grow strong with grain;
They depart and do not return to them.

5 "Who set the wild donkey free?
Who loosed the bonds of the [2]onager,
6 [c]Whose home I have made the wilderness,
And the [3]barren land his dwelling?
7 He scorns the tumult of the city;
He does not heed the shouts of the driver.
8 The range of the mountains *is* his pasture,
And he searches after [d]every green thing.

9 "Will the [e]wild ox be willing to serve you?
Will he bed by your manger?
10 Can you bind the wild ox in the furrow with ropes?
Or will he plow the valleys behind you?
11 Will you trust him because his strength *is* great?
Or will you leave your labor to him?
12 Will you trust him to bring home your [4]grain,
And gather it to your threshing floor?

13 "The wings of the ostrich wave proudly,

27 [s] Ps. 104:13, 14; 107:35
28 [t] Job 36:27, 28; [Ps. 147:8; Jer. 14:22]
29 [u] [Job 37:10]; Ps. 147:16, 17
30 [v] [Job 37:10] [6] Lit. *imprisoned*
31 [w] Job 9:9; Amos 5:8 [7] Or *the Seven Stars*
32 [8] Lit. *Constellations* [9] Or *Arcturus*
33 [x] [Ps. 148:6]; Jer. 31:35, 36
36 [y] [Job 9:4; 32:8; Ps. 51:6; Eccl. 2:26; James 1:5] [1] Lit. *the inward parts*
39 [z] Ps. 104:21
41 [a] Ps. 147:9; [Matt. 6:26; Luke 12:24]

CHAPTER 39

1 [a] Deut. 14:5; 1 Sam. 24:2; Ps. 104:18 [b] Ps. 29:9
3 [1] Lit. *pangs*
5 [2] A species of wild donkey
6 [c] Job 24:5; Jer. 2:24; Hos. 8:9 [3] Lit. *salt land*
8 [d] Gen. 1:29
9 [e] Num. 23:22; Deut. 33:17; Ps. 22:21; 29:6; 92:10; Is. 34:7
12 [4] Lit. *seed*

38:31,32 Pleiades…Orion…Mazzaroth…Great Bear. Stellar constellations (cf. Job 9:9) are in view.

38:33 ordinances of the heavens. The laws and powers that regulate all heavenly bodies.

38:36 wisdom…understanding. This is at the heart of the real issue. The wisdom of God which created and sustains the universe is at work in Job's suffering also. See also 39:17.

38:39–39:30 God asked Job the humiliating questions about whether he could take care of the animal kingdom. Job must have been feeling less and less significant under the crushing indictment of such comparisons with God.

39:5 onager. Another kind of donkey.

But are her wings and pinions *like the* kindly stork's?
14 For she leaves her eggs on the ground,
And warms them in the dust;
15 She forgets that a foot may crush them,
Or that a wild beast may break them.
16 She [f]treats her young harshly, as though *they were* not hers;
Her labor is in vain, without [5]concern,
17 Because God deprived her of wisdom,
And did not [g]endow her with understanding.
18 When she lifts herself on high,
She scorns the horse and its rider.

19 "Have you given the horse strength?
Have you clothed his neck with [6]thunder?
20 Can you [7]frighten him like a locust?
His majestic snorting strikes terror.
21 He paws in the valley, and rejoices in *his* strength;
[h]He gallops into the clash of arms.
22 He mocks at fear, and is not frightened;
Nor does he turn back from the sword.
23 The quiver rattles against him,
The glittering spear and javelin.
24 He devours the distance with fierceness and rage;
Nor does he come to a halt because the trumpet *has* sounded.
25 At *the blast of* the trumpet he says, 'Aha!'
He smells the battle from afar,
The thunder of captains and shouting.

26 "Does the hawk fly by your wisdom,
And spread its wings toward the south?
27 Does the [i]eagle mount up at your command,
And [j]make its nest on high?
28 On the rock it dwells and resides,
On the crag of the rock and the stronghold.
29 From there it spies out the prey;
Its eyes observe from afar.
30 Its young ones suck up blood;
And [k]where the slain *are*, there it *is*."

40

1 Moreover the LORD [a]answered Job, and said:

2 "Shall [b]the one who contends with the Almighty correct *Him?*
He who [c]rebukes God, let him answer it."

Job's Response to God

3 Then Job answered the LORD and said:

4 "Behold, [d] I am vile;
What shall I answer You?
[e]I lay my hand over my mouth.
5 Once I have spoken, but I will not answer;
Yes, twice, but I will proceed no further."

God's Challenge to Job

6 [f]Then the LORD answered Job out of the whirlwind, and said:

7 "Now[g] [1]prepare yourself like a man;
[h]I will question you, and you shall answer Me:

8 "Would[i] you indeed [2]annul My judgment?
Would you condemn Me that you may be justified?
9 Have you an arm like God?
Or can you thunder with [j]a voice like His?

16 [f] Lam. 4:3 [5] Lit. *fear*
17 [g] Job 35:11
19 [6] Or *a mane*
20 [7] *make him spring*
21 [h] Jer. 8:6
27 [i] Prov. 30:18, 19 [j] Jer. 49:16; Obad. 4
30 [k] Matt. 24:28; Luke 17:37

CHAPTER 40
1 [a] Job 38:1
2 [b] Job 9:3; 10:2; 33:13 [c] Job 13:3; 23:4
4 [d] Ezra 9:6; Job 42:6 [e] Job 29:9; Ps. 39:9
6 [f] Job 38:1
7 [g] Job 38:3 [h] Job 42:4 [1] Lit. *gird up your loins*
8 [i] Job 16:11; 19:6; [Ps. 51:4; Rom. 3:4] [2] *nullify*
9 [j] Job 37:4; [Ps. 29:3, 4]

39:13-18 ostrich. The silly bird that leaves her eggs on the ground lacks sense. God has not given her wisdom. She is almost a picture of Job, who is a mixture of foolishness and strength (v. 18).

39:19-25 Here is a magnificent, vivid picture of the war horse.

40:2 God challenged Job to answer all the questions he had posed. God didn't need to know the answer, but Job needed to admit his weakness, inferiority, and inability to even try to figure out God's infinite mind. God's wisdom was so superior, His sovereign control of everything so complete, that this was all Job needed to know.

40:3-5 Job's first response to God was "I am guilty as charged. I will say no more." He knows he should not have found fault with the Almighty. He should not have insisted on his own understanding. He should not have thought God unjust. So he was reduced to silence at last.

40:6–41:34 As if the first was not enough, God's second interrogation of Job commenced along the very same lines, only focusing on two unique animals in God's creation: Behemoth (40:15-24) and Leviathan (41:1-34), two creatures powerful and fearful who embodied all that is overwhelming, uncontrollable, and terrorizing in this world. Man can't control them, but God can.

40:8-14 God unleashed another torrent of crushing rebukes to Job, in which He mocked Job's questionings of Him by telling the sufferer that if he really thought he knew what was best for him rather than God (v. 8), then he should take over being God! (vv. 9-14).

10 [k]Then adorn yourself *with* majesty
and splendor,
And array yourself with glory and
beauty.
11 Disperse the rage of your wrath;
Look on everyone *who is* proud,
and humble him.
12 Look on everyone *who is* [l]proud,
and bring him low;
Tread down the wicked in their
place.
13 Hide them in the dust together,
Bind their faces in hidden
darkness.
14 Then I will also confess to you
That your own right hand can save
you.

15 "Look now at the [3]behemoth, which
I made *along* with you;
He eats grass like an ox.
16 See now, his strength *is* in his hips,
And his power *is* in his stomach
muscles.
17 He moves his tail like a cedar;
The sinews of his thighs are tightly
knit.
18 His bones *are like* beams of
bronze,
His ribs like bars of iron.
19 He *is* the first of the [m]ways of God;
Only He who made him can bring
near His sword.
20 Surely the mountains [n]yield food
for him,
And all the beasts of the field play
there.
21 He lies under the lotus trees,
In a covert of reeds and marsh.
22 The lotus trees cover him *with* their
shade;
The willows by the brook surround
him.
23 Indeed the river may rage,
Yet he is not disturbed;
He is confident, though the Jordan
gushes into his mouth,
24 *Though* he takes it in his eyes,
Or one pierces *his* nose with a
snare.

41 "Can you draw out [a]Leviathan[1]
with a hook,
Or *snare* his tongue with a line
which you lower?
2 Can you [b]put a reed through his
nose,
Or pierce his jaw with a [2]hook?
3 Will he make many supplications
to you?
Will he speak softly to you?
4 Will he make a covenant with
you?
Will you take him as a servant
forever?
5 Will you play with him as *with* a
bird,
Or will you leash him for your
maidens?
6 Will *your* companions [3]make a
banquet of him?
Will they apportion him among the
merchants?
7 Can you fill his skin with
harpoons,
Or his head with fishing spears?
8 Lay your hand on him;
Remember the battle—
Never do it again!
9 Indeed, *any* hope of *overcoming* him
is false;
Shall *one not* be overwhelmed at
the sight of him?
10 No one *is so* fierce that he would
dare stir him up.
Who then is able to stand against
Me?

10 [k]Ps. 93:1; 104:1
12 [l]1 Sam. 2:7; [Is. 2:12; 13:11]; Dan. 4:37
15 [3]A large animal, exact identity unknown
19 [m]Job 26:14
20 [n]Ps. 104:14

CHAPTER 41
1 [a]Ps. 74:14; 104:26; Is. 27:1 [1]A large sea creature, exact identity unknown
2 [b]2 Kin. 19:38; Is. 37:29 [2]thorn
6 [3]Or *bargain over him*

40:15-24 behemoth. While this is a generic term used commonly in the OT for large cattle or land animals, the description in this passage suggests an extraordinary creature. The hippopotamus has been suggested by the details in the passage (vv. 19-24). However, the short tail of a hippo is hardly consistent with v. 17, where tail could be translated "trunk." It could refer to an elephant, who could be considered "first" or chief of God's creatures whom only He can control (v. 19). Some believe God is describing His most impressive creation of land animals, the dinosaur species, which fit all the characteristics.

40:23 God was not saying this creature lived in the Jordan River, but rather, recognizing that the Jordan was familiar to Job, used it to illustrate how much water this beast could ingest. He could swallow the Jordan! It was a word used to refer to something of enormous size and threatening power.

41:1 Leviathan. This term appears in 4 other OT texts (Job 3:8; Pss. 74:14; 104:26; Is. 27:1). In each case Leviathan refers to some mighty creature who can overwhelm man but who is no match for God. Since this creature lives in the sea among ships (Ps. 104:26), some form of sea monster, possibly an ancient dinosaur, is in view. Some feel it was a crocodile, which had scaly hide (v. 15), terrible teeth (v. 14) and speed in the water (v. 32). But crocodiles are not sea creatures, and clearly this one was (v. 31). Some have thought it was a killer whale or a Great White Shark, because he is the ultimate killer beast over all other proud beasts (v. 34). It could also have been some sea-going dinosaur.

41:4 Will he make a covenant with you? "Will this monstrous creature need, for any reason, to come to terms with you, Job? Are you able to control him?" God asked.

41:10 Who then is able to stand against Me? This was the essential question being asked in both the Behemoth and Leviathan passages. God created these awesome creatures, and His might is far greater than theirs. If Job couldn't stand against them, what was he doing contending with God? He would be better off to fight a dinosaur or a killer shark.

11 [c]Who has preceded Me, that I
should pay *him*?
[d]Everything under heaven is Mine.

12 "I will not [4]conceal his limbs,
His mighty power, or his graceful
proportions.
13 Who can [5]remove his outer coat?
Who can approach *him* with a
double bridle?
14 Who can open the doors of his
face,
With his terrible teeth all around?
15 *His* rows of [6]scales are *his* pride,
Shut up tightly *as with* a seal;
16 One is so near another
That no air can come between
them;
17 They are joined one to another,
They stick together and cannot be
parted.
18 His sneezings flash forth light,
And his eyes *are* like the eyelids of
the morning.
19 Out of his mouth go burning
lights;
Sparks of fire shoot out.
20 Smoke goes out of his nostrils,
As *from* a boiling pot and burning
rushes.
21 His breath kindles coals,
And a flame goes out of his mouth.
22 Strength dwells in his neck,
And [7]sorrow dances before him.
23 The folds of his flesh are joined
together;
They are firm on him and cannot
be moved.
24 His heart is as hard as stone,
Even as hard as the lower *millstone.*
25 When he raises himself up, the
mighty are afraid;
Because of his crashings they [8]are
beside themselves.
26 *Though* the sword reaches him, it
cannot avail;
Nor does spear, dart, or javelin.
27 He regards iron as straw,
And bronze as rotten wood.
28 The arrow cannot make him flee;
Slingstones become like stubble to
him.
29 Darts are regarded as straw;
He laughs at the threat of javelins.
30 His undersides *are* like sharp
potsherds;
He spreads pointed *marks* in the
mire.
31 He makes the deep boil like a pot;
He makes the sea like a pot of
ointment.
32 He leaves a shining wake behind
him;
One would think the deep had
white hair.
33 On earth there is nothing like him,
Which is made without fear.
34 He beholds every high *thing;*
He *is* king over all the children of
pride."

Job's Repentance and Restoration

42 Then Job answered the LORD and
said:

2 "I know that You [a]can do
everything,
And that no purpose *of Yours* can
be withheld from You.
3 *You asked,* [b]'Who *is* this who hides
counsel without knowledge?'
Therefore I have uttered what I did
not understand,
[c]Things too wonderful for me,
which I did not know.
4 Listen, please, and let me speak;
You said, [d]'I will question you, and
you shall answer Me.'
5 "I have [e]heard of You by the hearing
of the ear,
But now my eye sees You.

11 [c][Rom. 11:35] [d]Ex. 19:5; [Deut. 10:14; Job 9:5-10; 26:6-14]; Ps. 24:1; 50:12; 1 Cor. 10:26, 28
12 [4]Lit. *keep silent about*
13 [5]Lit. *take off the face of his garment*
15 [6]Lit. *shields*
22 [7]*despair*
25 [8]*Or purify themselves*

CHAPTER 42
2 [a]Gen. 18:14; [Matt. 19:26; Mark 10:27; 14:36; Luke 18:27]
3 [b]Job 38:2 [c]Ps. 40:5; 131:1; 139:6
4 [d]Job 38:3; 40:7
5 [e]Job 26:14; [Rom. 10:17]

41:11 God did not need to buy anything; He already owned all things. Paul quoted this in Rom. 11:35.

42:1-6 Job's confession and repentance took place finally. He still did not know why he suffered so profoundly, but he was done complaining, questioning, and challenging God's wisdom and justice. He was reduced to such utter humility, crushed beneath the weight of God's greatness, that all he could do was repent for his insolence. Without answers to all of his questions, Job quietly bowed in humble submission before his Creator and admitted that God was sovereign (cf. Is. 14:24; 46:8-11). Most importantly for the message of the book, Job was still diseased and without his children and possessions, and God had not changed anything (except for the humbling of the heart of his servant). Satan had been proven completely wrong in the charges he brought against Job and in thinking he could destroy true saving faith; Job's companions were completely wrong in the charges they brought against him; but most critically, Job himself was completely wrong in the charges he had raised against God. He expressed his own sorrowful regret that he had not just accepted God's will without such ignorant complaints and questions.

42:3,4 ***You asked...You said.*** Job twice alluded to statements God had made in His interrogation of Job. The first allusion "Who *is* this who hides counsel without knowledge?" (38:2) indicted Job's pride and presumption regarding God's counsel. The second, "I will question you, and you shall answer Me" (38:3;40:7) expressed God's judicial authority to demand answers from His own accuser, Job. The two quotes manifested that Job understood the divine rebuke.

42:5 have heard...now my eye sees You. At last, Job said he understood God whom he had seen with the eyes of faith. He had never so well grasped the greatness, majesty, sovereignty, and independence of God as he did at that moment.

6 Therefore I [f]abhor[1] *myself,*
And repent in dust and ashes."

7 And so it was, after the LORD had spoken these words to Job, that the LORD said
to Eliphaz the Temanite, "My wrath is
aroused against you and your two friends,
for you have not spoken of Me *what is*
right, as My servant Job *has.* 8 Now therefore, take for yourselves [g]seven bulls and
seven rams, [h]go to My servant Job, and
offer up for yourselves a burnt offering;
and My servant Job shall [i]pray for you. For
I will accept [2]him, lest I deal with you *ac-*
cording to your folly; because you have not
spoken of Me *what is* right, as My servant
Job *has.*"

9 So Eliphaz the Temanite and Bildad the
Shuhite *and* Zophar the Naamathite went
and did as the LORD commanded them; for
the LORD had [3]accepted Job. 10 [j]And the
LORD [4]restored Job's losses when he
prayed for his friends. Indeed the LORD
gave Job [k]twice as much as he had before.
11 Then [l]all his brothers, all his sisters, and
all those who had been his acquaintances
before, came to him and ate food with him
in his house; and they consoled him and
comforted him for all the adversity that the
LORD had brought upon him. Each one
gave him a piece of silver and each a ring
of gold.

12 Now the LORD blessed [m]the latter
days of Job more than his beginning; for
he had [n]fourteen thousand sheep, six
thousand camels, one thousand yoke of
oxen, and one thousand female donkeys.
13 [o]He also had seven sons and three
daughters. 14 And he called the name of
the first [5]Jemimah, the name of the second [6]Keziah, and the name of the third
[7]Keren-Happuch. 15 In all the land were
found no women *so* beautiful as the
daughters of Job; and their father gave
them an inheritance among their brothers.

16 After this Job [p]lived one hundred and
forty years, and saw his children and
grandchildren *for* four generations. 17 So
Job died, old and [q]full of days.

6 [f] Ezra 9:6; Job 40:4 [1] *despise*
8 [g] Num. 23:1 [h] [Matt. 5:24] [i] Gen. 20:17; [James 5:15, 16; 1 John 5:16] [2] Lit. *his face*
9 [3] Lit. *lifted up the face of Job*
10 [j] Deut. 30:3; Ps. 14:7; 85:1-3; 126:1 [k] Is. 40:2 [4] Lit. *turned the captivity of Job,* what was captured from Job
11 [l] Job 19:13
12 [m] Job 1:10; 8:7; James 5:11 [n] Job 1:3
13 [o] Job 1:2
14 [5] Lit. *Handsome as the Day* [6] *Cassia,* a fragrance [7] Lit. *The Horn of Color* or *The Colorful Ray*
16 [p] Job 5:26; Prov. 3:16
17 [q] Gen. 15:15; 25:8; Job 5:26

42:6 repent in dust and ashes. All that was left to do was repent! The ashes upon which the broken man sat had not changed; but the heart of God's suffering servant had. Job did not need to repent of some sins which Satan or his accusers had raised. But Job had exercised presumption and allegations of unfairness against his Lord and hated himself for this in a way that called for brokenness and contrition.

42:7-17 The text goes back to prose, from the poetry begun in 3:1.

42:7,8 you have not spoken of Me *what is* right. God directly vindicated Job by saying that Job had spoken right about God in rejecting the error of his friends. They are then rebuked for those misrepresentations of insensitivity and arrogance. This does not mean that everything they said was incorrect, but they had made wrong statements about the character and works of God, and also had raised erroneous allegations against Job.

42:8 seven bulls and seven rams. This was the number of sacrifices specified in Num 23:1 by Balaam the prophet, so perhaps it was a traditional kind of burnt offering for sin.

42:8,9 As God had been gracious to Job, so He was to Job's friends, by means of sacrifice and prayer. Here the book points to the need for a sacrifice for sin, fulfilled in the Lord Jesus Christ who gave Himself as an offering for sins and ever lives to intercede (cf. 1 Tim. 2:5). Even before the Levitical priesthood, family heads acted as priests, offering sacrifices and mediating through prayer.

42:13 seven sons…three daughters. While the animals are double the number of Job 1:3, why are not the children? It is obvious that Job still had 7 sons and 3 daughters waiting for him in the presence of God (42:17).

42:14 These names are representative of the joys of restoration. Jemimah means "day light," Keziah means "sweet smelling," and Keren-Happuch describes a beautiful color ladies used to paint their eyelids.

42:15 gave them an inheritance. This was unusual in the East. By Jewish law, daughters only received an inheritance when there were no sons (Num. 27:8). Job had plenty for all.

42:17 So Job died, old and full of days. These concluding words take the reader back to where the account began (1:1). Job died in prosperity and his days were counted as a blessing. In the words of James (5:11), we have seen the outcome of the Lord's dealings, that the Lord is "very compassionate and merciful." But the "accuser of the brethren" (Rev. 12:10) is still "going to and fro on the earth" (1 Pet. 5:8) and God's servants are still learning to trust in the all-wise, all-powerful Judge of the universe for what they cannot understand.

The Book of

PSALMS

Title

The entire collection of Psalms is entitled "Praises" in the Hebrew text. Later, rabbis often designated it "The Book of Praises." The Septuagint (LXX), the Greek translation of the OT, labeled it "Psalms" (cf. "The book of Psalms" in the NT: Luke 20:42; Acts 1:20). The Greek verb from which the noun "psalms" comes basically denotes the "plucking or twanging of strings," so that an association with musical accompaniment is implied. The English title derives from the Greek term and its background. The Psalms constituted Israel's ancient, God-breathed (2 Tim. 3:16) "hymnbook," which defined the proper spirit and content of worship.

There are 116 psalms that have superscriptions or "titles." The Hebrew text includes these titles with the verses themselves. When the titles are surveyed individually and studied as a general phenomenon, there are significant indications that they were appended to their respective psalms shortly after composition and that they contain reliable information (cf. Luke 20:42).

These titles convey various kinds of information such as authorship, dedication, historical occasion, liturgical assignment to a worship director, liturgical instructions (e.g., what kind of song it is, whether it is to have a musical accompaniment, and what tune to use), plus other technical instructions of uncertain meaning due to their great antiquity. One very tiny, attached Hebrew preposition shows up in the majority of the Psalm titles. It may convey different relationships, e.g., "of," "from," "by," "to," "for," "in reference to," "about." Sometimes it occurs more than once, even in short headings, usually supplying "of," or "by," person X…"to," or "for," person Y information. However, this little preposition most frequently indicates the authorship of a psalm, whether "of" David, the accomplished psalmist of Israel, or "by" Moses, Solomon, Asaph, or the sons of Korah.

Authorship and Date

From the divine perspective, the Psalter points to God as its author. Approaching authorship from the human side one can identify a collection of more than 7 composers. King David wrote at least 75 of the 150 psalms; the sons of Korah accounted for 10 (Pss. 42,44–49,84,85,87); and Asaph contributed 12 (Pss. 50,73–83). Other penmen included Solomon (Pss. 72,127), Moses (Ps. 90), Heman (Ps. 88), and Ethan (Ps. 89). The remaining 48 psalms remain anonymous in their authorship, although Ezra is thought to be the author of some. The time range of the Psalms extends from Moses, ca. 1410 B.C. (Ps. 90), to the late sixth or early fifth century B.C. post-Exilic period (Ps. 126), which spans about 900 years of Jewish history.

Background and Setting

The backdrop for the Psalms is twofold: 1) the acts of God in creation and history, and 2) the history of Israel. Historically, the psalms range in time from the origin of life to the post-Exilic joys of the Jews liberated from Babylon. Thematically, the psalms cover a wide spectrum of topics, ranging from heavenly worship to earthly war. The collected psalms comprise the largest book in the Bible and the most frequently quoted OT book in the NT. Psalm 117 represents the middle chapter (out of 1,189) in the Bible. Psalm 119 is the largest chapter in the entire Bible. Through the ages, the psalms have retained their original primary purpose, i.e., to engender the proper praise and worship of God.

Historical and Theological Themes

The basic theme of Psalms is living real life in the real world, where two dimensions operate simultaneously: 1) a horizontal or temporal reality, and 2) a vertical or transcendent reality. Without denying the pain of the earthly dimension, the people of God are to live joyfully and dependently on the Person and promises standing behind the heavenly/eternal dimension. All cycles of human troubles and triumphs provide occasions for expressing human complaints, confidence, prayers, or praise, to Israel's sovereign Lord.

In view of this, Psalms presents a broad array of theology, practically couched in day-to-day reality. The sinfulness of man is documented concretely, not only through the behavioral patterns of the wicked, but also by the periodic stumblings of believers. The sovereignty of God is everywhere recognized, but not at the expense of genuine human responsibility. Life often seems to be out of control, and yet all events and situations are understood in the light of divine providence as being right on course according to God's timetable. Assuring glimpses of a future "God's day" bolsters the call for perseverance to the end. This book of praise manifests a very practical theology.

A commonly misunderstood phenomenon in Psalms is the association that often develops between the "one" (the psalmist) and the "many" (the theocratic people). Virtually all of the cases of this occur in the psalms of King David. There was an inseparable relationship between the mediatorial ruler and his people; as life went for the king, so it went for the people. Furthermore, at times this union accounted for the psalmist's apparent connection with Christ in the messianic psalms (or messianic portions of certain psalms). The so-called imprecatory (curse pronouncing) psalms may be better understood with this perspective. As God's mediatorial representative on earth, David prayed for judgment on his enemies, since these enemies were not only hurting him, but were primarily hurting God's people. Ultimately, they challenged the King of Kings, the God of Israel.

Interpretive Challenges

It is helpful to recognize certain recurring genres or literary types in the Psalter. Some of the most obvious are: 1) the wisdom type with instructions for right living; 2) lamentation patterns which deal with the pangs of life (usually arising from enemies without); 3) penitential psalms (mostly dealing with the "enemy" within, i.e., sin); 4) kingship emphases (universal or mediatorial; theocratic and/or messianic rule); and 5) thanksgiving psalms. A combination of style and subject matter help to identify such types when they appear.

The comprehensive literary characteristic of the psalms is that all of them are poetry par excellence. Unlike most English poetry, which is based on rhyme and meter, Hebrew poetry is essentially characterized by logical parallelisms. Some of the most important kinds of parallelisms are: 1) synonymous (the thought of the first line is restated with similar concepts in the second line, e.g., Ps. 2:1); 2) antithetic (the thought of the second line is contrasted with the first, e.g., Ps. 1:6); 3) climactic (the second and any subsequent lines pick up a crucial word, phrase, or concept and advance it in a stair-step fashion, e.g., Ps. 29:1,2); and 4) chiastic or introverted (the logical units are developed in an A...B...B'...A'...pattern, e.g., Ps. 1:2).

On a larger scale, some psalms in their development from the first to the last verse employ an acrostic or alphabetical arrangement. Psalms 9,10,25,34,37,111,112,119, and 145 are recognized as either complete or incomplete acrostics. In the Hebrew text, the first letter of the first word of every verse begins with a different Hebrew consonant, which advances in alphabetical order until the 22 consonants are exhausted. Such a literary vehicle undoubtedly aided in the memorization of the content and served to indicate that its particular subject matter had been covered from "A to Z." Psalm 119 stands out as the most complete example of this device, since the first letter of each of its 22, 8-verse stanzas moves completely through the Hebrew alphabet.

Outline

The 150 canonical psalms were organized quite early into 5 "books." Each of these books ends with a doxology (Pss. 41:13; 72:18-20; 89:52; 106:48; 150:6). Jewish tradition appealed to the number 5 and alleged that these divisions echoed the Pentateuch, i.e., the 5 books of Moses. It is true that there are clusters of psalms, such as 1) those drawn together by an association with an individual or group (e.g., "The sons of Korah," Pss. 42–49; Asaph, Pss. 73–83), 2) those dedicated to a particular function (e.g., "Songs of ascents," Pss. 120–134), or 3) those devoted explicitly to praise worship (Pss. 146–150). But no one configuration key unlocks the "mystery" as to the organizing theme of this 5-book arrangement. Thus, there is no identifiable thematic structure to the entire collection of psalms. A brief introduction and outline for each psalm will be provided with the study notes for individual psalms.

Book One: Psalms 1–41

PSALM 1

The Way of the Righteous and the End of the Ungodly

Blessed [a]*is* the man
Who walks not in the counsel of the [1]ungodly,
Nor stands in the path of sinners,
[b]Nor sits in the seat of the scornful;
2 But [c]his delight *is* in the law of the LORD,
[d]And in His law he [2]meditates day and night.
3 He shall be like a tree
[e]Planted by the [3]rivers of water,
That brings forth its fruit in its season,
Whose leaf also shall not wither;
And whatever he does shall [f]prosper.

4 The ungodly *are* not so,
But *are* [g]like the chaff which the wind drives away.
5 Therefore the ungodly shall not stand in the judgment,
Nor sinners in the congregation of the righteous.

6 For [h]the LORD knows the way of the righteous,
But the way of the ungodly shall perish.

PSALM 1

1 [a] Prov. 4:14 [b] Ps. 26:4, 5; Jer. 15:17 [1] *wicked*
2 [c] Ps. 119:14, 16, 35 [d] [Josh. 1:8] [2] *ponders* by talking to himself
3 [e] [Ps. 92:12-14]; Jer. 17:8; Ezek. 19:10 [3] *channels* [f] Gen. 39:2, 3, 23; Ps. 128:2
4 [g] Job 21:18; Ps. 35:5; Is. 17:13
6 [h] Ps. 37:18; [Nah. 1:7; John 10:14; 2 Tim. 2:19]

1:1-6 This wisdom psalm basically functions as an introduction to the entire book of Psalms. Its theme is as big as the whole Bible because it tells of people, paths, and ultimate destinations (for a significant parallel see Jer. 17:5-8). By two cycles of contrast, Ps. 1 separates all people into their respective spiritual categories:

- I. By observation, all people are separated ethically (1:1-4)
  - A. A picture of the godly (1:1-3)
  - B. A picture of the ungodly (1:4)
- II. By outcome, all people are separated judicially (1:5,6)
  - A. The failure of ungodly people (1:5)
  - B. The fruition of lifestyles (1:6)
    - 1. Recognition of the godly (1:6a)
    - 2. Ruination of the ungodly (1:6b)

1:1 Blessed. From the perspective of the individual, this is a deep-seated joy and contentment in God; from the perspective of the believing community, it refers to redemptive favor (cf. the blessings and cursings of Deut. 27:11–28:6). **walks not...Nor stands...Nor sits.** The "beatitude" man (cf. Matt. 5:3-11) is first described as one who avoids such associations as these which exemplify sin's sequential downward drag.

1:2 his delight...in the law. Switching to a positive description, the spiritually "happy" man is characterized by the consistent contemplation and internalization of God's Word for ethical direction and obedience.

1:3 like a tree. Because of the mostly arid terrain of Israel, a lush tree served as a fitting symbol of blessing in the OT. **Planted.** Lit. "transplanted." Trees do not plant themselves; neither do sinful people transport themselves into God's kingdom. Salvation is His marvelous work of grace (cf. Is. 61:3; Matt. 15:13). Yet, there is genuine responsibility in appropriating the abundant resources of God (cf. Jer. 17:8), which lead to eventual productivity.

1:4 The ungodly *are* not so. This is an abrupt contrast, lit. "Not so the wicked!" **chaff.** A frequent OT word picture from harvest time for what is unsubstantial, without value, and worthy only to be discarded.

1:5 Therefore...not stand. "Therefore" introduces the strong conclusion that the ungodly will not be approved by God's judgment.

1:6 the LORD knows. This is far more than recognition; the Lord "knows" everything. In this context, the reference is to personal intimacy and involvement with His righteous ones (contra. Matt. 7:23; cf. 2 Tim. 2:19). **the way of.** The repetition of this phrase picks up on the "path" imagery so characteristic of this psalm. It refers to one's total course of life, i.e., lifestyle. Here these two courses arrive at the ways of life and death, as in Deut. 30:19; Jer. 21:8; cf. Matt. 7:13,14. **shall perish.** One day the wicked person's way will end in ruin; a new order is coming and it will be a righteous order. So Ps. 1 begins with the "blessed" and ends with those who "perish" (cf. Pss. 9:5,6; 112:10).

Types of Psalms

Type	Psalms	Act of Worship
Individual and Communal Lament	3–7; 12; 13; 22; 25–28; 35; 38–40; 42–44; 51; 54–57; 59–61; 63; 64; 69–71; 74; 79; 80; 83; 85; 86; 88; 90; 102; 109; 120; 123; 130; 140–143	Express need for God's deliverance
Thanksgiving	8; 18; 19; 29; 30; 32–34; 36; 40; 41; 66; 103–106; 111; 113; 116; 117; 124; 129; 135; 136; 138; 139; 146–148; 150	Make aware of God's blessings Express thanks
Enthronement	47; 93; 96–99	Describe God's sovereign rule
Pilgrimage	43; 46; 48; 76; 84; 87; 120–134	Establish a mood of worship
Royal	2; 18; 20; 21; 45; 72; 89; 101; 110; 132; 144	Portray Christ the sovereign ruler
Wisdom	1; 37; 119	Instruct as to God's will
Imprecatory	7; 35; 40; 55; 58; 59; 69; 79; 109; 137; 139; 144	Invoke God's wrath and judgment against his enemies

PSALM 2

The Messiah's Triumph and Kingdom

Why [a]do the [1]nations [2]rage,
And the people plot a [3]vain thing?
2 The kings of the earth set themselves,
And the [b]rulers take counsel
together,
Against the LORD and against His
[c]Anointed,[4] *saying,*
3 "Let [d]us break Their bonds in pieces
And cast away Their cords from us."

4 He who sits in the heavens [e]shall
laugh;
The LORD shall hold them in derision.
5 Then He shall speak to them in His
wrath,
And distress them in His deep
displeasure:
6 "Yet I have [5]set My King
[6]On My holy hill of Zion."

7 "I will declare the [7]decree:
The LORD has said to Me,
[f]'You *are* My Son,
Today I have begotten You.
8 Ask of Me, and I will give *You*
The nations *for* Your inheritance,
And the ends of the earth *for* Your
possession.
9 [g]You shall [8]break them with a rod of
iron;
You shall dash them to pieces like a
potter's vessel.' "

10 Now therefore, be wise, O kings;
Be instructed, you judges of the earth.
11 Serve the LORD with fear,
And rejoice with trembling.
12 [9]Kiss the Son, lest [1]He be angry,
And you perish *in* the way,
When [h]His wrath is kindled but a
little.
[i]Blessed *are* all those who put their
trust in Him.

PSALM 2

1 [a] Acts 4:25,26 [1] *Gentiles* [2] *throng tumultuously* [3] *worthless or empty* **2** [b] [Matt. 12:14; 26:3, 4, 59-66; 27:1, 2; Mark 3:6; 11:18] [c] [John 1:41] [4] Christ, Commissioned One, Heb. *Messiah* **3** [d] Luke 19:14 **4** [e] Ps. 37:13 **6** [5] Lit. *installed* [6] Lit. *Upon Zion, the hill of My holiness* **7** [f] Matt. 3:17; Mark 1:1, 11; Luke 3:22; John 1:18; Acts 13:33; [Heb. 1:5; 5:5] [7] Or *decree of the LORD: He said to Me* **9** [g] Ps. 89:23; 110:5, 6; [Rev. 2:26, 27; 12:5; 19:15] [8] So with MT, Tg.; LXX, Syr., Vg. *rule* (cf. Rev. 2:27) **12** [h] [Rev. 6:16, 17] [i] [Ps. 5:11; 34:22] [9] LXX, Vg. *Embrace discipline;* Tg. *Receive instruction* [1] LXX *the LORD*

PSALM 3

title [a] 2 Sam. 15:13-17

PSALM 3

The LORD Helps His Troubled People

A Psalm of David [a]when he fled from
Absalom his son.

LORD, how they have increased who
trouble me!
Many *are* they who rise up against
me.
2 Many *are* they who say of me,
"*There is* no help for him in God."
Selah

2:1-12 Sometimes Ps. 2 is said to share with Ps. 1 in the role of introducing the Psalter (cf. "Blessed" in 1:1 and 2:12). Also, it seems that, while the function of Ps. 1 is to disclose the two different "ways" for individuals, Ps. 2 follows up with its application to nations. This psalm is normally termed "royal" and has had a long history of messianic interpretation. Although it has no title, it seems to bear the imprint of David's hand. As such, it fluidly moves from the lesser David through the Davidic dynasty to the Greater David—Jesus Christ. Psalm 2 progressively shines its poetic spotlight on 4 vivid scenes relating to the mutiny of mankind against God:

I. Scene One:
Human Rebellion (2:1-3)
II. Scene Two:
Divine Reaction (2:4-6)
III. Scene Three:
Divine Rule (2:7-9)
IV. Scene Four:
Human Responsibility (2:10-12)

2:1 plot a vain thing. This is the irony of man's depravity—devising, conspiring, and scheming emptiness (cf. Ps. 38:12; Prov. 24:2; Is. 59:3,13).

2:2 against...against. The nations and peoples, led by their kings and rulers (v. 1), direct their hostility toward the Lord and His anointed one. The consecrated and commissioned mediatorial representative referred to David in a near sense and Messiah, i.e., Christ, in the ultimate sense (cf. Acts 4:25,26).

2:3 Their bonds...Their cords. Mutinous mankind, instead of understanding that these are God's love-bonds (Hos. 11:4), view them as yoke-bonds (Jer. 5:5).

2:5 Then. After mocking them with the laughter of divine contempt, God speaks and acts from His perfectly balanced anger.

2:6 I have set. Their puny challenge (v. 3) is answered by this powerful pronouncement. It's as good as done: His king will be enthroned on Jerusalem's most prominent hill.

2:7 I will declare the decree. The installed mediator now recites the Lord's previously issued enthronement ordinance. **You *are* My Son.** This recalls 2 Sam. 7:8-16 as the basis for the Davidic king. It is also the only OT reference to the Father/Son relationship in the Trinity, a relationship planned in eternity past and realized in the incarnation, thus a major part of the NT. **Today I have begotten You.** This expresses the privileges of relationship, with its prophetic application to the Son—Messiah. This verse is quoted in the NT with reference to the birth of Jesus (Heb. 1:5,6) and also to His resurrection (Acts 13:33,34) as the ultimate fulfillments.

2:9 You shall...You shall. The supreme sovereignty of "the king of kings" is pictured in its subjugating might. The shepherd's "rod" and the king's "scepter" are the same word in the original. Shepherding and kingly imagery often merged in ancient Near Eastern thought (cf. Mic. 7:14).

2:10-12 The tone of these verses is surprising. Instead of immediate judgment, the Lord and His Anointed mercifully provide an opportunity for repentance. Five commands place responsibility on mutinous mankind.

2:12 Kiss the Son. This symbolic act would indicate allegiance and submission (cf. 1 Sam. 10:1; 1 Kin. 19:18). The word for "Son" here is not the Heb. word for "son" that was used in v. 7, but rather its Aram. counterpart (cf. Dan. 7:13), which is a term that would especially be suitable for these commands being addressed to "nations" (v. 1). **perish *in* the way.** These words pick up the major burden of Ps. 1.

3:1-8 This psalm intermingles both lament and confidence. In its sweeping scope, it becomes a pattern for praise, peace, and prayer amidst pressure. As it unfolds through 3 interrelated historical phenomena, David shares his theological "secret" of having assurance in the face of adversity.

3 But You, O LORD, *are* [b]a shield [1]for me,
My glory and [c]the One who lifts up
my head.
4 I cried to the LORD with my voice,
And [d]He heard me from His [e]holy
hill. Selah

5 [f]I lay down and slept;
I awoke, for the LORD sustained me.
6 [g]I will not be afraid of ten thousands
of people
Who have set *themselves* against me
all around.

7 Arise, O LORD;
Save me, O my God!
[h]For You have struck all my enemies
on the cheekbone;
You have broken the teeth of the
ungodly.
8 [i]Salvation *belongs* to the LORD.
Your blessing *is* upon Your people.
Selah

3 [b]Ps. 5:12; 28:7 [c]Ps. 9:13; 27:6 [1]Lit. *around*
4 [d]Ps. 4:3; 34:4 [e]Ps. 2:6; 15:1; 43:3
5 [f]Lev. 26:6; Ps. 4:8; Prov. 3:24
6 [g]Ps. 23:4; 27:3
7 [h]Job 16:10
8 [i]Ps. 28:8; 35:3; [Is. 43:11]

PSALM 4
title [1]*Choir Director*

PSALM 4

The Safety of the Faithful

To the [1]Chief Musician. With stringed instruments. A Psalm of David.

1 Hear me when I call, O God of my
righteousness!
You have relieved me in *my* distress;

I. The Psalmist's Predicament (3:1,2)
II. The Psalmist's Peace (3:3-6)
III. The Palmist's Prayer (3:7,8)

3:Title The first of 73 psalms attributed to David by superscription. Further information connects its occasion with the Absalom episode (2 Sam. 15–18), although many of its features are more descriptive of persecution in general.

3:1,2 increased...Many...Many. The psalmist begins on a low note with his multiplied miseries.

3:2,3 no help for him...But You...a shield for me. There is a strong contrast between the allegation and the psalmist's assurance. David's attitude and outlook embraces the theology that Paul summarized in Rom. 8:31. Psalm 3 also introduces Divine Warrior language (cf. Ex. 15 as a background).

3:5 I lay down and slept. Since God is known for His sustaining protection, David could relax in the most trying of circumstances.

3:7 Arise, O LORD. This is a battle cry for God to engage the enemy and defend His soldiers (cf. Num. 10:35; Ps. 68:1).

3:8 Salvation *belongs* to the LORD. This is a broad-sweeping, all-inclusive deliverance, whether in the temporal or eternal realm.

4:1-8 There are certain similarities between Pss. 3 and 4. For example, the former is sometimes labeled a morning psalm (cf. 3:5), while the latter has been called an evening psalm (cf. 4:8). In both, David is besieged with suffering, injustice, and oppression. Additionally, Ps. 4 also exhibits the changing attitudes of the worshiper in his most difficult circumstances. David's movement will be from anxiety to assurance, as he travels down the road of prayer and trust in God. At the end of yet another day of pressure, pain, and persecution, David engages in 3 conversations which ultimately lead to a point of blessed relaxation:

I. Praying to God for Preservation (4:1)
II. Reasoning with His enemies about Repentance (4:2-5)
III. Praising God for True Perspective (4:6-8)

4:Title Psalm 4 introduces the first of 55 assignments to the master, director, or chief overseer of worship services in its title. Further instruction is given in the direction "with stringed instruments." The chief musician, therefore, was to lead the great choir and the string portion of the orchestra in this celebration of worship.

4:1 O God of my righteousness. The ultimate basis for divine intervention resides in God, not in the psalmist. On union with God's righteousness based on His mercy, see Jer. 23:6 (cf. 1 Cor. 1:30). **distress.** This is an important word for trying circumstances in the psalms. It pictures the psalmist's plight as being in straits, i.e., painfully restricted. Here his testimony to God's historical salvation, "you have relieved me," conveys the picture that his Lord had provided space or room for him.

Historical Background to Psalms by David

Psalm	Historical Background	OT Text
Ps. 3	when David fled from Absalom his son	2 Sam. 15:13-17
Ps. 7	concerning the words of Cush a Benjamite	2 Sam. 16:5; 19:16
Ps. 18	the day the Lord delivered David from his enemies/Saul	2 Sam. 22:1-51
Ps. 30	at the dedication of the house of David	2 Sam. 5:11,12; 6:17
Ps. 34	when David pretended madness before Abimelech	1 Sam. 21:10-15
Ps. 51	when Nathan confronted David over sin with Bathsheba	2 Sam. 12:1-14
Ps. 52	when Doeg the Edomite warned Saul about David	1 Sam. 22:9,10
Ps. 54	when the Ziphites warned Saul about David	1 Sam. 23:19
Ps. 56	when the Philistines captured David in Gath	1 Sam. 21:10,11
Ps. 57	when David fled from Saul into the cave	1 Sam. 22:1; 24:3
Ps. 59	when Saul sent men to watch the house in order to kill David	1 Sam. 19:11
Ps. 60	when David fought against Mesopotamia and Syria	2 Sam. 8:3,13
Ps. 63	when David was in the wilderness of Judea	1 Sam. 23:14; or 2 Sam. 15:23-28
Ps. 142	when David was in a cave	1 Sam. 22:1; 24:3

[2]Have mercy on me, and hear my
prayer.

2 How long, O you sons of men,
Will you turn my glory to shame?
How long will you love
worthlessness
And seek falsehood? Selah
3 But know that [a]the LORD has [3]set
apart for Himself him who is
godly;
The LORD will hear when I call to
Him.

4 [b]Be[4] angry, and do not sin.
[c]Meditate within your heart on your
bed, and be still. Selah
5 Offer [d]the sacrifices of
righteousness,
And [e]put your trust in the LORD.

6 *There are* many who say,
"Who will show us *any* good?"
[f]LORD, lift up the light of Your
countenance upon us.
7 You have put [g]gladness in my
heart,
More than in the season that their
grain and wine
increased.
8 [h]I will both lie down in peace, and
sleep;
[i]For You alone, O LORD, make me
dwell in safety.

1 [2] *Be gracious to me*
3 [a] [2 Tim. 2:19]
[3] Many Heb. mss., LXX, Tg., Vg. *made wonderful*
4 [b] [Ps. 119:11; Eph. 4:26] [c] Ps. 77:6 [4] Lit. *Tremble* or *Be agitated*
5 [d] Deut. 33:19; Ps. 51:19 [e] Ps. 37:3, 5; 62:8
6 [f] Num. 6:26; Ps. 80:3, 7, 19
7 [g] Ps. 97:11, 12; Is. 9:3; Acts 14:17
8 [h] Job 11:19; Ps. 3:5 [i] [Lev. 25:18]; Deut. 12:10

PSALM 5
title [1] Heb. *nehiloth*
1 [a] Ps. 4:1 [2] Lit. *groaning*
3 [b] Ps. 55:17; 88:13
4 [3] Lit. *sojourn*
5 [c] [Hab. 1:13] [d] Ps. 1:5
6 [e] Ps. 55:23
7 [4] Lit. *the temple of Your holiness*
8 [f] Ps. 25:4, 5; 27:11; 31:3

PSALM 5

A Prayer for Guidance

To the Chief Musician. With [1]flutes.
A Psalm of David.

Give [a]ear to my words, O LORD,
Consider my [2]meditation.
2 Give heed to the voice of my cry,
My King and my God,
For to You I will pray.
3 My voice You shall hear in the
morning, O LORD;
[b]In the morning I will direct *it* to You,
And I will look up.

4 For You *are* not a God who takes
pleasure in wickedness,
Nor shall evil [3]dwell with You.
5 The [c]boastful shall not [d]stand in Your
sight;
You hate all workers of iniquity.
6 You shall destroy those who speak
falsehood;
The LORD abhors the [e]bloodthirsty
and deceitful man.

7 But as for me, I will come into Your
house in the multitude of
Your mercy;
In fear of You I will worship toward
[4]Your holy temple.
8 [f]Lead me, O LORD, in Your
righteousness because of my
enemies;

4:2,3 God's agenda for David (v. 3) is radically contrasted with that of his enemies (v. 2). The term for "godly" or "pious" in the OT is above all else indicating a person blessed by God's grace.

4:4 Be angry, and do not sin. In this context, the admonition means to tremble or shake in the fear of the Lord so as not to sin (cf. Is. 32:10,11; Hab. 3:16).

4:5 trust. This command reflects the primary word group in the OT for faith-commitment.

4:6-8 The taunting skeptics are cut off by the testimony of the psalmist to his rest because of God's personal blessings.

4:8 dwell in safety. The word "safety" introduces a play on words by going back to the term "trust" in v. 5. David evidences a total confidence in God amidst his crisis.

5:1–12 Psalm 5 is basically a lament with elements of declarations of innocence and confidence and prayers for protection. David was standing in the presence of the Lord when he put his enemies before his God. His prayers have two major concerns: "Help me and harm them!" Therefore, David releases his respective prayers for divine intervention and imprecation upon two rounds of contrast which differentiate the enemies of God from the children of God.

I. Round One: Theological Contrast of Retribution with Reconciliation (5:1-8)
   A. David's Prayer for Intervention Expressed (5:1-3)
   B. David's Prayer for Intervention Explained (5:4-8)
II. Round Two: Practical Contrast of the Wayward with the Worshipful (5:9-12)
   A. David's Prayer of Imprecation Expressed (5:10a-c)
   B. David's Prayer of Imprecation Explained (5:9,10d-12)

5:Title Whereas the instructions to the worship leader in Ps. 4 pertain to a stringed accompaniment, Ps. 5 is to be celebrated in community worship with flute accompaniment (cf. 1 Sam. 10:5; Kin. 1:40; Is. 30:29).

5:1 Give ear. This command is built upon the word for "ear." It takes its place alongside of parallel requests that God would pay careful attention to the supplicant and his sufferings (Pss. 17:1; 55:1,2).

5:2 My King and my God. David may have been the anointed theocratic king on earth, but he fully understood that the ultimate King of all Israel and of the whole earth is God (for God's conditional allowance for mediatorial kingship, see 1 Sam. 8:19ff.).

5:3 in the morning...In the morning. These words have led many to label this a morning psalm (cf. Pss. 3; 5:3).

5:4-6 not...Nor...not...hate...destroy...abhors. These 3 negatively phrased descriptions follow 3 directly stated affirmations. This reveals God's perfect standard of justice both in principle and in practice.

5:7 But as for me. The psalmist starkly contrasts himself with his enemies. They are haughty; he is humble.

5:8,9 To man's "hoof" problem, David exposes man's "mouth" problem, with special application to his slick-talking enemies. Proverbs is especially given to exposing the deadliness of mankind's spiritual "hoof" and "mouth" disease, i.e., one's walk and talk. Paul includes

Make Your way straight before my
face.

9 For *there is* no [5]faithfulness in their
mouth;
Their inward part *is* destruction;
[g]Their throat *is* an open tomb;
They flatter with their tongue.
10 Pronounce them guilty, O God!
Let them fall by their own counsels;
Cast them out in the multitude of
their transgressions,
For they have rebelled against You.

11 But let all those rejoice who put their
trust in You;
Let them ever shout for joy, because
You [6]defend them;
Let those also who love Your name
Be joyful in You.
12 For You, O LORD, will bless the
righteous;
With favor You will surround him as
with a shield.

PSALM 6

A Prayer of Faith in Time of Distress

To the Chief Musician. With stringed instruments. [a]On [1]an eight-stringed harp. A Psalm of David.

O LORD, [b]do not rebuke me in Your
anger,
Nor chasten me in Your hot
displeasure.
2 Have mercy on me, O LORD, for I *am*
weak;
O LORD, [c]heal me, for my bones are
troubled.
3 My soul also is greatly [d]troubled;
But You, O LORD—how long?

4 Return, O LORD, deliver me!
Oh, save me for Your mercies' sake!
5 [e]For in death *there is* no remembrance
of You;
In the grave who will give You
thanks?

6 I am weary with my groaning;
[2]All night I make my bed swim;
I drench my couch with my tears.
7 [f]My eye wastes away because of
grief;
It grows old because of all my
enemies.

8 [g]Depart from me, all you workers of
iniquity;
For the LORD has [h]heard the voice of
my weeping.
9 The LORD has heard my
supplication;
The LORD will receive my prayer.
10 Let all my enemies be ashamed and
greatly troubled;
Let them turn back *and* be ashamed
suddenly.

9 [g] Rom. 3:13
[5] *uprightness*
11 [6] *protect,* lit. *cover*

PSALM 6
title [a] Ps. 12:title
[1] Heb. *sheminith*
1 [b] Ps. 38:1; 118:18; [Jer. 10:24]
2 [c] Ps. 41:4; 147:3; [Hos. 6:1]
3 [d] Ps. 88:3; John 12:27
5 [e] Ps. 30:9; 88:10-12; 115:17; [Eccl. 9:10]; Is. 38:18
6 [2] Or *Every night*
7 [f] Job 17:7; Ps. 31:9
8 [g] [Matt. 25:41] [h] Ps. 3:4; 28:6

these assessments from Ps. 5:9 in his list of 14 terrible indictments of all mankind in Rom. 3:13.

5:8 Lead me…Make Your way straight. Disciples are to walk in God's way(s), being obedient to His direction(s) for their lives, yet they are fully dependent upon His grace for responsible progress (cf. Ps. 119:1-5,26,27,30,32,33).

5:10-12 He prays for the just ends of the wicked according to God's revealed standard of justice (Deut. 25:1), and contrastingly urges those who are regarded as righteous by the Lord's grace to joyfully celebrate His blessings.

6:1-10 This lament seems to be quite intensive, for apparently David is sleepless. His circumstances seem hopeless and helpless. The early Christian church regarded this psalm as the first among the "penitential psalms" (cf. Pss. 32,38,51,102,130,143). David's cries, coming up from the depths of his personal pit of persecution, indicate a radical change in his frame of mind as he addresses two different audiences.

I. Pouring out His Soul before God: A Defeatist Frame of Mind (6:1-7)
   A. A Tone of Helplessness (6:1-4)
   B. A Tone of Hopelessness (6:5-7)
II. Turning His Attention to His Enemies: A Defiant Frame of Mind (6:8-10)
   A. His Boldness about It (6:8a)
   B. His Basis for It (6:8b-10)

6: Title A new musical direction appears, lit. "Upon the eight," indicating either "on an eight-stringed harp" or "upon the octave" (i.e., a lower bass melody to accompany these lyrics of intense lament).

6:1 in Your anger…in Your hot displeasure. He does not ask for immunity from judgment, but for the tempering of God's discipline with mercy.

6:2,7 bones…eye. Many assume that because the psalmist mentions bodily "parts" his affliction was a grave physical illness. Obviously, his circumstances would have had an affect on his physical dimension. However, in OT anthropology such references are picturesque metaphors for an affliction of his total being (cf. all the parallel, personal references, e.g., "me," "my soul," i.e., my being or person, "I," etc.).

6:3 how long? This is a common exclamation of intense lament (cf. Ps. 90:13; Hab. 2:6; Rev. 6:10).

6:4 deliver me!…for Your mercies' sake. This introduces a new synonym for salvation, connoting an action of drawing off or out. He desires the Lord to graciously extricate him (cf. Job 36:15; Pss. 18:19; 116:8).

6:5 no remembrance of You. There is much about "death" and "the grave," i.e., Sheol, in Psalms. Such language as that of v. 5 does not imply annihilation, but inability to participate temporally in public praise offerings (cf. Hezekiah's reasoning in Is. 38:18).

6:6,7 Sleep has eluded him because of his severe sorrow.

6:8-10 Out of his dire straits, boldness surprisingly breaks through as he addresses his enemies. This boldness also has only one basis, that the psalmist's confidence is wholly grounded upon his Lord's attention and ultimate intervention.

PSALM 7

Prayer and Praise for Deliverance from Enemies

A [a]Meditation[1] of David, which he sang to the LORD [b]concerning the words of Cush, a Benjamite.

O LORD my God, in You I put my trust;
[c]Save me from all those who persecute me;
And deliver me,
2 [d]Lest they tear me like a lion,
[e]Rending *me* in pieces, while *there is* none to deliver.

3 O LORD my God, [f]if I have done this:
If there is [g]iniquity in my hands,
4 If I have repaid evil to him who was at peace with me,
Or [h]have plundered my enemy without cause,
5 Let the enemy pursue me and overtake *me;*
Yes, let him trample my life to the earth,
And lay my honor in the dust. Selah

6 Arise, O LORD, in Your anger;
[i]Lift Yourself up because of the rage of my enemies;
[j]Rise up [2]for me *to* the judgment You have commanded!
7 So the congregation of the peoples shall surround You;
For their sakes, therefore, return on high.
8 The LORD shall judge the peoples;
[k]Judge me, O LORD, [l]according to my righteousness,
And according to my integrity within me.

9 Oh, let the wickedness of the wicked come to an end,
But establish the just;
[m]For the righteous God tests the hearts and [3]minds.
10 [4]My defense *is* of God,
Who saves the [n]upright in heart.

11 God *is* a just judge,
And God is angry *with the wicked* every day.
12 If he does not turn back,
He will [o]sharpen His sword;
He bends His bow and makes it ready.
13 He also prepares for Himself instruments of death;
He makes His arrows into fiery shafts.

14 [p]Behold, *the wicked* brings forth iniquity;
Yes, he conceives trouble and brings forth falsehood.
15 He made a pit and dug it out,
[q]And has fallen into the ditch *which* he made.
16 [r]His trouble shall return upon his own head,
And his violent dealing shall come down on [5]his own crown.

17 I will praise the LORD according to His righteousness,
And will sing praise to the name of the LORD Most High.

PSALM 7
title [a] Hab. 3:1 [b] 2 Sam. 16 [1] Heb. *Shiggaion*
1 [c] Ps. 31:15
2 [d] Ps. 57:4; Is. 38:13 [e] Ps. 50:22
3 [f] 2 Sam. 16:7 [g] 1 Sam. 24:11
4 [h] 1 Sam. 24:7; 26:9
6 [i] Ps. 94:2 [j] Ps. 35:23; 44:23 [2] So with MT, Tg., Vg.; LXX *O LORD my God*
8 [k] Ps. 26:1; 35:24; 43:1 [l] Ps. 18:20; 35:24
9 [m] [1 Sam. 16:7] [3] Lit. *kidneys,* the most secret part of man
10 [n] Ps. 97:10, 11; 125:4 [4] Lit. *My shield is upon God*
12 [o] Deut. 32:41
14 [p] Job 15:35; Is. 59:4; [James 1:15]
15 [q] [Job 4:8]; Ps. 57:6
16 [r] Esth. 9:25; Ps. 140:9 [5] The crown of his own head

7:1-17 This psalm is basically a plea for divine vindication in the light of the oppressor's allegations and actions. David's confidence in the Divine Judge is the backbone of Ps. 7 (cf. Abraham in Gen. 18:25). As this truth grips him more and more, he will move from a tense anxiety to a transcendent assurance. This psalm follows David through 3 progressively calming stages of expression in response to the painfully false accusations that were being hurled against him.

I. Stage One: David's Concern as He Passionately Begs the Attention of the Divine Judge (7:1-5)
II. Stage Two: David's Court Appearance as He Painstakingly Argues His Case before the Divine Judge (7:6-16)
III. Stage Three: David's Composure as He Patiently Waits for the Verdict of the Divine Judge (7:17)

7:Title This title introduces one of the more enigmatic terms found in superscriptions of the psalms—"a *shiggaion* (Heb.) of David." It is probably related to the idea of wondering, reeling, veering, or weaving. Although the NKJV translates it "meditation," it more than likely conveys shifting emotions or movements of thought. Consequently, the term may also indicate the song's irregularity in rhythm (cf. Hab. 3:1). "He sang" also indicates that this was a vocal solo. The occasion, "concerning the words of Cush, a Benjamite," cannot be readily identified from the historical books; however, whoever this was or whatever the name represented, some enemy had obviously been falsely charging David (cf. Shimei—2 Sam. 16:5; 19:16).

7:2 Lest they tear me like a lion. Often the psalmist's enemies are symbolized by vicious, attacking animals, with "the king of beasts" occurring frequently (Pss. 10:9; 17:12; 22:13,16,21).

7:3-5 Such self-pronounced curses are powerful protestations of innocence (not sinlessness) in the context of being falsely charged (cf. the boldness of Job in 31:5ff.).

7:6 Arise. The battle cry relating back to Num. 10:35 recurs (cf. Pss. 9:19;10:12; 17:13; 44:26; 102:13).

7:8 my righteousness...my integrity. These are not declarations of sinlessness but of innocence in this "court case."

7:9 the righteous God tests the hearts and minds. The Just Judge has perfect insight (cf. God examining the heart and mind in Jer. 17:10; also cf. Acts 1:24; 15:8).

7:11-13 This shows yet another blending of the Divine Warrior and Divine Judge themes.

7:14-16 Often the principle of exact retribution surfaces in the psalms (cf. the maxim of Prov. 26:27 and the judgment of Hab. 2:15-18).

PSALM 8

The Glory of the LORD in Creation

To the Chief Musician. [1]On the instrument of Gath. A Psalm of David.

O LORD, our Lord,
How [a]excellent *is* Your name in all the earth,
Who have [b]set Your glory above the heavens!

2 [c]Out of the mouth of babes and nursing infants
You have [2]ordained strength,
Because of Your enemies,
That You may silence [d]the enemy and the avenger.

3 When I [e]consider Your heavens, the work of Your fingers,
The moon and the stars, which You have ordained,
4 [f]What is man that You are mindful of him,
And the son of man that You [g]visit[3] him?
5 For You have made him a little lower than [4]the angels,
And You have crowned him with glory and honor.

6 [h]You have made him to have dominion over the works of Your hands;
[i]You have put all *things* under his feet,
7 All sheep and oxen—
Even the beasts of the field,
8 The birds of the air,
And the fish of the sea
That pass through the paths of the seas.

9 [j]O LORD, our Lord,
How excellent *is* Your name in all the earth!

PSALM 9

Prayer and Thanksgiving for the LORD's Righteous Judgments

To the Chief Musician. To *the tune of* [1]"Death of the Son." A Psalm of David.

I will praise *You*, O LORD, with my whole heart;
I will tell of all Your marvelous works.
2 I will be glad and [a]rejoice in You;

PSALM 8
title [1] Heb. *Al Gittith*
1 [a] Ps. 148:13 [b] Ps. 113:4
2 [c] Matt. 21:16; [1 Cor. 1:27] [d] Ps. 44:16 [2] *established*
3 [e] Ps. 111:2
4 [f] Job 7:17, 18; [Heb. 2:6-8] [g] [Job 10:12] [3] *give attention to* or *care for*
5 [4] Heb. *Elohim, God;* LXX, Syr., Tg., Jewish tradition *angels*
6 [h] [Gen. 1:26, 28] [i] [1 Cor. 15:27; Eph. 1:22; Heb. 2:8]
9 [j] Ps. 8:1

PSALM 9
title [1] Heb. *Muth Labben*
2 [a] Ps. 5:11; 104:34

8:1-9 The beginning and ending of the psalm suggest that it is essentially a hymn of praise. Yet, a major portion qualifies it as a so-called nature psalm, i.e., a psalm of creation. Furthermore, there is a significant focus on the created dignity of man. Through this vehicle, the important subject of Adamic theology comes to the forefront, making this psalm ultimately suitable to the important association of the "One," the Last Adam, i.e., Christ and the "many" (cf. Heb. 2:6-8). Structurally, Ps. 8's beginning and concluding bursts of praise are driven by David's contemplation of two pairs of radical contrasts.

I. Introductory Praise (8:1)
II. Two Pairs of Radical Contrasts (8:2-8)
  A. Between the Nature of "Infants" and Infidels (8:2)
  B. Between Unaided General Revelation and Unveiled Special Revelation (8:3-8)
III. Concluding Praise (8:9)

8:Title Another instrument is referenced in this title, most probably a guitar-like harp associated with Gath in Philistia.

8:1 LORD...Lord. Of these twin nouns of direct address to God, the first is His specially revealed name Yahweh (Ex. 3:14) and the second puts an emphasis on His sovereignty. **Your name.** The name of God refers to the revealed Person of God, encompassing all of His attributes.

8:2 The introductory irony about infants set the stage for a contrast between the dependent and the foolishly self-sufficient.

8:3 Your heavens, the work of Your fingers. The heavens are created by God (Pss. 33:6,9; 102:25; 136:5). The anthropomorphism "Your fingers" miniaturizes the magnitude of the universe in the presence of the Creator.

8:4-6 Quoted in the NT at 1 Cor. 15:27,28; Eph. 1:22; Heb. 2:5-10.

8:4 What is man. If the whole universe is diminutive in the sight of the Divine Creator, how much less is the significance of mankind! Even the word for "man" used in v. 4 alludes to his weakness (cf. Pss. 9:19,20; 90:3a; 103:15, etc.). **and the son of man.** This phrase also looks upon man as insignificant and transitory (e.g., Ps. 90:3b). Yet, the Aram. counterpart of this phrase is found in Dan. 7:13, which has profound messianic overtones (cf. also Jesus' favorite self-designation in the NT, Son of Man).

8:5-8 These verses consistently emphasize the significance of man, who was created in the image and likeness of God to exercise dominion over the rest of creation (Gen. 1:26-28).

9:1-20 Psalms 9 and 10 go together, so much so that early Gr. and Lat. vss. treat and number them as one. However, Pss. 9 and 10 evidence two different forms: the first is an individual hymn while the second is an individual lament.

In the first part (vv. 1-12) praise is prominent, and in the second part (vv. 13-20) prayer is prominent. Many subtle patterns weave the thoughts of its verses and lines together. Shifting back and forth between the individual and corporate perspectives is characteristic, as are introverted (i.e., chiastic) structures. Basically, David's hymn in Ps. 9 ebbs and flows through two respective tides of prayer and praise.

I. First Tide: Divine Justice and Praise (9:1-12)
  A. Individual Praise and Divine Justice (9:1-4)
  B. Divine Justice and Corporate Praise (9:5-12)
II. Second Tide: Divine Justice and Prayer (9:13-20)
  A. Individual Prayer and Divine Justice (9:13-16)
  B. Divine Justice and Corporate Prayer (9:17-20)

9:Title The new element of this title lit. reads "upon death of a son." Many conjectures have arisen about this puzzling phrase, but it is safest to regard these words as designating a particular tune.

9:1,2 I will...I will...I will...I will. These 4 "I wills" launch Ps. 9 with David's dedication to exuberant worship of the Lord.

9:1 Your marvelous works. This especially references God's extraordinary interventions into history on behalf of His people (cf. the Exodus events).

I will sing praise to Your name,
[b]O Most High.

3 When my enemies turn back,
They shall fall and perish at Your presence.
4 For You have maintained my right and my cause;
You sat on the throne judging in righteousness.
5 You have rebuked the [2]nations,
You have destroyed the wicked;
You have [c]blotted out their name forever and ever.

6 O enemy, destructions are finished forever!
And you have destroyed cities;
Even their memory has [d]perished.
7 [e]But the LORD shall endure forever;
He has prepared His throne for judgment.
8 [f]He shall judge the world in righteousness,
And He shall administer judgment for the peoples in uprightness.

9 The LORD also will be a [g]refuge[3] for the oppressed,
A refuge in times of trouble.
10 And those who [h]know Your name will put their trust in You;
For You, LORD, have not forsaken those who seek You.

11 Sing praises to the LORD, who dwells in Zion!
[i]Declare His deeds among the people.
12 [j]When He avenges blood, He remembers them;
He does not forget the cry of the [4]humble.

13 Have mercy on me, O LORD!
Consider my trouble from those who hate me,
You who lift me up from the gates of death,
14 That I may tell of all Your praise
In the gates of [5]the daughter of Zion.
I will [k]rejoice in Your salvation.

15 [l]The [6]nations have sunk down in the pit *which* they made;
In the net which they hid, their own foot is caught.
16 The LORD is [m]known *by* the judgment He executes;
The wicked is snared in the work of his own hands.
[n]Meditation.[7] Selah

17 The wicked shall be turned into hell,
And all the [8]nations [o]that forget God.
18 [p]For the needy shall not always be forgotten;
[q]The expectation of the poor shall *not* perish forever.

19 Arise, O LORD,
Do not let man prevail;
Let the [9]nations be judged in Your sight.
20 Put them in fear, O LORD,
That the [1]nations may know themselves *to be but* men. Selah

2 [b][Ps. 83:18; 92:1]
5 [c]Prov. 10:7 [2]Gentiles
6 [d][Ps. 34:16]
7 [e]Ps. 102:12, 26; Heb. 1:11
8 [f][Ps. 96:13; 98:9; Acts 17:31]
9 [g]Ps. 32:7; 46:1; 91:2 [3]Lit. *secure height*
10 [h]Ps. 91:14
11 [i]Ps. 66:16; 107:22
12 [j][Gen. 9:5; Ps. 72:14] [4]*afflicted*
14 [k]Ps. 13:5; 20:5; 35:9 [5]Jerusalem
15 [l]Ps. 7:15, 16 [6]Gentiles
16 [m]Ex. 7:5 [n]Ps. 92:3 [7]Heb. *Higgaion*
17 [o]Job 8:13; Ps. 50:22 [8]Gentiles
18 [p]Ps. 9:12; 12:5 [q][Ps. 62:5; 71:5]; Prov. 23:18
19 [9]Gentiles
20 [1]Gentiles

PSALM 10

A Song of Confidence in God's Triumph over Evil

Why do You stand afar off, O LORD?
Why do You hide in times of trouble?
2 The wicked in *his* pride [1]persecutes the poor;

PSALM 10
2 [1]*hotly pursues*

9:4 You have maintained my right and my cause. This is exactly what God is known to do (cf. Deut. 10:18; 1 Kin. 8:45,49).

9:5-10 Verses 5 and 6 reveal the Just Judge's dealings with the godless, vv. 7,8, His dealings with all men in general, and vv. 9,10, His gracious dealings with dependent disciples.

9:11 the LORD, who dwells in Zion. There is a both/and tension running throughout the OT, i.e., God is enthroned in and above the heavens, and also, He symbolically dwells locally in His tabernacle (cf. 1 Kin. 8; Ps. 11:4).

9:12,18 the humble…the needy…the poor. These designations often stand for the individual psalmist and/or the corporate community of disciples he represents. The terms all point to those who are afflicted, vulnerable, and therefore totally dependent upon the Lord.

9:15,16 The "boomerang" principle of exact retribution returns.

9:17-20 Prominent theological themes from Pss. 1 and 2 also return as the psalmist draws this great hymn to a climax.

10:1-18 Whereas Ps. 9 started out with praise, Ps. 10 begins in despair. In Ps. 9 the psalmist was confident of the sure coming of Divine justice; in Ps. 10 injustice is rampant and God seems disinterested. However, the psalmist's walking more by sight than by faith will slowly turn around as he shifts his focus from empirical observations to theological facts. This is not an easy turn-around, especially since he is surrounded by so many practical atheists (cf. vv. 4,11,13). But hope will begin to dawn for the helpless (e.g., v. 12). In view of such kinds of general observations, the psalmist's expressions in Ps. 10 exemplify how true believers seem to live in two different worlds at the same time.

I. From His World of Hostility, Discouragement (10:1-11)
II. From His World of Hope, Encouragement (10:12-18)

10:1 Why?…*Why?* Two "whys" of lament boldly blurt out the psalmist's question: "God, why do You remain aloof?" (cf. Pss. 13:1; 22:11; 38:21; 44:24; 71:12; 88:14).

[a]Let them be caught in the plots which they have devised.
3 For the wicked [b]boasts of his heart's desire;
[2]He [c]blesses the greedy *and* renounces the LORD.
4 The wicked in his proud countenance does not seek *God;*
[3]God *is* in none of his [d]thoughts.

5 His ways [4]are always prospering;
Your judgments *are* far above, out of his sight;
As for all his enemies, he sneers at them.
6 [e]He has said in his heart, "I shall not be moved;
[f]I shall never be in adversity."
7 [g]His mouth is full of cursing and [h]deceit and oppression;
Under his tongue *is* trouble and iniquity.

8 He sits in the lurking places of the villages;
In the secret places he murders the innocent;
His eyes are secretly fixed on the helpless.
9 He lies in wait secretly, as a lion in his den;
He lies in wait to catch the poor;
He catches the poor when he draws him into his net.
10 So [5]he crouches, he lies low,
That the helpless may fall by his [6]strength.
11 He has said in his heart,
"God has forgotten;
He hides His face;
He will never see."

12 Arise, O LORD!
O God, [i]lift up Your hand!
Do not forget the [j]humble.
13 Why do the wicked renounce God?
He has said in his heart,
"You will not require *an account.*"

14 But You have [k]seen, for You observe trouble and grief,
To repay *it* by Your hand.
The helpless [l]commits[7] himself to You;
[m]You are the helper of the fatherless.
15 Break the arm of the wicked and the evil *man;*
Seek out his wickedness *until* You find none.

16 [n]The LORD *is* King forever and ever;
The nations have perished out of His land.
17 LORD, You have heard the desire of the humble;
You will prepare their heart;
You will cause Your ear to hear,
18 To [8]do justice to the fatherless and the oppressed,
That the man of the earth may [9]oppress no more.

2 [a] Ps. 7:16; 9:16
3 [b] Ps. 49:6; 94:3, 4 [c] Prov. 28:4 [2] Or *The greedy man curses and spurns the LORD*
4 [d] Ps. 14:1; 36:1 [3] Or *All his thoughts are, "There is no God"*
5 [4] Lit. *are strong*
6 [e] Ps. 49:11; [Eccl. 8:11] [f] Rev. 18:7
7 [g] [Rom. 3:14] [h] Ps. 55:10, 11
10 [5] Or *he is crushed, is bowed* [6] Or *mighty ones*
12 [i] Ps. 17:7; 94:2; Mic. 5:9 [j] Ps. 9:12
14 [k] [Ps. 11:4] [l] [2 Tim. 1:12] [m] Ps. 68:5; Hos. 14:3 [7] Lit. *leaves,* entrusts
16 [n] Ps. 29:10
18 [8] *vindicate* [9] *terrify*

PSALM 11
1 [a] Ps. 56:11
2 [b] Ps. 64:3, 4 [1] Lit. *in darkness*

PSALM 11

Faith in the LORD's Righteousness

To the Chief Musician. A Psalm of David.

In [a]the LORD I put my trust;
How can you say to my soul,
"Flee *as* a bird to your mountain"?
2 For look! [b]The wicked bend *their* bow,
They make ready their arrow on the string,
That they may shoot [1]secretly at the upright in heart.

10:3 blesses...renounces. The wicked's *modus operandi* is the opposite of what God demands (Deut. 25:1).

10:5 His ways are always prospering. God seems to be rewarding the ruthless. The psalmist's questioning insinuation is, "Has God also abandoned His own standards for retribution and reward?" Cf. other why-do-the-wicked-prosper inquiries in Job 20:2ff.; Jer. 12:1.

10:7-11 Evidences of "hoof" and "mouth" disease (walk/talk) return in application to the wicked. These are enhanced by a return also of the ungodly being described as stalking, rapacious beasts.

10:12 Arise. The battle cry of Num. 10:35 also comes back again (cf. Pss. 7:6; 9:19). **lift up Your hand.** This is an idiom for God's strength and power especially as it is used in the context of retaliation.

10:14 You are the helper of the fatherless. God is pictured as Helper or Advocate again, but this time in association with orphans. He is the Defender par excellence of the defenseless (on the imagery, cf. Ex. 22:21ff.; Deut. 10:18ff.; 1 Sam. 1:17; Jer. 7:6).

10:15 Break the arm of the wicked. The "hand" of God (vv. 12,14) is more than sufficiently strong to shatter the arm (another figure for power) of ungodly man.

10:16-18 The confident mood of this great climax outshines the psalm's introductory protestations. The psalmist's great Lord listens (v. 17) and acts (v. 18).

11:1-7 The panic that launched this psalm was not David's but that of his apparently well-meaning counselors. Their mood is panic, but David's is peace. In view of David's attitude, this psalm can be listed with the psalms of confidence (Pss. 4,16,23,27,62,125,131). Also, the solidarity of the theocratic king and the theocratic people is obvious, as indicated by the shifts back and forth between sing. and pl. phrasings. The developing verses and lines of this psalm reveal that, although two different "voices" were speaking to David in yet another context of personal and national crisis, he had made up his mind to trust only in the Lord.

I. Introductory Affirmation (11:1a)
II. The Two Voices
  A. The Voice Urging Flight (11:1b-3)
  B. The Voice Urging Faith (11:4-7)

11:1 In the LORD I put my trust. Lit. "I take refuge in the LORD." God is the exclusive refuge for His persecuted children (cf. Pss. 16:1; 36:7).

3 [c]If the foundations are destroyed,
What can the righteous do?

4 The LORD *is* in His holy temple,
The LORD's [d]throne *is* in heaven;
[e]His eyes behold,
His eyelids test the sons of men.
5 The LORD [f]tests the righteous,
But the wicked and the one who loves violence His soul hates.
6 Upon the wicked He will rain coals;
Fire and brimstone and a burning wind
[g]*Shall be* [2]the portion of their cup.

7 For the LORD *is* righteous,
He [h]loves righteousness;
[3]His countenance beholds the upright.

PSALM 12

Man's Treachery and God's Constancy

To the Chief Musician. [a]On [1]an eight-stringed harp. A Psalm of David.

Help,[2] LORD, for the godly man [b]ceases!
For the faithful disappear from among the sons of men.
2 [c]They speak idly everyone with his neighbor;
With flattering lips *and* [3]a double heart they speak.

3 May the LORD [4]cut off all flattering lips,
And the tongue that speaks [5]proud things,
4 Who have said,
"With our tongue we will prevail;
Our lips *are* our own;
Who *is* lord over us?"

5 "For the oppression of the poor, for the sighing of the needy,
Now I will arise," says the LORD;
"I will set *him* in the safety for which he yearns."

6 The words of the LORD *are* [d]pure words,
Like silver tried in a furnace of earth,
Purified seven times.
7 You shall keep them, O LORD,
You shall preserve them from this generation forever.

8 The wicked prowl on every side,
When vileness is exalted among the sons of men.

PSALM 13

Trust in the Salvation of the LORD

To the Chief Musician. A Psalm of David.

How long, O LORD? Will You forget me forever?

3 [c]Ps. 82:5; 87:1; 119:152
4 [d]Ps. 2:4; [Is. 66:1]; Matt. 5:34; 23:22; [Acts 7:49]; Rev. 4:2 [e][Ps. 33:18; 34:15, 16]
5 [f]Gen. 22:1; [James 1:12]
6 [g]1 Sam. 1:4; Ps. 75:8; Ezek. 38:22 [2]*Their allotted portion or serving*
7 [h]Ps. 33:5; 45:7 [3]*Or The upright beholds His countenance*

PSALM 12

title [a]Ps. 6:title [1]Heb. *sheminith*
1 [b][Is. 57:1]; Mic. 7:2 [2]*Save*
2 [c]Ps. 10:7; 41:6 [3]*An inconsistent mind*
3 [4]*destroy* [5]*great*
6 [d]2 Sam. 22:31; Ps. 18:30; 119:140; Prov. 30:5

11:3 These are the words of a committed but confused saint. His philosophical problem is, "In view of the crumbling of the theocratic society, what can one righteous person, out of a shrinking remnant, do?"

11:4a in His holy temple...in heaven. This emphasizes the transcendent throne room of God, yet God has sovereign sway over all the affairs of earth (cf. Hab. 2:20).

11:4b-5a His eyes behold...His eyelids test. His transcendence previously depicted does not negate His eminence here presented from the perspective of the divine scrutiny of all men, including the righteous (cf. Jer. 6:27-30; 17:10).

11:5b-6 His soul hates. This is undiluted, perfect retribution.

11:7a For the LORD *is* righteous. He loves righteousness. He Himself is the perfect norm or standard for all spiritual integrity.

11:7b His countenance. The marginal rendering is more suitable (cf. Pss. 17:15; 27:4; 63:2; 1 John 3:2).

12:1-8 Men's words do hurt, but the Lord's words heal. These thoughts preoccupy David in Ps. 12. The psalm begins and ends with the reality of the current reign of the wicked. Yet amidst this very black setting, the gemstone truth of v. 5 shines all the more brightly. These 8 verses are characterized by subtle repetitions and bold contrasts. In the development of Ps. 12, David provides a model for passing a spiritual hearing test, in that genuine disciples listen to and properly respond to two radically different sources of speech.

I. Surviving the Propaganda of Depraved Speech (12:1-4)
  A. By Prayer (12:1,2)
  B. By Petition (12:3,4)
II. Security in the Protection of Divine Speech (12:5-8)
  A. Its Divine Promises (12:5)
  B. Its Divine Purity (12:6)
  C. Its Divine Perseverance (12:7,8)

12:1 for the godly man ceases. His words and phraseology are deliberately hyperbolic, yet David's perception indeed was that the pious have perished!

12:2-4 These smooth-talking sinners verbally abuse the remnant (vv. 2,3) and verbally defy their Sovereign (v. 4).

12:3a May the LORD cut off all flattering lips. Here is a call for death in the light of sin. On the obnoxious sin of lying lips, cf. Ps. 5:9; Is. 30:10; Dan. 11:32; Rom. 3:13.

12:6 pure...purified. The Lord's perfect words present a most radical contrast with the profane words of arrogant sinners. The purity of God's Person assures the purity of His promises (cf. Ps. 19:7-10).

12:7,8 The hostile realities of v. 8 call for the heavenly resources of v. 7.

13:1-6 Psalm 13 launches with an explosion of 4 "How longs?" indicating another lament is about to begin. But David will shift radically from turmoil to tranquility in the space of 6 short verses through 3 levels of attitude.

I. Below "Sea Level" Expressions of Despair (13:1,2)
II. "Sea Level" Expressions of Desires (13:3,4)
III. "Mountaintop" Level Expressions of Delight (13:5,6)

13:1,2 These lines reintroduce the familiar triangle of the psalmist, his God, and his enemies. This 3-way relationship produces perplexity and pain. In view of God's apparent absence (v. 1), he seems left to his own resources which are unable to deal with the reality of his enemies (v. 2).

[a]How long will You hide Your face
from me?
2 How long shall I take counsel in my
soul,
Having sorrow in my heart daily?
How long will my enemy be exalted
over me?

3 Consider *and* hear me, O LORD my
God;
[b]Enlighten my eyes,
[c]Lest I sleep the *sleep of* death;
4 Lest my enemy say,
"I have prevailed against him";
Lest those who trouble me rejoice
when I am moved.

5 But I have trusted in Your mercy;
My heart shall rejoice in Your
salvation.
6 I will sing to the LORD,
Because He has dealt bountifully with
me.

PSALM 14

Folly of the Godless, and God's Final Triumph

To the Chief Musician. A Psalm of David.

The [a]fool has said in his heart,
"There is no God."
They are corrupt,
They have done abominable works,
There is none who does good.

2 [b]The LORD looks down from heaven
upon the children of men,
To see if there are any who
understand, who seek God.
3 [c]They have all turned aside,
They have together become corrupt;
There is none who does good,
No, not one.

4 Have all the workers of iniquity no
knowledge,
Who eat up my people *as* they eat
bread,
And [d]do not call on the LORD?
5 There they are in great fear,
For God *is* with the generation of the
righteous.
6 You shame the counsel of the poor,
But the LORD *is* his [e]refuge.

7 [f]Oh,[1] that the salvation of Israel *would*
come out of Zion!
[g]When the LORD brings back [2]the
captivity of His people,
Let Jacob rejoice *and* Israel be glad.

PSALM 15

The Character of Those Who May Dwell with the LORD

A Psalm of David.

LORD, [a]who may [1]abide in Your
tabernacle?
Who may dwell in Your holy hill?

PSALM 13
1 [a] Job 13:24; Ps. 89:46
3 [b] 1 Sam. 14:29; Ezra 9:8; Job 33:30; Ps. 18:28 [c] Jer. 51:39

PSALM 14
1 [a] Ps. 10:4; 53:1
2 [b] Ps. 33:13, 14; 102:19; Rom. 3:11
3 [c] Rom. 3:12
4 [d] Ps. 79:6; Is. 64:7; Jer. 10:25; Amos 8:4; Mic. 3:3
6 [e] Ps. 9:9; 40:17; 46:1; 142:5
7 [f] Ps. 53:6; [Rom. 11:25–27] [g] Deut. 30:3; Job 42:10 [1] Lit. *Who will give out of Zion the salvation of Israel?* [2] Or *His captive people*

PSALM 15
1 [a] Ps. 24:3–5 [1] sojourn

13:4b-5b rejoice...rejoice. Using the same verb, he deliberately contrasts his enemy's celebration with his own confidence in divine deliverance.

14:1-7 Psalm 14, a wisdom poem, along with its nearly identical twin Ps. 53, contains profound deliberations on human depravity. David's representative desire for deliverance (v. 7) provides the chorus to his two preceding dirges on depravity.

I. The Dirges on Depravity (14:1-6)
   A. The First Dirge: In the Form of a Round, Addresses the Universality of Depravity (14:1-3)
   B. The Second Dirge: In the Form of a Ballad, Addresses the Futility of Depravity (14:4-6)
II. The Chorus on Deliverance (14:7)
   A. The Wish for It (14:7a)
   B. The Worship Attending It (14:7b-c)

14:1 The fool. In the Bible, this designation carries moral rather than intellectual meaning (Is. 32:6).

14:1-3 The "alls" and "nones" of these lines make the indictments universally applicable. No wonder Paul included these indictments in Rom. 3:10-12. There is also a common scriptural association of doing with thinking.

14:4-6 The shift from third person affirmations about the wicked (vv. 4,5) to the second person (v. 6a) intensifies this confrontation with divine judgment.

14:7 Zion. The place on earth where God was pleased to reveal His presence, protection, and power (cf. Pss. 3:4; 20:2; 128:5; 132:13; 134:3).

15:1-5 Whereas Ps. 14 focused on the way of the wicked, Ps. 15 concentrates on the way of the righteous (cf. Ps. 1). The saved sinner is described as exhibiting indications of ethical integrity. These characteristics alternate in triplets of positive and negative descriptions. The whole psalm unfolds through a question-and-answer vehicle, and indeed it may be regarded as the ultimate Q and A session. With its focus on moral responsibility, the psalm offers a sequence of responses to the question of acceptable worship.

I. A Two-Part Question (15:1)
II. A Twelve-Part Response (15:2-5b)
   A. Three Positively-Phrased Ethical Characteristics (15:2)
      1. His lifestyle exhibits integrity
      2. His deeds exhibit justice
      3. His speed exhibits reliability
   B. Three Negatively Cast Ethical Characteristics (15:3)
      1. He does not tread over people with his tongue
      2. He does not harm his fellow man
      3. He does not dump reproach upon family or friend
   C. Three Positively Phrased Ethical Characteristics (15:4a-c)
      1. He views the reprobate as rejected
      2. He respects the people of God
      3. He holds himself accountable
   D. Three Negatively Cast Ethical Characteristics (15:4d-5b)
      1. He is not fickle
      2. He is not greedy
      3. He cannot be bought
III. A One-Part Guarantee (15:5c)

2 He who walks uprightly,
And works righteousness,
And speaks the [b]truth in his heart;
3 He *who* [c]does not backbite with his tongue,
Nor does evil to his neighbor,
[d]Nor does he [2]take up a reproach against his friend;
4 [e]In whose eyes a vile person is despised,
But he honors those who fear the LORD;
He *who* [f]swears to his own hurt and does not change;
5 He *who* does not put out his money at usury,
Nor does he take a bribe against the innocent.
He who does these *things* [g]shall never be moved.

2 [b] Zech. 8:16; [Eph. 4:25]
3 [c] [Lev. 19:16-18] [d] Ex. 23:1 [2] *receive*
4 [e] Esth. 3:2 [f] Lev. 5:4
5 [g] 2 Pet. 1:10

PSALM 16
title [a] Ps. 56–60
1 [1] *Watch over*

PSALM 16

The Hope of the Faithful, and the Messiah's Victory

A [a]Michtam of David.

1 Preserve[1] me, O God, for in You I put my trust.

2 *O my soul,* you have said to the LORD,
"You *are* my Lord,

15:1 Your tabernacle. Lit. "tent" (cf. Ps. 61:4; for possible background see 2 Sam. 6:12-17).

15:2-6 Notice the focus on life-and-lip qualities.

15:4 despised...honors. Whom God rejects, the psalmist rejects; whom God loves, he loves.

15:5 usury. Interest rates ran as high as 50 percent, but God's law put strict regulations on borrowing and lending (*see notes on Deut. 23:19,20; 24:10-13*). **he...shall never be moved.** This is an important promise in the light of its usage in Psalms and Proverbs (cf. Pss. 10:6; 13:4; 16:8; 46:5; 62:2,6; Prov. 10:30).

16:1-11 The only prayer of Ps. 16 comes in the first line. The rest of the psalm consists of David's weaving together his personal testimonies of trust in the Lord. In view of this, David's opening prayer is bolstered by two cycles of testimony.

I. David's Introductory Prayer (16:1)
II. David's Testimony (16:2-11)
  A. His Testimony of Communion (16:2-4)
    1. Its divine dimension (16:2)
    2. Its human dimension (16:3,4)
  B. His Testimony of Confidence (16:5-11)
    1. Its past and present dimensions (16:5-8)
    2. Its present and future dimensions (16:9-11)

16:Title. A Michtam of David. Cf. Pss. 56; 57; 58; 59; 60. In spite of many conjectures, this designation remains obscure.

16:1 Preserve me. This is a frequent request begging God to protect the psalmist (cf. Pss. 17:8; 140:4; 141:9).

16:2 *O my soul,* you have said. The words in italics are supplied because there is a variant in the Heb. Bible concerning the verb. It

Messianic Prophecies in the Psalms

Prophecy	Psalm	Fulfillment
1. God will announce Christ to be His Son	2:7	Matthew 3:17; Acts 13:33; Hebrews 1:5
2. All things will be put under Christ's feet	8:6	1 Cor. 15:27, Hebrews 2:8
3. Christ will be resurrected from the grave	16:10	Mark 16:6,7; Acts 13:35
4. God will forsake Christ in His moment of agony	22:1	Matthew 27:46; Mark 15:34
5. Christ will be scorned and ridiculed	22:7,8	Matthew 27:39-43; Luke 23:35
6. Christ's hands and feet will be pierced	22:16	John 20:25, 27; Acts 2:23
7. Others will gamble for Christ's clothes	22:18	Matthew 27:35,36
8. Not one of Christ's bones will be broken	34:20	John 19:32,33,36
9. Christ will be hated unjustly	35:19	John 15:25
10. Christ will come to do God's will	40:7,8	Hebrews 10:7
11. Christ will be betrayed by a friend	41:9	John 13:18
12. Christ's throne will be eternal	45:6	Hebrews 1:8
13. Christ will ascend to heaven	68:18	Ephesians 4:8
14. Zeal for God's temple will consume Christ	69:9	John 2:17
15. Christ will be given vinegar and gall	69:21	Matthew 27:34; John 19:28-30
16. Christ's betrayer will be replaced	109:8	Acts 1:20
17. Christ's enemies will bow down to Him	110:1	Acts 2:34,35
18. Christ will be a priest like Melchizedek	110:4	Hebrews 5:6; 6:20; 7:17
19. Christ will be the chief cornerstone	118:22	Matthew 21:42; Acts 4:11
20. Christ will come in the name of the Lord	118:26	Matthew 21:9

[b]My goodness is nothing apart from You."
3 As for the saints who *are* on the earth,
"They are the excellent ones, in [c]whom is all my delight."
4 Their sorrows shall be multiplied who hasten *after* another *god;*
Their drink offerings of [d]blood I will not offer,
[e]Nor take up their names on my lips.

5 O LORD, *You are* the portion of my inheritance and my cup;
You [2]maintain my lot.
6 The lines have fallen to me in pleasant *places;*
Yes, I have a good inheritance.

7 I will bless the LORD who has given me counsel;
My [3]heart also instructs me in the night seasons.
8 [f]I have set the LORD always before me;
Because *He is* at my right hand I shall not be moved.

9 Therefore my heart is glad, and my glory rejoices;
My flesh also will [4]rest in hope.
10 [g]For You will not leave my soul in [5]Sheol,
Nor will You allow Your Holy One to [6]see corruption.
11 You will show me the [h]path of life;
In Your presence *is* fullness of joy;
At Your right hand *are* pleasures forevermore.

2 [b]Job 35:7
3 [c]Ps. 119:63
4 [d]Ps. 106:37, 38 [e][Ex. 23:13]; Josh. 23:7
5 [2]Lit. *uphold*
7 [3]Mind, lit. *kidneys*
8 [f][Acts 2:25-28]
9 [4]Or *dwell securely*
10 [g]Ps. 49:15; 86:13; Acts 2:31, 32; Heb. 13:20 [5]The abode of the dead [6]*undergo*
11 [h]Ps. 139:24; [Matt. 7:14]

PSALM 17

Prayer with Confidence in Final Salvation

A Prayer of David.

Hear a just cause, O LORD,
Attend to my cry;
Give ear to my prayer *which is* not from deceitful lips.
2 Let my vindication come from Your presence;
Let Your eyes look on the things that are upright.

3 You have tested my heart;
You have visited *me* in the night;
[a]You have [1]tried me and have found [2]nothing;
I have purposed that my mouth shall not [b]transgress.
4 Concerning the works of men,
By the word of Your lips,
I have kept away from the paths of the destroyer.
5 [c]Uphold my steps in Your paths,
That my footsteps may not slip.

6 [d]I have called upon You, for You will hear me, O God;
Incline Your ear to me, *and* hear my speech.
7 Show Your marvelous lovingkindness by Your right hand,
O You who [3]save those who trust *in You*

PSALM 17
3 [a]Job 23:10; Ps. 66:10; Zech. 13:9; [1 Pet. 1:7] [b]Ps. 39:1 [1]*examined* [2]*Nothing evil*
5 [c]Job 23:11; Ps. 44:18; 119:133
6 [d]Ps. 86:7; 116:2
7 [3]*deliver*

may be just as well to regard the verb as a shortened form of "I said" (also occurring at 1Kin. 8:48; Job 42:2; Ps. 140:13; Ezek. 16:59). **My goodness is nothing apart from You.** I.e., "My well-being is entirely dependent upon You."

16:4 He will have nothing to do with false gods or the people pursuing them.

16:5,6 These lines use OT metaphors to describe the blessing of God.

16:9 my glory. Starting back at v. 7, the psalmist referred to his core of being as lit. "my kidneys," then "my heart," now "my glory," and next "my flesh" and "my soul." The anthropological terms stand for the whole person, so it is best to consider "my glory" as referring to that distinctive way in which man is created in the image of God, i.e., his intelligence and ability to speak.

16:10 These words expressed the confidence of the lesser David, but were applied messianically to the resurrection of the Greater David (the Lord Jesus Christ) both by Peter (Acts 2:25-28) and Paul (Acts 13:35).

17:1-15 This "prayer" of David brims with petitions, as many as seventeen of them depending upon the translation of certain Heb. verb forms. There are many literary parallels with Ps. 16. Although the psalm shows indications of mixed forms, it is essentially a prayer for protection. David is fond of using themes and phrases from the Exodus narrative (cf. Ex. 15; Deut. 32). A logical chiastic development is detected in its verses, with the focus shifting from the psalmist (vv. 1-8) to his enemies (vv. 9-12), remaining on his enemies in vv. 13,14, then shifting back to David (v. 15). Or viewing its development from another angle, David approaches the divine court with 3 clusters of appeals in seeking justice.

I. Appeals Dealing with Response and Recognition (17:1-5)
II. Appeals Dealing with Rescue and Relief (17:6-12)
   A. His Need for Rescue Is Presented (17:6-8)
   B. His Need for Relief Is Documented (17:9-12)
III. Appeals Dealing with Retribution and Rest (17:13-15)
   A. His Anticipation of Their Retribution (17:13,14)
   B. His Assurance of His Own Rest (17:15)

17:Title This is the first psalm simply entitled "a prayer" (cf. Pss. 86; 90; 102; 142).

17:1,2 The introductory language is that of the law court, and David stands before the ultimate Chief Justice to present his case.

17:3-5 His basic integrity (vv. 3,4) especially in view of the present case, was, is, and shall be dependent upon the grace of God (v. 5).

From those who rise up *against them.*
8 Keep me as the [4]apple of Your eye;
Hide me under the shadow of Your wings,
9 From the wicked who oppress me,
From my deadly enemies who surround me.

10 They have closed up their [e]fat *hearts;*
With their mouths they [f]speak proudly.
11 They have now surrounded us in our steps;
They have set their eyes, crouching down to the earth,
12 As a lion is eager to tear his prey,
And like a young lion lurking in secret places.

13 Arise, O LORD,
Confront him, cast him down;
Deliver my life from the wicked with Your sword,
14 With Your hand from men, O LORD,
From men of the world *who have* their portion in *this* life,
And whose belly You fill with Your hidden treasure.
They are satisfied with children,
And leave the rest of their *possession* for their babes.

15 As for me, [g]I will see Your face in righteousness;
[h]I shall be satisfied when I [i]awake in Your likeness.

8 [4]*pupil*
10 [e]Ezek. 16:49 [f][1 Sam. 2:3]
15 [g][1 John 3:2] [h]Ps. 4:6, 7; 16:11 [i][Is. 26:19]

PSALM 18
title [a]Ps. 36:title [b]2 Sam. 22
1 [c]Ps. 144:1
2 [d]Heb. 2:13 [1]Lit. *rock* [2]*Strength*
3 [e]Ps. 76:4; Rev. 5:12
4 [f]Ps. 116:3 [3]Lit. *Belial*
7 [g]Acts 4:31

PSALM 18

God the Sovereign Savior

To the Chief Musician. A Psalm of David [a]the servant of the LORD, who spoke to the LORD the words of [b]this song on the day that the LORD delivered him from the hand of all his enemies and from the hand of Saul. And he said:

I [c]will love You, O LORD, my strength.
2 The LORD is my rock and my fortress and my deliverer;
My God, my [1]strength, [d]in whom I will trust;
My shield and the [2]horn of my salvation, my stronghold.
3 I will call upon the LORD, [e]*who is worthy* to be praised;
So shall I be saved from my enemies.

4 [f]The pangs of death surrounded me,
And the floods of [3]ungodliness made me afraid.
5 The sorrows of Sheol surrounded me;
The snares of death confronted me.
6 In my distress I called upon the LORD,
And cried out to my God;
He heard my voice from His temple,
And my cry came before Him, *even* to His ears.

7 [g]Then the earth shook and trembled;
The foundations of the hills also quaked and were shaken,
Because He was angry.
8 Smoke went up from His nostrils,

17:8 the apple of Your eye. An expression meaning the pupil of the human eye. As a person protects that vital organ of vision, so God protects His people.

17:10 They have closed up their fat *hearts.* Lit. "They have closed their fat." This was a common OT idiom for insensitivity (cf. Deut. 32:15; Job 15:27; Ps. 73:7; Jer. 5:28).

17:13 Divine Warrior language.

17:14,15 The common grace of God is overlooked by those who are satisfied with temporal prosperities (v. 14), but David brings back the proper perspective on true satisfaction in v. 15. Cf. Jesus' teaching on these vital issues in Matt. 6:19-34.

18:1-50 Psalm 18 is clearly an individual psalm of thanksgiving, also bearing royal characteristics. Its poetry and themes resemble other ancient testimonies to God's great historical deliverances (e.g., Ex. 15; Judg. 5). Between David's opening (vv. 1-3) and closing (vv. 46-50) praises to God, his life with the Lord is described in 3 stages.

- I. Prelude: His Opening Praises (18:1-3)
- II. The Stages of His Life (18:4-45)
  - A. In the Pit of Peril (18:4-19)
    - 1. His desperation (18:4,5)
    - 2. His defender (18:6-15)
    - 3. His deliverance (18:16-19)
  - B. On a Course of Ethical Integrity (18:20-28)
    - 1. The principles of the Lord's direction (18:20-26)
    - 2. The privileges of the Lord's direction (18:27,28)
  - C. In the Turbulent Atmosphere of Leadership (18:29-45)
    - 1. Military leadership (18:29-42)
    - 2. Theocratic leadership (18:43-45)
- III. Postscript: His Closing Praises (18:46-50)

18:Title This large psalm bears a large title. Although the title seems to refer to only one specific occasion (e.g., "On the day"), it does state that God's deliverance was "from the hand of all his enemies and from the hand of Saul." Therefore, it is preferable that the language of this superscription be understood to summarize the testimony of David's whole life in retrospect.

18:1 love. This is not the normal word for love that often bears covenant meaning (e.g., Deut. 7:8; Ps. 119:97), but it is a rare verb form of a word group that expresses tender intimacy. David's choice of words intended to express very strong devotion, like Peter's in John 21:15-17.

18:2 Military metaphors for the Divine Warrior multiply in this verse. Both defensively and offensively, the Lord was all David needed in life's tough battles. On "the horn" (i.e., a symbol of power) of David's salvation, cf. Mary's testimony in Luke 1:47.

18:4 pangs Lit. "cords of death" (cf. Jon. 2:2-9).

18:7-15 This theophany, a vivid poetic picture of God's presence, rivals other biblical presentations (cf. Ex. 19:16ff.; Deut. 33:2ff.; Judg.

And devouring fire from His mouth;
Coals were kindled by it.
9 [h]He bowed the heavens also, and came down
With darkness under His feet.
10 [i]And He rode upon a cherub, and flew;
[j]He flew upon the wings of the wind.
11 He made darkness His secret place;
[k]His canopy around Him *was* dark waters
And thick clouds of the skies.
12 [l]From the brightness before Him,
His thick clouds passed with hailstones and coals of fire.

13 The LORD thundered from heaven,
And the Most High uttered [m]His voice,
[4]Hailstones and coals of fire.
14 [n]He sent out His arrows and scattered [5]the foe,
Lightnings in abundance, and He vanquished them.
15 Then the channels of the sea were seen,
The foundations of the world were uncovered
At Your rebuke, O LORD,
At the blast of the breath of Your nostrils.

16 [o]He sent from above, He took me;
He drew me out of many waters.
17 He delivered me from my strong enemy,
From those who hated me,
For they were too strong for me.
18 They confronted me in the day of my calamity,
But the LORD was my support.
19 [p]He also brought me out into a broad place;
He delivered me because He delighted in me.

20 [q]The LORD rewarded me according to my righteousness;
According to the cleanness of my hands
He has recompensed me.
21 For I have kept the ways of the LORD,
And have not wickedly departed from my God.
22 For all His judgments *were* before me,
And I did not put away His statutes from me.
23 I was also blameless [6]before Him,
And I kept myself from my iniquity.
24 [r]Therefore the LORD has recompensed me according to my righteousness,
According to the cleanness of my hands in His sight.

25 [s]With the merciful You will show Yourself merciful;
With a blameless man You will show Yourself blameless;
26 With the pure You will show Yourself pure;
And [t]with the devious You will show Yourself shrewd.
27 For You will save the humble people,
But will bring down [u]haughty looks.

28 [v]For You will light my lamp;
The LORD my God will enlighten my darkness.
29 For by You I can [7]run against a troop,
By my God I can leap over a wall.
30 *As for* God, [w]His way *is* perfect;
[x]The word of the LORD is [8]proven;
He *is* a shield [y]to all who trust in Him.

31 [z]For who *is* God, except the LORD?
And who *is* a rock, except our God?
32 *It is* God who [a]arms me with strength,
And makes my way perfect.
33 [b]He makes my feet like the *feet of* deer,
And [c]sets me on my high places.
34 [d]He teaches my hands to make war,
So that my arms can bend a bow of bronze.

35 You have also given me the shield of Your salvation;
Your right hand has held me up,
Your gentleness has made me great.
36 You enlarged my path under me,
[e]So my feet did not slip.

37 I have pursued my enemies and overtaken them;

9 [h]Ps. 144:5
10 [i]Ps. 80:1; 99:1 [j][Ps. 104:3]
11 [k]Ps. 97:2
12 [l]Ps. 97:3; 140:10; Hab. 3:11
13 [m][Ps. 29:3-9; 104:7] [4]So with MT, Tg., Vg.; a few Heb. mss., LXX omit *Hailstones and coals of fire*
14 [n]Josh. 10:10; Ps. 144:6; Is. 30:30; Hab. 3:11 [5]Lit. *them*
16 [o]Ps. 144:7
19 [p]Ps. 4:1; 31:8; 118:5
20 [q]1 Sam. 24:19; [Job 33:26]; Ps. 7:8
23 [6]*with*
24 [r]1 Sam. 26:23; Ps. 18:20
25 [s][1 Kin. 8:32; Ps. 62:12]; Matt. 5:7
26 [t][Lev. 26:23-28]; Prov. 3:34
27 [u][Ps. 101:5]; Prov. 6:17
28 [v]1 Kin. 15:4; Job 18:6; [Ps. 119:105]
29 [7]Or *run through*
30 [w][Deut. 32:4]; Rev. 15:3 [x]Ps. 12:6; 119:140; [Prov. 30:5] [y][Ps. 17:7] [8]Lit. *refined*
31 [z][Deut. 32:31, 39; 1 Sam. 2:2; Ps. 86:8-10; Is. 45:5]
32 [a][Ps. 91:2]
33 [b]2 Sam. 2:18; Hab. 3:19 [c]Deut. 32:13; 33:29
34 [d]Ps. 144:1
36 [e]Ps. 66:9; Prov. 4:12

4,5; Ps. 68:7,8; Mic. 1:3,4; Hab. 3; Rev. 19). His presence is largely described by various catastrophic responses by all creation.

18:16-19 His sheer power, exhibited so dramatically in vv. 7-15, is now amazingly attested as coming to rescue the psalmist personally.

18:20-24,37,38 These verses should not be taken out of context, making David look like an arrogant boaster. As in vv. 25-36 and 39-50, both David and the community, although responsible for living with integrity within the covenant relationship, are fully dependent on the resources of God to do so. Therefore, his "boasting" is biblical, since it is ultimately in the Lord (Jer. 9:23,24).

18:31 a rock. (cf. vv. 2,46). Moses, at the beginning of his great song about the Lord in Deut. 32, called God "The Rock" (v. 4). The Lord is indeed a massive, unshakable foundation and source of protection.

Neither did I turn back again till they
were destroyed.
38 I have wounded them,
So that they could not rise;
They have fallen under my feet.
39 For You have armed me with strength
for the battle;
You have [9]subdued under me those
who rose up against me.
40 You have also given me the necks of
my enemies,
So that I destroyed those who hated
me.
41 They cried out, but *there was* none to
save;
[f]*Even* to the LORD, but He did not
answer them.
42 Then I beat them as fine as the dust
before the wind;
I [g]cast them out like dirt in the streets.

43 You have delivered me from the
strivings of the people;
[h]You have made me the head of the
[1]nations;
[i]A people I have not known shall
serve me.
44 As soon as they hear of me they obey
me;
The foreigners [2]submit to me.
45 [j]The foreigners fade away,
And come frightened from their
hideouts.

46 The LORD lives!
Blessed *be* my Rock!
Let the God of my salvation be
exalted.
47 *It is* God who avenges me,
[k]And subdues the peoples under me;
48 He delivers me from my enemies.
[l]You also lift me up above those who
rise against me;
You have delivered me from the
violent man.
49 [m]Therefore I will give thanks to You,
O LORD, among the [3]Gentiles,
And sing praises to Your name.

50 [n]Great deliverance He gives to His
king,
And shows mercy to His anointed,
To David and his [4]descendants
forevermore.

39 [9] Lit. *caused to bow*
41 [f] Job 27:9; Prov. 1:28; Is. 1:15; Ezek. 8:18; Zech. 7:13
42 [g] Zech. 10:5
43 [h] 2 Sam. 8; Ps. 89:27 [i] Is. 52:15 [1] *Gentiles*
44 [2] *feign submission*
45 [j] Mic. 7:17
47 [k] Ps. 47:3
48 [l] Ps. 27:6; 59:1
49 [m] 2 Sam. 22:50; Rom. 15:9 [3] *nations*
50 [n] 2 Sam. 7:12; Ps. 21:1; 144:10 [4] Lit. *seed*

PSALM 19

The Perfect Revelation of the LORD

To the Chief Musician. A Psalm of David.

The [a]heavens declare the glory of
God;
And the [b]firmament[1] shows [2]His
handiwork.
2 Day unto day utters speech,
And night unto night reveals
knowledge.
3 *There is* no speech nor language
Where their voice is not heard.
4 [c]Their [3]line has gone out through all
the earth,
And their words to the end of the
world.

In them He has set a [4]tabernacle for
the sun,
5 Which *is* like a bridegroom coming
out of his chamber,
[d]*And* rejoices like a strong man to run
its race.
6 Its rising *is* from one end of heaven,
And its circuit to the other end;
And there is nothing hidden from its
heat.

PSALM 19

1 [a] Is. 40:22; [Rom. 1:19, 20] [b] Gen. 1:6, 7 [1] *expanse of heaven* [2] *the work of His hands*
4 [c] Rom. 10:18 [3] LXX, Syr., Vg. *sound;* Tg. *business* [4] *tent*
5 [d] Eccl. 1:5

18:50 This concluding verse is another royal messianic affirmation of the Davidic Covenant in 2 Sam. 7.

19:1-14 Because of its two distinct parts and two different names for God, some have tried to argue that Ps. 19 was really two compositions, one ancient and one more recent. However, the shorter form of the name "God" (cf. the longer form in Gen. 1:1) speaks of His power, especially power exhibited as Creator, while "LORD" fits the relational focus. Consequently, David depicted the LORD God as author of both His world and Word in a unified hymn. God has revealed Himself to mankind through these two avenues. The human race stands accountable to Him because of His non-verbal and verbal communications. In the light of these intentions, Ps. 19 eloquently summarizes two prominent vehicles of God's self-disclosure.

I. God's General Self-Disclosure in the World (19:1-6)
   A. The Publication of the Skies (19:1-4b)
   B. The Prominence of the Sun (19:4c-6)
II. God's Special Self-Disclosure in the Word (19:7-14)
   A. The Attributes of the Word (19:7,8)
   B. An Appreciation for the Word (19:9-11)
   C. The Application of the Word (19:12-14)

19:1-6 The testimony of the universe comes forth consistently and clearly, but sinful mankind persistently resists it. For this reason, general revelation cannot convert sinners, but it does make them highly accountable (cf. Rom. 1:18ff.). Salvation comes ultimately only through special revelation, i.e., as the Word of God is effectually applied by the Spirit of God.

19:1 heavens…firmament. Both are crucial elements of the creation in Gen. 1 (cf. vv. 1,8). **declare…shows.** Both verbs emphasize the continuity of these respective disclosures. **His handiwork.** An anthropomorphism illustrating God's great power (cf. the "work of His fingers" in Ps. 8:3).

19:2,3 speech…no speech. is not a contradiction, but shows that the constant communication of the heavens is not with words of a literal nature.

19:4 The message of the created world extends to everywhere.

19:4c-6 Neither the sun nor the heavens are deified as was the case in many pagan religions. In the Bible, God is the Creator and Ruler over all creation.

7 [e]The law of the LORD *is* perfect,
[5]converting the soul;
The testimony of the LORD *is* sure,
making [f]wise the simple;
8 The statutes of the LORD *are* right,
rejoicing the heart;
The commandment of the LORD *is*
pure, enlightening the eyes;
9 The fear of the LORD *is* clean,
enduring forever;
The judgments of the LORD *are* true
and righteous altogether.
10 More to be desired *are they* than [g]gold,
Yea, than much fine gold;
Sweeter also than honey and the
[6]honeycomb.
11 Moreover by them Your servant is
warned,
And in keeping them *there is* great
reward.

12 Who can understand *his* errors?
[h]Cleanse me from secret *faults.*
13 Keep back Your servant also from
[i]presumptuous *sins;*
Let them not have [j]dominion over me.
Then I shall be blameless,
And I shall be innocent of [7]great
transgression.

14 [k]Let the words of my mouth and the
meditation of my heart
Be acceptable in Your sight,
O LORD, my [8]strength and my
[l]Redeemer.

7 [e] Ps. 111:7; [Rom. 7:12] [f] Ps. 119:130 [5] *restoring*
10 [g] Ps. 119:72, 127; Prov. 8:10, 11, 19 [6] *honey in the combs*
12 [h] [Ps. 51:1, 2]
13 [i] Num. 15:30 [j] Ps. 119:133; [Rom. 6:12-14] [7] Or *much*
14 [k] Ps. 51:15 [l] Ps. 31:5; Is. 47:4 [8] Lit. *rock*

PSALM 20
1 [1] Lit. *set you on high*
4 [a] Ps. 21:2 [2] *counsel*
6 [3] Commissioned one, Heb. *messiah*
7 [b] Deut. 20:1; Ps. 33:16, 17; Prov. 21:31; Is. 31:1

PSALM 20

The Assurance of God's Saving Work

To the Chief Musician. A Psalm of David.

May the LORD answer you in the day
of trouble;
May the name of the God of Jacob
[1]defend you;
2 May He send you help from the
sanctuary,
And strengthen you out of Zion;
3 May He remember all your offerings,
And accept your burnt sacrifice. Selah

4 May He grant you according to your
heart's *desire,*
And [a]fulfill all your [2]purpose.
5 We will rejoice in your salvation,
And in the name of our God we will
set up *our* banners!
May the LORD fulfill all your petitions.

6 Now I know that the LORD saves His
[3]anointed;
He will answer him from His holy
heaven
With the saving strength of His right
hand.

7 Some *trust* in chariots, and some in
[b]horses;
But we will remember the name of
the LORD our God.
8 They have bowed down and fallen;

19:7-14 The scene shifts from God's world to God's Word.

19:7,8 Each of 4 parallel lines contains a word (a synonym) for God's Word; each describes what His Word is; and each pronounces what it effectually accomplishes.

19:7 law. This might better be translated, "His teaching," "a direction," or "instruction" (cf. Ps. 1:2). **testimony.** This word for the Word derives from the root "to bear witness." It, so to speak, bears testimony to its Divine Author.

19:8 statutes. This synonym looks upon God's Word as orders, charges, precepts, etc. They are viewed as the Governor's governings. **commandment.** This word is related to the verb "to command" or "order." The Word is therefore also perceived as divine orders.

19:9 fear. This is not technically a word for the Word, but it does reflect the reality that Scripture is the manual for worship of God. **judgments.** This term looks upon God's Word as conveying His judicial decisions.

19:12,13 The psalmist deals respectively with unintentional sins and high-handed infractions (cf. Lev. 4:1ff.; Num. 15:22ff.). David's concerns reflect the attitude of a maturing disciple who, by God's grace and provisions, deals with his sins and does not deny them.

19:14 Be acceptable. Using a term often associated with God's acceptance of properly offered, literal sacrifices, he asks for grace and enablement as he lays his "lip-and-life" sacrifices on the "altar" (cf. Josh. 1:8).

20:1-9 Psalms 20 and 21 are twin warfare events—Ps. 20 is mostly ceremony before a battle, while Ps. 21 is mostly celebration after a battle. In the theocracy, these were to be considered holy wars with the chain of command being as follows: the Lord is Commander-in-Chief over the anointed king-general and the theocratic people—soldiers. All holy convocations, both before and after battles, involved prayer and praise assemblies dedicated to God, who grants victories through the theocratic king-general. Psalm 20, in anticipation of a military campaign, commemorates a 3-phased ceremony regularly conducted by the people in the presence of the Commander-in-Chief on behalf of the king-general.

I. An Offering of Their Prayers (20:1-5)
II. A Confirmation of Their Confidence (20:6-8)
III. A Reaffirmation of Their Dependence (20:9)

20:1 May the LORD answer you in the day of trouble. This is the prayer of God's people for their king-general (cf. "His anointed," v. 6).

20:2 from the sanctuary...out of Zion. These are designations about the place of God's symbolic presence in the ark which David had recaptured and installed in a tabernacle on Mt. Zion. The people's wish was that the Lord Himself would uphold, support, and sustain the king-general with His extending, powerful presence throughout the military campaign.

20:5 your salvation. Here, by contrast, God's "salvation" is victory in battle.

20:7 Some *trust* in... Trust, boast, and praise must not be directed to the wrong objects but only to God Himself (cf., e.g., Deut. 17:16; 20:1-4; Lev. 26:7,8; Ps. 33:16,17; Is. 31:1-3; Jer. 9:23,24; Zech. 4:6).

But we have risen and stand upright.

9 Save, LORD!
May the King answer us when we
call.

PSALM 21

Joy in the Salvation of the LORD

To the Chief Musician. A Psalm of David.

The king shall have joy in Your
strength, O LORD;
And in Your salvation how greatly
shall he rejoice!
2 You have given him his heart's
desire,
And have not withheld the [a]request
of his lips. Selah
3 For You meet him with the blessings
of goodness;
You set a crown of pure gold upon his
head.
4 [b]He asked life from You, *and* You gave
it to him—
Length of days forever and ever.
5 His glory *is* great in Your salvation;
Honor and majesty You have placed
upon him.
6 For You have made him most blessed
forever;
[c]You have made him [1]exceedingly
glad with Your presence.
7 For the king trusts in the LORD,
And through the mercy of the Most
High he shall not be [2]moved.
8 Your hand will find all Your enemies;
Your right hand will find those who
hate You.
9 You shall make them as a fiery oven
in the time of Your anger;
The LORD shall swallow them up in
His wrath,
And the fire shall devour them.
10 Their offspring You shall destroy from
the earth,
And their [3]descendants from among
the sons of men.
11 For they intended evil against You;
They devised a plot *which* they are not
able *to* [d]*perform.*
12 Therefore You will make them turn
their back;
You will make ready *Your arrows* on
Your string toward their
faces.

13 Be exalted, O LORD, in Your own
strength!
We will sing and praise Your power.

PSALM 21

2 [a] 2 Sam. 7:26-29
4 [b] Ps. 61:5, 6; 133:3
6 [c] Ps. 16:11; 45:7
[1] Lit. *joyful with gladness*
7 [2] *shaken*
10 [3] Lit. *seed*
11 [d] Ps. 2:1-4

PSALM 22

The Suffering, Praise, and Posterity of the Messiah

To the Chief Musician. Set to [1]"The Deer of the Dawn." A Psalm of David.

My [a]God, My God, why have You
forsaken Me?
Why are You so far from helping Me,
And from the words of My groaning?

PSALM 22

title [1] Heb. *Aijeleth Hashahar*
1 [a] [Matt. 27:46; Mark 15:34]

20:9 This verse could also be rendered: "LORD, grant victory to the king! Answer us when we call!"

21:1-13 The first part of Ps. 21 is a thanksgiving for victory; the last part is an anticipation of future victories in the Lord through the king-general. Two scenarios of victory provide a context for praise and prayer to the Commander-in-Chief of Israel's king-general.

I. A Present-Past Scenario of Praise: Grounded upon Victories Accomplished in the Lord (21:1-6)
II. A Present-Future Scenario of Prayer and Praise: Grounded upon Victories Anticipated in the Lord (21:7-13)

21:2 Cf. Ps. 20:4, the before; Ps. 21:2, the after.

21:3 You set a crown of pure gold upon his head. This is symbolic of superlative blessing (note the reversal in Ezek. 21:25-27).

21:4 The first part of the verse most likely pertains to preservation of life in battle, and the second part to perpetuation of the dynasty (cf. 2 Sam. 7:13,16,29; Pss. 89:4; 132:12).

21:5,6 The King had given great prominence to the king-general.

21:7 For the king. The human responsibility dimension of the previous divine blessings is identified as the king-general's dependent trust in God. But the sovereign grace of God provides the ultimate basis for one not being "moved" or shaken (cf. Pss. 15:5; 16:8; 17:5; Prov. 10:30).

21:8 Your...You. Without denying the mediatorship of the king-general, these delineations obviously put the spotlight upon the Commander-in-Chief.

22:1-31 This psalm presents the reader with a great contrast in mood. Lament characterizes the first 21 verses, while praise and thanksgiving describe the last 10 verses. Prayer accounts for this dramatic shift from lament to praise. It is the story of first being God-forsaken and then God-found and filled. It was applied immediately to David and ultimately to the Greater David, Messiah. The NT contains 15 messianic quotations of or allusions to this psalm, leading some in the early church to label it "the fifth gospel."

I. The Psalmist's Hopelessness (22:1-10)
   A. His Hopelessness and National History (22:1-5)
   B. His Hopelessness and Natal History (22:6-10)
II. The Psalmist's Prayer (22:11-21)
   A. A No-Help Outlook (22:11-18)
   B. A Divine-Help Outlook (22:19-21)
III. The Psalmist's Testimonies and Worship (22:22-31)
   A. An Individual Precipitation of Praise (22:22-25)
   B. A Corporate Perpetuation of Praise (22:26-31)

22:Title. "The Deer of the Dawn." This unique phrase in the superscription is probably best taken as a tune designation.

22:1 This heavy lament rivals Job 3; Ps. 69; Jer. 20:14-18. **My God, My God, why have You forsaken Me?** The repeated noun of direct address to God reflects a personal molecule of hope in a seemingly hopeless situation. "Forsaken" is a strong expression for personal abandonment, intensely felt by David and supremely experienced by Christ on the cross (Matt. 27:46).

2 O My God, I cry in the daytime, but
You do not hear;
And in the night season, and am not
silent.

3 But You *are* holy,
Enthroned in the [b]praises of Israel.
4 Our fathers trusted in You;
They trusted, and You delivered
them.
5 They cried to You, and were
delivered;
[c]They trusted in You, and were not
ashamed.

6 But I *am* [d]a worm, and no man;
[e]A reproach of men, and despised by
the people.
7 [f]All those who see Me ridicule Me;
They [2]shoot out the lip, they shake
the head, *saying,*
8 "He[g] [3]trusted in the LORD, let Him
rescue Him;
[h]Let Him deliver Him, since He
delights in Him!"

9 [i]But You *are* He who took Me out of
the womb;
You made Me trust *while* on My
mother's breasts.
10 I was cast upon You from birth.
From My mother's womb
[j]You *have been* My God.
11 Be not far from Me,
For trouble *is* near;
For *there is* none to help.

12 [k]Many bulls have surrounded Me;
Strong *bulls* of [l]Bashan have encircled
Me.
13 [m]They [4]gape at Me *with* their
mouths,
Like a raging and roaring lion.

14 I am poured out like water,
[n]And all My bones are out of joint;
My heart is like wax;
It has melted [5]within Me.
15 [o]My strength is dried up like a
potsherd,
And [p]My tongue clings to My jaws;
You have brought Me to the dust of
death.

16 For dogs have surrounded Me;
The congregation of the wicked has
enclosed Me.
[q]They[6] pierced My hands and My
feet;
17 I can count all My bones.
[r]They look *and* stare at Me.
18 [s]They divide My garments among
them,
And for My clothing they cast lots.

19 But You, O LORD, do not be far from
Me;
O My Strength, hasten to help Me!
20 Deliver Me from the sword,
[t]My[7] precious *life* from the power of
the dog.
21 [u]Save Me from the lion's mouth
And from the horns of the wild oxen!

[v]You have answered Me.

22 [w]I will declare Your name to [x]My
brethren;
In the midst of the assembly I will
praise You.
23 [y]You who fear the LORD, praise Him!
All you [8]descendants of Jacob, glorify
Him,
And fear Him, all you offspring of
Israel!
24 For He has not despised nor
abhorred the affliction of the
afflicted;
Nor has He hidden His face from
Him;
But [z]when He cried to Him, He
heard.

3 [b] Deut. 10:21; Ps. 148:14
5 [c] Is. 49:23
6 [d] Job 25:6; Is. 41:14 [e] Ps. 109:25; [Is. 53:3]; Matt. 27:39-44
7 [f] Matt. 27:39; Mark 15:29 [2] Show contempt with their mouth
8 [g] Matt. 27:43; Luke 23:35 [h] Ps. 91:14 [3] LXX, Syr., Vg. *hoped;* Tg. *praised*
9 [i] [Ps. 71:5, 6]
10 [j] [Is. 46:3; 49:1]; Luke 1:35
12 [k] Ps. 22:21; 68:30 [l] Deut. 32:14
13 [m] Job 16:10; Ps. 35:21; Lam. 2:16; 3:46 [4] Lit. *have opened their mouths at Me*
14 [n] Ps. 31:10; Dan. 5:6
[5] Lit. *in the midst of My bowels*
15 [o] Prov. 17:22 [p] John 19:28
16 [q] Is. 53:7; Matt. 27:35; John 20:25 [6] So with some Heb. mss., LXX, Syr., Vg.; MT *Like a lion* instead of *They pierced*
17 [r] Luke 23:27, 35
18 [s] Matt. 27:35; Mark 15:24; Luke 23:34; John 19:24
20 [t] Ps. 35:17 [7] Lit. *My only one*
21 [u] 2 Tim. 4:17 [v] Is. 34:7
22 [w] Matt. 4:23; Mark 1:21, 39; Heb. 2:12 [x] [Rom. 8:29]
23 [y] Ps. 135:19, 20 [8] Lit. *seed*
24 [z] Ps. 31:22; Heb. 5:7

22:2-5 The thrust of these verses is "even though You have not responded to me, You remain the Holy One of Israel who has demonstrated His gracious attention time and time again to Your people."

22:6-8 Reproach and ridicule were overwhelming the psalmist. For messianic applications, cf. Matt. 27:39-44; Luke 23:35.

22:7 They shoot out the lip. Lit. "They separate the lip," an idiom for sneering (cf. Job 16:10; Ps. 35:21; Heb. 5:5).

22:8 He trusted in the LORD. Lit "he rolled to the LORD." The idea is that he turned his burden over to the Lord (cf. Ps. 37:5; Prov. 16:3).

22:9,10 The psalmist had a long history of reliance upon God.

22:12,13 This imagery of enemies as rapacious beasts returns (cf. vv. 16,20,21).

22:14,15 These are graphic images showing that his vitality and courage had left him.

22:16 They pierced My hands and My feet. The Heb. text reads "like a lion," i.e., these vicious attacking enemies, like animals, have torn me. Likely, a messianic prediction with reference to crucifixion (cf. Is. 53:5; Zech. 12:10).

22:17 This is a graphic picture of emaciation and exhaustion (cf. Job 33:21; Ps. 102:5).

22:18 They divide...they cast. All 4 gospel writers appeal to this imagery in describing Christ's crucifixion (Matt. 27:35; Mark 15:24; Luke 23:34; John 19:24).

22:21 You have answered Me. A welcomed breaking of God's silence finally arrives. This is fully in keeping with His character (cf. Pss. 20:6; 28:6; 31:22; 118:5).

22:22 The psalmist cannot contain himself; he must testify loudly in the great assembly of God's great mercies. His exuberance is meant to be contagious (cf. Heb. 2:12).

25 [a]My praise *shall be* of You in the great
assembly;
[b]I will pay My vows before those who
fear Him.
26 The poor shall eat and be satisfied;
Those who seek Him will praise the
LORD.
Let your heart live forever!

27 All the ends of the world
Shall remember and turn to the LORD,
And all the families of the [9]nations
Shall worship before [1]You.
28 [c]For the kingdom *is* the LORD's,
And He rules over the nations.

29 [d]All the prosperous of the earth
Shall eat and worship;
[e]All those who go down to [2]the dust
Shall bow before Him,
Even he who cannot keep himself
alive.

30 A posterity shall serve Him.
It will be recounted of the Lord to the
next generation,
31 They will come and declare His
righteousness to a people
who will be born,
That He has done *this*.

25 [a] Ps. 35:18; 40:9, 10 [b] Ps. 61:8; Eccl. 5:4
27 [9] *Gentiles* [1] So with MT, LXX, Tg.; Arab., Syr., Vg. *Him*
28 [c] [Ps. 47:7]; Obad. 21; [Zech. 14:9]; Matt. 6:13
29 [d] Ps. 17:10; 45:12; Hab. 1:16 [e] Ps. 28:1; [Is. 26:19] [2] Death

PSALM 23
1 [a] Ps. 78:52; 80:1; [Is. 40:11]; Ezek. 34:11, 12; [John 10:11; 1 Pet. 2:25; Rev. 7:16, 17] [b] [Ps. 34:9, 10; Phil. 4:19] [1] *lack*
2 [c] Ps. 65:11-13; Ezek. 34:14 [d] [Rev. 7:17] [2] Lit. *pastures of tender grass* [3] Lit. *waters of rest*
3 [e] Ps. 5:8; 31:3; Prov. 8:20
4 [f] Job 3:5; 10:21, 22; 24:17; Ps. 44:19 [g] [Ps. 3:6; 27:1] [h] Ps. 16:8; [Is. 43:2]
5 [i] Ps. 104:15 [j] Ps. 92:10; Luke 7:46
6 [4] So with LXX, Syr., Tg., Vg.; MT *return* [5] Or *To the end of my days*, lit. *For length of days*

PSALM 23

The LORD *the Shepherd of His People*

A Psalm of David.

1 The LORD *is* [a]my shepherd;
[b]I shall not [1]want.
2 [c]He makes me to lie down in [2]green
pastures;
[d]He leads me beside the [3]still waters.
3 He restores my soul;
[e]He leads me in the paths of
righteousness
For His name's sake.

4 Yea, though I walk through the valley
of [f]the shadow of death,
[g]I will fear no evil;
[h]For You *are* with me;
Your rod and Your staff, they comfort
me.

5 You [i]prepare a table before me in the
presence of my enemies;
You [j]anoint my head with oil;
My cup runs over.
6 Surely goodness and mercy shall
follow me
All the days of my life;
And I will [4]dwell in the house of the
LORD
[5]Forever.

22:27 His testimony expands by soliciting universal praises for universal divine blessings (cf. Pss. 67:7; 98:3).

23:1-6 This psalm is probably the best known passage of the OT. It is a testimony by David to the Lord's faithfulness throughout his life. As a hymn of confidence, it pictures the Lord as a disciple's Shepherd-King-Host. David, by using some common ancient Near Eastern images in Ps. 23, progressively unveils his personal relationship with the Lord in 3 stages.

I. David's Exclamation: "The Lord Is My Shepherd" (23:1a)
II. David's Expectations (23:1b-5b)
  A. "I Shall Not Want" (23:1b-3)
  B. "I Will Fear No Evil" (23:4,5b)
III. David's Exultation: "My Cup Runs Over" (23:5c-6)

23:1 The LORD *is* my shepherd. Cf. Gen. 48:15; 49:24; Deut 32:6-12; Pss. 28:9; 74:1; 77:20; 78:52; 79:13; 80:1; 95:7; 100:3; Is. 40:11; Jer. 23:3; Ezek. 34; Hos. 4:16; Mic. 5:4; 7:14; Zech. 9:16 on the image of the Lord as a Shepherd. This imagery was used commonly in kingly applications and is frequently applied to Jesus in the NT (e.g., John 10; Heb. 13:20; 1 Pet. 2:25; 5:4).

23:2,3 Four characterizing activities of the Lord as Shepherd (i.e., emphasizing His grace and guidance) are followed by the ultimate basis for His goodness, i.e., "His name's sake" (cf. Pss. 25:11; 31:3; 106:8; Is. 43:25; 48:9; Ezek. 36:22-32).

23:4 the valley of the shadow of death. Phraseology used to convey a perilously threatening environment (cf. Job 10:21,22; 38:17; Pss. 44:19; 107:10; Jer. 2:6; Luke. 1:79). **Your rod and Your staff.** The shepherd's club and crook are viewed as comforting instruments of protection and direction, respectively.

23:5,6 The able Protector (v. 4) is also the abundant Provider.

23:5 You anoint. The biblical imagery of anointing is frequently associated with blessing (Pss. 45:7; 92:10; 104:15; 133:2; Eccl. 9:8; Amos 6:6; Luke 7:46).

23:6 And I will dwell. There is some question concerning the form in the Heb. text (cf. also Ps. 27:4). Should it be rendered "I shall return" or "I shall dwell"? Whichever way it is taken, by the grace of his Lord, David is expecting ongoing opportunities of intimate fellowship.

Images of God in the Psalms

Images of God as	Reference in Psalms
Shield	3:3; 28:7; 119:114
Rock	18:2; 42:9; 95:1
King	5:2; 44:4; 74:12
Shepherd	23:1; 80:1
Judge	7:11
Refuge	46:1; 62:7
Fortress	31:3; 71:3
Avenger	26:1
Creator	8:1,6
Deliverer	37:39,40
Healer	30:2
Protector	5:11
Provider	78:23-29
Redeemer	107:2

PSALM 24

The King of Glory and His Kingdom

A Psalm of David.

1 The [a]earth *is* the LORD's, and all its
fullness,
The world and those who dwell
therein.
2 For He has [b]founded it upon the seas,
And established it upon the [1]waters.

3 [c]Who may ascend into the hill of the
LORD?
Or who may stand in His holy place?
4 He who has [d]clean hands and [e]a pure
heart,
Who has not lifted up his soul to an
idol,
Nor [f]sworn deceitfully.
5 He shall receive blessing from the
LORD,
And righteousness from the God of
his salvation.
6 This *is* Jacob, the generation of those
who [g]seek Him,
Who seek Your face. Selah

7 [h]Lift up your heads, O you gates!
And be lifted up, you everlasting
doors!
[i]And the King of glory shall come in.
8 Who *is* this King of glory?
The LORD strong and mighty,
The LORD mighty in [j]battle.
9 Lift up your heads, O you gates!
Lift up, you everlasting doors!
And the King of glory shall come in.
10 Who is this King of glory?
The LORD of hosts,
He *is* the King of glory. Selah

PSALM 24
1 [a] 1 Cor. 10:26, 28
2 [b] Ps. 89:11 [1] Lit. *rivers*
3 [c] Ps. 15:1-5
4 [d] [Job 17:9]; Ps. 26:6 [e] Ps. 51:10; 73:1; [Matt. 5:8] [f] Ps. 15:4
6 [g] Ps. 27:4, 8
7 [h] Ps. 118:20; Is. 26:2 [i] Ps. 29:2, 9; 97:6; Hag. 2:7; Acts 7:2; [1 Cor. 2:8]
8 [j] Rev. 19:13-16

PSALM 25

A Plea for Deliverance and Forgiveness

A Psalm of David.

1 To [a]You, O LORD, I lift up my soul.
2 O my God, I [b]trust in You;
Let me not be ashamed;
[c]Let not my enemies triumph over me.
3 Indeed, let no one who [1]waits on You
be ashamed;
Let those be ashamed who deal
treacherously without cause.

4 [d]Show me Your ways, O LORD;
Teach me Your paths.
5 Lead me in Your truth and teach me,
For You *are* the God of my salvation;
On You I wait all the day.

6 Remember, O LORD, [e]Your tender
mercies and Your
lovingkindnesses,
For they *are* from of old.

PSALM 25
1 [a] Ps. 86:4; 143:8
2 [b] Ps. 34:8 [c] Ps. 13:4; 41:11
3 [1] Waits for You in faith
4 [d] Ex. 33:13; Ps. 5:8; 27:11; 86:11; 119:27; 143:8
6 [e] Ps. 103:17; 106:1

24:1-10 The form of Ps. 24 has been disputed. For example, it has been labeled by some as an entrance ceremony (cf. Ps. 15), by others, a hymn of praise, and yet by others, a mixture of both elements. Its occasion has also been contended; however, the view that it might have been used at the time of the bringing of the ark to Jerusalem (2 Sam. 6:12-19; 1 Chr. 13) still has credible appeal. The early church designated it messianically as an ascension psalm (cf. v. 3). The movement of the psalm seems to follow the movement of the people. It traces the community's worship procession, both spatially and spiritually, through 3 progressive stages.

I. Stage One: Worship of the Creator through Contemplation (24:1,2)
II. Stage Two: Worship of the Savior through Consecration (24:3-6)
   A. The Probing Questions Inviting Consecration (24:3)
   B. The Proper Qualities Indicating Consecration (24:4-6)
III. Stage Three: Worship the King through Commemoration (24:7-10)

24:1 the LORD's. On His universal ownership, cf. Ex. 19:5; Deut. 10:14; Pss. 50:12; 89:11; in the NT, cf. 1 Cor. 3:21,23.

24:2 This is a poetic, not a scientific, picture of creation (cf. Gen. 1:9,10; 7:11; 49:25; Ex. 20:4; Deut. 33:13; Job 26:10; Pss. 74:13; 136:6; 2 Pet. 3:5).

24:3 In the liturgy, the questions were most likely asked by the priest. The worshipers would have then responded antiphonally with the "answers." On the form, cf. Ps. 15 and Is. 33:14-16.

24:4 These sample qualities do not signify sinless perfection, but rather basic integrity of inward motive and outward manner.

24:7-9 These are bold personifications indicating that the city gates need to stretch themselves to make way for the awesome entrance of the Great King. By so doing, they too participate in worshiping Him.

24:10 The LORD of hosts. The Divine Warrior possibly comes back into consideration; He, the Commander-in-Chief, is "the LORD of armies" (cf. 1 Sam. 17:45).

25:1-22 David grapples with the heavy issues of life, avoiding denial and affirming dependence. He must trust God in the face of his troubles and troublemakers. These 22 verses follow an acrostic development. On a larger scale, the psalm develops chiastically: Verses 1-7 and 16-22 are parallel sections of prayers for protection and/or deliverance, while the core, vv. 8-15, contains affirmations about God and about His dealings with believers.

I. Prayers in Times of Trial (25:1-7)
II. Praise in Periods of Confidence (25:8-15)
III. Petition for Help in Trouble (25:16-22)

25:1 I lift up my soul. This is a vivid picture of David's dependence (cf. Pss. 86:4; 143:8).

25:2,3 ashamed. The important phenomenon of shame for the wicked and no shame for the righteous returns (cf. a millennial expression of this great principle in Is. 49:23).

25:4,5 The noun and verb metaphors speak of direction for life's pathways (cf. the thrust of Ps. 1).

25:6,7 Remember…do not remember…remember. These are not concerns about God forgetting something, but the psalmist's prayer reminders about God's gracious covenant promises and provisions, all of which are grounded upon His "goodness sake" (cf. v. 11, "Your name's sake").

7 Do not remember [f]the sins of my youth, nor my transgressions;
[g]According to Your mercy remember me,
For Your goodness' sake, O LORD.

8 Good and upright *is* the LORD;
Therefore He teaches sinners in the way.
9 The humble He guides in justice,
And the humble He teaches His way.
10 All the paths of the LORD *are* mercy and truth,
To such as keep His covenant and His testimonies.
11 [h]For Your name's sake, O LORD,
Pardon my iniquity, for it *is* great.
12 Who *is* the man that fears the LORD?
[i]Him shall [2]He teach in the way [2]He chooses.
13 [j]He himself shall dwell in [3]prosperity,
And [k]his descendants shall inherit the earth.
14 [l]The secret of the LORD *is* with those who fear Him,
And He will show them His covenant.
15 [m]My eyes *are* ever toward the LORD,
For He shall [4]pluck my feet out of the net.

16 [n]Turn Yourself to me, and have mercy on me,
For I *am* [5]desolate and afflicted.
17 The troubles of my heart have enlarged;
Bring me out of my distresses!
18 [o]Look on my affliction and my pain,
And forgive all my sins.
19 Consider my enemies, for they are many;
And they hate me with [6]cruel hatred.
20 Keep my soul, and deliver me;
Let me not be ashamed, for I put my trust in You.
21 Let integrity and uprightness preserve me,
For I wait for You.

22 [p]Redeem Israel, O God,
Out of all their troubles!

7 [f]Job 13:26; [Jer. 3:25] [g]Ps. 51:1
11 [h]Ps. 31:3; 79:9; 109:21; 143:11
12 [i][Ps. 25:8; 37:23] [2]Or *he*
13 [j][Prov. 19:23] [k]Ps. 37:11; 69:36; Matt. 5:5 [3]Lit. *goodness*
14 [l][Prov. 3:32; John 7:17]
15 [m][Ps. 123:2; 141:8] [4]Lit. *bring out*
16 [n]Ps. 69:16 [5]*lonely*
18 [o]2 Sam. 16:12; Ps. 31:7
19 [6]*violent hatred*
22 [p][Ps. 130:8]

PSALM 26

A Prayer for Divine Scrutiny and Redemption

A Psalm of David.

Vindicate [a]me, O LORD,
For I have [b]walked in my integrity.
[c]I have also trusted in the LORD;
I shall not slip.
2 [d]Examine me, O LORD, and [1]prove me;
Try my mind and my heart.
3 For Your lovingkindness *is* before my eyes,
And [e]I have walked in Your truth.
4 I have not [f]sat with idolatrous mortals,
Nor will I go in with hypocrites.

PSALM 26
1 [a]Ps. 7:8 [b]2 Kin. 20:3; [Prov. 20:7] [c][Ps. 13:5; 28:7]
2 [d]Ps. 17:3; 139:23 [1]*test me*
3 [e]2 Kin. 20:3; Ps. 86:11
4 [f]Ps. 1:1; Jer. 15:17

25:8-10 More metaphors for life's paths are used for the purpose of begging divine direction (cf. vv. 4,5). The last line of v. 10 emphasizes covenant responsibilities on the human side (cf. the divine side in vv. 6,7).

25:11 Pardon my iniquity, for it *is* great. A maturing disciple develops an increasing sensitivity to sin which drives him more consistently to an appropriation of the promises of God's pardoning grace (cf. v. 18b).

25:12 Who…? This interrogative device (cf. Pss. 15; 24) serves as an introductory vehicle to the hallmarks of genuine discipleship.

25:14 The secret… This could well be rendered the "counsel" or intimate personal communion (cf. Job 29:4; Ps. 55:14; Prov. 3:32).

25:15 net. The snare of the hunter or fowler (cf. Ps. 31:4).

25:16-21 Ten rapid-fire prayer requests, asking for relief and encouragement, lie at the heart of these 6 verses.

25:16 desolate and afflicted. These terms speak of isolation and humiliation.

25:22 The shift from the individual to the community is really not surprising, since the welfare of the theocratic people is inextricably connected to the covenant individual (cf. Ps. 51:18-19).

26:1-12 Psalms 26, 27, and 28 mention the "house" of the Lord because public worship is the central interest. The form of Ps. 26 is mixed, i.e., containing elements of declarations of innocence, prayer, and confidence, (cf. v. 1 as a paradigm). Structurally, 4 intermingling prayers and proofs reveal the psalmist's passion to worship the Lord in spirit and in truth.

I. His Situation (26:1)
   A. His Prayer for Justice (26:1a)
   B. His Proofs of Commitment (26:1b)
II. His Transparency (26:2-8)
   A. His Prayer for Scrutiny (26:2)
   B. His Proofs of Loyalty (26:3-8)
III. His Eschatological Outlook (26:9-11a)
   A. His Prayers for Final Favor (26:9)
   B. His Proofs of Measurable Difference (26:10-11a)
IV. His Confidence (26:11b-12)
   A. His Prayers Show Confidence in the Person of God (26:11b)
   B. His Proofs Show Confidence in the Provision of God (26:12)

26:1 Vindicate me. Lit. "Judge me!" This refers to exoneration of some false accusations and/or charges under the protection of the covenant stipulations of the theocratic law (cf. Pss. 7:8; 35:24; 43:1). **my integrity.** Again, this is not a claim to perfection, but of innocence, particularly as viewed within the context of ungrounded "legal" charges (cf. Ps. 7:8; Prov. 10:9; 19:1; 20:7; 28:6). **I shall not slip.** Cf. Pss. 18:36; 37:31; contra. Ps. 73:18-20.

26:2 Examine…prove…Try. These 3 invitations to divine scrutiny are essentially synonymous ways of testing, refining, and purifying (cf. Pss. 11:4,5; 12:6; 17:3; 66:10; Jer. 17:9,10).

26:4,5 This language suggests that David is making a personal application of the characteristics of Ps. 1:1.

5 I have [g]hated the assembly of evildoers,
And will not sit with the wicked.

6 I will wash my hands in innocence;
So I will go about Your altar, O LORD,
7 That I may proclaim with the voice of thanksgiving,
And tell of all Your wondrous works.
8 LORD, [h]I have loved the habitation of Your house,
And the place [2]where Your glory dwells.

9 [i]Do[3] not gather my soul with sinners,
Nor my life with bloodthirsty men,
10 In whose hands *is* a sinister scheme,
And whose right hand is full of [j]bribes.

11 But as for me, I will walk in my integrity;
Redeem me and be merciful to me.
12 [k]My foot stands in an even place;
In the congregations I will bless the LORD.

PSALM 27

An Exuberant Declaration of Faith

A Psalm of David.

The LORD *is* my [a]light and my salvation;
Whom shall I fear?
The [b]LORD *is* the strength of my life;
Of whom shall I be afraid?
2 When the wicked came against me
To [c]eat[1] up my flesh,
My enemies and foes,
They stumbled and fell.
3 [d]Though an army may encamp against me,
My heart shall not fear;
Though war may rise against me,
In this I *will be* confident.

4 [e]One *thing* I have desired of the LORD,
That will I seek:
That I may [f]dwell in the house of the LORD
All the days of my life,
To behold the [2]beauty of the LORD,
And to inquire in His temple.
5 For [g]in the time of trouble
He shall hide me in His pavilion;
In the secret place of His tabernacle
He shall hide me;
He shall [h]set me high upon a rock.

6 And now [i]my head shall be [3]lifted up above my enemies all around me;
Therefore I will offer sacrifices of [4]joy in His tabernacle;
I will sing, yes, I will sing praises to the LORD.

7 Hear, O LORD, *when* I cry with my voice!
Have mercy also upon me, and answer me.
8 *When You said*, "Seek My face,"
My heart said to You, "Your face, LORD, I will seek."
9 [j]Do not hide Your face from me;
Do not turn Your servant away in anger;
You have been my help;
Do not leave me nor forsake me,
O God of my salvation.

5 [g]Ps. 31:6; 139:21
8 [h]Ps. 27:4; 84:1-4, 10 [2]Lit. *of the tabernacle of Your glory*
9 [i]Ps. 28:3 [3]*Do not take away*
10 [j]1 Sam. 8:3
12 [k]Ps. 40:2

PSALM 27

1 [a]Ps. 18:28; 84:11; [Is. 60:19, 20; Mic. 7:8] [b]Ex. 15:2; Ps. 62:7; 118:14; Is. 12:2; 33:2
2 [c]Ps. 14:4 [1]*devour*
3 [d]Ps. 3:6
4 [e]Ps. 26:8; 65:4 [f]Luke 2:37 [2]*delightfulness*
5 [g]Ps. 31:20; 91:1 [h]Ps. 40:2
6 [i]Ps. 3:3 [3]Lifted up in honor [4]*joyous shouts*
9 [j]Ps. 69:17; 143:7

26:6 Personal cleansing is a necessary prerequisite for acceptable worship (cf. Ps. 24:3,4).

26:7 That I may proclaim. The Heb. text reads "to hear the sound of praise and to proclaim…," a reference to the enjoyment of and participation in public worship.

26:8 Your glory. God's "glory" most frequently refers to His self-manifestation, e.g., His attributes revealed and exhibited. *See note on Lev. 9:23.*

26:9-11 This is another sharp contrast between the injurious and the innocent.

26:12 My foot stands. Cf. v. 1, "I shall not slip."

27:1-14 This psalm is characterized by strong contrasts such as lament and laud; persecution and praise; plus warfare and worship. In Ps. 27, the psalmist, in the presence of his Lord, engages in 3 conversations which help him balance the ups and downs of real life.

I. He Converses with Himself about Privileges (27:1-6)
II. He Converses with the Lord about Problems (27:7-12)
III. He Converses with Himself about Perseverance (27:13,14)

27:1 light. This important biblical word picture with exclusively positive connotations pictures the light of redemption in contrast to the darkness of condemnation (cf. Pss. 18:28; 36:9; 43:3; Is. 60:1,19,20; Mic. 7:8; John 8:12; 12:46; 1 John 1:5).

27:2 To eat up my flesh. An allusion to the psalmist's enemies being like vicious beasts (cf. Pss. 7:2; 14:4; 17:12; Job 19:22; Jer. 30:16; 50:7). This wording was also employed to describe slander and defamation (cf. a close Aram. parallel in Dan. 3:8; 6:24). **They stumbled and fell.** This doublet conveys thorough defeat (cf. Is. 3:8; 8:15; 31:3; Jer. 46:6).

27:4 One *thing*. The primary issue in David's life was to live in God's presence and by His purpose (cf. Pss. 15:1; 23:6; cf. Paul's "one thing" in Phil. 3:13).

27:5 His pavilion. David portrays the privileges of divine protection as being hidden in God's "booth" or "shelter," a term in parallelism with "tabernacle" or "tent."

27:8,9 "Seek My face," … Your face … Your face. God's "face" indicates His personal presence or simply His being (Pss. 24:6; 105:4); and seeking His face is a primary characteristic of true believers who desire fellowship with God (cf. Deut. 4:29; 2 Chr. 11:16; 20:4; Ps. 40:16; Jer. 50:4; Hos. 3:5; Zech. 8:22).

10 [k]When my father and my mother
forsake me,
Then the LORD will take care of me.

11 [l]Teach me Your way, O LORD,
And lead me in a smooth path,
because of my enemies.
12 Do not deliver me to the will of my
adversaries;
For [m]false witnesses have risen
against me,
And such as breathe out violence.
13 *I would have lost heart,* unless I had
believed
That I would see the goodness of the
LORD
[n]In the land of the living.

14 [o]Wait[5] on the LORD;
Be of good courage,
And He shall strengthen your heart;
Wait, I say, on the LORD!

PSALM 28

Rejoicing in Answered Prayer

A Psalm of David.

To You I will cry, O LORD my Rock:
[a]Do not be silent to me,
[b]Lest, if You *are* silent to me,
I become like those who go down to
the pit.
2 Hear the voice of my supplications
When I cry to You,
[c]When I lift up my hands [d]toward
Your holy sanctuary.

3 Do not [1]take me away with the
wicked
And with the workers of iniquity,
[e]Who speak peace to their neighbors,
But evil *is* in their hearts.
4 [f]Give them according to their deeds,
And according to the wickedness of
their endeavors;
Give them according to the work of
their hands;
Render to them what they deserve.
5 Because [g]they do not regard the
works of the LORD,
Nor the operation of His hands,
He shall destroy them
And not build them up.

6 Blessed *be* the LORD,
Because He has heard the voice of my
supplications!
7 The LORD *is* [h]my strength and my
shield;
My heart [i]trusted in Him, and I am
helped;
Therefore my heart greatly rejoices,
And with my song I will praise Him.

8 The LORD *is* [2]their strength,
And He *is* the [j]saving refuge of His
[3]anointed.
9 Save Your people,
And bless [k]Your inheritance;
Shepherd them also,
[l]And bear them up forever.

PSALM 29

Praise to God in His Holiness and Majesty

A Psalm of David.

Give[1] [a]unto the LORD, O you mighty
ones,
Give unto the LORD glory and
strength.
2 [2]Give unto the LORD the glory [3]due to
His name;

10 [k] Is. 49:15
11 [l] Ps. 25:4; 86:11; 119:33
12 [m] Deut. 19:18; Ps. 35:11; Matt. 26:60; Mark 14:56; John 19:33
13 [n] Job 28:13; Ps. 52:5; 116:9; 142:5; Is. 38:11; Jer. 11:19; Ezek. 26:20
14 [o] Ps. 25:3; 37:34; 40:1; 62:5; 130:5; Prov. 20:22; Is. 25:9; [Hab. 2:3] [5] Wait in faith

PSALM 28

1 [a] Ps. 35:22; 39:12; 83:1 [b] Ps. 88:4; 143:7; Prov. 1:12
2 [c] Ps. 5:7 [d] Ps. 138:2
3 [e] Ps. 12:2; 55:21; 62:4; Jer. 9:8 [1] *drag*
4 [f] [Ps. 62:12]; 2 Tim. 4:14; [Rev. 18:6; 22:12]
5 [g] Is. 5:12
7 [h] Ps. 18:2; 59:17 [i] Ps. 13:5; 112:7
8 [j] Ps. 20:6 [2] So with MT, Tg.; LXX, Syr., Vg. *the strength of His people* [3] Commissioned one, Heb. *messiah*
9 [k] [Deut. 9:29; 32:9; 1 Kin. 8:51; Ps. 33:12]; 106:40 [l] Deut. 1:31; Is. 63:9

PSALM 29

1 [a] 1 Chr. 16:28, 29 [1] *Ascribe*
2 [2] *Ascribe* [3] Lit. *of His name*

27:10 Even though those nearest and dearest to David might abandon him, his Lord would always be concerned about and care for him (cf. Deut. 31:6,8; Is. 49:14,15; Heb. 13:5).

27:14 Wait...Wait. This particular word for waiting connotes either a tense or eager and patient anticipation of the Lord (cf. Pss. 37:34; 40:1).

28:1-9 We encounter a radical shift from lamentation and prayer to thanksgiving. The psalmist, without regard for his unchanged circumstances, shows confidence in crisis. David, moving through two cycles of crisis and confidence, magnifies the justice of God.

I. First Cycle: Individual in Outlook, and Terminates in Praise (28:1-7)
   A. His Personal Crisis (28:1-5b)
   B. His Personal Confidence (28:5c-7)
II. Second Cycle: Corporate in Outlook, and Terminates in Prayer (28:8,9)
   A. His Reassurance in the Light of Corporate Confidence (28:8)
   B. His Request in the Face of Corporate Crisis (28:9)

28:1 silent...silent. On the striking picture of God being deaf and dumb regarding his situation, cf. Pss. 35:22; 83:1; 109:1; Is. 57:11; 64:12; 65:6; Hab. 1:13.

28:2 When I lift up my hands. On this symbolic "posture" representing the heart's attitude in dependent prayer, see Ex. 9:29; 17:11,12; Ps. 63:4; 1 Tim. 2:8.

28:3-5 The iniquities of the psalmist's (really God's) enemies bring forth sharp imprecations.

28:6 Because He has heard the voice of my supplications! Contrast vv. 1,2. Through faith, the psalmist will live his life as though God has already intervened.

28:8 His anointed. This is most likely a corporate reference to the people of God being anointed, not to an individual (cf. Hab. 3:13).

28:9 Your inheritance. God amazingly considers His people a most precious possession (cf. Deut. 7:6-16; 9:29; 1 Sam 10:1; Pss. 33:12; 94:5; Eph. 1:18).

29:1-11 This psalm has all the earmarks of the earliest Heb. poetry (cf. Ex. 15; Judg. 5). As to its general form, it is a hymn. Many of its images appear in parallel literature, especially in referencing pagan gods by various "forces of nature." However, the Lord is the unique Creator and supreme Sovereign over all these phenomena. He alone

Worship the LORD in [b]the [4]beauty of
holiness.

3 The voice of the LORD *is* over the
waters;
[c]The God of glory thunders;
The LORD *is* over many waters.
4 The voice of the LORD *is* powerful;
The voice of the LORD *is* full of
majesty.

5 The voice of the LORD breaks [d]the
cedars,
Yes, the LORD splinters the cedars of
Lebanon.
6 [e]He makes them also skip like a calf,
Lebanon and [f]Sirion like a young
wild ox.
7 The voice of the LORD [5]divides the
flames of fire.

8 The voice of the LORD shakes the
wilderness;
The LORD shakes the Wilderness of
[g]Kadesh.
9 The voice of the LORD makes the
[h]deer give birth,
And strips the forests bare;
And in His temple everyone says,
"Glory!"

10 The [i]LORD sat *enthroned* at the Flood,
And [j]the LORD sits as King forever.

2 [b] 2 Chr. 20:21; Ps. 110:3 [4] *majesty*
3 [c] [Job 37:4, 5]; Ps. 18:13; Acts 7:2
5 [d] Judg. 9:15; 1 Kin. 5:6; Ps. 104:16; Is. 2:13; 14:8
6 [e] Ps. 114:4 [f] Deut. 3:9
7 [5] *stirs up*, lit. *hews out*
8 [g] Num. 13:26
9 [h] Job 39:1
10 [i] Gen. 6:17; Job 38:8, 25 [j] Ps. 10:16
11 [k] Ps. 28:8; 68:35; [Is. 40:29]

PSALM 30
title [a] Deut. 20:5
1 [b] Ps. 28:9 [c] Ps. 25:2
2 [d] Ps. 6:2; 103:3; [Is. 53:5]
3 [e] Ps. 86:13 [1] So with Qr., Tg.; Kt., LXX, Syr., Vg. *from those who descend to the pit*
4 [f] Ps. 97:12 [2] Or *His holiness*
5 [g] Ps. 103:9; Is. 26:20; 54:7, 8 [h] Ps. 63:3 [3] *a shout of joy*
6 [4] *shaken*

11 [k]The LORD will give strength to His
people;
The LORD will bless His people with
peace.

PSALM 30

The Blessedness of Answered Prayer

A Psalm. A Song [a]at the dedication of the
house of David.

I will extol You, O LORD, for You have
[b]lifted me up,
And have not let my foes [c]rejoice over
me.
2 O LORD my God, I cried out to You,
And You [d]healed me.
3 O LORD, [e]You brought my soul up
from the grave;
You have kept me alive, [1]that I should
not go down to the pit.

4 [f]Sing praise to the LORD, you saints of
His,
And give thanks at the remembrance
of [2]His holy name.
5 For [g]His anger *is but for* a moment,
[h]His favor *is for* life;
Weeping may endure for a night,
But [3]joy *comes* in the morning.

6 Now in my prosperity I said,
"I shall never be [4]moved."

is "the God of gods" (Dan. 11:36). In view of these realities, 3 representative realms of the supremacy of God bring forth praise to Yahweh (Jehovah) alone.

I. The Lord's Supremacy over Heavenly Beings (29:1,2)
II. The Lord's Supremacy over the "Forces of Nature" (29:3-9)
III. The Lord's Supremacy over Humanity (29:10,11)

29:1 mighty ones. Lit "sons of God" (cf. Ps. 89:6 in its context of vv. 5-10; cf. the plural form of "gods" in Ex. 15:11). The reference here in Ps. 29 is most likely to Yahweh's mighty angels.

29:3-9 This is an awesome theophany, depicting dramatic movements in the powerful manifestations of the Lord God, which function to establish His supremacy as the only true God in comparison with any of the so-called gods of Israel's pagan neighbors.

29:3 The voice of the LORD. His voice is frequently associated with the thunder (cf., e.g., 1 Sam. 7:10; Job 37:4,5; Ps. 18:13; Is. 30:30, 31).

29:5 the cedars...the cedars of Lebanon. These are the grandest of forest trees, and those of Lebanon were especially impressive.

29:6 Sirion. This is the Phoenician name for Mt. Hermon to the N of Dan (cf. Deut. 3:9).

29:8 the Wilderness of Kadesh. Kadesh Barnea is in the southern desert country. For its importance in the history of Israel, *see note on Num. 20:1.*

29:10 the Flood. This refers to the universal flood of Gen. 6–8 (esp., Gen. 7:17)

30:1-12 A mixture of forms characterize Ps. 30. David speaks out of a cycle of life (i.e., lamentation and laud), especially moving through prayer to praise. In spite of great variety, the psalm is bonded together by praise emphases (cf. vv. 4,9,12). The psalmist's beginning and ending pledges to praise provide structure for his prayers and testimonies.

I. His Beginning Pledge of Praise (30:1a)
II. His Look Back upon Historic Prayers and Testimonies (30:1b-9)
   A. His Individual Remembrance (30:1b-3)
   B. His Public Reminders (30:4,5)
   C. His Individual Reflections (30:6-9)
III. His Look Ahead to Continuing Prayers and Testimonies (30:10-12a)
IV. His Concluding Pledge of Praise (30:12b)

30:Title The first and last parts of this title, i.e., "A Psalm...of David," are common notations in the superscriptions of many psalms. However, the middle words, "a song of dedication," or "consecration of the house," were probably added later, although they could have referenced David's temporary tent for the ark erected on Mt. Zion (2 Sam. 6:17) or his own house (2 Sam. 5:11,12).

30:2,3 You healed me. God alone is the unique healer (cf. Ex. 15:26; Deut. 32:39; Ps. 107:20). David is extolling God for bringing him back from a near-death experience.

30:5 This stark contrast constitutes one of the most worshipful testimonies from the Scriptures (cf. the principle in Is. 54:7,8; John 16:20-22; 2 Cor. 4:17).

30:6 David recalls his previous independent attitude and arrogant talk. God had warned the nation and its leaders about such sinfully

7 LORD, by Your favor You have made
my mountain stand strong;
[i]You hid Your face, *and* I was troubled.

8 I cried out to You, O LORD;
And to the LORD I made supplication:
9 "What profit *is there* in my blood,
When I go down to the pit?
[j]Will the dust praise You?
Will it declare Your truth?
10 Hear, O LORD, and have mercy on me;
LORD, be my helper!"

11 [k]You have turned for me my mourning
into dancing;
You have put off [5]my sackcloth and
clothed me with gladness,
12 To the end that *my* [6]glory may sing
praise to You and not be
silent.
O LORD my God, I will give thanks to
You forever.

PSALM 31

The LORD a Fortress in Adversity

To the Chief Musician. A Psalm of David.

In [a]You, O LORD, I [1]put my trust;
Let me never be ashamed;
Deliver me in Your righteousness.
2 [b]Bow down Your ear to me,
Deliver me speedily;
Be my rock of [2]refuge,
A [3]fortress of defense to save me.

3 [c]For You *are* my rock and my fortress;
Therefore, [d]for Your name's sake,
Lead me and guide me.
4 Pull me out of the net which they
have secretly laid for me,
For You *are* my strength.

5 [e]Into Your hand I commit my spirit;
You have redeemed me, O LORD God
of [f]truth.

6 I have hated those [g]who regard
useless idols;
But I trust in the LORD.
7 I will be glad and rejoice in Your
mercy,
For You have considered my trouble;
You have [h]known my soul in
[4]adversities,
8 And have not [i]shut[5] me up into the
hand of the enemy;
[j]You have set my feet in a wide place.

9 Have mercy on me, O LORD, for I am
in trouble;
[k]My eye wastes away with grief,
Yes, my soul and my [6]body!
10 For my life is spent with grief,
And my years with sighing;
My strength fails because of my
iniquity,
And my bones waste away.
11 [l]I am a [7]reproach among all my
enemies,
But [m]especially among my
neighbors,
And *am* repulsive to my
acquaintances;
[n]Those who see me outside flee from
me.
12 [o]I am forgotten like a dead man, out of
mind;
I am like a [8]broken vessel.
13 [p]For I hear the slander of many;
[q]Fear *is* on every side;
While they [r]take counsel together
against me,
They scheme to take away my life.

7 [i] [Deut. 31:17; Ps. 104:29; 143:7]
9 [j] [Ps. 6:5]
11 [k] Eccl. 3:4; Is. 61:3; Jer. 31:4 [5] The sackcloth of my mourning
12 [6] *soul*

PSALM 31

1 [a] Ps. 22:5 [1] *have taken refuge*
2 [b] Ps. 17:6; 71:2; 86:1; 102:2 [2] *strength* [3] Lit. *house of fortresses*
3 [c] [Ps. 18:2] [d] Ps. 23:3; 25:11
5 [e] Luke 23:46 [f] [Deut. 32:4]; Ps. 71:22
6 [g] Jon. 2:8
7 [h] [John 10:27] [4] *troubles*
8 [i] [Deut. 32:30]; Ps. 37:33 [j] [Ps. 4:1; 18:19] [5] *given me over*
9 [k] Ps. 6:7 [6] Lit. *belly*
11 [l] [Is. 53:4] [m] Job 19:13; Ps. 38:11; 88:8, 18 [n] Ps. 64:8 [7] *despised thing*
12 [o] Ps. 88:4, 5 [8] Lit. *perishing*
13 [p] Ps. 50:20; Jer. 20:10 [q] Lam. 2:22 [r] Ps. 62:4; Matt. 27:1

myopic outlooks (cf. Deut. 8:11-20; note sample failures in Deut. 32:15; 2 Chr. 32:25; Jer. 22:21; Hos. 13:6; Dan. 4:28-37). By the grace of God, David woke up to the fact that he was acting like his arrogant adversaries (cf. Ps. 10:6).

30:8-10 A familiar argument for preservation of life (cf. Pss. 6:5; 28:1; 88:10-12; 115:17; Is. 38:18,19).

30:12 *my* glory. Now with renewed perspective (contra. v. 6), he recognizes that all he is and has is due to God's unmerited grace (cf. v. 7a).

31:1-24 This psalm contains more of David's problems, prayers, and praises. David will again walk a road that takes him from anguish to assurance. Within the two settings of Ps. 31, the psalmist's testimonies passionately celebrate the sufficiencies of God.

I. The Originally Private Setting (31:1-18)
   A. His Testimony about Security and Salvation (31:1-5)
   B. His Testimony about Discernment and Deliverance (31:6-8)
   C. His Testimony about Reproach and Relief (31:9-18)
II. The Ultimately Public Setting (31:19-24)
   A. His Testimonies and Divine Exaltation (31:19-22)
   B. His Testimonies and Human Exhortation (31:23,24)

31:2 Bow down Your ear to me. This is a bold pay-attention-to-my-prayer demand (cf. Ps. 102:2).

31:3 The language resembles that of Ps. 23:1-3, except it now comes packaged in prayer requests.

31:5 Into Your hand. This is applied to both the lesser David and the Greater David (Luke 23:46); here it involves the common denominator of trust. This is a metaphor depicting God's power and control (cf. v. 15a; contra. vv. 8,15b).

31:6 I have hated. Cf. Ps. 26:5 on the proper basis for such hatred (cf. Ps. 139:21). **useless idols.** This is a common designation for false gods (cf. Deut. 32:21; 1 Kin. 16:13; Jer. 10:15; 14:22; 16:19; 18:15; Jon. 2:8). On the "idiocy" of idolatry, see Hab. 2:18-20.

31:9,10 These terms quite frequently are employed metaphysically to convey the non-physical impact of trials and tribulations.

31:11 He was a reproach to adversaries and personal acquaintances alike, a very painful alienation (cf. Ps. 88:8,18).

31:13 Fear *is* on every side. (cf. Jer. 6:25; 20:3,10; 46:5; 49:29; Lam. 2:22). **They scheme.** On such wicked plotting, cf. Jer. 11:19; 18:23.

14 But as for me, I trust in You, O LORD;
I say, "You *are* my God."
15 My times *are* in Your [s]hand;
Deliver me from the hand of my enemies,
And from those who persecute me.
16 [t]Make Your face shine upon Your servant;
Save me for Your mercies' sake.
17 [u]Do not let me be ashamed, O LORD, for I have called upon You;
Let the wicked be ashamed;
[v]Let them be silent in the grave.
18 [w]Let the lying lips be put to silence,
Which [x]speak insolent things proudly and contemptuously against the righteous.

19 [y]Oh, how great *is* Your goodness,
Which You have laid up for those who fear You,
Which You have prepared for those who trust in You
In the presence of the sons of men!
20 [z]You shall hide them in the secret place of Your presence
From the plots of man;
[a]You shall keep them secretly in a [9]pavilion
From the strife of tongues.

21 Blessed *be* the LORD,
For [b]He has shown me His marvelous kindness in a [1]strong city!
22 For I said in my haste,
"I am cut off from before Your eyes";
Nevertheless You heard the voice of my supplications
When I cried out to You.
23 Oh, love the LORD, all you His saints!
For the LORD preserves the faithful,
And fully repays the proud person.
24 [c]Be of good courage,
And He shall strengthen your heart,
All you who hope in the LORD.

PSALM 32

The Joy of Forgiveness

A Psalm of David. A [1]Contemplation.

Blessed *is he whose* [a]transgression *is* forgiven,
Whose sin *is* covered.
2 Blessed *is* the man to whom the LORD [b]does not [2]impute iniquity,
And [c]in whose spirit *there is* no deceit.

3 When I kept silent, my bones grew old
Through my groaning all the day long.
4 For day and night Your [d]hand was heavy upon me;
My vitality was turned into the drought of summer. Selah
5 I acknowledged my sin to You,
And my iniquity I have not hidden.
[e]I said, "I will confess my transgressions to the LORD,"
And You forgave the iniquity of my sin. Selah

6 [f]For this cause everyone who is godly shall [g]pray to You
In a time when You may be found;

15 [s][Job 14:5; 24:1]
16 [t]Ps. 4:6; 80:3
17 [u]Ps. 25:2, 20 [v][1 Sam. 2:9]; Ps. 94:17; 115:17
18 [w]Ps. 109:2; 120:2 [x][1 Sam. 2:3]; Ps. 94:4; [Jude 15]
19 [y]Ps. 145:7; [Rom. 2:4; 11:22]
20 [z][Ps. 27:5; 32:7] [a]Job 5:21 [9]*shelter*
21 [b][Ps. 17:7] [1]*fortified*
24 [c][Ps. 27:14]

PSALM 32

title [1]Heb. *Maschil*
1 [a][Ps. 85:2; 103:3]; Rom. 4:7, 8
2 [b][2 Cor. 5:19] [c]John 1:47 [2]*charge his account with*
4 [d]1 Sam. 5:6; Ps. 38:2; 39:10
5 [e]2 Sam. 12:13; Ps. 38:18; [Prov. 28:13; 1 John 1:9]
6 [f][1 Tim. 1:16] [g]Ps. 69:13; Is. 55:6

31:16 This is a request for a personal application of the blessing of Num. 6:25 (cf. Pss. 4:6; 67:1; 80:3,7,19; 119:135).

31:17 On their shame but not his, cf. Ps. 25:2,3,20; Jer. 17:18.

31:18,20 His enemies exhibit signs of "mouth" disease.

31:19 Your goodness. As in the case of His other attributes, God being perfectly good is the grounds for His doing good things (cf. Ps. 119:68).

31:23 love the LORD. Biblical love includes an attitudinal response and demonstrated obedience (cf. Deut. 6:4,5; 10:12; John 14:15,21; 15:10; 2 John 6). The assurance of both reward and retribution is a biblical maxim (e.g., Deut. 7:9,10).

31:24 Be of good courage. A sing. form of this pl. imperative was addressed to Joshua in 1:7. It is used nearly 20 times in the OT, particularly in anticipation of battle.

32:1-11 This psalm has been classified by the early church as one of 7 penitential psalms (cf. 6; 38; 51; 102; 130; 143). Among these, Pss. 32 and 51 stand out as confessional giants. As historically related to the life of David and especially in connection with the Bathsheba episode (cf. 2 Sam. 11–12), Ps. 51 would have preceded Ps. 32. The overall thrust, intent, and development of Ps. 32 may be summarized as follows: Life's most important lessons about sin, confession, and forgiveness are skillfully shared by David through two avenues of approach.

I. First Avenue: Remembering These Lessons (32:1-5)
   A. Lessons about Results (32:1,2)
   B. Lessons about Resistance (32:3,4)
   C. Lessons about Responses (32:5)
II. Second Avenue: Relaying These Lessons (32:6-11)
   A. Lessons about Responses (32:6,7)
   B. Lessons about Resistance (32:8,9)
   C. Lessons about Results (32:10-11)

32:Title "A contemplation" in the heading introduces a new technical term. It could indicate that Ps. 32 was a "*contemplative* poem," or a "psalm of *understanding,*" or a "*skillful* psalm."

32:1,2 transgression...sin...iniquity. Three key OT words for sin occur, viewing it respectively as rebellion, failure, and perversion.

32:3,4 These are vivid descriptions of the physical effects of his impenitent state.

32:5 David picks up the key terms that he had used to describe sin in vv. 1,2, but now, in a context of personal confession, he identifies those heinous affronts to the person of God as his own. On the priority of confession, cf. Prov. 28:13; 1 John 1:8-10.

32:6 David slips right back into teaching mode in this verse, emphasizing that every person who knows the grace of God should not presume upon that grace by putting off confession.

Surely in a flood of great waters
They shall not come near him.
7 [h]You *are* my hiding place;
You shall preserve me from trouble;
You shall surround me with [i]songs of deliverance. Selah

8 I will instruct you and teach you in the way you should go;
I will guide you with My eye.
9 Do not be like the [j]horse *or* like the mule,
Which have no understanding,
Which must be harnessed with bit and bridle,
Else they will not come near you.

10 [k]Many sorrows *shall be* to the wicked;
But [l]he who trusts in the LORD, mercy shall surround him.
11 [m]Be glad in the LORD and rejoice, you righteous;
And shout for joy, all *you* upright in heart!

PSALM 33

The Sovereignty of the LORD in Creation and History

Rejoice [a]in the LORD, O you righteous!
For praise from the upright is beautiful.
2 Praise the LORD with the harp;
[1]Make melody to Him with an instrument of ten strings.
3 Sing to Him a new song;
Play skillfully with a shout of joy.

4 For the word of the LORD *is* right,
And all His work *is done* in truth.
5 He loves righteousness and justice;
The earth is full of the goodness of the LORD.

6 [b]By the word of the LORD the heavens were made,
And all the [c]host of them [d]by the breath of His mouth.
7 [e]He gathers the waters of the sea together [2]as a heap;
He lays up the deep in storehouses.

8 Let all the earth fear the LORD;
Let all the inhabitants of the world stand in awe of Him.
9 For [f]He spoke, and it was *done;*
He commanded, and it stood fast.

10 [g]The LORD brings the counsel of the nations to nothing;
He makes the plans of the peoples of no effect.
11 [h]The counsel of the LORD stands forever,
The plans of His heart to all generations.
12 Blessed *is* the nation whose God *is* the LORD,
The people He has [i]chosen as His own inheritance.

13 [j]The LORD looks from heaven;
He sees all the sons of men.
14 From the place of His dwelling He looks
On all the inhabitants of the earth;
15 He fashions their hearts individually;
[k]He [3]considers all their works.

16 [l]No king *is* saved by the multitude of an army;

---

7 [h] Ps. 9:9 [i] Ex. 15:1; Judg. 5:1; [Ps. 40:3]
9 [j] Prov. 26:3
10 [k] Ps. 16:4; [Prov. 13:21; Rom. 2:9] [l] [Ps. 5:11, 12]; Prov. 16:20
11 [m] Ps. 64:10; 68:3; 97:12

PSALM 33

1 [a] Ps. 32:11; 97:12; Phil. 3:1; 4:4
2 [1] Lit. *Sing to Him*
6 [b] Gen. 1:6, 7; Ps. 148:5; [Heb. 11:3; 2 Pet. 3:5] [c] Gen. 2:1 [d] [Job 26:13]
7 [e] Gen. 1:9; Job 26:10; 38:8 [2] LXX, Tg., Vg. *in a vessel*
9 [f] Gen. 1:3; Ps. 148:5
10 [g] [Ps. 2:1-3]; Is. 8:10; 19:3
11 [h] [Job 23:13; Prov. 19:21]
12 [i] [Ex. 19:5; Deut. 7:6]; Ps. 28:9
13 [j] Job 28:24; [Ps. 14:2]
15 [k] [2 Chr. 16:9]; Job 34:21; [Jer. 32:19] [3] *understands*
16 [l] Ps. 44:6; 60:11; [Jer. 9:23, 24]

32:8 instruct…teach…guide. This terminology applies to biblical wisdom.

32:9 horse…mule. I.e., Don't be stubborn. Such animals are used as pointed illustrations of this sin (cf. Prov. 26:3; Is. 1:3; James 3:3).

33:1-22 This psalm is a general hymn of praise. Its two primary themes are: 1) Yahweh is the Lord of nature, and 2) He is Lord of history. In biblical thought, these realms are always related; the Creator sovereignly rules over His total creation, over all creatures throughout time.

- I. A Praise Prelude (33:1-3)
- II. The Rationale for Praise (33:4,5)
  - A. The Lord's Sovereign Power in Natural History (33:4)
  - B. The Lord's Sovereign Providence over Human History (33:5)
- III. The Response of Praise (33:6-19)
  - A. The Creator's Sovereign Power (33:6-9)
  - B. The Creator's Sovereign Providence (33:10-19)
- IV. A Prayer Finale (33:20-22)

33:1 beautiful. This means that praise to Him is proper, suitable, and fitting. On the propriety of praise, cf. Ps. 147:1.

33:3 a new song. I.e., a new occasion and impulse for expressing fresh praise to God (cf. Pss. 96:1; 98:1; 149:1).

33:6,9 God's utterances created a universe out of nothing (cf. "God said" in Gen. 1:3,6,9,11,14,20,24,26).

33:6 host. This designation refers to stellar and planetary bodies (cf. Is. 40:26; 45:12) and/or heaven's complement of angels (cf. Ps. 103:20-22). The former emphasis is more prominent in the immediate context.

33:7 He lays up. On this picturesque language of God's "heaping up" waters as a "pile" of dirt or sand, cf. Ex. 15:8; Josh. 3:13-16; Ps. 78:13.

33:10,11 A sharp contrast is drawn between mankind's shaky plans and the Lord's sovereign plans.

33:15 He fashions their hearts. This is the potter's word (cf. Gen. 2:7); for the significance of this statement, see Is. 29:15,16.

33:16-19 On the teaching of these verses, cf. the maxim of Zech. 4:6.

A mighty man is not delivered by
great strength.
17 [m]A horse *is* a [4]vain hope for safety;
Neither shall it deliver *any* by its
great strength.

18 [n]Behold, the eye of the LORD *is* on
those who fear Him,
On those who hope in His mercy,
19 To deliver their soul from death,
And [o]to keep them alive in famine.

20 Our soul waits for the LORD;
He *is* our help and our shield.
21 For our heart shall rejoice in Him,
Because we have trusted in His holy
name.
22 Let Your mercy, O LORD, be upon us,
Just as we hope in You.

PSALM 34

The Happiness of Those Who Trust in God

A Psalm of David [a]when he pretended
madness before Abimelech, who drove him
away, and he departed.

I will [b]bless the LORD at all times;
His praise *shall* continually *be* in my
mouth.
2 My soul shall make its boast in the
LORD;
The humble shall hear *of it* and be
glad.
3 Oh, magnify the LORD with me,
And let us exalt His name together.

4 I [c]sought the LORD, and He heard me,
And delivered me from all my fears.
5 They looked to Him and were
radiant,
And their faces were not ashamed.
6 This poor man cried out, and the
LORD heard *him*,
And saved him out of all his troubles.
7 [d]The [1]angel of the LORD [e]encamps all
around those who fear Him,
And delivers them.

8 Oh, [f]taste and see that the LORD *is*
good;
[g]Blessed *is* the man *who* trusts in Him!
9 Oh, fear the LORD, you His saints!
There is no [2]want to those who fear
Him.
10 The young lions lack and suffer
hunger;
[h]But those who seek the LORD shall not
lack any good *thing*.

11 Come, you children, listen to me;
[i]I will teach you the fear of the LORD.
12 [j]Who *is* the man *who* desires life,
And loves *many* days, that he may see
good?
13 Keep your tongue from evil,
And your lips from speaking [k]deceit.
14 [l]Depart from evil and do good;
[m]Seek peace and pursue it.

15 [n]The eyes of the LORD *are* on the
righteous,
And His ears *are open* to their cry.
16 [o]The face of the LORD *is* against those
who do evil,
[p]To [3]cut off the remembrance of them
from the earth.

17 *The righteous* cry out, and [q]the LORD
hears,
And delivers them out of all their
troubles.
18 [r]The LORD *is* near [s]to those who have a
broken heart,
And saves such as [4]have a contrite
spirit.

19 [t]Many *are* the afflictions of the
righteous,

17 [m] [Ps. 20:7; 147:10; Prov. 21:31] [4] *false*
18 [n] [Job 36:7]; Ps. 32:8; 34:15; [1 Pet. 3:12]
19 [o] Job 5:20; Ps. 37:19

PSALM 34

title [a] 1 Sam. 21:10-15
1 [b] [Eph. 5:20; 1 Thess. 5:18]
4 [c] [2 Chr. 15:2; Ps. 9:10; Matt. 7:7; Luke 11:9]
7 [d] [Ps. 91:11]; Dan. 6:22 [e] 2 Kin. 6:17 [1] Or *Angel*
8 [f] Ps. 119:103; [Heb. 6:5]; 1 Pet. 2:3 [g] Ps. 2:12
9 [2] *lack*
10 [h] [Ps. 84:11]
11 [i] Ps. 32:8
12 [j] [1 Pet. 3:10-12]
13 [k] [Eph. 4:25]
14 [l] Ps. 37:27; Is. 1:16, 17 [m] [Rom. 14:19; Heb. 12:14]
15 [n] Job 36:7; [Ps. 33:18]
16 [o] Lev. 17:10; Jer. 44:11; Amos 9:4 [p] Job 18:17; Ps. 9:6; 109:15; [Prov. 10:7] [3] *destroy*
17 [q] Ps. 34:6; 145:19
18 [r] [Ps. 145:18] [s] Ps. 51:17; [Is. 57:15] [4] *are crushed in spirit*
19 [t] Prov. 24:16

34:1-22 This acrostic psalm is quite similar to Ps. 25, not just in form, but also in major themes (e.g., the emphasis on redemption that brings each psalm to a close in 25:22 and 34:22). Individual and corporate applications of the Lord's deliverance are found throughout. This psalm unfolds with a praise mode followed by teaching.

I. Personal Testimony (34:1-10)

II. Personal Teaching (34:11-22)

34:Title The historical occasion to which this heading alludes is found in 1 Sam. 21:10-15; however, there is nothing obvious in the context of Ps. 34 to make such a specific connection. Abimelech, like Pharaoh, was a dynastic designation not a proper name.

34:1-3 This is one of the greatest invitations in the Psalms to all the people to join together in praise.

34:2 This is proper boasting because of the only proper object, God Himself (cf. Jer. 9:23,24).

34:7 The angel of the LORD. A special manifestation of Yahweh Himself at strategic historical junctures (cf. Gen. 16:7ff.; 18,19; 31:11ff.; Josh. 5; Judg. 6; 13). A strong case can be made that these were pre-incarnate appearances of the Lord Jesus Christ. *See note on Ex. 3:2.*

34:11 This solicitation to wisdom compares with Prov. 1–9.

34:12-14 This introduces some crucial character qualities of God's true people; cf. Ps. 15:1-5.

34:14 The pathway theme of Ps. 1; here the emphasis is on leaving the evil and doing good (cf. Job 28:28; Prov. 3:7; 16:6,17; Is. 1:16,17; etc.).

34:18 broken heart…contrite spirit. These are graphic idioms that describe dependent disciples (cf. Pss. 51:17; 147:3; Is. 57:15; 61:1; 66:2; Matt. 5:3).

34:19-22 The side-by-side realities of human persecution and divine preservation once again vividly depict real life in the real world.

[u]But the LORD delivers him out of them
all.
20 He guards all his bones;
[v]Not one of them is broken.
21 [w]Evil shall slay the wicked,
And those who hate the righteous
shall be [5]condemned.
22 The LORD [x]redeems the soul of His
servants,
And none of those who trust in Him
shall be condemned.

PSALM 35

The LORD the Avenger of His People

A Psalm of David.

Plead [1] *my cause,* O LORD, with those
who strive with me;
Fight against those who fight against
me.
2 Take hold of shield and [2]buckler,
And stand up for my help.
3 Also draw out the spear,
And stop those who pursue me.
Say to my soul,
"I *am* your salvation."

4 [a]Let those be put to shame and
brought to dishonor
Who seek after my life;
Let those be [b]turned back and
brought to confusion
Who plot my hurt.
5 [c]Let them be like chaff before the
wind,
And let the [3]angel of the LORD chase
them.
6 Let their way be [d]dark and slippery,
And let the angel of the LORD pursue
them.
7 For without cause they have [e]hidden
their net for me *in* a pit,
Which they have dug without cause
for my life.
8 [4]Let [f]destruction come upon him
unexpectedly,
And let his net that he has hidden
catch himself;
Into that very destruction let him fall.
9 And my soul shall be joyful in the
LORD;
It shall rejoice in His salvation.
10 [g]All my bones shall say,
"LORD, [h]who *is* like You,
Delivering the poor from him who is
too strong for him,
Yes, the poor and the needy from him
who plunders him?"

11 Fierce witnesses rise up;
They ask me *things* that I do not
know.
12 [i]They reward me evil for good,
To the sorrow of my soul.
13 But as for me, [j]when they were sick,
My clothing *was* sackcloth;
I humbled myself with fasting;
And my prayer would return to my
own [5]heart.
14 I paced about as though *he were* my
friend *or* brother;
I bowed down [6]heavily, as one who
mourns *for his* mother.
15 But in my [7]adversity they rejoiced
And gathered together;
Attackers gathered against me,
And I did not know *it;*
They tore *at me* and did not cease;
16 With ungodly mockers at feasts
They gnashed at me with their teeth.

17 Lord, how long will You [k]look on?

19 [u] Ps. 34:4, 6, 17
20 [v] John 19:33, 36
21 [w] Ps. 94:23; 140:11; Prov. 24:16 [5] *held guilty*
22 [x] 1 Kin. 1:29

PSALM 35

1 [1] *Contend for me*
2 [2] A small shield
4 [a] Ps. 40:14, 15; 70:2, 3 [b] Ps. 129:5
5 [c] Job 21:18; Ps. 83:13; Is. 29:5 [3] Or *Angel*
6 [d] Ps. 73:18; Jer. 23:12
7 [e] Ps. 9:15
8 [f] [Ps. 55:23]; Is. 47:11; [1 Thess. 5:3] [4] Lit. *Let destruction he does not know come upon him,*
10 [g] Ps. 51:8 [h] [Ex. 15:11]; Ps. 71:19; 86:8; [Mic. 7:18]
12 [i] Ps. 38:20; 109:5; Jer. 18:20; John 10:32
13 [j] Job 30:25 [5] Lit. *bosom*
14 [6] *in mourning*
15 [7] *limping, stumbling*
17 [k] Ps. 13:1; [Hab. 1:13]

35:1-28 Psalm 35, as to its form, is an individual lament. Its context of literal and legal warfare suggests a scenario of the theocratic king being accused, and about to be attacked, by a foreign power with whom he had previously entered into a covenant. David presents his "case" before the Divine Judge, moving from a complaint about the situation, to prayer about the situation, and finally, when the Lord would justly respond to the situation, praise for His righteous intervention. So, 3 cycles of exasperation and expectation in Ps. 35 convey the psalmist's prayers about his opponents to God.

I. First Cycle: The Attacks He Was Experiencing (35:1-10)
II. Second Cycle: The Perjury He Was Experiencing (35:11-18)
   A. He Prays that God Would Examine the Evidence (35:11-16)
   B. He Prays that God Would Act without Delay (35:17)
   C. He Pledges Praise (35:18)
III. Third Cycle: The Mockery He Was Anticipating (35:19-28)
   A. He Prays for Judgment concerning Them (35:19-21)
   B. He Prays for Justice concerning Himself (35:22-26)
   C. He Pledges Praise (35:27,28)

35:1 Plead *my cause*...Fight. The first bold prayer solicits the legal advocacy of God (cf. Prov. 25:8,9; Is. 3:13), while the second asks the Divine Warrior to fight his battles for him (e.g., Ex. 15:3; Deut. 32:41ff.).

35:3 Say to my soul, "I *am* your salvation." David is longing for reassurance (cf. Ps. 3:8a).

35:4-8 Cf. the imprecations of Pss. 7,69,109.

35:7 without cause...without cause. This adds to his defense; all their attacks, from a covenant or legal standpoint, have been unjustified.

35:10 LORD, who *is* like You. This had become a canonized expression of awe at the uniqueness of Israel's great God (cf. Ex. 15:11; Mic. 7:18).

35:11-14 A strong contrast is drawn between the psalmist's attitude about the covenant agreement and that of his treaty partner.

35:16 On the painful maimings of mockery, cf. Job 16:9; Pss. 37:12; 112:10; Lam. 2:16.

35:17 how long...? On laments, cf. Ps. 13:1; Hab. 1:2.

Rescue me from their destructions,
My precious *life* from the lions.
18 I will give You thanks in the great
assembly;
I will praise You among [8]many
people.

19 [l]Let them not rejoice over me who are
wrongfully my enemies;
Nor let them wink with the eye who
hate me without a cause.
20 For they do not speak peace,
But they devise deceitful matters
Against *the* quiet ones in the land.
21 They also opened their mouth wide
against me,
And said, "Aha, aha!
Our eyes have seen *it*."

22 *This* You have seen, O LORD;
Do not keep silence.
O Lord, do not be far from me.
23 Stir up Yourself, and awake to my
vindication,
To my cause, my God and my Lord.
24 Vindicate me, O LORD my God,
according to Your
righteousness;
And let them not rejoice over me.
25 Let them not say in their hearts, "Ah,
so we would have it!"
Let them not say, "We have
swallowed him up."

26 Let them be ashamed and brought to
mutual confusion
Who rejoice at my hurt;
Let them be [m]clothed with shame and
dishonor
Who exalt themselves against me.

27 [n]Let them shout for joy and be glad,
Who favor my righteous cause;
And let them say continually,
"Let the LORD be magnified,
Who has pleasure in the prosperity of
His servant."
28 And my tongue shall speak of Your
righteousness
And of Your praise all the day long.

18 [8] *a mighty*
19 [l] Ps. 69:4; 109:3; Lam. 3:52; [John 15:25]
26 [m] Ps. 109:29
27 [n] Rom. 12:15

PSALM 36

Man's Wickedness and God's Perfections

To the Chief Musician. A Psalm of David the servant of the LORD.

An oracle within my heart concerning
the transgression of the
wicked:
[a]*There is* no fear of God before his eyes.
2 For he flatters himself in his own
eyes,
When he finds out his iniquity *and*
when he hates.
3 The words of his mouth *are*
wickedness and deceit;
[b]He has ceased to be wise *and* to do
good.
4 [c]He devises wickedness on his bed;
He sets himself [d]in a way *that is* not
good;
He does not [1]abhor [e]evil.

5 Your mercy, O LORD, *is* in the
heavens;
Your faithfulness *reaches* to the clouds.
6 Your righteousness *is* like the [2]great
mountains;
[f]Your judgments *are* a great deep;
O LORD, You preserve man and
beast.

7 How precious *is* Your lovingkindness,
O God!

PSALM 36

1 [a] Rom. 3:18
3 [b] Ps. 94:8; Jer. 4:22
4 [c] Prov. 4:16; [Mic. 2:1] [d] Is. 65:2 [e] [Ps. 52:3; Rom. 12:9] [1] *reject, loathe*
6 [f] Job 11:8; Ps. 77:19; [Rom. 11:33] [2] *Lit. mountains of God*

35:19 wrongfully. Cf. "without cause" twice in v. 7.

35:21 "Aha, aha." This taunting chorus will return in v. 25.

35:21,22 Our eyes have seen *it*. *This* you have seen, O LORD. What David's enemy allegedly saw, the Lord has seen perfectly. David knew that his God would vindicate him based upon the true evidence, all in his favor.

35:23 To my cause. He brings back the advocacy theme of v. 1.

35:27 Cf. Ps. 40:16. **His servant.** Besides being a polite third person reference to the psalmist, the terminology was also used of an OT disciple regarding himself as bound to the Lord.

36:1-12 At least 3 themes may be detected in this psalm: 1) wisdom, vv. 1-4; 2) praise, vv. 5-9; and 3) prayer, vv. 10-12. Psalm 36 resembles Ps. 14 in its description of human depravity; it also brings to mind David's personal confession found in Ps. 32. Paul used Ps. 36:1 to summarize his list of 14 indictments against the whole race in Rom. 3:10-18. As to its overall structure, David's two different moods in Ps. 36 exemplify his continuing quest for balance concerning the realities of human wickedness and divine benevolence.

I. Mood of Deliberation (36:1-9)
   A. His Deliberations on Human Infidelity (36:1-4)
   B. His Deliberations on Divine Fidelity (36:5-9)
II. Mood of Dependence (36:10-12)
   A. Implemented through Prayer (36:10,11)
   B. Intimated through Perspective (36:12)

36:Title The term "servant," found in Ps. 35:27, appears in this title. It carries an association with covenant relationship emphasizing submission to and service for God. For its application to David within the texts of Psalms, cf. 78:70; 89:3.

36:1 no fear. This is the opposite of the attitude which characterizes true disciples. The word here is actually "dread" or "terror" (cf. Deut. 2:25; Ps. 119:120; Is. 2:10,19,21; etc.).

36:2 I.e., he flatters himself so much that he is unable to understand enough to hate his own iniquity.

36:3,4 Although Paul cites only Ps. 36:1b in Rom. 3, the same categories of characteristic sinfulness also show up in that context; cf. character: Ps. 36:2 with Rom. 3:10-12; communications: Ps. 36:39 with Rom. 3:13-14; and conduct: Ps. 36:3b-4 with Rom. 3:15-17.

36:5,6 These attributes of God are immeasurable.

Therefore the children of men [g]put
their trust under the shadow
of Your wings.
8 [h]They are abundantly satisfied with
the fullness of Your house,
And You give them drink from [i]the
river of Your pleasures.
9 [j]For with You *is* the fountain of life;
[k]In Your light we see light.

10 Oh, continue Your lovingkindness to
those who know You,
And Your righteousness to the
upright in heart.
11 Let not the foot of pride come against
me,
And let not the hand of the wicked
drive me away.
12 There the workers of iniquity have
fallen;
They have been cast down and are
not able to rise.

7 [g] Ruth 2:12; Ps. 17:8; 57:1; 91:4
8 [h] Ps. 63:5; 65:4; Is. 25:6; Jer. 31:12-14 [i] Ps. 46:4; Rev. 22:1
9 [j] [Jer. 2:13; John 4:10, 14] [k] [1 Pet. 2:9]

PSALM 37

The Heritage of the Righteous and the Calamity of the Wicked

A Psalm of David.

Do[a] not fret because of evildoers,
Nor be envious of the workers of
iniquity.
2 For they shall soon be cut down [b]like
the grass,
And wither as the green herb.

3 Trust in the LORD, and do good;
Dwell in the land, and feed on His
faithfulness.
4 [c]Delight yourself also in the LORD,
And He shall give you the desires of
your [d]heart.

5 [e]Commit[1] your way to the LORD,
Trust also in Him,
And He shall bring *it* to pass.
6 [f]He shall bring forth your
righteousness as the light,
And your justice as the noonday.

7 Rest in the LORD, [g]and wait patiently
for Him;
Do not fret because of him who
[h]prospers in his way,
Because of the man who brings
wicked schemes to pass.
8 [i]Cease from anger, and forsake
wrath;
[j]Do not fret—*it* only *causes* harm.

9 For evildoers shall be [2]cut off;
But those who wait on the LORD,
They shall [k]inherit the earth.
10 For [l]yet a little while and the wicked
shall be no *more;*
Indeed, [m]you will look carefully for
his place,
But it *shall be* no *more.*
11 [n]But the meek shall inherit the earth,
And shall delight themselves in the
abundance of peace.

12 The wicked plots against the just,
[o]And gnashes at him with his teeth.
13 [p]The Lord laughs at him,
For He sees that [q]his day is coming.
14 The wicked have drawn the sword
And have bent their bow,
To cast down the poor and needy,
To slay those who are of upright
conduct.
15 Their sword shall enter their own
heart,
And their bows shall be broken.

16 [r]A little that a righteous man has
Is better than the riches of many
wicked.

PSALM 37
1 [a] Ps. 73:3; [Prov. 23:17; 24:19]
2 [b] Job 14:2; Ps. 90:5, 6; 92:7; James 1:11
4 [c] Job 22:26; Ps. 94:19; Is. 58:14 [d] Ps. 21:2; 145:19; [Matt. 7:7,8]
5 [e] [Ps. 55:22; Prov. 16:3; 1 Pet. 5:7] [1] Lit. *Roll off onto*
6 [f] Job 11:17; [Is. 58:8, 10]
7 [g] Ps. 40:1; 62:5; [Lam. 3:26] [h] [Ps. 73:3-12]
8 [i] [Eph. 4:26] [j] Ps. 73:3
9 [k] Ps. 25:13; Prov. 2:21; [Is. 57:13; 60:21; Matt. 5:5] [2] *destroyed*
10 [l] [Heb. 10:37] [m] Job 7:10; Ps. 37:35, 36
11 [n] [Matt. 5:5]
12 [o] Ps. 35:16
13 [p] Ps. 2:4; 59:8 [q] 1 Sam. 26:10; Job 18:20
16 [r] Prov. 15:16; 16:8; [1 Tim. 6:6]

36:7 the shadow of Your wings. Although some would take this as referring to wings of the cherubim over the ark, it is probably more generally a reference to the protective care of a parent bird for its young (Deut. 32:11; Pss. 17:8; 91:4; Ruth 2:12; cf. Jesus' allusion to the word picture in Matt. 23:37).

36:9 In Your light we see light. It is likely that this phraseology bears both literal and figurative significance, i.e., God is the source of physical life and also of spiritual life. The Lord is the Source and Sustainer of all light and life.

36:11 the foot of pride. This is likely military imagery referring to the practice of a victorious king-general symbolically placing his foot upon the neck of a prostrated, defeated king-general.

36:12 Cf. Pss. 14:5a; 18:38; Prov. 24:16.

37:1-40 Psalm 37, an irregular acrostic, is a wisdom poem addressed to man, not God. Verses 12-24 sound very much like the maxims of proverbs. The covenant promises of the "land" for Israel are prominent in its verses (cf. vv. 3,9,11,22,29,34). Its basic theme deals with the age-old question "Why do the ungodly prosper while the godly painfully struggle through life?" An intricate arrangement puts forth David's answer. In Ps. 37, David mixes and matches 6 thoughts in order to advance his major message on the eventual arrival of divine justice.

I. An Introductory Overview (37:1,2)
II. An Initial Expansion (37:3-11)
III. Some Proverbial Perspectives (37:12-24)
IV. An Initial Testimony (37:25,26)
V. A Final Expansion (cf. vv. 3-11) (37:27-34)
VI. A Final Testimony (cf. vv. 25,26) (37:35-40)

37:2 Here-today-gone-tomorrow illustrations about the wicked characterize this psalm. On this theme, cf. Job 14:1,2; Pss. 90:5,6; 103:15,16; Is. 40:6-8; Matt. 6:30; James 1:10,11; 1 John 2:17.

37:7,8 The message of "Relax! Don't react!" returns (cf. v. 1).

37:10 yet a little while. Cf. similar terminology in Jer. 51:33; Hos. 1:4. The Lord's intervention is imminent.

17 For the arms of the wicked shall be broken,
But the LORD upholds the righteous.

18 The LORD knows the days of the upright,
And their inheritance shall be forever.
19 They shall not be ashamed in the evil time,
And in the days of famine they shall be satisfied.
20 But the wicked shall perish;
And the enemies of the LORD,
Like the splendor of the meadows, shall vanish.
Into smoke they shall vanish away.

21 The wicked borrows and does not repay,
But [s]the righteous shows mercy and gives.
22 [t]For *those* blessed by Him shall inherit the earth,
But *those* cursed by Him shall be [3]cut off.

23 [u]The steps of a *good* man are [4]ordered by the LORD,
And He delights in his way.
24 [v]Though he fall, he shall not be utterly cast down;
For the LORD upholds *him with* His hand.

25 I have been young, and *now* am old;
Yet I have not seen the righteous forsaken,
Nor his descendants begging bread.
26 [w]*He is* [5]ever merciful, and lends;
And his descendants *are* blessed.

27 Depart from evil, and do good;
And dwell forevermore.
28 For the LORD loves justice,
And does not forsake His saints;
They are preserved forever,
But the descendants of the wicked shall be cut off.
29 [x]The righteous shall inherit the land,
And dwell in it forever.

30 [y]The mouth of the righteous speaks wisdom,
And his tongue talks of justice.
31 The law of his God *is* in his heart;
None of his steps shall [6]slide.

32 The wicked [z]watches the righteous,
And seeks to slay him.
33 The LORD [a]will not leave him in his hand,
Nor condemn him when he is judged.

34 [b]Wait on the LORD,
And keep His way,
And He shall exalt you to inherit the land;
When the wicked are cut off, you shall see *it*.
35 I have seen the wicked in great power,
And spreading himself like a native green tree.
36 Yet [7]he passed away, and behold, he *was* no *more;*
Indeed I sought him, but he could not be found.

37 Mark the blameless *man*, and observe the upright;
For the future of *that* man *is* peace.
38 [c]But the transgressors shall be destroyed together;
The future of the wicked shall be cut off.

39 But the salvation of the righteous *is* from the LORD;
He is their strength [d]in the time of trouble.
40 And [e]the LORD shall help them and deliver them;
He shall deliver them from the wicked,
And save them,
[f]Because they trust in Him.

PSALM 38

Prayer in Time of Chastening

A Psalm of David. [a]To bring to remembrance.

O LORD, do not [b]rebuke me in Your wrath,
Nor chasten me in Your hot displeasure!

21 [s]Ps. 112:5, 9
22 [t][Prov. 3:33] [3]destroyed
23 [u][1 Sam. 2:9]; Ps. 40:2; 66:9; 119:5 [4]established
24 [v]Prov. 24:16
26 [w][Deut. 15:8]; Ps. 37:21 [5]Lit. *all the day*
29 [x]Ps. 37:9; Prov. 2:21
30 [y][Matt. 12:35]

31 [6]*slip*
32 [z]Ps. 10:8; 17:11
33 [a]Ps. 31:8; [2 Pet. 2:9]
34 [b]Ps. 27:14; 37:9
36 [7]So with MT, LXX, Tg.; Syr., Vg. *I passed by*
38 [c][Ps. 1:4-6; 37:20, 28]
39 [d]Ps. 9:9; 37:19
40 [e]Ps. 22:4; Is. 31:5; Dan. 3:17; 6:23 [f]1 Chr. 5:20; Ps. 34:22

PSALM 38
title [a]Ps. 70:title
1 [b]Ps. 6:1

37:17 the arms of the wicked shall be broken. Their members will be shattered for grabbing and getting wealth (v. 16b). Cf. Job 38:15; Ps. 10:15; Jer. 48:25; Ezek. 30:21.

37:18 Cf. Ps. 1:6.

37:21 The OT contains both precepts and proverbs about borrowing and lending; cf. Deut. 15:6; 28:12,44; Ps. 112:1-6; Prov. 22:7.

37:24 For corroborations of such divine comfort, cf. Ps. 145:14; Prov. 24:16; Mic. 7:8.

37:31 The law of his God *is* in his heart. On God's internalized instruction, cf. Deut. 6:6; Pss. 40:8; 119 (throughout); Jer. 31:33; Is. 51:7.

37:38 cut off. On this truth of judgment, cf. vv. 9,22,28,34, and Ps. 109:13. For a positive presentation in reference to the faithful, cf. Prov. 23:18; 24:14,20.

37:39 salvation...from the LORD. Since salvation belongs to Him (Ps. 3:8), He is the perennial Source of it (cf. Ps. 62:1,2).

38:1-22 Prayers surround a core of intense lament (vv. 2-20). In

2 For Your arrows pierce me deeply,
And Your hand presses me down.

3 *There is* no soundness in my flesh
Because of Your anger,
Nor *any* health in my bones
Because of my sin.
4 For my iniquities have gone over my
head;
Like a heavy burden they are too
heavy for me.
5 My wounds are foul *and* festering
Because of my foolishness.

6 I am [1]troubled, I am bowed down
greatly;
I go mourning all the day long.
7 For my loins are full of inflammation,
And *there is* no soundness in my flesh.
8 I am feeble and severely broken;
I groan because of the turmoil of my
heart.

9 Lord, all my desire *is* before You;
And my sighing is not hidden from
You.
10 My heart pants, my strength fails me;
As for the light of my eyes, it also has
gone from me.

11 My loved ones and my friends [c]stand
aloof from my plague,
And my relatives stand afar off.
12 Those also who seek my life lay
snares *for me;*
Those who seek my hurt speak of
destruction,
And plan deception all the day long.

13 But I, like a deaf *man*, do not hear;
And *I am* like a mute *who* does not
open his mouth.
14 Thus I am like a man who does not
hear,
And in whose mouth *is* no response.

15 For [2]in You, O LORD, [d]I hope;
You will [3]hear, O Lord my God.
16 For I said, "*Hear me,* lest they rejoice
over me,
Lest, when my foot slips, they exalt
themselves against me."

17 [e]For I *am* ready to fall,
And my sorrow *is* continually before
me.
18 For I will [f]declare my iniquity;
I will be [g]in [4]anguish over my sin.
19 But my enemies *are* vigorous, *and* they
are strong;
And those who hate me wrongfully
have multiplied.
20 Those also [h]who render evil for good,
They are my adversaries, because I
follow *what is* good.

21 Do not forsake me, O LORD;
O my God, [i]be not far from me!
22 Make haste to help me,
O Lord, my salvation!

PSALM 39

Prayer for Wisdom and Forgiveness

To the Chief Musician. To Jeduthun.
A Psalm of David.

1 I said, "I will guard my ways,
Lest I sin with my [a]tongue;
I will restrain my mouth with a
muzzle,
While the wicked are before me."

6 [1] Lit. *bent down*
11 [c] Ps. 31:11; 88:18
15 [d] [Ps. 39:7] [2] *I wait for You, O LORD* [3] *answer*
17 [e] Ps. 51:3
18 [f] Ps. 32:5 [g] [2 Cor. 7:9, 10] [4] *anxiety*
20 [h] Ps. 35:12
21 [i] Ps. 22:19; 35:22

PSALM 39
1 [a] Job 2:10; Ps. 34:13; [James 3:5-12]

many ways David's laments parallel those of Job. David's perspective is that his painful plight is due, at least in part, to his personal sin. Organizationally, David's opening and closing prayers in Ps. 38 relate to two onslaughts by enemies.

I. Introductory Prayer (38:1,2)
II. First Onslaught: The Enemy Within (38:3-10)
III. Second Onslaught: Enemies Without (38:11-20)
IV. Concluding Prayers (38:21,22)

38:Title. To bring to remembrance. Lit. "To cause to remember" (cf. the title to Ps. 70). The psalmist either 1) reminds God of his plight so that He might act, or 2) reminds himself and the community of his historic predicament so that both he and they would fervently pray in similar contexts of acute suffering.

38:1 Cf. Pss. 6:1; 39:11; Jer. 31:18.

38:2 Your arrows. The language relates to the Divine Warrior motif; on God as Archer, cf. Deut. 32:23; Job 6:4; 16:13; Ps. 7:12; Lam. 3:12,13; etc.

38:5 my foolishness. On culpable ethical folly, cf. Ps. 69:5. David views this as the reason for the divine chastisements of v. 3ff.

38:11 loved ones…friends…relatives. Those near and dear to him had abandoned him to his adversity, adding insult to injury.

38:13,14 The ultimate example of non-response to tauntings and torturings may be seen in the Suffering Servant of Is. 53:7; cf. 1 Pet. 2:23.

38:19,20 Although he had confessed personal sins, he remained legally innocent in comparison with his persecutors.

39:1-13 Psalm 39 is an exceptionally heavy lament, which compares with Job 7 and much of Ecclesiastes. It also carries on the here-today-gone-tomorrow emphasis of Ps. 37 with a new twist, an application to *all* men, especially the psalmist. In this intense lament, David will break his initial silence with two rounds of requests and reflections about the brevity and burdens of life.

I. Introduction: David's Silence (39:1-3)
II. Round One: The Brevity and Burdens of Life (39:4-6)
  A. His Request for Perspective (39:4)
  B. His Reflections on Perspective (39:5,6)
III. Round Two: The Brevity and Burdens of Life (39:7-13)
  A. His Reflection on Hope (39:7)

2 [b]I was mute with silence,
I held my peace *even* from good;
And my sorrow was stirred up.
3 My heart was hot within me;
While I was [1]musing, the fire burned.
Then I spoke with my tongue:

4 "LORD, [c]make me to know my end,
And what *is* the measure of my days,
That I may know how frail I *am.*
5 Indeed, You have made my days *as*
handbreadths,
And my age *is* as nothing before You;
Certainly every man at his best state
is but [d]vapor. Selah
6 Surely every man walks about like a
shadow;
Surely they [2]busy themselves in vain;
He heaps up *riches,*
And does not know who will gather
them.

7 "And now, Lord, what do I wait for?
My [e]hope *is* in You.
8 Deliver me from all my
transgressions;
Do not make me [f]the reproach of the
foolish.
9 [g]I was mute, I did not open my mouth,
Because it was [h]You who did *it.*
10 [i]Remove Your plague from me;
I am consumed by the blow of Your
hand.
11 When with rebukes You correct man
for iniquity,
You make his beauty [j]melt away like
a moth;
Surely every man *is* vapor. Selah

12 "Hear my prayer, O LORD,
And give ear to my cry;
Do not be silent at my tears;
For I *am* a stranger with You,
A sojourner, [k]as all my fathers *were.*
13 [l]Remove Your gaze from me, that I
may regain strength,
Before I go away and [m]am no more."

2 [b] Ps. 38:13
3 [1] *meditating*
4 [c] Ps. 90:12; 119:84
5 [d] Ps. 62:9; [Eccl. 6:12]
6 [2] *make an uproar for nothing*
7 [e] Ps. 38:15
8 [f] Ps. 44:13; 79:4; 119:22
9 [g] Ps. 39:2 [h] 2 Sam. 16:10; Job 2:10
10 [i] Job 9:34; 13:21
11 [j] Job 13:28; [Ps. 90:7]; Is. 50:9
12 [k] Gen. 47:9; Lev. 25:23; 1 Chr. 29:15; Ps. 119:19; Heb. 11:13; 1 Pet. 2:11
13 [l] Job 7:19; 10:20, 21; 14:6; Ps. 102:24 [m] [Job 14:10]

PSALM 40
1 [a] Ps. 25:5; 27:14; 37:7
2 [b] Ps. 69:2, 14; Jer. 38:6 [c] Ps. 27:5

PSALM 40

Faith Persevering in Trial

To the Chief Musician. A Psalm of David.

I [a]waited patiently for the LORD;
And He inclined to me,
And heard my cry.
2 He also brought me up out of a
horrible pit,
Out of [b]the miry clay,
And [c]set my feet upon a rock,
And established my steps.

B. His Requests and Reflections on Providence (39:8-11)
C. His Requests for Relief (39:12,13)

39:Title. To Jeduthun. This is most likely a specifically designated worship director (cf. 1 Chr. 9:16; 16:37ff.; 25:1-3; Neh. 11:17).

39:1 I will...I will. The form of these expressions intimate strong volitional commitments. **Lest I sin with my tongue.** This sinning could have been in one or both of two ways: 1) directly, by criticizing God for not bringing retribution on the wicked, and 2) indirectly, by complaining in the hearing of the wicked.

39:2 His silence did not ease his pain; it seemed to make it all the worse.

39:3 Cf. Jeremiah's predicament in Jer. 20:9. ***Then* I spoke with my tongue.** Contrast the silence of v. 1. Yet, he did not violate the conditions of his original commitment, since he did not vent before men, but unloaded his burdens before God (cf. vv. 4ff.)

39:4 For similar prayers about the brevity and burdens of life, cf. Job 6:11; 7:7; 14:13; 16:21,22; Ps. 90:12; Eccl. 2:3.

39:5 handbreadths. He measures the length of his life with the smallest popular measuring unit of ancient times (1 Kin. 7:26); cf. "four fingers" (i.e., about 2.9 in.) in Jer. 52:21. **and my age *is* as nothing before You.** On "measuring" God's age, cf. Ps. 90:2. **vapor.** For the same Heb. word, cf. Eccl. 1:2ff., "vanity" (a total of 31 occurrences of this term are in Eccl.); Ps. 144:4. On the concept in the NT, cf. James 4:14.

39:6 Surely they busy themselves in vain. On the futility and irony of this phenomenon, cf. Job 27:16 in context; Eccl. 2:18-23; Luke 12:16-20.

39:9 In this verse, the terminology of Pss. 38:13; 39:2 reappears, accompanied by the theology of Job 42.

39:11 like a moth. The moth normally represented one of the most destructive creatures, but here the delicacy of the moth is intended (cf. Job 13:28; Is. 50:9; 51:8; Matt. 6:19ff.).

39:12 stranger...sojourner. He considers himself to be a temporary guest and squatter in the presence of God; on the terminology, cf. Lev. 25:23; Deut. 24:19ff.; 1 Chr. 29:15; Ps. 119:19; and for the concept in the NT, cf. Heb. 11:13; 1 Pet. 2:11.

39:13 This stark request is parallel in its intention with v. 10.

40:1-17 Psalm 40 begins with a high-flight of thanksgiving and ends with a mixture of prayer and lament (cf. the movement of Ps. 27). Furthermore, the last 5 verses of Ps. 40 are nearly identical to Ps. 70. Crucial associations surface throughout this psalm. The first is between the theocratic king as an individual and the community of the theocratic people. Beyond this, from the vantage point of NT revelation, an association with the Greater David is contained in seed form in vv. 6-8 (cf. Heb. 10:5-7). Historical precedent and prayers for a present plight move the psalm along from beginning to end. Attitudinally, David understood the importance of what would be explicitly commanded through Paul in Rom. 12:1,2. These elements constitute only a part of the richness of Ps. 40. The following notes will help to follow David's mental movements through these 17 verses: Two situations constitute the framework for the psalmist's publicized expressions of worship in Ps. 40.

I. Precedent from a Past Situation (40:1-10)
A. The Merciful Rescue by God (40:1-3)
B. The Multiple Resources in God (40:4,5)
C. The Motivational Responses to God (40:6-10)
II. Prayers for a Present Situation (40:11-17)

40:2 a horrible pit...the miry clay. The imagery describes his past hopeless and helpless situation; cf. the language of Ps. 69:2,14; Jer. 38:6ff. God by His grace had taken him from no footing to sure footing.

3 [d]He has put a new song in my mouth—
Praise to our God;
Many will see *it* and fear,
And will trust in the LORD.

4 [e]Blessed *is* that man who makes the LORD his trust,
And does not respect the proud, nor such as turn aside to lies.

5 [f]Many, O LORD my God, *are* Your wonderful works
Which You have done;
[g]And Your thoughts toward us
Cannot be recounted to You in order;
If I would declare and speak *of them*,
They are more than can be numbered.

6 [h]Sacrifice and offering You did not desire;
My ears You have opened.
Burnt offering and sin offering You did not require.
7 Then I said, "Behold, I come;
In the scroll of the book *it is* written of me.
8 [i]I delight to do Your will, O my God,
And Your law *is* [j]within my heart."

9 [k]I have proclaimed the good news of righteousness
In the great assembly;
Indeed, [l]I do not restrain my lips,
O LORD, You Yourself know.
10 [m]I have not hidden Your righteousness within my heart;
I have declared Your faithfulness and Your salvation;
I have not concealed Your lovingkindness and Your truth
From the great assembly.

11 Do not withhold Your tender mercies from me, O LORD;
[n]Let Your lovingkindness and Your truth continually preserve me.
12 For innumerable evils have surrounded me;
[o]My iniquities have overtaken me, so that I am not able to look up;
They are more than the hairs of my head;
Therefore my heart fails me.

13 [p]Be pleased, O LORD, to deliver me;
O LORD, make haste to help me!
14 [q]Let them be ashamed and brought to mutual confusion
Who seek to destroy my [1]life;
Let them be driven backward and brought to dishonor
Who wish me evil.
15 Let them be [r]confounded because of their shame,
Who say to me, "Aha, aha!"

16 [s]Let all those who seek You rejoice and be glad in You;
Let such as love Your salvation [t]say continually,
"The LORD be magnified!"
17 [u]But I *am* poor and needy;
[v]*Yet* the LORD thinks upon me.
You *are* my help and my deliverer;
Do not delay, O my God.

PSALM 41

The Blessing and Suffering of the Godly

To the Chief Musician. A Psalm of David.

Blessed *is* he who considers the [1]poor;
The LORD will deliver him in time of trouble.

3 [d]Ps. 32:7; 33:3
4 [e]Ps. 34:8; 84:12
5 [f]Job 9:10 [g]Ps. 139:17; [Is. 55:8]
6 [h][1 Sam. 15:22]; Ps. 51:16; Is. 1:11; [Jer. 6:20; 7:22, 23]; Amos 5:22; [Mic. 6:6-8; Heb. 10:5-9]
8 [i][Matt. 26:39; John 4:34; 6:38]; Heb. 10:7 [j][Ps. 37:31; Jer. 31:33; 2 Cor. 3:3]
9 [k]Ps. 22:22, 25 [l]Ps. 119:13
10 [m]Acts 20:20, 27
11 [n]Ps. 61:7; Prov. 20:28
12 [o]Ps. 38:4; 65:3
13 [p]Ps. 70:1
14 [q]Ps. 35:4, 26; 70:2; 71:13 [1]Lit. *soul*
15 [r]Ps. 73:19
16 [s]Ps. 70:4 [t]Ps. 35:27
17 [u]Ps. 70:5; 86:1; 109:22 [v]Ps. 40:5; 1 Pet. 5:7

PSALM 41
1 [1]*helpless* or *powerless*

40:3 a new song. *See note on Ps. 33:3.*

40:3,4 trust in the LORD…the LORD his trust. The verb and the noun forms of this important Heb. root connote a faith of confident commitment, here in the right object, God alone (cf. the teaching of Jer. 17:7). David's desire was always to make such commitment contagious.

40:5 Cf. the psalmist's pleasant "frustration" in Ps. 139:12-18.

40:6-8 The author of Hebrews dramatically applies these verses to the Greater David (10:5-7).

40:6 Sacrifice and offering You did not desire. He is not negating the commandment to offer sacrifices, but is emphasizing their being offered with the right attitude of heart (contra. Saul, 1 Sam. 15:22,23; note the emphases on proper spiritual prerequisites for sacrifices in Pss. 19:14; 50:7-15; 51:15-17; 69:30-31; Is. 1:10-15; Jer. 7:21-26; Hos. 6:6; Amos 5:21-24; Mic. 6:6-8; Matt. 23:23). **My ears You have opened.** Lit. "ears" or "two ears You have dug for me." This pictures obedience and dedication.

40:7 In the scroll of the book *it is* written of me. Deuteronomy 17:14-20 would apply to the lesser David; cf. likely applications regarding the Greater David in passages like Luke 24:27; John 5:39,46.

40:9 the good news of righteous. This word for "good news" in Heb. (cf. the root in Is. 40:9; 41:27; 52:7; 60:6; 61:1) is the precursor of the NT terminology for the "gospel" and "preaching the gospel," i.e., "announcing the good news." "Righteousness" is identified as God's righteousness in the next verse (v. 10).

40:10 David's spirit here was encountered previously in Ps. 22:22,23.

40:12 Cf. Both external persecution and internal perversity in Ps. 38.

40:13-17 *See notes on Ps. 70.*

41:1-13 The words of this psalm are general and apply to anyone who might be considered "down." The most painful and specific factor addressed here is the insult which is being added to the psalmist's injury (cf. Pss. 6:38; and portions of Job and Jeremiah). While the form and structure of Ps. 41 is quite complex, "blessed" serves as bookends in vv. 1,13. Within these, other elements include 1) confidence (vv. 1b-3,11,12), 2) prayers (vv. 4,10), and 3) lament

2 The LORD will preserve him and keep
him alive,
And he will be blessed on the earth;
[a]You will not deliver him to the will of
his enemies.
3 The LORD will strengthen him on his
bed of illness;
You will [2]sustain him on his
sickbed.

4 I said, "LORD, be merciful to me;
[b]Heal my soul, for I have sinned
against You."
5 My enemies speak evil of me:
"When will he die, and his name
perish?"
6 And if he comes to see *me,* he speaks
[3]lies;
His heart gathers iniquity to itself;
When he goes out, he tells *it.*

7 All who hate me whisper together
against me;
Against me they [4]devise my hurt.
8 "An[5] evil disease," *they say,* "clings to
him.
And *now* that he lies down, he will
rise up no more."
9 [c]Even my own familiar friend in
whom I trusted,
[d]Who ate my bread,
Has [6]lifted up *his* heel against me.

10 But You, O LORD, be merciful to me,
and raise me up,
That I may repay them.
11 By this I know that You are well
pleased with me,
Because my enemy does not triumph
over me.
12 As for me, You uphold me in my
integrity,
And [e]set me before Your face forever.

13 [f]Blessed *be* the LORD God of Israel
From everlasting to everlasting!
Amen and Amen.

2 [a] Ps. 27:12
3 [2] *restore*
4 [b] Ps. 6:2; 103:3; 147:3
6 [3] *empty words*
7 [4] *plot*
8 [5] Lit. *A thing of Belial*
9 [c] 2 Sam. 15:12; Job 19:13, 19
[d] Ps. 55:12-14, 20; Jer. 20:10; Obad. 7; [Mic. 7:5]; Matt. 26:14-16, 21-25, 47-50; John 13:18, 21-30; Acts 1:16, 17 [6] Acted as a traitor
12 [e] [Job 36:7; Ps. 21:6; 34:15]
13 [f] Ps. 72:18, 19; 89:52; 106:48; 150:6

PSALM 42
title [1] Heb. *Maschil*
1 [2] Lit. *longs for*

Book Two: Psalms 42–72

PSALM 42

Yearning for God in the Midst of Distresses

To the Chief Musician. A [1]Contemplation of the sons of Korah.

As the deer [2]pants for the water
brooks,
So pants my soul for You, O God.

(vv. 5-9), with moments of wisdom and praise. David's message in Ps. 41 speaks of God's tender, loving care in the critical care unit of life.

I. Recognizes Human Compassion (41:1a)
II. Revels in God's Care for the Compassionate (41:1b-3)
III. Requests Grace, Health, and Forgiveness (41:4)
IV. Rehearses the Meanness that He Has Experienced (41:5-9)
V. Requests Grace, Health, and Retribution (41:10)
VI. Revels in God's Care for Him Personally (41:11,12)
VII. Recognizes Divine Compassion (41:13)

41:1 Blessed. On this "blessed," cf. Pss. 1:1; 2:12.

41:2 *And* he will be blessed on the earth. The verb "be blessed" is from the same Heb. root as the exclamatory description "blessed" of v. 1 (on other occurrences of the verb, cf. Prov. 3:18; 31:28; Song 6:9).

41:3 You will sustain him on his sickbed. This pictures God as Physician dispensing His tender, loving care

41:4 for I have sinned against You. The ancient Near Eastern association of sin and sickness returns (cf. Pss. 31:10; 32:5; 38:3,4,18; 40:12; etc.). On the explicit combination of "sinning against," cf. Ps. 51:4. This perspective of the psalmist does not negate the reference to his basic "integrity" in v. 12.

41:6 And if he comes...he goes out. This hypocritical "sick call" really adds insult to injury. The visitor lies to the sick one and gathers "information" for more slander.

41:9 Even my own familiar friend...lifted up *his* heel against me. David's close companion betrayed him; he kicked him while he was "down." The Greater David's experience and the employment of this reference in John 13:18 was to Judas (cf. Matt. 26:21ff.).

41:13 Blessed *be*. The essence of the Heb. root of "amen" is "it is true," i.e., reliable, confirmed, verified. Note that Book I of the Psalms (Pss. 1-41) closes with a doxology; cf. the endings of the other 4 books (Pss. 72:18,19; 89:52; 106:48; 150:6).

42:1-11 As in the case of Pss. 9 and 10, Pss. 42 and 43 were originally probably one. Some ancient manuscripts put them together; Ps. 43 has no title while the rest around it do. In form, Ps. 42 may be considered an individual lament. This psalm also exemplifies a primary characteristic of Book II of the Psalms, the preference of the ascription "God" (or parallels to it) for the Deity. The occasion and situation of Ps. 42 are historically unspecified; however, what is obvious is that the psalmist's situation was intense and greatly aggravated by his surrounding mockers. Consequently, Ps. 42 is a dirge of two stanzas.

I. Stanza One: The Psalmist Sings of His Drought (42:1-5)
   A. The Content of This Stanza (42:1-4)
   B. The Chorus of This Dirge (cf. v. 11) (42:5)
II. Stanza Two: The Psalmist Sings of His Drowning (42:6-11)
   A. The Content of This Stanza (42:6-10)
   B. The Chorus of This Dirge (cf. v. 5) (42:11)

42:Title The references to "the chief musician," i.e., the worship director, and Maskil, a "contemplation" or lesson (see marginal note; cf. Ps. 32:1) are not new, but the reference to "the sons of Korah" is. On the ancestry of "the sons of Korah," cf. Num. 26:10ff.; 1 Chr. 6:16ff.; 2 Chr. 20:19. A total of 11 psalms are associated with this group, and 7 of them are found in Book II (Pss. 42,44,45,46,47,48,49). These people are probably better regarded as the Levitical performers, rather than the authors of these psalms (i.e., "For the sons of Korah").

42:1 As the deer pants...so pants. On this simile from nature, cf. Joel 1:20. In the psalmist's estimation, he is facing a severe divine drought.

2 [a]My soul thirsts for God, for the [b]living God.
When shall I come and [3]appear before God?
3 [c]My tears have been my food day and night,
While they continually say to me,
[d]"Where *is* your God?"

4 When I remember these *things*,
[e]I pour out my soul within me.
For I used to go with the multitude;
[f]I went with them to the house of God,
With the voice of joy and praise,
With a multitude that kept a pilgrim feast.

5 [g]Why are you [4]cast down, O my soul?
And *why* are you disquieted within me?
[h]Hope in God, for I shall yet praise Him
[5]*For* the help of His countenance.

6 [6]O my God, my soul is cast down within me;
Therefore I will remember You from the land of the Jordan,
And from the heights of Hermon,
From [7]the Hill Mizar.
7 Deep calls unto deep at the noise of Your waterfalls;
[i]All Your waves and billows have gone over me.

2 [a]Ps. 63:1; 84:2; 143:6; [Jer. 10:10] [b]Rom. 9:26; 1 Thess. 1:9 [3]So with MT, Vg.; some Heb. mss., LXX, Syr., Tg. *I see the face of God*
3 [c]Ps. 80:5; 102:9 [d]Ps. 79:10; 115:2; Joel 2:17; Mic. 7:10
4 [e]1 Sam. 1:15; Job 30:16 [f]Ps. 55:14; 122:1; Is. 30:29
5 [g]Ps. 42:11; 43:5 [h]Ps. 71:14; Lam. 3:24 [4]Lit. *bowed down* [5]So with MT, Tg.; a few Heb. mss., LXX, Syr., Vg. *The help of my countenance, my God*
6 [6]So with MT, Tg.; a few Heb. mss., LXX, Syr., Vg. put *my God* at the end of v. 5 [7]Or *Mount*
7 [i]Ps. 69:1, 2; 88:7; Jon. 2:3
8 [j]Deut. 28:8 [k]Job 35:10; Ps. 149:5
9 [l]Ps. 38:6
10 [m]Ps. 42:3; Joel 2:17; Mic. 7:10 [8]Lit. *shattering* [9]*revile*
11 [n]Ps. 43:5 [1]Lit. *salvation*

PSALM 43
1 [a][Ps. 26:1; 35:24] [b]1 Sam. 24:15; Ps. 35:1
2 [c]Ps. 42:9

8 The LORD will [j]command His lovingkindness in the daytime,
And [k]in the night His song *shall be* with me—
A prayer to the God of my life.

9 I will say to God my Rock,
[l]"Why have You forgotten me?
Why do I go mourning because of the oppression of the enemy?"
10 *As* with a [8]breaking of my bones,
My enemies [9]reproach me,
[m]While they say to me all day long,
"Where *is* your God?"

11 [n]Why are you cast down, O my soul?
And why are you disquieted within me?
Hope in God;
For I shall yet praise Him,
The [1]help of my countenance and my God.

PSALM 43

Prayer to God in Time of Trouble

Vindicate [a]me, O God,
And [b]plead my cause against an ungodly nation;
Oh, deliver me from the deceitful and unjust man!
2 For You *are* the God of my strength;
Why do You cast me off?
[c]Why do I go mourning because of the oppression of the enemy?

42:2 My soul thirsts for God. On this desire for the water of God, cf. Ps. 36:8,9; Is. 41:17; 55:1; Jer. 2:13; 14:1-9; 17:13; John 4:10; 7:37,38; Rev. 7:17; 21:6; 22:1,17.

42:4 When I remember these *things*, I pour out my soul. Such language also characterizes Jeremiah's Lamentations, indicating a heavy dirge. On "pouring out one's soul" or "heart," cf. 1 Sam. 1:15; Ps. 62:8; Lam. 2:19. These are attempts at trying to unburden oneself from intolerable pain, grief, and agony.

42:5 Why are you cast down...and...disquieted...? In this active introspection the psalmist rebukes himself for his despondency.

42:6 the land of the Jordan...the heights of Hermon...the Hill Mizar. The Mt. Hermon and the Jordan notation refers to a location in northern Palestine, an area of head-waters which flow southward. These locations signal that a sharp contrast in the word pictures describing the psalmist's change in condition is imminent. He is about to move from drought to drowning (cf. vv. 7ff.). The location and significance of Mt. Mizar is not known.

42:7 Deep...Your waterfalls...Your waves and billows. He alleges that God is ultimately responsible for the oceans of trial in which he seems to be drowning.

42:8 The LORD will command His lovingkindness. This statement of confidence interrupts his laments (cf. their continuance in vv. 9,10), providing a few gracious gulps of divine "air" under the cascading inundations of his trials and tormentors.

43:1-5 Psalm 43 might be conceived of as an epilogue to Ps. 42. The psalmist moves away from introspection toward invocation. However, as v. 5 will indicate, the psalmist's problems had not ended, at least not fully and finally. Nevertheless, spiritual progress is evident. By interrelating the psalmist's two modes of communication in Ps. 43 and then by comparing them with the laments of Ps. 42, one observes indications of that progress as he continued to deal with his despondency.

I. Prayers to God (43:1-4)
   A. Righting Wrongs (43:1,2)
   B. Restoring "Rights" (i.e., proper or appropriate things) (43:3,4)
II. "Pep-talks" to Oneself (43:5)
   A. Exhortation (43:5a-b)
   B. Encouragement (43:5c-d)

43:1 Vindicate me...plead my cause. Lit. "Judge me, O God, and argue my case." This combination of legal terms demonstrates respectively that the psalmist was requesting God to be both his Divine Judge (cf. Judg. 11:27; 1 Sam. 24:12; Pss. 7:8; 26:1) and Defense Attorney (cf. Ps. 119:154; Prov. 22:23; 23:11; Jer. 50:34; Lam. 3:58). On both concepts together, as here, cf. 1 Sam. 24:15; Ps. 35:1, 24; Mic. 7:9.

43:2 Why...why...? Since God was his refuge of strength, the psalmist questioned why this divine rejection and why his dejection?

3 [d]Oh, send out Your light and Your truth!
Let them lead me;
Let them bring me to [e]Your holy hill
And to Your [1]tabernacle.
4 Then I will go to the altar of God,
To God my exceeding joy;
And on the harp I will praise You,
O God, my God.

5 [f]Why are you cast down, O my soul?
And why are you disquieted within me?
Hope in God;
For I shall yet praise Him,
The [2]help of my countenance and my God.

3 [d] [Ps. 40:11] [e] Ps. 3:4 [1] *dwelling places*
5 [f] Ps. 42:5, 11 [2] Lit. *salvation*

PSALM 44

Redemption Remembered in Present Dishonor

To the Chief Musician. A [a]Contemplation [1] of the sons of Korah.

We have heard with our ears, O God,
[b]Our fathers have told us,
The deeds You did in their days,
In days of old:
2 [c]You drove out the [2]nations with Your hand,
But them You planted;
You afflicted the peoples, and cast them out.
3 For [d]they did not gain possession of the land by their own sword,
Nor did their own arm save them;
But it was Your right hand, Your arm, and the light of Your countenance,
[e]Because You favored them.
4 [f]You are my King, [3]O God;
[4]Command victories for Jacob.
5 Through You [g]we will push down our enemies;
Through Your name we will trample those who rise up against us.
6 For [h]I will not trust in my bow,
Nor shall my sword save me.
7 But You have saved us from our enemies,
And have put to shame those who hated us.
8 [i]In God we boast all day long,
And praise Your name forever. Selah
9 But [j]You have cast *us* off and put us to shame,
And You do not go out with our armies.
10 You make us [k]turn back from the enemy,
And those who hate us have taken [5]spoil for themselves.
11 [l]You have given us up like sheep *intended* for food,
And have [m]scattered us among the nations.
12 [n]You sell Your people for *next to* nothing,
And are not enriched by selling them.
13 [o]You make us a reproach to our neighbors,

PSALM 44
title [a] Ps. 42:title [1] Heb. *Maschil*
1 [b] [Ex. 12:26, 27; Deut. 6:20]; Judg. 6:13; Ps. 78:3
2 [c] Ex. 15:17; 2 Sam. 7:10; Jer. 24:6; Amos 9:15 [2] *Gentiles, heathen*
3 [d] [Deut. 8:17, 18]; Josh. 24:12 [e] [Deut. 4:37; 7:7, 8]
4 [f] [Ps. 74:12] [3] So with MT, Tg.; LXX, Vg. *and my God* [4] So with MT, Tg.; LXX, Syr., Vg. *Who commands*
5 [g] Deut. 33:17; [Dan. 8:4]
6 [h] [1 Sam. 17:47]; Ps. 33:16; [Hos. 1:7]
8 [i] Ps. 34:2; [Jer. 9:24]
9 [j] Ps. 60:1
10 [k] Lev. 26:17; Josh. 7:8, 12; Ps. 89:43 [5] *plunder*
11 [l] Ps. 44:22; Rom. 8:36 [m] Lev. 26:33; Deut. 4:27; 28:64; Ps. 106:27; Ezek. 20:23
12 [n] Is. 52:3, 4; Jer. 15:13
13 [o] Ps. 79:4; 80:6; Jer. 24:9

43:3 Your light and Your truth! Let them lead me; Let them bring me. These are bold personifications for divine guidance. He desired that these "messenger-attributes" divinely direct (cf. such "leading" and "guiding" in Gen. 24:48; Pss. 78:14,53,72; 107:30; Is. 57:18) so as to bring him successfully to his destination, i.e., Israel's designated place for worship.

43:5 Why…why…Hope. Cf. Ps. 42:5,11.

44:1-26 Psalm 44 is a national lament following some great but historically unidentifiable defeat in battle. Throughout this psalm there are subtle shifts between speakers of the first person plural (i.e., "We" and "us"; cf. vv. 1-3,5,7,8,9-14,17-22) and the first person singular (i.e., "I" or "my"; cf. vv. 4,6,15-16). This may indicate that the psalm was originally sung antiphonally with alterations coming from both the beaten king-general and his defeated nation. The prayers of vv. 23-26 may have been offered in unison as a climax. By employing 3 historical centers in Ps. 44, the psalmist tries to understand and deal with a national tragedy.

I. Focus on Past History: The Shock of This National Tragedy (44:1-8)
II. Focus on Current History: The Inscrutability of This National Tragedy (44:9-22)
III. Focus on Future History: A Prayer for an End to This National Tragedy (44:23-26)

44:Title The words of this title are the same as those in the title of Ps. 42; however, in the Hebrew text their order is slightly different.

44:1 We have heard. There was a rich tradition about God's great acts which the nation's fathers had passed on. Indeed the rehearsal of holy history was commanded (cf. Ex. 10:1,2; 12:26ff.; 13:14ff.; Deut. 6:20ff.; Josh. 4:6ff.; Ps. 78:3).

44:2 You planted. On the imagery of God's planting His people, cf. 2 Sam. 7:10; Is. 5:1ff.; Jer. 12:2; also cf. their being planted and taking root in Ps. 80:8-11.

44:3 For they did not…But it was Your right hand. This is a brief historical summary of the theology of divine grace, intervention, and enablement (cf. Josh. 24:17,18).

44:4 Command victories for Jacob. If the division of the Heb. consonants is taken at a different point (as it is in some early versions) this line would better fit into the immediate context, reading: "You are my King, my God, who commands (or, orders) victories for Jacob." "Jacob," the original name of the ancient patriarch, is often used to designate the nation of Israel, especially in poetry.

44:5-8 Through You…For I will not trust in my bow…But You have saved us. The defeated king-general picks up the theology of v. 3 and adds his personal commitment to it.

44:9 But You…do not go out with our armies. The Lord God is viewed here as having resigned His commission as the nation's Divine Warrior.

44:11-16 You have given…You sell. These are graphic descriptions of God superintending the defeat and utter humiliation of the nation.

A scorn and a derision to those all
around us.
14 [p]You make us a byword among the
nations,
[q]A shaking of the head among the
peoples.
15 My dishonor *is* continually before me,
And the shame of my face has
covered me,
16 Because of the voice of him who
reproaches and reviles,
[r]Because of the enemy and the avenger.

17 [s]All this has come upon us;
But we have not forgotten You,
Nor have we dealt falsely with Your
covenant.
18 Our heart has not turned back,
[t]Nor have our steps departed from
Your way;
19 But You have severely broken us in
[u]the place of jackals,
And covered us [v]with the shadow of
death.

20 If we had forgotten the name of our
God,
Or [w]stretched[6] out our hands to a
foreign god,
21 [x]Would not God search this out?
For He knows the secrets of the heart.
22 [y]Yet for Your sake we are killed all day
long;
We are accounted as sheep for the
slaughter.

23 [z]Awake! Why do You sleep, O Lord?
Arise! Do not cast *us* off forever.
24 [a]Why do You hide Your face,
And forget our affliction and our
oppression?
25 For [b]our soul is bowed down to the
[7]dust;
Our body clings to the ground.
26 Arise for our help,
And redeem us for Your mercies'
sake.

14 [p] Deut. 28:37 [q] Job 16:4
16 [r] Ps. 8:2
17 [s] Dan. 9:13
18 [t] Job 23:11
19 [u] Is. 34:13 [v] [Ps. 23:4]
20 [w] [Deut. 6:14] [6] Worshiped
21 [x] Job 31:14; [Ps. 139:1, 2; Jer. 17:10]
22 [y] Rom. 8:36
23 [z] Ps. 7:6
24 [a] Job 13:24
25 [b] Ps. 119:25 [7] Ground, in humiliation

PSALM 45

The Glories of the Messiah and His Bride

To the Chief Musician. [a]Set to [1]"The Lilies."
A [2]Contemplation of the sons of Korah.
A Song of Love.

My heart is overflowing with a good
theme;
I recite my composition concerning
the King;
My tongue *is* the pen of a [3]ready
writer.

2 You are fairer than the sons of men;
[b]Grace is poured upon Your lips;
Therefore God has blessed You
forever.
3 [4]Gird Your [c]sword upon *Your* thigh,
[d]O Mighty One,
With Your [e]glory and Your majesty.
4 [f]And in Your majesty ride
prosperously because of truth,
humility, *and* righteousness;
And Your right hand shall teach You
awesome things.
5 Your arrows *are* sharp in the heart of
the King's enemies;
The peoples fall under You.

PSALM 45

title [a] Ps. 69:title [1] Heb. *Shoshannim* [2] Heb. *Maschil*
1 [3] *skillful*
2 [b] Luke 4:22
3 [c] [Is. 49:2; Heb. 4:12]; Rev. 1:16 [d] [Is. 9:6] [e] Jude 25 [4] *Belt on*
4 [f] Rev. 6:2

44:17-21 But we have not forgotten You…If we had forgotten the name of our God. The nation's recent defeat was painfully perplexing in view of their basic loyalty to God.

44:22 Yet for Your sake. They had no specific answers; only this inescapable conclusion that, by God's sovereign will, they were allowed to be destroyed by their enemies. Cf. Paul's quote of this verse in Rom. 8:36 and its general principle in Matt. 5:10-12; 1 Pet. 3:13-17; 4:12-16.

44:23 Awake!…arise! Cf. Ps. 35:23. God does not actually sleep. This is only in appearance to man's perception.

44:26 Arise. Cf. Num. 10:35; Pss. 3:7; 7:6. **And redeem us for Your mercies' sake.** The psalm therefore comes full circle from the history of God's gracious redemption (vv. 1-3) to the hope for the same in the near future (v. 26).

45:1-17 Some portions of Ps. 45 convey a secular emphasis, while others suggest a sacred extension. Upon the occasion of a royal wedding, the psalmist offers a 3-part song of celebration.

- I. Poetic Preface (45:1)
- II. Song of Celebration (45:2-16)
  - A. The King-Groom (45:2-9)
    1. Endowments of the king-groom (45:2)
    2. Exploits of the king-groom (45:3-5)
    3. Elevation of the king-groom (45:6,7)
    4. Eminence of the king-groom (45:8,9)
  - B. The Princess-Bride (45:10-15)
    1. A challenge to the princess-bride (45:10-12)
    2. The procession of the princess-bride (45:13-15)
  - C. Future Children from This Union (45:16)
- III. Poetic Postscript (45:17)

45:Title Two new notations are found, "Set to The Lilies" and "A Song of Love." The first most likely had to do with the tune used in accompaniment with its words. The second notation referring to its content probably indicated that this psalm was a wedding song, and even more specifically, a royal wedding composition.

45:1 My heart is overflowing…My tongue. The psalmist is overwhelmed with emotion upon the occasion of the king's marriage; consequently, he puts his stirred-up mind and feelings into words. In v. 2ff. his tongue is the brush that he uses to paint vivid word pictures.

45:2 You are fairer. I.e., you are "more beautiful than," or, "most handsome among" (cf. an ancient prerequisite for kingship; in the Bible note the comments, e.g., in 1 Sam. 9:2; 10:33; 16:12; 2 Sam. 14:25; 1 Kin. 1:6; Song 5:10; Is. 33:17). **Grace is poured upon Your lips.** The implication is that God has anointed the king's words (cf. Eccl. 10:12; Luke 4:22).

45:3-5 Gird Your sword. In these verses the psalmist wishes the king future victories in battle.

6 [g]Your throne, O God, *is* forever and
ever;
A [h]scepter of righteousness *is* the
scepter of Your kingdom.
7 You love righteousness and hate
wickedness;
Therefore God, Your God, has
[i]anointed You
With the oil of [j]gladness more than
Your companions.
8 All Your garments are [k]scented with
myrrh and aloes *and* cassia,
Out of the ivory palaces, by which
they have made You glad.
9 [l]Kings' daughters *are* among Your
honorable women;
[m]At Your right hand stands the queen
in gold from Ophir.

10 Listen, O daughter,
Consider and incline your ear;
[n]Forget your own people also, and
your father's house;
11 So the King will greatly desire your
beauty;
[o]Because He *is* your Lord, worship Him.
12 And the daughter of Tyre *will come*
with a gift;
[p]The rich among the people will seek
your favor.

13 The royal daughter *is* all glorious
within *the palace;*
Her clothing *is* woven with gold.
14 [q]She shall be brought to the King in
robes of many colors;
The virgins, her companions who
follow her, shall be brought to
You.
15 With gladness and rejoicing they shall
be brought;
They shall enter the King's palace.

16 Instead of Your fathers shall be Your
sons,
[r]Whom You shall make princes in all
the earth.
17 [s]I will make Your name to be
remembered in all
generations;
Therefore the people shall praise You
forever and ever.

6 [g] [Ps. 93:2]; Heb. 1:8, 9 [h] [Num. 24:17]
7 [i] Ps. 2:2 [j] Ps. 21:6; Heb. 1:8, 9
8 [k] Song 1:12, 13
9 [l] Song 6:8 [m] 1 Kin. 2:19
10 [n] Deut. 21:13; Ruth 1:16, 17
11 [o] Ps. 95:6; [Is. 54:5]
12 [p] Is. 49:23
14 [q] Song 1:4
16 [r] [1 Pet. 2:9; Rev. 1:6; 20:6]
17 [s] Mal. 1:11

PSALM 46

God the Refuge of His People and Conqueror of the Nations

To the Chief Musician. A Psalm of the sons of Korah. A Song [a]for Alamoth.

God *is* our [b]refuge and strength,
[c]A [1]very present help in trouble.
2 Therefore we will not fear,
Even though the earth be removed,
And though the mountains be carried
into the [2]midst of the sea;
3 [d]*Though* its waters roar *and* be
troubled,
Though the mountains shake with its
swelling. Selah

PSALM 46
title [a] 1 Chr. 15:20
1 [b] Ps. 62:7, 8 [c] [Deut. 4:7; Ps. 145:18] [1] *An abundantly available help*
2 [2] Lit. *heart*
3 [d] [Ps. 93:3, 4]

45:6,7 Your throne, O God. Since this king-groom was likely a member of the Davidic dynasty (e.g., 2 Sam. 7), there was a near and immediate application (cf. 1 Chr. 28:5; 29:23). Through progressive revelation (i.e., Heb. 1:8,9), we learn of the ultimate application to "a greater than Solomon" who is God—the Lord Jesus Christ.

45:9 Kings' daughters...Your honorable women...the queen. This court picture could refer to royal female guests, but also includes the other wives and concubines of the king-groom (cf. the situation with Solomon in 1 Kin. 11:1). Such polygamy of course was prohibited by God's Word; unfortunately, it was still common among the kings of Israel. **gold from Ophir.** Although its geographical location is not known, "Ophir" was well known as the location of the purest gold.

45:10-15 O daughter. The major emphasis of this portion is "Here comes the bride!" However, even in this section the focus still concentrates, according to ancient Near Eastern precedent, upon the royal groom.

45:16 Instead of Your fathers shall be Your sons. The loyal and joyful poet now speaks of the blessings of anticipated children from this union.

46:1-11 Psalm 46 was the scriptural catalyst for Martin Luther's great hymn, "A Mighty Fortress Is Our God." This psalm also launches a trilogy of psalms (i.e., 46,47,48); they are all songs of triumph. Furthermore, it has also been grouped among the so-called "songs of Zion" (cf. Pss. 48,76,84,87,122). Psalm 46 extols the adequacy of God in facing threats from nature and the nations. God indeed protects (cf. vv. 1,7,11) His people upon the earth (cf. vv. 2,6,8,9,10). The major burden of Ps. 46 is that God provides stability for His people who live in two exceedingly unstable environments.

I. The Unstable Environment of Nature (46:1-3)
  A. The Affirmation of His Stability (46:1)
  B. The Application of His Stability (46:2,3)
II. The Unstable Environment of the Nations (46:4-11)
  A. The First Chorus (46:4-7)
  B. The Follow-Up Chorus (46:8-11)

46:Title The new element in this title is "Alamoth." The early Gr. translation (LXX) interprets this technical term as "hidden things." However, the Heb. word normally has to do with "girls" or "young maidens." Consequently, the most likely conjecture about this phrase is that it is a technical musical notation, possibly indicating a song which was to be sung with female voices at a higher range.

46:2 Even though the earth be removed. I.e., "When earth changes and when mountains move (or) shake (or) totter (or) slip...," (cf. the language of Is. 24:19,20; 54:10; Hag. 2:6). These are poetic allusions to earthquakes. Since "the earth" and "mountains" are regarded by men as symbols of stability, when they "dance" great terror normally ensues. But when the most stable becomes unstable, there should be "no fear" because of the transcendent stability of God.

46:3 *Though* its waters roar. This is an illustration of powerfully surging and potentially destructive floods of waters. These will not erode God's protective fortifications.

4 *There is* a [e]river whose streams shall
make glad the [f]city of God,
The holy *place* of the [3]tabernacle of
the Most High.
5 God *is* [g]in the midst of her, she shall
not be [4]moved;
God shall help her, just [5]at the break
of dawn.
6 [h]The nations raged, the kingdoms
were moved;
He uttered His voice, the earth
melted.

7 The [i]LORD of hosts *is* with us;
The God of Jacob *is* our refuge. Selah

8 Come, behold the works of the LORD,
Who has made desolations in the
earth.
9 [j]He makes wars cease to the end of the
earth;
[k]He breaks the bow and cuts the spear
in two;
[l]He burns the chariot in the fire.

10 Be still, and know that I *am* God;
[m]I will be exalted among the nations,
I will be exalted in the earth!

11 The LORD of hosts *is* with us;
The God of Jacob *is* our refuge. Selah

4 [e][Ezek. 47:1-12] [f]Ps. 48:1, 8; Is. 60:14 [3]*dwelling places*
5 [g][Deut. 23:14; Is. 12:6]; Ezek. 43:7; Hos. 11:9; [Joel 2:27; Zeph. 3:15; Zech. 2:5, 10, 11; 8:3] [4]*shaken* [5]Lit. *at the turning of the morning*
6 [h]Ps. 2:1, 2
7 [i]Num. 14:9; 2 Chr. 13:12
9 [j]Is. 2:4 [k]Ps. 76:3 [l]Ezek. 39:9
10 [m][Is. 2:11, 17]

PSALM 47
2 [a]Deut. 7:21; Neh. 1:5; Ps. 76:12
3 [b]Ps. 18:47
4 [c][1 Pet. 1:4]
5 [d]Ps. 68:24, 25
7 [e]Zech. 14:9 [f]1 Cor. 14:15
8 [g]1 Chr. 16:31 [h]Ps. 97:2 [i]Ps. 48:1
9 [j][Rom. 4:11, 12] [k][Ps. 89:18]

PSALM 47

Praise to God, the Ruler of the Earth

To the Chief Musician. A Psalm of the sons of Korah.

Oh, clap your hands, all you peoples!
Shout to God with the voice of
triumph!
2 For the LORD Most High *is* awesome;
He is a great [a]King over all the earth.
3 [b]He will subdue the peoples under us,
And the nations under our feet.
4 He will choose our [c]inheritance for us,
The excellence of Jacob whom He
loves. Selah

5 [d]God has gone up with a shout,
The LORD with the sound of a trumpet.
6 Sing praises to God, sing praises!
Sing praises to our King, sing praises!
7 [e]For God *is* the King of all the earth;
[f]Sing praises with understanding.

8 [g]God reigns over the nations;
God [h]sits on His [i]holy throne.
9 The princes of the people have
gathered together,
[j]The people of the God of Abraham.
[k]For the shields of the earth *belong* to
God;
He is greatly exalted.

46:4 *There is* a river whose streams. These words about refreshing waters contrast with those about the threatening torrents of v. 3. Cf. the garden of paradise concept often mentioned in ancient Near Eastern literature, but most importantly, cf. the biblical revelation, noting especially the "bookends" of Gen. 2:10 and Rev. 22:1, 2. **the city of God.** These words in their present setting refer to Jerusalem, God's chosen earthly residence (cf. Ps. 48:1, 2; Is. 60:14).

46:5, 6 she shall not be moved. These verses pick up some of the key terms about moving, slipping, tottering, sliding, and roaring from vv. 1-3; however, here, because of the presence of God, the forces of nature and the nations are no longer a threat to the people of God who dwell with Him.

46:7 The LORD of hosts *is* with us. The precious personal presence (cf. "God with us" in Is. 7:14; 8:8, 10) of the Divine Warrior (cf. "LORD of hosts" or "armies," e.g., Pss. 24:10; 48:8; 59:5) secures the safety of His people.

46:8 desolations. This word not only characterizes God's past exploits but it is also employed in various "Day of the Lord" contexts (e.g., Is. 13:9; Hos. 5:9; Zeph. 2:15).

46:10 Be still, and know that I *am* God. This twin command to not panic and to recognize His sovereignty is probably directed to both His nation for comfort and all other nations for warning.

47:1-9 The main concepts of Ps. 47 develop around key words and phrases, e.g., "peoples" and "nations" (vv. 1, 3, 8, 9); "earth" and "all the earth" (vv. 2, 7, 9); and "king" or "reigning (as king)" (vv. 2, 6, 7, 8). The major message of this psalm is that God is the unique Sovereign over all. Structurally, there are two choruses of worship in Ps. 47 which celebrate this universal kingship of the Lord God Most High.

I. First Chorus: God as the Victorious King-Warrior (47:1-5)
   A. Its Call to Worship (47:1)
   B. Its Causes for Worship (47:2-5)
II. Second Chorus: God as the Sovereign King-Governor (47:6-9)
   A. Its Call to Worship (47:6)
   B. Its Causes for Worship (47:47:7-9b)
   C. Its Code of Worship (47:9c)

47:1 all you peoples. The call to worship is universal.

47:3 He will subdue. Or, "He subdues," i.e., an axiomatic truth about the past, present, and future.

47:4 He will choose. Again, "He chooses," serves as a timeless truth. Cf. the election of Israel in Deut. 7:6ff.; Ps. 135:4. On the land of promise as "inheritance," cf. Deut. 32:8, 9; Ps. 105:11. *See notes on Eph. 1:4; 1 Pet. 1:1, 2* for a discussion of the doctrine of divine election. **The excellence of Jacob whom He loves.** The "excellence" or "pride" of Jacob also refers to the land of Canaan (cf. the term illustratively in Is. 13:19; then in Is. 60:15; Nah. 2:2; etc.). "Whom He loves" is signal terminology for God's special, elective, covenantal "love" (cf., e.g., Mal. 1:2ff.). This special focus on God's covenant with Israel does not negate the bigger picture involving blessing to all nations sketched out in the original Abrahamic Covenant of Gen. 12:1-3.

47:5 God has gone up with a shout. The imagery likely refers to God's presence, after having gone into battle with His people, now ascending victoriously to His immanent "residence" on Mt. Zion and to His transcendent residence in heaven. This procession with the ark of God was accompanied by great shouts and blasts of celebration in vv. 5, 6.

47:9 the shields of the earth. This imagery stands parallel with "the princes of the people." Illustratively, there may be a loose analogy to God's sovereignly appointed human governors (cf. Rom. 13:1-7) as protectors for the masses.

PSALM 48

The Glory of God in Zion

A Song. A Psalm of the sons of Korah.

Great *is* the LORD, and greatly to be praised
In the [a]city of our God,
In His holy mountain.
2 [b]Beautiful in [1]elevation,
The joy of the whole earth,
Is Mount Zion *on* the sides of the north,
The city of the great King.
3 God *is* in her palaces;
He is known as her refuge.

4 For behold, [c]the kings assembled,
They passed by together.
5 They saw *it, and* so they marveled;
They were troubled, they hastened away.
6 Fear [d]took hold of them there,
And pain, as of a woman in birth pangs,
7 *As when* You break the [e]ships of Tarshish
With an east wind.

8 As we have heard,
So we have seen
In the city of the LORD of hosts,
In the city of our God:
God will [f]establish it forever. Selah

9 We have thought, O God, on [g]Your lovingkindness,
In the midst of Your temple.
10 According to [h]Your name, O God,
So *is* Your praise to the ends of the earth;
Your right hand is full of righteousness.
11 Let Mount Zion rejoice,
Let the daughters of Judah be glad,
Because of Your judgments.

12 Walk about Zion,
And go all around her.
Count her towers;
13 Mark well her bulwarks;
Consider her palaces;
That you may [i]tell *it* to the generation following.
14 For this *is* God,
Our God forever and ever;
[j]He will be our guide
[2]*Even* to death.

PSALM 48
1 [a]Ps. 46:4; 87:3; Matt. 5:35
2 [b]Ps. 50:2 [1]*height*
4 [c]2 Sam. 10:6, 14
6 [d]Ex. 15:15
7 [e]1 Kin. 10:22; Ezek. 27:25
8 [f][Ps. 87:5; Is. 2:2]; Mic. 4:1
9 [g]Ps. 26:3
10 [h][Deut. 28:58]; Josh. 7:9; Mal. 1:11
13 [i][Ps. 78:5-7]
14 [j]Is. 58:11 [2]So with MT, Syr.; LXX, Vg. *Forever*

PSALM 49

The Confidence of the Foolish

To the Chief Musician. A Psalm of the sons of Korah.

Hear this, all peoples;
Give ear, all inhabitants of the world,
2 Both low and high,
Rich and poor together.

48:1-14 In Ps. 48, it often appears that Zion itself is the object of praise. While referring to Zion, this hymn of confidence (cf. Pss. 46:47) contains several checks and balances showing that it is ultimately God, who dwells in Zion, who is to be praised. Therefore, this perspective must be kept in mind as the lines of Ps. 48 flow back and forth with respective emphases on the city and the great God of that city. This psalm, sung with orchestral accompaniment, therefore contrasts two different responses to the God of Zion and the Zion of God.

- I. Introduction (48:1-3)
- II. The Panic-Response of the Provokers of God (48:4-7)
  - A. The Chronicling of It (48:4-6)
  - B. The Cause of It (48:7)
- III. The Praise-Response of the People of God (48:8-14)
  - A. Their Celebration (48:8-13)
  - B. Their Conclusion (48:14)

48:2 The joy of the whole earth. Cf. the judgment context of Lam. 2:15. **the sides of the north.** "North" is an interpretive translation of a word term that occurs as a Semitic place name, i.e., "Zaphon." In Canaanite mythology Zaphon was an ancient Near Eastern equivalent to Mt. Olympus, the dwelling place of pagan gods. If this was the psalmist's intention in Ps. 48:2, the reference becomes a polemical description of the Lord; He is not only King of Kings but also is God of all so-called gods. **The city of the great King.** Cf. Ps. 47:2 and Matt. 5:34,35. God Himself has always been the King of Kings.

48:3 God *is* in her palaces. Better, "God is in her citadels." The context points to the military connotation of this word.

48:4-7 This dramatic, poetic rapid-fire, historical rehearsal of events chronicles some serious threat to Jerusalem from a hostile coalition of forces. They had come arrogantly to destroy Jerusalem, the Zion of God; but the God of Zion surprisingly and powerfully devastated them.

48:7 the ships of Tarshish. A notable Mediterranean port of uncertain location (cf. Jon. 1:3), possibly Spain.

48:8 As we have heard, so we have seen. Cf. the personal, individual testimony of Job (i.e., 42:5). The historical tradition of vv. 1-3 had been proven true once again in the events of vv. 4-7.

48:11 the daughters of Judah. This phrase would refer to the surrounding cities and villages.

48:14 For this *is* God. Other options for translating the Heb. text of this line are: 1) "For this God is our God," or 2) "For this is God, our God."

49:1-20 Psalm 49 deals with the most real thing about life—the certainty of death. One of its major lessons is that "you really can't take it with you." Containing these kinds of very practical lessons about life and death, it falls neatly into the category of a didactic or wisdom poem. At places it sounds very much like portions of Job, Proverbs, and Ecclesiastes. It contains warnings to the rich and famous and words of comfort for the poor. These timeless OT messages undergird many NT passages, such as the accounts about the rich fool in Luke 12:13-21 or the rich man and Lazarus in Luke 16. After a fairly lengthy introduction the body of the psalm falls into two parts as indicated by the climaxing refrain in vv. 12 and 20. The wisdom poet of Ps. 49 developed his somber theme in two stages, focusing on death as the universal experience of all men.

- I. Introduction (49:1-4)
- II. Stage One: The Common Experience *of* Death (49:5-12)

3 My mouth shall speak wisdom,
And the meditation of my heart *shall give* understanding.
4 I will incline my ear to a proverb;
I will disclose my [1]dark saying on the harp.

5 Why should I fear in the days of evil,
When the iniquity at my heels surrounds me?
6 Those who [a]trust in their wealth
And boast in the multitude of their riches,
7 None *of them* can by any means redeem *his* brother,
Nor [b]give to God a ransom for him—
8 For [c]the redemption of their souls *is* costly,
And it shall cease forever—
9 That he should continue to live eternally,
And [d]not [2]see the Pit.

10 For he sees wise men die;
Likewise the fool and the senseless person perish,
And leave their wealth to others.
11 [3]Their inner thought *is that* their houses *will last* forever,
Their dwelling places to all generations;
They [e]call *their* lands after their own names.
12 Nevertheless man, *though* in honor, does not [4]remain;
He is like the beasts *that* perish.

13 This is the way of those who *are* [f]foolish,
And of their posterity who approve their sayings. Selah
14 Like sheep they are laid in the grave;
Death shall feed on them;
[g]The upright shall have dominion over them in the morning;
[h]And their beauty shall be consumed in [5]the grave, far from their dwelling.
15 But God [i]will redeem my soul from the power of [6]the grave,
For He shall [j]receive me. Selah

16 Do not be afraid when one becomes rich,
When the glory of his house is increased;
17 For when he dies he shall carry nothing away;
His glory shall not descend after him.
18 Though while he lives [k]he blesses himself
(For *men* will praise you when you do well for yourself),
19 He shall go to the generation of his fathers;
They shall never see [l]light.[7]
20 A man *who is* in honor, yet does not understand,
[m]Is like the beasts *that* perish.

PSALM 49

4 [1] *riddle*
6 [a] Job 31:24; Ps. 52:7; [Prov. 11:28; Mark 10:23, 24]
7 [b] Job 36:18, 19
8 [c] [Matt. 16:26]
9 [d] Ps. 89:48 [2] *experience corruption*
11 [e] Gen. 4:17; Deut. 3:14 [3] LXX, Syr., Tg., Vg. *Their graves shall be their houses forever*
12 [4] So with MT, Tg.; LXX, Syr., Vg. *understand* (cf. v. 20)
13 [f] [Luke 12:20]
14 [g] Ps. 47:3; [Dan. 7:18; 1 Cor. 6:2; Rev. 2:26] [h] Job 4:21 [5] Or *Sheol*
15 [i] [Hos. 13:4]; Mark 16:6, 7; Acts 2:31, 32 [j] Ps. 73:24 [6] Or *Sheol*
18 [k] Deut. 29:19; Luke 12:19
19 [l] Job 33:30 [7] The light of life
20 [m] Eccl. 3:19

A. Applying His Teaching through an Important Reflection (49:5,6)
B. Explaining His Teaching through Important Reminders (49:7-12)

III. Stage Two: The Contrasting Experience *in* Death (49:13-20)
A. The Assurance of This Contrasting Experience in Death (49:13-15)
B. The Application of This Contrasting Experience in Death (49:16-20)

49:1 all peoples…all inhabitants. The scope of his message is geographically universal.

49:2 low and high, rich and poor. Note the chiastic order (i.e., A-B-B-A) of these descriptives. The scope of his message is also socially universal.

49:3,4 wisdom…understanding…proverb…dark saying. All these are wisdom terms (cf. respectively, Prov. 1:20; 9:1; 14:1; 24:7; then Prov. 2:3; 3:13; 5:1; 14:29; 18:2; 19:8; next Prov. 1:6; Ezek. 17:2; and finally, Judg. 14:12ff.).

49:5 the iniquity at my heels. This indicates evil chasing him.

49:6 Those who trust in their wealth. Mankind's propensity to trust in his own material goods is well attested in Scripture (e.g., Ps. 52:7; Jer. 17:5). Biblically this is exposed as the epitome of stupidity (cf., e.g., Prov. 23:4,5; Luke 12:16ff.).

49:7-9 None *of them* can. No person, regardless of his means, is able to escape death; it is inevitable (Heb. 9:27). This passage anticipates the second death of hell (cf. Rev. 20:11-15), except for those who by faith have repented of their sin and embraced the only adequate ransom—the one paid by the Lord Jesus Christ with his death on the cross (cf. Matt. 20:28; 1 Pet. 1:18,19).

49:9b-10a not see…For he sees. The irony is obvious; the wealthy person somehow hopes to get around death, yet he witnesses people constantly dying all around him, from the wise to the foolish.

49:12 Nevertheless man…does not remain. This refrain (cf. v. 20) is the main point of the psalm. Cf. this concept in Eccl. 3:19. While man and beast both die, man's spirit lives on eternally but beasts have no life after death.

49:14 Like sheep they are laid in the grave; Death shall feed on them. More irony; they are considered as sheep once noted for their grazing; now death shall graze on them. **The upright shall have dominion…in the morning.** This harbinger of good news to come (cf. v. 15) interrupts this long series of confirmations of the condemnation of the self-reliant.

49:15 But God will redeem my soul…He shall receive me. This is one of the greatest affirmations of confidence in God in the Psalms. Although the faithless person cannot buy his way out of death (v. 7ff.), the faithful one is redeemed by the only Redeemer, God Himself. On the significance of the word "receive," cf. Gen. 5:24; 2 Kin. 2:10; Ps. 73:24; Heb. 11:5. So in v. 15 the psalmist expresses his confidence in God, that He would raise him to eternal life.

49:17 he shall carry nothing away. An explicit you-can't-take-it-with-you attestation (cf. Job 1:21; Eccl. 5:15; 1 Tim. 6:6,7).

49:20 A man…yet does not understand. The refrain is similar to that of v. 12.

PSALM 50

God the Righteous Judge

A Psalm of Asaph.

The [a]Mighty One, God the LORD,
Has spoken and called the earth
From the rising of the sun to its going
down.
2 Out of Zion, the perfection of beauty,
[b]God will shine forth.
3 Our God shall come, and shall not
keep silent;
[c]A fire shall devour before Him,
And it shall be very tempestuous all
around Him.
4 [d]He shall call to the heavens from
above,
And to the earth, that He may judge
His people:
5 "Gather [e]My saints together to Me,
[f]Those who have [1]made a covenant
with Me by sacrifice."
6 Let the [g]heavens declare His
righteousness,
For [h]God Himself *is* Judge. Selah

7 "Hear, O My people, and I will speak,
O Israel, and I will testify against you;
[i]I *am* God, your God!
8 [j]I will not [2]rebuke you [k]for your
sacrifices
Or your burnt offerings,
Which are continually before Me.
9 [l]I will not take a bull from your
house,
Nor goats out of your folds.
10 For every beast of the forest *is* Mine,
And the cattle on a thousand hills.
11 I know all the birds of the mountains,
And the wild beasts of the field *are*
Mine.

12 "If I were hungry, I would not tell you;
[m]For the world *is* Mine, and all its
fullness.
13 [n]Will I eat the flesh of bulls,
Or drink the blood of goats?
14 [o]Offer to God thanksgiving,
And [p]pay your vows to the Most
High.
15 [q]Call upon Me in the day of trouble;
I will deliver you, and you shall
glorify Me."

16 But to the wicked God says:
"What *right* have you to declare My
statutes,
Or take My covenant in your mouth,
17 [r]Seeing you hate instruction
And cast My words behind you?
18 When you saw a thief, you
[s]consented [3] with him,
And have been a [t]partaker with
adulterers.
19 You give your mouth to evil,
And [u]your tongue frames deceit.
20 You sit *and* speak against your
brother;

PSALM 50

1 [a] Is. 9:6
2 [b] Deut. 33:2; Ps. 80:1
3 [c] Lev. 10:2; Num. 16:35; [Ps. 97:3]
4 [d] Deut. 4:26; 31:28; 32:1; Is. 1:2
5 [e] Deut. 33:3 [f] Ex. 24:7 [1] Lit. *cut*
6 [g] [Ps. 97:6] [h] Ps. 75:7
7 [i] Ex. 20:2
8 [j] Jer. 7:22 [k] Is. 1:11; [Hos. 6:6] [2] *reprove*
9 [l] Ps. 69:31
12 [m] Ex. 19:5; [Deut. 10:14; Job 41:11]; 1 Cor. 10:26
13 [n] [Ps. 51:15-17]
14 [o] Hos. 14:2; Heb. 13:15 [p] Num. 30:2; Deut. 23:21
15 [q] Job 22:27; [Zech. 13:9]
17 [r] Neh. 9:26; Rom. 2:21
18 [s] [Rom. 1:32] [t] 1 Tim. 5:22 [3] LXX, Syr., Tg., Vg. *ran*
19 [u] Ps. 52:2

50:1-23 God Himself is quoted throughout the psalm. Consequently, its form resembles the prophetic writings which specialized in delivering divine oracles. Its major burden is to delineate the nature of true worship (i.e., "worshiping in spirit and truth," cf. John 4:24). The psalmist skillfully develops this burden in a polemical fashion with its exposures of externalism and hypocrisy. The Lord God, the Supreme Judge, levels two felony charges against His professing people.

I. Introduction: The Supreme Judge Enters to Preside (50:1-6)
II. The Supreme Judge Levels Two Charges (50:7-21)
  A. First Charge: Ritualism (50:7-15)
  B. Second Charge: Rebellion (50:16-21)
III. The Supreme Judge Offers a Solution (50:22,23)

50:Title This is the first psalm entitled "a psalm of Asaph" (cf. Pss. 73–83 in Book III of Psalms). For references to "Asaph," cf. 1 Chr. 6:39; 15:16ff.; 16:5ff.; 25:1ff.; 2 Chr. 5:12; 29:30; Ezra 2:40; Neh. 12:46. Sometimes the simple "Asaph" may stand for the longer expression "the sons of Asaph." Each occasion needs to be examined to see what the relationship between a given psalm and "Asaph" might be, i.e., composed by, handed down by, sung by this special Levitical choir. Many older commentators feel that Ps. 50 was authored by the original "Asaph."

50:1 The Mighty One, God the LORD. The Divine Judge is introduced with three significant OT names. The first two are the short and longer forms of the most common word for "God" in the OT, and the third is the name for Israel's God par excellence, i.e., Yahweh (cf. its historical origin in Ex. 3:14). **From the rising of the sun to its going down.** A common OT idiom conveying from E to W, i.e., all over the planet.

50:2,3 God will shine forth. These verses utilize the language of theophany (cf. Ex. 19:16-19).

50:4,5 He shall call to the heavens…to the earth…His people…My saints. He summons the heavens and the earth as personified witnesses for these charges He is about to level concerning His professing people (cf., e.g., Deut. 32:1ff.; Is. 1:2ff.).

50:5 a covenant with Me by sacrifice. Such a ratification of covenant is serious, sacred business (cf. Ex. 24:3-8). This reference to "sacrifice" will set the stage for His first felony charge in v. 7ff.

50:8 I will not rebuke you for your sacrifices. The Divine Judge's condemnations are directed not at the act of sacrifice but at the people's attitude in sacrificing (cf. 1 Sam. 15:22; Pss. 40:6-8; 51:17; 69:30; Is. 1:12; Jer. 7:21-26; Hos. 6:6; Mic. 6:6-8).

50:9-13 will not take a bull from your house. God refuses mere ritual; it is an abomination to Him. He, unlike the pagan deities, needs nothing; He created everything and owns everything.

50:14 Offer to God thanksgiving. Here is the sacrifice that always pleases Him (cf. Ps. 51:18; Heb 13:15).

50:16-20 the wicked. Whereas the first charge dealt with a vertical relationship (cf. the first tablet of the Ten Commandments), this one in v. 16ff. focuses on evidences of horizontal violations of covenant (i.e., rebellion against God in the context of man to fellow man offenses; cf. the second half of the Ten Commandments).

You slander your own mother's son.
21 These *things* you have done, and I
kept silent;
[v]You thought that I was altogether like
you;
But I will rebuke you,
And [w]set *them* in order before your
eyes.

22 "Now consider this, you who [x]forget
God,
Lest I tear *you* in pieces,
And *there be* none to deliver:
23 Whoever offers praise glorifies Me;
And [y]to him who orders *his* conduct
aright
I will show the salvation of God."

21 [v][Rom. 2:4] [w][Ps. 90:8]
22 [x][Job 8:13]
23 [y]Gal. 6:16

PSALM 51
title [a]2 Sam. 12:1
1 [b][Is. 43:25; 44:22; Acts 3:19; Col. 2:14]
2 [c]Jer. 33:8; Ezek. 36:33; [Heb. 9:14; 1 John 1:7, 9]
4 [d]2 Sam. 12:13
[e][Luke 5:21]

PSALM 51

A Prayer of Repentance

To the Chief Musician. A Psalm of David
[a]when Nathan the prophet went to him,
after he had gone in to Bathsheba.

Have mercy upon me, O God,
According to Your lovingkindness;
According to the multitude of Your
tender mercies,
[b]Blot out my transgressions.
2 [c]Wash me thoroughly from my iniquity,
And cleanse me from my sin.

3 For I acknowledge my transgressions,
And my sin *is* always before me.
4 [d]Against You, You only, have I sinned,
And done *this* evil [e]in Your sight—

50:21 I kept silent…*But* I will rebuke you. God's longsuffering grace must never be looked upon as laxity (cf. 2 Pet. 3:3-10) nor abused. His reckoning for rebellion will indeed be manifested.

50:22 Now consider this. Before destruction, mercifully comes an opportunity for deliberation and repentance.

50:23 Whoever offers praise glorifies Me. Cf. v. 14. This remains the remedy for mere ritualism. The conclusions of vv. 22 and 23 came in chiastic order, heightening the total impact of the psalm's two felony charges (i.e., the recounting of *ritualism,* vv. 7-15; the recounting of *rebellion,* vv. 16-21; the remedy of repentance for *rebellion,* v. 22; the remedy of *repentance* for ritualism, v. 23).

51:1-19 This is the classic passage in the OT on man's repentance and God's forgiveness of sin. Along with Ps. 32, it was written by David after his affair with Bathsheba and his murder of Uriah, her husband (2 Sam. 11–12). It is one of 7 poems called penitential psalms (6, 32, 38, 51, 102, 130, 143). To David's credit, he recognized fully how horrendous his sin was against God, blamed no one but himself, and begged for divine forgiveness.

I. Plea for Forgiveness (51:1,2)
II. Proffer of Confession (51:3-6)
III. Prayer for Moral Cleanness (51:7-12)
IV. Promise of Renewed Service (51:13-17)
V. Petition for National Restoration (51:18,19)

51:1 lovingkindness. Even though he had sinned horribly, David knew that forgiveness was available, based on God's covenant love.

51:4 Against You, You only. David realized what every believer

Anointing of the Holy Spirit in the Old Testament

Old Testament Israel had mediators who stood between God and His people. To empower the OT mediators, the Holy Spirit gave special administrative ability to carry out the management of the nation and military skills which enabled them to defeat the theocracy's enemies. The Lord first anointed Moses with this ministry of the Spirit, and then in a truly dramatic scene, took some of this ministry of the Spirit and shared it with the 70 elders. Thus they were enabled to help Moses administer Israel (Num. 11:17-25).

Also Joshua (Deut. 34:9), the judges (Judg. 3:10; 6:34), and the kings of united Israel and the southern kingdom were anointed with this special ministry of the Spirit. When the Spirit of the Lord came upon King Saul, for example, he was in effect given "another heart" (1 Sam. 10:6-10). This does not mean that he was regenerated at this point in his life, but that he was given skills to be a king. Later the theocratic anointing was taken from Saul and given to David (1 Sam. 16:1-14). Saul, from that time on, became a totally incapable leader.

King David no doubt had this special ministry of the Spirit in mind in his prayer of repentance in Psalm 51. He was not afraid of losing his salvation when he prayed, "do not take your Holy Spirit from me" (Ps. 51:11), but rather was concerned that God would remove this spiritual wisdom and administrative skill from him. David had earlier seen such the tragedy in the life of Saul when that king of Israel lost the anointing of the Holy Spirit. David was thus pleading with God not to remove His hand of guidance.

King Solomon also perceived his youthful inabilities at the beginning of his reign and requested God to give him special wisdom in administering Israel. God was greatly pleased with this request and granted an extra measure to the young man (1 Kin. 3:7-12, 28; 4:29-34). Although the OT is silent in this regard about the kings who succeeded Solomon, the theocratic anointing of the Spirit likely came on all of the descendants of David in connection with the Davidic Covenant.

When the theocracy went out of existence as Judah was carried away into captivity, and the last Davidic king was disempowered, the theocratic anointing was no longer given (Ezek. 8–11). The kings of the northern tribes, on the other hand, being essentially apostate and not in the Davidic line, never had the benefit of this special ministry of the Spirit.

[f]That You may be found just [1]when
You speak,
And blameless when You judge.

5 [g]Behold, I was brought forth in
iniquity,
And in sin my mother conceived me.
6 Behold, You desire truth in the
inward parts,
And in the hidden *part* You will make
me to know wisdom.

7 [h]Purge me with hyssop, and I shall be
clean;
Wash me, and I shall be [i]whiter than
snow.
8 Make me hear joy and gladness,
That the bones You have broken [j]may
rejoice.
9 Hide Your face from my sins,
And blot out all my iniquities.

10 [k]Create in me a clean heart, O God,
And renew a steadfast spirit within
me.
11 Do not cast me away from Your
presence,
And do not take Your [l]Holy Spirit
from me.

12 Restore to me the joy of Your
salvation,
And uphold me *by Your* [m]generous
Spirit.
13 *Then* I will teach transgressors Your
ways,
And sinners shall be converted to
You.

14 Deliver me from the guilt of
bloodshed, O God,
The God of my salvation,
And my tongue shall sing aloud of
Your righteousness.

4 [f]Rom. 3:4 [1]LXX, Tg., Vg. *in Your words*
5 [g][Job 14:4; Ps. 58:3; John 3:6; Rom. 5:12]
7 [h]Ex. 12:22; Lev. 14:4; Num. 19:18; Heb. 9:19 [i][Is. 1:18]
8 [j][Matt. 5:4]
10 [k][Ezek. 18:31; Eph. 2:10]
11 [l][Luke 11:13]
12 [m][2 Cor. 3:17]
16 [n][1 Sam. 15:22]; Ps. 50:8-14; [Mic. 6:6-8]
17 [o]Ps. 34:18; [Is. 57:15]; 66:2
19 [p]Ps. 4:5

PSALM 52
title [a]1 Sam. 22:9 [b]Ezek. 22:9 [1]Heb. *Maschil*

15 O Lord, open my lips,
And my mouth shall show forth Your
praise.
16 For [n]You do not desire sacrifice, or
else I would give *it;*
You do not delight in burnt offering.
17 [o]The sacrifices of God *are* a broken
spirit,
A broken and a contrite heart—
These, O God, You will not despise.

18 Do good in Your good pleasure to
Zion;
Build the walls of Jerusalem.
19 Then You shall be pleased with [p]the
sacrifices of righteousness,
With burnt offering and whole burnt
offering;
Then they shall offer bulls on Your
altar.

PSALM 52

The End of the Wicked and the Peace of the Godly

To the Chief Musician. A [1]Contemplation of David [a]when Doeg the Edomite went and [b]told Saul, and said to him, "David has gone to the house of Ahimelech."

Why do you boast in evil, O mighty
man?
The goodness of God *endures*
continually.
2 Your tongue devises destruction,
Like a sharp razor, working deceitfully.
3 You love evil more than good,
Lying rather than speaking
righteousness. Selah
4 You love all devouring words,
You deceitful tongue.

5 God shall likewise destroy you
forever;

seeking forgiveness must, that even though he had tragically wronged Bathsheba and Uriah, his ultimate crime was against God and His holy law (cf. 2 Sam. 11:27). Romans 3:4 quotes Ps. 51:4.

51:5 brought forth in iniquity. David also acknowledged that his sin was not God's fault in any way (vv. 4b,6), nor was it some aberration. Rather, the source of David's sin was a fallen, sinful disposition, his since conception.

51:7 hyssop. Old Testament priests used hyssop, a leafy plant, to sprinkle blood or water on a person being ceremonially cleansed from defilements such as leprosy or touching a dead body (cf. Lev. 14:6ff.; Num. 19:16-19). Here hyssop is a figure for David's longing to be spiritually cleansed from his moral defilement. In forgiveness, God washes away sin (cf. Ps. 103:12; Is. 1:16; Mic. 7:19).

51:8 bones. A figure of speech for the framework of the entire person. He was experiencing personal collapse under guilt (cf. Ps. 32:3,4).

51:11 Your Holy Spirit from me. This is a reference to the special Holy Spirit anointing on theocratic mediators.

51:12 generous Spirit. The Holy Spirit is generous, willing, and eager to uphold the believer.

51:16 You do not desire sacrifice. Ritual without genuine repentance is useless. However, with a right heart attitude, sacrifices were acceptable (see v. 19).

52:1-9 This psalm is a poetic lesson about the futility of evil, the final triumph of righteousness, and the sovereign control of God over the moral events of history. The event in David's life which motivated him to write this psalm is recorded in 1 Sam. 21,22.

I. The Rashness of the Wicked (52:1-5)
II. The Reaction of the Righteous (52:6,7)
III. The Rejoicing of the Godly (52:8,9)

52:1 mighty man. A reference to Doeg, the chief of Saul's shepherds, who reported to Saul that the priests of Nob had aided David when he was a fugitive (cf. 1 Sam. 22:9,18,19).

52:5 God shall likewise destroy. Ultimately, the wicked are in the hands of a holy God (cf. Heb. 9:27).

He shall take you away, and pluck
you out of *your* dwelling
place,
And uproot you from the land of the
living. Selah
6 The righteous also shall see and fear,
And shall laugh at him, *saying,*
7 "Here is the man *who* did not make
God his strength,
But trusted in the abundance of his
riches,
And strengthened himself in his
[2]wickedness."

8 But I *am* [c]like a green olive tree in the
house of God;
I trust in the mercy of God forever
and ever.
9 I will praise You forever,
Because You have done *it;*
And in the presence of Your saints
I will wait on Your name, for *it* [3]*is*
good.

PSALM 53

Folly of the Godless, and the Restoration of Israel

To the Chief Musician. Set to "Mahalath."
A [1]Contemplation of David.

The [a]fool has said in his heart,
"*There is* no God."
They are corrupt, and have done
abominable iniquity;
[b]*There is* none who does good.

2 God looks down from heaven upon
the children of men,
To see if there are *any* who
understand, who [c]seek God.
3 Every one of them has turned aside;
They have together become corrupt;
There is none who does good,
No, not one.

4 Have the workers of iniquity [d]no
knowledge,
Who eat up my people *as* they eat
bread,
And do not call upon God?
5 [e]There they are in great fear
Where no fear was,
For God has scattered the bones of
him who encamps against
you;
You have put *them* to shame,
Because God has despised them.

6 [f]Oh, that the salvation of Israel would
come out of Zion!
When God brings back [2]the captivity
of His people,
Let Jacob rejoice *and* Israel be glad.

PSALM 54

Answered Prayer for Deliverance from Adversaries

To the Chief Musician. With [1]stringed
instruments. A [2]Contemplation of David
[a]when the Ziphites went and said to Saul,
"Is David not hiding with us?"

Save me, O God, by Your name,
And vindicate me by Your strength.
2 Hear my prayer, O God;
Give ear to the words of my mouth.

7 [2]Lit. *desire,* in evil sense
8 [c]Jer. 11:16
9 [3]Or *has a good reputation*

PSALM 53

title [1]Heb. *Maschil*
1 [a]Ps. 10:4 [b]Rom. 3:10-12
2 [c][2 Chr. 15:2]
4 [d]Jer. 4:22
5 [e]Lev. 26:17, 36; Prov. 28:1
6 [f]Ps. 14:7 [2]Or *His captive people*

PSALM 54

title [a]1 Sam. 23:19 [1]Heb. *neginoth* [2]Heb. *Maschil*

52:6 see and fear. God's punishment of the wicked serves as a reinforcement to the righteous to obey God. **shall laugh at him.** In the end, the wicked become a laughingstock in a universe controlled by God.

52:8 green olive tree. The psalmist exults (through this simile) that the one who trusts in the mercy of God is productive and secure.

53:1-6 This psalm is nearly identical to Ps. 14 (Ps. 53:1-5a is from Ps. 14:1-5a; Ps. 53:6 is from Ps. 4:7). The major difference is v. 5, in which the psalmist celebrates a military victory over an enemy. Apparently Ps. 14 is here rephrased to apply to a specified war event, earning it a distinct place in the canon.

I. The Description of Those Who Reject God and His People (53:1-5)
II. The Danger to Those Who Reject God and His People (53:5)
III. The Deliverance of His People (53:6)

53:Title. "Mahalath." The name of a tune or an instrument.

53:1-4 *See notes on Ps. 14.* Romans 3:10-12 quotes Ps. 53:1-3.

53:2 God. The reference to "God" rather than "LORD" is another difference between Ps. 14 and 53. "Elohim" is used 3 times in Ps. 14, but 7 times in Ps. 53.

53:5 in great fear. The verse describes a sudden reversal in the fortunes of war. The haughty enemy besieging Israel was suddenly terrified and utterly defeated. Historical examples of such unexpected terrors to Israel's enemy are recorded in 2 Chr. 20 and Is. 37. **scattered the bones.** Perhaps nothing was more disgraceful to a nation at war than to have the bones of its dead army scattered over the land rather than buried.

54:1-7 This psalm apparently comes from the same period of David's life as does Ps. 52. Even though David had recently rescued an Israelite border town from the Philistines, he was still considered a traitor to Saul (1 Sam. 23 and 26). In the wake of this emotional devastation, David prayed to God for vindication. The psalm provides encouragement to any believer who has been maligned.

I. The Prayer for Deliverance (54:1-3)
II. The Anticipation of Deliverance (54:4,5)
III. The Thanksgiving for Deliverance (54:6,7)

54:1 by Your name. In the ancient world, a person's name was essentially the person himself. Here, God's name includes His covenant protection. **vindicate.** David requests that God will execute justice for him, as in a court trial when a defendant is declared not guilty.

54:2 Give ear. An anthropomorphism meaning "listen," "pay attention."

54:3 strangers. Either non-Israelites or Israelites who had broken the covenant with God might be called strangers. Since in this case

3 For strangers have risen up against me,
And oppressors have sought after my life;
They have not set God before them. Selah

4 Behold, God *is* my helper;
The Lord *is* with those who [3]uphold my life.
5 He will repay my enemies for their evil.
[4]Cut them off in Your [5]truth.

6 I will freely sacrifice to You;
I will praise Your name, O LORD, for *it is* good.
7 For He has delivered me out of all trouble;
[b]And my eye has seen *its desire* upon my enemies.

PSALM 55

Trust in God Concerning the Treachery of Friends

To the Chief Musician. With [1]stringed instruments. A [2]Contemplation of David.

Give ear to my prayer, O God,
And do not hide Yourself from my supplication.
2 Attend to me, and hear me;
I [a]am [3]restless in my complaint, and moan noisily,
3 Because of the voice of the enemy,
Because of the oppression of the wicked;
[b]For they bring down trouble upon me,
And in wrath they hate me.

4 [c]My heart is severely pained within me,
And the terrors of death have fallen upon me.
5 Fearfulness and trembling have come upon me,
And horror has overwhelmed me.
6 So I said, "Oh, that I had wings like a dove!
I would fly away and be at rest.
7 Indeed, I would wander far off,
And remain in the wilderness. Selah
8 I would hasten my escape
From the windy storm *and* tempest."

9 Destroy, O Lord, *and* divide their [4]tongues,
For I have seen [d]violence and strife in the city.
10 Day and night they go around it on its walls;
[e]Iniquity and trouble *are* also in the midst of it.
11 Destruction *is* in its midst;
[f]Oppression and deceit do not depart from its streets.

12 [g]For *it is* not an enemy *who* reproaches me;
Then I could bear *it*.
Nor *is it* one *who* hates me who has [h]exalted *himself* against me;
Then I could hide from him.
13 But *it was* you, a man my equal,
[i]My companion and my acquaintance.
14 We took sweet counsel together,
And [j]walked to the house of God in the throng.

15 Let death seize them;
Let them [k]go down alive into [5]hell,
For wickedness *is* in their dwellings *and* among them.
16 As for me, I will call upon God,
And the LORD shall save me.
17 [l]Evening and morning and at noon
I will pray, and cry aloud,
And He shall hear my voice.
18 He has redeemed my soul in peace from the battle *that was* against me,
For [m]there were many against me.
19 God will hear, and afflict them,
[n]Even He who abides from of old. Selah
Because they do not change,

4 [3]*sustain my soul*
5 [4]*Destroy them* [5]Or *faithfulness*
7 [b]Ps. 59:10

PSALM 55
title [1]Heb. *neginoth* [2]Heb. *Maschil*
2 [a]Is. 38:14; 59:11; Ezek. 7:16 [3]*wander*
3 [b]2 Sam. 16:7, 8
4 [c]Ps. 116:3
9 [d]Jer. 6:7 [4]*speech, their counsel*
10 [e]Ps. 10:7
11 [f]Ps. 10:7
12 [g]Ps. 41:9 [h]Ps. 35:26; 38:16
13 [i]2 Sam. 15:12
14 [j]Ps. 42:4
15 [k]Num. 16:30, 33 [5]Or *Sheol*
17 [l]Dan. 6:10; Luke 18:1; Acts 3:1; 10:3, 30
18 [m]2 Chr. 32:7, 8
19 [n][Deut. 33:27]

Saul and the Ziphites are the oppressors, the strangers are apostate Israelites (cf. 1 Sam. 23:19; 26:1).

54:5 in Your truth. Since God is omniscient, He can execute perfect justice against the wicked.

54:7 seen *its desire*. David anticipates with confidence that which he has seen in the past—the defeat of his enemies.

55:1-23 In this individual lament, David pours out his heart to his Lord because a former close friend has betrayed him (vv. 12-14). There is a strong possibility that this psalm was occasioned by the betrayal of Absalom and/or Ahithophel (cf. 2 Sam. 5-18). Most of the psalm alternates between prayers for his enemy's ruin (vv. 9,15,19,23) and praises for God's blessings (vv. 16,18,22). The high point of the psalm for Christians who have been "stabbed in the back" by a confidant is v. 22. Though despairing, David expresses ultimate confidence in God.

I. The Prayer of Distress (55:1-8)
II. The Prayer for Justice (55:9-15)
III. The Prayer of Assurance (55:16-23)

55:3 bring down trouble. The verb pictures something being tipped over, crashing down on the victim.

55:6 wings like a dove. David expresses his escapist feelings.

55:9 divide their tongues. Perhaps this is an allusion to the Tower of Babel, where God destroyed the force of the movement against Him by multiplying languages (cf. Gen. 11:5-9).

55:15 go down alive into hell. Since God had done this once with the enemies of Moses (Num. 16:30), David asks Him to perform the same judgment on his enemies.

55:19 they do not change. David's enemies were too set in their ways and too secure to pay any attention to God.

Therefore they do not fear God.

20 He has [o]put forth his hands against
those who [p]were at peace
with him;
He has broken his [6]covenant.
21 [q]*The words* of his mouth were smoother
than butter,
But war *was* in his heart;
His words were softer than oil,
Yet they *were* drawn swords.

22 [r]Cast your burden on the LORD,
And [s]He shall sustain you;
He shall never permit the righteous to
be [7]moved.

23 But You, O God, shall bring them
down to the pit of destruction;
[t]Bloodthirsty and deceitful men [u]shall
not live out half their days;
But I will trust in You.

20 [o] Acts 12:1 [p] Ps. 7:4 [6] *treaty*
21 [q] Ps. 28:3; 57:4; [Prov. 5:3, 4; 12:18]
22 [r] [Ps. 37:5; Matt. 6:25-34; Luke 12:22-31; 1 Pet. 5:7] [s] Ps. 37:24 [7] *shaken*
23 [t] Ps. 5:6 [u] Prov. 10:27

PSALM 56

Prayer for Relief from Tormentors

To the Chief Musician. Set to [1]"The Silent Dove in Distant Lands." A Michtam of David when the [a]Philistines captured him in Gath.

Be [b]merciful to me, O God, for man
would swallow me up;
Fighting all day he oppresses me.
2 My enemies would [c]hound *me* all day,
For *there are* many who fight against
me, O Most High.

3 Whenever I am afraid,
I will trust in You.
4 In God (I will praise His word),
In God I have put my trust;
[d]I will not fear.
What can flesh do to me?
5 All day they twist my words;
All their thoughts *are* against me for
evil.
6 They gather together,
They hide, they mark my steps,
When they lie in wait for my life.
7 Shall they escape by iniquity?
In anger cast down the peoples,
O God!

8 You number my wanderings;
Put my tears into Your bottle;
[e]*Are they* not in Your book?
9 When I cry out *to You,*
Then my enemies will turn back;
This I know, because [f]God *is* for me.
10 In God (I will praise *His* word),
In the LORD (I will praise *His* word),
11 In God I have put my trust;
I will not be afraid.
What can man do to me?

12 Vows *made* to You *are binding* upon
me, O God;
I will render praises to You,
13 [g]For You have delivered my soul from
death.
Have You not *kept* my feet from falling,
That I may walk before God
In the [h]light of the living?

PSALM 56

title [a] 1 Sam. 21:11 [1] Heb. *Jonath Elem Rechokim*
1 [b] Ps. 57:1
2 [c] Ps. 57:3
4 [d] Ps. 118:6; Is. 31:3; [Heb. 13:6]
8 [e] [Mal. 3:16]
9 [f] [Ps. 118:6; Rom. 8:31]
13 [g] Ps. 116:8, 9 [h] Job 33:30

PSALM 57

Prayer for Safety from Enemies

To the Chief Musician. Set to [1]"Do Not Destroy." A Michtam of David [a]when he fled from Saul into the cave.

Be merciful to me, O God, be merciful
to me!

PSALM 57

title [a] 1 Sam. 22:1 [1] Heb. *Al Tashcheth*

55:20 broken his covenant. This enemy had broken a treaty in his treachery, even against his allies.

55:21 war *was* in his heart. Though the traitor talked peace, his intention was war.

55:22 Cast your burden on the LORD. The word for "burden" implies one's circumstances, one's lot. The psalmist promises that the Lord will uphold the believer in the struggles of life.

55:23 the pit of destruction. Compare the unusual death of Absalom (2 Sam. 18:9-15) and the suicide of Ahithophel (2 Sam. 17:23).

56:1-13 This psalm, apparently written when David had been endangered by the Philistines (1 Sam. 21:10-15), expresses the kind of confidence in the Lord that believers should exude when they find themselves in terrifying circumstances. David's natural reaction was to panic (vv. 3,4,11). But he demonstrates in this psalm that the believer can replace potential terror with the composure of trust.

I. Fear and Faith (56:1-4)
II. Destroyer and Deliverer (56:5-9)
III. Trust and Thanksgiving (56:10-13)

56:Title. "The Silent Dove in Distant Lands." Possibly a tune name which links Ps. 56 with Ps. 55 (cf. Ps. 55:6ff.). *See note on Ps. 16:Title.*

56:3 I will trust in You. Confidence in the Lord is a purposeful decision, replacing an emotional reaction to one's circumstances.

56:5 All day. Anguish is intensified by unceasing harassment.

56:7 In anger. The anger of God is not an emotional loss of temper, but a judicial outrage resulting from God's holy nature reacting to wickedness and ungodliness.

56:8 my tears...Your bottle. David asked God to keep a remembrance of all of his sufferings, so that God would eventually vindicate him.

56:11 What can man do to me? No human has the power to overcome God's providential control.

56:12 Vows. Confident that the Lord would deliver him, David had already vowed to present a thank offering to God (cf. Lev. 7:12; Ps. 50:14).

57:1-11 This is another lament expressing supreme confidence in the Lord in the midst of calamitous circumstances. Though David

For my soul trusts in You;
[b]And in the shadow of Your wings I
will make my refuge,
[c]Until *these* calamities have passed by.
2 I will cry out to God Most High,
To God [d]who performs *all things* for
me.
3 [e]He shall send from heaven and save
me;
He reproaches the one who [2]would
swallow me up. Selah
God [f]shall send forth His mercy and
His truth.

4 My soul *is* among lions;
I lie *among* the sons of men
Who are set on fire,
[g]Whose teeth *are* spears and arrows,
And their tongue a sharp sword.
5 [h]Be exalted, O God, above the heavens;
Let Your glory *be* above all the earth.

6 [i]They have prepared a net for my steps;
My soul is bowed down;
They have dug a pit before me;
Into the midst of it they *themselves*
have fallen. Selah

7 [j]My heart is steadfast, O God, my
heart is steadfast;
I will sing and give praise.
8 Awake, [k]my glory!

1 [b] Ruth 2:12; Ps. 17:8; 63:7 [c] Is. 26:20
2 [d] [Ps. 138:8]
3 [e] Ps. 144:5, 7 [f] Ps. 43:3 [2] *snaps at or hounds me, or crushes me*
4 [g] Prov. 30:14
5 [h] Ps. 108:5
6 [i] Ps. 9:15
7 [j] Ps. 108:1-5
8 [k] Ps. 16:9

Awake, lute and harp!
I will awaken the dawn.
9 [l]I will praise You, O Lord, among the
peoples;
I will sing to You among the [3]nations.
10 [m]For Your mercy reaches unto the
heavens,
And Your truth unto the clouds.
11 [n]Be exalted, O God, above the
heavens;
Let Your glory *be* above all the earth.

PSALM 58

The Just Judgment of the Wicked

To the Chief Musician. Set to [1]"Do Not
Destroy." A Michtam of David.

Do you indeed speak righteousness,
you silent ones?
Do you judge uprightly, you sons of
men?
2 No, in heart you work wickedness;
You weigh out the violence of your
hands in the earth.

3 [a]The wicked are estranged from the
womb;
They go astray as soon as they are
born, speaking lies.
4 [b]Their poison *is* like the poison of a
serpent;

9 [l] Ps. 108:3 [3] *Gentiles*
10 [m] Ps. 103:11
11 [n] Ps. 57:5

PSALM 58

title [1] Heb. *Al Taschcheth*
3 [a] [Ps. 53:3; Is. 48:8]
4 [b] Eccl. 10:11

finds himself hiding from Saul (see Title), he knows that his real refuge is not in the walls of the cave (cf. 1 Sam. 22:1; 24:3), but in the shadow of God's wings.

I. The Plea for Protection (57:1-6)
II. The Proffering of Praise (57:7-11)

57:Title. "Do Not Destroy." Possibly the opening words of a known song, implying that this psalm should be sung to the same tune. *See note on Ps. 16:Title.*

57:1 the shadow of Your wings. Metaphorically, God cares for His own as a mother bird protect its young. Symbolically, there may be a reference here to the cherubim wings on the ark of the covenant where God was specifically present (cf. Ex. 37:1-16; Pss. 17:8; 36:7; 61:4; 63:7; 91:1,4). **I will make my refuge.** When life becomes bizarre, only one's relationship with his God calms the soul.

57:2 God Most High. God is transcendent, elevated far above His creation and all powerful. **performs *all things* for me.** God's transcendence (v. 2a) never removes Him from intimate involvement in His peoples' lives.

57:4 lions. The wicked are pictured as menacing animals, ready to destroy their prey with their razor-edged teeth (cf. Pss. 7:2; 10:9; 17:12; 22:13). **set on fire.** The wicked are like a consuming fire.

57:5 Be exalted, O God. A truly godly person wants God's glory to be exhibited more than he wants his own personal problems to be solved.

57:6 a net…a pit. Set a trap, as a hunter might entangle an animal's feet with a net.

57:7-11 These verses were borrowed by David for Ps. 108:1-5.

57:8 my glory! The mind, that rational, intellectual, emotional part of a person which interacts with and praises God. *See note on 16:9.* **I will awaken the dawn.** He cannot wait until morning to praise the Lord for all of His blessings. He must wake up the personified dawn so that he can praise the Lord.

57:9 the peoples…nations. References to Gentiles, nations which would not normally know Jehovah God.

57:10 unto the heavens. David is thinking as broadly (v. 9) and as highly (vv. 10-11) as he can. God's mercy, truth, and glory are immense and unfathomable (cf. Rom. 11:33; Eph. 3:17,18).

58:1-11 As a lament against tyranny, the first half of the psalm rehearses a series of charges against wicked leaders and judges; and the second half is an imprecatory prayer that they be obliterated. In the end, the psalmist is certain that God will act with ultimate justice.

I. The Indictment of Unjust Leaders (58:1-5)
II. The Imprecation Against Unjust Leaders (58:6-11)

58:Title. "Do Not Destroy." *See note on Ps. 57. See note on Ps. 16:Title.*

58:1 silent ones. The leaders were silent when they should have spoken up for righteousness.

58:2 weigh out. These wicked rulers meditate on the strategy for wicked schemes.

58:3 as soon as they are born. All people are born totally depraved. Without being made new creatures in Christ by God's power, they are prevented by their wicked nature from pleasing God (cf. Ps. 51:5; Rom. 3:9-18; 2 Cor. 5:17).

58:4 Their poison. The words and actions of these tyrants are like

They are like the deaf cobra *that* stops
its ear,
5 Which will not [c]heed the voice of
charmers,
Charming ever so skillfully.

6 [d]Break[2] their teeth in their mouth,
O God!
Break out the fangs of the young
lions, O LORD!
7 [e]Let them flow away as waters *which*
run continually;
When he bends *his bow,*
Let his arrows be as if cut in
pieces.
8 *Let them be* like a snail which melts
away as it goes,
[f]*Like* a stillborn child of a woman, that
they may not see the sun.

9 Before your [g]pots can feel *the burning*
thorns,
He shall take them away [h]as with a
whirlwind,
As in His living and burning
wrath.
10 The righteous shall rejoice when he
sees the [i]vengeance;
[j]He shall wash his feet in the blood of
the wicked,
11 [k]So that men will say,
"Surely *there is* a reward for the
righteous;
Surely He is God who [l]judges in the
earth."

5 [c] Jer. 8:17
6 [d] Job 4:10 [2] *Break away*
7 [e] Josh. 2:11; 7:5; Ps. 112:10; Is. 13:7; Ezek. 21:7
8 [f] Job 3:16
9 [g] Ps. 118:12; Eccl. 7:6 [h] Job 27:21; Prov. 10:25
10 [i] [Deut. 32:43]; Jer. 11:20 [j] Ps. 68:23
11 [k] Ps. 92:15; Prov. 11:18; [2 Cor. 5:10] [l] Ps. 50:6; 75:7

PSALM 59

The Assured Judgment of the Wicked

To the Chief Musician. Set to [1]"Do Not Destroy." A Michtam of David [a]when Saul sent men, and they watched the house in order to kill him.

Deliver me from my enemies, O my
God;
[2]Defend me from those who rise up
against me.
2 Deliver me from the workers of
iniquity,
And save me from bloodthirsty men.

3 For look, they lie in wait for my life;
[b]The mighty gather against me,
Not *for* my transgression nor *for* my
sin, O LORD.
4 They run and prepare themselves
through no fault *of mine.*

[c]Awake to help me, and behold!
5 You therefore, O LORD God of hosts,
the God of Israel,
Awake to punish all the [3]nations;
Do not be merciful to any wicked
transgressors. Selah

6 [d]At evening they return,
They growl like a dog,
And go all around the city.
7 Indeed, they belch with their mouth;
[e]Swords *are* in their lips;
For *they say,* [f]"Who hears?"
8 But [g]You, O LORD, shall laugh at them;

PSALM 59

title [a] 1 Sam. 19:11 [1] Heb. *Al Tashcheth*
1 [2] Lit. *Set me on high*
3 [b] Ps. 56:6
4 [c] Ps. 35:23
5 [3] *Gentiles*
6 [d] Ps. 59:14
7 [e] Ps. 57:4; Prov. 12:18 [f] Job 22:13; Ps. 10:11
8 [g] Prov. 1:26

poisonous venom in a serpent's fangs. **deaf cobra.** Like a cobra which cannot hear its charmer are these stubborn rulers, who ignore all encouragements to righteousness.

58:6 Break their teeth...fangs. The psalmist prays that the means of doing evil would be destroyed.

58:7 flow away as waters. An imprecatory prayer that the tyrants would disappear like water seeping into sand in a dry wadi. **arrows...cut in pieces.** Apparently a prayer that the intentions of evil would be rendered as ineffective as broken arrows.

58:8 snail which melts away. A simile for that which is transitive, perhaps based facetiously on the idea that a snail depletes itself in its own trail as it moves along.

58:9 Before your pots...thorns. An obscure metaphor implying swiftness. The Lord will quickly destroy the wicked rulers.

58:10 wash his feet in the blood. The point of the figure is that the wicked will eventually be defeated and the righteous will share with the Lord in His victory.

58:11 God who judges in the earth. In the end, the righteous will see that Jehovah is not indifferent to injustices.

59:1-17 This is another in a series of laments in which the psalmist pleads for God to defend him against his oppressors. The psalm is a mixture of prayers, unfavorable descriptions of the adversary, imprecations, and praise to God. Though written when David was king of Israel, the psalm recalls an earlier time of anguish when Saul sought to kill David (1 Sam. 19:11). Ultimately David's strong confidence in God's sovereignty transforms the lament into a song of assurance.

I. Plea for God's Deliverance (59:1-15)
II. Praise for God's Defense (59:16,17)

59:Title. "Do Not Destroy." *See note Ps. 57:Title.* **Michtam.** *See note on Ps. 16:Title.* **Saul sent men...to kill him.** The setting for the psalm is 1 Sam. 19:11. David's wife (Saul's daughter) helped David escape through a window in the middle of the night.

59:5 God of hosts. "Hosts" represent God's angels as His army.

59:6 growl like a dog. Dogs of the ancient world were often wild scavengers. Here, they serve as a simile for the messengers of Saul outside David's house setting an ambush.

59:7 belch with their mouth. Pictures the coarse, uncouth character of Saul's henchmen (cf. v. 12). **swords *are* in their lips.** Their conversation was dedicated to the assassination of David. ***they say,* "Who hears?"** A blasphemy implying that God either doesn't exist or doesn't know what happens in the affairs of mankind.

59:8 all the nations. Gentiles (*see note on Ps. 57:9*). This phrase and "my people" in v. 11 imply that this psalm was written several years after the event when David was king and involved in international affairs. David wrote his psalms as a prophet under the superintendence of the Holy Spirit (2 Sam. 23:2).

You shall have all the [4]nations in
derision.
9 I will wait for You, O You [5]his
Strength;
[h]For God *is* my [6]defense.
10 [7]My God of mercy shall [i]come to meet
me;
God shall let [j]me see *my desire* on my
enemies.

11 Do not slay them, lest my people
forget;
Scatter them by Your power,
And bring them down,
O Lord our shield.
12 [k]*For* the sin of their mouth *and* the
words of their lips,
Let them even be taken in their pride,
And for the cursing and lying *which*
they speak.
13 [l]Consume *them* in wrath, consume *them*,
That they *may* not *be;*
And [m]let them know that God rules
in Jacob
To the ends of the earth. Selah

14 And [n]at evening they return,
They growl like a dog,
And go all around the city.
15 They [o]wander up and down for food,
And [8]howl if they are not satisfied.

16 But I will sing of Your power;
Yes, I will sing aloud of Your mercy in
the morning;
For You have been my defense
And refuge in the day of my trouble.
17 To You, [p]O my Strength, I will sing
praises;
For God *is* my defense,
My God of mercy.

8 [4] *Gentiles*
9 [h] [Ps. 62:2] [5] So with MT, Syr.; some Heb. mss., LXX, Tg., Vg. *my Strength* [6] Lit. *fortress*
10 [i] Ps. 21:3 [j] Ps. 54:7 [7] So with Qr.; some Heb. mss., LXX, Vg. *My God, His mercy;* Kt., some Heb. mss., Tg. *O God, my mercy;* Syr. *O God, Your mercy*
12 [k] Prov. 12:13
13 [l] Ps. 104:35 [m] Ps. 83:18
14 [n] Ps. 59:6
15 [o] Job 15:23 [8] So with LXX, Vg.; MT, Syr., Tg. *spend the night*
17 [p] Ps. 18:1

PSALM 60
title [a] Ps. 80 [b] 2 Sam. 8:3, 13; 1 Chr. 18:3 [1] Heb. *Shushan Eduth*
1 [c] Ps. 44:9
2 [d] [2 Chr. 7:14]; Is. 30:26
3 [e] Ps. 71:20 [f] Is. 51:17, 22; Jer. 25:15 [2] *staggering*
4 [g] Ps. 20:5; Is. 5:26; 11:12; 13:2
5 [h] Ps. 108:6-13
6 [i] Ps. 89:35 [j] Josh. 1:6 [k] Gen. 12:6 [l] Josh. 13:27
7 [m] Deut. 33:17 [n] [Gen. 49:10] [3] Lit. *protection*
8 [o] 2 Sam. 8:2

PSALM 60

Urgent Prayer for the Restored Favor of God

To the Chief Musician. [a]Set to [1]"Lily of the Testimony." A Michtam of David. For teaching. [b]When he fought against Mesopotamia and Syria of Zobah, and Joab returned and killed twelve thousand Edomites in the Valley of Salt.

O God, [c]You have cast us off;
You have broken us down;
You have been displeased;
Oh, restore us again!
2 You have made the earth tremble;
You have broken it;
[d]Heal its breaches, for it is shaking.
3 [e]You have shown Your people hard
things;
[f]You have made us drink the wine of
[2]confusion.

4 [g]You have given a banner to those who
fear You,
That it may be displayed because of
the truth. Selah
5 [h]That Your beloved may be delivered,
Save *with* Your right hand, and hear
me.

6 God has [i]spoken in His holiness:
"I will rejoice;
I will [j]divide [k]Shechem
And measure out [l]the Valley of
Succoth.
7 Gilead *is* Mine, and Manasseh *is*
Mine;
[m]Ephraim also *is* the [3]helmet for My
head;
[n]Judah *is* My lawgiver.
8 [o]Moab *is* My washpot;

59:11 lest my people forget. The psalmist thinks that if the Lord were to destroy the wicked too quickly, the lesson of God's hatred of evil might not be impressed on the minds of the people.

60:1-12 This psalm is a national lament written after the unexpected military setback alluded to in 2 Sam. 8:13 and 1 Chr. 18:12. While David and the main part of his army were fighting in the northern part of the country, one of Israel's other neighboring enemies, Edom, successfully attacked the southern part of Judah. David ultimately prevailed in victory. The psalm expresses the feelings of a people shocked and confused by a tragedy which suggested that God had abandoned them. Verses 5-12 are essentially repeated in Ps. 108:6-13.

I. The People's Contemplation of Abandonment (60:1-5)
II. The Lord's Control Over the Nations (60:6-8)
III. The People's Confidence in God (60:9-12)

60:Title. Joab...killed twelve thousand. The Lord soon rewarded their confidence in Him, enabling the armies of Israel to slaughter the Edomites.

60:2 earth tremble. Earthquake imagery is used to illustrate that what appears secure sometimes is not.

60:3 wine of confusion. This metaphor compares the impact of wine on the mind with the confusion which comes from a bewildering event in life.

60:4 banner. God and His truth serve as a rallying point for the perplexed people.

60:5 beloved. Probably a reference to David. There may be a play on words here in that the Heb. root for "David" and "beloved" is the same..

60:6 Shechem...Succoth. These are two territories on opposite sides of the Jordan, occupied by Israel. Jacob had settled in Succoth (E of the Jordan) when he returned from his sojourn with Laban (cf. Gen. 33:17).

60:7 Gilead...Judah. All of these key geographical locations in Israel ultimately belonged to God, who was more interested in their welfare than anyone else. **helmet.** Ephraim was the primary source of defense to the N of Israel. **lawgiver.** Judah was the tribe which was to govern Israel, from which David and his descendants came.

60:8 Moab...Edom...Philistia. The 3 principal enemies surrounding Israel to the NE, SE, and W, respectively. **Moab *is* My washpot.** The psalmist pictures Moab as a humble, menial servant to God,

[p]Over Edom I will cast My shoe;
[q]Philistia, shout in triumph because of Me."

9 Who will bring me *to* the strong city?
Who will lead me to Edom?
10 *Is it* not You, O God, [r]*who* cast us off?
And You, O God, *who* did [s]not go out with our armies?
11 Give us help from trouble,
[t]For the help of man *is* useless.
12 Through God [u]we will do valiantly,
For *it is* He *who* shall tread down our enemies.

PSALM 61

Assurance of God's Eternal Protection

To the Chief Musician. On [1]a stringed instrument. A Psalm of David.

Hear my cry, O God;
Attend to my prayer.
2 From the end of the earth I will cry to You,
When my heart is overwhelmed;
Lead me to the rock that is higher than I.

3 For You have been a shelter for me,
[a]A strong tower from the enemy.
4 I will abide in Your [2]tabernacle forever;
[b]I will trust in the shelter of Your wings. Selah

5 For You, O God, have heard my vows;
You have given *me* the heritage of those who fear Your name.
6 You will prolong the king's life,
His years as many generations.
7 He shall abide before God forever.
Oh, prepare mercy [c]and truth, *which* may [3]preserve him!

8 So I will sing praise to Your name forever,
That I may daily perform my vows.

PSALM 62

A Calm Resolve to Wait for the Salvation of God

To the Chief Musician. To [a]Jeduthun. A Psalm of David.

Truly [b]my soul silently *waits* for God;
From Him *comes* my salvation.
2 He only *is* my rock and my salvation;
He is my [1]defense;
I shall not be greatly [c]moved.[2]

3 How long will you attack a man?
You shall be slain, all of you,
[d]Like a leaning wall and a tottering fence.

---

8 [p]2 Sam. 8:14; Ps. 108:9 [q]2 Sam. 8:1
10 [r]Ps. 108:11 [s]Josh. 7:12
11 [t]Ps. 118:8; 146:3
12 [u]Num. 24:18

PSALM 61

title [1]Heb. *neginah*
3 [a]Prov. 18:10
4 [2]*tent*
[b]Ps. 91:4
7 [c]Ps. 40:11 [3]Lit. *guard or keep*

PSALM 62

title [a]1 Chr. 25:1
1 [b]Ps. 33:20
2 [c]Ps. 55:22 [1]*strong tower* [2]*shaken*
3 [d]Is. 30:13

---

either being or bringing a washbasin for His use. **Over Edom... shoe.** The picture is that of a man entering his house and throwing his shoes to his servant. Edom, like Moab, was a servant under God's sovereign control. **Philistia, shout in triumph.** Here is a victorious battle shout from the pagans, who must realize God's power is behind Israel's victory.

60:12 Through God...valiantly. The nation relearned the truth that only God gives victory.

61:1-8 David may have written this wonderful psalm when his own son, Absalom, temporarily drove him away from his throne in Israel (2 Sam. 15–18). The psalm is rich in metaphors and references to God's covenants with Israel. David once again demonstrates a godly response to overwhelming and depressing developments in life.

I. The Cry for Help (61:1,2)
II. The Confidence in God (61:3-7)
III. The Commitment to Loyalty (61:8)

61:2 From the end of the earth. David's absence from his homeland compounds his feelings of discouragement and exhaustion. The phrase also hints at feelings of estrangement from God. **my heart is overwhelmed.** David's hope and courage were failing. **the rock that is higher.** David expresses his disregard of personal autonomy and his reliance on his God in this metaphor for refuge.

61:3 strong tower. One of 4 figures of speech in vv. 3,4 for security; the strong towers stabilized the city walls and served as places of defense and refuge.

61:5 heritage. Refers to the benefits, including life in the Promised Land (cf. Deut. 28–30), of participating in a covenant with God.

61:6 prolong the king's life. In the immediate context, David prays for himself in his struggle with Absalom. Beyond this, here is a prayer for the continuity of the divinely established monarchy. Because he realized that one of his descendants would be the Messiah, David sometimes does not distinguish himself from the messianic dynasty.

61:7 forever. The Davidic Covenant guaranteed that on the basis of God's merciful and faithful dealings with David and the nation, David's descendants would rule on the throne of Israel forever (cf. 2 Sam. 7; Pss. 40:11; 89:4,33-37).

61:8 daily perform my vows. As a regular means of expressing thanksgiving for prayers answered, the psalmist promised daily obedience to his Lord (cf. Ps. 56:12).

62:1-12 Whether Absalom's rebellion is the setting or not (2 Sam. 15–18), David writes this psalm while facing treason from someone. David faces the problem of his adversaries forthrightly (vv. 3,4), but his thoughts focus primarily on God (cf. Phil. 4:4-13).

I. Affirming God's Covenant Relationship (62:1,2,5,6)
II. Confronting One's Treasonous Adversaries (62:3,4)
III. Trusting God's Sovereignty (62:7-10)
IV. Praising God's Power and Mercy (62:11,12)

62:Title. To Jeduthun. An official temple musician. *See note on Ps. 39:Title.*

62:1 silently *waits* for God. Silence indicates trust that is both patient and uncomplaining (cf. v. 5).

62:2 greatly moved. Means "shaken," or "demoralized."

62:3 leaning wall and a tottering fence. A metaphor for imminent collapse. Some apply it to the victim, but as translated here it refers to the attacker.

4 They only consult to cast *him* down
from his high position;
They [e]delight in lies;
They bless with their mouth,
But they curse inwardly. Selah

5 My soul, wait silently for God
alone,
For my [3]expectation *is* from Him.
6 He only *is* my rock and my
salvation;
He is my defense;
I shall not be [4]moved.
7 [f]In God *is* my salvation and my
glory;
The rock of my strength,
And my refuge, *is* in God.

8 Trust in Him at all times, you
people;
[g]Pour out your heart before Him;
God *is* a refuge for us. Selah

9 [h]Surely men of low degree *are* [5]a
vapor,
Men of high degree *are* a lie;
If they are weighed on the scales,
They *are* altogether *lighter* than
vapor.
10 Do not trust in oppression,
Nor vainly hope in robbery;
[i]If riches increase,
Do not set *your* heart *on them.*

11 God has spoken once,
Twice I have heard this:
That power *belongs* to God.
12 Also to You, O Lord, *belongs* mercy;
For [j]You [6]render to each one
according to his work.

4 [e]Ps. 28:3
5 [3]*hope*
6 [4]*shaken*
7 [f][Jer. 3:23]
8 [g]1 Sam. 1:15; Ps. 42:4; Lam. 2:19
9 [h]Job 7:16; Ps. 39:5; Is. 40:17 [5]*vanity*
10 [i]Job 31:25; [Mark 10:24; Luke 12:15; 1 Tim. 6:10]
12 [j][Matt. 16:27]; Rom. 2:6; 1 Cor. 3:8 [6]*reward*

PSALM 63
title [a]1 Sam. 22:5
1 [b]Ps. 42:2; [Matt. 5:6]
2 [c]Ps. 27:4
3 [d]Ps. 138:2
4 [e]Ps. 28:2; 143:6
5 [1]Lit. *fat* [2]*Abundance*
6 [f]Ps. 42:8
10 [3]Lit. *pour him out by the hand of the sword* [4]Prey

PSALM 63

Joy in the Fellowship of God

A Psalm of David [a]when he was in the
wilderness of Judah.

O God, You *are* my God;
Early will I seek You;
[b]My soul thirsts for You;
My flesh longs for You
In a dry and thirsty land
Where there is no water.
2 So I have looked for You in the
sanctuary,
To see [c]Your power and Your glory.

3 [d]Because Your lovingkindness *is* better
than life,
My lips shall praise You.
4 Thus I will bless You while I live;
I will [e]lift up my hands in Your name.
5 My soul shall be satisfied as with
[1]marrow and [2]fatness,
And my mouth shall praise You with
joyful lips.

6 When [f]I remember You on my bed,
I meditate on You in the *night*
watches.
7 Because You have been my help,
Therefore in the shadow of Your
wings I will rejoice.
8 My soul follows close behind You;
Your right hand upholds me.
9 But those *who* seek my life, to destroy
it,
Shall go into the lower parts of the
earth.
10 They shall [3]fall by the sword;
They shall be [4]a portion for jackals.
11 But the king shall rejoice in God;

62:6 I shall not be moved. David demonstrates his increased confidence in the Lord. At first he would not be "greatly moved" (v. 2). Here, on second thought, he would not be moved at all.

62:9 low degree…high degree. All men, regardless of social status, are woefully inadequate objects of trust.

63:1-11 In deepest words of devotion, this psalm expresses David's intense love for his Lord. The psalm was written while David was in the Judean wilderness, either during his flight from Saul (1 Sam. 23), or more likely from Absalom (2 Sam. 15; cf. 63:11 "the king"). David writes from the perspective of these tenses.

I. Present—Seeking God's Presence (63:1-5)
II. Past—Remembering God's Power (63:6-8)
III. Future—Anticipating God's Judgment (63:9-11)

63:1 Early will I seek You. Eagerness to be with the Lord in every situation is more in view than the time of day. **My soul thirsts.** David longs for God's presence like a wanderer in a desert longs for water. **In a dry and thirsty land.** David writes this psalm while hiding in the wilderness of Judea, but longing to be back worshiping in Jerusalem.

63:3 better than life. God's covenant love is more valuable to David than life itself (cf. Phil. 1:21; Acts 20:24).

63:4 lift up my hands. As an OT posture of prayer, the upheld hands pictured both the ascent of prayer and the readiness to receive every good gift which comes from God (cf. James 1:17). It was thus a posture of trust in God alone.

63:5 marrow and fatness. A metaphor comparing the spiritual and emotional satisfaction of the divine presence with the satisfaction of rich banquet food.

63:8 My soul follows close behind You. In response to God's repeated invitation to "hold fast" to Him (Deut. 4:4; 10:20; 13:4), the psalmist clings to God. This signifies David's unfailing commitment to his Lord.

63:9 into the lower parts of the earth. A reference to the realm of the dead. *See note on Eph. 4:9.*

63:10 jackals. Scavengers, feasting on unburied bodies. (*see note on Ps. 53:5*).

[g]Everyone who swears by Him shall glory;
But the mouth of those who speak lies shall be stopped.

11 [g]Deut. 6:13; [Is. 45:23; 65:16]

PSALM 64

Oppressed by the Wicked but Rejoicing in the LORD

To the Chief Musician. A Psalm of David.

Hear my voice, O God, in my [1]meditation;
Preserve my life from fear of the enemy.
2 Hide me from the secret plots of the wicked,
From the rebellion of the workers of iniquity,
3 Who sharpen their tongue like a sword,
[a]And bend *their bows to shoot* their arrows—bitter words,
4 That they may shoot in secret at the blameless;
Suddenly they shoot at him and do not fear.

5 They encourage themselves *in* an evil matter;
They talk of laying snares secretly;
[b]They say, "Who will see them?"
6 They devise iniquities:
"We have perfected a shrewd scheme."
Both the inward thought and the heart of man are deep.

7 But God shall shoot at them *with* an arrow;
Suddenly they shall be wounded.
8 So He will make them stumble over their own tongue;
[c]All who see them shall flee away.
9 All men shall fear,
And shall [d]declare the work of God;
For they shall wisely consider His doing.

10 [e]The righteous shall be glad in the LORD, and trust in Him.
And all the upright in heart shall glory.

PSALM 64
1 [1] complaint
3 [a] Ps. 58:7
5 [b] Ps. 10:11; 59:7
8 [c] Ps. 31:11
9 [d] Jer. 50:28; 51:10
10 [e] Job 22:19; Ps. 32:11

PSALM 65

Praise to God for His Salvation and Providence

To the Chief Musician. A Psalm of David. A Song.

Praise is awaiting You, O God, in Zion;
And to You the [1]vow shall be performed.
2 O You who hear prayer,
[a]To You all flesh will come.
3 Iniquities prevail against me;
As for our transgressions,
You will [b]provide atonement for them.

4 [c]Blessed *is the man* You [d]choose,
And cause to approach *You*,
That he may dwell in Your courts.
[e]We shall be satisfied with the goodness of Your house,
Of Your holy temple.

PSALM 65
1 [1] A promised deed
2 [a] [Is. 66:23]
3 [b] Ps. 51:2; 79:9; Is. 6:7; [Heb. 9:14; 1 John 1:7, 9]
4 [c] Ps. 33:12 [d] Ps. 4:3 [e] Ps. 36:8

63:11 who swears by Him. The Mosaic Covenant instructed this practice expressing loyalty to the true God alone (cf. Deut. 6:13; 10:20; 1 Kin. 8:31; Jer. 12:16).

64:1-10 This psalm begins with a vivid description of the devious ways of the wicked, especially their speech (vv. 3-5,8). Still, the psalmist does not fear that God will lose control of the situation. After seeing His justice at work, the righteous will be glad and trust all the more in Him (64:10).

I. The Malevolent Ingenuity of the Wicked (64:1-6)
II. The Memorable Reciprocation by the Lord (64:7-10)

64:1 Preserve...from fear. This word for "fear" means "dread," and is a different Heb. word than the "fear" in verses 4 and 9. The psalmist recognized that the fear of an enemy can be as destructive as an actual assault.

64:3 sharpen their tongue. Their intent was to slander with their speech (cf. Ps. 59:7).

64:4 in secret. Anonymously.

64:5 "Who will see them?" This was a question of brazen autonomy. They mock the omniscience of God (cf. Ps. 59:7).

64:6 inward thought...heart...deep. The evil intent of the unrighteous flows from inward depravity.

64:7 God shall shoot...arrow. The arrows of God, as OT history demonstrates, include natural judgments such as deadly disease, defeat, and calamity.

64:8 stumble...own tongue. God providentially steers the plots of the wicked to their own demise.

64:9 shall declare. Believers should glorify God, not only for His love and mercy, but also for His marvelous acts of judgment on the wicked.

65:1-13 This is a praise psalm, full of hopeful, confident, even enthusiastic feelings in response to God's goodness with no complaints or curses. The setting is a celebration at the tabernacle, perhaps at the Feast of Unleavened Bread in the spring, or the Feast of Tabernacles in the fall.

I. Praise for Spiritual Blessings (65:1-5)
II. Praise for Natural Blessings (65:6-13)

65:1 Zion. Specifically the hill in Jerusalem where Israel worshiped Jehovah, but also synonymous with the Promised Land (cf. Ps. 48:2; also Pss. 3:4; 9:12; 24:3; 68:5; 87). **vow...performed.** This is likely a reference to vows made by the farmers because of an abundant harvest (cf. Pss. 56:12; 61:8).

65:2 all flesh will come. Reference to the future millennial kingdom when all the world will worship the Lord (cf. Zech. 14:16-19).

65:3 atonement. The word, found 3 times in the Psalms (78:38; 79:9), means to cover away sin and its effects. In the OT, atonement was symbolized in sacrificial ritual (cf. Ex. 30:10; Lev. 16:10,11), though actual forgiveness of sin was ultimately based on the death of Christ applied to the penitent sinner (cf. Heb. 9).

5 *By* awesome deeds in righteousness
You will answer us,
O God of our salvation,
You who are the confidence of all the
ends of the earth,
And of the far-off seas;
6 Who established the mountains by
His strength,
[f]*Being* clothed with power;
7 [g]You who still the noise of the seas,
The noise of their waves,
[h]And the tumult of the peoples.
8 They also who dwell in the farthest
parts are afraid of Your signs;
You make the outgoings of the
morning and evening
[2]rejoice.

9 You [3]visit the earth and [i]water it,
You greatly enrich it;
[j]The river of God is full of water;
You provide their grain,
For so You have prepared it.
10 You water its ridges abundantly,
You settle its furrows;
You make it soft with showers,
You bless its growth.

11 You crown the year with Your
goodness,
And Your paths drip *with* abundance.
12 They drop *on* the pastures of the
wilderness,
And the little hills rejoice on every
side.
13 The pastures are clothed with flocks;
[k]The valleys also are covered with
grain;
They shout for joy, they also sing.

6 [f]Ps. 93:1
7 [g]Matt. 8:26 [h]Is. 17:12, 13
8 [2]*shout for joy*
9 [i][Deut. 11:12]; Jer. 5:24 [j]Ps. 46:4; 104:13; 147:8 [3]*give attention to*
13 [k]Is. 44:23; 55:12

PSALM 66
1 [a]Ps. 100:1
3 [b]Ps. 65:5 [c]Ps. 18:44
4 [d]Ps. 117:1; Zech. 14:16
6 [e]Ex. 14:21 [f]Josh. 3:14-16
9 [1]*slip*
10 [g]Job 23:10; Ps. 17:3 [h][Is. 48:10; Zech. 13:9; Mal. 3:3; 1 Pet. 1:7]
11 [i]Lam. 1:13; Ezek. 12:13

PSALM 66

Praise to God for His Awesome Works

To the Chief Musician. A Song. A Psalm.

Make [a]a joyful shout to God, all the
earth!
2 Sing out the honor of His name;
Make His praise glorious.
3 Say to God,
"How [b]awesome are Your works!
[c]Through the greatness of Your power
Your enemies shall submit themselves
to You.
4 [d]All the earth shall worship You
And sing praises to You;
They shall sing praises *to* Your name."
Selah

5 Come and see the works of God;
He is awesome *in His* doing toward
the sons of men.
6 [e]He turned the sea into dry *land;*
[f]They went through the river on foot.
There we will rejoice in Him.
7 He rules by His power forever;
His eyes observe the nations;
Do not let the rebellious exalt
themselves. Selah

8 Oh, bless our God, you peoples!
And make the voice of His praise to
be heard,
9 Who keeps our soul among the living,
And does not allow our feet to [1]be
moved.
10 For [g]You, O God, have tested us;
[h]You have refined us as silver is
refined.
11 [i]You brought us into the net;
You laid affliction on our backs.

65:5 confidence...earth...seas. Unlike local heathen gods, Jehovah God is not just the God of a single locality. The universal worship of the Lord is required of all men (cf. Rom. 1:18-32) and will be a reality in the messianic era when the kingdom of God will cover the earth (cf. Is. 2:1-4; Zech. 14:9).

65:8 outgoings...morning...evening. The nations who live in the E where the sun first makes its morning appearance, and those who live in the W where the sun disappears into darkness rejoice in the Lord.

65:11 paths drip *with* abundance. Like a farm wagon dropping its overflow along the cart path.

66:1-20 This joyful psalm begins with group praise and then focuses on the individual worship. The psalmist rehearses some of the major miracles in Israel's history and testifies that God has always been faithful in the midst of serious troubles.

I. Communal Hymn of Praise to God (66:1-12)
  A. For Future Glory (66:1-4)
  B. For Previous Faithfulness (66:5-7)
  C. For Continual Protection (66:8-12)
II. An Individual Hymn of Praise to God (66:13-20)
  A. Through Fulfilled Vows (66:13-15)
  B. For Answered Prayer (66:16-20)

66:1 joyful shout. A shout of loyalty and homage, as in 1 Sam. 10:24.

66:4 All the earth shall worship You. This praise is not only an acknowledgment of God's universal Lordship, but also an intimation of the people's belief in a future worldwide kingdom where God was worshiped (cf. Is. 66:23; Zech. 14:16; Phil. 2:10,11).

66:6 sea...river. A reference to the crossing of the Red Sea and possibly the Jordan River. The OT writers considered the Red Sea crossing the ultimate demonstration of God's power, as well as His care for Israel.

66:9 feet to be moved. God had prevented them from prematurely slipping into the realm of the dead.

66:10 refined us as silver. God had brought the nation through purifying trials.

66:11 brought us into the net. The psalmist speaks of a hunter's net or snare as a metaphor for some extremely difficult situations into which God had brought Israel.

12 [j]You have caused men to ride over our heads;
[k]We went through fire and through water;
But You brought us out to [2]rich *fulfillment*.

13 [l]I will go into Your house with burnt offerings;
[m]I will pay You my [3]vows,
14 Which my lips have uttered
And my mouth has spoken when I was in trouble.
15 I will offer You burnt sacrifices of fat animals,
With the sweet aroma of rams;
I will offer bulls with goats. Selah

16 Come *and* hear, all you who fear God,
And I will declare what He has done for my soul.
17 I cried to Him with my mouth,
And He was [4]extolled with my tongue.
18 [n]If I regard iniquity in my heart,
The Lord will not hear.
19 *But* certainly God [o]has heard *me;*
He has attended to the voice of my prayer.

20 Blessed *be* God,
Who has not turned away my prayer,
Nor His mercy from me!

PSALM 67
An Invocation and a Doxology

To the Chief Musician. On [1]stringed instruments. A Psalm. A Song.

God be merciful to us and bless us,
And [a]cause His face to shine upon us, Selah
2 That [b]Your way may be known on earth,
[c]Your salvation among all nations.
3 Let the peoples praise You, O God;
Let all the peoples praise You.
4 Oh, let the nations be glad and sing for joy!
For [d]You shall judge the people righteously,
And govern the nations on earth. Selah

5 Let the peoples praise You, O God;
Let all the peoples praise You.
6 [e]*Then* the earth shall [2]yield her increase;
God, our own God, shall bless us.
7 God shall bless us,
And all the ends of the earth shall fear Him.

PSALM 68
The Glory of God in His Goodness to Israel

To the Chief Musician. A Psalm of David. A Song.

Let [a]God arise,
Let His enemies be scattered;
Let those also who hate Him flee before Him.
2 [b]As smoke is driven away,
So drive *them* away;
[c]As wax melts before the fire,
So let the wicked perish at the presence of God.
3 But [d]let the righteous be glad;
Let them rejoice before God;
Yes, let them rejoice exceedingly.

4 Sing to God, sing praises to His name;
[e]Extol[1] Him who rides on the [2]clouds,
[f]By His name [3]YAH,
And rejoice before Him.

12 [j]Is. 51:23 [k]Is. 43:2 [2]*abundance*
13 [l]Ps. 100:4; 116:14, 17-19 [m][Eccl. 5:4] [3]Promised deeds
17 [4]*praised*
18 [n]Job 27:9; [Prov. 15:29; 28:9]; Is. 1:15; [John 9:31; James 4:3]
19 [o]Ps. 116:1, 2

PSALM 67
title [1]Heb. *neginoth*
1 [a]Num. 6:25
2 [b]Acts 18:25
[c]Is. 52:10; Titus 2:11
4 [d][Ps. 96:10, 13; 98:9]
6 [e]Lev. 26:4; Ps. 85:12; [Ezek. 34:27]; Zech. 8:12 [2]*give her produce*

PSALM 68
1 [a]Num. 10:35
2 [b][Is. 9:18]; Hos. 13:3 [c]Ps. 97:5; Mic. 1:4
3 [d]Ps. 32:11
4 [e]Deut. 33:26 [f][Ex. 6:3] [1]*Praise* [2]MT *deserts;* Tg. *heavens* (cf. v. 34 and Is. 19:1) [3]Lit. LORD, a shortened Heb. form

66:12 ride over our heads. A picture of a hostile army riding in victory over Israel's defeated troops.

66:13 pay You my vows. Paying the vows is spelled out in the following verses as offering sacrifices of dedication which had been previously promised God (cf. Lev. 1; 22:18,21; Pss. 56:12; 61:8; 65:1).

67:1-7 This brief psalm develops two optimistic themes: the need and result of God's mercy, and the future universal worship of God. The psalm reflects the promise to Abraham that God would bless his descendants, and in Abraham, "all the families of the earth" (Gen. 12:1-3).

I. The Prayer for Divine Mercy (67:1,2)
II. The Plea for Universal Worship (67:3-5)
III. The Prospect of Divine Blessings (67:6,7)

67:1 face to shine. When a king smiled on a supplicant with pleasure, the petitioner was likely to receive his request (cf. Num. 6:24-26; Pss. 31:16; 44:3; 80:3,7,19; 119:135; Prov. 16:15).

67:3 peoples. A reference to the inclusion of the Gentile nations in the millennial kingdom (cf. Is. 56:3-8; 60:1-14; Zech. 14:16-19; Matt. 8:11; 25:31-46; Rev. 20:1-10).

68:1-35 This exuberant psalm includes prayer, praise, thanksgiving, historical reminder, and imprecation. It expresses a pride in Jehovah God for His care over His people and His majesty in the universe. The writing of this psalm may have come out of David's jubilant restoration of the ark of the covenant to Jerusalem (cf. 2 Sam. 6:12-15).

I. A Fanfare of Commendation (68:1-6)
II. A Reflection on Faithfulness (68:7-18)
III. An Acclamation of Majesty (68:19-31)
IV. An Invitation to Praise (68:32-35)

68:1 Let God arise. The first sentence in this psalm is essentially the same as Num. 10:35. It was perhaps a fanfare of words announcing the movement of the ark of the covenant (cf. vv. 24-27; also 2 Sam. 6:12-15).

68:4 His name YAH. A shortened form of Yahweh, often translated LORD (cf. v. 16; Ex. 3:15). Other names for God in this psalm include God (Elohim, v. 1), Lord (Adonai, v. 11), Almighty (v. 14), LORD God (v. 18), God the Lord (v. 20), and King (v. 24).

5 [g]A father of the fatherless, a defender
of widows,
Is God in His holy habitation.
6 [h]God sets the solitary in families;
[i]He brings out those who are bound
into prosperity;
But [j]the rebellious dwell in a dry *land.*

7 O God, [k]when You went out before
Your people,
When You marched through the
wilderness, Selah
8 The earth shook;
The heavens also dropped *rain* at the
presence of God;
Sinai itself *was moved* at the presence
of God, the God of Israel.
9 [l]You, O God, sent a plentiful rain,
Whereby You confirmed Your
inheritance,
When it was weary.
10 Your congregation dwelt in it;
[m]You, O God, provided from Your
goodness for the poor.

11 The Lord gave the word;
Great *was* the [4]company of those who
proclaimed *it:*
12 "Kings[n] of armies flee, they flee,
And she who remains at home
divides the [5]spoil.
13 [o]Though you lie down among the
[6]sheepfolds,
[p]*You will be* like the wings of a dove
covered with silver,
And her feathers with yellow gold."
14 [q]When the Almighty scattered kings in
it,
It was *white* as snow in Zalmon.

15 A mountain of God *is* the mountain of
Bashan;
A mountain *of many* peaks *is* the
mountain of Bashan.
16 Why do you [7]fume with envy, you
mountains of *many* peaks?
[r]*This is* the mountain *which* God
desires to dwell in;
Yes, the LORD will dwell *in it* forever.

17 [s]The chariots of God *are* twenty
thousand,
Even thousands of thousands;
The Lord is among them *as in* Sinai, in
the Holy *Place.*
18 [t]You have ascended on high,
[u]You have led captivity captive;
[v]You have received gifts among men,
Even *from* [w]the rebellious,
[x]That the LORD God might dwell *there.*

19 Blessed *be* the Lord,
Who daily loads us *with benefits,*
The God of our salvation! Selah
20 Our God *is* the God of salvation;
And [y]to GOD the Lord *belong* escapes
from death.

21 But [z]God will wound the head of His
enemies,
[a]The hairy scalp of the one who still
goes on in his trespasses.
22 The Lord said, "I will bring [b]back
from Bashan,
I will bring *them* back [c]from the
depths of the sea,
23 [d]That [8]your foot may crush *them* in
blood,
[e]And the tongues of your dogs *may
have* their portion from *your*
enemies."

24 They have seen Your [9]procession,
O God,
The procession of my God, my King,
into the sanctuary.
25 [f]The singers went before, the players
on instruments *followed* after;
Among *them were* the maidens
playing timbrels.
26 Bless God in the congregations,
The Lord, from [g]the fountain of Israel.
27 [h]There *is* little Benjamin, their leader,

5 [g] [Ps. 10:14, 18; 146:9]
6 [h] Ps. 107:4-7 [i] Acts 12:6-11 [j] Ps. 107:34
7 [k] Ex. 13:21; [Hab. 3:13]
9 [l] Lev. 26:4; Deut. 11:11; Job 5:10; Ezek. 34:26
10 [m] Deut. 26:5; Ps. 74:19
11 [4] *host*
12 [n] Num. 31:8; Josh. 10:16; Judg. 5:19 [5] *plunder*
13 [o] Ps. 81:6 [p] Ps. 105:37 [6] Or *saddlebags*
14 [q] Josh. 10:10
16 [7] Lit. *stare*
[r] [Deut. 12:5]; 1 Kin. 9:3
17 [s] Deut. 33:2; Dan. 7:10
18 [t] Mark 16:19; Acts 1:9; Eph. 4:8; Phil. 2:9; Col. 3:1; Heb. 1:3 [u] Judg. 5:12 [v] Acts 2:4, 33; 10:44-46; [1 Cor. 12:4-11; Eph. 4:7-12] [w] [1 Tim. 1:13] [x] Ps. 78:60
20 [y] [Deut. 32:39]
21 [z] Hab. 3:13 [a] Ps. 55:23
22 [b] Num. 21:33; Deut. 30:1-9; Amos 9:1-3 [c] Ex. 14:22
23 [d] Ps. 58:10 [e] 1 Kin. 21:19; Jer. 15:3 [8] LXX, Syr., Tg., Vg. *you may dip your foot*
24 [9] Lit. *goings*
25 [f] 1 Chr. 13:8
26 [g] Deut. 33:28; Is. 48:1
27 [h] Judg. 5:14; 1 Sam. 9:21

68:6 solitary in families. God cares for those who have lost families, especially the orphans and widows (v. 5; cf. Ex. 22:22-24; Ps. 10:14; James 1:27). **brings out...bound.** Speaks of God's liberating prisoners of war.

68:9 confirmed Your inheritance. God sustains His covenant people.

68:14 snow in Zalmon. "Zalmon" means "black" or "dark mountain." The "snow" pictures the contrast of corpses or bones scattered over the mountain.

68:15 mountain of Bashan. A mountain across the Jordan to the E, here figuratively described as jealous of Mt. Zion (cf. v. 16), the place which had been chosen for the special presence of God (cf. Jer. 22:20,21).

68:17 Sinai, in the Holy *Place*. God's presence had been with the armies in the same way it had been on Mt. Sinai at the giving of the law (cf. Ex. 19).

68:18 ascended on high. Paul quotes this text in Eph. 4:8 where he applies it to Christ's ascending to the heavens in triumph.

68:22 Bashan...sea. Whether the enemy tries to escape by land (Bashan) or by sea, God will bring them back to be destroyed by His people (cf. Amos 9:2-4).

68:24 procession...sanctuary. A description of the celebration when the ark of the covenant, a symbol of God's presence, was brought to Mt. Zion (cf. 1 Chr. 15:16-28).

68:27 Benjamin...Naphtali. Representative tribes of Israel, two from the S (Benjamin and Judah) and two from the N (Zebulun and Naphtali).

The princes of Judah *and* their
[1] company,
The princes of Zebulun *and* the
princes of Naphtali.

28 [2] Your God has [i] commanded your
strength;
Strengthen, O God, what You have
done for us.
29 Because of Your temple at
Jerusalem,
[j] Kings will bring presents to You.
30 Rebuke the beasts of the reeds,
[k] The herd of bulls with the calves of
the peoples,
Till everyone [l] submits himself with
pieces of silver.
Scatter the peoples *who* delight in
war.
31 [m] Envoys will come out of Egypt;
[n] Ethiopia will quickly [o] stretch out her
hands to God.

32 Sing to God, you [p] kingdoms of the
earth;
Oh, sing praises to the Lord, Selah
33 To Him [q] who rides on the heaven
of heavens, *which were* of
old!
Indeed, He sends out His voice, a
[r] mighty voice.
34 [s] Ascribe strength to God;
His excellence *is* over Israel,
And His strength *is* in the clouds.
35 O God, [t] *You are* more awesome than
Your holy places.
The God of Israel *is* He who gives
strength and power to *His*
people.

Blessed *be* God!

27 [1] *throng*
28 [i] Ps. 42:8; Is. 26:12 [2] LXX, Syr., Tg., Vg. *Command, O God*
29 [j] 1 Kin. 10:10, 25; 2 Chr. 32:23; Ps. 45:12; 72:10; Is. 18:7
30 [k] Ps. 22:12 [l] 2 Sam. 8:2
31 [m] Is. 19:19-23 [n] Is. 45:14; Zeph. 3:10 [o] Ps. 44:20
32 [p] [Ps. 67:3, 4]
33 [q] Deut. 33:26; Ps. 18:10 [r] Ps. 46:6; Is. 30:30
34 [s] Ps. 29:1
35 [t] Ps. 76:12

PSALM 69

An Urgent Plea for Help in Trouble

To the Chief Musician. Set to [1] "The Lilies."
A Psalm of David.

Save me, O God!
For [a] the waters have come up to *my*
[2] neck.
2 [b] I sink in deep mire,
Where *there is* no standing;
I have come into deep waters,
Where the floods overflow me.
3 [c] I am weary with my crying;
My throat is dry;
[d] My eyes fail while I wait for my God.

4 Those who [e] hate me without a cause
Are more than the hairs of my head;
They are mighty who would destroy
me,
Being my enemies wrongfully;
Though I have stolen nothing,
I *still* must restore *it.*

5 O God, You know my foolishness;
And my sins are not hidden from You.
6 Let not those who [3] wait for You,
O Lord GOD of hosts, be
ashamed because of me;
Let not those who seek You be
[4] confounded because of me,
O God of Israel.
7 Because for Your sake I have borne
reproach;
Shame has covered my face.
8 [f] I have become a stranger to my
brothers,
And an alien to my mother's children;
9 [g] Because zeal for Your house has eaten
me up,
[h] And the reproaches of those who
reproach You have fallen on
me.

PSALM 69

title [1] Heb. *Shoshannim*
1 [a] Job 22:11; Jon. 2:5 [2] Lit. *soul*
2 [b] Ps. 40:2
3 [c] Ps. 6:6 [d] Deut. 28:32; Ps. 119:82, 123; Is. 38:14
4 [e] Ps. 35:19; John 15:25
6 [3] Wait in faith [4] *dishonored*
8 [f] Is. 53:3; Mark 3:21; Luke 8:19; John 7:3-5
9 [g] John 2:17 [h] Rom. 15:3

68:29 Kings...presents. This section of praise (vv. 28-35) looks forward to the Messiah's reign when the world will universally worship God in the temple in Jerusalem (cf. Is. 2:2-4; 18:7; 45:14; 60:3-7; Ezek. 40–48; Hag. 2:7; Zech. 2:11-13; 6:15; 8:21,22; 14:16-19).

68:30 pieces of silver. Tribute money, signifying subservience to God.

69:1-36 This psalm is a prayer of desperation. David realizes that because he is hated by others, he may shortly be killed. Though he begs for rescue, and calls down curses on his enemies, he concludes the psalm with a high note of praise, with inferences concerning the coming messianic kingdom when all enemies of God's people are dealt with swiftly and severely (cf. Rev. 2:27). Much of this psalm was applied to Christ by the NT writers. This psalm expresses the feelings of any believer who is being horribly ridiculed, but it uniquely refers to Christ.

I. The Prayer of Desperation (69:1-28)
   A. The Description of His Situation (69:1-3)
   B. The Reason for His Situation (69:4-12)
   C. The Hope for His Situation (69:13-18)
   D. The Reproach of His Situation (69:19-21)
   E. The Revenge for His Situation (69:22-28)
II. The Promise of Salvation (69:29-36)

69:Title. "The Lilies." The name of a tune. *See note on Ps. 45: Title.*

69:4 hate me. Quoted in John 15:25.

69:6 be ashamed. The psalmist fears that his dismal situation may be a stumbling block to other believers.

69:8 alien...children. Even his family rejected him (cf. Matt. 12:46-50; John 7:3-5).

69:9 has eaten me up. The psalmist has brought hatred and hostility on himself by his unyielding insistence that the behavior of the people measure up to their outward claim of devotion to God. Whenever God was dishonored he felt the pain, because he loved God so greatly. Jesus claimed for Himself this attitude, as indicated in John 2:17; Rom. 15:3.

10 When I wept *and chastened* my soul
with fasting,
That became my reproach.
11 I also [5]made sackcloth my garment;
I became a byword to them.
12 Those who [6]sit in the gate speak
against me,
And I *am* the song of the [i]drunkards.

13 But as for me, my prayer *is* to You,
O LORD, *in* the acceptable time;
O God, in the multitude of Your
mercy,
Hear me in the truth of Your
salvation.
14 Deliver me out of the mire,
And let me not sink;
Let me be delivered from those who
hate me,
And out of the deep waters.
15 Let not the floodwater overflow me,
Nor let the deep swallow me up;
And let not the pit shut its mouth on
me.

16 Hear me, O LORD, for Your
lovingkindness *is* good;
Turn to me according to the multitude
of Your tender mercies.
17 And do not hide Your face from Your
servant,
For I am in trouble;
Hear me speedily.
18 Draw near to my soul, *and* redeem it;
Deliver me because of my enemies.

19 You know [j]my reproach, my shame,
and my dishonor;
My adversaries *are* all before You.
20 Reproach has broken my heart,
And I am full of [7]heaviness;
[k]I looked *for someone* to take pity, but
there was none;
And for [l]comforters, but I found
none.
21 They also gave me gall for my food,
[m]And for my thirst they gave me
vinegar to drink.

22 [n]Let their table become a snare before
them,
And their well-being a trap.
23 [o]Let their eyes be darkened, so that
they do not see;
And make their loins shake
continually.
24 [p]Pour out Your indignation upon
them,
And let Your wrathful anger take
hold of them.
25 [q]Let their dwelling place be desolate;
Let no one live in their tents.
26 For they persecute the *ones* [r]You have
struck,
And talk of the grief of those You
have wounded.
27 [s]Add iniquity to their iniquity,
[t]And let them not come into Your
righteousness.
28 Let them [u]be blotted out of the book
of the living,
[v]And not be written with the
righteous.

29 But I *am* poor and sorrowful;
Let Your salvation, O God, set me up
on high.
30 [w]I will praise the name of God with a
song,
And will magnify Him with
thanksgiving.
31 [x]*This* also shall please the LORD better
than an ox *or* bull,
Which has horns and hooves.
32 [y]The humble shall see *this and* be glad;
And you who seek God, [z]your hearts
shall live.
33 For the LORD hears the poor,
And does not despise [a]His prisoners.

34 [b]Let heaven and earth praise Him,
The seas [c]and everything that moves
in them.
35 [d]For God will save Zion
And build the cities of Judah,
That they may dwell there and
possess it.

11 [5]Symbolic of sorrow
12 [i]Job 30:9 [6]Sit as judges
19 [j]Ps. 22:6, 7; Heb. 12:2
20 [k]Is. 63:5 [l]Job 16:2 [7]Lit. *sickness*
21 [m]Matt. 27:34, 48; Mark 15:23, 36; Luke 23:36; John 19:28-30
22 [n]Rom. 11:9, 10
23 [o]Is. 6:9, 10
24 [p][Jer. 10:25; 1 Thess. 2:16]
25 [q]Matt. 23:38; Luke 13:35; Acts 1:20
26 [r][Is. 53:4; 1 Pet. 2:24]
27 [s]Neh. 4:5; [Rom. 1:28] [t][Is. 26:10]
28 [u][Ex. 32:32]; Phil. 4:3; [Rev. 3:5; 13:8] [v]Ezek. 13:9; Luke 10:20; Heb. 12:23
30 [w][Ps. 28:7]
31 [x]Ps. 50:13, 14, 23; 51:16
32 [y]Ps. 34:2 [z]Ps. 22:26
33 [a][Ps. 68:6]; Eph. 3:1
34 [b]Ps. 96:11; Is. 44:23; 49:13 [c]Is. 55:12
35 [d]Ps. 51:18; Is. 44:26

69:11 sackcloth. David's wearing of sackcloth, a symbol of grief, brought even more ridicule.

69:12 sit in the gate. The highest in society, those who sat in the gate of a city, were usually governmental officials. Even there city leaders were gossiping about the psalmist. **song of the drunkards.** The dregs of society, the drunkards, ridiculed David in their raucous songs.

69:15 pit shut its mouth. The "pit" was another word for Sheol, the realm of the dead. The psalmist felt that death was imminent.

69:21 gall . . . vinegar. Gall was a poisonous herb. Here it serves as a metaphor for betrayal. Friends who should provide sustenance to the psalmist had turned against him. Gall in vinegar was actually offered to Christ while He was on the cross (Matt. 27:34).

69:22 table become a snare. A snare was a trap for birds. The psalmist prays that the plots of the wicked against him would backfire and destroy them instead.

69:22,23 Quoted in Rom. 11:9,10.

69:25 Quoted in Acts 1:20 with reference to Judas.

69:26 the *ones* You have struck. Those hostile to the psalmist were ridiculing him as one suffering from God's chastisement. In its messianic application, the suffering of the Messiah was a part of God's plan from eternity past (cf. Is. 53:10).

69:31 better than an ox *or* bull. See Ps. 51:16; also Heb. 9:11,12; 10:9-12. **horns and hooves.** Implies a grown animal, one that would be especially valuable.

36 Also, [e]the [8]descendants of His servants shall inherit it,
And those who love His name shall dwell in it.

PSALM 70

Prayer for Relief from Adversaries

To the Chief Musician. *A Psalm* of David.
[a]To bring to remembrance.

Make haste, [b]O God, to deliver me!
Make haste to help me, O LORD!

2 [c]Let them be ashamed and confounded
Who seek my life;
Let them be [1]turned back and confused
Who desire my hurt.
3 [d]Let them be turned back because of their shame,
Who say, [2]"Aha, aha!"

4 Let all those who seek You rejoice and be glad in You;
And let those who love Your salvation say continually,
"Let God be magnified!"

5 [e]But I *am* poor and needy;
[f]Make haste to me, O God!
You *are* my help and my deliverer;
O LORD, do not delay.

PSALM 71

God the Rock of Salvation

In [a]You, O LORD, I put my trust;
Let me never be put to shame.
2 [b]Deliver me in Your righteousness, and cause me to escape;
[c]Incline Your ear to me, and save me.
3 [d]Be my [1]strong refuge,
To which I may resort continually;
You have given the [e]commandment to save me,
For You *are* my rock and my fortress.

4 [f]Deliver me, O my God, out of the hand of the wicked,
Out of the hand of the unrighteous and cruel man.
5 For You are [g]my hope, O Lord GOD;
You are my trust from my youth.
6 [h]By You I have been [2]upheld from birth;
You are He who took me out of my mother's womb.
My praise *shall be* continually of You.

7 [i]I have become as a wonder to many,
But You *are* my strong refuge.
8 Let [j]my mouth be filled *with* Your praise
And with Your glory all the day.

9 Do not cast me off in the time of old age;
Do not forsake me when my strength fails.
10 For my enemies speak against me;
And those who lie in wait for my life [k]take counsel together,
11 Saying, "God has forsaken him;
Pursue and take him, for *there is* none to deliver *him*."

12 [l]O God, do not be far from me;
O my God, [m]make haste to help me!
13 Let them be [3]confounded *and* consumed
Who are adversaries of my life;
Let them be covered *with* reproach and dishonor
Who seek my hurt.

14 But I will hope continually,
And will praise You yet more and more.
15 My mouth shall tell of Your righteousness
And Your salvation all the day,
For I do not know *their* limits.
16 I will go in the strength of the Lord GOD;
I will make mention of Your righteousness, of Yours only.

17 O God, You have taught me from my [n]youth;

---

36 [e]Ps. 102:28 [8]Lit. *seed*

PSALM 70

title [a]Ps. 38:title
1 [b]Ps. 40:13-17
2 [c]Ps. 35:4, 26 [1]So with MT, LXX, Tg., Vg.; some Heb. mss., Syr. *appalled* (cf. 40:15)
3 [d]Ps. 40:15 [2]An expression of scorn
5 [e]Ps. 72:12, 13 [f]Ps. 141:1

PSALM 71

1 [a]Ps. 25:2, 3
2 [b]Ps. 31:1 [c]Ps. 17:6
3 [d]Ps. 31:2, 3 [e]Ps. 44:4 [1]Lit. *rock of refuge* or *rock of habitation*
4 [f]Ps. 140:1, 3
5 [g]Jer. 14:8; 17:7, 13, 17; 50:7
6 [h]Ps. 22:9, 10; Is. 46:3 [2]*sustained from the womb*
7 [i]Is. 8:18; Zech. 3:8; 1 Cor. 4:9
8 [j]Ps. 35:28
10 [k]2 Sam. 17:1
12 [l]Ps. 35:22 [m]Ps. 70:1
13 [3]*ashamed*
17 [n]Deut. 4:5; 6:7

70:1-5 This prayer for deliverance from one's enemies is nearly identical to Ps. 40:13-17 (*see outline and notes*). It substitutes "God" for "LORD" in vv. 1,4,5.

71:1-24 One of the features of the psalms is that they meet the circumstances of life. This psalm to God expresses the concerns of old age. At a time in his life when he thinks he should be exempt from certain kinds of troubles, he once again is personally attacked. Though his enemies conclude that God has abandoned him, the psalmist is confident that God will remain faithful.

I. Confidence in God Stated (71:1-8)
II. Confidence in God Practiced in Prayer (71:9-13)
III. Confidence in God Vindicated (71:14-24)

71:3 continually. Psalm 71:1-3 is almost the same as Ps. 31:1-3a. One difference, however, is the word "continually," which the elderly person writing this psalm wants to emphasize. God has "continually" been faithful (cf. vv. 6,14).

71:7 a wonder. A reference to his trials. People are amazed at this person's life, some interpreting his trials as God's care, and others as God's punishment.

71:15 *their* limits. The blessings of God's salvation and righteousness are innumerable.

And to this *day* I declare Your
wondrous works.
18 Now also [o]when *I am* old and
grayheaded,
O God, do not forsake me,
Until I declare Your strength to *this*
generation,
Your power to everyone *who* is to
come.

19 Also [p]Your righteousness, O God, *is*
[4]very high,
You who have done great things;
[q]O God, who *is* like You?
20 [r]*You,* who have shown me great and
severe troubles,
[s]Shall revive me again,
And bring me up again from the
depths of the earth.
21 You shall increase my greatness,
And comfort me on every side.

22 Also [t]with the lute I will praise You—
And Your faithfulness, O my God!
To You I will sing with the harp,
O [u]Holy One of Israel.
23 My lips shall greatly rejoice when I
sing to You,
And [v]my soul, which You have
redeemed.
24 My tongue also shall talk of Your
righteousness all the day long;
For they are confounded,
For they are brought to shame
Who seek my hurt.

PSALM 72

Glory and Universality of the Messiah's Reign

A Psalm [a]of Solomon.

Give the king Your judgments, O God,
And Your righteousness to the
king's Son.
2 [b]He will judge Your people with
righteousness,
And Your poor with justice.
3 [c]The mountains will bring peace to the
people,
And the little hills, by
righteousness.
4 [d]He will bring justice to the poor of the
people;
He will save the children of the
needy,
And will [1]break in pieces the
oppressor.

5 [2]They shall fear You
[e]As long as the sun and moon
endure,
Throughout all generations.
6 [f]He shall come down like rain upon
the grass before mowing,
Like showers *that* water the earth.
7 In His days the righteous shall
flourish,
[g]And abundance of peace,
Until the moon is no more.

8 [h]He shall have dominion also from sea
to sea,
And from the River to the ends of the
earth.
9 [i]Those who dwell in the wilderness
will bow before Him,
[j]And His enemies will lick the dust.
10 [k]The kings of Tarshish and of the
isles
Will bring presents;
The kings of Sheba and Seba
Will offer gifts.
11 [l]Yes, all kings shall fall down before
Him;
All nations shall serve Him.

12 For He [m]will deliver the needy when
he cries,

18 [o] [Is. 46:4] **19** [p] Deut. 3:24; Ps. 57:10 [q] Ps. 35:10 [4] *great,* lit. *to the height* of heaven **20** [r] Ps. 60:3 [s] Hos. 6:1, 2 **22** [t] Ps. 92:1-3 [u] 2 Kin. 19:22; Is. 1:4 **23** [v] Ps. 103:4

PSALM 72

title [a] Ps. 127:title

2 [b] [Is. 9:7; 11:2-5; 32:1] **3** [c] Ps. 85:10 **4** [d] Is. 11:4 [1] *crush* **5** [e] Ps. 72:7, 17; 89:36 [2] So with MT, Tg.; LXX, Vg. *They shall continue* **6** [f] Deut. 32:2; 2 Sam. 23:4; Hos. 6:3 **7** [g] Is. 2:4 **8** [h] Ex. 23:31; [Is. 9:6; Zech. 9:10] **9** [i] Ps. 74:14; Is. 23:13 [j] Is. 49:23; Mic. 7:17 **10** [k] 1 Kin. 10:2; 2 Chr. 9:21 **11** [l] Is. 49:23 **12** [m] Job 29:12

71:20 from the depths of the earth. Not actual resurrection, but rescue from near-death conditions and renewal of life's strength and meaning.

72:1-20 This is a Coronation Psalm, dedicated to the prosperity of Solomon at the beginning of his reign (1 Kin. 2). No NT writer applies any of the psalm to Christ. Still, since the Davidic kings and the Messiah's rule occasionally merge into each other in the OT literature, the messianic inferences here ought not to be missed (vv. 7,17; cf. Is. 11:1-5; 60-62). This psalm describes a reign when God, the king, nature, all classes of society, and foreign nations all live together in harmony.

I. A Just Reign (72:1-4)
II. A Universal Reign (72:5-11)
III. A Compassionate Reign (72:12-14)
IV. A Prosperous Reign (72:15-17)
V. A Glorious Reign (72:18-20)

72:1 Your judgments. A prayer that the king would faithfully mediate God's justice on the nation (cf. Deut. 17:18-20). **the king's Son.** A reference primarily to Solomon, emphasizing his bond with the Davidic dynasty; but it also anticipates Messiah's reign as the culmination of the Davidic Covenant (cf. 2 Sam. 7:12,13; Ps. 2:1-12).

72:3 mountains...peace. When the king rules with justice and compassion, the earth itself radiates well-being.

72:7 Until the moon is no more. Primarily referring to the length of the Davidic dynasty, and possibly also specifically to the messianic reign (2 Sam. 7:16; Ps. 89:3,4,29,36,37; Luke 1:30-33). Jeremiah also makes the same kind of observation (cf. Jer. 33:23-26).

72:8 the River. Israel's boundaries were to extend to the River Euphrates (cf. Ex. 23:31; 1 Kin. 4:21; Ps. 89:25).

72:10 Tarshish...Seba. Countries near and far which brought tribute to Solomon (cf. 1 Kin. 4:21; 10:1,23,24; Is. 60:4-7; Jer. 6:20). Tarshish is probably in Spain; Sheba, a kingdom in southern Arabia (modern Yemen); and Seba, a N African nation.

The poor also, and *him* who has no
helper.
13 He will spare the poor and needy,
And will save the souls of the
needy.
14 He will redeem their life from
oppression and violence;
And [n]precious shall be their blood in
His sight.

15 And He shall live;
And the gold of [o]Sheba will be given
to Him;
Prayer also will be made for Him
continually,
And daily He shall be praised.

16 There will be an abundance of grain
in the earth,
On the top of the mountains;
Its fruit shall wave like Lebanon;
[p]And *those* of the city shall flourish like
grass of the earth.

17 [q]His name shall endure forever;
His name shall continue as long as
the sun.
And [r]*men* shall be blessed in Him;
[s]All nations shall call Him blessed.

18 [t]Blessed *be* the LORD God, the God of
Israel,
[u]Who only does wondrous things!
19 And [v]blessed *be* His glorious name
forever!
[w]And let the whole earth be filled *with*
His glory.
Amen and Amen.

20 The prayers of David the son of Jesse
are ended.

14 [n] 1 Sam. 26:21; [Ps. 116:15]
15 [o] Is. 60:6
16 [p] 1 Kin. 4:20
17 [q] [Ps. 89:36] [r] [Gen. 12:3] [s] Luke 1:48
18 [t] 1 Chr. 29:10 [u] Ex. 15:11; Job 5:9
19 [v] [Neh. 9:5] [w] Num. 14:21; Hab. 2:14

Book Three: Psalms 73–89

PSALM 73

The Tragedy of the Wicked, and the Blessedness of Trust in God

A Psalm of [a]Asaph.

Truly God *is* good to Israel,
To such as are pure in heart.
2 But as for me, my feet had almost
stumbled;
My steps had nearly [b]slipped.
3 [c]For I *was* envious of the boastful,
When I saw the prosperity of the
[d]wicked.

4 For *there are* no [1]pangs in their death,
But their strength *is* firm.
5 [e]They *are* not in trouble *as other* men,
Nor are they plagued like *other* men.
6 Therefore pride serves as their
necklace;
Violence covers them [f]*like* a garment.
7 [g]Their [2]eyes bulge with abundance;
They have more than heart could
wish.
8 [h]They scoff and speak wickedly
concerning oppression;
They [i]speak [3]loftily.
9 They set their mouth [j]against the
heavens,
And their tongue walks through the
earth.

10 Therefore his people return here,
[k]And waters of a full *cup* are drained
by them.
11 And they say, [l]"How does God
know?
And is there knowledge in the Most
High?"
12 Behold, these *are* the ungodly,
Who are always at ease;
They increase *in* riches.

PSALM 73

title [a] Ps. 50:title
2 [b] Job 12:5
3 [c] Ps. 37:1, 7; [Prov. 23:17] [d] Job 21:5-16; Jer. 12:1
4 [1] *pains*
5 [e] Job 21:9
6 [f] Ps. 109:18
7 [g] Job 15:27; Jer. 5:28 [2] Tg. *face bulges;* LXX, Syr., Vg. *iniquity bulges*
8 [h] Ps. 53:1 [i] 2 Pet. 2:18; Jude 16 [3] Proudly
9 [j] Rev. 13:6
10 [k] [Ps. 75:8]
11 [l] Job 22:13

72:20 are ended. Asaph's psalms immediately follow after this (Pss. 73–83), though David did author some of the psalms included later in the collection (e.g., Pss. 86,101,103). This closes Book II (Pss. 42–72) of the Psalms.

73:1-28 This psalm illustrates the results of allowing one's faith in God to be buried under self-pity. The psalmist became depressed when he contrasted the seeming prosperity of the wicked with the difficulties of living a righteous life. Beginning in v. 15, however, his attitude changes completely. He looks at life from the perspective of being under the control of a sovereign, holy God, and concludes that it is the wicked, not the righteous, who have blundered.

I. Perplexity Over the Prosperity of the Wicked (73:1-14)
 A. Their Prosperity (73:1-5)
 B. Their Pride (73:6-9)
 C. Their Presumption (73:10-14)
II. Proclamation of the Justice of God (73:15-28)
 A. His Perspective (73:15-17)
 B. His Judgments (73:18-20)
 C. His Guidance (73:21-28)

73:Title. Asaph. Asaph was a Levite who led one of the temple choirs (1 Chr. 15:19; 25:1,2). His name is identified with Ps. 73–83, and also Ps. 50 (*see note there*). He either wrote these psalms, or his choir sang them, or later choirs in the tradition of Asaph sang them.

73:4 no pangs in their death. The wicked seem to go through life in good health, and then die a painless death.

73:9 tongue walks through the earth. The insolent speech of the wicked can be heard anywhere one goes.

73:10 are drained by them. Those who associate with the wicked person "drink in" everything he declares (cf. Ps. 1).

73:11 is there knowledge in the Most High? The wicked insist on living as if God is not omniscient and does not know what happens on earth.

13 Surely I have [4]cleansed my heart *in* [m]vain,
And washed my hands in innocence.
14 For all day long I have been plagued,
And chastened every morning.

15 If I had said, "I will speak thus,"
Behold, I would have been untrue to the generation of Your children.
16 When I thought *how* to understand this,
It *was* [5]too painful for me—
17 Until I went into the sanctuary of God;
Then I understood their [n]end.

18 Surely [o]You set them in slippery places;
You cast them down to destruction.
19 Oh, how they are *brought* to desolation, as in a moment!
They are utterly consumed with terrors.
20 As a dream when *one* awakes,
So, Lord, when You awake,
You shall despise their image.

21 Thus my heart was grieved,
And I was [6]vexed in my mind.
22 [p]I *was* so foolish and ignorant;
I was *like* a beast before You.
23 Nevertheless I *am* continually with You;
You hold *me* by my right hand.
24 [q]You will guide me with Your counsel,
And afterward receive me *to* glory.

25 [r]Whom have I in heaven *but You?*
And *there is* none upon earth *that* I desire besides You.
26 [s]My flesh and my heart fail;
But God *is* the [7]strength of my heart and my [t]portion forever.

13 [m] Job 21:15; 35:3; Mal. 3:14 [4] *kept my heart pure in vain*
16 [5] *troublesome in my eyes*
17 [n] [Ps. 37:38; 55:23]
18 [o] Ps. 35:6
21 [6] Lit. *pierced in my kidneys*
22 [p] Ps. 92:6
24 [q] Ps. 32:8; 48:14; Is. 58:11
25 [r] [Phil. 3:8]
26 [s] Ps. 84:2 [t] Ps. 16:5 [7] Lit. *rock*
27 [u] [Ps. 119:155] [8] Are unfaithful to You
28 [v] [Heb. 10:22; James 4:8] [w] Ps. 116:10; 2 Cor. 4:13

PSALM 74

title [1] Heb. *Maschil*
4 [a] Lam. 2:7 [b] Num. 2:2
8 [c] Ps. 83:4 [2] *oppress*

27 For indeed, [u]those who are far from You shall perish;
You have destroyed all those who [8]desert You for harlotry.
28 But *it is* good for me to [v]draw near to God;
I have put my trust in the Lord GOD,
That I may [w]declare all Your works.

PSALM 74

A Plea for Relief from Oppressors

A [1]Contemplation of Asaph.

O God, why have You cast *us* off forever?
Why does Your anger smoke against the sheep of Your pasture?
2 Remember Your congregation, *which* You have purchased of old,
The tribe of Your inheritance, *which* You have redeemed—
This Mount Zion where You have dwelt.
3 Lift up Your feet to the perpetual desolations.
The enemy has damaged everything in the sanctuary.
4 [a]Your enemies roar in the midst of Your meeting place;
[b]They set up their banners *for* signs.
5 They seem like men who lift up
Axes among the thick trees.
6 And now they break down its carved work, all at once,
With axes and hammers.
7 They have set fire to Your sanctuary;
They have defiled the dwelling place of Your name to the ground.
8 [c]They said in their hearts,
"Let us [2]destroy them altogether."
They have burned up all the meeting places of God in the land.

73:17 sanctuary of God. As the psalmist worshiped God at the worship center, he began to understand God's perspective on the fate of the wicked. This is the turning point of the psalm.

73:20 despise their image. The wicked are like a bad dream which one forgets as soon as he awakens. Their well-being is fleeting.

73:22 *like* a beast before You. The psalmist confesses his sin of evaluating life secularly and faithlessly.

73:27 perish...You have destroyed. The psalmist concludes that those who abandon God and attempt to live an autonomous life based on self-chosen idols will eventually endure eternal death.

74:1-23 This community lament expresses the agony of the people in the midst of the most excruciating of circumstances. It was bad enough that Israel's enemies had destroyed the temple (cf. 2 Kin. 25). But even worse, it seemed to the psalmist that God had abandoned them. In this prayer he reminds God of His bond with Israel, His past supernatural deeds in the protection of Israel, and begs God to save His covenant nation now (cf. Ps. 137 and Lamentations).

I. The Terror of Abandonment (74:1-11)
II. The Remembrance of Omnipotence (74:12-17)
III. The Plea for Help (74:18-23)

74:Title. Asaph. If this psalm reflects the destruction of the temple by Nebuchadnezzar in 586 B.C., Asaph would have been dead by then. Thus this title may mean that this psalm was written by or sung by a later Asaph choir (*see notes on Pss. 50,73:Title*).

74:2 tribe of Your inheritance. The psalmist laments that even though God possessed Israel, He had not protected it.

74:3 Lift up Your feet. An anthropomorphism meaning to hurry to come to examine the rubble.

74:4 their banners *for* signs. The ravagers had set up their military and pagan religious banners in God's temple.

74:5 lift up axes. Like lumberjacks surrounded by trees, the enemy had furiously destroyed everything in sight in the temple of God.

74:8 the meeting places. God allowed only one sanctuary and during Josiah's revival, the high places had been destroyed (cf. 2 Kin. 22,23). This may be a reference to the several rooms of the temple, or to nonsacrificial religious sites throughout the land.

9 We do not see our signs;
[d]*There is* no longer any prophet;
Nor *is there* any among us who knows
how long.
10 O God, how long will the adversary
[3]reproach?
Will the enemy blaspheme Your name
forever?
11 [e]Why do You withdraw Your hand,
even Your right hand?
Take it out of Your bosom and destroy
them.
12 For [f]God *is* my King from of old,
Working salvation in the midst of the
earth.
13 [g]You divided the sea by Your strength;
You broke the heads of the [4]sea
serpents in the waters.
14 You broke the heads of [5]Leviathan in
pieces,
And gave him *as* food to the people
inhabiting the wilderness.
15 [h]You broke open the fountain and the
flood;
[i]You dried up mighty rivers.
16 The day *is* Yours, the night also *is*
[j]Yours;
[k]You have prepared the light and the
sun.
17 You have [l]set all the borders of the
earth;
[m]You have made summer and winter.

18 Remember this, *that* the enemy has
reproached, O LORD,
And *that* a foolish people has
blasphemed Your name.
19 Oh, do not deliver the life of Your
turtledove to the wild beast!
Do not forget the life of Your poor
forever.
20 [n]Have respect to the covenant;
For the [6]dark places of the earth are
full of the [7]haunts of [8]cruelty.
21 Oh, do not let the oppressed return
ashamed!
Let the poor and needy praise Your
name.

22 Arise, O God, plead Your own cause;
Remember how the foolish man
[9]reproaches You daily.
23 Do not forget the voice of Your
enemies;
The tumult of those who rise up
against You increases
continually.

PSALM 75

Thanksgiving for God's Righteous Judgment

To the Chief Musician. Set to [a]"Do [1] Not Destroy." A Psalm of Asaph. A Song.

We give thanks to You, O God, we
give thanks!
For Your wondrous works declare *that*
Your name is near.

2 "When I choose the [2]proper time,
I will judge uprightly.
3 The earth and all its inhabitants are
dissolved;
I set up its pillars firmly. Selah

4 "I said to the boastful, 'Do not deal
boastfully,'
And to the wicked, [b]'Do not [3]lift up
the horn.
5 Do not lift up your horn on high;
Do *not* speak with [4]a stiff neck.' "
6 For exaltation *comes* neither from the
east

9 [d] 1 Sam. 3:1; Lam. 2:9; Ezek. 7:26; Amos 8:11
10 [3] *revile*
11 [e] Lam. 2:3
12 [f] Ps. 44:4
13 [g] Ex. 14:21 [4] *sea monsters*
14 [5] A large sea creature of unknown identity
15 [h] Ex. 17:5, 6; Num. 20:11; Ps. 105:41; Is. 48:21 [i] Ex. 14:21, 22; Josh. 2:10; 3:13
16 [j] Job 38:12 [k] Gen. 1:14-18
17 [l] Deut. 32:8; Acts 17:26 [m] Gen. 8:22
20 [n] Gen. 17:7, 8; Lev. 26:44, 45
[6] *hiding places* [7] *homes* [8] *violence*
22 [9] *reviles or taunts*

PSALM 75
title [a] Ps. 57:title [1] Heb. *Al Tashcheth*
2 [2] *appointed*
4 [b] [1 Sam. 2:3]; Ps. 94:4 [3] Raise the head proudly like a horned animal
5 [4] Insolent pride

74:9 our signs. While hostile and pagan signs were everywhere, signs of true Jehovah worship, such as the altars for sacrifice, were missing.

74:13 divided the sea. Most likely a reference to God's creation activity, rather than to the parting of the Red Sea (cf. Gen. 1:6-8; Ex. 14:26-31). **sea serpents.** This identifies whales, sharks, and other large sea creatures, including dinosaurs.

74:14 Leviathan. *See notes on Job 41:1.*

74:15 broke open the fountain...flood. This may be a reference to the universal flood (cf. Gen. 7:11), or it may describe creation (Gen. 1:6-8).

74:17 set all the borders. As Creator, God made day and night, the seasons (v. 16), he divided the land from the sea, and he even established national boundaries.

74:20 the covenant. The people had apostatized (cf. Ex. 16:3-8). God, however, was still in an eternal covenant (the Abrahamic Covenant) with the nation (cf. Gen. 17:1-8).

75:1-10 In this psalm, the believing community asserts that, in spite of physical, moral, and societal turmoil, God never loses control of the universe. He gives stability to earthly life, and He will judge the wicked at the appropriate time. Structurally, the psalm revolves around 3 metaphors: pillars of the earth (v. 3); horns (vv. 5,6,11); and God's cup of wrath (v. 8).

I. Divine Stability of the Universe (75:1-3)
II. Divine Justice over the World (75:4-10)

75:Title. "Do Not Destroy." *See note on Ps. 57:Title.*

75:1 Your name is near. God's name represents His presence. The history of God's supernatural interventions on behalf of His people demonstrated that God was personally immanent. But OT saints did not have the fullness from permanent, personal indwelling of the Holy Spirit (cf. John 14:1,16,17; 1 Cor. 3:16; 6:19).

75:3 I set up its pillars firmly. In uncertain times, God stabilizes societies through His common grace.

75:4 Do not lift up the horn. The horn symbolized an animal's or human's strength and majesty (cf. Deut. 33:17; Amos 6:13; Zech. 1:18-21). Lifting up the horn apparently described a stubborn animal who kept itself from entering a yoke by holding its head up as high as possible. The phrase thus symbolized insolence or rebellion.

Nor from the west nor from the
south.
7 But [c]God *is* the Judge:
[d]He puts down one,
And exalts another.
8 For [e]in the hand of the LORD *there is* a
cup,
And the wine is red;
It is fully mixed, and He pours it out;
Surely its dregs shall all the wicked of
the earth
Drain *and* drink down.

9 But I will declare forever,
I will sing praises to the God of Jacob.

10 "All[f] the [5]horns of the wicked I will
also cut off,
But [g]the horns of the righteous shall
be [h]exalted."

PSALM 76

The Majesty of God in Judgment

To the Chief Musician. On [1]stringed instruments. A Psalm of Asaph. A Song.

In [a]Judah God *is* known;
His name *is* great in Israel.
2 In [2]Salem also is His tabernacle,
And His dwelling place in Zion.
3 There He broke the arrows of the
bow,
The shield and sword of battle. Selah

4 You *are* more glorious and excellent
[b]*Than* the mountains of prey.
5 [c]The stouthearted were plundered;
[d]They [3]have sunk into their sleep;
And none of the mighty men have
found the use of their hands.
6 [e]At Your rebuke, O God of Jacob,
Both the chariot and horse were cast
into a dead sleep.

7 You, Yourself, *are* to be feared;
And [f]who may stand in Your presence
When once You are angry?
8 [g]You caused judgment to be heard
from heaven;
[h]The earth feared and was still,
9 When God [i]arose to judgment,
To deliver all the oppressed of the
earth. Selah

10 [j]Surely the wrath of man shall praise
You;
With the remainder of wrath You
shall gird Yourself.

11 [k]Make vows to the LORD your God,
and pay *them;*
[l]Let all who are around Him bring
presents to Him who ought to
be feared.
12 He shall cut off the spirit of princes;
[m]*He is* awesome to the kings of the earth.

PSALM 77

The Consoling Memory of God's Redemptive Works

To the Chief Musician. [a]To Jeduthun.
A Psalm of Asaph.

I cried out to God with my voice—
To God with my voice;
And He gave ear to me.
2 In the day of my trouble I sought the
Lord;
My hand was stretched out in the
night without ceasing;
My soul refused to be comforted.
3 I remembered God, and was troubled;

---

7 [c]Ps. 50:6 [d]1 Sam. 2:7; Ps. 147:6; Dan. 2:21
8 [e]Job 21:20; Ps. 60:3; Jer. 25:15; Rev. 14:10; 16:19
10 [f]Ps. 101:8; Jer. 48:25 [g]Ps. 89:17; 148:14 [h]1 Sam. 2:1 [5]Strength

PSALM 76

title [1]Heb. *neginoth*
1 [a]Ps. 48:1, 3
2 [2]Jerusalem
4 [b]Ezek. 38:12
5 [c]Is. 10:12; 46:12 [d]Ps. 13:3 [3]Lit. *have slumbered their sleep*
6 [e]Ex. 15:1-21; Ezek. 39:20; Nah. 2:13; Zech. 12:4
7 [f][Ezra 9:15; Nah. 1:6; Mal. 3:2; Rev. 6:17]
8 [g]Ex. 19:9 [h]1 Chr. 16:30; 2 Chr. 20:29
9 [i][Ps. 9:7-9]
10 [j]Ex. 9:16; Rom. 9:17
11 [k][Eccl. 5:4-6] [l]2 Chr. 32:22, 23
12 [m]Ps. 68:35

PSALM 77

title [a]Ps. 39:title

75:8 cup. The cup of wrath describes God's judgment which He forces down the throats of the wicked (cf. Job. 21:20; Is. 51:17; Jer. 25:15-29; Matt. 20:22; 26:39).

75:10 horns…cut off. To cut off the horns of the wicked would be to humble them (cf. v. 4).

76:1-12 This psalm teaches that God is willing to use His great power for His people. Some commentators, including the editors of the LXX, have suggested that this psalm was written to celebrate the destruction of Sennacherib's Assyrian army in 701 B.C., as well as the subsequent assassination of Sennacherib himself (vv. 5,6; cf. 2 Kin. 18,19; Is. 36,37). The psalm also includes eschatological overtones (especially vv. 8-12), when Jehovah will defeat His enemies and bring them into judgment.

I. God's Nearness to His People (76:1-3)
II. God's Deliverance of His People (76:4-9)
III. God's Majesty to His People (76:10-12)

76:Title. Asaph. *See notes on Pss. 50,73,74:Title.*

76:3 broke the arrows…shield…sword. God destroyed the enemy's weapons.

76:4 mountains of prey. Probably a poetic description of the attackers.

76:5 the use of their hands. God had crippled the enemy soldiers.

76:10 wrath of man shall praise You. The railings against God and His people are turned into praise to God when God providentially brings the wicked down (cf. Is. 36:4-20; Acts 2:23; Rom. 8:28).

76:12 cut off the spirit of princes. God shatters the attitude of proud governmental leaders who rebel against Him.

77:1-20 This psalm illustrates one cure for depression. The psalmist does not explain the cause of his despair, but he was definitely locked into gloom. When he thought about God, it only caused him to complain bitterly. But beginning in v. 10, the psalmist's mood starts to change because he commits himself to focusing on God's goodness and past acts of deliverance. His lament then changes into a hymn of praise.

I. The Irritations of a Depressed Soul (77:1-9)
II. The Intention to Refocus the Mind (77:10-15)
III. The Illustrations of God's Past Blessings (77:16-20)

77:Title. Jeduthun. *See note on Ps. 39:Title.*

77:2 hand was stretched out. This was the posture for prayer. The psalmist prayed throughout the night.

I complained, and my spirit was
overwhelmed. Selah

4 You hold my eyelids *open;*
I am so troubled that I cannot speak.
5 I have considered the days of old,
The years of ancient times.
6 I call to remembrance my song in the
night;
I meditate within my heart,
And my spirit [1]makes diligent search.

7 Will the Lord cast off forever?
And will He be favorable no more?
8 Has His mercy ceased forever?
Has *His* [b]promise failed
[2]forevermore?
9 Has God forgotten to be gracious?
Has He in anger shut up His tender
mercies? Selah

10 And I said, "This *is* my [3]anguish;
But I will remember the years of the
right hand of the Most High."
11 I will remember the works of the
LORD;
Surely I will remember Your wonders
of old.
12 I will also meditate on all Your work,
And talk of Your deeds.
13 Your way, O God, *is* in [4]the
[c]sanctuary;
Who *is* so great a God as *our* God?
14 You *are* the God who does wonders;
You have declared Your strength
among the peoples.
15 You have with *Your* arm redeemed
Your people,
The sons of Jacob and Joseph. Selah

16 The waters saw You, O God;
The waters saw You, they were
[d]afraid;
The depths also trembled.
17 The clouds poured out water;
The skies sent out a sound;
Your arrows also flashed about.
18 The voice of Your thunder *was* in the
whirlwind;
The lightnings lit up the world;
The earth trembled and shook.
19 Your way *was* in the sea,
Your path in the great waters,
And Your footsteps were not known.
20 You led Your people like a flock
By the hand of Moses and Aaron.

PSALM 78

God's Kindness to Rebellious Israel

A [a]Contemplation[1] of Asaph.

Give ear, O my people, *to* my law;
Incline your ears to the words of my
mouth.
2 I will open my mouth in a [b]parable;
I will utter [2]dark sayings of old,
3 Which we have heard and known,
And our fathers have told us.
4 [c]We will not hide *them* from their
children,
[d]Telling to the generation to come the
praises of the LORD,
And His strength and His wonderful
works that He has done.

5 For [e]He established a testimony in
Jacob,
And appointed a law in Israel,
Which He commanded our fathers,
That [f]they should make them known
to their children;
6 [g]That the generation to come might
know *them,*
The children *who* would be born,
That they may arise and declare *them*
to their children,
7 That they may set their hope in God,
And not forget the works of God,
But keep His commandments;
8 And [h]may not be like their fathers,
[i]A stubborn and rebellious generation,
A generation [j]*that* did not [3]set its
heart aright,

6 [1] *ponders diligently*
8 [b] [2 Pet. 3:8, 9] [2] Lit. *unto generation and generation*
10 [3] Lit. *infirmity*
13 [c] Ps. 73:17 [4] Or *holiness*
16 [d] Ex. 14:21; Hab. 3:8, 10

PSALM 78

title [a] Ps. 74:title [1] Heb. *Maschil*
2 [b] Matt. 13:34, 35 [2] *obscure sayings* or *riddles*
4 [c] Ex. 12:26, 27; Deut. 4:9; 6:7; Job 15:18; Is. 38:19; Joel 1:3 [d] Ex. 13:8, 14
5 [e] Ps. 147:19 [f] Deut. 4:9; 11:19
6 [g] Ps. 102:18
8 [h] 2 Kin. 17:14; 2 Chr. 30:7; Ezek. 20:18 [i] Ex. 32:9; Deut. 9:7, 24; 31:27; Judg. 2:19; Is. 30:9 [j] Job 11:13; Ps. 78:37 [3] Lit. *prepare its heart*

77:4 hold my eyelids *open.* The psalmist was so upset that he could neither sleep nor talk rationally.

77:6 my song in the night. The remembrance of happier times only deepened his depression. **spirit makes diligent search.** His spirit continually meditated on possible solutions to his problems.

77:10 years of the right hand of the Most High. The psalmist began to remember the times when God used His right hand (power) to strengthen and protect him.

77:16 waters...were afraid. A dramatic picture of God's parting the waters of the Red Sea (cf. v. 19; also Ex. 14:21-31; 15:1-19).

77:17 Your arrows. A metaphor for lightning flashes.

78:1-72 This didactic psalm was written to teach the children how gracious God had been in the past in spite of their ancestors' rebellion and ingratitude. If the children learn well the theological interpretation of their nation's history, hopefully they would "not be like their fathers" (v. 8). The psalmist especially focuses on the history of the Exodus.

I. Exhortation on the Instruction of Children (78:1-11)
II. Lecture on the Graciousness of God (78:12-72)
  A. Rehearsal of Israel's History (78:12-39)
  B. Reiteration of Historical Lessons (78:40-72)

78:2 parable. The word is used here in the broader sense of a story with moral and spiritual applications. **dark sayings.** Puzzling, ambiguous information. The lessons of history are not easily discerned correctly. For an infallible interpretation of history, there must be a prophet. The specific puzzle in Israel's history is the nation's rebellious spirit in spite of God's grace.

And whose spirit was not faithful to
God.

9 The children of Ephraim, *being* armed
and [4]carrying bows,
Turned back in the day of battle.
10 [k]They did not keep the covenant of
God;
They refused to walk in His law,
11 And [l]forgot His works
And His wonders that He had shown
them.

12 [m]Marvelous things He did in the sight
of their fathers,
In the land of Egypt, [n]*in* the field of
Zoan.
13 [o]He divided the sea and caused them
to pass through;
And [p]He made the waters stand up
like a heap.
14 [q]In the daytime also He led them with
the cloud,
And all the night with a light of fire.
15 [r]He split the rocks in the wilderness,
And gave *them* drink in abundance
like the depths.
16 He also brought [s]streams out of the
rock,
And caused waters to run down like
rivers.

17 But they sinned even more against
Him
By [t]rebelling against the Most High in
the wilderness.
18 And [u]they tested God in their heart
By asking for the food of their fancy.
19 [v]Yes, they spoke against God:
They said, "Can God prepare a table
in the wilderness?
20 [w]Behold, He struck the rock,
So that the waters gushed out,
And the streams overflowed.
Can He give bread also?
Can He provide meat for His
people?"

21 Therefore the LORD heard *this* and
[x]was furious;
So a fire was kindled against Jacob,
And anger also came up against
Israel,
22 Because they [y]did not believe in God,
And did not trust in His salvation.
23 Yet He had commanded the clouds
above,
[z]And opened the doors of heaven,
24 [a]Had rained down manna on them to
eat,
And given them of the [5]bread of
[b]heaven.
25 Men ate angels' food;
He sent them food to [6]the full.

26 [c]He caused an east wind to blow in the
heavens;
And by His power He brought in the
south wind.
27 He also rained meat on them like the
dust,
Feathered fowl like the sand of the
seas;
28 And He let *them* fall in the midst of
their camp,
All around their dwellings.
29 [d]So they ate and were well filled,
For He gave them their own desire.
30 They were not [7]deprived of their
craving;
But [e]while their food *was* still in their
mouths,
31 The wrath of God came against them,
And slew the stoutest of them,
And struck down the choice *men* of
Israel.

32 In spite of this [f]they still sinned,
And [g]did not believe in His
wondrous works.
33 [h]Therefore their days He consumed in
futility,
And their years in fear.

34 [i]When He slew them, then they
sought Him;
And they returned and sought
earnestly for God.
35 Then they remembered that [j]God *was*
their rock,
And the Most High God [k]their
Redeemer.

9 [4] Lit. *bow shooters*
10 [k] 2 Kin. 17:15
11 [l] Ps. 106:13
12 [m] Ex. 7–12 [n] Num. 13:22; Is. 19:11; 30:4; Ezek. 30:14
13 [o] Ex. 14:21 [p] Ex. 15:8
14 [q] Ex. 13:21
15 [r] Ex. 17:6; Num. 20:11; Is. 48:21; [1 Cor. 10:4]
16 [s] Num. 20:8, 10, 11
17 [t] Deut. 9:22; Is. 63:10; Heb. 3:16
18 [u] Ex. 16:2
19 [v] Ex. 16:3; Num. 11:4; 20:3; 21:5
20 [w] Num. 20:11
21 [x] Num. 11:1
22 [y] Deut. 1:32; 9:23; [Heb. 3:18]
23 [z] Gen. 7:11; [Mal. 3:10]
24 [a] Ex. 16:4 [b] John 6:31 [5] Lit. *grain*
25 [6] *satiation*
26 [c] Num. 11:31
29 [d] Num. 11:19, 20
30 [e] Num. 11:33 [7] Lit. *separated*
32 [f] Num. 14:16, 17 [g] Num. 14:11; Ps. 78:11, 22
33 [h] Num. 14:29, 35
34 [i] Num. 21:7; [Hos. 5:15]
35 [j] [Deut. 32:4, 15] [k] [Ex. 15:13]; Deut. 7:8; Is. 41:14; 44:6; 63:9

78:9 children of Ephraim. The act of treachery or apostasy of this largest of the northern tribes is not specifically identified in Israel's history.

78:12 field of Zoan. The regions of Zoan, an Egyptian city.

78:13 waters stand up like a heap. The parting of the Red Sea at the beginning of the Exodus, which allowed Israel to escape from the Egyptian armies, was always considered by the OT saints to be the most spectacular miracle of their history (cf. Ex. 14).

78:15 split the rocks. Twice in the wilderness, when Israel desperately needed a great water supply, God brought water out of rocks (cf. Ex. 17:6; Num. 20:11).

78:18 the food of their fancy. Instead of being grateful for God's marvelous provisions of manna, the Israelites complained against God and Moses. God sent them meat, but also judged them (Num. 11).

78:19 prepare a table in the wilderness. The answer was "yes," but the question implied a sarcastic lack of faith.

78:27 rained meat. A poetic description of the quail which dropped into Israel's camp in the wilderness (Num. 11:31-35).

36 Nevertheless they [l]flattered Him with their mouth,
And they lied to Him with their tongue;
37 For their heart was not steadfast with Him,
Nor were they faithful in His covenant.
38 [m]But He, *being* full of [n]compassion, forgave *their* iniquity,
And did not destroy *them.*
Yes, many a time [o]He turned His anger away,
And [p]did not stir up all His wrath;
39 For [q]He remembered [r]that they *were but* flesh,
[s]A breath that passes away and does not come again.

40 How often they [t]provoked[8] Him in the wilderness,
And grieved Him in the desert!
41 Yes, [u]again and again they tempted God,
And limited the Holy One of Israel.
42 They did not remember His [9]power:
The day when He redeemed them from the enemy,
43 When He worked His signs in Egypt,
And His wonders in the field of Zoan;
44 [v]Turned their rivers into blood,
And their streams, that they could not drink.
45 [w]He sent swarms of flies among them, which devoured them,
And [x]frogs, which destroyed them.
46 He also gave their crops to the caterpillar,
And their labor to the [y]locust.
47 [z]He destroyed their vines with hail,
And their sycamore trees with frost.
48 He also gave up their [a]cattle to the hail,
And their flocks to fiery [1]lightning.
49 He cast on them the fierceness of His anger,
Wrath, indignation, and trouble,
By sending angels of destruction *among them.*
50 He made a path for His anger;
He did not spare their soul from death,
But gave [2]their life over to the plague,

36 [l] Ex. 24:7, 8; Ezek. 33:31
38 [m] [Num. 14:18-20] [n] Ex. 34:6 [o] [Is. 48:9] [p] 1 Kin. 21:29
39 [q] Job 10:9; Ps. 103:14-16 [r] John 3:6 [s] [Job 7:7, 16; James 4:14]
40 [t] Ps. 95:8-10; [Eph. 4:30]; Heb. 3:16 [8] *rebelled against Him*
41 [u] Num. 14:22; Deut. 6:16
42 [9] Lit. *hand*
44 [v] Ex. 7:20
45 [w] Ex. 8:24 [x] Ex. 8:6
46 [y] Ex. 10:14
47 [z] Ex. 9:23-25
48 [a] Ex. 9:19 [1] *lightning bolts*
50 [2] *Or their beasts*

51 And destroyed all the [b]firstborn in Egypt,
The first of *their* strength in the tents of Ham.
52 But He [c]made His own people go forth like sheep,
And guided them in the wilderness like a flock;
53 And He [d]led them on safely, so that they did not fear;
But the sea [e]overwhelmed their enemies.
54 And He brought them to His [f]holy border,
This mountain [g]*which* His right hand had acquired.
55 [h]He also drove out the nations before them,
[i]Allotted them an inheritance by [3]survey,
And made the tribes of Israel dwell in their tents.

56 [j]Yet they tested and provoked the Most High God,
And did not keep His testimonies,
57 But [k]turned back and acted unfaithfully like their fathers;
They were turned aside [l]like a deceitful bow.
58 [m]For they provoked Him to anger with their [n]high places,
And moved Him to jealousy with their carved images.
59 When God heard *this,* He was furious,
And greatly abhorred Israel,
60 [o]So that He forsook the tabernacle of Shiloh,
The tent He had placed among men,
61 [p]And delivered His strength into captivity,
And His glory into the enemy's hand.
62 [q]He also gave His people over to the sword,
And was furious with His inheritance.
63 The fire consumed their young men,
And [r]their maidens were not given in marriage.
64 [s]Their priests fell by the sword,
And [t]their widows made no lamentation.

65 Then the Lord awoke as *from* sleep,

51 [b] Ex. 12:29, 30
52 [c] Ps. 77:20
53 [d] Ex. 14:19, 20 [e] Ex. 14:27, 28
54 [f] Ex. 15:17 [g] Ps. 44:3
55 [h] Josh. 11:16-23; Ps. 44:2 [i] Josh. 13:7; 19:51; 23:4 [3] *surveyed measurement,* lit. *measuring cord*
56 [j] Judg. 2:11-13
57 [k] Ezek. 20:27, 28 [l] Hos. 7:16
58 [m] Deut. 32:16, 21; Judg. 2:12; 1 Kin. 14:9; Is. 65:3 [n] Deut. 12:2
60 [o] 1 Sam. 4:11; Jer. 7:12-14; 26:6-9
61 [p] Judg. 18:30
62 [q] Judg. 20:21; 1 Sam. 4:10
63 [r] Jer. 7:34; 16:9; 25:10
64 [s] 1 Sam. 4:17; 22:18 [t] Job 27:15; Ezek. 24:23

78:41 limited the Holy One. The Israelites did this by doubting God's power.

78:42 did not remember His power. The generations of Israelites which left Egypt and eventually died in the wilderness were characterized by ignoring God's previous acts of power and faithfulness. The following verses (vv. 42-55) rehearse the plagues and miracles of the Exodus from Egypt, which marvelously demonstrated God's omnipotence and covenant love.

78:57 deceitful bow. This is a useless bow.

78:60 tabernacle of Shiloh. Shiloh was an early location of Jehovah worship in the Promised Land. The capture and removal of the ark from Shiloh by the Philistines symbolized God's judgment (cf. Josh. 18:1; 1 Sam. 1:9; 3:1; 4:1-22).

[u]Like a mighty man who shouts
because of wine.
66 And [v]He beat back His enemies;
He put them to a perpetual reproach.

67 Moreover He rejected the tent of
Joseph,
And did not choose the tribe of
Ephraim,
68 But chose the tribe of Judah,
Mount Zion [w]which He loved.
69 And He built His [x]sanctuary like the
heights,
Like the earth which He has
established forever.
70 [y]He also chose David His servant,
And took him from the sheepfolds;
71 From following [z]the ewes that had
young He brought him,
[a]To shepherd Jacob His people,
And Israel His inheritance.
72 So he shepherded them according to
the [b]integrity of his heart,
And guided them by the skillfulness
of his hands.

PSALM 79

A Dirge and a Prayer for Israel, Destroyed by Enemies

A Psalm of Asaph.

O God, the [1]nations have come into
[a]Your inheritance;
Your holy temple they have defiled;
[b]They have laid Jerusalem [2]in heaps.
2 [c]The dead bodies of Your servants
They have given *as* food for the birds
of the heavens,
The flesh of Your saints to the beasts
of the earth.
3 Their blood they have shed like water
all around Jerusalem,
And *there was* no one to bury *them*.
4 We have become a reproach to our
[d]neighbors,
A scorn and derision to those who are
around us.

5 [e]How long, LORD?
Will You be angry forever?
Will Your [f]jealousy burn like fire?
6 [g]Pour out Your wrath on the [3]nations
that [h]do not know You,
And on the kingdoms that [i]do not call
on Your name.
7 For they have devoured Jacob,
And laid waste his dwelling place.

8 [j]Oh, do not remember [4]former
iniquities against us!
Let Your tender mercies come
speedily to meet us,
For we have been brought very low.
9 Help us, O God of our salvation,
For the glory of Your name;
And deliver us, and provide
atonement for our sins,
[k]For Your name's sake!
10 [l]Why should the [5]nations say,
"Where *is* their God?"
Let there be known among the
nations in our sight
The avenging of the blood of Your
servants *which has been* shed.

11 Let [m]the groaning of the prisoner
come before You;
According to the greatness of Your
[6]power
Preserve those who are appointed to
die;
12 And return to our neighbors
[n]sevenfold into their bosom
[o]Their reproach with which they have
reproached You, O Lord.

13 So [p]we, Your people and sheep of
Your pasture,

65 [u]Is. 42:13
66 [v]1 Sam. 5:6
68 [w][Ps. 87:2]
69 [x]1 Kin. 6:1-38
70 [y]1 Sam. 16:11, 12; 2 Sam. 7:8
71 [z]2 Sam. 7:8; [Is. 40:11] [a]2 Sam. 5:2; 1 Chr. 11:2
72 [b]1 Kin. 9:4

PSALM 79
1 [a]Ps. 74:2 [b]2 Kin. 25:9, 10; 2 Chr. 36:17-19; Jer. 26:18; 52:12-14; Mic. 3:12
[1]*Gentiles* [2]*in ruins*
2 [c]Deut. 28:26; Jer. 7:33; 19:7; 34:20
4 [d]Ps. 44:13; [Dan. 9:16]
5 [e]Ps. 74:1, 9 [f][Zeph. 3:8]
6 [g]Jer. 10:25; [Zeph. 3:8] [h]Is. 45:4, 5; 1 Thess. 4:5; [2 Thess. 1:8] [i]Ps. 53:4
[3]*Gentiles*
8 [j]Is. 64:9 [4]Or *against us the iniquities of those who were before us*
9 [k]Jer. 14:7, 21
10 [l]Ps. 42:10
[5]*Gentiles*
11 [m]Ps. 102:20 [6]Lit. *arm*
12 [n]Gen. 4:15; Lev. 26:21; Prov. 6:31; Is. 30:26 [o]Ps. 74:10, 18, 22
13 [p]Ps. 74:1; 95:7

78:65 mighty man…wine. The picture is that of a furious, raging warrior entering the battle on Israel's side.

78:68 the tribe of Judah. Instead of the prestigious tribes, God chose Judah. In Judah was Mt. Zion where the central worship center of Jehovah was located. Also, David their king, as well as his royal descendants, were from this tribe.

79:1-13 The historical basis for this lament psalm was probably Nebuchadnezzar's destruction of the temple in 586 B.C. (cf. Ps. 74; 2 Kin. 25:8-21; Lam. 1-5). The psalm contains prayer for the nation's spiritual needs, curses against the enemies of God's people, and praises in anticipation of God's actions. The psalm helps the believer express his anguish in a disaster when it seems as though God is aloof.

I. The Lamentation Over the National Disaster (79:1-4)
II. The Supplication for Divine Intervention (79:5-13)
   A. The Prayer for Vindication (79:5-7)
   B. The Prayer for Forgiveness (79:8,9)
   C. The Prayer for Reprisal (79:10-12)
   D. The Praise for Response (79:13)

79:1 nations. In this context, the word refers to heathen, pagan people. **inheritance.** The inheritance of God was national Israel, and specifically its capital city, Jerusalem, where the temple was located.

79:9 atonement. See Ps. 65:3. **For Your name's sake.** A defeat of a nation was believed to be a defeat of its god. A mark of spiritual maturity is one's concern for the reputation of God.

79:10 "Where *is* their God?" The heathen were mocking Israel's God by saying that the destruction of the nation implied that its God was nonexistent.

79:11 appointed to die. A prayer for the preservation of the prisoners awaiting execution in the enemy's dungeon.

79:12 sevenfold into their bosom. A petition that God would restore His reputation by bringing a destruction of the enemies much worse than what had happened to Israel.

Will give You thanks forever;
[q]We will show forth Your praise to all generations.

PSALM 80

Prayer for Israel's Restoration

To the Chief Musician. [a]Set to [1]"The Lilies." A [2]Testimony of Asaph. A Psalm.

Give ear, O Shepherd of Israel,
[b]You who lead Joseph [c]like a flock;
You who dwell *between* the cherubim, [d]shine forth!
2 Before [e]Ephraim, Benjamin, and Manasseh,
Stir up Your strength,
And come *and* save us!

3 [f]Restore us, O God;
[g]Cause Your face to shine,
And we shall be saved!

4 O LORD God of hosts,
[h]How long will You be angry
Against the prayer of Your people?
5 [i]You have fed them with the bread of tears,
And given them tears to drink in great measure.
6 You have made us a strife to our neighbors,
And our enemies laugh among themselves.

7 Restore us, O God of hosts;
Cause Your face to shine,
And we shall be saved!

8 You have brought [j]a vine out of Egypt;
[k]You have cast out the [3]nations, and planted it.
9 You prepared *room* for it,
And caused it to take deep root,
And it filled the land.
10 The hills were covered with its shadow,
And the [4]mighty cedars with its [l]boughs.
11 She sent out her boughs to [5]the Sea,
And her branches to [6]the River.

12 Why have You [m]broken down her [7]hedges,
So that all who pass by the way pluck her *fruit?*
13 The boar out of the woods uproots it,
And the wild beast of the field devours it.

14 Return, we beseech You, O God of hosts;
[n]Look down from heaven and see,
And visit this vine
15 And the vineyard which Your right hand has planted,
And the branch *that* You made strong [o]for Yourself.
16 *It is* burned with fire, *it is* cut down;
[p]They perish at the rebuke of Your countenance.
17 [q]Let Your hand be upon the man of Your right hand,
Upon the son of man *whom* You made strong for Yourself.
18 Then we will not turn back from You;
Revive us, and we will call upon Your name.

19 Restore us, O LORD God of hosts;
Cause Your face to shine,
And we shall be saved!

PSALM 81

An Appeal for Israel's Repentance

To the Chief Musician. [a]On[1] an instrument of Gath. A Psalm of Asaph.

Sing aloud to God our strength;
Make a joyful shout to the God of Jacob.

13 [q]Is. 43:21

PSALM 80

title [a]Ps. 45:title [1]Heb. *Shoshannim* [2]Heb. *Eduth*
1 [b][Ex. 25:20-22]; 1 Sam. 4:4; 2 Sam. 6:2 [c]Ps. 77:20 [d]Deut. 33:2
2 [e]Ps. 78:9, 67
3 [f]Lam. 5:21 [g]Num. 6:25; Ps. 4:6
4 [h]Ps. 79:5
5 [i]Ps. 42:3; Is. 30:20
8 [j][Is. 5:1, 7]; Jer. 2:21; Ezek. 15:6; 17:6; 19:10 [k]Ps. 44:2; Acts 7:45 [3]*Gentiles*
10 [l]Lev. 23:40 [4]Lit. *cedars of God*
11 [5]The Mediterranean [6]The Euphrates
12 [m]Is. 5:5; Nah. 2:2 [7]*walls or fences*
14 [n]Is. 63:15
15 [o][Is. 49:5]
16 [p][Ps. 39:11]
17 [q]Ps. 89:21

PSALM 81

title [a]Ps. 8:title [1]Heb. *Al Gittith*

80:1-19 This psalm was probably written from Jerusalem in astonishment at the captivity of the 10 northern tribes in 722 B.C. The psalmist recognized that God's people had removed themselves through apostasy from the blessings of the Mosaic Covenant. So he begs God to act and to restore His people into covenant blessings (vv. 3,7,14,19).

I. Prayer for Divine Restoration (80:1-3)
II. Despair over God's Anger (80:4-7)
III. Description of God's Vine (80:8-16a)
IV. Prayer for Divine Restoration (80:16b-19)

80:Title. "The Lilies." The name of a tune. *See note on Ps. 45:Title.*

80:1 dwell *between* the cherubim. A reference to the ark of the covenant, a symbol for God's presence. The images of two cherubim sat on top of the ark, facing each other (cf. Ex. 37:1-9).

80:3 face to shine. *See note on Ps. 67:1*; cf. 80:7,19.

80:4 God of hosts. *See note on Ps. 59:5*; cf. 80:7,14.

80:8 vine out of Egypt. The vine is a metaphor for Israel, whom God delivered out of Egypt and nurtured into a powerful nation (cf. Is. 5:1-7; 27:2-6; Matt. 21:33-40).

80:17 son of man. In this context, this phrase is primarily a reference to Israel. In a secondary sense, the "son of man" may allude to the Davidic dynasty and even extend to the Messiah, since He is so frequently called by that title in the NT.

81:1-16 This psalm was intended to be used in the celebration of one of the feasts of Israel, most likely the Feast of Tabernacles. After the call to worship (vv. 1-5), the psalm presents a message from God in the first person (vv. 6-16). This oracle pleads with Israel to "listen" to Him (v. 13), so that He might pour out on the nation the blessings of the covenant.

I. A Call to Joyful Worship (81:1-5)
II. A Call to Godly Obedience (81:6-16)

2 Raise a song and strike the timbrel,
The pleasant harp with the lute.

3 Blow the trumpet at the time of the
New Moon,
At the full moon, on our solemn feast
day.
4 For [b]this *is* a statute for Israel,
A law of the God of Jacob.
5 This He established in Joseph *as* a
testimony,
When He went throughout the land
of Egypt,
[c]*Where* I heard a language I did not
understand.

6 "I removed his shoulder from the
burden;
His hands were freed from the baskets.
7 [d]You called in trouble, and I delivered
you;
[e]I answered you in the secret place of
thunder;
I [f]tested you at the waters of
[2]Meribah. Selah
8 "Hear,[g] O My people, and I will
admonish you!
O Israel, if you will listen to Me!
9 There shall be no [h]foreign god among
you;
Nor shall you worship any foreign
god.
10 [i]I *am* the LORD your God,
Who brought you out of the land of
Egypt;
[j]Open your mouth wide, and I will fill
it.

4 [b] Lev. 23:24; Num. 10:10
5 [c] Deut. 28:49; Ps. 114:1; Jer. 5:15
7 [d] Ex. 2:23; 14:10; Ps. 50:15 [e] Ex. 19:19; 20:18 [f] Ex. 17:6, 7; Num. 20:13 [2] Lit. *Strife* or *Contention*
8 [g] [Ps. 50:7]
9 [h] [Ex. 20:3; Deut. 5:7; 32:12]; Ps. 44:20; [Is. 43:12]
10 [i] Ex. 20:2; Deut. 5:6 [j] Ps. 103:5

11 [k] Ex. 32:1; Deut. 32:15
12 [l] [Job 8:4; Acts 7:42; Rom. 1:24, 26] [3] *the dictates of their heart*
13 [m] [Deut. 5:29; Is. 48:18]
15 [n] Rom. 1:30 [4] Lit. *time*
16 [o] Deut. 32:14 [p] Job 29:6 [5] Lit. *fat of wheat*

PSALM 82

1 [a] [2 Chr. 19:6; Eccl. 5:8] [b] Ps. 82:6 [1] Heb. *El*, lit. *God* [2] *Judges*; Heb. *elohim*, lit. *mighty ones* or *gods*
2 [c] [Deut. 1:17]; Prov. 18:5
3 [d] [Deut. 24:17; Is. 11:4; Jer. 22:16] [3] *Vindicate*

11 "But My people would not heed My
voice,
And Israel would *have* [k]none of Me.
12 [l]So I gave them over to [3]their own
stubborn heart,
To walk in their own counsels.

13 "Oh,[m] that My people would listen to
Me,
That Israel would walk in My ways!
14 I would soon subdue their enemies,
And turn My hand against their
adversaries.
15 [n]The haters of the LORD would pretend
submission to Him,
But their [4]fate would endure forever.
16 He would [o]have fed them also with
[5]the finest of wheat;
And with honey [p]from the rock I
would have satisfied you."

PSALM 82

A Plea for Justice

A Psalm of Asaph.

God [a]stands in the congregation of
[1]the mighty;
He judges among [b]the [2]gods.
2 How long will you judge unjustly,
And [c]show partiality to the wicked?
Selah
3 [3]Defend the poor and fatherless;
Do justice to the afflicted and [d]needy.
4 Deliver the poor and needy;
Free *them* from the hand of the wicked.

5 They do not know, nor do they
understand;

81:Title. an instrument of Gath. *See note on Ps. 8:Title.*

81:2 lute. A musical instrument with a long and narrow neck resembling a guitar.

81:3 New Moon…full moon. The seventh month of Israel's year (Tishri; Sept./Oct.) culminated the festival year with a succession of celebrations. The month began with the blowing of the trumpets, continued with the Day of Atonement on the tenth day, and celebrated the Feast of Tabernacles on the fifteenth day when the moon was full. The Feast of Tabernacles praised God for His care in the wilderness wanderings, and also pointed to the coming kingdom (Matt. 17:1-4).

81:5 language…not understand. Either the psalmist heard a message, the meaning of which he did not grasp, in which case this message is presented as an oracle in the following verses; or, the psalmist is referring to the Egyptian language, which the Jews did not know.

81:6 hands…freed…baskets. The Israelites in Egypt were forced to carry bricks and clay in baskets.

81:7 secret place of thunder. Probably a reference to God's presence on Mt. Sinai at the giving of the law (cf. Ex. 19:16ff.; 20:18ff.). **waters of Meribah.** Meribah, which means "strife" or "dispute," marked places where Israel tempted God (cf. Ex. 17:1-7; Num. 20:1-13; Pss. 95:8; 106:32).

81:14 soon subdue their enemies. One of the blessings of obedience promised to Israel in the Mosaic Covenant was victory over its enemies (cf. Num. 33:52-56; Deut. 6:16-19; 7:16-24).

81:16 honey from the rock. This phrase was first used by Moses in his song of praise (Deut. 32:13). Though honey is sometimes found in the clefts of rocks, the intent of the figure here is more likely to valuable food provided from unlikely places.

82:1-8 This psalm, like Pss. 2 and 58, focuses on the injustices of tyranny. The psalmist pictures God standing in the assembly of earthly leaders, to whom He has delegated authority, and condemning their injustices. The final prayer of the psalmist (v. 8) is that God Himself will take direct control of the affairs of this world.

I. The Assembly of World Leaders Before God (82:1)
II. The Evaluation of World Leaders by God (82:2-7)
III. The Replacement of World Leaders with God (82:8)

82:1 congregation of the mighty. The scene opens with God having called the world leaders together. **among the gods.** Some have taken this psalm to be about demons or false pagan gods. The best interpretation is that these "gods" are human leaders, such as judges, kings, legislators, and presidents (cf. Ex. 22:8,9,28; Judg. 5:8,9). God the Great Judge, presides over these lesser judges.

82:2-4 judge unjustly. God accuses the lesser human judges of social injustices which violate the Mosaic law (e.g., Deut. 24).

They walk about in darkness;
All the [e]foundations of the earth are
[4]unstable.

6 I said, [f]"You *are* [5]gods,
And all of you *are* children of the
Most High.
7 But you shall die like men,
And fall like one of the princes."

8 Arise, O God, judge the earth;
[g]For You shall inherit all nations.

5 [e]Ps. 11:3 [4]*moved*
6 [f]John 10:34
[5]Judges; Heb. *elohim*, lit. *mighty ones* or *gods*
8 [g]Ps. 2:8; [Rev. 11:15]

PSALM 83

Prayer to Frustrate Conspiracy Against Israel

A Song. A Psalm of Asaph.

Do[a] not keep silent, O God!
Do not hold Your peace,
And do not be still, O God!
2 For behold, [b]Your enemies make a
[1]tumult;
And those who hate You have [2]lifted
up their head.
3 They have taken crafty counsel
against Your people,
And consulted together [c]against Your
sheltered ones.
4 They have said, "Come, and [d]let us cut
them off from *being* a nation,
That the name of Israel may be
remembered no more."

5 For they have consulted together with
one [3]consent;
They [4]form a confederacy against
You:
6 [e]The tents of Edom and the
Ishmaelites;
Moab and the Hagrites;
7 Gebal, Ammon, and Amalek;
Philistia with the inhabitants of Tyre;
8 Assyria also has joined with them;
They have helped the children of Lot.
Selah

9 Deal with them as *with* [f]Midian,
As *with* [g]Sisera,
As *with* Jabin at the Brook Kishon,
10 Who perished at En Dor,
[h]*Who* became *as* refuse on the earth.
11 Make their nobles like [i]Oreb and like
Zeeb,
Yes, all their princes like [j]Zebah and
Zalmunna,
12 Who said, "Let us take for ourselves
The pastures of God for a
possession."

13 [k]O my God, make them like the
whirling dust,
[l]Like the chaff before the wind!

PSALM 83
1 [a]Ps. 28:1
2 [b]Ps. 81:15; Is. 17:12; Acts 4:25 [1]*uproar* [2]Exalted themselves
3 [c][Ps. 27:5]
4 [d]Esth. 3:6, 9; Jer. 11:19; 31:36
5 [3]Lit. *heart* [4]Lit. *cut a covenant*
6 [e]2 Chr. 20:1, 10, 11
9 [f]Num. 31:7; Judg. 7:22 [g]Judg. 4:15-24; 5:20, 21
10 [h]Zeph. 1:17
11 [i]Judg. 7:25 [j]Judg. 8:12-21
13 [k]Is. 17:13 [l]Job 21:18; Ps. 35:5; Is. 40:24; Jer. 13:24

82:5 darkness. Signifies both intellectual ignorance and moral iniquity. **foundations of the earth are unstable.** When leaders rule unjustly, the divinely established moral order which undergirds human existence is undermined.

82:6 I said. Kings and judges are set up ultimately by the decree of God (Ps. 2:6). God, in effect, invests His authority in human leaders for the stability of the universe (cf. Rom. 13:1-7). But God may revoke this authority (v. 7). **"You *are* gods."** Jesus, in quoting this phrase in John 10:34, supported the interpretation that the "gods" were human beings. In a play on words, he claims that if human leaders can be called "gods," certainly the Messiah can be called God. **children of the Most High.** Created by God for noble life.

82:7 die like men. In spite of being made in God's image, they were mortal and would die like human beings. **fall like...princes.** The unjust rulers would become vulnerable to the violent deaths which often accompanied tyranny.

82:8 You shall inherit all nations. The psalmist prayerfully anticipates the future when God will set up His kingdom and restore order and perfect justice to a sin-cursed world (cf. Pss. 96, 97; Is. 11:1-5).

83:1-18 This psalm, a national lament which includes prayer and imprecations, may be best studied with a map since several individual national enemies of Israel are noted. Second Chronicles 20:1-30 may record the specific historical event prompting this psalm, though some Bible students believe that the nations mentioned are only symbolic of all of Israel's enemies. The psalmist begs God to rescue Israel from its enemies as He had done so many times in the past.

I. A Plea for Help (83:1)
II. A Protest Against Israel's Enemies (83:2-8)
III. A Petition for Divine Judgment (83:9-18)

83:2 Your enemies. Throughout this psalm, the hostile nations are described as God's enemies.

83:4 cut them off. The hostile nations, under Satan's influence, repudiated God's promise to preserve forever the nation of Israel (cf. Gen. 17:7, 8; Ps. 89:34-37).

83:6 Edom...Hagrites. The list of nations represents Israel's enemies throughout its history. Edom descended from Esau and lived SE of Israel. The Ishmaelites, descendants from Abraham and Hagar, were Bedouin tribes. The Moabites descended from Lot (cf. v. 8) and were tribal people living E of the Jordan (cf. Judg. 11:17, 18; Is. 15, 16). The Hagrites were a nomadic tribe living E of the Jordan (1 Chr. 5:10, 19, 20).

83:7 Gebal...Tyre. Gebal was probably a community S of the Dead Sea, near Petra in Edom. Ammon, a nation descending from Lot, was located E of the Jordan River. The Amalekites, nomads living SE of the Jordan River, were descendants of Esau (cf. Gen. 36:12, 16; Ex. 17:8-13; Num. 24:20; Judg. 6:3; 1 Sam. 15:1-8). Philistia was located SW of Israel (Judg. 14–16). Tyre was NW of Israel (cf. Ezek. 27).

83:8 Assyria. This dominant nation of the eighth century B.C. took captive the northern 10 tribes of Israel in 722 B.C. Assyria used smaller nations, like Moab and Edom (the children of Lot; cf. Gen. 19:36-38), to accomplish its military goals.

83:9 Midian...Jabin. The psalmist reminded God of famous past victories. Gideon had defeated the Midianites (Judg. 7:19-25). Barak and Deborah defeated Jabin and his army commander, Sisera, near the Brook Kishon (Judg. 4, 5).

83:11 Oreb...Zalmunna. These men were chiefs of the Midianites when they were defeated by Gideon (cf. Judg. 6-8).

83:13-15 The psalmist uses several dramatic similes in his prayer for the destruction of Israel's enemies.

14 As the fire burns the woods,
And as the flame [m]sets the mountains on fire,
15 So pursue them with Your tempest,
And frighten them with Your storm.
16 Fill their faces with shame,
That they may seek Your name, O LORD.
17 Let them be [5]confounded and dismayed forever;
Yes, let them be put to shame and perish,
18 [n]That they may know that You, whose [o]name alone *is* the LORD,
Are [p]the Most High over all the earth.

PSALM 84

The Blessedness of Dwelling in the House of God

To the Chief Musician. [a]On [1] an instrument of Gath. A Psalm of the sons of Korah.

How [b]lovely [2]*is* Your tabernacle,
O LORD of hosts!
2 [c]My soul longs, yes, even faints
For the courts of the LORD;
My heart and my flesh cry out for the living God.

3 Even the sparrow has found a home,
And the swallow a nest for herself,
Where she may lay her young—
Even Your altars, O LORD of hosts,
My King and my God.
4 Blessed *are* those who dwell in Your [d]house;
They will still be praising You. Selah

5 Blessed *is* the man whose strength *is* in You,
Whose heart *is* set on pilgrimage.
6 *As they* pass through the Valley [e]of [3]Baca,
They make it a spring;
The rain also covers it with [4]pools.
7 They go [f]from strength to strength;
[5]*Each one* [g]appears before God in Zion.

8 O LORD God of hosts, hear my prayer;
Give ear, O God of Jacob! Selah
9 [h]O God, behold our shield,
And look upon the face of Your [6]anointed.

10 For a day in Your courts *is* better than a thousand.
I would rather [7]be a doorkeeper in the house of my God
Than dwell in the tents of wickedness.
11 For the LORD God *is* [i]a sun and [j]shield;
The LORD will give grace and glory;
[k]No good *thing* will He withhold
From those who walk uprightly.

12 O LORD of hosts,
[l]Blessed *is* the man who trusts in You!

14 [m] Ex. 19:18; Deut. 32:22
17 [5] *ashamed*
18 [n] Ps. 59:13 [o] Ex. 6:3 [p] [Ps. 92:8]

PSALM 84

title [a] Ps. 8:title [1] Heb. *Al Gittith*
1 [b] Ps. 27:4; 46:4, 5 [2] *are Your dwellings*
2 [c] Ps. 42:1, 2
4 [d] [Ps. 65:4]
6 [e] 2 Sam. 5:22-25 [3] Lit. *Weeping* [4] Or *blessings*
7 [f] Prov. 4:18; Is. 40:31; John 1:16; 2 Cor. 3:18 [g] Ex. 34:23; Deut. 16:16 [5] LXX, Syr., Vg. *The God of gods shall be seen*
9 [h] Gen. 15:1 [6] Commissioned one, Heb. *messiah*
10 [7] *stand at the threshold*
11 [i] Is. 60:19, 20; Mal. 4:2; Rev. 21:23 [j] Gen. 15:1 [k] Ps. 34:9, 10
12 [l] [Ps. 2:12; 40:4]

83:18 know...Most High. The purpose of the maledictions against the hostile nations is neither personal nor national, but spiritual: that the nations may know and glorify God. **whose name alone *is* the LORD.** "Alone" should precede "*are*" in the next phrase. The Gentile nations need to know that the God of the Bible is the only God.

84:1-12 This psalm, like other psalms of ascent (Pss. 120–134), expresses the joy of a pilgrim traveling up to Jerusalem, then up into the temple to celebrate one of the feasts. The pilgrim focuses his attention especially on the thought of being in the very presence of the Lord God. The NT believer-priest, in an even greater way, can come into the presence of the Lord (cf. Heb. 4:16; 10:19-22).

I. The Expectation of Worshiping God (84:1-4)
II. The Expedition to Worship God (84:5-7)
III. The Elation at Worshiping God (84:8-12)

84:Title. instrument of Gath. *See note on Ps. 8:Title.* **sons of Korah.** These descendants of Levi through Kohath were the gatekeepers and musicians in the temple at Jerusalem (1 Chr. 6:22; 9:17-32; 26:1; see all Pss. 42–49; 84,85; 87,88).

84:1 lovely *is* Your tabernacle. The temple worship center was "lovely" because it enabled the OT saint to come into the presence of God (cf. Pss. 27; 42:1,2 61:4; 63:1,2). **LORD of hosts.** "Hosts" represent God's angelic armies, thus God's omnipotence over all powers in heaven and on earth (cf. vv. 3,8,12).

84:2 longs...faints...cry out. The psalmist is consumed with his happy, but intense desire to worship God in the temple.

84:3 sparrow...swallow. The psalmist admires these birds who were able to build their nests in the temple courtyards, near the altars of God.

84:4 Blessed. This word is used 3 times (vv. 4,5,12) to describe the happiness of those who, like the sons of Korah, "lodged *all* around the house of God" (1 Chr. 9:27).

84:6 Valley of Baca. "Baca" can be translated as "weeping" or "balsam tree." The valley was an arid place on the way to Jerusalem. **They make it a spring.** The pilgrims traveling to a festival of worship at Jerusalem turn an arid valley into a place of joy.

84:7 strength to strength. Anticipation of joyous worship of God in Jerusalem overcame the pilgrims' natural weariness in their difficult journey. **Zion.** *See note on Ps. 87:2.*

84:9 behold our shield. A metaphor for the king, who also would have participated in a festival at the temple (cf. Ps. 47:9; Hos. 4:18). **the face of Your anointed.** The king is regularly described as God's "anointed" (Pss. 2:2; 18:50; 20:6; 28:8; 89:38,51). The psalmist thus prays that God would look upon the king with favor, blessing his reign with prosperity.

84:10 doorkeeper. One day standing at the door of the temple, or just being near even if not inside, was better than a thousand days fellowshiping with the wicked.

84:11 sun and shield. This pictures God's overall provision and protection.

PSALM 85

Prayer that the LORD Will Restore Favor to the Land

To the Chief Musician. A Psalm [a] of the sons of Korah.

LORD, You have been favorable to Your land;
You have [b] brought back the captivity of Jacob.
2 You have forgiven the iniquity of Your people;
You have covered all their sin. Selah
3 You have taken away all Your wrath;
You have turned from the fierceness of Your anger.
4 [c] Restore us, O God of our salvation,
And cause Your anger toward us to cease.
5 [d] Will You be angry with us forever?
Will You prolong Your anger to all generations?
6 Will You not [e] revive us again,
That Your people may rejoice in You?
7 Show us Your mercy, LORD,
And grant us Your salvation.

8 I will hear what God the LORD will speak,
For He will speak peace
To His people and to His saints;
But let them not turn back to [1] folly.
9 Surely [f] His salvation *is* near to those who fear Him,
[g] That glory may dwell in our land.
10 Mercy and truth have met together;
[h] Righteousness and peace have kissed.
11 Truth shall spring out of the earth,
And righteousness shall look down from heaven.
12 [i] Yes, the LORD will give *what is* good;
And our land will yield its increase.
13 Righteousness will go before Him,
And shall make His footsteps *our* pathway.

PSALM 85

title [a] Ps. 42:title
1 [b] Ezra 1:11–2:1; Ps. 14:7; Jer. 30:18; 31:23; Ezek. 39:25; Hos. 6:11; Joel 3:1
4 [c] Ps. 80:3, 7
5 [d] Ps. 79:5
6 [e] Hab. 3:2
8 [1] *foolishness*
9 [f] Is. 46:13
[g] Hag. 2:7; Zech. 2:5; [John 1:14]
10 [h] Ps. 72:3; [Is. 32:17]; Luke 2:14
12 [i] [Ps. 84:11; James 1:17]

PSALM 86

Prayer for Mercy, with Meditation on the Excellencies of the LORD

A Prayer of David.

Bow down Your ear, O LORD, hear me;
For I *am* poor and needy.
2 Preserve my [1] life, for I *am* holy;
You are my God;
Save Your servant who trusts in You!
3 Be merciful to me, O Lord,
For I cry to You all day long.
4 [2] Rejoice the soul of Your servant,
[a] For to You, O Lord, I lift up my soul.
5 For [b] You, Lord, *are* good, and ready to forgive,
And abundant in mercy to all those who call upon You.

6 Give ear, O LORD, to my prayer;
And attend to the voice of my supplications.

PSALM 86

2 [1] Lit. *soul*
4 [a] Ps. 25:1; 143:8
[2] *Make glad*
5 [b] Ps. 130:7; 145:9; [Joel 2:13]

85:1-13 The psalmist pledges that God will again demonstrate His covenant love to Israel. God has been merciful in the past; He is angry presently; but He will restore Israel in the future (cf. Deut. 30; Hos. 3:4,5). Though God judges, He is faithful to His promises. The feelings expressed in this psalm may describe those of the Jews returning from exile in Babylon. Though they were grateful for restoration to their land, they were disappointed that the conditions did not measure up to the glory of the pre-Exilic life there (cf. Ezra 3:12,13).

I. Review of God's Past Mercies (85:1-3)
II. Recognition of God's Present Anger (85:4-7)
III. Revelation of God's Future Salvation (85:8-13)

85:Title. sons of Korah. *See note on Ps. 84:Title.*

85:1 favorable to Your land. In the past, God deemed His nation, Israel, to be acceptable.

85:3 fierceness of Your anger. *See note on Ps. 56:7.*

85:7 mercy. The word means "loyal love" or "unfailing love," and specifies God's faithfulness to His people through His covenant relationship.

85:8 peace. Ultimately this comes in the Messiah's kingdom (cf. Matt. 10:34; Luke 2:14).

85:9 salvation…who fear Him. Only those who renounce their sinful autonomy and put their complete trust in the living God will participate in the blessings of salvation and the future kingdom (cf. John 3:3-5). **glory may dwell in our land.** The departure of the glory of God, which signified His presence, is described in Ezek. 10,11. He withdrew His glory because of the apostasy of the nation immediately preceding the Babylonian Exile (cf. Ezek. 8–11). The return of the glory of the Lord in the future millennial temple is foretold in Ezek. 43:1-4 (cf. Pss. 26:8; 63:2; Is. 40:3-5; 60:1-3; 62:1-5). *See note on Lev. 9:23.*

85:10 Mercy…truth…righteousness…peace. These 4 spiritual qualities characterizing the atmosphere of the future kingdom of Christ, will relate to each other in perfect harmony and will saturate kingdom life (cf. vv. 10,13).

85:12 our land…increase. Increase in the fertility and productivity of the land will also characterize the future kingdom of Christ (cf. Is. 4:2; 30:23-26; 32:15; Jer. 31:12; Ezek. 36:8-11; Amos 9:13-15; Zech. 8:11,12).

86:1-17 This psalm is an individual lament (cf. Ps. 56) in which David expresses his distress and overcomes that distress through praise and worship. There is a sense of urgency demonstrated by some 14 prayer requests. Undergirding the requests is the covenant relationship (vv. 2,5,13).

I. The Request for God's Attention (86:1-7)
II. The Testimony to God's Uniqueness (86:8-13)
III. The Plea for God's Deliverance (86:14-17)

86:2 I *am* holy. David, though recognizing his sinfulness (v. 1), insisted that by the grace of God he had not broken his covenant with the Lord.

86:4 soul…soul. The psalmist requests that his inner person would be preserved according to the covenant agreements (cf. Deut. 7,8,20).

7 In the day of my trouble I will call
upon You,
For You will answer me.

8 [c]Among the gods *there is* none like
You, O Lord;
Nor *are there any works* like Your
works.

9 All nations whom You have made
Shall come and worship before You,
O Lord,
And shall glorify Your name.

10 For You *are* great, and [d]do wondrous
things;
[e]You alone *are* God.

11 [f]Teach me Your way, O LORD;
I will walk in Your truth;
[3]Unite my heart to fear Your name.

12 I will praise You, O Lord my God,
with all my heart,
And I will glorify Your name
forevermore.

13 For great *is* Your mercy toward me,
And You have delivered my soul
from the depths of [4]Sheol.

14 O God, the proud have risen against
me,
And a mob of violent *men* have
sought my life,
And have not set You before them.

15 But [g]You, O Lord, *are* a God full of
compassion, and gracious,
Longsuffering and abundant in mercy
and truth.

16 Oh, turn to me, and have mercy on
me!
Give Your strength to Your servant,
And save the son of Your
maidservant.

17 Show me a sign for good,
That those who hate me may see *it*
and be ashamed,
Because You, LORD, have helped me
and comforted me.

8 [c][Ex. 15:11]; 2 Sam. 7:22; 1 Kin. 8:23; Ps. 89:6; Jer. 10:6
10 [d][Ex. 15:11]
[e]Deut. 6:4; Is. 37:16; Mark 12:29; 1 Cor. 8:4
11 [f]Ps. 27:11; 143:8
[3]Give me singleness of heart
13 [4]The abode of the dead
15 [g]Ex. 34:6; [Ps. 86:5]

PSALM 87

The Glories of the City of God

A Psalm of the sons of Korah. A Song.

His foundation *is* in the holy
mountains.

2 [a]The LORD loves the gates of Zion
More than all the dwellings of Jacob.

3 [b]Glorious things are spoken of you,
O city of God! Selah

4 "I will make mention of [1]Rahab and
Babylon to those who know
Me;
Behold, O Philistia and Tyre, with
Ethiopia:
'This *one* was born there.' "

5 And of Zion it will be said,
"This *one* and that *one* were born in her;

PSALM 87
2 [a]Ps. 78:67, 68
3 [b]Is. 60:1
4 [1]Egypt

86:8 Among the gods. David is here contrasting the true God with the imaginary deities of the heathen nations (cf. v. 10; also Ex. 15:11; Ps. 89:6; Is. 46:5-11).

86:9 All nations...worship. The psalmists and prophets often look into the future messianic age when all the nations of the world will worship the Lord (cf. Ps. 22:27; Is. 2:3; Zech. 8:21,22; 14:16-19; Rev. 15:4).

86:11 Unite my heart. The psalmist prays that he would have an undivided heart, single-heartedly loyal to his Lord (cf. Rom. 7:15; James 1:8).

86:14 the proud. The proud (i.e., arrogant, insolent) are those who act independently from God, rebelling against Him and His people (cf. Pss. 119:21,51,69,78,85,122).

86:16 the son of Your maidservant. David asks for special favor from God just as a servant born in the household would receive more than a servant brought in from outside the household (cf. Ps. 116:16).

86:17 a sign. A request for a favorable indication that would demonstrate that God was truly on David's side.

87:1-7 This psalm describes the Lord's love for Jerusalem and exalts this city as the religious center of the world in the coming messianic kingdom (cf. Ps. 48). Though the nations of the world (even including some of Israel's former enemies) will worship the Lord then, Israel will still be the favored nation (cf. Is. 2:2-4; 19:23-25; 45:22-25; 56:6-8; Zech. 8:20-23; 14:16-19).

I. The Lord's Love for Zion (87:1-3)
II. The Lord's Favor of Israel (87:4-6)
III. The Musicians' Exultation over Jerusalem (87:7)

87:Title. sons of Korah. *See note on Ps. 84:Title.*

87:1 His foundation...holy mountains. "His foundation" means "His founded city," namely Jerusalem, located in the hill country of Judea.

87:2 gates of Zion. Zion is a poetic description of Jerusalem, seemingly used by the OT writers when special spiritual and religious significance was being attached to the city. Though God certainly loved other cities in Israel, He did not choose any of them to be His worship center (cf. Pss. 122,125,132,133). The gates represent the access of the potential worshiper into the city where he could come into a special worshiping relationship with God. **More than all the dwellings of Jacob.** The other cities in Israel were not chosen by God to be the place of His special dwelling.

87:3 O city of God! Jerusalem was God's city because there God met His people in praise and offerings.

87:4 Rahab and Babylon. Rahab was a monster of ancient pagan mythology and symbolized Egypt in the OT (cf. Ps. 89:10; Is. 30:7; 51:9). Two of the superpowers of the ancient world, fierce enemies of Israel, will one day worship the Lord in Zion (cf. Is. 19:19-25). **Philistia...Tyre...Ethiopia.** Three more Gentile nations, ancient enemies of Israel, whose descendants will worship the Lord in Jerusalem (cf. Is. 14:28-32; 18:1-7). This multinational worship is pictured as a great joy to the Lord Himself. **This *one* was born there.** To be born in Jerusalem will be noted as a special honor in the messianic kingdom (cf. vv. 5,6; also Zech. 8:20-23).

And the Most High Himself shall establish her."
6 The LORD will record,
When He [c]registers the peoples:
"This *one* was born there." Selah
7 Both the singers and the players on instruments *say,*
"All my springs *are* in you."

PSALM 88
A Prayer for Help in Despondency

A Song. A Psalm of the sons of Korah. To the Chief Musician. Set to "Mahalath Leannoth." A [1]Contemplation of [a]Heman the Ezrahite.

O LORD, [b]God of my salvation,
I have cried out day and night before You.
2 Let my prayer come before You;
[2]Incline Your ear to my cry.

3 For my soul is full of troubles,
And my life [c]draws near to the grave.
4 I am counted with those who [d]go[3] down to the pit;
[e]I am like a man *who has* no strength,
5 [4]Adrift among the dead,
Like the slain who lie in the grave,
Whom You remember no more,
And who are cut off from Your hand.

6 You have laid me in the lowest pit,
In darkness, in the depths.
7 Your wrath lies heavy upon me,
And You have afflicted *me* with all [f]Your waves. Selah
8 [g]You have [5]put away my acquaintances far from me;
You have made me an abomination to them;
[h]*I am* shut up, and I cannot get out;
9 My eye wastes away because of affliction.

[i]LORD, I have called daily upon You;
I have stretched out my hands to You.
10 Will You work wonders for the dead?
Shall [6]the dead arise *and* praise You? Selah
11 Shall Your lovingkindness be declared in the grave?
Or Your faithfulness in the place of destruction?
12 Shall Your wonders be known in the dark?
And Your righteousness in the land of forgetfulness?

13 But to You I have cried out, O LORD,
And in the morning my prayer comes before You.
14 LORD, why do You cast off my soul?
Why do You hide Your face from me?
15 I *have been* afflicted and ready to die from *my* youth;
I suffer Your terrors;
I am distraught.
16 Your fierce wrath has gone over me;
Your terrors have [7]cut me off.
17 They came around me all day long like water;
They engulfed me altogether.
18 [j]Loved one and friend You have put far from me,
And my acquaintances into darkness.

6 [c]Is. 4:3

PSALM 88

title [a]1 Kin. 4:31; 1 Chr. 2:6 [1]Heb. *Maschil*
1 [b]Ps. 27:9; [Luke 18:7]
2 [2]Listen to
3 [c]Ps. 107:18
4 [d][Ps. 28:1] [e]Ps. 31:12 [3]Die
5 [4]Lit. *Free*
7 [f]Ps. 42:7
8 [g]Job 19:13, 19; Ps. 31:11; 142:4 [h]Lam. 3:7 [5]*taken away my friends*
9 [i]Ps. 86:3
10 [6]*shades, ghosts*
16 [7]*destroyed me*
18 [j]Job 19:13; Ps. 31:11; 38:11

87:7 "All my springs *are* in you." "Springs" is a metaphor for the source of joyful blessings. Eternal salvation, including the death and resurrection of Christ, is rooted in Jerusalem. The prophets also tell of a literal fountain flowing from the temple in Jerusalem which will water the surrounding land (cf. Joel 3:18; Ezek. 47:1-12).

88:1-18 This lament is unusual in that it does not end on a happy note. The psalmist has been ill or injured since the days of his youth (v. 15) and bemoans God's failure to hear his prayer for good health. He assumes that God is angry with him, but like Job, he knows of no cause for that anger. But though he does not understand God's ways, the psalmist does turn to God, thus indicating an underlying trust.

I. Complaints Against God's Action (88:1-9)
II. Challenges to God's Wisdom (88:10-12)
III. Charges Against God's Conduct (88:13-18)

88:Title. sons of Korah. *See note on Ps. 84:Title.* **"Mahalath Leannoth."** "Mahalath" is either the name of a tune or an instrument, possibly a reed pipe which was played on sad occasions. "Leannoth" may mean "to afflict" and describe the despair which permeates this psalm. **Contemplation.** *See note on Ps. 32:Title.* **Heman the Ezrahite.** Heman was a musician from the family of the Kohathites, who founded the Korahite choir (cf. 1 Chr. 6:33; 2 Chr. 5:12; 35:15). He may be the same person who was one of the wise men during Solomon's reign (1 Kin. 4:31). "Ezrahite" may mean "native born," or may be the name of a family clan (cf. 1 Chr. 2:6).

88:4 go down to the pit. "Pit" is one of several references to the grave in this psalm (cf. sheol, v. 3; the dead, vv. 5,10; the grave, vv. 5,11; place of destruction, v. 11).

88:5 Adrift among the dead. Expresses the idea that death cuts off all ties to friends and family as well as to God.

88:7 all Your waves. Like the waves rolling onto the seashore, so God has directed trouble after trouble on the psalmist (cf. v. 17).

88:8 put away my acquaintances. The psalmist claims that the Lord has turned his friends against him. Some see this as a quarantine experience, as from leprosy (cf. v. 18; also Job 19:13-20).

88:9 eye wastes away. This could be a description of the psalmist's tears, used as a figure for his entire collapse under this distress.

88:10 wonders for the dead. The psalmist reminds God, through a series of rhetorical questions, that the dead cannot testify to God's goodness.

88:14 hide Your face. That is, not answer prayer.

88:15 die from *my* youth. The psalmist has had some serious illness or injury from the time of his youth.

88:18 Loved one…friend…acquaintances. *See note on verse 8.*

PSALM 89

Remembering the Covenant with David, and Sorrow for Lost Blessings

A [1]Contemplation of [a]Ethan the Ezrahite.

I will sing of the mercies of the LORD forever;
With my mouth will I make known
Your faithfulness to all generations.
2 For I have said, "Mercy shall be built up forever;
[b]Your faithfulness You shall establish in the very heavens."

3 "I[c] have made a covenant with My chosen,
I have [d]sworn to My servant David:
4 'Your seed I will establish forever,
And build up your throne [e]to all generations.' " Selah

5 And [f]the heavens will praise Your wonders, O LORD;
Your faithfulness also in the assembly of the saints.
6 [g]For who in the heavens can be compared to the LORD?
Who among the sons of the mighty can be likened to the LORD?
7 [h]God is greatly to be feared in the assembly of the saints,
And to be held in reverence by all *those* around Him.
8 O LORD God of hosts,
Who *is* mighty like You, O LORD?
Your faithfulness also surrounds You.
9 [i]You rule the raging of the sea;
When its waves rise, You still them.
10 [j]You have broken [2]Rahab in pieces, as one who is slain;
You have scattered Your enemies with Your mighty arm.

11 [k]The heavens *are* Yours, the earth also *is* Yours;
The world and all its fullness, You have founded them.
12 The north and the south, You have created them;
[l]Tabor and [m]Hermon rejoice in Your name.
13 You have a mighty arm;
Strong is Your hand, *and* high is Your right hand.
14 Righteousness and justice *are* the foundation of Your throne;
Mercy and truth go before Your face.
15 Blessed *are* the people who know the [n]joyful sound!
They walk, O LORD, in the light of Your countenance.
16 In Your name they rejoice all day long,
And in Your righteousness they are exalted.
17 For You *are* the glory of their strength,
And in Your favor our [3]horn is [o]exalted.
18 For our shield *belongs* to the LORD,
And our king to the Holy One of Israel.

PSALM 89
title [a] 1 Kin. 4:31 [1] Heb. *Maschil*
2 [b] [Ps. 119:89, 90]
3 [c] 1 Kin. 8:16 [d] 2 Sam. 7:11; 1 Chr. 17:10-12
4 [e] [2 Sam. 7:13; Is. 9:7; Luke 1:33]
5 [f] [Ps. 19:1]
6 [g] Ps. 86:8; 113:5
7 [h] Ps. 76:7, 11
9 [i] Ps. 65:7; 93:3, 4; 107:29
10 [j] Ex. 14:26-28; Ps. 87:4; Is. 30:7; 51:9 [2] Egypt
11 [k] [Gen. 1:1; 1 Chr. 29:11]
12 [l] Josh. 19:22; Judg. 4:6; Jer. 46:18 [m] Deut. 3:8; Josh. 11:17; 12:1; Song 4:8
15 [n] Lev. 23:24; Num. 10:10; Ps. 98:6
17 [o] Ps. 75:10; 92:10; 132:17 [3] Strength

89:1-52 This psalm describes the author's attempt to reconcile the seeming contradictions between his theology and the reality of his nation's conditions. Through the first 37 verses, he rehearses what he knows to be theologically accurate: God has sovereignly chosen Israel to be His nation, and David's descendants to rule. The last third of the psalm reflects the psalmist's chagrin that the nation had been ravaged and the Davidic monarchy had apparently come to a disgraceful end. To his credit, the psalmist refuses to explain away his theology, but instead keeps the tension, hopefully to be resolved at a later time with the promised reestablishment of an earthly kingdom under one of David's descendants (cf. Pss. 110, 132).

- I. God's Manifest Faithfulness to the Davidic Covenant (89:1-37)
  - A. God's Covenant Love (89:1-4)
  - B. God's Praiseworthiness (89:5-18)
  - C. God's Covenant with David (89:19-37)
- II. God's Apparent Neglect of the Davidic Covenant (89:38-52)
  - A. The Psalmist's Lament (89:38-45)
  - B. The Psalmist's Consternation (89:46-51)
  - C. The Doxology (89:52)

89:Title. Ethan the Ezrahite. Possibly the Levitical singer mentioned in 1 Chr. 6:42 and 15:17,19 *(see note on Ps. 88:Title.)*.

89:1 mercies. *See note on Ps. 85:7* (cf. vv. 2,14,24,28,33,49).

89:2 You shall establish…heavens. The psalmist exults that the Lord Himself will guarantee the eternality of the Davidic dynasty (cf. 2 Sam. 23:5).

89:3 covenant with My chosen. The Davidic Covenant, culminating in Messiah's reign, was established in 2 Sam. 7 (cf. 1 Kin. 8:23; 1 Chr. 17; 2 Chr. 21:7; Pss. 110,132). The covenant was in the form of a royal grant covenant as God, the Great King, chose David as His servant king. In this type of covenant, the person with whom the Lord established the covenant could violate the terms of the covenant and the Lord would still be obligated to maintain the covenant.

89:4 seed…forever…throne. The covenant with David was extended to his descendants. The throne promise guaranteed that the rightful heir to the throne would always be a descendant of David (cf. vv. 29,36; see also 2 Sam. 7:13,16,18; Luke 1:31-33). The genealogies of Jesus qualify Him for the throne (cf. Matt. 1:1-17; Luke 3:23-38).

89:5 faithfulness. The word suggests constant and habitual actions, meaning here that God was reliable. For God to violate this consistency of actions would be to violate His very nature (cf. vv. 1,2,8,24,33,49).

89:6 sons of the mighty. Lit. "sons of God," i.e., angels.

89:7 assembly of the saints. Lit. "holy ones," which pictures a gathering of the angels around their sovereign Lord.

89:10 Rahab. A figurative term for Egypt. *See note on Ps. 87:4.*

89:12 Tabor and Hermon. Mountains in Israel pictured joining in praise with the rest of creation.

89:15 the joyful sound. Refers to a cheer, a shout of joyful homage to God (cf. Pss. 33:3; 47:5; 95:1; 98:4; 100:1. *See note on Ps. 66:1*).

89:17 our horn is exalted. *See note on Ps. 75:4* (cf. v. 24).

89:18 shield *belongs* to the LORD. The "shield" was a metaphor for the king (*see note on Ps. 84:9*).

19 Then You spoke in a vision to Your
[4]holy one,
And said: "I have given help to *one*
who is mighty;
I have exalted one [p]chosen from the
people.
20 [q]I have found My servant David;
With My holy oil I have anointed him,
21 [r]With whom My hand shall be
established;
Also My arm shall strengthen him.
22 The enemy shall not [5]outwit him,
Nor the son of wickedness afflict him.
23 I will beat down his foes before his
face,
And plague those who hate him.

24 "But My faithfulness and My mercy
shall be with him,
And in My name his horn shall be
exalted.
25 Also I will [s]set his hand over the sea,
And his right hand over the rivers.
26 He shall cry to Me, 'You *are* [t]my
Father,
My God, and [u]the rock of my
salvation.'
27 Also I will make him [v]*My* firstborn,
[w]The highest of the kings of the earth.
28 [x]My mercy I will keep for him forever,
And My covenant shall stand firm
with him.
29 His seed also I will make *to endure*
forever,
[y]And his throne [z]as the days of
heaven.

30 "If[a] his sons [b]forsake My law
And do not walk in My judgments,
31 If they [6]break My statutes
And do not keep My commandments,
32 Then I will punish their transgression
with the rod,
And their iniquity with stripes.
33 [c]Nevertheless My lovingkindness I will
not [7]utterly take from him,
Nor [8]allow My faithfulness to fail.
34 My covenant I will not break,
Nor [d]alter the word that has gone out
of My lips.
35 Once I have sworn [e]by My holiness;
I will not lie to David:
36 [f]His seed shall endure forever,
And his throne [g]as the sun before Me;
37 It shall be established forever like the
moon,
Even *like* the faithful witness in the
sky." Selah

38 But You have [h]cast off and
[i]abhorred,[9]
You have been furious with Your
[1]anointed.
39 You have renounced the covenant of
Your servant;
[j]You have [2]profaned his crown *by*
casting it to the ground.
40 You have broken down all his hedges;
You have brought his [3]strongholds to
ruin.
41 All who pass by the way [k]plunder
him;
He is a reproach to his neighbors.
42 You have exalted the right hand of his
adversaries;
You have made all his enemies rejoice.
43 You have also turned back the edge of
his sword,
And have not sustained him in the
battle.

19 [p] 1 Kin. 11:34 [4] So with many Heb. mss.; MT, LXX, Tg., Vg. *holy ones* **20** [q] 1 Sam. 13:14; 16:1-12; Acts 13:22 **21** [r] Ps. 80:17 **22** [5] Or *exact usury from him* **25** [s] Ps. 72:8 **26** [t] 2 Sam. 7:14; [1 Chr. 22:10]; Jer. 3:19 [u] 2 Sam. 22:47 **27** [v] Ex. 4:22; Ps. 2:7; Jer. 31:9; [Col. 1:15, 18] [w] Num. 24:7; [Ps. 72:11]; Rev. 19:16 **28** [x] Is. 55:3 **29** [y] [1 Kin. 2:4; Is. 9:7]; Jer. 33:17 [z] Deut. 11:21 **30** [a] [2 Sam. 7:14] [b] Ps. 119:53 **31** [6] *profane*

33 [c] 2 Sam. 7:14, 15 [7] Lit. *break off* [8] Lit. *deal falsely with My faithfulness* **34** [d] [Num. 23:19]; Jer. 33:20-22 **35** [e] [1 Sam. 15:29]; Amos 4:2; [Titus 1:2] **36** [f] [Luke 1:33] [g] Ps. 72:17 **38** [h] [1 Chr. 28:9] [i] Deut. 32:19 [9] *rejected* [1] Commissioned one, Heb. *messiah* **39** [j] Ps. 74:7; Lam. 5:16 [2] *defiled* **40** [3] *fortresses* **41** [k] Ps. 80:12

89:19 Your holy one. The "holy one" was the prophet, Nathan, whom the Lord used to tell David about His covenant with David (2 Sam. 7:4ff.).

89:25 hand…sea…rivers. A reference to the promise of Ex. 23:31 that the Lord would give Israel the land between the Red Sea and the Euphrates River.

89:27 *My* firstborn. The firstborn child was given a place of special honor and a double portion of the inheritance (Gen. 27; 2 Kin. 2:9). However, in a royal grant covenant, a chosen person could be elevated to the level of firstborn sonship and thus have title to a perpetual gift involving dynastic succession (cf. Ps. 2:7). Though not actually the first, Israel was considered the firstborn among nations (Ex. 4:22); Ephraim the younger was treated as the firstborn (Gen. 48:13-20); and David was the firstborn among kings. In this latter sense of prominent favor, Christ can be called the firstborn over all creation (Col. 1:15), in that He is given the preeminence over all created beings.

89:32 rod…stripes. The rod was an instrument for inflicting wounds, and the stripes were marks left by such a flogging. God's warning reflects His knowledge of the evident potential for disobedience among the descendants of David (cf. 2 Sam. 7:14). In the lifetime of David's grandsons, for example, the kingdom was split with the 10 northern tribes leaving the rulership of the Davidic line (cf. Jer. 31:31 and Ezek. 37:16,17 for the future reunification of the 12 tribes).

89:33 My lovingkindness. Though the Lord might have to severely discipline David's descendants, He would never remove His covenant from this family (cf. 2 Sam. 7:15). Thus the covenant could be conditional in any one or more generations and yet be unconditional in its final outcome (cf. Ezek. 37:24-28).

89:37 faithful witness in the sky. God's covenant with David regarding his descendants was as certain as the establishment of the sun (v. 36) and the moon in the heavens (cf. Jer. 33:14-26). The promise involved a kingdom "in the earth" (Jer. 33:15).

89:39 renounced the covenant. The Heb. word behind "renounced" is rare, and it may better be translated "disdained." It seemed to the psalmist that the condition of Israel indicated that God was neglecting His covenant with David (cf. Ezek. 37:1-14). **profaned his crown.** This depicts a serious insult to the dynasty because it is of divine origin.

89:40-45 The ruin is depicted in several images: left with broken hedges, thus defenseless; a stronghold whose ruins invite invaders; a weakling plundered by all his enemies; a soldier with a useless sword; and a youth prematurely old.

44 You have made his [4]glory cease,
And cast his throne down to the ground.
45 The days of his youth You have shortened;
You have covered him with shame. Selah

46 How long, LORD?
Will You hide Yourself forever?
Will Your wrath burn like fire?
47 Remember how short my time [l]is;
For what [m]futility have You created all the children of men?
48 What man can live and not [5]see [n]death?
Can he deliver his life from the power of [6]the grave? Selah

49 Lord, where *are* Your former lovingkindnesses,
Which You [o]swore to David [p]in Your truth?
50 Remember, Lord, the reproach of Your servants—
[q]*How* I bear in my bosom *the reproach of* all the many peoples,
51 [r]With which Your enemies have reproached, O LORD,
With which they have reproached the footsteps of Your [7]anointed.

52 [s]Blessed *be* the LORD forevermore!
Amen and Amen.

44 [4] *splendor* or *brightness*
47 [l] Ps. 90:9 [m] Ps. 62:9
48 [n] [Eccl. 3:19] [5] *experience death* [6] Or *Sheol*
49 [o] [2 Sam. 7:15]; Jer. 30:9; Ezek. 34:23 [p] Ps. 54:5
50 [q] Ps. 69:9, 19
51 [r] Ps. 74:10, 18, 22 [7] Commissioned one, Heb. *messiah*
52 [s] Ps. 41:13

Book Four: Psalms 90–106

PSALM 90

The Eternity of God, and Man's Frailty

A Prayer [a]of Moses the man of God.

LORD, [b]You have been our [1]dwelling place in all generations.
2 [c]Before the mountains were brought forth,
Or ever You [2]had formed the earth and the world,
Even from everlasting to everlasting, You *are* God.

3 You turn man to destruction,
And say, [d]"Return, O children of men."
4 [e]For a thousand years in Your sight
Are like yesterday when it is past,
And *like* a watch in the night.
5 You carry them away *like* a flood;
[f]*They are* like a sleep.
In the morning [g]they are like grass *which* grows up:
6 In the morning it flourishes and grows up;
In the evening it is cut down and withers.

7 For we have been consumed by Your anger,
And by Your wrath we are terrified.

PSALM 90

title [a] Deut. 33:1
1 [b] [Deut. 33:27; Ezek. 11:16] [1] LXX, Tg., Vg. *refuge*
2 [c] Job 15:7; [Prov. 8:25, 26] [2] Lit. *gave birth to*
3 [d] Gen. 3:19; Job 34:14, 15
4 [e] 2 Pet. 3:8
5 [f] Ps. 73:20 [g] Is. 40:6

89:45 days of his youth...shortened. This is a figure for the relative brevity of the Davidic dynasty. The dynasty was cut off in its youth.

89:46 hide Yourself forever. By God's seeming refusal to answer prayer and restore the Davidic kingship, it seemed as though God was hiding Himself. Of course, the discipline of disobedient kings had been foretold (v. 32). According to the prophets, God would eventually restore Israel and the Davidic throne in an earthly kingdom (cf. Hos. 3:4,5). Never in the OT is there a sense that this Davidic promise would be fulfilled by Christ with a spiritual and heavenly reign.

89:47. The prosperity of the Davidic kingdom is linked to the welfare of all people (cf. Ps. 72:17; Is. 9:7; 11:1-10). If the kingdom fails, who can survive? (v. 48).

89:49-51. Here is a final plea for God to come to the help of His people, so as to avoid reproach (cf. Is. 37:17-35).

89:52 Blessed *be* the LORD. This blessing, indicating returning confidence, closes not only Ps. 89, but all of Book III (Pss. 73–89) of the Psalms.

90:1-17 The thrust of this magnificent prayer is to ask God to have mercy on frail human beings living in a sin-cursed universe. Moses begins the psalm with a reflection on God's eternality, then expresses his somber thoughts about the sorrows and brevity of life in their relationship to God's anger, and concludes with a plea that God would enable his people to live a significant life. The psalm seems to have been composed as the older generation of Israelites who had left Egypt were dying off in the wilderness (Num. 14).

I. The Praise of God's Eternality (90:1,2)
II. The Perception of Man's Frailty (90:3-12)
III. The Plea for God's Mercy (90:13-17)

90:Title. Moses the man of God. Moses the prophet (Deut. 18:15-22) was unique in that the Lord knew him "face to face" (Deut. 34:10-12). "Man of God" (Deut. 33:1) is a technical term used over 70 times in the OT, always referring to one who spoke for God. It is used of Timothy in the NT (1 Tim. 6:11; 2 Tim. 3:17).

90:1 our dwelling place. God is our sanctuary for protection, sustenance, and stability (cf. Deut. 33:27; Ps. 91:9).

90:2 from everlasting to everlasting. God's nature is without beginning or end, free from all succession of time, and contains in itself the cause of time (cf. Ps. 102:27; Is. 41:4; 1 Cor. 2:7; Eph. 1:4; 1 Tim. 6:16; Rev. 1:8).

90:3 You turn man to destruction. The unusual word for destruction has the idea of crushed matter. Though different from the "dust" of Gen. 3:15, this phrase is no doubt a reference to that passage. Humanity lives under a sovereign decree of death and cannot escape it.

90:4 a watch in the night. A "watch" was a 4 hour period of time (cf. Ex. 14:24; Lam. 2:19; 2 Pet. 3:8).

90:5 *like* a flood. Humankind is snatched from the earth as though it were being swept away by floodwaters. **like a sleep.** Humanity lives its existence as though asleep or in a coma. People are insensitive to the brevity of life and the reality of God's wrath.

90:7 consumed by Your anger. The physical bodies of the human race wear out by the effects of God's judgment on sin in the universe (cf. Deut. 4:25-28; 11:16,17). Death is by sin (Rom. 5:12).

8 [h]You have set our iniquities before
You,
Our [i]secret *sins* in the light of Your
countenance.
9 For all our days have passed away in
Your wrath;
We finish our years like a sigh.
10 The days of our lives *are* seventy
years;
And if by reason of strength *they are*
eighty years,
Yet their boast *is* only labor and
sorrow;
For it is soon cut off, and we fly away.
11 Who knows the power of Your anger?
For as the fear of You, *so is* Your
wrath.
12 [j]So teach *us* to number our days,
That we may gain a heart of wisdom.

13 Return, O LORD!
How long?
And [k]have compassion on Your
servants.
14 Oh, satisfy us early with Your mercy,
[l]That we may rejoice and be glad all
our days!
15 Make us glad according to the days *in
which* You have afflicted us,
The years *in which* we have seen evil.
16 Let [m]Your work appear to Your
servants,
And Your glory to their children.
17 [n]And let the beauty of the LORD our
God be upon us,
And [o]establish the work of our hands
for us;
Yes, establish the work of our hands.

PSALM 91

Safety of Abiding in the Presence of God

He [a]who dwells in the secret place of
the Most High
Shall abide [b]under the shadow of the
Almighty.
2 [c]I will say of the LORD, "*He is* my
refuge and my fortress;
My God, in Him I will trust."

3 Surely [d]He shall deliver you from the
snare of the [1]fowler
And from the perilous pestilence.
4 [e]He shall cover you with His feathers,
And under His wings you shall take
refuge;
His truth *shall be your* shield and
[2]buckler.
5 [f]You shall not be afraid of the terror by
night,
Nor of the arrow *that* flies by day,
6 *Nor* of the pestilence *that* walks in
darkness,
Nor of the destruction *that* lays waste
at noonday.

7 A thousand may fall at your side,
And ten thousand at your right hand;
But it shall not come near you.
8 Only [g]with your eyes shall you look,

8 [h]Ps. 50:21; [Jer. 16:17] [i]Ps. 19:12; [Eccl. 12:14]
12 [j]Deut. 32:29; Ps. 39:4
13 [k]Ex. 32:12; Deut. 32:36
14 [l]Ps. 85:6
16 [m][Deut. 32:4]; Hab. 3:2
17 [n]Ps. 27:4 [o]Is. 26:12

PSALM 91
1 [a]Ps. 27:5; 31:20; 32:7 [b]Ps. 17:8; Is. 25:4; 32:2
2 [c]Ps. 142:5
3 [d]Ps. 124:7; Prov. 6:5 [1]One who catches birds in a trap or snare
4 [e]Ps. 17:8 [2]A small shield
5 [f][Job 5:19; Ps. 112:7; Is. 43:2]
8 [g]Ps. 37:34; Mal. 1:5

90:8 the light of Your countenance. All sin is in clear view to the "face" of God.

90:9 like a sigh. After struggling through his life of afflictions and troubles, a man's life ends with a moan of woe and weariness.

90:10 seventy years...eighty years. Though Moses lived to be 120 years old, and "His eyes were not dim nor his natural vigor diminished" (Deut. 34:7), human life was usually more brief and lived under the anger of God. Because of this certain and speedy end, life is sad.

90:11 as the fear of You...Your wrath. Instead of explaining away life's curses, a wise person will recognize God's wrath towards sin as the ultimate cause of all afflictions and consequently learn to fear God.

90:12 number our days. Evaluate the use of time in light of the brevity of life. **heart of wisdom.** Wisdom repudiates autonomy and focuses on the Lord's sovereignty and revelation.

90:14 Your mercy. *See note on Ps. 85:7.*

90:15 glad...afflicted us. A prayer that one's days of joy would equal his days of distress.

90:17 the beauty of the LORD. The Lord's beauty implies His delight, approval, and favor. **establish the work of our hands.** By God's mercy and grace, one's life can have value, significance, and meaning (cf. 1 Cor. 15:58).

91:1-16 This psalm describes God's ongoing sovereign protection of His people from the ever-present dangers and terrors which surround humanity. The original setting may be that of an army about to go to battle. Most of the terrors mentioned in this psalm are left undefined, no doubt intentionally, so that no kind of danger is omitted from application. Believers in every age can read this psalm to learn that nothing can harm a child of God unless the Lord permits it. However, in light of the many references in the Psalms to the future messianic kingdom (cf. especially Pss. 96–100), this psalm must be read as being literally fulfilled then.

I. The Lord's Protection (91:1-13)
   A. The Confidence (91:1,2)
   B. The Dangers (91:3-6)
   C. The Examples (91:7-13)
II. The Lord's Pledge (91:14-16)

91:1 secret place of the Most High. An intimate place of divine protection. The use of "Most High" for God emphasizes that no threat can ever overpower Him. **shadow of the Almighty.** In a land where the sun can be oppressive and dangerous, a "shadow" was understood as a metaphor for care and protection.

91:3 snare of the fowler. A fowler trapped birds. Here the metaphor represents any plots against the believer intended to endanger his life. **perilous pestilence.** The reference here and in v. 6 is specifically to dreaded diseases, plagues, and epidemics (cf. Jer. 14:12; Ezek. 5:12; 14:19).

91:4 under His wings. Pictures the protection of a parent bird (*see note on Ps. 57:1*).

91:8 Only with your eyes. The righteous are so safe in disaster all around them, that they are only spectators.

And see the reward of the wicked.

9 Because you have made the LORD,
who is [h]my refuge,
Even the Most High, [i]your dwelling
place,
10 [j]No evil shall befall you,
Nor shall any plague come near your
dwelling;
11 [k]For He shall give His angels charge
over you,
To keep you in all your ways.
12 In *their* hands they shall [3]bear you up,
[l]Lest you [4]dash your foot against a
stone.
13 You shall tread upon the lion and the
cobra,
The young lion and the serpent you
shall trample underfoot.

14 "Because he has set his love upon Me,
therefore I will deliver him;
I will [5]set him on high, because he
has [m]known My name.
15 He shall [n]call upon Me, and I will
answer him;
I *will be* [o]with him in trouble;
I will deliver him and honor him.
16 With [6]long life I will satisfy him,
And show him My salvation."

9 [h] Ps. 91:2 [i] Ps. 90:1
10 [j] [Prov. 12:21]
11 [k] Ps. 34:7; Matt. 4:6; Luke 4:10; [Heb. 1:14]
12 [l] Matt. 4:6; Luke 4:11 [3] *lift* [4] *strike*
14 [m] [Ps. 9:10] [5] *exalt him*
15 [n] Job 12:4; Ps. 50:15 [o] Is. 43:2
16 [6] Lit. *length of days*

PSALM 92

Praise to the LORD for His Love and Faithfulness

A Psalm. A Song for the Sabbath day.

It *is* [a]good to give thanks to the LORD,
And to sing praises to Your name,
O Most High;
2 To [b]declare Your lovingkindness in
the morning,
And Your faithfulness every night,
3 [c]On an instrument of ten strings,
On the lute,
And on the harp,
With harmonious sound.
4 For You, LORD, have made me glad
through Your work;
I will triumph in the works of Your
hands.

5 [d]O LORD, how great are Your works!
[e]Your thoughts are very deep.
6 [f]A senseless man does not know,
Nor does a fool understand this.
7 When [g]the wicked [1]spring up like
grass,
And when all the workers of iniquity
flourish,
It is that they may be destroyed
forever.

8 [h]But You, LORD, *are* on high
forevermore.
9 For behold, Your enemies, O LORD,
For behold, Your enemies shall perish;
All the workers of iniquity shall [i]be
scattered.

10 But [j]my [2]horn You have exalted like a
wild ox;
I have been [k]anointed with fresh oil.
11 [l]My eye also has seen *my desire* on my
enemies;
My ears hear *my desire* on the wicked
Who rise up against me.

12 [m]The righteous shall flourish like a
palm tree,
He shall grow like a cedar in Lebanon.
13 Those who are planted in the house of
the LORD

PSALM 92
1 [a] Ps. 147:1
2 [b] Ps. 89:1
3 [c] 1 Chr. 23:5
5 [d] Ps. 40:5; [Rev. 15:3] [e] Ps. 139:17, 18; [Is. 28:29; Rom. 11:33, 34]
6 [f] Ps. 73:22
7 [g] Job 12:6; Ps. 37:1, 2; Jer. 12:1, 2; [Mal. 3:15] [1] *sprout*
8 [h] [Ps. 83:18]
9 [i] Ps. 68:1
10 [j] Ps. 89:17 [k] Ps. 23:5 [2] Strength
11 [l] Ps. 54:7
12 [m] Num. 24:6; Ps. 52:8; Jer. 17:8; Hos. 14:5, 6

91:11,12 This promise of angelic protection was misquoted by Satan in his temptation of the Messiah (*see Matt. 4:6*).

91:13 tread...lion and the cobra. In general, a metaphor for God's protection from all deadly attacks (*see notes on Ps. 58:4ff.*).

91:14 set his love upon Me. God Himself is the speaker in this section (vv. 14–16) and He describes the blessing He gives to those who know and love Him. The word for "love" means a "deep longing" for God, or a "clinging" to God.

91:16 long life. Long life was a specific promise to the OT saint for obedience to the law (e.g., Ex. 20:12; Prov. 3:2). The prophets also promise it to God's people in the future messianic kingdom (cf. Is. 65:17-23).

92:1-15 This psalm expresses the exuberance of the psalmist as he recognizes that God is merciful in salvation, great in His works of creation, just in His dealings with the wicked, and faithful in prospering His children.

I. An Expression of Theistic Optimism (92:1-5)
II. An Observation concerning Righteous Sovereignty (92:6-9)
III. A Testimony to God's Goodness (92:10-15)

92:Title. for the Sabbath Day. In the post-Exilic community, some psalms were sung throughout the week in connection with the morning and evening sacrifice; others were designated especially for Sabbath worship.

92:2 lovingkindness...faithfulness. These attributes are constant themes of the psalms (*see notes on Pss. 85:7; 89:5;* see also Luke 10:2).

92:3 lute. *See note on Ps. 81:2.*

92:10 my horn. *See note on Ps. 75:4.* **anointed with fresh oil.** This figure is based on a practice of making an animal's horns gleam by rubbing oil on them. Thus God, in effect, had invigorated the psalmist (cf. Pss. 23:5; 133:2).

92:11 *my desire* on my enemies. God gratified the psalmist's desire by bringing his enemies to ruin.

92:12 flourish like a palm tree. The palm tree and the cedar symbolized permanence and strength (cf. v. 14). They are in contrast to the transience of the wicked, who are pictured as temporary as grass (v. 7). *See notes on Ps. 1.*

92:13 planted in the house of the LORD. A tree planted in the courtyard of the temple symbolized the thriving conditions of those who maintain a close relationship with the Lord (*see note on Ps. 52:8*).

Shall flourish in the courts of our
God.
14 They shall still bear fruit in old age;
They shall be [3]fresh and [4]flourishing,
15 To declare that the LORD is upright;
[n]*He is* my rock, and [o]*there is* no
unrighteousness in Him.

PSALM 93

The Eternal Reign of the LORD

The [a]LORD reigns, He is clothed with
majesty;
The LORD is clothed,
[b]He has girded Himself with strength.
Surely the world is established, so
that it cannot be [1]moved.
2 [c]Your throne *is* established from of old;
You *are* from everlasting.

3 The floods have [2]lifted up, O LORD,
The floods have lifted up their voice;
The floods lift up their waves.
4 [d]The LORD on high *is* mightier
Than the noise of many waters,
Than the mighty waves of the sea.

5 Your testimonies are very sure;
Holiness adorns Your house,
O LORD, [3]forever.

PSALM 94

God the Refuge of the Righteous

O LORD God, [a]to whom vengeance
belongs—
O God, to whom vengeance belongs,
shine forth!
2 Rise up, O [b]Judge of the earth;
[1]Render punishment to the proud.
3 LORD, [c]how long will the wicked,
How long will the wicked triumph?

4 They [d]utter speech, *and* speak insolent
things;
All the workers of iniquity boast in
themselves.
5 They break in pieces Your people,
O LORD,
And afflict Your heritage.
6 They slay the widow and the
stranger,
And murder the fatherless.
7 [e]Yet they say, "The LORD does not see,
Nor does the God of Jacob
[2]understand."

8 Understand, you senseless among the
people;
And *you* fools, when will you be
wise?
9 [f]He who planted the ear, shall He not
hear?
He who formed the eye, shall He not
see?
10 He who [3]instructs the [4]nations, shall
He not correct,
He who teaches man knowledge?
11 The LORD [g]knows the thoughts of
man,
That they *are* futile.

12 Blessed *is* the man whom You
[h]instruct, O LORD,
And teach out of Your law,
13 That You may give him [5]rest from the
days of adversity,
Until the pit is dug for the wicked.
14 For the LORD will not [6]cast off His
people,

14 [3] Full of oil or sap, lit. *fat* [4] *green*
15 [n] [Deut. 32:4] [o] [Rom. 9:14]

PSALM 93

1 [a] Ps. 96:10 [b] Ps. 65:6 [1] *shaken*
2 [c] Ps. 45:6; [Lam. 5:19]
3 [2] *raised up*
4 [d] Ps. 65:7
5 [3] Lit. *for length of days*

PSALM 94

1 [a] Deut. 32:35; [Is. 35:4; Nah. 1:2; Rom. 12:19]
2 [b] [Gen. 18:25] [1] *Repay with*
3 [c] [Job 20:5]
4 [d] Ps. 31:18; Jude 15
7 [e] Job 22:13; Ps. 10:11 [2] *pay attention*
9 [f] [Ex. 4:11; Prov. 20:12]
10 [3] *disciplines* [4] *Gentiles*
11 [g] Job 11:11; 1 Cor. 3:20
12 [h] [Deut. 8:5; Job 5:17; Ps. 119:71; Prov. 3:11, 12; Heb. 12:5, 6]
13 [5] *relief*
14 [6] *abandon*

93:1-5 Psalms 93 and 95–100 (cf. Ps. 47) are dedicated to celebrating God's sovereign kingship over the world. Psalm 93 glorifies God's eternal, universal kingdom which is providentially administered through His Son (Col. 1:17). Nothing is more powerful than the Lord; nothing is more steadfast than His reign, nothing is more sure than His revelation.

I. The Lord's Universal Kingdom (93:1-4)
A. Over the Earth (93:1,2)
B. Over the Sea (93:3,4)
II. The Lord's Authoritative Revelation (93:5)

93:1 The LORD reigns. An exclamation of the Lord's universal reign over the earth from the time of creation (v. 2; cf. Pss. 103:19; 145:13) and forever.

93:3,4 The sea with all its power is nothing in comparison to the power of God. The doubling and tripling of expressions throughout this psalm (vv. 1,3,4) are poetic means of generating literary energy and emphasis.

93:5 testimonies are very sure. As God's rule over the earth is stable, so His revelation given through Scripture is trustworthy (cf. Ps. 19:7).

94:1-23 The psalmist's urgent concern in this psalm is that the righteous are being oppressed, the wicked are prospering, and it does not look as though God cares. The psalmist thus pleads with God to punish the wicked (cf. Pss. 73,82).

I. Address to God (94:1,2)
II. Arrogance of the Wicked (94:3-7)
III. Admonition to the Foolish (94:8-11)
IV. Assurance for the Righteous (94:12-15)
V. Advocacy from God (94:16-23)

94:1 to whom vengeance belongs. Vengeance from God is not in the sense of uncontrolled vindictiveness, but in the sense of just retribution by the eternal Judge for trespasses against His law. **shine forth.** Make an appearance; he may even be asking for a theophany (cf. Pss. 50:2; 80:1).

94:7 The LORD does not see. An autonomous and atheistic attitude (*see note on Ps. 59:7*).

94:11 thoughts of man…*are* futile. The wicked designs of the human mind amount to nothing (cf. Ps. 92:5; 1 Cor. 3:20).

94:12 Blessed. To be blessed was to be wise and prosperous in life, as a result of the instruction of God (cf. Ps. 84:5,12).

94:14 will not cast off His people. God has a permanent commitment to His people, Israel, established through a covenant based

Nor will He forsake His inheritance.
15 But judgment will return to righteousness,
And all the upright in heart will follow it.

16 Who will rise up for me against the evildoers?
Who will stand up for me against the workers of iniquity?
17 Unless the LORD *had been* my help,
My soul would soon have settled in silence.
18 If I say, "My foot slips,"
Your mercy, O LORD, will hold me up.
19 In the multitude of my anxieties within me,
Your comforts delight my soul.

20 Shall [i]the throne of iniquity, which devises evil by law,
Have fellowship with You?
21 They gather together against the life of the righteous,
And condemn [j]innocent blood.
22 But the LORD has been my defense,
And my God the rock of my refuge.
23 He has brought on them their own iniquity,
And shall [7]cut them off in their own wickedness;
The LORD our God shall cut them off.

20 [i] Amos 6:3
21 [j] [Ex. 23:7]; Ps. 106:38; [Prov. 17:15]; Matt. 27:4
23 [7] *destroy them*

PSALM 95
2 [a] Eph. 5:19; James 5:13
3 [b] [Ps. 96:4; 1 Cor. 8:5, 6]
4 [1] In His possession
5 [c] Gen. 1:9, 10; Jon. 1:9
6 [d] 2 Chr. 6:13; Dan. 6:10; [Phil. 2:10]
7 [e] Ps. 79:13 [f] Heb. 3:7-11, 15; 4:7
[2] Under His care
8 [g] Ex. 17:2-7; Num. 20:13 [3] Or *Meribah*, lit. *Strife, Contention*
[4] Or *Massah*, lit. *Trial, Testing*
9 [h] Ps. 78:18; [1 Cor. 10:9] [i] Num. 14:22
10 [j] Acts 7:36; 13:18; Heb. 3:10, 17
[5] *disgusted*

PSALM 95

A Call to Worship and Obedience

Oh come, let us sing to the LORD!
Let us shout joyfully to the Rock of our salvation.
2 Let us come before His presence with thanksgiving;
Let us shout joyfully to Him with [a]psalms.
3 For [b]the LORD *is* the great God,
And the great King above all gods.
4 [1]In His hand *are* the deep places of the earth;
The heights of the hills *are* His also.
5 [c]The sea *is* His, for He made it;
And His hands formed the dry *land.*

6 Oh come, let us worship and bow down;
Let [d]us kneel before the LORD our Maker.
7 For He *is* our God,
And [e]we *are* the people of His pasture,
And the sheep [2]of His hand.

[f]Today, if you will hear His voice:
8 "Do not harden your hearts, as in the [3]rebellion,
[g]As *in* the day of [4]trial in the wilderness,
9 When [h]your fathers tested Me;
They tried Me, though they [i]saw My work.
10 For [j]forty years I was [5]grieved with *that* generation,

on His abiding love (Gen. 15; Jer. 12:15; Mic. 7:18). This important truth serves as a doctrinal basis for Pss. 93–100 and was intended to encourage the nation during difficult times. Paul refers to this in Rom. 11:1 as he assures the future salvation of Israel.

94:17 soul...settled in silence. "Silence" here is another term for sheol, the realm of the dead (cf. Ps. 31:17).

94:18 Your mercy. *See note on Ps. 85:7.*

94:20 throne of iniquity. A reference to a corrupt judge or ruler. **devises evil by law.** Corrupt judges and rulers counter the very divine moral order of the universe by using law for wickedness rather than for good.

94:23 cut them off in their own wickedness. Portrays destruction while they are sinning.

95:1-11 This psalm, with its references to the wilderness wanderings, may have been composed by David (Heb. 4:7) for the Feast of the Tabernacles (cf. Ps. 81). During this feast, the people of Israel lived in booths, remembering God's provisions for them in the wilderness. After a call to worship (95:1-7a), a prophecy in the voice of the Holy Spirit Himself (cf. Heb. 3:7) breaks in and reminds the people of the dangers of rebellion and tempting God. Verses 7b-11 are quoted verbatim in Heb. 3:7-11 (cf. Heb. 3:15; 4:3-7) with the warning that those vacillating Jews also were in danger of missing the promised "rest" (i.e., salvation).

I. Positive Call to Worship (95:1-7a)

II. Negative Warning of Wrath (95:7b-11)

95:1 Rock of our salvation. This metaphor for God was especially appropriate in this psalm, which refers (vv. 8,9) to the water that came from the rock in the wilderness (cf. Ex. 17:1-7; Num. 20:1-13; 1 Cor. 10:4).

95:3 the great King above all gods. This is a poetic way of denying the existence of other gods (cf. 96:5), which existed only as statues, not persons (cf. Jer. 10:1-10).

95:4 deep places of the earth. This refers to the depths of the seas, valleys, and caverns, and contrasts with the hills. The point (cf. v. 5) is that God was not a local god like the imaginary gods of the heathens, usually put up in high places, but the universal Creator and Ruler of the whole earth (*see note on Ps. 65:5*).

95:8 the rebellion. This is a reference to Meribah (translated "rebellion"), the place in the wilderness where the Israelites rebelled against the Lord. Their complaint about lack of water demonstrated their lack of faith in the Lord (Ex. 17:1-7; Num. 20:1-13; Ps. 81:7).

95:9 tested Me. This is a reference to the same event (v. 8), also called "Massah" (translated "testing"), when God brought water out of the rock (Ex. 17:7; cf. Deut. 6:16; 9:22; 33:8). The writer to the Hebrews applies the principle of this event to his readers, suggesting that their inclination to doubt the Lord and return to Judaism was parallel with their fathers' inclination to doubt the Lord and go back to Egypt.

And said, 'It *is* a people who go
astray in their hearts,
And they do not know My ways.'
11 So [k]I swore in My wrath,
'They shall not enter My rest.' "

PSALM 96

A Song of Praise to God Coming in Judgment

Oh, [a]sing to the LORD a new song!
Sing to the LORD, all the earth.
2 Sing to the LORD, bless His name;
Proclaim the good news of His
salvation from day to day.
3 Declare His glory among the [1]nations,
His wonders among all peoples.

4 For [b]the LORD *is* great and [c]greatly to
be praised;
[d]He *is* to be feared above all gods.
5 For [e]all the gods of the peoples *are*
idols,
[f]But the LORD made the heavens.
6 Honor and majesty *are* before Him;
Strength and [g]beauty *are* in His
sanctuary.

7 [h]Give[2] to the LORD, O families of the
peoples,
Give to the LORD glory and strength.
8 [3]Give to the LORD the glory *due* His
name;
Bring an offering, and come into His
courts.
9 Oh, worship the LORD [i]in the beauty
of holiness!
Tremble before Him, all the earth.

10 Say among the [4]nations, [j]"The LORD
reigns;
The world also is firmly established,
It shall not be [5]moved;
[k]He shall judge the peoples righteously."

11 [l]Let the heavens rejoice, and let the
earth be glad;
[m]Let the sea roar, and [6]all its fullness;
12 Let the field be joyful, and all that *is*
in it.
Then all the trees of the woods will
rejoice before the LORD.
13 For He is coming, for He is coming to
judge the earth.
[n]He shall judge the world with
righteousness,
And the peoples with His truth.

PSALM 97

A Song of Praise to the Sovereign LORD

The LORD [a]reigns;
Let the earth rejoice;
Let the multitude of [1]isles be glad!
2 [b]Clouds and darkness surround Him;

11 [k]Num. 14:23, 28-30; Deut. 1:35; Heb. 4:3, 5

PSALM 96

1 [a]1 Chr. 16:23-33
3 [1]*Gentiles*
4 [b]Ps. 145:3 [c]Ps. 18:3 [d]Ps. 95:3
5 [e]1 Chr. 16:26; [Jer. 10:11] [f]Ps. 115:15; Is. 42:5
6 [g]Ps. 29:2
7 [h]1 Chr. 16:28, 29; Ps. 29:1, 2 [2]*Ascribe*
8 [3]*Ascribe*
9 [i]1 Chr. 16:29; 2 Chr. 20:21; Ps. 29:2
10 [j]Ps. 93:1; 97:1; [Rev. 11:15; 19:6] [k]Ps. 67:4 [4]*Gentiles* [5]*shaken*
11 [l]Ps. 69:34; Is. 49:13 [m]Ps. 98:7 [6]*all that is in it*
13 [n][Rev. 19:11]

PSALM 97

1 [a][Ps. 96:10] [1]*Or coastlands*
2 [b]Ex. 19:9; Deut. 4:11; 1 Kin. 8:12; Ps. 18:11

95:10 go astray in their hearts. Their wanderings in the desert were the outworking of straying hearts.

95:11 My rest. The "rest" was originally the Promised Land, (i.e., Canaan), where the people came at the end of Israel's 40 year journey in the wilderness. It was analogously applied in the book of Hebrews to salvation by grace (Heb. 3:7–4:10; cf. Heb. 2:3).

96:1-13 The substance of this psalm, and portions of Pss. 97,98, and 100 are found in 1 Chr. 16, which was used by David's direction in the dedication of the tabernacle on Mt. Zion. The psalm has importance beyond that historical occasion, however, because it anticipates kingdom praise for the Lord from all the nations of the world (vv. 3,4,7,9-13; cf. Is. 2:2-4; Zech. 14:16-19), and even from nature itself. It also expresses the intense joy that will saturate the earth when the Messiah is ruling from Jerusalem (cf. Is. 25:9; 40:9,10).

I. The Proclamation of Praise (96:1-6)
 A. The Invitation to Praise (96:1-3)
 B. The Recipient of Praise (96:4-6)
II. The Exhortation to Worship (96:7-13)
 A. Worship from the Gentile Nations (96:7-10)
 B. Worship from Personified Nature (96:11-13)

96:1 a new song. This new song was intended for the future inauguration of the millennial rule of the Lord over the earth (cf. Pss. 144:9; 149:1; Rev. 5:9; 14:3).

96:2 Proclaim the good news. Genuine praise includes a testimony to others of God's plan of redemption.

96:3 His glory...nations. The glory of the Lord is more than just His majestic splendor. It includes all of the reasons for admiring and praising Him, such as His acts of creation (cf. Ps. 19:2) and redemption (v. 2). **all peoples.** *See note on Ps. 67:3.*

96:4 feared above all gods. *See note on Ps. 95:3.*

96:8 an offering. According to the psalmists and prophets, offerings and sacrifices will be presented to the Lord in the millennial kingdom (cf. Ps. 45:12; Ezek. 40–46).

96:9 the beauty of holiness. That is, "worship the LORD because of the splendor of His holiness" (cf. Pss. 29:2; 99; 110:3; also 1 Chr. 16:29). *See note on 2 Chr. 20:21.*

96:10 firmly established. Instead of the continuance of international chaos in human history, the world will be settled and efficiently managed by the Messiah in the millennial kingdom (cf. Ps. 2; Mic. 4:1-5). **judge the peoples righteously.** Not only will the Lord establish international peace and stability in the future messianic kingdom, but He will also rule the world with impeccable justice (cf. v. 13; Is. 11:1-5).

96:11,12 This is what even inanimate creation awaits (cf. Rom. 8:14-22).

96:13 He is coming. The rule of the Lord described in this psalm is not the present universal kingdom (Ps. 93), but one which will be established when Christ returns to earth.

97:1-12 The psalmist, though recognizing the Lord's universal rule at the present (v. 9), anticipates a new coming of the Lord to judge the earth. The imagery of the Lord's presence may, in fact, be the basis of some NT passages' descriptions of the second coming (cf. Matt. 24; Rev. 19). Special emphasis is also placed on the Lord's totally righteous judgments on the world in His kingdom, as well as His obliteration of false religions.

I. The Announcement of the Reign of the Lord (97:1,2)
II. The Effect of the Reign of the Lord (97:3-12)
 A. On His Foes (97:3-9)
 B. On His Friends (97:10-12)

[c]Righteousness and justice *are* the
foundation of His throne.
3 [d]A fire goes before Him,
And burns up His enemies round
about.
4 [e]His lightnings light the world;
The earth sees and trembles.
5 [f]The mountains melt like wax at the
presence of the LORD,
At the presence of the Lord of the
whole earth.
6 [g]The heavens declare His
righteousness,
And all the peoples see His glory.

7 [h]Let all be put to shame who serve
carved images,
Who boast of idols.
[i]Worship Him, all *you* gods.
8 Zion hears and is glad,
And the daughters of Judah rejoice
Because of Your judgments, O LORD.
9 For You, LORD, *are* [j]most high above
all the earth;
[k]You are exalted far above all gods.

10 You who love the LORD, [l]hate evil!
[m]He preserves the souls of His saints;
[n]He delivers them out of the hand of
the wicked.
11 [o]Light is sown for the righteous,
And gladness for the upright in heart.
12 [p]Rejoice in the LORD, you righteous,
[q]And give thanks [2]at the remembrance
of [3]His holy name.

2 [c][Ps. 89:14]
3 [d]Ps. 18:8; Dan. 7:10; Hab. 3:5
4 [e]Ex. 19:18
5 [f]Ps. 46:6; Amos 9:5; Mic. 1:4; Nah. 1:5
6 [g]Ps. 19:1
7 [h][Ex. 20:4] [i][Heb. 1:6]
9 [j]Ps. 83:18 [k]Ex. 18:11; Ps. 95:3; 96:4
10 [l][Ps. 34:14; Prov. 8:13; Amos 5:15; Rom. 12:9] [m]Ps. 31:23; 145:20; Prov. 2:8 [n]Ps. 37:40; Jer. 15:21; Dan. 3:28
11 [o]Job 22:28; Ps. 112:4; Prov. 4:18
12 [p]Ps. 33:1 [q]Ps. 30:4 [2]*Or for the memory* [3]*Or His holiness*

PSALM 98

A Song of Praise to the LORD for His Salvation and Judgment

A Psalm.

Oh, [a]sing to the LORD a new song!
For He has [b]done marvelous things;
His right hand and His holy arm have
gained Him the victory.
2 [c]The LORD has made known His
salvation;
[d]His righteousness He has revealed in
the sight of the [1]nations.
3 He has remembered His mercy and
His faithfulness to the house
of Israel;
[e]All the ends of the earth have seen
the salvation of our God.

4 Shout joyfully to the LORD, all the
earth;
Break forth in song, rejoice, and sing
praises.
5 Sing to the LORD with the harp,
With the harp and the sound of a
psalm,
6 With trumpets and the sound of a
horn;
Shout joyfully before the LORD, the
King.

7 Let the sea roar, and all its fullness,
The world and those who dwell in it;
8 Let the rivers clap *their* hands;

PSALM 98

1 [a]Ps. 33:3; Is. 42:10 [b]Ex. 15:11; Ps. 77:14
2 [c]Is. 52:10; [Luke 1:77; 2:30, 31] [d]Is. 62:2; Rom. 3:25 [1]*Gentiles*
3 [e][Is. 49:6]; Luke 3:6; [Acts 13:47; 28:28]

97:1 multitude of isles. Refers to all the continents, as well as islands of the world (cf. Is. 42:10; Dan. 2:34,35,44; Zech. 14:9).

97:2 Clouds and darkness. Such a description emphasizes the terrifying effect of the Lord's presence, both in the past (Ex. 19:16-18), and in the future Day of the Lord (Joel 2:2; Zeph. 1:15; Matt. 24:29,30).

97:3 burns up His enemies. The Lord will utterly destroy His enemies in the future Day of the Lord (cf. Zech. 14:12).

97:4 His lightnings. This is perhaps a reference to the Lord's awesome and public coming to rule the world (Matt. 24:26-30).

97:5 mountains melt. At the coming of the Lord, the mountains will fade away (cf. Is. 40:3-5; Zech. 14:4,10).

97:6 heavens declare His righteousness. See the parallel description of Christ's coming in glory in Is. 40:5 and Matt. 24:29-31 (cf. Rev. 19:11-15).

97:7 all *you* gods. No false gods or religions will be allowed in the messianic kingdom (cf. Zech. 13:2,3).

97:8 Zion. *See note on Ps. 87:2.* **Because of Your judgments.** A major reason for joy and well-being in the messianic kingdom will be the perfectly righteous judgments of Christ on the peoples of the world (cf. vv. 1-3; also Ps. 48:11; Is. 11:1-5; Zech. 8:3).

97:10 preserves the souls of His saints. Here the doctrine of eternal security is stated. Gratitude for such grace should motivate believers to holiness.

97:11 Light is sown. This is a poetic way of describing the ultimate triumph of righteousness and the righteous (cf. Is. 58:8,10; 60:19,20; Mal. 4:2).

98:1-9 Like the surrounding psalms, this psalm proclaims the excitement and joy of the whole earth over the rule of the Lord in the kingdom. This psalm is given over entirely to praise, with only a brief mention of the wicked.

I. Celebration of the Lord's Victorious Reign (98:1-6)
  A. Triumphs of the Lord (98:1-3)
  B. Praise to the Lord (98:4-6)
II. Exaltation of the Lord's Righteous Judgments (98:7-9)

98:1 a new song. *See note on Ps. 96:1.* **right hand...holy arm.** These are symbols of power. **the victory.** The Lord is often pictured in the OT as a divine warrior (Ex. 15:2,3; Pss. 18; 68:1-8; Is. 59:15ff.). According to the prophets, Christ will begin His millennial reign following His victory over the nations of the world which will gather against Israel in the end times (cf. Zech. 14:1-15; Rev. 19:11-21).

98:2 the nations. *See notes on Pss. 57:9; 67:3; 82:8.*

98:3 His mercy and His faithfulness. *See notes on Pss. 85:7 and 89:5.* **salvation.** These words are a metaphor for the Lord's establishment of His righteous kingdom on earth (cf. Is. 46:13; 51:5-8).

98:4 Shout joyfully. A great cheer, greeting and welcoming a king (cf. Zech. 9:9; Matt. 21:4-9). **Break forth.** The idea is that of an eruption of praise which could not be contained (cf. Is. 14:7; 44;23; 55:12).

98:5,6 harp...trumpets...horn. Instruments normally used in temple worship (cf. 1 Chr. 16:5,6; 2 Chr. 5:12,13; 29:25-30; Ezra 3:10-13).

98:8 rivers clap *their* hands. Different parts of nature are pictured as rejoicing in this universal scene of joy (cf. Is. 35:1,2; Rom. 8:19-21).

Let the hills be joyful together before
the LORD,
9 [f]For He is coming to judge the earth.
With righteousness He shall judge the
world,
And the peoples with [2]equity.

PSALM 99

Praise to the LORD for His Holiness

The LORD reigns;
Let the peoples tremble!
[a]He dwells *between* the cherubim;
Let the earth be [1]moved!
2 The LORD *is* great in Zion,
And He *is* high above all the peoples.
3 Let them praise Your great and
awesome name—
[2]He *is* holy.

4 The King's strength also loves justice;
You have established equity;
You have executed justice and
righteousness in Jacob.
5 Exalt the LORD our God,
And worship at His footstool—
He *is* holy.

6 Moses and Aaron were among His
priests,
And Samuel was among those who
[b]called upon His name;
They called upon the LORD, and He
answered them.
7 He spoke to them in the cloudy pillar;
They kept His testimonies and the
[3]ordinance He gave them.
8 You answered them, O LORD our God;
You were to them God-Who-Forgives,
Though You took vengeance on their
deeds.
9 Exalt the LORD our God,
And worship at His holy hill;
For the LORD our God *is* holy.

PSALM 100

A Song of Praise for the LORD's Faithfulness to His People

[a]A Psalm of Thanksgiving.

Make [b]a joyful shout to the LORD, [1]all
you lands!
2 Serve the LORD with gladness;
Come before His presence with
singing.
3 Know that the LORD, He *is* God;
[c]*It is* He *who* has made us, and [2]not we
ourselves;
[d]*We are* His people and the sheep of
His pasture.

4 [e]Enter into His gates with
thanksgiving,
And into His courts with praise.
Be thankful to Him, *and* bless His
name.
5 For the LORD *is* good;

9 [f][Ps. 96:10, 13] [2] *uprightness*

PSALM 99

1 [a] Ex. 25:22; 1 Sam. 4:4; Ps. 80:1 [1] *shaken*
3 [2] *Or It*
6 [b] 1 Sam. 7:9; 12:18
7 [3] *statute*

PSALM 100

title [a] Ps. 145:title
1 [b] Ps. 95:1 [1] Lit. *all the earth*
3 [c] Job 10:3, 8; Ps. 119:73; 139:13, 14; [Eph. 2:10] [d] Ps. 95:7; [Is. 40:11]; Ezek. 34:30, 31 [2] So with Kt., LXX, Vg.; Qr., many Heb. mss., Tg. *we are His*
4 [e] Ps. 66:13; 116:17-19

98:9 He is coming. *See note on Ps. 96:13.*

99:1-9 The theme of this psalm is summed up in its last phrase: "the LORD our God is holy" (v. 9). The psalmist encourages praise to the king for His holiness (vv. 3,5,9), which is the utter separateness of God's being from all other creatures and things, as well as His moral separateness from sin. The psalmist also exults in the truth that such a holy God has had an intimate saving relationship with Israel throughout her history (vv. 6-9).

I. Exaltation of the King's Holiness (99:1-5)
II. Examples of the King's Holiness (99:6-9)

99:1 ***between*** **the cherubim.** *See note on Ps. 80:1*; cf. Ps. 18:6-19; Ezek. 10:1ff.

99:2 Zion. *See note on Ps. 87:2*; cf. Heb. 12:22-24. **peoples.** *See notes on Pss. 57:9 and 67:3.*

99:4 King's strength also loves justice. "King's strength" may be a kind of epithet for God; or (combining this phrase with v. 3) the psalmist may be saying that a holy name is the strength of a just king. **equity.** That is, fairness (cf. Is. 11:1-5).

99:5 His footstool. In general, this is a metaphor for the temple in Jerusalem (cf. Is. 60:13; Lam. 2:1); but more specifically, for the ark of the covenant (1 Chr. 28:2). Footstools were included with the thrones of the kings of Israel (2 Chr. 9:8).

99:6 Moses...Aaron...Samuel. Using three of the nation's famous heroes for examples, the psalmist demonstrates that a holy God has had an enduring, intimate, and saving relationship with Israel.

99:7 cloudy pillar. This was a medium of divine direction (cf. Ex. 13:21,22; 33:9,10; Num. 12:5; Deut. 31:15ff.). **testimonies...ordinance.** Terms in Psalms for God's Word (see Ps. 119).

99:9 His holy hill. This is the hill in Jerusalem where the temple was (cf. Pss. 15:1; 24:3), and where it will be located in the future messianic kingdom (cf. Is. 24:23).

100:1-5 This well known psalm, emphasizing the universal nature of God's kingship, is a benediction to the series of psalms which are occupied with the Lord's kingdom rule (Pss. 93,95-100). Most of it is a call to praise and thanksgiving, while vv. 3 and 5 fix the reasons for that worship.

I. A Call to Praise the Lord (100:1-3)
II. A Call to Thank the Lord (100:4,5)

100:1 a joyful shout. *See note on Ps. 66:1.*

100:3 Know. In the sense of experiencing and being completely assured of the truth. **the LORD, He** ***is*** **God.** A confession that Israel's covenant God, Jehovah, is the only true God. **made us.** Though God's actual creation of every human being is understood here, this phrase seems to refer to God's making and blessing Israel as a nation (cf. Deut. 32:6,15; Ps. 95:6; Is. 29:22,23; 44:2). **His people...His pasture.** The shepherd image is often ascribed to the king of Israel, as well as to the Lord (cf. Ps. 78:70-72; Is. 44:28; Jer. 10:21; Zech. 10:3; 11:4-17; also Pss. 23:1; 28:9; 74:1; 77:20; 78:52,53; 80:1; 95:7). The figure suggests intimate care (cf. Luke 15:3-6). According to the NT, the Lord is also the Shepherd of saints in the church age (John 10:16).

100:4 His gates...courts. The gates and courts were those of the temple.

100:5 the LORD ***is*** **good.** God is the source and perfect example

[f]His mercy *is* everlasting,
And His truth *endures* to all generations.

PSALM 101

Promised Faithfulness to the LORD

A Psalm of David.

I will sing of mercy and justice;
To You, O LORD, I will sing praises.

2 I will behave wisely in a [1]perfect way.
Oh, when will You come to me?
I will [a]walk within my house with a perfect heart.

3 I will set nothing [2]wicked before my eyes;
[b]I hate the work of those [c]who fall away;
It shall not cling to me.
4 A perverse heart shall depart from me;
I will not [d]know wickedness.

5 Whoever secretly slanders his neighbor,
Him I will destroy;
[e]The one who has a haughty look and a proud heart,
Him I will not endure.

6 My eyes *shall be* on the faithful of the land,
That they may dwell with me;
He who walks in a [3]perfect way,
He shall serve me.
7 He who works deceit shall not dwell within my house;
He who tells lies shall not [4]continue in my presence.
8 [f]Early I will destroy all the wicked of the land,
That I may cut off all the evildoers [g]from the city of the LORD.

PSALM 102

The LORD'*s Eternal Love*

A Prayer of the afflicted, [a]when he is overwhelmed and pours out his complaint before the LORD.

Hear my prayer, O LORD,
And let my cry come to You.
2 [b]Do not hide Your face from me in the day of my trouble;
Incline Your ear to me;
In the day that I call, answer me speedily.

3 For my days [1]are [c]consumed like smoke,
And my bones are burned like a hearth.
4 My heart is stricken and withered like grass,
So that I forget to eat my bread.
5 Because of the sound of my groaning
My bones cling to my [2]skin.
6 I am like a pelican of the wilderness;
I am like an owl of the desert.

5 [f]Ps. 136:1

PSALM 101
2 [a]1 Kin. 11:4 [1]*blameless*
3 [b]Ps. 97:10 [c]Josh. 23:6 [2]*worthless*
4 [d][Ps. 119:115]
5 [e]Prov. 6:17
6 [3]*blameless*
7 [4]Lit. *be established*
8 [f][Ps. 75:10]; Jer. 21:12 [g]Ps. 48:2, 8

PSALM 102
title [a]Ps. 61:2
2 [b]Ps. 27:9; 69:17
3 [c]James 4:14 [1]Lit. *end in*
5 [2]*flesh*

of goodness. **His mercy.** *See note on Ps. 85:7.* **His truth.** In the sense of keeping His promises, i.e., His faithfulness.

101:1-8 This Davidic psalm expresses the righteous commitments of the mediatorial king (David) to his eternal king (the Lord) in regard to 1) his own personal life and 2) the lives of those who inhabit the kingdom. Possibly, this psalm was used later at the coronations of future kings over Israel. Ultimately, only King Jesus would perfectly fulfill these holy resolutions (cf. Is. 9:6,7; 11:1-5).

I. Personal Life of the King (101:1-4)
II. Personal Outcome of Kingdom Inhabitants (101:5-8)
  A. The just (101:6)
  B. The unjust (101:5,7,8)

101:2 perfect way. As the king goes, so go his followers (cf. v. 6). **when will You come to me?** This is not an eschatological expectation, but rather a personal expression of David's need for God's immanent involvement in his earthly kingship. **my house.** The king first starts with his own personal life (cf. v. 7), and then looks beyond to his kingdom (cf. vv. 5,8).

101:3,4 Similar to the "blessed man" in Ps. 1:1.

101:3 my eyes. The king desires to look at nothing but that which is righteous (cf. v. 6).

101:4 wickedness. The king will not engage in wickedness (cf. v. 8).

101:5 slanders...haughty look...proud heart. Neither character assassination nor pride will be tolerated in the kingdom.

101:6 the faithful of the land. Compare to "the wicked of the land" in v. 8.

101:7 deceit...lies. A premium is put on truth as foundational for a kingdom associated with the God of truth (cf. John 14:6).

101:8 the land...the city of the LORD. Israel and Jerusalem respectively.

102:1-28 The non-specific superscription is unique to this psalm which highlights the thoughts of one who is afflicted (cf. Pss. 22,69,79,102,130,142), perhaps expressing exilic lament (cf. Pss. 42,43,74,79,137). Like Job, whose troubles were not the result of God's judgment for personal sin, the psalmist cries out in pain. His only relief comes from refocusing on sovereign God and His eternal purposes. Messianic overtones are present as Heb. 1:10-12 quotes Ps. 102:25,26.

I. A Plea for Immediate Divine Help (102:1-11)
II. A Perspective of God's Sovereignty and Eternality (102:12-22)
III. A Prayer for Longer Life (102:23-28)

102:1,2 Frequently the Psalms begin with a cry for God's sovereign intervention when human resources have proved insufficient, e.g., Pss. 77:1; 142:1.

102:2 Your face...Your ear. Anthropomorphic language (i.e., a figure of speech that attributes human features to God) which points to God's attention and response respectively.

102:3-5 heart...bones. These terms describe the emotional and physical toll of the psalmist's ordeal.

102:6 pelican. Possibly a desert owl. The verse describes a desolate situation, extreme loneliness (cf. Is. 34:8-15; Zeph. 2:13-15). **owl.** Owls were unclean animals, cf. Lev. 11:16-18.

7 I lie awake,
And am like a sparrow alone on the housetop.
8 My enemies reproach me all day long;
Those who deride me swear an oath against me.
9 For I have eaten ashes like bread,
And mingled my drink with weeping,
10 Because of Your indignation and Your wrath;
For You have lifted me up and cast me away.
11 My days *are* like a shadow that lengthens,
And I wither away like grass.

12 But You, O LORD, shall endure forever,
And the remembrance of Your name to all generations.
13 You will arise *and* have mercy on Zion;
For the time to favor her,
Yes, the set time, has come.
14 For Your servants take pleasure in her stones,
And show favor to her dust.
15 So the [3]nations shall [d]fear the name of the LORD,
And all the kings of the earth Your glory.
16 For the LORD shall build up Zion;
[e]He shall appear in His glory.
17 [f]He shall regard the prayer of the destitute,
And shall not despise their prayer.

18 This will be [g]written for the generation to come,
That [h]a people yet to be created may praise the LORD.
19 For He [i]looked down from the height of His sanctuary;
From heaven the LORD viewed the earth,
20 [j]To hear the groaning of the prisoner,
To release those appointed to death,
21 To [k]declare the name of the LORD in Zion,
And His praise in Jerusalem,
22 [l]When the peoples are gathered together,
And the kingdoms, to serve the LORD.

23 He weakened my strength in the way;
He [m]shortened my days.
24 [n]I said, "O my God,
Do not take me away in the midst of my days;
[o]Your years *are* throughout all generations.
25 [p]Of old You laid the foundation of the earth,
And the heavens *are* the work of Your hands.
26 [q]They will perish, but You will [4]endure;
Yes, they will all grow old like a garment;
Like a cloak You will change them,
And they will be changed.
27 But [r]You *are* the same,
And Your years will have no end.
28 [s]The children of Your servants will continue,
And their descendants will be established before You."

15 [d] 1 Kin. 8:43 [3] Gentiles
16 [e] [Is. 60:1, 2]
17 [f] Neh. 1:6; Ps. 22:24
18 [g] Deut. 31:19; [Rom. 15:4; 1 Cor. 10:11] [h] Ps. 22:31
19 [i] Deut. 26:15; Ps. 14:2
20 [j] Ps. 79:11
21 [k] Ps. 22:22
22 [l] [Is. 2:2, 3; 49:22, 23; 60:3]; Zech. 8:20-23
23 [m] Job 21:21
24 [n] [Ps. 39:13]; Is. 38:10 [o] Job 36:26; [Ps. 90:2]; Hab. 1:12
25 [p] [Gen. 1:1; Neh. 9:6; Heb. 1:10-12]
26 [q] Is. 34:4; 51:6; Matt. 24:35; [2 Pet. 3:7, 10-12]; Rev. 20:11 [4] continue
27 [r] [Is. 41:4; 43:10; Mal. 3:6; Heb. 13:8]; James 1:17
28 [s] Ps. 69:36
PSALM 103
1 [a] Ps. 104:1, 35

PSALM 103

Praise for the LORD's Mercies

A Psalm of David.

Bless [a]the LORD, O my soul;
And all that is within me, *bless* His holy name!
2 Bless the LORD, O my soul,

102:7 sparrow. Feeling like a "lonely bird," the psalmist expresses his perceived abandonment by both God and man.

102:10,11 a shadow that lengthens. The time of sunset is used to describe the psalmist's desperate sense that his life will end shortly because God has punished him by withdrawing His presence and strength.

102:12-22 The psalmist radically shifts his focus from earth to heaven—from his dilemma to God—and basks in the eternal nature of God and the eternal outworking of God's redemptive plan.

102:13-16 Zion. Earthly Zion or Jerusalem is in view (cf. vv. 16,21, 22). Perhaps this points to the time of restoration after the Babylonian Exile (ca. 605–536 B.C.).

102:18 written. The psalmist had a sense of the perpetuation of his literary effort.

102:19 looked down…viewed. The transcendent omniscience of God is in view.

102:22 the peoples…the kingdoms. This will ultimately be fulfilled in Christ's messianic reign over the world (cf. Ps. 2).

102:23,24 The psalmist desires to live longer but acknowledges his mortality compared to God's eternality.

102:24 the midst of my days. Lit. at the halfway point of life.

102:25-27 Eternal God created the heavens and earth, which will one day perish (v. 26). Hebrews 1:10-12 applies this passage to the Lord Jesus Christ, who is superior to the angels because: 1) He is eternal, while they had a beginning; and 2) He created, but they were created. This passage clearly affirms the eternality and deity of Christ. The unchangeable God will outlast his creation, even into the new creation (cf. Mal. 3:6; James 1:17; 2 Pet. 3; Rev. 21,22).

102:28 The realistic hope of one who perceives that though he is about to die, God's purposes on earth will be accomplished in future generations.

103:1-22 Psalms 103 and 104 appear as an intentional pair designed to promote the blessing and exaltation of God. This psalm represents a soliloquy in which David surveys God's goodness and en-

And forget not all His benefits:
3 [b]Who forgives all your iniquities,
Who [c]heals all your diseases,
4 Who redeems your life from
destruction,
[d]Who crowns you with lovingkindness
and tender mercies,
5 Who satisfies your mouth with good
things,
So that [e]your youth is renewed like
the eagle's.

6 The LORD executes righteousness
And justice for all who are oppressed.
7 [f]He made known His ways to Moses,
His acts to the children of Israel.
8 [g]The LORD *is* merciful and gracious,
Slow to anger, and abounding in
mercy.
9 [h]He will not always strive *with us,*
Nor will He keep *His anger* forever.
10 [i]He has not dealt with us according to
our sins,
Nor punished us according to our
iniquities.

11 For as the heavens are high above the
earth,
So great is His mercy toward those
who fear Him;
12 As far as the east is from the west,
So far has He [j]removed our
transgressions from us.
13 [k]As a father pities *his* children,
So the LORD pities those who fear
Him.
14 For He [1]knows our frame;
He remembers that we *are* dust.

15 *As for* man, [l]his days *are* like grass;
As a flower of the field, so he
flourishes.
16 [m]For the wind passes over it, and it is
[2]gone,
And [n]its place remembers it no more.
17 But the mercy of the LORD *is* from
everlasting to everlasting
On those who fear Him,
And His righteousness to children's
children,
18 [o]To such as keep His covenant,
And to those who remember His
commandments to do them.

19 The LORD has established His throne
in heaven,
And [p]His kingdom rules over all.

20 [q]Bless the LORD, you His angels,
Who excel in strength, who [r]do His
word,
Heeding the voice of His word.
21 Bless the LORD, all *you* His hosts,
[s]*You* [3]ministers of His, who do His
pleasure.
22 Bless the LORD, all His works,
In all places of His dominion.

Bless the LORD, O my soul!

3 [b] Ps. 130:8; Is. 33:24 [c] [Ex. 15:26]; Ps. 147:3; [Is. 53:5]; Jer. 17:14
4 [d] [Ps. 5:12]
5 [e] [Is. 40:31]
7 [f] Ex. 33:12-17; Ps. 147:19
8 [g] [Ex. 34:6, 7; Num. 14:18]; Deut. 5:10; Neh. 9:17; Ps. 86:15; Jer. 32:18; Jon. 4:2; James 5:11
9 [h] [Ps. 30:5; Is. 57:16]; Jer. 3:5; [Mic. 7:18]
10 [i] [Ezra 9:13; Lam. 3:22]
12 [j] [2 Sam. 12:13; Is. 38:17; 43:25; Zech. 3:9; Heb. 9:26]
13 [k] Mal. 3:17
14 [1] Understands our constitution
15 [l] Is. 40:6-8; James 1:10, 11; 1 Pet. 1:24
16 [m] [Is. 40:7] [n] Job 7:10 [2] *not*
18 [o] [Deut. 7:9]; Ps. 25:10
19 [p] [Ps. 47:2; Dan. 4:17, 25]
20 [q] Ps. 148:2 [r] [Matt. 6:10]
21 [s] [Heb. 1:14] [3] *servants*

courages the angels and the works of God's creation to join him in divine praise.

I. A Call for Human Praise (103:1-19)
  A. Personally (103:1-5)
  B. Corporately (103:6-19)
II. A Call for Creation's Praise (103:20-22b)
  A. Angels (103:20-21)
  B. Works of Creation (103:22a-b)
III. A Refrain of Personal Praise (103:22c)

103:1 Bless the LORD. Cf. 103:2,22; 104:1,35

103:2 forget not all His benefits. These earthly gifts from God included: 1) forgiveness of sin (v. 3), 2) recovery from sickness (v. 3), 3) deliverance from death (v. 4), 4) abundant lovingkindness and mercy (v. 4), and 5) food to sustain life (v. 5).

103:3 diseases. This is not a promise, but rather a testimony which should be understood in the light of Deut. 32:39.

103:5 youth is renewed like the eagle's. The mysterious way of the long-lived eagle symbolized strength and speed (cf. Ex. 19:4; Jer. 48:40), which also characterizes human youth. As a general rule, a person blessed of God will grow weak and slow down less rapidly than otherwise (cf. Is. 40:29-31, which uses the same language).

103:6-19 The psalmist rehearses the attributes of God with which He blesses the saints.

103:7,8 His ways to Moses. Cf. Moses' request (Ex. 33:13) with God's answer (Ex. 34:6,7).

103:9 not always strive. There will be a final day of accountability, both at death (Luke 16:19-31) and the Great White Throne (Rev. 20:11-15). The Genesis flood served as a stark preview of this truth (cf. Gen. 6:3).

103:10 not dealt. God's great mercy (v. 11) and irreversible, complete justification (v. 12) have redemptively accomplished for us, by the death of Christ (cf. 2 Cor. 5:21; Phil. 3:9), what we ourselves could not do.

103:13 As a father. Unlike the pagan gods, who are apathetic or hostile.

103:14 dust. Physically speaking, as Adam was created of dust (Gen. 2:7), so mankind at death decomposes back into dust (Gen. 3:19).

103:15,16 days...like grass. Man's life is short and transitory (cf. Is. 40:8).

103:17,18 the mercy of the LORD. Those who appeal to God's mercy by proper fear (v. 17) and obedience (v. 18) will overcome the shortness of physical life with eternal life. Luke 1:50 quotes Ps. 103:17.

103:19 His throne in heaven. From everlasting to everlasting God has always ruled over all things (cf. Pss. 11:4; 47:1-9; 148:8-13). This universal kingdom is to be distinguished from God's mediatorial kingdom on earth.

103:20,21 His angels...His hosts. Unfallen, righteous angels who serve God night and day (cf. Ps. 148:2; Rev. 5:11-13).

103:22 His works. Refers to God's creation, which is also to His praise (cf. Pss. 148–150, also 1 Chr. 29:10-13).

PSALM 104

Praise to the Sovereign LORD for His Creation and Providence

Bless [a]the LORD, O my soul!
O LORD my God, You are very great:
You are clothed with honor and majesty,
2 Who cover *Yourself* with light as *with* a garment,
Who stretch out the heavens like a curtain.

3 [b]He lays the beams of His upper chambers in the waters,
Who makes the clouds His chariot,
Who walks on the wings of the wind,
4 Who makes His angels spirits,
His [1]ministers a flame of fire.

5 *You who* [2]laid the foundations of the earth,
So *that* it should not be moved forever,
6 You [c]covered it with the deep as *with* a garment;
The waters stood above the mountains.
7 At Your rebuke they fled;
At the voice of Your thunder they hastened away.
8 [3]They went up over the mountains;
They went down into the valleys,
To the place which You founded for them.
9 You have [d]set a boundary that they may not pass over,
[e]That they may not return to cover the earth.

10 He sends the springs into the valleys;
They flow among the hills.
11 They give drink to every beast of the field;
The wild donkeys quench their thirst.
12 By them the birds of the heavens have their home;
They sing among the branches.
13 [f]He waters the hills from His upper chambers;
The earth is satisfied with [g]the fruit of Your works.

14 [h]He causes the grass to grow for the cattle,
And vegetation for the service of man,
That he may bring forth [i]food from the earth,
15 And [j]wine *that* makes glad the heart of man,
Oil to make *his* face shine,
And bread *which* strengthens man's heart.
16 The trees of the LORD are full *of sap,*
The cedars of Lebanon which He planted,
17 Where the birds make their nests;
The stork has her home in the fir trees.
18 The high hills *are* for the wild goats;
The cliffs are a refuge for the [k]rock[4] badgers.

19 [l]He appointed the moon for seasons;
The [m]sun knows its going down.
20 [n]You make darkness, and it is night,
In which all the beasts of the forest creep about.
21 [o]The young lions roar after their prey,
And seek their food from God.
22 *When* the sun rises, they gather together

PSALM 104
1 [a] Ps. 103:1
3 [b] [Amos 9:6]
4 [1] *servants*
5 [2] Lit. *founded the earth upon her bases*
6 [c] Gen. 1:6
8 [3] Or *The mountains rose up; The valleys sank down*
9 [d] Job 26:10; Ps. 33:7; [Jer. 5:22] [e] Gen. 9:11-15
13 [f] Ps. 147:8 [g] Jer. 10:13
14 [h] Gen. 1:29 [i] Job 28:5
15 [j] Judg. 9:13; Ps. 23:5; Prov. 31:6; Eccl. 10:19
18 [k] Lev. 11:5 [4] *rock hyraxes*
19 [l] Gen. 1:14 [m] Job 38:12; Ps. 19:6
20 [n] [Ps. 74:16; Is. 45:7]
21 [o] Job 38:39

104:1-35 In vivid poetic detail, the psalmist sings of the Lord's glory in creation (cf. Gen. 1,2; Job 38–41; Pss. 19:1-6,148:1-6; Prov. 30:4; Is. 40:1-6; John 1:1-3; Rom. 1:18-25; Col. 1:16,17). He refers to the original creation (cf. 104:5) without forgetting the fall of man and the cursed earth (104:23,29,35). He alternates reciting God's greatness by 1) personal praise to the Creator (104:1,2,5-9,20-30), and 2) declaring God's handiwork to his human audience (104:3,4,10-19,31-35). The flow of the psalm loosely follows the order of creation as first reported in Gen. 1:1-31 but closes (v. 35) with an allusion to the end time events recorded in Rev. 20–22.

I. The Heavens and Earth Created (104:1-9)
II. The Needs of Creatures Met (104:10-18)
III. The Sun and Moon (104:19-23)
IV. The Sea and Its Inhabitants (104:24-26)
V. God's Providential Care (104:27-30)
VI. Benediction to the Creator (104:31-35)

104:1-9 This section approximates the first two days of creation (cf. Gen. 1:1-8).

104:1 very great. The Creator is greater than His creation. Therefore, the Creator is to be worshiped, not the creation (cf. Ex. 20:3,4; Rom. 1:29).

104:3 the waters. Refers to the original creation with the waters above the heaven (cf. Gen. 1:7,8).

104:4 spirits…flame of fire. Hebrews 1:7 attributes these characteristics to angels describing their swiftness and destructiveness as God's instruments of judgment.

104:5 foundations. Cf. Job 38:4

104:6-9 While this might sound like the worldwide flood of Gen. 6–9, it continues to refer to the creation, esp. Gen. 1:9,10 regarding the third day of creation.

104:10-18 With water (vv. 10-13), vegetation (v. 14), food-producing vines, trees and grain (v. 15), trees (vv. 16,17) and cliffs (v. 18), the Creator provides for the basic needs of His creation. This corresponds to the third day of creation (cf. Gen. 1:11-13).

104:13 upper chambers. Refers to rain clouds.

104:19-23 This section corresponds to the fourth day of creation in Gen. 1:14-19. The work period of predators (the night) is contrasted with the work time of humans (the day).

And lie down in their dens.
23 Man goes out to [p]his work
And to his labor until the evening.

24 [q]O LORD, how manifold are Your works!
In wisdom You have made them all.
The earth is full of Your [r]possessions—
25 This great and wide sea,
In which *are* innumerable teeming things,
Living things both small and great.
26 There the ships sail about;
There is that [s]Leviathan[5]
Which You have [6]made to play there.

27 [t]These all wait for You,
That You may give *them* their food in due season.
28 *What* You give them they gather in;
You open Your hand, they are filled with good.
29 You hide Your face, they are troubled;
[u]You take away their breath, they die and return to their dust.
30 [v]You send forth Your Spirit, they are created;
And You renew the face of the earth.

31 May the glory of the LORD endure forever;
May the LORD [w]rejoice in His works.
32 He looks on the earth, and it [x]trembles;
[y]He touches the hills, and they smoke.

33 [z]I will sing to the LORD as long as I live;
I will sing praise to my God while I have my being.
34 May my [a]meditation be sweet to Him;
I will be glad in the LORD.
35 May [b]sinners be consumed from the earth,
And the wicked be no more.

Bless the LORD, O my soul!
[7]Praise the LORD!

23 [p] Gen. 3:19
24 [q] Ps. 40:5; Prov. 3:19; [Jer. 10:12]; 51:15 [r] Ps. 65:9
26 [s] Job 41:1; Is. 27:1 [5] A large sea creature of unknown identity [6] Lit. *formed*
27 [t] Job 36:31; Ps. 136:25
29 [u] Job 34:15; [Eccl. 12:7]
30 [v] Is. 32:15
31 [w] Gen. 1:31; Prov. 8:31
32 [x] Hab. 3:10 [y] Ex. 19:18; Ps. 144:5
33 [z] Ps. 63:4
34 [a] Ps. 19:14
35 [b] Ps. 37:38 [7] Heb. *Hallelujah*

PSALM 105
1 [a] 1 Chr. 16:8-22, 34; Ps. 106:1; Is. 12:4 [b] Ps. 145:12
2 [c] Ps. 119:27
4 [d] Ps. 27:8
5 [e] Ps. 77:11
7 [f] [Is. 26:9]
8 [g] Luke 1:72

PSALM 105

The Eternal Faithfulness of the LORD

Oh, [a]give thanks to the LORD!
Call upon His name;
[b]Make known His deeds among the peoples!
2 Sing to Him, sing psalms to Him;
[c]Talk of all His wondrous works!
3 Glory in His holy name;
Let the hearts of those rejoice who seek the LORD!
4 Seek the LORD and His strength;
[d]Seek His face evermore!
5 [e]Remember His marvelous works which He has done,
His wonders, and the judgments of His mouth,
6 O seed of Abraham His servant,
You children of Jacob, His chosen ones!

7 He *is* the LORD our God;
[f]His judgments *are* in all the earth.
8 He [g]remembers His covenant forever,
The word *which* He commanded, for a thousand generations,

104:24-26 This portion corresponds to the fifth day of creation in Gen. 1:20-23.

104:26 Leviathan. This term appears in 4 other OT passages (Job 3:8; 41:1; Ps. 74:14; Is. 27:1). In each case, Leviathan refers to some mighty creature who can overwhelm man but who is no match for God. Some form of sea monster, probably a dinosaur, is in view. *See note on Job 41:1.*

104:27-30 All of creation waits upon God for his providential care. These verses allude to the sixth day of creation (cf. Gen. 1:24-31).

104:30 Your Spirit. This most likely should be translated "your breath," which corresponds to "the breath of life" in Gen. 2:7.

104:31-35 The psalmist closes with a benediction to the Creator in which he prays that the ungodly might no longer spiritually pollute God's universe (104:35). This prayer anticipates the new heaven and new earth (cf. Rev. 21,22).

104:32 trembles...smoke. Earthquakes and fires caused by lightning are in view.

104:35 sinners...wicked. Although God has been merciful to let His fallen human creation live on (cf. Gen. 3:1-24), those who bless and praise the Lord desire to see the day when 1) sinful men have been abolished from the earth (cf. Rev. 20:11-15), and 2) the curse of the earth is reversed (cf. Rev. 22:3).

105:1-45 Just as Pss. 103 and 104 were matched pairs; so are Pss. 105 and 106, as they look at Israel's history from God's perspective and then Israel's vantage respectively. This psalm possibly originated by command of David to Asaph on the occasion when the ark of the covenant was first brought to Jerusalem (2 Sam. 6:12-19; 1 Chr. 16:1-7). Psalm 105:1-15 repeats 1 Chr. 16:8-22.

I. Rejoicing in God's Works for Israel (105:1-3)
II. Remembering God's Works for Israel (105:4-6)
III. Recounting the Work of God for Israel (105:7-45)
  A. Abraham to Joseph (105:7-25)
  B. Moses to Joshua (105:26-45)

105:1-5 Ten imperatives call Israel to a time of remembering, celebrating, and spreading the report abroad of the work of God on Israel's behalf as a result of God's covenant with Abraham.

105:6 seed of Abraham...children of Jacob. Those who were to obey the commands of 105:1-5, i.e., the nation of Israel.

105:7-12 This section rehearses the Abrahamic Covenant.

105:8 a thousand generations. A reference to an exceedingly long time (a generation is normally 40 years) which would encompass the remainder of human history; i.e., forever (cf. Deut. 7:9; 1 Chr. 16:15).

9 [h]*The covenant* which He made with
Abraham,
And His oath to Isaac,
10 And confirmed it to Jacob for a
statute,
To Israel *as* an everlasting covenant,
11 Saying, [i]"To you I will give the land
of Canaan
As the allotment of your inheritance,"
12 [j]When they were few in number,
Indeed very few, [k]and strangers in it.

13 When they went from one nation to
another,
From *one* kingdom to another people,
14 [l]He permitted no one to do them
wrong;
Yes, [m]He rebuked kings for their
sakes,
15 *Saying,* "Do not touch My anointed
ones,
And do My prophets no harm."

16 Moreover [n]He called for a famine in
the land;
He destroyed all the [o]provision of
bread.
17 [p]He sent a man before them—
Joseph—*who* [q]was sold as a slave.
18 [r]They hurt his feet with fetters,
[1]He was laid in irons.
19 Until the time that his word came to
pass,
[s]The word of the LORD tested him.
20 [t]The king sent and released him,
The ruler of the people let him go
free.

9 [h] Gen. 17:2; Luke 1:73; [Gal. 3:17]; Heb. 6:17
11 [i] Gen. 13:15; 15:18
12 [j] Gen. 34:30; [Deut. 7:7] [k] Gen. 23:4; Heb. 11:9
14 [l] Gen. 35:5 [m] Gen. 12:17
16 [n] Gen. 41:54 [o] Lev. 26:26; Is. 3:1; Ezek. 4:16
17 [p] [Gen. 45:5] [q] Gen. 37:28, 36; Acts 7:9
18 [r] Gen. 40:15 [1] *His soul came into iron*
19 [s] Gen. 39:11-21; 41:25, 42, 43
20 [t] Gen. 41:14

21 [u] Gen. 41:40-44
22 [2] Bind as prisoners
23 [v] Gen. 46:6; Acts 7:15 [w] Ps. 78:51
24 [x] Ex. 1:7, 9
25 [y] Ex. 1:8-10; 4:21
26 [z] Ex. 3:10; 4:12-15
27 [a] Ex. 7–12; Ps. 78:43
29 [b] Ex. 7:20, 21; Ps. 78:44
30 [c] Ex. 8:6
31 [d] Ex. 8:16, 17
32 [e] Ex. 9:23-25
33 [f] Ps. 78:47
34 [g] Ex. 10:4

21 [u]He made him lord of his house,
And ruler of all his possessions,
22 To [2]bind his princes at his pleasure,
And teach his elders wisdom.

23 [v]Israel also came into Egypt,
And Jacob dwelt [w]in the land of Ham.
24 [x]He increased His people greatly,
And made them stronger than their
enemies.
25 [y]He turned their heart to hate His
people,
To deal craftily with His servants.

26 [z]He sent Moses His servant,
And Aaron whom He had chosen.
27 They [a]performed His signs among
them,
And wonders in the land of Ham.
28 He sent darkness, and made *it* dark;
And they did not rebel against His
word.
29 [b]He turned their waters into blood,
And killed their fish.
30 [c]Their land abounded with frogs,
Even in the chambers of their kings.
31 [d]He spoke, and there came swarms of
flies,
And lice in all their territory.
32 [e]He gave them hail for rain,
And flaming fire in their land.
33 [f]He struck their vines also, and their
fig trees,
And splintered the trees of their
territory.
34 [g]He spoke, and locusts came,
Young locusts without number,

105:9,10 The original covenant that God had made with Abraham. He later renewed it with Isaac and then Jacob (cf. Abraham—Gen. 12:1-3; 13:14-18; 15:18-21; 17:1-21;22:15-19; Isaac—26:23-25; and Jacob—35:9-12).

105:10 an everlasting covenant. From the time of the covenant until the end. Five OT covenants are spoken of as "everlasting": 1) the Noahic Covenant, Gen. 9:16; 2) the Abrahamic Covenant, Gen. 17:7,13, 19; 3) the Priestly Covenant, Lev. 24:8; 4) the Davidic Covenant, 2 Sam. 23:5; and 5) the New Covenant, Jer. 32:40.

105:11 Saying. This probably has God's promise to Abraham at Gen. 17:8 in view.

105:12 few in number. God promised Abraham that He would multiply his small number of descendants to be as numerous as the stars of heaven and the sand of the seashore (cf. Gen. 13:16; 15:5; 17:2,6; 22:17).

105:13 one nation to another. Abraham had migrated from Ur of the Chaldeans to Haran and finally to Canaan (Gen. 11:31). Later, he visited Egypt (Gen. 12:10–13:1).

105:14 He rebuked. The Lord struck Pharaoh and his house with great plagues when Sarai was taken to his quarters (Gen. 12:17). Abimelech, king of Gerar, was also rebuked by God (Gen. 20:3-7).

105:15 Do not touch...no harm. No one passage in the OT records this exact statement. The psalmist most likely is summarizing several occasions, such as Gen. 20:7; 26:11. **My anointed ones...My prophets.** With poetic parallelism, God's prophets are termed those whom He chose to represent Him on earth. In Gen. 20:7, Abraham is called a prophet. This title could also apply to Isaac and Jacob.

105:16-25 The history recorded in Gen. 37–50 is in view. Verses 16-22 refer to Joseph's experience in Egypt (cf. Gen. 37–41), while v. 23 looks to Jacob's trek to Egypt that resulted in a 430 year stay (Gen. 42–50; cf. Gen. 15:13,14; Ex. 12:40). Verses 24,25 give an overall summary of Israel's experience in Egypt (cf. Ex. 1:7-14).

105:23 the land of Ham. Another name for the area in Egypt where part of the descendants of Ham, the youngest son of Noah, settled (cf. Gen. 10; Ps. 78:51).

105:23-25 God sovereignly used Egypt to judge Israel (cf. Gen. 15:13).

105:26-36 God's deliverance of Israel from Egypt through the leadership of Moses and Aaron is rehearsed with a special emphasis on the 10 plagues, ending with the Passover (cf. Ex. 5–12).

105:28 darkness. The ninth plague (cf. Ex. 10:21-29).

105:29 waters into blood. The first plague (cf. Ex. 7:14-25).

105:30 frogs. The second plague (cf. Ex. 8:1-15).

105:31 swarms of flies...lice. The fourth and third plagues respectively (cf. Ex. 8:16-32). The fifth plague of pestilence (Ex. 9:1-7) and the sixth plague of boils (Ex. 9:8-12) are not mentioned.

105:32,33 hail...flaming fire. The seventh plague (cf. Ex. 9:13-35).

105:34,35 locusts. The eighth plague (cf. Ex. 10:1-20).

35 And ate up all the vegetation in their land,
And devoured the fruit of their ground.
36 [h]He also [3]destroyed all the firstborn in their land,
[i]The first of all their strength.
37 [j]He also brought them out with silver and gold,
And *there was* none feeble among His tribes.
38 [k]Egypt was glad when they departed,
For the fear of them had fallen upon them.
39 [l]He spread a cloud for a covering,
And fire to give light in the night.
40 [m]*The people* asked, and He brought quail,
And [n]satisfied them with the bread of heaven.
41 [o]He opened the rock, and water gushed out;
It ran in the dry places *like* a river.
42 For He remembered [p]His holy promise,
And Abraham His servant.
43 He brought out His people with joy,
His chosen ones with [4]gladness.
44 [q]He gave them the lands of the [5]Gentiles,
And they inherited the labor of the nations,
45 [r]That they might observe His statutes
And keep His laws.

[6]Praise the LORD!

36 [h] Ex. 12:29; 13:15; Ps. 135:8; 136:10 [i] Gen. 49:3 [3] Lit. *struck down*
37 [j] Ex. 12:35, 36
38 [k] Ex. 12:33
39 [l] Ex. 13:21; Neh. 9:12; Ps. 78:14; Is. 4:5
40 [m] Ex. 16:12 [n] Ps. 78:24
41 [o] Ex. 17:6; Num. 20:11; Ps. 78:15; 114:8; Is. 48:21; [1 Cor. 10:4]
42 [p] Gen. 15:13, 14; Ps. 105:8
43 [4] *a joyful shout*
44 [q] Josh. 11:16-23; 13:7; Ps. 78:55 [5] *nations*
45 [r] [Deut. 4:1, 40] [6] Heb. *Hallelujah*

PSALM 106
1 [a] 1 Chr. 16:34, 41 [1] Heb. *Hallelujah*
2 [2] *express*
3 [b] Ps. 15:2 [c] [Gal. 6:9] [3] LXX, Syr., Tg., Vg. *those who do*
4 [d] Ps. 119:132
5 [4] The people of Your inheritance
6 [e] 1 Kin. 8:47; [Ezra 9:7; Neh. 1:7; Jer. 3:25; Dan. 9:5]
7 [f] Ex. 14:11, 12

PSALM 106

Joy in Forgiveness of Israel's Sins

Praise[1] the LORD!
[a]Oh, give thanks to the LORD, for *He is* good!
For His mercy *endures* forever.
2 Who can [2]utter the mighty acts of the LORD?
Who can declare all His praise?
3 Blessed *are* those who keep justice,
And [3]he who [b]does righteousness at [c]all times!
4 [d]Remember me, O LORD, with the favor *You have toward* Your people.
Oh, visit me with Your salvation,
5 That I may see the benefit of Your chosen ones,
That I may rejoice in the gladness of Your nation,
That I may glory with [4]Your inheritance.
6 [e]We have sinned with our fathers,
We have committed iniquity,
We have done wickedly.
7 Our fathers in Egypt did not understand Your wonders;
They did not remember the multitude of Your mercies,
[f]But rebelled by the sea—the Red Sea.
8 Nevertheless He saved them for His name's sake,

105:36 destroyed...the firstborn. The tenth and final plague, which was death to the firstborn of man and beast (cf. Ex. 11:1–12:51).

105:37-41 The psalmist summarizes Israel's Exodus from Egypt. God provided for their financial and physical needs (cf. Ex. 11:2,3; 12:35 and Ex. 15:26); protection by day and night (cf. Ex. 14:19,20); food needs (Ex. 16:1-36); and water needs (cf. Ex. 17:6; Num. 20:1-11).

105:42-45 The psalmist concludes with a summary that alludes to Joshua's leading the nation back into the Land, first promised to Abraham, (Josh. 1–12) and then distributed to the 12 tribes of Israel (Josh. 13–24). What God promised (cf. 105:7-12) He delivered.

105:42 He remembered. As promised in v. 8.

105:45 observe...keep. This theme of obedience begins (1:6-9) and ends (24:14,15,16,18,21,24) the book of Joshua.

106:1-48 Psalm 106 rehearses God's mercy during Israel's history in spite of Israel's sinfulness (cf. Neh. 9:1-38; Ps. 78; Is. 63:7–64:12; Ezek. 20:1-44; Dan. 9:1-19; Acts 7:2-53; 1 Cor. 10:1-13). The occasion for this psalm is most likely the repentance (v. 6) of post-Exilic Jews who had returned to Jerusalem (vv. 46,47). Verses 1,47,48 seem to be borrowed from 1 Chr. 16:34-36, which was sung on the occasion of the ark's first being brought to Jerusalem by David (cf. 2 Sam. 6:12-19; 1 Chr. 16:1-7). True revival appears to be the psalmist's intention.

I. The Invocation (106:1-5)
II. The Identification with Israel's Sins (106:6)
III. The Confession of Israel's Sins (106:7-46)
  A. During Moses' Time (106:7-33)
  B. From Joshua to Jeremiah (106:34-46)
IV. The Plea for Salvation (106:47)
V. The Benediction (106:48)

106:1 good...mercy. These attributes of God are especially praiseworthy to the psalmist in light of Israel's historical sin pattern (cf. 106:6-46).

106:2,3 Verse 2 asks the question answered in v. 3.

106:4,5 The psalmist has the benefits of the Abrahamic Covenant in mind (*see note on Ps. 105:9,10*). He prays here for personal deliverance (v. 4) and later for national deliverance (v. 47).

106:6 We...fathers. The psalmist acknowledges the perpetual sinfulness of Israel, including that of his own generation.

106:7-12 This section recalls the crossing of the Red Sea during the Exodus by the nation, when Pharaoh and his army were in pursuit (cf. Ex. 14:1-31).

106:7 Red Sea. *See notes on Ex. 10:19; 13:18.*

106:8 His name's sake. The glory and reputation of God provide the highest motive for his actions. This frequent OT phrase appears 6 other places in the Psalms (cf. Pss. 23:3; 25:11; 31:3; 79:9; 109:21; 143:11).

[g]That He might make His mighty
power known.
9 [h]He rebuked the Red Sea also, and it
dried up;
So [i]He led them through the depths,
As through the wilderness.
10 He [j]saved them from the hand of him
who hated *them,*
And redeemed them from the hand of
the enemy.
11 [k]The waters covered their enemies;
There was not one of them left.
12 [l]Then they believed His words;
They sang His praise.

13 [m]They soon forgot His works;
They did not wait for His counsel,
14 [n]But lusted exceedingly in the
wilderness,
And tested God in the desert.
15 [o]And He gave them their request,
But [p]sent leanness into their soul.

16 When [q]they envied Moses in the
camp,
And Aaron the saint of the LORD,
17 [r]The earth opened up and swallowed
Dathan,
And covered the faction of Abiram.
18 [s]A fire was kindled in their company;
The flame burned up the wicked.

19 [t]They made a calf in Horeb,
And worshiped the molded image.
20 Thus [u]they changed their glory
Into the image of an ox that eats
grass.
21 They forgot God their Savior,
Who had done great things in Egypt,
22 Wondrous works in the land of Ham,
Awesome things by the Red Sea.
23 [v]Therefore He said that He would
destroy them,
Had not Moses His chosen one
[w]stood before Him in the
breach,
To turn away His wrath, lest He
destroy *them.*

24 Then they despised [x]the pleasant
land;
They [y]did not believe His word,
25 [z]But complained in their tents,
And did not heed the voice of the
LORD.
26 [a]Therefore He raised His hand *in an
oath* against them,
[b]To [5]overthrow them in the
wilderness,
27 [c]To [6]overthrow their descendants
among the [7]nations,
And to scatter them in the lands.

28 [d]They joined themselves also to Baal of
Peor,
And ate sacrifices [8]made to the dead.

8 [g]Ex. 9:16
9 [h]Ex. 14:21; Ps. 18:15; Is. 51:10; Nah. 1:4 [i]Is. 63:11-13
10 [j]Ex. 14:30
11 [k]Ex. 14:27, 28; 15:5
12 [l]Ex. 15:1-21
13 [m]Ex. 15:24; 16:2; 17:2
14 [n]Num. 11:4; 1 Cor. 10:6
15 [o]Num. 11:31 [p]Is. 10:16
16 [q]Num. 16:1-3
17 [r]Num. 16:31, 32; Deut. 11:6
18 [s]Num. 16:35, 46
19 [t]Ex. 32:1-4; Deut. 9:8; Acts 7:41
20 [u]Jer. 2:11; Rom. 1:23
23 [v]Ex. 32:10; Deut. 9:19 [w]Ezek. 22:30
24 [x]Deut. 8:7; Jer. 3:19; Ezek. 20:6 [y]Deut. 1:32; 9:23; [Heb. 3:18, 19]
25 [z]Num. 14:2, 27; Deut. 1:27
26 [a]Ezek. 20:15, 16; [Heb. 3:11, 18] [b]Num. 14:28-30 [5]*make them fall*
27 [c]Lev. 26:33; Ezek. 20:23 [6]*make their descendants fall also* [7]*Gentiles*
28 [d]Num. 25:3; Deut. 4:3; Hos. 9:10 [8]*offered*

106:9 He rebuked the Red Sea. This reliable historical account recalls a true supernatural miracle of God (cf. Ex. 14:21,22) just as He would later provide a way for the nation to cross the Jordan into the land (cf. Josh. 3:14-17).

106:10 Quoted in Luke 1:71.

106:11 not one of them left. As recorded in Ex. 14:28 (cf. Ps. 78:53).

106:12 They sang His praise. The Song of Moses is in view (cf. Ex. 15:1-21).

106:13-33 This section remembers the nation's wanderings in the wilderness (cf. Num. 14–Deut. 34).

106:13-15 The Jews forgot what God had most recently done on their behalf, but 1) remembered the basics of life that Egypt provided, and 2) doubted that they would have water (cf. Ex. 15:24) or food (cf. Ex. 16:2,3) in the future.

106:14 tested God. According to Num. 14:22, the nation tested God at least 10 times (cf. Ex. 5:21; 6:9; 14:11,12; 15:24; 16:2,3; 17:2,3; 32:1-6; Num. 11:1-6; 12:1,2; 14:2,3).

106:16-18 Korah, who is not named here, led the rebellion that is recounted (cf. Num. 16:1-35). God's judgment concluded with fire which consumed 250 men (cf. Num. 16:35).

106:19-23 This section remembers when the nation convinced Aaron to make a golden calf for idol worship while Moses was on the mountain receiving the commandments of God (cf. Ex. 32:1-14; Deut. 9:7-21).

106:19 Horeb. Most likely another name for Mt. Sinai (cf. Ex. 19:11). This special place, called "the mountain of God" (cf. Ex. 3:1; 1 Kin. 19:8), is where Moses received the commandments of God (Deut. 1:6; 5:2; 29:1; Mal. 4:4).

106:21 God their Savior. This title, common in the pastoral epistles, is seldom used in the OT outside of Isaiah (19:20; 43:3,11; 45:15,21;49:26; 60:16; 63:8). Here it refers to physical deliverance. It looks forward to Jesus Christ as spiritual redeemer (Luke 2:11).

106:22 Ham. Another name for the part of Egypt, which was settled by descendants of Ham, the second son of Noah (cf. Gen. 10:6-20).

106:23 Moses...in the breach. Moses pleaded with God, based on the Abrahamic Covenant promises, not to destroy the nation in spite of their idolatry and immoral behavior (cf. Ex. 32:11-14).

106:24-27 This portion recounts 1) the nation's rejection of Joshua's and Caleb's positive report from the Land, and 2) their desire to return to Egypt (cf. Num. 14:1-4). God responded with judgment (Num. 14:11-38).

106:24 the pleasant land. A term used of the Land God promised to Abraham for the nation Israel (cf. Jer. 3:19, Zech. 7:14).

106:28-31 This scene recounts Israel's encounter with the prophet Balaam who, on behalf of Balak, King of Moab, tried to curse Israel but was prevented from doing so by God (cf. Num. 22–24; Deut. 23:4; Josh. 24:9,10; Neh. 13:2). Having failed, Balaam advised Balak to entice Israel with immorality and idolatry (cf. Num. 31:16 with 25:1; 2 Pet. 2:15; Jude 11; Rev. 2:14). Israel sinned and God judged (Num. 25:1-13). Balaam was later slain by Israel (cf. Josh. 13:22).

106:28 Baal of Peor. Refers to Baal, a god of the Moabites, whose worship occurred at the location of the mountain called Peor (cf. Num. 23:28). **sacrifices made to the dead.** This most likely refers to sacrifices made to lifeless idols (cf. 1 Thess. 1:9). Israel should have been worshiping "the living God" (cf. Deut. 5:26; 1 Sam. 17:26,36; Pss. 42:2; 84:2; Jer. 10:3-10; Dan. 6:20,26).

29 Thus they provoked *Him* to anger
with their deeds,
And the plague broke out among
them.
30 [e]Then Phinehas stood up and
intervened,
And the plague was stopped.
31 And that was accounted to him [f]for
righteousness
To all generations forevermore.

32 [g]They angered *Him* also at the waters
of [9]strife,
[h]So that it went ill with Moses on
account of them;
33 [i]Because they rebelled against His
Spirit,
So that he spoke rashly with his lips.

34 [j]They did not destroy the peoples,
[k]Concerning whom the LORD had
commanded them,
35 [l]But they mingled with the Gentiles
And learned their works;
36 [m]They served their idols,
[n]Which became a snare to them.
37 [o]They even sacrificed their sons
And their daughters to [p]demons,
38 And shed innocent blood,
The blood of their sons and daughters,
Whom they sacrificed to the idols of
Canaan;
And [q]the land was polluted with
blood.
39 Thus they [1]were [r]defiled by their
own works,
And [s]played[2] the harlot by their own
deeds.

40 Therefore [t]the wrath of the LORD was
kindled against His people,
So that He abhorred [u]His own
inheritance.
41 And [v]He gave them into the hand of
the Gentiles,
And those who hated them ruled over
them.
42 Their enemies also oppressed them,
And they were brought into
subjection under their hand.
43 [w]Many times He delivered them;
But they rebelled in their counsel,
And were brought low for their
iniquity.

44 Nevertheless He regarded their
affliction,
When [x]He heard their cry;
45 [y]And for their sake He remembered
His covenant,
And [z]relented [a]according to the
multitude of His mercies.
46 [b]He also made them to be pitied
By all those who carried them away
captive.

47 [c]Save us, O LORD our God,
And gather us from among the
Gentiles,
To give thanks to Your holy name,
To triumph in Your praise.

30 [e] Num. 25:7, 8 **31** [f] Gen. 15:6; Num. 25:11-13 **32** [g] Num. 20:3-13; Ps. 81:7 [h] Deut. 1:37; 3:26 [9] Or *Meribah* **33** [i] Num. 20:3, 10 **34** [j] Judg. 1:21 [k] [Deut. 7:2, 16]; Judg. 2:2 **35** [l] Judg. 3:5, 6 **36** [m] Judg. 2:12 [n] Deut. 7:16 **37** [o] [Deut. 12:31; 32:17, 18]; 2 Kin. 16:3; 17:17; Ezek. 16:20, 21; [1 Cor. 10:20] [p] [Lev. 17:7] **38** [q] [Num. 35:33; Is. 24:5; Jer. 3:1, 2] **39** [r] [Lev. 18:24]; Ezek. 20:18 [1] *became unclean* [s] [Lev. 17:7; Num. 15:39]; Judg. 2:17; Hos. 4:12 [2] *Were unfaithful* **40** [t] Judg. 2:14; Ps. 78:59 [u] [Deut. 9:29; 32:9] **41** [v] Judg. 2:14; [Neh. 9:27] **43** [w] Judg. 2:16; [Neh. 9:27] **44** [x] Judg. 3:9; 6:7; 10:10 **45** [y] [Lev. 26:41, 42] [z] Judg. 2:18 [a] Ps. 69:16 **46** [b] 1 Kin. 8:50; [2 Chr. 30:9]; Ezra 9:9; Neh. 1:11; Jer. 42:12 **47** [c] 1 Chr. 16:35, 36

106:30 Phinehas. The son of Eleazar, son of Aaron (cf. Num. 25:7).

106:31 accounted to him for righteousness. This was a just and rewardable action, evidencing faith in God. As with Abraham (cf. Gen. 15:6 and Rom. 4:3; Gal. 3:6; James 2:23), so it was also with Phinehas. The everlasting covenant of perpetual priesthood through Aaron, from the house of Levi, was first made by God in Lev. 24:8,9 (cf. Jer. 33:17-22; Mal. 2:4-8). This covenant was reaffirmed in Num. 18:8,19. In this text, the covenant is further specified to be through the line of faithful Phinehas.

106:32-33 This scene looks back to Num. 20:1-13 when Moses, provoked by the continuing rebellion of Israel, nonetheless wrongly struck the rock in anger (cf. Ex. 11:8; 16:20) and thus offended God (cf. Num. 20:12). As a result, both Aaron (cf. Num. 20:22-29) and Moses (Deut. 34:1-8) died prematurely without entering the Promised Land.

106:32 the waters of strife. These are the waters of Meribah (cf. Num. 20:13).

106:33 His Spirit. This most likely refers to the Holy Spirit of God. The Spirit of God had an extensive ministry in the OT (cf. Gen. 1:2; 6:3; 2 Sam. 23:2; Neh. 9:30; Ps. 139:7; Is. 48:16; Ezek. 2:2; 3:12-14; 8:3; 11:1,5,24; Hag. 2:5, Zech. 7:12). Both Is. 63:10,11 and Acts 7:51 point to this particular event.

106:34-39 This section describes the general sins of Israel from the time they entered the Land (Josh. 3,4) until they were exiled to Assyria (2 Kin. 17) and Babylon (2 Kin. 24,25). They failed to expel the heathen and sadly conformed to their idolatry.

106:36-38 idols...demons...idols. Demons impersonate idols and encourage idol worship (cf. Deut. 32:17; 2 Chr. 33:5-7; 1 Cor. 10:14-21; Rev. 9:20). The sacrifice of children was not uncommon (cf. Deut. 12:31; 2 Kin. 17:17; Ezek. 16:20,21).

106:39 their own works...deeds. God held Israel directly responsible for their sin without excuse.

106:40-43 From the time of the judges until the Assyrian and Babylonian exiles, God used the hand of His enemies to discipline Israel for their sin.

106:44-46 This emphasizes the unconditional nature of God's covenant with Abraham.

106:45 for their sake. A secondary complement to God, who was primarily acting for His name's sake (cf. v. 8). **He remembered His covenant.** This answers the psalmist's prayer of vv. 4,5 with regard to the Abrahamic Covenant that 1) the descendants of Abraham would multiply, and 2) they would possess the Land (*see note on Ps. 105:9,10*; cf. Luke 1:72-75).

106:47 The psalmist pleads, on behalf of the nation and in light of the Abrahamic Covenant, for the nation to be regathered in Israel. He remembers what the men of Moses' day forgot, i.e., God as their Savior (cf. 106:21). Even though the tribes of Judah and Benjamin returned to Israel in Ezra and Nehemiah, this text looks ahead to the regathering of Israel at the time when the Lord Jesus Christ returns to rule over the promised Davidic (2 Sam. 7)/millennial kingdom (Rev. 20) on earth (cf. Ezek. 37:11-28; Hos. 14:4-8; Joel 3:18-21; Amos 9:7-15; Mic. 7:14-20; Zeph. 3:8-20; Zech. 12–14).

48 [d]Blessed *be* the LORD God of Israel
From everlasting to everlasting!
And let all the people say, "Amen!"
[3]Praise the LORD!

Book Five: Psalms 107–150

PSALM 107

Thanksgiving to the LORD for His Great Works of Deliverance

Oh, [a]give thanks to the LORD, for *He is* good!
For His [1]mercy *endures* forever.
2 Let the redeemed of the LORD say *so,*
Whom He has redeemed from the hand of the enemy,
3 And [b]gathered out of the lands,
From the east and from the west,
From the north and from the south.

4 They wandered in [c]the wilderness in a desolate way;
They found no city to dwell in.
5 Hungry and thirsty,
Their soul fainted in them.
6 [d]Then they cried out to the LORD in their trouble,
And He delivered them out of their distresses.
7 And He led them forth by the [e]right way,
That they might go to a city for a dwelling place.
8 [f]Oh, that *men* would give thanks to the LORD *for* His goodness,
And *for* His wonderful works to the children of men!
9 For [g]He satisfies the longing soul,
And fills the hungry soul with goodness.

10 Those who [h]sat in darkness and in the shadow of death,
[i]Bound[2] in affliction and irons—
11 Because they [j]rebelled against the words of God,
And [3]despised [k]the counsel of the Most High,
12 Therefore He brought down their heart with labor;
They fell down, and *there was* [l]none to help.
13 Then they cried out to the LORD in their trouble,
And He saved them out of their distresses.
14 [m]He brought them out of darkness and the shadow of death,
And broke their chains in pieces.
15 Oh, that *men* would give thanks to the LORD *for* His goodness,
And *for* His wonderful works to the children of men!
16 For He has [n]broken the gates of bronze,
And cut the bars of iron in two.

17 Fools, [o]because of their transgression,
And because of their iniquities, were afflicted.
18 [p]Their soul abhorred all manner of food,
And they [q]drew near to the gates of death.
19 Then they cried out to the LORD in their trouble,
And He saved them out of their distresses.
20 [r]He sent His word and [s]healed them,
And [t]delivered *them* from their destructions.
21 Oh, that *men* would give thanks to the LORD *for* His goodness,

48 [d]Ps. 41:13 [3]Heb. *Hallelujah*

PSALM 107

1 [a]1 Chr. 16:34; Ps. 106:1; Jer. 33:11 [1]Heb. same as *goodness,* vv. 8, 15, 21, 31, and *lovingkindness,* v. 43
3 [b]Is. 43:5, 6; Jer. 29:14; 31:8-10; [Ezek. 39:27, 28]
4 [c]Num. 14:33; 32:13; [Deut. 2:7; 32:10]; Josh. 5:6; 14:10
6 [d]Ps. 50:15; [Hos. 5:15]
7 [e]Ezra 8:21; Ps. 5:8; Jer. 31:9
8 [f]Ps. 107:15, 21
9 [g][Ps. 34:10; Luke 1:53]
10 [h][Is. 42:7; Mic. 7:8; Luke 1:79] [i]Job 36:8 [2]*Prisoners*
11 [j]Lam. 3:42 [k][Ps. 73:24] [3]*scorned*
12 [l]Ps. 22:11
14 [m]Ps. 68:6
16 [n]Is. 45:1, 2
17 [o][Is. 65:6, 7; Jer. 30:14, 15]; Lam. 3:39; Ezek. 24:23
18 [p]Job 33:20 [q]Job 33:22
20 [r]Matt. 8:8 [s]2 Kin. 20:5; Ps. 30:2 [t]Job 33:28, 30

106:48 From everlasting to everlasting. With the hopeful prayer of 106:47 on his lips, the psalmist closes the fourth book of the Psalms (Pss. 90–106) with a grand benediction focusing on the eternal character of God, Israel's Savior (cf. 1 Chr. 16:36; Pss. 41:13; 90:2).

107:1-43 The opening line of Pss. 105–107, "Oh, give thanks to the LORD," links together this trilogy of songs which praise God for His goodness and mercy to Israel. Most likely this psalm has a post-Exilic origin (cf. 107:3). The psalm develops two main themes: 1) praising God for His continual deliverance (107:4-32), and 2) remembering God's response to man's obedience/disobedience (107:33-42).

I. The Call to Praise (107:1-3)
II. The Cause of Rejoicing—Deliverance (107:4-32)
III. The Consequences of Obedience/Disobedience (107:33-42)
IV. The Commentary on Wisdom/Understanding (107:43)

107:1-3 All of those who have been delivered (redeemed) from the hand of Israel's enemy focus on God's goodness and everlasting mercy. They had been delivered through the centuries from Egypt to the S (cf. Ex. 12–14), Syria and Assyria to the N (cf. 2 Kin. 19:29-37), the Philistines to the W (cf. 2 Sam. 8:1; 2 King. 18:8), and Babylon to the E (cf. Ezra 1). Compare the psalmist's prayer in 106:47 with v. 3.

107:4-32 This portion contains four pictures or actual situations which illustrate the disastrous end of sin in the nation: 1) wandering in the wilderness (vv. 4-9), 2) languishing in prison (vv. 10-16); 3) enduring sickness (vv. 17-22); and 4) tossing on a stormy sea (vv. 23-32). Each picture follows the same sequence of four events: 1) man's predicament (vv. 4,5,10-12,17,18,23-27); 2) man's petition (vv. 6a,13a, 19a,28a); 3) God's pardon (vv. 6b,7),13b,14,19b,20,28b-30); and 4) man's praise (vv. 8,9,15,16,21,22,31,32).

107:4-9 Possibly the psalmist looked back at the desert wanderings of ungrateful, faithless Israel after the miraculous Exodus (Num. 14–Josh. 2).

107:10-16 Possibly the psalmist thought of the capture and imprisonment of King Zedekiah ca. 586 B.C. (cf. 2 Kin. 25:4-7; Jer. 39:4-8; Jer. 52:1-11).

107:17-22 Possibly the psalmist recalled the mass affliction and subsequent mass healing in Num. 21:4-9.

And *for* His wonderful works to the
children of men!
22 [u]Let them sacrifice the sacrifices of
thanksgiving,
And [v]declare His works with
[4]rejoicing.

23 Those who go down to the sea in
ships,
Who do business on great waters,
24 They see the works of the LORD,
And His wonders in the deep.
25 For He commands and [w]raises the
stormy wind,
Which lifts up the waves of the sea.
26 They mount up to the heavens,
They go down again to the depths;
[x]Their soul melts because of trouble.
27 They reel to and fro, and stagger like
a drunken man,
And [5]are at their wits' end.
28 Then they cry out to the LORD in their
trouble,
And He brings them out of their
distresses.
29 [y]He calms the storm,
So that its waves are still.
30 Then they are glad because they are
quiet;
So He guides them to their desired
haven.
31 [z]Oh, that *men* would give thanks to the
LORD *for* His goodness,
And *for* His wonderful works to the
children of men!
32 Let them exalt Him also [a]in the
assembly of the people,
And praise Him in the company of
the elders.

33 He [b]turns rivers into a wilderness,
And the watersprings into dry
ground;
34 A [c]fruitful land into [6]barrenness,
For the wickedness of those who
dwell in it.

22 [u] Lev. 7:12; Ps. 50:14; Heb. 13:15 [v] Ps. 9:11 [4] *joyful singing*
25 [w] Jon. 1:4
26 [x] Ps. 22:14
27 [5] Lit. *all their wisdom is swallowed up*
29 [y] Ps. 89:9; Matt. 8:26; Luke 8:24
31 [z] Ps. 107:8, 15, 21
32 [a] Ps. 22:22, 25
33 [b] 1 Kin. 17:1, 7; Is. 50:2
34 [c] Gen. 13:10; Deut. 29:23 [6] Lit. *a salty waste*
35 [d] Ps. 114:8; [Is. 41:17, 18]
38 [e] Gen. 12:2; 17:16, 20 [f] Ex. 1:7; [Deut. 7:14]
39 [g] 2 Kin. 10:32
40 [h] Job 12:21, 24
41 [i] 1 Sam. 2:8; [Ps. 113:7, 8] [j] Ps. 78:52
42 [k] Job 5:15, 16 [l] Job 5:16; Ps. 63:11; [Rom. 3:19]
43 [m] Ps. 64:9; Jer. 9:12; [Hos. 14:9]

PSALM 108
1 [a] Ps. 57:7-11
2 [b] Ps. 57:8-11
4 [1] *skies*

35 [d]He turns a wilderness into pools of
water,
And dry land into watersprings.
36 There He makes the hungry dwell,
That they may establish a city for a
dwelling place,
37 And sow fields and plant vineyards,
That they may yield a fruitful harvest.
38 [e]He also blesses them, and they
multiply greatly;
And He does not let their cattle
[f]decrease.

39 When they are [g]diminished and
brought low
Through oppression, affliction and
sorrow,
40 [h]He pours contempt on princes,
And causes them to wander in the
wilderness *where there is* no
way;
41 [i]Yet He sets the poor on high, far from
affliction,
And [j]makes *their* families like a flock.
42 [k]The righteous see *it* and rejoice,
And all [l]iniquity stops its mouth.

43 [m]Whoever *is* wise will observe these
things,
And they will understand the
lovingkindness of the LORD.

PSALM 108

Assurance of God's Victory over Enemies

A Song. A Psalm of David.

O [a]God, my heart is steadfast;
I will sing and give praise, even with
my glory.
2 [b]Awake, lute and harp!
I will awaken the dawn.
3 I will praise You, O LORD, among the
peoples,
And I will sing praises to You among
the nations.
4 For Your mercy *is* great above the
[1]heavens,

107:23-32 Possibly the psalmist had Jonah and the sailors bound for Tarshish in mind (cf. Jon. 1).

107:33,42 This section contrasts God's blessing in response to man's obedience with God's judgment on man's sin. The psalmist makes his point with 4 illustrations: 1) descending from prosperity to poverty (vv. 33,34); 2) being lifted up from barrenness to blessedness (vv. 35-38); 3) falling from the top to the bottom (vv. 39,40); and 4) being elevated from low to high (vv. 41,42).

107:33,34 Perhaps the 3 years of drought from Ahab's and Jezebel's sins are in view (cf. 1 Kin. 17:1; 18:18).

107:35-38 Perhaps the time of Abraham (Gen. 24:1,34,35) or Joshua (Josh. 24:13) is in view.

107:39,40 Perhaps the Assyrian Exile (2 Kin. 17:4-6) or the Babylonian Captivity (2 Kin. 24:14,15) is in view.

107:41,42 Perhaps the impoverished Jews in Egypt who were made rich with Egyptian gold and other treasures are in view (cf. Ex. 1:13,14 with 3:21,22; 11:2; 12:35,36).

107:43 Perhaps the psalmist has Prov. 8:1-36, Eccl. 12:13,14, or Hos. 14:9 in mind as he pens these concluding words.

108:1-13 David combines portions of his own previously written Pss. 57 and 60 to make up this psalm commemorating God's victories (vv. 1-5 are from 57:7-11; vv. 6-13 are from 60:5-12). He deleted the laments that began each psalm (57:1-6 and 60:1-4) while combining his own words of exaltation and confidence in God with only slight word variation. No specific historical occasion behind this psalm is given. *See notes on Ps. 57:7-11 and Ps. 60:5-12.*

I. Personal Exaltation of God (108:1-5)
II. Personal Confidence in God (108:6-13)

And Your truth *reaches* to the clouds.

5 [c]Be exalted, O God, above the heavens,
And Your glory above all the earth;
6 [d]That Your beloved may be delivered,
Save *with* Your right hand, and [2]hear me.

7 God has spoken in His holiness:
"I will rejoice;
I will divide Shechem
And measure out the Valley of Succoth.
8 Gilead *is* Mine; Manasseh *is* Mine;
Ephraim also *is* the [3]helmet for My head;
[e]Judah *is* My lawgiver.
9 Moab *is* My washpot;
Over Edom I will cast My shoe;
Over Philistia I will triumph."

10 [f]Who will bring me *into* the strong city?
Who will lead me to Edom?
11 *Is it* not *You*, O God, *who* cast us off?
And *You*, O God, *who* did not go out with our armies?
12 Give us help from trouble,
For the help of man is useless.
13 [g]Through God we will do valiantly,
For *it is* He *who* shall tread down our enemies.

PSALM 109

Plea for Judgment of False Accusers

To the Chief Musician. A Psalm of David.

Do[a] not keep silent,
O God of my praise!
2 For the mouth of the wicked and the mouth of the deceitful
Have opened against me;
They have spoken against me with a [b]lying tongue.
3 They have also surrounded me with words of hatred,
And fought against me [c]without a cause.
4 In return for my love they are my accusers,
But I *give myself to* prayer.
5 Thus [d]they have rewarded me evil for good,
And hatred for my love.

6 Set a wicked man over him,
And let [e]an [1]accuser stand at his right hand.
7 When he is judged, let him be found guilty,
And [f]let his prayer become sin.
8 Let his days be [g]few,
And [h]let another take his office.
9 [i]Let his children be fatherless,
And his wife a widow.
10 Let his children [2]continually be vagabonds, and beg;
Let them [3]seek *their bread* also from their desolate places.
11 [j]Let the creditor seize all that he has,
And let strangers plunder his labor.
12 Let there be none to extend mercy to him,
Nor let there be any to favor his fatherless children.
13 [k]Let his [4]posterity be cut off,
And in the generation following let their [l]name be blotted out.

14 [m]Let the iniquity of his fathers be remembered before the LORD,
And let not the sin of his mother [n]be blotted out.
15 Let them be continually before the LORD,

5 [c]Ps. 57:5, 11
6 [d]Ps. 60:5-12 [2]Lit. *answer*
8 [e][Gen. 49:10] [3]Lit. *protection*
10 [f]Ps. 60:9
13 [g]Ps. 60:12

PSALM 109

1 [a]Ps. 83:1
2 [b]Ps. 27:12
3 [c]Ps. 35:7; 69:4; John 15:25
5 [d]Ps. 35:7, 12; 38:20; Prov. 17:13
6 [e]Zech. 3:1 [1]Heb. *satan*
7 [f][Prov. 28:9]
8 [g][Ps. 55:23]; John 17:12 [h]Ps. 69:25; Acts 1:20
9 [i]Ex. 22:24
10 [2]*wander continuously* [3]So with MT, Tg.; LXX, Vg. *be cast out*
11 [j]Neh. 5:7; Job 5:5; 18:9
13 [k]Job 18:19; Ps. 37:28 [l]Prov. 10:7 [4]*descendants be destroyed*
14 [m][Ex. 20:5; Num. 14:18]; Is. 65:6; [Jer. 32:18] [n]Neh. 4:5; Jer. 18:23

109:1-31 This imprecatory psalm of David cannot be conclusively connected by the psalm's general details with any particular incident/person in the king's life as chronicled in 1, 2 Sam.; 1 Kin.; and 1 Chr. David responds here to those who have launched a vicious verbal assault of false accusations against him (cf. 109:2,3,20). This psalm is considered messianic in nature, since Acts 1:20 quotes v. 8 in reference to Judas' punishment for betraying Christ (cf. Pss. 41:9; 69:25). David reverses roles with his enemies by moving from being the accused in man's court to being the accuser/prosecutor before the bar of God.

I. The Plaintiff's Plea (109:1-5)
II. The Punishment Desired (109:6-20)
III. The Petition for Justice (109:21-29)
IV. The Praise of the Judge (109:30,31)

109:1 O God of my praise. David begins and ends (cf. v. 30) with praise for the Chief Justice of the universe. At v. 21, David addresses the Judge as "O GOD the Lord" and at v. 26 as "O LORD my God."

109:2-5 David's complaint was that the innocent were being accused by the guilty. He asserted that the charges were without cause (109:3). While Doeg the Edomite has been identified by some (cf. 1 Sam. 21,22; Ps. 52), the far more likely candidate would be Saul (cf. 1 Sam. 18–27). Eight of the 14 historical superscriptions in other psalms refer to the sufferings of David related to Saul's pursuits for the purpose of killing David (cf. Pss. 18,34,54,56,57,59,63,142).

109:2 In vv. 2-5,20,25,27-29, David refers to a group of accusers, in contrast to vv. 6-19 where an individual is mentioned. Most likely, the individual is the group leader.

109:6-20 The Mosaic law had anticipated false accusations and malicious witnesses (cf. Deut. 19:16-21) by decreeing that the false accuser was to be given the punishment intended for the accused. It would appear that David had this law in mind here and vv. 26-29. Thus, his imprecations are not malicious maledictions, but rather a call for justice according to the law. These severe words have respect not to the penitent, but to the impenitent and hard-hearted foes of God and His cause, whose inevitable fate is set.

109:8 The Apostle Peter cited this verse as justification for replacing Judas the betrayer with another apostle (cf. Acts. 1:20).

That He may [o]cut off the memory of
them from the earth;
16 Because he did not remember to show
mercy,
But persecuted the poor and needy
man,
That he might even slay the [p]broken
in heart.
17 [q]As he loved cursing, so let it come to
him;
As he did not delight in blessing, so
let it be far from him.
18 As he clothed himself with cursing as
with his garment,
So let it [r]enter his body like water,
And like oil into his bones.
19 Let it be to him like the garment
which covers him,
And for a belt with which he girds
himself continually.
20 *Let* this *be* the LORD's reward to my
accusers,
And to those who speak evil against
my person.

21 But You, O GOD the Lord,
Deal with me for Your name's sake;
Because Your mercy *is* good, deliver
me.
22 For I *am* poor and needy,
And my heart is wounded within me.
23 I am gone [s]like a shadow when it
lengthens;
I am shaken off like a locust.
24 My [t]knees are weak through fasting,
And my flesh is feeble from lack of
fatness.
25 I also have become [u]a reproach to
them;
When they look at me, [v]they shake
their heads.

26 Help me, O LORD my God!
Oh, save me according to Your
mercy,
27 [w]That they may know that this *is* Your
hand—
That You, LORD, have done it!
28 [x]Let them curse, but You bless;
When they arise, let them be
ashamed,
But let [y]Your servant rejoice.
29 [z]Let my accusers be clothed with
shame,
And let them cover themselves with
their own disgrace as with a
mantle.

30 I will greatly praise the LORD with my
mouth;
Yes, [a]I will praise Him among the
multitude.
31 For [b]He shall stand at the right hand
of the poor,
To save *him* from those [5]who
condemn him.

PSALM 110

Announcement of the Messiah's Reign

A Psalm of David.

1 The [a]LORD said to my Lord,
"Sit at My right hand,
Till I make Your enemies Your
[b]footstool."
2 The LORD shall send the rod of Your
strength [c]out of Zion.
[d]Rule in the midst of Your enemies!

15 [o] Job 18:17; [Ps. 34:16]
16 [p] [Ps. 34:18]
17 [q] Prov. 14:14; [Matt. 7:2]
18 [r] Num. 5:22
23 [s] Ps. 102:11
24 [t] Heb. 12:12
25 [u] Ps. 22:7; Jer. 18:16; Lam. 2:15
[v] Matt. 27:39; Mark 15:29
27 [w] Job 37:7
28 [x] 2 Sam. 6:11, 12
[y] Is. 65:14
29 [z] Job 8:22; Ps. 35:26
30 [a] Ps. 35:18; 111:1
31 [b] [Ps. 16:8] [5] Lit. *judging his soul*

PSALM 110

1 [a] Matt. 22:44; Mark 12:36; 16:19; Luke 20:42, 43; Acts 2:34, 35; Col. 3:1; Heb. 1:13
[b] [1 Cor. 15:25; Eph. 1:22]
2 [c] [Rom. 11:26, 27]
[d] [Ps. 2:9; Dan. 7:13, 14]

109:21-29 David petitioned the court for justice by asking for deliverance for the judge's sake (109:21) and then for his own sake (vv. 22-25). Afterwards, he requested that his enemies be rightfully punished (vv. 26-29).

109:30,31 David's praise for the Divine Magistrate (v. 30) was based on his confidence in the compassion and mercy of the judge (v. 31). Second Samuel 22 and Ps. 18 record the general outcome to David's case, which was tried in God's courtroom.

110:1-7 This psalm contains one of the most exalted prophetic portions of Scripture presenting Jesus Christ as both a holy king and a royal High-Priest—something that no human monarch of Israel ever experienced. It, along with Ps. 118, is by far the most quoted psalm in the NT (Matt. 22:44; 26:64; Mark 12:36; 14:62; Luke 20:42,43; 22:69; Acts 2:34,35; Heb. 1:13; 5:6; 7:17,21; 10:13). While portraying the perfect king, the perfect High-Priest, and the perfect government, Ps. 110 declares Christ's current role in heaven as the resurrected Savior (110:1) and His future role on earth as the reigning Monarch (110:2-7). This psalm is decidedly messianic and millennial in content. Jesus Christ (Matt. 22:43,44) verifies the Davidic authorship. The exact occasion of this psalm is unknown, but it could easily have been associated with God's declaration of the Davidic Covenant in 2 Sam. 7:4-17.

I. Christ the King (110:1-3)

II. Christ the High-Priest (110:4-7)

110:1 my Lord. Refers to the divine/human King of Israel—the Lord Jesus Christ. Christ's humanity descended from David, which is demanded by the Davidic promise of 2 Sam. 7:12. Using this passage, Christ also declared His deity in the Gospels (Matt. 22:44; Mark 12:36; Luke 20:42-43) by arguing that only God could have been lord to King David. **My right hand.** God the Father invited God the Son in His ascension to sit at the place of honor in the heavenly throne room (cf. Acts. 2:22-36; Heb. 10:10-12). **Your enemies Your footstool.** Footstool was an ancient Near Eastern picture of absolute victory portraying the idea that one's enemy was now underfoot (cf. Pss. 8:6,7; 47:3; Is. 66:1; 1 Cor. 15:27). This anticipates Christ's Second Advent (cf. Rev. 19:11-21) as a conquering king (cf. Heb. 10:13).

110:2 the rod. From the human side, the ancestral staff of Judah is in view (cf. Gen. 49:10). From the divine side, the rod of iron by which King Jesus will subdue the earth is intended (cf. Ps. 2:9). **Zion.** God intends to install His ultimate earthly king in Jerusalem (the SW side is Zion; cf. Ps. 132:13-18). The earthly Zion (cf. Ps. 2:6; Is. 59:20) is in view, not the heavenly Zion because 1) there are no enemies in heaven, and 2) none of the activities in vv. 5-7 will take place in heaven. **Rule.** Christ will rule on the earthly throne of His father David (cf. Luke 1:32), in fulfillment of Is. 9:6 and Zech. 14:9.

3 [e]Your people *shall be* volunteers
In the day of Your power;
[f]In the beauties of holiness, from the womb of the morning,
You have the dew of Your youth.
4 The LORD has sworn
And [g]will not relent,
"You *are* a [h]priest forever
According to the order of [i]Melchizedek."

3 [e] Judg. 5:2; Neh. 11:2 [f] 1 Chr. 16:29; Ps. 96:9
4 [g] [Num. 23:19] [h] [Zech. 6:13] [i] [Heb. 5:6, 10; 6:20]
5 [j] [Ps. 16:8] [k] Ps. 2:5, 12; [Rom. 2:5; Rev. 6:17] [1] Lit. *break kings in pieces*
6 [l] Ps. 68:21 [2] Lit. *break in pieces*
7 [m] [Is. 53:12]

5 The Lord *is* [j]at Your right hand;
He shall [1]execute kings [k]in the day of His wrath.
6 He shall judge among the nations,
He shall fill *the places* with dead bodies,
[l]He shall [2]execute the heads of many countries.
7 He shall drink of the brook by the wayside;
[m]Therefore He shall lift up the head.

110:3 volunteers. The redeemed inhabitants of earth will willingly serve the King of Kings and Lord of Lords. **the day of Your power.** Refers to the power displayed during the millennial reign of Jesus Christ (cf. Zech. 14:1-21; Rev. 19:11–20:6). **beauties...womb ...dew.** This seems to apply to the King and to represent Him as in the constant vigor of youth, a period distinguished by strength and activity, or it may refer to His holiness, eternality and deity.

110:4 You *are* a priest. The first time in the history of Israel when a king simultaneously served as High-Priest. Christ (a.k.a. "Branch," cf. Is. 4:2; Jer. 23:5,6; Zech. 3:8; 6:12,13) will build the temple at which the world will worship God (cf. 2 Sam. 7:13; Is. 2:2-4; Ezek. 40–48). **forever.** Christ represents the final and foremost High-Priest in the history of Israel. **the order of Melchizedek.** This High-Priest could not be of Aaron's lineage in that he would not be eternal, not be of Judah, not be a king, and not be of the New Covenant (Jer. 31:31-33; Heb. 8,9). Melchizedek, which means "king of righteousness," served as the human priest/king of Salem in Gen. 14:17-20 and provides a picture of the order of Christ's priesthood (cf. Heb. 5:6; 7:17,21). The sons of Zadok will serve with Christ in the Millennium as His human priestly associates (cf. Ezek. 44:15; 48:11).

110:5 Your right hand. The roles have here reversed—the Father now stands at the right hand of the Son. This pictures the Father supplying the needs of the Son (cf. Pss. 16:8; 109:31; Is. 41:13). The Father provides the defeat of His enemies on earth so that His Son can fulfill God's land and nation promises to Abraham (Gen. 12:1,2) and kingship promise to David (2 Sam. 7:12,13,16). **the day of His wrath.** This refers to the "Day of the LORD" (cf. v. 3 "the day of Your power"), which finds its global expression at the end of Daniel's 70th week (cf. Dan. 9:24-27). This term exclusively speaks of God's wrath, which will be poured out on an unrepentant world in order to set up Christ's 1,000 year (millennial) reign (cf. Joel 2:1,11,31; 3:14; Rev. 6:16,17; 14:19; 19:15).

110:6 judge...fill...execute. Cf. Pss. 2:8,9; 50:1-6; Is. 2:4; 9:6,7; Dan. 2:44,45; 7:26,27; Joel 3:2,12; Mic. 4:3; Matt. 25:32; Rev. 6:15-17; 14:20; 16:14; 19:19-21.

110:7 He shall drink. This pictures a refreshed conqueror who has kingly access to the whole world. This could anticipate the E-W flow of fresh water out of Jerusalem as recorded in Zech. 14:8. **He shall lift up.** The lifted head pictures Christ's strength in victory (cf. Pss. 3:3; 27:6; 75:10). As Ps. 22:28 reports, "For the kingdom *is* the LORD's, and He rules over the nations" (cf. Zech. 14:9).

Christ in the Psalms (Luke 24:44)

Psalms	NT Quote	Significance
2:1-12	Acts 4:25,26; 13:33; Heb. 1:5; 5:5	Incarnation, Crucifixion, Resurrection
8:3-8	1 Cor. 15:27,28; Eph. 1:22; Heb. 2:5-10	Creation
16:8-11	Acts 2:24-31; 13:35-37	Death, Resurrection
22:1-31	Matt. 27:35-46; John 19:23,24; Heb. 2:12; 5:5	Incarnation, Crucifixion, Resurrection
40:6-8	Heb. 10:5-9	Incarnation
41:9	John 13:18,21	Betrayal
45:6,7	Heb. 1:8,9	Deity
68:18	Eph. 4:8	Ascension, Enthronement
69:20,21, 25	Matt. 27:34, 48; Acts 1:15-20	Betrayal, Crucifixion
72:6-17	——	Millennial Kingship
78:1,2,15	Matt. 13:35; 1 Cor. 10:4	Theophany, Earthly teaching ministry
89:3-37	Acts 2:30	Millennial Kingship
102:25-27	Heb. 1:10-12	Creation, Eternality
109:6-19	Acts 1:15-20	Betrayal
110:1-7	Matt. 22:43-45; Acts. 2:33-35; Heb. 1:13; 5:6-10; 6:20; 7:24	Deity, Ascension, Heavenly Priesthood Millennial Kingship
118:22,23	Matt. 21:42; Mark 12:10,11; Luke 20:17; Acts 4:8-12; 1 Pet. 2:7	Rejection as Savior
132:12-18	Acts 2:30	Millennial Kingship

PSALM 111

Praise to God for His Faithfulness and Justice

Praise[1] the LORD!

[a]I will praise the LORD with *my* whole
heart,
In the assembly of the upright and *in*
the congregation.

2 [b]The works of the LORD *are* great,
[c]Studied by all who have pleasure in
them.
3 His work *is* [d]honorable and glorious,
And His righteousness endures
forever.
4 He has made His wonderful works to
be remembered;
[e]The LORD *is* gracious and full of
compassion.
5 He has given food to those who fear
Him;
He will ever be mindful of His
covenant.
6 He has declared to His people the
power of His works,
In giving them the [2]heritage of the
nations.

7 The works of His hands *are* [f]verity[3]
and justice;
All His precepts *are* sure.
8 [g]They stand fast forever and ever,
And are [h]done in truth and
uprightness.
9 [i]He has sent redemption to His
people;
He has commanded His covenant
forever:
[j]Holy and awesome *is* His name.
10 [k]The fear of the LORD *is* the beginning
of wisdom;

PSALM 111
1 [a] Ps. 35:18 [1] Heb. *Hallelujah*
2 [b] Ps. 92:5 [c] Ps. 143:5
3 [d] Ps. 145:4, 5
4 [e] [Ps. 86:5]
6 [2] *inheritance*
7 [f] [Rev. 15:3] [3] *truth*
8 [g] Is. 40:8; Matt. 5:18 [h] [Rev. 15:3]
9 [i] Luke 1:68 [j] Luke 1:49
10 [k] Job 28:28; [Prov. 1:7; 9:10]; Eccl. 12:13

PSALM 112
1 [a] Ps. 128:1 [1] Heb. *Hallelujah*
2 [b] [Ps. 102:28]
3 [c] Prov. 3:16; 8:18; [Matt. 6:33] [2] *stands*
4 [d] Job 11:17; Ps. 97:11
5 [e] Ps. 37:26; [Luke 6:35] [f] [Eph. 5:15; Col. 4:5]
6 [g] Prov. 10:7
7 [h] [Prov. 1:33]
8 [i] Heb. 13:9 [j] [Ps. 27:1; 56:11]; Prov. 1:33; 3:24; [Is. 12:2] [k] Ps. 59:10

A good understanding have all those
who do *His commandments.*
His praise endures forever.

PSALM 112

The Blessed State of the Righteous

Praise[1] the LORD!

Blessed *is* the man *who* fears the
LORD,
Who [a]delights greatly in His
commandments.

2 [b]His descendants will be mighty on
earth;
The generation of the upright will be
blessed.
3 [c]Wealth and riches *will be* in his
house,
And his righteousness [2]endures
forever.
4 [d]Unto the upright there arises light in
the darkness;
He is gracious, and full of
compassion, and righteous.
5 [e]A good man deals graciously and
lends;
He will guide his affairs [f]with
discretion.
6 Surely he will never be shaken;
[g]The righteous will be in everlasting
remembrance.
7 [h]He will not be afraid of evil tidings;
His heart is steadfast, trusting in the
LORD.
8 His [i]heart *is* established;
[j]He will not be afraid,
Until he [k]sees *his desire* upon his
enemies.
9 He has dispersed abroad,
He has given to the poor;

111:1-10 Psalms 111 and 112 are alike in that 1) they both begin with, "Praise the LORD!" (as does Ps. 113), and 2) they both are acrostics with 22 lines corresponding to the 22 letters of the Heb. alphabet. Psalm 111 exalts the works of God, while Ps. 112 extols the man who fears God. The author(s) and occasion(s) are unknown.

I. A Word of Praise (111:1)
II. Words about God's Works (111:2-9)
III. A Word of Wisdom (111:10)

111:1 whole heart. Jesus might have had this passage in mind when He stated that the greatest commandment was, "you shall love the Lord your God with all your heart…" (Matt. 22:37).

111:2-9 God's work(s) are mentioned 5 times (vv. 2,3,4,6,7). Overall, the greater work of redemption seems to be in view (v. 9) without excluding lesser works of a temporal nature (vv. 5,6).

111:5 food…His covenant. It is quite possible that the psalmist has alluded to God's faithfulness in providing food for Jacob through Joseph (Gen. 37–50) in fulfillment of the Abrahamic Covenant to make the nation like the stars of the sky (Gen. 15:5).

111:6 the heritage of the nations. It seems even more sure that the psalmist has the Abrahamic Covenant in view (cf. Gen. 15:18-21; 17:1-8), specifically the Exodus (Ex.–Deut.) and the conquering/dividing of the Land (Joshua). *See note on Deut. 7:1,2.*

111:9 commanded His covenant forever. In light of vv. 5,6 and Gal. 3:6-9, this appears to look at the redemption aspects of the Abrahamic Covenant, which was declared frequently to be an "everlasting" or "forever" covenant (cf. Gen. 17:7,13,19; 1 Chr. 16:15,17; Ps. 105:8,10; Is. 24:5).

111:10 The fear of the LORD. *See notes on Prov. 1:7; 9:10.*

112:1-10 *See note on Ps. 111:1-10.*

I. The Blessing of Obedience (112:1-9)
II. The Emptiness of Sin (112:10)

112:1 *who* fears the LORD. This psalm begins where 111:10 ended and links the two together.

112:2-9 The desire of every human for prosperity can only come through obedience to the commands of God (cf. Ps. 1:1-3).

112:9 dispersed abroad. Quoted by Paul in 2 Cor. 9:9.

His righteousness endures forever;
His [3]horn will be exalted with honor.
10 The wicked will see *it* and be grieved;
He will gnash his teeth and melt
away;
The desire of the wicked shall perish.

PSALM 113

The Majesty and Condescension of God

Praise[1] the LORD!

[a]Praise, O servants of the LORD,
Praise the name of the LORD!
2 [b]Blessed be the name of the LORD
From this time forth and forevermore!
3 [c]From the rising of the sun to its going
down
The LORD's name *is* to be praised.

4 The LORD *is* [d]high above all nations,
[e]His glory above the heavens.
5 [f]Who *is* like the LORD our God,
Who dwells on high,
6 [g]Who humbles Himself to behold
The things that are in the heavens and
in the earth?

7 [h]He raises the poor out of the dust,
And lifts the [i]needy out of the ash
heap,
8 That He may [j]seat *him* with princes—
With the princes of His people.
9 [k]He grants the [2]barren woman a
home,
Like a joyful mother of children.

Praise the LORD!

PSALM 114

The Power of God in His Deliverance of Israel

When [a]Israel went out of Egypt,
The house of Jacob [b]from a people
[1]of strange language,
2 [c]Judah became His sanctuary,
And Israel His dominion.

3 [d]The sea saw *it* and fled;
[e]Jordan turned back.
4 [f]The mountains skipped like rams,
The little hills like lambs.
5 [g]What ails you, O sea, that you fled?
O Jordan, *that* you turned back?
6 O mountains, *that* you skipped like
rams?
O little hills, like lambs?

9 [3] Strength

PSALM 113

1 [a] Ps. 135:1 [1] Heb. *Hallelujah*
2 [b] [Dan. 2:20]
3 [c] Is. 59:19; Mal. 1:11
4 [d] Ps. 97:9; 99:2 [e] [Ps. 8:1]
5 [f] Ps. 89:6; [Is. 57:15]
6 [g] [Ps. 11:4; Is. 57:15]
7 [h] 1 Sam. 2:8; Ps. 107:41
[i] Ps. 72:12
8 [j] [Job 36:7]
9 [k] 1 Sam. 2:5; Is. 54:1 [2] *childless*

PSALM 114

1 [a] Ex. 12:51; 13:3 [b] Ps. 81:5 [1] *who spoke unintelligibly*
2 [c] Ex. 6:7; 19:6; 25:8; 29:45, 46; Deut. 27:9
3 [d] Ex. 14:21; Ps. 77:16 [e] Josh. 3:13-16
4 [f] Ex. 19:18; Judg. 5:5; Ps. 29:6; Hab. 3:6
5 [g] Hab. 3:8

112:9 His horn. Horns on an animal were an indication of strength and prosperity. This is applied figuratively to the righteous.

112:10 In utter contrast to the righteous man of vv. 2-9, the wicked man lives a worthless existence without strength (cf. Ps. 1:4-6).

113:1-9 Psalms 113–118 comprise a rich 6-psalm praise to God commonly called the "Egyptian Hallel" ("hallel" meaning praise in Heb.). These were sung at Passover, Pentecost, and Tabernacles, but had the greatest significance at Passover, which celebrated the Jews' deliverance from Egypt (cf. Ex. 12–14). Traditionally Pss. 113,114 were sung before the Passover meal and Pss. 115–118 afterwards. Psalm 118 would most likely be what Christ and the disciples sang before they left the Upper Room the night Christ was betrayed (cf. Matt. 26:30; Mark 14:26). There are two other notable sets of praise in the Psalter: 1) The Great Hallel (Pss. 120–136) and 2) The Final Hallel (Pss. 145–150).

I. The Call to Praise (113:1-3)
II. The Cause for Praise (113:4-9)
  A. God's Transcendence (113:4,5)
  B. God's Immanence (113:6-9)

113:1 servants. Refers to the redeemed, all of whom should serve God with obedience. **the name.** The name of God represents all His attributes.

113:2 this time...forevermore. Praise is to be rendered always (cf. Eph. 5:20; 1 Thess. 5:18).

113:3 rising...going down. From the first moment of consciousness in the morning to the last waking moment before sleep.

113:4,5 Believers are to praise the only One worthy of praise for His transcendent sovereignty.

113:6-9 humbles. In appearance, God must figuratively lean over from the faraway heavens to examine the earth (cf. Is. 40:12-17). In a far greater way Christ humbled Himself in the incarnation (cf. Phil. 2:5-11).

113:7,8 the poor. This is borrowed almost exactly from Hannah's song in 1 Sam. 2:8. God is responsible for both the rich and the poor (Prov. 22:2). God's compassion reaches out to the poor and needy (cf. Ps. 72:12,13). Ultimately, Christ came to save those who are poor in spirit (cf. Is. 61:2; Luke 4:18).

113:9 the barren woman. Sarah (Gen. 21:2), Rebekah (Gen. 25:21), and Rachel (Gen. 30:23) would be the most significant since the outcome of the Abrahamic Covenant depended on these childless women being blessed by God to be mothers.

114:1-8 *See note on Ps. 113:1-9.* This psalm is the one most explicitly related to the Exodus (Ex. 12–14). It recounts God's response to a captive nation (Israel in Egypt) in order to honor His promises in the Abrahamic Covenant (Gen. 28:13-17) given to Jacob (cf. 114:1, "The house of Jacob;" 114:7, "the God of Jacob").

I. God Inhabits Israel (114:1,2)
II. God Intimidates Nature (114:3-6)
III. God Invites Trembling (114:7,8)

114:2 Judah...Israel. Judah/Benjamin and the northern ten tribes respectively. **sanctuary...dominion.** God dwelt among the peoples as a pillar of cloud by day and a pillar of fire by night (cf. Ex. 13:21,22; 14:19).

114:3 The sea...Jordan. Two miracles of God, i.e., separating the waters began and ended the Exodus. On the way out of Egypt, God parted the Red Sea (Ex. 14:15-31) and 40 years later He parted the Jordan River in order for the Jews to enter the Promised Land (Josh. 3:1-17).

114:4 mountains...little hills. Refers to the violent appearance of God to Israel at Sinai (cf. Ex. 19:18; Judg. 5:4,5; Ps. 68:17,18).

114:5,6 In poetic imagery, God questioned why the most fixed of geographical features, i.e., water and mountains, could not resist His power and will.

7 Tremble, O earth, at the presence of
the Lord,
At the presence of the God of Jacob,
8 [h]Who turned the rock *into* a pool of
water,
The flint into a fountain of waters.

PSALM 115

The Futility of Idols and the Trustworthiness of God

Not [a]unto us, O LORD, not unto us,
But to Your name give glory,
Because of Your mercy,
Because of Your truth.
2 Why should the [1]Gentiles say,
[b]"So where *is* their God?"

3 [c]But our God *is* in heaven;
He does whatever He pleases.
4 [d]Their idols *are* silver and gold,
The work of men's hands.
5 They have mouths, but they do not
speak;
Eyes they have, but they do not see;
6 They have ears, but they do not hear;
Noses they have, but they do not
smell;
7 They have hands, but they do not
handle;
Feet they have, but they do not walk;
Nor do they mutter through their
throat.
8 [e]Those who make them are like them;
So is everyone who trusts in them.

9 [f]O Israel, trust in the LORD;
[g]He *is* their help and their shield.
10 O house of Aaron, trust in the LORD;
He *is* their help and their shield.
11 You who fear the LORD, trust in the
LORD;
He *is* their help and their shield.

12 The LORD [2]has been mindful of *us;*
He will bless *us;*
He will bless the house of Israel;
He will bless the house of Aaron.
13 [h]He will bless those who fear the LORD,
Both small and great.

14 May the LORD give you increase more
and more,
You and your children.
15 *May* you *be* [i]blessed by the LORD,
[j]Who made heaven and earth.

16 The heaven, *even* the heavens, *are* the
LORD's;
But the earth He has given to the
children of men.
17 [k]The dead do not praise the LORD,
Nor any who go down into silence.
18 [l]But we will bless the LORD
From this time forth and forevermore.

Praise the LORD!

PSALM 116

Thanksgiving for Deliverance from Death

I [a]love the LORD, because He has heard
My voice *and* my supplications.
2 Because He has inclined His ear to me,
Therefore I will call *upon Him* as long
as I live.

3 [b]The [1]pains of death surrounded me,
And the [2]pangs of Sheol [3]laid hold of
me;
I found trouble and sorrow.

8 [h]Ex. 17:6; Num. 20:11; Ps. 107:35

PSALM 115

1 [a][Is. 48:11]; Ezek. 36:32
2 [b]Ps. 42:3, 10 [1]*nations*
3 [c][1 Chr. 16:26]
4 [d]Deut. 4:28; 2 Kin. 19:18; Is. 37:19; 44:10, 20; Jer. 10:3
8 [e]Ps. 135:18; Is. 44:9-11
9 [f]Ps. 118:2, 3 [g]Ps. 33:20
12 [2]*has remembered us*
13 [h]Ps. 128:1, 4
15 [i][Gen. 14:19] [j]Gen. 1:1; Acts 14:15; Rev. 14:7
17 [k]Ps. 6:5; 88:10-12; [Is. 38:18]
18 [l]Ps. 113:2; Dan. 2:20

PSALM 116

1 [a]Ps. 18:1
3 [b]Ps. 18:4-6 [1]Lit. *cords* [2]*distresses* [3]Lit. *found me*

114:7 Tremble. The only proper response of helpless nature before omnipotent God.

114:8 the rock. Refers to the first incident at Massah/Meribah (Ex. 17:5,6) and/or the second (Num. 20:8-11).

115:1-18 *See note on Ps. 113:1-9.* This praise psalm appears to be antiphonal in nature, following this outline and pattern: 1) the people (vv. 1-8); 2) the priests (vv. 9-11); 3) the people (vv. 12,13); 4) the priests (vv. 14,15); and 5) the people (vv. 16-18). Verses 4-11 are very similar to Ps. 135:15-20. It has been suggested that this psalm is post-Exilic (cf. v. 2) and could have first been sung at the dedication of the second temple (cf. Ezra 6:16).

115:1 to Your name give glory. God declared He would share His glory with no one (Is. 42:8; 48:11).

115:2 where *is* their God? (cf. Ps. 42:3,10; 79:10; Joel 2:17; Mic. 7:10). The Jews despised this Gentile taunt.

115:3 Israel's God is alive and rules the earth from His throne room above.

115:4-8 In contrast, Gentiles worship dead gods of their own making, fashioned in the image of the fallen creature (cf. Is. 44:9-20; 46:5-7; Jer. 10:3-16; Rom. 1:21-25). The idol worshiper becomes like the idol—spiritually useless.

115:9-11 This 3 verse, priestly admonition (cf. 118:2-4; 135:19,20) could apply to 3 different groups: 1) the nation Israel (115:9); 2) the Levitical priests from the house of Aaron (115:10); and 3) proselytes to Judaism who are God fearers (115:11). To all 3 groups, God is their help and shield.

115:16 the earth. Strong implications that planet earth alone is the dwelling place of life.

116:1-19 *See note on Ps. 113:1-9.* This is an intensely personal "thank you" psalm to the Lord for saving the psalmist from death (116:3,8). The occasion and author remain unknown, although the language used by Jonah in his prayer from the fish's stomach is remarkably similar. While this appears to deal with physical death, the same song could be sung by those who have been saved from spiritual death.

I. The Lord's Response to the Psalmist's Prayer for Deliverance from Death (116:1-11)
II. The Psalmist's Reaction to God's Deliverance of him from Death (116:12-19)

116:3 Sheol. Another term for grave/death.

4 Then I called upon the name of the
LORD:
"O LORD, I implore You, deliver my
soul!"

5 [c]Gracious *is* the LORD, and [d]righteous;
Yes, our God *is* merciful.
6 The LORD preserves the simple;
I was brought low, and He saved me.
7 Return to your [e]rest, O my soul,
For [f]the LORD has dealt bountifully
with you.

8 [g]For You have delivered my soul from
death,
My eyes from tears,
And my feet from falling.
9 I will walk before the LORD
[h]In the land of the living.
10 [i]I believed, therefore I spoke,
"I am greatly afflicted."
11 [j]I said in my haste,
[k]"All men *are* liars."

12 What shall I render to the LORD
For all His benefits toward me?
13 I will take up the cup of salvation,
And call upon the name of the LORD.
14 [l]I will pay my vows to the LORD
Now in the presence of all His
people.

15 [m]Precious in the sight of the LORD
Is the death of His saints.

16 O LORD, truly [n]I *am* Your servant;
I *am* Your servant, [o]the son of Your
maidservant;
You have loosed my bonds.
17 I will offer to You [p]the sacrifice of
thanksgiving,
And will call upon the name of the
LORD.

18 I will pay my vows to the LORD
Now in the presence of all His people,
19 In the [q]courts of the LORD's house,
In the midst of you, O Jerusalem.

[4]Praise the LORD!

PSALM 117

Let All Peoples Praise the LORD

Praise[a] the LORD, all you Gentiles!
[1]Laud Him, all you peoples!
2 For His merciful kindness is great
toward us,
And [b]the truth of the LORD *endures*
forever.

Praise the LORD!

PSALM 118

Praise to God for His Everlasting Mercy

Oh, [a]give thanks to the LORD, for *He is*
good!
[b]For His mercy *endures* forever.

5 [c][Ps. 103:8] [d][Ezra 9:15]; Neh. 9:8; [Ps. 119:137; 145:17; Jer. 12:1; Dan. 9:14]
7 [e][Jer. 6:16; Matt. 11:29] [f]Ps. 13:6
8 [g]Ps. 56:13
9 [h]Ps. 27:13
10 [i]2 Cor. 4:13
11 [j]Ps. 31:22 [k]Rom. 3:4
14 [l]Ps. 116:18
15 [m]Ps. 72:14; [Rev. 14:13]
16 [n]Ps. 119:125; 143:12 [o]Ps. 86:16
17 [p]Lev. 7:12; Ps. 50:14; 107:22
19 [q]Ps. 96:8 [4]Heb. *Hallelujah*

PSALM 117

1 [a]Rom. 15:11 [1]*Praise*
2 [b][Ps. 100:5]

PSALM 118

1 [a]1 Chr. 16:8, 34; Jer. 33:11 [b]2 Chr. 5:13; 7:3; Ezra 3:11; [Ps. 136:1-26]

116:9 I will walk. A vow of obedience.

116:10 I believed. Faith in God and His ability to deliver preceded the psalmist's prayer for deliverance. This verse is quoted by the Apostle Paul in 2 Cor. 4:13. It rehearses the principle of walking by faith, not by sight.

116:11 All men *are* liars. Either the psalmist is reacting to his false accusers or to men who say that they can deliver him but have not.

116:12 What shall I render. God needs nothing and puts no price on His free mercy and grace. The psalmist renders the only acceptable gift—obedience and thanksgiving.

116:13 the cup of salvation. This is the only place in the OT where this exact phrase is used. It probably has the meaning of the cup in Pss. 16:5; 23:5; i.e., the redeemed life circumstances provided by God, in contrast to Ps. 75:8, which speaks about the cup of God's wrath.

116:14 I will pay my vows. Most likely this refers to the vows made during the time of duress (cf. 116:18,19).

116:15,16 The psalmist realized what a special blessing his deliverance ("loosed my bonds") was in light of v. 15. Therefore, he reemphasized his role as a servant of God following the example of his mother.

116:17-19 These verses parallel v. 13,14. Jonah made an almost identical statement (Jon. 2:9).

116:17 the sacrifice of thanksgiving. Probably not a Mosaic sacrifice, but rather actual praise and thanksgiving rendered from the heart in the spirit of Pss. 136 and 138 (cf. Pss. 50:23; 100:4; 119:108).

116:19 the LORD's house. Refers to 1) the tabernacle in Jerusalem if written by David or before, or 2) the temple in Jerusalem if written by Solomon or later.

117:1,2 *See note on Ps. 113:1-9.* The seal of redemptive truth is bound up in this diminutive but seminal psalm—its profundity far outdistances its size. This pivotal psalm exhibits 3 distinguishing features: 1) it is the shortest psalm; 2) it is the shortest chapter in the Bible; and 3) it is the middle chapter of the Bible. That God looked redemptively beyond the borders of Israel in the OT is made clear here. The psalm looks back to God's intent for Adam and Eve in Eden (Gen. 1,2) and looks ahead to the ultimate fulfillment in the new heavens and earth (Rev. 21,22).

I. A Global Invitation (117:1)
II. A Grand Explanation (117:2)

117:1 Gentiles...peoples. Paul quoted this verse in Rom. 15:11 to make the point that from the very beginning of time God has pursued a worldwide redemptive purpose (cf. Rom. 15:7-13). Other passages quoted by Paul in Rom. 15 to make this point include: Deut. 32:43, 2 Sam. 22:50, and Is. 11:10. While not as obvious in the OT, the NT makes this point unmistakably clear (cf. Acts. 10:34,35; Rom. 1:16; 1 Cor. 12:13; Gal. 3:1-29, esp. 28; Col. 3:11).

117:2 The reasons for such exalted praise as that commanded in v. 1 are: 1) because of God's redemptive kindness, and 2) because of God's eternal truth. Therefore, what God has promised, He will provide (cf. John 6:37-40).

118:1-29 *See note on Ps. 113:1-9.* This psalm, along with Ps. 110, is intensely messianic and thus the most quoted by the NT (Matt. 21;9,42; 23:39; Mark 11:9,10; 12:10,11; Luke 13:35; 19:38; 20:17; John 12:13; Acts 4:11; Heb. 13:6; 1 Pet. 2:7). Neither the author nor the

2 [c]Let Israel now say,
"His mercy *endures* forever."
3 Let the house of Aaron now say,
"His mercy *endures* forever."
4 Let those who fear the LORD now say,
"His mercy *endures* forever."

5 [d]I called on the LORD in distress;
The LORD answered me *and* [e]*set me* in a broad place.
6 [f]The LORD *is* on my side;
I will not fear.
What can man do to me?
7 [g]The LORD is for me among those who help me;
Therefore [h]I shall see *my desire* on those who hate me.
8 [i]*It is* better to trust in the LORD
Than to put confidence in man.
9 [j]*It is* better to trust in the LORD
Than to put confidence in princes.

10 All nations surrounded me,
But in the name of the LORD I will destroy them.
11 They [k]surrounded me,
Yes, they surrounded me;
But in the name of the LORD I will destroy them.
12 They surrounded me [l]like bees;
They were quenched [m]like a fire of thorns;
For in the name of the LORD I will [1]destroy them.
13 You pushed me violently, that I might fall,
But the LORD helped me.
14 [n]The LORD *is* my strength and song,
And He has become my salvation.

15 The voice of rejoicing and salvation
Is in the tents of the righteous;
The right hand of the LORD does valiantly.
16 [o]The right hand of the LORD is exalted;
The right hand of the LORD does valiantly.
17 [p]I shall not die, but live,
And [q]declare the works of the LORD.
18 The LORD has [r]chastened[2] me severely,
But He has not given me over to death.

19 [s]Open to me the gates of righteousness;
I will go through them,
And I will praise the LORD.
20 [t]This is the gate of the LORD,
[u]Through which the righteous shall enter.

21 I will praise You,
For You have [v]answered me,
And have become my salvation.

22 [w]The stone *which* the builders rejected

2 [c][Ps. 115:9]
5 [d]Ps. 120:1 [e]Ps. 18:19
6 [f]Ps. 27:1; 56:9; [Rom. 8:31; Heb. 13:6]
7 [g]Ps. 54:4 [h]Ps. 59:10
8 [i]2 Chr. 32:7, 8; Ps. 40:4; Is. 31:1, 3; 57:13; Jer. 17:5
9 [j]Ps. 146:3
11 [k]Ps. 88:17
12 [l]Deut. 1:44 [m]Eccl. 7:6; Nah. 1:10

[1]*cut them off*
14 [n]Ex. 15:2; Is. 12:2
16 [o]Ex. 15:6
17 [p][Ps. 6:5]; Hab. 1:12 [q]Ps. 73:28
18 [r]Ps. 73:14; Jer. 31:18; [1 Cor. 11:32]; 2 Cor. 6:9
[2]*disciplined*
19 [s]Is. 26:2
20 [t]Ps. 24:7 [u]Is. 35:8; [Rev. 21:27; 22:14, 15]
21 [v]Ps. 116:1
22 [w]Matt. 21:42; Mark 12:10, 11; Luke 20:17; Acts 4:11; [Eph. 2:20; 1 Pet. 2:7, 8]

specific circumstances of the psalm are identified. Two reasonable possibilities could be entertained: 1) it was written during Moses' day in the Exodus, or 2) it was written sometime after the Jews returned to Jerusalem from Exile. Probably it was the former, given 1) the nature of the Egyptian Hallel (esp. Ps. 114); 2) its use by the Jewish community especially at Passover; 3) the close similarity to Moses' experience in the Exodus; 4) the striking similarity in language (Ps. 118:14 with Ex. 15:2; 118:15,16 with Ex. 15:6,12; 118:28 with Ex. 15:2); and 5) the particularly pointed messianic significance as it relates to the redemption provided by Christ our Passover (1 Cor. 5:7). It seems reasonable to propose that Moses possibly wrote this beautiful psalm to look back in worship at the historical Passover and look ahead in wonder to the spiritual Passover in Christ.

I. Call to Worship (118:1-4)
II. Personal Praise (118:5-21)
III. Corporate Praise (118:22-24)
IV. Commitment to Worship (118:25-29)

118:1 Oh, give thanks. Cf. Pss. 105–107,136. The psalm ends in v. 29 as it began here.

118:2-4 Israel…Aaron…those who fear the LORD. *See note on Ps. 115:9-11.* The phrase "His mercy endures forever" is repeated in all 26 verses of Ps. 136 (cf. 118:1,29).

118:5-21 This section contains individual praise by the psalmist, possibly Moses.

118:5-9 The psalmist focuses intensely on the Lord.

118:6 Hebrews 13:6 quotes this verse; cf. Ps. 56:4,11.

118:10-14 It seems obvious that the leader of the nation is speaking here.

118:12 a fire of thorns. Dried thorns burn easily and quickly.

118:13 You pushed me. Refers to the psalmist's enemy.

118:14 These words are identical to Moses' words in Ex. 15:2.

118:15-18 A declaration of victory.

118:15,16 The right hand. Very similar to Moses' words in Ex. 15:6,12.

118:18 This possibly refers to the incident at Meribah where Moses struck the rock (cf. Num. 20:8-13).

118:19-21 The victory against overwhelming odds elicits from the psalmist a great desire to praise God.

118:19 gates of righteousness. Most likely a figurative reference, i.e., spiritual gates through which the righteous pass (cf. Ps. 100:4), rather than to the gates of the temple, e.g., 1 Chr. 9:23.

118:20 the gate. This points to the entryway which leads to the presence of the Lord. Jesus may have had this psalm in mind when he taught about "the narrow gate" in Matt. 7:13,14.

118:21 my salvation. The Lord has delivered the psalmist from otherwise certain defeat and death (cf. 118:14,15).

118:22-26 The NT quotes of vv. 22,23 and vv. 25,26 lend strong messianic significance here. If Moses is the author, then the NT writers use a perfect analogy in connecting this passage to Christ. For example, Moses said that God would raise up another prophet like himself (Deut. 18:15). Peter identified this other prophet as the Lord Jesus Christ (cf. Acts 3:11-26). So Moses is a legitimate, biblically recognized type of Christ.

Has become the chief cornerstone.
23 [3]This was the LORD's doing;
It *is* marvelous in our eyes.
24 This *is* the day the LORD has made;
We will rejoice and be glad in it.

25 Save now, I pray, O LORD;
O LORD, I pray, send now prosperity.
26 [x]Blessed *is* he who comes in the name of the LORD!
We have blessed you from the house of the LORD.
27 God *is* the LORD,
And He has given us [y]light;
Bind the sacrifice with cords to the horns of the altar.
28 You *are* my God, and I will praise You;
[z]*You are* my God, I will exalt You.
29 Oh, give thanks to the LORD, for *He is* good!
For His mercy *endures* forever.

23 [3] Lit. *This is from the LORD*
26 [x] Matt. 21:9; 23:39; Mark 11:9; Luke 13:35; 19:38
27 [y] Esth. 8:16; [1 Pet. 2:9]
28 [z] Ex. 15:2; Is. 25:1

PSALM 119

Meditations on the Excellencies of the Word of God

א ALEPH

Blessed *are* the [1]undefiled in the way,
[a]Who walk in the law of the LORD!
2 Blessed *are* those who keep His testimonies,
Who seek Him with the [b]whole heart!
3 [c]They also do no iniquity;
They walk in His ways.
4 You have commanded *us*
To keep Your precepts diligently.
5 Oh, that my ways were directed
To keep Your statutes!
6 [d]Then I would not be ashamed,
When I look into all Your commandments.
7 I will praise You with uprightness of heart,
When I learn Your righteous judgments.
8 I will keep Your statutes;
Oh, do not forsake me utterly!

PSALM 119
1 [a] Ps. 128:1; [Ezek. 11:20; 18:17]; Mic. 4:2 [1] *blameless*
2 [b] Deut. 6:5; 10:12; 11:13; 13:3
3 [c] [1 John 3:9; 5:18]
6 [d] Job 22:26

118:22 stone…builders rejected…chief cornerstone. Peter identified the chief cornerstone in the NT as Christ (Acts 4:11; 1 Pet. 2:7). In the parable of the vineyard (Matt. 21:42; Mark 12:10-11; Luke 20:17), the rejected son of the vineyard owner is likened to the rejected stone which became the chief cornerstone. Christ was that rejected stone. Jewish leaders were pictured as builders of the nation. Now, this passage in v. 22 has a historical basis which is paralleled in its major features by analogy with the rejection of Christ who came to deliver/save the nation. Moses' experience, as a type of Christ, pictured Christ's rejection. On at least 3 occasions Moses (stone) was rejected by the Jews (builders) as their God sent the deliverer (chief cornerstone). For examples see Ex. 2:11-15, cf. Acts 7:35; Ex. 14:10-14,10; 16:1-3,11,12,20.

118:24 the day. Probably refers to 1) the day of deliverance and/or 2) the day the stone was made the chief cornerstone, which they now celebrate.

118:25 Save now, I pray. Transliterated from Heb., this becomes "Hosanna." These words were shouted by the crowd to Christ at the time of His triumphal entry to Jerusalem (Matt. 21:9; Mark 11:9,10; John 12:13). Days later they rejected Him because He did not provide military/political deliverance.

118:26 Blessed. Christ taught that the nation of Israel would not see Him again after his departure (ascension to heaven) until they could genuinely offer these words to Him at His second coming (cf. Matt. 23:39; Luke 13:35). In this historical text, it could have easily been sung by the Jews of Moses' day, especially at the end of the 40 years but prior to Moses' death (cf. Deut. 1–33). **the house of the LORD.** A phrase used in reference to the tabernacle of Moses (cf. Ex. 23:19; 34:26; Deut. 23:18) and later the temple (cf. 1 Kin. 6:1).

118:27 light. Similar to the Mosaic benediction of Num. 6:25. **the altar.** The altar of burnt offerings, which stood on the E in the court outside of the Holy Place (cf. Ex. 27:1-8; 38:1-7).

118:28 This bears a striking resemblance to Ex. 15:2.

118:29 A repetition of 118:1.

119:1-176 This longest of psalms and chapters in the Bible stands as the "Mt. Everest" of the Psalter. It joins Pss. 1 and 19 in exalting God's Word. The author is unknown for certain, although David, Daniel, or Ezra have reasonably been suggested. The psalmist apparently wrote while under some sort of serious duress (cf. vv. 23,42,51,61,67,71,78,86-87,95,110,121,134,139,143,146,153, 154,157,161,169). This is an acrostic psalm (cf. Pss. 9,10,25,34,37,111, 112,145) composed of 22 sections, each containing 8 lines. All 8 lines of the first section start with the first letter of the Heb. alphabet; thus the psalm continues until all 22 letters have been used in order. The 8 different terms referring to Scripture occurring throughout the psalm are: 1) law, 2) testimonies, 3) precepts, 4) statutes, 5) commandments, 6) judgments, 7) word, and 8) ordinances. From before sunrise to beyond sunset, the Word of God dominated the psalmist's life, e.g., 1) before dawn (v. 147), 2) daily (v. 97), 3) 7 times daily (v. 164), 4) nightly (vv. 55,148), and 5) at midnight (v. 62). Other than the acrostic form, Ps. 119 does not have an outline. Rather, there are many frequently recurring themes which will be delineated in the notes.

119:1,2 Blessed…Blessed. Similar to Ps. 1:1-3. Elsewhere, the psalmist declares that Scripture is more valuable than money (vv. 14,72,127,162) and brings more pleasure than the sweetness of honey (v. 103; cf. Prov. 13:13; 16:20; 19:16).

119:1 walk. An habitual pattern of living.

119:2 the whole heart. "Heart" refers to intellect, volition, and emotion (cf. vv. 7,10,11,32,34,36,58,69,70,80,111,112,145,161). Complete commitment or "whole heart" appears 6 times (vv. 2,10,34,58, 69,145).

119:4 To keep…diligently. The psalmist passionately desired to obey God's Word (cf. vv. 4,8,30-32,44,45,51,55,57,59-61,63,67,68,74, 83,87,101,102,106,110,112,129,141,157,167,168).

119:5,6 Oh. It is hard at times to distinguish where the psalmist's testimony ends and prayer begins (cf. vv. 29,36,58,133).

119:7 I will praise You. The Scriptures provoke singing, thanksgiving, rejoicing, and praise (cf. vv. 13,14,54,62,108,151,152,160,164, 171,172,175). **righteous.** God's Word reflects the character of God, especially righteousness (cf. vv. 7,62,75,106,123,138,144,160,164, 172).

ב BETH

9 How can a young man cleanse his way?
By taking heed according to Your word.
10 With my whole heart I have [e]sought You;
Oh, let me not wander from Your commandments!
11 [f]Your word I have hidden in my heart,
That I might not sin against You.
12 Blessed *are* You, O LORD!
Teach me Your statutes.
13 With my lips I have [g]declared
All the judgments of Your mouth.
14 I have rejoiced in the way of Your testimonies,
As *much as* in all riches.
15 I will meditate on Your precepts,
And [2]contemplate Your ways.
16 I will [h]delight myself in Your statutes;
I will not forget Your word.

ג GIMEL

17 [i]Deal bountifully with Your servant,
That I may live and keep Your word.
18 Open my eyes, that I may see
Wondrous things from Your law.
19 [j]I *am* a stranger in the earth;
Do not hide Your commandments from me.
20 [k]My soul [3]breaks with longing
For Your judgments at all times.
21 You rebuke the proud—the cursed,
Who stray from Your commandments.
22 [l]Remove from me reproach and contempt,
For I have kept Your testimonies.
23 Princes also sit *and* speak against me,
But Your servant meditates on Your statutes.
24 Your testimonies also *are* my delight
And my counselors.

ד DALETH

25 [m]My soul clings to the dust;
[n]Revive me according to Your word.
26 I have declared my ways, and You answered me;
[o]Teach me Your statutes.
27 Make me understand the way of Your precepts;
So [p]shall I meditate on Your wonderful works.
28 [q]My soul [4]melts from [5]heaviness;
Strengthen me according to Your word.
29 Remove from me the way of lying,
And grant me Your law graciously.
30 I have chosen the way of truth;
Your judgments I have laid *before me.*
31 I cling to Your testimonies;
O LORD, do not put me to shame!
32 I will run the course of Your commandments,
For You shall [r]enlarge my heart.

ה HE

33 [s]Teach me, O LORD, the way of Your statutes,
And I shall keep it *to* the end.
34 [t]Give me understanding, and I shall keep Your law;
Indeed, I shall observe it with *my* whole heart.
35 Make me walk in the path of Your commandments,
For I delight in it.
36 [6]Incline my heart to Your testimonies,
And not to [u]covetousness.
37 [v]Turn[7] away my eyes from [w]looking at worthless things,
And revive me in [8]Your way.

10 [e] 2 Chr. 15:15
11 [f] Ps. 37:31; Luke 2:19
13 [g] Ps. 34:11
15 [2] *look into*
16 [h] Ps. 1:2
17 [i] Ps. 116:7
19 [j] Gen. 47:9; Lev. 25:23; 1 Chr. 29:15; Ps. 39:12; Heb. 11:13
20 [k] Ps. 42:1, 2; 63:1; 84:2 [3] *is crushed*
22 [l] Ps. 39:8
25 [m] Ps. 44:25 [n] Ps. 143:11
26 [o] Ps. 25:4; 27:11; 86:11
27 [p] Ps. 145:5, 6
28 [q] Ps. 107:26 [4] Lit. *drops* [5] *grief*
32 [r] 1 Kin. 4:29; Is. 60:5; 2 Cor. 6:11, 13
33 [s] [Matt. 10:22; Rev. 2:26]
34 [t] [Prov. 2:6; James 1:5]
36 [u] Ezek. 33:31; [Mark 7:20-23]; Luke 12:15; [Heb. 13:5] [6] Cause me to long for
37 [v] Is. 33:15 [w] Prov. 23:5 [7] Lit. *Cause my eyes to pass away from* [8] So with MT, LXX, Vg.; Tg. *Your words*

119:9-11 Internalizing the Word is a believer's best weapon to defend against encroaching sin.

119:12 Teach me. The student/psalmist invites the Divine Author to be his instructor (cf. vv. 26,33,64,66,68,108,124,135) with the result that the psalmist did not turn aside from the Word (v. 102).

119:14 all riches. Cf. vv. 72,127.

119:15 meditate…contemplate. The psalmist reflected frequently on the Scriptures (cf. vv. 23,27,48,78,97,99,148).

119:16 I will delight. (cf. vv. 24,35,47,70,77,92,143,174). **I will not forget.** (cf. vv. 93,176).

119:18 Open my eyes. Perhaps this is the supreme prayer that a student of Scripture could speak since it confesses the student's inadequacy and the Divine Author's sufficiency (cf. vv. 98,99,105,130).

119:19 a stranger. As a citizen of God's kingdom, the psalmist was a mere sojourner in the kingdom of men.

119:20 breaks with longing. This expresses the psalmist's deep passion for the Word (cf. vv. 40,131).

119:21 the proud—the cursed. The psalmist identified with God's rebuke of those who disobey His Word (cf. vv. 53,104,113, 115,118,126).

119:24 my counselors. The chief means of biblical counseling is the application of God's Word by God's Spirit to the heart of a believer (cf. vv. 98-100).

119:25 Revive me. Revival is greatly desired by the psalmist, who realizes that God and God's Word alone are sufficient (cf. vv. 37,40, 50,88,93,107,149,154,156,159).

119:27 Make me understand. Philip asked the Ethiopian eunuch who was reading Is. 53, "Do you understand what you are reading?" (Acts 8:30). The psalmist understood God to be the best source of instruction (cf. vv. 34,73,100,125,144,169).

119:28 melts from heaviness. Refers to grief or sorrow over sin.

119:29,30 the way of lying…the way of truth. The psalmist desired to emulate the true character of God in contrast to the lying ways of Satan (cf. v. 163).

119:32 run the course. Reflects the energetic response of the psalmist to God's Word.

119:37 looking at worthless things. The psalmist desires to examine the things of greatest value, i.e., God's Word (cf. vv. 14,72,127).

38 [x]Establish Your word to Your servant,
Who *is devoted* to fearing You.
39 Turn away my reproach which I dread,
For Your judgments *are* good.
40 Behold, I long for Your precepts;
Revive me in Your righteousness.

ו WAW

41 Let Your mercies come also to me, O LORD—
Your salvation according to Your word.
42 So shall I have an answer for him who [9]reproaches me,
For I trust in Your word.
43 And take not the word of truth utterly out of my mouth,
For I have hoped in Your ordinances.
44 So shall I keep Your law continually,
Forever and ever.
45 And I will walk [1]at [y]liberty,
For I seek Your precepts.
46 [z]I will speak of Your testimonies also before kings,
And will not be ashamed.
47 And I will delight myself in Your commandments,
Which I love.
48 My hands also I will lift up to Your commandments,
Which I love,
And I will meditate on Your statutes.

ז ZAYIN

49 Remember the word to Your servant,
Upon which You have caused me to hope.
50 This *is* my [a]comfort in my affliction,
For Your word has given me life.
51 The proud have me in great derision,
Yet I do not turn aside from Your law.
52 I remembered Your judgments of old, O LORD,
And have comforted myself.
53 [b]Indignation has taken hold of me
Because of the wicked, who forsake Your law.
54 Your statutes have been my songs
In the house of my pilgrimage.
55 [c]I remember Your name in the night, O LORD,
And I keep Your law.
56 This has become mine,
Because I kept Your precepts.

ח HETH

57 [d]*You are* my portion, O LORD;
I have said that I would keep Your words.
58 I entreated Your favor with *my* whole heart;
Be merciful to me according to Your word.
59 I [e]thought about my ways,
And turned my feet to Your testimonies.
60 I made haste, and did not delay
To keep Your commandments.
61 The cords of the wicked have bound me,
But I have not forgotten Your law.
62 [f]At midnight I will rise to give thanks to You,
Because of Your righteous judgments.
63 I *am* a companion of all who fear You,
And of those who keep Your precepts.
64 [g]The earth, O LORD, is full of Your mercy;
Teach me Your statutes.

ט TETH

65 You have dealt well with Your servant,
O LORD, according to Your word.
66 Teach me good judgment and [h]knowledge,
For I believe Your commandments.
67 Before I was [i]afflicted I went astray,
But now I keep Your word.
68 You *are* [j]good, and do good;
Teach me Your statutes.
69 The proud have [k]forged[2] a lie against me,
But I will keep Your precepts with *my* whole heart.
70 [l]Their heart is [3]as fat as grease,
But I delight in Your law.
71 *It is* good for me that I have been afflicted,
That I may learn Your statutes.
72 [m]The law of Your mouth *is* better to me
Than thousands of *coins of* gold and silver.

38 [x] 2 Sam. 7:25
42 [9] *taunts*
45 [y] Prov. 4:12 [1] Lit. *in a wide place*
46 [z] Ps. 138:1; Matt. 10:18; Acts 26
50 [a] Job 6:10; [Rom. 15:4]
53 [b] Ex. 32:19; Ezra 9:3; Neh. 13:25
55 [c] Ps. 63:6
57 [d] Num. 18:20; Ps. 16:5; Jer. 10:16; Lam. 3:24
59 [e] Mark 14:72; Luke 15:17
62 [f] Acts 16:25
64 [g] Ps. 33:5
66 [h] Phil. 1:9
67 [i] Prov. 3:11; Jer. 31:18, 19; [Heb. 12:5-11]
68 [j] Ps. 106:1; 107:1; [Matt. 19:17]
69 [k] Job 13:4; Ps. 109:2 [2] Lit. *smeared me with a lie*
70 [l] Deut. 32:15; Job 15:27; Ps. 17:10; Is. 6:10; Jer. 5:28; Acts 28:27 [3] Insensible
72 [m] Ps. 19:10; Prov. 8:10, 11, 19

119:39 good. The very attributes of God (cf. v. 68) become the characteristics of Scripture: 1) trustworthy (v. 42); 2) true (vv. 43, 142,151,160); 3) faithful (v. 86); 4) unchangeable (v. 89); 5) eternal (vv. 90,152); 6) light (v. 105); and 7) pure (v. 140).

119:41 Your salvation. This reflects a repeated desire (cf. vv. 64,76,81,88,94,109,123,134,146,149,153,154,159,166).

119:43 hoped. The psalmist waits patiently for the working of God's Word (cf. vv. 49,74,81,114,147).

119:47,48 Which I love. The psalmist expresses his great affection for the Word (cf. vv. 97,113,127,140,159,163,165,167).

119:50 comfort. What the psalmist found in God's Word (cf. vv. 52,76,82).

119:68 You *are* good. The psalmist frequently appeals to the character of God: 1) His faithfulness (vv. 75,90); 2) His compassion (v. 77); 3) His righteousness (vv. 137,142); and 4) His mercy (v. 156).

119:70 fat as grease. Refers to the proud of v. 69 whose hearts are thick and thus the Word is unable to penetrate.

י YOD

73 [n]Your hands have made me and
fashioned me;
Give me understanding, that I may
learn Your commandments.
74 [o]Those who fear You will be glad
when they see me,
Because I have hoped in Your word.
75 I know, O LORD, [p]that Your judgments
are [4]right,
And *that* in faithfulness You have
afflicted me.
76 Let, I pray, Your merciful kindness be
for my comfort,
According to Your word to Your
servant.
77 Let Your tender mercies come to me,
that I may live;
For Your law *is* my delight.
78 Let the proud [q]be ashamed,
For they treated me wrongfully with
falsehood;
But I will meditate on Your precepts.
79 Let those who fear You turn to me,
Those who know Your testimonies.
80 Let my heart be blameless regarding
Your statutes,
That I may not be ashamed.

כ KAPH

81 [r]My soul faints for Your salvation,
But I hope in Your word.
82 My eyes fail *from searching* Your word,
Saying, "When will You comfort me?"
83 For [s]I have become like a wineskin in
smoke,
Yet I do not forget Your statutes.
84 [t]How many *are* the days of Your
servant?
[u]When will You execute judgment on
those who persecute me?
85 [v]The proud have dug pits for me,
Which *is* not according to Your law.
86 All Your commandments *are* faithful;
They persecute me [w]wrongfully;
Help me!
87 They almost made an end of me on
earth,
But I did not forsake Your precepts.
88 Revive me according to Your
lovingkindness,
So that I may keep the testimony of
Your mouth.

ל LAMED

89 [x]Forever, O LORD,
Your word [5]is settled in heaven.
90 Your faithfulness *endures* to all
generations;
You established the earth, and it
[6]abides.
91 They continue this day according to
[y]Your ordinances,
For all *are* Your servants.
92 Unless Your law *had been* my delight,
I would then have perished in my
affliction.
93 I will never forget Your precepts,
For by them You have given me life.
94 I *am* Yours, save me;
For I have sought Your precepts.
95 The wicked wait for me to destroy
me,
But I will [7]consider Your testimonies.
96 [z]I have seen the consummation of all
perfection,
But Your commandment *is*
exceedingly broad.

מ MEM

97 Oh, how I love Your law!
[a]It *is* my meditation all the day.
98 You, through Your commandments,
make me [b]wiser than my
enemies;
For they *are* ever with me.
99 I have more understanding than all
my teachers,
[c]For Your testimonies *are* my
meditation.
100 [d]I understand more than the [8]ancients,
Because I keep Your precepts.
101 I have restrained my feet from every
evil way,
That I may keep Your word.
102 I have not departed from Your
judgments,
For You Yourself have taught me.
103 [e]How sweet are Your words to my
taste,
Sweeter than honey to my mouth!
104 Through Your precepts I get
understanding;
Therefore I hate every false way.

נ NUN

105 [f]Your word *is* a lamp to my feet

73 [n] Job 10:8; 31:15; [Ps. 139:15, 16]
74 [o] Ps. 34:2
75 [p] [Heb. 12:10] [4] Lit. *righteous*
78 [q] Ps. 25:3
81 [r] Ps. 73:26; 84:2
83 [s] Job 30:30
84 [t] Ps. 39:4 [u] Rev. 6:10
85 [v] Ps. 35:7; Prov. 16:27; Jer. 18:22
86 [w] Ps. 35:19

89 [x] Ps. 89:2; Is. 40:8; Matt. 24:35; [1 Pet. 1:25] [5] Lit. *stands firm*
90 [6] Lit. *stands*
91 [y] Jer. 33:25
95 [7] *give attention to*
96 [z] Matt. 5:18
97 [a] Ps. 1:2
98 [b] Deut. 4:6
99 [c] [2 Tim. 3:15]
100 [d] [Job 32:7-9] [8] *aged*
103 [e] Ps. 19:10; Prov. 8:11
105 [f] Prov. 6:23

119:73 Your hands. Figuratively refers to God's involvement in human life (Ps. 139:13-16).

119:75 You have afflicted me. The psalmist expresses his confidence in God's sovereignty over human affliction referred to in 119:67,71 (cf. Deut. 32:39; Is. 45:7; Lam. 3:37,38).

119:83 a wineskin in smoke. Just as smoke will dry out, stiffen, and crack a wineskin thus making it useless, so the psalmist's affliction has debilitated him.

119:89 Forever...settled in heaven. God's Word will not change and is always spiritually relevant.

119:98-100 The wisdom of God always far surpasses the wisdom of man.

119:105 lamp...light. God's Word provides illumination to walk without stumbling.

And a light to my path.
106 [g]I have sworn and confirmed
That I will keep Your righteous
judgments.
107 I am afflicted very much;
Revive me, O LORD, according to Your
word.
108 Accept, I pray, [h]the freewill offerings
of my mouth, O LORD,
And teach me Your judgments.
109 [i]My life *is* continually [9]in my hand,
Yet I do not forget Your law.
110 [j]The wicked have laid a snare for me,
Yet I have not strayed from Your
precepts.
111 [k]Your testimonies I have taken as a
[1]heritage forever,
For they *are* the rejoicing of my heart.
112 I have inclined my heart to perform
Your statutes
Forever, to the very end.

ס SAMEK

113 I hate the [2]double-minded,
But I love Your law.
114 [l]You *are* my hiding place and my
shield;
I hope in Your word.
115 [m]Depart from me, you evildoers,
For I will keep the commandments of
my God!
116 Uphold me according to Your word,
that I may live;
And do not let me [n]be ashamed of
my hope.
117 [3]Hold me up, and I shall be safe,
And I shall observe Your statutes
continually.
118 You reject all those who stray from
Your statutes,
For their deceit *is* falsehood.
119 You [4]put away all the wicked of the
earth [o]*like* [5]dross;
Therefore I love Your testimonies.
120 [p]My flesh trembles for fear of You,
And I am afraid of Your judgments.

ע AYIN

121 I have done justice and righteousness;
Do not leave me to my oppressors.
122 Be [q]surety[6] for Your servant for good;
Do not let the proud oppress me.
123 My eyes fail *from seeking* Your
salvation
And Your righteous word.
124 Deal with Your servant according to
Your mercy,
And teach me Your statutes.
125 [r]I *am* Your servant;
Give me understanding,
That I may know Your testimonies.
126 *It is* time for *You* to act, O LORD,
For they have [7]regarded Your law as
void.
127 [s]Therefore I love Your commandments
More than gold, yes, than fine gold!
128 Therefore all *Your* precepts *concerning*
all *things*
I consider *to be* right;
I hate every false way.

פ PE

129 Your testimonies are wonderful;
Therefore my soul keeps them.
130 The entrance of Your words gives
light;
[t]It gives understanding to the [u]simple.
131 I opened my mouth and [v]panted,
For I longed for Your commandments.
132 [w]Look upon me and be merciful to me,
[x]As Your custom *is* toward those who
love Your name.
133 [y]Direct my steps by Your word,
And [z]let no iniquity have dominion
over me.
134 [a]Redeem me from the oppression of
man,
That I may keep Your precepts.
135 [b]Make Your face shine upon Your
servant,
And teach me Your statutes.
136 [c]Rivers of water run down from my
eyes,
Because *men* do not keep Your law.

צ TSADDE

137 [d]Righteous *are* You, O LORD,
And upright *are* Your judgments.
138 [e]Your testimonies, *which* You have
commanded,
Are righteous and very faithful.
139 [f]My zeal has [8]consumed me,
Because my enemies have forgotten
Your words.
140 [g]Your word *is* very [9]pure;
Therefore Your servant loves it.
141 I *am* small and despised,
Yet I do not forget Your precepts.

106 [g] Neh. 10:29
108 [h] Hos. 14:2; Heb. 13:15
109 [i] Judg. 12:3; Job 13:14 [9] *In danger*
110 [j] Ps. 140:5
111 [k] Deut. 33:4 [1] *inheritance*
113 [2] Lit. *divided* in heart or mind
114 [l] [Ps. 32:7]
115 [m] Ps. 6:8; Matt. 7:23
116 [n] Ps. 25:2; [Rom. 5:5; 9:33; 10:11; Phil. 1:20]
117 [3] *Uphold me*
119 [o] Is. 1:22, 25; Ezek. 22:18, 19 [4] *destroy*, lit. *cause to cease* [5] *slag* or *refuse*
120 [p] Job 4:14; Hab. 3:16
122 [q] Job 17:3; Heb. 7:22 [6] *guaranty*
125 [r] Ps. 116:16
126 [7] *broken Your law*
127 [s] Ps. 19:10
130 [t] Prov. 6:23 [u] [Ps. 19:7]; Prov. 1:4
131 [v] Ps. 42:1
132 [w] Ps. 106:4 [x] Ps. 51:1; [2 Thess. 1:6]
133 [y] Ps. 17:5 [z] [Ps. 19:13; Rom. 6:12]
134 [a] Luke 1:74
135 [b] Num. 6:25; Ps. 4:6
136 [c] Jer. 9:1, 18; 14:17; Lam. 3:48; Ezek. 9:4
137 [d] Ezra 9:15; Neh. 9:33; Jer. 12:1; Lam. 1:18; Dan. 9:7, 14
138 [e] [Ps. 19:7–9]
139 [f] Ps. 69:9; John 2:17 [8] *put an end to*
140 [g] Ps. 12:6 [9] Lit. *refined* or *tried*

119:111 rejoicing. The Word brings joy (cf. v. 162).

119:118,119 You reject...put away. God righteously judges the wicked by His Word.

119:128 *See note on v. 21.*

119:130 light...understanding. Refers to illumination in comprehending the meaning of Scripture.

119:131 panted. As after God Himself (cf. Ps. 42:1,2).

119:136 Rivers of water. The psalmist is brought to sobbing over the sin of others.

119:140 very pure. Like silver refined 7 times (cf. Ps. 12:6), the Word is without impurity, i.e., it is inerrant in all that it declares.

142 Your righteousness *is* an everlasting
righteousness,
And Your law *is* [h]truth.
143 Trouble and anguish have [1]overtaken
me,
Yet Your commandments *are* my
delights.
144 The righteousness of Your testimonies
is everlasting;
Give me understanding, and I shall
live.

ק QOPH

145 I cry out with *my* whole heart;
Hear me, O LORD!
I will keep Your statutes.
146 I cry out to You;
Save me, and I will keep Your
testimonies.
147 [i]I rise before the dawning of the
morning,
And cry for help;
I hope in Your word.
148 [j]My eyes are awake through the *night*
watches,
That I may meditate on Your word.
149 Hear my voice according to Your
lovingkindness;
O LORD, revive me according to Your
justice.
150 They draw near who follow after
wickedness;
They are far from Your law.
151 You *are* [k]near, O LORD,
And all Your commandments *are*
truth.
152 Concerning Your testimonies,
I have known of old that You have
founded them [l]forever.

ר RESH

153 [m]Consider my affliction and deliver me,
For I do not forget Your law.
154 [n]Plead my cause and redeem me;
Revive me according to Your word.
155 Salvation *is* far from the wicked,
For they do not seek Your statutes.
156 [2]Great *are* Your tender mercies,
O LORD;
Revive me according to Your
judgments.
157 Many *are* my persecutors and my
enemies,
Yet I do not [o]turn from Your
testimonies.
158 I see the treacherous, and [p]am
disgusted,
Because they do not keep Your word.
159 Consider how I love Your precepts;
Revive me, O LORD, according to Your
lovingkindness.
160 The entirety of Your word *is* truth,
And every one of Your righteous
judgments *endures* forever.

ש SHIN

161 [q]Princes persecute me without a cause,
But my heart stands in awe of Your
word.
162 I rejoice at Your word
As one who finds great treasure.
163 I hate and abhor lying,
But I love Your law.
164 Seven times a day I praise You,
Because of Your righteous judgments.
165 [r]Great peace have those who love Your
law,
And [3]nothing causes them to stumble.
166 [s]LORD, I hope for Your salvation,
And I do Your commandments.
167 My soul keeps Your testimonies,
And I love them exceedingly.
168 I keep Your precepts and Your
testimonies,
[t]For all my ways *are* before You.

ת TAU

169 Let my cry come before You, O LORD;
[u]Give me understanding according to
Your word.
170 Let my [4]supplication come before
You;
Deliver me according to Your word.
171 [v]My lips shall utter praise,
For You teach me Your statutes.
172 My tongue shall speak of Your word,
For all Your commandments *are*
righteousness.
173 Let Your hand become my help,
For [w]I have chosen Your precepts.
174 [x]I long for Your salvation, O LORD,
And [y]Your law *is* my delight.
175 Let my soul live, and it shall praise
You;
And let Your judgments help me.
176 [z]I have gone astray like a lost sheep;

142 [h] [Ps. 19:9; John 17:17]
143 [1] Lit. *found*
147 [i] Ps. 5:3
148 [j] Ps. 63:1, 6
151 [k] [Ps. 145:18]; Is. 50:8
152 [l] Luke 21:33
153 [m] Lam. 5:1
154 [n] 1 Sam. 24:15; Mic. 7:9
156 [2] Or *Many*
157 [o] Ps. 44:18
158 [p] Ezek. 9:4
161 [q] 1 Sam. 24:11; 26:18
165 [r] Prov. 3:2; [Is. 26:3; 32:17] [3] Lit. *they have no stumbling block*
166 [s] Gen. 49:18
168 [t] Job 24:23; Prov. 5:21
169 [u] Ps. 119:27, 144
170 [4] Prayer of supplication
171 [v] Ps. 119:7
173 [w] Josh. 24:22; Luke 10:42
174 [x] Ps. 119:166 [y] Ps. 119:16, 24
176 [z] [Is. 53:6]; Jer. 50:6; Matt. 18:12; Luke 15:4; [1 Pet. 2:25]

119:155 Salvation…far. Salvation is clearly revealed in the Scripture and nowhere else with such perspicuity.

119:160 The entirety…truth. There is not a speck of untruth in Scripture.

119:161 in awe. Just as one stands in awe of God Himself.

119:163 I hate…lying. Cf. vv. 29,30.

119:164 Seven times. Seven is perhaps used in the sense of perfection/completion meaning here that a continual attitude of praise characterizes the psalmist's life.

119:173 Your hand. An anthropomorphic figure of speech.

119:176 I have gone astray. In spite of all that he has affirmed regarding Scripture's power in his life, the psalmist confesses that sin has not yet been eliminated from his life (cf. Rom. 7:15-25). Any decrease of sin in his life should be attributed to the suppression of unrighteousness by the working of God's Word (cf. vv. 9-11).

Seek Your servant,
For I do not forget Your
commandments.

PSALM 120

Plea for Relief from Bitter Foes

A Song of Ascents.

In [a]my distress I cried to the LORD,
And He heard me.
2 Deliver my soul, O LORD, from lying
lips
And from a deceitful tongue.

3 What shall be given to you,
Or what shall be done to you,
You false tongue?
4 Sharp arrows of the [1]warrior,
With coals of the broom tree!

5 Woe is me, that I dwell in [b]Meshech,
[c]*That* I dwell among the tents of Kedar!
6 My soul has dwelt too long
With one who hates peace.
7 I *am for* peace;
But when I speak, they *are* for war.

PSALM 121

God the Help of Those Who Seek Him

A Song of Ascents.

I [a]will lift up my eyes to the hills—
From whence comes my help?
2 [b]My help *comes* from the LORD,
Who made heaven and earth.

PSALM 120

1 [a] Jon. 2:2
4 [1] *mighty one*
5 [b] Gen. 10:2; 1 Chr. 1:5; Ezek. 27:13; 38:2, 3; 39:1 [c] Gen. 25:13; Is. 21:16; 60:7; Jer. 2:10; 49:28; Ezek. 27:21

PSALM 121

1 [a] [Jer. 3:23]
2 [b] [Ps. 124:8]
3 [c] 1 Sam. 2:9; Prov. 3:23, 26 [d] [Ps. 127:1; Prov. 24:12]; Is. 27:3 [1] *slip*
5 [e] Is. 25:4 [f] Ps. 16:8 [2] *protector*
6 [g] Ps. 91:5; Is. 49:10; Jon. 4:8; Rev. 7:16
7 [h] Ps. 41:2 [3] *keep*
8 [i] Deut. 28:6; [Prov. 2:8; 3:6] [4] *keep*

PSALM 122

1 [a] [Is. 2:3; Mic. 4:2]; Zech. 8:21
3 [b] 2 Sam. 5:9
4 [c] Ex. 23:17; Deut. 16:16 [d] Ex. 16:34 [1] Or *As a testimony to*

3 [c]He will not allow your foot to [1]be
moved;
[d]He who keeps you will not slumber.
4 Behold, He who keeps Israel
Shall neither slumber nor sleep.

5 The LORD *is* your [2]keeper;
The LORD *is* [e]your shade [f]at your right
hand.
6 [g]The sun shall not strike you by day,
Nor the moon by night.

7 The LORD shall [3]preserve you from all
evil;
He shall [h]preserve your soul.
8 The LORD shall [i]preserve[4] your going
out and your coming in
From this time forth, and even
forevermore.

PSALM 122

The Joy of Going to the House of the LORD

A Song of Ascents. Of David.

I was glad when they said to me,
[a]"Let us go into the house of the LORD."
2 Our feet have been standing
Within your gates, O Jerusalem!

3 Jerusalem is built
As a city that is [b]compact together,
4 [c]Where the tribes go up,
The tribes of the LORD,
[1]To [d]the Testimony of Israel,

120:1-7 Psalms 120–136 comprise "The Great Hallel"; cf. "The Egyptian Hallel" (Pss. 113–118) and "The Final Hallel" (Pss. 145–150). Almost all these psalms (15 of 17) are "Songs of Ascent" (Pss. 120–134), which the Jewish pilgrims sang on their way up to Jerusalem (about 2,700 ft. in elevation) on 3 prescribed annual occasions. These feasts included: 1) Unleavened Bread; 2) Weeks/Pentecost/Harvest; and 3) Ingathering/Tabernacles/Booths. Cf. notes on Ex. 23:14-17; 34:22,23; Deut. 16:16. David authored 4 of these songs (Pss. 122,124, 131,133), Solomon one (Ps. 127), while 10 remain anonymous. When these psalms were assembled in this way is unknown. It appears that these songs begin far away from Jerusalem (cf. Meschech and Kedar in Ps. 120:5) and progressively move toward Jerusalem until the pilgrims have actually reached the temple and finished their worship (cf. Ps. 134:1,2). With regard to Ps. 120, the author and circumstances are unknown, although it seems as if the worshiper lives at a distance among unbelieving people (cf. Ps. 120:5).

I. Petition (120:1,2)
II. Indictment (120:3,4)
III. Lament (120:5-7)

120:2 lying lips...deceitful tongue. Cf. Pss. 109:2; 52:2-4; Rom. 3:9-18.

120:4 Sharp arrows...coals. Lies and false accusations are likened to 1) the pain/injury inflicted in battle by arrows, and 2) the pain of being burned with charcoal made from the wood of a broom tree (a desert bush that grows 10 to 15 ft. high).

120:5-7 The psalmist actually lives among pagans who do not embrace his desire for peace.

120:5 Meshech...Kedar. In Asia Minor (cf. Gen. 10:2) and Arabia (Is. 21:16) respectively.

121:1-8 *See note on Ps. 120:1-7.* The author and circumstances are unknown. This song strikes a strong note of assurance in 4 stages that God is help and protection to keep both Israel and individual believers safe from harm.

I. God—Helper (121:1,2)
II. God—Keeper (121:3,4)
III. God—Protector (121:5,6)
IV. God—Preserver (121:7,8)

121:1 hills. Most likely those in the distance as the pilgrim looks to Jerusalem, especially the temple.

121:2 My help. The psalmist does not look to the creation, but rather the Creator for his help.

121:3 be moved. Cf. Ps. 37:23,24.

121:3,4 slumber. Cf. the appearance of sleep, Ps. 44:23. The living God is totally unlike the pagan gods/dead idols (cf. 1 Kin. 18:27).

121:5 your right hand. This represents the place of human need.

121:6 by day...by night. Around the clock protection.

121:7,8 While this seems to have a temporal sense at first glance, there are indications that it looks beyond to eternal life, e.g., all evil (21:7) and forevermore (21:8).

122:1-9 *See note on Ps. 120:1-7.* David expressed his great joy over Jerusalem which he had settled by defeating the Jebusites (cf.

To give thanks to the name of the
LORD.
5 [e]For thrones are set there for
judgment,
The thrones of the house of David.

6 [f]Pray for the peace of Jerusalem:
"May they prosper who love you.
7 Peace be within your walls,
Prosperity within your palaces."
8 For the sake of my brethren and
companions,
I will now say, "Peace *be* within
you."
9 Because of the house of the LORD our
God
I will [g]seek your good.

PSALM 123

Prayer for Relief from Contempt

A Song of Ascents.

Unto You [a]I lift up my eyes,
O You [b]who dwell in the heavens.
2 Behold, as the eyes of servants *look* to
the hand of their masters,
As the eyes of a maid to the hand of
her mistress,
[c]So our eyes *look* to the LORD our
God,
Until He has mercy on us.

3 Have mercy on us, O LORD, have
mercy on us!
For we are exceedingly filled with
contempt.
4 Our soul is exceedingly filled
With the scorn of those who are at
ease,
With the contempt of the proud.

PSALM 124

The LORD the Defense of His People

A Song of Ascents. Of David.

"If it had not been the LORD who was
on our [a]side,"
[b]Let Israel now say—
2 "If it had not been the LORD who was
on our side,
When men rose up against us,
3 Then they would have [c]swallowed us
alive,
When their wrath was kindled
against us;
4 Then the waters would have
overwhelmed us,
The stream would have [1]gone over
our soul;
5 Then the swollen waters
Would have [2]gone over our soul."

6 Blessed *be* the LORD,
Who has not given us *as* prey to their
teeth.
7 [d]Our soul has escaped [e]as a bird from
the snare of the [3]fowlers;
The snare is broken, and we have
escaped.
8 [f]Our help *is* in the name of the LORD,
[g]Who made heaven and earth.

5 [e] Deut. 17:8; 2 Chr. 19:8
6 [f] Ps. 51:18
9 [g] Neh. 2:10; Esth. 10:3

PSALM 123

1 [a] Ps. 121:1; 141:8 [b] Ps. 2:4; 11:4; 115:3
2 [c] Ps. 25:15

PSALM 124

1 [a] Ps. 118:6; [Rom. 8:31] [b] Ps. 129:1
3 [c] Num. 16:30; Ps. 56:1, 2; 57:3; Prov. 1:12
4 [1] *swept over*
5 [2] *swept over*
7 [d] Ps. 91:3 [e] Prov. 6:5; Hos. 9:8 [3] Persons who catch birds in a trap or snare
8 [f] [Ps. 121:2] [g] Gen. 1:1; Ps. 134:3

2 Sam. 5) and bringing the tabernacle and ark for permanent residency (cf. 2 Sam. 6). David's desire/prayer was temporarily fulfilled in Solomon's reign (cf. 1 Kin. 4:24,25). It is ironic that Jerusalem, which means "city of peace," has been fought over through history more than any other city in the world. Prophetically, David's desire will not be experienced in its fullness until the Prince of Peace (Is. 9:6) comes to rule permanently (Zech. 14:9,11) as the promised Davidic King (cf. 2 Sam. 7:12,13,16; Ezek. 37:24-28).

I. Joy Over Worship (122:1-5)
II. Prayer Over Jerusalem (122:6-9)

122:1 the house of the LORD. A term used of the tabernacle (cf. Ex. 23:19; 34:26; 2 Sam. 12:20), not the temple that would be built later by Solomon.

122:2 standing within your gates. Sometime after the tabernacle and ark of the covenant had arrived in the city of David (2 Sam. 6). David's joy is that the ark has found its proper location.

122:3 compact together. The Jerusalem of David's day (Zion) was smaller than the enlargement by Solomon.

122:4 the Testimony of Israel. Refers to God's command to go up to Jerusalem 3 times annually (*see note on Ps. 120:1-7*).

122:6-9 A most appropriate prayer for a city whose name means peace and is the residency of the God of peace (Is. 9:6; Rom. 15:33; Heb. 13:20). Compare prayers for the peace of Israel (Pss. 125:5; 128:6) and other psalms which exalt Jerusalem (Pss. 128,132,147). History would prove that bad times had to come (Pss. 79,137) before the best of times (Rev. 21,22).

123:1-4 *See note on Ps. 120:1-7.* The author and situation are unknown.

I. Exalting God (123:1,2)
II. Enlisting God's Mercy (123:3,4)

123:1 my eyes. The progression from Ps. 121:1. **dwell in... heavens.** Cf. Pss. 11:4; 103:19; 113:5.

123:2 servants...masters. The psalmist reasons from the lesser to the greater (human to the divine; earthly to the heavenly). One's eyes should be on the Lord to mercifully meet one's needs.

123:3,4 contempt...scorn. From unbelieving pagans, perhaps the Samaritans (cf. Neh. 1:3; 2:19).

124:1-8 *See note on Ps. 120:1-7.* A Davidic psalm which generically recalls past deliverances, possibly the Exodus (v. 5).

I. God's Protection (124:1-5)
II. God's Provision (124:6-8)

124:1,2 God has preserved Israel from extinction.

124:2 When men rose up. A general statement which could cover the history of Israel from Abraham to David.

124:4,5 waters...stream...swollen waters. The Red Sea crossing (Ex. 14) and/or the Jordan crossing (Josh. 3) are pictured.

124:8 Our help. Cf. Ps. 121:1,2.

PSALM 125

The LORD *the Strength of His People*

A Song of Ascents.

Those who trust in the LORD
Are like Mount Zion,
Which cannot be moved, *but* abides
forever.
2 As the mountains surround Jerusalem,
So the LORD surrounds His people
From this time forth and forever.

3 For [a]the scepter of wickedness shall
not rest
On the land allotted to the righteous,
Lest the righteous reach out their
hands to iniquity.

4 Do good, O LORD, to *those who are*
good,
And to *those who are* upright in their
hearts.

5 As for such as turn aside to their
[b]crooked ways,
The LORD shall lead them away
With the workers of iniquity.

[c]Peace *be* upon Israel!

PSALM 126

A Joyful Return to Zion

A Song of Ascents.

When [a]the LORD brought back [1]the
captivity of Zion,
[b]We were like those who dream.
2 Then [c]our mouth was filled with
laughter,
And our tongue with singing.
Then they said among the [2]nations,
"The LORD has done great things for
them."
3 The LORD has done great things for
us,
And we are glad.

4 Bring back our captivity, O LORD,
As the streams in the South.

5 [d]Those who sow in tears
Shall reap in joy.
6 He who continually goes [3]forth
weeping,
Bearing [4]seed for sowing,
Shall doubtless come again [5]with
[e]rejoicing,
Bringing his sheaves *with him.*

PSALM 127

Laboring and Prospering with the LORD

A Song of Ascents. Of Solomon.

Unless the LORD builds the house,
They labor in vain who build it;
Unless [a]the LORD guards the city,
The watchman stays awake in vain.
2 *It is* vain for you to rise up early,
To sit up late,
To [b]eat the bread of sorrows;
For so He gives His beloved sleep.

PSALM 125
3 [a] Prov. 22:8; Is. 14:5
5 [b] Prov. 2:15; Is. 59:8 [c] Ps. 128:6; [Gal. 6:16]

PSALM 126
1 [a] Ps. 85:1; Jer. 29:14; Hos. 6:11; Joel 3:1 [1] *Those of the captivity* [b] Acts 12:9
2 [c] Job 8:21 [2] *Gentiles*
5 [d] Is. 35:10; 51:11; 61:7; Jer. 31:9; [Gal. 6:9]
6 [e] Is. 61:3 [3] *to and fro* [4] *Lit. a bag of seed for sowing* [5] *with shouts of joy*

PSALM 127
1 [a] [Ps. 121:3-5]
2 [b] [Gen. 3:17, 19]

125:1-5 *See note on Ps. 120:1-7.* The author and circumstances are unknown, although the times of Hezekiah (2 Kin. 18:27-35) or Nehemiah (Neh. 6:1-19) have been suggested.

I. The Security of Jerusalem (125:1-3)
II. The Spiritual Purity of Jerusalem (125:4,5)

125:1 Mount Zion. The SW mount representing Jerusalem and an emblem of permanence, supported by God's covenant promise.

125:1,2 forever. More than a temporal promise is involved here.

125:2 His people. Those who trust in the Lord (cf. v. 1).

125:3 scepter of wickedness. Assyrian rule if in Hezekiah's time, or Medo-Persian rule if in Nehemiah's day. **the land.** This would be the land promised to Abraham (Gen. 15:18-21).

125:4,5 The outcome of the upright (v. 4) is contrasted with the crooked (v. 5). The true Israel is distinguished from the false (cf. Rom. 2:28,29; 9:6,7).

125:5 lead them away. Eternal rather than temporal judgment seems to be in view. **Peace.** God will one day institute a lasting covenant of peace (cf. Ezek. 37:26).

126:1-6 *See note on Ps. 120:1-7.* The author and occasion are not named in the psalm. However, v. 1 points to a time of return from captivity. Most likely this refers to the Babylonian Captivity, from which there were 3 separate returns: 1) under Zerubbabel in Ezra 1–6 (ca. 538 B.C.); 2) under Ezra in Ezra 7–10 (ca. 458 B.C.); and 3) under Nehemiah in Neh. 1,2 (ca. 445 B.C.). The occasion could be 1) when the foundation for the second temple had been laid (cf. Ezra 3:8-10), or 2) when the Feast of Tabernacles was reinstated (cf. Neh. 8:13-14). This psalm is similar to Ps. 85 which rejoices over Israel's return from Egypt, but contrasts with Ps. 137 which laments the pain of the Babylonian captivity.

I. The Testimony of Restoration (126:1-3)
II. The Prayer for Riches (126:4)
III. The Wisdom of Righteousness (126:5,6)

126:1 those who dream. The actual experience of liberation, so unexpected, seemed more like a dream than reality.

126:2,3 The LORD has done. First recognized by the surrounding nations (v. 2) and then the returning remnant (v. 3).

126:4 Bring back. A prayer to restore the nation's fortunes at their best. **streams in the South.** The arid region S of Beersheba (called the Negev) which is utterly dry in the summer, but whose streams quickly fill and flood with the rains of spring. In this manner, the psalmist prays that Israel's fortunes will rapidly change from nothing to everything.

126:5,6 sow…reap. By sowing tears of repentance over sin, the nation reaped the harvest of a joyful return to the land of Israel.

127:1-5 *See note on Ps. 120:1-7.* The author is Solomon (cf. Eccl. 12:10), but the occasion is unknown. The major message of God's

3 Behold, [c]children *are* a heritage from
the LORD,
[d]The fruit of the womb *is* a [e]reward.
4 Like arrows in the hand of a warrior,
So *are* the children of one's youth.
5 [f]Happy *is* the man who has his quiver
full of them;
[g]They shall not be ashamed,
But shall speak with their enemies in
the gate.

PSALM 128

Blessings of Those Who Fear the LORD

A Song of Ascents.

Blessed [a]*is* every one who fears the
LORD,
Who walks in His ways.
2 [b]When you eat the [1]labor of your
hands,
You *shall be* happy, and *it shall be* [c]well
with you.
3 Your wife *shall be* [d]like a fruitful vine
In the very heart of your house,
Your [e]children [f]like olive plants
All around your table.
4 Behold, thus shall the man be blessed
Who fears the LORD.
5 [g]The LORD bless you out of Zion,
And may you see the good of
Jerusalem
All the days of your life.
6 Yes, may you [h]see your children's
children.

[i]Peace *be* upon Israel!

PSALM 129

Song of Victory over Zion's Enemies

A Song of Ascents.

"Many a time they have [a]afflicted [1]me
from [b]my youth,"
[c]Let Israel now say—
2 "Many a time they have afflicted me
from my youth;
Yet they have not prevailed against
me.
3 The plowers plowed on my back;
They made their furrows long."
4 The LORD *is* righteous;
He has cut in pieces the cords of the
wicked.

5 Let all those who hate Zion
Be put to shame and turned back.
6 Let them be as the [d]grass *on* the
housetops,
Which withers before it grows up,
7 With which the reaper does not fill his
hand,

3 [c][Gen. 33:5; Josh. 24:3, 4; Ps. 113:9] [d]Deut. 7:13; 28:4; Is. 13:18 [e][Ps. 113:9]
5 [f]Ps. 128:2, 3 [g]Job 5:4; Prov. 27:11

PSALM 128
1 [a]Ps. 119:1
2 [b]Is. 3:10 [c]Deut. 4:40 [1]Fruit of the labor
3 [d]Ezek. 19:10 [e]Ps. 127:3-5 [f]Ps. 52:8; 144:12
5 [g]Ps. 134:3
6 [h]Gen. 48:11; 50:23; Job 42:16; Ps. 103:17; [Prov. 17:6] [i]Ps. 125:5

PSALM 129
1 [a][Jer. 1:19; 15:20]; Matt. 16:18; 2 Cor. 4:8, 9 [b]Ezek. 23:3; Hos. 2:15 [c]Ps. 124:1 [1]*persecuted*
6 [d]Ps. 37:2

being central to and sovereign in life sounds much like portions of Solomon's Ecclesiastes (cf. Eccl. 2:24,25; 5:18-20; 7:13,14; 9:1). Psalms 112 and 128 also develop a strong message on the family.

I. God's Sovereignty in Everyday Life (127:1,2)
II. God's Sovereignty in Family Life (127:3-5)

127:1,2 God's sovereignty is seen in 3 realms: 1) building a house, 2) protecting a city, and 3) earning a living. In all 3 instances, the sovereign intention of God is far more crucial to the outcome than man's efforts. Otherwise, a man's endeavor is in vain (cf. Eccl. 1:2; 12:8).

127:2 the bread of sorrows. Food earned with painful labor.

127:3-5 The same principle of God's sovereignty applies to raising a family.

127:3 heritage...reward. Children are a blessing from the Lord. There are overtones of God's promise to Abraham to make his offspring like the stars of heaven and dust of the earth (Gen. 15:5; 13:16).

127:4,5 As arrows are indispensable for a warrior to succeed in battle, so children are invaluable as defenders of their father and mother in time of war or litigation. The more such defenders, the better.

128:1-6 *See note on Ps. 120:1-7.* The author and occasion are unknown. Psalms 112 and 127 also address issues of the home.

I. The Basics of Fearing the Lord (128:1,4)
II. The Blessings of Fearing the Lord (128:2,3,5,6)
A. In the Present (128:2,3)
B. In the Future (128:5,6)

128:1 who fears the LORD. *See notes on Prov. 1:7 and 9:10.* Psalm 112:1-6 also develops this theme. A good working definition is provided by the parallel line, "who walks in His ways." Fathers (Ps. 128:1,4), mothers (Prov. 31:30), and children (Ps. 34:11) are to fear the Lord. This psalm may have been the basis for Jesus' illustration of the two builders (cf. Matt. 7:24-27).

128:2,3 Four blessings are recounted: 1) provisions, 2) prosperity, 3) reproducing partner, and 4) flourishing progeny.

128:3 olive plants. Shoots grow off of the main root of an olive tree to reproduce.

128:5,6 Two realms of blessing are mentioned: 1) personal blessing and 2) national blessing.

128:6 children's children. Cf. Pss. 103:17; 112:2; Prov. 13:22; 17:6 on grandchildren. This is a prayer for prosperity for God's people.

129:1-8 *See note on Ps. 120:1-7.* The author and occasion are not specified. However, v. 4 indicates a release from captivity, most likely the Babylonian captivity.

I. Israel's Freedom Celebrated (129:1-4)
II. Israel's Foe Imprecated (129:5-8)

129:1 afflicted. From living in Egypt (ca. 1875–1445 B.C.), to enduring the Babylonian Captivity (ca. 605–538 B.C.), Israel had enjoyed little rest from her enemies.

129:2 prevailed. As the Lord had promised Abraham (cf. Gen. 12:1-3).

129:3 plowed on my back. A farming analogy used to describe the deep, but non-fatal, wounds inflicted on Israel by her enemies.

129:4 cut...the cords. These cords tied the ox to the plow, and refer to God ending the persecution (cf. Pss. 121,124).

129:5-8 A 3-part imprecatory prayer: 1) be put to shame and defeat (v. 5), 2) be few and short lived (vv. 6,7), and 3) be without God's blessing (v. 8).

129:6 grass...the housetops. Grass with shallow roots, which quickly dies with the first heat depicts the wicked.

Nor he who binds sheaves, his [2]arms.
8 Neither let those who pass by them say,
[e]"The blessing of the LORD *be* upon you;
We bless you in the name of the LORD!"

PSALM 130

Waiting for the Redemption of the LORD

A Song of Ascents.

Out [a]of the depths I have cried to You, O LORD;
2 Lord, hear my voice!
Let Your ears be attentive
To the voice of my supplications.

3 [b]If You, LORD, should [1]mark iniquities,
O Lord, who could [c]stand?
4 But *there is* [d]forgiveness with You,
That [e]You may be feared.

5 [f]I wait for the LORD, my soul waits,
And [g]in His word I do hope.
6 [h]My soul *waits* for the Lord
More than those who watch for the morning—
Yes, more than those who watch for the morning.
7 [i]O Israel, hope in the LORD;
For [j]with the LORD *there is* mercy,
And with Him *is* abundant redemption.
8 And [k]He shall redeem Israel
From all his iniquities.

PSALM 131

Simple Trust in the LORD

A Song of Ascents. Of David.

LORD, my heart is not [1]haughty,
Nor my eyes [2]lofty.
[a]Neither do I [3]concern myself with great matters,
Nor with things too [4]profound for me.

2 Surely I have calmed and quieted my soul,
[b]Like a weaned child with his mother;
Like a weaned child *is* my soul within me.

3 [c]O Israel, hope in the LORD
From this time forth and forever.

PSALM 132

The Eternal Dwelling of God in Zion

A Song of Ascents.

LORD, remember David
And all his afflictions;
2 How he swore to the LORD,

7 [2]*armsful*, lit. *bosom*
8 [e]Ruth 2:4

PSALM 130

1 [a]Lam. 3:55
3 [b][Ps. 143:2] [c][Nah. 1:6; Mal. 3:2]; Rev. 6:17 [1]*take note of*
4 [d][Ex. 34:7; Neh. 9:17; Ps. 86:5; Is. 55:7; Dan. 9:9] [e][1 Kin. 8:39, 40; Jer. 33:8, 9]
5 [f][Ps. 27:14] [g]Ps. 119:81
6 [h]Ps. 119:147
7 [i]Ps. 131:3 [j][Ps. 86:5, 15; Is. 55:7]
8 [k][Ps. 103:3, 4]; Luke 1:68; Titus 2:14

PSALM 131

1 [a]Jer. 45:5; [Rom. 12:16] [1]*Proud* [2]*Arrogant* [3]Lit. *walk in* [4]*difficult*
2 [b][Matt. 18:3; 1 Cor. 14:20]
3 [c][Ps. 130:7]

130:1-8 *See note on Ps. 120:1-7.* The author and occasion are not mentioned. This is the sixth of 7 penitential psalms (cf. Pss. 6, 32, 38, 51, 102, 143).

I. Urgent Prayer of the Psalmist (130:1,2)
II. Magnified Forgiveness of God (130:3,4)
III. Waiting Patience of the Psalmist (130:5,6)
IV. Unique Hope of Israel (130:7,8)

130:1 Out of the depths. A figurative expression of severe distress.

130:3,4 The psalmist basks in the glow of God's never ending forgiveness (cf. Ps. 143:2).

130:5 in His word I do hope. The psalmist expresses a certain hope since God's Word cannot fail (cf. Matt. 5:18; Luke 16:17; John 10:35).

130:6 watch for the morning. Probably refers to shepherds with a night watch which ends with the sun's rising.

130:7 hope in the LORD. The psalmist's hope in God's Word (v. 5) parallels Israel's hope in the Lord.

130:8 He shall redeem Israel. This can be taken in both a historical and a soteriological sense (cf. Matt. 1:21; Luke 1:68; Rom. 9–11).

131:1-3 *See note on Ps. 120:1-7.* David is the author, but the circumstances are not apparent.

I. A Personal Testimony (131:1,2)
II. A National Exhortation (131:3)

131:1 haughty…lofty. God gives grace to the humble (cf. Prov. 3:34; 16:5; James 4:6). David expresses the greatest of God's ways (cf. Ps. 139:6; Rom. 11:33-36).

131:2 Like a weaned child. David has been trained to trust God to supply his needs as a weaned child trusts his mother.

131:3 David exhorts the nation to forever embrace his own personal hope in the Lord.

132:1-18 *See note on Ps. 120:1-7.* The author and occasion are not specifically mentioned. However, the bringing of the tabernacle to Jerusalem in David's time seems likely (cf. 2 Sam. 6:12-19 with 132:6-9). Further, Solomon's quote of vv. 8-10 in his dedication of the temple (2 Chr. 6:41-42) makes that time probable. Psalm 132 has strong historical implications with regard to the Davidic Covenant (cf. 2 Sam. 7:10-14; 16; Pss. 89; 132:10,11) and pronounced messianic and millennial overtones (Ps. 132:12-18). Essentially, this psalm contains the nation's prayers for David's royal descendants which look ahead, even to Messiah.

I. Israel's First Prayer (132:1)
II. David's Vow to God (132:2-9)
III. Israel's Second Prayer (132:10)
IV. God's Vow to David (132:11-18)

132:1-9 This section focuses on David fulfilling his vow to God to bring the tabernacle to rest in Jerusalem and thus his descendants are to be remembered by the Lord.

132:1 his afflictions. This seems to be inclusive from the times of being pursued by Saul (cf. 1 Sam. 18–26) through God's judgment because David numbered the people (cf. 2 Sam. 24). Perhaps it focuses on David's greatest affliction, which came from not having the ark in Jerusalem.

132:2-5 Although this specific vow is not recorded elsewhere in Scripture, the historical circumstances can be found in 2 Sam. 6; 1 Chr. 13–16.

[a]*And* vowed to [b]the Mighty One of
Jacob:
3 "Surely I will not go into the chamber
of my house,
Or go up to the comfort of my bed;
4 I will [c]not give sleep to my eyes
Or slumber to my eyelids,
5 Until I [d]find a place for the LORD,
A dwelling place for the Mighty One
of Jacob."

6 Behold, we heard of it [e]in Ephrathah;
[f]We found it [g]in the fields of [1]the
woods.
7 Let us go into His tabernacle;
[h]Let us worship at His footstool.
8 [i]Arise, O LORD, to Your resting place,
You and [j]the ark of Your strength.
9 Let Your priests [k]be clothed with
righteousness,
And let Your saints shout for joy.

10 For Your servant David's sake,
Do not turn away the face of Your
[2]Anointed.

11 [l]The LORD has sworn *in* truth to
David;
He will not turn from it:
"I will set upon your throne [m]the [3]fruit
of your body.
12 If your sons will keep My covenant
And My testimony which I shall teach
them,
Their sons also shall sit upon your
throne forevermore."

13 [n]For the LORD has chosen Zion;
He has desired *it* for His [4]dwelling
place:
14 "This[o] *is* My resting place forever;
Here I will dwell, for I have desired it.
15 [p]I will abundantly bless her
[5]provision;
I will satisfy her poor with bread.
16 [q]I will also clothe her priests with
salvation,
[r]And her saints shall shout aloud for
joy.
17 [s]There I will make the [6]horn of David
grow;
[t]I will prepare a lamp for My
[7]Anointed.
18 His enemies I will [u]clothe with
shame,
But upon Himself His crown shall
flourish."

PSALM 132

2 [a]Ps. 65:1 [b]Gen. 49:24; Is. 49:26; 60:16
4 [c]Prov. 6:4
5 [d]1 Kin. 8:17; 1 Chr. 22:7; Ps. 26:8; Acts 7:46
6 [e]1 Sam. 17:12 [f]1 Sam. 7:1 [g]1 Chr. 13:5 [1]Heb. *Jaar,* lit. *Woods*
7 [h]Ps. 5:7; 99:5
8 [i]Num. 10:35 [j]Ps. 78:61
9 [k]Job 29:14
10 [2]Commissioned One, Heb. *Messiah*
11 [l][Ps. 89:3, 4, 33; 110:4] [m]2 Sam. 7:12; [1 Kin. 8:25; 2 Chr. 6:16; Luke 1:69; Acts 2:30] [3]*offspring*
13 [n][Ps. 48:1, 2] [4]*home*
14 [o]Ps. 68:16; Matt. 23:21
15 [p]Ps. 147:14 [5]*supply of food*
16 [q]2 Chr. 6:41; Ps. 132:9; 149:4 [r]1 Sam. 4:5; Hos. 11:12
17 [s]Ezek. 29:21; Luke 1:69 [t]1 Kin. 11:36; 15:4; 2 Kin. 8:19; 2 Chr. 21:7; Ps. 18:28 [6]Government [7]Heb. *Messiah*
18 [u]Job 8:22; Ps. 35:26

PSALM 133

Blessed Unity of the People of God

A Song of Ascents. Of David.

Behold, how good and how pleasant
it is
For [a]brethren to dwell together in
unity!

PSALM 133

1 [a]Gen. 13:8; Heb. 13:1

132:2 the Mighty One of Jacob. A title last used by Jacob in Gen. 49:24.

132:6-9 The ark was brought from Kiriath Jearim to Jerusalem (cf. 2 Sam. 6; 1 Chr. 13,15).

132:6 heard of it in Ephrathah. Probably referring to David's younger days in Ephrathah, which was an earlier name for Bethlehem (cf. Ruth 1:1,2; 4:11), when he and his family had heard of the ark but had not seen it. **found it in the fields of the woods.** After the ark of the covenant was returned by the Philistines in the days of Saul (cf. 1 Sam. 7:1,2), it rested at the house of Abinadab in Kiriath Jearim until David decided to move to Jerusalem (cf. 2 Sam. 6; 1 Chr. 13–16).

132:7 His footstool. God's throne is in heaven (cf. Is. 66:1) and His footstool is on earth (cf. Ps. 99:5), figuratively speaking. Thus to worship at the ark of the covenant on earth would be, so to speak, at God's footstool.

132:8 Arise, O LORD. Since the Holy Place contained the bread of the presence (Ex. 25:30; 1 Sam. 25:6), the psalmist refers to moving the ark to Jerusalem.

132:9 Describes the proper inward attire for the priests who would oversee the move.

132:10-18 This section focuses on God's fulfilling His vow to David to perpetuate the Davidic throne and thus his descendants are to be remembered by the Lord.

132:10 A prayer that God's promise and favor would not be withheld from David's descendants on the throne of Judah. **Your Anointed.** As David had been anointed king (1 Sam. 16:13), so a greater King had been anointed, namely Christ, but not yet seated on the throne (cf. Is. 61:1; Luke 4:18,19).

132:11,12 God's covenant with David (2 Sam. 23:5) is summarized here from 2 Sam. 7:11-16 and 1 Kin. 9:1-9.

132:12 This conditional aspect could interrupt the occupation of the throne, but it would not invalidate God's promise to one day seat the Messiah as king forever (cf. Ezek. 37:24-28).

132:13-18 This section looks forward prophetically to the day that Jesus Christ, the son of David and the son of Abraham (Matt. 1:1), will be installed by God on the throne of David in the city of God to rule and bring peace on earth, especially Israel (cf. Pss. 2,89,110; Is. 25,26; Jer. 23:5,6; 33:14-18; Ezek. 37; Dan. 2:44,45; Zech. 14:1-11).

132:13 Zion. Refers to earthly Jerusalem.

133:1-3 *See note on Ps. 120:1-7.* The occasion for this Davidic psalm is unknown. Perhaps it was prompted by the nation's coming together in unity at his coronation (cf. 2 Sam. 5:1-3; 1 Chr. 11:1-3). Its teaching on fraternal unity would have been instructive to David's sons, who were antagonistic towards one another, e.g., Absalom murdered Ammon (2 Sam. 13:28-33) and Adonijah tried to preempt Solomon's right to the throne (1 Kin. 1:5-53).

I. Praise of Unity (133:1)
II. Pictures of Unity (133:2,3)
 A. Oil on Aaron's head (133:2)
 B. Dew on Mt. Zion (133:3)

133:1 brethren. Those whose lineage can be traced to Abraham, Isaac, and Jacob. **unity.** While national unity might be on the surface, the foundation must always be spiritual unity. This would be the emphasis here, since these songs were sung by Jewish pilgrims traveling to the 3 great feasts.

2 *It is* like the precious oil upon the
head,
Running down on the beard,
The beard of Aaron,
Running down on the edge of his
garments.
3 *It is* like the dew of [b]Hermon,
Descending upon the mountains of
Zion;
For [c]there the LORD commanded the
blessing—
Life forevermore.

PSALM 134

Praising the LORD in His House at Night

A Song of Ascents.

Behold, bless the LORD,
All *you* servants of the LORD,
Who by night stand in the house of
the LORD!
2 [a]Lift up your hands *in* the sanctuary,
And bless the LORD.

3 The LORD who made heaven and earth
Bless you from Zion!

PSALM 135

Praise to God in Creation and Redemption

Praise the LORD!

3 [b]Deut. 4:48 [c]Lev. 25:21; Deut. 28:8; Ps. 42:8

PSALM 134

2 [a][1 Tim. 2:8]

PSALM 135

1 [a]Ps. 113:1
2 [b]Luke 2:37 [c]Ps. 116:19
3 [d][Ps. 119:68] [e]Ps. 147:1
4 [f][Ex. 19:5]; Mal. 3:17; [Titus 2:14; 1 Pet. 2:9] [1]*precious possession*
5 [g]Ps. 95:3; 97:9
6 [h]Ps. 115:3
7 [i]Jer. 10:13 [j]Job 28:25, 26; 38:24-28 [k]Jer. 51:16 [2]Water vapor
8 [l]Ex. 12:12; Ps. 78:51 [3]Lit. *struck down* [4]Lit. *From man to beast*
9 [m]Ex. 7:10; Deut. 6:22; Ps. 78:43 [n]Ps. 136:15
10 [o]Num. 21:24; Ps. 136:17

Praise the name of the LORD;
[a]Praise *Him,* O you servants of the
LORD!
2 [b]You who stand in the house of the
LORD,
In [c]the courts of the house of our
God,
3 Praise the LORD, for [d]the LORD *is*
good;
Sing praises to His name, [e]for *it is*
pleasant.
4 For [f]the LORD has chosen Jacob for
Himself,
Israel for His [1]special treasure.

5 For I know that [g]the LORD *is* great,
And our Lord *is* above all gods.
6 [h]Whatever the LORD pleases He does,
In heaven and in earth,
In the seas and in all deep places.
7 [i]He causes the [2]vapors to ascend from
the ends of the earth;
[j]He makes lightning for the rain;
He brings the wind out of His
[k]treasuries.

8 [l]He [3]destroyed the firstborn of Egypt,
[4]Both of man and beast.
9 [m]He sent signs and wonders into the
midst of you, O Egypt,
[n]Upon Pharaoh and all his servants.
10 [o]He defeated many nations
And slew mighty kings—

133:2 oil upon. Most likely refers to the anointing of Aaron as High-Priest of the nation (cf. Ex. 29:7; 30:30), which would picture a rich spiritual blessing as a first priority.

133:3 the dew of Hermon. Mt. Hermon, a 9,200 ft. peak at the extreme northern portion of Palestine, provided the major water supply for the Jordan River by its melting snow. This reference could be to the Jordan water supply or figuratively to the actual prevalent dew of Hermon being hypothetically transported to Zion. Either way, this pictures a refreshing material blessing as a second, lesser priority. **there.** Seems to refer to Zion. **Life forevermore.** cf. Ps. 21:4-6.

134:1-3 *See note on Ps. 120:1-7.* This final song in the "songs of ascent" seems to picture the worshipers exhorting the priests to continued faithfulness (134:1,2) while the priests bestow a final blessing on the faithful as the feast ends and the pilgrims depart Zion for home (134:3).

I. Exhortation to Faithfulness (134:1,2)
II. Solicitation of Blessing (134:3)

134:1 servants. Levites who ministered to God's people. **by night.** The burnt offerings continued day and night (cf. Lev. 6:8-13), as did the Levitical service (cf. 1 Chr. 9:33). **house of the LORD.** Refers to the tabernacle up to the time of David (Ex. 23:19; 2 Sam. 12:20) and to the temple from Solomon on (1 Kin. 9:10).

134:2 Lift up your hands. A common OT praise practice (cf. Pss. 28:2; 63:4; 119:48; 141:2; Lam. 2:19), which was understood figuratively in the NT (1 Tim. 2:8).

134:3 The LORD. The Creator blesses His human creation. **Bless you from Zion.** Since God's presence resided in the tabernacle/temple on Zion, from a human perspective it would be the source of divine blessing.

135:1-21 Psalms 135 and 136 conclude the "Great Hallel." The composer and occasion of Ps. 135 are unknown but likely post-Exilic. Psalms 135:15-20 is strikingly similar to Ps. 115:4-11.

I. Call to Praise (135:1,2)
II. Causes for Praise (135:3-18)
  A. God's Character (135:3)
  B. God's Choice of Jacob (135:4)
  C. God's Sovereignty in Creation (135:5-7)
  D. God's Deliverance of Israel (135:8-12)
  E. God's Unique Nature (135:13-18)
III. Concluding Praise (135:19-21)

135:1,2 servants...stand...in the courts. Addressed to the priests and Levites (cf. 134:1).

135:3 the LORD *is* good. A consistent theme in the psalms (cf. Pss. 16:2; 25:8; 34:8; 73:1; 86:5; 100:5; 106:1; 107:1; 118:1; 136:1; 145:9).

135:4 the LORD has chosen. Refers to God's unique selection of the offering of Abraham, Isaac, and Jacob to enjoy God's covenant blessing (cf. Deut. 7:6-8; 14:2; Ps. 105:6; Is. 41:8,9; 43:20; 44:1; 49:7). **His special treasure.** Cf. Deut. 26:18,19. *See note on Ps. 148:14.*

135:5 the LORD *is* great. A common superlative to distinguish the true God of Israel from the false gods of the other nations (cf. Deut. 7:21; Pss. 48:1; 77:13; 86:10; 95:3; 104:1; 145:3; 147:5).

135:7 vapors to ascend. Refers to the water cycle of earthly evaporation and condensation in the clouds.

135:8-12 In reference to God's deliverance of Israel from Egypt to the Promised Land.

135:8 destroyed. The final plague in Egypt (cf. Ex. 11).

135:9 signs and wonders. Cf. Deut. 26:8; 29:3; 34:11.

11 Sihon king of the Amorites,
Og king of Bashan,
And [p]all the kingdoms of Canaan—
12 [q]And gave their land *as* a [5]heritage,
A heritage to Israel His people.

13 [r]Your name, O LORD, *endures* forever,
Your fame, O LORD, throughout all
generations.
14 [s]For the LORD will judge His people,
And He will have compassion on His
servants.

15 [t]The idols of the nations *are* silver and
gold,
The work of men's hands.
16 They have mouths, but they do not
speak;
Eyes they have, but they do not see;
17 They have ears, but they do not hear;
Nor is there *any* breath in their
mouths.
18 Those who make them are like them;
So is everyone who trusts in them.

19 [u]Bless the LORD, O house of Israel!
Bless the LORD, O house of Aaron!
20 Bless the LORD, O house of Levi!
You who fear the LORD, bless the
LORD!
21 Blessed be the LORD [v]out of Zion,
Who dwells in Jerusalem!

Praise the LORD!

PSALM 136

Thanksgiving to God for His Enduring Mercy

Oh, [a]give thanks to the LORD, for *He is*
good!
[b]For His mercy *endures* forever.
2 Oh, give thanks to [c]the God of gods!
For His mercy *endures* forever.
3 Oh, give thanks to the Lord of lords!
For His mercy *endures* forever:

11 [p]Josh. 12:7-24
12 [q]Ps. 78:55; 136:21, 22 [5]*inheritance*
13 [r][Ex. 3:15; Ps. 102:12]
14 [s]Deut. 32:36
15 [t][Ps. 115:4-8]
19 [u][Ps. 115:9]
21 [v]Ps. 134:3

PSALM 136

1 [a]Ps. 106:1 [b]1 Chr. 16:34; Jer. 33:11
2 [c][Deut. 10:17]
4 [d]Deut. 6:22; Job 9:10; Ps. 72:18
5 [e]Gen. 1:1, 6-8; Prov. 3:19; Jer. 51:15
6 [f]Gen. 1:9; Ps. 24:2; [Is. 42:5]; Jer. 10:12
7 [g]Gen. 1:14-18
8 [h]Gen. 1:16
10 [i]Ex. 12:29; Ps. 135:8
11 [j]Ex. 12:51; 13:3, 16
12 [k]Ex. 6:6; Deut. 4:34; 5:15; 7:19; 9:29; 11:2; 2 Kin. 17:36; 2 Chr. 6:32; Jer. 32:17 [1]*Mighty power*
13 [l]Ex. 14:21
15 [m]Ex. 14:27
16 [n]Ex. 13:18; 15:22; Deut. 8:15
17 [o]Ps. 135:10-12
18 [p]Deut. 29:7
19 [q]Num. 21:21
20 [r]Num. 21:33
21 [s]Josh. 12:1 [2]*inheritance*

4 To Him [d]who alone does great
wonders,
For His mercy *endures* forever;
5 [e]To Him who by wisdom made the
heavens,
For His mercy *endures* forever;
6 [f]To Him who laid out the earth above
the waters,
For His mercy *endures* forever;
7 [g]To Him who made great lights,
For His mercy *endures* forever—
8 [h]The sun to rule by day,
For His mercy *endures* forever;
9 The moon and stars to rule by night,
For His mercy *endures* forever.

10 [i]To Him who struck Egypt in their
firstborn,
For His mercy *endures* forever;
11 [j]And brought out Israel from among
them,
For His mercy *endures* forever;
12 [k]With a strong hand, and with [1]an
outstretched arm,
For His mercy *endures* forever;
13 [l]To Him who divided the Red Sea in
two,
For His mercy *endures* forever;
14 And made Israel pass through the
midst of it,
For His mercy *endures* forever;
15 [m]But overthrew Pharaoh and his army
in the Red Sea,
For His mercy *endures* forever;
16 [n]To Him who led His people through
the wilderness,
For His mercy *endures* forever;
17 [o]To Him who struck down great kings,
For His mercy *endures* forever;
18 [p]And slew famous kings,
For His mercy *endures* forever—
19 [q]Sihon king of the Amorites,
For His mercy *endures* forever;
20 [r]And Og king of Bashan,
For His mercy *endures* forever—
21 [s]And gave their land as a [2]heritage,

135:11 Sihon. Cf. Num. 21:21,32, which recounts Israel's defeat of Sihon, king of the Amorites. **Og.** Cf. Num. 21:33-35, which recounts Israel's defeat of Og, king of Bashan. **kingdoms of Canaan.** Joshua 6–12 recounts Joshua's conquest of the Land.

135:12 gave their land…to Israel. As promised to Abraham (cf. Gen. 15:18-21).

135:13-18 The living God of Israel (vv. 13-14) stands decidedly superior to the imaginary gods of the nations (vv. 15-18).

135:18 make them…like them. Both are worthless and will know nothing of eternal life.

135:19-20 The categories 1) Israel, 2) Aaron, 3) Levi, and 4) you who fear the Lord, refer to the nation as a whole (Israel), the priesthood (Aaron and Levi), and the true believers (who fear the Lord).

136:1-26 This psalm, extremely similar to Ps. 135, closes the Great Hallel. Unique to all the psalms, Ps. 136 uses the antiphonal refrain "For His mercy *endures* forever" after each stanza, perhaps spoken by the people in responsive worship. The author and occasion remain unknown.

I. Call to Praise (136:1-3)
II. Causes for Praise (136:4-22)
  A. God's Creation (136:4-9)
  B. God's Deliverance (136:10-15)
  C. God's Care and Gift (136:16-22)
III. Concluding Praise (136:23-26)

136:1 *He is* good. *See note on Ps. 135:3.*

136:4-9 Cf. Gen. 1.

136:10-15 Cf. Ex. 11–14.

136:16-22 Cf. Num. 14–36.

136:19 Sihon. *See note on Ps. 135:11.*

136:20 Og. *See note on Ps. 135:11.*

For His mercy *endures* forever;
22 A heritage to Israel His servant,
For His mercy *endures* forever.

23 Who [t]remembered us in our lowly state,
For His mercy *endures* forever;
24 And [u]rescued us from our enemies,
For His mercy *endures* forever;
25 [v]Who gives food to all flesh,
For His mercy *endures* forever.

26 Oh, give thanks to the God of heaven!
For His mercy *endures* forever.

PSALM 137

Longing for Zion in a Foreign Land

By the rivers of Babylon,
There we sat down, yea, we wept
When we remembered Zion.
2 We hung our harps
Upon the willows in the midst of it.
3 For there those who carried us away captive asked of us a song,
And those who [a]plundered us *requested* mirth,
Saying, "Sing us *one* of the songs of Zion!"

4 How shall we sing the LORD's song
In a foreign land?
5 If I forget you, O Jerusalem,
Let my right hand forget *its skill!*
6 If I do not remember you,
Let my [b]tongue cling to the roof of my mouth—
If I do not exalt Jerusalem
Above my chief joy.

7 Remember, O LORD, against [c]the sons of Edom
The day of Jerusalem,
Who said, [1]"Raze *it,* raze *it,*
To its very foundation!"

8 O daughter of Babylon, [d]who are to be destroyed,
Happy the one [e]who repays you as you have served us!
9 Happy the one who takes and [f]dashes
Your little ones against the rock!

PSALM 138

The LORD's Goodness to the Faithful

A Psalm of David.

I will praise You with my whole heart;
[a]Before the gods I will sing praises to You.
2 [b]I will worship [c]toward Your holy temple,
And praise Your name
For Your lovingkindness and Your truth;
For You have [d]magnified Your word above all Your name.
3 In the day when I cried out, You answered me,

23 [t]Gen. 8:1; Deut. 32:36; Ps. 113:7
24 [u]Ps. 44:7
25 [v]Ps. 104:27; 145:15

PSALM 137

3 [a]Ps. 79:1
6 [b]Job 29:10; Ps. 22:15; Ezek. 3:26
7 [c]Jer. 49:7-22; Lam. 4:21; Ezek. 25:12-14; 35:2; Amos 1:11; Obad. 10-14 [1]Lit. *Make bare*
8 [d]Is. 13:1-6; 47:1 [e]Jer. 50:15; Rev. 18:6
9 [f]2 Kin. 8:12; Is. 13:16; Hos. 13:16; Nah. 3:10

PSALM 138

1 [a]Ps. 119:46
2 [b]Ps. 28:2 [c]1 Kin. 8:29 [d]Is. 42:21

136:23 lowly state. Cf. Deut. 7:7; 9:4,5; Ezek. 16:1-5.

137:1-9 A psalm, explicitly about the Babylonian captivity of Judah. Its author and date are unknown.

I. Lamentations (137:1-4)
II. Conditions (137:5,6)
III. Imprecations (137:7-9)

137:1 the rivers of Babylon. The Tigris and Euphrates Rivers. **we wept.** They even wept when the exile was over and the second temple was being built (cf. Ezra 3:12), so deep was their sorrow. **Zion.** The dwelling place of God on earth (Pss. 9:11; 76:2) which was destroyed by the Babylonians (2 Chr. 36:19; Pss. 74:6-8; 79:1; Is. 64:10, 11; Jer. 52:12-16; Lam. 2:4,6-9; Mic. 3:12).

137:2 hung our harps. In captivity, there was no use for an instrument of joy (cf. Is. 24:8).

137:3 those who carried us away. The Babylonians taunted the Jews to sing of their once beautiful, but now destroyed, Zion. **the songs of Zion.** Cf. Pss. 46,48,76,84,87,122.

137:4 How shall we sing. A rhetorical question whose answer is, "We can't!" **the LORD's song.** A unique way to refer to divine inspiration of the psalms.

137:5,6 Their refusal to sing was not caused by either of 2 unthinkable situations: 1) they forgot Jerusalem; 2) they did not have Jerusalem as their chief joy. The worst of punishments should be imposed if any one or a combination of these factors were to become true.

137:7 the sons of Edom. Edomites had been allied with the Babylonians in the fall and destruction of Jerusalem (cf. Is. 21:11,12; Jer. 49:7-12; Lam. 4:21; Ezek. 25:12-14; 35:1-15; Obad. 11-14). The psalmist only prayed for that which the Lord had always promised. **The day of Jerusalem.** The day Jerusalem was destroyed. *See notes on Ps. 137:1.*

137:8 destroyed. Cf. Is. 13:1–14:23,46,47; Jer. 50–51; Hab. 1:11; 2:6-17.

137:8,9 Happy the one. For these will be God's human instruments used to carry out His prophesied will for the destruction of Babylon.

138:1-8 The next 8 psalms were written by David (Pss. 138–145) and are his last in the Psalter. The occasion is unknown, although it's possible that David wrote them in response to the Davidic Covenant (cf. 2 Sam. 7:12-14,16).

I. Individual Praise (138:1-3)
II. International Praise (138:4,5)
III. Invincible Praise (138:6-8)

138:1 the gods. This can refer to either pagan royalty (cf. Ps. 82:1) and/or to the idols they worship.

138:2 holy temple. Refers to the tabernacle since Solomon's temple has not yet been built. **Your word above...Your name.** Most likely this means that God's latest revelation ("Your word") exceeded all previous revelation about God. This would be in concert with David's prayer (2 Sam. 7:18-29) after he received the Davidic promise (2 Sam. 7:12-14,16).

And made me bold *with* strength in
my soul.

4 [e] All the kings of the earth shall praise
You, O LORD,
When they hear the words of Your
mouth.
5 Yes, they shall sing of the ways of the
LORD,
For great *is* the glory of the LORD.
6 [f] Though the LORD *is* on high,
Yet [g] He regards the lowly;
But the proud He knows from afar.

7 [h] Though I walk in the midst of trouble,
You will revive me;
You will stretch out Your hand
Against the wrath of my enemies,
And Your right hand will save me.
8 [i] The LORD will [1] perfect *that which*
concerns me;
Your mercy, O LORD, *endures* forever;
[j] Do not forsake the works of Your
hands.

4 [e] Ps. 102:15
6 [f] [Ps. 113:4-7] [g] Prov. 3:34; [Is. 57:15]; Luke 1:48; [James 4:6; 1 Pet. 5:5]
7 [h] [Ps. 23:3, 4]
8 [i] Ps. 57:2; [Phil. 1:6] [j] Job 10:3, 8 [1] *complete*

PSALM 139
1 [a] Ps. 17:3; Jer. 12:3
2 [b] 2 Kin. 19:27 [c] Is. 66:18; Matt. 9:4
3 [d] Job 14:16; 31:4 [1] Lit. *winnow*
4 [e] [Heb. 4:13]

PSALM 139
God's Perfect Knowledge of Man

For the Chief Musician. A Psalm of David.

O LORD, [a] You have searched me and
known *me.*
2 [b] You know my sitting down and my
rising up;
You [c] understand my thought afar off.
3 [d] You [1] comprehend my path and my
lying down,
And are acquainted with all my ways.
4 For *there is* not a word on my tongue,
But behold, O LORD, [e] You know it
altogether.
5 You have [2] hedged me behind and
before,
And laid Your hand upon me.
6 [f] *Such* knowledge *is* too wonderful for
me;
It is high, I cannot *attain* it.

7 [g] Where can I go from Your Spirit?
Or where can I flee from Your
presence?
8 [h] If I ascend into heaven, You *are* there;
[i] If I make my bed in [3] hell, behold, You
are there.
9 *If* I take the wings of the morning,
And dwell in the uttermost parts of
the sea,
10 Even there Your hand shall lead me,
And Your right hand shall hold me.
11 If I say, "Surely the darkness shall
[4] fall on me,"
Even the night shall be light about
me;
12 Indeed, [j] the darkness [5] shall not hide
from You,
But the night shines as the day;
The darkness and the light *are* both
alike *to You.*

13 For You formed my inward parts;
You [6] covered me in my mother's
womb.
14 I will praise You, for [7] I am fearfully
and wonderfully made;
Marvelous are Your works,
And *that* my soul knows very well.
15 [k] My [8] frame was not hidden from You,
When I was made in secret,
And skillfully wrought in the lowest
parts of the earth.
16 Your eyes saw my substance, being
yet unformed.

5 [2] *enclosed*
6 [f] Job 42:3; Ps. 40:5
7 [g] [Jer. 23:24; Amos 9:2-4]
8 [h] [Amos 9:2-4] [i] [Job 26:6; Prov. 15:11] [3] Or *Sheol*
11 [4] Vg., Symmachus *cover*
12 [j] Job 26:6; 34:22; [Dan. 2:22; Heb. 4:13] [5] Lit. *is not dark*
13 [6] *wove*
14 [7] So with MT, Tg.; LXX, Syr., Vg. *You are fearfully wonderful*
15 [k] Job 10:8, 9; Eccl. 11:5 [8] Lit. *bones were*

138:4 All the kings. In contrast to Ps. 2:1-3, cf. Pss. 68:32; 72:11,12; 96:1,3,7,8; 97:1; 98:4; 100:1; 102:15; 148:11.

138:6,7 David sees himself as "the lowly" and his enemies as "the proud."

138:8 perfect. Refers to God's work in David's life, especially the Davidic Covenant (cf. 2 Sam. 7:12-14,16).

139:1-24 This intensely personal Davidic psalm expresses the psalmist's awe that God knew him, even to the minutest detail. David might have remembered the Lord's words, "…the LORD looks at the heart" (1 Sam. 16:7). The exact occasion is unknown.

I. God's Omniscience (139:1-6)
II. God's Omnipresence (139:7-12)
III. God's Omnipotence (139:13-18)
IV. David's Obeisance (139:19-24)

139:1-6 God knows everything about David.

139:1 searched me. As it has been in David's life, he prays later that it will continue to be (cf. vv. 23,24). David understands that nothing inside of him can be hidden from God.

139:5 hedged me. God used circumstances to limit David's actions.

139:6 too wonderful. Cf. Ps. 131:1; Rom. 11:33-36.

139:7-12 God was always watching over David and thus it was impossible to do anything over which God is not a spectator.

139:7 Your Spirit. A reference to the Holy Spirit (cf. Pss. 51:11; 143:10). See "The Anointing of the Holy Spirit in the OT" at Ps. 51.

139:9 the wings of the morning. In conjunction with "the uttermost parts of the sea," David uses this literary figure to express distance.

139:13-18 God's power is magnified in the development of human life before birth.

139:13 formed…covered. By virtue of the divinely designed period of pregnancy, God providentially watches over the development of the child while yet in the mother's womb.

139:15 secret…lowest parts. Used figuratively of the womb.

139:16 Your book. This figure of speech likens God's mind to a book of remembrance. **none of them.** God sovereignly ordained David's life before he was conceived.

And in Your book they all were
written,
The days fashioned for me,
When *as yet there were* none of them.

17 [l]How precious also are Your thoughts
to me, O God!
How great is the sum of them!
18 *If* I should count them, they would be
more in number than the sand;
When I awake, I am still with You.

19 Oh, that You would [m]slay the wicked,
O God!
[n]Depart from me, therefore, you
[9]bloodthirsty men.
20 For they [o]speak against You wickedly;
[1]Your enemies take *Your name* in vain.
21 [p]Do I not hate them, O LORD, who hate
You?
And do I not loathe those who rise up
against You?
22 I hate them with [2]perfect hatred;
I count them my enemies.

23 [q]Search me, O God, and know my
heart;
Try me, and know my anxieties;
24 And see if *there is any* wicked way in
me,
And [r]lead me in the way everlasting.

PSALM 140

Prayer for Deliverance from Evil Men

To the Chief Musician. A Psalm of David.

Deliver me, O LORD, from evil men;
Preserve me from violent men,
2 Who plan evil things in *their* hearts;
[a]They continually gather together *for*
war.
3 They sharpen their tongues like a
serpent;
The [b]poison of asps *is* under their
lips. Selah

4 [c]Keep me, O LORD, from the hands of
the wicked;
Preserve me from violent men,
Who have purposed to make my
steps stumble.
5 The proud have hidden a [d]snare for
me, and cords;
They have spread a net by the
wayside;
They have set traps for me. Selah

6 I said to the LORD: "You *are* my God;
Hear the voice of my supplications,
O LORD.
7 O GOD the Lord, the strength of my
salvation,
You have [1]covered my head in the
day of battle.
8 Do not grant, O LORD, the desires of
the wicked;
Do not further his *wicked* scheme,
[e]*Lest* they be exalted. Selah

9 "*As for* the head of those who surround
me,
Let the evil of their lips cover them;
10 [f]Let burning coals fall upon them;
Let them be cast into the fire,
Into deep pits, that they rise not up
again.
11 Let not a slanderer be established in
the earth;
Let evil hunt the violent man to
overthrow *him*."

12 I know that the LORD will [g]maintain
The cause of the afflicted,
And justice for the poor.
13 Surely the righteous shall give thanks
to Your name;

17 [l][Ps. 40:5; Rom. 11:33]
19 [m][Is. 11:4] [n]Ps. 119:115 [9]Lit. *men of bloodshed*
20 [o]Jude 15 [1]LXX, Vg. *They take your cities in vain*
21 [p]2 Chr. 19:2
22 [2]*complete*
23 [q]Job 31:6; Ps. 26:2
24 [r]Ps. 5:8; 143:10

PSALM 140
2 [a]Ps. 56:6
3 [b]Ps. 58:4; Rom. 3:13; James 3:8
4 [c]Ps. 71:4
5 [d]Ps. 35:7; Jer. 18:22
7 [1]*sheltered*
8 [e]Deut. 32:27
10 [f]Ps. 11:6
12 [g]1 Kin. 8:45; Ps. 9:4

139:17,18 David expresses his amazement at the infinite mind of God compared to the limited mind of man, especially as it relates to the physiology of human life (cf. vv. 13-16).

139:22 perfect hatred. David has no other response to God's enemies than that of hatred, i.e., he is not neutral towards them nor will he ever ally himself with them.

139:23,24 In light of vv. 19-22, David invites God to continue searching his heart to root out any unrighteousness, even when it is expressed against God's enemies.

139:24 the way everlasting. David expresses his desire/expectation of eternal life (*see note in Phil. 1:6*).

140:1-13 Davidic authorship is stated here, but the circumstances are unknown. It is like the psalms earlier in the Psalter that feature the usual complaint, prayer, and confident hope of relief.

I. Concerning David (140:1-5)
  A. "Deliver Me" (140:1-3)
  B. "Protect Me" (140:4,5)
II. Concerning David's Enemies (140:6-11)
  A. "Thwart Them" (140:6-8)
  B. "Punish Them" (140:9-11)
III. Concerning the Lord (140:12,13)

140:1-3 The emphasis here is deliverance from evil plans.

140:3 asps. A type of snake (cf. Rom. 3:13), signifying cunning and venom.

140:4,5 The emphasis here is protection from being captured.

140:6-8 The emphasis here is upon God's thwarting the plans of David's enemy.

140:7 covered my head. God has figuratively been David's helmet in battle.

140:9-11 The emphasis here is upon God's turning their evil plans back on them in judgment.

140:12,13 David expresses unshakeable confidence in the character of God and the outcome for the righteous (cf. Pss. 10:17,18; 74:21; 82:3,4).

The upright shall dwell in Your
presence.

PSALM 141

Prayer for Safekeeping from Wickedness

A Psalm of David.

LORD, I cry out to You;
Make haste to me!
Give ear to my voice when I cry out
to You.
2 Let my prayer be set before You [a]*as*
incense,
[b]The lifting up of my hands *as* [c]the
evening sacrifice.

3 Set a guard, O LORD, over my [d]mouth;
Keep watch over the door of my lips.
4 Do not incline my heart to any evil
thing,
To practice wicked works
With men who work iniquity;
[e]And do not let me eat of their
delicacies.

5 [f]Let the righteous strike me;
It shall be a kindness.
And let him rebuke me;
It shall be as excellent oil;
Let my head not refuse it.

For still my prayer *is* against the
deeds of the wicked.
6 Their judges are overthrown by the
sides of the [1]cliff,
And they hear my words, for they are
sweet.
7 Our bones are scattered at the mouth
of the grave,
As when one plows and breaks up
the earth.

8 But [g]my eyes *are* upon You, O GOD
the Lord;
In You I take refuge;
[2]Do not leave my soul destitute.
9 Keep me from [h]the snares they have
laid for me,
And from the traps of the workers of
iniquity.
10 [i]Let the wicked fall into their own
nets,
While I escape safely.

PSALM 142

A Plea for Relief from Persecutors

A [a]Contemplation[1] of David. A Prayer [b]when
he was in the cave.

I cry out to the LORD with my voice;
With my voice to the LORD I make my
supplication.
2 I pour out my complaint before Him;
I declare before Him my trouble.

3 When my spirit [2]was [c]overwhelmed
within me,
Then You knew my path.
In the way in which I walk
They have secretly [d]set a snare for
me.
4 Look on *my* right hand and see,
For *there is* no one who acknowledges
me;
Refuge has failed me;
No one cares for my soul.

5 I cried out to You, O LORD:
I said, "You *are* my refuge,
My portion in the land of the living.
6 [3]Attend to my cry,
For I am brought very low;
Deliver me from my persecutors,
For they are stronger than I.

PSALM 141
2 [a] [Ex. 30:8]; Luke 1:10; [Rev. 5:8; 8:3, 4] [b] Ps. 134:2; [1 Tim. 2:8] [c] Ex. 29:39, 41; 1 Kin. 18:29, 36; Dan. 9:21
3 [d] [Prov. 13:3; 21:23]
4 [e] Prov. 23:6
5 [f] [Prov. 9:8; Eccl. 7:5; Gal. 6:1]
6 [1] *rock*
8 [g] 2 Chr. 20:12; Ps. 25:15 [2] Lit. *Do not make my soul bare*
9 [h] Ps. 119:110
10 [i] Ps. 35:8

PSALM 142
title [a] Ps. 32:title [b] 1 Sam. 22:1; Ps. 57:title [1] Heb. *Maschil*
3 [c] Ps. 77:3 [d] Ps. 141:9 [2] Lit. *fainted*
6 [3] *Give heed*

141:1-10 Another psalm of lament by David whose occasion is unknown. This psalm is comprised of 4 prayers that have been combined into one.

I. Prayer for God's Haste (141:1,2)
II. Prayer for Personal Righteousness (141:3-5)
III. Prayer for Justice (141:6,7)
IV. Prayer for Deliverance (141:8-10)

141:2 incense...evening sacrifice. David desired that his prayers and stretching forth for God's help (Pss. 68:31; 77:2) be as disciplined and regular as the offering of incense (Ex. 30:7,8) and burnt offerings (Ex. 29:38,39) in the tabernacle.

141:3,4 David prayed that God would protect him from the kind of evil that characterized his own enemy.

141:5 David acknowledged that God would use other righteous men to answer his prayer in vv. 3,4 (cf. Prov. 9:8; 19:25; 27:6; 27:17).

141:6 judges...overthrown. That the leaders of the wicked would be punished by being thrown over a cliff (cf. Luke 4:28,29) is at the heart of David's prayer (cf. v. 5). **my words...sweet.** In the sense that David's words were true.

141:7 Our bones. The basis on which the judges were thrown over the cliff—they had first done this to the righteous (cf. 142:10).

141:10 fall into their own nets. David prays that the wicked will be destroyed by their own devices.

142:1-7 Under the same circumstances as Ps. 57 (according to the superscription), David recounted his desperate days hiding in the cave of Adullam (1 Sam. 22:1) while Saul sought him to take his life (1 Sam. 18–24). It appears that David's situation, for the moment at least, seems hopeless without God's intervention. Psalm 91 provides the truths that bring the solution.

I. Cry of David (142:1,2)
II. Circumstances of David (142:3,4)
III. Confidence of David (142:5-7)

142:4 no one. It appears to David that he has been totally abandoned.

142:5 You *are* my refuge. A frequent claim in the psalms (cf. Pss. 7:1; 11:1; 16:1; 18:2; 25:20; 31:1; 46:1; 57:1; 61:3; 62:7; 91:2; 94:22; 141:8; 143:9; 144:2).

7 Bring my soul out of prison,
That I may [e]praise Your name;
The righteous shall surround me,
For You shall deal bountifully with
me."

PSALM 143

An Earnest Appeal for Guidance and Deliverance

A Psalm of David.

Hear my prayer, O LORD,
Give ear to my supplications!
In Your faithfulness answer me,
And in Your righteousness.
2 Do not enter into judgment with Your
servant,
[a]For in Your sight no one living is
righteous.

3 For the enemy has persecuted my
soul;
He has crushed my life to the ground;
He has made me dwell in [1]darkness,
Like those who have long been dead.
4 [b]Therefore my spirit is overwhelmed
within me;
My heart within me is distressed.

5 [c]I remember the days of old;
I meditate on all Your works;
I [2]muse on the work of Your hands.
6 I spread out my hands to You;
[d]My soul *longs* for You like a thirsty
land. Selah

7 Answer me speedily, O LORD;
My spirit fails!
Do not hide Your face from me,
[e]Lest I [3]be like those who [4]go down
into the pit.
8 Cause me to hear Your
lovingkindness [f]in the
morning,
For in You do I trust;
[g]Cause me to know the way in which I
should walk,
For [h]I lift up my soul to You.

9 Deliver me, O LORD, from my
enemies;
[5]In You I take shelter.
10 [i]Teach me to do Your will,
For You *are* my God;
[j]Your Spirit *is* good.
Lead me in [k]the land of uprightness.

11 [l]Revive me, O LORD, for Your name's
sake!
For Your righteousness' sake bring
my soul out of trouble.
12 In Your mercy [m]cut[6] off my enemies,
And destroy all those who afflict my
soul;
For I *am* Your servant.

PSALM 144

A Song to the LORD Who Preserves and Prospers His People

A Psalm of David.

Blessed *be* the LORD my Rock,
[a]Who trains my hands for war,
And my fingers for battle—
2 My lovingkindness and my fortress,
My high tower and my deliverer,
My shield and *the One* in whom I take
refuge,
Who subdues [1]my people under me.

3 [b]LORD, what *is* man, that You take
knowledge of him?

7 [e] Ps. 34:1, 2

PSALM 143

2 [a] [Ex. 34:7]; Job 4:17; 9:2; 25:4; Ps. 130:3; Eccl. 7:20; [Rom. 3:20-23; Gal. 2:16]
3 [1] *dark places*
4 [b] Ps. 77:3
5 [c] Ps. 77:5, 10, 11 [2] *ponder*
6 [d] Ps. 63:1
7 [e] Ps. 28:1 [3] *become* [4] Die
8 [f] Ps. 46:5 [g] Ps. 5:8 [h] Ps. 25:1
9 [5] LXX, Vg. *To You I flee*
10 [i] Ps. 25:4, 5 [j] Neh. 9:20 [k] Is. 26:10
11 [l] Ps. 119:25
12 [m] Ps. 54:5 [6] *put an end to*

PSALM 144

1 [a] 2 Sam. 22:35; Ps. 18:34
2 [1] So with MT, LXX, Vg.; Syr., Tg. *the peoples* (cf. 18:47)
3 [b] Job 7:17; Ps. 8:4; Heb. 2:6

142:7 prison. The cave in which David was hidden.

143:1-12 No specific background is known for this Davidic psalm which is the final penitential psalm (cf. Pss. 6,32,38,51,102,130).

I. David's Passion (143:1,2)
II. David's Predicament (143:3-6)
II. David's Plea (143:7-12)

143:1 faithfulness...righteousness. David fervently appeals to God's character.

143:2 no one living is righteous. David admits his own unrighteousness and realizes that if he is to be delivered for righteousness sake, (cf. 143:11) it will be because of God's righteousness, not his own.

143:6 a thirsty land. As a drought-struck land yearns for life-giving water, so persecuted David longs for his life-giving Deliverer.

143:7 Your face. An anthropomorphism picturing God's attention to the psalmist's plight.

143:10 Your Spirit. Refers to the Holy Spirit (cf. Pss. 51:11; 139:7). *See note on Ps. 51:11.*

143:11 Your name's sake. David appeals to God's benefit and honor, not his own (cf. Pss. 23:3; 31:3; 79:9).

143:12 Your servant. To attack God's servant is to attack God, thus bringing God to the rescue.

144:1-15 This Davidic psalm, in part (144:1-8), is very similar to Ps. 18:1-15. It could be that this psalm was written under the same kind of circumstances as the former, i.e., on the day that the Lord delivered him from the hand of all his enemies and from the hand of Saul (cf. 2 Sam. 22:1-18).

I. God's Greatness (144:1,2)
II. Man's Insignificance (144:3,4)
III. God's Power (144:5-8)
IV. Man's Praise (144:9,10)
V. God's Blessing (144:11-15)

144:1 my Rock. David's foundation is God—solid and unshakeable (cf. Pss. 19:14; 31:3; 42:9; 62:2; 71:3; 89:26; 92:15; 95:1). **trains my hands for war.** David lived in the days of Israel's theocracy, not the NT church. God empowered the king to subdue His enemies.

144:2 God provided 6 benefits: 1) lovingkindness, 2) a fortress, 3) a high tower, 4) a deliverer, 5) a shield, and 6) a refuge.

144:3,4 Eternal God is contrasted with short-lived man (cf. Ps. 8:4).

Or the son of man, that You are
mindful of him?
4 [c]Man is like a breath;
[d]His days *are* like a passing shadow.
5 [e]Bow down Your heavens, O LORD,
and come down;
[f]Touch the mountains, and they shall
smoke.
6 [g]Flash forth lightning and scatter
them;
Shoot out Your arrows and destroy
them.
7 Stretch out Your hand from above;
Rescue me and deliver me out of
great waters,
From the hand of foreigners,
8 Whose mouth [h]speaks [2]lying words,
And whose right hand *is* a right hand
of falsehood.

9 I will [i]sing a new song to You, O God;
On a harp of ten strings I will sing
praises to You,
10 *The One* who gives [3]salvation to
kings,
[j]Who delivers David His servant
From the deadly sword.

11 Rescue me and deliver me from the
hand of foreigners,
Whose mouth speaks lying words,
And whose right hand *is* a right hand
of falsehood—
12 That our sons *may be* [k]as plants grown
up in their youth;
That our daughters *may be* as [4]pillars,
Sculptured in palace style;
13 *That* our barns *may be* full,
Supplying all kinds of produce;
That our sheep may bring forth
thousands
And ten thousands in our fields;
14 *That* our oxen *may be* well laden;
That there be no [5]breaking in or going
out;
That there be no outcry in our streets.
15 [l]Happy *are* the people who are in such
a state;
Happy *are* the people whose God *is*
the LORD!

PSALM 145

A Song of God's Majesty and Love

[a]A Praise of David.

I will [1]extol You, my God, O King;
And I will bless Your name forever
and ever.
2 Every day I will bless You,
And I will praise Your name forever
and ever.
3 [b]Great *is* the LORD, and greatly to be
praised;
And [c]His greatness *is* [2]unsearchable.

4 [d]One generation shall praise Your
works to another,
And shall declare Your mighty acts.
5 [3]I will meditate on the glorious
splendor of Your majesty,
And [4]on Your wondrous works.
6 *Men* shall speak of the might of Your
awesome acts,
And I will declare Your greatness.
7 They shall [5]utter the memory of Your
great goodness,
And shall sing of Your righteousness.
8 [e]The LORD *is* gracious and full of
compassion,
Slow to anger and great in mercy.
9 [f]The LORD *is* good to all,
And His tender mercies *are* over all
His works.

10 [g]All Your works shall praise You,
O LORD,
And Your saints shall bless You.
11 They shall speak of the glory of Your
kingdom,

4 [c]Ps. 39:11 [d]Job 8:9; 14:2; Ps. 102:11 **5** [e]Ps. 18:9; Is. 64:1 [f]Ps. 104:32 **6** [g]Ps. 18:13, 14 **8** [h]Ps. 12:2 [2]*empty or worthless* **9** [i]Ps. 33:2, 3; 40:3 **10** [j]Ps. 18:50 [3]*deliverance* **12** [k]Ps. 128:3 [4]*corner pillars* **14** [5]Lit. *breach* **15** [l]Deut. 33:29; [Ps. 33:12; Jer. 17:7]

PSALM 145

title [a]Ps. 100:title **1** [1]*praise* **3** [b][Ps. 147:5] [c]Job 5:9; 9:10; 11:7; Is. 40:28; [Rom. 11:33] [2]Beyond our understanding **4** [d]Is. 38:19 **5** [3]So with MT, Tg.; DSS, LXX, Syr., Vg. *They* [4]Lit. *on the words of Your wondrous works* **7** [5]*eagerly utter*, lit. *bubble forth* **8** [e][Ex. 34:6, 7; Num. 14:18]; Ps. 86:5, 15 **9** [f][Ps. 100:5]; Jer. 33:11; Nah. 1:7; [Matt. 19:17; Mark 10:18] **10** [g]Ps. 19:1

144:5-8 Highly figurative language is used to portray God as the heavenly warrior who comes to fight on earth on behalf of David against God's enemies.

144:9 a new song. A song of victory that celebrates deliverance/salvation (cf. Pss. 33:3; 40:3; 96:1; 98:1; 144:9; 149:1; Rev. 5:9; 14:3).

144:11 Cf. vv. 7,8.

144:12 sons...daughters. God's rescue of David's kingdom from foreigners would bring blessing on families.

144:13,14 barns...sheep...oxen. Blessing would also come to the agricultural efforts.

144:14 no breaking in...going out...outcry. Peace, not strife, would characterize the land.

145:1-21 David penned this most exquisite conclusion to his 75 psalms in the Psalter. Here, the king of Israel extols and celebrates the King of Eternity for who He is, what He has done, and what He has promised. Not only rich in content, this psalm also duplicates a majestic acrostic design using the 22 letters of the Heb. alphabet. Psalm 145 begins the great crescendo of praise that completes the psalter and might be called "The Final Hallel" (Pss. 145–150).

I. Commitment to Praise (145:1,2)
II. God's Awesome Greatness (145:3-7)
III. God's Great Grace (145:8-13)
IV. God's Unfailing Faithfulness (145:14-16)
V. God's Unblemished Righteousness (145:17-20)
VI. Recommitment/Exhortation to Praise (145:21)

145:1 my God, O King. David, king of Israel, recognized God as his sovereign (cf. Pss. 5:2; 84:3).

145:11-13 kingdom. David refers here to the broadest use of kingdom in Scripture—i.e., God the eternal king ruling over all from before creation and eternally thereafter (cf. Ps. 10:16; Dan. 4:3; 7:27).

And talk of Your power,
12 To make known to the sons of men
His mighty acts,
And the glorious majesty of His
kingdom.
13 [h]Your kingdom *is* an everlasting
kingdom,
And Your dominion *endures*
throughout all [6]generations.

14 The LORD upholds all who fall,
And [i]raises up all *who are* bowed
down.
15 [j]The eyes of all look expectantly to
You,
And [k]You give them their food in due
season.
16 You open Your hand
[l]And satisfy the desire of every living
thing.

17 The LORD *is* righteous in all His ways,
Gracious in all His works.
18 [m]The LORD *is* near to all who call upon
Him,
To all who call upon Him [n]in truth.
19 He will fulfill the desire of those who
fear Him;
He also will hear their cry and save
them.
20 [o]The LORD preserves all who love Him,
But all the wicked He will destroy.
21 My mouth shall speak the praise of
the LORD,
And all flesh shall bless His holy name
Forever and ever.

PSALM 146

The Happiness of Those Whose Help Is the LORD

Praise[1] the LORD!

[a]Praise the LORD, O my soul!
2 [b]While I live I will praise the LORD;
I will sing praises to my God while I
have my being.

3 [c]Do not put your trust in princes,
Nor in [2]a son of man, in whom *there is*
no [3]help.
4 [d]His spirit departs, he returns to his
earth;
In that very day [e]his plans perish.

5 [f]Happy *is he* who *has* the God of Jacob
for his help,
Whose hope *is* in the LORD his God,
6 [g]Who made heaven and earth,
The sea, and all that *is* in them;
Who keeps truth forever,
7 [h]Who executes justice for the
oppressed,
[i]Who gives food to the hungry.
[j]The LORD gives freedom to the
prisoners.

8 [k]The LORD opens *the eyes of* the blind;
[l]The LORD raises those who are bowed
down;
The LORD loves the righteous.
9 [m]The LORD watches over the strangers;
He relieves the fatherless and widow;
[n]But the way of the wicked He [4]turns
upside down.

10 [o]The LORD shall reign forever—
Your God, O Zion, to all generations.

Praise the LORD!

PSALM 147

Praise to God for His Word and Providence

Praise[1] the LORD!
For [a]*it is* good to sing praises to our
God;
[b]For *it is* pleasant, *and* [c]praise is
beautiful.

13 [h] Dan. 2:44; 4:3; [1 Tim. 1:17; 2 Pet. 1:11] [6] So with MT, Tg.; DSS, LXX, Syr., Vg. add *The LORD is faithful in all His words, And holy in all His works*
14 [i] Ps. 146:8
15 [j] Ps. 104:27 [k] Ps. 136:25
16 [l] Ps. 104:21, 28
18 [m] [Deut. 4:7] [n] [John 4:24]
20 [o] [Ps. 31:23]

PSALM 146

1 [a] Ps. 103:1 [1] Heb. *Hallelujah*
2 [b] Ps. 104:33
3 [c] [Is. 2:22] [2] A human being [3] *salvation*
4 [d] [Eccl. 12:7] [e] [Ps. 33:10; 1 Cor. 2:6]
5 [f] Jer. 17:7
6 [g] Gen. 1:1; Ex. 20:11; Acts 4:24; Rev. 14:7
7 [h] Ps. 103:6 [i] Ps. 107:9 [j] Ps. 107:10; Is. 61:1
8 [k] Matt. 9:30; [John 9:7, 32, 33] [l] Luke 13:13
9 [m] Deut. 10:18; Ps. 68:5 [n] Ps. 147:6 [4] Lit. *makes crooked*
10 [o] Ex. 15:18; Ps. 10:16; [Rev. 11:15]

PSALM 147

1 [a] Ps. 92:1 [b] Ps. 135:3 [c] Ps. 33:1 [1] Heb. *Hallelujah*

145:14-16 The emphasis is on God's common grace to all of humanity (cf. Matt. 5:45; Luke 6:35; Acts 14:17; 17:25).

145:20 the wicked…destroy. The wicked await an eternity of living forever, away from the presence of God in the lake of fire (cf. 2 Thess. 1:9; Rev. 20:11-15).

146:1-10 From this psalm to the conclusion of the Psalter, each psalm begins and ends with "Praise the LORD" (Pss. 146–150). Neither the composer nor the occasions are known. Psalm 146 appears similar in content to Pss. 113,145.

I. Commitment to Praise (146:1,2)
II. Misplaced Trust (146:3,4)
III. Blessed Hope (146:5-10)

146:1 O my soul. Cf. the beginnings and ends of Pss. 103,104.

146:3,4 Do not put…trust. This could be 1) a general principle, 2) a reference to the people wanting a human king like the nations (1 Sam. 8:5), or 3) Judah's later dependence on foreign kings for protection (2 Kin. 16:7-9).

146:5 the God of Jacob. Also the God of Abraham and Isaac, thus the recipients of God's blessing through the Abrahamic Covenant (cf. Gen. 12:1-3; Ps. 144:15).

146:6 Man's trust is best placed in the Creator of heaven and earth and the Revealer of all truth.

146:7-9b God righteously and mercifully reaches out to those in need.

146:9c the way of the wicked. Cf. Pss. 1:4-6; 145:20.

146:10 shall reign forever. In contrast to man who perishes (cf. 146:4), the truths of 146:5-9 are not faddish or temporal but rather eternal (cf. Rev. 22:5).

147:1-20 *See note on Ps. 146:1-10.* This seems to be a post-Exilic psalm (cf. 147:2,3) which might have been used to celebrate the rebuilt walls of Jerusalem (cf. Ps. 147:2,13; Neh. 12:27,43). The hard questions that God posed to Job (Job 38–41) and Israel (Is. 40), the

2 The LORD [d]builds up Jerusalem;
[e]He gathers together the outcasts of Israel.
3 [f]He heals the brokenhearted
And binds up their [2]wounds.
4 [g]He counts the number of the stars;
He calls them all by name.
5 [h]Great *is* our Lord, and [i]mighty in power;
[j]His understanding *is* infinite.
6 [k]The LORD lifts up the humble;
He casts the wicked down to the ground.

7 Sing to the LORD with thanksgiving;
Sing praises on the harp to our God,
8 [l]Who covers the heavens with clouds,
Who prepares rain for the earth,
Who makes grass to grow on the mountains.
9 [m]He gives to the beast its food,
And [n]to the young ravens that cry.
10 [o]He does not delight in the strength of the horse;
He takes no pleasure in the legs of a man.
11 The LORD takes pleasure in those who fear Him,
In those who hope in His mercy.

12 Praise the LORD, O Jerusalem!
Praise your God, O Zion!
13 For He has strengthened the bars of your gates;
He has blessed your children within you.
14 [p]He makes peace *in* your borders,
And [q]fills you with [3]the finest wheat.

15 [r]He sends out His command *to the* earth;
His word runs very swiftly.
16 [s]He gives snow like wool;
He scatters the frost like ashes;
17 He casts out His hail like [4]morsels;
Who can stand before His cold?
18 [t]He sends out His word and melts them;
He causes His wind to blow, *and* the waters flow.

19 [u]He declares His word to Jacob,
[v]His statutes and His judgments to Israel.
20 [w]He has not dealt thus with any nation;
And *as for His* judgments, they have not known them.

[5]Praise the LORD!

PSALM 148

Praise to the LORD from Creation

Praise[1] the LORD!

Praise the LORD from the heavens;
Praise Him in the heights!
2 Praise Him, all His angels;
Praise Him, all His hosts!
3 Praise Him, sun and moon;
Praise Him, all you stars of light!
4 Praise Him, [a]you heavens of heavens,
And [b]you waters above the heavens!

5 Let them praise the name of the LORD,
For [c]He commanded and they were created.
6 [d]He also established them forever and ever;

2 [d] Ps. 102:16 [e] Deut. 30:3; Is. 11:12; 56:8; Ezek. 39:28
3 [f] [Ps. 51:17]; Is. 61:1; Luke 4:18 [2] Lit. *sorrows*
4 [g] Is. 40:26
5 [h] Ps. 48:1 [i] Nah. 1:3 [j] Is. 40:28
6 [k] Ps. 146:8, 9
8 [l] Job 38:26; Ps. 104:13
9 [m] Job 38:41 [n] [Matt. 6:26]
10 [o] Ps. 33:16, 17
14 [p] Is. 54:13; 60:17, 18 [q] Ps. 132:15 [3] Lit. *fat of wheat*
15 [r] [Ps. 107:20]
16 [s] Job 37:6
17 [4] *fragments of food*
18 [t] Job 37:10
19 [u] Deut. 33:4; Ps. 103:7 [v] Mal. 4:4
20 [w] Deut. 4:32-34; [Rom. 3:1, 2] [5] Heb. *Hallelujah*

PSALM 148

1 [1] Heb. *Hallelujah*
4 [a] Deut. 10:14; 1 Kin. 8:27; [Neh. 9:6] [b] Gen. 1:7
5 [c] Gen. 1:1, 6
6 [d] Ps. 89:37; [Jer. 31:35, 36; 33:20, 25]

psalmist here turns into declarations worthy of praise. Verses 1,7,12 each introduce a stanza of praise in this 3-verse hymn. Verses 2,3,19,20 specifically speak of God's involvement with Israel.

I. Praise the Lord—Part 1 (147:1-6)
II. Praise the Lord—Part 2 (147:7-11)
III. Praise the Lord—Part 3 (147:12-20)

147:2 builds up Jerusalem. Ezra and Nehemiah chronicle this portion of Israel's history.

147:3 heals the brokenhearted. Cf. Ps. 137 (brokenhearted) with Ps. 126 (healed).

147:6 Each part of the psalm ends with a contrast—here the humble and the wicked (cf. 147:10,11,19,20).

147:13 He has strengthened. Refers to a means of defense, most likely in reference to the rebuilding of Jerusalem's walls in Nehemiah's time.

147:15-18 Describes the cold weather that Jerusalem can experience. God sovereignly oversees the normal and the extraordinary.

147:19,20 The psalmist acknowledges God's unique election of Israel from among all the nations (cf. Gen. 12:1-3; Ex. 19:5,6; Deut. 7:6-8; 14:2; 26:18,19; 2 Sam. 7:23,24; Ezek. 16:1-7).

148:1-14 *See note on Ps. 146:1-10.* The author and background for this psalm, which calls for all of God's creation to praise Him, is unknown. There is a connection between the creation praising God and His involvement with Israel.

I. Heaven's Praise (148:1-6)
   A. Who? (148:1-4)
   B. Why? (148:5,6)
II. Earth's Praise (148:7-14)
   A. Who? (148:7-12)
   B. Why? (148:13,14)

148:1-4 A representative sample of God's creation in the skies and heavens.

148:2 all His hosts. Another term for angels.

148:4 waters above the heavens. Cf. Gen. 1:7.

148:5,6 He emphatically ascribes creation to God alone.

148:6 Jeremiah 31:35-37; 33:20-22 might be in mind in the sense that the certain, fixed order of creation was a witness to God's unbreakable covenants with Abraham and David.

He made a decree which shall not
pass away.

7 Praise the LORD from the earth,
[e]You great sea creatures and all the
depths;
8 Fire and hail, snow and clouds;
Stormy wind, fulfilling His word;
9 [f]Mountains and all hills;
Fruitful trees and all cedars;
10 Beasts and all cattle;
Creeping things and flying fowl;
11 Kings of the earth and all peoples;
Princes and all judges of the earth;
12 Both young men and maidens;
Old men and children.

13 Let them praise the name of the LORD,
For His [g]name alone is exalted;
His glory *is* above the earth and
heaven.
14 And He [h]has exalted the [2]horn of His
people,
The praise of [i]all His saints—
Of the children of Israel,
[j]A people near to Him.

[3]Praise the LORD!

PSALM 149

Praise to God for His Salvation and Judgment

Praise[1] the LORD!

[a]Sing to the LORD a new song,
And His praise in the assembly of
saints.

2 Let Israel rejoice in their Maker;

7 [e] Is. 43:20
9 [f] Is. 44:23; 49:13
13 [g] Ps. 8:1
14 [h] 1 Sam. 2:1; Ps. 75:10 [i] Ps. 149:9 [j] Lev. 10:3; Eph. 2:17 [2] Strength or dominion [3] Heb. *Hallelujah*

PSALM 149

1 [a] Ps. 33:3 [1] Heb. *Hallelujah*

2 [b] Judg. 8:23; Zech. 9:9; Matt. 21:5
3 [c] Ex. 15:20; Ps. 81:2
4 [d] Ps. 35:27 [e] Ps. 132:16; Is. 61:3 [2] *meek*
5 [f] Job 35:10
6 [g] Heb. 4:12; Rev. 1:16
9 [h] Deut. 7:1,2; Ezek. 28:26 [i] Ps. 148:14; 1 Cor. 6:2 [3] Heb. *Hallelujah*

PSALM 150

1 [a] Ps. 145:5,6 [1] Heb. *Hallelujah* [2] *expanse of heaven*
2 [b] Deut. 3:24

Let the children of Zion be joyful in
their [b]King.
3 [c]Let them praise His name with the
dance;
Let them sing praises to Him with the
timbrel and harp.
4 For [d]the LORD takes pleasure in His
people;
[e]He will beautify the [2]humble with
salvation.

5 Let the saints be joyful in glory;
Let them [f]sing aloud on their beds.
6 *Let* the high praises of God *be* in their
mouth,
And [g]a two-edged sword in their
hand,
7 To execute vengeance on the nations,
And punishments on the peoples;
8 To bind their kings with chains,
And their nobles with fetters of iron;
9 [h]To execute on them the written
judgment—
[i]This honor have all His saints.

[3]Praise the LORD!

PSALM 150

Let All Things Praise the LORD

Praise[a 1] the LORD!

Praise God in His sanctuary;
Praise Him in His mighty
[2]firmament!

2 Praise Him for His mighty acts;
Praise Him according to His excellent
[b]greatness!

148:8 fulfilling His word. Another way of saying that God sovereignly oversees weather.

148:13,14 Two reasons are given for earth's praise: 1) His name alone is exalted in heaven (148:13) and 2) He has exalted Israel on earth (148:14).

148:14 the horn. Refers in general to the strength and prosperity of the nation, which became the cause of praise for Israel. This suggests that Israel enjoyed better times than in the past, e.g., during David's and Solomon's reigns or after returning from the Babylonian Captivity. **A people near to Him.** Cf. also "My chosen people" (Is. 43:20) and "His special treasure" (Ps. 135:4).

149:1-9 *See note on Ps. 146:1-10.* The composer and occasion for this psalm are unknown.

I. Israel's Praise of God (149:1-5)
II. Israel's Punishment of the Nations (149:6-9)

149:1 a new song. A song of testimony concerning salvation (cf. 149:4). **the assembly.** The gathering of the nation for worship.

149:3 the dance. Either individual or group, perhaps like David when he brought the Tabernacle to Jerusalem (2 Sam. 6:15-16). **the timbrel.** A tambourine-like instrument which accompanied dancing and singing (cf. Ex. 15:20; 1 Sam. 18:6). *See note on 2 Sam. 6:15,16.*

149:6-9 It would appear that this section is eschatological in nature and looks 1) to the Millennium when all nations and peoples will acknowledge Christ as king and 2) to Jerusalem as His royal capital (cf. Ezek. 28:25,26; Joel 3:9-17; Mic. 5:4-15).

149:9 the written judgment. Another way of saying "According to the Scriptures." as God has prophesied the subjection of the nations. **This honor.** The privilege of carrying out God's will.

150:1-6 *See note on Ps. 146:1-10.* This concluding psalm fitly caps the Psalter and the Final Hallel (Pss. 145-150) by raising and then answering some strategic questions about praise: 1) where? (150:1); 2) what for? (150:2); 3) with what? (150:3-5); and 4) who? (150:6). The author and occasion are unknown.

I. Place of Praise (150:1)
II. Points of Praise (150:2)
III. Proper Means of Praise (150:3-5)
IV. Practitioners of Praise (150:6)

150:1 sanctuary...mighty firmament. "Sanctuary" most likely refers to the temple in Jerusalem, so the sense would be "Praise God on earth and in heaven."

150:2 Praise should be for 1) what God has done and 2) who God is.

3 Praise Him with the sound of the [3]trumpet;
Praise Him with the lute and harp!
4 Praise Him with the timbrel and dance;
Praise Him with stringed instruments and flutes!
5 Praise Him with loud cymbals;
Praise Him with clashing cymbals!
6 Let everything that has breath praise the LORD.

[4]Praise the LORD!

3 [3] *cornet*
6 [4] Heb. *Hallelujah*

150:3 lute. A harp-like stringed instrument which was plucked with the finger rather than a plectrum (pick) like the harp.

150:4 timbrel and dance. *See note on Ps. 149:3.*

150:6 everything. All of God's living creation. This is the fitting conclusion to Book Five of the Psalms (Pss. 107–150) and to the entire Psalter.

The Book of PROVERBS

Title

The title in the Hebrew Bible is "The Proverbs of Solomon" (1:1), as also in the Greek Septuagint (LXX). Proverbs pulls together the most important 513 of the over 3,000 proverbs pondered by Solomon (1 Kin. 4:32; Eccl. 12:9), along with some proverbs of others whom Solomon likely influenced. The word "proverb" means "to be like," thus Proverbs is a book of comparisons between common, concrete images and life's most profound truths. Proverbs are simple, moral statements (or illustrations) that highlight and teach fundamental realities about life. Solomon sought God's wisdom (2 Chr. 1:8-12) and offered "pithy sayings" designed to make men contemplate 1) the fear of God and 2) living by His wisdom (1:7; 9:10). The sum of this wisdom is personified in the Lord Jesus Christ (1 Cor. 1:30).

Author and Date

The phrase "Proverbs of Solomon" is more a title than an absolute statement of authorship (1:1). While King Solomon, who ruled Israel from 971–931 B.C. and was granted great wisdom by God (see 1 Kin. 4:29-34), is the author of the didactic section (chaps. 1–9) and the proverbs of 10:1–22:16, he is likely only the compiler of the "sayings of the wise" in 22:17–24:34, which are of an uncertain date before Solomon's reign. The collection in chaps. 25–29 was originally composed by Solomon (25:1) but copied and included later by Judah's king Hezekiah (ca. 715–686 B.C.). Chapter 30 reflects the words of Agur and chap. 31 the words of Lemuel, who perhaps was Solomon. Proverbs was not assembled in its final form until Hezekiah's day or after. Solomon authored his proverbs before his heart was turned away from God (1 Kin. 11:1-11), since the book reveals a godly perspective and is addressed to the "naive" and "young" who need to learn the fear of God. Solomon also wrote Psalms 72 and 127, Ecclesiastes, and Song of Solomon. See Introduction: Author and Date for Ecclesiastes and Song of Solomon.

Background and Setting

The book reflects a 3-fold setting as: 1) general wisdom literature; 2) insights from the royal court; and 3) instruction offered in the tender relationship of a father and mother with their children, all designed to produce meditation on God. Since Proverbs is Wisdom literature, by nature it is sometimes difficult to understand (1:6). Wisdom literature is part of the whole of OT truth; the Priest gave the *Law,* the Prophet gave a *Word* from the Lord, and the Sage (or wise man) gave his wise *Counsel* (Jer. 18:18; Ezek. 7:26). In Proverbs, Solomon the Sage gives insight into the "knotty" issues of life (1:6) which are not directly addressed in the Law or the Prophets. Though it is practical, Proverbs is not superficial or external because it contains moral and ethical elements stressing upright living which flow out of a right relationship with God. In 4:1-4, Solomon connected 3 generations as he entrusted to his son Rehoboam what he learned at the feet of David and Bathsheba. Proverbs is both a pattern for the tender impartation of truth from generation to generation, as well as a vast resource for the content of the truth to be imparted. Proverbs contains the principles and applications of Scripture which the godly characters of the Bible illustrate in their lives.

Historical and Theological Themes

Solomon came to the throne with great promise, privilege, and opportunity. God had granted his request for understanding (1 Kin. 3:9-12; 1 Chr. 1:10,11), and his wisdom exceeded all others (1 Kin. 4:29-31). However, the shocking reality is that he failed to live out the truth that he knew and even taught his son Rehoboam (1 Kin. 11:1,4,6,7-11), who subsequently rejected his father's teaching (1 Kin. 12:6-11).

Proverbs contains a gold mine of biblical theology, reflecting themes of Scripture brought to the level of practical righteousness (1:3), by addressing man's ethical choices, calling into question how he thinks, lives, and manages his daily life in light of divine truth. More specifically, Proverbs calls man to live as the Creator intended him to live when He made man (Ps. 90:1,2,12).

The recurring promise of Proverbs is that generally the wise (the righteous who obey God) live longer (9:11), prosper (2:20-22), experience joy (3:13-18) and the goodness of God temporally (12:21), while fools suffer shame (3:35) and death (10:21). On the other hand, it must be remembered that this general principle is balanced by the reality that the wicked sometimes prosper (Ps. 73:3,12), though only temporarily (Ps. 73:17-19). Job illustrates that there are occasions when the godly wise are struck with disaster and suffering.

There are a number of important themes addressed in Proverbs, which are offered in random order and address different topics, so that it is helpful to study the proverbs thematically as illustrated.

I. Man's Relationship to God	
A. His Trust	Prov. 22:19
B. His Humility	Prov. 3:34
C. His Fear of God	Prov. 1:7
D. His Righteousness	Prov. 10:25
E. His Sin	Prov. 28:13
F. His Obedience	Prov. 6:23
G. Facing Reward	Prov. 12:28
H. Facing Tests	Prov. 17:3
I. Facing Blessing	Prov. 10:22
J. Facing Death	Prov. 15:11
II. Man's Relationship to Himself	
A. His Character	Prov. 20:11
B. His Wisdom	Prov. 1:5
C. His Foolishness	Prov. 26:10,11
D. His Speech	Prov. 18:21
E. His Self Control	Prov. 6:9-11
F. His Kindness	Prov. 3:3
G. His Wealth	Prov. 11:4
H. His Pride	Prov. 27:1
I. His Anger	Prov. 29:11
J. His Laziness	Prov. 13:4
III. Man's Relationship to Others	
A. His Love	Prov. 8:17
B. His Friends	Prov. 17:17
C. His Enemies	Prov. 19:27
D. His Truthfulness	Prov. 23:23
E. His Gossip	Prov. 20:19
F. As a Father	Prov. 20:7; 31:2-9
G. As a Mother	Prov. 31:10-31
H. As Children	Prov. 3:1-3
I. In Educating Children	Prov. 4:1-4
J. In Disciplining Children	Prov. 22:6

The two major themes which are interwoven and overlapping throughout Proverbs are wisdom and folly. Wisdom, which includes knowledge, understanding, instruction, discretion, and obedience, is built on the fear of the Lord and the Word of God. Folly is everything opposite to wisdom.

Interpretive Challenges

The first challenge is the generally elusive nature of Wisdom literature itself. Like the parables, the intended truths are often veiled from understanding if given only a cursory glance, and thus must be pondered in the heart (1:6; 2:1-4; 4:4-9).

Another challenge is the extensive use of parallelism, which is the placing of truths side by side so that the second line expands, completes, defines, emphasizes, or reaches the logical conclusion, the ultimate end, or, in some cases, the contrasting point of view. Often the actual parallel is only implied. For example, 12:13 contains an unstated, but clearly implied parallel, in that the righteous one comes through trouble because of his virtuous speech (cf. 28:7). In interpreting the Proverbs, one must: 1) determine the parallelism and often complete what is assumed and not stated by the author; 2) identify the figures of speech and rephrase the thought without those figures; 3) summarize the lesson or principle of the proverb in a few words; 4) describe the behavior that is taught; and 5) find examples inside Scripture.

Challenges are also found in the various contexts of Proverbs, all of which affect interpretation and understanding. First, there is the setting in which they were spoken; this is largely the context of the young men in the royal court of the king. Second, there is the setting of the book as a whole and how its teachings are to be understood in light of the rest of Scripture. For example, there is much to be gained by comparing the wisdom Solomon taught with the wisdom Christ personified. Third, there is the historical context in which the principles and truths draw on illustrations from their own day.

A final area of challenge comes in understanding that proverbs are divine guidelines and wise observations, i.e., teaching underlying principles (24:3,4) which are not always inflexible laws or absolute promises. These expressions of general truth (cf. 10:27; 22:4) generally do have "exceptions," due to the uncertainty of life and unpredictable behavior of fallen men. God does not guarantee uniform outcome or application for each proverb, but in studying them and applying them, one comes to contemplate the mind of God, His character, His attributes, His works, and His blessings. All of the treasures of wisdom and knowledge expressed in Proverbs are hidden in Christ (Col. 2:3).

Outline

I. Prologue (1:1-7)
   A. Title (1:1)
   B. Purpose (1:2-6)
   C. Theme (1:7)
II. Praise and Wisdom to the Young (1:8–9:18)
III. Proverbs for Everyone (10:1–29:27)
   A. From Solomon (10:1–22:16)
   B. From Wise Men (22:17–24:34)
   C. From Solomon Collected by Hezekiah (25:1–29:27)
IV. Personal Notes (30:1–31:31)
   A. From Agur (30:1-33)
   B. From Lemuel (31:1-31)

The Beginning of Knowledge

1 The [a]proverbs of Solomon the son of
David, king of Israel:

2 To know wisdom and instruction,
To [1]perceive the words of
understanding,
3 To receive the instruction of
wisdom,
Justice, judgment, and equity;
4 To give prudence to the [b]simple,
To the young man knowledge and
discretion—
5 [c]A wise *man* will hear and increase
learning,
And a man of understanding will
[2]attain wise counsel,
6 To understand a proverb and an
enigma,
The words of the wise and their
[d]riddles.

7 [e]The fear of the LORD *is* the
beginning of knowledge,
But fools despise wisdom and
instruction.

Shun Evil Counsel

8 [f]My son, hear the instruction of
your father,
And do not forsake the law of your
mother;
9 For they *will be* a [g]graceful
ornament on your head,
And chains about your neck.

10 My son, if sinners entice you,
[h]Do not consent.
11 If they say, "Come with us,
Let us [i]lie in wait to *shed* blood;
Let us lurk secretly for the innocent
without cause;
12 Let us swallow them alive like
[3]Sheol,
And whole, [j]like those who go
down to the Pit;
13 We shall find all *kinds* of precious
[4]possessions,

CHAPTER 1

1 [a] 1 Kin. 4:32; Prov. 10:1; 25:1; Eccl. 12:9
2 [1] *understand* or *discern*
4 [b] Prov. 9:4
5 [c] Prov. 9:9 [2] *acquire*
6 [d] Num. 12:8; Ps. 78:2; Dan. 8:23
7 [e] Job 28:28; Ps. 111:10; Prov. 9:10; 15:33; [Eccl. 12:13]
8 [f] Prov. 4:1
9 [g] Prov. 3:22
10 [h] Gen. 39:7-10; Deut. 13:8; Ps. 50:18; [Eph. 5:11]
11 [i] Prov. 12:6; Jer. 5:26
12 [j] Ps. 28:1 [3] Or *the grave*
13 [4] Lit. *wealth*

1:1-7 These verses form the Prologue, where the reader is called to serious study for his own benefit. In a few brief words, he is introduced to: 1) the genre of literature (v. 1); 2) a clear two-fold purpose (vv. 2-6); and 3) an all-important motto (v. 7).

1:1 proverbs. See Introduction: Title. The proverbs are short, pithy sayings which express timeless truth and wisdom. They arrest one's thoughts, causing the reader to reflect on how one might apply divine principles to life situations (e.g., 2:12). Proverbs contains insights both in poetry and prose; yet, at the same time, it includes commands to be obeyed. God's proverbs are not limited to this book alone (see Gen. 10:9; 1 Sam. 10:12; 24:13; Jer. 31:29; Ezek. 12:22; 18:2). **Solomon.** See Introduction: Author and Date. As Solomon became king of Israel, he sought and received wisdom and knowledge from the Lord (2 Chr 1:7-12), which led him to wealth, honor, and fame.

1:2-6 The two-fold purpose of the book is 1) to produce the skill of godly living by wisdom and instruction (v. 2a; expanded in vv. 3,4), and 2) to develop discernment (v. 2b, expanded in v. 5).

1:2 wisdom. See Introduction: Historical and Theological Themes. To the Hebrew mind, wisdom was not knowledge alone, but the skill of living a godly life as God intended man to live (cf. Deut. 4:5-8). **instruction.** This refers to the discipline of the moral nature. **understanding.** This word looks at the mental discipline which matures one for spiritual discernment.

1:3 wisdom, justice, judgment, and equity. Expanding the purpose and terms of v. 2a, Proverbs engages in a process of schooling a son in the disciplines of: 1) wisdom (a different Heb. word from that in v. 2) which means discreet counsel or the ability to govern oneself by choice; 2) justice, the ability to conform to the will and standard of God; a practical righteousness that matches one's positional righteousness; 3) judgment, the application of true righteousness in dealing with others; and 4) equity, the living of life in a fair, pleasing way.

1:4 prudence...simple. The purpose is to impart discernment to the naive and the ignorant. The root of "simple" is a word meaning "an open door," an apt description of the undiscerning, who do not know what to keep in or out of their minds. **young...knowledge and discretion.** To make one ponder before sinning, thus to make a responsible choice.

1:5 counsel. The wise believer will have the ability to guide or govern others with truth.

1:6 understand a proverb...enigma. Proverbs seeks to sharpen the mind by schooling one in "parabolic speech" and "dark sayings" that need reflection and interpretation. **riddles.** Study of the Scriptures is sufficient to provide the wisdom for the perplexities of life.

1:7 The fear of the LORD. The overarching theme of this book and particularly the first 9 chapters is introduced—reverence for God (see v. 29; 2:5; 3:7; 8:13; 9:10; 14:26,27; cf. also Job 28:28; Ps. 34:11; Acts 9:31). See Introduction: Historical and Theological Themes. This reverential awe and admiring, submissive fear is foundational for all spiritual knowledge and wisdom (cf. 2:4-6; 9:10; 15:33; Job 28:28; Ps. 111:10; Eccl. 12:13). While the unbeliever may make statements about life and truth, he does not have true or ultimate knowledge until he is in a redemptive relationship of reverential awe with God. Note the progression here: 1) teaching about God; 2) learning about God; 3) fearing God; 4) knowing God; and 5) imitating God's wisdom. The fear of the Lord is a state of mind in which one's own attitudes, will, feelings, deeds, and goals are exchanged for God's (cf. Ps. 42:1).

1:8–9:18 This lengthy section features parental praise of wisdom in the form of didactic addresses. These chapters prepare the reader for the actual proverbs that begin in 10:1ff.

1:10-19 Here is a warning against enticement by sinners who will succeed if his son fails to embrace wisdom (v. 8).

1:10 sinners. This term is reserved in Scripture to describe unbelievers for whom sin is continual and who endeavor to persuade even believers to sin with them (*see note on James 4:8*). The sins of murder and robbery are used as illustrations of such folly.

1:11 Come with us. The intimidating force of peer pressure is often the way to entice those who lack wisdom.

1:12 swallow. The wicked devise a plot of deception in which the innocent are captured and victimized like one who is taken by death itself—as with Joseph (Gen. 37:20ff.), Jeremiah (Jer. 38:6-13), and Daniel (Dan. 6:16,17). "Sheol" is the place of death. For the wicked it is a place of no return (Job 7:9), darkness (Ps. 143:3), and torment (Is. 14:11).

We shall fill our houses with
[5]spoil;
14 Cast in your lot among us,
Let us all have one purse"—
15 My son, [k]do not walk in the way
with them,
[l]Keep your foot from their path;
16 [m]For their feet run to evil,
And they make haste to shed
blood.
17 Surely, in [6]vain the net is spread
In the sight of any [7]bird;
18 But they lie in wait for their *own*
blood,
They lurk secretly for their *own*
lives.
19 [n]So *are* the ways of everyone who is
greedy for gain;
It takes away the life of its owners.

The Call of Wisdom

20 [o]Wisdom calls aloud [8]outside;
She raises her voice in the open
squares.
21 She cries out in the [9]chief
concourses,
At the openings of the gates in the
city
She speaks her words:
22 "How long, you [1]simple ones, will
you love [2]simplicity?
For scorners delight in their
scorning,
And fools hate knowledge.
23 Turn at my rebuke;
Surely [p]I will pour out my spirit on
you;
I will make my words known to
you.
24 [q]Because I have called and you
refused,
I have stretched out my hand and
no one regarded,
25 Because you [r]disdained all my
counsel,
And would have none of my
rebuke,
26 [s]I also will laugh at your calamity;
I will mock when your terror
comes,
27 When [t]your terror comes like a
storm,
And your destruction comes like a
whirlwind,
When distress and anguish come
upon you.

28 "Then[u] they will call on me, but I
will not answer;
They will seek me diligently, but
they will not find me.
29 Because they [v]hated knowledge
And did not [w]choose the fear of
the LORD,
30 [x]They would have none of my
counsel
And despised my every rebuke.
31 Therefore [y]they shall eat the fruit
of their own way,
And be filled to the full with their
own fancies.

13 [5] *plunder*
15 [k] Ps. 1:1; Prov. 4:14 [l] Ps. 119:101
16 [m] Prov. 6:17, 18; [Is. 59:7]; Rom. 3:15
17 [6] *futility* [7] Lit. *lord of the wing*
19 [n] Prov. 15:27; [1 Tim. 6:10]
20 [o] Prov. 8:1; 9:3; [John 7:37] [8] *in the street*
21 [9] LXX, Syr., Tg. *top of the walls*; Vg. *the head of multitudes*
22 [1] *naive* [2] *naivete*
23 [p] Is. 32:15; Joel 2:28; [John 7:39]
24 [q] Is. 65:12; 66:4; Jer. 7:13; Zech. 7:11
25 [r] Ps. 107:11; Luke 7:30
26 [s] Ps. 2:4
27 [t] [Prov. 10:24, 25]
28 [u] 1 Sam. 8:18; Job 27:9; 35:12; Ps. 18:41; Is. 1:15; Jer. 11:11; 14:12; Ezek. 8:18; Mic. 3:4; Zech. 7:13; [James 4:3]
29 [v] Job 21:14; Prov. 1:22 [w] Ps. 119:173
30 [x] Ps. 81:11; Prov. 1:25
31 [y] Job 4:8; Prov. 5:22, 23; 22:8; Is. 3:11; Jer. 6:19

1:13 We...spoil. This is the enlisting of the innocent without full disclosure of intent. Abundant spoil is promised by this outright robbery, which is made to appear easy and safe for the thieves and murderers.

1:15 do not walk. This directly confronts the invitation of v. 11. Sin must be rejected at the first temptation (cf. James 1:15; Ps. 119:114,115) by refusing even the association that can lead to sin (cf. Ps. 1:1-6). Avoid the beginnings of sin (see 4:14).

1:17 the net is spread. It would be ineffective to set up a net for catching a bird in full view of the bird. Taken with v. 18, this analogy means that the sinner sets up his trap for the innocent in secret, but in the end the trap is sprung on him (v. 19). This greed entraps him (cf. 1 Tim. 6:9-11). Stupid sinners rush to their own ruin.

1:20-33 In this section, wisdom is personified and speaks in the first person, emphasizing the serious consequences that come to those who reject it. Similar personifications of wisdom occur in 3:14-18; 8:1-36; 9:1-12.

1:21 cries out...in the city. While enticement is covert and secret (v. 10), wisdom, with nothing to hide, is available to everyone, being found in the most prominent of public places.

1:22 How long. Three questions reveal 3 classes of those needing wisdom, and the downward progression of sin: 1) the simple or naive, who are ignorant; 2) scorners or mockers, who commit more serious, determined acts; and 3) fools or obstinate unbelievers, who will not listen to the truth. Proverbs aims its wisdom primarily at the first group.

1:23 rebuke. God's wisdom brings to bear against the sinner indictments for sin that demand repentance. To the one who does repent, God promises the spirit or essence of true wisdom linked to divine revelation.

1:24-26 Sinners who respond with indifference and mockery at God's indictments increase their guilt (cf. Rom. 2:5) and bring upon themselves the wrath of God's mockery and indifference (vv. 26,27). Some wait to seek God until it is too late. See Deut. 1:45; 1 Sam. 28:6; Ps. 18:41.

1:26,27 calamity...terror...destruction...distress and anguish. All these terms describe the severe troubles of divine judgment. When sinners who have rejected wisdom call on God in the day of judgment, God will respond to their distress with derision.

1:28-32 God's rejection of sinners is carefully detailed. This is the aspect of God's wrath expressed in His abandonment of sinners. *See notes on Rom. 1:24-28.* No prayers or diligent seeking will help them (cf. 8:17).

1:28-30 I will not answer. God will withdraw His invitation to sinners because they have rejected Him. Note the rejection of knowledge (v. 22), fear of the Lord (vv. 7-9), counsel (v. 25), and reproof (v. 23).

1:31 eat the fruit of their own way. The ultimate punishment is God's giving a people up to the result of their wickedness. Cf. Rom. 1:24-28.

32 For the [3]turning away of the
simple will slay them,
And the complacency of fools will
destroy them;
33 But whoever listens to me will
dwell [z]safely,
And [a]will be [4]secure, without fear
of evil."

The Value of Wisdom

2 My son, if you receive my words,
And [a]treasure my commands
within you,
2 So that you incline your ear to
wisdom,
And apply your heart to
understanding;
3 Yes, if you cry out for discernment,
And lift up your voice for
understanding,
4 [b]If you seek her as silver,
And search for her as *for* hidden
treasures;
5 [c]Then you will understand the fear
of the LORD,
And find the knowledge of God.
6 [d]For the LORD gives wisdom;
From His mouth *come* knowledge
and understanding;
7 He stores up sound wisdom for the
upright;
[e]*He is* a shield to those who walk
uprightly;
8 He guards the paths of justice,
And [f]preserves the way of His
saints.
9 Then you will understand
righteousness and justice,
Equity *and* every good path.
10 When wisdom enters your heart,
And knowledge is pleasant to your
soul,
11 Discretion will preserve you;
[g]Understanding will keep you,
12 To deliver you from the way of
evil,
From the man who speaks
perverse things,
13 From those who leave the paths of
uprightness
To [h]walk in the ways of darkness;
14 [i]Who rejoice in doing evil,
And delight in the perversity of the
wicked;
15 [j]Whose ways *are* crooked,
And *who are* devious in their paths;
16 To deliver you from [k]the immoral
woman,
[l]From the seductress *who* flatters
with her words,
17 Who forsakes the companion of
her youth,
And forgets the covenant of her
God.
18 For [m]her house [1]leads down to
death,
And her paths to the dead;
19 None who go to her return,
Nor do they [2]regain the paths of
life—
20 So you may walk in the way of
goodness,

32 [3] waywardness
33 [z] Prov. 3:24-26 [a] Ps. 112:7 [4] at ease

CHAPTER 2

1 [a] [Prov. 4:21]
4 [b] [Prov. 3:14]
5 [c] [James 1:5, 6]
6 [d] 1 Kin. 3:9, 12; [Job 32:8; James 1:5]
7 [e] [Ps. 84:11]; Prov. 30:5
8 [f] [1 Sam. 2:9]; Ps. 66:9
11 [g] Prov. 4:6; 6:22
13 [h] Ps. 82:5; Prov. 4:19; [John 3:19, 20]
14 [i] Prov. 10:23; Jer. 11:15; [Rom. 1:32]
15 [j] Ps. 125:5; [Prov. 21:8]
16 [k] Prov. 5:20; 6:24; 7:5 [l] Prov. 5:3
18 [m] Prov. 7:27 [1] sinks
19 [2] Lit. reach

1:32 complacency. Willful carelessness or lack of appropriate care is intended.

2:1 my words. Solomon has taken God's law and made it his own by faith and obedience, as well as teaching. The wisdom of these words is available to those who, first of all, understand the rich value ("treasure") that wisdom possesses. Appropriating wisdom begins when one values it above all else.

2:2 ear...heart. *See note on 4:21-23.* Once wisdom is properly valued, both the ear and mind are captivated by it.

2:3 cry out for discernment. This shows the passionate pleading of one who is desperate to know and apply the truth of God. The least bit of indifference will leave one bereft of the fullness of wisdom.

2:4 seek...search. A desiring search, the most intensive of a lifetime. Cf. Job 28:1-28 for a parallel.

2:6 His mouth. The words of His mouth are contained in Scripture. It is there that God speaks (cf. Heb. 1:1,2; 2 Pet. 1:20,21). Wisdom comes only by revelation.

2:7,8 the upright. This identifies those who are true believers, who seek to know, love, and obey God and to live righteously. These covenant keepers alone can know wisdom and experience God's protection.

2:9 righteousness...justice, equity. The ethical triad of 1:3.

2:10 wisdom enters your heart. *See note on 4:21-23.*

2:11 Discretion...understanding. Truth is the protector from all evil (see Ps. 119:11,97-104).

2:12 speaks perverse things. Twisted speech is typical of those who reject wisdom (cf. Prov. 8:13; 10:31,32).

2:14 Fools love most what is worst.

2:16 immoral woman. She is the harlot repeatedly condemned in Proverbs (cf. 5:1-23; 6:20-29; 7:1-27; 22:14; 23:27), as in the rest of Scripture (Ex. 20:14; Lev. 20:10). Lit. she is "foreign" or "strange" because such women were at first from outside Israel, but came to include any prostitute or adulteress. Her words are the flattering or smooth words of Prov. 17:14-20.

2:17 forsakes the companion. She leaves the guidance and friendship of her husband (cf. 16:28; 17:9). **forgets the covenant.** In a wide sense this could be the covenant of Sinai (Ex 20:14), but specifically looks to the marriage covenant of Gen. 2:24, with its commitment to fidelity.

2:18 leads down to death. The destructive nature of this blinding sin leads one to walk alongside death (see vv. 8,9,12,15). Death in Proverbs is presented as both a gradual descent (5:23) and a sudden end (29:1).

2:19 None who go...return. The irreversible nature of continuing in this sin points to its devastating consequences. It leads to physical death, as expressed in the Heb. euphemisms of v. 22 ("cut off" and "uprooted"). After that comes the reality of eternal death.

And keep *to* the paths of
righteousness.
21 For the upright will dwell in the
[n]land,
And the blameless will remain in
it;
22 But the wicked will be [3]cut off
from the [4]earth,
And the unfaithful will be
uprooted from it.

Guidance for the Young

3 My son, do not forget my law,
[a]But let your heart keep my
commands;
2 For length of days and long life
And [b]peace they will add to you.

3 Let not mercy and truth forsake
you;
[c]Bind them around your neck,
[d]Write them on the tablet of your
heart,
4 [e]*And* so find favor and [1]high esteem
In the sight of God and man.

5 [f]Trust in the LORD with all your
heart,
[g]And lean not on your own
understanding;
6 [h]In all your ways acknowledge Him,
And He shall [2]direct your paths.

7 Do not be wise in your own [i]eyes;
Fear the LORD and depart from
evil.
8 It will be health to your [3]flesh,
And [j]strength[4] to your bones.

9 [k]Honor the LORD with your
possessions,
And with the firstfruits of all your
increase;
10 [l]So your barns will be filled with
plenty,
And your vats will overflow with
new wine.

11 [m]My son, do not despise the
chastening of the LORD,
Nor detest His correction;
12 For whom the LORD loves He
corrects,
[n]Just as a father the son *in whom* he
delights.

13 [o]Happy *is* the man *who* finds
wisdom,
And the man *who* gains
understanding;
14 [p]For her proceeds *are* better than the
profits of silver,
And her gain than fine gold.
15 She *is* more precious than rubies,
And [q]all the things you may desire
cannot compare with her.
16 [r]Length of days *is* in her right hand,
In her left hand riches and honor.
17 [s]Her ways *are* ways of pleasantness,
And all her paths *are* peace.
18 She *is* [t]a tree of life to those who
take hold of her,
And happy *are all* who [5]retain her.

19 [u]The LORD by wisdom founded the
earth;

21 [n] Ps. 37:3
22 [3] *destroyed* [4] *land*

CHAPTER 3

1 [a] Deut. 8:1
2 [b] Ps. 119:165; Prov. 4:10
3 [c] Ex. 13:9; Deut. 6:8; Prov. 6:21 [d] Prov. 7:3; Jer. 17:1; [2 Cor. 3:3]
4 [e] 1 Sam. 2:26; Luke 2:52; Rom. 14:18 [1] Lit. *good understanding*
5 [f] [Ps. 37:3, 5]; Prov. 22:19 [g] Prov. 23:4; [Jer. 9:23, 24]
6 [h] [1 Chr. 28:9]; Prov. 16:3; [Phil. 4:6; James 1:5] [2] Or *make smooth* or *straight*
7 [i] Rom. 12:16
8 [j] Job 21:24 [3] Body, lit. *navel* [4] Lit. *drink*
9 [k] Ex. 22:29; Deut. 26:2; [Mal. 3:10]
10 [l] Deut. 28:8
11 [m] Job 5:17; Ps. 94:12; Heb. 12:5, 6; Rev. 3:19
12 [n] Deut. 8:5; Prov. 13:24
13 [o] Prov. 8:32, 34, 35
14 [p] Job 28:13
15 [q] Matt. 13:44
16 [r] Prov. 8:18; [1 Tim. 4:8]
17 [s] [Matt. 11:29]
18 [t] Gen. 2:9; Prov. 11:30; 13:12; 15:4; Rev. 2:7 [5] *hold her fast*
19 [u] Ps. 104:24; Prov. 8:27

2:21 dwell in the land...remain. Exactly opposite to those who live in sexual sin and are headed for death, those who belong to the Lord will live. *See note on 8:18-21.*

3:1-35 Here the study of truth leading to wisdom is commended to all. This is enforced by a contrast of the destinies of the wise and wicked.

3:1-20 Solomon instructs that wisdom is: 1) rooted in sound teaching (vv. 1-4); 2) rests in trust in God (vv. 5,6), and 3) rewards those who obey (vv. 7-10). While wisdom demands chastening, it brings profound benefits (vv. 13-18), and its importance is clear since it undergirded God's creation (vv. 19,20).

3:1 my law. Heb. "Torah," from the verb "to throw, distribute, or teach," hence "teachings." It is used of God's law (29:18), but here, as in 2:1, it is used of the commands and principles that God gave through Solomon. **heart.** *See note on 4:21-23.*

3:3 neck...heart. The virtues of mercy (the Heb. word for lovingkindness and loyal love) and truth that come from God are to become part of us—outwardly in our behavior for all to see as an adornment of spiritual beauty, and inwardly as the subject of our meditation (cf. Deut. 6:4-9). Such inward and outward mercy and truth is evidence of New Covenant salvation (cf. Jer. 31:33,34)

3:4 God and man. Cf. Christ in Luke 2:52.

3:7 This is alluded to by Paul in Rom. 12:16.

3:8 health...strength. The strength here is in the marrow, the inner parts (Job 21:24). God is promising physical well-being for those who live wisely according to His will. Such physical well-being is what David forfeited before he confessed that he had sinned against Bathsheba and Uriah (see Pss. 32:3,4; 51:8).

3:9,10 Honor the LORD...possessions. A biblical view of possessions demands using them for honoring God. This is accomplished by trusting God (v. 5); by giving the first and best to God ("firstfruits"; cf. Ex. 22:29; 23:19; Deut. 18:4); by being fair (vv. 27,28); by giving generously (11:25); and by expressing gratitude for all He gives (Deut. 6:9-11). The result of such faithfulness to honor Him is prosperity and satisfaction.

3:11,12 not despise...chastening . Since even the wisest of God's children are subject to sin, there is necessity of God's fatherly discipline to increase wisdom and blessing. Such correction should not be resisted. *See notes on Heb. 12:5-11.*

3:14,15 Cf. Ps. 19:10,11. Divine wisdom yields the richest treasures, described in vv. 14-18 as "profits," "length of days," "riches," "honor," "pleasantness," "peace," "life," and happiness.

3:18 tree of life. This expression is a metaphor referring to temporal and spiritual renewal and refreshment (cf. 11:30; 13:12; 15:4).

3:19,20 Solomon is indicating that wisdom is basic to all of life, for by it God created everything. Since God used it to create the universe, how eager must we be to use it to live in this universe.

By understanding He established
the heavens;
20 By His knowledge the depths were
[v]broken up,
And clouds drop down the dew.

21 My son, let them not depart from
your eyes—
Keep sound wisdom and
discretion;
22 So they will be life to your soul
And grace to your neck.
23 [w]Then you will walk safely in your
way,
And your foot will not stumble.
24 When you lie down, you will not
be afraid;
Yes, you will lie down and your
sleep will be sweet.
25 [x]Do not be afraid of sudden
terror,
Nor of trouble from the wicked
when it comes;
26 For the LORD will be your
confidence,
And will keep your foot from
being caught.

27 [y]Do not withhold good from [6]those
to whom it is due,
When it is in the power of your
hand to do *so*.
28 [z]Do not say to your neighbor,
"Go, and come back,
And tomorrow I will give *it*,"
When *you have* it with you.
29 Do not devise evil against your
neighbor,
For he dwells by you for safety's
sake.
30 [a]Do not strive with a man without
cause,
If he has done you no harm.

31 [b]Do not envy the oppressor,
And choose none of his ways;
32 For the perverse *person is* an
abomination to the LORD,
[c]But His secret counsel *is* with the
upright.
33 [d]The curse of the LORD *is* on the
house of the wicked,
But [e]He blesses the home of the
just.
34 [f]Surely He scorns the scornful,
But gives grace to the humble.
35 The wise shall inherit glory,
But shame shall be the legacy of
fools.

Security in Wisdom

4 Hear, [a]*my* children, the instruction
of a father,
And give attention to know
understanding;
2 For I give you good doctrine:
Do not forsake my law.
3 When I was my father's son,
[b]Tender and the only one in the
sight of my mother,
4 [c]He also taught me, and said
to me:
"Let your heart retain my words;
[d]Keep my commands, and live.
5 [e]Get wisdom! Get understanding!
Do not forget, nor turn away from
the words of my mouth.
6 Do not forsake her, and she will
preserve you;
[f]Love her, and she will keep you.
7 [g]Wisdom *is* the principal thing;
Therefore get wisdom.
And in all your getting, get
understanding.
8 [h]Exalt her, and she will promote
you;
She will bring you honor, when
you embrace her.
9 She will place on your head [i]an
ornament of grace;

20 [v] Gen. 7:11
23 [w] [Ps. 37:24; 91:11, 12]; Prov. 10:9
25 [x] Ps. 91:5; 1 Pet. 3:14
27 [y] Rom. 13:7; [Gal. 6:10] [6] Lit. *its owners*
28 [z] Lev. 19:13; Deut. 24:15
30 [a] Prov. 26:17; [Rom. 12:18]
31 [b] Ps. 37:1; Prov. 24:1
32 [c] Ps. 25:14
33 [d] Lev. 26:14, 16; Deut. 11:28; Zech. 5:3, 4; Mal. 2:2 [e] Job 8:6; Ps. 1:3
34 [f] James 4:6; 1 Pet. 5:5

CHAPTER 4

1 [a] Ps. 34:11; Prov. 1:8
3 [b] 1 Chr. 29:1
4 [c] 1 Chr. 28:9; Eph. 6:4 [d] Prov. 7:2
5 [e] Prov. 2:2, 3
6 [f] 2 Thess. 2:10
7 [g] Prov. 3:13, 14; Matt. 13:44
8 [h] 1 Sam. 2:30
9 [i] Prov. 3:22

3:22 life to your soul. The association of wisdom with the inner spiritual life (*see notes on 3:2,16*) unfolds throughout the book (cf. 4:10,22; 7:2; 8:35; 9:11; 10:11,16,17; 11:19,30; 12:28; 13:14; 14:27; 15:4,24; 16:22; 19:23; 21:21; 22:4). **grace to your neck.** The wisdom of God will adorn one's life for all to see its beauty (cf. 1:9).

3:25,26 afraid...confidence. Living in God's wisdom provides the basis for the believer's peace of mind (v. 24) and removes fear (v. 25).

3:28 neighbor. A neighbor is anyone in need whom God brings across one's path. See Luke 10:29-37.

3:29 devise...dwells. Do not plan evil against one trusting in your protection.

3:30 strive. This can mean "come to hand blows," or, with legal overtones, "accuse a man."

3:31 envy. Many law-keepers wish they were law-breakers (Ps. 37:1-7). They would like to be oppressors rather than the oppressed.

3:32 abomination. Specifically, an abomination is an attitude or act that is incompatible with God's nature and intolerable to Him, leading to His anger and judgment. This is an important theme in Proverbs (*see note on 6:16-19*). **secret counsel.** This means that God discloses Himself and His truth to the upright (cf. Ps. 25:14).

3:34 humble. Lit. "he who bends himself" (James 4:6; 1 Pet. 5:5).

4:2 good doctrine...my law. There is no wisdom but that which is linked to good doctrine, which should be the focal point of all instruction (cf. 1 Tim. 1:10; 4:13,16; 5:17; 2 Tim. 3:10,16; 4:2; Titus 1:9; 2:1,10).

4:3-5 my father's son...my mother. This is Solomon's reference to David and Bathsheba (2 Sam. 12:24).

4:8 Exalt...embrace. The more highly one esteems wisdom, the more highly wisdom lifts that person.

4:9 head. *See notes on 1:9; 3:22.*

A crown of glory she will deliver
to you."
10 Hear, my son, and receive my
sayings,
[j]And the years of your life will be
many.
11 I have [k]taught you in the way of
wisdom;
I have led you in right paths.
12 When you walk, [l]your steps will
not be hindered,
[m]And when you run, you will not
stumble.
13 Take firm hold of instruction, do
not let go;
Keep her, for she *is* your life.

14 [n]Do not enter the path of the
wicked,
And do not walk in the way of
evil.
15 Avoid it, do not travel on it;
Turn away from it and pass on.
16 [o]For they do not sleep unless they
have done evil;
And their sleep is [1]taken away
unless they make *someone* fall.
17 For they eat the bread of
wickedness,
And drink the wine of violence.

18 [p]But the path of the just [q]*is* like the
shining [2]sun,
That shines ever brighter unto the
perfect day.
19 [r]The way of the wicked *is* like
darkness;
They do not know what makes
them stumble.

20 My son, give attention to my
words;
Incline your ear to my sayings.
21 Do not let them depart from your
eyes;
Keep them in the midst of your
heart;
22 For they *are* life to those who find
them,
And health to all their flesh.
23 Keep your heart with all
diligence,
For out of it *spring* the issues of
[s]life.
24 Put away from you a [3]deceitful
mouth,
And put perverse lips far from you.
25 Let your eyes look straight ahead,
And your eyelids look right before
you.
26 Ponder the path of your [t]feet,
And let all your ways be
established.
27 Do not turn to the right or the left;
Remove your foot from evil.

The Peril of Adultery

5 My son, pay attention to my
wisdom;
[1]Lend your ear to my
understanding,
2 That you may [2]preserve discretion,
And your lips [a]may keep
knowledge.
3 [b]For the lips of [3]an immoral woman
drip honey,
And her mouth *is* [c]smoother than
oil;
4 But in the end she is bitter as
wormwood,
Sharp as a two-edged sword.
5 Her feet go down to death,
[d]Her steps lay hold of [4]hell.
6 Lest you ponder *her* path of life—
Her ways are unstable;
You do not know *them*.

10 [j] Prov. 3:2
11 [k] 1 Sam. 12:23
12 [l] Job 18:7; Ps. 18:36 [m] [Ps. 91:11]; Prov. 3:23
14 [n] Ps. 1:1; Prov. 1:15
16 [o] Ps. 36:4; Mic. 2:1 [1] Lit. *robbed*
18 [p] Is. 26:7; Matt. 5:14, 45; Phil. 2:15 [q] 2 Sam. 23:4 [2] Lit. *light*
19 [r] 1 Sam. 2:9; [Job 18:5, 6]; Prov. 2:13; [Is. 59:9, 10; Jer. 23:12]; John 12:35
23 [s] [Matt. 12:34; 15:18, 19; Mark 7:21; Luke 6:45]
24 [3] *devious*
26 [t] Prov. 5:21; Heb. 12:13

CHAPTER 5

1 [1] Lit. *Bow*
2 [a] Mal. 2:7 [2] *appreciate good judgment*
3 [b] Prov. 2:16 [c] Ps. 55:21 [3] Lit. *a strange*
5 [d] Prov. 7:27 [4] Or *Sheol*

4:13 Take…not let go; Keep. The father commanded his son in v. 5 to "get wisdom"; here he commands him to hold on to it.

4:14 Do not enter the path of the wicked. Sin is best dealt with at its beginning by the application of necessary wisdom to suit the initial temptation (cf. Ps. 1:1).

4:15 Four verbs identify aspects necessary in urgently dealing with sin at its start (v. 14): 1) avoid the sinful situation; 2) travel as far from it as possible; 3) turn away from the sin; and 4) pass beyond or escape the sin. The plan here fits exactly with the pattern of sin's enticement outlined in James 1:13-15.

4:16,17 they do not sleep. Cf. 3:24. They have to sin before they can sleep, and they view their sin as food for their hungry, wicked souls.

4:18 path of the…shining sun. The path of the believer is one of increasing light, just as a sunrise begins with the faint glow of dawn and proceeds to the splendor of noonday.

4:21-23 heart. The "heart" commonly refers to the mind as the center of thinking and reason (3:3; 6:21; 7:3), but also includes the emotions (15:15,30), the will (11:20; 14:14), and thus, the whole inner being (3:5). The heart is the depository of all wisdom and the source of whatever affects speech (v. 24), sight (v. 25), and conduct (vv. 26,27).

5:1,2 pay attention. The wise father marshals all the essential terms to sum up his call to wisdom (cf. 1:2; 2:2; 3:13; 4:5).

5:3 lips…mouth. Seduction begins with deceptive flattery (cf. 2:16). Lips of honey should be part of true love in marriage (Song 4:11).

5:4,5 in the end. Lit. "the future" of tasting her lips is like "wormwood," a symbol of suffering (cf. Deut. 29:18), and a "sword," the symbol of death. She travels on the road to death and hell (cf. 2:18).

5:5 hell. *See note on 1:12.*

5:6 Her ways are unstable. Her steps willfully and predictably stagger here and there as she has no concern for the abyss ahead.

7 Therefore hear me now, *my* children,
And do not depart from the words of my mouth.
8 Remove your way far from her,
And do not go near the door of her house,
9 Lest you give your [5]honor to others,
And your years to the cruel *one;*
10 Lest aliens be filled with your [6]wealth,
And your labors *go* to the house of a foreigner;
11 And you mourn at last,
When your flesh and your body are consumed,
12 And say:
"How I have hated instruction,
And my heart despised correction!
13 I have not obeyed the voice of my teachers,
Nor inclined my ear to those who instructed me!
14 I was on the verge of total ruin,
In the midst of the assembly and congregation."

15 Drink water from your own cistern,
And running water from your own well.
16 Should your fountains be dispersed abroad,
[7]Streams of water in the streets?
17 Let them be only your own,
And not for strangers with you.
18 Let your fountain be blessed,
And rejoice with [e]the wife of your youth.
19 [f]*As a* loving deer and a graceful doe,
Let her breasts satisfy you at all times;
And always be [8]enraptured with her love.
20 For why should you, my son, be enraptured by [g]an immoral woman,
And be embraced in the arms of a seductress?

21 [h]For the ways of man *are* before the eyes of the LORD,
And He [9]ponders all his paths.
22 [i]His own iniquities entrap the wicked *man,*
And he is caught in the cords of his sin.
23 [j]He shall die for lack of instruction,
And in the greatness of his folly he shall go astray.

Dangerous Promises

6 My son, [a]if you become [1]surety for your friend,
If you have [2]shaken hands in pledge for a stranger,
2 You are snared by the words of your mouth;

9 [5] *vigor*
10 [6] Lit. *strength*
16 [7] *Channels*
18 [e] Deut. 24:5; Eccl. 9:9; Mal. 2:14
19 [f] Song 2:9 [8] Lit. *intoxicated*
20 [g] Prov. 2:16
21 [h] 2 Chr. 16:9; Job 31:4; 34:21; Prov. 15:3; Jer. 16:17; 32:19; Hos. 7:2; Heb. 4:13 [9] *observes,* lit. *weighs*
22 [i] Num. 32:23; Ps. 9:5; Prov. 1:31; Is. 3:11
23 [j] Job 4:21

CHAPTER 6

1 [a] Prov. 11:15 [1] *guaranty* or *collateral* [2] Lit. *struck*

5:7-14 These verses describe the high price of infidelity. The focus here is on the guilty suffering of the one who yields to lust rather than obeying God's law. Contrast the proper response to such temptation in the case of Joseph (Gen. 39:1-12).

5:9,10 your honor to others. The consequences of this sin may include slavery, as a commuted punishment, instead of death that should have come for adultery (Deut. 22:22). In that case, "the cruel one" was the judge and the "others" were the masters to whom all the energy of youth was directed in slavery. All personal wealth was lost to outsiders, and one served in a stranger's house helping him to prosper.

5:11 flesh and…body. This could be a reference to venereal disease (cf. 1 Cor. 6:18), or to the natural end of life. At that point, filled with an irreversible regret (v. 12), the ruined sinner vainly laments his neglect of warning and his sad disgrace.

5:14 midst of the assembly. A most painful loss in such a situation is public disgrace in the community. There can be public confession, discipline, and forgiveness, but not restoration to one's former place of honor and service. See 6:33.

5:15-19 Using the imagery of water, the joy of a faithful marriage is contrasted with the disaster of infidelity (vv. 9-14). "Cistern" and "well" refer to the wife from whom the husband is to draw all his satisfying refreshment, sexually and affectionately (v. 19; cf. 9:17,18; Song 4:9-11).

5:16,17 fountains…streams. The euphemism refers to the male procreation capacity with the idea of the foolish as a fountain scattering precious water—a picture of the wastefulness of sexual promiscuity. The result of such indiscriminate sin is called "streams of waters in the streets," a graphic description of the illegitimate street children of harlotry. Rather, says Solomon, "let them be only your own" and not the children of such immoral strangers.

5:18 fountain…blessed. God offers to bless male procreation when it is confined to one's wife. It should be noted that, in spite of the sinful polygamy of David and Solomon, as well as the disastrous polygamy of Rehoboam (cf. 2 Chr. 11:21), the instruction here identifies God's ideal as one wife from youth on.

5:19 graceful doe. The doe has graceful beauty in her face and form and is often used in the poetry of Bible times for the beauty of a woman. **breasts.** This is imagery of affection (cf. Song 1:13; 4:1-7; 7:7,8).

5:20 Such behavior is presented as having no benefit; thus, to justify such folly is senseless.

5:21,22 ponders…caught. The Lord sees all that man does and in mercy withholds immediate judgment, allowing the sinner time to repent or to be caught in his own sin (cf. Num. 32:23; Pss. 7:15,16; 57:6; Prov. 1:17; Gal. 6:7,8). Note the example of Haman (Esth. 5:9-14; 7:1-10).

5:23 He shall die. *See notes on 2:18; 5:5.*

6:1 surety…pledge. The foolishness here is making one's self responsible for another's debt and pledging to pay if the other defaults (cf. 11:15; 17:18; 20:16; 22:26). While there is precedent for such a practice, it is far better to give to those in need (see Deut. 15:1-15; 19:17) or lend without interest (see Lev. 25:35-38; 28:8).

6:2-4 snared…come into the hand. Cf. 22:26,27. Anyone who becomes responsible for another person's debt is trapped and con-

You are taken by the words of your mouth.
3 So do this, my son, and deliver yourself;
For you have come into the hand of your friend:
Go and humble yourself;
Plead with your friend.
4 [b]Give no sleep to your eyes,
Nor slumber to your eyelids.
5 Deliver yourself like a gazelle from the hand *of the hunter*,
And like a bird from the hand of the [3]fowler.

The Folly of Indolence

6 [c]Go to the ant, you sluggard!
Consider her ways and be wise,
7 Which, having no [4]captain,
Overseer or ruler,
8 Provides her [5]supplies in the summer,
And gathers her food in the harvest.
9 [d]How long will you [6]slumber, O sluggard?
When will you rise from your sleep?
10 A little sleep, a little slumber,
A little folding of the hands to sleep—
11 [e]So shall your poverty come on you like a prowler,
And your need like an armed man.

The Wicked Man

12 A worthless person, a wicked man,
Walks with a perverse mouth;
13 [f]He winks with his eyes,
He [7]shuffles his feet,
He points with his fingers;

4 [b] Ps. 132:4
5 [3] One who catches birds in a trap or snare
6 [c] Job 12:7
7 [4] Lit. *leader*
8 [5] Lit. *bread*
9 [d] Prov. 24:33, 34 [6] Lit. *lie down*
11 [e] Prov. 10:4
13 [f] Job 15:12; Ps. 35:19; Prov. 10:10 [7] *gives signals*, lit. *scrapes*

trolled because he has yielded control of what God has given him as a stewardship. The situation is so serious that it is imperative to take control of one's own God-given resources and get out of such an intolerable arrangement immediately ("deliver yourself," vv. 3,4) before coming to poverty or slavery. Cf. Gen 43:9; 44:32,33.

6:6-11 A warning against laziness is appropriate after the discussion on the folly of guaranteeing someone else's debt, since it is often lazy people who want sureties.

6:6 ant...sluggard. Cf. 30:25. The ant is an example of industry, diligence, and planning (vv. 7,8) and serves as a rebuke to a sluggard (a lazy one who lacks self control). Folly sends a lazy man to learn from an ant (see 10:4,26; 12:24; 13:4; 15:19; 19:15; 20:4; 26:14-16).

6:11 prowler...armed man. The lazy man, with his inordinate devotion to sleep rather than work (vv. 9,10), learns too late, thus coming to inescapable poverty just as a victim is overpowered by a robber (see 24:33,34). While laziness leads to poverty (cf. 10:4,5; 13:4; 20:4,13), laziness is not always the cause of poverty (cf. 14:31; 17:5; 19:1,17,22; 21:12; 28:3,11).

6:12 A worthless person. A scoundrel (1 Sam. 25:25; Job 34:18), lit. a "man of Belial" (useless; cf. 1 Sam. 2:12; 30:22), a term which came to be used of the Devil himself (see 2 Cor. 6:15).

6:13 winks...shuffles...points. Apparently this was common in the East. Fearing detection, and to hide his intention, the deceiver spoke lies to the victim while giving signals with his eyes, hands, and feet to someone else in on the deception to carry out the intrigue.

Symbols for the Bible

Symbol	Reality	Texts
1. Jesus Christ	Personification of the Word	John 1:1; Rev. 19:13
2. Valuable Metals	Incalculable worth	Ps. 12:6 (silver) Pss. 19:10; 119:27 (gold)
3. Seed	Source of new life	Matt. 13:10-23; James 1:18; 1 Pet. 1:23
4. Water	Cleansing from sin	Eph. 5:25-27; Rev. 21:6; 22:17
5. Mirror	Self-examination	James 1:22-25
6. Food	Nourishment to the soul	1 Cor. 3:3; 1 Pet. 2:1-3 (milk) Deut. 8:3; Matt. 4:4 (bread) 1 Cor. 3:3; Heb. 5:12-14 (meat) Ps. 19:10 (honey)
7. Clothing	A life dressed in truth	Titus 2:10; 1 Pet. 3:5
8. Lamp	Light for direction	Ps. 119:105; Prov. 6:23; 2 Pet. 1:19
9. Sword	Spiritual weapon	Eph. 6:17 (outwardly) Heb. 4:12 (inwardly)
10. Plumb line	Benchmark of spiritual reality	Amos 7:8
11. Hammer	Powerful judgment	Jer. 23:29
12. Fire	Painful judgment	Jer. 5:14; 20:9, 23:29

14 Perversity *is* in his heart,
[g]He devises evil continually,
[h]He sows discord.
15 Therefore his calamity shall come
[i]suddenly;
Suddenly he shall [j]be broken
[k]without remedy.

16 These six *things* the LORD hates,
Yes, seven *are* an abomination to
[8]Him:
17 [l]A [9]proud look,
[m]A lying tongue,
[n]Hands that shed innocent blood,
18 [o]A heart that devises wicked plans,
[p]Feet that are swift in running to
evil,
19 [q]A false witness *who* speaks lies,
And one who [r]sows discord
among brethren.

Beware of Adultery

20 [s]My son, keep your father's
command,
And do not forsake the law of your
mother.
21 [t]Bind them continually upon your
heart;
Tie them around your neck.
22 [u]When you roam, [1]they will lead
you;
When you sleep, [v]they will keep
you;
And *when* you awake, they will
speak with you.
23 [w]For the commandment *is* a lamp,
And the law a light;
Reproofs of instruction *are* the way
of life,
24 [x]To keep you from the evil woman,
From the flattering tongue of a
seductress.
25 [y]Do not lust after her beauty in
your heart,
Nor let her allure you with her
eyelids.
26 For [z]by means of a harlot
A man is reduced to a crust of bread;
[a]And [2]an adulteress will [b]prey
upon his precious life.
27 Can a man take fire to his bosom,
And his clothes not be burned?
28 Can one walk on hot coals,
And his feet not be seared?
29 So *is* he who goes in to his
neighbor's wife;
Whoever touches her shall not be
innocent.

30 *People* do not despise a thief
If he steals to satisfy himself when
he is starving.
31 Yet *when* he is found, [c]he must
restore sevenfold;
He may have to give up all the
substance of his house.
32 Whoever commits adultery with a
woman [d]lacks understanding;
He *who* does so destroys his own
soul.
33 Wounds and dishonor he will get,
And his reproach will not be
wiped away.

14 [g] Prov. 3:29; Mic. 2:1 [h] Prov. 6:19
15 [i] Prov. 24:22; Is. 30:13; 1 Thess. 5:3 [j] Jer. 19:11 [k] 2 Chr. 36:16
16 [8] Lit. *His soul*
17 [l] Ps. 101:5; Prov. 21:4 [m] Ps. 120:2; Prov. 12:22 [n] Deut. 19:10; Prov. 28:17; Is. 1:15 [9] Lit. *Haughty eyes*
18 [o] Gen. 6:5; Ps. 36:4; Prov. 24:2; Jer. 18:18; Mark 14:1, 43-46 [p] 2 Kin. 5:20-27; Is. 59:7; Rom. 3:15
19 [q] Ps. 27:12; Prov. 19:5, 9; Matt. 26:59-66 [r] Prov. 6:14; 1 Cor. 1:11-13; [Jude 3, 4, 16-19]
20 [s] Eph. 6:1
21 [t] Prov. 3:3
22 [u] [Prov. 3:23] [v] Prov. 2:11 [1] Lit. *it*
23 [w] Ps. 19:8; 2 Pet. 1:19
24 [x] Prov. 2:16
25 [y] Matt. 5:28
26 [z] Prov. 29:3 [a] Gen. 39:14 [b] Ezek. 13:18 [2] Wife of another, lit. *a man's wife*
31 [c] Ex. 22:1-4
32 [d] Prov. 7:7

6:14 discord. The sin of strife, dissent, or creating conflict intentionally recurs in Proverbs (15:18; 16:28; 17:14; 18:19; 21:9,19; 22:10; 23:29; 25:24; 26:21; 27:15; 28:25; 29:22).

6:15 without remedy. The results of iniquity can be irreversible. His punishment will fit his crime when God judges.

6:16-19 six...seven. The sequence of these two numbers was used both to represent totality and as a means of arresting attention (cf. 30:15,18; Job 5:19; Amos 1:3) These 7 detestable sins provide a profound glimpse into the sinfulness of man. These verses act as a summary of the previous warnings: 1) haughty eyes (v. 13a ,"winks"); 2) lying tongue (v. 12b,"perverse mouth"); 3) hands (v. 13c,"fingers"); 4) heart (v. 14a); 5) feet (v. 13b); 6) false witness (v. 12b); and 7) discord (v. 14c).

6:20,21 *See notes on 1:8,9; 3:1-3.*

6:22 roam...sleep...awake. Cf. 3:23,24. This parallels the 3 circumstances of life in Deut. 6:6-9; 11:18-20, for which wisdom provides direction, protection, and meditation. The biblical instruction for parents prevents the entrance of evil by supplying good and true thoughts, even when sleeping.

6:23 the commandment...the law...instruction. These all identify the Word of God, which provides the wisdom leading to abundant and eternal life.

6:24 *See notes on 2:16; 5:3.* Parental instruction in wisdom is crucial to strengthen a person against the strong attraction of sexual sin. By loving truth and being elevated to wisdom, men are not seduced by lying flattery.

6:25 lust. Sexual sin is rooted in lust (imagination of the sinful act), as implied in Ex. 20:17 and addressed by Christ in Matt. 5:28. This initial attraction must be consistently rejected (James 1:14,15).

6:26 crust of bread. Here the smallest piece of bread demonstrates how the prostitute reduces the life of a man to insignificance, including the loss of his wealth (see 29:3), freedom, family, purity, dignity, and even his soul (v. 32).

6:27-29 Powerful metaphors are given here to describe the obvious danger and destructive consequences of adultery, showing that punishment is a natural and expected consequence.

6:29 touches her. This refers to a touch intended to inflame sexual passion. Paul uses the same expression with the same meaning in 1 Cor. 7:1.

6:30-35 Adultery is compared to a thief. Unlike the pity extended to a starving thief, who, though it may cost all he has, can make restitution and put the crime behind him permanently (vv. 30,31), for the adulterer there is no restitution as he destroys his soul (v. 32; cf. Deut. 22:22). If he lives, he is disgraced for life (v. 33) with a reproach which will never go away. The jealous husband will have no mercy on him either (vv. 34,35; cf. 27:4; Song 8:6).

6:31 sevenfold. Varying measures of restitution occur in Scripture (cf. Ex. 22:1ff.; Lev. 6:5; Num. 5:7; 2 Sam. 12:6; Luke 19:8), but none are so severe as for the thief.

34 For [e]jealousy *is* a husband's fury;
Therefore he will not spare in the day of vengeance.
35 He will [3]accept no recompense,
Nor will he be appeased though you give many gifts.

7

1 My son, keep my words,
And [a]treasure my commands within you.
2 [b]Keep my commands and live,
[c]And my law as the apple of your eye.
3 [d]Bind them on your fingers;
Write them on the tablet of your heart.
4 Say to wisdom, "You *are* my sister,"
And call understanding *your* nearest kin,
5 [e]That they may keep you from the immoral woman,
From the seductress *who* flatters with her words.

The Crafty Harlot

6 For at the window of my house
I looked through my lattice,
7 And saw among the simple,
I perceived among the [1]youths,
A young man [f]devoid[2] of understanding,
8 Passing along the street near her corner;
And he took the path to her house
9 [g]In the twilight, in the evening,
In the black and dark night.

10 And there a woman met him,
With the attire of a harlot, and a crafty heart.
11 [h]She *was* loud and rebellious,
[i]Her feet would not stay at home.
12 At times *she was* outside, at times in the open square,
Lurking at every corner.
13 So she caught him and kissed him;
With an [3]impudent face she said to him:
14 "*I have* peace offerings with me;
Today I have paid my vows.
15 So I came out to meet you,
Diligently to seek your face,
And I have found you.
16 I have spread my bed with tapestry,
Colored coverings of [j]Egyptian linen.
17 I have perfumed my bed
With myrrh, aloes, and cinnamon.
18 Come, let us take our fill of love until morning;
Let us delight ourselves with love.
19 For [4]my husband *is* not at home;
He has gone on a long journey;
20 He has taken a bag of money [5]with him,
And will come home [6]on the appointed day."

21 [7]With [k]her enticing speech she caused him to yield,
[l]With her flattering lips she [8]seduced him.
22 Immediately he went after her, as an ox goes to the slaughter,
Or [9]as a fool to the correction of the [1]stocks,

34 [e] Prov. 27:4; Song 8:6
35 [3] Lit. *lift up the face of any*

CHAPTER 7

1 [a] Prov. 2:1
2 [b] Lev. 18:5; Prov. 4:4; [Is. 55:3] [c] Deut. 32:10; Ps. 17:8; Zech. 2:8
3 [d] Deut. 6:8; Prov. 6:21
5 [e] Prov. 2:16; 5:3
7 [f] [Prov. 6:32; 9:4, 16] [1] Lit. *sons* [2] *lacking*
9 [g] Job 24:15
11 [h] Prov. 9:13; 1 Tim. 5:13 [i] Titus 2:5
13 [3] *shameless*
16 [j] Is. 19:9; Ezek. 27:7
19 [4] Lit. *the man*
20 [5] Lit. *in his hand* [6] *at the full moon*
21 [k] Prov. 5:3 [l] Ps. 12:2 [7] *By the greatness of her words* [8] *compelled*
22 [9] LXX, Syr., Tg. *as a dog to bonds;* Vg. *as a lamb . . . to bonds* [1] *shackles*

7:1-4 Cf. 2:1-4; 3:1-3; 4:10.

7:2 apple of your eye. This expression refers to the pupil of the eye which, because it is the source of sight, is carefully protected (see Deut. 32:10; Ps. 17:8; Zech. 2:8). The son is to guard and protect his father's teachings because they give him spiritual and moral sight.

7:3 Bind. This is a call to give the truth of divine wisdom a permanent place in the mind and in conduct. Cf. 3:3; 6:21; Deut. 6:8.

7:6 The drama of seduction by the adulteress, introduced in v. 5 and unfolding to v. 23, is described from the viewpoint of one who is watching from his window.

7:7 simple...devoid of understanding. *See notes on 1:2-4.*

7:8 took the path. Against the advice of 4:14,15, he put himself right in the harlot's place. "Fleeing immorality" (1 Cor. 6:18) starts by not being in the harlot's neighborhood at night. Cf. v. 25.

7:10 a crafty heart. Lit. "hidden." This is an unfair contest between the simple young man, who lacks wisdom and is void of the truth, and the evil woman, who knows her goal, but hides her true intentions. *See notes on 6:26; 23:27,28.*

7:11,12 These verses break the narrative to describe the woman's modes of operation leading to her successful seduction of the simple man.

7:14 peace offerings. According to the law of peace offerings (Lev. 7:11-18), the meat left over after the sacrifice was to be eaten before the end of the day. She appears very religious in making the invitation that the man join her because she had made her offering and is bringing home the meat that must be eaten.

7:15 It is already night (v. 9) and the meal must be consumed. It cannot be left for morning. Such hypocrisy is concerned about the ceremonial law while aggressively seducing someone to violate God's moral law.

7:16,17 Egyptian linen. Fine linen was a sign of wealth (31:22; Is. 19:9; Ezek. 27:7). Here the solicitation is direct, as she describes the comfort of her bed with its aromatic spices (cf. Song 1:13; 3:6).

7:18 fill of love. Adultery is not true love, but mere physical gratification.

7:19,20 She gives the simple man the assurance that there is no fear of discovery of their act, since her husband has taken a large sum of cash, needed because he will be away for a long time (lit. "a full moon"), returning at a set time and not before.

7:21 When the location, time, and setting were allowed, the seduction was easy (cf. v. 26).

7:22 slaughter...stocks. Ignorant of the real danger and incapable of resistance, he quickly succumbs like a beast to be butchered or a criminal put in stocks.

23 Till an arrow struck his liver.
[m]As a bird hastens to the snare,
He did not know it [2]*would cost* his life.

24 Now therefore, listen to me, *my* children;
Pay attention to the words of my mouth:
25 Do not let your heart turn aside to her ways,
Do not stray into her paths;
26 For she has cast down many wounded,
And [n]all who were slain by her were strong *men.*
27 [o]Her house *is* the way to [3]hell,
Descending to the chambers of death.

The Excellence of Wisdom

8 Does not [a]wisdom cry out,
And understanding lift up her voice?
2 She takes her stand on the top of the [1]high hill,
Beside the way, where the paths meet.
3 She cries out by the gates, at the entry of the city,
At the entrance of the doors:
4 "To you, O men, I call,
And my voice *is* to the sons of men.
5 O you [2]simple ones, understand prudence,
And you fools, be of an understanding heart.
6 Listen, for I will speak of [b]excellent things,
And from the opening of my lips *will come* right things;
7 For my mouth will speak truth;
Wickedness *is* an abomination to my lips.
8 All the words of my mouth *are* with righteousness;
Nothing crooked or perverse *is* in them.
9 They *are* all plain to him who understands,
And right to those who find knowledge.
10 Receive my instruction, and not silver,
And knowledge rather than choice gold;
11 [c]For wisdom *is* better than rubies,
And all the things one may desire cannot be compared with her.

12 "I, wisdom, dwell with prudence,
And find out knowledge *and* discretion.
13 [d]The fear of the LORD *is* to hate evil;
[e]Pride and arrogance and the evil way
And [f]the perverse mouth I hate.
14 Counsel *is* mine, and sound wisdom;
I *am* understanding, [g]I have strength.
15 [h]By me kings reign,
And rulers decree justice.
16 By me princes rule, and nobles,
All the judges of [3]the earth.
17 [i]I love those who love me,
And [j]those who seek me diligently will find me.
18 [k]Riches and honor *are* with me,
Enduring riches and righteousness.
19 My fruit *is* better than gold, yes, than fine gold,
And my revenue than choice silver.
20 I [4]traverse the way of righteousness,
In the midst of the paths of justice,
21 That I may cause those who love me to inherit wealth,

23 [m]Eccl. 9:12 [2]Lit. *is for*
26 [n]Neh. 13:26
27 [o]Prov. 2:18; 5:5; 9:18; [1 Cor. 6:9, 10; Rev. 22:15] [3]Or *Sheol*

CHAPTER 8

1 [a]Prov. 1:20, 21; 9:3; [1 Cor. 1:24]
2 [1]Lit. *heights*
5 [2]*naive*
6 [b]Prov. 22:20
11 [c]Job 28:15; Ps. 19:10; 119:127; Prov. 3:14, 15; 4:5, 7; 16:16
13 [d]Prov. 3:7; 16:6 [e]1 Sam. 2:3; [Prov. 16:17, 18; Is. 13:11] [f]Prov. 4:24
14 [g]Eccl. 7:19; 9:16
15 [h]2 Chr. 1:10; Prov. 29:4; Dan. 2:21; [Matt. 28:18]; Rom. 13:1
16 [3]MT, Syr., Tg., Vg. *righteousness;* LXX, Bg., some mss. and editions *earth*
17 [i]1 Sam. 2:30; [Ps. 91:14]; Prov. 4:6; [John 14:21] [j]Prov. 2:4, 5; John 7:37; James 1:5
18 [k]Prov. 3:16; [Matt. 6:33]
20 [4]*walk about on*

7:23 arrow…bird. This refers to a mortal wound, as the liver represents the seat of life (Lam. 2:11) and the bird is snared to be eaten (cf. 6:26).

7:24 The appropriate application of this drama is made in the admonition of these verses to avoid her deadly seduction.

7:26 It is not just weak men who fall, but strong men in the wrong place at the wrong time with the wrong thoughts for the wrong reasons.

7:27 Cf. 5:5.

8:1-3 wisdom. *See notes on 1:20,21.* The openness and public exposure of wisdom contrasts with the secrecy and intrigues of the wicked adulterers in chap. 7.

8:4,5 simple ones. *See note on 1:4.*

8:6-8 The virtues of wisdom are summarized in all that is excellent, right, true, and righteous.

8:9 plain. Lit. "clear." The one who applies his mind to the wisdom of God will understand and gain moral knowledge and the insight to recognize truth. Cf. 1 Cor. 1:18-25.

8:10,11 The most valuable reality a young person can attain is the insight to order his life by the standard of truth (*see notes on 3:14,15; 8:19-21;* also Job 28:12-28; Ps. 19:10).

8:13 The fear of the LORD. *See notes on 1:7.* **arrogance…hate.** Wisdom hates what God hates (cf. 6:16-19; Ps. 5:5). The highest virtue is humility (submission to God), and thus wisdom hates pride and self-exaltation above all.

8:15,16 kings…rulers…princes…nobles. In this royal court setting, Solomon addresses his son as a future king. All these leaders should do their work by God's wisdom and justice.

8:17 love. Wisdom's love for the one who receives it is proven by the benefits mentioned in vv. 18-21.

8:18-21 Riches and honor. Cf. 3:16; 22:4. Solomon, who was given great wisdom, experienced its wealth of benefits firsthand as a young king (cf. 1 Kin. 3:12-14; 10:14-29).

That I may fill their treasuries.

22 "The [l] LORD possessed me at the
beginning of His way,
Before His works of old.
23 [m] I have been established from
everlasting,
From the beginning, before there
was ever an earth.
24 When *there were* no depths I was
brought forth,
When *there were* no fountains
abounding with water.
25 [n] Before the mountains were settled,
Before the hills, I was brought
forth;
26 While as yet He had not made the
earth or the [5] fields,
Or the [6] primal dust of the world.
27 When He prepared the heavens, I
was there,
When He drew a circle on the face
of the deep,
28 When He established the clouds
above,
When He strengthened the
fountains of the deep,
29 [o] When He assigned to the sea its
limit,
So that the waters would not
transgress His command,
When [p] He marked out the
foundations of the earth,
30 [q] Then I was beside Him *as* [7] a
master craftsman;
[r] And I was daily *His* delight,
Rejoicing always before Him,
31 Rejoicing in His inhabited world,
And [s] my delight *was* with the sons
of men.

22 [l] Job 28:26-28; Ps. 104:24; Prov. 3:19; [John 1:1]
23 [m] [Ps. 2:6]
25 [n] Job 15:7, 8
26 [5] *outer places* [6] Lit. *beginning of the dust*
29 [o] Gen. 1:9, 10; Job 38:8-11; Ps. 33:7; 104:9; Jer. 5:22 [p] Job 28:4, 6; Ps. 104:5
30 [q] [John 1:1-3, 18] [r] [Matt. 3:17] [7] A Jewish tradition *one brought up*
31 [s] Ps. 16:3; John 13:1

32 [t] Ps. 119:1, 2; 128:1; Prov. 29:18; Luke 11:28
34 [u] Prov. 3:13, 18
35 [v] Prov. 3:4; 12:2; [John 17:3]
36 [w] Prov. 20:2

CHAPTER 9

1 [a] [Matt. 16:18; 1 Cor. 3:9, 10; Eph. 2:20-22; 1 Pet. 2:5]
2 [b] Matt. 22:4 [c] Prov. 23:30 [1] *arranged*
4 [d] Ps. 19:7
5 [e] Song 5:1; Is. 55:1; [John 6:27]

32 "Now therefore, listen to me, *my*
children,
For [t] blessed *are those who* keep my
ways.
33 Hear instruction and be wise,
And do not disdain *it*.
34 [u] Blessed is the man who listens to
me,
Watching daily at my gates,
Waiting at the posts of my doors.
35 For whoever finds me finds life,
And [v] obtains favor from the LORD;
36 But he who sins against me
[w] wrongs his own soul;
All those who hate me love death."

The Way of Wisdom

9 Wisdom has [a] built her house,
She has hewn out her seven pillars;
2 [b] She has slaughtered her meat,
[c] She has mixed her wine,
She has also [1] furnished her table.
3 She has sent out her maidens,
She cries out from the highest
places of the city,
4 "Whoever [d] *is* simple, let him turn in
here!"
As for him who lacks
understanding, she says to
him,
5 "Come, [e] eat of my bread
And drink of the wine I have
mixed.
6 Forsake foolishness and live,
And go in the way of
understanding.

7 "He who corrects a scoffer gets
shame for himself,
And he who rebukes a wicked *man*
only harms himself.

8:22-31 The LORD possessed me. Cf. 3:19,20. Wisdom personified claims credit for everything that God created, so that wisdom was first, as God was eternally first. Christ used His eternal wisdom in creation (John 1:1-3; 1 Cor 1:24,30).

8:24-26 Note how these verses parallel the creation account. The earth (v. 23) with day one in Gen. 1:1-5; water (v. 24) with day two in Gen. 1:6-8; and land (vv. 25,26) with day three in Gen. 1:9-13.

8:27 circle on the face of the deep. The Heb. word for circle indicates that the earth is a globe; therefore the horizon is circular (cf. Is. 40:22). This "deep" that surrounds the earth is either the endless heavens or the sea, on which the circular horizon can best be seen.

8:29 sea its limit. In creation, God limited the waters on the earth (cf. Gen. 1:9; 7:11; 8:2), commanding into existence shorelines beyond which the oceans cannot go. **foundations.** This figuratively denotes the solid structure of the earth (cf. Job 38:4; Ps. 24:2).

8:30 master craftsman. As translated in Song 7:1 and Jer. 52:15, this term describes wisdom as competent and experienced in the craft of creation.

8:31 my delight. When God rejoiced over His creation (Gen. 1:31; Job 38:7), wisdom was also rejoicing, especially in the creation of mankind, who alone in the physical creation has the capacity to appreciate wisdom and truth.

8:36 hate me love death. Since wisdom is the source of life (see 3:18), anyone hating wisdom, so as to spurn it, is acting as if he loves death.

9:1 seven pillars. The significance of 7 is to convey the sufficiency of this house as full in size and fit for a banquet.

9:2 mixed her wine. Cf. 23:29,30. Wine was diluted with water as much as 1 to 8, to reduce its power to intoxicate. It was also mixed with spices for flavor (Song 8:20). Unmixed wine is called strong drink (cf. 20:1; 31:6; Lev. 10:9; Is. 28:7; Luke 1:15).

9:3-5 The call of wisdom is not secret, but public. *See note on 1:20,21.*

9:5 Come, eat...drink. Cf. God's banquet call (Is. 55:1-3; Luke 14:16-24; Rev. 22:17).

9:7-9 Wise people receive reproof and rebuke with appreciation; fools do not.

8 [f]Do not correct a scoffer, lest he hate you;
[g]Rebuke a wise *man*, and he will love you.
9 Give *instruction* to a wise *man*, and he will be still wiser;
Teach a just *man*, [h]and he will increase in learning.

10 "The[i] fear of the LORD *is* the beginning of wisdom,
And the knowledge of the Holy One *is* understanding.
11 [j]For by me your days will be multiplied,
And years of life will be added to you.
12 [k]If you are wise, you are wise for yourself,
And *if* you scoff, you will bear *it* alone."

The Way of Folly

13 [l]A foolish woman is [2]clamorous;
She is simple, and knows nothing.
14 For she sits at the door of her house,
On a seat [m]*by* the highest places of the city,
15 To call to those who pass by,
Who go straight on their way:
16 "Whoever[n] *is* [3]simple, let him turn in here";
And *as for* him who lacks understanding, she says to him,
17 "Stolen[o] water is sweet,
And bread *eaten* in secret is pleasant."
18 But he does not know that [p]the dead *are* there,
That her guests *are* in the depths of [4]hell.

Wise Sayings of Solomon

10

The proverbs of [a]Solomon:
[b]A wise son makes a glad father,
But a foolish son *is* the grief of his mother.

2 [c]Treasures of wickedness profit nothing,
[d]But righteousness delivers from death.
3 [e]The LORD will not allow the righteous soul to famish,
But He casts away the desire of the wicked.

4 [f]He who has a slack hand becomes poor,
But [g]the hand of the diligent makes rich.
5 He who gathers in [h]summer *is* a wise son;
He who sleeps in harvest *is* [i]a son who causes shame.

6 Blessings *are* on the head of the righteous,
But violence covers the mouth of the wicked.
7 [j]The memory of the righteous *is* blessed,
But the name of the wicked will rot.

8 The wise in heart will receive commands,
[k]But [1]a prating fool will [2]fall.

---

8 [f] Prov. 15:12; Matt. 7:6 [g] Ps. 141:5; Prov. 10:8
9 [h] [Matt. 13:12]
10 [i] Job 28:28; Ps. 111:10; Prov. 1:7
11 [j] Prov. 3:2, 16
12 [k] Job 35:6, 7; Prov. 16:26
13 [l] Prov. 7:11 [2] *boisterous*
14 [m] Prov. 9:3
16 [n] Prov. 7:7, 8 [3] *naive*
17 [o] Prov. 20:17
18 [p] Prov. 2:18; 7:27 [4] Or *Sheol*

CHAPTER 10

1 [a] Prov. 1:1; 25:1 [b] Prov. 15:20; 17:21, 25; 19:13; 29:3, 15
2 [c] Ps. 49:7; Prov. 11:4; 21:6; Ezek. 7:19; [Luke 12:19, 20] [d] Dan. 4:27
3 [e] Ps. 34:9, 10; 37:25; Prov. 28:25; [Matt. 6:33]
4 [f] Prov. 19:15 [g] Prov. 12:24; 13:4; 21:5
5 [h] Prov. 6:8 [i] Prov. 19:26
7 [j] Ps. 112:6; Eccl. 8:10
8 [k] Prov. 10:10 [1] Lit. *the foolish of lips* [2] *be thrust down* or *ruined*

9:10 The fear of the LORD. *See note on 1:7.*

9:11 See Introduction: Historical and Theological Themes.

9:12 Every individual is responsible for his own conduct, so that the choices we make affect our own lives.

9:13-18 The feast of folly is described as offered by the foolish hostess. Note the contrast with lady wisdom in vv. 1-6 and similarities to the immoral woman in 7:6-23.

9:13 clamorous. Cf. 7:11,12.

9:17 Forbidden delights sometimes seem sweeter and more pleasant because of their risk and danger.

9:18 hell. *See note on 1:12.* Like the adulterer, the flattering words of folly lead to death (see 2:18,19; 5:5; 7:21-23,26,27).

10:1–22:16 This large section contains 375 of Solomon's individual proverbs. They are in no apparent order, with only occasional grouping by subject, and are often without a context to qualify their application. They are based on Solomon's inspired knowledge of the Law and the Prophets. The parallel, two line proverbs of chaps. 10–15 are mostly contrasts or opposites (antithetical), while those of chaps. 16–22 are mostly similarities or comparisons (synthetical).

10:1 grief of his mother. *See note on 23:15,16.* This parental grief is most deeply felt by the mother, who plays a more intimate role in raising a child.

10:2 death. The greatest of all treasures, life, is gained by righteousness.

10:3 desire of the wicked. For a while, the wicked may seem to realize their desires; in the end, God removes their accomplishments because they are evil (cf. Ps. 37:16-20).

10:4 diligent. This is in contrast to the sluggard (*see notes on 6:6-11*). Poverty by itself is not evil, unless it is the product of laziness.

10:5 gathers...sleeps. Cf. 6:6-11; 13:4; 15:19; 24:30-34; 28:19,20. The timing necessary in agriculture can be applied to the general laying hold of life's opportunities.

10:6 violence. See 10:13; 12:13; 14:3; 18:6,7. The violence which has gone forth from the wicked, later falls back upon his foul mouth (cf. Hab. 2:17; Mal 2:16).

10:7 memory...name. This refers to the way a righteous person is remembered by man and God after his death.

10:8 receive commands. To finish the parallelism, the wise listens and is teachable and, therefore, will be lifted up. The fool, always talking, falls because he rejects God's commands.

9 [l]He who walks with integrity walks
securely,
But he who perverts his ways will
become known.

10 He who winks with the eye causes
trouble,
But a prating fool will fall.

11 The mouth of the righteous *is* a
well of life,
But violence covers the mouth of
the wicked.

12 Hatred stirs up strife,
But [m]love covers all sins.

13 Wisdom is found on the lips of him
who has understanding,
But [n]a rod *is* for the back of him
who [3]is devoid of
understanding.

14 Wise *people* store up knowledge,
But [o]the mouth of the foolish *is*
near destruction.

15 The [p]rich man's wealth *is* his
strong city;
The destruction of the poor *is* their
poverty.

16 The labor of the righteous *leads* to
[q]life,
The wages of the wicked to sin.

17 He who keeps instruction *is in* the
way of life,
But he who refuses correction
[4]goes astray.

18 Whoever [r]hides hatred *has* lying
lips,
And [s]whoever spreads slander *is* a
fool.

19 [t]In the multitude of words sin is not
lacking,
But [u]he who restrains his lips *is*
wise.

20 The tongue of the righteous *is*
choice silver;
The heart of the wicked *is worth*
little.

21 The lips of the righteous feed
many,
But fools die for lack of [5]wisdom.

22 [v]The blessing of the LORD makes *one*
rich,
And He adds no sorrow with it.

23 [w]To do evil *is* like sport to a fool,
But a man of understanding has
wisdom.

24 [x]The fear of the wicked will come
upon him,
And [y]the desire of the righteous
will be granted.

25 When the whirlwind passes by,
[z]the wicked *is* no *more,*
But [a]the righteous *has* an
everlasting foundation.

26 As vinegar to the teeth and smoke
to the eyes,

9 [l] [Ps. 23:4; Prov. 3:23; 28:18; Is. 33:15, 16]
12 [m] Prov. 17:9; [1 Cor. 13:4-7; James 5:20]; 1 Pet. 4:8
13 [n] Prov. 26:3 [3] Lit. *lacks heart*
14 [o] Prov. 18:7
15 [p] Job 31:24; Ps. 52:7; Prov. 18:11; [1 Tim. 6:17]
16 [q] Prov. 6:23
17 [4] *leads*
18 [r] Prov. 26:24 [s] Ps. 15:3; 101:5
19 [t] Job 11:2; [Prov. 18:21]; Eccl. 5:3 [u] Prov. 17:27; [James 1:19; 3:2]
21 [5] Lit. *heart*
22 [v] Gen. 24:35; 26:12; Deut. 8:18; Ps. 37:22; Prov. 8:21
23 [w] Prov. 2:14; 15:21
24 [x] Job 15:21; Prov. 1:27; Is. 66:4 [y] Ps. 145:19; Prov. 15:8; Matt. 5:6; [1 John 5:14, 15]
25 [z] Ps. 37:9, 10 [a] Ps. 15:5; Prov. 12:3; Matt. 7:24, 25

10:9 Those who have integrity (who live what they believe) exist without fear of some evil being discovered, while those who are perverse and have secret wickedness will not be able to hide it. Cf. 11:3; 19:1; 20:7.

10:10 winks with the eye. See 6:13,14.

10:11 well of life. The Lord is the source of this fountain (Ps. 36:9), which then springs up in the wise man as wise speech (10:11), wise laws (13:14), the fear of the Lord (12:27), and understanding (16:22). *See notes on 3:18; Ezek. 47:1-12; John 4:14; 7:38,39.* **violence.** *See note on 10:6.*

10:12 love. True love seeks the highest good for another (cf. 1 Cor. 14:4-7). First Peter 4:8 quotes this verse.

10:13 rod. This first reference to corporal punishment applied to the backside (cf. 19:29; 26:3) recommends it as the most effective way of dealing with children and fools. See also 13:24; 18:6; 19:29; 22:15; 23:13,14; 26:3; 29:15.

10:14 mouth of the foolish. The loose tongue of the fool is a recurring subject in Proverbs (cf. vv. 6,8,13,18,19,31,32; 12:23; 13:3; 15:1,2,23,26,28,31-33; 17:28; 18:2,6-8). James parallels this emphasis concerning the tongue (James 1:26; 3:1-12).

10:15 rich man's...poor. While the rich man thinks he has his walled city for protection (cf. 18:11; 28:11), the poor man knows he has nothing. Both should trust in the Lord as their only protection (cf. 3:5,6; 11:4,28; 18:10,11; Ps. 20:7; Eccl. 9:11-18; James 5:1-6).

10:16 wages. The industry alone of the righteous makes him truly successful, while the earnings of the wicked provide more opportunities for sinning.

10:18 hatred...slander. Both the harboring and venting of hatred are wrong and will be punished. Slander (gossip or lies) is forbidden (cf. 25:10; also 16:28; 18:8; 20:19; 26:20,22).

10:19 Wisdom is to restrain the tongue, since much speech risks sin. Cf. Ps. 39:1; James 1:26; 3:2-8.

10:20 tongue...heart. These words are used as parallel terms because they are inseparably linked. Cf. Matt. 15:18,19. **choice silver.** Good words are scarce, precious, and valuable (cf. 15:23; Is. 50:4).

10:21 feed...die. Sound teaching benefits many; the fool starves himself to death spiritually by his lack of wise teaching (cf. Hos 4:6).

10:22 rich. While having more than one needs is not the object of wisdom, it is generally the result (cf. Deut. 6:11-15;1 Kin. 3:10-14). See Introduction: Historical and Theological Themes. **no sorrow.** None of the sorrow that is associated with ill-gotten wealth (cf. 13:11; 15:6; 16:19; 21:6; 28:6) is associated with wealth provided by the Lord.

10:24 fear of the wicked. The righteous receive what they desire, while the wicked receive what they fear (cf. Heb. 10:26-29).

10:25 whirlwind. See 1:27; 6:15; 29:1.

So *is* the lazy *man* to those who
send him.

27 [b]The fear of the LORD prolongs days,
But [c]the years of the wicked will
be shortened.

28 The hope of the righteous *will be*
gladness,
But the [d]expectation of the wicked
will perish.

29 The way of the LORD *is* strength for
the upright,
But [e]destruction *will come* to the
workers of iniquity.

30 [f]The righteous will never be
removed,
But the wicked will not inhabit the
[6]earth.

31 [g]The mouth of the righteous brings
forth wisdom,
But the perverse tongue will be cut
out.

32 The lips of the righteous know
what is acceptable,
But the mouth of the wicked *what*
is perverse.

11 Dishonest[a1] scales *are* an
abomination to the LORD,
But a [2]just weight *is* His delight.

2 When pride comes, then comes
[b]shame;
But with the humble *is* wisdom.

3 The integrity of the upright will
guide [c]them,
But the perversity of the unfaithful
will destroy them.

4 [d]Riches do not profit in the day of
wrath,
But [e]righteousness delivers from
death.

5 The righteousness of the blameless
will [3]direct his way aright,
But the wicked will fall by his own
[f]wickedness.

6 The righteousness of the upright
will deliver them,
But the unfaithful will be caught
by *their* lust.

7 When a wicked man dies, *his*
expectation will [g]perish,
And the hope of the unjust
perishes.

8 [h]The righteous is delivered from
trouble,
And it comes to the wicked
instead.

9 The hypocrite with *his* mouth
destroys his neighbor,
But through knowledge the
righteous will be delivered.

10 [i]When it goes well with the
righteous, the city rejoices;
And when the wicked perish, *there*
is jubilation.

11 By the blessing of the upright the
city is [j]exalted,
But it is overthrown by the mouth
of the wicked.

12 He who [4]is devoid of wisdom
despises his neighbor,
But a man of understanding holds
his peace.

13 [k]A talebearer reveals secrets,
But he who is of a faithful spirit
[l]conceals a matter.

14 [m]Where *there is* no counsel, the
people fall;
But in the multitude of counselors
there is safety.

15 He who is [n]surety[5] for a stranger
will suffer,
But one who hates [6]being surety is
secure.

27 [b] Prov. 9:11 [c] Job 15:32
28 [d] Job 8:13
29 [e] Ps. 1:6
30 [f] Ps. 37:22; Prov. 2:21 [6] *land*
31 [g] Ps. 37:30; Prov. 10:13

CHAPTER 11

1 [a] Lev. 19:35, 36; Deut. 25:13-16; Prov. 20:10, 23; Mic. 6:11 [1] *deceptive* [2] Lit. *perfect stone*
2 [b] Prov. 16:18; 18:12; 29:23
3 [c] Prov. 13:6
4 [d] Prov. 10:2; Ezek. 7:19; Zeph. 1:18 [e] Gen. 7:1
5 [3] Or *make smooth or straight* [f] Prov. 5:22
7 [g] Prov. 10:28
8 [h] Prov. 21:18
10 [i] Prov. 28:12
11 [j] Prov. 14:34
12 [4] Lit. *lacks heart*
13 [k] Lev. 19:16; Prov. 20:19; 1 Tim. 5:13 [l] Prov. 19:11
14 [m] 1 Kin. 12:1
15 [n] Prov. 6:1, 2 [5] *guaranty* [6] *those pledging guaranty*, lit. *those who strike hands*

10:27 fear of the LORD. *See note on 1:7.*

10:29 The way of the LORD. This is the spiritual path in which God directs man to walk (*see note on Acts 18:25*).

10:30 Cf. Ps. 37:9-11.

11:1 Dishonest scales. Cf. 16:11; 20:10,23. As indicated in Lev. 19:35,36; Deut. 25:13-16; Ezek. 45:10; Amos 8:5; Mic. 6:10, God detests dishonesty.

11:2 pride. From a root meaning "to boil," or "to run over," indicating an overwhelmingly arrogant attitude or behavior. It is used of ordinary men (Deut. 17:12,13); kings (Neh. 9:10); Israel (Neh. 9:16,29); false prophets (Deut. 18:20); and murderers (Ex. 21:14). **the humble.** A rare word, which appears in Mic. 6:8: "walk humbly with your God." This humble and teachable spirit is first of all directed toward God (cf. 15:33; 16:18,19; 18:12; 22:4).

11:4 day of wrath. Money buys no escape from death in the day of final accounting to God, the divine Judge (cf. Is. 10:3; Ezek. 7:19; Zeph. 1:18; Luke 12:16-21).

11:11 Social influence for good or bad is in view.

11:12 despises. Lit. one who gossips, slanders, or destroys with words, in contrast to the silence of the wise. *See notes on 10:14,18.*

11:13 talebearer. This depicts someone who is a peddler in scandal, who speaks words deliberately intended to harm rather than merely unguarded speech (cf. Lev. 19:16).

11:14 multitude of counselors. As in 15:22; 20:18; 24:6, a good decision is made with multiple wise advisers. The more crucial the decision, the more appropriate is corporate wisdom. Note the example of David (2 Sam. 15:30–17:23).

11:15 *See note on 6:1.*

16 A gracious woman retains honor,
But ruthless *men* retain riches.
17 [o]The merciful man does good for his own soul,
But *he who is* cruel troubles his own flesh.
18 The wicked *man* does deceptive work,
But [p]he who sows righteousness *will have* a sure reward.
19 As righteousness *leads* to [q]life,
So he who pursues evil *pursues it* to his own [r]death.
20 Those who are of a perverse heart *are* an abomination to the LORD,
But *the* blameless in their ways *are* His delight.
21 [s]*Though they join* [7]forces, the wicked will not go unpunished;
But [t]the posterity of the righteous will be delivered.

22 *As* a ring of gold in a swine's snout,
So is a lovely woman who lacks [8]discretion.

23 The desire of the righteous *is* only good,
But the expectation of the wicked [u]*is* wrath.

24 There is *one* who [v]scatters, yet increases more;
And there is *one* who withholds more than is right,
But it *leads* to poverty.
25 [w]The generous soul will be made rich,
[x]And he who waters will also be watered himself.

26 The people will curse [y]him who withholds grain,
But [z]blessing *will be* on the head of him who sells *it*.

27 He who earnestly seeks good [9]finds favor,
[a]But trouble will come to him who seeks *evil*.

28 [b]He who trusts in his riches will fall,
But [c]the righteous will flourish like foliage.

29 He who troubles his own house [d]will inherit the wind,
And the fool *will be* [e]servant to the wise of heart.

30 The fruit of the righteous *is a* tree of life,
And [f]he who [1]wins souls *is* wise.

31 [g]If the righteous will be [2]recompensed on the earth,
How much more the ungodly and the sinner.

12

Whoever loves instruction loves knowledge,
But he who hates correction *is* stupid.

2 A good *man* obtains favor from the LORD,
But a man of wicked intentions He will condemn.

3 A man is not established by wickedness,
But the [a]root of the righteous cannot be moved.

17 [o] [Matt. 5:7; 25:34-36]
18 [p] Hos. 10:12; [Gal. 6:8, 9]; James 3:18
19 [q] Prov. 10:16; 12:28 [r] Prov. 21:16; [Rom. 6:23; James 1:15]
21 [s] Prov. 16:5 [t] Ps. 112:2; Prov. 14:26 [7] Lit. *hand to hand*
22 [8] *taste*
23 [u] Prov. 10:28; Rom. 2:8, 9
24 [v] Ps. 112:9; Prov. 13:7; 19:17
25 [w] Prov. 3:9, 10; [2 Cor. 9:6, 7] [x] [Matt. 5:7]
26 [y] Amos 8:5, 6 [z] Job 29:13
27 [a] Esth. 7:10; Ps. 7:15, 16; 57:6 [9] Lit. *seeks*
28 [b] Job 31:24 [c] Ps. 1:3; Jer. 17:8
29 [d] Eccl. 5:16 [e] Prov. 14:19
30 [f] Prov. 14:25; [Dan. 12:3; 1 Cor. 9:19-22; James 5:20] [1] Lit. *takes,* in the sense of *brings,* cf. 1 Sam. 16:11
31 [g] Jer. 25:29 [2] *rewarded*

CHAPTER 12
3 [a] [Prov. 10:25]

11:16 gracious woman...ruthless *men*. While evil men may grasp at wealth, they will never attain the honor due a gracious woman (cf. 31:30).

11:18 deceptive work. The efforts of the wicked deceiver do not yield the riches his deception seeks, but the righteous receive a reward from God.

11:20 abomination. Defined throughout Scripture as attitudes, this involves words and behaviors which God hates (see 6:16).

11:21 *Though they join* forces. The combined power of the wicked cannot free them from just punishment, while the unaided children of the righteous find deliverance by reason of their relationship with God.

11:22 ring of gold. A nose ring was an ornament intended to beautify a woman in OT times (cf. Gen. 24:47; Is. 3:21; Ezek. 16:12). It was as out of place in a pig's nose as the lack of discretion was in a lovely lady.

11:23 desire...expectation. These terms refer to outcomes from God's perspective.

11:24-26 scatters, yet increases. The principle here is that generosity, by God's blessing, secures increase, while stinginess leads to poverty instead of expected gain. The one who gives receives far more in return (Ps. 112:9; Eccl. 11:1; John 12:24,25; Acts 20:35; 2 Cor. 9:6-9).

11:28 trusts in his riches. Cf. 23:4,5; *see notes on 1 Tim. 6:17,19.*

11:29 inherit the wind. The one who mismanages his house will see all he has blown away, and he will have nothing left in the end. He will serve the one who manages well (15:27).

11:30 tree of life. *See note on 3:18.* **wins souls.** Lit. "to take lives," in the sense of doing them good or influencing them with wisdom's ways (cf. Luke 5:10). The word is also used for capturing people for evil purposes as in 6:25; Ps. 31:13; Ezek. 13:18.

11:31 recompensed. God's final blessing and reward to the "righteous," and His judgment and punishment of the "ungodly and sinners" come after life on this earth has ended. But there are foretastes of both during life on the earth, as the righteous experience God's personal care and goodness, while the wicked are void of it.

12:1 stupid. From the Heb. "to graze"; he is as stupid as the brute cattle (cf. Pss. 49:20; 73:22).

12:3 root. The familiar image is of the righteous being firm like a flourishing tree (Ps. 1; Jer. 17:7,8).

4 [b]An [1]excellent wife *is* the crown of
her husband,
But she who causes shame *is* [c]like
rottenness in his bones.

5 The thoughts of the righteous *are*
right,
But the counsels of the wicked *are*
deceitful.
6 [d]The words of the wicked *are*, "Lie
in wait for blood,"
[e]But the mouth of the upright will
deliver them.

7 [f]The wicked are overthrown and *are*
no more,
But the house of the righteous will
stand.

8 A man will be commended
according to his wisdom,
[g]But he who is of a perverse heart
will be despised.

9 [h]Better *is the one* who is [2]slighted
but has a servant,
Than he who honors himself but
lacks bread.

10 [i]A righteous *man* regards the life of
his animal,
But the tender mercies of the
wicked *are* cruel.

11 [j]He who [3]tills his land will be
satisfied with [k]bread,
But he who follows [4]frivolity [l]*is*
devoid of [5]understanding.

12 The wicked covet the catch of evil
men,
But the root of the righteous yields
fruit.
13 [m]The wicked is ensnared by the
transgression of *his* lips,
[n]But the righteous will come
through trouble.
14 [o]A man will be satisfied with good
by the fruit of *his* mouth,
[p]And the recompense of a man's
hands will be rendered to him.

15 [q]The way of a fool *is* right in his
own eyes,
But he who heeds counsel *is* wise.
16 [r]A fool's wrath is known at once,
But a prudent *man* covers shame.

17 [s]He *who* speaks truth declares
righteousness,
But a false witness, deceit.
18 [t]There is one who speaks like the
piercings of a sword,
But the tongue of the wise *promotes*
health.
19 The truthful lip shall be established
forever,
[u]But a lying tongue *is* but for a
moment.
20 Deceit is in the heart of those who
devise evil,
But counselors of peace have joy.
21 [v]No grave [6]trouble will overtake
the righteous,
But the wicked shall be filled with
evil.
22 [w]Lying lips *are* an abomination to
the LORD,
But those who deal truthfully *are*
His delight.

23 [x]A prudent man conceals
knowledge,

4 [b] Prov. 31:23; 1 Cor. 11:7 [c] Prov. 14:30; Hab. 3:16 [1] Lit. *A wife of valor*
6 [d] Prov. 1:11, 18 [e] Prov. 14:3
7 [f] Ps. 37:35-37; Prov. 11:21; Matt. 7:24-27
8 [g] 1 Sam. 25:17; Prov. 18:3
9 [h] Prov. 13:7 [2] *lightly esteemed*
10 [i] Deut. 25:4
11 [j] Gen. 3:19 [k] Prov. 28:19 [l] Prov. 6:32 [3] *works or cultivates* [4] Lit. *vain things* [5] Lit. *heart*
13 [m] Prov. 18:7 [n] [2 Pet. 2:9]
14 [o] Prov. 13:2; 15:23; 18:20 [p] Job 34:11; Prov. 1:31; 24:12; [Is. 3:10, 11]; Hos. 4:9
15 [q] Prov. 3:7; Luke 18:11
16 [r] Prov. 11:13; 29:11
17 [s] Prov. 14:5
18 [t] Ps. 57:4; Prov. 4:22; 15:4
19 [u] [Ps. 52:4, 5]; Prov. 19:9
21 [v] Ps. 91:10; Prov. 1:33; 1 Pet. 3:13 [6] *harm*
22 [w] Prov. 6:17; 11:20; Rev. 22:15
23 [x] Prov. 13:16

12:4 excellent wife. *See notes on 31:10; Ruth 3:11.* For the opposite see 19:13; 21:9,19; 25:24; 27:15. **rottenness in his bones.** This speaks of suffering that is like a painful and incurable condition.

12:6 Lie in wait. *See notes on 1:11,12.*

12:7 house. The rewards of wise living are not only to individuals, but extend to one's household or family.

12:9 Better…than. This is the first of several proverbs which makes a distinct comparison using "better…than" (cf. 15:16,17; 16:8,19,32; 17:1,12; 19:1; 21:9,19; 25:7,24; 27:5,10; 28:6). **slighted…honors himself.** The obscure one of lowly rank, who can at least afford to hire a servant because of his honest gain is better than the one who falsely boasts about his prominence but is really poor.

12:10 regards…cruel. Lit. he has concern for the condition of his beast, while the wicked has no concern for people.

12:11 frivolity. Energy expended in worthless pursuits and fantasies is as useless as outright laziness. *See notes on 6:6-11; 20:4; 24:30-34.*

12:12 covet the catch. This refers to the desire for booty gained by the schemes of the wicked, contrasted with a simple life of obedience that produces blessing.

12:14 fruit of *his* mouth. This deals with the power of words; the reward of wise words is like the reward for physical labor (cf. 10:11; 15:4; 18:4).

12:16 covers shame. A model of self-control, the prudent man ignores an insult (cf. 9:7; 10:12).

12:17 speaks truth. In the court, the truthful witness promotes justice.

12:18 speaks…piercings. The contrast here is between cutting words that are "blurted out"(Ps. 106:33) and thoughtful words that bring health. Cf. Eph. 4:29,30.

12:20 Deceit. The contrasting parallel is implied, not stated. Those who plan evil by deceit have no joy because of the risks and dangers in their plan, but the righteous who lead by peace fear nothing, and thus have joy.

12:23 conceals. Unlike the fool who makes all hear his folly, the wise person is a model of restraint and humility, speaking what he knows at an appropriate time (cf. 29:11). *See notes on 1:4; 10:14.*

But the heart of fools proclaims
foolishness.

24 [y]The hand of the diligent will rule,
But the lazy *man* will be put to
forced labor.

25 [z]Anxiety in the heart of man causes
depression,
But [a]a good word makes it glad.

26 The righteous should choose his
friends carefully,
For the way of the wicked leads
them astray.

27 The lazy *man* does not roast what
he took in hunting,
But diligence *is* man's precious
possession.

28 In the way of righteousness *is* life,
And in *its* pathway *there is* no
death.

13 A wise son *heeds* his father's
instruction,
[a]But a scoffer does not listen to
rebuke.

2 [b]A man shall eat well by the fruit of
his mouth,
But the soul of the unfaithful feeds
on violence.

3 [c]He who guards his mouth
preserves his life,
But he who opens wide his lips
shall have destruction.

4 [d]The soul of a lazy *man* desires, and
has nothing;
But the soul of the diligent shall be
made rich.

5 A righteous *man* hates lying,
But a wicked *man* is loathsome and
comes to shame.

6 [e]Righteousness guards *him whose*
way is blameless,
But wickedness overthrows the
sinner.

7 [f]There is one who makes himself
rich, yet *has* nothing;
And one who makes himself poor,
yet *has* great riches.

8 The ransom of a man's life *is* his
riches,
But the poor does not hear rebuke.

9 The light of the righteous rejoices,
[g]But the lamp of the wicked will be
put out.

10 By pride comes nothing but [h]strife,
But with the well-advised *is*
wisdom.

11 [i]Wealth *gained by* dishonesty will be
diminished,
But he who gathers by labor will
increase.

12 Hope deferred makes the heart
sick,
But [j]*when* the desire comes, *it is* a
tree of life.

13 He who [k]despises the word will be
destroyed,
But he who fears the
commandment will be
rewarded.

14 [l]The law of the wise *is* a fountain of
life,
To turn *one* away from [m]the snares
of death.

15 Good understanding [1]gains [n]favor,
But the way of the unfaithful *is*
hard.

16 [o]Every prudent *man* acts with
knowledge,

24 [y] Prov. 10:4
25 [z] Prov. 15:13 [a] Is. 50:4

CHAPTER 13

1 [a] Is. 28:14, 15
2 [b] Prov. 12:14
3 [c] Ps. 39:1; Prov. 21:23; [James 3:2]
4 [d] Prov. 10:4
6 [e] Prov. 11:3, 5, 6
7 [f] [Prov. 11:24; 12:9; Luke 12:20, 21]
9 [g] Job 18:5, 6; 21:17; Prov. 24:20
10 [h] Prov. 10:12
11 [i] Prov. 10:2; 20:21
12 [j] Prov. 13:19
13 [k] Num. 15:31; 2 Chr. 36:16; Is. 5:24
14 [l] Prov. 6:22; 10:11; 14:27 [m] 2 Sam. 22:6
15 [n] Ps. 111:10; Prov. 3:4 [1] *gives*
16 [o] Prov. 12:23

12:24 forced labor. Unlike the hardworking people who have charge over their work, the lazy are eventually forced to go to work for the diligent to survive.

12:26 astray. Cf. 1 Cor. 15:33. This verse could be understood as saying that the righteous "guides" his friends carefully, unlike the wicked who leads his companions astray.

12:27 does not roast. The sluggard lacks commitment to make something of his opportunities (cf. vv. 11,25).

13:2,3 The parallels here are implied. A man of good words prospers, but a man of evil words (thus unfruitful to God) provokes violence against himself.

13:4 *See notes on 6:6,11.*

13:7 makes himself rich...makes himself poor. The same pretense is presented in two contrasting weaknesses; one pretends to be rich while the other pretends to be poor. In contrast, men should be honest and unpretentious (cf. 11:24; 2 Cor 6:10).

13:8 ransom...riches...poor...rebuke. Riches deliver some from punishment, while others suffer, because they will not heed the rebuke of laziness, which keeps them poor.

13:9 light...lamp. This image of life, prosperity, and joy is contrasted with adversity and death (cf. Job 3:20).

13:10 The proud spurn advice from others; the wise accept it.

13:11 Cf. 20:21.

13:12 tree of life. *See note on 3:18.*

13:13 word...commandment. These terms refer to divine revelation.

13:14 fountain of life. The same Heb. word for "well of life." *See note on 10:11.*

But a fool lays open *his* folly.

17 A wicked messenger falls into
trouble,
But [p]a faithful ambassador *brings*
health.

18 Poverty and shame *will come* to
him who [2]disdains correction,
But [q]he who regards a rebuke will
be honored.

19 A desire accomplished is sweet to
the soul,
But *it is* an abomination to fools to
depart from evil.

20 He who walks with wise *men* will
be wise,
But the companion of fools will be
destroyed.

21 [r]Evil pursues sinners,
But to the righteous, good shall be
repaid.

22 A good *man* leaves an inheritance
to his children's children,
But [s]the wealth of the sinner is
stored up for the righteous.

23 [t]Much food *is in* the [3]fallow *ground*
of the poor,
And for lack of justice there is
[4]waste.

24 [u]He who spares his rod hates his
son,
But he who loves him disciplines
him [5]promptly.

25 [v]The righteous eats to the satisfying
of his soul,
But the stomach of the wicked
shall be in want.

14

The wise woman builds her house,
But the foolish pulls it down with
her hands.

2 He who walks in his uprightness
fears the LORD,
[a]But *he who is* perverse in his ways
despises Him.

3 In the mouth of a fool *is* a rod of
pride,
[b]But the lips of the wise will
preserve them.

4 Where no oxen *are*, the [1]trough *is*
clean;
But much increase *comes* by the
strength of an ox.

5 A [c]faithful witness does not lie,
But a false witness will utter [d]lies.

6 A scoffer seeks wisdom and does
not *find it*,
But [e]knowledge *is* easy to him who
understands.

7 Go from the presence of a foolish
man,
When you do not perceive *in him*
the lips of [f]knowledge.

8 The wisdom of the prudent *is* to
understand his way,
But the folly of fools *is* deceit.

9 [g]Fools mock at [2]sin,
But among the upright *there is*
favor.

17 [p] Prov. 25:13
18 [q] Prov. 15:5, 31, 32 [2] Lit. *ignores*
21 [r] Ps. 32:10; Is. 47:11
22 [s] Job 27:16, 17; Prov. 28:8; [Eccl. 2:26]
23 [t] Prov. 12:11 [3] *uncultivated* [4] Lit. *what is swept away*
24 [u] Prov. 19:18 [5] *early*
25 [v] Ps. 34:10; Prov. 10:3

CHAPTER 14

2 [a] [Rom. 2:4]
3 [b] Prov. 12:6
4 [1] *manger or feed trough*
5 [c] Rev. 1:5; 3:14 [d] Ex. 23:1; Deut. 19:16; Prov. 6:19; 12:17
6 [e] Prov. 8:9; 17:24
7 [f] Prov. 23:9
9 [g] Prov. 10:23 [2] Lit. *guilt*

13:16 lays open. The language vividly shows that a fool displays folly, like a peddler openly spreads out his wares for others to gaze upon. Cf. 12:23; 15:2.

13:19 The fool's relentless pursuit of evil and hatred of good does not ever let him taste the sweet blessings of obedience.

13:20 walks...companion. This speaks of the power of association to shape character. Cf. 1:10,18; 2:12; 4:14; 16:29; 22:24,25; 23:20; 28:7,19; Ps. 1.

13:21 This is a basic theme/general principle throughout Proverbs and is illustrated throughout the OT, which establishes that righteousness brings divine blessing and evil brings divine cursing.

13:22 leaves an inheritance. While good men's estates remain with their families, the wealth of the wicked does not. In the providence of God, it will ultimately belong to the righteous. Cf. 28:8; Job 27:16,17.

13:23 lack of justice. The contrast here is between the poor, but industrious, man who will be rewarded with provision from his efforts, and the rich man whose efforts are brought to ruin by his deeds of injustice (cf. James 5:1-6).

13:24 rod...disciplines...promptly. Early childhood teaching (*see note on 22:6*) requires both parental discipline, including corporal punishment (cf. 10:13; 19:18; 22:15; 29:15,17), and balanced kindness and love. There is great hope that the use of the "divine ordinance" of the rod will produce godly virtue (cf. 23:13,14) and parental joy (cf. 10:1; 15:20; 17:21; 23:15,16,24,25; 28:7; 29:1,15,17). Such discipline must have the right motivation (Heb. 12:5-11) and appropriate severity (Eph. 6:4). One who has genuine affection for his child, but withholds corporal punishment, will produce the same kind of child as a parent who hates his offspring.

13:25 This states more directly the teaching of vv. 13,18,21.

14:1 builds her house. Cf. the wise woman building her house (31:10-31) with lady wisdom building her house (9:1-6).

14:3 rod. A rare Heb. word that refers to a small shoot (see Is. 11:1). Here it is metaphoric for the proud, inflicting tongue in a fool's mouth, which destroys the fool and others (cf. 11:2; 16:18; 29:23).

14:7 Go. Avoid association with all who cannot teach you wisdom. Cf. 1 Tim 4:6,7; 6:3-5.

14:9 Fools mock at sin. While fools ridicule their impending judgment (cf. 1:26), the wise are promised favor with God (cf. Is. 1:11-20) and man (cf. 10:32; 11:27). Cf. 1 Sam. 2:26; Luke 2:40,52.

10 The heart knows its own bitterness,
And a stranger does not share its joy.

11 [h]The house of the wicked will be overthrown,
But the tent of the upright will flourish.

12 [i]There is a way *that seems* right to a man,
But [j]its end *is* the way of [k]death.

13 Even in laughter the heart may sorrow,
And [l]the end of mirth *may be* grief.

14 The backslider in heart will be [m]filled with his own ways,
But a good man *will be satisfied* [3]from [n]above.

15 The simple believes every word,
But the prudent considers well his steps.
16 [o]A wise *man* fears and departs from evil,
But a fool rages and is self-confident.
17 A quick-tempered *man* acts foolishly,
And a man of wicked intentions is hated.
18 The simple inherit folly,
But the prudent are crowned with knowledge.
19 The evil will bow before the good,
And the wicked at the gates of the righteous.

20 [p]The poor *man* is hated even by his own neighbor,
But [4]the rich *has* many [q]friends.

21 He who despises his neighbor sins;
[r]But he who has mercy on the poor, happy *is* he.

22 Do they not go astray who devise evil?
But mercy and truth *belong* to those who devise good.

23 In all labor there is profit,
But [5]idle chatter *leads* only to poverty.

24 The crown of the wise is their riches,
But the foolishness of fools *is* folly.

25 A true witness [6]delivers [s]souls,
But a deceitful *witness* speaks lies.

26 In the fear of the LORD *there is* strong confidence,
And His children will have a place of refuge.
27 [t]The fear of the LORD *is* a fountain of life,
To turn *one* away from the snares of death.

28 In a multitude of people *is* a king's honor,
But in the lack of people *is* the downfall of a prince.

29 [u]*He who is* slow to wrath has great understanding,
But *he who is* [7]impulsive exalts folly.

30 A sound heart *is* life to the body,
But [v]envy *is* [w]rottenness to the bones.

31 [x]He who oppresses the poor reproaches [y]his Maker,

11 [h]Job 8:15
12 [i]Prov. 16:25 [j]Rom. 6:21 [k]Prov. 12:15
13 [l]Prov. 5:4; Eccl. 2:1, 2
14 [m]Prov. 1:31; 12:15 [n]Prov. 13:2; 18:20 [3]Lit. *from above himself*
16 [o]Job 28:28; Ps. 34:14; Prov. 22:3
20 [p]Prov. 19:7 [q]Prov. 19:4 [4]Lit. *many are the lovers of the rich*
21 [r]Ps. 112:9; [Prov. 19:17]
23 [5]Lit. *talk of the lips*
25 [s][Ezek. 3:18-21] [6]*saves lives*
27 [t]Prov. 13:14
29 [u]Prov. 16:32; 19:11; Eccl. 7:9; James 1:19 [7]Lit. *short of spirit*
30 [v]Ps. 112:10 [w]Prov. 12:4; Hab. 3:16
31 [x]Prov. 17:5; Matt. 25:40; 1 John 3:17 [y][Job 31:15; Prov. 22:2]

14:10 At its depth, suffering and rejoicing are personal and private. No one is able to communicate them fully (1 Sam 1:10; 1 Kin. 8:38; Matt 2:18; 26:39-42,75).

14:12 way of death. *See notes on Matt. 7:13,14.*

14:14 backslider in heart. This term, so often used by the prophets (Is. 57:17; Jer. 3:6,8,11,12,14,32; 8:5; 31:22; 49:4; Hos. 11:7; 14:4), is here used in such a way as to clarify who is a backslider. He belongs in the category of the fool, the wicked, and the disobedient and he is contrasted with the godly wise. It is a word that the prophets used of apostate unbelievers.

14:17 quick-tempered...wicked intentions. The contrast is between the hasty anger that is labeled as folly and the deliberate malice which produces hatred (Ps. 37:7).

14:19 evil will bow. The ancient custom was for the inferior to prostrate himself before the superior or wait humbly before the great one's gate seeking favor. Good will humble evil.

14:20 This sad-but-true picture of human nature is not given approvingly, but only as a fact.

14:24 foolishness of fools *is* folly. This is emphatic language, playing on the word "fool" and showing that the only reward for fools is more folly.

14:25 The truth produces justice, on which the lives of people may depend.

14:26 fear of the LORD. *See note on 1:7.*

14:27 fountain of life. *See note on 10:11.*

14:28 multitude of people. This is a truism stating that a king's honor comes from the support of his people as they increase and prosper (cf. 30:29-31).

14:29 Cf. v. 17.

14:30 sound heart...body. A healthy mind filled with wisdom is associated with a healthy body (cf. 3:5-8; 17:22). **rottenness to the bones.** *See note on 12:4.*

14:31 oppresses the poor...Maker. It offends the Creator when one neglects the poor, who are part of His creation (cf. 14:21; 17:5; 19:17; 21:13; 22:2,7; 28:8; 29:13).

But he who honors Him has mercy
on the needy.

32 The wicked is banished in his
wickedness,
But [z]the righteous has a refuge in
his death.

33 Wisdom rests in the heart of him
who has understanding,
But [a]*what is* in the heart of fools is
made known.

34 Righteousness exalts a [b]nation,
But sin *is* a [8]reproach to *any* people.

35 [c]The king's favor *is* toward a wise
servant,
But his wrath *is against* him who
causes shame.

15 A [a]soft answer turns away wrath,
But [b]a harsh word stirs up anger.
2 The tongue of the wise uses
knowledge rightly,
[c]But the mouth of fools pours forth
foolishness.

3 [d]The eyes of the LORD *are* in every
place,
Keeping watch on the evil and the
good.

4 A [1]wholesome tongue *is* a tree of
life,
But perverseness in it breaks the
spirit.

5 [e]A fool despises his father's
instruction,
[f]But he who [2]receives correction is
prudent.

6 *In* the house of the righteous *there*
is much treasure,
But in the revenue of the wicked is
trouble.

7 The lips of the wise [3]disperse
knowledge,
But the heart of the fool *does* not *do*
so.

8 [g]The sacrifice of the wicked *is* an
abomination to the LORD,
But the prayer of the upright *is* His
delight.

9 The way of the wicked *is* an
abomination to the LORD,
But He loves him who [h]follows
righteousness.

10 [i]Harsh discipline *is* for him who
forsakes the way,
And [j]he who hates correction will
die.

11 [k]Hell[4] and [5]Destruction *are* before
the LORD;
So how much more [l]the hearts of
the sons of men.

12 [m]A scoffer does not love one who
corrects him,
Nor will he go to the wise.

13 [n]A merry heart makes a cheerful
[6]countenance,
But [o]by sorrow of the heart the
spirit is broken.

14 The heart of him who has
understanding seeks
knowledge,
But the mouth of fools feeds on
foolishness.

15 All the days of the afflicted *are* evil,
[p]But he who is of a merry heart *has*
a continual feast.

16 [q]Better *is* a little with the fear of the
LORD,
Than great treasure with trouble.

32 [z]Gen. 49:18; Job 13:15; [Ps. 16:11; 73:24]; 2 Cor. 1:9; 5:8; [2 Tim. 4:18]
33 [a]Prov. 12:16
34 [b]Prov. 11:11 [8]*shame* or *disgrace*
35 [c]Matt. 24:45-47

CHAPTER 15

1 [a]Prov. 25:15 [b]1 Sam. 25:10
2 [c]Prov. 12:23
3 [d]2 Chr. 16:9; Job 34:21; Prov. 5:21; Jer. 16:17; 32:19; Zech. 4:10; Heb. 4:13
4 [1]Lit. *healing*
5 [e]Prov. 10:1 [f]Prov. 13:18 [2]Lit. *keeps*
7 [3]*spread*
8 [g]Prov. 21:27; Eccl. 5:1; Is. 1:11; Jer. 6:20; Mic. 6:7
9 [h]Prov. 21:21
10 [i]1 Kin. 22:8 [j]Prov. 5:12
11 [k]Job 26:6; Ps. 139:8 [l]1 Sam. 16:7; 2 Chr. 6:30; Ps. 44:21; Acts 1:24 [4]Or *Sheol* [5]Heb. *Abaddon*
12 [m]Prov. 13:1; Amos 5:10; 2 Tim. 4:3
13 [n]Prov. 12:25 [o]Prov. 17:22 [6]*face*
15 [p]Prov. 17:22
16 [q]Ps. 37:16; Prov. 16:8; Eccl. 4:6; 1 Tim. 6:6

14:32 righteous…death. Cf. 23:18. Hope in death for the righteous is a central OT theme (cf. Job 19:25,26; Pss. 31:5; 49:14,15; 73:24; Eccl. 11:9; Is. 26:19; Dan. 12:1,2).

14:33 is made known. Wisdom is quietly preserved in the heart of the wise for the time of proper use, while fools are eager to blurt out their folly (cf. 12:23; 13:16; 15:2,14).

14:34 exalts. While just principles and actions preserve and even exalt a society, their absence shames a society (cf. 11:11).

14:35 causes shame. Cf. 10:5; 12:4.

15:2 *See note on 14:33.*

15:3 eyes of the LORD. Cf. 5:21. This refers to God's omniscience. Cf. 1 Sam 16:7; 2 Chr. 16:9; Job 24:23; Pss. 33:13-15; 139:1-16; Jer. 17:10.

15:4 tree of life. *See note on 3:18.* **breaks the spirit.** To crush or wound, thus to destroy one's morale (cf. Is. 65:14).

15:8 External acts of worship, though according to biblical prescription, are repulsive to God when the heart of the worshiper is wicked (cf. Is. 1:12-15; Amos 5:21; Mal. 1:11-14; Heb. 11:4,6).

15:10 the way. The way of truth and righteousness (see 2:13; 10:17).

15:11 Hell and Destruction. Cf. 27:20. Hell or Sheol is the place of the dead (*see note on 1:12*). "Destruction" refers to the experience of external punishment. Cf. Job 26:6.

15:13 Cf. v. 4.

15:15 continual feast. The joyous, inward condition of the wise man's heart (14:21) is described as a perpetual feast. Real happiness is always determined by the state of the heart (cf. Hab. 3:17,18; 1 Tim. 4:6-8).

15:16,17 *See note on 12:9* for other "better…than" references.

15:16 fear of the LORD. *See note on 1:7.*

17 [r]Better *is* a dinner of [7]herbs where
love is,
Than a fatted calf with hatred.

18 [s]A wrathful man stirs up strife,
But *he who is* slow to anger allays
contention.

19 [t]The way of the lazy *man is* like a
hedge of thorns,
But the way of the upright *is* a
highway.

20 [u]A wise son makes a father glad,
But a foolish man despises his
mother.

21 [v]Folly *is* joy *to him who is* destitute
of [8]discernment,
[w]But a man of understanding walks
uprightly.

22 [x]Without counsel, plans go awry,
But in the multitude of counselors
they are established.

23 A man has joy by the answer of his
mouth,
And [y]a word *spoken* [9]in due
season, how good *it is!*

24 [z]The way of life *winds* upward for
the wise,
That he may [a]turn away from [1]hell
below.

25 [b]The LORD will destroy the house of
the proud,
But [c]He will establish the
boundary of the widow.

26 [d]The thoughts of the wicked *are* an
abomination to the LORD,
[e]But *the words* of the pure *are*
pleasant.

27 [f]He who is greedy for gain troubles
his own house,
But he who hates bribes will live.

28 The heart of the righteous [g]studies
how to answer,
But the mouth of the wicked pours
forth evil.

29 [h]The LORD *is* far from the wicked,
But [i]He hears the prayer of the
righteous.

30 The light of the eyes rejoices the
heart,
And a good report makes the bones
[2]healthy.

31 The ear that hears the rebukes of life
Will abide among the wise.

32 He who disdains instruction
despises his own soul,
But he who heeds rebuke gets
understanding.

33 [j]The fear of the LORD *is* the
instruction of wisdom,
And [k]before honor *is* humility.

16

The [a]preparations[1] of the heart
belong to man,
[b]But the answer of the tongue *is*
from the LORD.

2 All the ways of a man *are* pure in
his own [c]eyes,
But the LORD weighs the spirits.

3 [d]Commit[2] your works to the LORD,
And your thoughts will be
established.

4 The [e]LORD has made all for Himself,

17 [r] Prov. 17:1 [7] Or *vegetables*
18 [s] Prov. 26:21
19 [t] Prov. 22:5
20 [u] Prov. 10:1
21 [v] Prov. 10:23 [w] Eph. 5:15 [8] Lit. *heart*
22 [x] Prov. 11:14
23 [y] Prov. 25:11; Is. 50:4 [9] Lit. *in its time*
24 [z] Phil. 3:20; [Col. 3:1, 2] [a] Prov. 14:16 [1] Or *Sheol*
25 [b] Prov. 12:7; Is. 2:11 [c] Ps. 68:5, 6
26 [d] Prov. 6:16, 18 [e] Ps. 37:30
27 [f] Is. 5:8; [Jer. 17:11]
28 [g] 1 Pet. 3:15
29 [h] Ps. 10:1; 34:16 [i] Ps. 145:18; [James 5:16]
30 [2] Lit. *fat*
33 [j] Prov. 1:7 [k] Prov. 18:12

CHAPTER 16
1 [a] Jer. 10:23 [b] Matt. 10:19 [1] *plans*
2 [c] Prov. 21:2
3 [d] Ps. 37:5; Prov. 3:6; [1 Pet. 5:7] [2] Lit. *Roll*
4 [e] Is. 43:7; Rom. 11:36

15:17 dinner of herbs. Vegetables are in view, the typical dinner of the poor.

15:18 "Hotheads" are contrasted with "peacemakers" (cf. 14:17,29; 15:1; 28:25; 29:11,22).

15:19 thorns. He is too lazy to remove them. *See notes on 6:6,11.*

15:22 *See note on 11:14.*

15:24 hell below. *See note on 1:12.*

15:25 When evil men try to take the property of widows, God will intervene (cf. 22:28; 23:10,11). The most desolate (widows) who have God's help possess a more permanent dwelling place than the prosperous and self-reliant sinners.

15:27 bribes. Cf. 18:5; 24:23; 29:4; Ex. 23:8; Deut. 16:19; Ecc. 7:7; Is. 1:23.

15:28 mouth...wicked pours forth. Wicked people don't guard their words. *See note on 12:23*; cf. Eph. 4:29.

15:30 light of the eyes. This is a comparison, so that the "good report" defines this term. Whatever is good, sound truth and wisdom stirs the heart by relieving anxiety and producing a cheerful face (cf. 14:30; 15:13; 17:22).

15:31 ear that hears...wise. The acquiring of wisdom demands a teachable spirit.

15:33 fear of the LORD. *See note on 1:7.*

16:1 preparations...answer. Human responsibility is always subject to God's absolute sovereignty (cf. 3:6; 16:2,9,33; 19:21; 20:24; 21:1,30,31).

16:2 spirits. While man can be self-deceived, God determines his true motives (cf. 21:2; 24:12; 1 Sam. 16:7; 1 Cor. 4:4).

16:3 Commit. Lit. "roll upon" in the sense of both total trust (3:5-6) and submission to the will of God (Pss. 22:8; 37:5; 119:133); He will fulfill your righteous plans.

16:4 The wicked will bring glory to God in the day of their judgment and eternal punishment. *See notes on Rom. 9:17-23.*

[f]Yes, even the wicked for the day of
[3]doom.

5 [g]Everyone proud in heart *is* an
abomination to the LORD;
Though they join [4]forces, none will
go unpunished.

6 [h]In mercy and truth
Atonement is provided for
iniquity;
And [i]by the fear of the LORD *one*
departs from evil.

7 When a man's ways please the
LORD,
He makes even his enemies to be
at peace with him.

8 [j]Better *is* a little with righteousness,
Than vast revenues without justice.

9 [k]A man's heart plans his way,
[l]But the LORD directs his steps.

10 Divination *is* on the lips of the
king;
His mouth must not transgress in
judgment.
11 [m]Honest weights and scales *are* the
LORD'S;
All the weights in the bag *are* His
[5]work.
12 *It is* an abomination for kings to
commit wickedness,
For [n]a throne is established by
righteousness.
13 [o]Righteous lips *are* the delight of
kings,
And they love him who speaks
what is right.
14 As messengers of death *is* the
king's wrath,
But a wise man will [p]appease it.
15 In the light of the king's face *is* life,
And his favor *is* like a [q]cloud of the
latter rain.

16 [r]How much better to get wisdom
than gold!
And to get understanding is to be
chosen rather than silver.
17 The highway of the upright *is* to
depart from evil;
He who keeps his way preserves
his soul.

18 Pride *goes* before destruction,
And a haughty spirit before [6]a fall.
19 Better *to be* of a humble spirit with
the lowly,
Than to divide the [7]spoil with the
proud.

20 He who heeds the word wisely
will find good,
And whoever [s]trusts in the LORD,
happy *is* he.

21 The wise in heart will be called
prudent,
And sweetness of the lips increases
learning.

22 Understanding *is* a wellspring of
life to him who has it.
But the correction of fools *is* folly.

23 The heart of the wise teaches his
mouth,
And adds learning to his lips.

24 Pleasant words *are like* a
honeycomb,

4 [f]Job 21:30; [Rom. 9:22] [3]Lit. *evil*
5 [g]Prov. 6:17; 8:13 [4]Lit. *hand to hand*
6 [h]Dan. 4:27; Luke 11:41 [i]Prov. 8:13; 14:16
8 [j]Ps. 37:16; Prov. 15:16
9 [k]Prov. 19:21 [l]Ps. 37:23; Prov. 20:24; Jer. 10:23
11 [m]Lev. 19:36 [5]*concern*
12 [n]Prov. 25:5
13 [o]Prov. 14:35
14 [p]Prov. 25:15
15 [q]Zech. 10:1
16 [r]Prov. 8:10, 11, 19
18 [6]*stumbling*
19 [7]*plunder*
20 [s]Ps. 34:8; Jer. 17:7

16:6 By God's "mercy and truth," He affects the "atonement" or covering of sin, which for the believing sinner inclines him to depart from evil. *See notes on Lev. 16:1-34; 17:11* for explanation of atonement. **fear of the LORD.** *See note on 1:7.*

16:7 This general rule does not preclude persecution from some. *See note on 2 Tim. 3:12.*

16:8 righteousness...justice. These words are synonyms here.

16:9 *See notes on vv. 1,2.* Sovereign God overrules the plans of men to fulfill His purposes. See Gen. 50:20; 1 Kin. 12:15; Ps. 119:133; Jer. 10:23; Dan. 5:23-30; 1 Cor. 3:19,20.

16:10 Divination. This does not imply any occultic practice forbidden in Lev. 19:26, but is literally a decision from divine wisdom, in the words of the king who represented God. The king was under mandate (Deut. 17:18-20) to seek out and speak God's wisdom (cf. David in 2 Sam. 14:17-20; Solomon in 1 Kin. 3:9-12; and Christ as King in Is. 11:2).

16:11 *See note on 11:1.*

16:12 *See note on 14:34.*

16:14 This points to the king's power of "life or death," which can be abused (cf. 1 Sam. 22:16-18; Esth. 7–10; Dan. 2:5) or used for good (cf. 2 Sam. 1:1-16; 4:5-12).

16:15 cloud of the latter rain. The late spring rain, which matured the crop, fell before the harvest (cf. 2 Sam. 23:3,4; Ps. 72:6) and is here compared to the king's power to grace his subjects with encouragement.

16:16 better. Cf. 3:13-16; 8:10,11,18,19.

16:17 A plain road represents the habitual course of the righteous in departing from evil. As long as he stays on it, he is safe.

16:19 The proud are those who have plundered the poor.

16:21 sweetness of the lips. "Honeyed words," which reflect intelligence, judiciousness, and discernment in speech. This refers to eloquent discourse from the wise (cf. v. 24).

16:22 wellspring of life. *See note on 10:11.* The advice of the understanding person brings blessing, while the correction offered by a fool is useless.

16:23 heart. *See note on 4:21-23.*

16:24 Pleasant words. *See note on v. 21*; cf. 24:13,14; Ps. 19:10.

Sweetness to the soul and health to
the bones.

25 There is a way *that seems* right to a
man,
But its end *is* the way of [t]death.

26 The person who labors, labors for
himself,
For his *hungry* mouth drives [u]him
on.

27 [8]An ungodly man digs up evil,
And *it is* on his lips like a burning
[v]fire.

28 A perverse man sows strife,
And [w]a whisperer separates the
best of friends.

29 A violent man entices his neighbor,
And leads him in a way *that is* not
good.

30 He winks his eye to devise
perverse things;
He [9]purses his lips *and* brings
about evil.

31 [x]The silver-haired head *is* a crown
of glory,
If it is found in the way of
righteousness.

32 [y]*He who is* slow to anger *is* better
than the mighty,
And he who rules his spirit than he
who takes a city.

33 The lot is cast into the lap,
But its every decision *is* from the
LORD.

17 Better *is* [a]a dry morsel with
quietness,
Than a house full of [1]feasting *with*
strife.

2 A wise servant will rule over [b]a
son who causes shame,
And will share an inheritance
among the brothers.

3 The refining pot *is* for silver and
the furnace for gold,
[c]But the LORD tests the hearts.

4 An evildoer gives heed to false
lips;
A liar listens eagerly to a [2]spiteful
tongue.

5 [d]He who mocks the poor reproaches
his Maker;
[e]He who is glad at calamity will not
go unpunished.

6 [f]Children's children *are* the crown
of old men,
And the glory of children *is* their
father.

7 Excellent speech is not becoming to
a fool,
Much less lying lips to a prince.

8 A present *is* a precious stone in the
eyes of its possessor;
Wherever he turns, he prospers.

9 [g]He who covers a transgression
seeks love,
But [h]he who repeats a matter
separates friends.

10 [i]Rebuke is more effective for a wise
man
Than a hundred blows on a fool.

25 [t] Prov. 14:12
26 [u] [Eccl. 6:7; John 6:35]
27 [v] [James 3:6] [8] Lit. *A man of Belial*
28 [w] Prov. 17:9
30 [9] Lit. *compresses*
31 [x] Prov. 20:29
32 [y] Prov. 14:29; 19:11

CHAPTER 17

1 [a] Prov. 15:17 [1] Or *sacrificial meals*
2 [b] Prov. 10:5
3 [c] 1 Chr. 29:17; Ps. 26:2; Prov. 15:11; Jer. 17:10; [Mal. 3:3]
4 [2] Lit. *destructive*
5 [d] Prov. 14:31 [e] Job 31:29; Prov. 24:17; Obad. 12; 1 Cor. 13:6
6 [f] [Ps. 127:3; 128:3]
9 [g] [Prov. 10:12; 1 Cor. 13:5-7; James 5:20] [h] Prov. 16:28
10 [i] Prov. 10:17; [Mic. 7:9]

16:25 way of death. Cf. 14:12.

16:26 labors for himself. Labor is hard and often grievous, but necessary, even for the lazy (cf. Eccl. 6:7; Eph. 4:28; 6:7; 2 Thess. 3:10-12).

16:27 ungodly man. *See note on 6:12.* He literally digs a pit for his neighbor as a hunter would for prey (cf. Pss. 7:15; 62:6), and his speech is incendiary (cf. James 3:6).

16:28 sows. The same root word is used for the release of flaming foxes in the grain fields of the Philistines (Judg. 15:4,5; cf. 17:9). **whisperer.** A slanderer or gossip. *See note on 6:14*; cf. 8:8; 26:20,22 for the same Heb. term.

16:30 purses. The idea of winking or squinting the eyes and compressing one's lips was to express the posture connoting deep thought and determined purpose.

16:31 This calls for respecting elders. Cf. 20:29.

16:32 slow to anger. *See notes on 14:17; 25:28.* Cf. Eccl. 9:17,18; James 1:19,20.

16:33 lot. *See note on 16:1.* Casting lots was a method often used to reveal God's purposes in a matter (cf. Josh. 14:1,2; 1 Sam. 14:38-43; 1 Chr. 25:8-31; Jon. 1:7; Acts 1:26). The High-Priest may have carried lots in his sacred vest, along with the Urim and Thummim (*see note on Ex. 28:30*).

17:1 Cf. 15:17.

17:2 wise servant...inheritance. A faithful servant will rise above an unworthy son and receive an inheritance (cf. 11:29; 1 Kin. 11:26,28-38; Matt. 8:11,12).

17:3 refining pot. This was a heated crucible used to test and refine precious metal. Cf. Ps. 66:10; Is. 1:25; 48:10; Jer. 6:29; Ezek. 22:17-22; Dan 12:10; Mal. 3:3.

17:5 Cf. 14:21,31.

17:6 Children's children. Godly influence generates mutual love and respect in a family, which extends from generation to generation (cf. Ps. 90 with Ex. 20:12).

17:8 present. This refers to a bribe that brings prosperity to its recipient (v. 23; 15:27).

17:9 Cf. 16:28; 18:8.

17:10 For the theme of a teachable spirit, cf. 9:7,8; 15:31-33.

11 An evil *man* seeks only rebellion;
Therefore a cruel messenger will be sent against him.

12 Let a man meet [j]a bear robbed of her cubs,
Rather than a fool in his folly.

13 Whoever [k]rewards evil for good,
Evil will not depart from his house.

14 The beginning of strife *is like* releasing water;
Therefore [l]stop contention before a quarrel starts.

15 [m]He who justifies the wicked, and he who condemns the just,
Both of them alike *are* an abomination to the LORD.

16 Why *is there* in the hand of a fool the purchase price of wisdom,
Since *he has* no heart *for it?*

17 [n]A friend loves at all times,
And a brother is born for adversity.

18 [o]A man devoid of [3]understanding [4]shakes hands in a pledge,
And becomes [5]surety for his friend.

19 He who loves transgression loves strife,
And [p]he who exalts his gate seeks destruction.

20 He who has a [6]deceitful heart finds no good,
And he who has [q]a perverse tongue falls into evil.

21 He who begets a scoffer *does so* to his sorrow,
And the father of a fool has no joy.

22 A [r]merry heart [7]does good, *like* medicine,
But a broken spirit dries the bones.

23 A wicked *man* accepts a bribe [8]behind the back
To pervert the ways of justice.

24 [s]Wisdom *is* in the sight of him who has understanding,
But the eyes of a fool *are* on the ends of the earth.

25 A [t]foolish son *is* a grief to his father,
And bitterness to her who bore him.

26 Also, to punish the righteous *is* not good,
Nor to strike princes for *their* uprightness.

27 [u]He who has knowledge spares his words,
And a man of understanding is of a calm spirit.

28 [v]Even a fool is counted wise when he holds his peace;
When he shuts his lips, *he is considered* perceptive.

18 A man who isolates himself seeks his own desire;
He rages against all [1]wise judgment.

2 A fool has no delight in understanding,
But in expressing his [a]own heart.

12 [j] 2 Sam. 17:8; Hos. 13:8
13 [k] Ps. 109:4, 5; Jer. 18:20; Rom. 12:17; 1 Thess. 5:15; [1 Pet. 3:9]
14 [l] [Prov. 20:3; 1 Thess. 4:11]
15 [m] Ex. 23:7; Prov. 24:24; Is. 5:23
17 [n] Ruth 1:16; Prov. 18:24
18 [o] Prov. 6:1 [3] Lit. *heart* [4] Lit. *strikes the hands* [5] *guaranty* or *collateral*
19 [p] Prov. 16:18
20 [q] James 3:8 [6] *crooked*
22 [r] Prov. 12:25; 15:13, 15 [7] Or *makes medicine even better*
23 [8] Under cover, lit. *from the bosom*
24 [s] Eccl. 2:14
25 [t] Prov. 10:1; 15:20; 19:13
27 [u] Prov. 10:19; James 1:19
28 [v] Job 13:5

CHAPTER 18

1 [1] *sound wisdom*
2 [a] Eccl. 10:3

17:11 Just retribution comes against people who rebel, and thus the king's messenger will have no mercy (cf. 16:14; 2 Sam. 20:1-22; 1 Kin. 2:25,29,34,46).

17:12 Fools are less rational in anger than wild bears.

17:13 evil for good. Solomon knew this proverb well since his father mistreated Uriah (cf. 2 Sam. 12:10-31). Contrast this with the man who repays evil with good (cf. 20:22; Matt. 5:43-48; 1 Pet. 3:9).

17:14 releasing water. The smallest break in the dam sets loose an uncontrollable flood force.

17:15 The unjust judge is controlled by his pride, prejudice, bribes, and passions. *See note on 24:23b-25*; cf. Ex. 23:7; Is. 5:23.

17:16 Even wealth cannot buy wisdom for those who do not love it. Cf. 4:7.

17:17 The difference between a friend and brother is noted here. A true friend is a constant source of love, while a brother in one's family may not be close, but is drawn near to help in trouble. Friends are closer than brothers because they are available all the time, not just in the crisis. Cf. 18:24.

17:18 *See notes on 6:1,2-4.*

17:19 exalts his gate. The image here is of the proud who flaunts his wealth with a huge house having a large front door and who thus invites death (cf. Jer. 22:13-19).

17:20 perverse. Cf. 10:31.

17:21 Cf. 10:1; 15:20; 17:25; 19:26.

17:22 Cf. 14:30; 15:13,30; 16:14; Job 29:24.

17:23 *See note on v. 8.*

17:24 ends of the earth. This refers to the fool's roving fixations in the absence of wisdom.

17:25 Cf. v. 21.

17:26 punish…strike. Here is a clear statement on political and religious injustice, focusing on the equally bad mistreatment of the innocent and the noble.

17:27 spares. Cf. 10:19; 14:29; 15:18; 16:27,32; 29:20.

17:28 fool is counted wise. This is not saying that fools show wisdom in their silence, but that silence conceals their folly.

18:1 isolates himself. This man seeks selfish gratification and accepts advice from no one.

18:2 Cf. Eccl. 10:12-14.

3 When the wicked comes, contempt
comes also;
And with dishonor *comes* reproach.

4 [b]The words of a man's mouth *are*
deep waters;
[c]The wellspring of wisdom *is* a
flowing brook.

5 *It is* not good to show partiality to
the wicked,
Or to overthrow the righteous in
[d]judgment.

6 A fool's lips enter into contention,
And his mouth calls for blows.
7 [e]A fool's mouth *is* his destruction,
And his lips *are* the snare of his
[f]soul.
8 [g]The words of a [2]talebearer *are* like
[3]tasty trifles,
And they go down into the
[4]inmost body.

9 He who is slothful in his work
Is a brother to him who is a great
destroyer.

10 The name of the LORD *is* a strong
[h]tower;
The righteous run to it and are [5]safe.
11 The rich man's wealth *is* his strong
city,
And like a high wall in his own
esteem.

12 [i]Before destruction the heart of a
man is haughty,
And before honor *is* humility.

13 He who answers a matter before he
hears *it*,
It *is* folly and shame to him.

14 The spirit of a man will sustain
him in sickness,
But who can bear a broken spirit?

15 The heart of the prudent acquires
knowledge,
And the ear of the wise seeks
knowledge.

16 [j]A man's gift makes room for him,
And brings him before great men.

17 The first *one* to plead his cause
seems right,
Until his neighbor comes and
examines him.

18 Casting [k]lots causes contentions to
cease,
And keeps the mighty apart.

19 A brother offended *is harder to win*
than a strong city,
And contentions *are* like the bars of
a castle.

20 [l]A man's stomach shall be satisfied
from the fruit of his mouth;
From the produce of his lips he
shall be filled.

21 [m]Death and life *are* in the power of
the tongue,
And those who love it will eat its
fruit.

22 [n]*He who* finds a wife finds a good
thing,
And obtains favor from the LORD.

23 The poor *man* uses entreaties,
But the rich answers [o]roughly.

4 [b] Prov. 10:11 [c] [James 3:17]
5 [d] Lev. 19:15; Deut. 1:17; 16:19; Ps. 82:2; Prov. 17:15
7 [e] Ps. 64:8; 140:9; Prov. 10:14 [f] Eccl. 10:12
8 [g] Prov. 12:18 [2] *gossip or slanderer* [3] A Jewish tradition *wounds* [4] Lit. *rooms of the belly*
10 [h] 2 Sam. 22:2, 3, 33; Ps. 18:2; 61:3; 91:2; 144:2 [5] *secure*, lit. *set on high*
12 [i] Prov. 15:33; 16:18
16 [j] Gen. 32:20, 21; 1 Sam. 25:27; Prov. 17:8; 21:14
18 [k] [Prov. 16:33]
20 [l] Prov. 12:14; 14:14
21 [m] Prov. 12:13; 13:3; Matt. 12:37
22 [n] Gen. 2:18; [Prov. 12:4; 19:14]
23 [o] James 2:3, 6

18:3 Sin and punishment are inseparably connected, as evil produces both the feeling of contempt in others and its manifestation, reproach.

18:4 words...deep waters. Wise speech is like a deep, inexhaustible stream of blessing.

18:5 Cf. 17:26; 28:21.

18:6,7 The fool self-destructs. Cf. 12:13; 17:14,19,28; 19:29; 20:3.

18:8 tasty trifles. This comes from a Heb. word, meaning "to swallow greedily." The proverb is repeated in 26:22.

18:9 slothful...destroyer. To leave a work half done or poorly done is to destroy it. *See notes on 6:1,11.*

18:10 The name of the LORD. This expression, found only here in Proverbs, stands for the manifest perfections of God such as faithfulness, power, mercy, and wisdom, on which the righteous rely for security (cf. Ex. 3:15; 15:1-3; Ps. 27:4,5)

18:11 This proverb repeats 10:15 and contrasts with v. 10.

18:12 Cf. 16:18.

18:14 broken spirit. Cf. 12:25; 15:13. When the spirit is broken, people lose hope.

18:16 man's gift. This is not the word for a bribe (cf. 17:23), but rather the word for a present given to someone (cf. Jacob's gift, Gen. 32:20,21; Joseph's gift, Gen. 43:11; David's gift, 1 Sam. 17:17,18; and Abigail's gift, 1 Sam. 25:27).

18:17 See v. 13. Cross-examination avoids hasty judgment.

18:18 lots. *See note on 16:33.*

18:19 There are no feuds as difficult to resolve as those with relatives; no barriers are so hard to bring down. Hence, great care should be taken to avoid such conflicts. **bars of a castle.** Cf. Judg. 16:3; 1 Kin. 4:13; Neh. 3:3; Is. 45:2.

18:20 the produce of his lips. *See notes on 12:14; 13:2,3.* The consequences of one's words should produce satisfaction and fulfillment.

18:21 Death and life. The greatest good and the greatest harm are in the power of the tongue (cf. James 3:6-10).

18:22 Cf. 12:4; 19:14; 31:10-31.

18:23 The rich do not need favors from others, so they do not care how they treat people.

24 A man *who has* friends [6]must
himself be friendly,
[p]But there is a friend *who* sticks
closer than a brother.

19

1 Better [a]*is* the poor who walks in
his integrity
Than *one who is* perverse in his lips,
and is a fool.

2 Also it is not good *for* a soul *to be*
without knowledge,
And he sins who hastens with *his*
feet.

3 The foolishness of a man twists his
way,
And his heart frets against the LORD.

4 [b]Wealth makes many friends,
But the poor is separated from his
friend.

5 A [c]false witness will not go
unpunished,
And *he who* speaks lies will not
escape.

6 Many entreat the favor of the
nobility,
And every man *is* a friend to one
who gives gifts.

7 [d]All the brothers of the poor hate
him;
How much more do his friends go
[e]far from him!
He may pursue *them with* words,
yet they [1]abandon *him.*

8 He who gets [2]wisdom loves his
own soul;
He who keeps understanding [f]will
find good.

9 A false witness will not go
unpunished,
And *he who* speaks lies shall perish.

10 Luxury is not fitting for a fool,
Much less [g]for a servant to rule
over princes.

11 [h]The discretion of a man makes him
slow to anger,
[i]And his glory *is* to overlook a
transgression.

12 [j]The king's wrath *is* like the roaring
of a lion,
But his favor *is* [k]like dew on the
grass.

13 [l]A foolish son *is* the ruin of his
father,
[m]And the contentions of a wife *are* a
continual [3]dripping.

14 [n]Houses and riches *are* an
inheritance from fathers,
But [o]a prudent wife *is* from the
LORD.

15 [p]Laziness casts *one* into a deep
sleep,
And an idle person will [q]suffer
hunger.

16 [r]He who keeps the commandment
keeps his soul,
But he who [4]is careless of his ways
will die.

17 [s]He who has pity on the poor lends
to the LORD,
And He will pay back what he has
given.

24 [p] Prov. 17:17; [John 15:14, 15] [6] So with Gr. mss., Syr., Tg., Vg.; MT *may come to ruin*

CHAPTER 19

1 [a] Prov. 28:6
4 [b] Prov. 14:20
5 [c] Ex. 23:1; Deut. 19:16-19; Prov. 6:19; 21:28
7 [d] Prov. 14:20 [e] Ps. 38:11 [1] Lit. *are not*
8 [f] Prov. 16:20 [2] Lit. *heart*
10 [g] Prov. 30:21, 22
11 [h] James 1:19 [i] Prov. 16:32; [Matt. 5:44]; Eph. 4:32; Col. 3:13
12 [j] Prov. 16:14 [k] Gen. 27:28; Deut. 33:28; Ps. 133:3; Hos. 14:5; Mic. 5:7
13 [l] Prov. 10:1 [m] Prov. 21:9, 19 [3] Irritation
14 [n] 2 Cor. 12:14 [o] Prov. 18:22
15 [p] Prov. 6:9 [q] Prov. 10:4
16 [r] Prov. 13:13; 16:17; Luke 10:28; 11:28 [4] Is reckless, lit. *despises*
17 [s] Deut. 15:7, 8; Job 23:12, 13; Prov. 28:27; Eccl. 11:1; Matt. 10:42; 25:40; [2 Cor. 9:6-8]; Heb. 6:10

18:24 must himself be friendly. The best text says "may come to ruin" (see margin) and warns that the person who makes friends too easily and indiscriminately does so to his own destruction. On the other hand, a friend chosen wisely is more loyal than a brother. **friend.** This is a strong word meaning "one who loves" and was used of Abraham, God's friend (2 Chr. 20:7; Is. 41:8; cf. 1 Sam. 18:1; 2 Sam. 1:26).

19:1 Integrity is better than wealth. Cf. 15:16,17; 16:8.

19:2 sins. Lit. "to miss the mark." **hastens with *his* feet.** Rashness, the result of ignorance, brings trouble.

19:3 his heart frets. The fool blames God for his troubles and failures (cf. Gen. 4:5; Is. 8:21; Lam. 3:39-41).

19:4 Wealth makes. Cf. v. 7; 14:20. Lit. wealth adds new friends while poverty alienates existing friends who grow weary of the demands of the poor.

19:5,9 For the sin of perjury, cf. 6:19; 12:17; 14:5,25; 19:9; Deut. 19:18-21.

19:6 Generosity or bribery could be the issue.

19:7 *See note on v. 4.*

19:10 Neither are suited for possessions or responsibilities beyond their capabilities of managing wisely (cf. 30:21-23).

19:11 slow to anger. *See note on 14:17.*

19:12 This is a call to submit to governmental authority. Cf. Rom. 13:1-4; 1 Pet. 2:13-17.

19:13 continual dripping. An obstinate, argumentative woman is literally like a leak so unrelenting that one has to run from it or go mad. Here are two ways to devastate a man: an ungodly son and an irritating wife.

19:14 One receives inheritance as a family blessing (a result of human birth), but a wise wife (cf. 31:10-31) is a result of divine blessing. Cf. 12:4; 18:22; 31:10-31.

19:15 *See notes on 6:6,11.*

19:16 commandment. Wisdom is equated with God's commandments. In a sense, Proverbs contain the applications and implications of all that is in God's moral law.

19:17 *See note on 14:31.*

18 [t]Chasten your son while there is hope,
And do not set your heart [5]on his destruction.

19 *A man of* great wrath will suffer punishment;
For if you rescue *him*, you will have to do it again.

20 Listen to counsel and receive instruction,
That you may be wise [u]in your latter days.

21 There are many plans in a man's heart,
[v]Nevertheless the LORD's counsel—that will stand.

22 What is desired in a man is [6]kindness,
And a poor man is better than a liar.

23 [w]The fear of the LORD *leads* to life,
And *he who has it* will abide in satisfaction;
He will not be visited with evil.

24 [x]A lazy *man* buries his hand in the [7]bowl,
And will not so much as bring it to his mouth again.

25 Strike a scoffer, and the simple [y]will become wary;
[z]Rebuke one who has understanding, *and* he will discern knowledge.

26 He who mistreats *his* father *and* chases away *his* mother
Is [a]a son who causes shame and brings reproach.

27 Cease listening to instruction, my son,
And you will stray from the words of knowledge.

28 A [8]disreputable witness scorns justice,
And [b]the mouth of the wicked devours iniquity.

29 Judgments are prepared for scoffers,
[c]And beatings for the backs of fools.

20 Wine [a]*is* a mocker,
Strong drink *is* a brawler,
And whoever is led astray by it is not wise.

2 The [1]wrath of a king *is* like the roaring of a lion;
Whoever provokes him to anger sins *against* his own life.

3 [b]*It is* honorable for a man to stop striving,
Since any fool can start a quarrel.

4 [c]The lazy *man* will not plow because of winter;
[d]He will beg during harvest and *have* nothing.

5 Counsel in the heart of man *is like* deep water,
But a man of understanding will draw it out.

6 Most men will proclaim each his own [2]goodness,

18 [t]Prov. 13:24 [5]Lit. *to put him to death;* a Jewish tradition *on his crying*
20 [u]Ps. 37:37
21 [v]Ps. 33:10, 11; Prov. 16:9; Is. 46:10; Heb. 6:17
22 [6]Lit. *lovingkindness*
23 [w]Prov. 14:27; [1 Tim. 4:8]
24 [x]Prov. 15:19 [7]LXX, Syr. *bosom;* Tg., Vg. *armpit*
25 [y]Deut. 13:11 [z]Prov. 9:8
26 [a]Prov. 17:2
28 [b]Job 15:16 [8]Lit. *witness of Belial,* worthless witness
29 [c]Prov. 26:3

CHAPTER 20

1 [a]Gen. 9:21; Prov. 23:29-35; Is. 28:7; Hos. 4:11
2 [1]Lit. *fear* or *terror,* produced by the king's wrath
3 [b]Prov. 17:14
4 [c]Prov. 10:4 [d]Prov. 19:15
6 [2]Lit. *mercy*

19:18 Chasten. *See notes on 3:11; 13:24; 22:6.*

19:19 Repeated acts of kindness are wasted on ill-natured people.

19:21 *See note on 16:1.*

19:22 Rich liars are not kind since their lies bring harm; a kind poor man is more desirable.

19:23 fear of the LORD. *See note on 1:7.*

19:24 The lazy man's lack of action to move his hand from the flat, metal food saucer up to his mouth is because he is too lazy, as explained in 26:15.

19:25 scoffer...simple...understanding. Three classes of people are noted: 1) scoffers are rebuked for learning nothing; 2) simpletons are warned by observing the rebuke of the scoffer; and 3) the understanding deepen their wisdom from any reproof.

19:26 mistreats. Cf. 10:1; 15:20; 17:21,25; 28:24. The son appears to come into possession of his father's property during his parents' lifetime, but rather than caring for them, he drives them out (cf. Ex. 20:12; 21:15,17).

19:28 disreputable witness. *See note on 12:17.*

19:29 *See note on 10:13.*

20:1 Wine...strong drink. This begins a new theme of temperance (see 23:20,21,29-35; 31:4,5). Wine was grape juice mixed with water to dilute it, but strong drink was unmixed (*see note on Eph. 5:18*). While the use of these beverages is not specifically condemned (Deut. 14:26), being intoxicated always is (Is. 28:7). Rulers were not to drink, so their judgment would not be clouded nor their behavior less than exemplary (see 31:4,5). *See note on 1 Tim 3:3.* **mocker...brawler.** "Mocker" is the same word as "scoffer" in 19:25,29; a brawler is violent, loud, and uncontrolled. Both words describe the personality of the drunkard.

20:2 *See notes on 16:14; 19:12.* Men who resist governmental authority injure themselves. *See notes on Rom. 13:1-5.*

20:3 Cf. 15:18; 17:14; 19:11.

20:4 lazy *man*. *See notes on 6:6,11.*

20:5 deep water. The wise man has keen discernment reaching to the deepest intentions of the heart to grasp wise counsel (cf. 18:4; Heb. 4:12).

20:6 There are a lot more people who are eager to brag about themselves than there are those who are truly faithful to testify of God's goodness.

But who can find a faithful man?

7 [e]The righteous *man* walks in his integrity;
[f]His children *are* blessed after him.

8 A king who sits on the throne of judgment
Scatters all evil with his eyes.

9 [g]Who can say, "I have made my heart clean,
I am pure from my sin"?

10 [h]Diverse weights *and* diverse measures,
They *are* both alike, an abomination to the LORD.

11 Even a child is [i]known by his deeds,
Whether what he does *is* pure and right.

12 [j]The hearing ear and the seeing eye,
The LORD has made them both.

13 [k]Do not love sleep, lest you come to poverty;
Open your eyes, *and* you will be satisfied with bread.

14 "*It is* [3]good for nothing," cries the buyer;
But when he has gone his way, then he boasts.

15 There is gold and a multitude of rubies,
But [l]the lips of knowledge *are* a precious jewel.

16 [m]Take the garment of one who is surety *for* a stranger,
And hold it as a pledge *when it* is for a seductress.

17 [n]Bread gained by deceit *is* sweet to a man,
But afterward his mouth will be filled with gravel.

18 [o]Plans are established by counsel;
[p]By wise counsel wage war.

19 [q]He who goes about *as* a talebearer reveals secrets;
Therefore do not associate with one [r]who flatters with his lips.

20 [s]Whoever curses his father or his mother,
[t]His lamp will be put out in deep darkness.

21 [u]An inheritance gained hastily at the beginning
[v]Will not be blessed at the end.

22 [w]Do not say, "I will [4]recompense evil";
[x]Wait for the LORD, and He will save you.

23 Diverse weights *are* an abomination to the LORD,
And dishonest scales *are* not good.

24 A man's steps *are* of the LORD;
How then can a man understand his own way?

25 *It is* a snare for a man to devote rashly *something as* holy,

7 [e] 2 Cor. 1:12 [f] Ps. 37:26
9 [g] [1 Kin. 8:46; 2 Chr. 6:36]; Job 9:30, 31; 14:4; [Ps. 51:5; Eccl. 7:20; Rom. 3:9; 1 John 1:8]
10 [h] Deut. 25:13
11 [i] Matt. 7:16
12 [j] Ex. 4:11; Ps. 94:9
13 [k] Rom. 12:11
14 [3] Lit. *evil, evil*
15 [l] [Job 28:12-19; Prov. 3:13-15]
16 [m] Prov. 22:26
17 [n] Prov. 9:17
18 [o] Prov. 24:6 [p] Luke 14:31
19 [q] Prov. 11:13 [r] Rom. 16:18
20 [s] Ex. 21:17; Lev. 20:9; Prov. 30:11; Matt. 15:4 [t] Job 18:5, 6; Prov. 24:20
21 [u] Prov. 28:20 [v] Hab. 2:6
22 [w] [Deut. 32:35]; Prov. 17:13; 24:29; [Rom. 12:17-19]; 1 Thess. 5:15; [1 Pet. 3:9] [x] 2 Sam. 16:12 [4] *repay*

20:7 integrity. *See note on 10:9.*

20:8 Scatters. The king as judge lit. "winnows" or "sifts" (as in v. 26) data as he discerns evil and good (cf. Is. 11:3,4).

20:9 No one can make himself sinless. Cf. Job 14:4; Rom. 3:10,23; 1 John 1:8. Those whose sin has been forgiven are pure before God (Ps. 51:1,2,9,10).

20:10 *See note on 11:1*; cf. 20:23.

20:12 Because God has given man the ability to hear and see, it should be obvious that He hears and sees everything (see Ps. 94:9).

20:13 *See notes on 6:6,11.*

20:14 The buyer purposely undervalues the thing he is negotiating to purchase, in order to bring down the price. Afterward, he brags about his cleverness.

20:15 Wealth is a blessing when honestly gained, but wisdom is more desirable. *See notes on 3:13-15; 8:10,11,18; 16:16.*

20:16 *See note on 6:1.* Garments were common security for a loan but they always had to be returned by sundown (Ex. 22:26,27; Deut. 24:10-13). "Seductress" is more likely "foreigner." Anyone who foolishly has taken on the responsibility for the debt of a stranger or an immoral woman will likely never be paid back, so he will never pay his creditor unless his own garment is taken as security.

20:18 wise counsel. Cf. 11:14; 15:22; Luke 14:28-32.

20:19 talebearer. Those who love to spread secrets will flatter to learn them.

20:20 lamp will be put out. Cf. 13:9. This grievous sin (cf. 30:11,17; Ex. 21:17; Lev. 20:9) will result in death.

20:21 gained hastily. This implies an unjust method in gaining the inheritance, so that it will be lost by the same unjust ways or by punishment (cf. 13:11; 21:5,6; 28:20,22).

20:22 "I will recompense evil." God, not man, avenges evil (cf. Deut. 32:35; Rom. 12:17,19; Heb. 10:30) and delivers from the wicked.

20:23 Cf. v. 10; *see note on 11:1.*

20:24 *See notes on 16:1,9,33.* Since a man cannot comprehend the unfolding purposes of God's providence in his life, he has to walk in faith.

20:25 to devote rashly. To declare something sacred, i.e., promising it to God in consecration as an offering, was irreversible and,

And afterward to reconsider *his*
vows.

26 [y]A wise king sifts out the wicked,
And brings the threshing wheel
over them.

27 [z]The spirit of a man *is* the lamp of
the LORD,
Searching all the [5]inner depths of
his heart.

28 [a]Mercy and truth preserve the king,
And by [6]lovingkindness he
upholds his throne.

29 The glory of young men *is* their
strength,
And [b]the splendor of old men *is*
their gray head.

30 Blows that hurt cleanse away evil,
As *do* stripes the [7]inner depths of
the heart.

CHAPTER 21

21 The king's heart *is* in the hand of
the LORD,
Like the [1]rivers of water; He turns
it wherever He wishes.

2 [a]Every way of a man *is* right in his
own eyes,
[b]But the LORD weighs the hearts.

3 [c]To do righteousness and justice
Is more acceptable to the LORD than
sacrifice.

4 [d]A haughty look, a proud heart,
And the [2]plowing of the wicked *are*
sin.

5 [e]The plans of the diligent *lead* surely
to plenty,
But *those of* everyone *who is* hasty,
surely to poverty.

6 [f]Getting treasures by a lying tongue
[3]*Is* the fleeting fantasy of those who
seek death.

7 The violence of the wicked will
[4]destroy them,
Because they refuse to do justice.

8 The way of [5]a guilty man *is*
perverse;
But *as for* the pure, his work *is* right.

9 Better to dwell in a corner of a
housetop,
Than in a house shared with [g]a
contentious woman.

10 [h]The soul of the wicked desires evil;
His neighbor finds no favor in his
eyes.

11 When the scoffer is punished, the
simple is made wise;
But when the [i]wise is instructed,
he receives knowledge.

12 The righteous *God* wisely considers
the house of the wicked,
Overthrowing the wicked for *their*
wickedness.

13 [j]Whoever shuts his ears to the cry
of the poor
Will also cry himself and not be
heard.

14 A gift in secret pacifies anger,
And a bribe [6]behind the back,
strong wrath.

15 *It is* a joy for the just to do justice,

26 [y]Ps. 101:8
27 [z]1 Cor. 2:11 [5]Lit. *rooms of the belly*
28 [a]Ps. 101:1; Prov. 21:21 [6]*mercy*
29 [b]Prov. 16:31
30 [7]Lit. *rooms of the belly*

CHAPTER 21
1 [1]*channels*
2 [a]Prov. 16:2 [b]Prov. 24:12; Luke 16:15
3 [c]1 Sam. 15:22; Prov. 15:8; Is. 1:11, 16, 17; Hos. 6:6; [Mic. 6:7, 8]
4 [d]Prov. 6:17 [2]Or *lamp*
5 [e]Prov. 10:4
6 [f]2 Pet. 2:3 [3]LXX *Pursue vanity on the snares of death;* Vg. *Is vain and foolish, and shall stumble on the snares of death;* Tg. *They shall be destroyed, and they shall fall who seek death*
7 [4]Lit. *drag them away*
8 [5]Or *The way of a man is perverse and strange;*
9 [g]Prov. 19:13
10 [h]James 4:5
11 [i]Prov. 19:25
13 [j][Matt. 7:2; 18:30-34]; James 2:13; 1 John 3:17
14 [6]Under cover, lit. *in the bosom*

therefore, serious. See Eccl. 5:4-6; cf. Num. 30:2; Deut. 23:21-23; Pss. 50:14; 78:11

20:26 *See note on v. 8.*

20:27 the lamp of the LORD. The "spirit" represents the conscience of man which searches every secret place. Cf. Rom. 2:15; *see note on 2 Cor. 1:12.*

20:28 Mercy and truth. *See note on 3:3.*

20:30 Wise use of corporal punishment deters evil behavior. *See note on 10:13.*

21:1 He turns it. *See notes on 16:1,9,33*; cf. 19:21; 20:24. Note the examples of the divine hand of God in the cases of Artaxerxes (Ezra 7:21-23), Tiglath-Pileser (Is. 10:5-7), Cyrus (Is. 45:1-4), and Nebuchadnezzar (Dan. 4:34; 5:23-25).

21:2 *See note on 16:2.*

21:3 *See notes on 15:8; 21:27* (cf. 1 Sam. 15:22; Is. 1:10-20; Hos. 6:6; Mic. 6:6-8).

21:4 plowing. Cf. 6:17; 30:13; Pss. 18:27; 131:1. This is best understood as the "lamp of the wicked" (see margin), "lamp" being used as a symbol for the eyes, which conveys their pride.

21:5-7 These verses address the evils of ill-gotten gain. They show 3 major defects in the way this gain is acquired: 1) hastily (v. 5; cf. 19:2; 28:20); 2) deceitfully (v. 6; cf. 13:11); and 3) violently (v. 7; cf. 12:6).

21:7 Cf. 1:18,19.

21:9 corner of a housetop. Since roofs were open like patios (cf. Deut. 22:8; 1 Sam. 9:25; 1 Kin. 4:10), a small arbor or enclosure in the corner of a flat roof was a very inconvenient place to live. **contentious woman.** Cf. v. 19; 19:13; 25:24; 27:15,16; *see note on 19:13.*

21:10 wicked desires evil. So strongly does he seek to do evil (cf. Eccl. 8:11) that he will not even spare his neighbor if he gets in his way.

21:11 *See note on 19:25.*

21:12 *See note on 20:22*; cf. 10:25; 14:11.

21:13 poor. *See note on 14:31.*

21:14 Cf. 17:8; 18:16; 19:6.

But destruction *will come* to the
workers of iniquity.

16 A man who wanders from the way
of understanding
Will rest in the assembly of the
[k]dead.

17 He who loves pleasure *will be* a
poor man;
He who loves wine and oil will not
be rich.

18 The wicked *shall be* a ransom for
the righteous,
And the unfaithful for the
upright.

19 Better to dwell [7]in the wilderness,
Than with a contentious and angry
woman.

20 [l]*There is* desirable treasure,
And oil in the dwelling of the
wise,
But a foolish man squanders it.

21 [m]He who follows righteousness and
mercy
Finds life, righteousness and
honor.

22 A [n]wise *man* [8]scales the city of the
mighty,
And brings down the trusted
stronghold.

23 [o]Whoever guards his mouth and
tongue
Keeps his soul from troubles.

24 A proud *and* haughty *man*—
"Scoffer" *is* his name;
He acts with arrogant pride.

25 The [p]desire of the lazy *man* kills
him,
For his hands refuse to labor.

26 He covets greedily all day long,
But the righteous [q]gives and does
not spare.

27 [r]The sacrifice of the wicked *is* an
abomination;
How much more *when* he brings it
with wicked intent!

28 A false witness shall perish,
But the man who hears *him* will
speak endlessly.

29 A wicked man hardens his face,
But *as for* the upright, he
[9]establishes his way.

30 [s]*There is* no wisdom or
understanding
Or counsel against the LORD.

31 The horse *is* prepared for the day
of battle,
But [t]deliverance *is* of the LORD.

22 A [a]*good* name is to be chosen rather
than great riches,
Loving favor rather than silver and
gold.

2 The [b]rich and the poor have this in
common,
The [c]LORD *is* the maker of them all.

3 A prudent *man* foresees evil and
hides himself,
But the simple pass on and are
[d]punished.

4 By humility *and* the fear of the
LORD
Are riches and honor and life.

5 Thorns *and* snares *are* in the way of
the perverse;
He who guards his soul will be far
from them.

16 [k]Ps. 49:14
19 [7]Lit. *in the land of the desert*
20 [l]Ps. 112:3; Prov. 8:21
21 [m]Prov. 15:9; Matt. 5:6; [Rom. 2:7]; 1 Cor. 15:58
22 [n]2 Sam. 5:6-9; Prov. 24:5; Eccl. 7:19; 9:15, 16 [8]Climbs over the walls of
23 [o]Prov. 12:13; 13:3; 18:21; [James 3:2]
25 [p]Prov. 13:4
26 [q][Prov. 22:9; Eph. 4:28]
27 [r]Prov. 15:8; Is. 66:3; Jer. 6:20; Amos 5:22
29 [9]Qr., LXX *understands*
30 [s]Is. 8:9, 10; [Jer. 9:23, 24]; Acts 5:39; 1 Cor. 3:19, 20
31 [t]Ps. 3:8; Jer. 3:23; [1 Cor. 15:57]

CHAPTER 22
1 [a][Prov. 10:7]; Eccl. 7:1
2 [b]Prov. 29:13 [c]Job 31:15; [Prov. 14:31]
3 [d]Prov. 27:12; Is. 26:20

21:16 This is proven in the account of the simple man who was seduced (2:18; 7:22,23; 9:18).

21:17 wine and oil. These are associated with unbridled luxury in feasting (Deut. 14:26; Neh. 8:12; Ps. 104:15; Amos 6:6; John 12:5). Costly indulgences impoverish.

21:18 By suffering the very thing they had devised for the righteous, or brought on them, the wicked became their ransom, in the sense of being a substitute in judgment.

21:19 *See note on 19:13.*

21:21 Those who pursue "righteousness" and "mercy" receive more than they seek (see Matt. 5:6,7; 6:33).

21:22 Cf. 24:5. Wisdom is better than strength (cf. Eccl. 7:19; 9:15).

21:26 The sin of covetousness marks the lazy man as the virtue of benevolence marks the righteous.

21:27 *See note on 15:8;* cf. v. 3; Is. 1:13-15.

21:28 false witness. *See note on 12:17.*

21:29 The wicked become obstinate, maintaining what suits them without regard for others or the truth, while good people proceed with integrity.

21:31 prepared...deliverance. This is not a condemnation of adequate preparation but rather of reliance on it for victory, instead of on the Lord (cf. Ezra 8:22; Ps. 20:7; Is. 31:1-3; Hos. 1:7).

22:3 Wise people see the approach of sin and remove themselves from it, while naive people walk right into it and suffer the consequences.

22:4 fear of the LORD. *See note on 1:7.*

6 [e]Train up a child in the way he
should go,
[1]And when he is old he will not
depart from it.

7 The [f]rich rules over the poor,
And the borrower *is* servant to the
lender.

8 He who sows iniquity will reap
[g]sorrow,[2]
And the rod of his anger will fail.

9 [h]He who has a [3]generous eye will
be [i]blessed,
For he gives of his bread to the poor.

10 [j]Cast out the scoffer, and contention
will leave;
Yes, strife and reproach will cease.

11 [k]He who loves purity of heart
And has grace on his lips,
The king *will be* his friend.

12 The eyes of the LORD preserve
knowledge,
But He overthrows the words of
the faithless.

13 [l]The lazy *man* says, "*There is* a lion
outside!
I shall be slain in the streets!"

14 [m]The mouth of an immoral woman
is a deep pit;
[n]He who is abhorred by the LORD
will fall there.

6 [e] Eph. 6:4; 2 Tim. 3:15 [1] *Even*
7 [f] Prov. 18:23; James 2:6
8 [g] Job 4:8 [2] *trouble*
9 [h] 2 Cor. 9:6 [i] [Prov. 19:17] [3] Lit. *good*
10 [j] Ps. 101:5
11 [k] Ps. 101:6
13 [l] Prov. 26:13
14 [m] Prov. 2:16; 5:3; 7:5 [n] Eccl. 7:26

15 Foolishness *is* bound up in the
heart of a child;
[o]The rod of correction will drive it
far from him.

16 He who oppresses the poor to
increase his *riches,*
And he who gives to the rich, *will*
surely *come* to poverty.

Sayings of the Wise

17 Incline your ear and hear the
words of the wise,
And apply your heart to my
knowledge;
18 For *it is* a pleasant thing if you
keep them within you;
Let them all be fixed upon your
lips,
19 So that your trust may be in the
LORD;
I have instructed you today, even
you.
20 Have I not written to you excellent
things
Of counsels and knowledge,
21 [p]That I may make you know the
certainty of the words of
truth,
[q]That you may answer words of
truth
To those who [4]send to you?

22 Do not rob the [r]poor because he *is*
poor,
Nor oppress the afflicted at the
gate;
23 [s]For the LORD will plead their cause,

15 [o] Prov. 13:24; 23:13, 14
21 [p] Luke 1:3, 4 [q] Prov. 25:13; 1 Pet. 3:15 [4] Or *send you*
22 [r] Ex. 23:6; Job 31:16-21; Zech. 7:10
23 [s] 1 Sam. 24:12; Ps. 12:5; 140:12

22:6 way he should go. There is only one right way, God's way, the way of life. That way is specified in great detail in Proverbs. Since it is axiomatic that early training secures lifelong habits, parents must insist upon this way, teaching God's Word and enforcing it with loving discipline consistently throughout the child's upbringing. *See note on 13:24.* Cf. Deut. 4:9; 6:6-8; 11:18-21; Josh. 24:15; Eph. 6:4.

22:7 rich rules. While this is naturally true, the Law and Prophets condemned those who were oppressive (cf. 22:22,23; Deut. 24:14-18; Is. 5:8; Jer. 34:13,17; Mic. 2:2).

22:8,9 generous eye. A reference to generosity in that he looks with a desire to give. The principle of sowing and reaping is emphasized. Cf. Job 4:8; Hos. 8:7; 10:13; 2 Cor. 9:6; Gal. 6:7-9.

22:11 Even the most powerful are drawn to the wise (cf. Eccl. 10:12).

22:12 the eyes of the LORD. *See note on 15:3.* God's sovereign omniscience protects the principles and possessors of divine knowledge.

22:13 a lion outside. Cf. 26:13. The lazy give lame excuses for not leaving the house to work. *See notes on 6:6,11.*

22:14 The flattering seductions of such a woman lure men into a pit as God makes their sin its own punishment. *See note on 2:16*; cf. 5:3; 7:5.

22:15 *See note on 13:24.*

22:16 These two vices reflect the same selfish attitude: withholding from the poor to keep what one has, and giving to the rich to induce them to give one more. Both are unacceptable to God and incur punishment.

22:17–24:34 Solomon did not author, but did compile, this collection containing 77 proverbs which were most likely spoken by godly men prior to Solomon's reign. The section begins with an introduction (22:17-21), followed by a collection of proverbs in random order, one, two or three verses each (as opposed to the one verse, two line proverbs in the previous section). This is followed by two collections of additional proverbs (22:22–24:22 and 24:23-34), which continue and enlarge upon the wisdom themes of this book.

22:17-21 This introductory section offers an exhortation, reminiscent of 2:1-5; 5:1,2, to be alert to hear and speak the wisdom of God.

22:20 excellent things. This term is lit. "chief proverbs" (cf. 8:6).

22:21 certainty. Solomon is especially concerned about accuracy so that his reader can teach others.

22:22–24:22 The first collection of words for wise men is recorded.

22:22,23 *See note on 14:31.*

22:22 gate. Beggars typically sat at the gate because of the large number of people passing by. The gate was also the place for civic

And plunder the soul of those who
plunder them.
24 Make no friendship with an angry
man,
And with a [t]furious man do not
go,
25 Lest you learn his ways
And set a snare for your soul.

26 [u]Do not be one of those who
[5]shakes hands in a pledge,
One of those who is [6]surety for
debts;
27 If you have nothing *with which* to
pay,
Why should he take away your
bed from under you?

28 [v]Do not remove the ancient
[7]landmark
Which your fathers have set.

29 Do you see a man *who* [8]excels in
his work?
He will stand before kings;
He will not stand before [9]unknown
men.

23 When you sit down to eat with a
ruler,
Consider carefully what *is* before
you;
2 And put a knife to your throat
If you *are* a man given to appetite.
3 Do not desire his delicacies,
For they *are* deceptive food.

4 [a]Do not overwork to be rich;
[b]Because of your own
understanding, cease!
5 [1]Will you set your eyes on that
which is not?
For *riches* certainly make
themselves wings;
They fly away like an eagle *toward*
heaven.

6 Do not eat the bread of [c]a [2] miser,
Nor desire his delicacies;
7 For as he thinks in his heart, so *is*
he.
"Eat and drink!" [d]he says to you,
But his heart is not with you.
8 The morsel you have eaten, you
will vomit up,
And waste your pleasant words.

9 [e]Do not speak in the hearing of a
fool,
For he will despise the wisdom of
your words.

10 Do not remove the ancient
[3]landmark,
Nor enter the fields of the
fatherless;
11 [f]For their Redeemer *is* mighty;
He will plead their cause against
you.

12 Apply your heart to instruction,
And your ears to words of
knowledge.

13 [g]Do not withhold correction from a
child,
For *if* you beat him with a rod, he
will not die.
14 You shall beat him with a rod,
And deliver his soul from [4]hell.

15 My son, if your heart is wise,
My heart will rejoice—indeed, I
myself;

24 [t] Prov. 29:22
26 [u] Prov. 11:15 [5] Lit. *strikes* [6] *guaranty*
28 [v] Deut. 19:14; 27:17; Job 24:2; Prov. 23:10 [7] *boundary*
29 [8] *is prompt in his business* [9] *obscure*

CHAPTER 23
4 [a] [Prov. 28:20; Matt. 6:19; 1 Tim. 6:9, 10; Heb. 13:5] [b] Rom. 12:16
5 [1] Lit. *Will you cause your eyes to fly upon it and it is not?*
6 [c] Deut. 15:9; Prov. 28:22 [2] Lit. *one who has an evil eye*
7 [d] Prov. 12:2
9 [e] Prov. 9:8; Matt. 7:6
10 [3] *boundary*
11 [f] Prov. 22:23
13 [g] Prov. 13:24
14 [4] Or *Sheol*

and legal issues to be settled (cf. 31:23). The "afflicted" were there begging or seeking justice or mercy and were to be fairly treated.

22:24,25 Cf. 12:26.

22:26,27 *See note on 6:1.*

22:28 landmark. This refers to stealing land by moving the boundaries. *See note on 15:25*; cf. Lev. 25:23; Deut. 19:14.

23:1-3 Here is a warning to exercise restraint when confronted with the luxuries of a wealthy ruler who seeks to lure you into his schemes and intrigues. Daniel is the classic illustration of one who lived by this proverb, refusing the allurements of the pagan monarch, which he knew could corrupt him (see Dan. 1:8ff.).

23:4,5 Cf. 11:28; 28:22; 1 Tim. 6:9,10,17. Rather than wearing one's self out pursuing wealth, pursue the wisdom of God and what glorifies Him, and He will bless with prosperity as He chooses. See 2:1-11; 3:5-10.

23:6-8 miser. This is the greedy one who, to be rich, hoards his riches, withholding from the poor and needy to keep and increase his own wealth. He invites someone to enjoy his courtesies, feigning generosity, while really being sickeningly hypocritical, as his real goal is to take advantage in some way so to increase his wealth at his guest's expense. Cf. 26:24-26.

23:9 This is true because fools hate wisdom (cf. 1:22; 9:8; 12:1).

23:10,11 ancient landmark. *See note on 15:25*; cf. 22:22,23.

23:11 Redeemer. In a normal situation the near kinsman would rescue the one who had fallen upon hard times (cf. Lev. 25:25; Ruth 2:20; 3:12,13; 4:1-12) or avenge in the case of a murder (Num. 35:19). "Redeemer" is applied to God as the Savior of His people (e.g., Gen. 48:16; Ex. 6:6; Job 19:25; Ps. 19:14; Is. 41:14; 43:14; 44:24) since the helpless had no voice.

23:13,14 correction. *See notes on 13:24; 22:6.* The child will survive the punishment and thus avoid an untimely or premature death due to sinful conduct (cf. Deut. 21:18-21).

23:14 hell. *See note on 1:12.*

23:15,16 son…wise. The result of correction (vv. 13,14) is the child's wise choices, bringing the parents joy (cf. vv. 24,25; 10:1; 15:20; 17:21; 28:7; 29:3).

16 Yes, my [5]inmost being will rejoice
When your lips speak right things.

17 [h]Do not let your heart envy sinners,
But [i]*be zealous* for the fear of the
LORD all the day;
18 [j]For surely there is a [6]hereafter,
And your hope will not be cut off.

19 Hear, my son, and be wise;
And guide your heart in the way.
20 [k]Do not mix with winebibbers,
Or with gluttonous eaters of meat;
21 For the drunkard and the glutton
will come to poverty,
And drowsiness will clothe *a man*
with rags.

22 [l]Listen to your father who begot
you,
And do not despise your mother
when she is old.

23 [m]Buy the truth, and do not sell *it*,
Also wisdom and instruction and
understanding.

24 [n]The father of the righteous will
greatly rejoice,
And he who begets a wise *child*
will delight in him.
25 Let your father and your mother
be glad,
And let her who bore you rejoice.

26 My son, give me your heart,
And let your eyes observe my ways.
27 [o]For a harlot *is* a deep pit,
And a seductress *is* a narrow well.

16 [5] Lit. *kidneys*
17 [h] Ps. 37:1; Prov. 24:1, 19 [i] Prov. 28:14
18 [j] [Ps. 37:37]
[6] Future, lit. *latter end*
20 [k] Prov. 20:1; 23:29, 30; Is. 5:22; Matt. 24:49; [Luke 21:34]; Rom. 13:13; [Eph. 5:18]
22 [l] Prov. 1:8; Eph. 6:1
23 [m] Prov. 4:7; 18:15; [Matt. 13:44]
24 [n] Prov. 10:1
27 [o] Prov. 22:14

28 [p] Prov. 7:12; Eccl. 7:26
29 [q] Is. 5:11, 22 [r] Gen. 49:12
30 [s] 1 Sam. 25:36; Prov. 20:1; 21:17; Is. 5:11; 28:7; [Eph. 5:18]
[t] Ps. 75:8
31 [7] *goes around*
34 [8] Lit. *heart*
35 [u] Prov. 27:22; Jer. 5:3 [v] Eph. 4:19

CHAPTER 24
1 [a] Ps. 1:1; 37:1; Prov. 23:17

28 [p]She also lies in wait as *for* a
victim,
And increases the unfaithful
among men.

29 [q]Who has woe?
Who has sorrow?
Who has contentions?
Who has complaints?
Who has wounds without cause?
Who [r]has redness of eyes?
30 [s]Those who linger long at the wine,
Those who go in search of [t]mixed
wine.
31 Do not look on the wine when it is
red,
When it sparkles in the cup,
When it [7]swirls around smoothly;
32 At the last it bites like a serpent,
And stings like a viper.
33 Your eyes will see strange things,
And your heart will utter perverse
things.
34 Yes, you will be like one who lies
down in the [8]midst of the sea,
Or like one who lies at the top of
the mast, *saying*:
35 "They [u] have struck me, *but* I was
not hurt;
They have beaten me, but I did not
feel *it*.
When shall [v]I awake, that I may
seek another *drink*?"

24 Do not be [a]envious of evil men,
Nor desire to be with them;
2 For their heart devises violence,
And their lips talk of
troublemaking.

23:16 inmost being. Lit. "the kidney," which, along with the heart (cf. 3:5; 4:21-23), are figurative expressions for the inner man or the seat of one's thoughts and feelings.

23:17 fear of the LORD. *See note on 1:7.*

23:18 there is a hereafter. Cf. v. 24. Anyone who might envy sinners needs to know that their prosperity is brief. They will die ("be cut off"); then there will be a time when all iniquities will be dealt with and divine justice will prevail (cf. Ps. 37:28-38). The righteous will live forever (*see note on 14:32*).

23:19 the way. The way of wisdom is the only right way (4:10,11).

23:20 winebibbers. Cf. vv. 29-35; Deut. 21:20.

23:22 Cf. 1:8; 2:1; 3:1; 4:1; 5:1; Eph. 6:1.

23:23 Buy the truth. Obtain the truth at all costs. *See notes on 4:5-7*; cf. Matt. 13:44-46. Then never relinquish it at any price (see Dan. 1:8ff.).

23:24,25 *See notes on v. 15; 13:24.*

23:27,28 harlot...seductress. Cf. 22:14. The terms refer to any immoral woman. *See notes on 2:16; 5:3-5; 7:5-27; 9:13-18.* Falling into her clutches should be as frightening as the prospect of falling into a deep pit or well, from which there is no escape.

23:29-35 This passage offers a powerful warning against drunkenness, presented as a riddle (v. 29) with its answer (v. 30). Following the riddle, come exhortations (vv. 31,32) and descriptions of the drunkard's delirious thoughts (vv. 33,35).

23:30 mixed wine. *See note on 20:1.* Lingering long at the wine is indicative of constant drinking, so as to induce drunkenness (cf. 1 Tim. 3:3; Titus 1:7). Searching for more to drink indicates the same pursuit.

23:31 wine when it is red. This describes wine when it is especially desirable and when it is most intoxicating, perhaps as "strong drink" or mixed with spices only and not water, as opposed to the "new wine" (3:10), which was fresh and unfermented or less fermented (cf. Hos. 4:11).

23:32 bites...stings. This recounts the hangover, but also the more than likely destructive consequences (cf. Is. 59:5; Jer. 8:17).

23:33 The delirium and distortion of reality are part of the drunkard's miserable experience (*see note on 1 Cor. 6:12*).

23:34 Here is the warning about the dizziness, sickness, and confusion of the drunkard, like being seasick at the top of the mast, the most agitated point on a ship in strong seas.

23:35 The drunkard's lack of sense is so severe that his first waking thought is to repeat his debauchery and dangerous sin.

24:1,2 Cf. 23:3,17.

3 Through wisdom a house is built,
And by understanding it is established;
4 By knowledge the rooms are filled
With all precious and pleasant riches.

5 [b]A wise man *is* strong,
Yes, a man of knowledge increases strength;
6 [c]For by wise counsel you will wage your own war,
And in a multitude of counselors *there is* safety.

7 [d]Wisdom *is* too lofty for a fool;
He does not open his mouth in the gate.

8 He who [e]plots to do evil
Will be called a [1]schemer.
9 The devising of foolishness *is* sin,
And the scoffer *is* an abomination to men.

10 *If* you [f]faint in the day of adversity,
Your strength *is* small.

11 [g]Deliver *those who* are drawn toward death,
And hold back *those* stumbling to the slaughter.
12 If you say, "Surely we did not know this,"
Does not [h]He who weighs the hearts consider *it?*
He who keeps your soul, does He *not* know *it?*
And will He *not* render to *each* man [i]according to his deeds?

13 My son, [j]eat honey because *it is* good,
And the honeycomb *which is* sweet to your taste;
14 [k]So *shall* the knowledge of wisdom *be* to your soul;
If you have found *it*, there is a [2]prospect,
And your hope will not be cut off.

15 Do not lie in wait, O wicked *man*, against the dwelling of the righteous;
Do not plunder his resting place;
16 [l]For a righteous *man* may fall seven times
And rise again,
[m]But the wicked shall fall by calamity.

17 [n]Do not rejoice when your enemy falls,
And do not let your heart be glad when he stumbles;
18 Lest the LORD see *it*, and [3]it displease Him,
And He turn away His wrath from him.

19 [o]Do not fret because of evildoers,
Nor be envious of the wicked;
20 For there will be no prospect for the evil *man;*
The lamp of the wicked will be put out.

21 My son, [p]fear the LORD and the king;
Do not associate with those given to change;
22 For their calamity will rise suddenly,
And who knows the ruin those two can bring?

5 [b] Prov. 21:22; Eccl. 9:16
6 [c] Luke 14:31
7 [d] Ps. 10:5; Prov. 14:6
8 [e] Prov. 6:14; 14:22; Rom. 1:30 [1] Lit. *master of evil plots*
10 [f] Deut. 20:8; Job 4:5; Jer. 51:46; Heb. 12:3
11 [g] Ps. 82:4; Is. 58:6, 7; 1 John 3:16
12 [h] 1 Sam. 16:7; Prov. 21:2 [i] Job 34:11; Ps. 62:12; Rev. 2:23; 22:12
13 [j] Ps. 19:10; 119:103; Prov. 25:16; Song 5:1
14 [k] Ps. 19:10; 58:11; Prov. 23:18 [2] Lit. *latter end*
16 [l] Job 5:19; [Ps. 34:19; 37:24; Mic. 7:8] [m] Esth. 7:10; Amos 5:2
17 [n] Job 31:29; Ps. 35:15, 19; [Prov. 17:5]; Obad. 12
18 [3] Lit. *it be evil in His eyes*
19 [o] Ps. 37:1
21 [p] [Rom. 13:7; 1 Pet. 2:17]

24:3,4 house is built. House can refer to a physical structure (cf. 14:1), a family (see Josh. 24:15), or even a dynasty (see 2 Sam. 7:11,12; 1 Kin 11:38; 1 Chr. 17:10).

24:5,6 Wisdom and wise counsel are associated with strength. *See notes on 11:14; 13:20*; cf. Eccl. 9:16-18.

24:7 the gate. *See note on 22:22.* Since the leading minds were there debating the issues of life, it was no place for fools.

24:11 The danger here may be from unjust treatment or violence. Deliverance can either be by giving a true testimony on their behalf, by providing what they need to survive, or by rescuing them from a fatal course.

24:12 He who weighs the hearts. *See note on 16:2.* God is the One who knows the truth about the motives of the heart and the excuses for failing to do what is right (cf. James 4:17). **render to *each* man according to his deeds.** Cf. v. 29; Job 34:11; Jer. 25:14; 50:29.

24:13,14 This is not a command to eat honey, but an analogy to seek the sweetness of wisdom's rewards (*see note on Ps. 19:10*).

24:14 hope...cut off. *See note on 23:18.*

24:15,16 seven times. This stands for "often" or "many" (see 26:26; Job 5:19). The plots of the wicked against the righteous, though partially and temporarily successful, shall not be ultimately successful; while the wicked will fall under God's eternal judgment and find no help or deliverance.

24:17,18 when your enemy falls. *See note on 25:21,22.* Gloating over a fallen enemy can be more serious than the sin the enemy committed.

24:19 Do not fret. Do not become angrily excited or envious at the apparent prosperity of the wicked. Cf. 3:31; 23:17,18; 24:1.

24:20 lamp of the wicked. *See note on 13:9.*

24:21 fear the LORD. *See note on 1:7.* **the king.** Loyalty to the king is proper because he is the agent of the Lord's wisdom (cf. Deut. 17:14-20; Rom. 13:1-7). That loyalty includes having no part with rebels who seek to subvert or overthrow him ("change"). Peter draws on this verse in his call to good citizenship in 1 Pet. 1:17; 2:17.

24:22 the ruin those two can bring. A reference to the retributive power of the king and the Lord (cf. Job 31:23).

Further Sayings of the Wise

23 These *things* also *belong* to the wise:

[q]*It is* not good to [4]show partiality in
judgment.
24 [r]He who says to the wicked, "You
are righteous,"
Him the people will curse;
Nations will abhor him.
25 But those who rebuke *the wicked*
will have [s]delight,
And a good blessing will come
upon them.

26 He who gives a right answer kisses
the lips.

27 [t]Prepare your outside work,
Make it fit for yourself in the field;
And afterward build your house.

28 [u]Do not be a witness against your
neighbor without cause,
[5]For would you deceive with your
lips?
29 [v]Do not say, "I will do to him just as
he has done to me;
I will render to the man according
to his work."

30 I went by the field of the lazy *man,*
And by the vineyard of the man
devoid of understanding;
31 And there it was, [w]all overgrown
with thorns;
Its surface was covered with
nettles;
Its stone wall was broken down.
32 When I saw *it,* I considered *it* well;
I looked on *it and* received
instruction:
33 [x]A little sleep, a little slumber,
A little folding of the hands to rest;
34 [y]So shall your poverty come *like* [6]a
prowler,
And your need like [7]an armed man.

Further Wise Sayings of Solomon

25 These[a] also *are* proverbs of Solomon
which the men of Hezekiah king of
Judah copied:

2 [b]*It is* the glory of God to conceal a
matter,
But the glory of kings *is* to search
out a matter.

3 *As* the heavens for height and the
earth for depth,
So the heart of kings *is*
unsearchable.

4 [c]Take away the dross from silver,
And it will go to the silversmith *for*
jewelry.
5 Take away the wicked from before
the king,
And his throne will be established
in [d]righteousness.

6 Do not exalt yourself in the
presence of the king,
And do not stand in the place of
the great;
7 [e]For *it is* better that he say to you,
"Come up here,"
Than that you should be put lower
in the presence of the prince,
Whom your eyes have seen.

8 [f]Do not go hastily to [1]court;
For what will you do in the end,

23 [q] Lev. 19:15; Deut. 1:17; 16:19; [John 7:24] [4] Lit. *recognize faces*
24 [r] Prov. 17:15; Is. 5:23
25 [s] Prov. 28:23
27 [t] 1 Kin. 5:17; Prov. 27:23-27
28 [u] Lev. 6:2, 3; 19:11; Eph. 4:25 [5] LXX, Vg. *Do not deceive*
29 [v] [Prov. 20:22; Matt. 5:39-44; Rom. 12:17-19]
31 [w] Gen. 3:18
33 [x] Prov. 6:9, 10
34 [y] Prov. 6:9-11 [6] Lit. *one who walks about* [7] Lit. *a man with a shield*

CHAPTER 25

1 [a] 1 Kin. 4:32
2 [b] Deut. 29:29; Rom. 11:33
4 [c] 2 Tim. 2:21
5 [d] Prov. 16:12; 20:8
7 [e] Luke 14:7-11
8 [f] Prov. 17:14; Matt. 5:25 [1] Lit. *contend* or *bring a lawsuit*

24:23a These words introduce a brief section forming an appendix of further wise sayings (vv. 23b-34) that finish the first group of proverbs compiled by Solomon to add to his own. *See note on 22:17–24:34.*

24:23b-25 partiality in judgment. Injustice is evil and destabilizes society. *See note on 17:15.*

24:26 kisses the lips. A just and righteous response is as desirable as this most intimate expression of friendship.

24:27 First, secure by diligent work and planning a good living in your fields, then build. In other words, provide a financial base so that all the necessities and contingencies are secured, then move from the tents (which were acceptable) to a house (which was desirable).

24:28,29 Avenging the evil done by one's neighbor by offering false witness (cf. 14:5; 19:5) against him is forbidden. *See notes on 6:19; 20:22.*

24:30-34. *See notes on 6:6,11.* Thorns also appear in his life in 15:19 (*see note there*).

25:1–29:27 Hezekiah's collection of Solomon's proverbs.

25:1 Hezekiah…copied. This collection of 137 proverbs was spoken by Solomon and most likely copied into a collection during the reign of Judah's king, Hezekiah (ca. 715–686 B.C.) over 200 years later. See Introduction: Author and Date. This is consistent with Hezekiah's efforts to bring revival to Judah (2 Chr. 29:30; 32:26), as he elevated the forgotten wisdom of David and Solomon (cf. 2 Chr. 29:31; 30:26).

25:2,3 God…kings. The roles of God and the king are compared. God, whose knowledge is above all human knowledge (cf. Ps. 92:5; Eccl. 3:11; Is. 46:10; Acts 15:18; Heb. 4:13), and whose ways are unsearchable (cf. Job 5:9; Ps. 145:3; Is. 40:28), keeps things to Himself because He needs no counsel (see Rom. 11:34). On the contrary, kings should rightly seek to know what they must know in order to rule righteously.

25:4,5 A nation is established as wisdom replaces and purifies wickedness (cf. 14:34; 16:12).

25:6,7 In the royal court as in all of life, self-seeking and pride bring one down. Do not intrude into such a place, for the elevating of the humble is honorable, but the humbling of the proud is disgraceful (cf. Luke 14:8-10; James 4:7-10).

25:8-10 go hastily to court. When conflict arises, the man with a contentious spirit is quick to go to court, but he is better off to talk it over with his neighbor than to expose himself to public shame in

When your neighbor has put you
to shame?
9 [g]Debate your case with your
neighbor,
And do not disclose the secret to
another;
10 Lest he who hears *it* expose your
shame,
And [2]your reputation be ruined.

11 A word fitly [h]spoken *is like* apples
of gold
In settings of silver.
12 *Like* an earring of gold and an
ornament of fine gold
Is a wise rebuker to an obedient ear.

13 [i]Like the cold of snow in time of
harvest
Is a faithful messenger to those
who send him,
For he refreshes the soul of his
masters.

14 [j]Whoever falsely boasts of giving
Is like [k]clouds and wind without
rain.

15 [l]By long forbearance a ruler is
persuaded,
And a gentle tongue breaks a bone.

16 Have you found honey?
Eat only as much as you need,
Lest you be filled with it and vomit.

17 Seldom set foot in your neighbor's
house,
Lest he become weary of you and
hate you.

18 [m]A man who bears false witness
against his neighbor
Is like a club, a sword, and a sharp
arrow.

19 Confidence in an unfaithful *man* in
time of trouble
Is like a bad tooth and a foot out of
joint.

20 *Like* one who takes away a garment
in cold weather,
And like vinegar on soda,
Is one who [n]sings songs to a heavy
heart.

21 [o]If your enemy is hungry, give him
bread to eat;
And if he is thirsty, give him water
to drink;
22 For *so* you will heap coals of fire on
his head,
[p]And the LORD will reward you.

23 The north wind brings forth rain,
And [q]a backbiting tongue an angry
countenance.

24 [r]*It is* better to dwell in a corner of a
housetop,
Than in a house shared with a
contentious woman.

25 *As* cold water to a weary soul,
So *is* [s]good news from a far
country.

26 A righteous *man* who falters before
the wicked
Is like a murky spring and a
[3]polluted well.

27 *It is* not good to eat much honey;
So [t]to seek one's own glory *is not*
glory.

28 [u]Whoever *has* no rule over his own
spirit
Is like a city broken down, without
walls.

9 [g] [Matt. 18:15]
10 [2] *the evil report concerning you not pass away*
11 [h] Prov. 15:23; Is. 50:4
13 [i] Prov. 13:17
14 [j] Prov. 20:6 [k] Jude 12
15 [l] Prov. 15:1
18 [m] Ps. 57:4; Prov. 12:18
20 [n] Dan. 6:18
21 [o] Ex. 23:4, 5; 2 Kin. 6:22; 2 Chr. 28:15; Matt. 5:44; Rom. 12:20
22 [p] 2 Sam. 16:12; [Matt. 6:4, 6]
23 [q] Ps. 101:5
24 [r] Prov. 19:13
25 [s] Prov. 15:30
26 [3] *ruined*
27 [t] Prov. 27:2; [Luke 14:11]
28 [u] Prov. 16:32

court, where everything will be told.

25:11,12 The imagery of beauty describes well chosen words, including words of rebuke. Cf. 15:23; 24:26.

25:13 cold of snow. A faithful messenger (cf. v. 25; 26:6) was as refreshing as snow would be in the heat of the summer harvest.

25:15 forbearance. Patience is a mighty weapon. See 15:1; 16:32.

25:16 This may be a parable that goes with v. 17, instructing the wise not to overdo anything that may lead to disgust and rejection, including overstaying or being overbearing with a friend who may begin to resent him.

25:18 He is as destructive to reputation as those weapons are to the body.

25:20 vinegar on soda. Pouring vinegar on an alkali (e.g., baking soda) produces a reaction like boiling or turning tranquility into agitation. So is the effect of singing joyful songs without sympathy to the sorrowful. Cf. Ps. 137:3,4.

25:21,22 As metals are melted by placing fiery coals on them, so is the heart of an enemy softened by such kindness. Contrast the coals of judgment in Ps. 140:10. Paul quotes this proverb in Rom. 12:20. Cf. Matt. 5:43-48.

25:23 The theme is cause and effect; as surely as a rain cloud brings the rain, slander produces anger.

25:24 *See note on 19:13; 21:9.*

25:25 *See note on v. 13.*

25:26 murky spring. The righteous one who sins muddies the water for the wicked who see him and for whom he should serve as an example of righteousness (cf. Ps. 17:5).

25:27 Eating honey is analogous to enjoying the sweetness of your own self-glory. *See notes on vv. 6,7,16.*

25:28 city broken down. Such are exposed and vulnerable to the incursion of evil thoughts and successful temptations. For the opposite, *see note on 16:32.*

26

As snow in summer [a]and rain in harvest,
So honor is not fitting for a fool.

2 Like a flitting sparrow, like a flying swallow,
So [b]a curse without cause shall not alight.

3 [c]A whip for the horse,
A bridle for the donkey,
And a rod for the fool's back.
4 Do not answer a fool according to his folly,
Lest you also be like him.
5 [d]Answer a fool according to his folly,
Lest he be wise in his own eyes.
6 He who sends a message by the hand of a fool
Cuts off *his own* feet *and* drinks violence.
7 *Like* the legs of the lame that hang limp
Is a proverb in the mouth of fools.
8 Like one who binds a stone in a sling
Is he who gives honor to a fool.
9 *Like* a thorn *that* goes into the hand of a drunkard
Is a proverb in the mouth of fools.
10 [1]The great *God* who formed everything
Gives the fool *his* hire and the transgressor *his* wages.
11 [e]As a dog returns to his own vomit,
[f]So a fool repeats his folly.
12 [g]Do you see a man wise in his own eyes?
There is more hope for a fool than for him.

13 The lazy *man* says, "*There is* a lion in the road!
A fierce lion *is* in the [2]streets!"
14 *As* a door turns on its hinges,
So *does* the lazy *man* on his bed.
15 The [h]lazy *man* buries his hand in the [3]bowl;
It wearies him to bring it back to his mouth.
16 The lazy *man is* wiser in his own eyes
Than seven men who can answer sensibly.

17 He who passes by *and* meddles in a quarrel not his own
Is like one who takes a dog by the ears.

18 Like a madman who throws firebrands, arrows, and death,
19 *Is* the man *who* deceives his neighbor,
And says, [i]"I was only joking!"

20 Where *there is* no wood, the fire goes out;
And where *there is* no [4]talebearer, strife ceases.
21 [j]*As* charcoal *is* to burning coals, and wood to fire,
So *is* a contentious man to kindle strife.

CHAPTER 26
1 [a] 1 Sam. 12:17
2 [b] Num. 23:8; Deut. 23:5; 2 Sam. 16:12
3 [c] Ps. 32:9; Prov. 19:29
5 [d] Matt. 16:1-4; Rom. 12:16
10 [1] Heb. difficult in v. 10; ancient and modern translators differ greatly
11 [e] 2 Pet. 2:22 [f] Ex. 8:15
12 [g] Prov. 29:20; Luke 18:11, 12; [Rev. 3:17]
13 [2] Or *plazas, squares*
15 [h] Prov. 19:24
[3] LXX, Syr. *bosom;* Tg., Vg. *armpit*
19 [i] Eph. 5:4
20 [4] *gossip* or *slanderer,* lit. *whisperer*
21 [j] Prov. 15:18

26:1-12 The fool is described in every verse. Most verses compare aspects of natural order that are violated with the behavior of a fool. The deteriorating nature of foolishness is seen as the description progresses from drink (v. 6) to vomit (v. 11).

26:1 These damaging incongruities of nature illustrate those in the moral realm. Cf. 17:7; 19:10.

26:2 curse without cause. A bird's aimless motion without landing is compared to a fool who utters an undeserved curse—it does not land either.

26:4,5 answer a fool. Taken together, these verses teach the appropriate way to answer a fool (e.g., an unbeliever who rejects truth). He should not be answered with agreement to his own ideas and presuppositions, or he will think he is right (v. 4), but rather he should be rebuked on the basis of his folly and shown the truth so he sees how foolish he is (v. 5).

26:6 Self-inflicted wounds come to the one who chooses to depend upon a fool (cf. 25:13).

26:7 Awkward and useless.

26:8 binds a stone. As it is nonsense to fasten a stone to a slingshot so that it will not release, so it is nonsense to honor a fool.

26:10 The Heb. language is obscure here, so as to produce many interpretations of what this is saying. Since it is impossible to know exactly what it said in the original, it is impossible to know exactly what it means. The translation might be: "Much brings forth from itself all; but the reward and the wages of the fool pass away." This could mean, reasonably, that although he who possesses much and has great ability may be able to accomplish all he wants, that is not the case when he makes use of the work of fools, who not only do not accomplish anything, but destroy everything.

26:11 Peter quotes this disgusting proverb in 2 Pet. 2:22.

26:12 wise in his own eyes. There are degrees of foolishness, with intellectual conceit being the most stupid and hard to remedy. This is applied to the lazy man in v. 16 and the rich in 28:11.

26:13-16 The lazy *man*. *See notes on 6:6,11; 22:13.*

26:16 The ignorant are ignorant of their ignorance. **seven.** *See note on 24:16.*

26:17-28 Here is a picturesque discourse on the evil speaking of fools and lazy people and its harmful effects.

26:17 meddles...dog by the ears. The dog was not domesticated in Palestine and thus to grab any dog was dangerous. The aggressor deserved to be bitten for his unprovoked act.

26:18,19 The serious damage done by deceit cannot be dismissed as a joke (cf. Is. 50:11).

26:20-22 talebearer. *See notes on 6:14; 16:28.* Slander fuels this fire.

22 The words of a [5]talebearer *are* like
[6]tasty trifles,
And they go down into the
[7]inmost body.

23 Fervent lips with a wicked heart
Are like earthenware covered with
silver dross.

24 He who hates, disguises *it* with his
lips,
And lays up deceit within himself;
25 [k]When [8]he speaks kindly, do not
believe him,
For *there are* seven abominations in
his heart;
26 *Though his* hatred is covered by
deceit,
His wickedness will be revealed
before the assembly.

27 [l]Whoever digs a pit will fall into it,
And he who rolls a stone will have
it roll back on him.

28 A lying tongue hates *those who are*
crushed by it,
And a flattering mouth works
[m]ruin.

27 Do[a] not boast about tomorrow,
For you do not know what a day
may bring forth.

2 [b]Let another man praise you, and
not your own mouth;
A stranger, and not your own lips.

3 A stone *is* heavy and sand *is*
weighty,
But a fool's wrath *is* heavier than
both of them.

4 Wrath *is* cruel and anger a torrent,
But [c]who *is* able to stand before
jealousy?

5 [d]Open rebuke *is* better
Than love carefully concealed.
6 Faithful *are* the wounds of a friend,
But the kisses of an enemy *are*
[e]deceitful.

7 A satisfied soul [1]loathes the
honeycomb,
But to a hungry soul every bitter
thing *is* sweet.

8 Like a bird that wanders from its
nest
Is a man who wanders from his
place.

9 Ointment and perfume delight the
heart,
And the sweetness of a man's friend
gives delight by [2]hearty counsel.

10 Do not forsake your own friend or
your father's friend,
Nor go to your brother's house in
the day of your calamity;
[f]Better *is* a neighbor nearby than a
brother far away.

11 My son, be wise, and make my
heart glad,
[g]That I may answer him who
reproaches me.

12 A prudent *man* foresees evil *and*
hides himself;
The simple pass on *and* are
[h]punished.

13 Take the garment of him who is
surety for a stranger,
And hold it in pledge *when* he is
surety for a seductress.

14 He who blesses his friend with a
loud voice, rising early in the
morning,

22 [5] *gossip* or *slanderer* [6] A Jewish tradition *wounds* [7] Lit. *rooms of the belly*
25 [k] Ps. 28:3; Prov. 26:23; Jer. 9:8 [8] Lit. *his voice is gracious*
27 [l] Esth. 7:10; Ps. 7:15; Prov. 28:10; Eccl. 10:8
28 [m] Prov. 29:5

CHAPTER 27

1 [a] Luke 12:19-21; James 4:13-16
2 [b] Prov. 25:27; 2 Cor. 10:12, 18; 12:11
4 [c] Prov. 6:34; 1 John 3:12
5 [d] [Prov. 28:23]; Gal. 2:14
6 [e] Matt. 26:49
7 [1] *tramples on*
9 [2] Lit. *counsel of the soul*
10 [f] Prov. 17:17; 18:24
11 [g] Prov. 10:1; 23:15-26
12 [h] Prov. 22:3

26:22 trifles. *See note on 18:8.*

26:23 earthenware covered. A cheap veneer of silver over a common clay pot hiding its commonness and fragility, is like the deception spoken by evil people. This thought is expanded in vv. 24-28.

26:27 The ruin intended for others will come back on the one who spoke it.

27:1 boast…tomorrow. Fools think they know the future or can affect its outcome, but the future rests with sovereign God. *See notes on 16:1,9*; cf. Ps. 37; James 4:13-16.

27:4 jealousy. Cf. 6:34; Song 8:6. The most uncontrollable sin.

27:5,6 Open rebuke. To genuinely love is to manifest the truth, even if it means to rebuke (cf. 28:23; Ps. 141:5; Gal. 4:16).

27:6 the kisses of an enemy. Cf. 5:3-5; 26:23,24.

27:7 The luxury and indolence of wealth make the best things tasteless, while the hard-working person who hungers finds every bitter thing sweet. This proverb extends beyond food to things in general, which means so much more to those with little.

27:8 man who wanders. Such are not only out of place, but off duty and in danger. Stay close to home.

27:10 Adhere to tried and true friends. The ties of blood may be less reliable than those of genuine friendship. *See notes on 17:17; 18:24.*

27:11 A wise son accredits his father and also aides him in difficulty with appropriate answers (cf. 10:1; 15:20). This proverb is true in reverse as well (cf. 17:25; 19:13; 22:21; 23:15).

27:12 Cf. 22:3.

27:13 *See note on 20:16.*

27:14 blesses his friend. Excessive flattery all day raises suspicion of selfishness.

It will be counted a curse to him.

15 A [i]continual dripping on a very rainy day
And a contentious woman are alike;
16 Whoever [3]restrains her restrains the wind,
And grasps oil with his right hand.
17 *As* iron sharpens iron,
So a man sharpens the countenance of his friend.

18 [j]Whoever [4]keeps the fig tree will eat its fruit;
So he who waits on his master will be honored.

19 As in water face *reflects* face,
So a man's heart *reveals* the man.

20 [k]Hell[5] and [6]Destruction are never full;
So [l]the eyes of man are never satisfied.

21 [m]The refining pot *is* for silver and the furnace for gold,
And a man *is valued* by what others say of him.

22 [n]Though you grind a fool in a mortar with a pestle along with crushed grain,
Yet his foolishness will not depart from him.

23 Be diligent to know the state of your [o]flocks,
And attend to your herds;
24 For riches *are* not forever,
Nor does a crown *endure* to all generations.
25 [p]*When* the hay is removed, and the tender grass shows itself,
And the herbs of the mountains are gathered in,
26 The lambs *will provide* your clothing,
And the goats the price of a field;
27 *You shall have* enough goats' milk for your food,
For the food of your household,
And the nourishment of your maidservants.

28 The [a]wicked flee when no one pursues,
But the righteous are bold as a lion.
2 Because of the transgression of a land, many *are* its princes;
But by a man of understanding *and* knowledge
Right will be prolonged.

3 [b]A poor man who oppresses the poor
Is like a driving rain [1]which leaves no food.

4 [c]Those who forsake the law praise the wicked,
[d]But such as keep the law contend with them.

5 [e]Evil men do not understand justice,
But [f]those who seek the LORD understand all.

6 Better *is* the poor who walks in his integrity
Than one perverse *in his* ways, though he *be* rich.

7 Whoever keeps the law *is* a discerning son,
But a companion of gluttons shames his father.

15 [i] Prov. 19:13
16 [3] Lit. *hides*
18 [j] 2 Kin. 18:31; Song 8:12; Is. 36:16; [1 Cor. 3:8; 9:7-13]; 2 Tim. 2:6 [4] *protects* or *tends*
20 [k] Prov. 30:15, 16; Hab. 2:5 [l] Eccl. 1:8; 4:8 [5] Or *Sheol* [6] Heb. *Abaddon*
21 [m] Prov. 17:3
22 [n] Prov. 23:35; 26:11; Jer. 5:3
23 [o] Prov. 24:27
25 [p] Ps. 104:14

CHAPTER 28

1 [a] Lev. 26:17, 36; Ps. 53:5
3 [b] Matt. 18:28 [1] Lit. *and there is no bread*
4 [c] Ps. 49:18; Rom. 1:32 [d] 1 Kin. 18:18; Neh. 13:11, 15; Matt. 3:7; 14:4; Eph. 5:11
5 [e] Ps. 92:6; Is. 6:9; 44:18 [f] Ps. 119:100; Prov. 2:9; John 17:17; 1 Cor. 2:15; [1 John 2:20, 27]

27:15,16 *See notes on 19:13; 21:9.* This kind of woman is impossible to restrain or tame.

27:17 iron sharpens iron. The benefits of intellectual and theological discussion encourage joy through a keener mind and the improvement of good character which the face will reveal.

27:20 Hell and Destruction. Man's desires are never filled up. They are as insatiable as the place of eternal punishment which never overfills (cf. 30:15,16).

27:21 refining pot...what others say. "Value" is not the best understanding. Popularity and praise "test" rather than "value" personal character in the crucible. *See note on 17:3.*

27:22 mortar...pestle. A bowl and rod of stone which were used to crush solid grain into powder.

27:23-27 This portion contrasts the common shepherd's labor and God's provision with the fleeting nature of uncertain riches and power (v. 24). Since all lands reverted to the original owners every 50 years, flocks were the staple wealth. Only by care and diligence could they be perpetuated and profitable. God's providence aids this effort (cf. Ps. 65:9-13) to properly use the blessings of the land (vv. 25-27).

28:1 A guilty conscience imagines accusers everywhere (cf. Num. 32:23; Ps. 53:5), while a clear conscience has boldness to face everyone.

28:2 many *are* its princes. Unrighteousness in a nation produces political instability with many vying for power, thus the tenure of each leader is shortened. Wisdom promotes social order and long rule.

28:3 oppresses the poor. When the poor come to power and oppress their own, it is as bad as a destructive storm washing the fields clean instead of watering the crop.

28:7 The son who obeyed God's law would not be a glutton and shame his father. Cf. 23:19-25.

8 One who increases his possessions
by usury and extortion
Gathers it for him who will pity
the poor.

9 One who turns away his ear from
hearing the law,
[g]Even his prayer *is* an abomination.

10 [h]Whoever causes the upright to go
astray in an evil way,
He himself will fall into his own
pit;
[i]But the blameless will inherit good.

11 The rich man *is* wise in his own
eyes,
But the poor who has
understanding searches him
out.

12 When the righteous rejoice, *there is*
great [j]glory;
But when the wicked arise, men
[2]hide themselves.

13 [k]He who covers his sins will not
prosper,
But whoever confesses and
forsakes *them* will have
mercy.

14 Happy *is* the man who is always
reverent,
But he who hardens his heart will
fall into calamity.

15 [l]*Like* a roaring lion and a charging
bear
[m]*Is* a wicked ruler over poor
people.

16 A ruler who lacks understanding *is*
a great [n]oppressor,
But he who hates covetousness will
prolong *his* days.

17 [o]A man burdened with bloodshed
will flee into a pit;
Let no one help him.

18 Whoever walks blamelessly will be
[3]saved,
But *he who is* perverse *in his* ways
will suddenly fall.

19 [p]He who tills his land will have
plenty of bread,
But he who follows frivolity will
have poverty enough!

20 A faithful man will abound with
blessings,
[q]But he who hastens to be rich will
not go unpunished.

21 [r]To [4]show partiality *is* not good,
[s]Because for a piece of bread a man
will transgress.

22 A man with an evil eye hastens
after riches,
And does not consider that
[t]poverty will come upon him.

23 [u]He who rebukes a man will find
more favor afterward
Than he who flatters with the
tongue.

24 Whoever robs his father or his
mother,
And says, "*It is* no transgression,"

9 [g] Ps. 66:18; 109:7; Prov. 15:8
10 [h] Ps. 7:15; Prov. 26:27 [i] [Matt. 6:33; Heb. 6:12; 1 Pet. 3:9]
12 [j] Prov. 11:10; 29:2 [2] Lit. *will be searched for*
13 [k] Ps. 32:3-5; 1 John 1:8-10
15 [l] Prov. 19:12; 1 Pet. 5:8 [m] Ex. 1:14; Prov. 29:2; Matt. 2:16
16 [n] Eccl. 10:16; Is. 3:12
17 [o] Gen. 9:6
18 [3] *delivered*
19 [p] Prov. 12:11; 20:13
20 [q] Prov. 13:11; 20:21; 23:4; 1 Tim. 6:9
21 [r] Prov. 18:5 [s] Ezek. 13:19 [4] Lit. *recognize faces*
22 [t] Prov. 21:5
23 [u] Prov. 27:5,6

28:8 usury and extortion. The law forbade the charging of interest to fellow Jews (see Deut. 23:19,20), but this was often violated (cf. Neh. 5:7,11; Ezek. 22:12). **Gathers it for him.** In the providence and justice of God, such wealth will be forfeited to someone who treats the poor fairly. *See notes on 13:22; 14:31.*

28:9 *See note on 15:8.*

28:10 The attempted corruption of the righteous is a wicked sin (Matt. 5:19; 18:6; 23:15). **fall into his own pit.** *See note on 26:27.*

28:11 rich man *is* wise in his own eyes. This contrasts the discerning poor with the rich man, who is deceived by his self-confidence. Riches are not always possessed by the unrighteous and wisdom by the poor, but, more often than not, this is the case due to the blinding nature of wealth (cf. 11:28; 18:23; Matt 19:23,24).

28:12 When wicked people come into power, the righteous "shout" (11:10), "groan" (29:2), and "hide" (28:28).

28:13 covers...confesses. Sin must not be covered but confessed. *See notes on Ps. 32:1-14; 1 John 1:6-9.*

28:14 hardens his heart. Cf. Ex. 7:13; 17:7; Ps. 95:8; Rom. 2:5.

28:16 great oppressor. The tyrannical leader who is covetous (implied) is foolish and short-lived.

28:17 Whoever is inwardly tormented by the murder of someone takes to ceaseless flight to escape the avenger of blood and the punishment of his crime. He flees and finds no rest until the grave receives him. The exhortation is to avoid helping a murderer with any support, refuge, or security against the vengeance which pursues him from the arm of justice.

28:20 abound with blessings. Blessings are the product of honest labor. See notes on 10:22; 11:24-26; cf. Gen. 49:25; Mal. 3:10. **hastens to be rich.** *See note on 20:21*; cf. 1 Tim. 6:9.

28:21 piece of bread. A small bribe. Cf. 15:27; 18:5; 24:23.

28:22 man with an evil eye. A miser is motivated by greed. *See notes on 21:5-7.*

28:23 Flattery has no value but reproof does, so it leads to gratitude. Cf. 16:13; 27:5,6.

28:24 robs his father...mother. *See note on 19:26.* To plunder one's own family is an unthinkable crime, but it is worse yet when denied.

The same [v]*is* companion to a
destroyer.

25 [w]He who is of a proud heart stirs up
strife,
[x]But he who trusts in the LORD will
be prospered.

26 He who [y]trusts in his own heart is
a fool,
But whoever walks wisely will be
delivered.

27 [z]He who gives to the poor will not
lack,
But he who hides his eyes will
have many curses.

28 When the wicked arise, [a]men hide
themselves;
But when they perish, the
righteous increase.

29 He[a] who is often rebuked, *and*
hardens *his* neck,
Will suddenly be destroyed, and
that without remedy.

2 When the righteous [1]are in
authority, the [b]people rejoice;
But when a wicked *man* rules, [c]the
people groan.

3 Whoever loves wisdom makes his
father rejoice,
But a companion of harlots wastes
his wealth.

4 The king establishes the land by
justice,
But he who receives bribes
overthrows it.

5 A man who [d]flatters his neighbor
Spreads a net for his feet.

6 By transgression an evil man is
snared,
But the righteous sings and
rejoices.

7 The righteous [e]considers the cause
of the poor,
But the wicked does not
understand *such* knowledge.

8 Scoffers [f]set a city aflame,
But wise *men* turn away wrath.

9 *If* a wise man contends with a
foolish man,
[g]Whether *the fool* rages or laughs,
there is no peace.

10 [h]The bloodthirsty hate the
blameless,
But the upright seek his [2]well-
being.

11 A fool vents all his [i]feelings,[3]
But a wise *man* holds them back.

12 If a ruler pays attention to lies,
All his servants *become* wicked.

13 The poor *man* and the oppressor
have this in common:
[j]The LORD gives light to the eyes of
both.

14 The king who judges the [k]poor
with truth,
His throne will be established
forever.

15 The rod and rebuke give [l]wisdom,
But a child left *to himself* brings
shame to his mother.

16 When the wicked are multiplied,
transgression increases;
But the righteous will see their
[m]fall.

17 Correct your son, and he will give
you rest;

24 [v]Prov. 18:9
25 [w]Prov. 13:10 [x]Prov. 29:25; 1 Tim. 6:6
26 [y]Prov. 3:5
27 [z]Deut. 15:7; Prov. 19:17; 22:9
28 [a]Job 24:4

CHAPTER 29

1 [a]2 Chr. 36:16; Prov. 6:15
2 [b]Esth. 8:15; Prov. 28:12 [c]Esth. 4:3 [1]*become great*
5 [d]Prov. 26:28
7 [e]Job 29:16; Ps. 41:1; Prov. 31:8, 9
8 [f]Prov. 11:11
9 [g]Matt. 11:17
10 [h]Gen. 4:5–8; 1 John 3:12 [2]Lit. *soul or life*
11 [i]Prov. 14:33 [3]Lit. *spirit*
13 [j][Matt. 5:45]
14 [k]Ps. 72:4; Is. 11:4
15 [l]Prov. 22:15
16 [m]Ps. 37:34; Prov. 21:12

28:25 proud heart…strife. This is arrogance that satisfies itself at the expense of conflict with others and never knows the prosperity of humble trust in God.

28:27 hides his eyes. This refers to one who does not respond to the needs of the poor. *See note on 14:31*; cf. 1 John 3:16–18.

28:28 *See note on v. 12.*

29:1 hardens *his* neck. This refers to a state of increasing obstinance, along with an unteachable spirit. *See note on 28:14.*

29:2 righteous…wicked. *See note on 28:12.* This could describe the political turmoil of the northern kingdom of Israel in the time of Hezekiah, who collected these proverbs (*see note on 25:1*).

29:4 bribes. *See note on 15:27.*

29:5 Flattery is a trap. Cf. 26:28; 28:23.

29:8 These angry, arrogant men fan the flames of strife that trap a city as if engulfed in flames (cf. 26:21).

29:9 contends. A fool may respond to wisdom with anger or laughter, but in either case, no agreement can be reached. Cf. 26:4,5.

29:12 ruler pays attention to lies. A corrupt leader will draw around him corrupt people. Allow lies and you will be surrounded by liars.

29:13 gives light to the eyes. This phrase means to sustain life. God gives life to both the poor and the rich oppressor, and He holds each responsible for His truth. Cf. 22:1.

29:15 *See notes on 13:24; 22:6.*

29:17 Correct your son. *See notes on 13:24; 22:6.*

Yes, he will give delight to your
soul.

18 [n]Where *there is* no [4]revelation, the
people cast off restraint;
But [o]happy *is* he who keeps the law.

19 A servant will not be corrected by
mere words;
For though he understands, he will
not respond.

20 Do you see a man hasty in his
words?
[p]*There is* more hope for a fool than
for him.

21 He who pampers his servant from
childhood
Will have him as a son in the end.

22 [q]An angry man stirs up strife,
And a furious man abounds in
transgression.

23 [r]A man's pride will bring him low,
But the humble in spirit will retain
honor.

24 Whoever is a partner with a thief
hates his own life;
[s]He [5]swears to tell the truth, but
reveals nothing.

25 [t]The fear of man brings a snare,
But whoever trusts in the LORD
shall be [6]safe.

26 [u]Many seek the ruler's [7]favor,
But justice for man *comes* from the
LORD.

27 An unjust man *is* an abomination
to the righteous,
And *he who is* upright in the way *is*
an abomination to the wicked.

The Wisdom of Agur

30 The words of Agur the son of Jakeh,
his utterance. This man declared to
Ithiel—to Ithiel and Ucal:

2 [a]Surely I *am* more stupid than *any*
man,
And do not have the
understanding of a man.
3 I neither learned wisdom
Nor have [b]knowledge of the Holy
One.

4 [c]Who has ascended into heaven, or
descended?
[d]Who has gathered the wind in His
fists?
Who has bound the waters in a
garment?
Who has established all the ends of
the earth?
What *is* His name, and what *is* His
Son's name,
If you know?

5 [e]Every word of God *is* [1]pure;
[f]He *is* a shield to those who put
their trust in Him.

18 [n] 1 Sam. 3:1; Ps. 74:9; Amos 8:11, 12 [o] Prov. 8:32; John 13:17 [4] *prophetic vision*
20 [p] Prov. 26:12
22 [q] Prov. 26:21
23 [r] Job 22:29; Prov. 15:33; 18:12; Is. 66:2; Dan. 4:30; Matt. 23:12; Luke 14:11; 18:14; Acts 12:23; [James 4:6-10; 1 Pet. 5:5, 6]
24 [s] Lev. 5:1 [5] Lit. *hears the adjuration or oath*
25 [t] Gen. 12:12; 20:2; Luke 12:4; John 12:42, 43 [6] *secure,* lit. *set on high*
26 [u] Ps. 20:9 [7] Lit. *face*

CHAPTER 30

2 [a] Ps. 73:22; Prov. 12:1
3 [b] [Prov. 9:10]
4 [c] [Ps. 68:18; John 3:13] [d] Job 38:4; Ps. 104:3; Is. 40:12
5 [e] Ps. 12:6; 19:8; 119:140 [f] Ps. 18:30; 84:11; 115:9-11 [1] *tested, refined, found pure*

29:18 no revelation. This proverb looks both to the lack of the Word (i.e., 1 Sam. 3:1) and the lack of hearing the Word (Amos 8:11, 12), which leads to lawless rebellion (cf. Ex. 32:25; Lev. 13:45; Num. 5:18). The proverb then contrasts the joy and glory of a lawful society (28:14; Mal. 4:4).

29:19 will not be corrected. This verse views the mind-set of an unprincipled and foolish slave who is unresponsive and irresponsible.

29:20 hasty in his words. *See note on 10:19.*

29:21 The idea is of overindulging a servant, so that the servant will ultimately want to be cared for like a son, rather than one who serves the master.

29:22 Cf. 15:18

29:23 Cf. 16:18, 19.

29:24 partner with a thief. By refusing to testify with full disclosure to avoid incrimination, one commits perjury which leads to punishment.

29:26 the ruler's favor. The moral is to seek the Lord's favor, since He alone can and will exact justice.

30:1-33 The words of Agur. This is a collection of proverbs written by an unknown sage who was likely a student of wisdom at the time of Solomon (cf. 1 Kin. 4:30, 31). Agur reflects humility (vv. 1-4), a deep hatred for arrogance (vv. 7-9), and a keen theological mind (vv. 5, 6).

30:1 utterance. This word is often used of a prophet (cf. Zech. 9:1; Mal. 1:1) and can be translated "burden" for its weighty character as a divine word or prophecy (cf. Mal. 1:1). **Ithiel and Ucal.** Agur addressed his wisdom perhaps to his favorite pupils, as Luke to Theophilus (Luke 1:1-4; Acts 1:1, 2).

30:2, 3 more stupid...neither learned. This is a statement of humility and a recognition of the reality that, apart from divine revelation, there would be no true wisdom at all (*see notes on 1:7; 9:10*). This is illustrated in the pursuits of Job (Job 3:3-26) and Solomon (Eccl. 3:1-15). Agur was wise because he first admitted what he could not know (1 Cor. 2:6-16).

30:3 knowledge of the Holy One. Agur knew that he could not gain wisdom through human searching alone. Understanding is here associated with the holiness of God. Cf. 9:10; 1 Cor. 8:2.

30:4 Who...what. These questions can be answered only by revelation from God. A man can know the "what" about creative wisdom through observation of the physical world and its inner workings, but cannot know the "who." The "who" can be known only when God reveals Himself, which He has in Scripture. This is the testimony and conclusion of Job (Job 42:1-6), Solomon (Eccl. 12:1-14), Isaiah (Is. 40:12-17; 46:8-11; 66:18, 19), and Paul (Rom. 8:18-39). **His Son's name.** Jesus Christ. Cf. John 1:1-18.

30:5, 6 These verses move from the uncertainty of human speculation to the certainty of divine revelation. Agur quotes from David (2 Sam 22:31; Ps. 18:30).

30:5 pure. Lit. "tried," and found to be without dross or error. Cf. Ps. 12:6.

6 [g]Do not add to His words,
Lest He rebuke you, and you be found a liar.

7 Two *things* I request of You
(Deprive me not before I die):
8 Remove falsehood and lies far from me;
Give me neither poverty nor riches—
[h]Feed me with the food allotted to me;
9 [i]Lest I be full and deny *You*,
And say, "Who *is* the LORD?"
Or lest I be poor and steal,
And profane the name of my God.

10 Do not malign a servant to his master,
Lest he curse you, and you be found guilty.

11 *There is* a generation *that* curses its [j]father,
And does not bless its mother.
12 *There is* a generation [k]*that is* pure in its own eyes,
Yet is not washed from its filthiness.
13 *There is* a generation—oh, how [l]lofty are their eyes!
And their eyelids are [2]lifted up.
14 [m]*There is* a generation whose teeth *are like* swords,
And whose fangs *are like* knives,
[n]To devour the poor from off the earth,
And the needy from *among* men.

15 The leech has two daughters—
Give *and* Give!

There are three *things that* are never satisfied,
Four never say, "Enough!":
16 [o]The[3] grave,
The barren womb,
The earth *that* is not satisfied with water—
And the fire never says, "Enough!"

17 [p]The eye *that* mocks *his* father,
And scorns obedience to *his* mother,
The ravens of the valley will pick it out,
And the young eagles will eat it.

18 There are three *things which* are too wonderful for me,
Yes, four *which* I do not understand:
19 The way of an eagle in the air,
The way of a serpent on a rock,
The way of a ship in the [4]midst of the sea,
And the way of a man with a virgin.

20 This *is* the way of an adulterous woman:
She eats and wipes her mouth,
And says, "I have done no wickedness."

21 For three *things* the earth is perturbed,
Yes, for four it cannot bear up:

6 [g] Deut. 4:2; 12:32; Rev. 22:18
8 [h] Job 23:12; Matt. 6:11; [Phil. 4:19]
9 [i] Deut. 8:12-14; Neh. 9:25, 26; Hos. 13:6
11 [j] Ex. 21:17; Prov. 20:20
12 [k] [Prov. 16:2]; Is. 65:5; Luke 18:11; [Titus 1:15, 16]
13 [l] Ps. 131:1; Prov. 6:17; Is. 2:11; 5:15
[2] In arrogance
14 [m] Job 29:17; Ps. 52:2 [n] Ps. 14:4; Amos 8:4
16 [o] Prov. 27:20; Hab. 2:5 [3] Or *Sheol*
17 [p] Gen. 9:22; Lev. 20:9; Prov. 20:20
19 [4] Lit. *heart*

30:6 Do not add. A powerful statement on the inspired nature of God's canonical Word to Israel. To add to God's Word is to deny God as the standard of truth (cf. Gen. 2:16,17 with 3:2,3). *See notes on Deut 4:2; 12:32; Rev. 22:18,19.*

30:7-9 The prayer of a true wisdom-seeker. He seeks from the Lord honesty in heart and sufficiency in Him (away from the dangers posed by the extremes of poverty or wealth). If he has too much, he could cease depending on God (*see Deut. 8:11-20; 10:15; 18:11*), and if he has too little, he could be tempted to be as the sluggard (6:6-11).

30:9 Who *is* the LORD? This is a question reflecting extreme arrogance, e.g., "Who *is* the Almighty, that we should serve Him?" (Job 21:14-16). Cf. Deut. 8:10-18; Luke 12:16-21.

30:11-14 *There is* a generation. These proverbs condemn various forms of unwise behavior and are connected with this common phrase which points to the fact that certain sins can uniquely permeate a whole society or time period.

30:11 *See note on 20:20.* Cf. Ex. 21:17; Pss. 14:5; 24:6.

30:12 *See notes on 16:2; 20:9*; cf. Matt. 23:23-26.

30:13 *See notes on 6:17; 21:4.*

30:14 *See note on 14:31.*

30:15,16 leech...Give *and* Give! These two blood-sucking mouths of the horse leech, which lived off the blood of its victim, are used to picture the insatiably greedy.

30:16 grave...fire. Four illustrations of the greedy are given, all of which are parasitic in nature and characterize the heart of human greed. Cf. Gen 16:2; 20:18; 30:1.

30:17 eye *that* mocks. This proverb vividly speaks to the tragic results of disregarding parental respect and authority and the destruction it brings. *See notes on 10:1; 17:21; 29:15,17*; cf. Ex. 20:12. **ravens...young eagles.** These birds scavenge the unburied corpse of a child who dies prematurely because of rebellion. Cf. 1 Sam. 17:44; 1 Kin. 14:11; Jer. 16:4; Ezek. 29:5; 39:7.

30:18-20 Hypocrisy is illustrated by 4 natural analogies of concealment: 1) an eagle leaves no trail in the air; 2) a slithering snake leaves no trail on the rock; 3) a ship leaves no trail in the sea; 4) a man leaves no marks after he has slept with a virgin. These actions are all concealed and thus serve to illustrate the hypocrisy of the adulterous woman who hides the evidences of her shame while professing innocence.

30:21-23 earth is perturbed. *See notes on 19:10; 28:3.* Society is greatly agitated when normal roles are overturned, e.g., servants reigning, fools made rich, hated women married, and maidservants becoming wives (cf. Gen. 16:1-6).

22 [q]For a servant when he reigns,
A fool when he is filled with food,
23 A [5]hateful *woman* when she is
married,
And a maidservant who succeeds
her mistress.

24 There are four *things which* are little
on the earth,
But they *are* exceedingly wise:
25 [r]The ants *are* a people not strong,
Yet they prepare their food in the
summer;
26 [s]The [6]rock badgers are a feeble folk,
Yet they make their homes in the
crags;
27 The locusts have no king,
Yet they all advance in ranks;
28 The [7]spider skillfully grasps with
its hands,
And it is in kings' palaces.

29 There are three *things which* are
majestic in pace,
Yes, four *which* are stately in walk:
30 A lion, *which is* mighty among
beasts
And does not turn away from
any;
31 A [8]greyhound,
A male goat also,
And [9]a king *whose* troops *are* with
him.

32 If you have been foolish in exalting
yourself,
Or if you have devised evil, [t]*put
your* hand on *your* mouth.
33 For *as* the churning of milk
produces butter,
And wringing the nose produces
blood,
So the forcing of wrath produces
strife.

The Words of King Lemuel's Mother

31 The words of King Lemuel, the utterance which his mother taught
him:

2 What, my son?
And what, son of my womb?
And what, [a]son of my vows?
3 [b]Do not give your strength to
women,
Nor your ways [c]to that which
destroys kings.

4 [d]*It is* not for kings, O Lemuel,
It is not for kings to drink wine,
Nor for princes intoxicating drink;
5 [e]Lest they drink and forget the law,
And pervert the justice of all [1]the
afflicted.
6 [f]Give strong drink to him who is
perishing,
And wine to those who are bitter
of heart.

22 [q] Prov. 19:10; Eccl. 10:7
23 [5] Or *hated*
25 [r] Prov. 6:6
26 [s] Lev. 11:5; Ps. 104:18 [6] *rock hyraxes*
28 [7] Or *lizard*
31 [8] Or perhaps *strutting rooster*, lit. *girded of waist* [9] A Jewish tradition *a king against whom there is no uprising*
32 [t] Job 21:5; 40:4; Mic. 7:16

CHAPTER 31
2 [a] Is. 49:15
3 [b] Prov. 5:9 [c] Deut. 17:17; 1 Kin. 11:1; Neh. 13:26; Prov. 7:26; Hos. 4:11
4 [d] Eccl. 10:17
5 [e] Hos. 4:11 [1] Lit. *sons of affliction*
6 [f] Ps. 104:15

30:24-28 four *things which* are little. These verses picture 4 creatures which survive due to natural instinct. The wisdom seen in each of these reveals the beauty of the wise Creator and His creation (cf. Ps. 8:3-9) and becomes a model for the principle that labor, diligence, organization, planning, and resourcefulness are better than strength, thus implying the superiority of wisdom over might.

30:25 ants. These survive through planning and labor. *See note on 6:6.*

30:26 rock badgers. Badgers, though weak, survive by being diligent enough to climb and find sanctuary in high places. Cf. Lev. 11:5; Ps. 104:18.

30:27 locusts. These survive through careful organization.

30:28 spider. These creatures are resourceful and can crawl and set up their webs even in a palace.

30:29-31 three *things*...majestic in pace...four. The 3 creatures and the king all picture wise, stately, and orderly deportment. Each offers a glimpse of the Creator's power and wisdom (cf. Job 38:1–42:6) and illustrates the dignity and confidence of those who walk wisely.

30:31 greyhound. The meaning in Heb. is uncertain. Other possibilities are 1) a strutting rooster or 2) a war-horse ready for battle. Cf. Job 39:19-25. **male goat.** This is the he-goat that was the leader of the flock. Cf Dan. 8:5.

30:32 *put your* hand on *your* mouth. Lit. "stop your scheming and talking"—a gesture of awestruck, self-imposed silence. Cf. Job 21:5; 29:9; 40:4.

30:33 produces. The verb is the same (pressing or squeezing) in all 3 instances. These are natural causes and effects to show that anger pressed beyond certain limits produces conflict.

31:1-31 This concluding chapter contains two poems: 1) The Wise King (31:2-9) and 2) The Excellent Wife (31:10-31). Both are the teachings of a godly mother (v. 1) to King Lemuel, whom ancient Jewish tradition identified as King Solomon, but who is otherwise unknown.

31:1 utterance. *See note on 30:1.* **mother taught him.** See 1:8.

31:2-9 The godly king is addressed (v. 2) and told that his reign should be characterized by: 1) holiness (v. 3); 2) sobriety (vv. 4-7); and 3) compassion (vv. 8,9). This section is filled with succinct and solemn warnings against vices to which kings are particularly susceptible—immorality, overindulgence, unrighteous rule, and indifference to those in need.

31:2 my son. The phrase is repeated 3 times to indicate the serious passion of a mother's heart. **son of my vows.** Like Hannah, she had dedicated her child to the Lord (cf. 1 Sam. 1:11,27-28).

31:3 Do not give your strength to women. Multiplying foreign wives destroys a king like it did Solomon (cf. Deut. 17:17; 1 Kin. 11:1-4). *See notes on 5:9-11.*

31:4,5 *See notes on 20:1; 23:29-35.* Intoxicating drinks can weaken reason and judgment, loosen convictions, or pervert the heart. They do not suit rulers who need clear, steady minds and keen judgment.

31:6,7 Give strong drink. Such extreme situations, possibly relating to a criminal on death row or someone agonizing in pain with a terminal illness or tragic circumstance, are in utter contrast to that of the king (cf. Ps. 104:15).

7 Let him drink and forget his
poverty,
And remember his misery no
more.

8 [g]Open your mouth for the
speechless,
In the cause of all *who are*
[2]appointed to die.

9 Open your mouth, [h]judge
righteously,
And [i]plead the cause of the poor
and needy.

The Virtuous Wife

10 [j]Who[3] can find a [4]virtuous wife?
For her worth *is* far above rubies.
11 The heart of her husband safely
trusts her;
So he will have no lack of gain.
12 She does him good and not evil
All the days of her life.
13 She seeks wool and flax,
And willingly works with her
hands.
14 She is like the merchant ships,
She brings her food from afar.
15 [k]She also rises while it is yet night,
And [l]provides food for her
household,
And a portion for her
maidservants.
16 She considers a field and buys it;
From [5]her profits she plants a
vineyard.
17 She girds herself with strength,
And strengthens her arms.
18 She perceives that her merchandise
is good,
And her lamp does not go out by
night.
19 She stretches out her hands to the
distaff,
And her hand holds the spindle.
20 [m]She extends her hand to the poor,
Yes, she reaches out her hands to
the needy.
21 She is not afraid of snow for her
household,
For all her household *is* clothed
with scarlet.
22 She makes tapestry for herself;
Her clothing *is* fine linen and
purple.
23 [n]Her husband is known in the
gates,
When he sits among the elders of
the land.
24 She makes linen garments and sells
them,

8 [g] Job 29:15, 16; Ps. 82 [2] Lit. *sons of passing away*
9 [h] Lev. 19:15; Deut. 1:16 [i] Job 29:12; Is. 1:17; Jer. 22:16
10 [j] Ruth 3:11; Prov. 12:4; 19:14 [3] Vv. 10-31 are an alphabetic acrostic in Hebrew; cf. Ps. 119 [4] Lit. *a wife of valor,* in the sense of all forms of excellence
15 [k] Prov. 20:13; Rom. 12:11 [l] Luke 12:42
16 [5] Lit. *the fruit of her hands*
20 [m] Deut. 15:11; Job 31:16-20; Prov. 22:9; Rom. 12:13; Eph. 4:28; Heb. 13:16
23 [n] Prov. 12:4

31:8,9 Open your mouth. Plead for those who cannot plead their own case, namely those who are otherwise ruined by their condition of weakness. The king's duty was to righteously uphold the case of the helpless in both physical (v. 6) and material (v. 9) crises. The monarch thus mediates the compassion of God. *See notes on 14:21,31.*

31:10-31 This poem offers a beautiful description of the excellent wife as defined by a wife and mother (v. 1). Spiritual and practical wisdom plus moral virtues mark the character of this woman in contrast to the immoral women of v. 3. While the scene here is of a wealthy home and the customs of the ancient Near East, the principles apply to every family. They are set forth as the prayer of every mother for the future wife of her son, and literarily arranged with each of the 22 verses beginning with the 22 letters of the Hebrew alphabet in consecutive order.

31:10-12 This section describes her marriage.

31:10 Who can find. She does exist, but is very hard to find. Cf. 18:22. **virtuous.** Excellent. *See note on 12:4*; cf. Ruth 3:11.

31:11 safely trusts her. He does not maintain jealous guard over her or keep his valuables locked up so that she cannot access them as was a common ancient practice in a house of distrust. She demonstrates impeccable loyalty to her husband, and her thrift and industry will add to his wealth.

31:13-24 This section describes her behavior.

31:13 seeks wool and flax. Excellent women gathered the material for making clothes (v. 19).

31:14 like the merchant ships. Excellent women would go far to secure the best food for their families.

31:15 rises while it is yet night. In order to have the food prepared for the family each day, she had to rise before dawn to begin the work, which she would do gladly.

31:16 considers a field. She was resourceful and entrepreneurial in her investing and reinvesting.

31:17 Such women were not soft, but by virtue of rigorous work, strong.

31:18 merchandise *is* good. That which she produced for the family of clothing, food, and wealth was good and profitable. **lamp...night.** Lamp is to be understood literally (cf. v. 15). She planted the vineyard during the day (v. 16), and wove late at night (v. 19). She rose early before dawn to prepare the food (v. 15), thus keeping a before-sunrise to after-dark schedule to care for her household, which was the foremost priority of her life (cf. Titus 2:5).

31:19 distaff...spindle. These tools are used to turn wool into thread for making clothing. Cf. Ex. 35:25.

31:20-24 Her activities, driven by the priority of caring for her family, resulted in multiplied fruitfulness for: 1) the poor and needy (v. 20); 2) her own household (v. 21); 3) herself (v. 22); 4) her husband (v. 23); and 5) the merchants (v. 24).

31:21 snow. Snow indicates the cold that occurs in the high altitudes of Palestine. Her labors anticipated her family's need for warm clothing in such cold places and seasons.

31:22 fine linen and purple. The efforts she makes to honor others are rewarded to her. These silk and purple garments are expensive evidences of the blessings returned to her by God's grace.

31:23 known in the gates. This woman made a significant contribution to her husband's position in the community and to his success (vv. 10-12). His domestic comfort promoted his advancement in public honor. A man's good reputation begins with his home and thus the virtue of his wife (cf 18:22).

31:24 makes...sells *them*. With all her other responsibilities faithfully discharged, she took time to make items of clothing for the purposes of trade.

And supplies sashes for the merchants.
25 Strength and honor *are* her clothing;
She shall rejoice in time to come.
26 She opens her mouth with wisdom,
And on her tongue *is* the law of kindness.
27 She watches over the ways of her household,
And does not eat the bread of idleness.
28 Her children rise up and call her blessed;
Her husband *also,* and he praises her:
29 "Many daughters have done well,
But you excel them all."
30 Charm *is* deceitful and beauty *is* passing,
But a woman *who* fears the LORD, she shall be praised.
31 Give her of the fruit of her hands,
And let her own works praise her in the gates.

31:25-27 This section emphasizes her character.

31:25 Strength and honor. These words describe the character of the woman who fears the Lord. Her inward clothing displays divine wisdom, giving her confidence to face the future with its unexpected challenges.

31:26 opens her mouth...law of kindness. Her teaching of wisdom and the law is tempered with mercy.

31:27 She was a skilled manager of the home. *See note on Titus 2:4,5.* **bread of idleness.** Lit. "eyes looking everywhere" as in the lazy man (cf. 6:6,9) of whom the same root word is used.

31:28,29 This section describes her family life.

31:28 rise up...call her blessed. She was greatly respected because she has earned the praise of her family. *See notes on 23:25; 29:17.* There can be no higher joy for a mother than for her children to grow up to praise her as the source of the wisdom that made them godly. *See note on 1 Tim. 2:15.*

31:29,30 you excel them all. This was her husband's superlative praise (v. 28) which was well-deserved, in which he used the same word for "excellent" found in v. 10.

31:30,31 This portion summarizes her spiritual life.

31:30 Charm...beauty. True holiness and virtue command permanent respect and affection, far more than charm and beauty of face and form. Cf. 1 Tim. 2:9,10; 1 Pet. 3:1-6. **a woman *who* fears the LORD.** Proverbs ends where it began with a reference to the fear of the Lord. *See note on 1:7.*

31:31 fruit...works. See vv. 10-29. While she receives material reward (v. 22), the praise and success she labored to bring to her family and community will be her praise. The result of all her efforts is her best eulogy.

The Book of ECCLESIASTES

Title

The English title, Ecclesiastes, comes from the Greek and Latin translations of Solomon's book. The LXX used the Greek term *ekklēsiastēs* for its title. It means "preacher," derived from the word *ekklēsia,* translated "assembly" or "congregation" in the NT. Both the Greek and Latin versions derive their titles from the Hebrew title, *Qoheleth,* which means "one who calls or gathers" the people. It refers to the one who addresses the assembly; hence, the preacher (cf. 1:1,2,12; 7:27; 12:8-10). Along with Ruth, Song of Solomon, Esther, and Lamentations, Ecclesiastes stands with the OT books of the Megilloth, or "five scrolls." Later rabbis read these books in the synagogue on 5 special occasions during the year—Ecclesiastes being read on Pentecost.

Author and Date

The autobiographical profile of the book's writer unmistakably points to Solomon. Evidence abounds such as: 1) the titles fit Solomon, "son of David, king in Jerusalem" (1:1) and "king over Israel in Jerusalem" (1:12); 2) the author's moral odyssey chronicles Solomon's life (1 Kin. 2–11); and 3) the role of one who "taught the people knowledge" and wrote "many proverbs" (12:9) corresponds to his life. All point to Solomon, the son of David, as the author.

Once Solomon is accepted as the author, the date and occasion become clear. Solomon was writing, probably in his latter years (no later than ca. 931 B.C.), primarily to warn the young people of his kingdom, without omitting others. He warned them to avoid walking through life on the path of human wisdom; he exhorted them to live by the revealed wisdom of God (12:9-14).

Background and Setting

Solomon's reputation for possessing extraordinary wisdom fits the Ecclesiastes profile. David recognized his son's wisdom (1 Kin. 2:6,9) before God gave Solomon an additional measure. After he received a "wise and understanding heart" from the Lord (1 Kin. 3:7-12), Solomon gained renown for being exceedingly wise by rendering insightful decisions (1 Kin. 3:16-28), a reputation that attracted "all the kings of the earth" to his courts (1 Kin. 4:34). In addition, he composed songs and proverbs (1 Kin. 4:32; cf. 12:9), activity befitting only the ablest of sages. Solomon's wisdom, like Job's wealth, surpassed the wisdom "of all the people of the east" (1 Kin. 4:30; Job 1:3).

The book is applicable to all who would listen and benefit, not so much from Solomon's experiences, but from the principles he drew as a result. Its aim is to answer some of life's most challenging questions, particularly where they seem contrary to Solomon's expectations. This has led some unwisely to take the view that Ecclesiastes is a book of skepticism. But in spite of amazingly unwise behavior and thinking, Solomon never let go of his faith in God (12:13,14).

Historical and Theological Themes

As is true with most biblical Wisdom literature, little historical narrative occurs in Ecclesiastes, apart from Solomon's own personal pilgrimage. The kingly sage studied life with high expectations but repeatedly bemoaned its shortcomings, which he acknowledged were due to the curse (Gen. 3:14-19). Ecclesiastes represents the painful autobiography of Solomon who, for much of his life, squandered God's blessings on his own personal pleasure rather than God's glory. He wrote to warn subsequent generations not to make the same tragic error, in much the same manner as Paul wrote to the Corinthians (cf. 1 Cor. 1:18-31; 2:13-16).

The key word is "vanity," which expresses the futile attempt to be satisfied apart from God. This word is used 37 times expressing the many things hard to understand about life. All earthly goals and ambitions when pursued as ends in themselves produce only emptiness. Paul was probably echoing Solomon's dissatisfaction when he wrote, "…the creation was subjected to futility" (Solomon's "vanity"; Rom. 8:19-21). Solomon's experience with the effects of the curse (see Gen. 3:17-19) led him to view life as "chasing after the wind."

Solomon asked, "What profit has a man from all his labor…?" (1:3), a question he repeated in 2:24

and 3:9. The wise king gave over a considerable portion of the book to addressing this dilemma. The impossibility of discovering both the inner workings of God's creation and the personal providence of God in Solomon's life were also deeply troubling to the king, as they were to Job. But the reality of judgment for all, despite many unknowns, emerged as the great certainty. In light of this judgment by God, the only fulfilled life is one lived in proper recognition of God and service to Him. Any other kind of life is frustrating and pointless.

A proper balance of the prominent "enjoy life" theme with that of "divine judgment" tethers the reader to Solomon's God with the sure chord of faith. For a time, Solomon suffered from the imbalance of trying to enjoy life without regard for the fear of Yahweh's judgment holding him on the path of obedience. In the end, he came to grasp the importance of obedience. The tragic results of Solomon's personal experience, coupled with the insight of extraordinary wisdom, make Ecclesiastes a book from which all believers can be warned and grow in their faith (cf. 2:1-26). This book shows that if one perceives each day of existence, labor, and basic provision as a gift from God, and accepts whatever God gives, then that person lives an abundant life (cf. John 10:10). However, one who looks to be satisfied apart from God will live with futility regardless of their accumulations.

Interpretive Challenges

The author's declaration that "all is vanity" envelops the primary message of the book (cf. 1:2; 12:8). The word translated "vanity" is used in at least 3 ways throughout the book. In each case, it looks at the nature of man's activity "under the sun" as: 1)"fleeting," which has in view the vapor-like (cf. James 4:14) or transitory nature of life; 2)"futile" or "meaningless," which focuses on the cursed condition of the universe and the debilitating effects it has on man's earthly experience; or 3) "incomprehensible" or "enigmatic," which gives consideration to life's unanswerable questions. Solomon draws upon all 3 meanings in Ecclesiastes.

While the context in each case will determine which meaning Solomon is focusing upon, the most recurring meaning of *vanity* is "incomprehensible" or "unknowable," referring to the mysteries of God's purposes. Solomon's conclusion to "fear God and keep His commandments" (12:13,14) is more than the book's summary; it is the only hope of the good life and the only reasonable response of faith and obedience to sovereign God. He precisely works out all activities under the sun, each in its time according to His perfect plan, but also discloses only as much as His perfect wisdom dictates and holds all men accountable. Those who refuse to take God and His Word seriously are doomed to lives of the severest vanity.

Outline

The book chronicles Solomon's investigations and conclusions regarding man's lifework, which combine all of his activity and its potential outcomes including limited satisfaction. The role of wisdom in experiencing success surfaces repeatedly, particularly when Solomon must acknowledge that God has not revealed all of the details. This leads Solomon to the conclusion that the primary issues of life after the Edenic fall involve divine blessings to be enjoyed and the divine judgment for which all must prepare.

Outline

I. Introduction
   A. Title (1:1)
   B. Poem—A Life of Activity That Appears Wearisome (1:2-11)
II. Solomon's Investigation (1:12–6:9)
   A. Introduction—The King and His Investigation (1:12-18)
   B. Investigation of Pleasure-Seeking (2:1-11)
   C. Investigation of Wisdom and Folly (2:12-17)
   D. Investigation of Labor and Rewards (2:18–6:9)
      1. One has to leave them to another (2:18-26)
      2. One cannot find the right time to act (3:1–4:6)
      3. One often must work alone (4:7-16)
      4. One can easily lose all he acquires (5:1–6:9)
III. Solomon's Conclusions (6:10–12:8)
   A. Introduction—The Problem of Not Knowing (6:10-12)
   B. Man Cannot Always Find Out Which Route is the Most Successful for Him to Take Because His Wisdom is Limited (7:1–8:17)
      1. On prosperity and adversity (7:1-14)
      2. On justice and wickedness (7:15-24)
      3. On women and folly (7:25-29)
      4. On the wise man and the king (8:1-17)
   C. Man Does Not Know What Will Come After Him (9:1–11:6)
      1. He knows he will die (9:1-4)
      2. He has no knowledge in the grave (9:5-10)
      3. He does not know his time of death (9:11,12)
      4. He does not know what will happen (9:13–10:15)
      5. He does not know what evil will come (10:16–11:2)
      6. He does not know what good will come (11:3-6)
   D. Man Should Enjoy Life, But Not Sin, Because Judgment Will Come to All (11:7–12:8)
IV. Solomon's Final Advice (12:9-14)

The Vanity of Life

1 The words of the Preacher, the son of David, [a]king in Jerusalem.

2 "Vanity[b] [1] of vanities," says the
Preacher;
"Vanity of vanities, [c]all *is* vanity."
3 [d]What profit has a man from all his
labor
In which he [2]toils under the sun?
4 *One* generation passes away, and
another generation comes;
[e]But the earth abides forever.
5 [f]The sun also rises, and the sun
goes down,
And [3]hastens to the place where it
arose.
6 [g]The wind goes toward the south,
And turns around to the north;
The wind whirls about continually,
And comes again on its circuit.
7 [h]All the rivers run into the sea,
Yet the sea *is* not full;
To the place from which the rivers
come,
There they return again.
8 All things *are* [4]full of labor;
Man cannot express *it*.
[i]The eye is not satisfied with seeing,
Nor the ear filled with hearing.
9 [j]That which has been *is* what will
be,
That which *is* done is what will be
done,
And *there is* nothing new under the
sun.
10 Is there anything of which it may
be said,
"See, this *is* new"?
It has already been in ancient times
before us.
11 *There is* [k]no remembrance of former
things,
Nor will there be any
remembrance of *things* that
are to come
By *those* who will come after.

The Grief of Wisdom

12 I, the Preacher, was king over Israel in
Jerusalem. 13 And I set my heart to seek
and [l]search out by wisdom concerning all
that is done under heaven; [m]this burdensome task God has given to the sons of
man, by which they may be [5]exercised. 14 I
have seen all the works that are done
under the sun; and indeed, all *is* vanity and
grasping for the wind.

CHAPTER 1

1 [a] Prov. 1:1
2 [b] Ps. 39:5, 6; 62:9; 144:4; Eccl. 12:8 [c] [Rom. 8:20, 21] [1] Or *Absurdity, Frustration, Futility, Nonsense;* and so throughout the book
3 [d] Eccl. 2:22; 3:9 [2] *labors*
4 [e] Ps. 104:5; 119:90
5 [f] Ps. 19:4–6 [3] Is *eager for,* lit. *panting*
6 [g] Eccl. 11:5; John 3:8
7 [h] [Ps. 104:8, 9; Jer. 5:22]
8 [i] Prov. 27:20; Eccl. 4:8 [4] *wearisome*
9 [j] Eccl. 3:15
11 [k] Eccl. 2:16
13 [l] [Eccl. 7:25; 8:16, 17] [m] Gen. 3:19; Eccl. 3:10 [5] Or *afflicted*

1:1 The words. The matters of the book are the crucial issues for Solomon's faith. They resemble the subject matter of Pss. 39; 49. **the Preacher.** The title of one who gathers the assembly together for instruction. See Introduction: Title.

1:2 Vanity of vanities. Solomon's way of saying "the greatest vanity." Cf. the discussion of "vanity" in Introduction: Interpretive Challenges.

1:3 profit. Advantage to or gain from one's labor. A very important and repeated word for Solomon (cf. 3:19; 5:9,11,16; 6:7,11; 7:11, 12; 10:10). Solomon looks at the fleeting moments of life and the seemingly small gain for man's activity under the sun. The only lasting efforts are those designed to accomplish God's purposes for eternity. **labor.** Labor is not just one's livelihood, but all of man's activity in life. **under the sun.** The phrase appears about 30 times to describe daily life.

1:4-7 These pictures from God's creation illustrate and underscore the futile repetition of human activity.

1:4 generation...earth. The essence of this comparison is permanence/impermanence without "profit" or "advantage." The observer perceives life as an endless cycle of activity which, by itself, does not bring security or meaning to man's experience.

1:8-11 This is a summary of sorts. Solomon looks at the effect of repetitious, enduring activity in God's creation over many generations as compared to the brief, comparatively profitless activity of one man which fails to produce an enduring satisfaction, and he concludes that it is wearisome. Another harsh reality comes with the realization that nothing is new and nothing will be remembered.

1:11 no remembrance. A written record or some other object which serves as a reminder of these events, people, and things will be short-lived.

1:12–6:9 This section records Solomon's ill-advised quest for greater wisdom.

1:12 king over Israel. See Introduction: Author and Date.

1:13 wisdom. Solomon's use of the term, in typical Hebrew fashion, is more practical than philosophical and implies more than knowledge. It carries notions of ability for proper behavior, success, common sense, and wit. **burdensome task.** Man's search to understand is at times difficult, yet God-given (cf. 2:26; 3:10; 5:16-19; 6:2; 8:11,15; 9:9; 12:11). **God.** The covenant name, LORD, is never used in Ecclesiastes. However, "God" is found almost 40 times. The emphasis is more on God's sovereignty in creation and providence than His covenant relationship through redemption.

1:14 grasping for the wind. One aspect of life's vanity is its fleeting character. Like the wind, much of what is desirable in life cannot be held in one's hand (cf. 1:14,17; 2:11,17,26; 4:4,6,16; 5:16; 6:9).

The "Vanities" of Ecclesiastes (1:2; 12:8)

1.	Human wisdom	2:14-16
2.	Human effort	2:18-23
3.	Human achievement	2:26
4.	Human life	3:18-22
5.	Human rivalry	4:4
6.	Human selfish sacrifice	4:7,8
7.	Human power	4:16
8.	Human greed	5:10
9.	Human accumulation	6:1-12
10.	Human religion	8:10-14

15 [n]*What is* crooked cannot be made
straight,
And what is lacking cannot be
numbered.

16 I communed with my heart, saying,
"Look, I have attained greatness, and have
gained [o]more wisdom than all who were
before me in Jerusalem. My heart has [6]un-
derstood great wisdom and knowledge."
17 [p]And I set my heart to know wisdom
and to know madness and folly. I perceived that this also is grasping for the
wind.

18 For [q]in much wisdom *is* much
grief,
And he who increases knowledge
increases sorrow.

The Vanity of Pleasure

2 I said [a]in my heart, "Come now, I will
test you with [b]mirth;[1] therefore enjoy
pleasure"; but surely, [c]this also *was* vanity.
2 I said of laughter—"Madness!"; and of
mirth, "What does it accomplish?" 3 [d]I
searched in my heart *how* [2]to gratify my
flesh with wine, while guiding my heart
with wisdom, and how to lay hold on folly,
till I might see what *was* [e]good for the sons
of men to do under heaven all the days of
their lives.
4 I made my works great, I built myself
[f]houses, and planted myself vineyards. 5 I
made myself gardens and orchards, and
I planted all *kinds* of fruit trees in them. 6 I
made myself water pools from which to
[3]water the growing trees of the grove. 7 I
acquired male and female servants, and
had [4]servants born in my house. Yes, I had
greater possessions of herds and flocks
than all who were in Jerusalem before me.
8 [g]I also gathered for myself silver and
gold and the special treasures of kings and
of the provinces. I acquired male and female singers, the delights of the sons of
men, *and* [5]musical instruments of all kinds.
9 [h]So I became great and [6]excelled [i]more
than all who were before me in Jerusalem.
Also my wisdom remained with me.

10 Whatever my eyes desired I did
not keep from them.
I did not withhold my heart from
any pleasure,
For my heart rejoiced in all my
labor;
And [j]this was my [7]reward from all
my labor.
11 Then I looked on all the works that
my hands had done
And on the labor in which I had
toiled;
And indeed all *was* [k]vanity and
grasping for the wind.
There was no profit under the sun.

The End of the Wise and the Fool

12 Then I turned myself to consider
wisdom [l]and madness and
folly;
For what *can* the man *do* who
succeeds the king?—
Only what he has already [m]done.
13 Then I saw that wisdom [n]excels
folly
As light excels darkness.
14 [o]The wise man's eyes *are* in his
head,
But the fool walks in darkness.

15 [n]Eccl. 7:13
16 [o]1 Kin. 3:12, 13; Eccl. 2:9 [6]Lit. *seen*
17 [p]Eccl. 2:3, 12; 7:23, 25; [1 Thess. 5:21]
18 [q]Eccl. 12:12

CHAPTER 2

1 [a]Luke 12:19 [b]Prov. 14:13; [Eccl. 7:4; 8:15] [c]Eccl. 1:2 [1]*gladness*
3 [d]Eccl. 1:17 [e][Eccl. 3:12, 13; 5:18; 6:12] [2]Lit. *to draw my flesh*
4 [f]1 Kin. 7:1-12
6 [3]*irrigate*
7 [4]Lit. *sons of my house*
8 [g]1 Kin. 9:28; 10:10, 14, 21 [5]Exact meaning unknown
9 [h]Eccl. 1:16 [i]2 Chr. 9:22 [6]Lit. *increased*
10 [j]Eccl. 3:22; 5:18; 9:9 [7]Lit. *portion*
11 [k]Eccl. 1:3, 14
12 [l]Eccl. 1:17; 7:25 [m]Eccl. 1:9
13 [n]Eccl. 7:11, 14, 19; 9:18; 10:10
14 [o]Prov. 17:24; Eccl. 8:1

1:15 crooked...lacking. With no necessarily moral implications being made, these words measure wisdom as the ability to resolve issues in life. In spite of man's grandest efforts, some crooked matters will remain unstraightened.

1:16 wisdom. Cf. Introduction: Background and Setting.

1:17 I set my heart to know. When Solomon depended on empirical research rather than divine revelation to understand life, he found it to be an empty experience.

1:18 wisdom...much grief. The expected outcome of wisdom is success. Success, in turn, should bring happiness. But Solomon concluded that there were no guarantees. This grieves the one who places his hope in human achievement alone.

2:1-11 Pleasure, although not necessarily evil, has its shortcomings, much like human wisdom. Solomon reflected upon his tragic experiences in attempting to draw satisfaction purely out of pleasure.

2:1,2 test. The investigation or test was crucial for Solomon. But the test was not scientific; rather it was a practical experiment to see what worked. He was interested in what a given act accomplished.

2:3 gratify. In further tests on the human level, Solomon overemphasized human gratification at the expense of God's glory.

2:4-8 Cf. 1 Kin. 4–10 for an amplified account of Solomon's riches.

2:8 musical instruments. This Heb. word occurs only here in the OT. The meaning is indicated in an early Egyptian letter that used a similar Canaanite word for "concubines." This fits Solomon's 700 wives and 300 concubines (1 Kin. 11:3). Most likely this should be translated "harem," which would refer to Solomon's many women (cf. 1 Kin. 11:3).

2:10 reward. Solomon's portion in life. This was what he received for all his activity and effort.

2:11 no profit. "Vanity" is defined in this context. The futility of the labor process is that Solomon had nothing of enduring and satisfying substance to show for it. Wisdom is no guarantee that one will achieve satisfaction, even in accomplishments comparable to Solomon's. To expend God-given resources for human accomplishment alone is empty.

2:12-17 Human wisdom suffers another crucial shortcoming—it leaves both the wise and the fool empty-handed at the threshold of death.

2:14 fool walks in darkness. The fool is not one who is mentally deficient, but is morally bankrupt. It is not that he cannot learn wisdom, but that he won't. He refuses to know, fear, and obey God.

Yet I myself perceived
That [p]the same event happens to
them all.

15 So I said in my heart,
"As it happens to the fool,
It also happens to me,
And why was I then more wise?"
Then I said in my heart,
"This also *is* vanity."
16 For *there is* [q]no more remembrance
of the wise than of the fool
forever,
Since all that now *is* will be
forgotten in the days to come.
And how does a wise *man* die?
As the fool!

17 Therefore I hated life because the work
that was done under the sun *was* distressing to me, for all *is* vanity and grasping for
the wind.
18 Then I hated all my labor in which I
had toiled under the sun, because [r]I must
leave it to the man who will come after me.
19 And who knows whether he will be wise
or a fool? Yet he will rule over all my labor
in which I toiled and in which I have shown
myself wise under the sun. This also *is* vanity. 20 Therefore I turned my heart and despaired of all the labor in which I had toiled
under the sun. 21 For there is a man whose
labor *is* with wisdom, knowledge, and skill;
yet he must leave his [8]heritage to a man
who has not labored for it. This also *is* vanity and a great evil. 22 [s]For what has man for
all his labor, and for the striving of his heart
with which he has toiled under the sun?
23 For all his days *are* [t]sorrowful, and his
work burdensome; even in the night his
heart takes no rest. This also is vanity.
24 [u]Nothing *is* better for a man *than* that
he should eat and drink, and *that* his soul
should enjoy good in his labor. This also, I
saw, was from the hand of God. 25 For who
can eat, or who can have enjoyment, [9]more
than I? 26 For *God* gives [v]wisdom and
knowledge and joy to a man who *is* good
in His sight; but to the sinner He gives the
work of gathering and collecting, that [w]he
may give to *him who is* good before God.
This also *is* vanity and grasping for the
wind.

14 [p] Ps. 49:10; Eccl. 9:2, 3, 11
16 [q] Eccl. 1:11; 4:16
18 [r] Ps. 49:10
21 [8] Lit. *portion*
22 [s] Eccl. 1:3; 3:9
23 [t] Job 5:7; 14:1
24 [u] Eccl. 3:12, 13, 22; Is. 56:12; Luke 12:19; 1 Cor. 15:32; [1 Tim. 6:17]
25 [9] So with MT, Tg., Vg.; some Heb. mss., LXX, Syr. *without Him*
26 [v] Job 32:8; Prov. 2:6; James 1:5
[w] Job 27:16, 17; Prov. 28:8

Everything Has Its Time

3 To everything *there is* a season,
A [a]time for every purpose under
heaven:

2 A time [1]to be born,
And [b]a time to die;
A time to plant,
And a time to pluck *what is*
planted;
3 A time to kill,
And a time to heal;
A time to break down,
And a time to build up;
4 A time to [c]weep,
And a time to laugh;
A time to mourn,
And a time to dance;
5 A time to cast away stones,
And a time to gather stones;
[d]A time to embrace,
And a time to refrain from
embracing;
6 A time to gain,
And a time to lose;
A time to keep,
And a time to throw away;
7 A time to tear,
And a time to sew;
[e]A time to keep silence,
And a time to [f]speak;
8 A time to love,
And a time to [g]hate;
A time of war,
And a time of peace.

The God-Given Task

9 [h]What profit has the worker from that
in which he labors? 10 [i]I have seen the
God-given task with which the sons of
men are to be occupied. 11 He has made
everything beautiful in its time. Also He

CHAPTER 3
1 [a] Eccl. 3:17; 8:6
2 [b] Job 14:5; Heb. 9:27
[1] Lit. *to bear*
4 [c] Rom. 12:15
5 [d] Joel 2:16; 1 Cor. 7:5
7 [e] Amos 5:13 [f] Prov. 25:11
8 [g] Prov. 13:5; Luke 14:26
9 [h] Eccl. 1:3
10 [i] Eccl. 1:13

2:17 because the work that was done. Since it had no more lasting value than the folly of a fool, Solomon viewed even the great reward of his labor as a source of pain.

2:18-22 Cf. 4:7,8

2:18 hated all my labor. Solomon left the kingdom divided to Jeroboam and his son Rehoboam, both of whom squandered their opportunities (1 Kin. 12–14).

2:21 heritage. The portion of one's life that he must leave behind at death.

2:24 Nothing *is* better. Even with the limitations of this present life (cf. 3:12,13,22; 5:18,19; 8:15; 9:7), humanity should rejoice in its temporal goodness. **from the hand of God.** Solomon's strong view of God's sovereignty brings comfort after an honest critique of what life in a cursed world entails.

2:25 more than I. Lit. "outside of Him" (i.e., God), or "without Him."

2:26 give to *him who is* good. The qualifier "in His sight" makes God's prerogative the standard.

3:1-8 a season, a time. Not only does God fix the standard and withhold or dispense satisfaction (2:26), but He also appoints "seasons" and "times." Earthly pursuits are good in their proper place and time, but unprofitable when pursued as the chief goal (cf. vv. 9,10).

3:9,10 Earthly pursuits (vv. 1-8) are unprofitable when considered as life's chief good, which was never intended by God.

3:11 everything. Every activity or event for which a culmination point may be fixed. **beautiful.** Fitting or appropriate. The phrase echoes "...and God saw that it was good" (Gen. 1:31). Even in a cursed

has put eternity in their hearts, except that
[j]no one can find out the work that God
does from beginning to end.
12 I know that nothing *is* [k]better for them
than to rejoice, and to do good in their
lives, 13 and also that [l]every man should
eat and drink and enjoy the good of all his
labor—it *is* the gift of God.

14 I know that whatever God does,
It shall be forever.
[m]Nothing can be added to it,
And nothing taken from it.
God does *it,* that men should fear
before Him.
15 [n]That which is has already been,
And what is to be has already
been;
And God [2]requires an account of
[3]what is past.

Injustice Seems to Prevail

16 Moreover [o]I saw under the sun:

In the place of [4]judgment,
Wickedness *was* there;
And *in* the place of righteousness,
[5]Iniquity *was* there.

17 I said in my heart,

[p]"God shall judge the righteous and
the wicked,
For *there is* a time there for every
[6]purpose and for every
work."

18 I said in my heart, "Concerning the condition of the sons of men, God tests them,
that they may see that they themselves are
like animals." 19 [q]For what happens to the
sons of men also happens to animals; one
thing befalls them: as one dies, so dies the
other. Surely, they all have one breath;
man has no advantage over animals, for
all *is* vanity. 20 All go to one place: [r]all are
from the dust, and all return to dust.
21 [s]Who[7] knows the spirit of the sons of
men, which goes upward, and the spirit of
the animal, which goes down to the earth?

11 [j] Job 5:9; Eccl. 7:23; 8:17; Rom. 11:33
12 [k] Eccl. 2:3, 24
13 [l] Eccl. 2:24
14 [m] James 1:17
15 [n] Eccl. 1:9 [2] Lit. *seeks* [3] *what is pursued*
16 [o] Eccl. 5:8 [4] *justice* [5] *Wickedness*
17 [p] Gen. 18:25; Ps. 96:13; Eccl. 11:9; [Matt. 16:27; Rom. 2:6-10; 2 Cor. 5:10; 2 Thess. 1:6-9] [6] *desire*
19 [q] Ps. 49:12, 20; 73:22; [Eccl. 2:16]
20 [r] Gen. 3:19; Ps. 103:14
21 [s] Eccl. 12:7 [7] LXX, Syr., Tg., Vg. *Who knows whether the spirit . . . goes upward, and whether . . . goes downward to the earth?*

universe, activity should not be meaningless. Its futility lies in the fickle satisfaction of man and his failure to trust the wisdom of sovereign God. **put eternity in their hearts.** God made men for His eternal purpose, and nothing in post-Fall time can bring them complete satisfaction.

3:12 to rejoice, and to do good. These words capture the goal of Solomon's message which he echoes and elaborates on in 11:9,10 and again in 12:13,14.

3:13 enjoy the good of all his labor. In accepting everything as a gift of his Creator, even in a cursed world, man is enabled to see "good" in all his work (cf. 2:24,25; 5:19).

3:14 fear before Him. Acknowledging God's enduring and perfect work becomes grounds for reverence, worship, and meaning. Apart from God, man's works are pitifully inadequate. The theme, "the fear of God," also appears in 5:7; 8:12,13; 12:13.

3:17 God shall judge...for *there is* a time. The culminating issue of Solomon's "appointed time" discussion is that there is a time for judgment (cf. John 5:28,29). God's judgment is a central theme in Solomon's message for this book (cf. 11:9; 12:14). Even where the word "judgment" is absent, the greater issue of divine retribution is often pervasive.

3:18,19 what happens. The ultimate fate of man and beast is to die. Solomon isn't looking at eternal destinies, but rather at what all earthly flesh shares in common.

3:20 from the dust...to dust. Genesis 3:19 is alluded to in the broadest sense, i.e., all of living creation will die and go to the grave. Neither heaven nor hell is considered here.

3:21 the spirit. Man's breath or physical life appears on the surface to be little different than that of an animal. In reality, man's soul differs in that God has made him eternal (cf. v. 11).

Solomon Reflects on Genesis

Toward the end of his life, the penitent King Solomon pondered life in the wake of the Fall and the outworking of man's sin. Solomon drew the following conclusions, possibly from his own study of Genesis:

1. God created the heavens and earth with laws of design and regularity (Eccl. 1:2-7; 3:1-8; cf. Gen. 1:1-31; 8:22).
2. Man is created from dust and returns to dust (Eccl. 3:20; 12:7; cf. Gen. 2:7; 3:19).
3. God placed in man His life-giving breath (Eccl. 12:7; cf. Gen. 2:7).
4. As God ordained it, marriage is one of life's most enjoyable blessings (Eccl. 9:9; cf. Gen. 2:18-25).
5. Divine judgment results from the Fall (Eccl. 3:14-22; 11:9; 12:14; cf. Gen. 2:17; 3:1-19).
6. The effect of the curse on creation is "vanity," i.e., futility (Eccl. 1:5-8; cf. Gen. 3:17-19).
7. Labor after the Fall is difficult and yields little profit (Eccl. 1:3, 13; 2:3; 3:9-11; cf. Gen. 3:17-19).
8. Death overcomes all creatures after the Fall (Eccl. 8:8; 9:4,5; cf. Gen. 2:17; 3:19).
9. After the Fall, man's heart is desperately wicked (Eccl. 7:20; 7:29; 8:11; 9:3; cf. Gen. 3:22; 6:5; 8:21).
10. God withholds certain knowledge and wisdom from man for His wise, but unspoken, reasons (Eccl. 6:12; 8:17; cf. Gen. 3:22).

22 [t]So I perceived that nothing *is* better
than that a man should rejoice in his own
works, for [u]that *is* his [8]heritage. [v]For who
can bring him to see what will happen
after him?

4 Then I returned and considered all the
[a]oppression that is done under the
sun:

And look! The tears of the
oppressed,
But they have no comforter—
[1]On the side of their oppressors
there is power,
But they have no comforter.
2 [b]Therefore I praised the dead who
were already dead,
More than the living who are still
alive.
3 [c]Yet, better than both *is he* who has
never existed,
Who has not seen the evil work
that is done under the sun.

The Vanity of Selfish Toil

4 Again, I saw that for all toil and every
skillful work a man is envied by his neighbor. This also *is* vanity and grasping for the
wind.

5 [d]The fool folds his hands
And consumes his own flesh.
6 [e]Better a handful *with* quietness
Than both hands full, *together with*
toil and grasping for the
wind.

7 Then I returned, and I saw vanity
under the sun:

8 There is one alone, without
[2]companion:
He has neither son nor brother.
Yet *there is* no end to all his labors,
Nor is his [f]eye satisfied with riches.
But [g]*he never asks,*
"For whom do I toil and deprive
myself of [h]good?"
This also *is* vanity and a [3]grave
misfortune.

The Value of a Friend

9 Two *are* better than one,
Because they have a good reward
for their labor.
10 For if they fall, one will lift up his
companion.
But woe to him *who is* alone when
he falls,
For *he has* no one to help him up.
11 Again, if two lie down together,
they will keep warm;
But how can one be warm *alone?*
12 Though one may be overpowered
by another, two can
withstand him.
And a threefold cord is not quickly
broken.

Popularity Passes Away

13 Better a poor and wise youth
Than an old and foolish king who
will be admonished no more.
14 For he comes out of prison to be
king,
Although [4]he was born poor in his
kingdom.
15 I saw all the living who walk
under the sun;
They were with the second youth
who stands in his place.
16 *There was* no end of all the people
[5]over whom he was made
king;
Yet those who come afterward will
not rejoice in him.
Surely this also *is* vanity and
grasping for the wind.

Fear God, Keep Your Vows

5 Walk [a]prudently when you go to the
house of God; and draw near to hear
rather [b]than to give the sacrifice of fools,
for they do not know that they do evil.

2 Do not be [c]rash with your mouth,

22 [t] Eccl. 2:24; 5:18 [u] Eccl. 2:10 [v] Eccl. 6:12; 8:7 [8] *portion or lot*

CHAPTER 4

1 [a] Job 35:9; Ps. 12:5; Eccl. 3:16; 5:8; Is. 5:7 [1] Lit. *At the hand*
2 [b] Job 3:17, 18
3 [c] Job 3:11-22; Eccl. 6:3; Luke 23:29
5 [d] Prov. 6:10; 24:33
6 [e] Prov. 15:16, 17; 16:8
8 [f] Prov. 27:20; Eccl. 5:10; [1 John 2:16] [g] Ps. 39:6 [h] Eccl. 2:18-21 [2] Lit. *a second* [3] Lit. *evil task*
14 [4] The youth
16 [5] Lit. *to all before whom he was to be*

CHAPTER 5

1 [a] Ex. 3:5; Is. 1:12 [b] [1 Sam. 15:22]; Ps. 50:8; Prov. 15:8; 21:27; [Hos. 6:6]
2 [c] Prov. 20:25

3:22 after him. Once again, death becomes the overshadowing reality.

4:1-3 The oppressiveness of some lives renders death more appealing.

4:3 evil work. Earthly life can be so disheartening as to make non-existence preferable.

4:4 envied by. The lack of satisfaction with life leads some to conclude that everyone else has it better.

4:5 folds his hands...consumes his own flesh. Even the man who settles into idleness, living on what he takes from others, is self-tormented, and never satisfied (cf. Is. 9:20; 44:20).

4:7-12 The futility of labor alone without satisfaction and without any heir to experience its value is addressed (cf. 2:18-22, a complementary message). Life is better with companionship.

4:13-16 The cherished popularity of kings is precarious and short-lived.

4:15 second youth. This refers to the legitimate successor to the "old king," as opposed to the "poor youth" who rises on his ability to reign.

5:1-7 A prelude to the book's concluding admonition to approach God with reverence.

5:1 the house of God. The temple Solomon built in Jerusalem (cf. 1 Kin. 8:15-21).

And let not your heart utter
anything hastily before God.
For God *is* in heaven, and you on
earth;
Therefore let your words [d]be few.
3 For a dream comes through much
activity,
And [e]a fool's voice *is known* by *his*
many words.

4 [f]When you make a vow to God, do
not delay to [g]pay it;
For *He has* no pleasure in fools.
Pay what you have vowed—
5 [h]Better not to vow than to vow and
not pay.

6 Do not let your [i]mouth cause your flesh
to sin, [j]nor say before the messenger *of God*
that it *was* an error. Why should God be
angry at your [1]excuse and destroy the
work of your hands? 7 For in the multitude
of dreams and many words *there is* also
vanity. But [k]fear God.

The Vanity of Gain and Honor

8 If you [l]see the oppression of the poor,
and the violent [2]perversion of justice and
righteousness in a province, do not marvel
at the matter; for [m]high official watches
over high official, and higher officials are
over them.
9 Moreover the profit of the land is for
all; *even* the king is served from the field.

10 He who loves silver will not be
satisfied with silver;
Nor he who loves abundance, with
increase.
This also *is* vanity.

11 When goods increase,
They increase who eat them;
So what profit have the owners
Except to see *them* with their
eyes?
12 The sleep of a laboring man *is*
sweet,
Whether he eats little or much;
But the abundance of the rich will
not permit him to sleep.

13 [n]There is a severe evil *which* I have
seen under the sun:
Riches kept for their owner to his
hurt.
14 But those riches perish through
[3]misfortune;
When he begets a son, *there is*
nothing in his hand.
15 [o]As he came from his mother's
womb, naked shall he return,
To go as he came;
And he shall take nothing from his
labor
Which he may carry away in his
hand.

16 And this also *is* a severe evil—
Just exactly as he came, so shall he
go.
And [p]what profit has he [q]who has
labored for the wind?
17 All his days [r]he also eats in
darkness,
And *he has* much sorrow and
sickness and anger.

18 Here is what I have seen: [s]*It is* good
and fitting *for one* to eat and drink, and to
enjoy the good of all his labor in which he
toils under the sun all the days of his life
which God gives him; [t]for it *is* his [4]heri-
tage. 19 As for [u]every man to whom God
has given riches and wealth, and given
him power to eat of it, to receive his [5]heri-
tage and rejoice in his labor—this *is* the
[v]gift of God. 20 For he will not dwell un-

2 [d] Prov. 10:19; Matt. 6:7
3 [e] Prov. 10:19
4 [f] Num. 30:2; Deut. 23:21-23; Ps. 50:14; 76:11 [g] Ps. 66:13, 14
5 [h] Prov. 20:25; Acts 5:4
6 [i] Prov. 6:2 [j] 1 Cor. 11:10 [1] Lit. *voice*
7 [k] [Eccl. 12:13]
8 [l] Eccl. 3:16 [m] [Ps. 12:5; 58:11; 82:1] [2] *wresting*
13 [n] Eccl. 6:1, 2
14 [3] Lit. *bad business*
15 [o] Job 1:21; Ps. 49:17; 1 Tim. 6:7
16 [p] Eccl. 1:3 [q] Prov. 11:29
17 [r] Ps. 127:2
18 [s] Eccl. 2:24; 3:12, 13; [1 Tim. 6:17] [t] Eccl. 2:10; 3:22 [4] Lit. *portion*
19 [u] [Eccl. 6:2] [v] Eccl. 2:24; 3:13 [5] Lit. *portion*

5:2 heaven…earth. Because God is in heaven and man is on earth, rash promises and arguments before Him are foolish.

5:4,5 vow and not pay. Promises made to God have serious implications. The OT background for this admonition is found in Deut. 23:21-23; Judg. 11:35. Ananias and Sapphira learned the hard way (cf. Acts 5:1-11).

5:6 mouth cause your flesh to sin. Don't vow something that your fleshly desire will cause you to break. **messenger.** The priest in the house of God (cf. Mal. 2:7). Both priests and prophets are called messengers, commissaries who deliver and report back messages for the Heavenly King (cf. Is. 6:1-13). Don't tell them your broken vow was a small thing.

5:7 fear God. Cf. 3:14; 8:12,13; 12:13.

5:8,9 Officials have an unfair advantage to attain wealth.

5:10 The love of money is never satisfied (cf. 1 Tim. 6:9,10).

5:11 They increase who eat them. This refers to the rich man's dependents.

5:12-17 Earthly treasures are precarious and bring disadvantages; they produce anxiety (v. 12) and pain (v. 13). They disappear through bad business (v. 14) and are left at death (v. 15). They can even produce fear (v. 17).

5:18-20 In contrast to the anxiety of those just described (vv. 12-17), for those who consider God as the source of wealth, there are pleasures, riches, and the ability to enjoy them (see 2:24).

5:18 fitting. The same word translated in 3:11 "beautiful." Once again, Solomon uses an admonition to enjoy the richness of life that God gives.

5:19 the gift of God. To understand this is to enjoy the satisfaction of His good gifts.

5:20 God keeps *him* busy. When a person recognizes the goodness of God, he rejoices and does not dwell unduly on the troubles detailed in the previous context.

duly on the days of his life, because God
keeps *him* busy with the joy of his heart.

6 There[a] is an evil which I have seen
under the sun, and it *is* common
among men: 2 A man to whom God has
given riches and wealth and honor, [b]so
that he lacks nothing for himself of all he
desires; [c]yet God does not give him power
to eat of it, but a foreigner consumes it.
This *is* vanity, and it *is* an evil [1]affliction.
3 If a man begets a hundred *children* and
lives many years, so that the days of his
years are many, but his soul is not satisfied
with goodness, or [d]indeed he has no burial, I say *that* [e]a [2]stillborn child *is* better
than he— 4 for it comes in vanity and departs in darkness, and its name is covered
with darkness. 5 Though it has not seen the
sun or known *anything,* this has more rest
than that man, 6 even if he lives a thousand
years twice—but has not seen goodness.
Do not all go to one [f]place?

7 [g]All the labor of man *is* for his
mouth,
And yet the soul is not satisfied.
8 For what more has the wise *man*
than the fool?
What does the poor man have,
Who knows *how* to walk before the
living?
9 Better *is* [3]the [h]sight of the eyes
than the wandering of
[4]desire.
This also *is* vanity and grasping for
the wind.

10 Whatever one is, he has been
named [i]already,
For it is known that he *is* man;
[j]And he cannot contend with Him
who is mightier than he.
11 Since there are many things that
increase vanity,
How *is* man the better?

12 For who knows what *is* good for man
in life, [5]all the days of his [6]vain life which
he passes like [k]a shadow? [l]Who can tell a
man what will happen after him under the
sun?

CHAPTER 6

1 [a] Eccl. 5:13
2 [b] Job 21:10; Ps. 17:14; 73:7 [c] Luke 12:20 [1] *disease*
3 [d] 2 Kin. 9:35; Is. 14:19, 20; Jer. 22:19 [e] Job 3:16; Ps. 58:8; Eccl. 4:3 [2] Or *miscarriage*
6 [f] Eccl. 2:14, 15
7 [g] Prov. 16:26
9 [h] Eccl. 11:9 [3] What the eyes see [4] Lit. *soul*
10 [i] Eccl. 1:9; 3:15 [j] Job 9:32; Is. 45:9; Jer. 49:19
12 [k] Ps. 102:11; James 4:14 [l] Ps. 39:6; Eccl. 3:22 [5] Lit. *the number of the days* [6] *futile*

CHAPTER 7

1 [a] Prov. 22:1 [b] Eccl. 4:2
2 [c] [Ps. 90:12]
3 [d] [2 Cor. 7:10] [1] *Vexation* or *Grief* [2] *well* or *pleasing*
5 [e] Ps. 141:5; [Prov. 13:18; 15:31, 32] [3] *listen to*
6 [f] Eccl. 2:2 [4] Lit. *sound*
7 [g] Ex. 23:8; Deut. 16:19; [Prov. 17:8, 23] [5] *destroys*
8 [h] Prov. 14:29; Gal. 5:22; Eph. 4:2
9 [i] Prov. 14:17; James 1:19
11 [j] Eccl. 11:7

The Value of Practical Wisdom

7 A [a]good name *is* better than
precious ointment,
And the day of death than the day
of one's [b]birth;
2 Better to go to the house of
mourning
Than to go to the house of feasting,
For that *is* the end of all men;
And the living will take *it* to [c]heart.
3 [1]Sorrow *is* better than laughter,
[d]For by a sad countenance the heart
is made [2]better.
4 The heart of the wise *is* in the
house of mourning,
But the heart of fools *is* in the
house of mirth.

5 [e]*It is* better to [3]hear the rebuke of
the wise
Than for a man to hear the song of
fools.
6 [f]For like the [4]crackling of thorns
under a pot,
So *is* the laughter of the fool.
This also is vanity.
7 Surely oppression destroys a wise
man's reason,
[g]And a bribe [5]debases the heart.
8 The end of a thing *is* better than its
beginning;
[h]The patient in spirit *is* better than
the proud in spirit.
9 [i]Do not hasten in your spirit to be
angry,
For anger rests in the bosom of
fools.
10 Do not say,
"Why were the former days better
than these?"
For you do not inquire wisely
concerning this.

11 Wisdom *is* good with an inheritance,
And profitable [j]to those who see
the sun.

6:2 God does not give him power to eat. The Lord gives and takes away for His own purposes. So, the blessings of God cannot be assumed or taken for granted. But they should be enjoyed with thankfulness while they are available.

6:3-6 Not having a burial, as in the case of King Jehoiakim (Jer. 22:18,19), indicated complete disrespect and disregard for one's life. To die without mourners or honors was considered worse than being born dead, even if one had many children and a full life.

6:3 This is hyperbole.

6:7-12 Lack of soul satisfaction comes from working only for what is consumed (v. 7), seeing little difference in the end between the wise and foolish (v. 8), not knowing the future (v. 9), realizing that God alone controls everything (v. 10), and true understanding of the present and future is limited (vv. 11,12).

7:1 good name. Where a man has so lived to earn a good reputation, the day of his death can be a time of honor.

7:2-6 The point of this section is to emphasize that more is learned from adversity than from pleasure. True wisdom is developed in the crucible of life's trials, though the preacher wishes that were not the case when he writes "this is also vanity" (v. 6).

7:10 former days. In the midst of trouble and discontent, it is easy to lose touch with reality.

12 For wisdom *is* [6]a [k]defense *as*
money *is* a defense,
But the [7]excellence of knowledge *is*
that wisdom gives [l]life to
those who have it.

13 Consider the work of God;
For [m]who can make straight what
He has made crooked?
14 [n]In the day of prosperity be joyful,
But in the day of adversity consider:
Surely God has appointed the one
[8]as well as the other,
So that man can find out nothing
that will come after him.

15 I have seen everything in my days of
vanity:
[o]There is a just *man* who perishes in
his righteousness,
And there is a wicked *man* who
prolongs *life* in his wickedness.

16 [p]Do not be overly righteous,
[q]Nor be overly wise:
Why should you destroy yourself?
17 Do not be overly wicked,
Nor be foolish:
[r]Why should you die before your
time?
18 *It is* good that you grasp this,
And also not remove your hand
from the other;
For he who [s]fears God will [9]escape
them all.

19 [t]Wisdom strengthens the wise
More than ten rulers of the city.

20 [u]For *there is* not a just man on earth
who does good
And does not sin.

21 Also do not take to heart
everything people say,
Lest you hear your servant cursing
you.
22 For many times, also, your own
heart has known
That even you have cursed others.

23 All this I have [1]proved by
wisdom.
[v]I said, "I will be wise";
But it *was* far from me.
24 [w]As for that which is far off and
[x]exceedingly deep,
Who can find it out?
25 [y]I applied my heart to know,
To search and seek out wisdom
and the reason *of things,*
To know the wickedness of folly,
Even of foolishness *and* madness.
26 [z]And I find more bitter than death
The woman whose heart *is* snares
and nets,
Whose hands *are* fetters.
[2]He who pleases God shall escape
from her,
But the sinner shall be trapped by
her.

27 "Here is what I have found," says
[a]the Preacher,
"*Adding* one thing to the other to
find out the reason,
28 Which my soul still seeks but I
cannot find:
[b]One man among a thousand I have
found,
But a woman among all these I
have not found.
29 Truly, this only I have found:
[c]That God made man upright,
But [d]they have sought out many
schemes."

12 [k]Eccl. 9:18 [l]Prov. 3:18 [6]A protective shade, lit. *shadow* [7]*advantage* or *profit*
13 [m]Job 12:14
14 [n]Deut. 28:47 [8]*alongside*
15 [o]Eccl. 8:12-14
16 [p]Prov. 25:16; Phil. 3:6 [q]Rom. 12:3
17 [r]Job 15:32; Ps. 55:23
18 [s]Eccl. 3:14; 5:7; 8:12, 13 [9]Lit. *come forth from all of them*
19 [t]Prov. 21:22; Eccl. 9:13-18
20 [u]1 Kin. 8:46; 2 Chr. 6:36; Prov. 20:9; Rom. 3:23; 1 John 1:8
23 [v]Rom. 1:22 [1]*tested*
24 [w]Job 28:12; 1 Tim. 6:16 [x]Rom. 11:33
25 [y]Eccl. 1:17
26 [z]Prov. 5:3, 4 [2]Lit. *He who is good before God*
27 [a]Eccl. 1:1, 2
28 [b]Job 33:23
29 [c]Gen. 1:27 [d]Gen. 3:6, 7

7:12 wisdom *is* a defense. Wisdom is better than money because it provides the fulfilled life.

7:13 make straight what He has made crooked. Man should consider God's activity because God is sovereign, decreeing and controlling everything under the sun (cf. 1:15).

7:14 prosperity...adversity. God ordains both kinds of days and withholds knowledge of the future.

7:15-18 The focus on the nature of righteousness is made clear in the statement "For he who fears God will escape them all" (v. 18).

7:15 perishes...prolongs. The fact that some righteous men die young and some wicked men live long is enigmatic (cf. 8:11,12).

7:16 overly righteous...overly wise. Solomon has already exhorted his readers to be righteous and wise (cf. v. 19). The warning here is against being self-righteous or pharisaical.

7:19 Wisdom strengthens. The measure of wisdom is its ability to bring good outcomes in life.

7:20 does good and does not sin. Solomon gave great emphasis to the general effects of sin (cf. Gen. 3:1-24) and also pointed out the universality of personal transgressions. Paul may have recalled this passage when he wrote Rom. 3:10.

7:21,22 people say. Since you have many offensive words to be forgiven, don't keep strict accounts of other's offensive words against you.

7:23,24 "I will be wise"...Who can find it out? The already wise king resolves to be even wiser. But upon further investigation, the limitations of wisdom become apparent. Some things are unknowable. This realization quickly dampens his enthusiasm.

7:26 The woman. This is the seductress about whom Solomon warns young men in Proverbs (Prov. 2:16-19; 5:1-14; 6:24-29; 7:1-27). Elsewhere, Solomon exalts the virtues of man's lifetime companion (Eccl. 9:9; cf. Prov. 5:15-23; 31:10-31).

7:27-29 Empirical acquisition of knowledge, that is man seeking righteousness through his many schemes, fails. Only God can make man upright.

7:29 many schemes. The same word is translated "intent" and reflects the evil imaginations of all human beings since Adam and Eve.

8 Who *is* like a wise *man?*
And who knows the interpretation
of a thing?
[a]A man's wisdom makes his face
shine,
And [b]the [1]sternness of his face is
changed.

Obey Authorities for God's Sake

2 I *say,* "Keep the king's commandment
[c]for the sake of your oath to God. 3 [d]Do not
be hasty to go from his presence. Do not
take your stand for an evil thing, for he
does whatever pleases him."

4 Where the word of a king *is, there is*
power;
And [e]who may say to him, "What
are you doing?"
5 He who keeps his command will
experience nothing harmful;
And a wise man's heart [2]discerns
both time and judgment,
6 Because [f]for every matter there is a
time and judgment,
Though the misery of man
[3]increases greatly.
7 [g]For he does not know what will
happen;
So who can tell him when it will
occur?
8 [h]No one has power over the spirit
to retain the spirit,
And no one has power in the day
of death.
There is [i]no release from that war,
And wickedness will not deliver
those who are given to it.

9 All this I have seen, and applied my
heart to every work that is done under the
sun: *There is* a time in which one man rules
over another to his own hurt.

CHAPTER 8

1 [a]Prov. 4:8, 9; Acts 6:15 [b]Deut. 28:50 [1]Lit. *strength*
2 [c]Ex. 22:11; 2 Sam. 21:7; 1 Chr. 29:24; Ezek. 17:18; [Rom. 13:5]
3 [d]Eccl. 10:4
4 [e]1 Sam. 13:11, 13; Job 34:18
5 [2]Lit. *knows*
6 [f]Eccl. 3:1, 17 [3]*is great upon him*
7 [g]Prov. 24:22; Eccl. 6:12
8 [h]Ps. 49:6, 7; Job 14:5 [i]Deut. 20:5-8
10 [j]Eccl. 2:16; 9:5 [4]Some Heb. mss., LXX, Vg. *praised*
11 [k]Ps. 10:6; 50:21; Is. 26:10
12 [l]Is. 65:20; [Rom. 2:5-7] [m][Deut. 4:40; Ps. 37:11, 18, 19; Prov. 1:32, 33; Is. 3:10; Matt. 25:34, 41]
14 [n]Ps. 73:14 [o]Eccl. 2:14; 7:15; 9:1-3
15 [p]Eccl. 2:24
17 [q]Job 5:9; Ps. 73:16; Eccl. 3:11; Rom. 11:33

CHAPTER 9

1 [a]Deut. 33:3; Job 12:10; Eccl. 8:14 [1]Lit. *put*
2 [b]Gen. 3:17-19; Job 21:7; Ps. 73:3, 12, 13; Mal. 3:15

Death Comes to All

10 Then I saw the wicked buried, who
had come and gone from the place of holiness, and they were [j]forgotten[4] in the city
where they had so done. This also *is* vanity. 11 [k]Because the sentence against an evil
work is not executed speedily, therefore
the heart of the sons of men is fully set in
them to do evil. 12 [l]Though a sinner does
evil a hundred *times,* and his *days* are prolonged, yet I surely know that [m]it will be
well with those who fear God, who fear before Him. 13 But it will not be well with the
wicked; nor will he prolong *his* days, *which*
are as a shadow, because he does not fear
before God.
14 There is a vanity which occurs on
earth, that there are just *men* to whom it
[n]happens according to the work of the
wicked; again, there are wicked *men* to
whom it happens according to the work
of the [o]righteous. I said that this also *is*
vanity.
15 [p]So I commended enjoyment, because
a man has nothing better under the sun
than to eat, drink, and be merry; for this
will remain with him in his labor *all* the
days of his life which God gives him under
the sun.
16 When I applied my heart to know
wisdom and to see the business that is
done on earth, even though one sees no
sleep day or night, 17 then I saw all the
work of God, that [q]a man cannot find out
the work that is done under the sun. For
though a man labors to discover *it,* yet he
will not find *it;* moreover, though a wise
man attempts to know *it,* he will not be
able to find *it.*

9 For I [1]considered all this in my heart,
so that I could declare it all: [a]that the
righteous and the wise and their works *are*
in the hand of God. People know neither
love nor hatred *by* anything *they see* before
them. 2 [b]All things *come* alike to all:

8:2,3 your oath to God. This refers to Israel's promises to serve King Solomon (1 Chr. 29:24).

8:5,6 time and judgment. Solomon returns to the message of 3:19 regarding a time for judgment. Knowing that God has appointed a time for judgment gives day to day living a clear purpose.

8:7 what...when. God has appointed a time for everything but man knows neither the time nor the outcome. These uncertainties can increase his misery.

8:8 spirit. "Wind" may be the better translation for the word "spirit." Death is as precarious and uncontrollable as the wind.

8:10 the place of holiness. This refers to the temple at Jerusalem (cf. 5:1). **vanity.** Lessons that should be gained from the death of the hypocritically wicked are quickly forgotten.

8:11 the sentence. The gracious delay of God's retribution leads to further disobedience. This delay, in actuality, in no way diminishes the certainty of final judgment.

8:12,13 those who fear God...the wicked. There is no real advantage for the wicked, although at times it might seem so (cf. 5:7; 12:13,14). Temporal patience does not eliminate eternal judgment.

8:14 vanity. Temporally speaking, God generally rewards obedience and punishes disobedience. Solomon regards the exceptions to this principle as vanity or enigmatic and discouraging (see Ps. 73).

8:15 enjoyment. In no way does Solomon commend unbridled, rampant indulgence in sin, which is implied in Christ's account of the man whose barns were full. That man may have justified his sin by quoting this passage (cf. Luke 12:19). His focus here is on the resolve to enjoy life in the face of the injustice which surrounded him (see 2:24).

8:16,17 the work of God. God's work is wonderful, but at times incomprehensible.

9:1 in the hand of God. There will be no inequities in the final judgment of the righteous or the wicked, because God remembers both in perfect detail.

One event *happens* to the righteous
and the wicked;
To the [2]good, the clean, and the
unclean;
To him who sacrifices and him
who does not sacrifice.
As is the good, so *is* the sinner;
He who takes an oath as *he* who
fears an oath.

3 This *is* an evil in all that is done under the
sun: that one thing *happens* to all. Truly the
hearts of the sons of men are full of evil;
madness *is* in their hearts while they live,
and after that *they go* to the dead. 4 But for
him who is joined to all the living there is
hope, for a living dog is better than a dead
lion.

5 For the living know that they will
die;
But [c]the dead know nothing,
And they have no more reward,
For [d]the memory of them is
forgotten.
6 Also their love, their hatred, and
their envy have now
perished;
Nevermore will they have a share
In anything done under the sun.

7 Go, [e]eat your bread with joy,
And drink your wine with a merry
heart;
For God has already accepted your
works.
8 Let your garments always be
white,
And let your head lack no oil.

9 [3]Live joyfully with the wife whom you
love all the days of your vain life which He
has given you under the sun, all your days
of vanity; [f]for that *is* your portion in life,
and in the labor which you perform under
the sun.
10 [g]Whatever your hand finds to do, do
it with your [h]might; for *there is* no work or
device or knowledge or wisdom in the
grave where you are going.
11 I returned [i]and saw under the sun
that—

The race *is* not to the swift,
Nor the battle to the strong,
Nor bread to the wise,
Nor riches to men of
understanding,
Nor favor to men of skill;
But time and [j]chance happen to
them all.
12 For [k]man also does not know his
time:
Like fish taken in a cruel net,
Like birds caught in a snare,
So the sons of men *are* [l]snared in
an evil time,
When it falls suddenly upon them.

Wisdom Superior to Folly

13 This wisdom I have also seen under
the sun, and it *seemed* great to me: 14 [m]*There
was* a little city with few men in it; and a
great king came against it, besieged it, and
built great [4]snares around it. 15 Now there
was found in it a poor wise man, and he by
his wisdom delivered the city. Yet no one
remembered that same poor man.
16 Then I said:

"Wisdom *is* better than [n]strength.
Nevertheless [o]the poor man's
wisdom *is* despised,
And his words are not heard.
17 Words of the wise, *spoken* quietly,
should be heard
Rather than the shout of a ruler of
fools.
18 Wisdom *is* better than weapons of
war;
But [p]one sinner destroys much
good."

10

1 Dead [1]flies [2]putrefy the perfumer's
ointment,
And cause it to give off a foul odor;
So does a little folly to one
respected for wisdom *and*
honor.
2 A wise man's heart *is* at his right
hand,
But a fool's heart at his left.
3 Even when a fool walks along the
way,
He lacks wisdom,

2 [2] LXX, Syr., Vg. *good and bad,*
5 [c] Job 14:21; Is. 63:16 [d] Job 7:8-10; Eccl. 1:11; 2:16; 8:10; Is. 26:14
7 [e] Eccl. 8:15
9 [f] Eccl. 2:10 [3] Lit. *See life*
10 [g] [Col. 3:17] [h] Rom. 12:11; Col. 3:23
11 [i] Jer. 9:23; Amos 2:14, 15 [j] 1 Sam. 6:9
12 [k] Eccl. 8:7 [l] Prov. 29:6; Luke 12:20, 39; 17:26; 1 Thess. 5:3
14 [m] 2 Sam. 20:16-22 [4] LXX, Syr., Vg. *bulwarks*
16 [n] Eccl. 7:12, 19 [o] Mark 6:2, 3
18 [p] Josh. 7:1-26; 2 Kin. 21:2-17

CHAPTER 10

1 [1] Lit. *Flies of death* [2] Tg., Vg. omit *putrefy*

9:2,3 one thing *happens* to all. Death because of universal depravity.

9:7 eat…drink. *See notes on 2:24.*

9:9 the wife. Cf. Prov. 5:15-19 and Solomon's Song.

9:11 time and chance. Wisdom cannot guarantee good outcomes because of what appear to be so many unpredictable contingencies.

9:12 his time. The time of his misfortune, especially death (cf. 11:8, "days of darkness"; 12:1, "difficult days").

9:13-15 Wisdom may not receive its due in this life.

9:16 This is true because he lacks status and position.

10:1-20 Solomon draws together assorted examples of the wisdom he has both scrutinized and touted.

10:2 right…left. This proverb is based on the fact that, commonly, the right hand is more deft than the left.

10:3 fool. *See note on 2:14.* **walks.** A person lacking wisdom will manifest that in daily conduct.

[a]And he shows everyone *that* he *is* a
fool.
4 If the spirit of the ruler rises
against you,
[b]Do not leave your post;
For [c]conciliation[3] pacifies great
offenses.

5 There is an evil I have seen under
the sun,
As an error proceeding from the
ruler:
6 [d]Folly is set in [4]great dignity,
While the rich sit in a lowly place.
7 I have seen servants [e]on horses,
While princes walk on the ground
like servants.

8 [f]He who digs a pit will fall into it,
And whoever breaks through a
wall will be bitten by a
serpent.
9 He who quarries stones may be
hurt by them,
And he who splits wood may be
endangered by it.
10 If the ax is dull,
And one does not sharpen the
edge,
Then he must use more strength;
But wisdom [5]brings success.

11 A serpent may bite [g]when *it is* not
charmed;
The [6]babbler is no different.
12 [h]The words of a wise man's mouth
are gracious,
But [i]the lips of a fool shall swallow
him up;
13 The words of his mouth begin with
foolishness,
And the end of his talk *is* raving
madness.
14 [j]A fool also multiplies words.
No man knows what is to be;
Who can tell him [k]what will be
after him?
15 The labor of fools wearies them,
For they do not even know how to
go to the city!

16 [l]Woe to you, O land, when your
king *is* a child,
And your princes feast in the
morning!
17 Blessed *are* you, O land, when your
king *is* the son of nobles,
And your [m]princes feast at the
proper time—
For strength and not for
drunkenness!
18 Because of laziness the [7]building
decays,
And [n]through idleness of hands
the house leaks.
19 A feast is made for laughter,
And [o]wine makes merry;
But money answers everything.

20 [p]Do not curse the king, even in your
thought;
Do not curse the rich, even in your
bedroom;
For a bird of the air may carry your
voice,
And a bird in flight may tell the
matter.

The Value of Diligence

11 Cast your bread [a]upon the waters,
[b]For you will find it after many
days.
2 [c]Give a serving [d]to seven, and also
to eight,
[e]For you do not know what evil
will be on the earth.

3 If the clouds are full of rain,
They empty *themselves* upon the
earth;
And if a tree falls to the south or
the north,
In the place where the tree falls,
there it shall lie.
4 He who observes the wind will not
sow,

3 [a]Prov. 13:16; 18:2 **4** [b]Eccl. 8:3 [c]1 Sam. 25:24-33; Prov. 25:15 [3]Lit. *healing, health* **6** [d]Esth. 3:1 [4]*exalted positions* **7** [e]Prov. 19:10; 30:22 **8** [f]Ps. 7:15; Prov. 26:27 **10** [5]Lit. *is a successful advantage* **11** [g]Ps. 58:4, 5; Jer. 8:17 [6]Lit. *master of the tongue* **12** [h]Prov. 10:32; Luke 4:22 [i]Prov. 10:14; Eccl. 4:5 **14** [j][Prov. 15:2]; Eccl. 5:3 [k]Eccl. 3:22; 8:7

16 [l]Is. 3:4, 5; 5:11 **17** [m]Prov. 31:4; Is. 5:11 **18** [n]Prov. 24:30-34 [7]Lit. *rafters sink* **19** [o]Judg. 9:13; Ps. 104:15; Eccl. 2:3 **20** [p]Ex. 22:28; Acts 23:5

CHAPTER 11

1 [a]Is. 32:20 [b][Deut. 15:10; Prov. 19:17; Matt. 10:42; 2 Cor. 9:8; Gal. 6:9, 10; Heb. 6:10] **2** [c]Ps. 112:9; Matt. 5:42; Luke 6:30; [1 Tim. 6:18, 19] [d]Mic. 5:5 [e]Eph. 5:16

10:5 It is a great and far-reaching evil when leaders make bad judgments.

10:6,7 the rich…princes. Life presents some strange ironies and is not, in this world, always fair.

10:8-10 digs…does not sharpen. Dangers and uncertainties abound in life.

10:10 wisdom brings success. A little wisdom will ease the efforts of life. Even though life's experiences often don't turn out the way one would have hoped, wise living usually produces a good outcome. This is a very important conclusion for Solomon's testing of wisdom.

10:12-14 words. Man demonstrates wisdom in words as well as works. Foolish words yield unfavorable outcomes.

10:15 to go to the city. A proverb for ignorance with regard to the most ordinary matters, which extends even to spiritual realities. If a fool can't find the town, how could he possibly locate God?

10:18 the building…the house. This is likely an analogy for the kingdom of a lazy monarch.

10:19 money answers everything. The partying king of v. 18 thinks he can fix all the disasters of his inept reign by raising taxes.

11:1 Cast your bread. Take a calculated and wise step forward in life, like a farmer who throws his seed on the wet or marshy ground and waits for it to grow (cf. Is. 32:20).

11:2 Give. Be generous while there is plenty, and make friends while time remains, because one never knows when he might need them to return the favor.

And he who regards the clouds
will not reap.

5 As [f]you do not know what *is* the
way of the [1]wind,
[g]*Or* how the bones *grow* in the womb
of her who is with child,
So you do not know the works of
God who makes everything.
6 In the morning sow your seed,
And in the evening do not
withhold your hand;
For you do not know which will
prosper,
Either this or that,
Or whether both alike *will be* good.

7 Truly the light is sweet,
And *it is* pleasant for the eyes [h]to
behold the sun;
8 But if a man lives many years
And [i]rejoices in them all,
Yet let him [j]remember the days of
darkness,
For they will be many.
All that is coming *is* vanity.

Seek God in Early Life

9 Rejoice, O young man, in your
youth,
And let your heart cheer you in the
days of your youth;
[k]Walk in the [2]ways of your heart,
And [3]in the sight of your eyes;
But know that for all these
[l]God will bring you into judgment.
10 Therefore remove [4]sorrow from
your heart,
And [m]put away evil from your flesh,
[n]For childhood and [5]youth *are*
vanity.

12 Remember [a] now your Creator in
the days of your youth,
Before the [1]difficult days come,
And the years draw near [b]when
you say,
"I have no pleasure in them":
2 While the sun and the light,
The moon and the stars,
Are not darkened,
And the clouds do not return after
the rain;
3 In the day when the keepers of the
house tremble,
And the strong men bow down;
When the grinders cease because
they are few,
And those that look through the
windows grow dim;
4 When the doors are shut in the
streets,
And the sound of grinding is low;
When one rises up at the sound of
a bird,
And all [c]the daughters of music
are brought low.
5 Also they are afraid of height,
And of terrors in the way;
When the almond tree blossoms,
The grasshopper is a burden,
And desire fails.
For man goes to [d]his eternal home,
And [e]the mourners go about the
streets.
6 *Remember your Creator* before the
silver cord is [2]loosed,

5 [f] John 3:8 [g] Ps. 139:14 [1] Or *spirit* **7** [h] Eccl. 7:11 **8** [i] Eccl. 9:7 [j] Eccl. 12:1 **9** [k] Num. 15:39; Job 31:7; Eccl. 2:10 [l] Eccl. 3:17; 12:14; [Rom. 14:10] [2] Impulses [3] As you see to be best **10** [4] *vexation* [m] 2 Cor. 7:1; 2 Tim. 2:22 [n] Ps. 39:5 [5] Prime of life

CHAPTER 12

1 [a] 2 Chr. 34:3; Prov. 22:6; Lam. 3:27 [b] 2 Sam. 19:35 [1] Lit. *evil* **4** [c] 2 Sam. 19:35 **5** [d] Job 17:13 [e] Gen. 50:10; Jer. 9:17 **6** [2] So with Qr., Tg.; Kt. *removed;* LXX, Vg. *broken*

11:7–12:8 Solomon crystallizes the book's message. Death is imminent and with it comes retribution. Enjoyment and judgment, though strange partners, come together in this section because both clamor for man's deepest commitment. Surprisingly, one does not win out over the other. In a world created for enjoyment but damaged by sin, judgment and enjoyment/pleasure are held in tension. With too much pleasure, judgment stands as a threatening force; with too much judgment, enjoyment suffers. In the final analysis, both are prominent themes of life that are resolved in our relationship to God, the primary issue of life and this book.

11:3-6 The world is full of things over which one has no control including the purposes of God. There is no virtue in wishful wondering, but there is hope for those who get busy and do their work.

11:7 light. Good times in contrast to "darkness" (v. 8), meaning bad times. Cf. 12:1.

11:9 Rejoice...judgment. The two terms seem to cancel out the other. How can this be explained? Enjoy life but do not commit iniquity. The balance that is called for insures that enjoyment is not reckless, sinful abandonment. Pleasure is experienced in faith and obedience, for as Solomon has said repeatedly, one can only receive true satisfaction as a gift from God.

11:10 vanity. Enjoy childhood and youth while you can because life is fleeting.

12:1 Remember...your Creator...difficult days. Remember you are God's property, so serve Him from the start of your years, not the end of your years, when service is very limited.

12:2-6 Solomon uses the imagery of aging, incorporating elements of a dilapidated house, nature, and a funeral procession to heighten the emphasis of 11:7–12:1.

12:2 sun...moon...clouds. Youth is typically the time of dawning light, old age the time of twilight's gloom.

12:3 keepers of the house tremble. The hands and arms which protect the body, as guards do a palace, shake in old age. **strong men bow down.** The legs, like supporting pillars, weaken. **grinders.** Teeth. **those that look through the windows.** Eyes.

12:4 doors. Lips that do not have much to say. **sound of grinding.** This refers to little eating, when the sound of masticating is low. **rises up.** Light sleep. **daughters of music.** The ear and voice that once loved music.

12:5 afraid of height. For fear of falling. **almond tree blossoms.** A white blossoming tree among dark trees speaks of hair. **mourners.** The funeral is near.

12:6,7 Here are the images of death.

12:6 silver cord is loosed. Perhaps this pictures a lamp hanging

Or the golden bowl is broken,
Or the pitcher shattered at the fountain,
Or the wheel broken at the well.
7 [f]Then the dust will return to the earth as it was,
[g]And the spirit will return to God
[h]who gave it.

8 "Vanity[i] of vanities," says the Preacher,
"All *is* vanity."

The Whole Duty of Man

9 And moreover, because the Preacher
was wise, he still taught the people knowledge; yes, he pondered and sought out *and*
[j]set[3] in order many proverbs. 10 The
Preacher sought to find [4]acceptable words;
and *what was* written *was* upright—words
of truth. 11 The words of the wise are like
goads, and the words of [5]scholars are like
well-driven nails, given by one Shepherd.
12 And further, my son, be admonished by
these. Of making many books *there is* no
end, and [k]much study *is* wearisome to the
flesh.
13 Let us hear the conclusion of the
whole matter:

[l]Fear God and keep His commandments,
For this is man's all.
14 For [m]God will bring every work into judgment,
Including every secret thing,
Whether good or evil.

7 [f]Gen. 3:19; Job 34:15; Ps. 90:3 [g]Eccl. 3:21 [h]Num. 16:22; 27:16; Job 34:14; Is. 57:16; Zech. 12:1
8 [i]Ps. 62:9
9 [j]1 Kin. 4:32 [3]*arranged*
10 [4]Lit. *delightful*
11 [5]Lit. *masters of assemblies*
12 [k]Eccl. 1:18
13 [l][Deut. 6:2; 10:12]; Mic. 6:8
14 [m]Eccl. 11:9; Matt. 12:36; [Acts 17:30, 31; Rom. 2:16; 1 Cor. 4:5; 2 Cor. 5:10]

from a silver chain, which breaks with age, smashing the lamp. Some suggest this refers to the spinal cord. **golden bowl.** Possibly this refers to the brain. **pitcher...fountain...wheel.** Wells required a wheel with a rope attached in order to lower the pitcher for water. Perhaps this pictures the fountain of blood, the heart. **loosed...broken...shattered...broken.** All of these actions portray death as tragic and irreversible.

12:7 dust...spirit. Solomon recalls Gen. 2:7 and 3:19 as he contemplates the end of the aging process. **spirit...who gave it.** The sage ends his message with the culmination of a human life. "The LORD gave and the LORD has taken away" (Job 1:21; 1 Tim. 6:7).

12:7,8 This gloomy picture of old age does not negate the truth that old age can be blessed for the godly (Prov. 16:31), but it does remind the young that they will not have the ability to enjoy that blessing of a godly old age and a life of strong service to God if they do not remember their Creator while young (v. 1).

12:9-14 Solomon's final words of advice.

12:11 goads...well-driven nails. Two shepherd's tools are in view: one used to motivate reluctant animals, the other to secure those who might otherwise wander into dangerous territory. Both goads and nails picture aspects of applied wisdom. **one Shepherd.** True wisdom has its source in God alone.

12:12 books. Books written on any other subject than God's revealed wisdom will only proliferate the uselessness of man's thinking.

12:13,14 Fear God. Solomon's final word on the issues raised in this book, as well as life itself, focus on one's relationship to God. All of the concern for a life under the sun, with its pleasures and uncertainties, was behind Solomon. Such things seemed comparatively irrelevant to him as he faced the end of his life. But death, in spite of the focused attention he had given to it in Ecclesiastes, was not the greatest equalizer. Judgment/retribution is the real equalizer as Solomon saw it, for God will bring every person's every act to judgment. Unbelievers will stand at the Great White Throne judgment (cf. Rev. 20:11-15) and believers before Christ at the Bema judgment (cf. 1 Cor. 3:10-15; 2 Cor. 5:9,10). When all is said and done, the certainty and finality of retribution give life the meaning for which David's ofttimes foolish son had been searching. Whatever may be one's portion in life, accountability to the God, whose ways are often mysterious, is both eternal and irrevocable.

The SONG OF SOLOMON

Title

The Greek Septuagint (LXX) and Latin Vulgate (Vg.) versions follow the Hebrew (Masoretic Text) with literal translations of the first two words in 1:1—"Song of Songs." Several English versions read "The Song of Solomon," thus giving the fuller sense of 1:1. The superlative, "Song of Songs" (cf. "Holy of Holies" in Ex. 26:33,34 and "King of Kings" in Rev. 19:16), indicates that this song is the best among Solomon's 1,005 musical works (1 Kin. 4:32). The word translated "song" frequently refers to music that honors the Lord (cf. 1 Chr. 6:31,32; Pss. 33:3; 40:3; 144:9).

Author and Date

Solomon, who reigned over the united kingdom 40 years (971–931 B.C.), appears 7 times by name in this book (1:1,5; 3:7,9,11; 8:11,12). In view of his writing skills, musical giftedness (1 Kin. 4:32), and the authorial, not dedicatory, sense of 1:1, this piece of Scripture could have been penned at any time during Solomon's reign. Since cities to the N and to the S are spoken of in Solomon's descriptions and travels, both the period depicted and the time of actual writing point to the united kingdom before it divided after Solomon's reign ended. Knowing that this portion of Scripture comprises one song by one author, it is best taken as a unified piece of poetic, Wisdom literature rather than a series of love poems without a common theme or author.

Background and Setting

Two people dominate this true-life, dramatic love song. Solomon, whose kingship is mentioned 5 times (1:4,12; 3:9,11; 7:5), appears as "the beloved." The Shulamite maiden (6:13) remains obscure; most likely she was a resident of Shunem, 3 mi. N of Jezreel in lower Galilee. Some suggest she is Pharaoh's daughter (1 Kin. 3:1), although the Song provides no evidence for this conclusion. Others favor Abishag, the Shunammite who cared for King David (1 Kin. 1:1-4,15). An unknown maiden from Shunem, whose family had possibly been employed by Solomon (8:11), seems most reasonable. She would have been Solomon's first wife (Eccl. 9:9), before he sinned by adding 699 other wives and 300 concubines (1 Kin. 11:3).

Minor roles feature several different groups in this book. First, note the not infrequent commentary by "the daughters of Jerusalem" (1:5; 2:7; 3:5; 5:8,16; 8:4), who might be part of Solomon's household staff (cf. 3:10). Second, Solomon's friends join in at 3:6-11; and third, so do the Shulamite's brothers (8:8,9). The affirmation of 5:1b would most likely be God's blessing on the couple's union. One can follow the narrative by noticing the suggested parts as indicated in headings throughout the song. Where possible variations are reasonable, they will be recognized in the study notes.

The setting combines both rural and urban scenes. Portions take place in the hill country N of Jerusalem, where the Shulamite lived (6:13) and where Solomon enjoyed prominence as a vinegrower and shepherd (Eccl. 2:4-7). The city section includes the wedding and time afterward at Solomon's abode in Jerusalem (3:6–7:13).

The first spring appears in 2:11-13 and the second in 7:12. Assuming a chronology without gaps, the Song of Solomon took place over a period of time at least one year in length, but probably no longer than two years.

Historical and Theological Themes

All 117 verses in Solomon's Song have been recognized by the Jews as a part of their sacred writings. Along with Ruth, Esther, Ecclesiastes, and Lamentations, it is included among the OT books of the Megilloth, or "five scrolls." The Jews read this song at Passover, calling it "the Holy of Holies." Surprisingly, God is not mentioned explicitly except possibly in 8:6. No formal theological themes emerge. The NT never quotes Solomon's Song directly (nor Esther, Obadiah, and Nahum).

In contrast to the two distorted extremes of ascetic abstinence and lustful perversion outside of marriage, Solomon's ancient love song exalts the purity of marital affection and romance. It parallels and enhances other portions of Scripture which portray God's plan for marriage, including the beauty and sanctity of sexual intimacy between husband and wife. The Song rightfully stands alongside other classic Scripture passages which expand on this theme, e.g., Gen. 2:24; Ps. 45; Prov. 5:15-23; 1 Cor. 7:1-5; 13:1-8; Eph. 5:18-33; Col. 3:18,19; and 1 Pet. 3:1-7. Hebrews 13:4 captures the heart of this song, "Marriage is honorable among all, and the bed undefiled; but fornicators and adulterers God will judge."

Interpretive Challenges

The Song has suffered strained interpretations over the centuries by those who use the "allegorical" method of interpretation, claiming that this song has no actual historical basis, but rather that it depicts God's love for Israel and/or Christ's love for the church. The misleading idea from hymnology that Christ is the rose of Sharon and the lily of the valleys results from this method (2:1). The "typological" variation admits the historical reality, but concludes that it ultimately pictures Christ's bridegroom love for His bride the church.

A more satisfying way to approach Solomon's Song is to take it at face value and interpret it in the normal historical sense, understanding the frequent use of poetic imagery to depict reality. To do so understands that Solomon recounts 1) his own days of courtship, 2) the early days of his first marriage, followed by 3) the maturing of this royal couple through the good and bad days of life. The Song of Solomon expands on the ancient marriage instructions of Gen. 2:24, thus providing spiritual music for a lifetime of marital harmony. It is given by God to demonstrate His intention for the romance and loveliness of marriage, the most precious of human relations and "the grace of life" (1 Pet. 3:7).

Outline

- I. The Courtship: "Leaving" (1:2–3:5)
  - A. The Lovers' Remembrances (1:2–2:7)
  - B. The Lovers' Expression of Reciprocal Love (2:8–3:5)
- II. The Wedding: "Cleaving" (3:6–5:1)
  - A. The Kingly Bridegroom (3:6-11)
  - B. The Wedding and First Night Together (4:1–5:1a)
  - C. God's Approval (5:1b)
- III. The Marriage: "Weaving" (5:2–8:14)
  - A. The First Major Disagreement (5:2–6:3)
  - B. The Restoration (6:4–8:4)
  - C. Growing in Grace (8:5-14)

1 The [a]song of songs, which *is* Solomon's.

The Banquet

THE [1]SHULAMITE

2 Let him kiss me with the kisses of
his mouth—
[b]For [2]your love *is* better than
wine.
3 Because of the fragrance of your
good ointments,
Your name *is* ointment poured
forth;
Therefore the virgins love you.
4 [c]Draw me away!

THE DAUGHTERS OF JERUSALEM

[d]We will run after [3]you.

THE SHULAMITE

The king [e]has brought me into his
chambers.

THE DAUGHTERS OF JERUSALEM

We will be glad and rejoice in
[4]you.

We will remember [3]your love more
than wine.

THE SHULAMITE

Rightly do they love [3]you.

5 I *am* dark, but lovely,
O daughters of Jerusalem,
Like the tents of Kedar,
Like the curtains of Solomon.
6 Do not look upon me, because I *am*
dark,
Because the sun has [5]tanned me.
My mother's sons were angry with
me;
They made me the keeper of the
vineyards,
But my own [f]vineyard I have not
kept.

(TO HER BELOVED)

7 Tell me, O you whom I love,
Where you feed *your flock,*
Where you make *it* rest at noon.
For why should I be as one who
[6]veils herself
By the flocks of your companions?

THE BELOVED

8 If you do not know, [g]O fairest
among women,
[7]Follow in the footsteps of the flock,
And feed your little goats
Beside the shepherds' tents.

CHAPTER 1

1 [a] 1 Kin. 4:32
2 [b] Song 4:10 [1] A Palestinian young woman, Song 6:13. The speaker and audience are identified according to the number, gender, and person of the Hebrew words. Occasionally the identity is not certain. [2] Masc. sing.: the Beloved
4 [c] Hos. 11:4; John 6:44; 12:32 [d] Phil. 3:12-14 [e] Ps. 45:14, 15; John 14:2; Eph. 2:6 [3] Masc. sing.: the Beloved [4] Fem. sing.: the Shulamite
6 [f] Song 8:11, 12 [5] Lit. *looked upon me*
7 [6] LXX, Syr., Vg. *wanders*
8 [g] Song 5:9 [7] Lit. *Go out*

1:1 See Introduction: Title; Author and Date.

1:2–3:5 In this first of 3 major sections to the Song, 32 out of 39 verses are spoken by the Shulamite, with brief interludes by her beloved and the daughters of Jerusalem. This portion most likely represents her remembrances of past events combined with the desires of her heart to marry the king, as she anticipates his arrival to take her to Jerusalem for the wedding in 3:6 ff.

1:2,3 Four features of Solomon attracted the beloved: 1) his lips, 2) his love, 3) his lotion, and 4) his pure lifestyle. Later Solomon noticed these same features in her (4:9-11).

1:3 the virgins. The daughters of Jerusalem (v. 5).

1:4 We will run. This is better understood as spoken by the Shulamite, rather than the daughters of Jerusalem, in the sense of "let us hurry/run." **The king has brought me.** This is better understood as the desire of her heart—"Let the king bring me into his chambers"—rather than a statement of fact. **We will remember your love.** The daughters of Jerusalem affirmed the Shulamite's praise in v. 2.

1:5,6 I *am* dark. The Shulamite was concerned that the sun (from working outdoors) had marred her complexion (cf. vineyard, 7:12; 8:11).

1:6 my own vineyard. Speaks of herself (cf. 8:12).

1:7 veils herself. Valuing purity, she disclaimed the veil of the prostitute, unlike Tamar (Gen. 38:14-16). Rather, she would go as a shepherdess to a shepherd.

1:8 This could have been spoken by the daughters of Jerusalem. **O fairest among women.** The Shulamite received accolades as the best (cf. 5:9; 6:1). This is reminiscent of the Prov. 31 woman (v. 29).

Local Color in the Song of Solomon

1:5	"tents of Kedar"	nomadic tribal tents made of dark goat hair
1:5	"curtains of Solomon"	most likely the beautiful curtains of Solomon's palace
1:9	"my filly"	a young, female horse
1:12; 4:13,14	"spikenard"	an aromatic oil taken from an Indian herb
1:13; 3:6; 4:6,14; 5:1,5,13	"myrrh"	an aromatic gum from the bark of a balsam tree made into perfume in either liquid or solid form
1:14; 4:13	"henna blooms"	a common shrub whose white, spring blossoms give off a fragrant scent
1:14	"En Gedi"	a lush oasis just west of the Dead Sea
1:15; 4:1; 5:12	"dove's eyes"	beautiful, deep, smoke gray eyes of the dove

9 I have compared you, [h]my love,
[i]To my filly among Pharaoh's
chariots.
10 [j]Your cheeks are lovely with
ornaments,
Your neck with chains *of gold.*

THE DAUGHTERS OF JERUSALEM

11 We will make [8]you ornaments of
gold
With studs of silver.

THE SHULAMITE

12 While the king *is* at his table,
My [9]spikenard sends forth its
fragrance.
13 A bundle of myrrh *is* my beloved
to me,
That lies all night between my
breasts.
14 My beloved *is* to me a cluster of
henna *blooms*
In the vineyards of En Gedi.

THE BELOVED

15 [k]Behold, you *are* fair, [1]my love!
Behold, you *are* fair!
You *have* dove's eyes.

THE SHULAMITE

16 Behold, you *are* [l]handsome, my
beloved!
Yes, pleasant!
Also our [2]bed *is* green.
17 The beams of our houses *are* cedar,
And our rafters of fir.

2 I *am* the rose of Sharon,
And the lily of the valleys.

THE BELOVED

2 Like a lily among thorns,
So is my love among the
daughters.

THE SHULAMITE

3 Like an apple tree among the trees
of the woods,
So *is* my beloved among the sons.
I sat down in his shade with great
delight,
And [a]his fruit *was* sweet to my
taste.

THE SHULAMITE TO THE DAUGHTERS OF JERUSALEM

4 He brought me to the [1]banqueting
house,
And his banner over me *was* love.
5 Sustain me with cakes of raisins,
Refresh me with apples,
For I *am* lovesick.

6 [b]His left hand *is* under my head,
And his right hand embraces me.
7 [c]I [2]charge you, O daughters of
Jerusalem,

9 [h] Song 2:2, 10, 13; 4:1, 7; John 15:14 [i] 2 Chr. 1:16
10 [j] Ezek. 16:11
11 [8] Fem. sing.: the Shulamite
12 [9] *perfume*
15 [k] Song 4:1; 5:12 [1] *my companion, friend*
16 [l] Song 5:10-16
[2] *couch*

CHAPTER 2

3 [a] Song 4:16; Rev. 22:1, 2
4 [1] Lit. *house of wine*
6 [b] Song 8:3
7 [c] Song 3:5; 8:4 [2] *adjure*

1:9 my love. The first of 9 uses (1:15; 2:2,10,13; 4:1,7; 5:2; 6:4) **my filly.** Coming from an accomplished horseman (1 Kin. 10:26-29), this speech figure makes perfect sense as a striking compliment of her dazzling beauty.

1:13 my beloved. The first of 24 appearances.

1:15 You *are* fair. Verbal affirmation fueled this romance. He used "fair" at least 10 times (1:15; 2:10,13; 4:1,7; 6:4,10; 7:6). **dove's eyes.** She returned the compliment in 5:12, which is best understood as beautiful eyes representing a beautiful personality.

1:16,17 Actually an outdoor setting in the forest.

2:3-6 This scene pictures the loving desire of the Shulamite rather than her actual experience.

2:4 banqueting house. The scene continues in the outdoors. This "house of wine" symbolizes the vineyard, just as the beams and rafters of 1:17 refer to the forest. **his banner.** As a military flag indicates location or possession, so Solomon's love flew over his beloved one (cf. Num. 1:52; Ps. 20:5).

2:7 I charge you. This refrain, which is repeated before the wedding (3:5) and also afterward (8:4), explicitly expresses her commitment to a chaste life before and during marriage. She invites

Local Color in the Song of Solomon

2:1	"rose of Sharon"	probably a bulb flower like crocus, narcissus, iris or daffodil growing in the low country (plain of Sharon), south of Mt. Carmel
2:1,16	"lily of the valleys"	possibly a six petaled flower that grew in the fertile, watered areas
2:3,5; 7:8; 8:5	"apple"	an aromatic, sweet fruit—possibly an apricot
2:5	"cakes of raisins"	a food associated with religious festivals, having possible erotic significance (cf. 2 Sam. 6:19; Hos. 3:1)
2:7,9,17; 3:5; 8:14	"gazelles"	a graceful member of the antelope family
2:7; 3:5	"does"	a female deer
2:9,17; 8:14	"stag"	a male deer
2:14; 5:2; 6:9	"dove"	a common symbol of love
2:17	"mountains of Bether"	a ravine or rugged hills in an unidentifiable location in Israel

By the gazelles or by the does of
the field,
Do not stir up nor awaken love
Until it pleases.

The Beloved's Request

THE SHULAMITE

8 The voice of my beloved!
Behold, he comes
Leaping upon the mountains,
Skipping upon the hills.
9 [d]My beloved is like a gazelle or a
young stag.
Behold, he stands behind our wall;
He is looking through the
windows,
Gazing through the lattice.

10 My beloved spoke, and said to me:
"Rise up, my love, my fair one,
And come away.
11 For lo, the winter is past,
The rain is over *and* gone.
12 The flowers appear on the earth;
The time of singing has come,
And the voice of the turtledove
Is heard in our land.
13 The fig tree puts forth her green
figs,
And the vines *with* the tender
grapes
Give a good smell.
Rise up, my love, my fair one,
And come away!

14 "O my [e]dove, in the clefts of the
rock,
In the secret *places* of the cliff,
Let me see your [3]face,
[f]Let me hear your voice;
For your voice *is* sweet,
And your face *is* lovely."

HER BROTHERS

15 Catch us [g]the foxes,
The little foxes that spoil the vines,
For our vines *have* tender grapes.

THE SHULAMITE

16 [h]My beloved *is* mine, and I *am* his.
He feeds *his flock* among the lilies.

(TO HER BELOVED)

17 [i]Until the day breaks
And the shadows flee away,
Turn, my beloved,
And be [j]like a gazelle
Or a young stag
Upon the mountains of [4]Bether.

A Troubled Night

THE SHULAMITE

3 By [a]night on my bed I sought the
one I love;
I sought him, but I did not find
him.
2 "I will rise now," *I said,*
"And go about the city;
In the streets and in the squares
I will seek the one I love."
I sought him, but I did not find
him.
3 [b]The watchmen who go about the
city found me;
I said,
"Have you seen the one I love?"
4 Scarcely had I passed by them,
When I found the one I love.

9 [d] Prov. 6:5; Song 2:17
14 [e] Song 5:2 [f] Song 8:13 [3] Lit. *appearance*
15 [g] Ps. 80:13; Ezek. 13:4; Luke 13:32
16 [h] Song 6:3
17 [i] Song 4:6 [j] Song 8:14 [4] Lit. *Separation*

CHAPTER 3

1 [a] Is. 26:9
3 [b] Song 5:7; Is. 21:6-8, 11, 12

accountability to the daughters of Jerusalem.

2:11-13 Winter past, rains over, flowers appearing, and vines blooming use springtime as a picture of their robust, growing love for one another.

2:14 This is best taken as a continuation of what Solomon said as quoted by the Shulamite (vv. 10-15).

2:15 Catch us the foxes. Perhaps, as she literally did in the vineyards, Solomon wanted her to do by analogy in their relationship, i.e., to remove those things in their relationship that would spoil their blossoming love. It could also be thought of as "Let us...."

2:16 My beloved *is* mine, and I *am* his. This clearly expresses the sanctity of a monogamous relationship that is built on mutual love (cf. 6:3; 7:10).

3:1-4 As the wedding time approaches, the Shulamite's expectations grew more intense. It's best to understand this as her dream, rather than a historical remembrance.

3:1 the one I love. She repeated this phrase once in each of the first 4 verses, expressing her exclusive love for Solomon.

3:3 watchmen. This imagined encounter resembles a later real experience (cf. 5:6-8).

Local Color in the Song of Solomon

3:6; 4:6,14	"frankincense"	amber resin extracted from trees and used for incense/spice
3:6	"fragrant powders"	various spices
3:7,9	"couch, palanquin"	a sedan chair that transported the king and his bride
3:9; 4:8,11,15; 5:15	"Lebanon"	a beautiful country, north of Israel on the coast, with rich natural resources

I held him and would not let him
go,
Until I had brought him to the
[c]house of my mother,
And into the [1]chamber of her who
conceived me.

5 [d]I [2]charge you, O daughters of
Jerusalem,
By the gazelles or by the does of
the field,
Do not stir up nor awaken love
Until it pleases.

The Coming of Solomon

THE SHULAMITE

6 [e]Who *is* this coming out of the
wilderness
Like pillars of smoke,
Perfumed with myrrh and
frankincense,
With all the merchant's fragrant
powders?
7 Behold, it *is* Solomon's couch,
With sixty valiant men around it,
Of the valiant of Israel.
8 They all hold swords,
Being expert in war.
Every man *has* his sword on his
thigh
Because of fear in the night.

4 [c]Song 8:2 [1]room
5 [d]Song 2:7; 8:4 [2]adjure
6 [e]Song 8:5

9 [3]A portable enclosed chair

CHAPTER 4

1 [a]Song 1:15; 5:12 [b]Song 6:5
2 [c]Song 6:6 [1]bereaved

9 Of the wood of Lebanon
Solomon the King
Made himself a [3]palanquin:
10 He made its pillars *of* silver,
Its support *of* gold,
Its seat *of* purple,
Its interior paved *with* love
By the daughters of Jerusalem.
11 Go forth, O daughters of Zion,
And see King Solomon with the
crown
With which his mother crowned
him
On the day of his wedding,
The day of the gladness of his
heart.

THE BELOVED

4 Behold, [a]you *are* fair, my love!
Behold, you *are* fair!
You *have* dove's eyes behind your
veil.
Your hair *is* like a [b]flock of goats,
Going down from Mount Gilead.
2 [c]Your teeth *are* like a flock of shorn
sheep
Which have come up from the
washing,
Every one of which bears twins,
And none *is* [1]barren among them.

3:4 The Shulamite finds Solomon in her dreams and brings him to where she actually resides—her mother's house.

3:5 As in 2:7, the beloved knows that the intensity of her love for Solomon cannot yet be experienced until the wedding, so she invites the daughters of Jerusalem to keep her accountable regarding sexual purity. Up to this point, the escalating desire of the Shulamite for Solomon has been expressed in veiled and delicate ways as compared to the explicit and open expressions which follow, as would be totally appropriate for a married couple (cf. 4:1 ff.).

3:6–5:1 This second major section portrays the king actually coming for his bride and their return to Jerusalem (3:6-11), the wedding (4:1-7), and the couple's consummation of their union (4:8–5:1). Unlike the previous section, Solomon does a majority of the speaking (15 of 23 verses).

3:6-11 This narrative would be better understood as spoken by the daughters of Jerusalem who are also called "the daughters of Zion" (v. 11).

4:1–5:1 Until 3:11, there has been no hint of a wedding or marriage; thus the scenario of events support the idea that 1:2–3:5 refers to premarital days, while 4:1ff. rehearses the wedding and their love life that followed. Several reasons support this explanation: 1) "wedding" is not mentioned before 3:11; 2) "bride" does not appear until 4:8, and then it is mentioned 6 times from 4:8 to 5:1; and 3) prior to 4:1 the beloved has a holy preoccupation with sexual restraint (cf. 2:7; 3:5), but not afterwards in the holy bonds of matrimony.

4:1-15 Possibly Solomon speaks vv. 1-7 in public and the far more intimate words of vv. 8-15 in private as they prepare to consummate their marriage in v. 16 and 5:1.

4:1-7 For other specific descriptions of the Shulamite's beauty, see

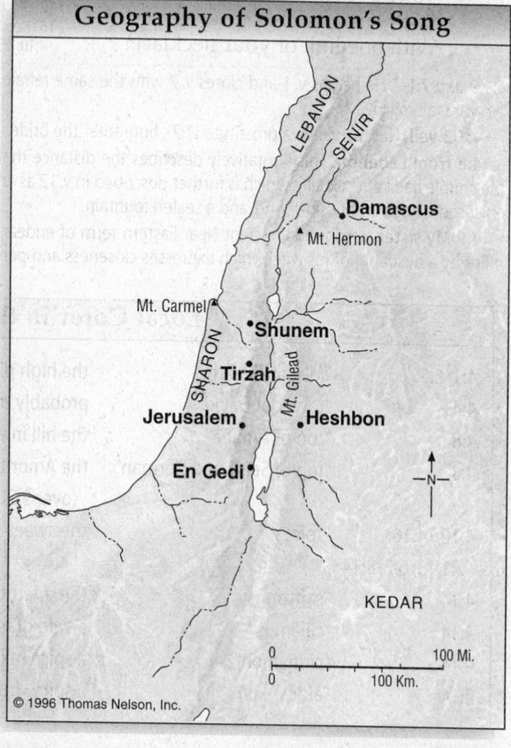

3 Your lips *are* like a strand of scarlet,
And your mouth is lovely.
[d]Your temples behind your veil
Are like a piece of pomegranate.
4 [e]Your neck *is* like the tower of David,
Built [f]for an armory,
On which hang a thousand
[2]bucklers,
All shields of mighty men.
5 [g]Your two breasts *are* like two fawns,
Twins of a gazelle,
Which feed among the lilies.

6 [h]Until the day breaks
And the shadows flee away,
I will go my way to the mountain
of myrrh
And to the hill of frankincense.

7 [i]You *are* all fair, my love,
And *there is* no spot in you.
8 Come with me from Lebanon, *my*
spouse,
With me from Lebanon.
Look from the top of Amana,
From the top of Senir [j]and
Hermon,
From the lions' dens,
From the mountains of the leopards.

9 You have ravished my heart,
My sister, *my* spouse;
You have ravished my heart
With one *look* of your eyes,
With one link of your necklace.

3 [d] Song 6:7
4 [e] Song 7:4 [f] Neh. 3:19 [2] Small shields
5 [g] Prov. 5:19; Song 7:3
6 [h] Song 2:17
7 [i] Song 1:15; Eph. 5:27
8 [j] Deut. 3:9; 1 Chr. 5:23; Ezek. 27:5

10 How fair is your love,
My sister, *my* spouse!
[k]How much better than wine is
your love,
And the [3]scent of your perfumes
Than all spices!
11 Your lips, O *my* spouse,
Drip as the honeycomb;
[l]Honey and milk *are* under your
tongue;
And the fragrance of your garments
Is [m]like the fragrance of Lebanon.

12 A garden [4]enclosed
Is my sister, *my* spouse,
A spring shut up,
A fountain sealed.
13 Your plants *are* an orchard of
pomegranates
With pleasant fruits,
Fragrant henna with spikenard,
14 Spikenard and saffron,
Calamus and cinnamon,
With all trees of frankincense,
Myrrh and aloes,
With all the chief spices—
15 A fountain of gardens,
A well of [n]living waters,
And streams from Lebanon.

10 [k] Song 1:2, 4 [3] *fragrance*
11 [l] Prov. 24:13, 14; Song 5:1 [m] Gen. 27:27; Hos. 14:6, 7
12 [4] *locked or barred*
15 [n] Zech. 14:8; John 4:10; 7:38

THE SHULAMITE

16 Awake, O north *wind*,
And come, O south!
Blow upon my garden,
That its spices may flow out.

6:4-9 and 7:1-7. He begins v. 1 and closes v. 7 with the same refrain, "you are fair my love."

4:1,3 veil. Not the veil of a prostitute (1:7), but rather the bride.

4:8 from Lebanon. This figuratively describes the distance that the couple had kept sexually, which is further described in v. 12 as an enclosed garden, a shut up spring, and a sealed fountain.

4:9 My sister. A common ancient Near Eastern term of endearment by a husband for his wife, which expresses closeness and permanence of relationship (cf. 4:10,12; 5:1,2).

4:15 a well of living waters. Solomon testified that whereas she was closed to his physical love before marriage (vv. 8,12), now she is appropriately open to it (cf. Prov. 5:15-20).

4:16 The Shulamite then portrays herself as an open garden, whereas before she was closed (4:12). She describes herself as "his garden" signifying voluntary sexual surrender (cf. 1 Cor. 7:3-5).

Local Color in the Song of Solomon

4:1; 6:5	"Mount Gilead"	the high plateau east of Galilee and Samaria
4:4	"tower of David"	probably the armory tower of Nehemiah 3:19,25
4:8	"top of Amana"	the hill in which the Amana River has its source in Syria
4:8	"top of Senir and Herman"	the Amorite and Hebrew names for the tallest summit in northern Israel (over 9,200 ft., cf. Deut. 3:9)
4:10,14,16; 5:1,13; 6:2; 8:14	"spices"	the sweet smelling oil from the balsam
4:14	"saffron"	the dried, powdered pistils and stamens of a small crocus
4:14	"calamus"	a wild grass with a gingery scent
4:14	"cinnamon"	a spice taken from the bark of a tree
4:14	"aloes"	a spicy drug with a strong scent

[o]Let my beloved come to his garden
And eat its pleasant [p]fruits.

THE BELOVED

5 I [a]have come to my garden, my
[b]sister, *my* spouse;
I have gathered my myrrh with my
spice;
[c]I have eaten my honeycomb with
my honey;
I have drunk my wine with my
milk.

(TO HIS FRIENDS)

Eat, O [d]friends!
Drink, yes, drink deeply,
O beloved ones!

The Shulamite's Troubled Evening

THE SHULAMITE

2 I sleep, but my heart is awake;
It is the voice of my beloved!
[e]He knocks, *saying,*
"Open for me, my sister, [1]my love,
My dove, my perfect one;
For my head is covered with dew,
My [2]locks with the drops of the
night."

3 I have taken off my robe;
How can I put it on *again?*
I have washed my feet;
How can I [3]defile them?
4 My beloved put his hand
By the [4]latch *of the door,*
And my heart yearned for him.
5 I arose to open for my beloved,
And my hands dripped *with*
myrrh,
My fingers with liquid myrrh,
On the handles of the lock.
6 I opened for my beloved,
But my beloved had turned away
and was gone.
My [5]heart leaped up when he
spoke.
[f]I sought him, but I could not find
him;
I called him, but he gave me no
answer.
7 [g]The watchmen who went about the
city found me.
They struck me, they wounded me;
The keepers of the walls
Took my veil away from me.
8 I charge you, O daughters of
Jerusalem,
If you find my beloved,
That you tell him I *am* lovesick!

THE DAUGHTERS OF JERUSALEM

9 What *is* your beloved
More than *another* beloved,
[h]O fairest among women?
What *is* your beloved
More than *another* beloved,
That you so [6]charge us?

THE SHULAMITE

10 My beloved *is* white and ruddy,
[7]Chief among ten thousand.
11 His head *is like* the finest gold;
His locks *are* wavy,
And black as a raven.
12 [i]His eyes *are* like doves
By the rivers of waters,
Washed with milk,
And [8]fitly set.
13 His cheeks *are* like a bed of spices,
Banks of scented herbs.
His lips *are* lilies,
Dripping liquid myrrh.
14 His hands *are* rods of gold
Set with beryl.
His body *is* carved ivory
Inlaid *with* sapphires.
15 His legs *are* pillars of marble
Set on bases of fine gold.
His countenance *is* like Lebanon,

16 [o]Song 5:1 [p]Song 7:13

CHAPTER 5

1 [a]Song 4:16 [b]Song 4:9 [c]Song 4:11 [d]Luke 15:7, 10; John 3:29
2 [e]Rev. 3:20 [1]*my companion, friend* [2]*curls* or *hair*
3 [3]*dirty*
4 [4]*opening*
6 [f]Song 3:1 [5]Lit. *soul*
7 [g]Song 3:3
9 [h]Song 1:8; 6:1 [6]*adjure*
10 [7]*Distinguished*
12 [i]Song 1:15; 4:1 [8]*sitting in a setting*

5:1 I have. While the guests feasted, the couple consummated their marriage (cf. Gen. 29:23; Deut. 22:13-21) and Solomon announced the blessing (cf. Gen. 2:25). **Eat, O friends!** Given the intimate and private nature of sexual union, it seems difficult to understand anyone but God speaking these words (cf. Prov. 5:21). This is the divine affirmation of sexual love between husband and wife as holy and beautiful.

5:2–8:14 This third major section features the couple's first argument (5:2–6:3) and their reconciliation (6:4–8:14).

5:2–6:3 Inevitable discord comes to even the most idyllic marriage. The "little foxes" of 2:15 have visited the home in this segment.

5:2 I sleep, but my heart is awake. Some have suggested the beloved dreams here, as in 3:1-4. However, she acknowledges "my heart is awake," indicating that she was not sound asleep. To make this a dream would make the rest of the book a dream, which is highly unlikely. **Open for me.** It appears that Solomon returned home earlier than expected and wanted to give his bride a romantic surprise.

5:3 How can I? Her groggy response to Solomon.

5:4-6 By the time she awakens fully and opens the door, Solomon has departed .

5:7 Unlike what happened in her dream (3:3), the watchmen treat her badly. Between the darkness and the unfamiliar features of the new bride, this could easily have happened.

5:9 The wise daughters of Jerusalem twice ask a question that prompts this bride to recall the superlative features of her new husband in vv. 10-16.

5:10-16 She responds that he is chief among ten thousand which is another way to say "He is the best of the best."

Excellent as the cedars.
16 His mouth *is* most sweet,
Yes, he *is* altogether lovely.
This *is* my beloved,
And this *is* my friend,
O daughters of Jerusalem!

THE DAUGHTERS OF JERUSALEM

6 Where has your beloved gone,
[a]O fairest among women?
Where has your beloved turned aside,
That we may seek him with you?

THE SHULAMITE

2 My beloved has gone to his [b]garden,
To the beds of spices,
To feed *his flock* in the gardens,
And to gather lilies.
3 [c]I *am* my beloved's,
And my beloved *is* mine.
He feeds *his flock* among the lilies.

Praise of the Shulamite's Beauty

THE BELOVED

4 O my love, you *are as* beautiful as Tirzah,
Lovely as Jerusalem,
Awesome as *an army* with banners!
5 Turn your eyes away from me,
For they have [1]overcome me.
Your hair *is* [d]like a flock of goats
Going down from Gilead.
6 [e]Your teeth *are* like a flock of sheep
Which have come up from the washing;
Every one bears twins,
And none *is* [2]barren among them.
7 [f]Like a piece of pomegranate
Are your temples behind your veil.

8 There are sixty queens
And eighty concubines,
And [g]virgins without number.
9 My dove, my [h]perfect one,
Is the only one,
The only one of her mother,
The favorite of the one who bore her.
The daughters saw her
And called her blessed,
The queens and the concubines,
And they praised her.

10 Who is she who looks forth as the morning,
Fair as the moon,
Clear as the sun,
[i]Awesome as *an army* with banners?

THE SHULAMITE

11 I went down to the garden of nuts
To see the verdure of the valley,
[j]To see whether the vine had budded
And the pomegranates had bloomed.

CHAPTER 6
1 [a] Song 1:8; 5:9
2 [b] Song 4:16; 5:1
3 [c] Song 2:16; 7:10
5 [d] Song 4:1
[1] *overwhelmed*

6 [e] Song 4:2
[2] *bereaved*
7 [f] Song 4:3
8 [g] Song 1:3
9 [h] Song 2:14; 5:2
10 [i] Song 6:4
11 [j] Song 7:12

6:1 Having established why they should look (5:9), the daughters ask a second question of "where to look?"

6:2,3 She believed Solomon had gone back to the garden and reaffirmed her exclusive love (cf. 2:16; 7:10).

6:4–8:4 The couple works through their difficulties and rekindles their love.

6:4-9 Apparently a reunion has occurred, and Solomon once again assured her of his love.

6:4 Lovely as Jerusalem. The nation's capital city was known as "the perfection of beauty, the joy of the whole earth" (cf. Ps. 48:1,2; Lam. 2:15).

6:8,9 Solomon reaches new heights in telling his bride she remains the best of the best (cf. 2:2; 4:7; 5:2).

6:8 queens…concubines…virgins. Are these Solomon's other women? There is no language of ownership or relationship. The numerical progression from 60 to 80 to "without number" points to the use of various categories for effect only. Solomon tells his beloved that she stands above all women.

6:10 This is better understood as being said by the daughters of Jerusalem as the third question in a series of 3 (cf. 5:9; 6:1). This time they exalt the Shulamite as one who ranks with the great beauties of God's creation.

6:11-13 This represents the most difficult portion to interpret in the entire song.

6:11,12 This is best understood as being spoken by the beloved. Solomon acknowledges that when he left home hastily (cf. 5:2-6), he returned to agricultural (v. 11) and military (v. 12) matters.

Local Color in the Song of Solomon

5:14	"beryl"	possibly a yellowish or greenish stone such as topaz
5:14	"sapphires"	the azure-blue lapis lazuli which was abundant in the East
6:4	"Tirzah"	a site known for its natural beauty and gardens located seven miles northeast of Shechem in Samaria
6:13	"the dance of the double camp"	literally "the dance of the two companies" which is possibly a dance of unknown origin associated with the place of Mahanaim (cf. Gen. 32:2)

12 Before I was even aware,
My soul had made me
As the chariots of [3]my noble
people.

THE BELOVED AND HIS FRIENDS

13 Return, return, O Shulamite;
Return, return, that we may look
upon you!

THE SHULAMITE

What would you see in the
Shulamite—
As it were, the dance of [4]the two
camps?

Expressions of Praise

THE BELOVED

7 How beautiful are your feet in
sandals,
[a]O prince's daughter!
The curves of your thighs *are* like
jewels,
The work of the hands of a skillful
workman.
2 Your navel *is* a rounded goblet;
It lacks no [1]blended beverage.
Your waist *is* a heap of wheat
Set about with lilies.
3 [b]Your two breasts *are* like two
fawns,
Twins of a gazelle.
4 [c]Your neck *is* like an ivory tower,
Your eyes *like* the pools in
Heshbon
By the gate of Bath Rabbim.
Your nose *is* like the tower of
Lebanon
Which looks toward Damascus.
5 Your head *crowns* you like *Mount*
Carmel,
And the hair of your head *is* like
purple;
A king *is* held captive by *your*
tresses.

6 How fair and how pleasant you
are,
O love, with your delights!
7 This stature of yours is like a palm
tree,
And your breasts *like* its clusters.
8 I said, "I will go up to the palm
tree,
I will take hold of its branches."
Let now your breasts be like
clusters of the vine,
The fragrance of your [2]breath like
apples,
9 And the roof of your mouth like
the best wine.

THE SHULAMITE

The wine goes down smoothly for
my beloved,
[3]Moving gently the [4]lips of
sleepers.
10 [d]I *am* my beloved's,
And [e]his desire *is* toward me.

11 Come, my beloved,
Let us go forth to the field;
Let us lodge in the villages.

12 [3] Heb. *Ammi Nadib*
13 [4] Heb. *Mahanaim*

CHAPTER 7

1 [a] Ps. 45:13
2 [1] Lit. *mixed or spiced drink*
3 [b] Song 4:5
4 [c] Song 4:4
8 [2] Lit. *nose*
9 [3] *Gliding over* [4] LXX, Syr., Vg. *lips and teeth.*
10 [d] Song 2:16; 6:3
[e] Ps. 45:11

6:13 Return, return. This is best understood as being spoken by the daughters of Jerusalem. In effect, they beckon the bride back to the royal palace. **Shulamite.** A variant spelling of Shunammite, i.e., a resident of Shunem, a part of the Land allotted to Issachar (cf. Josh. 19:18). **What would you see.** This is best understood as being spoken by the beloved. This probably refers to some form of marital dance associated with the city of Mahanaim which would be inappropriate for anyone other than Solomon to witness.

7:1-5 It is better to understand this as the friends answering Solomon. Verses 1 and 5 fit far better this way.

7:1 O prince's daughter. She appeared by beauty and dress to be of royal lineage, although she really came from a humble background.

7:6-9a Solomon and his bride start all over again. He picked up where he left off at 5:2.

7:9b–8:4 Unlike the response in 5:3, this time Solomon's beloved one responded with reciprocal love.

7:10 I *am* my beloved's. She expressed her loyal love for the third time (cf. 2:16; 6:3).

Local Color in the Song of Solomon

7:4	"the pools in Heshbon"	water reservoirs in the Moabite city of Heshbon near modern Amman
7:4	"the gate of Bath Rabbim"	possibly a gate name in Heshbon
7:4	"the tower of Lebanon"	most likely refers to the white color of the mountain rather than its elevation of 10,000 feet
7:4	"Damascus"	the capital city of Syria to the east of the Lebanon mountains
7:5	"Mount Carmel"	a prominent wooded mountain in northern Israel
7:13	"mandrakes"	a pungently fragrant herb considered to be an aphrodisiac (cf. Gen. 30:14)
8:11	"Baal Hamon"	an unknown location in the hill country north of Jerusalem

12 Let us get up early to the
vineyards;
Let us [f]see if the vine has budded,
Whether the grape blossoms are
open,
And the pomegranates are in
bloom.
There I will give you my love.
13 The [g]mandrakes give off a
fragrance,
And at our gates [h]*are* pleasant
fruits,
All manner, new and old,
Which I have laid up for you, my
beloved.

8 Oh, that you were like my brother,
Who nursed at my mother's breasts!
If I should find you outside,
I would kiss you;
I would not be despised.
2 I would lead you *and* bring you
Into the [a]house of my mother,
She *who* used to instruct me.
I would cause you to drink of
[b]spiced wine,
Of the juice of my pomegranate.

(TO THE DAUGHTERS OF JERUSALEM)

3 [c]His left hand *is* under my head,
And his right hand embraces me.
4 [d]I charge you, O daughters of
Jerusalem,
Do not stir up nor awaken love
Until it pleases.

Love Renewed in Lebanon

A RELATIVE

5 [e]Who *is* this coming up from the
wilderness,
Leaning upon her beloved?

I awakened you under the apple
tree.

12 [f]Song 6:11
13 [g]Gen. 30:14
[h]Song 2:3; 4:13, 16; Matt. 13:52

CHAPTER 8
2 [a]Song 3:4 [b]Prov. 9:2
3 [c]Song 2:6
4 [d]Song 2:7; 3:5
5 [e]Song 3:6

There your mother brought you
forth;
There she *who* bore you brought
you forth.

THE SHULAMITE TO HER BELOVED

6 [f]Set me as a seal upon your heart,
As a seal upon your arm;
For love *is as* strong as death,
[g]Jealousy *as* [1]cruel as [2]the grave;
Its flames *are* flames of fire,
[3]A most vehement flame.

7 Many waters cannot quench love,
Nor can the floods drown it.
[h]If a man would give for love
All the wealth of his house,
It would be utterly despised.

THE SHULAMITE'S BROTHERS

8 [i]We have a little sister,
And she has no breasts.
What shall we do for our sister
In the day when she is spoken
for?
9 If she *is* a wall,
We will build upon her
A battlement of silver;
And if she *is* a door,
We will enclose her
With boards of cedar.

THE SHULAMITE

10 I *am* a wall,
And my breasts like towers;
Then I became in his eyes
As one who found peace.
11 Solomon had a vineyard at Baal
Hamon;
[j]He leased the vineyard to
keepers;
Everyone was to bring for its fruit
A thousand silver coins.

6 [f]Is. 49:16; Jer. 22:24; Hag. 2:23 [g]Prov. 6:34, 35 [1]*severe*, lit. *hard* [2]Or *Sheol* [3]Lit. *A flame of* YAH, poetic form of *YHWH*, *the* LORD
7 [h]Prov. 6:35
8 [i]Ezek. 23:33
11 [j]Matt. 21:33

8:1 like my brother. This way she could have publicly bestowed her affection without embarrassment.

8:3,4 It will be just like it was when they courted (cf. 2:6,7). This time the restraint involves waiting for lovemaking until they are in private circumstances rather than public.

8:5-14 This final scene portrays the original "marriage encounter" where they reaffirm their love for one another.

8:5b I awakened you. This is better understood as being spoken by Solomon. The Shulamite's dream of 3:4 has actually been realized now in their marriage. **mother.** This is the sixth reference to the Shulamite's mother (cf. 1:6; 3:4; 6:9; 8:1; 8:2). In contrast, Solomon's mother Bathsheba is mentioned only once (cf. 3:11).

8:6 seal. The Shulamite is the seal and Solomon would do the sealing. This represents their publicly declared mutual love for one another.

8:6,7 For love. This represents the 1 Cor. 13:1-8 of the OT. Four qualities of love appear: 1) love is unyielding in marriage, as death is to life; 2) love is intense like the brightest flame, perhaps as bright as the glory of the Lord; 3) love is invincible or unquenchable, even when flooded by difficulty; and 4) love is so priceless that it cannot be bought, only given away.

8:8,9 The bride's brothers reminded everyone that they did their brotherly duty of keeping their sister pure before marriage (cf. the brothers of Rebekah in Gen. 24:50-60; Dinah in Gen. 34:13-27; and Tamar in 2 Sam. 13:1-22). The same standard of purity is taught in the NT (cf. 1 Thess. 4:1-8).

8:9 wall...door. Wall represents sexual purity; door portrays an openness to immorality.

8:10 wall. She reaffirmed that she lived a premarital life of a wall, successfully rebuffing all attempts on her honor. Thus her husband took great delight and contentment in her moral purity.

8:11,12 While Solomon might have leased out his real vineyard for profit, she gave the vineyard of her love to Solomon.

(TO SOLOMON)

12 My own vineyard *is* before me.
You, O Solomon, *may have* a thousand,
And those who tend its fruit two hundred.

THE BELOVED

13 You who dwell in the gardens,
The companions listen for your voice—
[k]Let me hear it!

THE SHULAMITE

14 [l]Make[4] haste, my beloved,
And [m]be like a gazelle
Or a young stag
On the mountains of spices.

13 [k] Song 2:14
14 [l] Rev. 22:17, 20
[m] Song 2:7, 9, 17
[4] Hurry, lit. *Flee*

8:13 The companions. These could be 1) Solomon's shepherd companions (cf. 1:7), 2) the daughters of Jerusalem (cf. 6:13), or 3) those who escorted the bride to Jerusalem (cf. 3:7).

The Book of
ISAIAH

Title

The book derives its title from the author, whose name means "The LORD is salvation," and is similar to the names Joshua, Elisha, and Jesus. Isaiah is quoted directly in the NT over 65 times, far more than any other OT prophet, and mentioned by name over 20 times.

Author and Date

Isaiah, the son of Amoz, ministered in and around Jerusalem as a prophet to Judah during the reigns of 4 kings of Judah: Uzziah (called "Azariah" in 2 Kings), Jotham, Ahaz, and Hezekiah (1:1), from ca. 739–686 B.C. He evidently came from a family of some rank, because he had easy access to the king (7:3) and intimacy with a priest (8:2). He was married and had two sons who bore symbolic names: "Shear-jashub" ("a remnant shall return," 7:3) and "Maher-shalal-hash-baz" ("hasting to the spoil, hurrying to the prey," 8:3). When called by God to prophesy, in the year of King Uzziah's death (ca. 739 B.C.), he responded with a cheerful readiness, though he knew from the beginning that his ministry would be one of fruitless warning and exhortation (6:9-13). Having been reared in Jerusalem, he was an appropriate choice as a political and religious counselor to the nation.

Isaiah was a contemporary of Hosea and Micah. His writing style has no rival in its versatility of expression, brilliance of imagery, and richness of vocabulary. The early church father Jerome likened him to Demosthenes, the legendary Greek orator. His writing features a range of 2,186 different words, compared to 1,535 in Ezekiel, 1,653 in Jeremiah, and 2,170 in the Psalms. Second Chronicles 32:32 records that he wrote a biography of King Hezekiah also. The prophet lived until at least 681 B.C. when he penned the account of Sennacherib's death (cf. 37:38). Tradition has it that he met his death under King Manasseh (ca. 695–642 B.C.) by being cut in two with a wooden saw (cf. Heb. 11:37).

Background and Setting

During Uzziah's prosperous 52 year reign (ca. 790–739 B.C.), Judah developed into a strong commercial and military state with a port for commerce on the Red Sea and the construction of walls, towers, and fortifications (2 Chr. 26:3-5,8-10,13-15). Yet the period witnessed a decline in Judah's spiritual status. Uzziah's downfall resulted from his attempt to assume the privileges of a priest and burn incense on the altar (2 Kin. 15:3,4; 2 Chr. 26:16-19). He was judged with leprosy, from which he never recovered (2 Kin. 15:5; 2 Chr 26:20,21).

His son Jotham (ca. 750–731 B.C.) had to take over the duties of king before his father's death. Assyria began to emerge as a new international power under Tiglath-Pileser (ca. 745–727 B.C.) while Jotham was king (2 Kin. 15:19). Judah also began to incur opposition from Israel and Syria to her north during his reign (2 Kin. 15:37). Jotham was a builder and a fighter like his father, but spiritual corruption still existed in the Land (2 Kin. 15:34,35; 2 Chr. 27:1,2).

Ahaz was 25 when he began to reign in Judah and he reigned until age 41 (2 Chr. 28:1,8; ca. 735–715 B.C.). Israel and Syria formed an alliance to combat the rising Assyrian threat from the E, but Ahaz refused to bring Judah into the alliance (2 Kin. 16:5; Is. 7:6). For this, the northern neighbors threatened to dethrone him, and war resulted (734 B.C.). In panic, Ahaz sent to the Assyrian king for help (2 Kin. 16:7) and the Assyrian king gladly responded, sacking Gaza, carrying all of Galilee and Gilead into captivity, and finally capturing Damascus (732 B.C.). Ahaz's alliance with Assyria led to his introduction of a heathen altar, which he set up in Solomon's temple (2 Kin. 16:10-16; 2 Chr. 28:3). During his reign (722 B.C.), Assyria captured Samaria, capital of the northern kingdom, and carried many of Israel's most capable people into captivity (2 Kin. 17:6,24).

Hezekiah began his reign over Judah in 715 B.C. and continued for 29 years to ca. 686 B.C. (2 Kin. 18:1,2). Reformation was a priority when he became king (2 Kin. 18:4,22; 2 Chr. 30:1). The threat of an Assyrian invasion forced Judah to promise heavy tribute to that eastern power. In 701 B.C. Hezekiah became very ill with a life-threatening disease, but he prayed and God graciously extended his life for 15 years (2 Kin. 20; Is. 38) until 686 B.C. The ruler of Babylon used the opportunity of his illness and recovery to send congratulations to him, probably seeking to form an alliance with Judah against Assyria at the same time (2 Kin. 20:12 ff.; Is. 39). When Assyria became weak through internal strife, Hezekiah refused to pay any further tribute to that power (2 Kin. 18:7). So in 701 B.C. Sennacherib, the Assyrian king, invaded the coastal areas of Israel, marching toward Egypt on Israel's southern flank. In the process he overran many Judean towns, looting and carrying many people back to Assyria. While besieging Lachish, he sent a contingent of forces to besiege Jerusalem (2 Kin 18:17–19:8; Is. 36:2–37:8). The side-expedition failed, however, so in a second attempt he sent messengers to Jerusalem demanding an immediate surrender of the city (2 Kin. 19:9ff.; Is. 37:9ff.). With Isaiah's encouragement, Hezekiah refused to surrender, and when Sennacherib's army fell prey to a sudden disaster, he returned to Nineveh and never threatened Judah again.

Historical and Theological Themes

Isaiah prophesied during the period of the divided kingdom, directing the major thrust of his message to the southern kingdom of Judah. He condemned the empty ritualism of his day (e.g., 1:10-15) and the idolatry into which so many of the people had fallen (e.g., 40:18-20). He foresaw the coming Babylonian captivity of Judah because of this departure from the Lord (39:6,7).

Fulfillment of some of his prophesies in his own lifetime provided his credentials for the prophetic office. Sennacherib's effort to take Jerusalem failed, just as Isaiah had said it would (37:6,7,36-38). The Lord healed Hezekiah's critical illness, as Isaiah had predicted (38:5; 2 Kin. 20:7). Long before Cyrus, king of Persia appeared on the scene, Isaiah named him as Judah's deliverer from the Babylonian captivity (44:28; 45:1). Fulfillment of his prophecies of Christ's first coming have given Isaiah further vindication (e.g., 7:14). The pattern of literal fulfillment of his already-fulfilled prophecies gives assurance that prophecies of Christ's second coming will also see literal fulfillment.

More than any other prophet, Isaiah provides data on the future day of the Lord and the time following. He details numerous aspects of Israel's future kingdom on earth not found elsewhere in the OT or NT, including changes in nature, the animal world, Jerusalem's status among the nations, the Suffering Servant's leadership, and others.

Through a literary device called "prophetic foreshortening," Isaiah predicted future events without delineating exact sequences of the events or time intervals separating them. For example, nothing in Isaiah reveals the extended period separating the two comings of the Messiah. Also, he does not provide as clear a distinction between the future temporal kingdom and the eternal kingdom as John does in Revelation 20:1-10; 21:1–22:5. In God's program of progressive revelation, details of these relationships awaited a prophetic spokesman of a later time.

Also known as the "evangelical Prophet," Isaiah spoke much about the grace of God toward Israel, particularly in his last 27 chapters. The centerpiece is Isaiah's unrivaled chap. 53, portraying Christ as the slain Lamb of God.

Interpretive Challenges

Interpretive challenges in a long and significant book such as Isaiah are numerous. The most critical of them focuses on whether Isaiah's prophecies will receive literal fulfillment or not, and on whether the Lord, in His program, has abandoned national Israel and permanently replaced the nation with the church, so that there is no future for national Israel.

On the latter issue, numerous portions of Isaiah support the position that God has not replaced ethnic Israel with an alleged "new Israel." Isaiah has too much to say about God's faithfulness to Israel, that He would not reject the people whom He has created and chosen (43:1). The nation is on the palms of His hands, and Jerusalem's walls are ever before His eyes (49:16). He is bound by His own Word to fulfill the promises He has made to bring them back to Himself and bless them in that future day (55:10-12).

On the former issue, literal fulfillment of many of Isaiah's prophecies has already occurred, as illustrated in Introduction: Historical and Theological Themes. To contend that those yet unfulfilled will see non-literal fulfillment is biblically groundless. This fact disqualifies the case for proposing that the church receives some of the promises made originally to Israel. The kingdom promised to David belongs to Israel, not the church. The future exaltation of Jerusalem will be on earth, not in heaven. Christ will reign personally on this earth as we know it, as well as in the new heavens and new earth (Rev. 22:1,3).

Outline

I. Judgment (1:1–35:10)
- A. Prophecies concerning Judah and Jerusalem (1:1–12:6)
  1. Judah's social sins (1:1–6:13)
  2. Judah's political entanglements (7:1–12:6)
- B. Oracles of Judgment and Salvation (13:1–23:18)
  1. Babylon and Assyria (13:1–14:27)
  2. Philistia (14:28-32)
  3. Moab (15:1–16:14)
  4. Syria and Israel (17:1-14)
  5. Ethiopia (18:1-7)
  6. Egypt (19:1–20:6)
  7. Babylon continued (21:1-10)
  8. Edom (21:11,12)
  9. Arabia (21:13-17)
  10. Jerusalem (22:1-25)
  11. Tyre (23:1-18)
- C. Redemption of Israel through World Judgment (24:1–27:13)
  1. God's devastation of the earth (24:1-23)
  2. First song of thanksgiving for redemption (25:1-12)
  3. Second song of thanksgiving for redemption (26:1-19)
  4. Israel's chastisements and final prosperity (26:20–27:13)
- D. Warnings against Alliance with Egypt (28:1–35:10)
  1. Woe to drunken politicians (28:1-29)
  2. Woe to religious formalists (29:1-14)
  3. Woe to those who hide plans from God (29:15-24)
  4. Woe to the pro-Egyptian party (30:1-33)
  5. Woe to those who trust in horses and chariots (31:1–32:20)
  6. Woe to the Assyrian destroyer (33:1-24)
  7. A cry for justice against the nations, particularly Edom (34:1–35:10)

II. Historical Interlude (36:1–39:8)
- A. Sennacherib's Attempt to Capture Jerusalem (36:1–37:38)
- B. Hezekiah's Sickness and Recovery (38:1-22)
- C. Babylonian Emissaries to Jerusalem (39:1-8)

III. Salvation (40:1–66:24)
- A. Deliverance from Captivity (40:1–48:22)
  1. Comfort to the Babylonian exiles (40:1-31)
  2. The end of Israel's misery (41:1–48:22)
- B. Sufferings of the Servant of the Lord (49:1–57:21)
  1. The Servant's mission (49:1–52:12)
  2. Redemption by the Suffering Servant (52:13–53:12)
  3. Results of the Suffering Servant's redemption (54:1–57:21)
- C. Future Glory of God's People (58:1–66:24)
  1. Two kinds of religion (58:1-14)
  2. Plea to Israel to forsake their sins (59:1-19)
  3. Future blessedness of Zion (59:20–61:11)
  4. Nearing of Zion's deliverance (62:1–63:6)
  5. Prayer for national deliverance (63:7–64:12)
  6. The Lord's answer to Israel's supplication (65:1–66:24)

1 The [a]vision of Isaiah the son of Amoz, which he saw concerning Judah and Jerusalem in the [b]days of Uzziah, Jotham, Ahaz, *and* Hezekiah, kings of Judah.

The Wickedness of Judah

2 [c]Hear, O heavens, and give ear,
O earth!
For the LORD has spoken:
"I have nourished and brought up
children,
And they have rebelled against
Me;
3 [d]The ox knows its owner
And the donkey its master's [1]crib;
But Israel [e]does not know,
My people do not [2]consider."

4 Alas, sinful nation,
A people [3]laden with iniquity,
[f]A [4]brood of evildoers,
Children who are corrupters!
They have forsaken the LORD,
They have provoked to anger
The Holy One of Israel,
They have turned away backward.

5 [g]Why should you be stricken again?
You will revolt more and more.
The whole head is sick,
And the whole heart faints.
6 From the sole of the foot even to
the head,
There is no soundness in it,
But wounds and bruises and
putrefying sores;
They have not been closed or
bound up,
Or soothed with ointment.

7 [h]Your country *is* desolate,
Your cities *are* burned with fire;
Strangers devour your land in your
presence;
And *it is* desolate, as overthrown
by strangers.
8 So the daughter of Zion is left [i]as a
[5]booth in a vineyard,
As a hut in a garden of cucumbers,
[j]As a besieged city.
9 [k]Unless the LORD of hosts
Had left to us a very small
remnant,
We would have become like
[l]Sodom,
We would have been made like
Gomorrah.

10 Hear the word of the LORD,
You rulers [m]of Sodom;
Give ear to the law of our God,
You people of Gomorrah:
11 "To what purpose *is* the multitude
of your [n]sacrifices to Me?"
Says the LORD.
"I have had enough of burnt
offerings of rams
And the fat of fed cattle.
I do not delight in the blood of
bulls,
Or of lambs or goats.

CHAPTER 1
1 [a] Num. 12:6 [b] 2 Chr. 26–32
2 [c] Jer. 2:12
3 [d] Jer. 8:7 [e] Jer. 9:3, 6 [1] *manger or feed trough* [2] *understand*
4 [f] Is. 57:3, 4; Matt. 3:7 [3] Lit. *heavy, weighed down* [4] *offspring, seed*
5 [g] Jer. 5:3
7 [h] Deut. 28:51, 52; 2 Chr. 36:19
8 [i] Job 27:18 [j] Jer. 4:17 [5] *shelter*
9 [k] 2 Kin. 25:11, 22; Lam. 3:22 [l] Gen. 19:24; Rom. 9:29
10 [m] Deut. 32:32
11 [n] [1 Sam. 15:22]

1:1 See Introduction: Title; Author and Date.

1:2-9 This is a courtroom scene in which the Lord is the plaintiff and the nation of Israel is the defendant. Instead of responding to God's ultimate care and provision for them, these people have failed to give Him the loving obedience that is His due.

1:2 heavens...earth. God intended Israel to be a channel of blessing to the nations (19:24,25; 42:6; Gen. 12:2,3), but instead He must call the nations to look on Israel's shame. **children.** The physical descendants of Abraham are God's chosen people, in spite of their disobedience (cf. Gen. 18:18,19).

1:3 ox...donkey. Animals appear to have more powers of reason than God's people who break fellowship with Him.

1:4 The Holy One of Israel. This is Isaiah's special title for God, found 25 times in this book (1:4; 5:19,24; 10:20; 12:6; 17:7; 29:19; 30:11,12,15; 31:1; 37:23; 41:14,16,20; 43:3,14; 45:11; 47:4; 48:17; 49:7; 54:5; 55:5; 60:9,14), but only 6 times in the rest of the OT (2 Kin. 19:22; Pss. 71:22; 78:41; 89:18; Jer. 50:29; 51:5). Isaiah also uses "Holy One" as a title 4 times (10:17; 40:25; 43:15; 49:7) and "Holy One of Jacob" once (29:23). In many contexts the name contrasts the holiness of God with the sinfulness of Israel.

1:5 Why...stricken again? Already in ruins because of rebellion against God (vv. 7,8), the nation behaved irrationally by continuing their rebellion.

1:8 daughter of Zion. The phrase occurs 28 times in the OT, 6 of which are in Isaiah (1:8; 10:32; 16:1; 37:22; 52:2; 62:11). It is a personification of Jerusalem, standing in this case for all of Judah.

1:9 LORD of hosts. Isaiah used this title or the similar "LORD God of hosts" 60 times. It pictured God as a mighty warrior, a leader of armies, capable of conquering all of Israel's enemies and providing for her survival. **remnant.** Sometimes rendered "survivors," this term designated the faithful among the Israelites. Paul cited this verse to prove the ongoing existence of faithful Israelites even in his day (Rom. 9:29). Such a remnant will constitute the nucleus of returning Israelites in the nation's regathering when the Messiah returns to earth. See 10:20,22; Hos. 1:10,11. **Sodom...Gomorrah.** In destroying them, God rained brimstone and fire on these two Canaanite cities because of their aggravated sinfulness (Gen. 18:20; 19:24,25,28). The two thereby became a proverbial expression for the ultimate in God's temporal judgment against any people (e.g., 13:19; Deut. 29:23; Jer. 23:14; 49:18; 50:40; Amos 4:11; Zeph. 2:9; Matt. 10:15; 2 Pet. 2:6; Jude 7). Had God's grace not intervened, He would have judged Israel in the same way.

1:10-17 The prophet applied the names of the sinful cities, Sodom and Gomorrah, to Judah and Jerusalem in decrying their empty formalism in worship. God found their activities utterly repulsive when they engaged in the rituals prescribed by Moses, because when doing so they persisted in iniquity.

1:11 I have had enough...I do not delight. Cf. 1 Sam. 15:22,23. God found all sacrifices meaningless and even abhorrent if the offerer failed in obedience to His laws. Rebellion is equated to the sin of witchcraft and stubbornness to iniquity and idolatry.

12 "When you come [o]to appear before
Me,
Who has required this from your
hand,
To trample My courts?
13 Bring no more [p]futile[6] sacrifices;
Incense is an abomination to Me.
The New Moons, the Sabbaths, and
[q]the calling of assemblies—
I cannot endure iniquity and the
sacred meeting.
14 Your [r]New Moons and your
[s]appointed feasts
My soul hates;
They are a trouble to Me,
I am weary of bearing *them.*
15 [t]When you [7]spread out your hands,
I will hide My eyes from you;
[u]Even though you make many
prayers,
I will not hear.
Your hands are full of [8]blood.

16 "Wash[v] yourselves, make
yourselves clean;
Put away the evil of your doings
from before My eyes.
[w]Cease to do evil,
17 Learn to do good;
Seek justice,
Rebuke [9]the oppressor;
[1]Defend the fatherless,
Plead for the widow.

18 "Come now, and let us [x]reason
together,"
Says the LORD,
"Though your sins are like scarlet,
[y]They shall be as white as snow;
Though they are red like crimson,
They shall be as wool.
19 If you are willing and obedient,
You shall eat the good of the land;
20 But if you refuse and rebel,
You shall be devoured by the
sword";
[z]For the mouth of the LORD has
spoken.

The Degenerate City

21 [a]How the faithful city has become a
[2]harlot!
It was full of justice;
Righteousness lodged in it,
But now [b]murderers.
22 [c]Your silver has become dross,
Your wine mixed with water.
23 [d]Your princes *are* rebellious,
And [e]companions of thieves;
[f]Everyone loves bribes,
And follows after rewards.
They [g]do not defend the fatherless,
Nor does the cause of the widow
come before them.

24 Therefore the Lord says,
The LORD of hosts, the Mighty One
of Israel,
"Ah, [h]I will [3]rid Myself of My
adversaries,
And [4]take vengeance on My
enemies.
25 I will turn My hand against you,

12 [o] Ex. 23:17
13 [p] Matt. 15:9 [q] Joel 1:14 [6] *worthless*
14 [r] Num. 28:11 [s] Lam. 2:6
15 [t] Prov. 1:28 [u] Ps. 66:18; Is. 59:1-3; Mic. 3:4 [7] *Pray* [8] *bloodshed*
16 [v] Jer. 4:14 [w] Rom. 12:9
17 [9] Some ancient vss. *the oppressed* [1] *Vindicate*
18 [x] Is. 43:26; Mic. 6:2
[y] Ps. 51:7; [Is. 43:25]; Rev. 7:14
20 [z] Is. 40:5; 58:14; Mic. 4:4; [Titus 1:2]
21 [a] Is. 57:3-9; Jer. 2:20 [b] Mic. 3:1-3 [2] *Unfaithful*
22 [c] Jer. 6:28
23 [d] Hos. 9:15 [e] Prov. 29:24 [f] Jer. 22:17 [g] Is. 10:2; Jer. 5:28; Ezek. 22:7; Zech. 7:10
24 [h] Deut. 28:63 [3] *be relieved of* [4] *avenge Myself*

1:13,14 The New Moons, the Sabbaths, and the calling of assemblies...appointed feasts. These were all occasions prescribed by the law of Moses (cf. Ex. 12:16; Lev. 23; Num. 10:10; 28:11–29:40; Deut. 16:1-17).

1:14 My soul hates. It is impossible to doubt the Lord's total aversion toward hypocritical religion. Other practices God hates include robbery for burnt offering (61:8), serving other gods (Jer. 44:4), harboring evil against a neighbor and love for a false oath (Zech. 8:16), divorce (Mal. 2:16), and the one who loves violence (Ps. 11:5).

1:16,17 Put away the evil...Seek justice. The outward evidence of the emptiness of Jerusalem's ritualism was the presence of evil works and the absence of good works.

1:17 the fatherless...the widow. Illustrative of good works are deeds done on behalf of those in need (v. 23; Deut. 10:17,18; 14:29; 24:17,19,20,21; 26:12,13; 27:19; James 1:27).

1:18-20 In developing His call for cleanliness in v. 16, the Lord pardoned the guilty who desire forgiveness and obedience. This section previews the last 27 chapters of Isaiah, which focus more on grace and forgiveness than on judgment.

1:18 scarlet...crimson. The two colors speak of the guilt of those whose hands were "full of blood" (v. 15). Fullness of blood speaks of extreme iniquity and perversity (cf. 59:3; Ezek. 9:9,10; 23:37,45). **white as snow...as wool.** Snow and wool are substances that are naturally white, and therefore portray what is clean, the blood-guilt (v. 15) having been removed (cf. Ps. 51:7). Isaiah was a prophet of grace, but forgiveness is not unconditional. It comes through repentance as v. 19 indicates.

1:19,20 willing and obedient...refuse and rebel. The prophet offered his readers the same choice God gave Moses in Deut. 28, a choice between a blessing and a curse. They may choose repentance and obedience and reap the benefits of the Land or refuse to do so and become victims of foreign oppressors. **eat...be devoured.** To accentuate the opposite outcomes, the Lord used the same Heb. word to depict both destinies. On one hand, they may eat the fruit of the Land; on the other, they may be eaten by conquering powers.

1:21-31 Verses 21-23 recount Jerusalem's current disobedience, with an account of God's actions to purge her in vv. 24-31.

1:21 harlot. Often in the OT, spiritual harlotry pictured the idolatry of God's people (e.g., Jer. 2:20; 3:1; Hos 2:2; 3:1; Ezek. 16:22-37). In this instance, however, Jerusalem's unfaithfulness incorporated a wider range of wrongs, including murders and general corruption (vv. 21,23). **justice; righteousness.** As Isaiah prophesied, ethical depravity had replaced the city's former virtues.

1:24 the Lord...the LORD of hosts, the Mighty One of Israel. The 3-fold title of God emphasized His role as the rightful judge of His sinful people. "The Mighty One of Israel" occurs only here in the Bible, though "the Mighty One of Jacob" appears 5 times (49:26; 60:16; Gen. 49:24; Ps. 132:2,5).

And [i]thoroughly[5] purge away
your dross,
And take away all your alloy.
26 I will restore your judges [j]as at the
first,
And your counselors as at the
beginning.
Afterward [k]you shall be called the
city of righteousness, the
faithful city."

27 Zion shall be redeemed with
justice,
And her [6]penitents with
righteousness.
28 The [l]destruction of transgressors
and of sinners *shall be*
together,
And those who forsake the LORD
shall be consumed.
29 For [7]they shall be ashamed of the
[8]terebinth trees
Which you have desired;
And you shall be embarrassed
because of the gardens
Which you have chosen.
30 For you shall be as a terebinth
whose leaf fades,
And as a garden that has no
water.
31 [m]The strong shall be as tinder,
And the work of it as a spark;
Both will burn together,
And no one shall [n]quench *them.*

25 [i] Is. 48:10; Ezek. 22:19-22; Mal. 3:3 [5] *refine with lye*
26 [j] Jer. 33:7-11 [k] Is. 33:5; Zech. 8:3
27 [6] Lit. *returners*
28 [l] Job 31:3; Ps. 9:5; [Is. 66:24; 2 Thess. 1:8, 9]
29 [7] So with MT, LXX, Vg.; some Heb. mss., Tg. *you* [8] Sites of pagan worship
31 [m] Ezek. 32:21 [n] Is. 66:24; Matt. 3:12; Mark 9:43

The Future House of God

2 The word that Isaiah the son of Amoz saw concerning Judah and Jerusalem.

2 Now [a]it shall come to pass [b]in the
latter days
[c]*That* the mountain of the LORD's
house
Shall be established on the top of
the mountains,
And shall be exalted above the
hills;
And all nations shall flow to it.
3 Many people shall come and say,
[d]"Come, and let us go up to the
mountain of the LORD,
To the house of the God of Jacob;
He will teach us His ways,
And we shall walk in His paths."
[e]For out of Zion shall go forth the
law,
And the word of the LORD from
Jerusalem.
4 He shall judge between the
nations,
And rebuke many people;
They shall beat their swords into
plowshares,
And their spears into pruning
[1]hooks;
Nation shall not lift up sword
against nation,
Neither shall they learn war
anymore.

CHAPTER 2

2 [a] Mic. 4:1 [b] Gen. 49:1 [c] Ps. 68:15
3 [d] Jer. 50:5; [Zech. 8:21-23; 14:16-21] [e] Luke 24:47
4 [1] *knives*

1:25,26 I will...thoroughly purge...I will restore. God's judgment of His people has future restoration as its goal. They were subsequently restored from the Babylonian captivity (Jer. 29:10), but this promise has in view a greater and more lasting restoration. It anticipates a complete and permanent restoration, which will make Jerusalem supreme among the nations (Jer. 3:17; Ezek. 5:5; Mic. 4:2; Zech. 8:22; 14:16). The only such purging and restoration in Scripture is that spoken of in conjunction with the yet-future "time of Jacob's trouble" (Jer. 30:6,7; i.e., Daniel's 70th week, cf. Dan. 9:24-27) and the second advent of the Messiah (Zech. 14:4).

1:27 Zion. Originally a designation for the hill Ophel, this name became a synonym for the entire city of Jerusalem. Isaiah always uses it that way. **be redeemed...penitents.** That remnant of the city who repented of their sins would find redemption in conjunction with God's future restoration of Israel's prosperity (cf. 59:20).

1:28 transgressors...sinners...those who forsake. Concurrent with the future blessing of the faithful remnant, the Lord will relegate the unrepentant to destruction. This is the only way Zion can become pure.

1:29 terebinth trees...gardens. These were settings where Israel practiced idolatrous worship. It is ironic that the Lord had chosen Israel while some citizens of Jerusalem have chosen the "gardens." When God calls them to account for their rebellious choice, they will be ashamed and embarrassed.

1:31 will burn...no one shall quench. Both the rebel and his works will perish. This is final judgment, not merely another captivity.

2:1–5:30 Chapters 2–5 comprise a single connected discourse.

2:1-5 The first of 3 pictures of Zion (Jerusalem) in this discourse that depicts her future exaltation.

2:2-4 The book of Micah contains this portion of Isaiah's prophecy almost word for word (Mic. 4:1-3), indicating that the younger contemporary of Isaiah may have obtained the words from him. Both passages present a prophetic picture of Zion in the future messianic kingdom when all people will recognize Jerusalem as the capital of the world.

2:2 in the latter days. The "latter (or last) days" is a time designation looking forward to the messianic era (Ezek. 38:16; Hos. 3:5; Mic. 4:1). The NT applied the expression to the period beginning with the first advent of Jesus Christ (Acts 2:17; 2 Tim. 3:1; Heb. 1:2; James 5:3; 2 Pet. 3:3). Old Testament prophets, being without a clear word regarding the time between the Messiah's two advents, linked the expression to the Messiah's return to establish His earthly kingdom, i.e., the millennial kingdom spoken about in Rev. 20:1-10. **the mountain of the LORD's house.** The reference is to Mt. Zion, the location of the temple in Jerusalem. The expression occurs two other times in the OT (2 Chr. 33:15; Mic. 4:1).

2:3 mountain of the LORD. Isaiah frequently calls Mt. Zion the "holy mountain" (11:9; 27:13; 56:7; 57:13; 65:11,25; 66:20).

2:4 swords into plowshares...spears into pruning hooks. With the Messiah on His throne in Jerusalem, the world will enjoy uninterrupted peaceful conditions. Warfare will continue to characterize human history until the Prince of Peace (9:6) returns to earth to put an end to it.

The Day of the LORD

5 O house of Jacob, come and let us
[f]walk
In the light of the LORD.

6 For You have forsaken Your
people, the house of Jacob,
Because they are filled [g]with
eastern ways;
They *are* [h]soothsayers like the
Philistines,
[i]And they [2]are pleased with the
children of foreigners.

7 [j]Their land is also full of silver and
gold,
And there is no end to their
treasures;
Their land is also full of horses,
And there is no end to their
chariots.

8 [k]Their land is also full of idols;
They worship the work of their
own hands,
That which their own fingers have
made.

9 People bow down,
And each man humbles himself;
Therefore do not forgive them.

10 [l]Enter into the rock, and hide in the
dust,
From the terror of the LORD
And the glory of His majesty.

11 The [3]lofty looks of man shall be
[m]humbled,
The haughtiness of men shall be
bowed down,
And the LORD alone shall be
exalted [n]in that day.

12 For the day of the LORD of hosts
Shall come upon everything proud
and lofty,
Upon everything lifted up—
And it shall be brought low—

13 Upon all [o]the cedars of Lebanon
that are high and lifted up,
And upon all the oaks of Bashan;

14 [p]Upon all the high mountains,
And upon all the hills *that are* lifted
up;

15 Upon every high tower,
And upon every fortified wall;

16 [q]Upon all the ships of Tarshish,
And upon all the beautiful sloops.

17 The [4]loftiness of man shall be
bowed down,
And the haughtiness of men shall
be brought low;
The LORD alone will be exalted in
that day,

18 But the idols [5]He shall utterly
abolish.

19 They shall go into the [r]holes of the
rocks,
And into the caves of the [6]earth,
[s]From the terror of the LORD
And the glory of His majesty,
When He arises [t]to shake the earth
mightily.

20 In that day a man will cast away
his idols of silver
And his idols of gold,
Which they made, *each* for himself
to worship,
To the moles and bats,

21 To go into the clefts of the rocks,
And into the crags of the rugged
rocks,
From the terror of the LORD
And the glory of His majesty,

5 [f]Eph. 5:8 **6** [g]Num. 23:7 [h]Deut. 18:14 [i]Ps. 106:35 [2]Or *clap, shake hands to make bargains with the children* **7** [j]Deut. 17:16; Is. 30:16; 31:1; Mic. 5:10 **8** [k]Is. 40:19, 20; Jer. 2:28 **10** [l]Is. 2:19, 21; Rev. 6:15, 16 **11** [m]Prov. 16:5; Is. 5:15 [n]Hos. 2:16 [3]*proud*

13 [o]Is. 14:8; Zech. 11:1, 2 **14** [p]Is. 30:25 **16** [q]1 Kin. 10:22; Is. 23:1, 14; 60:9 **17** [4]*pride* **18** [5]Or *shall utterly vanish* **19** [r]Hos. 10:8; [Rev. 9:6] [s][2 Thess. 1:9] [t]Ps. 18:7; Is. 2:21; 13:13; 24:1, 19, 20; Hag. 2:6, 7; Heb. 12:26 [6]Lit. *dust*

2:6–4:1 After a glimpse of Judah's glorious future (2:1-5), the prophet returned to the present for a scathing rebuke of her idolatry and the judgment of God it evokes.

2:6-9 Isaiah stated the Lord's formal charge against the people of Jerusalem.

2:6 eastern ways. Through caravans from the E, an influx of religious superstitions had filled Jerusalem and its environs.

2:8 full of idols. Jotham and Ahaz, two of the kings under whom Isaiah prophesied, failed to remove the idolatrous high places from the Land (2 Kin. 15:35; 16:4).

2:10-22 This section pictures conditions during the future day of the Lord. Though some elements of the description could fit what Judah experienced in the Babylonian captivity, the intensity of judgment predicted here could not have found fulfillment at that time. The tribulation period before Christ's return will be the time for these judgmental horrors.

2:12 the day of the LORD. The phrase "day of the LORD," (DOL) appears 19 times in the OT (Obad. 15; Joel 1:15; 2:1,11,31; 3:14; Amos 5:18,20; Is. 2:12; 13:6,9; Zeph. 1:7,14; Ezek. 13:5; 30:3; Zech. 14:1; Mal. 4:5) and 4 times in the NT (Acts 2:20; 1 Thess. 5:2; 2 Thess 2:2; 2 Pet. 3:10) to express the time of God's extreme wrath. The DOL can refer to a near future judgment (Ezek. 13:5; 30:3) or a far future judgment (Zech. 14:1; 2 Thess. 2:2). Two DOL expressions yet remain to be fulfilled: 1) at the end of Daniel's 70th week (see Joel 3:14; Mal. 4:5; 1 Thess. 5:2) and 2) at the end of the Millennium (see 2 Pet. 3:10). The DOL can occur through providential means (Ezek. 30:3) or directly at the hand of God (2 Pet. 3:10). At times, the near fulfillment (Joel 1:15) prefigures the far fulfillment (Joel 3:14); on other occasions, both kinds of fulfillment are included in one passage (13:6,9; Zeph 1:7,14). Here Isaiah looks to the far fulfillment at the end of the time of Jacob's trouble (Jer. 30:7).

2:13 cedars of Lebanon…oaks of Bashan. The cedars and oaks were objects of great admiration to people of OT times (Pss. 92:12; 104:16; Ezek. 27:6; 31:3). Yet even these impressive created objects would face destruction because of human rebellion.

2:19 holes of the rocks…caves of the earth. Revelation 6:12,15,16 uses this passage and 2:21 to describe man's flight from the terrors of tribulation during the period before Christ's personal return to earth. This shows that the final fulfillment of this prophecy will be during Daniel's 70th week.

When He arises to shake the earth
mightily.

22 [u]Sever[7] yourselves from such a
man,
Whose [v]breath *is* in his nostrils;
For [8]of what account is he?

Judgment on Judah and Jerusalem

3 For behold, the Lord, the LORD of
hosts,
[a]Takes away from Jerusalem and
from Judah
[b]The[1] stock and the store,
The whole supply of bread and the
whole supply of water;
2 [c]The mighty man and the man of
war,
The judge and the prophet,
And the diviner and the elder;
3 The captain of fifty and the
[2]honorable man,
The counselor and the skillful
artisan,
And the expert enchanter.

4 "I will give [d]children[3] *to be* their
princes,
And [4]babes shall rule over them.
5 The people will be oppressed,
Every one by another and every
one by his neighbor;
The child will be insolent toward
the [5]elder,
And the [6]base toward the
honorable."

6 When a man takes hold of his
brother
In the house of his father, *saying,*
"You have clothing;
You be our ruler,
And *let* these ruins *be* under your
[7]power,"
7 In that day he will protest, saying,
"I cannot cure *your* ills,
For in my house *is* neither food nor
clothing;
Do not make me a ruler of the
people."

8 For [e]Jerusalem stumbled,
And Judah is fallen,
Because their tongue and their
doings
Are against the LORD,
To provoke the eyes of His glory.
9 The look on their countenance
witnesses against them,
And they declare their sin as
[f]Sodom;
They do not hide *it.*
Woe to their soul!
For they have brought evil upon
themselves.

10 "Say to the righteous [g]that *it shall be*
well *with them,*
[h]For they shall eat the fruit of their
doings.
11 Woe to the wicked! [i]*It shall be* ill
with him,
For the reward of his hands shall
be [8]given him.
12 *As for* My people, children *are* their
oppressors,
And women rule over them.
O My people! [j]Those who lead you
[9]cause *you* to err,
And destroy the way of your
paths."

Oppression and Luxury Condemned

13 The LORD stands up [k]to [1]plead,
And stands to judge the people.
14 The LORD will enter into judgment
With the elders of His people
And His princes:
"For you have [2]eaten up [l]the
vineyard;
The plunder of the poor *is* in your
houses.
15 What do you mean by [m]crushing
My people
And grinding the faces of the
poor?"

22 [u]Ps. 146:3; Jer. 17:5 [v]Job 27:3 [7]Lit. *Cease yourselves from the man* [8]Lit. *in what is he to be esteemed*

CHAPTER 3

1 [a]2 Kin. 25:3; Is. 5:13; Jer. 37:21 [b]Lev. 26:26 [1]Every support
2 [c]2 Kin. 24:14; Is. 9:14, 15; Ezek. 17:12, 13
3 [2]Eminent looking men
4 [d]Eccl. 10:16 [3]*boys* [4]Or *capricious ones*
5 [5]*aged* [6]*despised, lightly esteemed*
6 [7]Lit. *hand*
8 [e]2 Chr. 36:16, 17; Mic. 3:12
9 [f]Gen. 13:13; Is. 1:10-15
10 [g][Deut. 28:1-14; Eccl. 8:12; Is. 54:17] [h]Ps. 128:2
11 [i][Ps. 11:6; Eccl. 8:12, 13] [8]*done to him*
12 [j]Is. 9:16 [9]*lead you astray*
13 [k]Is. 66:16; Hos. 4:1; Mic. 6:2 [1]*contend, plead His case*
14 [l]Matt. 21:33 [2]*burned*
15 [m]Mic. 3:2, 3

2:22 Sever yourselves. This calls readers to stop depending on other humans and to trust only in God who alone is worthy.

3:1–4:1 The Lord's indictment against and judgment of Jerusalem and Judah continued.

3:1 the Lord, the LORD of hosts. Emphasizing His ultimate authority, God refers to Himself by the title Adonai ("the Lord"), the sovereign Lord of all, and by the mighty and warlike "LORD of hosts."

3:1-3 Takes away…expert enchanter. God's judgment was to include a removal of the people's leadership.

3:4,5 children…honorable. Inexperience in government was to lead to degeneration and irresponsibility at every level of national life.

3:6,7 *let* these ruins…ruler of the people. Conditions of anarchy were to be so bad that no one would accept a position of authority over the people.

3:8 Jerusalem…Judah. The fall of Jerusalem in 586 B.C. was only a partial fulfillment of this prophecy. The final fulfillment awaits the times just prior to Christ's second coming. **against the LORD.** The root of Zion's problem surfaces: overt rebellion against the Lord. The people sinned shamelessly; they made no effort to conceal it (3:9).

3:12 children…women. Children and women were considered ill-suited for governmental leadership, so they figuratively depicted the incompetent rulers.

3:14 vineyard. The spoiling of the vineyard by the leaders amounts to their inequities in ruling the nation. Isaiah gave a more detailed comparison of God's people to a vineyard in 5:1-7.

Says the Lord GOD of hosts.

16 Moreover the LORD says:

"Because the daughters of Zion are
haughty,
And walk with [3]outstretched necks
And [4]wanton eyes,
Walking and [5]mincing *as* they go,
Making a jingling with their feet,
17 Therefore the Lord will strike with
[n]a scab
The crown of the head of the
daughters of Zion,
And the LORD will [o]uncover their
secret parts."

18 In that day the Lord will take away
the finery:
The jingling anklets, the [6]scarves,
and the [p]crescents;
19 The pendants, the bracelets, and
the veils;
20 The headdresses, the leg
ornaments, and the
headbands;
The perfume boxes, the charms,
21 and the rings;
The nose jewels,
22 the festal apparel, and the
mantles;
The outer garments, the purses,
23 and the mirrors;
The fine linen, the turbans, and the
robes.

24 And so it shall be:

Instead of a sweet smell there will
be a stench;
Instead of a sash, a rope;
Instead of well-set hair, [q]baldness;
Instead of a rich robe, a girding of
sackcloth;
And [7]branding instead of beauty.
25 Your men shall fall by the sword,
And your [8]mighty in the war.
26 [r]Her gates shall lament and mourn,
And she *being* desolate [s]shall sit on
the ground.

4 And [a]in that day seven women shall
take hold of one man, saying,
"We will [b]eat our own food and
wear our own apparel;
Only let us be called by your name,
To take away [c]our reproach."

The Renewal of Zion

2 In that day [d]the Branch of the LORD
shall be beautiful and glorious;
And the fruit of the earth *shall be*
excellent and appealing
For those of Israel who have
escaped.

3 And it shall come to pass that *he who is*
left in Zion and remains in Jerusalem [e]will
be called holy—everyone who is [f]recorded
among the living in Jerusalem. 4 When
[g]the Lord has washed away the filth of the
daughters of Zion, and purged the [1]blood
of Jerusalem from her midst, by the spirit
of judgment and by the spirit of burning,
5 then the LORD will create above every
dwelling place of Mount Zion, and above
her assemblies, [h]a cloud and smoke by day
and [i]the shining of a flaming fire by night.
For over all the glory there *will be* a [2]cover-
ing. 6 And there will be a tabernacle for
shade in the daytime from the heat, [j]for a
place of refuge, and for a shelter from
storm and rain.

God's Disappointing Vineyard

5 Now let me sing to my Well-beloved
A song of my Beloved [a]regarding
His vineyard:

My Well-beloved has a vineyard
[1]On a very fruitful hill.

16 [3] Head held high [4] *seductive, ogling* [5] *tripping or skipping* **17** [n] Deut. 28:27 [o] Jer. 13:22 **18** [p] Judg. 8:21, 26 [6] *headbands* **24** [q] Is. 22:12; Ezek. 27:31; Amos 8:10 [7] *burning scar*

25 [8] Lit. *strength* **26** [r] Jer. 14:2; Lam. 1:4 [s] Lam. 2:10

CHAPTER 4

1 [a] Is. 2:11, 17 [b] 2 Thess. 3:12 [c] Luke 1:25 **2** [d] Is. 12:1-6; [Jer. 23:5]; Zech. 3:8 **3** [e] Is. 60:21 [f] Phil. 4:3 **4** [g] Mal. 3:2, 3 [1] *bloodshed* **5** [h] Ex. 13:21, 22; Num. 9:15-23 [i] Zech. 2:5 [2] *canopy* **6** [j] Ps. 27:5; Is. 25:4

CHAPTER 5

1 [a] Ps. 80:8; Jer. 2:21; Matt. 21:33; Mark 12:1; Luke 20:9 [1] Lit. *In a horn, the son of fatness*

3:16 daughters of Zion. When women cultivate beauty for beauty's sake, they thereby reflect the moral decay of the nations and detract from the glory of God. Rather than emphasizing outward apparel and activities (vv. 16-24), ladies should cultivate the beauty of the inner person (1 Tim. 2:9,10; 1 Pet. 3:3,4). **mincing *as* they go.** Ornamental chains about the ankles necessitated shorter steps and produced tinkling sounds to attract attention.

4:1 seven women…one man. In the day of the Lord (*see note on 2:12*), He will judge wicked women indirectly by allowing a slaughtering of males, thereby producing a shortage of husbands.

4:2-6 The third picture of Zion resembles the first (2:1-5): an eventual purification and prosperity in the Land.

4:2 Branch. This messianic title occurs also in Jer. 23:5; 33:15; Zech. 3:8; 6:12. The thought behind the title relates to 2 Sam. 23:5, that of growth. The life of the Branch will bear spiritual fruit (cf. John 15:4,5).

4:3 *he who is* left…holy. "Holy" or "set apart" is another way of describing the remnant who will inherit God's prosperity in that day (cf. 1:9,27; 3:10).

4:4 spirit of burning. For other instances of purging by burning, see 1:25; 6:6,7.

4:5,6 covering…tabernacle. The future inhabitants of Jerusalem will enjoy the Lord's protective covering over the glory on Mt. Zion. This recalls Ezekiel's prophecy of the return of the Shekinah to the temple (Ezek. 43:2-5).

5:1-30 The conclusion of the extended discourse begun at 2:1 comes by way of a comparison of God's people to a vineyard which He cultivated, but which did not bear fruit.

5:1 Well-beloved. The Lord is the friend who is well-beloved by Isaiah. The vineyard belongs to Him (5:7).

2 He dug it up and cleared out its stones,
And planted it with the choicest vine.
He built a tower in its midst,
And also [2]made a winepress in it;
[b]So He expected *it* to bring forth *good* grapes,
But it brought forth wild grapes.

3 "And now, O inhabitants of Jerusalem and men of Judah,
[c]Judge, please, between Me and My vineyard.
4 What more could have been done to My vineyard
That I have not done in [d]it?
Why then, when I expected *it* to bring forth *good* grapes,
Did it bring forth wild grapes?
5 And now, please let Me tell you what I will do to My vineyard:
[e]I will take away its hedge, and it shall be burned;
And break down its wall, and it shall be trampled down.
6 I will lay it [f]waste;
It shall not be pruned or [3]dug,
But there shall come up briers and [g]thorns.
I will also command the clouds
That they rain no rain on it."

7 For the vineyard of the LORD of hosts *is* the house of Israel,
And the men of Judah are His pleasant plant.
He looked for justice, but behold, oppression;
For righteousness, but behold, [4]a cry *for help*.

2 [b] Deut. 32:6 [2] Lit. *hewed out*
3 [c] [Rom. 3:4]
4 [d] 2 Chr. 36:15, 16; Jer. 2:5; 7:25, 26; Mic. 6:3; Matt. 23:37
5 [e] 2 Chr. 36:19; Ps. 80:12; 89:40, 41
6 [f] 2 Chr. 36:19-21 [g] Is. 7:19-25; Jer. 25:11 [3] *hoed*
7 [4] *wailing*

8 [h] Jer. 22:13-17; Mic. 2:2; Hab. 2:9-12 [5] Accumulate houses
9 [i] Is. 22:14
10 [j] Ezek. 45:11 [6] 1 bath = 1/10 homer [7] 1 ephah = 1/10 homer
11 [k] Prov. 23:29, 30; Eccl. 10:16, 17; Is. 5:22 [8] *pursue*
12 [l] Amos 6:5 [m] Job 34:27; Ps. 28:5
13 [n] 2 Kin. 24:14-16 [o] Is. 1:3; 27:11; Hos. 4:6

Impending Judgment on Excesses

8 Woe to those who [5]join [h]house to house;
They add field to field,
Till *there is* no place
Where they may dwell alone in the midst of the land!
9 [i]In my hearing the LORD of hosts *said,*
"Truly, many houses shall be desolate,
Great and beautiful ones, without inhabitant.
10 For ten acres of vineyard shall yield one [j]bath,[6]
And a [7]homer of seed shall yield one ephah."

11 [k]Woe to those who rise early in the morning,
That they may [8]follow intoxicating drink;
Who continue until night, *till* wine inflames them!
12 [l]The harp and the strings,
The tambourine and flute,
And wine are in their feasts;
But [m]they do not regard the work of the LORD,
Nor consider the operation of His hands.

13 [n]Therefore my people have gone into captivity,
Because *they have* no [o]knowledge;
Their honorable men *are* famished,
And their multitude dried up with thirst.
14 Therefore Sheol has enlarged itself
And opened its mouth beyond measure;
Their glory and their multitude and their pomp,

5:2 *good* grapes…wild grapes. The owner made every conceivable provision for the vine's productivity and protection, illustrating the Lord's purely gracious choice of Israel. Justifiably, He expected a good yield from His investment, but the vine's produce was "sour berries," inedible and fit only for dumping.

5:5 burned…trampled down. As punishment for her unfruitfulness, Israel became desolate and accessible to any nation wishing to invade her, such as happened in the Babylonian invasion of 586 B.C., and will happen repeatedly until her national repentance at the second coming of the Messiah.

5:7 justice…oppression…righteousness…a cry. The Eng. words "equity…iniquity…right…riot" illustrate the effective play on words in the underlying Heb. behind v. 7.

5:8-23 The prophet pronounced 6 woes (judgments) against the unresponsive people of Israel.

5:8-10 The first woe was against real estate owners because of their greedy materialism.

5:8 house to house…field to field. God gave the land to the Israelites with the intention that the original allocation remain with each family (Lev. 25:23-25). By Isaiah's time, land speculators had begun putting together huge estates (Mic. 2:2,9), and the powerful rich used legal processes to deprive the poor of what was rightfully theirs (Amos 2:6,7).

5:10 one bath…one ephah. God judged the greedy rich by reducing the productivity of their land to a small fraction of what it would have been normally. One bath was roughly equivalent to 6 gallons (cf. marginal note). About one-half bushel would be produced from about 6 bushels of planted seed. Such amounts indicate famine conditions.

5:11,12 The second woe addressed the drunkards for their neglect of the Lord's work of judgment and redemption, and their devotion to pleasure.

5:14 Sheol. This term in this context pictures death as a great monster with wide-open jaws, ready to receive its victims. Such was to be the fate of those who perish in the captivity God will send to punish the people's sinfulness.

And he who is jubilant, shall
descend into it.
15 People shall be brought down,
[p]Each man shall be humbled,
And the eyes of the lofty shall be
humbled.
16 But the LORD of hosts shall be
[q]exalted in judgment,
And God who is holy shall be
hallowed in righteousness.
17 Then the lambs shall feed in their
pasture,
And in the waste places of [r]the [9]fat
ones strangers shall eat.

18 Woe to those who [1]draw iniquity
with cords of [2]vanity,
And sin as if with a cart rope;
19 [s]That say, "Let Him make speed *and*
hasten His work,
That we may see *it;*
And let the counsel of the Holy One
of Israel draw near and come,
That we may know *it.*"

20 Woe to those who call evil good,
and good evil;
Who put darkness for light, and
light for darkness;
Who put bitter for sweet, and
sweet for bitter!

21 Woe to *those who are* [t]wise in their
own eyes,
And prudent in their own sight!

22 Woe to men mighty at drinking
wine,
Woe to men valiant for mixing
intoxicating drink,
23 Who [u]justify the wicked for a bribe,
And take away justice from the
righteous man!

24 Therefore, [v]as the [3]fire devours the
stubble,
And the flame consumes the chaff,
So [w]their root will be as rottenness,
And their blossom will ascend like
dust;
Because they have rejected the law
of the LORD of hosts,
And despised the word of the Holy
One of Israel.
25 [x]Therefore the anger of the LORD is
aroused against His people;
He has stretched out His hand
against them
And stricken them,
And [y]the hills trembled.
Their carcasses *were* as refuse in the
midst of the streets.

[z]For all this His anger is not turned
away,
But His hand *is* stretched out still.

26 [a]He will lift up a banner to the
nations from afar,
And will [b]whistle to them from
[c]the end of the earth;
Surely [d]they shall come with
speed, swiftly.
27 No one will be weary or stumble
among them,
No one will slumber or sleep;
Nor [e]will the belt on their loins be
loosed,
Nor the strap of their sandals be
broken;
28 [f]Whose arrows *are* sharp,
And all their bows bent;
Their horses' hooves will [4]seem
like flint,
And their wheels like a whirlwind.
29 Their roaring *will be* like a lion,
They will roar like young lions;
Yes, they will roar
And lay hold of the prey;
They will carry *it* away safely,
And no one will deliver.
30 In that day they will roar against
them
Like the roaring of the sea.
And if *one* [g]looks to the land,
Behold, darkness *and* [5]sorrow;
And the light is darkened by the
clouds.

15 [p] Is. 2:9, 11 **16** [q] Is. 2:11 **17** [r] Is. 10:16 [9] Lit. *fatlings,* rich ones **18** [1] *drag* [2] *emptiness or falsehood* **19** [s] Jer. 17:15; Amos 5:18 **21** [t] Prov. 3:7; Rom. 1:22; 12:16; [1 Cor. 3:18-20] **23** [u] Ex. 23:8; Prov. 17:15; Is. 1:23; Mic. 3:11; 7:3 **24** [v] Ex. 15:7 [w] Job 18:16 [3] Lit. *tongue of fire*

25 [x] 2 Kin. 22:13, 17; Is. 66:15 [y] Ps. 18:7; Is. 64:3; Jer. 4:24; Nah. 1:5 [z] Is. 9:12, 17; Jer. 4:8; Dan. 9:16 **26** [a] Is. 11:10, 12 [b] Is. 7:18; Zech. 10:8 [c] Mal. 1:11 [d] Joel 2:7 **27** [e] Dan. 5:6 **28** [f] Jer. 5:16 [4] Lit. *be regarded as* **30** [g] Is. 8:22; Jer. 4:23-28; Joel 2:10; Luke 21:25, 26 [5] *distress*

5:18,19 The third woe was against those who defied the Lord and ridiculed His prophet.

5:19 Let Him make speed. The taunting unbelievers said, "Where is the judgment of which you have spoken, Isaiah? Bring it on. We will believe it when we see it." This challenge for God to hasten His judgment represented their disbelief that the Holy One of Israel would judge the people. See Isaiah's response in the naming of his son: "Speed the spoil, Hasten the Booty" (8:1; cf. 5:26).

5:20 evil good, and good evil. The fourth woe condemned the reversal of morality which dominated the nation. They utterly confused all moral distinctions.

5:21 wise in their own eyes. The object of the fifth woe was the people's arrogance. "Pride *goes* before destruction . . ." (cf. Prov. 16:18).

5:22,23 justify the wicked. The sixth woe pointed to the unjust sentences passed by drunken and bribed judges.

5:24-30 The conclusion of the discourse announced God's action in sending a mighty army against Judah to conquer and leave the land in darkness and distress.

5:26 nations from afar. Principal among the nations God would bring against Israel were: 1) Assyria, which conquered the northern kingdom in 722 B.C., and 2) Babylon, which completed its invasion of Jerusalem in 586 B.C. and destroyed the temple.

5:30 darkness. God's wrath against the people was to eliminate light (8:22; 42:7), but His promised deliverance of the remnant will

Isaiah Called to Be a Prophet

6 In the year that [a]King Uzziah died, I
[b]saw the Lord sitting on a throne, high
and lifted up, and the train of His *robe* filled
the temple. 2 Above it stood seraphim; each
one had six wings: with two he covered his
face, [c]with two he covered his feet, and
with two he flew. 3 And one cried to another and said:

> [d]"Holy, holy, holy *is* the LORD of
> hosts;
> [e]The whole earth *is* full of His
> glory!"

4 And the posts of the door were shaken by
the voice of him who cried out, and the
house was filled with smoke.
5 So I said:

> "Woe *is* me, for I am [1]undone!
> Because I *am* a man of [f]unclean
> lips,
> And I dwell in the midst of a
> people of unclean lips;
> For my eyes have seen the King,
> The LORD of hosts."

6 Then one of the seraphim flew to me,
having in his hand a live coal *which* he had
taken with the tongs from [g]the altar. 7 And
he [h]touched my mouth *with it,* and said:

> "Behold, this has touched your lips;
> Your iniquity is taken away,
> And your sin [2]purged."

8 Also I heard the voice of the Lord, saying:

> "Whom shall I send,
> And who will go for [i]Us?"

Then I said, "Here *am* I! Send me."
9 And He said, "Go, and [j]tell this people:

> 'Keep on hearing, but do not
> understand;
> Keep on seeing, but do not
> perceive.'
> 10 "Make [k]the heart of this people dull,
> And their ears heavy,
> And shut their eyes;
> [l]Lest they see with their eyes,
> And hear with their ears,
> And understand with their heart,
> And return and be healed."

11 Then I said, "Lord, how long?"

CHAPTER 6

1 [a] 2 Kin. 15:7; 2 Chr. 26:23; Is. 1:1 [b] John 12:41; Rev. 4:2, 3; 20:11
2 [c] Ezek. 1:11
3 [d] Rev. 4:8 [e] Num. 14:21; Ps. 72:19
5 [f] Ex. 6:12, 30
[1] *destroyed, cut off*
6 [g] Rev. 8:3
7 [h] Jer. 1:9; Dan. 10:16
[2] *atoned for*
8 [i] Gen. 1:26
9 [j] Is. 43:8; Matt. 13:14; Mark 4:12; Luke 8:10; John 12:40; Acts 28:26; Rom. 11:8
10 [k] Ps. 119:70; Mark 6:1-6; Acts 7:51; Rom. 10:1-4 [l] Jer. 5:21

ultimately turn that darkness into light at the coming of the Messiah (9:2; 42:16; 58:10; 60:2).

6:1-5 In preparation for calling Isaiah to be the prophet who would proclaim the coming judgment, God gave him a vision of His majestic holiness so overwhelming that it devastated him and made him realize his own sinfulness.

6:1 King Uzziah died. After 52 years of reigning, leprosy caused the death of Uzziah in 739 B.C. (cf. 2 Chr. 26:16-23). Isaiah began his prophetic ministry that year. He received the prophecies of the first 5 chapters after his call, but at 6:1 he returns to authenticate what he has already written by describing how he was called. **I saw.** The prophet became unconscious of the outside world and with his inner eye saw what God revealed to him. This experience recalls the experience of John's prophetic vision in Rev. 4:1-11. **high and lifted up.** The throne was greatly elevated, emphasizing the Most High God. **train.** This refers to the hem or fringe of the Lord's glorious robe that filled the temple. **temple.** Though Isaiah may have been at the earthly temple, this describes a vision which transcends the earthly. The throne of God is in the heavenly temple (Rev. 4:1-6; 5:1-7; 11:19; 15:5-8).

6:2 seraphim. The seraphim are an order of angelic creatures who bear a similarity to the 4 living creatures of Rev. 4:6, which in turn resemble the cherubim of Ezek. 10:1ff. **six wings.** Two wings covered the faces of the seraphim because they dared not gaze directly at God's glory. Two covered their feet, acknowledging their lowliness even though engaged in divine service. With two they flew in serving the One on the throne. Thus, 4 wings related to worship, emphasizing the priority of praise.

6:3 one cried to another. The seraphs were speaking to each other in antiphonal praise. **Holy, holy, holy.** The primary thrust of the 3-fold repetition of God's holiness (called the *trihagion*) is to emphasize God's separateness from and independence of His fallen creation, though it implies secondarily that God is 3 Persons. See Rev. 4:8, where the 4 living creatures utter the *trihagion.* **full of His glory.** The earth is the worldwide display of His immeasurable glory, perfections, and attributes as seen in creation (see Rom. 1:20). Fallen man has nevertheless refused to glorify Him as God (Rom. 1:23).

6:4 shaken...smoke. The shaking and smoke symbolize God's holiness as it relates to His wrath and judgment (cf. Ex. 19:16-20; Rev. 15:8).

6:5 unclean lips. If the lips are unclean, so is the heart. This vision of God's holiness vividly reminded the prophet of his own unworthiness which deserved judgment. Job (Job 42:6) and Peter (Luke 5:8) came to the same realization about themselves when confronted with the presence of the Lord (cf. Ezek. 1:28–2:7; Rev. 1:17).

6:6-13 Isaiah's vision has made him painfully aware of his sin and has broken him (cf. 66:2,5); in this way God has prepared him for his cleansing and his commission.

6:6 coal...altar. The hot coal taken from the altar of incense in heaven (cf. Rev. 8:3-5) is emblematic of God's purifying work. Repentance is painful.

6:7 taken away...purged. Spiritual cleansing for special service to the Lord, not salvation, is in view.

6:8 Us. This plural pronoun does not prove the doctrine of the Trinity, but does strongly imply it (see Gen. 1:26). **Here *am* I! Send me.** This response evidenced the humble readiness of complete trust. Though profoundly aware of his sin, he was available.

6:9,10 do not understand...do not perceive. Isaiah's message was to be God's instrument for hiding the truth from an unreceptive people. Centuries later, Jesus' parables were to do the same (Matt. 13:14,15; Mark 4:12; Luke 8:10; cf. 29:9,10; 42:18; 43:8; Deut. 29:4; John 12:40; Acts 28:26,27; Rom. 11:8).

6:11,12 how long? Because of such rejection from his people, the prophet asked how long he should preach this message of divine

And He answered:

[m]"Until the cities are laid waste and
without inhabitant,
The houses are without a man,
The land is utterly desolate,
12 [n]The LORD has removed men far
away,
And the forsaken places *are* many
in the midst of the land.
13 But yet a tenth *will be* in it,
And will return and be for
consuming,
As a terebinth tree or as an oak,
Whose stump *remains* when it is
cut down.
So [o]the holy seed *shall be* its
stump."

Isaiah Sent to King Ahaz

7 Now it came to pass in the days of
[a]Ahaz the son of Jotham, the son of Uzziah, king of Judah, *that* Rezin king of Syria
and Pekah the son of Remaliah, king of Israel, went up to Jerusalem to *make* war
against [b]it, but could not [1]prevail against
it. 2 And it was told to the house of David,
saying, "Syria's forces are [2]deployed in
Ephraim." So his heart and the heart of his
people were moved as the trees of the
woods are moved with the wind.
3 Then the LORD said to Isaiah, "Go out
now to meet Ahaz, you and [3]Shear-Jashub
your son, at the end of the aqueduct from
the upper pool, on the highway to the
Fuller's Field, 4 and say to him: '[4]Take
heed, and [5]be [c]quiet; do not fear or be
fainthearted for these two stubs of smoking firebrands, for the fierce anger of Rezin
and Syria, and the son of Remaliah. 5 Because Syria, Ephraim, and the son of Remaliah have plotted evil against you, saying,
6 "Let us go up against Judah and [6]trouble
it, and let us make a gap in its wall for ourselves, and set a king over them, the son of
Tabel"— 7 thus says the Lord GOD:

[d]"It shall not stand,
Nor shall it come to pass.
8 [e]For the head of Syria *is* Damascus,
And the head of Damascus *is*
Rezin.
Within sixty-five years Ephraim
will be [7]broken,
So that it will not *be* a people.
9 The head of Ephraim *is* Samaria,
And the head of Samaria *is*
Remaliah's son.
[f]If you will not believe,
Surely you shall not be
established."'"

The Immanuel Prophecy

10 Moreover the LORD spoke again to
Ahaz, saying, 11 [g]"Ask a sign for yourself
from the LORD your God; [8]ask it either in
the depth or in the height above."
12 But Ahaz said, "I will not ask, nor will
I test the LORD!"
13 Then he said, "Hear now, O house of
David! *Is it* a small thing for you to weary
men, but will you weary my God also?
14 Therefore the Lord Himself will give
you a sign: [h]Behold, the virgin shall conceive and bear [i]a Son, and shall call His
name [j]Immanuel. [9] 15 Curds and honey He
shall eat, that He may know to refuse the
evil and choose the good. 16 [k]For before the

11 [m]Mic. 3:12
12 [n]2 Kin. 25:21; Is. 5:9
13 [o]Deut. 7:6; Ezra 9:2

CHAPTER 7

1 [a]2 Chr. 28 [b]2 Kin. 16:5, 9 [1]*conquer it*
2 [2]Lit. *settled upon*
3 [3]Lit. *A Remnant Shall Return*
4 [c]Ex. 14:13; Is. 30:15; Lam. 3:26 [4]*Be careful* [5]*be calm*
6 [6]*cause a sickening dread*
7 [d]2 Kin. 16:5; Is. 8:10; Acts 4:25, 26
8 [e]2 Sam. 8:6; 2 Kin. 17:6 [7]Lit. *shattered*
9 [f]2 Chr. 20:20; Is. 5:24
11 [g]Matt. 12:38 [8]Lit. *make the request deep or make it high above*
14 [h]Matt. 1:23; Luke 1:31; John 1:45; Rev. 12:5 [i][Is. 9:6] [j]Is. 8:8, 10 [9]Lit. *God-With-Us*
16 [k]Is. 8:4

judgment. God replied that it must continue until the cities are desolate (v. 11) and the people have gone into exile (v. 12).

6:13 a tenth...will return. Though most will reject God, the tenth, also called "stumps" and "holy seed," represents the faithful remnant in Israel who will be the nucleus who hear and believe.

7:1,2 An unsuccessful invasion of Judah by Syria and Israel (i.e., the northern 10 tribes) led to a continued presence of King Tiglath-Pileser's Assyrian forces in Israel. Shortly after Ahaz assumed the throne (ca. 735 B.C.), this threat to Judah's security brought great fear to the king and the people of Judah. See 2 Chr. 28:5-8,17-19.

7:2 house of David. This expression refers to the Davidic dynasty, personified in the current king, Ahaz.

7:3 Shear-Jashub. The name means "a remnant shall return." The presence of Isaiah's son is an object lesson of God's faithfulness to believers among the people.

7:4 do not fear. Isaiah's message to Ahaz is one of reassurance. The two invading kings will not prevail.

7:8 Ephraim will be broken. This tribe represented all the northern 10 tribes. The prophet predicted the coming demise because of idolatry (cf. Hos. 4:17). In 65 years they would cease to be a people, first through the captivity of most of them in 722 B.C. (2 Kin. 17:6) and then with the importation of foreign settlers into the land in ca. 670 B.C. (2 Kin. 17:24; 2 Chr. 33:11; Ezra 4:2).

7:9 not believe...not be established. The choice belonged to Ahaz. He could trust the Lord's word or fall into the enemy's hands or, even worse, experience a final heart-hardening (6:9,10).

7:11 a sign. To encourage his faith, the Lord offered Ahaz a sign, but Ahaz feigned humility in refusing the sign (v. 10).

7:13 house of David. Upon hearing Ahaz's refusal, the prophet broadened his audience beyond Ahaz (see v. 2) to include the whole faithless house of David. The nation was guilty of wearying God (1:14).

7:14 sign. Since Ahaz refused to choose a sign (vv. 11,12), the Lord chose His own sign, whose implementation would occur far beyond Ahaz's lifetime. **the virgin.** This prophecy reached forward to the virgin birth of the Messiah, as the NT notes (Matt. 1:23). The Heb. word refers to an unmarried woman and means "virgin" (Gen. 24:43; Prov 30:19; Song 1:3; 6:8), so the birth of Isaiah's own son (8:3) could not have fully satisified the prophecy. Cf. Gen. 3:15. **Immanuel.** The title, applied to Jesus in Matt. 1:23, means "God with us."

7:15 Curds and honey. Curds result from coagulated milk, something like cottage cheese. This diet indicated the scarcity of provisions which characterized the period after foreign invaders had decimated the land.

Isaiah Fulfilled at Christ's First Advent

Reference	Fulfilled Literally	Fulfilled Typically
7:14	The virgin birth of Christ (Matt. 1:23)	
8:14,15		A stone of stumbling and a rock of offense (Rom. 9:33; 1 Pet. 2:8)
8:17		Christ's hope and trust in God (Heb. 2:13a)
8:18		The Son of God and the sons of God (Heb. 2:13b)
9:1,2		The arrival of Jesus in the area of Zebulun and Naphtali (Matt. 4:12-16)
9:6a	The birth of Immanuel (Matt. 1:23; Luke 1:31-33; 2:7,11)	
11:1	Revival of the Davidic dynasty (Matt. 1:6,16; Acts 13:23; Rev. 5:5; 22:16)	
12:3		Water from the wells of salvation (John 4:10,14)
25:8		The swallowing up of death (1 Cor. 15:54)
28:11		The gift of tongues as an authenticating sign of God's messengers (1 Cor. 14:21,22)
28:16	Incarnation of Jesus Christ (Matt. 21:42)	
29:18; 35:5		Jesus' healing of the physically deaf and blind (Matt. 11:5)
40:3-5	Preaching of John the Baptist (Matt. 3:3; Mark 1:3; Luke 3:4-6; John 1:23)	
42:1a, 2, 3	Christ at His baptism (Matt. 3:16,17) and transfiguration (Matt. 17:5) and His general demeanor throughout His first advent	
42:6		Christ extended the benefits of the New Covenant to the church (Heb. 8:6, 10-12)
42:7		Jesus healed physical blindness and provided liberty for the spiritual captives (Matt. 11:5; Luke 4:18)
42:7		Jesus removed spiritual darkness at His first coming (Matt. 4:16)
50:6	Jesus beaten and spat upon (Matt. 26:67; 27:26, 30; Mark 14:65; 15:19; Luke 22:63; John 18:22)	
50:7	Jesus resolutely setting His face to go to Jerusalem (Luke 9:51)	
53:1	Israel failed to recognize her Messiah (John 12:38)	
53:4		Jesus healed sick people as a symbol of His bearing of sin (Matt. 8:16,17)
53:7,8	Philip identifies Jesus as the one about whom the prophet wrote (Acts 8:32,33)	
53:7	Jesus remained silent at all phases of His trial (Matt. 26:63; 27:12-14; Mark 14:61; 15:5; Luke 23:9; John 19:9; 1 Pet. 2:23)	
53:7	Jesus was the Lamb of God who takes away the sin of the world (John 1:29; 1 Pet. 1:18,19; Rev. 5:6)	
53:9	Jesus was completely innocent of all charges against Him (1 Pet. 2:22)	
53:11	Jesus saw the need to be crucified between two criminals (Luke 22:37)	
54:13		Jesus saw those who came to Him at His first advent as taught by God (John 6:45)
55:3	Christ's resurrection was prerequisite to His some day occupying David's throne on earth (Acts 13:34)	
61:1,2a		Jesus saw His first-advent ministry as a spiritual counterpart of His second-advent deliverance of Israel (Luke 4:18,19)
62:11	Jesus fulfilled the call to the daughter of Zion in His triumphal entry (Matt. 21:5)	

Child shall know to refuse the evil and
choose the good, the land that you dread
will be forsaken by [l]both her kings.
17 [m]The LORD will bring the king of Assyria
upon you and your people and your father's house—days that have not come
since the day that [n]Ephraim departed from
Judah."

18 And it shall come to pass in that day
That the LORD [o]will whistle for the fly
That *is* in the farthest part of the rivers of Egypt,
And for the bee that *is* in the land of Assyria.
19 They will come, and all of them will rest
In the desolate valleys and in [p]the clefts of the rocks,
And on all thorns and in all pastures.

20 In the same day the Lord will shave with a [q]hired [r]razor,
With those from beyond [1]the River, with the king of Assyria,
The head and the hair of the legs,
And will also remove the beard.

21 It shall be in that day
That a man will keep alive a young cow and two sheep;
22 So it shall be, from the abundance of milk they give,
That he will eat curds;
For curds and honey everyone will eat who is left in the land.

23 It shall happen in that day,
That wherever there could be a thousand vines
Worth a thousand *shekels* of silver,
[s]It will be for briers and thorns.
24 With arrows and bows men will come there,
Because all the land will become briers and thorns.

25 And to any hill which could be dug with the hoe,
You will not go there for fear of briers and thorns;
But it will become a range for oxen
And a place for sheep to roam.

Assyria Will Invade the Land

8 Moreover the LORD said to me, "Take a
large scroll, and [a]write on it with a
man's pen concerning [1]Maher-Shalal-
Hash-Baz. 2 And I will take for Myself
faithful witnesses to record, [b]Uriah the
priest and Zechariah the son of Jebere-
chiah."
3 Then I went to the prophetess, and she
conceived and bore a son. Then the LORD
said to me, "Call his name Maher-Shalal-
Hash-Baz; 4 [c]for before the child [2]shall
have knowledge to cry 'My father' and
'My mother,' [d]the riches of Damascus and
the [3]spoil of Samaria will be taken away
before the king of Assyria."

16 [l]2 Kin. 15:30 **17** [m]2 Chr. 28:19, 20; Is. 8:7, 8; 10:5, 6 [n]1 Kin. 12:16 **18** [o]Is. 5:26 **19** [p]Is. 2:19; Jer. 16:16 **20** [q]Is. 10:5, 15 [r]2 Kin. 16:7; 2 Chr. 28:20 [1]The Euphrates **23** [s]Is. 5:6

CHAPTER 8

1 [a]Is. 30:8; Hab. 2:2 [1]Lit. *Speed the Spoil, Hasten the Booty* **2** [b]2 Kin. 16:10 **4** [c]2 Kin. 17:6; Is. 7:16 [d]2 Kin. 15:29 [2]*knows how* [3]*plunder*

7:16 refuse the evil. Before the promised son of Isaiah was old enough to make moral choices, the kings of Syria and Ephraim were to meet their doom at the hands of the Assyrians.

7:17 bring the king of Assyria upon you. Not only did the Lord use the Assyrians to judge the northern kingdom, He also used them to invade Ahaz's domain of Judah. This coming of the Assyrian king was the beginning of the end for the nation and eventually led to her captivity in Babylon.

7:18-25 The desolation prophesied in this section began in the days of Ahaz and reached its climax when the Babylonians conquered Judah. Its results continue to the time when the Messiah will return to deliver Israel and establish His kingdom on earth.

7:18 fly...bee. Egypt was full of flies, and Assyria was a country noted for beekeeping. These insects represented the armies from the powerful countries which the Lord would summon to overrun Judah and take the people into exile.

7:19 desolate valleys...clefts of the rocks. Not even inaccessible areas of the land were free from the invading armies.

7:20 hired razor. The Assyrians were the Lord's hired blade to shave and disgrace the entire body of Judah (cf. 1:6).

7:21,22 young cow and two sheep. The foreign invasion would cause a change from an agricultural economy to a pastoral one. Not enough men would remain in the land to farm. It was to be a time of great poverty.

7:23-25 briers and thorns. The presence of these uncultivated growths was a sign of desolation, as in 5:6.

8:1 large scroll. Isaiah was to prepare a large placard for public display. **Maher-Shalal-Hash-Baz.** *Maher-Shalal* told the Assyrian invaders to "speed to the spoil," with no doubt as to who was to win the battle. *Hash-Baz* invited them to "hasten the booty," i.e., to reap the benefits of the conquered land quickly (5:26). That placard reiterated, from another perspective, the prophecies just concluded in 7:18-25.

8:2 faithful witnesses. After the prophecy's fulfillment, the respected leaders Uriah and Zechariah verified to the people that Isaiah had spoken it on a given date before the Assyrian invasion. This verification accredited the Lord's word and upheld His honor (Deut. 18:21, 22; Jer. 28:9).

8:3 prophetess. Isaiah's wife was called a prophetess because the son to whom she gave birth was prophetic of the Assyrian conquest.

8:4 before the child. The time before the plunder of Syria and the northern kingdom of Israel began was very short. The Assyrians initiated their invasion before Isaiah's child learned to talk. That prophetic limit resembled the one set in 7:16, but there the prophecy was more far-reaching. Fulfillment of the closer prophecy verified the one relating to the distant future.

5 The LORD also spoke to me again, saying:

6 "Inasmuch as these people refused
The waters of [e]Shiloah that flow
softly,
And rejoice [f]in Rezin and in
Remaliah's son;
7 Now therefore, behold, the Lord
brings up over them
The waters of [4]the River, strong
and mighty—
The king of Assyria and all his
glory;
He will [5]go up over all his
channels
And go over all his banks.
8 He will pass through Judah,
He will overflow and pass over,
[g]He will reach up to the neck;
And the stretching out of his wings
Will [6]fill the breadth of Your land,
O [h]Immanuel.[7]

9 "Be [i] shattered, O you peoples, and
be broken in pieces!
Give ear, all you from far countries.
Gird yourselves, but be broken in
pieces;
Gird yourselves, but be broken in
pieces.
10 [j]Take counsel together, but it will
come to nothing;
Speak the word, [k]but it will not
stand,

6 [e] John 9:7 [f] Is. 7:1, 2
7 [4] The Euphrates
[5] Overflow
8 [g] Is. 30:28 [h] Is. 7:14; Matt. 1:23 [6] Lit. *be the fullness of* [7] Lit. *God-With-Us*
9 [i] Joel 3:9
10 [j] Is. 7:7; Acts 5:38
[k] Is. 7:14

[l] Rom. 8:31 [8] Heb. *Immanuel*
11 [9] Mighty power
12 [1] Lit. *fear or terror*
[2] Lit. *in dread*
14 [m] Is. 4:6; 25:4; Ezek. 11:16 [n] Luke 2:34; 20:17; Rom. 9:33; 1 Pet. 2:8 [3] *holy abode* [4] *stumbling over*
15 [o] Matt. 21:44
[5] *captured*
17 [p] Deut. 31:17; Is. 54:8 [q] Hab. 2:3
18 [r] Heb. 2:13

[l]For [8]God *is* with us."

Fear God, Heed His Word

11 For the LORD spoke thus to me with [9]a
strong hand, and instructed me that I should
not walk in the way of this people, saying:

12 "Do not say, 'A conspiracy,'
Concerning all that this people call
a conspiracy,
Nor be afraid of their [1]threats, nor
be [2]troubled.
13 The LORD of hosts, Him you shall
hallow;
Let Him *be* your fear,
And *let* Him *be* your dread.
14 [m]He will be as a [3]sanctuary,
But [n]a stone of stumbling and a
rock of [4]offense
To both the houses of Israel,
As a trap and a snare to the
inhabitants of Jerusalem.
15 And many among them shall
[o]stumble;
They shall fall and be broken,
Be snared and [5]taken."

16 Bind up the testimony,
Seal the law among my disciples.
17 And I will wait on the LORD,
Who [p]hides His face from the
house of Jacob;
And I [q]will hope in Him.
18 [r]Here am I and the children whom
the LORD has given me!

8:6 these people. Lit. "this people" (the Heb. is sing.). These were the people of Judah (cf. 6:9), but perhaps secondarily the whole nation of Israel. Ahaz had called on Assyria for help rather than relying on the Lord. **waters of Shiloah.** This was the stream from the Gihon Spring outside Jerusalem's city wall flowing to the Pool of Siloam inside the city which supplied the city's water (see 7:3). It symbolized the city's dependence on the Lord and His defense of the city, if they were to survive. First, the northern 10 tribes refused that dependence; later, King Ahaz of Judah in the S did the same.

8:7 waters of the River. In place of the waters of Shiloah, the waters of the River Euphrates were to overflow its banks and flood all the way to and including Judah. In other words, the King of Assyria was to sweep through the Land with his devastating destruction. Though outwardly Ahaz's submission to the Assyrians brought peace to Judah (2 Kin. 16:7-18), Isaiah saw the reality that David's throne was merely a hollow sham.

8:8 O Immanuel. Because of the Assyrian onslaught, the land of Immanuel (7:14) was to be stripped of all its earthly glory. What a pity that He who owns and will someday possess the land must see it in such a devastated condition!

8:9 be broken in pieces. Lest Assyria and other foreign powers think they conquered in their own strength, the prophet reminded them that they were only instruments for the Lord's use and would eventually come to nothing.

8:10 God *is* with us. The Heb. is *Immanuel*. The name of the virgin's child (7:14) guaranteed the eventual triumph of the faithful remnant of Israel.

8:11 with a strong hand. God inspired Isaiah with compelling power to speak a message that by its nature distanced him from the people he ministered to.

8:12 conspiracy. Many in Israel considered Isaiah, Jeremiah, and other prophets to be servants of the enemy when they advocated a policy of nonreliance on foreign powers and complete dependence on the Lord alone (see Jer. 37:13-15).

8:14 sanctuary...stone of stumbling. Isaiah found encouragement in the Lord as his holy place of protection from his accusers. The NT applies this verse to corporate Israel in her ongoing rejection of Jesus as Messiah (Luke 2:34; Rom. 9:32,33; 1 Pet. 2:8). **both the houses of Israel.** They will be collapsed until the return of the Messiah to the earth restores them.

8:15 many...shall stumble. Another prediction anticipated the stumbling of Israel, which included her rejection of her Messiah at His first advent (Luke 20:18; Rom. 9:32; cf. 28:16).

8:16 my disciples. These were God's faithful remnant, and hence disciples of Isaiah in a secondary sense. They had the responsibility of maintaining written records of his prophecies so that they could become public after the prophesied Assyrian invasion (see 8:2).

8:17 wait on...hope. The speaker is Isaiah whose disposition was to await the Lord's deliverance, the national salvation promised the faithful remnant (40:31; 49:23). *See note on Heb. 2:13.*

8:18 I and the children. In their historical setting, the words refer to Isaiah and his two sons, whose names had prophetic significance (i.e., as "signs and wonders"). *See note on Heb. 2:13.*

We [s]*are* for signs and wonders in
Israel
From the LORD of hosts,
Who dwells in Mount Zion.

19 And when they say to you, [t]"Seek
those who are mediums and wizards,
[u]who whisper and mutter," should not a
people seek their God? *Should they* [v]*seek* the
dead on behalf of the living? 20 [w]To the law
and to the testimony! If they do not speak
according to this word, *it is* because [x]*there*[6]
is no light in them.
21 They will pass through it hard-
pressed and hungry; and it shall happen,
when they are hungry, that they will be enraged and [y]curse [7]their king and their
God, and look upward. 22 Then they will
look to the earth, and see trouble and darkness, gloom of anguish; and *they will be*
driven into darkness.

18 [s]Ps. 71:7
19 [t]1 Sam. 28:8 [u]Is. 29:4 [v]Ps. 106:28
20 [w]Is. 1:10; 8:16; Luke 16:29 [x]Is. 8:22; Mic. 3:6 [6]Or *they have no dawn*
21 [y]Rev. 16:11 [7]Or *by their king and by their God*

The Government of the Promised Son

9 Nevertheless [a]the gloom *will* not *be*
upon her who *is* distressed,
As when at [b]first He lightly
esteemed
The land of Zebulun and the land
of Naphtali,
And [c]afterward more heavily
oppressed *her,*
By the way of the sea, beyond the
Jordan,
In Galilee of the Gentiles.
2 [d]The people who walked in
darkness
Have seen a great light;
Those who dwelt in the land of the
shadow of death,
Upon them a light has shined.
3 You have multiplied the nation
And [1]increased its joy;
They rejoice before You
According to the joy of harvest,
As *men* rejoice [e]when they divide
the spoil.
4 For You have broken the yoke of
his burden
And the staff of his shoulder,
The rod of his oppressor,
As in the day of [f]Midian.
5 For every warrior's [2]sandal from
the noisy battle,
And garments rolled in blood,
[g]Will be used for burning *and* fuel
[3]of fire.
6 [h]For unto us a Child is born,
Unto us a [i]Son is given;
And [j]the government will be upon
His shoulder.
And His name will be called
[k]Wonderful, Counselor, [l]Mighty
God,
Everlasting Father, [m]Prince of
Peace.
7 Of the increase of *His* government
and peace
[n]*There will be* no end,
Upon the throne of David and over
His kingdom,

CHAPTER 9

1 [a]Is. 8:22 [b]2 Kin. 15:29; 2 Chr. 16:4 [c]Matt. 4:13-16
2 [d]Matt. 4:16; Luke 1:79; 2 Cor. 4:6; Eph. 5:8
3 [e]Judg. 5:30 [1]So with Qr., Tg.; Kt., Vg. *not increased joy;* LXX *Most of the people You brought down in Your joy*
4 [f]Judg. 7:22
5 [g]Is. 66:15 [2]*boot* [3]*for the fire*
6 [h][Is. 7:14; Luke 2:11]; John 1:45 [i]Luke 2:7; [John 3:16; 1 John 4:9] [j][Matt. 28:18; 1 Cor. 15:25]; Rev. 12:5 [k]Judg. 13:18 [l]Titus 2:13 [m]Eph. 2:14
7 [n]Dan. 2:44; Matt. 1:1, 6; Luke 1:32, 33; John 7:42

8:19 *seek* the dead. People of Isaiah's day were using spiritualists to communicate with the dead as King Saul did through the medium at En Dor (1 Sam. 28:8-19). The law strictly forbade such consultations (Lev. 19:26; Deut. 18:10,11).

8:20 law…testimony. See 8:16. Light came through the prophecies of God's spokesman, Isaiah.

8:21,22 This is a dismal picture of those who were frustrated, desperate, and angry even to the point of cursing God, all because they refused to accept the truthfulness of what Isaiah had predicted regarding the nation's future hardships.

9:1 Zebulun…Naphtali…Galilee. Zebulun and Naphtali on the northern border in NE Galilee W of the Jordan River were the first to suffer from the invasion by the Assyrian king (2 Kin. 15:29), marking the beginning of dark days for Israel. **more heavily oppressed *her*.** A better translation is "will glorify her." "At first" the days were to be full of gloom, but "afterward" God would transform that gloom into honor. The NT applies this prophecy of Galilee's honor to the time of Jesus Christ's first advent (Matt. 4:12-16). Matthew 4:15,16 quotes Is. 9:1,2 directly. Ultimately, its fulfillment will come at His second advent when the area is freed from the yoke of foreign invaders.

9:2 a great light…light. The coming of the Messiah is synonymous with the coming of light to remove the darkness of captivity (42:16; 49:6; 58:8; 60:1,19,20).

9:3 multiplied the nation. Once again the Lord confirmed His covenant with Abraham to multiply his physical descendants as the sands of the seashore (Gen. 22:17).

9:4 broken the yoke. Eventually the Lord will free national Israel from bondage to Assyria, Babylon, and every other foreign power that has oppressed her.

9:5 burning *and* fuel of fire. The world will no longer need the accessories of warfare because a time of universal peace will follow the return of Christ.

9:6 Child…Son. These terms elaborate further on Immanuel, the child to be born to the virgin (7:14). The virgin's child will also be the royal Son of David, with rights to the Davidic throne (9:7; cf. Matt. 1:21; Luke 1:31-33; 2:7,11). **government.** In fulfillment of this verse and Ps. 2:9, the Son will rule the nations of the world (Rev. 2:27; 19:15). **Wonderful, Counselor.** The remaining 3 titles consist of two words each, so the intention was probably that each pair of words indicate one title: "Wonderful Counselor." In contrast to Ahaz, this King will implement supernatural wisdom in discharging His office (cf. 2 Sam. 16:23; 1 Kin. 3:28). **Mighty God.** As a powerful warrior, the Messiah will accomplish the military exploits mentioned in 9:3-5 (cf. 10:21; Deut. 10:17; Neh. 9:32). **Everlasting Father.** The Messiah will be a Father to His people eternally. As Davidic King, He will compassionately care for and discipline them (40:11; 63:16; 64:8; Pss. 68:5,6; 103:13; Prov. 3:12). **Prince of Peace.** The government of Immanuel will procure and perpetuate peace among the nations of the world (2:4; 11:6-9; Mic. 4:3).

9:7 throne of David. The virgin's Son will be the rightful heir to David's throne and will inherit the promises of the Davidic Covenant (2 Sam. 7:12-16; cf. Ps. 89:1-37; Matt. 1:1).

To order it and establish it with
judgment and justice
From that time forward, even
forever.
The [o]zeal of the LORD of hosts will
perform this.

The Punishment of Samaria

8 The Lord sent a word against
[p]Jacob,
And it has fallen on Israel.
9 All the people will know—
Ephraim and the inhabitant of
Samaria—
Who say in pride and arrogance of
heart:
10 "The bricks have fallen down,
But we will rebuild with hewn
stones;
The sycamores are cut down,
But we will replace *them* with
cedars."
11 Therefore the LORD shall set up
The adversaries of Rezin against
him,
And spur his enemies on,
12 The Syrians before and the
Philistines behind;
And they shall devour Israel with
an open mouth.

For all this His anger is not turned
away,
But His hand *is* [4]stretched out still.

13 For the people do not turn to Him
who strikes them,
Nor do they seek the LORD of
hosts.
14 Therefore the LORD will cut off
head and tail from Israel,
Palm branch and bulrush [q]in one
day.
15 The elder and honorable, he *is* the
head;
The prophet who teaches lies, he *is*
the tail.
16 For [r]the leaders of this people
cause *them* to err,
And *those who are* led by them are
destroyed.
17 Therefore the Lord [s]will have no
joy in their young men,
Nor have mercy on their fatherless
and widows;
For everyone *is* a hypocrite and an
evildoer,
And every mouth speaks [5]folly.

[t]For all this His anger is not turned
away,
But His hand *is* stretched out still.

18 For wickedness [u]burns as the fire;
It shall devour the briers and thorns,
And kindle in the thickets of the
forest;
They shall mount up *like* rising
smoke.
19 Through the wrath of the LORD of
hosts
[v]The land is burned up,
And the people shall be as fuel for
the fire;
[w]No man shall spare his brother.
20 And he shall [6]snatch on the right
hand
And be hungry;
He shall devour on the left hand
[x]And not be satisfied;
[y]Every man shall eat the flesh of his
own arm.
21 Manasseh *shall devour* Ephraim,
and Ephraim Manasseh;
Together they *shall be* [z]against
Judah.

[a]For all this His anger is not turned
away,
But His hand *is* stretched out still.

10 "Woe to those who [a]decree
unrighteous decrees,
Who write misfortune,
Which they have prescribed
2 To rob the needy of justice,
And to take what is right from the
poor of My people,

7 [o]Is. 37:32
8 [p]Gen. 32:28
12 [4]In judgment
14 [q]Rev. 18:8
16 [r]Is. 3:12; Mic. 3:1, 5, 9; Matt. 15:14
17 [s]Ps. 147:10 [t]Is. 5:25 [5]*foolishness*
18 [u]Ps. 83:14; [Is. 1:7; 10:17]; Nah. 1:10; Mal. 4:1
19 [v]Is. 8:22 [w]Mic. 7:2, 6
20 [x]Lev. 26:26 [y]Jer. 19:9 [6]*slice off* or *tear*
21 [z]2 Chr. 28:6, 8; Is. 11:13 [a]Is. 9:12, 17

CHAPTER 10

1 [a]Ps. 58:2

9:8–10:4 This poem tells of great warning calamities sent by the Lord that have gone unheeded by Israel. The same refrain recurs 4 times (9:12,17,21; 10:4), dividing it into 4 strophes.

9:9 pride and arrogance. Israel's downfall was her feeling of self-sufficiency whereby she thought she could handle any eventuality (v. 10).

9:11 adversaries of Rezin. The Syrian king's enemies were the Assyrians.

9:12 His hand *is* stretched out still. The outstretched hand will punish (cf. 5:25) beyond what the people had already experienced.

9:16 leaders…*those who are* led. The aggravated wickedness of Israel extended to all classes, even the fatherless and widows (v. 17) who often were the objects of special mercy (1:17).

9:19 No man…his brother. God's wrath allowed wickedness to cause the society to self-destruct. A senseless mutual exploitation resulted in anarchy and confusion (v. 20).

9:21 Manasseh…Ephraim…Judah. Descendants of Joseph's two sons (Manasseh and Ephraim) had engaged in civil war with one another before (see Judg. 12:4) and unite only in their opposition to Judah.

10:1,2 unrighteous decrees…rob the needy. The prophet returned to assign reasons for God's wrath again: 1) inequities in administering the laws, and 2) harsh treatment of those in need.

That widows may be their prey,
And *that* they may rob the
fatherless.
3 [b]What will you do in [c]the day of
punishment,
And in the desolation *which* will
come from [d]afar?
To whom will you flee for help?
And where will you leave your
glory?
4 Without Me they shall bow down
among the [e]prisoners,
And they shall fall [1]among the
slain."

[f]For all this His anger is not turned
away,
But His hand *is* stretched out still.

Arrogant Assyria Also Judged

5 "Woe to Assyria, [g]the rod of My
anger
And the staff in whose hand is My
indignation.
6 I will send him against [h]an
ungodly nation,
And against the people of My
wrath
I will [i]give him charge,
To seize the spoil, to take the prey,
And to tread them down like the
mire of the streets.
7 [j]Yet he does not mean so,
Nor does his heart think so;
But *it is* in his heart to destroy,
And cut off not a few nations.
8 [k]For he says,
'*Are* not my princes altogether
kings?
9 *Is* not [l]Calno [m]like Carchemish?
Is not Hamath like Arpad?
Is not Samaria [n]like Damascus?
10 As my hand has found the
kingdoms of the idols,
Whose carved images excelled
those of Jerusalem and
Samaria,
11 As I have done to Samaria and her
idols,
Shall I not do also to Jerusalem and
her idols?' "

12 Therefore it shall come to pass, when
the Lord has [2]performed all His work [o]on
Mount Zion and on Jerusalem, *that He will
say,* [p]"I will punish the fruit of the arrogant
heart of the king of Assyria, and the glory
of his haughty looks."
13 [q]For he says:

"By the strength of my hand I have
done *it,*
And by my wisdom, for I am
prudent;
Also I have removed the
boundaries of the people,
And have robbed their treasuries;
So I have put down the inhabitants
like a [3]valiant *man.*
14 [r]My hand has found like a nest the
riches of the people,
And as one gathers eggs *that are*
left,
I have gathered all the earth;
And there was no one who moved
his wing,
Nor opened *his* mouth with even a
peep."

15 Shall [s]the ax boast itself against
him who chops with it?
Or shall the saw exalt itself against
him who saws with it?
As if a rod could wield *itself*
against those who lift it up,
Or as if a staff could lift up, *as if it
were* not wood!
16 Therefore the Lord, the [4]Lord of
hosts,
Will send leanness among his fat
ones;
And under his glory
He will kindle a burning
Like the burning of a fire.

3 [b] Job 31:14 [c] Is. 13:6; Jer. 9:9; Hos. 9:7; Luke 19:44 [d] Is. 5:26
4 [e] Is. 24:22 [f] Is. 5:25 [1] Lit. *under*
5 [g] Jer. 51:20
6 [h] Is. 9:17 [i] 2 Kin. 17:6; Jer. 34:22
7 [j] Gen. 50:20; Mic. 4:11, 12; Acts 2:23, 24
8 [k] 2 Kin. 19:10
9 [l] Gen. 10:10; Amos 6:2 [m] 2 Chr. 35:20 [n] 2 Kin. 16:9
12 [o] 2 Kin. 19:31; Is. 28:21 [p] 2 Kin. 19:35; 2 Chr. 32:21; Jer. 50:18 [2] *completed*
13 [q] [2 Kin. 19:22-24]; Is. 37:24-27; Ezek. 28:4; Dan. 4:30 [3] *mighty*
14 [r] Job 31:25
15 [s] Jer. 51:20
16 [4] So with Bg.; MT, DSS *YHWH (the* LORD*)*

10:2 widows...fatherless. See 1:17.

10:3 day of punishment. The Assyrians were the first to invade, then Babylon and other foreign powers followed.

10:5 rod of My anger. God used Assyria as His instrument of judgment against Israel and Judah. He did the same with Babylon against Judah later on (Hab. 1:6).

10:6 an ungodly nation. "My people" (v. 2), the people of Israel and Judah.

10:7 he does not mean so. Assyria did not realize that she was the Lord's instrument, but thought her conquests were the result of her own power.

10:9 Calno...Damascus. These cities and territories all capitulated to the Assyrian invaders.

10:10,11 Shall I not do also. Proud Assyria warned Jerusalem that she would overcome that city just as she had been the instrument used by God against other nations.

10:12 punish...the king of Assyria. The Lord expressed His intention of punishing proud Assyria after He had finished using that nation to punish Jerusalem.

10:13,14 The prophet proved the Assyrian king's pride by reiterating his boast (cf. vv. 8-11).

10:15 ax...saw...rod...staff. Nothing more than an instrument of the Lord (vv. 5,24), Assyria had no power or wisdom of her own.

10:16-19 burning...burning...fire...flame...burn...consume. When He had finished using Assyria as His instrument, the Lord terminated the kingdom's existence (see v. 12).

17 So the Light of Israel will be for a fire,
And his Holy One for a flame;
[t]It will burn and devour
His thorns and his briers in one day.
18 And it will consume the glory of his forest and of [u]his fruitful field,
Both soul and body;
And they will be as when a sick man wastes away.
19 Then the rest of the trees of his forest
Will be so few in number
That a child may write them.

The Returning Remnant of Israel

20 And it shall come to pass in that day
That the remnant of Israel,
And such as have escaped of the house of Jacob,
[v]Will never again depend on him who [5]defeated them,
But will depend on the LORD, the Holy One of Israel, in truth.
21 The remnant will return, the remnant of Jacob,
To the [w]Mighty God.
22 [x]For though your people, O Israel, be as the sand of the sea,
[y]A remnant of them will return;
The destruction decreed shall overflow with righteousness.
23 [z]For the Lord GOD of hosts
Will make a determined end
In the midst of all the land.

24 Therefore thus says the Lord GOD of
hosts: "O My people, who dwell in Zion,
[a]do not be afraid of the Assyrian. He shall
strike you with a rod and lift up his staff
against you, in the manner of [b]Egypt.
25 For yet a very little while [c]and the
indignation will cease, as will My anger in
their destruction." 26 And the LORD of
hosts will [6]stir up [d]a scourge for him like
the slaughter of [e]Midian at the rock of
Oreb; [f]as His rod was on the sea, so will He
lift it up in the manner of Egypt.

27 It shall come to pass in that day
That his burden will be taken away from your shoulder,
And his yoke from your neck,
And the yoke will be destroyed because of [g]the anointing oil.

28 He has come to Aiath,
He has passed Migron;
At Michmash he has attended to his equipment.
29 They have gone [7]along [h]the ridge,
They have taken up lodging at Geba.
Ramah is afraid,
[i]Gibeah of Saul has fled.
30 [8]Lift up your voice,
O daughter [j]of Gallim!
Cause it to be heard as far as [k]Laish—
[9]O poor Anathoth!
31 [l]Madmenah has fled,
The inhabitants of Gebim seek refuge.
32 As yet he will remain [m]at Nob that day;
He will [n]shake his fist at the mount of [o]the daughter of Zion,
The hill of Jerusalem.

33 Behold, the Lord,
The LORD of hosts,
Will lop off the bough with terror;
[p]Those of high stature *will be* hewn down,
And the haughty will be humbled.
34 He will cut down the thickets of the forest with iron,
And Lebanon will fall by the Mighty One.

17 [t]Is. 9:18
18 [u]2 Kin. 19:23
20 [v]2 Kin. 16:7 [5]Lit. *struck*
21 [w][Is. 9:6]
22 [x]Rom. 9:27, 28 [y]Is. 6:13
23 [z]Is. 28:22; Dan. 9:27; Rom. 9:28
24 [a]Is. 7:4; 12:2 [b]Ex. 14
25 [c]Is. 10:5; 26:20; Dan. 11:36
26 [d]2 Kin. 19:35 [e]Judg. 7:25; Is. 9:4 [f]Ex. 14:26, 27 [6]*arouse*
27 [g]Ps. 105:15; [1 John 2:20]
29 [h]1 Sam. 13:23 [i]1 Sam. 11:4 [7]Or *over the pass*
30 [j]1 Sam. 25:44 [k]Judg. 18:7 [8]Or *Cry shrilly* [9]So with MT, Tg., Vg.; LXX, Syr. *Listen to her, O Anathoth*
31 [l]Josh. 15:31
32 [m]1 Sam. 21:1; Neh. 11:32 [n]Is. 13:2 [o]Is. 37:22
33 [p]Is. 37:24, 36-38; Ezek. 31:3; Amos 2:9

10:20 the remnant of Israel. Cf. 1:9. A small nucleus of God's people, preserved by His sovereign grace, form this righteous remnant in the midst of national apostasy. There were always the obedient few who preserved, obeyed, and passed on God's law. There will always be a remnant because God will never forsake the Abrahamic Covenant (cf. Mic. 2:12,13; Rom. 9:27; 11:5).

10:22 sand of the sea. Cf. Gen. 22:17.

10:23 a determined end. They must face the wrath of God. See Paul's use of this verse in Rom. 9:28.

10:25 the indignation. The indignation covers the entire period of Israel's exile (26:20; Dan. 11:36). Here is the promise that it will end with the return of the Messiah (11:1-16).

10:26 Midian…Egypt. Isaiah selected two examples from the past to illustrate the Lord's future deliverance of Israel: Gideon's victory over the Midianites (Judg. 7:25) and the slaughter of the Egyptians who pursued the Israelites through the Red Sea (Ex. 14:16,26,27).

10:27 burden…yoke. The removal of this yoke speaks of the future freeing of Israel from compulsion to render service to foreign oppressors.

10:28-32 Isaiah visualized the Assyrian army approaching Jerusalem from the N. The place names grew closer to Jerusalem as his vision progressed.

10:33 lop off…hewn down…humbled. Though the Assyrian army reached the walls of Jerusalem, the sovereign Lord, the Lord of hosts, intervened and sent them away in defeat. Later Isaiah recorded the literal fulfillment of this prophecy (37:24,36-38; cf. 2 Kin. 19:35-37; 2 Chr. 32:21).

10:34 Lebanon. The OT equates Assyria to Lebanon (Ezek. 31:3; cf. 2:13; 37:24).

The Reign of Jesse's Offspring

11 There [a]shall come forth a [1]Rod
from the [2]stem of [b]Jesse,
And [c]a Branch shall [3]grow out of
his roots.
2 [d]The Spirit of the LORD shall rest
upon Him,
The Spirit of wisdom and
understanding,
The Spirit of counsel and might,
The Spirit of knowledge and of the
fear of the LORD.

3 His delight *is* in the fear of the LORD,
And He shall not judge by the
sight of His eyes,
Nor decide by the hearing of His
ears;
4 But [e]with righteousness He shall
judge the poor,
And decide with equity for the
meek of the earth;
He shall [f]strike the earth with the
rod of His mouth,
And with the breath of His lips He
shall slay the wicked.
5 Righteousness shall be the belt of
His loins,
And faithfulness the belt of His
waist.

6 "The[g] wolf also shall dwell with the
lamb,
The leopard shall lie down with
the young goat,
The calf and the young lion and
the fatling together;
And a little child shall lead them.
7 The cow and the bear shall graze;
Their young ones shall lie down
together;
And the lion shall eat straw like
the ox.
8 The nursing child shall play by the
cobra's hole,
And the weaned child shall put his
hand in the viper's den.
9 [h]They shall not hurt nor destroy in
all My holy mountain,
For [i]the earth shall be full of the
knowledge of the LORD
As the waters cover the sea.

10 "And[j] in that day [k]there shall be a
Root of Jesse,
Who shall stand as a [l]banner to the
people;
For the [m]Gentiles shall seek Him,
And His resting place shall be
glorious."

11 It shall come to pass in that day
That the Lord shall set His hand
again the second time
To recover the remnant of His
people who are left,
[n]From Assyria and Egypt,
From Pathros and Cush,
From Elam and Shinar,
From Hamath and the [4]islands of
the sea.

12 He will set up a banner for the
nations,
And will [5]assemble the outcasts of
Israel,

CHAPTER 11

1 [a] [Zech. 6:12]; Rev. 5:5 [b] [Is. 9:7; 11:10]; Matt. 1:5; [Acts 13:23] [c] Is. 4:2 [1] *Shoot* [2] *stock or trunk* [3] *be fruitful*
2 [d] [Is. 42:1; 48:16; 61:1; Matt. 3:16]; Mark 1:10; Luke 3:22; [John 1:32]
4 [e] Rev. 19:11 [f] Job 4:9; Is. 30:28, 33; Mal. 4:6; 2 Thess. 2:8
6 [g] Hos. 2:18
9 [h] Job 5:23; Is. 65:25; Ezek. 34:25; Hos. 2:18 [i] Ps. 98:2, 3; Is. 45:6; Hab. 2:14
10 [j] Is. 2:11 [k] Is. 11:1; Rom. 15:12 [l] Is. 27:12, 13 [m] Rom. 15:10
11 [n] Is. 19:23-25; Hos. 11:11; Zech. 10:10 [4] *Or coastlands*
12 [5] *gather*

11:1 stem...roots. With the Babylonian captivity of 586 B.C., the Davidic dynasty appeared as decimated as the Assyrian army. A major difference between the two was the life remaining in the stump and roots of the Davidic line. That life was to manifest itself in new growth in the form of the Rod and Branch. **Jesse.** Jesse was David's father through whose line the messianic king was to come (Ruth 4:22; 1 Sam. 16:1,12,13). **Branch.** This is a title for the Messiah (see 4:2).

11:2 The Spirit of the LORD. As the Spirit of the Lord came upon David when he was anointed king (1 Sam 16:13; Ps. 51:11), so He will rest upon David's descendant, Christ, who will rule the world. **Spirit...the LORD...Him.** This verse refers to the 3 persons of the Holy Trinity (see 6:3). **wisdom and understanding...counsel and might...knowledge and...fear of the LORD.** These are Spirit-imparted qualifications that will enable the Messiah to rule justly and effectively. Compare the 7-fold Spirit in Rev. 1:4.

11:3 the sight of His eyes...the hearing of His ears. These are ordinary avenues for a king to obtain information needed to govern, but the future King will have supernatural perception beyond these usual sources.

11:4 poor...meek. The Messiah will reverse Israel's earlier dealings with the underprivileged (3:14,15; 10:2). **rod of His mouth.** The Branch's rule over the nations will be forceful. The NT uses equivalent terminology to describe the Warrior-King at His triumphant return to earth (Rev. 19:15; cf. 49:2; Ps. 2:9). **breath of His lips.** This is another figure for the Messiah's means of inflicting physical harm. Paul draws upon this to tell of the destruction of the man of lawlessness at Christ's second advent (2 Thess. 2:8).

11:5 belt...belt. The belt, which gathered the loose garments together, is figurative for the Messiah's readiness for conflict. Righteousness and faithfulness are His preparation. Cf. Eph. 6:14.

11:6-9 Conditions of peace will prevail to the extent that all enmity among men, among animals—rapacious or otherwise—and between men and animals will disappear. Such will characterize the future millennial kingdom in which the Prince of Peace (9:6) will reign.

11:9 full of the knowledge of the LORD. Everyone will know the Lord when He returns to fulfill His New Covenant with Israel (Jer. 31:34).

11:10 in that day. The time of universal peace will come in the future reign of the Lord (*see note on 2:12*). **Gentiles shall seek Him.** The Root of Jesse will also attract non-Jews who inhabit the future kingdom (49:6; 52:10; 60:3; 66:18). Paul saw God's ministry to Gentiles during the church age as an additional implication of this verse (Rom. 15:12).

11:11 second time. The first return of Israel to her Land was from Egyptian captivity (Ex. 14:26-29). The second will be from her worldwide dispersion (51:9-11; *see note on 10:20*).

And gather together [o]the dispersed
of Judah
From the four [6]corners of the earth.
13 Also [p]the envy of Ephraim shall
depart,
And the adversaries of Judah shall
be cut off;
Ephraim shall not envy Judah,
And Judah shall not harass
Ephraim.
14 But they shall fly down upon the
shoulder of the Philistines
toward the west;
Together they shall plunder the
[7]people of the East;
[q]They shall lay their hand on Edom
and Moab;
And the people of Ammon shall
obey them.
15 The LORD [r]will utterly [8]destroy the
tongue of the Sea of Egypt;
With His mighty wind He will
shake His fist over [9]the River,
And strike it in the seven streams,
And make *men* cross over [1]dryshod.
16 [s]There will be a highway for the
remnant of His people
Who will be left from Assyria,
[t]As it was for Israel
In the day that he came up from
the land of Egypt.

A Hymn of Praise

12 And [a]in that day you will say:

"O LORD, I will praise You;
Though You were angry with me,
Your anger is turned away, and
You comfort me.
2 Behold, God *is* my salvation,
I will trust and not be afraid;
[b]'For [c]YAH, the LORD, *is* my strength
and song;
He also has become my salvation.' "

3 Therefore with joy you will draw
[d]water
From the wells of salvation.

4 And in that day you will say:

[e]"Praise the LORD, call upon His
name;
[f]Declare His deeds among the
peoples,
Make mention that His [g]name is
exalted.
5 [h]Sing to the LORD,
For He has done excellent things;
This *is* known in all the earth.
6 [i]Cry out and shout, O inhabitant of
Zion,
For great *is* [j]the Holy One of Israel
in your midst!"

Proclamation Against Babylon

13 The [a]burden[1] against Babylon which Isaiah the son of Amoz saw.

2 "Lift[b] up a banner [c]on the high
mountain,
Raise your voice to them;

12 [o]John 7:35 [6]Lit. *wings*
13 [p]Is. 9:21; Jer. 3:18; Ezek. 37:16, 17, 22; Hos. 1:11
14 [q]Is. 63:1; Dan. 11:41; Joel 3:19; Amos 9:12 [7]Lit. *sons*
15 [r]Is. 50:2; 51:10, 11; Zech. 10:10, 11 [8]So with MT, Vg.; LXX, Syr., Tg. *dry up* [9]The Euphrates [1]Lit. *in sandals*
16 [s]Is. 19:23 [t]Ex. 14:29

CHAPTER 12
1 [a]Is. 2:11
2 [b]Ps. 83:18 [c]Ex. 15:2; Ps. 118:14
3 [d][John 4:10, 14; 7:37, 38]
4 [e]1 Chr. 16:8; Ps. 105:1 [f]Ps. 145:4-6 [g]Ps. 34:3
5 [h]Ex. 15:1; Ps. 98:1; Is. 24:14; 42:10, 11; 44:23
6 [i]Is. 52:9; 54:1; Zeph. 3:14, 15 [j]Ps. 89:18

CHAPTER 13
1 [a]Jer. 50; 51; Matt. 1:11; Rev. 14:8 [1]*oracle, prophecy*
2 [b]Is. 18:3 [c]Jer. 51:25

11:12 four corners of the earth. This figurative expression depicts the whole world (Rev. 20:8). The faithful remnant of Israel will return from a worldwide dispersion to their Land.

11:13 Ephraim...Judah. These were the two major divisions of Israel after the schism under Jeroboam (1 Kin. 12:16-20). Ephraim was the name representing the northern 10 tribes, and Judah the southern two. When the Messiah returns, they will reunite in a lasting peace.

11:14 west...East. In that day Israel will be free from all foreign oppression and will be the dominant political force.

11:15 the River. Just as He dried up the Red Sea in the deliverance from Egypt, the Lord will in the future dry up the Euphrates in connection with the final deliverance of His people. *See note on Rev. 16:12.*

11:16 highway. Isaiah has much to say about a way for the remnant returning to Jerusalem (35:8,9; 42:16; 43:19; 48:21; 49:11; 57:14; 62:10).

12:1-6 Two brief songs of praise (vv. 1-3,4-6) which redeemed Israel will sing at the outset of the millennial kingdom. They are the earthly counterpart to the heavenly doxology in Rev. 19:6,7.

12:1 Your anger is turned away. For the future remnant who will recognize the substitutionary death of Christ for their sins, Christ bore God's anger in their place. Otherwise, that anger against them would remain.

12:2 God *is* my salvation. God will deliver the faithful of Israel from both their political opponents and the spiritual consequences of their sins. **YAH, the LORD.** Rendered "the LORD JEHOVAH" in the original KJV, the doubling of the personal name of God serves to emphasize His role as the covenant-keeping One. **my strength and song...my salvation.** Moses and the Israelites sang a similar song to celebrate their deliverance from the Egyptians (Ex. 15:2; cf. Ps. 118:14).

12:3 water...wells. Isaiah's readers doubtless thought of how God satisfied the physical thirst of their ancestors in the Wilderness of Sin (Ex. 17:1-7). The same provision will apply for their descendants when the Messiah comes to deliver the nation (41:17,18; cf. 30:25; 35:6,7; 43:19; Ps. 107:35). The NT amplifies this provision to include the supply of spiritual water for the thirsty soul (John 4:10,14; 7:37; Rev. 7:16,17; 21:6; 22:17).

12:4,5 among the peoples...in all the earth. Following the future Day of the Lord, Israel will testify to the rest of the world about His greatness and majesty. This was His purpose for His earthly people from the beginning.

12:6 O inhabitant of Zion. The Heb. of this verse personifies Zion as a woman by commanding her to "cry out and shout" in celebration of the Lord's greatness.

13:1–23:18 These 11 chapters group together prophecies against foreign nations, much the same as those in Jer. 46–51 and Ezek. 25–32.

13:1–14:27 The section 13:1–14:24 deals specifically with Babylon and vv. 25-27 with Assyria, though Babylon was not yet a world power at the time of this prophecy. Isaiah foresaw a time when Babylon would overthrow the current dominant nation Assyria and be an international force.

13:1 burden. In the sense of his having heavy responsibility to

[d]Wave your hand, that they may
enter the gates of the nobles.
3 I have commanded My [2]sanctified
ones;
I have also called [e]My mighty ones
for My anger—
Those who [f]rejoice in My
exaltation."

2 [d]Is. 10:32
3 [e]Joel 3:11 [f]Ps. 149:2 [2]*consecrated or set apart*
4 [g]Is. 17:12; Joel 3:14

4 The [g]noise of a multitude in the
mountains,
Like that of many people!
A tumultuous noise of the
kingdoms of nations gathered
together!
The LORD of hosts musters
The army for battle.

deliver the message. It is used 15 other times in the OT in superscriptions like this (14:28; 15:1; 17:1; 19:1; 21:1,11,13; 22:1; 23:1; Lam. 2:14; Nah. 1:1; Hab. 1:1; Zech. 9:1; 12:1; Mal. 1:1). **Babylon…Isaiah…saw.** This chapter foretold the city's destruction. Even during the Assyrian Empire the city of Babylon was formidable and stood at the head in the list of Israel's enemies to be conquered.

13:2 Lift up a banner. As in 5:26, the Lord summoned foreign armies to conquer Babylon in all her greatness.

13:3 I have commanded…called. The Lord told of His gathering of armies to overcome Babylon. **My anger.** God's anger had turned away from Israel (12:1) and toward this oppressive foreign power.

13:4 The LORD of hosts musters the army. Lit. "the LORD of

God's Judgment on the Nations

	Obadiah	Amos	Isaiah	Jeremiah	Habakkuk	Ezekiel
Ammon		*1:13-15* Judgment		*49:1-6* Judgment; Restoration		*25:1-7* Judgment
Babylon			*13:1–14:23* Judgment	*50,51* Judgment	*2:6-17* Judgment	
Damascus		*1:3-5* Judgment	*17:1-3* Judgment; Remnant	*49:23-27* Judgment		
Edom	Judgment	*1:11,12* Judgment	*21:11,12* Judgment	*49:7-22* Judgment		*25:12-14* Judgment
Egypt			*19* Judgment	*46:1-26* Judgment		*29–32* Judgment
Moab		*2:1-3* Judgment	*15,16* Judgment; Remnant	*48* Judgment; Restoration		*25:8-11* Judgment
Philistia		*1:6-8* Judgment	*14:29-32* Judgment	*47* Judgment; Remnant		*25:15-17* Judgment
Tyre		*1:9,10* Judgment	*23* Judgment; Restoration			*26–28* Judgment

5 They come from a far country,
From the end of heaven—
The [h]LORD and His [3]weapons of
indignation,
To destroy the whole [i]land.

6 Wail, [j]for the day of the LORD *is* at
hand!
[k]It will come as destruction from
the Almighty.
7 Therefore all hands will be limp,
Every man's heart will melt,
8 And they will be afraid.
[l]Pangs[4] and sorrows will take hold
of *them;*
They will be in pain as a woman in
childbirth;
They will be amazed at one
another;
Their faces *will be like* flames.

9 Behold, [m]the day of the LORD
comes,
Cruel, with both wrath and fierce
anger,
To lay the land desolate;
And He will destroy [n]its sinners
from it.
10 For the stars of heaven and their
constellations
Will not give their light;
The sun will be [o]darkened in its
going forth,
And the moon will not cause its
light to shine.

11 "I will [p]punish the world for *its* evil,
And the wicked for their iniquity;
[q]I will halt the arrogance of the
proud,
And will lay low the haughtiness
of the [5]terrible.
12 I will make a mortal more rare
than fine gold,
A man more than the golden
wedge of Ophir.
13 [r]Therefore I will shake the heavens,
And the earth will move out of her
place,
In the wrath of the LORD of hosts
And in [s]the day of His fierce anger.
14 It shall be as the hunted gazelle,
And as a sheep that no man [6]takes
up;
[t]Every man will turn to his own
people,
And everyone will flee to his own
land.
15 Everyone who is found will be
thrust through,
And everyone who is captured will
fall by the sword.
16 Their children also will be [u]dashed
to pieces before their eyes;
Their houses will be plundered
And their wives [v]ravished.

17 "Behold, [w]I will stir up the Medes
against them,
Who will not [7]regard silver;
And *as for* gold, they will not
delight in it.
18 Also *their* bows will dash the
young men to pieces,

5 [h] Is. 42:13 [i] Is. 24:1; 34:2 [3] Or *instruments*
6 [j] Is. 2:12; Ezek. 30:3; Amos 5:18; Zeph. 1:7; Rev. 6:17 [k] Is. 10:25; Job 31:23; Joel 1:15
8 [l] Ps. 48:6 [4] *Sharp pains*
9 [m] Mal. 4:1 [n] Ps. 104:35; Prov. 2:22
10 [o] Is. 24:21-23; Ezek. 32:7; Joel 2:31; Matt. 24:29; Mark 13:24; Luke 21:25
11 [p] Is. 26:21 [q] [Is. 2:17] [5] Or *tyrants*
13 [r] Is. 34:4; 51:6; Hag. 2:6 [s] Ps. 110:5; Lam. 1:12
14 [t] Jer. 50:16; 51:9 [6] *gathers*
16 [u] Ps. 137:8, 9; Is. 13:18; 14:21; Hos. 10:14; Nah. 3:10 [v] Zech. 14:2
17 [w] Is. 21:2; Jer. 51:11, 28; Dan. 5:28, 31 [7] *esteem*

armies musters the army." *See note at 1:9.* This anticipated the end-time coming of the Lord to crush the final Babylon and to dash His enemies in pieces and establish a kingdom over all nations (Rev. 19:11-16).

13:5 From the end of heaven. The fall of Babylon to the Medes was merely a short-term glimpse of the ultimate fall of Babylon at the hands of the universal forces of God (Rev. 18:2).

13:6 the day of the LORD *is* at hand. The prophecy looked beyond the more immediate conquest of the city by the Medes to a greater day of the Lord and anticipated the final destruction of Babylon by the personal intervention of the Messiah. *See note on 2:12.*

13:7 heart will melt. Courage was to vanish (19:1; Ezek. 21:7; Nah. 2:10).

13:8 in pain as a woman in childbirth. The comparison of labor pains is often a figure to describe human sufferings in the period just before the final deliverance of Israel (21:3; 26:17,18; 66:7ff.; Jer. 4:31; 13:21; 22:23; Hos. 13:13; Mic. 4:10; 5:2,3; Matt. 24:8; 1 Thess. 5:3). Usually, it was the suffering of Israel, but here it pictured the misery of Babylon.

13:9 destroy its sinners. This occurs when Messiah returns in judgment of all living on earth. In this case the prophet moves forward to the Babylon which is the final evil world city to be destroyed with all its inhabitants (see Rev. 17,18).

13:10 stars...sun...moon. Scripture frequently associates cosmic upheavals with the period of tribulation just before Christ's return (24:23; Ezek. 32:7,8; Joel 2:10,30,31; Amos 8:9; Matt. 24:29; Mark 13:24,25; Luke 21:25; Rev. 6:12-14).

13:11 arrogance. The same sin of pride that led to Israel's judgment (5:21; 9:9) will cause Babylon's downfall (47:5,7,8; Rev. 18:7).

13:12 more rare. Because of this visitation human mortality will be extremely high, but not complete. God will spare a faithful remnant.

13:13 shake the heavens...earth will move. These upheavals are associated with the ones in v. 10 (Joel 2:10; Hag. 2:6; Rev. 6:12-14; cf. 2:19,21; 24:1,19,20; 34:4; 51:6).

13:14 gazelle...sheep. Humans are frightening to the shy gazelle, but indispensable to the helpless sheep. The Babylonians will find the Lord as their enemy and lose Him as their shepherd. All they can do is flee the land.

13:15,16 thrust through...captured...dashed to pieces...plundered...ravished. The prophet for the moment returned to the immediate future, when the Medes committed all those cruel atrocities in captured Babylon. For more brutal acts, see v. 18.

13:17 Medes. This people from an area SW of the Caspian Sea, N of Persia, E of Assyria, and NE of Babylon later allied themselves with the Babylonians to conquer Assyria ca. 610 B.C. and later with the Persians to cause the fall of Babylon (539 B.C.).

And they will have no pity on the
fruit of the womb;
Their eye will not spare children.
19 [x]And Babylon, the glory of
kingdoms,
The beauty of the Chaldeans'
pride,
Will be as when God overthrew
[y]Sodom and Gomorrah.
20 [z]It will never be inhabited,
Nor will it be settled from
generation to generation;
Nor will the Arabian pitch tents
there,
Nor will the shepherds make their
sheepfolds there.
21 [a]But wild beasts of the desert will
lie there,
And their houses will be full of
[8]owls;
Ostriches will dwell there,
And wild goats will caper there.
22 The hyenas will howl in their
citadels,
And jackals in their pleasant
palaces.
[b]Her time *is* near to come,
And her days will not be
prolonged."

Mercy on Jacob

14 For the LORD [a]will have mercy on
Jacob, and [b]will still choose Israel,
and settle them in their own land. [c]The
strangers will be joined with them, and
they will cling to the house of Jacob. 2 Then
people will take them [d]and bring them to
their place, and the house of Israel will
possess them for servants and maids in the
land of the LORD; they will take them captive whose captives they were, [e]and rule
over their oppressors.

Fall of the King of Babylon

3 It shall come to pass in the day the
LORD gives you rest from your sorrow, and
from your fear and the hard bondage in
which you were made to serve, 4 that you
[f]will take up this proverb against the king
of Babylon, and say:

"How the oppressor has ceased,
The [g]golden[1] city ceased!
5 The LORD has broken [h]the staff of
the wicked,
The scepter of the rulers;
6 He who struck the people in wrath
with a continual stroke,
He who ruled the nations in anger,
Is persecuted *and* no one hinders.
7 The whole earth is at rest *and* quiet;
They break forth into singing.
8 [i]Indeed the cypress trees rejoice
over you,
And the cedars of Lebanon,
Saying, 'Since you [2]were cut down,
No woodsman has come up
against us.'
9 "Hell[j][3] from beneath is excited
about you,
To meet *you* at your coming;
It stirs up the dead for you,
All the chief ones of the earth;

19 [x] Is. 14:4; Dan. 4:30; Rev. 18:11-16, 19, 21 [y] Gen. 19:24; Deut. 29:23; Jer. 50:40; Amos 4:11
20 [z] Jer. 50:3
21 [a] Is. 34:11-15; Zeph. 2:14; Rev. 18:2 [8] Or *howling creatures*
22 [b] Jer. 51:33

CHAPTER 14

1 [a] Ps. 102:13; Is. 49:13, 15; 54:7, 8 [b] Is. 41:8, 9; Zech. 1:17; 2:12 [c] Is. 60:4, 5, 10
2 [d] Is. 49:22; 60:9; 66:20 [e] Is. 60:14
4 [f] Is. 13:19; Hab. 2:6 [g] Rev. 18:16 [1] Or *insolent*
5 [h] Ps. 125:3
8 [i] Is. 55:12; Ezek. 31:16 [2] *have lain down*
9 [j] Ezek. 32:21 [3] Or *Sheol*

13:19-22 From the near future, Isaiah returned to the distant future. The ultimate fulfillment of these prophecies of Babylon's desolation will come in conjunction with Babylon's rebuilding and utter destruction when Christ returns (Rev. 14:8; 18:2). Obviously, Isaiah was unable to see the many centuries that separated Babylon's fall to the Medes from the destruction of the final Babylon by God (see Rev. 17,18).

13:19 Sodom and Gomorrah. God will overthrow rebuilt Babylon in the same supernatural way He did these two ancient cities (Gen. 19:24; Rev. 18:8).

13:20 never be inhabited. Though nothing like its glorious past, the site of Babylon has never been void of inhabitants. A city or town of one type or another has always existed there, so this prophecy must point toward a yet future desolation.

13:21,22 wild beasts...jackals. This is the utter devastation referred to in 21:9 and further described in Rev. 18:2 (cf. 34:11-17; Jer. 51:37).

13:22 near to come. As already noted in v. 6, once Babylon becomes great, her days are numbered.

14:1-3 While having some reference to the release from Babylonian captivity, the primary view in this chapter is identified in these opening verses. The prophet looked at the final Babylon at the end of the tribulation. The language is that which characterizes conditions during the millennial kingdom after the judgment of the final Babylon. The destruction of future Babylon is integrally connected with the deliverance of Israel from bondage. Babylon must perish so that the Lord may exalt His people. God's compassion for physical Israel receives fuller development in chaps. 40–46.

14:1 The strangers. These are Jewish proselytes who join themselves to the nation in the final earthly kingdom of Christ.

14:2 take them captive whose captives they were. Here is the great role reversal. Instead of their miserable state of captivity, endured in the tribulation under Antichrist, the Israelites will be the rulers of those nations that once dominated them.

14:3 rest. The future earthly kingdom of Messiah is in view. Cf. Acts 3:19-21.

14:4 you will take up this proverb. The prophet instructed the delivered nation to sing the song of vv. 4-21, celebrating the downfall of the king of Babylon. **the king of Babylon.** This could refer to the final Antichrist, who will rule Babylon, which will rule the earth (cf. Rev. 17:17,18) **oppressor has ceased.** The nation that made life bitter for God's people disappeared.

14:6 struck the people...ruled the nations. These picture the tyranny of the Babylonian king.

14:7 The whole earth...at rest *and* quiet. With the tyrant off the throne, the whole world will have peace. This has to be millennial.

14:9-11 Hell...Sheol. The two Eng. words represent the same Heb. word. Those kings of the nations already in the place of the dead stage a welcome party for the arriving king of Babylon.

It has raised up from their thrones
All the kings of the nations.
10 They all shall [k]speak and say to
you:
'Have you also become as weak as
we?
Have you become like us?
11 Your pomp is brought down to
Sheol,
And the sound of your stringed
instruments;
The maggot is spread under you,
And worms cover you.'

The Fall of Lucifer

12 "How[l] you are fallen from heaven,
O [4]Lucifer, son of the morning!
How you are cut down to the
ground,
You who weakened the nations!
13 For you have said in your heart:
[m]'I will ascend into heaven,
[n]I will exalt my throne above the
stars of God;
I will also sit on the [o]mount of the
congregation
[p]On the farthest sides of the north;
14 I will ascend above the heights of
the clouds,
[q]I will be like the Most High.'
15 Yet you [r]shall be brought down to
Sheol,
To the [5]lowest depths of the Pit.

16 "Those who see you will gaze at you,
And consider you, *saying:*
'*Is* this the man who made the earth
tremble,
Who shook kingdoms,
17 Who made the world as a
wilderness
And destroyed its cities,
Who [6]did not open the house of his
prisoners?'

18 "All the kings of the nations,
All of them, sleep in glory,
Everyone in his own house;
19 But you are cast out of your grave
Like an [7]abominable branch,
Like the garment of those who are
slain,
[8]Thrust through with a sword,
Who go down to the stones of the
pit,
Like a corpse trodden underfoot.
20 You will not be joined with them in
burial,
Because you have destroyed your
land
And slain your people.
[s]The brood of evildoers shall never
be named.
21 Prepare slaughter for his children
[t]Because of the iniquity of their
fathers,
Lest they rise up and possess the
land,
And fill the face of the world with
cities."

Babylon Destroyed

22 "For I will rise up against them,"
says the LORD of hosts,
"And cut off from Babylon [u]the
name and [v]remnant,
[w]And offspring and posterity," says
the LORD.
23 "I will also make it a possession for
the [x]porcupine,
And marshes of muddy water;
I will sweep it with the broom of
destruction," says the LORD of
hosts.

10 [k] Ezek. 32:21 **12** [l] Is. 34:4; Luke 10:18; [Rev. 12:7-9] [4] Lit. *Day Star* **13** [m] Ezek. 28:2; Matt. 11:23 [n] Dan. 8:10; 2 Thess. 2:4 [o] Ezek. 28:14 [p] Ps. 48:2 **14** [q] Is. 47:8; 2 Thess. 2:4 **15** [r] Ezek. 28:8; Matt. 11:23; Luke 10:15 [5] Lit. *recesses*

17 [6] Would not release **19** [7] *despised* [8] *Pierced* **20** [s] Job 18:19; Ps. 21:10; 109:13; Is. 1:4; 31:2 **21** [t] Ex. 20:5; Lev. 26:39; Is. 13:16; Matt. 23:35 **22** [u] Prov. 10:7; Is. 26:14; Jer. 51:62 [v] 1 Kin. 14:10 [w] Job 18:19; Is. 47:9 **23** [x] Is. 34:11; Zeph. 2:14

14:10 Have you become like us? The kings mock the king of Babylon, reminding him that human distinctions are meaningless among the dead.

14:11 maggot. Human pride vanishes for a rotting corpse covered with worms.

14:12-14 fallen from heaven...be like the Most High. Jesus' use of v. 12 to describe Satan's fall (Luke 10:18; cf. Rev. 12:8-10) has led many to see more than a reference to the king of Babylon. Just as the Lord addressed Satan in His words to the serpent (Gen. 3:14,15), this inspired dirge speaks to the king of Babylon and to the devil who energized him. See Ezek. 28:12-17 for similar language to the king of Tyre and Satan behind him.

14:12 heaven. The scene suddenly shifts from the underworld to heaven to emphasize the unbridled pride of the king and Satan energizing him. **Lucifer, son of the morning.** Lit. "Lucifer" means "shining one," but translators have often rendered it "morning star." Tradition of the time saw the stars as representing gods battling among themselves for places of preeminence.

14:13,14 I will. Five "I wills" emphasize the arrogance of the king of Babylon and of Satan from whom he takes his cue.

14:13 mount of the congregation. This was a mountain in northern Syria, according to local tradition, where the Canaanite gods assembled. The human king aspired to kingship over those gods.

14:15 Sheol...the Pit. Death awaits those who try to be like God (cf. vv. 9,11; Gen. 3:5,22).

14:16-21 The final section of the dirge elaborates on the disgrace of the king, on display before all as an unburied corpse.

14:16 *Is* this the man...? The complete role reversal from the most powerful to utter humiliation will provoke universal amazement.

14:18 All the kings...sleep in glory. The king of Babylon is the sole exception. The rest of the kings received honorable burials.

14:19 corpse trodden underfoot. Among the ancients, this was the deepest degradation. *See note on Eccl. 6:3-6.*

14:20 never be named. Because the king of Babylon was an evildoer, he had no monument or posterity to keep his memory alive.

14:22 cut off. Israel will have a remnant, but not Babylon, according the Lord's promise in vv. 22,23. Cf. Rev. 18:2,21

Assyria Destroyed

24 The LORD of hosts has sworn, saying,
"Surely, as I have thought, so it shall come to pass,
And as I have purposed, *so* it shall [y]stand:
25 That I will break the [z]Assyrian in My land,
And on My mountains tread him underfoot.
Then [a]his yoke shall be removed from them,
And his burden removed from their shoulders.
26 This *is* the [b]purpose that is purposed against the whole earth,
And this *is* the hand that is stretched out over all the nations.
27 For the LORD of hosts has [c]purposed,
And who will annul *it?*
His hand *is* stretched out,
And who will turn it back?"

Philistia Destroyed

28 This is the [9]burden which came in the year that [d]King Ahaz died.

29 "Do not rejoice, all you of Philistia,
[e]Because the rod that struck you is broken;
For out of the serpent's roots will come forth a viper,
[f]And its offspring *will be* a fiery flying serpent.
30 The firstborn of the poor will feed,
And the needy will lie down in safety;
I will kill your roots with famine,
And it will slay your remnant.
31 Wail, O gate! Cry, O city!
All you of Philistia *are* dissolved;
For smoke will come from the north,
And no one *will be* alone in his [1]appointed times."
32 What will they answer the messengers of the nation?
That [g]the LORD has founded Zion,
And [h]the poor of His people shall take refuge in it.

Proclamation Against Moab

15 The [a]burden[1] against Moab.

Because in the night [b]Ar of [c]Moab is laid waste
And destroyed,
Because in the night Kir of Moab is laid waste
And destroyed,
2 He has gone up to the [2]temple and Dibon,
To the high places to weep.
Moab will wail over Nebo and over Medeba;
[d]On all their heads *will be* baldness,
And every beard cut off.
3 In their streets they will clothe themselves with sackcloth;
On the tops of their houses
And in their streets
Everyone will wail, [e]weeping bitterly.
4 Heshbon and Elealeh will cry out,
Their voice shall be heard as far as [f]Jahaz;
Therefore the [3]armed soldiers of Moab will cry out;
His life will be burdensome to him.

24 [y]Is. 43:13
25 [z]Mic. 5:5, 6; Zeph. 2:13 [a]Is. 10:27; Nah. 1:13
26 [b]Is. 23:9; Zeph. 3:6, 8
27 [c]2 Chr. 20:6; Job 9:12; 23:13; Ps. 33:11; Prov. 19:21; 21:30; Is. 43:13; Dan. 4:31, 35
28 [d]2 Kin. 16:20; 2 Chr. 28:27 [9]*oracle, prophecy*
29 [e]2 Chr. 26:6 [f]2 Kin. 18:8

31 [1]Or *ranks*
32 [g]Ps. 87:1, 5 [h]Zech. 11:11

CHAPTER 15

1 [a]2 Kin. 3:4 [b]Deut. 2:9; Num. 21:28 [c]Is. 15:1–16:14; Jer. 25:21; 48:1-47; Amos 2:1-3; Zeph. 2:8-11 [1]*oracle, prophecy*
2 [d]Lev. 21:5; Jer. 48:37 [2]Heb. *bayith*, lit. *house*
3 [e]Jer. 48:38
4 [f]Num. 21:28; 32:3; Jer. 48:34 [3]So with MT, Tg., Vg.; LXX, Syr. *loins*

14:26 purpose that is purposed. The scope of this judgment against the whole earth represents His final wrath against the ungodly in Israel (5:25; 9:17) and the nations (23:11).

14:28 Ahaz died. The year of Ahaz's death is uncertain. It came when Hezekiah began his reign, either 727 B.C. (2 Kin. 18:1,9,10) or 716/15 B.C. (2 Kin. 18:13).

14:29 Philistia. Israel need not think an alliance with the Philistines would save them from the Assyrians, since Assyria would conquer this neighbor of Israel too. **rod...broken.** The prophet pictured the Assyrian weakness, their conquest of Philistia notwithstanding.

14:30-32 poor. The poor of Judah who depend on the Lord are to find Him to be a refuge, but the Philistine oppressors are to meet their doom.

14:32 messengers. These were the Philistine envoys who sought an alliance with Israel. Isaiah's answer saw the Lord as Zion's only security.

15:1–16:14. The demise of Moab taught Israel not to depend on that nation any more than others, but to depend on the Lord.

15:1 Moab. Moab was a country about 30 mi. sq., E of the Dead Sea, S of the Arnon River, and N of the Zered River. **Ar...Kir.** These were the two major cities of Moab.

15:2 Dibon. Moab chose the temple of the Moabite god Chemosh—3 mi. N of the Arnon—as the place of weeping because that god had failed to deliver the nation. **Nebo...Medeba.** Nebo is the mountain at the N end of the Dead Sea where the Lord took Moses to view the Promised Land (Deut. 34:1). Medeba is 5 mi. SE of Nebo. **baldness...every beard.** Shaving heads and beards expressed disgrace and humiliation (22:12; Lev. 21:5; Jer. 41:5; 48:37).

15:3 sackcloth. Wearing of sackcloth occurs 46 times in the Bible as a sign of mourning.

15:4 Heshbon...Elealeh...Jahaz. The city Heshbon was just under 20 mi. E of the northern end of the Dead Sea in a territory claimed by both Israel and Moab (Deut. 2:32,33). Elealeh was about a mi. away from Heshbon. The location of Jahaz was over 10 mi. S of Heshbon.

5 "My[g] heart will cry out for Moab;
His fugitives *shall flee* to Zoar,
Like [4]a three-year-old heifer.
For [h]by the Ascent of Luhith
They will go up with weeping;
For in the way of Horonaim
They will raise up a cry of
destruction,
6 For the waters [i]of Nimrim will be
desolate,
For the green grass has withered
away;
The grass fails, there is nothing
green.
7 Therefore the abundance they have
gained,
And what they have laid up,
They will carry away to the Brook
of the Willows.
8 For the cry has gone all around the
borders of Moab,
Its wailing to Eglaim
And its wailing to Beer Elim.
9 For the waters of [5]Dimon will be
full of blood;
Because I will bring more upon
[5]Dimon,
[j]Lions upon him who escapes from
Moab,
And on the remnant of the land."

Moab Destroyed

16 Send [a]the lamb to the ruler of the
land,
[b]From [1]Sela to the wilderness,
To the mount of the daughter of
Zion.
2 For it shall be as a [c]wandering bird
thrown out of the nest;
So shall be the daughters of Moab
at the fords of the [d]Arnon.

3 "Take counsel, execute judgment;
Make your shadow like the night
in the middle of the day;
Hide the outcasts,
Do not betray him who escapes.
4 Let My outcasts dwell with you,
O Moab;
Be a shelter to them from the face
of the [2]spoiler.
For the extortioner is at an end,
Devastation ceases,
The oppressors are consumed out
of the land.
5 In mercy [e]the throne will be
established;
And One will sit on it in truth, in
the tabernacle of David,
[f]Judging and seeking justice and
hastening [g]righteousness."

6 We have heard of the [h]pride of
Moab—
He is very proud—
Of his haughtiness and his pride
and his wrath;
[i]*But* his [3]lies *shall* not *be* so.
7 Therefore Moab shall [j]wail for
Moab;
Everyone shall wail.
For the foundations [k]of Kir
Hareseth you shall mourn;
Surely *they are* stricken.

8 For [l]the fields of Heshbon
languish,
And [m]the vine of Sibmah;
The lords of the nations have

5 [g] Is. 16:11; Jer. 48:31 [h] Jer. 48:5 [4] Or *The Third Eglath*, an unknown city, Jer. 48:34
6 [i] Num. 32:36
9 [j] 2 Kin. 17:25; Jer. 50:17 [5] So with MT, Tg.; DSS, Vg. *Dibon*; LXX *Rimon*

CHAPTER 16

1 [a] 2 Kin. 3:4; Ezra 7:17 [b] 2 Kin. 14:7; Is. 42:11 [1] Lit. *Rock*
2 [c] Prov. 27:8 [d] Num. 21:13
4 [2] *devastator*
5 [e] [Is. 9:6, 7; 32:1; 55:4; Dan. 7:14; Mic. 4:7; Luke 1:33; Rev. 11:15] [f] Ps. 72:2 [g] Is. 9:7
6 [h] Jer. 48:29; Amos 2:1; Obad. 3, 4; Zeph. 2:8, 10 [i] Is. 28:15 [3] Lit. *vain talk*
7 [j] Jer. 48:20 [k] 2 Kin. 3:25; Jer. 48:31
8 [l] Is. 24:7 [m] Is. 16:9

15:5 My heart will cry out. The prophecy expresses much greater sympathy for Moab's plight than for the other nations to be judged, even allowing for a surviving remnant (16:11,14). **a three-year-old heifer.** This phrase should not be translated, but rather is the proper name of "Eglath-shelishiyah," a city of unknown location. **Luhith...Horonaim.** These are two more cities whose location is unknown.

15:6 Nimrim. This is possibly the Wadi Numeira, the drying up of whose waters, along with the dead grass, pictures widespread devastation in Moab.

15:7 Brook of the Willows. Probably the Zered River; the refugees from Moab had to cross this to pass over into Edom to escape their invaders.

15:8 Eglaim...Beer Elim. The shouts of the fugitives reached all the way from the northern part of Edom (Eglaim) to its southern extremity (Beer Elim).

15:9 Dimon. Perhaps another spelling of "Dibon" (cf. v. 2), this religious center of heathendom is appropriate as a closing representation of the whole land of Moab. **Lions.** Flight from invading armies would not bring security, but new dangers from the beasts of the wilderness.

16:1 Send the lamb. This was an action showing submission to an overlord, as Mesha did to Omri, king of Israel (2 Kin. 3:4). **Sela.** This was a place in Edom not far from Petra (2 Kin. 14:7), from which fugitives of Moab were to send to Judah for help. **mount of the daughter of Zion.** This speaks figuratively of Jerusalem and her inhabitants.

16:2 fords of the Arnon. The fugitives fled to the S to escape the Assyrians entering Moab from the N.

16:3 night in the middle of the day. Moab asked Judah for shade from the wilting noonday sun, i.e., from their invaders.

16:4 My outcasts. These were likely the Moabites, the speaker being a personification of Moab. "Moab," defines who the outcasts were. **Be a shelter.** Moab continued its plea to Judah for refuge. **Devastation ceases.** The prophet anticipated the day when the oppression by the Assyrians would be no more.

16:5 throne...tabernacle of David. The Davidic king will some day sit on His throne in Zion (Amos 9:11,12), ending all injustices such as those committed by the Assyrians.

16:6 pride of Moab...very proud. Though a small nation, Moab's pride was well known (25:10,11; Jer. 48:29,42).

16:7 Kir Hareseth. This is probably the same city called Kir in 15:1.

16:8 Sibmah. Sibmah was a suburb of Heshbon (cf. Jer. 48:32).

broken down its choice
plants,
Which have reached to Jazer
And wandered through the
wilderness.
Her branches are stretched out,
They are gone over the [n]sea.
9 Therefore I will bewail the vine of
Sibmah,
With the weeping of Jazer;
I will drench you with my tears,
[o]O Heshbon and Elealeh;
For [4]battle cries have fallen
Over your summer fruits and your
harvest.

10 [p]Gladness is taken away,
And joy from the plentiful field;
In the vineyards there will be no
singing,
Nor will there be shouting;
No treaders will tread out wine in
the presses;
I have made their shouting cease.
11 Therefore [q]my [5]heart shall resound
like a harp for Moab,
And my inner being for [6]Kir
Heres.

12 And it shall come to pass,
When it is seen that Moab is weary
on [r]the high place,
That he will come to his sanctuary
to pray;
But he will not prevail.

13 This *is* the word which the LORD has
spoken concerning Moab since that time.
14 But now the LORD has spoken, saying,
"Within three years, [s]as the years of a hired
man, the glory of Moab will be despised

8 [n]Jer. 48:32
9 [o]Is. 15:4 [4]Or *shouting has*
10 [p]Is. 24:8; Jer. 48:33
11 [q]Is. 15:5; 63:15; Jer. 48:36; Hos. 11:8; Phil. 2:1 [5]Lit. *belly* [6]*Kir Hareseth*, v. 7
12 [r]Is. 15:2
14 [s]Job 7:1; 14:6; Is. 21:16

CHAPTER 17

1 [a]Gen. 14:15; 15:2; 2 Kin. 16:9; Jer. 49:23; Amos 1:3-5; Zech. 9:1; Acts 9:2 [1]*oracle, prophecy*
2 [b]Num. 32:34 [c]Jer. 7:33 [2]So with MT, Vg.; LXX *It shall be forsaken forever;* Tg. *Its cities shall be forsaken and desolate*
3 [d]Is. 7:16; 8:4
4 [e]Is. 10:16 [3]*fade*
5 [f]Is. 17:11; Jer. 51:33; Joel 3:13; Matt. 13:30
6 [g]Deut. 4:27; Is. 24:13; Obad. 5

with all that great multitude, and the remnant *will be* very small *and* feeble."

Proclamation Against Syria and Israel

17 The [a]burden [1]against Damascus.
"Behold, Damascus will cease from
being a city,
And it will be a ruinous heap.
2 [2]The cities of [b]Aroer *are* forsaken;
They will be for flocks
Which lie down, and [c]no one will
make *them* afraid.
3 [d]The fortress also will cease from
Ephraim,
The kingdom from Damascus,
And the remnant of Syria;
They will be as the glory of the
children of Israel,"
Says the LORD of hosts.

4 "In that day it shall come to pass
That the glory of Jacob will [3]wane,
And [e]the fatness of his flesh grow
lean.
5 [f]It shall be as when the harvester
gathers the grain,
And reaps the heads with his
arm;
It shall be as he who gathers heads
of grain
In the Valley of Rephaim.
6 [g]Yet gleaning grapes will be left in
it,
Like the shaking of an olive tree,
Two *or* three olives at the top of the
uppermost bough,
Four *or* five in its most fruitful
branches,"
Says the LORD God of Israel.

Jazer...sea. Moab's vines, rather than being on stakes, ran along the ground to Moab's extreme northern border, stretching from the desert on the E to the Dead Sea on the W. This perhaps signified the export of raisins and wine to Judah.

16:9 I will bewail. Isaiah displayed genuine emotion over the destruction of so rich an agricultural resource. This reflected the Lord's response too.

16:10 Gladness...joy. The normal celebration at harvest time is not to take place.

16:11 my heart...my inner being. The prophet and the Lord reflected deeply felt sorrow over this necessary judgment of Moab.

16:12 weary on the high place. Moab's religion had utterly failed. Rather than deliverance, the nation found weariness in their repeated rituals to their national god.

16:14 Within three years. Moab had 3 more years of "glory," perhaps till ca. 715 B.C., when the Assyrian king, Sargon, overran the country. **the remnant.** Assyria was not to completely obliterate Moab. Babylon received no such promise.

17:1 Damascus. This city served as the capital of Syria (sometimes called "Aram"). Its location NE of Mt. Hermon on the main land route between Mesopotamia and Egypt made it very influential. Its destruction by the Assyrians in 732 B.C. is the subject of this chapter.

17:2 Aroer. Syria's domain extended as far S as Aroer E of the Dead Sea, on the Arnon River (2 Kin. 10:32,33).

17:3 Ephraim. The northern 10 tribes, also known as "Israel," joined with Syria as objects of this oracle. They formed an alliance with Syria to combat the Assyrians, but many of their cites fell victim to the campaign in which Syria fell (see v. 1). **remnant of Syria.** Syria was to have a remnant, but not a kingdom, left after the Assyrian onslaught.

17:4 glory of Jacob. The waning of this glory pictured the judgment of God against the northern 10 tribes, descendants of Jacob.

17:5 Valley of Rephaim. As harvesters stripped bare that fertile valley W of Jerusalem, so God's judgment would leave nothing fruitful in the northern kingdom.

17:6 Two *or* three...Four *or* five. God's judgment against Ephraim was to leave only sparse pieces of her original abundance of olives.

7 In that day a man will [h]look to his
Maker,
And his eyes will have respect for
the Holy One of Israel.
8 He will not look to the altars,
The work of his hands;
He will not respect what his
[i]fingers have made,
Nor the [4]wooden images nor the
incense altars.

9 In that day his strong cities will be
as a forsaken [5]bough
And [6]an uppermost branch,
Which they left because of the
children of Israel;
And there will be desolation.

10 Because you have forgotten [j]the
God of your salvation,
And have not been mindful of the
Rock of your [7]stronghold,
Therefore you will plant pleasant
plants
And set out foreign seedlings;
11 In the day you will make your
plant to grow,
And in the morning you will make
your seed to flourish;
But the harvest *will be* a heap of
ruins
In the day of grief and desperate
sorrow.

12 Woe to the multitude of many
people
Who make a noise [k]like the roar of
the seas,
And to the rushing of nations
That make a rushing like the
rushing of mighty waters!
13 The nations will rush like the
rushing of many waters;
But *God* will [l]rebuke them and
they will flee far away,
And [m]be chased like the chaff of
the mountains before the
wind,
Like a rolling thing before the
whirlwind.
14 Then behold, at eventide, trouble!
And before the morning, he *is* no
more.
This *is* the portion of those who
plunder us,
And the lot of those who rob us.

Proclamation Against Ethiopia

18 Woe [a]to the land shadowed with
buzzing wings,
Which *is* beyond the rivers of
[1]Ethiopia,
2 Which sends ambassadors by sea,
Even in vessels of reed on the
waters, *saying,*
"Go, swift messengers, to a nation
tall and smooth *of skin,*
To a people terrible from their
beginning onward,
A nation powerful and treading
down,
Whose land the rivers divide."

3 All inhabitants of the world and
dwellers on the earth:
[b]When he lifts up a banner on the
mountains, you see *it;*
And when he blows a trumpet,
you hear *it.*
4 For so the LORD said to me,
"I will take My rest,
And I will [2]look from My dwelling
place
Like clear heat in sunshine,
Like a cloud of dew in the heat of
harvest."
5 For before the harvest, when the
bud is perfect
And the sour grape is ripening in
the flower,

7 [h] Is. 10:20; Hos. 3:5; Mic. 7:7
8 [i] Is. 2:8; 31:7 [4] Heb. *Asherim,* Canaanite deities
9 [5] LXX *Hivites;* Tg. *laid waste;* Vg. *as the plows* [6] LXX *Amorites;* Tg. *in ruins;* Vg. *corn*
10 [j] Ps. 68:19; Is. 51:13 [7] *refuge*
12 [k] Is. 5:30; Jer. 6:23; Ezek. 43:2; Luke 21:25
13 [l] Ps. 9:5; Is. 41:11 [m] Ps. 83:13; Hos. 13:3

CHAPTER 18

1 [a] 2 Kin. 19:9; Is. 20:4, 5; Ezek. 30:4, 5, 9; Zeph. 2:12; 3:10 [1] Heb. *Cush*
3 [b] Is. 5:26
4 [2] *watch*

17:7 look to his Maker. In the future, severe judgments are to awaken a remnant of Ephraim to their failure to depend on the Lord. Then they will repent.

17:8 work of his hands. Repentance is to lead to the forsaking of idolatry, which for so long beset the nation (see 2:6-22; 44:9-18).

17:10 forgotten the God of your salvation. Failure to remember God had left Israel unprotected.

17:11 make your plant to grow. The prophet reminded his readers of the futility of trying to meet their needs without the Lord's help.

17:12 multitude of many people. The prophet turned his attention to the coming armies of Judah's enemies and pronounced a "woe" upon them.

17:13 *God* will rebuke them. God's rebuke put those enemies to flight.

17:14 he *is* no more. When morning came, the invading force had disappeared. God protects His people.

18:1 buzzing wings. These may speak of Ethiopia's strong armada of ships. **Ethiopia.** "Cush" renders lit. the Heb. word for Ethiopia. The country was S of Egypt, including territory belonging to modern Ethiopia.

18:2 sea...waters...rivers. These all apparently refer to the Nile River and its tributaries.

18:3 All inhabitants...and dwellers. The prophet calls upon the whole human race to be alert for the signals that God is at work in the world.

18:4 I will take My rest. The Lord will wait patiently until the appropriate time to intervene in human affairs, until sunshine and dew have built to an opportune climactic moment.

He will both cut off the sprigs with
pruning hooks
And take away *and* cut down the
branches.
6 They will be left together for the
mountain birds of prey
And for the beasts of the earth;
The birds of prey will summer on
them,
And all the beasts of the earth will
winter on them.

7 In that time [c]a present will be
brought to the LORD of hosts
[3]From a people tall and smooth *of
skin,*
And from a people terrible from
their beginning onward,
A nation powerful and treading
down,
Whose land the rivers divide—
To the place of the name of the
LORD of hosts,
To Mount Zion.

Proclamation Against Egypt

19 The [a]burden[1] against Egypt.

Behold, the LORD [b]rides on a swift
cloud,
And will come into Egypt;
[c]The idols of Egypt will [2]totter at
His presence,
And the heart of Egypt will melt in
its midst.

2 "I will [d]set Egyptians against
Egyptians;
Everyone will fight against his
brother,
And everyone against his neighbor,
City against city, kingdom against
kingdom.
3 The spirit of Egypt will fail in its
midst;
I will destroy their counsel,
And they will [e]consult the idols
and the charmers,
The mediums and the sorcerers.
4 And the Egyptians I will give
[f]Into the hand of a cruel master,
And a fierce king will rule over
them,"
Says the Lord, the LORD of hosts.

5 [g]The waters will fail from the sea,
And the river will be wasted and
dried up.
6 The rivers will turn foul;
The brooks [h]of defense will be
emptied and dried up;
The reeds and rushes will wither.
7 The papyrus reeds by [3]the River,
by the mouth of the River,
And everything sown by the River,
Will wither, be driven away, and be
no more.
8 The fishermen also will mourn;
All those will lament who cast
hooks into the River,
And they will languish who spread
nets on the waters.
9 Moreover those who work in [i]fine
flax
And those who weave fine fabric
will be ashamed;
10 And its foundations will be broken.
All who make wages *will be*
troubled of soul.

11 Surely the princes of [j]Zoan *are* fools;

7 [c]Ps. 68:31; 72:10; Is. 16:1; Zeph. 3:10; Mal. 1:11; Acts 8:27-38 [3]So with DSS, LXX, Vg.; MT omits *From;* Tg. *To*

CHAPTER 19

1 [a]Jer. 9:25, 26; Ezek. 29:1–30:19; Joel 3:19 [b]Ps. 18:10; 104:3; Matt. 26:64; Rev. 1:7 [c]Ex. 12:12; Jer. 43:12 [1]*oracle, prophecy* [2]Lit. *shake*
2 [d]Judg. 7:22; 1 Sam. 14:16, 20; 2 Chr. 20:23; Matt. 10:21, 36
3 [e]1 Chr. 10:13; Is. 8:19; 47:12; Dan. 2:2
4 [f]Is. 20:4; Jer. 46:26; Ezek. 29:19
5 [g]Is. 50:2; Jer. 51:36; Ezek. 30:12
6 [h]2 Kin. 19:24
7 [3]The Nile
9 [i]1 Kin. 10:28; Prov. 7:16; Ezek. 27:7
11 [j]Num. 13:22; Ps. 78:12, 43; Is. 30:4

18:5 cut off...take away *and* cut down. As an all-wise farmer, God's pruning activity (i.e., His direct intervention) will be neither too early nor too late.

18:6 birds of prey. Dropping his metaphorical language, Isaiah describes in grotesque language the fallen carcasses of the victims of God's judgment.

18:7 place of the name of the LORD of hosts. Jerusalem was and remains the location on earth where the Lord has chosen to dwell (Deut. 12:5). Isaiah's prediction here extends to the future bringing of tribute to Jerusalem in the Messiah's kingdom.

19:1-4 Disunity and internal strife because of idolatry are to spell the end of Egypt's greatness.

19:1 rides on a swift cloud. Clouds are vehicles for the Lord's coming to execute judgment elsewhere (Pss. 18:10,11; 104:3; Dan. 7:13).

19:2 Egyptians against Egyptians. Noted for its internal strife through the centuries, the nation will experience even worse under God's judgment.

19:3 mediums...sorcerers. Internal strife will lead to disorientation and depression. With nowhere else to turn, the Egyptians will consult spiritualists. Israelites of Isaiah's day did the same (8:19).

19:4 fierce king. Egypt was subject to foreign rule beginning with the Assyrian conquest of the middle-seventh century B.C.

19:5-10 A disruption of the Nile River will wreak havoc in Egypt.

19:5,6 wasted and dried up...dried up. God will act to take away the country's only water resource, the Nile and its tributaries.

19:7 sown by the River. The alluvial deposits left by the flooding of the Nile yielded rich agricultural crops, permitting Egypt to export grain to the rest of the world.

19:8 cast hooks...spread nets. The loss of the Nile's important fishing business would mean a great loss to Egypt's population.

19:9 fine flax...fine fabric. Egypt was famous for its production of linen from flax. Both the growth of the plant and the manufacture of the cloth depended on water.

19:10 foundations. God was to remove the "pillars" on which the working class depended. The word refers either generally to the economic structure of the society or specifically to the upper class which organized the businesses of the land.

19:11-15 God's judgment was to confound Egypt's famed wisdom (cf. 1 Kin. 4:30).

Pharaoh's wise counselors give
foolish counsel.
[k]How do you say to Pharaoh, "I *am*
the son of the wise,
The son of ancient kings?"
12 [l]Where *are* they?
Where are your wise men?
Let them tell you now,
And let them know what the LORD
of hosts has [m]purposed
against Egypt.
13 The princes of Zoan have become
fools;
[n]The princes of [4]Noph are
deceived;
They have also [5]deluded Egypt,
Those who are the [6]mainstay of its
tribes.
14 The LORD has mingled [o]a perverse
spirit in her midst;
And they have caused Egypt to err
in all her work,
As a drunken man staggers in his
vomit.
15 Neither will there be *any* work for
Egypt,
Which [p]the head or tail,
Palm branch or bulrush, may do.

16 In that day Egypt will [q]be like
women, and will be afraid and fear because of the waving of the hand of the
LORD of hosts, [r]which He waves over it.
17 And the land of Judah will be a terror to
Egypt; everyone who makes mention of it
will be afraid in himself, because of the
counsel of the LORD of hosts which He has
[s]determined against it.

Egypt, Assyria, and Israel Blessed

18 In that day five cities in the land of
Egypt will [t]speak the language of Canaan
and [u]swear by the LORD of hosts; one will
be called the City of [7]Destruction.
19 In that day [v]there will be an altar to
the LORD in the midst of the land of Egypt,
and a pillar to the [w]LORD at its border.
20 And [x]it will be for a sign and for a witness to the LORD of hosts in the land of
Egypt; for they will cry to the LORD because of the oppressors, and He will send
them a [y]Savior and a Mighty One, and He
will deliver them. 21 Then the LORD will
be known to Egypt, and the Egyptians
will [z]know the LORD in that day, and [a]will
make sacrifice and offering; yes, they will
make a vow to the LORD and perform *it.*
22 And the LORD will strike Egypt, He will
strike and [b]heal *it;* they will return to the
LORD, and He will be entreated by them
and heal them.
23 In that day [c]there will be a highway
from Egypt to Assyria, and the Assyrian
will come into Egypt and the Egyptian into
Assyria, and the Egyptians will [d]serve
with the Assyrians.
24 In that day Israel will be one of three
with Egypt and Assyria—a blessing in the

11 [k]Gen. 41:38, 39; 1 Kin. 4:29, 30; Acts 7:22
12 [l]1 Cor. 1:20 [m]Ps. 33:11
13 [n]Jer. 2:16; Ezek. 30:13 [4]Ancient Memphis [5]Lit. *caused to stagger* [6]*cornerstone*
14 [o]1 Kin. 22:22; Is. 29:10
15 [p]Is. 9:14-16
16 [q]Jer. 51:30; Nah. 3:13 [r]Is. 11:15
17 [s]Is. 14:24; Dan. 4:35
18 [t]Zeph. 3:9 [u]Is. 45:23 [7]Some Heb. mss., Arab., DSS, Tg., Vg. *Sun;* LXX *Asedek,* lit. *Righteousness*
19 [v]Gen. 28:18; Ex. 24:4; Josh. 22:10, 26, 27; Is. 56:7; 60:7 [w]Ps. 68:31
20 [x]Josh. 4:20; 22:27 [y]Is. 43:11
21 [z][Is. 2:3, 4; 11:9] [a]Is. 56:7; 60:7; Zech. 14:16-18; Mal. 1:11
22 [b]Deut. 32:39; Is. 30:26; 57:18; [Heb. 12:11]
23 [c]Is. 11:16; 35:8; 49:11; 62:10 [d]Is. 27:13

19:11 Zoan. This major city of northern Egypt E of the Nile Delta region was the first large city a Semite would encounter in traveling toward the Nile. "Tanis" was also a name of this city that was a capital of northern Egypt at one point when the country split into two parts.

19:11,12 foolish counsel. Whatever wisdom Egypt's experts may have possessed formerly, they were helpless to deal with the crisis because they were ignorant of the Lord's judgment against the Land.

19:13 Noph. Another name for Memphis, the capital of northern Egypt at one time. This city had leaders who were in a state of confusion regarding a true perspective on Egypt's crisis. **mainstay of its tribes.** If the cornerstones of a society suffer from delusion, they can do nothing else than delude the people they lead.

19:14,15 The LORD has mingled. The Lord had caused dizziness that resulted in a complete loss of productivity, when the invaders came.

19:16-24 Turning from Egypt's destitution just described in vv. 1-15, the prophet proceeds to describe Egypt's eventual turning to the true God, "in that day" (v. 16), referring to the time of the millennial rule of Christ. These features have not been true of Egypt yet.

19:16 women...be afraid and fear. God's judgment will immobilize mighty Egypt to the point that the nation realizes it is defenseless and helpless.

19:17 Judah...a terror to Egypt. Instead of Judah fearing Egypt, the reverse will be true. God's great power on behalf of Israel will cause this to happen (cf. Ex. 10:7; 12:33). Such will occur at Christ's second advent.

19:18 five cities. Humanly speaking, the chances of even one Egyptian city turning to the Lord were remote, but divinely speaking, there will be 5 times that many. **language of Canaan.** Egypt is to speak the language of Judah. Not only are they to fear Judah (v. 17), they are also to convert to Judah's form of worship. **swear by the LORD of hosts.** Egypt will "in that day" turn to God in a dramatic way. This prophecy anticipates the personal reign of the Davidic King on earth. **City of Destruction.** More probably this was the "City of the Sun," i.e., Heliopolis, which was the home of the Egyptian sun-god (see "Beth Shemesh," Jer. 43:12,13).

19:19 altar...pillar. These speak figuratively of Egypt's conversion to the Lord "in that day" of the Messiah's reign on earth (cf. Gen. 28:22).

19:20 Savior. God is to act on behalf of Egypt as He did earlier in delivering Israel (Judg. 2:18; 3:9,15; 6:7-9; 10:11,12).

19:21 know the LORD in that day. The future kingdom will be a time when everyone will know the Lord, because the New Covenant will dominate (Jer. 31:31-34: Heb. 8:11; cf. 11:9; Hab. 2:14).

19:22 strike and heal. Just as a parent disciplines a child for purposes of betterment, so the Lord had dealt and would deal with Egypt (cf. Hos. 6:1).

19:23 a highway from Egypt to Assyria. The two great warring nations of Isaiah's time are to reach a lasting peace with each other during "that day" of Christ's reign (27:13; cf. 2:2-4).

19:24 a blessing in the midst of the land. Israel "in that day" will become what God intended her to be—a blessing to the rest of the world (Gen. 12:3; 42:6; contra 1:2).

midst of the land, 25 whom the LORD of
hosts shall bless, saying, "Blessed *is* Egypt
My people, and Assyria [e]the work of My
hands, and Israel My inheritance."

The Sign Against Egypt and Ethiopia

20 In the year that [a]Tartan[1] came to
Ashdod, when Sargon the king of
Assyria sent him, and he fought against
Ashdod and took it, 2 at the same time the
LORD spoke by Isaiah the son of Amoz,
saying, "Go, and remove [b]the sackcloth
from your [2]body, and take your sandals off
your feet." And he did so, [c]walking naked
and barefoot.
3 Then the LORD said, "Just as My servant Isaiah has walked naked and barefoot
three years [d]*for* a sign and a wonder
against Egypt and Ethiopia, 4 so shall the
[e]king of Assyria lead away the Egyptians
as prisoners and the Ethiopians as captives, young and old, naked and barefoot,
[f]with their buttocks uncovered, to the
shame of Egypt. 5 [g]Then they shall be
afraid and ashamed of Ethiopia their expectation and Egypt their glory. 6 And the
inhabitant of this territory will say in that
day, 'Surely such *is* our expectation, wherever we flee for [h]help to be delivered from
the king of Assyria; and how shall we escape?' "

25 [e] Deut. 14:2; Ps. 100:3; Is. 29:23; Hos. 2:23; [Eph. 2:10]

CHAPTER 20

1 [a] 2 Kin. 18:17 [1] Or *the Commander in Chief*
2 [b] Zech. 13:4; Matt. 3:4 [c] 1 Sam. 19:24; Mic. 1:8 [2] Lit. *loins*
3 [d] Is. 8:18
4 [e] Is. 19:4 [f] 2 Sam. 10:4; Is. 3:17; Jer. 13:22; Mic. 1:11
5 [g] 2 Kin. 18:21; Is. 30:3-5; 31:1; Ezek. 29:6,7
6 [h] Is. 30:5,7

CHAPTER 21

1 [a] Zech. 9:14 [1] *oracle, prophecy*
2 [b] Is. 33:1 [c] Is. 13:17; 22:6; Jer. 49:34
3 [d] Is. 15:5; 16:11 [e] Is. 13:8 [2] Lit. *bowed*
4 [f] Deut. 28:67
5 [g] Jer. 51:39; Dan. 5:5

The Fall of Babylon Proclaimed

21 The [1]burden against the Wilderness
of the Sea.

As [a]whirlwinds in the South pass
through,
So it comes from the desert, from a
terrible land.
2 A distressing vision is declared to
me;
[b]The treacherous dealer deals
treacherously,
And the plunderer plunders.
[c]Go up, O Elam!
Besiege, O Media!
All its sighing I have made to cease.

3 Therefore [d]my loins are filled with
pain;
[e]Pangs have taken hold of me, like
the pangs of a woman in
labor.
I was [2]distressed when *I* heard *it;*
I was dismayed when *I* saw *it.*
4 My heart wavered, fearfulness
frightened me;
[f]The night for which I longed He
turned into fear for me.
5 [g]Prepare the table,
Set a watchman in the tower,
Eat and drink.
Arise, you princes,
Anoint the shield!

19:25 My people...the work of My hands. Elsewhere Scripture uses these epithets to speak only of Israel (10:24; 29:23; 43:6,7; 45:11; 60:21; 64:8; Pss. 100:3; 110:3; 138:8; Jer. 11:4; Hos 1:10; 2:23). In the future kingdom, Israel is to be God's instrument for drawing other nations into His fold.

20:1 Tartan. The Heb. term is probably not a proper name, but a title designating a commander in the Assyrian army. **Ashdod... Sargon.** Ashdod was one of the 5 largest Philistine cities, all located SW of Jerusalem. Sargon, mentioned only here in the Bible, was Sargon II, king of Assyria from ca. 722–705 B.C. **took it.** The Assyrians captured Ashdod in 711 B.C., and so frightened the Egyptians that they backed away, thus teaching Judah the folly of reliance on a foreign power such as Egypt for protection.

20:2 at the same time. Isaiah began his object lesson 3 years (v. 3) before his speech in vv. 3-6, which came just prior to the Assyrian attack in 711 B.C. **sackcloth.** This apparel may denote Isaiah's mourning (Gen. 37:34; 2 Kin. 6:30) or it may signify his prophetic office (2 Kin. 1:8; Matt. 3:4). **naked and barefoot.** The Lord commanded stripping off all of his outer garments as an act denoting disgrace and humiliation.

20:3 My servant. This designation places Isaiah among a select group: Others include: Abraham (Gen. 26:24); Moses (Num. 12:7,8; Josh. 1:2,7; 2 Kin. 21:8; Mal. 4:4); Caleb (Num. 14:24); David (2 Sam. 3:18; 7:5,8; 1 Kin. 11:32,34,36,38; 14:8; 2 Kin. 19:34; 20:6; 1 Chr. 17:4,7; Ps. 89:3; Is. 37:35; Jer. 33:21,22,26; Ezek. 34:23,24; Ezek. 37:24,25); Job (Job 1:8; 2:3; 42:7,8); Eliakim (22:20); the Servant of the Lord (42:1; 49:5,6,7; 52:13; 53:11; Zech. 3:8; Matt. 12:18); Israel (41:8,9; 42:19; 43:10; 44:1,2,21,26; 44:21; 45:4; 48:20; 50:10; Jer. 30:10; 46:27,28; Ezek. 28:25; 37:25); Nebuchadnezzar (Jer. 25:9; 27:6; 43:10); Zerubbabel (Hag. 2:23); and Christ's follower (John 12:26). **sign...wonder.** Isaiah's nakedness and bare feet symbolized the coming desolation and shame of Egypt and Ethiopia at the hands of the Assyrians (cf. 19:4).

20:4 prisoners...captives. Esarhaddon, king of Assyria, fulfilled this prophecy in 671 B.C. (cf. 37:38; 2 Kin. 19:37; Ezra 4:2). Far from being a suitable object of Judah's trust, mighty Egypt will go off in shame.

20:6 how shall we escape? "We" refers to the people of Judah. Trust in Egypt has proven itself misplaced. Is there any adequate source of help?

21:1 Wilderness of the Sea. The prophet referred to an area of southern Babylon near the Persian Gulf known for its fertility. **As whirlwinds in the South.** The simile drew from the suddenness with which storm winds come from the Negev and sweep through the land of Israel. So sudden is to be Babylon's overthrow.

21:2 Elam...Media. The Elamites and Medes were part of the Persian army that defeated Babylon in 539 B.C.

21:3,4 pain...pangs...fearfulness...fear. The severity of the violence about which Isaiah must prophesy caused him extreme agitation.

21:5 eat and drink...anoint the shield! This part of the oracle recalled Belshazzar's feast in Dan. 5, when amid the celebration came a call to fight the attacking enemy invading the city.

6 For thus has the Lord said to me:
"Go, set a watchman,
Let him declare what he sees."
7 And he saw a chariot *with* a pair of
horsemen,
A chariot of donkeys, *and* a chariot
of camels,
And he listened earnestly with
great care.
8 [3]Then he cried, "A lion, my Lord!
I stand continually on the
[h]watchtower in the daytime;
I have sat at my post every night.
9 And look, here comes a chariot of
men *with* a pair of
horsemen!"
Then he answered and said,
[i]"Babylon is fallen, is fallen!
And [j]all the carved images of her
gods
He has broken to the ground."

10 [k]Oh, my threshing and the grain of
my floor!
That which I have heard from the
LORD of hosts,
The God of Israel,
I have declared to you.

Proclamation Against Edom

11 [l]The [4]burden against Dumah.

He calls to me out of [m]Seir,
"Watchman, what of the night?
Watchman, what of the night?"
12 The watchman said,
"The morning comes, and also the
night.
If you will inquire, inquire;
Return! Come back!"

Proclamation Against Arabia

13 [n]The [5]burden against Arabia.

In the forest in Arabia you will
lodge,
O you traveling companies [o]of
Dedanites.
14 O inhabitants of the land of Tema,
Bring water to him who is thirsty;
With their bread they met him who
fled.
15 For they fled from the swords,
from the drawn sword,
From the bent bow, and from the
distress of war.

16 For thus the LORD has said to me:
"Within a year, [p]according to the year of a
hired man, all the glory of [q]Kedar will fail;
17 and the remainder of the number of
archers, the mighty men of the people of
Kedar, will be diminished; for the LORD
God of Israel has spoken *it*."

Proclamation Against Jerusalem

22 The [1]burden against the Valley of
Vision.

What ails you now, that you have
all gone up to the housetops,
2 You who are full of noise,

8 [h] Hab. 2:1 [3] DSS *Then the observer cried, "My Lord!*
9 [i] Is. 13:19; 47:5, 9; 48:14; Jer. 51:8; Dan. 5:28, 31; Rev. 14:8; 18:2 [j] Is. 46:1; Jer. 50:2; 51:44
10 [k] Jer. 51:33; Mic. 4:13
11 [l] Gen. 25:14; 1 Chr. 1:30; Josh. 15:52 [m] Gen. 32:3; Jer. 49:7; Ezek. 35:2; Obad. 1 [4] *oracle, prophecy*
13 [n] Jer. 25:24; 49:28 [o] Gen. 10:7; 1 Chr. 1:9, 32; Jer. 25:23; Ezek. 27:15 [5] *oracle, prophecy*
16 [p] Is. 16:14 [q] Ps. 120:5; Song 1:5; Is. 42:11; 60:7; Ezek. 27:21

CHAPTER 22

1 [1] *oracle, prophecy*

21:6 set a watchman. Isaiah stationed a watchman on the city walls.

21:7 chariot...chariot...chariot. Isaiah heard the watchman warn of an approaching military force.

21:8 he cried, "A lion, my Lord." The Dead Sea Scrolls correctly read, "the watchman cried, my LORD." The watchman whom Isaiah had stationed (v. 6) continued his report.

21:9 Babylon is fallen, is fallen! The watchman proclaimed the tragic end of mighty Babylon, which initially fell to the Assyrians in 689 B.C. and again to the Persians in 539 B.C. Yet Isaiah's prediction looked forward to the ultimate fall of the great enemy of God, as verified by John's citation of this verse in Rev. 14:8; 18:2 (cf. Jer. 50:2; 51:8,49).

21:10 my threshing and the grain of my floor! The violent threshing of grain portrayed Babylon's oppression of Israel, and the resultant grain was Israel's deliverance by God. The concise saying offered God's people hope.

21:11 Dumah. This oasis in northern Arabia stood at the intersection of two important routes, one E-W from the Persian Gulf to Petra and the other N-S between the Red Sea and Tadmor. It was about 300 mi. S of Jerusalem. **Seir.** Another name for Edom—located S of the Dead Sea and the home of Esau's descendants—this is the source of an inquiry directed to Isaiah. **what of the night?** How long was the Assyrian oppression to last?

21:12 morning...night. The prophet promises a short-lived deliverance from Assyrian oppression, but quickly added the threat of Babylonian domination to follow soon.

21:13 forest. "Thicket," referring to scrub brush, is a better rendering since Arabia has few or no forests. **Dedanites.** Dedan was on the route to the Red Sea about 290 mi. SE of Dumah, in the northwestern part of the Arabian desert.

21:14 Tema. Tema was on the Red Sea route about 200 mi. SE of Dumah, in the northwestern part of the Arabian desert. **water... bread.** The prophet indicated that those fleeing the Assyrian army will need supplies.

21:15 they fled. The interior area of Arabia was a place of refuge for fugitives fleeing from the sophisticated armament of the Assyrians.

21:16 Kedar. Kedar covers the area in the northwestern part of the Arabian desert. **glory of Kedar will fail.** This prophecy anticipated the conquest of the region by Nebuchadnezzar, king of Babylon (Jer. 49:28).

22:1 Valley of Vision. This referred to Israel, since God often revealed Himself to Jerusalem in visions. However, the unrepentant inhabitants displayed a marked lack of vision in their oblivion to the destruction that awaited them. **What ails you...?** The prophet reproached the people for celebrating with wild parties when they should have been in deep repentance because of their sins. Apparently he anticipated a condition that arose in conjunction with Jerusalem's fall to the Babylonians in 586 B.C. But similar incursions by the Assyrians in either 711 or 701 B.C., from which the Lord delivered the city, had prompted the revelry among the people.

A [2]tumultuous city, [a]a joyous city?
Your slain *men are* not slain with
the sword,
Nor dead in battle.
3 All your rulers have fled together;
They are captured by the archers.
All who are found in you are
bound together;
They have fled from afar.
4 Therefore I said, "Look away from
me,
[b]I will weep bitterly;
Do not labor to comfort me
Because of the plundering of the
daughter of my people."

5 [c]For *it is* a day of trouble and
treading down and perplexity
[d]By the Lord GOD of hosts
In the Valley of Vision—
Breaking down the walls
And of crying to the mountain.
6 [e]Elam bore the quiver
With chariots of men *and*
horsemen,
And [f]Kir uncovered the shield.
7 It shall come to pass *that* your
choicest valleys
Shall be full of chariots,
And the horsemen shall set
themselves in array at the
gate.

8 [g]He removed the [3]protection of
Judah.
You looked in that day to the armor
[h]of the House of the Forest;
9 [i]You also saw the [4]damage to the
city of David,
That it was great;
And you gathered together the
waters of the lower pool.
10 You numbered the houses of
Jerusalem,
And the houses you broke down
To fortify the wall.
11 [j]You also made a reservoir between
the two walls
For the water of the old [k]pool.
But you did not look to its Maker,
Nor did you have respect for Him
who fashioned it long ago.

12 And in that day the Lord GOD of
hosts
[l]Called for weeping and for
mourning,
[m]For baldness and for girding with
sackcloth.
13 But instead, joy and gladness,
Slaying oxen and killing sheep,
Eating meat and [n]drinking wine:
[o]"Let us eat and drink, for tomorrow
we die!"

14 [p]Then it was revealed in my hearing
by the LORD of hosts,
"Surely for this iniquity there [q]will
be no atonement for you,
Even to your death," says the Lord
GOD of hosts.

The Judgment on Shebna

15 Thus says the Lord GOD of hosts:

"Go, proceed to this steward,
To [r]Shebna, *who is* over the house,
and say:

2 [a]Is. 32:13 [2]*boisterous*
4 [b]Jer. 4:19
5 [c]Is. 37:3 [d]Lam. 1:5; 2:2
6 [e]Jer. 49:35 [f]Is. 15:1
8 [g]2 Kin. 18:15, 16 [h]1 Kin. 7:2; 10:17 [3]Lit. *covering*
9 [i]2 Kin. 20:20; 2 Chr. 32:4; Neh. 3:16 [4]Lit. *breaches* in the city walls
11 [j]Neh. 3:16 [k]2 Kin. 20:20; 2 Chr. 32:3, 4
12 [l]Is. 32:11; Joel 1:13; 2:17 [m]Ezra 9:3; Is. 15:2; Mic. 1:16
13 [n]Is. 5:11, 22; 28:7, 8; Luke 17:26–29 [o]Is. 56:12; 1 Cor. 15:32
14 [p]Is. 5:9 [q]1 Sam. 3:14; Ezek. 24:13
15 [r]2 Kin. 18:37; Is. 36:3

22:2 sword...battle. Death came through starvation or disease as the Babylonians besieged the city.

22:3 rulers have fled. Rather than defend the city the way they ought, the leaders fled to save their own necks and in doing so, were captured (2 Kin. 25:4-7).

22:4 weep bitterly. Isaiah's pain was deep. He could not participate in the revelry because he saw the reality of the spiritual issues.

22:5 day...Lord GOD of hosts. On a former occasion when the city was about to fall, terror had reigned among the citizens. It was to occur again, leaving no room for merriment.

22:6 Elam...Kir. These lands had representatives in the Assyrian army that besieged Jerusalem.

22:7 choicest valleys. Valleys lying both in and around Jerusalem are to be full of enemy troops.

22:8 House of the Forest. Constructed by Solomon out of cedars (1 Kin. 7:2-6), the structure housed weaponry (1 Kin. 10:17) and other valuables (2 Chr. 9:20; Is. 39:2).

22:9 city of David. Jerusalem bore this name (2 Sam. 5:6,7,9). *See note on 29:1.* **lower pool.** The pool of Siloam furnished the city's water supply. Hezekiah's lengthy underground conduit fed the pool from the Gihon Spring.

22:10 fortify the wall. Hezekiah rebuilt the damaged wall (2 Chr. 32:5), but did so while trusting God. His faith contrasts with that of the people Isaiah currently addresses (v. 11b).

22:11 old pool. This refers to the Gihon Spring, which the prophet sometimes referred to as the "upper pool" (7:3; 36:2; cf. 2 Kin. 18:17). **did not look to its Maker.** Preparations for the city's defense were purely external. The people gave no thought to the Creator of the city, the pool, or the present crisis (cf. 31:1), against whom their physical defenses were useless.

22:12,13 sackcloth...joy and gladness. In the face of a crisis that required genuine repentance, the people responded with hilarity and self-indulgence. Contrast this spirit with the legitimate joy and gladness of God's people in 35:10; 51:11.

22:13 Let us eat and drink, for tomorrow we die! Paul cites the same philosophy (1 Cor. 15:32): If there is no resurrection, enjoyment in this life is all that matters. It utterly disregards God's eternal values.

22:14 no atonement. The Lord's prediction about the outcome of Isaiah's ministry (6:9,10) found fulfillment.

22:15 Shebna, who *is* over the house. Possibly of Egyptian extraction, this man was second in authority only to the king. Other OT references to Shebna refer to him as a "scribe" (36:22; 37:2; 2 Kin. 18:37; 19:2), his position after his demotion from steward as prophesied by Isaiah (see v. 19).

16 'What have you here, and whom
have you here,
That you have hewn a sepulcher
here,
As he [s]who hews himself a
sepulcher on high,
Who carves a tomb for himself in a
rock?
17 Indeed, the LORD will throw you
away violently,
O mighty man,
[t]And will surely seize you.
18 He will surely turn violently and
toss you like a ball
Into a large country;
There you shall die, and there
[u]your glorious chariots
Shall be the shame of your master's
house.
19 So I will drive you out of your
office,
And from your position [5]he will
pull you down.
20 'Then it shall be in that day,
That I will call My servant
[v]Eliakim the son of Hilkiah;
21 I will clothe him with your robe
And strengthen him with your belt;
I will commit your responsibility
into his hand.
He shall be a father to the
inhabitants of Jerusalem
And to the house of Judah.
22 The key of the house of David
I will lay on his [w]shoulder;
So he shall [x]open, and no one shall
shut;
And he shall shut, and no one shall
open.
23 I will fasten him *as* [y]a peg in a
secure place,
And he will become a glorious
throne to his father's house.

24 'They will hang on him all the glory of
his father's house, the offspring and the
posterity, all vessels of small quantity, from
the cups to all the pitchers. 25 In that day,'
says the LORD of hosts, 'the peg that is fastened in the secure place will be removed
and be cut down and fall, and the burden
that *was* on it will be cut off; for the LORD
has spoken.' "

Proclamation Against Tyre

23 The [a]burden[1] against Tyre.

Wail, you ships of Tarshish!
For it is laid waste,
So that there is no house, no
harbor;
From the land of [2]Cyprus it is
revealed to them.

2 Be still, you inhabitants of the
coastland,
You merchants of Sidon,
[3]Whom those who cross the sea
have filled.
3 And on great waters the grain of
Shihor,

16 [s] 2 Sam. 18:18; 2 Chr. 16:14; Matt. 27:60
17 [t] Esth. 7:8
18 [u] Is. 2:7
19 [5] LXX omits *he will pull you down;* Syr., Tg., Vg. *I will pull you down*
20 [v] 2 Kin. 18:18; Is. 36:3, 22; 37:2
22 [w] Is. 9:6
[x] Job 12:14; Rev. 3:7
23 [y] Ezra 9:8; Zech. 10:4

CHAPTER 23

1 [a] Jer. 25:22; 47:4; Ezek. 26–28; Amos 1:9; Zech. 9:2, 4
[1] oracle, prophecy
[2] Heb. *Kittim,* western lands, especially Cyprus
2 [3] So with MT, Vg.; LXX, Tg. *Passing over the water;* DSS *Your messengers passing over the sea*

22:16 hewn a sepulcher. Shebna arranged construction of a tomb fit for a king as a memorial for himself, when he should have been attending to the spiritual affairs of Judah. The prophet condemns his arrogance.

22:17 mighty man. Isaiah referred to Shebna's glorious estimate of himself.

22:18 large country...die...shame. Far from receiving a luxurious burial in Jerusalem, Shebna died a shameful death in a foreign country.

22:19 drive you out of your office. Arrogance caused Shebna's demotion from steward to scribe some time later in Hezekiah's reign but before 701 B.C. (36:1,2).

22:20 My servant Eliakim. Eliakim, who replaced Shebna as steward or prime minister, was highly honored in being called "My servant" (*see note on 20:3*).

22:21 father...Judah. The steward had supreme authority under the king's oversight.

22:22 key of the house of David. This authority to admit or refuse admittance into the king's presence evidenced the king's great confidence in Eliakim. Jesus applied this terminology to Himself as one who could determine who would enter His future Davidic kingdom (Rev. 3:7).

22:23 a glorious throne. The "throne" symbolized the honor Eliakim was to bring to his family.

22:24 hang on him. Returning to the figure of a peg (v. 23), Isaiah noted how Eliakim's posterity will use him to gain glory for themselves.

22:25 peg...removed. After a time of faithful service, Eliakim faltered and fell, and all "hanging" on him fell as well.

23:1 Tyre. A Phoenician seaport on the Mediterranean Sea, located about 35 mi. N of Mt. Carmel and 28 mi. W of Mt. Hermon, Tyre supplied lumber for King Solomon's temple (1 Kin. 5:1,7-12) and sailors for his navy (1 Kin. 9:26,27). **ships of Tarshish.** Tarshish was most likely in Spain, so "ships of Tarshish" were large trading vessels capable of making distant voyages on the open sea all the way to the port of Tyre. The OT refers to them frequently (2:16; 60:9; 1 Kin. 10:22; 22:48; Ps. 48:7; Ezek. 27:25; Jon. 1:3). **laid waste.** Tyre was under siege 5 times between this prophecy and 332 B.C. Only the last of these attacks (in 332 B.C., by Alexander the Great) completely leveled and subdued the city. Ezekiel prophesied this destruction in Ezek. 26:3–27:36. **no house, no harbor.** Weary from their long, difficult journey, sailors would find no customary haven of rest upon arrival at their destination, Tyre. **Cyprus.** Upon reaching this island in the eastern Mediterranean, the seamen would learn of Tyre's overthrow.

23:2 Sidon. Sidon was the other important Phoenician seaport, along with Tyre. Here it represented the rest of Phoenicia as reflecting the country's response to Tyre's overthrow.

23:3 Shihor...the River. Phoenicians carried much grain grown in Egypt—represented by "Shihor"—aboard their ships. They also bought and sold much of the commodity.

The harvest of [4]the River, *is* her
revenue;
And [b]she is a marketplace for the
nations.

4 Be ashamed, O Sidon;
For the sea has spoken,
The strength of the sea, saying,
"I do not labor, nor bring forth
children;
Neither do I rear young men,
Nor bring up virgins."
5 [c]When the report *reaches* Egypt,
They also will be in agony at the
report of Tyre.

6 Cross over to Tarshish;
Wail, you inhabitants of the
coastland!
7 *Is* this your [d]joyous *city,*
Whose antiquity *is* from ancient
days,
Whose feet carried her far off to
dwell?
8 Who has taken this counsel against
Tyre, [e]the crowning *city,*
Whose merchants *are* princes,
Whose traders *are* the honorable of
the earth?
9 The LORD of hosts has [f]purposed it,
To [5]bring to dishonor the [g]pride of
all glory,
To bring into contempt all the
honorable of the earth.

10 Overflow through your land like
[6]the River,
O daughter of Tarshish;
There is no more [7]strength.
11 He stretched out His hand over the
sea,
He shook the kingdoms;
The LORD has given a
commandment [h]against
Canaan
To destroy its strongholds.
12 And He said, "You will rejoice no
more,
O you oppressed virgin daughter
of Sidon.
Arise, [i]cross over to Cyprus;
There also you will have no rest."

13 Behold, the land of the [j]Chaldeans,
This people *which* was not;
Assyria founded it for [k]wild beasts
of the desert.
They set up its towers,
They raised up its palaces,
And brought it to ruin.

14 [l]Wail, you ships of Tarshish!
For your strength is laid waste.

15 Now it shall come to pass in that day
that Tyre will be forgotten seventy years,
according to the days of one king. At the
end of seventy years it will happen to Tyre
as *in* the song of the harlot:

16 "Take a harp, go about the city,
You forgotten harlot;
Make sweet melody, sing many
songs,
That you may be remembered."

17 And it shall be, at the end of seventy
years, that the LORD will deal with Tyre.
She will return to her hire, and [m]commit
fornication with all the kingdoms of the
world on the face of the earth. 18 Her gain
and her pay [n]will be set apart for the LORD;
it will not be treasured nor laid up, for her
gain will be for those who dwell before the
LORD, to eat sufficiently, and for [8]fine
clothing.

3 [b]Ezek. 27:3-23 [4]The Nile
5 [c]Is. 19:16
7 [d]Is. 22:2; 32:13
8 [e]Ezek. 28:2, 12
9 [f]Is. 14:26 [g]Job 40:11, 12; Is. 13:11; 24:4; Dan. 4:37 [5]*pollute*
10 [6]The Nile [7]*restraint,* lit. *belt*
11 [h]Zech. 9:2-4
12 [i]Ezek. 26:13, 14; Rev. 18:22
13 [j]Is. 47:1 [k]Ps. 72:9
14 [l]Ezek. 27:25-30
17 [m]Rev. 17:2
18 [n]Ex. 28:36; Zech. 14:20, 21 [8]*choice*

23:4 labor…bring forth children. Isaiah spoke of barrenness, labor, and childbirth frequently (7:14; 8:3; 9:6; 26:16-18; 37:3; 44:3-5; 45:10,11; 47:8; 49:21; 54:1-3; 66:9). Here the figure described Tyre, "the strength of the sea," bemoaning her desolate condition.

23:7 from ancient days. Tyre was a very old city, dating from about two millennia before Christ.

23:6,7 Tarshish…far off to dwell. Tyre's refugees had traveled throughout the Mediterranean world (see v. 1). They too lamented the city's fall.

23:8 crowning *city*…princes…honorable. Tyre had very high international prestige.

23:9 the pride of all glory. This furnished the reason the Lord of Hosts brought the overthrow of Tyre—their arrogance stemming from the city's prestige. They were foolish to rely on human glory.

23:10 no more strength. The oracle invited the colonies of Tyre to exercise their freedom in taking advantage of the city's fall.

23:11 the LORD has given a commandment against Canaan. The Lord had caused the downfall of the territory of Canaan, which included Tyre and Sidon.

23:12 virgin daughter of Sidon. A city once noted for its freshness and revelry (cf. v. 7) will become like a used-up old woman, piecing together what is left. God used the Assyrians to crush her (contrast the virgin daughter of Zion in 37:22).

23:13 Chaldeans…Assyria. The example of the Chaldeans, another name for the Babylonians, reminded Tyre of their hopelessness against Assyria. Assyria ravaged Babylon in 689 B.C.

23:15 seventy years. The devastation of Tyre was not permanent. A little village remains on the site of the ancient city to the present day. The time frame of the 70 years is obscure.

23:15,16 song of the harlot…forgotten…remembered. Harlots sang to draw attention to themselves, attention not so hard to obtain in ancient days. Like those harlots, the people of Tyre were invited to sing songs drawing attention to their earlier prosperity.

23:17 the LORD will deal. With God's help, the city was to return.

23:18 set apart for the LORD. Even Tyre's sinful gain was to support Judah as her colonies once supported her.

Impending Judgment on the Earth

24 Behold, the LORD makes the earth
empty and makes it waste,
Distorts its surface
And scatters abroad its inhabitants.
2 And it shall be:
As with the people, so with the
[a]priest;
As with the servant, so with his
master;
As with the maid, so with her
mistress;
[b]As with the buyer, so with the
seller;
As with the lender, so with the
borrower;
As with the creditor, so with the
debtor.
3 The land shall be entirely emptied
and utterly plundered,
For the LORD has spoken this word.

4 The earth mourns *and* fades away,
The world languishes *and* fades
away;
The [c]haughty[1] people of the earth
languish.
5 [d]The earth is also defiled under its
inhabitants,
Because they have [e]transgressed
the laws,
Changed the ordinance,
Broken the [f]everlasting covenant.
6 Therefore [g]the curse has devoured
the earth,
And those who dwell in it are
[2]desolate.
Therefore the inhabitants of the
earth are [h]burned,
And few men *are* left.

7 [i]The new wine fails, the vine
languishes,
All the merry-hearted sigh.
8 The mirth [j]of the tambourine
ceases,
The noise of the jubilant ends,
The joy of the harp ceases.
9 They shall not drink wine with a
song;
Strong drink is bitter to those who
drink it.
10 The city of confusion is broken
down;
Every house is shut up, so that
none may go in.
11 *There is* a cry for wine in the
streets,
All joy is darkened,
The mirth of the land is gone.
12 In the city desolation is left,
And the gate is stricken with
destruction.
13 When it shall be thus in the midst
of the land among the people,
[k]*It shall be* like the shaking of an
olive tree,
Like the gleaning of grapes when
the vintage is done.

14 They shall lift up their voice, they
shall sing;
For the majesty of the LORD
They shall cry aloud from the sea.
15 Therefore [l]glorify the LORD in the
dawning light,
[m]The name of the LORD God of Israel
in the coastlands of the sea.
16 From the ends of the earth we have
heard songs:
"Glory to the righteous!"
But I said, [3]"I am ruined, ruined!
Woe to me!

CHAPTER 24

2 [a] Hos. 4:9 [b] Ezek. 7:12, 13
4 [c] Is. 25:11 [1] *proud*
5 [d] Gen. 3:17; Num. 35:33; Is. 9:17; 10:6 [e] Is. 59:12 [f] 1 Chr. 16:14-19; Ps. 105:7-12
6 [g] Mal. 4:6 [h] Is. 9:19 [2] *Or held guilty*
7 [i] Is. 16:8-10; Joel 1:10, 12
8 [j] Is. 5:12, 14; Jer. 7:34; 16:9; 25:10; Ezek. 26:13; Hos. 2:11; Rev. 18:22
13 [k] [Is. 17:5, 6; 27:12]
15 [l] Is. 25:3 [m] Mal. 1:11
16 [3] Lit. *Leanness to me, leanness to me*

24:1–27:13 These 4 chapters give praise to God for His future victory over all enemies and the final deliverance of Israel in the Day of the Lord. The judgments in this chapter (24) look forward to the tribulation as described in Rev. 6ff.

24:1 empty...waste, distorts...scatters. The prophet generalized and broadened the destruction about which he had written more specifically in chaps. 13–23. The Lord is to deal with the whole earth more severely than He did at the tower of Babel or through the Noahic Flood.

24:2 people...priest...creditor...debtor. Neither rank, wealth, nor power were able to deliver from God's judgment.

24:3 the LORD has spoken. Isaiah used this expression or a comparable one 9 other times to emphasize the certainty of his predictions (1:20; 21:17; 22:25; 25:8; 37:22; 38:7; 38:15; 40:5; 58:14).

24:4 haughty people. The prophet again called attention to pride as the reason for God's judgment (cf. 23:9).

24:5 everlasting covenant. Likely, this referred to the Abrahamic Covenant, frequently referred to as "everlasting" (cf. Gen. 17:7,13,19; 1 Chr. 16:15,17; Pss. 105:8,10; 111:5,9), which contained devotion to God's moral law and salvation by faith in Him.

24:6 few men *are* left. This Gentile remnant differed from that of Israel. Presumably they will join in support of Israel when the Messiah returns.

24:7-9 merry-hearted sigh. The future day of judgment will terminate all merriment derived from natural sources. Cf. Rev. 18:22.

24:10 Every house. Houses normally provided security from outside harm, but they became inaccessible.

24:13 shaking of an olive tree. The same figure spoke of leanness in the judgment against Ephraim in 17:6.

24:14 lift up their voice...sing. The songs of the godly remnant (cf. v. 6), celebrating God's righteous judgment, replace the drunken music (cf. v. 9).

24:15 glorify the LORD. This call summoned all people worldwide to attribute to the Lord what was due Him.

24:16 Glory to the righteous! "Righteous" refers to God. **But I.** Isaiah could yet join in the celebration of God's glory because he pondered the grief and corruption in the world before that final celebration of God's victory.

[n]The treacherous dealers have dealt
treacherously,
Indeed, the treacherous dealers
have dealt very
treacherously."
17 [o]Fear and the pit and the snare
Are upon you, O inhabitant of the
earth.
18 And it shall be
That he who flees from the noise of
the fear
Shall fall into the pit,
And he who comes up from the
midst of the pit
Shall be [4]caught in the snare;
For [p]the windows from on high are
open,
And [q]the foundations of the earth
are shaken.
19 [r]The earth is violently broken,
The earth is split open,
The earth is shaken exceedingly.
20 The earth shall [s]reel[5] to and fro
like a drunkard,
And shall totter like a hut;
Its transgression shall be heavy
upon it,
And it will fall, and not rise again.
21 It shall come to pass in that day
That the LORD will punish on high
the host of exalted ones,
And on the earth [t]the kings of the
earth.
22 They will be gathered together,
As prisoners are gathered in the
[6]pit,
And will be shut up in the prison;
After many days they will be
punished.
23 Then the [u]moon will be disgraced
And the sun ashamed;
For the LORD of hosts will [v]reign
On [w]Mount Zion and in Jerusalem
And before His elders, gloriously.

16 [n] Is. 21:2; 33:1; Jer. 3:20; 5:11
17 [o] Jer. 48:43; Amos 5:19
18 [p] Gen. 7:11 [q] Ps. 18:7; 46:2; Is. 2:19, 21; 13:13 [4] Lit. *taken*
19 [r] Jer. 4:23
20 [s] Is. 19:14; 24:1; 28:7 [5] *stagger*
21 [t] Ps. 76:12
22 [6] *dungeon*
23 [u] Is. 13:10; 60:19; Ezek. 32:7; Joel 2:31; 3:15 [v] Rev. 19:4, 6 [w] [Heb. 12:22]

Praise to God

25 O LORD, You *are* my God.
[a]I will exalt You,
I will praise Your name,
[b]For You have done wonderful
things;
[c]*Your* counsels of old *are* faithfulness
and truth.
2 For You have made [d]a city a ruin,
A fortified city a ruin,
A palace of foreigners to be a city
no more;
It will never be rebuilt.
3 Therefore the strong people will
[e]glorify You;
The city of the [1]terrible nations
will fear You.
4 For You have been a strength to the
poor,
A strength to the needy in his
distress,
[f]A refuge from the storm,
A shade from the heat;
For the blast of the terrible ones *is*
as a storm *against* the wall.
5 You will reduce the noise of aliens,
As heat in a dry place;
As heat in the shadow of a cloud,
The song of the terrible ones will
be [2]diminished.
6 And in [g]this mountain

CHAPTER 25

1 [a] Ex. 15:2 [b] Ps. 98:1 [c] Num. 23:19
2 [d] Is. 21:9; 23:13; Jer. 51:37
3 [e] Is. 24:15; Rev. 11:13 [1] *terrifying*
4 [f] Is. 4:6
5 [2] *humbled*
6 [g] [Is. 2:2-4; 56:7]

24:17,18 pit…snare. The figure of an animal caught in a trap set by humans frequently symbolized the principle that life is a series of inescapable traps (2 Sam. 22:6; Job 18:8-10; 22:10; Pss. 18:5; 64:5; 106:36; 124:7; Jer. 48:43,44; Lam. 3:47; Amos 5:19).

24:18 windows from on high. In Noah's day, God judged with a flood (Gen. 7:11). He will judge again from heaven, but not with a flood. Cf. Rev. 6:13,14; 8:3-13; 16:1-21. **foundations of the earth.** Unparalleled earthquakes will mark the future visitation during and after the fulfillment of Daniel's 70-week prophecy (*see note on 13:13*; cf. Matt. 24:7; Rev. 6:12,14; 8:5; 11:19; 16:18).

24:20 drunkard…hut. Two more comparisons picture the ultimate collapse of the presumably strong and dependable planet earth: a staggering drunkard and a flimsy lean-to hut.

24:21 the host of exalted ones…kings. In the climactic phase of the Day of the Lord, He will strike against rebelling forces, both angelic (Eph. 6:12) and human. *See note on 2:12.*

24:22 shut up in the prison. The NT teaches more about the imprisonment of fallen angels before their final assignment to the lake of fire (2 Pet. 2:4; Jude 6; Rev. 9:2,3,11; 11:7; 17:8; 20:1-10). It does the same regarding unbelieving humans (Luke 16:19-31; Rev. 20:11-15).

24:23 moon…disgraced…sun ashamed. In the eternal state after Christ's millennial reign, the glory of God and of the Lamb will replace the sun and moon as sources of light (Rev. 21:23). **reign…in Jerusalem.** In Rev. 11:15-17; 19:6,16 (cf. Luke 1:31-33), John confirmed this clear prophecy of Messiah's future earthly reign in Jerusalem.

25:1 wonderful *things; Your* counsels of old. Isaiah responded to God's final judgment of the world (chap. 24) with praise to Him for planning His actions long before their implementation.

25:2 a city a ruin…never be rebuilt. The prophet did not stipulate which city, but a prophecy of Babylon's final destruction is in keeping with the context (21:9; cf. Jer. 51:37; Rev. 18).

25:3 strong people…terrible nations. When Christ reigns on earth, nations from the whole world will glorify and fear Him (see 24:14-16).

25:4 poor…needy. Another indicator of God's worthiness to be glorified is His upholding of the oppressed (cf. 11:4; 14:32).

25:4,5 storm…heat. Two weather extremes of Judah's climate illustrate how God will harbor the poor and needy: the sudden thunderstorm and the relentless heat.

25:6 this mountain. In the kingdom the Lord will host His great banquet on Mt. Zion for the faithful remnant (*see notes on 1:27; 2:2*).

[h]The LORD of hosts will make for
[i]all people
A feast of [3]choice pieces,
A feast of [4]wines on the lees,
Of fat things full of marrow,
Of well-refined wines on the lees.
7 And He will destroy on this
mountain
The surface of the covering cast
over all people,
And [j]the veil that is spread over all
nations.
8 He will [k]swallow up death forever,
And the Lord GOD will [l]wipe away
tears from all faces;
The rebuke of His people
He will take away from all the
earth;
For the LORD has spoken.

9 And it will be said in that day:
"Behold, this *is* our God;
[m]We have waited for Him, and He
will save us.
This *is* the LORD;
We have waited for Him;
[n]We will be glad and rejoice in His
salvation."

10 For on this mountain the hand of
the LORD will rest,
And [o]Moab shall be trampled
down under Him,
As straw is trampled down for the
refuse heap.
11 And He will spread out His hands
in their midst
As a swimmer reaches out to
swim,
And He will bring down their
[p]pride
Together with the trickery of their
hands.
12 The [q]fortress of the high fort of
your walls
He will bring down, lay low,
And bring to the ground, down to
the dust.

A Song of Salvation

26 In [a]that day this song will be sung
in the land of Judah:

"We have a strong city;
[b]*God* will appoint salvation *for* walls
and bulwarks.
2 [c]Open the gates,
That the righteous nation which
[1]keeps the truth may enter in.
3 You will keep *him* in perfect
[d]peace,
Whose mind *is* stayed *on You,*
Because he trusts in You.
4 Trust in the LORD forever,
[e]For in YAH, the LORD, *is*
[2]everlasting strength.
5 For He brings [3]down those who
dwell on high,
[f]The lofty city;
He lays it low,
He lays it low to the ground,
He brings it down to the dust.
6 The foot shall [4]tread it down—
The feet of the poor
And the steps of the needy."

7 The way of the just *is* uprightness;
[g]O Most Upright,
You [5]weigh the path of the just.

6 [h] Prov. 9:2; Matt. 22:4 [i] [Dan. 7:14; Matt. 8:11] [3] Lit. *fat things* [4] *wines matured on the sediment*
7 [j] 2 Cor. 3:15; [Eph. 4:18]
8 [k] [Hos. 13:14; 1 Cor. 15:54; Rev. 20:14] [l] Is. 30:19; Rev. 7:17; 21:4
9 [m] Gen. 49:18; Is. 8:17; 26:8; [Titus 2:13] [n] Ps. 20:5
10 [o] Is. 16:14; Jer. 48:1-47; Ezek. 25:8-11; Amos 2:1-3; Zeph. 2:9
11 [p] Is. 24:4; 26:5
12 [q] Is. 26:5

CHAPTER 26

1 [a] Is. 2:11; 12:1 [b] Is. 60:18
2 [c] Ps. 118:19, 20 [1] Or *remains faithful*
3 [d] Is. 57:19; [Phil. 4:6, 7]
4 [e] Is. 12:2; 45:17 [2] Or *Rock of Ages*
5 [f] Is. 25:11, 12 [3] *low*
6 [4] *trample*
7 [g] Ps. 37:23 [5] Or *make level*

25:7 covering…veil. God will remove the death shrouds from those in attendance at His banquet.

25:8 swallow up death. God will swallow up death, which itself functions as a swallower of human beings (5:14; Prov. 1:12). Paul notes the fulfillment of this promise in the resurrection of Christ (1 Cor. 15:54). **wipe away tears.** The Lord God will remove the sorrow associated with death (cf. 65:19). Revelation alludes to the tender action of this verse twice—once in 7:17 to describe the bliss of the redeemed in heaven, and once in 21:4 to describe ideal conditions in the New Jerusalem. **rebuke…He will take away.** Israel will be the head of the nations and no longer the tail (Deut. 28:13).

25:9 waited for Him. To wait for God entails an ultimate trust in Him, not becoming impatient when His timetable for final salvation differs from ours (cf. 26:8; 33:2; 40:31).

25:10 Moab. Moab represented the rest of the nations as does Edom elsewhere (34:5-15; 63:1-6; Obad. 1-9).

25:12 fortress…high fort…walls. Moabite cities had highly fortified and elevated walls. Even these will not withstand God's judgment.

26:1-4 The redeemed remnant will sing praise to God over their impregnable city, Jerusalem.

26:1 strong city. In contrast to the typical city of confusion (24:10; 25:2; 26:5) that was doomed, God has a future city of prominence, the millennial Jerusalem (Zech. 14:11).

26:2 Open the gates. Isaiah envisions the future Jerusalem, where only righteous Israel may enter. The redeemed remnant from other nations will come periodically to worship (Zech. 14:16-19).

26:3 perfect peace…trusts in You. A fixed disposition of trust in the Lord brings a peace that the wicked can never know (48:22; 57:21). Such reliance precludes double mindedness (James 1:6-8) and serving two masters (Matt. 6:24).

26:4 everlasting strength. Lit. the expression is "Rock of Ages," a rocky cliff where the trusting one may find shelter from attackers (cf. 12:2).

26:5,6 those who dwell on high…poor. The arrogant inhabit the lofty city during its overthrow; the humble inhabit the strong city (v. 1) in its exaltation (cf. James 1:9,10; 1 Pet. 5:5).

26:7 uprightness…weigh. The Heb. for "uprightness" means "straight," and the meaning of "weigh" is "make level." In a land of hilly, twisting roads, he spoke of a straight and level path for the feet of the poor and needy (cf. 40:3,4; 42:16; 45:13).

8 Yes, [h]in the way of Your
judgments,
O LORD, we have [i]waited for You;
The desire of *our* soul *is* for Your
name
And for the remembrance of You.
9 [j]With my soul I have desired You in
the night,
Yes, by my spirit within me I will
seek You early;
For when Your judgments *are* in
the earth,
The inhabitants of the world will
learn righteousness.

10 [k]Let grace be shown to the wicked,
Yet he will not learn righteousness;
In [l]the land of uprightness he will
deal unjustly,
And will not behold the majesty of
the LORD.
11 LORD, *when* Your hand is lifted up,
[m]they will not see.
But they will see and be ashamed
For [6]*their* envy of people;
Yes, the fire of Your enemies shall
devour them.

12 LORD, You will establish peace for
us,
For You have also done all our
works [7]in us.
13 O LORD our God, [n]masters besides
You
Have had dominion over us;
But by You only we make mention
of Your name.
14 *They are* dead, they will not live;
They are deceased, they will not
rise.
Therefore You have punished and
destroyed them,
And made all their memory to
[o]perish.

8 [h]Is. 64:5 [i]Is. 25:9; 33:2
9 [j]Ps. 63:6; Song 3:1; Is. 50:10; Luke 6:12
10 [k]Eccl. 8:12; [Rom. 2:4] [l]Ps. 143:10
11 [m]Job 34:27; Ps. 28:5; Is. 5:12 [6]Or *Your zeal for the people*
12 [7]Or *for us*
13 [n]2 Chr. 12:8
14 [o]Eccl. 9:5; Is. 14:22
15 [p]Is. 9:3 [8]Or *ends*
16 [q]Is. 37:3; Hos. 5:15
17 [r]Is. 13:8; [John 16:21] [9]*sharp pains*
18 [s]Ps. 17:14 [1]*given birth to*
19 [t]Is. 25:8; [Ezek. 37:1-14] [u][Dan. 12:2]; Hos. 13:14 [2]So with MT, Vg.; Syr., Tg. *their dead bodies;* LXX *those in the tombs*
20 [v]Ex. 12:22, 23; [Ps. 91:1, 4] [w][Ps. 30:5; Is. 54:7, 8; 2 Cor. 4:17]

15 You have increased the nation,
O LORD,
You have [p]increased the nation;
You are glorified;
You have expanded all the
[8]borders of the land.
16 LORD, [q]in trouble they have visited
You,
They poured out a prayer *when* Your
chastening *was* upon them.
17 As [r]a woman with child
Is in pain and cries out in her
[9]pangs,
When she draws near the time of
her delivery,
So have we been in Your sight,
O LORD.
18 We have been with child, we have
been in pain;
We have, as it were, [1]brought forth
wind;
We have not accomplished any
deliverance in the earth,
Nor have [s]the inhabitants of the
world fallen.

19 [t]Your dead shall live;
Together with [2]my dead body they
shall arise.
[u]Awake and sing, you who dwell in
dust;
For your dew *is like* the dew of
herbs,
And the earth shall cast out the
dead.

Take Refuge from the Coming Judgment

20 Come, my people, [v]enter your
chambers,
And shut your doors behind you;
Hide yourself, as it were, [w]for a
little moment,
Until the indignation is past.

26:8 waited for You. The future remnant divulges the key to its redemption—their complete dependence on the Lord, not humanly devised schemes.

26:9 in the night...early. The pious long for God at all times. **judgments...learn righteousness.** God's punishing hand benefits sinners in leading them to repentance.

26:10 not learn righteousness. God evidences His love and mercy toward other wicked ones, but they turn their back on it.

26:11 they will not see...they will see. The wicked, who are blind to God's authority and imminent judgment upon them, will be conscious of His compassion for His people Israel, to their own shame.

26:12 will establish peace. Though Israel's immediate future looks bleak, Isaiah expresses strong confidence that the nation will ultimately prosper.

26:13 masters besides You. Israel's history was replete with periods of foreign domination by the likes of Egypt and Assyria.

26:14 they will not rise. These foreign overlords are to be a thing of the past; they are not to appear again on the earthly scene.

26:15 have increased the nation. With prophetic certainty from the perspective of Israel's future restoration, Isaiah saw the expansion of Israel's borders as an accomplished fact.

26:16 trouble...chastening. The hard experiences of Israel's history drove her to call on God.

26:17,18 woman with child. Israel's tumultuous history is compared to a pregnant woman in labor.

26:18 not accomplished any deliverance. All the nation's effort was to no avail because they did not depend on the Lord.

26:19 dead shall live. This speaks of the raising of corporate Israel to participate in the great future banquet (cf. Ezek. 37). Daniel 12:2 speaks of the resurrection of individual OT saints.

26:20 for a little moment. Israel's final restoration was not immediately at hand. Hence she had to continue praying in solitude for that restoration until the time of God's indignation would pass.

21 For behold, the LORD [x]comes out of
His place
To punish the inhabitants of the
earth for their iniquity;
The earth will also disclose her
[3]blood,
And will no more cover her slain.

27 In that day the LORD with His severe
sword, great and strong,
Will punish Leviathan the fleeing
serpent,
[a]Leviathan that twisted serpent;
And He will slay [b]the reptile that *is*
in the sea.

The Restoration of Israel

2 In that day [c]sing to her,
[d]"A vineyard of [1]red wine!
3 [e]I, the LORD, keep it,
I water it every moment;
Lest any hurt it,
I keep it night and day.
4 Fury *is* not in Me.
Who would set [f]briers *and* thorns
Against Me in battle?
I would go through them,
I would burn them together.
5 Or let him take hold [g]of My
strength,
That he may [h]make peace with Me;
And he shall make peace with Me."

6 Those who come He shall cause [i]to
take root in Jacob;
Israel shall blossom and bud,
And fill the face of the world with
fruit.

7 [j]Has He struck [2]Israel as He struck
those who struck him?
Or has He been slain according to
the slaughter of those who
were slain by Him?
8 [k]In measure, by sending it away,
You contended with it.
[l]He removes *it* by His rough wind
In the day of the east wind.
9 Therefore by this the iniquity of
Jacob will be covered;
And this *is* all the fruit of taking
away his sin:
When he makes all the stones of
the altar
Like chalkstones that are beaten to
dust,
[3]Wooden images and incense altars
shall not stand.

10 Yet the fortified city *will be*
[m]desolate,
The habitation forsaken and left
like a wilderness;
There the calf will feed, and there
it will lie down
And consume its branches.
11 When its boughs are withered,
they will be broken off;
The women come *and* set them on
fire.
For [n]it *is* a people of no
understanding;
Therefore He who made them will
[o]not have mercy on them,
And [p]He who formed them will
show them no favor.

12 And it shall come to pass in that
day
That the LORD will thresh,
From the channel of [4]the River to
the Brook of Egypt;
And you will be [q]gathered one by
one,
O you children of Israel.

13 [r]So it shall be in that day:
[s]The great trumpet will be blown;
They will come, who are about to
perish in the land of Assyria,

21 [x]Mic. 1:3; [Jude 14] [3]Or *bloodshed*

CHAPTER 27

1 [a]Gen. 3:1; Ps. 74:13, 14; Rev. 12:9, 15 [b]Is. 51:9; Ezek. 29:3; 32:2
2 [c]Is. 5:1 [d]Ps. 80:8; Is. 5:7; Jer. 2:21 [1]So with MT (Kittel's *Biblia Hebraica*), Bg., Vg.; MT (*Biblia Hebraica Stuttgartensia*), some Heb. mss., LXX *delight*; Tg. *choice vineyard*
3 [e]1 Sam. 2:9; Ps. 121:4, 5; Is. 31:5; [John 10:28]
4 [f]2 Sam. 23:6; Is. 9:18
5 [g]Is. 25:4 [h]Job 22:21; Is. 26:3, 12; [Rom. 5:1; 2 Cor. 5:20]
6 [i]Is. 37:31; Hos. 14:5, 6
7 [j]Is. 10:12, 17; 30:30-33 [2]Lit. *him*
8 [k]Job 23:6; Ps. 6:1; Jer. 10:24; 30:11; 46:28; [1 Cor. 10:13]
[l][Ps. 78:38]
9 [3]Heb. *Asherim*, Canaanite deities
10 [m]Is. 5:6, 17; 32:14; Jer. 26:18
11 [n]Deut. 32:28; Is. 1:3 [o]Is. 9:17 [p]Deut. 32:18; Is. 43:1, 7; 44:2, 21, 24
12 [q][Is. 11:11; 56:8] [4]The Euphrates
13 [r]Is. 2:11 [s]Lev. 25:9; 1 Chr. 15:24; Matt. 24:31; Rev. 11:15

26:21 disclose her blood. The innocent killed by their oppressors are to come to life (cf. v. 19) and testify against their murderers.

27:1 Leviathan. *See note on Job 41:1.*

27:2-6 This vineyard of the Lord contrasts sharply with the one in 5:1-7. Far from a disappointment to the vinekeeper, this one bore abundant fruit (v. 6).

27:2 vineyard. Verse 6 identifies this vineyard as Israel.

27:3 I keep it night and day. God's future provisions for restored Israel will be complete.

27:4 Fury *is* not in Me. The time for Israel's punishment by God will pass. **briers *and* thorns...burn them.** I.e., the enemies of His people.

27:5 make peace with Me. The enemies of Israel may make peace with God.

27:6 fill the face of the world. In the future kingdom of the Messiah, restored Israel will rule with Him and fill the earth with the fruit of righteousness and peace.

27:7 struck Israel as He struck. God has tempered His dealings with Israel, but not so with those He used to punish Israel. His compassion for the other nations has come to an end.

27:8 sending it away. The Lord sent Judah into captivity to awaken the nation to trust in Him.

27:9 iniquity...covered. Jacob atoned for his iniquity by undergoing punishment from God.

27:10 fortified city. The city symbolized Judah's oppressors (cf. 24:10; 25:2; 26:5).

27:11 will not have mercy on them. In contrast with His dealings with Israel, the Creator will deal a fatal blow to her enemies.

27:12 gathered one by one. After the judgment of her enemies at the end of Daniel's 70th week, the faithful remnant of Israelites will return to their Land (Matt. 24:31).

And they who are outcasts in the land of [t]Egypt,
And shall [u]worship the LORD in the holy mount at Jerusalem.

Woe to Ephraim and Jerusalem

28 Woe to the crown of pride, to the drunkards of Ephraim,
Whose glorious beauty *is* a fading flower
Which *is* at the head of the [1]verdant valleys,
To those who are overcome with wine!
2 Behold, the Lord has a mighty and strong one,
[a]Like a tempest of hail and a destroying storm,
Like a flood of mighty waters overflowing,
Who will bring *them* down to the earth with *His* hand.
3 The crown of pride, the drunkards of Ephraim,
Will be trampled underfoot;
4 And the glorious beauty is a fading flower
Which *is* at the head of the [2]verdant valley,
Like the first fruit before the summer,
Which an observer sees;
He eats it up while it is still in his hand.
5 In that day the LORD of hosts will be
For a crown of glory and a diadem of beauty
To the remnant of His people,
6 For a spirit of justice to him who sits in judgment,
And for strength to those who turn back the battle at the gate.
7 But they also [b]have erred through wine,
And through intoxicating drink are out of the way;
[c]The priest and the prophet have erred through intoxicating drink,
They are swallowed up by wine,
They are out of the way through intoxicating drink;
They err in vision, they stumble *in* judgment.
8 For all tables are full of vomit *and* filth;
No place *is clean*.
9 "Whom[d] will he teach knowledge?
And whom will he make to understand the message?
Those *just* weaned from milk?
Those *just* drawn from the breasts?
10 [e]For precept *must be* upon precept, precept upon precept,
Line upon line, line upon line,
Here a little, there a little."
11 For with [f]stammering lips and another tongue
He will speak to this people,
12 To whom He said, "This *is* the [g]rest *with which*
You may cause the weary to rest,"

13 [t]Is. 19:21, 22 [u][Is. 2:3]; Zech. 14:16; [Heb. 12:22]

CHAPTER 28

1 [1]Lit. *valleys of fatness*
2 [a]Is. 30:30; Ezek. 13:11
4 [2]Lit. *valley of fatness*
7 [b]Prov. 20:1; Is. 5:11, 22; Hos. 4:11 [c]Is. 56:10, 12
9 [d]Jer. 6:10
10 [e][2 Chr. 36:15; Neh. 9:30; Jer. 25:3, 4; 35:15; 44:4]
11 [f]Is. 33:19; 1 Cor. 14:21
12 [g]Is. 30:15; Jer. 6:16; [Matt. 11:28, 29]

27:13 worship the LORD...at Jerusalem. The prophet reiterates one of his great themes: future worship of regathered Israel on Mt. Zion (24:23; 25:6,7,10).

28:1 Woe. The prominent thought in this word is impending disaster. **crown.** The walls of Samaria were the "crown" of a beautiful hill overlooking a lush valley leading toward the Mediterranean coast. **Ephraim.** The northern kingdom of Israel had fallen to the Assyrians, leaving a lesson for Jerusalem under similar circumstances to learn about foreign alliances. **overcome with wine.** Licentious living prevailed in Ephraim before her fall (vv. 3,7; Amos 4:1; 6:1,6).

28:2 a flood of mighty waters. Isaiah drew on forceful figures of speech to wake his readers from their lethargy in the face of the awfulness of an impending Assyrian invasion.

28:4 first fruit before the summer. Figs ripened before the end-of-summer harvest were devoured immediately. So the Assyrian conquest of Ephraim would be rapid.

28:5 crown of glory. The true crown will replace the fraudulent "crown of pride" (v. 1). **remnant of His people.** Isaiah again sounded the note of a faithful remnant in the Day of the Lord (cf. 10:20-22; 11:11,16; 37:31,32; 46:3).

28:6 spirit of justice. In that day of Messiah's reign, the empowering Spirit will prevail in bringing justice to the world (cf. 11:2).

28:7 priest...prophet...err. Drunkenness had infected even the religious leadership of the nation, resulting in false spiritual guidance of the people.

28:8 no place *is clean*. When leaders wallowed in filth, what hope did the nation have?

28:9 weaned from milk. The drunken leaders resented it when Isaiah and other true prophets treated them as toddlers, by reminding them of elementary truths of right and wrong.

28:10 precept upon precept...there a little. This is the drunkard's sarcastically mocking response to corrective advice from the prophet. Transliterated, the Hebrew monosyllables are *Sav lasav, sav lasav, Kav lakav, kav lakav, Ze'er sham, ze'er sham.* These imitations of a young child's babbling ridicule Isaiah's preaching.

28:11 another tongue. Since the drunkards would not listen to God's prophet, He responded to them by predicting their subservience to Assyrian taskmasters, who would give them instructions in a foreign language. The NT divulges an additional meaning of this verse that anticipates God's use of the miraculous gift of tongues as a credential of His NT messengers (*see note on 1 Cor. 14:21,22*; cf. Deut. 28:49; Jer. 5:15; 2 Cor. 12:12).

28:12 the rest...the refreshing...not hear. In simple language they could understand, God offered them relief from their oppressors, but they would not listen.

And, "This *is* the refreshing";
Yet they would not hear.
13 But the word of the LORD was to them,
"Precept upon precept, precept upon precept,
Line upon line, line upon line,
Here a little, there a little,"
That they might go and fall backward, and be broken
And snared and caught.

14 Therefore hear the word of the LORD, you scornful men,
Who rule this people who *are* in Jerusalem,
15 Because you have said, "We have made a covenant with death,
And with Sheol we are in agreement.
When the overflowing scourge passes through,
It will not come to us,
[h]For we have made lies our refuge,
And under falsehood we have hidden ourselves."

A Cornerstone in Zion

16 Therefore thus says the Lord GOD:

"Behold, I lay in Zion [i]a stone for a foundation,
A tried stone, a precious cornerstone, a sure foundation;
Whoever believes will not act hastily.
17 Also I will make justice the measuring line,
And righteousness the plummet;
The hail will sweep away the refuge of lies,
And the waters will overflow the hiding place.
18 Your covenant with death will be annulled,
And your agreement with Sheol will not stand;
When the overflowing scourge passes through,
Then you will be trampled down by it.
19 As often as it goes out it will take you;
For morning by morning it will pass over,
And by day and by night;
It will be a terror just to understand the report."

20 For the bed is too short to stretch out *on*,
And the covering so narrow that one cannot wrap himself *in it*.
21 For the LORD will rise up as *at* Mount [j]Perazim,
He will be angry as in the Valley of [k]Gibeon—
That He may do His work, [l]His awesome work,
And bring to pass His act, His [3]unusual act.
22 Now therefore, do not be mockers,
Lest your bonds be made strong;
For I have heard from the Lord GOD of hosts,
[m]A [4]destruction determined even upon the whole earth.

15 [h] Is. 9:15; Ezek. 13:22; Amos 2:4
16 [i] Gen. 49:24; Ps. 118:22; Is. 8:14, 15; Matt. 21:42; Mark 12:10; Luke 20:17; Acts 4:11; Rom. 9:33; 10:11; Eph. 2:20; 1 Pet. 2:6-8
21 [j] 2 Sam. 5:20; 1 Chr. 14:11 [k] Josh. 10:10, 12; 2 Sam. 5:25; 1 Chr. 14:16 [l] [Lam. 3:33; Luke 19:41-44] [3] Lit. *foreign*
22 [m] Is. 10:22; Dan. 9:27 [4] Lit. *complete end*

28:13 Precept upon precept…there a little. In light of their rejection, the Lord imitated the mockery of the drunkards in jabber they could not understand (see v. 10).

28:14 Therefore. In light of the tragedies that had befallen Ephraim (vv. 1-13), the scornful leaders in Jerusalem needed to steer a course different from relying on foreign powers for deliverance.

28:15 covenant with death. Scornful leaders in Jerusalem had made an agreement with Egypt to help defend themselves against the Assyrians. **overflowing scourge.** Combining images of an overflowing river and a whip, the people bragged about their invincibility to foreign invasion. **lies…falsehood.** Jerusalem's leaders yielded to expediency for the sake of security. Without directly admitting it, they had taken refuge in deceit and falsehood.

28:16 stone for a foundation…a sure foundation. The Lord God contrasted the only sure refuge with the false refuge of relying on foreigners (v. 15). This directly prophesied the coming of the Messiah (Matt. 21:42; Mark 12:10; Luke 20:17; Acts 4:11; Rom. 9:33; Eph. 2:20; 1 Pet. 2:6-8; cf. 8:14,15; Ps. 118:22). **will not act hastily.** The Greek OT interprets this Hebrew verb for "hurry" in the sense of "put to shame," furnishing the basis of the NT citations of this verse (Rom. 9:33; 10:11; 1 Pet. 2:6).

28:17 justice the measuring line. When the Messiah rules His kingdom, the system of justice will contrast strongly with the refuge of lies in which Jerusalem's leaders engaged (see v. 15).

28:18 covenant with death…will not stand. Trusting in foreign deliverers will utterly fail (see. v. 15).

28:19 morning by morning. The Assyrians repeatedly plundered the area around Jerusalem, provoking great terror among the city's inhabitants.

28:20 bed is too short…the covering so narrow. A proverbial expression about short beds and narrow sheets, telling Jerusalem that foreign alliances are inadequate preparations for the defense of the city.

28:21 Mount Perazim…Valley of Gibeon. Just as the Lord defeated the Philistines at Mt. Perazim (2 Sam. 5:19,20; 1 Chr. 14:10,11) and the Canaanites in the Valley of Gibeon (Josh. 10:6-11), He will do so against any who mock Him, even Jerusalemites.

28:22 destruction determined. God had decreed something unusual (v. 21), the destruction of His own wicked people. Yet, they could escape if they repented.

Listen to the Teaching of God

23 Give ear and hear my voice,
Listen and hear my speech.
24 Does the plowman keep plowing all day to sow?
Does he keep turning his soil and breaking the clods?
25 When he has leveled its surface,
Does he not sow the black cummin
And scatter the cummin,
Plant the wheat in rows,
The barley in the appointed place,
And the [5]spelt in its place?
26 For He instructs him in right judgment,
His God teaches him.

27 For the black cummin is not threshed with a threshing sledge,
Nor is a cartwheel rolled over the cummin;
But the black cummin is beaten out with a stick,
And the cummin with a rod.
28 Bread *flour* must be ground;
Therefore he does not thresh it forever,
Break *it with* his cartwheel,
Or crush it *with* his horsemen.
29 This also comes from the LORD of hosts,
[n]*Who* is wonderful in counsel *and* excellent in [6]guidance.

Woe to Jerusalem

29 "Woe [a]to [1]Ariel, to Ariel, the city [b]*where* David dwelt!
Add year to year;
Let feasts come around.
2 Yet I will distress Ariel;
There shall be heaviness and sorrow,
And it shall be to Me as Ariel.
3 I will encamp against you all around,
I will lay siege against you with a mound,
And I will raise siegeworks against you.
4 You shall be brought down,
You shall speak out of the ground;
Your speech shall be low, out of the dust;
Your voice shall be like a medium's, [c]out of the ground;
And your speech shall whisper out of the dust.

5 "Moreover the multitude of your [d]foes
Shall be like fine dust,
And the multitude of the terrible ones
Like [e]chaff that passes away;
Yes, it shall be [f]in an instant, suddenly.
6 [g]You will be punished by the LORD of hosts
With thunder and [h]earthquake and great noise,
With storm and tempest
And the flame of devouring fire.
7 [i]The multitude of all the nations who fight against [2]Ariel,
Even all who fight against her and her fortress,

25 [5]*rye*
29 [n]Ps. 92:5; Is. 9:6; Jer. 32:19 [6]*sound wisdom*

CHAPTER 29

1 [a]Ezek. 24:6, 9 [b]2 Sam. 5:9 [1]Jerusalem, lit. *Lion of God*
4 [c]Is. 8:19
5 [d]Is. 25:5 [e]Job 21:18; Is. 17:13 [f]Is. 30:13; 47:11; 1 Thess. 5:3
6 [g]Is. 28:2; 30:30 [h]1 Sam. 2:10; Zech. 14:4; Matt. 24:7; Mark 13:8; Luke 21:11; Rev. 16:18, 19
7 [i]Is. 37:36; Mic. 4:11, 12; Zech. 12:9 [2]Jerusalem

28:23 Give ear. The parable of a farmer underlined the lessons of judgment threats in vv. 18-22. As the farmer does his different tasks, each in the right season and proportion, so God adopts His measures to His purposes: now mercy, then judgment; punishing sooner, then later. His purpose was not to destroy His people, any more than the farmer's object in his threshing or plowing is to destroy his crop.

28:24 keep plowing...keep turning. No ordinary farmer plows and turns the soil endlessly. He sows also in accord with what is proper.

28:25 sow...scatter...plant. After preparing the soil, the farmer carefully places the seed.

28:26 God teaches him. Farming intelligently is a God-given instinct.

28:27,28 God-given understanding prevails in the threshing of various types of grain.

28:29 excellent in guidance. If God's way in the physical realm of farming is best, why did Jerusalem persist in refusing to accept His spiritual guidance?

29:1 Ariel. The word means "lion of God," referring to the city's strength, and perhaps "hearth of God," referring to the place where the altar of God always burns. Verses 7,8 show this to be a name for Jerusalem, and the chapter looks to the invasion of Jerusalem because of unbelief. ***where* David dwelt.** David named Jerusalem "the city of David" (22:9; 2 Sam. 5:7,9; cf. 2 Sam. 6:10,12,16; 1 Kin. 2:10; 3:1; 8:1; 9:24; 14:31; 15:8; 2 Kin. 8:24; 9:28; 12:21; 14:20; 15:7,38; 16:20; 1 Chr. 11:5,7; 13:13; 15:1,29; 2 Chr. 5:2; 8:11; 12:16; 14:1; 16:14; 21:1,20; 24:16,25; 27:9; 32:5,30; 33:14; Neh. 3:15; 12:37; Luke 2:4,11). **feasts.** Jerusalem's cycle of religious ceremonies were meaningless to God.

29:3 lay siege. God encamped against Jerusalem through His instruments, first the Assyrians (701 B.C.) and then the Babylonians (586 B.C.).

29:4 out of the ground...out of the dust. Jerusalem will be like a captive, humbled to the dust. Her voice will come from the earth like that of a medium spirit, like the voice of the dead was supposed to be. This would be fitting for her sins of necromancy.

29:5-8 In God's time, after Jerusalem's punishment, those who fought against the city will themselves come under God's judgment.

29:5 in an instant, suddenly. God's demolition of Israel's enemies will be very abrupt, as was the repulsion of the Assyrians from Jerusalem in 701 B.C.

29:6 thunder and earthquake and great noise. This terminology points to the storm theophany marking the termination of the seals, trumpets, and bowls in Revelation (Rev. 8:5; 11:19; 16:18).

And distress her,
Shall be [j]as a dream of a night
vision.
8 [k]It shall even be as when a hungry
man dreams,
And look—he eats;
But he awakes, and his soul is still
empty;
Or as when a thirsty man dreams,
And look—he drinks;
But he awakes, and indeed *he is*
faint,
And his soul still craves:
So the multitude of all the nations
shall be,
Who fight against Mount Zion."

The Blindness of Disobedience

9 Pause and wonder!
Blind yourselves and be blind!
[l]They are drunk, [m]but not with wine;
They stagger, but not with
intoxicating drink.
10 For [n]the LORD has poured out on
you
The spirit of deep sleep,
And has [o]closed your eyes, namely,
the prophets;
And He has covered your heads,
namely, [p]the seers.

11 The whole vision has become to you
like the words of a [3]book [q]that is sealed,
which *men* deliver to one who is literate,
saying, "Read this, please."
[r]And he says, "I cannot, for it *is* sealed."
12 Then the book is delivered to one who
[4]is illiterate, saying, "Read this, please."
And he says, "I am not literate."
13 Therefore the Lord said:

7 [j]Job 20:8
8 [k]Ps. 73:20
9 [l]Is. 28:7, 8 [m]Is. 51:21
10 [n]Ps. 69:23; Is. 6:9, 10; Mic. 3:6; Rom. 11:8 [o]Ps. 69:23; Is. 6:10 [p]1 Sam. 9:9; Is. 44:18; Mic. 3:6; [2 Thess. 2:9-12]
11 [q]Is. 8:16 [r]Dan. 12:4, 9; [Matt. 13:11-16]; Rev. 5:1-5, 9
[3] *scroll*
12 [4] Lit. *does not know books*
13 [s]Ps. 78:36; Ezek. 33:31; Matt. 15:8, 9; Mark 7:6, 7 [t]Col. 2:22
14 [u]Is. 6:9, 10; 28:21; Hab. 1:5 [v]Is. 44:25; Jer. 49:7; Obad. 8; 1 Cor. 1:19
15 [w]Is. 30:1 [x]Ps. 10:11; 94:7; Is. 47:10; Ezek. 8:12; Mal. 2:17
16 [y]Is. 45:9; Jer. 18:1-6; [Rom. 9:19-21]
17 [z]Is. 32:15

[s]"Inasmuch as these people draw
near with their mouths
And honor Me [t]with their lips,
But have removed their hearts far
from Me,
And their fear toward Me is taught
by the commandment of men,
14 [u]Therefore, behold, I will again do a
marvelous work
Among this people,
A marvelous work and a wonder;
[v]For the wisdom of their wise *men*
shall perish,
And the understanding of their
prudent *men* shall be
hidden."

15 [w]Woe to those who seek deep to
hide their counsel far from
the LORD,
And their works are in the dark;
[x]They say, "Who sees us?" and,
"Who knows us?"
16 Surely you have things turned
around!
Shall the potter be esteemed as the
clay;
For shall the [y]thing made say of
him who made it,
"He did not make me"?
Or shall the thing formed say of
him who formed it,
"He has no understanding"?

Future Recovery of Wisdom

17 *Is* it not yet a very little while
Till [z]Lebanon shall be turned into a
fruitful field,
And the fruitful field be esteemed
as a forest?

29:7 dream. All the threat to the city from enemy nations will fade like a bad dream when one awakens.

29:8 empty…faint. Jerusalem's attackers will frustrate themselves, as a dreamer who has the illusion that he eats and drinks, but awakens to find himself still hungry and thirsty.

29:9-14 The prophet returned to the theme of the blindness of mechanical religion.

29:9 blind…drunk. The blindness and drunkenness came from the people's inability to comprehend Isaiah's message about trusting God instead of Egypt.

29:10 spirit of deep sleep. Because Israel refused to hear her true prophets initially, their ability to hear has been impaired. God gave them up judicially to their own hardness of heart. Paul applied this verse specifically to the general condition of Israel's blindness during the age of the church (Rom. 11:8). **prophets…seers.** False prophets and seers have blinded their listeners with their false prophecies.

29:11 one who is literate. Those with ability to read could not do so because they had surrendered their spiritual sensitivity (cf. 6:9,10; Matt. 13:10-17).

29:12 one who is illiterate. The uneducated had two reasons for not knowing the book's contents: 1) the book was sealed, and 2) he could not read it even if it were not. It is deplorable when no one is capable of receiving God's rich revelation.

29:13 hearts far from Me. Empty ritualism does not bring closeness to God. Jesus used this verse to describe the Judaism of His day (Matt. 15:7-9; Mark 7:6,7).

29:14 wisdom…perish…understanding…hidden. The principle of resorting to human wisdom rather than divine wisdom was the spiritual plague of Jerusalem. The same principle was the downfall of the Greek world in Paul's day (1 Cor. 1:19).

29:15 hide…from the LORD. The prophet probably referred to a secret plan of the leaders to join with Egypt to combat the Assyrians. The Lord had counseled otherwise, so they hid their strategy from Him.

29:16 He did not make me. For man to make plans on his own without God is a rejection of God as Creator. Paul reasons that it is also a questioning of the sovereignty of God (Rom. 9:19-21). Does the clay think itself equal to the potter?

29:17 fruitful field…a forest. In the future, a reversal of roles between the mighty and the weak will transpire, when God intervenes to bless Jerusalem. The moral change in the Jewish nation will be as great as if the usually forested Lebanon were turned into a field and vice versa.

18 [a]In that day the deaf shall hear the
words of the book,
And the eyes of the blind shall see
out of obscurity and out of
darkness.
19 [b]The humble also shall increase *their*
joy in the LORD,
And [c]the poor among men shall
rejoice
In the Holy One of Israel.
20 For the [5]terrible one is brought to
nothing,
[d]The scornful one is consumed,
And all who [e]watch for iniquity
are cut off—
21 Who make a man an offender by a
word,
And [f]lay a snare for him who
reproves in the gate,
And turn aside the just [g]by empty
words.

22 Therefore thus says the LORD, [h]who
redeemed Abraham, concerning the house
of Jacob:

"Jacob shall not now be [i]ashamed,
Nor shall his face now grow pale;
23 But when he sees his children,
[j]The work of My hands, in his
midst,
They will hallow My name,
And hallow the Holy One of Jacob,
And fear the God of Israel.
24 These also [k]who erred in spirit will
come to understanding,
And those who complained will
learn doctrine."

18 [a] Is. 35:5; Matt. 11:5; Mark 7:37
19 [b] [Ps. 25:9; 37:11; Is. 11:4; 61:1; Matt. 5:5; 11:29] [c] Is. 14:30; [Matt. 5:3; 11:5; James 2:5]
20 [d] Is. 28:14 [e] Is. 59:4; Mic. 2:1 [5] *terrifying*
21 [f] Amos 5:10, 12 [g] Prov. 28:21
22 [h] Josh. 24:3 [i] Is. 45:17
23 [j] [Is. 45:11; 49:20-26; Eph. 2:10]
24 [k] Is. 28:7

CHAPTER 30

1 [a] Is. 29:15 [b] Deut. 29:19 [1] Lit. *weave a web*
2 [c] Is. 31:1; Jer. 43:7 [d] Num. 27:21; Josh. 9:14; 1 Kin. 22:7; Jer. 21:2; 42:2, 20
3 [e] Is. 20:5; Jer. 37:5, 7
4 [f] Is. 19:11
5 [g] Jer. 2:36
6 [h] Is. 57:9; Hos. 8:9; 12:1 [i] Deut. 8:15; Is. 14:29 [2] *oracle, prophecy*
7 [j] Jer. 37:7

Futile Confidence in Egypt

30 "Woe to the rebellious children,"
says the LORD,
[a]"Who take counsel, but not of Me,
And who [1]devise plans, but not of
My Spirit,
[b]That they may add sin to sin;
2 [c]Who walk to go down to Egypt,
And [d]have not asked My advice,
To strengthen themselves in the
strength of Pharaoh,
And to trust in the shadow of
Egypt!
3 [e]Therefore the strength of Pharaoh
Shall be your shame,
And trust in the shadow of Egypt
Shall be *your* humiliation.
4 For his princes were at [f]Zoan,
And his ambassadors came to
Hanes.
5 [g]They were all ashamed of a people
who could not benefit them,
Or be help or benefit,
But a shame and also a reproach."

6 [h]The [2]burden against the beasts of the
South.

Through a land of trouble and
anguish,
From which *came* the lioness and
lion,
[i]The viper and fiery flying serpent,
They will carry their riches on the
backs of young donkeys,
And their treasures on the humps
of camels,
To a people *who* shall not profit;
7 [j]For the Egyptians shall help in
vain and to no purpose.

29:18 deaf shall hear…blind shall see. The spiritual blindness of Israel will no longer exist. Jesus gives the words an additional meaning, applying it to His ministry of physical healing for the deaf and blind (Matt. 11:5; cf. 35:5).

29:19,20 increase *their* joy…cut off. The future messianic age will bring a reversal of status. Rejoicing will replace the hardships of the oppressed; the oppressors' dominance will end.

29:21 make a man an offender…turn aside the just. Those with political and judicial authority are no longer to misuse their power to oppress.

29:22 redeemed Abraham. God delivered Abraham from his pagan background when He brought him from beyond the Euphrates River into the land of Canaan (Josh. 24:2,3). Paul elaborates on this theme in Rom. 4:1-22. **not now be ashamed.** Israel in her history had frequently suffered disgrace, but the personal presence of the Messiah is to change that (45:17; 49:23; 50:7; 54:4). After the salvation of Israel in the end time, the children of Jacob will no longer cause their forefathers to blush over their wickedness.

29:23 hallow…hallow…fear. Jacob's descendants will marvel at the strong deliverance of the Lord and set Him apart as the only one worthy of utmost respect. God will cleanse Israel (cf. 54:13,14).

29:24 erred…complained. With their newfound respect for God, the formerly wayward ones were to gain the capacity for spiritual perception.

30:1 not of Me…not of My Spirit. Hezekiah's advisers urged him to turn to the Egyptians, not to God, for help against the invading Assyrians. Isaiah denounced this reliance on Egypt rather than God, who had forbidden such alliances.

30:2 not asked My advice. They had failed to consult God's prophet. **Egypt…Pharaoh…Egypt.** The Lord had warned Israel against returning to Egypt (Deut. 17:16). Now He warns them against an alliance with Egypt (31:1). Note the similar advice from the Assyrian Rabshakeh, while laying siege to Jerusalem (36:9).

30:3 shame…humiliation. The Assyrians had already defeated the Egyptian army only 100 mi. from the Egyptian border.

30:4 Zoan…Hanes. Judah's emissaries had penetrated from Zoan in the NE of Egypt to Hanes fifty mi. S of Memphis.

30:6 land of trouble and anguish…humps of camels. Isaiah pictured a rich caravan, trudging slowly through rugged territory fraught with dangers, on its way to Egypt to purchase assistance.

30:7 help in vain…Rahab-Hem-Shebeth. Egypt was unwilling to help so the prophet calls the powerful Egypt "Rahab," meaning

Therefore I have called her
[3]Rahah-Hem-Shebeth.

A Rebellious People

8 Now go, [k]write it before them on a tablet,
And note it on a scroll,
That it may be for time to come,
Forever and ever:
9 That [l]this *is* a rebellious people,
Lying children,
Children *who* will not hear the law of the LORD;
10 [m]Who say to the seers, "Do not see,"
And to the prophets, "Do not prophesy to us right things;
[n]Speak to us smooth things, prophesy deceits.
11 Get out of the way,
Turn aside from the path,
Cause the Holy One of Israel
To cease from before us."

12 Therefore thus says the Holy One of Israel:

"Because you [o]despise this word,
And trust in oppression and perversity,
And rely on them,
13 Therefore this iniquity shall be to you
[p]Like a breach ready to fall,
A bulge in a high wall,
Whose breaking [q]comes suddenly, in an instant.
14 And [r]He shall break it like the breaking of the potter's vessel,
Which is broken in pieces;
He shall not spare.
So there shall not be found among its fragments
[4]A shard to take fire from the hearth,
Or to take water from the cistern."

15 For thus says the Lord GOD, the Holy One of Israel:

[s]"In returning and rest you shall be saved;
In quietness and confidence shall be your strength."
[t]But you would not,
16 And you said, "No, for we will flee on horses"—
Therefore you shall flee!
And, "We will ride on swift *horses*"—
Therefore those who pursue you shall be swift!
17 [u]One thousand *shall flee* at the threat of one,
At the threat of five you shall flee,
Till you are left as a [5]pole on top of a mountain
And as a banner on a hill.

God Will Be Gracious

18 Therefore the LORD will wait, that He may be [v]gracious to you;
And therefore He will be exalted, that He may have mercy on you.
For the LORD *is* a God of justice;
[w]Blessed *are* all those who [x]wait for Him.

19 For the people [y]shall dwell in Zion at Jerusalem;
You shall [z]weep no more.
He will be very gracious to you at the sound of your cry;
When He hears it, He will [a]answer you.

7 [3] Lit. *Rahab Sits Idle*
8 [k] Hab. 2:2
9 [l] Deut. 32:20; Is. 1:2, 4; 65:2
10 [m] Is. 5:20; Jer. 11:21; Amos 2:12; Mic. 2:6 [n] 1 Kin. 22:8, 13; Jer. 6:14; 23:17, 26; Ezek. 13:7; Mic. 2:11; Rom. 16:18; 2 Tim. 4:3, 4
12 [o] Lev. 26:43; Num. 15:31; Prov. 1:30; 13:13; Is. 5:24; Ezek. 20:13, 16, 24; Amos 2:4
13 [p] 1 Kin. 20:30; Ps. 62:3, 4; Is. 58:12 [q] Is. 29:5
14 [r] Ps. 2:9; Jer. 19:11

[4] A piece of broken pottery
15 [s] Ps. 116:7; Is. 7:4; 28:12 [t] Matt. 23:37
17 [u] Lev. 26:36; Deut. 28:25; 32:30; Josh. 23:10; [Prov. 28:1]
[5] A tree stripped of branches
18 [v] Is. 33:2 [w] Ps. 2:12; 34:8; Prov. 16:20; Jer. 17:7 [x] Is. 26:8
19 [y] Is. 65:9; [Ezek. 37:25, 28] [z] Is. 25:8 [a] Ps. 50:15; Is. 65:24; [Matt. 7:7-11]

"strength," or "sitting idle" (Hebrew). "Rahab" is used of Egypt in Pss. 87:4; 89:10.

30:8 for time to come. The Lord's instruction to Isaiah was to make a permanent written record so that future generations could learn Israel's folly of trusting in Egypt instead of in the Lord.

30:9 rebellious people, lying children. The people's unwillingness to obey the Lord necessitated the keeping of a permanent record of their misdeeds.

30:10,11 prophesy deceits...turn aside from the path. Isaiah's listeners tired of hearing counsel that was contrary to the path they desired to follow and wanted him to change his message to accommodate them.

30:12-14 Since the people opted not to hear the word of the Lord's prophet, they will hear from the Lord's judgment.

30:12 this word. The reference is to the instruction of the Lord through Isaiah.

30:13,14 high wall...potter's vessel. Two comparisons portrayed the coming sudden disaster to befall the rebels, a high wall that collapses suddenly and a clay jug that shatters into many pieces when dropped.

30:15 rest...confidence. The Israelite rebels refused the true avenue of salvation and strength, i.e., resting and confidence in the Lord.

30:16 horses...swift *horses*. The people put their trust in Egypt's horses instead of the Lord. No horse could deliver them from their God-appointed oppressors (cf. Deut. 17:16; Pss. 33:17; 147:10).

30:17 One thousand...one. Similar figures elsewhere describe Israel's victories (Lev. 26:36; Josh. 23:10) and defeats (Deut. 32:30).

30:18 the LORD will wait. Since Judah would not wait on the Lord to deliver (25:9; 26:8; 33:2; cf. 30:15), He must wait to be gracious to the nation.

30:19 dwell in Zion at Jerusalem. The prophet emphatically pointed to a result of God's grace toward Israel—the survival of the city of Jerusalem as the center of her domain (65:9; Ezek. 37:25,28).

20 And *though* the Lord gives you
[b]The bread of adversity and the
water of [6]affliction,
Yet [c]your teachers will not be
moved into a corner anymore,
But your eyes shall see your
teachers.
21 Your ears shall hear a word behind
you, saying,
"This *is* the way, walk in it,"
Whenever you [d]turn to the right
hand
Or whenever you turn to the left.
22 [e]You will also defile the covering of
your images of silver,
And the ornament of your molded
images of gold.
You will throw them away as an
unclean thing;
[f]You will say to them, "Get away!"

23 [g]Then He will give the rain for your
seed
With which you sow the ground,
And bread of the increase of the
earth;
It will be [7]fat and plentiful.
In that day your cattle will feed
In large pastures.
24 Likewise the oxen and the young
donkeys that work the ground
Will eat cured fodder,
Which has been winnowed with
the shovel and fan.
25 There will be [h]on every high
mountain
And on every high hill
Rivers *and* streams of waters,
In the day of the [i]great slaughter,
When the towers fall.
26 Moreover [j]the light of the moon
will be as the light of the sun,
And the light of the sun will be
sevenfold,
As the light of seven days,
In the day that the LORD binds up
the bruise of His people
And heals the stroke of their
wound.

Judgment on Assyria

27 Behold, the name of the LORD
comes from afar,
Burning *with* His anger,
And *His* burden *is* heavy;
His lips are full of indignation,
And His tongue like a devouring
fire.
28 [k]His breath is like an overflowing
stream,
[l]Which reaches up to the neck,
To sift the nations with the sieve of
futility;
And *there shall be* [m]a bridle in the
jaws of the people,
Causing *them* to err.

29 You shall have a song
As in the night *when* a holy festival
is kept,
And gladness of heart as when one
goes with a flute,
To come into [n]the mountain of the
LORD,
To [8]the Mighty One of Israel.
30 [o]The LORD will cause His glorious
voice to be heard,
And show the descent of His arm,
With the indignation of *His* anger
And the flame of a devouring fire,
With scattering, tempest, [p]and
hailstones.
31 For [q]through the voice of the LORD
Assyria will be [9]beaten down,
As He strikes with the [r]rod.
32 And *in* every place where the staff
of punishment passes,
Which the LORD lays on him,

20 [b] 1 Kin. 22:27; Ps. 127:2 [c] Ps. 74:9; Amos 8:11 [6] *oppression*
21 [d] Josh. 1:7
22 [e] 2 Chr. 31:1; Is. 2:20; 31:7 [f] Hos. 14:8
23 [g] [Matt. 6:33]; 1 Tim. 6:8 [7] *rich*
25 [h] Is. 2:14, 15 [i] Is. 2:10-21; 34:2
26 [j] [Is. 60:19, 20; Rev. 21:23; 22:5]
28 [k] Is. 11:4; 2 Thess. 2:8 [l] Is. 8:8 [m] 2 Kin. 19:28; Is. 37:29
29 [n] [Is. 2:3] [8] Lit. *the Rock*
30 [o] Is. 29:6 [p] Is. 28:2
31 [q] Is. 14:25; 37:36 [r] Is. 10:5, 24 [9] Lit. *shattered*

30:20 eyes shall see. After their period of judgment because of disobedience, God is to open Israel's eyes to the soundness of the message of His prophets (29:24).

30:21 a word behind you. The teachers will be near and the pupils sensitive to the Lord's prophets, in strong contrast to the callousness formerly manifest (29:10,11).

30:22 throw them away. The Babylonian captivity rid Israel of her idolatry in fulfillment of this prophecy.

30:23-25 In the messianic kingdom of that future day, agriculture, cattle raising, food production, and water resources will prosper. The prophet predicted the redemption of nature (cf. Rom. 8:19-21).

30:25 towers fall. Powerful nations that oppress Israel will come to an end (contr. 29:17).

30:26 light of the moon...light of the sun. The benefits from the natural bodies of light will be much greater. Increase in the intensity of their light will work to people's advantage (60:19,20), not to their detriment as in Rev. 16:8,9.

30:27-33 Isaiah followed the promise of Judah's redemption (vv. 19-26) with a promise of Assyria's destruction.

30:27 the name of the LORD. His name focuses particularly on His revealed character as Sovereign and Savior (Deut. 12:5).

30:27,28 comes from afar...overflowing stream. The Lord will come suddenly upon His enemies as a great storm with its accompanying flood, to overwhelm them.

30:29 song...holy festival. While God's judgment devastated the Assyrians, the people of Jerusalem conducted a time of joyful celebration as at one of their feasts, perhaps a Passover.

30:30,31 Assyria...beaten down. Assyria in particular, but in the long range, any enemy of God's people will fall victim to divine storm and flood (vv. 27,28).

30:32 staff of punishment...tambourines and harps. With each blow of punishment against the Assyrians will come joyful celebration in Jerusalem.

It will be with tambourines and
harps;
And in battles of [s]brandishing He
will fight with it.
33 [t]For Tophet *was* established of old,
Yes, for the king it is prepared.
He has made *it* deep and large;
Its pyre *is* fire with much wood;
The breath of the LORD, like a
stream of brimstone,
Kindles it.

The Folly of Not Trusting God

31 Woe to those [a]who go down to
Egypt for help,
And [b]rely on horses,
Who trust in chariots because *they
are* many,
And in horsemen because they are
very strong,
But who do not look to the Holy
One of Israel,
[c]Nor seek the LORD!
2 Yet He also *is* wise and will bring
disaster,
And [d]will not [1]call back His
words,
But will arise against the house of
evildoers,
And against the help of those who
work iniquity.
3 Now the Egyptians *are* men, and
not God;
And their horses are flesh, and not
spirit.
When the LORD stretches out His
hand,
Both he who helps will fall,
And he who is helped will fall
down;
They all will perish [e]together.

God Will Deliver Jerusalem

4 For thus the LORD has spoken to me:

[f]"As a lion roars,
And a young lion over his prey
(When a multitude of shepherds is
summoned against him,
He will not be afraid of their voice
Nor be disturbed by their noise),
So the LORD of hosts will come
down
To fight for Mount Zion and for its
hill.
5 [g]Like birds flying about,
So will the LORD of hosts defend
Jerusalem.
Defending, He will also deliver *it;*
Passing over, He will preserve *it.*"

6 Return *to Him* against whom the children of Israel have [h]deeply revolted. 7 For
in that day every man shall [i]throw away
his idols of silver and his idols of gold—
[j]sin, which your own hands have made for
yourselves.

8 "Then Assyria shall [k]fall by a sword
not of man,
And a sword not of mankind shall
[l]devour him.
But he shall flee from the sword,
And his young men shall become
forced labor.
9 [m]He shall cross over to his
stronghold for fear,
And his princes shall be afraid of
the banner,"
Says the LORD,
Whose fire *is* in Zion
And whose furnace *is* in Jerusalem.

32 [s]Is. 11:15
33 [t]2 Kin. 23:10; Jer. 7:31

CHAPTER 31

1 [a]Is. 30:1, 2 [b]Deut. 17:16; Ps. 20:7; Is. 2:7; 30:16 [c]Is. 9:13; Dan. 9:13; Amos 5:4-8
2 [d]Num. 23:19; Jer. 44:29 [1]*retract*
3 [e]Is. 20:6
4 [f]Num. 24:9; Hos. 11:10; Amos 3:8
5 [g]Deut. 32:11; Ps. 91:4
6 [h]Hos. 9:9
7 [i]Is. 2:20; 30:22 [j]1 Kin. 12:30
8 [k]2 Kin. 19:35, 36 [l]Is. 37:36
9 [m]Is. 37:37

30:33 Tophet. Lit. a place of abomination. Idolatrous Israel had burned to death human victims in this valley just S of Jerusalem, an area sometimes called the Valley of Hinnom (2 Kin. 23:10; *see note on Jer. 19:6*). Later it became known as Gehenna, the place of refuse for the city, with constantly burning fires, symbolizing hell. The defeat was to be so complete that the fire burns continually.

31:1 horses...chariots. Egypt's horses and chariots were numerous (1 Kin. 10:28,29). Its flat topography was well suited for chariotry. They were be useful to Israel against the Assyrian cavalry. **Nor seek the LORD.** What made Israel's turning to Egypt most despicable was her accompanying turning away from the Lord.

31:2 He also *is* wise. Sarcastically, Isaiah countered the unwise royal counselors who had advised dependence on Egypt. **will not call back His words.** The implied exception is, of course, when the sinful nation repented, as in the case of Nineveh (Jon. 3:5-10).

31:3 flesh...spirit. For example, Hezekiah wisely chose to rely on the Lord, not on the arm of flesh (2 Chr. 32:8).

31:4 not be afraid...nor be disturbed. In His defense of Jerusalem, the Lord is to be like a strong and determined lion, unafraid of shepherds summoned against him.

31:5 birds flying about. The Lord is like a hovering mother bird with a strong attachment to her little ones and a willingness to do whatever is necessary for their safety.

31:6 Return *to Him.* The prophet called rebellious Israel to repent in light of God's gracious dealings with them (vv. 4,5; cf. 30:18, 19).

31:7 throw away his idols. The obvious helplessness of the idols to deliver rendered them completely useless.

31:8 Assyria shall fall. The defeat of Assyria by other-than-human means matched this prophecy well (see 37:36,37), but other such foreign oppressors meet the same fate in the distant future of Israel, during the time of Jacob's trouble (cf. Jer. 30:7).

31:9 fire *is* in Zion...furnace *is* in Jerusalem. Both in Isaiah's near future and in the distant future, Jerusalem was God's headquarters for bringing judgment on foreign nations. God Himself is the fire, waiting for all the enemies who attack Jerusalem.

A Reign of Righteousness

32 Behold, [a]a king will reign in
righteousness,
And princes will rule with justice.
2 A man will be as a hiding place
from the wind,
And [b]a [1]cover from the tempest,
As rivers of water in a dry place,
As the shadow of a great rock in a
weary land.
3 [c]The eyes of those who see will not
be dim,
And the ears of those who hear
will listen.
4 Also the heart of the [2]rash will
[d]understand knowledge,
And the tongue of the stammerers
will be ready to speak plainly.

5 The foolish person will no longer
be called [3]generous,
Nor the miser said *to be* bountiful;
6 For the foolish person will speak
foolishness,
And his heart will work [e]iniquity:
To practice ungodliness,
To utter error against the LORD,
To keep the hungry unsatisfied,
And he will cause the drink of the
thirsty to fail.
7 Also the schemes of the schemer
are evil;
He devises wicked plans
To destroy the poor with [f]lying
words,
Even when the needy speaks
justice.
8 But a [4]generous man devises
generous things,
And by generosity he shall stand.

Consequences of Complacency

9 Rise up, you women [g]who are at
ease,
Hear my voice;
You complacent daughters,
Give ear to my speech.
10 In a year and *some* days
You will be troubled, you
complacent women;
For the vintage will fail,
The gathering will not come.
11 Tremble, you *women* who are at
ease;
Be troubled, you complacent ones;
Strip yourselves, make yourselves
bare,
And gird *sackcloth* on *your* waists.

12 People shall mourn upon their
breasts
For the pleasant fields, for the
fruitful vine.
13 [h]On the land of my people will
come up thorns *and* briers,
Yes, on all the happy homes *in* [i]the
joyous city;
14 [j]Because the palaces will be
forsaken,
The bustling city will be deserted.
The forts and towers will become
lairs forever,
A joy of wild donkeys, a pasture of
flocks—
15 Until [k]the Spirit is poured upon us
from on high,
And [l]the wilderness becomes a
fruitful field,
And the fruitful field is counted as
a forest.

CHAPTER 32
1 [a] Ps. 45:1
2 [b] Is. 4:6 [1] *shelter*
3 [c] Is. 29:18; 35:5
4 [d] Is. 29:24 [2] *hasty*
5 [3] *noble*
6 [e] Prov. 24:7-9
7 [f] Jer. 5:26-28; Mic. 7:3
8 [4] *noble*
9 [g] Is. 47:8; Amos 6:1; Zeph. 2:15
13 [h] Is. 7:23-25; Hos. 9:6 [i] Is. 22:2
14 [j] Is. 27:10
15 [k] [Is. 11:2]; Ezek. 39:29; [Joel 2:28] [l] Ps. 107:35; Is. 29:17

32:1 a king...princes. In contrast to bad leaders already discussed (e.g., 28:14,15; 29:15), the prophet turned to the messianic king and His governmental assistants during the future day of righteousness. These will be the apostles (Luke 22:30) and the saints (1 Cor. 6:2; 2 Tim. 2:12; Rev. 2:26,27; 3:21).

32:2 shadow...land. During the millennial reign of Christ, leaders will provide protection like "the shadow of a mighty rock within a weary land," instead of posing threats to the people's well-being.

32:3 eyes...not...dim...ears...listen. A future generation of Israelites will experience a reversal of receptivity compared to Isaiah's generation (6:9,10; cf. 29:18,24; 30:20).

32:4 stammerers. The stammerers were former drunkards who uttered nonsense in their drunken stupor (28:7,8; 29:9).

32:5 foolish person...generous...miser...bountiful. In the future earthly kingdom envisioned by Isaiah, false appraisals of leadership qualities will be impossible, because everyone will see and speak clearly.

32:6-8 foolish person...generous man. An unwillingness to care for the needy reflects the character of a fool, but the generous person in dependence on God provides for the poor. These qualities will be evident to all in the age to come.

32:9-14 The prophet warns the women of Judah against complacency (cf. 3:16–4:1). God's eventual blessing on their nation gave no excuse for business as usual, i.e., dependence on Egypt instead of God.

32:9 at ease...complacent. "At ease" translates the word rendered "quiet" or "complacent" the word rendered "secure" in v. 18. The difference between the bad senses here and the good senses in v. 18 is the object of trust, Egypt or God. Ease and security in God are proper.

32:10 year and *some* days. Perhaps specifying a time when the Assyrian army came and pillaged the land, the prophet warned of how God's coming judgment was to spoil agricultural production.

32:11,12 Tremble...mourn. Present satisfaction with the status quo shortly gave way to an entirely different set of emotions.

32:13 thorns...briers. Without harmony with God, the land of God's people became just as desolate as any other forsaken territory (1:7; 5:6; 7:23).

32:14 bustling city. Jerusalem too was to become desolate through the Lord's purging judgments of the nation (Luke 21:24).

32:15-20 The promised kingdom was to eventually come to Israel with its accompanying fruitfulness, peace, and security.

32:15 the Spirit is poured upon us. The infusion of God's Spirit was to transform the land into productive fruitfulness (Joel 2:28–3:1).

The Peace of God's Reign

16 Then justice will dwell in the wilderness,
And righteousness remain in the fruitful field.
17 [m]The work of righteousness will be peace,
And the effect of righteousness, quietness and assurance forever.
18 My people will dwell in a peaceful habitation,
In secure dwellings, and in quiet [n]resting places,
19 [o]Though hail comes down [p]on the forest,
And the city is brought low in humiliation.
20 Blessed *are* you who sow beside all waters,
Who send out freely the feet of [q]the ox and the donkey.

A Prayer in Deep Distress

33 Woe to you [a]who plunder, though you *have* not *been* plundered;
And you who deal treacherously, though they have not dealt treacherously with you!
[b]When you cease plundering,
You will be [c]plundered;
When you make an end of dealing treacherously,
They will deal treacherously with you.

2 O LORD, be gracious to us;
[d]We have waited for You.
Be [1]their arm every morning,
Our salvation also in the time of trouble.

17 [m] Ps. 119:165; Is. 2:4; Rom. 14:17; James 3:18
18 [n] Is. 11:10; 14:3; 30:15; [Hos. 2:18-23; Zech. 2:5; 3:10]
19 [o] Is. 30:30 [p] Zech. 11:2
20 [q] [Eccl. 11:1]; Is. 30:23, 24

CHAPTER 33

1 [a] Is. 21:2; Hab. 2:8 [b] Rev. 13:10 [c] Is. 10:12; 14:25; 31:8
2 [d] Is. 25:9; 26:8 [1] LXX omits *their;* Syr., Tg., Vg. *our*
3 [e] Is. 17:13
5 [f] Ps. 97:9
7 [g] 2 Kin. 18:18, 37
8 [h] Judg. 5:6 [i] 2 Kin. 18:13-17 [2] Tg. *They have been removed from their cities* [3] So with MT, Vg.; DSS *witnesses;* LXX omits *cities*
9 [j] Is. 24:4
10 [k] Ps. 12:5; Is. 2:19, 21
11 [l] [Ps. 7:14; Is. 26:18; 59:4; James 1:15]

3 At the noise of the tumult the people [e]shall flee;
When You lift Yourself up, the nations shall be scattered;
4 And Your plunder shall be gathered
Like the gathering of the caterpillar;
As the running to and fro of locusts,
He shall run upon them.

5 [f]The LORD is exalted, for He dwells on high;
He has filled Zion with justice and righteousness.
6 Wisdom and knowledge will be the stability of your times,
And the strength of salvation;
The fear of the LORD *is* His treasure.

7 Surely their valiant ones shall cry outside,
[g]The ambassadors of peace shall weep bitterly.
8 [h]The highways lie waste,
The traveling man ceases.
[i]He has broken the covenant,
[2]He has despised the [3]cities,
He regards no man.
9 [j]The earth mourns *and* languishes,
Lebanon is shamed *and* shriveled;
Sharon is like a wilderness,
And Bashan and Carmel shake off *their fruits.*

Impending Judgment on Zion

10 "Now [k]I will rise," says the LORD;
"Now I will be exalted,
Now I will lift Myself up.
11 [l]You shall conceive chaff,
You shall bring forth stubble;

32:16 justice...righteousness. Noble spiritual values were to thrive in the future messianic reign.

32:18 My people...peaceful...secure...quiet. The people of Israel will enjoy lasting security with the Messiah personally present to ensure peace.

32:19 city is brought low. Jerusalem must learn humility before the prophesied ideal conditions can become reality.

32:20 Blessed. As with the beatitudes of Christ (Matt. 5:3-12), Isaiah pronounced the blessedness of those who participate in the future glory of Christ's kingdom.

33:1 you who plunder. Though the immediate reference is to Assyria (2 Kin. 18:13-16; 19:32-37), the prophecy looks beyond Assyria to any power that sets itself against Israel.

33:2 We have waited for You. Israel refused to do this earlier (30:15; 31:6), but had repented (25:9; 26:8; 33:2).

33:3,4 Just as Sennacherib took flight suddenly (cf. 37:37; 2 Chr. 32:21), so the nations will scatter before the Lord, leaving their spoils behind.

33:6 fear of the LORD. The same Spirit-imparted qualification possessed by the Messiah (11:2) will belong to His people when He returns.

33:7-9 From the vision of future glory, Isaiah returns to the disastrous present. Jerusalem's situation was hopeless when in 701 B.C. the Assyrian army had the city surrounded and was ready to move in.

33:7 valiant ones...ambassadors. Both men of war and diplomats had failed in their attempts to thwart the invaders.

33:8 highways lie waste. The enemy surrounding the city had cut off all travel and trade with the outside world.

33:9 Lebanon...Sharon...Bashan...Carmel. The enemy had spoiled places renowned for their lush fertility.

33:10 Now I will rise. When the oppressor's power had reached its zenith, the time had arrived for the Lord to assert Himself in judging the plunderer, in Isaiah's case the Assyrian troops.

33:11 chaff...stubble. References to Assyria, these reaffirm that the plunderer is to be plundered (v. 1).

Your breath, *as* fire, shall devour
you.
12 And the people shall be *like* the
burnings of lime;
[m]*Like* thorns cut up they shall be
burned in the fire.
13 Hear, [n]you *who are* afar off, what I
have done;
And you *who are* near,
acknowledge My might."

14 The sinners in Zion are afraid;
Fearfulness has seized the
hypocrites:
"Who among us shall dwell with
the devouring [o]fire?
Who among us shall dwell with
everlasting burnings?"
15 He who [p]walks righteously and
speaks uprightly,
He who despises the gain of
oppressions,
Who gestures with his hands,
refusing bribes,
Who stops his ears from hearing of
bloodshed,
And [q]shuts his eyes from seeing
evil:
16 He will dwell on [4]high;
His place of defense *will be* the
fortress of rocks;
Bread will be given him,
His water *will be* sure.

The Land of the Majestic King

17 Your eyes will see the King in His
[r]beauty;
They will see the land that is very
far off.
18 Your heart will meditate on terror:
[s]"Where *is* the scribe?
Where *is* he who weighs?
Where *is* he who counts the
towers?"

12 [m] Is. 9:18
13 [n] Ps. 48:10; Is. 49:1
14 [o] Is. 30:27, 30; Heb. 12:29
15 [p] Ps. 15:2; 24:3, 4; Is. 58:6-11 [q] Ps. 119:37
16 [4] Lit. *heights*
17 [r] Ps. 27:4
18 [s] 1 Cor. 1:20
19 [t] 2 Kin. 19:32 [u] Deut. 28:49, 50; Is. 28:11; Jer. 5:15 [5] Unintelligible speech
20 [v] Ps. 48:12 [w] Ps. 46:5; 125:1; Is. 32:18 [x] Is. 37:33 [y] Is. 54:2
21 [6] *ship*
22 [z] [Acts 10:42] [a] Is. 1:10; 51:4, 7; James 4:12 [b] Ps. 89:18; Is. 25:9; 35:4; Zech. 9:9
24 [c] Is. 40:2; Jer. 50:20; Mic. 7:18, 19; 1 John 1:7-9

CHAPTER 34

1 [a] Ps. 49:1; Is. 41:1; 43:9 [b] Deut. 32:1; Is. 1:2

19 [t]You will not see a fierce people,
[u]A people of obscure speech,
beyond perception,
Of a [5]stammering tongue *that you*
cannot understand.

20 [v]Look upon Zion, the city of our
appointed feasts;
Your eyes will see [w]Jerusalem, a
quiet home,
A tabernacle *that* will not be taken
down;
[x]Not one of [y]its stakes will ever be
removed,
Nor will any of its cords be broken.
21 But there the majestic LORD *will be*
for us
A place of broad rivers *and*
streams,
In which no [6]galley with oars will
sail,
Nor majestic ships pass by
22 (For the LORD *is* our [z]Judge,
The LORD *is* our [a]Lawgiver,
[b]The LORD *is* our King;
He will save us);
23 Your tackle is loosed,
They could not strengthen their
mast,
They could not spread the sail.

Then the prey of great plunder is
divided;
The lame take the prey.
24 And the inhabitant will not say, "I
am sick";
[c]The people who dwell in it *will be*
forgiven *their* iniquity.

Judgment on the Nations

34 Come [a]near, you nations, to hear;
And heed, you people!
[b]Let the earth hear, and all that is
in it,

33:12 lime…thorns. Burned limestone became dust; thorn bushes burned rapidly.

33:13 afar off…near. When God puts down the final enemies of Israel, He will receive worldwide acknowledgment of His might.

33:14 afraid; fearfulness. When sinners (false professors among the elect) comprehend the might of God, fear takes hold of their lives (Acts 5:11; Heb. 12:29).

33:15 righteously…uprightly. The only survivors in the presence of mighty God will be the righteous (Pss. 15:1-5; 24:3,4).

33:16 place of defense…bread…water. Those who are right with God will enjoy perfect security and ample provisions (32:15, 17,18).

33:17 King in His beauty. The prophecy moves beyond Hezekiah in his sackcloth, oppressed by his enemy, to Messiah in His beauty. Seeing Him in glory is another reward of the righteous. The near-future deliverance from Sennacherib anticipates a more distant wonder when the Messiah will sit on His throne.

33:18,19 In that future day God's people will remember past hardships under foreign domination.

33:20 tabernacle…not be taken down. God's presence is to permanently inhabit restored Jerusalem in the millennial kingdom.

33:21 broad rivers *and* streams. God is to restore wide rivers and streams as a means of defending the city.

33:22 He will save us. In explicit language, God, not the surrounding nations, is to deliver Israel.

33:23 tackle is loosed. In her own strength, Jerusalem is as helpless to defend herself as a ship deprived of its ropes and pulleys, that cannot sail.

33:23 lame take the prey. The weak city defeats the invaders with the Lord's enablement.

33:24 not say, "I am sick"…forgiven *their* iniquity. When Christ returns to rule, Jerusalem will be free of physical and spiritual problems.

34:1 Come near. Isaiah invited the nations to approach to hear God's sentence of judgment against them.

The world and all things that come
forth from it.
2 For the indignation of the LORD *is*
against all nations,
And *His* fury against all their
armies;
He has utterly destroyed them,
He has given them over to the
[c]slaughter.
3 Also their slain shall be thrown
out;
[d]Their stench shall rise from their
corpses,
And the mountains shall be melted
with their blood.
4 [e]All the host of heaven shall be
dissolved,
And the heavens shall be rolled up
like a scroll;
[f]All their host shall fall down
As the leaf falls from the vine,
And as [g]*fruit* falling from a fig tree.

5 "For [h]My sword shall be bathed in
heaven;
Indeed it [i]shall come down on
Edom,
And on the people of My curse, for
judgment.
6 The [j]sword of the LORD is filled
with blood,
It is made [1]overflowing with
fatness,
With the blood of lambs and goats,
With the fat of the kidneys of rams.
For [k]the LORD has a sacrifice in
Bozrah,
And a great slaughter in the land
of Edom.
7 The wild oxen shall come down
with them,
And the young bulls with the
mighty bulls;
Their land shall be soaked with
blood,
And their dust [2]saturated with
fatness."

8 For *it is* the day of the LORD's
[l]vengeance,
The year of recompense for the
cause of Zion.
9 [m]Its streams shall be turned into
pitch,
And its dust into brimstone;
Its land shall become burning
pitch.
10 It shall not be quenched night or
day;
[n]Its smoke shall ascend forever.
[o]From generation to generation it
shall lie waste;
No one shall pass through it
forever and ever.
11 [p]But the [3]pelican and the
[4]porcupine shall possess it,
Also the owl and the raven shall
dwell in it.
And [q]He shall stretch out over it
The line of confusion and the
stones of emptiness.
12 They shall call its nobles to the
kingdom,
But none *shall be* there, and all its
princes shall be nothing.

13 And [r]thorns shall come up in its
palaces,
Nettles and brambles in its
fortresses;
[s]It shall be a habitation of jackals,
A courtyard for ostriches.
14 The wild beasts of the desert shall
also meet with the [5]jackals,
And the wild goat shall bleat to its
companion;

2 [c]Is. 13:5
3 [d]Joel 2:20; Amos 4:10
4 [e]Ps. 102:26; Is. 13:13; Ezek. 32:7, 8; Joel 2:31; Matt. 24:29; 2 Pet. 3:10 [f]Is. 14:12 [g]Rev. 6:12-14
5 [h]Deut. 32:41, 42; Jer. 46:10; Ezek. 21:3-5 [i]Is. 63:1; Jer. 49:7, 8, 20; Ezek. 25:12-14; 35:1-15; Amos 1:11, 12; Obad. 1-14; Mal. 1:4
6 [j]Is. 66:16 [k]Zeph. 1:7 [1]Lit. *fat*
7 [2]Lit. *made fat*
8 [l]Is. 63:4
9 [m]Deut. 29:23; Ps. 11:6; Is. 30:33
10 [n]Rev. 14:11; 18:18; 19:3 [o]Is. 13:20-22; 24:1; 34:10-15; Mal. 1:3, 4
11 [p]Is. 14:23; Zeph. 2:14; Rev. 18:2 [q]2 Kin. 21:13; Lam. 2:8 [3]Or *owl* [4]Or *hedgehog*
13 [r]Is. 32:13; Hos. 9:6 [s]Is. 13:21
14 [5]Lit. *howling creatures*

34:3 Their stench. Prolonged exposure of dead corpses was and is repulsive and disgraceful (see 14:19).

34:4 heavens…scroll. Not even the heavens are to escape the effects of God's wrath. Revelation 6:14 affirms the future fulfillment of this prophecy during Daniel's 70th week (see 2:19; 13:10).

34:5 Edom. The prophet selects Edom as a representative of the rest of the nations (cf. 63:1; Gen. 25:23; Num. 20:14-21; Ezek. 35:1-15; Obad. 1-14; Mal. 1:2,3; cf. 25:10). **people of My curse.** Lit. "devoted people." The expression's negative connotation stems from their involuntary devotion to God.

34:6,7 lambs and goats…rams…wild oxen…bulls. Since the nations had not repented and obeyed God's way of sacrifice for sins, they became the sacrificial penalty for their own sins.

34:6 Bozrah. A chief city of Edom located about 20 mi. SE of the southern end of the Dead Sea.

34:8 day of the LORD's vengeance. *See note on 2:10-22.* God's day of vengeance on Edom (63:4) will be the same as on the rest of the nations (59:17,18; 61:2).

34:9,10 God's judgment is to reduce the nations to a state of perpetual volcanic waste.

34:9 brimstone…burning pitch. Genesis 19:24,28 describes Sodom in similar terms (cf. 30:33; Deut. 29:23; Ps. 11:6; Jer. 49:18; Ezek. 38:22).

34:10 smoke shall ascend forever. Revelation forecasts this destiny for final Babylon, the great end-time world empire (Rev. 14:10,11; 18:18; 19:3).

34:11-15 Various forms of animal and bird life symbolize the depopulated condition into which the nations fall after God's judgment upon them (13:21,22; 14:23).

34:11,13 pelican…owl…raven…ostriches. The presence of unclean birds was a sign of desolation and wilderness. Similar symbolism portrays the final state of Babylon in the future (Rev. 18:2; cf. 13:21; Jer. 50:39; Zeph. 2:13,14).

Also [6]the night creature shall rest
there,
And find for herself a place of rest.
15 There the arrow snake shall make
her nest and lay *eggs*
And hatch, and gather *them* under
her shadow;
There also shall the hawks be
gathered,
Every one with her mate.

16 "Search from [t]the book of the LORD,
and read:
Not one of these shall fail;
Not one shall lack her mate.
For My mouth has commanded it,
and His Spirit has gathered
them.
17 He has cast the lot for them,
And His hand has divided it
among them with a
measuring line.
They shall possess it forever;
From generation to generation they
shall dwell in it."

The Future Glory of Zion

35 The [a]wilderness and the [1]waste-
land shall be glad for them,
And the [b]desert[2] shall rejoice and
blossom as the rose;
2 [c]It shall blossom abundantly and
rejoice,
Even with joy and singing.
The glory of Lebanon shall be
given to it,
The excellence of Carmel and
Sharon.
They shall see the [d]glory of the
LORD,
The excellency of our God.
3 [e]Strengthen the [3]weak hands,
And make firm the [4]feeble knees.
4 Say to those *who are* fearful-hearted,
"Be strong, do not fear!
Behold, your God will come *with*
[f]vengeance,
With the recompense of God;
He will come and [g]save you."

5 Then the [h]eyes of the blind shall be
opened,
And [i]the ears of the deaf shall be
unstopped.
6 Then the [j]lame shall leap like a deer,
And the [k]tongue of the dumb sing.
For [l]waters shall burst forth in the
wilderness,
And streams in the desert.
7 The parched ground shall become
a pool,
And the thirsty land springs of
water;
In [m]the habitation of jackals, where
each lay,
There shall be grass with reeds and
rushes.

8 A [n]highway shall be there, and a
road,
And it shall be called the Highway
of Holiness.
[o]The unclean shall not pass over it,
But it *shall be* for others.
Whoever walks the road, although
a fool,
Shall not go astray.
9 [p]No lion shall be there,
Nor shall *any* ravenous beast go up
on it;

14 [6] Heb. *lilith*
16 [t] [Mal. 3:16]

CHAPTER 35

1 [a] Is. 32:15; 55:12 [b] Is. 41:19; 51:3 [1] *desert* [2] Heb. *arabah*
2 [c] Is. 32:15 [d] Is. 40:5
3 [e] Job 4:3, 4; Heb. 12:12 [3] Lit. *sinking* [4] *tottering* or *stumbling*
4 [f] Is. 34:8 [g] Ps. 145:19; Is. 33:22
5 [h] Is. 29:18; Matt. 9:27; John 9:6, 7 [i] [Matt. 11:5]
6 [j] Matt. 11:5; 15:30; John 5:8, 9; Acts 8:7 [k] Is. 32:4; Matt. 9:32; 12:22 [l] Is. 41:18; [John 7:38]
7 [m] Is. 34:13
8 [n] Is. 19:23 [o] Is. 52:1; Joel 3:17; [Matt. 7:13, 14]; 1 Pet. 1:15, 16; Rev. 21:27
9 [p] Lev. 26:6; [Is. 11:7, 9]; Ezek. 34:25

34:16 My mouth has commanded. The prophecies against the nation in vv. 1-15 were just as certain as God's sovereign command through His prophet.

34:17 divided it...with a measuring line. God had partitioned off Edom just as He once did Canaan (Num. 26:55,56; Josh. 18:4-6) and allotted it to the wild animals listed in vv. 11-15.

35:1-4 In contrast to luxuriant Edom that is to become a desert (34:1-17), during Messiah's reign on earth the whole world is to become a flourishing garden and this will offer encouragement to the weak.

35:1 desert...as the rose. Dramatic changes in the land are to come during the messianic age (see 30:23-25; 32:15-20).

35:2 Lebanon...Carmel and Sharon. Areas near the sea noted for their agricultural fertility. **They shall see.** Israel is to recognize the earth's newfound fruitfulness as coming from the Lord and attribute to Him the appropriate credit.

35:3 weak hands...feeble knees. The future change in Israel's international role is to serve to encourage the discouraged among the people. The writer of Hebrews gave an additional application of this verse to strengthen endurance among Christians suffering persecution for their faith (Heb. 12:12).

35:4 vengeance...save you. The vengeance of God (34:8) is to furnish the means to redeem His long-oppressed people of Israel.

35:5 eyes...opened...ears...unstopped. This is to reverse the spiritual condition of the immediate objects of Isaiah's ministry (see 29:18; 32:3).

35:6 lame...sing. God's restoration in the millennial age is to include physical restoration to the afflicted. Jesus' first coming gave a foretaste of that future day (Matt. 11:5; 12:22; Mark 7:37; Luke 7:21; Acts 3:8).

35:6,7 streams in the desert...springs of water. Water was and is a precious commodity in Israel (41:18). In the Millennium, there will be no scarcity.

35:7 habitation of jackals. The rocky crags normally inhabited by jackals (34:13) are to become splashy meadows.

35:8 Highway of Holiness. This refers to the way leading the redeemed back to Jerusalem, the throne of Messiah, literally and spiritually. Christ Himself is to be the leader on that way, called in 40:3, the "way of the LORD."

35:9 lion...ravenous beast. No ferocious beasts are to threaten the safety of those traveling the Highway of Holiness. **the redeemed.** Mentioned only rarely in chaps. 1–39 (1:27; 29:22) whose

It shall not be found there.
But the redeemed shall walk *there,*
10 And the [q]ransomed of the LORD
shall return,
And come to Zion with singing,
With everlasting joy on their heads.
They shall obtain joy and gladness,
And [r]sorrow and sighing shall flee
away.

Sennacherib Boasts Against the LORD

36 Now [a]it came to pass in the fourteenth year of King Hezekiah *that*
Sennacherib king of Assyria came up
against all the fortified cities of Judah and
took them. **2** Then the king of Assyria sent
the [1]Rabshakeh with a great army from
Lachish to King Hezekiah at Jerusalem.
And he stood by the aqueduct from the
upper pool, on the highway to the Fuller's
Field. **3** And [b]Eliakim the son of Hilkiah,
who was over the household, [c]Shebna the
scribe, and Joah the son of Asaph, the
recorder, came out to him.
4 [d]Then *the* Rabshakeh said to them,
"Say now to Hezekiah, 'Thus says the
great king, the king of Assyria: "What confidence is this in which you trust? **5** I say
you speak of having plans and power for
war; but *they are* [2]mere words. Now in
whom do you trust, that you rebel against
me? **6** Look! You are trusting in the [e]staff of
this broken reed, Egypt, on which if a man
leans, it will go into his hand and pierce it.
So *is* Pharaoh king of Egypt to all who
[f]trust in him.
7 "But if you say to me, 'We trust in the
LORD our God,' *is it* not He whose high
places and whose altars Hezekiah has
taken away, and said to Judah and Jerusalem, 'You shall worship before this
altar'?" ' **8** Now therefore, I urge you, give
a pledge to my master the king of Assyria,
and I will give you two thousand horses—
if you are able on your part to put riders on
them! **9** How then will you repel one captain of the least of my master's servants,
and put your trust in Egypt for chariots
and horsemen? **10** Have I now come up
without the LORD against this land to destroy it? The LORD said to me, 'Go up
against this land, and destroy it.' "
11 Then Eliakim, Shebna, and Joah said
to *the* Rabshakeh, "Please speak to your
servants in Aramaic, for we understand *it;*
and do not speak to us in [3]Hebrew in the
hearing of the people who *are* on the
wall."

10 [q] Is. 51:11 [r] Is. 25:8; 30:19; 65:19; [Rev. 7:17; 21:4]

CHAPTER 36

1 [a] 2 Kin. 18:13, 17; 2 Chr. 32:1
2 [1] A title, probably *Chief of Staff* or *Governor*
3 [b] Is. 22:20 [c] Is. 22:15
4 [d] 2 Kin. 18:19
5 [2] Lit. *a word of the lips*
6 [e] Ezek. 29:6 [f] Ps. 146:3; Is. 30:3, 5, 7
11 [3] Lit. *Judean*

theme is judgment; terms for redemption occur frequently in chaps. 40–66.

35:10 the ransomed…flee away. See 51:11 where the words occur again. Gladness is to replace sadness across the board in the day of Israel's restoration.

36:1–39:8 The 4 chapters duplicate almost verbatim 2 Kin. 18:13–20:19 (cf. 2 Chr. 32:1-23). *See 2 Kings notes* for amplification. Isaiah added this material to make the references to Assyria more understandable. It is most probable that Isaiah is the author of this section, since 2 Chr. 32:32 says Isaiah also wrote the acts of Hezekiah. Isaiah's record was incorporated into 2 Kings by the author of that record. These chapters form the transition closing the first division of Isaiah's prophecy. Chapters 36,37 are the historical consummation of chaps. 1–35—Jerusalem's deliverance from Assyria—and chaps. 38,39 the historical basis for chaps. 40–66—a preview of the Babylonian captivity.

36:1 fourteenth year of King Hezekiah. Since Sennacherib's attack came in 701 B.C., this places the beginning of Hezekiah's reign in 715 B.C. But since 2 Kin. 18:1 says he began to reign in the third year of Hoshea, ca. 729 B.C., Hezekiah served as co-regent with Ahaz (ca. 729–716 B.C.) before assuming the throne exclusively. It was customary for the later kings of Israel to assume their sons into partnership in the government during their lives. **Sennacherib.** The king of Assyria (ca. 705 to 681 B.C.). **fortified cities.** The discovery of the ancient *Annals of Sennacherib* reveals the cities he conquered in his campaign southward from Sidon on the Mediterranean coast.

36:2 Rabshakeh. The spokesman for Sennacherib's 3 highest officials, who represented the king against Jerusalem on this occasion, according to 2 Kin. 18:17. **great army.** This was a token force of the main army (37:36), with which Sennacherib hoped to bluff Judah into submitting. **Lachish.** A city about 25 mi. SW of Jerusalem. Sennacherib's conquest of this city was in its closing phase when he sent the messengers. **aqueduct from the upper pool.** Isaiah met Ahaz at the same spot to try unsuccessfully to dissuade him from trusting in foreign powers (7:3).

36:3 Eliakim…Shebna. *See notes on 22:19-22.* **Joah…the recorder.** The position was that of an intermediary between the king and the people.

36:4-10 Rabshakeh's logic was twofold: (1) Egypt was to be unable to deliver Jerusalem (vv. 4-6,8,9), and (2) the Lord had called on the Assyrians to destroy Judah (vv. 7,10).

36:4 great king, the king of Assyria. The self-appropriated title of Assyrian kings. In contrast, Rabshakeh rudely omitted any title for Hezekiah (vv. 4,14,15,16).

36:5 mere words. Words amounted to nothing when it came to warfare. In other words, Judah was defenseless.

36:6 broken reed, Egypt. The Assyrian's advice strongly resembled that of Isaiah (19:14-16; 30:7; 31:3).

36:7 He whose high places and whose altars. Rabshakeh mistakenly thought Hezekiah's reforms in removing idols (2 Kin. 18:4; 2 Chr. 31:1) had removed opportunities to worship the Lord. **this altar.** That all worship should center in Solomon's temple, was utterly foreign to the polytheistic Assyrians.

36:8,9 Rabshakeh taunted and minimized Judah's best defensive efforts, even with Egypt's help.

36:10 The LORD said. Rabshakeh's boastful claim of the authority from Judah's God for his mission may have been a ploy on his part to get a surrender, but it aligned with Isaiah's prophecy that the Assyrians would be His instrument to punish His people (8:7,8; 10:5,6). The Assyrians may have heard this from partisans or may not have known this, but Judah did.

36:11 Aramaic…Hebrew. Hezekiah's representatives, aware of the alarm created by the suggestion that the Lord was on the Assyrian side, asked Rabshekah to change from Hebrew to Aramaic, the language of diplomacy, so the people on the wall could not understand his words and be terrified.

12 But *the* Rabshakeh said, "Has my master sent me to your master and to you to
speak these words, and not to the men
who sit on the wall, who will eat and drink
their own waste with you?"
13 Then *the* Rabshakeh stood and called
out with a loud voice in Hebrew, and said,
"Hear the words of the great king, the king
of Assyria! 14 Thus says the king: 'Do not
let Hezekiah deceive you, for he will not be
able to deliver you; 15 nor let Hezekiah
make you trust in the LORD, saying, "The
LORD will surely deliver us; this city will
not be given into the hand of the king of
Assyria." ' 16 Do not listen to Hezekiah; for
thus says the king of Assyria: 'Make *peace*
with me *by a* present and come out to me;
[g]and every one of you eat from his own
vine and every one from his own fig tree,
and every one of you drink the waters of
his own cistern; 17 until I come and take
you away to a land like your own land, a
land of grain and new wine, a land of
bread and vineyards. 18 *Beware* lest Hezekiah persuade you, saying, "The LORD will
deliver us." Has any one of the [h]gods of
the nations delivered its land from the
hand of the king of Assyria? 19 Where *are*
the gods of Hamath and Arpad? Where *are*
the gods of Sepharvaim? Indeed, have they
delivered [i]Samaria from my hand? 20 Who
among all the gods of these lands have delivered their countries from my hand, that
the LORD should deliver Jerusalem from
my hand?' "
21 But they [4]held their peace and answered him not a word; for the king's commandment was, "Do not answer him."
22 Then Eliakim the son of Hilkiah, who
was over the household, Shebna the scribe,
and Joah the son of Asaph, the recorder,
came to Hezekiah with *their* clothes torn,
and told him the words of *the* Rabshakeh.

16 [g] 1 Kin. 4:25; Mic. 4:4; Zech. 3:10
18 [h] 2 Kin. 19:12; Is. 37:12
19 [i] 2 Kin. 17:6
21 [4] *were silent*

Isaiah Assures Deliverance

37 And [a]so it was, when King Hezekiah heard *it*, that he tore his
clothes, covered himself with sackcloth,
and went into the house of the LORD.
2 Then he sent Eliakim, who *was* over the
household, Shebna the scribe, and the elders of the priests, covered with sackcloth,
to Isaiah the prophet, the son of Amoz.
3 And they said to him, "Thus says Hezekiah: 'This day *is* a day of [b]trouble and rebuke and [1]blasphemy; for the children
have come to birth, but *there is* no strength
to bring them forth. 4 It may be that the
LORD your God will hear the words of *the*
Rabshakeh, whom his master the king of
Assyria has sent to [c]reproach the living
God, and will rebuke the words which the
LORD your God has heard. Therefore lift up
your prayer for the remnant that is left.' "
5 So the servants of King Hezekiah came
to Isaiah. 6 And Isaiah said to them, "Thus
you shall say to your master, 'Thus says the
LORD: "Do not be afraid of the words which
you have heard, with which the servants of
the king of Assyria have blasphemed Me.
7 Surely I will send a spirit upon him, and
he shall hear a rumor and return to his own
land; and I will cause him to fall by the
sword in his own land." ' "

Sennacherib's Threat and Hezekiah's Prayer

8 Then *the* Rabshakeh returned, and
found the king of Assyria warring against
Libnah, for he heard that he had departed

CHAPTER 37

1 [a] 2 Kin. 19:1-37; Is. 37:1-38
3 [b] Is. 22:5; 26:16; 33:2 [1] *contempt*
4 [c] Is. 36:15, 18, 20

36:12 men...on the wall. The foreign emissary continued his efforts to damage the city's morale by speaking of the horrors of famine that a long siege would entail.

36:13-17 Rabshakeh spoke longer and louder, suggesting that Hezekiah could not save the city, but the great king, the king of Assyria, would fill the people with abundance (vv. 16,17).

36:16 Make...present. Lit. "Make a blessing with me." The official invited the people to make a covenant with Assyria by surrendering.

36:17 take you away. Rabshakeh did not hide Assyria's well-known practice of deporting conquered peoples to distant places.

36:18-20 In Rabshakeh's eyes, the Lord was one of the many gods worshiped by nations conquered by the Assyrians (cf. 10:8-11).

36:21 held their peace. Hezekiah had apparently anticipated the ultimatum of the Assyrians and had told his representatives and the men on the wall not to respond.

36:22 clothes torn. The king's representatives reported to him in a state of grief and shock at the blasphemy they thought they had heard.

37:1 tore...sackcloth. A reaction that symbolized Hezekiah's grief, repentance and contrition. The nation was to repent and the king was to lead the way. **house of the LORD.** God designated the temple as His "house of prayer" (56:7; Matt. 21:13; Mark 11:17; Luke 19:46), so it was the proper place to go to confess sins and seek forgiveness (cf. Ps. 73:16,17).

37:2 elders of the priests. Senior religious leaders in Israel.

37:3 come to birth...no strength. Hezekiah compared his dilemma with a mother in labor unable to deliver her child. Jerusalem had to be delivered, but he was helpless to make it happen.

37:4 reproach the living God. Hezekiah received a report of Rabshakeh's belittling of the Lord by equating Him with other gods and points out the distinction between God who is living and gods who are lifeless and helpless (40:18-20; 46:5-7). **remnant that is left.** Only Jerusalem remained unconquered. Hezekiah asked Isaiah's prayer for the city.

37:6 Do not be afraid. The same assurance Isaiah had given Ahaz (7:4).

37:7 spirit. The Lord promised to incline Sennacherib's attitude in such a way that he would leave Jerusalem unharmed and return home.

37:8 Libnah. After conquering Lachish, Sennacherib moved on to this smaller town to the N of Lachish.

from Lachish. 9 And the king heard concerning Tirhakah king of Ethiopia, "He has
come out to make war with you." So when
he heard *it*, he sent messengers to Hezekiah, saying, 10 "Thus you shall speak to
Hezekiah king of Judah, saying: 'Do not let
your God in whom you trust deceive you,
saying, "Jerusalem shall not be given into
the hand of the king of Assyria." 11 Look!
You have heard what the kings of Assyria
have done to all lands by utterly destroying them; and shall you be delivered?
12 Have the [d]gods of the nations delivered
those whom my fathers have destroyed,
Gozan and Haran and Rezeph, and the
people of Eden who *were* in Telassar?
13 Where *is* the king of [e]Hamath, the king
of Arpad, and the king of the city of Sepharvaim, Hena, and Ivah?' "

14 And Hezekiah received the letter
from the hand of the messengers, and read
it; and Hezekiah went up to the house of
the LORD, and spread it before the LORD.
15 Then Hezekiah prayed to the LORD, saying: 16 "O LORD of hosts, God of Israel, *the
One* who dwells *between* the cherubim, You
are God, You [f]alone, of all the kingdoms of
the earth. You have made heaven and
earth. 17 [g]Incline Your ear, O LORD, and
hear; open Your eyes, O LORD, and see; and
[h]hear all the words of Sennacherib, which
he has sent to reproach the living God.
18 Truly, LORD, the kings of Assyria have
laid waste all the nations and their [i]lands,
19 and have cast their gods into the fire; for
they *were* [j]not gods, but the work of men's
hands—wood and stone. Therefore they
destroyed them. 20 Now therefore, O LORD
our God, [k]save us from his hand, that all
the kingdoms of the earth may [l]know that
You *are* the LORD, You alone."

12 [d]Is. 36:18, 19 **13** [e]Is. 49:23 **16** [f]Is. 43:10, 11 **17** [g]2 Chr. 6:40; Ps. 17:6; Dan. 9:18 [h]Ps. 74:22 **18** [i]2 Kin. 15:29; 16:9; 17:6, 24; 1 Chr. 5:26 **19** [j]Is. 40:19, 20 **20** [k]Is. 33:22 [l]Ps. 83:18

The Word of the LORD Concerning Sennacherib

21 Then Isaiah the son of Amoz sent to
Hezekiah, saying, "Thus says the LORD
God of Israel, 'Because you have prayed to
Me against Sennacherib king of Assyria,
22 this *is* the word which the LORD has spo-
ken concerning him:

"The virgin, the daughter of Zion,
Has despised you, laughed you to scorn;
The daughter of Jerusalem
Has shaken *her* head behind your back!

23 "Whom have you reproached and blasphemed?
Against whom have you raised *your* voice,
And lifted up your eyes on high?
Against the Holy One of Israel.
24 By your servants you have reproached the Lord,
And said, 'By the multitude of my chariots
I have come up to the height of the mountains,
To the limits of Lebanon;
I will cut down its tall cedars
And its choice cypress trees;
I will enter its farthest height,
To its fruitful forest.
25 I have dug and drunk water,
And with the soles of my feet I have dried up
All the brooks of [2]defense.'

26 "Did you not hear [m]long ago
How I made it,
From ancient times that I formed it?

25 [2]Or perhaps *Egypt* **26** [m]Is. 25:1; 40:21; 45:21

37:9 Tirhakah king of Ethiopia. Tirhakah did not become king of Ethiopia (and Egypt) until 11 years after the 701 B.C. siege, so Isaiah's use of "king" anticipates his future title. At that moment, however, he represented a threat to Sennacherib from the S that caused him to renew his call for Jerusalem's surrender to the N.

37:10-13 The king of Assyria sent messengers to summarize the arguments given in Rabshakeh's ultimatum of 36:4-19.

37:10 deceive. The accusation of deception was first against Hezekiah (36:14), then against the Lord.

37:11-13 The threat repeats the thrust of 36:18-20.

37:12 The conquered cities mentioned here lay between the Tigris and Euphrates Rivers in Mesopotamia.

37:13 These were cities of Syria that had fallen to the Assyrians recently.

37:14 house of the LORD. Godly Hezekiah returned to the house of the Lord (cf. v. 1) as he should have, in contrast to Ahab, who in a similar crisis refused even to ask a sign from the Lord (7:11,12).

37:16 *the One* who dwells...heaven and earth. The basis for Hezekiah's plea was God's role as the Sovereign and Creator of the universe, not Judah's worthiness to be delivered.

37:17 hear...see...hear. In contrast to the gods of other nations (Ps. 115:4-7), the God of Israel heard and saw all.

37:18,19 Hezekiah exploded the Assyrian theory that the Lord was no different from gods of the other nations that could not deliver their worshipers.

37:20 You alone. Hezekiah displayed the highest motivation of all in requesting the salvation of Jerusalem: that the world may know that the Lord alone is God (cf. Dan. 9:16-19).

37:21 Isaiah the son of Amoz. Immediately upon the conclusion of Hezekiah's prayer, Isaiah had a response from the Lord.

37:22 laughed you to scorn. Jerusalem, portrayed as a virgin helpless before a would-be rapist, had the "last laugh" against Sennacherib.

37:23 you reproached and blasphemed. The Lord had heard Sennacherib's reproach against Him (37:17).

37:24,25 Even the servants of Sennacherib had bragged about Assyria's being unstoppable.

Now I have brought it to pass,
That you should be
For crushing fortified cities *into*
heaps of ruins.
27 Therefore their inhabitants *had*
little power;
They were dismayed and
confounded;
They were *as* the grass of the field
And the green herb,
As the grass on the housetops
And grain blighted before it is
grown.

28 "But I know your dwelling place,
Your going out and your coming
in,
And your rage against Me.
29 Because your rage against Me and
your tumult
Have come up to My ears,
Therefore [n]I will put My hook in
your nose
And My bridle in your lips,
And I will [o]turn you back
By the way which you came." '

30 "This *shall be* a sign to you:

You shall eat this year such as
grows of itself,
And the second year what springs
from the same;
Also in the third year sow and
reap,
Plant vineyards and eat the fruit of
them.

31 And the remnant who have
escaped of the house of Judah
Shall again take root downward,
And bear fruit upward.
32 For out of Jerusalem shall go a
remnant,
And those who escape from Mount
Zion.
The [p]zeal of the LORD of hosts will
do this.

33 "Therefore thus says the LORD concerning the king of Assyria:

'He shall not come into this city,
Nor shoot an arrow there,
Nor come before it with shield,
Nor build a siege mound against it.
34 By the way that he came,
By the same shall he return;
And he shall not come into this
city,'
Says the LORD.
35 'For I will [q]defend this city, to save
it
For My own sake and for My
servant [r]David's sake.' "

Sennacherib's Defeat and Death

36 Then the [s]angel[3] of the LORD went
out, and [4]killed in the camp of the Assyrians one hundred and eighty-five thousand; and when *people* arose early in the
morning, there were the corpses—all dead.
37 So Sennacherib king of Assyria departed
and went away, returned *home,* and remained at Nineveh. 38 Now it came to
pass, as he was worshiping in the house of

29 [n] 2 Kin. 19:35-37; 2 Chr. 32:21; Is. 30:28; Ezek. 38:4 [o] Ezek. 38:4; 39:2
32 [p] 2 Kin. 19:31; Is. 9:7; 59:17; Joel 2:18; Zech. 1:14
35 [q] 2 Kin. 20:6; Is. 31:5; 38:6 [r] 1 Kin. 11:13
36 [s] 2 Kin. 19:35; Is. 10:12, 33, 34 [3] Or *Angel* [4] Lit. *struck*

37:26 I have brought it to pass. God corrected Sennacherib's vanity; he conquered nothing on his own, but was a mere instrument in the Lord's hand.

37:27 They were dismayed. Assyria had utterly overwhelmed populations included in their conquests.

37:28 your rage against Me. Sennacherib's ignorance of being a mere tool in the Lord's hand was bad, but his belittling of God, the source of his life, was far worse.

37:29 hook in your nose…bridle in your lips. In judging Sennacherib, the Lord treated him as a obstinate animal with a ring in his nose and/or a bridle in his mouth. Some ancient sources indicate that captives were led before a king by a cord attached to a hook or ring through the upper lip and nose. Thus, he was to be brought back to his own country.

37:30 sign. The two years in which they were sustained by the growth of the crops were the two in which Sennacherib ravaged them (cf. 32:10). He left immediately after the deliverance (37:37), so in the third year, the people left could plant again.

37:31,32 remnant…remnant. From the remnant of survivors in Jerusalem came descendants who covered the Land once again (1:9,27; 3:10; 4:3; 6:13; 8:16,17; 10:20,22; 11:12,16; 26:1-4,8; 27:12; 28:5; 37:4).

37:32 zeal of the LORD of hosts. The same confirmation of God's promise in 9:7 assured the future establishment of the messianic kingdom. Deliverance from Sennacherib in Hezekiah's day was a down payment on the literal, final restoration of Israel.

37:33 shall not come…build a siege mound. God promised that the Assyrians would not even pose a physical threat to Jerusalem. He came near, but never engaged in a true siege of the city.

37:34 shall he return. In contrast with his arrival in Judah as an overbearing, invincible monarch, he returned to Assyria as a defeated, dejected "has been." In his own *Annals* he claimed only to have "shut up" Jerusalem, not to have conquered it.

37:35 For My own sake. Since Sennacherib had directly challenged the Lord's faithfulness to His word (v. 10), the faithfulness of God was at stake in this contest with the Assyrians (cf. Ezek. 36:22, 23). **for My servant David's sake.** God pledged to perpetuate David's line on his throne (2 Sam. 7:16; cf. 9:6,7; 11:1; 55:3).

37:36 the angel of the LORD. This was Isaiah's only use of a title that is frequent in the OT, one referring to the Lord Himself. For identification, *see note on Ex. 3:2.* **killed.** Secular records also mention this massive slaughter of Assyrian troops, without noting its supernatural nature, of course (cf. Ex. 12:12,29).

37:37 Nineveh. The capital of Assyria.

Nisroch his god, that his sons Adrammelech and Sharezer struck him down with
the sword; and they escaped into the land
of Ararat. Then [t]Esarhaddon his son
reigned in his place.

Hezekiah's Life Extended

38 In [a]those days Hezekiah was sick
and near death. And Isaiah the
prophet, the son of Amoz, went to him and
said to him, "Thus says the LORD: [b]'Set
your house in order, for you shall die and
not live.' "
2 Then Hezekiah turned his face toward
the wall, and prayed to the LORD, 3 and
said, [c]"Remember now, O LORD, I pray,
how I have walked before You in truth and
with a [1]loyal heart, and have done *what is*
good in Your [d]sight." And Hezekiah wept
bitterly.
4 And the word of the LORD came to Isaiah, saying, 5 "Go and tell Hezekiah, 'Thus
says the LORD, the God of David your father: "I have heard your prayer, I have seen
your tears; surely I will add to your days
fifteen years. 6 I will deliver you and this
city from the hand of the king of Assyria,
and [e]I will defend this city." ' 7 And this *is*
[f]the sign to you from the LORD, that the
LORD will do this thing which He has spoken: 8 Behold, I will bring the shadow on
the sundial, which has gone down with the
sun on the sundial of Ahaz, ten degrees
backward." So the sun returned ten degrees on the dial by which it had gone
down.
9 This is the writing of Hezekiah king of
Judah, when he had been sick and had
recovered from his sickness:

10 I said,
"In the prime of my life
I shall go to the gates of Sheol;
I am deprived of the remainder of
my years."
11 I said,
"I shall not see [2]YAH,
The LORD [g]in the land of the living;
I shall observe man no more
[3]among the inhabitants of
[4]the world.
12 [h]My life span is gone,
Taken from me like a shepherd's
tent;
I have cut off my life like a weaver.
He cuts me off from the loom;
From day until night You make an
end of me.
13 I have considered until morning—
Like a lion,
So He breaks all my bones;
From day until night You make an
end of me.
14 Like a crane *or* a swallow, so I
chattered;
[i]I mourned like a dove;
My eyes fail *from looking* upward.
O [5]LORD, I am oppressed;
[6]Undertake for me!

15 "What shall I say?
[7]He has both spoken to me,
And He Himself has done *it*.
I shall walk carefully all my years
[j]In the bitterness of my soul.

38 [t]Ezra 4:2

CHAPTER 38

1 [a]2 Kin. 20:1-6, 9-11; 2 Chr. 32:24; Is. 38:1-8 [b]2 Sam. 17:23
3 [c]Neh. 13:14 [d]2 Kin. 18:5, 6; Ps. 26:3 [1]*whole or peaceful*
6 [e]2 Kin. 19:35-37; 2 Chr. 32:21; Is. 31:5; 37:35
7 [f]Judg. 6:17, 21, 36-40; 2 Kin. 20:8; Is. 7:11
11 [g]Ps. 27:13; 116:9 [2]Heb. *YAH, YAH* [3]LXX omits *among the inhabitants of the world* [4]So with some Heb. mss.; MT, Vg. *rest*; Tg. *land*
12 [h]Job 7:6
14 [i]Is. 59:11; Ezek. 7:16; Nah. 2:7 [5]So with Bg.; MT, DSS *Lord* [6]*Be my surety*
15 [j]Job 7:11; 10:1; Is. 38:17 [7]So with MT, Vg.; DSS, Tg. *And shall I say to Him*; LXX omits first half of this verse

37:38 his god. The place of Sennacherib's death (ca. 681 B.C.) recalled the impotence of his god, Nisroch, compared with the omnipotence of Hezekiah's God. **struck him down.** Sennacherib's pitiful death came 20 years after his confrontation with the Lord regarding the fate of Jerusalem. **Ararat.** Mountain region N of Israel, W of Assyria (cf. Gen. 8:4; 2 Kin. 19:37; Jer. 51:27). **Esarhaddon.** Successor to Sennacherib (ca. 681–669 B.C.).

38:1 In those days...sick. Hezekiah's sickness occurred before the Assyrian siege of Jerusalem described in chaps. 36,37. Isaiah placed the description of that illness here, along with chap. 39, to introduce chaps. 40–66. *See note on 2 Kin. 20:1.* **Set your house in order.** An instruction telling Hezekiah to make his final will known to his family (cf. 2 Sam. 17:23; 1 Kin. 2:1-9). **you shall die and not live.** The prediction sounded final, but Hezekiah knew God was willing to hear his appeal (cf. Ex. 32:7-14).

38:2,3 prayed...wept bitterly. *See note on 2 Kin. 20:2,3.*

38:3 loyal heart. Hezekiah's based his implied request for an extension of his life on an undivided desire to please the Lord.

38:5 fifteen years. The Lord's immediate (2 Kin. 20:4) response granted the king's request. Having to reverse a prophecy so quickly did not alarm Isaiah as it did Jonah later on (Jon. 4:2,3). Isaiah resembled Nathan in this respect (2 Sam. 7:3-6).

38:6 I will deliver...this city. The deliverance described in the previous chapter.

38:7,8 sign...ten degrees backward. Here is the first biblical mention of any means of marking time. According to 2 Kin. 20:8-10, Hezekiah requested this sign to confirm the Lord's promise of healing.

38:9 writing of Hezekiah. In response to his healing, Hezekiah wrote the record of his helplessness when facing death (vv. 10-14) and told of God's response to His condition (vv. 15-20). This poetry is missing from the parallel account in 2 Kings.

38:10 In the prime of my life. The king was probably in his thirties or forties when he fell sick.

38:11 I shall not see. Hezekiah feared that death would terminate his fellowship with the Lord. **YAH.** The Heb. repeats the name: "YAH, YAH." The KJV rendered it, "LORD, even the LORD." See 12:2; 26:4 for other such repetitions.

38:12 shepherd's tent...a weaver. Two comparisons with transient articles illustrate how death removes in a moment what may have seemed so permanent.

38:14 I mourned...Undertake for me! In his helplessness, Hezekiah pleaded with God to deliver him from impending death.

38:15 He Himself has done *it*. The king had complete confidence in God.

16 O Lord, by these *things men* live;
And in all these *things is* the life of my spirit;
So You will restore me and make me live.
17 Indeed *it was* for *my own* peace
That I had great bitterness;
But You have lovingly *delivered* my soul from the pit of corruption,
For You have cast all my sins behind Your back.
18 For [k]Sheol cannot thank You,
Death cannot praise You;
Those who go down to the pit cannot hope for Your truth.
19 The living, the living man, he shall praise You,
As I *do* this day;
[l]The father shall make known Your truth to the children.

20 "The LORD *was ready* to save me;
Therefore we will sing my songs with stringed instruments
All the days of our life, in the house of the LORD."

21 Now [m]Isaiah had said, "Let them take
a lump of figs, and apply *it* as a poultice on
the boil, and he shall recover."
22 And [n]Hezekiah had said, "What *is* the
sign that I shall go up to the house of the
LORD?"

18 [k]Ps. 6:5; 30:9; 88:11; 115:17; [Eccl. 9:10]
19 [l]Deut. 4:9; 6:7; Ps. 78:3, 4
21 [m]2 Kin. 20:7
22 [n]2 Kin. 20:8

CHAPTER 39
1 [a]2 Kin. 20:12-19; 2 Chr. 32:31; Is. 39:1-8 [1]Berodach-Baladan, 2 Kin. 20:12
2 [b]2 Chr. 32:25, 31; Job 31:25
3 [c]Deut. 28:49; Jer. 5:15
6 [d]2 Kin. 24:13; 25:13-15; Jer. 20:5
7 [e]Dan. 1:1-7
8 [f]1 Sam. 3:18

The Babylonian Envoys

39 At [a]that time [1]Merodach-Baladan
the son of Baladan, king of Babylon,
sent letters and a present to Hezekiah, for
he heard that he had been sick and had
recovered. 2 [b]And Hezekiah was pleased
with them, and showed them the house of
his treasures—the silver and gold, the
spices and precious ointment, and all his
armory—all that was found among his
treasures. There was nothing in his house
or in all his dominion that Hezekiah did
not show them.
3 Then Isaiah the prophet went to King
Hezekiah, and said to him, "What did
these men say, and from where did they
come to you?"
So Hezekiah said, "They came to me
from a [c]far country, from Babylon."
4 And he said, "What have they seen in
your house?"
So Hezekiah answered, "They have seen
all that *is* in my house; there is nothing
among my treasures that I have not shown
them."
5 Then Isaiah said to Hezekiah, "Hear the
word of the LORD of hosts: 6 'Behold, the
days are coming [d]when all that *is* in your
house, and what your fathers have accumulated until this day, shall be carried to Babylon; nothing shall be left,' says the LORD.
7 'And they shall take away *some* of your
[e]sons who will descend from you, whom
you will beget; and they shall be eunuchs in
the palace of the king of Babylon.' "
8 So Hezekiah said to Isaiah, [f]"The word
of the LORD which you have spoken *is*

38:16 restore me and make me live. The king's survival was God's accomplishment.

38:17 sins behind Your back. Hezekiah felt his sickness was somehow related to his sinfulness. To be rid of the latter was to be rid of the former also.

38:18 cannot hope. Hezekiah's understanding of the resurrection of believers was incomplete. The same was true of others throughout much of the OT. But he was right in recognizing that death ended his opportunity for earthly praise and worship in the presence of men.

38:19 father...children. Word about God's faithfulness passed from generation to generation (Deut. 4:9; 6:7; Ps. 78:3,4). If Hezekiah at this point had no heir, he had another reason for frustration over dying in the prime of life.

38:20 sing...in the house of the LORD. Hezekiah was so overwhelmed with gratitude to God that he felt compelled to express it appropriately throughout the 15 years he had left on earth.

38:21,22 These two verses furnish background details of the account in vv. 1-8.

38:21 poultice on the boil. The medicine for healing the king's sickness (2 Kin. 20:7).

38:22 sign. Hezekiah's request explained why the Lord gave him a sign that he would be healed (v. 7; cf. 2 Kin. 20:8). **the house of the LORD.** Hezekiah went to the temple (v. 20) as Isaiah had instructed him to do (2 Kin. 20:5,8).

39:1 At that time. Just after Hezekiah's sickness and recovery. **Merodach-Baladan.** *See note on 2 Kin. 20:12.*

39:2 Hezekiah was pleased. The text does not say whether it was because of flattery or of a desire for help against the increasing Assyrian threat. Cf. "attentive" in 2 Kin. 20:13. **treasures...treasures.** Doubtless to try and impress his visitors (2 Chr. 32:25), Hezekiah showed all he could contribute in an alliance against the Assyrians.

39:3 Isaiah the prophet went. God's spokesman showed up without being invited to confront the king, as often happened (e.g., 7:3; 2 Sam. 12:1; 1 Kin. 13:1; 18:16,17).

39:5,6 word of the LORD...carried to Babylon. Isaiah predicted the Babylonian captivity that would come over a century later (586 B.C.), another prophecy historically fulfilled in all of its expected detail.

39:6 nothing shall be left. Hezekiah's sin of parading his wealth before the visitors backfired, though this sin was only symptomatic of the ultimate reason for the captivity. The major cause was the corrupt leadership of Manasseh, Hezekiah's son (2 Kin. 21:11-15).

39:7 sons who will descend from you. To a king without an heir, this was good news (that he would have one some day) and bad news (that his sons must go into captivity). See 2 Kin. 24:12-16; 2 Chr. 33:11; Dan. 1:3,4,6 for the prophecy's fulfillment.

39:8 word of the LORD...good. A surprising response to the negative prophecy of vv. 5-7! It perhaps acknowledged Isaiah as

good!" For he said, "At least there will be
peace and truth in my days."

God's People Are Comforted

40 "Comfort, yes, comfort My people!"
Says your God.
2 "Speak [1]comfort to Jerusalem, and
cry out to her,
That her warfare is ended,
That her iniquity is pardoned;
[a]For she has received from the
LORD's hand
Double for all her sins."

3 [b]The voice of one crying in the
wilderness:
[c]"Prepare the way of the LORD;
[d]Make straight [2]in the desert
A highway for our God.
4 Every valley shall be exalted
And every mountain and hill
brought low;
[e]The crooked places shall be made
[3]straight
And the rough places smooth;
5 The [f]glory of the LORD shall be
revealed,
And all flesh shall see *it* together;
For the mouth of the LORD has
spoken."

6 The voice said, "Cry out!"
And [4]he said, "What shall I cry?"
[g]"All flesh *is* grass,
And all its loveliness *is* like the
flower of the field.
7 The grass withers, the flower fades,
Because the breath of the LORD
blows upon it;
Surely the people *are* grass.
8 The grass withers, the flower fades,
But [h]the word of our God stands
forever."

9 O Zion,
You who bring good tidings,
Get up into the high mountain;
O Jerusalem,
You who bring good tidings,
Lift up your voice with strength,
Lift *it* up, be not afraid;
Say to the cities of Judah, "Behold
your God!"

10 Behold, the Lord GOD shall come
[5]with a strong *hand*,
And [i]His arm shall rule for Him;
Behold, [j]His reward *is* with Him,
And His [6]work before Him.

CHAPTER 40
2 [a] Is. 61:7 [1] Lit. *to the heart of*
3 [b] Matt. 3:3; Mark 1:3; Luke 3:4-6; John 1:23 [c] [Mal. 3:1; 4:5, 6] [d] Ps. 68:4 [2] So with MT, Tg., Vg.; LXX omits *in the desert*
4 [e] Is. 45:2 [3] Or *a plain*
5 [f] Is. 35:2
6 [g] Job 14:2; James 1:10; 1 Pet. 1:24, 25 [4] So with MT, Tg.; DSS, LXX, Vg. *I*
8 [h] [John 12:34]
10 [i] Is. 59:16, 18 [j] Is. 62:11; Rev. 22:12 [5] *in strength* [6] *recompense*

God's faithful messenger. **peace and truth in my days.** Hezekiah perhaps reacted selfishly, or perhaps he looked for a bright spot to lighten the gloomy fate of his descendants.

40:1–66:24 The prophecies of chaps. 1–39 addressed Judah in her situation during Isaiah's ministry (739 B.C. until ca. 686 B.C.). The prophecies of chaps. 40–66 address Judah as though the prophesied Babylonian captivity (39:5-7) were already a present reality, though that captivity did not begin until 605–586 B.C. The words "'*There* is no peace,' says the LORD, 'for the wicked'" (48:22; 57:21) signal the divisions of this section into three parts: chaps. 40–48, chaps. 49–57, and chaps. 58–66.

40:1–48:22 This section looks at the hope and comfort of a blessed future subsequent to God's judgment in the forthcoming Babylonian captivity.

40:1,2 Comfort…comfort. The prophecy addressed God's prophets, instructing them to emphasize the theme of comfort to a captive people in a foreign land many mi. from their home city of Jerusalem. God has good plans for great blessing to Israel in the future because they are His covenant people, who are never to be permanently cast away (cf. Rom. 11:2).

40:2 iniquity is pardoned…double for all her sins. Cruel slaughter and captivity at the hands of the Babylonians was sufficient payment for past sins; so someday after worldwide dispersion, Israel will return to her land in peace and in the glory of Messiah's kingdom.

40:3-5 A prophetic exhortation told Israel to prepare for the revelation of the Lord's glory at the arrival of Messiah. Scripture sees John the Baptist in this role (Matt. 3:3; Mark; 1:3; Luke 3:4-6; John 1:23). It likewise sees the future forerunner who is to be like Elijah preparing for Christ's second coming (Mal. 3:1; 4:5,6).

40:3,4 Prepare the way. The remnant of Israel could remove obstacles from the coming Messiah's path through repentance from their sins. John the Baptist reminded his listeners of this necessity (Matt. 3:2), as did Jesus (Matt. 4:17; Mark 1:15). These verses reflect the custom of some eastern monarchs to send heralds before them to clear away obstacles, make causeways, straighten crooked roads and valleys, and level hills (cf. 45:1,2). John had the task of getting people ready for Messiah's arrival.

40:5 glory of the LORD…revealed. Jerusalem's misery is to end and the Lord's glory to replace it, so comfort will come to the city (v. 2), and every person will see God's glorious salvation (cf. 52:10) in Messiah's future kingdom (Hab. 2:14; Rev. 21:23; cf. 11:9). **mouth of the LORD has spoken.** Used for confirmations also in 1:20; 58:14; 62:2.

40:6-8 All flesh…flower fades. Isaiah elaborated on how transitory humanity is: here today, gone tomorrow. People pass away like plants under the hot breath of the withering E wind. James used this illustration to teach the folly of trusting in material wealth (James 1:10,11). Peter used it to illustrate the passing nature of everything related to humanity (1 Pet. 1:24,25).

40:8 the word of our God stands forever. The permanence of God's word guarantees against any deviation from the divine plan (55:11). He has promised Jerusalem's deliverance (v. 2) through His coming (vv. 3-5), so it must happen that way (cf. Matt. 5:18; Luke 16:17).

40:9 Zion…good tidings…Jerusalem…good tidings. Like a messenger on a mountain, to be seen and heard by all, the prophet called on the city to proclaim loudly to the rest of Judah's cities the good news of God's presence there (cf. 2:3). **"Behold, your God!"** The restoration of Israel to the Land is to include the resumption of God's presence in Jerusalem after many centuries (Ezek. 43:1-7; Rev. 21:22,23; cf. Ezek. 11:22,23).

40:10 the Lord God shall come with a strong *hand*. At His second coming, Christ returns with power to defeat His enemies and gather the dispersed of Israel to their Land (Matt. 24:31; Rev. 19:11-21).

11 He will [k]feed His flock like a shepherd;
He will gather the lambs with His arm,
And carry *them* in His bosom,
And gently lead those who are with young.

12 [l]Who has measured the [7]waters in the hollow of His hand,
Measured heaven with a [8]span
And calculated the dust of the earth in a measure?
Weighed the mountains in scales
And the hills in a balance?
13 [m]Who has directed the Spirit of the LORD,
Or *as* His counselor has taught Him?
14 With whom did He take counsel, and *who* instructed Him,
And [n]taught Him in the path of justice?
Who taught Him knowledge,
And showed Him the way of understanding?

15 Behold, the nations *are* as a drop in a bucket,
And are counted as the small dust on the scales;
Look, He lifts up the isles as a very little thing.
16 And Lebanon *is* not sufficient to burn,
Nor its beasts sufficient for a burnt offering.
17 All nations before Him *are* as [o]nothing,
And [p]they are counted by Him less than nothing and worthless.

18 To whom then will you [q]liken God?
Or what likeness will you compare to Him?
19 [r]The workman molds an image,
The goldsmith overspreads it with gold,
And the silversmith casts silver chains.
20 Whoever *is* too impoverished for *such* [9]a contribution
Chooses a tree *that* will not rot;
He seeks for himself a skillful workman
[s]To prepare a carved image *that* will not totter.

21 [t]Have you not known?
Have you not heard?
Has it not been told you from the beginning?
Have you not understood from the foundations of the earth?
22 *It is* He who sits above the circle of the earth,
And its inhabitants *are* like grasshoppers,
Who [u]stretches out the heavens like a curtain,
And spreads them out like a [v]tent to dwell in.
23 He [1]brings the [w]princes to nothing;
He makes the judges of the earth useless.

24 Scarcely shall they be planted,

11 [k] Jer. 31:10; [Ezek. 34:23, 31]; Mic. 5:4; [John 10:11, 14-16; Heb. 13:20; 1 Pet. 2:25]
12 [l] Prov. 30:4 [7] So with MT, LXX, Vg.; DSS adds *of the sea;* Tg. adds *of the world* [8] A span = ½ cubit, 9 inches; or the width of His hand
13 [m] Job 21:22; Rom. 11:34; [1 Cor. 2:16]
14 [n] Job 36:22, 23
17 [o] Dan. 4:35 [p] Ps. 62:9
18 [q] Ex. 8:10; 15:11; 1 Sam. 2:2; Is. 46:5; [Mic. 7:18]; Acts 17:29
19 [r] Ps. 115:4-8; Is. 41:7; 44:10; Hab. 2:18, 19
20 [s] 1 Sam. 5:3, 4; Is. 41:7; 46:7; Jer. 10:3 [9] *an offering*
21 [t] Ps. 19:1; Is. 37:26; Acts 14:17; Rom. 1:19
22 [u] Job 9:8; Ps. 104:2; Is. 42:5; 44:24; Jer. 10:12 [v] Job 36:29; Ps. 19:4
23 [w] Job 12:21; Ps. 107:40; Is. 34:12; [1 Cor. 1:26-29] [1] *reduces*

40:11 His arm. A picture of God's omnipotence. The same arm that powerfully scatters the Jews all over the earth in judgment is to overcome Israel's oppressors (v. 10) and to tenderly feed and lead His flock (Ps. 23:1,2; Jer. 31:10; Ezek. 34:11-16; Mic. 2:12).

40:12-14 By a series of questions, to which the implied answer is "no one," the prophet emphasized the omnipotence and omniscience of God, the God whose coming is to bring comfort to Israel according to vv. 1-11.

40:12 Who has measured...in a balance. God alone has power to create the physical universe and the earth in perfect balance, weighing mountains and seas perfectly, so that the earth moves perfectly in space. This matter of the amazing balance of our planet is called the science of isostasy.

40:13,14 directed the Spirit of the LORD. Isaiah pointed to the incomparable wisdom of God. Paul alluded to this verse in connection with God's wisdom in dealing with Jews and Gentiles (Rom. 11:34) and with God's impartation of wisdom to the spiritual believer (1 Cor. 2:16).

40:15-17 Since the surrounding nations who had oppressed Israel were utterly insignificant in comparison to the Lord's greatness and power, they could not prevent His purposes from being accomplished. His deliverance of Israel was certain.

40:16 burn...burnt offering. God is so great and worthy of so much worship, that even the large wood and animal resources of Lebanon were insufficient for appropriate offerings to Him.

40:18-20 The prophet sarcastically indicated the futility of trying to portray the immensity of God—His power, wisdom, and resources—in the form of a man-made idol, no matter how ornate, durable, and immovable.

40:21-31 Isaiah extolled God as Creator, in whom the Jews were to put their full trust.

40:21 told you...understood. Throughout human history people had heard by special revelation from God that the Lord, not idols, created all things. They had also understood it from natural revelation as reason looks at creation (cf. Rom. 1:20).

40:22 sits above the circle of the earth. The word "circle" is applicable to the spherical form of the earth, above which He sits. This implies that God upholds and maintains His creation on a continuing basis (Col. 1:17; Heb. 1:3). As He looks down, men seem like insects to the One who has stretched and spread out the universal heavens.

40:23 princes...judges. God disposes of human leaders according to His will (34:12; Job 12:17-21; Ps. 107:40; Dan. 2:21). Verse 24 expands on how suddenly God removes them.

Scarcely shall they be sown,
Scarcely shall their stock take root
in the earth,
When He will also blow on them,
And they will wither,
And the whirlwind will take them
away like stubble.

25 "To[x] whom then will you liken Me,
Or *to whom* shall I be equal?" says
the Holy One.
26 Lift up your eyes on high,
And see who has created these
things,
Who brings out their host by
number;
[y]He calls them all by name,
By the greatness of His might
And the strength of *His* power;
Not one is missing.

27 [z]Why do you say, O Jacob,
And speak, O Israel:
"My way is hidden from the LORD,
And my just claim is passed over
by my God"?
28 Have you not known?
Have you not heard?
The everlasting God, the LORD,
The Creator of the ends of the
earth,
Neither faints nor is weary.
[a]His understanding is unsearchable.
29 He gives power to the weak,
And to *those who have* no might He
increases strength.
30 Even the youths shall faint and be
weary,
And the young men shall utterly
fall,
31 But those who [b]wait on the LORD
[c]Shall renew *their* strength;
They shall mount up with wings
like eagles,
They shall run and not be weary,
They shall walk and not faint.

Israel Assured of God's Help

41 "Keep [a]silence before Me,
O coastlands,
And let the people renew *their*
strength!
Let them come near, then let them
speak;
Let us [b]come near together for
judgment.

2 "Who raised up one [c]from the
east?
Who in righteousness called him to
His feet?
Who [d]gave the nations before him,
And made *him* rule over kings?
Who gave *them* as the dust *to* his
sword,
As driven stubble to his bow?
3 Who pursued them, *and* passed
[1]safely
By the way *that* he had not gone
with his feet?
4 [e]Who has performed and done *it,*
Calling the generations from the
beginning?
'I, the LORD, am [f]the first;
And with the last I *am* [g]He.'"

25 [x] [Deut. 4:15]; Is. 40:18; [John 14:9; Col. 1:15]
26 [y] Ps. 147:4
27 [z] Is. 54:7, 8
28 [a] Ps. 147:5; Eccl. 11:5; Rom. 11:33
31 [b] Is. 30:15; 49:23 [c] [Job 17:9]; Ps. 103:5; [2 Cor. 4:8-10, 16]

CHAPTER 41

1 [a] Hab. 2:20; Zech. 2:13 [b] Is. 1:18
2 [c] Is. 46:11 [d] Gen. 14:14; Is. 45:1, 13
3 [1] Lit. *in peace*
4 [e] Is. 41:26 [f] Rev. 1:8, 17; 22:13 [g] Is. 43:10; 44:6

40:25 liken...be equal. Israel was foolish to compare such a sovereign, almighty Lord with the gods of their Babylonian captors (see v. 18).

40:26 created these *things.* Rather than worshiping the stars (47:13; Deut. 4:19; Jer. 7:18; 8:2; 44:17), Israel should have seen in them the evidence of God's creatorship (Ps. 19:1). As innumerable as the stars are, He knows every one and named each. Not one of the stars runs astray, but all are held by the forces with which He has endowed the universe to keep them in their orbit and place.

40:27-31 The prophet applied the comforting truths in vv. 1-26 about God to Israel's situation in Babylon during the coming captivity.

40:27 Why do you say...? In light of who God is, how could His people in exile have thought He had forgotten them or was ignorant of their condition?

40:28 Neither faints nor is weary. God was not too weak to act on their behalf, nor was fatigue an obstacle for the Creator in caring for His people (cf. vv. 29,30). Though even the young and strong become tired and fall, the Ancient of Days never does. **unsearchable.** To the human mind, God's wisdom is not fully comprehensible in how He chooses to fulfill His promises to deliver Israel. Paul saw a further illustration of this truth in God's plan for the final restoration of Israel (Rom. 11:33; see Is. 40:13).

40:31 wait on the LORD. See 8:17; 49:23. There is a general principle here that patient, praying believers are blessed by God with strength in their trials (cf. 2 Cor. 12:8-10). The Lord also expected His people to be patient and await His coming in glory at the end to fulfill the promises of national deliverance, when believing Israel would become stronger than they had ever been.

41:1 coastlands. The coasts of lands around the Mediterranean Sea and the islands represent the nations. **renew *their* strength.** The Lord challenged the nations that refused to wait on Him to be silent in awe and then move to renew their strength (cf. 40:31), meaning to collect their best arguments to plead their cause before Him.

41:2 one from the east. The Lord anointed Cyrus the Great, king of Persia, to accomplish His righteous will by conquering Babylon in 539 B.C. and allowing some of the Jewish exiles to return to Jerusalem (cf. 41:25; 44:28; 45:1). He founded the Persian Empire and ruled from ca. 550 to 530 B.C.

41:3 pursued...not gone with his feet. Cyrus accomplished his conquests with great ease in territories he had never before visited.

41:4 first...last. He existed before history and will exist after it (cf. 44:6; 48:12; Rev. 1:17; 2:8; 22:13). ***I am* He.** It is legitimate to translate the two Heb. words thus represented by "I am" (see also 42:8; 43:10,13; 46:4), a messianic title appropriated by Jesus frequently as explicit testimony to His deity (e.g., Mark 13:6; 14:62; Luke 21:8; John 8:28,58; 13:19). The title comes originally from the Lord's self-revelation to Moses in Ex. 3:14.

5 The coastlands saw *it* and feared,
The ends of the earth were afraid;
They drew near and came.
6 [h]Everyone helped his neighbor,
And said to his brother,
[2]"Be of good courage!"
7 [i]So the craftsman encouraged the
[j]goldsmith;[3]
He who smooths *with* the hammer
inspired him who strikes the
anvil,
Saying, [4]"It *is* ready for the
soldering";
Then he fastened it with pegs,
[k]*That* it might not totter.

8 "But you, Israel, *are* My servant,
Jacob whom I have [l]chosen,
The descendants of Abraham My
[m]friend.
9 *You* whom I have taken from the
ends of the earth,
And called from its farthest
regions,
And said to you,
'You *are* My servant,
I have chosen you and have not
cast you away:
10 [n]Fear not, [o]for I *am* with you;
Be not dismayed, for I *am* your
God.
I will strengthen you,
Yes, I will help you,
I will uphold you with My
righteous right hand.'

11 "Behold, all those who were
incensed against you
Shall be [p]ashamed and disgraced;
They shall be as nothing,
And those who strive with you
shall perish.
12 You shall seek them and not find
them—
[5]Those who contended with you.
Those who war against you
Shall be as nothing,
As a nonexistent thing.
13 For I, the LORD your God, will hold
your right hand,
Saying to you, 'Fear not, I will help
you.'

14 "Fear not, you [q]worm Jacob,
You men of Israel!
I will help you," says the LORD
And your Redeemer, the Holy One
of Israel.
15 "Behold, [r]I will make you into a
new threshing sledge with
sharp teeth;
You shall thresh the mountains and
beat *them* small,
And make the hills like chaff.
16 You shall [s]winnow them, the wind
shall carry them away,
And the whirlwind shall scatter
them;
You shall rejoice in the LORD,
And [t]glory in the Holy One of
Israel.

17 "The poor and needy seek water,
but *there is* none,
Their tongues fail for thirst.
I, the LORD, will hear them;
I, the God of Israel, will not
[u]forsake them.
18 I will open [v]rivers in desolate
heights,

6 [h]Is. 40:19 [2]Lit. *Be strong*
7 [i]Is. 44:13 [j]Is. 40:19 [k]Is. 40:20 [3]*refiner* [4]Or *The soldering is good*
8 [l]Deut. 7:6; 10:15; Ps. 135:4; [Is. 43:1] [m]2 Chr. 20:7; James 2:23
10 [n]Is. 41:13, 14; 43:5 [o][Deut. 31:6]
11 [p]Ex. 23:22; Is. 45:24; 60:12; Zech. 12:3
12 [5]Lit. *Men of your strife*
14 [q]Job 25:6; Ps. 22:6
15 [r]Mic. 4:13; Hab. 3:12; [2 Cor. 10:4]
16 [s]Jer. 51:2 [t]Is. 45:25
17 [u]Ps. 94:14; Rom. 11:2
18 [v]Is. 35:6, 7; 43:19; 44:3

41:5-7 Instead of turning to the Lord when they saw His anointed one, Cyrus, approaching, the nations turned to one another for help and made more idols. See 40:18-20 regarding Isaiah's description of idols and their makers.

41:8 Israel...My servant. The faithful of the nation receive the honored corporate designation as the servant of the Lord (*see note on 20:3*). As His servant, they stood in bold contrast to the rest of the nations (vv. 5-7). Cf. Israel as the servant in 42:18-25. **Abraham My friend.** "Friend" is an even higher designation than "servant" (John 15:14,15; cf. 2 Chr. 20:7; James 2:23) and speaks of a greater faithfulness.

41:9 taken from the ends of the earth. In the last days, God will regather Israel from her worldwide dispersion as He did from Egypt and Babylon because Israel is God's chosen nation (cf. 45:4; Amos 3:2).

41:10 Fear not. Israel need not fear God's destructive judgment, as the rest of the nations do (vv. 5,13,14; 43:1,5), because He is their God and faithful to His promise to restore the nation.

41:11-13 Through the Lord's help, the enemies of Israel were to be weakened and vanish (60:12; Zech. 12:3) while God strengthened Israel.

41:14 worm. This refers to the contempt of Israel by the ungodly nations, and the same term is used similarly of the Messiah on the cross (Ps. 22:6). **Redeemer, the Holy One of Israel.** The Heb. for "Redeemer" refers to a near relative who has the opportunity and responsibility to buy back what a relative has lost (*see note on Ruth 2:20*). The term occurs 5 more times in connection with the title "Holy One of Israel." (*See notes on 43:14; 47:4; 48:17; 49:7; 54:5*). As the Lord purchased His people from the bondage of Egypt by the blood of the Passover Lamb, He is to do the same from their worldwide exile by the blood of the True Lamb, Jesus Christ, when they turn to Him in faith (cf. Zech. 12:10–13:1).

41:15,16 mountains...hills. Figurative representations of foreign nations, whom Israel is to grind into nothingness in the time of her kingdom, when the Lord Jesus sets Himself up as King in Jerusalem.

41:17,18 poor and needy. Israel in her deprived state as a captive of foreign nations is spoken of as thirsty for blessing and joy. In the Messiah's future kingdom, the land of Israel will be well-watered (cf. 12:2,3; 35:6,7; 43:19-20; 44:3,4; 48:20-21), a real physical blessing, but symbolizing here the spiritual quenching that will be Israel's in the Millennium.

And fountains in the midst of the valleys;
I will make the [w]wilderness a pool of water,
And the dry land springs of water.
19 I will plant in the wilderness the cedar and the acacia tree,
The myrtle and the oil tree;
I will set in the [x]desert the cypress tree *and* the pine
And the box tree together,
20 [y]That they may see and know,
And consider and understand together,
That the hand of the LORD has done this,
And the Holy One of Israel has created it.

The Futility of Idols

21 "Present your case," says the LORD.
"Bring forth your strong *reasons*," says the [z]King of Jacob.
22 "Let[a] them bring forth and show us what will happen;
Let them show the [b]former things, what they *were*,
That we may [6]consider them,
And know the latter end of them;
Or declare to us things to come.
23 [c]Show the things that are to come hereafter,
That we may know that you *are* gods;
Yes, [d]do good or do evil,
That we may be dismayed and see *it* together.
24 Indeed [e]you *are* nothing,
And your work *is* nothing;
He who chooses you *is* an abomination.

18 [w]Ps. 107:35
19 [x]Is. 35:1
20 [y]Job 12:9; Is. 66:14
21 [z]Is. 43:15
22 [a]Is. 45:21 [b]Is. 43:9 [6]Lit. *set our heart on them*
23 [c]Is. 42:9; 44:7, 8; 45:3; [John 13:19] [d]Jer. 10:5
24 [e]Ps. 115:8; Is. 44:9; [Rom. 3:10-20; 1 Cor. 8:4]

25 "I have raised up one from the north,
And he shall come;
From the [7]rising of the sun [f]he shall call on My name;
[g]And he shall come against princes as *though* mortar,
As the potter treads clay.
26 [h]Who has declared from the beginning, that we may know?
And former times, that we may say, '*He is* righteous'?
Surely *there is* no one who shows,
Surely *there is* no one who declares,
Surely *there is* no one who hears your words.
27 [i]The first time [j]*I said* to Zion,
'Look, there they are!'
And I will give to Jerusalem one who brings good tidings.
28 [k]For I looked, and *there was* no man;
I looked among them, but *there was* no counselor,
Who, when I asked of them, could answer a word.
29 [l]Indeed they *are* all [8]worthless;
Their works *are* nothing;
Their molded images *are* wind and confusion.

25 [f]Ezra 1:2 [g]Is. 41:2; Jer. 50:3 [7]East
26 [h]Is. 43:9
27 [i]Is. 41:4 [j]Is. 40:9; Nah. 1:15
28 [k]Is. 63:5
29 [l]Is. 41:24 [8]So with MT, Vg.; DSS, Syr., Tg. *nothing*; LXX omits first line

The Servant of the LORD

42 "Behold! [a]My Servant whom I uphold,
My [1]Elect One *in whom* My soul [b]delights!
[c]I have put My Spirit upon Him;
He will bring forth justice to the Gentiles.
2 He will not cry out, nor raise *His* voice,

CHAPTER 42
1 [a]Is. 43:10; 49:3, 6; Matt. 12:18; [Phil. 2:7] [b]Matt. 3:17; 17:5; Mark 1:11; Luke 3:22; Eph. 1:6 [c][Is. 11:2]; Matt. 3:16; [Luke 4:18, 19, 21]; John 3:34 [1]Chosen

41:19 myrtle…oil tree…cypress tree…pine…box tree. Luxuriant vegetation will enrich the land when God redeems His creation (35:1,2,7; Rom. 8:19-21).

41:22,23 what will happen…come hereafter. God challenged the idols to prove their competence by predicting future events, as the Lord has done regarding "the former things," i.e., the raising of Cyrus (v. 2), the repulsion of the Assyrians from Jerusalem (chaps. 36,37), and the healing of Hezekiah (chap. 38).

41:23 do good or do evil. God invited the idols to proclaim and execute either deliverance or judgment, as He had done.

41:24 nothing…nothing. The idols were not what humans claimed they were, because they could not predict the future, nor could they judge or deliver. They were useless (44:9; Ps. 115:2-8; 1 Cor. 8:4; 10:19; Gal. 4:8).

41:25 from the north…from the rising of the sun. Cyrus, king of Persia, a land E of Babylon, approached Babylon from the N where he had conquered Media before coming to Babylon. **call on My name.** Apparently fulfilled by Cyrus' proclamation in Ezra 1:1-4.

41:26 no one. No soothsayer had predicted future happenings as the Lord had.

41:27-29 Idols were helpless in giving "good tidings" of future events (v. 27) and counsel to people (v. 28), and thus were useless.

42:1-9 This is the first of 4 Servant-Songs referring to Messiah (cf. 49:1-13; 50:4-11; 52:13–53:12). They speak of the Servant's gentle manner and worldwide mission. Verses 1-3 are applied to Jesus Christ at His first coming in Matt. 12:18-20.

42:1 My Servant. Others deserve the title "my servant" (*see note on 20:3*), but this personal Servant of the Lord is the Messiah, who was chosen (Luke 9:35; 1 Pet. 1:20; Rev. 13:8) because the Lord delights in Him (Matt. 3:17; 17:5) and puts His Spirit upon Him (11:2; 59:21; Matt. 3:16; Luke 4:18). **justice to the Gentiles.** At His second coming, Christ will rule over a kingdom in which justice prevails throughout the world. The millennial kingdom is not for Israel alone, though the Messiah will reign on the throne of David in Jerusalem, and Israel will be the glorious people. In fact, all the nations of the world will experience the righteousness and justice of the Messiah King.

42:2 not cry out…in the street. The quiet and submissive demeanor of Christ at His first advent fulfilled this prophecy (Matt. 11:28-30; 1 Pet. 2:23).

Nor cause His voice to be heard in
the street.
3 A bruised reed He will not break,
And [2]smoking flax He will not
[3]quench;
He will bring forth justice for truth.
4 He will not fail nor be discouraged,
Till He has established justice in
the earth;
[d]And the coastlands shall wait for
His law."

5 Thus says God the LORD,
[e]Who created the heavens and
stretched them out,
Who spread forth the earth and
that which comes from it,
[f]Who gives breath to the people on
it,
And spirit to those who walk on it:
6 "I,[g] the LORD, have called You in
righteousness,
And will hold Your hand;
I will keep You [h]and give You as a
covenant to the people,
As [i]a light to the Gentiles,
7 [j]To open blind eyes,
To [k]bring out prisoners from the
prison,
Those who sit in [l]darkness from
the prison house.
8 I *am* the LORD, that *is* My name;
And My [m]glory I will not give to
another,
Nor My praise to carved images.

3 [2] *dimly burning* [3] *extinguish*
4 [d] [Gen. 49:10]
5 [e] Is. 44:24; Zech. 12:1 [f] Job 12:10; 33:4; Is. 57:16; Dan. 5:23; Acts 17:25
6 [g] Is. 43:1 [h] Is. 49:8 [i] Is. 49:6; Luke 2:32; [Acts 10:45; 13:47; Gal. 3:14]
7 [j] Is. 35:5 [k] Is. 61:1; Luke 4:18; [2 Tim. 2:26; Heb. 2:14] [l] Is. 9:2
8 [m] Ex. 20:3-5; Is. 48:11

9 Behold, the former things have
come to pass,
And new things I declare;
Before they spring forth I tell you
of them."

Praise to the LORD

10 [n]Sing to the LORD a new song,
And His praise from the ends of
the earth,
[o]You who go down to the sea, and
[4]all that is in it,
You coastlands and you
inhabitants of them!
11 Let the wilderness and its cities lift
up *their voice,*
The villages *that* Kedar inhabits.
Let the inhabitants of Sela sing,
Let them shout from the top of the
mountains.
12 Let them give glory to the LORD,
And declare His praise in the
coastlands.
13 The LORD shall go forth like a
mighty man;
He shall stir up *His* zeal like a man
of war.
He shall cry out, [p]yes, shout aloud;
He shall prevail against His
enemies.

Promise of the LORD's Help

14 "I have held My peace a long time,
I have been still and restrained
Myself.

10 [n] Ps. 33:3; 40:3; 98:1 [o] Ps. 107:23 [4] Lit. *its fullness*
13 [p] Is. 31:4

42:3 bruised reed…smoking flax. The Servant will bring comfort and encouragement to the weak and oppressed. Cf. 40:11; 50:4; 61:1 and *see notes on Matt. 12:18-20.*

42:4 justice in the earth. Isaiah looked beyond the first coming of Christ to His second coming. Jesus fulfilled vv. 1a,2,3 at His first coming and will fulfill vv. 1b,4 at His second coming, when He rules the earth in perfect justice with "a rod of iron" (Ps. 2:8,9; Rev. 2:27).

42:5 Thus says God the LORD, who created…walk on it. Here God spoke directly to the Messiah, identified as "You" (v. 6). God's role as Creator of the universe (cf. 40:21,22) is the basis of certainty for the fulfilling of His will by His Servant the Messiah.

42:6 I, the LORD. Beginning with 41:13, the Lord's self-identification is frequent (41:13; 42:6,8; 43:3,11,15; 45:5,6,7,18; 48:17; 49:23; 51:15). His personal name is the one He explained to Moses as specially symbolic of the unique relationship He bore to Israel (Ex. 3:15; 6:3). Here that covenant name guarantees His ministry through the Messiah-Servant. **covenant to the people.** The Servant is a covenant in that He personifies and provides the blessings of salvation to God's people Israel. He is the Mediator of a better covenant than the one with Moses, i.e., the New Covenant (Jer. 31:31-34; Heb. 8:6,10-12). *See note on 49:8.* **light to the Gentiles.** Simeon saw the beginning of this fulfillment at Christ's first coming (Luke 2:32). He came as the Messiah of Israel, yet the Savior of the world, who revealed Himself to a non-Jewish immoral woman by the well in Samaria (cf. John 4:25,26) and commanded His followers to preach the gospel of salvation to everyone in the world (Matt. 28:19,20). Certainly the church, made up mostly of Gentiles grafted into the trunk of blessing (cf. Rom. 9:24-30; 11:11-24), fulfills this promise, as does the future kingdom on earth when the Servant will use Israel to shine and enlighten all the nations of the earth (49:6; cf. 19:24).

42:7 open blind eyes…bring out prisoners. Jesus fulfilled these words (9:1,2; Matt. 4:13-16) when He applied them to miracles of physical healing and freedom from spiritual bondage during His incarnation (Matt. 11:5; Luke 4:18). Under the Servant's millennial reign on earth, spiritual perception will replace Israel's spiritual blindness and her captives will receive their freedom (29:18; 32:3; 35:5; 61:1).

42:9 former things…new things. The "former things" are already fulfilled or about to be fulfilled prophecies of Isaiah (cf. 41:22). The "new things" pertain to the future accomplishments of the Lord through His Messiah-Servant when He comes.

42:10 new song, *and* His praise. This "new song" never before sung, called for by new manifestations of God's grace, will match the newness of conditions created by the Servant's work of redemption in the kingdom, for which earth's inhabitants will also sing "His praise." Cf. 2:2; 26:1; Rev. 4:11; 5:9.

42:11 Kedar…Sela. See 16:1 and 21:16.

42:13 mighty man…man of war. As a mighty warrior, the Lord will work through His Servant to overcome all enemies (40:10; cf. 9:7; 37:32; 59:17).

42:14 held My peace…been still and restrained Myself. From the beginning of creation God remained silent, until the time was ripe to intervene in human affairs. He has not been indifferent to wickedness in the world, but will send His Servant in "the fullness of the time" (Gal. 4:4).

Now I will cry like a woman in
[5]labor,
I will pant and gasp at once.
15 I will lay waste the mountains and
hills,
And dry up all their vegetation;
I will make the rivers coastlands,
And I will dry up the pools.
16 I will bring the blind by a way they
did not know;
I will lead them in paths they have
not known.
I will make darkness light before
them,
And crooked places straight.
These things I will do for them,
And not forsake them.
17 They shall be [q]turned back,
They shall be greatly ashamed,
Who trust in carved images,
Who say to the molded images,
'You *are* our gods.'

18 "Hear, you deaf;
And look, you blind, that you may
see.
19 [r]Who *is* blind but My servant,
Or deaf as My messenger *whom* I
send?
Who *is* blind as *he who is* perfect,
And blind as the LORD's servant?
20 Seeing many things, [s]but you do
not observe;
Opening the ears, but he does not
hear."

14 [5] *childbirth*
17 [q] Ps. 97:7; Is. 1:29; 44:11; 45:16
19 [r] Is. 43:8; Ezek. 12:2; [John 9:39, 41]
20 [s] Rom. 2:21

Israel's Obstinate Disobedience

21 The LORD is well pleased for His
righteousness' sake;
He will exalt the law and make *it*
honorable.
22 But this *is* a people robbed and
plundered;
All of them are [6]snared in holes,
And they are hidden in prison
houses;
They are for prey, and no one
delivers;
For plunder, and no one says,
"Restore!"

23 Who among you will give ear to
this?
Who will listen and hear for the
time to come?
24 Who gave Jacob for plunder, and
Israel to the robbers?
Was it not the LORD,
He against whom we have sinned?
[t]For they would not walk in His
ways,
Nor were they obedient to His law.
25 Therefore He has poured on him
the fury of His anger
And the strength of battle;
[u]It has set him on fire all around,
[v]Yet he did not know;
And it burned him,
Yet he did not take *it* to [w]heart.

22 [6] *Or trapped in caves*
24 [t] Is. 65:2
25 [u] 2 Kin. 25:9 [v] Is. 1:3; 5:13; Hos. 7:9 [w] Is. 29:13

The Redeemer of Israel

43 But now, thus says the LORD, who
created you, O Jacob,
And He who formed you, O Israel:

42:15 lay waste…dry up…dry up. God's judgment through His Servant will wreak devastation on the earth (cf. Rev. 6–19). The reverse of that will be His blessing through the same Messiah subsequently in the millennial kingdom (see 35:1-4; 41:18).

42:16 I will bring…lead…make…do. God's sovereignty will be evident to all as He guides the blind over previously uncharted courses (cf. Ex. 13:21,22). The spiritually blind (9:1,2) will see the way (see 42:7). Cf. Eph. 5:8.

42:17 carved images…molded images. God will utterly repudiate idolaters (cf. Ex. 32:4).

42:18-24 The Lord charged Israel, His servant, with unfaithfulness. In an important comparison, positive qualities of the Servant (42:1-7) are personified into an individual, the Messiah, but terms of reproach toward God's servant (42:18,19,22-24) are personified in the nation, Israel.

42:18-20 deaf…blind. Though they are called "My servant" (v. 19; 41:8; 44:21) and "My messenger" and were perfectly fitted with the truth, Isaiah's commission to prophesy highlighted the spiritual deafness and blindness of Israel (6:9,10; cf. 22:14; 29:11; 32:3). They were deaf to the voice of God and blind to spiritual reality and duty.

42:21 His righteousness' sake. In spite of Israel's deafness, blindness, and defective righteousness (v. 24), God will staunchly uphold His principles of righteousness. Cf. 59:14-17.

42:22 robbed and plundered…snared…hidden. Exiled and dispersed, Israel was like a caravan in the desert, attacked unmercifully by bandits and imprisoned in caves or dungeons, so that no human deliverer could restore them (cf. 63:5).

42:24 Was it not the LORD. The nation went into Babylonian exile and worldwide dispersion as punishment by God for their rebellion against Him (30:15; 57:17; 65:2).

42:25 the fury of His anger. The fall of Jerusalem to Babylon in 586 B.C. did not result from the strength of Babylon. Rather, Israel had to taste the wrath of God because they paid no attention to the Lord (1:3; 5:13; 29:13; 47:7; 51:1; Hos. 7:9). **set him on fire.** Nebuchadnezzar, king of Babylon, burned Jerusalem when he conquered the city (2 Kin. 25:8,9).

43:1 created…formed. The only explanation for the ongoing existence of the nation of Israel is God's sovereign grace, which brought her into existence from nothing (cf. Deut. 7:6-11) and sustains her. Since she was God's creation, she could find comfort in knowing that no one or nothing can destroy her, not even her own wickedness (cf. 43:18-25; Rom. 11:1,2,25-27). **Jacob…Israel.** This double designation (cf. Gen. 32:28) for God's chosen nation is used by Isaiah 21 times, 16 of them in chaps. 40–49 (9:8; 10:20; 14:1; 27:6; 29:23; 40:27; 41:8,14; 42:24; 43:1,22,28; 44:1,21,23; 45:4; 46:3; 48:1,12; 49:5,6). This speaks of the Lord's special attachment to Abraham's

"Fear not, [a]for I have redeemed you;
[b]I have called *you* by your name;
You *are* Mine.
2 [c]When you pass through the waters, [d]I *will be* with you;
And through the rivers, they shall not overflow you.
When you [e]walk through the fire, you shall not be burned,
Nor shall the flame scorch you.
3 For I *am* the LORD your God,
The Holy One of Israel, your Savior;
[f]I gave Egypt for your ransom,
Ethiopia and Seba in your place.
4 Since you were precious in My sight,
You have been honored,
And I have [g]loved you;
Therefore I will give men for you,
And people for your life.
5 [h]Fear not, for I *am* with you;
I will bring your descendants from the east,
And [i]gather you from the west;
6 I will say to the [j]north, 'Give them up!'
And to the south, 'Do not keep them back!'
Bring My sons from afar,
And My daughters from the ends of the earth—
7 Everyone who is [k]called by My name,
Whom [l]I have created for My glory;
I have formed him, yes, I have made him."
8 [m]Bring out the blind people who have eyes,
And the [n]deaf who have ears.
9 Let all the nations be gathered together,
And let the people be assembled.
[o]Who among them can declare this,
And show us former things?
Let them bring out their witnesses, that they may be justified;
Or let them hear and say, "*It is* truth."
10 "You[p] *are* My witnesses," says the LORD,
[q]"And My servant whom I have chosen,
That you may know and [r]believe Me,
And understand that I *am* He.
Before Me there was no God formed,
Nor shall there be after Me.
11 I, *even* I, [s]*am* the LORD,
And besides Me *there is* no savior.
12 I have declared and saved,
I have proclaimed,
And *there was* no [t]foreign *god* among you;
[u]Therefore you *are* My witnesses,"
Says the LORD, "that I *am* God.
13 [v]Indeed before the day *was*, I *am* He;

CHAPTER 43

1 [a]Is. 43:5; 44:6 [b]Is. 42:6; 45:4
2 [c][Ps. 66:12; 91:3] [d][Deut. 31:6]; Jer. 30:11 [e]Dan. 3:25
3 [f][Prov. 11:8; 21:18]
4 [g]Is. 63:9
5 [h]Is. 41:10; 44:2; Jer. 30:10; 46:27, 28 [i]Is. 54:7
6 [j]Is. 49:12
7 [k]Is. 63:19; James 2:7 [l]Ps. 100:3; Is. 29:23; [John 3:2, 3; 2 Cor. 5:17; Eph. 2:10]
8 [m]Is. 6:9; 42:19; Ezek. 12:2 [n]Is. 29:18
9 [o]Is. 41:21, 22, 26
10 [p]Is. 44:8 [q]Is. 55:4 [r]Is. 41:4; 44:6
11 [s]Is. 45:21; Hos. 13:4
12 [t]Deut. 32:16; Ps. 81:9 [u]Is. 44:8
13 [v]Ps. 90:2; Is. 48:16

physical seed. **Fear not.** The Lord repeated His word, relieving Israel's fear (35:4; 41:10,13,14; cf. 7:4). **redeemed.** God's redemption of His people from exile is not to be complete until His Servant returns to reign over the faithful remnant in the land of Israel who have believed on Jesus Christ (cf. Zech. 12:10–13:1; Rom. 11:25-27; Rev. 11:13). The limited return from Babylon only typified the final return. *See note on 43:14.*

43:2 waters…rivers…fire…flame. Many perils symbolized by these words have confronted the Israelites through the centuries and will continue to do so until the nation's final redemption, but the Lord promises the nation survival through them all. The passage of Moses' and Joshua's generations through the Red Sea (Ex. 14:21,22) and the Jordan River (Josh. 3:14-17) and the preservation of Shadrach, Meshach, and Abed-nego in the fiery furnace illustrate His care for Israel.

43:3 your Savior. God is by nature a Savior (v. 11; 45:21), both temporally and eternally (*see note on 1 Tim. 4:10*; cf. Titus 1:3; 2:10; 3:4). God delivered Israel from Egypt and will deliver her from Babylon and all future exiles, as well as bring her to spiritual salvation (Zech. 12:10–13:1; Rom. 11:25-27). **Ethiopia.** See 18:1. **Seba.** A country either in southern Arabia or across the Red Sea in NE Africa, near Ethiopia. Egypt, Ethiopia, and Seba became a vicarious compensation so that God could spare Israel. "Sabeans" is another name for the inhabitants of Seba (cf. 45:14).

43:5,6 east…west…north…south…ends of the earth. The Lord will regather to the land of Israel the faithful remnant of His people from their worldwide dispersion in conjunction with the institution of the Messiah's kingdom on earth (cf. 11:12).

43:7 called by My name…created for My glory. The faithful remnant of Israel will bear the Lord's name and exist for one primary purpose: to glorify Him (44:23).

43:8 blind…have eyes…deaf…have ears. Restored Israel (vv. 5-7) will have their spiritual eyesight and hearing restored (29:18; contra. 42:18,19).

43:9 their witnesses. Who among the idolatrous soothsayers could predict Cyrus would deliver Israel from Babylon, or make prophecies of any kind that already were fulfilled? The gods of the nations showed no ability to reveal accurately "the former things" (41:21-23) as the Lord had. So the nations had no witnesses to accredit that their gods could speak prophetic truth.

43:10 You *are* My witnesses…My servant. Israel's God repeatedly predicted the future accurately, enabling Israel to witness to His truthful accuracy (v. 13), and thus the reality that He was the only eternal, living God. This witnessing they will do again in the millennial kingdom (cf. Joel 2:28-32).

43:12 declared and saved…proclaimed. As in the deliverance from Egypt (Ex. 3,4), God declared in advance how He would redeem Israel from their captivity. Then came the actual events of the saving process, followed by the Lord's proclamation of that deliverance by way of reminder. The people, on the basis of such omniscience and omnipotence, gave testimony to the true and only living God.

43:13 before the day *was*. Before the first day of creation when time began and throughout all periods of history, God exists and

And *there is* no one who can
deliver out of My hand;
I work, and who will [w]reverse it?"

14 Thus says the LORD, your
Redeemer,
The Holy One of Israel:
"For your sake I will send to
Babylon,
And bring them all down as
fugitives—
The Chaldeans, who rejoice in their
ships.
15 I *am* the LORD, your Holy One,
The Creator of Israel, your [x]King."

16 Thus says the LORD, who [y]makes a
way in the sea
And a [z]path through the mighty
waters,
17 Who [a]brings forth the chariot and
horse,
The army and the power
(They shall lie down together, they
shall not rise;
They are extinguished, they are
quenched like a wick):
18 "Do[b] not remember the former
things,
Nor consider the things of old.
19 Behold, I will do a [c]new thing,
Now it shall spring forth;
Shall you not know it?
[d]I will even make a road in the
wilderness
And rivers in the desert.
20 The beast of the field will honor
Me,
The jackals and the ostriches,
Because [e]I give waters in the
wilderness
And rivers in the desert,
To give drink to My people, My
chosen.
21 [f]This people I have formed for
Myself;
They shall declare My [g]praise.

Pleading with Unfaithful Israel

22 "But you have not called upon Me,
O Jacob;
And you [h]have been weary of Me,
O Israel.
23 [i]You have not brought Me the
sheep for your burnt
offerings,
Nor have you honored Me with
your sacrifices.
I have not caused you to serve
with grain offerings,
Nor wearied you with incense.
24 You have bought Me no sweet cane
with money,
Nor have you satisfied Me with the
fat of your sacrifices;
But you have burdened Me with
your sins,
You have [j]wearied Me with your
iniquities.

25 "I, *even* I, *am* He who [k]blots out
your transgressions [l]for My
own sake;
[m]And I will not remember your sins.
26 Put Me in remembrance;
Let us contend together;
State your *case,* that you may be
[1]acquitted.

13 [w] Job 9:12; Is. 14:27
15 [x] Is. 41:20, 21
16 [y] Ex. 14:16, 21, 22; Ps. 77:19; Is. 51:10 [z] Josh. 3:13
17 [a] Ex. 14:4-9, 25
18 [b] Jer. 16:14
19 [c] Is. 42:9; 48:6; [2 Cor. 5:17; Rev. 21:5] [d] Ex. 17:6; Num. 20:11; Deut. 8:15; Ps. 78:16; Is. 35:1, 6
20 [e] Is. 48:21
21 [f] Ps. 102:18; Is. 42:12; [Luke 1:74, 75; Eph. 1:5, 6; 1 Pet. 2:9] [g] Jer. 13:11
22 [h] Mic. 6:3; Mal. 1:13; 3:14
23 [i] Amos 5:25
24 [j] Ps. 95:10; Is. 1:14; 7:13; Ezek. 6:9; Mal. 2:17
25 [k] Is. 44:22; Jer. 50:20; [Acts 3:19] [l] Ezek. 36:22 [m] Is. 1:18; Jer. 31:34
26 [1] *justified*

manifests His will and purpose. **no one...My hand.** The Heb. behind this clause is identical with the comparable clause in Deut. 32:39. God's actions are irreversible and can never end in frustration.

43:14 Redeemer, the Holy One of Israel. The former title characterizes the Lord's role in the salvation of His people in chaps. 40–66 (41:14; 43:14; 44:6,24; 47:4; 48:17; 49:7,26; 54:5,8; 59:20; 60:16; 63:16). The latter title represents his holiness throughout the book (*see note at 1:4*). The Lord's Servant retains His holiness in implementing His redemption of Israel. **Chaldeans...their ships.** When God sent a conqueror against Babylon (i.e., Cyrus, 45:1), the proud Babylonian fleet provided a means of flight for the country's fugitives. Babylon was accessible by ship through the Persian Gulf and the Tigris and Euphrates Rivers.

43:15 your King. The Lord was King over Israel from her inception, but the people asked for a human king instead (1 Sam. 8:4-7). The restoration will put Him back on the throne in the Person of His Servant the Messiah (Luke 1:31-33; cf. 6:1; 41:21).

43:16,17 sea...mighty waters...chariot and horse. To bring assurance of the greater future deliverance He will bring through His Servant, the Lord reminded Isaiah's readers of His deliverance of their ancestors from Egypt (Ex. 14:16,21,26-28; Josh. 3:13).

43:18,19 former things...things of old...new thing. Deliverances of the nation in the past will pale into insignificance in comparison with the future deliverance the Lord will give His people (42:9; 48:6; Jer. 16:14-15).

43:19,20 rivers...waters...rivers. In the Messiah's future kingdom, the barren places of Israel will be well-watered (41:18) and will supply refreshment for God's chosen people (43:1).

43:21 declare My praise. In the messianic age, Israel will finally give the Lord the credit that is due Him (contra. Jer. 13:11).

43:22-24 Even though the Lord has chosen Israel, Israel throughout her history has not chosen Him. Rather, they have wearied Him with their iniquities and empty ritualism (1:11-15).

43:25 I, *even* I...not remember your sins. This verse is probably the high point of grace in the OT. In spite of Israel's utter unworthiness, the Lord in His grace has devised a way that He can forgive their sins and grant righteousness (*see note on 61:10*), without compromising His holiness. This He would accomplish through the work of His Servant (53:6). In spite of her failures, Israel will always be God's chosen people.

43:26 State your *case.* God gives the nation opportunity to come into the court and plead her case. The strongest plea is not to claim personal worthiness, but to confess their sin and repent, thus pleading for mercy and forgiveness based on God's gracious promise in v. 25 and based on what Jesus Christ would do on the cross (cf. 55:6,7; Rom 3:21-26).

27 Your first father sinned,
And your [2]mediators have
transgressed against Me.
28 Therefore I will profane the princes
of the sanctuary;
[n]I will give Jacob to the curse,
And Israel to reproaches.

God's Blessing on Israel

44 "Yet hear me now, O Jacob My
servant,
And Israel whom I have chosen.
2 Thus says the LORD who made you
And formed you from the womb,
who will help you:
'Fear not, O Jacob My servant;
And you, Jeshurun, whom I have
chosen.
3 For I will pour water on him who
is thirsty,
And floods on the dry ground;
I will pour My Spirit on your
descendants,
And My blessing on your
offspring;
4 They will spring up among the
grass
Like willows by the watercourses.'
5 One will say, 'I *am* the LORD's';
Another will call *himself* by the
name of Jacob;
Another will write *with* his hand,
'The LORD's,'
And name *himself* by the name of
Israel.

There Is No Other God

6 "Thus says the LORD, the King of
Israel,
And his Redeemer, the LORD of
hosts:
[a]'I *am* the First and I *am* the Last;
Besides Me *there is* no God.
7 And [b]who can proclaim as I do?
Then let him declare it and set it in
order for Me,
Since I appointed the ancient
people.
And the things that are coming
and shall come,
Let them show these to them.
8 Do not fear, nor be afraid;
[c]Have I not told you from that time,
and declared *it?*
[d]You *are* My witnesses.
Is there a God besides Me?
Indeed [e]*there is* no other Rock;
I know not *one.*' "

Idolatry Is Foolishness

9 [f]Those who make an image, all of
them *are* useless,
And their precious things shall not
profit;
They *are* their own witnesses;
[g]They neither see nor know, that
they may be ashamed.
10 Who would form a god or mold an
image
[h]*That* profits him nothing?
11 Surely all his companions would
be [i]ashamed;
And the workmen, they *are* mere
men.
Let them all be gathered together,
Let them stand up;
Yet they shall fear,
They shall be ashamed together.

27 [2] *interpreters*
28 [n] Ps. 79:4; Jer. 24:9; Dan. 9:11; Zech. 8:13

CHAPTER 44

6 [a] Is. 41:4; [Rev. 1:8, 17; 22:13]
7 [b] Is. 41:4, 22, 26
8 [c] Is. 41:22 [d] Is. 43:10, 12 [e] Deut. 4:35; 32:39; 1 Sam. 2:2; 2 Sam. 22:32; Is. 45:5; Joel 2:27
9 [f] Is. 41:24 [g] Ps. 115:4
10 [h] Is. 41:29; Jer. 10:5; Hab. 2:18; Acts 19:26
11 [i] Ps. 97:7; Is. 1:29; 42:17

43:27 first father...mediators. Sins of even the respected patriarchal ancestors of the Jewish race, like Abraham, kept them from claiming personal merit (e.g., Gen. 12:11-13; 20:2). Even such honored intermediaries between God and Israel as the priests needed cleansing from sin (6:5-7).

43:28 Jacob to the curse...Israel to reproaches. Even though God will forgive the nation in the messianic age, she still must suffer in the intervening interval.

44:1-5 Under the shadow of more punishment to come (43:26-28), the prophet spoke of abundant blessing that was to be the nation's portion during the Millennium.

44:1,2 My servant...whom I have chosen...made you...formed you. God has chosen His servant Israel to be His own eternally (43:1,21,25), and they need not fear abandonment.

44:2 Jeshurun. An honored name for Israel whose root meaning is "right" or "straight," in contrast to the root of "Jacob" which means "over-reacher" or "deceiver" (cf. Deut. 32:15).

44:3 water...floods. The extensive blessing of physical conditions will favor the nation in the coming kingdom age (43:19,20); they were also symbolic of spiritual refreshment from the Holy Spirit and God Himself (32:15; Joel 2:28,29).

44:5 the LORD's...name of Jacob...The LORD's...name of Israel. In the future golden age of Israel, belonging to the Lord and belonging to God's chosen people will be synonymous, and it will be a badge of honor gladly worn without fear.

44:6 King...Redeemer...LORD of hosts...First...Last. The Lord identified Himself as Israel's King (43:15), Redeemer (43:14), Champion in battle (1:9), and Eternal One (41:4; cf. 48:12). Jesus, in a direct affirmation of His deity, called Himself the First and the Last (cf. Rev. 1:17; 2:8; 22:13). **Besides Me...no God.** God's exclusive claim to deity prepared the way for another challenge to false gods in vv. 7-20 (cf. 43:10).

44:7 let him declare...Let them show. If idols can foretell "the things that are coming and shall come," let them predict accurately, as the Lord has. Since the Jews have had predictions of the future ever since God chose them as His people, they are qualified to be His witnesses (v. 8).

44:9-11 ashamed...ashamed...ashamed. The workmen who manufactured idols were mere men and could make nothing as good as or greater than man. They and others who put their trust in idols had ample reason to fear and be ashamed of such folly (v. 11; contra. v. 8).

12 [j]The blacksmith with the tongs
works one in the coals,
Fashions it with hammers,
And works it with the strength of
his arms.
Even so, he is hungry, and his
strength fails;
He drinks no water and is faint.

13 The craftsman stretches out *his*
rule,
He marks one out with chalk;
He fashions it with a plane,
He marks it out with the compass,
And makes it like the figure of a
man,
According to the beauty of a man,
that it may remain in the
house.
14 He cuts down cedars for himself,
And takes the cypress and the oak;
He [1]secures *it* for himself among
the trees of the forest.
He plants a pine, and the rain
nourishes *it*.

15 Then it shall be for a man to burn,
For he will take some of it and
warm himself;
Yes, he kindles *it* and bakes bread;
Indeed he makes a god and
worships *it;*
He makes it a carved image, and
falls down to it.
16 He burns half of it in the fire;
With this half he eats meat;
He roasts a roast, and is satisfied.
He even warms *himself* and says,
"Ah! I am warm,
I have seen the fire."
17 And the rest of it he makes into a
god,
His carved image.
He falls down before it and
worships *it,*
Prays to it and says,
"Deliver me, for you *are* my god!"

18 [k]They do not know nor understand;
For [l]He has [2]shut their eyes, so
that they cannot see,
And their hearts, so that they
cannot [m]understand.
19 And no one [n]considers in his heart,
Nor *is there* knowledge nor
understanding to say,
"I have burned half of it in the fire,
Yes, I have also baked bread on its
coals;
I have roasted meat and eaten *it;*
And shall I make the rest of it an
abomination?
Shall I fall down before a block of
wood?"
20 He feeds on ashes;
[o]A deceived heart has turned him
aside;
And he cannot deliver his soul,
Nor say, "*Is there* not a [p]lie in my
right hand?"

Israel Is Not Forgotten

21 "Remember these, O Jacob,
And Israel, for you *are* My servant;
I have formed you, you *are* My
servant;
O Israel, you will not be [q]forgotten
by Me!
22 [r]I have blotted out, like a thick
cloud, your transgressions,
And like a cloud, your sins.
Return to Me, for [s]I have redeemed
you."

23 [t]Sing, O heavens, for the LORD has
done *it!*
Shout, you lower parts of the earth;
Break forth into singing, you
mountains,
O forest, and every tree in it!
For the LORD has redeemed Jacob,
And [u]glorified Himself in Israel.

12 [j] Is. 40:19; Jer. 10:3-5
14 [1] Lit. *appropriates*
18 [k] Is. 45:20 [l] [Ps. 81:12]; Is. 6:9, 10; 29:10; 2 Thess. 2:11 [m] Jer. 10:14 [2] Lit. *smeared over*
19 [n] Is. 46:8
20 [o] Job 15:31; Hos. 4:12; Rom. 1:21, 22; 2 Thess. 2:11; 2 Tim. 3:13 [p] Is. 57:11; 59:3, 4, 13; Rom. 1:25
21 [q] Is. 49:15
22 [r] Is. 43:25 [s] Is. 43:1; 1 Cor. 6:20; [1 Pet. 1:18, 19]
23 [t] Ps. 69:34; Is. 42:10; 49:13; Jer. 51:48; Rev. 18:20 [u] Is. 49:3; 60:21

44:12-19 Human workers expended all their energy to produce a beautiful idol, but the best they could make was the likeness of a man (Deut. 4:15-18; Rom. 1:23), and that could not renew their strength. Yet they who wait on the Lord will renew their strength (40:28-31). The same humanly nurtured trees used as fuel for fires to furnish warmth and to cook also provides wood for people to make idols, which they worship and to which they entrust their prayers and themselves. Nothing could be more foolish than worshiping as deity a piece of wood, while burning the same wood in a fire to keep warm. Idol-makers cannot comprehend the idiocy of creating gods from materials used for the most trivial domestic purposes. Cf. 6:9,10; Deut. 27:15.

44:20 deceived heart…lie. Like eating ashes, which provide no nourishment, idolatry is a deception, from which the sinner gets nothing but judgment (cf. Prov. 15:14; Hos. 12:1).

44:22 blotted out…your sins. Further reassurances of God's sovereign grace at work on behalf of Israel were given (43:25). God had blotted out their sins written in His book against them (cf. Rev. 20:12). As a person can't see what is ahead because it is blocked by a "thick cloud," so God obliterated the sins of those He redeemed. **Return to Me.** God has already provided for redemption, even before the cross, but based on it alone. For those who turn from sin and return to Him, there is redemption (because the purchase price for the sinner was paid by the sacrifice of Christ). The Lord calls on His people to repent so they may receive the promised redemption (cf. Neh. 1:9; Jer 4:1; 24:7; Joel 2:12; Zech. 1:3; Mal. 3:7; Matt. 3:2; 4:17; Rom. 3:25,26; Heb. 9:15).

44:23 heavens…every tree…redeemed Jacob. The national redemption of Israel at Christ's second coming entails also the redemption of all nature (Rom. 8:19-22), so the prophet calls on the whole creation to rejoice.

Judah Will Be Restored

24 Thus says the LORD, [v]your Redeemer,
And [w]He who formed you from the womb:
"I *am* the LORD, who makes all *things,*
[x]Who stretches out the heavens [3]all alone,
Who spreads abroad the earth by Myself;
25 Who [y]frustrates the signs [z]of the babblers,
And drives diviners mad;
Who turns wise men backward,
[a]And makes their knowledge foolishness;
26 [b]Who confirms the word of His servant,
And performs the counsel of His messengers;
Who says to Jerusalem, 'You shall be inhabited,'
To the cities of Judah, 'You shall be built,'
And I will raise up her waste places;
27 [c]Who says to the deep, 'Be dry!
And I will dry up your rivers';
28 Who says of [d]Cyrus, '*He is* My shepherd,
And he shall perform all My pleasure,
Saying to Jerusalem, [e]"You shall be built,"
And to the temple, "Your foundation shall be laid." '

24 [v]Is. 43:14 [w]Is. 43:1 [x]Job 9:8 [3]By Himself
25 [y]Is. 47:13 [z]Jer. 50:36 [a]2 Sam. 15:31; Job 5:12-14; Ps. 33:10; Is. 29:14; Jer. 51:57; 1 Cor. 1:20, 27
26 [b]Zech. 1:6; Matt. 5:18
27 [c]Jer. 50:38; 51:36
28 [d]2 Chr. 36:22; Ezra 1:1; Is. 45:13 [e]Ezra 6:7

CHAPTER 45

1 [a]Is. 44:28 [b]Ps. 73:23; Is. 41:13 [c]Dan. 5:30 [d]Job 12:21; Is. 45:5 [1]*strengthened* or *sustained*
2 [e]Is. 40:4 [f]Ps. 107:16 [2]Tg. *I will trample down the walls;* Vg. *I will humble the great ones of the earth* [3]DSS, LXX *mountains*
3 [g]Is. 41:23 [h]Ex. 33:12
4 [i]Is. 44:1
5 [j]Deut. 4:35; 32:39; Is. 44:8 [k]Is. 45:14, 18 [l]Ps. 18:32

Cyrus, God's Instrument

45 "Thus says the LORD to His anointed,
To [a]Cyrus, whose [b]right hand I have [1]held—
[c]To subdue nations before him
And [d]loose the armor of kings,
To open before him the double doors,
So that the gates will not be shut:
2 'I will go before you
[e]And[2] make the [3]crooked places straight;
[f]I will break in pieces the gates of bronze
And cut the bars of iron.
3 I will give you the treasures of darkness
And hidden riches of secret places,
[g]That you may know that I, the LORD,
Who [h]call *you* by your name,
Am the God of Israel.
4 For [i]Jacob My servant's sake,
And Israel My elect,
I have even called you by your name;
I have named you, though you have not known Me.
5 I *j am* the LORD, and [k]*there is* no other;
There is no God besides Me.
[l]I will gird you, though you have not known Me,

44:25 babblers...diviners. False prophets must suffer the consequences of their deceptive counsel (47:12-14; Deut. 13:1-5; Josh. 13:22; Jer. 27:9; 29:8; 50:36; Mic. 3:7).

44:26 His servant...His messengers. In contrast with His breaking the word of false prophets (v. 25), the Lord confirmed the word of His true prophets such as of Isaiah (Zech. 1:6). Most specially, God confirmed the Word of the Messiah, who is the consummate embodiment of all the prophets and messengers of God (Mal. 3:1; Matt. 21:34,36,37). **raise up her waste places.** The fall of Jerusalem came in 586 B.C. when the Babylonians invaded the Land. God promised to restore the Land to prosperity, the foretaste of restoration coming after 70 years with the help of the Persians (41:2), but the greater restoration to come in Messiah's kingdom.

44:27 Be dry! The Lord demonstrated His power by drying up the Red Sea and the Jordan River when delivering His people from Egypt (43:2).

44:28 Cyrus...My shepherd. The prophecy—given a century and a half before Cyrus lived and became king of Persia—predicted God's use of the Persian king to gather the faithful remnant of Israel back to the Land. In this role, Cyrus prefigured the Lord's Servant, who will shepherd the sheep of Israel in their final regathering (Mic. 5:4). The title "shepherd" applied to kings as leaders of God's people (2 Sam. 5:2; Jer. 3:15). In Acts 13:22, Paul compares David to the standard of Cyrus' obedience. **Jerusalem...the temple.** In 538 B.C. Cyrus decreed the rebuilding of the temple (Ezra 1:1,2; 6:3), thus fulfilling Isaiah's prophecy. The returning Jews completed the work in 516 B.C. (Ezra 6:15).

45:1 His anointed. This word is the one translated from the Heb. by the transliteration—"Messiah." It is the word used for the messianic Redeemer King in Ps. 2:2 and Dan. 9:25,26, but here refers to Cyrus, as the king set apart by God's providence for divine purposes. Though not a worshiper of the Lord, the Persian monarch played an unusual role as Israel's shepherd (44:28) and God's anointed judge on nations.

45:1,2 double doors...gates...gates of bronze. Probably this was a reference to the many gates in the city wall of Babylon which Cyrus entered with relative ease. The inner gates leading from the river to the city were left open, as were the palace doors. Herodotus, the Greek historian, reported that the openness of the city was so great that the Persians were taking prisoners as they moved to the palace in the center.

45:3 That you may know. God intended Cyrus to be aware that the God of the Jews was giving him victorious conquests. According to Josephus, the Jewish historian, who indicated that Daniel influenced Cyrus with the prophecy of Isaiah, the king did know that the God of Israel was with him.

45:4 For Jacob...have not known Me. For His servant Israel's sake, the Lord raised up Cyrus, calling him by name, even though Cyrus did not have a personal relationship to Him. At some point, Cyrus certainly became aware of the true God and His sovereign control over human affairs, perhaps through the influence of Daniel (cf. Ezra 1:1-4).

6 [m]That they may [n]know from the
rising of the sun to its setting
That *there is* none besides Me.
I *am* the LORD, and *there is* no other;
7 I form the light and create
darkness,
I make peace and [o]create calamity;
I, the LORD, do all these *things*.'

8 "Rain[p] down, you heavens, from
above,
And let the skies pour down
righteousness;
Let the earth open, let them bring
forth salvation,
And let righteousness spring up
together.
I, the LORD, have created it.

9 "Woe to him who strives with [q]his
Maker!
Let the potsherd *strive* with the
potsherds of the earth!
[r]Shall the clay say to him who
forms it, 'What are you
making?'
Or shall your handiwork *say*, 'He
has no hands'?
10 Woe to him who says to *his* father,
'What are you begetting?'
Or to the woman, 'What have you
brought forth?' "

11 Thus says the LORD,
The Holy One of Israel, and his
Maker:
[s]"Ask Me of things to come
concerning [t]My sons;
And concerning [u]the work of My
hands, you command Me.
12 [v]I have made the earth,
And [w]created man on it.
I—My hands—stretched out the
heavens,
And [x]all their host I have
commanded.
13 [y]I have raised him up in
righteousness,
And I will [4]direct all his ways;
He shall [z]build My city
And let My exiles go free,
[a]Not for price nor reward,"
Says the LORD of hosts.

The LORD, the Only Savior

14 Thus says the LORD:

[b]"The labor of Egypt and
merchandise of Cush
And of the Sabeans, men of stature,
Shall come over to you, and they
shall be yours;
They shall walk behind you,
They shall come over [c]in chains;
And they shall bow down to you.
They will make supplication to
you, *saying*, [d]'Surely God *is* in
you,
And *there is* no other;
[e]*There is* no other God.' "

15 Truly You *are* God, [f]who hide
Yourself,
O God of Israel, the Savior!
16 They shall be [g]ashamed
And also disgraced, all of them;
They shall go in confusion
together,
Who are makers of idols.
17 [h]*But* Israel shall be saved by the
LORD
With an [i]everlasting salvation;
You shall not be ashamed or
[j]disgraced
Forever and ever.

18 For thus says the LORD,
[k]Who created the heavens,

6 [m] Ps. 102:15; Is. 37:20; Mal. 1:11 [n] [Is. 11:9; 52:10] **7** [o] Is. 31:2; 47:11; Amos 3:6 **8** [p] Ps. 85:11 **9** [q] Is. 64:8 [r] Jer. 18:6; Rom. 9:20, 21 **11** [s] Is. 8:19 [t] Jer. 31:9 [u] Is. 29:23; 60:21; 64:8 **12** [v] Is. 42:5; Jer. 27:5 [w] Gen. 1:26 [x] Gen. 2:1; Neh. 9:6 **13** [y] Is. 41:2 [z] 2 Chr. 36:22; Is. 44:28 [a] [Rom. 3:24] [4] Or *make all his ways straight* **14** [b] Ps. 68:31; 72:10, 11; Is. 14:1; 49:23; 60:9, 10, 14, 16; Zech. 8:22, 23 [c] Ps. 149:8 [d] Jer. 16:19; Zech. 8:20-23; 1 Cor. 14:25 [e] Is. 45:5 **15** [f] Ps. 44:24; Is. 57:17 **16** [g] Is. 44:11 **17** [h] Is. 26:4; [Rom. 11:26] [i] Is. 51:6 [j] Is. 29:22 **18** [k] Is. 42:5

45:6 from the rising of the sun to its setting. This expression, meaning the whole earth, points to the fact that through the eventual, final regathering of Israel (of which Cyrus' exploits were a foretaste), the whole earth will know the Lord alone is God (cf. 43:10; 44:6).

45:8 righteousness...salvation...righteousness. Eventually the Lord will cause righteous goodness to prevail throughout the world, just as He has promised Israel that it would (v. 13; Hos. 10:12).

45:9,10 Woe...Woe. Figures of the potter and the clay and of parent and child show how absurd it is to contend with God over His plans for the future. This anticipated the objections by the Jews against 1) their captivity and restoration by a pagan king, and 2) ultimately God's sovereign plan to redeem Gentiles as well as Jews worldwide (cf. Rom. 9:20-24).

45:11 Ask Me of things to come. The Lord commands Israel to seek information about what He will do for the nation in the future, for He will reveal it.

45:12,13 I have made...He shall build My city. As the omnipotent Creator, God can save the nation through Cyrus as He has promised.

45:14 Egypt...Cush...Sabeans. Three countries to the S (cf. 43:3) illustrate the worldwide submission to Israel that will prevail during the messianic kingdom age. **Surely God *is* in you.** All nations will acknowledge the presence of the one true God among His people Israel (49:23; 60:14). Paul the apostle found a fuller sense in these words when he advised the Corinthians on exercising prophecy rather than tongues in their meetings. This brought an acknowledgment from visitors of God's presence among them (1 Cor. 14:25).

45:15 hide Yourself. The contemporary situation hid God's purposes of mercy toward Israel, i.e., that they would repent and He would eventually regather them and make Jerusalem the center of world attention (cf. 8:17; 54:8; 57:17; Ps. 44:24).

45:16,17 Israel shall be saved. Makers of idols are to find disillusionment because of the failure of their gods to deliver, but Israel is to find eternal salvation in the Lord (44:9-11; Rom. 11:25-27).

Who is God,
Who formed the earth and made it,
Who has established it,
Who did not create it [5]in vain,
Who formed it to be [l]inhabited:
[m]"I *am* the LORD, and *there is* no other.
19 I have not spoken in [n]secret,
In a dark place of the earth;
I did not say to the seed of Jacob,
'Seek Me [6]in vain';
[o]I, the LORD, speak righteousness,
I declare things that are right.

20 "Assemble yourselves and come;
Draw near together,
You *who have* escaped from the nations.
[p]They have no knowledge,
Who carry the wood of their carved image,
And pray to a god *that* cannot save.
21 Tell and bring forth *your case;*
Yes, let them take counsel together.
[q]Who has declared this from ancient time?
Who has told it from that time?
Have not I, the LORD?
[r]And *there is* no other God besides Me,
A just God and a Savior;
There is none besides Me.

22 "Look to Me, and be saved,
[s]All you ends of the earth!
For I *am* God, and *there is* no other.
23 [t]I have sworn by Myself;
The word has gone out of My mouth *in* righteousness,
And shall not return,
That to Me every [u]knee shall bow,
[v]Every tongue shall take an oath.
24 He shall say,
[7]'Surely in the LORD I have [w]righteousness and strength.
To Him *men* shall come,
And [x]all shall be ashamed
Who are incensed against Him.
25 [y]In the LORD all the descendants of Israel
Shall be justified, and [z]shall glory.' "

Dead Idols and the Living God

46 Bel [a]bows down, Nebo stoops;
Their idols were on the beasts and on the cattle.
Your carriages *were* heavily loaded,
[b]A burden to the weary *beast.*
2 They stoop, they bow down together;
They could not deliver the burden,
[c]But have themselves gone into captivity.

3 "Listen to Me, O house of Jacob,
And all the remnant of the house of Israel,
[d]Who have been upheld *by Me* from [1]birth,
Who have been carried from the womb:
4 Even to *your* old age, [e]I *am* He,
And *even* to gray hairs [f]I will carry *you!*
I have made, and I will bear;
Even I will carry, and will deliver *you.*

18 [l]Gen. 1:26; Ps. 115:16; Acts 17:26 [m]Is. 45:5 [5]*Or empty, a waste*
19 [n]Deut. 30:11 [o]Ps. 19:8; Is. 45:23; 63:1 [6]*Or in a waste place*
20 [p]Is. 44:9; 46:7; Jer. 10:5
21 [q]Is. 41:22; 43:9 [r]Is. 44:8
22 [s]Ps. 22:27; 65:5
23 [t]Gen. 22:16; Is. 62:8; [Heb. 6:13] [u]Rom. 14:11; [Phil. 2:10] [v]Deut. 6:13; Ps. 63:11; Is. 19:18; 65:16
24 [w]Is. 54:17; [Jer. 23:5; 1 Cor. 1:30] [x]Is. 41:11 [7]*Or Only in the LORD are all righteousness and strength*
25 [y]Is. 45:17 [z]1 Cor. 1:31

CHAPTER 46

1 [a]Is. 21:9; Jer. 50:2 [b]Jer. 10:5
2 [c]Judg. 18:17, 18, 24; 2 Sam. 5:21; Jer. 48:7; Hos. 10:5, 6
3 [d]Deut. 32:11; Ps. 71:6; Is. 63:9 [1]*Lit. the belly*
4 [e]Mal. 3:6 [f]Ps. 48:14

45:19 not spoken in secret. Unlike mysterious utterances of the false gods (8:19; 29:4), God's revelations through His true prophets are open and accessible.

45:21 Who has declared this from ancient time? The Lord's case to prove He is the only true God is unanswerable; only He foretold the captivity of Judah and the deliverance from that captivity, as well as other future events that happened just as He had predicted.

45:21 *there is* no other...*There is* none. The Lord restated the truth expressed by Moses in Deut. 4:35 (cf. 43:10; 44:6; 45:6). The scribe who asked Jesus about the greatest commandment cited this same principle in agreeing with Jesus' answer to his question (Mark 12:32).

45:22 be saved, all you ends of the earth! When the Messiah sits on His throne in Jerusalem, all people will enjoy His temporal salvation in the physical blessings of the millennial earth and will have opportunity for spiritual salvation (49:6).

45:23 every knee shall bow. In the kingdom age, all nations will worship the one true God of Israel. A further meaning, justified by the NT, applies this verse to believers' accountability to God when He evaluates their works (Rom. 14:11). In assigning the words another meaning, Paul relates the words to the coming universal acknowledgment that "Jesus Christ *is* Lord, to the glory of God the Father" (Phil. 2:10,11).

45:25 all the descendants of Israel. Physical descent from Abraham alone cannot bring justification. Only the faithful remnant of Israel will be saved (v. 17; Rom. 11:25-27). "Justified" means to be declared righteous, to be treated as if one is not sinful, but holy through the application of Christ's righteousness to the one who believes (cf. 61:10; 2 Cor. 5:21).

46:1 Bel...Nebo. The two most prominent gods in Babylon. "Bel" is another spelling for "Baal," the Phoenician chief god of Babylon. That "Nebo" was extensively worshiped is shown by the proper names compounded from his: Nebuchadnezzar, Nabopolassar, and Nebuzaradan.

46:2 gone into captivity. When Cyrus came, even the gods were taken into exile. These idols couldn't save themselves from being laid down on the backs of beasts and hauled away, let alone save the people who worshiped them.

46:3,4 all the remnant of the house of Israel. The God of Israel is not helpless like idols. In His strength He has sustained and will sustain helpless Israel through every circumstance. In v. 4, the Lord uses the first person pronoun 5 times to emphasize His personal involvement in delivering Israel.

5 "To[g] whom will you liken Me, and
make *Me* equal
And compare Me, that we should
be alike?
6 [h]They lavish gold out of the bag,
And weigh silver on the scales;
They hire a [i]goldsmith, and he
makes it a god;
They prostrate themselves, yes,
they worship.
7 [j]They bear it on the shoulder, they
carry it
And set it in its place, and it stands;
From its place it shall not move.
Though [k]*one* cries out to it, yet it
cannot answer
Nor save him out of his trouble.

8 "Remember this, and [2]show
yourselves men;
[l]Recall to mind, O you transgressors.
9 [m]Remember the former things of old,
For I *am* God, and [n]*there is* no
other;
I am God, and *there is* none like Me,
10 [o]Declaring the end from the
beginning,
And from ancient times *things* that
are not *yet* done,
Saying, [p]'My counsel shall stand,
And I will do all My pleasure,'
11 Calling a bird of prey [q]from the
east,
The man [r]who executes My
counsel, from a far country.
Indeed [s]I have spoken *it;*
I will also bring it to pass.
I have purposed *it;*
I will also do it.

12 "Listen to Me, you [t]stubborn-
hearted,
[u]Who *are* far from righteousness:
13 [v]I bring My righteousness near, it
shall not be far off;
My salvation [w]shall not [3]linger.
And I will place [x]salvation in Zion,
For Israel My glory.

The Humiliation of Babylon

47 "Come [a]down and [b]sit in the dust,
O virgin daughter of [c]Babylon;
Sit on the ground without a throne,
O daughter of the Chaldeans!
For you shall no more be called
Tender and [1]delicate.
2 [d]Take the millstones and grind meal.
Remove your veil,
Take off the skirt,
Uncover the thigh,
Pass through the rivers.
3 [e]Your nakedness shall be uncovered,
Yes, your shame will be seen;
[f]I will take vengeance,
And I will not arbitrate with a
man."

4 *As for* [g]our Redeemer, the LORD of
hosts *is* His name,
The Holy One of Israel.

5 "Sit in [h]silence, and go into darkness,
O daughter of the Chaldeans;
[i]For you shall no longer be called
The Lady of Kingdoms.
6 [j]I was angry with My people;
[k]I have profaned My inheritance,
And given them into your hand.
You showed them no mercy;
[l]On the elderly you laid your yoke
very heavily.
7 And you said, 'I shall be [m]a lady
forever,'

5 [g] Is. 40:18, 25
6 [h] Is. 40:19; 41:6; Jer. 10:4 [i] Is. 44:12
7 [j] Is. 45:20; 46:1; Jer. 10:5 [k] Is. 45:20
8 [l] Is. 44:19 [2] *be men,* take courage
9 [m] Deut. 32:7; Is. 42:9; 65:17 [n] Is. 45:5, 21
10 [o] Is. 45:21; 48:3 [p] Ps. 33:11; Prov. 19:21; 21:30; Is. 14:24; 25:1; Acts 5:39; Heb. 6:17
11 [q] Is. 41:2, 25 [r] Is. 44:28 [s] Num. 23:19
12 [t] Ps. 76:5; Is. 48:4; Zech. 7:11, 12; Mal. 3:13 [u] [Rom. 10:3]
13 [v] [Rom. 1:17] [w] Hab. 2:3 [x] Is. 62:11; Joel 3:17; [1 Pet. 2:6] [3] *delay*

CHAPTER 47

1 [a] Jer. 48:18 [b] Is. 3:26 [c] Is. 14:18-23; Jer. 25:12; 50:1–51:64 [1] *dainty*
2 [d] Ex. 11:5; Jer. 25:10
3 [e] Is. 3:17; 20:4 [f] [Rom. 12:19]
4 [g] Jer. 50:34
5 [h] 1 Sam. 2:9 [i] Is. 13:19; [Dan. 2:37]; Rev. 17:18
6 [j] 2 Sam. 24:14 [k] Is. 43:28 [l] Deut. 28:49, 50
7 [m] Rev. 18:7

46:5-8 The human origin and utter impotence of idols renders them unfit for comparison with the God of Israel (40:18-20). In v. 8, the prophet calls on the readers to recall the impotence of the idols they worship in transgression of God's law.

46:9 Remember the former things of old. The readers are to recall: 1) all the past history of fulfilled prophecies, as well as 2) miraculous deliverances such as that from Egypt, and 3) providential blessings Israel has experienced. All of these are ample evidence that He alone is God.

46:11 man…from a far country. Cyrus was this man whom God summoned to conquer Babylon and return a remnant of Israel to end the 70 year captivity a century and a half after Isaiah wrote this prophecy (44:28; 45:1).

46:13 righteousness…salvation in Zion. At God's appointed time, the salvation of Israel will become reality and result in the Messiah's righteous kingdom (61:3; 62:11; Joel 3:17; Zech. 12:10–13:1; Rom. 11:25-27).

47:1-3 O virgin daughter of Babylon. The prophet depicted Babylon as a virgin in the sense of never before having been captured. Babylon sat like a royal virgin in the dust, experiencing complete humiliation. The "throne" was gone, taken by Persian power, and the empire never recovered from being robbed of its power, its people, and its name. The former royal virgin is depicted as a slave woman forced to exchange royal garments for working clothes, who must lift her garment to wade through the water as she serves like a slave traversing the river in her duties. Such duties in the E belonged to women of low rank, fitting imagery for Babylon's fall into degradation.

47:5 Lady of Kingdoms. The title continues the analogy of v. 1 and speaks of the exalted position from which Babylon was to fall. She was mistress of the world, but would later become a slave woman (cf. v. 7), degraded by pride and false security (v. 8).

47:6 showed them no mercy. Though God was punishing Israel in captivity, Babylon's cruel oppression of the captive Israelites was cause for the kingdom's overthrow. Cf. Jer. 50:17,18; 51:33-40; Zech. 1:15.

47:7-9 In Rev. 18:7,8,10,16,19, John alludes to these verses in describing the downfall of Babylon just before Christ's return. Compare "a lady forever" with 18:7, "am no widow" with 18:7, and "in one day" with 18:8.

So that you did not [n]take these *things* to heart,
[o]Nor remember the latter end of them.

8 "Therefore hear this now, *you who are* given to pleasures,
Who dwell securely,
Who say in your heart, 'I *am,* and *there is* no one else besides me;
I shall not sit *as* a widow,
Nor shall I know the loss of children';

9 But these two *things* shall come to you
[p]In a moment, in one day:
The loss of children, and widowhood.
They shall come upon you in their fullness
Because of the multitude of your sorceries,
For the great abundance of your enchantments.

10 "For you have trusted in your wickedness;
You have said, 'No one [q]sees me';
Your wisdom and your knowledge have [2]warped you;
And you have said in your heart,
'I *am,* and *there is* no one else besides me.'

11 Therefore evil shall come upon you;
You shall not know from where it arises.
And trouble shall fall upon you;
You will not be able [3]to put it off.
And [r]desolation shall come upon you [s]suddenly,
Which you shall not know.

12 "Stand now with your enchantments
And the multitude of your sorceries,
In which you have labored from your youth—
Perhaps you will be able to profit,
Perhaps you will prevail.

13 [t]You are wearied in the multitude of your counsels;
Let now [u]the [4]astrologers, the stargazers,
And [5]the monthly prognosticators
Stand up and save you
From what shall come upon you.

14 Behold, they shall be [v]as stubble,
The fire shall [w]burn them;
They shall not deliver themselves
From the power of the flame;
It shall not *be* a coal to be warmed by,
Nor a fire to sit before!

15 Thus shall they be to you
With whom you have labored,
[x]Your merchants from your youth;
They shall wander each one to his [6]quarter.
No one shall save you.

Israel Refined for God's Glory

48 "Hear this, O house of Jacob,
Who are called by the name of Israel,
And have come forth from the wellsprings of Judah;

7 [n]Is. 42:25; 46:8 [o]Deut. 32:29; Jer. 5:31; Ezek. 7:2, 3
9 [p]Ps. 73:19; 1 Thess. 5:3; Rev. 18:8
10 [q]Is. 29:15; Ezek. 8:12; 9:9 [2]*led you astray*
11 [3]Lit. *to cover it or atone for it*
[r]Is. 13:6; Jer. 51:8, 43; Luke 17:27; 1 Thess. 5:3 [s]Is. 29:5
13 [t]Is. 57:10 [u]Is. 8:19; 44:25; 47:9; Dan. 2:2, 10 [4]Lit. *viewers of the heavens* [5]Lit. *those giving knowledge for new moons*
14 [v]Is. 5:24; Nah. 1:10; Mal. 4:1 [w][Is. 10:17]; Jer. 51:58
15 [x]Rev. 18:11 [6]*own side or way*

47:8 no one else besides me. This pinnacle of Babylon's pride was mockery of the true God in its frivolous presumption of deity (v. 10; cf. 44:6).

47:9 In a moment, in one day. Babylon did not decay slowly, but went from being the wealthy lady, the unconquered virgin, the proud, invincible mother of many to a degraded, slave woman in the dust, who lost her throne, her children, and her very life. It happened in one night, suddenly and unexpectedly, when Cyrus and the Persian army entered the city (cf. Dan. 5:28,30). **loss of children, and widowhood.** Babylon did lose its inhabitants, many of whom were killed and taken captive under Cyrus. This prophecy was fulfilled again when Babylon revolted against Darius; and in order to hold out in the siege, each man chose one woman of his family and strangled the rest to save provisions. Darius impaled 3,000 of the revolters.

47:10 Sinners foolishly think they are safe, and there is none to judge them. Cf. Pss. 10:11; 94:7.

47:11 evil...trouble...desolation. The Persians under Cyrus suddenly initiated (cf. v. 9) the visitation that ultimately obliterated Babylon. Its culmination is to come in conjunction with the destruction of a revived Babylon, the world headquarters of evil at the second coming of Christ (51:8; Rev. 18:2-24).

47:12 enchantments...sorceries. The magical practices of Babylon, designed to aid against enemies (also v. 9), will characterize the Babylon of the future also (Rev. 18:23).

47:13 Let now the astrologers...save you. Babylon relied heavily on those who looked for combinations of stars, who watched conjunctions of heavenly bodies, who made much of months of birth, and who relied on the movements of stars to predict the future (Dan. 2:2,10). The prophet sarcastically points out the futility of such trust. This ancient deception is still popular today in the widespread use of horoscopes.

47:14 They shall not deliver themselves. The astrologers were helpless to save themselves, much less the Babylonians who depended on them, or anyone else. The divine fire that came was not to be a fire to warm them, but to consume them.

47:15 No one shall save you. When judgment comes, the astrologers with whom the people trafficked and spent their money, will run to their homes, unable to save themselves or anyone else.

48:1,2 swear by the name of the LORD...not in truth. The people were nominally Israelites, but their hearts were far from God. This hypocrisy was common all through Israel's history, even to the time of the Lord Jesus. Cf. Matt. 23:3,13-39.

Who swear by the name of the
LORD,
And make mention of the God of
Israel,
But [a]not in truth or in
righteousness;
2 For they call themselves [b]after the
holy city,
And [c]lean on the God of Israel;
The LORD of hosts *is* His name:

3 "I have [d]declared the former things
from the beginning;
They went forth from My mouth,
and I caused them to hear it.
Suddenly I did *them,* [e]and they
came to pass.
4 Because I knew that you *were*
[1]obstinate,
And [f]your neck *was* an iron sinew,
And your brow bronze,
5 Even from the beginning I have
declared *it* to you;
Before it came to pass I proclaimed
it to you,
Lest you should say, 'My idol has
done them,
And my carved image and my
molded image
Have commanded them.'

6 "You have heard;
See all this.
And will you not declare *it?*
I have made you hear new things
from this time,
Even hidden things, and you did
not know them.
7 They are created now and not from
the beginning;
And before this day you have not
heard them,
Lest you should say, 'Of course I
knew them.'
8 Surely you did not hear,
Surely you did not know;
Surely from long ago your ear was
not opened.
For I knew that you would deal
very treacherously,
And were called [g]a transgressor
from the womb.

9 "For[h] My name's sake [i]I will [2]defer
My anger,
And *for* My praise I will restrain it
from you,
So that I do not cut you off.
10 Behold, [j]I have refined you, but
not as silver;
I have tested you in the [k]furnace of
affliction.
11 For My own sake, for My own
sake, I will do *it;*
For [l]how should *My name* be
profaned?
And [m]I will not give My glory to
another.

God's Ancient Plan to Redeem Israel

12 "Listen to Me, O Jacob,
And Israel, My called:
I *am* He, [n]I *am* the [o]First,
I *am* also the Last.
13 Indeed [p]My hand has laid the
foundation of the earth,
And My right hand has stretched
out the heavens;
When [q]I call to them,
They stand up together.

14 "All of you, assemble yourselves,
and hear!
Who among them has declared
these *things?*
[r]The LORD loves him;
[s]He shall do His pleasure on
Babylon,

CHAPTER 48

1 [a] Is. 58:2; Jer. 4:2; 5:2
2 [b] Is. 52:1; 64:10 [c] Is. 10:20; Jer. 7:4; 21:2; Mic. 3:11; Rom. 2:17
3 [d] Is. 44:7, 8; 46:10 [e] Josh. 21:45; Is. 42:9
4 [f] Ex. 32:9; Deut. 31:27; Ezek. 2:4; 3:7 [1] Heb. *hard*
8 [g] Deut. 9:7, 24; Ps. 58:3; Is. 46:3, 8
9 [h] Ps. 79:9; 106:8; Is. 43:25; Ezek. 20:9, 14, 22, 44 [i] [Neh. 9:30, 31]; Ps. 78:38; Is. 30:18; 65:8 [2] *delay*
10 [j] Ps. 66:10; Jer. 9:7 [k] Deut. 4:20; 1 Kin. 8:51; Jer. 11:4
11 [l] Lev. 22:2, 32; Deut. 32:26, 27; Ezek. 20:9 [m] Is. 42:8
12 [n] Deut. 32:39 [o] Is. 44:6; [Rev. 22:13]
13 [p] Ex. 20:11; Ps. 102:25; Is. 42:5; 45:12, 18; Heb. 1:10-12 [q] Is. 40:26
14 [r] Is. 45:1 [s] Is. 44:28; 47:1-15

48:3-5 The Lord predicted events that have happened as He predicted them (41:2-4; 46:10), so the people would not ascribe these events to other gods.

48:3 former things. *See note on 46:9.*

48:6 new things. From this point onward, the prophecies of Messiah's first and second coming and the restoration of Israel have a new distinctiveness. Babylon becomes the Babylon of Revelation (v. 20), and God uses Isaiah to communicate truths about the messianic kingdom on earth and the new heavens and new earth that follow it (e.g., 11:1-5; 65:17). Verse 7 indicates that God had never before revealed these features about the future.

48:9 For My name's sake. The nation Israel had no merit to prompt God's favor toward them (v. 8). They deserved wrath and death, but His mercy toward them originates in His desire to be glorified and His desire to display the integrity of His own name.

48:10,11 refined...tested. Since Isaiah's time, Israel's testings have included the Babylonian captivity and present worldwide dispersion from her Land; unlike silver purged in the furnace, the purging of Israel is not complete, and they are not refined. But God keeps up the afflictions until they are, so His name is not defamed through the destruction of Israel. The nation will be purged (cf. Zech. 13:1). God's plan is such that He alone, not man or man-made idols, will receive credit for Israel's salvation (42:8; cf. Rom. 11:25-27,33-36). The adversaries of God are never to be given legitimate reasons for scoffing at God and His work.

48:14,15 him; He...His arm...him...him...his way. Beginning with v. 6, the prophet began to write of the new things. Babylon is the final one of Rev. 18, and the instrument of God's judgment is Messiah. The pronouns refer to Jesus Christ whom the Lord will anoint to defeat the final Babylon at His second coming and bring Israel to her land and kingdom. That it is not Cyrus is also clear from the statement, "The LORD loves him," which is too strong to apply to the pagan king—but not to God's Beloved, the Lord Jesus.

And His arm *shall be against* the
Chaldeans.
15 I, *even* I, have spoken;
Yes, [t]I have called him,
I have brought him, and his way
will prosper.

16 "Come near to Me, hear this:
[u]I have not spoken in secret from
the beginning;
From the time that it was, I *was*
there.
And now [v]the Lord GOD and His
Spirit
[3]Have sent Me."

17 Thus says [w]the LORD, your
Redeemer,
The Holy One of Israel:
"I *am* the LORD your God,
Who teaches you to profit,
[x]Who leads you by the way you
should go.
18 [y]Oh, that you had heeded My
commandments!
[z]Then your peace would have been
like a river,
And your righteousness like the
waves of the sea.
19 [a]Your descendants also would have
been like the sand,
And the offspring of your body
like the grains of sand;
His name would not have been cut
off
Nor destroyed from before Me."

20 [b]Go forth from Babylon!
Flee from the Chaldeans!
With a voice of singing,
Declare, proclaim this,
Utter it to the end of the earth;
Say, "The LORD has [c]redeemed
His servant Jacob!"
21 And they [d]did not thirst
When He led them through the
deserts;
He [e]caused the waters to flow from
the rock for them;
He also split the rock, and the
waters gushed out.

22 "*There*[f] *is* no peace," says the LORD,
"for the wicked."

15 [t]Is. 45:1, 2
16 [u]Is. 45:19 [v]Is. 61:1; Zech. 2:8, 9, 11 [3]Heb. verb is sing.; or *Has sent Me and His Spirit*
17 [w]Is. 43:14 [x]Ps. 32:8; Is. 49:9, 10
18 [y]Deut. 5:29; Ps. 81:13 [z]Deut. 28:1-14; Ps. 119:165; Is. 32:16-18; 66:12
19 [a]Gen. 22:17; Is. 10:22; 44:3, 4; 54:3; Jer. 33:22; Hos. 1:10
20 [b]Jer. 50:8; 51:6, 45; Zech. 2:6, 7; Rev. 18:4 [c][Ex. 19:4-6]
21 [d][Is. 41:17, 18] [e]Ex. 17:6; Ps. 105:41
22 [f][Is. 57:21]

CHAPTER 49

1 [a]Is. 41:1 [b]Jer. 1:5; Matt. 1:20; Luke 1:35; John 1:14; 10:36 [1]Lit. *inward parts*
2 [c]Is. 11:4; Hos. 6:5; [Heb. 4:12]; Rev. 1:16; 2:12

The Servant, the Light to the Gentiles

49 "Listen, [a]O coastlands, to Me,
And take heed, you peoples from
afar!
[b]The LORD has called Me from the
womb;
From the [1]matrix of My mother He
has made mention of My
name.
2 And He has made [c]My mouth like
a sharp sword;

48:16 sent Me. Here it was not the prophet who spoke, but the Messiah, the Servant of the Lord whom the Lord God and the Holy Spirit will send for the final regathering of Israel and establishment of His kingdom as described in 61:1-7.

48:17-19 Chastisements of Israel by the Redeemer and Holy One of Israel are for discipline (42:18–43:13; cf. Heb. 12:10). Some day they will end, when Israel heeds the Lord's commandments and God's punishments will turn to prosperity. A future generation will do so and enjoy the refreshment of a continuous stream of God's peace and righteousness that rolls over them like the relentless sea (65:18).

48:19 like the sand…like the grains of sand. Because of Israel's disobedience, God's promise to Abraham to multiply his descendants (Gen. 22:17) has not yet been finally fulfilled. Even though the nation was temporarily set aside during the Babylonian captivity and during the dispersion before 1948 A.D., and will suffer deadly assaults in the coming time of Jacob's trouble (cf. Jer. 30:7), God will be true to His promise.

48:20 Go forth from Babylon! The worldwide proclamation of deliverance, along with the statement that "the LORD has redeemed…Jacob" shows that it is not the return of a meager 50,000 Jews from historic Babylon while most stayed in that pagan land, but the final redemption of the nation as Zechariah spoke of it in Zech. 12:10–13:1 and Paul in Rom. 11:1,2,25-27. A redeemed Israel is to make a complete separation from the final Babylon and its wicked system, and proclaim to the world the Lord's grace toward the nation. John repeats this command in Rev. 18:4.

48:21 they did not thirst. Isaiah pointed to the way that God miraculously provided for Moses' generation, after He delivered them from Egypt (Ex. 17:6; cf. Is. 41:17,18), as an illustration of how He will provide for redeemed Israel when they escape the final world empire of Babylon.

48:22 no peace…for the wicked. Cf. 57:21. Not every Israelite will enjoy the Lord's salvation, but only the faithful remnant who have turned from their wicked ways. The wicked will be purged out before the kingdom of peace is established (cf. Zech. 13:7-9).

49:1–57:21 This section defines the Messiah/Servant's prophetic and priestly functions, His equipment for His task, His sufferings and humiliation, and His final exaltation. The word "servant" occurs about 20 times in this portion, which magnifies Jesus Christ as the Lamb of God who was slain to redeem God's elect.

49:1-13 The second of 4 Servant-songs (cf. 42:1-9; 50:4-11; 52:13–53:12). This one tells of the Servant's mission and spiritual success.

49:1 from the womb; from the matrix of My mother. The whole world, including Gentiles ("coastlands," "people from afar") are called to recognize two significant points: (1) the Messiah/Servant will be a human being, born as others are of a woman, yet virgin born (cf. 7:14; Luke 1:30-33), and (2) He will be an individual as distinct from a personified group such as the nation of Israel, which has also been called the Lord's servant (41:8,9; 42:19; 43:10; 44:1,2,21,26; 45:4; 48:20; 50:10).

49:2 My mouth like a sharp sword. The Lord has given power to His Servant to speak effectively and thereby to conquer His enemies (11:4; cf. Ps. 2:9; Rev. 1:16; 2:12,16; 19:15). His Word is always

[d]In the shadow of His hand He has
hidden Me,
And made Me [e]a polished shaft;
In His quiver He has hidden Me."

3 "And He said to me,
[f]'You *are* My servant, O Israel,
[g]In whom I will be glorified.'
4 [h]Then I said, 'I have labored in vain,
I have spent my strength for
nothing and in vain;
Yet surely my [2]just reward *is* with
the LORD,
And my [3]work with my God.' "

5 "And now the LORD says,
Who formed Me from the womb *to*
be His Servant,
To bring Jacob back to Him,
So that Israel [i]is [4]gathered to Him
(For I shall be glorious in the eyes
of the LORD,
And My God shall be My strength),
6 Indeed He says,
'It is too small a thing that You
should be My Servant
To raise up the tribes of Jacob,
And to restore the preserved ones
of Israel;
I will also give You as a [j]light to
the Gentiles,
That You should be My salvation
to the ends of the earth.' "

7 Thus says the LORD,
The Redeemer of Israel, [5]their
Holy One,
[k]To Him [6]whom man despises,
To Him whom the nation abhors,
To the Servant of rulers:
[l]"Kings shall see and arise,
Princes also shall worship,
Because of the LORD who is
faithful,
The Holy One of Israel;
And He has chosen You."

8 Thus says the LORD:

"In an [m]acceptable[7] time I have
heard You,
And in the day of salvation I have
helped You;
I will [8]preserve You [n]and give You
As a covenant to the people,
To restore the earth,
To cause them to inherit the
desolate [9]heritages;
9 That You may say [o]to the
prisoners, 'Go forth,'
To those who *are* in darkness,
'Show yourselves.'

"They shall feed along the roads,
And their pastures *shall be* on all
desolate heights.
10 They shall neither [p]hunger nor
thirst,
[q]Neither heat nor sun shall strike
them;

2 [d]Is. 51:16 [e]Ps. 45:5
3 [f][Is. 41:8; 42:1; Zech. 3:8] [g]Is. 44:23; Matt. 12:18; [John 13:31, 32; 14:13; 15:8; 17:4; Eph. 1:6]
4 [h][Ezek. 3:19] [2]*justice* [3]*recompense*
5 [i]Matt. 23:37; [Rom. 11:25-29] [4]Qr., DSS, LXX *gathered to Him;* Kt. *not gathered*
6 [j]Is. 42:6; 51:4; [Luke 2:32]; Acts 13:47; [Gal. 3:14]
7 [k][Ps. 22:6; Is. 53:3; Matt. 26:67; 27:41]; Mark 15:29; Luke 23:35 [l][Is. 52:15] [5]Lit. *his or its* [6]Lit. *who is despised of soul*
8 [m]Ps. 69:13; 2 Cor. 6:2 [n]Is. 42:6 [7]*favorable* [8]*keep* [9]*inheritances*
9 [o]Is. 61:1; Zech. 9:12; Luke 4:18
10 [p]Is. 33:16; 48:21; Rev. 7:16 [q]Ps. 121:6

effective (55:11; Eph. 6:17; Heb. 4:12) **hidden Me.** Messiah, before His appearing, was hidden with God, ready to be drawn out at the precise moment (cf. Gal. 4:4,5).

49:3 You *are* my servant, O Israel. That the Lord's use of the name Israel refers here to Messiah (42:1; 49:5,6,7; 52:13; 53:11) is explainable through the intimate relationship that exists between the nation and her King.

49:4 in vain…for nothing and in vain. At His first coming, the Servant met with rejection by His nation. It may have appeared to some that His mission was a failure because of the suffering and rejection He endured (cf. John 1:9-11). The last two Servant-songs also emphasize the Servant's suffering (50:4-11; 52:13–53:12). But, though rejected by men, the Servant expresses His strong assurance that He is doing God's work and will be rewarded with complete success.

49:5 back to Him…gathered to Him. The Servant's mission will include the priority of bringing Israel to the Lord. Cf. Matt. 10:5,6; 15:24; Rom. 1:16; 11:25-27. He will complete this at His second advent (cf. Zech. 12:10–13:1).

49:6 raise up the tribes of Jacob…My salvation to the ends of the earth. The Servant's goal is the salvation and restoration of Israel for the fulfillment of the covenant promise. But not limited to Israel, He is to function as a light bringing salvation to the Gentiles. Israel's mission had always been to bring the nations to God (19:24; 42:6). This she will finally do very effectively in the tribulation after the conversion of the 144,000 witnesses (Rev. 7:1-10; 14:1-5) and when she is restored to her Land at the Servant's return to earth. Cf. 9:2; 11:10; 42:6; 45:22; Luke 2:32. Paul applied this verse to his ministry to the Gentiles on his first missionary journey (Acts 13:47).

49:7 man despises…nation abhors. This speaks to the humiliating treatment of the Servant at His first advent, a theme emphasized by Isaiah (50:6-9; 52:14,15; 53:3). The "nation" is used collectively for all who reject Him, particularly Gentiles, who are the rulers, kings, and princes referred to as someday giving exalted treatment to the Servant at His second advent. Former oppressors will bow down to Him as in 52:15, because of the salvation of Israel.

49:8 acceptable time…day of salvation. Messiah is represented as asking for the grace of God to be given to sinners. God gives His favorable answer in a time of grace (cf. 61:1) when salvation's day comes to the world (cf. Gal. 4:4,5; Heb. 4:7). At His appointed time in the future, the Lord will, by His Servant, accomplish the final deliverance of Israel. Paul applied these words to his ministry of proclaiming the gospel of God's grace to all people (2 Cor. 6:2). **a covenant to the people.** *See note at 42:6.* When the Lord saves and regathers Israel, they will return to the Land, to which Joshua brought their ancestors after their exit from Egypt, now restored and glorious (44:26; Josh. 13:1-8).

49:9,10 prisoners…darkness…feed…pastures. At the Messiah's second advent, Israel's condition will change from captivity and oppression to contentment and prosperity such as that enjoyed by a well-fed, protected, and watered flock of sheep. These ideal conditions will be enjoyed by the faithful remnant returning for their kingdom in Israel. John reveals that this condition is a foretaste of heaven (Rev. 7:16,17).

For He who has mercy on them
[r]will lead them,
Even by the springs of water He
will guide them.
11 [s]I will make each of My mountains
a road,
And My highways shall be elevated.
12 Surely [t]these shall come from afar;
Look! Those from the north and
the west,
And these from the land of Sinim."

13 [u]Sing, O heavens!
Be joyful, O earth!
And break out in singing,
O mountains!
For the LORD has comforted His
people,
And will have mercy on His
afflicted.

God Will Remember Zion

14 [v]But Zion said, "The LORD has
forsaken me,
And my Lord has forgotten me."

15 "Can[w] a woman forget her nursing
child,
[1]And not have compassion on the
son of her womb?
Surely they may forget,
[x]Yet I will not forget you.
16 See, [y]I have inscribed you on the
palms *of My hands;*
Your walls *are* continually before
Me.
17 Your [2]sons shall make haste;
Your destroyers and those who laid
you waste
Shall go away from you.
18 [z]Lift up your eyes, look around and
see;
All these gather together *and* come
to you.
As I live," says the LORD,
"You shall surely clothe yourselves
with them all [a]as an ornament,
And bind them *on you* as a bride
does.

19 "For your waste and desolate
places,
And the land of your destruction,
[b]Will even now be too small for the
inhabitants;
And those who swallowed you up
will be far away.
20 [c]The children you will have,
[d]After you have lost the others,
Will say again in your ears,
'The place *is* too small for me;
Give me a place where I may
dwell.'
21 Then you will say in your heart,
'Who has begotten these for me,
Since I have lost my children and
am desolate,
A captive, and wandering to and
fro?
And who has brought these up?
There I was, left alone;
But these, where *were* they?' "

22 [e]Thus says the Lord GOD:

"Behold, I will lift My hand in an
oath to the nations,
And set up My [3]standard for the
peoples;
They shall bring your sons in *their*
[4]arms,
And your daughters shall be
carried on *their* shoulders;
23 [f]Kings shall be your foster fathers,
And their queens your nursing
mothers;
They shall bow down to you with
their faces to the earth,
And [g]lick up the dust of your feet.
Then you will know that I *am* the
LORD,
[h]For they shall not be ashamed who
wait for Me."

10 [r] Ps. 23:2; Is. 40:11; 48:17 **11** [s] Is. 40:4 **12** [t] Is. 43:5, 6 **13** [u] Is. 44:23 **14** [v] Is. 40:27 **15** [w] Ps. 103:13; Mal. 3:17 [x] Rom. 11:29 [1] Lit. *From having compassion* **16** [y] Ex. 13:9; Song 8:6; Hag. 2:23 **17** [2] DSS, LXX, Tg., Vg. *builders* **18** [z] Is. 60:4; John 4:35 [a] Prov. 17:6 **19** [b] Is. 54:1, 2; Zech. 10:10 **20** [c] Is. 60:4 [d] [Matt. 3:9; Rom. 11:11] **22** [e] Is. 60:4 [3] *banner* [4] Lit. *bosom* **23** [f] Ps. 72:11; Is. 52:15 [g] Ps. 72:9; Mic. 7:17 [h] Ps. 34:22; [Rom. 5:5]

49:12 come from afar. Israel's regathering will be from a worldwide exile (43:5,6), even far away places like Sinim, probably an ancient name for what is China.

49:13 Cf. Rev. 12:12.

49:14 Here is the summary of the history of lament by the nation during its long period of suffering. Verses 15-23 follow with words of assurance responding to the despondency.

49:16 The Lord is referring here to the Jews' custom, perhaps drawn from Ex. 13:9, of puncturing their hands with a symbol of their city and temple, as a sign of devotion (cf. Song 8:6).

49:17,18 Your sons...bind them *on you.* Zion's sons will return as the city's destroyers depart and will adorn the city. Israel will be the means of the conversion of the nations in the end (cf. Rom 11:11,12,15).

49:19-21 After the faithful remnant is regathered in salvation, and Gentiles come to faith in the kingdom through Jewish witnesses, millennial Jerusalem will not be large enough to contain all her inhabitants.

49:22 nations...shall bring your sons...and your daughters. The promise will find literal fulfillment as the nations of the world assist the faithful remnant of Israel to their land (14:2; 43:6; 60:4; 66:20). At the outset of the kingdom, when this regathering takes place, all the Gentiles will be believers in Jesus Christ who, by faith, escaped the wrath of the Lamb on the Day of the Lord and entered the kingdom (*see notes on Matt. 25:31-46*). Nations and leaders, that in history oppressed Israel, will humble themselves before the redeemed people of God's covenant, and Israel will know that waiting on the Lord will not disappoint (8:17; 40:31).

24 [i]Shall the prey be taken from the mighty,
Or the captives [5]of the righteous be delivered?

25 But thus says the LORD:

"Even the captives of the mighty shall be taken away,
And the prey of the terrible be delivered;
For I will contend with him who contends with you,
And I will save your children.
26 I will [j]feed those who oppress you with their own flesh,
And they shall be drunk with their own [k]blood as with sweet wine.
All flesh [l]shall know
That I, the LORD, *am* your Savior,
And your Redeemer, the Mighty One of Jacob."

The Servant, Israel's Hope

50 Thus says the LORD:

"Where *is* [a]the certificate of your mother's divorce,
Whom I have put away?
Or which of My [b]creditors *is it* to whom I have sold you?
For your iniquities [c]you have sold yourselves,
And for your transgressions your mother has been put away.
2 Why, when I came, *was there* no man?
Why, when I called, *was there* none to answer?
Is My hand shortened at all that it cannot redeem?
Or have I no power to deliver?
Indeed with My [d]rebuke I dry up the sea,
I make the rivers a wilderness;
Their fish stink because *there is* no water,
And die of thirst.
3 [e]I clothe the heavens with blackness,
[f]And I make sackcloth their covering."

4 "The[g] Lord GOD has given Me
The tongue of the learned,
That I should know how to speak
A word in season to *him who is* [h]weary.
He awakens Me morning by morning,
He awakens My ear
To hear as the learned.
5 The Lord GOD [i]has opened My ear;
And I was not [j]rebellious,
Nor did I turn away.
6 [k]I gave My back to those who struck *Me*,
And [l]My cheeks to those who plucked out the beard;
I did not hide My face from shame and [m]spitting.

7 "For the Lord GOD will help Me;
Therefore I will not be disgraced;
Therefore [n]I have set My face like a flint,
And I know that I will not be ashamed.

24 [i] Matt. 12:29; Luke 11:21,22 [5] So with MT, Tg.; DSS, Syr., Vg. *of the mighty;* LXX *unjustly*
26 [j] Is. 9:20 [k] Rev. 14:20 [l] Ps. 9:16; Is. 60:16

CHAPTER 50

1 [a] Deut. 24:1; Jer. 3:8 [b] Deut. 32:30; 2 Kin. 4:1; Neh. 5:5 [c] Is. 52:3
2 [d] Ps. 106:9; Nah. 1:4
3 [e] Ex. 10:21 [f] Is. 13:10; Rev. 6:12
4 [g] Ex. 4:11 [h] Matt. 11:28
5 [i] Ps. 40:6; Is. 35:5 [j] Matt. 26:39; Mark 14:36; Luke 22:42; John 8:29; 14:31; 15:10; Acts 26:19; [Phil. 2:8; Heb. 5:8; 10:7]
6 [k] Matt. 27:26; John 18:22 [l] Matt. 26:67; 27:30; Mark 14:65; 15:19 [m] Lam. 3:30
7 [n] Ezek. 3:8, 9; Luke 9:51

49:24 prey be taken...captives...be delivered. As in v. 14, Isaiah speaks of Zion again expressing her despondency over her captivity and wondering about deliverance. The Lord replies again with encouraging words in vv. 25,26.

49:25,26 feed...with their own flesh...drunk with their own blood. Strong language against Israel's enemies reassures her of eventual deliverance from her exile. The angel of the waters draws on this terminology in celebrating the third bowl judgment in Rev. 16:6. The destruction of Israel's enemies, led by Satan in the tribulation (cf. Rev. 12:15,16), also fulfills this pledge.

49:26 All flesh shall know. God's deliverance of Israel will be so dramatic that the world will recognize that the Lord, the Savior, Redeemer, and Mighty One of Israel is the true God (11:9; 45:6; Ezek. 39:7; Hab. 2:14).

50:1 certificate of your mother's divorce...My creditors. Though the sufferings of Judah were the necessary result of sin, no certificate of divorce or sale to creditors occurred because Zion's separation from the Lord was only temporary. In fact, God gave the non-Davidic northern kingdom a certificate of divorce (*see note on Jer. 3:8*). However, the unconditional promises of the Davidic Covenant (2 Sam. 7) precluded such a divorce for Judah, although there would be a time of separation (cf. 54:6,7).

50:2 Why...? God asked why no one was willing to believe and obey Him, even after all had seen His redemptive power in Egypt, when He dried up the Red Sea (Ex. 14:21), opened the river Jordan by turning it into dry land (Josh. 4:23), and killed the fish in Egypt (Ex. 7:18-21). The Lord's power to redeem was indisputable (59:1). He proved it by His deliverance from Egypt (43:16,17; 44:27; 46:9; 48:3,21).

50:4-11 This is the third of 4 Servant-songs (cf. 42:1-9; 49:1-13; 52:13–53:12), and it is Messiah's soliloquy about being perfected through obedience (vv. 4,5) and sufferings (v. 6). The Apostle John writes much about Jesus' obedience to God in fulfilling His will (cf. John 5:19,36; 6:38; 7:16,29; 12:49,50). Cf. Phil. 2:8; Heb. 5:8; 10:7.

50:6 My back...My cheeks...My face. The Servant remained obedient though provoked to rebel by excessively vile treatment. Jesus fulfilled this prophecy by remaining submissive to the Father's will (Matt. 26:67; 27:26,30; Mark 14:65; 15:19; Luke 22:63; John 18:22).

50:7 set My face like a flint. So sure was He of the Lord God's help that He resolutely determined to remain unswayed by whatever hardship might await Him (cf. Ezek. 3:8,9). Jesus demonstrated this determination in setting His face to go to Jerusalem to be crucified (Luke 9:51).

8 [o]*He is* near who justifies Me;
Who will contend with Me?
Let us stand together.
Who *is* [1]My adversary?
Let him come near Me.
9 Surely the Lord GOD will help Me;
Who *is* he *who* will condemn Me?
[p]Indeed they will all grow old like a
garment;
[q]The moth will eat them up.

10 "Who among you fears the LORD?
Who obeys the voice of His
Servant?
Who [r]walks in darkness
And has no light?
[s]Let him trust in the name of the
LORD
And rely upon his God.
11 Look, all you who kindle a fire,
Who encircle *yourselves* with
sparks:
Walk in the light of your fire and in
the sparks you have
kindled—
[t]This you shall have from My hand:
You shall lie down [u]in torment.

The LORD Comforts Zion

51 "Listen to Me, [a]you who [1]follow
after righteousness,
You who seek the LORD:
Look to the rock *from which* you
were hewn,
And to the hole of the pit *from*
which you were dug.
2 [b]Look to Abraham your father,
And to Sarah *who* bore you;
[c]For I called him alone,
And [d]blessed him and increased
him."
3 For the LORD will [e]comfort Zion,
He will comfort all her waste
places;
He will make her wilderness like
Eden,
And her desert [f]like the garden of
the LORD;
Joy and gladness will be found in
it,
Thanksgiving and the voice of
melody.

4 "Listen to Me, My people;
And give ear to Me, O My nation:
[g]For law will proceed from Me,
And I will make My justice rest
[h]As a light of the peoples.
5 [i]My righteousness *is* near,
My salvation has gone forth,
[j]And My arms will judge the
peoples;
[k]The coastlands will wait upon Me,
And [l]on My arm they will trust.
6 [m]Lift up your eyes to the heavens,
And look on the earth beneath.
For [n]the heavens will vanish away
like smoke,
[o]The earth will grow old like a
garment,
And those who dwell in it will die
in like manner;
But My salvation will be [p]forever,
And My righteousness will not be
[2]abolished.

7 "Listen to Me, you who know
righteousness,
You people [q]in whose heart *is* My
law:
[r]Do not fear the reproach of men,
Nor be afraid of their insults.
8 For [s]the moth will eat them up like
a garment,

8 [o] Acts 2:24; [Rom. 8:32-34] [1] Lit. *master of My judgment*
9 [p] Job 13:28; Ps. 102:26; Heb. 1:11 [q] Is. 51:6, 8
10 [r] Ps. 23:4 [s] 2 Chr. 20:20
11 [t] [John 9:39] [u] Ps. 16:4

CHAPTER 51

1 [a] [Rom. 9:30-32] [1] *pursue*
2 [b] Rom. 4:1-3; Heb. 11:11 [c] Gen. 12:1 [d] Gen. 24:35; Deut. 1:10; Ezek. 33:24
3 [e] Is. 40:1; 52:9; Ps. 102:13 [f] Gen. 13:10; Joel 2:3
4 [g] Is. 2:3 [h] Is. 42:6
5 [i] Is. 46:13 [j] Ps. 67:4 [k] Is. 60:9 [l] [Rom. 1:16]
6 [m] Is. 40:26 [n] Ps. 102:25, 26; Is. 13:13; 34:4; Matt. 24:35; Heb. 1:10-12; 2 Pet. 3:10 [o] Is. 24:19, 20; 50:9; Heb. 1:10-12 [p] Is. 45:17 [2] *broken*
7 [q] Ps. 37:31; Jer. 31:33; [Heb. 10:16] [r] Is. 25:8; 54:4; [Matt. 5:11, 12; 10:28; Acts 5:41]
8 [s] Is. 50:9

50:8,9 No matter how He was mistreated, mocked, and repudiated, the Servant has full confidence of the Lord God's support, so He welcomed an adversary to come.

50:10,11 Here was a call to the unconverted to believe and be saved, along with a warning that those who tried to escape moral, spiritual darkness by lighting their own fire (man-made religion, works righteousness) were to end up in eternal torment.

51:1,2 The prophet assured the nation of deliverance by pointing to God's past covenant with Abraham (Gen. 12:13), who was the rock in the quarry from which they were hewn as a people. Originally, Abraham was but one person, but God multiplied his descendants as He had promised (Gen. 13:16; 15:5; 17:5; 22:17).

51:3 waste places…Eden…desert…garden of the LORD. The same God whose power fulfilled His promises to Abraham is to transform Israel's desolation into a primeval paradise, both nationally and spiritually, causing joy and songs of thanksgiving to ring from it.

51:4 law…justice…light of the peoples. The Servant's rule over Israel's earthly kingdom is to cause righteousness to prevail for the benefit of all nations.

51:5 near…gone forth. The Servant's power to restore His people and bring justice, righteousness, and salvation to the world was at work, but God's perspective differs from man's reckoning of time. Though near by God's reckoning in timeless eternity, the fruition of His deliverance was yet many centuries from Isaiah's day. The nations who survive judgment will trust in Him and enter His kingdom.

51:6 heavens will vanish…earth will grow old. This begins to take place in the time of tribulation (cf. Rev. 6:12-14; 8:12,13; 16:8-10,21), setting the stage, along with the earthly judgments on land, sea, and fresh water (cf. Rev. 6:14; 8:6-11; 16:3-5), for a renewed earth during the Millennium. The actual "uncreation" or destruction of the present universe, of which Peter wrote (2 Pet. 3:10-13), occurs at the end of Christ's millennial reign on the earth, when a new heavens and a new earth will replace the present creation (2 Pet. 3:10; Rev. 21:1).

51:7,8 Israel's enemies will perish, but the Servant's salvation will be permanent.

And the worm will eat them like wool;
But My righteousness will be forever,
And My salvation from generation to generation."

9 [t]Awake, awake, [u]put on strength,
O arm of the LORD!
Awake [v]as in the ancient days,
In the generations of old.
[w]*Are* You not *the arm* that cut [x]Rahab apart,
And wounded the [y]serpent?

10 *Are* You not *the One* who [z]dried up the sea,
The waters of the great deep;
That made the depths of the sea a road
For the redeemed to cross over?
11 So [a]the ransomed of the LORD shall return,
And come to Zion with singing,
With everlasting joy on their heads.
They shall obtain joy and gladness;
Sorrow and sighing shall flee away.

12 "I, *even* I, *am* He [b]who comforts you.
Who *are* you that you should be afraid
[c]Of a man *who* will die,
And of the son of a man *who* will be made [d]like grass?
13 And [e]you forget the LORD your Maker,
[f]Who stretched out the heavens
And laid the foundations of the earth;
You have feared continually every day
Because of the fury of the oppressor,
When *he has* prepared to destroy.
[g]And where *is* the fury of the oppressor?
14 The captive exile hastens, that he may be loosed,
[h]That he should not die in the pit,
And that his bread should not fail.
15 But I *am* the LORD your God,
Who [i]divided the sea whose waves roared—
The LORD of hosts *is* His name.
16 And [j]I have put My words in your mouth;
[k]I have covered you with the shadow of My hand,
[l]That I may [3]plant the heavens,
Lay the foundations of the earth,
And say to Zion, 'You *are* My people.' "

God's Fury Removed

17 [m]Awake, awake!
Stand up, O Jerusalem,
You who [n]have drunk at the hand of the LORD
The cup of His fury;
You have drunk the dregs of the cup of trembling,
And drained *it* out.
18 *There is* no one to guide her
Among all the sons she has brought forth;
Nor *is there any* who takes her by the hand
Among all the sons she has brought up.
19 [o]These two *things* have come to you;
Who will be sorry for you?—
Desolation and destruction, famine and sword—
[p]By whom will I comfort you?
20 [q]Your sons have fainted,
They lie at the head of all the streets,
Like an antelope in a net;
They are full of the fury of the LORD,
The rebuke of your God.

21 Therefore please hear this, you afflicted,
And drunk [r]but not with wine.

9 [t]Ps. 44:23 [u]Ps. 93:1 [v]Ps. 44:1 [w]Job 26:12; Ps. 89:10; Is. 30:7 [x]Ps. 87:4 [y]Ps. 74:13; Is. 27:1
10 [z]Ex. 14:21; Is. 63:11-13
11 [a]Is. 35:10; Jer. 31:11, 12
12 [b]2 Cor. 1:3 [c]Ps. 118:6; Is. 2:22 [d]Is. 40:6, 7; James 1:10; 1 Pet. 1:24
13 [e]Deut. 6:12; 8:11; Is. 17:10; Jer. 2:32 [f]Ps. 104:2 [g]Job 20:7
14 [h]Zech. 9:11
15 [i]Job 26:12
16 [j]Deut. 18:18; Is. 59:21; John 3:34 [k]Ex. 33:22; Is. 49:2 [l]Is. 65:17 [3]*establish*
17 [m]Is. 52:1 [n]Job 21:20; Is. 29:9; Jer. 25:15; Rev. 14:10; 16:19
19 [o]Is. 47:9 [p]Amos 7:2
20 [q]Lam. 2:11
21 [r]Lam. 3:15

51:9,10 This prayer for deliverance in the future was based on times past when the Lord overcame Rahab, which was a term widely used to refer to things that wreak havoc, often, as in this case, Egypt (see Ps. 87:4).

51:11-16 Again, Isaiah summarized a constant theme, that instead of hearing dying men (v. 12), Israel should trust the Creator of all things. He had delivered Israel in the past and is to do so permanently in the future before the nations can be destroyed (v. 14), so they have no need to fear oppressors. The blessing of restored Israel will be evidenced in the joy of v. 11.

51:16 My words in your mouth. Israel had been the unfaithful depository of divine revelation (cf. Rom. 9:1-5), but the time is coming when God will put words into the mouths of His future faithful remnant (59:21) when He sets up the kingdom of Messiah in Zion on a renewed earth. Cf. 51:6; 65:17; 66:22.

51:17,18 Jerusalem, you who have drunk. Jerusalem experienced the Lord's anger through her extended subservience to foreign powers with no human to deliver her (v. 18), but the punishment will end (v. 22; 40:1,2; cf. 29:9). On the other hand, Babylon will drink from the cup of His anger forever (Rev. 14:8-11; 16:19).

51:19 two *things*. The city of Jerusalem (v. 17) had suffered the twofold loss of property ("desolation and destruction") and human life ("famine and sword").

51:20 Your sons have fainted. The city's inhabitants lay helpless in the streets, having expended all their strength in fighting unsuccessfully against the Lord's fury (40:30).

51:21,22 drunk but not with wine. Jerusalem was drunk through drinking the cup of God's wrath (63:6). But, in contrast to

22 Thus says your Lord,
The LORD and your God,
Who [s]pleads the cause of His people:
"See, I have taken out of your hand
The cup of trembling,
The dregs of the cup of My fury;
You shall no longer drink it.
23 [t]But I will put it into the hand of
those who afflict you,
Who have said to [4]you,
'Lie down, that we may walk over
you.'
And you have laid your body like
the ground,
And as the street, for those who
walk over."

God Redeems Jerusalem

52 Awake, awake!
Put on your strength, O Zion;
Put on your beautiful garments,
O Jerusalem, the holy city!
For the uncircumcised [a]and the
unclean
Shall no longer come to you.
2 [b]Shake yourself from the dust, arise;
Sit down, O Jerusalem!
[c]Loose yourself from the bonds of
your neck,
O captive daughter of Zion!

3 For thus says the LORD:

[d]"You have sold yourselves for
nothing,
And you shall be redeemed
[e]without money."

4 For thus says the Lord GOD:

22 [s] Is. 3:12, 13; 49:25; Jer. 50:34
23 [t] Is. 14:2; Jer. 25:17, 26-28; Zech. 12:2 [4] Lit. *your soul*

CHAPTER 52

1 [a] Neh. 11:1; Is. 48:2; 64:10; Zech. 14:20, 21; Matt. 4:5; [Rev. 21:2-27]
2 [b] Is. 3:26 [c] Is. 9:4; 10:27; 14:25; Zech. 2:7
3 [d] Ps. 44:12; Jer. 15:13 [e] Is. 45:13

"My people went down at first
Into [f]Egypt to [1]dwell there;
Then the Assyrian oppressed them
without cause.
5 Now therefore, what have I here,"
says the LORD,
"That My people are taken away for
nothing?
Those who rule over them
[2]Make them wail," says the LORD,
"And My name *is* [g]blasphemed
continually every day.
6 Therefore My people shall know
My name;
Therefore *they shall know* in that
day
That I *am* He who speaks:
'Behold, *it is* I.' "

7 [h]How beautiful upon the mountains
Are the feet of him who brings
good news,
Who proclaims peace,
Who brings glad tidings of good
things,
Who proclaims salvation,
Who says to Zion,
[i]"Your God reigns!"
8 Your watchmen shall lift up *their*
voices,
With their voices they shall sing
together;
For they shall see eye to eye
When the LORD brings back Zion.
9 Break forth into joy, sing together,
You waste places of Jerusalem!
For the LORD has comforted His
people,
He has redeemed Jerusalem.

4 [f] Gen. 46:6 [1] As resident aliens
5 [g] Ezek. 36:20, 23; Rom. 2:24 [2] DSS *Mock;* LXX *Marvel and wail;* Tg. *Boast themselves;* Vg. *Treat them unjustly*
7 [h] Is. 40:9; 61:1; Nah. 1:15; Rom. 10:15; Eph. 6:15 [i] Ps. 93:1; Is. 24:23

Babylon, which drank the fury of God's wrath to the last drop (v. 17; Rev. 18:6), Israel will have the cup removed before all the wrath is consumed. It will be handed to Israel's oppressors for them to drink the full fury (49:26; Jer. 25:15,26,28; Zech. 12:2).

52:1,2 your strength…beautiful garments. A call is given for Zion to awake from drunkenness and clothe herself in garments of honor and dignity provided by the Lord. Foreign invaders will no longer control the city at the time of her final restoration.

52:3 sold yourselves for nothing…redeemed without money. The Jews became the servants of their foreign conquerors, who paid nothing for Israel, so the Lord will redeem Israel gratuitously from sin (45:13; 55:1).

52:5 Those who rule over them. A reference to the Babylonians and their cruelty to captive Israelites. **My name *is* blasphemed.** Foreign rulers despised the God of Israel as long as His people were in bondage. God delivered His people, not for their goodness, but for the sake of His holy name—to prove He was truthful, faithful, and powerful (Ezek. 20:9,14). Paul cited the blasphemy to Israel's God that resulted from the hypocrisy of first-century Jews not applying to themselves the standards of God that they knew and taught others (Rom. 2:24).

52:6 in that day that I *am* He. After the Day of the Lord, when Israel experiences deliverance from her worldwide dispersion, she will recognize the fulfillment of prophecies through Isaiah and others and enjoy full assurance that the Lord had spoken and fulfilled His promises of deliverance. They will connect these events with the great "I AM" (43:11; Ex. 3:13-15).

52:7 How beautiful…good news. Messengers will traverse the mountains around Jerusalem to spread the good news of the return of redeemed Israel to the Land (40:9; 61:1; Nah. 1:15). Paul broadened this millennial reference to the preaching of the gospel in the kingdom to include spreading the gospel of God's grace from the time of Jesus Christ on (Rom. 10:15; cf. Eph. 6:15). **good *things*…salvation…"Your God reigns!"** The good news pertains to the ideal conditions of Israel's golden age, during which Christ will reign personally over His kingdom (24:23; Ps. 93:1).

52:8 eye to eye. See Num 14:14. This Heb. expression portrayed two people so close to each other that they can look into one another's eyes. The point is that the messengers of the truth ("watchmen") will see the Lord return to Zion (a better translation) as vividly as they see each other looking eye to eye.

52:9,10 comforted…redeemed. The ruined city will respond to the call to sing for joy because the Lord has provided comfort (40:1,2; 49:13; 51:12) and redemption (41:14; 43:1,12,14; 44:6,23,24; 47:4).

10 [j]The LORD has [3]made bare His holy
arm
In the eyes of [k]all the nations;
And all the ends of the earth shall
see
The salvation of our God.

11 [l]Depart! Depart! Go out from there,
Touch no unclean *thing;*
Go out from the midst of her,
[m]Be clean,
You who bear the vessels of the
LORD.
12 For [n]you shall not go out with
haste,
Nor go by flight;
[o]For the LORD will go before you,
[p]And the God of Israel *will be* your
rear guard.

The Sin-Bearing Servant

13 Behold, [q]My Servant shall [4]deal
prudently;
[r]He shall be exalted and [5]extolled
and be very high.
14 Just as many were astonished at
you,
So His [s]visage[6] was marred more
than any man,
And His form more than the sons
of men;
15 [t]So shall He [7]sprinkle many
nations.
Kings shall shut their mouths at
Him;
For [u]what had not been told them
they shall see,
And what they had not heard they
shall consider.

53 Who [a]has believed our report?
And to whom has the arm of the
LORD been revealed?
2 For He shall grow up before Him
as a tender plant,
And as a root out of dry ground.
He has no [1]form or [2]comeliness;
And when we see Him,
There is no [3]beauty that we should
desire Him.
3 [b]He is despised and [4]rejected by
men,
A Man of [5]sorrows and
[c]acquainted with [6]grief.
And we hid, as it were, *our* faces
from Him;
He was despised, and [d]we did not
esteem Him.

10 [j]Ps. 98:1-3 [k]Luke 3:6 [3]Revealed His power
11 [l]Is. 48:20; Jer. 50:8; Zech. 2:6, 7; 2 Cor. 6:17 [m]Lev. 22:2; [Is. 1:16]
12 [n]Ex. 12:11, 33; Deut. 16:3 [o]Mic. 2:13 [p]Ex. 14:19, 20; Is. 58:8
13 [q]Is. 42:1 [r]Is. 57:15; Phil. 2:9 [4]*prosper* [5]Lit. *be lifted up*
14 [s]Ps. 22:6, 7; Matt. 26:67; 27:30; John 19:3 [6]*appearance*
15 [t]Num. 19:18-21; Ezek. 36:25 [u]Rom. 15:21; [Eph. 3:5, 9]; 1 Pet. 1:2 [7]Or *startle*

CHAPTER 53
1 [a]John 12:38; Rom. 10:16
2 [1]Stately form [2]*splendor* [3]Lit. *appearance*
3 [b]Ps. 22:6; [Is. 49:7; Matt. 27:30, 31; Luke 18:31-33; 23:18] [c][Heb. 4:15] [d][John 1:10, 11] [4]Or *forsaken* [5]Lit. *pains* [6]Lit. *sickness*

52:11 Depart! Depart! The prophet commands the Israelites to leave the lands of their exiles to return to Jerusalem (48:20; Jer. 50:8; Zech. 2:6,7; Rev. 18:4). Under Cyrus there was only a limited return (50,000), but the final fulfillment in view here is in the future. **Touch no unclean *thing*...be clean.** Returning exiles were not to defile themselves by taking property home from their exile (cf. Josh. 6:18; 7:1). The NT gave these prophetic words an application in principle by using them as an exhortation forbidding Christians to involve themselves with spiritual ties to forces of heathendom (2 Cor. 6:17).

52:12 not...with haste. Delivered captives will not have to hurry in their return to Jerusalem, as their ancestors did when delivered from Egypt (Ex. 12:11,33,39; Deut. 16:3). They can move deliberately and safely, with the Messiah in front and God in back. Cf. 58:8.

52:13–53:12 This is the last and most memorable of the 4 Messiah/Servant songs (cf. 42:1-9; 49:1-13; 50:4-11). This section contains unarguable, incontrovertible proof that God is the author of Scripture and Jesus the fulfillment of messianic prophecy. The details are so minute that no human could have predicted them by accident and no imposter fulfilled them by cunning. Clearly this refers to Messiah Jesus, as the NT attests (cf. Matt 8:17; Mark 15:28; Luke 22:37; John 12:38; Acts 8:28-35; Rom. 10:16; 1 Pet. 2:21-25). It is often alluded to without being quoted (cf. Mark 9:12; Rom. 4:25; 1 Cor. 15:3; 2 Cor. 5:21; 1 Pet. 1:19; 1 John 3:5).

52:13-15 Here is a summary and preview of the humiliation and exaltation of the Servant, described in more detail in 53:1-12. The details cover the work of Christ in His substitutionary death, His burial, His resurrection, His saving of sinners, His intercession, and His kingdom.

52:13 exalted...extolled...very high. Ultimately, when the Servant rules over His kingdom, He will receive international recognition for the effectiveness of His reign (cf. Phil 2:9).

52:14 His visage was marred. The Servant must undergo inhuman cruelty to the point that He no longer looks like a human being. His appearance is so awful that people look at Him in astonishment (53:2,3; Ps. 22:6; Matt. 26:67; 27:30; John 19:3).

52:15 sprinkle many nations. In His disfigured state, the Servant will perform a priestly work of cleansing not just Israel, but many outside the nation (Ex. 29:21; Lev. 4:6; 8:11; 14:7; Num. 8:7; 19:18,19; Heb. 9:13). **shut their mouths.** At His exaltation, human leaders in the highest places will be speechless and in awe before the once-despised Servant (cf. Ps. 2). When He takes His throne, they will see the unfolding of power and glory such as they have never heard. Paul applied the principle in this verse to his apostolic mission of preaching the gospel of Christ where Christ was yet unknown (Rom. 15:21).

53:1 Who has believed our report? The question implied that, in spite of these and other prophecies, only a few would recognize the Servant when He appeared. This anticipation found literal fulfillment at Christ's first advent. Israel did not welcome Him at His first advent (John 1:9-11; 12:38). Paul applied the same prophecy to the world at large (Rom. 10:16). **the arm of the LORD.** At His first coming, the nation did not recognize the mighty, incarnate power of God in the person of Jesus, their Deliverer.

53:2 before Him. Though unrecognized by the world (v. 1), Messiah Jesus was observed carefully by God, who ordered every minute circumstance of His life. **dry ground...no beauty that we should desire Him.** The Servant will arise in lowly conditions and wear none of the usual emblems of royalty, making His true identity visible only to the discerning eye of faith.

53:3 despised...rejected...despised. The prophet foresees the hatred and rejection by mankind toward the Messiah/Servant, who suffered not only external abuse, but also internal grief over the lack of response from those He came to save (e.g., Matt. 23:37; Luke 13:34). **we hid...we did not esteem.** By using the first person, the prophet spoke for his unbelieving nation's aversion to a crucified Messiah and their lack of respect for the incarnate Son of God.

4 Surely [e]He has borne our [7]griefs
And carried our [8]sorrows;
Yet we [9]esteemed Him stricken,
[1]Smitten by God, and afflicted.
5 But He *was* [f]wounded [2] for our
transgressions,
He was [3]bruised for our iniquities;
The chastisement for our peace *was*
upon Him,
And by His [g]stripes[4] we are healed.
6 All we like sheep have gone astray;
We have turned, every one, to his
own way;
And the LORD [5]has laid on Him the
iniquity of us all.

7 He was oppressed and He was
afflicted,
Yet [h]He opened not His mouth;
[i]He was led as a lamb to the
slaughter,
And as a sheep before its shearers
is silent,
So He opened not His mouth.
8 He was [j]taken from [6]prison and
from judgment,
And who will declare His
generation?
For [k]He was cut off from the land
of the living;
For the transgressions of My
people He was stricken.
9 [l]And [7]they made His grave with
the wicked—
But with the rich at His death,
Because He had done no violence,
Nor *was any* [m]deceit in His mouth.

10 Yet it pleased the LORD to [8]bruise
Him;
He has put *Him* to grief.
When You make His soul [n]an
offering for sin,
He shall see *His* seed, He shall
prolong *His* days,
And the pleasure of the LORD shall
prosper in His hand.
11 [9]He shall see the labor of His soul,
and be satisfied.
By His knowledge [o]My righteous
[p]Servant shall [q]justify many,
For He shall bear their iniquities.

4 [e] [Matt. 8:17; Heb. 9:28; 1 Pet. 2:24] [7] Lit. *sicknesses* [8] Lit. *pains* [9] *reckoned* [1] *Struck down*
5 [f] [Is. 53:10; Rom. 4:25; 1 Cor. 15:3, 4] [g] [1 Pet. 2:24, 25] [2] Or *pierced through* [3] *crushed* [4] Blows that cut in
6 [5] Lit. *has caused to land on Him*
7 [h] Matt. 26:63; 27:12-14; Mark 14:61; 15:5; Luke 23:9; John 19:9 [i] Acts 8:32, 33; Rev. 5:6
8 [j] Matt. 27:11-26; Luke 23:1-25 [6] *confinement*
[k] [Dan. 9:26]
9 [l] Matt. 27:57-60; Luke 23:33 [m] 1 Pet. 2:22; 1 John 3:5 [7] Lit. *he* or *He*
10 [n] John 1:29; Acts 2:24; [2 Cor. 5:21] [8] *crush*
11 [o] [1 John 2:1] [p] Is. 42:1 [q] [Acts 13:38, 39; Rom. 5:15-18] [9] So with MT, Tg., Vg.; DSS, LXX *From the labor of His soul He shall see light*

53:4 borne…carried. Cf. vv. 11,12. Even though the verbs are past tense, they predict happenings future to Isaiah's time, i.e., "prophetic perfects" in Heb. here and elsewhere in this Servant-song. Isaiah was saying that the Messiah would bear the consequences of the sins of men, namely the griefs and sorrows of life, though incredibly the Jews who watched Him die thought He was being punished by God for His own sins. Matthew found an analogical fulfillment of these words in Jesus' healing ministry (*see notes on Matt. 8:16,17*), because sickness results from sin for which the Servant paid with His life (vv. 7,8; cf. 1 Pet. 2:24). In eternity, all sickness will be removed, so ultimately it is included in the benefits of the atonement.

53:5 wounded for our transgressions…bruised for our iniquities. This verse is filled with the language of substitution. The Servant suffered not for His own sin, since He was sinless (cf. Heb. 4:15; 7:26), but as the substitute for sinners. The emphasis here is on Christ being the substitute recipient of God's wrath on sinners (cf. 2 Cor. 5:21; Gal. 1:3,4; Heb. 10:9,10). **chastisement for our peace.** He suffered the chastisement of God in order to procure our peace with God. **by His stripes we are healed.** The stripe (the Heb. noun is singular) that caused His death has brought salvation to those for whose sins He died. Peter confirms this in 1 Pet. 2:24.

53:6 All we…every one…us all. Every person has sinned (Rom. 3:9,23), but the Servant has sufficiently shouldered the consequences of sin and the righteous wrath deserved by sinners (cf. 1 Tim. 2:5,6; 4:10; 1 John 2:2). The manner in which God laid our iniquity on Him was that God treated Him as if He had committed every sin ever committed by every person who would ever believe, though He was perfectly innocent of any sin. God did so to Him, so that wrath being spent and justice satisfied, God could then give to the account of sinners who believe, the righteousness of Christ, treating them as if they had done only the righteous acts of Christ. In both cases, this is substitution. *See notes on 2 Cor. 5:21.*

53:7,8 This is the portion of Scripture read by the Ethiopian eunuch and subsequently explained to him by Philip as referring to Jesus (Acts 8:32,33).

53:7 opened not His mouth. The Servant will utter no protest and will be utterly submissive to those who oppress Him. Jesus fulfilled this (Matt. 26:63; 27:12-14; Mark 14:61; 15:5; Luke 23:9; John 19:9; 1 Pet. 2:23). **lamb to the slaughter.** The Servant was to assume the role of a sacrificial lamb (Ex. 12:3,6). Jesus fulfilled this figurative role literally (John 1:29; 1 Pet. 1:18,19; Rev. 5:6).

53:8 cut off…for the transgressions of My people. The Servant lost His life to be the substitute object of wrath in the place of the Jews, who by that substitution will receive salvation and the righteousness of God imputed to them. Similar terminology applies to the Messiah in Dan. 9:26.

53:9 with the wicked…with the rich. Because of His disgraceful death, the Jews intended the Servant to have a disgraceful burial along with the thieves (cf. John 19:31), but instead He was buried with "the rich" in an honorable burial through the donated tomb of rich Joseph of Arimathea (Matt. 27:57-60; Mark 15:42-46; Luke 23:50-53; John 19:38-40). **no violence, nor…deceit.** The Servant's innocence meant that His execution was totally undeserved. Peter notes the fulfillment of this in 1 Pet. 2:22.

53:10 it pleased the LORD. Though the Servant did not deserve to die, it was the Lord's will for Him to do so (Matt. 26:39; Luke 22:42; John 12:27; Acts 2:23). **an offering for sin.** Fulfilled by the Servant as the lamb of God (v. 7; John 1:29). Christ is the Christian's Passover (1 Cor. 5:7). This conclusively eliminates the error that Christ's atonement provides present day healing for those who pray in faith. His death was an atonement for sin, not sickness. *See note on 53:4.* **see *His* seed…prolong *His* days.** To see His seed, the Servant must rise from the dead. He will do this and live to reign forever (2 Sam. 7:13,16; Pss. 21:4; 89:4; 132:12).

53:11 He shall…be satisfied. The one sacrifice of the Servant will provide complete satisfaction in settling the sin issue (1 John 2:2; cf. 1:11). **By His knowledge.** The Servant knew exactly what needed to be done to solve the sin problem. **justify many.** Through the divine "knowledge" of how to justify sinners, the plan was accomplished that by His one sacrifice He declared many righteous before God (Rom. 5:19; 2 Cor. 5:21).

12 [r]Therefore I will divide Him a
portion with the great,
[s]And He shall divide the [1]spoil
with the strong,
Because He [t]poured out His soul
unto death,
And He was [u]numbered with the
transgressors,
And He bore the sin of many,
And [v]made intercession for the
transgressors.

A Perpetual Covenant of Peace

54 "Sing, O [a]barren,
You *who* have not borne!
Break forth into singing, and cry
aloud,
You *who* have not labored with
child!
For more *are* the children of the
desolate
Than the children of the married
woman," says the LORD.
2 "Enlarge[b] the place of your tent,
And let them stretch out the
curtains of your dwellings;
Do not spare;
Lengthen your cords,
And strengthen your stakes.
3 For you shall expand to the right
and to the left,
And your descendants will [c]inherit
the nations,
And make the desolate cities
inhabited.
4 "Do[d] not fear, for you will not be
ashamed;
Neither be disgraced, for you will
not be put to shame;
For you will forget the shame of
your youth,
And will not remember the
reproach of your widowhood
anymore.
5 [e]For your Maker *is* your husband,
The LORD of hosts *is* His name;
And your Redeemer *is* the Holy
One of Israel;
He is called [f]the God of the whole
earth.
6 For the LORD [g]has called you
Like a woman forsaken and
grieved in spirit,
Like a youthful wife when you
were refused,"
Says your God.
7 "For[h] a mere moment I have
forsaken you,
But with great mercies [i]I will
gather you.
8 With a little wrath I hid My face
from you for a moment;
[j]But with everlasting kindness I
will have mercy on you,"
Says the LORD, your Redeemer.

9 "For this *is* like the waters of [k]Noah
to Me;
For as I have sworn
That the waters of Noah would no
longer cover the earth,
So have I sworn
That I would not be angry with
[l]you, nor rebuke you.
10 For [m]the mountains shall depart
And the hills be removed,
[n]But My kindness shall not depart
from you,
Nor shall My covenant of peace be
removed,"

12 [r] Ps. 2:8 [s] Col. 2:15 [t] Is. 50:6; [Rom. 3:25] [u] Matt. 27:38; Mark 15:28; Luke 22:37; 2 Cor. 5:21 [v] Luke 23:34 [1] *plunder*

CHAPTER 54

1 [a] Gal. 4:27
2 [b] Is. 49:19, 20
3 [c] Is. 14:2; 49:22, 23; 60:9
4 [d] Is. 41:10
5 [e] Jer. 3:14; Hos. 2:19 [f] Zech. 14:9; Rom. 3:29
6 [g] Is. 62:4
7 [h] Ps. 30:5; Is. 26:20; 60:10; 2 Cor. 4:17 [i] [Is. 43:5; 56:8]
8 [j] Is. 55:3; Jer. 31:3
9 [k] Gen. 8:21; 9:11; [2 Pet. 3:6, 7] [l] Is. 12:1; Ezek. 39:29
10 [m] Ps. 46:2; Is. 51:6; Matt. 5:18 [n] 2 Sam. 23:5; Ps. 89:33, 34; Is. 55:3; 59:21; 61:8

53:12 portion with the great...spoil with the strong. The Servant's reward for His work will be to enjoy the "spoils" of His spiritual victories during His millennial reign. **numbered with the transgressors.** The Servant assumes a role among sinful human beings, fulfilled by Jesus when He was crucified between two criminals (Luke 22:37). **made intercession for the transgressors.** This speaks of the office of intercessory High-Priest, which began on the cross (Luke 23:34) and continues in heaven (cf. Heb. 7:25; 9:24).

54:1 barren...have not borne...have not labored...desolate. In her exile and dispersion, Israel has been destitute, disgraced as a woman who had borne no children (49:21). The prophet calls for singing, however, because of the Lord's promise of future fruitfulness for the nation (49:19,20). The NT supplies an additional application of the principle in this verse, citing it as evidence that the Jerusalem above, mother of the children of promise through Sarah, will enjoy great fruitfulness (Gal. 4:27).

54:2 Enlarge...stretch out...Lengthen. The prophet commanded barren Israel to prepare for the day when her numerous inhabitants will require larger space to dwell in (26:15; 49:19,20).

54:3 expand...inherit the nations. The Messiah's future kingdom is to be worldwide, far greater in extent than the former kingdoms of David and Solomon.

54:4 shame of your youth...reproach of your widowhood. Israel's sins brought on the Egyptian captivity, the Babylonian exile, and her current dispersion, but the glories of the future kingdom will be so great that they will overshadow past failures.

54:5 husband...Redeemer. The basis for forgetting past failures is Israel's relationship to the Lord as her husband (62:4,5) and Redeemer (41:14).

54:6-8 forsaken...grieved...refused. Israel in exile and dispersion has been like a wife whose husband has rejected her. But this is only for a brief time compared to the everlasting kindness she will enjoy when the Messiah returns to gather the woeful wife (26:20).

54:9 waters of Noah. Just as God swore He would never again judge the whole earth with a flood (Gen. 8:21; 9:11), so He has taken an oath never to be angry with His people again. He will fulfill this promise after their final restoration.

54:10 mountains...hills...My kindness...My covenant. In the Millennium (48:6,7; 51:6,16) topography will change (see Ezek. 38:20; Mic. 1:4; Zech. 14:4,10), but not God's pledge of well-being for Israel as a result of the New Covenant (55:3; 59:21; 61:8).

Says the LORD, who has mercy on
you.

11 "O you afflicted one,
Tossed with tempest, *and* not
comforted,
Behold, I will lay your stones with
[o]colorful gems,
And lay your foundations with
sapphires.
12 I will make your pinnacles of rubies,
Your gates of crystal,
And all your walls of precious
stones.
13 All your children *shall be* [p]taught
by the LORD,
And [q]great *shall be* the peace of
your children.
14 In righteousness you shall be
established;
You shall be far from oppression,
for you shall not fear;
And from terror, for it shall not
come near you.
15 Indeed they shall surely assemble,
but not because of Me.
Whoever assembles against you
shall [r]fall for your sake.

16 "Behold, I have created the
blacksmith
Who blows the coals in the fire,
Who brings forth an [1]instrument
for his work;
And I have created the [2]spoiler to
destroy.
17 No weapon formed against you
shall [s]prosper,
And every tongue *which* rises
against you in judgment
You shall condemn.

11 [o] 1 Chr. 29:2; Job 28:16; Rev. 21:18, 19
13 [p] Jer. 31:34; [John 6:45; 1 Cor. 2:10]; 1 Thess. 4:9; [1 John 2:20] [q] Ps. 119:165
15 [r] Is. 41:11-16
16 [1] Or *weapon* [2] *destroyer*
17 [s] Is. 17:12-14; 29:8
[t] Is. 45:24, 25; 54:14

CHAPTER 55

1 [a] [Matt. 5:6; John 4:14; 7:37; Rev. 21:6; 22:17] [b] [Matt. 13:44; Rev. 3:18]
2 [1] Lit. *weigh out silver*
3 [c] Matt. 11:28 [d] Is. 54:8; 61:8; Jer. 32:40 [e] 2 Sam. 7:8; Ps. 89:28; [Acts 13:34]
4 [f] [John 18:37; Rev. 1:5] [g] [Jer. 30:9; Ezek. 34:23; Dan. 9:25]
5 [h] Is. 52:15; Eph. 2:11, 12 [i] Is. 60:5 [j] Is. 60:9
6 [k] Matt. 5:25; 25:11; John 7:34; 8:21; 2 Cor. 6:2; [Heb. 3:13] [l] Ps. 32:6; Is. 49:8

This *is* the heritage of the servants
of the LORD,
[t]And their righteousness *is* from
Me,"
Says the LORD.

An Invitation to Abundant Life

55 "Ho! [a]Everyone who thirsts,
Come to the waters;
And you who have no money,
[b]Come, buy and eat.
Yes, come, buy wine and milk
Without money and without price.
2 Why do you [1]spend money for
what is not bread,
And your wages for *what* does not
satisfy?
Listen carefully to Me, and eat *what*
is good,
And let your soul delight itself in
abundance.
3 Incline your ear, and [c]come to Me.
Hear, and your soul shall live;
[d]And I will make an everlasting
covenant with you—
The [e]sure mercies of David.
4 Indeed I have given him *as* [f]a
witness to the people,
[g]A leader and commander for the
people.
5 [h]Surely you shall call a nation you
do not know,
[i]And nations *who* do not know you
shall run to you,
Because of the LORD your God,
And the Holy One of Israel;
[j]For He has glorified you."

6 [k]Seek the LORD while He may be
[l]found,

54:11,12 colorful gems...sapphires...rubies...crystal...precious stones. The elaborate ornamentation will outfit Jerusalem to be the center of the future, eternal messianic reign following the Millennium (Rev. 21:18-21). As magnificent as this is, it is not as important as the spiritual richness of the kingdom, when truth and peace (v. 13) prevail along with righteousness (v. 14). The Lord Himself will teach everyone during the messianic kingdom, so everyone will know His righteousness (11:9; Jer. 31:34). Jesus gave this verse an additional focus, applying it to those with spiritual insight to come to Him during His first advent (John 6:45).

54:15-17 Whoever assembles against you shall fall. In the millennial kingdom this will occur, as prophesied by John in Rev. 20:7-9. The Lord will burn up all Israel's enemies The heritage of the Lord's servants in the Messiah's kingdom will include His protection from would-be conquerors. It should be noted that after the Servant-song of Isaiah 53, Israel is always referrred to as God's "servants" (plural) rather than His servant (54:17; 56:6; 63:17; 65:8,9,13,14,15; 66:14).

55:1 Everyone. The Servant's redemptive work and glorious kingdom is for the benefit of all who are willing to come (53:6). The prophet invites his readers to participate in the benefits obtained by the suffering of the Servant in chap. 53 and described in chap. 54. **no money...without money and without price.** Benefits in the Servant's kingdom will be free because of His redemptive work (53:6,8,11; Eph. 2:8,9). **wine and milk.** Symbols for abundance, satisfaction, and prosperity (Song 5:1; Joel 3:18).

55:2 not bread. This is the "bread of deceit" (Prov. 20:17) and not the "bread of life" (John 6:32-35).

55:3 everlasting covenant. The New Covenant that God will give to Israel (54:8; 61:8; Jer. 31:31-34; 32:40; 50:5; Ezek. 16:60; 37:26; Heb. 13:20). **sure mercies of David.** The Davidic Covenant promised David that his seed would be ruler over Israel in an everlasting kingdom (2 Sam. 7:8,16; Ps. 89:27-29). Paul connected the resurrection of Christ with this promise (Acts 13:34), since it was an essential event in fulfilling this promise. If He had not fully satisfied God by His atoning death, He would not have risen; if He had not risen from the dead, He could not eventually sit on David's earthly throne. But He did rise and will fulfill the kingly role (v. 4). Cf. Jer. 30:9; Ezek. 34:23,24; 37:24,25; Dan. 9:25; Hos. 3:5; Mic. 5:2. The whole world will come to Him as the Great King (v. 5).

55:6,7 Here is one of the clearest OT invitations to salvation now and kingdom blessing later. It gives an excellent example of how

Call upon Him while He is near.
7 [m]Let the [2]wicked forsake his way,
And the unrighteous man [n]his thoughts;
Let him return to the LORD,
[o]And He will have mercy on him;
And to our God,
For He will abundantly pardon.

8 "For[p] My thoughts *are* not your thoughts,
Nor *are* your ways My ways," says the LORD.
9 "For[q] *as* the heavens are higher than the earth,
So are My ways higher than your ways,
And My thoughts than your thoughts.

10 "For [r]as the rain comes down, and the snow from heaven,
And do not return there,
But water the earth,
And make it bring forth and bud,
That it may give seed to the sower
And bread to the eater,
11 [s]So shall My word be that goes forth from My mouth;
It shall not return to Me [3]void,
But it shall accomplish what I please,
And it shall [t]prosper *in the thing* for which I sent it.

12 "For[u] you shall go out with joy,
And be led out with peace;
The mountains and the hills
Shall [v]break forth into singing before you,
And [w]all the trees of the field shall clap *their* hands.
13 [x]Instead of [y]the thorn shall come up the cypress tree,
And instead of the brier shall come up the myrtle tree;
And it shall be to the LORD [z]for a name,
For an everlasting sign *that* shall not be cut off."

Salvation for the Gentiles

56 Thus says the LORD:
"Keep justice, and do righteousness,
[a]For My salvation *is* about to come,
And My righteousness to be revealed.
2 Blessed *is* the man *who* does this,
And the son of man *who* lays hold on it;
[b]Who keeps from defiling the Sabbath,
And keeps his hand from doing any evil."

3 Do not let [c]the son of the foreigner
Who has joined himself to the LORD
Speak, saying,
"The LORD has utterly separated me from His people";
Nor let the [d]eunuch say,
"Here I am, a dry tree."
4 For thus says the LORD:
"To the eunuchs who keep My Sabbaths,
And choose what pleases Me,
And hold fast My covenant,

7 [m]Is. 1:16 [n]Is. 59:7; Zech. 8:17 [o]Ps. 130:7; Jer. 3:12 [2]Lit. *man of iniquity*
8 [p]2 Sam. 7:19
9 [q]Ps. 103:11
10 [r]Deut. 32:2
11 [s]Is. 45:23; Matt. 24:35 [t]Is. 46:9-11 [3]*empty,* without fruit
12 [u]Is. 35:10 [v]Ps. 98:8 [w]1 Chr. 16:33
13 [x]Is. 41:19 [y]Mic. 7:4 [z]Jer. 13:11

CHAPTER 56

1 [a]Is. 46:13; Matt. 3:2; 4:17; Rom. 13:11, 12
2 [b]Ex. 20:8-11; 31:13-17; Is. 58:13; Jer. 17:21, 22; Ezek. 20:12, 20
3 [c]Is. 14:1; [Eph. 2:12-19] [d]Deut. 23:1; Jer. 38:7; Acts 8:27

people were saved during the OT period. Salvation grace and mercy were available to the soul that was willing to 1) seek the Lord (Deut. 4:29; 2 Chr. 15:4) and 2) call on Him while He is still available (65:1; Ps. 32:6; Prov. 8:17; Matt. 25:1-13; John 7:34; 8:21; 2 Cor. 6:2; Heb. 2:3; 3:13,15). Such true seeking in faith is accompanied by repentance, which is described as forsaking ways and thoughts and turning from sinful living to the Lord. A sinner must come, believing in God, recognizing his sin and desiring forgiveness and deliverance from that sin. At the same time he must recognize his own inability to be righteous or to satisfy God and cast himself on God's mercy. It is then that he receives a complete pardon. His sin has been covered by the substitution of the Messiah in his place (chap. 53). This OT pattern of salvation is illustrated in Luke 18:9-14.

55:7 forsake. An integral part of seeking the Lord (v. 6) is a turning from sin (1:16).

55:8,9 My thoughts...My ways. Some may doubt such willingness as is described in v. 7, but God's grace is far beyond human comprehension, especially as manifested toward Israel.

55:10,11 rain...snow...My word. Moisture from heaven invariably accomplishes its intended purpose in helping meet human physical needs. The Word of God will likewise produce its intended results in fulfilling God's spiritual purposes, especially the establishment of the Davidic kingdom on earth (vv. 1-5).

55:12 go out with joy...led out with peace. Exiled Israel will return from her dispersion rejoicing in her deliverance and unbothered by her enemies.

55:13 Instead of the thorn...myrtle tree. In the Davidic kingdom positive changes in nature, including the reverse of the curse (Gen. 3:17), will be an ongoing testimony to the Lord's redemption of His people (44:23; Rom. 8:19-23).

56:1 about to come...to be revealed. Incentives to comply with 55:6,7 include the nearness of God's kingdom of salvation and righteousness (51:5).

56:2 keeps from defiling the Sabbath. Sabbath observance, established after the deliverance from Egypt (Ex. 20:8-11), became a sign of fulfilling the covenant God made with Moses (Ex. 31:13-17).

56:3 foreigner...eunuch. Such individuals, excluded from Israel by the law (Ex. 12:43; Deut. 23:1,3,7,8), will find in the coming of the messianic kingdom the removal of such exclusions.

56:4,5 hold fast My covenant...an everlasting name. Eunuchs with hearts inclined to comply with the Mosaic Covenant may anticipate an endless posterity. It is never works that save (cf. Rom. 3:20; Eph. 2:8,9); rather, obeying God's law, doing what pleases Him or

5 Even to them I will give in [e]My house
And within My walls a place [f]and a name
Better than that of sons and daughters;
I will give [1]them an everlasting name
That shall not be cut off.

6 "Also the sons of the foreigner
Who join themselves to the LORD, to serve Him,
And to love the name of the LORD, to be His servants—
Everyone who keeps from defiling the Sabbath,
And holds fast My covenant—
7 Even them I will [g]bring to My holy mountain,
And make them joyful in My [h]house of prayer.
[i]Their burnt offerings and their sacrifices
Will be [j]accepted on My altar;
For [k]My house shall be called a house of prayer [l]for all nations."
8 The Lord GOD, [m]who gathers the outcasts of Israel, says,
[n]"Yet I will gather to him
Others besides those who are gathered to him."

Israel's Irresponsible Leaders

9 [o]All you beasts of the field, come to devour,
All you beasts in the forest.
10 His watchmen *are* [p]blind,
They are all ignorant;
[q]They *are* all dumb dogs,
They cannot bark;
[2]Sleeping, lying down, loving to slumber.
11 Yes, *they are* [r]greedy [3]dogs
Which [s]never [4]have enough.
And they *are* shepherds
Who cannot understand;
They all look to their own way,
Every one for his own gain,
From his *own* territory.
12 "Come," *one says,* "I will bring wine,
And we will fill ourselves with intoxicating [t]drink;
[u]Tomorrow will be [v]as today,
And much more abundant."

Israel's Futile Idolatry

57 The righteous perishes,
And no man takes *it* to heart;
[a]Merciful men *are* taken away,
[b]While no one considers
That the righteous is taken away from [1]evil.
2 He shall enter into peace;
They shall rest in [c]their beds,
Each one walking *in* his uprightness.

3 "But come here,
[d]You sons of the sorceress,
You offspring of the adulterer and the harlot!
4 Whom do you ridicule?
Against whom do you make a wide mouth
And stick out the tongue?
Are you not children of transgression,
Offspring of falsehood,
5 Inflaming yourselves with gods
[e]under every green tree,

5 [e]1 Tim. 3:15 [f][1 John 3:1, 2] [1]Lit. *him*
7 [g][Is. 2:2, 3; 60:11; Mic. 4:1, 2] [h]Matt. 21:13; Mark 11:17; Luke 19:46 [i][Rom. 12:1; Heb. 13:15; 1 Pet. 2:5] [j]Is. 60:7 [k]Matt. 21:13 [l][Mal. 1:11]
8 [m]Ps. 147:2; Is. 11:12; 27:12; 54:7 [n]Is. 60:3-11; 66:18-21; [John 10:16]
9 [o]Jer. 12:9
10 [p]Matt. 15:14 [q]Phil. 3:2
[2]Or *Dreaming*
11 [r]Is. 28:7; Ezek. 13:19; [Mic. 3:5, 11] [s]Ezek. 34:2-10 [3]Lit. *strong of soul* [4]Lit. *do not know satisfaction*
12 [t]Is. 28:7 [u]Ps. 10:6; Prov. 23:35; Is. 22:13; Luke 12:19; 1 Cor. 15:32 [v]2 Pet. 3:4

CHAPTER 57

1 [a]Ps. 12:1 [b]1 Kin. 14:13 [1]Lit. *the face of evil*
2 [c]2 Chr. 16:14
3 [d]Is. 1:4; Matt. 16:4
5 [e]2 Kin. 16:4

desiring to keep the promises of obedience are the evidences that one has been saved, and will thus enjoy all salvation blessings.

56:6,7 holds fast My covenant...accepted on My altar. The sacrifices of a foreigner who loves God, whose heart is inclined to serve Him and obey the Mosaic law, will find his sacrifices welcome, in the coming kingdom as well.

56:7 My house...for all nations. In the kingdom of the Messiah, the Jerusalem temple will be the focal point for worship of the Lord by people of all ethnic backgrounds. Jesus cited a violation of this anticipation by His contemporaries in His second cleansing of the temple: Jewish leaders had made the temple a commercial venture (Matt. 21:13; Mark 11:17; Luke 19:46).

56:8 *Others* besides those...gathered. Besides gathering Israel's exiles into His kingdom, the Lord will bring in non-Jews also (49:6).

56:9-12 A commentary on Israel's false prophets and irresponsible leaders who led them astray.

56:9-11 beasts...watchmen...shepherds. These titles identify the wicked; other prophets refer to Israel's enemies as beasts (Jer. 12:9; Ezek. 34:5,8). Prophets, who should have been watchmen and warned Israel to repent, ignored their responsibility (cf. Ezek. 3:17). Priests also failed to lead Israel in paths of righteousness (Ezek. 34:1-6; Zech. 11:15-17).

56:12 wine...intoxicating drink. This is indicative of the self-indulgent irresponsibility of the leaders. Drunkenness completely obliterated any concern that leaders had for their people. *See notes on Prov. 31:4-7.*

57:1,2 In contrast to the evil leaders, who were engaged in debauchery and self-indulgence, were the righteous who were removed from impending divine judgments. The righteous do suffer by oppression and distress at what is going on around them, but they die in faith and enjoy their eternal reward.

57:3 sorceress...adulterer...harlot. Sorcery and adultery were figurative designations for idolatry. God summoned the wicked to give an account.

57:4 stick out the tongue. The ungodly blatantly ridiculed God's messengers (e.g., 28:9,10).

57:5,6 These verses feature elements of idolatry such as child sacrifice, which were a part of worshiping the Ammonite god Molech (Jer. 32:35; Ezek. 20:26,31). In response to Israel's offerings to idols,

[f]Slaying the children in the valleys,
Under the clefts of the rocks?
6 Among the smooth [g]*stones* of the stream
Is your portion;
They, they, *are* your lot!
Even to them you have poured a drink offering,
You have offered a grain offering.
Should I receive comfort in [h]these?

7 "On[i] a lofty and high mountain
You have set [j]your bed;
Even there you went up
To offer sacrifice.
8 Also behind the doors and their posts
You have set up your remembrance;
For you have uncovered yourself *to those other* than Me,
And have gone up to them;
You have enlarged your bed
And [2]made *a covenant* with them;
[k]You have loved their bed,
Where you saw *their* [3]nudity.
9 [l]You went to the king with ointment,
And increased your perfumes;
You sent your [m]messengers far off,
And *even* descended to Sheol.
10 You are wearied in the length of your way;
[n]*Yet* you did not say, 'There is no hope.'
You have found the life of your hand;
Therefore you were not grieved.

11 "And [o]of whom have you been afraid, or feared,
That you have lied
And not remembered Me,
Nor taken *it* to your heart?
Is it not because [p]I have [4]held My peace from of old
That you do not fear Me?

5 [f]2 Kin. 23:10; Ps. 106:37, 38; Jer. 7:31; Ezek. 16:20
6 [g]Jer. 3:9; Hab. 2:19 [h]Jer. 5:9, 29; 9:9
7 [i]Jer. 3:6; Ezek. 16:16 [j]Ezek. 23:41
8 [k]Ezek. 16:26 [2]Lit. *cut* [3]Lit. *hand,* a euphemism
9 [l]Hos. 7:11 [m]Ezek. 23:16, 40
10 [n]Jer. 2:25; 18:12
11 [o]Prov. 29:25; Is. 51:12, 13 [p]Ps. 50:21; Eccl. 8:11; Is. 42:14 [4]*remained silent*

14 [q]Is. 40:3; 62:10; Jer. 18:15
15 [r]Job 6:10; Luke 1:49 [s]Ps. 68:35; Zech. 2:13 [t]Ps. 34:18; 51:17; Is. 66:2 [u]Ps. 147:3; Is. 61:1-3
16 [v]Ps. 85:5; 103:9; [Mic. 7:18] [w]Num. 16:22; Job 34:14; Heb. 12:9
17 [x]Is. 2:7; 56:11; Jer. 6:13 [y]Is. 8:17; 45:15; 59:2 [z]Is. 9:13 [5]Or *turning back*
18 [a]Jer. 3:22 [b]Is. 61:2

12 I will declare your righteousness
And your works,
For they will not profit you.
13 When you cry out,
Let your collection *of idols* deliver you.
But the wind will carry them all away,
A breath will take *them.*
But he who puts his trust in Me shall possess the land,
And shall inherit My holy mountain."

Healing for the Backslider

14 And one shall say,
[q]"Heap it up! Heap it up!
Prepare the way,
Take the stumbling block out of the way of My people."
15 For thus says the High and Lofty One
Who inhabits eternity, [r]whose name *is* Holy:
[s]"I dwell in the high and holy *place,*
[t]With him *who* has a contrite and humble spirit,
[u]To revive the spirit of the humble,
And to revive the heart of the contrite ones.
16 [v]For I will not contend forever,
Nor will I always be angry;
For the spirit would fail before Me,
And the souls [w]*which* I have made.
17 For the iniquity of [x]his covetousness
I was angry and struck him;
[y]I hid and was angry,
[z]And he went on [5]backsliding in the way of his heart.
18 I have seen his ways, and [a]will heal him;
I will also lead him,
And restore comforts to him
And to [b]his mourners.

what was the Lord's appropriate response—to be satisfied or to take vengeance? Jeremiah had the answer (Jer. 5:9,29; 9:9).

57:7,8 The location of idol altars where Israel committed spiritual adultery in offering sacrifices (Jer. 3:6; Ezek. 16:16) to Baal and Astarte.

57:9 went to the king. An example of this was Ahaz, who called on the king of Assyria for help and spared no expense in copying the idolatry of Assyria (2 Kin. 16:7-18).

57:10 found the life of your hand. Rather than recognizing the hopelessness of idolatry, and in spite of the weariness of idol worship, the Israelites found renewed strength to pursue their idolatrous course.

57:11 you have lied. These wicked people feared false gods more than the true God to whom they played the hypocrite, trading on God's patience.

57:12,13 I will declare your righteousness. God will break His silence by elaborating on Israel's sham righteousness, a sarcastic way of saying they have no real righteousness. The folly of such devotion to non-existent gods will show up when judgment comes and they all are blown away, while the worshipers of the true God enjoy the blessings of the kingdom. See Ps. 37:11; Matt. 5:5.

57:14-20 In contrast with the threats of judgment for idolatry (vv. 3-13), vv. 14-20 give promises of blessing.

57:14 Take the stumbling block. The command is to remove all barriers to prepare the way for God's people to return to Him (62:10).

57:15,18 revive the spirit...revive the heart. The Lord sends true revival, which comes to the humble and contrite (61:1-3; contra. v. 10). After all the years of Israel's sin and backsliding, and of Israel's punishment, God's grace will prevail (43:25) and spiritual healing and restoration will come.

57:17 backsliding. *See note on Prov. 14:14.*

19 "I create [c]the fruit of the lips:
Peace, peace [d]to *him who is* far off
and to *him who is* near,"
Says the LORD,
"And I will heal him."
20 [e]But the wicked *are* like the troubled
sea,
When it cannot rest,
Whose waters cast up mire and
dirt.
21 "*There*[f] *is* no peace,"
Says my God, "for the wicked."

Fasting that Pleases God

58 "Cry aloud, [1]spare not;
Lift up your voice like a trumpet;
[a]Tell My people their transgression,
And the house of Jacob their sins.
2 Yet they seek Me daily,
And delight to know My ways,
As a nation that did righteousness,
And did not forsake the ordinance
of their God.
They ask of Me the ordinances of
justice;
They take delight in approaching
God.
3 'Why[b] have we fasted,' *they say,*
'and You have not seen?
Why have we [c]afflicted our souls,
and You take no notice?'

"In fact, in the day of your fast you
find pleasure,
And [2]exploit all your laborers.
4 [d]Indeed you fast for strife and
debate,
And to strike with the fist of
wickedness.
You will not fast as *you do* this day,
To make your voice heard on high.
5 Is [e]it a fast that I have chosen,
[f]A day for a man to afflict his soul?
Is it to bow down his head like a
bulrush,
And [g]to spread out sackcloth and
ashes?
Would you call this a fast,
And an acceptable day to the
LORD?

6 "*Is* this not the fast that I have
chosen:
To [h]loose the bonds of wickedness,
[i]To undo the [3]heavy burdens,
[j]To let the oppressed go free,
And that you break every yoke?
7 *Is it* not [k]to share your bread with
the hungry,
And that you bring to your house
the poor who are [4]cast out;
[l]When you see the naked, that you
cover him,
And not hide yourself from [m]your
own flesh?
8 [n]Then your light shall break forth
like the morning,
Your healing shall spring forth
speedily,
And your righteousness shall go
before you;
[o]The glory of the LORD shall be your
rear guard.
9 Then you shall call, and the LORD
will answer;
You shall cry, and He will say,
'Here I *am.*'

"If you take away the yoke from
your midst,
The [5]pointing of the finger, and
[p]speaking wickedness,
10 *If* you extend your soul to the
hungry
And satisfy the afflicted soul,
Then your light shall dawn in the
darkness,

19 [c]Is. 6:7; 51:16; 59:21; Heb. 13:15 [d]Acts 2:39; Eph. 2:17
20 [e]Job 15:20; Prov. 4:16; Jude 13
21 [f]Is. 48:22

CHAPTER 58

1 [a]Mic. 3:8 [1]*do not hold back*
3 [b]Mal. 3:13-18; Luke 18:12 [c]Lev. 16:29; 23:27 [2]Lit. *drive hard*
4 [d]1 Kin. 21:9
5 [e]Zech. 7:5 [f]Lev. 16:29 [g]Esth. 4:3; Job 2:8; Dan. 9:3
6 [h]Luke 4:18, 19 [i]Neh. 5:10-12 [j]Jer. 34:9 [3]Lit. *bonds of the yoke*
7 [k]Ezek. 18:7; Matt. 25:35 [l]Job 31:19-22; James 2:14-17 [m]Gen. 29:14; Neh. 5:5 [4]*wandering*
8 [n]Job 11:17 [o]Ex. 14:19; Is. 52:12
9 [p]Ps. 12:2; Is. 59:13 [5]Lit. *sending out of*

57:19 fruit of the lips. According to Heb. 13:15, this phrase refers to praising and thanking God. Cf. Hos. 14:2. In this context, it is the voice crying "peace, peace" in a call to people far and near to come to the Lord and receive spiritual healing.

57:20,21 like the troubled sea. In contrast to those in v. 19, the wicked enjoy anything but peace (Jude 13). Cf. 48:22.

58:1–66:24 This section describes the future glory for God's people Israel.

58:1-5 A description of religious formalism that manifests itself in improper fasting.

58:1 Cry aloud. The prophet was to tell the people of Israel in plain language those areas of their behavior with which the Lord was displeased.

58:2 take delight in approaching God. Israel was merely "going through the motions." Their appearance of righteousness was mere pretense (1:11).

58:3-7 Why. The people complained when God did not recognize their religious actions, but God responded that their fastings had been only half-hearted. Hypocritical fasting resulted in contention, quarreling, and pretense, excluding the possibility of genuine prayer to God. Fasting consisted of more than just an outward ritual and a mock repentance, it involved penitence over sin and consequent humility, disconnecting from sin and oppression of others, feeding the hungry, and acting humanely toward those in need.

58:8 your righteousness...rear guard. When Israel learned the proper way to fast, she would enjoy the blessings of salvation and the Messiah's kingdom (52:12).

58:9 Here I *am*. See 65:1. In contrast with the complaint of v. 3, a time will come when the Lord will be completely responsive to the prayers of His people (65:24). This will be done when they are converted and giving evidence of the transformation in the kind of works that reflect a truly repentant heart (vv. 9,10). At the time of Christ's return, Israel will demonstrate true repentance and the fullness of blessing will be poured out (vv. 10b,11).

And your [6]darkness shall *be* as the
noonday.
11 The LORD will guide you
continually,
And satisfy your soul in drought,
And strengthen your bones;
You shall be like a watered garden,
And like a spring of water, whose
waters do not fail.
12 Those from among you
[q]Shall build the old waste places;
You shall raise up the foundations
of many generations;
And you shall be called the
Repairer of the Breach,
The Restorer of [7]Streets to Dwell In.

13 "If [r]you turn away your foot from
the Sabbath,
From doing your pleasure on My
holy day,
And call the Sabbath a delight,
The holy *day* of the LORD
honorable,
And shall honor Him, not doing
your own ways,
Nor finding your own pleasure,
Nor speaking *your own* words,
14 [s]Then you shall delight yourself in
the LORD;
And I will cause you to [t]ride on
the high hills of the earth,
And feed you with the heritage of
Jacob your father.
[u]The mouth of the LORD has
spoken."

Separated from God

59 Behold, the LORD's hand is not
[a]shortened,
That it cannot save;
Nor His ear heavy,
That it cannot hear.
2 But your iniquities have separated
you from your God;
And your sins have hidden *His*
face from you,
So that He will [b]not hear.
3 For [c]your hands are defiled with
[1]blood,
And your fingers with iniquity;
Your lips have spoken lies,
Your tongue has muttered
perversity.
4 No one calls for justice,
Nor does *any* plead for truth.
They trust in [d]empty words and
speak lies;
[e]They conceive [2]evil and bring forth
iniquity.
5 They hatch vipers' eggs and weave
the spider's web;
He who eats of their eggs dies,
And *from* that which is crushed a
viper breaks out.
6 [f]Their webs will not become
garments,
Nor will they cover themselves
with their works;
Their works *are* works of iniquity,
And the act of violence *is* in their
hands.
7 [g]Their feet run to evil,
And they make haste to shed
[h]innocent blood;
[i]Their thoughts *are* thoughts of
iniquity;
Wasting and [j]destruction *are* in
their paths.
8 The way of [k]peace they have not
known,
And *there is* no justice in their
ways;
[l]They have made themselves
crooked paths;
Whoever takes that way shall not
know peace.

Sin Confessed

9 Therefore justice is far from us,
Nor does righteousness overtake
us;

10 [6] Or *gloom*
12 [q] Is. 61:4 [7] Lit. *Paths*
13 [r] Ex. 31:16, 17; 35:2, 3; Is. 56:2, 4, 6; Jer. 17:21-27
14 [s] Job 22:26; Is. 61:10 [t] Deut. 32:13; 33:29; Is. 33:16; Hab. 3:19 [u] Is. 1:20; 40:5; Mic. 4:4

CHAPTER 59

1 [a] Num. 11:23; Is. 50:2; Jer. 32:17
2 [b] Is. 1:15
3 [c] Is. 1:15, 21; Jer. 2:30, 34; Ezek. 7:23; Hos. 4:2 [1] *bloodshed*
4 [d] Is. 30:12; Jer. 7:4 [e] Job 15:35; Ps. 7:14; Is. 33:11 [2] *trouble*
6 [f] Job 8:14
7 [g] Prov. 1:16; Rom. 3:15 [h] Prov. 6:17 [i] Is. 55:7 [j] Rom. 3:16, 17
8 [k] Is. 57:20, 21 [l] Ps. 125:5; Prov. 2:15

58:12 build the old waste places. In view here is the final restoration of the millennial Jerusalem, of which Nehemiah's rebuilding of the walls (Neh. 2:17) was only a foretaste (61:4; Amos 9:11).

58:13 turn away your foot from the Sabbath. The Sabbath was holy ground on which no one should walk. Keeping the Sabbath was symbolic of obedience to all the law of Moses (56:2). For the setting aside of Sabbath law in the NT, *see notes on Rom. 14:5,6 and Col. 2:16,17*.

58:14 delight yourself in the LORD. Repentant ones walking in fellowship with the Lord experience satisfaction of soul (Ps. 37:4). Their satisfaction will not come from material goods (contra. 55:2).

59:1 LORD's hand...His ear. The Lord's strength is more than adequate to bring deliverance to captive Israel (50:2). His ear is attuned to the call of His repentant people (58:9; 65:24).

59:2 iniquities...sins. Abraham's physical lineage had not yet experienced the Lord's deliverance because of the barrier created by their wrong-doing. This is a universal truth applying to all men—sin separates people from God (cf. Rom 3:23).

59:5 vipers' eggs...spider's web. It is sad when persons do evil, but even sadder when they delight in poisoning or ensnaring others with their evil habits (Rom. 1:32). Israel had reached this latter state.

59:6 webs...works. Just as spiders' webs are too flimsy to serve as clothing, so were Israel's evil works. Spiritually, they did not suffice.

59:7,8 Their feet...shall not know peace. From Isaiah's pen, the words focused on the national depravity of Israel that stood in the way of God's deliverance. Paul showed that what was true of sinful Israel is indicative of the depravity of all mankind, (Rom. 3:15-17).

[m]We look for light, but there is darkness!
For brightness, *but* we walk in blackness!
10 [n]We grope for the wall like the blind,
And we grope as if *we had* no eyes;
We stumble at noonday as at twilight;
We are as dead *men* in desolate places.
11 We all growl like bears,
And [o]moan sadly like doves;
We look for justice, but *there is* none;
For salvation, *but* it is far from us.
12 For our [p]transgressions are multiplied before You,
And our sins testify against us;
For our transgressions *are* with us,
And *as for* our iniquities, we know them:
13 In transgressing and lying against the LORD,
And departing from our God,
Speaking oppression and revolt,
Conceiving and uttering [q]from the heart words of falsehood.
14 Justice is turned back,
And righteousness stands afar off;
For truth is fallen in the street,
And equity cannot enter.
15 So truth fails,
And he *who* departs from evil makes himself a [r]prey.

The Redeemer of Zion

Then the LORD saw *it*, and [3]it displeased Him
That *there was* no justice.
16 [s]He saw that *there was* no man,
And [t]wondered that *there was* no intercessor;
[u]Therefore His own arm brought salvation for Him;
And His own righteousness, it sustained Him.
17 [v]For He put on righteousness as a breastplate,
And a helmet of salvation on His head;
He put on the garments of vengeance for clothing,
And was clad with zeal as a cloak.
18 [w]According to *their* deeds, accordingly He will repay,
Fury to His adversaries,
Recompense to His enemies;
The coastlands He will fully repay.
19 [x]So shall they fear
The name of the LORD from the west,
And His glory from the rising of the sun;
When the enemy comes in [y]like a flood,
The Spirit of the LORD will lift up a standard against him.

20 "The[z] Redeemer will come to Zion,
And to those who turn from transgression in Jacob,"
Says the LORD.

21 "As[a] for Me," says the LORD, "this *is*
My covenant with them: My Spirit who *is*
upon you, and My words which I have put
in your mouth, shall not depart from your
mouth, nor from the mouth of your descendants, nor from the mouth of your descendants' descendants," says the LORD,
"from this time and forevermore."

9 [m]Jer. 8:15
10 [n]Deut. 28:29; Job 5:14; Amos 8:9
11 [o]Is. 38:14; Ezek. 7:16
12 [p]Is. 24:5; 58:1
13 [q]Matt. 12:34
15 [r]Is. 5:23; 10:2; 29:21; 32:7 [3]Lit. *it was evil in His eyes*
16 [s]Is. 41:28; 63:5; 64:7; Ezek. 22:30 [t]Mark 6:6 [u]Ps. 98:1; Is. 63:5
17 [v]Eph. 6:14, 17; 1 Thess. 5:8
18 [w]Is. 63:6; Rom. 2:6
19 [x]Ps. 113:3; Mal. 1:11 [y]Rev. 12:15
20 [z]Rom. 11:26
21 [a][Heb. 8:10; 10:16]

59:10,11 grope...stumble. Here is a picture of men seeking unsuccessfully to escape their depraved condition through their own strength. They wind up growling and lamenting their inability to gain salvation (Deut. 28:29).

59:12-14 transgressions...sins. The prophet supplies the answer to the nation's frustrations: their sins and transgressions remain as an obstacle to God's deliverance. Though their external rituals may be proper, the hindrance of impure motives remains between God and His people (Matt. 12:34; Mark 7:21,22). The presence of iniquity eliminates righteousness.

59:15 makes himself a prey. In an environment where evil prevailed, anyone who departed from it became a victim of his environment because he did not fit in.

59:15,16 the LORD saw...no intercessor. The Lord was aware of Israel's tragic condition and of the absence of anyone to intervene on His behalf. The Lord took it on Himself to change Israel's condition through the intervention of His Suffering Servant (53:12).

59:17 righteousness as a breastplate...helmet of salvation. Figuratively speaking, the Lord armed Himself for the deliverance of His people and for taking vengeance on enemies who would seek His destruction. Paul drew on this terminology in describing a believer's spiritual preparation for warding off the attacks of Satan (Eph. 6:14,17; 1 Thess. 5:8).

59:17,18 garments of vengeance...Recompense to His enemies. In the process of delivering the faithful remnant of Israel, the Lord executes decisive judgment against all rebellious nations ("coastlands") as well as the wicked Israelites (63:1-6).

59:19 shall they fear. All surviving peoples throughout the world are to have added reason to worship the Lord, seeing how He defeated all enemies by the power of His Spirit in bringing salvation to His people Israel. All over the earth, submission to Him is to be the only path to survival in the coming kingdom.

59:20,21 The Redeemer will come. The Messiah, the Suffering Servant, will redeem Zion and all faithful Israelites. This unalterable promise to the nation was the basis for Paul's reassurance of the future salvation of Israel (Rom. 11:26,27).

59:21 My covenant...forevermore. Because God's New Covenant with Israel is "everlasting" (55:3; cf. Jer. 31:31-34), God's Spirit and His words are to remain objects of their attention continually.

The Gentiles Bless Zion

60 Arise, [a]shine;
For your light has come!
And [b]the glory of the LORD is risen upon you.
2 For behold, the darkness shall cover the earth,
And deep darkness the people;
But the LORD will arise over you,
And His glory will be seen upon you.
3 The [c]Gentiles shall come to your light,
And kings to the brightness of your rising.

4 "Lift[d] up your eyes all around, and see:
They all gather together, [e]they come to you;
Your sons shall come from afar,
And your daughters shall be nursed at *your* side.
5 Then you shall see and become radiant,
And your heart shall swell with joy;
Because [f]the abundance of the sea shall be turned to you,
The wealth of the Gentiles shall come to you.
6 The multitude of camels shall cover your *land,*
The dromedaries of Midian and [g]Ephah;
All those from [h]Sheba shall come;
They shall bring [i]gold and incense,
And they shall proclaim the praises of the LORD.
7 All the flocks of [j]Kedar shall be gathered together to you,
The rams of Nebaioth shall minister to you;
They shall ascend with [k]acceptance on My altar,
And [l]I will glorify the house of My glory.

8 "Who *are* these *who* fly like a cloud,
And like doves to their roosts?
9 [m]Surely the coastlands shall wait for Me;
And the ships of Tarshish *will come* first,
[n]To bring your sons from afar,
[o]Their silver and their gold with them,
To the name of the LORD your God,
And to the Holy One of Israel,
[p]Because He has glorified you.

10 "The[q] sons of foreigners shall build up your walls,
[r]And their kings shall minister to you;
For [s]in My wrath I struck you,
[t]But in My favor I have had mercy on you.
11 Therefore your gates [u]shall be open continually;
They shall not be shut day or night,
That *men* may bring to you the wealth of the Gentiles,
And their kings in procession.
12 [v]For the nation and kingdom which will not serve you shall perish,

CHAPTER 60

1 [a]Eph. 5:14 [b]Mal. 4:2
3 [c]Is. 49:6, 23; Rev. 21:24
4 [d]Is. 49:18 [e]Is. 49:20-22
5 [f][Rom. 11:25-27]
6 [g]Gen. 25:4 [h]Gen. 25:3; Ps. 72:10 [i]Is. 61:6; Matt. 2:11
7 [j]Gen. 25:13 [k]Is. 56:7 [l]Is. 60:13; Hag. 2:7, 9
9 [m]Ps. 72:10 [n][Gal. 4:26] [o]Jer. 3:17 [p]Is. 55:5
10 [q]Is. 14:1, 2; 61:5; Zech. 6:15 [r]Is. 49:23; Rev. 21:24 [s]Is. 57:17 [t]Is. 54:7, 8
11 [u]Is. 26:2; 60:18; 62:10; Rev. 21:25, 26
12 [v]Is. 14:2; Zech. 14:17; Matt. 21:44

60:1,2 glory of the LORD...darkness...deep darkness...His glory. Addressing Zion (59:20; 60:14), Isaiah told the city and thus the nation Israel that her light has come, putting her in contrast with the rest of the darkened world. This expressed the glory of Jerusalem during the millennial kingdom.

60:3 Gentiles shall come. Jerusalem's light will attract other nations seeking relief from their darkness (2:3). Only believing Jews and Gentiles will enter the earthly kingdom after the Day of the Lord, but as the 1,000 years goes along children will be born and nations will become populated by those who reject Jesus Christ. The glory of the King in Jerusalem, and His mighty power will draw those Gentiles to His light.

60:4 gather...sons...daughters. Another promise of the regathering of Israel's faithful remnant (49:18,22).

60:5 joy...wealth. Two more benefits of Israel's future kingdom will be rejoicing and an abundance of material possessions as symbolized in vv. 6,7 (23:18; 24:14; 61:6).

60:6 Midian...Ephah...Sheba. The descendants of Midian, Abraham's son through Keturah (Gen. 25:1,2), inhabited the desert areas E of the Jordan River. Ephah was one of the sons of Midian (Gen. 25:4) whose ancestors settled on the E coast of the Elanitic Gulf. Sheba was a district in Arabia noted for its wealth (1 Kin. 10:1,2).

60:7 Kedar...Nebaioth. The descendants of Kedar, a son of Ishmael (Gen. 25:13), lived in the desert between Syria and Mesopotamia. The Nabateans, inhabitants of the Arabian city Petra, were probably the descendants of Nebaioth, the oldest son of Ishmael (Gen. 25:13). **acceptance on My altar.** Animal sacrifices brought by other nations during the millennial kingdom will glorify the house of God's glory even more (v. 13). *See notes on Ezek. 40–48* for the description of the operation of sacrifices in the millennial temple.

60:8 fly like a cloud...doves. Figurative language to describe the rapid influx of Gentiles into Jerusalem.

60:9 coastlands...ships of Tarshish...your sons...silver ...gold. Because of the Lord's favor toward Zion, the city will attract worldwide attention (23:1; 41:1). Trading vessels will return Israel's faithful remnant as they bring rich treasures to Jerusalem.

60:10 build up your walls. The rebuilding of Jerusalem's walls, helped by Persian kings, was merely a foretaste of the final rebuilding of the city assisted by Gentiles when Christ returns to earth. **in My wrath...in My favor.** God's past dealings with Israel have been largely in wrath, but His future merciful work will demonstrate His favor.

60:11 gates...open continually. Unrestricted access to Jerusalem will prevail in the future kingdom (26:2; 62:10; Rev. 21:25,26).

60:12 nation...perish. Survival in the future kingdom will be impossible for those nations who do not come to terms with Israel (11:13,14; 14:2; 49:23). The Lord will rule the nations with a rod of iron (cf. Ps. 2:7-12).

And *those* nations shall be utterly
ruined.

13 "The [w]glory of Lebanon shall come
to you,
The cypress, the pine, and the box
tree together,
To beautify the place of My
sanctuary;
And I will make [x]the place of My
feet glorious.
14 Also the sons of those who
afflicted you
Shall come [y]bowing to you,
And all those who despised you
shall [z]fall prostrate at the
soles of your feet;
And they shall call you The City of
the LORD,
[a]Zion of the Holy One of Israel.

15 "Whereas you have been forsaken
and hated,
So that no one went through *you,*
I will make you an eternal
excellence,
A joy of many generations.
16 You shall drink the milk of the
Gentiles,
[b]And milk the breast of kings;
You shall know that [c]I, the LORD,
am your Savior
And your Redeemer, the Mighty
One of Jacob.

17 "Instead of bronze I will bring gold,
Instead of iron I will bring silver,
Instead of wood, bronze,
And instead of stones, iron.
I will also make your officers
peace,

13 [w] Is. 35:2 [x] 1 Chr. 28:2; Ps. 132:7
14 [y] Is. 45:14 [z] Is. 49:23; Rev. 3:9 [a] [Heb. 12:22; Rev. 14:1]
16 [b] Is. 49:23 [c] Is. 43:3

And your magistrates
righteousness.
18 Violence shall no longer be heard
in your land,
Neither [1]wasting nor destruction
within your borders;
But you shall call [d]your walls
Salvation,
And your gates Praise.

God the Glory of His People

19 "The [e]sun shall no longer be your
light by day,
Nor for brightness shall the moon
give light to you;
But the LORD will be to you an
everlasting light,
And [f]your God your glory.
20 [g]Your sun shall no longer go down,
Nor shall your moon withdraw
itself;
For the LORD will be your
everlasting light,
And the days of your mourning
shall be ended.
21 [h]Also your people *shall* all *be*
righteous;
[i]They shall inherit the land forever,
[j]The branch of My planting,
[k]The work of My hands,
That I may be glorified.
22 [l]A little one shall become a
thousand,
And a small one a strong nation.
I, the LORD, will hasten it in its
time."

The Good News of Salvation

61 "The [a]Spirit of the Lord GOD *is*
upon Me,
Because the LORD [b]has anointed
Me

18 [d] Is. 26:1 [1] *devastation*
19 [e] Rev. 21:23; 22:5 [f] Is. 41:16; 45:25; Zech. 2:5
20 [g] Amos 8:9
21 [h] Is. 52:1; Rev. 21:27 [i] Ps. 37:11; Matt. 5:5 [j] Is. 61:3; [Matt. 15:13; John 15:2] [k] Is. 29:23; [Eph. 2:10]
22 [l] Matt. 13:31, 32

CHAPTER 61

1 [a] Is. 11:2; Matt. 3:17; Luke 4:18, 19; John 1:32; 3:34 [b] Ps. 45:7; Matt. 11:5; Luke 7:22

60:13 glory of Lebanon. Timber was Lebanon's claim to fame. As in Solomon's temple (1 Kin. 5:10,18), but even more so, the timber taken from Lebanon's forests will enrich the Lord's temple in Jerusalem.

60:14 The City of the LORD. Nations which formerly were oppressors of Israel will acknowledge Zion's supremacy as the city that belongs to the Lord.

60:15 forsaken and hated…eternal excellence. Jerusalem will switch roles from having been despised to being exalted forever.

60:16 milk…milk. As a mother feeds her infant, so Gentiles and kings will provide wealth and power to Zion. The city will recognize the Lord as her Savior and Redeemer, "the Mighty One of Jacob," as will "all flesh" (49:26).

60:17 gold…silver…peace…righteousness. Jerusalem in the future kingdom will be a place of beauty and peace where right will prevail.

60:18 Salvation…Praise. The walls and gates of the city that will take on those names refer to the divine protection the Lord provides from any form of violence or destruction.

60:19 sun shall no longer…everlasting light. Isaiah, looking beyond the millennial kingdom, sees a view of the new Jerusalem following the Millennium (Rev. 21:23; 22:5). His prophetic perspective did not allow him to distinguish the eternal phase of the future kingdom from the temporal one, just as the OT prophets could not distinguish between the first and second advent of Christ (cf. 1 Pet. 1:10,11).

60:20 mourning…ended. In the eternal kingdom of the new creation, subjects will shed no more tears (Rev. 21:4).

60:21 inherit the land forever. Israel will inherit the land promised to Abraham (Gen. 12:1,7; 13:15; 15:18). During the millennial kingdom, that will be the land of Israel as we know it today. In the eternal kingdom, it will be the New Jerusalem, capital of the new creation. **I may be glorified.** The ultimate mission of Israel is to glorify the Lord (49:3; 61:3).

60:22 little one…strong nation. Israel's great increase in numbers and power resulting from the Lord's working will bring them into never before experienced world prominence.

61:1,2a The Spirit…acceptable year of the LORD. The Servant of the Lord (42:1) will be the ultimate Preacher and the Redeemer of

To preach good tidings to the poor;
He has sent Me [c]to [1]heal the brokenhearted,
To proclaim [d]liberty to the captives,
And the opening of the prison to *those who are* bound;
2 [e]To proclaim the acceptable year of the LORD,
And [f]the day of vengeance of our God;
[g]To comfort all who mourn,
3 To [2]console those who mourn in Zion,
[h]To give them beauty for ashes,
The oil of joy for mourning,
The garment of praise for the spirit of heaviness;
That they may be called trees of righteousness,
[i]The planting of the LORD, [j]that He may be glorified."

4 And they shall [k]rebuild the old ruins,
They shall raise up the former desolations,
And they shall repair the ruined cities,
The desolations of many generations.
5 [l]Strangers shall stand and feed your flocks,
And the sons of the foreigner
Shall be your plowmen and your vinedressers.
6 [m]But you shall be named the priests of the LORD,
They shall call you the servants of our God.
[n]You shall eat the riches of the Gentiles,
And in their glory you shall boast.
7 [o]Instead of your shame *you shall have* double *honor*,
And *instead of* confusion they shall rejoice in their portion.
Therefore in their land they shall possess double;
Everlasting joy shall be theirs.

8 "For [p]I, the LORD, love justice;
[q]I hate robbery [3]for burnt offering;
I will direct their work in truth,
[r]And will make with them an everlasting covenant.
9 Their descendants shall be known among the Gentiles,
And their offspring among the people.
All who see them shall acknowledge them,
[s]That they *are* the posterity *whom* the LORD has blessed."

10 [t]I will greatly rejoice in the LORD,
My soul shall be joyful in my God;
For [u]He has clothed me with the garments of salvation,
He has covered me with the robe of righteousness,
[v]As a bridegroom decks *himself* with ornaments,
And as a bride adorns *herself* with her jewels.
11 For as the earth brings forth its bud,
As the garden causes the things that are sown in it to spring forth,
So the Lord GOD will cause
[w]righteousness and [x]praise to spring forth before all the nations.

1 [c] Ps. 147:3 [d] Is. 42:7; [Acts 10:43] [1] Lit. *bind up*
2 [e] Lev. 25:9 [f] Is. 34:8; Mal. 4:1, 3; [2 Thess. 1:7] [g] Is. 57:18; Jer. 31:13; Matt. 5:4
3 [h] Ps. 30:11 [i] Is. 60:21; [Jer. 17:7, 8] [j] [John 15:8] [2] Lit. *appoint*
4 [k] Is. 49:8; 58:12; Ezek. 36:33; Amos 9:14
5 [l] [Eph. 2:12]
6 [m] Ex. 19:6 [n] Is. 60:5, 11
7 [o] Is. 40:2; Zech. 9:12
8 [p] Ps. 11:7 [q] Is. 1:11, 13 [r] Gen. 17:7; Ps. 105:10; Is. 55:3; Jer. 32:40 [3] Or *in*
9 [s] Is. 65:23
10 [t] Hab. 3:18 [u] Ps. 132:9, 16 [v] Is. 49:18; Rev. 21:2
11 [w] Ps. 72:3; 85:11 [x] Is. 60:18; 62:7

Israel who rescues them. Jesus speaks of the initial fulfillment of this promise, referring it to His ministry of providing salvation's comfort to the spiritually oppressed (Luke 4:18,19). He says specifically, "Today this Scripture is fulfilled in your hearing" (Luke 4:21). The Jews that were saved during Christ's ministry, and those being saved during this church age, still do not fulfill the promise of the salvation of the nation to come in the end time (cf. Zech. 12:10–13:1; Rom. 11:25-27).

61:1 Spirit…Lord God…Me. The 3 persons of the Holy Trinity function together in this verse (6:8; cf. Matt. 3:16,17). **liberty to the captives.** The "captives" are Israelites remaining in the dispersion following the Babylonian captivity (42:7).

61:2 acceptable year. The same as "the day of salvation" (49:8) and "the year of My redeemed" (63:4). This is where Jesus stopped reading in the synagogue (Luke 4:19), indicating that the subsequent writing in the rest of the chapter (vv. 3-11) awaited the second coming of Christ. **day of vengeance.** As part of His deliverance of Israel, the Lord will pour out wrath on all who oppose Him (59:17-18). Cf. Rev. 6–19.

61:3 console…glorified. The purpose of the Lord's consolation of the mourners after centuries of suffering (60:20) will be to glorify Himself (60:21).

61:4 rebuild. The rebuilding of Israel's cities is part of God's future plan for the nation (49:8; 58:12; 60:10).

61:6 priests of the LORD. In fulfillment of Ex. 19:6, Israel will be a kingdom of priests when Christ establishes His kingdom. In the meantime, Peter applied the same terminology to the church (1 Pet. 2:9).

61:7 double *honor*. Israel will receive double portions of blessing to replace the double punishment of her exile (40:2).

61:8 everlasting covenant. This refers to the New Covenant. *See note on 55:3.*

61:10 clothed me…covered me. Here is the OT picture of imputed righteousness, the essential heart of the New Covenant. When a penitent sinner recognizes he can't achieve his own righteousness by works (*see notes on Rom. 3:19-22; 2 Cor. 5:21; Phil. 3:8,9*), and repents and calls on the mercy of God, the Lord covers him with His own divine righteousness by grace through his faith.

Assurance of Zion's Salvation

62 For Zion's sake I will not [1]hold My peace,
And for Jerusalem's sake I will not rest,
Until her righteousness goes forth as brightness,
And her salvation as a lamp *that* burns.
2 [a]The Gentiles shall see your righteousness,
And all [b]kings your glory.
[c]You shall be called by a new name,
Which the mouth of the LORD will name.
3 You shall also be [d]a crown of glory
In the hand of the LORD,
And a royal diadem
In the hand of your God.
4 [e]You shall no longer be termed [f]Forsaken,[2]
Nor shall your land any more be termed [g]Desolate;[3]
But you shall be called [4]Hephzibah, and your land [5]Beulah;
For the LORD delights in you,
And your land shall be married.
5 For *as* a young man marries a virgin,
So shall your sons marry you;
And *as* the bridegroom rejoices over the bride,
[h]*So* shall your God rejoice over you.
6 [i]I have set watchmen on your walls, O Jerusalem;
They shall [6]never hold their peace day or night.
You who [7]make mention of the LORD, do not keep silent,
7 And give Him no rest till He establishes
And till He makes Jerusalem [j]a praise in the earth.
8 The LORD has sworn by His right hand
And by the arm of His strength:
"Surely I will no longer [k]give your grain
As food for your enemies;
And the sons of the foreigner shall not drink your new wine,
For which you have labored.
9 But those who have gathered it shall eat it,
And praise the LORD;
Those who have brought it together shall drink it [l]in My holy courts."
10 Go through,
Go through the gates!
[m]Prepare the way for the people;
Build up,
Build up the highway!
Take out the stones,
[n]Lift up a banner for the peoples!
11 Indeed the LORD has proclaimed
To the end of the world:
[o]"Say to the daughter of Zion,
'Surely your salvation is coming;
Behold, His [p]reward *is* with Him,
And His [8]work before Him.' "
12 And they shall call them The Holy People,
The Redeemed of the LORD;
And you shall be called Sought Out,
A City Not Forsaken.

The LORD in Judgment and Salvation

63 Who *is* this who comes from Edom,
With dyed garments from Bozrah,
This *One who is* [1]glorious in His apparel,

CHAPTER 62

1 [1] *keep silent* **2** [a] Is. 60:3 [b] Ps. 102:15, 16; 138:4, 5; 148:11, 13 [c] Is. 62:4, 12; 65:15 **3** [d] Is. 28:5; Zech. 9:16; 1 Thess. 2:19 **4** [e] Hos. 1:10; 1 Pet. 2:10 [f] Is. 49:14; 54:6, 7 [g] Is. 54:1 [2] Heb. *Azubah* [3] Heb. *Shemamah* [4] Lit. *My Delight Is in Her* [5] Lit. *Married* **5** [h] Is. 65:19 **6** [i] Is. 52:8; Jer. 6:17; Ezek. 3:17; 33:7 [6] *not be silent* [7] *remember*

7 [j] Is. 60:18; 61:11; Jer. 33:9; Zeph. 3:19, 20 **8** [k] Lev. 26:16; Deut. 28:31, 33; Judg. 6:3-6; Is. 1:7; Jer. 5:17 **9** [l] Deut. 12:12; 14:23, 26 **10** [m] Is. 40:3; 57:14 [n] Is. 11:12 **11** [o] Zech. 9:9; Matt. 21:5; John 12:15 [p] Is. 40:10; [Rev. 22:12] [8] *recompense*

CHAPTER 63

1 [1] *Or adorned*

62:1 not hold My peace…not rest. The Lord expresses His determination to make Jerusalem a lighthouse for the world (58:8; 60:1-3).

62:2 new name. Jerusalem's new name will reflect Israel's new favored status (vv. 4,12; 65:15).

62:4 Hephzibah…Beulah. The terms mean "My delight is in her" and "Married," reflecting a full restored relationship with the Lord.

62:5 sons marry you. "Marry" in the sense of occupying and possessing the city.

62:6,7 never hold their peace…do not keep silent…give Him no rest. The prophets of Israel issued constant warnings about lurking enemies and prayed for Jerusalem to be "a praise" (60:18; 61:11). There will be more prophets in the kingdom who continually proclaim the honor of the Lord.

62:8,9 The LORD has sworn. The end of foreign domination over Jerusalem is as certain as the oath of God.

62:9 My holy courts. This refers to the millennial temple (cf. Ezek. 40–46).

62:10 Prepare. This and the accompanying commands prepare the people for the exaltation of Zion and the manifestation of her salvation (11:12; 40:3; 57:14).

62:11 Say to the daughter…Behold. Matthew may also have alluded to these words when he was quoting from Zech. 9:9 as it related to Jesus' triumphal entry into Jerusalem (see Matt. 21:5). **His reward…His work.** See 40:9,10.

62:12 A City Not Forsaken. See v. 4 and cf. Zion's complaint in 49:14.

63:1 Edom…Bozrah. Edom represents a God-hating world (34:5). Bozrah was a capital city in Edom at one time (34:6). Messiah, coming as the avenger approaching Jerusalem to reign after having avenged His people on His and their enemies, is presented in imagery taken from the destruction of Edom, the representative in this picture of the last and most bitter foes of God and His people. He alone is "mighty to save."

Traveling in the greatness of His strength?—
"I who speak in righteousness, mighty to save."

2 Why [a]*is* Your apparel red,
And Your garments like one who treads in the winepress?

3 "I have [b]trodden the winepress alone,
And from the peoples no one *was* with Me.
For I have trodden them in My anger,
And trampled them in My fury;
Their blood is sprinkled upon My garments,
And I have stained all My robes.

4 For the [c]day of vengeance *is* in My heart,
And the year of My redeemed has come.

5 [d]I looked, but [e]*there was* no one to help,
And I wondered
That *there was* no one to uphold;
Therefore My own [f]arm brought salvation for Me;
And My own fury, it sustained Me.

6 I have trodden down the peoples in My anger,
Made them drunk in My fury,
And brought down their strength to the earth."

God's Mercy Remembered

7 I will mention the lovingkindnesses of the LORD
And the praises of the LORD,
According to all that the LORD has bestowed on us,
And the great goodness toward the house of Israel,
Which He has bestowed on them according to His mercies,
According to the multitude of His lovingkindnesses.

8 For He said, "Surely they *are* My people,
Children *who* will not lie."
So He became their Savior.

9 [g]In all their affliction He was [2]afflicted,
[h]And the Angel of His Presence saved them;
[i]In His love and in His pity He redeemed them;
And [j]He bore them and carried them
All the days of old.

10 But they [k]rebelled and [l]grieved His Holy Spirit;
[m]So He turned Himself against them as an enemy,
And He fought against them.

11 Then he [n]remembered the days of old,
Moses *and* his people, *saying:*
"Where *is* He who [o]brought them up out of the sea

2 [a][Rev. 19:13, 15] 3 [b]Lam. 1:15; Rev. 14:19, 20; 19:15 4 [c]Is. 34:8; 35:4; 61:2; Jer. 51:6 5 [d]Is. 41:28; 59:16 [e][John 16:32] [f]Ps. 98:1; Is. 59:16

9 [g]Judg. 10:16 [h]Ex. 14:19 [i]Deut. 7:7 [j]Ex. 19:4 [2]Kt., LXX, Syr. *not afflicted* 10 [k]Ex. 15:24 [l]Num. 14:11; Ps. 78:40; Acts 7:51; 1 Cor. 10:1-11 [m]Ex. 23:21; Ps. 106:40 11 [n]Ps. 106:44, 45 [o]Ex. 14:30

63:3 anger...fury...blood. The Savior explains the red coloring of His clothing (v. 2) as resulting from His judgmental activity against Israel's enemies (61:2). The splattered grape juice staining His clothing is, in reality, "blood" from those destroyed in judgment. John alludes to vv. 1-3 in describing the second coming of Christ, the Warrior-King. *See notes on Rev. 19:13,15.*

63:4 day of vengeance...year of My redeemed. The Messiah's future reckoning with the wicked will coincide with His redemption of Israel (61:2).

63:5 no one to help...My own arm. The future salvation of Israel will be a single-handed accomplishment of the Lord (v. 3; 59:15,16).

63:6 Made them drunk. See 51:17,21-23. Revelation compares God's wrath to wine several times (e.g., Rev. 14:10,19; 16:19; 19:15). "Brought down their strength" is lit. saying "spilled their blood."

63:7–64:12 As one of Israel's watchmen, Isaiah, on behalf of the faithful remnant, prays this penitential confession and prayer for Israel's restoration (cf. 62:6,7).

63:7-14 The prayer reviews God's compassionate acts toward His people in spite of their unfaithfulness to Him.

63:7,8 lovingkindnesses...lovingkindnesses. All the plurals in this verse imply that language is inadequate to recite all the goodness and undeserved mercies God has showered on the nation time after time because of His everlasting covenant with them. By His elective choice, they became His people and He their Savior (43:1,3); this guarantees that they will not always be false ("lie"), but someday true and faithful to God because of His sovereign election of them. Cf. Eph. 1:3,4.

63:9 Angel of His Presence. The angel, who delivered the Israelites from Egypt, was none other than the Lord Himself (Ex. 14:19; 23:20-23; 33:12,14,15; Num. 20:16). He is sometimes identified as the Angel of the Lord. He was close enough to His people that He felt their afflictions as if they were His own. *See note on Ex. 3:2.*

63:10 rebelled and grieved His Holy Spirit. In spite of the Lord's loving choice and sympathy, Israel continually turned their backs on Him and spurned His lovingkindnesses toward them (Num. 20:10; Pss. 78:40; 106:33; Acts 7:51; cf. Eph. 4:30). Here is an illustration of the reality that the Holy Spirit is a Person, since only a person can be grieved.

63:11-13 he remembered...might not stumble. The Lord, in spite of their perversity, did not forget His covenant nor fully forsake them (Lev. 26:40-45; Ps. 106:45,46). In contrasting their present state of destitution with that of blessing experienced by Moses' generation, the people of Israel lamented the loss of God's mighty works on their behalf and pleaded with the Lord that He would not forsake them. **brought them up out of the sea...put His Holy Spirit within them...Dividing the water.** Typical mighty works of God were letting the people pass through the sea as on dry ground (Ex. 14:29,30) and the ministry of the Holy Spirit among them (Num. 11:17,25,29). "Within" does not refer to individual indwelling but rather would best be translated with a corporate sense of "among" or "in the midst." Another reference is made to the miracle of the Red Sea (Ex 14:21,22).

With the [3]shepherd of His flock?
[p]Where *is* He who put His Holy
Spirit within them,
12 Who led *them* by the right hand of
Moses,
[q]With His glorious arm,
[r]Dividing the water before them
To make for Himself an everlasting
name,
13 [s]Who led them through the deep,
As a horse in the wilderness,
That they might not stumble?"

14 As a beast goes down into the
valley,
And the Spirit of the LORD causes
him to rest,
So You lead Your people,
[t]To make Yourself a glorious name.

A Prayer of Penitence

15 [u]Look down from heaven,
And see [v]from Your habitation,
holy and glorious.
Where *are* Your zeal and Your
strength,
The yearning [w]of Your heart and
Your mercies toward me?
Are they restrained?
16 [x]Doubtless You *are* our Father,
Though Abraham [y]was ignorant of
us,
And Israel does not acknowledge
us.
You, O LORD, *are* our Father;
Our Redeemer from Everlasting *is*
Your name.
17 O LORD, why have You [z]made us
stray from Your ways,
And hardened our heart from Your
fear?
Return for Your servants' sake,
The tribes of Your inheritance.
18 [a]Your holy people have possessed *it*
but a little while;
[b]Our adversaries have trodden
down Your sanctuary.
19 We have become *like* those of old,
over whom You never ruled,
Those who were never called by
Your name.

64 Oh, that You would [1]rend the
heavens!
That You would come down!
That the mountains might shake at
Your [a]presence—
2 As fire burns brushwood,
As fire causes water to boil—
To make Your name known to Your
adversaries,
That the nations may tremble at
Your presence!
3 When [b]You did awesome things *for
which* we did not look,
You came down,
The mountains shook at Your
presence.
4 For since the beginning of the world
[c]*Men* have not heard nor perceived
by the ear,
Nor has the eye seen any God
besides You,
Who acts for the one who waits for
Him.
5 You meet him who rejoices and
does righteousness,
Who remembers You in Your ways.

11 [p]Num. 11:17, 25, 29; Hag. 2:5 [3]MT, Vg. *shepherds*
12 [q]Ex. 15:6 [r]Ex. 14:21, 22; Josh. 3:16; Is. 11:15; 51:10
13 [s]Ps. 106:9
14 [t]2 Sam. 7:23
15 [u]Deut. 26:15; Ps. 80:14 [v]Ps. 33:14 [w]Jer. 31:20; Hos. 11:8
16 [x]Deut. 32:6 [y]Job 14:21
17 [z]Is. 6:9, 10; John 12:40
18 [a]Deut. 7:6 [b]Ps. 74:3-7; Is. 64:11

CHAPTER 64

1 [a]Ex. 19:18; Ps. 18:9; 144:5; Mic. 1:3, 4; [Hab. 3:13] [1]*tear open*
3 [b]Ex. 34:10
4 [c]Ps. 31:19

63:14 make Yourself a glorious name. The Lord's purpose for Israel was and is to make them great so as to magnify His name in the world. Cf. v. 12.

63:15-19 After having extolled God's goodness (vv. 7-9) and rehearsed God's past faithfulness to Israel for the sake of His glory (vv. 11-13), the prophet offered a prayer of repentance by the nation in its desolate condition.

63:15 Where...Your mercies toward me? On behalf of the people, Isaiah asked if God had changed how He felt about Israel and prayed for new mercies such as He had exhibited toward the nation in the past.

63:16 Abraham...Israel. The nation's physical ancestors, Abraham and Jacob (Israel) played a crucial role in Jewish thinking. It had been the besetting temptation and sin of the Jews to rest on the mere privilege of descent from Abraham and Jacob (cf. Matt. 3:9; John 4:12; 8:39), but at last they renounce that to trust God alone as Father.

63:17 made us stray...hardened our heart. The sense is that God allowed them to stray and be burdened in their hearts. They were not denying their own guilt, but confessing that because of it, God gave them up to the consequences of their iniquitous choices. Cf. 6:9,10; Ps. 81:11,12; Hos. 4:17; Rom. 1:24-28.

63:18 trodden down Your sanctuary. The Babylonians, among others, had possessed the land given to Israel and desecrated God's sanctuary (Ps. 74:3-7).

63:19 never...never. Israel's complaint was that her desolate condition was comparable to that of nations who had no unique relationship with the Lord.

64:1-5 A plea for the Lord to demonstrate His power as He did in earlier days.

64:1,2 rend the heavens...shake at Your presence. Israel's response to her own complaint (63:19) was a plea that God would burst forth to execute vengeance suddenly on His people's foes (cf. Pss. 18:7-9; 144:5; Hab. 3:5,6), manifesting Himself in judgment again as He did at Mt. Sinai (Ex. 19:18; Judg. 5:5; Ps. 68:8; Heb. 12:18-20). As God's name is to receive glory through His redemption of Israel (63:14), it also is to have widespread recognition because of His judgment against Israel's enemies (Ps. 99:1).

64:3 awesome things. Another reference to God's acts at Sinai (Deut. 10:21).

64:4 ear...eye. God's judgmental manifestations are unique. No one has witnessed the likes of His awesome works on behalf of His own. Paul adapts words from this verse to speak of direct revelation of God imparted to His apostles and prophets and pertaining to mysteries hidden from mankind before the birth of the church (1 Cor. 2:9).

You are indeed angry, for we have
sinned—
[d]In these ways we continue;
And we need to be saved.
6 But we are all like an unclean *thing*,
And all [e]our righteousnesses *are*
like [2]filthy rags;
We all [f]fade as a leaf,
And our iniquities, like the wind,
Have taken us away.
7 And *there is* no one who calls on
Your name,
Who stirs himself up to take hold
of You;
For You have hidden Your face
from us,
And have [3]consumed us because
of our iniquities.

8 But now, O LORD,
You *are* our Father;
We *are* the clay, and You our
[g]potter;
And all we *are* the work of Your
hand.
9 Do not be furious, O LORD,
Nor remember iniquity forever;
Indeed, please look—we all *are*
Your people!
10 Your holy cities are a wilderness,
Zion is a wilderness,
Jerusalem a desolation.
11 Our holy and beautiful [4]temple,
Where our fathers praised You,
Is burned up with fire;
And all [h]our pleasant things [5]are
laid waste.

12 [i]Will You restrain Yourself because
of these *things*, O LORD?
[j]Will You [6]hold Your peace, and
afflict us very severely?

The Righteousness of God's Judgment

65 "I was [a]sought by *those who* did not
ask *for Me;*
I was found by *those who* did not
seek Me.
I said, 'Here I am, here I am,'
To a nation *that* [b]was not called by
My name.
2 [c]I have stretched out My hands all
day long to a [d]rebellious
people,
Who [e]walk in a way *that is* not
good,
According to their own thoughts;
3 A people [f]who provoke Me to
anger continually to My face;
[g]Who sacrifice in gardens,
And burn incense on altars of
brick;
4 [h]Who sit among the graves,
And spend the night in the tombs;
[i]Who eat swine's flesh,
And the broth of [1]abominable
things is *in* their vessels;
5 [j]Who say, 'Keep to yourself,
Do not come near me,
For I am holier than you!'
These [2]*are* smoke in My nostrils,
A fire that burns all the day.

6 "Behold, [k]*it is* written before Me:
[l]I will not keep silence, [m]but will
repay—

5 [d]Mal. 3:6
6 [e][Phil. 3:9] [f]Ps. 90:5, 6; Is. 1:30 [2]Lit. *a filthy garment*
7 [3]Lit. *caused us to melt*
8 [g]Is. 29:16; 45:9; Jer. 18:6; [Rom. 9:20, 21]
11 [h]Ezek. 24:21 [4]Lit. *house* [5]*have become a ruin*
12 [i]Is. 42:14 [j]Ps. 83:1 [6]*keep silent*

CHAPTER 65

1 [a]Rom. 9:24; 10:20 [b]Is. 63:19
2 [c]Rom. 10:21 [d]Is. 1:2, 23 [e]Is. 42:24
3 [f]Deut. 32:21 [g]Is. 1:29
4 [h]Deut. 18:11 [i]Lev. 11:7; Is. 66:17 [1]Unclean meats, Lev. 7:18; 19:7
5 [j]Matt. 9:11; Luke 7:39; 18:9-12 [2]Cause My wrath to smoke
6 [k]Deut. 32:34 [l]Ps. 50:3 [m]Ps. 79:12

64:5 we need to be saved. Direct exposure to the awesome character of God's judgment brings a realization of sinners' need of salvation (cf. Acts 16:26-30).

64:6 unclean *thing*...filthy rags. As in 53:6, the prophet included himself among those confessing their utter unworthiness to be in God's presence. Isaiah employed the imagery of menstrual cloths used during a woman's period to picture uncleanness (cf. Lev. 15:19-24). This is true of the best behavior of unbelievers (cf. Phil. 3:5-8).

64:7-9 no one who calls. The prophet finds no exception among a people whose iniquities had separated them from God. *See notes on Rom. 3:10-18.* Such seeking and calling on the Lord as Isaiah describes in 55:6,7 cannot occur apart from the powerful conviction and awakening of the sinful heart by the Holy Spirit. Thus the prayer recognizes God as a potter in control of clay and pleads for Him to do a saving work (v. 8). Cf. 45:9,10; 60:21; 63:16. Such a work is what God promised to end His fury (54:7,8) and His memory of sin (v. 9; 43:25).

64:11 burned up with fire...laid waste. Through prophetic revelation Isaiah uttered these words many years before the fall of Jerusalem and the destruction of the temple in 586 B.C. Yet, he lamented over the fallen state as though it had already occurred. God's people were in desperate straits and their prayers urgent and persistent: "How can You stand by when Your people and Your land are so barren?"

65:1-7 In response to the prayer of 63:7–64:12, the Lord repeated the warnings of His judgment.

65:1 not ask...not seek...not called. Though Israel sought the Lord, they did so only superficially. They did not genuinely seek Him. The NT assigns an additional sense to the words in Rom. 10:20, applying them to Gentiles who find Him through the work of His sovereign grace.

65:2 I have stretched out...rebellious people. God had continually taken the initiative in inviting His people Israel to walk in His ways, but time after time they rebuffed Him. Using this verse, Paul concurred in citing the rebelliousness of his fellow Jews (Rom. 10:21).

65:3,4 Here Isaiah gave more references to Israel's sin, such as defiance in practicing idolatry, communing with the spirits of the dead (a forbidden practice according to Deut. 18:10,11), eating in ways forbidden by the Mosaic law (Lev. 11:7,8), consuming food connected with "abominable" idol sacrifices, and the arrogance of self-righteousness (cf. Matt. 9:11; Luke 5:30; 18:11).

65:5 smoke in My nostrils. This alluded to the smoke of their self-righteous sacrifices, an endless irritation to God who responds in judgment.

65:6 I will not keep silence. The Lord's response to the prayer asking Him not to restrain Himself in granting deliverance (64:12) was that He will act in judgment, not deliverance, to punish sin (v. 7).

Even repay into their bosom—
7 Your iniquities and [n]the iniquities
of your fathers together,"
Says the LORD,
[o]"Who have burned incense on the
mountains
[p]And blasphemed Me on the hills;
Therefore I will measure their
former work into their
bosom."

8 Thus says the LORD:

"As the new wine is found in the
cluster,
And *one* says, 'Do not destroy it,
For [q]a blessing *is* in it,'
So will I do for My servants' sake,
That I may not destroy them [r]all.
9 I will bring forth descendants from
Jacob,
And from Judah an heir of My
mountains;
My [s]elect shall inherit it,
And My servants shall dwell there.
10 [t]Sharon shall be a fold of flocks,
And [u]the Valley of Achor a place
for herds to lie down,
For My people who have [v]sought
Me.

11 "But you *are* those who forsake the
LORD,
Who forget [w]My holy mountain,
Who prepare [x]a table for [3]Gad,
And who furnish a drink offering
for [4]Meni.
12 Therefore I will number you for
the sword,
And you shall all bow down to the
slaughter;
[y]Because, when I called, you did not
answer;
When I spoke, you did not hear,
But did evil before My eyes,
And chose *that* in which I do not
delight."

13 Therefore thus says the Lord GOD:

"Behold, My servants shall eat,
But you shall be hungry;
Behold, My servants shall drink,
But you shall be thirsty;
Behold, My servants shall rejoice,
But you shall be ashamed;
14 Behold, My servants shall sing for
joy of heart,
But you shall cry for sorrow of
heart,
And [z]wail for [5]grief of spirit.
15 You shall leave your name [a]as a
curse to [b]My chosen;
For the Lord GOD will slay you,
And [c]call His servants by another
name;
16 [d]So that he who blesses himself in
the earth
Shall bless himself in the God of
truth;
And [e]he who swears in the earth
Shall swear by the God of truth;
Because the former troubles are
forgotten,
And because they are hidden from
My eyes.

The Glorious New Creation

17 "For behold, I create [f]new heavens
and a new earth;

7 [n]Ex. 20:5 [o]Ezek. 18:6 [p]Is. 57:7; Ezek. 20:27, 28
8 [q]Joel 2:14 [r]Is. 1:9; Amos 9:8, 9
9 [s]Matt. 24:22
10 [t]Is. 33:9 [u]Josh. 7:24; Hos. 2:15 [v]Is. 55:6
11 [w]Is. 56:7 [x]Ezek. 23:41; [1 Cor. 10:21] [3]Lit. *Troop* or *Fortune;* a pagan deity [4]Lit. *Number* or *Destiny;* a pagan deity
12 [y]2 Chr. 36:15, 16; Prov. 1:24; Is. 41:28; 50:2; 66:4; Jer. 7:13
14 [z]Matt. 8:12; Luke 13:28 [5]Or *a broken spirit*
15 [a]Jer. 29:22; Zech. 8:13 [b]Is. 65:9, 22 [c][Acts 11:26]
16 [d]Ps. 72:17; Jer. 4:2 [e]Deut. 6:13; Zeph. 1:5
17 [f]Is. 51:16; 66:22; [2 Pet. 3:13]; Rev. 21:1

65:8-10 In the midst of the final fury of judgment when the time of Jacob's trouble comes (cf. Jer. 30:7) and God purges out the rebels in Israel (cf. Ezek. 20:38), there will also be the restoration of the faithful remnant to the Land. Though judgment comes to the nation as a whole, God will spare and save (cf. Zech. 12:10–13:1; Rom. 11:25-27) the faithful remnant, "My servants" (1:9), in the future kingdom. This will include a physical return of God's elect, believing Jews, to the land of Israel (57:13).

65:10 Sharon…Valley of Achor. Sharon was the western fertile territory on the Mediterranean coast, S of Mt. Carmel (35:2). The eastern Valley of Achor was near Jericho and the Jordan River (Josh. 7:24,26). Together they represented the whole land.

65:11,12 Another pronouncement of judgment was given on the rebellious Israelites, who resorted to the worship of pagan gods, like "Gad" and "Meni," and had no one to blame but themselves for the sword of damnation that fell on them.

65:13,14 Continuing to address the rebel idolaters, the Lord Himself gave contrasts between the faithful and unfaithful of Israel.

65:15 your name as a curse…another name. Israel's new name was to reflect her favored status among the nations (62:2-4). Delinquent Israelites, on the other hand, were to endure the reproach of men, so that the very name "Jew" would be disclaimed.

65:16 God of truth. Lit. this is "God of Amen," referring to the very God, the True God, who will honor His promises to Israel, thus vindicating Himself in the eyes of all people. Someday the rebels will be purged out and the redeemed remnant will be left. In that time, all blessing and swearing will be by the one and only True God, because all idols will be vanquished and forgotten in the glory of the kingdom of Messiah.

65:17-25 The blessings of faithful Israel in the coming kingdom are described.

65:17 new heavens and a new earth. Israel's future kingdom will include a temporal kingdom of a thousand years (*see notes on Rev. 20:1-10*) and an eternal kingdom in God's new creation (51:6,16; 54:10; 66:22; cf. Rev. 21:1-8). The prophet uses the eternal kingdom here as a reference point for both. Isaiah's prophecy does not make clear the relationship between the kingdom's two aspects as does later prophecy (Rev. 20:1–21:8). This is similar to the compression of Christ's first and second advents, so that in places they are indistinguishable (cf. 61:1,2).

And the former shall not be
remembered or [6]come to mind.
18 But be glad and rejoice forever in
what I create;
For behold, I create Jerusalem *as* a
rejoicing,
And her people a joy.
19 [g]I will rejoice in Jerusalem,
And joy in My people;
The [h]voice of weeping shall no
longer be heard in her,
Nor the voice of crying.
20 "No more shall an infant from there
live but a few days,
Nor an old man who has not
fulfilled his days;
For the child shall die one hundred
years old,
[i]But the sinner *being* one hundred
years old shall be accursed.
21 [j]They shall build houses and
inhabit *them;*
They shall plant vineyards and eat
their fruit.

17 [6] Lit. *come upon the heart* **19** [g] Is. 62:4, 5 [h] Is. 35:10; 51:11; Rev. 7:17; 21:4 **20** [i] Eccl. 8:12, 13; Is. 3:11; 22:14 **21** [j] Ezek. 28:26; 45:4; Hos. 11:11; Amos 9:14

65:20 No more shall an infant…Nor an old man. Long life will prevail in the millennial kingdom. In the temporal phase of the kingdom, death will happen, but not nearly so early as in the time of Isaiah. **sinner…accursed.** In the millennial phase of Israel's kingdom, a sinful person may die at age 100, but will be considered a mere youth at the time of his premature death. Having died an untimely death at such a youthful time, it will be assumed that God has taken his life for sin. The curse will be reversed in the Millennium, but it will not be removed until the eternal state (cf. Rev. 22:3).

65:21,22 build…inhabit…plant…eat. Social justice will prevail in Israel's kingdom. No enemies will deprive people of what is rightfully theirs (contra. Deut. 28:30).

Isaiah's Description of Israel's Future Kingdom

Description	Isaiah passages
1. The Lord will restore the faithful remnant of Israel to the Land to inhabit the kingdom at its beginning.	1:9,25-27; 3:10; 4:3; 6:13; 8:10; 9:1; 10:20,22,25,27; 11:11,12,16; 14:1,2; 14:22,26; 26:1-4; 27:12; 28:5; 35:9; 37:4,31,32; 40:2,3; 41:9; 43:5,6; 46:3,4; 49:5,8; 49:12,22; 51:11; 54:7-10; 55:12; 57:13,18; 60:4,9; 61:1-4,7; 65:8-10; 66:8,9,19
2. As the Lord defeats Israel's enemies, He will provide protection for His people.	4:5,6; 9:1,4; 12:1-6; 13:4; 14:2; 21:9; 26:4,5; 27:1-4; 30:30,31; 32:2; 33:16,22; 35:4; 99:8,9; 49:17,18; 52:6; 54:9,10; 55:10,11; 58:12; 60:10,12,18; 62:9; 66:16
3. In her kingdom, Israel will enjoy great prosperity of many kinds.	26:15,19; 27:2,13; 29:18-20; 22:22,23; 30:20; 32:3; 32:15-20; 33:6,24; 35:3,5,6,8-10; 40:11; 42:6,7,16; 43:5,6,8,10,21; 44:5,14; 46:13; 48:6; 49:10; 52:9; 54:2,3; 55:1,12; 58:9,14; 60:5,16,21; 61:4,6-10; 62:5; 65:13-15,18,24; 66:21,22
4. The city of Jerusalem will rise to world preeminence in the kingdom.	2:2-4; 18:7; 25:6; 40:5,9; 49:19-21; 60:1-5,13-15,17; 62:3,4
5. Israel will be the center of world attention in the kingdom.	23:18; 54:1-3; 55:5; 56:6-8; 60:5-9; 66:18-21
6. Israel's mission in the kingdom will be to glorify the Lord.	60:21; 61:3
7. Gentiles in the kingdom will receive blessing through the channel of faithful Israel.	11:10; 19:18,24,25; 42:6; 45:22,23; 49:6; 51:5; 56:3,6-8; 60:3,7,8; 61:5; 66:19
8. Worldwide peace will prevail in the kingdom under the rule of the Prince of Peace.	2:4; 9:5,6; 11:10; 19:23; 26:12; 32:18; 54:14; 57:19; 66:12
9. Moral and spiritual conditions in the kingdom will reach their highest plane since the Fall of Adam.	27:6; 28:6,17; 32:16; 42:7; 44:3; 45:8; 51:4; 61:11; 65:21,22
10. Governmental leadership in the kingdom will be superlative with the Messiah heading it up.	9:6,7; 11:2,3; 16:5; 24:23; 25:3; 32:1; 32:5; 33:22; 42:1,4; 43:15; 52:13; 53:12; 55:3-5
11. Humans will enjoy long life in the kingdom.	65:20,22
12. Knowledge of the Lord will be universal in the kingdom.	11:9; 19:21; 33:13; 40:5; 41:20; 45:6,14; 49:26; 52:10,13,15; 54:13; 66:23
13. The world of nature will enjoy a great renewal in the kingdom.	12:3; 30:23-26; 32:15; 35:1-4,6,7; 41:18,19; 43:19,20; 44:3,23; 55:1,2,13; 58:10,11
14. "Wild" animals will be tame in the kingdom.	11:6-9; 35:9; 65:25
15. Sorrow and mourning will not exist in the kingdom.	25:8; 60:20
16. An eternal kingdom, as a part of God's new creation, will follow the millennial kingdom.	24:23; 51:6; 51:16; 54:11,12; 60:11,19; 65:17
17. The King will judge overt sin in the kingdom.	66:24

22 They shall not build and another inhabit;
They shall not plant and [k]another eat;
For [l]as the days of a tree, *so shall be* the days of My people,
And [m]My elect shall long enjoy the work of their hands.
23 They shall not labor in vain,
[n]Nor bring forth children for trouble;
For [o]they *shall be* the descendants of the blessed of the LORD,
And their offspring with them.

24 "It shall come to pass
That [p]before they call, I will answer;
And while they are still speaking, I will [q]hear.
25 The [r]wolf and the lamb shall feed together,
The lion shall eat straw like the ox,
[s]And dust *shall be* the serpent's food.
They shall not hurt nor destroy in all My holy mountain,"
Says the LORD.

True Worship and False

66 Thus says the LORD:
[a]"Heaven *is* My throne,
And earth *is* My footstool.
Where *is* the house that you will build Me?
And where *is* the place of My rest?
2 For all those *things* My hand has made,
And all those *things* exist,"
Says the LORD.
[b]"But on this *one* will I look:
[c]On *him who is* poor and of a contrite spirit,
And who trembles at My word.
3 "He[d] who kills a bull *is as if* he slays a man;
He who sacrifices a lamb, *as if* he [e]breaks a dog's neck;
He who offers a grain offering, *as if he offers* swine's blood;
He who burns incense, *as if* he blesses an idol.
Just as they have chosen their own ways,
And their soul delights in their abominations,
4 So will I choose their delusions,
And bring their fears on them;
[f]Because, when I called, no one answered,
When I spoke they did not hear;
But they did evil before My eyes,
And chose *that* in which I do not delight."

The LORD Vindicates Zion

5 Hear the word of the LORD,
You who tremble at His word:
"Your brethren who [g]hated you,
Who cast you out for My name's sake, said,
[h]'Let the LORD be glorified,
That [i]we may see your joy.'
But they shall be ashamed."
6 The sound of noise from the city!
A voice from the temple!
The voice of the LORD,
Who fully repays His enemies!

22 [k]Is. 62:8, 9 [l]Ps. 92:12 [m]Is. 65:9, 15
23 [n]Hos. 9:12 [o]Is. 61:9; [Jer. 32:38, 39; Acts 2:39]
24 [p]Ps. 91:15; Is. 58:9 [q]Is. 30:19; Dan. 9:20-23
25 [r]Is. 11:6-9 [s]Gen. 3:14; Mic. 7:17

CHAPTER 66

1 [a]1 Kin. 8:27; 2 Chr. 6:18; Ps. 11:4; Matt. 5:34; Acts 17:24
2 [b]Ps. 34:18; [Is. 57:15; 61:1; Matt. 5:3, 4; Luke 18:13, 14] [c]Ps. 34:18; 51:17
3 [d][Is. 1:10-17; 58:1-7; Mic. 6:7, 8] [e]Deut. 23:18
4 [f]Prov. 1:24; Is. 65:12; Jer. 7:13
5 [g]Ps. 38:20; Is. 60:15; [Luke 6:22, 23] [h]Is. 5:19 [i][2 Thess. 1:10; Titus 2:13]

65:23 Nor...for trouble. Lit. this means "for sudden death." Subjects in the kingdom will enjoy freedom from ordinary misfortunes related to premature death of infants. There will be the lowest infant mortality rate ever. Along with longer life (v. 20), this means the earth will be greatly populated at an exponential rate of reproduction. Cf. Rev. 20:7-9 for the massive collection of people at the end of the kingdom who come against Christ.

65:24 before they call...while they are still speaking. Relationship with the Lord will be so close that He will anticipate and provide for every need (58:9).

65:25 wolf...lamb...lion...ox...serpent's. Dangers from the animal world will be nonexistent during the reign of the Servant of the Lord (11:6-9).

66:1,2 Isaiah began the final summary of his prophecy with a reminder that God is not looking for a temple of stone, since as Creator of all things, the whole universe is His dwelling place. Stephen cited this passage before the Sanhedrin to point out their error in limiting God to a temple made with hands (Acts 7:49,50). On the contrary, God is looking for a heart to dwell in, a heart that is tender and broken, not one concerned with the externalities of religion (cf. Matt. 5:3-9). God is looking to dwell in the heart of a person who takes His Word seriously (cf. 66:5; John 14:23).

66:3 *as if* he slays a man. God loathes even the sacrifices of the wicked (cf. Prov. 15:8; 28:9). They often killed children to offer in sacrifice (cf. Ezek. 23:39). Some of the Jews were offering bulls as sacrifices with the same empty heartedness as the pagans offering "a man" on the altar. **breaks a dog's neck.** This refers to offering dogs in sacrifice, which, as unclean (Jer. 15:3; cf. 56:10,11), are associated with swine (Matt. 7:6; 2 Pet. 2:22). To sacrifice a lamb with an attitude no different than if it were a dog betrayed the empty heartedness of the offerer. All of these images are meant to illustrate the shallow hypocrisy of one who makes an offering to God, but with no more heartbrokenness than a pagan who kills a child, offers a dog, sacrifices pig's blood, blesses an idol, and loves such abominations. God will judge such (v. 4).

66:5 Your brethren who hated you. The apostate Israelites intensified their rivalry with the faithful remnant (65:11-15) and blasphemously said, "Let the LORD be glorified," words uttered in the sarcastic spirit of 5:19 by these apostates. In the end, "they shall be ashamed" because God's judgment will fall.

7 "Before she was in labor, she gave birth;
Before her pain came,
She delivered a male child.
8 Who has heard such a thing?
Who has seen such things?
Shall the earth be made to give birth in one day?
Or shall a nation be born at once?
For as soon as Zion was in labor,
She gave birth to her children.
9 Shall I bring to the time of birth, and not cause delivery?" says the LORD.
"Shall I who cause delivery shut up *the womb?*" says your God.
10 "Rejoice with Jerusalem,
And be glad with her, all you who love her;
Rejoice for joy with her, all you who mourn for her;
11 That you may feed and be satisfied
With the consolation of her bosom,
That you may drink deeply and be delighted
With the abundance of her glory."

12 For thus says the LORD:

"Behold, [j]I will extend peace to her like a river,
And the glory of the Gentiles like a flowing stream.
Then you shall [k]feed;
On *her* sides shall you be [l]carried,
And be dandled on *her* knees.
13 As one whom his mother comforts,
So I will [m]comfort you;
And you shall be comforted in Jerusalem."

The Reign and Indignation of God

14 When you see *this,* your heart shall rejoice,
And [n]your bones shall flourish like grass;
The hand of the LORD shall be known to His servants,
And *His* indignation to His enemies.
15 [o]For behold, the LORD will come with fire
And with His chariots, like a whirlwind,
To render His anger with fury,
And His rebuke with flames of fire.
16 For by fire and by [p]His sword
The LORD will judge all flesh;
And the slain of the LORD shall be [q]many.

17 "Those[r] who sanctify themselves and purify themselves,
To go to the gardens
[1]After an *idol* in the midst,
Eating swine's flesh and the abomination and the mouse,
Shall [2]be consumed together," says the LORD.

18 "For I *know* their works and their
[s]thoughts. It shall be that I will [t]gather all
nations and tongues; and they shall come
and see My glory. 19 [u]I will set a sign
among them; and those among them who
escape I will send to the nations: *to*
Tarshish and [3]Pul and Lud, who draw the
bow, and Tubal and Javan, *to* the coastlands afar off who have not heard My fame
nor seen My glory. [v]And they shall declare
My glory among the Gentiles. 20 Then they
shall [w]bring all your brethren [x]for an offering to the LORD out of all nations, on horses and in chariots and in litters, on mules

12 [j] Is. 48:18; 60:5 [k] Is. 60:16 [l] Is. 49:22; 60:4
13 [m] Is. 51:3; [2 Cor. 1:3, 4]
14 [n] Ezek. 37:1
15 [o] Is. 9:5; [2 Thess. 1:8]
16 [p] Is. 27:1 [q] Is. 34:6
17 [r] Is. 65:3-8 [1] Lit. *After one* [2] *come to an end*
18 [s] Is. 59:7 [t] Is. 45:22-25; Jer. 3:17
19 [u] Luke 2:34 [v] Mal. 1:11 [3] So with MT, Tg.; LXX *Put* (cf. Jer. 46:9)
20 [w] Is. 49:22 [x] Is. 18:7; [Rom. 15:16]

66:7-9 Here is another comparison with the human birth process (see 13:8), this time to teach two lessons: 1) no birth can come until labor pains have occurred (vv. 7,8); and 2) when labor occurs, birth will surely follow (v. 9). Cf. Jer. 30:6,7; Matt. 24:8; 1 Thess. 5:3. The point is that Israel's suffering will end with a delivery! The Lord will not impose travail on the remnant without bringing them to the kingdom (v. 10).

66:11 feed and be satisfied. The prophet compares Jerusalem to a nursing mother.

66:12 peace...like a river. The picture is of abundant peace that compares to a wadi filled with a rushing torrent of water.

66:14 to His servants...to His enemies. Prosperity will belong to the faithful remnant, but wrath to those who oppose the Lord.

66:15 whirlwind...flames of fire. That the wrath of God will come to the rebels is expressed in language describing the end-time judgment (cf. 29:6).

66:16 the slain...many. The many who fight against the Lord when He comes to establish His kingdom will die (34:6,7; Rev. 19:21).

66:17 sanctify themselves and purify themselves. Sanctification and purification for right purposes are right, but when done for purposes of idol worship, will draw judgment from the one true God.

66:18 their works and their thoughts. The Lord was aware of the motivations behind the actions of apostate Israelites (v. 17). **gather all nations and tongues.** See 2:2-4. Jerusalem will be the center of world attention because of the presence of the Messiah there.

66:19 those...who escape. The faithful remnant of Israel are in view, who had escaped both the persecutions of their enemies and the judgment of God against those enemies (v. 16). **Tarshish and Pul and Lud...Tubal and Javan.** Tarshish was possibly in Spain, Pul and Lud in North Africa, Tubal in NE Asia Minor, and Javan in Greece. These were representative Gentile populations that will hear of God's glory through the faithful remnant.

66:20 bring all your brethren. As their offering to the Lord, the Gentiles who hear of God's glory will expedite the return of Israel's faithful remnant (43:6; 49:22).

and on camels, to My holy mountain Jerusalem," says the LORD, "as the children of
Israel bring an offering in a clean vessel
into the house of the LORD. 21 And I will
also take some of them for [y]priests *and*
Levites," says the LORD.

22 "For as [z]the new heavens and the
new earth
Which I will make shall remain
before Me," says the LORD,
"So shall your descendants and
your name remain.
23 And [a]it shall come to pass
That from one New Moon to
another,
And from one Sabbath to another,
[b]All flesh shall come to worship
before Me," says the LORD.

24 "And they shall go forth and look
Upon the corpses of the men
Who have transgressed against
Me.
For their [c]worm does not die,
And their fire is not quenched.
They shall be an abhorrence to all
flesh."

21 [y]Ex. 19:6; Is. 61:6; 1 Pet. 2:9; Rev. 1:6
22 [z]Is. 65:17; Heb. 12:26, 27; 2 Pet. 3:13; Rev. 21:1
23 [a]Zech. 14:16
[b]Zech. 14:17-21
24 [c]Is. 14:11; Mark 9:44, 46, 48

66:21 priests *and* Levites. Some of the returning remnant will function in these specialized roles in the services of the millennial temple and memorial sacrifices (cf. Ezek. 44–46).

66:22 your descendants…remain. National Israel will have a never-ending existence through the Millennium, and on into the new heavens and the new earth throughout eternity.

66:23 All flesh…worship before Me. All humanity will participate in worshiping the Lord at stipulated times during the temporal phase of the messianic kingdom.

66:24 worm does not die…fire is not quenched. The corpses of those enduring everlasting torment will serve as a vivid reminder to all of the grievous nature and terrible consequences of rebellion against God. In referring to this verse, Jesus referred to the Valley of Hinnom—i.e., Gehenna—where a continually burning trash-heap pictured the never-ending pain of the lost (Mark 9:47,48). *See note on Jer. 19:6.*

The Book of
JEREMIAH

Title

This book gains its title from the human author, who begins with "the words of Jeremiah…" (1:1). Jeremiah recounts more of his own life than any other prophet, telling of his ministry, the reactions of his audiences, testings, and his personal feelings. His name means "Jehovah throws," in the sense of laying down a foundation, or "Jehovah establishes, appoints, or sends."

Seven other Jeremiahs appear in Scripture (2 Kin. 23:31; 1 Chr. 5:24; 1 Chr. 12:4; 1 Chr. 12:10; 1 Chr. 12:13; Neh. 10:2; Neh. 12:1), and Jeremiah the prophet is named at least 9 times outside of his book (cf. 2 Chr. 35:25; 36:12; 36:21,22; Dan. 9:2; Ezra 1:1; Matt. 2:17; 16:14; 27:9). The Old and New Testaments quote Jeremiah at least 7 times: 1) Dan. 9:2 (25:11,12; 29:10); 2) Matt. 2:18 (31:15); 3) Matt. 27:9 (18:2; 19:2,11; 32:6-9); 4) 1 Cor. 1:31 (9:24); 5) 2 Cor. 10:17 (9:24); 6) Heb. 8:8-12 (31:31-34); and 7) Heb. 10:16,17 (31:33,34).

Author and Date

Jeremiah, who served as both a priest and a prophet, was the son of a priest named Hilkiah (not the High-Priest of 2 Kin. 22:8 who discovered the book of the law). He was from the small village of Anathoth (1:1), today called Anata, about 3 mi. NE of Jerusalem in Benjamin's tribal inheritance. As an object lesson to Judah, Jeremiah remained unmarried (16:1-4). He was assisted in ministry by a scribe, named Baruch, to whom Jeremiah dictated and who copied and had custody over the writings compiled from the prophet's messages (36:4,32; 45:1). Jeremiah has been known as "the weeping prophet" (cf. 9:1; 13:17; 14:17), living a life of conflict because of his predictions of judgment by the invading Babylonians. He was threatened, tried for his life, put in stocks, forced to flee from Jehoiakim, publicly humiliated by a false prophet, and thrown into a pit.

Jeremiah carried out a ministry directed mostly to his own people in Judah, but which expanded to other nations at times. He appealed to his countrymen to repent and avoid God's judgment via an invader (chaps. 7,26). Once invasion was certain after Judah refused to repent, he pled with them not to resist the Babylonian conqueror in order to prevent total destruction (chap. 27). He also called on delegates of other nations to heed his counsel and submit to Babylon (chap. 27), and he predicted judgments from God on various nations (25:12-38; chaps. 46–51).

The dates of his ministry, which spanned 5 decades, are from the Judean king Josiah's 13th year, noted in 1:2 (627 B.C.), to beyond the fall of Jerusalem to Babylon in 586 B.C. (Jer. 39,40,52). After 586 B.C., Jeremiah was forced to go with a fleeing remnant of Judah to Egypt (Jer. 43,44). He was possibly still ministering in 570 B.C. (*see note on 44:30*). A rabbinic note claims that when Babylon invaded Egypt in 568/67 B.C. Jeremiah was taken captive to Babylon. He could have lived even to pen the book's closing scene ca. 561 B.C. in Babylon, when Judah's king Jehoiachin, captive in Babylon since 597 B.C., was allowed liberties in his last days (52:31-34). Jeremiah, if still alive at that time, was between 85 and 90 years old.

Background and Setting

Background details of Jeremiah's times are portrayed in 2 Kin. 22–25 and 2 Chr. 34–36. Jeremiah's messages paint pictures of: 1) his people's sin; 2) the invader God would send; 3) the rigors of siege; and 4) calamities of destruction. Jeremiah's message of impending judgment for idolatry and other sins was preached over a period of 40 years (ca. 627–586 B.C. and beyond). His prophecy took place during the reigns of Judah's final 5 kings (Josiah 640–609 B.C., Jehoahaz 609 B.C., Jehoiakim 609–598 B.C., Jehoiachin 598–597 B.C., and Zedekiah 597–586 B.C.).

The spiritual condition of Judah was one of flagrant idol worship (cf. chap. 2). King Ahaz, preceding his son Hezekiah long before Jeremiah in Isaiah's day, had set up a system of sacrificing children to the god Molech in the Valley of Hinnom just outside Jerusalem (735–715 B.C.). Hezekiah led in reforms and clean-up (Is. 36:7), but his son Manasseh continued to foster child sacrifice along with gross idolatry, which continued into Jeremiah's time (7:31; 19:5; 32:35). Many also worshiped the "queen of heaven" (7:18; 44:19). Josiah's reforms, reaching their apex in 622 B.C., forced a repressing of the worst practices outwardly, but the deadly cancer of sin was deep and flourished quickly again after a shallow revival.

Religious insincerity, dishonesty, adultery, injustice, tyranny against the helpless, and slander prevailed as the norm not the exception.

Politically momentous events occurred in Jeremiah's day. Assyria saw its power wane gradually; then Ashurbanipal died in 626 B.C. Assyria grew so feeble that in 612 B.C. her seemingly invincible capital, Nineveh, was destroyed (cf. the book of Nahum). The Neo-Babylonian empire under Nabopolassar (625–605 B.C.) became dominant militarily with victories against Assyria (612 B.C.), Egypt (609–605 B.C.), and Israel in 3 phases (605 B.C., as in Dan. 1; 597 B.C., as in 2 Kin. 24:10-16; and 586 B.C., as in Jer. 39,40,52).

While Joel and Micah had earlier prophesied of Judah's judgment, during Josiah's reign, God's leading prophets were Jeremiah, Habakkuk, and Zephaniah. Later, Jeremiah's contemporaries, Ezekiel and Daniel, played prominent prophetic roles.

Historical and Theological Themes

The main theme of Jeremiah is judgment upon Judah (chaps. 1–29) with restoration in the future messianic kingdom (23:3-8; 30–33). Whereas Isaiah devoted many chapters to a future glory for Israel (Is. 40–66), Jeremiah gave far less space to this subject. Since God's judgment was imminent he concentrated on current problems as he sought to turn the nation back from the point of no return.

A secondary theme is God's willingness to spare and bless the nation only if the people repent. Though this is a frequent emphasis, it is most graphically portrayed at the potter's shop (18:1-11). A further focus is God's plan for Jeremiah's life, both in his proclamation of God's message and in his commitment to fulfill all of His will (1:5-19; 15:19-21). Other themes include: 1) God's longing for Israel to be tender toward Him, as in the days of first love (2:1-3); 2) Jeremiah's servant tears, as "the weeping prophet" (9:1; 14:17); 3) the close, intimate relationship God had with Israel and that He yearned to keep (13:11); 4) suffering, as in Jeremiah's trials (11:18-23; 20:1-18) and God's sufficiency in all trouble (20:11-13); 5) the vital role that God's Word can play in life (15:16); 6) the place of faith in expecting restoration from the God for whom nothing is too difficult (chap. 32, especially vv. 17,27); and 7) prayer for the coordination of God's will with God's action in restoring Israel to its land (33:3,6-18).

Interpretive Challenges

A number of questions arise, such as: 1) How can one explain God's forbidding prayer for the Jews (7:16) and saying that even Moses' and Samuel's advocacy could not avert judgment (15:1)? 2) Did Jeremiah make an actual trek of several hundred miles to the Euphrates River, or did he bury his loin cloth nearby (13:4-7)? 3) How could he utter such severe things about the man who announced his birth (20:14-18)? 4) Does the curse on Jeconiah's kingly line relate to Christ (22:30)? 5) How is one to interpret the promises of Israel's return to its ancient land (chaps. 30–33)? and 6) How will God fulfill the New Covenant in relation to Israel and the church (31:31-34)? The answers to these will be included in the study notes at the appropriate passages.

A frequent challenge is to understand the prophet's messages in their right time setting, since the book of Jeremiah is not always chronological, but loosely arranged, moving back and forth in time for thematic effect. Ezekiel, by contrast, usually places his material in chronological order.

Outline

I. Preparation of Jeremiah (1:1-19)
  A. The Context of Jeremiah (1:1-3)
  B. The Choice of Jeremiah (1:4-10)
  C. The Charge to Jeremiah (1:11-19)

II. Proclamations to Judah (2:1–45:5)
  A. Condemnation of Judah (2:1–29:32)
    1. First message (2:1–3:5)
    2. Second message (3:6–6:30)
    3. Third message (7:1–10:25)
    4. Fourth message (11:1–13:27)
    5. Fifth message (14:1–17:18)
    6. Sixth message (17:19-27)
    7. Seventh message (18:1–20:18)
    8. Eight message (21:1-14)
    9. Ninth message (22:1–23:40)
    10. Tenth message (24:1-10)
    11. Eleventh message (25:1-38)
    12. Twelfth message (26:1-24)
    13. Thirteenth message (27:1–28:17)
    14. Fourteenth message (29:1-32)
  B. Consolation to Judah—New Covenant (30:1–33:26)
    1. The forecast of restoration (30:1–31:40)
    2. The faith in restoration (32:1-44)
    3. The forecast of restoration—Part 2 (33:1-26)
  C. Calamity on Judah (34:1–45:5)
    1. Before Judah's fall (34:1–38:28)
    2. During Judah's fall (39:1-18)
    3. After Judah's fall (40:1–45:5)

III. Proclamations of Judgment on the Nations (46:1–51:64)
  A. Introduction (46:1; cf. 25:15-26)
  B. Against Egypt (46:2-28)
  C. Against Philistia (47:1-7)
  D. Against Moab (48:1-47)
  E. Against Ammon (49:1-6)
  F. Against Edom (49:7-22)
  G. Against Damascus (49:23-27)
  H. Against Kedar and Hazor [Arabia] (49:28-33)
  I. Against Elam (49:34-39)
  J. Against Babylon (50:1–51:64)

IV. The Fall of Jerusalem (52:1-34)
  A. The Destruction of Jerusalem (52:1-23)
  B. The Deportation of Jews (52:24-30)
  C. The Deliverance of Jehoiachin (52:31-34)

1 The words of Jeremiah the son of Hilkiah, of the priests who *were* [a]in Anathoth in the land of Benjamin, 2 to whom
the word of the LORD came in the days of
[b]Josiah the son of Amon, king of Judah, [c]in
the thirteenth year of his reign. 3 It came
also in the days of [d]Jehoiakim the son of Josiah, king of Judah, [e]until the end of the
eleventh year of Zedekiah the son of Josiah,
king of Judah, [f]until the carrying away of
Jerusalem captive [g]in the fifth month.

The Prophet Is Called

4 Then the word of the LORD came to me, saying:

5 "Before I [h]formed you in the womb
[i]I knew you;
Before you were born I [j]sanctified[1] you;
I [2]ordained you a prophet to the nations."

6 Then said I:

[k]"Ah, Lord GOD!
Behold, I cannot speak, for I *am* a youth."

7 But the LORD said to me:

"Do not say, 'I *am* a youth,'
For you shall go to all to whom I send you,
And [l]whatever I command you, you shall speak.
8 [m]Do not be afraid of their faces,
For [n]I *am* with you to deliver you,"
says the LORD.

9 Then the LORD put forth His hand and
[o]touched my mouth, and the LORD said to
me:

"Behold, I have [p]put My words in your mouth.
10 [q]See, I have this day set you over
the nations and over the kingdoms,
To [r]root out and to pull down,
To destroy and to throw down,
To build and to plant."

11 Moreover the word of the LORD came
to me, saying, "Jeremiah, what do you
see?"
And I said, "I see a [3]branch of an almond tree."
12 Then the LORD said to me, "You have
seen well, for I am [4]ready to perform My
word."

CHAPTER 1
1 [a] Josh. 21:18; 1 Kin. 2:26; 1 Chr. 6:60; Is. 10:30; Jer. 29:27
2 [b] 1 Kin. 13:2; 2 Kin. 21:24; 2 Chr. 34:1; Jer. 3:6; 36:2 [c] Jer. 25:3
3 [d] 2 Kin. 23:34; 1 Chr. 3:15; 2 Chr. 36:5-8; Jer. 25:1 [e] 2 Kin. 24:17; 1 Chr. 3:15; 2 Chr. 36:11-13; Jer. 39:2 [f] Jer. 52:12 [g] 2 Kin. 25:8
5 [h] Is. 49:1, 5 [i] Ex. 33:12 [j] [Luke 1:15]; Gal. 1:15 [1] *set you apart* [2] *appointed*
6 [k] Ex. 4:10; 6:12, 30
7 [l] Num. 22:20, 38; Jer. 1:17; Matt. 28:20
8 [m] Ezek. 2:6; 3:9 [n] Ex. 3:12; Deut. 31:6; Josh. 1:5; Jer. 15:20; Heb. 13:6
9 [o] Is. 6:7; Mark 7:33-35 [p] Ex. 4:11-16; Deut. 18:18; Is. 51:16
10 [q] 1 Kin. 19:17 [r] Jer. 18:7-10; Ezek. 22:18; [2 Cor. 10:4, 5]
11 [3] Lit. *rod*
12 [4] Lit. *watching*

Illustrations of God's Judgment

An Almond Branch (1:11,12)
A Boiling Caldron (1:13-16)
Lions (2:15, 4:7, 5:6, 50:17).
A Scorching Storm Wind (4:11,12, 18:17, 23:19, 25:32)
Wolf (5:6)
Leopard (5:6)
Stripping Away Judah's Branches (5:10)
Fire (5:14)
Making This House (Worship Center) like Shiloh (7:14)
Serpents, Adders (8:17)
Destroying Olive Branches (11:16-17)
Uprooting (12:17)
Linen Sash Made Worthless (13:1-11)
Bottles Filled with Wine and Dashed Against One Another (13:12-14)
A Potter's Jar Shattered (19:10,11; cf. 22:28)
A Hammer [God's Word] Crushing a Rock (23:29)
A Cup of Wrath (25:15)
Zion Plowed as a Field (26:18)
Wearing Yokes of Wood and Iron (27:2; 28:13)
A Hammer [Babylon] (50:23)
A Mountain of Destruction [Babylon] (51:25)

1:1 Anathoth. A town in the territory of Benjamin, 3 mi. N of Jerusalem, assigned to the Levites (cf. Josh. 21:18) where Abiathar had once lived (1 Kin. 2:26).

1:2 in the days of. Jeremiah's ministry spanned at least 5 decades—from Judah's king Josiah (13th year, 627 B.C.) to the final king, Zedekiah, in his last year (586 B.C.).

1:3 fifth month. Babylonian conquerors began deporting Judeans into captivity in the Heb. month Ab (July–Aug.) in 586 B.C. (52:12; 2 Kin. 25:8-11), shortly after breaking into Jerusalem on the fourth month and ninth day (39:2; 52:6).

1:5 Before I formed you… This is not reincarnation; it is God's all-knowing cognizance of Jeremiah and sovereign plan for him before he was conceived (cf. Paul's similar realization, Gal. 1:15).

1:6 Jeremiah's response points out his inability and his inexperience. If as a young man he was 20–25 years old in 626 B.C., he was 60–65 in 586 B.C. when Jerusalem fell (chap. 39), and 85–90 if he lived to the time of 52:31-34 (ca. 561 B.C.).

1:7-10 The power backing Jeremiah's service was God's presence and provision (cf. 2 Cor. 3:5).

1:9 My words in your mouth. God used him as His mouthpiece, speaking His message (15:19); thus, Jeremiah's fitting response was to receive God's Word (15:16).

1:10 set you over. Because God spoke through Jeremiah, the message has divine authority.

1:11-16 Illustrations of God's charge were twofold. First, there was the sign of the almond rod. The almond tree was literally "the wakeful tree," because it awakened from the sleep of winter earlier than the other trees, blooming in Jan. It was a symbol of God's early judgment, as Jeremiah announced (605–586 B.C.). Second, the boiling cauldron pictured the Babylonian invaders bringing judgment on Judah (cf. 20:4).

13 And the word of the LORD came to me the second time, saying, "What do you see?"

And I said, "I see [s]a boiling pot, and it is facing away from the north."

14 Then the LORD said to me:

"Out of the [t]north calamity shall
break forth
On all the inhabitants of the land.
15 For behold, I am [u]calling
All the families of the kingdoms of
the north," says the LORD;
"They shall come and [v]each one set
his throne
At the entrance of the gates of
Jerusalem,
Against all its walls all around,
And against all the cities of Judah.
16 I will utter My judgments
Against them concerning all their
wickedness,
Because [w]they have forsaken Me,
Burned [x]incense to other gods,
And worshiped the works of their
own [y]hands.

17 "Therefore [z]prepare yourself and
arise,
And speak to them all that I
command you.
[a]Do not be dismayed before their
faces,
Lest I dismay you before them.
18 For behold, I have made you this
day
[b]A fortified city and an iron pillar,
And bronze walls against the
whole land—
Against the kings of Judah,
Against its princes,
Against its priests,
And against the people of the land.
19 They will fight against you,
But they shall not prevail against
you.
For I *am* with you," says the LORD,
"to deliver you."

God's Case Against Israel

2 Moreover the word of the LORD came to me, saying, 2 "Go and cry in the hearing of Jerusalem, saying, 'Thus says the LORD:

"I remember you,
The kindness of your [a]youth,
The love of your betrothal,
[b]When you [1]went after Me in the
wilderness,
In a land not sown.
3 [c]Israel *was* holiness to the LORD,
[d]The firstfruits of His increase.
[e]All that devour him will offend;
Disaster will [f]come upon them,"
says the LORD.' "

4 Hear the word of the LORD, O house of Jacob and all the families of the house of Israel. 5 Thus says the LORD:

[g]"What injustice have your fathers
found in Me,
That they have gone far from Me,
[h]Have followed [2]idols,
And have become idolaters?
6 Neither did they say, 'Where *is* the
LORD,
Who [i]brought us up out of the
land of Egypt,
Who led us through [j]the
wilderness,
Through a land of deserts and pits,
Through a land of drought and the
shadow of death,
Through a land that no one crossed
And where no one dwelt?'

13 [s] Ezek. 11:3; 24:3 **14** [t] Jer. 6:1 **15** [u] Jer. 6:22; 25:9 [v] Is. 22:7; Jer. 39:3 **16** [w] Deut. 28:20; Jer. 17:13 [x] Is. 65:3, 4; Jer. 7:9 [y] Is. 37:19; Jer. 2:28 **17** [z] 1 Kin. 18:46; 2 Kin. 4:29; Job 38:3; Luke 12:35; [1 Pet. 1:13] [a] Ezek. 2:6 **18** [b] Is. 50:7; Jer. 6:27; 15:20

CHAPTER 2

2 [a] Ezek. 16:8; Hos. 2:15 [b] Deut. 2:7; Jer. 2:6 [1] *followed* **3** [c] [Ex. 19:5, 6; Deut. 7:6; 14:2] [d] James 1:18; Rev. 14:4 [e] Jer. 12:14 [f] Gen. 12:3; Is. 41:11; Jer. 30:15, 16; 50:7 **5** [g] Is. 5:4; Mic. 6:3 [h] 2 Kin. 17:15; Jer. 8:19; [Jon. 2:8]; Rom. 1:21 [2] *vanities* or *futilities* **6** [i] Ex. 20:2; Is. 63:11 [j] Deut. 8:15; 32:10

1:17-19 Jeremiah's part was proclamation, as God's mouthpiece (v. 17); God's part was preservation in defending the prophet (vv. 18, 19). God did protect him often, e.g., 11:18-23; 20:1ff., and 38:7-13.

2:1-3 Jerusalem…Israel. Jeremiah pointed to the sensitivity of the Lord and His care for them in the early history (v. 21). After centuries, many were: 1) far from God, whom they had forsaken (vv. 5, 31); 2) deep in idolatry (vv. 11, 27, 28); and 3) without true salvation (as v. 8; 5:10a).

2:3 firstfruits. Israel was first to worship the true God (Ex. 19:5, 6) through His covenant with Abraham (Gen. 12:1-3), which also assured His intent to bless peoples from all nations (16:19-21; Dan. 7:27).

Major Trials of Jeremiah

1. Trial By Death Threats (11:18-23)
2. Trial By Isolation (15:15-21)
3. Trial By Stocks (19:14–20:18)
4. Trial By Arrest (26:7-24)
5. Trial By Challenge (28:10-16)
6. Trial By Destruction (36:1-32)
7. Trial By Violence and Imprisonment (37:15)
8. Trial By Starvation (38:1-6)
9. Trial By Chains (40:1)
10. Trial By Rejection (42:1–43:4)

Jeremiah faced life-threatening trials throughout his ministry as a prophet of the Lord.

7 I brought you into [k]a bountiful country,
To eat its fruit and its goodness.
But when you entered, you [l]defiled My land
And made My heritage an abomination.
8 The priests did not say, 'Where *is* the LORD?'
And those who handle the [m]law did not know Me;
The rulers also transgressed against Me;
[n]The prophets prophesied by Baal,
And walked after *things that* do not profit.

9 "Therefore [o]I will yet [3]bring charges against you," says the LORD,
"And against your children's children I will bring charges.
10 For pass beyond the coasts of [4]Cyprus and see,
Send to [5]Kedar and consider diligently,
And see if there has been such *a* [p]*thing.*
11 [q]Has a nation changed *its* gods,
Which *are* [r]not gods?
[s]But My people have changed their Glory
For *what* does not profit.
12 Be astonished, O heavens, at this,
And be horribly afraid;
Be very desolate," says the LORD.
13 "For My people have committed two evils:
They have forsaken Me, the [t]fountain of living waters,
And hewn themselves cisterns—broken cisterns that can hold no water.
14 "*Is* Israel [u]a servant?
Is he a homeborn *slave?*
Why is he plundered?
15 [v]The young lions roared at him, *and* growled;
They made his land waste;
His cities are burned, without inhabitant.
16 Also the people of [6]Noph and [w]Tahpanhes
Have [7]broken the crown of your head.
17 [x]Have you not brought this on yourself,
In that you have forsaken the LORD your God
When [y]He led you in the way?
18 And now why take [z]the road to Egypt,
To drink the waters of [a]Sihor?
Or why take the road to [b]Assyria,
To drink the waters of [8]the River?
19 Your own wickedness will [c]correct you,
And your backslidings will rebuke you.
Know therefore and see that *it is* an evil and bitter *thing*
That you have forsaken the LORD your God,
And the [9]fear of Me *is* not in you,"
Says the Lord GOD of hosts.

20 "For of old I have [d]broken your yoke *and* burst your bonds;
And [e]you said, 'I will not [1]transgress,'
When [f]on every high hill and under every green tree
You lay down, [g]playing the harlot.
21 Yet I had [h]planted you a noble vine, a seed of highest quality.
How then have you turned before Me
Into [i]the degenerate plant of an alien vine?
22 For though you wash yourself with lye, and use much soap,
Yet your iniquity is [j]marked[2] before Me," says the Lord GOD.

23 "How[k] can you say, 'I am not [3]polluted,
I have not gone after the Baals'?
See your way in the valley;

7 [k]Num. 13:27 [l]Num. 35:33; Is. 24:5; Hos. 4:3
8 [m]Rom. 2:20 [n]Jer. 23:13
9 [o]Jer. 2:35; Ezek. 20:35, 36; Mic. 6:2 [3]*contend with*
10 [p]Jer. 18:13 [4]Heb. *Kittim,* representatative of western cultures [5]In northern Arabian desert, representative of eastern cultures
11 [q]Mic. 4:5 [r]Ps. 115:4; Is. 37:19 [s]Ps. 106:20; Rom. 1:23
13 [t]Ps. 36:9; Jer. 17:13; [John 4:14]
14 [u][Ex. 4:22]
15 [v]Is. 1:7; Jer. 50:17
16 [w]2 Kin. 23:29-37; Jer. 43:7-9 [6]Memphis in ancient Egypt [7]Or *grazed*
17 [x]Jer. 4:18 [y]Deut. 32:10
18 [z]Is. 30:1-3 [a]Josh. 13:3 [b]Hos. 5:13 [8]The Euphrates
19 [c]Is. 3:9; Jer. 4:18; Hos. 5:5 [9]*dread*
20 [d]Lev. 26:13 [e]Ex. 19:8; Josh. 24:18; Judg. 10:16; 1 Sam. 12:10 [f]Deut. 12:2; Is. 57:5, 7; Jer. 3:6 [g]Ex. 34:15 [1]Kt. *serve*
21 [h]Ex. 15:17; Ps. 44:2; 80:8; Is. 5:2 [i]Deut. 32:32; Is. 5:4
22 [j]Job 14:16, 17; Jer. 17:1, 2; Hos. 13:12 [2]*stained*
23 [k]Prov. 30:12 [3]*defiled*

2:8 priests...prophets. Leaders, who did not really know the Lord, set the idolatrous pattern for others (cf. Hos. 4:6).

2:13 two evils. First, Israel had abandoned the Lord, the source of spiritual salvation and sustenance (cf. 17:8; Ps. 36:9; John 4:14). Second, Israel turned to idolatrous objects of trust; Jeremiah compared these with underground water storage devices for rainwater, which were broken and let water seep out, thus proving useless.

2:14 How is it that a people under God's special care are left at the mercy of an enemy, like a worthless slave?

2:15 young lions. The figure represents invading soldiers that burned cities (cf. 4:7), perhaps a reference to the disaster from the Babylonians during Jehoiakim's fourth year, and again 3 years later when he relied on Egypt (cf. 20:4; 46:2; 2 Kin. 24:1,2).

2:16 Noph...Tahpanhes. These two cities in Egypt stood for the country itself.

2:18 Dependence on alliances with Egypt and Assyria was part of national undoing, a source of shame (vv. 36,37). **Sihor.** Refers to the Nile River.

2:19 backslidings. Cf. 3:6,8,11,12,14,22; 8:5; 31:22; 49:4; Is. 57:17; Hos. 11:7; 14:4. For clarification of the meaning, *see note on Prov. 14:14.*

2:23 the Baals. An inclusive term referring collectively to false

Know what you have done:
You are a swift dromedary breaking
loose in her ways,
24 A wild donkey used to the
wilderness,
That sniffs at the wind in her
desire;
In her time of mating, who can
turn her away?
All those who seek her will not
weary themselves;
In her month they will find her.
25 Withhold your foot from being
unshod, and your throat from
thirst.
But you said, [l]'There is no hope.
No! For I have loved [m]aliens, and
after them I will go.'

26 "As the thief is ashamed when he is
found out,
So is the house of Israel ashamed;
They and their kings and their
princes, and their priests and
their [n]prophets,
27 Saying to a tree, 'You *are* my father,'
And to a [o]stone, 'You gave birth to
me.'
For they have turned *their* back to
Me, and not *their* face.
But in the time of their [p]trouble
They will say, 'Arise and save us.'
28 But [q]where *are* your gods that you
have made for yourselves?
Let them arise,
If they [r]can save you in the time of
your [4]trouble;
For [s]*according to* the number of
your cities
Are your gods, O Judah.

29 "Why will you plead with Me?
You all have transgressed against
Me," says the LORD.
30 "In vain I have [t]chastened your
children;
They [u]received no correction.
Your sword has [v]devoured your
prophets
Like a destroying lion.

31 "O generation, see the word of the
LORD!
Have I been a wilderness to Israel,
Or a land of darkness?
Why do My people say, 'We [5]are
lords;
[w]We will come no more to You'?
32 Can a virgin forget her ornaments,
Or a bride her attire?
Yet My people [x]have forgotten Me
days without number.

33 "Why do you beautify your way to
seek love?
Therefore you have also taught
The wicked women your ways.
34 Also on your skirts is found
[y]The blood of the lives of the poor
innocents.
I have not found it by [6]secret
search,
But plainly on all these things.
35 [z]Yet you say, 'Because I am
innocent,
Surely His anger shall turn from
me.'
Behold, [a]I will plead My case
against you,
[b]Because you say, 'I have not
sinned.'
36 [c]Why do you gad about so much to
change your way?
Also [d]you shall be ashamed of
Egypt [e]as you were ashamed
of Assyria.
37 Indeed you will go forth from him
With your hands on [f]your head;
For the LORD has rejected your
trusted allies,
And you will [g]not prosper by
them.

Israel Is Shameless

3 "They say, 'If a man divorces his wife,
And she goes from him
And becomes another man's,
[a]May he return to her again?'
Would not that [b]land be greatly
polluted?
But you have [c]played the harlot
with many lovers;
[d]Yet return to Me," says the LORD.

2 "Lift up your eyes to [e]the desolate
heights and see:
Where have you not [1]lain *with*
men?
[f]By the road you have sat for them
Like an Arabian in the wilderness;

25 [l]Is. 57:10; Jer. 18:12 [m]Jer. 3:13
26 [n]Is. 28:7; Jer. 5:31
27 [o]Jer. 3:9 [p]Judg. 10:10; Is. 26:16; Hos. 5:15
28 [q]Deut. 32:37; Judg. 10:14 [r]Is. 45:20 [s]2 Kin. 17:30, 31; Jer. 11:13 [4]Or *evil*
30 [t]Is. 9:13 [u]Is. 1:5; Jer. 5:3; 7:28 [v]Neh. 9:26; Jer. 26:20-24; Acts 7:52; 1 Thess. 2:15
31 [w]Deut. 32:15; Jer. 2:20, 25 [5]*have dominion*
32 [x]Ps. 106:21; Is. 17:10; Jer. 3:21; 13:25; Hos. 8:14
34 [y]2 Kin. 21:16; 24:4; Ps. 106:38; Jer. 7:6; 19:4 [6]*digging*
35 [z]Jer. 2:23, 29; Mal. 2:17; 3:8 [a]Jer. 2:9 [b][Prov. 28:13; 1 John 1:8, 10]
36 [c]Jer. 31:22; Hos. 5:13; 12:1 [d]Is. 30:3 [e]2 Chr. 28:16
37 [f]2 Sam. 13:19; Jer. 14:3, 4 [g]Jer. 37:7-10

CHAPTER 3

1 [a]Deut. 24:1-4 [b]Jer. 2:7 [c]Jer. 2:20; Ezek. 16:26 [d]Jer. 4:1; [Zech. 1:3]
2 [e]Deut. 12:2; Jer. 2:20; 3:21; 7:29 [f]Prov. 23:28 [1]Lit. *been violated*

deities. **dromedary.** The nation, in chasing other idols, is depicted as a female camel pursuing its instinct, and as a wild ass in heat sniffing the wind to find a mate, craving to attract others of its kind. Other pictures of Israel are that of a thief, who is ashamed when exposed (v. 26), and that of a maid or a bride who forgets what beautifies her (v. 32).

3:1 If a man divorces. Such a man was not to take that woman as his wife again, for this would defile her (Deut. 24:4) and be a scandal. Jeremiah used this analogy to picture Israel as a harlot in the spiritual realm, with many lovers, i.e., nations (2:18,25) and idols (2:23-25; 3:2,6-9). Yet, the Lord would graciously receive Israel or Judah back as His wife if she would repent (3:12-14).

[g]And you have polluted the land
With your harlotries and your
wickedness.
3 Therefore the [h]showers have been
withheld,
And there has been no latter rain.
You have had a [i]harlot's forehead;
You refuse to be ashamed.
4 Will you not from this time cry to
Me,
'My Father, You *are* [j]the guide of
[k]my youth?
5 [l]Will He remain angry forever?
Will He keep it to the end?'
Behold, you have spoken and done
evil things,
As you were able."

A Call to Repentance

6 The LORD said also to me in the days of
Josiah the king: "Have you seen what
[m]backsliding Israel has done? She has
[n]gone up on every high mountain and
under every green tree, and there played
the harlot. 7 [o]And I said, after she had done
all these *things,* 'Return to Me.' But she did
not return. And her treacherous [p]sister Judah saw it. 8 Then I saw that [q]for all the
causes for which backsliding Israel had
committed adultery, I had [r]put her away
and given her a certificate of divorce; [s]yet
her treacherous sister Judah did not fear,
but went and played the harlot also. 9 So it
came to pass, through her casual harlotry,
that she [t]defiled the land and committed
adultery with [u]stones and trees. 10 And yet
for all this her treacherous sister Judah has
not turned to Me [v]with her whole heart,
but in pretense," says the LORD.
11 Then the LORD said to me, [w]"Backsliding Israel has shown herself more righteous than treacherous Judah. 12 Go and
proclaim these words toward [x]the north,
and say:

'Return, backsliding Israel,' says the
LORD;
'I will not cause My anger to fall on
you.
For I *am* [y]merciful,' says the LORD;
'I will not remain angry forever.
13 [z]Only acknowledge your iniquity,
That you have transgressed against
the LORD your God,
And have [a]scattered your [2]charms
To [b]alien deities [c]under every
green tree,
And you have not obeyed My
voice,' says the LORD.

14 "Return, O backsliding children,"
says the LORD; [d]"for I am married to you. I
will take you, [e]one from a city and two
from a family, and I will bring you to [f]Zion.
15 And I will give you [g]shepherds according to My heart, who will [h]feed you with
knowledge and understanding.
16 "Then it shall come to pass, when you
are multiplied and [i]increased in the land in
those days," says the LORD, "that they will
say no more, 'The ark of the covenant of
the LORD.' [j]It shall not come to mind, nor
shall they remember it, nor shall they visit
it, nor shall it be made anymore.
17 "At that time Jerusalem shall be
called The Throne of the LORD, and all the
nations shall be gathered to it, [k]to the
name of the LORD, to Jerusalem. No more
shall they [l]follow [3] the dictates of their evil
hearts.
18 "In those days [m]the house of Judah
shall walk with the house of Israel, and
they shall come together out of the land of
[n]the north to [o]the land that I have given as
an inheritance to your fathers.
19 "But I said:

'How can I put you among the
children
And give you [p]a pleasant land,
A beautiful heritage of the hosts of
nations?'

"And I said:

'You shall call Me, [q]"My Father,"
And not turn away from Me.'

2 [g] Jer. 2:7
3 [h] Lev. 26:19; Jer. 14:3-6 [i] Zeph. 3:5
4 [j] Ps. 71:17; Prov. 2:17 [k] Jer. 2:2; Hos. 2:15
5 [l] Ps. 103:9; [Is. 57:16]; Jer. 3:12
6 [m] Jer. 7:24 [n] Jer. 2:20
7 [o] 2 Kin. 17:13 [p] Jer. 3:11; Ezek. 16:47, 48
8 [q] Ezek. 23:9 [r] 2 Kin. 17:6; Is. 50:1 [s] Ezek. 23:11
9 [t] Jer. 2:7 [u] Is. 57:6; Jer. 2:27
10 [v] Jer. 12:2; Hos. 7:14
11 [w] Ezek. 16:51, 52
12 [x] 2 Kin. 17:6
[y] Ps. 86:15; Jer. 12:15; 31:20; 33:26
13 [z] Lev. 26:40; Deut. 30:1, 2; [Prov. 28:13; 1 John 1:9] [a] Ezek. 16:15 [b] Jer. 2:25 [c] Deut. 12:2 [2] Lit. *ways*
14 [d] Jer. 31:32; Hos. 2:19, 20 [e] Jer. 31:6 [f] [Rom. 11:5]
15 [g] Jer. 23:4; 31:10; [Ezek. 34:23]; Eph. 4:11 [h] Acts 20:28
16 [i] Is. 49:19; Jer. 23:3 [j] Is. 65:17
17 [k] Is. 60:9 [l] Deut. 29:19; Jer. 7:24 [3] *walk after the stubbornness* or *imagination*
18 [m] Is. 11:13; Jer. 50:4; Ezek. 37:16-22; Hos. 1:11 [n] Jer. 31:8 [o] Amos 9:15
19 [p] Ps. 106:24 [q] Is. 63:16; Jer. 3:4

3:6 backsliding. Also 3:8,11,12,14. *See note on Prov. 14:14.*

3:8 I had put her away and given her a certificate of divorce. Though God hates divorce (Mal. 2:16), it is tolerated for unrepentant adultery (*see notes on Matt. 5:32; 19:8,9*), as indicated by this analogy of God's divorcing Israel for that continual sin in the spiritual realm. God had divorced Israel but not yet Judah (cf. Is. 50:1). Cf. Ezra 10:3, where divorce is the right action of God's people to separate from idolatrous wives.

3:14 I am married to you. God pictured His covenant relationship with Israel as a marriage, and pleaded with mercy for Judah to repent and return. He will take her back. Cf. Hosea's restoration of Gomer as a picture of God taking back His wicked, adulterous people.

3:16-18 it shall come to pass…in those days. When Israel repents (vv. 13,14,22), which has not happened, but will in the millennial era of God's restoration that the prophets often describe (Jer. 23:5,6; 30–33; Ezek. 36), God will bring these blessings: 1) shepherds to teach them the truth; 2) His own immediate presence on the throne in Jerusalem, not just the ark of His covenant; 3) allegiance even of Gentile nations; 4) righteousness; 5) genuineness in worship; 6) unity of Israel (north) and Judah (south) into one kingdom; and 7) reestablishment in their own Promised Land.

3:19 put you among the children. Here is a reference to adoption into God's family, when the people turn back from idols to acknowledge Him as "Father."

20 Surely, *as* a wife treacherously
departs from her [4]husband,
So [r]have you dealt treacherously
with Me,
O house of Israel," says the LORD.

21 A voice was heard on [s]the desolate
heights,
Weeping *and* supplications of the
children of Israel.
For they have perverted their way;
They have forgotten the LORD their
God.

22 "Return, you backsliding children,
And I will [t]heal your backslidings."

"Indeed we do come to You,
For You are the LORD our God.
23 [u]Truly, in vain *is salvation hoped for*
from the hills,
And from the multitude of
mountains;
[v]Truly, in the LORD our God
Is the salvation of Israel.
24 [w]For shame has devoured
The labor of our fathers from our
youth—
Their flocks and their herds,
Their sons and their daughters.
25 We lie down in our shame,
And our [5]reproach covers us.
[x]For we have sinned against the
LORD our God,
We and our fathers,
From our youth even to this day,
And [y]have not obeyed the voice of
the LORD our God."

4 "If you will return, O Israel," says
the LORD,
[a]"Return to Me;
And if you will put away your
abominations out of My sight,
Then you shall not be moved.
2 [b]And you shall swear, 'The LORD
lives,'
[c]In truth, in [1]judgment, and in
righteousness;
[d]The nations shall bless themselves
in Him,
And in Him they shall [e]glory."

3 For thus says the LORD to the men of
Judah and Jerusalem:

[f]"Break up your [2]fallow ground,
And [g]do not sow among thorns.
4 [h]Circumcise yourselves to the LORD,
And take away the foreskins of
your hearts,
You men of Judah and inhabitants
of Jerusalem,
Lest My fury come forth like fire,
And burn so that no one can
quench *it*,
Because of the evil of your doings."

An Imminent Invasion

5 Declare in Judah and proclaim in Jerusalem, and say:

[i]"Blow the trumpet in the land;
Cry, 'Gather together,'
And say, [j]'Assemble yourselves,
And let us go into the fortified
cities.'
6 Set up the [3]standard toward Zion.
Take refuge! Do not delay!
For I will bring disaster from the
[k]north,
And great destruction."

7 [l]The lion has come up from his
thicket,
And [m]the destroyer of nations is
on his way.
He has gone forth from his place
[n]To make your land desolate.
Your cities will be laid waste,
Without inhabitant.
8 For this, [o]clothe yourself with
sackcloth,

20 [r] Is. 48:8 [4] Lit. *companion*
21 [s] Is. 15:2
22 [t] Jer. 30:17; 33:6; Hos. 6:1; 14:4
23 [u] Ps. 121:1, 2 [v] Ps. 3:8; Prov. 21:31; Jer. 17:14; 31:7; Jon. 2:9
24 [w] Jer. 11:13; 14:20; Hos. 9:10
25 [x] Ezra 9:6, 7 [y] Jer. 22:21 [5] *disgrace*

CHAPTER 4

1 [a] Jer. 3:1, 22; 15:19; Joel 2:12
2 [b] Deut. 10:20; Is. 45:23; 65:16; Jer. 12:16
[c] Is. 48:1; Zech. 8:8 [d] [Gen. 22:18]; Ps. 72:18; Is. 65:16; Jer. 3:17; [Gal. 3:8] [e] Is. 45:25; Jer. 9:24; 1 Cor. 1:31; 2 Cor. 10:17 [1] *justice*
3 [f] Hos. 10:12 [g] Matt. 13:7 [2] *untilled*
4 [h] Deut. 10:16; 30:6; Jer. 9:25, 26; [Rom. 2:28, 29; Col. 2:11]
5 [i] Jer. 6:1; Hos. 8:1 [j] Josh. 10:20; Jer. 8:14
6 [k] Jer. 1:13-15; 6:1, 22; 50:17 [3] *banner*
7 [l] 2 Kin. 24:1; Dan. 7:4 [m] Jer. 25:9; Ezek. 26:7-10 [n] Is. 1:7; 6:11; Jer. 2:15
8 [o] Is. 22:12; Jer. 6:26

3:20 a wife treacherously departs. Hosea had earlier used this same imagery (ca. 755–710 B.C.). Thus God had given the divorce because the spiritual adultery was unrepentant. But when repentance comes, He will take Israel back (cf. 3:1). **O...Israel.** Since the irretrievable dispersion of Israel in the N (722 B.C.) Judah alone was left to be called by the name Israel, as Jeremiah sometimes chose to do (i.e., 3:20-23).

4:3 "Break up..." Jeremiah appealed for a spiritual turnabout from sinful, wasteful lives. He pictured this as the plowing of ground, formerly hard and unproductive due to weeds, in order to make it useful for sowing (cf. Matt. 13:18-23).

4:4 Circumcise. This surgery (Gen. 17:10-14) was to cut away flesh that could hold disease in its folds and could pass the disease on to wives. It was important for the preservation of God's people physically. But it was also a symbol of the need for the heart to be cleansed from sin's deadly disease. The really essential surgery needed to happen on the inside, where God calls for taking away fleshly things that keep the heart from being spiritually devoted to Him and from true faith in Him and His will. Jeremiah later expanded on this theme (31:31-34; cf. Deut. 10:16; 30:6; Rom. 2:29). God selected the reproductive organ as the location of the symbol for man's need of cleansing for sin, because it is the instrument most indicative of his depravity, since by it he reproduces generations of sinners.

4:6,7 disaster from the north. This evil is Babylon's army, which would invade from that direction. The "lion" on the prowl fit Babylon because of its conquering power, and Babylon was symbolized by the winged lions guarding its royal court. Babylon is later identified in 20:4. Many details in chap. 4 graphically depict warriors in conquest (vv. 7,13,29).

Lament and wail.
For the fierce anger of the LORD
Has not turned back from us.

9 "And it shall come to pass in that day," says the LORD,
"*That* the heart of the king shall perish,
And the heart of the princes;
The priests shall be astonished,
And the prophets shall wonder."

10 Then I said, "Ah, Lord GOD!
[p]Surely You have greatly deceived this people and Jerusalem,
[q]Saying, 'You shall have peace,'
Whereas the sword reaches to the [4]heart."

11 At that time it will be said
To this people and to Jerusalem,
[r]"A dry wind of the desolate heights *blows* in the wilderness
Toward the daughter of My people—
Not to fan or to cleanse—
12 A wind too strong for these will come for Me;
Now [s]I will also speak judgment against them."

13 "Behold, he shall come up like clouds,
And [t]his chariots like a whirlwind.
[u]His horses are swifter than eagles.
Woe to us, for we are plundered!"

14 O Jerusalem, [v]wash your heart from wickedness,
That you may be saved.
How long shall your evil thoughts lodge within you?
15 For a voice declares [w]from Dan
And proclaims [5]affliction from Mount Ephraim:
16 "Make mention to the nations,
Yes, proclaim against Jerusalem,
That watchers come from a [x]far country
And raise their voice against the cities of Judah.

10 [p] 2 Kin. 25:10-12; Ezek. 14:9; 2 Thess. 2:11 [q] Jer. 5:12; 14:13 [4] Lit. *soul*
11 [r] Jer. 51:1; Ezek. 17:10; Hos. 13:15
12 [s] Jer. 1:16
13 [t] Is. 5:28 [u] Deut. 28:49; Lam. 4:19; Hos. 8:1; Hab. 1:8
14 [v] Prov. 1:22; Is. 1:16; Jer. 13:27; James 4:8
15 [w] Jer. 8:16; 50:17 [5] Or *wickedness*
16 [x] Is. 39:3; Jer. 5:15

17 [y]Like keepers of a field they are against her all around,
Because she has been rebellious against Me," says the LORD.
18 "Your[z] ways and your doings
Have procured these *things* for you.
This *is* your wickedness,
Because it is bitter,
Because it reaches to your heart."

Sorrow for the Doomed Nation

19 O my [a]soul, my soul!
I am pained in my very heart!
My heart makes a noise in me;
I cannot hold my peace,
Because you have heard, O my soul,
The sound of the trumpet,
The alarm of war.
20 [b]Destruction upon destruction is cried,
For the whole land is plundered.
Suddenly [c]my tents are plundered,
And my curtains in a moment.
21 How long will I see the [6]standard,
And hear the sound of the trumpet?

22 "For My people *are* foolish,
They have not known Me.
They *are* [7]silly children,
And they have no understanding.
[d]They *are* wise to do evil,
But to do good they have no knowledge."

23 [e]I beheld the earth, and indeed *it was* [f]without form, and void;
And the heavens, they *had* no light.
24 [g]I beheld the mountains, and indeed they trembled,
And all the hills moved back and forth.
25 I beheld, and indeed *there was* no man,
And [h]all the birds of the heavens had fled.
26 I beheld, and indeed the fruitful land *was* a [i]wilderness,
And all its cities were broken down

17 [y] 2 Kin. 25:1, 4
18 [z] Ps. 107:17; Is. 50:1; Jer. 2:17, 19
19 [a] 2 Kin. 25:11; 2 Chr. 36:20; Is. 15:5; 16:11; 21:3; 22:4; Jer. 9:1, 10; 20:9
20 [b] Ps. 42:7; Ezek. 7:26 [c] Jer. 10:20
21 [6] *banner*
22 [d] Jer. 9:3; 13:23; Rom. 16:19; 1 Cor. 14:20 [7] *foolish*
23 [e] Is. 24:19 [f] Gen. 1:2
24 [g] Is. 5:25; Jer. 10:10; Ezek. 38:20
25 [h] Jer. 9:10; 12:4; Zeph. 1:3
26 [i] Jer. 9:10

4:10 deceived. Like Habakkuk (1:12-17), Jeremiah was horrified at these words of judgment, contrasting the prevailing hope of peace. God is sometimes described as if doing a thing He merely permits, such as allowing false prophets who delude themselves to also deceive a sinful people into thinking peace would follow (cf. 6:14; 8:11; 1 Kin. 22:21-24). God sees how people insist on their delusions, and lets it happen.

4:14 wash. Jeremiah continued to appeal for a dealing with sin so that national destruction might be averted (v. 20), while there was still time to repent (cf. chaps. 7,26).

4:22 wise to do evil. Israelites were wise in doing evil but were dull in knowing to do the good, i.e., God's will. Paul, applying the principle but turning it to the positive, wanted the believers at Rome to be wise to do good but unlearned in the skill of doing evil (Rom. 16:19).

4:23 without form. Jeremiah may be borrowing the language, but the description in its context is not of creation in Gen. 1:2, but of judgment on the land of Israel and its cities (v. 20). The invader left it desolate of the previous form and void of inhabitants due to slaying and flight (v. 25). The heavens gave no light, possibly due to smoke from fires that were destroying cities (vv. 7,20).

At the presence of the LORD,
By His fierce anger.

27 For thus says the LORD:

"The whole land shall be desolate;
[j]Yet I will not make a full end.
28 For this [k]shall the earth mourn,
And [l]the heavens above be black,
Because I have spoken.
I have [m]purposed and [n]will not
relent,
Nor will I turn back from it.
29 The whole city shall flee from the
noise of the horsemen and
bowmen.
They shall go into thickets and
climb up on the rocks.
Every city *shall be* forsaken,
And not a man shall dwell in it.

30 "And *when* you *are* plundered,
What will you do?
Though you clothe yourself with
crimson,
Though you adorn *yourself* with
ornaments of gold,
[o]Though you enlarge your eyes
with paint,
In vain you will make yourself fair;
[p]*Your* lovers will despise you;
They will seek your life.

31 "For I have heard a voice as of a
woman in [8]labor,
The anguish as of her who brings
forth her first child,
The voice of the daughter of Zion
bewailing herself;
She [q]spreads her hands, *saying*,
'Woe *is* me now, for my soul is
[9]weary
Because of murderers!'

The Justice of God's Judgment

5 "Run to and fro through the streets
of Jerusalem;
See now and know;
And seek in her open places
[a]If you can find a man,
[b]If there is *anyone* who executes
[1]judgment,
Who seeks the truth,
[c]And I will pardon her.

2 [d]Though they say, '*As* [e]the LORD
lives,'
Surely they [f]swear falsely."

3 O LORD, *are* not [g]Your eyes on the
truth?
You have [h]stricken them,
But they have not grieved;
You have consumed them,
But [i]they have refused to receive
correction.
They have made their faces harder
than rock;
They have refused to return.

4 Therefore I said, "Surely these *are*
poor.
They are foolish;
For [j]they do not know the way of
the LORD,
The judgment of their God.
5 I will go to the great men and
speak to them,
For [k]they have known the way of
the LORD,
The judgment of their God."
But these have altogether [l]broken
the yoke
And burst the bonds.
6 Therefore [m]a lion from the forest
shall slay them,
[n]A wolf of the deserts shall destroy
them;
[o]A leopard will watch over their
cities.
Everyone who goes out from there
shall be torn in pieces,
Because their transgressions are
many;
Their backslidings have increased.

7 "How shall I pardon you for this?
Your children have forsaken Me
And [p]sworn by *those* [q]*that are* not
gods.
[r]When I had fed them to the full,
Then they committed adultery
And assembled themselves by
troops in the harlots' houses.
8 [s]They were *like* well-fed lusty
stallions;
Every one neighed after his
neighbor's wife.

27 [j] Jer. 5:10, 18; 30:11; 46:28 **28** [k] Jer. 12:4, 11; 14:2; Hos. 4:3 [l] Is. 5:30; 50:3; Joel 2:30, 31 [m] Is. 46:10, 11; [Dan. 4:35] [n] [Num. 23:19]; Jer. 7:16; 23:30; 30:24 **30** [o] 2 Kin. 9:30; Ezek. 23:40 [p] Jer. 22:20, 22; Lam. 1:2, 19; Ezek. 23:9, 10, 22 **31** [q] Is. 1:15; Lam. 1:17 [8] *childbirth* [9] *faint*

CHAPTER 5

1 [a] Ezek. 22:30 [b] Gen. 18:23-32 [c] Gen. 18:26 [1] *justice*

2 [d] Is. 48:1; Titus 1:16 [e] Jer. 4:2 [f] Jer. 7:9 **3** [g] 2 Kin. 25:1; [2 Chr. 16:9; Jer. 16:17] [h] Is. 1:5; 9:13; Jer. 2:30 [i] Is. 9:13; Jer. 7:28; Zeph. 3:2 **4** [j] Is. 27:11; Jer. 8:7; Hos. 4:6 **5** [k] Mic. 3:1 [l] Ex. 32:25; Ps. 2:3; Jer. 2:20 **6** [m] Jer. 4:7 [n] Ps. 104:20; Ezek. 22:27; Hab. 1:8; Zeph. 3:3 [o] Hos. 13:7 **7** [p] Josh. 23:7; Jer. 12:16; Zeph. 1:5 [q] Deut. 32:21; Jer. 2:11; Gal. 4:8 [r] Deut. 32:15 **8** [s] Jer. 13:27; 29:23; Ezek. 22:11

5:1 find a man. The city was too sinful to have even one man who, by truth and justice, could qualify to be an advocate to secure pardon for Judah. Refusal to repent was the norm (v. 3) for the common people (v. 4) and for the leaders (v. 5).

5:6 lion. Three animals which tear and eat their victims represented the invader: the lion (*see note on 4:6,7*), the wolf, and the leopard, picturing vicious judgment on both poor (v. 4) and rich (v. 5).

5:7 adultery. Often the idea of adultery is figurative for idolatry or political alliances (*see note on 3:1*), but the language here refers to physical adultery by men seeking out a harlot or going to neighbors' wives (v. 8), thus violating the seventh commandment (Ex. 20:14).

9 Shall I not punish *them* for these
things?" says the LORD.
"And shall I not [t]avenge Myself on
such a nation as this?

10 "Go up on her walls and destroy,
But do not [2]make a [u]complete end.
Take away her branches,
For they *are* not the LORD's.
11 For [v]the house of Israel and the
house of Judah
Have dealt very treacherously with
Me," says the LORD.

12 [w]They have lied about the LORD,
And said, [x]"*It is* not He.
[y]Neither will [3]evil come upon us,
Nor shall we see sword or famine.
13 And the prophets become wind,
For the word *is* not in them.
Thus shall it be done to them."

14 Therefore thus says the LORD God of
hosts:

"Because you speak this word,
[z]Behold, I will make My words in
your mouth fire,
And this people wood,
And it shall devour them.
15 Behold, I will bring a [a]nation
against you [b]from afar,
O house of Israel," says the LORD.
"It *is* a mighty nation,
It *is* an ancient nation,
A nation whose language you do
not know,
Nor can you understand what they
say.
16 Their quiver *is* like an open tomb;
They *are* all mighty men.
17 And they shall eat up your
[c]harvest and your bread,
Which your sons and daughters
should eat.
They shall eat up your flocks and
your herds;
They shall eat up your vines and
your fig trees;
They shall destroy your fortified
cities,
In which you trust, with the sword.

18 "Nevertheless in those days," says the
LORD, "I [d]will not [4]make a complete end of
you. 19 And it will be when you say, [e]'Why
does the LORD our God do all these *things*
to us?' then you shall answer them, 'Just as
you have [f]forsaken Me and served foreign
gods in your land, so [g]you shall serve
aliens in a land *that is* not yours.'

20 "Declare this in the house of Jacob
And proclaim it in Judah, saying,
21 'Hear this now, O [h]foolish people,
Without [5]understanding,
Who have eyes and see not,
And who have ears and hear not:
22 [i]Do you not fear Me?' says the
LORD.
'Will you not tremble at My
presence,
Who have placed the sand as the
[j]bound of the sea,
By a perpetual decree, that it
cannot pass beyond it?
And though its waves toss to and
fro,
Yet they cannot prevail;
Though they roar, yet they cannot
pass over it.
23 But this people has a defiant and
rebellious heart;
They have revolted and departed.
24 They do not say in their heart,
"Let us now fear the LORD our God,
[k]Who gives rain, both the [l]former
and the latter, in its season.
[m]He reserves for us the appointed
weeks of the harvest."
25 [n]Your iniquities have turned these
things away,
And your sins have withheld good
from you.

26 'For among My people are found
wicked *men;*
They [o]lie in wait as one who sets
snares;
They set a trap;
They catch men.
27 As a cage is full of birds,
So their houses *are* full of deceit.
Therefore they have become great
and grown rich.

9 [t] Jer. 9:9
10 [u] Jer. 4:27 [2] *completely destroy*
11 [v] Jer. 3:6, 7, 20
12 [w] 2 Chr. 36:16; Jer. 4:10 [x] Is. 28:15; 47:8; Jer. 23:17 [y] Jer. 14:13 [3] *disaster*
14 [z] Is. 24:6; Jer. 1:9; 23:29; Hos. 6:5; Zech. 1:6
15 [a] Deut. 28:49; Is. 5:26; Jer. 1:15; 6:22 [b] Is. 39:3; Jer. 4:16
17 [c] Lev. 26:16; Deut. 28:31, 33; Jer. 8:16; 50:7, 17
18 [d] Jer. 30:11; Amos 9:8 [4] *completely destroy*
19 [e] Deut. 29:24-29; 1 Kin. 9:8, 9; Jer. 13:22; 16:10-13 [f] Jer. 1:16; 2:13 [g] Deut. 28:48; Jer. 16:13
21 [h] Is. 6:9; Jer. 6:10; Ezek. 12:2; Matt. 13:14; John 12:40; Acts 28:26; Rom. 11:8 [5] Lit. *heart*
22 [i] Deut. 28:58; Ps. 119:120; Jer. 2:19; 10:7; [Rev. 15:4] [j] Job 26:10
24 [k] Ps. 147:8; Jer. 14:22; [Matt. 5:45]; Acts 14:17 [l] Deut. 11:14; Joel 2:23; James 5:7 [m] [Gen. 8:22]
25 [n] Jer. 3:3
26 [o] Ps. 10:9; Prov. 1:11; Jer. 18:22; Hab. 1:15

5:10 not the LORD's. The people, depicted as vine branches to be destroyed (cf. 11:16,17), did not genuinely know the Lord in a saving relationship, but had forsaken Him and given allegiance to other gods. The description of having eyes but not seeing, and ears but not hearing (v. 21) is used by Isaiah (6:9) and Jesus Christ (Matt. 13:13) for such false professors as these branches. Jesus also referred to false branches in John 15:2,6 which were burned.

5:14 My words...fire. The judgment of Judah prophesied in God's Word by Jeremiah will bring destruction, but not elimination (v. 18), to the nation, cf. 23:29.

5:22 sand...of the sea. God's providential acts in the natural world such as 1) creating the seashore to prevent flooding, 2) giving rain at the appropriate times (v. 24), and 3) providing time for harvest (v. 24) are witness enough to the Lord's reality and grace. As the nation turns away from God, He will take these unappreciated gifts away (v. 25).

28 They have grown [p]fat, they are
sleek;
Yes, they [6]surpass the deeds of the
wicked;
They do not plead [q]the cause,
The cause of the fatherless;
[r]Yet they prosper,
And the right of the needy they do
not defend.
29 [s]Shall I not punish *them* for these
things?' says the LORD.
'Shall I not avenge Myself on such a
nation as this?'

30 "An astonishing and [t]horrible thing
Has been committed in the land:
31 The prophets prophesy [u]falsely,
And the priests rule by their *own*
power;
And My people [v]love *to have it* so.
But what will you do in the end?

Impending Destruction from the North

6 "O you children of Benjamin,
Gather yourselves to flee from the
midst of Jerusalem!
Blow the trumpet in Tekoa,
And set up a signal-fire in [a]Beth
Haccerem;
[b]For disaster appears out of the
north,
And great destruction.
2 I have likened the daughter of Zion
To a lovely and delicate woman.
3 The [c]shepherds with their flocks
shall come to her.
They shall pitch *their* tents against
her all around.
Each one shall pasture in his own
place."

4 "Prepare[d] war against her;
Arise, and let us go up [e]at noon.
Woe to us, for the day goes away,
For the shadows of the evening are
lengthening.
5 Arise, and let us go by night,
And let us destroy her palaces."

6 For thus has the LORD of hosts said:

"Cut down trees,
And build a mound against
Jerusalem.

This *is* the city to be punished.
She *is* full of oppression in her
midst.
7 [f]As a fountain [1]wells up with water,
So she wells up with her
wickedness.
[g]Violence and plundering are heard
in her.
Before Me continually *are* [2]grief
and wounds.
8 Be instructed, O Jerusalem,
Lest [h]My soul depart from you;
Lest I make you desolate,
A land not inhabited."

9 Thus says the LORD of hosts:

"They shall thoroughly glean as a
vine the remnant of Israel;
As a grape-gatherer, put your hand
back into the branches."

10 To whom shall I speak and give
warning,
That they may hear?
Indeed their [i]ear *is* uncircumcised,
And they cannot give heed.
Behold, [j]the word of the LORD is a
reproach to them;
They have no delight in it.
11 Therefore I am full of the fury of
the LORD.
[k]I am weary of holding *it* in.
"I will pour it out [l]on the children
outside,
And on the assembly of young
men together;
For even the husband shall be
taken with the wife,
The aged with *him who is* full of
days.
12 And [m]their houses shall be turned
over to others,
Fields and wives together;
For I will stretch out My hand
Against the inhabitants of the
land," says the LORD.
13 "Because from the least of them
even to the greatest of them,
Everyone *is* given to
[n]covetousness;
And from the prophet even to the
[o]priest,
Everyone deals falsely.

28 [p] Deut. 32:15 [q] Is. 1:23; Jer. 7:6; 22:3; Zech. 7:10 [r] Job 12:6; Ps. 73:12 [6] Or *pass over* or *overlook*
29 [s] Jer. 5:9; Mal. 3:5
30 [t] Jer. 23:14; Hos. 6:10; 2 Tim. 4:3
31 [u] Jer. 14:14; Ezek. 13:6 [v] Mic. 2:11

CHAPTER 6

1 [a] Neh. 3:14 [b] Jer. 4:6
3 [c] 2 Kin. 25:1-4; Jer. 4:17; 12:10
4 [d] Jer. 51:27; Joel 3:9 [e] Jer. 15:8; Zeph. 2:4
7 [f] Is. 57:20 [g] Ps. 55:9 [1] *gushes* [2] *sickness*
8 [h] Ezek. 23:18; Hos. 9:12
10 [i] Ex. 6:12; Jer. 5:21; 7:26; [Acts 7:51] [j] Jer. 8:9; 20:8
11 [k] Jer. 20:9 [l] Jer. 9:21
12 [m] Deut. 28:30; Jer. 8:10; 38:22
13 [n] Is. 56:11; Jer. 8:10; 22:17 [o] Jer. 5:31; 23:11; Mic. 3:5, 11

5:31 prophesy falsely. These included prophets with bogus messages, priests who asserted their own authority, and also followers who indulged such falseness. All are guilty before God.

6:1 Tekoa...Beth Haccerem. Tekoa, the home of Amos, is 6 mi. S of Bethlehem. The location of Beth Haccerem ("vineyard house") is unknown, but probably near Tekoa. As the enemy came from the N, the people would flee S. **north.** *See note on 4:6,7.*

6:3 shepherds. These were hostile leaders of the invading Babylonians, whose soldiers were compared with flocks.

6:6 Cut down trees. A besieging tactic is described in which trees were used to build up ramps against the city walls.

6:9 thoroughly glean. Unlike the benevolent practice of leaving food in the field for the poor to glean (Lev. 19:9,10; Ruth 2:5-18), the Babylonians will leave no one when they "harvest" Judah.

14 They have also [p]healed the [3]hurt of
My people [4]slightly,
[q]Saying, 'Peace, peace!'
When *there is* no peace.
15 Were they [r]ashamed when they
had committed abomination?
No! They were not at all ashamed;
Nor did they know how to blush.
Therefore they shall fall among
those who fall;
At the time I punish them,
They shall be cast down," says the
LORD.

16 Thus says the LORD:

"Stand in the ways and see,
And ask for the [s]old paths, where
the good way *is*,
And walk in it;
Then you will find [t]rest for your
souls.
But they said, 'We will not walk *in*
it.'
17 Also, I set [u]watchmen over you,
saying,
[v]'Listen to the sound of the trumpet!'
But they said, 'We will not listen.'
18 Therefore hear, you nations,
And know, O congregation, what *is*
among them.
19 [w]Hear, O earth!
Behold, I will certainly bring
[x]calamity on this people—
[y]The fruit of their thoughts,
Because they have not heeded My
words
Nor My law, but rejected it.
20 [z]For what purpose to Me
Comes frankincense [a]from Sheba,
And [b]sweet cane from a far
country?
[c]Your burnt offerings *are* not
acceptable,
Nor your sacrifices sweet to Me."

21 Therefore thus says the LORD:

"Behold, I will lay stumbling blocks
before this people,
And the fathers and the sons
together shall fall on them.
The neighbor and his friend shall
perish."

22 Thus says the LORD:

"Behold, a people comes from the
[d]north country,
And a great nation will be raised
from the farthest parts of the
earth.
23 They will lay hold on bow and
spear;
They *are* cruel and have no mercy;
Their voice [e]roars like the sea;
And they ride on horses,
As men of war set in array against
you, O daughter of Zion."

24 We have heard the report of it;
Our hands grow feeble.
[f]Anguish has taken hold of us,
Pain as of a woman in [5]labor.
25 Do not go out into the field,
Nor walk by the way.
Because of the sword of the enemy,
Fear *is* on every side.
26 O daughter of my people,
[g] Dress in sackcloth
[h]And roll about in ashes!
[i]Make mourning *as for* an only son,
most bitter lamentation;
For the plunderer will suddenly
come upon us.

27 "I have set you *as* an assayer *and* [j]a
fortress among My people,
That you may know and test their
way.
28 [k]They *are* all stubborn rebels,
[l]walking as slanderers.
They are [m]bronze and iron,
They *are* all corrupters;
29 The bellows blow fiercely,
The lead is consumed by the fire;
The smelter refines in vain,
For the wicked are not drawn off.
30 *People* will call them [n]rejected
silver,
Because the LORD has rejected
them."

14 [p] Jer. 8:11-15; Ezek. 13:10 [q] Jer. 4:10; 23:17 [3] Lit. *crushing* [4] Superficially
15 [r] Jer. 3:3; 8:12
16 [s] Is. 8:20; Jer. 18:15; Mal. 4:4; Luke 16:29 [t] Matt. 11:29
17 [u] Is. 21:11; 58:1; Jer. 25:4; Ezek. 3:17; Hab. 2:1 [v] Deut. 4:1
19 [w] Is. 1:2 [x] Jer. 19:3, 15 [y] Prov. 1:31
20 [z] Ps. 40:6; 50:7-9; Is. 1:11; 66:3; Amos 5:21; Mic. 6:6, 7 [a] Is. 60:6 [b] Is. 43:24 [c] Jer. 7:21-23
22 [d] Jer. 1:15; 10:22; 50:41-43
23 [e] Is. 5:30
24 [f] Jer. 4:31; 13:21; 49:24 [5] *childbirth*
26 [g] Jer. 4:8 [h] Jer. 25:34; Mic. 1:10 [i] Amos 8:10; [Zech. 12:10]
27 [j] Jer. 1:18
28 [k] Jer. 5:23 [l] Jer. 9:4 [m] Ezek. 22:18
30 [n] Is. 1:22; Jer. 7:29

6:14 'Peace, peace!' Wicked leaders among the prophets and priests (v. 13) proclaimed peace falsely and gave weak and brief comfort. They provided no true healing from the spiritual wound, not having discernment to deal with the sin and its effects (v. 15). The need was to return to obedience (v. 16). Cf. 8:11.

6:16 Here is the image of travelers who are lost, stopping to inquire about the right way they once knew before they wandered so far off it.

6:17 watchmen. Prophets.

6:20 not acceptable. Using imported fragrances in their offerings did not make them sweetly acceptable to God when the worshipers rejected His word (v. 19).

6:21 stumbling blocks. Cf. Matt. 21:44; Is. 8:14; 1 Pet. 2:8.

6:22,23 A description of the Babylonians.

6:27-30 I have set you. God placed Jeremiah as a kind of assayer to test the people's obedience. He also was a "fortress," meaning a "tester" who works with metals. Their sin prevented them from being pure silver, but rather they were bronze, iron, lead, even impure silver, so that they failed the test.

Trusting in Lying Words

7 The word that came to Jeremiah from
the LORD, saying, 2 [a]"Stand in the gate
of the LORD's house, and proclaim there
this word, and say, 'Hear the word of the
LORD, all *you of* Judah who enter in at these
gates to worship the LORD!' " 3 Thus says
the LORD of hosts, the God of Israel:
[b]"Amend your ways and your doings, and
I will cause you to dwell in this place.
4 [c]Do not trust in these lying words, saying, 'The temple of the LORD, the temple of
the LORD, the temple of the LORD *are* these.'
5 "For if you thoroughly amend your
ways and your doings, if you thoroughly
[d]execute [1]judgment between a man and
his neighbor, 6 *if* you do not oppress the
stranger, the fatherless, and the widow,
and do not shed innocent blood in this
place, [e]or walk after other gods to your
hurt, 7 [f]then I will cause you to dwell in
this place, in [g]the land that I gave to your
fathers forever and ever.
8 "Behold, you trust in [h]lying words that
cannot profit. 9 [i]Will you steal, murder,
commit adultery, swear falsely, burn incense to Baal, and [j]walk after other gods
whom you do not know, 10 [k]and *then* come
and stand before Me in this house [l]which
is called by My name, and say, 'We are delivered to do all these abominations'?
11 Has [m]this house, which is called by My
name, become a [n]den of thieves in your
eyes? Behold, I, even I, have seen *it*," says
the LORD.
12 "But go now to [o]My place which *was*
in Shiloh, [p]where I set My name at the first,
and see [q]what I did to it because of the
wickedness of My people Israel. 13 And
now, because you have done all these
works," says the LORD, "and I spoke to you,
[r]rising up early and speaking, but you did
not hear, and I [s]called you, but you did not
answer, 14 therefore I will do to the house
which is called by My name, in which you
trust, and to this place which I gave to you
and your fathers, as I have done to [t]Shiloh.
15 And I will cast you out of My sight, [u]as I
have cast out all your brethren—[v]the
whole posterity of Ephraim.
16 "Therefore [w]do not pray for this people, nor lift up a cry or prayer for them, nor
make intercession to Me; [x]for I will not
hear you. 17 Do you not see what they do
in the cities of Judah and in the streets of
Jerusalem? 18 [y]The children gather wood,
the fathers kindle the fire, and the women
knead dough, to make cakes for the queen
of heaven; and *they* [z]pour out drink offerings to other gods, that they may provoke
Me to anger. 19 [a]Do they provoke Me to
anger?" says the LORD. "*Do they* not *provoke*
themselves, to the shame of their own
faces?"
20 Therefore thus says the Lord GOD:
"Behold, My anger and My fury will be
poured out on this place—on man and on
beast, on the trees of the field and on the
fruit of the ground. And it will burn and
not be quenched."
21 Thus says the LORD of hosts, the God
of Israel: [b]"Add your burnt offerings to
your sacrifices and eat meat. 22 [c]For I did
not speak to your fathers, or command
them in the day that I brought them out of
the land of Egypt, concerning burnt offerings or sacrifices. 23 But this is what I commanded them, saying, [d]'Obey My voice,
and [e]I will be your God, and you shall be
My people. And walk in all the ways that I
have commanded you, that it may be well
with you.' 24 [f]Yet they did not obey or in-

CHAPTER 7
2 [a] Jer. 17:19; 26:2
3 [b] Jer. 4:1; 18:11; 26:13
4 [c] Jer. 7:8; Mic. 3:11
5 [d] 1 Kin. 6:12; Jer. 21:12; 22:3 [1] *justice*
6 [e] Deut. 6:14, 15; Jer. 13:10
7 [f] Deut. 4:40 [g] Jer. 3:18
8 [h] Jer. 5:31; 14:13, 14
9 [i] 1 Kin. 18:21; Hos. 4:1, 2; Zeph. 1:5 [j] Ex. 20:3; Jer. 7:6; 19:4
10 [k] Ezek. 23:39 [l] Jer. 7:11, 14; 32:34; 34:15
11 [m] Is. 56:7 [n] Matt. 21:13; Mark 11:17; Luke 19:46
12 [o] Josh. 18:1; Judg. 18:31 [p] Deut. 12:11 [q] 1 Sam. 4:10; Ps. 78:60; Jer. 26:6
13 [r] 2 Chr. 36:15; Jer. 11:7 [s] Prov. 1:24; Is. 65:12; 66:4
14 [t] 1 Sam. 4:10, 11; Ps. 78:60; Jer. 26:6, 9
15 [u] 2 Kin. 17:23 [v] Ps. 78:67; Hos. 7:13; 9:13; 12:1
16 [w] Ex. 32:10; Deut. 9:14; Jer. 11:14 [x] Jer. 15:1
18 [y] Jer. 44:17 [z] Jer. 19:13
19 [a] Deut. 32:16, 21
21 [b] Is. 1:11; Jer. 6:20; Hos. 8:13; Amos 5:21, 22
22 [c] 1 Sam. 15:22; Ps. 51:16; [Hos. 6:6]
23 [d] Ex. 15:26; 16:32; Deut. 6:3 [e] [Ex. 19:5, 6]; Lev. 26:12; [Jer. 11:4; 13:11]
24 [f] Ps. 81:11; Jer. 11:8

7:1 The word that came. This was Jeremiah's first temple sermon (v. 2); another is found in chap. 26. God was aroused against the sins He names (vv. 6,19), especially at His temple becoming a den of thieves (v. 11). The point of this message, however, was that if Israel would repent, even at this late hour, God would still keep the conqueror from coming (vv. 3,7). They must reject lies such as the false hope that peace is certain, based on the reasoning that the Lord would never bring calamity on His own temple (v. 4). They must turn from their sins (v. 3,5,9), and end their hypocrisy (v. 10).

7:7 the land…I gave…forever. God refers to the unconditional element of the land promise in the Abrahamic Covenant (Gen. 12,15,17,22).

7:12 go…to…Shiloh. God calls them to return to Shiloh where the tabernacle dwelt along with the ark of the covenant. He permitted the Philistines to devastate that place (1 Sam. 4), and He is ready to do similarly with Jerusalem, the place of His temple (vv. 13,14).

7:13 rising up early. This refers to the daily ministry of the prophets (cf. v. 25).

7:15 as I have cast out…Ephraim. Ephraim represents the northern kingdom of Israel, since it was the leading tribe (cf. 2 Kin. 17:23). As God exiled them to Assyria (ca. 722 B.C.), though they were more in number and power, so He will do to the southern kingdom.

7:16 do not pray. God told His spokesman not to pray for the people (cf. 11:14). He did not find Judah inclined to repent. Instead, He found the glib use of self-deluding slogans, such as in 7:4, and flagrant idol worship in v. 18 from a people insistent on not hearing (v. 27; 19:15). Cf. 1 John 5:16.

7:18 the queen of heaven. Cf. 44:17-19,25. The Jews were worshiping Ishtar, an Assyrian and Babylonian goddess also called Ashtoreth and Astarte, the wife of Baal or Molech. Because these deities symbolized generative power, their worship involved prostitution.

7:22 I did not…command. Bible writers sometimes use apparent negation to make a comparative emphasis. What God commanded His people at the Exodus was not so much the offerings, as it was the heart obedience which prompted the offerings. See this comparative sense used elsewhere (Deut. 5:3; Hos. 6:6; 1 John 3:18).

7:22,23 offerings…sacrifices…Obey. Here is a crucial emphasis on internal obedience. Cf. Josh. 1:8; 1 Sam. 15:22; Prov. 15:8; 21:3; Is. 1:11-17; Hos. 6:6; Matt. 9:13.

cline their ear, but [g]followed[2] the counsels
and the [3]dictates of their evil hearts, and
[h]went[4] backward and not forward.
25 Since the day that your fathers came out
of the land of Egypt until this day, I have
even [i]sent to you all My servants the
prophets, daily rising up early and sending *them.* **26** [j]Yet they did not obey Me or
incline their ear, but [k]stiffened their neck.
[l]They did worse than their fathers.
27 "Therefore [m]you shall speak all these
words to them, but they will not obey you.
You shall also call to them, but they will
not answer you.

Judgment on Obscene Religion

28 "So you shall say to them, 'This *is* a
nation that does not obey the voice of the
LORD their God [n]nor receive correction.
[o]Truth has perished and has been cut off
from their mouth. **29** [p]Cut off your hair and
cast *it* away, and take up a lamentation on
the desolate heights; for the LORD has rejected and forsaken the generation of His
wrath.' **30** For the children of Judah have
done evil in My sight," says the LORD.
[q]"They have set their abominations in the
house which is called by My name, to [5]pol-
lute it. **31** And they have built the [r]high
places of Tophet, which *is* in the Valley of
the Son of Hinnom, to [s]burn their sons and
their daughters in the fire, [t]which I did not
command, nor did it come into My heart.
32 "Therefore behold, [u]the days are coming," says the LORD, "when it will no more
be called Tophet, or the Valley of the Son of
Hinnom, but the Valley of Slaughter; [v]for
they will bury in Tophet until there is no
room. **33** The [w]corpses of this people will
be food for the birds of the heaven and for
the beasts of the earth. And no one will
frighten *them away.* **34** Then I will cause to
[x]cease from the cities of Judah and from
the streets of Jerusalem the voice of mirth
and the voice of gladness, the voice of the
bridegroom and the voice of the bride. For
[y]the land shall be desolate.

8 "At that time," says the LORD, "they
shall bring out the bones of the kings
of Judah, and the bones of its princes, and
the bones of the priests, and the bones of
the prophets, and the bones of the inhabitants of Jerusalem, out of their graves.
2 They shall spread them before the sun
and the moon and all the host of heaven,
which they have loved and which they
have served and after which they have
walked, which they have sought and
[a]which they have worshiped. They shall
not be gathered [b]nor buried; they shall be
like refuse on the face of the earth. **3** Then
[c]death shall be chosen rather than life by
all the [1]residue of those who remain of this
evil family, who remain in all the places
where I have driven them," says the LORD
of hosts.

The Peril of False Teaching

4 "Moreover you shall say to them,
'Thus says the LORD:

"Will they fall and not rise?
Will one turn away and not return?
5 Why has this people [d]slidden back,
Jerusalem, in a perpetual
backsliding?
[e]They hold fast to deceit,
[f]They refuse to return.
6 [g]I listened and heard,
But they do not speak aright.
[h]No man repented of his
wickedness,
Saying, 'What have I done?'
Everyone turned to his own
course,
As the horse rushes into the battle.

7 "Even [i]the stork in the heavens
Knows her appointed times;
And the turtledove, the swift, and
the swallow
Observe the time of their coming.
But [j]My people do not know the
judgment of the LORD.

8 "How can you say, 'We *are* wise,
[k]And the law of the LORD *is* with
us'?
Look, the false pen of the scribe
certainly works falsehood.

24 [g]Deut. 29:19; Jer. 9:14 [h]Jer. 32:33 [2]*walked in* [3]*stubbornness* or *imagination* [4]Lit. *they were*
25 [i]2 Chr. 36:15; Jer. 25:4; 29:19; Mark 12:1-10; Luke 11:47-49
26 [j]Jer. 11:8 [k]Neh. 9:17 [l]Jer. 16:12; Matt. 23:32
27 [m]Jer. 1:7; 26:2; 37:14, 15; 43:1-4; Ezek. 2:7
28 [n]Jer. 5:3 [o]Jer. 9:3
29 [p]Job 1:20; Is. 15:2; Jer. 48:37; Mic. 1:16
30 [q]2 Kin. 21:4; 2 Chr. 33:3-5, 7; Jer. 32:34, 35; Ezek. 7:20; Dan. 9:27; 11:31 [5]*defile*
31 [r]2 Kin. 23:10; Jer. 19:5; 32:35 [s]Lev. 18:21; 2 Kin. 17:17; Ps. 106:38 [t]Deut. 17:3
32 [u]Jer. 19:6 [v]2 Kin. 23:10; Jer. 19:11
33 [w]Jer. 9:22; 19:11; Ezek. 6:5
34 [x]Is. 24:7, 8; Jer. 16:9; 25:10; Ezek. 26:13; Hos. 2:11; Rev. 18:23 [y]Lev. 26:33; Is. 1:7; Jer. 4:27

CHAPTER 8
2 [a]2 Kin. 23:5; Jer. 19:13; Ezek. 8:16; Zeph. 1:5; Acts 7:42 [b]Jer. 22:19
3 [c]Job 3:21, 22; 7:15, 16; Jon. 4:3; Rev. 9:6 [1]*remnant*
5 [d]Jer. 7:24 [e]Jer. 9:6 [f]Jer. 5:3
6 [g]Ps. 14:2; [Is. 30:18; Mal. 3:16; 2 Pet. 3:9] [h]Ezek. 22:30; Mic. 7:2; Rev. 9:20
7 [i]Prov. 6:6-8; Song 2:12; Is. 1:3; Matt. 16:2, 3 [j]Jer. 5:4; 9:3
8 [k]Rom. 2:17

7:25 Cf. v. 13.

7:29 Cut off your hair. This is a sign depicting God's cutting the nation off and casting them into exile. Ezekiel used a similar illustration by cutting his hair (Ezek. 5:1-4). God never casts away the genuinely saved from spiritual salvation (John 6:37; 10:28,29).

7:31 burn their sons. Though God forbade this atrocity (Lev. 18:21; 20:2-5; Deut. 12:31), Israelites still offered babies as sacrifices at the high places of idol worship (Tophet) in the valley of Hinnom (S end of Jerusalem). They offered them to the fire god Molech, under the delusion that this god would reward them. *See note on 19:6.*

7:32 Valley of Slaughter. God renamed the place because great carnage would be forthcoming in the Babylonian invasion.

8:1 bring out the bones. Conquerors would ransack all the tombs to gain treasures and then humiliate the Jews by scattering the bones of the rich and honored in open spaces as a tribute to the superiority of their gods (v. 2).

8:4 Jeremiah spoke of the natural instinct of one who falls, to get up, and one who leaves, to return, but Judah did not possess this instinct.

8:5 backsliding. *See note on 2:19.*

8:7 The instinct of the migratory birds leads them with unfailing regularity to return every spring from their winter homes. But God's people will not return, though the winter of divine wrath is arriving.

9 [l]The wise men are ashamed,
They are dismayed and taken.
Behold, they have rejected the word of the LORD;
So [m]what wisdom do they have?
10 Therefore [n]I will give their wives to others,
And their fields to those who will inherit *them;*
Because from the least even to the greatest
Everyone is given to [o]covetousness;
From the prophet even to the priest
Everyone deals falsely.
11 For they have [p]healed the hurt of the daughter of My people [2]slightly,
Saying, [q]'Peace, peace!'
When *there is* no peace.
12 Were they [r]ashamed when they had committed abomination?
No! They were not at all ashamed,
Nor did they know how to blush.
Therefore they shall fall among those who fall;
In the time of their punishment
They shall be cast down," says the LORD.

13 "I will surely [3]consume them," says the LORD.
"No grapes *shall be* [s]on the vine,
Nor figs on the [t]fig tree,
And the leaf shall fade;
And *the things* I have given them shall [u]pass away from them." ' "

14 "Why do we sit still?
[v]Assemble yourselves,
And let us enter the fortified cities,
And let us be silent there.
For the LORD our God has put us to silence
And given us [w]water[4] of gall to drink,
Because we have sinned against the LORD.

15 "*We* [x]looked for peace, but no good *came;*
And for a time of health, and there was trouble!
16 The snorting of His horses was heard from [y]Dan.
The whole land trembled at the sound of the neighing of His [z]strong ones;
For they have come and devoured the land and all that is in it,
The city and those who dwell in it."

17 "For behold, I will send serpents among you,
Vipers which cannot be [a]charmed,
And they shall bite you," says the LORD.

The Prophet Mourns for the People

18 I would comfort myself in sorrow;
My heart *is* faint in me.
19 Listen! The voice,
The cry of the daughter of my people
From [b]a far country:
"*Is* not the LORD in Zion?
Is not her King in her?"

"Why have they provoked Me to anger
With their carved images—
With foreign idols?"

20 "The harvest is past,
The summer is ended,
And we are not saved!"

21 [c]For the hurt of the daughter of my people I am hurt.
I am [d]mourning;
Astonishment has taken hold of me.
22 *Is there* no [e]balm in Gilead,
Is there no physician there?
Why then is there no recovery
For the health of the daughter of my people?

9 Oh, [a]that my head were waters,
And my eyes a fountain of tears,
That I might weep day and night
For the slain of the daughter of my people!

9 [l]Is. 19:11; Jer. 6:15; [1 Cor. 1:27] [m]Is. 44:25; Jer. 4:22
10 [n]Deut. 28:30; Amos 5:11; Zeph. 1:13 [o]Is. 56:11; 57:17; Jer. 6:13
11 [p]Jer. 6:14 [q]Ezek. 13:10 [2]Superficially
12 [r]Ps. 52:1, 7; Is. 3:9; Jer. 3:3; 6:15; Zeph. 3:5
13 [s]Jer. 5:17; 7:20; Joel 1:17 [t]Matt. 21:19; Luke 13:6 [u]Deut. 28:39, 40 [3]Or *take them away*
14 [v]Jer. 4:5 [w]Deut. 29:18; Ps. 69:21; Jer. 9:15; Lam. 3:19; Matt. 27:34 [4]Bitter or poisonous water
15 [x]Jer. 14:19
16 [y]Judg. 18:29; Jer. 4:15 [z]Jer. 47:3
17 [a]Ps. 58:4, 5
19 [b]Is. 39:3; Jer. 5:15
21 [c]Jer. 9:1 [d]Jer. 14:2; Joel 2:6; Nah. 2:10
22 [e]Gen. 37:25; Jer. 46:11

CHAPTER 9
1 [a]Is. 22:4; Jer. 10:19; Lam. 2:18

8:11 Cf. 4:10; 6:14.

8:16 Dan. The territory of this tribe was on the northern border of the land, where the invasion would begin and sweep S.

8:17 send serpents. This is a figurative picture of the Babylonian victors.

8:19 far country. This is the cry of the exiled Jews that will come after they are taken captive into Babylon. They will wonder why God would let this happen to His land and people.

8:20-22 we are not saved! The coming devastation is compared with the hopeless anguish when harvest time has passed but people are still in desperate need. Jeremiah identified with his people's suffering (v. 21) as a man of tears (cf. 9:1), but saw a doom so pronounced that there was no remedy to soothe. There was no healing balm, the kind in abundance in Gilead (E of the Sea of Galilee), and no physician to cure (cf. Gen. 37:25; 43:11).

9:1 waters...tears. Jeremiah cared so greatly that he longed for the relief of flooding tears or a place of retreat to be free of the burden of Judah's sins for a while.

2 Oh, that I had in the wilderness
A lodging place for travelers;
That I might leave my people,
And go from them!
For [b]they *are* all adulterers,
An assembly of treacherous men.

3 "And *like* their bow [c]they have bent
their tongues *for* lies.
They are not valiant for the truth
on the earth.
For they proceed from [d]evil to evil,
And they [e]do not know Me," says
the LORD.
4 "Everyone[f] take heed to his
[1]neighbor,
And do not trust any brother;
For every brother will utterly
supplant,
And every neighbor will [g]walk
with slanderers.
5 Everyone will [h]deceive his
neighbor,
And will not speak the truth;
They have taught their tongue to
speak lies;
They weary themselves to commit
iniquity.
6 Your dwelling place *is* in the midst
of deceit;
Through deceit they refuse to
know Me," says the LORD.

7 Therefore thus says the LORD of hosts:

"Behold, [i]I will refine them and [2]try
them;
[j]For how shall I deal with the
daughter of My people?
8 Their tongue *is* an arrow shot out;
It speaks [k]deceit;
One speaks [l]peaceably to his
neighbor with his mouth,
But [3]in his heart he [4]lies in wait.
9 [m]Shall I not punish them for these
things?" says the LORD.
"Shall I not avenge Myself on such a
nation as this?"

10 I will take up a weeping and
wailing for the mountains,
And [n]for the [5]dwelling places of
the wilderness a lamentation,
Because they are burned up,
So that no one can pass through;
Nor can *men* hear the voice of the
cattle.
[o]Both the birds of the heavens and
the beasts have fled;
They are gone.

11 "I will make Jerusalem [p]a heap of
ruins, [q]a den of jackals.
I will make the cities of Judah
desolate, without an
inhabitant."

12 [r]Who *is* the wise man who may understand this? And *who is he* to whom the
mouth of the LORD has spoken, that he may
declare it? Why does the land perish *and*
burn up like a wilderness, so that no one
can pass through?
13 And the LORD said, "Because they
have forsaken My law which I set before
them, and have [s]not obeyed My voice, nor
walked according to it, 14 but they have
[t]walked according to the [6]dictates of their
own hearts and after the Baals, [u]which
their fathers taught them," 15 therefore
thus says the LORD of hosts, the God of Israel: "Behold, I will [v]feed them, this people, [w]with wormwood, and give them
[7]water of gall to drink. 16 I will [x]scatter
them also among the Gentiles, whom neither they nor their fathers have known.
[y]And I will send a sword after them until I
have consumed them."

The People Mourn in Judgment

17 Thus says the LORD of hosts:

"Consider and call for [z]the
mourning women,
That they may come;
And send for skillful wailing
women,
That they may come.
18 Let them make haste
And take up a wailing for us,
That [a]our eyes may run with tears,
And our eyelids gush with water.
19 For a voice of wailing is heard
from Zion:
'How we are plundered!
We are greatly ashamed,
Because we have forsaken the land,
Because we have been cast out of
[b]our dwellings.' "

2 [b] Jer. 5:7, 8; 23:10; Hos. 4:2 **3** [c] Ps. 64:3; Is. 59:4; Jer. 9:8; Hos. 4:1, 2 [d] Jer. 4:22; 13:23 [e] Judg. 2:10; 1 Sam. 2:12; Jer. 4:22; Hos. 4:1; 1 Cor. 15:34 **4** [f] Ps. 12:2; Prov. 26:24, 25; Jer. 9:8; Mic. 7:5, 6 [g] Ps. 15:3; Prov. 10:18; Jer. 6:28 [1] *friend* **5** [h] Ps. 36:3, 4; Is. 59:4 **7** [i] Is. 1:25; Jer. 6:27; Mal. 3:3 [j] Hos. 11:8 [2] *test* **8** [k] Ps. 12:2 [l] Ps. 55:21 [3] Inwardly he [4] *sets his ambush* **9** [m] Is. 1:24; Jer. 5:9, 29 **10** [n] Jer. 4:26; Hos. 4:3 [5] Or *pastures*

[o] Jer. 4:25; Hos. 4:3 **11** [p] Is. 25:2; Jer. 19:3, 8; 26:9 [q] Is. 13:22; 34:13 **12** [r] Ps. 107:43; Is. 42:23; Hos. 14:9 **13** [s] Jer. 3:25; 7:24 **14** [t] Jer. 7:24; 11:8; Rom. 1:21-24 [u] Gal. 1:14; 1 Pet. 1:18 [6] *stubbornness* or *imagination* **15** [v] Ps. 80:5 [w] Deut. 29:18; Jer. 8:14; 23:15; Lam. 3:15 [7] Bitter or poisonous water **16** [x] Lev. 26:33; Deut. 28:64; Jer. 15:2-4 [y] Lev. 26:33; Jer. 44:27; Ezek. 5:2 **17** [z] 2 Chr. 35:25; Job 3:8; Eccl. 12:5; Amos 5:16; Matt. 9:23 **18** [a] Is. 22:4; Jer. 9:1; 14:17 **19** [b] Lev. 18:28

9:2 A lodging place for travelers. Simple square buildings with an open court were built in remote areas to accommodate caravans. Though it would be lonely and filthy in the wilderness, Jeremiah preferred it to Jerusalem so as to be removed from the moral pollution of the people, which he described in vv. 3-8.

9:3 do not know Me. *See note on 5:10.*

9:15 wormwood. The Lord pictured the awful suffering of the judgment as wormwood, which had very bitter leaves. Their food would be bitterness, and their water as foul as gall, a poisonous herb.

20 Yet hear the word of the LORD,
O women,
And let your ear receive the word
of His mouth;
Teach your daughters wailing,
And everyone her neighbor a
lamentation.
21 For death has come through our
windows,
Has entered our palaces,
To kill off [c]the children—[8]*no longer*
to be outside!
And the young men—[9]*no longer* on
the streets!

22 Speak, "Thus says the LORD:

'Even the carcasses of men shall fall
[d]as refuse on the open field,
Like cuttings after the harvester,
And no one shall gather *them.*' "

23 Thus says the LORD:

[e]"Let not the wise *man* glory in his
wisdom,
Let not the mighty *man* glory in his
[f]might,
Nor let the rich *man* glory in his
riches;
24 But [g]let him who glories glory in
this,
That he understands and knows
Me,
That I *am* the LORD, exercising
lovingkindness, [1]judgment,
and righteousness in the
earth.
[h]For in these I delight," says the
LORD.

25 "Behold, the days are coming," says
the LORD, "that [i]I will punish all *who are*
circumcised with the uncircumcised—
26 Egypt, Judah, Edom, the people of
Ammon, Moab, and all *who are* in the [j]far-
thest corners, who dwell in the wilderness.
For all *these* nations *are* uncircumcised, and
all the house of Israel *are* [k]uncircumcised in
the heart."

21 [c] 2 Chr. 36:17; Jer. 6:11; 18:21; Ezek. 9:5, 6 [8] Lit. *from outside* [9] Lit. *from the square*
22 [d] Ps. 83:10; Is. 5:25; Jer. 8:1, 2
23 [e] [Eccl. 9:11; Is. 47:10]; Ezek. 28:3-7 [f] Ps. 33:16-18
24 [g] Ps. 20:7; 44:8; Is. 41:16; Jer. 4:2; 1 Cor. 1:31; 2 Cor. 10:17; [Gal. 6:14] [h] Is. 61:8; Mic. 7:18 [1] *justice*
25 [i] [Jer. 4:4; Rom. 2:28, 29]
26 [j] Jer. 25:23 [k] Lev. 26:41; Jer. 4:4; 6:10; Ezek. 44:7; [Rom. 2:28]

CHAPTER 10
2 [a] [Lev. 18:3; 20:23; Deut. 12:30]
3 [b] Is. 40:19; 45:20 [1] Lit. *vanity*
4 [c] Is. 41:7
5 [d] Ps. 115:5; Is. 46:7; Jer. 10:5; 1 Cor. 12:2 [e] Ps. 115:7; Is. 46:1, 7 [f] Is. 41:23, 24
6 [g] Ex. 15:11; Deut. 33:26; Ps. 86:8, 10; Is. 46:5-9; Jer. 10:16
7 [h] Jer. 5:22; Rev. 15:4 [i] Ps. 89:6
8 [j] Ps. 115:8; Hab. 2:18 [2] *vain teaching*
9 [k] Dan. 10:5

Idols and the True God

10 Hear the word which the LORD
speaks to you, O house of Israel.
2 Thus says the LORD:

[a]"Do not learn the way of the
Gentiles;
Do not be dismayed at the signs of
heaven,
For the Gentiles are dismayed at
them.
3 For the customs of the peoples *are*
[1]futile;
For [b]*one* cuts a tree from the forest,
The work of the hands of the
workman, with the ax.
4 They decorate it with silver and
gold;
They [c]fasten it with nails and
hammers
So that it will not topple.
5 They *are* upright, like a palm tree,
And [d]they cannot speak;
They must be [e]carried,
Because they cannot go *by*
themselves.
Do not be afraid of them,
For [f]they cannot do evil,
Nor can they do any good."

6 Inasmuch as *there is* none [g]like You,
O LORD
(You *are* great, and Your name *is*
great in might),
7 [h]Who would not fear You, O King
of the nations?
For this is Your rightful due.
For [i]among all the wise *men* of the
nations,
And in all their kingdoms,
There is none like You.
8 But they are altogether [j]dull-
hearted and foolish;
A wooden idol *is* a [2]worthless
doctrine.
9 Silver is beaten into plates;
It is brought from Tarshish,
And [k]gold from Uphaz,
The work of the craftsman
And of the hands of the
metalsmith;

9:22 How galling to the Jews to hear that their carcasses will be trampled contemptuously.

9:24 understands and knows Me. Nothing but a true knowledge of God can save the nation. Paul refers to this passage twice (cf. 1 Cor. 1:31; 2 Cor. 10:17).

9:26 Egypt...wilderness. A preview of God's judgment of the nations detailed in chaps. 46–51. **uncircumcised...heart.** *See note on 4:4.*

10:2 the signs of heaven. Gentiles worshiped celestial bodies, including the sun, moon, and stars.

10:4 decorate. Idols were often carved from wood (v. 3) and ornamented with gold or silver (cf. v. 9). Some were molded from clay (Judg. 18:17; Is. 42:17). The context points out the impossibility (vv. 3-5) of such non-existent gods punishing or rewarding humans.

10:7 King. God, who sovereignly created and controls all things (cf. vv. 12,16; Deut. 4:35), is alone the eternal, living God (cf. Pss. 47, 145) worthy of trust. By contrast, earthly idols have to be fashioned by men (v. 9), and will perish (v. 15).

10:9 Tarshish. Possibly a commercial port in southern Spain or on the island of Sardinia. Cf. Jon. 1:3. **Uphaz.** Location is uncertain.

Blue and purple *are* their clothing;
They *are* all [l]the work of skillful
men.
10 But the LORD *is* the true God;
He *is* [m]the living God and the
[n]everlasting King.
At His wrath the earth will
tremble,
And the nations will not be able to
endure His indignation.

11 Thus you shall say to them: [o]"The
gods that have not made the heavens and
the earth [p]shall perish from the earth and
from under these heavens."

12 He [q]has made the earth by His
power,
He has [r]established the world by
His wisdom,
And [s]has stretched out the heavens
at His discretion.
13 [t]When He utters His voice,
There is a [3]multitude of waters in
the heavens:
[u]"And He causes the vapors to
ascend from the ends of the
earth.
He makes lightning for the rain,
He brings the wind out of His
treasuries."

14 [v]Everyone is [w]dull-hearted, without
knowledge;
[x]Every metalsmith is put to shame
by an image;
[y]For his molded image *is* falsehood,
And *there is* no breath in them.
15 They *are* futile, a work of errors;
In the time of their punishment
they shall perish.
16 [z]The Portion of Jacob *is* not like
them,
For He *is* the Maker of all *things,*
And [a]Israel *is* the tribe of His
inheritance;
[b]The LORD of hosts *is* His name.

The Coming Captivity of Judah

17 [c]Gather up your wares from the
land,
O [4]inhabitant of the fortress!

18 For thus says the LORD:
"Behold, I will [d]throw out at this
time
The inhabitants of the land,
And will distress them,
[e]That they may find *it so.*"

19 [f]Woe is me for my hurt!
My wound is severe.
But I say, [g]"Truly this *is* an
infirmity,
And [h]I must bear it."
20 [i]My tent is plundered,
And all my cords are broken;
My children have gone from me,
And they *are* [j]no more.
There is no one to pitch my tent
anymore,
Or set up my curtains.

21 For the shepherds have become
dull-hearted,
And have not sought the LORD;
Therefore they shall not prosper,
And all their flocks shall be
[k]scattered.
22 Behold, the noise of the report has
come,
And a great commotion out of the
[l]north country,
To make the cities of Judah
desolate, a [m]den of jackals.

23 O LORD, I know the [n]way of man *is*
not in himself;
It is not in man who walks to direct
his own steps.
24 O LORD, [o]correct me, but with
justice;
Not in Your anger, lest You bring
me to nothing.
25 [p]Pour out Your fury on the Gentiles,
[q]who do not know You,
And on the families who do not
call on Your name;
For they have eaten up Jacob,
[r]Devoured him and consumed him,
And made his dwelling place
desolate.

9 [l]Ps. 115:4
10 [m]1 Tim. 6:17 [n]Ps. 10:16
11 [o]Ps. 96:5 [p]Is. 2:18; Zeph. 2:11
12 [q]Gen. 1:1, 6, 7; Jer. 51:15 [r]Ps. 93:1 [s]Job 9:8; Ps. 104:2; Is. 40:22
13 [t]Job 38:34 [u]Ps. 135:7 [3]Or *noise*
14 [v]Jer. 51:17 [w]Prov. 30:2 [x]Is. 42:17; 44:11 [y]Hab. 2:18
16 [z]Ps. 16:5; Jer. 51:19; Lam. 3:24 [a]Deut. 32:9; Ps. 74:2 [b]Is. 47:4
17 [c]Jer. 6:1 [4]*Or you who dwell under siege*
18 [d]1 Sam. 25:29; 2 Chr. 36:20 [e]Ezek. 6:10
19 [f]Jer. 8:21 [g]Ps. 77:10 [h]Mic. 7:9
20 [i]Jer. 4:20; Lam. 2:4 [j]Jer. 31:15; Lam. 1:5
21 [k]Jer. 23:2
22 [l]Jer. 5:15 [m]Jer. 9:11
23 [n]Prov. 16:1; 20:24
24 [o]Ps. 6:1; 38:1; Jer. 30:11
25 [p]Ps. 79:6, 7; Zeph. 3:8 [q]Job 18:21; 1 Thess. 4:5; [2 Thess. 1:8] [r]Jer. 8:16

10:11-16 The true and living Creator God is again contrasted with dead idols.

10:16 Portion of Jacob. God is the all sufficient source for His people (Num. 18:20), and He will not fail them as idols do (11:12). **Israel *is* the tribe of His inheritance.** To this nation, God gave His inheritance in covenant love.

10:20 My tent is plundered. Jeremiah, using a nomadic metaphor, shifted into words that Israelites will speak when the invaders attack. They will feel "woe" due to their "wound," and cry out over their homes being plundered and their children being slain or scattered to exile.

10:23 the way...*is* not in himself. Man is incapable of guiding his own life adequately. This prayer shifts to his need of God (Prov. 3:5,6; 16:9), who had a plan for Jeremiah before he was even born (1:5).

10:24,25 Jeremiah saw himself ("correct me") in solidarity with his people (cf. Dan. 9:1ff.) and understood the nation must be punished, but desired some mercy and moderation; he prayed that God's full fury be poured on the nations that induced the Jews into idolatry.

The Broken Covenant

11 The word that came to Jeremiah
from the LORD, saying, 2 "Hear the
words of this covenant, and speak to the
men of Judah and to the inhabitants of Jerusalem; 3 and say to them, 'Thus says the
LORD God of Israel: [a]"Cursed *is* the man
who does not obey the words of this
covenant 4 which I commanded your fathers in the day I brought them out of the
land of Egypt, [b]from the iron furnace, saying, [c]'Obey My voice, and do according to
all that I command you; so shall you be My
people, and I will be your God,' 5 that I
may establish the [d]oath which I have
sworn to your fathers, to give them [e]'a
land flowing with milk and honey,' as *it is*
this day." ' "
And I answered and said, [1]"So be it,
LORD."
6 Then the LORD said to me, "Proclaim
all these words in the cities of Judah and in
the streets of Jerusalem, saying: 'Hear the
words of this covenant [f]and do them. 7 For
I earnestly exhorted your fathers in the day
I brought them up out of the land of Egypt,
until this day, [g]rising early and exhorting,
saying, "Obey My voice." 8 [h]Yet they did
not obey or incline their ear, but [i]everyone
[2]followed the dictates of his evil heart;
therefore I will bring upon them all the
words of this covenant, which I commanded *them* to do, but *which* they have not
done.' "
9 And the LORD said to me, [j]"A conspiracy has been found among the men of Judah and among the inhabitants of Jerusalem. 10 They have turned back to [k]the
iniquities of their forefathers who refused
to hear My words, and they have gone
after other gods to serve them; the house of
Israel and the house of Judah have broken
My covenant which I made with their fathers."
11 Therefore thus says the LORD: "Behold, I will surely bring calamity on them
which they will not be able to [3]escape; and
[l]though they cry out to Me, I will not listen
to them. 12 Then the cities of Judah and the
inhabitants of Jerusalem will go and [m]cry
out to the gods to whom they offer incense,
but they will not save them at all in the
time of their trouble. 13 For *according to* the
number of your [n]cities were your gods, O
Judah; and *according to* the number of the
streets of Jerusalem you have set up altars
to *that* shameful thing, altars to burn incense to Baal.
14 "So [o]do not pray for this people, or lift
up a cry or prayer for them; for I will not
hear *them* in the time that they cry out to
Me because of their trouble.

15 "What[p] has My beloved to do in My
house,
Having [q]done lewd deeds with
many?
And [r]the holy flesh has passed
from you.
When you do evil, then you
[s]rejoice.
16 The LORD called your name,
[t]Green Olive Tree, Lovely *and* of
Good Fruit.
With the noise of a great tumult
He has kindled fire on it,
And its branches are broken.

17 "For the LORD of hosts, [u]who planted
you, has pronounced doom against you for
the evil of the house of Israel and of the
house of Judah, which they have done
against themselves to provoke Me to anger
in offering incense to Baal."

Jeremiah's Life Threatened

18 Now the LORD gave me knowledge *of*
it, and I know *it;* for You showed me their
doings. 19 But I *was* like a docile lamb
brought to the slaughter; and I did not
know that they had devised schemes
against me, *saying,* "Let us destroy the tree
with its fruit, [v]and let us cut him off from

CHAPTER 11
3 [a]Deut. 27:26; [Jer. 17:5]; Gal. 3:10
4 [b]Deut. 4:20; 1 Kin. 8:51 [c]Lev. 26:3; Deut. 11:27; Jer. 7:23
5 [d]Ex. 13:5; Deut. 7:12; Ps. 105:9; Jer. 32:22 [e]Ex. 3:8 [1]Heb. *Amen*
6 [f]Deut. 17:19; [Rom. 2:13]; James 1:22
7 [g]Jer. 35:15
8 [h]Jer. 7:26 [i]Jer. 13:10 [2]*walked in the stubbornness* or *imagination*
9 [j]Ezek. 22:25; Hos. 6:9
10 [k]1 Sam. 15:11; Jer. 3:10, 11; Ezek. 20:18
11 [3]Lit. *go out*
[l]Ps. 18:41; Prov. 1:28; Is. 1:15; Jer. 14:12; Ezek. 8:18; Mic. 3:4; Zech. 7:13
12 [m]Deut. 32:37; Jer. 44:17
13 [n]2 Kin. 23:13; Jer. 2:28
14 [o]Ex. 32:10; Jer. 7:16; 14:11; [1 John 5:16]
15 [p]Ps. 50:16 [q]Ezek. 16:25 [r][Titus 1:15] [s]Prov. 2:14
16 [t]Ps. 52:8; [Rom. 11:17]
17 [u]Is. 5:2; Jer. 2:21; 12:2
19 [v]Ps. 83:4; Jer. 18:18

11:2 this covenant. The reference is to God's covenant, summarized in vv. 3-5, which promised curses for disobeying and blessings for obeying (cf. Deut. 27:26–28:68).

11:4 the iron furnace. A metaphor for the hardship of Egyptian bondage hundreds of years earlier (cf. Ex. 1:8-14).

11:9 A conspiracy. This refers to a deliberate resisting of God's appeals for repentance and an insistence upon trusting their own "peace" message and idols.

11:13 Judah was so filled with idolatry that there were false deities for every city and a polluted altar on every street.

11:14 do not pray. Cf. 7:16 and *see note there.* Their own prayers, as long as they rejected God, could not gain the answer they desired (v. 11; Ps. 66:18), and the same was true of another's prayers for them.

11:15 My beloved. A phrase showing God's sensitive regard for His relationship to Israel as a nation (cf. 2:2; 12:7). It does not carry the assumption, however, that every individual is spiritually saved (cf. 5:10a). **lewd deeds.** Shameful idolatry that defiled all that befits true temple worship, such as the examples in Ezek. 8:6-13. These were gross violations of the first 3 commandments (cf. Ex. 20:2-7). **holy flesh.** In some way, they corrupted the animal sacrifices by committing sin which they enjoyed (cf. 7:10).

11:16,17 Green Olive Tree. Israel was pictured as a grapevine (2:21), then an olive tree meant to bear good fruit. However, they produced fruit that calls only for the fire of judgment (as 5:10).

11:18-23 You showed me. Jeremiah's fellow townsmen from Anathoth, one of the 48 cities throughout the land dedicated to the Levites, plotted his death. Their words, "Let us destroy the tree…," indicate their desire to silence Jeremiah by murder.

[w]the land of the living, that his name may be remembered no more."

20 But, O LORD of hosts,
You who judge righteously,
[x]Testing the [4]mind and the heart,
Let me see Your [y]vengeance on
them,
For to You I have revealed my
cause.

21 "Therefore thus says the LORD concerning the men of [z]Anathoth who seek
your life, saying, [a]'Do not prophesy in the
name of the LORD, lest you die by our
hand'— 22 therefore thus says the LORD of
hosts: 'Behold, I will punish them. The
young men shall die by the sword, their
sons and their daughters shall [b]die by
famine; 23 and there shall be no remnant of
them, for I will bring catastrophe on the
men of Anathoth, *even* [c]the year of their
punishment.' "

Jeremiah's Question

12 Righteous [a]*are* You, O LORD, when
I plead with You;
Yet let me talk with You about *Your*
judgments.
[b]Why does the way of the wicked
prosper?
Why are those happy who deal so
treacherously?
2 You have planted them, yes, they
have taken root;
They grow, yes, they bear fruit.
[c]You *are* near in their mouth
But far from their [1]mind.

3 But You, O LORD, [d]know me;
You have seen me,
And You have [e]tested my heart
toward You.
Pull them out like sheep for the
slaughter,
And prepare them for [f]the day of
slaughter.
4 How long will [g]the land mourn,

19 [w]Ps. 27:13
20 [x]1 Sam. 16:7; 1 Chr. 28:9; Ps. 7:9 [y]Jer. 15:15 [4]Most secret parts, lit. *kidneys*
21 [z]Jer. 1:1; 12:5, 6 [a]Is. 30:10; Amos 2:12; Mic. 2:6
22 [b]Jer. 9:21
23 [c]Jer. 23:12; Hos. 9:7; Mic. 7:4

CHAPTER 12

1 [a]Ezra 9:15; Ps. 51:4; Jer. 11:20 [b]Job 12:6; Jer. 5:27, 28; Hab. 1:4; Mal. 3:15
2 [c]Is. 29:13; Ezek. 33:31; Matt. 15:8; Mark 7:6 [1]Most secret parts, lit. *kidneys*
3 [d]Ps. 17:3 [e]Ps. 7:9; 11:5; Jer. 11:20 [f]Jer. 17:18; 50:27; James 5:5
4 [g]Jer. 23:10; Hos. 4:3
[h]Jer. 9:10; Hos. 4:3; Hab. 3:17 [i]Ps. 107:34
5 [j]Josh. 3:15; 1 Chr. 12:15 [2]Or *thicket*
6 [k]Gen. 37:4-11; Job 6:15; Ps. 69:8; Jer. 9:4, 5 [l]Ps. 12:2; Prov. 26:25 [3]Or *abundantly* [4]Lit. *good*
8 [m]Hos. 9:15; Amos 6:8
9 [n]Lev. 26:22 [5]*inheritance*
10 [o]Jer. 6:3; 23:1 [p]Ps. 80:8-16; Is. 5:1-7 [6]Lit. *shepherds* or *pastors*

And the herbs of every field
wither?
[h]The beasts and birds are
consumed,
[i]For the wickedness of those who
dwell there,
Because they said, "He will not see
our final end."

The LORD Answers Jeremiah

5 "If you have run with the footmen,
and they have wearied you,
Then how can you contend with
horses?
And *if* in the land of peace,
In which you trusted, *they wearied*
you,
Then how will you do in [j]the
[2]floodplain of the Jordan?
6 For even [k]your brothers, the house
of your father,
Even they have dealt treacherously
with you;
Yes, they have called [3]a multitude
after you.
[l]Do not believe them,
Even though they speak [4]smooth
words to you.

7 "I have forsaken My house, I have
left My heritage;
I have given the dearly beloved of
My soul into the hand of her
enemies.
8 My heritage is to Me like a lion in
the forest;
It cries out against Me;
Therefore I have [m]hated it.
9 My [5]heritage *is* to Me *like* a
speckled vulture;
The vultures all around *are* against
her.
Come, assemble all the beasts of
the field,
[n]Bring them to devour!
10 "Many [o]rulers[6] have destroyed [p]My
vineyard,

11:20 Let me see Your vengeance. Jeremiah pleaded for God's defense on his behalf, actually guaranteed in 1:8,18,19.

12:1 Why. The issue of why the wicked escape for a time unscathed has often been raised by God's people (cf. Ps. 73; Hab. 1:2-4).

12:3 Pull them out...for the slaughter. The prophet here turned from the sadness of pleading for his people to calling on God to punish them. Such imprecatory prayers are similar to prayers throughout the Psalms.

12:4 He will not see our final end. Here is the foolish idea that Jeremiah was wrong and didn't know how things would happen.

12:5 If you have run. The Lord replied to Jeremiah telling him that if he grew faint with lesser trials and felt like quitting, what would he do when the battle got even harder? **floodplain of the Jordan.** The river in flood stage overflowed its banks into a plain that grew up as a thicket. The point is that Jeremiah needed to be ready to deal with tougher testings, pictured by the invader's overwhelming the land like a flood, or posing high danger as in the Jordan thicket where concealed wild animals could terrify a person.

12:6 even your brothers. Jeremiah met antagonism not only from fellow townsmen (cf. 11:18-23 and *see note there*), but from his own family! He was separated from them (v. 7).

12:8 like a lion. Jeremiah's own people collectively are like a lion acting ferociously against him.

12:9 a speckled vulture. God's people, speckled with sin and compromise, are opposed by other vultures, i.e., enemy nations.

They have [q]trodden My portion underfoot;
They have made My [7]pleasant portion a desolate wilderness.
11 They have made it [r]desolate;
Desolate, it mourns to Me;
The whole land is made desolate,
Because [s]no one takes *it* to heart.
12 The plunderers have come
On all the desolate heights in the wilderness,
For the sword of the LORD shall devour
From *one* end of the land to the *other* end of the land;
No flesh shall have peace.
13 [t]They have sown wheat but reaped thorns;
They have [8]put themselves to pain *but* do not profit.
But be ashamed of your harvest
Because of the fierce anger of the LORD."

14 Thus says the LORD: "Against all My
evil neighbors who [u]touch the inheritance
which I have caused My people Israel to
inherit—behold, I will [v]pluck them out of
their land and pluck out the house of Judah from among them. 15 [w]Then it shall be,
after I have plucked them out, that I will
return and have compassion on them [x]and
bring them back, everyone to his heritage
and everyone to his land. 16 And it shall
be, if they will learn carefully the ways of
My people, [y]to swear by My name, 'As the
LORD lives,' as they taught My people to
swear by Baal, then they shall be [z]estab-
lished in the midst of My people. 17 But if
they do not [a]obey, I will utterly pluck up
and destroy that nation," says the LORD.

Symbol of the Linen Sash

13 Thus the LORD said to me: "Go and
get yourself a linen sash, and put it
[1]around your waist, but do not put it in
water." 2 So I got a [2]sash according to the
word of the LORD, and put *it* around my
waist.
3 And the word of the LORD came to me
the second time, saying, 4 "Take the [3]sash
that you acquired, which *is* [4]around your
waist, and arise, go to the [5]Euphrates, and
hide it there in a hole in the rock." 5 So I
went and hid it by the Euphrates, as the
LORD commanded me.
6 Now it came to pass after many days
that the LORD said to me, "Arise, go to the
Euphrates, and take from there the sash
which I commanded you to hide there."
7 Then I went to the Euphrates and dug,
and I took the [6]sash from the place where I
had hidden it; and there was the sash, ruined. It was profitable for nothing.
8 Then the word of the LORD came to me,
saying, 9 "Thus says the LORD: 'In this
manner [a]I will ruin the pride of Judah and
the great [b]pride of Jerusalem. 10 This evil
people, who [c]refuse to hear My words,
who [d]follow [7]the dictates of their hearts,
and walk after other gods to serve them
and worship them, shall be just like this
sash which is profitable for nothing. 11 For
as the sash clings to the waist of a man, so
I have caused the whole house of Israel
and the whole house of Judah to cling to
Me,' says the LORD, 'that [e]they may become My people, [f]for renown, for praise,
and for [g]glory; but they would [h]not hear.'

Symbol of the Wine Bottles

12 "Therefore you shall speak to them
this word: 'Thus says the LORD God of Israel: "Every bottle shall be filled with
wine." '
"And they will say to you, 'Do we not
certainly know that every bottle will be
filled with wine?'
13 "Then you shall say to them, 'Thus
says the LORD: "Behold, I will fill all the inhabitants of this land—even the kings who
sit on David's throne, the priests, the
prophets, and all the inhabitants of Jerusalem—[i]with drunkenness! 14 And [j]I will
dash them [8]one against another, even the

10 [q]Is. 63:18 [7]*desired portion of land*
11 [r]Jer. 10:22; 22:6 [s]Is. 42:25
13 [t]Lev. 26:16; Deut. 28:38; Mic. 6:15; Hag. 1:6 [8]Or *strained*
14 [u]Jer. 2:3; 50:11, 12; Zech. 2:8 [v]Deut. 30:3; Ps. 106:47; Is. 11:11-16; Jer. 32:37
15 [w]Jer. 31:20; Lam. 3:32; Ezek. 28:25 [x]Amos 9:14
16 [y][Jer. 4:2]; Zeph. 1:5 [z][Eph. 2:20, 21; 1 Pet. 2:5]
17 [a]Ps. 2:8-12; Is. 60:12

CHAPTER 13

1 [1]Lit. *upon your loins*
2 [2]*waistband*

4 [3]*waistband* [4]Lit. *upon your loins* [5]Heb. *Perath*
7 [6]*waistband*
9 [a]Lev. 26:19 [b][Is. 2:10-17; 23:9]; Zeph. 3:11
10 [c]Jer. 16:12 [d]Jer. 7:24; 16:12 [7]*walk in the stubbornness* or *imagination*
11 [e][Ex. 19:5, 6; Deut. 32:10, 11] [f]Jer. 33:9 [g]Is. 43:21 [h]Ps. 81:11; Jer. 7:13, 24, 26
13 [i]Ps. 60:3; 75:8; Is. 51:17; 63:6; Jer. 25:27; 51:7, 57
14 [j]2 Chr. 36:17; Ps. 2:9; Is. 9:20, 21; Jer. 19:9-11 [8]Lit. *a man against his brother*

12:12 sword of the LORD. God's strength can be for defending (cf. 47:6; Judg. 7:20) or in this case, condemning. The Babylonians were God's sword doing His will.

12:14 evil neighbors. Other nations which hurt Israel will, in their turn, also receive judgment from the Lord (cf. 9:26; 25:14-32; chaps. 46–51).

12:15 bring them back. God will restore His people to the land of Israel in a future millennial day, as indicated in chaps. 30–33.

13:1 a linen sash. One of several signs Jeremiah enacted to illustrate God's message (cf. Introduction) involved putting a linen sash (generally the inner garment against the skin) around his waist. This depicted Israel's close intimacy with God in the covenant, so that they could glorify Him (v. 11). **do not put it in water.** Signified the moral filth of the nation. Buried and allowed time to rot (v. 7), the sash pictured Israel as useless to God due to sin (v. 10). Hiding it by the Euphrates (v. 6) pointed to the land of Babylon, where God would exile Israel to deal with her pride (cf. v. 9).

13:4 Euphrates. This refers literally to a site on the Euphrates River because: 1) the Euphrates is the area of exile (20:4); 2) "many days" fits the round trip of well over 1,000 mi. (v. 6); and 3) the ruining of the nation's pride (v. 9) relates to judgment by Babylon (vv. 10,11).

13:12-14 Every bottle. God pictured inhabitants of Israel in Babylon's invasion as bottles or skins of wine. As wine causes drunkenness, they will be dazed, stumbling in darkness (cf. v. 16), out of control, and victims of destruction (v. 14).

fathers and the sons together," says the LORD. "I will not pity nor spare nor have mercy, but will destroy them." ' "

Pride Precedes Captivity

15 Hear and give ear:
Do not be proud,
For the LORD has spoken.
16 [k]Give glory to the LORD your God
Before He causes [l]darkness,
And before your feet stumble
On the dark mountains,
And while you are [m]looking for
light,
He turns it into [n]the shadow of
death
And makes *it* dense darkness.
17 But if you will not hear it,
My soul will [o]weep in secret for
your pride;
My eyes will weep bitterly
And run down with tears,
Because the LORD's flock has been
taken captive.

18 Say to [p]the king and to the queen
mother,
"Humble yourselves;
Sit down,
For your rule shall collapse, the
crown of your glory."
19 The cities of the South shall be shut
up,
And no one shall open *them;*
Judah shall be carried away
captive, all of it;
It shall be wholly carried away
captive.

20 Lift up your eyes and see
Those who come from the [q]north.
Where *is* the flock *that* was given to
you,
Your beautiful sheep?
21 What will you say when He
punishes you?
For you have taught them
To be chieftains, to be head over you.
Will not [r]pangs seize you,
Like a woman in [9]labor?
22 And if you say in your heart,
[s]"Why have these things come upon
me?"
For the greatness of your iniquity
[t]Your skirts have been uncovered,
Your heels [1]made bare.
23 Can the Ethiopian change his skin
or the leopard its spots?
Then may you also do good who
are accustomed to do evil.

24 "Therefore I will [u]scatter them [v]like
stubble
That passes away by the wind of
the wilderness.
25 [w]This is your lot,
The portion of your measures from
Me," says the LORD,
"Because you have forgotten Me
And trusted in [x]falsehood.
26 Therefore [y]I will uncover your
skirts over your face,
That your shame may appear.
27 I have seen your adulteries
And your *lustful* [z]neighings,
The lewdness of your harlotry,
Your abominations [a]on the hills in
the fields.
Woe to you, O Jerusalem!
Will you still not be made clean?"

Sword, Famine, and Pestilence

14 The word of the LORD that came to Jeremiah concerning the droughts.

2 "Judah mourns,
And [a]her gates languish;
They [b]mourn for the land,

16 [k]Josh. 7:19; Ps. 96:8; Mal. 2:2 [l]Is. 5:30; 8:22; Amos 8:9 [m]Is. 59:9 [n]Ps. 44:19; Jer. 2:6
17 [o]Ps. 119:136; Jer. 9:1; 14:17; Luke 19:41, 42
18 [p]2 Kin. 24:12; Jer. 22:26
20 [q]Jer. 10:22; 46:20
21 [r]Jer. 6:24 [9]*childbirth*
22 [s]Jer. 16:10 [t]Is. 47:2; Ezek. 16:37; Nah. 3:5 [1]Lit. *suffer violence*
24 [u]Lev. 26:33; Jer. 9:16; Ezek. 5:2, 12 [v]Ps. 1:4; Hos. 13:3
25 [w]Job 20:29; Ps. 11:6; Matt. 24:51 [x]Jer. 10:14
26 [y]Lam. 1:8; Ezek. 16:37; Hos. 2:10
27 [z]Jer. 5:7, 8 [a]Is. 65:7; Jer. 2:20; Ezek. 6:13

CHAPTER 14

2 [a]2 Kin. 25:3; Is. 3:26 [b]Jer. 8:21

13:16 Give glory to the LORD. Show by repentance and obedience to God that you respect His majesty.

13:18 king...queen mother. Jehoiachin and Nehushta, ca. 597 B.C. (cf. 22:24-26; 29:2; 2 Kin. 24:8-17). Because the king was only 18 years old, she held the real power.

13:19 wholly carried away. "All" and "wholly" do not require absolutely every individual, for Jeremiah elsewhere explains that some were to be slain and a remnant left in the land or fleeing to Egypt (chaps. 39–44).

13:23 Ethiopian...leopard. The vivid analogy assumes that sinners cannot change their sinful natures (cf. "incurably sick," 17:9, marginal note). Only God can change the heart (31:18, 31-34).

13:26 uncover your skirts over your face. This was done to shame captive women and prostitutes (cf. Nah. 3:5).

13:27 *lustful* neighings. Refers to desire at an animal level, without conscience.

14:1 droughts. Jeremiah seems to actually give the prophecy of this chapter during a drought in Judah (vv. 2-6).

14:2 gates languish. The "gates" were the place of public concourse, which during drought and consequent famine were empty or occupied by mourners.

Object Lessons

- The Linen Sash (13:1-11)
- The Vessel Marred and Remade (18:1-11)
- The Vessel Dashed upon the Rocks (19:10-11)
- Two Baskets of Figs (24:1-10)
- The Wooden and Iron Yokes (chaps. 27, 28)
- The Purchase of Land (32:6-44)
- The Stones in Egypt (43:8-10)

And [c]the cry of Jerusalem has gone up.
3 Their nobles have sent their lads for water;
They went to the cisterns *and* found no water.
They returned with their vessels empty;
They were [d]ashamed and confounded
[e]And covered their heads.
4 Because the ground is parched,
For there was [f]no rain in the land,
The plowmen were ashamed;
They covered their heads.
5 Yes, the deer also gave birth in the field,
But [1]left because there was no grass.
6 And [g]the wild donkeys stood in the desolate heights;
They sniffed at the wind like jackals;
Their eyes failed because *there was* no grass."

7 O LORD, though our iniquities testify against us,
Do it [h]for Your name's sake;
For our backslidings are many,
We have sinned against You.
8 [i]O the Hope of Israel, his Savior in time of trouble,
Why should You be like a stranger in the land,
And like a traveler *who* turns aside to tarry for a night?
9 Why should You be like a man astonished,
Like a mighty one [j]*who* cannot save?
Yet You, O LORD, [k]*are* in our midst,
And we are called by Your name;
Do not leave us!

10 Thus says the LORD to this people:

[l]"Thus they have loved to wander;
They have not restrained their feet.
Therefore the LORD does not accept them;
[m]He will remember their iniquity now,
And punish their sins."

11 Then the LORD said to me, [n]"Do not
pray for this people, for *their* good.
12 [o]When they fast, I will not hear their cry;
and [p]when they offer burnt offering and
grain offering, I will not accept them. But
[q]I will consume them by the sword, by the
famine, and by the pestilence."
13 [r]Then I said, "Ah, Lord GOD! Behold,
the prophets say to them, 'You shall not see
the sword, nor shall you have famine, but
I will give you [2]assured [s]peace in this
place.'"
14 And the LORD said to me, [t]"The
prophets prophesy lies in My name. [u]I
have not sent them, commanded them, nor
spoken to them; they prophesy to you a
false vision, [3]divination, a worthless thing,
and the [v]deceit of their heart. 15 Therefore
thus says the LORD concerning the prophets who prophesy in My name, whom I did
not send, [w]and who say, 'Sword and
famine shall not be in this land'—'By
sword and famine those prophets shall be
consumed! 16 And the people to whom
they prophesy shall be cast out in the
streets of Jerusalem because of the famine
and the sword; [x]they will have no one to
bury them—them nor their wives, their
sons nor their daughters—for I will pour
their wickedness on them.'
17 "Therefore you shall say this word to
them:

[y]'Let my eyes flow with tears night and day,
And let them not cease;
[z]For the virgin daughter of my people
Has been broken with a mighty stroke, with a very severe blow.
18 If I go out to [a]the field,
Then behold, those slain with the sword!

2 [c] 1 Sam. 5:12; Jer. 11:11; 46:12; Zech. 7:13
3 [d] Job 6:20; Ps. 40:14 [e] 2 Sam. 15:30
4 [f] Jer. 3:3; Ezek. 22:24
5 [1] *abandoned* her young
6 [g] Job 39:5, 6; Jer. 2:24
7 [h] Ps. 25:11; Jer. 14:21
8 [i] Jer. 17:13
9 [j] Is. 59:1 [k] Ex. 29:45; Lev. 26:11; Ps. 46:5; Jer. 8:19
10 [l] Jer. 2:23-25 [m] [Jer. 44:21-23]; Hos. 8:13
11 [n] Ex. 32:10; Jer. 7:16; 11:14
12 [o] Prov. 1:28; [Is. 1:15; 58:3-6]; Ezek. 8:18; Mic. 3:4; Zech. 7:13 [p] Jer. 6:20 [q] Jer. 9:16
13 [r] Jer. 4:10 [s] Jer. 8:11; 23:17 [2] *true*
14 [t] Jer. 27:10 [u] Jer. 29:8, 9 [v] Jer. 23:16; Ezek. 12:24 [3] Telling the future by signs and omens
15 [w] Jer. 5:12; Ezek. 14:10
16 [x] Ps. 79:2, 3; Jer. 7:32; 15:2, 3
17 [y] Jer. 9:1; 13:17; Lam. 1:16 [z] Is. 37:22; Jer. 8:21; Lam. 1:15; 2:13
18 [a] Jer. 6:25; Lam. 1:20; Ezek. 7:15

14:7 O LORD. Jeremiah from 14:7–15:21, pursues a series of prayers in which he dialogues with the Lord, who hears and responds (as 1:7; 12:5-17, etc.). Five rounds or exchanges occur (14:7-12; 14:13-18; 14:19–15:9; 15:10-14; 15:15-21).

14:7-9 our backslidings. The prophet confesses Judah's guilt but reminds God that His reputation is tied up with what happens to His people (vv. 7,9). He asks that the Lord be not indifferent as a foreigner or overnight visitor (v. 8).

14:10-12 God responded in this first exchange that 1) He must judge Judah for chronic sinfulness, and 2) Jeremiah is not to pray for the sparing of Judah nor will He respond to their prayers since unrepentance must be punished (cf. 11:14, and *see note there*).

14:13 the prophets say. Jeremiah seemed to put forth the excuse that the people cannot help it since the false prophets deluded them with lying assurances of peace.

14:14-18 The excuse was not valid. These were deceits spawned from the prophets' lying hearts. The prophets would suffer for their own sins (vv. 14,15), but so would the people for "their wickedness" (vv. 16-18; 5:31).

14:17 virgin daughter. Judah is so called, having never before been under foreign bondage.

And if I enter the city,
Then behold, those sick from famine!
Yes, both prophet and [b]priest go about in a land they do not know.' "

The People Plead for Mercy

19 [c]Have You utterly rejected Judah?
Has Your soul loathed Zion?
Why have You stricken us so that [d]*there is* no healing for us?
[e]We looked for peace, but *there was* no good;
And for the time of healing, and there was trouble.
20 We acknowledge, O LORD, our wickedness
And the iniquity of our [f]fathers,
For [g]we have sinned against You.
21 Do not abhor *us*, for Your name's sake;
Do not disgrace the throne of Your glory.
[h]Remember, do not break Your covenant with us.
22 [i]Are there any among [j]the idols of the nations that can cause [k]rain?
Or can the heavens give showers?
[l]*Are* You not He, O LORD our God?
Therefore we will wait for You,
Since You have made all these.

The LORD Will Not Relent

15 Then the LORD said to me, [a]"*Even* if
[b]Moses and [c]Samuel stood before
Me, My [1]mind *would* not *be* favorable toward this people. Cast *them* out of My
sight, and let them go forth. 2 And it shall
be, if they say to you, 'Where should we
go?' then you shall tell them, 'Thus says
the LORD:

[d]"Such as *are* for death, to death;
And such as *are* for the sword, to the sword;
And such as *are* for the famine, to the famine;
And such as *are* for the [e]captivity, to the captivity."

18 [b] Jer. 23:11 **19** [c] Jer. 6:30; 7:29; 12:7; Lam. 5:22 [d] Jer. 15:18 [e] Job 30:26; Jer. 8:15; 1 Thess. 5:3 **20** [f] Neh. 9:2; Ps. 32:5; Jer. 3:25 [g] Ps. 106:6; Jer. 8:14; 14:7; Dan. 9:8 **21** [h] Ps. 106:45 **22** [i] Zech. 10:1 [j] Deut. 32:21 [k] 1 Kin. 17:1; Jer. 5:24 [l] Ps. 135:7

CHAPTER 15

1 [a] Ps. 99:6; Ezek. 14:14 [b] Ex. 32:11-14; Num. 14:13-20; Ps. 99:6 [c] 1 Sam. 7:9 [1] Lit. *soul was not toward* **2** [d] Jer. 43:11; Ezek. 5:2, 12; Zech. 11:9; [Rev. 13:10] [e] Jer. 9:16; 16:13

3 "And I will [f]appoint over them four
forms *of destruction*," says the LORD: "the
sword to slay, the dogs to drag, [g]the birds
of the heavens and the beasts of the earth
to devour and destroy. 4 I will hand them
over to [h]trouble, to all kingdoms of the
earth, because of [i]Manasseh the son of
Hezekiah, king of Judah, for what he did in
Jerusalem.

5 "For who will have pity on you, O Jerusalem?
Or who will bemoan you?
Or who will turn aside to ask how you are doing?
6 [j]You have forsaken Me," says the LORD,
"You have [k]gone backward.
Therefore I will stretch out My hand against you and destroy you;
[l]I am [2]weary of relenting!
7 And I will winnow them with a winnowing fan in the gates of the land;
I will [m]bereave *them* of children;
I will destroy My people,
Since they [n]do not return from their ways.
8 Their widows will be increased to Me more than the sand of the seas;
I will bring against them,
Against the mother of the young men,
A plunderer at noonday;
I will cause anguish and terror to fall on them [o]suddenly.

9 "She[p] languishes who has borne seven;
She has breathed her last;
[q]Her sun has gone down
While *it was* yet day;
She has been ashamed and confounded.
And the remnant of them I will deliver to the sword
Before their enemies," says the LORD.

3 [f] Lev. 26:16, 21, 25; Jer. 12:3; Ezek. 14:21 [g] Jer. 7:33 **4** [h] Deut. 28:25 [i] 2 Kin. 24:3, 4 **6** [j] Jer. 2:13 [k] Is. 1:4; Jer. 7:24 [l] Jer. 20:16; Zech. 8:14 [2] *tired* **7** [m] Jer. 18:21; Hos. 9:12-16 [n] Is. 9:13; Jer. 5:3; Amos 4:10, 11 **8** [o] Is. 29:5 **9** [p] 1 Sam. 2:5; Is. 47:9 [q] Jer. 6:4; Amos 8:9

14:18 a land they do not know. Babylon.

14:19,20 Have You utterly rejected Judah? Lest the Lord be casting Judah off forever, the prophet in deep contrition confesses the nation's sin (cf. Dan. 9:4ff.).

14:21 the throne of Your glory. Jerusalem, place of the temple.

15:1-9 It was ineffective at this point to intercede for the nation. Even prayers by Moses (cf. Num. 14:11-25) and Samuel (cf. 1 Sam. 12:19-25), eminent in intercession, would not defer judgment, where unrepentance persists (cf. 18:8; 26:3). Chief among things provoking judgment was the intense sin of King Manasseh (695–642 B.C.). Noted in v. 4., this provocation is recounted in 2 Kin. 21:1-18, cf. 2 Kin. 23:26, which says the Lord did not relent from His anger because of this (see also 2 Kin. 24:3,4).

15:6 I am weary of relenting! God often withholds the judgment He threatens (cf. 26:19; Ex. 32:14; 1 Chr. 21:15), sparing men so that His patience might lead them to repentance (cf. Rom. 2:4,5; 3:25).

15:9 sun...gone down while...yet day. Young mothers die in youth and their children are killed.

Jeremiah's Dejection

10 [r]Woe is me, my mother,
That you have borne me,
A man of strife and a man of
contention to the whole [3]earth!
I have neither lent for interest,
Nor have men lent to me for
interest.
Every one of them curses me.

11 The LORD said:

"Surely it will be well with your
remnant;
Surely I will cause [s]the enemy to
intercede with you
In the time of adversity and in the
time of affliction.
12 Can anyone break iron,
The northern iron and the bronze?
13 Your wealth and your treasures
I will give as [t]plunder without
price,
Because of all your sins,
Throughout your territories.
14 And I will [4]make *you* cross over
with your enemies
[u]Into a land *which* you do not know;
For a [v]fire is kindled in My anger,
Which shall burn upon you."

15 O LORD, [w]You know;
Remember me and [5]visit me,
And [x]take vengeance for me on my
persecutors.
In Your enduring patience, do not
take me away.
Know that [y]for Your sake I have
suffered rebuke.
16 Your words were found, and I [z]ate
them,
And [a]Your word was to me the joy
and rejoicing of my heart;
For I am called by Your name,
O LORD God of hosts.

10 [r] Job 3:1; Jer. 20:14 [3] Or *land*
11 [s] Jer. 40:4, 5
13 [t] Ps. 44:12; Is. 52:3
14 [u] Deut. 28:36, 64; Jer. 16:13 [v] Deut. 32:22; Ps. 21:9; Jer. 17:4 [4] So with MT, Vg.; LXX, Syr., Tg. *cause you to serve* (cf. 17:4)
15 [w] Jer. 12:3 [x] Jer. 20:12 [y] Ps. 69:7-9; Jer. 20:8 [5] *attend to*
16 [z] Ezek. 3:1, 3; Rev. 10:9 [a] [Job 23:12; Ps. 119:72]
17 [b] Ps. 26:4, 5
18 [c] Job 34:6; Jer. 10:19; 30:15; Mic. 1:9 [d] Job 6:15 [6] Or *cannot be trusted*
19 [e] Jer. 4:1; Zech. 3:7 [f] 1 Kin. 17:1; Jer. 15:1 [g] Jer. 6:29; Ezek. 22:26; 44:23
20 [h] Jer. 1:18; 6:27; Ezek. 3:9 [i] Ps. 46:7; Is. 41:10; Jer. 1:8, 19; 20:11; 37:21; 38:13; 39:11, 12

17 [b]I did not sit in the assembly of the
mockers,
Nor did I rejoice;
I sat alone because of Your hand,
For You have filled me with
indignation.
18 Why is my [c]pain perpetual
And my wound incurable,
Which refuses to be healed?
Will You surely be to me [d]like an
unreliable stream,
As waters *that* [6]fail?

The LORD Reassures Jeremiah

19 Therefore thus says the LORD:

[e]"If you return,
Then I will bring you back;
You shall [f]stand before Me;
If you [g]take out the precious from
the vile,
You shall be as My mouth.
Let them return to you,
But you must not return to them.
20 And I will make you to this people
a fortified bronze [h]wall;
And they will fight against you,
But [i]they shall not prevail against
you;
For I *am* with you to save you
And deliver you," says the LORD.
21 "I will deliver you from the hand of
the wicked,
And I will redeem you from the
grip of the terrible."

Jeremiah's Life-Style and Message

16 The word of the LORD also came to
me, saying, 2 "You shall not take a
wife, nor shall you have sons or daughters
in this place." 3 For thus says the LORD concerning the sons and daughters who are
born in this place, and concerning their
mothers who bore them and their fathers
who begot them in this land: 4 "They shall

15:10 Woe is me. Overcome by grief (cf. 9:1), Jeremiah wished that he had not been born (as 20:14-18). He had not been a bad or disagreeable creditor or debtor, either of whom kindle hatred. Yet his people cursed him, and he felt the sting.

15:11-14 In the midst of judgment, the Lord promised protection for the obedient remnant in Judah (cf. Mal. 3:16,17). The Babylonians permitted some to stay in the land when they departed (40:5-7). Jeremiah personally received kind treatment from the invader (40:1-6), and his enemies in Judah would later appeal to him (21:1-6; 37:3; 42:1-6). Ultimately, a band of renegade Judeans took Jeremiah to Egypt against God's will (cf. 43:1-7).

15:15-18 O LORD, You know. Jeremiah, in a mood of self-pity, reminded the Lord of his faithfulness in bearing reproach, his love for His word, and his separation from evil men to stand alone.

15:18 an unreliable stream. He asked that the Lord not fail him like a wadi that has dried up (v. 18). The answer to this concern is in 2:13 (the Lord is his fountain), 15:19-21, and 17:5-8.

15:19 The Lord reprimanded Jeremiah for self-pity and impatience. He had to have the proper posture before God and repent. If he did so, he would discern true values ("take out the precious," a figure drawn from removing pure metal from dross), and have the further privilege of being God's mouthpiece. Let sinners change to his values, but let him never compromise to theirs. As a man who is to assay and test others (6:27-30), he must first assay himself (cf. Moses, in Ex. 4:22-26).

15:20,21 When Jeremiah repents, God will protect him (vv. 20,21, as 1:18,19).

16:2 You shall not take a wife. Since destruction and exile are soon to fall on Judah, the prophet must not have a wife and family. God's kindness will keep him from anxiety over them in the awful situation of suffering and death (v. 4). Cf. 15:9 and 1 Cor. 7:26.

die [a]gruesome deaths; they shall not be
[b]lamented nor shall they be [c]buried, *but*
they shall be [d]like refuse on the face of the
earth. They shall be consumed by the
sword and by famine, and their [e]corpses
shall be meat for the birds of heaven and
for the beasts of the earth."
5 For thus says the LORD: [f]"Do not enter
the house of mourning, nor go to lament or
bemoan them; for I have taken away My
peace from this people," says the LORD,
"lovingkindness and mercies. 6 Both the
great and the small shall die in this land.
They shall not be buried; [g]neither shall
men lament for them, [h]cut themselves, nor
[i]make themselves bald for them. 7 Nor
shall *men* break *bread* in mourning for
them, to comfort them for the dead; nor
shall *men* give them the cup of consolation
to [j]drink for their father or their mother.
8 Also you shall not go into the house of
feasting to sit with them, to eat and drink."
9 For thus says the LORD of hosts, the
God of Israel: "Behold, [k]I will cause to
cease from this place, before your eyes and
in your days, the voice of [1]mirth and the
voice of gladness, the voice of the bridegroom and the voice of the bride.
10 "And it shall be, when you show this
people all these words, and they say to you,
[l]'Why has the LORD pronounced all this
great disaster against us? Or what *is* our iniquity? Or what *is* our sin that we have
committed against the LORD our God?'
11 then you shall say to them, [m]'Because
your fathers have forsaken Me,' says the
LORD; 'they have walked after other gods
and have served them and worshiped
them, and have forsaken Me and not kept
My law. 12 And you have done [n]worse than
your fathers, for behold, [o]each one [2]follows
the dictates of his own evil heart, so that no
one listens to Me. 13 [p]Therefore I will cast
you out of this land [q]into a land that you do
not know, neither you nor your fathers; and
there you shall serve other gods day and
night, where I will not show you favor.'

CHAPTER 16

4 [a]Jer. 15:2 [b]Jer. 22:18; 25:33 [c]Jer. 14:16; 19:11 [d]Ps. 83:10; Jer. 8:2; 9:22 [e]Ps. 79:2; Is. 18:6; Jer. 7:33; 34:20
5 [f]Ezek. 24:17, 22, 23
6 [g]Jer. 22:18 [h]Lev. 19:28; Deut. 14:1; Jer. 41:5; 47:5 [i]Is. 22:12; Jer. 7:29
7 [j]Prov. 31:6
9 [k]Is. 24:7, 8; Jer. 7:34; 25:10; Ezek. 26:13; Hos. 2:11; Rev. 18:23 [1]*rejoicing*
10 [l]Deut. 29:24; 1 Kin. 9:8; Jer. 5:19
11 [m]Deut. 29:25; 1 Kin. 9:9; 2 Chr. 7:22; Neh. 9:26-29; Jer. 22:9
12 [n]Jer. 7:26 [o]Jer. 3:17; 18:12 [2]*walks after the stubbornness* or *imagination*
13 [p]Deut. 4:26; 28:36, 63 [q]Jer. 15:14
14 [r]Is. 43:18; Jer. 23:7, 8; [Ezek. 37:21-25]
15 [s]Jer. 3:18 [t]Jer. 24:6; 30:3; 32:37
16 [u]Amos 4:2; Hab. 1:15
17 [v]2 Chr. 16:9; Job 34:21; Ps. 90:8; Prov. 5:21; Jer. 23:24; 32:19; Zech. 4:10; [Luke 12:2; 1 Cor. 4:5]; Heb. 4:13
18 [w]Is. 40:2; Jer. 17:18; Rev. 18:6 [x][Ezek. 43:7]
19 [y]Ps. 18:1, 2; Is. 25:4 [z]Jer. 17:17 [a]Is. 44:10
20 [b]Ps. 115:4-8; Is. 37:19; Jer. 2:11; 5:7; Hos. 8:4-6; Gal. 4:8
21 [c]Ex. 15:3; Ps. 83:18; Is. 43:3; Jer. 33:2; Amos 5:8

CHAPTER 17

1 [a]Jer. 2:22 [b]Job 19:24 [c]Prov. 3:3; 7:3; Is. 49:16; 2 Cor. 3:3

God Will Restore Israel

14 "Therefore behold, the [r]days are coming," says the LORD, "that it shall no more be
said, 'The LORD lives who brought up the
children of Israel from the land of Egypt,'
15 but, 'The LORD lives who brought up the
children of Israel from the land of the [s]north
and from all the lands where He had driven
them.' For [t]I will bring them back into their
land which I gave to their fathers.
16 "Behold, I will send for many [u]fisher-
men," says the LORD, "and they shall fish
them; and afterward I will send for many
hunters, and they shall hunt them from
every mountain and every hill, and out of
the holes of the rocks. 17 For My [v]eyes *are*
on all their ways; they are not hidden from
My face, nor is their iniquity hidden from
My eyes. 18 And first I will repay [w]double
for their iniquity and their sin, because
[x]they have defiled My land; they have
filled My inheritance with the carcasses of
their detestable and abominable idols."

19 O LORD, [y]my strength and my fortress,
[z]My refuge in the day of affliction,
The Gentiles shall come to You
From the ends of the earth and say,
"Surely our fathers have inherited lies,
Worthlessness and [a]unprofitable *things*."
20 Will a man make gods for himself,
[b]Which *are* not gods?

21 "Therefore behold, I will this once cause them to know,
I will cause them to know
My hand and My might;
And they shall know that [c]My name *is* the LORD.

Judah's Sin and Punishment

17 "The sin of Judah *is* [a]written with a [b]pen of iron;
With the point of a diamond *it is* [c]engraved

16:5 house of mourning. This was a home where friends prepared a meal for a bereaved family. Don't mourn with them or rejoice, he is told (cf. v. 8).

16:6 cut...bald. These acts indicated extreme grief.

16:10-13 Why...? Jeremiah was to explain the reason for the judgment, i.e., their forsaking God and worshiping false gods (v. 11; 2:13). They would get their fill of idols in Babylon (v. 13).

16:14,15 no more be said. In view of the Lord's promise of restoration from Babylon, the proof of God's redemptive power and faithfulness in the deliverance from Egypt would give way to a greater demonstration in the deliverance of His people from Babylon. That bondage was to be so severe that deliverance from Babylon was a greater relief than from Egypt.

16:15 all the lands. This reference is extensive enough to be fully realized only in the final gathering into Messiah's earthly kingdom.

16:16 many fishermen...hunters. These are references to Babylonian soldiers, who were doing God's judgment work (v. 17).

16:18 repay double. The word for "double" signified "full or complete," a fitting punishment for such severe sins.

16:19-21 The result of God's judgment on the Jews will be the end of idolatry; even some Gentiles, witnessing the severity, will renounce idols. After the return from Babylon, this was partly fulfilled as the Jews entirely and permanently renounced idols, and many Gentiles turned from their idols to Jehovah. However, the complete fulfillment will come in the final restoration of Israel (cf. Is. 2:1-4; 49:6; 60:3).

17:1 The sin of Judah. Reasons for the judgment (chap. 16) con-

On the tablet of their heart,
And on the horns of your altars,
2 While their children remember
Their altars and their [d]wooden[1] images
By the green trees on the high hills.
3 O My mountain in the field,
I will give as plunder your wealth, all your treasures,
And your high places of sin within all your borders.
4 And you, even yourself,
Shall let go of your heritage which I gave you;
And I will cause you to serve your enemies
In [e]the land which you do not know;
For [f]you have kindled a fire in My anger *which* shall burn forever."

5 Thus says the LORD:

[g]"Cursed *is* the man who trusts in man
And makes [h]flesh his [2]strength,
Whose heart departs from the LORD.
6 For he shall be [i]like a shrub in the desert,
And [j]shall not see when good comes,
But shall inhabit the parched places in the wilderness,
[k]*In* a salt land *which is* not inhabited.
7 "Blessed[l] *is* the man who trusts in the LORD,
And whose hope is the LORD.
8 For he shall be [m]like a tree planted by the waters,
Which spreads out its roots by the river,
And will not [3]fear when heat comes;
But its leaf will be green,
And will not be anxious in the year of drought,
Nor will cease from yielding fruit.

9 "The [n]heart *is* deceitful above all *things*,
And [4]desperately wicked;
Who can know it?
10 I, the LORD, [o]search the heart,
I test the [5]mind,
[p]Even to give every man according to his ways,
According to the fruit of his doings.

11 "*As* a partridge that [6]broods but does not hatch,
So is he who gets riches, but not by right;
It [q]will leave him in the midst of his days,
And at his end he will be [r]a fool."

12 A glorious high throne from the beginning
Is the place of our sanctuary.
13 O LORD, [s]the hope of Israel,
[t]All who forsake You shall be ashamed.

"Those who depart from Me
Shall be [u]written in the earth,
Because they have forsaken the LORD,
The [v]fountain of living waters."

Jeremiah Prays for Deliverance

14 Heal me, O LORD, and I shall be healed;
Save me, and I shall be saved,
For [w]You *are* my praise.
15 Indeed they say to me,
[x]"Where *is* the word of the LORD?
Let it come now!"

2 [d] Judg. 3:7 [1] Heb. *Asherim*, Canaanite deities
4 [e] Jer. 16:13 [f] Is. 5:25; Jer. 15:14
5 [g] Ps. 146:3; Is. 30:1, 2; 31:1 [h] Is. 31:3 [2] Lit. *arm*
6 [i] Jer. 48:6 [j] Job 20:17 [k] Deut. 29:23; Job 39:6
7 [l] Ps. 2:12; 34:8; 125:1; 146:5; Prov. 16:20; [Is. 30:18]; Jer. 39:18
8 [m] Job 8:16; [Ps. 1:3; Ezek. 31:3-9]
[3] Qr., Tg. *see*
9 [n] [Eccl. 9:3]; Matt. 15:19; [Mark 7:21, 22] [4] Or *incurably sick*
10 [o] 1 Sam. 16:7; 1 Chr. 28:9; Ps. 7:9; 139:23, 24; Prov. 17:3; Jer. 11:20; 20:12; Rom. 8:27; Rev. 2:23 [p] Ps. 62:12; Jer. 32:19; Rom. 2:6 [5] Most secret parts, lit. *kidneys*
11 [q] Ps. 55:23 [r] Luke 12:20 [6] Sits on eggs
13 [s] Jer. 14:8 [t] [Ps. 73:27; Is. 1:28] [u] Luke 10:20 [v] Jer. 2:13
14 [w] Deut. 10:21; Ps. 109:1
15 [x] Is. 5:19; Ezek. 12:22; 2 Pet. 3:4

tinue here: 1) idolatry (vv. 1-4), 2) relying on the flesh (v. 5), and 3) dishonesty in amassing wealth (v. 11). **pen of iron.** The names of idols were engraved on the horns of their altars with such a tool. The idea is that Judah's sin was permanent, etched in them as if into stone. How much different to have God's word written on the heart (31:33).

17:3 My mountain in the field. Jerusalem in Judah.

17:4 land…you do not know. Babylon.

17:5-8 Cursed *is* the man. Jeremiah contrasted the person who experiences barrenness (vv. 5,6) with the one who receives blessing (vv. 7,8). The difference in attitude is in "trust" placed in man or "trust" vested in the Lord (vv. 5,7). And the contrast in vitality is between being like a parched dwarf juniper in the desert (v. 6) or a tree drawing sustenance from a stream to bear fruit (v. 8; cf. Ps. 1:1-3).

17:10 I…search the heart. For the sin of man (vv. 1-4), for the barren man (vv. 5,6), or the blessed man (vv. 7,8), God is the final Judge and renders His judgment for their works (cf. Rev. 20:11-15). By Him, actions are weighed (1 Sam. 2:3).

17:11 a partridge. This referred to a sand grouse which invaded and brooded over a nest not its own, but was forced to leave before the eggs hatched. It depicted a person who unjustly took possession of things he had no right to take and couldn't enjoy the benefits, despite all the effort.

17:14-18 Jeremiah voiced the prayerful cry that God would deliver him from his enemies (v. 14). Surrounded by ungodly people (vv. 1-6,11,13), he showed qualities of godliness: 1) God was his praise (v. 14); 2) he had a shepherd's heart to follow God (v. 16); 3) he was a man of prayer open to God's examination (v. 16); 4) God was his hope (v. 17); and 5) he trusted God's delivering faithfulness even in judgment (v. 18).

16 As for me, [y]I have not hurried
away from *being* a shepherd
who follows You,
Nor have I desired the woeful day;
You know what came out of my
lips;
It was right there before You.
17 Do not be a terror to me;
[z]You *are* my hope in the day of
doom.
18 [a]Let them be ashamed who
persecute me,
But [b]do not let me be put to shame;
Let them be dismayed,
But do not let me be dismayed.
Bring on them the day of doom,
And [c]destroy[7] them with double
destruction!

Hallow the Sabbath Day

19 Thus the LORD said to me: "Go and
stand in the gate of the children of the people, by which the kings of Judah come in
and by which they go out, and in all the
gates of Jerusalem; 20 and say to them,
[d]'Hear the word of the LORD, you kings of
Judah, and all Judah, and all the inhabitants of Jerusalem, who enter by these
gates. 21 Thus says the LORD: [e]"Take heed
to yourselves, and bear no burden on the
Sabbath day, nor bring *it* in by the gates of
Jerusalem; 22 nor carry a burden out of
your houses on the Sabbath day, nor do
any work, but hallow the Sabbath day, as I
[f]commanded your fathers. 23 [g]But they did
not obey nor incline their ear, but [8]made
their neck stiff, that they might not hear
nor receive instruction.
24 "And it shall be, [h]if you heed Me carefully," says the LORD, "to bring no burden
through the gates of this city on the [i]Sab-
bath day, but hallow the Sabbath day, to do
no work in it, 25 [j]then shall enter the gates
of this city kings and princes sitting on the
throne of David, riding in chariots and on
horses, they and their princes, accompanied by the men of Judah and the inhabitants of Jerusalem; and this city shall remain forever. 26 And they shall come from
the cities of Judah and from [k]the places
around Jerusalem, from the land of Benjamin and from [l]the [9]lowland, from the
mountains and from [m]the [1]South, bringing
burnt offerings and sacrifices, grain offerings and incense, bringing [n]sacrifices of
praise to the house of the LORD.
27 "But if you will not heed Me to hallow
the Sabbath day, such as not carrying a
burden when entering the gates of Jerusalem on the Sabbath day, then [o]I will kindle
a fire in its gates, [p]and it shall devour the
palaces of Jerusalem, and it shall not be
[q]quenched." ' "

16 [y] Jer. 1:4-12
17 [z] Jer. 16:19; Nah. 1:7
18 [a] Ps. 35:4; 70:2; Jer. 15:10; 18:18 [b] Ps. 25:2 [c] Jer. 11:20 [7] Lit. *crush*
20 [d] Ps. 49:1, 2; Jer. 19:3, 4
21 [e] Num. 15:32; Neh. 13:19; [John 5:9-12, 17; 7:22-24]
22 [f] Ex. 20:8; 31:13; Ezek. 20:12
23 [g] Jer. 7:24, 26 [8] Were stubborn
24 [h] Jer. 11:4; 26:3 [i] Ex. 16:23-30; 20:8-10; Num. 15:32-36; Deut. 5:12-14; Neh. 13:15; [Is. 58:13]
25 [j] Jer. 22:4
26 [k] Jer. 33:13 [l] Zech. 7:7 [m] Judg. 1:9 [n] Ps. 107:22; 116:17; Jer. 33:11 [9] Heb. *shephelah* [1] Heb. *Negev*
27 [o] Jer. 21:14; Lam. 4:11; Amos 1:4, 7, 10, 12 [p] 2 Kin. 25:9; 2 Chr. 36:19; Jer. 39:8; 52:13; Amos 2:5 [q] Jer. 7:20; Ezek. 20:47

CHAPTER 18

3 [1] Potter's wheel
4 [2] *was making* [3] *ruined*
6 [a] Is. 45:9; Rom. 9:20, 21 [b] Is. 64:8
7 [c] Jer. 1:10
8 [d] Jer. 7:3-7; 12:16; [Ezek. 18:21; 33:11] [e] [Ps. 106:45]; Jer. 26:3; [Hos. 11:8; Joel 2:13]; Jon. 3:10

The Potter and the Clay

18 The word which came to Jeremiah
from the LORD, saying: 2 "Arise and
go down to the potter's house, and there I
will cause you to hear My words." 3 Then I
went down to the potter's house, and there
he was, making something at the [1]wheel.
4 And the vessel that he [2]made of clay was
[3]marred in the hand of the potter; so he
made it again into another vessel, as it
seemed good to the potter to make.
5 Then the word of the LORD came to me,
saying: 6 "O house of Israel, [a]can I not do
with you as this potter?" says the LORD.
"Look, [b]as the clay *is* in the potter's hand,
so *are* you in My hand, O house of Israel!
7 The instant I speak concerning a nation
and concerning a kingdom, to [c]pluck up,
to pull down, and to destroy *it*, 8 [d]if that
nation against whom I have spoken turns
from its evil, [e]I will relent of the disaster
that I thought to bring upon it. 9 And the
instant I speak concerning a nation and
concerning a kingdom, to build and to
plant *it*, 10 if it does evil in My sight so that
it does not obey My voice, then I will relent
concerning the good with which I said I
would benefit it.
11 "Now therefore, speak to the men of
Judah and to the inhabitants of Jerusalem,

17:21-24 Sabbath day. Not only had the Jews failed to observe Sabbath days, but also the required Sabbath year of rest for the Land (Lev. 25:1-7) was regularly violated. God had warned that such disobedience would bring judgment (Lev. 26:34,35,43; 2 Chr. 36:20,21). The 70 year captivity was correlated to the 490 years from Saul to the captivity, which included 70 Sabbath years. When the Jews were restored from captivity, special stress was placed on Sabbath faithfulness (cf. Neh. 13:19).

17:25-27 For obedience, God would assure the dynasty of David perpetual rule in Jerusalem, safety for the city, and worship at the temple (vv. 25,26). Continued disobedience would meet with destruction of the city (v. 27).

18:1–20:18 A close link exists between chap. 17 and chaps. 18–20. Destruction is in view (chap. 17), but repentance can yet prevent that (18:7,8). However, repentance was not present (18:12), so Jeremiah's shattered flask illustrated God's dashing Israel in judgment (chap. 19). Then the rejection spirit (cf. 19:15) led to persecution against God's mouthpiece (chap. 20).

18:2-6 potter's house. God sent Jeremiah to a potter, who gave him an illustration by shaping a vessel. The prophet secured a vessel and used it for his own illustration (19:1ff.). Jeremiah watched the potter at his wheel. The soft clay became misshapen, but the potter shaped it back into a good vessel. God will so do with Judah if she repents.

18:8-10 Though He had announced impending judgment, the "marred" nation can be restored as a good vessel by God, who will hold off the judgment (vv. 8,11). By contrast, if the nation followed sin, He would not bring the blessing desired (vv. 9,10).

saying, 'Thus says the LORD: "Behold, I am fashioning a disaster and devising a plan against you. [f]Return now every one from his evil way, and make your ways and your doings [g]good." ' "

God's Warning Rejected

12 And they said, [h]"That is hopeless! So we will walk according to our own plans, and we will every one [4]obey the [i]dictates[5] of his evil heart."

13 Therefore thus says the LORD:

[j]"Ask now among the Gentiles,
Who has heard such things?
The virgin of Israel has done [k]a
very horrible thing.
14 Will *a man* [6]leave the snow water
of Lebanon,
Which comes from the rock of the
field?
Will the cold flowing waters be
forsaken for strange waters?

15 "Because My people have forgotten
[l]Me,
They have burned incense to
worthless idols.
And they have caused themselves
to stumble in their ways,
From the [m]ancient paths,
To walk in pathways and not on a
highway,
16 To make their land [n]desolate *and* a
perpetual [o]hissing;
Everyone who passes by it will be
astonished
And shake his head.
17 [p]I will scatter them [q]as with an east
wind before the enemy;
[r]I will [7]show them the back and
not the face
In the day of their calamity."

Jeremiah Persecuted

18 Then they said, [s]"Come and let us devise plans against Jeremiah; [t]for the law shall not perish from the priest, nor counsel from the wise, nor the word from the prophet. Come and let us attack him with the tongue, and let us not give heed to any of his words."

19 Give heed to me, O LORD,
And listen to the voice of those
who contend with me!
20 [u]Shall evil be repaid for good?
For they have [v]dug a pit for my life.
Remember that I [w]stood before You
To speak good [8]for them,
To turn away Your wrath from
them.
21 Therefore [x]deliver up their
children to the famine,
And pour out their *blood*
By the force of the sword;
Let their wives *become* widows
And [y]bereaved of their children.
Let their men be put to death,
Their young men *be* slain
By the sword in battle.
22 Let a cry be heard from their houses,
When You bring a troop suddenly
upon them;
For they have dug a pit to take me,
And hidden snares for my feet.
23 Yet, LORD, You know all their
counsel
Which is against me, to slay *me*.
[z]Provide no atonement for their
iniquity,
Nor blot out their sin from Your
sight;
But let them be overthrown before
You.
Deal *thus* with them
In the time of Your [a]anger.

The Sign of the Broken Flask

19 Thus says the LORD: "Go and get a potter's earthen flask, and *take* some of the elders of the people and some

11 [f]2 Kin. 17:13; Is. 1:16-19; Jer. 4:1; Acts 26:20 [g]Jer. 7:3-7
12 [h]Is. 57:10; Jer. 2:25 [i]Jer. 3:17; 23:17 [4]Lit. *do* [5]*stubbornness* or *imagination*
13 [j]Is. 66:8; Jer. 2:10, 11; 1 Cor. 5:1 [k]Jer. 5:30; Hos. 6:10
14 [6]*forsake*
15 [l]Jer. 2:13, 32 [m]Jer. 6:16
16 [n]Jer. 19:8 [o]1 Kin. 9:8; Lam. 2:15; Mic. 6:16
17 [p]Jer. 13:24 [q]Ps. 48:7 [r]Jer. 2:27 [7]So with LXX, Syr., Tg., Vg.; MT *look them in*
18 [s]Jer. 11:19 [t]Lev. 10:11; Mal. 2:7; [John 7:48]
20 [u]Ps. 109:4 [v]Ps. 35:7; 57:6; Jer. 5:26 [w]Jer. 14:7–15:1 [8]*concerning*
21 [x]Ps. 109:9-20; Jer. 11:22; 14:16 [y]Jer. 15:7, 8; Ezek. 22:25
23 [z]Neh. 4:5; Ps. 35:14; 109:14; Is. 2:9; Jer. 11:20 [a]Jer. 7:20

18:12 That is hopeless! Jeremiah brought them to the point where they actually stated their condition honestly. The prophet's threats were useless because they were so far gone—abandoned to their sins and the penalty. All hypocrisy was abandoned in favor of honesty, without repentance. Repentance was not in Israel (as v. 18; 19:15). This explains a seeming paradox, that Israel can repent and avert judgment, yet Jeremiah is not to pray for Israel (7:16; 11:14). It would do no good to pray for their change since they steeled themselves against any change.

18:13 virgin of Israel. It enhanced their guilt that Israel was the virgin whom God had chosen (cf. 2 Kin. 19:21).

18:14 snow water...cold flowing waters. No reasonable man would forsake such for "the rock of the field," perhaps a poetic term for Mt. Lebanon, from which the high mountain streams flowed. Yet Israel forsook God, the fountain of living waters, for broken foreign cisterns (cf. 2:13).

18:18 plans against Jeremiah. Plans to indict the prophet with their "tongues" and then to slay him (v. 23) were based on the promise that his message of doom was not true. The business of the priests, the wise, and the prophets continued as usual since God made them lasting institutions (cf. Lev. 6:18; 10:11).

18:19-23 Give heed to me. This is one of many examples of prayer aligning with God's will as Jeremiah prays for God's work of judgment to be done (vv. 11,15-17).

18:22 dug a pit. Cf. 38:6.

19:1 elders of the people...the priests. These were chosen to be credible witnesses of the symbolic action with the "earthen flask," so no one could plead ignorance of the prophesy. The 72 elders who made up the Sanhedrin were partly from the "priests" and the other tribes ("people").

of the elders of the priests. 2 And go out to
[a]the Valley of the Son of Hinnom, which *is*
by the entry of the Potsherd Gate; and proclaim there the words that I will tell you,
3 [b]and say, 'Hear the word of the LORD, O
kings of Judah and inhabitants of Jerusalem. Thus says the LORD of hosts, the God
of Israel: "Behold, I will bring such a catastrophe on this place, that whoever hears
of it, his ears will [c]tingle.
4 "Because they [d]have forsaken Me and
made this an alien place, because they
have burned incense in it to other gods
whom neither they, their fathers, nor the
kings of Judah have known, and have
filled this place with [e]the blood of the innocents 5 [f](they have also built the high
places of Baal, to burn their sons with fire
for burnt offerings to Baal, [g]which I did not
command or speak, nor did it come into
My mind), 6 therefore behold, the days are
coming," says the LORD, "that this place
shall no more be called Tophet or [h]the Valley of the Son of Hinnom, but the Valley of
Slaughter. 7 And I will make void the
counsel of Judah and Jerusalem in this
place, [i]and I will cause them to fall by the
sword before their enemies and by the
hands of those who seek their lives; their
[j]corpses I will give as meat for the birds of
the heaven and for the beasts of the earth.
8 I will make this city [k]desolate and a hissing; everyone who passes by it will be astonished and hiss because of all its
plagues. 9 And I will cause them to eat the
[l]flesh of their sons and the flesh of their
daughters, and everyone shall eat the flesh
of his friend in the siege and in the desperation with which their enemies and those
who seek their lives shall drive them to despair."'
10 [m]"Then you shall break the flask in
the sight of the men who go with you,
11 and say to them, 'Thus says the LORD of
hosts: [n]"Even so I will break this people
and this city, as *one* breaks a potter's vessel,
which cannot be [1]made whole again; and
they shall [o]bury *them* in Tophet till *there is*
no place to bury. 12 Thus I will do to this
place," says the LORD, "and to its inhabitants, and make this city like Tophet.
13 And the houses of Jerusalem and the
houses of the kings of Judah shall be defiled [p]like the place of Tophet, because of
all the houses on whose [q]roofs they have
burned incense to all the host of heaven,
and [r]poured out drink offerings to other
gods."'"
14 Then Jeremiah came from Tophet,
where the LORD had sent him to prophesy;
and he stood in [s]the court of the Lord's
house and said to all the people, 15 "Thus
says the LORD of hosts, the God of Israel:
'Behold, I will bring on this city and on all
her towns all the doom that I have pronounced against it, because [t]they have
stiffened their necks that they might not
hear My words.'"

The Word of God to Pashhur

20 Now [a]Pashhur the son of [b]Immer,
the priest who *was* also chief governor in the house of the LORD, heard that
Jeremiah prophesied these things. 2 Then
Pashhur struck Jeremiah the prophet, and
put him in the stocks that *were* in the high
[c]gate of Benjamin, which *was* by the house
of the LORD.
3 And it happened on the next day that
Pashhur brought Jeremiah out of the
stocks. Then Jeremiah said to him, "The
LORD has not called your name Pashhur,
but [1]Magor-Missabib. 4 For thus says the
LORD: 'Behold, I will make you a terror to
yourself and to all your friends; and they
shall fall by the sword of their enemies,
and your eyes shall see *it*. I will [d]give all
Judah into the hand of the king of Babylon,

CHAPTER 19

2 [a] Josh. 15:8; 2 Kin. 23:10; Jer. 7:31; 32:35
3 [b] Jer. 17:20 [c] 1 Sam. 3:11; 2 Kin. 21:12
4 [d] Deut. 28:20; Is. 65:11; Jer. 2:13, 17, 19; 15:6; 17:13 [e] 2 Kin. 21:12; Jer. 2:34; 7:6
5 [f] Num. 22:41; Jer. 7:31; 32:35 [g] Lev. 18:21; 2 Kin. 17:17; Ps. 106:37, 38
6 [h] Josh. 15:8; Jer. 7:32
7 [i] Lev. 26:17; Deut. 28:25; Jer. 15:2, 9 [j] Ps. 79:2; Jer. 7:33; 16:4; 34:20
8 [k] Jer. 18:16; 49:13; 50:13
9 [l] Lev. 26:29; Deut. 28:53, 55; Is. 9:20; Lam. 4:10; Ezek. 5:10
10 [m] Jer. 51:63, 64
11 [n] Ps. 2:9; Is. 30:14; Jer. 13:14; Lam. 4:2; Rev. 2:27 [o] Jer. 7:32 [1] *restored*
13 [p] 2 Kin. 23:10; Ps. 74:7; 79:1; Jer. 52:13; Ezek. 7:21, 22 [q] 2 Kin. 23:12; Jer. 32:29; Zeph. 1:5 [r] Jer. 7:18; Ezek. 20:28
14 [s] 2 Chr. 20:5; Jer. 26:2-8
15 [t] Neh. 9:17, 29; Jer. 7:26; 17:23

CHAPTER 20

1 [a] Ezra 2:37, 38 [b] 1 Chr. 24:14
2 [c] Jer. 37:13; Zech. 14:10
3 [1] Lit. *Fear on Every Side*
4 [d] Jer. 21:4-10

19:2 Valley...Hinnom. *See note on 19:6.* **Potsherd Gate.** The gate of "broken pottery" was on the S wall of Jerusalem where the potters formed pottery for use in the temple nearby.

19:6 Tophet. Hebrew uses the word *toph* for "drum." This was another name for the Valley of Hinnom, an E-W valley at the S end of Jerusalem where, when children were burned in sacrifice to idols (cf. vv. 4,5), drums were beaten to drown their cries. Rubbish from Jerusalem was dumped there and continually burned. The place became a symbol for the burning fires of hell, called Gehenna (Matt. 5:22). Cf. 7:30-32; Is. 30:33. It was to become a place of massacre.

19:9 eat the flesh. Desperate for food during a long siege, some would resort to cannibalism, eating family members and friends (Lam. 4:10).

19:10 Cf. v. 1.

19:13 defiled. With dead bodies (cf. 2 Kin. 23:10). **incense to...host of heaven.** Refers to worship of the sun, planets, and stars from flat housetops (cf. 32:29; 2 Kin. 23:11,12; Zeph. 1:5).

20:1 Pashhur. The meaning is either "ease," or "deliverance is round about," both in contrast to the new name God assigns him in v. 3. He was one of several men so named (cf. 21:1; 38:1). **Immer.** He was one of the original "governors of the sanctuary" (cf. 1 Chr. 24:14). **chief governor.** He was not the High-Priest, but the chief official in charge of temple police, who were to maintain order.

20:2 struck Jeremiah. He or others acting on his authority, delivered 40 lashes (see Deut. 25:3) to the prophet. **put him in the stocks.** Hands, feet, and neck were fastened in holes, bending the body to a distorted posture, causing excruciating pain. **high gate.** The northern gate of the upper temple court.

20:3 Magor-Missabib. "Terror on every side" is the fitting name which the Lord reckons for the leader. The details of that terror are in vv. 4,6 (cf. 6:25).

20:4 Babylon. This was Jeremiah's direct identification of the conqueror who would come out of the "north" (1:13), from "a far country" (4:16).

and he shall carry them captive to Babylon
and slay them with the sword. 5 Moreover
I [e]will deliver all the wealth of this city, all
its produce, and all its precious things; all
the treasures of the kings of Judah I will
give into the hand of their enemies, who
will plunder them, seize them, and [f]carry
them to Babylon. 6 And you, Pashhur, and
all who dwell in your house, shall go into
captivity. You shall go to Babylon, and
there you shall die, and be buried there,
you and all your friends, to whom you
have [g]prophesied lies.'"

Jeremiah's Unpopular Ministry

7 O LORD, You [2]induced me, and I
was persuaded;
[h]You are stronger than I, and have
prevailed.
[i]I am [3]in derision daily;
Everyone mocks me.
8 For when I spoke, I cried out;
[j]I shouted, "Violence and plunder!"
Because the word of the LORD was
made to me
A reproach and a derision daily.
9 Then I said, "I will not make
mention of Him,
Nor speak anymore in His name."
But *His word* was in my heart like a
[k]burning fire
Shut up in my bones;
I was weary of holding *it* back,
And [l]I could not.
10 [m]For I heard many [4]mocking:
"Fear on every side!"
"Report," *they say,* "and we will
report it!"
[n]All my acquaintances watched for
my stumbling, *saying,*
"Perhaps he can be induced;
Then we will prevail against him,
And we will take our revenge on
him."
11 But the LORD *is* [o]with me as a
mighty, awesome One.
Therefore my persecutors will
stumble, and will not
[p]prevail.
They will be greatly ashamed, for
they will not prosper.
Their [q]everlasting confusion will
never be forgotten.
12 But, O LORD of hosts,
You who [r]test the righteous,
And see the [5]mind and heart,
[s]Let me see Your vengeance on
them;
For I have pleaded my cause
before You.

13 Sing to the LORD! Praise the LORD!
For [t]He has delivered the life of the
poor
From the hand of evildoers.

14 [u]Cursed *be* the day in which I was
born!
Let the day not be blessed in which
my mother bore me!
15 Let the man *be* cursed
Who brought news to my father,
saying,
"A male child has been born to
you!"
Making him very glad.
16 And let that man be like the cities
Which the LORD [v]overthrew, and
did not relent;
Let him [w]hear the cry in the
morning
And the shouting at noon,
17 [x]Because he did not kill me from the
womb,
That my mother might have been
my grave,
And her womb always enlarged
with me.
18 [y]Why did I come forth from the
womb to [z]see [6]labor and
sorrow,
That my days should be consumed
with shame?

Jerusalem's Doom Is Sealed

21 The word which came to Jeremiah
from the LORD when [a]King Zedekiah sent to him [b]Pashhur the son of Mel-
chiah, and [c]Zephaniah the son of Maa-

5 [e] 2 Kin. 20:17; 2 Chr. 36:10; Jer. 3:24; 27:21, 22 [f] Is. 39:6
6 [g] Jer. 14:13-15; Lam. 2:14
7 [h] Jer. 1:6, 7 [i] Job 12:4; Lam. 3:14 [2] *enticed* or *persuaded* [3] Lit. *a laughingstock all the day*
8 [j] Jer. 6:7
9 [k] Job 32:18-20; Ps. 39:3; Jer. 4:19; 23:9; [Ezek. 3:14]; Acts 4:20 [l] Job 32:18; Jer. 6:11; Acts 18:5
10 [m] Ps. 31:13 [n] Job 19:19; Ps. 41:9; 55:13, 14; Luke 11:53, 54 [4] *slandering*
11 [o] Jer. 1:18, 19 [p] Jer. 15:20; 17:18
[q] Jer. 23:40
12 [r] Ps. 7:9; 11:5; 17:3; 139:23; [Jer. 11:20; 17:10] [s] Ps. 54:7; 59:10; Jer. 15:15 [5] Most secret parts, lit. *kidneys*
13 [t] Ps. 35:9, 10; 109:30, 31
14 [u] Job 3:3; Jer. 15:10
16 [v] Gen. 19:25 [w] Jer. 18:22
17 [x] Job 3:10, 11
18 [y] Job 3:20; Jer. 15:10 [z] Lam. 3:1 [6] *toil*

CHAPTER 21

1 [a] 2 Kin. 24:17, 18; Jer. 32:1-3; 37:1; 52:1-3 [b] 1 Chr. 9:12; Jer. 38:1 [c] 2 Kin. 25:18; Jer. 29:25; 37:3

20:8 derision daily. In vv. 7-18, Jeremiah prayerfully lamented the ridicule he was experiencing because of God's role for his life. His feelings wavered between quitting (v. 9a), being encouraged (vv. 9c,11), petitioning for help (v. 12), praise (v. 13), and waves of depression (vv. 14-18; cf. 11:18-23; 15:10,15-18).

20:9 I will not make mention. A surge of dejection swept over Jeremiah, making him long to say no more. But he was compelled inside (cf. Job 32:18,19; Ps. 39:3; Acts 18:5; 1 Cor. 9:16,17) because he did not want his enemies to see him fail (v. 10), he felt the powerful presence of the Lord (v. 11), and he remembered God's previous deliverances (v. 13).

20:14 Cursed *be* the day. Another tide of depression engulfed the prophet, perhaps when he was in the painful stocks (v. 2). His words are like Job's (Job 3:3,10,11).

20:15 Let the man *be* cursed. The servant of God fell into sinful despair, and he questioned the wisdom and purpose of God, for which he should have been thankful.

20:16 the cities which the LORD overthrew. Sodom and Gomorrah (Gen. 19:25).

21:1 King Zedekiah. Cf. 2 Kin. 24:17–25:7 for details of his reign ca. 597–586 B.C. **Pashhur.** This priest was different from the man by this name in 20:1-6. Cf. 38:1.

seiah, the priest, saying, 2 [d]"Please inquire
of the LORD for us, for [1]Nebuchadnezzar
king of Babylon makes war against us. Perhaps the LORD will deal with us according
to all His wonderful works, that *the king*
may go away from us."
3 Then Jeremiah said to them, "Thus you
shall say to Zedekiah, 4 'Thus says the
LORD God of Israel: "Behold, I will turn
back the weapons of war that *are* in your
hands, with which you fight against the
king of Babylon and the [2]Chaldeans who
besiege you outside the walls; and [e]I will
assemble them in the midst of this city. 5 I
[f]Myself will fight against you with an
[g]outstretched hand and with a strong arm,
even in anger and fury and great wrath. 6 I
will strike the inhabitants of this city, both
man and beast; they shall die of a great
pestilence. 7 And afterward," says the
LORD, [h]"I will deliver Zedekiah king of Judah, his servants and the people, and such
as are left in this city from the pestilence
and the sword and the famine, into the
hand of Nebuchadnezzar king of Babylon,
into the hand of their enemies, and into the
hand of those who seek their life; and he
shall strike them with the edge of the
sword. [i]He shall not spare them, or have
pity or mercy." '
8 "Now you shall say to this people,
'Thus says the LORD: "Behold, [j]I set before
you the way of life and the way of death.
9 He who [k]remains in this city shall die by
the sword, by famine, and by pestilence; but
he who goes out and [3]defects to the Chaldeans who besiege you, he shall [l]live, and
his life shall be as a prize to him. 10 For I
have [m]set My face against this city for adversity and not for good," says the LORD.
[n]"It shall be given into the hand of the king
of Babylon, and he shall [o]burn it with fire." '

Message to the House of David

11 "And concerning the house of the
king of Judah, *say,* 'Hear the word of the
LORD, 12 O house of David! Thus says the
LORD:

[p]"Execute[4] judgment [q]in the morning;
And deliver *him who is* plundered
Out of the hand of the oppressor,
Lest My fury go forth like fire
And burn so that no one can
quench *it,*
Because of the evil of your doings.

13 "Behold, [r]I *am* against you,
O [5]inhabitant of the valley,
And rock of the plain," says the
LORD,
"Who say, [s]'Who shall come down
against us?
Or who shall enter our dwellings?'
14 But I will punish you according to
the [t]fruit of your [6]doings,"
says the LORD;
"I will kindle a fire in its forest,
And [u]it shall devour all things
around it." ' "

22 Thus says the LORD: "Go down to
the house of the king of Judah, and
there speak this word, 2 and say, [a]'Hear the
word of the LORD, O king of Judah, you
who sit on the throne of David, you and
your servants and your people who enter
these gates! 3 Thus says the LORD: [b]"Execute[1] judgment and righteousness, and deliver the plundered out of the hand of the
oppressor. Do no wrong and do no violence to the stranger, the [c]fatherless, or the
widow, nor shed innocent blood in this
place. 4 For if you indeed do this thing,
[d]then shall enter the gates of this house,
riding on horses and in chariots, accompanied by servants and people, kings who sit
on the throne of David. 5 But if you will not
[2]hear these words, [e]I swear by Myself,"
says the LORD, "that this house shall become a desolation." ' "
6 For thus says the LORD to the house of
the king of Judah:

2 [d] Ex. 9:28; 1 Sam. 9:9; Jer. 37:3, 7; Ezek. 14:7; 20:1-3 [1] Heb. *Nebuchadrezzar,* and so elsewhere in the book
4 [e] Is. 13:4; Jer. 39:3; Lam. 2:5, 7; Zech. 14:2 [2] Or *Babylonians,* and so elsewhere in the book
5 [f] Jer. 32:24; 33:5; Is. 63:10 [g] Ex. 6:6; Deut. 4:34; Jer. 6:12
7 [h] 2 Kin. 25:5-7, 18-21; Jer. 37:17; 39:5; 52:9 [i] Deut. 28:50; 2 Chr. 36:17; Jer. 13:14; Ezek. 7:9; Hab. 1:6-10
8 [j] Deut. 30:15, 19; Is. 1:19, 20
9 [k] Jer. 38:2 [l] Jer. 39:18 [3] Lit. *falls away to*
10 [m] Lev. 17:10; Jer. 44:11, 27; Amos 9:4 [n] Jer. 38:3 [o] 2 Kin. 25:9; 2 Chr. 36:19; Jer. 34:2, 22; 37:10
12 [p] Ps. 72:1; Is. 1:17; Jer. 22:3; Zech. 7:9 [q] Ps. 101:8; Zeph. 3:5 [4] *Dispense justice*
13 [r] [Jer. 23:30-32; Ezek. 13:8] [s] 2 Sam. 5:6, 7; Jer. 49:4; Lam. 4:12; Obad. 3, 4 [5] *dweller*
14 [t] Prov. 1:31; Is. 3:10, 11; Jer. 17:10; 32:19 [u] 2 Chr. 36:19; Is. 10:16, 18; Jer. 11:16; 17:27; 52:13; Ezek. 20:47, 48 [6] *deeds*

CHAPTER 22

2 [a] Jer. 17:20
3 [b] Is. 58:6; Jer. 21:12; [Mic. 6:8]; Zech. 7:9; 8:16; Matt. 23:23 [c] Jer. 7:6; Zech. 7:10 [1] *Dispense justice*
4 [d] Jer. 17:25
5 [e] Matt. 23:38; Heb. 6:13, 17 [2] Obey

21:2 war against us. This was during the last siege by Babylon (v. 4), ca. 587/86 B.C., resulting in the third deportation of Jews. Zedekiah hoped for God's intervention, such as Hezekiah received against Sennacherib (2 Kin. 19:35,36).

21:4 turn back the weapons...assemble them. The Jews were already fighting the invaders by going outside the walls of the city to battle them on the hillsides and in the valleys as they approached. However, they would soon be driven back into the city where the enemy would collect all their weapons and execute many with those very weapons.

21:5 I Myself will fight. God used an invader as His judging instrument (v. 7). The Jews have not only the Babylonians as their enemy, but God.

21:7 strike them...sword. This was the fate of Zedekiah's son and many nobles. Zedekiah died of grief (cf. 34:4; 2 Kin. 25:6-8).

21:8,9 life and...death. Since a persistent lack of repentance had led to the conquest, Jeremiah urged the Jews to submit and surrender to the besieger so as to be treated as captives of war and live rather than be killed.

21:12 O house of David! The royal family and all connected were called to enact justice and righteousness promptly ("morning"). There was still time for them to escape the destruction if there was repentance.

21:13 inhabitant of the valley...rock of the plain. Jerusalem personified, situated among rocks, hills, and valleys.

21:14 I will punish. During the siege Jerusalem will be burned (v. 10), as will the land in general.

22:2,4 throne of David. Refers to the Davidic Covenant of 2 Sam. 7:3-17, in which God promised David that his heirs will rule over Israel.

"You *are* [f]Gilead to Me,
The head of Lebanon;
Yet I surely will make you a
wilderness,
Cities *which* are not inhabited.
7 I will prepare destroyers against
you,
Everyone with his weapons;
They shall cut down [g]your choice
cedars
[h]And cast *them* into the fire.

8 And many nations will pass by this city;
and everyone will say to his neighbor,
[i]'Why has the LORD done so to this great
city?' 9 Then they will answer, [j]'Because
they have forsaken the covenant of the
LORD their God, and worshiped other gods
and served them.' "

10 Weep not for [k]the dead, nor
bemoan him;
Weep bitterly for him [l]who goes
away,
For he shall return no more,
Nor see his native country.

Message to the Sons of Josiah

11 For thus says the LORD concerning
[m]Shallum[3] the son of Josiah, king of Judah,
who reigned instead of Josiah his father,
[n]who went from this place: "He shall not
return here anymore, 12 but he shall die in
the place where they have led him captive,
and shall see this land no more.

13 "Woe[o] to him who builds his house
by unrighteousness
And his [4]chambers by injustice,
[p]*Who* uses his neighbor's service
without wages
And gives him nothing for his
work,
14 Who says, 'I will build myself a
wide house with spacious
[5]chambers,
And cut out windows for it,
Paneling *it* with cedar
And painting *it* with vermilion.'

15 "Shall you reign because you
enclose *yourself* in cedar?
Did not your father eat and drink,
And do justice and righteousness?
Then [q]*it was* well with him.
16 He [6]judged the cause of the poor
and needy;
Then *it was* well.
Was not this knowing Me?" says
the LORD.
17 "Yet[r] your eyes and your heart *are*
for nothing but your
covetousness,
For shedding innocent blood,
And practicing oppression and
violence."

18 Therefore thus says the LORD concerning Jehoiakim the son of Josiah, king of Judah:

[s]"They shall not lament for him,
Saying, [t]'Alas, my brother!' or
'Alas, my sister!'
They shall not lament for him,
Saying, 'Alas, master!' or 'Alas, his
glory!'
19 [u]He shall be buried with the burial
of a donkey,
Dragged and cast out beyond the
gates of Jerusalem.

20 "Go up to Lebanon, and cry out,
And lift up your voice in Bashan;
Cry from Abarim,
For all your lovers are destroyed.
21 I spoke to you in your prosperity,
But you said, 'I will not hear.'
[v]This *has been* your manner from
your youth,
That you did not obey My voice.
22 The wind shall eat up all [w]your
[7]rulers,
And your lovers shall go into
captivity;
Surely then you will be ashamed
and humiliated
For all your wickedness.
23 O inhabitant of Lebanon,

6 [f] Gen. 37:25; Num. 32:1; Song 4:1
7 [g] Is. 37:24 [h] Jer. 21:14
8 [i] Deut. 29:24-26; 1 Kin. 9:8, 9; 2 Chr. 7:20-22; Jer. 16:10
9 [j] 2 Kin. 22:17; 2 Chr. 34:25; Jer. 11:3
10 [k] 2 Kin. 22:20 [l] Jer. 14:17; 22:11; Lam. 3:48
11 [m] 1 Chr. 3:15 [n] 2 Kin. 23:34; 2 Chr. 36:4; Ezek. 19:4 [3] Or *Jehoahaz*
13 [o] 2 Kin. 23:35; Jer. 17:11; Ezek. 22:13 [p] Lev. 19:13; Deut. 24:14, 15; Mic. 3:10; Hab. 2:9; James 5:4 [4] Lit. *roof chambers, upper chambers*
14 [5] Lit. *roof chambers, upper chambers*
15 [q] 2 Kin. 23:25; Ps. 128:2; Is. 3:10; Jer. 7:23; 42:6
16 [6] Defended
17 [r] Jer. 6:13; 8:10; Ezek. 19:6; [Luke 12:15-20]
18 [s] Jer. 16:4, 6 [t] 1 Kin. 13:30
19 [u] 1 Kin. 21:23, 24; 2 Chr. 36:6; Jer. 36:30; Dan. 1:2
21 [v] Jer. 3:24, 25; 32:30
22 [w] Jer. 23:1 [7] Lit. *shepherds*

22:6 Gilead…Lebanon. The beautiful high mountains of the land.

22:7 cut down…choice cedars. This could primarily refer to the palaces and great houses built from such timber (cf. Song 1:17).

22:10 the dead. Probably a reference to Josiah who died before the destruction (2 Kin. 22:20; Is. 57:1). Dying saints are to be envied, living sinners pitied. When Josiah died, and on each anniversary of his death, there was open public weeping in which Jeremiah participated (2 Chr. 35:24,25).

22:11,12 Shallum. This is another name for King Jehoahaz (3 month reign, 609 B.C., 2 Kin. 23:31) the fourth son of Josiah (cf. 1 Chr. 3:15). It was given to him in irony, because the people called him Shalom ("peace"), but Shallum means "retribution."

22:13-17 Woe to him. This message indicted Jehoahaz (vv. 13,14,17), who was unlike his father, the good king, Josiah (vv. 15,16).

22:18-19 Jehoiakim. Ruling from 609 to 598 B.C., he was also wicked in taxing the people (2 Kin. 23:35) and making them build his splendid palace without pay, violating God's law in Lev. 19:13 and Deut. 24:14,15 (cf. Mic. 3:10; Hab. 2:9; James 5:4). He was slain in Babylon's second siege and his corpse dishonored, being left like a dead donkey on the ground for scavengers to feed on.

22:20 Go up to Lebanon. Sinners dwelling in the NW in Lebanon's cedar land and others to the NE beyond the Sea of Galilee in Bashan will suffer in the invasion. The entirety of the land will come under judgment as Abarim in the SE.

Making your nest in the cedars,
How gracious will you be when
pangs come upon you,
Like [x]the pain of a woman in
[8]labor?

Message to Coniah

24 "*As* I live," says the LORD, [y]"though
[9]Coniah the son of Jehoiakim, king of Judah, [z]were the [1]signet on My right hand,
yet I would pluck you off; 25 [a]and I will
give you into the hand of those who seek
your life, and into the hand of *those* whose
face you fear—the hand of Nebuchadnezzar king of Babylon and the hand of the
[2]Chaldeans. 26 [b]So I will cast you out, and
your mother who bore you, into another
country where you were not born; and
there you shall die. 27 But to the land to
which they desire to return, there they
shall not return.

28 "Is this man [3]Coniah a despised,
broken idol—
[c]A vessel in which *is* no pleasure?
Why are they cast out, he and his
descendants,
And cast into a land which they do
not know?
29 [d]O earth, earth, earth,
Hear the word of the LORD!
30 Thus says the LORD:
'Write this man down as [e]childless,
A man *who* shall not prosper in his
days;
For [f]none of his descendants shall
prosper,
Sitting on the throne of David,
And ruling anymore in Judah.' "

23 [x]Jer. 6:24 [8]*childbirth*
24 [y]2 Kin. 24:6, 8; 1 Chr. 3:16; 2 Chr. 36:9; Jer. 37:1 [z]Song 8:6; Is. 49:16; Hag. 2:23 [9]Or *Jeconiah* or *Jehoiachin* [1]*signet ring*
25 [a]2 Kin. 24:15, 16; Jer. 34:20 [2]Or *Babylonians*
26 [b]2 Kin. 24:15; Jer. 10:18; 16:13
28 [c]Ps. 31:12; Jer. 48:38; Hos. 8:8 [3]See note at v. 24
29 [d]Deut. 32:1; Is. 1:2; 34:1; Mic. 1:2
30 [e]1 Chr. 3:16, 17; Matt. 1:12 [f]Ps. 94:20; Jer. 36:30

CHAPTER 23

1 [a]Is. 56:9-12; Jer. 10:21
2 [b]Ex. 32:34
3 [c]Is. 11:11, 12, 16; Jer. 32:37
4 [d]Jer. 3:15; [Ezek. 34:23]
5 [e]Is. 4:2; 11:1; 40:10, 11; Jer. 33:14; [Dan. 9:24; Zech. 6:12]; Matt. 1:1, 6; Luke 3:31; [John 1:45; 7:42] [f]Ps. 72:2; Is. 9:7; 32:1, 18; [Dan. 9:24] [1]*act wisely* [2]*justice* [3]*land*
6 [g]Deut. 33:28; Jer. 30:10; Zech. 14:11 [h]Jer. 32:37 [i]Is. 45:24; Jer. 33:16; [Dan. 9:24; Rom. 3:22; 1 Cor. 1:30] [4]Heb. *YHWH Tsidkenu*
7 [j]Is. 43:18, 19; Jer. 16:14

The Branch of Righteousness

23 "Woe [a]to the shepherds who destroy and scatter the sheep of My
pasture!" says the LORD. 2 Therefore thus
says the LORD God of Israel against the
shepherds who feed My people: "You have
scattered My flock, driven them away, and
not attended to them. [b]Behold, I will attend to you for the evil of your doings,"
says the LORD. 3 "But [c]I will gather the
remnant of My flock out of all countries
where I have driven them, and bring them
back to their folds; and they shall be fruitful and increase. 4 I will set up [d]shepherds
over them who will feed them; and they
shall fear no more, nor be dismayed, nor
shall they be lacking," says the LORD.

5 "Behold, [e]*the* days are coming," says
the LORD,
"That I will raise to David a Branch
of righteousness;
A King shall reign and [1]prosper,
[f]And execute [2]judgment and
righteousness in the [3]earth.
6 [g]In His days Judah will be saved,
And Israel [h]will dwell safely;
Now [i]this *is* His name by which
He will be called:

[4]THE LORD OUR RIGHTEOUSNESS.

7 "Therefore, behold, [j]*the* days are coming," says the LORD, "that they shall no
longer say, 'As the LORD lives who brought
up the children of Israel from the land of
Egypt,' 8 but, 'As the LORD lives who
brought up and led the descendants of the

22:24-26 Coniah. A short form of Jeconiah, perhaps used in contempt, who was also called Jehoiachin. He ruled only 3 months and 10 days (2 Chr. 36:9) in 598–597 B.C., and was taken into captivity, where he lived out his life.

22:24 signet. A ring with a personal insignia on it (cf. Hag. 2:23).

22:28 Questions the people who idolized Jeconiah were asking.

22:30 Write...as childless. Jeconiah did have offspring (1 Chr. 3:17,18), but he was reckoned childless in the sense that he had no sons who would reign ("Sitting on the throne..."). The curse continued in his descendants down to Joseph, the husband of Mary. How could Jesus then be the Messiah when His father was under this curse? It was because Joseph was not involved in the blood line of Jesus since He was virgin born (Matt. 1:12). Jesus' blood right to the throne of David came through Mary from Nathan, Solomon's brother, not Solomon (Jeconiah's line) thus bypassing this curse (Luke 3:31, 32). Cf. 36:30.

23:1,2 Woe to the shepherds. These were false leaders who failed in their duty to assure the people's welfare (as v. 2), starting with the kings in chap. 22 and other civil heads, as well as prophets and priests (cf. v. 11). They stood in utter contrast to the shepherds God would later give the nation (v. 4; 3:15). Other significant chapters which condemn evil shepherds and false prophets include chaps. 14,27,28; Is. 28; Ezek. 13, 34; Mic. 3; Zech. 11.

23:3,4 I will gather. God pledged to restore exiled Israelites to their ancient soil. Cf. similar promises in chaps. 30–33, and 16:14,15. The land in view was lit. Palestine, being contrasted with all the other countries (v. 3), thus assuring that the regathering would be as literal as the scattering. The restoration of Judah from Babylon is referred to in language which in its fullness can only refer to the final restoration of God's people ("out of all countries" and v. 8), under Messiah. "Neither shall they be lacking" indicates that no one will be missing or detached. These are prophecies not yet fulfilled. Cf. 32:37,38; Is. 60:21; Ezek 34:11-16.

23:4 shepherds...will feed them. Cf. Ezek 34:23-31. Zerubbabel, Ezra, Nehemiah, and others were small fulfillments compared to the consummate shepherding of the Messiah Jesus.

23:5 Branch. The Messiah is pictured as a branch (lit. "shoot") out of David's family tree (cf. 23:5; 33:15,16; Is. 4:2; 11:1-5; Zech. 3:8; 6:12, 13), who will rule over God's people in the future. Cf. 33:14-17 where the same promise is repeated.

23:6 THE LORD OUR RIGHTEOUSNESS. This emphasis is stated 3 times in vv. 5,6. Messiah's shepherding is contrasted with that of the false shepherds (vv. 1,2,11,14). Judah and Israel will be reunited (cf. Ezek. 37:15-23).

23:7,8 *See note on 16:14,15.*

house of Israel from the north country
[k]and from all the countries where I had
driven them.' And they shall dwell in their
own [l]land."

False Prophets and Empty Oracles

9 My heart within me is broken
Because of the prophets;
[m]All my bones shake.
I am like a drunken man,
And like a man whom wine has overcome,
Because of the LORD,
And because of His holy words.
10 For [n]the land is full of adulterers;
For [o]because of a curse the land mourns.
[p]The pleasant places of the wilderness are dried up.
Their course of life is evil,
And their might *is* not right.

11 "For [q]both prophet and priest are profane;
Yes, [r]in My house I have found their wickedness," says the LORD.
12 "Therefore[s] their way shall be to them
Like slippery *ways;*
In the darkness they shall be driven on
And fall in them;
For I [t]will bring disaster on them,
The year of their punishment,"
says the LORD.
13 "And I have seen [5]folly in the prophets of Samaria:
[u]They prophesied by Baal
And [v]caused My people Israel to err.
14 Also I have seen a horrible thing in the prophets of Jerusalem:
[w]They commit adultery and walk in lies;
They also [x]strengthen the hands of evildoers,
So that no one turns back from his wickedness.
All of them are like [y]Sodom to Me,
And her inhabitants like Gomorrah.

15 "Therefore thus says the LORD of hosts
concerning the prophets:

'Behold, I will feed them with
[z]wormwood,
And make them drink the water of gall;
For from the prophets of Jerusalem
[6]Profaneness has gone out into all the land.' "

16 Thus says the LORD of hosts:

"Do not listen to the words of the prophets who prophesy to you.
They make you worthless;
[a]They speak a vision of their own heart,
Not from the mouth of the LORD.
17 They continually say to those who despise Me,
'The LORD has said, [b]"You shall have peace" ';
And *to* everyone who [c]walks according to the [7]dictates of his own heart, they say,
[d]'No evil shall come upon you.' "

18 For [e]who has stood in the counsel of the LORD,
And has perceived and heard His word?
Who has marked His word and heard *it?*
19 Behold, a [f]whirlwind of the LORD has gone forth in fury—
A violent whirlwind!
It will fall violently on the head of the wicked.
20 The [g]anger of the LORD will not turn back
Until He has executed and performed the thoughts of His heart.
[h]In the latter days you will understand it perfectly.

21 "I[i] have not sent these prophets, yet they ran.
I have not spoken to them, yet they prophesied.
22 But if they had stood in My counsel,
And had caused My people to hear My words,

8 [k]Is. 43:5, 6; Ezek. 34:13; Amos 9:14, 15 [l]Gen. 12:7; Jer. 16:14, 15; 31:8
9 [m]Jer. 8:18; Hab. 3:16
10 [n]Jer. 9:2 [o]Hos. 4:2; Mal. 3:5 [p]Ps. 107:34; Jer. 9:10
11 [q]Jer. 6:13; Zeph. 3:4 [r]Jer. 7:30; 32:34; Ezek. 8:11; 23:39
12 [s]Ps. 35:6; [Prov. 4:19]; Jer. 13:16 [t]Jer. 11:23
13 [u]1 Kin. 18:18-21; Jer. 2:8 [v]Is. 9:16 [5]Lit. *distastefulness*
14 [w]Jer. 29:23 [x]Jer. 23:22; Ezek. 13:22, 23 [y]Gen. 18:20; Deut. 32:32; Is. 1:9, 10
15 [z]Deut. 29:18; Jer. 9:15 [6]Or *Pollution*
16 [a]Jer. 14:14; Ezek. 13:3, 6
17 [b]Jer. 8:11; Ezek. 13:10; Zech. 10:2 [c]Deut. 29:19; Jer. 3:17 [d]Jer. 5:12; Amos 9:10; Mic. 3:11 [7]*stubbornness* or *imagination*
18 [e]Job 15:8, 9; [Jer. 23:22; 1 Cor. 2:16]
19 [f]Jer. 25:32; 30:23; Amos 1:14
20 [g]2 Kin. 23:26, 27; Jer. 30:24 [h]Gen. 49:1
21 [i]Jer. 14:14; 23:32; 27:15

23:13,14 Jerusalem and Judah were worse than Samaria and Israel.

23:14 a horrible thing in the prophets. The false shepherds told lies, committed adultery, and declared vain dreams (vv. 25,27). They became like chaff rather than grain (v. 28), while promising peace (v. 17) to those whose sins provoke God to bring calamity, not comfort. The scene was like Sodom and Gomorrah, whose sin so grieved God that He destroyed them by fire (cf. Gen. 19:13,24,25).

23:18 Here was the reason not to listen to the false prophets (cf. v. 16)—they didn't speak God's Word.

23:20 latter days. They wouldn't listen, but the day would come (v. 12) when the judgment would fall and then they would "understand."

23:21,22 According to the Mosaic law, these false prophets should have been stoned (cf. Deut. 13:1-5; 18:20-22).

Then they would have [j]turned
them from their evil way
And from the evil of their doings.

23 "*Am* I a God near at hand," says the
LORD,
"And not a God afar off?
24 Can anyone [k]hide himself in secret
places,
So I shall not see him?" says the
LORD;
[l]"Do I not fill heaven and earth?"
says the LORD.

25 "I have heard what the prophets have
said who prophesy lies in My name, saying,
'I have dreamed, I have dreamed!' 26 How
long will *this* be in the heart of the prophets
who prophesy lies? Indeed *they are* prophets
of the deceit of their own heart, 27 who try
to make My people forget My name by their
dreams which everyone tells his neighbor,
[m]as their fathers forgot My name for Baal.

28 "The prophet who has a dream, let
him tell a dream;
And he who has My word, let him
speak My word faithfully.
What *is* the chaff to the wheat?"
says the LORD.
29 "*Is* not My word like a [n]fire?" says
the LORD,
"And like a hammer *that* breaks the
rock in pieces?

30 "Therefore behold, [o]I *am* against the
prophets," says the LORD, "who steal My
words every one from his neighbor. 31 Behold, I *am* [p]against the prophets," says the
LORD, "who use their tongues and say, 'He
says.' 32 Behold, I *am* against those who
prophesy false dreams," says the LORD,
"and tell them, and cause My people to err
by their [q]lies and by [r]their recklessness. Yet
I did not send them or command them;
therefore they shall not [s]profit this people
at all," says the LORD.
33 "So when these people or the prophet
or the priest ask you, saying, 'What is [t]the
[8]oracle of the LORD?' you shall then say to
them, [9]'What oracle?' I will even forsake
you," says the LORD. 34 "And *as for* the
prophet and the priest and the people who
say, 'The [1]oracle of the LORD!' I will even
punish that man and his house. 35 Thus
every one of you shall say to his neighbor,
and every one to his brother, 'What has the
LORD answered?' and, 'What has the LORD
spoken?' 36 And the [2]oracle of the LORD you
shall mention no more. For every man's
word will be his oracle, for you have [u]per-
verted the words of the living God, the LORD
of hosts, our God. 37 Thus you shall say to
the prophet, 'What has the LORD answered
you?' and, 'What has the LORD spoken?'
38 But since you say, 'The [3]oracle of the
LORD!' therefore thus says the LORD: 'Because you say this word, "The oracle of the
LORD!" and I have sent to you, saying, "Do
not say, 'The oracle of the LORD!' " 39 therefore behold, I, even I, [v]will utterly forget you
and forsake you, and the city that I gave you
and your fathers, and *will cast you* out of My
presence. 40 And I will bring [w]an everlasting
reproach upon you, and a perpetual
[x]shame, which shall not be forgotten.' "

The Sign of Two Baskets of Figs

24 The [a]LORD showed me, and there
were two baskets of figs set before
the temple of the LORD, after Nebuchadnezzar [b]king of Babylon had carried away
captive [c]Jeconiah the son of Jehoiakim,
king of Judah, and the princes of Judah
with the craftsmen and smiths, from Jerusalem, and had brought them to Babylon.
2 One basket *had* very good figs, like the
figs *that are* first ripe; and the other basket
had very bad figs which could not be eaten,
they were so [d]bad. 3 Then the LORD said to
me, "What do you see, Jeremiah?"
And I said, "Figs, the good figs, very
good; and the bad, very bad, which cannot
be eaten, they are so bad."
4 Again the word of the LORD came to
me, saying, 5 "Thus says the LORD, the God
of Israel: 'Like these good figs, so will I [1]ac-
knowledge those who are carried away

22 [j]Jer. 25:5
24 [k][Ps. 139:7]; Amos 9:2, 3 [l][1 Kin. 8:27]; Ps. 139:7
27 [m]Judg. 3:7
29 [n]Jer. 5:14
30 [o]Deut. 18:20; Ps. 34:16; Jer. 14:14, 15; Ezek. 13:8, 9
31 [p]Ezek. 13:9
32 [q]Jer. 20:6; 27:10; Lam. 2:14; 3:37 [r]Zeph. 3:4 [s]Jer. 7:8; Lam. 2:14
33 [t]Is. 13:1; Nah. 1:1; Hab. 1:1; Zech. 9:1; Mal. 1:1
[8]*burden, prophecy*
[9]LXX, Tg., Vg. *'You are the burden.'*
34 [1]*burden, prophecy*
36 [u]Deut. 4:2
[2]*burden, prophecy*
38 [3]*burden, prophecy*
39 [v]Hos. 4:6
40 [w]Jer. 20:11; Ezek. 5:14, 15 [x]Mic. 3:5-7

CHAPTER 24

1 [a]Amos 7:1, 4; 8:1 [b]2 Kin. 24:12-16; 2 Chr. 36:10 [c]Jer. 22:24-28; 29:2
2 [d]Is. 5:4, 7; Jer. 29:17
5 [1]*regard*

23:23,24 God near...God afar off. Let not false prophets think they can hide their devices from God, who declares Himself omnipresent and omniscient, in both an immanent and transcendent sense.

23:25 I have dreamed. Here was a claim to divine revelation through dreams (cf. Num. 12:6). But such claims were a deception (vv. 26,27), utterly unequal in power to God's Word (vv. 28,29).

23:29 like a fire...hammer. God's Word has irresistible qualities to prevail over the deception in the shepherd's false messages.

23:33 the oracle of the LORD...What oracle? The people asked, in mockery, for Jeremiah to give them his latest prophecy ("oracle"). This ridicule of Jeremiah's faithful preaching demanded a response, and God told the prophet to repeat the question and reply simply "I will even forsake you," meaning judgment from God was coming.

23:34-40 The oracle of the LORD! When a person falsely claimed to have a word from God, he would be punished for perverting God's truth. Claiming to have prophecies from God, when not true, is dangerous.

24:1 after Nebuchadnezzar...carried away. Babylon's second deportation of Judeans in 597 B.C. (cf. 2 Kin. 24:10-17).

24:5 Like these good figs. The object lesson of v. 2 is explained. Deported Judeans, captive in Babylon, will have good treatment, not death as shown in 29:5-7,10. They will be granted privileges as colonists rather than being enslaved as captives.

captive from Judah, whom I have sent out of this place for *their own* good, into the land of the Chaldeans. [6] For I will set My eyes on them for good, and [e]I will bring them back to this land; [f]I will build them and not pull *them* down, and I will plant them and not pluck *them* up. [7] Then I will give them [g]a heart to know Me, that I *am* the LORD; and they shall be [h]My people, and I will be their God, for they shall return to Me [i]with their whole heart.

[8] 'And as the bad [j]figs which cannot be eaten, they are so bad'—surely thus says the LORD—'so will I give up Zedekiah the king of Judah, his princes, the [k]residue of Jerusalem who remain in this land, and [l]those who dwell in the land of Egypt. [9] I will deliver them to [m]trouble into all the kingdoms of the earth, for *their* harm, [n]*to be* a reproach and a byword, a taunt and a curse, in all places where I shall drive them. [10] And I will send the sword, the famine, and the pestilence among them, till they are [2]consumed from the land that I gave to them and their fathers.' "

Seventy Years of Desolation

25 The word that came to Jeremiah concerning all the people of Judah, [a]in the fourth year of [b]Jehoiakim the son of Josiah, king of Judah (which *was* the first year of Nebuchadnezzar king of Babylon), [2] which Jeremiah the prophet spoke to all the people of Judah and to all the inhabitants of Jerusalem, saying: [3] [c]"From the thirteenth year of Josiah the son of Amon, king of Judah, even to this day, this *is* the twenty-third year in which the word of the LORD has come to me; and I have spoken to you, rising early and speaking, [d]but you have not listened. [4] And the LORD has sent to you all His servants the prophets, [e]rising early and sending *them,* but you have not listened nor inclined your ear to hear. [5] They said, [f]'Repent now everyone of his evil way and his evil doings, and dwell in the land that the LORD has given to you and your fathers forever and ever. [6] Do not go after other gods to serve them and worship them, and do not provoke Me to anger with the works of your hands; and I will not harm you.' [7] Yet you have not listened to Me," says the LORD, "that you might [g]provoke Me to anger with the works of your hands to your own hurt.

[8] "Therefore thus says the LORD of hosts: 'Because you have not heard My words, [9] behold, I will send and take [h]all the families of the north,' says the LORD, 'and Nebuchadnezzar the king of Babylon, [i]My servant, and will bring them against this land, against its inhabitants, and against these nations all around, and will utterly destroy them, and [j]make them an astonishment, a hissing, and perpetual desolations. [10] Moreover I will [1]take from them the [k]voice of mirth and the voice of gladness, the voice of the bridegroom and the voice of the bride, [l]the sound of the millstones and the light of the lamp. [11] And this whole land shall be a desolation *and* an astonishment, and these nations shall serve the king of Babylon seventy [m]years.

[12] 'Then it will come to pass, [n]when [2]seventy years are completed, *that* I will punish the king of Babylon and that nation, the land of the Chaldeans, for their iniquity,' says the LORD; [o]'and I will make it a perpetual desolation. [13] So I will bring on that land all My words which I have pronounced against it, all that is written in this book, which Jeremiah has prophesied concerning all the nations. [14] [p](For many nations [q]and great kings shall [r]be served by them also; [s]and I will repay them according to their deeds and according to the works of their own hands.)' "

6 [e] Jer. 12:15; 29:10; Ezek. 11:17 [f] Jer. 32:41; 33:7; 42:10
7 [g] [Deut. 30:6; Jer. 32:39; Ezek. 11:19; 36:26, 27] [h] Is. 51:16; Jer. 30:22; 31:33; 32:38; Ezek. 14:11; Zech. 8:8; [Heb. 8:10] [i] 1 Sam. 7:3; Ps. 119:2; Jer. 29:13
8 [j] Jer. 29:17 [k] Jer. 39:9 [l] Jer. 44:1, 26-30
9 [m] Deut. 28:25, 37; 1 Kin. 9:7; 2 Chr. 7:20; Jer. 15:4; 29:18; 34:17 [n] Ps. 44:13, 14
10 [2] *destroyed*

CHAPTER 25

1 [a] Jer. 36:1 [b] 2 Kin. 24:1, 2; 2 Chr. 36:4-6; Dan. 1:1, 2
3 [c] Jer. 1:2 [d] Jer. 7:13; 11:7, 8, 10
4 [e] Jer. 7:13, 25
5 [f] 2 Kin. 17:13; [Is. 55:6, 7]; Jer. 18:11; Ezek. 18:30; [Jon. 3:8-10]
7 [g] Deut. 32:21; Jer. 7:19; 32:30
9 [h] Jer. 1:15 [i] Is. 45:1; Jer. 27:6 [j] Jer. 18:16
10 [k] Is. 24:7-11; Jer. 7:34; 16:9; Ezek. 26:13; Hos. 2:11; Rev. 18:23 [l] Eccl. 12:4; Is. 47:2 [1] Lit. *cause to perish from them*
11 [m] 2 Chr. 36:21; Jer. 29:10; Dan. 9:2; Zech. 7:5
12 [n] 2 Chr. 36:21, 22; Ezra 1:1; Jer. 29:10; Dan. 9:2 [o] Is. 13:20; Jer. 50:3 [2] Beginning circa 605 B.C. (2 Kin. 24:1) and ending circa 536 B.C. (Ezra 1:1)
14 [p] Jer. 50:9; 51:27, 28 [q] Jer. 51:27 [r] Jer. 27:7 [s] Jer. 50:29; 51:6, 24

24:6,7 While it is true that a remnant returned to Judah in 538 B.C., this promise had greater overtones in regard to the ultimate fulfillment of the Abrahamic (Gen. 12), Davidic (2 Sam. 7), and New (Jer. 31) Covenants in the day of Messiah's coming and kingdom (cf. 32:41; 33:7). Their conversion (v. 7) from idolatry to the one true God is expressed in language which, in its fullness, applies to the complete conversion in the final Kingdom after the present dispersion (cf. Rom. 11:1-5,25-27).

24:8-10 as the bad figs. Those remaining at Jerusalem during the 11 years (597–586 B.C.) of Zedekiah's vassal reign would soon face hardship from further scattering to other countries, violent death, famine, and disease; cf. Jer. 29:17. See 25:9 and *note there.* These verses quote the curses of Deut. 28:25,37 (cf. Jer. 29:18,22; Ps. 44:13,14) and are also fulfilled in the history of the long dispersion until Messiah returns.

25:1 fourth year. The date is 605/04 B.C., as Jehoiakim reigned in 609–598 B.C. **first year.** Nebuchadnezzar reigned 605–562 B.C.

25:3 thirteenth year. The time is ca. 627/626 B.C. Josiah ruled in 640–609 B.C. **twenty-third year.** Jeremiah began his ministry in the 13th year of Josiah (cf. 1:2) and had been faithful to preach repentance and judgment for 23 years (ca. 605/604 B.C.).

25:9 My servant. God used a pagan king, Nebuchadnezzar, to accomplish His will (cf. Cyrus in Is. 45:1).

25:10 Cf. 7:34; Rev. 18:23.

25:11 seventy years. Here is the first specific statement on the length of the exile (cf. 29:10). This period probably began in the fourth year of Jehoiakim, when Jerusalem was first captured and the temple treasures were taken. It ends with the decree of Cyrus to let the Jews return, spanning from ca. 605/04 B.C. to 536/35 B.C. The exact number of Sabbath years is 490 years, the period from Saul to the Babylonian captivity. This was retribution for their violation of the Sabbath law (cf. Lev. 26:34,35; 2 Chr. 36:21).

25:13 all the nations. Jeremiah prophesied judgments on surrounding nations (cf. chaps. 46–49), while Babylon is the focus of judgment in chaps. 50–51.

25:14 be served by them. The Babylonians, who made other nations their slaves, would become the servants of nations.

Judgment on the Nations

15 For thus says the LORD God of Israel
to me: "Take this [t]wine cup of [3]fury from
My hand, and cause all the nations, to
whom I send you, to drink it. 16 And [u]they
will drink and stagger and go mad because
of the sword that I will send among them."
17 Then I took the cup from the LORD's
hand, and made all the nations drink, to
whom the LORD had sent me: 18 Jerusalem
and the cities of Judah, its kings and its
princes, to make them [v]a desolation, an astonishment, a hissing, and [w]a curse, as *it is*
this day; 19 Pharaoh king of Egypt, his servants, his princes, and all his people; 20 all
the mixed multitude, all the kings of [x]the
land of Uz, all the kings of the land of the
[y]Philistines (namely, Ashkelon, Gaza,
Ekron, and [z]the remnant of Ashdod);
21 [a]Edom, Moab, and the people of
Ammon; 22 all the kings of [b]Tyre, all the
kings of Sidon, and the kings of the coastlands which *are* across the [c]sea; 23 [d]Dedan,
Tema, Buz, and all *who are* in the farthest
corners; 24 all the kings of Arabia and all
the kings of the [e]mixed multitude who
dwell in the desert; 25 all the kings of
Zimri, all the kings of [f]Elam, and all the
kings of the [g]Medes; 26 [h]all the kings of the
north, far and near, one with another; and
all the kingdoms of the world which *are* on
the face of the earth. Also the king of [4]She-
shach shall drink after them.
27 "Therefore you shall say to them,
'Thus says the LORD of hosts, the God of Israel: [i]"Drink, [j]be drunk, and vomit! Fall
and rise no more, because of the sword
which I will send among you."' 28 And it
shall be, if they refuse to take the cup from
your hand to drink, then you shall say to
them, 'Thus says the LORD of hosts: "You
shall certainly drink! 29 For behold, [k]I
begin to bring calamity on the city [l]which
is called by My name, and should you be
utterly unpunished? You shall not be
unpunished, for [m]I will call for a sword on
all the inhabitants of the earth," says the
LORD of hosts.'
30 "Therefore prophesy against them all
these words, and say to them:

'The LORD will [n]roar from on high,
And utter His voice from [o]His holy
habitation;
He will roar mightily against [p]His
fold.
He will give [q]a shout, as those who
tread *the grapes*,
Against all the inhabitants of the
earth.
31 A noise will come to the ends of
the earth—
For the LORD has [r]a controversy
with the nations;
[s]He will plead His case with all
flesh.
He will give those *who are* wicked
to the sword,' says the LORD."

32 Thus says the LORD of hosts:

"Behold, disaster shall go forth
From nation to nation,
And [t]a great whirlwind shall be
raised up
From the farthest parts of the earth.

33 [u]"And at that day the slain of the LORD
shall be from *one* end of the earth even to
the *other* end of the earth. They shall not be
[v]lamented, [w]or gathered, or buried; they
shall become refuse on the ground.

34 "Wail, [x]shepherds, and cry!
Roll about *in the ashes*,
You leaders of the flock!
For the days of your slaughter and
your dispersions are fulfilled;
You shall fall like a precious vessel.
35 And the shepherds will have no
[5]way to flee,
Nor the leaders of the flock to
escape.
36 A voice of the cry of the shepherds,
And a wailing of the leaders to the
flock *will be heard*.
For the LORD has plundered their
pasture,
37 And the peaceful dwellings are cut
down
Because of the fierce anger of the
LORD.
38 He has left His lair like the lion;
For their land is desolate
Because of the fierceness of the
Oppressor,
And because of His fierce anger."

15 [t] Job 21:20; Ps. 75:8; Is. 51:17; Rev. 14:10 [3] *wrath*
16 [u] Jer. 51:7; Ezek. 23:34; Nah. 3:11
18 [v] Jer. 25:9, 11 [w] Jer. 24:9
20 [x] Job 1:1; Lam. 4:21 [y] Jer. 47:1-7; Ezek. 25:16, 17 [z] Is. 20:1
21 [a] Jer. 49:7
22 [b] Jer. 47:4; Zech. 9:2-4 [c] Jer. 49:23
23 [d] Is. 21:13; Jer. 49:7, 8
24 [e] Jer. 25:20; 50:37; Ezek. 30:5
25 [f] Gen. 10:22; Is. 11:11; Jer. 49:34 [g] Is. 13:17; Jer. 51:11, 28
26 [h] Jer. 50:9 [4] A code word for Babylon, Jer. 51:41
27 [i] Jer. 25:16; Hab. 2:16 [j] Is. 63:6
29 [k] [Prov. 11:31]; Is. 10:12; Jer. 13:13; Ezek. 9:6; [Luke 23:31; 1 Pet. 4:17] [l] Dan. 9:18 [m] Ezek. 38:21
30 [n] Is. 42:13; Joel 3:16; Amos 1:2 [o] Ps. 11:4 [p] 1 Kin. 9:3; Ps. 132:14 [q] Is. 16:9; Jer. 48:33
31 [r] Hos. 4:1; Mic. 6:2 [s] Is. 66:16; Joel 3:2
32 [t] Jer. 23:19; 30:23
33 [u] Is. 34:2, 3; 66:16 [v] Jer. 16:4, 6; Ezek. 39:4, 17 [w] Ps. 79:3; Jer. 8:2; Rev. 11:9
34 [x] Jer. 4:8; 6:26; Ezek. 27:30
35 [5] Or *refuge*

25:15 this wine cup. A symbol for stupefying judgments (v. 16).

25:17 made all the nations drink. Obviously Jeremiah could not visit all the places listed from vv. 18-26, but in this vision he acted as if representatives from all those nations were present so he could make them drink in the message of wrath (v. 27), and understand there was no escape (vv. 28,29).

25:29 the city...called by My name. Jerusalem (cf. Dan. 9:18).

25:30-33 While embracing the judgments soon to come to Judah and other nations, this has end-time language ("one end of the earth...to the other") and must be ultimately fulfilled in the time of tribulation described in Rev. 6–19.

Jeremiah Saved from Death

26 In the beginning of the reign of Jehoiakim the son of Josiah, king of
Judah, this word came from the LORD, saying, 2 "Thus says the LORD: 'Stand in [a]the
court of the LORD's house, and speak to all
the cities of Judah, which come to worship
in the LORD's house, [b]all the words that I
command you to speak to them. [c]Do not
diminish a word. 3 [d]Perhaps everyone will
listen and turn from his evil way, that I
may [e]relent concerning the calamity which
I purpose to bring on them because of the
evil of their doings.' 4 And you shall say to
them, 'Thus says the LORD: [f]"If you will
not listen to Me, to walk in My law which
I have set before you, 5 to heed the words
of My servants the prophets [g]whom I sent
to you, both rising up early and sending
them (but you have not heeded), 6 then I
will make this house like [h]Shiloh, and will
make this city [i]a curse to all the nations of
the earth."'"
7 So the priests and the prophets and all
the people heard Jeremiah speaking these
words in the house of the LORD. 8 Now it
happened, when Jeremiah had made an
end of speaking all that the LORD had commanded *him* to speak to all the people, that
the priests and the prophets and all the
people seized him, saying, "You will surely die! 9 Why have you prophesied in the
name of the LORD, saying, 'This house shall
be like Shiloh, and this city shall be [j]deso-
late, without an inhabitant'?" And all the
people were gathered against Jeremiah in
the house of the LORD.
10 When the princes of Judah heard
these things, they came up from the king's
house to the house of the LORD and sat
down in the entry of the New Gate of
the LORD's *house*. 11 And the priests and the
prophets spoke to the princes and all the
people, saying, [1]"This man deserves to
[k]die! For he has prophesied against this
city, as you have heard with your ears."
12 Then Jeremiah spoke to all the princes
and all the people, saying: "The LORD sent
me to prophesy against this house and
against this city with all the words that you
have heard. 13 Now therefore, [l]amend
your ways and your doings, and obey the
voice of the LORD your God; then the LORD
will relent concerning the doom that He
has pronounced against you. 14 As for me,
here [m]I am, in your hand; do with me as
seems good and [2]proper to you. 15 But
know for certain that if you put me to
death, you will surely bring innocent
blood on yourselves, on this city, and on its
inhabitants; for truly the LORD has sent me
to you to speak all these words in your
hearing."
16 So the princes and all the people said
to the priests and the prophets, "This man
does not deserve to die. For he has spoken
to us in the name of the LORD our God."
17 [n]Then certain of the elders of the land
rose up and spoke to all the assembly of
the people, saying: 18 [o]"Micah of Moresheth prophesied in the days of Hezekiah
king of Judah, and spoke to all the people
of Judah, saying, 'Thus says the LORD of
hosts:

[p]" Zion shall be plowed *like* a field,
Jerusalem shall become [q]heaps of
ruins,
And the mountain of the [3]temple
Like the [4]bare hills of the forest."'

19 Did Hezekiah king of Judah and all Judah ever put him to death? [r]Did he not
fear the LORD and [s]seek the LORD's favor?
And the LORD [t]relented concerning the
doom which He had pronounced against
them. [u]But we are doing great evil against
ourselves."
20 Now there was also a man who
prophesied in the name of the LORD, Urijah
the son of Shemaiah of Kirjath Jearim, who
prophesied against this city and against
this land according to all the words of Jeremiah. 21 And when Jehoiakim the king,
with all his mighty men and all the princes,
heard his words, the king sought to put

CHAPTER 26

2 [a] 2 Chr. 24:20, 21; Jer. 19:14 [b] Deut. 4:2; Jer. 43:1; Ezek. 3:10; Matt. 28:20; [Rev. 22:19] [c] Acts 20:27
3 [d] Is. 1:16-19; Jer. 36:3-7 [e] Jer. 18:8; Jon. 3:9
4 [f] Lev. 26:14, 15; Deut. 28:15; 1 Kin. 9:6; Is. 1:20; Jer. 17:27; 22:5
5 [g] Jer. 25:4; 29:19
6 [h] 1 Sam. 4:10, 11; Ps. 78:60; Jer. 7:12, 14 [i] 2 Kin. 22:19; Is. 65:15; Jer. 24:9
9 [j] Jer. 9:11
11 [k] Jer. 38:4 [1] Lit. *A judgment of death to this man*
13 [l] Jer. 7:3; [Joel 2:13]; Jon. 3:8
14 [m] Jer. 38:5 [2] *right*
17 [n] Acts 5:34
18 [o] Mic. 1:1 [p] Mic. 3:12 [q] Neh. 4:2; Ps. 79:1; Jer. 9:11 [3] Lit. *house* [4] Lit. *high places*
19 [r] 2 Chr. 32:26; Is. 37:1, 4, 15-20 [s] 2 Kin. 20:1-19 [t] Ex. 32:14; 2 Sam. 24:16; Jer. 18:8 [u] [Acts 5:39]

26:1 In the beginning. The time was 609 B.C. The message is about 4 years earlier than that in 25:1 and about 11 years before 24:1.

26:2 Stand in the court. This was the largest public gathering place at the temple.

26:6 like Shiloh. The former dwelling place of God before Jerusalem. Cf. 7:12 and *see note there*.

26:11 Jeremiah was accused of treason. Cf. Paul's arrest in Acts 21:27,28.

26:12 Jeremiah spoke. Leaders and people threatened to kill him (v. 8). The prophet defended himself while in extreme danger. He did not compromise, but displayed tremendous spiritual courage. He was ready to die (v. 14), yet warned the crowd that God would hold the guilty accountable (v. 15).

26:15 put me to death. Cf. Matt. 23:31-37.

26:17-19 elders...spoke. These spokesmen cited the prophet Micah (cf. Mic. 3:12), who before and during Hezekiah's reign (ca. 715–686 B.C.) prophesied the destruction of Jerusalem and its temple. They reasoned that because they didn't kill Micah, God rescinded the judgment. They must not kill Jeremiah so God might change His mind. Micah's prophecy and Jeremiah's would come true in time.

26:20-22 also a man...prophesied. Urijah, like Micah and Jeremiah, had warned of doom on Jerusalem, speaking in Jehoiakim's day only a bit earlier than Jeremiah's present warning (609 B.C.). He was executed. The decision could have gone either way since there was precedent for killing and for sparing.

him to death; but when Urijah heard *it*, he
was afraid and fled, and went to Egypt.
22 Then Jehoiakim the king sent men to
Egypt: Elnathan the son of Achbor, and
other men *who went* with him to Egypt.
23 And they brought Urijah from Egypt
and brought him to Jehoiakim the king,
who killed him with the sword and cast his
dead body into the graves of the [5]common
people.
24 Nevertheless [v]the hand of Ahikam the
son of Shaphan was with Jeremiah, so that
they should not give him into the hand of
the people to put him to death.

Symbol of the Bonds and Yokes

27 In[1] the beginning of the reign of [2]Je-
hoiakim the son of Josiah, [a]king of
Judah, this word came to Jeremiah from
the LORD, saying, 2 "Thus says the LORD to
me: 'Make for yourselves bonds and
yokes, [b]and put them on your neck, 3 and
send them to the king of Edom, the king of
Moab, the king of the Ammonites, the king
of Tyre, and the king of Sidon, by the hand
of the messengers who come to Jerusalem
to Zedekiah king of Judah. 4 And command them to say to their masters, "Thus
says the LORD of hosts, the God of Israel—
thus you shall say to your masters: 5 [c]'I
have made the earth, the man and the
beast that *are* on the ground, by My great
power and by My outstretched arm, and
[d]have given it to whom it seemed proper
to Me. 6 [e]And now I have given all these
lands into the hand of Nebuchadnezzar
the king of Babylon, [f]My servant; and [g]the
beasts of the field I have also given him to
serve him. 7 [h]So all nations shall serve him
and his son and his son's son, [i]until the
time of his land comes; [j]and then many nations and great kings shall make him serve
them. 8 And it shall be, *that* the nation and
kingdom which will not serve Nebuchadnezzar the king of Babylon, and which will
not put its neck under the yoke of the king
of Babylon, that nation I will punish,' says
the LORD, 'with the sword, the famine, and
the pestilence, until I have consumed them
by his hand. 9 Therefore do not listen to
your prophets, your diviners, your
[3]dreamers, your soothsayers, or your sorcerers, who speak to you, saying, "You
shall not serve the king of Babylon." 10 For
they prophesy a [k]lie to you, to remove you
far from your land; and I will drive you
out, and you will perish. 11 But the nations
that bring their necks under the yoke of the
king of Babylon and serve him, I will let
them remain in their own land,' says the
LORD, 'and they shall till it and dwell in
it.' " ' "
12 I also spoke to [l]Zedekiah king of Judah according to all these words, saying,
"Bring your necks under the yoke of the
king of Babylon, and serve him and his
people, and live! 13 [m]Why will you die,
you and your people, by the sword, by the
famine, and by the pestilence, as the LORD
has spoken against the nation that will not
serve the king of Babylon? 14 Therefore
[n]do not listen to the words of the prophets
who speak to you, saying, 'You shall not
serve the king of Babylon,' for they prophesy [o]a lie to you; 15 for I have [p]not sent
them," says the LORD, "yet they prophesy a
lie in My name, that I may drive you out,
and that you may perish, you and the
prophets who prophesy to you."
16 Also I spoke to the priests and to all
this people, saying, "Thus says the LORD:
'Do not listen to the words of your prophets
who prophesy to you, saying, "Behold, [q]the
vessels of the LORD's house will now shortly be brought back from Babylon"; for they
prophesy a lie to you. 17 Do not listen to
them; serve the king of Babylon, and live!
Why should this city be laid waste? 18 But if
they *are* prophets, and if the word of the
LORD is with them, let them now make intercession to the LORD of hosts, that the vessels which are left in the house of the LORD,
in the house of the king of Judah, and at Jerusalem, do not go to Babylon.'
19 "For thus says the LORD of hosts [r]con-
cerning the pillars, concerning the Sea,

23 [5] Lit. *sons of the people*
24 [v] 2 Kin. 22:12-14; Jer. 39:14; 40:5-7

CHAPTER 27

1 [a] Jer. 27:3, 12, 20; 28:1 [1] LXX omits v. 1. [2] So with MT, Tg., Vg.; some Heb. mss., Arab., Syr. *Zedekiah* (cf. 27:3, 12; 28:1)
2 [b] Jer. 28:10, 12; Ezek. 4:1; 12:3; 24:3
5 [c] Ps. 115:15; 146:6; Is. 45:12 [d] Deut. 9:29; Ps. 115:16; Jer. 32:17; Dan. 4:17, 25, 32
6 [e] Jer. 28:14 [f] Jer. 25:9; 43:10; Ezek. 29:18, 20 [g] Jer. 28:14; Dan. 2:38
7 [h] 2 Chr. 36:20 [i] Jer. 25:12; 50:27; [Dan. 5:26]; Zech. 2:8, 9 [j] Jer. 25:14
9 [3] Lit. *dreams*
10 [k] Jer. 23:16, 32; 28:15
12 [l] Jer. 28:1; 38:17
13 [m] [Prov. 8:36]; Jer. 27:8; 38:23; [Ezek. 18:31]
14 [n] Jer. 23:16 [o] Jer. 14:14; 23:21; 29:8, 9; Ezek. 13:22
15 [p] Jer. 23:21; 29:9
16 [q] 2 Kin. 24:13; 2 Chr. 36:7, 10; Jer. 28:3; Dan. 1:2
19 [r] 1 Kin. 7:15; 2 Kin. 25:13-17; Jer. 52:17, 20, 21

26:22 Elnathan. A high ranking official who on another occasion sided with Jeremiah (cf. 36:12,25).

26:23 the graves. In the Kidron Valley, to the E of the temple (cf. 2 Kin. 23:6).

26:24 Ahikam. He used his strategic influence to spring Jeremiah free of the death threat. This civil leader under King Josiah (cf. 2 Kin. 22:12,14) and father of Gedaliah, was appointed governor over Judah by the Babylonians after Jerusalem's final fall in 586 B.C. (39:14; 40:13–41:3).

27:1 reign of Jehoiakim. This may refer to Jehoiakim around 609/608 B.C. (as chap. 26). Or, possibly, the correct reading is "Zedekiah" as in vv. 3,12, and 28:1, which would put the date at the outset of his 597–586 B.C. reign.

27:2 Make...bonds and yokes. This object lesson symbolized bondage to Babylon. The yoke was bound on Jeremiah's neck to picture Judah's captivity (v. 12), then sent to 6 kings of nearby nations who would also be under Babylon's power (v. 3). Cf. Jer. 28:10-12.

27:7 Cf. 25:13,14.

27:8 yoke of...Babylon. The point of the object lesson is simple. Any nation that will serve Babylon willingly may stay in their own land, but nations that will not submit voluntarily to Babylon will suffer destruction. Consequently, Judah should submit and not be removed from the land (vv. 9-18).

27:18 make intercession. God would not answer such a prayer, as proven by vv. 19-22. This revealed His indifference to the prayers of these false prophets.

concerning the carts, and concerning the
remainder of the vessels that remain in this
city, 20 which Nebuchadnezzar king of
Babylon did not take, when he carried
away [s]captive Jeconiah the son of Jehoiakim, king of Judah, from Jerusalem to
Babylon, and all the nobles of Judah and
Jerusalem— 21 yes, thus says the LORD of
hosts, the God of Israel, concerning the
[t]vessels that remain in the house of the
LORD, and in the house of the king of Judah
and of Jerusalem: 22 'They shall be [u]carried
to Babylon, and there they shall be until
the day that I [v]visit them,' says the LORD.
'Then [w]I will bring them up and restore
them to this place.' "

Hananiah's Falsehood and Doom

28 And [a]it happened in the same year,
at the beginning of the reign of Zedekiah king of Judah, in the [b]fourth year *and*
in the fifth month, *that* Hananiah the son of
[c]Azur the prophet, who *was* from Gibeon,
spoke to me in the house of the LORD in the
presence of the priests and of all the people, saying, 2 "Thus speaks the LORD of
hosts, the God of Israel, saying: 'I have broken [d]the yoke of the king of Babylon.
3 [e]Within two full years I will bring back to
this place all the vessels of the LORD's
house, that Nebuchadnezzar king of Babylon [f]took away from this place and carried to Babylon. 4 And I will bring back to
this place [1]Jeconiah the son of Jehoiakim,
king of Judah, with all the captives of Judah who went to Babylon,' says the LORD,
'for I will break the yoke of the king of
Babylon.' "
5 Then the prophet Jeremiah spoke to
the prophet Hananiah in the presence of
the priests and in the presence of all the
people who stood in the house of the LORD,
6 and the prophet Jeremiah said, [g]"Amen!
The LORD do so; the LORD perform your
words which you have prophesied, to
bring back the vessels of the LORD's house
and all who were carried away captive,
from Babylon to this place. 7 Nevertheless
hear now this word that I speak in your
hearing and in the hearing of all the people: 8 The prophets who have been before
me and before you of old prophesied
against many countries and great kingdoms—of war and disaster and pestilence.
9 As for [h]the prophet who prophesies of
[i]peace, when the word of the prophet
comes to pass, the prophet will be known
as one whom the LORD has truly sent."
10 Then Hananiah the prophet took the
[j]yoke off the prophet Jeremiah's neck and
broke it. 11 And Hananiah spoke in the
presence of all the people, saying, "Thus
says the LORD: 'Even so I will break the
yoke of Nebuchadnezzar king of Babylon
[k]from the neck of all nations within the
space of two full years.' " And the prophet
Jeremiah went his way.
12 Now the word of the LORD came to
Jeremiah, after Hananiah the prophet had
broken the yoke from the neck of the
prophet Jeremiah, saying, 13 "Go and tell
Hananiah, saying, 'Thus says the LORD:
"You have broken the yokes of wood, but
you have made in their place yokes of
iron." 14 For thus says the LORD of hosts,
the God of Israel: [l]"I have put a yoke of
iron on the neck of all these nations, that
they may serve Nebuchadnezzar king of
Babylon; and they shall serve him. [m]I have
given him the beasts of the field also." ' "
15 Then the prophet Jeremiah said to
Hananiah the prophet, "Hear now, Hananiah, the LORD has not sent you, but [n]you
make this people trust in a [o]lie. 16 Therefore thus says the LORD: 'Behold, I will cast
you from the face of the earth. This year
you shall [p]die, because you have taught
[q]rebellion against the LORD.' "
17 So Hananiah the prophet died the
same year in the seventh month.

20 [s]2 Kin. 24:14, 15; 2 Chr. 36:10, 18; Jer. 24:1
21 [t]Jer. 20:5
22 [u]2 Kin. 25:13; 2 Chr. 36:18 [v]2 Chr. 36:21; Jer. 29:10; 32:5 [w]Ezra 1:7; 7:19

CHAPTER 28

1 [a]Jer. 27:1 [b]Jer. 51:59 [c]Ezek. 11:1
2 [d]Jer. 27:12
3 [e]Jer. 27:16 [f]2 Kin. 24:13; Dan. 1:2
4 [1]*Jehoiachin,* 2 Kin. 24:12
6 [g]1 Kin. 1:36; Ps. 41:13; Jer. 11:5
9 [h]Deut. 18:22 [i]Jer. 23:17; Ezek. 13:10, 16
10 [j]Jer. 27:2
11 [k]Jer. 27:7
14 [l]Deut. 28:48; Jer. 27:7, 8 [m]Jer. 27:6
15 [n]Jer. 20:6; 29:31; Lam. 2:14; Ezek. 13:22; Zech. 13:3 [o]Jer. 27:10; 29:9
16 [p]Jer. 20:6 [q]Deut. 13:5; Jer. 29:32

27:20 Ca. 597 B.C.

27:21,22 vessels. Jeremiah revealed that Judah's temple vessels taken to Babylon (cf. 2 Kin. 24:13; Dan. 1:1,2) would be restored to the temple. Fulfillment around 536 B.C. was spoken of in Ezra 5:13-15. About 516/515 B.C. these articles were placed in the rebuilt temple (Ezra 6:15).

28:1 reign of Zedekiah. Cf. 27:1 and *see note there*. The fourth year would be about 593 B.C. **Hananiah.** This man was one of several by this name in Scripture, in this case a foe of God's true prophet, distinct from the loyal Hananiah of Dan. 1:6.

28:2,3 I have broken the yoke. The false prophet, of the kind Jeremiah warned of in 27:14-16, boldly predicted victory over Babylon and the return of the temple vessels within two years. In actuality, Babylon achieved its third and final step in conquering Judah 11 years later (586 B.C.) as in chaps. 39,40,52. As to the vessels, *see note on 27:21,22.*

28:4 bring back...Jeconiah. This rash, false claim fell into ignominy. Jeconiah, soon taken to Babylon in 597 B.C., would live out his years there and not return to Jerusalem (52:31-34). Other captives either died in captivity, or didn't return until 61 years later. Cf. 22:24-26.

28:10 took the yoke off. The phony prophet, in foolishness, removed the object lesson from the true spokesman and broke it as a sign of his own prediction coming true (cf. vv. 2-4,11).

28:13 Go and tell Hananiah. Jeremiah apparently left the meeting, and later God sent him back to confront the liar, likely wearing yokes of iron (which Hananiah could not break!) to replace the wooden ones (v. 14) and to illustrate his message.

28:15-17 the LORD has not sent you. Jeremiah told Hananiah that 1) God had not approved his message; 2) he was guilty of encouraging the people to trust in a lie, even rebellion; and 3) God would require his life that very year, 597 B.C. The true prophet's word was authenticated in Hananiah's death in two months (cf. v. 17).

Jeremiah's Letter to the Captives

29 Now these *are* the words of the letter that Jeremiah the prophet sent
from Jerusalem to the remainder of the elders who were [a]carried away captive—to
the priests, the prophets, and all the people
whom Nebuchadnezzar had carried away
captive from Jerusalem to Babylon. 2 (This
happened after [b]Jeconiah[1] the king, the
[c]queen mother, the [2]eunuchs, the princes
of Judah and Jerusalem, the craftsmen, and
the smiths had departed from Jerusalem.)
3 *The letter was sent* by the hand of Elasah
the son of [d]Shaphan, and Gemariah the
son of Hilkiah, whom Zedekiah king of Judah sent to Babylon, to Nebuchadnezzar
king of Babylon, saying,

4 Thus says the LORD of hosts, the
God of Israel, to all who were
carried away captive, whom I have
caused to be carried away from Jerusalem to Babylon:

5 Build houses and dwell *in them;*
plant gardens and eat their fruit.
6 Take wives and beget sons and
daughters; and take wives for your
sons and give your daughters to
husbands, so that they may bear
sons and daughters—that you may
be increased there, and not
diminished. 7 And seek the peace
of the city where I have caused you
to be carried away captive, [e]and
pray to the LORD for it; for in its
peace you will have peace. 8 For
thus says the LORD of hosts, the
God of Israel: Do not let your
prophets and your diviners who
are in your midst [f]deceive you, nor
listen to your dreams which you
cause to be dreamed. 9 For they
prophesy [g]falsely to you in My
name; I have not sent them, says
the LORD.

10 For thus says the LORD: After [h]sev-
enty years are completed at
Babylon, I will visit you and
perform My good word toward
you, and cause you to [i]return to
this place. 11 For I know the
thoughts that I think toward you,
says the LORD, thoughts of peace
and not of evil, to give you a future
and a hope. 12 Then you will [j]call
upon Me and go and pray to Me,
and I will [k]listen to you. 13 And
[l]you will seek Me and find *Me,*
when you search for Me [m]with all
your heart. 14 [n]I will be found by
you, says the LORD, and I will
bring you back from your
captivity; [o]I will gather you from
all the nations and from all the
places where I have driven you,
says the LORD, and I will bring you
to the place from which I cause
you to be carried away captive.

15 Because you have said, "The LORD
has raised up prophets for us in
Babylon"— 16 [p]therefore thus says
the LORD concerning the king who
sits on the throne of David,
concerning all the people who
dwell in this city, and concerning
your brethren who have not gone
out with you into captivity—
17 thus says the LORD of hosts:
Behold, I will send on them the
sword, the famine, and the
pestilence, and will make them like
[q]rotten figs that cannot be eaten,
they are so bad. 18 And I will
pursue them with the sword, with
famine, and with pestilence; and I
[r]will deliver them to trouble
among all the kingdoms of the
earth—to be [s]a curse, an
astonishment, a hissing, and a
reproach among all the nations
where I have driven them, 19 because they have not heeded My
words, says the LORD, which [t]I sent
to them by My servants the
prophets, rising up early and
sending *them;* neither would you

CHAPTER 29

1 [a]Jer. 27:20
2 [b]2 Kin. 24:12-16; 2 Chr. 36:9, 10; Jer. 22:24-28 [c]2 Kin. 24:12, 15; Jer. 13:18 [1]*Jehoiachin,* 2 Kin. 24:12; 2 Chr. 36:10 [2]Or *officers*
3 [d]2 Chr. 34:8
7 [e]Ezra 6:10; Neh. 1:4-11; Dan. 9:16; 1 Tim. 2:2
8 [f]Jer. 14:14; 23:21; 27:14, 15; Eph. 5:6
9 [g]Jer. 28:15; 37:19
10 [h]2 Chr. 36:21-23; Ezra 1:1-4; Jer. 25:12; 27:22; Dan. 9:2; Zech. 7:5 [i][Jer. 24:6, 7]; Zeph. 2:7
12 [j]Ps. 50:15; Jer. 33:3; Dan. 9:3 [k]Ps. 145:19
13 [l]Lev. 26:39-42; Deut. 30:1-3 [m]1 Chr. 22:19; 2 Chr. 22:9; Jer. 24:7
14 [n][Deut. 4:7]; Ps. 32:6; 46:1; [Is. 55:6, 7]; Jer. 24:7 [o]Is. 43:5, 6; Jer. 23:8; 32:37
16 [p]Jer. 38:2, 3, 17-23
17 [q]Jer. 24:3, 8-10
18 [r]Deut. 28:25; 2 Chr. 29:8; Jer. 15:4; 24:9; 34:17; Ezek. 12:15 [s]Jer. 26:6; 42:18
19 [t]Jer. 25:4; 26:5; 35:15

29:1 the letter. Jeremiah, shortly after the 597 B.C. deportation of many countrymen (cf. v. 2), wrote to comfort them in exile.

29:4-10 Jeremiah's counsel to Israelites in Babylon was to take all the steps in living as colonists planning to be there for a long time (70 years, 29:10, as 25:11). Further, they were to seek Babylon's peace and intercede in prayer for it, their own welfare being bound with it (v. 7; cf. Ezra 6:10; 7:23).

29:11 thoughts of peace. This assured God's intentions to bring about blessing in Israel's future (cf. chaps. 30–33).

29:12-14 you will call. What God planned, He also gave the people opportunity to participate in by sincere (v. 13) prayer. Cf. 1 John 5:14,15.

29:14 I will be found by you. The Lord would answer their prayer, by returning the Jews to their land, cf. Daniel's example and God's response (Dan. 9:4-27). Fulfillment would occur in the era of Ezra and Nehemiah, and beyond this in even fuller measure after the Second Advent of their Messiah (cf. Dan. 2:35,45; 7:13,14,27; 12:1-3,13).

29:15-19 Because you have said. Amazingly still rejecting God's true message, Jewish captives listened to false prophets among them (cf. vv. 8,9,21-23). This was the very sin which would cause God to send a further deportation to those still in Judah (586 B.C.).

29:17 like rotten figs. Cf. the principle of Jer. 24.

heed, says the LORD. 20 Therefore
hear the word of the LORD, all you
of the captivity, whom I have sent
from Jerusalem to Babylon.

21 Thus says the LORD of hosts, the
God of Israel, concerning Ahab the
son of Kolaiah, and Zedekiah the
son of Maaseiah, who prophesy a
[u]lie to you in My name: Behold, I
will deliver them into the hand of
Nebuchadnezzar king of Babylon,
and he shall slay them before your
eyes. 22 [v]And because of them a
curse shall be taken up by all the
captivity of Judah who *are* in
Babylon, saying, "The LORD make
you like Zedekiah and Ahab,
[w]whom the king of Babylon
roasted in the fire"; 23 because
[x]they have done disgraceful things
in Israel, have committed adultery
with their neighbors' wives, and
have spoken lying words in My
name, which I have not
commanded them. Indeed I [y]know,
and *am* a witness, says the LORD.

24 You shall also speak to Shemaiah
the Nehelamite, saying, 25 Thus
speaks the LORD of hosts, the God of
Israel, saying: You have sent letters
in your name to all the people who
are at Jerusalem, [z]to Zephaniah the
son of Maaseiah the priest, and to
all the priests, saying, 26 "The LORD
has made you priest instead of Jehoiada the priest, so that there
should be [a]officers *in* the house of
the LORD over every man *who* is [b]de-
mented and considers himself a
prophet, that you should [c]put him
in prison and in the stocks. 27 Now
therefore, why have you not
rebuked Jeremiah of Anathoth who
makes himself a prophet to you?
28 For he has sent to us *in* Babylon,
saying, 'This *captivity is* long; build
houses and dwell *in them,* and plant
gardens and eat their fruit.' "

21 [u]Jer. 14:14, 15; Lam. 2:14; 2 Pet. 2:1
22 [v]Gen. 48:20; Is. 65:15 [w]Dan. 3:6, 21
23 [x]Jer. 23:14 [y][Prov. 5:21; Jer. 16:17]; Mal. 3:5; [Heb. 4:13]
25 [z]2 Kin. 25:18; Jer. 21:1
26 [a]Jer. 20:1 [b]2 Kin. 9:11; Hos. 9:7; Mark 3:21; John 10:20; Acts 26:24; [2 Cor. 5:13] [c]Jer. 20:1, 2; Acts 16:24
31 [d]Jer. 28:15 [e]Ezek. 13:8-16, 22, 23
32 [f]Jer. 28:16 [3]*descendants,* lit. *seed*

CHAPTER 30

3 [a]Ps. 53:6; Jer. 29:14; 30:18; 32:44; Ezek. 39:25; Amos 9:14; Zeph. 3:20 [b]Jer. 16:15; Ezek. 20:42; 36:24
5 [1]*dread*
6 [c]Jer. 4:31; 6:24 [2]Lit. *male can give birth* [3]*childbirth*
7 [d][Is. 2:12]; Hos. 1:11; Joel 2:11; Amos 5:18; Zeph. 1:14 [e]Lam. 1:12; Dan. 9:12; 12:1

29 Now Zephaniah the priest read
this letter in the hearing of Jeremiah the prophet. 30 Then the
word of the LORD came to Jeremiah, saying: 31 Send to all those in
captivity, saying, Thus says the
LORD concerning Shemaiah the Nehelamite: Because Shemaiah has
prophesied to you, [d]and I have not
sent him, and he has caused you to
trust in a [e]lie— 32 therefore thus
says the LORD: Behold, I will
punish Shemaiah the Nehelamite
and his [3]family: he shall not have
anyone to dwell among this
people, nor shall he see the good
that I will do for My people, says
the LORD, [f]because he has taught
rebellion against the LORD.

Restoration of Israel and Judah

30 The word that came to Jeremiah
from the LORD, saying, 2 "Thus
speaks the LORD God of Israel, saying:
'Write in a book for yourself all the words
that I have spoken to you. 3 For behold, the
days are coming,' says the LORD, 'that [a]I
will bring back from captivity My people
Israel and Judah,' says the LORD. [b]'And I
will cause them to return to the land that
I gave to their fathers, and they shall possess it.' "
4 Now these *are* the words that the LORD
spoke concerning Israel and Judah.
5 "For thus says the LORD:

'We have heard a voice of
trembling,
Of [1]fear, and not of peace.
6 Ask now, and see,
Whether a [2]man is ever in [3]labor
with child?
So why do I see every man *with* his
hands on his loins
[c]Like a woman in labor,
And all faces turned pale?
7 [d]Alas! For that day *is* great,
[e]So that none *is* like it;
And it *is* the time of Jacob's trouble,
But he shall be saved out of it.

29:21-23 Ahab...and Zedekiah. Two captive, false Israelite prophets, who had been misleading exiles in Babylon (v. 15), will stir up the wrath of their captor king, who will cast them into a furnace (as in Dan. 3). They aroused not only the Babylonian potentate's enmity, but God's also, because of prophecies against His word and physical adultery (cf. 5:7).

29:24-32 The judgment against Shemaiah, the otherwise unknown prophet, who opposed Jeremiah, was similar to that experienced by Hananiah (cf. 28:15-17).

29:28 This referred to Jeremiah's letter mentioned in v. 5.

30:3 I will bring back. This theme verse gives in capsule form the pledge of chaps. 30–33. God's restoration of the whole nation to their own land (cf. 29:10; Amos 9:14,15; Rom. 11:26) has in view a final regathering never to be removed again (*see note on 16:15*) and not just a return in the time of Ezra and Nehemiah (vv. 8,9; 31:31ff.; 32:39,40; 33:8,9,15,16). This verse is a summary of the prophecy given in vv. 4-9.

30:7 time of Jacob's trouble. This period of unprecedented difficulty for Israel, as the verse defines, is set in a context of Israel's final restoration. It is best equated with the time of tribulation (cf. vv. 8,9) just before Christ's Second Advent, mentioned elsewhere (Dan. 12:1; Matt. 24:21,22) and described in detail of Rev. 6–19.

8 'For it shall come to pass in that
day,'
Says the LORD of hosts,
'*That* I will break his yoke from
your neck,
And will burst your bonds;
Foreigners shall no more enslave
them.
9 But they shall serve the LORD their
God,
And [f]David their king,
Whom I will [g]raise up for them.

10 'Therefore [h]do not fear, O My
servant Jacob,' says the LORD,
'Nor be dismayed, O Israel;
For behold, I will save you from
afar,
And your seed [i]from the land of
their captivity.
Jacob shall return, have rest and be
quiet,
And no one shall make *him* afraid.
11 For I *am* with [j]you,' says the LORD,
'to save you;
[k]Though I make a full end of all
nations where I have
scattered you,
[l]Yet I will not make a complete end
of you.
But I will correct you [m]in justice,
And will not let you go altogether
unpunished.'

12 "For thus says the LORD:

[n]'Your affliction *is* incurable,
Your wound *is* severe.
13 *There is* no one to plead your cause,
That you may be bound up;
[o]You have no healing medicines.
14 [p]All your lovers have forgotten you;
They do not seek you;
For I have wounded you with the
wound [q]of an enemy,
With the chastisement [r]of a cruel
one,
For the multitude of your
iniquities,
[s]*Because* your sins have increased.
15 Why [t]do you cry about your
affliction?
Your sorrow *is* incurable.
Because of the multitude of your
iniquities,
Because your sins have increased,
I have done these things to you.

16 'Therefore all those who devour
you [u]shall be devoured;
And all your adversaries, every
one of them, shall go into
[v]captivity;
Those who plunder you shall
become [w]plunder,
And all who prey upon you I will
make a [x]prey.
17 [y]For I will restore health to you
And heal you of your wounds,'
says the LORD,
'Because they called you an outcast
saying:
"This *is* Zion;
No one seeks her." '

18 "Thus says the LORD:

'Behold, I will bring back the
captivity of Jacob's tents,
And [z]have mercy on his dwelling
places;
The city shall be built upon its own
[4]mound,
And the palace shall remain
according to its own plan.
19 Then [a]out of them shall proceed
thanksgiving
And the voice of those who make
merry;
[b]I will multiply them, and they shall
not diminish;
I will also glorify them, and they
shall not be small.
20 Their children also shall be [c]as
before,
And their congregation shall be
established before Me;
And I will punish all who oppress
them.
21 Their nobles shall be from among
them,
[d]And their governor shall come
from their midst;
Then I will [e]cause him to draw
near,
And he shall approach Me;

9 [f] Is. 55:3; Ezek. 34:23; 37:24; Hos. 3:5 [g] [Luke 1:69; Acts 2:30; 13:23]
10 [h] Is. 41:13; 43:5; 44:2; Jer. 46:27, 28 [i] Jer. 3:18
11 [j] [Is. 43:2-5] [k] Amos 9:8 [l] Jer. 4:27; 46:27, 28 [m] Ps. 6:1; Is. 27:8; Jer. 10:24; 46:28
12 [n] 2 Chr. 36:16; Jer. 15:18
13 [o] Jer. 8:22
14 [p] Jer. 22:20, 22; Lam. 1:2 [q] Job 13:24; 16:9; 19:11 [r] Job 30:21 [s] Jer. 5:6
15 [t] Jer. 15:18
16 [u] Ex. 23:22; Is. 41:11; Jer. 10:25 [v] Is. 14:2; Joel 3:8 [w] Is. 33:1; Ezek. 39:10 [x] Jer. 2:3
17 [y] Ex. 15:26; Ps. 107:20; Is. 30:26; Jer. 33:6
18 [z] Ps. 102:13 [4] *ruins*
19 [a] Ps. 126:1, 2; Is. 51:11; Jer. 31:4; Zeph. 3:14 [b] Is. 49:19-21; Jer. 23:3; 33:22; Zech. 10:8
20 [c] Is. 1:26
21 [d] Gen. 49:10 [e] Num. 16:5; Ps. 65:4

30:9 David their king. The Messiah, the greater David in David's dynasty, ultimately fulfills this promise (2 Sam. 7:16). He is the great king often promised as Israel's hope (23:5,6; Is. 9:7; Ezek. 37:24,25; Dan. 2:35,45; 7:13,14,27; Matt. 25:34; 26:64; Luke 1:32; Rev. 17:14; 19:16). No king of David's seed has held the scepter since the captivity. Zerubbabel, of David's line, never claimed the title of king (cf. Hag. 2:2).

30:11 not make a complete end of you. Israel will endure as a people until Messiah's kingdom (cf. Rom 11:1-29).

30:12-15 Judah had no reason to complain.

30:16-24 These absolute and extensive promises have yet to be fulfilled in history; they look forward to the reign of Christ, the greater David, in the millennial kingdom of the "latter days."

30:21 their governor. This refers to the Messiah, the king of v. 9 and 23:5,6, springing up from within Israel (cf. Is. 11:1), able to approach God as a priest.

For who *is* this who pledged his
heart to approach Me?' says
the LORD.
22 'You shall be [f]My people,
And I will be your God.' "

23 Behold, the [g]whirlwind of the
LORD
Goes forth with fury,
A [5]continuing whirlwind;
It will fall violently on the head of
the wicked.
24 The fierce anger of the LORD will
not return until He has done
it,
And until He has performed the
intents of His heart.

[h]In the latter days you will consider
it.

The Remnant of Israel Saved

31 "At [a]the same time," says the LORD,
[b]"I will be the God of all the families of Israel, and they shall be My people."
2 Thus says the LORD:

"The people who survived the
sword
Found grace in the wilderness—
Israel, when [c]I went to give him
rest."

3 The LORD has appeared [1]of old to
me, *saying:*
"Yes, [d]I have loved you with [e]an
everlasting love;
Therefore with lovingkindness I
have [f]drawn you.
4 Again [g]I will build you, and you
shall be rebuilt,
O virgin of Israel!
You shall again be adorned with
your [h]tambourines,
And shall go forth in the dances of
those who rejoice.
5 [i]You shall yet plant vines on the
mountains of Samaria;
The planters shall plant and [2]eat
them as ordinary food.
6 For there shall be a day
When the watchmen will cry on
Mount Ephraim,
[j]'Arise, and let us go up *to* Zion,
To the LORD our God.' "

7 For thus says the LORD:

22 [f]Ex. 6:7; Jer. 32:38; Ezek. 36:28; Hos. 2:23; Zech. 13:9
23 [g]Jer. 23:19, 20; 25:32 [5]Or *sweeping*
24 [h]Gen. 49:1

CHAPTER 31

1 [a]Jer. 30:24 [b]Jer. 30:22
2 [c]Ex. 33:14; Num. 10:33; Deut. 1:33; Josh. 1:13; Ps. 95:11; Is. 63:14
3 [d]Deut. 4:37; 7:8; Mal. 1:2 [e]Is. 43:4; Rom. 11:28 [f]Hos. 11:4 [1]Lit. *from afar*
4 [g]Jer. 33:7 [h]Ex. 15:20; Judg. 11:34; Ps. 149:3
5 [i]Ps. 107:37; Is. 65:21; Ezek. 28:26; Amos 9:14 [2]Lit. *treat them as common*
6 [j][Is. 2:3; Jer. 31:12; 50:4, 5; Mic. 4:2]
7 [k]Is. 12:5, 6
8 [l]Jer. 3:12, 18; 23:8 [m]Deut. 30:4; Is. 43:6; Ezek. 20:34, 41; 34:13
9 [n][Ps. 126:5; Jer. 50:4] [o]Is. 35:8; 43:19; 49:10, 11 [p]Ex. 4:22
10 [q]Is. 40:11; Ezek. 34:12-14 [3]Or *coastlands*
11 [r]Is. 44:23; 48:20; Jer. 15:21; 50:19 [s]Is. 49:24
12 [t]Ezek. 17:23 [u]Hos. 3:5 [v]Is. 58:11 [w]Is. 35:10; 65:19; [John 16:22; Rev. 21:4]

[k]"Sing with gladness for Jacob,
And shout among the chief of the
nations;
Proclaim, give praise, and say,
'O LORD, save Your people,
The remnant of Israel!'
8 Behold, I will bring them [l]from the
north country,
And [m]gather them from the ends
of the earth,
Among them the blind and the
lame,
The woman with child
And the one who labors with child,
together;
A great throng shall return there.
9 [n]They shall come with weeping,
And with supplications I will lead
them.
I will cause them to walk [o]by the
rivers of waters,
In a straight way in which they
shall not stumble;
For I am a Father to Israel,
And Ephraim *is* My [p]firstborn.

10 "Hear the word of the LORD,
O nations,
And declare *it* in the [3]isles afar off,
and say,
'He who scattered Israel [q]will
gather him,
And keep him as a shepherd *does*
his flock.'
11 For [r]the LORD has redeemed Jacob,
And ransomed him [s]from the hand
of one stronger than he.
12 Therefore they shall come and sing
in [t]the height of Zion,
Streaming to [u]the goodness of the
LORD—
For wheat and new wine and oil,
For the young of the flock and the
herd;
Their souls shall be like a [v]well-
watered garden,
[w]And they shall sorrow no more at
all.

13 "Then shall the virgin rejoice in the
dance,
And the young men and the old,
together;
For I will turn their mourning to
joy,
Will comfort them,
And make them rejoice rather than
sorrow.

31:1 At the same time. Equated with the latter days in 30:24. In this chapter, prophecies of the restoration of the nation are continued.

31:2-14 Here are messianic kingdom conditions.

14 I will [4]satiate the soul of the priests
with abundance,
And My people shall be satisfied
with My goodness, says the
LORD."

Mercy on Ephraim

15 Thus says the LORD:

[x]"A voice was heard in [y]Ramah,
Lamentation *and* bitter [z]weeping,
Rachel weeping for her children,
Refusing to be comforted for her
children,
Because [a]they *are* no more."

16 Thus says the LORD:

"Refrain your voice from [b]weeping,
And your eyes from tears;
For your work shall be rewarded,
says the LORD,
And they shall come back from the
land of the enemy.
17 There is [c]hope in your future, says
the LORD,
That *your* children shall come back
to their own border.

18 "I have surely heard Ephraim
bemoaning himself:
'You have [d]chastised me, and I was
chastised,
Like an untrained bull;
[e]Restore me, and I will return,
For You *are* the LORD my God.
19 Surely, [f]after my turning, I
repented;
And after I was instructed, I struck
myself on the thigh;
I was [g]ashamed, yes, even
humiliated,
Because I bore the reproach of my
youth.'
20 *Is* Ephraim My dear son?
Is he a pleasant child?
For though I spoke against him,
I earnestly remember him still;
[h]Therefore My [5]heart yearns for him;
[i]I will surely have mercy on him,
says the LORD.

21 "Set up signposts,
Make landmarks;
[j]Set your heart toward the highway,
The way in *which* you went.
[6]Turn back, O virgin of Israel,
Turn back to these your cities.
22 How long will you [k]gad about,
O you [l]backsliding daughter?
For the LORD has created a new
thing in the earth—
A woman shall encompass a man."

Future Prosperity of Judah

23 Thus says the LORD of hosts, the God
of Israel: "They shall again use this speech
in the land of Judah and in its cities, when
I bring back their captivity: [m]'The LORD
bless you, O home of justice, *and* [n]moun-
tain of holiness!' 24 And there shall dwell in
Judah itself, and [o]in all its cities together,
farmers and those going out with flocks.
25 For I have [7]satiated the weary soul, and
I have replenished every sorrowful soul."
26 After this I awoke and looked around,
and my sleep was [p]sweet to me.
27 "Behold, the days are coming, says the
LORD, that [q]I will sow the house of Israel and
the house of Judah with the seed of man and
the seed of beast. 28 And it shall come to
pass, *that* as I have [r]watched over them [s]to
pluck up, to break down, to throw down, to
destroy, and to afflict, so I will watch over
them [t]to build and to plant, says the LORD.
29 [u]In those days they shall say no more:

'The fathers have eaten sour grapes,
And the children's teeth are set on
edge.'

14 [4]Fill to the full **15** [x]Matt. 2:17, 18 [y]Josh. 18:25; Judg. 4:5; Is. 10:29; Jer. 40:1 [z]Gen. 37:35 [a]Jer. 10:20 **16** [b][Is. 25:8; 30:19] **17** [c]Jer. 29:11 **18** [d]Job 5:17; Ps. 94:12 [e]Ps. 80:3, 7, 19; Jer. 17:4; Lam. 5:21; [Acts 3:26] **19** [f]Deut. 30:2 [g]Ezek. 36:31; [Zech. 12:10] **20** [h]Gen. 43:30; Deut. 32:36; Judg. 10:16; Is. 63:15; Hos. 11:8 [i]Is. 57:18; Jer. 3:12; 12:15; [Hos. 14:4]; Mic. 7:18 [5]Lit. *inward parts* **21** [j]Jer. 50:5 [6]Or *Return* **22** [k]Jer. 2:18, 23, 36 [l]Jer. 3:6, 8, 11, 12, 14, 22 **23** [m]Ps. 122:5-8; Is. 1:26 [n][Zech. 8:3] **24** [o]Jer. 33:12 **25** [7]*fully satisfied* **26** [p]Prov. 3:24 **27** [q]Ezek. 36:9-11; Hos. 2:23 **28** [r]Jer. 44:27; Dan. 9:14 [s]Jer. 1:10; 18:7 [t]Jer. 24:6 **29** [u]Lam. 5:7; Ezek. 18:2, 3

31:15 A voice...in Ramah. The reflection, for a moment, is on the distress of an Israelite mother for her children slain in the Babylonian invasion. This was a backdrop for the many contrasting promises of restoration to a joyful time (as vv. 12-14,16,17) in the messianic day. Matthew saw the same description of sadness as apt, in principle, to depict something of the similar weeping of Jewish mothers when King Herod had babies slain at Bethlehem in a bid to kill the Messiah as a child (Matt. 2:17,18).

31:18-20 Restore me. Jeremiah wrote of Israel (the 10 tribes called Ephraim) as finally recognizing, in humility, the need for the Lord to move them to repentance and forgiveness. Cf. Ps. 102:13-17 for the relation of Israel's restoration to their prayers; see also 24:6,7; Lam. 5:21; cf. John 6:44,65).

31:22 backsliding. *See note on 2:19.* **A woman shall encompass a man.** Here is one of the most puzzling statements in Jeremiah. Some see the virgin birth of Christ (but "woman" means a woman, not a virgin, and "encompass" or "surround" does not suggest conceiving). Possibly it refers to the formerly virgin Israel (v. 21), who is now a disgraced, divorced wife (v. 22; 3:8). She will one day in the future reembrace her former husband, the Lord, and He will receive her back, fully forgiven. That would be "a new thing on the earth."

31:26 my sleep was sweet. The hope of Israel's restoration brought a moment of peace in Jeremiah's otherwise tumultuous ministry.

31:28 build and...plant. The Lord repeated what He at first told Jeremiah in 1:10 regarding His two works of judging and blessing. The latter is in two images, architectural (building) and agricultural (planting).

31:29 eaten sour grapes. This was apparently a proverb among the exiles' children born in Babylon, to express that they suffered the consequences of their fathers' sins rather than their own (Lam. 5:7; Ezek. 18:2,3).

30 [v]But every one shall die for his own iniquity; every man who eats the sour
grapes, his teeth shall be set on edge.

A New Covenant

31 "Behold, the [w]days are coming, says
the LORD, when I will make a new covenant
with the house of Israel and with the house
of Judah— 32 not according to the covenant
that I made with their fathers in the day
that [x]I took them by the hand to lead them
out of the land of Egypt, My covenant
which they broke, [8]though I was a husband
to them, says the LORD. 33 [y]But this *is* the
covenant that I will make with the house of
Israel after those days, says the LORD: [z]I
will put My law in their minds, and write it
on their [9]hearts; [a]and I will be their God,
and they shall be My people. 34 No more
shall every man teach his neighbor, and
every man his brother, saying, 'Know the
LORD,' for [b]they all shall know Me, from the
least of them to the greatest of them, says
the LORD. For [c]I will forgive their iniquity,
and their sin I will remember no more."

35 Thus says the LORD,
[d]Who gives the sun for a light by
day,
The ordinances of the moon and
the stars for a light by night,
Who disturbs [e]the sea,
And its waves roar
[f](The LORD of hosts *is* His name):

36 "If [g]those ordinances depart
From before Me, says the LORD,
Then the seed of Israel shall also
cease
From being a nation before Me
forever."

37 Thus says the LORD:
[h]"If heaven above can be measured,
And the foundations of the earth
searched out beneath,
I will also [i]cast off all the seed of
Israel
For all that they have done, says
the LORD.

38 "Behold, the days are coming, says
the LORD, that the city shall be built for the
LORD [j]from the Tower of Hananel to the
Corner Gate. 39 [k]The surveyor's line shall
again extend straight forward over the hill
Gareb; then it shall turn toward Goath.
40 And the whole valley of the dead bodies
and of the ashes, and all the fields as far as
the Brook Kidron, [l]to the corner of the
Horse Gate toward the east, [m]*shall be* holy
to the LORD. It shall not be plucked up or
thrown down anymore forever."

Jeremiah Buys a Field

32 The word that came to Jeremiah
from the LORD [a]in the tenth year of
Zedekiah king of Judah, which was the
eighteenth year of Nebuchadnezzar. 2 For
then the king of Babylon's army besieged
Jerusalem, and Jeremiah the prophet was
shut up [b]in the court of the prison, which
was in the king of Judah's house. 3 For Zedekiah king of Judah had shut him up, saying, "Why do you [c]prophesy and say,
'Thus says the LORD: [d]"Behold, I will give
this city into the hand of the king of Babylon, and he shall take it; 4 and Zedekiah
king of Judah [e]shall not escape from the
hand of the Chaldeans, but shall surely be
delivered into the hand of the king of
Babylon, and shall speak with him [1]face to

30 [v]Deut. 24:16; 2 Chr. 25:4; Is. 3:11; [Ezek. 18:4, 20; Gal. 6:5, 7]
31 [w]Jer. 32:40; 33:14; Ezek. 37:26; Heb. 8:8-12; 10:16, 17
32 [x]Deut. 1:31; Is. 63:12 [8]So with MT, Tg., Vg.; LXX, Syr. *and I turned away from them*
33 [y]Jer. 32:40; Heb. 10:16 [z]Ps. 40:8; [Ezek. 11:19; 36:26, 27; 2 Cor. 3:3] [a]Jer. 24:7; 30:22; 32:38 [9]Lit. *inward parts*
34 [b]Is. 11:9; 54:13; Jer. 24:7; Hab. 2:14; [John 6:45; 1 Cor. 2:10; 1 John 2:20] [c]Jer. 33:8; 50:20; Mic. 7:18; [Acts 10:43; 13:39; Rom. 11:27]
35 [d]Gen. 1:14-18; Deut. 4:19; Ps. 72:5, 17; 89:2, 36; 119:91 [e]Is. 51:15 [f]Jer. 10:16
36 [g]Ps. 148:6; Is. 54:9, 10; Jer. 33:20
37 [h]Is. 40:12; Jer. 33:22 [i]Jer. 33:24-26; [Rom. 11:2-5, 26, 27]
38 [j]Neh. 3:1; 12:39; Zech. 14:10
39 [k]Ezek. 40:8; Zech. 2:1, 2
40 [l]2 Kin. 11:16; 2 Chr. 23:15; Neh. 3:28 [m][Joel 3:17]; Zech. 14:20

CHAPTER 32

1 [a]2 Kin. 25:1, 2; Jer. 39:1, 2
2 [b]Neh. 3:25; Jer. 33:1; 37:21; 39:14
3 [c]Jer. 26:8, 9 [d]Jer. 21:3-7; 34:2
4 [e]2 Kin. 25:4-7; Jer. 34:3; 38:18, 23; 39:5; 52:9 [1]Lit. *mouth to mouth*

31:31-34 a new covenant. In contrast to the Mosaic Covenant under which Israel failed, God promised a New Covenant with a spiritual, divine dynamic by which those who know Him would participate in the blessings of salvation. The fulfillment was to individuals, yet also to Israel as a nation (v. 36; Rom. 11:16-27). It is set 1) in the framework of a reestablishment in their land (e.g., chaps. 30–33 and in vv. 38-40) and 2) in the time after the ultimate difficulty (30:7). In principle, this covenant, also announced by Jesus Christ (Luke 22:20), begins to be exercised with spiritual aspects realized for Jewish and Gentile believers in the church era (1 Cor. 11:25; Heb. 8:7-13; 9:15; 10:14-17; 12:24; 13:20). It has already begun to take effect with "the remnant according to the election of grace" (Rom. 11:5). It will be also realized by the people of Israel in the last days, including the regathering to their ancient land, Palestine (chaps. 30–33). The streams of the Abrahamic, Davidic, and New Covenants find their confluence in the millennial kingdom ruled over by the Messiah.

31:35-37 These verses emphasize the certainty with which Israel can expect God to fulfill the New Covenant (cf. 33:17-22; 25,26).

31:38-40 The tower was in the NE corner of the city (cf. Neh. 3:1; 12:39). When New Covenant promises are ultimately fulfilled to Israel in its regathering to its land, rebuilt Jerusalem will meet certain specifications. The "Corner Gate" is at the NW corner (2 Kin. 14:13; 2 Chr. 26:9). "The surveyor's line" marks out the area for rebuilding. It will point over the hill Gareb and then toward Goath; both places are impossible to identify today. "The valley of...dead bodies" is the valley of Hinnom, a place of refuse and burning fires (cf. 7:31, and *see note there*). The "Horse Gate" was at the SE corner of the temple courts (2 Kin. 11:16; Neh. 3:28).

32:1 tenth year. The time is 587 B.C., the tenth year in Zedekiah's reign (597–586 B.C.), the eighteenth of Nebuchadnezzar's rule, during Babylon's siege of Jerusalem.

32:2 Babylon's army besieged. The siege, set up in the tenth month (Jan.) of 588 B.C., lasted at least 30 months to the fourth month (July) of 586 B.C. (39:1,2). Cf. 34:1 and *see note there*. The events of the chapter occurred in this setting of Judah's imminent loss of its land, only about a year before Babylon's final takeover detailed in chaps. 39,40,52.

32:2-5 shut up in...prison. Judah's final king put Jeremiah into prison on the charge of preaching treason, against nation and king, whereas Zedekiah savored positive talk to spark new morale to hold out.

face, and see him [f]eye to eye; 5 then he
shall [g]lead Zedekiah to Babylon, and there
he shall be [h]until I visit him," says the
LORD; [i]"though you fight with the Chaldeans, you shall not succeed" '?"
6 And Jeremiah said, "The word of the
LORD came to me, saying, 7 'Behold, Hanamel the son of Shallum your uncle will
come to you, saying, "Buy my field which
is in Anathoth, for the [j]right of redemption
is yours to buy *it*." ' 8 Then Hanamel my
uncle's son came to me in the court of the
prison according to the word of the LORD,
and said to me, 'Please buy my field that *is*
in Anathoth, which *is* in the country of
Benjamin; for the right of inheritance *is*
yours, and the redemption yours; buy *it*
for yourself.' Then I knew that this was the
word of the LORD. 9 So I bought the field
from Hanamel, the son of my uncle who
was in Anathoth, and [k]weighed *out to* him
the money—seventeen shekels of silver.
10 And I signed the [2]deed and sealed *it*,
took witnesses, and weighed the money on
the scales. 11 So I took the purchase deed,
both that which was sealed *according* to the
law and custom, and that which was open;
12 and I gave the purchase deed to [l]Baruch
the son of Neriah, son of Mahseiah, in the
presence of Hanamel my uncle's *son*, and
in the presence of the [m]witnesses who
signed the purchase deed, before all the
Jews who sat in the court of the prison.
13 "Then I charged [n]Baruch before them,
saying, 14 'Thus says the LORD of hosts, the
God of Israel: "Take these deeds, both this
purchase deed which is sealed and this
deed which is open, and put them in an
earthen vessel, that they may last many
days." 15 For thus says the LORD of hosts,
the God of Israel: "Houses and fields and
vineyards shall be [o]possessed again in this
land." '

Jeremiah Prays for Understanding

16 "Now when I had delivered the purchase deed to Baruch the son of Neriah, I
prayed to the LORD, saying: 17 'Ah, Lord
GOD! Behold, [p]You have made the heavens
and the earth by Your great power and outstretched arm. [q]There is nothing too [3]hard
for You. 18 *You* show [r]lovingkindness to
thousands, and repay the iniquity of the fathers into the bosom of their children after
them—the Great, [s]the Mighty God, whose
name *is* [t]the LORD of hosts. 19 *You are* [u]great
in counsel and mighty in [4]work, for your
[v]eyes *are* open to all the ways of the sons of
men, [w]to give everyone according to his
ways and according to the fruit of his doings. 20 You have set signs and wonders in
the land of Egypt, to this day, and in Israel
and among *other* men; and You have made
Yourself [x]a name, as it is this day. 21 You
[y]have brought Your people Israel out of
the land of Egypt with signs and wonders,
with a strong hand and an outstretched
arm, and with great terror; 22 You have
given them this land, of which You swore
to their fathers to give them—[z]"a land
flowing with milk and honey." 23 And they
came in and took possession of it, but
[a]they have not obeyed Your voice or
walked in Your law. They have done nothing of all that You commanded them to do;
therefore You have caused all this calamity
to come upon them.
24 'Look, the siege mounds! They have
come to the city to take it; and the city has
been given into the hand of the Chaldeans
who fight against it, because of [b]the sword
and famine and pestilence. What You have
spoken has happened; there You see *it!*
25 And You have said to me, O Lord GOD,
"Buy the field for money, and take witnesses"!—yet the city has been given into
the hand of the Chaldeans.' "

God's Assurance of the People's Return

26 Then the word of the LORD came to
Jeremiah, saying, 27 "Behold, I *am* the
LORD, the [c]God of all flesh. Is there anything too hard for Me? 28 Therefore thus
says the LORD: 'Behold, I will give this city
into the hand of the Chaldeans, into the
hand of Nebuchadnezzar king of Babylon,
and he shall take it. 29 And the Chaldeans
who fight against this city shall come and
[d]set fire to this city and burn it, with the
houses [e]on whose roofs they have offered
incense to Baal and poured out drink offerings to other gods, to provoke Me to anger;

4 [f] Jer. 39:5
5 [g] Jer. 27:22; 39:7; Ezek. 12:12, 13 [h] Jer. 27:22 [i] Jer. 21:4; 33:5
7 [j] Lev. 25:24, 25, 32; Ruth 4:4
9 [k] Gen. 23:16; Zech. 11:12
10 [2] Lit. *book*
12 [l] Jer. 36:4 [m] Is. 8:2
13 [n] Jer. 36:4
15 [o] Ezra 2:1; [Jer. 31:5, 12, 14]; Amos 9:14, 15; Zech. 3:10
17 [p] 2 Kin. 19:15; Ps. 102:25; Is. 40:26-29; Jer. 27:5 [q] Gen. 18:14; Jer. 32:27; Zech. 8:6; Matt. 19:26; Mark 10:27; Luke 18:27 [3] *difficult*
18 [r] Ex. 20:6; 34:7; Deut. 5:9, 10 [s] Ps. 50:1; [Is. 9:6]; Jer. 20:11 [t] Jer. 10:16
19 [u] Is. 28:29 [v] Job 34:21; Ps. 33:13; Prov. 5:21; Jer. 16:17 [w] Ps. 62:12; Jer. 17:10; [Matt. 16:27; John 5:29] [4] *deed*
20 [x] Ex. 9:16; 1 Chr. 17:21; Is. 63:12; Jer. 13:11; Dan. 9:15
21 [y] Ex. 6:6; 2 Sam. 7:23; 1 Chr. 17:21; Ps. 136:11, 12
22 [z] Ex. 3:8, 17; Deut. 1:8; Ps. 105:9-11; Jer. 11:5
23 [a] [Neh. 9:26]; Jer. 11:8; [Dan. 9:10-14]
24 [b] Jer. 14:12; Ezek. 14:21
27 [c] [Num. 16:22]
29 [d] 2 Chr. 36:19; Jer. 21:10; 37:8, 10; 52:13 [e] Jer. 19:13

32:8 the right of inheritance. A man facing hardship could sell property, and the right to redeem it until the Jubilee year belonged to the closest blood relative. If a stranger had taken it due to unpaid debt, the relative could redeem it as a family possession (Lev. 25:25). Levite land could be sold only to a Levite (Lev. 25:32-34), such as Jeremiah. He did as the Lord told him (vv. 9-12).

32:14 Take these deeds. Title deeds to the land, kept for security reasons in a pottery jar, would attest in a future day to one's claim of possession. Men of Anathoth did return to Jerusalem from Babylon (Ezra 2:23). Also, some of the poor of the land, left by the Babylonians (chap. 39), could have included certain inhabitants of Anathoth. In a still future day, God will be able (vv. 17,27) to make this land good to a resurrected Jeremiah and confirm to the right people that they are the prophet/priest's descendants.

32:16-25 With the immense sovereign power God possesses to do whatever He wishes in the present captivity and the future return, Jeremiah wondered why God had him redeem the field.

32:26-35 God reviewed Judah's sins and affirmed to Jeremiah that the Babylonians would prevail over Jerusalem ("this city" in v. 28, etc.).

30 because the children of Israel and the
children of Judah [f]have done only evil before Me from their youth. For the children
of Israel have provoked Me only to anger
with the work of their hands,' says the
LORD. 31 'For this city has been to Me *a*
provocation of My anger and My fury from
the day that they built it, even to this day;
[g]so I will remove it from before My face
32 because of all the evil of the children of
Israel and the children of Judah, which
they have done to provoke Me to anger—
[h]they, their kings, their princes, their
priests, [i]their prophets, the men of Judah,
and the inhabitants of Jerusalem. 33 And
they have turned to Me the [j]back, and not
the face; though I taught them, [k]rising up
early and teaching *them,* yet they have not
listened to receive instruction. 34 But they
[l]set their abominations in [5]the house
which is called by My name, to defile it.
35 And they built the high places of Baal
which *are* in the Valley of the Son of Hinnom, to [m]cause their sons and their daughters to pass through *the fire* to [n]Molech,
[o]which I did not command them, nor did it
come into My mind that they should do
this abomination, to cause Judah to sin.'
36 "Now therefore, thus says the LORD,
the God of Israel, concerning this city of
which you say, 'It shall be delivered into
the hand of the king of Babylon by the
sword, by the famine, and by the pestilence: 37 Behold, I will [p]gather them out of
all countries where I have driven them in
My anger, in My fury, and in great wrath; I
will bring them back to this place, and I
will cause them [q]to dwell safely. 38 They
shall be [r]My people, and I will be their
God; 39 then I will [s]give them one heart
and one way, that they may fear Me forever, for the good of them and their children
after them. 40 And [t]I will make an everlasting covenant with them, that I will not turn
away from doing them good; but [u]I will
put My fear in their hearts so that they will
not depart from Me. 41 Yes, [v]I will rejoice
over them to do them good, and [w]I will
[6]assuredly plant them in this land, with all
My heart and with all My soul.'

42 "For thus says the LORD: [x]'Just as I
have brought all this great calamity on this
people, so I will bring on them all the good
that I have promised them. 43 And fields
will be bought in this land [y]of which you
say, "*It is* desolate, without man or beast; it
has been given into the hand of the Chaldeans." 44 Men will buy fields for money,
sign deeds and seal *them,* and take witnesses, in [z]the land of Benjamin, in the
places around Jerusalem, in the cities of Judah, in the cities of the mountains, in the
cities of the [7]lowland, and in the cities of
the [8]South; for [a]I will cause their captives
to return,' says the LORD."

Excellence of the Restored Nation

33 Moreover the word of the LORD
came to Jeremiah a second time,
while he was still [a]shut up in the court of
the prison, saying, 2 "Thus says the LORD
[b]who made it, the LORD who formed it to
establish it [c](the[1] LORD *is* His name):
3 [d]'Call to Me, and I will answer you, and
show you great and [2]mighty things, which
you do not know.'
4 "For thus says the LORD, the God of Israel, concerning the houses of this city and
the houses of the kings of Judah, which
have been pulled down *to fortify* against
[e]the siege mounds and the sword: 5 'They
come to fight with the Chaldeans, but *only*
to [f]fill their places with the dead bodies of
men whom I will slay in My anger and My
fury, all for whose wickedness I have hidden My face from this city. 6 Behold, [g]I will
bring it health and healing; I will heal them
and reveal to them the abundance of peace
and truth. 7 And [h]I will cause the captives
of Judah and the captives of Israel to return, and will rebuild those places [i]as at
the first. 8 I will [j]cleanse them from all their
iniquity by which they have sinned against
Me, and I will pardon all their iniquities by
which they have sinned and by which they
have transgressed against Me. 9 [k]Then it
shall be to Me a name of joy, a praise, and
an honor before all nations of the earth,

30 [f]Deut. 9:7-12; Is. 63:10; Jer. 2:7; 3:25; 7:22-26; Ezek. 20:28
31 [g]2 Kin. 23:27; 24:3; Jer. 27:10
32 [h]Ezra 9:7; Is. 1:4, 6; Dan. 9:8 [i]Jer. 23:14
33 [j]Jer. 2:27; 7:24 [k]Jer. 7:13
34 [l]2 Kin. 21:1-7; Jer. 7:10-12, 30; 23:11; Ezek. 8:5, 6 [5]The temple
35 [m]2 Chr. 28:2, 3; 33:6; Jer. 7:31; 19:5 [n]Lev. 18:21; 1 Kin. 11:33; 2 Kin. 23:10; Acts 7:43 [o]Jer. 7:31
37 [p]Deut. 30:3; Jer. 23:3; 29:14; 31:10; 50:19; Ezek. 37:21 [q]Jer. 33:16
38 [r][Jer. 24:7; 30:22; 31:33]
39 [s][Jer. 24:7; Ezek. 11:19]
40 [t]Is. 55:3; Jer. 31:31; Ezek. 37:26 [u]Deut. 31:6, 8; [Ezek. 39:29; Jer. 31:33]
41 [v]Deut. 30:9; Is. 62:5; 65:19; Zeph. 3:17 [w]Jer. 24:6; 31:28; Amos 9:15 [6]*truly*
42 [x]Jer. 31:28; Zech. 8:14, 15
43 [y]Jer. 33:10
44 [z]Jer. 17:26 [a]Jer. 33:7, 11 [7]Heb. *shephelah* [8]Heb. *Negev*

CHAPTER 33

1 [a]Jer. 32:2, 3
2 [b]Is. 37:26 [c]Ex. 15:3; [Jer. 10:16]; Amos 5:8; 9:6 [1]Heb. *YHWH*
3 [d]Ps. 91:15; [Is. 55:6, 7]; Jer. 29:12 [2]*inaccessible*
4 [e]Is. 22:10; Jer. 32:24; Ezek. 4:2; 21:22; Hab. 1:10
5 [f]2 Kin. 23:14; Jer. 21:4-7; 32:5
6 [g]Jer. 30:17; Hos. 6:1
7 [h]Ps. 85:1; Jer. 30:3; 32:44; Amos 9:14 [i]Is. 1:26; Jer. 24:6; 30:20; 31:4, 28; 42:10; Amos 9:14, 15
8 [j]Ps. 51:2; Is. 44:22; Jer. 50:20; Ezek. 36:25, 33; Mic. 7:18, 19; Zech. 13:1; [Heb. 9:11-14]
9 [k]Is. 62:7; Jer. 13:11

32:36-41 However, one day God will restore Israel to the Land and provide the blessing of salvation.

32:37 I will bring them back to this place. God pledged to restore Israelites to the very land of Israel (cf. v. 44). It is natural to expect His fulfillment of this blessing to be just as literal as the reverse—His scattering from the Land (cf. v. 42).

32:38,39 This speaks of spiritual salvation, i.e., the true knowledge and worship of God.

32:40 an everlasting covenant. The ultimate fulfillment of a future in the Land was not fulfilled in the Ezra/Nehemiah return. This occurs in the time when God gives the people of Israel a new heart in eternal salvation along with their return to the ancient land (cf. 33:8,9, and Ezek. 36:26).

32:42-44 In the millennial kingdom, land will again be bought and sold in Israel.

33:3 Call…I will answer. God invited Jeremiah's prayer, which appeals to Him to fulfill the aspects of His promises which He guarantees He will attend to (as 29:11-14; Dan. 9:4-19; cf. John 15:7). His answer to the prayer was assured in vv. 4-26 here (cf. v. 14).

33:8 Again the Lord emphasized the individual spiritual salvation associated with the New Covenant restoration to the land.

who shall hear all the good that I do to
them; they shall [l]fear and tremble for all
the goodness and all the prosperity that I
provide for it.'
10 "Thus says the LORD: 'Again there
shall be heard in this place—[m]of which
you say, "It *is* desolate, without man and
without beast"—in the cities of Judah, in
the streets of Jerusalem that are desolate,
without man and without inhabitant and
without beast, 11 the [n]voice of joy and the
voice of gladness, the voice of the bridegroom and the voice of the bride, the voice
of those who will say:

[o]"Praise the LORD of hosts,
For the LORD *is* good,
For His mercy *endures* forever"—

and of those *who will* bring [p]the sacrifice of
praise into the house of the LORD. For I will
cause the captives of the land to return as
at the first,' says the LORD.
12 "Thus says the LORD of hosts: [q]'In this
place which is desolate, without man and
without beast, and in all its cities, there
shall again be a dwelling place of shepherds causing *their* flocks to lie down.
13 [r]In the cities of the mountains, in the
cities of the lowland, in the cities of the
South, in the land of Benjamin, in the
places around Jerusalem, and in the cities
of Judah, the flocks shall again [s]pass under
the hands of him who counts *them*,' says
the LORD.
14 [t]'Behold, the days are coming,' says
the LORD, 'that [u]I will perform that good
thing which I have promised to the house
of Israel and to the house of Judah:

15 'In those days and at that time
I will cause to grow up to David
A [v]Branch of righteousness;
He shall execute judgment and
righteousness in the earth.
16 In those days Judah will be saved,
And Jerusalem will dwell safely.
And this *is the name* by which she
will be called:

[3]THE LORD OUR RIGHTEOUSNESS.'

17 "For thus says the LORD: 'David shall
never [w]lack a man to sit on the throne of
the house of Israel; 18 nor shall the [x]priests,
the Levites, lack a man to [y]offer burnt offerings before Me, to [4]kindle grain offerings, and to sacrifice continually.' "

The Permanence of God's Covenant

19 And the word of the LORD came to Jeremiah, saying, 20 "Thus says the LORD: 'If
you can break My covenant with the day
and My covenant with the night, so that
there will not be day and night in their season, 21 then [z]My covenant may also be broken with David My servant, so that he
shall not have a son to reign on his throne,
and with the Levites, the priests, My ministers. 22 As [a]the host of heaven cannot be
numbered, nor the sand of the sea measured, so will I [b]multiply the descendants
of David My servant and the [c]Levites who
minister to Me.' "
23 Moreover the word of the LORD came
to Jeremiah, saying, 24 "Have you not considered what these people have spoken,
saying, 'The two families which the LORD
has chosen, He has also cast them off '?
Thus they have [d]despised My people, as if
they should no more be a nation before
them.
25 "Thus says the LORD: 'If [e]My covenant
is not with day and night, *and if* I have not
[f]appointed the ordinances of heaven and
earth, 26 [g]then I will [h]cast away the descendants of Jacob and David My servant,
so that I will not take *any* of his descendants *to be* rulers over the descendants of
Abraham, Isaac, and Jacob. For I will cause
their captives to return, and will have
mercy on them.' "

Zedekiah Warned by God

34 The word which came to Jeremiah
from the LORD, [a]when Nebuchadnezzar king of Babylon and all his army,
[b]all the kingdoms of the earth under his
dominion, and all the people, fought
against Jerusalem and all its cities, saying,
2 "Thus says the LORD, the God of Israel:
'Go and [c]speak to Zedekiah king of Judah
and tell him, "Thus says the LORD: 'Behold,

9 [l]Is. 60:5
10 [m]Jer. 32:43
11 [n]Jer. 7:34; 16:9; 25:10; Rev. 18:23 [o]1 Chr. 16:8; 2 Chr. 5:13; Ezra 3:11; Ps. 136:1; Is. 12:4 [p]Lev. 7:12; Ps. 107:22; 116:17; Heb. 13:15
12 [q]Is. 65:10; [Jer. 31:24; 50:19; Ezek. 34:12-15; Zeph. 2:6, 7]
13 [r]Jer. 17:26; 32:44 [s]Lev. 27:32; [Luke 15:4]
14 [t]Jer. 23:5; 31:27, 31 [u]Is. 32:1; Jer. 29:10; 32:42; Ezek. 34:23-25; Hag. 2:6-9
15 [v]Is. 4:2; 11:1; Jer. 23:5; Zech. 3:8; 6:12, 13
16 [3]Heb. *YHWH Tsidkenu*; cf. Jer. 23:5, 6
17 [w]2 Sam. 7:16; 1 Kin. 2:4; Ps. 89:29; [Luke 1:32]
18 [x]Num. 3:5-10; Deut. 18:1; 24:8; Josh. 3:3; Ezek. 44:15 [y][Rom. 12:1; 15:16; 1 Pet. 2:5, 9; Rev. 1:6] [4]*burn*
21 [z]2 Sam. 23:5; 2 Chr. 7:18; 21:7; Ps. 89:34
22 [a]Gen. 15:5; 22:17; Jer. 31:37 [b]Jer. 30:19; Ezek. 36:10, 11 [c]Is. 66:21; Jer. 33:18
24 [d]Neh. 4:2-4; Esth. 3:6-8; Ps. 44:13, 14; 83:4; Ezek. 36:2
25 [e]Gen. 8:22; Jer. 33:20 [f]Ps. 74:16; 104:19
26 [g]Jer. 31:37 [h]Rom. 11:1, 2

CHAPTER 34

1 [a]2 Kin. 25:1; Jer. 32:1, 2; 39:1; 52:4 [b]Jer. 1:15; 25:9; Dan. 2:37, 38
2 [c]2 Chr. 36:11, 12; Jer. 22:1, 2; 37:1, 2

33:11 Praise the LORD. These are the words of Ps. 136:1, actually used by the Jews at their return from Babylon (Ezra 3:11).

33:15 A Branch. This is the Messiah King in David's lineage, as in 23:5,6. He is the King whose reign immediately follows the second coming when He appears in power (Dan. 2:35,45; 7:13,14,27; Matt. 16:27-28; 24:30; 26:64).

33:17-22 God promised to fulfill the Davidic (2 Sam. 17) and Priestly/Levitical (Num. 25:10-13) Covenants without exception. The promise was as certain as the sure appearance of night and day and the incalculable number of stars or sand grains (cf. 31:35-37; 33:25,26).

33:24 two families. Judah and Israel. **He has also cast them off.** Many, even today, believe Israel as a nation has no future. In vv. 25,26 God emphatically denies that notion (cf. 31:35,36; Ps. 74:16,17; Rom. 11:1,2).

34:1 when Nebuchadnezzar...fought. The siege began ca. Jan. 15, 588 B.C. (39:1), and ended ca. July 18, 586 (39:2; 52:5,6). This chapter was set in Zedekiah's reign, during the siege of 588–586 B.C., and was an amplification of 32:1-5, the message that resulted in Jeremiah's incarceration. **against Jerusalem.** Babylon's destruction of Jerusalem began Aug. 14, 586 (2 Kin. 25:8,9).

[d]I will give this city into the hand of the
king of Babylon, and he shall burn it with
fire. 3 And [e]you shall not escape from his
hand, but shall surely be taken and delivered into his hand; your eyes shall see the
eyes of the king of Babylon, he shall speak
with you [f]face[1] to face, and you shall go to
Babylon.' " ' 4 Yet hear the word of the
LORD, O Zedekiah king of Judah! Thus says
the LORD concerning you: 'You shall not
die by the sword. 5 You shall die in peace;
as in [g]the ceremonies of your fathers, the
former kings who were before you, [h]so
they shall burn incense for you and [i]la-
ment for you, *saying,* "Alas, lord!" For I
have pronounced the word, says the
LORD.' "
6 Then Jeremiah the prophet spoke all
these words to Zedekiah king of Judah in
Jerusalem, 7 when the king of Babylon's
army fought against Jerusalem and all the
cities of Judah that were left, against
Lachish and Azekah; for *only* [j]these fortified cities remained of the cities of Judah.

Treacherous Treatment of Slaves

8 *This is* the word that came to Jeremiah
from the LORD, after King Zedekiah had
made a covenant with all the people who
were at Jerusalem to proclaim [k]liberty to
them: 9 [l]that every man should set free his
male and female slave—a Hebrew man or
woman—[m]that no one should keep a Jewish brother in bondage. 10 Now when all
the princes and all the people, who had entered into the covenant, heard that everyone should set free his male and female
slaves, that no one should keep them in
bondage anymore, they obeyed and let
them go. 11 But afterward they changed
their minds and made the male and female
slaves return, whom they had set free, and
brought them into subjection as male and
female slaves.
12 Therefore the word of the LORD came
to Jeremiah from the LORD, saying,
13 "Thus says the LORD, the God of Israel:
'I made a [n]covenant with your fathers in
the day that I brought them out of the land
of Egypt, out of the house of bondage, saying, 14 "At the end of [o]seven years let
every man set free his Hebrew brother,
who [2]has been sold to him; and when he
has served you six years, you shall let him
go free from you." But your fathers did
not obey Me nor incline their ear. 15 Then
you [3]recently turned and did what was
right in My sight—every man proclaiming
liberty to his neighbor; and you [p]made a
covenant before Me [q]in the house which is
called by My name. 16 Then you turned
around and [r]profaned My name, and
every one of you brought back his male
and female slaves, whom he had set at liberty, at their pleasure, and brought them
back into subjection, to be your male and
female slaves.'
17 "Therefore thus says the LORD: 'You
have not obeyed Me in proclaiming liberty,
every one to his brother and every one to
his neighbor. [s]Behold, I proclaim liberty to
you,' says the LORD—[t]'to the sword, to
pestilence, and to famine! And I will deliver you to [u]trouble among all the kingdoms
of the earth. 18 And I will give the men
who have transgressed My covenant, who
have not performed the words of the
covenant which they made before Me,
when [v]they cut the calf in two and passed
between the parts of it— 19 the princes of
Judah, the princes of Jerusalem, the [4]eu-
nuchs, the priests, and all the people of the
land who passed between the parts of the
calf— 20 I will [w]give them into the hand of
their enemies and into the hand of those
who seek their life. Their [x]dead bodies
shall be for meat for the birds of the heav-
en and the beasts of the earth. 21 And I will
give Zedekiah king of Judah and his
princes into the hand of their enemies, into
the hand of those who seek their life, and
into the hand of the king of Babylon's
army [y]which has gone back from you.
22 [z]Behold, I will command,' says the
LORD, 'and cause them to return to this city.
They will fight against it [a]and take it and

2 [d]2 Kin. 25:9; Jer. 21:10; 32:3, 28
3 [e]2 Kin. 25:4, 5; Jer. 21:7; 52:7-11 [f]2 Kin. 25:6, 7; Jer. 32:4; 39:5, 6 [1]Lit. *mouth to mouth*
5 [g]2 Chr. 16:14; 21:19 [h]Dan. 2:46 [i]Jer. 22:18
7 [j]2 Kin. 18:13; 19:8; 2 Chr. 11:5, 9
8 [k]Ex. 21:2; Lev. 25:10; Neh. 5:1-13; Is. 58:6; Jer. 34:14, 17
9 [l]Neh. 5:11 [m]Lev. 25:39-46
13 [n]Ex. 24:3, 7, 8; Deut. 5:2, 3, 27; Jer. 31:32
14 [o]Ex. 21:2; 23:10; Deut. 15:12; 1 Kin. 9:22 [2]Or *sold himself*
15 [p]2 Kin. 23:3; Neh. 10:29 [q]Jer. 7:10 [3]Lit. *today*
16 [r]Ex. 20:7; Lev. 19:12
17 [s]Lev. 26:34, 35; Esth. 7:10; Dan. 6:24; [Matt. 7:2; Gal. 6:7]; James 2:13 [t]Jer. 32:24, 36 [u]Deut. 28:25, 64; Jer. 29:18
18 [v]Gen. 15:10, 17
19 [4]Or *officers*
20 [w]2 Kin. 25:19-21; Jer. 22:25 [x]Deut. 28:26; 1 Sam. 17:44, 46; 1 Kin. 14:11; 16:4; Ps. 79:2; Jer. 7:33; 16:4; 19:7
21 [y]Jer. 37:5-11; 39:4-7
22 [z]Jer. 37:8, 10 [a]Jer. 38:3; 39:1, 2, 8; 52:7, 13

34:3 This prophecy about Zedekiah (cf. 32:1-5) was fulfilled as reported in 2 Kin. 25:6,7; Jer. 52:7-11.

34:8-10 a covenant...to proclaim liberty. Zedekiah's pact to free slaves met with initial compliance. The covenant followed the law of release in Lev. 25:39-55; Deut. 15:12-18 in hopes of courting God's favor and ending His judgment.

34:11 they changed their minds. Former slave masters treacherously went back on their agreement and recalled the slaves. Some suggest that this treachery came when the Egyptian army approached and Babylon's forces withdrew temporarily (37:5,11) and the inhabitants believed that danger was past.

34:12-16 Therefore the word...came. God reminded the unfaithful Jews of His own covenant, when He freed Israelites from Egyptian bondage (cf. Ex. 21:2; Deut. 15:12-15). He had commanded that Hebrew slaves should serve only 6 years, then be set free in the seventh (vv. 13,14).

34:17-22 You have not obeyed. Due to recent duplicity (v. 16), God promised only one kind of liberty to the offenders, liberty to judgment by sword, pestilence, and famine (v. 17).

34:18,21 cut the calf in two. God will give the guilty over to death before the conqueror, for they denied the covenant ratified by blood (v. 21). In this custom, as in Gen. 15:8-17, two parties laid out parts of a sacrifice on two sides, then walked between the parts. By that symbolic action each pledged to fulfill his promise, agreeing in effect, "May my life (represented by the blood) be poured out if I fail to honor my part."

burn it with fire; and [b]I will make the
cities of Judah a desolation without inhabitant.' "

The Obedient Rechabites

35 The word which came to Jeremiah
from the LORD in the days of Jehoiakim the son of Josiah, king of Judah, saying, 2 "Go to the house of the [a]Rechabites,
speak to them, and bring them into the
house of the LORD, into one of [b]the chambers, and give them wine to drink."
3 Then I took Jaazaniah the son of Jeremiah, the son of Habazziniah, his brothers
and all his sons, and the whole house of
the Rechabites, 4 and I brought them into
the house of the LORD, into the chamber of
the sons of Hanan the son of Igdaliah, a
man of God, which *was* by the chamber of
the princes, above the chamber of Maaseiah the son of Shallum, [c]the keeper of the
[1]door. 5 Then I set before the sons of the
house of the Rechabites bowls full of wine,
and cups; and I said to them, "Drink
wine."
6 But they said, "We will drink no wine,
for [d]Jonadab the son of Rechab, our father,
commanded us, saying, 'You shall drink
[e]no wine, you nor your sons, forever. 7 You
shall not build a house, sow seed, plant a
vineyard, nor have *any of these;* but all your
days you shall dwell in tents, [f]that you
may live many days in the land where you
are sojourners.' 8 Thus we have [g]obeyed
the voice of Jonadab the son of Rechab, our
father, in all that he charged us, to drink no
wine all our days, we, our wives, our sons,
or our daughters, 9 nor to build ourselves
houses to dwell in; nor do we have vineyard, field, or seed. 10 But we have dwelt
in tents, and have obeyed and done according to all that Jonadab our father commanded us. 11 But it came to pass, when
Nebuchadnezzar king of Babylon came up
into the land, that we said, 'Come, let us
[h]go to Jerusalem for fear of the army of the
Chaldeans and for fear of the army of the
Syrians.' So we dwell at Jerusalem."
12 Then came the word of the LORD to Jeremiah, saying, 13 "Thus says the LORD of
hosts, the God of Israel: 'Go and tell the
men of Judah and the inhabitants of Jerusalem, "Will you not [i]receive instruction to
[2]obey My words?" says the LORD. 14 "The
words of Jonadab the son of Rechab, which
he commanded his sons, not to drink wine,
are performed; for to this day they drink
none, and obey their father's commandment. [j]But although I have spoken to you,
[k]rising early and speaking, you did not
[3]obey Me. 15 I have also sent to you all My
[l]servants the prophets, rising up early and
sending *them,* saying, [m]'Turn now everyone
from his evil way, amend your doings, and
do not go after other gods to serve them;
then you will [n]dwell in the land which I
have given you and your fathers.' But you
have not inclined your ear, nor obeyed Me.
16 Surely the sons of Jonadab the son of
Rechab have performed the commandment
of their [o]father, which he commanded
them, but this people has not obeyed Me." '
17 "Therefore thus says the LORD God of
hosts, the God of Israel: 'Behold, I will
bring on Judah and on all the inhabitants
of Jerusalem all the doom that I have pronounced against them; [p]because I have
spoken to them but they have not heard,
and I have called to them but they have not
answered.' "
18 And Jeremiah said to the house of the
Rechabites, "Thus says the LORD of hosts,
the God of Israel: 'Because you have
obeyed the commandment of Jonadab
your father, and kept all his precepts and
done according to all that he commanded
you, 19 therefore thus says the LORD of
hosts, the God of Israel: "Jonadab the son
of Rechab shall not lack a man to [q]stand
before Me forever." ' "

The Scroll Read in the Temple

36 Now it came to pass in the [a]fourth
year of Jehoiakim the son of Josiah,
king of Judah, *that* this word came to Jeremiah from the LORD, saying: 2 "Take a

22 [b] Jer. 9:11; 44:2, 6

CHAPTER 35

2 [a] 2 Sam. 4:2; 2 Kin. 10:15; 1 Chr. 2:55 [b] 1 Kin. 6:5, 8; 1 Chr. 9:26, 33
4 [c] 2 Kin. 12:9; 25:18; 1 Chr. 9:18, 19 [1] Lit. *threshold*
6 [d] 2 Kin. 10:15, 23 [e] Lev. 10:9; Num. 6:2–4; Judg. 13:7, 14; Prov. 31:4; Ezek. 44:21; Luke 1:15
7 [f] Ex. 20:12; Eph. 6:2, 3
8 [g] [Prov. 1:8, 9; 4:1, 2, 10; 6:20; Eph. 6:1; Col. 3:20]
11 [h] Jer. 4:5–7; 8:14
13 [i] [Is. 28:9–12]; Jer. 6:10; 17:23; 32:33 [2] *listen to*
14 [j] 2 Chr. 36:15 [k] Jer. 7:13; 25:3 [3] *listen to*
15 [l] Jer. 26:4, 5; 29:19 [m] [Is. 1:16, 17]; Jer. 18:11; 25:5, 6; [Ezek. 18:30–32]; Acts 26:20 [n] Jer. 7:7; 25:5, 6
16 [o] [Heb. 12:9]
17 [p] Prov. 1:24; Is. 65:12; 66:4; Jer. 7:13
19 [q] [Ex. 20:12]; Jer. 15:19; [Luke 21:36; Eph. 6:2, 3]

CHAPTER 36

1 [a] 2 Kin. 24:1; 2 Chr. 36:5–7; Jer. 25:1, 3; 45:1; Dan. 1:1

35:1-19 This chapter provided a description of the commitment to obedience by a group of people to their father, in contrast to the Jews' disobedience to God.

35:1 days of Jehoiakim. 609–597 B.C. This backed up to several years before 34:1, possibly for a thematic reason—to cite a case of obedience after the episode of treachery in chap. 34.

35:2 The Rechabites. These were a semi-nomadic Kenite group, related to Moses' father-in-law (Judg. 1:16; 4:11), descended from those in 1 Chr. 2:55. The originator of their rules was Jonadab (35:6,14; 2 Kin. 10:15,23). They derived their name from Rechab (v. 8) and were not of Jacob's seed, but "strangers" in Israel.

35:8 obeyed. What was commended here was not the father's specific commands about nomadic life, but the steadfast obedience of the sons. Their obedience was unreserved in all aspects, at all times, on the part of all, without exception; in all these respects Israel was lacking (v. 14).

35:13-17 The prophet indicted the Jews for flagrant disobedience.

35:18,19 Because you have obeyed. God will bless the Rechabites not in spiritually saving them all, but in preserving a posterity in which some can have a place in His service. A Rechabite still has a role in Neh. 3:14. Also, the title over Ps. 71 in the LXX (Gr. translation of the OT) was addressed for use by the sons of Jonadab and the earliest captives.

36:1 fourth year of Jehoiakim. This chapter, like chap. 35, goes back several years earlier than chaps. 32–34, before or shortly after the first of 3 deportations from Jerusalem to Babylon in 605 B.C.

[b]scroll of a book and [c]write on it all the
words that I have spoken to you against Israel, against Judah, and against [d]all the nations, from the day I spoke to you, from the
days of [e]Josiah even to this day. **3** It [f]may
be that the house of Judah will hear all the
adversities which I purpose to bring upon
them, that everyone may [g]turn from his
evil way, that I may forgive their iniquity
and their sin."
4 Then Jeremiah [h]called Baruch the son
of Neriah; and [i]Baruch wrote on a scroll of
a book, [1]at the instruction of Jeremiah, all
the words of the LORD which He had spoken to him. **5** And Jeremiah commanded
Baruch, saying, "I *am* confined, I cannot go
into the house of the LORD. **6** You go, therefore, and read from the scroll which you
have written [2]at my instruction, the words
of the LORD, in the hearing of the people in
the LORD's house on [j]the day of fasting.
And you shall also read them in the hearing of all Judah who come from their cities.
7 It may be that they will present their supplication before the LORD, and everyone
will turn from his evil way. For great *is* the
anger and the fury that the LORD has pronounced against this people." **8** And
Baruch the son of Neriah did according to
all that Jeremiah the prophet commanded
him, reading from the book the words of
the LORD in the LORD's house.
9 Now it came to pass in the fifth year of
Jehoiakim the son of Josiah, king of Judah,
in the ninth month, *that* they proclaimed a
fast before the LORD to all the people in Jerusalem, and to all the people who came
from the cities of Judah to Jerusalem.
10 Then Baruch read from the book the
words of Jeremiah in the house of the
LORD, in the chamber of Gemariah the son
of Shaphan the scribe, in the upper court at
the [k]entry of the New Gate of the LORD's
house, in the [3]hearing of all the people.

The Scroll Read in the Palace

11 When Michaiah the son of Gemariah,
the son of Shaphan, heard all the words of
the LORD from the book, **12** he then went
down to the king's house, into the scribe's
chamber; and there all the princes were sitting—[l]Elishama the scribe, Delaiah the son
of Shemaiah, [m]Elnathan the son of Achbor,
Gemariah the son of Shaphan, Zedekiah
the son of Hananiah, and all the princes.
13 Then Michaiah declared to them all the
words that he had heard when Baruch
read the book in the hearing of the people.
14 Therefore all the princes sent Jehudi the
son of Nethaniah, the son of Shelemiah,
the son of Cushi, to Baruch, saying, "Take
in your hand the scroll from which you
have read in the hearing of the people, and
come." So Baruch the son of Neriah took
the scroll in his hand and came to them.
15 And they said to him, "Sit down now,
and read it in our hearing." So Baruch read
it in their hearing.
16 Now it happened, when they had
heard all the words, that they looked in
fear from one to another, and said to
Baruch, "We will surely tell the king of all
these words." **17** And they asked Baruch,
saying, "Tell us now, how did you write all
these words—[4]at his instruction?"
18 So Baruch answered them, "He proclaimed with his mouth all these words to
me, and I wrote *them* with ink in the book."
19 Then the princes said to Baruch, "Go
and hide, you and Jeremiah; and let no one
know where you are."

The King Destroys Jeremiah's Scroll

20 And they went to the king, into the
court; but they stored the scroll in the
chamber of Elishama the scribe, and told
all the words in the hearing of the king.
21 So the king sent Jehudi to bring the
scroll, and he took it from Elishama the
scribe's chamber. And Jehudi read it in the
hearing of the king and in the hearing of all
the princes who stood beside the king.
22 Now the king was sitting in [n]the winter
house in the ninth month, with *a fire* burning on the hearth before him. **23** And it
happened, when Jehudi had read three or

2 [b] Is. 8:1; Ezek. 2:9; Zech. 5:1 [c] Jer. 30:2; Hab. 2:2 [d] Jer. 25:15 [e] Jer. 25:3
3 [f] Jer. 26:3; Ezek. 12:3 [g] [Deut. 30:2, 8; 1 Sam. 7:3]; Is. 55:7; Jer. 18:8; Jon. 3:8
4 [h] Jer. 32:12 [i] Jer. 45:1 [1] Lit. *from Jeremiah's mouth*
6 [j] Lev. 16:29; 23:27-32; Acts 27:9 [2] Lit. *from my mouth*
10 [k] Jer. 26:10 [3] Lit. *ears*
12 [l] Jer. 41:1 [m] Jer. 26:22
17 [4] Lit. *with his mouth*
22 [n] Judg. 3:20; Amos 3:15

36:2 write on it. The command was to record in one volume all the messages since the outset of Jeremiah's ministry in 627 B.C. (1:2) up to 605/604 B.C., to be read to the people in the temple (v. 6.).

36:4 Baruch wrote. Jeremiah's recording secretary (cf. 32:12) wrote the prophet's messages (cf. 45:1), and penned them a second time after the first scroll was burned (cf. 36:32). He also read the messages in the temple (v. 10) and in the palace (v. 15). Later, Jehudi read a small part of the first scroll before King Jehoiakim (vv. 21-23).

36:5 confined. The word means "restricted, hindered, shut up," and is the same term used for imprisonment in 33:1 and 39:15. The fact that princes allowed Jeremiah to depart into hiding (v. 19) may indicate that he was curtailed in some ways without being in prison. There is no record of his being imprisoned in Jehoiakim's rule.

36:6 the day of fasting. Cf. v. 9. Here was a special fast day, appointed to avert the impending calamity, which would make the Jews more open to the message of the prophet (v. 7).

36:9 fifth year. This year (604 B.C.) was the next year after that of v. 1, which may suggest that it took some part of a year to repeat and record the long series of messages so far given (cf. v. 18). **ninth month.** Nov./ Dec. (cf. vv. 22,23).

36:10 chamber. On the N side, above the wall overlooking the temple court, where the people gathered, Baruch read from a window or balcony.

36:17,18 They asked if Baruch had written these words from memory or actual dictation from the inspired prophet. The latter was true. They were concerned it might be God's Word (cf. vv. 16,25).

four columns, *that the king* cut it with the
scribe's knife and cast *it* into the fire that
was on the hearth, until all the scroll was
consumed in the fire that *was* on the
hearth. 24 Yet they were [o]not afraid, nor
did they [p]tear their garments, the king nor
any of his servants who heard all these
words. 25 Nevertheless Elnathan, Delaiah,
and Gemariah implored the king not to
burn the scroll; but he would not listen to
them. 26 And the king commanded Jerahmeel [5]the king's son, Seraiah the son of
Azriel, and Shelemiah the son of Abdeel, to
seize Baruch the scribe and Jeremiah the
prophet, but the LORD hid them.

Jeremiah Rewrites the Scroll

27 Now after the king had burned the
scroll with the words which Baruch had
written [6]at the instruction of Jeremiah, the
word of the LORD came to Jeremiah, saying: 28 "Take yet another scroll, and write
on it all the former words that were in the
first scroll which Jehoiakim the king of Judah has burned. 29 And you shall say to Jehoiakim king of Judah, 'Thus says the
LORD: "You have burned this scroll, saying,
[q]'Why have you written in it that the king
of Babylon will certainly come and destroy
this land, and cause man and beast to
[r]cease from here?' " 30 Therefore thus says
the LORD concerning Jehoiakim king of Judah: [s]"He shall have no one to sit on the
throne of David, and his dead body shall
be [t]cast out to the heat of the day and the
frost of the night. 31 I will punish him, his
[7]family, and his servants for their iniquity;
and I will bring on them, on the inhabitants of Jerusalem, and on the men of Judah all the doom that I have pronounced
against them; but they did not heed." ' "
32 Then Jeremiah took another scroll and
gave it to Baruch the scribe, the son of Neriah, who wrote on it [8]at the instruction of
Jeremiah all the words of the book which
Jehoiakim king of Judah had burned in the
fire. And besides, there were added to
them many similar words.

Zedekiah's Vain Hope

37 Now King [a]Zedekiah the son of Josiah reigned instead of Coniah the
son of Jehoiakim, whom Nebuchadnezzar
king of Babylon made king in the land of
Judah. 2 [b]But neither he nor his servants
nor the people of the land gave heed to the
words of the LORD which He spoke by the
prophet Jeremiah.
3 And Zedekiah the king sent Jehucal
the son of Shelemiah, and [c]Zephaniah the
son of Maaseiah, the priest, to the prophet
Jeremiah, saying, [d]"Pray now to the LORD
our God for us." 4 Now Jeremiah was coming and going among the people, for they
had not *yet* put him in prison. 5 Then
[e]Pharaoh's army came up from Egypt; and
when the Chaldeans who were besieging
Jerusalem heard news of them, they departed from Jerusalem.
6 Then the word of the LORD came to the
prophet Jeremiah, saying, 7 "Thus says the
LORD, the God of Israel, 'Thus you shall say
to the king of Judah, [f]who sent you to Me to
inquire of Me: "Behold, Pharaoh's army
which has come up to help you will return
to Egypt, to their own land. 8 [g]And the Chaldeans shall come back and fight against this
city, and take it and burn it with fire." '
9 Thus says the LORD: 'Do not deceive yourselves, saying, "The Chaldeans will surely
depart from us," for they will not depart.
10 [h]For though you had defeated the whole
army of the Chaldeans who fight against
you, and there remained *only* wounded men
among them, they would rise up, every man
in his tent, and burn the city with fire.' "

Jeremiah Imprisoned

11 And it happened, when the army of
the Chaldeans left *the siege* of Jerusalem for
fear of Pharaoh's army, 12 that Jeremiah
went out of Jerusalem to go into the land of

24 [o][Ps. 36:1]; Jer. 36:16 [p]Gen. 37:29, 34; 2 Sam. 1:11; 1 Kin. 21:27; 2 Kin. 19:1, 2; 22:11; Is. 36:22; 37:1; Jon. 3:6
26 [5]Or *son of Hammelech*
27 [6]Lit. *from Jeremiah's mouth*
29 [q]Jer. 32:3 [r]Jer. 25:9-11; 26:9
30 [s]Jer. 22:30 [t]Jer. 22:19
31 [7]Lit. *seed*
32 [8]Lit. *from Jeremiah's mouth*

CHAPTER 37

1 [a]2 Kin. 24:17; 1 Chr. 3:15; 2 Chr. 36:10; Jer. 22:24
2 [b]2 Kin. 24:19, 20; 2 Chr. 36:12-16; [Prov. 29:12]
3 [c]Jer. 21:1, 2; 29:25; 52:24 [d]1 Kin. 13:6; Jer. 42:2; Acts 8:24
5 [e]2 Kin. 24:7; Jer. 37:7; Ezek. 17:15
7 [f]Is. 36:6; Jer. 21:2; Ezek. 17:17
8 [g]2 Chr. 36:19; Jer. 34:22
10 [h]Lev. 26:36-38; Is. 30:17; Jer. 21:4, 5

36:23 cut it. As often as Jehudi read "three or four columns," the king cut it up, doing so all the way through the whole scroll because he rejected the message (cf. v. 29). Jehoiakim is the king who sent men to Egypt (chap. 26) to bring back God's faithful prophet, Urijah, so that he could execute him.

36:24 not afraid. The king's servants were more hardened than the princes (v. 16).

36:26 the LORD hid them. God, who guides (cf. 1:8,19; 10:23), gave Jeremiah and Baruch safety (cf. 36:19; Ps. 32:8; Prov. 3:5,6).

36:27 Cf. Is. 40:18; 55:11; Matt. 5:18.

36:31 I will punish him. Consequences followed Jehoiakim's defiance. In 598 B.C. he met his own death (22:18,19; 2 Kin. 23:36; 2 Chr. 36:5). He had none to occupy the throne (v. 30). Jehoiachin or Jeconiah (Coniah in 22:24), his son, did succeed him, but with virtually no rule at all, lasting only 3 months and 10 days in 597 B.C. (22:24-30; 2 Chr. 36:9,10). Babylon deported him for the rest of his life (cf. 52:31-34) and none of his descendants ruled (cf. 22:30, and *see note there*).

37:1 Zedekiah...reigned. Zedekiah, an uncle of Jeconiah, was raised to the throne by Nebuchadnezzar in contempt for Jehoiakim and Jeconiah. His 11 year vassal rule was from 597–586 B.C. The message of the king to Jeremiah in this chapter is somewhat earlier than that in chap. 21, when Zedekiah was afraid of the Chaldean's (Babylonian's) defeating Egypt and returning to besiege Jerusalem (vv. 3,5).

37:4 The prophet was no longer in the prison court as he had been (32:2; 33:1).

37:7-10 say to the king. Babylon, which temporarily ended the siege to deal with an Egyptian advance, would return and destroy Jerusalem.

37:12 Jeremiah went out. He returned to his hometown to claim the property he had purchased in 32:6-12.

Benjamin to claim his property there
among the people. 13 And when he was in
the Gate of Benjamin, a captain of the
guard *was* there whose name *was* Irijah the
son of Shelemiah, the son of Hananiah;
and he seized Jeremiah the prophet, saying, "You are defecting to the Chaldeans!"
14 Then Jeremiah said, [1]"False! I am not
defecting to the Chaldeans." But he did not
listen to him.

So Irijah seized Jeremiah and brought
him to the princes. 15 Therefore the princes
were angry with Jeremiah, and they struck
him [i]and put him in prison in the [j]house of
Jonathan the scribe. For they had made
that the prison.
16 When Jeremiah entered [k]the dungeon
and the cells, and Jeremiah had remained
there many days, 17 then Zedekiah the
king sent and took him *out*. The king asked
him secretly in his house, and said, "Is
there *any* word from the LORD?"

And Jeremiah said, "There is." Then he
said, "You shall be [l]delivered into the hand
of the king of Babylon!"
18 Moreover Jeremiah said to King Zedekiah, "What offense have I committed
against you, against your servants, or
against this people, that you have put me
in prison? 19 Where now *are* your prophets
who prophesied to you, saying, 'The king
of Babylon will not come against you or
against this land?' 20 Therefore please hear
now, O my lord the king. Please, let my petition be accepted before you, and do not
make me return to the house of Jonathan
the scribe, lest I die there."
21 Then Zedekiah the king commanded
that they should commit Jeremiah [m]to the
court of the prison, and that they should
give him daily a piece of bread from the
bakers' street, [n]until all the bread in the
city was gone. Thus Jeremiah remained in
the court of the prison.

Jeremiah in the Dungeon

38 Now Shephatiah the son of Mattan,
Gedaliah the son of Pashhur, [a]Jucal[1]
the son of Shelemiah, and [b]Pashhur the
son of Malchiah [c]heard the words that Jeremiah had spoken to all the people, saying,
2 "Thus says the LORD: [d]'He who remains
in this city shall die by the sword, by
famine, and by pestilence; but he who goes
over to the Chaldeans shall live; his life
shall be as a prize to him, and he shall live.'
3 Thus says the LORD: [e]'This city shall surely be [f]given into the hand of the king of
Babylon's army, which shall take it.' "
4 Therefore the princes said to the king,
"Please, [g]let this man be put to death, for
thus he [2]weakens the hands of the men of
war who remain in this city, and the hands
of all the people, by speaking such words
to them. For this man does not seek the
[3]welfare of this people, but their harm."
5 Then Zedekiah the king said, "Look,
he *is* in your hand. For the king can *do*
nothing against you." 6 [h]So they took Jeremiah and cast him into the dungeon of
Malchiah [4]the king's son, which *was* in the
court of the prison, and they let Jeremiah
down with ropes. And in the dungeon
there was no water, but mire. So Jeremiah
sank in the mire.
7 [i]Now Ebed-Melech the Ethiopian, one
of the [5]eunuchs, who was in the king's
house, heard that they had put Jeremiah in
the dungeon. When the king was sitting at
the Gate of Benjamin, 8 Ebed-Melech went
out of the king's house and spoke to the
king, saying: 9 "My lord the king, these
men have done evil in all that they have
done to Jeremiah the prophet, whom they
have cast into the dungeon, and he is likely
to die from hunger in the place where he is.
For *there is* [j]no more bread in the city."
10 Then the king commanded Ebed-Melech
the Ethiopian, saying, "Take from here thirty men with you, and lift Jeremiah the
prophet out of the dungeon before he dies."

14 [1] *a lie*
15 [i] Jer. 20:2; [Matt. 21:35] [j] Gen. 39:20; 2 Chr. 16:10; 18:26; Jer. 38:26; Acts 5:18
16 [k] Jer. 38:6
17 [l] 2 Kin. 25:4-7; Jer. 21:7; Ezek. 12:12, 13; 17:19-21
21 [m] Jer. 32:2; 38:13, 28 [n] 2 Kin. 25:3; Jer. 38:9; 52:6

CHAPTER 38

1 [a] Jer. 37:3 [b] Jer. 21:1 [c] Jer. 21:8 [1] *Jehucal,* Jer. 37:3
2 [d] Jer. 21:9
3 [e] Jer. 21:10; 32:3 [f] Jer. 34:2
4 [g] Jer. 26:11 [2] Is discouraging [3] Well-being; lit. *peace*
6 [h] Jer. 37:21; Lam. 3:55 [4] Or *son of Hammelech*
7 [i] Jer. 39:16 [5] Or *officers*
9 [j] Jer. 37:21

37:13 Hananiah. Jeremiah had predicted his death (28:16) and thus the grandson took revenge with a false accusation (cf. 38:19; 52:15).

37:15 struck him. Jeremiah often absorbed blows, threats, or other mistreatment for proclaiming the truth from God (11:21; 20:2; 26:8; 36:26; 38:6,25).

37:17 This showed Zedekiah's willful rejection. He knew Jeremiah spoke for God.

37:19 prophets. They were shown to be liars who said the "king of Babylon" would not come. He had come and would return.

37:21 bread. The king showed a measure of kindness by returning Jeremiah to "the court of the prison" (cf. 32:2; 33:1), promising "bread" as long as it lasted in the siege (cf. 38:9). He remained there until Jerusalem was taken soon after the food was gone (38:28), with only a brief trip to a pit (38:6-13).

38:4 let this man be put to death. Cf. 26:11 and *see note there.* **he weakens the hands.** They charged that Jeremiah's urging to submit to Babylon (v. 2) undermined the defenders' morale and will. By proclaiming Babylon's victory, he was viewed as a traitor to Judah.

38:5 the king can *do* nothing. This is a spineless evasion of courage and decency by a leader who rejected God's Word.

38:6 no water, but mire. The murderous princes (cf. v. 4) would let God's spokesman die of thirst, hunger, hypothermia, or suffocation if he sank too deeply into the bottom of the cistern. Cf. Ps. 69:2,14, a reference to Messiah.

38:7-13 Ebed-Melech. An Ethiopian, Gentile stranger acted decisively to deliver Jeremiah from his own people who were seeking to kill him. Perhaps a keeper of the royal harem ("eunuch"), this man later received God's deliverance of his own life and His tribute for his faith (39:15-18).

11 So Ebed-Melech took the men with him
and went into the house of the king under
the treasury, and took from there old
clothes and old rags, and let them down
by ropes into the dungeon to Jeremiah.
12 Then Ebed-Melech the Ethiopian said to
Jeremiah, "Please put these old clothes and
rags under your armpits, under the ropes."
And Jeremiah did so. 13 So they pulled Jeremiah up with ropes and lifted him out of
the dungeon. And Jeremiah remained [k]in
the court of the prison.

Zedekiah's Fears and Jeremiah's Advice

14 Then Zedekiah the king sent and had
Jeremiah the prophet brought to him at the
third entrance of the house of the LORD.
And the king said to Jeremiah, "I will [l]ask
you something. Hide nothing from me."
15 Jeremiah said to Zedekiah, "If I declare *it* to you, will you not surely put me
to death? And if I give you advice, you will
not listen to me."
16 So Zedekiah the king swore secretly to
Jeremiah, saying, "*As* the LORD lives, [m]who
made our very souls, I will not put you to
death, nor will I give you into the hand of
these men who seek your life."
17 Then Jeremiah said to Zedekiah,
"Thus says the LORD, the God of hosts, the
God of Israel: 'If you surely [n]surrender[6]
[o]to the king of Babylon's princes, then
your soul shall live; this city shall not be
burned with fire, and you and your house
shall live. 18 But if you do not [7]surrender
to the king of Babylon's princes, then this
city shall be given into the hand of the
Chaldeans; they shall burn it with fire, and
[p]you shall not escape from their hand.' "
19 And Zedekiah the king said to Jeremiah, "I am afraid of the Jews who have
[q]defected to the Chaldeans, lest they deliver me into their hand, and they [r]abuse me."
20 But Jeremiah said, "They shall not deliver *you*. Please, obey the voice of the
LORD which I speak to you. So it shall be
[s]well with you, and your soul shall live.
21 But if you refuse to [8]surrender, this *is* the
word that the LORD has shown me:
22 'Now behold, all the [t]women who are
left in the king of Judah's house *shall be*
surrendered to the king of Babylon's
princes, and those *women* shall say:

"Your close friends have [9]set upon
you
And prevailed against you;
Your feet have sunk in the mire,
And they have [1]turned away
again."

23 'So they shall surrender all your wives
and [u]children to the Chaldeans. [v]You shall
not escape from their hand, but shall be
taken by the hand of the king of Babylon.
And you shall cause this city to be burned
with fire.' "
24 Then Zedekiah said to Jeremiah, "Let
no one know of these words, and you shall
not die. 25 But if the princes hear that I
have talked with you, and they come to
you and say to you, 'Declare to us now
what you have said to the king, and also
what the king said to you; do not hide *it*
from us, and we will not put you to death,'
26 then you shall say to them, [w]'I presented
my request before the king, that he would
not make me return [x]to Jonathan's house
to die there.' "
27 Then all the princes came to Jeremiah
and asked him. And he told them according to all these words that the king had
commanded. So they stopped speaking
with him, for the conversation had not
been heard. 28 Now [y]Jeremiah remained in
the court of the prison until the day that Jerusalem was taken. And he was *there* when
Jerusalem was taken.

The Fall of Jerusalem

39 In the [a]ninth year of Zedekiah king
of Judah, in the tenth month, Nebuchadnezzar king of Babylon and all his
army came against Jerusalem, and besieged it. 2 In the [b]eleventh year of Zedekiah, in the fourth month, on the ninth *day*
of the month, the [1]city was penetrated.
3 [c]Then all the princes of the king of
Babylon came in and sat in the Middle
Gate: Nergal-Sharezer, Samgar-Nebo, Sar-

13 [k] Neh. 3:25; Jer. 37:21; Acts 23:35; 24:27; 28:16, 30
14 [l] Jer. 21:1, 2; 37:17
16 [m] Num. 16:22; Is. 57:16; Zech. 12:1; [Acts 17:25, 28]
17 [n] 2 Kin. 24:12 [o] Jer. 39:3 [6] Lit. *go out*
18 [p] Jer. 32:4; 34:3 [7] Lit. *go out*
19 [q] Jer. 39:9 [r] 1 Sam. 31:4
20 [s] Jer. 40:9
21 [8] Lit. *go out*
22 [t] Jer. 8:10
[9] Or *misled*
[1] Deserted you
23 [u] Jer. 39:6; 41:10 [v] Jer. 39:5
26 [w] Jer. 37:20 [x] Jer. 37:15
28 [y] [Ps. 23:4]; Jer. 37:21; 39:14

CHAPTER 39

1 [a] 2 Kin. 25:1-12; Jer. 52:4; Ezek. 24:1, 2
2 [b] Jer. 1:3 [1] *city wall was breached*
3 [c] Jer. 1:15; 38:17

38:14-23 I will ask you. This is one of several queries as Zedekiah wanted to hear God's Word but rejected it. God's Word was surrender, and His answer for rejection was calamity for Jerusalem, capture of the king, and tragedy for his family plus others of the palace. For the fulfillment to Zedekiah, cf. 39:4-8.

38:22 close friends have set upon you. Palace women, taken over by Babylonians, heaped cutting ridicule on Zedekiah for listening to friends whose counsel failed him, who left him helpless as one with his feet stuck in mire.

38:27 these words...the king...commanded. Jeremiah did not fall into lying deception here. What he said was true though he did not divulge all details of the conversation, to which the princes had no right.

39:1,2 In the ninth year...the eleventh year. Cf. 34:1, and *see note there*. Cf. 52:1-7; 2 Kin. 25:1-4. This siege of 30 months involved the enemy's surrounding the city walls, cutting off all entrances and exits, all food supplies, and as much water as possible, so that famine, thirst, and disease would eventually weaken the beleaguered city dwellers and they could be easily conquered.

39:3 sat in the Middle Gate. This expressed full military occupation of the city, since this gate was between the upper city (Mt. Zion) and the lower city to the N.

sechim, [2]Rabsaris, Nergal-Sarezer, [3]Rabmag, with the rest of the princes of the king of Babylon.

4 [d]So it was, when Zedekiah the king of Judah and all the men of war saw them, that they fled and went out of the city by night, by way of the king's garden, by the gate between the two walls. And he went out by way of the [4]plain. 5 But the Chaldean army pursued them and [e]overtook Zedekiah in the plains of Jericho. And when they had captured him, they brought him up to Nebuchadnezzar king of Babylon, to [f]Riblah in the land of Hamath, where he pronounced judgment on him. 6 Then the king of Babylon killed the sons of Zedekiah before his [g]eyes in Riblah; the king of Babylon also killed all the [h]nobles of Judah. 7 Moreover [i]he put out Zedekiah's eyes, and bound him with bronze [5]fetters to carry him off to Babylon. 8 [j]And the Chaldeans burned the king's house and the houses of the people with [k]fire, and broke down the [l]walls of Jerusalem. 9 [m]Then Nebuzaradan the captain of the guard carried away captive to Babylon the remnant of the people who remained in the city and those who [n]defected to him, with the rest of the people who remained. 10 But Nebuzaradan the captain of the guard left in the land of Judah the [o]poor people, who had nothing, and gave them vineyards and fields [6]at the same time.

Jeremiah Goes Free

11 Now Nebuchadnezzar king of Babylon gave charge concerning Jeremiah to Nebuzaradan the captain of the guard, saying, 12 "Take him and look after him, and do him no [p]harm; but do to him just as he says to you." 13 So Nebuzaradan the captain of the guard sent Nebushasban, Rabsaris, Nergal-Sharezer, Rabmag, and all the king of Babylon's chief officers; 14 then they sent *someone* [q]to take Jeremiah from the court of the prison, and committed him [r]to Gedaliah the son of [s]Ahikam, the son of Shaphan, that he should take him home. So he dwelt among the people.

15 Meanwhile the word of the LORD had come to Jeremiah while he was shut up in the court of the prison, saying, 16 "Go and speak to [t]Ebed-Melech the Ethiopian, saying, 'Thus says the LORD of hosts, the God of Israel: "Behold, [u]I will bring My words upon this city for adversity and not for good, and they shall be *performed* in that day before you. 17 But I will deliver you in that day," says the LORD, "and you shall not be given into the hand of the men of whom you *are* afraid. 18 For I will surely deliver you, and you shall not fall by the sword; but [v]your life shall be as a prize to you, [w]because you have put your trust in Me," says the LORD.' "

Jeremiah with Gedaliah the Governor

40 The word that came to Jeremiah from the LORD [a]after Nebuzaradan the captain of the guard had let him go from Ramah, when he had taken him bound in chains among all who were carried away captive from Jerusalem and Judah, who were carried away captive to Babylon.

2 And the captain of the guard took Jeremiah and [b]said to him: "The LORD your God has pronounced this doom on this place. 3 Now the LORD has brought *it,* and has done just as He said. [c]Because you *people* have sinned against the LORD, and not obeyed His voice, therefore this thing has come upon you. 4 And now look, I free you this day from the chains that [1]*were* on your hand. [d]If it seems good to you to come with me to Babylon, come, and I will look after you. But if it seems wrong for you to come with me to Babylon, remain here. See, [e]all the land *is* before you; wherever it seems good and convenient for you to go, go there."

5 Now while Jeremiah had not yet gone back, *Nebuzaradan said,* "Go back to [f]Gedaliah the son of Ahikam, the son of Shaphan, [g]whom the king of Babylon has made governor over the cities of Judah, and dwell with him among the people. Or go wherever it seems convenient for you to

3 [2] A title, probably *Chief Officer;* also v. 13 [3] A title, probably *Troop Commander;* also v. 13
4 [d] 2 Kin. 25:4; Is. 30:16; Jer. 52:7; Amos 2:14 [4] Or *Arabah;* the Jordan Valley
5 [e] Jer. 21:7; 32:4; 38:18, 23 [f] 2 Kin. 23:33; Jer. 52:9, 26, 27
6 [g] Deut. 28:34 [h] Jer. 34:19-21
7 [i] 2 Kin. 25:7; Jer. 52:11; Ezek. 12:13 [5] *chains*
8 [j] 2 Kin. 25:9; Jer. 38:18; 52:13 [k] Jer. 21:10 [l] 2 Kin. 25:10; Neh. 1:3; Jer. 52:14
9 [m] 2 Kin. 25:8, 11, 12, 20 [n] Jer. 38:19
10 [o] Jer. 40:7 [6] Lit. *on that day*
12 [p] Jer. 1:18, 19; 15:20, 21
14 [q] Jer. 38:28 [r] Jer. 40:5 [s] 2 Kin. 22:12, 14; 2 Chr. 34:20; Jer. 26:24
16 [t] Jer. 38:7, 12 [u] Jer. 21:10; [Dan. 9:12; Zech. 1:6]
18 [v] Jer. 21:9; 45:5 [w] 1 Chr. 5:20; Ps. 37:40; [Jer. 17:7, 8]

CHAPTER 40

1 [a] Jer. 39:9, 11
2 [b] Jer. 50:7
3 [c] Deut. 29:24, 25; Jer. 50:7; Dan. 9:11; [Rom. 2:5]
4 [d] Jer. 39:12 [e] Gen. 20:15 [1] Or *are*
5 [f] Jer. 39:14 [g] 2 Kin. 25:22; Jer. 41:10

39:5 Riblah in…Hamath. Nebuchadnezzar's command headquarters were 230 mi. to the N of Jerusalem. **pronounced judgment.** He dealt with the king as a common criminal. The king had violated his oath (cf. 2 Chr. 36:13; Ezek. 17:13-19).

39:6-10 Cf. 52:12-16; 2 Kin. 25:8-12.

39:7 put out Zedekiah's eyes. This reconciles 32:4 with Ezek. 12:13.

39:11,12 Jeremiah's prophecies were known to Nebuchadnezzar through defectors (v. 9; 38:19), and also through Jews taken to Babylon with Jeconiah (cf. 40:2).

39:14 take Jeremiah from the court. This was given as a general summary, whereas 40:1-6 gave more detail concerning the prophet who was first carried to Ramah (40:1) with the other captives before being released (40:2-5). "Gedaliah" was a former supporter of Jeremiah (26:24) and chief among the defectors, loyal to Nebuchadnezzar, so was made governor (40:5) over the remnant left in the land.

39:15-18 Cf. 38:7-13, and *see note there.*

40:2,3 The pagan captain understood the judgment of God better than the leaders of Judah.

40:4,5 The captain did exactly as Nebuchadnezzar had told him in 39:12.

40:5,6 Jeremiah chose to go to Gedaliah, the newly appointed governor at Mizpah several mi. N of Jerusalem. Gedaliah was soon be assassinated (cf. 41:1-3).

go." So the captain of the guard gave him rations and a gift and let him go. 6 [h]Then Jeremiah went to Gedaliah the son of Ahikam, to [i]Mizpah, and dwelt with him among the people who were left in the land.

7 [j]And when all the captains of the armies who *were* in the fields, they and their men, heard that the king of Babylon had made Gedaliah the son of Ahikam governor in the land, and had committed to him men, women, children, and [k]the poorest of the land who had not been carried away captive to Babylon, 8 then they came to Gedaliah at Mizpah—[l]Ishmael the son of Nethaniah, [m]Johanan and Jonathan the sons of Kareah, Seraiah the son of Tanhumeth, the sons of Ephai the Netophathite, and [n]Jezaniah[2] the son of a [o]Maachathite, they and their men. 9 And Gedaliah the son of Ahikam, the son of Shaphan, took an oath before them and their men, saying, "Do not be afraid to serve the Chaldeans. Dwell in the land and serve the king of Babylon, and it shall be [p]well with you. 10 As for me, I will indeed dwell at Mizpah and serve the Chaldeans who come to us. But you, gather wine and summer fruit and oil, put *them* in your vessels, and dwell in your cities that you have taken." 11 Likewise, when all the Jews who *were* in Moab, among the Ammonites, in Edom, and who *were* in all the countries, heard that the king of Babylon had left a remnant of Judah, and that he had set over them Gedaliah the son of Ahikam, the son of Shaphan, 12 then all the Jews [q]returned out of all places where they had been driven, and came to the land of Judah, to Gedaliah at Mizpah, and gathered wine and summer fruit in abundance.

13 Moreover Johanan the son of Kareah and all the captains of the forces that *were* in the fields came to Gedaliah at Mizpah, 14 and said to him, [3]"Do you certainly know that [r]Baalis the king of the Ammonites has sent Ishmael the son of Nethaniah to murder you?" But Gedaliah the son of Ahikam did not believe them.

15 Then Johanan the son of Kareah spoke secretly to Gedaliah in Mizpah, saying, "Let me go, please, and I will kill Ishmael the son of Nethaniah, and no one will know *it*. Why should he murder you, so that all the Jews who are gathered to you would be scattered, and the [s]remnant in Judah perish?"

16 But Gedaliah the son of Ahikam said to Johanan the son of Kareah, "You shall not do this thing, for you speak falsely concerning Ishmael."

Insurrection Against Gedaliah

41 Now it came to pass in the seventh month [a]*that* Ishmael the son of Nethaniah, the son of Elishama, of the royal [1]family and of the officers of the king, came with ten men to Gedaliah the son of Ahikam, at [b]Mizpah. And there they ate bread together in Mizpah. 2 Then Ishmael the son of Nethaniah, and the ten men who were with him, arose and [c]struck Gedaliah the son of [d]Ahikam, the son of Shaphan, with the sword, and killed him whom the king of Babylon had made [e]governor over the land. 3 Ishmael also struck down all the Jews who were with him, *that is,* with Gedaliah at Mizpah, and the Chaldeans who were found there, the men of war.

4 And it happened, on the second day after he had killed Gedaliah, when as yet no one knew *it,* 5 that certain men came from Shechem, from Shiloh, and from Samaria, eighty men [f]with their beards shaved and their clothes torn, having cut themselves, with offerings and incense in their hand, to bring *them* to [g]the house of the LORD. 6 Now Ishmael the son of Nethaniah went out from Mizpah to meet them, weeping as he went along; and it happened as he met them that he said to them, "Come to Gedaliah the son of Ahikam!" 7 So it was, when they came into the midst of the city, that Ishmael the son of Nethaniah [h]killed them *and cast them* into the midst of a [2]pit, he and the men who were with him. 8 But ten men were found among them who said to Ishmael, "Do not kill us, for we have treasures of wheat, barley, oil, and honey in the field." So he desisted and did not kill them among their brethren. 9 Now the [3]pit into which Ishmael had cast all the dead bodies of the men whom he had slain, because of Gedaliah, *was* [i]the same one Asa the king had made

6 [h] Jer. 39:14 [i] Judg. 20:1; 1 Sam. 7:5; 2 Chr. 16:6
7 [j] 2 Kin. 25:23, 24 [k] Jer. 39:10
8 [l] Jer. 41:1-10 [m] Jer. 41:11; 43:2 [n] Jer. 42:1 [o] Deut. 3:14; Josh. 12:5; 2 Sam. 10:6 [2] *Jaazaniah,* 2 Kin. 25:23
9 [p] Jer. 27:11; 38:17-20
12 [q] Jer. 43:5
14 [r] Jer. 41:10 [3] Or *Certainly you know that*
15 [s] Jer. 42:2

CHAPTER 41

1 [a] 2 Kin. 25:25 [b] Jer. 40:6, 10 [1] Lit. *seed*
2 [c] 2 Sam. 3:27; 20:9, 10; 2 Kin. 25:25; Ps. 41:9; 109:5; John 13:18 [d] Jer. 26:24 [e] Jer. 40:5
5 [f] Lev. 19:27, 28; Deut. 14:1; Is. 15:2 [g] 1 Sam. 1:7; 2 Kin. 25:9; Neh. 10:34, 35
7 [h] Ps. 55:23; Is. 59:7; Ezek. 22:27; 33:24, 26 [2] Or *cistern*
9 [i] 1 Kin. 15:22; 2 Chr. 16:6 [3] Or *cistern*

40:7 captains…in the fields. The leaders of Judah's army scattered in fear.

40:9-12 God had tempered the severity of judgment by allowing a remnant to prosper.

40:13-16 Johanan. This man's fair warning to Gedaliah of Ishmael's death plot went unheeded.

41:1-4 In the second month after the city of Jerusalem had been burned, the careless governor entertained Ishmael's group and invited a massacre.

41:5 eighty men. Most likely, this group had come in mourning over the destruction of Jerusalem, and so servants (v. 8) were led to slaughter. He did amazing damage with only 10 men (v. 1). Eventually they must have acquired more to do than what is described in v. 10.

41:9 Asa. He ruled Judah (ca. 911–873 B.C.). Cf. 1 Kin. 15:16-22.

for fear of Baasha king of Israel. Ishmael
the son of Nethaniah filled it with *the* slain.
10 Then Ishmael carried away captive all
the [j]rest of the people who *were* in Mizpah,
[k]the king's daughters and all the people
who remained in Mizpah, [l]whom Nebuzaradan the captain of the guard had committed to Gedaliah the son of Ahikam. And
Ishmael the son of Nethaniah carried them
away captive and departed to go over to
[m]the Ammonites.
11 But when [n]Johanan the son of Kareah
and all the captains of the forces that *were*
with him heard of all the evil that Ishmael
the son of Nethaniah had done, 12 they
took all the men and went to fight with
Ishmael the son of Nethaniah; and they
found him by [o]the great pool that *is* in
Gibeon. 13 So it was, when all the people
who *were* with Ishmael saw Johanan the
son of Kareah, and all the captains of the
forces who *were* with him, that they were
glad. 14 Then all the people whom Ishmael
had carried away captive from Mizpah
turned around and came back, and went to
Johanan the son of Kareah. 15 But Ishmael
the son of Nethaniah escaped from Johanan with eight men and went to the
Ammonites.
16 Then Johanan the son of Kareah, and
all the captains of the forces that were with
him, took from Mizpah all the [p]rest of the
people whom he had recovered from
Ishmael the son of Nethaniah after he had
murdered Gedaliah the son of Ahikam—
the mighty men of war and the women
and the children and the eunuchs, whom
he had brought back from Gibeon. 17 And
they departed and dwelt in the habitation
of [q]Chimham, which is near Bethlehem, as
they went on their way to [r]Egypt, 18 because of the Chaldeans; for they were
afraid of them, because Ishmael the son of
Nethaniah had murdered Gedaliah the son
of Ahikam, [s]whom the king of Babylon
had made governor in the land.

The Flight to Egypt Forbidden

42 Now all the captains of the forces,
[a]Johanan the son of Kareah, Jezaniah the son of Hoshaiah, and all the people, from the least to the greatest, came
near 2 and said to Jeremiah the prophet,
[b]"Please, let our petition be acceptable to
you, and [c]pray for us to the LORD your
God, for all this remnant (since we are left
but [d]a few of many, as you can see), 3 that
the LORD your God may show us [e]the way
in which we should walk and the thing we
should do."
4 Then Jeremiah the prophet said to
them, "I have heard. Indeed, I will pray to
the LORD your God according to your
words, and it shall be, *that* [f]whatever the
LORD answers you, I will declare *it* to you.
I will [g]keep nothing back from you."
5 So they said to Jeremiah, [h]"Let the
LORD be a true and faithful witness between us, if we do not do according to
everything which the LORD your God
sends us by you. 6 Whether *it is* [1]pleasing
or [2]displeasing, we will [i]obey the voice of
the LORD our God to whom we send you,
[j]that it may be well with us when we obey
the voice of the LORD our God."
7 And it happened after ten days that the
word of the LORD came to Jeremiah. 8 Then
he called Johanan the son of Kareah, all the
captains of the forces which *were* with him,
and all the people from the least even to
the greatest, 9 and said to them, "Thus says
the LORD, the God of Israel, to whom you
sent me to present your petition before
Him: 10 'If you will still remain in this land,
then [k]I will build you and not pull *you*
down, and I will plant you and not pluck
you up. For I [l]relent concerning the disaster
that I have brought upon you. 11 Do not be
afraid of the king of Babylon, of whom you
are afraid; do not be afraid of him,' says the
LORD, [m]'for I *am* with you, to save you and
deliver you from his hand. 12 And [n]I will
show you mercy, that he may have mercy
on you and cause you to return to your
own land.'
13 "But if [o]you say, 'We will not dwell in
this land,' disobeying the voice of the LORD
your God, 14 saying, 'No, but we will go to
the land of [p]Egypt where we shall see no
war, nor hear the sound of the trumpet,
nor be hungry for bread, and there we will
dwell'— 15 Then hear now the word of the
LORD, O remnant of Judah! Thus says the
LORD of hosts, the God of Israel: 'If you

10 [j]Jer. 40:11, 12 [k]Jer. 43:6 [l]Jer. 40:7 [m]Jer. 40:14
11 [n]Jer. 40:7, 8, 13-16
12 [o]2 Sam. 2:13
16 [p]Jer. 40:11, 12; 43:4-7
17 [q]2 Sam. 19:37, 38 [r]Jer. 43:7
18 [s]Jer. 40:5

CHAPTER 42

1 [a]Jer. 40:8, 13; 41:11
2 [b]Jer. 15:11 [c]Ex. 8:28; 1 Sam. 7:8; 12:19; 1 Kin. 13:6; Is. 37:4; Jer. 37:3; Acts 8:24; [James 5:16] [d]Lev. 26:22; Deut. 28:62; Is. 1:9; Lam. 1:1
3 [e]Ezra 8:21
4 [f]1 Kin. 22:14; Jer. 23:28 [g]1 Sam. 3:17, 18; Ps. 40:10; Acts 20:20
5 [h]Gen. 31:50; Judg. 11:10; Jer. 43:2; Mic. 1:2; Mal. 2:14; 3:5
6 [i]Ex. 24:7; Deut. 5:27; Josh. 24:24 [j]Deut. 5:29, 33; 6:3; Jer. 7:23 [1]Lit. *good* [2]Lit. *evil*
10 [k]Jer. 24:6; 31:28; 33:7; Ezek. 36:36 [l]Deut. 32:36; [Jer. 18:8]
11 [m]Num. 14:9; 2 Chr. 32:7, 8; Is. 8:9, 10; 43:2, 5; Jer. 1:19; 15:20; Rom. 8:31
12 [n]Neh. 1:11; Ps. 106:46; Prov. 16:7
13 [o]Jer. 44:16
14 [p]Is. 31:1; Jer. 41:17; 43:7

41:12-15 went to fight with Ishmael. Johanan heard of Ishmael's murders and taking people captive, and brought men to stop him. They freed the captives (vv. 13,14), but Ishmael and his men escaped (v. 15).

41:12 pool...Gibeon. Cf. 2 Sam. 2:13.

42:1,2 Jeremiah. He probably was one carried off from Mizpah, freed, and dwelt with Johanan (41:16).

42:1-6 pray for us. The remnant in Judah asked Jeremiah to pray to God and find His will on what they should do. They promised to obey (v. 6).

42:7-12 After 10 days of prayer Jeremiah reported God's Word, telling them to remain in the land under God's protection (v. 10).

42:10 I relent. By this God means "I am satisfied with the punishment inflicted if you do not add new offenses."

42:13-19 The prophet gave explicit warning (v. 19) not to go to Egypt where they would be exposed to corrupting paganism.

42:20 They were hypocrites who already desired Egypt.

[q]wholly[3] set [r]your faces to enter Egypt,
and go to dwell there, 16 then it shall be
that the [s]sword which you feared shall
overtake you there in the land of Egypt;
the famine of which you were afraid shall
follow close after you there *in* Egypt; and
there you shall die. 17 So shall it be with all
the men who set their faces to go to Egypt
to dwell there. They shall die by the sword,
by famine, and by pestilence. And [t]none of
them shall remain or escape from the disaster that I will bring upon them.'
18 "For thus says the LORD of hosts, the
God of Israel: 'As My anger and My fury
have been [u]poured out on the inhabitants
of Jerusalem, so will My fury be poured
out on you when you enter Egypt. And
[v]you shall be an oath, an astonishment, a
curse, and a reproach; and you shall see
this place no more.'
19 "The LORD has said concerning you, O
remnant of Judah, [w]'Do not go to Egypt!'
Know certainly that I have [4]admonished
you this day. 20 For you [5]were hypocrites
in your hearts when you sent me to the
LORD your God, saying, 'Pray for us to the
LORD our God, and according to all that
the LORD your God says, so declare to us
and we will do *it*.' 21 And I have this day
declared *it* to you, but you have [x]not
obeyed the voice of the LORD your God, or
anything which He has sent you by me.
22 Now therefore, know certainly that you
[y]shall die by the sword, by famine, and by
pestilence in the place where you desire to
go to dwell."

Jeremiah Taken to Egypt

43 Now it happened, when Jeremiah
had stopped speaking to all the
people all the [a]words of the LORD their
God, for which the LORD their God had
sent him to them, all these words, 2 [b]that
Azariah the son of Hoshaiah, Johanan the
son of Kareah, and all the proud men
spoke, saying to Jeremiah, "You speak
falsely! The LORD our God has not sent you
to say, 'Do not go to Egypt to dwell there.'
3 But [c]Baruch the son of Neriah has [1]set
you against us, to deliver us into the hand
of the Chaldeans, that they may put us to
death or carry us away captive to Babylon." 4 So Johanan the son of Kareah, all
the captains of the forces, and all the people would [d]not obey the voice of the LORD,
to remain in the land of Judah. 5 But Johanan the son of Kareah and all the captains of the forces took [e]all the remnant of
Judah who had returned to dwell in the
land of Judah, from all nations where they
had been driven— 6 men, women, children, [f]the king's daughters, [g]and every
person whom Nebuzaradan the captain of
the guard had left with Gedaliah the son of
Ahikam, the son of Shaphan, and Jeremiah
the prophet and Baruch the son of Neriah.
7 [h]So they went to the land of Egypt, for
they did not obey the voice of the LORD.
And they went as far as [i]Tahpanhes.
8 Then the [j]word of the LORD came to
Jeremiah in Tahpanhes, saying, 9 "Take
large stones in your hand, and hide them
in the sight of the men of Judah, in the
[2]clay in the brick courtyard which *is* at the
entrance to Pharaoh's house in Tahpanhes;
10 and say to them, 'Thus says the LORD of
hosts, the God of Israel: "Behold, I will
send and bring Nebuchadnezzar the king
of Babylon, [k]My servant, and will set his
throne above these stones that I have hidden. And he will spread his royal pavilion
over them. 11 [l]When he comes, he shall
strike the land of Egypt *and deliver* to death
[m]*those appointed* for death, and to captivity
those appointed for captivity, and to the
sword *those appointed* for the sword. 12 [3]I
will kindle a fire in the houses of [n]the gods
of Egypt, and he shall burn them and carry
them away captive. And he shall array
himself with the land of Egypt, as a shepherd puts on his garment, and he shall go
out from there in peace. 13 He shall also
break the sacred pillars of [4]Beth Shemesh
that *are* in the land of Egypt; and the houses of the gods of the Egyptians he shall
burn with fire."' '"

15 [q] Deut. 17:16; Jer. 44:12-14 [r] Luke 9:51 [3] Or *surely*
16 [s] Jer. 44:13, 27; Ezek. 11:8; Amos 9:1-4
17 [t] Jer. 44:14, 28
18 [u] 2 Chr. 36:16-19; Jer. 7:20 [v] Deut. 29:21; Is. 65:15; Jer. 18:16; 24:9; 26:6; 29:18, 22; 44:12
19 [w] Deut. 17:16; Is. 30:1-7 [4] *warned*
20 [5] Lit. *used deceit against your souls*
21 [x] Is. 30:1-7
22 [y] Jer. 42:17; Ezek. 6:11

CHAPTER 43

1 [a] Jer. 42:9-18
2 [b] Jer. 42:1
3 [c] Jer. 36:4; 45:1 [1] Or *incited*
4 [d] 2 Kin. 25:26
5 [e] Jer. 40:11, 12
6 [f] Jer. 41:10 [g] Jer. 39:10; 40:7
7 [h] Jer. 42:19 [i] Jer. 2:16; 44:1
8 [j] Jer. 44:1-30
9 [2] Or *mortar*
10 [k] Jer. 25:9; 27:6; Ezek. 29:18, 20
11 [l] Is. 19:1-25; Jer. 25:15-19; 44:13; 46:1, 2, 13-26; Ezek. 29:19, 20 [m] Jer. 15:2; Zech. 11:9
12 [n] Ex. 12:12; Is. 19:1; Jer. 46:25; Ezek. 30:13 [3] So with MT, Tg.; LXX, Syr., Vg. *He*
13 [4] Lit. *House of the Sun*, ancient On, later called Heliopolis

43:1-7 when Jeremiah...stopped speaking. The incorrigible, disobedient leaders accused him of deceit and forced Jeremiah and the remnant to go to Egypt, despite the fact that all his prophecies regarding Babylon had come to pass. In so doing, they went out of God's protection into His judgment, as all who are disobedient to His Word do.

43:3,6 Baruch. The faithful recorder of chap. 36 was still with Jeremiah, kept safe as God promised him at least 20 years earlier (45:5; cf. 605 B.C. in v. 1).

43:7 Tahpanhes. A location in the eastern delta region of Egypt.

43:9-13 Take large stones. Stones, placed in the mortar of the brick pavement in the courtyard entrance of the Pharaoh's house, signaled the place where the conquering king of Babylon would bring devastation on Egypt and establish his throne. This was fulfilled in an invasion ca. 568/67 B.C.

43:12 as a shepherd puts on his garment. A very simple and easy task describes how quickly and easily Nebuchadnezzar will conquer Egypt.

43:13 sacred pillars of Beth Shemesh. Heb. "house of the sun." This refers to a temple for the worship of the sun. Located N of Memphis, E of the Nile, these pillars were said to be 60–100 ft. high.

Israelites Will Be Punished in Egypt

44 The word that came to Jeremiah
concerning all the Jews who dwell
in the land of Egypt, who dwell at [a]Migdol,
at [b]Tahpanhes, at [c]Noph,[1] and in the country of [d]Pathros, saying, 2 "Thus says the
LORD of hosts, the God of Israel: 'You have
seen all the calamity that I have brought on
Jerusalem and on all the cities of Judah; and
behold, this day they *are* [e]a desolation, and
no one dwells in them, 3 because of their
wickedness which they have committed to
provoke Me to anger, in that they went [f]to
burn incense *and* to [g]serve other gods
whom they did not know, they nor you nor
your fathers. 4 However [h]I have sent to you
all My servants the prophets, rising early
and sending *them,* saying, "Oh, do not do
this abominable thing that I hate!" 5 But
they did not listen or incline their ear to
turn from their wickedness, to burn no incense to other gods. 6 So My fury and My
anger were poured out and kindled in the
cities of Judah and in the streets of Jerusalem; and they [2]are wasted *and* desolate, as
it is this day.'

7 "Now therefore, thus says the LORD, the
God of hosts, the God of Israel: 'Why do
you commit *this* great evil [i]against yourselves, to cut off from you man and
woman, child and infant, out of Judah,
leaving none to remain, 8 in that you [j]pro-
voke Me to wrath with the works of your
hands, burning incense to other gods in the
land of Egypt where you have gone to
dwell, that you may cut yourselves off and
be [k]a curse and a reproach among all the
nations of the earth? 9 Have you forgotten
the wickedness of your fathers, the wickedness of the kings of Judah, the wickedness
of their wives, your own wickedness, and
the wickedness of your wives, which they
committed in the land of Judah and in the
streets of Jerusalem? 10 They have not been
[l]humbled,[3] to this day, nor have they
[m]feared; they have not walked in My law
or in My statutes that I set before you and
your fathers.'

11 "Therefore thus says the LORD of
hosts, the God of Israel: 'Behold, [n]I will set
My face against you for catastrophe and
for [4]cutting off all Judah. 12 And I will take
the remnant of Judah who have set their
faces to go into the land of Egypt to dwell
there, and [o]they shall all be consumed *and*
fall in the land of Egypt. They shall be consumed by the sword *and* by famine. They
shall die, from the least to the greatest, by
the sword and by famine; and [p]they shall
be an oath, an astonishment, a curse and a
reproach! 13 [q]For I will punish those who
dwell in the land of Egypt, as I have punished Jerusalem, by the sword, by famine,
and by pestilence, 14 so that none of the
remnant of Judah who have gone into the
land of Egypt to dwell there shall escape or
survive, lest they return to the land of Judah, to which they [r]desire[5] to return and
dwell. For [s]none shall return except those
who escape.'"

15 Then all the men who knew that their
wives had burned incense to other gods,
with all the women who stood by, a great
multitude, and all the people who dwelt in
the land of Egypt, in Pathros, answered
Jeremiah, saying: 16 "*As for* the word that
you have spoken to us in the name of the
LORD, [t]we will not listen to you! 17 But we
will certainly do [u]whatever has gone out
of our own mouth, to burn incense to the
[v]queen of heaven and pour out drink offerings to her, as we have done, we and our
fathers, our kings and our princes, in the
cities of Judah and in the streets of Jerusalem. For *then* we had plenty of [6]food, were
well-off, and saw no trouble. 18 But since
we stopped burning incense to the queen
of heaven and pouring out drink offerings
to her, we have lacked everything and
have been consumed by the sword and by
famine."

19 *The women also said,* [w]"And when we
burned incense to the queen of heaven and
poured out drink offerings to her, did we
make cakes for her, to worship her, and
pour out drink offerings to her without our
husbands' *permission?*"

20 Then Jeremiah spoke to all the people—the men, the women, and all the people who had given him *that* answer—saying: 21 "The incense that you burned in the

CHAPTER 44

1 [a] Ex. 14:2; Jer. 46:14 [b] Jer. 43:7; Ezek. 30:18 [c] Is. 19:13; Jer. 2:16; 46:14; Ezek. 30:13, 16; Hos. 9:6 [d] Is. 11:11; Ezek. 29:14; 30:14 [1] Ancient Memphis
2 [e] Is. 6:11; Jer. 4:7; 9:11; 34:22; Mic. 3:12
3 [f] Jer. 19:4 [g] Deut. 13:6; 32:17
4 [h] 2 Chr. 36:15; Jer. 7:25; 25:4; 26:5; 29:19; Zech. 7:7
6 [2] Or *became a ruin*
7 [i] Num. 16:38; Jer. 7:19; [Ezek. 33:11]; Hab. 2:10
8 [j] 2 Kin. 17:15-17; Jer. 25:6, 7; 44:3; 1 Cor. 10:21, 22 [k] 1 Kin. 9:7, 8; 2 Chr. 7:20; Jer. 42:18
10 [l] 2 Chr. 36:12; Jer. 6:15; 8:12; Dan. 5:22 [m] [Prov. 28:14] [3] Lit. *crushed*
11 [n] Lev. 17:10; 20:5, 6; Jer. 21:10; Amos 9:4 [4] *destroying*
12 [o] Jer. 42:15-17, 22 [p] Is. 65:15; Jer. 42:18
13 [q] Jer. 43:11
14 [r] Jer. 22:26, 27 [s] [Is. 4:2; 10:20]; Jer. 44:28; [Rom. 9:27] [5] Lit. *lift up their soul*
16 [t] Jer. 6:16
17 [u] Num. 30:12; Deut. 23:23; Judg. 11:36 [v] 2 Kin. 17:16; Jer. 7:18 [6] Lit. *bread*
19 [w] Jer. 7:18

44:1 The word that came. The unrelenting iniquity of the Jews called for yet another prophecy of judgment on them in Egypt.

44:2-6 The prophet summarized what had occurred in Judah as a basis for what he predicted coming on the refugees in Egypt.

44:7,9,10 Incredibly, after being spared death in Judah, they pursued it by their sin in Egypt.

44:11-14 Ironically, the Jews taken to Babylon were weaned from idolatry and restored to their land; those taken to Egypt for their obstinate idolatry, perished there.

44:14 except those who escape. A small number (v. 28) who fled before the arrival of Babylonian armies were spared.

44:15 wives. The idolatry apparently began with the women.

44:17-19 queen of heaven. *See note on 7:18.* This is a title Roman Catholicism erroneously attributes to Mary, the mother of Jesus, in a blending of Christianity with paganism. The Jews' twisted thinking credits the idol with the prosperity of pre-captivity Judah, further mocking the goodness of God.

44:20-23 Jeremiah set the record straight, saying the idol was not the source of their prosperity, but it was the cause of their calamity.

cities of Judah and in the streets of Jerusalem, you and your fathers, your kings and
your princes, and the people of the land,
did not the LORD remember them, and did
it *not* come into His mind? 22 So the LORD
could no longer bear *it,* because of the evil
of your doings *and* because of the
abominations which you committed.
Therefore your land is a desolation, an astonishment, a curse, and without an inhabitant, [x]as *it is* this day. 23 Because you have
burned incense and because you have
sinned against the LORD, and have not
obeyed the voice of the LORD or walked in
His law, in His statutes or in His testimonies, [y]therefore this calamity has happened to you, as *at* this day."
24 Moreover Jeremiah said to all the people and to all the women, "Hear the word
of the LORD, all Judah who *are* in the land
of Egypt! 25 Thus says the LORD of hosts,
the God of Israel, saying: 'You and your
wives have spoken with your mouths and
fulfilled with your hands, saying, "We will
surely keep our vows that we have made,
to burn incense to the queen of heaven and
pour out drink offerings to her." You will
surely keep your vows and perform your
vows!' 26 Therefore hear the word of the
LORD, all Judah who dwell in the land of
Egypt: 'Behold, [z]I have sworn by My
[a]great name,' says the LORD, 'that [b]My
name shall no more be named in the
mouth of any man of Judah in all the land
of Egypt, saying, "The Lord GOD lives."
27 Behold, I will watch over them for adversity and not for good. And all the men
of Judah who *are* in the land of Egypt [c]shall
be consumed by the sword and by famine,
until there is an end to them. 28 Yet [d]a
small number who escape the sword shall
return from the land of Egypt to the land of
Judah; and all the remnant of Judah, who
have gone to the land of Egypt to dwell
there, shall know whose words will stand,
Mine or theirs. 29 And this *shall be* a sign to
you,' says the LORD, 'that I will punish you
in this place, that you may know that My
words will surely [e]stand against you for
adversity.'
30 "Thus says the LORD: 'Behold, [f]I will
give Pharaoh Hophra king of Egypt into
the hand of his enemies and into the hand
of those who seek his life, as I gave [g]Zede-
kiah king of Judah into the hand of Nebuchadnezzar king of Babylon, his enemy
who sought his life.' "

Assurance to Baruch

45 The [a]word that Jeremiah the
prophet spoke to [b]Baruch the son of
Neriah, when he had written these words
in a book [1]at the instruction of Jeremiah, in
the [c]fourth year of Jehoiakim the son of Josiah, king of Judah, saying, 2 "Thus says
the LORD, the God of Israel, to you, O
Baruch: 3 'You said, "Woe is me now! For
the LORD has added grief to my sorrow. I
[d]fainted in my sighing, and I find no
rest." '
4 "Thus you shall say to him, 'Thus says
the LORD: "Behold, [e]what I have built I will
break down, and what I have planted I will
pluck up, that is, this whole land. 5 And do
you seek great things for yourself? Do not
seek *them;* for behold, [f]I will bring adversity on all flesh," says the LORD. "But I will
give your [g]life to you as a prize in all
places, wherever you go." ' "

Judgment on Egypt

46 The word of the LORD which came
to Jeremiah the prophet against [a]the
nations. 2 Against [b]Egypt.
[c]Concerning the army of Pharaoh
Necho, king of Egypt, which was by the
River Euphrates in Carchemish, and which
Nebuchadnezzar king of Babylon [d]de-
feated in the [e]fourth year of Jehoiakim the
son of Josiah, king of Judah:

3 "Order[1] the [2]buckler and shield,
And draw near to battle!
4 Harness the horses,

22 [x]Jer. 25:11, 18, 38
23 [y]1 Kin. 9:9; Neh. 13:18; Jer. 44:2; Dan. 9:11, 12
26 [z]Gen. 22:16; Deut. 32:40, 41; Jer. 22:5; Amos 6:8; Heb. 6:13 [a]Jer. 10:6 [b]Neh. 9:5; Ps. 50:16; Ezek. 20:39
27 [c]Jer. 1:10; 31:28; Ezek. 7:6
28 [d]Is. 10:19; 27:12, 13
29 [e][Ps. 33:11]
30 [f]Jer. 46:25, 26; Ezek. 29:3; 30:21 [g]2 Kin. 25:4-7; Jer. 39:5

CHAPTER 45

1 [a]Jer. 36:1, 4, 32 [b]Jer. 32:12, 16; 43:3 [c]Jer. 25:1; 36:1; 46:2 [1]Lit. *from Jeremiah's mouth*
3 [d]Ps. 6:6; 69:3; [2 Cor. 4:1, 16; Gal. 6:9]
4 [e]Is. 5:5; Jer. 1:10; 11:17; 18:7-10; 31:28
5 [f]Jer. 25:17-26 [g]Jer. 21:9; 38:2; 39:18

CHAPTER 46

1 [a]Jer. 25:15
2 [b]Jer. 25:17-19; Ezek. 29:2–32:32 [c]2 Kin. 23:33-35 [d]2 Kin. 23:29; 24:7; 2 Chr. 35:20 [e]Jer. 45:1
3 [1]*Set in order* [2]A small shield

44:24-28 Jeremiah repeated the doom stated in vv. 11-14.

44:29,30 sign. The "sign" of punishment was described in v. 30 as the strangulation of Pharaoh Hophra in 570 B.C. by Amasis, which paved the way for Nebuchadnezzar's invasion in the 23rd year of his reign (568/67 B.C.).

45:1 fourth year of Jehoiakim. The year was 605 B.C. (chap. 36), when the recording of God's messages to Jeremiah was in view.

45:3 Woe is me now! Baruch felt anxiety as his own cherished plans of a bright future were apparently dashed; even death became a darkening peril (cf. v. 5). Also, he was possibly pressed by human questionings about God carrying through with such calamity (cf. v. 4). Jeremiah spoke to encourage him (v. 2).

45:4 say to him. God will judge this whole nation (the Jews).

45:5 you seek great things. Baruch had his expectations far too high and that made the disasters harder to bear. It is enough that he be content just to live. Jeremiah, who once also complained, learned by his own suffering to encourage complainers.

46:1 against the nations. Jeremiah had already proclaimed that all the nations at some time are to "drink the cup" of God's wrath (25:15-26). In chaps. 46–51 God selected certain nations and forecast their doom. Likely given to Jeremiah at different times, the prophecies were collected according to the nations, not the chronology.

46:2-26 Against Egypt. Cf. Is. 19,20; Ezek. 29–32. Verses 2-12 depict Pharaoh Necho's overthrow by the Babylonians at Carchemish by the Euphrates River in 605 B.C., in which Egypt lost all its territory W of the river.

46:3-6 Here was a derisive call to Egypt to ready itself for defeat.

And mount up, you horsemen!
Stand forth with *your* helmets,
Polish the spears,
[f]Put on the armor!
5 Why have I seen them dismayed
and turned back?
Their mighty ones are beaten
down;
They have speedily fled,
And did not look back,
For [g]fear *was* all around," says the
LORD.
6 "Do not let the swift flee away,
Nor the mighty man escape;
They will [h]stumble and fall
Toward the north, by the River
Euphrates.

7 "Who *is* this coming up [i]like a
flood,
Whose waters move like the
rivers?
8 Egypt rises up like a flood,
And *its* waters move like the
rivers;
And he says, 'I will go up *and*
cover the earth,
I will destroy the city and its
inhabitants.'
9 Come up, O horses, and rage,
O chariots!
And let the mighty men come
forth:
[3]The Ethiopians and [4]the Libyans
who handle the shield,
And the Lydians [j]who handle *and*
bend the bow.
10 For this *is* [k]the day of the Lord GOD
of hosts,
A day of vengeance,
That He may avenge Himself on
His adversaries.
[l]The sword shall devour;
It shall be [5]satiated and made
drunk with their blood;
For the Lord GOD of hosts [m]has a
sacrifice
In the north country by the River
Euphrates.

11 "Go[n] up to Gilead and take balm,
[o]O virgin, the daughter of Egypt;
In vain you will use many
medicines;
[p]You shall not be cured.
12 The nations have heard of your
[q]shame,
And your cry has filled the land;
For the mighty man has stumbled
against the mighty;
They both have fallen together."

Babylonia Will Strike Egypt

13 The word that the LORD spoke to Jeremiah the prophet, how Nebuchadnezzar
king of Babylon would come *and* [r]strike
the land of Egypt.

14 "Declare in Egypt, and proclaim in
[s]Migdol;
Proclaim in [6]Noph and in
[t]Tahpanhes;
Say, 'Stand fast and prepare
yourselves,
For the sword devours all around
you.'
15 Why are your valiant *men* swept
away?
They did not stand
Because the LORD drove them
away.
16 He made many fall;
Yes, [u]one fell upon another.
And they said, 'Arise!
[v]Let us go back to our own people
And to the land of our nativity
From the oppressing sword.'
17 They cried there,
'Pharaoh, king of Egypt, *is but* a
noise.
He has passed by the appointed
time!'

18 "*As* I live," says the King,
[w]Whose name *is* the LORD of hosts,
"Surely as Tabor *is* among the
mountains
And as Carmel by the sea, *so* he
shall come.
19 O [x]you daughter dwelling in Egypt,
Prepare yourself [y]to go into
captivity!
For [7]Noph shall be waste and
desolate, without inhabitant.

20 "Egypt *is* a very pretty [z]heifer,
But destruction comes, it comes
[a]from the north.

4 [f] Is. 21:5; Jer. 51:11, 12; Joel 3:9; Nah. 2:1; 3:14
5 [g] Jer. 49:29
6 [h] Jer. 46:12, 16; Dan. 11:19
7 [i] Is. 8:7, 8; Jer. 47:2; Dan. 11:22
9 [j] Is. 66:19 [3] Heb. *Cush* [4] Heb. *Put*
10 [k] Is. 13:6; Joel 1:15 [l] Deut. 32:42; Is. 31:8; Jer. 12:12 [m] Is. 34:6; Zeph. 1:7; Ezek. 39:17 [5] Filled to the full
11 [n] Jer. 8:22 [o] Is. 47:1; Jer. 31:4, 21 [p] Ezek. 30:21
12 [q] Jer. 2:36; Nah. 3:8-10
13 [r] Is. 19:1; Jer. 43:10, 11; Ezek. 29:1-21
14 [s] Jer. 44:1 [t] Ezek. 30:18 [6] Ancient Memphis
16 [u] Lev. 26:36, 37; Jer. 46:6 [v] Jer. 51:9
18 [w] Is. 47:4; Jer. 48:15; Mal. 1:14
19 [x] Jer. 48:18 [y] Is. 20:4 [7] Ancient Memphis
20 [z] Hos. 10:11 [a] Jer. 1:14

46:10 the day of the Lord. While this phrase often refers to an eschatological judgment on earth (such as in Joel 1:15; Zeph. 1:7; Mal. 4:5; 1 Thess. 5:2; 2 Pet. 3:10), it also may refer to a historical day. In this case it refers to the Egyptian defeat (cf. Lam. 2:22). *See note on Is. 2:12.*

46:11 Gilead. *See note on 8:22.*

46:13-26 Babylon's invasion of Egypt, 15 or 16 years before the destruction of Jerusalem is here detailed (601 B.C.; cf. v. 13). Having spent 13 years in a siege of Tyre, Nebuchadnezzar was promised Egypt as a reward for humbling Tyre (cf. Ezek. 29:17-20).

46:18 Tabor...Carmel. As those two mountains rise above the hills of Palestine, so Nebuchadnezzar will be superior.

46:20,21 a very pretty heifer...fat bulls. Fat and untamed, ready to kill.

21 Also her mercenaries are in her
midst like [8]fat bulls,
For they also are turned back,
They have fled away together.
They did not stand,
For [b]the day of their calamity had
come upon them,
The time of their punishment.
22 [c]Her noise shall go like a serpent,
For they shall march with an army
And come against her with axes,
Like those who chop wood.

23 "They shall [d]cut down her forest,"
says the LORD,
"Though it cannot be searched,
Because they *are* innumerable,
And more numerous than
[e]grasshoppers.
24 The daughter of Egypt shall be
ashamed;
She shall be delivered into the
hand
Of [f]the people of the north."

25 The LORD of hosts, the God of Israel,
says: "Behold, I will bring punishment on
[9]Amon of [g]No,[1] and Pharaoh and Egypt,
[h]with their gods and their kings—Pharaoh
and those who [i]trust in him. 26 [j]And I will
deliver them into the hand of those who
seek their lives, into the hand of Nebuchadnezzar king of Babylon and the hand
of his servants. [k]Afterward it shall be inhabited as in the days of old," says the
LORD.

God Will Preserve Israel

27 "But[l] do not fear, O My servant
Jacob,
And do not be dismayed, O Israel!
For behold, I will [m]save you from
afar,
And your offspring from the land
of their captivity;
Jacob shall return, have rest and be
at ease;
No one shall make *him* afraid.
28 Do not fear, O Jacob My servant,"
says the LORD,
"For I *am* with you;
For I will make a complete end of
all the nations
To which I have driven you,
But I will not make [n]a complete
end of you.
I will rightly [o]correct you,
For I will not leave you wholly
unpunished."

Judgment on Philistia

47 The word of the LORD that came to
Jeremiah the prophet [a]against the
Philistines, [b]before Pharaoh attacked Gaza.
2 Thus says the LORD:

"Behold, [c]waters rise [d]out of the
north,
And shall be an overflowing flood;
They shall overflow the land and
all that is in it,
The city and those who dwell
within;
Then the men shall cry,
And all the inhabitants of the land
shall wail.
3 At the [e]noise of the stamping
hooves of his strong horses,
At the rushing of his chariots,
At the rumbling of his wheels,
The fathers will not look back for
their children,
[1]Lacking courage,
4 Because of the day that comes to
plunder all the [f]Philistines,
To cut off from [g]Tyre and Sidon
every helper who remains;
For the LORD shall plunder the
Philistines,
[h]The remnant of the country of
[i]Caphtor.[2]
5 [j]Baldness has come upon Gaza,
[k]Ashkelon is cut off
With the remnant of their valley.
How long will you cut yourself?

6 "O you [l]sword of the LORD,
How long until you are quiet?
Put yourself up into your scabbard,
Rest and be still!
7 How can [3]it be quiet,
Seeing the LORD has [m]given it a
charge
Against Ashkelon and against the
seashore?
There He has [n]appointed it."

21 [b][Ps. 37:13]; Jer. 50:27 [8]Lit. *calves of the stall*
22 [c][Is. 29:4]
23 [d]Is. 10:34 [e]Judg. 6:5; 7:12; Joel 2:25
24 [f]Jer. 1:15
25 [g]Ezek. 30:14-16; Nah. 3:8 [h]Ex. 12:12; Jer. 43:12, 13; Ezek. 30:13; Zeph. 2:11 [i]Is. 30:1-5; 31:1-3 [9]A sun god [1]Ancient Thebes
26 [j]Jer. 44:30; Ezek. 32:11 [k]Ezek. 29:8-14
27 [l]Is. 41:13, 14; 43:5; 44:2; Jer. 30:10, 11 [m]Is. 11:11; Jer. 23:3, 4; Mic. 7:12
28 [n]Jer. 10:24; Amos 9:8, 9 [o]Jer. 30:11

CHAPTER 47

1 [a]Is. 14:29-31; Ezek. 25:15-17; Zeph. 2:4, 5; Zech. 9:6 [b]Amos 1:6
2 [c]Is. 8:7, 8; Jer. 46:7, 8 [d]Jer. 1:14
3 [e]Judg. 5:22; Jer. 8:16; Nah. 3:2 [1]Lit. *From sinking hands*
4 [f]Is. 14:29-31 [g]Is. 23:1-18; Jer. 25:22; Ezek. 26:1-21; 28:20-24; Amos 1:9, 10; Zech. 9:2-4 [h]Ezek. 25:16; Amos 1:8 [i]Gen. 10:14; Deut. 2:23; Amos 9:7 [2]Cappadocia in Asia Minor
5 [j]Jer. 48:37; Mic. 1:16; Zeph. 2:4 [k]Judg. 1:18; Jer. 25:20; Amos 1:7, 8; Zech. 9:5
6 [l]Deut. 32:41; Judg. 7:20; Jer. 12:12; Ezek. 21:3-5
7 [m]Is. 10:6; Ezek. 14:17 [n]Mic. 6:9 [3]Lit. *you*

46:26 Afterward. Forty years after Nebuchadnezzar's conquest of Egypt, it threw off the Babylonian yoke but never regained its former glory (Ezek 29:11-15).

46:27,28 do not fear…Jacob. Though Israel has been scattered to the nations, the nations will receive their judgments, and the Lord will restore Israel (repeated from 30:10,11) from dispersion to its own land (as in Jer. 23:5-8; 30–33). No matter what judgments fall on Israel, they will not be destroyed, as Paul reiterates in Rom. 11:1,2,15,25-27.

47:1-5 against the Philistines. Cf. Is. 14:29-32; Ezek. 25:15-17; Amos 1:6-8; Zeph. 2:4-7. Although Egypt's Pharaoh Hophra conquered the Philistines (who lived on the coastal plain of Palestine) in Gaza and Phoenicia around 587 B.C. (v. 1), Babylon appears to be the conqueror in this scene, ("out of the N") at the same time as the invasion of Judah (588-586 B.C.; cf. 39:1,2).

47:6,7 sword of the LORD. Cf. Judg. 7:18,20.

Judgment on Moab

48 Against [a]Moab.
Thus says the LORD of hosts, the God of Israel:

"Woe to [b]Nebo!
For it is plundered,
[c]Kirjathaim is shamed *and* taken;
[1]The high stronghold is shamed and dismayed—
2 [d]No more praise of Moab.
In [e]Heshbon they have devised evil against her:
'Come, and let us cut her off as a nation.'
You also shall be cut down,
O [f]Madmen![2]
The sword shall pursue you;
3 A voice of crying *shall be* from [g]Horonaim:
'Plundering and great destruction!'

4 "Moab is destroyed;
[3]Her little ones have caused a cry to be heard;
5 [h]For in the Ascent of Luhith they ascend with continual weeping;
For in the descent of Horonaim the enemies have heard a cry of destruction.

6 "Flee, save your lives!
And be like [4]the [i]juniper in the wilderness.
7 For because you have trusted in your works and your [j]treasures,
You also shall be taken.
And [k]Chemosh shall go forth into captivity,
His [l]priests and his princes together.
8 And [m]the plunderer shall come against every city;
No one shall escape.
The valley also shall perish,
And the plain shall be destroyed,
As the LORD has spoken.

9 "Give[n] wings to Moab,
That she may flee and get away;
For her cities shall be desolate,
Without any to dwell in them.
10 [o]Cursed *is* he who does the work of the LORD deceitfully,
And cursed *is* he who keeps back his sword from blood.

11 "Moab has been at ease from [5]his youth;
He [p]has settled on his dregs,
And has not been emptied from vessel to vessel,
Nor has he gone into captivity.
Therefore his taste remained in him,
And his scent has not changed.

12 "Therefore behold, the days are coming," says the LORD,
"That I shall send him [6]wine-workers
Who will tip him over
And empty his vessels
And break the bottles.
13 Moab shall be ashamed of [q]Chemosh,
As the house of Israel [r]was ashamed of [s]Bethel, their confidence.

14 "How can you say, [t]'We *are* mighty
And strong men for the war'?
15 Moab is plundered and gone up *from* her cities;
Her chosen young men have [u]gone down to the slaughter," says [v]the King,
Whose name *is* the LORD of hosts.

16 "The calamity of Moab *is* near at hand,
And his affliction comes quickly.
17 Bemoan him, all you who are around him;
And all you who know his name,
Say, [w]'How the strong staff is broken,
The beautiful rod!'

CHAPTER 48

1 [a] Is. 15:1–16:14; 25:10; Ezek. 25:8-11; Amos 2:1-3; Zeph. 2:8-11 [b] Is. 15:2 [c] Num. 32:37; Jer. 48:23; Ezek. 25:9 [1] Heb. *Misgab*
2 [d] Is. 16:14 [e] Is. 15:4; Jer. 49:3 [f] Is. 10:31 [2] A city of Moab
3 [g] Is. 15:5; Jer. 48:5, 34
4 [3] So with MT, Tg., Vg.; LXX *Proclaim it in Zoar*
5 [h] Is. 15:5
6 [i] Jer. 17:6 [4] Or *Aroer,* a city of Moab
7 [j] Ps. 52:7; Is. 59:4; Jer. 9:23; [1 Tim. 6:17] [k] Num. 21:29; Judg. 11:24; Jer. 48:13 [l] Jer. 49:3
8 [m] Jer. 6:26
9 [n] Ps. 55:6
10 [o] Judg. 5:23; 1 Sam. 15:3, 9; 1 Kin. 20:42
11 [p] Zeph. 1:12 [5] Heb. uses masc. and fem. pronouns interchangeably in this chapter.
12 [6] Lit. *tippers* of wine bottles
13 [q] 1 Kin. 11:7 [r] Hos. 10:6 [s] 1 Kin. 12:29; 13:32-34; Hos. 8:5, 6
14 [t] Is. 16:6
15 [u] [Is. 40:30, 31]; Jer. 50:27 [v] Jer. 46:18; 51:57; Mal. 1:14
17 [w] Is. 9:4; 14:4, 5

48:1 Against Moab. Various sites of unknown location in Moab are to be destroyed (vv. 1-5). The judgment is framed in similar words or some of the same words as in other passages (Is. 15:1-9; 16:6-14; 25:10-12; Ezek. 25:8-11; Amos 2:1-3; Zeph. 2:8-11). Desolation overtook different parts of Moab at various times, but Babylon in 588–86 B.C. or 582–81 B.C. is likely the main destroyer (cf. 48:40). The Moabites were Lot's descendants (cf. Gen. 19:37), who lived E of the Dead Sea and often fought with Israel.

48:7 Chemosh. He was the leading god of Moab (cf. Num. 21:29; Judg. 11:24; 1 Kin. 11:7; 2 Kin. 23:13).

48:10 Cursed *is* he. God's aim to judge Moab was so intense that He pronounced a curse on whatever instrument (army) He would use if they should carry it out "deceitfully" i.e., "carelessly," or "with slackness," or "being remiss" (Prov. 10:4; cf. 12:24).

48:11,12 This wine making imagery is vivid. In the production of sweet wine, the juice was left in a wineskin until the sediment or dregs settled onto the bottom. Then it was poured into another skin until more dregs were separated. This process continued until the dregs were all removed and a pure, sweet wine obtained. Moab was not taken from suffering to suffering so that her bitter dregs would be removed though the purging of pain. Thus the nation was settled into the thickness and bitterness of its own sin. Judgment from God was coming to smash them.

18 "O [x]daughter inhabiting [y]Dibon,
Come down from *your* glory,
And sit in thirst;
For the plunderer of Moab has
come against you,
He has destroyed your
strongholds.
19 O inhabitant of [z]Aroer,
[a]Stand by the way and watch;
Ask him who flees
And her who escapes;
Say, 'What has happened?'
20 Moab is shamed, for he is broken
down.
[b]Wail and cry!
Tell it in [c]Arnon, that Moab is
plundered.

21 "And judgment has come on the
plain country:
On Holon and Jahzah and
Mephaath,
22 On Dibon and Nebo and Beth
Diblathaim,
23 On Kirjathaim and Beth Gamul
and Beth Meon,
24 On [d]Kerioth and Bozrah,
On all the cities of the land of
Moab,
Far or near.
25 [e]The [7]horn of Moab is cut off,
And his [f]arm is broken," says the
LORD.

26 "Make[g] him drunk,
Because he exalted *himself* against
the LORD.
Moab shall wallow in his vomit,
And he shall also be in derision.
27 For [h]was not Israel a derision to
you?
[i]Was he found among thieves?
For whenever you speak of him,
You shake *your head in* [j]*scorn.*
28 You who dwell in Moab,
Leave the cities and [k]dwell in the
rock,
And be like [l]the dove *which* makes
her nest
In the sides of the cave's mouth.

29 "We have heard the [m]pride of Moab
(He *is* exceedingly proud),
Of his loftiness and arrogance and
[n]pride,
And of the haughtiness of his
heart."
30 "I know his wrath," says the LORD,
"But it *is* not right;
[o]His [8]lies have made nothing right.
31 Therefore [p]I will wail for Moab,
And I will cry out for all Moab;
[q]I will mourn for the men of Kir
Heres.
32 [q]O vine of Sibmah! I will weep for
you with the weeping of
[r]Jazer.
Your plants have gone over the sea,
They reach to the sea of Jazer.
The plunderer has fallen on your
summer fruit and your
vintage.
33 [s]Joy and gladness are taken
From the plentiful field
And from the land of Moab;
I have caused wine to [1]fail from
the winepresses;
No one will tread with joyous
shouting—
Not joyous shouting!

34 "From[t] the cry of Heshbon to
[u]Elealeh and to Jahaz
They have uttered their voice,
[v]From Zoar to Horonaim,
Like [2]a three-year-old heifer;
For the waters of Nimrim also shall
be desolate.

35 "Moreover," says the LORD,
"I will cause to cease in Moab
[w]The one who offers *sacrifices* in the
[3]high places
And burns incense to his gods.
36 Therefore [x]My heart shall wail like
flutes for Moab,
And like flutes My heart shall wail
For the men of Kir Heres.
Therefore [y]the riches they have
acquired have perished.

37 "For [z]every head *shall be* bald, and
every beard clipped;
On all the hands *shall be* cuts, and
[a]on the loins sackcloth—
38 A general lamentation
On all the [b]housetops of Moab,
And in its streets;

18 [x] Is. 47:1 [y] Num. 21:30; Josh. 13:9, 17; Is. 15:2; Jer. 48:22
19 [z] Deut. 2:36; Josh. 12:2; Is. 17:2 [a] 1 Sam. 4:13, 14, 16
20 [b] Is. 16:7 [c] Num. 21:13
24 [d] Jer. 48:41; Amos 2:2
25 [e] Ps. 75:10; Zech. 1:19-21 [f] Ezek. 30:21 [7] Strength
26 [g] Jer. 25:15
27 [h] Zeph. 2:8 [i] Jer. 2:26 [j] Lam. 2:15; [Mic. 7:8-10]
28 [k] Ps. 55:6, 7 [l] Song 2:14
29 [m] Is. 16:6; Zeph. 2:8, 10 [n] Jer. 49:16
30 [o] Is. 16:6; Jer. 50:36 [8] *idle talk*
31 [p] Is. 15:5; 16:7, 11 [9] So with DSS, LXX, Vg.; MT *He*
32 [q] Is. 16:8, 9 [r] Num. 21:32; Is. 16:10
33 [s] Is. 16:10; Jer. 25:10; Joel 1:12 [1] *cease*
34 [t] Is. 15:4-6 [u] Num. 32:3, 37 [v] Is. 15:5, 6 [2] Or *The Third Eglath,* an unknown city, Is. 15:5
35 [w] Is. 15:2; 16:12 [3] Places for pagan worship
36 [x] Is. 15:5; 16:11 [y] Is. 15:7
37 [z] Is. 15:2, 3; Jer. 16:6; 41:5; 47:5 [a] Gen. 37:34; Is. 15:3; 20:2
38 [b] Is. 15:3

48:18-20 Dibon...Aroer. These places were on the Arnon River, but would be thirsty.

48:24 Kerioth. Likely the city of Judas Iscariot. Cf. Josh. 15:25.

48:25 horn...is cut off. An example of the OT use of "horn" as as a symbol of military power, as an animal uses horns to hook, gouge, or ram. Moab is to be dehorned.

48:26 Here is as a vivid picture of humiliation.

48:29 Suffering didn't come to humble Moab (*see note on vv. 11,12*), so she remained proud.

For I have [c]broken Moab like a
vessel in which *is* no
pleasure," says the LORD.
39 "They shall wail:
'How she is broken down!
How Moab has turned her back
with shame!'
So Moab shall be a derision
And a dismay to all those about
her."
40 For thus says the LORD:

"Behold, [d]one shall fly like an eagle,
And [e]spread his wings over Moab.
41 Kerioth is taken,
And the strongholds are surprised;
[f]The mighty men's hearts in Moab
on that day shall be
Like the heart of a woman in birth
pangs.
42 And Moab shall be destroyed [g]as a
people,
Because he exalted *himself* against
the LORD.
43 [h]Fear and the pit and the snare *shall
be* upon you,
O inhabitant of Moab," says the
LORD.
44 "He who flees from the fear shall
fall into the pit,
And he who gets out of the pit
shall be caught in the [i]snare.
For upon Moab, upon it [j]I will bring
The year of their punishment,"
says the LORD.

45 "Those who fled stood under the
shadow of Heshbon
Because of exhaustion.
But [k]a fire shall come out of
Heshbon,
A flame from the midst of [l]Sihon,
And [m]shall devour the brow of
Moab,
The crown of the head of the sons
of tumult.
46 [n]Woe to you, O Moab!
The people of Chemosh perish;
For your sons have been taken
captive,
And your daughters captive.

38 [c] Jer. 22:28
40 [d] Deut. 28:49; Jer. 49:22; Hos. 8:1; Hab. 1:8 [e] Is. 8:8
41 [f] Is. 13:8; 21:3; Jer. 30:6; Mic. 4:9, 10
42 [g] Ps. 83:4; Jer. 48:2
43 [h] Is. 24:17, 18; Lam. 3:47
44 [i] 1 Kin. 19:17; Is. 24:18; Amos 5:19 [j] Jer. 11:23
45 [k] Num. 21:28, 29 [l] Num. 21:21, 26; Ps. 135:11 [m] Num. 24:17
46 [n] Num. 21:29
47 [o] Jer. 49:6, 39

CHAPTER 49

1 [a] Deut. 23:3, 4; 2 Chr. 20:1; Jer. 25:21; Ezek. 21:28-32; 25:1-7 [b] Amos 1:13-15; Zeph. 2:8-11 [1] Heb. *Malcam*, lit. *their king;* an Ammonite god, 1 Kin. 11:5; *Molech*, Lev. 18:21
2 [c] Amos 1:13-15 [d] Ezek. 25:5 [2] Lit. *daughters*
3 [e] Jer. 48:2 [f] Is. 32:11; Jer. 48:37 [g] Jer. 48:7 [3] See v. 1
4 [h] Jer. 9:23 [i] Jer. 3:14 [j] Jer. 48:7 [k] Jer. 21:13 [4] Lit. *Your valley is flowing*
6 [l] Jer. 48:47

47 "Yet I will bring back the captives of
Moab
[o]In the latter days," says the LORD.

Thus far *is* the judgment of Moab.

Judgment on Ammon

49 Against the [a]Ammonites.
Thus says the LORD:

"Has Israel no sons?
Has he no heir?
Why *then* does [1]Milcom inherit
[b]Gad,
And his people dwell in its cities?
2 [c]Therefore behold, the days are
coming," says the LORD,
"That I will cause to be heard an
alarm of war
In [d]Rabbah of the Ammonites;
It shall be a desolate mound,
And her [2]villages shall be burned
with fire.
Then Israel shall take possession of
his inheritance," says the
LORD.

3 "Wail, O [e]Heshbon, for Ai is
plundered!
Cry, you daughters of Rabbah,
[f]Gird yourselves with sackcloth!
Lament and run to and fro by the
walls;
For [3]Milcom shall go into captivity
With his [g]priests and his princes
together.
4 Why [h]do you boast in the valleys,
[4]Your flowing valley, O [i]backsliding
daughter?
Who trusted in her [j]treasures,
[k]*saying,*
'Who will come against me?'
5 Behold, I will bring fear upon you,"
Says the Lord GOD of hosts,
"From all those who are around you;
You shall be driven out, everyone
headlong,
And no one will gather those who
wander off.
6 But [l]afterward I will bring back
The captives of the people of
Ammon," says the LORD.

48:47 I will bring back. God will allow a remnant of Moab to return to the land (cf. 12:14-17; 46:26; 48:47; 49:6,39), through their descendants in the messianic era ("the latter days").

49:1-6 Against the Ammonites. Cf. Ezek. 25:1-7; Amos 1:13-15; Zeph. 2:8-11. These people descended from Lot (cf. Gen. 19:38) and lived N of Moab. Though Israel had people who were heirs to Transjordan, i.e., Gad, Reuben, and one half of Manasseh (cf. Josh. 22:1-9), the Ammonites, whose god was Milcham or Molech, were chided for having usurped the area (v. 1), when the northern kingdom was taken captive by Shalmaneser.

49:2 an alarm of war. Nebuchadnezzar defeated Ammon in the fifth year after the destruction of Jerusalem, around 582/81 B.C.

49:4 flowing valley. Flowing with the blood of the slain. **backsliding.** *See note on Prov. 14:14.*

49:6 I will bring back. As with Moab (cf. 48:47 and *see note there*), God promised that captives would have an opportunity to return. This was partially fulfilled under Cyrus, but will be more fully in the coming kingdom of Messiah (cf. 48:47).

Judgment on Edom

7 [m]Against Edom.
Thus says the LORD of hosts:

[n]"*Is* wisdom no more in Teman?
[o]Has counsel perished from the prudent?
Has their wisdom [p]vanished?
8 Flee, turn back, dwell in the depths, O inhabitants of [q]Dedan!
For I will bring the calamity of Esau upon him,
The time *that* I will punish him.
9 [r]If grape-gatherers came to you,
Would they not leave *some* gleaning grapes?
If thieves by night,
Would they not destroy until they have enough?
10 [s]But I have made Esau bare;
I have uncovered his secret places,
And he shall not be able to hide himself.
His descendants are plundered,
His brethren and his neighbors,
And [t]he *is* no more.
11 Leave your fatherless children,
I will preserve *them* alive;
And let your widows trust in Me."

12 For thus says the LORD: "Behold,
[u]those whose judgment *was* not to drink of
the cup have assuredly drunk. And *are* you
the one who will altogether go unpunished? You shall not go unpunished, but
you shall surely drink *of it.* 13 For [v]I have
sworn by Myself," says the LORD, "that
[w]Bozrah shall become a desolation, a reproach, a [5]waste, and a curse. And all its
cities shall be perpetual [6]wastes."

14 [x]I have heard a message from the LORD,
And an ambassador has been sent to the nations:
"Gather together, come against her,
And rise up to battle!
15 "For indeed, I will make you small among nations,
Despised among men.
16 Your fierceness has deceived you,
The [y]pride of your heart,
O you who dwell in the clefts of the rock,
Who hold the height of the hill!
[z]Though you make your [a]nest as high as the eagle,
[b]I will bring you down from there,"
says the LORD.

17 "Edom also shall be an astonishment;
[c]Everyone who goes by it will be astonished
And will hiss at all its plagues.
18 [d]As in the overthrow of Sodom and Gomorrah
And their neighbors," says the LORD,
"No one shall remain there,
Nor shall a son of man dwell in it.

19 "Behold, [e]he shall come up like a lion from [f]the [7]floodplain of the Jordan
Against the dwelling place of the strong;
But I will suddenly make him run away from her.
And who *is* a chosen *man that* I may appoint over her?
For [g]who *is* like Me?
Who will arraign Me?
And [h]who *is* that shepherd
Who will withstand Me?"

20 [i]Therefore hear the counsel of the LORD that He has taken against Edom,
And His purposes that He has proposed against the inhabitants of Teman:
Surely the least of the flock shall [8]draw them out;
Surely He shall make their dwelling places desolate with them.

7 [m] Gen. 25:30; 32:3; Is. 34:5, 6; Jer. 25:21; Ezek. 25:12-14; 35:1-15; Joel 3:19; Amos 1:11, 12; Obad. 1-9, 15, 16 [n] Gen. 36:11; Job 2:11 [o] Is. 19:11 [p] Jer. 8:9
8 [q] Is. 21:13; Jer. 25:23
9 [r] Obad. 5, 6
10 [s] Obad. 5, 6; Mal. 1:3 [t] Is. 17:14
12 [u] Jer. 25:29; Obad. 16
13 [v] Gen. 22:16; Is. 45:23; Jer. 44:26; Amos 6:8 [w] Gen. 36:33; 1 Chr. 1:44; Is. 34:6; 63:1; Amos 1:12 [5] *ruin* [6] *ruins*
14 [x] Obad. 1-4
16 [y] Jer. 48:29 [z] Obad. 3, 4 [a] Job 39:27; Is. 14:13-15 [b] Amos 9:2
17 [c] Jer. 18:16; 49:13; 50:13; Ezek. 35:7
18 [d] Gen. 19:24, 25; Deut. 29:23; Jer. 50:40; Amos 4:11; Zeph. 2:9
19 [e] Jer. 50:44 [f] Josh. 3:15; Jer. 12:5 [g] Ex. 15:11; Is. 46:9 [h] Job 41:10 [7] Or *thicket*
20 [i] Is. 14:24, 27; Jer. 50:45 [8] Or *drag them away*

49:7-22 Against Edom. Cf. Is. 21:11,12; Ezek. 25:12-14; Amos 1:11,12; Obad. 1. This prophecy is closely related to Obadiah. These people descended from Esau (cf. Gen. 36:1-19) and lived S of the Dead Sea. Perpetual desolation is ahead for Edom (v. 13). God will make it bare (vv. 10,18). The destroyer is probably Babylon in 588–586 B.C. or 582–581 B.C. as v. 19 has descriptions used of Babylon against Judah (lion, 4:7; flooding of the Jordan, 12:5). Also "fly like an eagle" (v. 22) is used of Babylon (Hab. 1:8). There is no prophecy of a future restoration.

49:8 Esau. He was cursed for his godlessness and his punishment was perpetuated in his descendants (cf. Heb. 12:11,17).

49:9 *See notes on Obad. 5.*

49:10 he *is* no more. Edom was politically extinct after the Roman conquest.

49:11 This was because no adult men will be left to care for them.

49:12 those...not to drink...have...drunk. This refers to the Jews who had a covenant relation to God. What will happen to a nation that has no such pledge?

49:16,17 Edom was situated in high and rugged mountains and thus convinced it was invincible. But the ruin will come and be irreversible.

49:19-21 These words are repeated in 50:44-46, where they refer to Babylon.

49:20 the least of the flock. The weakest of the Chaldeans shall drag them away captive.

21 [j]The earth shakes at the noise of their fall;
At the cry its noise is heard at the Red Sea.
22 Behold, [k]He shall come up and fly like the eagle,
And spread His wings over Bozrah;
The heart of the mighty men of Edom in that day shall be
Like the heart of a woman in birth pangs.

Judgment on Damascus

23 [l]Against Damascus.

[m]"Hamath and Arpad are shamed,
For they have heard bad news.
They are fainthearted;
[n]*There is* [9]trouble on the sea;
It cannot be quiet.
24 Damascus has grown feeble;
She turns to flee,
And fear has seized *her.*
[o]Anguish and sorrows have taken her like a woman in [1]labor.
25 Why is [p]the city of praise not deserted, the city of My joy?
26 [q]Therefore her young men shall fall in her streets,
And all the men of war shall be cut off in that day," says the LORD of hosts.
27 "I[r] will kindle a fire in the wall of Damascus,
And it shall consume the palaces of Ben-Hadad."

Judgment on Kedar and Hazor

28 [s]Against Kedar and against the kingdoms of Hazor, which Nebuchadnezzar king of Babylon shall strike.
Thus says the LORD:

"Arise, go up to Kedar,
And devastate [t]the men of the East!
29 Their [u]tents and their flocks they shall take away.
They shall take for themselves their curtains,
All their vessels and their camels;
And they shall cry out to them,
[v]'Fear *is* on every side!'

30 "Flee, get far away! Dwell in the depths,
O inhabitants of Hazor!" says the LORD.
"For Nebuchadnezzar king of Babylon has taken counsel against you,
And has conceived a plan against you.

31 "Arise, go up to [w]the wealthy nation that dwells securely,"
says the LORD,
"Which has neither gates nor bars,
[x]Dwelling alone.
32 Their camels shall be for booty,
And the multitude of their cattle for plunder.
I will [y]scatter to all winds those [2]in the farthest corners,
And I will bring their calamity from all its sides," says the LORD.
33 "Hazor [z]shall be a dwelling for jackals, a desolation forever;
No one shall reside there,
Nor son of man dwell in it."

Judgment on Elam

34 The word of the LORD that came to Jeremiah the prophet against [a]Elam, in the [b]beginning of the reign of Zedekiah king of Judah, saying, 35 "Thus says the LORD of hosts:

21 [j] Jer. 50:46; Ezek. 26:15, 18
22 [k] Jer. 48:40, 41
23 [l] Is. 17:1-3; Amos 1:3, 5; Zech. 9:1, 2 [m] Jer. 39:5; Zech. 9:2 [n] [Is. 57:20] [9] *anxiety*
24 [o] Is. 13:8; Jer. 4:31; 6:24; 48:21 [1] *childbirth*
25 [p] Jer. 33:9
26 [q] Jer. 50:30; Amos 4:10
27 [r] Amos 1:4
28 [s] Gen. 25:13; Ps. 120:5; Is. 21:16, 17; Jer. 2:10; Ezek. 27:21 [t] Judg. 6:3; Job 1:3
29 [u] Ps. 120:5 [v] Jer. 46:5
31 [w] Ezek. 38:11 [x] Num. 23:9; Deut. 33:28; Mic. 7:16
32 [y] Ezek. 5:10 [2] Lit. *cut off at the corner,* Jer. 9:26; 25:23
33 [z] Jer. 9:11; 10:22; Zeph. 2:9, 12-15; Mal. 1:3
34 [a] Gen. 10:22; Jer. 25:25; Ezek. 32:24; Dan. 8:2 [b] 2 Kin. 24:17, 18; Jer. 28:1

49:23-27 Against Damascus. Cf. Is. 17:1-3; Amos 1:3-5. Hamath, a city on the Orontes River that marked the northern limit of Solomon's rule (2 Chr. 8:4), 110 mi. N of Damascus in southern Syria, and Arpad, 105 mi. SW of the modern Aleppo in Northern Syria, were to fall, as well as Damascus, Syria's capital. Nebuchadnezzar conquered them in 605 B.C.

49:25 city of praise...My joy. Could be translated, "the city of renown," famous due to its situation in a spacious oasis and its trade, as in Ezek. 27:18.

49:27 palaces of Ben-Hadad. Here was the place where so many cruel evils against Israel were devised, thus the reason for its overthrow. The name is common among Syrian kings, meaning Son of Hadad, an idol, so it does not refer to the Ben-Hadad of 2 Kin. 13:3 and Amos 1:4.

49:28-33 Against Kedar...Hazor. Cf. Is. 21:13-17. These areas in the Arabian desert E of Judah were to be laid waste (as a different Hazor was a few mi. NW of the Sea of Galilee). Kedar was an Ishmaelite tribe (cf. Gen. 25:13; Ezek. 27:21). The conqueror was Nebuchadnezzar in 599/98 B.C. as recounted in an ancient record, the Babylonian Chronicle. It was shortly after this that Babylon seized Jerusalem in 598/97 B.C.

49:31 neither gates nor bars. These nomads were out of the way of contending powers in Asia and Africa.

49:34-39 against Elam. As in 25:25, Elam (200 mi. E of Babylon and W of the Tigris River) was to be subjugated. Babylon fulfilled this in 596 B.C. Later, Cyrus of Persia conquered Elam and incorporated Elamites into the Persian forces that conquered Babylon in 539 B.C. Its capital, Susa, was the residence of Darius and became the center of the Persian Empire (Neh. 1:1; Dan. 8:2).

49:34 reign of Zedekiah. Jeremiah speaks of this judgment in 597 B.C.

'Behold, I will break [c]the [3]bow of
Elam,
The foremost of their might.
36 Against Elam I will bring the four
winds
From the four quarters of heaven,
And scatter them toward all those
winds;
There shall be no nations where the
outcasts of Elam will not go.
37 For I will cause Elam to be
dismayed before their
enemies
And before those who seek their
life.
[d]I will bring disaster upon them,
My fierce anger,' says the LORD;
'And I will send the sword after
them
Until I have consumed them.
38 I will [e]set My throne in Elam,
And will destroy from there the
king and the princes,' says
the LORD.

39 'But it shall come to pass [f]in the
latter days:
I will bring back the captives of
Elam,' says the LORD."

Judgment on Babylon and Babylonia

50 The word that the LORD spoke
[a]against Babylon *and* against the
land of the Chaldeans by Jeremiah the
prophet.

2 "Declare among the nations,
Proclaim, and [1]set up a standard;
Proclaim—do not conceal *it*—
Say, 'Babylon is [b]taken, [c]Bel is
shamed.
[2]Merodach is broken in pieces;
[d]Her idols are humiliated,
Her images are broken in pieces.'
3 [e]For out of the north [f]a nation
comes up against her,
Which shall make her land
desolate,

35 [c] Ps. 46:9; Is. 22:6 [3] Power
37 [d] Jer. 9:16
38 [e] Jer. 43:10
39 [f] Jer. 48:47

CHAPTER 50

1 [a] Gen. 10:10; 11:9; 2 Kin. 17:24; Is. 13:1; 47:1; Dan. 1:1; Rev. 14:8
2 [b] Is. 21:9 [c] Is. 46:1; Jer. 51:44 [d] Jer. 43:12, 13 [1] *lift* [2] Or *Marduk;* a Babylonian god
3 [e] Jer. 51:48; Dan. 5:30, 31 [f] Is. 13:17, 18, 20

[3] Or *wander*
4 [g] Ezra 2:1; Is. 11:12, 13; Jer. 3:18; 31:31; 33:7; Hos. 1:11 [h] Ezra 3:12, 13; [Ps. 126:5]; Jer. 31:9; [Zech. 12:10] [i] Hos. 3:5
5 [j] Jer. 31:31
6 [k] Is. 53:6; [Ezek. 34:15, 16]; Matt. 9:36; 10:6; 1 Pet. 2:25 [l] Jer. 23:1; Ezek. 34:2 [m] [Jer. 2:20; 3:6, 23]
7 [n] Ps. 79:7 [o] Jer. 40:2, 3; Zech. 11:5 [p] Jer. 2:3; Dan. 9:16 [q] [Ps. 90:1; 91:1] [r] Ps. 22:4; Jer. 14:8; 17:13
8 [s] Is. 48:20; Jer. 51:6, 45; Zech. 2:6, 7; [Rev. 18:4] [4] *male goats*
9 [t] Jer. 15:14; 51:27

And no one shall dwell therein.
They shall [3]move, they shall
depart,
Both man and beast.
4 "In those days and in that time,"
says the LORD,
"The children of Israel shall come,
[g]They and the children of Judah
together;
[h]With continual weeping they shall
come,
[i]And seek the LORD their God.
5 They shall ask the way to Zion,
With their faces toward it, *saying,*
'Come and let us join ourselves to
the LORD
In [j]a perpetual covenant
That will not be forgotten.'

6 "My people have been [k]lost sheep.
Their shepherds have led them
[l]astray;
They have turned them away *on*
[m]the mountains.
They have gone from mountain to
hill;
They have forgotten their resting
place.
7 All who found them have
[n]devoured them;
And [o]their adversaries said, [p]'We
have not offended,
Because they have sinned against
the LORD, [q]the habitation of
justice,
The LORD, [r]the hope of their
fathers.'

8 "Move[s] from the midst of Babylon,
Go out of the land of the
Chaldeans;
And be like the [4]rams before the
flocks.
9 [t]For behold, I will raise and cause
to come up against Babylon
An assembly of great nations from
the north country,

49:35 break the bow. Elamites were famous archers (cf. Is. 22:6).

49:39 I will bring back. As with certain other peoples in this section of nations, God would allow Elamites to return to their homeland. In Acts 2:9, Elamites were among the group present at the Pentecost event. This has eschatological implications as well.

50:1 against Babylon. The subject of chaps. 50 and 51 (cf. Is. 13:1–14:23; Hab. 2:6-17). Judgment focuses on Media Persia's conquest of Babylon in 539 B.C. The prediction of elements of violent overthrow, which was not the case when Cyrus conquered since there was not even a battle, point to greater fulfillment near the coming of Messiah in glory when events more fully satisfy the description (cf. Rev. 17,18).

50:2 idols. First the idols of Babylon are discredited by Jeremiah's using an unusual word for idols, meaning in Hebrew "dung pellets."

50:3 no one shall dwell. The far view in the v. 1 note cites this as not yet fulfilled in a sudden way (cf. 51:8). Media Persia came down from the N in 539 B.C. and armies in the years that followed, but only gradually brought the past Babylon to complete desolation (cf. vv. 12,13).

50:4-10 children of Israel shall come. Jeremiah predicted a return for exiled Israel and Judah (vv. 17-20, as chaps. 30–33) as the scattered and penitent people were given opportunity to escape Babylon's doom and return to Jerusalem and to the Lord in an eternal covenant (v. 5).

50:5 *In* a perpetual covenant. This is the New Covenant summarized in 31:31.

And they shall array themselves
against her;
From there she shall be captured.
Their arrows *shall be* like *those* of
[5]an expert warrior;
[u]None shall return in vain.
10 And Chaldea shall become
plunder;
[v]All who plunder her shall be
satisfied," says the LORD.

11 "Because[w] you were glad, because
you rejoiced,
You destroyers of My heritage,
Because you have grown fat [x]like a
heifer threshing grain,
And you [6]bellow like bulls,
12 Your mother shall be deeply
ashamed;
She who bore you shall be
ashamed.
Behold, the least of the nations
shall be a [y]wilderness,
A dry land and a desert.
13 Because of the wrath of the LORD
She shall not be inhabited,
[z]But she shall be wholly desolate.
[a]Everyone who goes by Babylon
shall be horrified
And hiss at all her plagues.

14 "Put[b] yourselves in array against
Babylon all around,
All you who bend the bow;
Shoot at her, spare no arrows,
For she has sinned against the
LORD.
15 Shout against her all around;
She has [c]given her hand,
Her foundations have fallen,
[d]Her walls are thrown down;
For [e]it *is* the vengeance of the
LORD.
Take vengeance on her.
As she has done, so do to her.
16 Cut off the sower from Babylon,
And him who handles the sickle at
harvest time.
For fear of the oppressing sword
[f]Everyone shall turn to his own
people,
And everyone shall flee to his own
land.

17 "Israel *is* like [g]scattered sheep;
[h]The lions have driven *him* away.
First [i]the king of Assyria devoured
him;
Now at last this [j]Nebuchadnezzar
king of Babylon has broken
his bones."

18 Therefore thus says the LORD of hosts,
the God of Israel:

"Behold, I will punish the king of
Babylon and his land,
As I have punished the king of
[k]Assyria.
19 [l]But I will bring back Israel to his
home,
And he shall feed on Carmel and
Bashan;
His soul shall be satisfied on
Mount Ephraim and Gilead.
20 In those days and in that time,"
says the LORD,
[m]"The iniquity of Israel shall be
sought, but *there shall be* none;
And the sins of Judah, but they
shall not be found;
For I will pardon those [n]whom I
preserve.

21 "Go up against the land of
Merathaim, against it,
And against the inhabitants of
[o]Pekod.
[7]Waste and utterly destroy them,"
says the LORD,
"And do [p]according to all that I
have commanded you.
22 [q]A sound of battle *is* in the land,
And of great destruction.
23 How [r]the hammer of the whole
earth has been cut apart and
broken!
How Babylon has become a
desolation among the nations!
I have laid a snare for you;
24 You have indeed been [s]trapped,
O Babylon,
And you were not aware;
You have been found and also
caught,
Because you have [t]contended
against the LORD.

9 [u]2 Sam. 1:22 [5]So with some Heb. mss., LXX, Syr.; MT, Tg., Vg. *a warrior who makes childless*
10 [v][Rev. 17:16]
11 [w]Is. 47:6 [x]Hos. 10:11 [6]Or *neigh like steeds*
12 [y]Jer. 51:43
13 [z]Jer. 25:12 [a]Jer. 49:17
14 [b]Jer. 51:2
15 [c]1 Chr. 29:24; 2 Chr. 30:8; Lam. 5:6; Ezek. 17:18 [d]Jer. 51:58 [e]Jer. 51:6, 11
16 [f]Is. 13:14; Jer. 51:9
17 [g]2 Kin. 24:10, 14 [h]Jer. 2:15 [i]2 Kin. 15:29; 17:6; 18:9-13 [j]2 Kin. 24:10-14; 25:1-7
18 [k]Is. 10:12; Ezek. 31:3, 11, 12; Nah. 3:7, 18, 19
19 [l]Is. 65:10; Jer. 33:12; Ezek. 34:13
20 [m]Num. 23:21; Is. 43:25; [Jer. 31:34; Mic. 7:19] [n]Is. 1:9
21 [o]Ezek. 23:23 [p]2 Sam. 16:11; 2 Kin. 18:25; 2 Chr. 36:23; Is. 10:6; 44:28; 48:14 [7]Or *Attack* with the sword
22 [q]Jer. 51:54
23 [r]Is. 14:6; Jer. 51:20-24
24 [s]Jer. 51:8, 31; Dan. 5:30 [t][Is. 45:9]

50:11-16 Judgment on Babylon is the vengeance of God (v. 15) for her treatment of his people.

50:17-20 This section summarized the divine interpretation of Israel's history: 1) suffering and judgment on her (v. 17); 2) judgment on those who afflicted Israel (v. 18); 3) her return in peace and plenty (v. 19); and 4) the pardon of her iniquity (v. 20) under Messiah.

50:21 Merathaim…Pekod. This was a dramatic play on words emphasizing cause and effect. The first means "double rebellion" and named a region in southern Babylon near the Persian Gulf; the latter, meaning "punishment," was also in southern Babylon on the E bank of the Tigris River.

50:23 hammer of the whole earth. The description was of Babylon's former conquering force, and God's breaking the "hammer" He had once used. The fact that God used Babylon as His executioner was no commendation of that nation (cf. Hab. 1:6,7).

25 The LORD has opened His armory,
And has brought out [u]the weapons
of His indignation;
For this *is* the work of the Lord
GOD of hosts
In the land of the Chaldeans.
26 Come against her from the farthest
border;
Open her storehouses;
Cast her up as heaps of ruins,
And destroy her utterly;
Let nothing of her be left.
27 Slay all her [v]bulls,
Let them go down to the slaughter.
Woe to them!
For their day has come, the time of
[w]their punishment.
28 The voice of those who flee and
escape from the land of
Babylon
[x]Declares in Zion the vengeance of
the LORD our God,
The vengeance of His temple.

29 "Call together the archers against
Babylon.
All you who bend the bow,
encamp against it all around;
Let none of them [8]escape.
[y]Repay her according to her work;
According to all she has done, do
to her;
[z]For she has been proud against the
LORD,
Against the Holy One of Israel.
30 [a]Therefore her young men shall fall
in the streets,
And all her men of war shall be cut
off in that day," says the LORD.
31 "Behold, I *am* against you,
O most haughty one!" says the
Lord GOD of hosts;
"For your day has come,
[9]The time *that* I will punish you.
32 The most [b]proud shall stumble and
fall,
And no one will raise him up;
[c]I will kindle a fire in his cities,
And it will devour all around
him."

33 Thus says the LORD of hosts:

"The children of Israel *were*
oppressed,
Along with the children of Judah;
All who took them captive have
held them fast;
They have refused to let them go.
34 [d]Their Redeemer *is* strong;
[e]The LORD of hosts *is* His name.
He will thoroughly plead their
[f]case,
That He may give rest to the land,
And disquiet the inhabitants of
Babylon.

35 "A sword *is* against the Chaldeans,"
says the LORD,
"Against the inhabitants of Babylon,
And [g]against her princes and [h]her
wise men.
36 A sword *is* [i]against the
soothsayers, and they will be
fools.
A sword *is* against her mighty
men, and they will be
dismayed.
37 A sword *is* against their horses,
Against their chariots,
And against all [j]the mixed peoples
who *are* in her midst;
And [k]they will become like
women.
A sword *is* against her treasures,
and they will be robbed.
38 [l]A [1]drought *is* against her waters,
and they will be dried up.
For it *is* the land of carved images,
And they are insane with *their*
idols.

39 "Therefore [m]the wild desert beasts
shall dwell *there* with the
jackals,
And the ostriches shall dwell in it.
[n]It shall be inhabited no more
forever,
Nor shall it be dwelt in from
generation to generation.
40 [o]As God overthrew Sodom and
Gomorrah
And their neighbors," says the
LORD,
"*So* no one shall reside there,
Nor son of man [p]dwell in it.

25 [u] Is. 13:5
27 [v] Ps. 22:12; Is. 34:7; Jer. 46:21 [w] Ps. 37:13; Jer. 48:44; Ezek. 7:7
28 [x] Ps. 149:6-9; Jer. 51:10
29 [y] Ps. 137:8; Jer. 51:56; [2 Thess. 1:6]; Rev. 18:6 [z] [Is. 47:10] [8] Qr., some Heb. mss., LXX, Tg. add *to her*
30 [a] Is. 13:18; Jer. 49:26; 51:4
31 [9] So with MT, Tg.; LXX, Vg. *The time of your punishment*
32 [b] Is. 26:5; Mal. 4:1 [c] Jer. 21:14
34 [d] Prov. 23:11; Is. 43:14; Jer. 15:21; 31:11; Rev. 18:8 [e] Is. 47:4 [f] Jer. 51:36; Mic. 7:9
35 [g] Dan. 5:30 [h] Is. 47:13; Jer. 51:57
36 [i] Is. 44:25; Jer. 48:30
37 [j] Jer. 25:20; Ezek. 30:5 [k] Jer. 51:30; Nah. 3:13
38 [l] Is. 44:27; Jer. 51:36; Rev. 16:12 [1] So with MT, Tg., Vg.; Syr. *sword;* LXX omits *A drought is*
39 [m] Is. 13:21, 22; 34:14; Jer. 51:37; Rev. 18:2 [n] Is. 13:20; Jer. 25:12
40 [o] Gen. 19:24, 25; Is. 13:19; Jer. 49:18; [Luke 17:28-30]; 2 Pet. 2:6; Jude 7 [p] Is. 13:20

50:28 vengeance of His temple. This refers to their burning the temple in the destruction of Jerusalem (cf. 51:11).

50:29 Repay her. God aimed to bless Israel and curse all who curse her (cf. Gen. 12:1-3, Abrahamic Covenant). The judgment on Babylon, as in Hab. 2, was a repayment in view of Babylon's wrongs as God defends Israel's case (v. 34; 51:36,56), particularly God's vengeance on her arrogance ("proud against the LORD" cf. vv. 31,32).

50:34 Redeemer. The OT concept of kinsmen-redeemer included the protection of a relative's person and property, the avenging of a relative's murder, the purchase of alienated property, and even the marriage of his widow (cf. Lev. 25:25; Num. 35:21; Ruth 4:4).

50:35-38 The "sword" is mentioned 5 times (cf. Ezek. 21).

50:40 As God overthrew Sodom. Cf. 50:1. What befell Sodom (cf. Gen. 19) was sudden and total destruction, not like the Media Persia takeover, but like an example for the future devastation that will overtake the final Babylon (cf. Rev. 17,18).

41 "Behold,[q] a people shall come from
the north,
And a great nation and many kings
Shall be raised up from the ends of
the earth.
42 [r]They shall hold the bow and the
lance;
[s]They *are* cruel and shall not show
mercy.
[t]Their voice shall roar like the sea;
They shall ride on horses,
Set in array, like a man for the battle,
Against you, O daughter of
Babylon.

43 "The king of Babylon has [u]heard the
report about them,
And his hands grow feeble;
Anguish has taken hold of him,
Pangs as of a woman in [v]childbirth.

44 "Behold,[w] he shall come up like a
lion from the [2]floodplain of
the Jordan
Against the dwelling place of the
strong;
But I will make them suddenly run
away from her.
And who *is* a chosen *man that* I
may appoint over her?
For who *is* like Me?
Who will arraign Me?
And [x]who *is* that shepherd
Who will withstand Me?"

45 Therefore hear [y]the counsel of the
LORD that He has taken
against Babylon,
And His [z]purposes that He has
proposed against the land of
the Chaldeans:
[a]Surely the least of the flock shall
draw them out;
Surely He will make their dwelling
place desolate with them.
46 [b]At the noise of the taking of Babylon
The earth trembles,
And the cry is heard among the
nations.

The Utter Destruction of Babylon

51 Thus says the LORD:

"Behold, I will raise up against
[a]Babylon,
Against those who dwell in [1]Leb
Kamai,
[b]A destroying wind.
2 And I will send [c]winnowers to
Babylon,
Who shall winnow her and empty
her land.
[d]For in the day of doom
They shall be against her all
around.
3 Against *her* [e]let the archer bend his
bow,
And lift himself up against *her* in
his armor.
Do not spare her young men;
[f]Utterly destroy all her army.
4 Thus the slain shall fall in the land
of the Chaldeans,
[g]And *those* thrust through in her
streets.
5 For Israel is [h]not forsaken, nor
Judah,
By his God, the LORD of hosts,
Though their land was filled with
sin against the Holy One of
Israel."

6 [i]Flee from the midst of Babylon,
And every one save his life!
Do not be cut off in her iniquity,
For [j]this *is* the time of the LORD's
vengeance;
[k]He shall recompense her.
7 [l]Babylon *was* a golden cup in the
LORD's hand,
That made all the earth drunk.
[m]The nations drank her wine;
Therefore the nations [n]are
deranged.
8 Babylon has suddenly [o]fallen and
been destroyed.
[p]Wail for her!
[q]Take balm for her pain;
Perhaps she may be healed.

9 We would have healed Babylon,
But she is not healed.
Forsake her, and [r]let us go
everyone to his own country;
[s]For her judgment reaches to heaven
and is lifted up to the skies.
10 The LORD has [t]revealed our
righteousness.
Come and let us [u]declare in Zion
the work of the LORD our God.

41 [q] Is. 13:2-5; Jer. 6:22; 25:14; 51:27
42 [r] Jer. 6:23 [s] Is. 13:18 [t] Is. 5:30
43 [u] Jer. 51:31 [v] Jer. 6:24
44 [w] Jer. 49:19-21 [x] Job 41:10; Jer. 49:19 [2] Or *thicket*
45 [y] [Ps. 33:11; Is. 14:24]; Jer. 51:10, 11 [z] Jer. 51:29 [a] Jer. 49:19, 20
46 [b] Rev. 18:9

CHAPTER 51

1 [a] Is. 47:1; Jer. 50:1 [b] 2 Kin. 19:7; Jer. 4:11; Hos. 13:15 [1] Lit. *The Midst of Those Who Rise Up Against Me;* a code word for Chaldea, Babylonia
2 [c] Is. 41:16; Jer. 15:7; Matt. 3:12 [d] Jer. 50:14
3 [e] Jer. 50:14, 29 [f] Jer. 50:21
4 [g] Jer. 49:26; 50:30, 37
5 [h] [Is. 54:7, 8; Jer. 33:24-26; 46:28]
6 [i] Jer. 50:8; Rev. 18:4 [j] Jer. 50:15 [k] Jer. 25:14
7 [l] Jer. 25:15; Hab. 2:16; Rev. 17:4 [m] Rev. 14:8 [n] Jer. 25:16
8 [o] Is. 21:9; Jer. 50:2; Rev. 14:8; 18:2 [p] [Is. 48:20]; Rev. 18:9, 11, 19 [q] Jer. 46:11
9 [r] Is. 13:14; Jer. 46:16; 50:16 [s] Ezra 9:6; Rev. 18:5
10 [t] Ps. 37:6; Mic. 7:9 [u] [Is. 40:2]; Jer. 50:28

50:41 from the north. Media Persia in 539 B.C.

50:41-46 Cf. 6:22-24; 49:19-21. The "lion" is Cyrus.

51:1-4 the day of doom. The coming of the northern invader is in view.

51:5 Here is a reminder that God will not utterly forget or destroy His people. Cf. Rom. 11:1,2,29.

51:8 suddenly fallen. The focus was first on Babylon's sudden fall on one night in 539 B.C. (Dan. 5:30). The far view looks at the destruction of the final Babylon near the Second Advent when it will be absolutely sudden (Rev. 18).

11 [v]Make[2] the arrows bright!
Gather the shields!
[w]The LORD has raised up the spirit
of the kings of the Medes.
[x]For His plan *is* against Babylon to
destroy it,
Because it *is* [y]the vengeance of the
LORD,
The vengeance for His temple.
12 [z]Set up the standard on the walls of
Babylon;
Make the guard strong,
Set up the watchmen,
Prepare the ambushes.
For the LORD has both devised and
done
What He spoke against the
inhabitants of Babylon.
13 [a]O you who dwell by many waters,
Abundant in treasures,
Your end has come,
The measure of your covetousness.
14 [b]The LORD of hosts has sworn by
Himself:
"Surely I will fill you with men, [c]as
with locusts,
And they shall lift [d]up a shout
against you."

15 [e]He has made the earth by His
power;
He has established the world by
His wisdom,
And [f]stretched out the heaven by
His understanding.
16 When He utters *His* voice—
There is a multitude of waters in
the heavens:
[g]"He causes the vapors to ascend
from the ends of the earth;
He makes lightnings for the rain;
He brings the wind out of His
treasuries."

17 [h]Everyone is dull-hearted, without
knowledge;
Every metalsmith is put to shame
by the carved image;
[i]For his molded image *is* falsehood,
And *there is* no breath in them.
18 They *are* futile, a work of errors;
In the time of their punishment
they shall perish.

11 [v]Jer. 46:4, 9; Joel 3:9, 10 [w]Is. 13:17 [x]Jer. 50:45 [y]Jer. 50:28 [2]*Polish the arrows!*
12 [z]Nah. 2:1; 3:14
13 [a]Rev. 17:1, 15
14 [b]Jer. 49:13; Amos 6:8 [c]Jer. 51:27; Nah. 3:15 [d]Jer. 50:15
15 [e]Gen. 1:1, 6; Jer. 10:12-16 [f]Job 9:8; Ps. 104:2; Is. 40:22
16 [g]Ps. 135:7; Jer. 10:13
17 [h][Is. 44:18-20]; Jer. 10:14 [i]Jer. 50:2

19 The Portion of Jacob *is* not like
them,
For He *is* the Maker of all things;
And *Israel is* the tribe of His
inheritance.
The LORD of hosts *is* His name.

20 "You[j] *are* My battle-ax *and* weapons
of war:
For with you I will break the
nation in pieces;
With you I will destroy kingdoms;
21 With you I will break in pieces the
horse and its rider;
With you I will break in pieces the
chariot and its rider;
22 With you also I will break in pieces
man and woman;
With you I will break in pieces [k]old
and young;
With you I will break in pieces the
young man and the maiden;
23 With you also I will break in pieces
the shepherd and his flock;
With you I will break in pieces the
farmer and his yoke of oxen;
And with you I will break in pieces
governors and rulers.

24 "And[l] I will repay Babylon
And all the inhabitants of Chaldea
For all the evil they have done
In Zion in your sight," says the
LORD.

25 "Behold, I *am* against you,
[m]O destroying mountain,
Who destroys all the earth," says
the LORD.
"And I will stretch out My hand
against you,
Roll you down from the rocks,
[n]And make you a burnt mountain.
26 They shall not take from you a
stone for a corner
Nor a stone for a foundation,
[o]But you shall be desolate forever,"
says the LORD.

27 [p]Set up a banner in the land,
Blow the trumpet among the
nations!
[q]Prepare the nations against her,

20 [j]Is. 10:5, 15; Jer. 50:23
22 [k]2 Chr. 36:17; Is. 13:15, 16
24 [l]Jer. 50:15, 29
25 [m]Is. 13:2; Zech. 4:7 [n]Rev. 8:8
26 [o]Jer. 50:26, 40
27 [p]Is. 13:2; Jer. 50:2; 51:12 [q]Jer. 25:14

51:11 kings of the Medes. The aggressor was specifically identified (cf. v. 28) as the leader of the Medes, assisted by Persia (539 B.C.).

51:15-19 He has made the earth. God's almighty power and wisdom in creation are evidences of His superiority to all idols (vv. 17, 18), who along with their worshipers will all be destroyed by His mighty power (vv. 15, 16, 19), as in Babylon's case.

51:20-23 You *are* My battle-ax. Cyrus of Persia was God's war club. Ten times the phrase "with you" hits with the force of a hammer.

51:25 destroying mountain. Though Babylon existed on a plain, this phrase was meant as a portrayal of Babylon's looming greatness and power in devastating nations (cf. also 50:23, and *see note there*). **a burnt mountain.** Babylon will be like a volcano that is extinct, never to be rebuilt (v. 26).

51:27 Here are listed the people N of Babylon who were conquered by the Medes early in the sixth century B.C. They assisted the Medes against Babylon.

Call [r]the kingdoms together
against her:
Ararat, Minni, and Ashkenaz.
Appoint a general against her;
Cause the horses to come up like
the bristling locusts.
28 Prepare against her the nations,
With the kings of the Medes,
Its governors and all its rulers,
All the land of his dominion.
29 And the land will tremble and
sorrow;
For every [s]purpose of the LORD
shall be performed against
Babylon,
[t]To make the land of Babylon a
desolation without
inhabitant.
30 The mighty men of Babylon have
ceased fighting,
They have remained in their
strongholds;
Their might has failed,
[u]They became *like* women;
They have burned her dwelling
places,
[v]The bars of her *gate* are broken.
31 [w]One runner will run to meet
another,
And one messenger to meet
another,
To show the king of Babylon that
his city is taken on *all* sides;
32 [x]The passages are blocked,
The reeds they have burned with
fire,
And the men of war are terrified.

33 For thus says the LORD of hosts, the
God of Israel:

"The daughter of Babylon *is* [y]like a
threshing floor
When [z]*it is* time to thresh her;
Yet a little while
[a]And the time of her harvest will
come."
34 "Nebuchadnezzar the king of
Babylon
Has [b]devoured me, he has crushed
me;
He has made me an [c]empty vessel,
He has swallowed me up like a
monster;
He has filled his stomach with my
delicacies,
He has spit me out.
35 Let the violence *done* to me and my
flesh *be* upon Babylon,"
The inhabitant of Zion will say;
"And my blood be upon the
inhabitants of Chaldea!"
Jerusalem will say.

36 Therefore thus says the LORD:

"Behold, [d]I will plead your case and
take vengeance for you.
[e]I will dry up her sea and make her
springs dry.
37 [f]Babylon shall become a heap,
A dwelling place for jackals,
[g]An astonishment and a hissing,
Without an inhabitant.
38 They shall roar together like lions,
They shall growl like lions' whelps.
39 In their excitement I will prepare
their feasts;
[h]I will make them drunk,
That they may rejoice,
And sleep a perpetual sleep
And not awake," says the LORD.
40 "I will bring them down
Like lambs to the slaughter,
Like rams with male goats.

41 "Oh, how [i]Sheshach[3] is taken!
Oh, how [j]the praise of the whole
earth is seized!
How Babylon has become desolate
among the nations!
42 [k]The sea has come up over Babylon;
She is covered with the multitude
of its waves.
43 [l]Her cities are a desolation,
A dry land and a wilderness,
A land where [m]no one dwells,
Through which no son of man
passes.
44 I will punish [n]Bel[4] in Babylon,
And I will bring out of his mouth
what he has swallowed;
And the nations shall not stream to
him anymore.
Yes, [o]the wall of Babylon shall fall.

27 [r] Jer. 50:41, 42
29 [s] Jer. 50:45 [t] Is. 13:19, 20; 47:11; Jer. 50:13; 51:26, 43
30 [u] Is. 19:16; Jer. 48:41 [v] Is. 45:1, 2; Lam. 2:9; Amos 1:5; Nah. 3:13
31 [w] Jer. 50:24
32 [x] Jer. 50:38
33 [y] Is. 21:10; Dan. 2:35; Amos 1:3; Mic. 4:13 [z] Is. 41:15; Hab. 3:12 [a] Is. 17:15; Hos. 6:11; Joel 3:13; Rev. 14:15
34 [b] Jer. 50:17 [c] Is. 24:1-3
36 [d] [Ps. 140:12]; Jer. 50:34 [e] Jer. 50:38
37 [f] Is. 13:22; Jer. 50:39; [Rev. 18:2] [g] Jer. 25:9, 11
39 [h] Jer. 51:57
41 [i] Jer. 25:26 [j] Is. 13:19; Jer. 49:25; [Dan. 4:30] [3] A code word for Babylon, Jer. 25:26
42 [k] Is. 8:7, 8; Jer. 51:55; Dan. 9:26
43 [l] Jer. 50:39, 40 [m] Is. 13:20
44 [n] Jer. 50:2; Is. 46:1 [o] Jer. 50:15 [4] A Babylonian god

51:31 To show the king of Babylon. Couriers brought the report of the city's fall. Since Belshazzar was slain in the city on the night of the fall (Dan. 5:30), reference may be to runners speeding the news to his co-ruler Nabonidus, who was away from Babylon or possibly to Daniel, the third ruler in the kingdom (Dan. 5:29).

51:32 The method of capturing the city was to block off the Euphrates River and dry up the river bed under the city wall, then march in. The "fire" was set to frighten and it did.

51:39 drunk. The allusion is possibly to Belshazzar's drunken feast, recorded in Dan. 5:1-4 (cf. v. 57).

51:41 Sheshach is taken! This is another name for Babylon (cf. 25:26).

45 "My[p] people, go out of the midst of
her!
And let everyone deliver [5]himself
from the fierce anger of the
LORD.
46 And lest your heart faint,
And you fear [q]for the rumor that
will be heard in the land
(A rumor will come *one* year,
And after that, in *another* year
A rumor *will come,*
And violence in the land,
Ruler against ruler),
47 Therefore behold, the days are
coming
That I will bring judgment on the
carved images of Babylon;
Her whole land shall be ashamed,
And all her slain shall fall in her
midst.
48 Then [r]the heavens and the earth
and all that *is* in them
Shall sing joyously over Babylon;
[s]For the plunderers shall come to
her from the north," says the
LORD.

49 As Babylon *has caused* the slain of
Israel to fall,
So at Babylon the slain of all the
earth shall fall.
50 [t]You who have escaped the sword,
Get away! Do not stand still!
[u]Remember the LORD afar off,
And let Jerusalem come to your
mind.

51 [v]We are ashamed because we have
heard reproach.
Shame has covered our faces,
For strangers [w]have come into the
[6]sanctuaries of the LORD's
house.

52 "Therefore behold, the days are
coming," says the LORD,
"That I will bring judgment on her
carved images,
And throughout all her land the
wounded shall groan.
53 [x]Though Babylon were to [7]mount
up to heaven,
And though she were to fortify the
height of her strength,
Yet from Me plunderers would
come to her," says the LORD.

54 [y]The sound of a cry *comes* from
Babylon,
And great destruction from the
land of the Chaldeans,
55 Because the LORD is plundering
Babylon
And silencing her loud voice,
Though her waves roar like great
waters,
And the noise of their voice is
uttered,
56 Because the plunderer comes
against her, against Babylon,
And her mighty men are taken.
Every one of their bows is broken;
[z]For the LORD *is* the God of
recompense,
He will surely repay.

57 "And I will make drunk
Her princes and [a]wise men,
Her governors, her deputies, and
her mighty men.
And they shall sleep a perpetual
sleep
And not awake," says [b]the King,
Whose name *is* the LORD of hosts.

58 Thus says the LORD of hosts:

"The broad walls of Babylon shall
be utterly [c]broken,[8]
And her high gates shall be burned
with fire;
[d]The people will labor in vain,
And the nations, because of the
fire;
And they shall be weary."

Jeremiah's Command to Seraiah

59 The word which Jeremiah the prophet
commanded Seraiah the son of [e]Neriah,
the son of Mahseiah, when he went with
Zedekiah the king of Judah to Babylon in
the fourth year of his reign. And Seraiah
was the quartermaster. 60 So Jeremiah
[f]wrote in a book all the evil that would
come upon Babylon, all these words that
are written against Babylon. 61 And Jeremiah said to Seraiah, "When you arrive in
Babylon and see it, and read all these
words, 62 then you shall say, 'O LORD, You
have spoken against this place to cut it off,
so that [g]none shall remain in it, neither
man nor beast, but it shall be desolate forever.' 63 Now it shall be, when you have

45 [p] Is. 48:20; [Jer. 50:8, 28; 51:6; Rev. 18:4] [5] Lit. *his soul*
46 [q] 2 Kin. 19:7; Is. 13:3-5
48 [r] Is. 44:23; 48:20; 49:13; Rev. 18:20 [s] Jer. 50:3, 41
50 [t] Jer. 44:28 [u] [Deut. 4:29-31]; Ezek. 6:9
51 [v] Ps. 44:15; 79:4 [w] Ps. 74:3-8; Jer. 52:13; Lam. 1:10 [6] *holy places*
53 [x] Gen. 11:4; Job 20:6; [Ps. 139:8-10; Is. 14:12-14]; Jer. 49:16; Amos 9:2; Obad. 4 [7] *ascend*
54 [y] Jer. 50:22
56 [z] Ps. 94:1; Jer. 50:29
57 [a] Jer. 50:35 [b] Jer. 46:18; 48:15
58 [c] Jer. 50:15 [d] Hab. 2:13 [8] Lit. *laid utterly bare*
59 [e] Jer. 32:12
60 [f] Is. 30:8; Jer. 36:2
62 [g] Is. 13:20; 14:22, 23; Jer. 50:3, 39

51:45-50 Again the Lord's people were warned to flee.

51:58 labor in vain. People from many nations enslaved in Babylon had built the wall for nothing.

51:59 Seraiah…the quartermaster. This man looked after the comfort of the king. He may have been the brother of Baruch, Jeremiah's secretary (cf. 32:12).

51:60-63 This royal official carried the scroll (v. 60) to read (v. 61) in Babylon and then dramatically illustrate the coming destruction.

finished reading this book, [h]*that* you shall
tie a stone to it and throw it out into the
Euphrates. 64 Then you shall say, 'Thus
Babylon shall sink and not rise from the
catastrophe that I will bring upon her. And
they shall be weary.' "
Thus far *are* the words of Jeremiah.

The Fall of Jerusalem Reviewed

52 Zedekiah *was* [a]twenty-one years
old when he became king, and he
reigned eleven years in Jerusalem. His
mother's name *was* Hamutal the daughter
of Jeremiah of [b]Libnah. 2 He also did evil
in the sight of the LORD, according to all
that Jehoiakim had done. 3 For because of
the anger of the LORD *this* happened in Jerusalem and Judah, till He finally cast
them out from His presence. Then Zedekiah [c]rebelled against the king of Babylon.
4 Now it came to pass in the [d]ninth year
of his reign, in the tenth month, on the
tenth *day* of the month, *that* Nebuchadnezzar king of Babylon and all his army
came against Jerusalem and encamped
against it; and *they* built a siege wall
against it all around. 5 So the city was besieged until the eleventh year of King Zedekiah. 6 By the fourth month, on the ninth
day of the month, the famine had become
so severe in the city that there was no food
for the people of the land. 7 Then the city
wall was broken through, and all the men
of war fled and went out of the city at
night by way of the gate between the two
walls, which *was* by the king's garden,
even though the Chaldeans *were* near the
city all around. And they went by way of
the [1]plain.
8 But the army of the Chaldeans pursued the king, and they overtook Zedekiah in the plains of Jericho. All his army
was scattered from him. 9 [e]So they took
the king and brought him up to the king
of Babylon at Riblah in the land of
Hamath, and he pronounced judgment on
him. 10 [f]Then the king of Babylon killed
the sons of Zedekiah before his eyes. And
he killed all the princes of Judah in Riblah. 11 He also [g]put out the eyes of Zedekiah; and the king of Babylon bound him
in [2]bronze fetters, took him to Babylon,
and put him in prison till the day of his
death.

The Temple and City Plundered and Burned

12 [h]Now in the fifth month, on the tenth
day of the month ([i]which *was* the nineteenth year of King Nebuchadnezzar king
of Babylon), [j]Nebuzaradan, the captain of
the guard, *who* served the king of Babylon,
came to Jerusalem. 13 He burned the
house of the LORD and the king's house; all
the houses of Jerusalem, that is, all the
houses of the great, he burned with fire.
14 And all the army of the Chaldeans who
were with the captain of the guard broke
down all the walls of Jerusalem all
around. 15 [k]Then Nebuzaradan the captain of the guard carried away captive
some of the poor people, the rest of the
people who remained in the city, the defectors who had deserted to the king of
Babylon, and the rest of the craftsmen.
16 But Nebuzaradan the captain of the
guard left *some* of the poor of the land as
vinedressers and farmers.
17 [l]The [m]bronze pillars that *were* in the
house of the LORD, and the carts and the
bronze Sea that *were* in the house of the
LORD, the Chaldeans broke in pieces, and
carried all their bronze to Babylon. 18 They
also took away [n]the pots, the shovels, the
trimmers, the [3]bowls, the spoons, and all
the bronze utensils with which the priests
ministered. 19 The basins, the firepans, the
bowls, the pots, the lampstands, the
spoons, and the cups, whatever *was* solid
gold and whatever *was* solid silver, the captain of the guard took away. 20 The two pillars, one Sea, the twelve bronze bulls which
were under *it, and* the carts, which King Solomon had made for the house of the
LORD—[o]the bronze of all these articles was
beyond measure. 21 Now *concerning* the
[p]pillars: the height of one pillar *was* eighteen [4]cubits, a measuring line of twelve cubits could measure its circumference, and
its thickness *was* [5]four fingers; *it was* hollow. 22 A capital of bronze *was* on it; and the

63 [h] Jer. 19:10, 11; Rev. 18:21

CHAPTER 52

1 [a] 2 Kin. 24:18; 2 Chr. 36:11 [b] Josh. 10:29; 2 Kin. 8:22; Is. 37:8
3 [c] 2 Chr. 36:13
4 [d] 2 Kin. 25:1; Jer. 39:1; Ezek. 24:1, 2; Zech. 8:19
7 [1] Or *Arabah;* the Jordan Valley
9 [e] 2 Kin. 25:6; Jer. 32:4; 39:5
10 [f] Ezek. 12:13
11 [g] Ezek. 12:13
[2] *shackles*
12 [h] 2 Kin. 25:8-21 [i] Jer. 52:29 [j] Jer. 39:9
15 [k] Jer. 39:9
17 [l] Jer. 27:19 [m] 1 Kin. 7:15, 23, 27, 50
18 [n] Ex. 27:3; 1 Kin. 7:40, 45; 2 Kin. 25:14 [3] *basins*
20 [o] 1 Kin. 7:47; 2 Kin. 25:16
21 [p] 1 Kin. 7:15; 2 Kin. 25:17; 2 Chr. 3:15 [4] 18 inches each [5] 3 inches

52:1-34 This chapter is almost identical to 2 Kin. 24:18–25:30, and it is a historical supplement detailing Jerusalem's fall (as chap. 39). It fittingly opens with her last king and his sin (597–586 B.C.). The purpose of this chapter is to show how accurate Jeremiah's prophecies were concerning Jerusalem and Judah.

52:1 Jeremiah. A different man from the author (cf. 1:1).

52:4-11 *See note on 34:1.* This narrative rehearses the account of the fall of Jerusalem. So crucial was this event that the OT records it 4 times (see also 39:1-14; 2 Kin. 25; 2 Chr. 36:11-21).

52:4 ninth year…tenth month. For vv. 4-6, *see notes on 34:1 and 39:1.*

52:12 tenth *day*. The parallel phrase in 2 Kin. 25:8 reads "seventh day." Nebuzaradan (v. 12), "captain of the guard," started from Riblah on the seventh day and arrived in Jerusalem on the tenth day. **nineteenth year.** 586 B.C.

52:18,19 They also took. The conquerors plundered the magnificent Solomonic temple and took the articles to Babylon. First Kings 6–8 describes these articles. Later, Belshazzar would use some of

height of one capital *was* five cubits, with a
network and pomegranates all around the
capital, all of bronze. The second pillar,
with pomegranates was the same. **23** There
were ninety-six pomegranates on the sides;
[q]all the pomegranates, all around on the
network, *were* one hundred.

The People Taken Captive to Babylonia

24 [r]The captain of the guard took Seraiah
the chief priest, [s]Zephaniah the second
priest, and the three doorkeepers. **25** He
also took out of the city an [6]officer who
had charge of the men of war, seven men
of the king's close associates who were
found in the city, the principal scribe of the
army who mustered the people of the land,
and sixty men of the people of the land
who were found in the midst of the city.
26 And Nebuzaradan the captain of the
guard took these and brought them to the
king of Babylon at Riblah. **27** Then the king
of Babylon struck them and put them to
death at Riblah in the land of Hamath.
Thus Judah was carried away captive from
its own land.
28 [t]These *are* the people whom Nebuchadnezzar carried away captive: [u]in the
seventh year, [v]three thousand and twenty-
three Jews; **29** [w]in the eighteenth year of
Nebuchadnezzar he carried away captive
from Jerusalem eight hundred and thirty-
two persons; **30** in the twenty-third year of
Nebuchadnezzar, Nebuzaradan the captain of the guard carried away captive of
the Jews seven hundred and forty-five persons. All the persons *were* four thousand
six hundred.

Jehoiachin Released from Prison

31 [x]Now it came to pass in the thirty-seventh year of the captivity of Jehoiachin
king of Judah, in the twelfth month, on the
twenty-fifth *day* of the month, *that* [7]Evil-
Merodach king of Babylon, in the first *year*
of his reign, [y]lifted[8] up the head of Jehoiachin king of Judah and brought him out of
prison. **32** And he spoke kindly to him and
gave him a more prominent seat than those
of the kings who *were* with him in Babylon.
33 So [9]Jehoiachin changed from his prison
garments, [z]and he ate bread regularly before the king all the days of his life. **34** And
as for his provisions, there was a regular
ration given him by the king of Babylon, a
portion for each day until the day of his
death, all the days of his life.

23 [q]1 Kin. 7:20
24 [r]2 Kin. 25:18; 1 Chr. 6:14; Ezra 7:1 [s]Jer. 21:1; 29:25
25 [6]Lit. *eunuch*
28 [t]2 Kin. 24:2 [u]2 Kin. 24:12 [v]2 Kin. 24:14
29 [w]2 Kin. 25:11; Jer. 39:9
31 [x]2 Kin. 25:27-30 [y]Gen. 40:13, 20; Ps. 3:3; 27:6 [7]Or *Awil-Marduk;* lit. *The Man of Marduk* [8]Showed favor to
33 [z]2 Sam. 9:7, 13; 1 Kin. 2:7 [9]Lit. *he*

these at his immoral banquet, gloating over victory he wrongly attributed to his gods (Dan. 5; cf. Dan. 1:2).

52:22 five. Second Kings 25:17 reads "three." There may have been two parts to the capitals, the lower part of two cubits and the upper part, carved ornately, of 3 cubits. The lower may be omitted in 2 Kin. 25:17 as belonging to the shaft of the pillar.

52:24-27 Babylon executed some Judean leaders as an act of power, of resentment over the 18 month resistance (cf. 52:4-6), and of intimidation to prevent future plots.

52:25 seven. Second Kings 25:19 reads "five." *See note on 52:12.*

52:28-30 carried away. The stages of deportation to Babylon are: 1) in 605 B.C. under Jehoiakim which marked the beginning of the 70 years of exile, 2) in 597 B.C. under Jehoiachin, 3) in 586 B.C. under Zedekiah, and 4) a mopping up campaign in 582–81 B.C. The number may include only males.

52:31-34 captivity of Jehoiachin. A captive since 597 B.C., he appears here in 561 B.C., after Nebuchadnezzar's death when Evil-Merodach ruled Babylon. Though detained, the former king was kindly freed to enjoy previously denied privileges. The Lord did not forget the Davidic line even in exile.

52:31 twenty-fifth. Second Kings 25:27 reads "twenty-seventh." Probably the decree was on the 25th day and carried out on the 27th.

The Book of
LAMENTATIONS

Title

"Lamentations" was derived from a translation of the title as found in the Latin Vulgate (Vg.) translation of the Greek OT, the Septuagint (LXX), and conveys the idea of "loud cries." The Hebrew exclamation *'ekah* ("How,"which expresses "dismay"), used in 1:1; 2:1, and 4:1, gives the book its Hebrew title. However, the rabbis began early to call the book "loud cries" or "lamentations" (cf. Jer. 7:29). No other entire OT book contains only laments, as does this distressful dirge, marking the funeral of the once beautiful city of Jerusalem (cf. 2:15). This book keeps alive the memory of that fall and teaches all believers how to deal with suffering.

Author and Date

The author of Lamentations is not named within the book, but there are internal and historical indications that it was Jeremiah. The LXX introduces Lam. 1:1, "And it came to pass, after Israel had been carried away captive…Jeremiah sat weeping [cf. 3:48,49, etc.]…lamented…and said…." God had told Jeremiah to have Judah lament (Jer. 7:29), and Jeremiah also wrote laments for Josiah (2 Chr. 35:25).

Jeremiah wrote Lamentations as an eyewitness (cf. 1:13-15; 2:6,9; 4:1-12), possibly with Baruch's secretarial help (cf. Jer. 36:4; 45:1), during or soon after Jerusalem's fall in 586 B.C. It was mid-July when the city fell and mid-August when the temple was burned. Likely, Jeremiah saw the destruction of walls, towers, homes, palace, and temple; he wrote while the event remained painfully fresh in his memory, but before his forced departure to Egypt ca. 583 B.C. (cf. Jer. 43:1-7). The language used in Lamentations closely parallels that used by Jeremiah in his much larger prophetic book (cf. 1:2 with Jer. 30:14; 1:15 with Jer. 8:21; 1:6 and 2:11 with Jer. 9:1,18; 2:22 with Jer. 6:25; 4:21 with Jer. 49:12).

Background and Setting

The prophetic seeds of Jerusalem's destruction were sown through Joshua 800 years in advance (Josh. 23:15,16). Now, for over 40 years, Jeremiah had prophesied of coming judgment and been scorned by the people for preaching doom (ca. 645–605 B.C.). When that judgment came on the disbelieving people from Nebuchadnezzar and the Babylonian army, Jeremiah still responded with great sorrow and compassion toward his suffering and obstinate people. Lamentations relates closely to the book of Jeremiah, describing the anguish over Jerusalem's receiving God's judgment for unrepentant sins. In the book that bears his name, Jeremiah had predicted the calamity in chaps. 1–29. In Lamentations, he concentrates in more detail on the bitter suffering and heartbreak that was felt over Jerusalem's devastation (cf. Ps. 46:4,5). So critical was Jerusalem's destruction, that the facts are recorded in 4 separate OT chapters: 2 Kin. 25; Jer. 39:1-11; 52; and 2 Chr. 36:11-21.

All 154 verses have been recognized by the Jews as a part of their sacred canon. Along with Ruth,

Second Kings, Jeremiah, and Lamentations Compared

	2 Kings 25 (See also 2 Chr. 36:11-21)	Jeremiah	Lamentations
1. The siege of Jerusalem	1,2	39:1-3; 52:4,5	2:20-22; 3:5,7
2. The famine in the city	3	37:21; 52:6	1:11,19; 2:11,12; 2:19,20; 4:4,5,9,10; 5:9,10
3. The flight of the army and the king	4-7	39:4-7; 52:8-11	1:3,6; 2:2; 4:19,20
4. The burning of the palace, temple, and city	8,9	39:8; 52:13	2:3-5; 4:11; 5:18
5. The breaching of the city walls	10	33:4,5; 52:7	2:7-9
6. The exile of the populace	11,12	28:3,4,14; 39:9,10	1:1,4,5,18; 2:9,14; 3:2,19; 4:22; 5:2
7. The looting of the temple	13-15	51:51	1:10; 2:6,7
8. The execution of the leaders	18-21	39:6	1:15; 2:2,20
9. The vassal status of Judah	22-25	40:9	1:1; 5:8,9
10. The collapse of the expected foreign help	24:7	27:1-11; 37:5-10	4:17; 5:6

Esther, Song of Solomon, and Ecclesiastes, Lamentations is included among the OT books of the Megilloth, or "five scrolls," which were read in the synagogue on special occasions. Lamentations is read on the 9th of Ab (July/Aug.) to remember the date of Jerusalem's destruction by Nebuchadnezzar. Interestingly, this same date later marked the destruction of Herod's temple by the Romans in A.D. 70.

Historical and Theological Themes

The chief focus of Lamentations is on God's judgment in response to Judah's sin. This theme can be traced throughout the book (1:5,8,18,20; 3:42; 4:6,13,22; 5:16). A second theme which surfaces is the hope found in God's compassion (as in 3:22-24,31-33; cf. Ps. 30:3-5). Though the book deals with disgrace, it turns to God's great faithfulness (3:22-25) and closes with grace as Jeremiah moves from lamentation to consolation (5:19-22).

God's sovereign judgment represents a third current in the book. His holiness was so offended by Judah's sin that He ultimately brought the destructive calamity. Babylon was chosen to be His human instrument of wrath (1:5,12,15; 2:1,17; 3:37,38; cf. Jer. 50:23). Jeremiah mentions Babylon more than 150 times from Jer. 20:4 to 52:34, but in Lamentations he never once explicitly names Babylon or its king, Nebuchadnezzar. Only the Lord is identified as the One who dealt with Judah's sin.

Fourth, because the sweeping judgment seemed to be the end of every hope of Israel's salvation and the fulfillment of God's promises (cf. 3:18), much of the book appears in the mode of prayer: 1) 1:11, which represents a wailing confession of sin (cf. v. 18); 2) 3:8, with its anguish when God "shuts out my prayer" (cf. Jer. 7:16; Lam. 3:43-54); 3) 3:55-59, where Jeremiah cries to God for relief, or 3:60-66, where he seeks for recompense to the enemies (which Jer. 50,51 guarantees); and 4) 5:1-22, with its appeal to heaven for restored mercy (which Jer. 30–33 assures), based on the confidence that God is faithful (3:23).

A fifth feature relates to Christ. Jeremiah's tears (3:48,49) compare with Jesus' weeping over the same city of Jerusalem (Matt. 23:37-39; Luke 19:41-44). Though God was the judge and executioner, it was a grief to Him to bring this destruction. The statement "In all their affliction, He [God] was afflicted" (Is. 63:9) was true in principle. God will one day wipe away all tears (Is. 25:8; Rev. 7:17; 21:4) when sin shall be no more.

A sixth theme is an implied warning to all who read this book. If God did not hesitate to judge His beloved people (Deut. 32:10), what will He do to the nations of the world who reject His Word?

Interpretive Challenges

Certain details pose initial difficulties. Among them are: 1) imprecatory prayers for judgment on other sinners (1:21-22; 3:64-66); 2) the reason for God shutting out prayer (3:8); and 3) the necessity of judgment that is so severe (cf. 1:1,14; 3:8).

Outline

In the first 4 chapters, each verse begins in an acrostic pattern, i.e., using the 22 letters of the Hebrew alphabet in sequence. Chapters 1, 2, and 4 have 22 verses corresponding to 22 letters, while chap. 3 employs each letter for 3 consecutive verses until there are 22 trios, or 66 verses. Chapter 5 is not written alphabetically, although it simulates the pattern in that it has 22 verses. An acrostic order, such as in Ps. 119 (where all 22 Hebrew letters are used in series of 8 verses each), was used to aid memorization. The structure of the book ascends and descends from the great confession in 3:22-24, "Great is His faithfulness," which is the literal center of the book.

Outline

I. The First Lament: Jerusalem's Devastation (1:1-22)
  A. Jeremiah's Sorrow (1:1-11)
  B. Jerusalem's Sorrow (1:12-22)
II. The Second Lament: The Lord's Anger Explained (2:1-22)
  A. The Lord's Perspective (2:1-10)
  B. A Human Perspective (2:11-19)
  C. Jeremiah's Prayer (2:20-22)
III. The Third Lament: Jeremiah's Griefs Expressed (3:1-66)
  A. His Distress (3:1-20)
  B. His Hope (3:21-38)
  C. His Counsel/Prayer (3:39-66)
IV. The Fourth Lament: God's Wrath Detailed (4:1-22)
  A. For Jerusalem (4:1-20)
  B. For Edom (4:21,22)
V. The Fifth Lament: The Remnant's Prayers (5:1-22)
  A. To Be Remembered by the Lord (5:1-18)
  B. To Be Restored by the Lord (5:19-22)

Jerusalem in Affliction

1 How lonely sits the city
That was full of people!
[a]*How* like a widow is she,
Who *was* great among the nations!
The [b]princess among the provinces
Has become a [1]slave!

2 She [c]weeps bitterly in the [d]night,
Her tears *are* on her cheeks;
Among all her lovers
She has none to comfort *her.*
All her friends have dealt
treacherously with her;
They have become her enemies.

3 [e]Judah has gone into captivity,
Under affliction and hard
servitude;
[f]She dwells among the [2]nations,
She finds no [g]rest;
All her persecutors overtake her in
dire straits.

4 The roads to Zion mourn
Because no one comes to the [3]set
feasts.
All her gates are [h]desolate;
Her priests sigh,
Her virgins are afflicted,
And she *is* in bitterness.

5 Her adversaries [i]have become [4]the
master,
Her enemies prosper;
For the LORD has afflicted her
[j]Because of the multitude of her
transgressions.
Her [k]children have gone into
captivity before the enemy.

6 And from the daughter of Zion
All her splendor has departed.
Her princes have become like deer
That find no pasture,
That [5]flee without strength
Before the pursuer.

7 In the days of her affliction and
roaming,
Jerusalem [l]remembers all her
pleasant things
That she had in the days of old.
When her people fell into the hand
of the enemy,
With no one to help her,
The adversaries saw her
And mocked at her [6]downfall.

8 [m]Jerusalem has sinned gravely,
Therefore she has become [7]vile.
All who honored her despise her
Because [n]they have seen her
nakedness;
Yes, she sighs and turns away.

9 Her uncleanness *is* in her skirts;
She [o]did not consider her destiny;
Therefore her collapse was
awesome;
She had no comforter.
"O LORD, behold my affliction,
For *the* enemy is exalted!"

10 The adversary has spread his hand
Over all her [8]pleasant things;
For she has seen [p]the nations enter
her [9]sanctuary,
Those whom You commanded
[q]Not to enter Your assembly.

11 All her people sigh,
[r]They [1]seek bread;

CHAPTER 1

1 [a] Is. 47:7-9 [b] 1 Kin. 4:21; Ezra 4:20; Jer. 31:7 [1] Lit. *forced laborer*
2 [c] Jer. 13:17 [d] Job 7:3
3 [e] Jer. 52:27 [f] Lam. 2:9 [g] Deut. 28:65 [2] *Gentiles*
4 [h] Is. 27:10 [3] *appointed*
5 [i] Deut. 28:43 [j] Jer. 30:14, 15; Dan. 9:7, 16 [k] Jer. 52:28 [4] Lit. *her head*
6 [5] Lit. *are gone*
7 [l] Ps. 137:1 [6] Vg. *Sabbaths*
8 [m] [1 Kin. 8:46] [n] Jer. 13:22; Ezek. 16:37; Hos. 2:10 [7] LXX, Vg. *moved or removed*
9 [o] Deut. 32:29; Is. 47:7; Jer. 5:31
10 [p] Ps. 74:4-8; Is. 64:10, 11; Jer. 51:51 [q] Deut. 23:3; Neh. 13:1 [8] *desirable* [9] *holy place,* the temple
11 [r] Jer. 38:9; 52:6 [1] *hunt food*

1:1-22 How lonely sits the city. Jerusalem was lonely, its people mourning (v. 2), forsaken by formerly friendly nations (v. 2), in captivity (v. 3), uprooted from their land (v. 3), their temple violated (v. 10). The multitude of sins (vv. 5,8) had brought this judgment from the righteous God (v. 18).

1:1 *How* like a widow. Verses 1-11 vividly portray the city like a bereft and desolate woman, as often in other Scriptures (cf. Ezek. 16,23; Mic. 4:10,13). **a slave.** Judah was taken captive to serve as slaves in Babylon.

1:2 She has none to comfort *her*. This ominous theme is mentioned 4 other times (vv. 9,16,17,21). **lovers…friends…have become her enemies.** This refers to the heathen nations allied to Judah, and their idols whom Judah "loved" (Jer. 2:20-25). Some later joined as enemies against her (2 Kin. 24:2,7; Ps. 137:7).

1:3 captivity. Ca. 586 B.C. as in Jer. 39,40,52. There had been two deportations earlier, in 605 B.C. and 597 B.C. (cf. Introduction: Author and Date).

1:4 Zion. This represents the place where Jehovah dwells, the mount on which the temple was built. **set feasts.** Passover, Pentecost (Feast of Weeks) and Tabernacles (cf. Ex. 23; Lev. 23). **priests sigh.** These were among those left in Judah before fleeing to Egypt (Jer. 43), or possibly exiles in Babylon who mourned from afar (cf. v. 3).

1:5 the multitude of her transgressions. This was the cause of the judgment (cf. Jer. 40:3; Dan. 9:7,16).

1:8 become vile. This could refer to either the vile, wretched estate of continued sin and its ruinous consequences through judgment, or to being "moved, removed," as the LXX and Vg. translate it. Probably the former is correct, as befits the third and fourth lines, i.e., a despised, shameful, naked condition in contrast to her former splendor (cf. v. 6b).

1:9 Her uncleanness *is* in her skirts. A graphic description of the flow of spiritual uncleanness reaching the bottom of her dress (cf. Lev. 15:19-33).

1:10 enter her sanctuary. This was true of the Ammonites and Moabites (Deut. 23:3; Neh. 13:1,2). If the heathen were not allowed to enter for worship, much less were they tolerated to loot and destroy. On a future day, the nations will come to worship (Zech. 14:16).

They have given their [2]valuables
for food to restore life.
"See, O LORD, and consider,
For I am scorned."

12 "*Is it* nothing to you, all you who
[3]pass by?
Behold and see
[s]If there is any sorrow like my
sorrow,
Which has been brought on me,
Which the LORD has inflicted
In the day of His fierce anger.

13 "From above He has sent fire into
my bones,
And it overpowered them;
He has [t]spread a net for my feet
And turned me back;
He has made me desolate
And faint all the day.

14 "The[u] yoke of my transgressions
was [4]bound;
They were woven together by His
hands,
And thrust upon my neck.
He made my strength fail;
The Lord delivered me into the
hands of *those whom* I am not
able to withstand.

15 "The Lord has trampled underfoot all
my mighty *men* in my midst;
He has called an assembly against
me
To crush my young men;
[v]The Lord trampled *as* in a winepress
The virgin daughter of Judah.

16 "For these *things* I weep;
My eye, [w]my eye overflows with
water;
Because the comforter, who should
restore my life,
Is far from me.
My children are desolate
Because the enemy prevailed."

17 [x]Zion [5]spreads out her hands,
But no one comforts her;
The LORD has commanded
concerning Jacob
That those [y]around him *become* his
adversaries;
Jerusalem has become an unclean
thing among them.

18 "The LORD is [z]righteous,
For I [a]rebelled against His
[6]commandment.
Hear now, all peoples,
And behold my sorrow;
My virgins and my young men
Have gone into captivity.

19 "I called for my lovers,
But they deceived me;
My priests and my elders
Breathed their last in the city,
While they sought food
To restore their life.

20 "See, O LORD, that I *am* in distress;
My [b]soul[7] is troubled;
My heart is overturned within me,
For I have been very rebellious.
[c]Outside the sword bereaves,
At home *it is* like death.

21 "They have heard that I sigh,
But no one comforts me.
All my enemies have heard of my
trouble;
They are [d]glad that You have done
it.
Bring on [e]the day You have
[8]announced,
That they may become like me.

22 "Let[f] all their wickedness come
before You,
And do to them as You have done
to me
For all my transgressions;
For my sighs *are* many,
And my heart *is* faint."

11 [2] *desirable things*
12 [s] Dan. 9:12 [3] Lit. *pass by this way*
13 [t] Ezek. 12:13; 17:20
14 [u] Deut. 28:48 [4] So with MT, Tg.; LXX, Syr., Vg. *watched over*
15 [v] Is. 63:3; [Rev. 14:19]
16 [w] Ps. 69:20; Eccl. 4:1; Jer. 13:17; Lam. 2:18
17 [x] [Is. 1:15]; Jer. 4:31 [y] 2 Kin. 24:2-4; Jer. 12:9 [5] Prays
18 [z] Neh. 9:33; Ps. 119:75; Dan. 9:7, 14 [a] 1 Sam. 12:14, 15; Jer. 4:17 [6] Lit. *mouth*
20 [b] Job 30:27; Is. 16:11; Jer. 4:19; Lam. 2:11; Hos. 11:8 [c] Deut. 32:25; Ezek. 7:15 [7] Lit. *inward parts*
21 [d] Ps. 35:15; Jer. 48:27; 50:11; Lam. 2:15; Obad. 12 [e] Is. 13; [Jer. 46] [8] *proclaimed*
22 [f] Neh. 4:4, 5; Ps. 109:15; 137:7, 8; Jer. 30:16

1:11 See, O LORD. The description of the devastated widow ends with a plea for God's mercy.

1:12 all you who pass by. Here was the pathetic appeal of Jerusalem for some compassion even from strangers!

1:13 fire into my bones. This emphasizes the penetrating depth of the judgment. **turned me back.** God's purpose was to bring repentance.

1:14 yoke of my transgressions...by His hands. Once the farmer had put the yoke on the animal's neck, he would control it with the reins in his hands. So God, who has brought Jerusalem under yoke-bondage to Babylon, still controlled His people.

1:15 an assembly against me. Not the usual assembly for a solemn feast; rather the army of Babylon for destruction. **in a winepress.** Speaks of forcing blood to burst forth like juice from crushed grapes. Comparable language is used in Rev. 14:20 and 19:15 in regard to God's final wrath.

1:17 unclean. This refers to a menstruous woman, shamed, separated from her husband and the temple (cf. vv. 8,9 and Lev. 15:19ff.).

1:18 The LORD is righteous...I rebelled. The true sign of repentance was to justify God and condemn oneself.

1:21,22 Bring on the day. A prayer that God will likewise bring other ungodly people into judgment, especially Babylon (cf. 2:20-22; 3:64-66; 4:21,22). Such prayers are acceptable against the enemies of God (cf. Ps. 109:14,15).

1:22 come before You. Cf. Rev. 16:19.

God's Anger with Jerusalem

2 How the Lord has covered the daughter of Zion
With a [a]cloud in His anger!
[b]He cast down from heaven to the earth
[c]The beauty of Israel,
And did not remember [d]His footstool
In the day of His anger.

2 The Lord has swallowed up and has [e]not pitied
All the dwelling places of Jacob.
He has thrown down in His wrath
The strongholds of the daughter of Judah;
He has brought *them* down to the ground;
[f]He has profaned the kingdom and its princes.

3 He has cut off in fierce anger
Every [1]horn of Israel;
[g]He has drawn back His right hand
From before the enemy.
[h]He has blazed against Jacob like a flaming fire
Devouring all around.

4 [i]Standing like an enemy, He has bent His bow;
With His right hand, like an adversary,
He has slain [j]all *who were* pleasing to His eye;
On the tent of the daughter of Zion,
He has poured out His fury like fire.

5 [k]The Lord was like an enemy.
He has swallowed up Israel,
He has swallowed up all her palaces;
[l]He has destroyed her strongholds,
And has increased mourning and lamentation
In the daughter of Judah.

6 He has done violence [m]to His [2]tabernacle,
[n]*As if it were* a garden;
He has destroyed His place of assembly;
The LORD has caused
The appointed feasts and Sabbaths to be forgotten in Zion.
In His burning indignation He has [o]spurned the king and the priest.

7 The Lord has spurned His altar,
He has [p]abandoned His sanctuary;
He has [3]given up the walls of her palaces
Into the hand of the enemy.
[q]They have made a noise in the house of the LORD
As on the day of a set feast.

8 The LORD has [4]purposed to destroy
The [r]wall of the daughter of Zion.
[s]He has stretched out a line;
He has not withdrawn His hand from destroying;
Therefore He has caused the rampart and wall to lament;
They languished together.

9 Her gates have sunk into the ground;
He has destroyed and [t]broken her bars.
[u]Her king and her princes *are* among the [5]nations;
[v]The Law *is* no *more*,
And her [w]prophets find no [6]vision from the LORD.

10 The elders of the daughter of Zion
[x]Sit on the ground *and* keep silence;
[7]They [y]throw dust on their heads
And [z]gird themselves with sackcloth.
The virgins of Jerusalem
Bow their heads to the ground.

CHAPTER 2

1 [a][Lam. 3:44] [b]Matt. 11:23 [c]2 Sam. 1:19 [d]1 Chr. 28:2; Ps. 99:5; Ezek. 43:7
2 [e]Ps. 21:9; Lam. 3:43 [f]Ps. 89:39, 40; Is. 43:28
3 [g]Ps. 74:11; Jer. 21:4, 5 [h]Ps. 89:46 [1]Strength
4 [i]Is. 63:10 [j]Ezek. 24:25
5 [k]Jer. 30:14 [l]2 Kin. 25:9; Jer. 52:13; Lam. 2:2
6 [m]Ps. 80:12; 89:40; Is. 5:5; Jer. 7:14 [n]Is. 1:8; Jer. 52:13 [o]Is. 43:28 [2]Lit. *booth*
7 [p]Ezek. 24:21 [q]Ps. 74:3-8 [3]*delivered*
8 [r]Jer. 52:14 [s][2 Kin. 21:13; Is. 34:11; Amos 7:7-9] [4]*determined*
9 [t]Jer. 51:30 [u]Deut. 28:36; 2 Kin. 24:15; 25:7; Lam. 1:3; 4:20 [v]2 Chr. 15:3 [w]Ps. 74:9; Mic. 3:6 [5]*Gentiles* [6]Prophetic revelation
10 [x]Job 2:13; Is. 3:26 [y]Job 2:12; Ezek. 27:30 [z]Is. 15:3; Jon. 3:6-8 [7]A sign of mourning

2:1 How the Lord has. Much in Lam. 2 depicts God's judgment in vivid portrayals. He covered the Judeans with a cloud (v. 1), withdrew His hand of protection (v. 3), bent His bow and had slain with His arrows (v. 4), and stretched out a surveyor's line to mark walls to be destroyed (v. 8). He will work a rebuilding of Jerusalem in the future kingdom (Zech. 2:1-13). **The beauty of Israel.** Likely refers to Mt. Zion and the temple (cf. Pss. 48:2; 50:2; Is. 60:13; 64:11; Ezek. 16:14; Dan. 11:45). **His footstool.** Refers to the ark of the covenant as indicated by 1 Chr. 28:2 and Pss. 99:5; 132:7.

2:2 He has thrown down. The Lord had cast down the bastions of Judah's defense, as He told Jeremiah He would do from the outset of his ministry (Jer. 1:10).

2:3 Every horn. Serves as an emblem of power, as exemplified in animals.

2:6-11 Tragedy comes to everything and everyone through sin. The account mentions the temple where Israelites came to worship (v. 6), feasts and Sabbaths (v. 6), leaders such as the king and priests (v. 6), His altar and holy places (v. 7), city walls (v. 8), the law (v. 9), and children in the family (v. 11).

2:6,7 Cf. 1:4.

2:7 noise in the house of the LORD as on the day of a set feast. A shout of triumph in the captured temple resembled the joyous celebrations in the same place at the solemn feasts.

11 [a]My eyes fail with tears,
My [8]heart is troubled;
[b]My [9]bile is poured on the ground
Because of the destruction of the daughter of my people,
Because [c]the children and the infants
Faint in the streets of the city.

12 They say to their mothers,
"Where *is* grain and wine?"
As they swoon like the wounded
In the streets of the city,
As their life is poured out
In their mothers' bosom.

13 How shall I [d]console[1] you?
To what shall I liken you,
O daughter of Jerusalem?
What shall I compare with you,
that I may comfort you,
O virgin daughter of Zion?
For your ruin *is* spread wide as the sea;
Who can heal you?

14 Your [e]prophets have seen for you
False and deceptive visions;
They have not [f]uncovered your iniquity,
To bring back your captives,
But have envisioned for you false
[g]prophecies and delusions.

15 All who [2]pass by [h]clap *their* hands at you;
They hiss [i]and shake their heads
At the daughter of Jerusalem:
"*Is* this the city that is called
[j]'The perfection of beauty,
The joy of the whole earth'?"

16 [k]All your enemies have opened their mouth against you;
They hiss and gnash *their* teeth.
They say, [l]"We have swallowed *her* up!
Surely this *is* the [m]day we have waited for;
We have found *it*, [n]we have seen *it!*"

11 [a] Ps. 6:7; Lam. 3:48 [b] Job 16:13; Ps. 22:14 [c] Lam. 4:4 [8] Lit. *inward parts* [9] Lit. *liver* **13** [d] Lam. 1:12; Dan. 9:12 [1] Or *bear witness to* **14** [e] Jer. 2:8; 23:25-29; 29:8, 9; 37:19; Ezek. 13:2 [f] Is. 58:1; Ezek. 23:36; Mic. 3:8 [g] Jer. 23:33-36; Ezek. 22:25, 28 **15** [h] 1 Kin. 9:8; Job 27:23; Jer. 18:16; Ezek. 25:6; Nah. 3:19 [i] 2 Kin. 19:21; Ps. 44:14 [j] [Ps. 48:2; 50:2]; Ezek. 16:14 [2] Lit. *pass by this way* **16** [k] Job 16:9, 10; Ps. 22:13; Lam. 3:46 [l] Ps. 56:2; 124:3; Jer. 51:34 [m] Lam. 1:21; [Obad. 12-15] [n] Ps. 35:21

17 The LORD has done what He [o]purposed;
He has fulfilled His word
Which He commanded in days of old.
He has thrown down and has not pitied,
And He has caused an enemy to
[p]rejoice over you;
He has exalted the [3]horn of your adversaries.

18 Their heart cried out to the Lord,
"O wall of the daughter of Zion,
[q]Let tears run down like a river day and night;
Give yourself no relief;
Give [4]your eyes no rest.

19 "Arise, [r]cry out in the night,
At the beginning of the watches;
[s]Pour out your heart like water
before the face of the Lord.
Lift your hands toward Him
For the life of your young children,
Who faint from hunger [t]at the head of every street."

20 "See, O LORD, and consider!
To whom have You done this?
[u]Should the women eat their offspring,
The children [5]they have cuddled?
Should the priest and prophet be slain
In the sanctuary of the Lord?

21 "Young [v] and old lie
On the ground in the streets;
My virgins and my young men
Have fallen by the [w]sword;
You have slain *them* in the day of Your anger,
You have slaughtered *and* not pitied.

22 "You have invited as to a feast day
[x]The terrors that surround me.
In the day of the LORD's anger
There was no refugee or survivor.
[y]Those whom I have borne and brought up
My enemies have [z]destroyed."

17 [o] Lev. 26:16 [p] Ps. 38:16 [3] Strength **18** [q] Jer. 14:17; Lam. 1:16 [4] Lit. *the daughter of your eye* **19** [r] Ps. 119:147 [s] 1 Sam. 1:15; Ps. 42:4; 62:8 [t] Is. 51:20 **20** [u] Lev. 26:29; Deut. 28:53; Jer. 19:9; Lam. 4:10; Ezek. 5:10 [5] Vg. *a span long* **21** [v] 2 Chr. 36:17; Jer. 6:11 [w] Jer. 18:21 **22** [x] Ps. 31:13; Is. 24:17; Jer. 6:25 [y] Hos. 9:12 [z] Jer. 16:2-4; 44:7

2:11,12 This description of Babylon's invasion depicted the reality of a hungry child dying in its mother's arms as a result.

2:14 False and deceptive visions. As Jer. 23:16,17 indicates, these lies spoke of peace and comfort, not judgment. Cf. Jer. 23:30-40 to see how such lying led to destruction.

2:17 He has fulfilled his Word. The enemy that gloats in vv. 15,16 should recognize that the destruction was the work of a sovereign God. This verse is the focal point of the chapter (cf. Jer. 51:12).

2:18 wall of the daughter of Zion. The penetrated walls of Jerusalem cried out in anguish that they had been broached by the Babylonians.

2:20 See, O LORD, and consider! The chapter closes by placing the issue before God. **women eat their offspring.** Hunger became so desperate in the 18-month siege that women resorted to the unbelievable—even eating their children (cf. 4:10; Lev. 26:29; Deut. 28:53,56,57; Jer. 19:9).

2:21 the day of Your anger. This describes the complete slaughter, as does 2 Chr. 36:17.

The Prophet's Anguish and Hope

3 I *am* the man *who* has seen affliction
by the rod of His wrath.
2 He has led me and made *me* walk
In darkness and not *in* light.
3 Surely He has turned His hand
against me
Time and time again throughout
the day.

4 He has aged [a]my flesh and my
skin,
And [b]broken my bones.
5 He has besieged me
And surrounded *me* with bitterness
and [1]woe.
6 [c]He has set me in dark places
Like the dead of long ago.

7 [d]He has hedged me in so that I
cannot get out;
He has made my chain heavy.
8 Even [e]when I cry and shout,
He shuts out my prayer.
9 He has blocked my ways with
hewn stone;
He has made my paths crooked.

10 [f]He *has been* to me a bear lying in
wait,
Like a lion in [2]ambush.
11 He has turned aside my ways and
[g]torn me in pieces;
He has made me desolate.
12 He has bent His bow
And [h]set me up as a target for the
arrow.

13 He has caused [i]the [3]arrows of His
quiver
To pierce my [4]loins.
14 I have become the [j]ridicule of all
my people—
[k]Their taunting song all the day.
15 [l]He has filled me with bitterness,
He has made me drink
wormwood.

16 He has also broken my teeth [m]with
gravel,
And [5]covered me with ashes.
17 You have moved my soul far from
peace;
I have forgotten [6]prosperity.
18 [n]And I said, "My strength and my
hope
Have perished from the LORD."

19 Remember my affliction and
roaming,
[o]The wormwood and the [7]gall.
20 My soul still remembers
And [8]sinks within me.
21 This I recall to my mind,
Therefore I have [p]hope.

22 [q]*Through* the LORD's mercies we are
not consumed,
Because His compassions [r]fail not.
23 *They are* new [s]every morning;
Great *is* Your faithfulness.
24 "The LORD *is* my [t]portion," says my
soul,
"Therefore I [u]hope in Him!"

25 The LORD *is* good to those who
[v]wait for Him,
To the soul *who* seeks Him.
26 *It is* good that *one* should [w]hope
[x]and wait quietly
For the salvation of the LORD.
27 [y]*It is* good for a man to bear
The yoke in his youth.

28 [z]Let him sit alone and keep silent,
Because *God* has laid *it* on him;
29 [a]Let him put his mouth in the
dust—
There may yet be hope.

CHAPTER 3
4 [a]Job 16:8 [b]Ps. 51:8; Is. 38:13
5 [1]*hardship* or *weariness*
6 [c][Ps. 88:5, 6; 143:3]
7 [d]Job 3:23; 19:8; Hos. 2:6
8 [e]Job 30:20; Ps. 22:2
10 [f]Is. 38:13 [2]Lit. *secret places*
11 [g]Job 16:12, 13; Jer. 15:3; Hos. 6:1
12 [h]Job 7:20; 16:12; Ps. 38:2
13 [i]Job 6:4 [3]Lit. *sons of* [4]Lit. *kidneys*
14 [j]Ps. 22:6, 7; 123:4; Jer. 20:7 [k]Job 30:9; Ps. 69:12; Lam. 3:63
15 [l]Jer. 9:15
16 [m][Prov. 20:17] [5]Lit. *bent me down in*
17 [6]Lit. *good*
18 [n]Ps. 31:22
19 [o]Jer. 9:15; Lam. 3:5, 15 [7]*bitterness*
20 [8]Lit. *bowed down*
21 [p]Ps. 130:7
22 [q][Mal. 3:6] [r]Ps. 78:38; [Jer. 3:12; 30:11]
23 [s]Is. 33:2; Zeph. 3:5
24 [t]Ps. 16:5; 73:26; 119:57; Jer. 10:16 [u]Jer. 17:17; Mic. 7:7
25 [v]Ps. 130:6; Is. 30:18
26 [w][Rom. 4:16-18] [x]Ex. 14:13; Ps. 37:7; Is. 7:4
27 [y]Ps. 94:12
28 [z]Jer. 15:17
29 [a]Job 42:6

3:1-20 the man *who* has seen affliction. Jeremiah's distress in such tragedy comes from God, referred to as "He" throughout this section. Even the righteous experience "the rod of God's wrath."

3:8 He shuts out my prayer. Cf. v. 44. God's non-response to Jeremiah's prayers was not because Jeremiah was guilty of personal sin (cf. Ps. 66:18); rather, it was due to Israel's perpetual sin without repentance (Jer. 19:15). God's righteousness to judge that sin must pursue its course (Jer. 7:16, and *see note there*; 11:14). Jeremiah knew that, yet prayed, wept (vv. 48-51), and longed to see repentance.

3:16 broken my teeth with gravel. This refers to the grit that often mixed with bread baked in ashes as was common in the E (cf. Prov. 20:17).

3:21 This I recall. The prophet referred to what followed as he reviewed God's character.

3:21-33 The relentless sorrow over Judah's judgment drove Jeremiah to consider the grace, mercy, and compassion of God. The tone of his thinking changed dramatically.

3:22 mercies. This Heb. word, used about 250 times in the OT, refers to God's gracious love. It is a comprehensive term that encompasses love, grace, mercy, goodness, forgiveness, truth, compassion, and faithfulness.

3:22-24 His compassions fail not. As bleak as the situation of judgment had become, God's covenant lovingkindness was always present (cf. vv. 31,32), and His incredible faithfulness always endured so that Judah would not be destroyed forever (cf. Mal. 3:6).

3:23 Great *is* Your faithfulness. The bedrock of faith is the reality that God keeps all His promises according to His truthful, faithful character.

3:27 The yoke in his youth. This speaks of the duty from God, including disciplinary training, that Jeremiah received in his youth (cf. Jer. 1:6,7).

3:29 mouth in the dust. A term which pictures submission.

30 [b]Let him give *his* cheek to the one
who strikes him,
And be full of reproach.

31 [c]For the Lord will not cast off
forever.
32 Though He causes grief,
Yet He will show compassion
According to the multitude of His
mercies.
33 For [d]He does not afflict [9]willingly,
Nor grieve the children of men.

34 To crush under one's feet
All the prisoners of the earth,
35 To turn aside the justice *due* a man
Before the face of the Most High,
36 Or subvert a man in his cause—
[e]The Lord does not approve.

37 Who *is* he [f]*who* speaks and it
comes to pass,
When the Lord has not commanded
it?
38 *Is it* not from the mouth of the
Most High
That [g]woe and well-being proceed?
39 [h]Why should a living man
[1]complain,
[i]A man for the punishment of his
sins?

40 Let us search out and examine our
ways,
And turn back to the LORD;
41 [j]Let us lift our hearts and hands
To God in heaven.
42 [k]We have transgressed and rebelled;
You have not pardoned.

43 You have covered *Yourself* with
anger
And pursued us;
You have slain *and* not pitied.
44 You have covered Yourself with a
cloud,
That prayer should not pass
through.
45 You have made us an [l]offscouring
and refuse
In the midst of the peoples.

46 [m]All our enemies
Have opened their mouths against
us.
47 [n]Fear and a snare have come upon
us,
[o]Desolation and destruction.
48 [p]My eyes overflow with rivers of
water
For the destruction of the daughter
of my people.

49 [q]My eyes flow and do not cease,
Without interruption,
50 Till the LORD from heaven
[r]Looks down and sees.
51 My eyes bring suffering to my soul
Because of all the daughters of my
city.

52 My enemies [s]without cause
Hunted me down like a bird.
53 They [2]silenced my life [t]in the pit
And [u]threw [3]stones at me.
54 [v]The waters flowed over my head;
[w]I said, "I am cut off!"

55 [x]I called on Your name, O LORD,
From the lowest [y]pit.
56 [z]You have heard my voice:
"Do not hide Your ear
From my sighing, from my cry for
help."
57 You [a]drew near on the day I called
on You,
And said, [b]"Do not fear!"

58 O Lord, You have [c]pleaded the
case for my soul;
[d]You have redeemed my life.
59 O LORD, You have seen [4]*how* I am
wronged;

30 [b] Job 16:10; Is. 50:6; [Matt. 5:39; 26:67]; Mark 14:65; Luke 22:63
31 [c] Ps. 77:7; 94:14; [Is. 54:7-10]
33 [d] [Ps. 119:67, 71, 75; Is. 28:21; Ezek. 33:11; Heb. 12:10] [9] Lit. *from His heart*
36 [e] [Jer. 22:3; Hab. 1:13]
37 [f] [Ps. 33:9-11]
38 [g] Job 2:10; [Is. 45:7]; Jer. 32:42; Amos 3:6; [James 3:10, 11]
39 [h] Prov. 19:3 [i] Jer. 30:15; Mic. 7:9; [Heb. 12:5, 6] [1] Or *murmur*
41 [j] Ps. 86:4
42 [k] Neh. 9:26; Jer. 14:20; Dan. 9:5
45 [l] 1 Cor. 4:13
46 [m] Job 30:9, 10; Ps. 22:6-8; Lam. 2:16
47 [n] Is. 24:17, 18; Jer. 48:43, 44 [o] Is. 51:19
48 [p] Jer. 4:19; 14:17; Lam. 2:11
49 [q] Ps. 77:2; Jer. 14:17
50 [r] Ps. 80:14; Is. 63:15; Lam. 5:1
52 [s] Ps. 35:7, 19
53 [t] Jer. 37:16 [u] Dan. 6:17 [2] LXX *put to death* [3] Lit. *a stone on*
54 [v] Ps. 69:2; Jon. 2:3-5 [w] Is. 38:10
55 [x] Ps. 130:1; Jon. 2:2 [y] Jer. 38:6-13
56 [z] Ps. 3:4
57 [a] James 4:8 [b] Is. 41:10, 14; Dan. 10:12
58 [c] Ps. 35:1; Jer. 51:36 [d] Ps. 71:23
59 [4] Lit. *my wrong*

3:30 give *his* cheek. The Lord Jesus did this (cf. Is. 50:6; 1 Pet. 2:23).

3:33-47 God had a just basis for judgment.

Other Laments

Job 3:3-26; 7:1-21; 10:1-22
Psalms (over 40) e.g. Pss. 3, 120
Jeremiah 15:15-18; 17:14-18; 18:19-23
Ezek. 19:1-14; 27:1-36; 32:1-21

3:38 This contrasted God's sovereign bestowal of judgment with blessing.

3:40,41 turn back to the LORD. The solution to Judah's judgment was to repent, looking to God for relief and restoration.

3:42 not pardoned. God judged their sin righteously.

3:48-51 My eyes. The summary of Jeremiah's sorrow.

3:52-63 My enemies. Jeremiah's description of persecution sounded much like the time when his enemies at the palace had cast him into a cistern (cf. v. 53; Jer. 38:4-6). God reassured him in answer to prayer (v. 57), and redeemed him (v. 58) by sending Ebed-melech to rescue him (cf. Jer. 38:7-13). Jeremiah pleads for justice to be rendered on those enemies (vv. 59-63).

3:58 You have redeemed my life. Jeremiah said this to encourage others to trust God.

[e]Judge my case.
60 You have seen all their vengeance,
All their [f]schemes against me.

61 You have heard their reproach, O LORD,
All their schemes against me,
62 The lips of my enemies
And their whispering against me all the day.
63 Look at their [g]sitting down and their rising up;
I *am* their taunting song.

64 [h]Repay them, O LORD,
According to the work of their hands.
65 Give them [5]a veiled heart;
Your curse *be* upon them!
66 In Your anger,
Pursue and destroy them
[i]From under the heavens of the [j]LORD.

The Degradation of Zion

4 How the gold has become dim!
How changed the fine gold!
The stones of the sanctuary are [1]scattered
At the head of every street.

2 The precious sons of Zion,
[2]Valuable as fine gold,
How they are [3]regarded [a]as clay pots,
The work of the hands of the potter!

3 Even the jackals present their breasts
To nurse their young;
But the daughter of my people *is* cruel,
[b]Like ostriches in the wilderness.

4 The tongue of the infant clings
To the roof of its mouth for thirst;
[c]The young children ask for bread,
But no one breaks *it* for them.

5 Those who ate delicacies
Are desolate in the streets;
Those who were brought up in scarlet
[d]Embrace ash heaps.

6 The punishment of the iniquity of the daughter of my people
Is greater than the punishment of the [e]sin of Sodom,
Which was [f]overthrown in a moment,
With no hand to help her!

7 Her [4]Nazirites were [5]brighter than snow
And whiter than milk;
They were more ruddy in body than rubies,
Like sapphire in their [6]appearance.

8 *Now* their appearance is blacker than soot;
They go unrecognized in the streets;
[g]Their skin clings to their bones,
It has become as dry as wood.

9 *Those* slain by the sword are better off
Than *those* who die of hunger;
For these [h]pine away,
Stricken *for lack* of the fruits of the [i]field.

10 The hands of the [j]compassionate women
Have [7]cooked their [k]own children;
They became [l]food for them
In the destruction of the daughter of my people.

11 The LORD has fulfilled His fury,
[m]He has poured out His fierce anger.
[n]He kindled a fire in Zion,
And it has devoured its foundations.

12 The kings of the earth,
And all inhabitants of the world,
Would not have believed
That the adversary and the enemy
Could [o]enter the gates of Jerusalem—

59 [e] Ps. 9:4
60 [f] Jer. 11:19
63 [g] Ps. 139:2
64 [h] Ps. 28:4; Jer. 11:20; 2 Tim. 4:14
65 [5] A Jewish tradition *sorrow of*
66 [i] Deut. 25:19; Jer. 10:11 [j] Ps. 8:3

CHAPTER 4

1 [1] Lit. *poured out*
2 [a] Is. 30:14; Jer. 19:11; [2 Cor. 4:7] [2] Lit. *Weighed against* [3] *reckoned*
3 [b] Job 39:14-17
4 [c] Ps. 22:15
5 [d] Job 24:8
6 [e] Ezek. 16:48 [f] Gen. 19:25; Jer. 20:16
7 [4] Or *nobles* [5] Or *purer* [6] Lit. *polishing*
8 [g] Job 19:20; Ps. 102:5
9 [h] Lev. 26:39; Ezek. 24:23 [i] Jer. 16:4
10 [j] Lev. 26:29; Deut. 28:57; 2 Kin. 6:29; Jer. 19:9; Lam. 2:20; Ezek. 5:10 [k] Is. 49:15 [l] Deut. 28:57 [7] *boiled*
11 [m] Jer. 7:20; Lam. 2:17; Ezek. 22:31 [n] Deut. 32:22; Jer. 21:14
12 [o] Jer. 21:13

3:64-66 Repay them. This imprecatory prayer for divine vengeance would be answered in Babylon's fall (cf. Is. 46,47; Jer. 50,51; Dan. 5). It would also have its ultimate answer at the Great White Throne (Rev. 20:11-15).

4:1 gold has become dim. The gold adornment of the temple, looted by the conquerors, lost its luster with a coating of dust where they scattered the remains.

4:3 nurse their young. Even worthless jackals by nature nurse their young, but under the severities of conquest, Israelite women were unable to nurse their babies (cf. v. 4). **Like ostriches.** Birds which are notable for ignoring their young (cf. Job 39:14-16).

4:6 the sin of Sodom. Their sin was homosexuality. The fact that the suffering of Jerusalem was prolonged, while that of even Sodom was swift, marks it as the greater punishment (cf. 1 Pet. 4:17).

4:7,8 Nazirites. Those who were the purest, most devout (cf. Num. 6), strong, healthy, and noble of the people became dirty, weak and ignoble.

4:10 cooked...children. Cf. 2:20, and *see note there.*

13 [p]Because of the sins of her prophets
And the iniquities of her priests,
[q]Who shed in her midst
The blood of the just.

14 They wandered blind in the streets;
[r]They have defiled themselves with
blood,
[s]So that no one would touch their
garments.

15 They cried out to them,
"Go away, [t]unclean!
Go away, go away,
Do not touch us!"
When they fled and wandered,
Those among the nations said,
"They shall no longer dwell *here.*"

16 The [8]face of the LORD scattered
them;
He no longer regards them.
[u]*The people* do not respect the priests
Nor show favor to the elders.

17 Still [v]our eyes failed us,
Watching vainly for our help;
In our watching we watched
For a nation *that* could not save *us.*

18 [w]They [9]tracked our steps
So that we could not walk in our
streets.
[x]Our end was near;
Our days were over,
For our end had come.

19 Our pursuers were [y]swifter
Than the eagles of the heavens.
They pursued us on the mountains
And lay in wait for us in the
wilderness.

13 [p] Jer. 5:31; Ezek. 22:26, 28; Zeph. 3:4 [q] Jer. 2:30; 26:8, 9; Matt. 23:31
14 [r] Jer. 2:34 [s] Num. 19:16
15 [t] Lev. 13:45, 46
16 [u] Lam. 5:12 [8] Tg. *anger*
17 [v] 2 Kin. 24:7
18 [w] 2 Kin. 25:4 [x] Ezek. 7:2, 3, 6; Amos 8:2 [9] Lit. *hunted*
19 [y] Deut. 28:49
20 [z] Gen. 2:7 [a] Jer. 52:9; Ezek. 12:13
21 [b] Ps. 83:3-6 [c] Jer. 25:15; Obad. 10
22 [d] [Is. 40:2; Jer. 33:7, 8] [e] Ps. 137:7 [1] *has been completed*

CHAPTER 5

1 [a] Ps. 89:50 [b] Ps. 79:4; Lam. 2:15
2 [c] Ps. 79:1
3 [d] Ex. 22:24; Jer. 15:8; 18:21
5 [e] Deut. 28:48; Jer. 28:14 [1] Lit. *necks*
6 [f] Gen. 24:2 [g] Hos. 9:3; 12:1 [h] Jer. 2:18; Hos. 5:13

20 The [z]breath of our nostrils, the
anointed of the LORD,
[a]Was caught in their pits,
Of whom we said, "Under his
shadow
We shall live among the nations."

21 Rejoice and be glad, O daughter of
[b]Edom,
You who dwell in the land of Uz!
[c]The cup shall also pass over to
you
And you shall become drunk and
make yourself naked.

22 [d]*The punishment of* your iniquity [1]is
accomplished,
O daughter of Zion;
He will no longer send you into
captivity.
[e]He will punish your iniquity,
O daughter of Edom;
He will uncover your sins!

A Prayer for Restoration

5 Remember, [a]O LORD, what has
come upon us;
Look, and behold [b]our reproach!
2 [c]Our inheritance has been turned
over to aliens,
And our houses to foreigners.
3 We have become orphans and
waifs,
Our mothers *are* like [d]widows.
4 We pay for the water we drink,
And our wood comes at a price.
5 [e]*They* pursue at our [1]heels;
We labor *and* have no rest.
6 [f]We have given our hand [g]*to* the
Egyptians
And the [h]Assyrians, to be satisfied
with bread.

Beyond Lamentations

Hope of Restoration

1. Isaiah 35:1-10
2. Jeremiah 30:1–31:40
3. Ezekiel 37:1-28
4. Hosea 3:5, 14:1-9
5. Joel 3:18-21
6. Amos 9:11-15
7. Micah 7:14-20
8. Zephaniah 3:14-20
9. Zechariah 14:1-11
10. Malachi 4:1-6

4:15 Go away. The people chased the false leaders away.

4:16 The face of the LORD. This was symbolic of divine anger. The Jews had to face up to God.

4:20 The breath of our nostrils. This was a term for God, the life-giver.

4:21,22 Edom...land of Uz. In effect God said, "Laugh all you want now. Your judgment will come" (cf. Jer. 25:15-29).

5:1 Remember, O LORD. Jeremiah prayed for mercy on his people. He summed up the nation's wounds and woes (vv. 1-10), recalled woes of specific groups (vv. 11-14), showed why God judged (vv. 15-18), and interceded for the renewal of Israel (vv. 19-22; cf. Mic. 7:18-20).

5:6 the Egyptians...the Assyrians. The Jews submitted to unholy alliances, thus expressing trust in men for protection and goods (cf. Jer. 2:18,36).

7 [i]Our fathers sinned *and are* no more,
But we bear their iniquities.
8 Servants rule over us;
There is none to deliver *us* from
their hand.
9 We get our bread *at the risk* of our
lives,
Because of the sword in the
wilderness.

10 Our skin is hot as an oven,
Because of the fever of famine.
11 They [j]ravished the women in Zion,
The maidens in the cities of Judah.
12 Princes were hung up by their
hands,
And elders were not respected.
13 Young men [k]ground at the
millstones;
Boys staggered under *loads of* wood.
14 The elders have ceased *gathering at*
the gate,
And the young men from their
[l]music.

15 The joy of our heart has ceased;
Our dance has turned into
[m]mourning.
16 [n]The crown has fallen *from* our
head.
Woe to us, for we have sinned!
17 Because of this our heart is faint;
[o]Because of these *things* our eyes
grow dim;
18 Because of Mount Zion which is
[p]desolate,
With foxes walking about on it.

19 You, O LORD, [q]remain forever;
[r]Your throne from generation to
generation.
20 [s]Why do You forget us forever,
And forsake us for so long a time?
21 [t]Turn us back to You, O LORD, and
we will be [2]restored;
Renew our days as of old,
22 Unless You have utterly rejected
us,
And are very angry with us!

7 [i] Jer. 31:29
11 [j] Is. 13:16; Zech. 14:2
13 [k] Judg. 16:21
14 [l] Is. 24:8; Jer. 7:34
15 [m] Jer. 25:10; Amos 8:10
16 [n] Job 19:9; Ps. 89:39; Jer. 13:18
17 [o] Ps. 6:7
18 [p] Is. 27:10
19 [q] Ps. 9:7; Hab. 1:12 [r] Ps. 45:6
20 [s] Ps. 13:1; 44:24
21 [t] Ps. 80:3, 7, 19; Jer. 31:18 [2] *returned*

5:7 This is a cynical proverb from Jer. 31:29 and Ezek. 18:2.

5:8-18 A list of horrors that had befallen Judah.

5:16 The crown has fallen. Israel lost its line of kings wearing the crown. The Davidic monarchy was temporarily over and will not be resumed until Christ comes as King (Jer. 23:5-8; Ezek. 37:24-28; Rev. 19:1-21).

5:19 Your throne from generation. Here is the high point of this chapter. Jeremiah was consoled by the fact that God always sits on His sovereign throne ruling over the universe from heaven (Pss. 45:6; 93:2; 102:12; 103:19; Dan. 4:3,34,35).

5:21 Turn us back to You. God must Himself initiate and enable any return to Him (cf. Ps. 80:3,7,19; Jer. 24:7; 31:18; John 6:44,65). **Renew our days.** The intercessions of vv. 19-22 will yet be fulfilled in the New Covenant restoration of Israel (cf. Jer. 30–33, and *see notes there*).

5:21,22 This plea was not made with anger. The humble closing prayer sought God, who can never reject His people forever, to be faithful in restoring them (cf. Jer. 31:35-37; 33:25,26). In fact, their godly sorrow over sin was the beginning of that restoration, which would be completed by turning to God in faith and obedience.

The Book of
EZEKIEL

Title

The book has always been named for its author, Ezekiel (1:3; 24:24), who is nowhere else mentioned in Scripture. His name means "strengthened by God," which, indeed, he was for the prophetic ministry to which God called him (3:8,9). Ezekiel uses visions, prophecies, parables, signs, and symbols to proclaim and dramatize the message of God to His exiled people.

Author and Date

If the "thirtieth year" of 1:1 refers to Ezekiel's age, he was 25 when taken captive and 30 when called into ministry. Thirty was the age when priests commenced their office, so it was a notable year for Ezekiel. His ministry began in 593/92 B.C. and extended at least 22 years until 571/70 B.C. (cf. 25:17). He was a contemporary of both Jeremiah (who was about 20 years older) and Daniel (who was the same age), whom he names in 14:14,20; 28:3 as an already well known prophet. Like Jeremiah (Jer. 1:1) and Zechariah (cf. Zech. 1:1 with Neh. 12:16), Ezekiel was both a prophet and a priest (1:3). Because of his priestly background, he was particularly interested in and familiar with the temple details; so God used him to write much about them (8:1–11:25; 40:1–47:12).

Ezekiel and his wife (who is mentioned in 24:15-27) were among 10,000 Jews taken captive to Babylon in 597 B.C. (2 Kin. 24:11-18). They lived in Tel-Abib (3:15) on the bank of the Chebar River, probably SE of Babylon. Ezekiel writes of his wife's death in exile (Ezek. 24:18), but the book does not mention Ezekiel's death, which rabbinical tradition suggests occurred at the hands of an Israelite prince whose idolatry he rebuked around 560 B.C.

The author received his call to prophesy in 593 B.C. (1:2), in Babylon ("the land of the Chaldeans"), during the fifth year of King Jehoiachin's captivity, which began in 597 B.C. Frequently, Ezekiel dates his prophecies from 597 B.C. (8:1; 20:1; 24:1; 26:1; 29:1; 30:20; 31:1; 32:1,17; 33:21; 40:1). He also dates the message in 40:1 as 573/72, the 14th year after 586 B.C., i.e., Jerusalem's final fall. The last dated utterance of Ezekiel was in 571/70 B.C. (29:17).

Prophecies in chaps. 1–28 are in chronological order. In 29:1, the prophet regresses to a year earlier than in 26:1. But from 30:1 on (cf. 31:1; 32:1,17), he is close to being strictly chronological.

Background and Setting

From the historical perspective, Israel's united kingdom lasted more than 110 years (ca. 1043–931 B.C.), through the reigns of Saul, David, and Solomon. Then the divided kingdom, Israel (north) and Judah (south), extended from 931 B.C. to 722/21 B.C. Israel fell to Assyria in 722/21 B.C. leaving Judah, the surviving kingdom for 135 years, which fell to Babylon in 605–586 B.C.

In the more immediate setting, several features were strategic. Politically, Assyria's vaunted military might crumbled after 626 B.C., and the capital, Nineveh, was destroyed in 612 B.C. by the Babylonians and Medes (cf. Nahum). The neo-Babylonian empire had flexed its muscles since Nabopolassar took the throne in 625 B.C., and Egypt, under Pharaoh Necho II, was determined to conquer what she could. Babylon smashed Assyria in 612–605 B.C., and registered a decisive victory against Egypt in 605 B.C. at Carchemish, leaving, according to the Babylonian Chronicle, no survivors. Also in 605 B.C., Babylon, led by Nebuchadnezzar, began the conquest of Jerusalem and the deportation of captives, among them Daniel (Dan. 1:2). In Dec., 598 B.C., he again besieged Jerusalem, and on Mar. 16, 597 B.C. took possession. This time, he took captive Jehoiachin and a group of 10,000, including Ezekiel (2 Kin. 24:11-18). The final destruction of Jerusalem and the conquest of Judah, including the third deportation, came in 586 B.C.

Religiously, King Josiah (ca. 640–609 B.C.) had instituted reforms in Judah (cf. 2 Chr. 34). Tragically, despite his effort, idolatry had so dulled the Judeans that their awakening was only "skin deep" overall. The Egyptian army killed Josiah as it crossed Palestine in 609 B.C., and the Jews plunged on in sin toward judgment under Jehoahaz (609 B.C.), Jehoiakim [Eliakim] (609–598 B.C.), Jehoiachin (598–597 B.C.), and Zedekiah (597–586 B.C.).

Domestically, Ezekiel and the 10,000 lived in exile in Babylonia (2 Kin. 24:14), more as colonists than captives, being permitted to farm tracts of land under somewhat favorable conditions (Jer. 29). Ezekiel even had his own house (3:24; 20:1).

Prophetically, false prophets deceived the exiles with assurances of a speedy return to Judah (13:3,16; Jer. 29:1). From 593–585 B.C., Ezekiel warned that their beloved Jerusalem would be destroyed and their exile prolonged, so there was no hope of immediate return. In 585 B.C., an escapee from Jerusalem, who had evaded the Babylonians, reached Ezekiel with the first news that the city had fallen in 586 B.C., about 6 months earlier (33:21). That dashed the false hopes of any immediate deliverance for the exiles, so the remainder of Ezekiel's prophecies related to Israel's future restoration to its homeland and the final blessings of the messianic kingdom.

Historical and Theological Themes

The "glory of the Lord" is central to Ezekiel, appearing in 1:28; 3:12,23; 10:4,18; 11:23; 43:4,5; 44:4. The book includes graphic descriptions of the disobedience of Israel and Judah, despite God's kindness (chap. 23; cf. chap. 16). It shows God's desire for Israel to bear fruit which He can bless; however, selfish indulgence had left Judah ready for judgment, like a torched vine (chap. 15). References are plentiful to Israel's idolatry and its consequences, such as Pelatiah dropping dead (11:13), a symbolic illustration of overall disaster for the people.

Many picturesque scenes illustrate spiritual principles. Among these are Ezekiel eating a scroll (chap. 2); the faces on 4 angels representing aspects of creation over which God rules (1:10); a "barbershop" scene (5:1-4); graffiti on temple walls reminding readers of what God really wants in His dwelling place, namely holiness and not ugliness (8:10); and sprinkled hot coals depicting judgment (10:2,7).

Chief among the theological themes are God's holiness and sovereignty. These are conveyed by frequent contrast of His bright glory against the despicable backdrop of Judah's sins (1:26-28; often in chaps. 8–11; and 43:1-7). Closely related is God's purpose of glorious triumph so that all may "know that I am the LORD." This divine monogram, God's signature authenticating His acts, is mentioned more than 60 times, usually with a judgment (6:7; 7:4), but occasionally after the promised restoration (34:27; 36:11,38; 39:28).

Another feature involves God's angels carrying out His program behind the scenes (1:5-25; 10:1-22). A further important theme is God's holding each individual accountable for pursuing righteousness (18:3-32).

Ezekiel also stresses sinfulness in Israel (2:3-7; 8:9,10) and other nations (throughout chaps. 25–32). He deals with the necessity of God's wrath to deal with sin (7:1-8; 15:8); God's frustration of man's devices to escape from besieged Jerusalem (12:1-13; cf. Jer. 39:4-7); and God's grace pledged in the Abrahamic Covenant (Gen. 12:1-3) being fulfilled by restoring Abraham's people to the land of the covenant (chaps. 34,36–48; cf. Gen. 12:7). God promises to preserve a remnant of Israelites through whom He will fulfill His restoration promises and keep His inviolate Word.

Interpretive Challenges

Ezekiel uses extensive symbolic language, as did Isaiah and Jeremiah. This raises the question as to whether certain portions of Ezekiel's writings are to be taken literally or figuratively, e.g., being bound with ropes, 3:25; whether the prophet was taken bodily to Jerusalem, 8:1-3; how individual judgment can be worked out in chap. 18 when the wicked elude death in 14:22,23 and some of the godly die in an invasion, 21:3,4; how God would permit a faithful prophet's wife to die (24:15-27); when some of the judgments on other nations will occur (chaps. 25–32); whether the temple in chaps. 40–46 will be a literal one and in what form; and how promises of Israel's future relate to God's program with the church. These issues will be treated in the study notes.

Outline

The book can be largely divided into sections about condemnation/retribution and then consolation/restoration. A more detailed look divides the book into 4 sections. First, are prophecies on the ruin of Jerusalem (chaps. 1–24). Second, are prophecies of retribution on nearby nations (chaps. 25–32), with a glimpse at God's future restoration of Israel (28:25,26). Thirdly, there is a transition chapter (33) which gives instruction concerning a last call for Israel to repent. Finally, the fourth division includes rich expectations involving God's future restoration of Israel (chaps. 34–48).

Outline

- I. Prophecies of Jerusalem's Ruin (1:1–24:27)
  - A. Preparation and Commission of Ezekiel (1:1–3:27)
    - 1. Divine appearance to Ezekiel (1:1-28)
    - 2. Divine assignment to Ezekiel (2:1–3:27)
  - B. Proclamation of Jerusalem's Condemnation (4:1–24:27)
    - 1. Signs of coming judgment (4:1–5:4)
    - 2. Messages concerning judgment (5:5–7:27)
    - 3. Visions concerning abomination in the city and temple (8:1–11:25)
    - 4. Explanations of judgment (12:1–24:27)
- II. Prophecies of Retribution to the Nations (25:1–32:32)
  - A. Ammon (25:1-7)
  - B. Moab (25:8-11)
  - C. Edom (25:12-14)
  - D. Philistia (25:15-17)
  - E. Tyre (26:1–28:19)
  - F. Sidon (28:20-24)
    - Excursus: The Restoration of Israel (28:25,26)
  - G. Egypt (29:1–32:32)
- III. Provision for Israel's Repentance (33:1-33)
- IV. Prophecies of Israel's Restoration (34:1-48:35)
  - A. Regathering of Israel to the Land (34:1–37:28)
    - 1. Promise of a True Shepherd (34:1-31)
    - 2. Punishment of the nations (35:1–36:7)
    - 3. Purposes of restoration (36:8-38)
    - 4. Pictures of restoration—dry bones and two sticks (37:1-28)
  - B. Removal of Israel's Enemies from the Land (38:1–39:29)
    - 1. Invasion of Gog to plunder Israel (38:1-16)
    - 2. Intervention of God to protect Israel (38:17–39:29)
  - C. Reinstatement of True Worship in Israel (40:1–46:24)
    - 1. New temple (40:1–43:12)
    - 2. New worship (43:13–46:24)
  - D. Redistribution of the Land in Israel (47:1–48:35)
    - 1. Position of the river (47:1-12)
    - 2. Portions for the tribes (47:13–48:35)

Ezekiel's Vision of God

1 Now it came to pass in the thirtieth
year, in the fourth *month*, on the fifth
day of the month, as I *was* among the captives by [a]the River Chebar, *that* [b]the heavens were opened and I saw [c]visions[1] of
God. 2 On the fifth *day* of the month, which
was in the fifth year of King Jehoiachin's
captivity, 3 the word of the LORD came expressly to Ezekiel the priest, the son of
Buzi, in the land of the [2]Chaldeans by the
River Chebar; and [d]the hand of the LORD
was upon him there.
4 Then I looked, and behold, [e]a whirlwind
was coming [f]out of the north, a great cloud
with raging fire engulfing itself; and brightness *was* all around it and radiating out of its
midst like the color of amber, out of the
midst of the fire. 5 [g]Also from within it *came*
the likeness of four living creatures. And
[h]this *was* their appearance: they had [i]the
likeness of a man. 6 Each one had four faces,
and each one had four wings. 7 Their [3]legs
were straight, and the soles of their feet *were*
like the soles of calves' feet. They sparkled
[j]like the color of burnished bronze. 8 [k]The
hands of a man *were* under their wings on
their four sides; and each of the four had
faces and wings. 9 Their wings touched one
another. *The creatures* did not turn when they
went, but each one went straight [l]forward.
10 As for [m]the likeness of their faces, *each*
[n]had the face of a man; each of the four
had [o]the face of a lion on the right side,
[p]each of the four had the face of an ox on
the left side, [q]and each of the four had the
face of an eagle. 11 Thus *were* their faces.
Their wings stretched upward; two *wings*
of each one touched one another, and [r]two
covered their bodies. 12 And [s]each one
went straight forward; they went wherever the spirit wanted to go, and they did not
turn when they went.
13 As for the likeness of the living creatures, their appearance *was* like burning
coals of fire, [t]like the appearance of torches going back and forth among the living
creatures. The fire was bright, and out of
the fire went lightning. 14 And the living
creatures ran back and forth, [u]in appearance like a flash of lightning.
15 Now as I looked at the living creatures, behold, [v]a wheel *was* on the earth beside each living creature with its four faces.
16 [w]The appearance of the wheels and their
workings *was* [x]like the color of beryl, and
all four had the same likeness. The appearance of their workings *was*, as it were, a
wheel in the middle of a wheel. 17 When
they moved, they went toward any one of
four directions; they did not turn aside
when they went. 18 As for their rims, they
were so high they were awesome; and
their rims *were* [y]full of eyes, all around the

CHAPTER 1

1 [a]Ezek. 3:15, 23; 10:15 [b]Matt. 3:16; Mark 1:10; Luke 3:21; Acts 7:56; 10:11; Rev. 4:1; 19:11 [c]Ex. 24:10; Num. 12:6; Is. 1:1; 6:1; Ezek. 8:3; Dan. 8:1, 2 [1]So with MT, LXX, Vg.; Syr., Tg. *a vision*
3 [d]1 Kin. 18:46; 2 Kin. 3:15; Ezek. 3:14, 22 [2]Or *Babylonians*, and so elsewhere in the book
4 [e]Is. 21:1; Jer. 23:19; 25:32; Ezek. 13:11, 13 [f]Jer. 1:14
5 [g]Ezek. 10:15, 17, 20; Rev. 4:6-8 [h]Ezek. 10:8 [i]Ezek. 10:14
7 [j]Dan. 10:6; Rev. 1:15 [3]Lit. *feet*
8 [k]Ezek. 10:8, 21
9 [l]Ezek. 1:12; 10:20-22
10 [m]Ezek. 10:14; Rev. 4:7
[n]Num. 2:10 [o]Num. 2:3 [p]Num. 2:18 [q]Num. 2:25
11 [r]Is. 6:2; Ezek. 1:23
12 [s]Ezek. 10:11, 22
13 [t]Ps. 104:4; Rev. 4:5
14 [u]Zech. 4:10; [Matt. 24:27; Luke 17:24]
15 [v]Ezek. 10:9
16 [w]Ezek. 10:9, 10 [x]Dan. 10:6
18 [y]Ezek. 10:12; [Zech. 4:10]; Rev. 4:6, 8

1:1 thirtieth year. Most likely this was Ezekiel's age, since the date relative to the king's reign is given in 1:2. Thirty was the age when a priest (cf. v. 3 with Num. 4) began his priestly duties. **River Chebar.** A major canal off of the Euphrates River, S of Babylon. **visions of God.** This scene has similarities to the visions of God's throne in Rev. 4,5, where the emphasis is also on a glimpse of that throne just before judgment is released in Rev. 6–19.

1:2 fifth year. This is 593 B.C. The king, Ezekiel, and 10,000 others (2 Kin. 24:14) had been deported to Babylon in 597 B.C., Ezekiel at the age of 25.

1:3 word of the LORD...hand of the LORD. As God prepared Isaiah (Is. 6:5-13) and Jeremiah (Jer. 1:4-19), so the Lord prepares Ezekiel to receive revelation and strengthens him for his high and arduous task to speak as His prophet. **Ezekiel the priest.** *See note on v. 1.*

1:4-14 The opening vision focuses on angels surrounding God's presence.

1:4 whirlwind...fire. Judgment on Judah in a further and totally devastating phase (beyond the 597 B.C. deportation) is to come out of the N, and did come from Babylon in 588–586 (as Jer. 39,40). Its terror is depicted by a fiery whirlwind emblematic of God's judgments and the golden brightness signifying dazzling glory.

1:5 four living creatures. Four angels, most likely the cherubs in 10:1-22, appearing in the erect posture and figure of man (note face, legs, feet, hands in vv. 6-8) emerge to serve God who judges. The number 4 may have respect to the 4 corners of the earth, implying that God's angels execute His commands everywhere.

1:6 four faces. *See note on v. 10.* **four wings.** Four wings instead of two symbolize speed in performing God's will (cf. v. 14).

1:7 legs. They were not bent like an animal's, but "straight" like pillars, showing strength. **calves' feet.** This points to their stability and firm stance.

1:8 hands of a man. This is a symbol of their skillful service.

1:9 did not turn. They were able to move in any direction without needing to turn, giving swift access to do God's will. Apparently all were in harmony as to the way they moved (v. 12).

1:10 faces. These symbols identify the angels as intelligent ("man"), powerful ("lion"), servile ("ox"), and swift ("eagle").

1:12 the spirit. This refers to the divine impulse by which God moved them to do His will (cf. 1:20).

1:13 like...fire...torches. Their appearance conveyed God's glory and pure, burning justice (cf. Is. 6); judgment which they assisted in carrying out even on Israel, who had for so long hardened themselves against His patience.

1:14 Intense, relentless motion signifies God's constant work of judgment.

1:15-25 This section looks at the glory of God's throne in heaven.

1:15 a wheel. This depicts God's judgment as a war machine (like a massive chariot) moving where He is to judge. The cherubim above the ark are called chariots in 1 Chr. 28:18.

1:16 wheel in the middle of a wheel. This depicted the gigantic (v. 15, "on the earth" and "so high," v. 18) energy of the complicated revolutions of God's massive judgment machinery bringing about His purposes with unerring certainty.

1:17 did not turn aside. Cf. vv. 9,12. The judgment machine moved where the angels went (cf. vv. 19,20).

1:18 eyes. These may picture God's omniscience, i.e., perfect knowledge, given to these angelic servants so that they can act in judgment unerringly. God does nothing by blind impulse.

four of them. 19 [z]When the living creatures
went, the wheels went beside them; and
when the living creatures were lifted up
from the earth, the wheels were lifted up.
20 Wherever the spirit wanted to go, they
went, *because* there the spirit went; and the
wheels were lifted together with them, [a]for
the spirit of the [4]living creatures *was* in the
wheels. 21 When those went, *these* went;
when those stood, *these* stood; and when
those were lifted up from the earth, the
wheels were lifted up together with them,
for the spirit of the [5]living creatures *was* in
the wheels.
22 [b]The likeness of the [6]firmament above
the heads of the [7]living creatures *was* like
the color of an awesome [c]crystal, stretched
out [d]over their heads. 23 And under the firmament their wings *spread out* straight, one
toward another. Each one had two which
covered one side, and each one had two
which covered the other side of the body.
24 [e]When they went, I heard the noise of
their wings, [f]like the noise of many waters,
like [g]the voice of the Almighty, a tumult
like the noise of an army; and when they
stood still, they let down their wings. 25 A
voice came from above the firmament that
was over their heads; whenever they stood,
they let down their wings.
26 [h]And above the firmament over their
heads *was* the likeness of a throne, [i]in appearance like a sapphire stone; on the likeness of the throne *was* a likeness with the
appearance of a man high above [j]it. 27 Also
from the appearance of His waist and upward [k]I saw, as it were, the color of amber
with the appearance of fire all around
within it; and from the appearance of His
waist and downward I saw, as it were, the
appearance of fire with brightness all
around. 28 [l]Like the appearance of a rainbow in a cloud on a rainy day, so *was* the
appearance of the brightness all around it.
[m]This *was* the appearance of the likeness of
the glory of the LORD.

Ezekiel Sent to Rebellious Israel

So when I saw *it*, [n]I fell on my face, and
I heard a voice of One speaking.
2 And He said to me, "Son of man,
[a]stand on your feet, and I will speak to
you." 2 Then [b]the Spirit entered me when
He spoke to me, and set me on my feet;
and I heard Him who spoke to me. 3 And
He said to me: "Son of man, I am sending

19 [z] Ezek. 10:16, 17
20 [a] Ezek. 10:17 [4] Lit. *living creature;* LXX, Vg. *spirit of life;* Tg. *creatures*
21 [5] See note at v. 20
22 [b] Ezek. 10:1 [c] Rev. 4:6 [d] Ezek. 10:1 [6] Or *expanse* [7] So with LXX, Tg., Vg.; MT *living creature*
24 [e] Ezek. 3:13; 10:5 [f] Ezek. 43:2; Dan. 10:6; Rev. 1:15 [g] Job 37:4, 5; Ps. 29:3, 4; 68:33
26 [h] Ezek. 10:1 [i] Ex. 24:10, 16; Ezek. 8:4; 11:22, 23; 43:4, 5 [j] Ezek. 8:2
27 [k] Ezek. 8:2
28 [l] [Gen. 9:13]; Rev. 4:3; 10:1 [m] Ezek. 3:23; 8:4 [n] Gen. 17:3; Ezek. 3:23; Dan. 8:17; Acts 9:4; Rev. 1:17

CHAPTER 2

1 [a] Dan. 10:11; Acts 9:6
2 [b] Ezek. 3:24; Dan. 8:18

1:19,20 spirit. *See note on 1:12.*

1:24 noise of many waters. This imagery could have in mind a thunderous rush of heavy rain or the washing of surf on rocks (cf. 43:2; Rev. 1:15; 14:2; 19:6).

1:25 voice. No doubt this is the "voice of the Almighty" (v. 24), since God's throne (v. 25) was "over their heads."

1:26 a throne. Cf. Ps. 103:19; Rev. 4:2-8. **a man.** The Godhead appears in the likeness of humanity, though God is a spirit (John 4:24). The Messiah, God incarnate, is the representative of the "fullness of the Godhead" (Col. 2:9), so this can be a prelude to the incarnation of Messiah in His character as Savior and Judge (cf. Rev. 19:11-16).

1:28 the glory of the LORD. That glory shines fully in the person of Jesus Christ (cf. 2 Cor. 4:6), which is a constant theme in Ezekiel.

2:1 fell on my face. John, in Rev. 1:17, had the same reaction to seeing the glory of the Lord. **Son of man.** A term used over 90 times by Ezekiel to indicate his humanness.

2:2 the Spirit entered me. What God commands a servant to do (v. 1), He gives power to fulfill by His Spirit (cf. 3:14; Zech. 4:6). This pictures the selective empowering by the Holy Spirit to enable an individual for special service to the Lord, which occurred frequently in the OT. For examples see 11:5; 37:1; Num. 24:2; Judg. 3:10; 6:34; 11:29; 13:25; 1 Sam. 10:10; 16:13,14; 19:20; 2 Chr. 15:1; Luke 4:18.

Dates in Ezekiel

Event/Verse	Year	Month/Day	Date	Year
1. Call (1:2)	5	4/5	July 31	593
2. Temple tour (8:1)	6	6/5	Sept. 17	592
3. Elders' visit (20:1)	7	5/10	Aug. 17	591
4. Siege begins (24:1)	9	10/10	Jan. 15	588
5. Against Tyre (26:1)	11	?/1	?	587/586
6. Against Egypt (29:1)	10	10/12	Jan. 7	587
7. Against Tyre, Egypt (29:17)	27	1/1	April 26	571
8. Against Pharaoh (30:20)	11	1/7	April 29	587
9. Against Pharaoh (31:1)	11	3/1	June 21	587
10. Lament for Pharaoh (32:1)	12	12/1	March 3	585
11. Pharaoh to Sheol (32:17)	12	?/15	?	586/585
12. Refugee report on Fall of Jerusalem (33:21)	12	10/5	Jan. 8	585
13. Vision of Future Temple Begins (40:1)	25	1/10	April 28	573

you to the children of Israel, to a rebellious
nation that has [c]rebelled against Me; [d]they
and their fathers have transgressed against
Me to this very day. **4** [e]For *they are* [1]impu-
dent and stubborn children. I am sending
you to them, and you shall say to them,
'Thus says the Lord GOD.' **5** [f]As for them,
whether they hear or whether they
refuse—for they *are* a [g]rebellious house—
yet they [h]will know that a prophet has
been among them.
6 "And you, son of man, [i]do not be
afraid of them nor be afraid of their words,
though [j]briers and thorns *are* with you and
you dwell among scorpions; [k]do not be
afraid of their words or dismayed by their
looks, [l]though they *are* a rebellious house.
7 [m]You shall speak My words to them,
whether they hear or whether they refuse,
for they *are* rebellious. **8** But you, son of
man, hear what I say to you. Do not be rebellious like that rebellious house; open
your mouth and [n]eat what I give you."
9 Now when I looked, there was [o]a hand
stretched out to me; and behold, [p]a scroll
of a book *was* in it. **10** Then He spread it before me; and *there was* writing on the inside
and on the outside, and written on it *were*
lamentations and mourning and woe.

3

Moreover He said to me, "Son of man,
eat what you find; [a]eat this scroll, and
go, speak to the house of Israel." **2** So I
opened my mouth, and He caused me to
eat that scroll.
3 And He said to me, "Son of man, feed
your belly, and fill your stomach with this
scroll that I give you." So I [b]ate, and it was
in my mouth [c]like honey in sweetness.
4 Then He said to me: "Son of man, go to
the house of Israel and speak with My

3 [c]Ezek. 5:6; 20:8, 13, 18 [d]1 Sam. 8:7, 8; Jer. 3:25; Ezek. 20:18, 21, 30
4 [e]Ps. 95:8; Is. 48:4; Jer. 5:3; 6:15; Ezek. 3:7 [1]Lit. *stiff-faced and hard-hearted sons*
5 [f]Is. 6:9, 10; Ezek. 3:11, 26, 27; [Matt. 10:12-15; Acts 13:46] [g]Ezek. 3:26 [h]Ezek. 33:33; [Luke 10:10, 11; John 15:22]
6 [i]Is. 51:12; Jer. 1:8, 17; Ezek. 3:9; Luke 12:4 [j][2 Sam. 23:6, 7; Is. 9:18]; Jer. 6:28; Ezek. 28:24; Mic. 7:4 [k]Ezek. 3:9; [1 Pet. 3:14] [l]Ezek. 3:9, 26, 27
7 [m]Jer. 1:7, 17; [Ezek. 3:10, 17]
8 [n]Ezek. 3:1-3; Rev. 10:9
9 [o]Jer. 1:9; [Ezek. 8:3] [p]Jer. 36:2; Ezek. 3:1; Rev. 5:1-5; 10:8-11

CHAPTER 3

1 [a]Ezek. 2:8, 9
3 [b]Jer. 15:16; Rev. 10:9 [c]Ps. 19:10; 119:103
6 [d]Jon. 3:5-10; Matt. 11:21
7 [e]John 15:20, 21 [f]Ezek. 2:4 [1]Lit. *strong of forehead*
9 [g]Is. 50:7; Jer. 1:18; Mic. 3:8 [h]Jer. 1:8, 17; Ezek. 2:6
11 [i]Ezek. 2:5, 7
12 [j]1 Kin. 18:12; Ezek. 8:3; Acts 8:39 [k]Ezek. 1:28; 8:4
13 [l]Ezek. 1:24; 10:5
14 [m]2 Kin. 3:15; Ezek. 1:3; 8:1 [2]Or *anger*
15 [n]Job 2:13; Ps. 137:1

words to them. **5** For you *are* not sent to a
people of unfamiliar speech and of hard
language, *but* to the house of Israel, **6** not to
many people of unfamiliar speech and of
hard language, whose words you cannot
understand. Surely, [d]had I sent you to
them, they would have listened to you.
7 But the house of Israel will not listen to
you, [e]because they will not listen to Me;
[f]for all the house of Israel *are* [1]impudent
and hard-hearted. **8** Behold, I have made
your face strong against their faces, and
your forehead strong against their foreheads. **9** [g]Like adamant stone, harder than
flint, I have made your forehead; [h]do not
be afraid of them, nor be dismayed at their
looks, though they *are* a rebellious house."
10 Moreover He said to me: "Son of man,
receive into your heart all My words that I
speak to you, and hear with your ears.
11 And go, get to the captives, to the children of your people, and speak to them
and tell them, [i]'Thus says the Lord GOD,'
whether they hear, or whether they
refuse."
12 Then [j]the Spirit lifted me up, and I
heard behind me a great thunderous voice:
"Blessed *is* the [k]glory of the LORD from His
place!" **13** *I* also *heard* the [l]noise of the
wings of the living creatures that touched
one another, and the noise of the wheels
beside them, and a great thunderous noise.
14 So the Spirit lifted me up and took me
away, and I went in bitterness, in the [2]heat
of my spirit; but [m]the hand of the LORD
was strong upon me. **15** Then I came to the
captives at Tel Abib, who dwelt by the
River Chebar; and [n]I sat where they sat,
and remained there astonished among
them seven days.

2:5 The people cannot plead ignorance.

2:6 briers and thorns…scorpions. Cf. 3:7,9; 22:29. These are figures of speech God used to describe the people of Judah whose obstinate rejection of His Word was like the barbs of thorns and stings of scorpions to Ezekiel. The wicked were often so called (cf. 2 Sam. 23:6; Song 2:2; Is. 9:18).

2:8 open your mouth and eat. Ezekiel was to obey the command, not literally eating a scroll (vv. 9,10), but in a spiritual sense by receiving God's message so that it became an inward passion. Cf. also 3:1-3,10 and Jer. 15:16.

2:10 writing on the inside and…outside. Scrolls were normally written on one side only, but this judgment message was so full it required all the available space (cf. Zech. 5:3; Rev. 5:1) to chronicle the suffering and sorrow that sin had brought, as recorded in chaps. 2–32.

3:1-3 eat this scroll…So I ate. God's messenger must first internalize God's truth for himself, then preach it.

3:3 like honey. Even though the message was judgment on Israel, the scroll was sweet because it was God's Word (cf. Pss. 19:10; 119:103) and because it vindicated God in holiness, righteousness, glory, and faithfulness, in which Jeremiah also delighted (Jer. 15:16). Bitterness also was experienced by the prophet (3:14) in this message of judgment confronting Judah's rebellion (v. 9). The Apostle John records a similar bittersweet experience with the Word of God in Rev. 10:9,10.

3:7 Cf. John 15:20.

3:8,9 I have made your face strong. What God commands ("do not be afraid") He gives sufficiency to do ("I have made") so God will enable the prophet to live up to his name (which means "strengthened by God"). Cf. 2:2; 3:14,24; Is. 41:10; Jer. 1:8,17.

3:9 rebellious. It is sad to observe that the exile and affliction did not make the Jews more responsive to God; rather, they were hardened by their sufferings. God gave Ezekiel a "hardness" to surpass the people and sustain his ministry as prophet to the exiles.

3:12,14 the Spirit lifted me up. This is a phrase used to describe the prophet being elevated to a heavenly vision, as in the experiences of 8:3 and 11:1.

3:14 bitterness. *See note on 3:3.*

3:15 the captives. Tel Abib was the main city for the Jewish captives, who may have included some of the 10 tribes taken long before in the conquering of the northern kingdom of Israel in 722 B.C., as 2 Kin. 17:6 may indicate ("Habor" is the same river as Chebar). **remained…seven days.** Ezekiel sat with the sorrowing people for 7

Ezekiel Is a Watchman

16 Now it [o]came to pass at the end of
seven days that the word of the LORD came
to me, saying, 17 [p]"Son of man, I have
made you [q]a watchman for the house of Israel; therefore hear a word from My
mouth, and give them [r]warning from Me:
18 When I say to the wicked, 'You shall
surely die,' and you give him no warning,
nor speak to warn the wicked from his
wicked way, to save his life, that same
wicked *man* [s]shall die in his iniquity; but
his blood I will require at your hand.
19 Yet, if you warn the wicked, and he does
not turn from his wickedness, nor from his
wicked way, he shall die in his iniquity;
[t]but you have delivered your soul.

20 "Again, when a [u]righteous *man* turns
from his righteousness and commits iniquity, and I lay a stumbling block before
him, he shall die; because you did not give
him warning, he shall die in his sin, and
his righteousness which he has done shall
not be remembered; but his blood I will require at your hand. 21 Nevertheless if you
warn the righteous *man* that the righteous
should not sin, and he does not sin, he
shall surely live because he took warning;
also you will have delivered your soul."
22 [v]Then the hand of the LORD was upon
me there, and He said to me, "Arise, go out
[w]into the plain, and there I shall talk with
you."
23 So I arose and went out into the plain,

16 [o] Jer. 42:7
17 [p] Ezek. 33:7-9 [q] Is. 52:8; 56:10; Jer. 6:17 [r] [Lev. 19:17; Prov. 14:25]; Is. 58:1
18 [s] Ezek. 33:6; [John 8:21, 24]
19 [t] Is. 49:4, 5; Ezek. 14:14, 20; Acts 18:6; 20:26; 1 Tim. 4:16
20 [u] Ps. 125:5; Ezek. 18:24; 33:18; Zeph. 1:6
22 [v] Ezek. 1:3 [w] Ezek. 8:4

days, the usual period for manifesting deep grief (cf. Job 2:13). He identified with them in their suffering (cf. Ps. 137:1), thus trying to win their trust when he spoke God's Word.

3:17 a watchman. This role was spiritually analogous to the role of watchmen on a city wall, vigilant to spot the approach of an enemy and warn the residents to muster a defense. The prophet gave timely warnings of approaching judgment. The work of a watchman is vividly set forth in 2 Sam. 18:24-27 and 2 Kin. 9:17-20. *See notes on 33:1-16.*

3:18-21 Cf. chap. 18, and *see notes there.*

3:18 the wicked...him...his. The emphasis of singular pronouns was on individuals. The ministry of Habakkuk (2:1), Jeremiah (6:17), and Isaiah (56:10) were more national than individual. Ezekiel's ministry was more personal, focused on individual responsibility to trust and obey God. Disobedience or obedience to God's messages was a matter of life or death; Ezek. 18:1-20 is particularly devoted to this emphasis. **no warning...die.** Men are not to assume that ignorance, even owing to the negligence of preachers, will be any excuse to save them from divine punishment. Cf. Rom. 2:12. **save his life.** This refers to physical death, not eternal damnation, though that would be a consequence for many. In the Pentateuch, God had commanded death for many violations of His law and warned that it could be a consequence of any kind of consistent sin (cf. Josh. 1:16-18). The people of Israel had long abandoned that severe standard of purification, so God took execution back into His own hands, as in the destruction of Israel, Judah, and Jerusalem. On the other hand, God had also promised special protection and life to the obedient. Cf. 18:9-32; 33:11-16; Prov. 4:4; 7:2; Amos 5:4,6.

3:18,20 his blood I will require. Though each sinner is responsible for his own sin (cf. 18:1-20), the prophet who is negligent in his duty to proclaim the warning message becomes, in God's sight, a manslayer when God takes that person's life. The responsibility of the prophet is serious (cf. James 3:1), and he is responsible for that person's death in the sense of Gen. 9:5. The Apostle Paul had this passage (and Ezek. 33:6,8) in view in Acts 18:6 and 20:26. Even for preachers today, there is such a warning in Heb. 13:17. Certainly the consequence for such unfaithfulness on the preacher's part includes divine chastening and loss of eternal reward (cf. 1 Cor. 4:1-5).

3:20 a righteous *man*. Here is a person who was obeying God by doing what was right, but fell into sin and God took his life in chastisement. The "stumbling block" was a stone of judgment that kills. Ps. 119:165 says: "Great peace have those who love Your law, and nothing causes them to stumble." The crushing stone always falls on the disobedient. Hebrews 12:9 says it is better to obey and "live." Cf. 1 Cor. 11:30; James 1:21, 1 John 5:16.

3:21 delivered your soul. The prophet had done his duty.

Ezekiel's Sign Experiences

(cf. Ezek. 24:24, 27)

1. Ezekiel was housebound, tied up, and mute (3:23-27).
2. Ezekiel used a clay tablet and an iron plate as illustrations in his preaching (4:1-3).
3. Ezekiel had to lie on his left side for 390 days and his right side for 40 days (4:4-8).
4. Ezekiel had to eat in an unclean manner (4:9-17).
5. Ezekiel had to shave his head and beard (5:1-4).
6. Ezekiel had to pack his bags and dig through the wall of Jerusalem (12:1-14).
7. Ezekiel had to eat his bread with quaking and drink water with trembling (12:17-20).
8. Ezekiel brandished a sharp sword and struck his hands together (21:8-17).
9. Ezekiel portrayed Israel in the smelting furnace (22:17-22).
10. Ezekiel had to cook a pot of stew (24:1-14).
11. Ezekiel could not mourn at the death of his wife (24:15-24).
12. Ezekiel was mute for a season (24:25-27).
13. Ezekiel put two sticks together and they became one (37:15-28).

and behold, [x]the glory of the LORD stood
there, like the glory which I [y]saw by the
River Chebar; [z]and I fell on my face.
24 Then [a]the Spirit entered me and set me
on my feet, and spoke with me and said to
me: "Go, shut yourself inside your house.
25 And you, O son of man, surely [b]they
will put ropes on you and bind you with
them, so that you cannot go out among
them. 26 [c]I will make your tongue cling to
the roof of your mouth, so that you shall be
mute and [d]not be [3]one to rebuke them, [e]for
they *are* a rebellious house. 27 [f]But when I
speak with you, I will open your mouth,
and you shall say to them, [g]'Thus says the
Lord GOD.' He who hears, let him hear;
and he who refuses, let him refuse; for they
are a rebellious house.

The Siege of Jerusalem Portrayed

4 "You also, son of man, take a clay
tablet and lay it before you, and portray on it a city, Jerusalem. 2 [a]Lay siege
against it, build a [b]siege wall against it,
and heap up a mound against it; set camps
against it also, and place battering rams
against it all around. 3 Moreover take for
yourself an iron plate, and set it *as* an iron
wall between you and the city. Set your
face against it, and it shall be [c]besieged,
and you shall lay siege against it. [d]This *will*
be a sign to the house of Israel.
4 "Lie also on your left side, and lay the
iniquity of the house of Israel upon it. *Ac-*
cording to the number of the days that you
lie on it, you shall bear their iniquity. 5 For
I have laid on you the years of their iniquity, according to the number of the days,
three hundred and ninety days; [e]so you
shall bear the iniquity of the house of Israel.
6 And when you have completed them, lie
again on your right side; then you shall
bear the iniquity of the house of Judah forty
days. I have laid on you a day for each year.
7 "Therefore you shall set your face toward the siege of Jerusalem; your arm *shall*
be uncovered, and you shall prophesy
against it. 8 [f]And surely I will [1]restrain you
so that you cannot turn from one side to
another till you have ended the days of
your siege.
9 "Also take for yourself wheat, barley,
beans, lentils, millet, and spelt; put them
into one vessel, and make bread of them
for yourself. *During* the number of days
that you lie on your side, three hundred
and ninety days, you shall eat it. 10 And
your food which you eat *shall be* by weight,
twenty shekels a day; from time to time
you shall eat it. 11 You shall also drink
water by measure, one-sixth of a hin; from
time to time you shall drink. 12 And you
shall eat it *as* barley cakes; and bake it
using fuel of human waste in their sight."
13 Then the LORD said, "So [g]shall the children of Israel eat their defiled bread among
the Gentiles, where I will drive them."
14 So I said, [h]"Ah, Lord GOD! Indeed I
have never defiled myself from my youth
till now; I have never eaten [i]what died of

23 [x] Ezek. 1:28; Acts 7:55 [y] Ezek. 1:1 [z] Ezek. 1:28
24 [a] Ezek. 2:2
25 [b] Ezek. 4:8
26 [c] Ezek. 24:27; Luke 1:20, 22 [d] Hos. 4:17; Amos 8:11 [e] Ezek. 2:5-7 [3] Lit. *one who rebukes*
27 [f] Ex. 4:11, 12; Ezek. 24:27; 33:22 [g] Ezek. 3:11

CHAPTER 4

2 [a] Jer. 6:6; Ezek. 21:22 [b] 2 Kin. 25:1
3 [c] Jer. 39:1, 2; Ezek. 5:2 [d] Ezek. 12:6, 11; 24:24, 27
5 [e] Num. 14:34
8 [f] Ezek. 3:25 [1] Lit. *put ropes on*
13 [g] Dan. 1:8; Hos. 9:3
14 [h] Acts 10:14 [i] Ex. 22:31; Lev. 17:15; 22:8; Ezek. 44:31

3:23 the glory of the LORD. See Introduction: Historical and Theological Themes.

3:24 shut yourself inside your house. He was to fulfill much of his ministry at home (8:1; 12:1-7), thereby limiting it to those who came to hear him there.

3:25 they will put ropes on you. These were not literal, but spiritual. On one hand, they could be the inner ropes of depressing influence which the rebellious Jews exerted on his spirit. Their perversity, like ropes, would repress his freedom in preaching. More likely, they imply the restraint that God placed on him by supernational power, so that he could only go and speak where and when God chose (cf. vv. 26,27).

3:26,27 you shall be mute. He was not to speak primarily, but to act out God's message. The prohibition was only partial, for on any occasion (v. 27) when God did open his mouth, as He often did in chaps. 5–7, he was to speak (3:22; 11:25; 12:10,19,23,28). The end of such intermittent dumbness with regard to his own people closely synchronized with Ezekiel's receiving a refugee's report of Jerusalem's fall (24:25-27; 33:21,22). He also spoke with regard to judgments on other nations (chaps. 25–32).

4:1–7:27 Here is the first series of prophecies given over a year's time, of Jerusalem's conquest by the Babylonians in 586 B.C.

4:1-3 portray…Jerusalem. Ezekiel's object lesson was to use a soft tile to create a miniature city layout of Jerusalem with walls and siege objects to illustrate Babylon's final coming siege of Jerusalem (588–586 B.C.).

4:4-6 Lie…on your left side…right side. Lying on his side, likely facing N, illustrated God's applying judgment to Israel, and facing S pointed to judgment on Judah. It is not necessary to assume that Ezekiel was in the prone position all the time. It was doubtless part of each day, as his need for preparing food (v. 9) indicates.

4:4,6 you shall bear their iniquity. Ezekiel's action was not to represent the time of Israel's sinning, but the time of its punishment.

4:5 three hundred and ninety. Each day symbolized a year (v. 6). Israel in the N was accountable during this span of time whose beginning and end is uncertain.

4:6 forty. Judah was also guilty, but the 40 cannot represent less guilt (cf. 23:11). It may extend the time beyond the 390 to 430 or they may run concurrently, but the exact timing is uncertain.

4:7 arm…uncovered. A symbol for being ready for action, as a soldier would do (cf. Is. 52:10).

4:8 I will restrain you. This was to symbolize the impossibility of the Jews being able to shake off their punishment.

4:9-13 make bread. Scarcity of food in the 18 month siege especially made necessary the mixing of all kinds of grain for bread. The "20 shekels" would be about 8 ounces, while "one-sixth of a hin" would be less than a quart. There would be minimums for daily rations. It must be noted that the command of v. 12 regarding "human waste" relates only to the fuel used to prepare the food. Bread was baked on hot stones (cf. 1 Kin. 19:6) heated by human waste because no other fuel was available. This was repulsive and polluting (cf. Deut. 23:12-14) and the Lord calls it "defiled bread" (v. 13).

4:14,15 never defiled. Ezekiel, like Daniel, had convictions to be

itself or was torn by beasts, nor has [j]abom-
inable[2] flesh ever come into my mouth."
15 Then He said to me, "See, I am giving
you cow dung instead of human waste,
and you shall prepare your bread over it."
16 Moreover He said to me, "Son of man,
surely I will cut off the [k]supply of bread in
Jerusalem; they shall [l]eat bread by weight
and with anxiety, and shall [m]drink water
by measure and with dread, 17 that they
may lack bread and water, and be dismayed with one another, and [n]waste away
because of their iniquity.

A Sword Against Jerusalem

5 "And you, son of man, take a sharp
sword, take it as a barber's razor, [a]and
pass *it* over your head and your beard;
then take scales to weigh and divide the
hair. 2 [b]You shall burn with fire one-third
in the midst of [c]the city, when [d]the days of
the siege are finished; then you shall take
one-third and strike around *it* with the
sword, and one-third you shall scatter in
the wind: I will draw out a sword after
[e]them. 3 [f]You shall also take a small number of them and bind them in the edge of
your *garment*. 4 Then take some of them
again and [g]throw them into the midst of
the fire, and burn them in the fire. From
there a fire will go out into all the house of
Israel.
5 "Thus says the Lord GOD: 'This *is* Jerusalem; I have set her in the midst of the nations and the countries all around her.
6 She has rebelled against My judgments
by doing wickedness more than the nations, and against My statutes more than
the countries that *are* all around her; for
they have refused My judgments, and they
have not walked in My statutes.' 7 Therefore thus says the Lord GOD: 'Because you
have [1]multiplied *disobedience* more than
the nations that *are* all around you, have
not walked in My statutes [h]nor kept My
judgments, [2]nor even done according to
the judgments of the nations that *are* all
around you'— 8 therefore thus says the
Lord GOD: 'Indeed I, even I, *am* against you
and will execute judgments in your midst
in the sight of the nations. 9 [i]And I will do
among you what I have never done, and
the like of which I will never do again, because of all your abominations. 10 Therefore fathers [j]shall eat *their* sons in your
midst, and sons shall eat their fathers; and
I will execute judgments among you, and
all of you who remain I will [k]scatter to all
the winds.
11 'Therefore, *as* I live,' says the Lord
GOD, 'surely, because you have [l]defiled My
sanctuary with all your [m]detestable things
and with all your abominations, therefore I
will also diminish *you;* [n]My eye will not
spare, nor will I have any pity. 12 [o]One-
third of you shall die of the pestilence, and
be consumed with famine in your midst;
and one-third shall fall by the sword all
around you; and [p]I will scatter another
third to all the winds, and I will draw out
a sword after [q]them.
13 'Thus shall My anger [r]be spent, and I
will [s]cause My fury to rest upon them,
[t]and I will be avenged; [u]and they shall
know that I, the LORD, have spoken *it* in
My zeal, when I have spent My fury upon
them. 14 Moreover [v]I will make you a
waste and a reproach among the nations
that *are* all around you, in the sight of all
who pass by.

14 [j] Deut. 14:3; Is. 65:4; 66:17 [2] Ritually unclean flesh, Lev. 7:18
16 [k] Lev. 26:26; Ps. 105:16; Is. 3:1; Ezek. 5:16; 14:13 [l] Ezek. 4:10, 11; 12:19 [m] Ezek. 4:11
17 [n] Lev. 26:39; Ezek. 24:23

CHAPTER 5

1 [a] Lev. 21:5; Is. 7:20; Ezek. 44:20
2 [b] Ezek. 5:12 [c] Ezek. 4:1 [d] Ezek. 4:8, 9 [e] Lev. 26:25; Lam. 1:20
3 [f] Jer. 40:6; 52:16
4 [g] Jer. 41:1, 2; 44:14
7 [h] 2 Kin. 21:9-11; 2 Chr. 33:9; Jer. 2:10, 11; Ezek. 16:47 [1] Or *raged* [2] So with MT, LXX, Tg., Vg.; many Heb. mss., Syr. *but have done* (cf. 11:12)
9 [i] Lam. 4:6; Dan. 9:12; [Amos 3:2]; Matt. 24:21
10 [j] Lev. 26:29; Deut. 28:53; 2 Kin. 6:29; Jer. 19:9; Lam. 2:20; 4:10 [k] Lev. 26:33; Deut. 28:64; Ps. 44:11; Ezek. 5:2, 12; 6:8; 12:14; Amos 9:9; Zech. 2:6; 7:14
11 [l] 2 Chr. 36:14; [Jer. 7:9-11]; Ezek. 8:5, 6, 16 [m] Ezek. 11:21 [n] Ezek. 7:4, 9; 8:18; 9:10
12 [o] Jer. 15:2; 21:9; Ezek. 6:12 [p] Jer. 9:16; [Ezek. 6:8] [q] Jer. 43:10, 11; 44:27; Ezek. 5:2; 12:14
13 [r] Lam. 4:11; Ezek. 6:12; 7:8 [s] Ezek. 21:17 [t] [Deut. 32:36]; Is. 1:24 [u] Is. 59:17; Ezek. 36:6; 38:19 **14** [v] Lev. 26:31; Neh. 2:17

undefiled even in his food (cf. Dan. 1:8 and *see note there*). God permitted fuel of dried cow chips for cooking his food in gracious deference to His spokesman's sensitivity (cf. 44:31).

4:16,17 They were soon to have neither bread nor water in any amount, and they were to grieve over the famine and their iniquity (cf. Lev. 26:21-26).

5:1-4 a barber's razor. The sign in shaving his hair illustrated the severe humiliation to come at the hand of enemies, emphasizing calamities to three segments of Jerusalem due to the Babylonian conquest. Some were punished by fire, i.e., pestilence and famine (v. 12), others died by the enemy's sword, and some were dispersed and pursued by death (cf. v. 12). A small part of his hair clinging to his garment (v. 3) depicted a remaining remnant, some of whom were subject to further calamity (v. 4; cf. 6:8; Jer. 41–44).

5:5 Jerusalem. Here the great city alone was not meant, but was used as a representative of the whole land which, despite its strategic opportunity and responsibility, rejected God (vv. 6,7).

5:7 Instead of being a witness to the heathen nations, Israel had exceeded them in idolatrous practices. The nations maintained their familiar idols, while Israel defected from their true and living God. God's people were worse than the pagans in proportion to spiritual knowledge and privileges. The judgments of God are always relative to light and privilege granted. Since Ezekiel's people were unique in their disobedience, they were to be outstanding in their punishment.

5:8-10 The book of Lamentations reveals how literally these promises were realized when parents ate their children and sons ate their fathers in the times of starvation. Down through the centuries had come the threats of Lev. 26:29 and Deut. 28:53, taken up by Jeremiah (Jer. 19:9; Lam. 2:22; 4:10; cf. Is. 9:20), and sealed in the life of the disobedient nation. Even the remnant would be scattered and suffer.

5:11 *as* I live. Here was a solemn oath pledging the very existence of God for the fulfillment of the prophecy. It is found 14 times in this book. Their greatest sin was defiling the sanctuary, showing the height of their wickedness.

5:12 The 4 well known judgments (cf. vv. 2-4) of pestilence, famine, sword, and scattering were their judgment. They had no place to offer atoning blood, thus bearing their sins without relief.

5:13-15 Ezekiel's purpose was to impress on Israel's conscience God's intense hatred of idolatry and apostasy. "Fury" and "anger" are repeated 6 times.

15 'So [3]it shall be a [w]reproach, a taunt, a
[x]lesson, and an astonishment to the nations that *are* all around you, when I execute judgments among you in anger and in
fury and in [y]furious rebukes. I, the LORD,
have spoken. 16 When I [z]send against them
the terrible arrows of famine which shall
be for destruction, which I will send to destroy you, I will increase the famine upon
you and cut off your [a]supply of bread.
17 So I will send against you famine and
[b]wild beasts, and they will bereave you.
[c]Pestilence and blood shall pass through
you, and I will bring the sword against
you. I, the LORD, have spoken.' "

Judgment on Idolatrous Israel

6 Now the word of the LORD came to me,
saying: 2 "Son of man, [a]set your face
toward the [b]mountains of Israel, and
prophesy against them, 3 and say, 'O
mountains of Israel, hear the word of the
Lord GOD! Thus says the Lord GOD to the
mountains, to the hills, to the ravines, and
to the valleys: "Indeed I, *even* I, will bring a
sword against you, and [c]I will destroy
your [1]high places. 4 Then your altars shall
be desolate, your incense altars shall be
broken, and [d]I will cast down your slain
men before your idols. 5 And I will lay the
corpses of the children of Israel before their
idols, and I will scatter your bones all
around your altars. 6 In all your dwelling
places the cities shall be laid waste, and the
[2]high places shall be desolate, so that your
altars may be laid waste and made desolate, your idols may be broken and made
to cease, your incense altars may be cut
down, and your works may be abolished.
7 The slain shall fall in your midst, and
[e]you shall know that I *am* the LORD.
8 [f]"Yet I will leave a remnant, so that you
may have *some* who escape the sword
among the nations, when you are [g]scat-
tered through the countries. 9 Then those of
you who escape will [h]remember Me among
the nations where they are carried captive,
because [i]I was crushed by their adulterous
heart which has departed from Me, and [j]by
their eyes which play the harlot after their
idols; [k]they will loathe themselves for the
evils which they committed in all their
abominations. 10 And they shall know that
I *am* the LORD; I have not said in vain that I
would bring this calamity upon them."
11 'Thus says the Lord GOD: [l]"Pound[3]
your fists and stamp your feet, and say,
'Alas, for all the evil abominations of the
house of Israel! [m]For they shall fall by the
sword, by famine, and by pestilence. 12 He
who is far off shall die by the pestilence, he
who is near shall fall by the sword, and he
who remains and is besieged shall die by
the famine. [n]Thus will I spend My fury
upon them. 13 Then you shall know that I
am the LORD, when their slain are among
their idols all around their altars, [o]on every
high hill, [p]on all the mountaintops, [q]under
every green tree, and under every thick
oak, wherever they offered sweet incense
to all their idols. 14 So I will [r]stretch out My
hand against them and make the land desolate, yes, more desolate than the wilderness toward [s]Diblah, in all their dwelling
places. Then they shall know that I *am* the
LORD.' " ' "

Judgment on Israel Is Near

7 Moreover the word of the LORD came to
me, saying, 2 "And you, son of man,
thus says the Lord GOD to the land of Israel:

[a]'An end! The end has come upon
the four corners of the land.
3 Now the end *has come* upon you,
And I will send My anger against
you;
I will judge you [b]according to your
ways,
And I will repay you for all your
abominations.
4 [c]My eye will not spare you,
Nor will I have pity;
But I will repay your ways,
And your abominations will be in
your midst;
[d]Then you shall know that I *am* the
LORD!'

---

15 [w]Deut. 28:37; 1 Kin. 9:7; Ps. 79:4; Jer. 24:9; Lam. 2:15 [x][Is. 26:9]; Jer. 22:8, 9; 1 Cor. 10:11 [y]Is. 66:15, 16; Ezek. 5:8; 25:17 [3]LXX, Syr., Tg., Vg. *you*
16 [z]Deut. 32:23 [a]Lev. 26:26; Ezek. 4:16; 14:13
17 [b]Lev. 26:22; Deut. 32:24; Ezek. 14:21; 33:27; 34:25; Rev. 6:8 [c]Ezek. 38:22

CHAPTER 6

2 [a]Ezek. 20:46; 21:2; 25:2 [b]Ezek. 36:1
3 [c]Lev. 26:30 [1]Places for pagan worship
4 [d]Lev. 26:30
6 [2]Places for pagan worship
7 [e]Ezek. 7:4, 9
8 [f]Jer. 44:28; Ezek. 5:2, 12; 12:16; 14:22 [g]Ezek. 5:12
9 [h][Deut. 4:29]; Ps. 137; Jer. 51:50 [i]Ps. 78:40; Is. 7:13; 43:24; Hos. 11:8 [j]Num. 15:39; Ezek. 20:7, 24 [k]Lev. 26:39; Job 42:6; Ezek. 20:43; 36:31
11 [l]Ezek. 21:14 [m]Ezek. 5:12 [3]Lit. *Strike your hands*
12 [n]Lam. 4:11, 22; Ezek. 5:13
13 [o]Jer. 2:20; 3:6 [p]1 Kin. 14:23; 2 Kin. 16:4; Ezek. 20:28; Hos. 4:13 [q]Is. 57:5
14 [r]Is. 5:25; Ezek. 14:13; 20:33, 34 [s]Num. 33:46

CHAPTER 7

2 [a]Ezek. 7:3, 5, 6; 11:13; Amos 8:2, 10; [Matt. 24:6, 13, 14]
3 [b][Rom. 2:6]
4 [c]Ezek. 5:11 [d]Ezek. 12:20

5:16 arrows of famine. The evil arrows included hail, rain, mice, locusts, and mildew (cf. Deut. 32:23,24).

5:17 I, the LORD, have spoken. Cf. vv. 13,15 for the same expression, which was God's personal signature on their doom.

6:3 says the Lord…to the mountains. God had the prophet do this because the people worshiped at idol altars in the "high places" (cf. Lev. 26:30-33; Is. 65:7; Jer. 3:6; Hos. 4:13; Mic. 6:1,2).

6:7 you shall know that I *am* the LORD. This clause recurs in vv. 10,13,14 and 60 times elsewhere in the book. It shows that the essential reason for judgment is the violation of the character of God. This is repeatedly acknowledged in Lev. 18–26, where the motive for all obedience to God's law is the fact that He is the Lord God.

6:8-10 The mass of people was rejected, but grace and mercy were given to a godly group in the nation. There never has been nor ever will be a complete end to Israel. The doctrine of the remnant can be studied in Is. 1:9; 10:20; Jer. 43:5; Zeph. 2:7; 3:13; Zech. 10:9; Rom. 9:6-13; 11:5.

6:14 Diblah. A reference to Diblathaim, a city on the eastern edge of Moab (Num. 33:46; Jer. 48:22), near the desert E and S of the Dead Sea.

7:1-9 This lament declared that the entire land of Israel was ripe for judgment. God's patience had ended. The final destruction of Jerusalem by Nebuchadnezzar was in view (586 B.C.).

5 "Thus says the Lord GOD:

'A disaster, a singular [e]disaster;
Behold, it has come!
6 An end has come,
The end has come;
It has dawned for you;
Behold, it has come!
7 [f]Doom has come to you, you who
dwell in the land;
[g]The time has come,
A day of trouble *is* near,
And not of rejoicing in the
mountains.
8 Now upon you I will soon [h]pour
out My fury,
And spend My anger upon you;
I will judge you according to your
ways,
And I will repay you for all your
abominations.

9 'My eye will not spare,
Nor will I have pity;
I will [1]repay you according to your
ways,
And your abominations will be in
your midst.
Then you shall know that I *am* the
LORD who strikes.

10 'Behold, the day!
Behold, it has come!
[i]Doom has gone out;
The rod has blossomed,
Pride has budded.
11 [j]Violence has risen up into a rod of
wickedness;
None of them *shall remain*,
None of their multitude,
None of [2]them;
[k]Nor *shall there be* wailing for them.
12 The time has come,
The day draws near.

'Let not the buyer [l]rejoice,
Nor the seller [m]mourn,
For wrath *is* on their whole
multitude.
13 For the seller shall not return to
what has been sold,
Though he may still be alive;
For the vision concerns the whole
multitude,
And it shall not turn back;
No one will strengthen himself
Who lives in iniquity.

14 'They have blown the trumpet and
made everyone ready,
But no one goes to battle;
For My wrath *is* on all their
multitude.
15 [n]The sword *is* outside,
And the pestilence and famine
within.
Whoever *is* in the field
Will die by the sword;
And whoever *is* in the city,
Famine and pestilence will devour
him.

16 'Those who [o]survive will escape
and be on the mountains
Like doves of the valleys,
All of them mourning,
Each for his iniquity.
17 Every [p]hand will be feeble,
And every knee will be *as* weak *as*
water.
18 They will also [q]be girded with
sackcloth;
Horror will cover them;
Shame *will be* on every face,
Baldness on all their heads.

19 'They will throw their silver into
the streets,
And their gold will be like refuse;
Their [r]silver and their gold will not
be able to deliver them
In the day of the wrath of the
LORD;
They will not satisfy their souls,
Nor fill their stomachs,
Because it became their stumbling
block of iniquity.

20 'As for the beauty of his ornaments,
He set it in majesty;
[s]But they made from it
The images of their abominations—
Their detestable things;
Therefore I have made it
Like refuse to them.

5 [e] 2 Kin. 21:12, 13; Nah. 1:9
7 [f] Ezek. 7:10 [g] Zeph. 1:14, 15
8 [h] Ezek. 20:8, 21
9 [1] Lit. *give*
10 [i] Ezek. 7:7
11 [j] Jer. 6:7 [k] Jer. 16:5, 6; Ezek. 24:16, 22 [2] Or *their wealth*
12 [l] Prov. 20:14; 1 Cor. 7:30 [m] Is. 24:2
15 [n] Deut. 32:25; Jer. 14:18; Lam. 1:20; Ezek. 5:12
16 [o] Ezra 9:15; Is. 37:31; Ezek. 6:8; 14:22
17 [p] Is. 13:7; Jer. 6:24; Ezek. 21:7; Heb. 12:12
18 [q] Is. 3:24; 15:2, 3; Jer. 48:37; Ezek. 27:31; Amos 8:10
19 [r] Prov. 11:4; Jer. 15:13; Zeph. 1:18
20 [s] Jer. 7:30

7:10 rod has blossomed. Verse 11 explains this. Violence had grown up into a rod of wickedness, which likely refers to Nebuchadnezzar, the instrument of God's vengeance (cf. Is. 10:5; Jer. 51:20).

7:12 buyer rejoice...seller mourn. Such matters of business were meaningless because the Chaldeans (Babylonians) took all the land and killed those they didn't take captive (v. 15) and the rest escaped (v. 16). Wealth was useless (vv. 19,20).

7:13 seller shall not return to...sold. There was to be no Jubilee year in which all lands were returned to their original owners (cf. Lev. 25).

7:17-22 This section described the mourning of the helpless and frightened people. In distress, they recognized the uselessness of the things in which they trusted. Their wealth provided nothing. Their "silver and gold" (v. 19), their "ornaments" (v. 20) were as useless as the idols they made with them.

21 I will give it as [t]plunder
Into the hands of strangers,
And to the wicked of the earth as
spoil;
And they shall defile it.
22 I will turn My face from them,
And they will defile My secret place;
For robbers shall enter it and defile
it.

23 'Make a chain,
For [u]the land is filled with crimes
of blood,
And the city is full of violence.
24 Therefore I will bring the [v]worst of
the Gentiles,
And they will possess their houses;
I will cause the pomp of the strong
to cease,
And their holy places shall be
[w]defiled.
25 [3]Destruction comes;
They will seek peace, but *there shall*
be none.
26 [x]Disaster will come upon disaster,
And rumor will be upon rumor.
[y]Then they will seek a vision from a
prophet;
But the law will perish from the
priest,
And counsel from the elders.

27 'The king will mourn,
The prince will be clothed with
desolation,
And the hands of the common
people will tremble.
I will do to them according to their
way,
And according to what they
deserve I will judge them;
Then they shall know that I *am* the
LORD!' "

21 [t]2 Kin. 24:13; Jer. 20:5
23 [u]2 Kin. 21:16
24 [v]Ezek. 21:31; 28:7 [w]2 Chr. 7:20; Ezek. 24:21
25 [3]Lit. *Shuddering*
26 [x]Deut. 32:23; Is. 47:11; Jer. 4:20 [y]Ps. 74:9; Lam. 2:9; Ezek. 20:1, 3; Mic. 3:6

Abominations in the Temple

8 And it came to pass in the sixth year, in
the sixth *month,* on the fifth *day* of the
month, as I sat in my house with [a]the elders of Judah sitting before me, that [b]the
hand of the Lord GOD fell upon me there.
2 [c]Then I looked, and there was a likeness,
like the appearance of fire—from the appearance of His waist and downward, fire;
and from His waist and upward, like the
appearance of brightness, [d]like the color of
amber. 3 He [e]stretched out the form of a
hand, and took me by a lock of my hair;
and [f]the Spirit lifted me up between earth
and heaven, and [g]brought me in visions of
God to Jerusalem, to the door of the north
gate of the inner *court,* [h]where the seat of
the image of jealousy *was,* which [i]pro-
vokes[1] to jealousy. 4 And behold, the
[j]glory of the God of Israel *was* there, like
the vision that I [k]saw in the plain.
5 Then He said to me, "Son of man, lift
your eyes now toward the north." So I lifted my eyes toward the north, and there,
north of the altar gate, was this image of
jealousy in the entrance.
6 Furthermore He said to me, "Son of
man, do you see what they are doing, the
great [l]abominations that the house of Israel commits here, to make Me go far away
from My sanctuary? Now turn again, you
will see greater abominations." 7 So He
brought me to the door of the court; and
when I looked, there was a hole in the wall.
8 Then He said to me, "Son of man, dig
into the wall"; and when I dug into the
wall, there was a door.
9 And He said to me, "Go in, and see the
wicked abominations which they are
doing there." 10 So I went in and saw, and
there—every [m]sort of [n]creeping thing,
abominable beasts, and all the idols of the
house of Israel, [2]portrayed all around on

CHAPTER 8

1 [a]Ezek. 14:1; 20:1; 33:31 [b]Ezek. 1:3; 3:22
2 [c]Ezek. 1:26, 27 [d]Ezek. 1:4, 27
3 [e]Dan. 5:5 [f]Ezek. 3:14; Acts 8:39 [g]Ezek. 11:1, 24; 40:2 [h]Jer. 7:30; 32:34; Ezek. 5:11 [i]Ex. 20:4; Deut. 32:16, 21 [1]Arouses the LORD's jealousy
4 [j]Ezek. 3:12; 9:3 [k]Ezek. 1:28; 3:22, 23
6 [l]2 Kin. 23:4, 5; Ezek. 5:11; 8:9, 17
10 [m]Ex. 20:4; Deut. 4:16-18 [n]Rom. 1:23 [2]Or *carved*

7:22 My secret place. The Holy of Holies in the temple will be desecrated by pagans, that place where only once a year the High-Priest could enter to make atonement in God's presence.

7:23 Make a chain. Ezekiel is to perform another emblematic act of captivity (cf. Jer. 27:2; Nah. 3:10).

7:24 the worst of the Gentiles. Babylonian pagans.

7:27 according to what they deserve. Cf. Gen. 18:25.

8:1 the sixth year. 592 B.C. (cf. 1:2) in Aug./Sep., a year and two months after the first vision (1:1). **the hand of the Lord.** This ushered the prophet into a series of visions (v. 3) stretching to the end of chap. 11.

8:2 a likeness. He saw the glory of the Lord (v. 4) as in 1:26-28.

8:3 in visions of God. Ezekiel 8–11 deals with details conveyed only to Ezekiel in visions. Ezekiel's trip to Jerusalem was in spirit only, while his body physically remained in his house. In visions, he went to Jerusalem and in visions he returned to Babylon (11:24). After God finished the visions, Ezekiel told his home audience what he had seen. The visions are not a description of deeds done in the past in Israel, but a survey of Israel's current condition, as they existed at that very time. **the seat…image of jealousy.** God represents to Ezekiel the image of an idol (cf. Deut. 4:16) in the entrance to the inner court of the temple. It is called "the image of jealousy" because it provoked the Lord to jealousy (5:13; 16:38; 36:6; 38:19; Ex. 20:5).

8:4 the glory of…God. God was also there in glory, but was ignored while the people worshiped the idol (v. 6).

8:6 to make Me go far away. Sin would expel the people from their land and God from His sanctuary.

8:7-12 This section describes "greater abominations" (v. 6) of idolatry, namely a secret cult of idolatrous elders.

8:8 dig into the wall…a door. This indicates the clandestine (cf. v. 12) secrecy of these idolaters, practicing their cult in hiding.

8:10 portrayed…on the walls. The temple's walls are ugly with graffiti featuring creatures linked with Egyptian animal cults (cf. Rom 1:23) and other idols. Leaders of Israel, who should be worshiping the God of the temple, are offering incense to them (v. 11).

the walls. 11 And there stood before them
[o]seventy men of the elders of the house of
Israel, and in their midst stood Jaazaniah
the son of Shaphan. Each man had a censer
in his hand, and a thick cloud of incense
went up. 12 Then He said to me, "Son of
man, have you seen what the elders of the
house of Israel do in the dark, every man
in the room of his idols? For they say, [p]'The
LORD does not see us, the LORD has forsak-
en the land.' "
13 And He said to me, "Turn again, *and*
you will see greater abominations that
they are doing." 14 So He brought me to
the door of the north gate of the LORD's
house; and to my dismay, women were sitting there weeping for [3]Tammuz.
15 Then He said to me, "Have you seen
this, O son of man? Turn again, you will see
greater abominations than these." 16 So He
brought me into the inner court of the
LORD's house; and there, at the door of the
temple of the LORD, [q]between the porch and
the altar, [r]*were* about twenty-five men [s]with
their backs toward the temple of the LORD
and their faces toward the east, and they
were worshiping [t]the sun toward the east.
17 And He said to me, "Have you seen
this, O son of man? Is it a trivial thing to the
house of Judah to commit the abominations which they commit here? For they
have [u]filled the land with violence; then
they have returned to provoke Me to
anger. Indeed they put the branch to their
nose. 18 [v]Therefore I also will act in fury.
My [w]eye will not spare nor will I have pity;
and though they [x]cry in My ears with a
loud voice, I will not hear them."

The Wicked Are Slain

9 Then He called out in my hearing with
a loud voice, saying, "Let those who
have charge over the city draw near, each
with a [1]deadly weapon in his hand." 2 And
suddenly six men came from the direction
of the upper gate, which faces north, each
with his [2]battle-ax in his hand. [a]One man
among them *was* clothed with linen and
had a writer's inkhorn [3]at his side. They
went in and stood beside the bronze altar.
3 Now [b]the glory of the God of Israel had
gone up from the cherub, where it had been,
to the threshold of the [4]temple. And He
called to the man clothed with linen, who
had the writer's inkhorn at his side; 4 and
the LORD said to him, "Go through the
midst of the city, through the midst of Jerusalem, and put [c]a mark on the foreheads of
the men [d]who sigh and cry over all the
abominations that are done within it."
5 To the others He said in my [5]hearing,
"Go after him through the city and [e]kill;[6]
[f]do not let your eye spare, nor have any
pity. 6 [g]Utterly[7] slay old *and* young men,
maidens and little children and women;
but [h]do not come near anyone on whom *is*
the mark; and [i]begin at My sanctuary." [j]So
they began with the elders who *were* before

11 [o] Num. 11:16, 25; Luke 10:1
12 [p] Ps. 14:1; Is. 29:15; Ezek. 9:9
14 [3] A Sumerian fertility god similar to the Gr. god Adonis
16 [q] Joel 2:17 [r] Ezek. 11:1 [s] 2 Chr. 29:6; Jer. 2:27; 32:33; Ezek. 23:39 [t] Deut. 4:19; 2 Kin. 23:5, 11; Job 31:26; Jer. 44:17
17 [u] Ezek. 9:9; Amos 3:10; Mic. 2:2
18 [v] Ezek. 5:13; 16:42; 24:13

[w] Ezek. 5:11; 7:4, 9; 9:5, 10 [x] Prov. 1:28; Is. 1:15; Jer. 11:11; 14:12; Mic. 3:4; Zech. 7:13

CHAPTER 9

1 [1] Or *destroying*
2 [a] Lev. 16:4; Ezek. 10:2; Rev. 15:6 [2] Lit. *shattering weapon* [3] Lit. *upon his loins*
3 [b] Ezek. 3:23; 8:4; 10:4, 18; 11:22, 23 [4] Lit. *house*
4 [c] Ex. 12:7, 13; Ezek. 9:6; [2 Cor. 1:22; 2 Tim. 2:19]; Rev. 7:2, 3; 9:4; 14:1 [d] Ps. 119:53, 136; Jer. 13:17; Ezek. 6:11; 21:6; 2 Cor. 12:21; 2 Pet. 2:8
5 [e] Ezek. 7:9 [f] Ezek. 5:11 [5] Lit. *ears* [6] Lit. *strike*
6 [g] 2 Chr. 36:17 [h] Ex. 12:23; Rev. 9:4 [i] Jer. 25:29; Amos 3:2; [Luke 12:42; 1 Pet. 4:17] [j] Ezek. 8:11, 12, 16 [7] Lit. *Slay to destruction*

8:11 seventy...elders. Obviously not the Sanhedrin, since it was not formed until after the restoration from Babylon, though the pattern had been suggested much earlier (cf. Ex. 24:9,10; Num. 11:16). These men were appointed to guard against idolatry! **Jaazaniah...son of Shaphan.** If he was the son of the Shaphan who read God's Word to Josiah (2 Kin. 22:8-11), we have some concept of the depth of sin to which the leaders had fallen. He is not to be confused with the man in 11:1, who had a different father.

8:14 weeping for Tammuz. Yet a greater abomination than the secret cult was Israel's engaging in the Babylonian worship of Tammuz or Dumuzi (Duzu), beloved of Ishtar, the god of spring vegetation. Vegetation burned in the summer, died in the winter, and came to life in the spring. The women mourned over the god's demise in July and longed for his revival. The fourth month of the Hebrew calendar still bears the name Tammuz. With the worship of this idol were connected the basest immoralities.

8:16 worshiping the sun. In the most sacred inner court where only priests could go (Joel 2:17), there was the crowning insult to God. Twenty-five men were worshiping the sun as an idol (cf. Deut 4:19; 2 Kin. 23:5,11; Job 31:26; Jer. 44:17). These 25 represent the 24 orders of priests plus the High-Priest.

8:17 put the branch to their nose. The meaning is uncertain, but it seems to have been some act of contempt toward God. The Gr. OT translators rendered it, "they are as mockers."

8:18 I...will act in fury. God must judge intensely due to such horrible sins (cf. 24:9,10).

9:1 charge over the city. God summoned His servant angels to carry out His judgments. These angelic executioners (cf. Dan. 4:13, 17,23) came equipped with weapons of destruction.

9:2 six men. Angels can appear like men when ministering on earth (cf. Gen. 18:1; Dan. 9:20-23). **One man.** He was superior to the others. Linen indicates high rank (cf. Dan. 10:5; 12:6). Perhaps this was the Angel of the Lord, the pre-incarnate Christ (*see note on Ex. 3:2*). He had all the instruments of an oriental scribe to carry out His task (vv. 4,11).

9:3 the glory...had gone up. The glory of God departs before the destruction of the city and temple. The gradual departure of God from His temple is depicted in stages: the glory resides in the temple's Most Holy Place, between the wings of the cherubs on each side of the ark of the covenant over the mercy seat, then leaves to the front door (9:3; 10:4), later to the E gate by the outer wall (10:18,19), and finally to the Mt. of Olives to the E, having fully departed (11:22,23). The glory will return in the future kingdom of Messiah (43:2-7).

9:4 a mark on the foreheads. Since God's departure removed all protection and gave the people over to destruction, it was necessary for the angelic scribe (Angel of the Lord) to mark for God's preservation the righteous who had been faithful to Him. Those left unmarked were subject to death in Babylon's siege (v. 5). The mark was the indication of God's elect, identified personally by the pre-incarnate Christ. He was marking the elect (cf. Ex. 12:7). Malachi 3:16-18 indicates a similar idea. Cf. Rev. 7:3; 9:4. The marked ones were penitent and were identified for protection. Here was a respite of grace for the remnant. The rest were to be killed (vv. 5-7).

the [8]temple. **7** Then He said to them, "Defile the [9]temple, and fill the courts with the
slain. Go out!" And they went out and
killed in the city.
8 So it was, that while they were killing
them, I was left *alone;* and I [k]fell on my face
and cried out, and said, [l]"Ah, Lord GOD!
Will You destroy all the remnant of Israel
in pouring out Your fury on Jerusalem?"
9 Then He said to me, "The iniquity of
the house of Israel and Judah *is* exceedingly great, and [m]the land is full of bloodshed,
and the city full of perversity; for they say,
[n]'The LORD has forsaken the land, and [o]the
LORD does not see!' **10** And as for Me also,
My [p]eye will neither spare, nor will I have
pity, *but* [q]I will recompense their deeds on
their own head."
11 Just then, the man clothed with linen,
who *had* the inkhorn at his side, reported
back and said, "I have done as You commanded me."

The Glory Departs from the Temple

10 And I looked, and there in the [a]fir-
mament[1] that was above the head
of the cherubim, there appeared something
like a sapphire stone, having the appearance of the likeness of a throne. **2** [b]Then He
spoke to the man clothed with linen, and
said, "Go in among the wheels, under the
cherub, fill your hands with [c]coals of fire
from among the cherubim, and [d]scatter
them over the city." And he went in as I
watched.
3 Now the cherubim were standing on
the [2]south side of the [3]temple when the
man went in, and the [e]cloud filled the
inner court. **4** [f]Then the glory of the LORD
went up from the cherub, *and paused* over
the threshold of the [4]temple; and [g]the
house was filled with the cloud, and the
court was full of the brightness of the
LORD's [h]glory. **5** And the [i]sound of the
wings of the cherubim was heard *even* in
the outer court, like [j]the voice of Almighty
God when He speaks.
6 Then it happened, when He commanded the man clothed in linen, saying, "Take
fire from among the wheels, from among
the cherubim," that he went in and stood
beside the wheels. **7** And the cherub
stretched out his hand from among the
cherubim to the fire that *was* among the
cherubim, and took *some of it* and put *it*
into the hands of the *man* clothed with
linen, who took *it* and went out. **8** [k]The
cherubim appeared to have the form of a
man's hand under their wings.
9 [l]And when I looked, there were four
wheels by the cherubim, one wheel by one
cherub and another wheel by each other
cherub; the wheels appeared *to have* the
color of a [m]beryl stone. **10** *As for* their appearance, all four looked alike—as it were,
a wheel in the middle of a wheel. **11** [n]When
they went, they went toward *any of* their
four directions; they did not turn aside
when they went, but followed in the direction the head was facing. They did not turn
aside when they went. **12** And their whole
body, with their back, their hands, their
wings, and the wheels that the four had,
were [o]full of eyes all around. **13** As for the
wheels, they were called in my [5]hearing,
"Wheel."
14 [p]Each one had four faces: the first face
was the face of a cherub, the second face
the face of a man, the third the face of a
lion, and the fourth the face of an eagle.
15 And the cherubim were lifted up. This
was [q]the living creature I saw by the River
Chebar. **16** [r]When the cherubim went, the
wheels went beside them; and when the

6 [8] Lit. *house*
7 [9] Lit. *house*
8 [k] Num. 14:5; 16:4, 22, 45; Josh. 7:6 [l] Ezek. 11:13; Amos 7:2-6
9 [m] 2 Kin. 21:16; Jer. 2:34; Ezek. 8:17 [n] Job 22:13; Ezek. 8:12 [o] Ps. 10:11; Is. 29:15
10 [p] Is. 65:6; Ezek. 5:11; 7:4; 8:18 [q] Ezek. 11:21; Hos. 9:7

CHAPTER 10

1 [a] Ezek. 1:22, 26 [1] *expanse*
2 [b] Ezek. 9:2, 3; Dan. 10:5 [c] Ps. 18:10-13; Is. 6:6; Ezek. 1:13 [d] Rev. 8:5
3 [e] 1 Kin. 8:10, 11 [2] Lit. *right* [3] Lit. *house*
4 [f] Ezek. 1:28 [g] 1 Kin. 8:10; Ezek. 43:5 [4] Lit. *house*
[h] Ezek. 11:22, 23
5 [i] [Job 40:9]; Ezek. 1:24; [Rev. 10:3] [j] [Ps. 29:3]
8 [k] Ezek. 1:8; 10:21
9 [l] Ezek. 1:15 [m] Ezek. 1:16
11 [n] Ezek. 1:17
12 [o] Rev. 4:6, 8
13 [5] Lit. *ears*
14 [p] 1 Kin. 7:29, 36; Ezek. 1:6, 10, 11; Rev. 4:7
15 [q] Ezek. 1:3, 5
16 [r] Ezek. 1:19

9:8 Will You destroy all? Ezekiel is fearfully aroused in prayer because the judgment on Jerusalem and Israel is so vast. God replies that pervasive sin demands thorough judgment (vv. 9,10), yet comforts him by the report that the faithful had been marked to be spared (v. 11). Cf. Rom 11:1,2,25-27.

10:1 a throne. It rises above God's angelic servants, the same 4 as in chap. 1 (10:20,22), and is the throne of 1:26-28 on which God sits (cf. 10:20). From it, He directs the operation of His war machine ("wheels," *see note on 1:15,16*) on Jerusalem (v. 2). The throne is like a sapphire shining forth representing God's glory and holiness (11:22).

10:2 fill...with coals. God specifies that the marking angel (9:2,11) reach into the war machine and fill his hands with fiery coals in the presence of the angels of chap. 1. These coals picture the fires of judgment which God's angels are to "scatter" on Jerusalem. In Is. 6, "coals" were used for the purification of the prophet; here they were for the destruction of the wicked (cf. Heb. 12:29). Fire did destroy Jerusalem in 586 B.C.

10:3 cherubim. These were different from the cherubim of chap. 1 and here in v. 4.

10:4 This verse explains how the "cloud" of v. 3 "filled the inner court." It repeats what is first described in 9:3.

10:6,7 These verses picked up the action of the angelic scribe from v. 2.

10:7 cherub...put *it* into the hands. One of the 4 cherubim of 1:5ff. and v. 1 puts the fiery coals into the marking angel's hand.

10:9-17 wheels by the cherubim. This whole section is similar to 1:4-21. Four wheels on God's chariot mingled with the 4 angels (cf. 1:15-21) coordinated with each other in precision, and each with a different one of the cherubim. All looked so much alike that it was as if one wheel blended entirely with another (v. 10). As their appearance was so unified, their action was in unison, and instant (v. 11). The cherubim had bodies like men and their chariot wheels were full of eyes denoting full perception both to see the sinners and their fitting judgment. The color beryl is a sparkling yellow or gold.

10:14 the face of a cherub. This description of one cherub in 1:10 indicates this was the face of an ox.

10:15 lifted up. They were all ready to move in unison (vv. 16,17) as the Shekinah glory of God departed (v. 18).

cherubim lifted their wings to mount up
from the earth, the same wheels also did
not turn from beside them. 17 [s]When [6]*the
cherubim* stood still, *the wheels* stood still,
and when [7]*one* was lifted up, [8]*the other* lifted itself up, for the spirit of the living creature *was* in them.
18 Then [t]the glory of the LORD [u]departed
from the threshold of the [9]temple and
stood over the cherubim. 19 And [v]the
cherubim lifted their wings and mounted
up from the earth in my sight. When they
went out, the wheels *were* beside them; and
they stood at the door of the [w]east gate of
the LORD's house, and the glory of the God
of Israel *was* above them.
20 [x]This *is* the living creature I saw
under the God of Israel [y]by the River
Chebar, and I knew they *were* cherubim.
21 [z]Each one had four faces and each one
four wings, and the likeness of the hands
of a man *was* under their wings. 22 And
[a]the likeness of their faces *was* the same *as*
the faces which I had seen by the River
Chebar, their appearance and their persons. [b]They each went straight forward.

Judgment on Wicked Counselors

11 Then [a]the Spirit lifted me up and
brought me to [b]the East Gate of the
LORD's house, which faces eastward; and
there [c]at the door of the gate were twenty-
five men, among whom I saw Jaazaniah
the son of Azzur, and Pelatiah the son of
Benaiah, princes of the people. 2 And He
said to me: "Son of man, these *are* the men
who devise iniquity and give wicked
[1]counsel in this city, 3 who say, *'The time is*
not [d]near to build houses; [e]this *city is* the
[2]caldron, and we *are* the meat.' 4 Therefore
prophesy against them, prophesy, O son of
man!"
5 Then [f]the Spirit of the LORD fell upon
me, and said to me, "Speak! 'Thus says the
LORD: "Thus you have said, O house of Israel; for [g]I know the things that come into
your mind. 6 [h]You have multiplied your
slain in this city, and you have filled its
streets with the slain." 7 Therefore thus
says the Lord GOD: [i]"Your slain whom you
have laid in its midst, they *are* the meat,
and this *city is* the caldron; [j]but I shall
bring you out of the midst of it. 8 You have
[k]feared the sword; and I will bring a sword
upon you," says the Lord GOD. 9 "And I
will bring you out of its midst, and deliver
you into the hands of strangers, and [l]exe-
cute judgments on you. 10 [m]You shall fall
by the sword. I will judge you at [n]the border of Israel. [o]Then you shall know that I
am the LORD. 11 [p]This *city* shall not be your
[3]caldron, nor shall you be the meat in its
midst. I will judge you at the border of Israel. 12 And you shall know that I *am* the
LORD; for you have not walked in My
statutes nor executed My judgments, but
[q]have done according to the customs of the
Gentiles which *are* all around you."' "
13 Now it happened, while I was prophesying, that [r]Pelatiah the son of Benaiah
died. Then [s]I fell on my face and cried with
a loud voice, and said, "Ah, Lord GOD!
Will You make a complete end of the remnant of Israel?"

God Will Restore Israel

14 Again the word of the LORD came to
me, saying, 15 "Son of man, your brethren,
your relatives, your countrymen, and all
the house of Israel in its entirety, *are* those

17 [s]Ezek. 1:12, 20, 21 [6]Lit. *they* [7]Lit. *they were* [8]Lit. *they lifted them*
18 [t]Ezek. 10:4 [u]Hos. 9:12 [9]Lit. *house*
19 [v]Ezek. 11:22 [w]Ezek. 11:1
20 [x]Ezek. 1:22 [y]Ezek. 1:1
21 [z]Ezek. 1:6, 8; 10:14; 41:18, 19
22 [a]Ezek. 1:10 [b]Ezek. 1:9, 12

CHAPTER 11

1 [a]Ezek. 3:12, 14 [b]Ezek. 10:19 [c]Ezek. 8:16
2 [1]Advice
3 [d]Ezek. 12:22, 27; 2 Pet. 3:4 [e]Jer. 1:13; Ezek. 11:7, 11; 24:3, 6 [2]Pot
5 [f]Ezek. 2:2; 3:24 [g][Jer. 16:17; 17:10]
6 [h]Is. 1:15; Ezek. 7:23; 22:2-6, 9, 12, 27
7 [i]Ezek. 24:3, 6; Mic. 3:2, 3 [j]2 Kin. 25:18-22; Jer. 52:24-27; Ezek. 11:9
8 [k]Jer. 42:16
9 [l]Ezek. 5:8
10 [m]2 Kin. 25:19-21; Jer. 39:6; 52:10 [n]1 Kin. 8:65; 2 Kin. 14:25 [o]Ps. 9:16; Ezek. 6:7; 13:9, 14, 21, 23
11 [p]Ezek. 11:3, 7 [3]Pot
12 [q]Lev. 18:3, 24; Deut. 12:30, 31; Ezek. 8:10, 14, 16
13 [r]Acts 5:5 [s]Ezek. 9:8

10:18,19 glory...departed. There were several stages: 9:3; 10:1, 3,4; 10:18,19; 11:22,23. There was thus written over the entire structure, as well as Israel's spiritual life, "Ichabod" (the glory has departed). Cf. 1 Sam. 4:21; 10:18,19.

11:1 twenty-five men. Ezekiel, though at the temple only in the vision (cf. 8:3, and *see note there*), saw because God, who was everywhere present and all-knowing, impressed specific details on him in the vision. The wicked leaders (cf. v. 2) were part of God's reason for the judgment (vv. 8,10). Ezekiel was taken in spirit to the very place which the glory of God had left in 10:19 and was given a vision of "twenty-five men," who represented, not priests, but influential leaders among the people, who gave fatal advice to the people (v. 2). **Jaazaniah the son of Azzur.** *See note on 8:11.*

11:3 caldron...meat. Though this is obscure, it may be that the bad advice these leaders were giving was that the people should not be engaged in business as usual, "building houses" or taking care of their comfort and futures, when they were about to be cooked like meat in a pot over a blazing fire. The idea must have been that the people should get ready for battle, and be prepared to fight, not focusing on comfort, but survival. Jeremiah had told the people to surrender to the Babylonians and save their lives, rather than fight and be killed (cf. Jer. 27:9-17). These false leaders, like the prophets and priests whom Jeremiah confronted for telling the people not to submit, scorned Jeremiah's words from God and would pay for it (v. 4). Cf. 24:1-14.

11:6 multiplied your slain. Leaders who misled Israel by inciting false expectations of a victorious defense, rather than peaceful surrender, were responsible for the deadly results. Many people died in resisting Babylon.

11:7 I shall bring you out. The false leaders thought that unless they fought, they would all be in a caldron, i.e., the city. But here the Lord promised that some would be delivered from the city, only to die on Israel's border in the wilderness (vv. 8-11). This was literally fulfilled at Riblah (cf. 2 Kin. 25:18-21; Jer. 52:24-27).

11:13 Pelatiah...died. The death of one leader from v. 1 was a sign that God would indeed carry out His word. Apparently this leader did die suddenly at the time Ezekiel was shown the vision, so that the prophet feared that this death meant death for all Israelites (9:8).

11:14,15 Ezekiel was told he had a new family, not the priests at Jerusalem to whom he was tied by blood, but his fellow exiles in Babylon, identified as those who were treated as outcasts. The priesthood was about to be ended and he was to have a new family.

about whom the inhabitants of Jerusalem
have said, 'Get far away from the LORD;
this land has been given to us as a possession.' 16 Therefore say, 'Thus says the Lord
GOD: "Although I have cast them far off
among the Gentiles, and although I have
scattered them among the countries, [t]yet
I shall be a little [4]sanctuary for them in
the countries where they have gone."'
17 Therefore say, 'Thus says the Lord GOD:
[u]"I will gather you from the peoples, assemble you from the countries where you
have been scattered, and I will give you the
land of Israel."' 18 And they will go there,
and they will take away all its [v]detestable
things and all its abominations from there.
19 Then [w]I will give them one heart, and I
will put [x]a new spirit within [5]them, and
take [y]the stony heart out of their flesh, and
give them a heart of flesh, 20 [z]that they
may walk in My statutes and keep My
judgments and do them; [a]and they shall be
My people, and I will be their God. 21 But
as for those whose hearts follow the desire
for their detestable things and their
abominations, [b]I will recompense their
deeds on their own heads," says the Lord
GOD.
22 So the cherubim [c]lifted up their
wings, with the wheels beside them, and
the glory of the God of Israel *was* high
above them. 23 And [d]the glory of the LORD
went up from the midst of the city and
stood [e]on the mountain, [f]which *is* on the
east side of the city.
24 Then [g]the Spirit took me up and
brought me in a vision by the Spirit of God
into [6]Chaldea, to those in captivity. And
the vision that I had seen went up from

16 [t] Ps. 90:1; 91:9; Is. 8:14; Jer. 29:7, 11 [4] *holy place*
17 [u] Is. 11:11-16; Jer. 3:12, 18; 24:5; Ezek. 20:41, 42; 28:5
18 [v] Ezek. 37:23
19 [w] Jer. 32:39; Ezek. 36:26; Zeph. 3:9 [x] Ps. 51:10; [Jer. 31:33]; Ezek. 18:31 [y] Zech. 7:12; [Rom. 2:4, 5] [5] Lit. *you* (pl.)
20 [z] Ps. 105:45 [a] Jer. 24:7; Ezek. 14:11; 36:28; 37:27
21 [b] Ezek. 9:10
22 [c] Ezek. 1:19
23 [d] Ezek. 8:4; 9:3 [e] Zech. 14:4 [f] Ezek. 43:2
24 [g] Ezek. 8:3; 2 Cor. 12:2-4 [6] Or *Babylon*, and so elsewhere in the book

CHAPTER 12

2 [a] Is. 1:23; Ezek. 2:3, 6-8 [b] Is. 6:9; 42:20; Jer. 5:21; Matt. 13:13, 14; Mark 4:12; 8:18; [Luke 8:10; John 9:39-41; 12:40]; Acts 28:26; Rom. 11:8 [c] Ezek. 2:5
6 [d] Is. 8:18; Ezek. 4:3; 24:24
9 [e] Ezek. 2:5 [f] Ezek. 17:12; 24:19
10 [g] Mal. 1:1 [1] *oracle, prophecy*

me. 25 So I spoke to those in captivity of all
the things the LORD had shown me.

Judah's Captivity Portrayed

12 Now the word of the LORD came to
me, saying: 2 "Son of man, you
dwell in the midst of [a]a rebellious house,
which [b]has eyes to see but does not see,
and ears to hear but does not hear; [c]for
they *are* a rebellious house.
3 "Therefore, son of man, prepare your
belongings for captivity, and go into captivity by day in their sight. You shall go
from your place into captivity to another
place in their sight. It may be that they will
consider, though they *are* a rebellious
house. 4 By day you shall bring out your
belongings in their sight, as though going
into captivity; and at evening you shall go
in their sight, like those who go into captivity. 5 Dig through the wall in their sight,
and carry your belongings out through it.
6 In their sight you shall bear *them* on *your*
shoulders *and* carry *them* out at twilight;
you shall cover your face, so that you cannot see the ground, [d]for I have made you a
sign to the house of Israel."
7 So I did as I was commanded. I
brought out my belongings by day, as
though going into captivity, and at evening
I dug through the wall with my hand. I
brought *them* out at twilight, *and* I bore
them on *my* shoulder in their sight.
8 And in the morning the word of the
LORD came to me, saying, 9 "Son of man,
has not the house of Israel, [e]the rebellious
house, said to you, [f]'What are you doing?'
10 Say to them, 'Thus says the Lord GOD:
"This [g]burden[1] *concerns* the prince in Jeru-

11:15 Get far away. The contemptuous words of those still left in Jerusalem at the carrying away of Jeconiah and the exiles indicated that they felt smugly secure and believed the land was their possession.

11:16 little sanctuary. This is better rendered "for a little while," i.e., however long the captivity lasted. God was to be the protection and provision for those who had been scattered through all the 70 years until they were restored. The exiles may have cast off the Jews, but God had not (Is. 8:14). This holds true for the future restoration of the Jews (vv. 17,18).

11:19,20 a new spirit. God pledged not only to restore Ezekiel's people to their ancient land, but to bring the New Covenant with its blessings. Cf. 36:25-28, and *see notes on Jer. 31:31ff.*

11:23 the mountain...east. The glory of God moved to the Mt. of Olives to which the glorious Son of God will return at the Second Advent (cf. 43:1-5; Zech. 14:4).

11:24 brought me in a vision. Again, Ezekiel has remained bodily in his Babylonian house, seen by his visitors (v. 25; 8:1). God, who supernaturally showed him a vision in Jerusalem, caused his sense of awareness to return to Chaldea, thus ending the vision state. Once the vision was completed, Ezekiel was able to tell his exiled countrymen what God had shown him (v. 25).

12:2 a rebellious house. The message of Ezekiel was addressed to his fellow exiles who were as hardened as those still in Jerusalem. They were so intent on a quick return to Jerusalem, that they would not accept his message of Jerusalem's destruction. Their rebellion is described in familiar terms (Deut. 29:1-4; Is. 6:9,10; Jer. 5:21; cf. Matt. 13:13-15; Acts 28:26,27).

12:3 prepare...for captivity. This dramatic object lesson by the prophet called for carrying belongings out in a stealthy way as an act that depicted baggage for exile, just the bare necessities. His countrymen carried out such baggage when they went into captivity, or sought to escape during Babylon's takeover of Jerusalem (vv. 7,11). Some attempting to escape were caught as in a net, like King Zedekiah who was overtaken, blinded, and forced into exile (vv. 12,13; 2 Kin. 24:18–25:7; Jer. 39:4-7; 52:1-11). Verse 9 indicates that Ezekiel actually did what he was told.

12:5 This section depicts those in desperation trying to escape from their sun-dried brick homes.

12:6 cover your face. This was to avoid recognition.

12:10-13 the prince. This is a reference to King Zedekiah, who was always referred to by Ezekiel as prince, never king. Jehoiachin was regarded as the true king (cf. 17:13), because the Babylonians never deposed him formally. All the house of Israel, however, shared the calami-

salem and all the house of Israel who are
among them." ' 11 Say, [h]'I *am* a sign to you.
As I have done, so shall it be done to them;
[i]they shall be carried away into captivity.'
12 And [j]the prince who *is* among them
shall bear *his belongings* on *his* shoulder at
twilight and go out. They shall dig through
the wall to carry *them* out through it. He
shall cover his face, so that he cannot see
the ground with *his* eyes. 13 I will also
spread My [k]net over him, and he shall be
caught in My snare. [l]I will bring him to
Babylon, *to* the land of the Chaldeans; yet
he shall not see it, though he shall die
there. 14 [m]I will scatter to every wind all
who *are* around him to help him, and all
his troops; and [n]I will draw out the sword
after them.
15 [o]"Then they shall know that I *am* the
LORD, when I scatter them among the nations and disperse them throughout the
countries. 16 [p]But I will spare a few of their
men from the sword, from famine, and
from pestilence, that they may declare all
their abominations among the Gentiles
wherever they go. Then they shall know
that I *am* the LORD."

Judgment Not Postponed

17 Moreover the word of the LORD came
to me, saying, 18 "Son of man, [q]eat your
bread with [2]quaking, and drink your
water with trembling and anxiety. 19 And
say to the people of the land, 'Thus says
the Lord GOD to the inhabitants of Jerusalem *and* to the land of Israel: "They shall
eat their bread with anxiety, and drink
their water with dread, so that her land
may [r]be emptied of all who are in it, [s]be-
cause of the violence of all those who dwell
in it. 20 Then the cities that are inhabited
shall be laid waste, and the land shall become desolate; and you shall know that I
am the LORD." ' "
21 And the word of the LORD came to me,
saying, 22 "Son of man, what *is* this
proverb *that* you *people* have about the land
of Israel, which says, [t]'The days are prolonged, and every vision fails'? 23 Tell
them therefore, 'Thus says the Lord GOD:
"I will lay this proverb to rest, and they
shall no more use it as a proverb in Israel."
But say to them, [u]"The days are at hand,
and the [3]fulfillment of every vision. 24 For
[v]no more shall there be any [w]false[4] vision
or flattering divination within the house of
Israel. 25 For I *am* the LORD. I speak, and
[x]the word which I speak will come to pass;
it will no more be postponed; for in your
days, O rebellious house, I will say the
word and [y]perform it," says the Lord
GOD.' "
26 Again the word of the LORD came to
me, saying, 27 [z]"Son of man, look, the
house of Israel is saying, 'The vision that
he sees *is* [a]for many days *from now,* and he
prophesies of times far off.' 28 [b]Therefore
say to them, 'Thus says the Lord GOD:
"None of My words will be postponed any
more, but the word which I speak [c]will be
done," says the Lord GOD.' "

Woe to Foolish Prophets

13 And the word of the LORD came to
me, saying, 2 "Son of man, prophesy [a]against the prophets of Israel who
prophesy, and say to [b]those who prophesy
out of their own [c]heart,[1] 'Hear the word of
the LORD!' "
3 Thus says the Lord GOD: "Woe to the
foolish prophets, who follow their own
spirit and have seen [2]nothing! 4 O Israel,
your prophets are [d]like foxes in the
deserts. 5 You [e]have not gone up into the
[3]gaps to build a wall for the house of Israel to stand in battle on the day of the
LORD. 6 [f]They have envisioned futility and
false divination, saying, 'Thus says the
LORD!' But the LORD has [g]not sent them;
yet they hope that the word may [4]be confirmed. 7 Have you not seen a futile vision,
and have you not spoken false divination?

11 [h] Ezek. 12:6 [i] 2 Kin. 25:4, 5, 7
12 [j] 2 Kin. 25:4; Jer. 39:4; 52:7; Ezek. 12:6
13 [k] Job 19:6; Jer. 52:9; Lam. 1:13; Ezek. 17:20 [l] 2 Kin. 25:7; Jer. 52:11; Ezek. 17:16
14 [m] 2 Kin. 25:4; Ezek. 5:10 [n] Ezek. 5:2, 12
15 [o] [Ps. 9:16]; Ezek. 6:7, 14; 12:16, 20
16 [p] 2 Kin. 25:11, 22; Ezek. 6:8-10
18 [q] Lam. 5:9; Ezek. 4:16 [2] *shaking*
19 [r] Jer. 10:22; Ezek. 6:6, 7, 14; Mic. 7:13; Zech. 7:14 [s] Ps. 107:34
22 [t] Jer. 5:12; Ezek. 11:3; 12:27; Amos 6:3; 2 Pet. 3:4
23 [u] Ps. 37:13; Joel 2:1; Zeph. 1:14 [3] Lit. *word*
24 [v] Jer. 14:13-16; Ezek. 13:6; Zech. 13:2-4 [w] Lam. 2:14 [4] Lit. *vain*
25 [x] [Is. 55:11]; Dan. 9:12; [Luke 21:33] [y] Num. 23:19; [Is. 14:24]
27 [z] Ezek. 12:22 [a] Dan. 10:14
28 [b] Ezek. 12:23, 25 [c] Jer. 4:7

CHAPTER 13

2 [a] Is. 28:7; Jer. 23:1-40; Lam. 2:14; Ezek. 22:25-28 [b] Ezek. 13:17 [c] Jer. 14:14; 23:16, 26 [1] Inspiration
3 [2] No vision
4 [d] Song 2:15
5 [e] Ps. 106:23; [Jer. 23:22]; Ezek. 22:30 [3] *breaches*
6 [f] Jer. 29:8; Ezek. 22:28 [g] Jer. 27:8-15 [4] Come true

ty to fall on Zedekiah. How literally these prophecies were fulfilled can be seen from the account in 2 Kin. 25:1-7. The "net" and "snare" (v. 13) were the Babylonian army. He was taken captive to Babylon, but he never saw it because his eyes had been put out at Riblah.

12:14-16 God's hand was to be with the enemy as His rod of correction, with only a few left.

12:22 this proverb. Delay had given the people the false impression that the stroke of judgment would never come. In fact, a saying had become popular, no doubt developed by false prophets who caused the people to reject Ezekiel's visions and prophecies (cf. v. 27) and gave "false divinations" (vv. 23,24).

12:25 in your days. The prophet is explicit about the present time for fulfillment, i.e., in their lifetime.

13:2 against the prophets. False prophets had long flourished in Judah and had been transported to Babylon as well. Here God directs Ezekiel to indict those false prophets for futile assurances of peace (as Jer. 23) in vv. 1-16. Then His attention turns to lying prophetesses in vv. 17-23. The test of a prophet is found in Deut. 13:1-5 and 18:21,22.

13:2,3 heart...spirit. Spurious spokesmen prophesy subjectively out of their minds while claiming to have revelation and authority from the Lord (cf. v. 7).

13:4 like foxes. False prophets did not do anything helpful. Rather, like foxes, they were mischievous and destructive.

13:5 to build a wall. The false prophets did nothing to shore up the spiritual defenses the people so needed in the face of judgment. The enemy had made "gaps" but the false prophets never encouraged the people to repent and return to the Lord. Those who would were called for in 22:30. The "day of the Lord" came in 586 B.C. when the theocracy fell. *See note on Is. 2:12.*

You say, 'The LORD says,' but I have not spoken."

8 Therefore thus says the Lord GOD: "Because you have spoken nonsense and envisioned lies, therefore I *am* indeed against you," says the Lord GOD. 9 "My hand will be [h]against the prophets who envision futility and who [i]divine lies; they shall not be in the assembly of My people, [j]nor be written in the record of the house of Israel, [k]nor shall they enter into the land of Israel. [l]Then you shall know that I *am* the Lord GOD.

10 "Because, indeed, because they have seduced My people, saying, [m]'Peace!' when *there is* no peace—and one builds a wall, and they [n]plaster[5] it with untempered *mortar*— 11 say to those who plaster *it* with untempered *mortar,* that it will fall. [o]There will be flooding rain, and you, O great hailstones, shall fall; and a stormy wind shall tear *it* down. 12 Surely, when the wall has fallen, will it not be said to you, 'Where *is* the mortar with which you plastered *it?*' "

13 Therefore thus says the Lord GOD: "I will cause a stormy wind to break forth in My fury; and there shall be a flooding rain in My anger, and great hailstones in fury to consume *it.* 14 So I will break down the wall you have plastered with untempered *mortar,* and bring it down to the ground, so that its foundation will be uncovered; it will fall, and you shall be consumed in the midst of it. [p]Then you shall know that I *am* the LORD.

15 "Thus will I accomplish My wrath on the wall and on those who have plastered it with untempered *mortar;* and I will say to you, 'The wall *is* no *more,* nor those who plastered it, 16 *that is,* the prophets of Israel who prophesy concerning Jerusalem, and who [q]see visions of peace for her when *there is* no peace,' " says the Lord GOD.

17 "Likewise, son of man, [r]set your face against the daughters of your people, [s]who prophesy out of their own [6]heart; prophesy against them, 18 and say, 'Thus says the Lord GOD: "Woe to the *women* who sew *magic* charms [7]on their sleeves and make veils for the heads of people of every height to hunt souls! Will you [t]hunt the souls of My people, and keep yourselves alive? 19 And will you profane Me among My people [u]for handfuls of barley and for pieces of bread, killing people who should not die, and keeping people alive who should not live, by your lying to My people who listen to lies?"

20 'Therefore thus says the Lord GOD: "Behold, I *am* against your *magic* charms by which you hunt souls there like [8]birds. I will tear them from your arms, and let the souls go, the souls you hunt like birds. 21 I will also tear off your veils and deliver My people out of your hand, and they shall no longer be as prey in your hand. [v]Then you shall know that I *am* the LORD.

22 "Because with [w]lies you have made the heart of the righteous sad, whom I have not made sad; and you have [x]strengthened the hands of the wicked, so that he does not turn from his wicked way to save his life. 23 Therefore [y]you shall no longer envision futility nor practice divination; for I will deliver My people out of your hand, and you shall know that I *am* the LORD." ' "

Idolatry Will Be Punished

14 Now [a]some of the elders of Israel came to me and sat before me. 2 And the word of the LORD came to me, saying, 3 "Son of man, these men have set up their idols in their hearts, and put

9 [h] Jer. 23:30 [i] Jer. 20:3-6 [j] Ezra 2:59, 62; Neh. 7:5; [Ps. 69:28] [k] Jer. 20:3-6 [l] Ezek. 11:10, 12
10 [m] Jer. 6:14; 8:11 [n] Ezek. 22:28 [5] Or *whitewash*
11 [o] Ezek. 38:22
14 [p] Ezek. 13:9, 21, 23; 14:8
16 [q] Jer. 6:14; 8:11; 28:9; Ezek. 13:10
17 [r] Ezek. 20:46; 21:2 [s] Ezek. 13:2; Rev. 2:20 [6] Inspiration
18 [t] [2 Pet. 2:14] [7] Lit. *over all the joints of My hands;* Vg. *under every elbow;* LXX, Tg. *on all elbows of the hands*
19 [u] 1 Sam. 2:15-17; Prov. 28:21; Mic. 3:5; Rom. 16:18; 1 Pet. 5:2
20 [8] Lit. *flying ones*
21 [v] Ezek. 13:9
22 [w] Jer. 28:15 [x] Jer. 23:14
23 [y] Ezek. 12:24; 13:6; Mic. 3:5, 6; Zech. 13:3

CHAPTER 14

1 [a] 2 Kin. 6:32; Ezek. 8:1; 20:1; 33:31

13:9 A 3-fold judgment is given to the false prophets: 1) they would not be in the council of God's people; 2) their names would be wiped from the register of Israel (Ezra 2:62); and 3) they would never return to the Land (cf. 20:38).

13:10,11 builds a wall. False prophets had lulled the people into false security. Phony "peace" promises, while sin continued on the brink of God's judgment, was a way, so to speak, of erecting a defective "wall" and whitewashing it to make it look good. Such an unsafe "wall" was doomed to collapse (v. 11) when God would bring His storm, picturing the invaders' assault (v. 11).

13:11-16 These descriptions are all images belonging to the illustration of the wall, not meant to convey real wind, flood, and hail. The Babylonians were the actual destroyers of Israel's hypocritical false spirituality.

13:17-23 Although women are rebuked by Isaiah (3:16–4:1; 32:9-13) and Amos (4:1-3), this is the only OT text where false prophetesses are mentioned. Sorcery was practiced mainly by women. Jezebel is called a false prophetess in Rev. 2:20.

13:18,19 charms...veils...handfuls of barley...bread. Apparently these sorceresses employed all these things in their divinations, hunting down souls for their advantage (v. 20).

13:22 with lies. Predators had saddened the righteous by a false message leading to calamity which involved great loss even for them (cf. 21:3,4). They had encouraged the wicked to expect a bright future, and saw no need to repent to avoid death.

13:23 I will deliver My people. Certainly this was true in the restoration after the 70 years in Babylon, but will be fully true in Messiah's kingdom. God's true promise will bring an end to sorcery and false prophecy (cf. Mic. 3:6,7; Zech. 13:1-6).

14:1-3 elders...came. These leaders came insincerely seeking God's counsel (v. 3; cf. Ps. 66:18), as God reveals to the prophet, who thus saw through their facade and indicted them for determining to pursue their evil way and defy God's will. False prophets of chap. 13 were thriving, as the civil leaders and populace whom they represented set a welcoming climate and inclination for the delusions.

before them [b]that which causes them to
stumble into iniquity. [c]Should I let Myself
be inquired of at all by them?
4 "Therefore speak to them, and say to
them, 'Thus says the Lord GOD: "Everyone
of the house of Israel who sets up his idols
in his heart, and puts before him what
causes him to stumble into iniquity, and
then comes to the prophet, I the LORD will
answer him who comes, according to the
multitude of his idols, 5 that I may seize the
house of Israel by their heart, because they
are all estranged from Me by their idols."'
6 "Therefore say to the house of Israel,
'Thus says the Lord GOD: "Repent, turn
away from your idols, and [d]turn your
faces away from all your abominations.
7 For anyone of the house of Israel, or of
the strangers who dwell in Israel, who
separates himself from Me and sets up his
idols in his heart and puts before him
what causes him to stumble into iniquity,
then comes to a prophet to inquire of him
concerning Me, I the LORD will answer
him by Myself. 8 [e]I will set My face against
that man and make him a [f]sign and a
proverb, and I will cut him off from the
midst of My people. [g]Then you shall know
that I *am* the LORD.
9 "And if the prophet is induced to
speak anything, I the LORD [h]have induced
that prophet, and I will stretch out My
hand against him and destroy him from
among My people Israel. 10 And they shall
bear their iniquity; the punishment of the
prophet shall be the same as the punishment of the one who inquired, 11 that the
house of Israel may [i]no longer stray from
Me, nor be profaned anymore with all their
transgressions, [j]but that they may be My
people and I may be their God," says the
Lord GOD.'"

Judgment on Persistent Unfaithfulness

12 The word of the LORD came again to
me, saying: 13 "Son of man, when a land
sins against Me by persistent unfaithfulness, I will stretch out My hand against it;
I will cut off its [k]supply of bread, send
famine on it, and cut off man and beast
from it. 14 [l]Even *if* these three men, Noah,
Daniel, and Job, were in it, they would deliver *only* themselves [m]by their righteousness," says the Lord GOD.
15 "If I cause [n]wild beasts to pass
through the land, and they [1]empty it, and
make it so desolate that no man may pass
through because of the beasts, 16 *even*
[o]*though* these three men *were* [2]in it, *as* I
live," says the Lord GOD, "they would deliver neither sons nor daughters; only they
would be delivered, and the land would be
[p]desolate.
17 "Or *if* [q]I bring a sword on that land,
and say, 'Sword, go through the land,' and
I [r]cut off man and beast from it, 18 even
[s]*though* these three men *were* in it, *as* I live,"
says the Lord GOD, "they would deliver
neither sons nor daughters, but only they
themselves would be delivered.
19 "Or *if* I send [t]a pestilence into that
land and [u]pour out My fury on it in blood,
and cut off from it man and beast, 20 even
[v]*though* Noah, Daniel, and Job *were* in it, *as*
I live," says the Lord GOD, "they would deliver neither son nor daughter; they would
deliver *only* themselves by their righteousness."
21 For thus says the Lord GOD: "How
much more it shall be when [w]I send My
four [3]severe judgments on Jerusalem—the
sword and famine and wild beasts and
pestilence—to cut off man and beast from
it? 22 [x]Yet behold, there shall be left in it a
remnant who will be [y]brought out, *both*

3 [b] Ezek. 7:19; Zeph. 1:3 [c] 2 Kin. 3:13; Is. 1:15; Jer. 11:11; Ezek. 20:3, 31
6 [d] 1 Sam. 7:3; Neh. 1:9; Is. 2:20; 30:22; 55:6, 7; Ezek. 18:30
8 [e] Lev. 17:10; 20:3, 5, 6; Jer. 44:11; Ezek. 15:7 [f] Num. 26:10; Deut. 28:37; Ezek. 5:15 [g] Ezek. 6:7; 13:14
9 [h] 1 Kin. 22:23; Job 12:16; Is. 66:4; Jer. 4:10; 2 Thess. 2:11
11 [i] Ps. 119:67, 71; Jer. 31:18, 19; [Heb. 12:11]; 2 Pet. 2:15 [j] Ezek. 11:20; 37:27
13 [k] Lev. 26:26; 2 Kin. 25:3; Is. 3:1; Jer. 52:6; Ezek. 4:16; 5:16
14 [l] Jer. 15:1 [m] [Prov. 11:4]
15 [n] Lev. 26:22; Num. 21:6; Ezek. 5:17; 14:21 [1] Lit. *bereave it of children*
16 [o] Ezek. 14:14, 18, 20 [p] Ezek. 15:8; 33:28, 29 [2] Lit. *in the midst of it*
17 [q] Lev. 26:25; Ezek. 5:12; 21:3, 4; 29:8; 38:21 [r] Ezek. 25:13; Zeph. 1:3
18 [s] Ezek. 14:14
19 [t] 2 Sam. 24:15; Ezek. 38:22 [u] Ezek. 7:8
20 [v] Ezek. 14:14
21 [w] Ezek. 5:17; 33:27; Amos 4:6-10; Rev. 6:8 [3] Lit. *evil*
22 [x] 2 Kin. 25:11, 12; Ezra 2:1; Ezek. 12:16; 36:20 [y] Ezek. 6:8

14:4 I the LORD will answer. They received no verbal answer, but an answer directly from the Lord in the action of judgment.

14:6 turn away. The Lord answered the two-faced inquiry in only one way, by a call to repent. The seekers were turned away from Him to idols (v. 6b), and He must be turned away from them (v. 8a). The guilty, including both those back at Jerusalem and the exiles tolerating the same things, were to repent, turning away from idols to God.

14:8 The punishment echoed the warnings of Lev. 20:3,5,6 and Deut. 28:27.

14:9 induced. God will deceive (entice) a false prophet only in a qualified sense. When one willfully rejects His Word, He places a resulting cloud of darkness, or permits it to continue, hiding the truth so that the person is deceived by his own obstinate self-will. This fits with the same principle as when God gives up Israel to evil statutes (20:25,26), counsel that they insist on as they spurn His Word (20:24,26). When people refuse the truth, He lets them seek after their own inclinations and gives them over to falsehood (20:39). This is the wrath of abandonment noted in Rom. 1:18-32 (cf. 1 Kin. 22:20-23; 2 Thess. 2:11).

14:12 The word...came again. Ezekiel answered a deception that God would never judge the people of Judah, since some righteous were among them. God would honor the presence of the godly (vv. 14,20).

14:13-20 My hand against. God promised 4 acts in His drama of judgment (cf. summary, v. 21). In none could the 3 heroes avert tragedy as advocates. These were: 1) famine; 2) ravages by wild beasts; 3) the sword; and 4) pestilence.

14:14-20 Noah, Daniel, and Job. Jeremiah 7:16 and 15:1-4 provide a close parallel to this passage. According to Jeremiah, even Moses and Samuel, well known for their power in intercessory prayer, would not prevail to deliver Jerusalem and the people. The 3 OT heroes mentioned in this section exhibited power in intercession on behalf of others (cf. Gen. 6:18; Job 42:7-10; Dan. 1,2) at strategic points in redemptive history, and even they could not deliver anyone but themselves if they were there praying earnestly. Even the presence and prayers of the godly could not stop the coming judgment. Genesis 18:22-32 and Jer. 5:1-4 provide rare exceptions to the principle that one man's righteousness is no protection for others.

sons and daughters; surely they will come
out to you, and [z]you will see their ways
and their doings. Then you will be comforted concerning the disaster that I have
brought upon Jerusalem, all that I have
brought upon it. 23 And they will comfort
you, when you see their ways and their doings; and you shall know that I have done
nothing [a]without cause that I have done in
it," says the Lord GOD.

The Outcast Vine

15 Then the word of the LORD came to
me, saying: 2 "Son of man, how is
the wood of the vine *better* than any other
wood, the vine branch which is among the
trees of the forest? 3 Is wood taken from it
to make any object? Or can *men* make a peg
from it to hang any vessel on? 4 Instead, [a]it
is thrown into the fire for fuel; the fire devours both ends of it, and its middle is
burned. Is it useful for *any* work? 5 Indeed,
when it was whole, no object could be
made from it. How much less will it be
useful for *any* work when the fire has devoured it, and it is burned?
6 "Therefore thus says the Lord GOD: 'Like
the wood of the vine among the trees of the
forest, which I have given to the fire for fuel,
so I will give up the inhabitants of Jerusalem; 7 and [b]I will set My face against them.
[c]They will go out from *one* fire, but *another*
fire shall devour them. [d]Then you shall
know that I *am* the LORD, when I set My face
against them. 8 Thus I will make the land
desolate, because they have persisted in
unfaithfulness,' says the Lord GOD."

God's Love for Jerusalem

16 Again the word of the LORD came to
me, saying, 2 "Son of man, [a]cause
Jerusalem to know her abominations,
3 and say, 'Thus says the Lord GOD to Jerusalem: "Your [1]birth [b]and your nativity *are*
from the land of Canaan; [c]your father *was*
an Amorite and your mother a Hittite. 4 *As
for* your nativity, [d]on the day you were
born your navel cord was not cut, nor were
you washed in water to cleanse *you;* you
were not rubbed with salt nor wrapped in
swaddling cloths. 5 No eye pitied you, to
do any of these things for you, to have
compassion on you; but you were thrown
out into the open field, when you yourself
were [2]loathed on the day you were born.
6 "And when I passed by you and saw
you struggling in your own blood, I said to
you in your blood, 'Live!' Yes, I said to you
in your blood, 'Live!' 7 [e]I made you [3]thrive
like a plant in the field; and you grew, matured, and became very beautiful. *Your*
breasts were formed, your hair grew, but
you *were* naked and bare.
8 "When I passed by you again and
looked upon you, indeed your time *was* the
time of love; [f]so I spread [4]My wing over
you and covered your nakedness. Yes, I
[g]swore an oath to you and entered into a
[h]covenant with you, and [i]you became
Mine," says the Lord GOD.
9 "Then I washed you in water; yes, I
thoroughly washed off your blood, and I
anointed you with oil. 10 I clothed you in
embroidered cloth and gave you sandals of
[5]badger skin; I clothed you with fine linen

22 [z] Ezek. 20:43
23 [a] Jer. 22:8, 9

CHAPTER 15

4 [a] [John 15:6]
7 [b] Lev. 26:17; [Ps. 34:16]; Jer. 21:10; Ezek. 14:8 [c] Is. 24:18 [d] Ezek. 7:4

CHAPTER 16

2 [a] Is. 58:1; Ezek. 20:4; 22:2
3 [b] Ezek. 21:30 [c] Gen. 15:16; Deut. 7:1; Josh. 24:15; Ezek. 16:45 [1] *origin and your birth*
4 [d] Hos. 2:3
5 [2] *abhorred*
7 [e] Ex. 1:7; Deut. 1:10 [3] Lit. *a myriad*
8 [f] Ruth 3:9; Jer. 2:2 [g] Gen. 22:16-18 [h] Ex. 24:6-8 [i] [Ex. 19:5]; Jer. 2:2; Ezek. 20:5; [Hos. 2:19, 20] [4] Or *the corner of My garment*
10 [5] Or *dolphin or dugong*

14:22,23 their ways. An ungodly Jerusalem remnant, brought as captives to join exiled Jews in Babylon, were to be very wicked. Exiles already there, repulsed by this evil, were to realize God's justness in His severe judgment on Jerusalem.

15:1-3 Then the word…came. Israel, often symbolized by a vine (17:6-10; Gen. 49:22; Jer. 2:21), had become useful for nothing. Failing to do the very thing God set her apart to do—bear fruit—she no longer served any purpose and was useless (v. 2). Other trees can be used for construction of certain things, but a fruitless vine is useless (v. 3). It has no value. In every age the people of God have their value in their fruitfulness.

15:4,5 thrown into the fire. The burning of the fruitless vine symbolized judgment in the deportations of 605 B.C. and 597 B.C. leading up to the final conquest in 586 B.C. Isaiah made the same analogy in his prophecy (Is. 5:1-7), saying Israel produced only useless sour berries.

15:6-8 Therefore. The prophet applies the symbol to Israel and predicts the desolation of the city and the land. In the time of the Great Tribulation, it will be so again (cf. Rev. 14:18).

16:1-7 This section covers the period from Abraham entering Canaan (cf. Gen. 12) through the exile in Egypt (cf. Ex. 12).

16:1 the word. This longest chapter in Ezekiel is similar to chap. 23, in that both indict Judah as spiritually immoral (v. 2). The story of Israel's sin and unfaithfulness to the love of God is told in all its sordid, vile character. The chap. is so sad and indicting that some of the ancient rabbis did not allow it to be read in public.

16:3-5 Israel was like an abandoned child. In 16:4-14 we see the history of Israel from her conception to her glory under Solomon.

16:3 birth…Amorite…Hittite. Cf. 16:45. These names identify the residents of Canaan who occupied the land when Abraham migrated there (cf. Gen. 12:5,6). Jerusalem had the same moral character as the rest of Canaan.

16:4,5 Israel, in the day of its birth, was unwanted and uncared for.

16:6 Live! The time intended here is probably the patriarchal period of Abraham, Isaac, and Jacob, when God formed His people.

16:7 thrive. This refers more to the people than to the land. It seems to refer to the time of Israel's growth during the 430 year stay in Egypt; wild but flourishing and beautiful Israel was "naked," without the benefits of culture and civilization (Gen. 46–Ex. 12; cf. Ex. 1:7,9,12).

16:8-14 This is best taken as the time from the Exodus (Ex. 12ff.) through David's reign (1 Kin. 2).

16:8 the time of love. This refers to the marriageable state. Spreading his "wing" was a custom of espousal (cf. Ruth 3:9) and indicates that God entered into a covenant with the young nation at Mt. Sinai (cf. Ex. 19:5-8). Making a covenant signifies marriage, the figure of God's relation to Israel (cf. Jer. 2:2; 3:1ff.; Hos. 2:2-23).

16:9-14 These gifts were marriage gifts customarily presented to a queen. The crowning may refer to the reigns of David and

and covered you with silk. 11 I adorned
you with ornaments, [j]put bracelets on
your wrists, [k]and a chain on your neck.
12 And I put a [6]jewel in your nose, earrings
in your ears, and a beautiful crown on
your head. 13 Thus you were adorned with
gold and silver, and your clothing *was of*
fine linen, silk, and embroidered cloth.
[l]You ate *pastry of* fine flour, honey, and oil.
You were exceedingly [m]beautiful, and succeeded to royalty. 14 [n]Your fame went out
among the nations because of your beauty,
for it *was* perfect through My splendor
which I had bestowed on you," says the
Lord GOD.

Jerusalem's Harlotry

15 [o]"But you trusted in your own beauty,
[p]played the harlot because of your fame,
and poured out your harlotry on everyone
passing by who *would have* it. 16 [q]You took
some of your garments and adorned multicolored [7]high places for yourself, and
played the harlot on them. *Such* things
should not happen, nor be. 17 You have
also taken your beautiful jewelry from My
gold and My silver, which I had given you,
and made for yourself male images and
played the harlot with them. 18 You took
your embroidered garments and covered
them, and you set My oil and My incense
before them. 19 Also [r]My food which I
gave you—the pastry of fine flour, oil, and
honey *which* I fed you—you set it before
them as [8]sweet incense; and *so* it was,"
says the Lord GOD.
20 [s]"Moreover you took your sons and
your daughters, whom you bore to Me,
and these you sacrificed to them to be devoured. *Were* your *acts* of harlotry a small
matter, 21 that you have slain My children
and offered them up to them by causing
them to pass through *the* [t]*fire?* 22 And in all
your abominations and acts of harlotry
you did not remember the days of your
[u]youth, [v]when you were naked and bare,
struggling in your blood.
23 "Then it was so, after all your wickedness—'Woe, woe to you!' says the Lord
GOD— 24 *that* [w]you also built for yourself a
shrine, and [x]made a [9]high place for yourself in every street. 25 You built your high
places [y]at the head of every road, and
made your beauty to be abhorred. You offered yourself to everyone who passed by,
and multiplied your acts of harlotry. 26 You
also committed harlotry with [z]the Egyptians, your very fleshly neighbors, and increased your acts of harlotry to [a]provoke
Me to anger.
27 "Behold, therefore, I stretched out My
hand against you, diminished your [1]allot-
ment, and gave you up to the will of those
who hate you, [b]the daughters of the Philistines, who were ashamed of your lewd
behavior. 28 You also played the harlot
with the [c]Assyrians, because you were insatiable; indeed you played the harlot with
them and still were not satisfied. 29 Moreover you multiplied your acts of harlotry
as far as the land of the trader, [d]Chaldea;
and even then you were not satisfied.
30 "How degenerate is your heart!" says
the Lord GOD, "seeing you do all these
things, the deeds of a brazen harlot.

Jerusalem's Adultery

31 [e]"You erected your shrine at the head
of every road, and built your [2]high place in
every street. Yet you were not like a harlot,
because you scorned [f]payment. 32 *You are*
an adulterous wife, *who* takes strangers instead of her husband. 33 Men make payment to all harlots, but [g]you made your
payments to all your lovers, and [3]hired
them to come to you from all around for
your harlotry. 34 You are the opposite of
other women in your harlotry, because no
one solicited you to be a harlot. In that you
gave payment but no payment was given
you, therefore you are the opposite."

11 [j]Gen. 24:22, 47; Is. 3:19; Ezek. 23:42 [k]Gen. 41:42; Prov. 1:9
12 [6]Lit. *ring*
13 [l]Deut. 32:13, 14 [m]Ps. 48:2
14 [n]Ps. 50:2; Lam. 2:15
15 [o]Deut. 32:15; Jer. 7:4; Mic. 3:11 [p]Is. 1:21; 57:8; Jer. 2:20; 3:2, 6, 20; Ezek. 23:11-20; Hos. 1:2
16 [q]2 Kin. 23:7; Ezek. 7:20; Hos. 2:8 [7]Places for pagan worship
19 [r]Hos. 2:8 [8]Or *a sweet aroma*
20 [s]2 Kin. 16:3; Ps. 106:37; Is. 57:5; Jer. 7:31; Ezek. 20:26
21 [t]2 Kin. 17:17; Jer. 19:5; Ezek. 20:31; 23:37
22 [u]Jer. 2:2; Hos. 11:1 [v]Ezek. 16:4-6
24 [w]Jer. 11:13; Ezek. 16:31, 39; 20:28, 29 [x]Ps. 78:58; Is. 57:7; Jer. 2:20; 3:2 [9]Place for pagan worship
25 [y]Prov. 9:14
26 [z]Ezek. 16:26; 20:7, 8 [a]Deut. 31:20
27 [b]2 Chr. 28:18; Is. 9:12; Ezek. 16:57 [1]Allowance of food
28 [c]2 Kin. 16:7, 10-18; 2 Chr. 28:16, 20-23; Jer. 2:18, 36; Ezek. 23:12; Hos. 10:6
29 [d]Ezek. 23:14-17
31 [e]Ezek. 16:24, 39 [f]Is. 52:3 [2]Place for pagan worship
33 [g]Is. 30:6; 57:9; Ezek. 16:41; Hos. 8:9, 10 [3]Or *bribed*

Solomon, when Jerusalem became the royal city. Israel was actually a small kingdom but with a great reputation (cf. 1 Kin. 10). This refers to the time from Joshua's conquest of Canaan (Josh. 3ff.) through David's reign (cf. 1 Kin. 2) and into Solomon's time (before 1 Kin. 11).

16:14 My splendor. The nation was truly a trophy of God's grace (cf. Deut. 7:6-8). The presence and glory of the Lord provided Jerusalem with her beauty and prominence.

16:15-34 Continuing the marriage metaphor, this section describes the spiritual harlotry of Israel from Solomon (cf. 1 Kin. 11:1) all the way to Ezekiel's time.

16:15-19 A general summary of the nation's idolatry as she gave herself to the religious practices of the Canaanites. Every gracious gift from God was devoted to idols.

16:20-22 sons…daughters. This refers to the sacrifices of children to pagan gods (cf. 20:25,26,31; 2 Kin. 16:3; 21:6; 23:10; 24:4). God had expressly forbidden this (cf. Deut. 12:31; 18:10). Still, the children were first slain, then burned (cf. Jer. 7:31; 19:5; 32:35; Mic. 6:7) until Josiah's abolition of it. It had been reinstated in Ezekiel's day.

16:23-30 This section, partly woe and partly lament, spoke to Judah's obsession with idolatry and her being influenced by Egypt (v. 26), the Philistines (v. 27), Assyria (v. 28), and Babylon (v. 29).

16:27 ashamed. The wickedness and gross evil of the Jews even scandalized pagan Philistines.

16:29 Chaldea. They even prostituted themselves with the Babylonians (cf. 2 Kin. 20:12-19).

16:31-34 It is wicked to be solicited and then paid for immorality. Israel engaged in far worse behavior—she solicited and even paid her idol consorts. This refers to the heavy tribute Israel had to pay to the godless nations.

Jerusalem's Lovers Will Abuse Her

35 'Now then, O harlot, hear the word
of the LORD! 36 Thus says the Lord GOD:
"Because your filthiness was poured out
and your nakedness uncovered in your
harlotry with your lovers, and with all
your abominable idols, and because of
[h]the blood of your children which you
gave to them, 37 surely, therefore, [i]I will
gather all your lovers with whom you
took pleasure, all those you loved, *and* all
those you hated; I will gather them from
all around against you and will uncover
your nakedness to them, that they may
see all your nakedness. 38 And I will
judge you as [j]women who break wedlock
or [k]shed blood are judged; I will bring
blood upon you in fury and jealousy. 39 I
will also give you into their hand, and
they shall throw down your shrines and
break down [l]your [4]high places. [m]They
shall also strip you of your clothes, take
your beautiful jewelry, and leave you
naked and bare.
40 [n]"They shall also bring up an assembly against you, [o]and they shall stone you
with stones and thrust you through with
their swords. 41 They shall [p]burn your
houses with fire, and [q]execute judgments
on you in the sight of many women; and I
will make you [r]cease playing the harlot,
and you shall no longer hire lovers. 42 So
[s]I will lay to rest My fury toward you, and
My jealousy shall depart from you. I will
be quiet, and be angry no more. 43 Because [t]you did not remember the days of
your youth, but [5]agitated Me with all
these *things,* surely [u]I will also recompense your [6]deeds on *your own* head,"
says the Lord GOD. "And you shall not
commit lewdness in addition to all your
abominations.

More Wicked than Samaria and Sodom

44 "Indeed everyone who quotes
proverbs will use *this* proverb against you:
'Like mother, like daughter!' 45 You *are*
your mother's daughter, [7]loathing husband and children; and you *are* the [v]sister
of your sisters, who loathed their husbands and children; [w]your mother *was* a
Hittite and your father an Amorite.
46 "Your elder sister *is* Samaria, who
dwells with her daughters to the north of
you; and [x]your younger sister, who dwells
to the south of you, *is* Sodom and her
daughters. 47 You did not walk in their
ways nor act according to their abominations; but, as *if that were* too little, [y]you became more corrupt than they in all your
ways.
48 "*As* I live," says the Lord GOD, "neither [z]your sister Sodom nor her daughters
have done as you and your daughters have
done. 49 Look, this was the iniquity of your
sister Sodom: She and her daughter had
pride, [a]fullness of food, and abundance of
idleness; neither did she strengthen the
hand of the poor and needy. 50 And they
were haughty and [b]committed abomination before Me; therefore [c]I took them
away as [8]I saw *fit.*
51 "Samaria did not commit [d]half of
your sins; but you have multiplied your
abominations more than they, and [e]have
justified your sisters by all the abominations which you have done. 52 You who
judged your sisters, bear your own shame
also, because the sins which you committed were more abominable than theirs;
they are more righteous than you. Yes, be
disgraced also, and bear your own shame,
because you justified your sisters.
53 [f]"When I bring back their captives,
the captives of Sodom and her daughters,
and the captives of Samaria and her
daughters, then *I will also bring back* [g]the
captives of your captivity among them,
54 that you may bear your own shame and
be disgraced by all that you did when
[h]you comforted them. 55 When your sisters, Sodom and her daughters, return to
their former state, and Samaria and her
daughters return to their former state,
then you and your daughters will return
to your former state. 56 For your sister
Sodom was not a byword in your mouth
in the days of your pride, 57 before your
wickedness was uncovered. It was like
the time of the [i]reproach of the daughters
of [9]Syria and all *those* around her, and of
[j]the daughters of the Philistines, who despise you everywhere. 58 [k]You have paid
for your lewdness and your abominations," says the LORD. 59 For thus says the
Lord GOD: "I will deal with you as you
have done, who [l]despised [m]the oath by
breaking the covenant.

36 [h] Jer. 2:34; Ezek. 16:20
37 [i] Jer. 13:22, 26; Lam. 1:8; Ezek. 23:9, 10, 22, 29; Hos. 2:10; 8:10; Nah. 3:5
38 [j] Lev. 20:10; Deut. 22:22; Ezek. 23:45 [k] Gen. 9:6; Ex. 21:12; Ezek. 16:20, 36
39 [l] Ezek. 16:24, 31 [m] Ezek. 23:26; Hos. 2:3 [4] Places for pagan worship
40 [n] Ezek. 23:45-47; Hab. 1:6-10 [o] John 8:5, 7
41 [p] Deut. 13:16; 2 Kin. 25:9; Jer. 39:8; 52:13 [q] Ezek. 5:8; 23:10, 48 [r] Ezek. 23:27
42 [s] 2 Sam. 24:25; Ezek. 5:13; 21:17; Zech. 6:8
43 [t] Ps. 78:42; Ezek. 16:22 [u] Ezek. 9:10; 11:21; 22:31 [5] So with LXX, Syr., Tg., Vg.; MT *were agitated with Me* [6] Lit. *way*
45 [v] Ezek. 23:2-4 [w] Ezek. 16:3 [7] Or *despising*
46 [x] Deut. 32:32; Is. 1:10
47 [y] 2 Kin. 21:9; Ezek. 5:6, 7
48 [z] Is. 3:9; Lam. 4:6; Matt. 10:15; 11:24; Rev. 11:8
49 [a] Gen. 13:10; Is. 22:13; Amos 6:4-6
50 [b] Gen. 13:13; 18:20; 19:5 [c] Gen. 19:24 [8] Vg. *you saw;* LXX *he saw;* Tg. *as was revealed to Me*
51 [d] Ezek. 23:11 [e] Jer. 3:8-11; Matt. 12:41
53 [f] Is. 1:9; [Ezek. 16:60] [g] Jer. 20:16
54 [h] Ezek. 14:22
57 [i] 2 Kin. 16:5; 2 Chr. 28:18; Is. 7:1; Ezek. 5:14, 15; 22:4 [j] Ezek. 16:27 [9] Heb. *Aram;* so with MT, LXX, Tg., Vg.; many Heb. mss., Syr. *Edom*
58 [k] Ezek. 23:49
59 [l] Ezek. 17:13 [m] Deut. 29:12

16:35-40 I...will uncover your nakedness. Public exposure of profligate women and the stoning of them were well-known customs in ancient Israel, making them a shameful spectacle.

16:42 By exacting the full penalty on Israel's sins in the destruction by Babylon, God's wrath was to be satisfied.

16:44-45 Like mother, like daughter! Judah has followed in the pagan footsteps of her beginnings (cf. 16:3).

16:46-59 Judah is compared to Samaria and Sodom, whose judgment for sin was great. Judah was more corrupt (v. 47), multiplied Samaria's and Sodom's sin (v. 51), and committed more abominable sin (v. 52).

An Everlasting Covenant

60 "Nevertheless I will [n]remember My
covenant with you in the days of your
youth, and I will establish [o]an everlasting
covenant with you. 61 Then [p]you will remember your ways and be ashamed, when
you receive your older and your younger
sisters; for I will give them to you for
[q]daughters, [r]but not because of My
covenant with you. 62 [s]And I will establish
My covenant with you. Then you shall
know that I *am* the LORD, 63 that you may
[t]remember and be ashamed, [u]and never
open your mouth anymore because of
your shame, when I provide you an atonement for all you have done," says the Lord
GOD.' "

The Eagles and the Vine

17 And the word of the LORD came to
me, saying, 2 "Son of man, pose a
riddle, and speak a [a]parable to the house
of Israel, 3 and say, 'Thus says the Lord
GOD:

[b]"A great eagle with large wings and
long pinions,
Full of feathers of various colors,
Came to Lebanon
And [c]took from the cedar the
highest branch.
4 He cropped off its topmost young
twig
And carried it to a land of trade;
He set it in a city of merchants.
5 Then he took some of the seed of
the land
And planted it in [d]a fertile field;
He placed *it* by abundant waters
And set it [e]like a willow tree.
6 And it grew and became a
spreading vine [f]of low
stature;
Its branches turned toward him,
But its roots were under it.
So it became a vine,
Brought forth branches,
And put forth shoots.

7 "But there was [1]another great eagle
with large wings and many
feathers;
And behold, [g]this vine bent its
roots toward him,
And stretched its branches toward
him,
From the garden terrace where it
had been planted,
That he might water it.
8 It was planted in [2]good soil by
many waters,
To bring forth branches, bear fruit,
And become a majestic vine." '

9 "Say, 'Thus says the Lord GOD:

"Will it thrive?
[h]Will he not pull up its roots,
Cut off its fruit,
And leave it to wither?
All of its spring leaves will wither,
And no great power or many
people
Will be needed to pluck it up by its
roots.
10 Behold, *it is* planted,
Will it thrive?
[i]Will it not utterly wither when the
east wind touches it?
It will wither in the garden terrace
where it grew." ' "

11 Moreover the word of the LORD came
to me, saying, 12 "Say now to [j]the rebellious house: 'Do you not know what these
things mean?' Tell *them,* 'Indeed [k]the king of

60 [n]Lev. 26:42-45; Ps. 106:45 [o]Is. 55:3; Jer. 32:40; 50:5; Ezek. 37:26
61 [p]Jer. 50:4, 5; Ezek. 20:43; 36:31 [q]Is. 54:1; 60:4; [Gal. 4:26] [r]Jer. 31:31
62 [s]Hos. 2:19, 20
63 [t]Ezek. 36:31, 32; Dan. 9:7, 8 [u]Ps. 39:9; [Rom. 3:19]

CHAPTER 17
2 [a]Ezek. 20:49; 24:3
3 [b]Jer. 48:40; Ezek. 17:12; Hos. 8:1 [c]2 Kin. 24:12
5 [d]Deut. 8:7-9 [e]Is. 44:4
6 [f]Ezek. 17:14
7 [g]Ezek. 17:15 [1]So with LXX, Syr., Vg.; MT, Tg. *one*
8 [2]Lit. *a good field*
9 [h]2 Kin. 25:7
10 [i]Ezek. 19:12; Hos. 13:15
12 [j]Ezek. 2:3-5; 12:9 [k]2 Kin. 24:11-16; Ezek. 1:2; 17:3

16:60 I will remember My covenant. God is gracious and He always finds a covenant basis on which He can exercise His grace. The Lord will remember the Abrahamic Covenant (cf. Gen. 12:1ff.) made with Israel in her youth. Restoration will be by grace, not merit. **an everlasting covenant.** This is the New Covenant, which is unconditional, saving, and everlasting (cf. 37:26; Is. 59:21; 61:8; Jer. 31:31-34; Heb. 8:6-13). The basis of God's grace will not be the Mosaic Covenant, which the Jews could never fulfill, even with the best intentions (cf. Ex. 24:1ff.). When God establishes His eternal covenant, Israel will know that God is the Lord because of His grace.

16:63 an atonement. This looks to the cross of Christ (cf. Is. 53), by which God's just wrath on sin was satisfied so that He could grant grace to all who believe (cf. 2 Cor. 5:21).

17:1 This chap. is dated about 588 B.C. (two years before the destruction of Jerusalem). The history of the period is in 2 Kin. 24; 2 Chr. 36; Jer. 36,37,52.

17:3 A great eagle. The king of Babylon, in view here, took royal captives and others (vv. 4,12,13). **the cedar.** The kingdom of Judah.

17:4 topmost young twig. This is Jehoiachin, the king, exiled in 597 B.C. (2 Kin. 24:11-16). Babylon is the "land of trade" (16:29).

17:5,6 seed. Those whom Babylon left in Judah in 597 B.C., who could prosper as a tributary to the conqueror, turned toward him (v. 6).

17:6 a spreading vine. Refers to Zedekiah (ca. 597–586 B.C.), the youngest son of Josiah whom Nebuchadnezzar appointed king in Judah. The benevolent attitude of Nebuchadnezzar helped Zedekiah to prosper, and if he had remained faithful to his pledge to Nebuchadnezzar, Judah would have continued as a tributary kingdom. Instead, he began courting help from Egypt (2 Chr. 36:13), which Jeremiah protested (Jer. 37:5-7).

17:7 another great eagle. Egypt is meant (v. 15), specifically Pharaoh Apries, a.k.a. Hophra (588–568 B.C.). Zedekiah turned to him to help revolt against Babylon.

17:9,10 wither. Zedekiah's treachery would not prosper. The king was captured in the plains of Jericho (Jer. 52:8). The dependence on Egypt would fail, and Judah would wither as the E wind (a picture of Babylon, cf. 13:11-13) blasted her.

Babylon went to Jerusalem and took its
king and princes, and led them with him to
Babylon. 13 [l]And he took the king's offspring, made a covenant with him, [m]and
put him under oath. He also took away the
mighty of the land, 14 that the kingdom
might be [n]brought low and not lift itself
up, *but* that by keeping his covenant it
might stand. 15 But [o]he rebelled against
him by sending his ambassadors to Egypt,
[p]that they might give him horses and
many people. [q]Will he prosper? Will he
who does such *things* escape? Can he break
a covenant and still be delivered?

16 '*As* I live,' says the Lord GOD, 'surely
[r]in the place *where* the king *dwells* who
made him king, whose oath he despised
and whose covenant he broke—with him
in the midst of Babylon he shall die.
17 [s]Nor will Pharaoh with *his* mighty army
and great company do anything in the war,
[t]when they heap up a siege mound and
build a [3]wall to cut off many persons.
18 Since he despised the oath by breaking
the covenant, and in fact [u]gave[4] his hand
and still did all these *things*, he shall not escape.' "

19 Therefore thus says the Lord GOD: "*As*
I live, surely My oath which he despised,
and My covenant which he broke, I will
recompense on his own head. 20 I will
[v]spread My net over him, and he shall be
taken in My snare. I will bring him to
Babylon and [w]try him there for the [5]trea-
son which he committed against Me.
21 [x]All his [6]fugitives with all his troops
shall fall by the sword, and those who remain shall be [y]scattered to every wind;
and you shall know that I, the LORD, have
spoken."

13 [l] 2 Kin. 24:17; Jer. 37:1; Ezek. 17:5 [m] 2 Chr. 36:13
14 [n] Ezek. 29:14
15 [o] 2 Kin. 24:20; 2 Chr. 36:13; Jer. 52:3; Ezek. 17:7 [p] Deut. 17:16; Is. 31:1, 3; 36:6, 9 [q] Ezek. 17:9
16 [r] Jer. 52:11; Ezek. 12:13
17 [s] Jer. 37:7; Ezek. 29:6 [t] Jer. 52:4; Ezek. 4:2 [3] Or *siege wall*
18 [u] 1 Chr. 29:24; Lam. 5:6 [4] Took an oath
20 [v] Ezek. 12:13 [w] Jer. 2:35; Ezek. 20:36 [5] Lit. *unfaithful act*
21 [x] Ezek. 12:14 [y] Ezek. 12:15; 22:15 [6] So with MT, Vg.; many Heb. mss., Syr. *choice men*; Tg. *mighty men*; LXX omits *All his fugitives*

22 [z] [Is. 11:1; Jer. 23:5; Zech. 3:8] [a] Is. 53:2 [b] [Ps. 2:6]
23 [c] [Is. 2:2, 3]; Ezek. 20:40; [Mic. 4:1] [d] Ezek. 31:6; Dan. 4:12
24 [e] Ezek. 37:3; Amos 9:11; Luke 1:52; [Rom. 11:23, 24] [f] Ezek. 22:14

CHAPTER 18

2 [a] Jer. 31:29; Lam. 5:7
4 [b] Num. 16:22; 27:16; Is. 42:5; 57:16 [c] Ezek. 18:20; [Rom. 6:23]
6 [d] Ezek. 22:9 [1] At the mountain shrines

Israel Exalted at Last

22 Thus says the Lord GOD: "I will take
also *one* of the highest [z]branches of the
high cedar and set *it* out. I will crop off
from the topmost of its young twigs [a]a tender one, and will [b]plant *it* on a high and
prominent mountain. 23 [c]On the mountain
height of Israel I will plant it; and it will
bring forth boughs, and bear fruit, and be
a majestic cedar. [d]Under it will dwell birds
of every sort; in the shadow of its branches
they will dwell. 24 And all the trees of the
field shall know that I, the LORD, [e]have
brought down the high tree and exalted
the low tree, dried up the green tree and
made the dry tree flourish; [f]I, the LORD,
have spoken and have done *it*."

A False Proverb Refuted

18 The word of the LORD came to me
again, saying, 2 "What do you mean
when you use this proverb concerning the
land of Israel, saying:

'The [a]fathers have eaten sour
grapes,
And the children's teeth are set on
edge'?

3 "*As* I live," says the Lord GOD, "you
shall no longer use this proverb in Israel.

4 "Behold, all souls are [b]Mine;
The soul of the father
As well as the soul of the son is
Mine;
[c]The soul who sins shall die.
5 But if a man is just
And does what is lawful and right;
6 [d]If he has not eaten [1]on the
mountains,

17:11-21 put him under oath. The parable is explained in detail. Babylon (v. 12) made Zedekiah a vassal subject to her, took captives, and left Judah weak (vv. 13,14). Zedekiah broke the agreement (v. 15) in which he swore by the Lord to submit to Babylon (2 Chr. 36:13), and sought Egypt's help, thus he was taken to Babylon to live out his life (v. 16,19; Jer. 39:4-7). Egypt was to be no help to him (v. 17) or any protector of his army (v. 21).

17:22,23 *one* of the highest branches. This is messianic prophecy stating that God will provide the Messiah from the royal line of David ("the high cedar") and establish Him in His kingdom (like a mountain, cf. Dan. 2:35,44,45). He will be "a high branch" reigning in the height of success. "Branch" is a name for Messiah (cf. 34:23, 24; 37:24,25; Is. 4:2; Jer. 23:5; 33:15; Zech. 3:8; 6:12). Messiah will be "a tender one" (v. 22) growing into a "majestic cedar" (v. 23). Under His kingdom rule, all nations will be blessed and Israel restored.

17:24 made the dry tree flourish. The Messiah would grow out of the dry tree left after humbling judgment, i.e., Judah's remnant from which He came of a lowly family (cf. Is. 6:13), yet would prosper.

18:1-32 One of the foundational principles of Scripture is presented in this chap. (also taught in Deut. 24:16; 2 Kin. 14:6): Judgment is according to individual faith and conduct. He had foretold national punishment, but the reason was individual sin (cf. 3:16-21; 14:12-20; 33:1-20).

18:2 eaten sour grapes. The people of Judah would not acknowledge their guilt worthy of judgment. Though they were themselves wicked and idolatrous, they blamed their forefathers for their state (cf. 2 Kin. 21:15). The rationalizing is expressed in a current proverb (cf. Jer. 31:29) which means, in effect, "They sinned (ate sour grapes); we inherit the bitterness" (teeth set on edge).

18:3 no longer use this proverb. God rejected their blame shifting and evasion of responsibility.

18:4 The soul who sins shall die. God played no favorites, but was fair in holding each individual accountable for his own sin. The death is physical death which, for many, results in eternal death.

18:5-18 Two scenarios are proposed to clarify the matter of personal guilt: 1) a just father of an unjust son (vv. 5-13); and 2) an unjust father of a just son (vv. 14-18).

18:5 if a man is just. The definition of "just" or righteous is given in specifics in vv. 6-9. Such behavior could only characterize a genuine believer who was "faithful" from the heart.

Nor lifted up his eyes to the idols
of the house of Israel,
Nor [e]defiled his neighbor's wife,
Nor approached [f]a woman during
her impurity;
7 If he has not [g]oppressed anyone,
But has restored to the debtor his
[h]pledge;
Has robbed no one by violence,
But has [i]given his bread to the
hungry
And covered the naked with
[j]clothing;
8 If he has not [2]exacted [k]usury
Nor taken any increase,
But has withdrawn his hand from
iniquity
And [l]executed true [3]judgment
between man and man;
9 *If* he has walked in My statutes
And kept My judgments
faithfully—
He *is* just;
He shall surely [m]live!"
Says the Lord GOD.

10 "If he begets a son *who is* a robber
Or [n]a shedder of blood,
Who does any of these *things*
11 And does none of those *duties*,
But has eaten [4]on the mountains
Or defiled his neighbor's wife;
12 If he has oppressed the poor and
needy,
Robbed by violence,
Not restored the pledge,
Lifted his eyes to the idols,
Or [o]committed abomination;
13 If he has exacted usury
Or taken increase—
Shall he then live?
He shall not live!
If he has done any of these
abominations,
He shall surely die;
[p]His blood shall be upon him.

14 "*If,* however, he begets a son
Who sees all the sins which his
father has done,
And considers but does not do
likewise;
15 [q]*Who* has not eaten [5]on the
mountains,
Nor lifted his eyes to the idols of
the house of Israel,
Nor defiled his neighbor's wife;
16 Has not oppressed anyone,
Nor withheld a pledge,
Nor robbed by violence,
But has given his bread to the
hungry
And covered the naked with
clothing;
17 *Who* has withdrawn his hand from
[6]the poor
And not received usury or increase,
But has executed My judgments
And walked in My statutes—
He shall not die for the iniquity of
his father;
He shall surely live!

18 "*As for* his father,
Because he cruelly oppressed,
Robbed his brother by violence,
And did what *is* not good among
his people,
Behold, [r]he shall die for his
iniquity.

Turn and Live

19 "Yet you say, 'Why [s]should the son
not bear the guilt of the father?' Because
the son has done what is lawful and right,
and has kept all My statutes and observed
them, he shall surely live. 20 [t]The soul who
sins shall die. [u]The son shall not bear the
guilt of the father, nor the father bear the
guilt of the son. [v]The righteousness of
the righteous shall be upon himself, [w]and
the wickedness of the wicked shall be
upon himself.
21 "But [x]if a wicked man turns from all
his sins which he has committed, keeps all
My statutes, and does what is lawful and
right, he shall surely live; he shall not die.

6 [e] Lev. 18:20; 20:10 [f] Lev. 18:19; 20:18
7 [g] Ex. 22:21; Lev. 19:15; 25:14 [h] Ex. 22:26; Deut. 24:12 [i] Deut. 15:7, 11; Ezek. 18:16; [Matt. 25:35–40]; Luke 3:11 [j] Is. 58:7
8 [k] Ex. 22:25; Lev. 25:36; Deut. 23:19; Neh. 5:7; Ps. 15:5 [l] Deut. 1:16; Zech. 8:16 [2] Lent money at interest [3] *justice*
9 [m] Ezek. 20:11; Amos 5:4; [Hab. 2:4; Rom. 1:17]
10 [n] Gen. 9:6; Ex. 21:12; Num. 35:31
11 [4] At the mountain shrines
12 [o] 2 Kin. 21:11; Ezek. 8:6, 17
13 [p] Lev. 20:9, 11-13, 16, 27; Ezek. 3:18; Acts 18:6
15 [q] Ezek. 18:6 [5] At the mountain shrines
17 [6] So with MT, Tg., Vg.; LXX *iniquity* (cf. v. 8)
18 [r] Ezek. 3:18
19 [s] Ex. 20:5; Deut. 5:9; 2 Kin. 23:26; 24:3, 4
20 [t] 2 Kin. 14:6; 22:18-20; Ezek. 18:4 [u] Deut. 24:16; 2 Kin. 14:6; 2 Chr. 25:4; Jer. 31:29, 30 [v] 1 Kin. 8:32; Is. 3:10, 11; [Matt. 16:27] [w] Rom. 2:6-9
21 [x] Ezek. 18:27; 33:12, 19

18:8 exacted usury. This refers to interest on loans (*see notes on Deut. 23:19,20; 24:10-13*).

18:9 He shall surely live! The righteous do die physically for many reasons that do not contradict this principle, e.g., old age, martyrdom, or death in battle. While there are exceptions to "surely live" as to temporal life (cf. 21:3,4), and sometimes the ungodly survive, unlike 18:13 (cf. 14:22,23), there can be absolutely no exceptions in God's ultimate spiritual reckoning. In every case, the just die to live eternally and the unjust, who never possessed spiritual life, shall perish physically and eternally (John 5:28,29; Rev. 20:11-15). The just will live no matter what the character of his parents or children. For an explanation of Ex. 20:5, *see the note there.*

18:10-13 son...a robber. Could such a sinful son claim the merits of his father's righteousness and live? No! Each person is responsible for his own personal sin.

18:14-18 he shall die for his iniquity. This part features an unjust father and a just son to make the same point. The righteous son shall "surely live" (v. 17).

18:19,20 The prophet restated the principle of personal accountability.

18:19-29 Cf. 33:12-20.

18:21,22 if a wicked man turns. The next case involves an unjust person turning to righteousness. He received a clean slate in forgiveness (v. 22), and spiritual life forever.

22 [y]None of the transgressions which he
has committed shall be remembered
against him; because of the righteousness
which he has done, he shall [z]live. 23 [a]Do I
have any pleasure at all that the wicked
should die?" says the Lord GOD, "*and* not
that he should turn from his ways and
live?
24 "But [b]when a righteous man turns
away from his righteousness and commits
iniquity, and does according to all the
abominations that the wicked *man* does,
shall he live? [c]All the righteousness which
he has done shall not be remembered; because of the unfaithfulness of which he is
guilty and the sin which he has committed,
because of them he shall die.
25 "Yet you say, [d]'The way of the Lord is
not fair.' Hear now, O house of Israel, is it
not My way which is fair, and your ways
which are not fair? 26 [e]When a righteous
man turns away from his righteousness,
commits iniquity, and dies in it, it is because of the iniquity which he has done
that he dies. 27 Again, [f]when a wicked *man*
turns away from the wickedness which he
committed, and does what is lawful and
right, he preserves himself alive. 28 Because he [g]considers and turns away from
all the transgressions which he committed,
he shall surely live; he shall not die. 29 [h]Yet
the house of Israel says, 'The way of the
Lord is not fair.' O house of Israel, is it not
My ways which are fair, and your ways
which are not fair?
30 [i]"Therefore I will judge you, O house
of Israel, every one according to his ways,"
says the Lord GOD. [j]"Repent, and turn from
all your transgressions, so that iniquity will
not be your ruin. 31 [k]Cast away from you
all the transgressions which you have committed, and get yourselves a [l]new heart
and a new spirit. For why should you die,
O house of Israel? 32 For [m]I have no pleasure in the death of one who dies," says the
Lord GOD. "Therefore turn and [n]live!"

Israel Degraded

19 "Moreover [a]take up a lamentation
for the princes of Israel, 2 and say:

'What *is* your mother? A lioness:
She lay down among the lions;
Among the young lions she
nourished her cubs.
3 She brought up one of her cubs,
And [b]he became a young lion;
He learned to catch prey,
And he devoured men.
4 The nations also heard of him;
He was trapped in their pit,
And they brought him with chains
to the land of [c]Egypt.

5 'When she saw that she waited, *that*
her hope was lost,
She took [d]another of her cubs *and*
made him a young lion.
6 [e]He roved among the lions,
And [f]became a young lion;
He learned to catch prey;
He devoured men.
7 [1]He knew their desolate places,
And laid waste their cities;
The land with its fullness was
desolated
By the noise of his roaring.
8 [g]Then the nations set against him
from the provinces on every
side,

22 [y] Is. 43:25; Jer. 50:20; Ezek. 18:24; 33:16; Mic. 7:19 [z] [Ps. 18:20-24]
23 [a] Lam. 3:33; [Ezek. 18:32; 33:11; 1 Tim. 2:4; 2 Pet. 3:9]
24 [b] 1 Sam. 15:11; 2 Chr. 24:2, 17-22; Ezek. 3:20; 18:26; 33:18 [c] [2 Pet. 2:20]
25 [d] Ezek. 18:29; 33:17, 20; Mal. 2:17; 3:13-15
26 [e] Ezek. 18:24
27 [f] Ezek. 18:21
28 [g] Ezek. 18:14
29 [h] Ezek. 18:25
30 [i] Ezek. 7:3; 33:20 [j] Matt. 3:2; Rev. 2:5
31 [k] Is. 1:16; 55:7; Eph. 4:22, 23 [l] Ps. 51:10; Jer. 32:39; Ezek. 11:19; 36:26
32 [m] Lam. 3:33; Ezek. 33:11; [2 Pet. 3:9] [n] [Prov. 4:2, 5, 6]

CHAPTER 19

1 [a] Ezek. 26:17; 27:2
3 [b] Ezek. 19:2; 2 Kin. 23:31, 32
4 [c] 2 Kin. 23:33, 34; 2 Chr. 36:4
5 [d] 2 Kin. 23:34
6 [e] 2 Kin. 24:8, 9 [f] Ezek. 19:3
7 [1] LXX *He stood in insolence;* Tg. *He destroyed its palaces;* Vg. *He learned to make widows*
8 [g] 2 Kin. 24:2, 11

18:23 Do I have…pleasure. God takes no willful pleasure in the death of the unrighteous (cf. John 5:40; 1 Tim. 2:4; 2 Pet. 3:9).

18:24 a righteous man turns. The next scenario is a righteous man turning to a life of sin. His former, apparent righteousness was not genuine (cf. 1 John 2:19), and God did not remember it as a valid expression of faith.

18:25-29 Yet you say. God applied the principle in summary to Israel's sin problem (cf. vv. 2-4). They, not He, must acknowledge their lack of equity (cf. vv. 25,29).

18:30 Therefore I will judge. The conclusion is that the just God must judge each person for his own life. But He invites repentance, so that hope may replace ruin (cf. 33:10,11).

18:31 get…a new heart. The key to life eternal and triumph over death is conversion. This involves repentance from sin (vv. 30, 31a) and receiving the new heart which God gives with a new spirit, wrought by the Holy Spirit (36:24-27; Jer. 31:34; John 3:5-8).

18:32 I have no pleasure. The death of His saints is precious to God (Ps. 116:15). By contrast, He has no such pleasure when a person dies without repentance. While God is sovereign in salvation, man is responsible for his own sin. **turn and live.** This was a call to repent and avoid physical and eternal death (cf. Pss. 23:6; 73:24; Is. 26:19-21; Dan. 12:2,3,13). Ezekiel was a preacher of repentance and of God's offer of mercy to the penitent.

19:1-14 lamentation. This is an elegy in typical lamentation meter (v. 14b), dealing with the captivity of Kings Jehoahaz (609 B.C.) and Jehoiachin (597 B.C.), and the collapse of the Davidic dynasty under Zedekiah (586 B.C.).

19:1 the princes of Israel. This refers to the kings of Judah just mentioned.

19:1-9 What *is* your mother? Judah is the "lioness," just as in v. 10 she is the "vine." Her cubs symbolize kings who were descendants of David exposed to the corrupting influences of heathen kings ("young lions").

19:3,4 one of her cubs. This refers to Jehoahaz (Shallum), who ruled in 609 B.C. and was deposed by Egypt's Pharaoh Necho after reigning only 3 months (v. 4; 2 Kin. 23:32-34; 2 Chr. 36:2).

19:5-9 another of her cubs. This refers to Jehoiachin, who in 597 B.C. was carried to Babylon in a cage as in v. 9 (2 Kin. 24:6-15). Though he reigned only 3 months, he was oppressive and unjust. God used the pagan nations of Egypt and Babylon to judge these wicked kings. The Babylonians kept Jehoiachin imprisoned for 37 years, releasing him at the age of 55 (2 Kin. 25:27-30; Jer. 52:31,32).

And spread their net over him;
[h]He was trapped in their pit.
9 [i]They put him in a cage with [2]chains,
And brought him to the king of Babylon;
They brought him in nets,
That his voice should no longer be heard on [j]the mountains of Israel.

10 'Your mother *was* [k]like a vine in your [3]bloodline,
Planted by the waters,
[l]Fruitful and full of branches
Because of many waters.
11 She had strong branches for scepters of rulers.
[m]She towered in stature above the thick branches,
And was seen in her height amid the [4]dense foliage.
12 But she was [n]plucked up in fury,
She was cast down to the ground,
And the [o]east wind dried her fruit.
Her strong branches were broken and withered;
The fire consumed them.
13 And now she *is* planted in the wilderness,
In a dry and thirsty land.
14 [p]Fire has come out from a rod of her branches
And devoured her fruit,
So that she has no strong branch—a scepter for ruling.' "

[q]This *is* a lamentation, and has become a lamentation.

The Rebellions of Israel

20 It came to pass in the seventh year,
in the fifth *month,* on the tenth *day*
of the month, *that* [a]certain of the elders of
Israel came to inquire of the LORD, and sat
before me. 2 Then the word of the LORD
came to me, saying, 3 "Son of man, speak
to the elders of Israel, and say to them,
'Thus says the Lord GOD: "Have you come
to inquire of Me? *As* I live," says the Lord
GOD, [b]"I will not be inquired of by you." '
4 Will you judge them, son of man, will
you judge *them?* Then [c]make known to
them the abominations of their fathers.
5 "Say to them, 'Thus says the Lord GOD:
"On the day when [d]I chose Israel and
raised My hand in an oath to the descendants of the house of Jacob, and made Myself [e]known to them in the land of Egypt, I
raised My hand in an oath to them, saying,
[f]'I *am* the LORD your God.' 6 On that day I
raised My hand in an oath to them, [g]to
bring them out of the land of Egypt into a
land that I had searched out for them,
[h]'flowing with milk and honey,' [i]the glory
of all lands. 7 Then I said to them, 'Each of
you, [j]throw away [k]the abominations
which are before his eyes, and do not defile
yourselves with [l]the idols of Egypt. I *am*
the LORD your God.' 8 But they rebelled
against Me and would not [1]obey Me. They
did not all cast away the abominations
which were before their eyes, nor did they
forsake the idols of Egypt. Then I said, 'I
will [m]pour out My fury on them and fulfill
My anger against them in the midst of the
land of Egypt.' 9 [n]But I acted for My
name's sake, that it should not be profaned
before the Gentiles among whom they
were, in whose sight I had made Myself
[o]known to them, to bring them out of the
land of Egypt.
10 "Therefore I [p]made them go out of the
land of Egypt and brought them into the
wilderness. 11 [q]And I gave them My
statutes and [2]showed them My judgments,
[r]'which, *if* a man does, he shall live by
them.' 12 Moreover I also gave them My
[s]Sabbaths, to be a sign between them and
Me, that they might know that I *am* the
LORD who sanctifies them. 13 Yet the house
of Israel [t]rebelled against Me in the wilderness; they did not walk in My statutes;
they [u]despised My judgments, [v]'which, *if* a
man does, he shall live by them'; and they
greatly [w]defiled My Sabbaths. Then I said I
would pour out My fury on them in the
[x]wilderness, to consume them. 14 [y]But I

8 [h] Ezek. 19:4
9 [i] 2 Chr. 36:6; Jer. 22:18 [j] Ezek. 6:2 [2] Or *hooks*
10 [k] Ezek. 17:6 [l] Deut. 8:7-9 [3] Lit. *blood,* so with MT, Syr., Vg.; LXX *like a flower on a pomegranate tree;* Tg. *in your likeness*
11 [m] Ezek. 31:3; Dan. 4:11 [4] Or *many branches*
12 [n] Jer. 31:27, 28 [o] Ezek. 17:10; Hos. 13:5
14 [p] Judg. 9:15; 2 Kin. 24:20; Ezek. 17:18 [q] Lam. 2:5

CHAPTER 20

1 [a] Ezek. 8:1, 11, 12; 14:1
3 [b] Ezek. 7:26; 14:3
4 [c] Ezek. 16:2; 22:2; Matt. 23:32
5 [d] Ex. 6:6-8; Deut. 7:6 [e] Ex. 3:8; 4:31; Deut. 4:34 [f] Ex. 20:2
6 [g] Ex. 3:8, 17; Deut. 8:7-9; Jer. 32:22 [h] Ex. 3:8 [i] Ex. 3:8, 17; 13:5; 33:3; Ps. 48:2; Jer. 11:5; 32:22; Ezek. 20:15; Dan. 8:9; Zech. 7:14
7 [j] Ezek. 18:31 [k] 2 Chr. 15:8 [l] Lev. 18:3; Deut. 29:16; Josh. 24:14
8 [m] Ezek. 7:8 [1] Lit. *listen to*
9 [n] Num. 14:13 [o] Josh. 2:10; 9:9, 10
10 [p] Ex. 13:18
11 [q] Deut. 4:8; Neh. 9:13; Ps. 147:19 [r] Lev. 18:5; Ezek. 20:13; Rom. 10:5; [Gal. 3:12] [2] Lit. *made known to*
12 [s] Ex. 20:8; Deut. 5:12; Neh. 9:14
13 [t] Num. 14:22; Ps. 78:40; Ezek. 20:8 [u] Prov. 1:25 [v] Lev. 18:5 [w] Ex. 16:27 [x] Num. 14:29; Ps. 106:23
14 [y] Ezek. 20:9, 20

19:10-14 Your mother...like a vine. Judah prospered as a luxuriant vine (v. 10), with strong power and eminence (v. 11). God plucked up the vine in judgment, desolating her (v. 12; cf. 13:11-13), exiling her (v. 13), and leaving no strong king (v. 14).

19:14 a rod. The blame for the catastrophe that came to Judah is laid on one ruler, King Zedekiah who was responsible for the burning of Jerusalem because of his treachery (cf. Jer. 38:20-23). The house of David ended in shame and, for nearly 2,600 years since, Israel has had no king of David's line. When Messiah came, they rejected Him and preferred Caesar. Messiah still became their Savior and will return as their King.

20:1 the seventh year. Ca. 591 B.C.

20:3-44 elders...come to inquire. Cf. the similarity in 14:1-3. The prophet responds with a message from the Lord that gives a historical survey of Israel, featuring its uniform pattern of sin. Israel rebelled in Egypt (vv. 5-9), then in the wilderness trek (vv. 10-26), and the entry into the Land of Promise (vv. 27-32). Through all this, God kept delivering them to save His reputation (vv. 9, 14, 22). Yet sinful obstinacy finally led to His judging them (vv. 45-49). Verses 33-44 speak of His regathering Israel to their land in the future time of Christ's Second Advent.

20:5 raised My hand...oath. Cf. vv. 5, 6, 15, 23, 28, 42. God promised Israel deliverance from Egypt (cf. Ex. 6:2-8).

acted for My name's sake, that it should
not be profaned before the Gentiles, in
whose sight I had brought them out. 15 So
[z]I also raised My hand in an oath to them
in the wilderness, that I would not bring
them into the land which I had given *them,*
[a]'flowing with milk and honey,' [b]the glory
of all lands, 16 [c]because they despised My
judgments and did not walk in My
statutes, but profaned My Sabbaths; for
[d]their heart went after their idols. 17 [e]Nev-
ertheless My eye spared them from destruction. I did not make an end of them in
the wilderness.

18 "But I said to their children in the
wilderness, 'Do not walk in the statutes of
your fathers, nor observe their judgments,
nor defile yourselves with their idols. 19 I
am the LORD your God: [f]Walk in My
statutes, keep My judgments, and do them;
20 [g]hallow My Sabbaths, and they will be a
sign between Me and you, that you may
know that I *am* the LORD your God.'

21 "Notwithstanding, [h]the children rebelled against Me; they did not walk in My
statutes, and were not careful to observe
My judgments, [i]'which, *if* a man does, he
shall live by them'; but they profaned My
Sabbaths. Then I said I would pour out My
fury on them and fulfill My anger against
them in the wilderness. 22 Nevertheless I
[3]withdrew My hand and acted for My
name's sake, that it should not be profaned
in the sight of the Gentiles, in whose sight
I had brought them out. 23 Also I raised
My hand in an oath to those in the wilderness, that [j]I would scatter them among the
Gentiles and disperse them throughout the
countries, 24 [k]because they had not executed My judgments, but had despised My
statutes, profaned My Sabbaths, and [l]their
eyes were fixed on their fathers' idols.

25 "Therefore [m]I also gave them up to
statutes *that were* not good, and judgments
by which they could not live; 26 and I pronounced them unclean because of their ritual gifts, in that they caused all [4]their firstborn to pass [n]through *the fire,* that I might
make them desolate and that they [o]might
know that I am the LORD."'

27 "Therefore, son of man, speak to the
house of Israel, and say to them, 'Thus says
the Lord GOD: "In this too your fathers
have [p]blasphemed Me, by being unfaithful
to Me. 28 When I brought them into the
land *concerning* which I had raised My
hand in an oath to give them, and [q]they
saw all the high hills and all the thick trees,
there they offered their sacrifices and provoked Me with their offerings. There they
also sent up their [r]sweet aroma and
poured out their drink offerings. 29 Then I
said to them, 'What *is* this [5]high place to
which you go?' So its name is called
[6]Bamah to this day."' 30 Therefore say to
the house of Israel, 'Thus says the Lord
GOD: "Are you defiling yourselves in the
manner of your [s]fathers, and committing
harlotry according to their [t]abominations?
31 For when you offer [u]your gifts and
make your sons pass through the fire, you
defile yourselves with all your idols, even
to this day. So shall I be inquired of by you,
O house of Israel? *As* I live," says the Lord
GOD, "I will [v]not be inquired of by you.
32 [w]What you have in your mind shall
never be, when you say, 'We will be like
the Gentiles, like the families in other
countries, serving wood and stone.'

God Will Restore Israel

33 "*As* I live," says the Lord GOD, "surely with a mighty hand, [x]with an outstretched arm, and with fury poured out, I
will rule over you. 34 I will bring you out
from the peoples and gather you out of the
countries where you are scattered, with a
mighty hand, with an outstretched arm,
and with fury poured out. 35 And I will
bring you into the wilderness of the peoples, and there [y]I will plead My case with
you face to face. 36 [z]Just as I pleaded My
case with your fathers in the wilderness of
the land of Egypt, so I will plead My case
with you," says the Lord GOD.

37 "I will make you [a]pass under the rod,
and I will bring you into the bond of the
[b]covenant; 38 [c]I will purge the rebels from
among you, and those who transgress
against Me; I will bring them out of the

15 [z]Num. 14:28; Ps. 95:11; 106:26 [a]Ex. 3:8 [b]Ezek. 20:6
16 [c]Ezek. 20:13, 24 [d]Num. 15:39; Ps. 78:37; Amos 5:25; Acts 7:42
17 [e][Ps. 78:38]
19 [f]Deut. 5:32
20 [g]Is. 58:13, 14; Jer. 17:22
21 [h]Num. 25:1; Deut. 9:23 [i]Lev. 18:5
22 [3]Refrained from judgment
23 [j]Lev. 26:33; Deut. 28:64; Ps. 106:27; Jer. 15:4
24 [k]Ezek. 20:13, 16 [l]Ezek. 6:9
25 [m]Ps. 81:12; Rom. 1:24; 2 Thess. 2:11
26 [n]2 Kin. 17:17; 2 Chr. 28:3; Jer. 32:35; Ezek. 16:20 [o]Ezek. 6:7; 20:12, 20 [4]Lit. *that open the womb*
27 [p]Num. 15:30; Is. 65:7; Rom. 2:24
28 [q]1 Kin. 14:23; Ps. 78:58; Is. 57:5-7; Jer. 3:6; Ezek. 6:13 [r]Ezek. 16:19
29 [5]Place for pagan worship [6]Lit. *High Place*
30 [s]Judg. 2:19 [t]Jer. 7:26; 16:12
31 [u]Ps. 106:37-39; Jer. 7:31; Ezek. 16:20; 20:26 [v]Ezek. 20:3
32 [w]Ezek. 11:5
33 [x]Jer. 21:5
35 [y]Jer. 2:9, 35; Ezek. 17:20
36 [z]Num. 14:21-23, 28
37 [a]Lev. 27:32; Jer. 33:13 [b]Ps. 89:30-34; Ezek. 16:60, 62
38 [c]Ezek. 34:17; Amos 9:9, 10; Zech. 13:8, 9; [Mal. 3:3; 4:1-3; Matt. 25:32]

20:25,26 I...gave them up. God allowed the Jews to live in sin. Cf. v. 32, "We will be like the Gentiles...." Cf. Ps. 81:11,12; Rom 1:24-28. Like all human beings, the story of the Jews is one long history of rebellion.

20:34 Paul quotes this in 2 Cor. 6:17. God will someday rule over Israel in the glorious kingdom of Messiah, after the people have repented and been saved (cf. Zech. 12–14).

20:35 wilderness of the peoples. Other lands where the scattered people of Israel live are pictured as a wilderness in which the Jews will suffer. This is analogous to God's bringing His people from Egypt through the wilderness long ago, before thrusting them into the Promised Land (v. 36).

20:37 pass under the rod. God used a shepherd figure here, apt since He was their Great Shepherd (34:11-13; Jer. 23:5-8). As a shepherd, God brings his sheep home to their fold (cf. Jer. 33:13), has them file in, separating sheep from goats (cf. Matt. 25), passing under his shepherd's rod to be noted and checked for injury. He will bring them into the bond of the New Covenant by giving them His Spirit with life (36:24-27; 37:14; 39:29). This is Israel's final salvation (Rom. 11:26-33).

20:38 I will purge the rebels. God will see that no rebel, no one without the renewing by His Spirit in salvation, will come back to

country where they dwell, but [d]they shall
not enter the land of Israel. Then you will
know that I *am* the LORD.
39 "As for you, O house of Israel," thus
says the Lord GOD: [e]"Go, serve every one
of you his idols—and hereafter—if you
will not obey Me; [f]but profane My holy
name no more with your gifts and your
idols. 40 For [g]on My holy mountain, on the
mountain height of Israel," says the Lord
GOD, "there [h]all the house of Israel, all of
them in the land, shall serve Me; there [i]I
will accept them, and there I will require
your offerings and the firstfruits of your
[7]sacrifices, together with all your holy
things. 41 I will accept you as a [j]sweet
aroma when I bring you out from the peoples and gather you out of the countries
where you have been scattered; and I will
be hallowed in you before the Gentiles.
42 [k]Then you shall know that I *am* the
LORD, [l]when I bring you into the land of Israel, into the country *for* which I raised My
hand in an oath to give to your fathers.
43 And [m]there you shall remember your
ways and all your doings with which you
were defiled; and [n]you shall [8]loathe yourselves in your own sight because of all the
evils that you have committed. 44 [o]Then
you shall know that I *am* the LORD, when I
have dealt with you [p]for My name's sake,
not according to your wicked ways nor according to your corrupt doings, O house of
Israel," says the Lord GOD.' "

Fire in the Forest

45 Furthermore the word of the LORD
came to me, saying, 46 [q]"Son of man, set
your face toward the south; [9]preach
against the south and prophesy against the
forest land, the [1]South, 47 and say to the
forest of the South, 'Hear the word of the
LORD! Thus says the Lord GOD: "Behold, [r]I
will kindle a fire in you, and it shall devour
[s]every green tree and every dry tree in
you; the blazing flame shall not be
quenched, and all faces [t]from the south to
the north shall be scorched by it. 48 All
flesh shall see that I, the LORD, have kindled it; it shall not be quenched." ' "
49 Then I said, "Ah, Lord GOD! They say
of me, 'Does he not speak [u]parables?' "

Babylon, the Sword of God

21 And the word of the LORD came to
me, saying, 2 [a]"Son of man, set your
face toward Jerusalem, [b]preach[1] against
the holy places, and prophesy against the
land of Israel; 3 and say to the land of Israel, 'Thus says the LORD: "Behold, I *am*
[c]against you, and I will draw My sword
out of its sheath and cut off both [d]righ-
teous and wicked from you. 4 Because I
will cut off both righteous and wicked
from you, therefore My sword shall go out
of its sheath against all flesh [e]from south *to*
north, 5 that all flesh may know that I, the
LORD, have drawn My sword out of its
sheath; it [f]shall not return anymore." '
6 [g]Sigh therefore, son of man, with [2]a
breaking heart, and sigh with bitterness
before their eyes. 7 And it shall be when
they say to you, 'Why are you sighing?'
that you shall answer, 'Because of the
news; when it comes, every heart will melt,
[h]all hands will be feeble, every spirit will
faint, and all knees will be weak *as* water.
Behold, it is coming and shall be brought
to pass,' says the Lord GOD."
8 Again the word of the LORD came to

38 [d] Jer. 44:14
39 [e] Judg. 10:14; Ps. 81:12; Amos 4:4 [f] Is. 1:13-15; Ezek. 23:38
40 [g] Is. 2:2, 3; Ezek. 17:23; Mic. 4:1 [h] Ezek. 37:22 [i] Is. 56:7; 60:7; Ezek. 43:27; Zech. 8:20-22; Mal. 3:4; [Rom. 12:1] [7] *offerings*
41 [j] Eph. 5:2; Phil. 4:18
42 [k] Ezek. 36:23; 38:23 [l] Ezek. 11:17; 34:13; 36:24
43 [m] Ezek. 16:61 [n] Lev. 26:39; Ezek. 6:9; Hos. 5:15 [8] Or *despise*
44 [o] Ezek. 24:24 [p] Ezek. 36:22
46 [q] Ezek. 21:2; Amos 7:16 [9] *proclaim,* lit. *drop*

[1] Heb. *Negev*
47 [r] Is. 9:18, 19; Jer. 21:14 [s] Luke 23:31 [t] Ezek. 21:4
49 [u] Ezek. 12:9; 17:2; Matt. 13:13; John 16:25

CHAPTER 21

2 [a] Ezek. 20:46 [b] Amos 7:16 [1] *proclaim,* lit. *drop*
3 [c] Jer. 21:13; Ezek. 5:8; Nah. 2:13; 3:5 [d] Job 9:22
4 [e] Jer. 12:12; Ezek. 20:47
5 [f] [Is. 45:23; 55:11]
6 [g] Is. 22:4; Jer. 4:19; Luke 19:41 [2] Emotional distress, lit. *the breaking of your loins*
7 [h] Ezek. 7:17

Palestine to have a part in the messianic kingdom. All whom He permits to return will serve Him (v. 40), in contrast to those who serve idols (v. 39). The purging takes place during the "time of Jacob's trouble" (Jer. 30:7), during the Great Tribulation (Matt. 24:21).

20:39 If they persist in their stubborn idolatry, God will allow them to follow it to their doom. He would also rather have them as out-and-out idolaters rather than hypocritical patronizers of His worship like they had been (cf. Amos 5:21-26).

20:40-42 all…in the land. The promised regathering in Messiah's earthly kingdom is to the very same land—literal Palestine—from which they were scattered (v. 41), expressly the land given to their fathers (36:28; Gen. 12:7). They will "all" be there, repentant (v. 43) and saved (Rom. 11:26,27), serving the Lord wholeheartedly, a united nation engaged in purified worship (cf. 27:22,23; Is. 11:13).

20:44 you shall know. God purposed all of this great restoration so that repentant, renewed Israel knew that He is the Lord, a key theme, as in v. 38. Also, those of other nations will know by this who He is and render Him due reverence (v. 41; 36:23,36).

20:46-48 preach against the south. The S is Palestine, particularly Judah, usually invaded from the N. Though Babylonia was to the E (19:12), its army would swing W toward the Mediterranean Sea and then come S out of the N to invade Judah. The invader (Nebuchadnezzar in 586 B.C.) will overwhelm the land as a sweeping fire (cf. 15:1-8; 19:12; Zech. 11:1-3), devouring trees indiscriminately, green or dry (cf. 21:3,4). Palestine had much more "forest" in biblical times.

20:49 This demonstrates the elders' (v. 1) refusal to comprehend Ezekiel's clear message. To the unwilling heart, there was no understanding.

21:1-7 the word…came. This is the sign of the sword against Jerusalem (vv. 1-17). God depicts His judgment in terms of a man unsheathing his polished sword for deadly thrusts. God is the swordsman (vv. 3,4), but Babylon is His sword (v. 19). The historical background for this prophecy is Nebuchadnezzar's 588 B.C. campaign to quell revolts in Judah, as well as Tyre and Ammon.

21:3,4 righteous and wicked. In Babylon's indiscrimination as an invader, people in the army's path die, whether righteous or wicked. This occurs from N to S, through the whole span of Israel's land, tying in with the judgment pictured by fire (20:45-49). Trees green or dry (20:47) probably depict people whether righteous or wicked (21:3,4; cf. Luke 23:31).

21:8-17 The sword (Babylon) was "sharpened."

me, saying, 9 "Son of man, prophesy and
say, 'Thus says the LORD!' Say:

[i]'A sword, a sword is sharpened
And also polished!
10 Sharpened to make a dreadful
slaughter,
Polished to flash like lightning!
Should we then make mirth?
It despises the scepter of My son,
As it does all wood.
11 And He has given it to be polished,
That it may be handled;
This sword is sharpened, and it is
polished
To be given into the hand of [j]the
slayer.'

12 "Cry and wail, son of man;
For it will be against My people,
Against all the princes of Israel.
Terrors including the sword will be
against My people;
Therefore [k]strike *your* thigh.

13 "Because *it is* [l]a testing,
And what if *the sword* despises
even the scepter?
[m]*The scepter* shall be no *more*,"

says the Lord GOD.

14 "You therefore, son of man,
prophesy,
And [n]strike *your* hands together.
The third time let the sword do
double *damage*.
It *is* the sword *that* slays,
The sword that slays the great *men*,
That enters their [o]private
chambers.
15 I have set the point of the sword
against all their gates,
That the heart may melt and many
may stumble.
Ah! [p]*It is* made bright;
It is grasped for slaughter:

16 "Swords[q] [3] at the ready!
Thrust right!
Set your blade!
Thrust left—
Wherever your [4]edge is ordered!

17 "I also will [r]beat My fists together,
And [s]I will cause My fury to rest;
I, the LORD, have spoken."

18 The word of the LORD came to me
again, saying: 19 "And son of man, appoint
for yourself two ways for the sword of the
king of Babylon to go; both of them shall
go from the same land. Make a sign; put *it*
at the head of the road to the city. 20 Appoint a road for the sword to go to [t]Rabbah
of the Ammonites, and to Judah, into fortified Jerusalem. 21 For the king of Babylon
stands at the parting of the road, at the fork
of the two roads, to use divination: he
shakes the arrows, he consults the [5]im-
ages, he looks at the liver. 22 In his right
hand is the divination for Jerusalem: to set
up battering rams, to call for a slaughter, to
[u]lift the voice with shouting, [v]to set battering rams against the gates, to heap up a
siege mound, and to build a wall. 23 And it
will be to them like a false divination in the
eyes of those who [w]have sworn oaths with
them; but he will bring their iniquity to remembrance, that they may be taken.
24 "Therefore thus says the Lord GOD:
'Because you have made your iniquity to
be remembered, in that your transgressions are uncovered, so that in all your doings your sins appear—because you have
come to remembrance, you shall be taken
in hand.
25 'Now to you, O [x]profane, wicked
prince of Israel, [y]whose day has come,

9 [i] Deut. 32:41; Ezek. 5:1; 21:15, 28
11 [j] Ezek. 21:19
12 [k] Jer. 31:19
13 [l] Job 9:23; 2 Cor. 8:2 [m] Ezek. 21:27
14 [n] Num. 24:10; Ezek. 6:11 [o] 1 Kin. 20:30
15 [p] Ezek. 21:10, 28
16 [q] Ezek. 14:17 [3] Lit. *Sharpen yourself!* or *Unite yourself!* [4] Lit. *face*
17 [r] Ezek. 22:13 [s] Ezek. 5:13; 16:42; 24:13
20 [t] Deut. 3:11; Jer. 49:2; Ezek. 25:5; Amos 1:14
21 [5] Heb. *teraphim*
22 [u] Jer. 51:14 [v] Ezek. 4:2
23 [w] Ezek. 17:16, 18
25 [x] 2 Chr. 36:13; Jer. 52:2; Ezek. 12:10; 17:19 [y] Ezek. 21:29

21:10 It despises the scepter. Cf. also v. 13. Possibly this affirmed that God's sword, so overwhelming in v. 10a, was to despise the Judean royal scepter (cf. Gen. 49:9,10), which was powerless to stop it and would soon pass away (vv. 25-27). God's judgment was too strong for this object made of (or partly of) wood, as it holds in contempt all such items of wood. "My son" may refer to Judah (cf. Ex. 4:22,23), or to the king as God's "son," such as was Solomon (1 Chr. 28:6).

21:11 the slayer. God is always the judge and executioner, no matter what He uses.

21:12 strike *your* thigh. Or it can be translated, "beat your breast." In either wording, it is an emphatic gesture of grief that the prophet acts out. This accompanies further symbols of grief in his "cry," "wail" (v. 12), clapping of hands (v. 14), and "beating of fists" (v. 17).

21:18-20 This imagery sees Babylon's army on the march coming to a crossroads. The sword is the king of Babylon, Nebuchadnezzar, who is faced with a decision. One sign points to Jerusalem and Judah, the other to Rabbah, the capital of Ammon. In 593 B.C. Ammon had conspired with Judah against Babylon. The king had to decide which place to attack, so he sought his gods through divination (v. 21).

21:21 the king...stands...to use divination. This means to "seek an omen," to gain guidance from superstitious devices (cf. Is. 47:8-15). Three methods are available to Babylon's leader. He shook arrows and let them fall, then read a conclusion from the pattern. He looked at Teraphim (idols), or examined an animal liver to gain help from his gods. Actually, the true God controlled this superstition to achieve His will, the attack on Jerusalem and Judah. Later, Nebuchadnezzar attacked Rabbah in Ammon E of the Jordan (vv. 28-32).

21:22 All the paraphernalia of war were prepared.

21:23 false divination. The people of Jerusalem thought this superstitious decision was not a true divination and would fail. They were wrong (vv. 24,25).

21:25 wicked prince. Zedekiah.

whose iniquity *shall* end, 26 thus says the
Lord GOD:

"Remove the turban, and take off
the crown;
Nothing *shall remain* the same.
[z]Exalt the humble, and humble the
exalted.
27 [6]Overthrown, overthrown,
I will make it overthrown!
[a]It shall be no *longer,*
Until He comes whose right it is,
And I will give it *to* [b]*Him.*" '

A Sword Against the Ammonites

28 "And you, son of man, prophesy and
say, 'Thus says the Lord GOD [c]concerning
the Ammonites and concerning their reproach,' and say:

'A sword, a sword *is* drawn,
Polished for slaughter,
For consuming, for flashing—
29 While they [d]see false visions for
you,
While they divine a lie to you,
To bring you on the necks of the
wicked, the slain
[e]Whose day has come,
Whose iniquity *shall* end.
30 'Return[f] *it* to its sheath.
[g]I will judge you
In the place where you were
created,
[h]In the land of your [7]nativity.
31 I will [i]pour out My indignation on
you;
I will [j]blow against you with the
fire of My wrath,
And deliver you into the hands of
brutal men *who are* skillful to

26 [z] Luke 1:52
27 [a] Gen. 49:10; [Luke 1:32, 33; John 1:49] [b] Ps. 2:6; 72:7, 10; [Jer. 23:5, 6; Ezek. 34:24; 37:24] [6] Or *Distortion, Ruin*
28 [c] Jer. 25:21; 49:1-6; Ezek. 25:1-7; Amos 1:13; Zeph. 2:8-11
29 [d] Jer. 27:9; Ezek. 12:24; 13:6-9; 22:28 [e] Job 18:20; Ps. 37:17; Is. 10:3; Ezek. 7:2, 3, 7
30 [f] Jer. 47:6, 7 [g] Gen. 15:14 [h] Ezek. 16:3 [7] Or *origin*
31 [i] Ezek. 7:8 [j] Ps. 18:15; Is. 30:33; Ezek. 22:20, 21; Hag. 1:9
[k] Jer. 6:22, 23; 51:20, 21; Hab. 1:6-10
32 [l] Ezek. 25:10

CHAPTER 22

2 [a] Ezek. 20:4 [b] Nah. 3:1
3 [c] Ezek. 24:6, 7
4 [d] 2 Kin. 21:16; Ezek. 24:7, 8 [e] Deut. 28:37; 1 Kin. 9:7; Ezek. 5:14; Dan. 9:16
5 [1] Lit. *defiled of name*
6 [f] Is. 1:23; Ezek. 22:27; Mic. 3:1-3; Zeph. 3:3 [2] Lit. *arm*
7 [g] Ex. 20:12; Lev. 20:9; Deut. 5:16; 27:16 [h] Ex. 22:22; Jer. 5:28; Ezek. 22:25; Mal. 3:5 [3] Lit. *orphan*
8 [i] Lev. 19:30
9 [j] Lev. 19:16; Jer. 9:4 [k] Ezek. 18:6, 11
10 [l] Lev. 18:7, 8 [m] Lev. 18:19; 20:18; Ezek. 18:6
11 [n] Lev. 18:20; Jer. 5:8; Ezek. 18:11

[k]destroy.
32 You shall be fuel for the fire;
Your blood shall be in the midst of
the land.
[l]You shall not be remembered,
For I the LORD have spoken.' "

Sins of Jerusalem

22 Moreover the word of the LORD
came to me, saying, 2 "Now, son of
man, [a]will you judge, will you judge [b]the
bloody city? Yes, show her all her
abominations! 3 Then say, 'Thus says the
Lord GOD: "The city sheds [c]blood in her
own midst, that her time may come; and
she makes idols within herself to defile
herself. 4 You have become guilty by the
blood which you have [d]shed, and have defiled yourself with the idols which you
have made. You have caused your days to
draw near, and have come to *the end of*
your years; [e]therefore I have made you a
reproach to the nations, and a mockery to
all countries. 5 *Those* near and *those* far
from you will mock you as [1]infamous *and*
full of tumult.
6 "Look, [f]the princes of Israel: each one
has used his [2]power to shed blood in you.
7 In you they have [g]made light of father
and mother; in your midst they have [h]op-
pressed the stranger; in you they have mistreated the [3]fatherless and the widow.
8 You have despised My holy things and
[i]profaned My Sabbaths. 9 In you are [j]men
who slander to cause bloodshed; [k]in you
are those who eat on the mountains; in
your midst they commit lewdness. 10 In
you men [l]uncover their fathers' nakedness; in you they violate women who are
[m]set apart during their impurity. 11 One
commits abomination [n]with his neighbor's
wife; [o]another lewdly defiles his daughter-

21:26 Remove...turban...crown. God, in the coming judgment on Judah in 588–586 B.C., removed the turban representing the priestly leadership, and the crown picturing the succession of kings. Neither office was fully restored after the captivity. This marked the commencement of "the times of the Gentiles" (Luke 21:24).

21:27 Until He comes. The 3-fold mention of "overthrown" expresses the severest degree of unsettled and chaotic conditions. Israel was to experience severe instability and even the kingly privilege will not be Israel's again until the Messiah comes, "to whom it rightly belongs," or "whose right it is" (cf. Gen. 49:10). God will give the kingship to Him (cf. Jer. 23:5-8), the greater "David" (Ezek. 37:24). His "right" is that perfect combination of priestly and royal offices (cf. Heb. 5–7).

21:28-32 concerning the Ammonites. The Babylonian armies also were to conquer this people in 582/81 B.C. (cf. 25:1-7). Their "reproach" was the gleeful disdain they heaped on Jerusalem when the city fell, the temple was profaned, and Judeans were taken captive (25:3).

21:30 Return *it* to its sheath. This called the Ammonites not to resist Babylon, which would be useless, for they would be slaughtered in their own land.

21:32 You shall not be remembered. Israel had a future (v. 27), but God would not give Ammon mercy at the time and let the devastation occur. After this, they were further devastated by Judas Maccabeus' army, according to an ancient source (1 Macc. 5:6,7). Later, according to Jeremiah 49:6, God permitted exiles to return to their land. Finally, they disappeared from the family of nations altogether.

22:2 the bloody city. Cf. vv. 3,4,6,9,12,13. This refers to Jerusalem because of her judicial murders (vv. 6,9; 23:27), her sacrifice of children, and her rebellion against Babylon (cf. 24:6).

22:4-13 become guilty. At least 17 kinds of sin appear in this indictment of Jerusalem's blood guiltiness, and more in vv. 25-29. The only restraint on their evil was their ability. They did all the evil they could, and shedding blood seemed to be the most popular.

22:5 Cf. Rom. 2:24. God links His honor to the behavior of His people.

22:9 eat on the mountains. This meant idol worship which the passage clarifies (v. 4), i.e., eating meals at idol shrines, accompanied by sexual sins, such as those described in vv. 10,11.

in-law; and another in you violates his sister, his father's [p]daughter. 12 In you [q]they take bribes to shed blood; [r]you take usury and increase; you have made profit from your neighbors by extortion, and [s]have forgotten Me," says the Lord GOD.

13 "Behold, therefore, I [t]beat My fists at the dishonest profit which you have made, and at the bloodshed which has been in your midst. 14 [u]Can your heart endure, or can your hands remain strong, in the days when I shall deal with you? [v]I, the LORD, have spoken, and will do *it.* 15 [w]I will scatter you among the nations, disperse you throughout the countries, and [x]remove your filthiness completely from you. 16 You shall defile yourself in the sight of the nations; then [y]you shall know that I *am* the LORD." ' "

Israel in the Furnace

17 The word of the LORD came to me, saying, 18 "Son of man, [z]the house of Israel has become dross to Me; they *are* all bronze, tin, iron, and lead, in the midst of a [a]furnace; they have become dross from silver. 19 Therefore thus says the Lord GOD: 'Because you have all become dross, therefore behold, I will gather you into the midst of Jerusalem. 20 *As men* gather silver, bronze, iron, lead, and tin into the midst of a furnace, to blow fire on it, to [b]melt *it;* so I will gather *you* in My anger and in My fury, and I will leave *you there* and melt you. 21 Yes, I will gather you and blow on you with the fire of My wrath, and you shall be melted in its midst. 22 As silver is melted in the midst of a furnace, so shall you be melted in its midst; then you shall know that I, the LORD, have [c]poured out My fury on you.' "

11 [o]Lev. 18:15 [p]Lev. 18:9
12 [q]Ex. 23:8; Deut. 16:19; 27:25; Mic. 7:2, 3 [r]Ex. 22:25 [s]Deut. 32:18; Ps. 106:21; Jer. 3:21; Ezek. 23:35
13 [t]Ezek. 21:17
14 [u]Ezek. 21:7 [v]Ezek. 17:24
15 [w]Deut. 4:27; Neh. 1:8; Ezek. 20:23; Zech. 7:14 [x]Ezek. 23:27, 48
16 [y]Ps. 9:16
18 [z]Ps. 119:119; Is. 1:22; Jer. 6:28; Lam. 4:1 [a]Prov. 17:3; Is. 48:10
20 [b]Is. 1:25; Jer. 9:7
22 [c]Ezek. 20:8, 33; Hos. 5:10
24 [d]Is. 9:13; Jer. 2:30; Ezek. 24:13; Zeph. 3:2 [4]So with MT, Syr., Vg.; LXX *showered upon*
25 [e]Jer. 11:9; Hos. 6:9 [f]Matt. 23:14 [g]Mic. 3:11; Zeph. 3:3, 4 [5]So with MT, Vg.; LXX *princes;* Tg. *scribes* [6]Lit. *souls*
26 [h]Jer. 32:32; Lam. 4:3; Mal. 2:8 [i]1 Sam. 2:29 [j]Lev. 10:10 [7]Lit. *done violence to*
27 [k]Is. 1:23; Ezek. 22:6; Mic. 3:1-3, 9-11; Zeph. 3:3 [8]Lit. *souls*
28 [l]Ezek. 13:10 [m]Ezek. 13:6, 7 [n]Jer. 23:25-32; Ezek. 21:29
29 [o]Ex. 23:9; Lev. 19:33
30 [p]Is. 59:16; 63:5; Jer. 5:1 [q]Ezek. 13:5 [r]Ps. 106:23; Jer. 15:1
31 [s]Ezek. 22:22 [t]Ezek. 9:10; [Rom. 2:8, 9]

CHAPTER 23
2 [a]Jer. 3:7, 8; Ezek. 16:44-46

Israel's Wicked Leaders

23 And the word of the LORD came to me, saying, 24 "Son of man, say to her: 'You *are* a land that is [d]not [4]cleansed or rained on in the day of indignation.' 25 [e]The conspiracy of her [5]prophets in her midst is like a roaring lion tearing the prey; they [f]have devoured [6]people; [g]they have taken treasure and precious things; they have made many widows in her midst. 26 [h]Her priests have [7]violated My law and [i]profaned My holy things; they have not [j]distinguished between the holy and unholy, nor have they made known *the difference* between the unclean and the clean; and they have hidden their eyes from My Sabbaths, so that I am profaned among them. 27 Her [k]princes in her midst *are* like wolves tearing the prey, to shed blood, to destroy [8]people, and to get dishonest gain. 28 [l]Her prophets plastered them with untempered *mortar,* [m]seeing false visions, and divining [n]lies for them, saying, 'Thus says the Lord GOD,' when the LORD had not spoken. 29 The people of the land have used oppressions, committed robbery, and mistreated the poor and needy; and they wrongfully [o]oppress the stranger. 30 [p]So I sought for a man among them who would [q]make a wall, and [r]stand in the gap before Me on behalf of the land, that I should not destroy it; but I found no one. 31 Therefore I have [s]poured out My indignation on them; I have consumed them with the fire of My wrath; and I have recompensed [t]their deeds on their own heads," says the Lord GOD.

Two Harlot Sisters

23 The word of the LORD came again to me, saying:

2 "Son of man, there were [a]two
women,

22:14-16 Ezekiel saw not only the punishment in the immediate future, but the worldwide dispersion of the Jews still going on today, which continues for the purging of Israel's sins.

22:16 then you shall know. After the defiling dispersion, when the sin has been purged, Israel will come to know the Lord. Many Jews do know Him now, but the nation will be saved in the future (cf. Rom. 11:25-27; Zech. 12–14).

22:17-22 bronze, tin, iron, and lead. This pictures God's judgment of Jerusalem as a smelting furnace (cf. Is. 1:22; Jer. 6:28-30; Zech. 13:9; Mal. 3:2,3) which burns away dross and impurities, resulting in purified metal. His wrath was the fire (v. 21; an apt term for Babylon's fiery destruction of the city), and His people were to be refined (v. 20), with the sinful ones removed (cf. 21:13-22). Even in the ultimate day, God will follow this principle in purging His creation of sin (2 Pet. 3:9-14).

22:25-29 conspiracy. The whole nation was wicked. First, all leaders are indicted for their vicious sin: prophets, priests, princes, then the people in general.

22:30 So I sought for a man. Ezekiel and Jeremiah were faithful, but apart from them God sought a man capable of advocacy for Israel when its sin had gone so far. But no one could lead the people to repentance and draw the nation back from the brink of the judgment that came in 586 B.C. (Jer. 7:26,36; 19:15). Only God's Messiah, God Himself, will have the character and the credentials sufficient to do what no man can do, intercede for Israel (cf. Is. 59:16-19; 63:5; Rev. 5). He was rejected by them in His earthly ministry, so the effects of this judgment continue today, until they turn to Him in faith (cf. Zech. 12:10; 13:1).

23:2-4 two women. This chap. describes the spiritual infidelity of Israel and Judah, pictured as two sisters, to convey the gravity of sin in Judah. "One mother" refers to the united kingdom, while "two women" refers to the divided kingdom. Oholah, meaning "Her own tabernacle," as she had her separate dwelling-place apart from the temple, represents Samaria. In the northern kingdom, Jeroboam had set up worship, which God rejected. Oholibah, "My tabernacle is in her," represents Jerusalem, where God did establish worship.

The daughters of one mother.
3 [b]They committed harlotry in Egypt,
They committed harlotry in [c]their youth;
Their breasts were there embraced,
Their virgin bosom was there pressed.
4 Their names: [1]Oholah the elder and [2]Oholibah [d]her sister;
[e]They were Mine,
And they bore sons and daughters.
As for their names,
Samaria *is* Oholah, and Jerusalem *is* Oholibah.

The Older Sister, Samaria

5 "Oholah played the harlot even though she was Mine;
And she lusted for her lovers, the neighboring [f]Assyrians,
6 *Who were* clothed in purple,
Captains and rulers,
All of them desirable young men,
Horsemen riding on horses.
7 Thus she committed her harlotry with them,
All of them choice men of Assyria;
And with all for whom she lusted,
With all their idols, she defiled herself.
8 She has never given up her harlotry *brought* [g]from Egypt,
For in her youth they had lain with her,
Pressed her virgin bosom,
And poured out their immorality upon her.

9 "Therefore I have delivered her
Into the hand of her lovers,
Into the hand of the [h]Assyrians,
For whom she lusted.
10 They uncovered her nakedness,
Took away her sons and daughters,
And slew her with the sword;
She became a byword among women,
For they had executed judgment on her.

The Younger Sister, Jerusalem

11 "Now [i]although her sister Oholibah saw *this*, [j]she became more corrupt in her lust than she, and in her harlotry more corrupt than her sister's harlotry.

12 "She lusted for the neighboring [k]Assyrians,
[l]Captains and rulers,
Clothed most gorgeously,
Horsemen riding on horses,
All of them desirable young men.
13 Then I saw that she was defiled;
Both *took* the same way.
14 But she increased her harlotry;
She looked at men portrayed on the wall,
Images of [m]Chaldeans portrayed in vermilion,
15 Girded with belts around their waists,
Flowing turbans on their heads,
All of them looking like captains,
In the manner of the Babylonians of Chaldea,
The land of their nativity.
16 [n]As soon as her eyes saw them,
She lusted for them
And sent [o]messengers to them in Chaldea.

17 "Then the [3]Babylonians came to her, into the bed of love,
And they defiled her with their immorality;
So she was defiled by them, [p]and alienated herself from them.
18 She revealed her harlotry and uncovered her nakedness.
Then [q]I [r]alienated Myself from her,
As I had alienated Myself from her sister.

19 "Yet she multiplied her harlotry
In calling to remembrance the days of her youth,
[s]When she had played the harlot in the land of Egypt.
20 For she lusted for her [4]paramours,
Whose flesh *is like* the flesh of donkeys,
And whose issue *is like* the issue of horses.

3 [b] Lev. 17:7; Josh. 24:14; Jer. 3:9 [c] Ezek. 16:22
4 [d] Jer. 3:6, 7 [e] Ezek. 16:8, 20 [1] Lit. *Her Own Tabernacle* [2] Lit. *My Tabernacle Is in Her*
5 [f] 2 Kin. 15:19; 16:7; 17:3; Ezek. 16:28; Hos. 5:13; 8:9, 10
8 [g] Ex. 32:4; 1 Kin. 12:28; 2 Kin. 10:29; 17:16; Ezek. 23:3, 19
9 [h] 2 Kin. 17:3
11 [i] Jer. 3:8
[j] Jer. 3:8-11; Ezek. 16:51, 52
12 [k] 2 Kin. 16:7, 8; Ezek. 16:28 [l] Ezek. 23:6, 23
14 [m] Jer. 50:2; Ezek. 8:10; 16:29
16 [n] 2 Kin. 24:1 [o] Is. 57:9
17 [p] Ezek. 23:22, 28 [3] Lit. *sons of Babel*
18 [q] Jer. 6:8 [r] Ps. 78:59; 106:40; Jer. 12:8
19 [s] Lev. 18:3; Ezek. 23:2
20 [4] Illicit lovers

23:5-10 Oholah played the harlot. The northern kingdom of Israel was a harlot, in a spiritual sense, by seeking union for fulfillment and security with idolatrous, young, wealthy, attractive Assyria. Assyria turned on her (v. 10), conquered her, and deported Israel in 722 B.C. (2 Kin. 17).

23:11-21 more corrupt. Cf. 16:47. The focus is Judah's (the southern kingdom) craving for Babylonian idolatry that alienated her from God. Judah learned nothing from Israel's punishment (v. 13).

23:12 Assyrians. Ahaz placed Judah under the protection of Assyria (2 Kin. 16:7-10), a political move denounced by Isaiah (Is. 7:13-17).

23:14-16 Chaldeans. Judah was drawn to portraits of Babylonian men, done in brilliant colors, lusting for the Chaldean lifestyle. Social and political alliance led to spiritual defection.

23:17 into the bed of love. The description portrays spiritual unfaithfulness graphically (v. 30).

23:19 Judah renewed her old sins from the days of Egypt, returning to her first degradation.

21 Thus you called to remembrance
the lewdness of your youth,
When the [t]Egyptians pressed your
bosom
Because of your youthful breasts.

Judgment on Jerusalem

22 "Therefore, Oholibah, thus says the Lord GOD:

[u]'Behold, I will stir up your lovers
against you,
From whom you have alienated
yourself,
And I will bring them against you
from every side:
23 The Babylonians,
All the Chaldeans,
[v]Pekod, Shoa, Koa,
[w]All the Assyrians with them,
All of them desirable young men,
Governors and rulers,
Captains and men of renown,
All of them riding on horses.
24 And they shall come against you
With chariots, wagons, and war-
horses,
With a horde of people.
They shall array against you
Buckler, shield, and helmet all
around.

'I will delegate judgment to them,
And they shall judge you
according to their judgments.
25 I will set My [x]jealousy against you,
And they shall deal furiously with
you;
They shall remove your nose and
your ears,
And your remnant shall fall by the
sword;
They shall take your sons and your
daughters,
And your remnant shall be
devoured by fire.
26 [y]They shall also strip you of your
clothes
And take away your beautiful
jewelry.

27 'Thus [z]I will make you cease your
lewdness and your [a]harlotry
Brought from the land of Egypt,
So that you will not lift your eyes
to them,
Nor remember Egypt anymore.'

28 "For thus says the Lord GOD: 'Surely I
will deliver you into the hand of [b]those
you hate, into the hand *of those* [c]from
whom you alienated yourself. 29 [d]They
will deal hatefully with you, take away all
you have worked for, and [e]leave you
naked and bare. The nakedness of your
harlotry shall be uncovered, both your
lewdness and your harlotry. 30 I will do
these *things* to you because you have [f]gone
as a harlot after the Gentiles, because you
have become defiled by their idols. 31 You
have walked in the way of your sister;
therefore I will put her [g]cup in your hand.'
32 "Thus says the Lord GOD:

'You shall drink of your sister's
cup,
The deep and wide one;
[h]You shall be laughed to scorn
And held in derision;
It contains much.
33 You will be filled with
drunkenness and sorrow,
The cup of horror and desolation,
The cup of your sister Samaria.
34 You shall [i]drink and drain it,
You shall break its [5]shards,
And tear at your own breasts;
For I have spoken,'
Says the Lord GOD.

35 "Therefore thus says the Lord GOD:

'Because you [j]have forgotten Me and
[k]cast Me behind your back,
Therefore you shall bear the *penalty*
Of your lewdness and your
harlotry.'"

Both Sisters Judged

36 The LORD also said to me: "Son of
man, will you [l]judge Oholah and Oholibah? Then [m]declare to them their abominations. 37 For they have committed adultery,
and [n]blood *is* on their hands. They have
committed adultery with their idols, and
even sacrificed their sons [o]whom they bore
to Me, passing them through *the fire,* to devour *them.* 38 Moreover they have done

21 [t]Ezek. 16:26
22 [u]Ezek. 16:37-41; 23:28
23 [v]Jer. 50:21 [w]Ezek. 23:12
25 [x]Ex. 34:14; Ezek. 5:13; 8:17, 18; Zeph. 1:18
26 [y]Is. 3:18-23; Ezek. 16:39
27 [z]Ezek. 16:41; 22:15 [a]Ezek. 23:3, 19
28 [b]Jer. 21:7-10; Ezek. 16:37-41 [c]Ezek. 23:17
29 [d]Deut. 28:48; Ezek. 23:25, 26, 45-47 [e]Ezek. 16:39
30 [f]Ezek. 6:9
31 [g]2 Kin. 21:13; Jer. 7:14, 15; 25:15; Ezek. 23:33
32 [h]Ezek. 22:4, 5
34 [i]Ps. 75:8; Is. 51:17 [5]Earthenware fragments
35 [j]Is. 17:10; Jer. 3:21; Ezek. 22:12; Hos. 8:14; 13:6 [k]1 Kin. 14:9; Jer. 2:27; 32:33; Neh. 9:26
36 [l]Jer. 1:10; Ezek. 20:4; 22:2 [m]Is. 58:1; Ezek. 16:2; Mic. 3:8
37 [n]Ezek. 16:38 [o]Ezek. 16:20, 21, 36, 45; 20:26, 31

23:22-35 stir up your lovers. God's anger at Judah's sin prompted His bringing Babylonians and others to deal severely with her. The passage sets forth how Judah's companion nations were the instruments of her judgment.

23:23 Pekod, Shoa, Koa. Three different Aramean tribes.

23:25 remove your nose...your ears. Atrocities by Babylonians would include facial dismemberment, ancient punishment for an adulteress practiced in Egypt, Chaldea, and elsewhere.

23:32-34 drink of your sister's cup. Judah was to experience the "cup" of God's judgment as Samaria had in 722 B.C. (cf. 23:46-49). Often the idea of "drinking a cup" is symbolic of receiving God's wrath (cf. Ps. 75:8; Is. 51:17-22; Jer. 25:15-29; Matt. 20:22).

23:36-42 The prophet detailed a shameful summary of God's case against the nation—a double arraignment calling for judgment.

this to Me: They have [p]defiled My sanctuary on the same day and [q]profaned My
Sabbaths. 39 For after they had slain their
children for their idols, on the same day
they came into My sanctuary to profane it;
and indeed [r]thus they have done in the
midst of My house.
40 "Furthermore you sent for men to
come from afar, [s]to whom a messenger *was*
sent; and there they came. And you
[t]washed yourself for them, [u]painted your
eyes, and adorned yourself with ornaments. 41 You sat on a stately [v]couch, with
a table prepared before it, [w]on which you
had set My incense and My oil. 42 The
sound of a carefree multitude *was* with her,
and [6]Sabeans *were* brought from the
wilderness with men of the common sort,
who put bracelets on their [7]wrists and
beautiful crowns on their heads. 43 Then I
said concerning *her who had grown* old in
adulteries, 'Will they commit harlotry with
her now, and she *with them?*' 44 Yet they
went in to her, as men go in to a woman
who plays the harlot; thus they went in to
Oholah and Oholibah, the lewd women.
45 But righteous men will [x]judge them
after the manner of adulteresses, and after
the manner of women who shed blood, because they *are* adulteresses, and [y]blood *is*
on their hands.
46 "For thus says the Lord GOD: [z]'Bring
up an assembly against them, give them
up to trouble and plunder. 47 [a]The assembly shall stone them with stones and [8]exe-
cute them with their swords; [b]they shall
slay their sons and their daughters, and
burn their houses with fire. 48 Thus [c]I will
cause lewdness to cease from the land,
[d]that all women may be taught not to practice your lewdness. 49 They shall repay
you for your lewdness, and you shall [e]pay
for your idolatrous sins. [f]Then you shall
know that I *am* the Lord GOD.' "

Symbol of the Cooking Pot

24 Again, in the ninth year, in the tenth
month, on the tenth *day* of the
month, the word of the LORD came to me,
saying, 2 "Son of man, write down the
name of the day, this very day—the king of
Babylon started his siege against Jerusalem
[a]this very day. 3 [b]And utter a parable to the
rebellious house, and say to them, 'Thus
says the Lord GOD:

[c]"Put on a pot, set *it* on,
And also pour water into it.
4 Gather pieces *of meat* in it,
Every good piece,
The thigh and the shoulder.
Fill *it* with choice [1]cuts;
5 Take the choice of the flock.
Also pile *fuel* bones under it,
Make it boil well,
And let the cuts simmer in it."

6 'Therefore thus says the Lord GOD:

"Woe to [d]the bloody city,
To the pot whose scum *is* in it,
And whose scum is not gone from it!
Bring it out piece by piece,
On which no [e]lot has fallen.
7 For her blood is in her midst;
She set it on top of a rock;
[f]She did not pour it on the ground,
To cover it with dust.
8 That it may raise up fury and take vengeance,
[g]I have set her blood on top of a rock,
That it may not be covered."

9 'Therefore thus says the Lord GOD:

[h]"Woe to the bloody city!
I too will make the pyre great.
10 Heap on the wood,
Kindle the fire;
Cook the meat well,
Mix in the spices,
And let the [2]cuts be burned up.

11 "Then set the pot empty on the coals,

38 [p]2 Kin. 21:4, 7; Ezek. 5:11; 7:20 [q]Ezek. 22:8
39 [r]2 Kin. 21:2-8
40 [s]Is. 57:9 [t]Ruth 3:3 [u]2 Kin. 9:30; Jer. 4:30
41 [v]Esth. 1:6; Is. 57:7; Amos 2:8; 6:4 [w]Prov. 7:17; Ezek. 16:18, 19; Hos. 2:8
42 [6]Or *drunkards* [7]Lit. *hands*
45 [x]Ezek. 16:38 [y]Ezek. 23:37
46 [z]Ezek. 16:40
47 [a]Lev. 20:10; Ezek. 16:40 [b]2 Chr. 36:17, 19; Ezek. 24:21 [8]Lit. *cut down*
48 [c]Ezek. 22:15 [d]Deut. 13:11; Ezek. 22:15; 2 Pet. 2:6
49 [e]Is. 59:18; Ezek. 23:35 [f]Ezek. 20:38, 42, 44; 25:5

CHAPTER 24

2 [a]2 Kin. 25:1; Jer. 39:1; 52:4
3 [b]Ezek. 17:12 [c]Jer. 1:13; Ezek. 11:3
4 [1]Lit. *bones*
6 [d]2 Kin. 24:3, 4; Ezek. 22:2, 3, 27; Mic. 7:2; Nah. 3:1 [e]2 Sam. 8:2; Joel 3:3; Obad. 11; Nah. 3:10
7 [f]Lev. 17:13; Deut. 12:16
8 [g][Matt. 7:2]
9 [h]Ezek. 24:6; Nah. 3:1; Hab. 2:12
10 [2]Lit. *bones*

23:45 righteous men. This likely refers to the remnant of godly people in the nation who would affirm the justice of judgment.

24:1,2 this very day. The time was Jan. 15, 588 B.C. (dating from 597 as in 1:2). The Babylonians began the 18 month siege of Jerusalem (Jer. 39:1,2; 52:4-12).

24:3-5 utter a parable. The choice cuts of lamb picture God's flock being boiled in a pot, symbolizing Jerusalem in the heat of the siege. Cf. 11:3. Animal bones were frequently used for fuel.

24:6 Woe to the bloody city. Jerusalem's populace was guilty of bloody corruption, which was pictured by the boiled scum or rust in the pot (cf. 22:2).

24:7 her blood. The city's blood (a general symbol of sin) was blatantly open, not hidden, as depicted by exposure on top of a rock. When blood was not covered with dust, the law was violated (Lev. 17:13). God's vengeance would come by Babylon's army.

24:9,10 the pyre great...cuts be burned up. Intensely provoked by sin, God wanted Ezekiel to picture the fire as furious judgment that kills the people.

24:11,12 set the pot empty. After all pieces (people) were burned up, then the pot was heated empty. This portrayed the Lord's thorough follow-through by the besieger to totally destroy the city and the temple, with all its residue (cf. the treatment of a leprous house in Lev. 14:34-45).

That it may become hot and its
bronze may burn,
That [i]its filthiness may be melted
in it,
That its scum may be consumed.
12 She has [3]grown weary with [4]lies,
And her great scum has not gone
from her.
Let her scum *be* in the fire!
13 In your [j]filthiness *is* lewdness.
Because I have cleansed you, and
you were not cleansed,
You will [k]not be cleansed of your
filthiness anymore,
[l]Till I have caused My fury to rest
upon you.
14 [m]I, the LORD, have spoken *it;*
[n]It shall come to pass, and I will
do *it;*
I will not hold back,
[o]Nor will I spare,
Nor will I relent;
According to your ways
And according to your deeds
[5]They will judge you,"
Says the Lord GOD.' "

The Prophet's Wife Dies

15 Also the word of the LORD came to
me, saying, 16 "Son of man, behold, I take
away from you the desire of your eyes
with one stroke; yet you shall [p]neither
mourn nor weep, nor shall your tears run
down. 17 Sigh in silence, [q]make no mourning for the dead; [r]bind your turban on
your head, and [s]put your sandals on your
feet; [t]do not cover *your* [6]lips, and do not
eat man's bread *of sorrow."*
18 So I spoke to the people in the morning, and at evening my wife died; and the
next morning I did as I was commanded.
19 And the people said to me, [u]"Will you
not tell us what these *things signify* to us,
that you behave so?"
20 Then I answered them, "The word of
the LORD came to me, saying, 21 'Speak to
the house of Israel, "Thus says the Lord
GOD: 'Behold, [v]I will profane My sanctuary, [7]your arrogant boast, the desire of
your eyes, the [8]delight of your soul; [w]and
your sons and daughters whom you left
behind shall fall by the sword. 22 And you
shall do as I have done; [x]you shall not
cover *your* [9]lips nor eat man's bread *of sorrow.* 23 Your turbans shall be on your heads
and your sandals on your feet; [y]you shall
neither mourn nor weep, but [z]you shall
pine away in your iniquities and mourn
with one another. 24 Thus [a]Ezekiel is a sign
to you; according to all that he has done
you shall do; [b]and when this comes, [c]you
shall know that I *am* the Lord GOD.' "
25 'And you, son of man—*will it* not *be* in
the day when I take from them [d]their
stronghold, their joy and their glory, the
desire of their eyes, and [1]that on which
they set their minds, their sons and their
daughters: 26 on that day [e]one who escapes will come to you to let *you* hear *it*
with *your* ears; 27 [f]on that day your mouth
will be opened to him who has escaped;
you shall speak and no longer be mute.
Thus you will be a sign to them, and they
shall know that I *am* the LORD.' "

Proclamation Against Ammon

25 The word of the LORD came to me,
saying, 2 "Son of man, [a]set your
face [b]against the Ammonites, and prophesy against them. 3 Say to the Ammonites,
'Hear the word of the Lord GOD! Thus says
the Lord GOD: [c]"Because you said, 'Aha!'
against My sanctuary when it was profaned, and against the land of Israel when
it was desolate, and against the house of

11 [i]Ezek. 22:15
12 [3]Or *wearied Me* [4]Or *toil*
13 [j]Ezek. 23:36-48 [k]Jer. 6:28-30; Ezek. 22:24 [l]Ezek. 5:13; 8:18; 16:42
14 [m][1 Sam. 15:29] [n]Num. 23:19; Ps. 33:9; Is. 55:11 [o]Ezek. 5:11 [5]LXX, Syr., Tg., Vg. *I*
16 [p]Jer. 16:5
17 [q]Jer. 16:5 [r]Lev. 10:6; 21:10 [s]2 Sam. 15:30 [t]Mic. 3:7 [6]Lit. *moustache*
19 [u]Ezek. 12:9; 37:18
21 [v]Jer. 7:14; Lam. 2:7; Ezek. 7:20, 24 [w]Jer. 6:11; 16:3, 4; Ezek. 23:25, 47 [7]Lit. *the pride of your strength* [8]Lit. *compassion*
22 [x]Jer. 16:6, 7 [9]Lit. *moustache*
23 [y]Job 27:15; Ps. 78:64 [z]Lev. 26:39; Ezek. 33:10
24 [a]Is. 20:3; Ezek. 4:3; 12:6, 11; Luke 11:29, 30 [b]Jer. 17:15; John 13:19; 14:29 [c]Ezek. 6:7; 25:5
25 [d]Ps. 48:2; 50:2; Ezek. 24:21 [1]Lit. *the lifting up of their soul*
26 [e]Ezek. 33:21
27 [f]Ezek. 3:26; 33:22

CHAPTER 25

2 [a]Ezek. 35:2 [b]Jer. 49:1; Ezek. 21:28; Amos 1:13-15; Zeph. 2:9
3 [c]Ps. 70:2, 3; [Prov. 17:5]; Ezek. 26:2

24:16-27 Ezekiel's wife died as a sign to Israel. All personal sorrow was eclipsed in the universal calamity. Just as Ezekiel was not to mourn the death of his wife (v. 17), so Israel was not to mourn the death of her families (vv. 19-24). Though the text emphasizes how precious his wife was, the "desire of his eyes" (vv. 16,21), his "boast" and "delight" (v. 21), he was obedient and submitted to God's will. He became a heartbreaking sign to his people.

24:25 in the day. This refers to the destruction of the temple.

24:26,27 on that day. One who escaped the destruction of Jerusalem (586 B.C.) would come to Ezekiel in Babylon and report the story. From that day forward, he was to be silent until the captives arrived; then he could speak of Judah (cf. 3:26,27). This was about a two year period (cf. 33:21; Jer. 52:5-7), when there was no need to preach judgment because it had come. He did speak of other nations (as recorded beginning in chap. 25).

25:1 The word of the LORD came. Ezekiel 25:1–32:32 proclaims judgments on 7 other nations, similar to the series in Jer. 46–51. Four of them are singled out in this chap. for vindictive jealousy and hate toward Israel. It is fitting, after devoting chaps. 1–24 to calamity on His chosen nation, that God should reveal His impartiality toward all sinners and give the prophet judgments to proclaim on Gentiles. Israel's sinful failure had profaned God's honor in the eyes of these peoples (36:21-23), but these nations had falsely assumed that, when Israel was exiled, their God was defeated.

25:2,3 against the Ammonites. These people lived on the edge of the desert E of the Jordan River and N of Moab. They had joined Babylon against Judah about 600 B.C. (2 Kin. 24:2ff.). In 594 B.C., together with other nations, they tried to influence Judah to ally with them against Babylon (Jer. 27:2ff.). Ezekiel 21:18-20 indicates that Babylon came after them. There is no record of an attack, so they must have surrendered (21:28; Zeph. 2:8-11). They were of incestuous origin (cf. Gen. 19:37,38) and often hostile toward Judah (cf. Judg. 10; 1 Sam. 11; 2 Sam. 10,12; Jer. 49:1-6; Lam. 2:15; Amos 1:13-15). God judged this people because of their enmity against Israel (vv. 3,6). They expressed malicious pleasure at the dishonoring of the temple, desolation of the land, and dispersion of the inhabitants.

Judah when they went into captivity, 4 indeed, therefore, I will deliver you as a possession to the [1]men of the East, and they
shall set their encampments among you
and make their dwellings among you; they
shall eat your fruit, and they shall drink
your milk. 5 And I will make [d]Rabbah [e]a
stable for camels and Ammon a resting
place for flocks. [f]Then you shall know that
I *am* the LORD."

6 'For thus says the Lord GOD: "Because
you [g]clapped *your* hands, stamped your
feet, and [h]rejoiced in heart with all your
disdain for the land of Israel, 7 indeed,
therefore, I will [i]stretch out My hand
against you, and give you as plunder to the
nations; I will cut you off from the peoples,
and I will cause you to perish from the
countries; I will destroy you, and you shall
know that I *am* the LORD."

4 [1] Lit. *sons*
5 [d] Deut. 3:11; 2 Sam. 12:26; Jer. 49:2; Ezek. 21:20 [e] Is. 17:2 [f] Ezek. 24:24
6 [g] Job 27:23; Lam. 2:15; Nah. 3:19; Zeph. 2:15 [h] Ezek. 36:5
7 [i] Ezek. 35:3
8 [j] Is. 15:6; Jer. 48:1; Amos 2:1, 2 [k] Ezek. 35:2, 5
9 [l] Num. 32:3, 38; Josh. 13:17; 1 Chr. 5:8; Jer. 48:23
10 [m] Ezek. 25:4 [n] Ezek. 21:32
12 [o] 2 Chr. 28:17; Ps. 137:7; Jer. 49:7, 8; Amos 1:11; Obad. 10-14

Proclamation Against Moab

8 'Thus says the Lord GOD: "Because
[j]Moab and [k]Seir say, 'Look! The house of
Judah *is* like all the nations,' 9 therefore,
behold, I will clear the territory of Moab of
cities, of the cities on its frontier, the glory
of the country, Beth Jeshimoth, Baal Meon,
and [l]Kirjathaim. 10 [m]To the men of the East
I will give it as a possession, together with
the Ammonites, that the Ammonites [n]may
not be remembered among the nations.
11 And I will execute judgments upon
Moab, and they shall know that I *am* the
LORD."

Proclamation Against Edom

12 'Thus says the Lord GOD: [o]"Because of
what Edom did against the house of Judah
by taking vengeance, and has greatly of-

25:4 I will deliver you…to the men of the East. Perhaps this meant the coming of Babylon from the E which would devastate Ammon in either 588–86 B.C. or 582/81 B.C. Or it could refer to their land being occupied by the various nomadic tribes living beyond the Jordan.

25:5 Rabbah. This important Ammonite capitol (cf. Amos 1:14), now called Amman, is about 25 mi. NE of the upper tip of the Dead Sea, E of the Jordan River.

25:7 cause you to perish. Ammonites would be destroyed and eliminated from their land. Yet, Jer. 49:6 assures a later return of a remnant of these scattered people.

25:8-11 Moab and Seir. The origin of these people is given in Gen. 19:37,38. Their land was the area S of the Arnon River along the lower region of the Dead Sea. Cf. Is. 15,16; Jer. 48; Amos 2:1-3. The Babylonians destroyed cities there in 582/81 B.C. The reason for judgment (v. 8) also included their gloating over Israel's fall, as well as their scorn in saying Israel was like all other people with no privileged position before God. Both Ammonites and Moabites became absorbed into the Arabian peoples.

25:8 Seir. Another name for the adjacent Edomite area (Gen. 32:3; 36:20,21,30), dominated by Mt. Seir and a mountainous, extremely rugged, rocky country. Her judgments are given in 25:12-14.

25:12 Edom. Cf. chap. 35; Is. 21:11,12; Jer. 49:7-22; Amos 1:11,12; Obadiah; Mal. 1:3-5. These people lived S of Moab from the Dead Sea to the Gulf of Aqabah. These people had been almost annihilated by David (2 Sam. 8:14), but won back independence during the reign of Ahaz (ca. 735–715 B.C.). Their revenge was hostility to Israel constantly (cf. Gen. 27:27-41; Is. 34:5-7). The reason for judgment is Edom's disdain when the Israelites were devastated in 588–86 B.C. They acted like a cheering section for Babylon, "raze it, raze it" (Ps. 137:7; Lam. 4:21,22; Obad. 10-14).

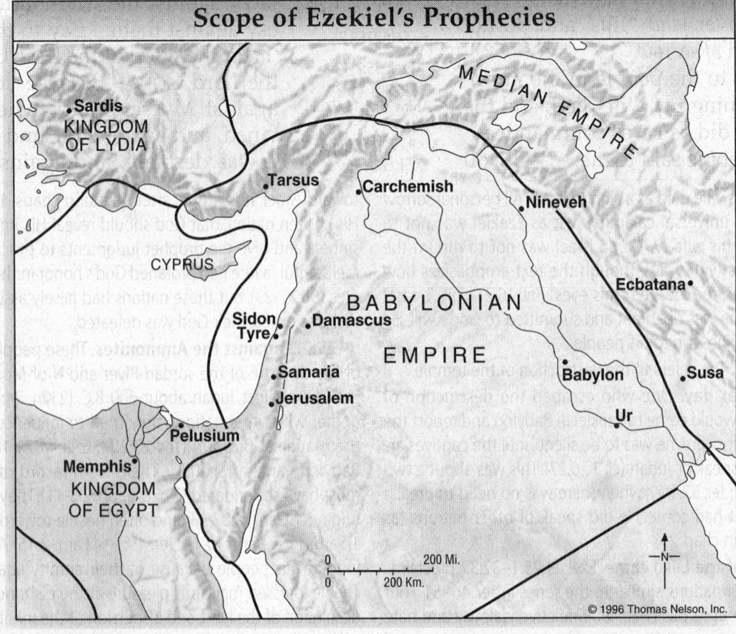

fended by avenging itself on them," 13 therefore thus says the Lord GOD: "I will also
stretch out My hand against Edom, cut off
man and beast from it, and make it desolate
from Teman; [2]Dedan shall fall by the sword.
14 [p]I will lay My vengeance on Edom by the
hand of My people Israel, that they may do
in Edom according to My anger and according to My fury; and they shall know My
vengeance," says the Lord GOD.

Proclamation Against Philistia

15 'Thus says the Lord GOD: [q]"Because
[r]the Philistines dealt vengefully and took
vengeance with [3]a spiteful heart, to destroy because of the [4]old hatred," 16 therefore thus says the Lord GOD: [s]"I will stretch
out My hand against the Philistines, and I
will cut off the [t]Cherethites [u]and destroy
the remnant of the seacoast. 17 I will [v]exe-
cute great vengeance on them with furious
rebukes; [w]and they shall know that I *am*
the LORD, when I lay My vengeance upon
them." ' "

Proclamation Against Tyre

26 And it came to pass in the eleventh
year, on the first *day* of the month,
that the word of the LORD came to me, saying, 2 "Son of man, [a]because Tyre has said
against Jerusalem, [b]'Aha! She is broken
who *was* the gateway of the peoples; now
she is turned over to me; I shall be filled;
she is laid waste.'
3 "Therefore thus says the Lord GOD:

13 [2]Or *even to Dedan they shall fall*
14 [p]Is. 11:14
15 [q]Jer. 25:20; Amos 1–6 [r]2 Chr. 28:18 [3]Lit. *spite in soul* [4]Or *perpetual*
16 [s]Zeph. 2:4 [t]1 Sam. 30:14 [u]Jer. 47:4
17 [v]Ezek. 5:15 [w]Ps. 9:16

CHAPTER 26

2 [a]2 Sam. 5:11; Is. 23:1; Jer. 25:22; Amos 1:9; Zech. 9:2 [b]Ezek. 25:3
4 [c]Ezek. 26:14
5 [d]Ezek. 27:32
6 [e]Ezek. 25:5
7 [f]Jer. 27:3-6; Ezek. 29:18 [g]Ezra 7:12; Is. 10:8; Jer. 52:32; Dan. 2:37, 47 [1]Heb. *Nebuchadrezzar,* and so elsewhere in the book
8 [h]Jer. 52:4; Ezek. 21:22 [2]Lit. *a large shield*
11 [i]Hab. 1:8

'Behold, I *am* against you, O Tyre, and will
cause many nations to come up against
you, as the sea causes its waves to come
up. 4 And they shall destroy the walls of
Tyre and break down her towers; I will
also scrape her dust from her, and [c]make
her like the top of a rock. 5 It shall be *a place*
for spreading nets [d]in the midst of the sea,
for I have spoken,' says the Lord GOD; 'it
shall become plunder for the nations.
6 Also her daughter *villages* which *are* in
the fields shall be slain by the sword.
[e]Then they shall know that I am the LORD.'
7 "For thus says the Lord GOD: 'Behold,
I will bring against Tyre from the north
[f]Nebuchadnezzar[1] king of Babylon, [g]king
of kings, with horses, with chariots, and
with horsemen, and an army with many
people. 8 He will slay with the sword your
daughter *villages* in the fields; he will
[h]heap up a siege mound against you, build
a wall against you, and raise a [2]defense
against you. 9 He will direct his battering
rams against your walls, and with his axes
he will break down your towers. 10 Because of the abundance of his horses, their
dust will cover you; your walls will shake
at the noise of the horsemen, the wagons,
and the chariots, when he enters your
gates, as men enter a city that has been
breached. 11 With the hooves of his [i]horses
he will trample all your streets; he will slay
your people by the sword, and your strong
pillars will fall to the ground. 12 They will
plunder your riches and pillage your mer-

25:13,14 against Edom…by the hand of My people Israel. The Arab tribe called Nabateans invaded Edom in 325 B.C.; but it was the Jewish forces of Judas Maccabeus in 164 B.C. and John Hyrcanus in 126 B.C. which fully subjugated Edom. Jews even compelled Edomites to submit to their religion. All 3 of these nations (Ammon, Moab, and Edom) have disappeared as separate nations into the Arab peoples.

25:13 Teman; Dedan. Reference is to key Edomite towns. Teman (Teima) was possibly 200 mi. E of the Dead Sea in the Arabian Desert in the northern expanse of Edom's territory. Dedan was maybe located 100 mi. S of Teman, yet far E of the Red Sea.

25:15-17 the Philistines. Cf. Is. 14:29-33; Jer. 47; Joel 3:4; Amos 1:6-8; Obad. 19; Zeph. 2:4-7; Zech. 9:5. The reason for their judgment was perpetual enmity, and vengefulness against Israel, which perpetuated the "old hatred" from as far back as Judg. 13–16. They constantly harassed and oppressed Israel until David broke their power during Saul's reign (1 Sam. 17). They repeatedly rose up and were subdued by Israel. Nebuchadnezzar invaded their land (Jer. 47).

25:16 Cherethites. They originated in Crete and became part of the Philistine nation (*see note on 1 Sam. 30:14*), with some serving in David's bodyguard (2 Sam. 8:18; 15:18).

25:17 great vengeance. This was fulfilled at the time of Babylon's invasion of 588–86 B.C. or 582/81 B.C. (cf. Jer. 25:20; 47:1-7).

26:1 the eleventh year. In 586 B.C., the 11th year of Jehoiachin's captivity, on the tenth day of the fifth month, Jerusalem was captured.

26:3,4 I *am* against you, O Tyre. The judgment of this city covers 3 chaps. (26–28), indicating its importance to God. Cf. Is. 23; Amos 1:9,10. Tyre was an ancient city of the Phoenicians, appearing for the first time in Josh. 19:29. During the reigns of David and Solomon it had great influence. Hiram, its king, was a friend to David (2 Sam. 5:11), who helped him and Solomon in building operations (cf. 1 Kin. 5:1-12; 1 Chr. 14:1; 2 Chr. 2:3,11). Later, Tyrians sold Jews into slavery (cf. Joel 3:4-8; Amos 1:9,10). God would move "many nations" to invade Tyre, the commercial center of the Mediterranean (cf. 27:3), in successive attacks pictured by wave following wave. Babylon (v. 7) besieged Tyre from 585–573 B.C.; later came Alexander's Grecian army in 332 B.C. Babylon had devastated the coastal city, but many Tyrians escaped to an island fortress which withstood attack. The later Grecian attackers "scraped" all the remaining "dust" and rubble and dumped it into the sea, building a causeway to the island nearly a half mile out. They also brought ships and overcame the fortress defenders in a devastating assault on Tyre. The predictions in chaps. 26–28 have been fulfilled with amazing literal accuracy.

26:5,14 *for* spreading nets. Tyre became a fishing city, a place to spread fishing nets for centuries, until the Saracens finally destroyed what was left in the fourth century. Since then the once great center of Mediterranean commerce has been a nondescript village.

26:7-14 Here is a vivid description of the original devastation by Babylon's King Nebuchadnezzar called "king of kings" (v. 7) because so many other rulers were subject to him. God had given him universal rule (cf. Dan. 2:37). Verses 8 and 9 describe the siege, vv. 10-14, the devastation.

26:12 They will plunder. After Nebuchadnezzar in v. 7 and "he" and "his" in vv. 8-11, "they" in v. 12 appears to broaden the reference

chandise; they will break down your walls
and destroy your pleasant houses; they
will lay your stones, your timber, and your
soil in the [j]midst of the water. 13 [k]I will put
an end to the sound of [l]your songs, and the
sound of your harps shall be heard no
more. 14 [m]I will make you like the top of a
rock; you shall be *a place for* spreading nets,
and you shall never be rebuilt, for I the
LORD have spoken,' says the Lord GOD.
15 "Thus says the Lord GOD to Tyre: 'Will
the coastlands not [n]shake at the sound of
your fall, when the wounded cry, when
slaughter is made in the midst of you?
16 Then all the [o]princes of the sea will
[p]come down from their thrones, lay aside
their robes, and take off their embroidered
garments; they will clothe themselves with
trembling; [q]they will sit on the ground,
[r]tremble *every* moment, and [s]be astonished
at you. 17 And they will take up a [t]lamen-
tation for you, and say to you:

"How you have perished,
O one inhabited by seafaring men,
O renowned city,
Who was [u]strong at sea,
She and her inhabitants,
Who caused their terror *to be* on all
her inhabitants!
18 Now [v]the coastlands tremble on
the day of your fall;
Yes, the coastlands by the sea are
troubled at your departure." '

19 "For thus says the Lord GOD: 'When I
make you a desolate city, like cities that are
not inhabited, when I bring the deep upon
you, and great waters cover you, 20 then I
will bring you down [w]with those who descend into the Pit, to the people of old, and
I will make you dwell in the lowest part of
the earth, in places desolate from antiquity,
with those who go down to the Pit, so that
you may never be inhabited; and I shall establish glory [x]in the land of the living. 21 [y]I
will make you a terror, and you *shall be* no
more; [z]though you are sought for, you will
never be found again,' says the Lord GOD."

12 [j] Ezek. 27:27, 32
13 [k] Is. 14:11; 24:8; Jer. 7:34; 25:10; Amos 6:5 [l] Is. 23:16; Ezek. 28:13; Rev. 18:22
14 [m] Ezek. 26:4, 5
15 [n] Jer. 49:21; Ezek. 27:28
16 [o] Is. 23:8 [p] Jon. 3:6 [q] Job 2:13 [r] Ezek. 32:10; Hos. 11:10 [s] Ezek. 27:35
17 [t] Ezek. 27:2-36; Rev. 18:9 [u] Josh. 19:29; Is. 23:4
18 [v] Ezek. 26:15
20 [w] Ezek. 32:18 [x] Ezek. 32:23
21 [y] Ezek. 27:36; 28:19 [z] Ps. 37:10, 36; Ezek. 28:19

CHAPTER 27

2 [a] Ezek. 26:17
3 [b] Ezek. 26:17; 28:2 [c] Is. 23:3 [d] Ezek. 28:12 [1] Lit. *sit* or *dwell*
5 [e] Deut. 3:9; 1 Chr. 5:23; Song 4:8 [2] *built*
6 [f] Is. 2:12, 13; Zech. 11:2 [g] Gen. 10:4; Is. 23:1, 12; Jer. 2:10 [3] Heb. *Kittim,* western lands, especially Cyprus
9 [h] Josh. 13:5; 1 Kin. 5:18; Ps. 83:7
10 [4] Heb. *Lud* [5] Heb. *Put*

Lamentation for Tyre

27 The word of the LORD came again to
me, saying, 2 "Now, son of man,
[a]take up a lamentation for Tyre, 3 and say
to Tyre, [b]'You who [1]are situated at the entrance of the sea, [c]merchant of the peoples
on many coastlands, thus says the Lord
GOD:

"O Tyre, you have said,
[d]'I *am* perfect in beauty.'
4 Your borders *are* in the midst of the
seas.
Your builders have perfected your
beauty.
5 They [2]made all *your* planks of fir
trees from [e]Senir;
They took a cedar from Lebanon to
make you a mast.
6 *Of* [f]oaks from Bashan they made
your oars;
The company of Ashurites have
inlaid your planks
With ivory from [g]the coasts of
[3]Cyprus.
7 Fine embroidered linen from Egypt
was what you spread for
your sail;
Blue and purple from the coasts of
Elishah was what covered
you.

8 "Inhabitants of Sidon and Arvad
were your oarsmen;
Your wise men, O Tyre, were in you;
They became your pilots.
9 Elders of [h]Gebal and its wise men
Were in you to caulk your seams;
All the ships of the sea
And their oarsmen were in you
To market your merchandise.

10 "Those from Persia, [4]Lydia, and
[5]Libya
Were in your army as men of war;
They hung shield and helmet in
you;
They gave splendor to you.

to others among the "many nations" (v. 3). At this point, "they" are not only Babylonians, but also Alexander's army which later heaped debris from the ruins into the sea to advance to the island stronghold (cf. Zech. 9:3,4).

26:13 songs…harps. According to Is. 23:16, Tyre was famous for musicians.

26:15-18 So important a center of commerce could not be destroyed without affecting all the nearby nations. All the nations around the Mediterranean would consider Tyre's fall a calamity. According to customs of mourning, rulers would descend from their thrones and disrobe.

26:19-21 Tyre's destruction is compared to a dead person placed in the grave.

27:1-11 a lamentation for Tyre. The whole chap. is a lamentation, describing Tyre as a great trade ship destroyed on the high seas. The proper names indicate the participants in commerce with Tyre.

27:5-9 fir trees from Senir. The area is the Amorite designation for Mt. Hermon, to the NE from the northern tip of the Sea of Galilee. Lesser known places were: Elishah (v. 7), believed to be in Cyprus; Arvad (v. 8), an island city off the Mediterranean coast N of Byblos; and Gebal (v. 9), a name also used for Byblos, N of today's Beirut. "Ashurites" (v. 6) were the Assyrians, who had skilled wood workers.

27:10,11 men of war. These places provided mercenary soldiers for the Phoenician army to defend Tyre.

11 Men of Arvad with your army *were*
on your walls *all* around,
And the men of Gammad were in
your towers;
They hung their shields on your
walls *all* around;
They made [i]your beauty perfect.

12 [j]"Tarshish *was* your merchant because
of your many luxury goods. They gave
you silver, iron, tin, and lead for your
goods. 13 [k]Javan, Tubal, and Meshech *were*
your traders. They bartered [l]human lives
and vessels of bronze for your merchandise. 14 Those from the house of [m]To-
garmah traded for your wares with horses,
steeds, and mules. 15 The men of [n]Dedan
were your traders; many isles *were* the market of your hand. They brought you ivory
tusks and ebony as payment. 16 Syria *was*
your merchant because of the abundance
of goods you made. They gave you for
your wares emeralds, purple, embroidery,
fine linen, corals, and rubies. 17 Judah and
the land of Israel *were* your traders. They
traded for your merchandise wheat of
[o]Minnith, millet, honey, oil, and [p]balm.
18 Damascus *was* your merchant because of
the abundance of goods you made, because of your many luxury items, with the
wine of Helbon and with white wool.
19 Dan and Javan paid for your wares, [6]tra-
versing back and forth. Wrought iron, cassia, and cane were among your merchandise. 20 [q]Dedan *was* your merchant in
saddlecloths for riding. 21 Arabia and all
the princes of [r]Kedar *were* your regular
merchants. They traded with you in lambs,
rams, and goats. 22 The merchants of
[s]Sheba and Raamah *were* your merchants.
They traded for your wares the choicest
spices, all kinds of precious stones, and
gold. 23 [t]Haran, Canneh, Eden, the merchants of [u]Sheba, Assyria, *and* Chilmad
were your merchants. 24 These *were* your
merchants in choice items—in purple
clothes, in embroidered garments, in
chests of multicolored apparel, in sturdy
woven cords, which were in your marketplace.

25 "The [v]ships of Tarshish were
carriers of your merchandise.
You were filled and very glorious
[w]in the midst of the seas.
26 Your oarsmen brought you into
many waters,
But [x]the east wind broke you in
the midst of the seas.

27 "Your [y]riches, wares, and
merchandise,
Your mariners and pilots,
Your caulkers and merchandisers,
All your men of war who *are* in
you,
And the entire company which *is*
in your midst,
Will fall into the midst of the seas
on the day of your ruin.
28 The [z]common-land[7] will shake at
the sound of the cry of your
pilots.

29 "All [a]who handle the oar,
The mariners,
All the pilots of the sea
Will come down from their ships
and stand on the [8]shore.
30 They will make their voice heard
because of you;
They will cry bitterly and [b]cast
dust on their heads;
They [c]will roll about in ashes;
31 They will [d]shave themselves
completely bald because of
you,
Gird themselves with sackcloth,

11 [i]Ezek. 27:3
12 [j]Gen. 10:4; 2 Chr. 20:36; Ezek. 38:13
13 [k]Gen. 10:2; Is. 66:19; Ezek. 27:19 [l]Joel 3:3-6; Rev. 18:13
14 [m]Gen. 10:3; Ezek. 38:6
15 [n]Gen. 10:7; Is. 21:13
17 [o]Judg. 11:33; 1 Kin. 5:9, 11; Ezra 3:7; Acts 12:20 [p]Jer. 8:22
19 [6]LXX, Syr. *from Uzal*
20 [q]Gen. 25:3
21 [r]Gen. 25:13; Is. 60:7; Jer. 49:28
22 [s]Gen. 10:7; 1 Kin. 10:1, 2; Ps. 72:10; Is. 60:6; Ezek. 38:13
23 [t]Gen. 11:31; 2 Kin. 19:12; Is. 37:12 [u]Gen. 25:3
25 [v]Ps. 48:7; Is. 2:16 [w]Ezek. 27:4
26 [x]Ps. 48:7; Jer. 18:17; Acts 27:14
27 [y][Prov. 11:4]
28 [z]Ezek. 26:15 [7]*open lands* or *pasturelands*
29 [a]Rev. 18:17 [8]Lit. *land*
30 [b]1 Sam. 4:12; 2 Sam. 1:2; Job 2:12; Lam. 2:10; Rev. 18:19 [c]Esth. 4:1, 3; Jer. 6:26; Jon. 3:6
31 [d]Is. 15:2; Jer. 16:6; Ezek. 29:18

27:11 Arvad. *See note on vv. 5-9.* **Gammad.** A place often identified as northern Syria.

27:12 Tarshish. This verse begins the description of the commercial glory of Tyre. Most likely this place refers to Tarshishah in southern Spain, a Phoenician colony famous for silver (Jer. 10:9).

27:13 Javan, Tubal, and Meshech. Javan was Ionia, a large area in Greece. The other two, in Asia Minor, may be the Tibarenoi and Moschoi mentioned by the writer Herodotus, or slave-trading cities called Tabal and Mushku by the Assyrians.

27:14 house of Togarmah. Beth-Togarmah is identified with Armenia in NE Asia Minor, which is modern Turkey.

27:15 Dedan. Probably Rhodes.

27:17 Minnith. An Ammonite town (Judg. 11:33).

27:18 Helbon. Today it is called Halbun, 13 mi. N of Damascus.

27:19 Dan. A Danite area is meant; but translators are not sure which areas are designated by this and Javan. **cassia.** A perfume.

27:21 Kedar. Refers to nomadic Bedouin tribes.

27:22 Sheba and Raamah. These were cities in the SW extremity of Arabia (Gen. 10:7; 1 Chr. 1:9).

27:23 Haran, Canneh, Eden. All were Mesopotamian towns; Canneh may have been in northern Syria, the Calneh of Amos 6:2, or the Caino of Is. 10:9. **Assyria…Chilmad.** These were also in Mesopotamia.

27:25 ships of Tarshish. The large cargo carrying sea ships that sailed across the Mediterranean.

27:26,27 the east wind broke. This pictures Tyre's fall aptly as a shipwreck on the seas. The sea, the place of her glory, will be her grave. "The east wind" is a picture of Babylon in its power from the E (cf. 13:11-13).

27:28-35 the cry. This maintains the metaphor of Tyre as a ship and turns particularly to men lamenting her ruin, for their livelihood has been tied to the commerce she represents. Verses 30-32 describe common actions signifying mourning.

And weep for you
With bitterness of heart *and* bitter
wailing.
32 In their wailing for you
They will [e]take up a lamentation,
And lament for you:
[f]What *city is* like Tyre,
Destroyed in the midst of the sea?
33 'When[g] your wares went out by
sea,
You satisfied many people;
You enriched the kings of the earth
With your many luxury goods and
your merchandise.
34 But [h]you are broken by the seas in
the depths of the waters;
[i]Your merchandise and the entire
company will fall in your
midst.
35 [j]All the inhabitants of the isles will
be astonished at you;
Their kings will be greatly afraid,
And *their* countenance will be
troubled.
36 The merchants among the peoples
[k]will hiss at you;
[l]You will become a horror, and *be*
no [m]more forever.' " ' "

Proclamation Against the King of Tyre

28 The word of the LORD came to me
again, saying, 2 "Son of man, say to
the prince of Tyre, 'Thus says the Lord
GOD:

"Because your heart *is* [a]lifted[1] up,
And [b]you say, 'I *am* a god,
I sit *in* the seat of gods,
[c]In the midst of the seas,'
[d]Yet you *are* a man, and not a god,
Though you set your heart as the
heart of a god
3 (Behold, [e]you *are* wiser than
Daniel!
There is no secret that can be
hidden from you!
4 With your wisdom and your
understanding
You have gained [f]riches for
yourself,
And gathered gold and silver into
your treasuries;
5 [g]By your great wisdom in trade you
have increased your riches,
And your heart is lifted up because
of your riches),"
6 'Therefore thus says the Lord GOD:

"Because you have set your heart as
the heart of a god,
7 Behold, therefore, I will bring
[h]strangers against you,
[i]The most terrible of the nations;
And they shall draw their swords
against the beauty of your
wisdom,
And defile your splendor.
8 They shall throw you down into
the [j]Pit,
And you shall die the death of the
slain
In the midst of the seas.
9 "Will you still [k]say before him who
slays you,
'I *am* a god'?
But you *shall be* a man, and not a
god,
In the hand of him who slays you.
10 You shall die the death of [l]the
uncircumcised
By the hand of aliens;
For I have spoken," says the Lord
GOD.' "

Lamentation for the King of Tyre

11 Moreover the word of the LORD came
to me, saying, 12 "Son of man, [m]take up a
lamentation for the king of Tyre, and say to
him, 'Thus says the Lord GOD:

[n]"You *were* the seal of perfection,

32 [e] Ezek. 26:17 [f] Ezek. 26:4, 5; Rev. 18:18
33 [g] Rev. 18:19
34 [h] Ezek. 26:19 [i] Ezek. 27:27
35 [j] Is. 23:6; Ezek. 26:15, 16
36 [k] Jer. 18:16; Zeph. 2:15 [l] Ezek. 26:2 [m] Ps. 37:10, 36; Ezek. 28:19

CHAPTER 28

2 [a] Jer. 49:16; Ezek. 31:10 [b] Is. 14:14; 47:8; Ezek. 28:9; 2 Thess. 2:4 [c] Ezek. 27:3, 4 [d] Is. 31:3; Ezek. 28:9 [1] Proud
3 [e] Ezek. 14:14; Dan. 1:20; 2:20-23, 28; 5:11, 12; Zech. 9:3
4 [f] Ezek. 27:33; Zech. 9:1-3
5 [g] Ps. 62:10; Zech. 9:3
7 [h] Ezek. 26:7 [i] Ezek. 7:24; 21:31; 30:11; Hab. 1:6-8
8 [j] Is. 14:15
9 [k] Ezek. 28:2
10 [l] 1 Sam. 17:26, 36; Ezek. 31:18; 32:19, 21, 25, 27
12 [m] Ezek. 27:2 [n] Ezek. 27:3; 28:3

27:36 There will be some who scorn with malicious joy.

28:1-19 This section concerning the king of Tyre is similar to Is. 14:3-23 referring to the king of Babylon. In both passages, some of the language best fits Satan. Most likely, both texts primarily describe the human king who is being used by Satan, much like Peter when Jesus said to him, "Get behind Me, Satan!" (Matt. 16:23). The judgment can certainly apply to Satan also.

28:2 to the prince of Tyre. Since "prince" is sometimes used to mean "the king" (37:24,25), the "prince" in v. 2 is the "king" in v. 12, Ittobaal II. The prophet is dealing with the spirit of Tyre more than just the king. This prophecy is dated shortly before the siege of Tyre by Nebuchadnezzar (585–573 B.C.). **I *am* a god.** Many ancient kings claimed to be a god, and acted as if they were (v. 6). When this king claimed to be a god, he was displaying the same proud attitude as the serpent who promised Adam and Eve they could be like God (Gen. 3:5).

28:3-5 wiser than Daniel. This is said in sarcastic derision of the leader's own exaggerated claims. Here is an indicator that Daniel, who had been captive for years in Babylon, had become well known.

28:6-10 strangers against you…aliens. The reference is to invading Babylonians, and later the Greeks. (cf. chap. 26). God was the true executioner.

28:11-19 This lament over "the king of Tyre" reached behind to the real supernatural source of wickedness, Satan. Cf. Matt. 16:21-23, where Peter was rebuked by the Lord, as under Satanic control and motivation.

28:12 the seal of perfection. The Lord led Ezekiel to address the king as the one to be judged, but clearly the power behind him was

Full of wisdom and perfect in
beauty.
13 You were in [o]Eden, the garden of
God;
Every precious stone *was* your
covering:
The sardius, topaz, and diamond,
Beryl, onyx, and jasper,
Sapphire, turquoise, and emerald
with gold.
The workmanship of [p]your
timbrels and pipes
Was prepared for you on the day
you were created.

14 "You *were* the anointed [q]cherub who
covers;
I established you;
You were on [r]the holy mountain of
God;
You walked back and forth in the
midst of fiery stones.
15 You *were* perfect in your ways from
the day you were created,
Till [s]iniquity was found in you.

16 "By the abundance of your trading
You became filled with violence
within,
And you sinned;
Therefore I cast you as a profane
thing
Out of the mountain of God;
And I destroyed you, [t]O covering
cherub,
From the midst of the fiery stones.

13 [o]Gen. 2:8; Is. 51:3; Ezek. 31:8, 9; 36:35 [p]Ezek. 26:13
14 [q]Ex. 25:20; Ezek. 28:16 [r]Is. 14:13; Ezek. 20:40
15 [s][Is. 14:12]
16 [t]Ezek. 28:14
17 [u]Ezek. 28:2, 5 [2]Proud
19 [v]Ezek. 26:21 [w]Ezek. 27:36
21 [x]Ezek. 6:2; 25:2; 29:2 [y]Gen. 10:15, 19; Is. 23:2, 4, 12; Ezek. 27:8; 32:30
22 [z]Ex. 14:4, 17; Ezek. 39:13 [a]Ps. 9:16 [b]Ezek. 28:25
23 [c]Ezek. 38:22

17 "Your [u]heart was [2]lifted up because
of your beauty;
You corrupted your wisdom for
the sake of your splendor;
I cast you to the ground,
I laid you before kings,
That they might gaze at you.

18 "You defiled your sanctuaries
By the multitude of your iniquities,
By the iniquity of your trading;
Therefore I brought fire from your
midst;
It devoured you,
And I turned you to ashes upon
the earth
In the sight of all who saw you.
19 All who knew you among the
peoples are astonished at you;
[v]You have become a horror,
And *shall be* no [w]more forever." ' "

Proclamation Against Sidon

20 Then the word of the LORD came to
me, saying, 21 "Son of man, [x]set your face
[y]toward Sidon, and prophesy against her,
22 and say, 'Thus says the Lord GOD:

[z]"Behold, I *am* against you, O Sidon;
I will be glorified in your midst;
And [a]they shall know that I *am* the
LORD,
When I execute judgments in her
and am [b]hallowed in her.
23 [c]For I will send pestilence upon her,
And blood in her streets;

Satan. This phrase must be associated with Satan as one perfect in angelic beauty before he rebelled against God. But, it can also relate to "perfection" in the same context of Tyre's enterprise, topmost in its trade to the ancient world (27:3,4,11), glorious in her seafaring efforts (27:24), and the crowning city (Is. 23:8), i.e., "perfect" as Jerusalem also is said to be (16:14; Lam. 2:15). **Full of wisdom.** This referred to Satan's wisdom as an angel and to Tyre's wisdom (skill) in trade (cf. 27:8,9; 28:4).

28:13 You were in Eden. This could be Satan in the Garden of Eden (Gen. 3:1-15), or it might refer to Tyre's king in a beautiful environment, a kind of Eden. **Every precious stone.** This depicts Satan's rich investiture (Gen. 2:12), and/or Tyre's king possessing every beautiful stone as Solomon had (1 Kin. 10:10). **workmanship of your timbrels.** This could refer both to Satan's once being in charge of heavenly praise and to Tyre's beautiful musical instruments used in celebration (26:13). **you were created.** Satan, however, is more likely to have such wealth and beauty, wisdom, and perfection at his creation than this earthly king would have at his birth.

28:14 anointed cherub. This refers to Satan in his exalted privilege as an angel guarding (i.e., covering) God's throne, as cherubim guarded Eden (Gen. 3:24). Satan originally had continuous and unrestricted access to the glorious presence of God. **I established you.** This was true of both Satan, by God's sovereign permission, and Tyre's king. **You were on the holy mountain.** A high privilege is meant, whether referring to Satan before God in His kingdom (mountain, cf. Dan. 2:35), or Tyre's monarch described in a picturesque analogy, as Assyria can be described as a cedar in Lebanon (31:3) to convey a picture of towering height.

28:15 perfect in your ways. This verse was not completely true of the king, but it was accurate of Satan before he sinned. **Till iniquity was found in you.** Satan's sin of pride (cf. Is. 14:14; 1 Tim. 3:6) is in view here.

28:16 The description transitions to feature the king of Tyre, describing his demise, as he followed the pattern of Satan himself.

28:17-19 I laid you before kings. It would be difficult to relate this to Satan. The earthly king of Tyre, in his downfall, would be knocked or cast to the ground, cut down, and lie before the gaze of other kings. From Is. 23:17 there is the implication of a revival under Persian rule (Neh. 13:16). Two hundred and fifty years after Nebuchadnezzar, Tyre was strong enough to hold off Alexander for 7 years. The Romans made it a capital of the province. Gradually it disappeared and its location is not prominent.

28:21 Sidon. Sidon (vv. 20-24) is a sister seaport to Tyre in Phoenicia, 23 mi. N. Even in the time of the judges (Judg. 10:6), the corrupting influence of this place had begun. It was the headquarters for Baal worship.

28:22,23 judgments in her. God is to bring bloodshed and pestilence on people there, probably at the time He brings an invasion against Tyre.

The wounded shall be judged in
her midst
By the sword against her on every
side;
Then they shall know that I *am* the
LORD.

24 "And there shall no longer be a pricking brier or [d]a painful thorn for the house
of Israel from among all *who are* around
them, who [e]despise them. Then they shall
know that I *am* the Lord GOD."

Israel's Future Blessing

25 'Thus says the Lord GOD: "When I
have [f]gathered the house of Israel from the
peoples among whom they are scattered,
and am [g]hallowed in them in the sight of
the Gentiles, then they will dwell in their
own land which I gave to My servant Jacob. 26 And they will [h]dwell [3]safely there,
[i]build houses, and [j]plant vineyards; yes,
they will dwell securely, when I execute
judgments on all those around them who
despise them. Then they shall know that I
am the LORD their God."' "

Proclamation Against Egypt

29 In the tenth year, in the tenth *month*,
on the twelfth *day* of the month, the
word of the LORD came to me, saying,
2 "Son of man, [a]set your face against Pharaoh king of Egypt, and prophesy against
him, and [b]against all Egypt. 3 Speak, and
say, 'Thus says the Lord GOD:

[c]"Behold, I *am* against you,
O Pharaoh king of Egypt,
O great [d]monster who lies in the
midst of his rivers,
[e]Who has said, 'My [1]River *is* my
own;
I have made *it* for myself.'
4 But [f]I will put hooks in your jaws,
And cause the fish of your rivers to
stick to your scales;
I will bring you up out of the midst
of your rivers,
And all the fish in your rivers will
stick to your scales.
5 I will leave you in the wilderness,
You and all the fish of your rivers;
You shall fall on the [2]open [g]field;
[h]You shall not be picked up or
[3]gathered.
[i]I have given you as food
To the beasts of the field
And to the birds of the heavens.

6 "Then all the inhabitants of Egypt
Shall know that I *am* the LORD,
Because they have been a [j]staff of
reed to the house of Israel.
7 [k]When they took hold of you with
the hand,
You broke and tore all their
[4]shoulders;
When they leaned on you,
You broke and made all their backs
quiver."

8 'Therefore thus says the Lord GOD:
"Surely I will bring [l]a sword upon you and
cut off from you man and beast. 9 And the
land of Egypt shall become [m]desolate and
waste; then they will know that I *am* the
LORD, because he said, 'The River *is* mine,
and I have made *it*.' 10 Indeed, therefore, I
am against you and against your rivers,
[n]and I will make the land of Egypt utterly
waste and desolate, [o]from [5]Migdol *to* Syene, as far as the border of Ethiopia.
11 [p]Neither foot of man shall pass through
it nor foot of beast pass through it, and it

24 [d] Num. 33:55; Josh. 23:13; Is. 55:13; Ezek. 2:6 [e] Ezek. 16:57; 25:6, 7
25 [f] Ps. 106:47; Is. 11:12, 13; Jer. 32:37; Ezek. 11:17; 20:41; 34:13; 37:21 [g] Ezek. 28:22
26 [h] Jer. 23:6; Ezek. 36:28 [i] Is. 65:21; Jer. 32:15, 43, 44; Amos 9:13, 14 [j] Jer. 31:5; Amos 9:14 [3] *securely*

CHAPTER 29

2 [a] Ezek. 28:21 [b] Is. 19:1; Jer. 25:19; 46:2, 25; Ezek. 30:1–32:32; Joel 3:19
3 [c] Jer. 44:30; Ezek. 28:22; 29:10 [d] Ps. 74:13, 14; Is. 37:1; 51:9; Ezek. 32:2 [e] Ezek. 28:2 [1] The Nile
4 [f] 2 Kin. 19:28; Is. 37:29; Ezek. 38:4
5 [g] Ezek. 32:4-6 [h] Jer. 8:2; 16:4; 25:33 [i] Jer. 7:33; 34:20; Ezek. 39:4 [2] Lit. *face of the field* [3] So with MT, LXX, Vg.; some Heb. mss., Tg. *buried*
6 [j] 2 Kin. 18:21; Is. 36:6; Ezek. 17:15
7 [k] Jer. 37:5, 7, 11; Ezek. 17:17 [4] So with MT, Vg.; LXX, Syr. *hand*
8 [l] Jer. 46:13; Ezek. 14:17; 32:11-13
9 [m] Ezek. 30:7, 8
10 [n] Ezek. 30:12 [o] Ezek. 30:6 [5] Or *the tower*
11 [p] Jer. 43:11, 12; 46:19; Ezek. 32:13

28:24 no longer…a pricking brier. This is a summary of the judgment scenarios so far revealed (chaps. 25–28). The enemies of Israel would be so devastated by God that 1) they would no longer be pestering Israel, and 2) they would see that the God who judges them is the true God of Israel.

28:25,26 When I have gathered. In this brief excursus of hope, God promised to restore Israel to the land of Palestine (cf. chaps. 34,36–39; Is. 65:21; Jer. 30–33; Amos 9:14,15). This looks to Messiah's earthly kingdom.

29:1 the tenth year. 587 B.C. is the 10th year after Jehoiachin's deportation. It is a year and two days after Nebuchadnezzar had come to Jerusalem (24:1,2; 2 Kin. 25:1) and 7 months before its destruction (2 Kin. 25:3-8). This is the first of 7 oracles against Egypt (cf. 29:17; 30:1; 32:1; 32:17).

29:2 against all Egypt. Cf. Is. 19; Jer. 46:1-26. Egypt was to fall, even though it could be pictured as a water monster (vv. 3-5), a towering tree like Assyria (31:3), a young lion (32:2), and a sea monster (32:2-8). The judgment looks ahead to 570 B.C. when the Greeks of Cyrene defeated Pharaoh (Apries) Hophra and 568/67 B.C. when Babylon conquered Egypt.

29:3 great monster. Most likely the crocodile is the figure used for the king. Crocodiles were worshiped by the Egyptians, and lived in their rivers. "Rahab" a general term used for a monster which often symbolized Egypt. *See notes on Pss. 87:4; 89:10; Is. 30:7.*

29:4 fish of your rivers. This figuratively represents the people who followed Pharaoh and who were a part of God's judgment on Egypt as a whole (v. 5,6a).

29:6 a staff of reed. The Israelites had depended on Egyptians in military alliances as people lean on a staff that gives way, failing them. Egypt had betrayed the confidence of Israel as God said they would (cf. Jer. 17:5,7). Because Israel never should have trusted Egypt does not lessen Egypt's judgment.

29:9 The River. The Nile River was the water supply for all Egypt's crops. *See note on v. 18.*

29:10 from Migdol *to* Syene. This covered the entirety of Egypt, since Migdol (Ex. 14:2) was in the N and Syene in the southern border of "Ethiopia."

shall be uninhabited forty years. **12** [q]I will
make the land of Egypt desolate in the
midst of the countries *that are* desolate; and
among the cities *that are* laid waste, her
cities shall be desolate forty years; and I
will [r]scatter the Egyptians among the nations and disperse them throughout the
countries."
13 'Yet, thus says the Lord GOD: "At the
[s]end of forty years I will gather the Egyptians from the peoples among whom they
were scattered. **14** I will bring back the captives of Egypt and cause them to return to
the land of Pathros, to the land of their origin, and there they shall be a [t]lowly kingdom. **15** It shall be the lowliest of kingdoms; it shall never again exalt itself above
the nations, for I will diminish them so that
they will not rule over the nations anymore. **16** No longer shall it be [u]the confidence of the house of Israel, but will remind them of *their* iniquity when they
turned to follow them. Then they shall
know that I *am* the Lord GOD." ' "

Babylonia Will Plunder Egypt

17 And it came to pass in the twenty-seventh year, in the first *month,* on the first *day*
of the month, *that* the word of the LORD
came to me, saying, **18** "Son of man, [v]Neb-
uchadnezzar king of Babylon caused his
army to labor strenuously against Tyre;
every head *was* made [w]bald, and every
shoulder rubbed raw; yet neither he nor
his army received wages from Tyre, for the
labor which they expended on it. **19** Therefore thus says the Lord GOD: 'Surely I will
give the land of Egypt to [x]Nebuchad-
nezzar king of Babylon; he shall take away
her wealth, carry off her spoil, and remove
her pillage; and that will be the wages for
his army. **20** I have given him the land of
Egypt *for* his labor, because they [y]worked
for Me,' says the Lord GOD.
21 'In that day [z]I will cause the [6]horn of
the house of Israel to spring forth, and I
will [a]open your mouth to speak in their
midst. Then they shall know that I *am* the
LORD.' "

12 [q] Jer. 25:15-19; 27:6-11; Ezek. 30:7, 26 [r] Jer. 46:19; Ezek. 30:23, 26
13 [s] Is. 19:23; Jer. 46:26
14 [t] Ezek. 17:6, 14
16 [u] Is. 30:2, 3; 36:4, 6; Lam. 4:17; Ezek. 17:15; 29:6
18 [v] Jer. 25:9; 27:6; Ezek. 26:7-12 [w] Jer. 48:37; Ezek. 27:31
19 [x] Jer. 43:10-13; Ezek. 30:10
20 [y] Is. 10:6, 7; 45:1-3; Jer. 25:9
21 [z] 1 Sam. 2:10; Ps. 92:10; 132:17 [a] Ezek. 24:27; Amos 3:7, 8; [Luke 21:15] [6] Strength

CHAPTER 30

2 [a] Is. 13:6; 15:2; Ezek. 21:12; Joel 1:5, 11, 13
3 [b] Ezek. 7:7, 12; Joel 2:1; Obad. 15; Zeph. 1:7
4 [c] Ezek. 29:19 [d] Jer. 50:15 [1] Heb. *Cush*
5 [e] Jer. 25:20, 24 [2] Heb. *Put* [3] Heb. *Lud*
6 [f] Ezek. 29:10 [4] Or *the tower*

Egypt and Her Allies Will Fall

30 The word of the LORD came to me
again, saying, **2** "Son of man,
prophesy and say, 'Thus says the Lord
GOD:

[a]"Wail, 'Woe to the day!'
3 For [b]the day *is* near,
Even the day of the LORD *is* near;
It will be a day of clouds, the time
of the Gentiles.
4 The sword shall come upon Egypt,
And great anguish shall be in
[1]Ethiopia,
When the slain fall in Egypt,
And they [c]take away her wealth,
And [d]her foundations are broken
down.

5 "Ethiopia, [2]Libya, [3]Lydia, [e]all the mingled people, Chub, and the men of the
lands who are allied, shall fall with them
by the sword."
6 'Thus says the LORD:

"Those who uphold Egypt shall fall,
And the pride of her power shall
come down.
[f]From [4]Migdol *to* Syene
Those within her shall fall by the
sword,"
Says the Lord GOD.

29:11,12 uninhabited forty years. Although difficult to pinpoint, one possibility is that this period was when Babylon, under Nebuchadnezzar, reigned supreme in Egypt (vv. 19,20), from ca. 568/67 B.C. to 525 B.C. until Cyrus gained Persian control.

29:13-16 I will gather the Egyptians. Egypt regained normalcy as is currently true, but never again reached the pinnacle of international prominence she once enjoyed.

29:17 the twenty-seventh year. This is 571/70 B.C. as counted from the captivity of Jehoiachin in 597 B.C., about 17 years after the prophecy in vv. 1-16.

29:18 labor…against Tyre. In ca. 585–573 B.C., Nebuchadnezzar besieged Tyre for 13 years before subduing the city (cf. Ezek. 26:1–28:19). Tyrians retreated to an island bastion out in the sea and survived, not giving Babylon full satisfaction in spoils ("wages") equal to such long struggle.

29:19 I will give the land of Egypt. To make up for Babylon's lack of sufficient reward from Tyre, God allowed a Babylonian conquest of Egypt in 568/67 B.C. Babylon's army had worked as an instrument which God used to bring down Egypt.

29:21 I will cause the horn…to spring forth. Cf. 23:25,26. God caused Israel's power to return and restored her authority as the power in an animal's horn (cf. 1 Sam. 2:1). Though other nations subdued her, her latter end in messianic times will be blessed. **I will open your mouth.** Most likely this refers to the day when Ezekiel's writings would be understood by looking back at their fulfillment. His muteness had already ceased in 586/585 B.C. when Jerusalem fell (cf. 33:21,22).

30:3 the day of the LORD *is* near. This is a common expression for God's judgment, especially His future judgment (cf. Joel 1:15; 2:1,11; 3:14; Zech. 14:1; 1 Thess. 5:2; 2 Thess. 2:2; 2 Pet. 3:10). God's judgment "day" for Egypt embraces a near fulfillment in Babylon's 568/67 invasion (v. 10; 32:11), as well as the distant day of the Lord in the future tribulation period when God calls all nations to judgment (Dan. 11:42,43). *See note on Is. 2:12.*

30:5 Ethiopia, Libya, Lydia. *See notes on 27:10 and 29:10.* **Chub.** An unidentified nation, along with the "mingled people" and "men of the lands." These also may have been mercenaries in Egypt's army, like the previous ones in this verse.

30:6 Migdol…Syene. *See note on 29:10.*

7 "They[g] shall be desolate in the midst of the desolate countries,
And her cities shall be in the midst of the cities *that are* laid waste.
8 Then they will know that I *am* the LORD,
When I have set a fire in Egypt
And all her helpers are destroyed.
9 On that day [h]messengers shall go forth from Me in ships
To make the [5]careless Ethiopians afraid,
And great anguish shall come upon them,
As on the day of Egypt;
For indeed it is coming!"

10 'Thus says the Lord GOD:

[i]"I will also make a multitude of Egypt to cease
By the hand of Nebuchadnezzar king of Babylon.
11 He and his people with him, [j]the most terrible of the nations,
Shall be brought to destroy the land;
They shall draw their swords against Egypt,
And fill the land with the slain.
12 [k]I will make the rivers dry,
And [l]sell the land into the hand of the wicked;
I will make the land waste, and all that is in it,
By the hand of aliens.
I, the LORD, have spoken."

13 'Thus says the Lord GOD:

"I will also [m]destroy the idols,
And cause the images to cease from [6]Noph;
[n]There shall no longer be princes from the land of Egypt;
[o]I will put fear in the land of Egypt.
14 I will make [p]Pathros desolate,
Set fire to [q]Zoan,
[r]And execute judgments in [7]No.
15 I will pour My fury on [8]Sin, the strength of Egypt;
[s]I will cut off the multitude of [9]No,
16 And [t]set a fire in Egypt;
Sin shall have great pain,
No shall be split open,
And Noph *shall be in* distress daily.
17 The young men of [1]Aven and Pi Beseth shall fall by the sword,
And these *cities* shall go into captivity.
18 [u]At [2]Tehaphnehes the day shall also be [3]darkened,
When I break the yokes of Egypt there.
And her arrogant strength shall cease in her;
As for her, a cloud shall cover her,
And her daughters shall go into captivity.
19 Thus I will [v]execute judgments on Egypt,
Then they shall know that I *am* the LORD." ' "

Proclamation Against Pharaoh

20 And it came to pass in the eleventh
year, in the first *month*, on the seventh *day*
of the month, *that* the word of the LORD
came to me, saying, 21 "Son of man, I have
[w]broken the arm of Pharaoh king of Egypt;
and see, [x]it has not been bandaged for
healing, nor a [4]splint put on to bind it, to
make it strong enough to hold a sword.
22 Therefore thus says the Lord GOD: 'Surely I *am* [y]against Pharaoh king of Egypt,
and will [z]break his arms, both the strong
one and the one that was broken; and I will
make the sword fall out of his hand. 23 [a]I
will scatter the Egyptians among the nations, and disperse them throughout the
countries. 24 I will strengthen the arms of
the king of Babylon and put My sword in
his hand; but I will break Pharaoh's arms,

7 [g] Jer. 25:18-26; Ezek. 29:12
9 [h] Is. 18:1, 2 [5] Or *secure*
10 [i] Ezek. 29:19
11 [j] Ezek. 28:7; 31:12
12 [k] Is. 19:5, 6 [l] Is. 19:4
13 [m] Is. 19:1; Jer. 43:12; 46:25; Zech. 13:2 [n] Zech. 10:11 [o] Is. 19:16 [6] Ancient Memphis
14 [p] Is. 11:11; Jer. 44:1, 15; Ezek. 29:14 [q] Ps. 78:12, 43; Is. 19:11, 13 [r] Jer. 46:25; Ezek. 30:15, 16; Nah. 3:8-10 [7] Ancient Thebes
15 [s] Jer. 46:25 [8] Ancient Pelusium [9] Ancient Thebes
16 [t] Ezek. 30:8
17 [1] Ancient On, Heliopolis
18 [u] Jer. 2:16 [2] *Tahpanhes,* Jer. 43:7 [3] So with many Heb. mss., Bg., LXX, Syr., Tg., Vg.; MT *refrained*
19 [v] [Ps. 9:16]; Ezek. 5:8; 25:11
21 [w] Jer. 48:25 [x] Jer. 46:11 [4] Lit. *bandage*
22 [y] Jer. 46:25; Ezek. 29:3 [z] Ps. 37:17
23 [a] Ezek. 29:12; 30:17, 18, 26

30:8 helpers. All Egypt's alliances and their arms will be useless in the day of God's judgment.

30:9 Apparently, the Egyptians will flee the horrors to Ethiopia and increase that nations fear of its own inevitable judgment.

30:10,11 Nebuchadnezzar was God's instrument.

30:12 rivers dry. Apart from the Nile and its branches, Egypt was a barren desert. Her life depended on an annual inundation of the land by the flooding Nile.

30:14 Pathros. The large region S of Memphis. **Zoan.** This key city of the Nile Delta's eastern portion was called Tanis by Greeks.

30:15 Sin. The name referred to ancient Pelusium, a key city at the tip of the Nile's eastern arm near the Mediterranean Sea. Since "No" (Thebes) and "Sin" were at opposite borders of Egypt and so many cities are named, the passage speaks of judgment on the entire land.

30:17 Pi Beseth. The city was on the NE branch of the Nile where cats were mummified in honor of the cat-headed goddess, Ugastet.

30:18 Tehaphnehes. This city, named after the Egyptian queen, was a residence of the pharaohs.

30:20 the eleventh year. Ca. 587 B.C., counted from the deportation of Judah in 597 B.C.

30:21 I have broken the arm. God figuratively depicted His act of taking power from Egypt through Nebuchadnezzar, resulting in defeat and dispersion (vv. 23,26).

30:22 break his arms. Both the defeat of Pharaoh Hophra (cf. Jer. 37:5ff.) and the earlier defeat of Pharaoh Necho at Carchemish (cf. 2 Kin. 24:7; Jer. 46:2) are in view.

and he will groan before him with the groanings of a mortally wounded *man.*
25 Thus I will strengthen the arms of the king of Babylon, but the arms of Pharaoh shall fall down; [b]they shall know that I *am* the LORD, when I put My sword into the hand of the king of Babylon and he stretches it out against the land of Egypt.
26 [c]I will scatter the Egyptians among the nations and disperse them throughout the countries. Then they shall know that I *am* the LORD.' "

Egypt Cut Down Like a Great Tree

31 Now it came to pass in the [a]eleventh year, in the third *month,* on the first *day* of the month, *that* the word of the LORD came to me, saying, 2 "Son of man, say to Pharaoh king of Egypt and to his multitude:

[b]'Whom are you like in your greatness?
3 [c]Indeed Assyria *was* a cedar in Lebanon,
With fine branches that shaded the forest,
And of high stature;
And its top was among the thick boughs.
4 [d]The waters made it grow;
Underground waters gave it height,
With their rivers running around the place where it was planted,
And sent out [1]rivulets to all the trees of the field.
5 'Therefore [e]its height was exalted above all the trees of the field;
Its boughs were multiplied,
And its branches became long because of the abundance of water,
As it sent them out.
6 All the [f]birds of the heavens made their nests in its boughs;
Under its branches all the beasts of the field brought forth their young;
And in its shadow all great nations [2]made their home.
7 'Thus it was beautiful in greatness and in the length of its branches,
Because its roots reached to abundant waters.
8 The cedars in the [g]garden of God could not hide it;
The fir trees were not like its boughs,
And the [3]chestnut trees were not like its branches;
No tree in the garden of God was like it in beauty.
9 I made it beautiful with a multitude of branches,
So that all the trees of Eden envied it,
That *were* in the garden of God.'

10 "Therefore thus says the Lord GOD: 'Because you have increased in height, and it set its top among the thick boughs, and [h]its heart was [4]lifted up in its height,
11 therefore I will deliver it into the hand of the [i]mighty one of the nations, and he shall surely deal with it; I have driven it out for its wickedness.
12 And aliens, [j]the most terrible of the nations, have cut it down and left it; its branches have fallen [k]on the mountains and in all the valleys; its boughs lie [l]broken by all the rivers of the land; and all the peoples of the earth have gone from under its shadow and left it.

13 'On [m]its ruin will remain all the birds of the heavens,
And all the beasts of the field will come to its branches—

14 'So that no trees by the waters may ever again exalt themselves for their height, nor set their tops among the thick boughs, that no tree which drinks water may ever be high enough to reach up to them.

25 [b]Ps. 9:16
26 [c]Ezek. 29:12

CHAPTER 31

1 [a]Jer. 52:5, 6; Ezek. 30:20; 32:1
2 [b]Ezek. 31:18
3 [c]Is. 10:33, 34; Ezek. 17:3, 4, 22; 31:16; Dan. 4:10, 20-23
4 [d]Jer. 51:36; Ezek. 29:3-9 [1]Or *channels*
5 [e]Dan. 4:11
6 [f]Ezek. 17:23; 31:13; Dan. 4:12, 21; Matt. 13:32

[2]Lit. *dwelled*
8 [g]Gen. 2:8, 9; 13:10; Is. 51:3; Ezek. 28:13; 31:16, 18 [3]Or *plane,* Heb. *armon*
10 [h]2 Chr. 32:25; Is. 10:12; 14:13, 14; Ezek. 28:17; Dan. 5:20 [4]Proud
11 [i]Ezek. 30:10; Dan. 5:18, 19
12 [j]Ezek. 28:7; 30:11; 32:12 [k]Ezek. 32:5; 35:8 [l]Ezek. 30:24, 25
13 [m]Is. 18:6; Ezek. 32:4

30:26 People often don't learn that God is Lord until judgment falls.

31:1 the eleventh year. 587 B.C. Two months after the oracle of 30:20-26.

31:2-18 Whom are you like...? Ezekiel filled this chap. with a metaphor/analogy comparing Egypt to a huge tree that dominates a forest to a king/nation that dominates the world (cf. 17:22-24; Dan. 4:1-12,19-27). He reasoned that just as a strong tree like Assyria (v. 3) fell (ca. 609 B.C.), so will Egypt (ca. 568 B.C.). If the Egyptians tend to be proud and feel invincible, let them remember how powerful Assyria had fallen already.

31:3 cedar in Lebanon. The trees were as high as 80 ft. and were an example of supreme power and domination, particularly the great cedars which grew in the mountains N of Israel.

31:8,9 garden of God...trees of Eden. (36:35; Gen. 13:10; Is. 51:3; Joel 2:3). Since Assyria was in the area of the Garden of Eden, Ezekiel used the ultimate of gardens as a point of relative reference by which to describe tree-like Assyria.

31:10 Because you. Ezekiel shifted from the historical illustration of Assyria's pride and fall to the reality of Egypt. God was using Assyria to teach the nations the folly of earthly power and might.

31:14-16 the Pit. The scene shifts from earth and the garden of God to the grave (cf. 32:18), as God again refers to the destruction of Assyria and all her allies ("all the trees," "all that drink water").

'For [n]they have all been delivered
to death,
[o]To the depths of the earth,
Among the children of men who
go down to the Pit.'

15 "Thus says the Lord GOD: 'In the day
when it [p]went down to [5]hell, I caused
mourning. I covered the deep because of it.
I restrained its rivers, and the great waters
were held back. I caused Lebanon to
[6]mourn for it, and all the trees of the field
wilted because of it. 16 I made the nations
[q]shake at the sound of its fall, when I [r]cast
it down to [7]hell together with those who
descend into the Pit; and [s]all the trees of
Eden, the choice and best of Lebanon, all
that drink water, [t]were comforted in the
depths of the earth. 17 They also went
down to hell with it, with those *slain* by the
sword; and *those who were* its *strong* arm
[u]dwelt in its shadows among the nations.
18 [v]'To which of the trees in Eden will
you then be likened in glory and greatness? Yet you shall be brought down with
the trees of Eden to the depths of the earth;
[w]you shall lie in the midst of the uncircumcised, with *those* slain by the sword. This *is*
Pharaoh and all his multitude,' says the
Lord GOD."

Lamentation for Pharaoh and Egypt

32 And it came to pass in the twelfth
year, in the [a]twelfth *month,* on the
first *day* of the month, *that* the word of the
LORD came to me, saying, 2 "Son of man,
[b]take up a lamentation for Pharaoh king of
Egypt, and say to him:

[c]'You are like a young lion among
the nations,
And [d]you *are* like a monster in the
seas,
[e]Bursting forth in your rivers,
Troubling the waters with your feet,
And [f]fouling their rivers.'

3 "Thus says the Lord GOD:

'I will therefore [g]spread My net
over you with a company of
many people,
And they will draw you up in My
net.
4 Then [h]I will leave you on the land;
I will cast you out on the open
fields,
[i]And cause to [1]settle on you all the
birds of the heavens.
And with you I will fill the beasts
of the whole earth.
5 I will lay your flesh [j]on the
mountains,
And fill the valleys with your
carcass.

6 'I will also water the land with the
flow of your blood,
Even to the mountains;
And the riverbeds will be full of
you.
7 When *I* put out your light,
[k]I will cover the heavens, and make
its stars dark;
I will cover the sun with a cloud,
And the moon shall not give her
light.
8 All the [2]bright lights of the
heavens I will make dark
over you,
And bring darkness upon your
land,'
Says the Lord GOD.

9 'I will also trouble the hearts of many
peoples, when I bring your destruction
among the nations, into the countries
which you have not known. 10 Yes, I will
make many peoples astonished at you, and
their kings shall be horribly afraid of you
when I brandish My sword before them;
and [l]they shall tremble *every* moment,
every man for his own life, in the day of
your fall.'
11 [m]"For thus says the Lord GOD: 'The
sword of the king of Babylon shall come
upon you. 12 By the swords of the mighty
warriors, all of them [n]the most terrible of
the nations, I will cause your multitude to
fall.

[o]'They shall plunder the pomp of
Egypt,

14 [n]Ps. 82:7 [o]Ezek. 32:18
15 [p]Ezek. 32:22, 23 [5]Or *Sheol* [6]Lit. *be darkened*
16 [q]Ezek. 26:15; Hag. 2:7 [r]Is. 14:15; Ezek. 32:18 [s]Is. 14:8; Hab. 2:17 [t]Ezek. 32:31 [7]Or *Sheol*
17 [u]Lam. 4:20
18 [v]Ezek. 32:19 [w]Jer. 9:25, 26; Ezek. 28:10; 32:19, 21

CHAPTER 32

1 [a]Ezek. 31:1; 33:21
2 [b]Ezek. 27:2 [c]Jer. 4:7; Ezek. 19:2-6; Nah. 2:11-13 [d]Is. 27:1; Ezek. 29:3 [e]Jer. 46:7, 8 [f]Ezek. 34:18
3 [g]Ezek. 12:13; 17:20
4 [h]Ezek. 29:5 [i]Is. 18:6; Ezek. 31:13 [1]Lit. *sit* or *dwell*
5 [j]Ezek. 31:12
7 [k]Is. 13:10; Joel 2:31; 3:15; Amos 8:9; Matt. 24:29; Mark 13:24; Luke 21:25; Rev. 6:12, 13; 8:12
8 [2]Or *shining*
10 [l]Ezek. 26:16
11 [m]Jer. 46:26; Ezek. 30:4
12 [n]Ezek. 28:7; 30:11; 31:12 [o]Ezek. 29:19

31:18 will you...be likened...? Egypt, like all the other great nations, including Assyria, will be felled by God.

32:1 the twelfth year. 585 B.C., 12 years from the deportation of Judah in 597 B.C.

32:2 like a young lion. The picture describes Egypt's deadly energetic stalking power in her dealings with other nations. She was also violent like the crocodile (cf. 29:3).

32:3-6 spread My net over you. God will entrap Egypt as a net ensnares a lion or crocodile, using many people (soldiers). Egyptians will fall, their corpses gorge birds and beasts, their blood soak the earth and waters.

32:7,8 light. This is likely a reference to Pharaoh, whose life and power is extinguished, and all the rest of the leaders and people basking in his light are plunged into darkness.

32:11,12 The sword of...Babylon. This is the definite identification of the conqueror, as in 30:10 when Nebuchadnezzar is actually named (cf. 21:19; 29:19; Jer. 46:26).

And all its multitude shall be
destroyed.
13 Also I will destroy all its animals
From beside its great waters;
[p]The foot of man shall muddy them
no more,
Nor shall the hooves of animals
muddy them.
14 Then I will make their waters [3]clear,
And make their rivers run like oil,'
Says the Lord GOD.

15 'When I make the land of Egypt
desolate,
And the country is destitute of all
that once filled it,
When I strike all who dwell in it,
[q]Then they shall know that I *am* the
LORD.

16 'This *is* the [r]lamentation
With which they shall lament her;
The daughters of the nations shall
lament her;
They shall lament for her, for
Egypt,
And for all her multitude,'
Says the Lord GOD."

Egypt and Others Consigned to the Pit

17 It came to pass also in the twelfth year,
on the fifteenth *day* of the month, [s]*that* the
word of the LORD came to me, saying:

18 "Son of man, wail over the
multitude of Egypt,
And [t]cast them down to the depths
of the earth,
Her and the daughters of the
famous nations,
With those who go down to the Pit:
19 'Whom [u]do you surpass in beauty?
[v]Go down, be placed with the
uncircumcised.'

20 "They shall fall in the midst of *those*
slain by the sword;
She is delivered to the sword,
[w]Drawing her and all her multitudes.
21 [x]The strong among the mighty
Shall speak to him out of the midst
of hell
With those who help him:
'They have [y]gone down,
They lie with the uncircumcised,
slain by the sword.'

22 "Assyria [z] *is* there, and all her
company,
With their graves all around her,
All of them slain, fallen by the
sword.
23 [a]Her graves are set in the recesses of
the Pit,
And her company is all around her
grave,
All of them slain, fallen by the
sword,
Who [b]caused terror in the land of
the living.

24 "There *is* [c]Elam and all her
multitude,
All around her grave,
All of them slain, fallen by the
sword,
Who have [d]gone down
uncircumcised to the lower
parts of the earth,
[e]Who caused their terror in the land
of the living;
Now they bear their shame with
those who go down to the Pit.
25 They have set her [f]bed in the midst
of the slain,
With all her multitude,
With her graves all around it,
All of them uncircumcised, slain by
the sword;
Though their terror was caused
In the land of the living,
Yet they bear their shame
With those who go down to the Pit;
It was put in the midst of the slain.

26 "There *are* [g]Meshech and Tubal and
all their multitudes,
With all their graves around it,
All of them [h]uncircumcised, slain
by the sword,
Though they caused their terror in
the land of the living.
27 [i]They do not lie with the mighty
Who are fallen of the
uncircumcised,

13 [p] Ezek. 29:11
14 [3] Lit. *sink;* settle, grow clear
15 [q] Ex. 7:5; 14:4, 18; Ps. 9:16; Ezek. 6:7
16 [r] 2 Sam. 1:17; 2 Chr. 35:25; Jer. 9:17; Ezek. 26:17
17 [s] Ezek. 32:1; 33:21
18 [t] Ezek. 26:20; 31:14
19 [u] Jer. 9:25, 26; Ezek. 31:2, 18 [v] Ezek. 28:10
20 [w] Ps. 28:3
21 [x] Is. 1:31; 14:9, 10; Ezek. 32:27
[y] Ezek. 32:19, 25
22 [z] Ezek. 31:3, 16
23 [a] Is. 14:15 [b] Ezek. 32:24-27, 32
24 [c] Gen. 10:22; 14:1; Is. 11:11; Jer. 25:25; 49:34-39 [d] Ezek. 32:21 [e] Ezek. 32:23
25 [f] Ps. 139:8
26 [g] Gen. 10:2; Ezek. 27:13; 38:2, 3; 39:1 [h] Ezek. 32:19
27 [i] Is. 14:18, 19

32:13,14 With no men or beasts to stir up the mud in the Nile and its branches, the water will be clear and flow smoothly. Since the river was the center of all life, this pictures the devastation graphically.

32:17 the twelfth year. 585 B.C. reckoned from 597 B.C.

32:18 the famous nations. All other countries which have been conquered. **the Pit.** Refers to Sheol/grave (cf. 31:14-16).

32:19-21 The prophet followed Egypt and her people beyond the grave. The king of Egypt is addressed by the other nations in "hell," taunting him as he is on the same level with them. This shows that there is conscious existence and fixed destiny beyond death. See Luke 16:19-31.

32:22 Assyria *is* there. The slain of several nations are pictured in the afterlife: Assyria (vv. 22,23), Elam (vv. 24,25), Meshech and Tubal (vv. 26-28; cf. 38:1,2, and *see notes there*), and Edom (vv. 29-30). Although mighty for a time on earth, the fallen lie as defeated equals in death, all conquered by God and consigned to eternal hell (v. 21).

Who have gone down to hell with
their weapons of war;
They have laid their swords under
their heads,
But their iniquities will be on their
bones,
Because of the terror of the mighty
in the land of the living.
28 Yes, you shall be broken in the
midst of the uncircumcised,
And lie with *those* slain by the
sword.

29 "There *is* [j]Edom,
Her kings and all her princes,
Who despite their might
Are laid beside *those* slain by the
sword;
They shall lie with the
uncircumcised,
And with those who go down to
the Pit.
30 [k]There *are* the princes of the north,
All of them, and all the [l]Sidonians,
Who have gone down with the
slain
In shame at the terror which they
caused by their might;
They lie uncircumcised with *those*
slain by the sword,
And bear their shame with those
who go down to the Pit.

31 "Pharaoh will see them
And be [m]comforted over all his
multitude,
Pharaoh and all his army,
Slain by the sword,"
Says the Lord GOD.

32 "For I have caused My terror in the
land of the living;
And he shall be placed in the midst
of the uncircumcised
With *those* slain by the sword,
Pharaoh and all his multitude,"
Says the Lord GOD.

The Watchman and His Message

33 Again the word of the LORD came to
me, saying, 2 "Son of man, speak to
[a]the children of your people, and say to
them: [b]'When I bring the sword upon a
land, and the people of the land take a man
from their territory and make him their
[c]watchman, 3 when he sees the sword
coming upon the land, if he blows the
trumpet and warns the people, 4 then whoever hears the sound of the trumpet and
does [d]not take warning, if the sword
comes and takes him away, [e]his blood shall
be on his *own* head. 5 He heard the sound
of the trumpet, but did not take warning;
his blood shall be upon himself. But he
who takes warning will [1]save his life. 6 But
if the watchman sees the sword coming
and does not blow the trumpet, and the
people are not warned, and the sword
comes and takes *any* person from among
them, [f]he is taken away in his iniquity; but
his blood I will require at the watchman's
hand.'

7 [g]"So you, son of man: I have made you
a watchman for the house of Israel; therefore you shall hear a word from My mouth
and warn them for Me. 8 When I say to the
wicked, 'O wicked *man*, you shall surely
die!' and you do not speak to warn the
wicked from his way, that wicked *man*
shall die in his iniquity; but his blood I will
require at your hand. 9 Nevertheless if you
warn the wicked to turn from his way, and
he does not turn from his way, he shall die
in his iniquity; but you have [2]delivered
your soul.

10 "Therefore you, O son of man, say to
the house of Israel: 'Thus you say, "If our
transgressions and our sins *lie* upon us,

29 [j] Is. 9:25, 26; 34:5, 6; Jer. 49:7-22; Ezek. 25:12-14
30 [k] Jer. 1:15; 25:26; Ezek. 38:6, 15; 39:2 [l] Jer. 25:22; Ezek. 28:21-23
31 [m] Ezek. 14:22; 31:16

CHAPTER 33

2 [a] Ezek. 3:11 [b] Ezek. 14:17 [c] 2 Sam. 18:24, 25; 2 Kin. 9:17; Hos. 9:8
4 [d] 2 Chr. 25:16; Jer. 6:17; Zech. 1:4 [e] Ezek. 18:13; 35:9; [Acts 18:6]
5 [1] *Or deliver his soul*
6 [f] Ezek. 33:8
7 [g] Is. 62:6; Ezek. 3:17-21
9 [2] *Or saved your life*

32:31,32 Pharaoh...comforted. A strange comfort coming from the recognition that he and his people were not alone in misery and doom.

33:1-33 Again the word...came. This chap. is a transition between God's judgments against Jerusalem and the nations (chaps. 1–32) and Israel's bright future when she is restored to her land (chaps. 34–48). It provided God's instructions for national repentance, and is thus the preface to the prophecies of comfort and salvation which follow (chaps. 34–39).

33:2-20 speak to...your people. This was given to prepare the exiles' minds to look on the awful calamity in Jerusalem as a just act by God (cf. 14:21-23). He had faithfully warned, but they did not pay heed. Ezekiel had been forbidden to speak to his people from 24:26,27, until Jerusalem was captured. Meanwhile, he had spoken to the foreign nations (chaps. 25–32).

33:2-9 watchman. Such men as Jeremiah and Ezekiel (cf. 3:16-21) were spiritual watchmen (33:7-9), warning that God would bring a sword on His people so that they had opportunity to prepare and be safe. This analogy came from the custom of putting guards on the city wall watching for the approach of danger, then trumpeting the warning. For the function of a watchman, cf. 2 Sam. 18:24,25; 2 Kin. 9:17; Jer. 4:5; 6:1; Hos. 8:1; Amos 3:6; Hab. 2:1.

33:4 his blood...on his *own* head. Once the watchman did his duty, the responsibility passed to each person. *See the notes on chap. 18*, where each person is accountable for his own response to God's warnings, whether to die in judgment or to live as one who heeded and repented. Ezekiel had been a very faithful and obedient "watchman."

33:8,9 his blood I will require. A prophet who sounded the warning of repentance for sin was not to be judged (v. 9), but the one who failed to deliver the message was held accountable (v. 8). This referred to unfaithfulness on the part of the prophet for which he bore responsibility and was chastened by God. *See the notes on chap. 18 and Acts 20:26.*

and we [h]pine[3] away in them, [i]how can we
then live?" ' 11 Say to them: '*As* I live,' says
the Lord GOD, [j]'I have no pleasure in the
death of the wicked, but that the wicked
[k]turn from his way and live. Turn, turn
from your evil ways! For [l]why should you
die, O house of Israel?'

The Fairness of God's Judgment

12 "Therefore you, O son of man, say to
the children of your people: 'The [m]righ-
teousness of the righteous man shall not
deliver him in the day of his transgression; as for the wickedness of the wicked,
[n]he shall not fall because of it in the day
that he turns from his wickedness; nor
shall the righteous be able to live because
of *his righteousness* in the day that he sins.'
13 When I say to the righteous *that* he shall
surely live, [o]but he trusts in his own righteousness and commits iniquity, none of
his righteous works shall be remembered;
but because of the iniquity that he has
committed, he shall die. 14 Again, [p]when I
say to the wicked, 'You shall surely die,' if
he turns from his sin and does [4]what is
lawful and [5]right, 15 *if* the wicked [q]re-
stores the pledge, [r]gives back what he has
stolen, and walks in [s]the statutes of life
without committing iniquity, he shall
surely live; he shall not die. 16 [t]None of
his sins which he has committed shall be
remembered against him; he has done
what is lawful and right; he shall surely
live.
17 [u]"Yet the children of your people say,
'The way of the LORD is not [6]fair.' But it is
their way which is not fair! 18 [v]When the
righteous turns from his righteousness and
commits iniquity, he shall die because of it.
19 But when the wicked turns from his
wickedness and does what is lawful and
right, he shall live because of it. 20 Yet you
say, [w]'The way of the LORD is not [7]fair.' O
house of Israel, I will judge every one of
you according to his own ways."

The Fall of Jerusalem

21 And it came to pass in the twelfth year
[x]of our captivity, in the tenth *month,* on the
fifth *day* of the month, [y]*that* one who had
escaped from Jerusalem came to me and
said, [z]"The city has been [8]captured!"
22 Now [a]the hand of the LORD had been
upon me the evening before the man came
who had escaped. And He had [b]opened
my mouth; so when he came to me in the
morning, my mouth was opened, and I
was no longer mute.

The Cause of Judah's Ruin

23 Then the word of the LORD came to
me, saying: 24 "Son of man, [c]they who inhabit those [d]ruins in the land of Israel are
saying, [e]'Abraham was only one, and he
inherited the land. [f]But we *are* many; the
land has been given to us as a [g]posses-
sion.'
25 "Therefore say to them, 'Thus says the
Lord GOD: [h]"You eat *meat* with blood, you
[i]lift up your eyes toward your idols, and
[j]shed blood. Should you then possess the
[k]land? 26 You rely on your sword, you
commit abominations, and you [l]defile one
another's wives. Should you then possess
the land?" '
27 "Say thus to them, 'Thus says the
Lord GOD: "*As* I live, surely [m]those who *are*
in the ruins shall fall by the sword, and the
one who *is* in the open field [n]I will give to

10 [h] Lev. 26:39; Ezek. 24:23 [i] Is. 49:14; Ezek. 37:11 [3] Or *waste away*
11 [j] [2 Sam. 14:14; Lam. 3:33]; Ezek. 18:23, 32; Hos. 11:8; [2 Pet. 3:9] [k] Ezek. 18:21, 30; [Hos. 14:1, 4; Acts 3:19] [l] [Is. 55:6, 7]; Jer. 3:22; Ezek. 18:30, 31; Hos. 14:1; [Acts 3:19]
12 [m] Ezek. 3:20; 18:24, 26 [n] [2 Chr. 7:14]; Ezek. 8:21; 33:19
13 [o] Ezek. 3:20; 18:24
14 [p] [Is. 55:7]; Jer. 18:7, 8; Ezek. 3:18, 19; 18:27; Hos. 14:1, 4 [4] *justice* [5] *righteousness*
15 [q] Ezek. 18:7 [r] Ex. 22:1-4; Lev. 6:2, 4, 5; Num. 5:6, 7; Luke 19:8 [s] Lev. 18:5; Ps. 119:59; 143:8; Ezek. 20:11, 13, 21
16 [t] [Is. 1:18; 43:25]; Ezek. 18:22
17 [u] Ezek. 18:25, 29 [6] Or *equitable*
18 [v] Ezek. 18:26
20 [w] Ezek. 18:25, 29 [7] Or *equitable*
21 [x] Ezek. 1:2 [y] Ezek. 24:26 [z] 2 Kin. 25:4 [8] Lit. *struck down*
22 [a] Ezek. 1:3; 8:1; 37:1 [b] Ezek. 24:27
24 [c] Ezek. 34:2 [d] Ezek. 36:4 [e] Is. 51:2; [Acts 7:5; Rom. 4:12] [f] Mic. 3:11; [Matt. 3:9; John 8:39] [g] Ezek. 11:15
25 [h] Gen. 9:4; Lev. 3:17; 7:26; 17:10-14; 19:26; Deut. 12:16, 23; 15:23 [i] Ezek. 18:6 [j] Ezek. 22:6, 9 [k] Deut. 29:28
26 [l] Ezek. 18:6; 22:11
27 [m] Ezek. 33:24 [n] Ezek. 39:4

33:10-11 how can we then live? The Israelites reasoned that if they were liable to death in judgment that was inevitable, they were in a hopeless condition and had no future. God replied that He had no pleasure in seeing the wicked go into death for their sin, but desired them to repent and live (cf. 2 Pet. 3:9). The divine answer to the human question is "Repent and be saved!" (cf. 18:23,30-32). Here was a blending of compassion with the demands of God's holiness. Repentance and forgiveness were offered to all.

33:12-20 *See notes on 18:19-29.* One of the basic principles of God's dealing with His people is presented here: judgment is according to personal faith and conduct. The discussion is not about eternal salvation and eternal death, but physical death in judgment for sin which, for believers, could not result in eternal death. The righteous behavior in v. 15 could only characterize a true believer, who was faithful from the heart. There is no distinction made as to the matter of who is a true believer in God. There is only a discussion of the issue of behavior as a factor in physical death. For those who were apostate idolaters, physical death would lead to eternal death. For believers who were lovers of the true God, their sin would lead only to physical punishment (cf. 1 Cor. 11:28-31; 1 John 5:16,17). "Righteous" and "wicked" are terms describing behavior, not one's position before God. It is not the "righteousness of God" imputed as illustrated in the case of Abraham (Gen. 15:6; Rom. 4:3-5), but rather one's deeds that are in view (vv. 15-19).

33:17,20 not fair. They blamed God for their calamities when actually they were being judged for their sins.

33:21 "The city has been captured!" A fugitive or fugitives (the Heb. could be a collective noun) who escaped from Jerusalem reached Ezekiel with the report on Jan. 8, 585 B.C., almost 6 months after the fall on July 18, 586 (Jer. 39:1,2; 52:5-7). Ezekiel 24:1,2 and 33:21 show a 36 month span from the outset of the siege on Jan. 15, 588, to the report in 33:21.

33:22 opened my mouth. God exercised control over the mouth of Ezekiel (*see note on 3:26*).

33:23-29 There is no date attached to the prophecies from 33:23–39:29, but the first message after the fall of Jerusalem was a rebuke of Israel's carnal confidence. This prophecy was against the remnant of Judah who remained in the Land of Promise after the fall of Jerusalem. Ezekiel warns the survivors that more judgment will come on them if they do not obey God. By some strange reasoning, they thought that if God had given the Land to Abraham when he was alone, it would be more securely theirs because they were many in number, a claim based on quantity rather than quality (v. 24). But judgment will come if they turn and reject God again (vv. 25-29).

the beasts to be devoured, and those who
are in the strongholds and [o]caves shall die
of the pestilence. 28 [p]For I will make the
land most desolate, [9]her [q]arrogant
strength shall cease, and [r]the mountains
of Israel shall be so desolate that no one
will pass through. 29 Then they shall know
that I *am* the LORD, when I have made the
land most desolate because of all their
abominations which they have committed." '

Hearing and Not Doing

30 "As for you, son of man, the children
of your people are talking about you beside the walls and in the doors of the houses; and they [s]speak to one another, everyone saying to his brother, 'Please come and
hear what the word is that comes from the
LORD.' 31 So [t]they come to you as people
do, they [u]sit before you *as* My people, and
they [v]hear your words, but they do not do
them; [w]for with their mouth they show
much love, *but* [x]their hearts pursue their
own gain. 32 Indeed you *are* to them as a
very lovely song of one who has a pleasant
voice and can play well on an instrument;
for they hear your words, but they do [y]not
do them. 33 [z]And when this comes to
pass—surely it will come—then [a]they will
know that a prophet has been among
them."

Irresponsible Shepherds

34 And the word of the LORD came to
me, saying, 2 "Son of man, prophesy against the shepherds of Israel, prophesy and say to them, 'Thus says the Lord
GOD to the shepherds: [a]"Woe to the shepherds of Israel who feed themselves!
Should not the shepherds feed the flocks?
3 [b]You eat the fat and clothe yourselves
with the wool; you [c]slaughter the fatlings,
but you do not feed the flock. 4 [d]The weak
you have not strengthened, nor have you
healed those who were sick, nor bound
up the broken, nor brought back what

27 [o] Judg. 6:2; 1 Sam. 13:6; Is. 2:19
28 [p] Jer. 44:2, 6, 22; Ezek. 36:34, 35 [q] Ezek. 7:24; 24:21 [r] Ezek. 6:2, 3, 6 [9] Lit. *pride of her strength*
30 [s] Is. 29:13; Ezek. 14:3; 20:3, 31
31 [t] Ezek. 14:1 [u] Ezek. 8:1 [v] Is. 58:2 [w] Ps. 78:36, 37; Is. 29:13; Jer. 12:2; 1 John 3:18 [x] [Matt. 13:22]
32 [y] [Matt. 7:21-28; James 1:22-25]
33 [z] 1 Sam. 3:20 [a] Ezek. 2:5

CHAPTER 34

2 [a] Jer. 23:1; Ezek. 22:25; Mic. 3:1-3, 11; Zech. 11:17
3 [b] Is. 56:11; Zech. 11:16 [c] Ezek. 33:25, 26; Mic. 3:1-3; Zech. 11:5
4 [d] Zech. 11:16 [e] Matt. 9:36; 10:16; 18:12, 13; Luke 15:4 [f] [1 Pet. 5:3] [1] *harshness* or *rigor*
5 [g] Ezek. 33:21 [h] Num. 27:17; 1 Kin. 22:17; Jer. 10:21; Matt. 9:36; Mark 6:34 [i] Is. 56:9; Jer. 12:9
6 [j] Jer. 40:11, 12; 50:6; Ezek. 7:16; 1 Pet. 2:25
8 [k] Ezek. 34:5, 6 [l] Ezek. 34:2, 10
10 [m] Jer. 21:13; 52:24-27; Ezek. 5:8; 13:8; Zech. 10:3 [n] Ezek. 3:18; Heb. 13:17 [o] Ezek. 34:2, 8 [p] Ps. 72:12-14; Ezek. 13:23
12 [q] Jer. 31:10 [r] Jer. 13:16; Ezek. 30:3; Joel 2:2
13 [s] Is. 65:9, 10; Jer. 23:3; Ezek. 11:17; 20:41; 28:25; 36:24; 37:21, 22 [2] Or *by the streams*
14 [t] Ps. 23:2; Jer. 3:15; [John 10:9] [u] Jer. 33:12

was driven away, nor [e]sought what was
lost; but with [f]force and [1]cruelty you have
ruled them. 5 [g]So they were [h]scattered because *there was* no shepherd; [i]and they became food for all the beasts of the field
when they were scattered. 6 My sheep
[j]wandered through all the mountains,
and on every high hill; yes, My flock was
scattered over the whole face of the earth,
and no one was seeking or searching *for*
them."
7 'Therefore, you shepherds, hear the
word of the LORD: 8 "*As* I live," says the
Lord GOD, "surely because My flock became a prey, and My flock [k]became food
for every beast of the field, because *there*
was no shepherd, nor did My shepherds
search for My flock, [l]but the shepherds fed
themselves and did not feed My flock"—
9 therefore, O shepherds, hear the word of
the LORD! 10 Thus says the Lord GOD: "Behold, I *am* [m]against the shepherds, and [n]I
will require My flock at their hand; I will
cause them to cease feeding the sheep, and
the shepherds shall [o]feed themselves no
more; for I will [p]deliver My flock from
their mouths, that they may no longer be
food for them."

God, the True Shepherd

11 'For thus says the Lord GOD: "Indeed
I Myself will search for My sheep and seek
them out. 12 As a [q]shepherd seeks out his
flock on the day he is among his scattered
sheep, so will I seek out My sheep and deliver them from all the places where they
were scattered on [r]a cloudy and dark day.
13 And [s]I will bring them out from the
peoples and gather them from the countries, and will bring them to their own
land; I will feed them on the mountains of
Israel, [2]in the valleys and in all the inhabited places of the country. 14 [t]I will feed
them in good pasture, and their fold shall
be on the high mountains of Israel. [u]There
they shall lie down in a good fold and feed
in rich pasture on the mountains of Israel.

33:30-33 Here was a message to exiles, who had no intention of obeying the prophet's messages. They liked to listen, but not apply the prophet's words. They finally knew by bitter experience that he had spoken the truth of God. The people appreciated the eloquence of Ezekiel, but not the realty of his message.

34:1 From this chap. on, Ezekiel's messages are mostly comforting, telling of God's grace and faithfulness to His covenant promises.

34:2 prophesy against the shepherds. The reference was to preexilic leaders such as kings, priests, and prophets, i.e., false ones who fleeced the flock for personal gain (vv. 3,4) rather than fed or led righteously (as 22:25-28; Jer. 14,23; Zech. 11). This stands in contrast to the Lord as Shepherd in Pss. 23; 80:1; Is. 40:11; Jer. 31:10; Luke 15:4,5; John 10:1ff.

34:5 food for all the beasts. The beasts pictured nations that prey on Israel (cf. Dan. 7:3-7), though it could possibly include actual wild beasts, as in 14:21. Cf. 34:25,28 and *see notes there.*

34:9,10 This was no idle threat, as proven by the case of King Zedekiah (cf. Jer. 52:10,11).

34:11 I...will search. God, the true Shepherd, would search out and find His sheep in order to restore Israel to their land for the kingdom which the Messiah leads (vv. 12-14).

34:12 a cloudy and dark day. This refers to the "day of the Lord" judgment on Israel (cf. Jer. 30:4-7).

34:12-14 Here is the promise of a literal regathering and restoration of the people of Israel to their own land from their worldwide dispersion. Since the scattering was literal, the regathering must also be literal. Once they are regathered in Messiah's kingdom, they will no longer want (vv. 15,16).

15 I will feed My flock, and I will make
them lie down," says the Lord GOD. 16 [v]"I
will seek what was lost and bring back
what was driven away, bind up the broken
and strengthen what was sick; but I will
destroy [w]the fat and the strong, and feed
them [x]in judgment."
17 'And *as for* you, O My flock, thus says
the Lord GOD: [y]"Behold, I shall judge between sheep and sheep, between rams and
goats. 18 *Is it* too little for you to have eaten
up the good pasture, that you must tread
down with your feet the [3]residue of your
pasture—and to have drunk of the clear
waters, that you must foul the residue with
your feet? 19 And *as for* My flock, they eat
what you have trampled with your feet,
and they drink what you have fouled with
your feet."
20 'Therefore thus says the Lord GOD to
them: [z]"Behold, I Myself will judge between the fat and the lean sheep. 21 Because you have pushed with side and
shoulder, butted all the weak ones with
your horns, and scattered them abroad,
22 therefore I will save My flock, and they
shall no longer be a prey; and I will judge
between sheep and sheep. 23 I will establish one [a]shepherd over them, and he shall
feed them—[b]My servant David. He shall
feed them and be their shepherd. 24 And [c]I,
the LORD, will be their God, and My servant David [d]a prince among them; I, the
LORD, have spoken.
25 [e]"I will make a covenant of peace
with them, and [f]cause wild beasts to cease
from the land; and they [g]will dwell safely
in the wilderness and sleep in the woods.
26 I will make them and the places all
around [h]My hill [i]a blessing; and I will
[j]cause showers to come down in their season; there shall be [k]showers of blessing.
27 Then [l]the trees of the field shall yield
their fruit, and the earth shall yield her increase. They shall be safe in their land; and
they shall know that I *am* the LORD, when
I have [m]broken the bands of their yoke
and delivered them from the hand of those
who [n]enslaved them. 28 And they shall no
longer be a prey for the nations, nor shall
beasts of the land devour them; but [o]they
shall dwell safely, and no one shall make
them afraid. 29 I will raise up for them a
[p]garden[4] of renown, and they shall [q]no
longer be consumed with hunger in the
land, [r]nor bear the shame of the Gentiles
anymore. 30 Thus they shall know that [s]I,
the LORD their God, *am* with them, and
they, the house of Israel, *are* [t]My people,"
says the Lord GOD.' "
31 "You are My [u]flock, the flock of My
pasture; you *are* men, *and* I *am* your God,"
says the Lord GOD.

Judgment on Mount Seir

35 Moreover the word of the LORD
came to me, saying, 2 "Son of man,
set your face against [a]Mount Seir and
[b]prophesy against it, 3 and say to it, 'Thus
says the Lord GOD:

"Behold, O Mount Seir, I *am* against
you;
[c]I will stretch out My hand against
you,
And make you [1]most desolate;
4 I shall lay your cities waste,
And you shall be desolate.
Then you shall know that I *am* the
LORD.

16 [v] Is. 40:11; Mic. 4:6; [Matt. 18:11; Mark 2:17; Luke 5:32] [w] Is. 10:16; Amos 4:1 [x] Jer. 10:24
17 [y] Ezek. 20:37; Mal. 4:1; [Matt. 25:32]
18 [3] *remainder*
20 [z] Ezek. 34:17
23 [a] [Is. 40:11; Jer. 23:4, 5]; Hos. 1:11; [John 10:11; Heb. 13:20; 1 Pet. 2:25; 5:4] [b] Jer. 30:9; Ezek. 37:24; Hos. 3:5
24 [c] Ex. 29:45; Ezek. 37:25 [d] Is. 55:3; Jer. 30:9; Ezek. 37:24, 25; Hos. 3:5
25 [e] Ezek. 37:26 [f] Lev. 26:6; Job 5:22, 23; Is. 11:6-9; Hos. 2:18 [g] Jer. 23:6
26 [h] Is. 56:7 [i] Gen. 12:2; Is. 19:24; Zech. 8:13 [j] Lev. 26:4 [k] Ps. 68:9
27 [l] Lev. 26:4; Ps. 85:12; Is. 4:2 [m] Lev. 26:13; Is. 52:2, 3; Jer. 2:20 [n] Jer. 25:14
28 [o] Jer. 30:10; Ezek. 39:26
29 [p] [Is. 11:1] [q] Ezek. 36:29 [r] Ezek. 36:3, 6, 15 [4] Lit. *planting place*
30 [s] Ezek. 34:24 [t] Ps. 46:7, 11; Ezek. 14:11; 36:28
31 [u] Ps. 100:3; Jer. 23:1; [John 10:11]

CHAPTER 35

2 [a] Gen. 36:8; Deut. 2:5; Jer. 25:21; 49:7-22; Ezek. 25:12-14; Joel 3:19; Amos 1:11, 12; Obad. 1-9, 15, 16 [b] Amos 1:11
3 [c] Ezek. 6:14 [1] Lit. *a desolation and a waste*

34:15,16 I will feed My flock. In contrast to self-indulgent leaders who took advantage of the sheep, God will meet the needs of His sheep (people). This is clearly reminiscent of Ps. 23 and will be fulfilled by the Good Shepherd (John 10:1ff.), who will reign as Israel's Shepherd.

34:17-22 judge between. Once He has judged the leaders, God will also judge the abusive members of the flock as to their true spiritual state. This passage anticipates the judgment of the people given by Jesus Christ in Matt. 25:31-46. The ungodly are known because they trample the poor. The Lord alone is able to sort out the true from the false (cf. parables of Matt. 13), and will do so in the final kingdom.

34:23 one shepherd...David. This refers to the greater One in David's dynasty (cf. 2 Sam. 7:12-16), the Messiah, who will be Israel's ultimate king over the millennial kingdom (31:24-26; Jer. 30:9; Hos. 3:5; Zech. 14:9). The Lord in v. 24 is God the Father.

34:24 a prince. The word can at times be used of the king himself (37:34,35; cf. 28:2,12), as here.

34:25 covenant of peace. Refers to the New Covenant of Jer. 31:31-34 (cf. 37:26) in full operation during the millennial kingdom. **wild beasts.** This refers to actual animals that will be tamed in the kingdom, see Is. 11:6-9; 35:9 and Hos. 2:18.

34:26 My hill. A reference to Jerusalem and Zion in particular, where the Jews will come to worship the Lord. **showers of blessing.** Cf. the "times of refreshing" in Acts 3:19,20, when the curses of Deut. 28:15-68 are lifted.

34:27 The faithfulness of the Land is also indicated in Amos 9:13.

34:28,29 no longer be a prey. God will stop other nations from subjugating the people of Israel.

34:30 I...their God. An oft-repeated OT theme (cf. Gen. 17:7,8). This speaks of the ultimate salvation of Israel as in Rom. 11:25-27.

35:2 against Mount Seir. Cf. Is. 21:11,12; Jer. 49:7-22; Amos 1:11,12; Obadiah. This is another name for Edom (cf. v. 15; Gen. 32:3; 38:6), also threatened with judgment in 25:12-14 (*see notes there*). Edom was considered Israel's most inveterate and bitter enemy (cf. Ps. 137:7; Mal. 1:2-5) and was located E of the Arabah from the Dead Sea to the Gulf of Aqabah. The main cities were Teman and Petra, now in ruins.

35:3,4 This prediction (cf. vv. 6-9) came to pass literally, first by Nebuchadnezzar and later in 126 B.C. by John Hyrcanus. There is no trace of Edomites now, though their desolate cities can be identified as predicted by Obadiah (Obad. 18) and Jeremiah (Jer. 49:13). Cf. vv. 6-9.

5 [d]"Because you have had an [2]ancient
hatred, and have shed *the blood of* the children of Israel by the power of the sword
at the time of their calamity, [e]*when* their
iniquity *came to an* end, 6 therefore, *as* I
live," says the Lord GOD, "I will prepare
you for [f]blood, and blood shall pursue
you; [g]since you have not hated [3]blood,
therefore blood shall pursue you. 7 Thus I
will make Mount Seir [4]most desolate,
and cut off from it the [h]one who leaves
and the one who returns. 8 And I will fill
its mountains with the slain; on your hills
and in your valleys and in all your
ravines those who are slain by the sword
shall fall. 9 [i]I will make you [5]perpetually
desolate, and your cities shall be uninhabited; [j]then you shall know that I *am*
the LORD.
10 "Because you have said, 'These two
nations and these two countries shall be
mine, and we will [k]possess them,' although [l]the LORD was there, 11 therefore, *as*
I live," says the Lord GOD, "I will do [m]ac-
cording to your anger and according to the
envy which you showed in your hatred
against them; and I will make Myself
known among them when I judge you.
12 [n]Then you shall know that I *am* the
LORD. I have [o]heard all your [p]blasphemies
which you have spoken against the mountains of Israel, saying, 'They are desolate;
they are given to us to consume.' 13 Thus
[q]with your mouth you have [6]boasted
against Me and multiplied your [r]words
against Me; I have heard *them*."
14 'Thus says the Lord GOD: [s]"The whole
earth will rejoice when I make you desolate. 15 [t]As you rejoiced because the inheritance of the house of Israel was desolate,
[u]so I will do to you; you shall be desolate,
O Mount Seir, as well as all of Edom—all
of it! Then they shall know that I *am* the
LORD."'

Blessing on Israel

36 "And you, son of man, prophesy to
the [a]mountains of Israel, and say,
'O mountains of Israel, hear the word of
the LORD! 2 Thus says the Lord GOD: "Because [b]the enemy has said of you, 'Aha!
[c]The [1]ancient heights [d]have become our
possession,'"' 3 therefore prophesy, and
say, 'Thus says the Lord GOD: "Because
they made *you* desolate and swallowed
you up on every side, so that you became
the possession of the rest of the nations,
[e]and you are taken up by the lips of [f]talk-
ers and slandered by the people"—
4 therefore, O mountains of Israel, hear
the word of the Lord GOD! Thus says the
Lord GOD to the mountains, the hills, the
[2]rivers, the valleys, the desolate wastes,
and the cities that have been forsaken,
which [g]became plunder and [h]mockery to
the rest of the nations all around—
5 therefore thus says the Lord GOD:
[i]"Surely I have spoken in My burning
jealousy against the rest of the nations
and against all Edom, [j]who gave My land
to themselves as a possession, with
wholehearted joy *and* [3]spiteful minds, in
order to plunder its open country."'
6 "Therefore prophesy concerning the
land of Israel, and say to the mountains,
the hills, the rivers, and the valleys, 'Thus
says the Lord GOD: "Behold, I have spoken
in My jealousy and My fury, because you
have [k]borne the shame of the nations."
7 Therefore thus says the Lord GOD: "I
have [l]raised My hand in an oath that surely the nations that *are* around you shall

5 [d] Ezek. 25:12 [e] Ps. 137:7; Dan. 9:24; Amos 1:11; Obad. 10 [2] Or *everlasting*
6 [f] Is. 63:1-6; Ezek. 16:38; 32:6 [g] Ps. 109:17 [3] Or *bloodshed*
7 [h] Judg. 5:6 [4] Lit. *a waste and a desolation*
9 [i] Jer. 49:13; Ezek. 25:13 [j] Ezek. 36:11 [5] Lit. *desolated forever*
10 [k] Ps. 83:4-12; Ezek. 36:2, 5 [l] [Ps. 48:1-3; 132:13, 14]; Is. 12:6; Ezek. 48:35; Zeph. 3:15
11 [m] [Matt. 7:2; James 2:13]
12 [n] Ps. 9:16 [o] Zeph. 2:8 [p] Is. 52:5
13 [q] [1 Sam. 2:3] [r] Ezek. 36:3 [6] Lit. *made yourself great*
14 [s] Is. 65:13, 14
15 [t] Obad. 12, 15 [u] Jer. 50:11; Lam. 4:21

CHAPTER 36

1 [a] Ezek. 6:2, 3
2 [b] Jer. 33:24; Ezek. 25:3; 26:2 [c] Deut. 32:13; Ps. 78:69; Is. 58:14; Hab. 3:19 [d] Ezek. 35:10 [1] Or *everlasting*
3 [e] Deut. 28:37; 1 Kin. 9:7; Lam. 2:15; Dan. 9:16 [f] Ps. 44:13, 14; Jer. 18:16; Ezek. 35:13
4 [g] Ezek. 34:8, 28 [h] Ps. 79:4; Jer. 48:27 [2] Or *ravines*
5 [i] Deut. 4:24; Ezek. 38:19 [j] Ezek. 35:10, 12 [3] Lit. *scorning souls*
6 [k] Ps. 74:10; 123:3, 4; Ezek. 34:29
7 [l] Ezek. 20:5

35:5 Because. God will judge Edom because of 1) her perpetual enmity against Israel since Esau's hatred of Jacob (Gen. 25–28), and 2) Edom's spiteful bloodshed against the Israelites trying to escape the Babylonians in 586 B.C.

35:10 Because. A further reason for Edom's doom is her design to snatch control of the territory occupied by "two nations," i.e., Israel (N) and Judah (S). They plotted to take over these nations for their own gain (v. 12), but were prevented and destroyed because "the LORD was there."

35:11,12 anger...envy...blasphemies. Here were more reasons for Edom's destruction.

35:13 you...boasted against Me. Still another reason for judgment was Edom's proud ambitions that were really against God (cf. v. 10, "although the LORD was there").

35:15 As you rejoiced. This final reason for doom was Edom's joy over Israel's calamity. **they shall know.** The ultimate aim in Edom's judgment is that "the whole earth" may know He is the Lord and see His glory. Sadly, sinners find this out only in their own destruction. Cf. Heb. 10:31.

36:1 This chap. presents the prerequisite regeneration which Israel must experience before they can nationally enter into the promised blessings. This chap. must be understood to speak of a literal Israel, a literal land, and a literal regeneration, leading to a literal kingdom under Messiah. **prophesy to the mountains.** Cf. vv. 1,4,6,8. Ezekiel addresses Israel's mountains, as symbolic of the whole nation. He promises: 1) to give these mountains again to dispersed Israel (v. 12); 2) to cause fruit to grow on them (v. 8); 3) to rebuild cities and to multiply people there (v. 10); and 4) to bless in a greater way than in the past (v. 11). This promise can only be fulfilled in future millennial blessing to Israel that she has not yet experienced, because it includes the salvation of the New Covenant (vv. 25-27,29,31,33).

36:2-15 This section continues the prophecy against Edom from chap. 35.

36:2 Because the enemy has said. God will restore these areas to Israel which their enemies claim to possess (cf. Gen. 12:7). They will pay for their spite against Israel.

36:7 raised My hand in an oath. God testifies, as a formal pledge, that he will bring a turnabout in which the nations that seized the land will be shamed.

[m]bear their own shame. 8 But you, O
mountains of Israel, you shall shoot forth
your branches and yield your fruit to My
people Israel, for they are about to come.
9 For indeed I *am* for you, and I will turn to
you, and you shall be tilled and sown. 10 I
will multiply men upon you, all the house
of Israel, all of it; and the cities shall be inhabited and [n]the ruins rebuilt. 11 [o]I will
multiply upon you man and beast; and
they shall increase and [4]bear young; I will
make you inhabited as in former times,
and do [p]better *for you* than at your beginnings. [q]Then you shall know that I *am* the
LORD. 12 Yes, I will cause men to walk on
you, My people Israel; [r]they shall take possession of you, and you shall be their inheritance; no more shall you [s]bereave
them *of children.*"

13 'Thus says the Lord GOD: "Because
they say to you, [t]'You devour men and bereave your nation *of children,*' 14 therefore
you shall devour men no more, nor bereave your nation anymore," says the Lord
GOD. 15 [u]Nor will I let you hear the taunts
of the nations anymore, nor bear the reproach of the peoples anymore, nor shall
you cause your nation to stumble anymore," says the Lord GOD.' "

The Renewal of Israel

16 Moreover the word of the LORD came
to me, saying: 17 "Son of man, when the
house of Israel dwelt in their own land,
[v]they defiled it by their own ways and
deeds; to Me their way was like [w]the
uncleanness of a woman in her customary
impurity. 18 Therefore I poured out My
fury on them [x]for the blood they had shed
on the land, and for their idols *with which*
they had defiled it. 19 So I [y]scattered them
among the nations, and they were dispersed throughout the countries; I judged
them [z]according to their ways and their
deeds. 20 When they came to the nations,
wherever they went, they [a]profaned My
holy name—when they said of them,
'These *are* the people of the LORD, *and* yet
they have gone out of His land.' 21 But I
had concern [b]for My holy name, which the
house of Israel had profaned among the
nations wherever they went.

22 "Therefore say to the house of Israel,
'Thus says the Lord GOD: "I do not do *this*
for your sake, O house of Israel, [c]but for
My holy name's sake, which you have profaned among the nations wherever you
went. 23 And I will sanctify My great
name, which has been profaned among the
nations, which you have profaned in their
midst; and the nations shall know that I *am*
the LORD," says the Lord GOD, "when I am
[d]hallowed in you before their eyes. 24 For
[e]I will take you from among the nations,
gather you out of all countries, and bring
you into your own land. 25 [f]Then I will
sprinkle clean water on you, and you shall
be clean; I will cleanse you [g]from all your

7 [m] Jer. 25:9, 15, 29
10 [n] Is. 58:12; 61:4; Amos 9:14
11 [o] Jer. 31:27; 33:12 [p] Job 42:12; Is. 51:3 [q] Ezek. 35:9; 37:6, 13 [4] Lit. *be fruitful*
12 [r] Obad. 17 [s] Jer. 15:7; Ezek. 22:12, 27
13 [t] Num. 13:32
15 [u] Is. 60:14; Ezek. 34:29
17 [v] Lev. 18:25, 27, 28; Jer. 2:7 [w] Lev. 15:19
18 [x] Ezek. 16:36, 38; 23:37
19 [y] Deut. 28:64; Ezek. 5:12; 22:15; Amos 9:9 [z] Ezek. 7:3; 18:30; 39:24; [Rom. 2:6]
20 [a] Is. 52:5; Ezek. 12:16; Rom. 2:24
21 [b] Ezek. 20:9, 14
22 [c] Ps. 106:8; Ezek. 20:44
23 [d] Is. 5:16; Ezek. 20:41; 28:22
24 [e] Is. 43:5, 6; Ezek. 34:13; 37:21
25 [f] Num. 19:17-19; Ps. 51:7; Is. 52:15; Heb. 9:13, 19; 10:22 [g] Jer. 33:8

36:8-15 Israel's land will be productive (vv. 8,9), populated (vv. 10,11), and peaceful (vv. 12-15). These features will be fully realized in the Messiah's kingdom. The return from Babylon was only a partial fulfillment and foreshadowing of the fullness to come in the future kingdom.

36:16-19 Ezekiel gives a backward look to underscore why Israel had suffered the past judgments by the Lord. It was because the Jews had "defiled" their land by their sins that the Lord purged it. He likened such a defilement to a menstrual condition (v. 17).

36:20 they profaned My holy name. Even in dispersion, Israelites tainted God's honor in the sight of the heathen, who concluded that the Lord of this exiled people was not powerful enough to keep them in their land.

36:21-23 for My holy name's sake. Restoring Israel to the land that God pledged in covenant (Gen. 12:7) will sanctify His great name, and move other peoples to "know that I am the LORD." This glory for God is the primary reason for Israel's restoration (cf. v. 32).

36:24 bring you into your own land. God assured Israel that He will bring them out of other lands back to the Promised Land (v. 24), the very land from which He scattered them (v. 20). It is the same "land that I gave to your fathers" (v. 28), a land distinct from those of other nations (v. 36), and a land whose cities will be inhabited by those who return (vv. 33,36,38). The establishment of the modern state of Israel indicates this has initially begun.

36:25-27 I will cleanse you. Along with the physical reality of a return to the Land, God pledged spiritual renewal: 1) cleansing from sin; 2) a new heart of the New Covenant (cf. Jer. 31:31-34); 3) a new spirit or disposition inclined to worship Him; and 4) His Spirit dwelling in them, enabling them to walk in obedience to His word. This has not happened, because Israel has not trusted Jesus Christ as Messiah and Savior, but it will before the kingdom of Messiah (cf. Zech. 12–14; Rom. 11:25-27; Rev. 11:13).

36:25-31 This section is among the most glorious in all Scripture on the subject of Israel's restoration to the Lord and national salvation. This salvation is described in v. 25 as a cleansing that will wash away sin. Such washing was symbolized in the Mosaic rites of purification (cf. Num. 19:17-19; Ps. 119:9; Is. 4:4; Zech. 13:1). For the concept of sprinkling in cleansing, see Ps. 51:7,10; Heb. 9:13; 10:22. This is the washing Paul wrote of in Eph. 5:26 and Titus 3:5. Jesus had this very promise in mind in John 3:5.

What was figuratively described in v. 25 is explained as literal in vv. 26,27. The gift of the "new heart" signifies the new birth, which is regeneration by the Holy Spirit (cf. 11:18-20). The "heart" stands for the whole nature. The "spirit" indicates the governing power of the mind which directs thought and conduct. A "stony heart" is stubborn and self-willed. A "heart of flesh" is pliable and responsive. The evil inclination is removed and a new nature replaces it. This is New Covenant character as in Jer. 31:31-34.

The Lord will also give His "Spirit" to the faithful Jews (cf. 39:29; Is. 44:3; 59:21; Joel 2:28,29; Acts 2:16ff.). When Israel becomes the true people of God (v. 28), the judgment promise of Hosea 1:9 is nullified. All nature will experience the blessings of Israel's salvation (vv. 29,30). When the Jews have experienced such grace, they will be even more repentant—a sign of true conversion (v. 31).

Ezekiel profoundly proclaims the doctrines of conversion and spiritual life. He includes forgiveness (v. 25), regeneration (v. 26), the in-

filthiness and from all your idols. 26 I will
give you a [h]new heart and put a new spirit within you; I will take the heart of stone
out of your flesh and give you a heart of
flesh. 27 I will put My [i]Spirit within you
and cause you to walk in My statutes, and
you will keep My judgments and do *them.*
28 [j]Then you shall dwell in the land that I
gave to your fathers; [k]you shall be My
people, and I will be your God. 29 I will
[l]deliver you from all your uncleannesses.
[m]I will call for the grain and multiply it,
and [n]bring no famine upon you. 30 [o]And I
will multiply the fruit of your trees and the
increase of your fields, so that you need
never again bear the reproach of famine
among the nations. 31 Then [p]you will remember your evil ways and your deeds
that *were* not good; and you [q]will [5]loathe
yourselves in your own sight, for your iniquities and your abominations. 32 [r]Not for
your sake do I do *this,*" says the Lord GOD,
"let it be known to you. Be ashamed and
confounded for your own ways, O house
of Israel!"
33 'Thus says the Lord GOD: "On the day
that I cleanse you from all your iniquities,
I will also enable *you* to dwell in the cities,
[s]and the ruins shall be rebuilt. 34 The desolate land shall be tilled instead of lying
desolate in the sight of all who pass by.
35 So they will say, 'This land that was desolate has become like the garden of [t]Eden;
and the wasted, desolate, and ruined cities
are now fortified *and* inhabited.' 36 Then the
nations which are left all around you shall
know that I, the LORD, have rebuilt the ruined places *and* planted what was desolate.
[u]I, the LORD, have spoken *it,* and I will do
it."
37 'Thus says the Lord GOD: [v]"I will also
let the house of Israel inquire of Me to do
this for them: I will [w]increase their men
like a flock. 38 Like a [6]flock *offered as* holy
sacrifices, like the flock at Jerusalem on its
[7]feast days, so shall the ruined cities be
filled with flocks of men. Then they shall
know that I *am* the LORD." ' "

The Dry Bones Live

37 The [a]hand of the LORD came upon
me and brought me out [b]in the Spirit of the LORD, and set me down in the
midst of the valley; and it *was* full of bones.
2 Then He caused me to pass by them all
around, and behold, *there were* very many
in the open valley; and indeed *they were*
very dry. 3 And He said to me, "Son of
man, can these bones live?"
So I answered, "O Lord GOD, [c]You
know."
4 Again He said to me, "Prophesy to
these bones, and say to them, 'O dry bones,
hear the word of the LORD! 5 Thus says the
Lord GOD to these bones: "Surely I will
[d]cause breath to enter into you, and you
shall live. 6 I will put sinews on you and
bring flesh upon you, cover you with skin
and put breath in you; and you shall live.
[e]Then you shall know that I *am* the
LORD." ' "
7 So I prophesied as I was commanded;
and as I prophesied, there was a noise, and
suddenly a rattling; and the bones came together, bone to bone. 8 Indeed, as I looked,
the sinews and the flesh came upon them,
and the skin covered them over; but *there
was* no breath in them.
9 Also He said to me, "Prophesy to the
breath, prophesy, son of man, and say to
the [1]breath, 'Thus says the Lord GOD:
[f]"Come from the four winds, O breath, and

26 [h] Ps. 51:10; Jer. 32:39; Ezek. 11:19; [John 3:3]
27 [i] Is. 44:3; 59:21; Ezek. 11:19; 37:14; [Joel 2:28, 29]
28 [j] Ezek. 28:25; 37:25 [k] Jer. 30:22; Ezek. 11:20; 37:27
29 [l] Zech. 13:1; [Matt. 1:21; Rom. 11:26] [m] Ps. 105:16 [n] Ezek. 34:27, 29; Hos. 2:21-23
30 [o] Lev. 26:4; Ezek. 34:27
31 [p] Ezek. 16:61, 63 [q] Lev. 26:39; Ezek. 6:9; 20:43 [5] *despise*
32 [r] Deut. 9:5
33 [s] Ezek. 36:10
35 [t] Is. 51:3; Ezek. 28:13; Joel 2:3
36 [u] Ezek. 17:24; 22:14; 37:14; Hos. 14:4-9
37 [v] Ezek. 14:3; 20:3, 31
[w] Ezek. 36:10
38 [6] Lit. *holy flock* [7] *appointed feasts*

CHAPTER 37

1 [a] Ezek. 1:3 [b] Ezek. 3:14; 8:3; 11:24; Acts 8:39
3 [c] [Deut. 32:39; 1 Sam. 2:6; John 5:21; Rom. 4:17; 2 Cor. 1:9]
5 [d] Gen. 2:7; Ps. 104:29, 30; Ezek. 37:9, 10, 14
6 [e] Is. 49:23; Ezek. 6:7; 35:12; Joel 2:27; 3:17
9 [f] [Ps. 104:30] [1] Breath of life

dwelling Holy Spirit (v. 27), and the responsive obedience to God's law (v. 27). These are all clearly presented as he prophesies Israel's conversion. As a nation, they will truly know their God (v. 38), hate their sin (vv. 31,32), and glorify their Savior (v. 32).

36:32 Not for your sake. God's glory and reputation among the nations, not Israel's, causes this restoration to be promised (cf. Ps. 115:1; Acts 5:41; Rom. 1:5; 3 John 7).

36:35 the garden. Millennial conditions will be similar (not identical) to those in Eden (cf. 47:1-12; Is. 35:1,2; 55:13; Zech. 8:12).

36:37 inquire of Me to do this. God will sovereignly work this return/renewal, yet give Israelites the human privilege of praying for it to be realized. This prophecy was to stir up the people's prayers.

36:37,38 increase their men. There will be an increase in the population during the Millennium. When the male population came to Jerusalem, they brought vast numbers of animals for sacrifice. That was small compared to future kingdom conditions.

37:1 brought me...in the Spirit. 37:1-14 involves another vision. God does not change Ezekiel's location but gives him a vivid inward sense that he has been taken to a valley "full of bones." (For other visions, cf. 1:1–3:15; 8:1–11:24; 40:1–48:35.) This passage, part of a series of revelations received during the night before the messenger came with the news of the destruction of Jerusalem, was to ease the gloom of the people. **in the midst of the valley.** It no doubt represents the world area wherever Israelites were scattered (cf. v. 12).

37:2 very dry. This pictures the dead nation lifeless, scattered, and bleached, just as a dry tree (17:24) pictures a dead nation, to which only God can give life.

37:3 "...can these bones live?" The many dry bones (v. 2) picture the nation Israel (v. 11) as apparently dead in their dispersion, and waiting for national resurrection. The people knew about the doctrine of individual resurrection, otherwise this prophecy would have had no meaning (cf. 1 Kin. 17; 2 Kin. 4; 13:21; Is. 25:8; 26:19; Dan. 12:2; Hos. 13:14).

37:4-6 Prophesy to these bones. Ezekiel is to proclaim God's pledge to reassemble Israelites from the world and restore the nation of Israel to life (v. 5) and give them His Spirit (v. 14) in true salvation and spiritual life. Clearly, God is promising the resurrection of the nation of Israel and its spiritual regeneration (cf. 36:25-27).

37:7-10 In the vision, Ezekiel did as he was told and the dead bones became a living nation (v. 10).

breathe on these slain, that they may
live."[1] " 10 So I prophesied as He commanded me, [g]and [2]breath came into them,
and they lived, and stood upon their feet,
an exceedingly great army.
11 Then He said to me, "Son of man, these
bones are the [h]whole house of Israel. They
indeed say, [i]'Our bones are dry, our hope is
lost, and we ourselves are cut off!' 12 Therefore prophesy and say to them, 'Thus says
the Lord GOD: "Behold, [j]O My people, I will
open your graves and cause you to come up
from your graves, and [k]bring you into the
land of Israel. 13 Then you shall know that I
am the LORD, when I have opened your
graves, O My people, and brought you up
from your graves. 14 I [l]will put My Spirit in
you, and you shall live, and I will place you
in your own land. Then you shall know that
I, the LORD, have spoken *it* and performed
it," says the LORD.' "

One Kingdom, One King

15 Again the word of the LORD came to
me, saying, 16 "As for you, son of man,
[m]take a stick for yourself and write on it:
'For Judah and for [n]the children of Israel,
his companions.' Then take another stick
and write on it, 'For Joseph, the stick of
Ephraim, and *for* all the house of Israel, his
companions.' 17 Then [o]join them one to another for yourself into one stick, and they
will become one in your hand.
18 "And when the children of your people speak to you, saying, [p]'Will you not
show us what you *mean* by these?'—
19 [q]say to them, 'Thus says the Lord GOD:
"Surely I will take [r]the stick of Joseph,
which *is* in the hand of Ephraim, and the
tribes of Israel, his companions; and I will
join them with it, with the stick of Judah,
and make them one stick, and they will be
one in My hand." ' 20 And the sticks on
which you write will be in your hand [s]be-
fore their eyes.
21 "Then say to them, 'Thus says the Lord
GOD: "Surely [t]I will take the children of Israel from among the nations, wherever they
have gone, and will gather them from every
side and bring them into their own land;
22 and [u]I will make them one nation in the
land, on the mountains of Israel; and [v]one
king shall be king over them all; they shall
no longer be two nations, nor shall they ever
be divided into two kingdoms again.
23 [w]They shall not defile themselves anymore with their idols, nor with their detestable things, nor with any of their transgressions; but [x]I will deliver them from all their
dwelling places in which they have sinned,
and will cleanse them. Then they shall be
My people, and I will be their God.
24 "[y]David My servant *shall be* king over
them, and [z]they shall all have one shepherd; [a]they shall also walk in My judgments
and observe My statutes, and do them.
25 [b]Then they shall dwell in the land that I
have given to Jacob My servant, where your
fathers dwelt; and they shall dwell there,
they, their children, and their children's
children, [c]forever; and [d]My servant David
shall be their prince forever. 26 Moreover I
will [3]make [e]a covenant of peace with them,
and it shall be an everlasting covenant with
them; I will establish them and [f]multiply
them, and I will set My [g]sanctuary in their

10 [g] Rev. 11:11 [2] Breath of life
11 [h] Jer. 33:24; Ezek. 36:10 [i] Ps. 141:7; Is. 49:14
12 [j] Deut. 32:39; 1 Sam. 2:6; Is. 26:19; 66:14; [Dan. 12:2]; Hos. 13:14 [k] Ezek. 36:24
14 [l] Is. 32:15; Ezek. 36:27; [Joel 2:28, 29]; Zech. 12:10
16 [m] Num. 17:2, 3 [n] 2 Chr. 11:12, 13, 16; 15:9; 30:11, 18
17 [o] Is. 11:13; Jer. 50:4; Ezek. 37:22-24; Hos. 1:11; Zeph. 3:9
18 [p] Ezek. 12:9; 24:19
19 [q] Zech. 10:6 [r] Ezek. 37:16, 17
20 [s] Ezek. 12:3
21 [t] Is. 43:5, 6; Jer. 32:37; Ezek. 36:24; Amos 9:14, 15
22 [u] Is. 11:13; Jer. 3:18; Hos. 1:11 [v] Ezek. 34:23; John 10:16
23 [w] Ezek. 36:25 [x] Ezek. 36:28, 29
24 [y] Is. 40:11; [Jer. 23:5; 30:9]; Ezek. 34:23, 24; Hos. 3:5; [Luke 1:32] [z] [John 10:16] [a] Ezek. 36:27
25 [b] Ezek. 36:28 [c] Is. 60:21; Joel 3:20; Amos 9:15 [d] Ps. 89:3, 4; John 12:34
26 [e] Ps. 89:3; Is. 55:3; [Jer. 32:40] [f] Jer. 30:19; Ezek. 36:10 [g] [2 Cor. 6:16] [3] Lit. *cut*

37:11-13 This is the key to the interpretation of the vision. It is the resurrection and salvation of Israel.

37:14 I will put My Spirit in you. *See note on 36:25-27.* **performed *it*.** God's reputation is at stake in the restoration and regeneration of Israel into the Land. He must do what He promised so all know that He is Lord.

37:15-23 The vision ended and Ezekiel was given an object lesson which his people observed (vv. 18,20). This drama of uniting two sticks offered a second illustration that God will not only regather Israelites to their land, but will for the first time since 931 B.C. (the end of Solomon's reign, 1 Kin. 11:26-40) restore union between Israel and Judah (vv. 19,21,22) in the messianic reign (cf. Is. 11:12,13; Jer. 3:18; Hos. 1:11).

37:21-23 God made 3 promises that summarized His future plans for Israel: 1) restoration, v. 21; 2) unification, v. 22; and 3) purification, v. 23. These promises bring to fulfillment: 1) the Abrahamic Covenant (cf. Gen. 12); 2) the Davidic Covenant (2 Sam. 7); and 3) the New Covenant (cf. Jer. 31), respectively.

37:22 one king. This leader (cf. vv. 24,25) is the Messiah-King-Shepherd often promised for David's dynasty (34:23,24; Jer. 23:5-8; 30:9; Dan. 2:35,45; 7:13,14,27), who is the one king of Zech. 14:9 (cf. Matt. 25:31,34,40).

37:23 cleanse them. This is provided by the provisions of the New Covenant (cf. 36:27; 37:14; Jer. 31:31-34).

37:24,25 David. This is to be understood as Jesus Christ the Messiah, descendant of David (cf. 2 Sam. 7:8-17; Is. 7:14; 9:6,7; Mic. 5:2; Matt. 1:1,23; Luke 1:31-33).

37:25 land that I have given to Jacob. It is natural to see this physical land, so clarified, as the very land God gave to Abraham, Isaac, and Jacob (Gen. 12:7; 26:24; 35:12).

37:26 covenant of peace. Cf. 34:25. This is the New Covenant in full force. Israel has never yet been in a state of perpetual salvation peace; this awaits fulfillment in the future kingdom of the Messiah who is the "Prince of Peace" (Is. 9:6). **an everlasting covenant.** The everlasting nature of the Abrahamic (cf. Gen. 17:7), Levitic (Lev. 24:8), Davidic (2 Sam. 23:5), and New (Jer. 50:5) Covenants are joined together in the redeemed who experience the millennial kingdom "forever" (used 4 times in vv. 25-28). The Heb. word for "everlasting" may refer to a long time or eternity. It is also true that these covenants will continue to be fulfilled after the Millennium in the eternal state. **My sanctuary.** The Spirit of God begins to prepare for the great reality that God will have a sanctuary in the midst of His people and will dwell with them (cf. Zech. 6:12,13). God promised to dwell with man on earth (47:1-12). This has been God's desire in all epochs: 1) before Moses (Gen. 17:7,8); 2) in the Mosaic era (Lev. 26:11-13); 3) in the church era (1 Cor. 3:16; 6:19); 4) in the Millennium (Ezek. 37:26-28); and 5) in eternity future (Rev. 21:3).

midst forevermore. 27 [h]My tabernacle also
shall be with them; indeed I will be [i]their
God, and they shall be My people. 28 [j]The
nations also will know that I, the LORD,
[k]sanctify Israel, when My sanctuary is in
their midst forevermore." ' "

Gog and Allies Attack Israel

38 Now the word of the LORD came to
me, saying, 2 [a]"Son of man, [b]set
your face against [c]Gog, of the land of
[d]Magog, [1]the prince of Rosh, [e]Meshech,
and Tubal, and prophesy against him,
3 and say, 'Thus says the Lord GOD: "Behold, I *am* against you, O Gog, the prince of
Rosh, Meshech, and Tubal. 4 [f]I will turn
you around, put hooks into your jaws, and
[g]lead you out, with all your army, horses,
and horsemen, [h]all splendidly clothed, a
great company *with* bucklers and shields,
all of them handling swords. 5 Persia,
[2]Ethiopia, and [3]Libya are with them, all of
them *with* shield and helmet; 6 [i]Gomer and
all its troops; the house of [j]Togarmah *from*
the far north and all its troops—many people *are* with you.
7 [k]"Prepare yourself and be ready, you
and all your companies that are gathered
about you; and be a guard for them. 8 [l]Af-
ter many days [m]you will be visited. In the
latter years you will come into the land of
those brought back from the sword [n]*and*
gathered from many people on [o]the mountains of Israel, which had long been desolate; they were brought out of the nations,
and now all of them [p]dwell safely. 9 You
will ascend, coming [q]like a storm, covering
the [r]land like a cloud, you and all your
troops and many peoples with you."
10 'Thus says the Lord GOD: "On that
day it shall come to pass *that* thoughts will
arise in your mind, and you will make an

27 [h] Lev. 26:11; [John 1:14]; Rev. 21:3 [i] Ezek. 11:20
28 [j] Ezek. 36:23 [k] Ex. 31:13; Ezek. 20:12

CHAPTER 38

2 [a] Ezek. 39:1 [b] Ezek. 35:2,3 [c] Ezek. 38:1–39:24; Rev. 20:8 [d] Gen. 10:2; Ezek. 39:6; Rev. 20:8 [e] Ezek. 32:26 [1] Tg., Vg., Aquila *the chief prince of Meshech,* also v. 3
4 [f] 2 Kin. 19:28; Ezek. 29:4 [g] Is. 43:17 [h] Ezek. 23:12
5 [2] Heb. *Cush* [3] Heb. *Put*
6 [i] Gen. 10:2 [j] Gen. 10:3; Ezek. 27:14
7 [k] Is. 8:9, 10; Jer. 46:3, 4
8 [l] Deut. 4:30; Is. 24:22 [m] Is. 29:6 [n] Ezek. 34:13 [o] Ezek. 36:1, 4 [p] Jer. 23:6; Ezek. 34:25; 39:26 9 [q] Is. 28:2 [r] Jer. 4:13

37:27 Paul quotes this in 2 Cor. 6:16.

38:1–39:29 These chaps. tell of a coming northern confederacy of nations who will invade the Promised Land.

38:2 against Gog. This name is found in 1 Chr. 5:4. The LXX used "Gog" to render names such as Agag (Num. 24:7) and Og (Deut. 3:1), possibly showing that though it was a proper name, it came to be used as a general title for an enemy of God's people. "Gog" most likely carries the idea "high" or "supreme one," based on the comparison in Num. 24:7. It refers to a person, described as a "prince" from the land of Magog, who is the final Antichrist. *See note on Rev. 20:8-10*, where Gog and Magog are referred to again. These titles are used there symbolically of the final world uprising against Jerusalem, its people and Messiah King. This attack comes not just from the N but the 4 corners of the world, as a world of sinners at the end of the 1,000 year kingdom come to fight the saints in the "beloved city" of Jerusalem. On that occasion, there is only one weapon used—divine fire. This is the climax to the last battle with Satan and his armies, whose eternal destiny is set. It is followed by the final judgment of all the ungodly before the Lord (Rev. 20:11-15) and the creation of the eternal, sinless state (Rev. 21:1). *See notes on chap. 39.* **Magog.** Some see this people as derived from Japheth (Gen. 10:2), later called the Scythians. Others propose a people in SE Anatolia, later known as Asiatic people such as the Mongols and Huns. Others see Magog as an overall term for barbarians, N of Palestine, around the Caspian and Black Seas. **the prince of Rosh, Meshech, and Tubal.** Should be translated "chief prince of Meshech and Tubal..." because: 1) Rosh (more than 600 times) in the Heb. OT is an adjective, "chief," often in references to the "chief priest" (2 Kin. 25:18); 2) most ancient versions took it to mean "chief" or "head"; and 3) in all places other than chaps. 38 and 39 where both Meshech and Tubal are mentioned, Rosh is not listed as a third people (27:13; 32:26; Gen. 10:2; 1 Chr. 1:5). This is also descriptive of the Antichrist, who rises to world dominance in the coming time of tribulation (cf. Dan. 9:24-27; 11:36-45; Rev. 13:1-17; 19:20). **Meshech, and Tubal.** Two peoples were recognized in ancient Assyrian monuments: one called Mushki (Mushku) and the other Tubali (Tabal). Both were in Asia Minor, the area of Magog, modern-day Turkey. Summing up, a chief prince, who is the enemy of God's people, will lead a coalition of nations against Jerusalem. The details of this enemy force and its destruction are given by Ezekiel in the rest of chaps. 38,39.

38:4 I will...lead you out. Just as God used Assyria (Is. 8) and Babylon (21:19) as human invaders for His judgments, He aims to use this army. In this case, He brings the invader to Palestine so that He may visit judgment (v. 8) on the invader itself (38:18-23; 39:1-10). He thus uses the language of hooks in the jaws, as in judging Egypt (29:4). From the aggressors' perspective, they think that it is their plan only to seize the spoil which draws them to Palestine (vv. 11,12).

38:5 Persia, Ethiopia, and Libya. The invasion involves a coalition of powers from the E and S of Palestine. Persia is modern Iran, Libya is in N Africa, W of Egypt; and Ethiopia is S of Egypt.

38:6 Gomer. Today the area is Armenia, which also was known as Cappodocia, having a people called Gomer in Assyrian inscriptions. **Togarmah.** Today's eastern Turkey (*see note on 27:14*).

38:7,8 This is the great time of Israel's cleansing, salvation, and spiritual life (cf. vv. 22,27,28; Zech 12:10–13:9), getting them ready for Messiah's return and kingdom (Zech. 14).

38:8 In the latter years. In the context of Israel's restoration (Ezek. 34–39), the invader will make its final bid for the Land. **those brought back from the sword.** This refers to Israelites who have been returned to their land, after the sword had killed or scattered many of their people. The Heb. word for "brought back" means "to return" or "restore" (Gen. 40:13; 41:13). **gathered.** This word also frequently refers to God's final regathering of Israel (37:21; Is. 11:12; 43:5; Jer. 32:37). It has begun historically and will continue until the latter days. In the final millennial kingdom, there will occur the full and spiritual regathering, when all Israel is saved to enter their promised kingdom (cf. Zech. 12–14; Rom. 11:25-27). **dwell safely.** This term occurs in several contexts devoted to the Israelites' blessed estate after God has brought them back to their land (28:26; 34:25,28; 39:26; Jer. 32:37; Zech. 14:11).

38:9 You will ascend. The time of the invasion is best understood as the end of the future tribulation period of 7 years. Israel will have been under a false peace in treaty with the Antichrist (Dan. 9:27; 11:22,24), before he turns on them in the "abomination of desolation" (Dan. 9:27; Matt. 29:15). The false peace will end in hostility lasting to the completion of the 7 years (Zech. 14:1-3). When this final war occurs (cf. Rev. 16:12-16), Christ will ultimately conquer the beast, the false prophet, and all the ungodly forces (Rev. 19:11-21) in order to establish His millennial kingdom (Rev. 20:1-10).

38:10-13 This describes the peace in Israel during the period of Antichrist's short-lived treaty with them (Dan. 9:27) in the first half of

evil plan: 11 You will say, 'I will go up
against a land of [s]unwalled villages; I will
[t]go to a peaceful people, [u]who dwell [4]safe-
ly, all of them dwelling without walls, and
having neither bars nor gates'— 12 to take
plunder and to take booty, to stretch out
your hand against the waste places *that are
again* inhabited, [v]and against a people
gathered from the nations, who have acquired livestock and goods, who dwell in
the midst of the land. 13 [w]Sheba, [x]Dedan,
the merchants [y]of Tarshish, and all [z]their
young lions will say to you, 'Have you
come to take plunder? Have you gathered
your army to take booty, to carry away silver and gold, to take away livestock and
goods, to take great plunder?' " '

14 "Therefore, son of man, prophesy and
say to Gog, 'Thus says the Lord GOD: [a]"On
that day when My people Israel [b]dwell
safely, will you not know *it?* 15 [c]Then you
will come from your place out of the far
north, you and many peoples with you, all
of them riding on horses, a great company
and a mighty army. 16 You will come up
against My people Israel like a cloud, to
cover the land. It will be in the latter days
that I will bring you against My land, so
that the nations may [d]know Me, when I am
[e]hallowed in you, O Gog, before their
eyes." 17 Thus says the Lord GOD: "Are *you*
he of whom I have spoken in former days
by My servants the prophets of Israel, who
prophesied for years in those days that I
would bring you against them?

Judgment on Gog

18 "And it will come to pass at the same
time, when Gog comes against the land of
Israel," says the Lord GOD, "*that* My fury
will show in My face. 19 For [f]in My jealousy [g]*and* in the fire of My wrath I have
spoken: [h]'Surely in that day there shall be
a great [5]earthquake in the land of Israel,
20 so that [i]the fish of the sea, the birds of
the heavens, the beasts of the field, all
creeping things that creep on the earth,
and all men who *are* on the face of the earth
shall shake at My presence. [j]The mountains shall be thrown down, the steep
places shall fall, and every wall shall fall to
the ground.' 21 I will [k]call for [l]a sword
against Gog throughout all My mountains," says the Lord GOD. [m]"Every man's
sword will be against his brother. 22 And I
will [n]bring him to judgment with [o]pesti-
lence and bloodshed; [p]I will rain down on
him, on his troops, and on the many peoples who *are* with him, flooding rain,
[q]great hailstones, fire, and brimstone.
23 Thus I will magnify Myself and [r]sanctify
Myself, [s]and I will be known in the eyes of
many nations. Then they shall know that I
am the LORD." '

Gog's Armies Destroyed

39 "And [a]you, son of man, prophesy
against Gog, and say, 'Thus says the
Lord GOD: "Behold, I *am* against you, O
Gog, [1]the prince of Rosh, Meshech, and
Tubal; 2 and I will [b]turn you around and
lead you on, [c]bringing you up from the far
north, and bring you against the mountains of Israel. 3 Then I will knock the bow
out of your left hand, and cause the arrows
to fall out of your right hand. 4 [d]You shall
[2]fall upon the mountains of Israel, you and
all your troops and the peoples who *are*
with you; [e]I will give you to birds of prey
of every sort and *to* the beasts of the field

11 [s]Zech. 2:4 [t]Jer. 49:31 [u]Ezek. 38:8 [4]*securely*
12 [v]Ezek. 38:8
13 [w]Ezek. 27:22 [x]Ezek. 27:15, 20 [y]Ezek. 27:12 [z]Ezek. 19:3, 5
14 [a]Is. 4:1 [b]Jer. 23:6; Ezek. 38:8, 11; [Zech. 2:5, 8]
15 [c]Ezek. 39:2
16 [d]Ezek. 35:11 [e]Is. 5:16; 8:13; 29:23; Ezek. 28:22
19 [f]Deut. 32:21, 22; Ps. 18:7, 8; Ezek. 36:5, 6; [Nah. 1:2]; Heb. 12:29 [g]Ps. 89:46 [h]Joel 3:16; Hag. 2:6, 7; Rev. 16:18 [5]Lit. *shaking*
20 [i]Hos. 4:3 [j]Jer. 4:24; Nah. 1:5, 6
21 [k]Ps. 105:16 [l]Ezek. 14:17 [m]Judg. 7:22; 1 Sam. 14:20; 2 Chr. 20:23; Hag. 2:22
22 [n]Is. 66:16; Jer. 25:31 [o]Ezek. 5:17 [p]Ps. 11:6; Is. 30:30; Ezek. 13:11 [q]Rev. 16:21
23 [r]Ezek. 36:23 [s]Ps. 9:16; Ezek. 37:28; 38:16

CHAPTER 39

1 [a]Ezek. 38:2, 3 [1]Tg., Vg., Aquila *the chief prince of Meshech*
2 [b]Ezek. 38:8 [c]Ezek. 38:15
4 [d]Ezek. 38:4, 21 [e]Ezek. 33:27 [2]Be slain

Daniel's 70th week. References to "unwalled villages," refer to that period of 3½ years when Israel is secure under the protection of the world-ruling "prince that shall come," called Antichrist (cf. Dan. 9:27). After Antichrist turns on Israel, there is an escalation of hostility until the end of the 7 year time when this great force comes to plunder Jerusalem and the Promised Land (v. 12).

38:12 to take plunder…booty. Antichrist takes over the world for his own power and possession. The wealth of his empire is described in Rev. 18.

38:13 Dedan, Tarshish. *See note on Jon 1:3.*

38:15 riding on horses. These could be actual horses used in war, if tribulation judgments (seals, trumpets, vials) in Rev. 6–16 have dealt drastic blows to industries producing war vehicles and weaponry. Or, some see horses and weapons here (39:3,9) being used symbolically to represent meaning which would be easy to grasp in Ezekiel's day, but which would be fulfilled in the future time with different war forms suitable to that time.

38:16 that the nations may know Me. The phrase, frequent in Ezekiel, is part of the theme to glorify God and show His sovereign power (cf. Introduction: Historical and Theological Themes). God is the victor, who will be "hallowed" by fire (cf. v. 19).

38:17 Are *you* he…? *See notes on 38:2.* This refers to the general references to this time and the participants (cf. Joel 3:9-17; Amos 5:11,12; Zeph. 3:8). Even Daniel (Dan. 2:41-44) referred to this time at least 3 decades prior to Ezek. 38. The nature of the question presupposes that the previous generalities are now being particularized in the person of Gog.

38:18-23 My fury will show. God's patience will be exhausted with the repeated attempts to annihilate Israel since the "abomination" by Antichrist (Dan. 9:27; Matt. 24:15), and He will employ a great earthquake in Israel; panic will seize the invading soldiers (v. 21) who will turn and use their weapons against one another (cf. 2 Chr. 20:22, 23). He will further decimate the ranks by pestilence, a deluge of rain, large hailstones, plus fire and brimstone. The descriptions here are identical to that of the last half of the 7 year tribulation in Rev. 6:12-17; 11:19; 16:17-21; 19:11-21.

39:1-10 bring you. This scene of the army's ruin adds detail to 38:18-23 such as: 1) the disarming of soldiers (v. 3); 2) their fall in death (vv. 4,5); 3) the gorging of birds and beasts on the corpses (v. 4); 4) fire sent also on others besides the army (v. 6); and 5) burning of weapons by Israelites (vv. 9,10).

to be devoured. 5 You shall [3]fall on [4]the
open field; for I have spoken," says the
Lord GOD. 6 [f]"And I will send fire on
Magog and on those who live [5]in security
in [g]the coastlands. Then they shall know
that I *am* the LORD. 7 [h]So I will make My
holy name known in the midst of My people Israel, and I will not *let them* [i]profane
My holy name anymore. [j]Then the nations
shall know that *I am* the LORD, the Holy
One in Israel. 8 [k]Surely it is coming, and it
shall be done," says the Lord GOD. "This *is*
the day [l]of which I have spoken.
9 "Then those who dwell in the cities of
Israel will go out and set on fire and burn
the weapons, both the shields and bucklers, the bows and arrows, the [6]javelins
and spears; and they will make fires with
them for seven years. 10 They will not take
wood from the field nor cut down *any* from
the forests, because they will make fires
with the weapons; [m]and they will plunder
those who plundered them, and pillage
those who pillaged them," says the Lord
GOD.

The Burial of Gog

11 "It will come to pass in that day *that* I
will give Gog a burial place there in Israel,
the valley of those who pass by east of the
sea; and it will obstruct travelers, because
there they will bury Gog and all his multitude. Therefore they will call *it* the Valley
of [7]Hamon Gog. 12 For seven months the
house of Israel will be burying them, [n]in
order to cleanse the land. 13 Indeed all the
people of the land will be burying, and
they will gain [o]renown for it on the day
that [p]I am glorified," says the Lord GOD.
14 "They will set apart men regularly employed, with the help of [8]a search party, to
pass through the land and bury those bodies remaining on the ground, in order [q]to
cleanse it. At the end of seven months they
will make a search. 15 The search party will
pass through the land; and *when anyone*
sees a man's bone, he shall [9]set up a marker by it, till the buriers have buried it in the
Valley of Hamon Gog. 16 *The* name of *the*
city *will* also *be* [1]Hamonah. Thus they shall
[r]cleanse the land."'

A Triumphant Festival

17 "And as for you, son of man, thus
says the Lord GOD, [s]'Speak to every sort of
bird and to every beast of the field:

[t]"Assemble yourselves and come;
Gather together from all sides to
My [u]sacrificial meal
Which I am sacrificing for you,
A great sacrificial meal [v]on the
mountains of Israel,
That you may eat flesh and drink
blood.
18 [w]You shall eat the flesh of the
mighty,
Drink the blood of the princes of
the earth,
Of rams and lambs,
Of goats and bulls,
All of them [x]fatlings of Bashan.
19 You shall eat fat till you are full,
And drink blood till you are
drunk,
At My sacrificial meal
Which I am sacrificing for you.
20 [y]You shall be filled at My table
With horses and riders,
[z]With mighty men
And with all the men of war," says
the Lord GOD.

Israel Restored to the Land

21 [a]"I will set My glory among the nations; all the nations shall see My judgment
which I have executed, and [b]My hand
which I have laid on them. 22 [c]So the house
of Israel shall know that I *am* the LORD their
God from that day forward. 23 [d]The Gentiles shall know that the house of Israel
went into captivity for their iniquity; because they were unfaithful to Me, therefore
[e]I hid My face from them. I [f]gave them into

5 [3] Be slain [4] Lit. *the face of the field*
6 [f] Ezek. 38:22; Amos 1:4, 7, 10; Nah. 1:6 [g] Ps. 72:10; Is. 66:19; Jer. 25:22 [5] *securely* or *confidently*
7 [h] Ezek. 39:25 [i] Lev. 18:21; Ezek. 36:23 [j] Ezek. 38:16
8 [k] Rev. 16:17; 21:6 [l] Ezek. 38:17
9 [6] Lit. *hand staffs*
10 [m] Is. 14:2; 33:1; Mic. 5:8; Hab. 2:8
11 [7] Lit. *The Multitude of Gog*
12 [n] Deut. 21:23; Ezek. 39:14, 16
13 [o] Jer. 33:9; Zeph. 3:19, 20 [p] Ezek. 28:22
14 [q] Ezek. 39:12 [8] Lit. *those who pass through*
15 [9] *build*
16 [r] Ezek. 39:12 [1] Lit. *Multitude*
17 [s] Is. 56:9; [Jer. 12:9]; Ezek. 39:4; Rev. 19:17, 18 [t] Is. 18:6 [u] Is. 34:6, 7; Jer. 46:10; Zeph. 1:7 [v] Ezek. 39:4
18 [w] Ezek. 29:5; Rev. 19:18 [x] Deut. 32:14; Ps. 22:12
20 [y] Ps. 76:5, 6; Ezek. 38:4; Hag. 2:22 [z] Rev. 19:18
21 [a] Ex. 9:16; Is. 37:20; Ezek. 36:23; 38:23 [b] Ex. 7:4
22 [c] Ex. 39:7, 28
23 [d] Jer. 22:8, 9; 44:22; Ezek. 36:18-20, 23 [e] Deut. 31:17; Is. 1:15; 59:2; Ezek. 39:29 [f] Lev. 26:25

39:9,10 burn the weapons. There is enough equipment to provide fuel for 7 years.

39:9 seven years. A vast army (cf. "many," 38:15) would have much weaponry, requiring 7 years to burn. Since this is likely at the end of the time of tribulation, synonymous with the battle of Armageddon (Rev. 16:16; 19:19-21), the burials would extend into the millennial kingdom.

39:11-16 give Gog a burial place. Israelites moving E from the Mediterranean, with the sea to their backs and the Jezreel Valley before them, bury bodies. Further, people in the whole land help in the interment, which consumes 7 months. The description fits the time after Christ's Second Advent extending into the 1,000 millennial era as those who go into His kingdom do the work (cf. Rev. 20:1-10).

39:11,16 Hamon Gog. Lit. "the multitude of Gog." In v. 16, a city in the area will be named Hamonah, "multitude" (cf. a similar idea in Joel 3:14).

39:17-20 Speak to...bird and...beast. God's word summons carrion birds and carnivorous animals to consume the fallen flesh as described in Rev. 19:21.

39:17,18 My sacrificial meal. Since God describes the feast by the imagery of a sacrificial meal, the warriors who fell (v. 19) are described figuratively in words such as rams and other animals used in sacrifice.

39:21-29 I will set My glory. God vanquishes Israel's foes to show His glory so that His enemies and Israel will all know that He is the Lord (vv. 6,22). This is Israel's salvation spoken of in Zech. 12:10–13:9 and Rom. 11:25-27.

the hand of their enemies, and they all fell
by the sword. 24 [g]According to their
uncleanness and according to their transgressions I have dealt with them, and hidden My face from them." '

25 "Therefore thus says the Lord GOD:
[h]'Now I will bring back the captives of Jacob, and have mercy on the [i]whole house
of Israel; and I will be jealous for My holy
name— 26 [j]after they have borne their
shame, and all their unfaithfulness in
which they were unfaithful to Me, when
they [k]dwelt safely in their *own* land and no
one made *them* afraid. 27 [l]When I have
brought them back from the peoples and
gathered them out of their enemies' lands,
and I [m]am hallowed in them in the sight of
many nations, 28 [n]then they shall know
that I *am* the LORD their God, who sent
them into captivity among the nations, but
also brought them back to their land, and
left none of them [2]captive any longer.
29 [o]And I will not hide My face from them
anymore; for I shall have [p]poured out My
Spirit on the house of Israel,' says the Lord
GOD."

24 [g] 2 Kin. 17:7; Jer. 2:17, 19; 4:18; Ezek. 36:19
25 [h] Is. 27:12, 13; Jer. 30:3, 18; Ezek. 34:13; 36:24 [i] Jer. 31:1; Ezek. 20:40; Hos. 1:11
26 [j] Dan. 9:16 [k] Lev. 26:5, 6
27 [l] Ezek. 28:25, 26 [m] Ezek. 36:23, 24; 38:16
28 [n] Ezek. 34:30

[2] Lit. *there*

29 [o] Is. 54:8, 9 [p] Is. 32:15; Ezek. 36:27; 37:14; [Joel 2:28; Zech. 12:10]; Acts 2:17

A New City, a New Temple

40 In the twenty-fifth year of our captivity, at the beginning of the year,
on the tenth *day* of the month, in the fourteenth year after [a]the city was [1]captured,
on the very same day [b]the hand of the
LORD was upon me; and He took me there.
2 [c]In the visions of God He took me into
the land of Israel and [d]set me on a very

CHAPTER 40

1 [a] 2 Kin. 25:1-4; Jer. 39:2, 3; 52:4-7; Ezek. 33:21 [b] Ezek. 1:3; 3:14, 22; 37:1 [1] Lit. *struck* 2 [c] Ezek. 1:1; 3:14; 8:3; 37:1; Dan. 7:1, 7 [d] [Is. 2:2, 3]; Ezek. 17:23; 20:40; 37:22; [Mic. 4:1]; Rev. 21:10

39:29 poured out My Spirit. God's provision of His Spirit at the Second Advent complements the regathering (cf. 36:27; 37:14; Joel 2:28). The Gog and Magog assault in Rev. 20:7-9 at the end of the Millennium is another assault on Jerusalem patterned after certain images of the invasion here (chaps. 38,39), but it is a distinct event one thousand years after the millennial kingdom begins. *See note on Rev. 20:8,9.*

40:1–48:35 Following this great battle at the end of the time of tribulation, this section provides explicit details concerning Christ's millennial reign which follows, giving more detail about the 1,000 year kingdom than all other OT prophecies put together. It is the "holy of holies" among millennial forecasts. As has been done with the previous 39 chaps., this concluding portion will also be approached in a literal, historical manner which best serves the interpreter in all Scripture. In many ways these chaps. are the most important in the book since they form the crowning reality, the climax of Ezekiel's prophecy and Israel's restoration. The section includes: 1) the new temple (40:1–43:12); 2) the new worship (43:13–46:24); and 3) the new apportionment of the Land (47:1–48:35).

40:1 the twenty-fifth year. 573 B.C., in the first month of the ecclesiastical year, Nisan. The tenth day was the start of preparations for Passover.

40:2 In the visions of God He took me. Ezekiel 40–48 narrates another vision, as did 1:1–3:27; 8–11; and 37:1-14. The characterization of the prophecy as a vision in no way detracts from its literal

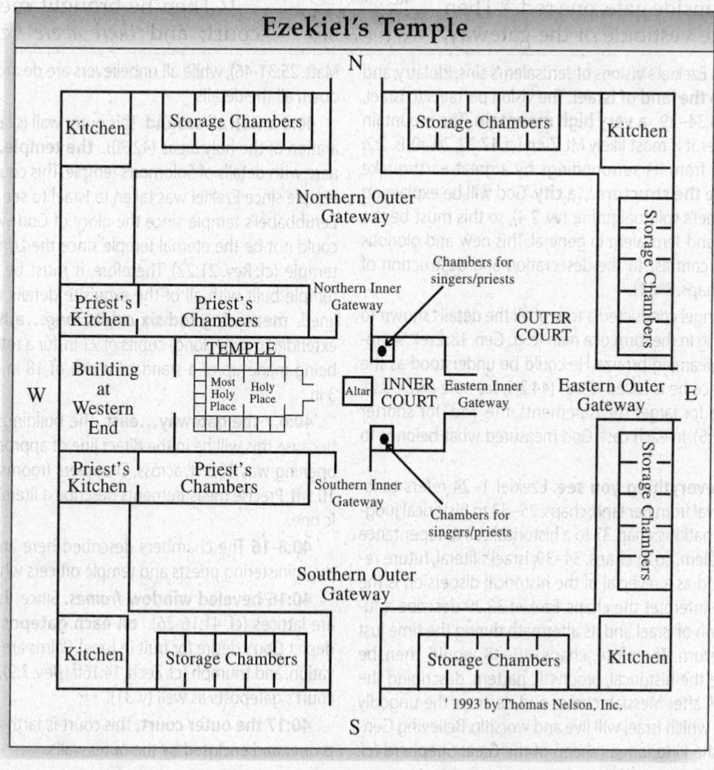

high mountain; on it toward the south *was*
something like the structure of a city. 3 He
took me there, and behold, *there was* a man
whose appearance *was* [e]like the appearance of bronze. [f]He had a line of flax [g]and
a measuring rod in his hand, and he stood
in the gateway.
4 And the man said to me, [h]"Son of man,
look with your eyes and hear with your
ears, and [2]fix your mind on everything I
show you; for you *were* brought here so
that I might show *them* to you. [i]Declare to
the house of Israel everything you see."
5 Now there was [j]a wall all around the outside of the [3]temple. In the man's hand was
a measuring rod six [4]cubits *long, each being*
a cubit and a handbreadth; and he measured the width of the wall structure, one
rod; and the height, one rod.

The Eastern Gateway of the Temple

6 Then he went to the gateway which
faced [k]east; and he went up its stairs and
measured the threshold of the gateway,
which was one rod wide, and the other
threshold *was* one rod wide. 7 Each gate
chamber *was* one rod long and one rod
wide; between the gate chambers *was a*
space of five cubits; and the threshold of the
gateway by the vestibule of the inside gate
was one rod. 8 He also measured the
vestibule of the inside gate, one rod. 9 Then
he measured the vestibule of the gateway,
eight cubits; and the gateposts, two cubits.
The vestibule of the gate *was* on the inside.
10 In the eastern gateway *were* three gate
chambers on one side and three on the
other; the three *were* all the same size; also
the gateposts were of the same size on this
side and that side.
11 He measured the width of the entrance to the gateway, ten cubits; *and* the
length of the gate, thirteen cubits. 12 *There*
was a [5]space in front of the gate chambers,
one cubit *on this side* and one cubit on that
side; the gate chambers *were* six cubits on
this side and six cubits on that side.
13 Then he measured the gateway from the
roof of *one* gate chamber to the roof of the
other; the width *was* twenty-five cubits, as
door faces door. 14 He measured the
gateposts, sixty cubits high, and the court
all around the gateway *extended* to the
gatepost. 15 *From* the front of the entrance
gate to the front of the vestibule of the
inner gate *was* fifty cubits. 16 *There were*
[l]beveled window *frames* in the gate chambers and in their intervening archways on
the inside of the gateway all around, and
likewise in the vestibules. *There were* windows all around on the inside. And on
each gatepost *were* [m]palm trees.

The Outer Court

17 Then he brought me into [n]the outer
court; and *there were* [o]chambers and a

3 [e]Ezek. 1:7; Dan. 10:6; Rev. 1:15 [f]Ezek. 47:3; Zech. 2:1, 2 [g]Rev. 11:1; 21:15
4 [h]Ezek. 44:5 [i]Ezek. 43:10 [2]Lit. *set your heart*
5 [j][Is. 26:1]; Ezek. 42:20 [3]Lit. *house* [4]A royal cubit of about 21 inches
6 [k]Ezek. 43:1
12 [5]Lit. *border*
16 [l]1 Kin. 6:4; Ezek. 41:16, 26 [m]1 Kin. 6:29, 32, 35; 2 Chr. 3:5; Ezek. 40:22, 26, 31, 34, 37; 41:18-20, 25, 26
17 [n]Ezek. 10:5; 42:1; 46:21; Rev. 11:2 [o]1 Kin. 6:5; 2 Chr. 31:11; Ezek. 40:38

reality any more than Ezekiel's visions of Jerusalem's sins, idolatry, and destruction did. **into the land of Israel.** The vision pertains to Israel, as did chaps. 1–24,33,34–39. **a very high mountain.** The mountain is not named; however, it is most likely Mt. Zion (cf. 17:22; 20:40; Is. 2:2; Micah 4:1), lifted up from its surroundings by a great earthquake (Zech. 14:4,5,10). **like the structure…a city.** God will be explaining details relating to Israel's spiritual future (vv. 2,4), so this must be the temple in particular and Jerusalem in general. This new and glorious temple will stand in contrast to the desecration and destruction of Solomon's temple (chaps. 8–11).

40:3 a man. An angel conducted a tour of all the details shown to the prophet, appearing in the form of a man (e.g., Gen. 18; Ezek. 9), appearing like bright, gleaming bronze. He could be understood as the Angel of the Lord since he is called "LORD" (44:2,5; *see note on Ex. 3:2*). His "line of flax" was for larger measurements, the "rod" for shorter ones (cf. Rev. 11:1; 21:5). In each case God measured what belongs to Him.

40:4 Declare…everything you see. Ezekiel 1–24 refers to Israel's historical removal from her land; chaps. 25–32 to historical judgments against other nations; chap. 33 to a historical call to repentance and the fall of Jerusalem. So in chaps. 34–39, Israel's literal, future return to the same Land as a reversal of the historical dispersion is the most natural way to interpret the chaps. Ezekiel 38,39 describe a future, historical invasion of Israel and its aftermath during the time just before Messiah's return. Therefore, chaps. 40–48 would then be thought to continue the historical, prophetic pattern, describing the millennial conditions after Messiah comes and destroys the ungodly (Rev. 19:11ff.), under which Israel will live and worship. Believing Gentiles will also be in the kingdom as sheep of the Great Shepherd (cf. Matt. 25:31-46), while all unbelievers are destroyed. Ezekiel is to write down all the details.

40:5 a wall all around. This outer wall is later described as a separation of the holy areas (42:20). **the temple.** See 1 Kin. 6,7 to compare with details of Solomon's temple. This could not be the heavenly temple since Ezekiel was taken to Israel to see it (v. 2). It could not be Zerubbabel's temple since the glory of God was not present then. It could not be the eternal temple since the Lord and the Lamb are its temple (cf. Rev. 21:22). Therefore, it must be the earthly millennial temple built with all of the exquisite details that are yet to be outlined. **measuring rod six cubits *long*…a handbreadth.** The rod extended 6 royal (long) cubits of 21 in. for a total of 10.5 ft., each cubit being made up of a standard width of 18 in. and a handbreadth of 3 in.

40:6,7 the gateway…east. The buildings of the E gate are first because this will be in the direct line of approach to the temple. Each opening was 10.5 ft. across. Chambers (rooms) in the wall are 10.5 x 10.5 ft. Precise measurements describe a literal temple, not a symbolic one.

40:8-16 The chambers described here are accommodations for the ministering priests and temple officers who care for the temple.

40:16 beveled window *frames*. Since they had no glass, these are lattices (cf. 41:16-26). **on each gatepost…palm trees.** These depict God's desire for fruit in Israel. Palms are symbols of beauty, salvation, and triumph (cf. Zech. 14:16ff.; Rev. 7:9). Palms are on the inner court's gateposts as well (v. 31).

40:17 the outer court. This court is farthest out from the temple proper and enclosed by the outer walls.

pavement made all around the court; [p]thir-
ty chambers faced the pavement. 18 The
pavement was by the side of the gateways,
corresponding to the length of the gateways; *this was* the lower pavement. 19 Then
he measured the width from the front of
the lower gateway to the front of the inner
court exterior, one hundred cubits toward
the east and the north.

The Northern Gateway

20 On the outer court was also a gateway
facing north, and he measured its length
and its width. 21 Its gate chambers, three
on this side and three on that side, its
gateposts and its archways, had the same
measurements as the first gate; its length
was fifty cubits and its width twenty-five
cubits. 22 Its windows and those of its archways, and also its palm trees, *had* the same
measurements as the gateway facing east;
it was ascended by seven steps, and its
archway *was* in front of it. 23 A gate of the
inner court was opposite the northern
gateway, just as the eastern *gateway;* and he
measured from gateway to gateway, one
hundred cubits.

The Southern Gateway

24 After that he brought me toward the
south, and there a gateway was facing
south; and he measured its gateposts and
archways according to these same measurements. 25 *There were* windows in it and
in its archways all around like those windows; its length *was* fifty cubits and its
width twenty-five cubits. 26 Seven steps
led up to it, and its archway *was* in front of
them; and it had palm trees on its
gateposts, one on this side and one on that
side. 27 *There was* also a gateway on the
inner court, facing south; and he measured
from gateway to gateway toward the
south, one hundred cubits.

17 [p] Ezek. 45:5
30 [q] Ezek. 40:21, 25, 33, 36
38 [r] 2 Chr. 4:6

Gateways of the Inner Court

28 Then he brought me to the inner court
through the southern gateway; he measured the southern gateway according to
these same measurements. 29 Also its gate
chambers, its gateposts, and its archways
were according to these same measurements; *there were* windows in it and in its
archways all around; *it was* fifty cubits long
and twenty-five cubits wide. 30 *There were*
archways all around, [q]twenty-five cubits
long and five cubits wide. 31 Its archways
faced the outer court, palm trees *were* on its
gateposts, and going up to it *were* eight
steps.
32 And he brought me into the inner
court facing east; he measured the gateway according to these same measurements. 33 Also its gate chambers, its
gateposts, and its archways *were* according to these same measurements; and
there were windows in it and in its archways all around; *it was* fifty cubits long
and twenty-five cubits wide. 34 Its archways faced the outer court, and palm
trees *were* on its gateposts on this side and
on that side; and going up to it *were* eight
steps.
35 Then he brought me to the north gateway and measured *it* according to these
same measurements— 36 also its gate
chambers, its gateposts, and its archways.
It had windows all around; its length *was*
fifty cubits and its width twenty-five cubits. 37 Its gateposts faced the outer court,
palm trees *were* on its gateposts on this side
and on that side, and going up to it *were*
eight steps.

Where Sacrifices Were Prepared

38 *There was* a chamber and its entrance
by the gateposts of the gateway, where
they [r]washed the burnt offering. 39 In the
vestibule of the gateway *were* two tables on
this side and two tables on that side, on

40:17-37 Here is a further blueprint for the temple area, with more precise measurements. The numbers 5, 25, 50 and 100 are frequently used. The sanctuary formed a square of some 500 cubits.

40:38-47 This section describes "chambers" for the priests, and raises the question of sacrifices in the millennial kingdom. They will exist as vv. 39-43 indicate, but will be no more efficacious then than they were in OT times. No sacrifice before or after Christ saves. They only point to Him as the one true Lamb who takes away sin. The Lord's Supper is a memorial that looks back to Calvary and in no way diminishes the cross. Israel rejected their Messiah, but when they have received Him and are in His kingdom, they will have a memorial of sacrifices that point to Him. They will have missed the memorial of the Lord's Supper, but will then have their own memorial sacrifices for 1,000 years.

Millennial Sacrifices

Levitical	Millennial*
1. Burnt—Lev. 1:3-17	1. Burnt—Ezek. 40:39
2. Grain—Lev. 2:1-16	2. Grain—Ezek. 45:15
3. Peace—Lev. 3:1-17	3. Peace—Ezek. 45:15
4. Sin—Lev. 4:1-35	4. Sin—Ezek. 40:39
5. Trespass—Lev. 5:1–6:7	5. Trespass—Ezek. 40:39
6. Drink—Lev. 23:13, 37	6. Drink—Ezek. 45:17

*** Is. 56:7, 66:20-23; Jer. 33:18 further confirm the burnt and grain offerings.**

which to slay the burnt offering, [s]the sin
offering, and [t]the trespass offering. 40 At
the outer side of the vestibule, as one goes
up to the entrance of the northern gateway,
were two tables; and on the other side of
the vestibule of the gateway *were* two tables. 41 Four tables *were* on this side and
four tables on that side, by the side of the
gateway, eight tables on which they
slaughtered *the sacrifices.* 42 *There were* also
four tables of hewn stone for the burnt offering, one cubit and a half long, one cubit
and a half wide, and one cubit high; on
these they laid the instruments with which
they slaughtered the burnt offering and the
sacrifice. 43 Inside *were* hooks, a handbreadth wide, fastened all around; and the
flesh of the sacrifices *was* on the tables.

Chambers for Singers and Priests

44 Outside the inner gate *were* the chambers for [u]the singers in the inner court, one
facing south at the side of the northern
gateway, and the other facing north at the
side of the southern gateway. 45 Then he
said to me, "This chamber which faces
south *is* for [v]the priests who have charge of
the temple. 46 The chamber which faces
north *is* for the priests [w]who have charge
of the altar; these *are* the sons of [x]Zadok,
from the sons of Levi, who come near the
LORD to minister to Him."

Dimensions of the Inner Court and Vestibule

47 And he measured the court, one hundred cubits long and one hundred cubits
wide, foursquare. The altar *was* in front of
the temple. 48 Then he brought me to the
[y]vestibule of the temple and measured the
doorposts of the vestibule, five cubits on
this side and five cubits on that side; and
the width of the gateway was three cubits
on this side and three cubits on that side.
49 [z]The length of the vestibule *was* twenty
cubits, and the width eleven cubits; and by
the steps which led up to it *there were* [a]pil-
lars by the doorposts, one on this side and
another on that side.

Dimensions of the Sanctuary

41 Then he [a]brought me into the [1]sanc-
tuary and measured the doorposts,
six cubits wide on one side and six cubits
wide on the other side—the width of the
tabernacle. 2 The width of the entryway
was ten cubits, and the side walls of the entrance *were* five cubits on this side and five
cubits on the other side; and he measured
its length, forty cubits, and its width, twenty cubits.
3 Also he went inside and measured the
doorposts, two cubits; and the entrance,
six cubits *high;* and the width of the entrance, seven cubits. 4 [b]He measured the
length, twenty cubits; and the width, twenty cubits, beyond the sanctuary; and he
said to me, "This *is* the Most Holy *Place.*"

The Side Chambers on the Wall

5 Next, he measured the wall of the
[2]temple, six cubits. The width of each side
chamber all around the temple *was* four
cubits on every side. 6 [c]The side chambers
were in three stories, one above the other,
thirty chambers in each story; they rested
on [3]ledges which *were* for the side chambers all around, that they might be supported, but [d]not fastened to the wall of the
temple. 7 As one went up from story to
story, the side chambers [e]became wider all
around, because their supporting ledges in
the wall of the temple ascended like steps;
therefore the width of the structure increased as one went up *from* the lowest
story to the highest by way of the middle
one. 8 I also saw an elevation all around
the temple; it was the foundation of the
side chambers, [f]a full rod, *that is,* six cubits
high. 9 The thickness of the outer wall of

39 [s] Lev. 4:2, 3 [t] Lev. 5:6; 6:6; 7:1
44 [u] 1 Chr. 6:31, 32; 16:41-43; 25:1-7
45 [v] Lev. 8:35; Num. 3:27, 28, 32, 38; 18:5; 1 Chr. 9:23; 2 Chr. 13:11; Ps. 134:1
46 [w] Lev. 6:12, 13; Num. 18:5; Ezek. 44:15 [x] 1 Kin. 2:35; Ezek. 43:19; 44:15, 16
48 [y] 1 Kin. 6:3; 2 Chr. 3:4
49 [z] 1 Kin. 6:3
[a] 1 Kin. 7:15-22; 2 Chr. 3:17; Jer. 52:17-23; [Rev. 3:12]

CHAPTER 41

1 [a] Ezek. 40:2, 3, 17 [1] Heb. *heykal;* the main room in the temple, the holy place, Ex. 26:33
4 [b] 1 Kin. 6:20; 2 Chr. 3:8
5 [2] Lit. *house*
6 [c] 1 Kin. 6:5-10 [d] 1 Kin. 6:6, 10 [3] Lit. *the wall*
7 [e] 1 Kin. 6:8
8 [f] Ezek. 40:5

40:39 burnt…sin…trespass offering. For OT background see 1) Lev. 1:1-17; 6:8-13; 2) Lev. 4:1-35; 6:24-30; and 3) Lev. 5:1–6:7; 7:1-10 respectively. cf. Ezek. 43:18-27; 45:13-25; 46:1-15,19-24.

40:41 tables on which they slaughtered. Four tables are on either side of the inner court's N gate, used for commemorating the death of Christ by slaying burnt, sin, and trespass offerings.

40:44 singers. Provision is made for the praises of the redeemed in music.

40:46 sons of Zadok. Proper names tie the vision to historical reality, calling for literal interpretation. This Levitical family descended from Levi, Aaron, Eleazar and Phinehas (1 Chr. 6:3-8). In accord with God's covenant with Phinehas (Num. 25:10-13), and because of Eli's unfaithfulness (cf. 1 Sam. 1,2) and Zadok's faithfulness to David and Solomon (1 Kin. 1:32-40), Zadok's sons serve as priests in the millennial temple. Other references to sons of Zadok are in 43:19; 44:15 and 48:11.

40:47 measured the court. The court around the temple was a square, around the square temple (41:1). **The altar.** This is the bronze altar where offerings occur. Cf. 43:13-27.

40:48,49 vestibule. This refers to the temple porch and is similar to that of Solomon's temple.

41:1 into the sanctuary. Precise descriptions continue for the temple proper, its sanctuary or holy place (here called "tabernacle"), and side chambers for priests' quarters (vv. 5-11). This chap. can be studied in the light of 1 Kin. 6,7 to note differences from Solomon's temple.

41:4 the Most Holy *Place*. The Holy of Holies, which the High-Priest entered annually on the Day of Atonement (cf. Lev. 16). These dimensions are identical to Solomon's (1 Kin. 6:20), and twice those of the tabernacle in the wilderness.

41:5-11 This section describes the "wall" and "side chambers."

the side chambers *was* five cubits, and so
also the remaining terrace by the place of
the side chambers of the [4]temple. 10 And
between *it and* the *wall* chambers was a
width of twenty cubits all around the temple on every side. 11 The doors of the side
chambers opened on the terrace, one door
toward the north and another toward the
south; and the width of the terrace *was* five
cubits all around.

The Building at the Western End

12 The building that faced the separating
courtyard at its western end *was* seventy
cubits wide; the wall of the building *was*
five cubits thick all around, and its length
ninety cubits.

Dimensions and Design of the Temple Area

13 So he measured the temple, one [g]hun-
dred cubits long; and the separating courtyard with the building and its walls *was*
one hundred cubits long; 14 also the width
of the eastern face of the temple, including
the separating courtyard, *was* one hundred
cubits. 15 He measured the length of the
building behind it, facing the separating
courtyard, with its [h]galleries on the one
side and on the other side, one hundred cubits, as well as the inner [5]temple and the
porches of the court, 16 their doorposts and
[i]the beveled window frames. And the galleries all around their three stories opposite
the threshold were paneled with [j]wood
from the ground to the windows—the windows were covered— 17 from the space
above the door, even to the inner [6]room, as
well as outside, and on every wall all
around, inside and outside, by measure.
18 And *it was* made [k]with cherubim and
[l]palm trees, a palm tree between cherub
and cherub. *Each* cherub had two faces,
19 [m]so that the face of a man *was* toward a
palm tree on one side, and the face of a
young lion toward a palm tree on the other
side; thus *it was* made throughout the temple all around. 20 From the floor to the
space above the door, and on the wall of
the sanctuary, cherubim and palm trees
were carved.
21 The [n]doorposts of the temple *were*
square, *as was* the front of the sanctuary;
their appearance was similar. 22 [o]The altar
was of wood, three cubits high, and its
length two cubits. Its corners, its length,
and its sides *were* of wood; and he said to
me, "This *is* [p]the table that *is* [q]before the
LORD."
23 [r]The temple and the sanctuary had
two doors. 24 The doors had two [s]panels
apiece, two folding panels: two *panels* for
one door and two panels for the other *door.*
25 Cherubim and palm trees *were* carved on
the doors of the temple just as they *were*
carved on the walls. A wooden canopy *was*
on the front of the vestibule outside.
26 *There were* [t]beveled window *frames* and
palm trees on one side and on the other, on
the sides of the vestibule—also on the side
chambers of the temple and on the
canopies.

The Chambers for the Priests

42 Then he [a]brought me out into the
outer court, by the way toward the
[b]north; and he brought me into [c]the chamber which *was* opposite the separating
courtyard, and which *was* opposite the
building toward the north. 2 Facing the
length, *which was* one hundred cubits (the
width was fifty cubits), was the north door.
3 Opposite the inner court of twenty *cubits,*
and opposite the [d]pavement of the outer
court, *was* [e]gallery against gallery in three
stories. 4 In front of the chambers, toward
the inside, *was* a walk ten cubits wide, at a
distance of one cubit; and their doors faced
north. 5 Now the upper chambers *were*
shorter, because the galleries took away
space from them more than from the lower
and middle stories of the building. 6 For
they *were* in three *stories* and did not have
pillars like the pillars of the courts; therefore *the upper level* was [1]shortened more
than the lower and middle levels from the
ground up. 7 And a wall which *was* outside
ran parallel to the chambers, at the front of
the chambers, toward the outer court; its
length *was* fifty cubits. 8 The length of the
chambers toward the outer court *was* fifty
cubits, whereas that facing the temple *was*
one [f]hundred cubits. 9 At the lower cham-

9 [4] Lit. *house*
13 [g] Ezek. 40:47
15 [h] Ezek. 42:3, 5 [5] Or *sanctuary*
16 [i] 1 Kin. 6:4; Ezek. 40:16, 25 [j] 1 Kin. 6:15
17 [6] Lit. *house;* the Most Holy Place
18 [k] 1 Kin. 6:29; 2 Chr. 3:7 [l] 2 Chr. 3:5; Ezek. 40:16
19 [m] Ezek. 1:10; 10:14
21 [n] 1 Kin. 6:33; Ezek. 40:9, 14, 16; 41:1
22 [o] Ex. 30:1-3; 1 Kin. 6:20; Rev. 8:3 [p] Ex. 25:23, 30; Lev. 24:6; Ezek. 23:41; 44:16; Mal. 1:7, 12 [q] Ex. 30:8
23 [r] 1 Kin. 6:31-35
24 [s] 1 Kin. 6:34
26 [t] Ezek. 40:16

CHAPTER 42

1 [a] Ezek. 41:1 [b] Ezek. 40:20 [c] Ezek. 41:12, 15
3 [d] Ezek. 40:17 [e] Ezek. 41:15, 16; 42:5
6 [1] Or *narrowed*
8 [f] Ezek. 41:13, 14

41:12 building…at its western end. Beyond the western end of the temple proper was a distinct building with space that serves the temple, possibly housing supplies.

41:13 measured the temple. Cf. 40:47. It was about 175 ft. square.

41:15 galleries. These were terraced buildings with decorations (vv. 18-20).

41:18 cherubim and palm trees. Figures of angels (cf. chaps. 1,10) with palms between them (possibly to depict life and fruitfulness of God's servants) were on the walls of the temple proper and on the doors (v. 25). Each cherub (unlike that of chaps. 1,10 which had 4 faces) had the face of a man and of a lion, possibly to represent the humanity and kingship of Messiah.

41:22 This was the altar of incense (cf. Ex. 30:1-3; 1 Kin. 7:48).

42:3 gallery against gallery. Priestly rooms are described (vv. 3-12), situated along the S, N, and W walls of the sanctuary and Most Holy Place, in 3 stories. Priests eat the holy offerings (cf. Lev. 2:3,10; 6:9-11; 10:12): and dress there (vv. 13,14).

bers *was* the entrance on the east side, as
one goes into them from the outer court.
10 Also *there were* chambers in the thickness of the wall of the court toward the
east, opposite the separating courtyard
and opposite the building. 11 [g]*There was* a
walk in front of them also, and their appearance *was* like the chambers which *were*
toward the north; they *were* as long and as
wide as the others, and all their exits and
entrances *were* according to plan. 12 And
corresponding to the doors of the chambers that *were* facing south, as one enters
them, *there was* a door in front of the walk,
the way directly in front of the wall toward
the east.
13 Then he said to me, "The north chambers *and* the south chambers, which *are* opposite the separating courtyard, *are* the
holy chambers where the priests who approach the LORD [h]shall eat the most holy
offerings. There they shall lay the most
holy offerings—[i]the grain offering, the sin
offering, and the trespass offering—for the
place *is* holy. 14 [j]When the priests enter
them, they shall not go out of the holy
chamber into the outer court; but there they
shall leave their garments in which they
minister, for they *are* holy. They shall put
on other garments; then they may approach *that* which *is* for the people."

Outer Dimensions of the Temple

15 Now when he had finished measuring the inner [2]temple, he brought me out
through the gateway that faces toward the
[k]east, and measured it all around. 16 He
measured the east side with the [3]measur-
ing rod, five hundred rods by the measuring rod all around. 17 He measured the
north side, five hundred rods by the measuring rod all around. 18 He measured the
south side, five hundred rods by the measuring rod. 19 He came around to the west
side *and* measured five hundred rods by
the measuring rod. 20 He measured it on
the four sides; [l]it had a wall all around,
[m]five hundred *cubits* long and five hundred wide, to separate the holy areas from
the [4]common.

The Temple, the LORD's Dwelling Place

43 Afterward he brought me to the
gate, the gate [a]that faces toward the
east. 2 [b]And behold, the glory of the God of
Israel came from the way of the east. [c]His
voice *was* like the sound of many waters;
[d]and the earth shone with His glory. 3 *It
was* [e]like the appearance of the vision
which I saw—like the vision which I saw
when [1]I came [f]to destroy the city. The visions *were* like the vision which I saw [g]by
the River Chebar; and I fell on my face.
4 [h]And the glory of the LORD came into the
[2]temple by way of the gate which faces toward the east. 5 [i]The Spirit lifted me up
and brought me into the inner court; and
behold, [j]the glory of the LORD filled the
[3]temple.
6 Then I heard *Him* speaking to me from
the temple, while [k]a man stood beside me.
7 And He said to me, "Son of man, *this is*
[l]the place of My throne and [m]the place of
the soles of My feet, [n]where I will dwell in
the midst of the children of Israel forever.
[o]No more shall the house of Israel defile
My holy name, they nor their kings, by
their [4]harlotry or with [p]the carcasses of
their kings on their high places. 8 [q]When
they set their threshold by My threshold,
and their doorpost by My doorpost, with a
wall between them and Me, they defiled
My holy name by the abominations which
they committed; therefore I have con-

11 [g] Ezek. 42:4
13 [h] Lev. 6:16, 26; 24:9; Ezek. 43:19 [i] Lev. 2:3, 10; 6:14, 17, 25
14 [j] Ezek. 44:19
15 [k] Ezek. 40:6; 43:1 [2] Lit. *house*
16 [3] About 10.5 feet, Ezek. 40:5
20 [l] [Is. 60:18]; Ezek. 40:5; Zech. 2:5 [m] Ezek. 45:2; Rev. 21:16 [4] Or *profane*

CHAPTER 43

1 [a] Ezek. 10:19; 46:1
2 [b] Ezek. 11:23 [c] Ezek. 1:24; Rev. 1:15; 14:2 [d] Ezek. 10:4; Rev. 18:1
3 [e] Ezek. 1:4-28 [f] Jer. 1:10; Ezek. 9:1, 5; 32:18 [g] Ezek. 1:28; 3:23 [1] Some Heb. mss., Vg. *He*
4 [h] Ezek. 10:19; 11:23 [2] Lit. *house*
5 [i] Ezek. 3:12, 14; 8:3; 2 Cor. 12:2-4 [j] Ezek. 40:34; 1 Kin. 8:10, 11 [3] Lit. *house*
6 [k] Ezek. 1:26; 40:3
7 [l] Ps. 99:1; Is. 60:13 [m] 1 Chr. 28:2; Ps. 99:5 [n] Ex. 29:45; Ps. 68:16; 132:14; Ezek. 37:26-28; Joel 3:17; [John 1:14; 2 Cor. 6:16] [o] Ezek. 39:7 [p] Lev. 26:30; Jer. 16:18; Ezek. 6:5, 13 [4] Unfaithful idolatry
8 [q] 2 Kin. 16:14; 21:4, 5, 7; Ezek. 8:3; 23:39; 44:7

42:15-20 out through the gateway. The angel measured the height and thickness of the outside wall (40:5); then the outer court (40:6-27); next the inner court with the chambers (40:28–42:14); finally, the extent of all the temple buildings outside. Measurements of the outer wall, 500 rods each way, were approximately one mi. on each of the 4 sides. Much too large for Mt. Moriah, this scheme will require changes in the topography of Jerusalem, as Zechariah predicted (14:9-11).

43:2 the glory of the God of Israel. In earlier chaps. of this prophecy, emphasis was given to the departure of God's glory from the temple (see chaps. 8–11). Thus the Lord abandoned His people to destruction and dispersion. Here, in the millennial temple, the glory of God returns to dwell. His glory will be manifest in fullness in the future kingdom, after the Lord's Second Advent, which is also to be glorious (Matt. 16:27; 25:31). Verses 1-12 describe God's glorious entrance into the sanctuary. **came from...the east.** The glory had been in the tabernacle (Ex. 40:34,35) and the temple (1 Kin. 8:10,11), though not in Zerubbabel's temple. Here, the Lord returns to be Israel's King. The glory departed to the E from Israel (11:23) when God judged them, so the glory returns from the E when He has regathered them, and is restoring their worship.

43:3 like the...vision. This vision appearance of God to Ezekiel is glorious, just as the vision in chaps. 8–11, which pictures His coming, by angels, to judge Jerusalem (cf. 9:3-11; 10:4-7). **like the vision...by the River Chebar.** God's appearance is also glorious as in the vision of 1:3-28. **I fell on my face.** Just as in the other visions of God's glory (1:28; 9:8). Cf. Rev. 1:12-17.

43:5 the glory...filled the temple. The future kingdom glory of God will fill His temple (Zech. 2:5), as He filled the tabernacle (Ex. 40:34) and later Solomon's temple (1 Kin. 8:11; Ps. 29:9).

43:7 the place of My throne. The King of Glory (Ps. 24:7-10) claims the millennial temple as His place to dwell. Cf. 1 Chr. 29:23; Zech. 6:13. There will be human, unresurrected people in the kingdom, who entered when Christ returned and destroyed all the wicked. They will worship at this actual temple.

43:8,9 The future temple will be most holy, protected from 1) harlotry such as the Israelites had engaged in (2 Kin. 23:7) and 2) defiling tombs of kings that Israel had allowed in the sacred temple area (Ezek. 21:18).

sumed them in My anger. 9 Now let them
put their harlotry and the carcasses of their
kings far away from Me, and I will dwell in
their midst forever.
10 "Son of man, [r]describe the [5]temple to
the house of Israel, that they may be
ashamed of their iniquities; and let them
measure the pattern. 11 And if they are
ashamed of all that they have done, make
known to them the design of the [6]temple
and its arrangement, its exits and its entrances, its entire design and all its [s]ordi-
nances, all its forms and all its laws. Write
it down in their sight, so that they may
keep its whole design and all its ordinances, and [t]perform them. 12 This *is* the
law of the [7]temple: The whole area surrounding [u]the mountaintop *is* most holy.
Behold, this *is* the law of the temple.

Dimensions of the Altar

13 "These are the measurements of the
[v]altar in cubits [w](the [8]*cubit is* one cubit and
a handbreadth): the base one cubit high
and one cubit wide, with a rim all around
its edge of one span. This *is* the height of
the altar: 14 from the base on the ground to
the lower ledge, two cubits; the width of
the ledge, one cubit; from the smaller ledge
to the larger ledge, four cubits; and the
width of the ledge, *one* cubit. 15 The altar
hearth *is* four cubits high, with four [x]horns
extending upward from the [9]hearth. 16 The
altar hearth *is* twelve cubits long, twelve
wide, [y]square at its four corners; 17 the
ledge, fourteen *cubits* long and fourteen
wide on its four sides, with a rim of half a
cubit around it; its base, one cubit all
around; and [z]its steps face toward the
east."

Consecrating the Altar

18 And He said to me, "Son of man, thus
says the Lord GOD: 'These *are* the ordinances for the altar on the day when it is
made, for sacrificing [a]burnt offerings on it,
and for [b]sprinkling blood on it. 19 You shall
give [c]a young bull for a sin offering to [d]the
priests, the Levites, who are of the seed of
[e]Zadok, who approach Me to minister to
Me,' says the Lord GOD. 20 You shall take
some of its blood and put *it* on the four
horns of the altar, on the four corners of the
ledge, and on the rim around it; thus you
shall cleanse it and make atonement for it.
21 Then you shall also take the bull of the
sin offering, and [f]burn it in the appointed
place of the [1]temple, [g]outside the sanctuary. 22 On the second day you shall offer a
kid of the goats without blemish for a sin
offering; and they shall cleanse the altar, as
they cleansed *it* with the bull. 23 When you
have finished cleansing *it*, you shall offer a
young bull without blemish, and a ram
from the flock without blemish. 24 When
you offer them before the LORD, [h]the
priests shall throw salt on them, and they
will offer them up *as* a burnt offering to the
LORD. 25 Every day for [i]seven days you
shall prepare a goat *for* a sin offering; they
shall also prepare a young bull and a ram
from the flock, both without blemish.
26 Seven days they shall make atonement
for the altar and purify it, and so [2]conse-
crate [3]*it*. 27 [j]When these days are over it
shall be, on the eighth day and thereafter,
that the priests shall offer your burnt offerings and your peace offerings on the altar;
and I will [k]accept you,' says the Lord
GOD."

The East Gate and the Prince

44 Then He brought me back to the
outer gate of the sanctuary [a]which
faces toward the east, but it *was* shut.
2 And the LORD said to me, "This gate shall
be shut; it shall not be opened, and no man
shall enter by it, [b]because the LORD God of

10 [r] Ezek. 40:4 [5] Lit. *house*
11 [s] Ezek. 44:5 [t] Ezek. 11:20 [6] Lit. *house*
12 [u] Ezek. 40:2 [7] Lit. *house*
13 [v] Ex. 27:1-8; 2 Chr. 4:1 [w] Ezek. 41:8 [8] A royal cubit of about 21 inches
15 [x] Ex. 27:2; Lev. 9:9; 1 Kin. 1:50 [9] Heb. *ariel*
16 [y] Ex. 27:1
17 [z] Ex. 20:26
18 [a] Ex. 40:29 [b] Lev. 1:5, 11; [Heb. 9:21, 22]
19 [c] Ex. 29:10; Lev. 8:14; Ezek. 45:18, 19 [d] Ezek. 44:15, 16 [e] 1 Kin. 2:35; Ezek. 40:46
21 [f] Ex. 29:14; Lev. 4:12 [g] Heb. 13:11 [1] Lit. *house*
24 [h] Lev. 2:13; Num. 18:19; [Mark 9:49, 50; Col. 4:6]
25 [i] Ex. 29:35; Lev. 8:33
26 [2] Lit. *fill its hands* [3] LXX, Syr. *themselves*
27 [j] Lev. 9:1-4 [k] Ezek. 20:40, 41; [Rom. 12:1; 1 Pet. 2:5]

CHAPTER 44
1 [a] Ezek. 43:1
2 [b] Ezek. 43:2-4

43:10-12 Here is the key to the entire vision of chaps. 40–48. These glorious future plans show how much Israel forfeited by their sins. Every detail should produce repentance in Ezekiel's hearers and readers.

43:13-27 the altar. The measurements of the altar of burnt offering are given in vv. 13-17, then the offerings are described (vv. 18-27). These offerings are not efficacious, nor were the OT sacrifices. They were all symbolic of death for sin. They do not take away sin (cf. Heb. 10:4). They were prospective; these will be retrospective.

43:19 a young bull for a sin offering. Exact offerings, in language just as definitive as the literal descriptions in Moses' day, are also just as literal here. They are of a memorial nature; they are not efficacious any more than OT sacrifices were. As OT sacrifices pointed forward to Christ's death, so these are tangible expressions, not competing with, but pointing back to the value of Christ's completely effective sacrifice, once for all (Heb. 9:28; 10:10). God at that time endorsed OT offerings as tokens of forgiving and cleansing worshipers on the basis and credit of the great Lamb they pointed to, who alone could take away sins (John 1:29). The tangible expressions of worship, which the Israelites for so long failed to offer validly (cf. Is. 1:11-15), will at last be offered acceptably, then with full understanding about the Lamb of God to whom they point. The bread and the cup, which believers today find meaningful, do not compete with Christ's cross but are tangible memorials of its glory. So will these sacrifices be. **seed of Zadok.** Cf. 40:46 and 44:10, and *see notes there.*

43:24 salt. Cf. Lev. 2:13. **burnt offering.** As the sin offering is a part of future millennial worship (v. 19), so there are other offerings also (cf. Lev. 1–7). The burnt offering, denoting full consecration to God is one; the peace offering expressing gratitude for peace with God in covenant bonds is another (v. 27).

43:25 without blemish. Commemorative of Christ's unblemished perfection.

44:1,2 the outer gate...*was* shut. The Lord has returned from the direction in which He departed (10:18,19). It is kept closed, in

Israel has entered by it; therefore it shall be
shut. 3 *As for* the [c]prince, *because* he *is* the
prince, he may sit in it to [d]eat bread before
the LORD; he shall enter by way of the
vestibule of the gateway, and go out the
same way."

Those Admitted to the Temple

4 Also He brought me by way of the
north gate to the front of the [1]temple; so I
looked, and [e]behold, the glory of the LORD
filled the house of the LORD; [f]and I fell on
my face. 5 And the LORD said to me, [g]"Son
of man, [2]mark well, see with your eyes
and hear with your ears, all that I say to
you concerning all the [h]ordinances of the
house of the LORD and all its laws. Mark
well who may enter the house and all who
go out from the sanctuary.
6 "Now say to the [i]rebellious, to the
house of Israel, 'Thus says the Lord GOD:
"O house of Israel, [j]let Us have no more of
all your abominations. 7 [k]When you
brought in [l]foreigners, [m]uncircumcised in
heart and uncircumcised in flesh, to be in
My sanctuary to defile it—My house—and
when you offered [n]My food, [o]the fat and
the blood, then they broke My covenant
because of all your abominations. 8 And
you have not [p]kept charge of My holy
things, but you have set *others* to keep
charge of My sanctuary for you." 9 Thus
says the Lord GOD: [q]"No foreigner, uncircumcised in heart or uncircumcised in
flesh, shall enter My sanctuary, including
any foreigner who *is* among the children of
Israel.

3 [c]Gen. 31:54; Ex. 24:9-11; [1 Cor. 10:18] [d]Ezek. 46:2, 8
4 [e]Is. 6:3; Ezek. 3:23; 43:5 [f]Ezek. 1:28; 43:3 [1]Lit. *house*
5 [g]Deut. 32:46; Ezek. 40:4 [h]Deut. 12:32; Ezek. 43:10, 11 [2]Lit. *set your heart*
6 [i]Ezek. 2:5 [j]Ezek. 45:9; 1 Pet. 4:3
7 [k]Ezek. 43:8; Acts 21:28 [l]Lev. 22:25 [m]Lev. 26:41; Deut. 10:16; Jer. 4:4; 9:26; [Acts 7:51] [n]Lev. 21:17 [o]Lev. 3:16
8 [p]Lev. 22:2; Num. 18:7
9 [q]Ezek. 44:7; Joel 3:17; Zech. 14:21
10 [r]2 Kin. 23:8; Ezek. 48:11
11 [s]1 Chr. 26:1-19 [t]2 Chr. 29:34; 30:17 [u]Num. 16:9
12 [v]Is. 9:16; Mal. 2:8 [w]Ps. 106:26 [3]Lit. *became a stumbling block of iniquity to the house of Israel*
13 [x]Num. 18:3; 2 Kin. 23:9 [y]Ezek. 32:30
14 [z]Num. 18:4; 1 Chr. 23:28-32; Ezek. 44:11
15 [a]Ezek. 40:46 [b][1 Sam. 2:35]; 2 Sam. 15:27; Ezek. 43:19; 48:11 [c]Ezek. 44:10 [d]Deut. 10:8 [e]Lev. 3:16, 17; 17:5, 6; Ezek. 44:7
16 [f]Num. 18:5, 7, 8 [g]Ezek. 41:22; Mal. 1:7, 12
17 [h]Ex. 28:39-43; 39:27-29; Rev. 19:8
18 [i]Ex. 28:40; 39:28; Is. 3:20; Ezek. 24:17, 23

Laws Governing Priests

10 [r]"And the Levites who went far from
Me, when Israel went astray, who strayed
away from Me after their idols, they shall
bear their iniquity. 11 Yet they shall be ministers in My sanctuary, [s]*as* gatekeepers of
the house and ministers of the house; [t]they
shall slay the burnt offering and the sacrifice for the people, and [u]they shall stand
before them to minister to them. 12 Because
they ministered to them before their idols
and [v]caused[3] the house of Israel to fall into
iniquity, therefore I have [w]raised My hand
in an oath against them," says the Lord
GOD, "that they shall bear their iniquity.
13 [x]And they shall not come near Me to
minister to Me as priest, nor come near any
of My holy things, nor into the Most Holy
Place; but they shall [y]bear their shame and
their abominations which they have committed. 14 Nevertheless I will make them
[z]keep charge of the temple, for all its work,
and for all that has to be done in it.
15 [a]"But the priests, the Levites, [b]the
sons of Zadok, who kept charge of My
sanctuary [c]when the children of Israel
went astray from Me, they shall come near
Me to minister to Me; and they [d]shall stand
before Me to offer to Me the [e]fat and the
blood," says the Lord GOD. 16 "They shall
[f]enter My sanctuary, and they shall come
near [g]My table to minister to Me, and they
shall keep My charge. 17 And it shall be,
whenever they enter the gates of the inner
court, that [h]they shall put on linen garments; no wool shall come upon them
while they minister within the gates of the
inner court or within the house. 18 [i]They

---

honor of the Lord's glory having returned through it for the millennial worship and indicating that the Lord will not depart again as in chaps. 8–11 (cf. 43:1-5). This eastern gate of the temple should not be confused with the modern sealed eastern gate of the city (cf. 45:6-8).

44:3 the prince...may sit in it. The designation "prince" is used at least 14 times in chaps. 44–47. He is not the Lord Jesus Christ, but someone distinct from Him (cf. "eat bread before the LORD"); he has sins for which he offers sacrifice (45:22), and fathers sons (46:16-18). He cannot enter by the E gate which the Lord used, but he is allowed to come in and go out by the gate's vestibule, and eat bread by the gateway. He cannot perform priestly duties (45:19) as Messiah will (cf. Ps. 110:4; Zech. 6:12,13), and he must worship the Lord (46:2). Most likely "the prince" is one who is neither a priest nor the king, but rather one who administrates the kingdom, representing the King (the Lord Jesus Christ) on one hand, and also the princes (14:8,9) who individually lead the 12 tribes. Possibly, he will be a descendant of David.

44:5-9 Mark well who may enter. Since the Lord's glory fills the temple, it is sanctified (v. 4), and God is particular about what kind of people worship there. Sins of the past, as in chaps. 8–11, must not be repeated and if they are, will exclude their perpetrators from the temple. Only the circumcised in heart may enter (Deut. 30:6; Jer. 4:4; Rom. 2:25-29), whether of Israel or another nation (vv. 7,9). Many other peoples than Jews will go into the kingdom in unresurrected bodies, because they have believed in Jesus Christ and were ready for His coming. They will escape His deadly judgment and populate and reproduce in the 1,000 year kingdom. Such circumcision pertains to a heart which is sincere about removing sin and being devoted to the Lord (cf. Jer. 29:13). In the Millennium, a Jew with an uncircumcised heart will be considered a foreigner (v. 9). "Uncircumcised in flesh" refers to sinners and "foreigner" identifies rejecters of the true God.

44:10 Levites...shall bear their iniquity. God makes distinctions. Levites in the line of those unfaithful in days before the judgment can minister in temple services but they cannot make offerings or enter the Most Holy Place (vv. 11-14). Only Zadok's line can fulfill these ministries (vv. 15,16). The reason for this is the value which God attaches to the faithfulness of Zadok in the past (1 Sam. 2:35; 2 Sam. 15:24ff.; 1 Kin. 1:32-40; 2:26-35). *See note on 40:46.*

44:16 My table. This is the altar of burnt offering (cf. 40:46; 41:22).

44:17-27 it shall be. Various standards govern priestly service, such as moderation (v. 20) and sobriety (v. 21). They will model holy behavior as they teach the people to live their lives set apart to God (vv. 23,24). Minutia about dress (such as forbidding the uncleanness of sweat resulting from wearing wool), marriage (cf. Lev. 21:14), contact with dead bodies, etc. point more naturally to a literal fulfillment than to a generalized blurring of details in a symbolical interpretation.

shall have linen turbans on their heads and
linen trousers on their bodies; they shall
not clothe themselves with *anything that
causes* sweat. **19** When they go out to the
outer court, to the *outer* court to the people,
[j]they shall take off their garments in which
they have ministered, leave them in the
holy chambers, and put on other garments;
and in their holy garments they shall [k]not
sanctify the people.
20 [l]"They shall neither shave their heads,
nor let their hair grow [m]long, but they shall
keep their hair well trimmed. **21** [n]No priest
shall drink wine when he enters the inner
court. **22** They shall not take as wife a
[o]widow or a divorced woman, but take
virgins of the descendants of the house of
Israel, or widows of priests.
23 "And [p]they shall teach My people *the
difference* between the holy and the unholy,
and cause them to [q]discern between the
unclean and the clean. **24** [r]In controversy
they shall stand as judges, *and* judge it according to My judgments. They shall keep
My laws and My statutes in all My appointed meetings, [s]and they shall hallow
My Sabbaths.
25 "They shall not defile *themselves* by
coming near a dead person. Only for father
or mother, for son or daughter, for brother
or unmarried sister may they defile themselves. **26** [t]After he is cleansed, they shall
count seven days for him. **27** And on the
day that he goes to the sanctuary to minister in the sanctuary, [u]he must offer his sin
offering [v]in the inner court," says the Lord
GOD.
28 "It shall be, in regard to their inheritance, *that* I [w]*am* their inheritance. You
shall give them no [x]possession in Israel,
for I *am* their possession. **29** [y]They shall eat
the grain offering, the sin offering, and the
trespass offering; [z]every dedicated thing in
Israel shall be theirs. **30** The [a]best[4] of all
firstfruits of any kind, and every sacrifice
of any kind from all your sacrifices, shall
be the priest's; also you [b]shall give to the
priest the first of your ground meal, [c]to
cause a blessing to rest on your house.
31 The priests shall not eat anything, bird
or beast, that [d]died naturally or was torn
by wild beasts.

The Holy District

45 "Moreover, when you [a]divide the
land by lot into inheritance, you
shall [b]set apart a district for the LORD, a
holy section of the land; its length *shall be*
twenty-five thousand *cubits,* and the width
ten thousand. It *shall be* holy throughout its
territory all around. **2** Of this there shall be
a square plot for the sanctuary, [c]five hundred by five hundred *rods,* with fifty cubits
around it for an open space. **3** So this is the
district you shall measure: twenty-five
thousand *cubits* long and ten thousand
wide; [d]in it shall be the sanctuary, the Most
Holy *Place.* **4** It shall be [e]a holy *section* of the
land, belonging to the priests, the ministers
of the sanctuary, who come near to minister to the LORD; it shall be a place for their
houses and a holy place for the sanctuary.
5 [f]*An area* twenty-five thousand *cubits* long
and ten thousand wide shall belong to the
Levites, the ministers of the [1]temple; they
shall have [g]twenty[2] chambers as a possession.

Properties of the City and the Prince

6 [h]"You shall appoint as the property of
the city *an area* five thousand *cubits* wide
and twenty-five thousand long, adjacent to
the district of the holy *section;* it shall belong to the whole house of Israel.
7 [i]"The prince shall have *a section* on one
side and the other of the holy district and
the city's property; and bordering on the
holy district and the city's property, extending westward on the west side and
eastward on the east side, the length *shall
be* side by side with one of the *tribal* por-

19 [j]Lev. 6:10; 16:4, 23, 24; Ezek. 42:14 [k]Ex. 30:29; Lev. 6:27; Ezek. 46:20; [Matt. 23:17]
20 [l]Lev. 21:5 [m]Num. 6:5
21 [n]Lev. 10:9
22 [o]Lev. 21:7, 13, 14
23 [p]Lev. 10:10, 11; Ezek. 22:26; Hos. 4:6; Mic. 3:9-11; Zeph. 3:4; Hag. 2:11-13; Mal. 2:6-8 [q]Lev. 20:25
24 [r]Deut. 17:8, 9; 1 Chr. 23:4; 2 Chr. 19:8-10 [s]Ezek. 22:26
26 [t]Num. 6:10; 19:11, 13-19
27 [u]Lev. 5:3, 6; Num. 6:9-11 [v]Ezek. 44:17
28 [w]Num. 18:20; Deut. 10:9; 18:1, 2; Josh. 13:14, 33 [x]Ezek. 45:4
29 [y]Lev. 7:6 [z]Lev. 27:21, 28; Num. 18:14
30 [a]Ex. 13:2; 22:29; 23:19; Num. 3:13; 18:12 [4]Lit. *first*
[b]Num. 15:20; Neh. 10:37 [c]Prov. 3:9; [Mal. 3:10]
31 [d]Ex. 22:31; Lev. 22:8; Deut. 14:21; Ezek. 4:14

CHAPTER 45

1 [a]Num. 26:52-56; Ezek. 47:22 [b]Ezek. 48:8, 9
2 [c]Ezek. 42:20
3 [d]Ezek. 48:10
4 [e]Ezek. 48:10, 11
5 [f]Ezek. 48:13 [g]Ezek. 40:17 [1]Lit. *house* [2]So with MT, Tg., Vg.; LXX *a possession, cities of dwelling*
6 [h]Ezek. 48:15
7 [i]Ezek. 48:21

44:28-31 I *am* their possession. As the priests had no possession in the Land when it was originally apportioned, so in the future God will be their portion.

45:1-5 a district for the LORD. This sacred land, set apart at the heart (center) of Palestine, is separate from allotments designated for various tribes, seven to the N and five to the S (cf. chap. 48). Though the whole earth is the Lord's (Ps. 24:1), this area is meaningful to Him in a special sense, as providing for special purposes which 45:2-8 goes on to define. This holy rectangle (8.5 mi. by 3.3 mi.) (vv. 1,3) corresponds to 48:8-22, which describes this portion as between Judah to the N and Benjamin to the S extending from the Mediterranean E to the eastern border. It is the area for the priestly homes (v. 4) particularly, but is also for the benefit of all worshipers.

45:2 a…plot for the sanctuary. At the heart of the special allotment is the temple area (48:10), which serves all Israelite tribes, and also is the worship center for those of the whole world, who visit (Is. 4:2,3; Zech. 14:16-19). It is one mi. square (cf. 42:15-20). As a center, not only for those in Palestine but for the world, the area is appropriately larger than past temples that served Israel.

45:5 to the Levites. Distinct from the land devoted to temple and priestly homes is another portion for Levites, who assist in temple service. This portion is also about 8.5 x 3.3 mi. and lies N of the temple/priest allotment. Cf. 48:13,14 for more details.

45:6 property of the city. On the S of the central sanctuary plot is the city of Jerusalem with an area of about 8.5 x 1.65 mi. Cf. 48:15-20 for more details.

45:7 The prince shall have *a section*. *See note on 44:3.* This administrator of the kingdom under Christ will have his territory in two parts, one to the W and the other to the E of the temple/priest and city portions in vv. 1-6. Cf. 48:21,22 for more details.

tions, from the west border to the east border. 8 The land shall be his possession in Israel; and [j]My princes shall no more oppress My people, but they shall give *the rest*
of the land to the house of Israel, according
to their tribes."

Laws Governing the Prince

9 'Thus says the Lord GOD: [k]"Enough, O
princes of Israel! [l]Remove violence and
plundering, execute justice and righteousness, and stop dispossessing My people,"
says the Lord GOD. 10 "You shall have
[m]honest scales, an honest ephah, and an
honest bath. 11 The ephah and the bath
shall be of the same measure, so that the
bath contains one-tenth of a homer, and
the ephah one-tenth of a homer; their measure shall be according to the homer.
12 The [n]shekel *shall be* twenty gerahs;
twenty shekels, twenty-five shekels, *and*
fifteen shekels shall be your mina.

13 "This *is* the offering which you shall
offer: you shall give one-sixth of an ephah
from a homer of wheat, and one-sixth of an
ephah from a homer of barley. 14 The ordinance concerning oil, the bath of oil, *is* one-
tenth of a bath from a kor. A kor *is* a homer
or ten baths, for ten baths *are* a homer.
15 And one lamb shall be given from a flock

8 [j] [Is. 11:3-5]; Jer. 22:17; Ezek. 22:27
9 [k] Ezek. 44:6 [l] Jer. 22:3; Zech. 8:16
10 [m] Lev. 19:36; Deut. 25:15; Prov. 16:11; Amos 8:4-6; Mic. 6:10, 11
12 [n] Ex. 30:13; Lev. 27:25; Num. 3:47

45:8 My princes shall no more oppress. God pledges a kingdom era free from civil leaders selfishly taking advantage of the people, i.e., seizing their land (cf. 22:27; 1 Kin. 21; Num. 36:7-9; Is. 5:8; Hos. 5:10; Mic. 2:1,2). The princes most likely are the leaders of each tribe. No one will be deprived of his possession under Messiah's rule.

45:9-12 The leaders of the land are urged to be thoroughly honest in their commercial dealings. This warning shows that there will be sin in the Millennium. The believing Jews who entered the 1,000 year reign of Christ on earth and inherited the promised kingdom will be fully human and capable of such sins. There also will be children who do not necessarily believe, as the final rebellion against King Messiah and His temple proves (cf. Rev. 20:7-9).

45:10 scales. Relates to selling by weight. **ephah.** Relates to selling by dry volume. **bath.** Relates to selling by liquid volume.

45:11 ephah. About .75 bu. **bath.** About 6 gal. **homer.** In liquid volume about 60 gal. and in dry volume about 7.5 bu.

45:12 shekel. By weight about .4 oz. made up of 20 gerahs (.02 oz./each). Sixty shekels (20+25+15) equal a "mina" or about 24 oz. (1.5 lbs.).

45:13-17 Here are the offerings for Israel's prince (v. 16). Because of what the people will give him, he will provide for public sacrifices (v. 17).

45:13 They will give 1/60th of their grain.

45:14 kor. *See note on homer in 45:11.* They will give one percent of their oil.

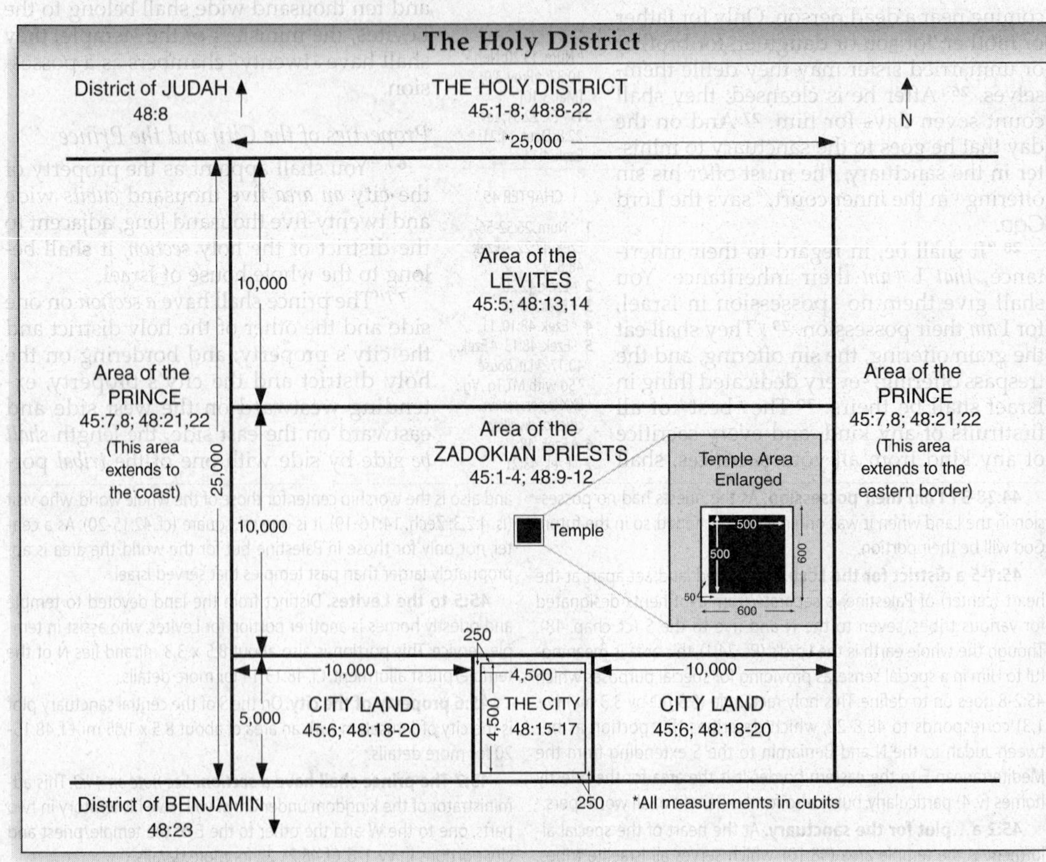

of two hundred, from the rich pastures of
Israel. These shall be for grain offerings,
burnt offerings, and peace offerings, [o]to
make atonement for them," says the Lord
GOD. 16 "All the people of the land shall
give this offering for the prince in Israel.
17 Then it shall be the [p]prince's part *to give*
burnt offerings, grain offerings, and drink
offerings, at the feasts, the New Moons, the
Sabbaths, and at all the appointed seasons
of the house of Israel. He shall prepare the
sin offering, the grain offering, the burnt offering, and the peace offerings to make
atonement for the house of Israel."

Keeping the Feasts

18 'Thus says the Lord GOD: "In the first
month, on the first *day* of the month, you
shall take a young bull without blemish
and [q]cleanse the sanctuary. 19 [r]The priest
shall take some of the blood of the sin offering and put *it* on the doorposts of the
[3]temple, on the four corners of the ledge of
the altar, and on the gateposts of the gate
of the inner court. 20 And so you shall do
on the seventh *day* of the month [s]for everyone who has sinned unintentionally or in
ignorance. Thus you shall make atonement
for the temple.
21 [t]"In the first *month,* on the fourteenth
day of the month, you shall observe the
Passover, a feast of seven days; unleavened
bread shall be eaten. 22 And on that day the
prince shall prepare for himself and for all
the people of the land [u]a bull *for* a sin offering. 23 On the [v]seven days of the feast he
shall prepare a burnt offering to the LORD,
seven bulls and seven rams without blemish, daily for seven days, [w]and a kid of the
goats daily *for* a sin offering. 24 [x]And he
shall prepare a grain offering of one ephah
for each bull and one ephah for each ram,
together with a hin of oil for each ephah.
25 "In the seventh *month,* on the fifteenth
day of the month, at the [y]feast, he shall do
likewise for seven days, according to the
sin offering, the burnt offering, the grain
offering, and the oil."

The Manner of Worship

46 'Thus says the Lord GOD: "The gateway of the inner court that faces toward the east shall be shut the six [a]work-
ing days; but on the Sabbath it shall be
opened, and on the day of the New Moon

15 [o]Lev. 1:4; 6:30
17 [p]Ezek. 46:4-12
18 [q]Lev. 16:16, 33; Ezek. 43:22, 26
19 [r]Lev. 16:18-20; Ezek. 43:20 [3]Lit. *house*
20 [s]Lev. 4:27; Ps. 19:12
21 [t]Ex. 12:18; Lev. 23:5, 6; Num. 9:2, 3; 28:16, 17; Deut. 16:1
22 [u]Lev. 4:14
23 [v]Lev. 23:8 [w]Num. 28:15, 22, 30; 29:5, 11, 16, 19
24 [x]Num. 28:12-15; Ezek. 46:5, 7
25 [y]Lev. 23:34; Num. 29:12; Deut. 16:13; 2 Chr. 5:3; 7:8, 10

CHAPTER 46

1 [a]Ex. 20:9

45:15 They will give one lamb for every 200 in the flocks or one-half of one percent.

45:16,17 prince. *See note on 44:3.*

45:17 feasts...New Moons...Sabbaths...appointed seasons. These will be discussed in notes on 45:18–46:15.

45:18-25 The annual feasts for the nations are outlined. The millennial feasts include 3 of the 6 Levitical feasts: 1) Passover; 2) Unleavened Bread; and 3) Tabernacles. Three Levitical feasts are not celebrated: 1) Pentecost; 2) Trumpets; and 3) Atonement. Most likely they are excluded because what they had looked forward to prophetically have been fulfilled and now serve no significant remembrance purpose such as Passover and Tabernacle will continue to provide.

45:18-20 atonement. The day of atonement is never mentioned, but God institutes a never-before-celebrated festival to start the "new year" with an emphasis on holiness in the temple. The first month, Abib, would be in Mar./Apr. The feast appears to last 7 days (v. 20). It indicates that there will be sin in the kingdom, committed by those who entered alive and their offspring.

45:21-24. Passover and Unleavened Bread are combined as in the NT and focus on remembering God's deliverance of the nation from Egypt and Christ's death providing deliverance from sin. They continue on into the Millennium as a week long feast of remembrance, which will serve much the same purpose then as the bread and cup do now (cf. Ex. 12–15 for details). The 3 annual pilgrimage feasts with required attendance under Mosaic legislation were: 1) Unleavened Bread, 2) Pentecost, and 3) Tabernacles (cf. Ex. 23:14-17; Num. 28:16–29:40; Deut. 16:1-17). They have been modified with the 3 in 45:18-25. Pentecost is replaced by the new feast of vv. 18-20. There are also portion differences from the Mosaic law (cf. Num. 28:19-21), plus the millennial offerings are richer and more abundant, in general.

45:22,23 the prince. *See note on 44:3.* Here he sacrifices for his own sin.

45:24 hin. About one gal.

45:25 The Feast of Tabernacles continues on into the Millennium as confirmed by Zech. 14:16-21. This would be a remembrance of God's sustaining provision in the wilderness. The seventh month, Tishri, would be in Sep./Oct. and this feast will last for one week, as do the previous two. The prince ("he," v. 25) once again offers sacrifice.

46:1-15 This section further discusses offerings and deals with: 1) Sabbath and New Moon (vv. 1-8); 2) appointed feast days (9-11); 3) voluntary offerings (v. 12); and 4) daily sacrifices (vv. 13-15). Cf. Num. 28:1-15 for a summary of former Mosaic details.

46:1 The gateway...shall be shut. Shutting the gate 6 days seems to serve the purpose of giving special distinction to the Sabbath and New Moon, when it is open and in use. Israel largely failed

Millennial Feasts

Levitical	Millennial
1. N/A	1. New Year—Ezek. 45:18-20
2. Passover—Lev. 23:5	2. Passover—Ezek. 45:21-24
3. Unleavened Bread—Lev. 23:6-8	3. Unleavened Bread—Ezek. 45:21-24
4. Pentecost—Lev. 23:9-22	4. N/A
5. Trumpets—Lev. 23:23-25	5. N/A
6. Atonement—Lev. 23:26-32	6. N/A
7. Tabernacles—Lev. 23:33-44	7. Tabernacles—Ezek. 45:25

it shall be opened. **2** [b]The prince shall enter
by way of the vestibule of the gateway
from the outside, and stand by the
gatepost. The priests shall prepare his
burnt offering and his peace offerings. He
shall worship at the threshold of the gate.
Then he shall go out, but the gate shall not
be shut until evening. **3** Likewise the people of the land shall worship at the entrance to this gateway before the LORD on
the Sabbaths and the New Moons. **4** The
burnt offering that [c]the prince offers to the
LORD on the [d]Sabbath day *shall be* six lambs
without blemish, and a ram without blemish; **5** [e]and the grain offering *shall be one*
ephah for a ram, and the grain offering for
the lambs, [1]as much as he wants to give, as
well as a hin of oil with every ephah. **6** On
the day of the New Moon *it shall be* a
young bull without blemish, six lambs,
and a ram; they shall be without blemish.
7 He shall prepare a grain offering of an
ephah for a bull, an ephah for a ram, [2]as
much as he wants to give for the lambs,
and a hin of oil with every ephah. **8** [f]When
the prince enters, he shall go in by way of
the vestibule of the gateway, and go out
the same way.

9 "But when the people of the land
[g]come before the LORD on the appointed
feast days, whoever enters by way of the
north [h]gate to worship shall go out by way
of the south gate; and whoever enters by
way of the south gate shall go out by way
of the north gate. He shall not return by
way of the gate through which he came,
but shall go out through the opposite gate.
10 The prince shall then be in their midst.
When they go in, he shall go in; and when
they go out, he shall go out. **11** At the festivals and the appointed feast days [i]the
grain offering shall be an ephah for a bull,
an ephah for a ram, as much as he wants to
give for the lambs, and a hin of oil with
every ephah.

12 "Now when the prince makes a voluntary burnt offering or voluntary peace
offering to the LORD, the gate that faces toward the east [j]shall then be opened for
him; and he shall prepare his burnt offering and his peace offerings as he did on the
Sabbath day. Then he shall go out, and
after he goes out the gate shall be shut.

13 [k]"You shall daily make a burnt offering to the LORD *of* a lamb of the first year
without blemish; you shall prepare it
[3]every morning. **14** And you shall prepare a
grain offering with it every morning, a
sixth of an ephah, and a third of a hin of oil
to moisten the fine flour. This grain offering
is a perpetual ordinance, to be made regularly to the LORD. **15** Thus they shall prepare
the lamb, the grain offering, and the oil, *as*
a [l]regular burnt offering every morning."

The Prince and Inheritance Laws

16 'Thus says the Lord GOD: "If the
prince gives a gift *of some* of his inheritance
to any of his sons, it shall belong to his
sons; it is their possession by inheritance.
17 But if he gives a gift of some of his inheritance to one of his servants, it shall be
his until [m]the year of liberty, after which it
shall return to the prince. But his inheritance shall belong to his sons; it shall become theirs. **18** Moreover [n]the prince shall
not take any of the people's inheritance by
evicting them from their property; he shall
provide an inheritance for his sons from
his own property, so that none of My people may be scattered from his property." ' "

How the Offerings Were Prepared

19 Now he brought me through the entrance, which *was* at the side of the gate,
into the holy [o]chambers of the priests

2 [b] Ezek. 44:3
4 [c] Ezek. 45:17 [d] Num. 28:9, 10
5 [e] Num. 28:12; Ezek. 45:24; 46:7, 11 [1] Lit. *the gift of his hand*
7 [2] Lit. *as much as his hand can reach*
8 [f] Ezek. 44:3; 46:2
9 [g] Ex. 23:14-17; 34:23; Deut. 16:16, 17; Ps. 84:7; Mic. 6:6 [h] Ezek. 48:31, 33
11 [i] Ezek. 46:5, 7
12 [j] Ezek. 44:3; 46:1, 2, 8
13 [k] Ex. 29:38; Num. 28:3-5 [3] Lit. *morning by morning*
15 [l] Ex. 29:42; Num. 28:6
17 [m] Lev. 25:10
18 [n] Ezek. 45:8
19 [o] Ezek. 42:13

and was judged in ancient times in regard to these days (Jer. 17:22-27; cf. 2 Chr. 36:21). The Sabbath will be reinstated for a restored and regenerated Israel. Note here that modern day sabbatarians fail to realize that the Sabbath consisted of far more than just rest from labor, but included specific sacrifices. It is inconsistent to take one part of the Sabbath observance and discard the others.

46:2 The prince. *See note on 44:3.* He appears 5 times (vv. 2,4,8,10,12) in regard to sacrifices. He is to be an example of spiritual integrity to the people (cf. v. 10).

46:6,7 New Moon. Israel's calendar was lunar, so the feasts were reckoned according the phases of the moon.

46:8 When the prince enters. He does not normally use the eastern gate itself, which is for the Lord (44:2). Rather, he enters and exits by the gate's vestibule. However, v. 12 permits his use of the gate for free will offerings.

46:9 the people. The people's entrance and exit for temple worship is to be done in an orderly flow to prevent congestion, since all will be present (cf. Deut. 16:16).

46:10-12 The prince. He sets the example of worship for the people.

46:13-15 daily. The testimony of the OT is that to remove the continual burnt offering meant an abolition of public worship (cf. Dan. 8:11-13; 11:31; 12:11).

46:16,17 a gift. This explains inheritance laws governing the prince. A gift to one of his sons is permanent (v. 16), but a gift to a servant lasts only to the year of Jubilee, the 50th year (cf. Lev. 25:10-13), and then returns to him (v. 17).

46:17 the year of liberty. The year of Jubilee.

46:18 the prince shall not take any…inheritance. As in 45:8,9, the prince is not to confiscate others' property to enlarge his own holdings, as often occurred in Israel's history when rulers became rich by making others poor (cf. 1 Kin. 21).

46:19-24 chambers. The priests' kitchen chambers are convenient for managing their parts of the offerings and cooking sacrificial meals for worshipers, possibly close to the inner E gate. The "ministers of the temple" (v. 24) are not the priests, but temple servants.

which face toward the north; and there a place *was* situated at their extreme western end. 20 And he said to me, "This *is* the place where the priests shall [p]boil the trespass offering and the sin offering, *and* where they shall [q]bake the grain offering, so that they do not bring *them* out into the outer court [r]to sanctify the people."

21 Then he brought me out into the outer court and caused me to pass by the four corners of the court; and in fact, in every corner of the court *there was another* court. 22 In the four corners of the court *were* enclosed courts, forty *cubits* long and thirty wide; all four corners *were* the same size. 23 *There was* a row *of building stones* all around in them, all around the four of them; and [4]cooking hearths were made under the rows of stones all around. 24 And he said to me, "These *are* the [5]kitchens where the ministers of the [6]temple shall [s]boil the sacrifices of the people."

The Healing Waters and Trees

47 Then he brought me back to the door of the [1]temple; and there was [a]water, flowing from under the threshold of the temple toward the east, for the front of the temple faced east; the water was flowing from under the right side of the temple, south of the altar. 2 He brought me out by way of the north gate, and led me around on the outside to the outer gateway that faces [b]east; and there was water, running out on the right side.

3 And when [c]the man went out to the east with the line in his hand, he measured one thousand cubits, and he brought me through the waters; the water *came up to my* ankles. 4 Again he measured one thousand and brought me through the waters; the water *came up to my* knees. Again he measured one thousand and brought me through; the water *came up to my* waist. 5 Again he measured one thousand, *and it was* a river that I could not cross; for the water was too deep, water in which one must swim, a river that could not be crossed. 6 He said to me, "Son of man, have you seen *this?*" Then he brought me and returned me to the bank of the river.

7 When I returned, there, along the bank of the river, *were* very many [d]trees on one side and the other. 8 Then he said to me: "This water flows toward the eastern region, goes down into the [2]valley, and enters the sea. *When it* reaches the sea, *its* waters are healed. 9 And it shall be *that* every living thing that moves, wherever [3]the rivers go, will live. There will be a very great multitude of fish, because these waters go there; for they will be healed, and everything will live wherever the river goes. 10 It shall be *that* fishermen will stand by it from En Gedi to En Eglaim; they will be *places* for spreading their nets. Their fish will be of the same kinds as the fish [e]of the Great Sea, exceedingly many. 11 But its swamps and marshes will not be healed; they will be given over to salt. 12 [f]Along the bank of the river, on this side and that, will grow all *kinds of* trees used for food; [g]their leaves will not wither, and their fruit will not fail. They will bear fruit every month, because their water flows from the sanctuary. Their fruit will be for food, and their leaves for [h]medicine."[4]

Borders of the Land

13 Thus says the Lord GOD: "These *are* the [i]borders by which you shall divide the

20 [p] 2 Chr. 35:13 [q] Lev. 2:4, 5, 7 [r] Ezek. 44:19
23 [4] Lit. *boiling places*
24 [s] Ezek. 46:20 [5] Lit. *house of those who boil* [6] Lit. *house*

CHAPTER 47

1 [a] Ps. 46:4; Is. 30:25; 55:1; [Jer. 2:13]; Joel 3:18; Zech. 13:1; 14:8; [Rev. 22:1, 17] [1] Lit. *house*
2 [b] Ezek. 44:1, 2
3 [c] Ezek. 40:3
7 [d] [Is. 60:13, 21; 61:3; Ezek. 47:12; Rev. 22:2]
8 [2] Or *Arabah*, the Jordan Valley
9 [3] Lit. *two rivers*
10 [e] Num. 34:3; Josh. 23:4; Ezek. 48:28
12 [f] Ezek. 47:7; [Rev. 22:2] [g] Job 18:16; [Ps. 1:3; Jer. 17:8] [h] [Rev. 22:2] [4] Or *healing*
13 [i] Num. 34:1-29

47:1-12 This section reinforces the constant emphasis of the prophets that in the final kingdom amazing physical and geographical changes will occur on the earth, and especially the land of Israel. This chap. deals mainly with changes in the water.

47:1,2 water, flowing...east. A stream of water flows up from underneath the temple (cf. Joel 3:18), going E to the Jordan, then curving S through the Dead Sea area (vv. 7,8). Zechariah 14:8 refers to this stream as flowing from Jerusalem to the W (Mediterranean Sea) as well as to the E (Dead Sea). Its origin coincides with Christ's Second Advent arrival on the Mt. of Olives (cf. Zech. 14:4; Acts 1:11), which will trigger a massive earthquake, thus creating a vast E-W valley running through Jerusalem and allowing for the water flow. *See note on Zech. 14:3,4.*

47:3-5 he measured. The escorting angel, wanting to reveal the size of the river, took Ezekiel, in the vision, to four different distances from the temple, where the stream was found to be at increasing depths until it was over his head. Cf. Is. 35:1-7, where the prophet says the "desert will blossom like a rose."

47:7 very many trees. Lush growth from the river.

47:8 waters are healed. The flow E, then S, runs into the Dead Sea and renders good the salty water (more than 6 times as salty as the sea) that formerly would not support life because of its high mineral content. The Dead Sea is transformed into a "living sea" of fresh water.

47:9 multitude of fish. These fish are said to be the same kinds in the Mediterranean (v. 10), probably referring to volume rather than species, since the river and the Dead Sea are fresh water.

47:10 En Gedi. The site is on the Dead Sea's W bank, about halfway along its length, near Masada. **En Eglaim.** Possibly it is Ein-Feska near Qumran at the northwestern extremity of the sea. Some argue for a site on the E bank, so that fishermen on both sides are in view.

47:11 swamps and marshes. This could supply salt for the temple offerings (cf. 43:24), as well as for food.

47:12 all *kinds of* trees. Cf. v. 7. The scene describes the blessing of returning to Eden-like abundance (Gen. 2:8,9,16). **leaves...fruit.** Cf. v. 7. The fruit is for food and the leaves serve a medicinal purpose, probably both in preventative and corrective senses. The fruit is perpetual, kept so by a continual and lavish supply of spring water from the temple.

47:13-23 These *are* the borders. The picture is that of an enlarged Canaan for all to inhabit. The boundaries are substantially

land as an inheritance among the twelve
tribes of Israel. [j]Joseph *shall have two* portions. 14 You shall inherit it equally with
one another; for I [k]raised My hand in an
oath to give it to your fathers, and this land
shall [l]fall to you as your inheritance.
15 "This *shall be* the border of the land on
the north: from the Great Sea, *by* [m]the road
to Hethlon, as one goes to [n]Zedad,
16 [o]Hamath, [p]Berothah, Sibraim (which *is*
between the border of Damascus and the
border of Hamath), to Hazar Hatticon
(which *is* on the border of Hauran). 17 Thus
the boundary shall be from the Sea to
[q]Hazar Enan, the border of Damascus; and
as for the north, northward, it is the border
of Hamath. *This is* the north side.
18 "On the east side you shall mark out
the border from between Hauran and Damascus, and between Gilead and the land
of Israel, along the Jordan, and along the
eastern side of the sea. *This is* the east side.
19 "The south side, toward the [5]South,
shall be from Tamar to [r]the waters of [6]Meri-
bah by Kadesh, along the brook to the
Great Sea. *This is* the south side, toward the
South.
20 "The west side *shall be* the Great Sea,
from the *southern* boundary until one
comes to a point opposite Hamath. This *is*
the west side.
21 "Thus you shall [s]divide this land
among yourselves according to the tribes
of Israel. 22 It shall be that you will divide
it by [t]lot as an inheritance for yourselves,
[u]and for the strangers who dwell among
you and who bear children among you.
[v]They shall be to you as native-born
among the children of Israel; they shall
have an inheritance with you among the
tribes of Israel. 23 And it shall be *that* in
whatever tribe the stranger dwells, there
you shall give *him* his inheritance," says
the Lord GOD.

Division of the Land

48 "Now these *are* the names of the
tribes: [a]From the northern border
along the road to Hethlon at the entrance
of Hamath, to Hazar Enan, the border of
Damascus northward, in the direction of
Hamath, *there shall be* one *section for* [b]Dan
from its east to its west side; 2 by the border of Dan, from the east side to the west,
one *section for* [c]Asher; 3 by the border of
Asher, from the east side to the west, one
section for [d]Naphtali; 4 by the border of
Naphtali, from the east side to the west,
one *section for* [e]Manasseh; 5 by the border

13 [j]Gen. 48:5; 1 Chr. 5:1; Ezek. 48:4, 5
14 [k]Gen. 12:7; 13:15; 15:7; 17:8; 26:3; 28:13; Deut. 1:8; Ezek. 20:5, 6, 28, 42 [l]Ezek. 48:29
15 [m]Ezek. 48:1 [n]Num. 34:7, 8
16 [o]Num. 34:8 [p]2 Sam. 8:8
17 [q]Num. 34:9; Ezek. 48:1
19 [r]Num. 20:13; Deut. 32:51; Ps. 81:7; Ezek. 48:28 [5]Heb. *Negev* [6]Lit. *Strife*

21 [s]Ezek. 45:1
22 [t]Num. 26:55, 56 [u][Eph. 3:6; Rev. 7:9, 10] [v][Acts 11:18; 15:9; Gal. 3:28; Eph. 2:12-14; Col. 3:11]

CHAPTER 48

1 [a]Ezek. 47:15 [b]Josh. 19:40-48
2 [c]Josh. 19:24-31
3 [d]Josh. 19:32-39
4 [e]Josh. 13:29-31; 17:1-11, 17, 18

larger than those given to Moses in Num. 34:1-15. Palestine, promised in God's covenant with Abraham (v. 14; Gen. 12:7), has specific geographical limits within which Israel will finally occupy tribal areas which differ from the occupation in Joshua's day (cf. Josh. 13–22). This is the complete fulfillment of the promise of the land in the Abrahamic Covenant.

47:13 Joseph...*two* portions. This is in keeping with the promise of Jacob to Joseph (Gen. 48:5,6,22; 49:22-26).

47:15-20 The borders of the millennial Promised Land are described 1) to the N (vv. 15-17), 2) to the E (v. 18); 3) to the S (v. 19); and 4) to the W (v. 20).

47:22 bear children. This reminds us that children will be born all through the 1,000 year rule of Messiah. Not all will believe and be saved, as evidenced by the final rebellion (cf. Rev. 20:8,9).

47:23 stranger. This provision is in keeping with Lev. 19:34.

48:1-7,23-29 the tribes. The land pledged to each tribe within the total area described in 47:13-23 fulfills God's promises to actually restore Israel's people from around the world to the Promised Land just as they were actually scattered from it (28:25,26; 34–37; 39:21-29; Jer. 31:33). Dan is first mentioned. Though omitted from the 144,000 in Rev. 7, probably because of severe idolatry, Dan is restored in grace.

The millennial allotments of land to the tribes of Israel.

of Manasseh, from the east side to the
west, one *section for* [f]Ephraim; 6 by the border of Ephraim, from the east side to the
west, one *section for* [g]Reuben; 7 by the border of Reuben, from the east side to the
west, one *section for* [h]Judah; 8 by the border
of Judah, from the east side to the west,
shall be [i]the district which you shall set
apart, twenty-five thousand *cubits* in
width, and *in* length the same as one of the
other portions, from the east side to the
west, with the [j]sanctuary in the center.
9 "The district that you shall set apart for
the LORD *shall be* twenty-five thousand *cubits* in length and ten thousand in width.
10 To these—to the priests—the holy district shall belong: on the north twenty-five
thousand *cubits in length,* on the west ten
thousand in width, on the east ten thousand in width, and on the south twenty-
five thousand in length. The sanctuary of
the LORD shall be in the center. 11 [k]*It shall be*
for the priests of the sons of Zadok, who
are sanctified, who have kept My charge,
who did not go astray when the children of
Israel went astray, [l]as the Levites went
astray. 12 And *this* district of land that is set
apart shall be to them a thing most [m]holy
by the border of the Levites.
13 "Opposite the border of the priests,
the [n]Levites *shall have an area* twenty-five
thousand *cubits* in length and ten thousand
in width; its entire length *shall be* twenty-
five thousand and its width ten thousand.
14 [o]And they shall not sell or exchange any
of it; they may not alienate this best *part* of
the land, for *it is* holy to the LORD.
15 [p]"The five thousand *cubits* in width
that remain, along the edge of the twenty-
five thousand, shall be [q]for general use by
the city, for dwellings and common-land;
and the city shall be in the center. 16 These
shall be its measurements: the north side
four thousand five hundred *cubits,* the
south side four thousand five hundred, the
east side four thousand five hundred, and
the west side four thousand five hundred.
17 The common-land of the city shall be: to
the north two hundred and fifty *cubits,* to
the south two hundred and fifty, to the east
two hundred and fifty, and to the west two
hundred and fifty. 18 The rest of the length,
alongside the district of the holy *section,*
shall be ten thousand *cubits* to the east and
ten thousand to the west. It shall be adjacent to the district of the holy *section,* and
its produce shall be food for the workers of
the city. 19 [r]The workers of the city, from all
the tribes of Israel, shall cultivate it. 20 The
entire district *shall be* twenty-five thousand
cubits by twenty-five thousand *cubits,*
foursquare. You shall set apart the holy
district with the property of the city.
21 [s]"The rest *shall belong* to the prince, on
one side and on the other of the holy district and of the city's property, next to the
twenty-five thousand *cubits* of the *holy* district as far as the eastern border, and westward next to the twenty-five thousand as
far as the western border, adjacent to the
tribal portions; *it shall belong* to the prince.
It shall be the holy district, [t]and the sanctuary of the [1]temple *shall be* in the center.
22 Moreover, apart from the possession of
the Levites and the possession of the city
which are in the midst of what *belongs* to the
prince, *the area* between the border of Judah and the border of [u]Benjamin shall belong to the prince.
23 "As for the rest of the tribes, from the
east side to the west, Benjamin *shall have*
one *section;* 24 by the border of Benjamin,
from the east side to the west, [v]Simeon
shall have one *section;* 25 by the border of
Simeon, from the east side to the west,
[w]Issachar *shall have* one *section;* 26 by the
border of Issachar, from the east side to the
west, [x]Zebulun *shall have* one *section;* 27 by
the border of Zebulun, from the east side
to the west, [y]Gad *shall have* one *section;*
28 by the border of Gad, on the south side,
toward the [2]South, the border shall be
from Tamar *to* [z]the waters of [3]Meribah *by*
Kadesh, along the brook to the [a]Great Sea.
29 [b]This *is* the land which you shall divide
by lot as an inheritance among the tribes of
Israel, and these *are* their portions," says
the Lord GOD.

The Gates of the City and Its Name

30 "These *are* the exits of the city. On the
north side, measuring four thousand five
hundred *cubits* 31 [c](the gates of the city
shall be named after the tribes of Israel), the
three gates northward: one gate for Reuben, one gate for Judah, and one gate for
Levi; 32 on the east side, four thousand five
hundred *cubits,* three gates: one gate for Joseph, one gate for Benjamin, and one gate
for Dan; 33 on the south side, measuring

5 [f]Josh. 16:5-10; 17:8-10, 14-18
6 [g]Josh. 13:15-23
7 [h]Josh. 15:1-63; 19:9
8 [i]Ezek. 45:1-6 [j][Is. 12:6; 33:20-22]; Ezek. 45:3, 4
11 [k]Ezek. 40:46; 44:15 [l]Ezek. 44:10, 12
12 [m]Ezek. 45:4
13 [n]Ezek. 45:5
14 [o]Ex. 22:29; Lev. 27:10, 28, 33; Ezek. 44:30
15 [p]Ezek. 45:6 [q]Ezek. 42:20
19 [r]Ezek. 45:6
21 [s]Ezek. 34:24; 45:7; 48:22 [t]Ezek. 48:8, 10 [1]Lit. *house*
22 [u]Josh. 18:21-28
24 [v]Josh. 19:1-9
25 [w]Josh. 19:17-23
26 [x]Josh. 19:10-16
27 [y]Josh. 13:24-28
28 [z]Gen. 14:7; 2 Chr. 20:2; Ezek. 47:19 [a]Ezek. 47:10, 15, 19, 20 [2]Heb. *Negev* [3]Lit. *Strife*
29 [b]Ezek. 47:14, 21, 22
31 [c][Rev. 21:10-14]

48:8-22 the district. Already described in 45:1-8, this unique area includes land allotment for the sentry and the Zadokian priests (vv. 8-12); the Levites (vv. 13-14); the city (vv. 15-20); and the prince (vv. 21,22).

48:30-35 These *are* the exits. Twelve city gates, 3 in each cardinal direction, bear the names of Israel's tribes, one on each gate.

48:30 four thousand five hundred *cubits*. All 4 sides when added together equal 18,000 cubits (cf. v. 16), which is nearly 6 mi. around. Josephus, a Jewish historian, reported in the first century A.D. that Jerusalem was approximately 4 mi. in perimeter.

four thousand five hundred *cubits,* three
gates: one gate for Simeon, one gate for
Issachar, and one gate for Zebulun; **34** on
the west side, four thousand five hundred
cubits with their three gates: one gate for
Gad, one gate for Asher, and one gate for
Naphtali. **35** All the way around *shall be*
eighteen thousand *cubits;* [d]and the name of
the city from *that* day *shall be:* [e]THE[4] LORD
IS THERE."

35 [d] Jer. 23:6; 33:16 [e] Is. 12:6; 14:32; 24:23; Jer. 3:17; 8:19; 14:9; Ezek. 35:10; Joel 3:21; Zech. 2:10; Rev. 21:3; 22:3 [4] Heb. *YHWH Shammah*

48:35 the name. The city is called YHWH Shammah, "The LORD is There." The departed glory of God (chaps. 8–11) has returned (chaps. 44:1,2), and His dwelling, the temple, is in the very center of the district given over to the Lord. With this final note, all of the unconditional promises which God had made to Israel in the Abrahamic Covenant (Gen. 12); the Levitic Covenant (Num. 25); the Davidic Covenant (2 Sam. 7); and the New Covenant (Jer. 31) have been fulfilled. So this final verse provides the consummation of Israel's history—the returned presence of God!

The Book of DANIEL

Title

According to Hebrew custom, the title is drawn from the prophet who throughout the book received revelations from God. Daniel bridges the entire 70 years of the Babylonian captivity (ca. 605–536 B.C.; cf. 1:1 and 9:1-3). Nine of the 12 chapters relate revelation through dreams/visions. Daniel was God's mouthpiece to the Gentile and Jewish world, declaring God's current and future plans. What Revelation is to the NT prophetically and apocalyptically, Daniel is to the OT.

Author and Date

Several verses indicate that the writer is Daniel (8:15,27; 9:2; 10:2,7; 12:4,5), whose name means "God is my Judge." He wrote in the autobiographical first person from 7:2 on, and is to be distinguished from the other 3 Daniel's of the OT (cf. 1 Chr. 3:1; Ezra 8:2; Neh. 10:6). As a teenager, possibly about 15 years old, Daniel was kidnaped from his noble family in Judah and deported to Babylon to be brainwashed into Babylonian culture for the task of assisting in dealing with the imported Jews. There he spent the remainder of a long life (85 years or more). He made the most of the exile, successfully exalting God by his character and service. He quickly rose to the role of statesman by official royal appointment and served as a confidante of kings as well as a prophet in two world empires, i.e., the Babylonian (2:48) and the Medo-Persian (6:1,2). Christ confirmed Daniel as the author of this book (cf. Matt. 24:15).

Daniel lived beyond the time described in Dan. 10:1 (ca. 536 B.C.). It seems most probable that he wrote the book shortly after this date but before ca. 530 B.C. Daniel 2:4b–7:28, which prophetically describes the course of Gentile world history, was originally and appropriately written in Aramaic, the contemporary language of international business. Ezekiel, Habakkuk, Jeremiah, and Zephaniah were Daniel's prophetic contemporaries.

Background and Setting

The book begins in 605 B.C. when Babylon conquered Jerusalem and exiled Daniel, his 3 friends, and others. It continues to the eventual demise of Babylonian supremacy in 539 B.C., when Medo-Persian besiegers conquered Babylon (5:30,31), and goes even beyond that to 536 B.C. (10:1). After Daniel was transported to Babylon, the Babylonian victors conquered Jerusalem in two further stages (597 B.C. and 586 B.C.). In both takeovers, they deported more Jewish captives. Daniel passionately remembered his home, particularly the temple at Jerusalem, almost 70 years after having been taken away from it (6:10).

Daniel's background is alluded to in part by Jeremiah, who names 3 of the last 5 kings in Judah before captivity (cf. Jer. 1:1-3): Josiah (ca. 641–609 B.C.), Jehoiakim (ca. 609–597 B.C.) and Zedekiah (597–586 B.C.). Jehoahaz (ca. 609 B.C.) and Jehoiachin (ca. 598–597 B.C.) are not mentioned (cf. Jeremiah Introduction: Background and Setting). Daniel is also mentioned by Ezekiel (cf. 14:14,20; 28:3) as being righteous and wise. He is alluded to by the writer of Hebrews as one of "…the prophets: who through faith…stopped the mouths of lions" (Heb. 11:32,33).

The long-continued sin of the Judeans without national repentance eventually led to God's judgment for which Jeremiah, Habakkuk, and Zephaniah had given fair warning. Earlier, Isaiah and other faithful prophets of God had also trumpeted the danger. When Assyrian power had ebbed by 625 B.C., the Neo-Babylonians conquered: 1) Assyria with its capital Nineveh in 612 B.C.; 2) Egypt in the following years; and 3) Judah in 605 B.C. when they overthrew Jerusalem in the first of 3 steps (also 597 B.C., 586 B.C.). Daniel was one of the first groups of deportees, and Ezekiel followed in 597 B.C.

Israel of the northern kingdom had earlier fallen to Assyria in 722 B.C. With Judah's captivity, the judgment was complete. In Babylon, Daniel received God's word concerning successive stages of Gentile world domination through the centuries until the greatest Conqueror, Messiah, would put down all Gentile lordship. He then will defeat all foes and raise His covenant people to blessing in His glorious millennial kingdom.

Historical and Theological Themes

Daniel was written to encourage the exiled Jews by revealing God's program for them, both during and after the time of Gentile power in the world. Prominent above every other theme in the book is God's sovereign control over the affairs of all rulers and nations, and their final replacement with the True King. The key verses are 2:20-22,44 (cf. 2:28,37; 4:34-35; 6:25-27). God had not suffered defeat in allowing Israel's fall (Dan. 1), but was providentially working His sure purposes toward an eventual full display of His King, the exalted Christ. He sovereignly allowed Gentiles to dominate Israel, i.e., Babylon (605–539 B.C.), Medo-Persia (539–331 B.C.), Greece (331–146 B.C.), Rome (146 B.C.–A.D. 476), and all the way to the Second Advent of Christ. These stages in Gentile power are set forth in chaps. 2 and 7. This same theme also embraces Israel's experience both in defeat and finally in her kingdom blessing in chaps. 8–12 (cf. 2:35,45; 7:27). A key aspect within the over-arching theme of God's kingly control is Messiah's coming to rule the world in glory over all men (2:35,45; 7:13,14,27). He is like a stone in chap. 2, and like a son of man in chap. 7. In addition, He is the Anointed One (Messiah) in chap. 9:26. Chapter 9 provides the chronological framework from Daniel's time to Christ's kingdom.

A second theme woven into the fabric of Daniel is the display of God's sovereign power through miracles. Daniel's era is one of 6 in the Bible with a major focus on miracles by which God accomplished His purposes. Other periods include: 1) the Creation and Flood (Gen. 1–11); 2) the patriarchs and Moses (Gen. 12–Deut.); 3) Elijah and Elisha (1 Kin. 19–2 Kin. 13); 4) Jesus and the apostles (Gospels, Acts); and 5) the time of the Second Advent (Revelation). God, who has everlasting dominion and ability to work according to His will (4:34,35), is capable of miracles, all of which would be lesser displays of power than was exhibited when He acted as Creator in Gen. 1:1. Daniel chronicles the God-enabled recounting and interpreting of dreams which God used to reveal His will (chaps. 2,4,7). Other miracles included: 1) His writing on the wall and Daniel's interpreting it (chap. 5); 2) His protection of the 3 men in a blazing furnace (chap. 3); 3) His provision of safety for Daniel in a lions' den (chap. 6); and 4) supernatural prophecies (chaps. 2; 7; 8; 9:24–12:13).

Interpretive Challenges

The main challenges center on interpreting passages about future tribulation and kingdom promises. Though the use of Imperial Aramaic and archeology have confirmed the early date of writing, some skeptical interpreters, unwilling to acknowledge supernatural prophecies that came to pass (there are over 100 in chap. 11 alone that were fulfilled), place these details in the intertestamental times. They see these prophecies, not as miraculously foretelling the future, but as simply the observations of a later writer, who is recording events of his own day. Thus, they date Daniel in the days of Antiochus IV Epiphanes (175–164 B.C., chap. 8; 11:21-45). According to this scheme, the expectation of the Stone and Son of Man (chaps. 2,7) turned out to be a mistaken notion that did not actually come to pass, or the writer was being intentionally deceptive. Actually, a future 7 year judgment period (cf. 7:21,22; 11:36-45; 12:1) and a literal 1,000 year kingdom (cf. Rev. 20) after Christ's second coming when He will reign over Israelites and Gentiles (7:27) is taught. This will be an era before and distinct from the final, absolutely perfect, ultimate state, i.e., the new heaven and the new earth with its capital, the New Jerusalem (Rev. 21,22). The literal interpretation of prophecy, including Daniel, leads to the premillennial perspective.

Many other aspects of interpretation challenge readers: e.g., interpreting numbers (1:12,20; 3:19; 9:24-27); identifying the one like a Son of Man (7:13,14); determining whether to see Antiochus of the past or Antichrist of the far future in 8:19-23; explaining the "seventy sevens" in 9:24-27; and deciding whether Antiochus of 11:21-35 is still meant in 11:36-45, or whether it is the future Antichrist.

Outline

- I. The Personal Background of Daniel (1:1-21)
  - A. Conquest of Jerusalem (1:1,2)
  - B. Conscription of Jews for Training (1:3-7)
  - C. Courage of Four Men in Trial (1:8-16)
  - D. Choice of Four Men for Royal Positions (1:17-21)
- II. The Prophetic Course of Gentile Dominion (2:1–7:28)
  - A. Dilemmas of Nebuchadnezzar (2:1–4:37)
  - B. Debauchery and Demise of Belshazzar (5:1-31)
  - C. Deliverance of Daniel (6:1-28)
  - D. Dream of Daniel (7:1-28)
- III. The Prophetic Course of Israel's Destiny (8:1–12:13)
  - A. Prophecy of the Ram and Male Goat (8:1-27)
  - B. Prophecy of the Seventy Weeks (9:1-27)
  - C. Prophecy of Israel's Humiliation and Restoration (10:1–12:13)

Daniel and His Friends Obey God

1 In the third year of the reign of [a]Jehoia-
kim king of Judah, Nebuchadnezzar
king of Babylon came to Jerusalem and besieged it. **2** And the Lord gave Jehoiakim
king of Judah into his hand, with [b]some of
the articles of [1]the house of God, which he
carried [c]into the land of Shinar to the
house of his god; [d]and he brought the articles into the treasure house of his god.
3 Then the king instructed Ashpenaz,
the master of his eunuchs, to bring [e]some
of the children of Israel and some of the
king's descendants and some of the nobles,
4 young men [f]in whom *there was* no blemish, but good-looking, gifted in all wisdom, possessing knowledge and quick to
understand, who *had* ability to serve in the
king's palace, and [g]whom they might
teach the language and [2]literature of the
Chaldeans. **5** And the king appointed for
them a daily provision of the king's delicacies and of the wine which he drank, and
three years of training for them, so that at
the end of *that time* they might [h]serve before the king. **6** Now from among those of
the sons of Judah were Daniel, Hananiah,
Mishael, and Azariah. **7** [i]To them the chief
of the eunuchs gave names: [j]he gave Daniel *the name* Belteshazzar; to Hananiah,
Shadrach; to Mishael, Meshach; and to Azariah, Abed-Nego.
8 But Daniel purposed in his heart that
he would not defile himself [k]with the portion of the king's delicacies, nor with the
wine which he drank; therefore he requested of the chief of the eunuchs that he might
not defile himself. **9** Now [l]God had
brought Daniel into the favor and [3]good-
will of the chief of the eunuchs. **10** And the
chief of the eunuchs said to Daniel, "I fear
my lord the king, who has appointed your
food and drink. For why should he see
your faces looking worse than the young
men who *are* your age? Then you would
endanger my head before the king."
11 So Daniel said to [4]the steward whom
the chief of the eunuchs had set over Daniel, Hananiah, Mishael, and Azariah,
12 "Please test your servants for ten days,
and let them give us vegetables to eat and
water to drink. **13** Then let our appearance
be examined before you, and the appearance of the young men who eat the portion
of the king's delicacies; and as you see fit,
so deal with your servants." **14** So he consented with them in this matter, and tested
them ten days.
15 And at the end of ten days their features appeared better and fatter in flesh
than all the young men who ate the portion of the king's delicacies. **16** Thus [5]the
steward took away their portion of delicacies and the wine that they were to drink,
and gave them vegetables.
17 As for these four young men, [m]God
gave them [n]knowledge and skill in all literature and wisdom; and Daniel had [o]un-
derstanding in all visions and dreams.
18 Now at the end of the days, when the
king had said that they should be brought
in, the chief of the eunuchs brought them
in before Nebuchadnezzar. **19** Then the
king [6]interviewed them, and among them
all none was found like Daniel, Hananiah,
Mishael, and Azariah; therefore [p]they
served before the king. **20** [q]And in all matters of wisdom *and* understanding about
which the king examined them, he found

CHAPTER 1

1 [a]2 Kin. 24:1, 2; 2 Chr. 36:5-7; Jer. 25:1; 52:12-30
2 [b]2 Chr. 36:7; Jer. 27:19, 20; Dan. 5:2 [c]Gen. 10:10; 11:2; Is. 11:11; Zech. 5:11 [d]2 Chr. 36:7 [1]The temple
3 [e]2 Kin. 20:17, 18; Is. 39:7
4 [f]Lev. 24:19, 20 [g]Acts 7:22 [2]Lit. *writing* or *book*
5 [h]Gen. 41:46; 1 Sam. 16:22; 1 Kin. 10:8; Dan. 1:19
7 [i]Gen. 41:45; 2 Kin. 24:17 [j]Dan. 2:26; 4:8; 5:12
8 [k]Lev. 11:47; Deut. 32:38; Ezek. 4:13; Hos. 9:3
9 [l]Gen. 39:21; 1 Kin. 8:50; [Job 5:15, 16]; Ps. 106:46; [Prov. 16:7]; Acts 7:10; 27:3 [3]*kindness*
11 [4]Or *Melzar*
16 [5]Or *Melzar*
17 [m]1 Kin. 3:12, 28; 2 Chr. 1:10-12; [Luke 21:15; James 1:5-7] [n]Acts 7:22 [o]Num. 12:6; 2 Chr. 26:5; Dan. 5:11, 12, 14; 10:1
19 [p]Gen. 41:46; [Prov. 22:29]; Dan. 1:5 [6]Lit. *talked with them*
20 [q]1 Kin. 10:1

1:1 third year. 606–605 B.C. It was the third year by Babylonian dating, which did not count a king's initial (accession) year, but began with the following year. So the "third year" is in harmony with the same year labeled as "fourth" by the Judean system of dating (cf. Jer. 46:2). **Jehoiakim.** Son of Josiah who ruled (ca. 609–597 B.C.) when Nebuchadnezzar first plundered Jerusalem. **Nebuchadnezzar.** Son of Nabopolassar who ruled Babylon (ca. 605–562 B.C.).

1:2 Shinar. A term for Babylon. **his god.** Bel or Marduk (same as Merodach). Babylonian religion recognized other gods too (cf. 1:7 and *see note there*). To conquer another nation's deities was thought to prove the superiority of the victor's god.

1:4. Qualifications for Jews to be trained in affairs of state included being: 1) *physically* free from bodily blemish or handicap and handsome, i.e., a pleasing appearance in the public eye; 2) *mentally* sharp; and 3) *socially* poised and polished for representing the leadership. The ages of the trainees was most likely 14-17.

1:5 three years of training. Cf. 2:1 and *see note there.*

1:7 names. A key factor in the "brainwashing" process of the Babylonian training was a name switch. This was to link the inductees to local gods rather than to support their former religious loyalty. Daniel means "God is my judge," but became Belteshazzar, or "Bel Protect the King." Hananiah, "the Lord is Gracious," was changed to Shadrach, "Command of Aku," another Babylonian god. Mishael, meaning "Who is like the Lord?" was given the name Meshach, "Who is what Aku Is?" Finally, Azariah, "the Lord is my Helper," became Abed-nego, "Servant of Nego," also called Nebo, a god of vegetation (cf. Is. 46:1).

1:8 Daniel purposed. The pagan food and drink was devoted to idols. To indulge was to be understood as honoring these deities. Daniel "purposed in his heart" (cf. Prov. 4:23) not to engage in compromise by being untrue to God's call of commitment (cf. Ex. 34:14, 15). Also, foods that God's law prohibited (Lev. 1:1) were items that pagans consumed; to partake entailed direct compromise (cf. Dan. 1:12). Moses took this stand (Heb. 11:24-26), as did the psalmist (Ps. 119:115), and Jesus (Heb. 7:26). Cf. 2 Cor. 6:14-18; 2 Tim 2:20.

1:9. God honored Daniel's trust and allegiance by sovereignly working favorably for him among the heathen leaders. In this instance, it prevented persecution and led to respect, whereas later on God permitted opposition against Daniel which also elevated him (Dan. 3,6). One way or another, God honors those who honor Him (1 Sam. 2:30; 2 Chr. 16:9).

1:12 vegetables. This Heb. word appears in a plural form in the OT, only here and in v. 16. It might refer to wheat or barley, or it could be fresh vegetables.

1:15 fatter in flesh. Indicates healthiness.

them ten times better than all the magicians *and* astrologers who *were* in all his
realm. 21 [r]Thus Daniel continued until the
first year of King Cyrus.

Nebuchadnezzar's Dream

2 Now in the second year of Nebuchadnezzar's reign, Nebuchadnezzar had
dreams; [a]and his spirit was *so* troubled that
[b]his sleep left him. 2 [c]Then the king gave
the command to call the magicians, the astrologers, the sorcerers, and the Chaldeans
to tell the king his dreams. So they came
and stood before the king. 3 And the king
said to them, "I have had a dream, and my
spirit is anxious to [1]know the dream."
4 Then the Chaldeans spoke to the king
in Aramaic, [d]"O[2] king, live forever! Tell
your servants the dream, and we will give
the interpretation."
5 The king answered and said to the
Chaldeans, "My [3]decision is firm: if you
do not make known the dream to me, and
its interpretation, you shall be [e]cut in
pieces, and your houses shall be made an
ash heap. 6 [f]However, if you tell the dream
and its interpretation, you shall receive
from me gifts, rewards, and great honor.
Therefore tell me the dream and its interpretation."
7 They answered again and said, "Let
the king tell his servants the dream, and
we will give its interpretation."
8 The king answered and said, "I know
for certain that you would gain time, because you see that my decision is firm: 9 if
you do not make known the dream to me,
there is only one decree for you! For you
have agreed to speak lying and corrupt
words before me till the [4]time has
changed. Therefore tell me the dream, and
I shall know that you can [5]give me its interpretation."
10 The Chaldeans answered the king,
and said, "There is not a man on earth who
can tell the king's matter; therefore no
king, lord, or ruler has *ever* asked such
things of any magician, astrologer, or Chaldean. 11 *It is* a [6]difficult thing that the king
requests, and there is no other who can tell
it to the king [g]except the gods, whose
dwelling is not with flesh."
12 For this reason the king was angry
and very furious, and gave the command
to destroy all the wise *men* of Babylon.
13 So the decree went out, and they began
killing the wise *men;* and they sought
[h]Daniel and his companions, to kill *them.*

God Reveals Nebuchadnezzar's Dream

14 Then with counsel and wisdom Daniel
answered Arioch, the captain of the king's
guard, who had gone out to kill the wise
men of Babylon; 15 he answered and said to
Arioch the king's captain, "Why is the decree from the king so [7]urgent?" Then Arioch made the decision known to Daniel.
16 So Daniel went in and asked the king

21 [r] Dan. 6:28; 10:1

CHAPTER 2

1 [a] Gen. 40:5-8; 41:1, 8; Job 33:15-17; Dan. 2:3; 4:5 [b] Esth. 6:1; Dan. 6:18
2 [c] Gen. 41:8; Ex. 7:11; Is. 47:12, 13; Dan. 1:20; 2:10, 27; 4:6; 5:7
3 [1] Or *understand*
4 [d] 1 Kin. 1:31; Dan. 3:9; 5:10; 6:6, 21 [2] The original language of Daniel 2:4b through 7:28 is Aramaic.
5 [e] 2 Kin. 10:27; Ezra 6:11; Dan. 3:29 [3] The command
6 [f] Dan. 5:16
9 [4] Situation [5] Or *declare to me*
11 [g] Gen. 41:39; Dan. 5:11 [6] Or *rare*
13 [h] Dan. 1:19, 20
15 [7] Or *harsh*

1:20 ten times better. This probably uses the number qualitatively to signify fullness or completeness, i.e., they displayed incredible skill in answering, beyond the performance of other men who spoke without God's help. Compare this with "ten days" (vv. 12-15) which is quantitative, since it refers to an actual passage of time.

1:21 first year. Cyrus of Persia conquered Babylon in 539 B.C. His third year, in 10:1, is the latest historical year that Daniel mentions (cf. Ezra 1:1–2:1).

An Overview of Daniel's Kingdoms

I. Daniel 2/Daniel 7	
A. Babylon	2:32, 37,38; 7:4, 17
B. Medo-Persia	2:32, 39; 7:5, 17
C. Greece	2:32, 39; 7:6, 17
D. Rome	2:33, 40; 7:7, 17, 23
E. Revived Rome	2:33, 41-43; 7:7,8, 11, 24,25
F. Millennium	2:34,35, 44,45; 7:13,14, 26,27
II. Daniel 8/Daniel 11	
A. Medo-Persia	8:3-8, 20,21; 10:20,21, 11:2-35
B. Greece	8:3-8, 20,21; 10:20,21, 11:2-35
C. Revived Rome	8:9-12, 23-26; 11:36-45.

2:1 second year. Promotion of the 4 Hebrews after 3 years (1:5,18) agrees with the year of promotion after the dream in the "second year." *See note on 1:1.* **dreams.** In the time of revelation, God spoke through the interpretation of dreams that He induced (cf. v. 29).

2:2 Chaldeans. This could refer to all people native to Chaldea (1:4; 3:8), or, as here, to a special class of soothsayers who taught Chaldean culture.

2:4 Aramaic. This language, to which Daniel suddenly switches in v. 4b and retains through 7:28, was written with an alphabet like Hebrew, yet had distinctive differences. Aramaic was the popular language of the Babylonian, Assyrian, and Persian areas, and was useful in governmental and trade relations. Daniel 1:1–2:4a and 8:1–12:13 were written in Hebrew, possibly because the focus was more directly on Hebrew matters. Daniel 2:4b–7:28 switches to Aramaic because the subject matter is centered more on other nations and matters largely involving them.

2:5 My decision is firm. The king shrewdly withheld the dream, though he remembered it, to test his experts. He was anxious for a straight interpretation, with no deception.

2:7 Let the king tell. The worldly men of human skill failed (cf. the magicians in Pharaoh's court, Ex. 8:16-19, with Joseph, Gen. 41:1ff.). Verses 8-13 show how impossible it is for humans to truly interpret dreams from God (cf. v. 27). But Daniel, who trusted God in prayer (v. 18), received His supernatural interpretation (vv. 19,30). He gave credit to God in his prayer (vv. 20-23) and his testimony before Nebuchadnezzar (vv. 23,45). Later the king, too, gave God the glory (v. 47).

to give him time, that he might tell the king
the interpretation. 17 Then Daniel went to
his house, and made the decision known to
Hananiah, Mishael, and Azariah, his companions, 18 [i]that they might seek mercies
from the God of heaven concerning this secret, so that Daniel and his companions
might not perish with the rest of the wise
men of Babylon. 19 Then the secret was revealed to Daniel [j]in a night vision. So Daniel blessed the God of heaven.
20 Daniel answered and said:

[k]"Blessed be the name of God forever
and ever,
[l]For wisdom and might are His.
21 And He changes [m]the times and
the seasons;
[n]He removes kings and raises up
kings;
[o]He gives wisdom to the wise
And knowledge to those who have
understanding.
22 [p]He reveals deep and secret things;
[q]He knows what *is* in the darkness,
And [r]light dwells with Him.

23 "I thank You and praise You,
O God of my fathers;
You have given me wisdom and
might,
And have now made known to me
what we [s]asked of You,
For You have made known to us
the king's [8]demand."

Daniel Explains the Dream

24 Therefore Daniel went to Arioch,
whom the king had appointed to destroy
the wise *men* of Babylon. He went and said
thus to him: "Do not destroy the wise *men*
of Babylon; take me before the king, and I
will tell the king the interpretation."
25 Then Arioch quickly brought Daniel
before the king, and said thus to him, "I
have found a man of the [9]captives of Judah, who will make known to the king the
interpretation."
26 The king answered and said to Daniel,
whose name *was* Belteshazzar, "Are you
able to make known to me the dream
which I have seen, and its interpretation?"
27 Daniel answered in the presence of
the king, and said, "The secret which the
king has demanded, the wise *men*, the astrologers, the magicians, and the soothsayers cannot declare to the king. 28 [t]But there
is a God in heaven who reveals secrets, and
He has made known to King Nebuchadnezzar [u]what will be in the latter days.
Your dream, and the visions of your head
upon your bed, were these: 29 As for you,
O king, thoughts came *to* your *mind while*
on your bed, *about* what would come to
pass after this; [v]and He who reveals secrets
has made known to you what will be.
30 [w]But as for me, this secret has not been
revealed to me because I have more wisdom than anyone living, but for *our* sakes
who make known the interpretation to the
king, [x]and that you may [1]know the
thoughts of your heart.
31 "You, O king, were watching; and behold, a great image! This great image,
whose splendor *was* excellent, stood before
you; and its form *was* awesome. 32 [y]This
image's head *was* of fine gold, its chest and
arms of silver, its belly and [2]thighs of
bronze, 33 its legs of iron, its feet partly of
iron and partly of [3]clay. 34 You watched
while a stone was cut out [z]without hands,
which struck the image on its feet of iron
and clay, and broke them in pieces. 35 [a]Then
the iron, the clay, the bronze, the silver, and
the gold were crushed together, and became
[b]like chaff from the summer threshing
floors; the wind carried them away so that
[c]no trace of them was found. And the stone
that struck the image [d]became a great
mountain [e]and filled the whole earth.
36 "This *is* the dream. Now we will tell
the interpretation of it before the king.
37 [f]You, O king, *are* a king of kings. [g]For the
God of heaven has given you a kingdom,
power, strength, and glory; 38 [h]and wherever the children of men dwell, or the
beasts of the field and the birds of the
heaven, He has given *them* into your hand,
and has made you ruler over them all—
[i]you *are* this head of gold. 39 But after you
shall arise [j]another kingdom [k]inferior to

18 [i][Dan. 9:9; Matt. 18:19]
19 [j]Num. 12:6; Job 33:15; [Prov. 3:32]; Amos 3:7
20 [k]Ps. 113:2 [l][1 Chr. 29:11, 12; Job 12:13; Ps. 147:5; Jer. 32:19; Matt. 6:13; Rom. 11:33]
21 [m]Ps. 31:15; Esth. 1:13; Dan. 2:9; 7:25 [n]Job 12:18; [Ps. 75:6, 7; Jer. 27:5; Dan. 4:35] [o]1 Kin. 3:9, 10; 4:29; [James 1:5]
22 [p]Job 12:22; Ps. 25:14; [Prov. 3:22] [q]Job 26:6; Ps. 139:12; [Is. 45:7; Jer. 23:24; Heb. 4:13] [r][Ps. 36:9]; Dan. 5:11, 14; [1 Tim. 6:16; James 1:17; 1 John 1:5]
23 [s]Ps. 21:2, 4; Dan. 2:18, 29, 30 [8]Lit. *word*
25 [9]Lit. *sons of the captivity*
28 [t]Gen. 40:8; Amos 4:13 [u]Gen. 49:1; Is. 2:2; Dan. 10:14; Mic. 4:1
29 [v][Dan. 2:22, 28]
30 [w]Acts 3:12 [x]Dan. 2:47 [1]Understand
32 [y]Dan. 2:38, 45 [2]Or *sides*
33 [3]Or *baked clay*, also vv. 34, 35, 42
34 [z]Dan. 8:25; [Zech. 4:6]; 2 Cor. 5:1; Heb. 9:24
35 [a]Dan. 7:23–27; [Rev. 16:14] [b]Ps. 1:4; Is. 17:13; 41:15, 16; Hos. 13:3 [c]Ps. 37:10, 36 [d][Is. 2:2, 3]; Mic. 4:1 [e]Ps. 80:9
37 [f]Ezra 7:12; Is. 47:5; Jer. 27:6, 7; Ezek. 26:7; Hos. 8:10 [g]Ezra 1:2
38 [h]Ps. 50:10, 11; Jer. 27:6; Dan. 4:21, 22 [i]Dan. 2:32
39 [j]Dan. 5:28, 31 [k]Dan. 2:32

2:20-23 This praise to God sums up the theme of the whole book, namely that God is the One who controls all things and grants all wisdom and might.

2:28 God…reveals secrets. Just as He did during Joseph's time in Egypt (cf. Gen. 40:8; 41:16).

2:36-45 we will tell the interpretation. Five empires in succession would rule over Israel, here pictured by parts of a statue (body). In Dan. 7, the same empires are represented by 4 great beasts. These empires are Babylon, Medo-Persia, Greece, Rome, and the later revived Rome (cf. Introduction: Background and Setting), each one differentiated from the previous as indicated by the declining quality of the metal. A stone picturing Christ (Luke 20:18) at His second coming (as the Son of Man also does in Dan. 7:13,14) will destroy the fourth empire in its final phase with catastrophic suddenness (2:34,35,44, 45). Christ's total shattering of Gentile power will result in the establishment of His millennial kingdom, the ultimate empire, and then continuing on eternally (2:44; 7:27).

2:39 inferior. This probably means "lower" (lit. "earthward") on the image of a man as Daniel guides Nebuchadnezzar's thoughts downward on the body from his own empire (the head) to the one that

yours; then another, a third kingdom of
bronze, which shall rule over all the earth.
40 And [l]the fourth kingdom shall be as
strong as iron, inasmuch as iron breaks in
pieces and shatters everything; and like
iron that crushes, *that kingdom* will break in
pieces and crush all the others. 41 Whereas
you saw the feet and toes, partly of potter's clay and partly of iron, the kingdom
shall be divided; yet the strength of the
iron shall be in it, just as you saw the iron
mixed with ceramic clay. 42 And *as* the toes
of the feet *were* partly of iron and partly of
clay, [m]so the kingdom shall be partly
strong and partly [4]fragile. 43 As you saw
iron mixed with ceramic clay, they will
mingle with the seed of men; but they will
not adhere to one another, just as iron does
not mix with clay. 44 And in the days of
these kings [n]the God of heaven will set up
a kingdom [o]which shall never be destroyed; and the kingdom shall not be left
to other people; [p]it shall [5]break in pieces
and [6]consume all these kingdoms, and it
shall stand forever. 45 [q]Inasmuch as you
saw that the stone was cut out of the
mountain without hands, and that it broke
in pieces the iron, the bronze, the clay, the
silver, and the gold—the great God has
made known to the king what will come to
pass after this. The dream is certain, and its
interpretation is sure."

Daniel and His Friends Promoted

46 [r]Then King Nebuchadnezzar fell on
his face, prostrate before Daniel, and commanded that they should present an offering [s]and incense to him. 47 The king answered Daniel, and said, "Truly [t]your God
is the God of [u]gods, the Lord of kings, and
a revealer of secrets, since you could reveal
this secret." 48 [v]Then the king promoted
Daniel [w]and gave him many great gifts;
and he made him ruler over the whole
province of Babylon, and [x]chief administrator over all the wise *men* of Babylon.
49 Also Daniel petitioned the king, [y]and he
set Shadrach, Meshach, and Abed-Nego
over the affairs of the province of Babylon;
but Daniel [z]*sat* in [7]the gate of the king.

The Image of Gold

3 Nebuchadnezzar the king made an
image of gold, whose height *was* [1]sixty
cubits *and* its width six cubits. He set it up
in the plain of Dura, in the province of
Babylon. 2 And King Nebuchadnezzar
sent *word* to gather together the satraps,
the administrators, the governors, the
counselors, the treasurers, the judges, the
magistrates, and all the officials of
the provinces, to come to the dedication of
the image which King Nebuchadnezzar
had set up. 3 So the satraps, the administrators, the governors, the counselors, the
treasurers, the judges, the magistrates, and
all the officials of the provinces gathered
together for the dedication of the image
that King Nebuchadnezzar had set up; and
they stood before the image that Nebuchadnezzar had set up. 4 Then a herald
cried [2]aloud: "To you it is commanded, [a]O
peoples, nations, and languages, 5 *that* at
the time you hear the sound of the horn,

40 [l] Dan. 7:7, 23
42 [m] Dan. 7:24 [4] Or *brittle*
44 [n] Dan. 2:28, 37 [o] Is. 9:6, 7; Ezek. 37:25; Dan. 4:3, 34; 6:26; 7:14, 27; Mic. 4:7; [Luke 1:32, 33] [p] Ps. 2:9; Is. 60:12; Dan. 2:34, 35; [1 Cor. 15:24] [5] Or *crush* [6] Lit. *put an end to*
45 [q] Dan. 2:35; Is. 28:16
46 [r] Dan. 3:5, 7; Acts 10:25; 14:13; Rev. 19:10; 22:8 [s] Lev. 26:31; Ezra 6:10
47 [t] Dan. 3:28, 29; 4:34-37 [u] [Deut. 10:17]
48 [v] [Prov. 14:35; 21:1] [w] Dan. 2:6 [x] Dan. 4:9; 5:11
49 [y] Dan. 1:7; 3:12 [z] Esth. 2:19, 21; 3:2; Amos 5:15 [7] The king's court

CHAPTER 3

1 [1] About 90 feet
4 [a] Dan. 4:1; 6:25 [2] Lit. *with strength*

would succeed it. Medo-Persia, though lacking the glory of Babylon (silver as compared to gold), was not inferior in strength to Babylon when its day of power came; it actually conquered Babylon (7:5). Also in the case of Greece, bronze is less glorious (valuable) than silver, but stronger. **rule over all the earth.** Alexander the Great became the ruler of the world, including Israel, from Europe to Egypt to India.

2:40 strong as iron. This metal fittingly represents the Roman Empire which would be characterized by the description predicted. It did have armies in iron armor known as the Iron Legions of Rome, and it had strength and invincibility.

2:41 toes. Ten toes represent the same kings as the 10 horns in 7:24. They will rule in the final time of the Gentile empire, which Christ destroys in violent abruptness at His second coming.

2:41-43 clay and…iron. The iron in the 10 toes (kings) represents the Roman Empire in its revived form, prior to the second coming of Christ, as having iron-like strength for conquest (cf. Rev. 13:4,5). But the clay mixed in depicts that the union (federation) of kings and nations would have fatal flaws of human weakness, so that it is inherently vulnerable.

2:44 stand forever. God's kingdom ruled by Messiah is the final rule, never to be replaced. It has a millennial phase and an eternal future, but it is the same king who rules both.

2:45 stone…mountain. The stone is Messiah (cf. Ps. 118:22,23; Is. 28:16; Rom. 9:33; 1 Pet. 2:6; esp. Luke 20:18). The mountain pictures God's all-transcending government that looms over weak earthly powers (4:17,25; Pss. 47:8; 103:19; 145:13; Rev. 17:9). Messiah is "cut out" of this sovereign realm by God, which accords with the Son of Man coming (7:13,14); "without hands" denotes that the Messiah comes from God and is not of human origin or power (cf. the same idea in 8:25). The virgin birth and the resurrection, as well as the second coming, could be encompassed in this reference to supernatural origin.

3:1 image of gold. The statue, which the king arrogantly made, represented himself as an expression of his greatness and glory and reflected the dream where he was the head of gold (2:38). It was not necessarily made of solid gold, but more likely would have been overlaid with gold, like many objects found in the ruins of Babylon. The word for "image" usually means a human form. The height of the figure was about 90 ft. and the width 9 ft.; it would have been comparable in height to date palms found in that area. The self-deifying statue of the king need not have been grotesquely thin in proportion to the height since a massive base could have contributed to the height. This established the worship of Nebuchadnezzar and the nation under his power, in addition to the other gods.

3:2. Leaders attending the "summit conference" for Nebuchadnezzar's display are: satraps, or leaders over regions; administrators, or military chiefs; governors, or civil administrators; counselors, or lawyers; treasurers; judges, or government arbiters; magistrates, or judges in our sense today; officials, or other civil leaders.

flute, harp, lyre, *and* psaltery, in symphony
with all kinds of music, you shall fall down
and worship the gold image that King
Nebuchadnezzar has set up; 6 and whoever does not fall down and worship shall
[b]be cast immediately into the midst of a
burning fiery furnace."
7 So at that time, when all the people
heard the sound of the horn, flute, harp,
and lyre, in symphony with all kinds of
music, all the people, nations, and languages fell down *and* worshiped the gold
image which King Nebuchadnezzar had
set up.

Daniel's Friends Disobey the King

8 Therefore at that time certain Chaldeans [c]came forward and accused the
Jews. 9 They spoke and said to King Nebuchadnezzar, [d]"O king, live forever! 10 You,
O king, have made a decree that everyone
who hears the sound of the horn, flute,
harp, lyre, *and* psaltery, in symphony with
all kinds of music, shall fall down and
worship the gold image; 11 and whoever
does not fall down and worship shall be
cast into the midst of a burning fiery furnace. 12 [e]There are certain Jews whom you
have set over the affairs of the province of
Babylon: Shadrach, Meshach, and Abed-
Nego; these men, O king, have [f]not paid
due regard to you. They do not serve your
gods or worship the gold image which you
have set up."
13 Then Nebuchadnezzar, in [g]rage and
fury, gave the command to bring Shadrach,
Meshach, and Abed-Nego. So they
brought these men before the king. 14 Nebuchadnezzar spoke, saying to them, "*Is it*
true, Shadrach, Meshach, and Abed-Nego,
that you do not serve my gods or worship
the gold image which I have set up?
15 Now if you are ready at the time you
hear the sound of the horn, flute, harp,
lyre, *and* psaltery, in symphony with all
kinds of music, and you fall down and
worship the image which I have made,
[h]*good!* But if you do not worship, you shall
be cast immediately into the midst of a
burning fiery furnace. [i]And who *is* the god
who will deliver you from my hands?"
16 Shadrach, Meshach, and Abed-Nego
answered and said to the king, "O Nebuchadnezzar, [j]we have no need to answer
you in this matter. 17 If that *is the case,* our
[k]God whom we serve is able to [l]deliver us
from the burning fiery furnace, and He
will deliver *us* from your hand, O king.
18 But if not, let it be known to you, O king,
that we do not serve your gods, nor will
we [m]worship the gold image which you
have set up."

Saved in Fiery Trial

19 Then Nebuchadnezzar was full of
fury, and the expression on his face
changed toward Shadrach, Meshach, and
Abed-Nego. He spoke and commanded
that they heat the furnace seven times
more than it was usually heated. 20 And he
commanded certain mighty men of valor
who *were* in his army to bind Shadrach,
Meshach, and Abed-Nego, *and* cast *them*
into the burning fiery furnace. 21 Then
these men were bound in their coats, their
trousers, their turbans, and their *other* garments, and were cast into the midst of the
burning fiery furnace. 22 Therefore, because the king's command was [3]urgent,
and the furnace exceedingly hot, the flame
of the fire killed those men who took up
Shadrach, Meshach, and Abed-Nego.

6 [b] Jer. 29:22; Ezek. 22:18-22; Matt. 13:42, 50; Rev. 9:2; 13:15; 14:11
8 [c] Ezra 4:12-16; Esth. 3:8, 9; Dan. 6:12, 13
9 [d] Dan. 2:4; 5:10; 6:6, 21
12 [e] Dan. 2:49 [f] Dan. 1:8; 6:12, 13
13 [g] Dan. 2:12; 3:19
15 [h] Ex. 32:32; Luke 13:9 [i] Ex. 5:2; 2 Kin. 18:35; Is. 36:18-20; Dan. 2:47
16 [j] [Matt. 10:19]
17 [k] Job 5:19; [Ps. 27:1, 2; Is. 26:3, 4]; Jer. 1:8; 15:20, 21; Dan. 6:19-22 [l] 1 Sam. 17:37; Jer. 1:8; 15:20, 21; 42:11; Dan. 6:16, 19-22; Mic. 7:7; 2 Cor. 1:10
18 [m] Job 13:15
22 [3] Or *harsh*

3:5 lyre. Like a harp, possibly square or rectangular, with strings to pluck with a plectrum (pick), yielding high tones. **psaltery.** An instrument plucked with the fingers rather than a plectrum (pick), yielding low tones.

3:6 furnace. Some ancient kilns were found to have been shaped like a vertical tunnel open only at the top, with a dome supported by columns. Charcoal normally served as fuel.

3:8 certain Chaldeans. These are most likely the priests of Bel-Merodach who were envious of these young Jews, and sought their death.

3:12 They do not serve your gods or worship the gold image. Enemies of God's servants witnessed such a clear-cut testimony that they were in no doubt about their rejection of idolatry and unshakeable allegiance to the God of Israel.

3:13 these men. Daniel is not mentioned as being part of the refusal to worship witnessed by the Chaldeans. If present, he surely would have joined these others in faithfulness to God.

3:15 who *is* the god? The king's challenge would return to embarrass him. The true God was able to deliver, just as He was able to reveal a dream and its meaning. Nebuchadnezzar had earlier called him "the God of gods" (2:47), but having let that fade from his attention, he soon would be shocked and humiliated when God took up his challenge (3:28,29).

3:16 we have no need to answer. The 3 men meant no disrespect. They did not have any defense, nor did they need to reconsider their commitment, since they stood fast for their God as the only true and living God. Their lives were in His hands as they indicated in vv. 17,18 (cf. Isa. 43:1,2).

3:19 seven times more. The king's fury at being defied to his face led him to cry for an intensification of the heat. He was not literally requiring the fire to be 7 times hotter as a gauge would indicate, or requiring 7 times as long to heat, or 7 times the amount of fuel (cf. v. 6, "cast immediately"). The king in anger means "intensely hot," using "seven" figuratively to denote completeness (as Lev. 26:18-28; Prov. 6:31; 24:16), similar to "ten" in Dan. 1:20. Cf. "exceedingly hot" (3:22). A stone or brick furnace with an air draft could be made hotter by more fuel and air.

3:22 took up. Refers to being taken upward on some kind of ramp to a spot near enough to the top to be thrown in (cf. v. 26). The fire was so hot it incinerated the king's men.

23 And these three men, Shadrach, Meshach, and Abed-Nego, fell down bound
into the midst of the burning fiery furnace.
24 Then King Nebuchadnezzar was astonished; and he rose in haste *and* spoke,
saying to his [4]counselors, "Did we not cast
three men bound into the midst of the fire?"
They answered and said to the king,
"True, O king."
25 "Look!" he answered, "I see four men
loose, [n]walking in the midst of the fire; and
they are not hurt, and the form of the
fourth is like [o]the[5] Son of God."

Nebuchadnezzar Praises God

26 Then Nebuchadnezzar went near the
[6]mouth of the burning fiery furnace *and*
spoke, saying, "Shadrach, Meshach, and
Abed-Nego, servants of the [p]Most High
God, come out, and come *here.*" Then
Shadrach, Meshach, and Abed-Nego came
from the midst of the fire. 27 And the
satraps, administrators, governors, and the
king's counselors gathered together, and
they saw these men [q]on whose bodies the
fire had no power; the hair of their head was
not singed nor were their garments affected,
and the smell of fire was not on them.
28 Nebuchadnezzar spoke, saying,
"Blessed be the God of Shadrach, Meshach, and Abed-Nego, who sent His [r]An-
gel[7] and delivered His servants who trusted in Him, and they have frustrated the
king's word, and yielded their bodies, that
they should not serve nor worship any god
except their own God! 29 [s]Therefore I make
a decree that any people, nation, or language which speaks anything amiss
against the [t]God of Shadrach, Meshach,
and Abed-Nego shall be [u]cut in pieces, and
their houses shall be made an ash heap;
[v]because there is no other God who can
deliver like this."
30 Then the king [8]promoted Shadrach,
Meshach, and Abed-Nego in the province
of Babylon.

24 [4] High officials
25 [n] [Ps. 91:3-9]; Is. 43:2 [o] Job 1:6; 38:7; [Ps. 34:7]; Dan. 3:28 [5] Or *a son of the gods*
26 [p] [Dan. 4:2, 3, 17, 34, 35] [6] Lit. *door*
27 [q] [Is. 43:2]; Heb. 11:34
28 [r] [Ps. 34:7, 8]; Is. 37:36; [Jer. 17:7]; Dan. 6:22, 23; Acts 5:19; 12:7 [7] Or *angel*
29 [s] Dan. 6:26 [t] Dan. 2:46, 47; 4:34-37 [u] Ezra 6:11; Dan. 2:5 [v] Dan. 6:27
30 [8] Lit. *caused to prosper*

CHAPTER 4

1 [a] Ezra 4:17; Dan. 3:4; 6:25
2 [b] Dan. 3:26
3 [c] 2 Sam. 7:16; Ps. 89:35-37; Dan. 6:27; 7:13, 14; [Luke 1:31-33] [d] [Dan. 2:44; 4:34; 6:26]
5 [e] Dan. 2:28, 29 [f] Dan. 2:1
7 [g] Dan. 2:2
8 [h] Dan. 1:7 [i] Is. 63:11; Dan. 2:11; 4:18; 5:11, 14
9 [j] Dan. 2:48; 5:11

Nebuchadnezzar's Second Dream

4 Nebuchadnezzar the king,

[a]To all peoples, nations, and
languages that dwell in all the
earth:

Peace be multiplied to you.

2 I thought it good to declare the
signs and wonders [b]that the Most
High God has worked for me.

3 [c]How great *are* His signs,
And how mighty His wonders!
His kingdom *is* [d]an everlasting
kingdom,
And His dominion *is* from
generation to generation.

4 I, Nebuchadnezzar, was at rest in
my house, and flourishing in my
palace. 5 I saw a dream which
made me afraid, [e]and the thoughts
on my bed and the visions of my
head [f]troubled me. 6 Therefore I
issued a decree to bring in all the
wise *men* of Babylon before me,
that they might make known to me
the interpretation of the dream.
7 [g]Then the magicians, the
astrologers, the Chaldeans, and the
soothsayers came in, and I told
them the dream; but they did not
make known to me its
interpretation. 8 But at last Daniel
came before me [h](his name *is* Belteshazzar, according to the name of
my god; [i]in him *is* the Spirit of the
Holy God), and I told the dream
before him, *saying:* 9 "Belteshazzar,
[j]chief of the magicians, because I
know that the Spirit of the Holy
God *is* in you, and no secret
troubles you, explain to me the

3:23 fell down. A shaft directed them into the furnace bottom, on top of the fuel.

3:25 four men loose. The king seemed only to have known that the fourth person was a heavenly being. He called him a son of the gods (a pagan reference to one who appeared supernatural) and an "Angel" (v. 28). The fourth person could possibly have been the second person of the Godhead (Jesus Christ) in a pre-incarnate appearance (*see notes on Josh. 5:13-15; Judg. 6:11ff.*).

3:27 the fire had no power. When God enacts a miracle, He supernaturally controls all details so that His power is unmistakable, and there is no other explanation.

3:28-30 The king was convinced and eager to add the God of these men to his panoply of deities. Soon he learned that God was not one of many, but the only God (Dan. 4).

4:1-3 Nebuchadnezzar's praise of God in 4:1-3 and 34b-37 is the theme that brackets the experience the king reiterates in the first person (vv. 4-34). He began and ended the narrative with praise, and in between told why he converted to such worship of the true God! (Cf. Rom. 11:33.)

4:6 wise *men* of Babylon. The king gave them another try (cf. 2:2-13) and they were again unable.

4:8 at last Daniel came. Daniel alone interpreted the tree vision (v. 10), enabled by God. **my god.** As the story began, he depicted himself still as a worshipper of Bel-Merodach.

4:9 chief of the magicians. Here was the title the pagans gave him (cf. 5:11). **Spirit.** The meaning here and in v. 18 (as well as 5:11,14) is rightly translated as "the Spirit of the holy God." Wording for the true God in the Heb. of Josh. 24:19 is equivalent to the Aram.

visions of my dream that I have
seen, and its interpretation.

10 These *were* the visions of my head
while on my bed:

I was looking, and behold,
[k]A tree in the midst of the earth,
And its height was great.
11 The tree grew and became strong;
Its height reached to the heavens,
And it could be seen to the ends of
all the earth.
12 Its leaves *were* lovely,
Its fruit abundant,
And in it *was* food for all.
[l]The beasts of the field found shade
under it,
The birds of the heavens dwelt in
its branches,
And all flesh was fed from it.

13 "I saw in the visions of my head
while on my bed, and there was [m]a
watcher, [n]a holy one, coming
down from heaven. 14 He cried
[1]aloud and said thus:

[o]'Chop down the tree and cut off its
branches,
Strip off its leaves and scatter its
fruit.
[p]Let the beasts get out from under
it,
And the birds from its branches.
15 Nevertheless leave the stump and
roots in the earth,
Bound with a band of iron and
bronze,
In the tender grass of the field.
Let it be wet with the dew of
heaven,
And *let* him graze with the beasts
On the grass of the earth.
16 Let his heart be changed from *that*
of a man,
Let him be given the heart of a
beast,
And let seven [q]times[2] pass over
him.
17 'This decision *is* by the decree of the
watchers,
And the sentence by the word of
the holy ones,
In order [r]that the living may
know
[s]That the Most High rules in the
kingdom of men,
[t]Gives it to whomever He will,
And sets over it the [u]lowest of
men.'

18 "This dream I, King Nebuchadnezzar, have seen. Now you, Belteshazzar, declare its interpretation,
[v]since all the wise *men* of my
kingdom are not able to make
known to me the interpretation;
but you *are* able, [w]for the Spirit of
the Holy God *is* in you."

Daniel Explains the Second Dream

19 Then Daniel, [x]whose name was
Belteshazzar, was astonished for a
time, and his thoughts [y]troubled
him. *So* the king spoke, and said,
"Belteshazzar, do not let the dream
or its interpretation trouble you."
Belteshazzar answered and said,
"My lord, *may* [z]the dream [3]concern
those who hate you, and its
interpretation [4]concern your
enemies!

20 [a]"The tree that you saw, which
grew and became strong, whose
height reached to the heavens and
which *could be seen* by all the earth,
21 whose leaves *were* lovely and its
fruit abundant, in which *was* food
for all, under which the beasts of
the field dwelt, and in whose
branches the birds of the heaven
had their home— 22 [b]it *is* you, O
king, who have grown and become

10 [k]Ezek. 31:3; Dan. 4:20
12 [l]Jer. 27:6; Ezek. 17:23; 31:6; Lam. 4:20
13 [m][Dan. 4:17, 23] [n]Deut. 33:2; Ps. 89:7; Dan. 8:13; Zech. 14:5; Jude 14
14 [o]Ezek. 31:10-14; Dan. 4:23; [Matt. 3:10; 7:19; Luke 13:7-9] [p]Ezek. 31:12, 13; Dan. 4:12 [1]Lit. *with strength*
16 [q]Dan. 11:13; 12:7 [2]Possibly *years*
17 [r]Ps. 9:16; 83:18 [s]Dan. 2:21; 4:25, 32; 5:21 [t]Jer. 27:5-7; Ezek. 29:18-20; Dan. 2:37; 5:18 [u]1 Sam. 2:8; Dan. 11:21
18 [v]Gen. 41:8, 15; Dan. 5:8, 15 [w]Dan. 4:8, 9; 5:11, 14
19 [x]Dan. 4:8 [y]Jer. 4:19; Dan. 7:15, 28; 8:27 [z]2 Sam. 18:32; Jer. 29:7; Dan. 4:24; 10:16 [3]*be for* [4]*for*
20 [a]Dan. 4:10-12
22 [b]Dan. 2:37, 38

here (*see note on 2:4*). Some believe he meant "a spirit of the holy gods." This is unlikely, since no pagan worshipers claimed purity or holiness for their deities. In fact, just the opposite was believed. And since Nebuchadnezzar was rehearsing his conversion, he could genuinely identify the true Spirit of God.

4:10-17 A tree. This pictures Nebuchadnezzar after 605 B.C. (cf. 4:20-22). The creatures in v. 12 represent people under his rule (v. 22). The fall of the tree represents the coming time of God's judgment on him (cf. 4:23-25).

4:13 a watcher, a holy one. This was an angel (cf. v. 23), a servant of God, who controlled a nation's rise or fall (cf. Dan. 10:13). Angels often have roles administering God's judgment, as shown also in Gen. 18, Is. 37, and Rev. 16.

4:15 stump. The basis (nucleus) of the kingdom, still in existence in v. 26 (as Is. 6:13), will later sprout as in nature (Job 14:7-9). The band is a guarantee that God will protect what remains intact and preserve the king's rule (v. 26).

4:16 heart of a beast. Some form of the disease called lycanthropy, in which a person thinks he is an animal and lives wildly, caused him to eat grass, have thick and unkept nails, shaggy hair, and behave inhumanly. **seven times.** (cf. also 4:23,25,32). Probably "years" are meant, not "months." which is used v. 29. Daniel uses the same term clearly to mean "years" in 7:25.

4:19 astonished. Daniel's compassionate alarm at the coming calamity.

strong; for your greatness has
grown and reaches to the heavens,
[c]and your dominion to the end of
the earth.

23 [d]"And inasmuch as the king saw a
watcher, a holy one, coming down
from heaven and saying, 'Chop
down the tree and destroy it, but
leave its stump and roots in the
earth, *bound* with a band of iron
and bronze in the tender grass of
the field; let it be wet with the dew
of heaven, [e]and let him graze with
the beasts of the field, till seven
[5]times pass over him'; 24 this is the
interpretation, O king, and this is
the decree of the Most High, which
has come upon my lord the king:
25 They shall [f]drive you from men,
your dwelling shall be with the
beasts of the field, and they shall
make you [g]eat grass like oxen.
They shall wet you with the dew of
heaven, and seven [6]times shall
pass over you, [h]till you know that
the Most High rules in the
kingdom of men, and [i]gives it to
whomever He chooses.

26 "And inasmuch as they gave the
command to leave the stump *and*
roots of the tree, your kingdom
shall be assured to you, after you
come to know that [j]Heaven[7] rules.
27 Therefore, O king, let my advice
be acceptable to you; [k]break off
your sins by *being* righteous, and
your iniquities by showing mercy
to *the* poor. [l]Perhaps there may be
[m]a [8]lengthening of your
prosperity."

Nebuchadnezzar's Humiliation

28 All *this* came upon King Nebuchadnezzar. 29 At the end of the
twelve months he was walking
[9]about the royal palace of Babylon.
30 The king [n]spoke, saying, "Is not
this great Babylon, that I have built
for a royal dwelling by my mighty
power and for the honor of my
majesty?"

31 [o]While the word *was still* in the
king's mouth, [p]a voice fell from
heaven: "King Nebuchadnezzar, to
you it is spoken: the kingdom has
departed from you! 32 And [q]they
shall drive you from men, and
your dwelling *shall be* with the
beasts of the field. They shall make
you eat grass like oxen; and seven
[1]times shall pass over you, until
you know that the Most High rules
in the kingdom of men, and gives
it to whomever He chooses."

33 That very hour the word was
fulfilled concerning Nebuchadnezzar; he was driven from men
and ate grass like oxen; his body
was wet with the dew of heaven
till his hair had grown like eagles'
feathers and his nails like birds'
claws.

Nebuchadnezzar Praises God

34 And [r]at the end of the [2]time I,
Nebuchadnezzar, lifted my eyes to
heaven, and my understanding
returned to me; and I blessed the
Most High and praised and
honored Him [s]who lives forever:

For His dominion *is* [t]an everlasting
dominion,
And His kingdom *is* from
generation to generation.
35 [u]All the inhabitants of the earth *are*
reputed as nothing;
[v]He does according to His will in
the army of heaven
And *among* the inhabitants of the
earth.
[w]No one can restrain His hand
Or say to Him, [x]"What have You
done?"

36 At the same time my reason
returned to me, [y]and for the glory
of my kingdom, my honor and
splendor returned to me. My
counselors and nobles resorted to
me, I was [z]restored to my
kingdom, and excellent majesty
was [a]added to me. 37 Now I, Nebu-

22 [c]Jer. 27:6-8
23 [d]Dan. 4:13-15 [e]Dan. 5:21 [5]Possibly *years*
25 [f]Dan. 4:32; 5:21 [g]Ps. 106:20 [h]Ps. 83:18; Dan. 4:2, 17, 32 [i]Jer. 27:5 [6]Possibly *years*
26 [j]Matt. 21:25; Luke 15:18 [7]God
27 [k][Prov. 28:13]; Is. 55:7; Ezek. 18:21, 22; [Rom. 2:9-11; 1 Pet. 4:8] [l][Ps. 41:1-3]; Is. 58:6, 7, 10 [m]1 Kin. 21:29 [8]*prolonging*
29 [9]Or *upon*
30 [n]Prov. 16:18; Is. 13:19; Dan. 5:20

31 [o]Dan. 5:5; Luke 12:20 [p]Dan. 4:24
32 [q][Dan. 4:25] [1]Possibly *years*
34 [r]Dan. 4:26 [s]Ps. 102:24-27; Dan. 6:26; 12:7; [Rev. 4:10] [t][Ps. 10:16]; Dan. 2:44; 7:14; Mic. 4:7; [Luke 1:33] [2]Lit. *days*
35 [u]Ps. 39:5; Is. 40:15, 17 [v]Ps. 115:3; 135:6; Dan. 6:27 [w]Job 34:29; Is. 43:13 [x]Job 9:12; Is. 45:9; Jer. 18:6; Rom. 9:20; [1 Cor. 2:16]
36 [y]Dan. 4:26 [z]2 Chr. 20:20 [a]Job 42:12; [Prov. 22:4; Matt. 6:33]

4:26 Heaven rules. God is synonymous with His abode.

4:27 break off your sins. Daniel called for a recognition of sin and repentance (cf. Is. 55:7). He was not presenting a works salvation, but treating the issue of sin exactly as Jesus did with the rich young ruler in Matt. 19:16-23. The king failed to repent at this point (v. 30).

4:30 I have built. Nebuchadnezzar was known for his building projects, such as a 400 foot high mountain terraced with flowing water and hanging gardens for his wife (one of the 7 wonders of the ancient world) as a place for cool refreshment. For such pride, judgment fell (vv. 31-33).

4:34 lifted my eyes. God's grace enables a person to do this (John 6:44,65). "For those who honor Me I will honor" (1 Sam. 2:30); and "Surely He [God] scorns the scornful, but gives grace to the humble" (Prov. 3:34). The praise of vv. 34b-37 and 1-3 came as a result (cf. Jer. 9:23,24).

chadnezzar, [b]praise and extol and
honor the King of heaven, [c]all of
whose works *are* truth, and His
ways justice. [d]And those who walk
in pride He is able to put down.

Belshazzar's Feast

5 Belshazzar the king [a]made a great feast
for a thousand of his lords, and drank
wine in the presence of the thousand.
2 While he tasted the wine, Belshazzar
gave the command to bring the gold and
silver vessels [b]which his [1]father Nebuchadnezzar had taken from the temple
which *had been* in Jerusalem, that the king
and his lords, his wives, and his concubines might drink from them. **3** Then they
brought the gold [c]vessels that had been
taken from the temple of the house of God
which *had been* in Jerusalem; and the king
and his lords, his wives, and his concubines drank from them. **4** They drank wine,
[d]and praised the gods of gold and silver,
bronze and iron, wood and stone.
5 [e]In the same hour the fingers of a
man's hand appeared and wrote opposite
the lampstand on the plaster of the wall of
the king's palace; and the king saw the part
of the hand that wrote. **6** Then the king's
countenance changed, and his thoughts
troubled him, so that the joints of his hips
were loosened and his [f]knees knocked
against each other. **7** [g]The king cried
[2]aloud to bring in [h]the astrologers, the
Chaldeans, and the soothsayers. The king
spoke, saying to the wise *men* of Babylon,
"Whoever reads this writing, and tells me
its interpretation, shall be clothed with
purple and *have* a chain of gold around his
neck; [i]and he shall be the third ruler in the
kingdom." **8** Now all the king's wise *men*
came, [j]but they could not read the writing,
or make known to the king its interpretation. **9** Then King Belshazzar was greatly
[k]troubled, his countenance was changed,
and his lords were [3]astonished.
10 The queen, because of the words of
the king and his lords, came to the banquet
hall. The queen spoke, saying, "O king,
live forever! Do not let your thoughts trouble you, nor let your countenance change.
11 [l]There is a man in your kingdom in
whom *is* the Spirit of the Holy God. And in
the days of your [4]father, light and understanding and wisdom, like the wisdom of
the gods, were found in him; and King
Nebuchadnezzar your [4]father—your father the king—made him chief of the magicians, astrologers, Chaldeans, *and* soothsayers. **12** Inasmuch as an excellent spirit,
knowledge, understanding, interpreting
dreams, solving riddles, and [5]explaining
enigmas were found in this Daniel,
[m]whom the king named Belteshazzar, now
let Daniel be called, and he will give the interpretation."

The Writing on the Wall Explained

13 Then Daniel was brought in before the
king. The king spoke, and said to Daniel,
"*Are* you that Daniel [6]who is one of the
captives from Judah, whom my [7]father the
king brought from Judah? **14** I have heard
of you, that [n]the [8]Spirit of God *is* in you,
and *that* light and understanding and excellent wisdom are found in you. **15** Now
[o]the wise *men,* the astrologers, have been
brought in before me, that they should
read this writing and make known to me
its interpretation, but they could not give
the interpretation of the thing. **16** And I
have heard of you, that you can give interpretations and [9]explain enigmas. [p]Now if
you can read the writing and make known
to me its interpretation, you shall be
clothed with purple and *have* a chain of
gold around your neck, and shall be the
third ruler in the kingdom."
17 Then Daniel answered, and said before the king, "Let your gifts be for yourself, and give your rewards to another; yet
I will read the writing to the king, and
make known to him the interpretation.
18 O king, [q]the Most High God gave Nebuchadnezzar your [1]father a kingdom and
majesty, glory and honor. **19** And because
of the majesty that He gave him, [r]all peoples, nations, and languages trembled and

37 [b] Dan. 2:46, 47; 3:28, 29 [c] Deut. 32:4; [Ps. 33:4]; Is. 5:16; [Rev. 15:3] [d] Ex. 18:11; Job 40:11, 12; Dan. 5:20

CHAPTER 5

1 [a] Esth. 1:3; Is. 22:12-14
2 [b] 2 Kin. 24:13; 25:15; Ezra 1:7-11; Jer. 52:19; Dan. 1:2 [1] Or *ancestor*
3 [c] 2 Chr. 36:10
4 [d] Is. 42:8; Dan. 5:23; Rev. 9:20
5 [e] Dan. 4:31
6 [f] Ezek. 7:17; 21:7
7 [g] Dan. 4:6, 7; 5:11, 15 [h] Is. 47:13 [i] Dan. 6:2, 3 [2] Lit. *with strength*
8 [j] Gen. 41:8; Dan. 2:27; 4:7; 5:15
9 [k] Job 18:11; Is. 21:2-4; Jer. 6:24; Dan. 2:1; 5:6 [3] *perplexed*
11 [l] Dan. 2:48; 4:8, 9, 18 [4] Or *ancestor*
12 [m] Dan. 1:7; 4:8 [5] Lit. *untying knots*
13 [6] Lit. *who is of the sons of the captivity* [7] Or *ancestor*
14 [n] Dan. 4:8, 9, 18; 5:11, 12 [8] Or *spirit of the gods*
15 [o] Dan. 5:7, 8
16 [p] Dan. 5:7, 29 [9] Lit. *untie knots*
18 [q] Jer. 27:5-7; Dan. 2:37, 38; 4:17, 22, 25 [1] Or *ancestor*
19 [r] Jer. 27:7

5:1 Belshazzar. These events occurred in 539 B.C., over two decades after his father, Nebuchadnezzar's death (ca. 563/2 B.C.). This king, whose name (similar to Daniel's, cf. 4:8), means "Bel, protect the king," is about to be conquered by the Medo-Persian army.

5:2 vessels. The celebration was designed to boost morale and break the feelings of doom, because at this very time, armies of Medo-Persia (cf. v. 30) had Babylon helplessly under siege.

5:4 This exercise was a call for their deities to deliver them.

5:5 man's hand. Babylonian hands had taken God's vessels (mentioned twice) and held them in contempt to dishonor and challenge Him. Now the Hand that controls all men, and which none can restrain, challenged them (4:35). God's answer to their challenge was clear, as in vv. 23-28.

5:7-9 they could not. Without God's help, the experts again failed (cf. chaps. 2, 4), but God's man Daniel would not.

5:10 The queen spoke. Possibly she was a surviving wife or a daughter of Nebuchadnezzar. If the latter, she was a wife of Nabonidus who co-ruled with Belshazzar (cf. "third ruler," v. 16). She, like Nebuchadnezzar in chap. 4, has confidence in Daniel (vv. 11, 12).

5:13 father. Used in the same sense of grandfather (cf. 5:18).

5:16 the third ruler. This trio included Daniel, along with Belshazzar, Nebuchadnezzar's grandson (ruled 553–539 B.C.), and Nabonidus (ruled 556–539 B.C.). The prizes turned out to be non-existent in light of the city's conquest that very night (vv. 29, 30).

feared before him. Whomever he wished,
he [s]executed; whomever he wished, he
kept alive; whomever he wished, he set up;
and whomever he wished, he put down.
20 [t]But when his heart was lifted up, and
his spirit was hardened in pride, he was
deposed from his kingly throne, and they
took his glory from him. 21 Then he was
[u]driven from the sons of men, his heart
was made like the beasts, and his dwelling
was with the wild donkeys. They fed him
with grass like oxen, and his body was wet
with the dew of heaven, [v]till he [2]knew that
the Most High God rules in the kingdom of
men, and appoints over it whomever He
chooses.
22 "But you his son, Belshazzar, [w]have
not humbled your heart, although you
knew all this. 23 [x]And you have [3]lifted
yourself up against the Lord of heaven.
They have brought the [y]vessels of [4]His
house before you, and you and your lords,
your wives and your concubines, have
drunk wine from them. And you have
praised the gods of silver and gold, bronze
and iron, wood and stone, [z]which do not
see or hear or know; and the God who
holds your breath in His hand [a]and owns
all your ways, you have not glorified.
24 Then the [5]fingers of the hand were sent
from Him, and this writing was written.
25 "And this is the inscription that was
written:

[6]MENE, MENE, [7]TEKEL, [8]UPHARSIN.

26 This *is* the interpretation of *each* word.
MENE: God has numbered your kingdom,
and finished it; 27 TEKEL: [b]You have been
weighed in the balances, and found wanting; 28 PERES: Your kingdom has been divided, and given to the [c]Medes and [d]Per-
sians."[9] 29 Then Belshazzar gave the
command, and they clothed Daniel with
purple and *put* a chain of gold around his
neck, and made a proclamation concerning
him [e]that he should be the third ruler in
the kingdom.

Belshazzar's Fall

30 [f]That very night Belshazzar, king of
the Chaldeans, was slain. 31 [g]And Darius
the Mede received the kingdom, *being*
about sixty-two years old.

The Plot Against Daniel

6 It pleased Darius to set over the kingdom one hundred and twenty satraps,
to be over the whole kingdom; 2 and over
these, three governors, of whom Daniel
was one, that the satraps might give account to them, so that the king would suffer no loss. 3 Then this Daniel distinguished himself above the governors and
satraps, [a]because an excellent spirit *was* in
him; and the king gave thought to setting
him over the whole realm. 4 [b]So the governors and satraps sought to find *some*
charge against Daniel concerning the kingdom; but they could find no charge or
fault, because he *was* faithful; nor was
there any error or fault found in him.
5 Then these men said, "We shall not find
any charge against this Daniel unless we
find *it* against him concerning the law of
his God."
6 So these governors and satraps
thronged before the king, and said thus to

19 [s] Dan. 2:12, 13; 3:6 **20** [t] Ex. 9:17; Job 15:25; Is. 14:13-15; Dan. 4:30, 37 **21** [u] Job 30:3-7; Dan. 4:32, 33 [v] Ex. 9:14-16; Ps. 83:17, 18; Ezek. 17:24; [Dan. 4:17, 34, 35] [2] Recognized **22** [w] Ex. 10:3; 2 Chr. 33:23; 36:12 **23** [x] Dan. 5:3, 4 [y] Ex. 40:9; Num. 18:3; Is. 52:11; Heb. 9:21 [z] Ps. 115:5, 6; Is. 37:19; Hab. 2:18, 19; Acts 17:24-26; Rom. 1:21 [a] Ps. 139:3; Prov. 20:24; [Jer. 10:23] [3] Exalted [4] The temple **24** [5] Lit. *palm* **25** [6] Lit. *a mina* (50 shekels) from the verb "to number" [7] Lit. *a shekel* from the verb "to weigh" [8] Lit. *and half-shekels* from the verb "to divide"; pl. of *Peres,* v. 28 **27** [b] Job 31:6; Ps. 62:9; Jer. 6:30

28 [c] Is. 21:2; Dan. 5:31; 9:1 [d] Dan. 6:28; Acts 2:9 [9] Aram. *Paras,* consonant with *Peres* **29** [e] Dan. 5:7, 16 **30** [f] Jer. 51:31, 39, 57 **31** [g] Dan. 2:39; 9:1

CHAPTER 6

3 [a] Dan. 5:12 **4** [b] Eccl. 4:4

5:25-29 MENE, MENE. This means "counted," or "appointed," and is doubled for stronger emphasis. *Tekel* means "weighed" or "assessed," by the God who weighs actions (1 Sam. 2:3; Ps. 62:9). *Peres* denotes "divided," i.e., to the Medes and Persians. *Pharsin* in v. 25 is the plural of *peres,* possibly emphasizing the parts in the division. The "U" prefix on *pharsin* has the idea of the English "and."

5:30 That very night. One ancient account alleged that Persia's General Ugbaru had troops dig a trench to divert and thus lower the waters of the Euphrates River. Since the river flowed through the city of Babylon, the lowered water enabled besiegers to unexpectedly invade via the waterway under the thick walls and reach the palace before the city was aware. The end then came quickly, as guards, Belshazzar, and others were slain on Oct. 16, 539 B.C.

5:31 Darius the Mede. Possibly Darius is not a name, but an honored title for Cyrus, who with his army entered Babylon Oct. 29, 539 B.C. It is used in inscriptions for at least 5 Persian rulers. History mentions no specific man named Darius the Mede. In 6:28 it is possible to translate, "Darius even . . . Cyrus." A less likely possibility is that Darius is a second name for Gubaru, Cyrus' appointed king to head up the Babylonian sector of his empire. Gubaru (or Gobryas) is distinct from Ugbaru, the general, who died soon after conquering Babylon. As previously prophesied, Babylon met God's judgment (cf. Is. 13,47; Jer. 50,51; Hab. 2:5-19).

6:1 satraps. Each is a provincial administrator under the king. Daniel's eminent appointment was to a post as "governor" (v. 2), assisting the king as his vice-regent.

6:2 suffer no loss. They were responsible to prevent loss from military revolts, tax evasion, or fraud.

6:3 an excellent spirit. Daniel, over 80, had enjoyed God's blessing throughout his life (cf. 1:20,21; 2:49; 4:8; 5:12). **over the whole realm.** Daniel was the favorite of the king. He had experience, wisdom, a sense of history, leadership, a good reputation, ability, attitude, and revelation from the God of heaven. Apparently, God wanted him in the place of influence to encourage and assist in the Jews' return to Judah, since the return was made in Cyrus' first year (539–537 B.C.), right before the lions' den incident. From the record of Ezra 1 and 6, all the basic elements of the return appear: 1) the temple was to be rebuilt with the cost paid from Cyrus' treasury; 2) all Jews who visited could return, and those who stayed were urged to assist financially; and 3) the gold and silver vessels stolen from the temple by Nebuchadnezzar were to be taken back. To account for such favor toward the Jews, it is easy to think of Daniel not only influencing Cyrus to write such a decree, but even formulating it for him (cf. Prov. 21:1).

6:4 charge against Daniel. The jealous plot, not unlike the effort against Daniel's 3 friends in 3:8ff., was also similar to that by Joseph's brothers (cf. Gen. 37:18-24).

him: [c]"King Darius, live forever! 7 All the
governors of the kingdom, the administrators and satraps, the counselors and advisors, have [d]consulted together to establish
a royal statute and to make a firm decree,
that whoever petitions any god or man for
thirty days, except you, O king, shall be
cast into the den of lions. 8 Now, O king,
establish the decree and sign the writing,
so that it cannot be changed, according to
the [e]law of the Medes and Persians, which
[1]does not alter." 9 Therefore King Darius
signed the written decree.

Daniel in the Lions' Den

10 Now when Daniel knew that the writing was signed, he went home. And in his
upper room, with his windows open [f]to-
ward Jerusalem, he knelt down on his
knees [g]three times that day, and prayed
and gave thanks before his God, as was his
custom since early days.
11 Then these men assembled and found
Daniel praying and making supplication
before his God. 12 [h]And they went before
the king, and spoke concerning the king's
decree: "Have you not signed a decree that
every man who petitions any god or man
within thirty days, except you, O king,
shall be cast into the den of lions?"
The king answered and said, "The thing
is true, [i]according to the law of the Medes
and Persians, which [2]does not alter."
13 So they answered and said before the
king, "That Daniel, [j]who is [3]one of the captives from Judah, [k]does not show due regard for you, O king, or for the decree that
you have signed, but makes his petition
three times a day."
14 And the king, when he heard *these*
words, [l]was greatly displeased with himself, and set *his* heart on Daniel to deliver
him; and he [4]labored till the going down of
the sun to deliver him. 15 Then these men
[5]approached the king, and said to the king,
"Know, O king, that *it is* [m]the law of the
Medes and Persians that no decree or
statute which the king establishes may be
changed."
16 So the king gave the command, and
they brought Daniel and cast *him* into the
den of lions. *But* the king spoke, saying to
Daniel, "Your God, whom you serve continually, He will deliver you." 17 [n]Then a
stone was brought and laid on the mouth
of the den, [o]and the king sealed it with his
own signet ring and with the signets of his
lords, that the purpose concerning Daniel
might not be changed.

Daniel Saved from the Lions

18 Now the king went to his palace and
spent the night fasting; and no [6]musicians
were brought before him. [p]Also his sleep
[7]went from him. 19 Then the [q]king arose
very early in the morning and went in
haste to the den of lions. 20 And when he
came to the den, he cried out with a [8]la-
menting voice to Daniel. The king spoke,
saying to Daniel, "Daniel, servant of the
living God, [r]has your God, whom you
serve continually, been able to deliver you
from the lions?"
21 Then Daniel said to the king, [s]"O
king, live forever! 22 [t]My God sent His
angel and [u]shut the lions' mouths, so that
they have not hurt me, because I was
found innocent before Him; and also, O
king, I have done no wrong before you."
23 Now the king was exceedingly glad
for him, and commanded that they should
take Daniel up out of the den. So Daniel
was taken up out of the den, and no injury
whatever was found on him, [v]because he
believed in his God.

Darius Honors God

24 And the king gave the command,
[w]and they brought those men who had accused Daniel, and they cast *them* into the

6 [c] Neh. 2:3; Dan. 2:4; 6:21
7 [d] Ps. 59:3; 62:4; 64:2-6
8 [e] Esth. 1:19; 8:8; Dan. 6:12, 15 [1] Lit. *does not pass away*
10 [f] 1 Kin. 8:29, 30, 46-48; Ps. 5:7; Jon. 2:4 [g] Ps. 55:17; Acts 2:1, 2, 15; [Phil. 4:6]; 1 Thess. 5:17, 18
12 [h] Dan. 3:8-12; Acts 16:19-21 [i] Esth. 1:19; Dan. 6:8, 15 [2] Lit. *does not pass away*
13 [j] Dan. 1:6; 5:13 [k] Esth. 3:8; Dan. 3:12; Acts 5:29 [3] Lit. *of the sons of the captivity*
14 [l] Mark 6:26 [4] *strove*
15 [5] Lit. *thronged before*
[m] Esth. 8:8; Ps. 94:20, 21; Dan. 6:8, 12
17 [n] Lam. 3:53 [o] Matt. 27:66
18 [p] Esth. 6:1; Ps. 77:4; Dan. 2:1 [6] Exact meaning unknown [7] Or *fled*
19 [q] Dan. 3:24
20 [r] Gen. 18:14; Num. 11:23; Jer. 32:17; Dan. 3:17; [Luke 1:37] [8] Or *grieved*
21 [s] Dan. 2:4; 6:6
22 [t] Num. 20:16; Is. 63:9; Dan. 3:28; Acts 12:11; [Heb. 1:14] [u] Ps. 91:11-13; 2 Tim. 4:17; Heb. 11:33
23 [v] Heb. 11:33
24 [w] Deut. 19:18, 19; Esth. 7:10

6:7 except you, O king. A deceptive stroke of the king's ego secured his injunction, which was designed to benefit Daniel's peers. Ancient kings were frequently worshiped as gods. Pagans had such inferior views of their gods that such homage was no problem.

6:8 law…which does not alter. Once enacted, Medo-Persian law could not be changed, even by the king (cf. 6:12,15; Esth. 1:19; 8:8).

6:10 toward Jerusalem. Daniel's uncompromising pattern of prayer toward God's temple conformed to Solomon's prayer that the Lord's people would do so (1 Kin. 8:44,45). Three times a day was also the pattern established by David (Ps. 55:16,17).

6:13 one of the captives from Judah. Daniel had lived over 60 years in Babylon. His loyalty to the rulers was well known (5:13); in spite of that loyalty, his consistent faithfulness to God brought this threat.

6:14 He went from a self-styled god to a fool in one day.

6:16 den of lions. The word "den" is related to the Heb. term meaning "to dig," so it refers to an underground pit which likely had 1) a hole at the top from which to drop food into the pit, and 2) a door at the foot of a ramp or on a hillside through which the lions could enter.

6:22 His angel. In this miracle, the angel was possibly the same person as the fourth person in the fiery furnace (cf. 3:25 and *see note there*). **innocent before Him.** That is the supreme commendation of Daniel as blameless before God and unworthy of such a death.

6:23 no injury…on him. God openly honored Daniel's faith for the purpose of showing His glory (cf. 3:26,27). That is not always the case, as God may choose to be glorified by permitting a trusted servant to be martyred (cf. Daniel in Heb. 11:33 with others in 11:35-38).

6:24 the king gave the command. Like the sin of Achan (Josh. 7:20-26), this sin against God, Darius, and Daniel cost the men and their families their lives. This judgment of God was also an important detail in the miracle, lest some critic suggest the lions were tame or toothless or not hungry.

den of lions—them, [x]their children, and
their wives; and the lions overpowered
them, and broke all their bones in pieces
before they ever came to the bottom of the
den.
25 [y]Then King Darius wrote:

To all peoples, nations, and
languages that dwell in all the
earth:

Peace be multiplied to you.

26 [z]I make a decree that in every
dominion of my kingdom *men
must* [a]tremble and fear before the
God of Daniel.

[b]For He *is* the living God,
And steadfast forever;
His kingdom *is the one* which shall
not be [c]destroyed,
And His dominion *shall endure* to
the end.
27 He delivers and rescues,
[d]And He works signs and wonders
In heaven and on earth,
Who has delivered Daniel from the
[9]power of the lions.

28 So this Daniel prospered in the reign
of Darius [e]and in the reign of [f]Cyrus the
Persian.

Vision of the Four Beasts

7 In the first year of Belshazzar king of
Babylon, [a]Daniel [1]had a dream and
[b]visions of his head *while* on his bed. Then
he wrote down the dream, telling [2]the
main facts.

24 [x]Deut. 24:16; 2 Kin. 14:6; Esth. 9:10
25 [y]Ezra 1:1, 2; Esth. 3:12; 8:9; Dan. 4:1
26 [z]Ezra 6:8-12; 7:13; Dan. 3:29 [a]Ps. 99:1 [b]Dan. 4:34; 6:20; Hos. 1:10; Rom. 9:26 [c]Dan. 2:44; 4:3; 7:14, 27; [Luke 1:33]
27 [d]Dan. 4:2, 3 [9]Lit. *hand*
28 [e]Dan. 1:21 [f]Ezra 1:1, 2

CHAPTER 7

1 [a]Num. 12:6; [Amos 3:7] [b][Dan. 2:28] [1]Lit. *saw* [2]Lit. *the head* or *chief of the words*

3 [c]Dan. 7:17; Rev. 13:1; 17:8
4 [d]Deut. 28:49; 2 Sam. 1:23; Jer. 48:40; Ezek. 17:3; Hab. 1:8 [e]Dan. 4:16, 34
5 [f]Dan. 2:39
6 [g]Dan. 8:8, 22
7 [h]Dan. 2:40 [i]Dan. 2:41; Rev. 12:3; 13:1
8 [j]Dan. 8:9 [k]Rev. 9:7 [l]Ps. 12:3; Rev. 13:5, 6 [3]Lit. *great things*
9 [m][Rev. 20:4] [n]Ps. 90:2 [o]Ps. 104:2; Rev. 1:14 [4]Or *set up*

2 Daniel spoke, saying, "I saw in my vision by night, and behold, the four winds
of heaven were stirring up the Great Sea.
3 And four great beasts [c]came up from the
sea, each different from the other. 4 The
first *was* [d]like a lion, and had eagle's
wings. I watched till its wings were
plucked off; and it was lifted up from the
earth and made to stand on two feet like a
man, and a [e]man's heart was given to it.
5 [f]"And suddenly another beast, a second, like a bear. It was raised up on one
side, and *had* three ribs in its mouth between its teeth. And they said thus to it:
'Arise, devour much flesh!'
6 "After this I looked, and there was another, like a leopard, which had on its back
four wings of a bird. The beast also had
[g]four heads, and dominion was given to it.
7 "After this I saw in the night visions,
and behold, [h]a fourth beast, dreadful and
terrible, exceedingly strong. It had huge
iron teeth; it was devouring, breaking in
pieces, and trampling the residue with its
feet. It *was* different from all the beasts that
were before it, [i]and it had ten horns. 8 I was
considering the horns, and [j]there was another horn, a little one, coming up among
them, before whom three of the first horns
were plucked out by the roots. And there,
in this horn, *were* eyes like the eyes [k]of a
man, [l]and a mouth speaking [3]pompous
words.

Vision of the Ancient of Days

9 "I [m]watched till thrones were [4]put
in place,
And [n]the Ancient of Days was
seated;
[o]His garment *was* white as snow,

6:25-27 King Darius wrote. Impacted by Daniel and by the Lord, he expressed himself as if he had come to a point of personal trust in God for his salvation such as Nebuchadnezzar (cf. 4:1-3,34-37). Daniel illustrated the evangelistic potency of a godly, uncompromising life. Cf. Matt. 5:48.

7:1 first year. This represented a flashback to 553 B.C., 14 years before the feast of 5:1-3. Chapters 7,8 occur after chap. 4, but before chap. 5. The dream of Dan. 7 moves far beyond Daniel's day to the coming of Israel's king to end all Gentile kingdoms and to establish His eternal kingdom (7:13,14,27; as 2:35,45).

7:2 Great Sea. This superlative refers to the Mediterranean, much greater in size than other bodies of water in that area of the world. Here this "sea" is used to represent nations and peoples (cf. Dan. 7:3,17; Rev. 13:1).

7:3 four…beasts. These beasts represent the same empires as the individual parts of the image in chap. 2. Christ the King, the Son of Man from heaven (vv. 13,14), corresponds to the Stone in 2:35,45.

7:4 lion…wings. The vicious, powerful, swift king of beasts represents Babylon. Winged lions guarded the gates of the royal palaces of Babylon. Daniel's contemporaries, Jeremiah, Ezekiel, and Habakkuk, used animals to describe Nebuchadnezzar.

7:5 a bear. This is Medo-Persia, with the greater "side" being Persia and "ribs" referring to vanquished nations.

7:6 a leopard. This represents Greece with its fleetness in conquest under Alexander the Great (born in 356 B.C.). He ruled from Europe to Africa to India. The "four heads" represent the 4 generals who divided the kingdom after Alexander's death at age 33 (323 B.C.). They ruled Macedonia, Asia Minor, Syria, and Egypt (cf. 8:8).

7:7 fourth beast. No such animal exists; rather this is a unique beast pointing to the Roman Empire, already represented by iron in 2:40, devastating in conquest. Roman dominion fell apart in A.D. 476, yet it lived on in a divided status (Europe), but will be revived and return to great unified strength near Christ's second coming. Then it will be comprised of the 10 parts under kings (vv. 7,24), as well as an 11th king, the Antichrist (vv. 8,24; 2 Thess. 2:3-10; Rev. 13:1-10).

7:8 another horn. This describes the rise of Antichrist (cf. v. 20). This beast is human ("eyes like a man" and a "mouth speaking") and is proud (cf. Rev. 13:5,6).

7:9,10 I watched. Daniel's vision flashes forward to the divine throne from which judgment will come on the fourth kingdom (cf. Rev. 20:11-15).

And the hair of His head *was* like
pure wool.
His throne *was* a fiery flame,
[p]Its wheels a burning fire;
10 [q]A fiery stream issued
And came forth from before Him.
[r]A thousand thousands ministered
to Him;
Ten thousand times ten thousand
stood before Him.
[s]The [5]court was seated,
And the books were opened.

11 "I watched then because of the sound
of the [6]pompous words which the horn
was speaking; [t]I watched till the beast was
slain, and its body destroyed and given to
the burning flame. 12 As for the rest of the
beasts, they had their dominion taken
away, yet their lives were prolonged for a
season and a time.

13 "I was watching in the night
visions,
And behold, [u]*One* like the Son of
Man,
Coming with the clouds of heaven!
He came to the Ancient of Days,
And they brought Him near before
Him.
14 [v]Then to Him was given dominion
and glory and a kingdom,
That all [w]peoples, nations, and
languages should serve Him.
His dominion *is* [x]an everlasting
dominion,
Which shall not pass away,
And His kingdom *the one*
Which shall not be destroyed.

Daniel's Visions Interpreted

15 "I, Daniel, was grieved in my spirit
[7]within *my* body, and the visions of my
head troubled me. 16 I came near to one of

9 [p]Ezek. 1:15
10 [q]Ps. 50:3; Is. 30:33; 66:15 [r]Deut. 33:2; 1 Kin. 22:19; Ps. 68:17; Rev. 5:11 [s]Dan. 12:1; [Rev. 20:11-15] [5]Or *judgment*
11 [t][Rev. 19:20; 20:10] [6]Lit. *great*
13 [u]Ezek. 1:26; [Matt. 24:30; 26:64; Mark 13:26; 14:62; Luke 21:27; Rev. 1:7, 13; 14:14]
14 [v]Ps. 2:6-8; Dan. 7:27; [Matt. 28:18; John 3:35, 36; 1 Cor. 15:27; Eph. 1:22; Phil. 2:9-11; Rev. 1:6; 11:15] [w]Dan. 3:4 [x]Ps. 145:13; Mic. 4:7; [Luke 1:33]; John 12:34; Heb. 12:28
15 [7]Lit. *in the midst of its sheath*

7:11,12 the beast was slain. Reference is to the fourth beast (i.e., the Roman sphere), headed up by the "little horn" or Antichrist (vv. 7,24). He will be destroyed at Christ's second coming (cf. Rev. 19:20; 20:10); cf. the smashing by the Stone, Dan. 2:35,45.

7:12 rest of the beasts. These are the 3 earlier beasts (empires of chaps. 2,7). Each successively lost its chief dominance when it was conquered in history. Yet each was amalgamated into the empire that gained ascendancy, and survived in its descendants. As the second advent draws near, all 3 empires in their descendants will be a part of the Roman phase in its final form (Rev. 13:2). Survival will *not* be possible for the final and revived phase of the fourth empire after Christ's second coming, for catastrophic devastation (cf. 2:35) will utterly destroy it, and Christ's kingdom will replace it.

7:13,14 Son of Man. The Messiah (cf. 9:26), Christ is meant; He often designated Himself by this phrase (Matt. 16:26; 19:28; 26:64). "The clouds of heaven" are seen again in Rev. 1:7. Here He is distinct from the Ancient of Days, or Eternal One, the Father, who will coronate Him for the kingdom (2:44). The picture of old age is not that of being feeble, rather it highlights eternality and divine wisdom to judge (as 7:9,10).

7:14 all peoples, nations, and languages. These distinctions are earthly and speak of the promise of an earthly kingdom, ruled by Christ, that merges into the eternal kingdom (cf. vv. 18,27; Rev. 20:1-4,21,22).

7:15 grieved in my spirit. Coming judgment made him sad, because it meant that history to its end would be a story of sin and judgment (cf. v. 28).

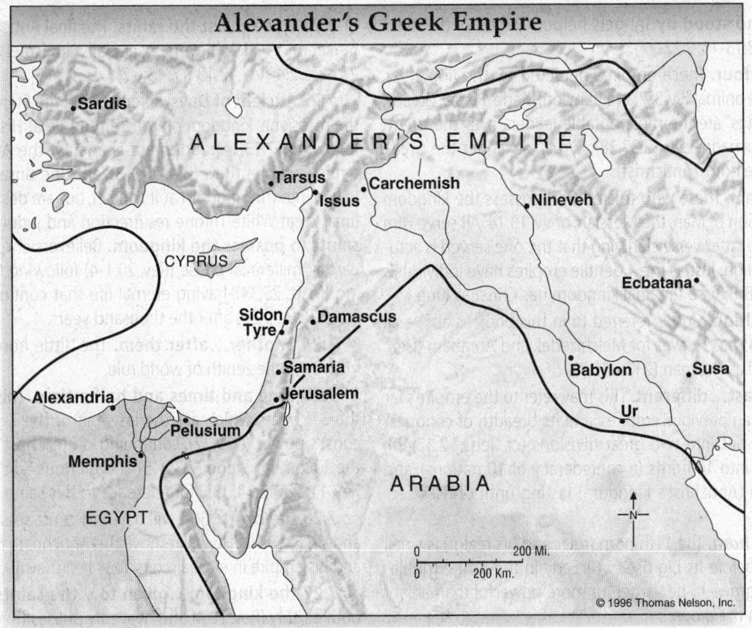

those who stood by, and asked him the
truth of all this. So he told me and made
known to me the interpretation of these
things: 17 'Those great beasts, which are
four, *are* four [8]kings *which* arise out of the
earth. 18 But [y]the saints of the Most High
shall receive the kingdom, and possess
the kingdom forever, even forever and
ever.'
19 "Then I wished to know the truth
about the fourth beast, which was different
from all the others, exceedingly dreadful,
with its teeth of iron and its nails of bronze,
which devoured, broke in pieces, and trampled the residue with its feet; 20 and the ten
horns that *were* on its head, and the other
horn which came up, before which three
fell, namely, that horn which had eyes and
a mouth which spoke [9]pompous words,
whose appearance *was* greater than his fellows.
21 "I was watching; [z]and the same horn
was making war against the saints, and
prevailing against them, 22 until the Ancient of Days came, [a]and a judgment was
made *in favor* of the saints of the Most
High, and the time came for the saints to
possess the kingdom.
23 "Thus he said:

'The fourth beast shall be
[b]A fourth kingdom on earth,
Which shall be different from all
other kingdoms,
And shall devour the whole earth,
Trample it and break it in pieces.
24 [c]The ten horns *are* ten kings
Who shall arise from this kingdom.
And another shall rise after them;
He shall be different from the first
ones,
And shall subdue three kings.
25 [d]He shall speak *pompous* words
against the Most High,
Shall [e]persecute[1] the saints of the
Most High,
And shall [f]intend to change times
and law.
Then [g]*the saints* shall be given into
his hand
[h]For a time and times and half a
time.

26 'But[i] the court shall be seated,
And they shall [j]take away his
dominion,
To consume and destroy *it* forever.
27 Then the [k]kingdom and dominion,
And the greatness of the kingdoms
under the whole heaven,
Shall be given to the people, the
saints of the Most High.
[l]His kingdom *is* an everlasting
kingdom,
[m]And all dominions shall serve and
obey Him.'

28 "This *is* the end of the [2]account. As for
me, Daniel, [n]my thoughts greatly troubled
me, and my countenance changed; but I
[o]kept the matter in my heart."

17 [8] Representing their kingdoms, v. 23
18 [y] Ps. 149:5-9; Is. 60:12-14; Dan. 7:14; [2 Tim. 2:11; Rev. 2:26, 27; 20:4; 22:5]
20 [9] Lit. *great things*
21 [z] Rev. 11:7; 13:7; 17:14
22 [a] [Rev. 1:6]
23 [b] Dan. 2:40
24 [c] Dan. 7:7; Rev. 13:1; 17:12
25 [d] Is. 37:23; Dan. 11:36; Rev. 13:1-6 [e] Rev. 17:6 [f] Dan. 2:21 [g] Rev. 13:7; 18:24 [h] Dan. 12:7; Rev. 12:14 [1] Lit. *wear out*
26 [i] [Dan. 2:35; 7:10, 22] [j] Rev. 19:20
27 [k] Is. 54:3; Dan. 7:14, 18, 22; Rev. 20:4 [l] 2 Sam. 7:16; Ps. 89:35-37; Is. 9:7; Dan. 2:44; 4:34; 7:14; [Luke 1:33, 34]; John 12:34; [Rev. 11:15; 22:5] [m] Ps. 2:6-12; 22:27; 72:11; 86:9; Is. 60:12; Rev. 11:1
28 [n] Dan. 8:27 [o] Luke 2:19, 51 [2] Lit. *word*

7:16 those who stood by. Angels helped Daniel understand God's revelations (8:13-16; 9:22-27).

7:17 beasts…four. These empires depicted by the lion, bear, leopard, and bizarre animal (vv. 3-7) are Babylon, Medo-Persia, Greece, and Rome. The "kings" are the most notable leaders over these empires, such as Nebuchadnezzar (2:37,38), Cyrus, Alexander the Great, and finally the "little horn" (Antichrist).

7:18,22,27 saints. These who trusted God possess the kingdom headed up by the Son of Man, the Messiah, of vv. 13,14. All serve Him in vv. 14 and 27, the latter verse clarifying that the one served is actually God the Most High. Just as the 4 Gentile empires have individuals as kings (cf. 2:38; 7:8; 8:8), so the final kingdom has Christ as King.

7:18 the Most High. God is referred to in this book as above all gods (2:47; 3:29; 4:35), as He was for Melchizedek and Abraham (Gen. 14:19,20,22) as well as Naaman (2 Kin. 5:17).

7:19 fourth beast…different. This may refer to the empire's far greater diversity than previous empires, and its breadth of conquest (v. 24). It branches out into two great divisions (cf. "legs," 2:33,40), then near the end into 10 horns (a confederacy of 10 nations), and even an 11th horn (Antichrist's kingdom) lasting until Christ's second coming.

7:20 the other *horn*. The 11th horn (ruler and his realm) is small and less powerful before its big rise (v. 8). Early in the future tribulation period, it (he) grows to be "larger" or more powerful than any of the horns (rulers) in the group.

7:21 war against the saints. The final Antichrist will lead a great persecution of believers, especially in Israel (cf. Matt. 24:15-22; 2 Thess. 2:4; Rev. 12:13-17; 13:6,7).

7:22 Ancient of Days. Refers to God the Eternal One, who confers the messianic kingdom on the Son to rule at His second coming and following (7:13,14). Judgment is against the Antichrist, Satan who empowers him (Rev. 13:4; 20:1-3), and the unsaved who are not allowed into the kingdom at its outset, but are destroyed and await the final, Great White Throne resurrection and judgment (Rev. 20:11-15). **saints to possess the kingdom.** Believers enter the kingdom in its earthly, millennial phase (Rev. 20:1-4) following Christ's second coming (Matt. 25:34), having eternal life that continues into the eternal state (Rev. 21,22) after the thousand years.

7:24 another…after them. The "little horn" (Antichrist) blasts his way to the zenith of world rule.

7:25 time and times and half a time. This obviously refers to the 3½ years which are the last half of the 7 year period of Antichrist's power (cf. 9:27), continuing on to Christ's second coming as the Judgment Stone (2:35,45) and glorious Son of Man (7:13,14). Cf. Rev. 11:2,3; 12:14; 13:5 for reference to this same period.

7:26 the court. God will have his court session to judge sinners and sin (vv. 9,10). He will remove the Antichrist's rule, and destroy him and his empire in eternal, conscious hell (Rev. 19:20; 20:10).

7:27 the kingdom…given to…the saints. God's kingdom in both earthly (Rev. 20:4) and heavenly phases (Rev. 21:27; 22:3,4,14).

Vision of a Ram and a Goat

8 In[1] the third year of the reign of King
Belshazzar a vision appeared *to* me—
to me, Daniel—after the one that appeared
to me [a]the first time. 2 I saw in the vision,
and it so happened while I was looking,
that I *was* in [b]Shushan,[2] the [3]citadel, which
is in the province of Elam; and I saw in the
vision that I was by the River Ulai. 3 Then
I lifted my eyes and saw, and there, standing beside the river, was a ram which had
two horns, and the two horns *were* high;
but one *was* [c]higher than the other, and the
higher *one* came up last. 4 I saw the ram
pushing westward, northward, and southward, so that no animal could [4]withstand
him; nor *was there any* that could deliver
from his hand, [d]but he did according to his
will and became great.

5 And as I was considering, suddenly a
male goat came from the west, across the
surface of the whole earth, without touching the ground; and the goat *had* a notable
[e]horn between his eyes. 6 Then he came to
the ram that had two horns, which I had
seen standing beside the river, and ran at
him with furious power. 7 And I saw him
confronting the ram; he was moved with
rage against him, [5]attacked the ram, and
broke his two horns. There was no power
in the ram to withstand him, but he cast
him down to the ground and trampled
him; and there was no one that could deliver the ram from his hand.

8 Therefore the male goat grew very
great; but when he became strong, the
large horn was broken, and in place of it
[f]four notable ones came up toward the
four winds of heaven. 9 [g]And out of one of
them came a little horn which grew exceedingly great toward the south, [h]toward
the east, and toward the [i]Glorious *Land.*
10 [j]And it grew up to [k]the host of heaven;
and [l]it cast down *some* of the host and *some*
of the stars to the ground, and trampled
them. 11 [m]He even exalted *himself* as high
as [n]the Prince of the host; [o]and by him
[p]the daily *sacrifices* were taken away, and
the place of [6]His sanctuary was cast
down. 12 Because of transgression, [q]an
army was given over *to the horn* to oppose
the daily *sacrifices;* and he cast [r]truth down
to the ground. He [s]did *all this* and prospered.

13 Then I heard [t]a holy one speaking;
and *another* holy one said to that certain *one*
who was speaking, "How long *will* the vision *be, concerning* the daily *sacrifices* and
the transgression [7]of desolation, the giving
of both the sanctuary and the host to be
trampled underfoot?"

14 And he said to me, "For two thousand
three hundred [8]days; then the sanctuary
shall be cleansed."

Gabriel Interprets the Vision

15 Then it happened, when I, Daniel, had
seen the vision and [u]was seeking the
meaning, that suddenly there stood before
me [v]one having the appearance of a man.
16 And I heard a man's voice [w]between *the
banks of* the Ulai, who called, and said,
[x]"Gabriel, make this *man* understand the
vision." 17 So he came near where I stood,

CHAPTER 8
1 [a]Dan. 7:1 [1]The Hebrew language resumes in Dan. 8:1.
2 [b]Neh. 1:1; Esth. 1:2; 2:8 [2]Or *Susa* [3]Or *fortified palace*
3 [c]Dan. 7:5
4 [d]Dan. 5:19 [4]Lit. *stand before him*
5 [e]Dan. 8:8, 21; 11:3
7 [5]Lit. *struck*
8 [f]Dan. 7:6; 8:22; 11:4
9 [g]Dan. 11:21 [h]Dan. 11:25 [i]Ps. 48:2
10 [j]Dan. 11:28 [k]Is. 14:13; Jer. 48:26 [l]Rev. 12:4
11 [m]2 Kin. 19:22, 23; 2 Chr. 32:15-17; Is. 37:23; Dan. 8:25; 11:36, 37 [n]Josh. 5:14 [o]Ezek. 46:14; Dan. 11:31; 12:11 [p]Ex. 29:38 [6]The temple
12 [q]Dan. 11:31 [r]Ps. 119:43; Is. 59:14 [s]Dan. 8:4; 11:36
13 [t]Dan. 4:13, 23; 1 Pet. 1:12 [7]Or *making desolate*
14 [8]Lit. *evening-mornings*
15 [u]1 Pet. 1:10 [v]Ezek. 1:26
16 [w]Dan. 12:6, 7 [x]Dan. 9:21; Luke 1:19, 26

8:1 third year. Ca. 551 B.C., two years after the dream of chap. 7 but before chap. 5. **the first time.** Looks back to chap. 7.

8:2 Shushan. Called Susa by the Greeks, this was a chief city of the Medo-Persian Empire, about 250 mi. E of Babylon. Since Daniel saw himself in a vision, he may not have been bodily in that place (cf. Ezekiel's vision of being at the Jerusalem temple, though bodily still with the elders in Babylon, Ezek. 8–11).

8:3-9 This imagery unfolded historically. The ram pictures the Medo-Persian Empire, as a whole, its two horns standing for the two entities (the Medes and the Persians) that merged into one. The history of this empire is briefly noted in v. 4, as it is seen conquering from the E to the W, S and N, under Cyrus, as predicted also by Isaiah 150 years earlier (Is. 45:1-7). The higher horn, which appeared last, represents Persia. The goat (v. 5) represents Greece with its great horn Alexander, who with his army of 35,000, moved with such speed that he is pictured as not even touching the ground. The broken horn is Alexander in his death; the 4 horns are generals who became kings over 4 sectors of the Grecian empire after Alexander (cf. 7:6). The small horn is Antiochus Epiphanes, who rose from the third empire to rule the Syrian division in 175–164 B.C. and is the same king dominant in 11:21-35. Cf. 7:8,24-26 where a similar "little horn" clearly represents the final Antichrist. The reason both are described as "little horns" is because one prefigures the other. A far more detailed summary will come later in 11:2-35.

8:9 Glorious *Land.* Palestine. Cf. 11:16,41.

8:10 host of heaven. Picturesque language portrays Antiochus' persecution against Jewish people using the figure of stars (as Gen. 12:3; 15:5; 22:17; Ex. 12:41; Deut. 1:10). When defeated, the "stars" (Jewish people) will fall under the tyrant's domination.

8:11 Prince. In addition to the desecration of the temple (cf. 1 Macc. 1:20-24,41-50), Antiochus blasphemed Christ to whom ultimately the host of Jewish people sacrifice and to whom the sanctuary belongs. He is later the "Prince of princes" (v. 25).

8:13 holy one. Angels are in view here.

8:14 two thousand three hundred days. These are 2,300 evenings/mornings, with no "and" in between, which refers to 2,300 total units or days. Genesis 1:15 does use "and," i.e., "Evening and morning, one day." The period runs to about 6⅓ years of sacrificing a lamb twice a day, morning and evening (Ex. 29:38,39). The prophecy was precise in identifying the time as that of Antiochus' persecution, ca. Sept. 6, 171 B.C. to Dec. 25, 165/4 B.C. After his death, Jews celebrated the cleansing of their holy place in the Feast of Lights, or Hanukkah, in celebration of the restoration led by Judas Maccabeus.

8:15 appearance of a man. The word for man meaning "a mighty man" is the linguistic framework for "Gabriel," which means "mighty one of God." This is the first mention of an angel by name in the Bible.

8:16 a man's voice. God spoke with a human voice. **the Ulai.** A river E of the Persian city of Susa.

and when he came I was afraid and [y]fell on
my face; but he said to me, "Understand,
son of man, that the vision *refers* to the time
of the end."

18 [z]Now, as he was speaking with me, I
was in a deep sleep with my face to the
ground; [a]but he touched me, and stood me
upright. 19 And he said, "Look, I am making known to you what shall happen in the
latter time of the indignation; [b]for at the
appointed time the end *shall be.* 20 The ram
which you saw, having the two horns—
they are the kings of Media and Persia.
21 And the [9]male goat *is* the [1]kingdom of
Greece. The large horn that *is* between its
eyes [c]*is* the first king. 22 [d]As for the broken
horn and the four that stood up in its place,
four kingdoms shall arise out of that nation, but not with its power.

23 "And in the latter time of their
kingdom,
When the transgressors have
reached their fullness,
A king shall arise,
[e]Having fierce [2]features,
Who understands sinister schemes.
24 His power shall be mighty, [f]but not
by his own power;
He shall destroy [3]fearfully,
[g]And shall prosper and thrive;
[h]He shall destroy the mighty, and
also the holy people.
25 "Through[i] his cunning
He shall cause deceit to prosper
under his [4]rule;
[j]And he shall exalt *himself* in his
heart.
He shall destroy many in *their*
prosperity.
[k]He shall even rise against the
Prince of princes;
But he shall be [l]broken without
human [4]means.

26 "And the vision of the evenings and
mornings
Which was told is true;
[m]Therefore seal up the vision,
For *it refers* to many days *in the
future.*"

27 [n]And I, Daniel, fainted and was sick
for days; afterward I arose and went about
the king's business. I was [5]astonished by
the vision, but no one understood it.

Daniel's Prayer for the People

9 In the first year [a]of Darius the son of
Ahasuerus, of the lineage of the
Medes, who was made king over the realm
of the Chaldeans— 2 in the first year of his
reign I, Daniel, understood by the books
the number of the years *specified* by the
word of the LORD through [b]Jeremiah the
prophet, that He would accomplish seventy years in the desolations of Jerusalem.
3 [c]Then I set my face toward the Lord
God to make request by prayer and supplications, with fasting, sackcloth, and

17 [y]Ezek. 1:28; 44:4; Dan. 2:46; Rev. 1:17
18 [z]Dan. 10:9; Luke 9:32 [a]Ezek. 2:2; Dan. 10:10, 16, 18
19 [b]Hab. 2:3
21 [c]Dan. 11:3 [9]*shaggy male* [1]Lit. *king,* representing his kingdom, Dan. 7:17, 23
22 [d]Dan. 11:4
23 [e]Deut. 28:50 [2]Lit. *countenance*
24 [f]Rev. 17:13 [g]Dan. 11:36 [h]Dan. 7:25 [3]Or *extraordinarily*
25 [i]Dan. 11:21 [j]Dan. 8:11-13; 11:36; 12:7 [k]Dan. 11:36; Rev. 19:19, 20 [l]Job 34:20; Lam. 4:6 [4]Lit. *hand*
26 [m]Ezek. 12:27; Dan. 12:4, 9; Rev. 22:10
27 [n]Dan. 7:28; 8:17; Hab. 3:16 [5]*amazed*

CHAPTER 9

1 [a]Dan. 1:21
2 [b]2 Chr. 36:21; Ezra 1:1; Jer. 25:11, 12; 29:10; Zech. 7:5
3 [c]Neh. 1:4; Dan. 6:10; 10:15

8:17 afraid and fell. Loss of consciousness is a common reaction to heavenly visitation (cf. Ezek. 1; Is. 6; Rev. 1). **time of the end.** This term likely has a double sense of fulfillment. First, the "end" (as v. 19), "latter time" (vv. 19,23), and "appointed time" (v. 19) refer to time late in the specific span that the historical prophecy has in view. That time is the period defined by the empires in these verses, Persia (Ram) and Greece (Goat), when the Grecian sector will be divided into 4 parts (v. 8). One of these, the Syrian under Seleucus (*see note on v. 22*), will eventually lead to Antiochus Epiphanes (175–164 B.C.) as the "little horn" meant in v. 9, who persecutes the people of Israel (v. 10) and defies God (v. 11). Cf. 11:21-35 and *see notes there.* Secondly, this "little horn" in v. 9, the Antichrist in the last days at the time of the eschatological fulfillment, sees Antiochus as a pattern of the Antichrist, who in many ways will be like him, though far greater in power, and will exercise his career in the end of the age just before Christ's return.

8:21 male goat...large horn. This is the third Gentile world power, the kingdom of Greece, and specifically Alexander the Great, the notable and "first king" after conquering Medo-Persia. Cf. 11:3.

8:22 broken *horn* and...four. Alexander died at age 33 in 323 B.C., leaving no heir ready to reign. So 4 men, after 22 years of fighting, assumed rule over 4 Grecian sectors: 1) Cassander, Macedonia; 2) Lysimachus, Thrace and Asia Minor; 3) Seleucus, Syria, and Babylonia; 4) Ptolemy, Egypt, and Arabia. These are the 4 referred to in "toward the four winds" (v. 8). The phrase "not with its power" indicates they did not have Alexander's power or direct family lineage.

8:23-25 A king shall arise. The near fulfillment views Antiochus as the historical persecutor as in vv. 9-14. His career down to 164 B.C. was "in the latter time of their kingdom," that of the male goat in the Syrian territory. Rome conquered Greece by 146 B.C., only a few years later, and became the next dominant empire. Antiochus died, "broken without *human* means," due to insanity and disease of the bowels. The far fulfillment sees Antiochus in vv. 23-25 as prophetically illustrating the final tribulation period and the Antichrist. In such a view, the king here is also the "little horn," as in 7:7; 8:9 and the willful king in 11:36-45.

8:25 Prince of princes. *See note on 8:11.*

8:26 seal up the vision. Since he told it here, this did not mean to shut it up to secrecy but to preserve it as truth even if not to be fulfilled for a long time.

9:1 the first year. Ca. 539 B.C. **made king.** This may mean that Darius (a title, not a proper name, *see note on 5:31*) refers to Cyrus who was made king by God's allowance (cf. Ps. 75:6,7). Since Cyrus was the first monarch of the Medo-Persian empire, this time note was also the first year after the death of Belshazzar, when Babylon fell.

9:2 seventy years. Daniel's study of "the books" (OT scrolls) focused on the years prophesied for the captivity by Jeremiah in Jer. 25:11,12 and 29:10. Since the end of that span was near, he prayed for God's next move on behalf of Israel. Cf. 2 Chr. 36:21, where it is indicated that the 70 years of exile was intended to restore the Sabbath rests that Israel had ignored for so many years (cf. Lev. 25:4,5; 26:34-43).

ashes. 4 And I prayed to the LORD my God,
and made confession, and said, "O [d]Lord,
great and awesome God, who keeps His
covenant and mercy with those who love
Him, and with those who keep His commandments, 5 [e]we have sinned and committed iniquity, we have done wickedly
and rebelled, even by departing from Your
precepts and Your judgments. 6 [f]Neither
have we heeded Your servants the
prophets, who spoke in Your name to our
kings and our princes, to our fathers and
all the people of the land. 7 O Lord, [g]righ-
teousness *belongs* to You, but to us shame
of face, as *it is* this day—to the men of Judah, to the inhabitants of Jerusalem and all
Israel, those near and those far off in all the
countries to which You have driven them,
because of the unfaithfulness which they
have committed against You.

8 "O Lord, to us *belongs* shame of face, to
our kings, our princes, and our fathers, because we have sinned against You. 9 [h]To the
Lord our God *belong* mercy and forgiveness, though we have rebelled against Him.
10 We have not obeyed the voice of the
LORD our God, to walk in His laws, which
He set before us by His servants the
prophets. 11 Yes, [i]all Israel has transgressed
Your law, and has departed so as not to
obey Your voice; therefore the curse and the
oath written in the [j]Law of Moses the servant of God have been poured out on us,
because we have sinned against Him.
12 And He has [k]confirmed His words,
which He spoke against us and against our
judges who judged us, by bringing upon us
a great disaster; [l]for under the whole heav-
en such has never been done as what has
been done to Jerusalem.

13 [m]"As *it is* written in the Law of Moses,
all this disaster has come upon us; [n]yet we
have not made our prayer before the LORD
our God, that we might turn from our iniquities and understand Your truth.
14 Therefore the LORD has [o]kept the disaster in mind, and brought it upon us; for
[p]the LORD our God *is* righteous in all the
works which He does, though we have not
obeyed His voice. 15 And now, O Lord our
God, [q]who brought Your people out of the
land of Egypt with a mighty hand, and
made Yourself [r]a name, as *it is* this day—
we have sinned, we have done wickedly!

16 "O Lord, [s]according to all Your righteousness, I pray, let Your anger and Your
fury be turned away from Your city Jerusalem, [t]Your holy mountain; because for our
sins, [u]and for the iniquities of our fathers,
[v]Jerusalem and Your people [w]*are* a reproach to all *those* around us. 17 Now
therefore, our God, hear the prayer of Your
servant, and his supplications, [x]and [y]for
the Lord's sake [1]cause Your face to shine
on [2]Your sanctuary, [z]which is desolate.
18 [a]O my God, incline Your ear and hear;
open Your eyes [b]and see our desolations,
and the city [c]which is called by Your name;
for we do not present our supplications before You because of our righteous deeds,
but because of Your great mercies. 19 O
Lord, hear! O Lord, forgive! O Lord, listen
and act! Do not delay for Your own sake,
my God, for Your city and Your people are
called by Your name."

The Seventy-Weeks Prophecy

20 Now while I *was* speaking, praying,
and confessing my sin and the sin of my
people Israel, and presenting my supplication before the LORD my God for the holy
mountain of my God, 21 yes, while I *was*
speaking in prayer, the man [d]Gabriel,
whom I had seen in the vision at the beginning, [3]being caused to fly swiftly,
reached me about the time of the evening
offering. 22 And he informed *me*, and
talked with me, and said, "O Daniel, I have
now come forth to give you skill to understand. 23 At the beginning of your supplications the [4]command went out, and I
have come to tell *you*, for you *are* greatly
[e]beloved; therefore [f]consider the matter,
and understand the vision:

24 "Seventy [5]weeks are determined
For your people and for your holy
city,

4 [d] Ex. 20:6
5 [e] 1 Kin. 8:47, 48; Neh. 9:33; Ps. 106:6; Is. 64:5-7; Jer. 14:7
6 [f] 2 Chr. 36:15; Jer. 44:4, 5
7 [g] Neh. 9:33
9 [h] [Neh. 9:17; Ps. 130:4, 7]
11 [i] Is. 1:3-6; Jer. 8:5-10 [j] Lev. 26:14; Neh. 1:6; Ps. 106:6
12 [k] Is. 44:26; Jer. 44:2-6; Lam. 2:17; Zech. 1:6 [l] Lam. 1:12; 2:13; Ezek. 5:9; [Amos 3:2]
13 [m] Lev. 26:14-45; Deut. 28:15-68; Lam. 2:17 [n] Job 36:13; Is. 9:13; Jer. 2:30; Hos. 7:7
14 [o] Jer. 31:28; 44:27 [p] Neh. 9:33
15 [q] Ex. 32:11; 1 Kin. 8:51; Neh. 1:10 [r] Ex. 14:18; Neh. 9:10; Jer. 32:20
16 [s] 1 Sam. 12:7; Ps. 31:1; Mic. 6:4, 5 [t] Ps. 87:1-3; Dan. 9:20; Joel 3:17; Zech. 8:3 [u] Ex. 20:5 [v] Ps. 122:6; Jer. 29:7; Lam. 2:16 [w] Ps. 79:4
17 [x] Num. 6:24-26; Ps. 80:3, 7, 19 [y] Lam. 5:18 [z] [John 16:24] [1] Be gracious [2] The temple
18 [a] Is. 37:17 [b] Ex. 3:7 [c] Jer. 25:29
21 [d] Dan. 8:16; Luke 1:19, 26 [3] Or *being weary with weariness*
23 [e] Dan. 10:11, 19 [f] Matt. 24:15 [4] Lit. *word*
24 [5] Lit. *sevens,* and so throughout the chapter

9:4-19 I prayed. Various aspects of the passage give rich instruction regarding prayer. True prayer is: in response to the Word (v. 2), characterized by fervency (v. 3) and self-denial (v. 4), identified unselfishly with God's people (v. 5), strengthened by confession (vv. 5-15), dependent on God's character (vv. 4,7,9,15), and has as its goal, God's glory (vv. 16-19).

9:11 the curse. This refers to the judgment that God brought, as promised, for Israel's disobedience in the Land (Lev. 26:21-42; Deut. 28:15-68). This is in contrast to the blessings associated with faith and obedience (Lev. 26:3-20; Deut. 28:1-14). God had given the promise that even in a time of judgment, if Israel would confess their sin, He would bring blessing again (Lev. 26:40-42).

9:16. Daniel prayed for restoration in 3 aspects. In effect he asked God to bring back "Your city" (vv. 16,18), "Your sanctuary (v. 17), and "Your people" (v. 19). God's answer embraced all three (v. 24).

9:21 the man Gabriel. This angel, called a "man" because he appeared in the form of a man, appeared also in 8:16. Cf. the angel Michael in 10:13,20; 12:1. **the evening offering.** This was the second lamb of two offered daily (cf. 8:14 and *see note there*), this one at 3 p.m., a common time for prayer (Ezra 9:5).

9:24-26 Seventy weeks from...Until. These are weeks of years, whereas weeks of days are described in a different way (10:2,3). The time spans from the Persian Artaxerxes' decree to rebuild Jerusalem, ca. 445 B.C. (Neh. 2:1-8), to the Messiah's kingdom. This panorama in-

To finish the transgression,
[6]To make an end of sins,
[g]To make reconciliation for iniquity,
[h]To bring in everlasting
righteousness,
To seal up vision and prophecy,
[i]And to anoint [7]the Most Holy.

25 "Know therefore and understand,
That from the going forth of the
command
To restore and build Jerusalem
Until [j]Messiah [k]the Prince,
There shall be seven weeks and
sixty-two weeks;
The [8]street shall be built again, and
the [9]wall,
Even in troublesome times.

26 "And after the sixty-two weeks
[l]Messiah shall [1]be cut off, [m]but not
for Himself;
And [n]the people of the prince who
is to come
[o]Shall destroy the city and the
sanctuary.
The end of it *shall be* with a flood,
And till the end of the war
desolations are determined.
27 Then he shall confirm [p]a [2]covenant
with [q]many for one week;
But in the middle of the week
He shall bring an end to sacrifice
and offering.
And on the wing of abominations
shall be one who makes
desolate,
[r]Even until the consummation,
which is determined,
Is poured out on the [3]desolate."

Vision of the Glorious Man

10 In the third year of Cyrus king of
Persia a message was revealed to
Daniel, whose [a]name was called Belteshazzar. The message *was* true, [1]but the appointed time *was* long; and he understood
the message, and had understanding of the
vision. 2 In those days I, Daniel, was
mourning three full weeks. 3 I ate no
[2]pleasant food, no meat or wine came into
my mouth, nor did I anoint myself at all,
till three whole weeks were fulfilled.
4 Now on the twenty-fourth day of the
first month, as I was by the side of the

24 [g] 2 Chr. 29:24; [Is. 53:10]; Acts 10:43; [Rom. 5:10]; Heb. 9:12, 14 [h] Rev. 14:6 [i] Ps. 45:7 [6] So with Qr., LXX, Syr., Vg.; Kt., Theodotion *To seal up* [7] The Most Holy Place
25 [j] Luke 2:1, 2; John 1:41; 4:25 [k] Is. 55:4 [8] Or *open square* [9] Or *moat*
26 [l] [Is. 53:8]; Matt. 27:50; Mark 9:12; 15:37; [Luke 23:46; 24:26]; John 19:30; Acts 8:32 [m] [1 Pet. 2:21] [n] Matt. 22:7 [o] Matt. 24:2; Mark 13:2; Luke 19:43, 44 [1] Suffer the death penalty
27 [p] Is. 42:6 [q] [Matt. 26:28] [r] Dan. 11:36 [2] Or *treaty* [3] Or *desolator*

CHAPTER 10

1 [a] Dan. 1:7 [1] Or *and of great conflict;*
3 [2] *desirable*

cludes: 1) 7 weeks or 49 years, possibly closing Nehemiah's career in the rebuilding of the "street and wall," as well as the end of the ministry of Malachi and the close of the OT; 2) 62 weeks or 434 more years for a total of 483 years to the first advent of Messiah. This was fulfilled at the triumphal entry on 9 Nisan, A.D. 30 (*see notes on Matt. 21:1-11*). The Messiah will be "cut off," (a common reference to death); and 3) the final 7 years or 70th week of the time of Antichrist (cf. v. 27). Roman people, from whom the Antichrist will come, will "destroy the city" of Jerusalem and its temple in A.D. 70.

9:24. This highly complex and startlingly accurate prophecy answers Daniel's prayer, not with reference to near history, but by giving the future of Israel in the final end of the age. God promises 2 sets of 3 accomplishments each. First, those related to sin are: 1) **finish the transgression,** i.e., restrain sin and Israel's in particular in its long trend of apostasy, as in v. 11; 2) **make an end of sins,** i.e., to judge it with finality (cf. Heb. 9:26); and 3) **make reconciliation for iniquity,** signifies to furnish the actual basis of covering sin by full atonement, the blood of the crucified Messiah who is "cut off" (v. 26), which affects the first two realities (cf. the fountain, Zech. 13:1).

Second, those accomplishments related to righteousness are: 1) **bring in...righteousness,** the eternal righteousness of Daniel's people in their great change from centuries of apostasy; 2) **seal up vision...,** i.e., no more revelation is needed and God will bring these anticipations to completion by their fulfillment in Israel's blessing as a nation; and 3) **anoint the Most Holy,** consecrate the Holy Place in a temple of the future that will be the center of worship in the millennial kingdom (cf. Ezek. 40–48). Clearly this must be understood to sweep to the end of Gentile power and the time of Antichrist right before Christ's return. Summing up, the first 3 are fulfilled in principle at Christ's first coming, in full at His return. The last 3 complete the plan at His Second Advent.

9:27 Then. This is clearly the end of the age, the Second Advent judgment, because the bringing in of righteousness did not occur 7 years after the death of the Messiah, nor did the destruction of Jerusalem fit the 7 year period (occurring 37 years later). This is the future 7 year period which ends with sin's final judgment and Christ's reign of righteousness; i.e., the return of Christ and the establishment of His rule. These 7 years constitute the 70th week of Daniel. **he shall confirm.** "He" is the last-mentioned prince (v. 26), leader of the Roman sphere (cf. chaps. 2 and 7), the Antichrist who comes in the latter days. The time is in the future tribulation period of "one week," i.e., the final 7 years of v. 24. He confirms (lit., causes to prevail) a 7 year covenant, his own pact with Israel for what will turn out actually to be for a shorter time. The leader in this covenant is the "little horn" of 7:7,8,20,21,24-26, and the evil leader of NT prophecy (Mark 13:14; 2 Thess. 2:3-10; Rev. 13:1-10). That he is in the future, even after Christ's First Advent, is shown by 1) Matt. 24:15; 2) by the time references that match (7:25; Rev. 11:2,3; 12:14; 13:5); and 3) by the end here extending to the Second Advent, matching the duration elsewhere mentioned in Daniel (2:35,45; 7:15ff.; 12:1-3) and Rev. 11:2; 12:14; 13:5. **middle of the week.** This is the halfway point of the 70th week of years, i.e., 7 years leading to Christ's second coming. The Antichrist will break his covenant with Israel (v. 27a), which has resumed its ancient sacrificial system. Three and a half years of tribulation remain, agreeing with the time in other Scriptures (7:25; Rev. 11:2,3; 12:14; 13:5, called "Great Tribulation," cf. Matt. 24:21) as God's wrath intensifies. **abominations...one who makes desolate** The Antichrist will cause abomination against Jewish religion. This violation will desolate or ruin what Jews regard as sacred, namely their holy temple and the honoring of God's presence there (cf. 1 Kin. 9:3; 2 Thess. 2:4). Jesus refers directly to this text in His Olivet discourse (Matt. 24:15). *See note on 11:31.* **the consummation.** God permits this tribulation under the Antichrist's persecutions and ultimately triumphs, achieving judgment of the sin and sinners in Israel (12:7) and in the world (cf. Jer. 25:31). This includes the Antichrist (11:45; Rev. 19:20), and all who deserve judgment (9:24; Matt. 13:41-43).

10:1 third year. Ca. 536 B.C. Two years had passed since the first decree to let Israel return (cf. Ezra 1:1–2:1; 2:64–3:1).

great river, that *is,* the [3]Tigris, 5 I lifted my
eyes and looked, and behold, a certain
man clothed in [b]linen, whose waist *was*
[c]girded with gold of Uphaz! 6 His body
was like beryl, his face like the appearance
of lightning, his eyes like torches of fire, his
arms and feet like burnished bronze in
color, [d]and the sound of his words like the
voice of a multitude.
7 And I, Daniel, alone saw the vision, for
the men who were with me did not see the
vision; but a great terror fell upon them, so
that they fled to hide themselves. 8 Therefore I was left alone when I saw this great
vision, and no strength remained in me; for
my [4]vigor was turned to [5]frailty in me,
and I retained no strength. 9 Yet I heard the
sound of his words; and while I heard the
sound of his words I was in a deep sleep
on my face, with my face to the ground.

Prophecies Concerning Persia and Greece

10 [e]Suddenly, a hand touched me, which
made me tremble on my knees and *on* the
palms of my hands. 11 And he said to me,
"O Daniel, [f]man greatly beloved, understand the words that I speak to you, and
stand upright, for I have now been sent to
you." While he was speaking this word to
me, I stood trembling.
12 Then he said to me, [g]"Do not fear,
Daniel, for from the first day that you set
your heart to understand, and to humble
yourself before your God, [h]your words
were heard; and I have come because of
your words. 13 [i]But the prince of the kingdom of Persia withstood me twenty-one
days; and behold, [j]Michael, one of the
chief princes, came to help me, for I had
been left alone there with the kings of Persia. 14 Now I have come to make you understand what will happen to your people
[k]in the latter days, [l]for the vision *refers* to
many days yet *to come.*"
15 When he had spoken such words to
me, [m]I [6]turned my face toward the ground
and became speechless. 16 And suddenly,
[n]*one* having the likeness of the [7]sons of
men [o]touched my lips; then I opened my
mouth and spoke, saying to him who
stood before me, "My lord, because of the
vision [p]my sorrows have [8]overwhelmed
me, and I have retained no strength. 17 For
how can this servant of my lord talk with
you, my lord? As for me, no strength remains in me now, nor is any breath left in
me."
18 Then again, *the one* having the likeness of a man touched me and strengthened me. 19 [q]And he said, "O man greatly
beloved, [r]fear not! Peace *be* to you; be
strong, yes, be strong!"
So when he spoke to me I was strengthened, and said, "Let my lord speak, for you
have strengthened me."
20 Then he said, "Do you know why I
have come to you? And now I must return
to fight [s]with the prince of Persia; and
when I have gone forth, indeed the prince
of Greece will come. 21 But I will tell you
what is noted in the Scripture of Truth. (No
one upholds me against these, [t]except Michael your prince.

11 "Also [a]in the first year of [b]Darius
the Mede, I, *even* I, stood up to confirm and strengthen him.) 2 And now I will

4 [3] Heb. *Hiddekel*
5 [b] Ezek. 9:2; 10:2 [c] Rev. 1:13; 15:6
6 [d] [Rev. 1:15]
8 [4] Lit. *splendor* [5] Lit. *ruin*
10 [e] Dan. 9:21
11 [f] Dan. 9:23
12 [g] Rev. 1:17 [h] Dan. 9:3, 4, 22, 23; Acts 10:4
13 [i] Dan. 10:20 [j] Dan. 10:21; 12:1; Jude 9; [Rev. 12:7]
14 [k] Gen. 49:1; Deut. 31:29; Dan. 2:28 [l] Dan. 8:26; 10:1
15 [m] Dan. 8:18; 10:9 [6] Lit. *set*
16 [n] Dan. 8:15 [o] Jer. 1:9; Dan. 10:10 [p] Dan. 10:8, 9 [7] Theodotion, Vg. *the son;* LXX *a hand* [8] Or *turned upon*
19 [q] Dan. 10:11 [r] Judg. 6:23; Is. 43:1; Dan. 10:12
20 [s] Dan. 10:13
21 [t] Dan. 10:13; Jude 9; [Rev. 12:7]

CHAPTER 11

1 [a] Dan. 9:1 [b] Dan. 5:31

10:6 His body...like beryl. The messenger whom Daniel sees in a vision (vv. 1,7) was distinct from the angel Michael, from whom he needed assistance (v. 13). The description of such glory has led some to see him as Christ in a pre-incarnate appearance (such as Josh. 5:13-15; 6:2; Judg. 6:11-23). He is described almost identically to Christ (Rev. 1:13,14) and Daniel's reaction is similar to John's (Rev. 1:17).

10:10 a hand touched me. Most likely this was Gabriel, who interpreted other revelations to Daniel (cf. 8:16) and spoke similarly of Daniel's being beloved in 9:20-23.

10:12 your words were heard. This was a great encouragement from God who was attentive to prayer and acted to answer it (cf. 9:20-27).

10:13 prince of...Persia. The 3 week delay was due to an evil angel opposing Gabriel in heavenly warfare (cf. Rev. 16:12-14). This angel was specially anointed with Persian power in an effort to thwart the work of God. This tells us that Satan engages in heavenly warfare to influence generations and nations against God and His people (cf. Eph. 6:10ff.). **Michael.** This is the chief angel of heaven (cf. 10:21; 12:1; Jude 9; Rev. 12:7). Michael remained to assure that the Jews would be free to return to their land.

10:14 *many* days yet *to come.* This refers to the future plan of God for His people, extending from Daniel's time to that of the Antichrist.

10:19 I was strengthened. This was the third time (vv. 10,16), showing the overwhelming trauma of divine presence and revelation.

10:20 prince of Greece. An evil angel contesting for the kingdom of Greece.

10:21 Scripture of Truth. God's plan of certain and true designs for men and nations, which He can reveal according to His discretion (11:2; Is. 46:9-11). **except Michael.** The angel with Michael intended to handle the demons of Persia and Greece. This actually forms the heavenly basis for the earthly unfolding of history in 11:2-35.

11:1 first year. Ca. 539 B.C. (cf. 6:1ff.; 9:1). **I, stood up to... strengthen him.** The messenger of 10:10ff. continues to speak of assisting Michael (even as Michael had strengthened him in the battle with demons in 10:21), confirming Darius in his purpose of kindness to Israel in decreeing their return.

11:2-45 As in 8:3-26, this prophecy sweeps all the way from the history of spiritual conflict in Israel (11:2-35) to the tribulation (vv. 36-42) when Michael aids in fully delivering Israel (12:1). The detail of this history is so minute and accurate, so confirmed by history, that unbelieving critics have, without evidence, insisted that it was actually written 400 years later than Daniel, after it had happened which would make the prophet a deceiver. The prophecy actually looks ahead from Daniel to the final Antichrist.

11:2-35 This section unfolds the near fulfillment of the Persian kingdom and the reign of Greece through Antiochus Epiphanes.

tell you the truth: Behold, three more kings
will arise in Persia, and the fourth shall be
far richer than *them* all; by his strength,
through his riches, he shall stir up all
against the realm of Greece. 3 Then [c]a
mighty king shall arise, who shall rule
with great dominion, and [d]do according to
his will. 4 And when he has arisen, [e]his
kingdom shall be broken up and divided
toward the four winds of heaven, but not
among his posterity [f]nor according to his
dominion with which he ruled; for his
kingdom shall be uprooted, even for others besides these.

Warring Kings of North and South

5 "Also the king of the South shall become strong, as well as *one* of his princes;
and he shall gain power over him and
have dominion. His dominion *shall be* a
great dominion. 6 And at the end of *some*
years they shall join forces, for the daughter of the king of the South shall go to the
king of the North to make an agreement;
but she shall not retain the power of her
[1]authority, and neither he nor his [1]authority shall stand; but she shall be given up,
with those who brought her, and with him
who begot her, and with him who
strengthened her in *those* times. 7 But from
a branch of her roots *one* shall arise in his
place, who shall come with an army, enter
the fortress of the king of the North, and
deal with them and prevail. 8 And he shall
also carry their gods captive to Egypt, with
their [2]princes *and* their precious articles of
silver and gold; and he shall continue *more*
years than the king of the North.

9 "Also *the king of the North* shall come to
the kingdom of the king of the South, but
shall return to his own land. 10 However
his sons shall stir up strife, and assemble a
multitude of great forces; and *one* shall certainly come [g]and overwhelm and pass
through; then he shall return [h]to his
fortress and stir up strife.

11 "And the king of the South shall be
[i]moved with rage, and go out and fight
with him, with the king of the North, who
shall muster a great multitude; but the
[j]multitude shall be given into the hand of
his *enemy*. 12 When he has taken away the
multitude, his heart will be [3]lifted up; and
he will cast down tens of thousands, but he
will not prevail. 13 For the king of the
North will return and muster a multitude
greater than the former, and shall certainly
come at the end of some years with a great
army and much equipment.

14 "Now in those times many shall rise
up against the king of the South. Also, [4]violent men of your people shall exalt themselves [5]in fulfillment of the vision, but they
shall [k]fall. 15 So the king of the North shall
come and [l]build a siege mound, and take a
fortified city; and the [6]forces of the South
shall not withstand *him*. Even his choice
troops *shall have* no strength to resist. 16 But
he who comes against him [m]shall do according to his own will, and [n]no one shall
stand against him. He shall stand in the
Glorious Land with destruction in his
[7]power.

17 "He shall also [o]set his face to enter
with the strength of his whole kingdom,
and [8]upright ones with him; thus shall he

3 [c]Dan. 7:6; 8:5 [d]Dan. 8:4; 11:16, 36
4 [e]Jer. 49:36; Ezek. 37:9; Dan. 7:2; 8:8; Zech. 2:6; Rev. 7:1 [f]Dan. 8:22
6 [1]Lit. *arm*
8 [2]Or *molded images*
10 [g]Is. 8:8; Jer. 46:7, 8; 51:42; Dan. 9:26; 11:26, 40 [h]Dan. 11:7
11 [i]Prov. 16:14 [j][Ps. 33:10, 16]
12 [3]Proud
14 [k]Job 9:13 [4]Or *robbers*, lit. *sons of breakage* [5]Lit. *to establish*
15 [l]Jer. 6:6; Ezek. 4:2; 17:17 [6]Lit. *arms*
16 [m]Dan. 8:4, 7 [n]Josh. 1:5 [7]Lit. *hand*
17 [o]2 Kin. 12:17; 2 Chr. 20:3; Ezek. 4:3, 7 [8]Or *bring equitable terms*

11:2 three more kings...and the fourth. The 3 in the Persian sphere, after Cyrus (10:1), were Cambyses (ca. 530–522 B.C.), Psuedo-Smerdis (ca. 522 B.C.), and Darius I Hystaspes (ca. 522–486 B.C.). The fourth is Xerxes I, called Ahasuerus in Esther (486–465 B.C.). Kings after Xerxes are not included, probably because Xerxes' failed military campaign against the Greeks (481–479 B.C.) sounded the beginning of the end for Persia, which finally fell ca. 331 B.C. to Alexander the Great.

11:3 a mighty king. Alexander the Great (cf. 8:5).

11:4 After Alexander's death (ca. 323 B.C.), 4 who were not of his posterity took sectors of his wide empire (*see notes on 7:6; 8:3-9*). The king of the South (Egypt) and king of the North (Syria), receive emphasis in v. 5 and after. As time moved on, other leaders ruled, crossing and recrossing Palestine.

11:5,6 king of the South...king of the North. King of the South represents the Ptolomies, the leaders of Egypt, contrasted often in vv. 5ff. with the king of the North, the Seleucids, leaders of Syria (v. 6). South and N are in relation to Palestine, for which the angel Gabriel, speaking in this passage, is so concerned. Verses 5-20 cover almost 200 years of wars between these bordering powers.

11:6 join forces. Berenice, daughter of Egypt's Ptolemy II Philadelphus (285–246 B.C.), married Syria's King Antiochus II Theos (261–246 B.C.). The latter part of the verse refers to the political advantage they hoped the alliance would produce. Antiochus divorced his wife to marry Berenice. Later that divorced wife murdered Berenice, her baby son, and even Antiochus by poisoning him. Thus she brought her own son, Seleucus II Callinicus, to the throne.

11:7 from a branch of her roots. The murdered Berenice's brother stood in his father's place. His name was Ptolemy III Euergetes of Egypt (246–222 B.C.), and in reverse he conquered Syria, sacking their great treasure (v. 8).

11:9 *king of the North* shall come. Syria's Callinicus attacked Egypt ca. 240 B.C. but retreated, soundly beaten.

11:10 his sons. Seleucus' sons (successors) kept up war against Egypt, as described in vv. 11-35.

11:11 king of the South. Ptolemy IV Philopator (222–203 B.C.) devastated the Syrian army under Antiochus III the Great (223–187 B.C.). Egypt's advantage would be brief (v. 12).

11:13-16 king of the North. Thirteen years later Antiochus returned with a great army, and in a series of strikes against Egypt brought Palestine ("the Glorious Land") into his control as far S as Gaza.

11:14 violent men of your people. Violent Jews wanted Judean independence from Egypt, but failed in their revolt.

11:16 he who comes against him. Antiochus III the Great took lasting dominion over Israel. **Glorious Land** Palestine (cf. 8:9).

do. And he shall give him the daughter of
women to destroy it; but she shall not
stand *with him*, [p]or be for him. 18 After this
he shall turn his face to the coastlands, and
shall take many. But a ruler shall bring the
reproach against them to an end; and with
the reproach removed, he shall turn back
on him. 19 Then he shall turn his face toward the fortress of his own land; but he
shall [q]stumble and fall, [r]and not be found.
20 "There shall arise in his place one who
imposes taxes *on* the glorious kingdom;
but within a few days he shall be destroyed, but not in anger or in battle.
21 And in his place [s]shall arise a vile person, to whom they will not give the honor
of royalty; but he shall come in peaceably,
and seize the kingdom by intrigue. 22 With
the [9]force of a [t]flood they shall be swept
away from before him and be broken, [u]and
also the prince of the covenant. 23 And
after the league *is made* with him [v]he shall
act deceitfully, for he shall come up and become strong with a small *number of* people.
24 He shall enter peaceably, even into the
richest places of the province; and he shall
do *what* his fathers have not done, nor his
forefathers: he shall disperse among them
the plunder, [1]spoil, and riches; and he shall
devise his plans against the strongholds,
but *only* for a time.
25 "He shall stir up his power and his
courage against the king of the South with
a great army. And the king of the South
shall be stirred up to battle with a very
great and mighty army; but he shall not
stand, for they shall devise plans against
him. 26 Yes, those who eat of the portion of
his delicacies shall destroy him; his army
shall [2]be swept away, and many shall fall
down slain. 27 Both these kings' hearts
shall be bent on evil, and they shall speak
lies at the same table; but it shall not prosper, for the end *will* still *be* at the [w]ap-
pointed time. 28 While returning to his
land with great riches, his heart shall be
moved against the holy covenant; so he
shall do *damage* and return to his own land.

The Northern King's Blasphemies

29 "At the appointed time he shall return
and go toward the south; but it shall not be
like the former or the latter. 30 [x]For ships
from [3]Cyprus shall come against him;

17 [p] Dan. 9:26
19 [q] Ps. 27:2; Jer. 46:6 [r] Job 20:8; Ps. 37:36; Ezek. 26:21
21 [s] Dan. 7:8
22 [t] Dan. 9:26 [u] Dan. 8:10, 11 [9] Lit. *arms*
23 [v] Dan. 8:25
24 [1] *booty*
26 [2] Or *overflow*
27 [w] Dan. 8:19; Hab. 2:3
30 [x] Gen. 10:4; Num. 24:24; Is. 23:1, 12; Jer. 2:10 [3] Heb. *Kittim*, western lands, especially Cyprus

11:17 give...the daughter. Antiochus, feeling pressure from Rome (fourth empire, 2:40; 7:7) to make peace with Egypt, offered his daughter Cleopatra to marry Ptolemy V Epiphanes (ca. 192 B.C.). The Syrian thus hoped his daughter would spy to help him to "destroy" or weaken Egypt and bring it under his power. Cleopatra, instead of helping her father, favored her Egyptian mate.

11:18 a ruler. Antiochus had set his sights to conquer Greece, along the Mediterranean coastlands. But this brought him into conflict with Rome, so that a Roman, Lucius Scipio Asiaticus, repaid the Syrian aggression against Roman rights in the area with a resounding defeat (ca. 191–190 B.C.).

11:19 fall. Antiochus returned from defeat to his own land compelled by Rome to relinquish all his territory W of the Taurus and to repay the costs of war. He was likely killed by defenders of a Persian temple he tried to plunder at night in Elymais (to get money to pay reparations required by Rome).

11:20 one who imposes taxes. Rome required Seleucus IV Philopator to render tribute, for Rome was increasingly powerful. The Syrian set out to tax his subjects heavily to raise the tribute. Soon, he died after being poisoned. The "glorious kingdom" possibly refers to Israel ("the Glorious Land") with its splendid temple.

11:21 a vile person. In vv. 21-35, the most cruel king of the North was Seleucid, the Syrian persecutor of Israel named Antiochus IV Epiphanes (cf. 8:9-14, 23-25). He came to the throne when his brother Seleucus was murdered and a son of the dead king who might succeed him, Demetrius I Soter, was held hostage in Rome. In the vacuum, Antiochus seized power in Syria.

11:22 they shall be swept away. Egypt's armies were swept away by Antiochus' invading forces as by a flood (cf. "flood" for military onslaught, 9:26). Israel's "prince of the covenant," Onias III, was murdered by his own defecting brother Menelaus at the request of Antiochus (171 B.C.).

11:23 the league. In an Egyptian struggle for the throne, Antiochus developed an alliance with Ptolemy VI Philometer over his rival Ptolemy VII Euergetes II (distinct from the leader in v. 7). By this league, Antiochus deceitfully plotted to gain greater power in Egypt. "With a small" force, he conquered Memphis and the rest of Egypt all the way to Alexandria.

11:24 enter peaceably. Antiochus, under the guise of friendship, plundered the richest Egyptian places he could strike. To gain support, he gave lavish gifts, possibly battle spoils. **devise his plans against the strongholds.** He formed a scheme to take over Egypt.

11:25 his power...against the...South. Antiochus attacked Philometer, who had become an enemy. The latter fell due to treachery by trusted supporters (v. 26a), and became Antiochus' captive.

11:26 those who eat. Betraying counselors whom Philometer fed, led him to attack Syria to secure his defeat and death for him and his men.

11:27 shall speak lies. Antiochus feigned help to reinstate Ptolemy Philometer to Egypt's throne, occupied then by Ptolemy Euergetes. Both kings lied at the conference, and Antiochus set Philometer up as king at Memphis, whereas Euergetes reigned at Alexandria. The two Egyptians soon agreed on a joint rule, frustrating the Syrian.

11:28 against the holy covenant. En route N through Israel to Syria with riches, Antiochus met a revolt, as sources outside Scripture mention. He struck Jerusalem's temple, profaned the sacrificial system, massacred 80,000 men, took 40,000 prisoners, sold 40,000 as slaves, and squelched a Jewish bid to depose his own designated priest, Menelaus.

11:29 toward the south. Antiochus, for the third time, invaded Egypt against the joint rulership (ca. 168 B.C.); however, with much less success.

11:30 ships...come against him. A Roman fleet from Cyprus sided with Egypt, thwarting Antiochus' attack. Backing down from engaging Rome in war, Antiochus left Egypt, taking out his rage on Israelites in his path. He opposed God's Mosaic Covenant that some Jews kept, despite Syrian policies and some Jewish compromise. Antiochus showed favors to Jewish apostates ("who forsake the holy covenant") as non-biblical writings attest.

therefore he shall be grieved, and return in
rage against the holy covenant, and do
damage.
"So he shall return and show regard for
those who forsake the holy covenant.
31 And [4]forces shall be mustered by him,
[y]and they shall defile the sanctuary fortress; then they shall take away the daily
sacrifices, and place *there* the abomination
of desolation. 32 Those who do wickedly
against the covenant he shall [5]corrupt with
flattery; but the people who know their
God shall be strong, and carry out *great ex-*
ploits. 33 And those of the people who understand shall instruct many; yet *for many*
days they shall fall by sword and flame, by
captivity and plundering. 34 Now when
they fall, they shall be aided with a little
help; but many shall join with them by
[6]intrigue. 35 And *some* of those of understanding shall fall, [z]to refine them, purify
them, and make *them* white, *until* the time
of the end; because *it is* still for the appointed time.
36 "Then the king shall do according to
his own will: he shall [a]exalt and magnify
himself above every god, shall speak blasphemies against the God of gods, and
shall prosper till the wrath has been accomplished; for what has been determined shall be done. 37 He shall regard
neither the [7]God of his fathers nor the desire of women, [b]nor regard any god; for
he shall exalt himself above *them* all.
38 But in their place he shall honor a god
of fortresses; and a god which his fathers
did not know he shall honor with gold
and silver, with precious stones and
pleasant things. 39 Thus he shall act
against the strongest fortresses with a foreign god, which he shall acknowledge,
and advance *its* glory; and he shall cause
them to rule over many, and divide the
land for [8]gain.

The Northern King's Conquests

40 "At the [c]time of the end the king of
the South shall attack him; and the king
of the North shall come against him [d]like
a whirlwind, with chariots, [e]horsemen,
and with many ships; and he shall enter
the countries, overwhelm *them,* and pass
through. 41 He shall also enter the Glorious Land, and many *countries* shall be
overthrown; but these shall escape from
his hand: [f]Edom, Moab, and the [9]promi-

31 [y]Dan. 8:11-13; 12:11 [4]Lit. *arms*
32 [5]*pollute*
34 [6]Or *slipperiness, flattery*
35 [z][Deut. 8:16; Prov. 17:3]; Dan. 12:10; Zech. 13:9; Mal. 3:2, 3
36 [a]Dan. 7:8, 25
37 [b]Is. 14:13; 2 Thess. 2:4 [7]Or *gods*
39 [8]*profit*
40 [c]Dan. 11:27, 35; 12:4, 9 [d]Is. 21:1 [e]Ezek. 38:4; Rev. 9:16
41 [f]Is. 11:14 [9]Lit. *chief of the sons of Ammon*

11:31 defile the sanctuary. Antiochus' soldiers, no doubt working with apostate Jews, guarded the temple, halting all worship, while others attacked the city on the Sabbath slaughtering men, women, and children. Soldiers desecrated Israel's temple, banned circumcision and daily sacrifices (1 Macc. 1:44-54), and sacrificed a pig on the altar. The Syrians on Chislev (Dec. 15, 167 B.C.), even imposed an idol statue in honor of the Olympian god Zeus into the temple. Jews called it "the abomination that causes desolation," i.e., emptying or ruining for Jewish worship. **abomination of desolation.** Antiochus' soldiers profaned God's temple by spreading sow's broth on the altar and banning daily sacrifices (cf. 8:14 and *see note there*) as described in 1 Macc. 1:44-54. Both Daniel and Jesus said this atrocity was only a preview of the abomination that would happen later under the final Antichrist (9:27; Matt. 24:15).

11:32-34 Those who do wickedly. Compromisers (cf. v. 30) among the Jews were enticed by flattery to side with Antiochus and be corrupted (cf. 1 Macc. 1:11-15).

11:32 the people who know their God. Jews loyal to God (called Hasideans) stood on firm convictions, suffering death rather than compromising (v. 33; as also 1 Macc. 1:62,63). Judas Maccabeus, helped by Rome, led them in a successful revolt.

11:33 instruct many. Jews who "cause to be wise," that is those who believe and know the truth, instructed others in the Scriptures, while also suffering continued persecution.

11:34 a little help. Many would fall away, and Jews committed to the covenant would have little help, humanly speaking. Some, fearing the faithful remnant's dealing with apostates, pretended loyalty.

11:35 to refine them. Faced by persecution, some who remained true to God's "understanding" (any true believers, 12:3) were to fall as martyrs. The gracious design of such suffering was to sanctify them. The persecution pattern continues until the final "end" that God appointed, at Christ's second coming. Reference to this "end" prepares for a transition in v. 36 to final tribulation times when the Antichrist, whom Antiochus prefigures, will be in power. **time of the end...appointed time.** These two eschatological terms point to a forward leap across thousands of years of history from Antiochus to a future similar trial when the willful king (vv. 36-45) rules. The willful king is the "little horn," the Antichrist (7:7,8,20,21,24-26), the persecutor of 9:27 (*see note there*).

11:36-45 This section is the far fulfillment of God's prophetic plan. It summarizes details of Daniel's 70th week which are found nowhere else in Scripture. Antiochus Epiphanes, a type of Antichrist, is the perfect transition point to the actual Antichrist.

11:36 Then. This word points to the future "time of the end" mentioned in v. 35. Verses 36-45 discuss the career of the final Antichrist in the last 7 years before Christ's millennial kingdom. This willful king is the final Antichrist (*see notes on 7:8,11-12,25; 9:27*; cf. Rev. 13:4-7).

11:37 God of his fathers. The word for "God" is "Elohim," a word that is plural, thus in this context probably refers to "gods." Pagan Gentiles have had traditional gods passed down from their fathers, but this king has no regard for any of them. His only god is power (v. 38, "god of fortresses"). **desire of women.** This could mean that Antichrist will be a homosexual; but it surely means he has no normal desire for or, interest in, women, e.g., as one who is celibate.

11:38 god of fortresses. The term for fortress is used 5 other times in this chapter (vv. 7,10,19,31,39) and each time means "a strong place." Power is to be his god, and he spends all his treasures to become powerful and to finance wars. With this power, he will attack every stronghold (v. 39).

11:40 king of...South...North. Here is the final N/S conflict. The S was Egypt in the earlier context. Here is the last great battle with the final army from the N retaliating against the attack of the final southern African power. Antichrist will not allow this without striking back and winning, defeating both as recorded in v. 41ff. The willful king, Antichrist, withstands onslaughts from both, and prevails, entering Israel ("the Glorious Land") and, perhaps, committing at that time the abomination of desolation (9:23; Matt. 24:15). With this victory, he will be established in power for a time.

nent people of Ammon. 42 He shall
stretch out his hand against the countries,
and the land of [g]Egypt shall not escape.
43 He shall have power over the treasures
of gold and silver, and over all the precious things of Egypt; also the Libyans
and Ethiopians *shall follow* [h]at his heels.
44 But news from the east and the north
shall trouble him; therefore he shall go
out with great fury to destroy and annihilate many. 45 And he shall plant the tents
of his palace between the seas and [i]the
glorious holy mountain; [j]yet he shall
come to his end, and no one will help
him.

Prophecy of the End Time

12 "At that time Michael shall stand
up,
The great prince who stands *watch*
over the sons of your people;
[a]And there shall be a time of
trouble,
Such as never was since there was
a nation,
Even to that time.
And at that time your people [b]shall
be delivered,
Every one who is found [c]written in
the book.
2 And many of those who sleep in
the dust of the earth shall
awake,
[d]Some to everlasting life,
Some to shame [e]*and* everlasting
[1]contempt.
3 Those who are wise shall [f]shine
Like the brightness of the
firmament,
[g]And those who turn many to
righteousness
[h]Like the stars forever and ever.

4 "But you, Daniel, [i]shut up the words,
and seal the book until the time of the end;
many shall [j]run to and fro, and knowledge
shall increase."
5 Then I, Daniel, looked; and there
stood two others, one on this riverbank
and the other on that [k]riverbank. 6 And
one said to the man clothed in [l]linen, who
was above the waters of the river, [m]"How
long shall the fulfillment of these wonders *be?*"
7 Then I heard the man clothed in linen,
who *was* above the waters of the river,
when he [n]held up his right hand and his
left hand to heaven, and swore by Him
[o]who lives forever, [p]that *it shall be* for a
time, times, and half *a time;* [q]and when the
power of [r]the holy people has been completely shattered, all these *things* shall be
finished.
8 Although I heard, I did not understand. Then I said, "My lord, what *shall be*
the end of these *things?*"
9 And he said, "Go *your way,* Daniel, for
the words *are* closed up and sealed till the
time of the end. 10 [s]Many shall be purified,
made white, and refined, [t]but the wicked
shall do wickedly; and none of the wicked
shall understand, but [u]the wise shall understand.

42 [g]Joel 3:19
43 [h]Ex. 11:8
45 [i]Ps. 48:2 [j]Rev. 19:20

CHAPTER 12
1 [a]Is. 26:20; Jer. 30:7; Ezek. 5:9; Dan. 9:12; Matt. 24:21; Mark 13:19 [b]Rom. 11:26 [c]Ex. 32:32; Ps. 56:8
2 [d][Matt. 25:46; John 5:28, 29; Acts 24:15] [e][Is. 66:24; Rom. 9:21] [1]Lit. *abhorrence*
3 [f]Prov. 3:35; Dan. 11:33, 35; Matt. 13:43 [g]Prov. 11:30; [James 5:19, 20] [h]1 Cor. 15:41
4 [i]Is. 8:16; Dan. 12:9; Rev. 22:10 [j]Amos 8:12
5 [k]Dan. 10:4
6 [l]Ezek. 9:2; Dan. 10:5 [m]Dan. 8:13; 12:8; Matt. 24:3; Mark 13:4
7 [n]Deut. 32:40 [o]Dan. 4:34 [p]Dan. 7:25; Rev. 12:14 [q]Luke 21:24 [r]Dan. 8:24
10 [s]Zech. 13:9 [t]Is. 32:6, 7; Rev. 22:11 [u]Dan. 12:3; Hos. 14:9; John 7:17; 8:47

11:44 news from...east and...north. Military bulletins alert the willful king, in his victories, of other sectors of the world deploying troops to the Palestinian theater (cf. Rev. 9:16; 16:12).

11:45 his end. To face the latest threats, the willful king sets up his command post between the Mediterranean Sea and the Dead Sea (and/or Sea of Galilee) and the holy mountain of Jerusalem, his troops filling the land (cf. Zech. 12:2,3; 14:2,3; Rev. 19:17-21). No one is able to help him against God, who, by the return of Christ, brings him to his end (cf. Rev. 19:20).

12:1 that time. This points back to 11:36-45, the time of the ascendancy of Antichrist during the final tribulation period. During that period, Michael the archangel (cf. Jude 9) of 10:13, 21 ministers with special attention to protecting Israel during that Gentile time (cf. Is. 26:20,21; Jer. 30:7; Matt. 24:21). "Your people" means Daniel's Israelite people, who can have hope, even in the distress of an unprecedented kind set for the Great Tribulation (Matt. 24:21; cf. Rev. 12:12-17; 13:7). The book is the book of the saved (Mal. 3:16–4:3; Luke 10:20; Rev. 13:8; 17:8; 20:12,15; 21:27).

12:2 many...Some...Some. Two groups will arise from death constituting the "many" meaning all, as in John 5:29. Those of faith will rise to eternal life, the rest of the unsaved to eternal torment. The souls of OT saints are already with the Lord; at that time, they will receive glorified bodies (cf. Rev. 20:4-6).

12:3 wise. Those having true knowledge, by faith in God's Word, not only leaders (as 11:33), but others (11:35; 12:10). To *shine* in glory is a privilege of all the saved (cf. the principle in 1 Thess. 2:12; 1 Pet. 5:10). Any who influence others for righteousness shine like stars in varying capacities of light as their reward (as in 1 Cor. 3:8). The faithfulness of the believer's witness will determine one's eternal capacity to reflect God's glory.

12:4 the time of the end. Refers to the 70th week of tribulation (cf. 11:35,40). **run to and fro.** This Heb. verb form always refers to the movement of a person searching for something. In the tribulation, people will search for answers to the devastation and discover increased knowledge through Daniel's preserved book.

12:5 two others. Two angels.

12:6 man...in linen. *See note on 10:6.*

12:7 a time, times, and half *a time.* This answers the question of v. 6. Adding these (one, two, and one-half) come to the final 3½ years of Daniel's 70th week (9:27), the time of trouble when the "little horn," or willful king, persecutes the saints (7:25; cf. 11:36-39 and Rev. 12:14; the same span is described by other phrases in Rev. 11:2,3; 13:5).

12:10 Many...purified. Salvation will come to many Jews during the Great Tribulation (cf. Zech. 13:8,9, where the prophet speaks of one-third; Rom. 11:26; Rev. 11:13). The truly saved develop in godliness through trials. The unsaved pursue false values.

11 "And from the time *that* the daily *sac-*
rifice is taken away, and the abomination
of desolation is set up, *there shall be* one
thousand two hundred and ninety days.
12 Blessed *is* he who waits, and comes to
the one thousand three hundred and thirty-five days.
13 "But you, go *your way* till the end; [v]for
you shall rest, [w]and will arise to your inheritance at the end of the days."

13 [v] Is. 57:2; Rev. 14:13 [w] Ps. 1:5

12:11 the daily *sacrifice*. This reference is to the end of daily temple sacrifice, previously allowed under a covenant which the Antichrist formed with Israel, which he later causes to cease in the middle of the final 7 years (9:27). Then, favorable relations give way to persecution. Even his abomination that desecrates the temple (as 9:27; Matt. 24:1; Mark. 13:14; 2 Thess. 2:3,4) is accompanied with persecution. **one thousand two hundred and ninety days.** From the intrusion of the abomination, there follow 1,290 days, including 1,260 which make up the last 3 ½ years of the final 7 years (*see note on v. 7*), then 30 days more, possibly to allow for the judgment of the living subsequent to Christ's return (cf. Matt. 24:29-31; 25:31-46), before millennial kingdom blessings begin.

12:12 Blessed. This is in the kingdom (2:35,45; 7:13,14,27) that gives blessedness after the subjugation to Gentile empires in chaps. 2,7,8. **one thousand three hundred and thirty-five days.** Forty-five more days, even beyond the 1,290 days, allows for transition between Israel's time of being shattered (v. 7) and God's setting up of His kingdom (cf. 7:13,14,27).

12:13 go. Daniel's own career would soon involve death. **will arise.** In resurrection (cf. 12:2; John 5:28-29). **at the end of the days.** The kingdom will ensue after the prophesied days of 9:24-27; 12:11,12.

The Book of HOSEA

Title

The title is derived from the main character and author of the book. The meaning of his name, "salvation," is the same as that of Joshua (cf. Num. 13:8,16) and Jesus (Matt. 1:21). Hosea is the first of the 12 Minor Prophets. "Minor" refers to the brevity of the prophecies, as compared to the length of the works of Isaiah, Jeremiah, and Ezekiel.

Author and Date

The book of Hosea is the sole source of information about the author. Little is known about him, and even less about his father, Beeri (1:1). Hosea was probably a native of the northern kingdom of Israel, since he shows familiarity with the history, circumstances, and topography of the north (cf. 4:15; 5:1,13; 6:8,9; 10:5; 12:11,12; 14:6). This would make him and Jonah the only writing prophets from the northern kingdom. Although he addressed both Israel (the northern kingdom) and Judah (the southern kingdom), he identified the king of Israel as "our king" (7:5).

Hosea had a lengthy period of ministry, prophesying ca. 755–710 B.C., during the reigns of Uzziah (790–739 B.C.), Jotham (750–731 B.C.), Ahaz (735–715 B.C.), and Hezekiah (715–686 B.C.) in Judah, and Jeroboam II (793–753 B.C.) in Israel (1:1). His long career spanned the last 6 kings of Israel from Zechariah (753–752 B.C.) to Hoshea (732–722 B.C.). The overthrow of Zechariah (the last of the dynasty of Jehu) in 752 B.C. is depicted as yet future (1:4). Thus he followed Amos' preaching in the north, and was a contemporary of Isaiah and Micah as well, both of whom prophesied in Judah. Second Kings 14–20 and 2 Chronicles 26–32 record the historical period of Hosea's ministry.

Background and Setting

Hosea began his ministry to Israel (also called Ephraim, after its largest tribe) during the final days of Jeroboam II, under whose guidance Israel was enjoying both political peace and material prosperity as well as moral corruption and spiritual bankruptcy. Upon Jeroboam II's death (753 B.C.), however, anarchy prevailed and Israel declined rapidly. Until her overthrow by Assyria 20 years later, 4 of Israel's 6 kings were assassinated by their successors. Prophesying during the days surrounding the fall of Samaria, Hosea focuses on Israel's moral waywardness (cf. the book of Amos) and her breach of the covenantal relationship with the Lord, announcing that judgment was imminent.

Circumstances were not much better in the southern kingdom. Usurping the priestly function, Uzziah had been struck with leprosy (2 Chr. 26:16-21); Jotham condoned idolatrous practices, opening the way for Ahaz to encourage Baal worship (2 Chr. 27:1–28:4). Hezekiah's revival served only to slow Judah's acceleration toward a fate similar to that of her northern sister. Weak kings on both sides of the border repeatedly sought out alliances with their heathen neighbors (7:11; cf. 2 Kin. 15:19; 16:7) rather than seeking the Lord's help.

Historical and Theological Themes

The theme of Hosea is God's loyal love for His covenant people, Israel, in spite of their idolatry. Thus Hosea has been called the St. John (the apostle of love) of the OT. The Lord's true love for His people is unending and will tolerate no rival. Hosea's message contains much condemnation, both national and individual, but at the same time, he poignantly portrays the love of God toward His people with passionate emotion. Hosea was instructed by God to marry a certain woman, and experience with her a domestic life which was a dramatization of the sin and unfaithfulness of Israel. The marital life of Hosea and his wife, Gomer, provide the rich metaphor which clarifies the themes of the book: sin, judgment, and forgiving love.

Interpretive Challenges

That the faithless wife, Gomer, is symbolic of faithless Israel is without doubt; but questions remain. First, some suggest that the marital scenes in chaps. 1–3 should be taken only as allegory. However, there is nothing in the narrative, presented in simple prose, which would even question its literal occurrence.

Much of its impact would be lost if not literal. When non-literal elements within the book are introduced, they are prefaced with "saw" (5:13; 9:10,13), the normal Hebraic means of introducing non-literal scenes. Furthermore, there is no account of a prophet ever making himself the subject of an allegory or parable.

Second, what are the moral implications of God's command for Hosea to marry a prostitute? It appears best to see Gomer as chaste at the time of marriage to Hosea, only later having become an immoral woman. The words "take yourself a wife of harlotry" are to be understood proleptically, i.e., looking to the future. An immoral woman could not serve as a picture of Israel coming out of Egypt (2:15; 9:10), who then later wandered away from God (11:1). Chapter 3 describes Hosea taking back his wife, who had been rejected because of adultery, a rejection that was unjustifiable if Hosea had married a prostitute with full knowledge of her character.

A third question arises concerning the relationship between chap. 1 and chap. 3 and whether the woman of chap. 3 is Gomer or another woman. There are a number of factors which suggest that the woman of chap. 3 is Gomer. In 1:2, God's command is to "Go, take;" in 3:1, however, His command is to "Go again, love," suggesting that Hosea's love was to be renewed to the same woman. Furthermore, within the analogy of chap. 1, Gomer represents Israel. As God renews His love toward faithless Israel, so Hosea is to renew his love toward faithless Gomer. For Hos. 3 to denote a different woman would confuse the analogy.

Outline

I. Adulterous Wife and Faithful Husband (1:1–3:5)
   A. Hosea and Gomer (1:1-11)
   B. God and Israel (2:1-23)
   C. Both Parties Reconciled (3:1-5)

II. Adulterous Israel and Faithful Lord (4:1–14:9)
   A. Adulterous Israel Found Guilty (4:1–6:3)
   B. Adulterous Israel Put Away (6:4–10:15)
   C. Adulterous Israel Restored to the Lord (11:1–14:9)

1 The word of the LORD that came to Hosea the son of Beeri, in the days of [a]Uzziah, [b]Jotham, [c]Ahaz, *and* [d]Hezekiah, kings of Judah, and in the days of [e]Jeroboam the son of Joash, king of Israel.

The Family of Hosea

2 When the LORD began to speak by Hosea, the LORD said to Hosea:

[f]"Go, take yourself a wife of harlotry
And children of harlotry,
For [g]the land has committed great
[1]harlotry
By departing from the LORD."

3 So he went and took Gomer the daughter of Diblaim, and she conceived and bore him a son. 4 Then the LORD said to him:

"Call his name Jezreel,
For in a little *while*
[h]I will avenge the bloodshed of
Jezreel on the house of Jehu,
[i]And bring an end to the kingdom
of the house of Israel.
5 [j]It shall come to pass in that day
That I will break the bow of Israel
in the Valley of Jezreel."

6 And she conceived again and bore a daughter. Then *God* said to him:

"Call her name [2]Lo-Ruhamah,
[k]For I will no longer have mercy on
the house of Israel,
[3]But I will utterly take them away.
7 [l]Yet I will have mercy on the house
of Judah,
Will save them by the LORD their
God,
And [m]will not save them by bow,
Nor by sword or battle,
By horses or horsemen."

8 Now when she had weaned Lo-Ruhamah, she conceived and bore a son. 9 Then *God* said:

"Call his name [4]Lo-Ammi,
For you *are* not My people,
And I will not be your *God*.

The Restoration of Israel

10 "Yet [n]the number of the children of
Israel
Shall be as the sand of the sea,
Which cannot be measured or
numbered.

CHAPTER 1

1 [a] 2 Chr. 26; Is. 1:1; Amos 1:1 [b] 2 Kin. 15:5, 7, 32-38; 2 Chr. 27; Mic. 1:1 [c] 2 Kin. 16:1-20; 2 Chr. 28 [d] 2 Kin. 18–20; 2 Chr. 29:1–32:33; Mic. 1:1 [e] 2 Kin. 13:13; 14:23-29; Amos 1:1
2 [f] Hos. 3:1 [g] Deut. 31:16; Judg. 2:17; Ps. 73:27; Jer. 2:13; Ezek. 16:1-59; 23:1-49 [1] Spiritual adultery
4 [h] 2 Kin. 10:11 [i] 2 Kin. 15:8-10; 17:6, 23; 18:11
5 [j] 2 Kin. 15:29
6 [k] 2 Kin. 17:6 [2] Lit. *No-Mercy* [3] Or *That I may forgive them at all*
7 [l] 2 Kin. 19:29-35; Is. 30:18; 37:36, 37 [m] Ps. 44:3-7; [Zech. 4:6]
9 [4] Lit. *Not-My-People*
10 [n] Gen. 22:17; 32:12; Jer. 33:22

1:1 The Word of the LORD. Cf. 6:5. This kind of introduction, expressing the prophet's divine authority and message source, appears also in Joel 1:1; Mic. 1:1; Zeph. 1:1; Zech. 1:1; Mal. 1:1. Similar statements appear in Amos 1:3; Obad. 1; Jon. 1:1; Hag. 1:2.

1:2 wife of harlotry. See Introduction: Interpretive Challenges. **children of harlotry.** This points to the future unfaithfulness of their mother. The children were possibly not fathered by Hosea. That Hosea's marriage to Gomer was to depict God's marriage to Israel is clearly set forth and becomes the key to the theme of the book.

1:4 Jezreel. Meaning "God will scatter" (cf. Zech. 10:9), the name is given to the child so named, as a prediction of judgment (cf. 2 Kin. 9:7–10:28). **I will avenge the bloodshed of Jezreel.** It was at the city of Jezreel where Jehu slaughtered the house of Ahab (cf. 2 Kin. 9:7–10:28). **bring an end.** Looks forward to the exile of Israel to Assyria in 722 B.C., from which she never returned.

1:5 the Valley of Jezreel. Jezreel, called Esdraelon, extends 10 mi. in breadth from the Jordan to the Mediterranean Sea, near Carmel; it was the great battlefield (see Rev. 16:14-16) adjoining the Valley of Megiddo, which will become an avenue of blessing (cf. v. 11) when Christ returns in triumph. **break the bow.** The bow was a common euphemism denoting military strength, the principle instrument of warfare in Israel. Fulfillment came in 722 B.C. when Assyria invaded.

1:6 Lo-Ruhamah. Lit. "not pitied," this daughter is named to symbolize God bringing judgment on Israel, no longer extending His favor towards them.

1:7 I will have mercy on...Judah. God chose to intervene on behalf of Hezekiah when Jerusalem was besieged at the hands of the Assyrians in 701 B.C. (cf. 2 Kin. 19; Is. 37).

1:9 Lo-Ammi. The name means "not My people" and symbolizes God's rejection of Israel. **I will not be your *God*.** Lit. "I will not be 'I am' to you." The phrase gives the breaking of the covenant, a kind of divorce formula, in contrast to the covenant or marriage formula "I am that I am" given in Ex. 3:14.

1:10–2:1 In spite of the waywardness of Israel, God preserved a remnant for Himself from both Israel and Judah. Speaking of millennial blessings, God promised national increase (cf. Is. 54:1), national conversion and reunion (cf. Ezek. 37:15-23), national leadership (3:5), and national restoration (2:23).

1:10 number. A reaffirmation of the Abrahamic Covenant, not to be fulfilled in this generation but in the future (cf. Gen. 22:17).

God's Lovingkindness to Israel

	HOSEA and GOMER	GOD and ISRAEL
BETROTHAL	Hos. 1:2	Assumed; Jer. 2:2; Ezek. 16:8
ONE FLESH	Hos. 1:3	Assumed; Jer. 3:1; Ezek. 16:9-14
ADULTERY	Hos. 2:2; 3:1	Hos. 2:5; 4:12; Jer. 3:6; 5:7; Ezek. 16:15-34
DIVORCE	Hos. 3:1	Hos. 2:2; Jer. 3:8-10, 20; Ezek. 16:35-59
REMARRIAGE	Hos. 3:3-5	Hos. 1:10,11; 2:14-23; 14:4-9; Jer. 3:22-4:2; Ezek. 16:60-63

[o]And it shall come to pass
In the place where it was said to them,
'You *are* [5]not My [p]people,'
There it shall be said to them,
'*You are* [q]sons of the living God.'
11 [r]Then the children of Judah and the children of Israel
Shall be gathered together,
And appoint for themselves one head;
And they shall come up out of the land,
For great *will be* the day of Jezreel!

2 Say to your brethren, [1]'My people,'
And to your sisters, [2]'Mercy *is* shown.'

God's Unfaithful People

2 "Bring[3] charges against your mother, [4]bring charges;
For [a]she *is* not My wife, nor *am* I her Husband!
Let her put away her [b]harlotries from her sight,
And her adulteries from between her breasts;
3 Lest [c]I strip her naked
And expose her, as in the day she was [d]born,
And make her like a wilderness,
And set her like a dry land,
And slay her with [e]thirst.

4 "I will not have mercy on her children,
For they *are* the [f]children of harlotry.
5 For their mother has played the harlot;
She who conceived them has behaved shamefully.
For she said, 'I will go after my lovers,
[g]Who give *me* my bread and my water,
My wool and my linen,
My oil and my drink.'

6 "Therefore, behold,
[h]I will hedge up your way with thorns,
And [5]wall her in,
So that she cannot find her paths.
7 She will [6]chase her lovers,
But not overtake them;
Yes, she will seek them, but not find *them*.
Then she will say,
[i]'I will go and return to my [j]first husband,
For then *it was* better for me than now.'
8 For she did not [k]know
That I gave her grain, new wine, and oil,
And multiplied her silver and gold—
Which they prepared for Baal.

9 "Therefore I will return and take away
My grain in its time
And My new wine in its season,
And will take back My wool and My linen,
Given to cover her nakedness.
10 Now [l]I will uncover her lewdness in the sight of her lovers,
And no one shall deliver her from My hand.
11 [m]I will also cause all her mirth to cease,
Her feast days,
Her New Moons,
Her Sabbaths—
All her appointed feasts.

12 "And I will destroy her vines and her fig trees,
Of which she has said,
'These *are* my wages that my lovers have given me.'
So I will make them a forest,
And the beasts of the field shall eat them.

10 [o]1 Pet. 2:10 [p]Rom. 9:26 [q]Is. 63:16; 64:8; [John 1:12] [5]Heb. *lo-ammi*, v. 9
11 [r]Is. 11:11-13; Jer. 3:18; 50:4; [Ezek. 34:23; 37:15-28]

CHAPTER 2

1 [1]Heb. *Ammi*, Hos. 1:9, 10 [2]Heb. *Ruhamah*, Hos. 1:6
2 [a]Is. 50:1 [b]Ezek. 16:25 [3]Or *Contend with* [4]Or *contend*
3 [c]Jer. 13:22, 26; Ezek. 16:37-39 [d]Ezek. 16:4-7, 22 [e]Jer. 14:3; Amos 8:11-13
4 [f]John 8:41
5 [g]Ezek. 23:5; Hos. 2:8, 12
6 [h]Job 19:8; Lam. 3:7, 9 [5]Lit. *wall up her wall*
7 [i]Luke 15:17, 18 [j]Is. 54:5-8; Jer. 2:2; 3:1; Ezek. 16:8; 23:4 [6]Or *pursue*
8 [k]Is. 1:3; Ezek. 16:19
10 [l]Ezek. 16:37
11 [m]Jer. 7:34; 16:9; Hos. 3:4; Amos 5:21; 8:10

not My people. Quoted by Paul in Rom. 9:26.

1:11 one head. Refers to Messiah (cf. 3:5). **day of Jezreel.** Here used positively in the sense of divine blessing (cf. 2:22).

2:2 Bring charges against your mother. Although the language is applicable to Gomer, it depicts a courtroom scene in which the Lord, as the plaintiff, brings charges against the defendant. Individual Israelites, depicted as the children, are commanded to bring charges against their mother, Israel as a nation. The physical immorality of Gomer pictures the spiritual idolatry of Israel.

2:5 I will go. Lit. "Let me go," it denotes strong desire and bent. Israel attributed her prosperity to the idols of her heathen neighbors, "her lovers" (cf. vv. 7, 10, 12). She would not be deterred from pursuing them.

2:8-13 God withheld rain and productivity to show Israel that the Canaanite god Baal was not the god of rain and fertility.

2:8 prepared for Baal. Baal (the Phoenician sun-god) worship, already present during the time of the judges (cf. Judg. 2:17; 3:3; 8:33), became established in Israel when king Ahab married Jezebel, who attempted to obliterate Israelite worship of the true God (cf. 1 Kin. 19). Offerings to Baal actually came from God's dowry to Israel (cf. Ezek. 16:10-14).

2:10 I will uncover her lewdness. God pledged to expose Israel's wickedness. The phrase is linked to being taken forcibly into captivity in Ezek. 16:37-40. **her lovers.** The idols were personified as if they could see, though they could offer no help.

2:11 feast days. Ever since the Exodus from Egypt, Israel had intermingled the worship of the Lord with the worship of false gods (cf. Amos 5:26; Acts 7:43).

13 I will punish her
For the days of the Baals to which
she burned incense.
She decked herself with her
earrings and jewelry,
And went after her lovers;
But Me she forgot," says the LORD.

God's Mercy on His People

14 "Therefore, behold, I will allure her,
Will bring her into the wilderness,
And speak [7]comfort to her.
15 I will give her her vineyards from
there,
And [n]the Valley of Achor as a door
of hope;
She shall sing there,
As in [o]the days of her youth,
[p]As in the day when she came up
from the land of Egypt.

16 "And it shall be, in that day,"
Says the LORD,
"*That* you will call Me [8]'My
Husband,'
And no longer call Me [9]'My Master,'
17 For [q]I will take from her mouth the
names of the Baals,
And they shall be remembered by
their name no more.
18 In that day I will make a [r]covenant
for them
With the beasts of the field,
With the birds of the air,
And *with* the creeping things of the
ground.
Bow and sword of battle [s]I will
shatter from the earth,
To make them [t]lie down safely.

14 [7] Lit. *to her heart*
15 [n] Josh. 7:26 [o] Jer. 2:1-3; Ezek. 16:8-14 [p] Ex. 15:1
16 [8] Heb. *Ishi* [9] Heb. *Baali*
17 [q] Ex. 23:13; Josh. 23:7; Ps. 16:4
18 [r] Job 5:23; Is. 11:6-9; Ezek. 34:25 [s] Is. 2:4; Ezek. 39:1-10 [t] Lev. 26:5; Is. 32:18; Jer. 23:6; Ezek. 34:25

19 "I will betroth you to Me forever;
Yes, I will betroth you to Me
In righteousness and justice,
In lovingkindness and mercy;
20 I will betroth you to Me in
faithfulness,
And [u]you shall know the LORD.

21 "It shall come to pass in that day
That [v]I will answer," says the LORD;
"I will answer the heavens,
And they shall answer the earth.
22 The earth shall answer
With grain,
With new wine,
And with oil;
They shall answer [1]Jezreel.
23 Then [w]I will sow her for Myself in
the earth,
[x]And I will have mercy on *her who
had* [2]not obtained mercy;
Then [y]I will say to *those who were*
[3]not My people,
'You *are* [4]My people!'
And they shall say, *'You are* my
God!' "

Israel Will Return to God

3 Then the LORD said to me, "Go again,
love a woman *who is* loved by a [a]lover[1]
and is committing adultery, just like the
love of the LORD for the children of Israel,
who look to other gods and love *the* raisin
cakes *of the pagans*."
2 So I bought her for myself for fifteen
shekels of silver, and one and one-half
homers of barley. 3 And I said to her, "You
shall [b]stay with me many days; you shall

20 [u] [Jer. 31:33, 34]; Hos. 6:6; 13:4; [John 17:3]
21 [v] Is. 55:10; Zech. 8:12; [Mal. 3:10, 11]
22 [1] Lit. *God Will Sow*
23 [w] Jer. 31:27; Amos 9:15 [x] Hos. 1:6 [y] Hos. 1:10; Zech. 13:9; Rom. 9:25, 26; [Eph. 2:11-22]; 1 Pet. 2:10 [2] Heb. *lo-ruhamah* [3] Heb. *lo-ammi* [4] Heb. *ammi*

CHAPTER 3

1 [a] Jer. 3:20 [1] Lit. *friend or husband*
3 [b] Deut. 21:13

2:13 Me she forgot. Cf. 2 Kin. 17:7-18 for a detailed description of what their abandonment of God involved.

2:14 speak comfort to her. The phrase was used of wooing (Gen. 34:3; Judg. 19:3; Ruth 2:13). God will restore Israel to Himself.

2:15 Valley of Achor. Lit. "Valley of Trouble," near Jericho where Achan and his family were judged (Josh. 7:24). This reference alerts Israel that her discipline and judgment would not last forever because there is a "door of hope."

2:16 My Husband...My Master. The former (lit. "my ishi") denotes affection and intimacy, while the latter (lit. "my baali") speaks of rulership.

2:17 In v. 13, Israel forgot her true God; God said she would forget her false gods. What the outward conformity to the Mosaic Covenant could not do, God does through a new, regenerated heart in the New Covenant (Jer. 31:31-34; Zech. 13:1,2).

2:18 a covenant. This depicts a millennial scene (cf. Is. 2:4; 11:6-9; Mic. 4:3) when God's people become subject to God and creation becomes subject to them.

2:19,20 I will betroth you. Repeated 3 times, the term emphasizes the intensity of God's restoring love for the nation. In that day, Israel will be no longer be thought of as a prostitute. Israel brings nothing to the marriage; God makes all the promises and provides all the dowry. These verses are recited by every orthodox Jew as he places the phylacteries on his hand and forehead (cf. Deut. 11:18). The regeneration/conversion of the nation is much like that of an individual (cf. 2 Cor. 5:16-19).

2:22,23 A reversal of circumstances (cf. 1:4,6,9).

2:22 Jezreel. As in 1:11, used here in the positive sense of scattering seed to sow it.

2:23 Quoted by Paul in Rom. 9:25 as analogous to the conversion of Gentiles.

3:1 Go again, love. Having been previously separated, Hosea was commanded to pursue his estranged wife Gomer (cf. Introduction: Interpretive Challenges), thereby illustrating God's unquenchable love for faithless Israel. **raisin cakes.** Eaten as a part of special occasions (cf. 2 Sam. 6:19), they may have been used in idolatrous ceremonies, possibly as an aphrodisiac (cf. Song 2:5).

3:2 bought her. Probably from a slave auction, Hosea purchased Gomer for 15 shekels of silver and 1½ homers of barley. Together, the total may have equaled 30 pieces of silver, the price paid for a common slave (cf. Ex. 21:32). Barley was the offering of one accused of adultery (Num. 5:15).

3:3-5 Gomer would not be allowed conjugal relations for "many days," with any man, including Hosea. As a further element of the pic-

not play the harlot, nor shall you have a
man—so, too, *will* I *be* toward you."
4 For the children of Israel shall abide
many days [c]without king or prince, without sacrifice or sacred pillar, without
[d]ephod or [e]teraphim. 5 Afterward the children of Israel shall return and [f]seek the
LORD their God and [g]David their king.
They shall fear the LORD and His goodness
in the [h]latter days.

God's Charge Against Israel

4 Hear the word of the LORD,
You children of Israel,
For the LORD *brings* a [a]charge[1]
against the inhabitants of the
land:

"There is no truth or mercy
Or [b]knowledge of God in the land.
2 *By* swearing and lying,
Killing and stealing and
committing adultery,
They break all restraint,
With bloodshed [2]upon bloodshed.
3 Therefore [c]the land will mourn;
And [d]everyone who dwells there
will waste away
With the beasts of the field
And the birds of the air;
Even the fish of the sea will be
taken away.

4 "Now let no man contend, or
rebuke another;
For your people *are* like those [e]who
contend with the priest.
5 Therefore you shall stumble [f]in the
day;
The prophet also shall stumble
with you in the night;
And I will destroy your mother.

6 [g]My people are destroyed for lack
of knowledge.
Because you have rejected
knowledge,
I also will reject you from being
priest for Me;
[h]Because you have forgotten the
law of your God,
I also will forget your children.

7 "The more they increased,
The more they sinned against Me;
[i]I[3] will change [4]their glory into
shame.
8 They eat up the sin of My people;
They set their [5]heart on their
iniquity.
9 And it shall be: [j]like people, like
priest.
So I will punish them for their
ways,
And [6]reward them for their deeds.
10 For [k]they shall eat, but not have
enough;
They shall commit harlotry, but not
increase;
Because they have ceased obeying
the LORD.

The Idolatry of Israel

11 "Harlotry, wine, and new wine
[l]enslave the heart.
12 My people ask counsel from their
[m]wooden *idols*,
And their [7]staff informs them.
For [n]the spirit of harlotry has
caused *them* to stray,
And they have played the harlot
against their God.
13 [o]They offer sacrifices on the
mountaintops,
And burn incense on the hills,

4 [c] Hos. 10:3 [d] Ex. 28:4-12; 1 Sam. 23:9-12 [e] Gen. 31:19, 34; Judg. 17:5; 18:14, 17; [1 Sam. 15:23]
5 [f] Jer. 50:4 [g] Jer. 30:9; Ezek. 34:24 [h] [Is. 2:2, 3]; Jer. 31:9

CHAPTER 4

1 [a] Is. 1:18; Hos. 12:2; Mic. 6:2 [b] Jer. 4:22 [1] A legal complaint
2 [2] Lit. *touching*
3 [c] Is. 24:4; 33:9; Jer. 4:28; 12:4; Amos 5:16; 8:8 [d] Zeph. 1:3
4 [e] Deut. 17:12
5 [f] Jer. 15:8; Hos. 2:2, 5
6 [g] Is. 5:13 [h] Ezek. 22:26
7 [i] 1 Sam. 2:30; Mal. 2:9 [3] So with MT, LXX, Vg.; scribal tradition, Syr., Tg. *They will change* [4] So with MT, LXX, Syr., Tg., Vg.; scribal tradition *My glory*
8 [5] Desires
9 [j] Is. 24:2; Jer. 5:30, 31; 2 Tim. 4:3, 4 [6] *repay*
10 [k] Lev. 26:26; Is. 65:13; Mic. 6:14; Hag. 1:6
11 [l] Prov. 20:1; Is. 5:12; 28:7
12 [m] Jer. 2:27 [n] Is. 44:19, 20 [7] Diviner's rod
13 [o] Is. 1:29; 57:5, 7; Jer. 2:20; Ezek. 6:13; 20:28

ture of God's dealings with His covenant people during the present age, Israel would exist without her existing political and religious (both true and false) relations until Messiah returns at the Second Advent to set up His millennial reign (cf. Ezek. 40–48; Zech. 12–14).

3:4 without ephod or teraphim. Idolatrous items of priestly clothing and objects of worship.

3:5 David. Cf. 1:11. This must refer to Messiah during the Millennium, as "in the latter days" specifies (cf. Is. 55:3,4; Jer. 30:9; Ezek. 34:23, 24; 37:24,25). The Jews did not seek after Christ at His first advent. This reference has the Davidic Covenant as its background (cf. 2 Sam. 7:12-17; Pss. 39; 132).

4:1 the LORD *brings* a charge. Turning from the analogy of his own marriage, the prophet made the judicial charge in God's indictment against Israel.

4:2 Note the many infractions of the Ten Commandments (cf. Ex. 20:3-17).

4:3 Sin plays havoc with lower creation and nature (cf. Joel 1:17-20; Rom. 8:19-22).

4:4 let no man contend. Rationalizing and denying their wrongs, the people protested their innocence, like those who would not humbly accept the decision of the priests (cf. Deut 17:8-13).

4:5 your mother. The Israelite state of which the people are the children (cf. 2:2).

4:6 reject you from being priest for Me. Having rejected the Lord's instruction, Israel could no longer serve as His priest to the nations (cf. Ex. 19:6; James 3:1).

4:7-10 Their position of power and glory, abused in succeeding generations by the eating of the sin offerings, would be turned to shame. Being no different than the people, the priests, who should have been faithful, would share their punishment (cf. Is. 24:1-3).

4:11 Here is a moral truth applicable to all people and times. Verses 12,13 are illustrations of the enslavement in Israel.

4:12 spirit of harlotry. A prevailing mindset and inclination to worldly spiritual immorality, i.e., idolatry (cf. 5:4).

4:13 Bereft of righteous teaching and understanding, they sacrificed to idols. Hilltops and groves of trees were favorite places for idolatrous worship (cf. Deut. 12:2; Jer. 2:20; Ezek. 6:13), including religious prostitution.

Under oaks, poplars, and
terebinths,
Because their shade *is* good.
[p]Therefore your daughters commit
harlotry,
And your brides commit adultery.

14 "I will not punish your daughters
when they commit harlotry,
Nor your brides when they commit
adultery;
For *the men* themselves go apart
with harlots,
And offer sacrifices with a [q]ritual
harlot.
Therefore people *who* do not
understand will be trampled.

15 "Though you, Israel, play the harlot,
Let not Judah offend.
[r]Do not come up to Gilgal,
Nor go up to [s]Beth[8] Aven,
[t]Nor swear an oath, *saying,* 'As the
LORD lives'—

16 "For Israel [u]is stubborn
Like a stubborn calf;
Now the LORD will let them forage
Like a lamb in [9]open country.

17 "Ephraim *is* joined to idols,
[v]Let him alone.
18 Their drink [1]is rebellion,
They commit harlotry continually.
[w]Her [2]rulers [3]dearly love dishonor.
19 [x]The wind has wrapped her up in
its wings,
And [y]they shall be ashamed
because of their sacrifices.

13 [p] Amos 7:17; [Rom. 1:28-32]
14 [q] Deut. 23:18
15 [r] Hos. 9:15; 12:11 [s] 1 Kin. 12:29; Josh. 7:2; Hos. 10:8 [t] Jer. 5:2; 44:26; Amos 8:14 [8] Lit. *House of Idolatry* or *Wickedness*
16 [u] Jer. 3:6; 7:24; 8:5; Zech. 7:11 [9] Lit. *a large place*
17 [v] Matt. 15:14
18 [w] Mic. 3:11 [1] Or *has turned aside* [2] Lit. *shields* [3] Heb. difficult; a Jewish tradition *shamefully love, 'Give!'*
19 [x] Jer. 51:1 [y] Is. 1:29

Impending Judgment on Israel and Judah

5 "Hear this, O priests!
Take heed, O house of Israel!
Give ear, O house of the king!
For [1]yours *is* the judgment,
Because [a]you have been a snare to
Mizpah
And a net spread on Tabor.
2 The revolters are [b]deeply involved
in slaughter,
Though I rebuke them all.
3 [c]I know Ephraim,
And Israel is not hidden from Me;
For now, O Ephraim, [d]you commit
harlotry;
Israel is defiled.

4 "They[2] do not direct their deeds
Toward turning to their God,
For [e]the spirit of harlotry is in their
midst,
And they do not know the LORD.
5 The [f]pride of Israel testifies to his
face;
Therefore Israel and Ephraim
stumble in their iniquity;
Judah also stumbles with them.

6 "With their flocks and herds
[g]They shall go to seek the LORD,
But they will not find *Him;*
He has withdrawn Himself from
them.
7 They have [h]dealt treacherously
with the LORD,
For they have begotten [3]pagan
children.
Now a New Moon shall devour
them and their heritage.

8 "Blow[i] the ram's horn in Gibeah,
The trumpet in Ramah!

CHAPTER 5

1 [a] Hos. 6:9 [1] Or *to you*
2 [b] Is. 29:15; Hos. 4:2; 6:9
3 [c] Amos 3:2; 5:12 [d] Hos. 4:17
4 [e] Hos. 4:12 [2] Or *Their deeds will not allow them to turn*
5 [f] Hos. 7:10
6 [g] Prov. 1:28; Is. 1:15; Jer. 11:11; Ezek. 8:18; Mic. 3:4; John 7:34
7 [h] Is. 48:8; Jer. 3:20; Hos. 6:7 [3] Lit. *strange*
8 [i] Hos. 8:1; Joel 2:1

4:14 Although all who sin will be judged, God forbade punishing the adulteresses alone and leaving the men who patronized them to go free. The heaviest punishment would not be on the women who sin, but the fathers and husbands who set such a bad example by their engagement with prostitutes. **do not understand.** Cf. 4:6.

4:15 Gilgal. Between Jordan and Jericho in the area of Samaria, this was once a holy place to God (Josh. 5:10-15; 1 Sam. 10:8; 15:21), afterwards desecrated by idol worship (cf. 9:15; 12:11; Amos 4:4; 5:5). **Beth Aven.** Judah was to stay away from Israel's centers of false worship, including Beth Aven ("house of wickedness/deceit"). This was a deliberate substitution for the name Bethel ("house of God"), once sacred to God (Gen. 28:17,19), but made by Jeroboam a place to worship calves (cf. 1 Kin. 12:28-33; 13:1; Jer. 48:13; Amos 3:14; 7:13).

4:16 Because Israel was like a stubborn calf, God no longer attempted to corral her, abandoning her as a lamb in a vast wilderness.

4:17 Ephraim...Let him alone. As the largest and most influential of the northern 10 tribes, Ephraim's name was often used as representative of the northern nation. This was an expression of God's wrath of abandonment. When sinners reject Him and are bent on fulfilling their wicked purposes, God removes restraining grace and turns them over to the results of their own perverse choices. This kind of wrath is that in Rom. 1:18-32 (cf. Judg. 10:13; 2 Chr. 15:2; 24:20; Ps. 81:11,12).

5:1 Hosea addressed the priests, the people, and the royal family; the 3 imperatives demand attention. The religious and civil leaders had entrapped the people (cf. 6:9; 7:7). **Mizpah...Tabor.** Mizpah of Gilead, lying E of the Jordan (Judg. 10:17; 11:29), and Tabor, SW of the Sea of Galilee, were likely places for false worship.

5:5 pride of Israel testifies to his face. Israel's pride in idolatry provided self-incrimination (cf. 7:10).

5:6,7 Her religious sacrifices and monthly festivals no longer brought divine favor, only judgment. God "has withdrawn Himself from them." *See note on 4:17.*

5:8 The enemy was already upon them and thus her watchmen were to sound the alarm (cf. Num. 10:9). **Gibeah...Ramah.** Located

[j]Cry aloud *at* [k]Beth Aven,
'*Look* behind you, O Benjamin!'
9 Ephraim shall be desolate in the day of rebuke;
Among the tribes of Israel I make known what is sure.

10 "The princes of Judah are like those who [l]remove a landmark;
I will pour out my wrath on them like water.
11 Ephraim is [m]oppressed *and* broken in judgment,
Because he willingly walked by [n]*human* precept.
12 Therefore I *will be* to Ephraim like a moth,
And to the house of Judah [o]like rottenness.

13 "When Ephraim saw his sickness,
And Judah *saw* his [p]wound,
Then Ephraim went [q]to Assyria
And sent to King Jareb;
Yet he cannot cure you,
Nor heal you of your wound.
14 For [r]I *will be* like a lion to Ephraim,
And like a young lion to the house of Judah.
[s]I, *even* I, will tear *them* and go away;
I will take *them* away, and no one shall rescue.
15 I will return again to My place
Till they [4]acknowledge their offense.
Then they will seek My face;
In their affliction they will earnestly seek Me."

A Call to Repentance

6 Come,[a] and let us return to the LORD;
For [b]He has torn, but [c]He will heal us;
He has stricken, but He will [1]bind us up.
2 [d]After two days He will revive us;
On the third day He will raise us up,
That we may live in His sight.
3 [e]Let us know,
Let us pursue the knowledge of the LORD.
His going forth is established [f]as the morning;
[g]He will come to us [h]like the rain,
Like the latter *and* former rain to the earth.

Impenitence of Israel and Judah

4 "O Ephraim, what shall I do to you?
O Judah, what shall I do to you?
For your faithfulness is like a morning cloud,
And like the early dew it goes away.
5 Therefore I have hewn *them* by the prophets,
I have slain them by [i]the words of My mouth;
And [2]your judgments *are like* light *that* goes forth.
6 For I desire [j]mercy[3] and [k]not sacrifice,
And the [l]knowledge of God more than burnt offerings.

7 "But like [4]men they transgressed the covenant;
There they dealt treacherously with Me.
8 [m]Gilead *is* a city of evildoers
And [5]defiled with blood.
9 As bands of robbers lie in wait for a man,
So the company of [n]priests
[o]murder on the way to Shechem;
Surely they commit [p]lewdness.
10 I have seen a horrible thing in the house of Israel:
There *is* the [6]harlotry of Ephraim;
Israel is defiled.

8 [j] Is. 10:30 [k] Josh. 7:2
10 [l] Deut. 19:14; 27:17
11 [m] Deut. 28:33 [n] Mic. 6:16
12 [o] Prov. 12:4
13 [p] Jer. 30:12-15 [q] 2 Kin. 15:19; Hos. 7:11; 10:6
14 [r] Ps. 7:2; Lam. 3:10; Hos. 13:7, 8 [s] Ps. 50:22
15 [4] Lit. *become guilty or bear punishment*

CHAPTER 6

1 [a] Is. 1:18; Acts 10:43 [b] Deut. 32:39; Hos. 5:14 [c] Jer. 30:17; Hos. 14:4 [1] Bandage
2 [d] Luke 24:46; Acts 10:40; [1 Cor. 15:4]
3 [e] Is. 54:13 [f] 2 Sam. 23:4 [g] Ps. 72:6; Joel 2:23 [h] Job 29:23
5 [i] [Jer. 23:29] [2] Or *the judgments on you*
6 [j] Matt. 9:13; 12:7 [k] Is. 1:12, 13; [Mic. 6:6-8] [l] [John 17:3] [3] Or *faithfulness* or *loyalty*
7 [4] Or *Adam*
8 [m] Hos. 12:11 [5] Lit. *foot-tracked*
9 [n] Hos. 5:1 [o] Jer. 7:9, 10; Hos. 4:2 [p] Ezek. 22:9; 23:27; Hos. 2:10
10 [6] Spiritual adultery

on Judah's northern border with Israel. **Beth Aven.** (Bethel) situated in southern Israel (cf. 4:15). All three were strategic defense cities. **Benjamin.** Used to refer to the whole southern kingdom.

5:10 remove a landmark. Boundaries, marked by stones, could be easily moved at night. Moving them was tantamount to stealing land from a neighbor (cf. Deut. 19:14; 27:17; Prov. 22:28; 23:10). Worse, Israel's leaders were moving spiritual lines established by God (cf. v. 11).

5:12 moth...rottenness. God will be destructive to Israel.

5:13 King Jareb. "Jareb" means "warrior" and refers to king of Assyria, to whom Israel (cf. 2 Kin. 15:19,20) and later Judah (cf. 2 Kin. 16:5-9) turned for help.

5:14,15 Foreign assistance would be of no value, since the Lord was orchestrating punishment at the hands of the Assyrians. He would remove Himself "till they acknowledge their offense" and "seek My face" (cf. 3:5).

6:1-3 Coming with the beginning of Christ's millennial reign (cf. Zech. 12:10–13:1; Is. 43:1-6), Hosea records Israel's future words of repentance (cf. 5:15).

6:2 After two days...On the third day. Not a reference to the resurrection of Christ (illness, not death, is in the context), but to the quickness of healing and restoration (cf. the quickness with which the dry bones of Ezek. 37 respond). Numbers are used similarly elsewhere (e.g., Job 5:19; Prov. 6:16; 30:15,18; Amos 1:3).

6:6 I desire mercy...not sacrifice. Cf. Matt. 9:13; 12:7.

6:4-7 Because Israel's commitment to the Lord was fleeting and superficial, He had to send prophets with stern words (vv. 4,5), calling for a covenantal loyalty befitting a marriage relationship (v. 6). But they violated the marriage vows (v. 7).

6:7 men...covenant. A reference to the Mosaic Covenant (cf. 8:1; Ex. 19:5,6).

11 Also, O Judah, a harvest is
appointed for you,
When I return the captives of My
people.

7 "When I would have healed Israel,
Then the iniquity of Ephraim was
uncovered,
And the wickedness of Samaria.
For [a]they have committed fraud;
A thief comes in;
A band of robbers [1]takes spoil
outside.
2 They [2]do not consider in their
hearts
That [b]I remember all their
wickedness;
Now their own deeds have
surrounded them;
They are before My face.
3 They make a [c]king glad with their
wickedness,
And princes [d]with their lies.

4 "They[e] *are* all adulterers.
Like an oven heated by a baker—
He ceases stirring *the fire* after
kneading the dough,
Until it is leavened.
5 In the day of our king
Princes have made *him* sick,
[3]inflamed with [f]wine;
He stretched out his hand with
scoffers.
6 They prepare their heart like an
oven,
While they lie in wait;
[4]Their baker sleeps all night;
In the morning it burns like a
flaming fire.
7 They are all hot, like an oven,
And have devoured their judges;
All their kings have fallen.
[g]None among them calls upon Me.

8 "Ephraim [h]has mixed himself
among the peoples;
Ephraim is a cake unturned.
9 [i]Aliens have devoured his strength,
But he does not know *it;*
Yes, gray hairs are here and there
on him,
Yet he does not know *it.*
10 And the [j]pride of Israel testifies to
his face,
But [k]they do not return to the LORD
their God,
Nor seek Him for all this.

Futile Reliance on the Nations

11 "Ephraim[l] also is like a silly dove,
without [5]sense—
[m]They call to Egypt,
They go to [n]Assyria.
12 Wherever they go, I will [o]spread
My net on them;
I will bring them down like birds
of the air;
I will chastise them
[p]According to what their
congregation has heard.

13 "Woe to them, for they have fled
from Me!
Destruction to them,
Because they have transgressed
against Me!
Though [q]I redeemed them,
Yet they have spoken lies against
Me.
14 [r]They did not cry out to Me with
their heart
When they wailed upon their beds.

"They [6]assemble together for grain
and new [s]wine,
[7]They rebel against Me;
15 Though I disciplined *and*
strengthened their arms,
Yet they devise evil against Me;
16 They return, *but* not [8]to the Most
High;
[t]They are like a treacherous bow.
Their princes shall fall by the
sword
For the [u]cursings of their tongue.

CHAPTER 7
1 [a]Ezek. 23:4-8; Hos. 5:1 [1]*plunders*
2 [b]Ps. 25:7; Jer. 14:10; 17:1; Hos. 8:13; 9:9; Amos 8:7 [2]Lit. *do not say to*
3 [c]Hos. 1:1 [d]Mic. 7:3; [Rom. 1:32]
4 [e]Jer. 9:2; 23:10
5 [f]Is. 28:1, 7 [3]Lit. *with the heat of*
6 [4]So with MT, Vg.; Syr., Tg. *Their anger;* LXX *Ephraim*
7 [g]Is. 64:7
8 [h]Ps. 106:35
9 [i]Is. 1:7; 42:25; Hos. 8:7
10 [j]Hos. 5:5 [k]Is. 9:13
11 [l]Hos. 11:11 [m]Is. 30:3 [n]Hos. 5:13; 8:9 [5]Lit. *heart*
12 [o]Ezek. 12:13 [p]Lev. 26:14; Deut. 28:15; 2 Kin. 17:13
13 [q]Ex. 18:8; Mic. 6:4
14 [r]Job 35:9, 10; Ps. 78:36; Jer. 3:10; Zech. 7:5 [s]Judg. 9:27; Amos 2:8 [6]So with MT, Tg.; Vg. *thought upon;* LXX *slashed themselves for* (cf. 1 Kin. 18:28) [7]So with MT, Syr., Tg.; LXX omits *They rebel against Me;* Vg. *They departed from Me*
16 [t]Ps. 78:57 [u]Ps. 73:9; Dan. 7:25; Mal. 3:13, 14 [8]Or *upward*

6:11 Lest Judah feel smug at her neighbor's demise, the prophet reminds them that they have a day of reckoning awaiting them (cf. Jer. 51:13; Joel 2:1-3).

7:1 Samaria. As the capital, Samaria represents the northern kingdom.

7:4-7 The civil leaders' evil lust burned so passionately all night, that the prophet repeatedly described it like a consuming oven (cf. vv. 4,6,7), so hot that the baker could forego stirring the fire during the entire night and still have adequate heat for baking the next morning.

7:7 All their kings have fallen. Four of Israel's final 6 kings were murdered by usurpers.

7:8,9 At Israel's invitation, foreign nations made debilitating inroads into her national and religious life. This intrusion was making her like "a cake unturned," burned on one side and raw on the other. Payment for this foreign assistance was "devouring her strength" (v. 9) and making her old and feeble without noticing it.

7:11,12 Like a dove, reputed to be easily lured and captured (cf. Matt. 10:16), so Israel had been enticed by Egypt and Assyria, who ultimately trapped her.

7:13 redeemed them. From Egypt and their other enemies.

7:14 wailed upon their beds...assemble together. The former phrase may speak of appeals to pagan fertility gods upon beds of sacred prostitution, while the latter, if the marginal reading is correct, harkens to Elijah's encounter with the prophets of Baal on Mt. Carmel (cf. 1 Kin. 18:28).

This *shall be* their derision [v]in the
land of Egypt.

The Apostasy of Israel

8 "*Set* the [1]trumpet to your mouth!
He shall come [a]like an eagle against
the house of the LORD,
Because they have transgressed My
covenant
And rebelled against My law.
2 [b]Israel will cry to Me,
'My God, [c]we know You!'
3 Israel has rejected the good;
The enemy will pursue him.

4 "They[d] set up kings, but not by Me;
They made princes, but I did not
acknowledge *them.*
From their silver and gold
They made idols for themselves—
That they might be cut off.
5 Your [2]calf [3]is rejected, O Samaria!
My anger is aroused against
them—
[e]How long until they attain to
innocence?
6 For from Israel *is* even this:
A [f]workman made it, and it *is* not
God;
But the calf of Samaria shall be
broken to pieces.

7 "They[g] sow the wind,
And reap the whirlwind.
The stalk has no bud;
It shall never produce meal.
If it should produce,
[h]Aliens would swallow it up.
8 [i]Israel is swallowed up;
Now they are among the Gentiles
[j]Like a vessel in which *is* no
pleasure.
9 For they have gone up to Assyria,
Like [k]a wild donkey alone by itself;
Ephraim [l]has hired lovers.
10 Yes, though they have hired among
the nations,
Now [m]I will gather them;
And they shall [4]sorrow a little,
Because of the [5]burden of [n]the
king of princes.

11 "Because Ephraim has made many
altars for sin,
They have become for him altars
for sinning.
12 I have written for him [o]the great
things of My law,
But they were considered a strange
thing.
13 *For* the sacrifices of My offerings
[p]they sacrifice flesh and eat *it*,
[q]*But* the LORD does not accept them.
[r]Now He will remember their
iniquity and punish their sins.
They shall return to Egypt.

14 "For[s] Israel has forgotten [t]his
Maker,
And has built [6]temples;
Judah also has multiplied [u]fortified
cities;
But [v]I will send fire upon his cities,
And it shall devour his [7]palaces."

Judgment of Israel's Sin

9 Do[a] not rejoice, O Israel, with joy
like *other* peoples,
For you have played the harlot
against your God.
You have made love *for* [b]hire on
every threshing floor.
2 The threshing floor and the
winepress
Shall not feed them,
And the new wine shall fail in her.
3 They shall not dwell in [c]the LORD's
land,
[d]But Ephraim shall return to Egypt,

16 [v]Deut. 28:68; Ezek. 23:32; Hos. 8:13; 9:3

CHAPTER 8

1 [a]Deut. 28:49; Jer. 4:13 [1]*ram's horn,* Heb. *shophar*
2 [b]Ps. 78:34; Hos. 5:15; 7:14 [c]Titus 1:16
4 [d]1 Kin. 12:20; 2 Kin. 15:23, 25; Hos. 13:10, 11
5 [e]Ps. 19:13; Jer. 13:27 [2]Golden calf image [3]Or *has rejected you*
6 [f]Is. 40:19
7 [g]Prov. 22:8 [h]Hos. 7:9
8 [i]2 Kin. 17:6; Jer. 51:34 [j]Jer. 22:28; 25:34
9 [k]Hos. 7:11; 12:1; Jer. 2:24 [l]Ezek. 16:33, 34
10 [m]Ezek. 16:37; 22:20 [n]Is. 10:8; Ezek. 26:7; Dan. 2:37 [4]Or *begin to diminish* [5]Or *oracle* or *proclamation*
12 [o][Deut. 4:6-8]; Ps. 119:18; 147:19, 20
13 [p]Zech. 7:6 [q]Jer. 14:10; Hos. 6:6; 9:4; 1 Cor. 4:5 [r]Hos. 9:9; Amos 8:7; Luke 12:2
14 [s]Deut. 32:18; [Hos. 2:13; 4:6; 13:6] [t]Is. 29:23 [u]Num. 32:17; 2 Kin. 18:13 [v]Jer. 17:27 [6]Or *palaces* [7]Or *citadels*

CHAPTER 9

1 [a]Is. 22:12, 13; Hos. 10:5 [b]Jer. 44:17
3 [c][Lev. 25:23]; Jer. 2:7 [d]Hos. 7:16; 8:13

8:1 like an eagle. Lit. a "vulture," Assyria was ready to descend quickly upon Israel to devour her (cf. Deut. 28:49). **transgressed My covenant.** *See note on 6:7.*

8:2 we know You! Israel's syncretistic worship wherein she practiced idolatry while crying out to God.

8:5 Your calf is rejected. Calf worship was the national religion of the northern kingdom (cf. 1 Kin. 12:25-33; Ex. 32).

8:7 sow the wind...whirlwind. This indicates the escalating uselessness of all their false religion.

8:9 they have gone up to Assyria. As the context notes, this is not a reference to the captivity, but to the alliance she made with Assyria. "Like a wild donkey," Israel has stubbornly pursued foreign assistance rather than depending on the Lord.

8:12 Israel has been duly warned; she is without excuse (cf. 6:7; 8:1).

8:13 shall return to Egypt. Recalling the place of Israel's former bondage, Hosea reminds them that Assyria will be their future "Egypt" (cf. 9:3; 11:5; Deut. 28:68). A few Judean refugees actually did go to Egypt (cf. 2 Kin. 25:26). Isaiah used "Sodom" in a similar representative fashion (Is. 1:9,10).

8:14 Judah...fortified cities. Though less idolatrous than Israel, Judah showed lack of trust in God by trusting more in fortifications. Instead of drawing near to God, Judah multiplied human defenses (cf. Is. 22:8; Jer. 5:17).

9:1-17 Hosea enumerates the features of the Lord's banishment to Assyria: loss of joy (vv. 1,2); exile (vv. 3-6); loss of spiritual discernment (vv. 7-9); declining birth rate (vv. 10–16); and abandonment by God (v. 17).

9:1,2 threshing floor...winepress. These were the very places where sacred prostitution took place in an attempt to cause Baal to bring prosperity.

9:3 the LORD's land. Cf. Lev. 25:23. **Egypt.** *See note on 8:13* (cf. 11:3).

And [e]shall eat unclean *things* in
Assyria.
4 They shall not offer wine *offerings*
to the LORD,
Nor [f]shall their [g]sacrifices be
pleasing to Him.
It shall be like bread of mourners to
them;
All who eat it shall be defiled.
For their bread *shall be* for their
own life;
It shall not come into the house of
the LORD.

5 What will you do in the appointed
day,
And in the day of the feast of the
LORD?
6 For indeed they are gone because
of destruction.
Egypt shall gather them up;
Memphis shall bury them.
[h]Nettles shall possess their
valuables of silver;
Thorns *shall be* in their tents.

7 The [i]days of punishment have
come;
The days of recompense have come.
Israel knows!
The prophet *is* a [j]fool,
[k]The spiritual man *is* insane,
Because of the greatness of your
iniquity and great enmity.
8 The [l]watchman of Ephraim *is* with
my God;
But the prophet *is* a [1]fowler's snare
in all his ways—
Enmity in the house of his God.
9 [m]They are deeply corrupted,
As in the days of [n]Gibeah.
He will remember their iniquity;
He will punish their sins.

10 "I found Israel
Like grapes in the [o]wilderness;
I saw your fathers
As the [p]firstfruits on the fig tree in
its first season.
But they went to [q]Baal Peor,
And [2]separated themselves *to that*
shame;
[r]They became an abomination like
the thing they loved.
11 *As for* Ephraim, their glory shall fly
away like a bird—
No birth, no pregnancy, and no
conception!
12 Though they bring up their
children,
Yet I will bereave them to the last
man.
Yes, [s]woe to them when I depart
from them!
13 Just [t]as I saw Ephraim like Tyre,
planted in a pleasant place,
So Ephraim will bring out his
children to the murderer."

14 Give them, O LORD—
What will You give?
Give them [u]a miscarrying womb
And dry breasts!

15 "All their wickedness *is* in [v]Gilgal,
For there I hated them.
Because of the evil of their deeds
I will drive them from My house;
I will love them no more.
[w]All their princes *are* rebellious.
16 Ephraim is [x]stricken,
Their root is dried up;
They shall bear no fruit.
Yes, were they to bear children,
I would kill the darlings of their
womb."

17 My God will [y]cast them away,
Because they did not obey Him;
And they shall be [z]wanderers
among the nations.

Israel's Sin and Captivity

10 Israel [a]empties *his* vine;
He brings forth fruit for himself.
According to the multitude of his
fruit
[b]He has increased the altars;

3 [e]Ezek. 4:13
4 [f]Jer. 6:20 [g]Hos. 8:13; Amos 5:22
6 [h]Is. 5:6; 7:23; Hos. 10:8
7 [i]Is. 10:3; Jer. 10:15; Mic. 7:4; Luke 21:22 [j]Lam. 2:14; [Ezek. 13:3, 10] [k]Mic. 2:11
8 [l]Jer. 6:17; 31:6; Ezek. 3:17; 33:7 [1]One who catches birds in a trap or snare
9 [m]Hos. 10:9 [n]Judg. 19:22
10 [o]Jer. 2:2 [p]Is. 28:4; Mic. 7:1 [q]Num. 25:3; Ps. 106:28 [r]Ps. 81:12 [2]Or *dedicated*
12 [s]Deut. 31:17; Hos. 7:13
13 [t]Ezek. 26–28
14 [u]Luke 23:29
15 [v]Hos. 4:15; 12:11 [w]Is. 1:23; Hos. 5:2
16 [x]Hos. 5:11
17 [y]2 Kin. 17:20; [Zech. 10:6] [z]Lev. 26:33

CHAPTER 10

1 [a]Nah. 2:2 [b]Jer. 2:28; Hos. 8:11; 12:11

9:4 bread of mourners...defiled. Food eaten on the occasion of mourning was considered unclean, defiling anyone eating it (cf. Deut. 26:12-15).

9:6 Memphis. An ancient capital of Egypt known for its tombs and pyramids.

9:7,8 The prophets were God's inspired messengers and watchmen (cf. Ezek. 3:17; 33:1-7), yet Israel considered them fools and madmen.

9:9 Gibeah. Cf. 10:9. Israel's sin is likened to the gross evil of the men of Gibeah, a reference to their heinous rape of the concubine (Judg. 19:22-25), an infamous and unforgettable crime (cf. Judg. 19:30).

9:10 grapes in the wilderness. A rare and refreshing find (cf. Deut. 32:10). **Baal Peor.** Prior to entering the Promised Land, Israel fell into worship of Baal at Baal Peor (Num. 25:3-18).

9:11-14 Reminiscent of the imprecatory psalms, Hosea prayed that God's blessing would be withdrawn, in the figure of withholding children, the ultimate earthly blessing.

9:15 Gilgal. As a center of idol worship (cf. 4:15), the place was representative of Israel's spiritual adultery; therefore He had rejected them from intimate fellowship.

9:17 wanderers. God promised global dispersion for disobedience (cf. Lev. 26:33; Deut. 28:64,65).

10:1 Agricultural prosperity had resulted in spiritual corruption (cf. Ezek. 16:10-19).

According to the bounty of his land
They have embellished *his* sacred pillars.
2 Their heart is [c]divided;[1]
Now they are held guilty.
He will break down their altars;
He will ruin their sacred pillars.

3 For now they say,
"We have no king,
Because we did not fear the LORD.
And as for a king, what would he do for us?"
4 They have spoken words,
Swearing falsely in making a covenant.
Thus judgment springs up [d]like hemlock in the furrows of the field.

5 The inhabitants of Samaria fear
Because of the [e]calf[2] of Beth Aven.
For its people mourn for it,
And [3]its priests shriek for it—
Because its [f]glory has departed from it.
6 *The idol* also shall be carried to Assyria
As a present for King [g]Jareb.
Ephraim shall receive shame,
And Israel shall be ashamed of his own counsel.

7 *As for* Samaria, her king is cut off
Like a twig on the water.
8 Also the [h]high places of [4]Aven,
[i]the sin of Israel,
Shall be destroyed.
The thorn and thistle shall grow on their altars;
[j]They shall say to the mountains,
"Cover us!"
And to the hills, "Fall on us!"

9 "O Israel, you have sinned from the days of [k]Gibeah;
There they stood.
The [l]battle in Gibeah against the children of [5]iniquity
Did not [6]overtake them.
10 When *it is* My desire, I will chasten them.
[m]Peoples shall be gathered against them
When I bind them [7]for their two transgressions.
11 Ephraim *is* [n]a trained heifer
That loves to thresh *grain;*
But I harnessed her fair neck,
I will make Ephraim [8]pull *a plow.*
Judah shall plow;
Jacob shall break his clods."

12 Sow for yourselves righteousness;
Reap in mercy;
[o]Break up your fallow ground,
For *it is* time to seek the LORD,
Till He [p]comes and rains righteousness on you.

13 [q]You have plowed wickedness;
You have reaped iniquity.
You have eaten the fruit of lies,
Because you trusted in your own way,
In the multitude of your mighty men.
14 Therefore tumult shall arise among your people,
And all your fortresses shall be plundered
As Shalman plundered Beth Arbel in the day of battle—
A mother dashed in pieces upon *her* children.
15 Thus it shall be done to you,
O Bethel,
Because of your great wickedness.
At dawn the king of Israel
Shall be cut off utterly.

God's Continuing Love for Israel

11 "When Israel *was* a [1]child, I loved him,
And out of Egypt [a]I called My [b]son.

2 [c] 1 Kin. 18:21; Zeph. 1:5; [Matt. 6:24] [1] Divided in loyalty
4 [d] Deut. 31:16, 17; 2 Kin. 17:3, 4; Amos 5:7
5 [e] 1 Kin. 12:28, 29; Hos. 8:5, 6; 13:2 [f] Hos. 9:11 [2] Lit. *calves,* images [3] *idolatrous priests*
6 [g] Hos. 5:13
8 [h] Hos. 4:15 [i] Deut. 9:21; 1 Kin. 13:34 [j] Is. 2:19; Luke 23:30; Rev. 6:16 [4] Lit. *Idolatry* or *Wickedness*
9 [k] Hos. 9:9 [l] Judg. 20 [5] So with many Heb. mss., LXX, Vg.; MT *unruliness* [6] Or *overcome*
10 [m] Jer. 16:16 [7] Or *in their two habitations*
11 [n] [Jer. 50:11; Hos. 4:16; Mic. 4:13] [8] Lit. *to ride*
12 [o] Jer. 4:3 [p] Hos. 6:3
13 [q] [Job 4:8; Prov. 22:8; Gal. 6:7, 8]

CHAPTER 11

1 [a] Matt. 2:15 [b] Ex. 4:22, 23 [1] Or *youth*

10:3,4 The last 5 kings of Israel were usurpers. Impotent and unworthy of respect, they were incapable of enforcing the laws of the land.

10:5 the calf of Beth Aven. *See notes on 4:15; 8:5.*

10:8 Cover us...Fall on us. The captivity would be so severe that the people would pray for the mountains and hills to fall on them, similar to the last days (cf. Luke 23:30; Rev. 6:16).

10:10 two transgressions. Israel would receive a double portion of judgment for her multiplied iniquity (cf. Is. 40:2; Jer. 16:18).

10:11 a trained heifer that loves to thresh *grain*. This was a far easier work than plowing, since cattle were not bound together under a yoke, but tread on the grain singly and were free to eat some of it, as the law required that they be unmuzzled (Deut. 25:4; 1 Cor. 9:9).

10:14 Shalman plundered Beth Arbel. Shalman was probably Shalmaneser V, king of Assyria (727–722 B.C.), who played a role in Israel's demise (cf. 2 Kin. 17:3-6). Although the location of Beth Arbel is uncertain, the memory of the heinous crimes committed there were vividly etched into their minds.

10:15 king. Hoshea, ca. 732–722 B.C.

11:1 In tender words reminiscent of the Exodus from Egypt (cf. Ex. 4:22,23), the Lord reassured Israel of His intense love for her. His compassion for her was aroused (cf. Is. 12:1; 40:1,2; 49:13; Jer. 31:10-14; Zech. 1:12-17). See Matt. 2:15 for Matthew's analogical use of this verse in relationship to Jesus Christ.

2 [2]*As* they called them,
So they [c]went [3]from them;
They sacrificed to the Baals,
And burned incense to carved images.

3 "I[d] taught Ephraim to walk,
Taking them by [4]their arms;
But they did not know that [e]I healed them.
4 I drew them with [5]gentle cords,
With bands of love,
And [f]I was to them as those who take the yoke from their [6]neck.
[g]I stooped *and* fed them.

5 "He shall not return to the land of Egypt;
But the Assyrian shall be his king,
Because they refused to repent.
6 And the sword shall slash in his cities,
Devour his districts,
And consume *them*,
Because of their own counsels.
7 My people are bent on [h]backsliding from Me.
Though [7]they call [8]to the Most High,
None at all exalt *Him*.

8 "How[i] can I give you up, Ephraim?
How can I hand you over, Israel?
How can I make you like [j]Admah?
How can I set you like Zeboiim?
My heart [9]churns within Me;
My sympathy is stirred.
9 I will not execute the fierceness of My anger;
I will not again destroy Ephraim.
[k]For I *am* God, and not man,
The Holy One in your midst;
And I will not [1]come with terror.

10 "They shall walk after the LORD.
[l]He will roar like a lion.
When He roars,
Then *His* sons shall come trembling from the west;
11 They shall come trembling like a bird from Egypt,
[m]Like a dove from the land of Assyria.
[n]And I will let them dwell in their houses,"
Says the LORD.

God's Charge Against Ephraim

12 "Ephraim has encircled Me with lies,
And the house of Israel with deceit;
But Judah still walks with God,
Even with the [2]Holy One *who is* faithful.

12 "Ephraim [a]feeds on the wind,
And pursues the east wind;
He daily increases lies and [1]desolation.
[b]Also they make a [2]covenant with the Assyrians,
And [c]oil is carried to Egypt.

2 "The[d] LORD also *brings* a [3]charge against Judah,
And will punish Jacob according to his ways;
According to his deeds He will recompense him.
3 He took his brother [e]by the heel in the womb,
And in his strength he [f]struggled with God.
4 Yes, he struggled with the Angel and prevailed;
He wept, and sought favor from Him.
He found Him *in* [g]Bethel,
And there He spoke to us—

2 [c]2 Kin. 17:13-15 [2]So with MT, Vg.; LXX *Just as I called them;* Tg. interprets as *I sent prophets to a thousand of them.* [3]So with MT, Tg., Vg.; LXX *from My face*
3 [d]Deut. 1:31; 32:10, 11 [e]Ex. 15:26 [4]Some Heb. mss., LXX, Syr., Vg. *My arms*
4 [f]Lev. 26:13 [g]Ex. 16:32; Ps. 78:25 [5]Lit. *cords of a man* [6]Lit. *jaws*
7 [h]Jer. 3:6, 7; 8:5 [7]The prophets [8]Or *upward*
8 [i]Jer. 9:7 [j]Gen. 14:8; 19:24, 25; Deut. 29:23 [9]Lit. *turns over*
9 [k]Num. 23:19 [1]Or *enter a city*
10 [l]Is. 31:4; [Joel 3:16]; Amos 1:2
11 [m]Is. 11:11; 60:8; Hos. 7:11 [n]Ezek. 28:25, 26; 34:27, 28
12 [2]Or *holy ones*

CHAPTER 12

1 [a]Job 15:2, 3; Hos. 8:7 [b]2 Kin. 17:4; Hos. 8:9 [c]Is. 30:6 [1]*ruin* [2]Or *treaty*
2 [d]Hos. 4:1; Mic. 6:2 [3]A legal complaint
3 [e]Gen. 25:26 [f]Gen. 32:24-28
4 [g][Gen. 28:12-19; 35:9-15]

11:3,4 The Lord's endearing word pictures are reflected in Ezekiel's touching descriptions of Israel's early years (cf. Ezek. 16).

11:5 shall not return to...Egypt. *See notes on 8:13.*

11:5-7 In spite of His tender care, Israel was ungrateful, demanding punishment (cf. Rom. 1:21).

11:7 backsliding. *See note on Prov. 14:14.*

11:8 Admah...Zeboiim. Because of the Lord's great love for Ephraim, it was painful to punish her as He did these two cities, which were destroyed with Sodom and Gomorrah (cf. Gen. 10:19; 19:23-25; Deut. 29:23).

11:9 I will not again destroy Ephraim. The destruction referred to that inflicted by Assyrian King Tiglath-Pileser, who deprived Israel of Gilead, Galilee, and Naphtali (2 Kin. 15:29). Ultimately, it referred to the promise that after the long dispersion God would, in mercy, restore His people in the kingdom, never to be destroyed again.

11:10 will roar like a lion. Though the Lord would, as a lion, roar against Israel in judgment (cf. Amos 1:2), He would also roar for the purpose of calling, protecting, and blessing (cf. Joel 3:16). **from the west.** Returns from Assyrian and Babylonian captivities were from the E. This undoubtedly has reference to His return at the Second Advent to set up the millennial kingdom (cf. Is. 11:11,12) when He calls Israel from their worldwide dispersion and reverses the judgment of 9:17.

12:1 Israel's attempted alliances with heathen neighbors were of no worth. This prophecy was delivered at about the time of Israel's seeking the aid of the Egyptian king.

12:2 Jacob. Frequently used interchangeably with "Israel" (cf. 10:11; Gen. 32:28).

12:3-6 He exhorted them to follow their father Jacob's persevering prayerfulness, which brought God's favor on him. As God is unchanging, He would show the same favor to Jacob's posterity as He did to Jacob, if, like him, they sought God.

5 That is, the LORD God of hosts.
The LORD *is* His [h]memorable name.
6 [i]So you, by *the help of* your God,
return;
Observe mercy and justice,
And wait on your God continually.

7 "A cunning [4]Canaanite!
[j]Deceitful scales *are* in his hand;
He loves to oppress.
8 And Ephraim said,
[k]'Surely I have become rich,
I have found wealth for myself;
In all my labors
They shall find in me no iniquity
that *is* sin.'

9 "But I *am* the LORD your God,
Ever since the land of Egypt;
[l]I will again make you dwell in
tents,
As in the days of the appointed
feast.
10 [m]I have also spoken by the prophets,
And have multiplied visions;
I have given [5]symbols [6]through
the witness of the prophets."

11 Though [n]Gilead *has* idols—
Surely they are [7]vanity—
Though they sacrifice bulls in
[o]Gilgal,
Indeed their altars *shall be* heaps in
the furrows of the field.

12 Jacob [p]fled to the country of Syria;
[q]Israel served for a spouse,
And for a wife he tended *sheep.*
13 [r]By a prophet the LORD brought
Israel out of Egypt,
And by a prophet he was
preserved.
14 Ephraim [s]provoked *Him* to anger
most bitterly;
Therefore his Lord will leave the
guilt of his bloodshed upon
him,
[t]And return his reproach upon him.

Relentless Judgment on Israel

13 When Ephraim spoke, trembling,
He exalted *himself* in Israel;
But when he offended through
Baal *worship,* he died.
2 Now they sin more and more,
And have made for themselves
molded images,
Idols of their silver, according to
their skill;
All of it *is* the work of craftsmen.
They say of them,
"Let [1]the men who sacrifice [2]kiss
the calves!"
3 Therefore they shall be like the
morning cloud
And like the early dew that passes
away,
[a]Like chaff blown off from a
threshing floor
And like smoke from a chimney.

4 "Yet [b]I *am* the LORD your God
Ever since the land of Egypt,
And you shall know no God but
Me;
For [c]*there is* no savior besides Me.
5 [d]I [3]knew you in the wilderness,
[e]In the land of [4]great drought.
6 [f]When they had pasture, they were
filled;
They were filled and their heart
was exalted;
Therefore they forgot Me.

7 "So [g]I will be to them like a lion;
Like [h]a leopard by the road I will
lurk;
8 I will meet them [i]like a bear
deprived *of her cubs;*
I will tear open their rib cage,

5 [h]Ex. 3:15
6 [i]Hos. 14:1; Mic. 6:8
7 [j]Prov. 11:1; Amos 8:5; Mic. 6:11 [4]Or *merchant*
8 [k]Ps. 62:10; Hos. 13:6; Rev. 3:17
9 [l]Lev. 23:42
10 [m]2 Kin. 17:13; Jer. 7:25 [5]Or *parables* [6]Lit. *by the hand*
11 [n]Hos. 6:8 [o]Hos. 9:15 [7]*worthless*
12 [p]Gen. 28:5; Deut. 26:5 [q]Gen. 29:20, 28
13 [r]Ex. 12:50, 51; 13:3; Ps. 77:20; Is. 63:11, 12; Mic. 6:4
14 [s]Ezek. 18:10-13
[t]Dan. 11:18; Mic. 6:16

CHAPTER 13

2 [1]Or *those who offer human sacrifice* [2]Worship with kisses
3 [a]Ps. 1:4; Is. 17:13; Dan. 2:35
4 [b]Is. 43:11 [c]Is. 43:11; 45:21, 22; [1 Tim. 2:5]
5 [d]Deut. 2:7; 32:10 [e]Deut. 8:15 [3]Cared for you [4]Lit. *droughts*
6 [f]Deut. 8:12, 14; 32:13-15; Jer. 5:7
7 [g]Lam. 3:10; Hos. 5:14 [h]Jer. 5:6
8 [i]2 Sam. 17:8; Prov. 17:12

12:7 Canaanite. Because the Canaanites were known as traders, the word came to be used synonymously with "merchant" (cf. Ezek. 16:29; 17:4; Zeph. 1:11). Though she denied it (v. 8), Israel had become materialistic, filled with greed, and fond of dishonest gain.

12:9 At the annual Feast of Tabernacles, also called "booths" (cf. Num. 29:12-38), Israel dwelt in tents to commemorate her 40 years of wilderness wanderings. In captivity, she would be forced to live in them permanently.

12:10 I have also spoken. Here is an aggravation of their guilt, that it was not through ignorance that they sinned, but in defiance of God's revealed Word.

12:11 heaps in the furrows. As gathered and piled stones would dot a farmer's field, so Israel multiplied her stone altars across the land. "Gilgal" means "a heap of stones," so this is a play on words.

12:12-14 The reference to Jacob's wanderings to Syria and Israel's sojourn in Egypt should cause Ephraim to confess her pride, recognize her humble origins, and acknowledge that only by God's gracious power were they made a nation.

13:1 trembling. When Ephraim, the most powerful tribe, spoke early in Israel's history, it was with authority and produced fear. **he died.** Because of his sins and in spite of being feared, Ephraim died, spiritually and now nationally.

13:2 kiss the calves! An act of devotion to their idols (cf. 1 Kin. 19:18).

13:4-6 Having entered into a marriage covenant with the Lord, Israel was to remain faithful to Him alone (cf. Ex. 20:2,3); yet she forgot Him.

13:7,8 The lion, leopard, and bear are all native to Israel. Her Protector would now become to her as a wild beast, tearing and devouring (cf. Lev. 26:21,22; Deut. 32:24; Ezek. 14:21).

And there I will devour them like a
lion.
The [5]wild beast shall tear them.

9 "O Israel, [6]you are destroyed,
But [7]your help *is* from Me.
10 [8]I will be your King;
[j]Where *is any other,*
That he may save you in all your
cities?
And your judges to whom [k]you
said,
'Give me a king and princes'?
11 [l]I gave you a king in My anger,
And took *him* away in My wrath.

12 "The [m] iniquity of Ephraim *is* bound
up;
His sin *is* stored up.
13 [n]The sorrows of a woman in
childbirth shall come upon
him.
He *is* an unwise son,
For he should not stay long where
children are born.

14 "I will ransom them from the
[9]power of [1]the grave;
I will redeem them from death.
[o]O Death, [2]I will be your plagues!
O [3]Grave, [4]I will be your
destruction!
[p]Pity is hidden from My eyes."

15 Though he is fruitful among *his*
brethren,
[q]An east wind shall come;
The wind of the LORD shall come
up from the wilderness.
Then his spring shall become dry,
And his fountain shall be dried up.
He shall plunder the treasury of
every desirable prize.

16 Samaria [5]is held guilty,
For she has [r]rebelled against her
God.
They shall fall by the sword,
Their infants shall be dashed in
pieces,
And their women with child
[s]ripped open.

Israel Restored at Last

14 O Israel, [a]return to the LORD your
God,
For you have stumbled because of
your iniquity;
2 Take words with you,
And return to the LORD.
Say to Him,
"Take away all iniquity;
Receive *us* graciously,
For we will offer the [b]sacrifices[1] of
our lips.
3 Assyria shall [c]not save us,
[d]We will not ride on horses,
Nor will we say anymore to the
work of our hands, '*You are*
our gods.'
[e]For in You the fatherless finds
mercy."

4 "I will heal their [f]backsliding,
I will [g]love them freely,
For My anger has turned away
from him.
5 I will be like the [h]dew to Israel;
He shall [2]grow like the lily,
And [3]lengthen his roots like
Lebanon.
6 His branches shall [4]spread;
[i]His beauty shall be like an olive
tree,
And [j]his fragrance like Lebanon.
7 [k]Those who dwell under his
shadow shall return;

8 [5] Lit. *beast of the field*
9 [6] Lit. *it* or *he destroyed you* [7] Lit. *in your help*
10 [j] Deut. 32:38 [k] 1 Sam. 8:5, 6 [8] LXX, Syr., Tg., Vg. *Where is your king?*
11 [l] 1 Sam. 8:7; 10:17-24
12 [m] Deut. 32:34, 35; Job 14:17; [Rom. 2:5]
13 [n] Is. 13:8; Mic. 4:9, 10
14 [o] [1 Cor. 15:54, 55] [p] Jer. 15:6 [9] Lit. *hand* [1] Or *Sheol* [2] LXX *where is your punishment?* [3] Or *Sheol* [4] LXX *where is your sting?*
15 [q] Gen. 41:6; Jer. 4:11, 12; Ezek. 17:10; 19:12
16 [r] 2 Kin. 18:12 [s] 2 Kin. 15:16 [5] LXX *shall be disfigured*

CHAPTER 14

1 [a] Hos. 12:6; [Joel 2:13]
2 [b] [Ps. 51:16, 17; Hos. 6:6; Heb. 13:15] [1] Lit. *bull calves;* LXX *fruit*
3 [c] Hos. 7:11; 10:13; 12:1 [d] [Ps. 33:17]; Is. 31:1 [e] Ps. 10:14; 68:5
4 [f] Jer. 14:7 [g] [Eph. 1:6]
5 [h] Job 29:19; Prov. 19:12; Is. 26:19 [2] Lit. *bud or sprout* [3] Lit. *strike*
6 [i] Ps. 52:8; 128:3 [j] Gen. 27:27 [4] Lit. *go*
7 [k] Dan. 4:12

13:12 bound up...stored up. Israel's sins are all well-documented and safely preserved for the day of reckoning (cf. 7:2; Deut. 32:34, 35; Job 14:17).

13:13 where children are born. This refers to the birth canal. Employing this figure of giving birth, the Lord likens Ephraim to an unwise child, unwilling to move through to birth. By long deferring a "new birth" with repentance, the nation was like a child remaining in the canal dangerously long and risking death (cf. 2 Kin. 19:3; Is. 37:3; 66:9).

13:14 Placing the strong affirmation of deliverance so abruptly after a denunciation intensified the wonder of His unrequited love (cf. 11:8,9; Lev. 26:44). This can apply to God's restoration of Israel from Assyria, and in future times from all the lands of the dispersion, preserving them and bringing them back to their land for the kingdom of Messiah (Ezek. 37). It also speaks of the time of personal resurrection as in Dan. 12:2,3. Repentant Israelites will be restored to the land and even raised from death to glory. Paul uses this text in 1 Cor. 15:55 (quoting the LXX) to celebrate the future resurrection of the church. The Messiah's great victory over death and the grave is the firstfruits of the full harvest to come, when all believers will likewise experience the power of His resurrection.

13:15 east wind. Refers to Assyria.

13:16 The shocking atrocities mentioned were in keeping with brutalities characteristic of the Assyrians (cf. 2 Kin. 17:5; Is. 13:6; Amos 1:13; Nah. 3:10).

14:1,2 Israel was invited to return, bringing words of repentance accompanied with obedience, repaying God's gracious acceptance of them with "sacrifices of our lips."

14:3 fatherless. God repeatedly demanded mercy for the orphan (cf. Ex. 22:22; Deut. 10:18); consequently, Israel could expect to receive His compassion (cf. Luke 15:17-20).

14:4-8 The ultimate fulfillment of these blessings must be millennial, since Israel has not nor will not repent in the manner of vv. 2,3 until the end of the Great Tribulation (cf. Zech. 12:10–13:1). The Lord's love is beautifully presented in metaphors taken from the lily, the cedars of Lebanon, and the olive tree.

14:4 backsliding. *See note on Prov. 14:14.*

They shall be revived *like* grain,
And [5]grow like a vine.
Their [6]scent *shall be* like the wine of
Lebanon.

8 "Ephraim *shall say,* 'What have I to
do anymore with idols?'
I have heard and observed him.
I *am* like a green cypress tree;
[l]Your fruit is found in Me."

9 Who *is* wise?
Let him understand these things.
Who is prudent?
Let him know them.
For [m]the ways of the LORD *are* right;
The righteous walk in them,
But transgressors stumble in them.

7 [5] Lit. *bud* or *sprout* [6] Lit. *remembrance*
8 [l] [John 15:4]
9 [m] [Ps. 111:7, 8; Prov. 10:29]; Zeph. 3:5

14:7 Their scent…like the wine of Lebanon. Their "scent" (lit. "remembrance") denotes worldwide fame and admiration.

14:8 The Lord, not idols, will care for Israel. He, not Israel, is the tree providing shelter and prosperity, the "green cypress tree" from whom her fruitfulness would come.

14:9 Representative of the theme of the book, Hosea's epilogue concludes the prophecy by presenting the reader with two ways of living (cf. Deut. 30:19,20; Ps. 1). He appeals to all readers to be wise, to choose the Lord's way, for His ways are right (cf. Ps. 107:43; Eccl. 12:13,14).

The Book of JOEL

Title

The Greek Septuagint (LXX) and Latin Vulgate (Vg.) versions follow the Hebrew Masoretic Text (MT), titling this book after Joel the prophet, the recipient of the message from God (1:1). The name means "the LORD is God" and refers to at least a dozen men in the OT. Joel is referred to only once in the NT (Acts 2:16-21).

Author and Date

The author identified himself only as "Joel the son of Pethuel" (1:1). The prophecy provides little else about the man. Even the name of his father is not mentioned elsewhere in the OT. Although he displayed a profound zeal for the temple sacrifices (1:9; 2:13-16), his familiarity with pastoral and agricultural life and his separation from the priests (1:13,14; 2:17) suggest he was not a Levite. Extrabiblical tradition records that he was from the tribe of Reuben, from the town of Bethom or Bethharam, located NE of the Dead Sea on the border of Reuben and Gad. The context of the prophecy, however, hints that he was a Judean from the Jerusalem vicinity, since the tone of a stranger is absent.

Dating the book relies solely on canonical position, historical allusions, and linguistic elements. Because of: 1) the lack of any mention of later world powers (Assyria, Babylon, or Persia); 2) the fact that Joel's style is like that of Hosea and Amos rather than of the post-Exilic prophets; and 3) the verbal parallels with other early prophets (Joel 3:16/Amos 1:2; Joel 3:18/Amos 9:13), a late ninth century B.C. date, during the reign of Joash (ca. 835–796 B.C.), seems most convincing. Nevertheless, while the date of the book cannot be known with certainty, the impact on its interpretation is minimal. The message of Joel is timeless, forming doctrine which could be repeated and applied in any age.

Background and Setting

Tyre, Sidon, and Philistia had made frequent military incursions into Israel (3:2ff.). An extended drought and massive invasion of locusts had stripped every green thing from the Land and brought severe economic devastation (1:7-20), leaving the southern kingdom weak. This physical disaster gives Joel the illustration for God's judgment. As the locusts were a judgment on sin, God's future judgments during the Day of the Lord will far exceed them. In that day, God will judge His enemies and bless the faithful. No mention is made of specific sins, nor is Judah rebuked for idolatry. Yet, possibly due to a calloused indifference, the prophet calls them to a bona fide repentance, admonishing them to "rend your heart, and not your garments" (2:13).

Historical and Theological Themes

The theme of Joel is the Day of the Lord. It permeates all parts of Joel's message, making it the most sustained treatment in the entire OT (1:15; 2:1; 2:11; 2:31; 3:14). The phrase is employed 19 times by 8 different OT authors (Is. 2:12; 13:6,9; Ezek. 13:5; 30:3; Joel 1:15; 2:1,11,31; 3:14; Amos 5:18 [2x],20; Obad. 15; Zeph. 1:7,14 [2x]; Zech. 14:1; Mal. 4:5). The phrase does not have reference to a chronological time period, but to a general period of wrath and judgment uniquely belonging to the Lord. It is exclusively the day which unveils His character—mighty, powerful, and holy, thus terrifying His enemies. The Day of the Lord does not always refer to an eschatological event; on occasion it has a near historical fulfillment, as seen in Ezek. 13:5, where it speaks of the Babylonian conquest and destruction of Jerusalem. As is common in prophecy, the near fulfillment is an historic event upon which to comprehend the more distant, eschatological fulfillment.

The Day of the Lord is frequently associated with seismic disturbances (e.g., 2:1-11; 2:31; 3:16), violent weather (Ezek. 13:5ff.), clouds and thick darkness (e.g., 2:2; Zeph. 1:7ff.), cosmic upheaval (2:3,30), and as a "great and very terrible" (2:11) day that would "come as destruction from the Almighty" (1:15). The latter half of Joel depicts time subsequent to the Day of the Lord in terms of promise and hope. There will be a pouring out of the Spirit on all flesh, accompanied by prophetic utterances, dreams, visions (2:28,29), as well as the coming of Elijah, an epiphany bringing restoration and hope (Mal. 4:5,6). As a result of the Day of the Lord there will be physical blessings, fruitfulness, and prosperity (2:21ff.; 3:16-21).

It is a day when judgment is poured out on sinners that subsequently leads to blessings on the penitent, and reaffirmation of God's covenant with His people. *See note on 1 Thess. 5:2.*

Interpretive Challenges

It is preferable to view chap. 1 as describing an actual invasion of locusts that devastated the Land. In chap. 2, a new level of description meets the interpreter. Here the prophet is projecting something beyond the locust plague of chap. 1, elevating the level of description to new heights, with increased intensity that is focused on the plague and the immediate necessity for true repentance. The prophet's choice of similes, such as "like the appearance of horses" (2:4) and "like mighty men" (2:7), suggests that he is still using the actual locusts to illustrate an invasion which can only be the massive overtaking of the final Day of the Lord.

A second issue confronting the interpreter is Peter's quotation from Joel 2:28-32 in Acts 2:16-21. Some have viewed the phenomena of Acts 2 and the destruction of Jerusalem in A.D. 70 as the fulfillment of the Joel passage, while others have reserved its fulfillment to the final Day of the Lord only—but clearly Joel is referring to the final terrible Day of the Lord. The pouring out of the Holy Spirit at Pentecost not a fulfillment, but a preview and sample of the Spirit's power and work, to be released fully and finally in the Messiah's kingdom after the Day of the Lord. *See note on Acts 2:16-21.*

Outline

Following 1:1, the contents of the book are arranged under 3 basic categories. In the first section (1:2-20) the prophet describes the contemporary Day of the Lord. The land is suffering massive devastation caused by a locust plague and drought. The details of the calamity (1:2-12) are followed by a summons to communal penitence and reformation (1:13-20).

The second section (2:1-17) provides a transition from the historical plague of locusts described in chap. 1 to the eschatological Day of the Lord in 2:18–3:21. Employing the contemporary infestation of locusts as a backdrop, the prophet, with an increased level of intensity, paints a vivid and forceful picture of the impending visitation of the Lord (2:1-11) and, with powerful and explicit terminology, tenaciously renews the appeal for repentance (2:12-17).

In the third section (2:18–3:21), the Lord speaks directly, assuring His people of His presence among them (2:27; 3:17,21). This portion of the book assumes that the repentance solicited (2:12-17) had occurred and describes the Lord's zealous response (2:18,19a) to their prayer. Joel 2:18-21 forms the transition in the message from lamentation and woe to divine assurances of God's presence and the reversal of the calamities, with 2:19b,20 introducing the essence and nature of that reversal. The Lord then gives 3 promises to assure the penitents of His presence: material restoration through the divine healing of their land (2:21-27), spiritual restoration through the divine outpouring of His Spirit (2:28-32), and national restoration through the divine judgment on the unrighteous (3:1-21).

Outline

I. Day of the Lord Experienced: Historical (1:1-20)
   - A. Source of the Message (1:1)
   - B. Command to Contemplate the Devastation (1:2-4)
   - C. Completeness of the Devastation (1:5-12)
   - D. Call to Repent in Light of the Devastation (1:13-20)

II. Day of the Lord Illustrated: Transitional (2:1-17)
   - A. Alarm Sounds (2:1)
   - B. Army Invades (2:2-11)
   - C. Admonition to Repent (2:12-17)

III. Day of the Lord Described: Eschatological (2:18–3:21)
   - A. Introduction (2:18-20)
   - B. Material Restoration (2:21-27)
   - C. Spiritual Restoration (2:28-32)
   - D. National Restoration (3:1-21)

1 The word of the LORD that came to
[a]Joel the son of Pethuel.

The Land Laid Waste

2 Hear this, you elders,
And give ear, all you inhabitants of
the land!
[b]Has *anything like* this happened in
your days,
Or even in the days of your
fathers?
3 [c]Tell your children about it,
Let your children *tell* their children,
And their children another
generation.

4 [d]What the chewing [1]locust left, the
[e]swarming locust has eaten;
What the swarming locust left, the
crawling locust has eaten;
And what the crawling locust left,
the consuming locust has
eaten.

5 Awake, you [f]drunkards, and weep;
And wail, all you drinkers of wine,
Because of the new wine,
[g]For it has been cut off from your
mouth.
6 For [h]a nation has come up against
My land,
Strong, and without number;
[i]His teeth *are* the teeth of a lion,
And he has the fangs of a [2]fierce
lion.
7 He has [j]laid waste My vine,
And [3]ruined My fig tree;
He has stripped it bare and thrown
it away;
Its branches are made white.

8 [k]Lament like a virgin girded with
sackcloth
For [l]the husband of her youth.
9 [m]The grain offering and the drink
offering

CHAPTER 1

1 [a] Acts 2:16
2 [b] Jer. 30:7; Joel 2:2
3 [c] Ex. 10:2; Ps. 78:4; Is. 38:19
4 [d] Deut. 28:38; Joel 2:25; Amos 4:9 [e] Is. 33:4 [1] Exact identity of these locusts unknown
5 [f] Is. 5:11; 28:1; Hos. 7:5 [g] Is. 32:10
6 [h] Prov. 30:25; Joel 2:2, 11, 25 [i] Rev. 9:8 [2] Or *lioness*
7 [j] Is. 5:6; Amos 4:9 [3] Or *splintered*
8 [k] Is. 22:12 [l] Prov. 2:17; Jer. 3:4
9 [m] Hos. 9:4; Joel 1:13; 2:14

1:1 The word of the LORD. This introductory phrase is commonly employed by the prophets to indicate that the message was divinely commissioned. Cf. Hos. 1:1; Mic. 1:1; Zeph. 1:1. Slightly varied forms are found in 1 Sam. 15:10; 2 Sam 24:11; Jer. 1:2; Ezek. 1:3; Jon. 1:1; Zech. 1:1; Mal. 1:1. **LORD.** A distinctively Israelitish designation for God, the name speaks of intimacy and a relationship bonded metaphorically through the covenant likened to marriage and thus carries special significance to Israel (Ex. 3:14). **Joel.** His name means "the LORD is God." **Pethuel.** His name means "openheartedness of/toward God" and is the only occurrence of this name in the Bible.

1:2-20 The prophet described the contemporary Day of the Lord. The land was suffering massive devastation caused by a locust plague and drought. The details of the calamity (vv. 2-12) are followed by a summons to communal penitence and reformation (vv. 13-20).

1:2 Hear...give ear. The gravity of the situation demanded the undivided focus of their senses, emphasizing the need to make a conscious, purposeful decision in the matter. The terminology was commonly used in "lawsuit" passages (cf. Is. 1:2; Hos. 4:1), intimating that Israel was found guilty and that the present judgment was her "sentence." **elders...all you inhabitants.** The former term refers to the civil and religious leaders, who, in light of their position, were exhorted to lead by example the entire population toward repentance.

1:3 Tell...children...another generation. The pedagogical importance of reciting the Lord's mighty acts to subsequent generations is heavily underscored by the 3-fold injunction (cf. Ex. 10:1-6; Deut. 4:9; 6:6,7; 11:19; 32:7; Pss. 78:5-7; 145:4-7; Prov. 4:1ff.).

1:4 locust. The 4 kinds of locusts refer to their species or their stages of development. Cf. 2:25, where the writer mentions them in different order. The total destruction caused by their voracious appetites demands repentance (cf. Deut. 28:38; Is. 33:4; Amos 7:1).

1:5-12 Total destruction affected all social and economic levels. Affected were the drunkards who delighted in the abundance of the vine (vv. 5-7), the priests who utilized the produce in the offerings (vv. 8-10), and the farmers who planted, cultivated, and reaped the harvest (vv. 11,12). As if building toward a crescendo, the prophet noted in the first stanza that the luxuries of life were withdrawn. In the second, the elements needed to worship were interrupted. In the third, the essentials for living were snatched away. To lose the enjoyment of wine was one thing; to no longer be able to outwardly worship God was another; but to have nothing to eat was the sentence of death!

1:5 Awake...weep...wail. The drunkards were to awaken to the realization that their wine would be no more. They were to weep bitterly and to wail. The severity of the devastation called for public, communal mourning. **new wine.** Occasionally translated "sweet wine," the term can denote either freshly squeezed grape juice or newly fermented wine (cf. Is. 49:26).

1:6,7 My land...vine...fig tree. The possessive pronoun refers to the Lord. He is the owner of the land (cf. Lev. 25:23; Num. 36:2; Ezek. 38:16), the vine, and the fig tree (cf. Hos. 2:9). Instead of symbols of prosperity and peace (1 Kin. 4:25; Mic. 4:4; Zech. 3:10), the vine and fig tree had become visual reminders of divine judgment.

1:6 a nation. A literal invasion of locusts pictured the kind of destruction and judgment inflicted by human armies. **teeth of a lion.** Joel described these hostile, countless locusts as possessing the "fangs of a fierce lion," so able were they to devour anything in their path. They are occasionally used as symbolic of violence (Gen. 49:9; Num. 23:24) and of the violent, awesome nature of God's judgment (Is. 30:6; Hos. 13:8).

1:8 Lament like a virgin. As with the drunkards, the religious leaders were to lament as a young maiden would upon the death of her youthful husband, wherein she exchanged the silky fabric of a wedding dress and the joy of a wedding feast for the scratchy, coarse clothing of goat's hair and the cry of a funeral dirge. The term "virgin" lacks the notion of virginity in many cases (e.g., Esth. 2:17; Ezek. 23:3), and when coupled together with the term "husband," points to a young maiden widowed shortly after marriage. **sackcloth.** Fabric generally made of goat's hair, usually black or dark in color (cf. Rev. 6:12), and usually placed on the bare body around the hips (Gen. 37:34; 1 Kin. 21:27), leaving the chest free for "beating" (Is. 32:11,12), was used in the ancient world to depict sorrow and penitence (Neh. 9:1; Is. 37:1; Matt. 11:21). Because the prophets' message usually dealt with a call to repentance, it became the principle garment worn by prophets (Matt. 3:4; Rev. 11:3).

1:8,9 The metaphor is significant because the OT speaks of the Lord as the husband of Israel, His wife (Is. 54:5-8; Jer. 31:32). The covenantal offerings and libations could not be carried out; Israel, the wife of the Lord, was to repent, lest her relationship with the Lord became like that of the young widowed maiden.

1:9 grain offering...drink offering Have been cut off. To cut off these offerings, sacrificed each morning and evening (Ex. 29:38-

Have been cut off from the house
of the LORD;
The priests [n]mourn, who minister
to the LORD.
10 The field is wasted,
[o]The land mourns;
For the grain is ruined,
[p]The new wine is dried up,
The oil fails.

11 [q]Be ashamed, you farmers,
Wail, you vinedressers,
For the wheat and the barley;
Because the harvest of the field has
perished.
12 [r]The vine has dried up,
And the fig tree has withered;
The pomegranate tree,
The palm tree also,
And the apple tree—
All the trees of the field are
withered;
Surely [s]joy has withered away
from the sons of men.

Mourning for the Land

13 [t]Gird yourselves and lament, you
priests;
Wail, you who minister before the
altar;
Come, lie all night in sackcloth,
You who minister to my God;
For the grain offering and the
drink offering
Are withheld from the house of
your God.
14 [u]Consecrate a fast,
Call [v]a sacred assembly;
Gather the elders
And [w]all the inhabitants of the land
Into the house of the LORD your
God,
And cry out to the LORD.

15 [x]Alas for the day!
For [y]the day of the LORD *is* at hand;
It shall come as destruction from
the Almighty.
16 Is not the food [z]cut off before our
eyes,
[a]Joy and gladness from the house of
our God?
17 The seed shrivels under the clods,
Storehouses are in shambles;
Barns are broken down,
For the grain has withered.

9 [n] Joel 2:17 **10** [o] Jer. 12:11; Hos. 3:4 [p] Is. 24:7 **11** [q] Jer. 14:3, 4; Amos 5:16 **12** [r] Joel 1:10; Hab. 3:17 [s] Is. 16:10; 24:11; Jer. 48:33 **13** [t] Jer. 4:8; Ezek. 7:18

14 [u] 2 Chr. 20:3; Joel 2:15, 16 [v] Lev. 23:36 [w] 2 Chr. 20:13 **15** [x] [Is. 13:9; Jer. 30:7]; Amos 5:16 [y] Is. 13:6; Ezek. 7:2-12 **16** [z] Is. 3:1; Amos 4:6 [a] Deut. 12:7; Ps. 43:4

42; Lev. 23:13), was to cut off the people from the covenant. The gravity of the situation was deepened by the fact that it threatened the livelihood of the priests, who were given a portion of most sacrifices.

1:11 Be ashamed, you farmers. The primary emphasis of the Heb. term connotes a public disgrace, a physical state to which the guilty party has been forcibly brought.

1:12 All the trees…are withered. The picture was bleak, for even the deep roots of the trees could not withstand the torturous treatment administered by the locusts, especially when accompanied by an extended drought. **joy has withered.** Human joy and delight had departed from all segments of society; none had escaped the grasp of the locusts. The joy that normally accompanied the time of harvest had been replaced with despair.

1:14 Consecrate a fast. The prophet called the priests to take action, first by example (v. 13) and then by proclamation (v. 14). As the official leaders, it was their duty to proclaim a public fast so that the entire nation could repent and petition the Lord to forgive and restore. Here they were admonished to "consecrate" a fast, denoting its urgent, sacred character. **Call a sacred assembly.** Directives for calling an assembly, generally for festive purposes (cf. 2 Chr. 7:9; Neh 8:18), are given in Num. 10:3. Parallel in thought to "consecrate a fast," no work was permitted on such days (Lev. 23:36; Num. 29:35; Deut. 16:8).

1:15 the day of the LORD *is* at hand. This is the first occurrence of the theme. Later in the book (2:18ff.; 3:1,18-21), the Day of the Lord (the occasion when God pours out His wrath on man) results in blessing and exoneration for God's people and judgment toward Gentiles (Is. 13:6; Ezek. 30:3), but here Joel directs the warning toward his own people. The Day of the Lord is speedily approaching; unless sinners repent, dire consequences await them. **destruction from the Almighty.** The Heb. term "destruction" forms a powerful play on words with the "Almighty." The notion of invincible strength is foremost; destruction at the hand of omnipotent God is coming.

1:17,18 seed shrivels…animals groan. From the spiritual realm to the physical realm, all was in shambles. Though innocent, in judgment even the animals suffered (cf. Rom. 8:18-22) the loss of food.

Day of the Lord

NINETEEN EXPLICIT MENTIONS OF "DAY OF THE LORD" IN THE OLD TESTAMENT

1. Obad. 15	6. Joel 3:14	11. Is. 13:6	16. Ezek. 13:5
2. Joel 1:15	7. Amos 5:18	12. Is. 13:9	17. Ezek. 30:3
3. Joel 2:1	8. Amos 5:18	13. Zeph. 1:7	18. Zech. 14:1
4. Joel 2:11	9. Amos 5:20	14. Zeph. 1:14	19. Mal. 4:5
5. Joel 2:31	10. Is. 2:12	15. Zeph. 1:14	

FOUR EXPLICIT MENTIONS OF "DAY OF THE LORD" IN THE NEW TESTAMENT

1. Acts 2:20	2. 1 Thess. 5:2	3. 2 Thess. 2:2	4. 2 Pet. 3:10

18 How [b]the animals groan!
The herds of cattle are restless,
Because they have no pasture;
Even the flocks of sheep [4]suffer
punishment.

19 O LORD, [c]to You I cry out;
For [d]fire has devoured the [5]open
pastures,
And a flame has burned all the
trees of the field.
20 The beasts of the field also [e]cry out
to You,
For [f]the water brooks are dried up,
And fire has devoured the [6]open
pastures.

The Day of the LORD

2 Blow [a]the [1]trumpet in Zion,
And [b]sound an alarm in My holy
mountain!
Let all the inhabitants of the land
tremble;
For [c]the day of the LORD is coming,
For it is at hand:
2 [d]A day of darkness and gloominess,
A day of clouds and thick
darkness,
Like the morning *clouds* spread
over the mountains.
[e]A people *come,* great and strong,
[f]The like of whom has never been;
Nor will there ever be any *such*
after them,
Even for many successive
generations.

3 A fire devours before them,
And behind them a flame burns;
The land *is* like [g]the Garden of
Eden before them,
[h]And behind them a desolate
wilderness;
Surely nothing shall escape them.

4 [i]Their appearance is like the
appearance of horses;
And like [2]swift steeds, so they run.
5 [j]With a noise like chariots
Over mountaintops they leap,
Like the noise of a flaming fire that
devours the stubble,
Like a strong people set in battle
array.

6 Before them the people writhe in
pain;
[k]All faces [3]are drained of color.
7 They run like mighty men,
They climb the wall like men of
war;
Every one marches in formation,
And they do not break [l]ranks.
8 They do not push one another;
Every one marches in his own
[4]column.
Though they lunge between the
weapons,
They are not [5]cut down.
9 They run to and fro in the city,
They run on the wall;
They climb into the houses,
They [m]enter at the windows [n]like a
thief.

10 [o]The earth quakes before them,
The heavens tremble;
[p]The sun and moon grow dark,
And the stars diminish their
brightness.
11 [q]The LORD gives voice before His
army,
For His camp is very great;
[r]For strong *is the One* who executes
His word.
For the [s]day of the LORD *is* great
and very terrible;
[t]Who can endure it?

18 [b] 1 Kin. 8:5; Jer. 12:4; 14:5, 6; Hos. 4:3 [4] LXX, Vg. *are made desolate*
19 [c] [Ps. 50:15]; Mic. 7:7 [d] Jer. 9:10; Amos 7:4 [5] Lit. *pastures of the wilderness*
20 [e] Job 38:41; Ps. 104:21; 147:9; Joel 1:18 [f] 1 Kin. 17:7; 18:5 [6] Lit. *pastures of the wilderness*

CHAPTER 2

1 [a] Jer. 4:5; Joel 2:15; Zeph. 1:16 [b] Num. 10:5 [c] Joel 1:15; 2:11, 31; 3:14; [Obad. 15]; Zeph. 1:14 [1] *ram's horn*
2 [d] Joel 2:10, 31; Amos 5:18; Zeph. 1:15 [e] Joel 1:6; 2:11, 25 [f] Ex. 10:14; Lam. 1:12; Dan. 9:12; 12:1; Joel 1:2
3 [g] Gen. 2:8; Is. 51:3; Ezek. 36:35 [h] Ex. 10:5, 15; Ps. 105:34, 35; Zech. 7:14
4 [i] Rev. 9:7 [2] Or *horsemen*
5 [j] Rev. 9:9
6 [k] Is. 13:8; Jer. 8:21; Lam. 4:8; Nah. 2:10 [3] LXX, Tg., Vg. *gather blackness*
7 [l] Prov. 30:27
8 [4] Lit. *highway* [5] Halted by losses
9 [m] Jer. 9:21 [n] John 10:1
10 [o] Ps. 18:7; Joel 3:16; Nah. 1:5 [p] Is. 13:10; 34:4; Jer. 4:23; Ezek. 32:7, 8; Joel 2:31; 3:15; Matt. 24:29; Rev. 8:12
11 [q] Jer. 25:30; Joel 3:16; Amos 1:2 [r] Jer. 50:34; Rev. 18:8 [s] Jer. 30:7; Amos 5:18; Zeph. 1:15 [t] [Mal. 3:2]

1:19 to You I cry out. As the first to call to repentance, the prophet had to be the first to heed the warning. He had to lead by example and motivate the people to respond. In the midst of proclaiming judgment, God's prophets often led in intercessory prayer for mercy and forgiveness (cf. Ex. 32:11-14; Jer. 42:1-4; Dan. 9:1-19; Amos 7:1-6).

2:1-17 With an increased level of intensity, Joel utilized the metaphor of the locust plague and drought as a backdrop from which to launch an intensified call to repent in view of the coming invasion of Judah and the Day of the Lord, present and future.

2:1 Blow the trumpet. In the ancient world, horns were used to gather people for special occasions or to warn of danger (Ex. 19:13,16,19; 20:18; Num. 10:1-10; Is. 27:13; Amos 3:6; Zeph. 1:14-16; Zech. 9:14; 1 Thess. 4:16). The term here refers to a ram's horn.

2:2-11 In dramatic and vivid language, Joel compared the drought and locusts to fire, horses, and an invading army.

2:2 darkness and gloominess...clouds and thick darkness. These features describe the blackness of a locust invasion, so thick that it blots out the sun with its deadly living cloud of insects. Such terms are also often common figures for misery and calamity in the OT (Is. 8:22; 60:2; Jer. 13:16; Amos 5:18,20; Zeph. 1:15) and past visitations of the Lord (Ex. 10:12ff.; 19:16-19; 24:16; Deut 4:12; 5:22,23).

2:4 Their appearance is like...horses. The resemblance of the locust's head to that of a horse is striking, so much so that the prophet reiterates the word "appearance." Horses were not used for agricultural purposes in ancient times, but were the most feared military equipment (Ex. 15:1ff.,19; Deut. 20:1; Josh. 11:4). The simile continues with "like chariots" (v. 5); "like a strong people" (v. 5); "like mighty men" (v. 7); and "like men of war" (v. 7).

2:10 earth quakes...sun and moon grow dark. The ground trembles as dust flies along with the growing devastation. Earthquakes and cosmic disruptions are well attested elsewhere as signs accompanying divine appearances (Judg. 5:4; Ps. 18:7; Jer. 4:23-26; Nah. 1:5,6; Matt. 24:7). Joel later refers to these signs (cf. 2:31; 3:15).

A Call to Repentance

12 "Now, therefore," says the LORD,
[u]"Turn to Me with all your heart,
With fasting, with weeping, and
with mourning."
13 So [v]rend your heart, and not [w]your
garments;
Return to the LORD your God,
For He *is* [x]gracious and merciful,
Slow to anger, and of great
kindness;
And He relents from doing harm.
14 [y]Who knows *if* He will turn and
relent,
And leave [z]a blessing behind Him—
[a]A grain offering and a drink
offering
For the LORD your God?

15 [b]Blow the [6]trumpet in Zion,
[c]Consecrate a fast,
Call a sacred assembly;
16 Gather the people,
[d]Sanctify the congregation,
Assemble the elders,
Gather the children and nursing
babes;
[e]Let the bridegroom go out from his
chamber,
And the bride from her dressing
room.
17 Let the priests, who minister to the
LORD,
Weep [f]between the porch and the
altar;
Let them say, [g]"Spare Your people,
O LORD,
And do not give Your heritage to
reproach,
That the nations should [7]rule over
them.
[h]Why should they say among the
peoples,
'Where *is* their God?' "

The Land Refreshed

18 Then the LORD will [i]be zealous for
His land,
And pity His people.

12 [u][Deut. 4:29]; Jer. 4:1; Ezek. 33:11; Hos. 12:6; 14:1
13 [v][Ps. 34:18; 51:17; Is. 57:15] [w]Gen. 37:34; 2 Sam. 1:11; Job 1:20; Jer. 41:5 [x][Ex. 34:6]
14 [y]Josh. 14:12; 2 Sam. 12:22; 2 Kin. 19:4; Jer. 26:3; Jon. 3:9 [z]Hag. 2:19 [a]Joel 1:9, 13
15 [b]Num. 10:3; 2 Kin. 10:20 [c]Joel 1:14 [6]*ram's horn*
16 [d]Ex. 19:10 [e]Ps. 19:5
17 [f]Matt. 23:35 [g]Ex. 32:11, 12; [Is. 37:20]; Amos 7:2, 5 [h]Ps. 42:10 [7]Or *speak a proverb against them*
18 [i][Is. 60:10; 63:9, 15]
19 [j]Jer. 31:12; Hos. 2:21, 22; Joel 1:10; [Mal. 3:10]
20 [k]Ex. 10:19 [l]Jer. 1:14, 15 [m]Deut. 11:24 [8]Lit. *great*
21 [9]Lit. *great*
22 [n]Joel 1:19
23 [o]Deut. 11:14; Is. 41:16; Jer. 5:24; Hab. 3:18; Zech. 10:7 [p]Lev. 26:4; Hos. 6:3; Zech. 10:1; James 5:7 [1]Or *teacher of righteousness*
25 [q]Joel 1:4-7; 2:2-11 [2]Exact identity of these locusts unknown

19 The LORD will answer and say to
His people,
"Behold, I will send you [j]grain and
new wine and oil,
And you will be satisfied by them;
I will no longer make you a
reproach among the nations.

20 "But [k]I will remove far from you
[l]the northern *army,*
And will drive him away into a
barren and desolate land,
With his face toward the eastern sea
And his back [m]toward the western
sea;
His stench will come up,
And his foul odor will rise,
Because he has done [8]monstrous
things."

21 Fear not, O land;
Be glad and rejoice,
For the LORD has done [9]marvelous
things!
22 Do not be afraid, you beasts of the
field;
For [n]the open pastures are
springing up,
And the tree bears its fruit;
The fig tree and the vine yield their
strength.
23 Be glad then, you children of Zion,
And [o]rejoice in the LORD your God;
For He has given you the [1]former
rain faithfully,
And He [p]will cause the rain to
come down for you—
The former rain,
And the latter rain in the first *month.*
24 The threshing floors shall be full of
wheat,
And the vats shall overflow with
new wine and oil.

25 "So I will restore to you the years
[q]that the swarming [2]locust
has eaten,
The crawling locust,
The consuming locust,

2:12-14 Even in the midst of judgment, opportunity to repent was given. If they would demonstrate genuine repentance, the Lord stood ready to forgive and bless.

2:16 From oldest to youngest they were to come. The situation is so grave that even the groom and bride were exhorted to assemble (cf. Deut. 24:5); consummation of the marriage could wait.

2:18–3:21 With the advent of v. 18, the text makes a decisive transition, devoting the remainder of the book to restoration. It assumes an interval of time between v. 17 and v. 18 during which Israel repented. As a result of her repentance, the 3 major concerns of 1:1–2:17 are answered by the Lord: physical restoration (2:21-27), spiritual restoration (2:28-32), and national restoration (3:1-21).

2:20 northern *army.* Although some have viewed this as a reference to the locusts, it is more likely referring to a military invasion by a country coming down from the N of Israel (cf. Ezek. 38:6,15; 39:2). That future army will be driven into the eastern sea (Dead Sea) and the western sea (Mediterranean Sea).

2:21-24 Reminiscent of 1:18-20, the former situation had been reversed. The animals were admonished to be afraid no longer.

2:23,24 former...latter rain. The former rains came in Oct.-Dec. to prepare the seed-bed and assist germination, while the latter rains came in Mar.-May to provide ample moisture for the grain and fruit crops to be rich and full.

And the chewing locust,
My great army which I sent among
you.
26 You shall [r]eat in plenty and be
satisfied,
And praise the name of the LORD
your God,
Who has dealt wondrously with
you;
And My people shall never be put
to [s]shame.
27 Then you shall know that I *am* [t]in
the midst of Israel:
[u]I *am* the LORD your God
And there is no other.
My people shall never be put to
shame.

God's Spirit Poured Out

28 "And[v] it shall come to pass afterward
That [w]I will pour out My Spirit on
all flesh;
[x]Your sons and your [y]daughters
shall prophesy,
Your old men shall dream dreams,
Your young men shall see visions.
29 And also on *My* [z]menservants and
on *My* maidservants
I will pour out My Spirit in those
days.

30 "And [a]I will show wonders in the
heavens and in the earth:
Blood and fire and pillars of smoke.
31 [b]The sun shall be turned into
darkness,
And the moon into blood,
[c]Before the coming of the great and
awesome day of the LORD.
32 And it shall come to pass
That [d]whoever calls on the name of
the LORD
Shall be [3]saved.

26 [r] Lev. 26:5; Deut. 11:15; Is. 62:9 [s] Is. 45:17
27 [t] Lev. 26:11, 12; [Joel 3:17, 21] [u] [Is. 45:5, 6]
28 [v] Ezek. 39:29; Acts 2:17-21 [w] Zech. 12:10 [x] Is. 54:13 [y] Acts 21:9
29 [z] [1 Cor. 12:13; Gal. 3:28]
30 [a] Matt. 24:29; Mark 13:24, 25; Luke 21:11, 25, 26; Acts 2:19
31 [b] Is. 13:9, 10; 34:4; Joel 2:10; 3:15; Matt. 24:29; Mark 13:24; Luke 21:25; Acts 2:20; Rev. 6:12, 13 [c] Is. 13:9; Zeph. 1:14-16; [Mal. 4:1, 5, 6]
32 [d] Jer. 33:3; Acts 2:21; Rom. 10:13 [3] Or *delivered*

[e] Is. 46:13; [Rom. 11:26] [f] Is. 11:11; Jer. 31:7; [Mic. 4:7]; Rom. 9:27 [4] Or *salvation*

CHAPTER 3

1 [a] Jer. 30:3; Ezek. 38:14
2 [b] Is. 66:18; Mic. 4:12; Zech. 14:2 [c] Is. 66:16; Jer. 25:31; Ezek. 38:22
3 [d] Obad. 11; Nah. 3:10
4 [e] Is. 14:29-31; Jer. 47:1-7; Ezek. 25:15-17; Amos 1:6-8; Zech. 9:5-7 [1] Or *render Me repayment* [2] Or *repay Me* [3] Or *repayment*
5 [4] Lit. *precious good things*

For [e]in Mount Zion and in
Jerusalem there shall be
[4]deliverance,
As the LORD has said,
Among [f]the remnant whom the
LORD calls.

God Judges the Nations

3 "For behold, [a]in those days and at
that time,
When I bring back the captives of
Judah and Jerusalem,
2 [b]I will also gather all nations,
And bring them down to the
Valley of Jehoshaphat;
And I [c]will enter into judgment
with them there
On account of My people, My
heritage Israel,
Whom they have scattered among
the nations;
They have also divided up My land.
3 They have [d]cast lots for My people,
Have given a boy *as payment* for a
harlot,
And sold a girl for wine, that they
may drink.

4 "Indeed, what have you to do with
Me,
[e]O Tyre and Sidon, and all the
coasts of Philistia?
Will you [1]retaliate against Me?
But if you [2]retaliate against Me,
Swiftly and speedily I will return
your [3]retaliation upon your
own head;
5 Because you have taken My silver
and My gold,
And have carried into your temples
My [4]prized possessions.
6 Also the people of Judah and the
people of Jerusalem
You have sold to the Greeks,

2:27 I *am* in the midst of Israel. This return promised a reversal of the Lord's departure (cf. Ezek. 8–11).

2:28-32 See Introduction: Interpretive Challenges; *see notes on Acts 2:16-21.*

2:28 afterward. The abundance of material blessings would be followed by the outpouring of spiritual blessings. When coupled with the other temporal phrases within the passage ("in those days" [v. 29] and "before the coming of the great and awesome Day of the LORD" [v. 31]), the term points to a Second Advent fulfillment time frame. **all flesh.** Since the context is "your sons and your daughters," "all flesh" best refers to the house of Israel only. The nations are the recipients of God's wrath, not the effusion of His Spirit (cf. 3:2,9ff.).

2:30,31 Before...day of the LORD. Unmistakable heavenly phenomena will signal the imminent arrival of God's wrath in the Day of the Lord (cf. v. 10).

2:32 whoever calls. Quoted by Paul in Rom. 10:13. **remnant.** In spite of the nation's sin, God promised to fulfill His unconditional covenants (Noahic, Abrahamic, Davidic, and New). A future remnant of Jews will inherit God's promised blessings (cf. Is. 10:20-22; 11:11,16; Jer. 31:7; Mic. 2:12; Zeph. 3:13; Rom. 9:27).

3:1-21 Joel notes the national restoration of Israel, in which the people will be regathered to Palestine (Is. 11:15,16; Matt. 24:31).

3:2 gather all nations. The nations of the world will be gathered to Jerusalem to the battle of Armageddon (Zech. 12:3; 14:2; Rev. 16:16; 19:11-21). **Valley of Jehoshaphat.** The name means "Yahweh judges" (cf. 3:12,14) and although the exact location is unknown, other prophets spoke of this judgment as occurring near Jerusalem (Ezek. 38,39; Dan. 11:45; Zech. 9:14ff.; 12:1ff.). This judgment of the nations includes the event of Matt. 25:31-46.

3:5,6 The exact historical event referred to here is uncertain. Slave trading was a common practice among the Phoenicians and Philistines.

3:6 the Greeks. Although not prominent militarily, the Greeks were active in commerce on the Mediterranean in the 9th century B.C.

That you may remove them far
from their borders.

7 "Behold, [f]I will raise them
Out of the place to which you have
sold them,
And will return your [5]retaliation
upon your own head.
8 I will sell your sons and your
daughters
Into the hand of the people of
Judah,
And they will sell them to the
[g]Sabeans,[6]
To a people [h]far off;
For the LORD has spoken."

9 [i]Proclaim this among the nations:
"Prepare for war!
Wake up the mighty men,
Let all the men of war draw near,
Let them come up.
10 [j]Beat your plowshares into swords
And your [7]pruning hooks into
spears;
[k]Let the weak say, 'I *am* strong.' "
11 Assemble and come, all you nations,
And gather together all around.
Cause [l]Your mighty ones to go
down there, O LORD.

12 "Let the nations be wakened, and
come up to the Valley of
Jehoshaphat;
For there I will sit to [m]judge all the
surrounding nations.
13 [n]Put in the sickle, for [o]the harvest is
ripe.
Come, go down;
For the [p]winepress is full,
The vats overflow—
For their wickedness *is* great."

14 Multitudes, multitudes in the
valley of decision!
For [q]the day of the LORD *is* near in
the valley of decision.
15 The sun and moon will grow dark,
And the stars will diminish their
brightness.
16 The LORD also will roar from Zion,
And utter His voice from Jerusalem;
The heavens and earth will shake;
[r]But the LORD will be a shelter for
His people,
And the strength of the children of
Israel.

17 "So you shall know that I *am* the
LORD your God,
Dwelling in Zion My [s]holy
mountain.
Then Jerusalem shall be holy,
And no aliens shall ever pass
through her again."

God Blesses His People

18 And it will come to pass in that day
That the mountains shall drip with
new wine,
The hills shall flow with milk,
And all the brooks of Judah shall
be flooded with water;
A [t]fountain shall flow from the
house of the LORD
And water the Valley of [8]Acacias.

19 "Egypt shall be a desolation,
And Edom a desolate wilderness,
Because of violence *against* the
people of Judah,
For they have shed innocent blood
in their land.
20 But Judah shall abide forever,
And Jerusalem from generation to
generation.
21 For I will [u]acquit them of the guilt
of bloodshed, whom I had
not acquitted;
For the LORD dwells in Zion."

7 [f] Is. 43:5, 6; Jer. 23:8; Zech. 9:13 [5] Or *repayment*
8 [g] Ezek. 23:42 [h] Jer. 6:20 [6] Lit. *Shebaites,* Is. 60:6; Ezek. 27:22
9 [i] Jer. 6:4; Ezek. 38:7; Mic. 3:5
10 [j] [Is. 2:4; Mic. 4:3] [k] Zech. 12:8 [7] *pruning knives*
11 [l] Ps. 103:20; Is. 13:3
12 [m] [Ps. 96:13]; Is. 2:4
13 [n] [Matt. 13:39]; Rev. 14:15 [o] Jer. 51:33; Hos. 6:11 [p] [Is. 63:3]; Lam. 1:5; Rev. 14:19
14 [q] Joel 2:1
16 [r] [Is. 51:5, 6]
17 [s] Obad. 16; Zech. 8:3
18 [t] Ps. 46:4; Ezek. 47:1; Zech. 14:8; [Rev. 22:1] [8] Heb. *Shittim*
21 [u] Is. 4:4

3:7,8 The reversal of fortunes will be startling. The victims themselves will be called upon to be the instruments and avengers of the Lord's wrath (cf. Is 11:12-14; Zech. 12:8).

3:8 Sabeans. Trading merchants who lived in Arabia (1 Kin. 10; Jer. 6:20).

3:9-17 Joel resumes the theme of vv. 1-3, the gathering of the nations to the earthly courtroom, the Valley of Jehoshaphat. The sentence has been handed down and the Judge orders His agents to ready the scene for the execution.

3:14 valley of decision. This location is the same as the Valley of Jehoshaphat where the sentence of judgment will be carried out (cf. 3:2,12). *See note on 3:2.*

3:15,16 The sun…moon. Cf. 2:10,30,31. These are signs that precede the coming eschatological Day of the Lord at the end of the Great Tribulation (cf. Matt. 24:29,30).

3:17 Zion My holy mountain. This will be the earthly location of God's presence in the millennial temple (cf. Ezek. 40–48) at Jerusalem. **ever pass through her again.** God has promised a future time when His glory in Judah will not be eclipsed. This time of ultimate peace and prosperity will be experienced after Christ conquers the world and sets up His millennial kingdom on earth (cf. Ezek. 37:24-28; Matt. 24,25; Rev. 19).

3:18 Valley of Acacias. Known for its acacia trees, the valley was situated on the northern shores of the Dead Sea and served as the final stopover for Israel prior to her entrance into the Promised Land (Num. 25:1; Josh. 2:1; 3:1). This valley is also the place to which the millennial river will flow (Ezek. 47:1-12; Zech. 14:8).

3:20 Judah…forever. This is in reference to Christ's millennial kingdom on earth, which is yet to be fulfilled.

The Book of

AMOS

Title

As with each of the Minor Prophets, the title comes from the name of the prophet to whom God gave His message (1:1). Amos' name means "burden" or "burden-bearer." He is not to be confused with Amoz ("stout, strong"), the father of Isaiah (Is. 1:1).

Author and Date

Amos was from Tekoa, a small village 10 mi. S of Jerusalem. He was the only prophet to give his occupation before declaring his divine commission. He was not of priestly or noble descent, but worked as a "sheepbreeder" (1:1; cf. 2 Kin. 3:4) and a "tender of sycamore fruit" (7:14) and was a contemporary of Jonah (2 Kin. 14:25), Hosea (Hos. 1:1), and Isaiah (Is. 1:1). The date of writing is mid-eighth century B.C., during the reigns of Uzziah, king of Judah (ca. 790–739 B.C.) and Jeroboam II, king of Israel (ca. 793–753 B.C.), two years before a memorable earthquake (1:1; cf. Zech. 14:5, ca. 760 B.C.).

Background and Setting

Amos was a Judean prophet called to deliver a message primarily to the northern tribes of Israel (7:15). Politically, it was a time of prosperity under the long and secure reign of Jeroboam II who, following the example of his father Joash (2 Kin. 13:25), significantly "restored the territory of Israel" (2 Kin. 14:25). It was also a time of peace with both Judah (cf. 5:5) and her more distant neighbors; the ever-present menace of Assyria was subdued earlier that century because of Nineveh's repentance at the preaching of Jonah (Jon. 3:10). Spiritually, however, it was a time of rampant corruption and moral decay (4:1; 5:10-13; 2 Kin. 14:24).

Historical and Theological Themes

Amos addresses Israel's two primary sins: 1) an absence of true worship, and 2) a lack of justice. In the midst of their ritualistic performance of worship, they were not pursuing the Lord with their hearts (4:4,5; 5:4-6) nor following His standard of justice with their neighbors (5:10-13; 6:12). This apostasy, evidenced by continual, willful rejection of the prophetic message of Amos, is promised divine judgment. Because of His covenant, however, the Lord will not abandon Israel altogether, but will bring future restoration to the righteous remnant (9:7-15).

Interpretive Challenges

In 9:11, the Lord promised that He "will raise up the tabernacle of David, which has fallen down." At the Jerusalem Council, convened to discuss whether Gentiles should be allowed into the church without requiring circumcision, James quotes this passage (Acts 15:15,16) to support Peter's report of how God had "visited the Gentiles to take out of them a people for His name" (Acts 15:14). Some have thus concluded that the passage was fulfilled in Jesus, the greater Son of David, through whom the dynasty of David was reestablished. The Acts reference, however, is best seen as an illustration of Amos' words and not the fulfillment. The temporal allusions to a future time ("On that day," 9:11), when Israel will "possess the remnant of Edom, and all the Gentiles" (9:12), when the Lord "will plant them in their land, and no longer shall they be pulled up from the land I have given them" (9:15), all make it clear that the prophet is speaking of Messiah's return at the Second Advent to sit upon the throne of David (cf. Is. 9:7), not the establishment of the church by the apostles.

Outline

I. Judgments Against the Nations (1:1–2:16)
 A. Introduction (1:1,2)
 B. Against Israel's Enemies (1:3–2:3)
 C. Against Judah (2:4,5)
 D. Against Israel (2:6-16)

II. Condemnations Against Israel ((3:1–6:14)
 A. Sin of Irresponsibility (3:1-15)
 B. Sin of Idolatry (4:1-13)
 C. Sin of Moral/Ethical Decay (5:1–6:14)

III. Visions of Judgment and Restoration (7:1–9:15)
 A. The Lord Will Spare (7:1-6)
  1. Vision of locusts (7:1-3)
  2. Vision of fire (7:4-6)
 B. The Lord Will No Longer Spare (7:7–9:10)
  1. Vision of the plumb line (7:7-9)
  2. Historical interlude (7:10-17)
  3. Vision of the fruit basket (8:1-14)
  4. Vision of the altar (9:1-10)
 C. The Lord Will Restore (9:11-15)

1

The words of Amos, who was among
the [a]sheepbreeders of [b]Tekoa, which
he saw concerning Israel in the days of
[c]Uzziah king of Judah, and in the days of
[d]Jeroboam the son of Joash, king of Israel,
two years before the [e]earthquake.
2 And he said:

"The LORD [f]roars from Zion,
And utters His voice from
Jerusalem;
The pastures of the shepherds
mourn,
And the top of [g]Carmel withers."

Judgment on the Nations

3 Thus says the LORD:

"For three transgressions of
[h]Damascus, and for four,
I will not turn away its *punishment*,
Because they have [i]threshed Gilead
with implements of iron.
4 [j]But I will send a fire into the house
of Hazael,
Which shall devour the palaces of
[k]Ben-Hadad.
5 I will also break the *gate* [l]bar of
Damascus,
And cut off the inhabitant from the
Valley of Aven,
And the one who [1]holds the
scepter from [2]Beth Eden.
The people of Syria shall go
captive to Kir,"
Says the LORD.

6 Thus says the LORD:

"For three transgressions of [m]Gaza,
and for four,
I will not turn away its *punishment*,
Because they took captive the
whole captivity
To deliver *them* up to Edom.
7 [n]But I will send a fire upon the wall
of Gaza,
Which shall devour its palaces.
8 I will cut off the inhabitant [o]from
Ashdod,
And the one who holds the scepter
from Ashkelon;
I will [p]turn My hand against
Ekron,
And [q]the remnant of the Philistines
shall perish,"
Says the Lord GOD.

9 Thus says the LORD:

"For three transgressions of [r]Tyre,
and for four,
I will not turn away its *punishment*,
Because they delivered up the
whole captivity to Edom,
And did not remember the
covenant of brotherhood.
10 But I will send a fire upon the wall
of Tyre,
Which shall devour its palaces."

11 Thus says the LORD:

CHAPTER 1

1 [a] 2 Kin. 3:4; Amos 7:14 [b] 2 Sam. 14:2; Jer. 6:1 [c] 2 Kin. 15:1-7; 2 Chr. 26:1-23; Is. 1:1; Hos. 1:1 [d] 2 Kin. 14:23-29; Amos 7:10 [e] Zech. 14:5
2 [f] Is. 42:13; Jer. 25:30; Joel 3:16 [g] 1 Sam. 25:2; Is. 33:9
3 [h] Is. 8:4; 17:1-3; Jer. 49:23-27; Zech. 9:1 [i] 2 Kin. 10:32, 33
4 [j] Jer. 49:27; 51:30 [k] 1 Kin. 20:1; 2 Kin. 6:24
5 [l] 2 Kin. 14:28; Is. 8:4; Jer. 51:30; Lam. 2:9 [1] Rules [2] Lit. *House of Eden*
6 [m] 1 Sam. 6:17; Jer. 47:1, 5; Zeph. 2:4
7 [n] Jer. 47:1
8 [o] Jer. 47:5; Zeph. 2:4 [p] Ps. 81:14 [q] Is. 14:29-31; Jer. 47:1-7; Ezek. 25:16; Joel 3:4-8; Zeph. 2:4-7; Zech. 9:5-7
9 [r] Is. 23:1-18; Jer. 25:22; Ezek. 26:2-4; Joel 3:4-8

1:1 the earthquake. Mentioned by Zechariah (14:5), Josephus (*Antiquities,* IX:10:4) connects it with Uzziah's sin of usurping the role of a priest (2 Chr. 26:16-23). An earthquake of severe magnitude occurred ca. 760 B.C.

1:2 roars. In Joel 3:16, the Lord "roars" against the nations; here His wrath was directed primarily toward Israel (cf. Jer. 25:30). Amos, a shepherd, courageously warned the flock of God's pasture that they were in imminent danger from a roaring lion who turned out to be the ultimate Shepherd of the flock (cf. 3:8). **Carmel.** Known for its bountiful trees and lush gardens, "Carmel" means "fertility" or "garden land" and refers to the mountain range that runs E to W in northern Israel and juts out into the Mediterranean Sea (cf. 9:3).

1:3–2:3 Amos began with Israel's enemies, and thereby gained an initial hearing. When he turned to God's judgment on Israel, the leaders tried to silence him (cf. 7:10-17).

1:3 For three transgressions…for four. This rhetorical device is repeated in each of the 8 messages, differing from a similar pattern used elsewhere. There they are specific mathematical enumerations (e.g., Prov. 30:15,18,21,29), emphasizing that each nation was being visited for an incalculable number of infractions. With 3, the cup of iniquity was full; with 4 it overflowed. This judgment was to fall on Syria, whose capital is Damascus. **threshed Gilead.** Large threshing sleds which, when dragged over grain, would both thresh the grain and cut the straw. Gilead, located in the northeastern, Golan Heights region of Israel, was vulnerable to Syria's cruel attacks (cf. 2 Kin. 13:7; 18:12).

1:4 Ben-Hadad. Apparently a throne name, meaning "son of (the god) Hadad." Ben-Hadad II was a son of Syrian king Hazael (841–801 B.C.).

1:5 Valley of Aven. Meaning "valley of wickedness," it may refer to Baalbek, the center of sun worship, located N of Damascus. **Beth Eden.** "House of pleasure." It was located in eastern Syria across the Euphrates. **Kir.** Apparently the original home of the Syrians. It was a region to which they were later exiled (2 Kin. 16:9). Its exact location is unknown.

1:6 Gaza. Philistia's most prominent merchant city, ideally situated between Egypt and Israel, here used to refer to the Philistine nation. **took captive the whole captivity.** They deported an entire population (cf. Jer. 13:19), possibly during the reign of Jehoram (2 Chr. 21:16,17; Joel 3:3), ca. 853–841 B.C.

1:7,8 Four of the 5 major cities of Philistia. The fifth, Gath, was not mentioned because it had been destroyed earlier by Uzziah (2 Chr. 26:6).

1:9 covenant of brotherhood. A longstanding brotherly relationship existed between Phoenicia and Israel, beginning with King Hiram's assistance to David and Solomon in the building of the temple (2 Sam. 5:11; 1 Kin. 5:1-12; 9:11-14), and later cemented through the marriage of Jezebel to Ahab (1 Kin. 16:31). No king of Israel ever made war against Phoenicia, especially the two major cities, Tyre and Sidon.

1:10 Tyre. Alexander the Great conquered this stronghold ca. 330 B.C. (cf. Ezek. 26:1-18).

"For three transgressions of [s]Edom,
and for four,
I will not turn away its *punishment,*
Because he pursued his [t]brother
with the sword,
And cast off all pity;
His anger tore perpetually,
And he kept his wrath forever.
12 But [u]I will send a fire upon Teman,
Which shall devour the palaces of
Bozrah."

13 Thus says the LORD:

"For three transgressions of [v]the
people of Ammon, and for
four,
I will not turn away its *punishment,*
Because they ripped open the
women with child in Gilead,
That they might enlarge their
territory.
14 But I will kindle a fire in the wall
of [w]Rabbah,
And it shall devour its palaces,
[x]Amid shouting in the day of battle,
And a tempest in the day of the
whirlwind.
15 [y]Their king shall go into captivity,
He and his princes together,"
Says the LORD.

2 Thus says the LORD:

[a]"For three transgressions of Moab,
and for four,
I will not turn away its *punishment,*
Because he [b]burned the bones of
the king of Edom to lime.
2 But I will send a fire upon Moab,
And it shall devour the palaces of
[c]Kerioth;

11 [s]Is. 21:11; Jer. 49:8; Ezek. 25:12-14; Mal. 1:2-5 [t]Num. 20:14-21; 2 Chr. 28:17; Obad. 10-12
12 [u]Jer. 49:7, 20; Obad. 9, 10
13 [v]Jer. 49:1; Ezek. 25:2; Zeph. 2:8, 9
14 [w]Deut. 3:11; 1 Chr. 20:1; Jer. 49:2 [x]Ezek. 21:22; Amos 2:2
15 [y]Jer. 49:3

CHAPTER 2

1 [a]Is. 15:1-16; Jer. 25:21; Ezek. 25:8-11; Zeph. 2:8-11 [b]2 Kin. 3:26, 27
2 [c]Jer. 48:24, 41
3 [d]Num. 24:17; Jer. 48:7
4 [e]2 Kin. 17:19; Hos. 12:2; Amos 3:2 [f]Lev. 26:14 [g]Is. 9:15, 16; 28:15; Jer. 16:19; Hab. 2:18 [h]Jer. 9:14; 16:11, 12; Ezek. 20:13, 16, 18
5 [i]Jer. 17:27; Hos. 8:14
6 [j]Judg. 2:17-20; 2 Kin. 17:7-18; 18:12; Ezek. 22:1-13, 23-29 [k]Is. 29:21 [l]Joel 3:3; Amos 4:1; 5:11; 8:6; Mic. 2:2; 3:3
7 [m]Amos 5:12 [n]Lev. 18:6-8; Ezek. 22:11 [o]Lev. 20:3; Ezek. 36:20-22 [1]Or *trample on*
8 [p]1 Cor. 8:10 [q]Ex. 22:26

Moab shall die with tumult,
With shouting *and* trumpet sound.
3 And I will cut off [d]the judge from
its midst,
And slay all its princes with him,"
Says the LORD.

Judgment on Judah

4 Thus says the LORD:

"For three transgressions of [e]Judah,
and for four,
I will not turn away its *punishment,*
[f]Because they have despised the
law of the LORD,
And have not kept His
commandments.
[g]Their lies lead them astray,
Lies [h]which their fathers followed.
5 [i]But I will send a fire upon Judah,
And it shall devour the palaces of
Jerusalem."

Judgment on Israel

6 Thus says the LORD:

"For three transgressions of [j]Israel,
and for four,
I will not turn away its *punishment,*
Because [k]they sell the righteous for
silver,
And the [l]poor for a pair of
sandals.
7 They [1]pant after the dust of the
earth *which is* on the head of
the poor,
And [m]pervert the way of the
humble.
[n]A man and his father go in to the
same girl,
[o]To defile My holy name.
8 They lie down [p]by every altar on
clothes [q]taken in pledge,

1:11 pursued…cast off all pity. More than mere fighting, Edom pursued his brother, stifling any feelings of compassion. *See notes on Obadiah* for a more complete description of Edom's judgment.

1:12 Teman. The grandson of Esau (Gen. 36:11), after whom this town in northern Edom was named. **Bozrah.** A fortress city of northern Edom, about 35 mi. N of Petra.

1:13 people of Ammon. Descendants of Ben-Ammi, the son of Lot and his younger daughter (Gen. 19:34-38). **Rabbah.** Situated E of the Jordan river, this was the capital city. **ripped open the women with child.** Such inhumane treatment in wartime was not an uncommon practice (cf. 2 Kin. 8:12; 15:16; Hos. 13:16).

2:1 Moab. Descendants of Lot and his elder daughter (Gen. 19:37). **burned the bones.** This event, where vengeance didn't stop at death, is not recorded elsewhere in Scripture.

2:2 Kerioth. An important Moabite city, either as a capital or center of worship.

2:3 judge. Possibly denoting the king, who was often so designated (2 Kin. 15:5; Dan. 9:12).

2:4 Judah. With the judgments against the nations finished, the prophet proceeded to address Judah, moving ever closer to his ultimate target of Israel. **despised the law of the LORD.** The nations were judged because they had sinned against the law of God, which was written in the heart and conscience (cf. Rom. 2:24,25). Judah and Israel were judged because they sinned against God's revealed, written law.

2:5 fire upon Judah. The Babylonian King Nebuchadnezzar fulfilled this judgment, ca. 605–586 B.C. (cf. 2 Kin. 24,25).

2:6,7 Greed, so all-consuming that for insignificant debts they would sell another into slavery (cp. Matt. 18:23-35), was accompanied by uncontained sexual passion. Care for the poor is a prominent OT theme (e.g., Prov. 14:31; 17:5) and sexual purity is mandated repeatedly. Violations of both are an affront to God's holy name.

2:7 go in to the *same* girl. In the context of oppressing the helpless, the reference was probably to a slave girl (cf. Ex. 21:7-11).

2:8 clothes taken in pledge. Outer garments used to secure a loan were to be returned before sunset (Ex. 22:25-27; Deut. 24:12,13); instead, they used them to engage in idolatrous acts.

And drink the wine of [2]the
condemned *in* the house of
their god.

9 "Yet *it was* I *who* destroyed the
[r]Amorite before them,
Whose height *was* like the [s]height
of the cedars,
And he *was as* strong as the oaks;
Yet I [t]destroyed his fruit above
And his roots beneath.
10 Also *it was* [u]I *who* brought you up
from the land of Egypt,
And [v]led you forty years through
the wilderness,
To possess the land of the Amorite.
11 I raised up some of your sons as
[w]prophets,
And some of your young men as
[x]Nazirites.
Is it not so, O you children of
Israel?"
Says the LORD.
12 "But you gave the Nazirites wine to
drink,
And commanded the prophets
[y]saying,
'Do not prophesy!'

13 "Behold,[z] I am [3]weighed down by
you,
As a cart full of sheaves [4]is
weighed down.
14 [a]Therefore [5]flight shall perish from
the swift,
The strong shall not strengthen his
power,
[b]Nor shall the mighty [6]deliver
himself;
15 He shall not stand who handles the
bow,
The swift of foot shall not [7]escape,
Nor shall he who rides a horse
deliver himself.
16 The most [8]courageous men of
might
Shall flee naked in that day,"
Says the LORD.

8 [2] Or *those punished by fines*
9 [r] Gen. 15:16; Num. 21:25; Deut. 2:31; Josh. 10:12 [s] Ezek. 31:3 [t] Is. 5:24; Ezek. 17:9; [Mal. 4:1]
10 [u] Ex. 12:51; Amos 3:1; 9:7 [v] Deut. 2:7
11 [w] Num. 12:6 [x] Num. 6:2, 3; Judg. 13:5
12 [y] Is. 30:10; Jer. 11:21; Amos 7:13, 16; Mic. 2:6
13 [z] Is. 1:14 [3] Or *tottering under* [4] Or *totters*
14 [a] Jer. 46:6 [b] Ps. 33:16; Jer. 9:23 [5] Or *the place of refuge* [6] Lit. *save his soul* or *life*
15 [7] Or *save*
16 [8] Lit. *strong of his heart among the mighty*

CHAPTER 3
2 [a] [Gen. 18:19; Ex. 19:5, 6; Deut. 7:6; Ps. 147:19] [b] Jer. 14:10; Ezek. 20:36; Dan. 9:12; Matt. 11:22; [Rom. 2:9]
4 [1] Lit. *give his voice*
5 [2] Or *bait or lure*
6 [c] Is. 45:7 [3] *ram's horn*
7 [d] Gen. 6:13; 18:17; [Jer. 23:22]; Dan. 9:22; [John 15:15]
8 [e] Jer. 20:9; [Mic. 3:8]; Acts 4:20; 1 Cor. 9:16
9 [4] So with MT; LXX *Assyria* [5] Or *oppression*
10 [f] Ps. 14:4; Jer. 4:22; Amos 5:7; 6:12

Authority of the Prophet's Message

3 Hear this word that the LORD has spoken against you, O children of Israel, against the whole family which I brought up from the land of Egypt, saying:

2 "You[a] only have I known of all the
families of the earth;
[b]Therefore I will punish you for all
your iniquities."

3 Can two walk together, unless they
are agreed?
4 Will a lion roar in the forest, when
he has no prey?
Will a young lion [1]cry out of his
den, if he has caught nothing?
5 Will a bird fall into a snare on the
earth, where there is no [2]trap
for it?
Will a snare spring up from the
earth, if it has caught nothing
at all?
6 If a [3]trumpet is blown in a city, will
not the people be afraid?
[c]If there is calamity in a city, will
not the LORD have done *it?*

7 Surely the Lord GOD does nothing,
Unless [d]He reveals His secret to
His servants the prophets.
8 A lion has roared!
Who will not fear?
The Lord GOD has spoken!
[e]Who can but prophesy?

Punishment of Israel's Sins

9 "Proclaim in the palaces at
[4]Ashdod,
And in the palaces in the land of
Egypt, and say:
'Assemble on the mountains of
Samaria;
See great tumults in her midst,
And the [5]oppressed within her.
10 For they [f]do not know to do right,'
Says the LORD,

2:9 Amorite. The pre-Conquest inhabitants of Canaan, whom God defeated for the Jews (cf. Josh. 10:12-15). Their giant stature was said to make the spies look like grasshoppers (Num. 13:32,33).

2:11 Nazirites. See Num. 6:1-21.

2:14-16 Neither personal strength nor military armament was sufficient to prevent the Lord's hand of judgment by the Assyrians ca. 722 B.C. (cf. 2 Kin. 17).

3:1 the whole family. The primary recipient of these messages was Israel; Judah was not excluded.

3:2 You only have I known. This "knowing" refers to an intimate relationship, not just awareness. Cf. Gen. 4:1,17; Matt. 1:25; John 10:14,15. But, God's sovereign choice of Israel did not exempt her from punishment for disobedience.

3:3-8 The Lord posed a series of questions to show that, as some things are certain in nature, surely nothing happens in Israel that is outside His sovereignty. Certain actions have certain results! The Lord had spoken a word, and therefore the prophet was to speak, and the people were to listen with trembling. Instead, they tried to silence the prophet (cf. 2:12; 7:12,13).

3:7 Judgment is coming, but the Lord graciously warned the nation in advance through His prophets (e.g., Noah, Gen. 6; Abraham, Gen. 18).

3:9 The heathen nations, such as the Philistines and Egyptians, were rhetorically summoned to witness God's judgment. If they condemn Israel, how much more will a righteous God?

'Who store up violence and
[6]robbery in their palaces.' "

11 Therefore thus says the Lord GOD:

"An adversary *shall be* all around
the land;
He shall sap your strength from
you,
And your palaces shall be
plundered."

12 Thus says the LORD:

"As a shepherd [7]takes from the
mouth of a lion
Two legs or a piece of an ear,
So shall the children of Israel be
taken out
Who dwell in Samaria—
In the corner of a bed and [8]on the
edge of a couch!
13 Hear and testify against the house
of Jacob,"
Says the Lord GOD, the God of
hosts,
14 "That in the day I punish Israel for
their transgressions,
I will also visit *destruction* on the
altars of [g]Bethel;
And the horns of the altar shall be
cut off
And fall to the ground.
15 I will [9]destroy [h]the winter house
along with [i]the summer
house;
The [j]houses of ivory shall perish,
And the great houses shall have an
end,"
Says the LORD.

4 Hear this word, you [a]cows of
Bashan, who *are* on the
mountain of Samaria,
Who oppress the [b]poor,
Who crush the needy,
Who say to [1]your husbands,
"Bring *wine*, let us [c]drink!"
2 [d]The Lord GOD has sworn by His
holiness:
"Behold, the days shall come upon
you
When He will take you away [e]with
fishhooks,
And your posterity with fishhooks.
3 [f]You will go out *through* broken
walls,
Each one straight ahead of her,
And you will [2]be cast into
Harmon,"
Says the LORD.

4 "Come[g] to Bethel and transgress,
At [h]Gilgal multiply transgression;
[i]Bring your sacrifices every morning,
[j]Your tithes every three [3]days.
5 [k]Offer a sacrifice of thanksgiving
with leaven,
Proclaim *and* announce [l]the
freewill offerings;
For this you love,
You children of Israel!"
Says the Lord GOD.

Israel Did Not Accept Correction

6 "Also I gave you [4]cleanness of teeth
in all your cities.
And lack of bread in all your
places;
[m]Yet you have not returned to Me,"
Says the LORD.

7 "I also withheld rain from you,
When *there were* still three months
to the harvest.
I made it rain on one city,
I withheld rain from another city.
One part was rained upon,
And where it did not rain the part
withered.
8 So two *or* three cities wandered to
another city to drink water,

10 [6] Or *devastation*
12 [7] Or *snatches* [8] Heb. uncertain, possibly *on the cover*
14 [g] 2 Kin. 23:15; Hos. 10:5-8, 14, 15; Amos 4:4
15 [h] Jer. 36:22 [i] Judg. 3:20 [j] 1 Kin. 22:39; Ps. 45:8 [9] Lit. *strike*

CHAPTER 4

1 [a] Ps. 22:12; Ezek. 39:18 [b] Amos 2:6 [c] Prov. 23:20 [1] Lit. *their masters* or *lords*
2 [d] Ps. 89:35 [e] Jer. 16:16; Ezek. 29:4; Hab. 1:15
3 [f] Ezek. 12:5 [2] Or *cast them*
4 [g] Ezek. 20:39; Amos 3:14 [h] Hos. 4:15 [i] Num. 28:3; Amos 5:21, 22 [j] Deut. 14:28 [3] Or *years*, Deut. 14:28
5 [k] Lev. 7:13 [l] Lev. 22:18; Deut. 12:6
6 [m] 2 Chr. 28:22; Is. 26:11; Jer. 5:3; Hag. 2:17 [4] Hunger

3:11 An adversary. The Assyrians who captured and deported Israel in 722 B.C.

3:12 The Lord gives a vivid description of the small remnant left in Israel after the Assyrian invasion.

3:13 Hear and testify. As in v. 9, the heathen nations were once again called upon to witness and testify.

3:14 Bethel. The principal place of idol worship in Israel (cf. 1 Kin. 12:25-33).

4:1 cows of Bashan. A description of the women of Samaria who lived luxurious lives (cf. Is. 3:16-26; 32:9-13; Jer. 4:30). Bashan was a fertile region below Mt. Hermon E of the Jordan River known for its lush pastures. Under Jeroboam II, Israel was enjoying great prosperity.

4:2,3 *through* broken *walls*...into Harmon. Captives will be led out of the city through breaches in the walls, depicting massive overthrow. The location of Harmon is unknown.

4:4,5 With poignant sarcasm, Amos indicted Israel for idolatrous sacrifices and ritualistic religion.

4:4 Bethel...Gilgal. Bethel, the place of Jacob's dream (Gen. 28), and Gilgal, where Israel was circumcised before surrounding Jericho (Josh. 5:1-9), were sacred to Israel.

4:5 sacrifice...with leaven. Though prohibited from most offerings, leaven was required as a part of the thanksgiving offering (Lev. 7:11-15).

4:6-11 Past warnings were futile, a fact repeatedly emphasized by "Yet you have not returned to Me" (vv. 6,8,9,10,11).

4:6 cleanness of teeth. Amos employed this euphemism to depict the absence of food during famine and drought sent by God to warn Israel, which he described in vv. 6-9 (cf. Deut. 28:22,23,24,47,48; Lev. 26:18).

But they were not satisfied;
Yet you have not returned to Me,"
Says the LORD.

9 "I[n] blasted you with blight and mildew.
When your gardens increased,
Your vineyards,
Your fig trees,
And your olive trees,
[o]The locust devoured *them;*
Yet you have not returned to Me,"
Says the LORD.

10 "I sent among you a plague [p]after the manner of Egypt;
Your young men I killed with a sword,
Along with your captive horses;
I made the stench of your camps come up into your nostrils;
Yet you have not returned to Me,"
Says the LORD.

11 "I overthrew *some* of you,
As God overthrew [q]Sodom and Gomorrah,
And you were like a firebrand plucked from the burning;
Yet you have not returned to Me,"
Says the LORD.

12 "Therefore thus will I do to you,
O Israel;
Because I will do this to you,
[r]Prepare to meet your God,
O Israel!"

13 For behold,
He who forms mountains,
And creates the [5]wind,
[s]Who declares to man what [6]his thought *is,*
And makes the morning darkness,
[t]Who treads the high places of the earth—
[u]The LORD God of hosts *is* His name.

9 [n] Deut. 28:22; Hag. 2:17 [o] Joel 1:4, 7; Amos 7:1, 2 **10** [p] Ex. 9:3, 6; Lev. 26:25; Deut. 28:27, 60; Ps. 78:50 **11** [q] Gen. 19:24, 25; Deut. 29:23; Is. 13:19; Jer. 49:18; Lam. 4:6 **12** [r] Jer. 5:22 **13** [s] Ps. 139:2; Dan. 2:28 [t] Mic. 1:3 [u] Is. 47:4; Jer. 10:16 [5] Or *spirit* [6] Or *His*

CHAPTER 5

1 [a] Jer. 7:29; 9:10, 17; Ezek. 19:1 **4** [b] [Deut. 4:29; 2 Chr. 15:2; Jer. 29:13] [c] [Is. 55:3] **5** [d] 1 Kin. 12:28, 29; Amos 4:4 [e] Gen. 21:31-33; Amos 8:14 [f] Hos. 4:15 **6** [g] [Is. 55:3, 6, 7; Amos 5:14] **7** [h] Amos 6:12 **8** [i] Job 9:9; 38:31 [j] Ps. 104:20 [k] Job 38:34 [l] [Amos 4:13]

A Lament for Israel

5 Hear this word which I [a]take up against you, a lamentation, O house of Israel:

2 The virgin of Israel has fallen;
She will rise no more.
She lies forsaken on her land;
There is no one to raise her up.

3 For thus says the Lord GOD:

"The city that goes out by a thousand
Shall have a hundred left,
And that which goes out by a hundred
Shall have ten left to the house of Israel."

A Call to Repentance

4 For thus says the LORD to the house of Israel:

[b]"Seek Me [c]and live;
5 But do not seek [d]Bethel,
Nor enter Gilgal,
Nor pass over to [e]Beersheba;
For Gilgal shall surely go into captivity,
And [f]Bethel shall come to nothing.
6 [g]Seek the LORD and live,
Lest He break out like fire *in* the house of Joseph,
And devour *it,*
With no one to quench *it* in Bethel—
7 You who [h]turn justice to wormwood,
And lay righteousness to rest in the earth!"

8 He made the [i]Pleiades and Orion;
He turns the shadow of death into morning
[j]And makes the day dark as night;
He [k]calls for the waters of the sea
And pours them out on the face of the earth;
[l]The LORD *is* His name.

4:11 firebrand plucked from the burning. Only because of God's mercy was Israel saved from extinction (cf. Zech 3:2; Jude 23).

4:12 Prepare to meet your God. The general concept was first used of Israel's preparation to receive the covenant at Sinai (Ex. 19:11,15); here she was implored to prepare for His judgment.

4:13 This is the God whom they were to be prepared to face. He is the Lord God Almighty.

5:1,2 A funeral dirge was taken up for Israel, likened to a young woman who had died.

5:3 Many were to be killed in battle or taken captive; only a handful would return (cf. 3:12; Is. 6:11-13).

5:5 Bethel...Gilgal. *See note on 4:4.* **Beersheba.** Located in southern Judah, 50 mi. SW of Jerusalem, Beersheba had a rich Israelite history (cf. Gen. 21:33; 26:23; 1 Sam. 8:1-3; 1 Kin. 19:3-7). Apparently, people from the N crossed over the border to worship there (cf. 8:14).

5:6 house of Joseph. Refers to the northern kingdom, since Ephraim and Manasseh, sons of Joseph, were two of its largest tribes.

5:7 justice to wormwood. Justice was so perverted that it was like wormwood, an herb known for its bitter taste (cf. Rev. 8:11).

5:8 Pleiades and Orion. Pleiades, part of the constellation Taurus, and Orion depict God's creative power and wisdom (cf. Job 9:9; 38:31-35). Israel was guilty of worshiping the stars (cf. v. 26) instead of their Creator.

9 He [1]rains ruin upon the strong,
So that fury comes upon the
fortress.

10 [m]They hate the one who rebukes in
the gate,
And they [n]abhor the one who
speaks uprightly.
11 [o]Therefore, because you [2]tread
down the poor
And take grain [3]taxes from him,
Though [p]you have built houses of
hewn stone,
Yet you shall not dwell in them;
You have planted [4]pleasant
vineyards,
But you shall not drink wine from
them.
12 For I [q]know your manifold
transgressions
And your mighty sins:
[r]Afflicting the just *and* taking bribes;
[s]Diverting the poor *from justice* at
the gate.
13 Therefore [t]the prudent keep silent
at that time,
For it *is* an evil time.

14 Seek good and not evil,
That you may live;
So the LORD God of hosts will be
with you,
[u]As you have spoken.
15 [v]Hate evil, love good;
Establish justice in the gate.
[w]It may be that the LORD God of
hosts
Will be gracious to the remnant of
Joseph.

The Day of the LORD

16 Therefore the LORD God of hosts, the
Lord, says this:

"*There shall be* wailing in all streets,
And they shall say in all the
highways,
'Alas! Alas!'
They shall call the farmer to
mourning,

9 [1]Or *flashes forth destruction*
10 [m]Is. 29:21; 66:5; Amos 5:15 [n]1 Kin. 22:8; Is. 59:15; Jer. 17:16-18
11 [o]Amos 2:6 [p]Deut. 28:30, 38, 39; Mic. 6:15; Zeph. 1:13; Hag. 1:6 [2]*trample* [3]Or *tribute* [4]*desirable*
12 [q]Hos. 5:3 [r]Is. 1:23; 5:23; Amos 2:6 [s]Is. 29:21
13 [t]Amos 6:10
14 [u]Mic. 3:11
15 [v]Ps. 97:10; Rom. 12:9 [w]Joel 2:14
16 [x]2 Chr. 35:25; Jer. 9:17
17 [y]Ex. 12:12
18 [z]Is. 5:19; Jer. 17:15; Joel 1:15; 2:1, 11, 31 [a]Is. 5:30; Joel 2:2
19 [b]Job 20:24; Is. 24:17, 18; Jer. 48:44
21 [c]Is. 1:11-16; Amos 4:4, 5; 8:10 [d]Lev. 26:31; Jer. 14:12; Hos. 5:6
22 [e]Is. 66:3; Mic. 6:6, 7
24 [f]Jer. 22:3; Ezek. 45:9; Hos. 6:6; Mic. 6:8
25 [g]Deut. 32:17; Josh. 24:14; Neh. 9:18-21; Acts 7:42, 43
26 [h]1 Kin. 11:33 [5]LXX, Vg. *tabernacle of Moloch* [6]A pagan deity

[x]And skillful lamenters to wailing.
17 In all vineyards *there shall be*
wailing,
For [y]I will pass through you,"
Says the LORD.

18 [z]Woe to you who desire the day of
the LORD!
For what good *is* [a]the day of the
LORD to you?
It *will be* darkness, and not light.
19 It *will be* [b]as though a man fled
from a lion,
And a bear met him!
Or *as though* he went into the
house,
Leaned his hand on the wall,
And a serpent bit him!
20 *Is* not the day of the LORD
darkness, and not light?
Is it not very dark, with no
brightness in it?

21 "I[c] hate, I despise your feast days,
And [d]I do not savor your sacred
assemblies.
22 [e]Though you offer Me burnt
offerings and your grain
offerings,
I will not accept *them,*
Nor will I regard your fattened
peace offerings.
23 Take away from Me the noise of
your songs,
For I will not hear the melody of
your stringed instruments.
24 [f]But let justice run down like water,
And righteousness like a mighty
stream.

25 "Did[g] you offer Me sacrifices and
offerings
In the wilderness forty years,
O house of Israel?
26 You also carried [5]Sikkuth[6] [h]your
king
And [6]Chiun, your idols,
The star of your gods,
Which you made for yourselves.

5:10-13 The fabric of justice had been destroyed, causing pervasive corruption "in the gates," the place where justice was administered (cf. v. 15; Deut. 21:19; Josh. 20:4).

5:16,17 Looking back at the accusations made earlier, Amos pictured the people mourning as the Lord passed through their midst, executing His sentence of judgment (cf. Ex. 11:3ff.).

5:18-20 Even the wicked wanted the Day of the Lord to come, mistakenly thinking that it would bring victory instead of judgment (cf. Zeph. 1:14-18).

5:21-24 When performed with a corrupt heart, even the "savored" festivals and offerings were despised by the Lord (cf. Lev. 26:27,31; Ps. 51:16,17,19).

5:25,26 In addition to worshiping the Lord in the wilderness, Israel also worshiped other gods, carrying along "Sikkuth (or "tabernacle") your king (or "Molech") and Chiun, your idols." Molech worship included the astrological worship of Saturn and the host of heaven and the actual sacrificing of children (2 Kin. 17:16,17). Warned against Molech worship (Deut. 18:9-13), Israel nevertheless pursued all facets of it, continuing with Solomon (1 Kin. 11:7) and his descendants (1 Kin. 12:28; 2 Kin. 17:16,17; Jer. 32:35) until Josiah (2 Kin. 23:10). Stephen recited Amos 5:25-27 when he recounted the sins of Israel in Acts 7:42,43.

27 Therefore I will send you into
captivity [i]beyond Damascus,"
Says the LORD, [j]whose name *is* the
God of hosts.

Warnings to Zion and Samaria

6 Woe [a]to you *who are* at [b]ease in
Zion,
And [c]trust in Mount Samaria,
Notable persons in the [d]chief
nation,
To whom the house of Israel
comes!
2 [e]Go over to [f]Calneh and see;
And from there go to [g]Hamath the
great;
Then go down to Gath of the
Philistines.
[h]*Are you* better than these
kingdoms?
Or is their territory greater than
your territory?

3 *Woe to* you who [i]put far off the day
of [j]doom,
[k]Who cause [l]the seat of violence to
come near;
4 Who lie on beds of ivory,
Stretch out on your couches,
Eat lambs from the flock
And calves from the midst of the
stall;
5 [m]Who sing idly to the sound of
stringed instruments,
And invent for yourselves [n]musical
instruments [o]like David;
6 Who [p]drink wine from bowls,
And anoint yourselves with the
best ointments,
[q]But are not grieved for the
affliction of Joseph.
7 Therefore they shall now go
[r]captive as the first of the
captives,
And those who recline at banquets
shall be removed.

27 [i] 2 Kin. 17:6; Amos 7:11, 17; Mic. 4:10 [j] Amos 4:13

CHAPTER 6

1 [a] Luke 6:24 [b] Ps. 123:4; Is. 32:9-11; Zeph. 1:12 [c] Is. 31:1; Jer. 49:4 [d] Ex. 19:5; Amos 3:2
2 [e] Jer. 2:10 [f] Gen. 10:10; Is. 10:9 [g] 1 Kin. 8:65; 2 Kin. 18:34 [h] Nah. 3:8
3 [i] Is. 56:12; Ezek. 12:27; Amos 9:10; Matt. 24:37-39 [j] Amos 5:18 [k] Amos 5:12 [l] Ps. 94:20
5 [m] Is. 5:12; Amos 5:23 [n] 1 Chr. 15:16; 16:42 [o] 1 Chr. 23:5
6 [p] Amos 2:8; 4:1 [q] Gen. 37:25
7 [r] Amos 5:27
8 [s] Gen. 22:16; Jer. 51:14; Amos 4:2; 8:7; Heb. 6:13-17 [t] Ps. 47:4; Ezek. 24:21; Amos 8:7
10 [u] Amos 5:13 [v] Amos 8:3 [1] Lit. *his loved one* or *uncle* [2] Lit. *bones*
11 [w] Is. 55:11 [x] 2 Kin. 25:9; Amos 3:15
12 [y] 1 Kin. 21:7-13; Is. 59:13, 14; Hos. 10:4; Amos 5:7, 11, 12
13 [3] Lit. *Nothing* [4] Lit. *Horns,* a symbol of strength
14 [z] Jer. 5:15 [a] Num. 34:7, 8; 1 Kin. 8:65; 2 Kin. 14:25

8 [s]The Lord GOD has sworn by
Himself,
The LORD God of hosts says:
"I abhor [t]the pride of Jacob,
And hate his palaces;
Therefore I will deliver up *the* city
And all that is in it."

9 Then it shall come to pass, that if ten
men remain in one house, they shall die.
10 And when [1]a relative *of the dead,* with
one who will burn *the bodies,* picks up the
[2]bodies to take them out of the house, he
will say to one inside the house, *"Are there*
any more with you?"
Then someone will say, "None."
And he will say, [u]"Hold your tongue!
[v]For we dare not mention the name of the
LORD."

11 For behold, [w]the LORD gives a
command:
[x]He will break the great house into
bits,
And the little house into pieces.

12 Do horses run on rocks?
Does *one* plow *there* with oxen?
Yet [y]you have turned justice into
gall,
And the fruit of righteousness into
wormwood,
13 You who rejoice over [3]Lo Debar,
Who say, "Have we not taken
[4]Karnaim for ourselves
By our own strength?"

14 "But, behold, [z]I will raise up a
nation against you,
O house of Israel,"
Says the LORD God of hosts;
"And they will afflict you from the
[a]entrance of Hamath
To the Valley of the Arabah."

5:27 Assyria conquered Damascus in 732 B.C., then overtook Israel in 722 B.C.

6:1,2 The two capitals of Judah and Israel, Zion and Samaria, were invited to look around. If Calneh (possibly the Calno of Is. 10:9) and Hamath (Syria) and Gath (Philistia) could not put off judgment, how could they?

6:6 drink wine from bowls. These large bowls, usually used for sacrificial purposes, here typify the excesses of their lifestyle.

6:8 sworn by Himself. Cf. Gen. 22:16; Heb. 6:13,14.

6:9,10 The judgment was so comprehensive that even small remnants were sought out and killed.

6:10 one who will burn. This could refer to cremation, demanded by the excessive number killed and because of fear of epidemics. With rare exceptions (cf. 1 Sam. 31:12), corpses were buried in ancient Israel. **dare not mention...the LORD.** Previously welcomed as a friend, the Lord came in judgment as a foe; survivors would not want to invoke His name out of fear.

6:12 Israel's exercise of justice was as absurd as running horses on rocks or plowing rocks with oxen.

6:13 Lo Debar...Karnaim. These were, apparently, two Syrian sites captured by Jeroboam II (cf. 2 Kin. 14:25). "Lo Debar" means "nothing" and sarcastically points out that Israel's "great" gain will amount to nothing. "Karnaim" means "horns" which symbolizes the strength of an animal. Israel foolishly believed they had conquered in their own strength.

6:14 a nation. Assyria in 722 B.C. **Hamath to the Valley of the Arabah.** These represent the northern and southern perimeters of the kingdom as reestablished by Jeroboam II (cf. 2 Kin. 14:25).

Vision of the Locusts

7 Thus the Lord GOD showed me: Behold, He formed locust swarms at the [1]beginning of the late crop; indeed *it was* the late crop after the king's mowings.
2 And so it was, when they had finished eating the grass of the land, that I said:

"O Lord GOD, forgive, I pray!
[a]Oh,[2] that Jacob may stand,
For he *is* small!"
3 *So* [b]the LORD relented concerning this.
"It shall not be," said the LORD.

Vision of the Fire

4 Thus the Lord GOD showed me: Behold, the Lord GOD called [3]for conflict by fire, and it consumed the great deep and devoured the [4]territory. **5** Then I said:

"O Lord GOD, cease, I pray!
[c]Oh, that Jacob may stand,
For he *is* small!"
6 *So* the LORD relented concerning this.
"This also shall not be," said the Lord GOD.

Vision of the Plumb Line

7 Thus He showed me: Behold, the Lord stood on a wall *made* with a plumb line, with a plumb line in His hand. **8** And the LORD said to me, "Amos, what do you see?"

And I said, "A plumb line."
Then the Lord said:

"Behold, [d]I am setting a plumb line
In the midst of My people Israel;
[e]I will not pass by them anymore.
9 [f]The [5]high places of Isaac shall be desolate,
And the [6]sanctuaries of Israel shall be laid waste.
[g]I will rise with the sword against the house of Jeroboam."

Amaziah's Complaint

10 Then Amaziah the [h]priest of [i]Bethel sent to [j]Jeroboam king of Israel, saying, "Amos has conspired against you in the midst of the house of Israel. The land is not able to [7]bear all his words. **11** For thus Amos has said:

'Jeroboam shall die by the sword,
And Israel shall surely be led away [k]captive
From their own land.' "

12 Then Amaziah said to Amos:

"Go, you seer!
Flee to the land of Judah.
There eat bread,
And there prophesy.
13 But [l]never again prophesy at Bethel,
[m]For it *is* the king's [8]sanctuary,
And it *is* the royal [9]residence."

14 Then Amos answered, and said to Amaziah:

"I *was* no prophet,
Nor *was* I [n]a son of a prophet,
But I *was* a [o]sheepbreeder
And a tender of sycamore fruit.
15 Then the LORD took me [1]as I followed the flock,
And the LORD said to me,
'Go, [p]prophesy to My people Israel.'
16 Now therefore, hear the word of the LORD:
You say, 'Do not prophesy against Israel,

CHAPTER 7
1 [1] Lit. *beginning of the sprouting of*
2 [a] Is. 51:19 [2] Or *How shall Jacob stand*
3 [b] Deut. 32:36; Jer. 26:19; Hos. 11:8; Amos 5:15; Jon. 3:10; [James 5:16]
4 [3] *to contend* [4] Lit. *portion*
5 [c] Amos 7:2, 3
8 [d] 2 Kin. 21:13; Is. 28:17; 34:11; Lam. 2:8 [e] Mic. 7:18
9 [f] Gen. 46:1; Hos. 10:8; Mic. 1:5 [5] Places of pagan worship
[g] 2 Kin. 15:8–10; Amos 7:11 [6] Or *holy places*
10 [h] 1 Kin. 12:31, 32; 13:33 [i] 1 Kin. 13:32; Amos 4:4 [j] 2 Kin. 14:23 [7] Or *endure*
11 [k] Amos 5:27; 6:7
13 [l] Amos 2:12; Acts 4:18 [m] 1 Kin. 12:29, 32; Amos 7:9 [8] Or *holy place* [9] Lit. *house*
14 [n] 1 Kin. 20:35; 2 Kin. 2:5; 2 Chr. 19:2 [o] 2 Kin. 3:4; Amos 1:1; Zech. 13:5
15 [p] Amos 3:8 [1] Lit. *from behind*

7:1–9:10 Amos introduced 5 visions, with an historical interlude (7:10-17). The first two depict the Lord's commitment to spare a remnant, while the last 3 announce the inevitability of judgment.

7:1-3 The first vision, symbolizing God's action, saw a swarm of locusts devouring the people's portion of the later cuttings, after the king had taken the first cutting (cf. Joel 1:2-12).

7:3 The LORD relented. Much like He did at Abraham's pleading over Sodom in Gen. 18:22,23.

7:4-6 Under the figure of fire, the second vision concerns a devastating drought, causing the underground water supplies to dry up and the fields to be consumed (cf. Deut. 32:22). Amos again pleaded Israel's cause (cf. vv. 2,3).

7:7-9 The true spiritual nature of Israel was here tested (and found wanting) by God's plumb line of righteousness in this third of 5 visions. The sword of judgment was to come from Assyria.

7:10-17 The words of Amos cut deep into the heart of Israel's leadership, causing them to accuse him of conspiracy against the king (cf. Jer. 26:11; 37:11-13; 38:1-6).

7:11 Amos has said. This most likely refers to v. 9.

Five Visions of Amos
1. Vision of Locusts (7:1-3)
2. Vision of Fire (7:4-6)
3. Vision of the Plumb Line (7:7-9)
4. Vision of the Summer Fruit (8:1-14)
5. Vision of the Lord (9:1-10)

And [q]do not [2]spout against the
house of Isaac.'
17 "Therefore [r]thus says the LORD:

[s]'Your wife shall be a harlot in the
city;
Your sons and daughters shall fall
by the sword;
Your land shall be divided by
survey line;
You shall die in a [t]defiled land;
And Israel shall surely be led away
captive
From his own land.' "

Vision of the Summer Fruit

8 Thus the Lord GOD showed me: Behold, a basket of summer fruit. 2 And
He said, "Amos, what do you see?"
So I said, "A basket of summer fruit."
Then the LORD said to me:

[a]"The end has come upon My people
Israel;
[b]I will not pass by them anymore.
3 And [c]the songs of the temple
Shall be wailing in that day,"
Says the Lord GOD—
"Many dead bodies everywhere,
[d]They shall be thrown out in
silence."

4 Hear this, you who [1]swallow up
the needy,
And make the poor of the land fail,

5 Saying:

"When will the New Moon be past,
That we may sell grain?
And [e]the Sabbath,
That we may [2]trade wheat?
[f]Making the ephah small and the
shekel large,
Falsifying the scales by [g]deceit,
6 That we may buy the poor for
[h]silver,
And the needy for a pair of
sandals—
Even sell the bad wheat?"

7 The LORD has sworn by [i]the pride
of Jacob:
"Surely [j]I will never forget any of
their works.
8 [k]Shall the land not tremble for this,
And everyone mourn who dwells
in it?
All of it shall swell like [3]the River,
Heave and subside
[l]Like the River of Egypt.

9 "And it shall come to pass in that
day," says the Lord GOD,
[m]"That I will make the sun go down
at noon,
And I will darken the earth in
[4]broad daylight;
10 I will turn your feasts into
[n]mourning,
[o]And all your songs into
lamentation;
[p]I will bring sackcloth on every
waist,
And baldness on every head;
I will make it like mourning for an
only *son*,
And its end like a bitter day.

11 "Behold, the days are coming," says
the Lord GOD,
"That I will send a famine on the
land,
Not a famine of bread,
Nor a thirst for water,
But [q]of hearing the words of the
LORD.
12 They shall wander from sea to sea,
And from north to east;
They shall run to and fro, seeking
the word of the LORD,
But shall [r]not find *it*.

13 "In that day the fair virgins
And strong young men

16 [q]Deut. 32:2; Ezek. 21:2; Mic. 2:6 [2]Lit. *drip*
17 [r]Jer. 28:12; 29:21, 32 [s]Is. 13:16; Lam. 5:11; Hos. 4:13; Zech. 14:2 [t]2 Kin. 17:6; Ezek. 4:13; Hos. 9:3

CHAPTER 8

2 [a]Ezek. 7:2 [b]Amos 7:8
3 [c]Amos 5:23 [d]Amos 6:9, 10
4 [1]Or *trample on*, Amos 2:7
5 [e]Ex. 31:13-17; Neh. 13:15 [f]Mic. 6:10, 11 [g]Lev. 19:35, 36; Deut. 25:13-15 [2]Lit. *open*
6 [h]Amos 2:6
7 [i]Deut. 33:26, 29; Ps. 68:34; Amos 6:8 [j]Ps. 10:11; Hos. 7:2; 8:13
8 [k]Hos. 4:3 [l]Jer. 46:7, 8; Amos 9:5 [3]The Nile; some Heb. mss., LXX, Tg., Syr., Vg. *River* (cf. 9:5); MT *the light*
9 [m]Job 5:14; Is. 13:10; 59:9, 10; Jer. 15:9; [Mic. 3:6]; Matt. 27:45; Mark 15:32; Luke 23:44 [4]Lit. *a day of light*
10 [n]Lam. 5:15; Ezek. 7:18 [o]Is. 15:2, 3; Jer. 48:37; Ezek. 27:31 [p]Jer. 6:26; [Zech. 12:10]
11 [q]1 Sam. 3:1; 2 Chr. 15:3; Ps. 74:9; Ezek. 7:26; Mic. 3:6
12 [r]Hos. 5:6

7:17 led away captive. To Assyria ca. 722 B.C.

8:1 summer fruit. In this fourth vision, as fruit was fully ripened by the summer's sun, so Israel was ripe for judgment

8:5 New Moon. Based on a lunar calendar, Israel would celebrate the day with a festival. Like the Sabbath, no work was to be done (1 Sam. 20:5,6; 2 Kin. 4:23; Ezek. 46:3). The merchants' eagerness for the day to end revealed their appetite for greed. **ephah small...shekel large.** By dishonest weighing, the merchant decreased the actual amount received and increased the cost of the merchandise. *See note on Prov. 11:1* for other passages on dishonest measures.

8:6 bad wheat. This denotes the chaff, which was mixed into the good wheat to cheat the buyer.

8:7 pride of Jacob. As surely as the nation was filled with pride, so the Lord would not forget her works (cf. 6:8).

8:8 Heave and subside like the River of Egypt. Like the Nile, which annually provided water and rich soil deposits for farmers by greatly overflowing its banks, so judgment would overflow the land.

8:9 the sun go down at noon. Probably referring to the total eclipse of the sun ca. 763 B.C. as a picture of God's coming judgment.

8:10 sackcloth. *See note on Joel 1:8.*

8:11,12 During prosperity, the nation rejected the prophets (cf. 7:10-17); in captivity no word from the Lord could be found (cf. 1 Sam. 28:6ff.).

Shall faint from thirst.

14 Those who [s]swear by [t]the [5]sin of Samaria,
Who say,
'As your god lives, O Dan!'
And, 'As the way of [u]Beersheba lives!'
They shall fall and never rise again."

The Destruction of Israel

9 I saw the Lord standing by the altar, and He said:

"Strike the [1]doorposts, that the thresholds may shake,
And [a]break them on the heads of them all.
I will slay the last of them with the sword.
[b]He who flees from them shall not get away,
And he who escapes from them shall not be delivered.

2 "Though[c] they dig into [2]hell,
From there My hand shall take them;
[d]Though they climb up to heaven,
From there I will bring them down;
3 And though they [e]hide themselves on top of Carmel,
From there I will search and take them;
Though they hide from My sight at the bottom of the sea,
From there I will command the serpent, and it shall bite them;
4 Though they go into captivity before their enemies,
From there [f]I will command the sword,
And it shall slay them.
[g]I will set My eyes on them for harm and not for good."

5 The Lord GOD of hosts,
He who touches the earth and it [h]melts,
[i]And all who dwell there mourn;
All of it shall swell like [3]the River,
And subside like the River of Egypt.
6 He who builds His [j]layers[4] in the sky,
And has founded His strata in the earth;
Who [k]calls for the waters of the sea,
And pours them out on the face of the earth—
[l]The LORD *is* His name.

7 "*Are* you not like the [5]people of Ethiopia to Me,
O children of Israel?" says the LORD.
"Did I not bring up Israel from the land of Egypt,
The [m]Philistines from [n]Caphtor,[6]
And the Syrians from [o]Kir?

8 "Behold, [p]the eyes of the Lord GOD *are* on the sinful kingdom,
And I [q]will destroy it from the face of the earth;
Yet I will not utterly destroy the house of Jacob,"
Says the LORD.

9 "For surely I will command,
And will [7]sift the house of Israel among all nations,
As *grain* is sifted in a sieve;
[r]Yet not the smallest [8]grain shall fall to the ground.
10 All the sinners of My people shall die by the sword,
[s]Who say, 'The calamity shall not overtake nor confront us.'

Israel Will Be Restored

11 "On[t] that day I will raise up
The [9]tabernacle of David, which has fallen down,

14 [s]Hos. 4:15 [t]Deut. 9:21 [u]Amos 5:5 [5]Or *Ashima*, a Syrian goddess

CHAPTER 9

1 [a]Ps. 68:21; Hab. 3:13 [b]Amos 2:14 [1]Capitals of the pillars
2 [c]Ps. 139:8; Jer. 23:24 [d]Job 20:6; Jer. 51:53; Obad. 4; Matt. 11:23 [2]Or *Sheol*
3 [e]Jer. 23:24
4 [f]Lev. 26:33 [g]Lev. 17:10; Jer. 21:10; 39:16; 44:11
5 [h]Ps. 104:32; 144:5; Is. 64:1; Mic. 1:4 [i]Amos 8:8 [3]The Nile
6 [j]Ps. 104:3, 13 [k]Amos 5:8 [l]Amos 4:13; 5:27 [4]Or *stairs*
7 [m]Jer. 47:4 [n]Deut. 2:23 [o]Amos 1:5 [5]Lit. *sons of the Ethiopians* [6]Crete
8 [p]Jer. 44:27; Amos 9:4 [q]Jer. 5:10; 30:11; [Joel 2:32]; Amos 3:12; [Obad. 16, 17]
9 [r][Is. 65:8-16] [7]*shake* [8]Lit. *pebble*
10 [s][Is. 28:15]; Jer. 5:12; Amos 6:3
11 [t]Acts 15:16-18 [9]Lit. *booth;* a figure of a deposed dynasty

8:14 Samaria...Dan. Jeroboam I built altars at both locations in an effort to keep Israel from going to Jerusalem to worship (1 Kin. 12:26-29). **Beersheba.** *See note on 5:5.*

9:1 The fifth vision opens with the Lord standing beside the altar in Bethel, commanding that the temple be torn down, thus falling upon the worshipers. He would spare none.

9:2-4 Desperate to escape, none will successfully hide from the hand of judgment. Righteous David found solace in the omnipresence of God (Ps. 139:7-10; cf. Jer. 23:23,24); the wicked find only His wrath (cf. Rev. 20:13).

9:3 Carmel. A mountainous region, rising 1800 feet above the Mediterranean, known for its many caves and forests. *See note on 1:2.*

9:5-9 Lest any one question the Lord's power, they are reminded of His omnipotence revealed in creation and in His sovereign rulership of the nations. Other nations have been transplanted from their homelands; why not Israel?

9:5 the River. *See note on 8:8.*

9:7 Kir. *See note on 1:5.*

9:9 sift...among all nations. Only the chaff was to be punished; His remnant was to be preserved to inherit the blessings spoken of in the following verses.

9:11-15 Millennial blessings await the final faithful remnant, when Messiah personally reigns over all nations in Jerusalem upon the throne of David, and the Jews are never again pulled up from their divinely inherited land (9:15).

9:11 tabernacle of David. A reference to the dynasty of David

And [1]repair its damages;
I will raise up its ruins,
And rebuild it as in the days of
old;
12 [u]That they may possess the remnant
of [v]Edom,[2]
And all the Gentiles who are called
by My name,"
Says the LORD who does this thing.

13 "Behold, [w]the days are coming,"
says the LORD,
"When the plowman shall overtake
the reaper,
And the treader of grapes him who
sows seed;
[x]The mountains shall drip with
sweet wine,
And all the hills shall flow *with it.*
14 [y]I will bring back the captives of My
people Israel;
[z]They shall build the waste cities
and inhabit *them;*
They shall plant vineyards and
drink wine from them;
They shall also make gardens and
eat fruit from them.
15 I will plant them in their land,
[a]And no longer shall they be pulled
up
From the land I have given them,"
Says the LORD your God.

11 [1] Lit. *wall up its breaches*
12 [u] Obad. 19 [v] Num. 24:18; Is. 11:14 [2] LXX *mankind*
13 [w] Lev. 26:5 [x] Joel 3:18
14 [y] Ps. 53:6; Is. 60:4; Jer. 30:3, 18 [z] Is. 61:4
15 [a] Is. 60:21; Ezek. 34:28; 37:25

(cf. Introduction: Interpretive Challenges). God will "raise up" and "rebuild" this tabernacle on earth for Christ to rule in His millennial kingdom (cf. Zech. 14:9-11). The apostles used this passage to illustrate that Gentiles could thus be a part of God's redemption. *See notes on Acts 15:13-18.*

9:13,14 Prosperity, in hyperbolic fashion, is here described (cf. Lev. 26:5; Joel 3:18; contra. Is. 5). Fruitfulness is so enormous that planting and reaping seasons overlap. This prosperity will encourage massive repatriation (cf. Is. 11:15,16) and reconstruction (cf. Zech. 2:1-5).

9:15 no longer shall they be pulled up from the land. The ultimate fulfillment of God's land promise to Abraham (cf. Gen. 12:7; 15:7; 17:8) will occur during Christ's millennial reign on earth (cf. Joel 2:26,27).

The Ultimate Restoration of Israel

1. Is. 27; 42–44; 65; 66	8. Obad. 17,21
2. Jer. 30–33	9. Micah 7:14-20
3. Ezek. 36; 37; 40–48	10. Zeph. 3:14-20
4. Dan. 9:20-27; 12:1-3	11. Hag. 2:20-23
5. Hosea 2:14-23; 14:4-7	12. Zech. 13;14
6. Joel 3:18-21	13. Mal. 4:1-3
7. Amos 9:11-15	

The Book of
OBADIAH

Title

The book is named after the prophet who received the vision (1:1). Obadiah means "servant of the LORD" and occurs 20 times in the OT, referring to at least 20 other OT individuals. Obadiah is the shortest book in the OT and is not quoted in the NT.

Author and Date

Nothing is known for certain about the author. Other OT references to men of this name do not appear to be referring to this prophet. His frequent mentions of Jerusalem, Judah, and Zion suggest that he belonged to the southern kingdom (cf. vv. 10-12,17,21). Obadiah was probably a contemporary of Elijah and Elisha.

The date of writing is equally difficult to determine, though we know it is tied to the Edomite assault on Jerusalem described in vv. 10-14. Obadiah apparently wrote shortly after the attack. There were 4 significant invasions of Jerusalem in OT history: 1) by Shishak, king of Egypt, ca. 925 B.C. during the reign of Rehoboam (1 Kin. 14:25,26; 2 Chr. 12); 2) by the Philistines and Arabians between 848–841 B.C. during the reign of Jehoram of Judah (2 Chr. 21:8-20); 3) by Jehoash, king of Israel, ca. 790 B.C. (2 Kin. 14; 2 Chr. 25); and 4) by Nebuchadnezzar, king of Babylon, in the fall of Jerusalem in 586 B.C. Of these 4, only the second and the fourth are possible fits with historical data. Number two is preferable, since Obadiah's description does not indicate the total destruction of the city, which took place under Nebuchadnezzar's attack. Also, although the Edomites were involved in Nebuchadnezzar's destruction of Jerusalem (Ps. 137; Lam. 4:21), it is significant that Obadiah does not mention the Babylonians by name (as with all the other prophets who wrote about Jerusalem's fall), nor is there any reference to the destruction of the temple or the deportation of the people; in fact, the captives appear to have been taken to the SW, not E to Babylon (cf. v. 20).

Background and Setting

The Edomites trace their origin to Esau, the firstborn (twin) son of Isaac and Rebekah (Gen. 25:24-26), who struggled with Jacob even while in the womb (Gen. 25:22). Esau's name means "hairy," because "he was like a hairy garment all over" (Gen. 25:25). He is also called Edom, meaning "red," owing to the sale of his birthright in exchange for some "red stew" (Gen. 25:30). He showed a disregard for the covenant promises by marrying two Canaanite women (Gen. 26:34) and later the daughter of Ishmael (Gen. 28:9). He loved the out-of-doors and, after having his father's blessing stolen from him by Jacob, was destined to remain a man of the open spaces (Gen. 25:27; 27:38-40). Esau settled in a region of mostly rugged mountains S of the Dead Sea (Gen. 33:16; 36:8,9; Deut. 2:4,5) called Edom (Gr., "Idumea"), the 40 mi. wide area which stretches approximately 100 mi. S to the Gulf of Aqabah. The fabled King's Highway, an essential caravan route linking North Africa with Europe and Asia, passes along the eastern plateau (Num. 20:17). The struggle and birth of Jacob and Esau (Gen. 25) form the ultimate background to the prophecy of Gen. 25:23, "two nations are in your womb." Their respective descendants, Israel and Edom, were perpetual enemies. When Israel came out from Egypt, Edom denied their brother Jacob passage through their land, located S of the Dead Sea (Num. 20:14-21). Nevertheless, Israel was instructed by God to be kind to Edom (Deut. 23:7,8). Obadiah, having received a vision from God, was sent to describe their crimes and to pronounce total destruction upon Edom because of their treatment of Israel.

The Edomites opposed Saul (ca. 1043–1011 B.C.) and were subdued under David (ca. 1011–971 B.C.) and Solomon (ca. 971–931 B.C.). They fought against Jehoshaphat (ca. 873–848 B.C.) and successfully rebelled against Jehoram (ca. 853–841 B.C.). They were again conquered by Judah under Amaziah (ca. 796–767 B.C.), but they regained their freedom during the reign of Ahaz (ca. 735–715 B.C.). Edom was later controlled by Assyria and Babylon; and in the fifth century B.C. the Edomites were forced by the Nabateans to leave their territory. They moved to the area of southern Palestine and became known as Idumeans. Herod the Great, an Idumean, became king of Judea under Rome in 37 B.C. In a sense, the enmity between Esau and Jacob was continued in Herod's attempt to murder Jesus. The Idumeans participated in the rebellion of Jerusalem against Rome and were defeated along with the Jews by Titus in

A.D. 70. Ironically, the Edomites applauded the destruction of Jerusalem in 586 B.C. (cf. Ps. 137:7) but died trying to defend it in A.D. 70. After that time they were never heard of again. As Obadiah predicted, they would be "cut off forever" (v. 10); "and no survivor shall *remain* of the house of Esau" (v. 18).

Historical and Theological Themes

The book is a case study of Gen. 12:1-3, with two interrelated themes: 1) the judgment of Edom by God for cursing Israel. This was apparently told to Judah, thereby providing reassurance to Judah that the Day of the Lord (v. 15) would bring judgment upon Edom for her pride and for her participation in Judah's downfall; 2) Judah's restoration. This would even include the territory of the Edomites (vv. 19-21; Is. 11:14). Obadiah's blessing includes the near fulfillment of Edom's demise (vv. 1-15) under the assault of the Philistines and Arabians (2 Chr. 21:8-20) and the far fulfillment of the nation's judgment in the first century A.D. and Israel's final possession of Edom (vv. 15-21).

Interpretive Challenges

The striking similarity between Obad. 1-9 and Jer. 49:7-22 brings up the question: Who borrowed from whom? Assuming there was not a third common source, it appears that Jeremiah borrowed, where appropriate, from Obadiah, since the shared verses form one unit in Obadiah, while in Jeremiah they are scattered among other verses.

Outline

I. God's Judgment on Edom (1-14)
   A. Edom's Punishment (1-9)
   B. Edom's Crimes (10-14)
II. God's Judgment on the Nations (15,16)
III. God's Restoration of Israel (17-21)

The Coming Judgment on Edom

1 The vision of Obadiah.

Thus says the Lord GOD
[a]concerning Edom
[b](We have heard a report from the LORD,
And a messenger has been sent among the nations, *saying,*
"Arise, and let us rise up against her for battle"):

2 "Behold, I will make you small among the nations;
You shall be greatly despised.
3 The [c]pride of your heart has deceived you,
You who dwell in the clefts of the rock,
Whose habitation is high;
[d]*You* who say in your heart, 'Who will bring me down to the ground?'
4 [e]Though you ascend *as* high as the eagle,
And though you [f]set your nest among the stars,
From there I will bring you down," says the LORD.

5 "If [g]thieves had come to you,
If robbers by night—
Oh, how you will be cut off!—
Would they not have stolen till they had enough?
If grape-gatherers had come to you,
[h]Would they not have left *some* gleanings?

1 [a]Is. 21:11; Ezek. 25:12; Joel 3:19; Mal. 1:3 [b]Jer. 49:14-16; Obad. 1-4
3 [c]Is. 16:6; Jer. 49:16 [d]Is. 14:13-15; Rev. 18:7
4 [e]Job 20:6 [f]Hab. 2:9; Mal. 1:4
5 [g]Jer. 49:9 [h]Deut. 24:21
7 [i]Jer. 38:22 [j]Is. 19:11; Jer. 49:7 [1]Or *wound or plot* [2]Or *There is no understanding in him*
8 [k][Job 5:12-14]; Is. 29:14
9 [l]Ps. 76:5 [m]Gen. 36:11; 1 Chr. 1:45; Job 2:11; Jer. 49:7
10 [n]Gen. 27:41; Ezek. 25:12; Amos 1:11 [o]Ezek. 35:9; Joel 3:19
11 [p]Ps. 83:5-8; Amos 1:6, 9 [q]Joel 3:3; Nah. 3:10
12 [r]Mic. 4:11; 7:10 [3]Gloated over [4]Lit. *On the day he became a foreigner*

6 "Oh, how Esau shall be searched out!
How his hidden treasures shall be sought after!
7 All the men in your confederacy
Shall force you to the border;
[i]The men at peace with you
Shall deceive you *and* prevail against you.
Those who eat your bread shall lay a [1]trap for you.
[j]No[2] one is aware of it.

8 "Will[k] I not in that day," says the LORD,
"Even destroy the wise *men* from Edom,
And understanding from the mountains of Esau?
9 Then your [l]mighty men,
O [m]Teman, shall be dismayed,
To the end that everyone from the mountains of Esau
May be cut off by slaughter.

Edom Mistreated His Brother

10 "For [n]violence against your brother Jacob,
Shame shall cover you,
And [o]you shall be cut off forever.
11 In the day that you [p]stood on the other side—
In the day that strangers carried captive his forces,
When foreigners entered his gates
And [q]cast lots for Jerusalem—
Even you *were* as one of them.

12 "But you should not have [r]gazed[3] on the day of your brother
[4]In the day of his captivity;

1 The vision. The prophetic word often came from God in the form of a vision (cf. Hab. 1:1). **Thus says the Lord GOD.** Although the background of the prophet is obscure, the source of his message is not. It was supernaturally given by God, and was not motivated by unholy vengeance. **Edom.** Descendants of Esau (Gen. 25:30; 36:1ff.), the Edomites settled in the region S of the Dead Sea. See Introduction: Background and Setting. **Arise...rise up against her.** The prophet heard of an international plot to overthrow Edom. The selfish motives of Edom's enemies were divinely controlled by the Lord's "messengers" to serve His sovereign purposes (cf. Ps. 104:4).

3,4 Who will bring me down...I will bring you down. Edom's pride was answered decisively by the Sovereign Ruler (cf. Matt. 23:12). The calamity against Edom, though brought about by her enemies, was truly God's judgment of her pride (cf. Prov. 16:18; 1 Cor. 10:12).

3 the clefts of the rock. Dwelling in difficult mountain terrain, Edom's imposing, impregnable capital city of Petra was virtually inaccessible, giving her a sense of security and self-sufficiency. Deep, terrifying gorges emanating from peaks reaching 5,700 ft. surrounded her like a fortress, generating a proud, false sense of security.

5 robbers by night. Because of the rugged terrain and very narrow access through the gorges, predatory attack could only come at night.

5,6 Edom's attackers, by divine judgment, would not stop where normal thieves would when they have enough. Instead, they would leave nothing.

7 Those conspiring against Edom (v. 1) were her allies ("men in your confederacy"), her neighbors ("men at peace with you"), and even the outlying tribes who benefited from Edom's prosperity ("those who eat your bread").

8 wise *men*. Edom was known for her wise men and sages (Jer. 49:7). Her location on the King's Highway provided her with intellectual stimulation with India, Europe, and North Africa.

9 Teman. A name derived from a descendant of Esau (Gen. 36:11), it refers to a region in the northern part of Edom which was the home of Job's friend, Eliphaz (Job 4:1).

10 violence against...Jacob. Edom's opposition is in view, which began as Israel approached the land (cf. Num. 20:14-21) and continued to Habakkuk's day. "Slaughter" (v. 9) and shame for Edom will be just retribution for Edom's violence and slaughter against her brother's people.

11-14 The charge of v. 10 is here amplified: 1) they "stood," withholding assistance (v. 11); 2) they "rejoiced" over Judah's downfall (v. 12; cf. Pss. 83:4-6; 137:4-6); 3) they plundered the city (v. 13); and 4) they prevented the escape of her fugitives (v. 14).

Nor should you have [s]rejoiced
over the children of Judah
In the day of their destruction;
Nor should you have spoken
proudly
In the day of distress.
13 You should not have entered the
gate of My people
In the day of their calamity.
Indeed, you should not have
[5]gazed on their affliction
In the day of their calamity,
Nor laid *hands* on their substance
In the day of their calamity.
14 You should not have stood at the
crossroads
To cut off those among them who
escaped;
Nor should you have [6]delivered
up those among them who
remained
In the day of distress.

15 "For[t] the day of the LORD upon all
the nations *is* near;
[u]As you have done, it shall be done
to you;
Your [7]reprisal shall return upon
your own head.
16 [v]For as you drank on My holy
mountain,
So shall all the nations drink
continually;
Yes, they shall drink, and swallow,
And they shall be as though they
had never been.

12 [s][Prov. 17:5]; Ezek. 35:15; 36:5
13 [5]Gloated over
14 [6]Handed over to the enemy
15 [t]Ezek. 30:3; [Joel 1:15; 2:1, 11, 31; Amos 5:18, 20] [u]Jer. 50:29; 51:56; Hab. 2:8 [7]Or *reward*
16 [v]Joel 3:17

Israel's Final Triumph

17 "But on Mount Zion there [w]shall be
[8]deliverance,
And there shall be holiness;
The house of Jacob shall possess
their possessions.
18 The house of Jacob shall be a fire,
And the house of Joseph [x]a flame;
But the house of Esau *shall be*
stubble;
They shall kindle them and devour
them,
And no survivor shall *remain* of the
house of Esau,"
For the LORD has spoken.

19 The [9]South [y]shall possess the
mountains of Esau,
[z]And the Lowland shall possess
Philistia.
They shall possess the fields of
Ephraim
And the fields of Samaria.
Benjamin *shall possess* Gilead.
20 And the captives of this host of the
children of Israel
Shall possess the land of the
Canaanites
As [a]far as Zarephath.
The captives of Jerusalem who are
in Sepharad
[b]Shall possess the cities of the [1]South.
21 Then [c]saviors[2] shall come to
Mount Zion
To judge the mountains of Esau,
And the [d]kingdom shall be the
LORD's.

17 [w]Is. 14:1, 2; Joel 2:32; Amos 9:8 [8]Or *salvation*
18 [x]Is. 5:24; 9:18, 19; Zech. 12:6
19 [y]Is. 11:14; Amos 9:12 [z]Zeph. 2:7 [9]Heb. *Negev*
20 [a]1 Kin. 17:9; Luke 4:26 [b]Jer. 32:44 [1]Heb. *Negev*
21 [c][James 5:20] [d]Ps. 22:28; [Dan. 2:44; 7:14; Zech. 14:9; Rev. 11:15] [2]*deliverers*

15 day of the LORD. God's near judgment of Edom in history (vv. 1-14) was a preview of His far judgment on all nations (vv. 15,16) who refuse to bow to His sovereignty (cf. discussion of "Day of the Lord" in Introduction to Joel).

16 My holy mountain. Zion, referring to Jerusalem (cf. v. 17). **drink, and swallow.** Compare Zech. 12:2, where the Lord will make His people as a "cup of drunkenness" from which His enemies will be made to drink. This refers to the cup of God's wrath. Judah drank temporarily of judgment, Edom will drink "continually."

17 A reversal of Judah's plight in vv. 10-14 will come about when Messiah intercedes and establishes His millennial kingdom and "holiness" prevails.

18-20 Those of Judah who remain (v. 14) will be divinely empowered to "devour" (v. 18) and completely wipe out the "house of Esau" (Zech. 12:6; cf. Is. 11:14; 34:5-17). When Messiah sets up His kingdom, the boundaries of the Davidic and Solomonic kingdoms will once again expand to include that promised to Jacob in his dream at Bethel (Gen. 28:14) which reaffirmed God's promise to Abraham (cf. Gen. 12). This could include the S (mountains of Esau); the W (Philistia); the N (Ephraim…Samaria); and the E (Gilead).

18 house of Jacob…house of Joseph. Representatives of Abraham's seed.

20 Canaanites. Those peoples who occupied the land before the Exodus. **Zarephath.** Also known as Sarepta (cf. Luke 4:26), this town was located on the Phoenician coast between Tyre and Sidon. **Sepharad.** Not mentioned elsewhere in Bible, the location is uncertain. Most rabbis identify it with Spain; others have suggested Sparta or Sardis.

21 saviors shall come…to judge. Just as the Lord raised up judges to deliver His people (cf. Neh. 9:27), so will He establish similar leaders to help rule in the millennial kingdom (cf. 1 Cor. 6:2; Rev. 20:4). **the kingdom shall be the LORD's.** When the nations are judged in the Day of the Lord, He will then set up His millennial kingdom, a theocracy in which He rules His people directly on earth (Zech. 14:4-9; Rev. 11:15).

God's Judgment on Edom

More than any other nation mentioned in the OT, Edom is the supreme object of God's wrath.

- Pss. 83:5-18; 137:7
- Is. 11:14; 21:11,12; 34:5; 63:1-6
- Jer. 49:7-22
- Lam. 4:21,22
- Ezek. 25:12-14; 35:1-15
- Joel 3:19
- Amos 1:11,12; 9:11,12
- Mal. 1:2-5

The Book of JONAH

Title

Following the lead of the Hebrew Masoretic text (MT), the title of the book is derived from the principal character, Jonah (meaning "dove"), the son of Amittai (1:1). Both the Septuagint (LXX) and the Latin Vulgate (Vg.) ascribe the same name.

Author and Date

The book makes no direct claim regarding authorship. Throughout the book, Jonah is repeatedly referred to in the third person, causing some to search for another author. It was not an uncommon OT practice, however, to write in the third person (e.g., Ex. 11:3; 1 Sam. 12:11). Furthermore, the autobiographical information revealed within its pages clearly points to Jonah as the author. The firsthand accounts of such unusual events and experiences would be best recounted from the hand of Jonah himself. Nor should the introductory verse suggest otherwise, since other prophets such as Hosea, Joel, Micah, Zephaniah, Haggai, and Zechariah have similar openings.

According to 2 Kin. 14:25, Jonah came from Gath-hepher near Nazareth. The context places him during the long and prosperous reign of Jeroboam II (ca. 793–758 B.C.), making him a prophet to the northern tribes just prior to Amos during the first half of the eighth century B.C., ca. 760 B.C. The Pharisees were wrong when they said "no prophet has arisen out of Galilee" (John 7:52), because Jonah was a Galilean. An unverifiable Jewish tradition says Jonah was the son of the widow of Zarephath whom Elijah raised from the dead (1 Kin. 17:8-24).

Background and Setting

As a prophet to the 10 northern tribes of Israel, Jonah shares a background and setting with Amos. The nation enjoyed a time of relative peace and prosperity. Both Syria and Assyria were weak, allowing Jeroboam II to enlarge the northern borders of Israel to where they had been in the days of David and Solomon (2 Kin. 14:23-27). Spiritually, however, it was a time of poverty; religion was ritualistic and increasingly idolatrous, and justice had become perverted. Peacetime and wealth had made her bankrupt spiritually, morally, and ethically (cf. 2 Kin. 14:24; Amos 4:1ff.; 5:10-13). As a result, God was to punish her by bringing destruction and captivity from the Assyrians in 722 B.C. Nineveh's repentance may have been aided by the two plagues (765 and 759 B.C.) and a solar eclipse (763 B.C.), preparing them for Jonah's judgment message.

Historical and Theological Themes

Jonah, though a prophet of Israel, is not remembered for his ministry in Israel which could explain why the Pharisees erringly claimed in Jesus' day that no prophet had come from Galilee (cf. John 7:52). Rather, the book relates the account of his call to preach repentance to Nineveh and his refusal to go. Nineveh, the capital of Assyria and infamous for its cruelty, was an historical nemesis of Israel and Judah. The focus of this book is on that Gentile city, which was founded by Nimrod, great-grandson of Noah (Gen. 10:6-12). Perhaps the largest city in the ancient world (1:2; 3:2,3; 4:11), it was nevertheless destroyed about 150 years after the repentance of the generation in the time of Jonah's visit (612 B.C.), as Nahum prophesied (Nah. 1:1ff.). Israel's political distaste for Assyria, coupled with a sense of spiritual superiority as the recipient of God's covenant blessing, produced a recalcitrant attitude in Jonah toward God's request for missionary service. Jonah was sent to Nineveh in part to shame Israel by the fact that a pagan city repented at the preaching of a stranger, whereas Israel would not repent though preached to by many prophets. He was soon to learn that God's love and mercy extends to all of His creatures (4:2,10,11), not just His covenant people (cf. Gen. 9:27; 12:3; Lev. 19:33,34; 1 Sam. 2:10; Is. 2:2; Joel 2:28-32).

The book of Jonah reveals God's sovereign rule over man and all creation. Creation came into being through Him (1:9) and responds to His every command (1:4,17; 2:10; 4:6,7; cf. Mark 4:41). Jesus employed the repentance of the Ninevites to rebuke the Pharisees, thereby illustrating the hardness of the Pharisees' hearts and their unwillingness to repent (Matt. 12:38-41; Luke 11:29-32). The heathen city of Nineveh repented at the preaching of a reluctant prophet, but the Pharisees would not repent at the preaching of the greatest of all prophets, in spite of overwhelming evidence that He was actually their Lord and Messiah. Jonah is a picture of Israel, who was chosen and commissioned by God to be His witness (Is. 43:10-12; 44:8), who rebelled against His will (Ex. 32:1-4; Judg. 2:11-19; Ezek. 6:1-5; Mark 7:6-9), but who has been miraculously preserved by God through centuries of exile and dispersion to finally preach His truth (Jer. 30:11; 31:35-37; Hos. 3:3-5; Rev. 7:1-8; 14:1-3).

Interpretive Challenges

The primary challenge is whether the book is to be interpreted as historical narrative or as allegory/parable. The grand scale of the miracles, such as being kept alive 3 days and nights in a big fish, has led some skeptics and critics to deny their historical validity and substitute spiritual lessons, either to the constituent parts (allegory) or to the book as a whole (parable). But however grandiose and miraculous the events may have been, the narrative must be viewed as historical. Centered on an historically identifiable OT prophet who lived in the eighth century B.C., the account of whom has been recorded in narrative form, there is no alternative but to understand Jonah as historical. Furthermore, Jesus did not teach the story of Jonah as a parable but as an actual account firmly rooted in history (Matt. 12:38-41; 16:4; Luke 11:29-32).

Outline

- I. Running from God's Will (1:1-17)
  - A. The Commission of Jonah (1:1,2)
  - B. The Flight of Jonah (1:3)
  - C. The Pursuit of Jonah (1:4-16)
  - D. The Preservation of Jonah (1:17)
- II. Submitting to God's Will (2:1-10)
  - A. The Helplessness of Jonah (2:1-3)
  - B. The Prayer of Jonah (2:4-7)
  - C. The Repentance of Jonah (2:8,9)
  - D. The Deliverance of Jonah (2:10)
- III. Fulfilling God's Will (3:1-10)
  - A. The Commission Renewed (3:1,2)
  - B. The Prophet Obeys (3:3,4)
  - C. The City Repents (3:5-9)
  - D. The Lord Relents (3:10)
- IV. Questioning God's Will (4:1-11)
  - A. The Prophet Displeased (4:1-5)
  - B. The Prophet Rebuked (4:6-11)

Jonah's Disobedience

1 Now the word of the LORD came to [a]Jo-
nah the son of Amittai, saying,
2 "Arise, go to [b]Nineveh, that [c]great city,
and cry out against it; for [d]their wickedness has come up before Me." 3 But Jonah
arose to flee to Tarshish from the presence
of the LORD. He went down to [e]Joppa, and
found a ship going to Tarshish; so he paid
the fare, and went down into it, to go with
them to [f]Tarshish [g]from the presence of the
LORD.

The Storm at Sea

4 But [h]the LORD [1]sent out a great wind
on the sea, and there was a mighty tempest
on the sea, so that the ship was about to be
broken up.
5 Then the mariners were afraid; and
every man cried out to his god, and threw
the cargo that *was* in the ship into the sea,
to lighten [2]the load. But Jonah had gone
down [i]into the lowest parts of the ship,
had lain down, and was fast asleep.
6 So the captain came to him, and said to
him, "What do you mean, sleeper? Arise,
[j]call on your God; [k]perhaps your God will
consider us, so that we may not perish."
7 And they said to one another, "Come,
let us [l]cast lots, that we may know for
whose cause this trouble *has come* upon
us." So they cast lots, and the lot fell on Jonah. 8 Then they said to him, [m]"Please tell
us! For whose cause *is* this trouble upon
us? What is your occupation? And where
do you come from? What is your country?
And of what people are you?"
9 So he said to them, "I *am* a Hebrew;
and I fear [3]the LORD, the God of heaven,
[n]who made the sea and the dry *land*."

CHAPTER 1

1 [a] 2 Kin. 14:25; Matt. 12:39-41; 16:4; Luke 11:29, 30, 32
2 [b] Is. 37:37 [c] Gen. 10:11, 12; 2 Kin. 19:36; Jon. 4:11; Nah. 1:1; Zeph. 2:13 [d] Gen. 18:20; Hos. 7:2
3 [e] Josh. 19:46; 2 Chr. 2:16; Ezra 3:7; Acts 9:36, 43 [f] Is. 23:1 [g] Gen. 4:16; Job 1:12; 2:7
4 [h] Ps. 107:25 [1] Lit. *hurled*
5 [i] 1 Sam. 24:3 [2] Lit. *from upon them*
6 [j] Ps. 107:28 [k] Joel 2:14
7 [l] Josh. 7:14; 1 Sam. 14:41, 42; Prov. 16:33
8 [m] Josh. 7:19; 1 Sam. 14:43
9 [n] [Neh. 9:6]; Ps. 146:6; Acts 17:24 [3] Heb. *YHWH*

1:1 Jonah the son of Amittai. Jonah's name is Heb. for "dove," while that of his father means "truthful" or "loyal."

1:2 Arise, go to Nineveh. While other prophets prophesied against Gentile nations, this is the only case of a prophet actually being sent to a foreign nation to deliver God's message against them. This was for the salvation of that city and for the shame and jealousy of Israel, as well as a rebuke to the reluctance of the Jews to bring Gentiles to the true God. Nineveh, which dates back to Nimrod (Gen. 10:11), was located on the banks of the Tigris River approximately 500 mi. NE of Israel. It was always one of Assyria's royal cities and for many years served as the capital. The name Nineveh, is thought to derive from "ninus," i.e., Nimrod, and means the residence of Nimrod or "nunu" (Akkadian for "fish"). The people worshiped the fish goddess Nanshe (the daughter of Ea, the goddess of fresh water) and Dagon the fish god who was represented as half man and half fish. **that great city.** Nineveh was great both in size (3:3) and in power, exerting significant influence over the Middle East until her destruction by Nebuchadnezzar in 612 B.C. It was possibly the largest city in the world at this time. According to historians, magnificent walls almost 8 mi. long enveloped the inner city, with the rest of the city/district occupying an area with a circumference of some 60 miles. Its population could have approached 600,000 (cf. 4:11). **their wickedness has come up before Me.** Nineveh was the center of idolatrous worship of Assur and Ishtar. A century later, Nahum pronounced doom upon Assyria for her evil ways and cruelty (Nah. 3), which was carried out by Nebuchadnezzar in 612 B.C.

1:3 But Jonah arose to flee to Tarshish. This is the only recorded instance of a prophet refusing God's commission (cf. Jer. 20:7-9). The location of Tarshish, known for its wealth (Ps. 72:10; Jer. 10:9; Ezek. 27:12,25), is uncertain. The Gr. historian Herodotus identified it with Tartessus, a merchant city in southern Spain. The prophet went as far W in the opposite direction as possible, showing his reluctance to bring salvation blessing to Gentiles. **from the presence of the LORD.** While no one can escape from the Lord's omnipresence (Ps. 139:7-12), it is thought that the prophet was attempting to flee His manifest presence in the temple at Jerusalem (cf. Gen. 4:16; Jon. 2:4). **Joppa.** Joppa (today Jaffa), located on the Mediterranean coast near the border of Judah and Samaria, was also the location of Peter's vision in preparation for his visit to Cornelius, a Gentile (Acts 10).

1:4 a great wind. This is not an ordinary storm, but an extreme one sent (lit. "hurled") from God. Sailors, accustomed to storms, were afraid of this one (v. 5), a fear which served God's purpose (cf. Ps. 104:4).

1:7 cast lots. The last resort is to ascertain whose guilt has caused such divine anger. God could reveal His will by controlling the lots, which He did. This method of discernment by casting lots, the exact procedure of which is not known, was not forbidden in Israel (cf. Prov. 16:33; Josh. 7:14ff.; 15:1; 1 Sam 14:36-45; Acts 1:26).

1:9 I *am* a Hebrew. Jonah identified himself by the name that Israelites used among Gentiles (cf. 1 Sam. 4:6,9; 14:11). **the God of heaven.** This title, in use from earliest times (Gen. 24:3,7), may have been specifically chosen by Jonah to express the sovereignty of the Lord in contrast to Baal, who was a sky god (cf. 1 Kin. 18:24). Spoken to sailors who were most likely from Phoenicia, the center of Baal worship, the title bears significant weight, especially when coupled with the phrase "who made the sea and the dry land." This was the appropriate identification when introducing the true and living God to pagans who didn't have Scripture, but whose reason led them to recognize the fact that there had to be a Creator (cf. Rom 1:18-23). To begin with creation, as in Acts 14:14-17 and 17:23b-29, was the proper starting point. To evangelize Jews, one can begin with the OT Scripture.

Ten Miracles in Jonah

1. 1:4 "the LORD sent out a great wind on the sea"
2. 1:7 "the lot fell on Jonah"
3. 1:15 "the sea ceased from its raging"
4. 1:17 "the LORD had prepared a great fish"
5. 1:17 "to swallow Jonah (alive)"
6. 2:10 "the LORD spoke to the fish...it vomited Jonah onto dry *land*"
7. 3:10 "God saw their works...they turned from their evil way"
8. 4:6 "the LORD God prepared a plant"
9. 4:7 "God prepared a worm"
10. 4:8 "God prepared a vehement east wind"

Jonah Thrown into the Sea

10 Then the men were exceedingly
afraid, and said to him, "Why have you
done this?" For the men knew that he fled
from the presence of the LORD, because he
had told them. 11 Then they said to him,
"What shall we do to you that the sea may
be calm for us?"—for the sea was growing
more tempestuous.

12 And he said to them, [o]"Pick me up
and [4]throw me into the sea; then the sea
will become calm for you. For I know that
this great tempest *is* because of me."
13 Nevertheless the men rowed hard to
return to land, [p]but they could not, for the
sea continued to grow more tempestuous
against them. 14 Therefore they cried out to
the LORD and said, "We pray, O LORD,
please do not let us perish for this man's
life, and [q]do not charge us with innocent
blood; for You, O LORD, [r]have done as it
pleased You." 15 So they picked up Jonah
and threw him into the sea, [s]and the sea
ceased from its raging. 16 Then the men
[t]feared the LORD exceedingly, and offered a
sacrifice to the LORD and took vows.

Jonah's Prayer and Deliverance

17 Now the LORD had prepared a great
fish to swallow Jonah. And [u]Jonah was in
the belly of the fish three days and three
nights.

2 Then Jonah prayed to the LORD his God
from the fish's belly. 2 And he said:

"I [a]cried out to the LORD because of
my affliction,
[b]And He answered me.

"Out of the belly of Sheol I cried,
And You heard my voice.
3 [c]For You cast me into the deep,
Into the heart of the seas,
And the floods surrounded me;
[d]All Your billows and Your waves
passed over me.
4 [e]Then I said, 'I have been cast out of
Your sight;
Yet I will look again [f]toward Your
holy temple.'
5 The [g]waters surrounded me, *even*
to my soul;
The deep closed around me;
Weeds were wrapped around my
head.
6 I went down to the [1]moorings of
the mountains;
The earth with its bars *closed*
behind me forever;
Yet You have brought up my [h]life
from the pit,
O LORD, my God.

7 "When my soul fainted within me,
I remembered the LORD;
[i]And my prayer went *up* to You,
Into Your holy temple.

8 "Those who regard [j]worthless idols
Forsake their own [2]Mercy.
9 But I will [k]sacrifice to You
With the voice of thanksgiving;
I will pay what I have [l]vowed.
[m]Salvation *is* of the [n]LORD."

10 So the LORD spoke to the fish, and it
vomited Jonah onto dry *land*.

Jonah Preaches at Nineveh

3 Now the word of the LORD came to Jonah the second time, saying, 2 "Arise,

12 [o] John 11:50 [4] Lit. *hurl*
13 [p] [Prov. 21:30]
14 [q] Deut. 21:8 [r] Ps. 115:3; [Dan. 4:35]
15 [s] [Ps. 89:9; 107:29]; Luke 8:24
16 [t] Mark 4:41; Acts 5:11
17 [u] [Matt. 12:40; Luke 11:30]

CHAPTER 2

2 [a] 1 Sam. 30:6; Ps. 120:1; Lam. 3:55 [b] Ps. 65:2
3 [c] Ps. 88:6 [d] Ps. 42:7
4 [e] Ps. 31:22; Jer. 7:15 [f] 1 Kin. 8:38; 2 Chr. 6:38; Ps. 5:7
5 [g] Ps. 69:1; Lam. 3:54
6 [h] Job 33:28; [Ps. 16:10; Is. 38:17] [1] *foundations* or *bases*
7 [i] 2 Chr. 30:27; Ps. 18:6
8 [j] 2 Kin. 17:15; Ps. 31:6; Jer. 10:8 [2] Or *Lovingkindness*
9 [k] Ps. 50:14, 23; Jer. 33:11; Hos. 14:2 [l] Job 22:27; [Eccl. 5:4, 5] [m] Ps. 3:8; [Is. 45:17] [n] [Jer. 3:23]

1:11,12 Unwilling to go to Nineveh and feeling guilty, Jonah was willing to sacrifice himself in an effort to save the lives of others. Apparently, he would rather have died than go to Nineveh.

1:13,14 Heathen sailors had more concern for one man than Jonah had for tens of thousands in Nineveh. The storm, Jonah's words, and the lots all indicated to the sailors that the Lord was involved; thus they offered sacrifices to Him and made vows, indicating Jonah had told them more about God than is recorded here.

1:15 the sea ceased. This was similar to Christ's quieting the storm on the Sea of Galilee (cf. Matt. 8:23-27).

1:17 a great fish. The species of fish is uncertain; the Heb. word for whale is not here employed. God sovereignly prepared (lit. "appointed") a great fish to rescue Jonah. Apparently Jonah sank into the depth of the sea before the fish swallowed him (cf. 2:3,5,6). **three days and three nights.** *See note on Matt. 12:40; 16:4.*

2:1-9 Jonah acknowledged God's sovereignty (vv. 1-3) and submitted to it (vv. 2:4-9).

2:2 Out of the belly of Sheol. The phrase does not necessarily indicate that Jonah actually died. "Sheol" frequently has a hyperbolic meaning in contexts where it denotes a catastrophic condition near death (Ps. 30:3). Later Jonah expressed praise for his deliverance "from the pit," speaking of his escape from certain death.

2:3 In describing his watery experience, Jonah acknowledged that his circumstances were judgment from the Lord.

2:4 I have been cast out of Your sight. In 1:3, Jonah ran from the Lord's presence; here he realizes that the Lord has temporarily expelled him.

2:5 my soul. This describes Jonah's total person—both physically and spiritually (cf. v. 7).

2:9 I have vowed. Jonah found himself in the same position as the mariners: offering sacrifices and making vows (cf. 1:16). In light of 3:1-4, Jonah's vow could well have been to carry out God's ministry will for him by preaching in Nineveh (Pss. 50:14; 66:13,14).

2:10 the LORD spoke. Just as God calls the stars by name (Is. 40:26; cf. Ps. 147:4), so He speaks to His creation in the animal world (cf. Num. 22:28-30). Most likely, Jonah was vomited upon the shore near Joppa.

3:1,2 Gracious in giving Jonah a second chance, God again commissioned him to go to Nineveh. Jonah is the only prophet actually sent by God to preach repentance in a foreign land.

go to Nineveh, that great city, and preach
to it the message that I tell you." 3 So Jonah arose and went to Nineveh, according to the word of the LORD. Now Nineveh was an exceedingly great city, [1]a
three-day journey *in extent.* 4 And Jonah
began to enter the city on the first day's
walk. Then [a]he cried out and said, "Yet
forty days, and Nineveh shall be overthrown!"

The People of Nineveh Believe

5 So the [b]people of Nineveh believed
God, proclaimed a fast, and put on sackcloth, from the greatest to the least of them.
6 Then word came to the king of Nineveh;
and he arose from his throne and laid aside
his robe, covered *himself* with sackcloth
[c]and sat in ashes. 7 [d]And he caused *it* to be
proclaimed and published throughout
Nineveh by the decree of the king and his
[2]nobles, saying,

> Let neither man nor beast, herd
> nor flock, taste anything; do not
> let them eat, or drink water. 8 But
> let man and beast be covered with
> sackcloth, and cry mightily to
> God; yes, [e]let every one turn from
> his evil way and from [f]the
> violence that is in his hands.
> 9 [g]Who can tell *if* God will turn
> and relent, and turn away from
> His fierce anger, so that we may
> not perish?

10 [h]Then God saw their works, that they
turned from their evil way; and God relented from the disaster that He had said
He would bring upon them, and He did
not do it.

Jonah's Anger and God's Kindness

4 But it displeased Jonah exceedingly,
and he became angry. 2 So he prayed
to the LORD, and said, "Ah, LORD, was not
this what I said when I was still in my
country? Therefore I [a]fled previously to
Tarshish; for I know that You *are* a [b]gra-
cious and merciful God, slow to anger
and abundant in lovingkindness, One
who relents from doing harm. 3 [c]There-
fore now, O LORD, please take my life
from me, for [d]*it is* better for me to die than
to live!"
4 Then the LORD said, "*Is it* right for you
to be angry?"
5 So Jonah went out of the city and sat
on the east side of the city. There he
made himself a shelter and sat under it in
the shade, till he might see what would
become of the city. 6 And the LORD God
prepared a [1]plant and made it come up
over Jonah, that it might be shade for his
head to deliver him from his misery. So
Jonah [2]was very grateful for the plant.
7 But as morning dawned the next day
God prepared a worm, and it *so* damaged
the plant that it withered. 8 And it happened, when the sun arose, that God prepared a vehement east wind; and the sun
beat on Jonah's head, so that he grew
faint. Then he wished death for himself,
and said, [e]"*It is* better for me to die than
to live."
9 Then God said to Jonah, "*Is it* right for
you to be angry about the plant?"
And he said, "*It is* right for me to be
angry, even to death!"

CHAPTER 3

3 [1] Exact meaning unknown
4 [a] [Deut. 18:22]
5 [b] [Matt. 12:41; Luke 11:32]
6 [c] Job 2:8
7 [d] 2 Chr. 20:3; Dan. 3:29; Joel 2:15 [2] Lit. *great ones*
8 [e] Is. 58:6 [f] Is. 59:6
9 [g] 2 Sam. 12:22; Joel 2:14; Amos 5:15
10 [h] Ex. 32:14; Jer. 18:8; Amos 7:3, 6

CHAPTER 4

2 [a] Jon. 1:3 [b] Ex. 34:6; Num. 14:18; Ps. 86:5, 15; Joel 2:13
3 [c] 1 Kin. 19:4; Job 6:8, 9 [d] Jon. 4:8
6 [1] Heb. *kikayon,* exact identity unknown [2] Lit. *rejoiced with great joy*
8 [e] Jon. 4:3

3:3 an exceedingly great city, a three-day journey. Lit. "a great city to God," the text emphasizes not only its size (cf. 1:2) but its importance (cf. 4:11). A metropolitan city the size of Nineveh, with a circumference of about 60 mi., would require 3 days just to get around it. These dimensions are confirmed by historians. Stopping to preach would only add to the time requirement.

3:4 Yet forty days. The time frame may harken back to Moses' supplication for 40 days and nights at Sinai (Deut. 9:18,25). Jonah's message, while short, accomplishes God's intended purpose.

3:5 the people...believed God. Jonah's experience with the fish (2:1-10), in light of the Ninevites pagan beliefs (*see note on 1:2*), certainly gained him an instant hearing. From the divine side, this wholesale repentance was a miraculous work of God. Pagan sailors and a pagan city responded to the reluctant prophet, showing the power of God in spite of the weakness of His servant.

3:6 The king of Nineveh, thought to be either Adad-nirari III (ca. 810–783) or Assurdan III (ca. 772–755), exchanged his royal robes for sackcloth and ashes (cf. Job 42:6; Is. 58:5). Reports of Jonah's miraculous fish experience may have preceded him to Nineveh, accounting for the swift and widespread receptivity of his message (cf. 1:2). It is generally believed that acid from the fish's stomach would have bleached Jonah's face, thus validating the experience.

3:7-9 man nor beast. It was a Persian custom to use animals in mourning ceremonies.

3:10 God saw...God relented. *See note on Gen. 6:6* (cf. Jer. 18:7,8). The Ninevites truly repented.

4:1,2 Jonah, because of his rejection of Gentiles and distaste for their participation in salvation, was displeased at God's demonstration of mercy towards the Ninevites, thereby displaying the real reason for his original flight to Tarshish. From the very beginning, Jonah had clearly understood the gracious character of God (cf. 1 Tim. 2:4; 2 Pet. 3:9). He had received pardon, but didn't want Nineveh to know God's mercy (cf. a similar attitude in Luke 15:25ff.).

4:3 better...to die than to live! Perhaps Jonah was expressing the reality of breaking his vow (2:9) to God a second time (cf. Num. 30:2; Eccl. 5:1-6).

4:6 a plant. The identity is uncertain, but it possibly could be the fast growing castor oil plant, which in hot climates grows rapidly to give shade with its large leaves.

4:8 vehement east wind. A hot, scorching wind, normally called "sirocco," blowing off the Arabian desert. The shelter Jonah made for himself (v. 5) would not exclude this "agent" of God's sovereignty.

10 But the LORD said, "You have had
pity on the plant for which you have not
labored, nor made it grow, which [3]came
up in a night and perished in a night.
11 And should I not pity Nineveh, [f]that
great city, in which are more than one
hundred and twenty thousand persons
[g]who cannot discern between their right
hand and their left—and much livestock?"

10 [3] Lit. *was a son of a night*
11 [f] Jon. 1:2; 3:2, 3
[g] Deut. 1:39; Is. 7:16

4:10,11 God's love for the people of Nineveh, whom He had created, is far different from Jonah's indifference to their damnation and greater than Jonah's warped concern for a wild plant for which he had done nothing. God was ready to spare Sodom for 10 righteous; how much more a city which includes 120,000 small children, identified as those who cannot discern the right hand from the left (cf. Gen. 18:22,23). With that many 3 or 4 year old children, it is reasonable to expect a total population in excess of 600,000.

The Book of MICAH

Title

The name of the book is derived from the prophet who, having received the word of the Lord, was commissioned to proclaim it. Micah, whose name is shared by others in the OT (e.g., Judg. 17:1; 2 Chr. 13:2; Jer. 36:11), is a shortened form of Micaiah (or Michaiah) and means "Who is like the LORD?" In 7:18, Micah uses a play on his own name, saying "Who is a God like You?"

Author and Date

The first verse establishes Micah as the author. Beyond that, little is known about him. His parentage is not given, but his name suggests a godly heritage. He traces his roots to the town of Moresheth (1:1,14), located in the foothills of Judah, approximately 25 mi. SW of Jerusalem, on the border of Judah and Philistia, near Gath. From a productive agricultural area, he was like Amos, a country resident removed from the national politics and religion, yet chosen by God (3:8) to deliver a message of judgment to the princes and people of Jerusalem.

Micah places his prophecy during the reigns of Jotham (750–731 B.C.), Ahaz (731–715 B.C.), and Hezekiah (715–686 B.C.). His indictments of social injustices and religious corruption renew the theme of Amos (mid-eighth century B.C.) and his contemporaries, Hosea in the N (ca. 755–710 B.C.) and in the S Isaiah (ca. 739–690 B.C.). This fits that which is known about the character of Ahaz (2 Kin. 16:10-18) and his son Hezekiah prior to his sweeping spiritual reformations (2 Chr. 29; 31:1). His references to the imminent fall of Samaria (1:6) clearly position him before 722 B.C., at approximately 735–710 B.C.

Background and Setting

Because the northern kingdom was about to fall to Assyria during Micah's ministry in 722 B.C., Micah dates his message with the mention of Judean kings only. While Israel was an occasional recipient of his words (cf. 1:5-7), his primary attention was directed toward the southern kingdom in which he lived. The economic prosperity and the absence of international crises which marked the days of Jeroboam II (793–753 B.C.), during which the borders of Judah and Israel rivaled those of David and Solomon (cf. 2 Kin. 14:23-27), were slipping away. Syria and Israel invaded Judah, taking the wicked Ahaz temporarily captive (cf. 2 Chr. 28:5-16; Is. 7:1,2). After Assyria had overthrown Syria and Israel, the good king Hezekiah withdrew his allegiance to Assyria, causing Sennacherib to besiege Jerusalem in 701 B.C. (cf. 2 Kin. 18,19; 2 Chr. 32). The Lord then sent His angel to deliver Judah (2 Chr. 32:21). Hezekiah was used by God to lead Judah back to true worship.

After the prosperous reign of Uzziah, who died in 739 B.C., his son Jotham continued the same policies, but failed to remove the centers of idolatry. Outward prosperity was only a facade masking rampant social corruption and religious syncretism. Worship of the Canaanite fertility god Baal was increasingly integrated with the OT sacrificial system, reaching epidemic proportions under the reign of Ahaz (cf. 2 Chr. 28:1-4). When Samaria fell, thousands of refugees swarmed into Judah, bringing their religious syncretism with them. But while Micah (like Hosea) addressed this issue, it was the disintegration of personal and social values to which he delivered his most stinging rebukes and stern warnings (e.g., 7:5,6). Assyria was the dominant power and a constant threat to Judah, so Micah's prediction that Babylon, then under Assyrian rule, would conquer Judah (4:10) seemed remote. Thus, as the prophet Amos was to Israel, Micah was to Judah.

Historical and Theological Themes

Primarily, Micah proclaimed a message of judgment to a people persistently pursuing evil. Similar to other prophets (cf. Hos. 4:1; Amos 3:1), Micah presented his message in lawsuit/courtroom terminology (1:2; 6:1,2). The prophecy is arranged in 3 oracles or cycles, each beginning with the admonition to "hear" (1:2; 3:1; 6:1). Within each oracle, he moves from doom to hope—doom because they have broken God's law given at Sinai; hope because of God's unchanging covenant with their forefathers (7:20). One third of the book targets the sins of his people; another third looks at the punishment of God to come; and another third promises hope for the faithful after the judgment. Thus, the theme of the inevitability of divine judgment for sin is coupled together with God's immutable commitment to His covenant promises. The combination of God's 1) absolute consistency in judging sin and 2) unbending commitment to His covenant through the remnant of His people provides the hearers with a clear disclosure of the character of the Sovereign of the universe. Through divine intervention, He will bring about both judgment on sinners and blessing on those who repent.

Interpretive Challenges

The verbal similarity between Mic. 4:1-3 and Is. 2:2-4 raises the question of who quoted whom. Interpreters are divided, with no clear-cut answers on either side. Because the two prophets lived in close proximity to each other, prophesying during the same period, this similarity is understandable. God gave the same message through two preachers. The introductory phrase, "in the latter days" (4:1), removes these verses from any post-Exilic fulfillment and requires an eschatological timeframe surrounding the Second Advent of Christ and the beginning of the Millennium.

Apart from Is. 2:2-4, three other passages from Micah are quoted elsewhere in Scripture. Micah 3:12 is quoted in Jer. 26:18, thereby saving Jeremiah's life from King Jehoiakim's death sentence. Micah 5:2 is quoted by the chief priests and scribes (Matt. 2:6) in response to Herod's query about the birthplace of the Messiah. Micah 7:6 is employed by Jesus in Matt. 10:35,36 when commissioning His disciples.

Outline

- I. Superscription (1:1)
- II. God Gathers to Judge and Deliver (1:2–2:13)
  - A. Samaria and Judah Punished (1:2-16)
  - B. Oppressors Judged (2:1-5)
  - C. False Prophets Renounced (2:6-11)
  - D. Promise of Deliverance (2:12,13)
- III. God Judges Rulers and Comes to Deliver (3:1–5:15)
  - A. The Contemporary Leaders are Guilty (3:1-12)
  - B. The Coming Leader Will Deliver and Restore (4:1–5:15)
- IV. God Brings Indictments and Ultimate Deliverance (6:1–7:20)
  - A. Messages of Reproof and Lament (6:1–7:6)
  - B. Messages of Confidence and Victory (7:7-20)

CHAPTER 1

1 The word of the LORD that came to [a]Micah of Moresheth in the days of [b]Jotham, Ahaz, *and* Hezekiah, kings of Judah, which he saw concerning Samaria and Jerusalem.

The Coming Judgment on Israel

2 Hear, all you peoples!
Listen, O earth, and all that is in it!
Let the Lord GOD be a witness against you,
The Lord from [c]His holy temple.

3 For behold, the LORD is coming out of His place;
He will come down
And tread on the high places of the earth.
4 [d]The mountains will melt under Him,
And the valleys will split
Like wax before the fire,
Like waters poured down a steep place.
5 All this is for the transgression of Jacob
And for the sins of the house of Israel.
What *is* the transgression of Jacob?
Is it not Samaria?
And what *are* the [e]high places of Judah?
Are they not Jerusalem?

6 "Therefore I will make Samaria [f]a heap of ruins in the field,
Places for planting a vineyard;
I will pour down her stones into the valley,
And I will [g]uncover her foundations.
7 All her carved images shall be beaten to pieces,
And all her [h]pay as a harlot shall be burned with the fire;
All her idols I will lay desolate,
For she gathered *it* from the pay of a harlot,
And they shall return to the [i]pay of a harlot."

Mourning for Israel and Judah

8 Therefore I will wail and howl,
I will go stripped and naked;
[j]I will make a wailing like the jackals
And a mourning like the ostriches,
9 For her wounds *are* incurable.
For [k]it has come to Judah;
It has come to the gate of My people—
To Jerusalem.

10 [l]Tell *it* not in Gath,
Weep not at all;
In [1]Beth Aphrah
Roll yourself in the dust.
11 Pass by in naked shame, you inhabitant of [2]Shaphir;
The inhabitant of [3]Zaanan does not go out.
Beth Ezel mourns;
Its place to stand is taken away from you.
12 For the inhabitant of [4]Maroth [5]pined for good,
But [m]disaster came down from the LORD

1 [a][2 Pet. 1:21]; Jer. 26:18 [b]2 Kin. 15:5, 7, 32-38; 2 Chr. 27:1-9; Is. 1:1; Hos. 1:1
2 [c][Ps. 11:4]
4 [d]Amos 9:5
5 [e]Deut. 32:13; 33:29; Amos 4:13
6 [f]2 Kin. 19:25; Mic. 3:12 [g]Ezek. 13:14
7 [h]Hos. 2:5 [i]Deut. 23:18; Is. 23:17
8 [j]Ps. 102:6
9 [k]2 Kin. 18:13; Is. 8:7, 8
10 [l]2 Sam. 1:20 [1]Lit. *House of Dust*
11 [2]Lit. *Beautiful* [3]Lit. *Going Out*
12 [m]Is. 59:9-11; Jer. 14:19; Amos 3:6 [4]Lit. *Bitterness* [5]Lit. *was sick*

1:1 Moresheth. Located SW of Jerusalem, near the Philistine city of Gath (cf. 1:14).

1:2-7 The prophet summons all the nations (v. 2) of the world into court to hear charges against Samaria and Judah (vv. 5-7; cf. Is. 3:13,14). Their destruction was to be a warning example to the nations, prefiguring God's judgment on all who sin against Him. As an omnipotent Conqueror, the Sovereign over all creation is assured of victory (vv. 3,4).

1:2 His holy temple. Context points to God's heavenly throne (cf. Ps. 11:4; Is. 6:1,4).

1:3,4 high places...mountains. These could refer to key military positions, so crucial to Israel's defense, or to the pagan places of worship in the land (cf. v. 5). When fortifications disappeared like melted wax, people were gripped by the terrifying reality that they were to answer to the Judge of all the earth (Gen. 18:25; Amos 4:12,13).

1:3 the LORD is coming...down. A warning of impending divine judgment by One who sits in the ultimate High Place.

1:5 Samaria...Jerusalem. The two capitals, of Israel and Judah, here representative of their respective nations.

1:6,7 The Lord spoke directly of the fall of Samaria at the hands of the Assyrians (ca. 722 B.C.).

1:7 pay as a harlot. Centers of idolatry were financed primarily through payments of money, food, and clothing (cf. Gen. 38:17,18; Ezek. 16:10,11; Hos. 2:8,9; 3:1) to cultic prostitutes, who were strictly forbidden in Israel (Deut. 23:17,18). Precious gold and silver, taken from Israel's temples, was used by the Assyrian invaders for their own idol worship.

1:8-16 The judgment was so grave that even the prophet lamented as he traced the enemy's irreversible (v. 9) invasion.

1:9 to the gate of My people. Assyria, under Sennacherib, came close to toppling Judah in 701 B.C. (cf. 2 Kin. 18:13-27). It is best to see "my" in reference to Micah, not God, contra. the NKJV translation.

1:10-15 Eleven towns W of Jerusalem are mentioned, some with a play on words as explained in the marginal references.

1:10 Tell *it* not in Gath. Reflective of David's dirge at Saul's death (cf. 2 Sam. 1:20), Micah admonished them not to tell the Philistines, lest they would be glad and rejoice. Micah, because of the location of his upbringing, knew how they would react.

1:11 Zaanan does not go out. These inhabitants, in danger and fear, would not go out to console their neighbors who had been overrun.

1:12 disaster came down. This points to the Lord as the source of judgment (cf. vv. 3,4).

To the gate of Jerusalem.
13 O inhabitant of [n]Lachish,
Harness the chariot to the swift
steeds
(She *was* the beginning of sin to the
daughter of Zion),
For the transgressions of Israel
were [o]found in you.

14 Therefore you shall [p]give presents
to [6]Moresheth Gath;
The houses of [q]Achzib[7] *shall be* a
lie to the kings of Israel.
15 I will yet bring an heir to you,
O inhabitant of [r]Mareshah;[8]
The glory of Israel shall come to
[s]Adullam.[9]
16 Make yourself [t]bald and cut off
your hair,
Because of your [u]precious children;
Enlarge your baldness like an
eagle,
For they shall go from you into
[v]captivity.

Woe to Evildoers

2 Woe to those who devise iniquity,
And [1]work out evil on their beds!
At [a]morning light they practice it,
Because it is in the power of their
hand.
2 They [b]covet fields and take *them* by
violence,
Also houses, and seize *them.*
So they oppress a man and his
house,
A man and his inheritance.

3 Therefore thus says the LORD:

"Behold, against this [c]family I am
devising [d]disaster,
From which you cannot remove
your necks;
Nor shall you walk haughtily,
For this *is* an evil time.
4 In that day *one* shall take up a
proverb against you,
And [e]lament with a bitter
lamentation, saying:
'We are utterly destroyed!
He has changed the [2]heritage of
my people;
How He has removed *it* from me!
To [3]a turncoat He has divided our
fields.' "

5 Therefore you will have no [4]one to
determine boundaries by lot
In the assembly of the LORD.

Lying Prophets

6 "Do not prattle," *you say to those*
who [5]prophesy.
So they shall not prophesy [6]to you;
[7]They shall not return insult for
insult.
7 *You who are* named the house of
Jacob:
"Is the Spirit of the LORD restricted?
Are these His doings?
Do not My words do good
To him who walks uprightly?

8 "Lately My people have risen up as
an enemy—
You pull off the robe with the
garment
From those who trust *you,* as they
pass by,

13 [n]Josh. 10:3; 2 Kin. 14:19; 18:14; Is. 36:2 [o]Ezek. 23:11
14 [p]2 Sam. 8:2 [q]Josh. 15:44 [6]Lit. *Possession of Gath* [7]Lit. *Lie*
15 [r]Josh. 15:44 [s]2 Chr. 11:7 [8]Lit. *Inheritance* [9]Lit. *Refuge*
16 [t]Job 1:20 [u]Lam. 4:5 [v]2 Kin. 17:6; Amos 7:11, 17; [Mic. 4:10]

CHAPTER 2

1 [a]Hos. 7:6, 7 [1]Plan
2 [b]Is. 5:8
3 [c]Ex. 20:5; Jer. 8:3; Amos 3:1, 2 [d]Amos 5:13
4 [e]2 Sam. 1:17 [2]Lit. *portion* [3]Lit. *one turning back,* an apostate
5 [4]Lit. *one casting a surveyor's line*
6 [5]Or *preach,* lit. *drip words* [6]Lit. *to these* [7]Vg. *He shall not take shame*

1:13 Lachish...sin to the daughter of Zion. Located SW of Jerusalem, Lachish was a key military fortress whose "sin" was dependence on military might.

1:14 give presents. As parting gifts were given to brides (cf. 1 Kin. 9:16), this was a symbol of the departure of Moresheth Gath into captivity.

1:15 glory of Israel...Adullam. The people of Israel (i.e., her "glory;" cf. Hos. 9:11-13) were to flee to the caves, as David did to the cave at Adullam (2 Sam 23:13).

1:16 Make yourself bald. Priests were forbidden to make themselves bald (Lev. 21:5), nor were the people to imitate the heathen practice of doing so (Deut. 14:1). But here it would be acceptable as a sign of deep mourning (Ezra 9:3; Job 1:20; Is. 22:12; Ezek. 7:18).

2:1-11 As chapter one denounced sin against God; chapter two denounces sin against man. In vv. 1-5, Micah decried the corrupt practices of the affluent; in vv. 6-11 he attacked the false prophets and those who would silence the true prophets.

2:1,2 The courtroom scene continues, with the accusations being read against the affluent: they had violated the tenth commandment (Ex. 20:17; cf. 22:26; 23:4-9). The poor, unable to defend themselves, were at the mercy of the wealthy.

2:2 his inheritance. Property in Israel was ultimately to be permanent (Lev. 25:10,13; Num. 36:1-12; cf. 1 Kin. 21).

2:3-5 As a result of sin, God would allow foreign invaders to divide their land; none of them would have the inheritance apportioned to them. As the rich took from the poor, so God would take back that which He gave as judgment on the nation.

2:6-11 False prophets, commanding Micah to cease prophesying, would certainly not prophesy against the people's evil doing; they would not confront them with the divine standard of holiness. Rather, their false message (v. 7) had stopped the mouths of the true prophets and had permitted the rulers to engage in social atrocities (vv. 8,9), leading the people to destruction (v. 10). They didn't want true prophecies; therefore, they got what they wanted (cf. Is. 30:10). It is best to understand that Micah speaks in v. 6 and God in vv. 7-11.

2:6 Do not prattle. The true prophet was accused of childish babbling, when the real babblers were the false prophets (cf. v. 11).

2:7 Spirit of the LORD. God responded to the evil prophets that their message affirming sin in the nation was inconsistent with the Holy Spirit and His true message to Micah (cf. 3:8). God's words do reward the righteous, but they also rebuke those engaging in evil deeds.

Like men returned from war.
9 The women of My people you cast
out
From their pleasant houses;
From their children
You have taken away My glory
forever.

10 "Arise and depart,
For this *is* not *your* [f]rest;
Because it is [g]defiled, it shall
destroy,
Yes, with utter destruction.
11 If a man should walk in a false
spirit
And speak a lie, *saying,*
'I will [8]prophesy to you [9]of wine
and drink,'
Even he would be the [h]prattler of
this people.

Israel Restored

12 "I[i] will surely assemble all of you,
O Jacob,
I will surely gather the remnant of
Israel;
I will put them together [j]like sheep
of [1]the fold,
Like a flock in the midst of their
pasture;
[k]They shall make a loud noise
because of *so many* people.
13 The one who breaks open will
come up before them;
They will break out,
Pass through the gate,
And go out by it;
[l]Their king will pass before them,
[m]With the LORD at their head."

Wicked Rulers and Prophets

3 And I said:

"Hear now, O heads of Jacob,
And you [a]rulers of the house of
Israel:
[b]*Is it* not for you to know justice?
2 You who hate good and love evil;
Who strip the skin from [1]My
people,
And the flesh from their bones;
3 Who also [c]eat the flesh of My
people,
Flay their skin from them,
Break their bones,
And chop *them* in pieces
Like *meat* for the pot,
[d]Like flesh in the caldron."

4 Then [e]they will cry to the LORD,
But He will not hear them;
He will even hide His face from
them at that time,
Because they have been evil in
their deeds.

5 Thus says the LORD [f]concerning the
prophets
Who make my people stray;
Who chant [2]"Peace"
[3]While they [g]chew with their teeth,
But who prepare war against him
[h]Who puts nothing into their
mouths:
6 "Therefore [i] you shall have night
without [4]vision,
And you shall have darkness
without divination;
The sun shall go down on the
prophets,
And the day shall be dark for
[j]them.
7 So the seers shall be ashamed,
And the diviners abashed;
Indeed they shall all cover their
lips;
[k]For *there is* no answer from God."

8 But truly I am full of power by the
Spirit of the LORD,
And of justice and might,
[l]To declare to Jacob his
transgression
And to Israel his sin.
9 Now hear this,
You heads of the house of Jacob
And rulers of the house of Israel,

10 [f]Deut. 12:9 [g]Lev. 18:25
11 [h]Is. 30:10; Jer. 5:30, 31; 2 Tim. 4:3, 4 [8]Or *preach,* lit. *drip* [9]*concerning*
12 [i][Mic. 4:6, 7] [j]Jer. 31:10 [k]Ezek. 33:22; 36:37 [1]Heb. *Bozrah*
13 [l][Hos. 3:5] [m]Is. 52:12

CHAPTER 3

1 [a]Ezek. 22:27 [b]Ps. 82:1-5; Jer. 5:4, 5
2 [1]Lit. *them*
3 [c]Ps. 14:4; 27:2; Zeph. 3:3 [d]Ezek. 11:3, 6, 7
4 [e]Ps. 18:41; Prov. 1:28; Is. 1:15; Jer. 11:11
5 [f]Is. 56:10, 11; Jer. 6:13; Ezek. 13:10, 19 [g]Matt. 7:15 [h]Ezek. 13:18 [2]All is well [3]For those who feed them
6 [i]Is. 8:20-22; 29:10-12 [j]Is. 29:10; [Jer. 23:33-40]; Ezek. 13:23 [4]Prophetic revelation
7 [k]Amos 8:11
8 [l]Is. 58:1

2:9 women of My people. Most likely a reference to widows.

2:11 The people accepted any "prophet" who would tailor his message to their greed, wealth, and prosperity. This false prophet is the real "prattler."

2:12,13 Messiah will make ready the way, removing the obstacles which might hinder His remnant's deliverance and return at the Second Advent (cf. Is. 11:15,16; 52:12).

2:12 remnant. Cf. 4:7; 5:7; 5:8; 7:18. *See note on Is. 10:20.*

3:1-4 In beginning the second oracle, Micah first addressed Israel's corrupt rulers, as in 2:1,2, who should be aware of injustice. Yet their conduct toward the poor was like the butchering of animals (vv. 2,3). Therefore, when judgment came and they cried for help, God didn't answer (v. 4).

3:5-7 False prophets (cf. 2:6-11) also stood guilty before the Judge because they misled the people, prophesying peace when they were fed, but predicting war when they were not (v. 5). Like the rulers, they too were motivated by greed. Therefore, having blinded others, they would be struck with blindness and silence (vv. 6,7).

3:8 Micah, in contrast to the false prophets, spoke by the power of God's Holy Spirit (cf. 2:7). Therefore his message was authoritative and true.

3:9-12 All ruling classes are guilty: rulers judged for reward (v. 9-11a), priests taught for hire (v. 11b), prophets divined for money (v. 11c). All the while, they were self-deceived into thinking the Lord

Who abhor justice
And [5]pervert all equity,
10 [m]Who build up Zion with
[n]bloodshed
And Jerusalem with iniquity:
11 [o]Her heads judge for a bribe,
[p]Her priests teach for pay,
And her prophets divine for
[6]money.
[q]Yet they lean on the LORD, and say,
"Is not the LORD among us?
No harm can come upon us."
12 Therefore because of you
Zion shall be [r]plowed *like* a field,
[s]Jerusalem shall become heaps of
ruins,
And [t]the mountain of the [7]temple
Like the bare hills of the forest.

9 [5]Lit. *twist*
10 [m]Jer. 22:13, 17 [n]Ezek. 22:27; Hab. 2:12
11 [o]Is. 1:23; Mic. 7:3 [p]Jer. 6:13 [q]Is. 48:2; Jer. 7:4 [6]Lit. *silver*
12 [r]Jer. 26:18 [s]Ps. 79:1; Jer. 9:11 [t]Mic. 4:1, 2 [7]Lit. *house*

CHAPTER 4

1 [a]Is. 2:2-4; Ezek. 17:22; Dan. 2:28; 10:14; Hos. 3:5

The LORD's Reign in Zion

4 Now [a]it shall come to pass in the
latter days
That the mountain of the LORD's
house
Shall be established on the top of
the mountains,
And shall be exalted above the
hills;
And peoples shall flow to it.
2 Many nations shall come and say,
"Come, and let us go up to the
mountain of the LORD,
To the house of the God of Jacob;
He will teach us His ways,
And we shall walk in His paths."
For out of Zion the law shall go
forth,
And the word of the LORD from
Jerusalem.
3 He shall judge between many
peoples,
And rebuke strong nations afar off;
They shall beat their swords into
[b]plowshares,
And their spears into [1]pruning
hooks;
Nation shall not lift up sword
against nation,
[c]Neither shall they learn war
anymore.
4 [d]But everyone shall sit under his
vine and under his fig tree,
And no one shall make *them* afraid;
For the mouth of the LORD of hosts
has spoken.
5 For all people walk each in the
name of his god,
But [e]we will walk in the name of
the LORD our God
Forever and ever.

Zion's Future Triumph

6 "In that day," says the LORD,
[f]"I will assemble the lame,
[g]I will gather the outcast
And those whom I have afflicted;
7 I will make the lame [h]a remnant,
And the outcast a strong nation;
So the LORD [i]will reign over them
in Mount Zion
From now on, even forever.
8 And you, O tower of the flock,
The stronghold of the daughter of
Zion,
To you shall it come,
Even the former dominion shall
come,
The kingdom of the daughter of
Jerusalem."
9 Now why do you cry aloud?
[j]*Is there* no king in your midst?
Has your counselor perished?

3 [b]Is. 2:4; Joel 3:10 [c]Ps. 72:7 [1]*pruning knives*
4 [d]1 Kin. 4:25; Zech. 3:10
5 [e]Zech. 10:12
6 [f]Ezek. 34:16 [g]Ps. 147:2
7 [h]Mic. 2:12 [i][Is. 9:6; 24:23; Luke 1:33; Rev. 11:15]
9 [j]Jer. 8:19

would give them favor because they identified themselves with Him. Consequently, the nation would be destroyed (fulfilled by Nebuchadnezzar in 586 B.C.).

3:12 Cf. Jer. 26:18.

4:1-3 Cf. Is. 2:2-4.

4:1 In a reversal of 3:12, Micah shifted from impending judgment to prophesies of the future millennial kingdom ("the latter days") in which Mt. Zion (v. 3), the center of Messiah's coming earthly kingdom, shall be raised both spiritually and physically (cf. Zech. 14:9,10). This discussion continues to 5:15.

4:2 Many nations. People throughout the earth, not just Israel, will come as a spontaneous "flow" (cf. v. 1) to worship the Lord in Jerusalem during the Millennium (cf. Zech. 8:20-23).

4:3 beat their swords into plowshares. Because the Almighty One is ruling in Jerusalem with a rod of iron (cf. Rev. 2:27; 12:5; 19:15), and because of the unprecedented fruitfulness of the land (cf. Amos 9:13), military hardware will no longer be needed.

4:4 under his vine…fig tree. Once employed as a description of the peaceful era of Solomon (cf. 1 Kin. 4:25), this phrase looks forward to greater peace and prosperity in the Millennium (cf. Zech. 3:10).

4:5 Even if all others were walking after other gods at the present, the godly remnant of Israel would no longer pursue other gods but would walk after the true God in the millennial kingdom (cf. Josh. 24:15).

4:6-8 Micah continued to describe the wonderful conditions of the coming earthly kingdom of Messiah. Repeating the figure of sheep (cf. 2:12,13), the "tower of the flock" depicted the city of Jerusalem, the future dwelling place of Messiah, as watching over the people.

4:7 forever. The Heb. term does not always mean "without end," but signifies a long, indefinite period of time, the length of which is always determined by the context. Here it refers to the 1,000 year reign of Messiah on earth (cf. Rev. 20).

4:9,10 Judah will be taken captive to Babylon (vv. 9,10a), but the Lord will release them from there (v. 10b), by the edict of Persian king Cyrus (ca. 538 B.C.), allowing them to return to Jerusalem (cf. Ezra 1:2-4).

For [k]pangs have seized you like a
woman in [2]labor.
10 Be in pain, and labor to bring forth,
O daughter of Zion,
Like a woman in birth pangs.
For now you shall go forth from
the city,
You shall dwell in the field,
And to [l]Babylon you shall go.
There you shall be delivered;
There the [m]LORD will [n]redeem you
From the hand of your enemies.

11 [o]Now also many nations have
gathered against you,
Who say, "Let her be defiled,
And let our eye [p]look upon Zion."
12 But they do not know [q]the
thoughts of the LORD,
Nor do they understand His
counsel;
For He will gather them [r]like
sheaves to the threshing floor.

13 "Arise[s] and [t]thresh, O daughter of
Zion;
For I will make your horn iron,
And I will make your hooves
bronze;
You shall [u]beat in pieces many
peoples;
[v]I will consecrate their gain to the
LORD,
And their substance to [w]the Lord
of the whole earth."

5 Now gather yourself in troops,
O daughter of troops;
He has laid siege against us;
They will [a]strike the judge of Israel
with a rod on the cheek.

The Coming Messiah

2 "But you, [b]Bethlehem [c]Ephrathah,
Though you are little [d]among the
[e]thousands of Judah,
Yet out of you shall come forth to
Me
The One to be [f]Ruler in Israel,
[g]Whose goings forth *are* from of old,
From [1]everlasting."

3 Therefore He shall give them up,
Until the time *that* [h]she who is in
labor has given birth;
Then [i]the remnant of His brethren
Shall return to the children of
Israel.
4 And He shall stand and [j]feed [2] *His
flock*
In the strength of the LORD,
In the majesty of the name of the
LORD His God;
And they shall abide,
For now He [k]shall be great
To the ends of the earth;
5 And this *One* [l]shall be peace.

Judgment on Israel's Enemies

When the Assyrian comes into our
land,
And when he treads in our palaces,
Then we will raise against him
Seven shepherds and eight
princely men.
6 They shall [3]waste with the sword
the land of Assyria,
And the land of [m]Nimrod at its
entrances;
Thus He shall [n]deliver *us* from the
Assyrian,
When he comes into our land
And when he treads within our
borders.

9 [k]Is. 13:8; Jer. 30:6 [2]*childbirth*
10 [l]2 Chr. 36:20; Amos 5:27 [m][Is. 45:13; Mic. 7:8-12] [n]Ezra 1:1-3; 2:1; Ps. 18:17
11 [o]Lam. 2:16 [p]Obad. 12
12 [q][Is. 55:8, 9] [r]Is. 21:10
13 [s]Jer. 51:33; [Zech. 12:1-8; 14:14] [t]Is. 41:15 [u]Dan. 2:44 [v]Is. 18:7 [w]Zech. 4:14

CHAPTER 5

1 [a]1 Kin. 22:24; Job 16:10; Lam. 3:30; Matt. 27:30; Mark 15:19
2 [b]Is. 11:1; Matt. 2:6; Luke 2:4, 11; John 7:42 [c]Gen. 35:19; 48:7; Ruth 4:11 [d]1 Sam. 23:23 [e]Ex. 18:25 [f][Gen. 49:10; Is. 9:6] [g]Ps. 90:2; [John 1:1] [1]Lit. *the days of eternity*
3 [h]Hos. 11:8; Mic. 4:10 [i]Mic. 4:7; 7:18
4 [j][Is. 40:11; 49:9; Ezek. 34:13-15, 23, 24]; Mic. 7:14 [k]Ps. 72:8; Is. 52:13; Zech. 9:10; [Luke 1:32] [2]*shepherd*
5 [l][Is. 9:6]; Luke 2:14; [Eph. 2:14; Col. 1:20]
6 [m]Gen. 10:8-11 [n]Is. 14:25; Luke 1:71 [3]*devastate*

4:11-13 Micah switched again to the time of the Second Advent. The gathering of "many nations" and "many peoples" depicts that future battle of Armageddon (Zech. 12; 14). In that day, the Lord will empower His people (cf. 5:7-9; Is. 11:14; Zech. 14:14).

4:13 horn iron...hooves bronze. Using the figurative language of an animal with metal features, the Lord looked to a day when Israel will permanently defeat their enemies.

5:1 strike the judge of Israel. A reference to the capture of King Zedekiah at the hands of Babylon in 586 B.C. (cf. 2 Kin. 24,25).

5:2-4 This passage looked forward to Christ's First Advent (5:2), an intervening time (5:3a), and beyond to the Second Advent (5:3b,4).

5:2 Bethlehem Ephrathah. The town S of Jerusalem which was the birthplace of David and later Jesus Christ (1 Sam. 16; Matt. 2:5; Luke 2:4-7). The name Bethlehem means "house of bread" because the area was a grain producing region in OT times. The name Ephrathah ("fruitful") differentiates it from the Galilean town by the same name. The town, known for her many vineyards and olive orchards, was small in size but not in honor. **from of old, From everlasting.** This speaks of eternal God's incarnation in the person of Jesus Christ. It points to His millennial reign as King of Kings (cf. Is. 9:6).

5:3 give them up. A reference to the interval between Messiah's rejection at His First Advent and His Second Advent, during the times of the Gentiles when Israel rejects Christ and is under the domination of enemies. Regathering of the "remnant of His brethren" did not occur at the First Advent but is slated for the Second Advent (cf. Is. 10:20-22; 11:11-16). Nor can "return" speak of Gentiles, since it cannot be said that they "returned" to the Lord. Rather, the context of 5:3,4 is millennial and cannot be made to fit the First Advent. Thus, "she who is in labor" must denote the nation of Israel (cf. Rev. 12:1-6).

5:4 The millennial rule of Christ, sitting upon the throne of David (cf. Is. 6:13).

5:5,6 Assyrian. Assyria, God's instrument against Israel (722 B.C.) and Judah (Sennacherib's siege in 701 B.C.) is here used as a representative of enemy nations in opposition to the Lord.

5:5 Seven...eight. An idiom for a full and sufficient number of leaders, more than enough for the task (cf. Eccl. 11:2).

5:6 Nimrod. A reference to Assyria (cf. Gen. 10:11) that could possibly also include Babylon (cf. Gen. 10:10).

7 Then [o]the remnant of Jacob
Shall be in the midst of many
peoples,
[p]Like dew from the LORD,
Like showers on the grass,
That [4]tarry for no man
Nor [5]wait for the sons of men.
8 And the remnant of Jacob
Shall be among the Gentiles,
In the midst of many peoples,
Like a [q]lion among the beasts of
the forest,
Like a young lion among flocks of
sheep,
Who, if he passes through,
Both treads down and tears in
pieces,
And none can deliver.
9 Your hand shall be lifted against
your adversaries,
And all your enemies shall be [6]cut
off.

10 "And it shall be in that day," says
the LORD,
"That I will [r]cut[7] off your [s]horses
from your midst
And destroy your [t]chariots.
11 I will cut off the cities of your land
And throw down all your
strongholds.
12 I will cut off sorceries from your
hand,
And you shall have no
[u]soothsayers.
13 [v]Your carved images I will also cut
off,
And your sacred pillars from your
midst;

7 [o] Mic. 5:3 [p] Gen. 27:28; Deut. 32:2; Ps. 72:6; Hos. 14:5 [4] wait [5] delay
8 [q] Gen. 49:9; Num. 24:9
9 [6] destroyed
10 [r] Zech. 9:10 [s] Deut. 17:16 [t] Is. 2:7; 22:18; Hos. 14:3 [7] destroy
12 [u] Deut. 18:10-12; Is. 2:6
13 [v] Zech. 13:2

You shall [w]no more worship the
work of your hands;
14 I will pluck your [8]wooden images
from your midst;
Thus I will destroy your cities.
15 And I will [x]execute vengeance in
anger and fury
On the nations that have not
[9]heard."

[w] Is. 2:8
14 [8] Heb. *Asherim*, Canaanite deities
15 [x] [2 Thess. 1:8] [9] obeyed

God Pleads with Israel

6 Hear now what the LORD says:
"Arise, plead your case before the
mountains,
And let the hills hear your voice.
2 [a]Hear, O you mountains, [b]the
LORD's complaint,
And you strong foundations of the
earth;
For [c]the LORD has a complaint
against His people,
And He will [1]contend with Israel.

3 "O My people, what [d]have I done to
you?
And how have I [e]wearied you?
Testify against Me.
4 [f]For I brought you up from the land
of Egypt,
I redeemed you from the house of
bondage;
And I sent before you Moses,
Aaron, and Miriam.
5 O My people, remember now
What [g]Balak king of Moab
counseled,
And what Balaam the son of Beor
answered him,
From [2]Acacia Grove to Gilgal,

CHAPTER 6
2 [a] Ps. 50:1, 4 [b] [Is. 1:18]; Hos. 12:2 [c] [Is. 1:18] [1] *bring charges against*
3 [d] Is. 5:4; Jer. 2:5, 31 [e] Is. 43:22, 23; Mal. 1:13
4 [f] [Deut. 4:20]
5 [g] Num. 22:5, 6; Josh. 24:9 [2] Heb. *Shittim*, Num. 25:1; Josh. 2:1; 3:1

5:7-9 Israel's presence in the midst of many peoples would be to some a source of blessing (cf. Zech. 8:22,23); to others, she would be like a lion—a source of fear and destruction (cf. Is. 11:14; Zech 12:2,3,6; 14:14).

5:9 all your enemies. This absolute and complete peace has never yet been experienced by Israel. This points to the millennial kingdom when the Prince of Peace shall reign, having conquered the nations (cf. v.15).

5:10 in that day. The future kingdom is in view. Israel had been forbidden the use of cavalry (Deut. 17:16), lest they trust in earthly forces, rather than God (1 Kin. 10:26,28). God will remove all implements in which they trust so the people, stripped of all human resources, rest only on Him. War instruments will have no place in that time of peace.

5:11-14 cut off the cities...strongholds. Continuing the thought from v. 10, fortified cities were designed for defense; their strength tempted people to put their trust in them rather than in God alone (cf. 1:13; Ps. 27:1; Hos. 10:13,14). People will live in peace in unwalled villages (Ezek. 38:11). The cities are also associated with centers of pagan worship (v. 14; cf. Deut. 16:21:), the worship of Asherah (Canaanite goddess of fertility and war). All forms of self-reliance in war and idolatrous worship will be removed so that the nation must rely solely on Christ their King for deliverance and worship Him alone.

6:1 Micah opens this third cycle of oracles (6:1–7:20) with a dramatic courtroom motif moving back and forth between 3 speakers: the Lord pleading His case, the people responding under conviction, and the prophet as the lawyer for the plaintiff.

6:1,2 The Lord commanded Micah (v. 1), as His advocate, to plead His case before the mountains and hills, which were to act as witnesses against His people (cf. Deut. 4:25,26; Is. 1:2). The mountains and hills were present at Sinai when the Lord made His covenant with Israel and when the commandments were written and placed in the ark of the covenant as a permanent witness (cf. Deut. 31:26).

6:3-5 This was the Lord's appeal. With tenderness and emotion, the divine Plaintiff recalled His many gracious acts toward them, almost to the point of assuming the tone of a defendant. Noting their trek from bondage in Egypt to their own homeland, God had provided leadership (v. 4), reversed the attempts of Balaam to curse the people (v. 5a; cf. Num. 22–24), and miraculously parted the Jordan River (v. 5b) so they could cross over from Acacia Grove, located E of the Jordan, to Gilgal on the W side near Jericho. God had faithfully kept all His promises to them.

That you may know [h]the
righteousness of the LORD."

6 With what shall I come before the
LORD,
And bow myself before the High
God?
Shall I come before Him with burnt
offerings,
With calves a year old?
7 [i]Will the LORD be pleased with
thousands of rams,
Ten thousand [j]rivers of oil?
[k]Shall I give my firstborn *for* my
transgression,
[3]The fruit of my body *for* the sin of
my soul?

8 He has [l]shown you, O man, what
is good;
And what does the LORD require of
you
But [m]to do justly,
To love [4]mercy,
And to walk humbly with your
God?

Punishment of Israel's Injustice

9 The LORD's voice cries to the city—
Wisdom shall see Your name:

"Hear the rod!
Who has appointed it?
10 Are there yet the treasures of
wickedness
In the house of the wicked,
And the short measure *that is* an
abomination?
11 Shall I count pure *those* with [n]the
wicked scales,
And with the bag of deceitful
weights?
12 For her rich men are full of
[o]violence,
Her inhabitants have spoken lies,
And [p]their tongue is deceitful in
their mouth.

13 "Therefore I will also [q]make *you* sick
by striking you,
By making *you* desolate because of
your sins.
14 [r]You shall eat, but not be satisfied;
[5]Hunger *shall be* in your midst.
[6]You may carry *some* away, but shall
not save *them;*
And what you do rescue I will give
over to the sword.

15 "You shall [s]sow, but not reap;
You shall tread the olives, but not
anoint yourselves with oil;
And *make* sweet wine, but not
drink wine.
16 For the statutes of [t]Omri are [u]kept;
All the works of Ahab's house *are*
done;
And you walk in their counsels,
That I may make you a
[7]desolation,
And your inhabitants a hissing.
Therefore you shall bear the
[v]reproach of [8]My people."

Sorrow for Israel's Sins

7 Woe is me!
For I am like those who gather
summer fruits,
Like those who [a]glean vintage
grapes;
There is no cluster to eat
Of the first-ripe fruit *which* [b]my
soul desires.
2 The [c]faithful [1] *man* has perished
from the earth,
And *there is* no one upright among
men.
They all lie in wait for blood;
[d]Every man hunts his brother with
a net.

5 [h]Judg. 5:11
7 [i]Ps. 50:9; Is. 1:11 [j]Job 29:6 [k]Lev. 18:21; 20:1-5; 2 Kin. 16:3; Jer. 7:31; Ezek. 23:37 [3]My own child
8 [l][Deut. 10:12; 1 Sam. 15:22]; Hos. 6:6; 12:6 [m]Gen. 18:19; Is. 1:17 [4]Or *lovingkindness*
11 [n]Lev. 19:36; Hos. 12:7
12 [o]Is. 1:23; 5:7; Amos 6:3, 4; Mic. 2:1, 2
[p]Jer. 9:2-6, 8; Hos. 7:13; Amos 2:4
13 [q]Lev. 26:16; Ps. 107:17
14 [r]Lev. 26:26 [5]Or *Emptiness* or *Humiliation* [6]Tg., Vg. *You shall take hold*
15 [s]Deut. 28:38-40; Amos 5:11; Zeph. 1:13; Hag. 1:6
16 [t]1 Kin. 16:25, 26 [u]1 Kin. 16:30; 21:25, 26; 2 Kin. 21:3; Hos. 5:11 [v]Is. 25:8 [7]Or *object of horror* [8]So with MT, Tg., Vg.; LXX *nations*

CHAPTER 7
1 [a]Is. 17:6 [b]Is. 28:4; Hos. 9:10
2 [c]Ps. 12:1; Is. 57:1 [d]Hab. 1:15 [1]Or *loyal*

6:6,7 Micah, as though speaking on behalf of the people, asked rhetorically how, in light of God's faithfulness toward them, they could continue their hypocrisy by being outwardly religious but inwardly sinful.

6:8 Micah's terse response (v. 8) indicated they should have known the answer to the rhetorical question. Spiritual blindness had led them to offer everything except the one thing He wanted—a spiritual commitment of the heart from which right behavior would ensue (cf. Deut. 10:12-19; Matt. 22:37-39). This theme is often represented in the OT (cf. 1 Sam. 15:22; Is. 1:11-20; Jer. 7:21-23; Hos. 6:6; Amos 5:15).

6:9-16 The Lord was sending judgment; God Himself had appointed the "rod" that would punish His people. The Lord spoke, noting that their corrupt deeds perpetrated on the poor were still continuing, in spite of His warnings and discipline (vv. 10-12). Therefore, a severe judgment was coming (vv. 13-15); it would happen to them just as it did to their northern neighbor, Israel (v. 16) when led by the counsel of wicked kings.

6:9 Hear the rod! Listen for the description of the coming punishment (cf. vv. 13-15; Is. 10:5,24).

6:16 statues of Omri. Ca. 885–874 B.C. He was the founder of Samaria and of Ahab's wicked house as well as a supporter of Jeroboam's superstitions (cf. 1 Kin. 16:16-28). **works of Ahab's house.** Cf. 1 Kin. 21:25,26. (ca. 874–853 B.C.)

7:1-6 Micah lamented the circumstances of his day. In his vain search for an upright person (cf. v. 2), he compared himself to the vinedresser who enters his vineyard late in the season and finds no fruit. The leaders conspired together to get what they wanted (v. 3). No one could be trusted (vv. 5,6). Christ used v. 6 as an illustration when He commissioned the twelve (Matt. 10:1,35,36).

7:1 Woe is me! Micah sounded like Isaiah (cf. Is. 6:5).

3 That they may successfully do evil
with both hands—
The prince asks *for gifts*,
The judge *seeks* a [e]bribe,
And the great *man* utters his evil
desire;
So they scheme together.
4 The best of them *is* [f]like a brier;
The most upright *is sharper* than a
thorn hedge;
The day of your watchman and
your punishment comes;
Now shall be their perplexity.

5 [g]Do not trust in a friend;
Do not put your confidence in a
companion;
Guard the doors of your mouth
From her who lies in your [h]bosom.
6 For [i]son dishonors father,
Daughter rises against her mother,
Daughter-in-law against her
mother-in-law;
A man's enemies *are* the men of his
own household.
7 Therefore I will look to the LORD;
I will [j]wait for the God of my
salvation;
My God will hear me.

Israel's Confession and Comfort

8 [k]Do not rejoice over me, my enemy;
[l]When I fall, I will arise;
When I sit in darkness,
The LORD *will be* a light to me.
9 [m]I will bear the indignation of the
LORD,
Because I have sinned against Him,
Until He pleads my [n]case
And executes justice for me.
He will bring me forth to the light;
I will see His righteousness.
10 Then *she who is* my enemy will see,
And [o]shame will cover her who
said to me,
[p]"Where is the LORD your God?"
My eyes will see her;
Now she will be trampled down
Like mud in the streets.

11 *In* the day when your [q]walls are to
be built,
In that day [2]the decree shall go far
and wide.
12 *In* that day [r]they[3] shall come to
you
From Assyria and the [4]fortified
cities,
From the [5]fortress to [6]the River,
From sea to sea,
And mountain *to* mountain.
13 Yet the land shall be desolate
Because of those who dwell in it,
And [s]for the fruit of their deeds.

God Will Forgive Israel

14 Shepherd Your people with Your
staff,
The flock of Your heritage,
Who dwell [7]solitarily *in* a
[t]woodland,
In the midst of Carmel;
Let them feed *in* Bashan and
Gilead,
As in days of old.

15 "As[u] in the days when you came
out of the land of Egypt,
I will show [8]them [v]wonders."

16 The nations [w]shall see and be
ashamed of all their might;

3 [e] Amos 5:12; Mic. 3:11
4 [f] Is. 55:13; Ezek. 2:6
5 [g] Jer. 9:4 [h] Deut. 28:56
6 [i] Matt. 10:36; Mark 3:21; Luke 8:19; John 7:5
7 [j] Ps. 130:5; Is. 25:9; Lam. 3:24, 25
8 [k] Prov. 24:17; Obad. 12; [Acts 10:43] [l] Ps. 37:24; [Prov. 24:16]; 2 Cor. 4:9
9 [m] Lam. 3:39, 40; [2 Cor. 5:21] [n] Jer. 50:34
10 [o] Ps. 35:26 [p] Ps. 42:3
11 [q] Is. 54:11; [Amos 9:11] [2] Or *the boundary shall be extended*
12 [r] [Is. 11:16; 19:23-25] [3] Lit. *he*, collective of the captives [4] Heb. *arey mazor*, possibly *cities of Egypt* [5] Heb. *mazor*, possibly *Egypt* [6] The Euphrates
13 [s] Jer. 21:14
14 [t] Is. 37:24 [7] Alone
15 [u] Ps. 68:22; 78:12 [v] Ex. 34:10 [8] Lit. *him*, collective for the captives
16 [w] Is. 26:11

7:7 In spite of his dire circumstances, Micah, as a watchman (cf. v. 4) would intently look for evidence of God's working, trusting God to act in His own time and way (cf. Hab. 3:16-19).

7:8-10 Israel confessed her faith in the Lord , warning her enemies that she will rise again (vv. 8, 10). She confessed her sin, acknowledging the justice of God's punishment and anticipating His restoration.

7:10 Where is the LORD your God? Cf. Ps. 42:3,10; Matt. 27:43.

7:11-13 Micah again spoke, recounting the many blessings awaiting the faithful remnant in Messiah's millennial rule. It would include unprecedented expansion (cf. Zech. 2:1-5) and massive infusion of immigrants (cf. Is. 11:15,16). For those who defied Messiah's millennial rulership, their land would become desolate (v. 13; cf. Zech. 14:16-19).

7:14-17 Micah petitioned the Lord (v. 14) to shepherd, feed, and protect His people like a flock (cf. Ps. 23). The Lord answered, reiterating that He would demonstrate His presence and power among them as He did in the Exodus from Egypt (v. 15). As a result (cf. v. 10), the vaunted pride and power of the nations would be rendered powerless (cf. Josh. 2:9-11) and, having been humbled (v. 17), they would no longer listen to or engage in the taunting of His people (v. 16b; cf. Gen. 12:3; Is 52:15).

7:15 wonders. These miracles will be fulfilled in God's judgment on the earth which precedes the Second Advent of Messiah (cf. Rev. 6–19).

God's Forgiveness of Sin

1. God removes our sins as far as the E is from the W (Ps. 103:12)
2. God completely cleanses us from the stain of our sins (Is. 1:18)
3. God throws our sins behind His back (Is. 38:17)
4. God remembers our sins no more (Jer. 31:34)
5. God treads our sins underfoot (Mic. 7:19)
6. God casts our sins into the depths of the sea (Mic. 7:19)

[x]They shall put *their* hand over *their* mouth;
Their ears shall be deaf.
17 They shall lick the [y]dust like a serpent;
[z]They shall crawl from their holes like [9]snakes of the earth.
[a]They shall be afraid of the LORD our God,
And shall fear because of You.
18 [b]Who *is* a God like You,
[c]Pardoning iniquity
And passing over the transgression of [d]the remnant of His heritage?
[e]He does not retain His anger forever,
Because He delights *in* [f]mercy.[1]
19 He will again have compassion on us,
And will subdue our iniquities.

You will cast all [2]our sins
Into the depths of the sea.
20 [g]You will give truth to Jacob
And [3]mercy to Abraham,
[h]Which You have sworn to our fathers
From days of old.

16 [x] Job 21:5 **17** [y] Ps. 72:9; [Is. 49:23] [z] Ps. 18:45 [a] Jer. 33:9 [9] Lit. *crawlers* **18** [b] Ex. 15:11 [c] Ex. 34:6, 7, 9; Is. 43:25; Jer. 50:20 [d] Mic. 4:7 [e] Ps. 103:8, 9, 13; [Is. 57:16] [f] [Ezek. 33:11] [1] Or *lovingkindness* **19** [2] Lit. *their* **20** [g] Luke 1:72, 73 [h] Ps. 105:9 [3] Or *lovingkindness*

7:18-20 In response to the gracious, forgiving character displayed toward Israel by their Master, the repentant remnant of the people extolled His incomparable grace and mercy (cf. Ps. 130:3,4).

7:18 Who *is* a God like You? Micah began this final section with a play on words involving his name. See Introduction: Title.

7:20 sworn to our fathers. In spite of Israel's unfaithfulness to God, the Lord intends to fulfill His unconditional promises in the Abrahamic Covenant made with Abraham and confirmed with Isaac and Jacob (cf. Gen. 12,15,17,22,26,28,35). When enacted in conjunction with the Davidic Covenant, Israel will again be restored as a people and a nation to the land originally promised to Abraham. Jesus Christ, the ultimate descendant of David, will rule from Jerusalem over the world as King of Kings and Lord of Lords (cf. Rev. 17:14; 19:16).

The Book of NAHUM

Title

The book's title is taken from the prophet of God's oracle against Nineveh, the capital of Assyria. Nahum means "comfort" or "consolation" and is a short form of Nehemiah ("comfort of Yahweh"). Nahum is not quoted in the NT, although there may be an allusion to Nah. 1:15 in Rom. 10:15 (cf. Is. 52:7).

Author and Date

The significance of the writing prophets was not their personal lives; it was their message. Thus, background information about the prophet from within the prophecy is rare. Occasionally one of the historical books will shed additional light. In the case of Nahum, nothing is provided except that he was an Elkoshite (1:1), referring either to his birthplace or his place of ministry. Attempts to identify the location of Elkosh have been unsuccessful. Suggestions include Al Qosh, situated in northern Iraq (thus Nahum would have been a descendant of the exiles taken to Assyria in 722 B.C.), Capernaum ("town of Nahum"), or a location in southern Judah (cf. 1:15). His birthplace or locale is not significant to the interpretation of the book.

With no mention of any kings in the introduction, the date of Nahum's prophecy must be implied by historical data. The message of judgment against Nineveh portrays a nation of strength, intimating a time not only prior to her fall in 612 B.C. but probably before the death of Ashurbanipal in 626 B.C., after which Assyria's power fell rapidly. Nahum's mention of the fall of No Amon, also called Thebes (3:8-10), in 663 B.C. (at the hands of Ashurbanipal) appears to be fresh in their minds and there is no mention of the rekindling that occurred ten years later, suggesting a mid-seventh century B.C. date during the reign of Manasseh (ca. 695–642 B.C.; cf. 2 Kin. 21:1-18).

Background and Setting

A century after Nineveh repented at the preaching of Jonah, she returned to idolatry, violence, and arrogance (3:1-4). Assyria was at the height of her power, having recovered from Sennacherib's defeat (701 B.C.) at Jerusalem (cf. Is. 37:36-38). Her borders extended all the way into Egypt. Esarhaddon had recently transplanted conquered peoples into Samaria and Galilee in 670 B.C. (cf. 2 Kin. 17:24; Ezra 4:2), leaving Syria and Palestine very weak. But God brought Nineveh down under the rising power of Babylon's king Nabopolassar and his son, Nebuchadnezzar (ca. 612 B.C.). Assyria's demise turned out just as God had prophesied.

Historical and Theological Themes

Nahum forms a sequel to the book of Jonah, who prophesied over a century earlier. Jonah recounts the remission of God's promised judgment toward Nineveh, while Nahum depicts the later execution of God's judgment. Nineveh was proud of her invulnerable city, with her walls reaching 100 ft. high and with a moat 150 ft. wide and 60 ft. deep; but Nahum established the fact that the sovereign God (1:2-5) would bring vengeance upon those who violated His law (1:8,14; 3:5-7). The same God had a retributive judgment against evil which is also redemptive, bestowing His loving kindnesses upon the faithful (cf. 1:7,12,13,15; 2:2). The prophecy brought comfort to Judah and all who feared the cruel Assyrians. Nahum said Nineveh would end "with an overflowing flood" (1:8); and it happened when the Tigris River overflowed to destroy enough of the walls to let the Babylonians through. Nahum also predicted that the city would be hidden (3:11). After its destruction in 612 B.C., the site was not rediscovered until 1842 A.D.

Interpretive Challenges

Apart from the uncertain identity of Elkosh (cf. Introduction: Author and Date), the prophecy presents no real interpretive difficulties. The book is a straightforward prophetic announcement of judgment against Assyria and her capital Nineveh for cruel atrocities and idolatrous practices.

Outline

I. Superscription (1:1)

II. Destruction of Nineveh Declared (1:2-15)

- A. God's Power Illustrated (1:2-8)
- B. God's Punishment Stated (1:9-15)

III. Destruction of Nineveh Detailed (2:1-13)

- A. The City is Assaulted (2:1-10)
- B. The City is Discredited (2:11-13)

IV. Destruction of Nineveh Demanded (3:1-19)

- A. The First Charge (3:1-3)
- B. The Second Charge (3:4-7)
- C. The Third Charge (3:8-19)

1 The [1]burden [a]against Nineveh. The book of the vision of Nahum the Elkoshite.

God's Wrath on His Enemies

2 God *is* [b]jealous, and the LORD
avenges;
The LORD avenges and *is* furious.
The LORD will take vengeance on
His adversaries,
And He reserves *wrath* for His
enemies;
3 The LORD *is* [c]slow to anger and
[d]great in power,
And will not at all acquit *the*
wicked.

[e]The LORD has His way
In the whirlwind and in the storm,
And the clouds *are* the dust of His
feet.
4 [f]He rebukes the sea and makes it
dry,
And dries up all the rivers.
[g]Bashan and Carmel wither,
And the flower of Lebanon wilts.
5 The mountains quake before Him,
The hills melt,
And the earth [2]heaves at His
presence,
Yes, the world and all who dwell
in it.
6 Who can stand before His
indignation?
And [h]who can endure the
fierceness of His anger?
His fury is poured out like fire,
And the rocks are thrown down by
Him.

7 [i]The LORD *is* good,
A stronghold in the day of
trouble;
And [j]He knows those who trust in
Him.
8 But with an overflowing flood
He will make an utter end of its
place,
And darkness will pursue His
enemies.

9 [k]What do you [3]conspire against the
LORD?
[l]He will make an utter end *of it.*
Affliction will not rise up a second
time.
10 For while tangled [m]*like* thorns,
[n]And while drunken *like*
drunkards,
[o]They shall be devoured like
stubble fully dried.
11 From you comes forth *one*
Who plots evil against the LORD,
A [4]wicked counselor.

CHAPTER 1

1 [a] 2 Kin. 19:36; Jon. 1:2; Nah. 2:8; Zeph. 2:13 [1] *oracle, prophecy*
2 [b] Ex. 20:5; Josh. 24:19
3 [c] Ex. 34:6, 7; Neh. 9:17; Ps. 103:8 [d] [Job 9:4] [e] Ps. 18:17
4 [f] Josh. 3:15, 16; Ps. 106:9; Is. 50:2; Matt. 8:26 [g] Is. 33:9
5 [2] Tg. *burns*
6 [h] Jer. 10:10; [Mal. 3:2]
7 [i] Ps. 25:8; 37:39, 40; 100:5; [Jer. 33:11]; Lam. 3:25 [j] Ps. 1:6; John 10:14; 2 Tim. 2:19
9 [k] Ps. 2:1; Nah. 1:11 [l] 1 Sam. 3:12 [3] Or *devise*
10 [m] 2 Sam. 23:6; Mic. 7:4 [n] Is. 56:12; Nah. 3:11 [o] Is. 5:24; 10:17; Mal. 4:1
11 [4] Lit. *counselor of Belial*

1:1 burden. The prophecy is heavy because it is a message of doom. He was only the messenger of this divine oracle of judgment on Nineveh.

1:2-15 The destruction of Nineveh was announced.

1:2-8 Nahum, defining God's power in general, establishes the fact that He is omnipotent, a holy and jealous God who will punish the wicked and avenge His own.

1:2 jealous. This attribute, often used of God's burning zeal for His wife, Israel, emphasizes His passionate reaction against anyone guilty of spiritual adultery. Possibly the captivity of the 10 northern tribes (722 B.C.) or the invasion of Sennacherib (701 B.C.) is in view here.

1:3 slow to anger. The jealousy of v. 2 should not suggest that God is quick to anger; rather He is longsuffering (cf. Ex. 34:6; Num. 14:18). God had extended His forbearance to Nineveh at least a century earlier in response to their repentance at Jonah's preaching (cf. Jon. 3:10; 4:2). But although patient, His justice will eventually punish the wicked. **whirlwind...storm...clouds.** These figures frequently describe the Lord's appearances (theophanies), often in judgment (cf. Ex. 19:9,16; Ps. 83:15; Is. 29:6; Joel 2:2; 1 Thess. 4:17). Nature is the theater in which His power and majesty is showcased.

1:4 His mighty power is revealed when He rebukes the sea, as in the crossing of the Red Sea (Ex. 14:15-25) and when He withholds His rain from the fertile valleys and coastal highlands. **Bashan... Carmel...Lebanon.** Bashan, located below Mt. Hermon, E of the Jordan was known for her lush pastures (Mic. 7:14). Carmel, along the coast of Canaan, became synonymous with fruitfulness (Song 7:5). Lebanon was renowned for her beautiful cedars (1 Kin. 5:14-18). Yet, they too would wither before the infinite strength of the omnipotent Judge.

1:5 The violent shaking of the earth provides another evidence of the Lord's awesome power, as even that which seems to be most stable trembles.

1:6 This series of rhetorical questions summarizes vv. 2-5; His power and resolve to spew His wrath on Nineveh is irresistible, melting all opposition before it.

1:7 In contrast to v. 6, Nahum eased the fury by adding that God was compassionate, a mighty fortress (cf. Ps. 46:1) to those who put their hope in Him (cf. Is. 33:2-4; 37:3-7,29-38). The verse foreshadowed the vindication of Judah in vv. 12b,13,15; 2:2.

1:8 flood...darkness. Nahum described Nineveh's judgment metaphorically as an engulfing flood and darkness from which none can escape.

1:9-15 Having established God's power and sovereign right to judge generally, Nahum announced specifically God's judgment upon Nineveh, interweaving expressions of blessing and hope for Israel within the oracles of doom upon the wicked nation. The sovereign Judge not only punishes (vv. 9-12a,14) but also saves (vv. 12b, 13,15).

1:9 conspire. All Assyrian attempts to foil God's judgment would end in futility (cf. Ps. 2). Their affliction of His people would not be allowed to occur again (cf. v. 12). Their end was determined.

1:11 wicked counselor. The phrase, lit. "counselor of Belial," suggests Satanic influence on the leadership, identified as the king of Assyria (cf. 3:18). Specific reference could be to Ashurbanipal (669–633 B.C.) or more likely to Sennacherib (705-681 B.C.), who invaded Judah in 701 B.C. and of whom Isaiah speaks in similar language (Is. 10:7).

12 Thus says the LORD:

"Though *they are* [5]safe, and likewise many,
Yet in this manner they will be [p]cut down
When he passes through.
Though I have afflicted you,
I will afflict you no more;
13 For now I will break off his yoke from you,
And burst your bonds apart."

14 The LORD has given a command concerning you:
[6]"Your name shall be perpetuated no longer.
Out of the house of your gods
I will cut off the carved image and the molded image.
I will dig your [q]grave,
For you are [r]vile."[7]

15 Behold, on the mountains
The [s]feet of him who brings good tidings,
Who proclaims peace!
O Judah, keep your appointed feasts,
Perform your vows.
For the [8]wicked one shall no more pass through you;
He is [t]utterly cut off.

The Destruction of Nineveh

2

He[1] who scatters has come up before your face.
Man the fort!
Watch the road!
Strengthen *your* flanks!
Fortify *your* power mightily.

2 For the LORD will restore the excellence of Jacob
Like the excellence of Israel,
For the emptiers have emptied them out
And ruined their vine branches.

3 The shields of his mighty men *are* made red,
The valiant men *are* in scarlet.
The chariots *come* with flaming torches
In the day of his preparation,
And [2]the spears are brandished.
4 The chariots rage in the streets,
They jostle one another in the broad roads;
They seem like torches,

12 [p] [Is. 10:16-19, 33, 34] [5] Or *at peace* or *complete*
14 [q] Ezek. 32:22, 23 [r] Nah. 3:6 [6] Lit. *No more of your name shall be fruitful* [7] Or *contemptible*
15 [s] Is. 40:9; 52:7; Rom. 10:15
[t] Is. 29:7, 8 [8] Lit. *one of Belial*

CHAPTER 2

1 [1] Vg. *He who destroys*
3 [2] Lit. *the cypresses are shaken*; LXX, Syr. *the horses rush about*; Vg. *the drivers are stupefied*

1:12 Thus says the LORD. Used as a common prophetic formula introducing God's unequivocal message, it occurs only here in the book. Verse 12a is related in the third person, denoting the enemy, while in v. 12b the chosen people of God are spoken of in the second person. The safety of a walled city and massive numbers ("many") would not be a sufficient defense. "In this manner" harkens back to vv. 7-10.

1:12b,13 I will afflict you no more. Judah was to be no longer afflicted by Assyria.

1:14 Three judgments were pronounced. First, the king of Assyria, representing the nation, would become destitute of descendants. Second, the gods by which they received their authority would be destroyed. Third, the king would be put to death (cf. the fall of Nineveh in 612 B.C.).

1:15 mountains...feet. The verse echoes Is. 52:7, where it refers to those who announced the deliverance from Babylon. The theme of good tidings and peace reverberates throughout the message of the NT (cf. Luke 2:10; Is. 61:1 with Luke 4:16-21; Rom. 10:15; Eph. 2:14-18). **appointed feasts.** During a siege, people were prevented from going up to Jerusalem to celebrate her annual feasts (cf. Num. 28,29). With the destruction of Assyria, Judah was called upon to celebrate her feasts and to pay the vows made while under siege (cf. Ps. 116:14,17,18).

2:1-13 Nineveh's fall in 612 B.C. at the hands of Nebuchadnezzar of Babylon, though still future in Nahum's day, is described vividly in present tense terms.

2:1 scatters. Assyria had made a practice of dispersing captives to many nations; now she would receive similar judgment. **Man... Watch...Strengthen!** The prophet, with irony and satire, ordered the Assyrians to prepare for the coming invasion from Babylon.

2:2 excellence of Jacob...Israel. This is not a reference to the southern and northern tribes, since the northern tribes had been overrun by Assyria almost a century earlier; but these are titles of honor for Judah, remembering the day when Jacob received God's blessing at Peniel (Gen. 32:27,28) and had his name changed to Israel. Together, they signify the nation's restoration to the promised position. **emptiers have emptied them...** Assyria had repeatedly "emptied" the land, destroying its fruitful vineyards and economic lifeblood.

2:3 shields...made red. Shields were either overlaid with copper, whose reflections of sunshine would make the army appear larger and strike terror in the enemy, or they were covered with hide that was dyed red, so as to extinguish fiery arrows and to minimize the sight of blood. "Scarlet" clothing would have similar benefits. **spears are brandished.** Warriors, denoting their eagerness and readiness for battle, would wave their weapons.

2:4 Confusion reigned in Nineveh, where battle preparations were hurriedly made.

God's Judgment Against Assyria/Nineveh

IN RETROSPECT—Fulfilled

1. Jer. 50:17,18	2. Ezek. 32:22,23

IN PROSPECT—Prophesied

1. Is. 10:5	6. Mic. 5:5,6
2. Is. 10:24-27	7. Nah. 1:1
3. Is. 14:24,25	8. Nah. 2:8
4. Is. 30:31-33	9. Nah. 3:7,18
5. Is. 31:8,9	10. Zeph. 2:13-15

They run like lightning.

5 He remembers his nobles;
They stumble in their walk;
They make haste to her walls,
And the defense is prepared.
6 The gates of the rivers are opened,
And the palace is dissolved.
7 [3]It is decreed:
She shall be led away captive,
She shall be brought up;
And her maidservants shall lead
her as with the voice of doves,
Beating their breasts.

8 Though Nineveh of old *was* like a
pool of water,
Now they flee away.
[4]"Halt! Halt!" *they cry;*
But no one turns back.
9 [5]Take spoil of silver!
Take spoil of [a]gold!
There is no end of treasure,
Or wealth of every desirable prize.
10 She is empty, desolate, and waste!
The heart melts, and the knees
shake;
Much pain *is* in every side,
And all their faces [6]are drained of
color.

11 Where *is* the dwelling of the [b]lions,
And the feeding place of the young
lions,
Where the lion walked, the lioness
and lion's cub,
And no one made *them* afraid?
12 The lion tore in pieces enough for
his cubs,
[7]Killed for his lionesses,
[c]Filled his caves with prey,
And his dens with [8]flesh.

13 "Behold, [d]I *am* against you," says the
LORD of hosts, "I will burn [9]your chariots
in smoke, and the sword shall devour your
young lions; I will cut off your prey from
the earth, and the voice of your [e]messen-
gers shall be heard no more."

The Woe of Nineveh

3 Woe to the [a]bloody city!
It *is* all full of lies *and* robbery.
Its [1]victim never departs.
2 The noise of a whip
And the noise of rattling wheels,
Of galloping horses,
Of [2]clattering chariots!
3 Horsemen charge with bright
sword and glittering spear.
There is a multitude of slain,
A great number of bodies,
Countless corpses—
They stumble over the corpses—
4 Because of the multitude of
[3]harlotries of the [4]seductive
harlot,
[b]The mistress of sorceries,
Who sells nations through her
harlotries,
And families through her sorceries.

7 [3]Heb. *Huzzab*
8 [4]Lit. *Stand*
9 [a]Ezek. 7:19; Zeph. 1:18 [5]*Plunder*
10 [6]LXX, Tg., Vg. *gather blackness;* Joel 2:6
11 [b]Job 4:10, 11; Ezek. 19:2-7
12 [c]Is. 10:6; Jer. 51:34 [7]Lit. *Strangled* [8]Torn flesh
13 [d]Jer. 21:13; Ezek. 5:8; Nah. 3:5 [e]2 Kin. 18:17-25; 19:9-13, 23 [9]Lit. *her*

CHAPTER 3

1 [a]Ezek. 22:2, 3; 24:6-9; Hab. 2:12 [1]Lit. *prey*
2 [2]*bounding* or *jolting*
4 [b]Is. 47:9-12; Rev. 18:2, 3 [3]Spiritual unfaithfulness [4]Lit. *goodly charm,* in a bad sense

2:5 They make haste to her walls. This may continue the thought of v. 4, depicting Nineveh's royalty and military leaders dashing to one of her many defense towers which, according to the Greek historian Diodorus Siculus, numbered 1,500 and reached a height of 200 ft.. It is also possible that the latter part of the verse is a description of the attackers preparing to erect a "mantelet," a small fortress type box in which soldiers rode for protection as they advanced to the wall.

2:6 gates of the rivers. Nineveh, lying at the confluence of 3 rivers (the Tigris and two smaller rivers), constructed dams to minimize the damage of seasonal flooding to her walls. The latter part of v. 6 suggests that these dam gates were opened, causing the walls to be dissolved and the palace to be taken (cf. Introduction: Historical and Theological Themes; Nah. 1:8).

2:7 She shall be led away captive. The goddess of Nineveh, probably Ishtar, was taken by her attackers to demonstrate the superiority of their gods (cf. 1 Sam. 4:1-11). The temple prostitutes ("maidservants") mourned the fate of their goddess.

2:8 pool of water. Though Nineveh was like an oasis in the desert that attracted many people, they fled from the devastation.

2:9 Take spoil. Spoils abounded in Nineveh, but it was her turn to be plundered.

2:10 heart melts. The great city of Nineveh, lying in ruin, evoked fear and terror in those who observed it (cf. Dan. 5:6).

2:11-13 Where *is*. Archeologists have found a carving from a palace showing an Assyrian king on a lion hunt. Nahum rhetorically asks where Nineveh has gone. No longer describing Nineveh's fall, he taunted her, ridiculing her fall from power and glory. Like a pride of lions, with plenty to eat and in fear of no enemy, Nineveh ruthlessly "tore in pieces" her prey. She herself will become prey for another nation, under the sovereign direction of God. "I *am* against you" should be the most feared words a nation could receive from God.

2:13 burn your chariots. Nineveh, known for burning the captured cities, would receive the same fate. **your messengers.** The voice of the messengers who carried the edicts of the mighty king of Assyria to the captured nations would become mute.

3:1-19 The prophet Nahum, asserting that the destruction of Nineveh was justly deserved, makes 3 charges against her (vv. 1,4,8-10), followed by the consequences (vv. 2,3,5-7,11-19).

3:1 bloody city. The first accusation was a charge well documented in history. Assyria proved to be an unusually cruel, bloodthirsty nation. **lies.** Assyria employed falsehood and treachery to subdue her enemies (cf. 2 Kin. 18:28-32). **robbery.** See 2:11,12. Preying upon her victims, she filled her cities with the goods of other nations.

3:2,3 These verses reach back to the scene portrayed in 2:3-5. Assyria was so overrun that she is filled with corpses, causing the defenders to stumble over them.

3:4 The second charge against Nineveh was spiritual and moral harlotry. The nation was likened to a beautiful prostitute who seduced the nations with her illicit enticements.

5 "Behold, I *am* [c]against you," says
the LORD of hosts;
[d]"I will lift your skirts over your face,
I will show the nations your
nakedness,
And the kingdoms your shame.
6 I will cast abominable filth upon
you,
Make you [e]vile,[5]
And make you [f]a spectacle.
7 It shall come to pass *that* all who
look upon you
[g]Will flee from you, and say,
[h]'Nineveh is laid waste!
[i]Who will bemoan her?'
Where shall I seek comforters for
you?"

8 [j]Are you better than [k]No[6] Amon
That was situated by the [7]River,
That had the waters around her,
Whose rampart *was* the sea,
Whose wall *was* the sea?
9 Ethiopia and Egypt *were* her
strength,
And *it was* boundless;
[l]Put and Lubim were [8]your helpers.
10 Yet she *was* carried away,
She went into captivity;
[m]Her young children also were
dashed to pieces
[n]At the head of every street;
They [o]cast lots for her honorable
men,
And all her great men were bound
in chains.
11 You also will be [p]drunk;
You will be hidden;
You also will seek refuge from the
enemy.
12 All your strongholds *are* [q]fig trees
with ripened figs:
If they are shaken,
They fall into the mouth of the eater.
13 Surely, [r]your people in your midst
are women!
The gates of your land are wide
open for your enemies;
Fire shall devour the [s]bars of your
gates.

14 Draw your water for the siege!
[t]Fortify your strongholds!
Go into the clay and tread the
mortar!
Make strong the brick kiln!
15 There the fire will devour you,
The sword will cut you off;
It will eat you up like a [u]locust.

Make yourself many—like the
locust!
Make yourself many— like the
swarming locusts!
16 You have multiplied your
[v]merchants more than the
stars of heaven.
The locust plunders and flies away.
17 [w]Your commanders *are* like
swarming locusts,
And your generals like great
grasshoppers,
Which camp in the hedges on a
cold day;
When the sun rises they flee away,
And the place where they *are* is not
known.

18 [x]Your shepherds slumber, O [y]king
of Assyria;
Your nobles rest *in the dust.*

5 [c] Jer. 50:31; Ezek. 26:3; Nah. 2:13 [d] Is. 47:2, 3; Jer. 13:26 **6** [e] Nah. 1:14 [f] Heb. 10:33 [5] *despicable* **7** [g] Rev. 18:10 [h] Jon. 3:3; 4:11 [i] Is. 51:19; Jer. 15:5 **8** [j] Amos 6:2 [k] Jer. 46:25; Ezek. 30:14-16 [6] Ancient Thebes; Tg., Vg. *populous Alexandria* [7] Lit. *rivers,* the Nile and the surrounding canals **9** [l] Gen. 10:6; Jer. 46:9; Ezek. 27:10 [8] LXX *her* **10** [m] Ps. 137:9; Is. 13:16; Hos. 13:16 [n] Lam. 2:19 [o] Joel 3:3; Obad. 11 **11** [p] Is. 49:26; Jer. 25:27; Nah. 1:10 **12** [q] Rev. 6:12, 13 **13** [r] Is. 19:16; Jer. 50:37; 51:30 [s] Ps. 147:13; Jer. 51:30 **14** [t] Nah. 2:1 **15** [u] Joel 1:4 **16** [v] Rev. 18:3, 11-19 **17** [w] Rev. 9:7 **18** [x] Ex. 15:16; Ps. 76:5, 6; Is. 56:10; Jer. 51:57 [y] Jer. 50:18; Ezek. 31:3

3:5,6 Nineveh would be publicly exposed, resulting in shame and humiliation.

3:7 Nineveh is laid waste! Instead of mourning, there would be rejoicing at her fall. None would be found to comfort her; she would bear her misery alone.

3:8-10 Nahum sets forth the third and final charge against Nineveh: they hadn't learned from No Amon. Also known as Thebes, No Amon was the great capital of southern Egypt, 400 mi. S of Cairo. One of the most magnificent ancient civilizations of the world, it was renowned for its 100 gates, a temple measuring 330 ft. long and 170 ft. wide, and its network of canals. It fell to Ashurbanipal of Assyria in 663 B.C. Like No Amon by the Nile, Nineveh was situated by the Tigris River, enjoying the security of conquered nations around her. However, her end would be like that of No Amon.

3:9 Ethiopia...Egypt...Put...Lubim. No Amon was well protected on all sides, nestled between lower Egypt on the N and Ethiopia on the S. The location of Put is best identified in the general vicinity of North Africa. Josephus says that Put, the third son of Ham (Gen. 10:6), was the founder of Libya. Lubim has been identified with the area of modern Libya as well.

3:11 drunk. As predicted (cf. 1:10), Nineveh would be made to drink of God's wrath, making her drunk and defenseless to His judgment.

3:12,13 Nahum employed a series of metaphors to emphasize that Nineveh's strong defenses would be easily overrun. Their walls would be like ripe fruit that falls at the slightest shaking and their battle forces like weak women.

3:14,15 The prophet taunted the people with sarcasm, urging them to prepare for battle, to fortify the city's defenses, only to be destroyed. As the locust leaves nothing, stripping all the foliage, so there would be nothing left of Nineveh (cf. Amos 7:1).

3:16 multiplied your merchants. Nineveh had multiplied her merchants, bringing immense wealth, which is just more to destroy.

3:17 locusts. Not only was Nineveh's commercial strength gone (v. 16), but her governing resources disappeared as well. After camping for the night within the massive walls of this great citadel, the locusts, depicting Assyria's leadership, flew away with the first rays of warm sunshine in search of food.

Your people are [z]scattered on the
mountains,
And no one gathers them.
19 Your injury *has* no healing,
[a]Your wound is severe.
[b]All who hear news of you
Will clap *their* hands over you,
For upon whom has not your
wickedness passed
continually?

18 [z] 1 Kin. 22:17; Is. 13:14

19 [a] Jer. 46:11; Mic. 1:9
[b] Job 27:23; Lam. 2:15; Zeph. 2:15

3:18,19 The destiny of Nineveh was certain. She had received the death blow; she would not recover. And all who hear of it would rejoice. Assyria had devastated the nations with her atrocities and cruelties; the news of her downfall brought happiness and mirth among the nations.

3:18 slumber…rest The Assyrian leaders and army, described in terms of exhaustion and sleep, were dead; the people were scattered. There were none left to help against the invasion of the Babylonians, to whom they fell in 612 B.C.

The Book of HABAKKUK

Title

This prophetic book takes its name from its author and possibly means "one who embraces" (1:1; 3:1). By the end of the prophecy, this name becomes appropriate as the prophet clings to God regardless of his confusion about God's plans for his people.

Author and Date

As with many of the Minor Prophets, nothing is known about the prophet except that which can be inferred from the book. In the case of Habakkuk, internal information is virtually nonexistent, making conclusions about his identity and life conjectural. His simple introduction as "the prophet Habakkuk" may imply that he needed no introduction since he was a well known prophet of his day. It is certain that he was a contemporary of Jeremiah, Ezekiel, Daniel, and Zephaniah.

The mention of the Chaldeans (1:6) suggests a late seventh century B.C. date, shortly before Nebuchadnezzar commenced his military march through Nineveh (612 B.C.), Haran (609 B.C.), and Carchemish (605 B.C.), on his way to Jerusalem (605 B.C.). Habakkuk's bitter lament (1:2-4) may reflect a time period shortly after the death of Josiah (609 B.C.), days in which the godly king's reforms (cf. 2 Kin. 23) were quickly overturned by his successor, Jehoiakim (Jer. 22:13-19).

Background and Setting

Habakkuk prophesied during the final days of the Assyrian Empire and the beginning of Babylonia's world rulership under Nabopolassar and his son Nebuchadnezzar. When Nabopolassar ascended to power in 626 B.C., he immediately began to expand his influence to the N and W. Under the leadership of his son, the Babylonian army overthrew Nineveh in 612 B.C., forcing the Assyrian nobility to take refuge first in Haran and then Carchemish. Nebuchadnezzar pursued them, overrunning Haran in 609 B.C. and Carchemish in 606 B.C.

The Egyptian king Necho, traveling through Judah in 609 B.C. to assist the fleeing Assyrian king, was opposed by King Josiah at Megiddo (2 Chr. 35:20-24). Josiah was killed in the ensuing battle, leaving his throne to a succession of 3 sons and a grandson. Earlier, as a result of discovering the Book of the Law in the temple (622 B.C.), Josiah had instituted significant spiritual reforms in Judah (2 Kin. 22,23), abolishing many of the idolatrous practices of his father Amon (2 Kin. 21:20-22) and grandfather Manasseh (2 Kin. 21:11-13). Upon his death, however, the nation quickly reverted to her evil ways (cf. Jer. 22:13-19), causing Habakkuk to question God's silence and apparent lack of punitive action (1:2-4) to purge His covenant people.

Historical and Theological Themes

The opening verses reveal a historical situation similar to the days of Amos and Micah. Justice had essentially disappeared from the Land; violence and wickedness were pervasive, existing unchecked. In the midst of these dark days, the prophet cried out for divine intervention (1:2-4). God's response, that He was sending the Chaldeans to judge Judah (1:5-11), creates an even greater theological dilemma for Habakkuk: Why didn't God purge His people and restore their righteousness? How could God use the Chaldeans to judge a people more righteous than they (1:12–2:1)? God's answer that He would judge the Chaldeans also (2:2-20), did not fully satisfy the prophet's theological quandary; in fact, it only intensified it. In Habakkuk's mind, the issue crying for resolution is no longer God's righteous response toward evil (or lack thereof), but the vindication of God's character and covenant with His people (1:13). Like Job, the prophet argued with God, and through that experience he achieved a deeper understanding of God's sovereign character and a firmer faith in Him (cf. Job 42:5,6; Is. 55:8,9). Ultimately, Habakkuk realized that God was not to be worshiped merely because of the temporal blessings He bestowed, but for His own sake (3:17-19).

Interpretive Challenges

The queries of the prophet represent some of the most fundamental questions in all of life, with the answers providing crucial foundation stones on which to build a proper understanding of God's character and His sovereign ways in history. The core of his message lies in the call to trust God (2:4), "the just shall live by his faith." The NT references ascribe unusual importance theologically to Habakkuk. The writer of Hebrews quotes Hab. 2:4 to amplify the believer's need to remain strong and faithful in the midst of affliction and trials (Heb. 10:38). The apostle Paul, on the other hand, employs the verse twice (Rom. 1:17; Gal. 3:11) to accentuate the doctrine of justification by faith. There need not be any interpretive conflict, however, for the emphasis in both Habakkuk and the NT references goes beyond the act of faith to include the continuity of faith. Faith is not a one-time act, but a way of life. The true believer, declared righteous by God, will habitually persevere in faith throughout all his life (cf. Col. 1:22,23; Heb. 3:12-14). He will trust the sovereign God who only does what is right.

Outline

- I. Superscription (1:1)
- II. The Prophet's Perplexities (1:2–2:20)
  - A. His first complaint (1:2-4)
  - B. God's first response (1:5-11)
  - C. His second complaint (1:12–2:1)
  - D. God's second response (2:2-20)
- III. The Prophet's Prayer (3:1-19)
  - A. Petition for God's mercy (3:1,2)
  - B. Praise of God's power (3:3-15)
  - C. Promise of God's sufficiency (3:16-19)

1

The [1]burden which the prophet Habakkuk saw.

The Prophet's Question

2 O LORD, how long shall I cry,
[a]And You will not hear?
Even cry out to You, [b]"Violence!"
And You will [c]not save.
3 Why do You show me iniquity,
And cause *me* to see [2]trouble?
For plundering and violence *are* before me;
There is strife, and contention arises.
4 Therefore the law is powerless,
And justice never goes forth.
For the [d]wicked surround the righteous;
Therefore perverse judgment proceeds.

The LORD's Reply

5 "Look[e] among the nations and watch—
Be utterly astounded!
For *I will* work a work in your days
Which you would not believe,
though it were told *you*.
6 For indeed I am [f]raising up the Chaldeans,
A bitter and hasty [g]nation
Which marches through the breadth of the earth,
To possess dwelling places *that are* not theirs.
7 They are terrible and dreadful;
Their judgment and their dignity proceed from themselves.
8 Their horses also are [h]swifter than leopards,
And more fierce than evening wolves.
Their [3]chargers [4]charge ahead;
Their cavalry comes from afar;
They fly as the [i]eagle *that* hastens to eat.

9 "They all come for violence;
Their faces are set *like* the east wind.
They gather captives like sand.
10 They scoff at kings,
And princes are scorned by them.
They deride every stronghold,
For they heap up earthen *mounds* and seize it.

CHAPTER 1

1 [1] *oracle, prophecy*
2 [a] Lam. 3:8 [b] Mic. 2:1, 2; 3:1-3 [c] [Job 21:5-16]
3 [2] Or *toil*
4 [d] Jer. 12:1
5 [e] Is. 29:14; Ezek. 12:22-28
6 [f] Deut. 28:49, 50; 2 Kin. 24:2; 2 Chr. 36:17; Jer. 4:11-13; Mic. 4:10 [g] Ezek. 7:24; 21:31
8 [h] Jer. 4:13 [i] Job 9:26; 39:29, 30; Lam. 4:19; Ezek. 17:3; Hos. 8:1; Matt. 24:28; Luke 17:37 [3] Lit. *horsemen* [4] Lit. *spring about*

1:1 burden. A weighty, heavy oracle of judgment (cf. 1:5-11; 2:2-20) is often depicted by this term when employed by the prophets to announce God's wrath against sin (e.g., Is. 13:1; 15:1; 17:1; 19:1; Nah. 1:1; Zech. 9:1; 12:1; Mal. 1:1). **saw.** God's message to Habakkuk took the form of a vision.

1:2-4 In Habakkuk's first complaint, he perceived that God appeared indifferent to Judah's sin. Jealous for His righteousness and knowing that a breach of the covenant required judgment (cf. Deut. 28), Habakkuk questioned God's wisdom, expressing bewilderment at His seeming inactivity in the face of blatant violation of His law. The Jews had sinned by violence and injustice and should have been punished by the same.

1:2 how long shall I cry. The phrase, reflecting the prophet's impatience, is frequently used by the psalmist to express similar thoughts of perplexity (cf. Pss. 13:1,2; 62:3; Jer. 14:9; Matt. 27:46).

Other Psalms

1.	"The Song of Deliverance"	Exodus 15:1-18
2.	"The Song of Moses"	Deuteronomy 32:1-43
3.	"The Song of Deborah"	Judges 5:1-31
4.	"The Song of Hannah"	1 Samuel 2:1-10
5.	"The Song of the Women"	1 Samuel 18:6,7
6.	"The Song of David"	2 Samuel 22:1-51
7.	"The Song of Hezekiah"	Isaiah 38:9-20
8.	"The Song of Jonah"	Jonah 2:1-9
9.	"The Song of Habakkuk"	Habakkuk 3:1-19
10.	"The Song of Mary"	Luke 1:46-55

1:2,3 Violence...iniquity...trouble...plundering. Judah's society is defined with 4 terms denoting malicious wickedness by which one morally and ethically oppresses his neighbor, resulting in contention and strife.

1:2 And You will not save. The prophet wanted a cleansing, purging, chastening, and revival among the people that would return them to righteousness.

1:4 law is powerless. Lit. the "law is chilled, numbed" (cf. Gen. 45:26; Ps. 77:2). It had no respect, was given no authority. As hands rendered useless by cold, the impact and effectiveness of the law was paralyzed by the corruption of Judah's leaders (cf. Eccl. 8:11).

1:5-11 In response to Habakkuk's perplexity and pleading, God broke His silence, informing him that He was not indifferent to Judah's sin; but rather than revival, He was sending the "terrible and dreadful" judgment (v. 7).

1:5 Look...watch...Be utterly astounded! The series of commands is plural, indicating that the wider community of Judah and Jerusalem were to take note of this imminent invasion. Paul quotes this text in Acts 13:41.

1:6-8 The Chaldeans (Babylonians) would come at the behest of the divine Commander. He is the Sovereign who brings this people of ruthless character and conduct to invade Judah. The Chaldeans are described as self-assured, self-sufficient, self-deified, and deadly (cf. Jer. 51:20).

1:8 evening wolves. These were wolves who had suffered hunger all day long and were forced to prowl into the night for food. Like wolves, Babylon's army displayed extraordinary stamina and an undaunted eagerness to attack for the purpose of devouring the spoils of victory.

1:10 Whether it be royal authority or physical obstacles, the Babylonian army marched forward with nothing but scorn for those in their path. **heap up earthen *mounds*.** Rubble and dirt piled up against the fortress or city wall as a ramp to gain entry.

11 Then *his* [5]mind changes, and he
transgresses;
He commits offense,
[j]*Ascribing* this power to his god."

The Prophet's Second Question

12 Are You not [k]from everlasting,
O LORD my God, my Holy One?
We shall not die.
O LORD, [l]You have appointed them
for judgment;
O Rock, You have marked them for
[m]correction.
13 *You are* of purer eyes than to
behold evil,
And cannot look on wickedness.
Why do You look on those who
deal treacherously,
And hold Your tongue when the
wicked devours
A *person* more righteous than he?
14 *Why* do You make men like fish of
the sea,
Like creeping things *that have* no
ruler over them?
15 They take up all of them with a
hook,
They catch them in their net,
And gather them in their dragnet.
Therefore they rejoice and are glad.
16 Therefore [n]they sacrifice to their
net,
And burn incense to their
dragnet;
Because by them their share *is*
[6]sumptuous
And their food plentiful.
17 Shall they therefore empty their
net,
And continue to slay nations
without pity?

2 I will [a]stand my watch
And set myself on the rampart,
And watch to see what He will say
to me,
And what I will answer when I am
corrected.

The Just Live by Faith

2 Then the LORD answered me and said:

[b]"Write the vision
And make *it* plain on tablets,
That he may run who reads it.
3 For [c]the vision *is* yet for an
appointed time;
But at the end it will speak, and it
will [d]not lie.
Though it tarries, [e]wait for it;
Because it will [f]surely come,
It will not tarry.

11 [j]Dan. 5:4 [5]Lit. *spirit* or *wind*
12 [k]Deut. 33:27; Ps. 90:2; 93:2; Mal. 3:6 [l]Is. 10:5-7; Mal. 3:5 [m]Jer. 25:9
16 [n]Deut. 8:17 [6]Lit. *fat*

CHAPTER 2

1 [a]Is. 21:8, 11
2 [b]Is. 8:1
3 [c]Dan. 8:17, 19; 10:14 [d]Ezek. 12:24, 25 [e][Heb. 10:37, 38] [f]Ps. 27:13, 14; [James 5:7, 8; 2 Pet. 3:9]

1:11 to his god. Though the Chaldeans were God's instruments of judgment, their self-sufficiency and self-adulation planted the seeds for their own destruction (described in 2:2-20), as they stood guilty of idolatry and blasphemy before the sovereign Lord.

1:12–2:1 Habakkuk, in his reaction to the perplexing revelation (vv. 5-11), declared his confidence in the Lord (v. 12), then unveiled his second complaint, namely, how could the Lord use a wicked nation (the Chaldeans) to judge a nation (Judah) more righteous than they (vv. 13-17)? The prophet ended by expressing his determination to wait for an answer (2:1).

1:12 O LORD my God...Holy One. Although the prophet could not fully comprehend the sovereign workings of His righteous God, he expressed his complete faith and trust. As he rehearsed the unchangeable character of God as eternal, sovereign, and holy, he became assured that Judah would not be completely destroyed (cf. Jer. 31:35-40; 33:23-26). Under the faithful hand of God, he realized that the Chaldeans were coming to correct, not annihilate. **O Rock.** A title for God which expresses His immovable and unshakeable character (cf. Pss. 18:2,31,46; 31:2,3; 62:2,6,7; 78:16,20,35).

1:13 purer eyes. In spite of the prophet's expressions of faith and trust, he found himself in even further perplexity. The essence of Habakkuk's next quandary is expressed in this verse: If God is too pure to behold evil, then how can He use the wicked to devour a person more righteous than he? Would not God's use of the Chaldeans result in even greater damage to His righteous character?

1:14-17 Lest God had forgotten just how wicked the Chaldeans were, Habakkuk drew attention to their evil character and behavior. Life was cheap to the Chaldeans. In the face of their ruthless tactics of war, other societies were "like fish of the sea, like creeping things that have no ruler over them." In light of their reputation (vv. 6-10), how could God have unleashed this ruthless force upon another helpless people?

1:16 sacrifice...burn incense to their dragnet. If that is not enough, the prophet added that they attributed their gain to their own military might rather than to the true God.

1:17 empty their net. How long will the aggressor (the Chaldeans) be permitted to pursue injustice and engage in such wickedness? Can God tolerate it indefinitely?

2:1 stand my watch. Comparing himself to a watchman (cf. Ezek. 3,33), standing as a sentinel upon the city walls, Habakkuk prepared to wait for God's answer and to ponder his reply.

2:2-20 In response to Habakkuk's second complaint (1:12–2:1), the Lord announced that He would judge the Chaldeans as well for their wickedness. His reply included: 1) the instructions to write it down, as a reminder that it would surely occur (vv. 2,3); 2) a description of the character of the wicked in comparison to the righteous (vv. 4,5); and 3) the pronouncement of 5 woes describing the Chaldeans' demise (vv. 6-20).

2:2,3 Write the vision. Habakkuk was to record the vision to preserve it for posterity, so that all who read it would know of the certainty of its fulfillment (cf. similar language in Dan. 12:4,9). The prophecy had lasting relevance and thus had to be preserved. Although a period of time would occur before its fulfillment, all were to know that it would occur at God's "appointed time" (cf. Is. 13; Jer. 50,51). Babylon would fall to the Medo-Persian kingdom of Cyrus ca. 539 B.C. (cf. Dan. 5).

2:2 That he may run who reads it. Perhaps referring 1) to clarity of form, so even the one who runs by it may easily absorb its meaning, or 2) to clarity of content, so that the courier could easily transmit the message to others.

4 "Behold the proud,
His soul is not upright in him;
But the [g]just shall live by his
faith.

Woe to the Wicked

5 "Indeed, because he transgresses by
wine,
He is a proud man,
And he does not stay at home.
Because he [h]enlarges his desire as
[1]hell,
And he *is* like death, and cannot be
satisfied,
He gathers to himself all nations
And heaps up for himself all
peoples.

6 "Will not all these [i]take up a
proverb against him,
And a taunting riddle against him,
and say,
'Woe to him who increases
What is not his—how long?
And to him who loads himself
with [2]many pledges'?
7 Will not [3]your creditors rise up
suddenly?
Will they not awaken who oppress
you?
And you will become their booty.
8 [j]Because you have plundered many
nations,
All the remnant of the people shall
plunder you,
Because of men's [4]blood
And the violence of the land *and*
the city,
And of all who dwell in it.

9 "Woe to him who covets evil gain
for his house,
That he may [k]set his nest on high,
That he may be delivered from the
[5]power of disaster!
10 You give shameful counsel to your
house,
Cutting off many peoples,
And sin *against* your soul.
11 For the stone will cry out from the
wall,
And the beam from the timbers
will answer it.

12 "Woe to him who builds a town
with bloodshed,
Who establishes a city by iniquity!
13 Behold, *is it* not of the LORD of
hosts
That the peoples labor [6]to feed the
fire,
And nations weary themselves in
vain?
14 For the earth will be filled
With the knowledge of the glory of
the LORD,
As the waters cover the sea.

4 [g] [John 3:36]; Rom. 1:17; Heb. 10:38
5 [h] Prov. 27:20; 30:16; Is. 5:11-15 [1] Or *Sheol*
6 [i] Mic. 2:4 [2] Syr., Vg. *thick clay*
7 [3] Lit. *those who bite you*
8 [j] Is. 33:1; Jer. 27:7; Ezek. 39:10; Zech. 2:8

[4] Or *bloodshed*
9 [k] Jer. 49:16; Obad. 4 [5] Lit. *hand of evil*
13 [6] Lit. *for what satisfies fire,* for what is of no lasting value

2:4 the proud. While the context makes this an obvious reference to the Chaldeans, the passage introduces the marks which distinguish all wicked from all righteous, regardless of ethnic origin. Two opposing characteristics are here contrasted. The proud trusts in himself; the just lives by his faith. **the just shall live by his faith.** In contrast to the proud, the just will be truly preserved through his faithfulness to God. This is the core of God's message to/through Habakkuk. Both the aspect of justification by faith, as noted by Paul's usage in Rom. 1:17 and Gal. 3:11, as well as the aspect of sanctification by faith, as employed by the writer of Hebrews (10:38) reflect the essence of Habakkuk; no conflict exists. The emphasis in both Habakkuk and the NT references goes beyond the act of faith to include the continuity of faith. Faith is not a one-time act, but a way of life. The true believer, declared righteous by God, will persevere in faith as the pattern of his life (cf. Col. 1:22,23; Heb. 3:12-14).

2:5 The diatribe against the Chaldeans served as the basis for the denunciations described in vv. 6-20. They were proud and greedy. Like hell and death (cf. Prov. 1:12; 27:20; 30:15,16), they were never satisfied but always wanted more.

2:6-20 Five woes, in the form of a taunt song, were pronounced upon the Chaldeans in anticipation of their eventual judgment. Presented in 5 stanzas of 3 verses each, the 5 woes were directed at 5 different classes of evildoers.

2:6-8 The first woe charged extortion, i.e., plundering nations under threat of great bodily harm for the purpose of making themselves rich. As a result, they were to become plunder for those nations who remained.

2:6 all these. A reference to all the nations who suffered at the hands of the Babylonians. **Woe.** An interjection often used in prophetic literature to introduce a judicial indictment or a sentence of judgment (Is. 5:8,11,18,20-22; Jer. 22:13; 23:1; Amos 5:18; 6:1). **many pledges.** The Babylonians exacted heavy taxation of conquered nations. Such action often accompanied loans with excessive interest made to the poor (cf. Deut. 24:10-13; 2 Kin. 4:1-7; Neh. 5:1-13).

2:7 your creditors. The survivor nations, from whom taxation was extorted (cf. v. 8).

2:9-11 The second charge, of premeditated exploitation borne out of covetousness, was a continuation of vv. 6-8. The walls of their houses, built with stones and timbers taken from others, testified against them (v. 11).

2:9 set his nest on high. Wanting to protect themselves from any recriminations their enemies might seek to shower upon them, the Chaldeans had sought to make their cities impregnable and inaccessible to the enemy (cf. Is. 14:13,14).

2:10 You give shameful counsel. The Chaldean leaders by counseling to kill, shamed themselves and harmed their souls.

2:12-14 The third woe accuses them of being ruthless despots, building luxurious palaces by means of bloodshed and forced labor. Like a fire that burns everything given to it, their labors would all be futile, having no lasting value (v. 13; cf. Mic. 3:10).

2:14 filled. In contrast to the self-exaltation of the Chaldeans, whose efforts come to naught, God promised that the whole earth would recognize His glory at the establishment of His millennial kingdom (cf. Num. 14:21; Ps. 72:19; Is. 6:3; 11:9).

15 "Woe to him who gives drink to his
neighbor,
[7]Pressing *him to* your [l]bottle,
Even to make *him* drunk,
That you may look on [8]his
nakedness!
16 You are filled with shame instead
of glory.
You also—drink!
And [9]be exposed as
uncircumcised!
The cup of the LORD's right hand
will be turned against you,
And utter shame will be on your
glory.
17 For the violence *done to* Lebanon
will cover you,
And the plunder of beasts *which*
made them afraid,
Because of men's blood
And the violence of the land *and*
the city,
And of all who dwell in it.

18 "What profit is the image, that its
maker should carve it,
The molded image, a teacher of
lies,
That the maker of its mold should
trust in it,
To make mute idols?
19 Woe to him who says to wood,
'Awake!'
To silent stone, 'Arise! It shall
teach!'
Behold, it is overlaid with gold and
silver,
Yet in it there is no breath at all.

20 "But[m] the LORD is in His holy
temple.
Let all the earth keep silence before
Him."

The Prophet's Prayer

3 A prayer of Habakkuk the prophet, on
[1]Shigionoth.

2 O LORD, I have heard Your speech
and was afraid;
O LORD, revive Your work in the
midst of the years!
In the midst of the years make *it*
known;
In wrath remember mercy.

3 God came from Teman,
The Holy One from Mount Paran.
Selah

15 [l] Hos. 7:5 [7] Lit. *Attaching* or *Joining* [8] Lit. *their*
16 [9] DSS, LXX *reel!*; Syr., Vg. *fall fast asleep!*
20 [m] Zeph. 1:7; Zech. 2:13

CHAPTER 3

1 [1] Exact meaning unknown

2:15-17 The fourth charge is debauchery, wherein Babylon forced others to become intoxicated and poisoned, making them behave shamefully and become easy prey. As a result, they too would be forced to drink the cup of God's wrath and exposed to public shame (cf. Jer. 49:12).

2:16 uncircumcised. This word refers to "foreskin," expressing in Heb. thought the greatest contempt, the sign of being an alien from God. *See note on Jer. 4:4.* **cup of the LORD's right hand.** A metaphor referring to divine retribution, served up by His powerful right hand (cf. Ps. 21:8). What the Chaldeans did to others, would also be done to them (vv. 7,8). **shame will be on your glory.** Carrying out the metaphor of drunkenness, here is a reference to the humiliation of "shameful spewing." The very thing in which they gloried would become the object of their shame. While the Lord's glory would be "as the waters cover the seas" (v. 14), Babylon's glory would be covered with shame.

2:17 violence. The reference may be to the ruthless exploitation of trees and animals, providing building materials, firewood, and food, which often accompanied military campaigns. Lebanon's beautiful cedars were plundered for selfish purposes (cf. Is. 14:7,8; 37:24). It also includes the slaughter of men. Verse 17b suggests that it may symbolize Israel and her inhabitants, whom Nebuchadnezzar conquered (cf. 2 Kin. 14:9; Jer. 22:6,23; Ezek. 17:3).

2:18-20 The fifth accusation is idolatry, exposing the folly of following other gods (cf. Is. 41:24; 44:9). The destruction of the Chaldeans would demonstrate the superiority of the Lord over all gods.

2:19 'Awake!'...'Arise!' Compare the sarcasm with that of Elijah's words to the prophets of Baal on Mt. Carmel (1 Kin. 18:27; cf. Jer. 2:27).

2:20 holy temple. A reference to heaven, from where the Lord rules (Ps. 11:4) and answers the prayers of those who seek Him (1 Kin. 8:28-30; Ps. 73:17). **keep silence.** In contrast to the silence of the idols (v. 19), the living, Sovereign Ruler of the universe calls all the earth to be silent before Him. None can assert his independence from Him; all the earth must worship in humble submission (cf. Ps. 46:10; Is. 52:15).

3:1-19 The reference to "Habakkuk the prophet" (cf. 1:1) marks a transition. The argumentative tone of the previous chapters, in which he cried for divine interference, is transformed into a plea for God's mercy (v. 2), a review of God's power (vv. 3-15), and a chorus of praise for God's sustaining grace and sufficiency (vv. 16-19). But while the tone changes, a strong, thematic connection remains. Having been informed of God's plan of judgment, Habakkuk returns to the matter of Judah's judgment, pleading for mercy.

3:1 Shigionoth. The precise meaning is unknown (its singular form occurs in the heading to Ps. 7). In light of the musical notation at the end of chap. 3, it is thought that it has a musical-liturgical significance, and that this chapter was sung.

3:2 Your speech. A reference back to 1:5-11 and 2:2-20, where the Lord informed Habakkuk of His plans for judging Judah and the Chaldeans. **revive Your work.** Knowledge of the severity of God's judgment struck Habakkuk with fear. As though God's power had not been used in a long time, the prophet asked the Lord to "revive" (lit. "to quicken"), to repeat His mighty saving works on behalf of His people, Israel. **In the midst of the years.** In the midst of His punishment of Judah at the hand of the Chaldeans, the prophet begged that God would remember mercy.

3:3-15 Employing figures from God's past intervention on Israel's behalf, taken from the deliverance of His people from Egypt and the conquest of Canaan, Habakkuk painted a picture of their future redemption. The Exodus from Egypt is often used as an analogy of the future redemption of Israel at the beginning of the Millennium (cf. Is. 11:16).

3:3 Teman...Mount Paran. Teman, named after a grandson of Esau, was an Edomite city (Amos 1:12; Obad. 9). Mount Paran was located in the Sinai peninsula. Both allude to the theater in which God

His glory covered the heavens,
And the earth was full of His
praise.
4 *His* brightness was like the light;
He had rays *flashing* from His
hand,
And there His power *was* hidden.
5 Before Him went pestilence,
And fever followed at His feet.

6 He stood and measured the earth;
He looked and startled the nations.
[a]And the everlasting mountains
were scattered,
The perpetual hills bowed.
His ways *are* everlasting.
7 I saw the tents of Cushan in
affliction;
The curtains of the land of Midian
trembled.

8 O LORD, were *You* displeased with
the rivers,
Was Your anger against the rivers,
Was Your wrath against the sea,
That You rode on Your horses,
Your chariots of salvation?
9 Your bow was made quite ready;
Oaths were sworn over *Your*
[2]arrows. Selah

You divided the earth with rivers.
10 The mountains saw You *and*
trembled;
The overflowing of the water
passed by.
The deep uttered its voice,
And [b]lifted its hands on high.
11 The [c]sun and moon stood still in
their habitation;
At the light of Your arrows they
went,
At the shining of Your glittering
spear.

12 You marched through the land in
indignation;
You [3]trampled the nations in
anger.
13 You went forth for the salvation of
Your people,
For salvation with Your Anointed.
You struck the head from the
house of the wicked,
By laying bare from foundation to
neck. Selah

14 You thrust through with his own
arrows
The head of his villages.
They came out like a whirlwind to
scatter me;
Their rejoicing was like feasting on
the poor in secret.
15 [d]You walked through the sea with
Your horses,
Through the heap of great waters.

16 When I heard, [e]my body trembled;
My lips quivered at *the* voice;
Rottenness entered my bones;
And I trembled in myself,

6 [a] Nah. 1:5
9 [2] Lit. *tribes or rods*, cf. v. 14
10 [b] Ex. 14:22
11 [c] Josh. 10:12-14
12 [3] Or *threshed*
15 [d] Ps. 77:19; Hab. 3:8
16 [e] Ps. 119:120

displayed great power when He brought Israel into the land of Canaan (cf. Deut. 33:2; Judg. 5:4).

3:3,4 The Shekinah glory, which protected and led Israel from Egypt through the wilderness (cf. Ex. 40:34-38), was the physical manifestation of His presence. Like the sun, He spread His radiance throughout the heavens and the earth.

3:5 pestilence...fever. Recalling the judgment attending Israel's disobedience to the covenant given at Sinai (Ex. 5:3; Num. 14:12; Deut. 28:21,22; 32:24), Habakkuk accentuated the sovereign agency of God's judgments. Both were a part of the divine entourage.

3:6,7 The entire universe responds in fear at the approach of Almighty God (cf. Ex. 15:14). As at the Creation (Is. 40:12), the earth and its inhabitants are at His disposal.

3:7 Cushan...Midian. Probably referring to one people living in the Sinai peninsula region (cf. Ex. 2:16-22; 18:1-5; Num. 12:1, where Moses' wife was identified as being both Midianite and Cushite).

3:8-15 With rhetorical vividness, Habakkuk addressed the Lord directly, rehearsing His judicial actions against anything that opposes His will.

3:8 Your horses...Your chariots. Symbolic descriptions of God defeating the enemy (cf. 3:11,15).

3:9 Oaths were sworn over *Your* arrows. The Lord's arrows were commissioned under divine oaths (cf. Jer. 47:6,7).

3:11 sun and moon stood still. As prominent symbols of God's created order, the sun and moon are subservient to His beckoning. The imagery is reminiscent of Israel's victory over the Amorites at Gibeon (Josh. 10:12-14).

3:12 trampled. Lit. "threshed," the term is often used to depict military invasions and the execution of judgment (cf. Judg. 8:7; 2 Kin. 13:7; Is. 21:10; 25:10; Dan. 7:23; Amos 1:3).

3:13 salvation with Your Anointed. Both the parallelism with v. 13a ("Your people") and the numerous contextual allusions to the Exodus make this a likely reference to Moses and the chosen people of Israel, who, as God's anointed, achieved victory over Pharaoh and the armies of Egypt (cf. Ps. 105:15). Ultimately, it foreshadows a subsequent, future deliverance in anticipation of the Messiah (cf. Ps. 132:10-12) promised in the Davidic Covenant (cf. 2 Sam. 7:11-16). **struck the head from the house of the wicked.** Possible reference to either the pharaoh of the Exodus, whose firstborn was slain, or to the king of the Chaldeans, whose house was built by unjust gain (2:9-11).

3:14 They came out...to scatter. A possible reference to the pursuit of fleeing Israel at the Red Sea by Pharaoh's army (Ex. 14:5-9). Like the poor, Israel appeared to be easy prey for the pursuing Egyptians.

3:15 You walked through the sea. Another reference to God's miraculous, protective intervention on behalf of Israel at the Red Sea. The historical event demonstrates His sovereign rulership of the universe and provides assurance to the troubled prophet that the Lord could be counted on to save once more His people.

3:16-19 Habakkuk ended the prophecy with renewed commitment and affirmation of faith, expressing unwavering confidence in God.

That I might rest in the day of
trouble.
When he comes up to the people,
He will invade them with his
troops.

A Hymn of Faith

17 Though the fig tree may not
blossom,
Nor fruit be on the vines;
Though the labor of the olive may
fail,
And the fields yield no food;
Though the flock may be cut off
from the fold,
And there be no herd in the
stalls—
18 Yet I will [f]rejoice in the LORD,
I will joy in the God of my
salvation.

19 [4]The LORD God is my strength;
He will make my feet like [g]deer's
feet,
And He will make me [h]walk on
my high hills.

To the Chief Musician. With my stringed instruments.

18 [f]Is. 41:16; 61:10
19 [g]2 Sam. 22:34; Ps. 18:33 [h]Deut. 32:13; 33:29 [4]Heb. *YHWH Adonai*

3:16 rest. The Lord had answered his prayer (v. 1); the Lord would vindicate His righteousness and ultimately restore a truly repentant people (cf. 2:4). While the answer satisfied Habakkuk, the thought of a Chaldean invasion of his people has also left him physically exhausted and overwhelmed (cf. Jer. 4:19). Nevertheless, the prophet could "rest in the day of trouble" because he knew the Lord would judge righteously.

3:17,18 I will rejoice in the LORD. If everything that was normal and predictable collapsed, the prophet would still rejoice. Obedience to the covenant was a requisite element to the enjoyment of agricultural and pastoral prosperity (Deut. 28:1-14). Though disobedience would initiate the covenant curses (Deut. 28:31-34,49-51), the prophet affirmed his commitment to the Lord; his longing and joyful desire was for God Himself.

3:19 The LORD God is my strength. God's response to Habakkuk's perplexities not only promised divine wrath but also provided assurance of divine favor and hope. Security and hope were not based on temporal blessings but on the Lord Himself. This is the essence of 2:4: "the just shall live by his faith." **like deer's *feet*.** As the sure-footed deer scaled the precipitous mountain heights without slipping, so Habakkuk's faith in the Lord enabled him to endure the hardships of the imminent invasion, and all of his perplexing questions. **To the Chief Musician.** Habakkuk 3 possibly served as a psalm for temple worship (cf. 3:1).

The Book of ZEPHANIAH

Title

As with each of the 12 Minor Prophets, the prophecy bears the name of its author, which is generally thought to mean "the LORD hides" (cf. 2:3).

Author and Date

Little is known about the author, Zephaniah. Three other OT individuals share his name. He traces his genealogy back 4 generations to King Hezekiah (ca. 715–686 B.C.), standing alone among the prophets descended from royal blood (1:1). Royal genealogy would have given him the ear of Judah's king, Josiah, during whose reign he preached.

The prophet himself dates his message during the reign of Josiah (640–609 B.C.). The moral and spiritual conditions detailed in the book (cf. 1:4-6; 3:1-7) seem to place the prophecy prior to Josiah's reforms, when Judah was still languishing in idolatry and wickedness. It was in 628 B.C. that Josiah tore down all the altars to Baal, burned the bones of false prophets, and broke the carved idols (2 Chr. 34:3-7); and in 622 B.C. the Book of the Law was found (2 Chr. 34:8–35:19). Consequently, Zephaniah most likely prophesied from 635–625 B.C., and was a contemporary of Jeremiah.

Background and Setting

Politically, the imminent transfer of Assyrian world power to the Babylonians weakened Nineveh's hold on Judah, bringing an element of independence to Judah for the first time in 50 years. King Josiah's desire to retain this newfound freedom from taxation and subservience undoubtedly led him to interfere later with Egypt's attempt to interdict the fleeing king of Nineveh in 609 B.C. (cf. 2 Chr. 35:20-27). Spiritually, the reigns of Hezekiah's son Manasseh (ca. 695–642 B.C.), extending over 4 decades, and his grandson Amon (ca. 642–640 B.C.), lasting only two years, were marked by wickedness and apostasy (2 Kin. 21; 2 Chr. 33). The early years of Josiah's reign were also characterized by the evil from his fathers (2 Kin. 23:4). In 622 B.C., however, while repairing the house of the Lord, Hilkiah the High-Priest found the Book of the Law (2 Kin. 22:8). Upon reading it, Josiah initiated extensive reforms (2 Kin. 23). It was during the early years of Josiah's reign, prior to the great revival, that this 11th hour prophet, Zephaniah, prophesied and no doubt had an influence on the sweeping reforms Josiah brought to the nation. But the evil kings before Josiah (55 years) had had such an effect on Judah that it never recovered. Josiah's reforms were too late and didn't outlast his life.

Historical and Theological Themes

Zephaniah's message on the Day of the Lord warned Judah that the final days were near, through divine judgment at the hands of Nebuchadnezzar, ca. 605–586 B.C. (1:4-13). Yet, it also looks beyond to the far fulfillment in the judgments of Daniel's 70th week (1:18; 3:8). The expression "Day of the Lord" is employed by the author more often than by any other OT writer, and is described as a day that is near (1:7), and as a day of wrath, trouble, distress, devastation, desolation, darkness, gloominess, clouds, thick darkness, trumpet, and alarm (1:15,16,18). Yet even within these oracles of divine wrath, the prophet exhorted the people to seek the Lord, offering a shelter in the midst of judgment (2:3), and proclaiming the promise of eventual salvation for His believing remnant (2:7; 3:9-20).

Interpretive Challenges

The book presents an unambiguous denunciation of sin and warning of imminent judgment on Judah. Some have referred the phrase "I will restore to the peoples a pure language" (3:9) to the restoration of a universal language, similar to the days prior to confusion of languages at the Tower of Babel (Gen. 11:1-9). They point out that the word "language" is also used in Gen. 11:7. It is better, however, to understand the passage as pointing to a purification of heart and life. This is confirmed by the context (cf. 3:13) and corroborated by the fact that the word "language" is most commonly translated "lip." When combined with "pure," the reference to speech speaks of inward cleansing from sin (Is. 6:5) manifested in speech (cf. Matt. 12:34), including the removal of the names of false gods from their lips (Hos. 2:17). It does not imply a one world language.

Outline

- I. Superscription (1:1)
- II. The Lord's Judgment (1:2–3:8)
  - A. On the Whole Earth (1:2,3)
  - B. On Judah (1:4–2:3)
  - C. On the Surrounding Nations (2:4-15)
    - 1. Philistia (2:4-7)
    - 2. Moab/Ammon (2:8-11)
    - 3. Ethiopia (2:12)
    - 4. Assyria (2:13-15)
  - D. On Jerusalem (3:1-7)
  - E. On All Nations (3:8)
- III. The Lord's Blessing (3:9-20)
  - A. For the Nations (3:9,10)
  - B. For Judah (3:11-20)

1 The word of the LORD which came to
Zephaniah the son of Cushi, the son
of Gedaliah, the son of Amariah, the son of
Hezekiah, in the days of [a]Josiah the son of
Amon, king of Judah.

The Great Day of the LORD

2 "I will [1]utterly consume
everything
From the face of the land,"
Says the LORD;
3 "I [b] will consume man and beast;
I will consume the birds of the
heavens,
The fish of the sea,
And the [2]stumbling blocks along
with the wicked.
I will cut off man from the face of
the [3]land,"
Says the LORD.

4 "I will stretch out My hand against
Judah,
And against all the inhabitants of
Jerusalem.
[4]I will cut off every trace of Baal
from this place,
The names of the [c]idolatrous[5]
priests with the *pagan*
priests—
5 Those [d]who worship the host of
heaven on the housetops;
Those who worship and swear
oaths by the LORD,
But who *also* swear [e]by [6]Milcom;
6 [f]Those who have turned back from
following the LORD,
And [g]have not sought the LORD,
nor inquired of Him."

7 [h]Be silent in the presence of the
Lord GOD;
[i]For the day of the LORD *is* at
hand,
For [j]the LORD has prepared a
sacrifice;
He has [7]invited His guests.

8 "And it shall be,
In the day of the LORD's sacrifice,
That I will punish [k]the princes and
the king's children,
And all such as are clothed with
foreign apparel.

CHAPTER 1

1 [a] 2 Kin. 22:1, 2; 2 Chr. 34:1-33; Jer. 1:2; 22:11
2 [1] Lit. *make a complete end of*, Jer. 8:13
3 [b] Hos. 4:3 [2] Idols [3] *ground*
4 [4] Fulfilled in 2 Kin. 23:4, 5
[c] 2 Kin. 23:5; Hos. 10:5 [5] Heb. *chemarim*
5 [d] 2 Kin. 23:12; Jer. 19:13 [e] Josh. 23:7 [6] Or *Malcam*, an Ammonite god, 1 Kin. 11:5; Jer. 49:1; *Molech*, Lev. 18:21
6 [f] Is. 1:4; Jer. 2:13 [g] Hos. 7:7
7 [h] Hab. 2:20; Zech. 2:13 [i] Is. 13:6 [j] Deut. 28:26; Is. 34:6; Jer. 46:10; Ezek. 39:17-19 [7] Lit. *set apart, consecrated*
8 [k] Jer. 39:6

1:1 Hezekiah...Josiah. Zephaniah traced his royal lineage back to his great-great-grandfather Hezekiah (ca. 715–686 B.C.) and placed his ministry contemporaneous with Josiah (ca. 640–609 B.C.).

1:2,3 The prophet began by noting the far fulfillment of the Day of the Lord, when even animal and physical creation will be affected by His judgment of the earth (cf. Gen. 3:17-19; Ex. 12:29; Josh. 7:24,25; Rom. 8:22).

1:2 face of the land. Generally translated "ground," the term is used in reference to the whole earth (1:18). The phraseology is reminiscent of the Noahic Flood (Gen. 6:7,17; 7:21-23).

1:3 Comparisons with the Genesis Flood continue with "man and beast" and "birds of the heavens" (Gen. 6:7; 7:23). The prophet also alluded to the creation, pairing man and beast (sixth day of creation) and birds with fish (fifth day of creation). **stumbling blocks.** Whatever alienates man from God will be removed.

1:4-9 The Lord narrowed His words of judgment to specifically focus on Judah, specifying the causes of judgment as apostasy and idolatry (vv. 4-6), as always coupled with moral and ethical corruption (vv. 7-9).

1:4 cut off every trace of Baal. The worship of Baal, the Canaanite god of fertility, was a constant source of temptation to Israel (cf. Num. 25:1-5; Judg. 2:13), as people tried worshiping him alongside the worship of the Lord (Jer. 7:9; 23:25-29). This mix became a primary cause for judgment (Hos. 2:8; 2 Kin. 17:16-20; Jer. 11:13-17) which would forever excise the worship of Baal from Israel.

1:5 worship the host of heaven. Astrology was also a prominent part of Israel's idolatrous practices; they worshiped the host of heaven from as early as the Exodus (cf. Deut. 4:19; Amos 5:25,26; Acts 7:40-43). God warned them repeatedly, but they rebelled (2 Kin. 23:5,6; Jer. 7:17,18; 8:2; 44:17-25). Altars were often erected on housetop roofs to provide a clear view of the sky (Jer. 8:2; 19:13; 32:29). **swear by Milcom.** Judah's syncretistic worship was reflected in swearing by the Lord and, at the same time, by Milcom, who may be either the Ammonite deity of 1 Kin. 11:5,33, or Molech, the worship of whom included child sacrifice, astrology, and sacred prostitution (cf. Lev. 18:21; 2 Kin. 17:16,17; Ezek. 23:37; Amos 5:25,26; Acts 7:40-43).

1:6 Zephaniah lastly mentioned those who had at first heeded calls to repentance but later had willfully turned away.

1:7 Be silent. In view of the just judgment, there was no defense to be spoken and in view of the devastation only shocked and mute wonder (cf. Hab. 2:20; Zech. 2:13). **day of the LORD.** *See notes on Joel 1:15.* **prepared a sacrifice...invited His guests.** God's judgment on Israel was viewed as His sacrifice. The guests were the dreaded Babylonians, who as "priests" were invited to slay the sacrifice, i.e., Judah (cf. Is. 13:3; 34:6; Jer. 46:10; Ezek. 39:17; Hab. 1:6; Rev. 19:17,18).

1:8 the princes...king's children. Judgment began with the royal house. Lacking commitment to God's covenant, they had adopted the customs and idolatrous practices of the heathen. Since Josiah was only 8 years old when he assumed rulership (ca. 640 B.C.), the reference would not be to his children but to the princes of the royal house or to the children of the king who would be ruling when the prophecy was fulfilled (cf. 2 Kin. 25:7; Jer. 39:6).

"Day of the Lord" Fulfillments

Near	Far
Obadiah 1-14	Obadiah 15-21
Joel 1:15, 2:1, 11	Joel 2:31 (3:1), 3:14
Amos 5:18-20	——
——	Isaiah 2:12
Isaiah 13:6	Isaiah 13:9
Zephaniah 1:7	Zephaniah 1:14
Ezekiel 13:5, 20:3	——
——	Zechariah 14:1
——	Malachi 4:5

9 In the same day I will punish
All those who [l]leap over the
threshold,
Who fill their masters' houses with
violence and deceit.

10 "And there shall be on that day,"
says the LORD,
"The sound of a mournful cry from
[m]the Fish Gate,
A wailing from the Second Quarter,
And a loud crashing from the hills.
11 [n]Wail, you inhabitants of [8]Maktesh!
For all the merchant people are cut
down;
All those who handle money are
cut off.

12 "And it shall come to pass at that
time
That I will search Jerusalem with
lamps,
And punish the men
Who are [o]settled[9] in complacency,
[p]Who say in their heart,
'The LORD will not do good,
Nor will He do evil.'
13 Therefore their goods shall become
booty,
And their houses a desolation;
They shall build houses, but not
inhabit *them;*
They shall plant vineyards, but
[q]not drink their wine."

14 [r]The great day of the LORD *is* near;
It is near and hastens quickly.
The noise of the day of the LORD is
bitter;
There the mighty men shall cry
out.
15 [s]That day *is* a day of wrath,
A day of trouble and distress,
A day of devastation and
desolation,
A day of darkness and gloominess,
A day of clouds and thick
darkness,
16 A day of [t]trumpet and alarm
Against the fortified cities
And against the high towers.

17 "I will bring distress upon men,
And they shall [u]walk like blind
men,
Because they have sinned against
the LORD;
Their blood shall be poured out
like dust,
And their flesh like refuse."

18 [v]Neither their silver nor their gold
Shall be able to deliver them
In the day of the LORD's wrath;
But the whole land shall be
devoured
By the fire of His jealousy,
For He will make speedy
riddance
Of all those who dwell in the
land.

A Call to Repentance

2 Gather[a] yourselves together, yes,
gather together,
O [1]undesirable nation,
2 Before the decree is issued,
Or the day passes like chaff,
Before the LORD's fierce anger
comes upon you,
Before the day of the LORD's anger
comes upon you!
3 [b]Seek the LORD, [c]all you meek of the
earth,
Who have upheld His justice.
Seek righteousness, seek humility.

9 [l] 1 Sam. 5:5 **10** [m] 2 Chr. 33:14; Neh. 3:3; 12:39 **11** [n] James 5:1 [8] A market district of Jerusalem, lit. *Mortar* **12** [o] Jer. 48:11; Amos 6:1 [p] Ps. 94:7 [9] Lit. *on their lees;* like the dregs of wine **13** [q] Deut. 28:39 **14** [r] Jer. 30:7; Joel 2:1, 11 **15** [s] Is. 22:5

16 [t] Is. 27:13; Jer. 4:19 **17** [u] Deut. 28:29 **18** [v] Ezek. 7:19

CHAPTER 2

1 [a] 2 Chr. 20:4; Joel 1:14; 2:16 [1] Or *shameless* **3** [b] Ps. 105:4; Amos 5:6 [c] Ps. 76:9

1:9 leap over the threshold. This describes the eagerness with which the rich hurried from their homes to plunder the poor.

1:10,11 The merchants, made wealthy from dishonest gain (cf. v. 9), were singled out to depict the anguish of the coming judgment. The Fish Gate, known today as the Damascus Gate, is located on the N side. The Second Quarter was a district within the city walls. Maktesh, meaning "mortar," was a name applied to the Valley of Siloam from its shape; it was a district where merchants carried on business.

1:12 I will search. None would escape the punishment of the Lord (Amos 9:1-4). **settled in complacency.** See marginal note. With this term referring to a thickened crust which forms on wine when left undisturbed for a long period of time, the prophet described the people's indifference and slothfulness toward God. Their indifference led them to regard God as morally indifferent.

1:14-18 Zephaniah vividly described the Day of the Lord in staccato fashion, rehearsing the ominous conditions characterizing that day. This section seems to point to the near fulfillment when Babylon subdued Judah (vv. 4-13), as well as a far fulfillment which will involve the whole earth (v. 18).

1:16 day of trumpet and alarm. In accordance with God's instructions, a trumpet was fashioned for the purpose of sounding an alarm (Num. 10:1-10).

1:17,18 As though worthless, their blood and flesh was discarded as dust. Their silver and gold, corruptly gained (cf. vv. 9-13), would be of no avail to protect them from the wrath of holy God (cf. Jer. 46:28).

1:17 walk like blind men. As blind men, they would grope unsuccessfully for escape routes (Deut. 28:29).

1:18 the whole land. The discussion expands to include the whole earth as in vv. 2,3.

2:1-3 With the announcement of coming judgment, God mercifully invited His people to repent. They were to assemble to entreat the favor of the Lord and avert His wrath (cf. Joel 2:16).

2:1 undesirable nation. See marginal note. No longer sensitive to God's call to repentance through His many prophets, Judah had sunk to shamelessness.

[d]It may be that you will be hidden
In the day of the LORD's anger.

Judgment on Nations

4 For [e]Gaza shall be forsaken,
And Ashkelon desolate;
They shall drive out Ashdod [f]at noonday,
And Ekron shall be uprooted.
5 Woe to the inhabitants of [g]the seacoast,
The nation of the Cherethites!
The word of the LORD *is* against you,
O [h]Canaan, land of the Philistines:
"I will destroy you;
So there shall be no inhabitant."

6 The seacoast shall be pastures,
With [2]shelters for shepherds [i]and folds for flocks.
7 The coast shall be for [j]the remnant of the house of Judah;
They shall feed *their* flocks there;
In the houses of Ashkelon they shall lie down at evening.
For the LORD their God will [k]intervene[3] for them,
And [l]return their captives.

8 "I[m] have heard the reproach of Moab,
And [n]the insults of the people of Ammon,
With which they have reproached My people,
And [o]made arrogant threats against their borders.
9 Therefore, as I live,"
Says the LORD of hosts, the God of Israel,
"Surely [p]Moab shall be like Sodom,
And [q]the people of Ammon like Gomorrah—
[r]Overrun[4] with weeds and saltpits,
And a [5]perpetual desolation.
The residue of My people shall plunder them,
And the remnant of My people shall possess them."

10 This they shall have [s]for their pride,
Because they have reproached and made arrogant threats
Against the people of the LORD of hosts.
11 The LORD *will be* awesome to them,
For He will reduce to nothing all the gods of the earth;
[t]*People* shall worship Him,
Each one from his place,
Indeed all [u]the shores of the nations.

12 "You[v] Ethiopians also,
You shall be slain by [w]My sword."

13 And He will stretch out His hand against the north,
[x]Destroy Assyria,
And make Nineveh a desolation,
As dry as the wilderness.
14 The herds shall lie down in her midst,
[y]Every beast of the nation.
Both the [z]pelican and the bittern
Shall lodge on the capitals *of* her *pillars;*
Their voice shall sing in the windows;
Desolation *shall be* at the threshold;
For He will lay bare the [a]cedar work.
15 This is the rejoicing city
[b]That dwelt securely,

3 [d] Joel 2:14; Amos 5:14, 15 **4** [e] Jer. 47:1, 5; Amos 1:7, 8; Zech. 9:5 [f] Jer. 6:4 **5** [g] Ezek. 25:15-17 [h] Josh. 13:3 **6** [i] Is. 17:2 [2] Underground huts or cisterns, lit. *excavations* **7** [j] [Mic. 5:7, 8] [k] Luke 1:68 [l] Jer. 29:14 [3] Lit. *visit them* **8** [m] Jer. 48:27; Amos 2:1-3 [n] Ezek. 25:3; Amos 1:13 [o] Jer. 49:1 **9** [p] Is. 15:1-9; Jer. 48:1-47

[q] Amos 1:13 [r] Deut. 29:23 [4] Lit. *Possessed by nettles* [5] Or *permanent ruin* **10** [s] Is. 16:6 **11** [t] Mal. 1:11 [u] Gen. 10:5 **12** [v] Is. 18:1-7; Ezek. 30:4, 5 [w] Ps. 17:13 **13** [x] Is. 10:5-27; 14:24-27; Mic. 5:5, 6 **14** [y] Is. 13:21 [z] Is. 14:23; 34:11 [a] Jer. 22:14 **15** [b] Is. 47:8

2:3 It may be that you will be hidden. Even the meek, those who had followed the law of the Lord, were encouraged to continue to manifest fruits of repentance, so they would be sheltered in the day of His judgment (Is. 26:20).

2:4-15 God used the heathen nations to punish His people, but He would not permit those nations to go unpunished. To illustrate this, 4 representative nations were chosen from the 4 points of the compass.

2:4-7 The first nation to be judged was Philistia, to the W of Israel. Judgment was to come swiftly and unexpectedly, even at noonday when it was least expected. Of the 5 Philistine cities, only Gath was omitted (cf. Amos 1:6-8).

2:5 Cherethites. Occasionally a synonym for Philistia, this term represented a branch from Crete *(see note on Amos 9:7)*. David's bodyguard was comprised of both Cherethites and Pelethites (2 Sam. 8:18; 1 Kin. 1:38,44). *See note on 1 Sam. 30:14.*

2:7 return their captives. The Lord would initiate the physical return of Israel's exiles to occupy the land vacated by judgment on Philistia.

2:8-11 To the E, the descendants of Lot by his daughters through incest, Moab and Ammon (Gen. 19:30-38), are mentioned. They had reproached and reviled God's people, incurring divine wrath (cf. Gen. 12:3). Like Sodom and Gomorrah in the days of their ancestor Lot, they too would come to ruin and desolation.

2:11 worship Him...all the shores of the nations. The final fulfillment of these predictions is yet future, depicting the Millennium when all the gods of the nations will be reduced to nothing and the Lord Himself will be worshiped universally (Is. 66:18-21; Zech. 14:16; Mal. 1:11).

2:12 Ethiopia lay to the S of Israel. She would be judged by His sword, fulfilled in Nebuchadnezzar's invasion and conquest of Egypt (Ezek. 30:24,25).

2:13-15 Assyria, located NW of Israel, would be desolated as well. Nineveh fell, shortly after this prophecy, to the Babylonians in 612 B.C. Famed for her irrigation system, she would be left dry.

2:15 In language similar to that of the king of Babylon (Is. 14:13, 14; 47:8) and the prince of Tyre (Ezek. 28:2), Assyria had claimed for herself divine attributes. For this she would be brought to ruin.

[c]That said in her heart,
"I *am it*, and *there is* none besides
me."
How has she become a desolation,
A place for beasts to lie down!
Everyone who passes by her
[d]Shall hiss and [e]shake his fist.

The Wickedness of Jerusalem

3 Woe to her who is rebellious and
polluted,
To the oppressing city!
2 She has not obeyed *His* voice,
She has not received correction;
She has not trusted in the LORD,
She has not drawn near to her
God.

3 [a]Her princes in her midst *are*
roaring lions;
Her judges *are* [b]evening wolves
That leave not a bone till morning.
4 Her [c]prophets are insolent,
treacherous people;
Her priests have [1]polluted the
sanctuary,
They have done [d]violence to the
law.
5 The LORD *is* righteous in her
midst,
He will do no unrighteousness.
[2]Every morning He brings His
justice to light;
He never fails,
But [e]the unjust knows no shame.

6 "I have cut off nations,
Their fortresses are devastated;
I have made their streets desolate,
With none passing by.
Their cities are destroyed;
There is no one, no inhabitant.
7 [f]I said, 'Surely you will fear Me,
You will receive instruction'—
So that her dwelling would not be
cut off,
Despite everything for which I
punished her.
But [3]they rose early and
[g]corrupted all their deeds.

A Faithful Remnant

8 "Therefore [h]wait for Me," says the
LORD,
"Until the day I rise up [4]for
plunder;
My determination *is* to [i]gather the
nations
To My assembly of kingdoms,
To pour on them My indignation,
All My fierce anger;
All the earth [j]shall be devoured
With the fire of My jealousy.

9 "For then I will restore to the
peoples [k]a pure [5]language,
That they all may call on the name
of the LORD,
To serve Him with one accord.
10 [l]From beyond the rivers of
Ethiopia
My worshipers,
The daughter of My dispersed
ones,
Shall bring My offering.

15 [c]Rev. 18:7 [d]Lam. 2:15 [e]Nah. 3:19

CHAPTER 3

3 [a]Ezek. 22:27 [b]Jer. 5:6; Hab. 1:8
4 [c]Hos. 9:7 [d]Ezek. 22:26; Mal. 2:7, 8 [1]*Or profaned*
5 [e]Jer. 3:3 [2]Lit. *Morning by morning*
7 [f]Jer. 8:6 [g]Gen. 6:12 [3]*They were eager*
8 [h]Prov. 20:22; Mic. 7:7; Hab. 2:3 [i]Is. 66:18; Ezek. 38:14-23; Joel 3:2; Mic. 4:12; Matt. 25:32 [j]Zeph. 1:18 [4]LXX, Syr. *for witness*; Tg. *for the day of My revelation for judgment*; Vg. *for the day of My resurrection that is to come*
9 [k]Is. 19:18; 57:19 [5]Lit. *lip*
10 [l]Ps. 68:31; Is. 18:1; Acts 8:27

3:1-7 After pronouncing judgment on the nations, the prophet returned to again pronounce woe upon Jerusalem. Because of that city's favored position among the nations (cf. Ex. 19:5), more was expected.

3:2 She has not received correction. Jerusalem was soon to learn that to reject God's correction leads to destruction (Prov. 5:23). **She has not drawn near to her God.** The Lord had taken up residence in that city, making Him easily accessible (Deut. 4:7), yet they had refused to draw near to Him in proper worship.

3:3-5 Four classes of leadership were singled out for condemnation: The political leaders, i.e., the 1) princes and 2) judges; who are both likened to ravenous wolves, endlessly searching for more prey (cf. 1:8,9). The spiritual leaders, i.e., the 3) prophets and 4) priests, were unfaithful to the Lord whom they claimed to represent. By contrast, the Lord never failed to manifest a faithful standard of justice and righteousness.

3:6,7 The desolations brought by the Lord on surrounding nations were to serve as warnings to Judah, meant to turn His people back to Him. But instead, enticed by the fruits of corruption, the people rose early to zealously and deliberately pursue the way of sin.

3:8 The prophet transitions from the historical invasion of Judah by Babylon to the future day of the Lord. He speaks of the Great Tribulation, when the Lord will gather all the nations for judgment (cf. Joel 3:1,2,12-17; Zech. 12:2,3; 14:2; Matt. 24:21). The faithful remnant, presumably the meek of 2:1-3, are exhorted to wait in trust for Him to carry out His judgment.

3:9-20 The final section unveils the blessings of restoration for God's people and the nations.

3:9 pure language. See Introduction: Interpretive Challenges. A remnant of the nations, converted to the Lord, will worship Him in righteousness and truth (Zech. 8:20-23; 14:16). Pure speech will come from purified hearts (cf. Luke 6:45).

3:10 They will return from distant places (cf. Is. 11:11,15,16; 27:13).

God's "I Wills" of Restoration

Zephaniah 3:18-20

1. I will gather	3:18
2. I will deal	3:19
3. I will save	3:19
4. I will appoint	3:19
5. I will bring you back	3:20
6. I will give you	3:20

11 In that day you shall not be
shamed for any of your deeds
In which you transgress against
Me;
For then I will take away from
your midst
Those who [m]rejoice in your pride,
And you shall no longer be
haughty
In My holy mountain.
12 I will leave in your midst
[n]A meek and humble people,
And they shall trust in the name of
the LORD.
13 [o]The remnant of Israel [p]shall do no
unrighteousness
[q]And speak no lies,
Nor shall a deceitful tongue be
found in their mouth;
For [r]they shall feed *their* flocks and
lie down,
And no one shall make *them*
afraid."

Joy in God's Faithfulness

14 [s]Sing, O daughter of Zion!
Shout, O Israel!
Be glad and rejoice with all *your*
heart,
O daughter of Jerusalem!
15 The LORD has taken away your
judgments,
He has cast out your enemy.
[t]The King of Israel, the LORD, [u]*is* in
your midst;
You shall [6]see disaster no more.
16 In that day [v]it shall be said to
Jerusalem:
"Do not fear;
Zion, [w]let not your hands be weak.
17 The LORD your God [x]in your
midst,
The Mighty One, will save;
[y]He will rejoice over you with
gladness,
He will quiet *you* with His love,
He will rejoice over you with
singing."
18 "I will gather those who [z]sorrow
over the appointed assembly,
Who are among you,
To whom its reproach *is* a burden.
19 Behold, at that time
I will deal with all who afflict you;
I will save the [a]lame,
And gather those who were driven
out;
I will appoint them for praise and
fame
In every land where they were put
to shame.
20 At that time [b]I will bring you back,
Even at the time I gather you;
For I will give you [7]fame and
praise
Among all the peoples of the earth,
When I return your captives before
your eyes,"
Says the LORD.

11 [m]Is. 2:12; 5:15; Matt. 3:9 **12** [n]Is. 14:32; Zech. 13:8, 9 **13** [o]Is. 10:20-22; [Mic. 4:7] [p]Is. 60:21 [q]Zech. 8:3, 16; Rev. 14:5 [r]Ezek. 34:13-15, 28 **14** [s]Is. 12:6 **15** [t][John 1:49] [u]Ezek. 48:35; [Rev. 7:15]

[6]So with Heb. mss., LXX, Bg.; MT, Vg. *fear* **16** [v]Is. 35:3, 4 [w]Job 4:3; Heb. 12:12 **17** [x]Zeph. 3:5, 15 [y]Deut. 30:9; Is. 62:5; 65:19; Jer. 32:41 **18** [z]Lam. 2:6 **19** [a][Ezek. 34:16; Mic. 4:6, 7] **20** [b]Is. 11:12; Ezek. 28:25; Amos 9:14 [7]Lit. *a name*

3:11-13 The Lord will purge the proud and ungodly from among them (Zech. 13:1-6), leaving a meek and humble people. Material prosperity and peace will accompany them as well, allowing them to enjoy the rich blessings of God undisturbed (Joel 3:18-20; Mic. 4:4).

3:14-20 The messianic era of millennial blessing and restoration is described.

3:15-17 The basis for rejoicing in v. 14 is that Israel's day of judgment is past and her King is residing in her midst. His departure just prior to Nebuchadnezzar's destruction of the temple is graphically depicted in Ezek. 8–11; but He will return as Lord and Messiah, a fact so glorious that it is repeated in v. 17.

3:17 As a bridegroom rejoices over his bride (cf. Is. 62:4), the Lord will exult over His people with gladness and song, resting in quiet ecstasy over His people in whom is all His delight (cf. Deut. 30:9; Is. 54).

3:18 those who sorrow over the appointed assembly. Unable to celebrate the appointed feasts (cf. Ex. 23:14-17) while in exile, the godly remnant sorrowed. But the Lord will remove their sorrow, giving them praise and fame (v. 19).

3:19,20 at that time. The time of the return of the King, Messiah, when the Jews will be regathered and become a source of blessing to the world, fulfilling Israel's original destiny (Deut. 26:18,19; Is. 62:7).

The Book of HAGGAI

Title

The prophecy bears the name of its author. Because his name means "festal one," it is suggested that Haggai was born on a feast day. Haggai is the second shortest book in the OT (Obadiah is shorter) and is quoted by the NT once (cf. Heb. 12:26).

Author and Date

Little is known about Haggai apart from this short prophecy. He is mentioned briefly in Ezra 5:1 and 6:14, on both occasions in conjunction with the prophet Zechariah. The lists of refugees in Ezra mention nothing of Haggai; there are no indications of his parentage or tribal ancestry. Nor does history provide any record of his occupation. He is the only person in the OT with the name, although similar names occur (cf. Gen. 46:16; Num. 26:15; 2 Sam. 3:4; 1 Chr. 6:30). Furthermore, Hag. 2:3 may suggest that he too had seen the glory of Solomon's temple before it was destroyed, making him at least 70 years of age when writing his prophecy.

There is no ambiguity or controversy about the date of the prophecy. The occasion of each of his 4 prophecies is clearly specified (1:1; 2:1; 2:10; 2:20), occurring within a 4 month span of time in the second year (ca. 520 B.C.) of Persian king Darius Hystaspes (ca. 521–486 B.C.). Haggai most likely had returned to Jerusalem from Babylon with Zerubbabel 18 years earlier in 538 B.C.

Background and Setting

In 538 B.C., as a result of the proclamation of Cyrus the Persian (cf. Ezra 1:1-4), Israel was allowed to return from Babylon to her homeland under the civil leadership of Zerubbabel and the spiritual guidance of Joshua the High-Priest (cf. Ezra 3:2). About 50,000 Jews returned. In 536 B.C., they began to rebuild the temple (cf. Ezra 3:1–4:5) but opposition from neighbors and indifference by the Jews caused the work to be abandoned (cf. Ezra 4:1-24). Sixteen years later Haggai and Zechariah were commissioned by the Lord to stir up the people to 1) not only rebuild the temple, but also to 2) reorder their spiritual priorities (cf. Ezra 5:1–6:22). As a result, the temple was completed 4 years later (ca. 516 B.C.; cf. Ezra 6:15).

Historical and Theological Themes

The primary theme is the rebuilding of God's temple, which had been lying in ruins since its destruction by Nebuchadnezzar in 586 B.C. By means of 5 messages from the Lord, Haggai exhorted the people to renew their efforts to build the house of the Lord. He motivated them by noting that the drought and crop failures were caused by misplaced spiritual priorities (1:9-11).

But to Haggai, the rebuilding of the temple was not an end in itself. The temple represented God's dwelling place, His manifest presence with His chosen people. The destruction of the temple by Nebuchadnezzar followed the departure of God's dwelling glory (cf. Ezek. 8–11); to the prophet, the rebuilding of the temple invited the return of God's presence to their midst. Using the historical situation as a springboard, Haggai reveled in the supreme glory of the ultimate messianic temple yet to come (2:7), encouraging them with the promise of even greater peace (2:9), prosperity (2:19), divine rulership (2:21,22), and national blessing (2:23) during the Millennium.

Interpretive Challenges

The most prominent interpretive ambiguity within the prophecy is the phrase "the Desire of All Nations" (2:7). Although many translations exist, there are essentially only two interpretations. Pointing to "The silver is Mine, and the gold is Mine" (2:8), as well as to Is. 60:5 and Zech. 14:14, some contend that it refers to Jerusalem, to which the wealth of other nations will be brought during the Millennium (cf. Is. 60:11; 61:6). It seems preferable, however, to see a reference here to the Messiah, a Deliverer for whom all the nations ultimately long. Not only is this interpretation supported by the ancient rabbis and the early church, the mention of "glory" in the latter part of the verse suggests a personal reference to the Messiah (cf. Is. 40:5; 60:1; Luke 2:32).

Outline and Chronology

		Year	Month	Day
I. Rebuke for Disobedience	1:1-11	2	6	1
II. Remnant Responds and Rebuilds	1:12-15	2	6	24
III. Return of God's Glory	2:1-9	2	7	21
IV. Religious Questions	2:10-19	2	9	24
V. Reign of the Lord	2:20-23	2	9	24

The Command to Build God's House

1 In [a]the second year of King Darius, in
the sixth month, on the first day of the
month, the word of the LORD came by
[b]Haggai the prophet to [c]Zerubbabel the
son of Shealtiel, governor of Judah, and to
[d]Joshua the son of [e]Jehozadak, the high
priest, saying, 2 "Thus speaks the LORD of
hosts, saying: 'This people says, "The time
has not come, the time that the LORD's
house should be built." ' "
3 Then the word of the LORD [f]came by
Haggai the prophet, saying, 4 "*Is it* [g]time
for you yourselves to dwell in your paneled houses, and this [1]temple *to lie* in
ruins?" 5 Now therefore, thus says the
LORD of hosts: [h]"Consider your ways!

6 "You have [i]sown much, and bring
in little;
You eat, but do not have
enough;
You drink, but you are not filled
with drink;
You clothe yourselves, but no one
is warm;
And [j]he who earns wages,
Earns wages *to put* into a bag with
holes."

7 Thus says the LORD of hosts: "Consider
your ways! 8 Go up to the [k]mountains and
bring wood and build the [2]temple, that I
may take pleasure in it and be glorified,"
says the LORD. 9 [l]"*You* looked for much, but
indeed *it came to* little; and when you
brought it home, [m]I blew it away. Why?"
says the LORD of hosts. "Because of My
house that *is in* ruins, while every one of
you runs to his own house. 10 Therefore
[n]the heavens above you withhold the dew,
and the earth withholds its fruit. 11 For I
[o]called for a drought on the land and the
mountains, on the grain and the new wine
and the oil, on whatever the ground brings
forth, on men and livestock, and on [p]all the
labor of *your* hands."

The People's Obedience

12 [q]Then Zerubbabel the son of Shealtiel,
and Joshua the son of Jehozadak, the high
priest, with all the remnant of the people,
obeyed the voice of the LORD their God,
and the words of Haggai the prophet, as
the LORD their God had sent him; and the

CHAPTER 1

1 [a]Ezra 4:24; Hag. 2:10; Zech. 1:1,7 [b]Ezra 5:1; 6:14 [c]1 Chr. 3:19; Ezra 2:2; Neh. 7:7; Zech. 4:6; Matt. 1:12, 13 [d]Ezra 5:2, 3; Zech. 6:11 [e]1 Chr. 6:15
3 [f]Ezra 5:1
4 [g]2 Sam. 7:2 [1]Lit. *house*
5 [h]Lam. 3:40
6 [i]Deut. 28:38-40; Hos. 8:7; Hag. 1:9, 10; 2:16, 17 [j]Zech. 8:10
8 [k]Ezra 3:7 [2]Lit. *house*
9 [l]Hag. 2:16 [m]Hag. 2:17
10 [n]Lev. 26:19; Deut. 28:23; 1 Kin. 8:35; Joel 1:18-20
11 [o]1 Kin. 17:1; 2 Kin. 8:1 [p]Hag. 2:17
12 [q]Ezra 5:2

1:1-11 Discouraged by the opposition of her neighbors (Ezra 4:1-5,24), the people had wrongly concluded that it was not yet time for them to rebuild the temple (v. 2). With a biting query, the Lord reminded them that it was not right for them to live in paneled houses while the temple lay in ruins (v. 4) and urged them to consider carefully the consequences of their indifference (vv. 5-11).

1:1 second year of King Darius. Not to be confused with Darius the Mede (cf. Dan. 5:31), Darius I (Hystaspes) became king of Persia in 521 B.C., having ascended to the throne after the death of Cambyses. As an officer of Cambyses and the great-grandson of Cyrus the Great's brother, Darius retained the loyalty of the Persian army and thereby defeated other contenders for the throne. He reigned until his death in 486 B.C. **sixth month...first day.** The first day of the month of Elul corresponds to Aug. 29, 520 B.C. **Zerubbabel.** Zerubbabel was the grandson of Jehoiachin (Jeconiah in Matt. 1:12; cf. 1 Chr. 3:17,19) and thus he was in the Davidic line. Though it is highly questionable if he is to be identified with Sheshbazzar (Ezra 1:8,11; 5:14,16), his role as civil leader (Ezra 2:2) and overseer of the temple rebuilding project (Zech. 4:6-10) is certain. He reestablished the Davidic throne, even though it will not again be occupied until the time of Messiah (cf. Pss. 2;110). **Joshua...the high priest.** Spelled Jeshua in Ezra 3:2, Joshua was a descendant of Zadok (1 Chr. 6:15) and the religious leader of the exilic community that returned to Jerusalem. He reestablished the high-priestly line of Aaron though Eleazar. **Jehozadak.** One of Nebuchadnezzar's captives (cf. 1 Chr. 6:15)

1:2 This people says. Haggai begins his message by quoting a popular expression of the people, saying it was not time to build the temple. Though propelled by the hostile opposition of their neighbors (Ezra 4:1-5,24) and the lack of economic prosperity (cf. vv. 9-11), the roots of their reluctance lay ultimately in their selfish indifference to the Lord. God's displeasure is noted in His reference to them as "This people" and not "My people." They wanted their wealth for themselves, not a temple.

1:4 temple...ruins. Cf. Ezra 3:1-13 for the start of the second temple. Selfish indulgence, revealed by the prophet's rhetorical query, demonstrated their hypocrisy and misplaced priorities. Walls and ceilings overlaid with cedar were common in wealthy residences (cf. 1 Kin. 7:3,7; Jer. 22:14).

1:6 Using 5 pairs of poetic contrasts, each concluding essentially the same thing, Haggai painted a vivid picture of their economic and social distress. Their selfish lack of concern for God's house had only caused them more hardship (cf. Matt. 6:33). This was Solomon's message in Ecclesiastes, restated, "All is vanity."

1:8 Go up...bring wood...build. Three imperatives give the remedy for their trouble. The long captivity of 70 years had let the forests grow so there was ample wood. They were to use it to rebuild the house of the Lord, and therein He would be glorified. By putting God first, He would then be honored in their worship and they would be blessed in the secondary matters of life. Compare this pitiful project (Ezra 3:12; Hag. 2:3) to the opulence of Solomon's first temple (cf. 1 Chr. 28,29; 2 Chr. 2–6).

1:9 runs to his own house. Because the Jews were zealous to pursue their own interests, the prophet drew a contrast between the one who eagerly ran to care for "his own house," while disregarding God's house ("My house").

1:10,11 Economic catastrophe, resulting from God's withholding of the summer dew, was the price for their disobedience (cf. Deut. 7:13). Grain, wine, and oil were the primary crops of the land. Cattle, also, languished because of the absence of spiritual health (cf. Joel 1:18-20).

1:12-15 Haggai's second message came 23 days after the first one (v. 15), around Sep. 21, 520 B.C. The Lord's call to "Consider your ways" (vv. 5,7) caused the people to respond in repentance and obedience (v. 12). This new message "I *am* with you" further stirred the Jews to action (vv. 13,14).

1:12,14 the remnant of the people. The exiles who returned from Babylon took the message to heart. Realizing that the words of the prophet were from the Lord, they "obeyed" and "feared," knowing that God was present.

people feared the presence of the LORD.
13 Then Haggai, the LORD's messenger,
spoke the LORD's message to the people,
saying, [r]"I *am* with you, says the LORD."
14 So [s]the LORD stirred up the spirit of Zerubbabel the son of Shealtiel, [t]governor of
Judah, and the spirit of Joshua the son of
Jehozadak, the high priest, and the spirit of
all the remnant of the people; [u]and they
came and worked on the house of the LORD
of hosts, their God, 15 on the twenty-fourth
day of the sixth month, in the second year
of King Darius.

The Coming Glory of God's House

2 In the seventh *month*, on the twenty-
first of the month, the word of the LORD
came [1]by Haggai the prophet, saying:
2 "Speak now to Zerubbabel the son of Shealtiel, governor of Judah, and to Joshua the
son of Jehozadak, the high priest, and to
the remnant of the people, saying: 3 [a]'Who
is left among you who saw this [2]temple in
its former glory? And how do you see it
now? In comparison with it, [b]*is this* not in
your eyes as nothing? 4 Yet now [c]be strong,
Zerubbabel,' says the LORD; 'and be strong,
Joshua, son of Jehozadak, the high priest;
and be strong, all you people of the land,'
says the LORD, 'and work; for I *am* with
you,' says the LORD of hosts. 5 [d]'*According to*
the word that I covenanted with you when
you came out of Egypt, so [e]My Spirit remains among you; do not fear!'
6 "For thus says the LORD of hosts:
[f]'Once more (it *is* a little while) [g]I will
shake heaven and earth, the sea and dry
land; 7 and I will shake all nations, and
they shall come to [h]the [3]Desire of All Nations, and I will fill this [4]temple with
[i]glory,' says the LORD of hosts. 8 'The silver
is Mine, and the gold *is* Mine,' says the

13 [r] [Matt. 28:20; Rom. 8:31]
14 [s] 2 Chr. 36:22; Ezra 1:1 [t] Hag. 2:21 [u] Ezra 5:2, 8; Neh. 4:6

CHAPTER 2

1 [1] Lit. *by the hand of*
3 [a] Ezra 3:12, 13 [b] Zech. 4:10 [2] Lit. *house*
4 [c] Deut. 31:23; 1 Chr. 22:13; 28:20; Zech. 8:9; Eph. 6:10
5 [d] Ex. 29:45, 46 [e] [Neh. 9:20]; Is. 63:11, 14
6 [f] Heb. 12:26 [g] [Joel 3:16]
7 [h] Gen. 49:10; Mal. 3:1 [i] 1 Kin. 8:11; Is. 60:7; Zech. 2:5 [3] Or *desire of all nations* [4] Lit. *house*

1:13 I *am* with you. Oppressed by hostilities from without and famine from within, the Lord responded to their genuine repentance and obedience, assuring them of His presence with them. This should have evoked a memory of God's Word to Joshua and the returning people centuries before (cf. Josh. 1:5).

1:14 stirred up the spirit. The Lord energized the leaders and the people through His Word to carry on the work of rebuilding the temple. God had sovereignly moved in the heart of Cyrus 16 years earlier (cf. 2 Chr. 36:22,23; Ezra 1:1-3). The people's response of repentance and obedience allowed God's Spirit to energize them for the task.

2:1-9 With building operations in full swing, the Lord gave a strong message of encouragement, especially to the elderly among them who had seen Solomon's temple. Though the temple of Solomon was of greater magnificence, the Lord urged the people to be courageous, assuring them of His presence (v. 4), His faithfulness to His covenant promises (v. 5), and promises of a greater, more glorious temple in the future (vv. 6-9).

2:1 seventh *month*...twenty-first. This day in the month of Tishri corresponds to Oct. 17, 520 B.C. Leviticus 23:39-44 indicates that this was the final day of the Feast of Tabernacles, a feast to celebrate God's provision for Israel during her 40 years of wilderness wanderings and give thanks for a bountiful harvest. On this occasion the Lord gave Haggai the third message.

2:2 The first message was directed toward the leaders, Zerubbabel and Joshua (*see notes on 1:1*). Here the prophet includes the remainder of the exiles who returned from Babylon.

2:3 you who saw. Some remained, perhaps even Haggai, who had seen the temple of Solomon before its destruction (cf. Ezra 3:12,13). With 3 rhetorical questions, the Lord through His prophet Haggai drew attention to the fact that this temple was inferior to Solomon's temple (cf. Ezra 3:8-13), which caused many to be discouraged by its lack of splendor.

2:4 be strong. To counteract the discouragement, the Lord repeated the command to "be strong" and to "work," assuring them of God's presence. This was the second reminder from the Lord, "I *am* with you" (cf. 1:13).

2:5 Spoken at the close of the feast commemorating God's provision during the wilderness wanderings, His covenant commitment and the promise that His Spirit would be with them as "when you came out of Egypt" would be most reassuring (ca. 1445 B.C.). He had not forgotten them over the last 9 centuries (Ex. 33:14). **My Spirit.** The third Person of the Triune Godhead (cf. Num. 11:16,17).

2:6,7 I will shake. The shaking of the cosmic bodies and the nations goes beyond the historical removal of kingdoms and the establishment of others, such as the defeat of Persia by Greece (Dan. 7). Rather, the text looks to the cataclysm in the universe described in Rev. 6–19, the subjugation of the nations by the Messiah, and the setting up of His kingdom which will never be destroyed (cf. Dan. 2:44; 7:27; Zech. 14:16-21; Matt. 25:32; Luke 21:26; Heb. 12:26; Rev. 19:19-21).

2:7 Desire of All Nations. See Introduction: Interpretive Challenges. While some view the phrase as referring to Jerusalem (e.g., Ezra 6:3-9), it seems preferable to see a reference here to the Messiah, the Deliverer for whom all the nations ultimately long. **I will fill this temple with glory.** There is no Scripture to indicate that God's glory ever did come to Zerubbabel's temple, as the first temple was filled with the Shekinah glory (cf. 1 Kin. 8:10,11; 2 Chr. 5:13,14). However, His glory will fill the millennial temple (Ezek. 43:5). This glorification cannot refer to Christ's physical presence in Herod's temple, for the events of vv. 6-9 cannot be accounted for historically. The context speaks of the establishment of His earthly, Davidic, millennial kingdom and His presence in the temple during that kingdom.

2:8 silver...gold. Economically destitute, the people were reassured that He is the possessor of all things (cf. Ps. 50:12).

Zerubbabel

DAVID
SOLOMON
NATHAN
ZERUBBABEL
(Matt. 1:12)
(Luke 3:27)
JOSEPH
MARY

LORD of hosts. 9 [j]'The glory of this latter
[5]temple shall be greater than the former,'
says the LORD of hosts. 'And in this place I
will give [k]peace,' says the LORD of hosts."

The People Are Defiled

10 On the twenty-fourth *day* of the ninth
month, in the second year of Darius, the
word of the LORD came by Haggai the
prophet, saying, 11 "Thus says the LORD of
hosts: 'Now, [l]ask the priests *concerning the*
law, saying, 12 "If one carries holy meat in
the fold of his garment, and with the edge
he touches bread or stew, wine or oil, or
any food, will it become holy?" ' "

Then the priests answered and said,
"No."

13 And Haggai said, "If *one who is* [m]un-

9 [j] [John 1:14] [k] Ps. 85:8, 9; Luke 2:14; [Eph. 2:14] [5] Lit. *house*
11 [l] Lev. 10:10, 11; Deut. 33:10; Mal. 2:7
13 [m] Lev. 22:4-6; Num. 19:11, 22

2:9 this latter temple. The Jews viewed the temple in Jerusalem as one temple existing in different forms at different times. The rebuilt temple was considered a continuation of Solomon's temple (cf. v. 3). However, the eschatological glory of the millennial temple, i.e., the latter temple, will far surpass even the grandeur of Solomon's temple (the former temple). Cf. Ezek. 40–48 for the detailed description of the millennial temple. **I will give peace.** This peace is not limited to that peace which He gives to believers (e.g., Rom. 5:1), but looks ahead to that ultimate peace when He returns to rule as the Prince of Peace upon the throne of David in Jerusalem (Is. 9:6,7; Zech. 6:13; Acts 2:30).

2:10-19 The fourth message of Haggai occurred 2 months after the third, on the 24th day of the month of Chislev, corresponding to Dec. 18, 520 B.C. Only one month earlier, Zechariah began his prophetic ministry (Zech. 1:1). The message sought to demonstrate that while their disobedience caused God's blessings to be withheld, their obedience would cause His blessings to be released.

2:11-14 To provide an analogy or object lesson for the people, two questions were asked of the priests relative to ceremonial law. The first question was intended to show that ceremonial cleanness cannot be transferred (v. 12), while the second question showed that ceremonial uncleanness can be transferred (v. 13). Haggai then applied the lesson (v. 14). Even though the people had been bringing their offerings while neglecting the rebuilding of the temple, their offerings had not been acceptable. Their sin had caused their sacrifices to be contaminated and ineffectual. And their good works, their offerings, could not transmit cleanness. In other words, sin is contagious, righteousness is not (cf. 1 Sam. 15:22; Hos. 6:6).

The Temples of the Bible

Identification	Date	Description	References
The Tabernacle (mobile Temple)	about 1444 B.C.	Detailed plan received by Moses from the Lord Constructed by divinely appointed artisans Desecrated by Nadab and Abihu	Ex. 25–30; 35:30–40:38; Lev. 10:1-7
Solomon's Temple	966–586 B.C.	Planned by David Constructed by Solomon Destroyed by Nebuchadnezzar	2 Sam. 7:1-29; 1 Kin. 8:1-66; Jer. 32:28-44
Zerubbabel's Temple	516–169 B.C.	Envisioned by Zerubbabel Constructed by Zerubbabel and the elders of the Jews Desecrated by Antiochus Epiphanes	Ezra 6:1-22; 3:1-8; 4:1-14;
Herod's Temple	19 B.C.–A.D. 70	Zerubbabel's temple restored by Herod the Great Destroyed by the Romans	Mark 13:2, 14-23; Luke 1:11-20; 2:22-38; 2:42-51; 4:21-24; Acts 21:27-33
The Present Temple	Present Age	Found in the heart of the believer The body of the believer is the Lord's only temple until the Messiah returns	1 Cor. 6:19,20; 2 Cor. 6:16-18
The Temple of Revelation 11	Tribulation Period	To be constructed during the Tribulation by the Antichrist To be desecrated and destroyed	Dan. 9:2; Matt. 24:15; 2 Thess. 2:4; Rev. 17:18
Ezekiel's (Millennial) Temple	Millennium	Envisioned by the prophet Ezekiel To be built by the Messiah during His millennial reign	Ezek. 40:1–42:20; Zech. 6:12,13
The Eternal Temple of His Presence	The Eternal Kingdom	The greatest temple of all ("The Lord God Almighty and the Lamb are its temple") A spiritual temple	Rev. 21:22; 22:1-21

The temple (Gr. *hieron*) is a place of worship, a sacred or holy space built primarily for the national worship of God.

clean *because* of a dead body touches any of
these, will it be unclean?"
So the priests answered and said, "It
shall be unclean."
14 Then Haggai answered and said,
[n]" 'So is this people, and so is this nation
before Me,' says the LORD, 'and so is every
work of their hands; and what they offer
there is unclean.

Promised Blessing

15 'And now, carefully [o]consider from
this day forward: from before stone was
laid upon stone in the temple of the
LORD— 16 since those *days,* [p]when *one*
came to a heap of twenty ephahs, there
were *but* ten; when *one* came to the wine
vat to draw out fifty baths from the press,
there were *but* twenty. 17 [q]I struck you with
blight and mildew and hail [r]in all the
labors of your hands; [s]yet you did not *turn*
to Me,' says the LORD. 18 'Consider now
from this day forward, from the twenty-
fourth day of the ninth month, from [t]the
day that the foundation of the LORD's temple was laid—consider it: 19 [u]Is the seed
still in the barn? As yet the vine, the fig
tree, the pomegranate, and the olive tree
have not yielded *fruit. But* from this day I
will [v]bless *you.*' "

Zerubbabel Chosen as a Signet

20 And again the word of the LORD came
to Haggai on the twenty-fourth day of the
month, saying, 21 "Speak to Zerubbabel,
[w]governor of Judah, saying:

[x]'I will shake heaven and earth.
22 [y]I will overthrow the throne of
kingdoms;
I will destroy the strength of the
Gentile kingdoms.
[z]I will overthrow the chariots
And those who ride in them;
The horses and their riders shall
come down,
Every one by the sword of his
brother.

23 'In that day,' says the LORD of hosts, 'I
will take you, Zerubbabel My servant, the
son of Shealtiel,' says the LORD, [a]'and will
make you like a signet *ring;* for [b]I have chosen you,' says the LORD of hosts."

14 [n][Titus 1:15]
15 [o]Hag. 1:5, 7; 2:18
16 [p]Hag. 1:6, 9; Zech. 8:10
17 [q]Deut. 28:22; 1 Kin. 8:37; Amos 4:9 [r]Hag. 1:11 [s]Jer. 5:3; Amos 4:6-11
18 [t]Ezra 5:1, 2, 16; Zech. 8:9
19 [u]Zech. 8:12 [v]Ps. 128:1-6; Jer. 31:12, 14; [Mal. 3:10]
21 [w]Ezra 5:2; Hag. 1:1, 14; Zech. 4:6-10 [x]Hag. 2:6, 7; [Heb. 12:26, 27]
22 [y][Dan. 2:44; Rev. 19:11-21] [z]Ps. 46:9; Ezek. 39:20; Mic. 5:10; Zech. 9:10
23 [a]Song 8:6; Jer. 22:24 [b]Is. 42:1; 43:10

2:15-18 The Lord called the people to again consider their situation prior to the resumption of the temple building. In those days, the farmer found less than expected (cf. 1:6,9-11).

2:16 ephahs…baths. Four to 6 gal., respectively. Between 50 to 60 percent of the expected harvest had been lost.

2:19 *But* from this day I will bless *you*. As a result of their obedience, God promised to bless them from that day forth (cf. v. 10).

2:20-23 The fifth message to Zerubbabel the governor of Judah (v. 20) came on the same day as the fourth, and he returned to the theme of vv. 6-9 and the millennial reign of the Messiah. Once again, it depicted the overthrow of the kingdoms of the world and the establishment of the messianic kingdom (cf. Dan. 2:44; 7:27). As the events predicted did not transpire historically, the promise pertains to the royal line through whom the Messiah would come. It looked to the ultimate day when Messiah reigns on earth (cf. Ps. 2; Rev. 19,20).

2:23 In that day. The day of Messiah's triumph (cf. Zech. 12–14). **My servant.** A distinctly Davidic and messianic title (cf. 2 Sam. 3:18; 1 Kin. 11:34; Is. 42:1-9; Ezek. 37:24,25). **signet *ring*.** The signet ring was a symbol of honor, authority, and power (cf. Song 8:6). It corresponded to a king's scepter which was used to seal letters and decrees (cf. 1 Kin. 21:8; Esth. 8:8; Dan. 6:17). Zerubbabel, as God's signet ring, stands as the official representative of the Davidic dynasty and represents the resumption of the messianic line interrupted by the Exile. Just as Pharaoh gave Joseph his signet ring and made him second in the kingdom (Gen. 41:41-43), so God will do for the Davidic line of kings. The pre-Exilic signet of Jehoiachin was removed by God (Jer. 22:24) and renewed here in his grandson, Zerubbabel, who reestablished the Davidic line of kings, which would culminate in the millennial reign of Christ. Possibly through a levirate marriage, Zerubbabel appears in the line of Christ on both Joseph's side (Matt. 1:12) and Mary's side (Luke 3:27), thus bypassing God's curse on the lines of Jehoiakim and Jehoiachin (cf. Jer. 22:24-30; 36:27-32).

The Book of ZECHARIAH

Title

The universal tradition of both Jews and Christians endorses the prophet Zechariah as author. His name, common to more than 29 OT men, means "The LORD remembers." This book is second only to Isaiah in the breadth of the prophet's writings about Messiah.

Author and Date

Like Jeremiah and Ezekiel, Zechariah was also a priest (Neh. 12:12-16) According to tradition, he was a member of the Great Synagogue, a council of 120 originated by Nehemiah and presided over by Ezra. This council later developed into the ruling elders of the nation, called the Sanhedrin. He was born in Babylon and joined his grandfather, Iddo, in the group of exiles who first returned to Jerusalem under the leadership of Zerubbabel and Joshua the High-Priest (cf. Neh. 12:4). Because he is occasionally mentioned as the son of his grandfather (cf. Ezra 5:1; 6:14; Neh. 12:16), it is thought that his father, Berechiah, died at an early age before he could succeed his father into the priesthood.

Zechariah's opening words are dated from 520 B.C., the second year of Darius I (cf. 1:1). The Persian emperor Cyrus had died and was succeeded by Cambyses (ca. 530–521 B.C.) who conquered Egypt. He had no son, he killed himself, and Darius rose to the throne by quelling a revolution. He was a contemporary of Haggai, and began his prophesying 2 months after him (cf. Haggai Introduction). He is called a young man in 2:4, suggesting that Zechariah was younger than Haggai. The length of his ministry is uncertain; the last dated prophecy (7:1) came approximately two years after the first, making them identical in time with Haggai's prophecy (520–518 B.C.). Chapters 9–14 are generally thought to come from a later period of his ministry. Differences in style and references to Greece indicate a date of ca. 480–470 B.C., after Darius I (ca. 521–486 B.C.) and during Xerxes' reign (ca. 486–464 B.C.), the king who made Esther queen of Persia. According to Matt. 23:35, he was murdered between the temple and the altar, a fate similar to an earlier Zechariah (cf. 2 Chr. 24:20,21), who had been stoned to death.

Background and Setting

The historical background and setting of Zechariah are the same as that of his contemporary, Haggai (cf. Haggai Introduction). In 538 B.C., Cyrus the Persian freed the captives from Israel to resettle their homeland (cf. Ezra 1:1-4) and about 50,000 returned from Babylon. They immediately began to rebuild the temple (cf. Ezra 3:1–4:5), but opposition from neighbors, followed by indifference from within, caused the work to be abandoned (cf. Ezra 4:24). Sixteen years later (cf. Ezra 5:1,2), Zechariah and Haggai were commissioned by the Lord to stir up the people to rebuild the temple. As a result, the temple was completed 4 years later in 516 B.C. (Ezra 6:15).

Historical and Theological Themes

Zechariah joined Haggai in rousing the people from their indifference, challenging them to resume the building of the temple. Haggai's primary purpose was to rebuild the temple; his preaching has a tone of rebuke for the people's indifference, sin, and lack of trust in God. He was used to start the revival, while Zechariah was used to keep it going strong with a more positive emphasis, calling the people to repentance and reassuring them regarding future blessings. Zechariah sought to encourage the people to build the temple in view of the promise that someday Messiah would come to inhabit it. The people were not just building for the present, but with the future hope of Messiah in mind. He encouraged the people, still downtrodden by the Gentile powers (1:8-12), with the reality that the Lord remembers His covenant promises to them and that He would restore and bless them. Thus the name of the book (which means "The LORD remembers") contains in seed form the theme of the prophecy.

This "apocalypse of the OT" as it is often called, relates both to Zechariah's immediate audience as well as to the future. This is borne out in the structure of the prophecy itself, since in each of the 3 major sections (chaps. 1–6,7,8,9-14), the prophet begins historically and then moves forward to the time of the Second Advent, when Messiah returns to His temple to set up His earthly kingdom. The prophet reminded the people that Messiah had both an immediate and long-term commitment to His people. Thus the prophet's words were "good *and* comforting" (1:13), both to the exiles of Zechariah's day as well as to the remnant of God's chosen people in that future day.

This book is the most messianic, apocalyptic, and eschatological in the OT. Primarily, it is a prophecy about Jesus Christ, focusing on His coming glory as a means to comfort Israel (cf. 1:13,17). While the book is filled with visions, prophecies, signs, celestial visitors, and the voice of God, it is also practical, dealing with issues like repentance, divine care, salvation, and holy living. Prophecy was soon to be silent for more than 400 years until John the Baptist, so God used Zechariah to bring a rich, abundant outburst of promise for the future to sustain the faithful remnant through those silent years.

Interpretive Challenges

While there are numerous challenges to the reader, two passages within the prophecy present notable interpretive difficulty. In 11:8, the Good Shepherd "dismissed the three shepherds in one month." The presence of the definite article points to familiarity, so that the Jews would have understood the identity of these shepherds without further reference. It is not so easy for modern readers to understand. Numerous alternatives concerning their identity have been suggested. One of the oldest, and probably the correct, view identifies them as three orders of leaders: the priests, elders, and scribes of Israel. During His earthly ministry, Jesus also confronted the hypocrisy of Israel's religious leaders (cf. Matt. 23), disowning them with scathing denunciations, followed by destruction of the whole nation in A.D. 70. Since His coming, the Jewish people have had no other prophet, priest, or king.

Considerable discussion also surrounds the identity of the individual who possessed "wounds between your arms" (13:6). Some have identified him with Christ, the wounds supposedly referring to His crucifixion. But Christ could neither have denied that He was a prophet, nor could He have claimed that He was a farmer, or that He was wounded in the house of His friends. Obviously, it is a reference to a false prophet (cf. vv. 4,5) who was wounded in his idolatrous worship. The zeal for the Lord will be so great in the kingdom of Messiah that idolaters will make every attempt to hide their true identity, but their scars will be the telltale evidence of their iniquity.

Outline

I. Call to Repentance (1:1-6)

II. Eight Night Visions of Zechariah (1:7–6:15)
- A. Man Among the Myrtle Trees (1:7-17)
- B. Four Horns and Four Craftsmen (1:18-21)
- C. Man with Measuring Line (2:1-13)
- D. Cleansing of High-Priest (3:1-10)
- E. Gold Lampstand and Two Olive Trees (4:1-14)
- F. Flying Scroll (5:1-4)
- G. Woman in Basket (5:5-11)
- H. Four Chariots (6:1-8)
- I. Appendix: Coronation of Joshua the High-Priest (6:9-15)

III. Four Messages of Zechariah (7:1–8:23)
- A. Question about Fasting (7:1-3)
- B. Four Responses (7:4–8:23)
  1. Rebuke for wrong motives (7:4-7)
  2. Repentance required (7:8-14)
  3. Restoration of favor (8:1-17)
  4. Fasts become feasts (8:18-23)

IV. Two Burdens of Zechariah (9:1–14:21)
- A. Messiah's Rejection at First Advent (9:1–11:17)
- B. Messiah's Acceptance at Second Advent (12:1–14:21)

A Call to Repentance

CHAPTER 1

1 In the eighth month [a]of the second
year of Darius, the word of the LORD
came [b]to Zechariah the son of Berechiah,
the son of [c]Iddo the prophet, saying,
2 "The LORD has been very angry with
your fathers. 3 Therefore say to them,
'Thus says the LORD of hosts: "Return [d]to
Me," says the LORD of hosts, "and I will return to you," says the LORD of hosts. 4 "Do
not be like your fathers, [e]to whom the former prophets preached, saying, 'Thus says
the LORD of hosts: [f]"Turn now from your
evil ways and your evil deeds." ' But they
did not hear nor heed Me," says the LORD.

5 "Your fathers, where *are* they?
And the prophets, do they live
forever?
6 Yet surely [g]My words and My
statutes,
Which I commanded My servants
the prophets,
Did they not overtake your
fathers?

"So they returned and said:

[h]'Just as the LORD of hosts
determined to do to us,
According to our ways and
according to our deeds,
So He has dealt with us.' " ' "

Vision of the Horses

7 On the twenty-fourth day of the
eleventh month, which is the month She-
bat, in the second year of Darius, the word
of the LORD came to Zechariah the son of
Berechiah, the son of Iddo the prophet: 8 I
saw by night, and behold, [i]a man riding on
a red horse, and it stood among the myrtle
trees in the hollow; and behind him *were*

1 [a] Ezra 4:24; 6:15; Hag. 1:1; Zech. 7:1 [b] Ezra 5:1; 6:14; Zech. 7:1; Matt. 23:35; Luke 11:51 [c] Neh. 12:4, 16
3 [d] Is. 31:6; 44:22; [Mic. 7:19; Mal. 3:7-10; Luke 15:20; James 4:8]
4 [e] 2 Chr. 36:15, 16 [f] Is. 31:6; Jer. 3:12; 18:11; Ezek. 18:30; [Hos. 14:1]
6 [g] [Is. 55:11] [h] Lam. 1:18; 2:17
8 [i] Is. 55:13; Zech. 6:2; [Rev. 6:4]

1:1-6 The opening 6 verses provide an introduction to the entire prophecy in which the prophet calls upon the people to repent and never again repeat the past sins of their fathers (cf. 1 Cor. 10:11).

1:1 eighth month of the second year of Darius. Ca. Oct./Nov. 520 B.C. See Introduction: Author and Date. Zechariah began his ministry two months after the start of Haggai's ministry (cf. Hag. 1:1) and the resumption of the rebuilding of the temple (cf. Hag. 1:12-15). The OT prophets who dated their prophecies did so according to the reign of a king in Israel, Judah, or both. Only Haggai and Zechariah date their prophecies according to the reign of the Gentile king, indicating that the times of the Gentiles (Luke 21:24) had begun. **Zechariah.** See Introduction: Author and Date.

1:2 The LORD has been very angry. This actually means "to break out in long-controlled indignation," reminding the people of the severity of God's wrath and the necessity of His judgment on their past sins in pre-Exilic times.

1:3 the LORD of hosts. This frequently used name for God shows His might as the commander of the hosts, whether they are the armies of Israel (cf. 2 Chr. 26:11), the armies of the heathen nations (cf. Judg. 4:2), or the heavenly inhabitants (cf. 1 Kin. 22:19). **Return to Me.** Though primarily a book of consolation, the prophet begins with a call to repentance, to preclude any false security on the part of Israel, i.e., thinking that God would bless His chosen people regardless of their spiritual condition. This expresses the ongoing desire of God (cf. Gen. 17:7; Lev. 26:12; Ezek. 37:27; 2 Cor. 6:6; James 4:8; Rev. 21:3), and the constant condition for blessing.

1:4 Do not be like your fathers. The disobedient, obstinate behavior of their fathers was not so much directed toward the prophets, but at God Himself. The people were well aware of their fathers' sins (cf. Ezra 9:7) and could look around them and see the results. History should have taught them to repent. **the former prophets.** A reference to the pre-Exilic prophets who all preached the same message of repentance before the Exile, e.g., Isaiah and Jeremiah. Cf. "My servants" (v. 6).

1:5 While both their fathers and the former prophets were dead, the legacy of their fathers' failure to heed the prophets' warnings was vividly before them, exemplified by the city of Jerusalem and the temple lying in ruins, needing to be rebuilt.

1:6 God's Word accomplishes all which He designs (Is. 55:10,11), in blessing and in judgment. His warnings, so precisely fulfilled, overtook and destroyed their fathers, who recognized God's hand in the judgment (cf. Lam. 2:17; Ezra 9:6ff.). The Exile was positive proof that God punishes those who sin and reject His warnings. **they returned.** This would better be translated "they repented" (cf. Dan. 9:1-19).

1:7–6:15 God gave Zechariah these visions for the comfort of the post-Exilic remnant of Israel who had been commissioned to return from Persia to the land promised to Abraham (cf. Gen. 12). They were to rebuild the temple (cf. 1 and 2 Chr.) and to anticipate the day of Messiah's return, when all of God's promises to Israel would finally, fully, and ultimately be fulfilled. Some portions of the visions have been fulfilled, but the large number await the Second Advent of Jesus Christ. The following summary will help to distinguish the contribution of individual visions and clarify the whole. Vision 1—Man among the myrtle trees (1:7-17), God promises prosperity to Israel. Vision 2—Four horns and four craftsmen (1:18-21), God judges the nations who attacked Israel. Vision 3—Man with a measuring line (2:1-13), God rebuilds Jerusalem. Vision 4—Cleansing of the High-Priest (3:1-10), God purifies both High-Priest and people. Vision 5—Golden lampstand and two olives trees (4:1-14), God rebuilds the temple. Vision 6—Flying scroll (5:1-4), God removes imparted sin/idolatry. Vision 7—Woman in basket (5:5-11), God removes the system of false religion. Vision 8—Four chariots (6:1-8), God brings peace and rest to Israel. Appendix—Coronation of the High-Priest (6:9-15), Messiah assumes the office of both King and Priest.

1:7-17 This is the first of 8 night visions which Zechariah saw in a single night. It summarized all the other 7 by giving the general theme, leaving the details to the other visions. Reassuring words are provided to the exiles by revealing God's purpose for the future of His chosen people.

1:7 the twenty-fourth day of the eleventh month. Ca. Jan./Feb. 519 B.C. Approximately 3 months after Zechariah's opening call to repentance.

1:8 I saw by night. This is the first vision revealing God's plan for Jerusalem, which begins with the sight of "a man riding on a red horse." The man is identified as the Angel of the Lord (cf. v. 11). The other riders report to Him, indicating His authority over them. Because of the strength of horses, they became symbols of war. Red is often the symbol of blood, hence judgment (cf. Is. 63:1-4; Rev. 6:3ff.). **among the myrtle trees in the hollow.** Myrtle trees were associated with booth-making at the Feast of Tabernacles (Lev. 23:33-44; Neh 8:15) and with messianic blessing (cf. Is. 41:19; 55:13), and thereby possibly speak of restoration and blessing. Their location in the hollow has

[j]horses: red, sorrel, and white. 9 Then I
said, [k]"My lord, what *are* these?" So the
angel who talked with me said to me, "I
will show you what they *are*."
10 And the man who stood among the
myrtle trees answered and said, [l]"These
are the ones whom the LORD has sent to
walk to and fro throughout the earth."
11 [m]So they answered the Angel of the
LORD, who stood among the myrtle trees,
and said, "We have walked to and fro
throughout the earth, and behold, all the
earth is [1]resting quietly."

The LORD Will Comfort Zion

12 Then the Angel of the LORD answered
and said, "O LORD of hosts, [n]how long will
You not have mercy on Jerusalem and on
the cities of Judah, against which You were
angry [o]these seventy years?"
13 And the LORD answered the angel
who talked to me, *with* [p]good *and* comforting words. 14 So the angel who spoke with
me said to me, [2]"Proclaim, saying, 'Thus
says the LORD of hosts:

"I am [q]zealous[3] for Jerusalem
And for Zion with great [4]zeal.
15 I am exceedingly angry with the
nations at ease;
For [r]I was a little angry,
And they helped—*but* with evil
intent."

16 'Therefore thus says the LORD:

[s]"I am returning to Jerusalem with
mercy;
My [t]house [u]shall be built in it,"
says the LORD of hosts,
"And [v]a *surveyor's* line shall be
stretched out over
Jerusalem." '

17 "Again proclaim, saying, 'Thus says
the LORD of hosts:

"My cities shall again [5]spread out
through prosperity;
[w]The LORD will again comfort Zion,
And [x]will again choose
Jerusalem." ' "

Vision of the Horns

18 Then I raised my eyes and looked,
and there *were* four [y]horns. 19 And I said to

8 [j][Zech. 6:2-7; Rev. 6:2]
9 [k]Zech. 4:4, 5, 13; 6:4
10 [l][Heb. 1:14]
11 [m][Ps. 103:20, 21] [1]Lit. *sitting and quiet*
12 [n]Ps. 74:10; Jer. 12:4; Hab. 1:2 [o]2 Chr. 36:21; Jer. 25:11, 12; 29:10; Dan. 9:2; Zech. 7:5
13 [p]Jer. 29:10
14 [q]Joel 2:18; Zech. 8:2 [2]Lit. *Cry out* [3]Or *jealous* [4]Or *jealousy*
15 [r]Is. 47:6
16 [s][Is. 12:1; 54:8; Zech. 2:10; 8:3] [t]Ezra 6:14, 15; Hag. 1:4; Zech. 4:9 [u]2 Chr. 36:23; Ezra 1:2, 3; Is. 44:28 [v]Zech. 2:1-3
17 [w][Is. 40:1, 2; 51:3] [x]Is. 14:1; Zech. 2:12 [5]Or *overflow with good*
18 [y][Lam. 2:17]

been thought to refer to a low place where such shrubs would flourish. Because of the lowliness (these shrubs would never exceed 8 ft. in height), commonness, fragrance (from white blossoms), and abundance in flourishing places, it is best to see these as representing Israel, God's people. They are the lowly and yet enriched people. Their lowliness in the hollow could also refer to Israel's current humiliation. **red, sorrel, and white.** Presumably these other horses had riders as well. The colors may speak of the work of the riders: red speaking of bloodshed and judgment (cf. Is. 63:1,2), white speaking of victory (cf. Rev. 19:11), and sorrel or a brownish color is possibly a combination of the others. A similar picture is found in Rev. 6:1-8. These horses are about to gain a victorious judgment. Since they are messengers of vengeance, they likely represent angels, so frequently employed as God's instruments of judgment.

1:9 the angel who talked with me. This interpreting angel (1:13,14,19; 2:3; 3:1; 4:1) is to be distinguished from the Angel of the Lord (vv. 11,12).

1:10 walk to and fro. A symbolic military description of angelic movement patrolling and reconnoitering on a global scale. The purpose is to ascertain the state of the enemy and to respond to God's will in engaging that enemy triumphantly.

1:11 the Angel of the LORD. Elsewhere the Angel of the Lord is frequently identified with the pre-incarnate Lord Himself (e.g., Gen. 16:11,13; 18:1,2,13,17; 22:11-18; Ex. 3:2,4; Josh. 5:13; 6:2; Judg. 6:12,14; 13:21,22). In v. 13, this Angel is called Lord, and is the divine commander-in-chief of this angelic army. **all the earth is resting quietly.** In contrast to the difficulties facing the exiles, without temple or city walls, the heathen nations were superficially at rest, occupied with their own selfish interests (cf. v. 15). This was generally the condition in the second year of Darius. The contrast makes the plight of Israel all the more distressing and the hope for the fulfillment of Hag. 2:7,22 more intense.

1:12 The Angel of the Lord interceded to God the Father on behalf of Israel, pleading for the withdrawal of God's chastening hand. The "seventy years" refers to God's words to Jeremiah concerning the length of Judah's exile (Jer. 25:11,12; 29:10).

1:13 good *and* comforting words. The content of these words is given in vv. 14-17: God still loved Jerusalem (v. 14), He was angry with the nations who afflicted them (v. 15), and He will bring prosperity to Jerusalem (vv. 16,17).

1:14 I am zealous for Jerusalem. God first described Himself as jealous when making His covenant with Israel (Ex. 20:5; 34:14). This same jealousy had been experienced by Israel in punishment (cf. Deut. 29:18-28; Ezek. 5:13). That same jealous love is expressed emphatically in the city's defense.

1:15 Moved by His great love for His people, the Lord acted in anger (cf. v. 2) against the nations which mistreated His people. Although they were His instrument of judgment against Israel, they had exceeded God's instructions in meting out punishment. They did not understand that God's intention was to punish for a time and then show compassion (cf. Is. 54:7,8).

1:16,17 Not only would the temple be rebuilt which at that time had only foundations (cf. Hag. 2:18), but the city itself would again expand due to the prosperity (cf. Is. 40:9,10). The wall was completed 75 years later. God would again comfort Jerusalem (cf. Is. 40:1,2; 51:3,12) and would again choose it as the place of His earthly throne (cf. Ps. 132:13). This will be fulfilled in the millennial kingdom of Messiah (cf. Rev. 20). Given the fact that the returning Jews lost sight of their priorities (cf. Hag. 1:1-12), this message reaffirmed God's plan. It should be noted that the millennial kingdom will provide the presence of God in Jerusalem (Ezek. 48:35), a glorious temple (Ezek. 40–48), a rebuilt Jerusalem (Jer. 31:38-40), the nations punished (Matt. 25:31-46), the prosperity of Judah's cities (Is. 60:4-9) the blessedness of the people (Zech. 9:17), and the comfort of Zion (Is. 14:1).

1:18-21 The second of 8 night visions adds details to the judgment of the nations who persecuted His Israel, building upon God's promise to comfort His people (1:13,17).

1:18 four horns. Horns were symbols of power and pride (cf. Pss.

the angel who talked with me, "What *are*
these?"
So he answered me, [z]"These *are* the
[6]horns that have scattered Judah, Israel,
and Jerusalem."
20 Then the LORD showed me four craftsmen. 21 And I said, "What are these coming to do?"
So he said, "These *are* the [a]horns that
scattered Judah, so that no one could lift
up his head; but [7]the craftsmen are coming
to terrify them, to cast out the horns of the
nations that [b]lifted up *their* horn against
the land of Judah to scatter it."

Vision of the Measuring Line

2 Then I raised my eyes and looked, and
behold, [a]a man with a measuring line
in his hand. 2 So I said, "Where are you
going?"
And he said to me, [b]"To measure Jerusalem, to see what *is* its width and what *is* its
length."
3 And there *was* the angel who talked
with me, going out; and another angel was
coming out to meet him, 4 who said to him,
"Run, speak to this young man, saying:
[c]'Jerusalem shall be inhabited *as* towns
without walls, because of the multitude of
men and livestock in it. 5 For I,' says the
LORD, 'will be [d]a wall of fire all around her,
[e]and I will be the glory in her midst.' "

Future Joy of Zion and Many Nations

6 "Up, up! Flee [f]from the land of the
north," says the LORD; "for I have [g]spread
you abroad like the four winds of heaven,"
says the LORD. 7 "Up, Zion! [h]Escape, you
who dwell with the daughter of Babylon."
8 For thus says the LORD of hosts: "He
sent Me after glory, to the nations which
plunder you; for he who [i]touches you
touches the [1]apple of His eye. 9 For surely
I will [j]shake My hand against them, and
they shall become [2]spoil for their servants.
Then [k]you will know that the LORD of
hosts has sent Me.
10 [l]"Sing and rejoice, O daughter of
Zion! For behold, I am coming and I [m]will
dwell in your midst," says the LORD.
11 [n]"Many nations shall be joined to the
LORD [o]in that day, and they shall become
[p]My people. And I will dwell in your
midst. Then [q]you will know that the LORD
of hosts has sent Me to you. 12 And the
LORD will [r]take possession of Judah as His

19 [z]Ezra 4:1, 4, 7 [6]Kingdoms or powers
21 [a][Ps. 75:10] [b]Ps. 75:4, 5 [7]Lit. *these*

CHAPTER 2

1 [a]Jer. 31:39; Ezek. 40:3; 47:3; Zech. 1:16
2 [b]Rev. 11:1
4 [c]Jer. 31:27
5 [d][Is. 26:1] [e][Is. 60:19]
6 [f]Is. 48:20 [g]Deut. 28:64
7 [h]Is. 48:20; Jer. 51:6; [Rev. 18:4]
8 [i]Deut. 32:10; Ps. 17:8 [1]Lit. *pupil*
9 [j]Is. 19:16 [k]Zech. 4:9 [2]*booty* or *plunder*
10 [l]Is. 12:6 [m][Lev. 26:12]
11 [n][Is. 2:2, 3] [o]Zech. 3:10 [p]Ex. 12:49 [q]Ezek. 33:33
12 [r][Deut. 32:9]; Ps. 33:12; Jer. 10:16

75:10; 89:17; 92:10; Dan. 7:24; 8:20,21; Mic. 4:13). In the context of judgment each symbolizes either a nation or the head of that nation (cf. Dan. 7:21,24; 8:3; Rev. 17:12). Here the horns represent nations that attacked God's people (vv. 19,21), referring either to Egypt, Assyria, Babylonia, and Medo-Persia or perhaps, more likely, to the 4 world empires of Dan. 2,7: Babylonia, Medo-Persia, Greece, and Rome, all of which oppressed Israel.

1:20 four craftsmen. The word is literally the term for stone workers, metal workers, and wood workers—those who shape material with hammers and chisels. These "hammers" represent the nations which overthrow the 4 horns (v. 18). As with the 4 beasts of Dan. 7, each empire is overthrown by the subsequent one, the last being replaced by Messiah's kingdom (cf. Dan. 2:44; 7:9-14,21,22). Babylon was hammered in a night attack by the Medo-Persians (539 B.C.). With the victory of Alexander over Darius in 333 B.C. at Issus, the Greeks hammered the Medo-Persian "horn." In the second century B.C., the Roman hammer fell and one by one the nations fell (Israel in 63 B.C.). The Roman Empire, revived in the last days, according to Daniel, will be hammered by the returning Messiah (cf. Dan. 2:34,35,45).

2:1-13 The third vision reveals a man with a measuring line. Like the second vision, it too builds on God's promise to comfort His people (1:13,17). The restoration of Jerusalem after the return from Babylon is only a foretaste of the future messianic kingdom, for the language of the vision cannot be fulfilled historically. Its scope extends beyond the time of Zechariah to the rule of the Messiah on earth.

2:1 a man with a measuring line. The restoration and rebuilding of Jerusalem is symbolized. It is very possible that the surveyor is the Angel of the Lord (cf. 1:11; 6:12; Ezek. 40:2,3), who is laying out the future dimensions of the city.

2:3 angel...talked with me. This is the instructing angel of 1:9.

2:4 The news was so wonderful that it was to be heralded immediately. An angel arrived to explain that Jerusalem will become so large that it will extend beyond any walls (cf. Is. 49:19,20; Ezek. 38:11). The conditions here described have at no time been true historically (cf. Neh. 7:4; 11:1,2); full realization must be assigned to a future earthly kingdom (cf. Is. 49:19,20). A counterfeit of this unwalled safety will exist under Antichrist in the time of tribulation *(see notes on Ezek. 38:8-12)*.

2:5 a wall of fire all around her. Though without walls, Jerusalem will dwell securely because of divine protection. The phrase is reminiscent of the pillar of fire at the Exodus (cf. Ex. 13:21; 2 Kin. 6:15-17; Is. 4:5,6). **I will be the glory in her midst.** More than protection, the glory depicts the Messiah's blessing and personal presence in His earthly kingdom (cf. Is. 4:2-6; 40:5; 60:17,18; Ezek. 42:1-7).

2:6-9 The prophet turned from the distant future (vv. 4,5) to the present, summoning those Israelites still in Babylon (referred to as the land of the north, cf. v. 7, because of the direction from which it invaded Israel) to flee before God poured out His judgment on it. This also implied a future call to leave a future Babylon (cf. Rev. 17:3-5; 18:1-8).

2:6 I have spread you. According to 2 Kin. 17:6, they were scattered from the Gozan River, 200 mi. W of Nineveh, to Media, 300 mi. E. Some had even taken refuge in Moab, Ammon, Edom, and Egypt (cf. Jer. 40:11,12; 43:7).

2:8 He sent Me after glory. The Messiah is sent by the "LORD of Hosts" (v. 9) to procure His glory and to vindicate Him in the nations who have spoiled Israel. **the apple of His eye.** *See note on Deut. 32:10.* Harming God's chosen people is like striking the pupil of God's eye.

2:10-13 The language is once again messianic, describing the personal presence of the Messiah, dwelling on the throne of David in Jerusalem during the Millennium.

2:11,12 Echoing the promise to Abraham (Gen. 12:3), many nations will join themselves to the Lord (cf. 6:15; Zech. 8:20-23; Is. 2:2-4; 56:6,7; 60:3). But this will not alter God's choice of His people, they will still be "His inheritance in the Holy Land" (cf. Deut. 32:9).

inheritance in the Holy Land, and will
again choose Jerusalem. 13 [s]Be silent, all
flesh, before the LORD, for He is aroused
[t]from His holy habitation!"

Vision of the High Priest

3 Then he showed me [a]Joshua the high
priest standing before the Angel of the
LORD, and [b]Satan[1] standing at his right
hand to oppose him. 2 And the LORD said
to Satan, [c]"The LORD rebuke you, Satan!
The LORD who [d]has chosen Jerusalem rebuke you! [e]*Is* this not a brand plucked
from the fire?"
3 Now Joshua was clothed with [f]filthy
garments, and was standing before the
Angel.
4 Then He answered and spoke to those
who stood before Him, saying, "Take away
the filthy garments from him." And to him
He said, "See, I have removed your iniquity from you, [g]and I will clothe you with
rich robes."
5 And I said, "Let them put a clean [h]tur-
ban on his head."
So they put a clean turban on his head,
and they put the clothes on him. And the
Angel of the LORD stood by.

The Coming Branch

6 Then the Angel of the LORD admonished Joshua, saying, 7 "Thus says the
LORD of hosts:

'If you will walk in My ways,
And if you will [i]keep My
command,
Then you shall also [j]judge My
house,
And likewise have charge of My
courts;
I will give you places to walk
Among these who [k]stand here.

8 'Hear, O Joshua, the high priest,
You and your companions who sit
before you,
For they are [l]a[2] wondrous sign;
For behold, I am bringing forth
[m]My Servant the [n]BRANCH.
9 For behold, the stone
That I have laid before Joshua:

13 [s]Hab. 2:20; Zeph. 1:7 [t]Ps. 68:5

CHAPTER 3

1 [a]Ezra 5:2; Hag. 1:1; Zech. 6:11 [b]1 Chr. 21:1; Job 1:6; Ps. 109:6; [Rev. 12:9, 10] [1]Lit. *the Adversary*
2 [c]Mark 9:25; [Jude 9] [d][Rom. 8:33] [e]Amos 4:11; Jude 23
3 [f]Ezra 9:15; Is. 64:6
4 [g]Gen. 3:21; Is. 61:10
5 [h]Ex. 29:6
7 [i]Lev. 8:35; Ezek. 44:16 [j]Deut. 17:9, 12 [k]Zech. 3:4
8 [l]Ps. 71:7 [m]Is. 42:1 [n]Is. 11:1; 53:2; Jer. 23:5; 33:15; Zech. 6:12 [2]Lit. *men of a sign* or *wonder*

2:12 Holy Land. Used only here, the expression is made not because it is the Promised Land but because it will be the site of Messiah's earthly throne when the land has been cleansed. A holy land is appropriate and expected for its holy Lord (Is. 6:1-5).

2:13 His holy habitation. God's dwelling in heaven (cf. Pss. 15:1; 24:3).

3:1-10 The fourth night vision emphasizes Israel's cleansing and restoration as a priestly nation. The vision itself is given in vv. 1-5, followed by the explanation and significance in vv. 6-10. The revealer was most likely God Himself.

3:1 The scene is invested with a judicial character as Joshua, the High-Priest of the restoration who came back in the first group with Zerubbabel (cf. Ezra 3:2; 5:2; Hag. 1:1), was accused by Satan, who was standing at the right side, the place of accusation under the law (cf. Ps. 109:6). That Joshua was representative of the nation is evident from: 1) the emphasis on the nation in these visions; 2) the fact that the rebuke in v. 2 is based on God's choice of Jerusalem, not Joshua; 3) the identification in v. 8 of Joshua and his fellow priests as symbolic of future Israel; and 4) its application to the land in v. 9. **Satan.** This could also be translated "adversary" and thus the person's identity would be unknown. However, because the activity of accusation is so in keeping with Satan (cf. Job 1,2; Rev. 12:10), his identification is preferable. The malicious adversary stands in the presence of the Lord to proclaim Israel's sins and their unworthiness of God's favor. The situation is crucial: If Joshua is vindicated, Israel is accepted; If Joshua is rejected, Israel is rejected. The entire plan of God for the nation was revealed in the outcome. Israel's hopes would either be destroyed or confirmed.

3:2 the LORD said. The Angel of the Lord is identified as the Lord, thus verifying this "messenger" as deity. *See notes on Judg. 1:11; 6:11.* And the message was crucial in confirming that 1) God had not cast off the Jews, but was consistent with His covenants with them in Abraham and David, and 2) His election takes their side against Satan's accusations. God will do this rebuking, as reported in Rev. 20:10. *See note on Jude 9.* **chosen Jerusalem.** God's favor rested on Israel above any nation on earth (cf. Deut. 7:6-11). He snatched them from potential disappearance in their captivity, like pulling a stick out of the fire just before it is torched (cf. Amos 4:11). Thus, God confirmed His purposes for Israel, sweeping from Zechariah's time to the consummation of human history (cf. Rev. 12:3-17).

3:3 filthy garments. Employing the most loathsome, vile term for filth, the phrase pictures the habitual condition of defilement of the priesthood and the people (cf. Is. 4:4; 64:6), which became the basis of Satan's accusation that the nation is morally impure and unworthy of God's protection and blessing.

3:4 The removal of filthy garments by the angels ("who stood before him") depicted the promised future forensic justification, the salvation of the nation (cf. v. 9; 12:10–13:1; Rom. 11:25-27). The High-Priest was symbolically clothed with rich robes, which spoke of righteousness imputed (cf. Is. 61:10) and the restoration of Israel to her original calling (cf. Ex. 19:6; Is. 61:6; Rom. 11:1,2).

3:5 a clean turban. The turban, part of the High-Priest's dress, was inscribed with the words: "Holiness to the LORD" (Ex. 28:36,37; 39:30,31). Zechariah joined the scene, calling for this because it strongly symbolized that Israel's priestly place with God was restored.

3:6,7 Although God will keep His promise to justify Israel, reinstate the nation as His priestly people to serve in His house, keep His courts, and have complete access to His presence—all based on His sovereign, electing love and not by merit or works of man—that will not be fulfilled until Israel is faithful to the Lord. It awaits the fulfillment of 12:10–13:1.

3:8 they are a wondrous sign. The companion priests sitting before Joshua were symbols of future Israel, foreshadowing the coming Messiah. **My Servant the BRANCH.** Two messianic phrases are here combined. "My Servant" is used by earlier prophets to depict the Messiah (Is. 42:1; 49:3,5; 52:13; 53:11; Ezek. 34:23,24) and speaks of His complete obedience and His humble estate. "Branch" also points to the Messiah (cf. 6:12,13; Is. 4:2; Jer. 23:5; 33:15) and denotes His rise from humble beginnings (Is. 11:1; Jer. 23:5,6) and His fruitfulness (6:12; Is. 11:1).

3:9 the stone. Here is another reference to Messiah. In Ps. 118:22,23; Is. 8:13-15; 28:16; Dan. 2:35,45; Matt. 21:42; Eph. 2:19-22;

[o]Upon the stone *are* [p]seven eyes.
Behold, I will engrave its inscription,'
Says the LORD of hosts,
'And [q]I will remove the iniquity of that land in one day.
10 [r]In that day,' says the LORD of hosts,
'Everyone will invite his neighbor
[s]Under his vine and under his fig tree.' "

Vision of the Lampstand and Olive Trees

4 Now [a]the angel who talked with me
came back and wakened me, [b]as a man
who is wakened out of his sleep. 2 And he
said to me, "What do you see?"
So I said, "I am looking, and there *is* [c]a
lampstand of solid gold with a bowl on top
of it, [d]and on the *stand* seven lamps with
seven pipes to the seven lamps. 3 [e]Two
olive trees *are* by it, one at the right of the
bowl and the other at its left." 4 So I answered and spoke to the angel who talked
with me, saying, "What *are* these, my
lord?"
5 Then the angel who talked with me answered and said to me, "Do you not know
what these are?"
And I said, "No, my lord."
6 So he answered and said to me:

"This *is* the word of the LORD to
[f]Zerubbabel:
[g]'Not by might nor by power, but by My Spirit,'
Says the LORD of hosts.
7 'Who *are* you, [h]O great mountain?
Before Zerubbabel *you shall become* a plain!
And he shall bring forth [i]the capstone
[j]With shouts of "Grace, grace to it!" ' "

8 Moreover the word of the LORD came
to me, saying:

9 "The hands of Zerubbabel
[k]Have laid the foundation of this [1]temple;
His hands [l]shall also finish *it*.
Then [m]you will know
That the [n]LORD of hosts has sent Me to you.
10 For who has despised the day of [o]small things?

9 [o][Zech. 4:10; Rev. 5:6] [p]Ps. 118:22 [q]Jer. 31:34; 50:20; Zech. 3:4
10 [r]Zech. 2:11 [s]1 Kin. 4:25; Is. 36:16; Mic. 4:4

CHAPTER 4

1 [a]Zech. 1:9; 2:3 [b]Dan. 8:18
2 [c]Rev. 1:12 [d]Ex. 25:37; [Rev. 4:5]
3 [e]Rev. 11:3, 4
6 [f]Hag. 1:1 [g]Is. 30:1; Hos. 1:7; Hag. 2:4, 5
7 [h]Ps. 114:4, 6; Is. 40:4; Jer. 51:25; Nah. 1:5; Zech. 14:4, 5; [Matt. 21:21] [i]Ps. 118:22 [j]Ezra 3:10, 11, 13; Ps. 84:11
9 [k]Ezra 3:8-10; 5:16; Hag. 2:18 [l]Ezra 6:14, 15; Zech. 6:12, 13 [m]Zech. 2:9, 11; 6:15 [n][Is. 43:16]; Zech. 2:8 [1]Lit. *house*
10 [o]Neh. 4:2-4; Amos 7:2, 5; Hag. 2:3

1 Pet. 2:6-8, He is a rejected stone, a stone of stumbling, a stone of refuge, a destroying stone, and a foundation stone. Here He is the precious foundation stone, with "7 eyes" symbolic of His omniscience and infinite intelligence (cf. 4:10; Is. 11:2; Col. 2:3; Rev. 5:6). The engraving may be a reference to the cornerstone of the temple building, on which will be engraved an inscription attesting to the Divine Builder and the purpose for which the building was erected. As such, it is closely tied to the removal of "the iniquity of that land in one day," symbolized by the removal of filthy garments in v. 4. The phrase looks to the future day when there will cleansing and forgiveness for the nation as a whole (12:10–13:1; Rom. 11:25-27), made possible through Christ's redemptive provision at Calvary.

3:10 invite his neighbor under. A common expression in Israel for peace and prosperity (cf. 1 Kin. 4:25; Mic. 4:4), here depicting the peace during the millennial rule of Messiah.

4:1-14 The fourth vision focused on Joshua the High-Priest and, by extension, the cleansing and restoration of the nation to her divinely appointed role as priest. This fifth vision focuses on the civil leader Zerubbabel, a descendant of David, to encourage him in the work of rebuilding the temple. The faithful completion of the work would then enable Israel to again bear light of God's grace (testimony) to the world.

4:1 as a man who is wakened. Once again the interpreting angel comes to awaken the prophet out of spiritual exhaustion from the holy trauma of the previous vision. Cf. Dan. 10:9.

4:2 seven pipes to the seven lamps. The lampstand is the 7-branched kind used in the tabernacle, with the addition of a bowl on the top of it in order to maintain an abundant supply of oil and pipes to carry the oil to keep the 7 lamps burning. The picture is of an abundant supply.

4:3 Two olive trees. Olive oil, was used in those days to fuel the lamps. The two olive trees supply oil to the bowl. The graphic picture is of limitless oil, supplied automatically without human agency, flowing from the trees down to the bowl, down to the lamps.

4:4 What *are* these. Zechariah wanted to know the meaning of the two olive trees. Because of Zechariah's priestly background, his query surprised the interpreting angel (v. 5). His question goes unanswered until later (v. 14).

4:6 This *is* the word of the LORD to Zerubbabel. The purpose of the vision was to encourage Zerubbabel to complete the temple rebuilding, to assure him of divine enablement for that venture and the endless supply for the future glory of Messiah's kingdom and temple. The lampstand pictured Israel fully supplied by God to be His light then and in the future. It must be noted that the church has temporarily taken this role presently (cf. Eph. 5:8,9; Rev. 1:12,13,20), until Israel's salvation and restoration to covenant blessing and usefulness. Cf. Rom. 11:11-24. **Not by might...power, but by My Spirit.** Neither human might, wealth, or physical stamina would be sufficient to complete the work. Only an abundant supply of the power of the Holy Spirit, pictured by the "bowl" (v. 2) would enable him to carry out the task, and enable Israel in the Messiah's kingdom to be a light again to the world by the operation of the Spirit (cf. Ezek. 36:24).

4:7 Who *are* you, O great mountain? Because the outcome is guaranteed (vv. 6,9), any mountain-like opposition will be leveled by God to become like a flat surface. No obstacle will be able to stop the completion of the temple in Zerubbabel's time or in the final kingdom of Messiah (cf. Ezek. 40–48). **the capstone.** The final stone of the building will be put into place, signifying its completion. **Grace, grace to it!** This blessing signifying shouts of joy and thanksgiving came to pass (cf. Ezra 3:11-13) over the completion of the temple. Contrast this attitude with that of the people seeing the unfinished temple (Hag. 2:3).

4:9 Me. This is the Angel of the Lord (*see note on 1:11*), the Protector, Deliverer, Defender of Israel, sent to bring this to fulfillment. In the future, He will come as Messiah to set up worship in the temple in His kingdom.

4:10 the day of small things. Though the rebuilding of a temple smaller than Solomon's may have been discouraging to some (cf. Ezra

For these seven rejoice to see
The [2]plumb line in the hand of
Zerubbabel.
[p]They are the eyes of the LORD,
Which scan to and fro throughout
the whole earth."

11 Then I answered and said to him,
"What *are* these [q]two olive trees—at the
right of the lampstand and at its left?"
12 And I further answered and said to him,
"What *are these* two olive branches that *drip*
[3]into the receptacles of the two gold pipes
from which the golden *oil* drains?"
13 Then he answered me and said, "Do
you not know what these *are?*"
And I said, "No, my lord."
14 So he said, [r]"These *are* the two
[4]anointed ones, [s]who stand beside the
Lord of the whole earth."

Vision of the Flying Scroll

5 Then I turned and raised my eyes, and
saw there a flying [a]scroll.
2 And he said to me, "What do you see?"
So I answered, "I see a flying scroll. Its
length *is* twenty cubits and its width ten
cubits."
3 Then he said to me, "This *is* the [b]curse
that goes out over the face of the whole
earth: 'Every thief shall be expelled,' according *to* this side of *the scroll;* and, 'Every
perjurer shall be expelled,' according *to*
that side of it."

4 "I will send out *the curse,*" says the
LORD of hosts;
"It shall enter the house of the [c]thief
And the house of [d]the one who
swears falsely by My name.
It shall remain in the midst of his
house
And consume [e]it, with its timber
and stones."

Vision of the Woman in a Basket

5 Then the angel who talked with me
came out and said to me, "Lift your eyes
now, and see what this *is* that goes forth."
6 So I asked, "What *is* it?" And he said,
"It *is* a [1]basket that is going forth."
He also said, "This *is* their resemblance
throughout the earth: 7 Here *is* a lead disc
lifted up, and this *is* a woman sitting inside
the basket"; 8 then he said, "This *is*
Wickedness!" And he thrust her down into
the basket, and threw the lead [2]cover over
its mouth. 9 Then I raised my eyes and
looked, and there *were* two women, coming with the wind in their wings; for they

10 [p] 2 Chr. 16:9; Prov. 15:3; Zech. 3:9 [2] Lit. *plummet stone*
11 [q] Zech. 4:3; Rev. 11:4
12 [3] Lit. *into the hands of*
14 [r] Rev. 11:4 [s] Zech. 3:1-7 [4] Lit. *sons of fresh oil*

CHAPTER 5

1 [a] Jer. 36:2; Ezek. 2:9; Rev. 5:1
3 [b] Mal. 4:6
4 [c] Ex. 20:15; Lev. 19:11 [d] Ex. 20:7; Lev. 19:12; Is. 48:1; Jer. 5:2; Zech. 8:17; Mal. 3:5 [e] Lev. 14:34, 35; Job 18:15
6 [1] Heb. *ephah*, a measuring container, and so elsewhere
8 [2] Lit. *stone*

3:12; Hag. 2:3), the Lord announced that His pleasure was upon this work, and that His omniscient care ("7 eyes") was watching over and taking pleasure in its completion. He said in effect, "Don't despise what God is pleased with." This was only a picture of the glorious restoration when Messiah comes to reign. That temple will make all others pale by comparison (cf. Ezek. 40–48).

4:14 These *are* the two anointed ones. The two olives trees (v. 4,11) represent the kingly and priestly offices in Israel through which the blessing of God was to flow. The two olive branches (v. 12) are the two men who occupied the supreme positions in those offices at that time: Zerubbabel, as a descendant of David, and Joshua, the High-Priest, a descendant of Eleazar. Together, they foreshadow the Messiah, in whom these two offices are combined (cf. 6:13; Ps. 119) and who is the true source of blessing to make Israel the light to the nations (cf. Is. 60:1-3). They had positions of responsibility in service to "the LORD of the whole earth," a millennial term that points to the final kingdom (cf. Mic. 5:4).

5:1-4 This sixth vision of the flying scroll depicts the Word of God which has been disobeyed by Israel and the entire world. It calls for God's righteous judgment of the sinner according to His standard, clearly set forth in His Word.

5:1,2 This flying scroll, unfurled for all to read both sides, measured 30 ft. long and 15 ft. wide (a cubit being 18 in.), exactly the size of the Holy Place in the tabernacle. The scroll represents, then, a divine standard, by which man is to be measured.

5:3 curse. The scroll, symbolizing the law of God, is a figure for a curse or punishment on all who disobeyed it and for blessing on all who obeyed it (cf. Deut. 27:26; 28:15-68). A similar picture is presented in Rev. 5:1-9; 10:1-11. **Every thief...Every perjurer.** Written on both sides, the scroll probably contained the Ten Commandments, not just two. The two singled out, the third and eighth, are most likely representative of all commands of God's law, for which Israel was guilty of violations (cf. James 2:10). It has an immediate message to those of Zechariah's time that God will root out and destroy the sinners who reject His Word; but it also has a future message for Israel and the world prior to Messiah's kingdom (cf. Ezek. 20:33-38; Matt. 25:31-46).

5:4 There is no escape from the judgment of God. His Word will enter the place of sinners and remain there until it has accomplished its purpose (Is. 55:10,11), which will be particularly true in the kingdom. The promise of the land in Deut. 30:1-10 will be fulfilled in the future day, as will consuming judgment (cf. Rev. 6–19).

5:5-11 The previous vision dealt with the purging of sinners from the land. This seventh vision of a woman in a basket continues the theme, focusing on the removal of the whole sinful system from Israel, which will happen before the kingdom comes (cf. Ezek. 20:38).

5:5,6 The wicked system is represented as a basket with a woman held captive inside under a lead lid. An ephah (basket) was smaller than a bushel, holding about 5 gallons. Like the flying scroll (cf. vv. 1-4), this was obviously enlarged for the purpose of the vision. The people of Israel are seen as pieces of grain, perhaps indicating that the wickedness is particularly materialistic. This was a sin that Israel picked up in Babylon and it has influenced them through the centuries until removed by the Messiah in the last days. This secular commercialism is central to the final world system (cf. Rev. 18).

5:7,8 woman. Inside the basket was sitting a woman, personifying this final wickedness (cf. Rev. 17:3-5), which is not dormant, since the lead cover is required to restrain it in the basket (cf. 2 Thess. 2:6-8).

5:9 two women...wind in their wings. Since storks are unclean birds (Lev. 11:19; Deut. 14:18) these must be agents of evil, demonic forces, protective of the wicked secularism, who set up the final system of evil. God allows them to set up the world system that the Lord destroys when He returns (cf. Rev. 19:11-16).

had wings like the wings of a [f]stork, and
they lifted up the basket between earth
and heaven.
10 So I said to the [g]angel who talked
with me, "Where are they carrying the basket?"
11 And he said to me, "To [h]build a house
for it in [i]the land of [3]Shinar; when it is
ready, *the basket* will be set there on its
base."

Vision of the Four Chariots

6 Then I turned and raised my eyes and
looked, and behold, four chariots *were*
coming from between two mountains, and
the mountains *were* mountains of bronze.
2 With the first chariot *were* [a]red horses,
with the second chariot [b]black horses,
3 with the third chariot white horses, and
with the fourth chariot dappled horses—
strong *steeds.* 4 Then I answered [c]and said
to the angel who talked with me, "What *are*
these, my lord?"
5 And the angel answered and said to
me, [d]"These *are* four spirits of heaven, who
go out from *their* [e]station before the Lord of
all the earth. 6 [1]The one with the black
horses is going to [f]the north country, the
white are going after them, and the dappled are going toward the south country."
7 Then the strong *steeds* went out, eager to
go, that they might [g]walk to and fro
throughout the earth. And He said, "Go,
walk to and fro throughout the earth." So
they walked to and fro throughout the
earth. 8 And He called to me, and spoke to
me, saying, "See, those who go toward the
north country have given rest to My [h]Spir-
it in the north country."

The Command to Crown Joshua

9 Then the word of the LORD came to me,
saying: 10 "Receive *the gift* from the captives—from Heldai, Tobijah, and Jedaiah,
who have come from Babylon—and go the
same day and enter the house of Josiah the
son of Zephaniah. 11 Take the silver and
gold, make [i]an [2] elaborate crown, and set *it*
on the head of [j]Joshua the son of Jehozadak,
the high priest. 12 Then speak to him, saying, 'Thus says the LORD of hosts, saying:

"Behold, [k]the Man whose name *is*
the [l]BRANCH!

9 [f] Lev. 11:13, 19; Ps. 104:17; Jer. 8:7
10 [g] Zech. 5:5
11 [h] Jer. 29:5, 28 [i] Gen. 10:10; Is. 11:11; Dan. 1:2 [3] Babylon

CHAPTER 6

2 [a] Zech. 1:8; Rev. 6:4 [b] Rev. 6:5
4 [c] Zech. 5:10
5 [d] [Ps. 104:4; Heb. 1:7, 14] [e] 1 Kin. 22:19; Dan. 7:10; Zech. 4:14; Luke 1:19
6 [1] The chariot [f] Jer. 1:14; Ezek. 1:4
7 [g] Gen. 13:17; Zech. 1:10
8 [h] Eccl. 10:4
11 [i] Ex. 29:6 [j] Ezra 3:2; Hag. 1:1; Zech. 3:1 [2] Lit. *crowns*
12 [k] John 1:45 [l] Is. 4:2; 11:1; Jer. 23:5; 33:15; Zech. 3:8

5:11 Shinar. The destination of the women bearing the basket was Shinar, an older word designating Babylon (cf. Gen. 10:10). The older word is used possibly to recall the Tower of Babel as a symbol of opposition against God (cf. Gen. 11:2). There it will be placed in a "house," possibly referring to a temple, in which it would be set on a base or pedestal as an idol. Again the vision is unmistakably looking forward to the final Babylon of Rev. 17,18 at the second coming of Christ (cf. Mal. 4:1-3).

6:1-8 The eighth and final vision completes the cycle and connects with the first vision. It pictures 4 chariots with the horses introduced in the first vision (1:8), symbolizing God's angelic agents (cf. v. 5) swiftly carrying out His judgment on the nations just prior to the establishment of the messianic kingdom.

6:1 two mountains...of bronze. Representing the reality of God's judgment on the nations who attack Israel, the two mountains are probably Mt. Zion and the Mt. of Olives, where the Lord will return and judge (cf. Joel 3:2,12,14; Zech. 14:4). This valley, called Jehoshaphat ("Jehovah judges") could refer to the Kidron Valley between these two mountains. Jews, Christians, and even Muslims have long taught that the last judgment will be there. The bronze has a symbolic relationship to judgment as in the case of the bronze serpent (Num. 21:9) and/or the bronze altar (Ex. 27:2), where sin was dealt with by God.

6:2,3 The judgment scene is further dramatized by these chariots and horses. For the significance of the horses' colors, *see note on 1:8.* The addition of "black" horses may represent famine and death. The "sorrel" horse has been replaced with "dappled" (i.e., spotted) horses. A similar picture is found in Rev. 6:1-8, where the horsemen of the apocalypse appear in judgment imagery, riding forth in vengeance on the nations.

6:5 four spirits of heaven. This imagery represents divine angelic agents sent out to execute judgment on behalf of the "LORD of all the earth," a millennial title designating the universal rule of the Messiah in the kingdom age (cf. 4:14; Mic. 4:13).

6:6,7 going...throughout the earth. These angelic judgment carriers unleash catastrophic judgment on the earth (cf. Rev. 6:1–19:16 for similarities). Nothing is said about going E and W because of the sea and the desert. Israel's enemies came from the N (Assyria, Babylon, Seleucids, and Romans) and the S (Egyptians). This N, S exit leads to a worldwide unleashing of judgment on the nations all over the earth (cf. Matt. 25:31-46).

6:8 rest to My Spirit. As a result of God's judgment of His enemies, His wrath can rest. God has been avenged by this action, particularly in regard to the power from the N being judged finally. This likely refers to the final Babylon (cf. Rev. 17,18). Until this judgment is done and God's wrath rests, the kingdom can't be established (Rev. 19,20) with the Messiah on His throne.

6:9-15 Joshua served as an illustration of the Messiah in this passage in that Zechariah's crowning of Joshua, the High-Priest, was a miniature, advance illustration of the future coronation of Messiah, the Branch, who will unite the two offices of priest and king (v. 13). This appendix supplements visions 4 and 5 (3:1-10; 4:1-14) and culminates the series of 8 visions with the climax of history—the coronation of the Lord Jesus Christ.

6:10 *gift* from the captives. Jewish exiles who remained in Babylon, but who had come bearing gifts for the building of the temple are identified. Zechariah was told to meet them that same day and receive their gifts.

6:11 an elaborate crown. Zechariah was to make not a High-Priest's crown or turban, but an ornate crown, one constructed of many circlets, a majestic crown (like the one on the returning Messiah in Rev. 19:12). This crown was to be set on the head of the High-Priest, Joshua. In the OT, the kingly and priestly offices were kept rigidly distinct. The office of king belonged only to the house of David, while the office of priest was only for the house of Levi. Uzziah's mingling of the two brought about his death (cf. 2 Chr. 26:16-23). But here this act is ordered by God to depict the coming King/Priest Messiah.

6:12 the BRANCH. Though the crown was placed on the head of Joshua, the High-Priest (v. 11), the act was a symbol of that future crowning of Messiah, the BRANCH (cf. 3:8). In Messiah, the offices of king and priest will be united.

From His place He shall [3]branch
out,
[m]And He shall build the temple of
the LORD;
13 Yes, He shall build the temple of
the LORD.
He [n]shall bear the glory,
And shall sit and rule on His
throne;
So [o]He shall be a priest on His
throne,
And the counsel of peace shall
be between [4]them
both." '

14 "Now the [5]elaborate crown shall be
[p]for a memorial in the temple of the LORD
[6]for Helem, Tobijah, Jedaiah, and Hen the
son of Zephaniah. 15 Even [q]those from afar
shall come and build the temple of the
LORD. Then you shall know that the LORD
of hosts has sent Me to you. And *this* shall
come to pass if you diligently obey the
voice of the LORD your God."

12 [m] [Matt. 16:18; Eph. 2:20; Heb. 3:3] [3] Lit. *sprout up*
13 [n] Is. 22:24 [o] Ps. 110:4; [Heb. 3:1] [4] Both offices
14 [p] Ex. 12:14; Mark 14:9 [5] Lit. *crowns* [6] So with MT, Tg., Vg.; Syr. *for Heldai* (cf. v. 10); LXX *for the patient ones*
15 [q] Is. 57:19; [Eph. 2:13]

CHAPTER 7

2 [1] Lit. *they*, cf. v. 5 [2] Or *Sar-Ezer* [3] Heb. *Bethel* [4] Or *to entreat the favor of*
3 [a] Deut. 17:9; Mal. 2:7 [b] Zech. 8:19 [5] Lit. *consecrate myself*
5 [c] [Is. 58:1-9] [d] Jer. 41:1 [e] Zech. 1:12 [f] [Rom. 14:6]
6 [g] Deut. 12:7; 14:26; 1 Chr. 29:22
7 [h] Is. 1:16-20; Jer. 7:5, 23; Zech. 1:4 [i] Jer. 17:26 [6] Heb. *Negev*

Obedience Better than Fasting

7 Now in the fourth year of King Darius
it came to pass *that* the word of the
LORD came to Zechariah, on the fourth day
of the ninth month, Chislev, 2 when [1]*the
people* sent [2]Sherezer, with Regem-Melech
and his men, *to* [3]the house of God, [4]to pray
before the LORD, 3 *and* to [a]ask the priests
who *were* in the house of the LORD of hosts,
and the prophets, saying, "Should I weep
in [b]the fifth month and [5]fast as I have done
for so many years?"
4 Then the word of the LORD of hosts
came to me, saying, 5 "Say to all the people
of the land, and to the priests: 'When you
[c]fasted and mourned in the fifth [d]and seventh *months* [e]during those seventy years,
did you really fast [f]for Me—for Me?
6 [g]When you eat and when you drink, do
you not eat and drink *for yourselves?*
7 *Should you* not *have obeyed* the words
which the LORD proclaimed through the
[h]former prophets when Jerusalem and the
cities around it were inhabited and prosperous, and [i]the [6]South and the Lowland
were inhabited?' "

6:12-15 In this brief section, 8 facts are given about Messiah, the BRANCH: 1) He will come from Israel ("His place," v. 12); 2) He will build the millennial temple (vv. 12b,13a); 3) He will be glorious (v. 13); 4) He will be king and priest (v. 13); 5) He makes peace (v. 13); 6) He opens the kingdom to Gentiles (v. 15a); 7) He will corroborate God's Word (v. 15b); and 8) He demands obedience (v. 15c). This, as always, is the essential matter. After Israel believes, the Messiah will come to set up His kingdom (cf. 12:10–13:1; 14:9-21). Faith and cleansing must come first.

6:12,13 He shall build the temple. The building of the restoration temple was promised to Zerubbabel (cf. 4:9,10). The building of this temple, promised to Messiah, points to the construction of the millennial temple (cf. Is. 2:2-4; Ezek. 40–43; Hag. 2:6-9).

6:14 The crown was not to be kept by Joshua, but was to serve as both a memorial to the devotion of the men who came from Babylon and, more importantly, as a reminder of the coming of Messiah and the ultimate hope of Israel. **Helem...Hen.** Helem is apparently another name of Heldai, and Hen another name for Josiah the son of Zephaniah (see v. 10).

7:1–8:23 As a result of the night visions which described the future of Israel, including the subjugation of her enemies, the final regathering to the Land, her cleansing, restoration, and the coming of Messiah and His kingdom, the Jews were greatly encouraged and comforted. The temple was more than half done, all obstacles to the construction were removed by the decree of Darius confirming the decree of Cyrus (cf. Ezra 6:1-14), and all was going very well. This gave rise to a question by the delegation from Bethel. The question involved the continuation of a national fast to mourn the fall of Jerusalem and the destruction of the temple. Though Jerusalem had no walls yet and there were many ruins (cf. Hag. 1:4), now that the temple was being finished, they were sent to inquire of the Lord and the priests whether they needed to continue the fast. The question is answered negatively in chap. 7 with two messages and positively in chap. 8 with two messages. Each of the 4 messages was given to impress upon the people the need to live righteously. As with chaps. 1–6, the prophet began historically and then moved prophetically to the time of the Second Advent of Christ.

7:1 the fourth year of King Darius. Nov./Dec. 518 B.C., two years after Zechariah's first message (cf. 1:1) and the night visions (cf. 1:7), and two years before the temple was completed.

7:2 *to* the house of God. While "house of the LORD" is used of the temple about 250 times in the OT, nowhere else in the OT does the Heb. word Bethel (which means "house of God") refer to the temple. The word is best viewed as a reference to a city and not the temple. These men came "from" rather than "to" Bethel, a town 12 mi. N of Jerusalem. Since the return from Babylon, the Jews had rebuilt and reinhabited Bethel (cf. Ezra 2:28; Neh. 7:32).

7:3 weep in the fifth month and fast. The Day of Atonement was the only annual fast required by God's law (Lev. 23:27), and other occasional fasts were called for by God (cf. Joel 1:12,14). The fall of Jerusalem was remembered by 4 fasts (cf. 2 Kin. 25; Jer. 39:1-4; 41; 52:13), in the fourth, fifth, seventh and tenth months *(see note on 8:19)*. Because the temple was burned in the fifth month (July–Aug.), that fast was considered the most serious and thus the delegation uses it as the test case (cf. 2 Kin. 25:8; Jer. 52:12). They had kept this wailing and fasting for "many years," but it seemed only a wearisome ritual in light of the present prosperity.

7:5 seventh *months.* This fast mourned the death of Gedaliah, the governor appointed by Nebuchadnezzar (2 Kin. 25:22-26; Jer. 41) after the fall of Jerusalem in 586 B.C.

7:5,6 did you really fast for Me. Zechariah pointed out that they were not fasting out of genuine sorrow and repentance, but out of self-pity (cf. Is. 1:10-15; 58:3-9).

7:7 *obeyed* the words. The important matter is not ritual, but obedience. It is obedience to God's Word that brought in the past great joy, peace, and prosperity to Israel, and that covered the Land during the time of David and Solomon. If the present generation in Zechariah's time substitutes ritual for obedience, they too will lose the joy, peace, and prosperity they were enjoying. **South...Lowland.** A reference to the area S of Beersheba and the Mediterranean coastal plain, encompassing the land from S to W.

Disobedience Resulted in Captivity

8 Then the word of the LORD came to
Zechariah, saying, 9 "Thus says the LORD
of hosts:

[j]'Execute true justice,
Show [7]mercy and compassion
Everyone to his brother.
10 [k]Do not oppress the widow or the fatherless,
The alien or the poor.
[l]Let none of you plan evil in his heart
Against his brother.'

11 But they refused to heed, [m]shrugged[8]
their shoulders, and [n]stopped[9] their ears
so that they could not hear. 12 Yes, they
made their [o]hearts like flint, [p]refusing to
hear the law and the words which the
LORD of hosts had sent by His Spirit
through the former prophets. [q]Thus great
wrath came from the LORD of hosts.
13 Therefore it happened, *that* just as He
proclaimed and they would not hear, so
[r]they called out and I would not listen,"
says the LORD of hosts. 14 "But [s]I scattered
them with a whirlwind among all the nations which they had not known. Thus the land became desolate after them, so that no one passed through or returned; for they made the pleasant land desolate."

Jerusalem, Holy City of the Future

8 Again the word of the LORD of hosts
came, saying, 2 "Thus says the LORD of
hosts:

[a]'I am [1]zealous for Zion with great [2]zeal;
With great [3]fervor I am zealous for her.'

3 "Thus says the LORD:

[b]'I will return to Zion,
And [c]dwell in the midst of Jerusalem.
Jerusalem [d]shall be called the City of Truth,
[e]The Mountain of the LORD of hosts,
[f]The Holy Mountain.'

4 "Thus says the LORD of hosts:

[g]'Old men and old women shall again sit
In the streets of Jerusalem,
Each one with his staff in his hand
Because of [4]great age.
5 The streets of the city
Shall be [h]full of boys and girls
Playing in its streets.'

6 "Thus says the LORD of hosts:

'If it is [5]marvelous in the eyes of the remnant of this people in these days,
[i]Will it also be marvelous in My eyes?'
Says the LORD hosts.

7 "Thus says the LORD of hosts:

9 [j] Is. 58:6, 7; Jer. 7:28 [7] Or *lovingkindness*
10 [k] Ex. 22:22; Ps. 72:4; Is. 1:17; Jer. 5:28 [l] Ps. 36:4; Ezek. 38:10; 45:9; Mic. 2:1; Zech. 8:16, 17
11 [m] Neh. 9:29 [n] Jer. 17:23; Acts 7:57 [8] Lit. *gave a stubborn or rebellious shoulder* [9] Lit. *made their ears heavy*
12 [o] Ezek. 11:19 [p] Neh. 9:29, 30 [q] 2 Chr. 36:16; Dan. 9:11, 12
13 [r] Prov. 1:24-28; Is. 1:15; Jer. 11:11; Mic. 3:4
14 [s] Lev. 26:33; Deut. 4:27; 28:64; Neh. 1:8

CHAPTER 8

2 [a] Joel 2:18; Nah. 1:2; Zech. 1:14 [1] Or *jealous* [2] Or *jealousy* [3] Lit. *heat* or *rage*
3 [b] Zech. 1:16 [c] Zech. 2:10, 11 [d] Is. 1:21 [e] [Is. 2:2, 3] [f] Jer. 31:23
4 [g] 1 Sam. 2:31; Is. 65:20 [4] Lit. *many days*
5 [h] Jer. 30:19, 20
6 [i] [Gen. 18:14; Luke 1:37] [5] Or *wonderful*

7:8-14 This is the second of the 4 messages in answer to the question (v. 3). Harkening back to his opening call (1:4) and to the warnings of earlier prophets (cf. Is. 1:11-17; 58:1-7; Amos 5:10-15), the prophet alerts the delegation to produce the fruits of righteousness that demonstrate obedience to God's Word (vv. 9,10) and to revisit the actions of their fathers who deliberately rejected God's Word (vv. 11,12a) which activated the fury of God against them (v. 12b). Cf. Deut. 28:15-68; 2 Chr. 36:14-16.

7:12 by His Spirit. The Holy Spirit served a vital function in the revelation and inspiration of God's Word through human authors (cf. 1 Cor. 2:10; 2 Pet. 1:21).

7:13 I would not listen. This reflects a severe form of God's wrath by which He abandons disobedient sinners. *See notes on 11:9*; cf. Judg. 10:13,14; 16:18-21; Prov. 1:24-31; Hos. 4:17; Matt. 15:14; Rom. 1:18-32.

7:14 I scattered them. This refers to the captivity and dispersion of the people and the desolation of the land in their absence (cf. Deut. 30:3-10).

8:1-23 Continuing his response to the delegation from Bethel, Zechariah contrasted Israel's past judgment with the promised future restoration. In light of past captivity, the nation was to repent and live righteously; in light of promised future blessings, Israel is to repent and live righteously. The last two messages (vv. 1-17 and 18-23) look positively to the future, when Israel will be brought to a place of special blessing and fasts will become feasts.

8:2 zealous. *See note on 1:14.* This very strong language expresses the idea that God can't bear the estrangement from His chosen people brought about by their sin, nor can he always tolerate the enemies of Israel. His love for Israel is so great that he will come in full presence to Israel again and dwell with His people. Ezekiel had the vision of God leaving Jerusalem (Ezek. 8–11) and of His presence returning (43:1-5). **Zion.** The mountain on which ancient Jerusalem was built, which became a name for the city.

8:3 City of Truth. A city which is characterized by truth, both in word and in deed (vv. 8,16) because it is ruled over by Messiah who is characterized by truth (John 14:6). **The Holy Mountain.** Zion is holy because the King who lives there is holy (Is. 6:3).

8:4,5 The most defenseless of society will live in tranquility, peace, and security (cf. Is. 65:20-22).

8:6 Men tend to limit God (cf. Ps. 78:19,20,41), but nothing is too hard for the Lord (cf. Gen. 18:14; Jer. 32:17,27). "Just because they seem too difficult for you," the Lord asks, in effect, "must they be too hard for Me?"

8:7,8 east…west. The context assures that this return speaks of a worldwide regathering at the Second Advent of Christ. The return from Babylon cannot be in view also, since Israel had not been scattered to the W until the diaspora engineered by the Romans in the first century A.D.

'Behold, [j]I will save My people
from the land of the [6]east
And from the land of the [7]west;
8 I will [k]bring them *back*,
And they shall dwell in the midst
of Jerusalem.
[l]They shall be My people
And I will be their God,
[m]In truth and righteousness.'

9 "Thus says the LORD of hosts:

[n]'Let your hands be strong,
You who have been hearing in
these days
These words by the mouth of [o]the
prophets,
Who *spoke* in [p]the day the
foundation was laid
For the house of the LORD of
hosts,
That the temple might be built.
10 For before these days
There were no [q]wages for man nor
any hire for beast;
There was no peace from the enemy
for whoever went out or
came in;
For I set all men, everyone, against
his neighbor.

11 [r]But now I *will* not *treat* the remnant of
this people as in the former days,' says the
LORD of hosts.

12 'For [s] the [8]seed *shall be* prosperous,
The vine shall give its fruit,
[t]The ground shall give her increase,
And [u]the heavens shall give their
dew—
I will cause the remnant of this
people
To possess all these.
13 And it shall come to pass
That just as you were [v]a curse
among the nations,
O house of Judah and house of
Israel,
So I will save you, and [w]you shall
be a blessing.
Do not fear,
Let your hands be strong.'

14 "For thus says the LORD of hosts:

[x]'Just as I determined to [9]punish
you
When your fathers provoked Me to
wrath,'
Says the LORD of hosts,
[y]'And I would not relent,
15 So again in these days
I am determined to do good
To Jerusalem and to the house of
Judah.
Do not fear.
16 These *are* the things you shall [z]do:
[a]Speak each man the truth to his
neighbor;

7 [j]Ps. 107:3; Is. 11:11; Ezek. 37:21 [6]Lit. *rising sun* [7]Lit. *setting sun*
8 [k]Zeph. 3:20; Zech. 10:10 [l][Jer. 30:22; 31:1, 33; Zech. 13:9] [m]Jer. 4:2
9 [n]1 Chr. 22:13; Is. 35:4; Hag. 2:4 [o]Ezra 5:1, 2; 6:14; Zech. 4:9 [p]Hag. 2:18
10 [q]Hag. 1:6, 9
11 [r][Ps. 103:9]; Is. 12:1; Hag. 2:15-19
12 [s]Joel 2:22 [t]Ps. 67:6 [u]Hag. 1:10 [8]Lit. *seed of peace*
13 [v]Jer. 42:18 [w]Gen. 12:2; Ruth 4:11, 12; Is. 19:24, 25; Ezek. 34:26; [Zeph. 3:20]
14 [x]Jer. 31:28 [y][2 Chr. 36:16] [9]Lit. *bring calamity to you*
16 [z]Zech. 7:9, 10 [a]Ps. 15:2; [Prov. 12:17-19]; Zech. 8:3; [Eph. 4:25]

Other Names for Jerusalem

Lit. "The city of peace"

- The city of our God (Ps. 48:1)
- The city of the great King (Ps. 48:2)
- The city of the Lord of hosts (Ps. 48:8)
- Salem (Ps. 76:2)
- Zion (Ps. 76:2)
- The city of righteousness (Is. 1:26)
- The faithful city (Is. 1:26)
- Ariel, i.e., Lion of God (Is. 29:1)
- The holy city (Is. 52:1)
- City of the Lord (Is. 60:14)
- Hephzibah ["My delight is in her"] (Is. 62:4)
- The Throne of the Lord (Jer. 3:17)
- THE LORD OUR RIGHTEOUSNESS (Jer. 33:16)
- The perfection of beauty (Lam. 2:15)
- The joy of the whole earth (Lam. 2:15)
- THE LORD IS THERE [YHWH Shammah] (Ezek. 48:35)
- City of truth (Zech. 8:3)
- The Holy Mountain (Zech. 8:3)

8:8 *See note on Zech. 1:3.* This refers to Israel's national conversion, spoken of in 12:10–13:1, and by Jeremiah (32:38-41) and Paul (Rom. 11:25-27).

8:9-17 The practical results of vv. 1-8 were laid out for the people. In view of such a glorious future, the people were exhorted to renew their energy toward the building of the temple and toward righteous living.

8:9 the prophets. This refers to Haggai and Zechariah for sure; possibly there were non-writing prophets also.

8:10,11 Zechariah recalled the immediate years prior to 520 B.C., described in Hag. 1:6-11, when their hassles and intrigues with the Samaritans and their love of ease and comfort developed indifference toward building the temple, resulting in divine punishment. But, since they had begun again to build the temple, God would not treat the people as He had those described in v. 10.

8:12,13 The richness and comprehensiveness of these promises of prosperity look beyond the historical moment to the time when Messiah reigns in His millennial kingdom. This will be a reversal of Deut. 28:15-68 and Jer. 24:9; 25:18; 29:22.

8:14,15 The sorrows of past judgment became the pledges of future blessings (cf. Jer. 32:42).

8:16,17 As always, the promised blessings are connected with obedience to His righteous standards. Such obedience can only be brought about by the power of the Spirit in the life of one who has been transformed by God's grace through faith. These standards are reminisient of Pss. 15:1-5; 24:4; Prov. 6:20-22.

Give judgment in your gates for
truth, justice, and peace;
17 [b]Let none of you think evil in [1]your
heart against your neighbor;
And do not love a false oath.
For all these *are things* that I hate,'
Says the LORD."

18 Then the word of the LORD of hosts
came to me, saying, 19 "Thus says the LORD
of hosts:

[c]'The fast of the fourth *month*,
[d]The fast of the fifth,
[e]The fast of the seventh,
[f]And the fast of the tenth,
Shall be [g]joy and gladness and
cheerful feasts
For the house of Judah.
[h]Therefore love truth and peace.'

20 "Thus says the LORD of hosts:

'Peoples shall yet come,
Inhabitants of many cities;
21 The inhabitants of one *city* shall go
to another, saying,
[i]"Let us continue to go and pray
before the LORD,
And seek the LORD of hosts.
I myself will go also."
22 Yes, [j]many peoples and strong
nations
Shall come to seek the LORD of
hosts in Jerusalem,
And to pray before the LORD.'

23 "Thus says the LORD of hosts: 'In those
days ten men [k]from every language of the
nations shall [l]grasp the [2]sleeve of a Jewish
man, saying, "Let us go with you, for we
have heard [m]*that* God *is* with you." ' "

Israel Defended Against Enemies

9 The [1]burden of the word of the LORD
Against the land of Hadrach,
And [a]Damascus its resting place
(For [b]the eyes of men
And all the tribes of Israel
Are on the LORD);
2 Also *against* [c]Hamath, *which*
borders on it,
And *against* [d]Tyre and [e]Sidon,
though they are very [f]wise.
3 For Tyre built herself a tower,
Heaped up silver like the dust,

17 [b] Prov. 3:29; Jer. 4:14; Zech. 7:10 [1] Lit. *his*
19 [c] Jer. 52:6 [d] Jer. 52:12 [e] 2 Kin. 25:25; Jer. 41:1, 2 [f] Jer. 52:4 [g] Esth. 8:17 [h] Zech. 8:16; Luke 1:74, 75
21 [i] [Is. 2:2, 3; Mic. 4:1, 2]
22 [j] Is. 60:3; 66:23; [Zech. 14:16-21]
23 [k] Is. 3:6 [l] [Is. 45:14] [m] 1 Cor. 14:25 [2] Lit. *wing,* corner of a garment

CHAPTER 9

1 [a] Is. 17:1; Jer. 23:33 [b] Amos 1:3-5 [1] *oracle, prophecy*
2 [c] Jer. 49:23 [d] Is. 23; Jer. 25:22; 47:4; Ezek. 26; Amos 1:9, 10 [e] 1 Kin. 17:9 [f] Ezek. 28:3

8:18,19 The fourth and final response to the delegation from Bethel notes how national days of fasting and mourning will be transformed into joyous feasts. This was really the answer to the original question in 7:3. Turn the fasts into feasts of joy in light of the promised blessings of God.

8:19 In addition to the fasts of the fifth and seventh months *(see notes on 7:3,5)*, two additional fasts were held. In the fourth month they commemorated the breaching of the wall of Jerusalem (2 Kin. 25:3; Jer. 39:2-4) and in the tenth month they remembered the beginning of the final siege of Jerusalem which began in 588 B.C. (2 Kin. 25:1; Jer. 39:1).

8:20-22 Israel restored in millennial glory will be the means of blessing to all the world (cf. Is. 2:2-4; Mic. 4:1-5). Gentiles from around the world will make a pilgrimage to Jerusalem to entreat the Lord. This signifies salvation of people from all over the world during the kingdom, fulfilling Ps. 122.

8:23 In those days. In the days in which the messianic kingdom on earth is inaugurated (*see note on Joel 3:18*), the Jews will truly be God's messengers as originally intended, and will bring multitudes to Christ. The 10 to 1 ratio represents a vast number of Gentiles who will come (cf. Gen. 31:7; Lev. 26:26; Num. 14:22; 1 Sam. 1:8; Neh. 4:12). The Messiah, in the midst of millennial Israel, will be the attraction of the world. People, seeing the Jews so blessed in their kingdom will demand to go and meet the Savior King.

9:1–14:21 Employing the phrase "in that day" 18 times, Zechariah places primary focus in his final two undated oracles on: 1) the downfall of the nation; 2) the salvation of Israel; and 3) the establishment of the Messiah as King. The first oracle (9:1–11:17) deals with the first and third features and ends with prophecies of the rejection of Christ at His first coming; the second oracle (12:1–14:21) deals with the second and third culminating with the kingdom of Messiah Christ.

9:1-8 This oracle features a series of judgments announced against the nations surrounding Israel (vv. 1-7), with deliverance promised for His people (v. 8). Most understand this to be a prophecy of the famous Greek conqueror, Alexander the Great's victories, given approximately 200 years before he marched through Palestine. He provides an analogy of Christ returning to judge the nations and save Israel at the end of the Great Tribulation (cf. Matt. 24:21).

9:1 burden. A heavy, burdensome message (i.e., oracle), the prediction of a threatening event, in this case the judgment of the nations. **Hadrach.** The location is uncertain. Possibly it is ancient Hatarika, a city mentioned in the annals of Assyrian Kings, in the vicinity of Hamath. The old Jewish tradition made it a compound name, *Had* meaning sharp and *rach* meaning soft. The sharp/soft land could be a reference to the dual Medo-Persian kingdom. Media was thought to be the sharp side because of its powerful conquerors like Cyrus, and Persia the soft side because of its debauchery. The cities in vv. 1,2 were major cities under Medo-Persian power. **Damascus.** This city was to be the main target of the judgment of God through Alexander upon the capital of Syria, one of Israel's worst enemies from ca. 900–722 B.C. **the eyes of men...are on the LORD.** God's judgment through Alexander the Great would be visible to all mankind, especially Israel.

9:2 Hamath. A major city, 125 mi. N of Damascus on the Orontes River. Alexander conquered these cities of the Syrian interior under Medo-Persian control, then turned to the coast moving S, conquering the cities of the Phoenicians and Philistines on the way to Egypt. **Tyre and Sidon...are very wise.** Phoenician cities on the Mediterranean coast, were known for their skill and wisdom (cf. Ezek. 28:12-15) and Satanic influence (Ezek. 28:11-19).

9:3,4 Tyre. This city was occupying an island one-half mile offshore, and thought itself to be invincible (cf. Is. 23:1-4). With walls 150 ft. high in some places, it was such an impregnable city that the Assyrian Shalmaneser besieged it for 5 years and failed to conquer it. Nebuchadnezzar tried for 13 years unsuccessfully. But Alexander, God's judgment instrument, using the rubble of the mainland city destroyed by Nebuchadnezzar, built a causeway out to the island and destroyed it in 7 months (ca. 334–332 B.C.).

And gold like the mire of the
streets.
4 Behold, [g]the LORD will cast her out;
He will destroy [h]her power in the
sea,
And she will be devoured by fire.

5 Ashkelon shall see *it* and fear;
Gaza also shall be very sorrowful;
And [i]Ekron, for He dried up her
expectation.
The king shall perish from Gaza,
And Ashkelon shall not be
inhabited.

6 "A [2] mixed race shall settle [j]in
Ashdod,
And I will cut off the pride of the
[k]Philistines.
7 I will take away the blood from his
mouth,
And the abominations from
between his teeth.
But he who remains, even he *shall
be* for our God,
And shall be like a leader in Judah,
And Ekron like a Jebusite.
8 [l]I will camp around My house
Because of the army,
Because of him who passes by and
him who returns.
No more shall an oppressor pass
through them,
For now I have seen with My eyes.

4 [g] Is. 23:1 [h] Ezek. 26:17
5 [i] Zeph. 2:4, 5
6 [j] Amos 1:8; Zeph. 2:4 [k] Ezek. 25:15-17 [2] Lit. *An illegitimate one*
8 [l] [Ps. 34:7]

The Coming King

9 "Rejoice [m]greatly, O daughter of
Zion!
Shout, O daughter of Jerusalem!
Behold, [n]your King is coming to
you;
He *is* just and having salvation,
Lowly and riding on a donkey,
A colt, the foal of a donkey.
10 I [o]will cut off the chariot from
Ephraim
And the horse from Jerusalem;
The [p]battle bow shall be cut off.
He shall speak peace to the
nations;
His dominion *shall be* [q]'from sea to
sea,
And from the River to the ends of
the earth.'

God Will Save His People

11 "As for you also,
Because of the blood of your
covenant,
I will set your [r]prisoners free from
the waterless pit.
12 Return to the stronghold,
[s]You prisoners of hope.
Even today I declare
That I will restore [t]double to you.
13 For I have bent Judah, My *bow,*
Fitted the bow with Ephraim,
And raised up your sons, O Zion,
Against your sons, O Greece,

9 [m] Zeph. 3:14, 15; Zech. 2:10 [n] [Ps. 110:1; Is. 9:6, 7; Jer. 23:5, 6]; Matt. 21:5; Mark 11:7, 9; Luke 19:38; John 12:15
10 [o] Hos. 1:7; Mic. 5:10 [p] Ps. 46:9; Is. 2:4; Hos. 2:18; Mic. 4:3 [q] Ps. 72:8
11 [r] Is. 42:7
12 [s] Is. 49:9; Jer. 17:13; Heb. 6:18-20 [t] Is. 61:7

9:5,6 The cities of Philistia were terrified at the swiftness with which Alexander the Great's army was able to conquer Tyre. Then, Alexander marched S, conquering all these Philistine cities and killing their national pride.

9:7 This judgment put an end to idolatry for many Philistines who turned to the God of Israel. In the imagery of this verse, the nation is seen as a man with blood in his mouth (from eating sacrifices to idols) and abominations (the other defiled food of idol worship) which are removed. The picture is of conversion to worship the true God. **like a Jebusite.** These ancient inhabitants of Jerusalem were conquered by David (cf. 2 Sam. 5:6-11) and amalgamated into Israel. So it will be with these Philistines.

9:8 This is the pledge of God's protection of Jerusalem from Alexander. It came true when, on his way S, Alexander treated Jerusalem with kindness. After having subjugated Egypt, he returned through Palestine again without doing Israel harm. **No more shall an oppressor pass through.** The supernatural and lasting protection here promised must anticipate the Second Advent of Messiah, whose coming is the subject through the rest of this message. The transition from Alexander to Christ can be understood in this way: If God can use a pagan king to judge the nations and save Israel, how much more will He use His righteous Messiah? So v. 8 bridges to the final judgment and deliverance of Messiah.

9:9,10 The two advents of Christ are here compressed as though they were one as in Is. 61:1-3 (cf. Luke 4:16,21). Actually, v. 9 refers to His first coming and v. 10 is His second. OT prophets didn't see the great time period between the two comings. The church age was a "mystery" hidden from them (cf. Eph. 3:1-9; Col. 1:27).

9:9 King...riding on a donkey. Unlike Alexander the Great, this King comes riding on a donkey (cf. Jer. 17:25). This was fulfilled at Christ's triumphal entry (Matt. 21:1-5; John 12:12-16). The Jews should have been looking for someone from the line of David (cf. 2 Sam. 7; 1 Chr. 17). Four elements in this verse describe Messiah's character: 1) He is King; 2) He is just; 3) He brings salvation; and 4) He is humble.

9:10-15 Zechariah moves to the Second Advent of Christ and the establishment of His universal kingdom (*see notes on 9:9,10; 11:15, 16*). Not characterized by bloodshed, Messiah's rule will be a kingdom of peace in which weapons of warfare will be destroyed or converted to peaceful uses (cf. Is. 2:4; 9:5-7; 11:1-10; Mic. 5:2,10-15), and peace spreads from the Euphrates River (the terminus of civilization) to the world.

9:10 Ephraim. This is another name for Israel, used often in the OT for the northern kingdom and occasionally for the whole nation.

9:11 blood of your covenant. Why is Israel to be so blessed? It is not because of her faithfulness through the centuries, but because of God's unfailing devotion to His covenant of blood made with Abraham (Gen. 15:1-10), which is in force as long as God lives. **from the waterless pit.** Prisoners in ancient times were often kept in dry wells or pits, like Joseph was (Gen. 37:24,28). The exiles of Israel, pictured as being in a dry well of captivity, suffering, and despair, will be freed because of His unbreakable covenant with them. They are thus called "prisoners of hope" (v. 12) who are to receive "double" blessing (cf. Is. 61:7).

9:13-15 Reminiscent of the Exodus (Ex. 19:16-19; Hab. 3:3-15), the Lord will protect and empower them (cf. Is. 11:11-16; Zech. 12:6,8).

And made you like the sword of a
mighty man."

14 Then the LORD will be seen over
them,
And [u]His arrow will go forth like
lightning.
The Lord GOD will blow the
trumpet,
And go [v]with whirlwinds from the
south.
15 The LORD of hosts will [w]defend
them;
They shall devour and subdue
with slingstones.
They shall drink *and* roar as if with
wine;
They shall be filled *with blood* like
[3]basins,
Like the corners of the altar.
16 The LORD their God will [x]save
them in that day,
As the flock of His people.
For [y]they *shall be like* the [4]jewels of
a crown,
[z]Lifted like a banner over His
land—
17 For [a]how great is [5]its goodness
And how great [5]its [b]beauty!
[c]Grain shall make the young men
thrive,
And new wine the young women.

Restoration of Judah and Israel

10 Ask [a]the LORD for [b]rain
In [c]the time of the [1]latter rain.
The LORD will make [2]flashing
clouds;
He will give them showers of rain,
Grass in the field for everyone.

2 For the [d]idols[3] speak delusion;
The diviners envision [e]lies,
And tell false dreams;
They [f]comfort in vain.
Therefore *the people* wend their
way like [g]sheep;
They are [4]in trouble [h]because *there
is* no shepherd.

3 "My anger is kindled against the
[i]shepherds,
[j]And I will punish the [5]goatherds.
For the LORD of hosts [k]will visit
His flock,
The house of Judah,
And [l]will make them as His royal
horse in the battle.
4 From him comes [m]the cornerstone,
From him [n]the tent peg,
From him the battle bow,
From him every [6]ruler together.
5 They shall be like mighty men,
Who [o]tread down *their enemies*
In the mire of the streets in the
battle.
They shall fight because the LORD
is with them,
And the riders on horses shall be
put to shame.

6 "I will strengthen the house of
Judah,
And I will save the house of
Joseph.
[p]I will bring them back,

14 [u] Ps. 18:14; Hab. 3:11 [v] Is. 21:1 **15** [w] Is. 37:35; Zech. 12:8 [3] Sacrificial basins **16** [x] Jer. 31:10, 11 [y] Is. 62:3; Mal. 3:17 [z] Is. 11:12 [4] Lit. *stones* **17** [a] [Ps. 31:19] [b] [Ps. 45:1-16] [c] Joel 3:18 [5] Lit. *His*

CHAPTER 10

1 [a] [Jer. 14:22] [b] [Deut. 11:13, 14] [c] [Joel 2:23] [1] Spring rain [2] Or *lightning flashes*

2 [d] Jer. 10:8 [e] Jer. 27:9; [Ezek. 13] [f] Job 13:4 [g] Jer. 50:6, 17 [h] Ezek. 34:5-8; Matt. 9:36; Mark 6:34 [3] Heb. *teraphim* [4] *afflicted* **3** [i] Jer. 25:34-36; Ezek. 34:2; Zech. 11:17 [j] Ezek. 34:17 [k] Luke 1:68 [l] Song 1:9 [5] Leaders **4** [m] Is. 28:16 [n] Is. 22:23 [6] Or *despot* **5** [o] Ps. 18:42 **6** [p] Jer. 3:18; Ezek. 37:21

The initial historical fulfillment of this prophecy came when the Maccabees defeated the Greeks ca. 167 B.C.; the final, complete fulfillment will occur at His Second Advent. The Maccabean triumph is only a pledge and a preview of final triumph over all enemies.

9:15 subdue with slingstones. This may mean the Jews will easily subdue their enemies as David did Goliath (Judg. 20:16). Or better, it should be rendered "trample or sling stones," meaning that they will contemptuously tread on the harmless missiles cast at them by their enemies. This could depict the futility of Armageddon when the armies of the God-hating world gathers in Israel and is destroyed by the Messiah (cf. Rev. 16:12-16; 19:11-16). The bloodshed of the godless will be visible in that day, from one end of the land of Palestine to the other, like blood splattered on the corners of the altar of sacrifice from basins which caught it when the animal was slain (cf. Rev. 14:20). **drink *and* roar.** This describes Israel's excitement and exuberance over their victory.

9:16,17 Abundant prosperity, such as the world has never seen, results in excessive rejoicing and praise results from God "saving" His people, Israel (cf. Deut. 33:28; Ps. 4:7,8).

10:1 Ask the LORD for rain. In light of the promised blessings of 9:17, the prophet encourages the people to request these blessings from the Lord, with confidence. There will be literal rain and latter rain (Apr./May) in the kingdom (cf. Is. 35:1-7) making the land flourish, but the promise here extends to refer to spiritual blessings (cf Hos. 6:1-3). The "latter rain" of spiritual grace and goodness from God will bring refreshment to people's souls (cf. Is. 44:3).

10:2 idols...diviners. In contrast to God who provides abundance, idols or household gods (cf. Gen. 31:19,34) and demonic fortunetellers left Israel as sheep without a shepherd (cf. Ezek. 34:6-10). God will judge them all for that false leadership (v. 3). The implications of these words is that a similar deception will occur in the end times. The NT confirms this (cf. Matt. 24:5,11,22-28; 2 Thess. 1:8-12).

10:3 royal horse. Though like sheep, Israel will become like an invincible royal war-horse when strengthened by the Lord to conquer His foes (12:8).

10:4 cornerstone. A frequently used messianic title (cf. Is. 28:16; Eph. 2:20; 1 Pet. 2:6-8). Christ is the foundation on which His kingdom rests. **tent peg.** This may refer to a peg attached to the tent's center pole on which utensils and valuables were hung. Messiah is the peg in the midst of His kingdom, for all the glory of the kingdom will hang on Him (cf. 6:13; Is. 22:23-24). **battle bow...ruler.** Another reference to the Messiah (cf. 9:13; Rev. 19:11-16), under whose authority every ruler will be sanctioned.

10:5 the LORD is with them. The prophet pictured foot soldiers overpowering the cavalry (cf. 12:1-9) in battle. This analogy was to illustrate the power of God's people when He is "with them."

10:6 house of Judah...Joseph. Both the southern and northern kingdoms of Israel will be restored to a position of blessing, as the

Because I [q]have mercy on them.
They shall be as though I had not
cast them aside;
For I *am* the LORD their God,
And I [r]will hear them.
7 *Those of* Ephraim shall be like a
mighty man,
And their [s]heart shall rejoice as if
with wine.
Yes, their children shall see *it* and
be glad;
Their heart shall rejoice in the
LORD.
8 I will [t]whistle for them and gather
them,
For I will redeem them;
[u]And they shall increase as they
once increased.

9 "I[v] will [7]sow them among the
peoples,
And they shall [w]remember Me in
far countries;
They shall live, together with their
children,
And they shall return.
10 [x]I will also bring them back from
the land of Egypt,
And gather them from Assyria.
I will bring them into the land of
Gilead and Lebanon,
[y]Until no *more room* is found for
them.

11 [z]He shall pass through the sea with
affliction,
And strike the waves of the sea:
All the depths of [8]the River shall
dry up.
Then [a]the pride of Assyria shall be
brought down,
And [b]the scepter of Egypt shall
depart.

12 "So I will strengthen them in the
LORD,
And [c]they shall walk up and down
in His name,"
Says the LORD.

Desolation of Israel

11 Open [a]your doors, O Lebanon,
That fire may devour your cedars.
2 Wail, O cypress, for the [b]cedar has
fallen,
Because the mighty *trees* are
ruined.
Wail, O oaks of Bashan,
[c]For the thick forest has come
down.
3 *There is* the sound of wailing
[d]shepherds!
For their glory is in ruins.
There is the sound of roaring lions!
For the [1]pride of the Jordan is in
ruins.

6 [q]Hos. 1:7; Zech. 1:16 [r]Zech. 13:9
7 [s]Ps. 104:15
8 [t]Is. 5:26 [u]Is. 49:19; Ezek. 36:37; Zech. 2:4
9 [v]Hos. 2:23 [w]Deut. 30:1 [7]Or *scatter*
10 [x]Is. 11:11; Hos. 11:11 [y]Is. 49:19, 20
11 [z]Is. 11:15 [a]Is. 14:25; Zeph. 2:13 [b]Ezek. 30:13 [8]The Nile
12 [c]Mic. 4:5

CHAPTER 11

1 [a]Zech. 10:10
2 [b]Ezek. 31:3 [c]Is. 32:19
3 [d]Jer. 25:34-36 [1]Or *floodplain, thicket*

whole nation is restored in millennial blessing (cf. Jer. 32:37). **I *am* the LORD their God.** The reason for Israel's restoration was because of God, the covenant keeper, who gave a strong reiteration of His continuing, unconditional commitment to them. The curses of Deut. 28:15-68 expressed in the Assyrian and Babylonian deportations did not abrogate God's promised blessings to Israel nor transfer them to another people. Even after they had crucified the Messiah, Peter told them they were still able to receive the promise (cf. Acts 2:39) because the Abrahamic Covenant was still in place and they were the people of God's promise (Acts 3:25).

10:7 The joy of the restored nation of Israel at the beginning of the Millennium is likened to those who have been drinking wine (cf. Is. 66:10-14; Zeph. 3:14-20).

10:8 I will whistle for them. The prophecy summarized what had been said, namely the Messiah's call for Israel to be redeemed and for them to regather in His land (cf. Is. 5:26). As in Egypt (cf. Ex. 1:8-22), those of Israel who are protected by God because of their faith in Messiah will survive the Tribulation and enter the Millennium to multiply greatly (cf. 2:4; Is. 54:1-3).

10:9,10 Another summary is given stating that as God had previously scattered them all over the world (A.D. 70), He would bring them back to populate His messianic kingdom (cf. Is. 11:11,12; 49:20-22).

10:11 Similar to Israel crossing the Red Sea, God will remove both geographical and political obstacles to Israel's return for the Kingdom of Messiah. Assyria and Egypt, traditional enemies of Israel, symbolize any nation that would try to withhold God from fulfilling His will (cf. Is. 11:11,12).

10:12 walk...in His name. The people of Israel will be the messengers of their Messiah in the millennial kingdom. This is the complete spiritual restoration spoken of by Ezekiel (cf. Ezek. 36:21-38; 37:1-14,22-28).

11:1-17 In stark contrast to chaps. 9,10, in which Messiah is pictured as a wonderful Shepherd, this passage presents an ugly picture of the rejection of the Messiah, the true Shepherd. The prophet turns from the glories of the accepted Messiah at His second coming to the national apostasy and rejection of Messiah at His first coming.

11:1-3 As a fire sweeping down to ravage the whole land of Israel, Zechariah described a fire of judgment that would consume the ungodly as a conflagration consumes trees. The devastation is not limited to spiritual judgment only, but includes the death of people as the land of Israel is judged. The language is the book's most poetic. "Lebanon," "Bashan," and "Jordan" represent the whole land as judgment sweeps from top to bottom covering the entire nation from the north, inland, and down the Jordan Valley to the southern border.

11:2 Wail, O cypress. If the mighty cedars have fallen, surely the more vulnerable smaller trees will be unable to stand. **oaks of Bashan.** The poem moves from Lebanon, on the northern border of Israel, to Bashan, E of the Sea of Galilee, known for its oaks and lush pastures (cf. Amos 4:1; Mic. 7:14).

11:3 wailing shepherds. The shepherds lament the loss of their pastures, and the young lions their homes and food. Both are poetic figures of the misery that will occur in the land under the ravaging judgment. As the chapter unfolds, it becomes clear that this most likely prophesies the destruction of Jerusalem in A.D. 70. and the subsequent devastation of the whole land, which resulted in the dissolution of the Jewish state.

Prophecy of the Shepherds

4 Thus says the LORD my God, "Feed the
flock for slaughter, 5 whose owners
slaughter them and [e]feel no guilt; those
who sell them [f]say, 'Blessed be the LORD,
for I am rich'; and their shepherds do [g]not
pity them. 6 For I will no longer pity the inhabitants of the land," says the LORD. "But
indeed I will give everyone into his neighbor's hand and into the hand of his king.
They shall [2]attack the land, and I will not
deliver *them* from their hand."
7 So I fed the flock for slaughter, [3]in particular [h]the poor of the flock. I took for myself two staffs: the one I called [4]Beauty, and
the other I called [5]Bonds; and I fed the
flock. 8 I [6]dismissed the three shepherds
[i]in one month. My soul loathed them, and
their soul also abhorred me. 9 Then I said,
"I will not feed you. [j]Let what is dying die,
and what is perishing perish. Let those that
are left eat each other's flesh." 10 And I
took my staff, [7]Beauty, and cut it in two,
that I might break the covenant which I
had made with all the peoples. 11 So it was
broken on that day. Thus [k]the [8] poor of the
flock, who were watching me, knew that it
was the word of the LORD. 12 Then I said to
them, "If it is [9]agreeable to you, give *me*
my wages; and if not, refrain." So they
[l]weighed out for my wages thirty *pieces* of
silver.
13 And the LORD said to me, "Throw it to
the [m]potter"—that princely price they set
on me. So I took the thirty *pieces* of silver
and threw them into the house of the LORD
for the potter. 14 Then I cut in two my other
staff, [1]Bonds, that I might break the brotherhood between Judah and Israel.
15 And the LORD said to me, [n]"Next, take
for yourself the implements of a foolish
shepherd. 16 For indeed I will raise up a
shepherd in the land *who* will not care for
those who are cut off, nor seek the young,

5 [e][Jer. 2:3]; 50:7 [f]Deut. 29:19; Hos. 12:8; 1 Tim. 6:9 [g]Ezek. 34:2, 3
6 [2]Lit. *strike*
7 [h]Jer. 39:10; Zeph. 3:12; Matt. 11:5 [3]So with MT, Tg., Vg.; LXX *for the Canaanites* [4]Or *Grace* [5]Or *Unity*
8 [i]Hos. 5:7 [6]Or *destroyed,* lit. *cut off*
9 [j]Jer. 15:2
10 [7]Or *Grace*
11 [k]Zeph. 3:12; Matt. 27:50; Mark 15:37; Luke 23:46; Acts 8:32 [8]So with MT, Tg., Vg.; LXX *the Canaanites*
12 [l]Gen. 37:28; Ex. 21:32; Matt. 26:15; 27:9, 10 [9]*good in your sight*
13 [m]Matt. 27:3-10; Acts 1:18, 19
14 [1]Or *Unity*
15 [n]Is. 56:11; Ezek. 34:2

11:4-14 The cause for the calamity of vv. 1-3 is here given: the rejection of the true Shepherd. God used the prophet Zechariah as an actor playing the part of a shepherd to illustrate the true Shepherd, Jesus Christ, and the rejection He encountered. Instructions given in vv. 4-6 are enacted in vv. 7-14.

11:4-6 The Lord God said that His people were to be treated like sheep fattened for the slaughter, whose shepherds have no pity, but are only interested in money for the meat. Thus God will serve up His sheep for slaughter without pity. With God's pity (cf. Hos. 1:6) and protection withdrawn, they will be given over to their Roman "neighbors" and to their "King" Caesar (cf. John 19:14,15), who will ultimately lead them to their destruction in A.D. 70 by the Roman army (cf. John 11:47-50). Over one million Jews were slaughtered in that assault, and almost half a million in subsequent Roman attacks in Palestine.

11:7-14 Here is the record of Zechariah playing a dramatic role to act out the rejection of Christ that will lead to the judgment of Israel outlined in vv. 1-3.

11:7 I fed the flock. The prophet did feed the truth of God to his people as a picture of what Messiah would do when He came. **the poor of the flock.** Only the poor responded when Jesus came to feed the flock (cf. Matt. 11:5; 1 Cor. 1:26). They were the lowly who would not follow the pride of the priest, scribes, and Pharisees, but believed on Jesus. **Beauty...Bonds.** The prophet's symbolic act called for him to take "two staffs." Eastern shepherds often carried two sticks, a rod to ward off wild beasts and a staff to guide and retrieve wayward sheep (cf. Ps. 23:4). The staff speaks of Christ the Good Shepherd who expressed the love and grace of God by tenderly leading and protecting His people (Mark 6:34), while the rod speaks of His unifying ministry, binding together the scattered house of Israel into one fold (cf. v. 14; Matt. 15:24).

11:8 dismissed the three shepherds. Though difficult to identify, one of the oldest interpretation is that this refers to the priests, elders, and scribes of Israel (see Introduction: Interpretive Challenges). Jesus bestowed grace and unity upon the populace, but confronted the hypocrisy of these religious leaders, and because they rejected Him all 3 offices were obliterated in a short time. God ended the traditional offices of the mediators and in its place brought a new priesthood of believers (cf. 1 Pet. 2:5,9; Rev. 1:6; 5:10; 20:6). **My soul loathed them.** Lit. it means "My soul was short with them," referring to the limits of God's patience toward the unrepentant.

11:9 eat each other's flesh. *See note on 7:13.* In this drama, Zechariah played the unnatural role of a shepherd who abandons his sheep and stops teaching and protecting them. Those who refused to believe were to be given over to pursue their own desires and left exposed to deadly enemies. In the Roman siege of A.D. 70, some of the starving inhabitants did resort to cannibalism (cf. Jer. 19:9).

11:10 break the covenant. Apparently this refers to God's promise to restrain the nations from decimating Israel. God set aside His kind and gracious protection and His providential care for His people, allowing Rome to invade and destroy Israel (cf. Luke 19:41-44; 21:24).

11:11 The believing remnant of Christ's day knew God's Word was being fulfilled. They knew judgment was coming, but avoided the long term consequences by faith in Christ.

11:12 thirty *pieces* of silver. Zechariah carried on the drama by symbolically picturing Jesus asking those He came to shepherd what they felt He was worth to them. In a mocking response, the leaders offered 30 silver pieces which was the amount of compensation paid for a slave gored by an ox (cf. Ex. 21:32). This is exactly what Judas Iscariot was paid to betray the Great Shepherd (Matt. 26:14-16). The Jews of Jesus' day who offered that amount were saying He was worth no more than a common slave.

11:13 The prophet received further instruction in acting out the drama that pictures the rejection of Ch rist, namely to throw the 30 pieces into the temple. This was fulfilled when Judas Iscariot, laden with guilt, went back and threw the blood money on the temple floor. The priests gathered the money and used it to buy a field from a potter (cf. Matt. 27:3-10). **princely price.** This ultimate sarcasm from God greeted the ultimate insult from humanity.

11:14 The breaking of the first staff (v. 10) preceded the Jews' rejection of the Shepherd, while the breaking of this rod once symbolizing the nation's unity (v. 7) followed His rejection, being fulfilled in the Roman breakup of the Jewish commonwealth. Josephus recorded that in the Roman conquering, the internal dissension among the people in their conflicting parties set Jew against Jew so that they struck each other as cruelly as the Romans struck them.

11:15,16 With the removal of the true Shepherd, the drama called for the prophet to play a foolish shepherd, who depicted the Antichrist of Daniel's 70th week (cf. 2 Thess. 2:3; John 5:43; Dan. 9:27). Zechariah's prophecy jumped from the first century A.D. to the last days before the second coming, omitting the present mystery of the

nor heal those that are broken, nor feed
those that still stand. But he will eat the flesh
of the fat and tear their hooves in [o]pieces.

17 "Woe[p] to the worthless shepherd,
Who leaves the flock!
A sword *shall be* against his arm
And against his right eye;
His arm shall completely wither,
And his right eye shall be totally
blinded."

The Coming Deliverance of Judah

12 The [1]burden of the word of the LORD
against Israel. Thus says the LORD,
[a]who stretches out the heavens, lays the
foundation of the earth, and [b]forms the
spirit of man within him: 2 "Behold, I will
make Jerusalem [c]a cup of [2]drunkenness to
all the surrounding peoples, when they lay
siege against Judah and Jerusalem. 3 [d]And
it shall happen in that day that I will make
Jerusalem [e]a very heavy stone for all peoples; all who would heave it away will
surely be cut in pieces, though all nations of
the earth are gathered against it. 4 In that
day," says the LORD, [f]"I will strike every
horse with confusion, and its rider with
madness; I will open My eyes on the house
of Judah, and will strike every horse of the
peoples with blindness. 5 And the governors of Judah shall say in their heart, 'The
inhabitants of Jerusalem *are* my strength in
the LORD of hosts, their God.' 6 In that day I
will make the governors of Judah [g]like a
firepan in the woodpile, and like a fiery
torch in the sheaves; they shall devour all
the surrounding peoples on the right hand
and on the left, but Jerusalem shall be inhabited again in her own place—Jerusalem.
7 "The LORD will save the tents of Judah
first, so that the glory of the house of David and the glory of the inhabitants of Jerusalem shall not become greater than that of
Judah. 8 In that day the LORD will defend
the inhabitants of Jerusalem; the one who
is feeble among them in that day shall be
like David, and the house of David *shall be*
like God, like the Angel of the LORD before
them. 9 It shall be in that day *that* I will
seek to [h]destroy all the nations that come
against Jerusalem.

Mourning for the Pierced One

10 [i]"And I will pour on the house of David and on the inhabitants of Jerusalem the
Spirit of grace and supplication; then they
will [j]look on Me whom they pierced. Yes,

16 [o]Ezek. 34:1-10; Mic. 3:1-3
17 [p]Jer. 23:1; Ezek. 34:2; Zech. 10:2; 11:15; John 10:12, 13

CHAPTER 12

1 [a]Is. 42:5; 44:24 [b]Num. 16:22; [Eccl. 12:7; Is. 57:16]; Heb. 12:9 [1]*oracle, prophecy*
2 [c]Is. 51:17 [2]Lit. *reeling*
3 [d]Zech. 12:4, 6, 8; 13:1 [e]Matt. 21:44
4 [f]Ps. 76:6; Ezek. 38:4
6 [g]Is. 10:17, 18; Obad. 18; Zech. 11:1
9 [h]Hag. 2:22
10 [i]Jer. 31:9; 50:4; Ezek. 39:29; [Joel 2:28, 29] [j]John 19:34, 37; 20:27; [Rev. 1:7]

church age *(see notes on 9:9,10; 9:10-15)*. This foolish (wicked) shepherd had a broken staff or club which he used to beat stubborn sheep into submission, something clearly inappropriate for a shepherd who thoughtfully and tenderly cared for his sheep. God permitted this wicked shepherd to arise, to destroy the sheep. Because they did not choose the Good Shepherd, Israel will receive a foolish one who will do absolutely the opposite of what is expected of shepherds, he will destroy the sheep (v. 16). This is exactly what Antichrist does (cf. Dan. 9:27; Matt. 24:15-22).

11:17 His arm...right eye. Zechariah condemned the worthless shepherd, noting that his strength ("arm") and his intelligence ("eye") would be taken away from him (cf. Dan. 7:9-14; 24-27; 8:23-25; 2 Thess. 2:8; Rev. 19:20; 20:10).

12:1–14:21 The second and final burden of Zechariah presents the familiar theme of Israel's ultimate deliverance and salvation. In contrast to initial judgment, he now encourages God's covenant people with a description of her restoration and blessing in the millennial kingdom, as true to His character and Zechariah's name, "the LORD remembers."

12:1 burden...against Israel. *See note on 9:1.* The prophecy described a future siege against the nation, indicating that there would be significant devastation before there was repentance and conversion in Israel (cf. 14:1,2). **stretches...lays...forms.** The God who performed the work of creation will ultimately do the work of consummation.

12:2 cup of drunkenness. Jerusalem is pictured as a large basin from which the nations will figuratively drink with eagerness, only to find themselves becoming intoxicated, disoriented, and thus easy prey for divine judgment at the end of Daniel's 70th week in the battle of Armageddon when nations gather to attack Jerusalem (cf. Ezek. 38:1-6,14-16; Dan. 11:40-44; Rev. 9:13-16; 14:20; 16:12-16).

12:3 will surely be cut in pieces. Like lifting a heavy weight, Jerusalem will "seriously injure" (lit.) any people that try to gain victory over it. This is due to divine intervention (cf. vv. 4,5).

12:4 Horses, ancient symbols of strength, emphasizes God's superior power over Israel's enemies. Confusion, madness, and blindness are noted as curses on Israel in Deut. 28:28; here they are promised to Israel's enemies.

12:5 Knowing that God had chosen Jerusalem as the city of His special affection will give confidence to the "governors" (leaders) all over the land (cf. Ps 46:5). This verse has overtones indicating the saving faith of the Jews in that day, since they are claiming to have trust in God.

12:6 Two similes describe the operation of God's power: a "firepan" used to carry hot coals to start a wood fire and a "torch" used to light dry grain. Thus will the power of God devour the armies that attack Israel in the latter days.

12:7 Judah first. God will first deliver the defenseless country people before the well-fortified capital, demonstrating that the battle was not won by military might or strategy.

12:8 The Lord will make the feeble like David, the greatest soldier in Israel's history (cf. 1 Sam. 18:7). And the "house of David," like the "Angel of the LORD," are most likely references to the Messiah Himself, who will be the strength of His people.

12:9 *See note on 12:2* for important cross references.

12:10 I will pour. God, in His own perfect time and by His own power, will sovereignly act to save Israel. This was prophesied by other prophets (cf. Ezek. 39:29; Joel 2:28-32), and by the Apostle Paul (cf. Rom. 11:25-27). **Spirit of grace and supplication.** The Holy Spirit is so identified because He brings saving grace and because that grace produces sorrow that will result in repentant prayer to God for forgiveness (cf. Matt. 5:4; Heb. 10:29). **look on Me whom they pierced.** Israel's repentance will come because they look to Jesus, the One whom they rejected and crucified (cf. Is. 53:5; John 19:37), in faith at the Second Advent (Rom. 11:25-27). When God says they pierced "Me," He is certainly affirming the incarnation of deity—Jesus was God. *See note on John 10:30.*

they will mourn for Him [k]as one mourns
for *his* only *son,* and grieve for Him as one
grieves for a firstborn. 11 In that day there
shall be a great [l]mourning in Jerusalem,
[m]like the mourning at Hadad Rimmon in
the plain of [3]Megiddo. 12 [n]And the land
shall mourn, every family by itself: the
family of the house of David by itself, and
their wives by themselves; the family of
the house of [o]Nathan by itself, and their
wives by themselves; 13 the family of the
house of Levi by itself, and their wives by
themselves; the family of Shimei by itself,
and their wives by themselves; 14 all the
families that remain, every family by itself,
and their wives by themselves.

Idolatry Cut Off

13 "In that [a]day [b]a fountain shall be
opened for the house of David and
for the inhabitants of Jerusalem, for sin and
for [c]uncleanness.
2 "It shall be in that day," says the LORD
of hosts, "*that* I will [d]cut off the names of
the idols from the land, and they shall no
longer be remembered. I will also cause
[e]the prophets and the unclean spirit to depart from the land. 3 It shall come to pass

10 [k] Jer. 6:26; Amos 8:10
11 [l] [Matt. 24:30]; Acts 2:37; [Rev. 1:7] [m] 2 Kin. 23:29 [3] Heb. *Megiddon*
12 [n] [Matt. 24:30; Rev. 1:7] [o] Luke 3:31

CHAPTER 13

1 [a] Acts 10:43; [Rev. 21:6, 7] [b] Ps. 36:9; [Heb. 9:14; 1 John 1:7] [c] Num. 19:17; Is. 4:4; Ezek. 36:25
2 [d] Ex. 23:13; Hos. 2:17 [e] Jer. 23:14, 15; 2 Pet. 2:1
3 [f] Deut. 18:20; [Ezek. 14:9] [g] Deut. 13:6-11; [Matt. 10:37]
4 [h] Jer. 6:15; 8:9; [Mic. 3:6, 7] [i] 2 Kin. 1:8; Is. 20:2; Matt. 3:4
5 [j] Amos 7:14
6 [1] Or *hands*
7 [k] Is. 40:11; Ezek. 34:23, 24; 37:24; Mic. 5:2, 4 [l] [John 10:30] [m] Matt. 26:31, 56, 67; Mark 14:27; 1 Pet. 5:4; Rev. 7:16, 17 [n] Luke 12:32

that if anyone still prophesies, then his father and mother who begot him will say to
him, 'You shall [f]not live, because you have
spoken lies in the name of the LORD.' And
his father and mother who begot him [g]shall
thrust him through when he prophesies.
4 "And it shall be in that day *that* [h]every
prophet will be ashamed of his vision
when he prophesies; they will not wear [i]a
robe of coarse hair to deceive. 5 [j]But he will
say, 'I *am* no prophet, I *am* a farmer; for a
man taught me to keep cattle from my
youth.' 6 And *one* will say to him, 'What
are these wounds between your [1]arms?'
Then he will answer, '*Those* with which I
was wounded in the house of my friends.'

The Shepherd Savior

7 "Awake, O sword, against [k]My
Shepherd,
Against the Man [l]who is My
Companion,"
Says the LORD of hosts.
[m]"Strike the Shepherd,
And the sheep will be scattered;
Then I will turn My hand against
[n]the little ones.

12:11 Hadad Rimmon...Megiddo. The bitter mourning of that day is likened to the death of righteous king Josiah at Hadad Rimmon in the Megiddo plain (cf. 2 Chr. 35:20-24), located NW of Jerusalem (cf. James 4:8,9).

12:12-14 The royal (David and his son Nathan) and priestly lines (Levi and his grandson Shimei), who in the past had set an evil example, were foremost in their contrition and mourning (cf. 2 Sam. 5:14; Num. 3:17-21). It is possible that Is. 53:1-9 comprises the content of their confession. This mourning and deep penitence is not some corporate emotion, but each person individually is brought to sorrow and faith in the Lord Jesus Christ. *See note on Rev. 11:13.*

13:1 house of David...inhabitants of Jerusalem. The totality of cleansing is noted by its effect on both royalty and commoners. **a fountain...for sin and for uncleanness.** A symbolic reference to the means of cleansing and purification through the atoning death of the pierced One (cf. 1 John 1:7). This has direct reference to the New Covenant of Jer. 31:31-34; Ezek. 36:25-32; Rom. 11:26-29. So the storm that broke upon Israel for the crime of Calvary and has raged with unmitigated fury for long, tragic centuries, will suddenly end and salvation will turn sin into righteousness in the gladness and glory of the kingdom of Messiah Jesus.

13:2-6 When Christ returns and cleanses Israel from her defilement, He is also going to cleanse the nation from the deception of false prophets and their demonic religion.

13:2 unclean spirit. The agents of idolatry are false prophets, but the spiritual power behind it is demonic. The wicked spirits who energize false prophets are unclean because they hate God and holiness and drive their victims into moral impurities and false religion (cf. Deut. 32:17; 1 Kin. 22:19-23; Ps. 106:34-39; 1 Cor. 10:20).

13:3 Because of the salvation of God which has cleansed God's people and made them love Him and His truth, hatred of false prophecy will overrule normal human feelings, causing even a father and mother to put their own apostate child to death (cf. Deut. 13:6-9,12-15; Deut. 18:18-22). This is a stern reminder of how God feels about and will eventually treat those preachers who misrepresent the truth.

13:4,5 a robe of coarse hair. Because of these stern measures, false prophets will cease wearing the traditional clothing of a prophet (cf. 2 Kin. 1:8; Matt. 3:4). They will adopt a clandestine approach to propagating their demon-inspired lies (cf. Jer. 22:22; Mic. 3:7), and lie if they are asked whether they are prophets, claiming to be farmers.

13:6 wounds between your arms. The phrase cannot refer to Messiah, but is a continuation of the false prophet's behavior in vv. 4,5. When the false prophet denies any association with pagan practices, others will challenge him to explain the suspicious wounds on his body. False prophets would cut themselves to arouse prophetic ecstasy in idolatrous rites (cf. Lev. 19:28; Deut. 14:1; 1 Kin. 18:28; Jer. 16:6; 48:37), but they will claim the scars represent some attack they suffered from friends. See Introduction: Interpretive Challenges.

13:7-9 Zechariah turned from the false prophets wounded in "friends'" houses to the true prophet wounded in the house of His friends, Israel. He compressed events of both the First (13:7) and Second (13:8,9) Advents into this brief section. It spoke of Christ's crucifixion (v. 7) and the Jewish remnant at His second coming (vv. 8,9).

13:7 My Shepherd...the Man who is My Companion. God spoke of the True Shepherd, that mighty Man who is His intimate associate, thus He identified Christ as His co-equal, affirming the deity of Christ (cf. John 1:1; 10:30; 14:9). **Strike the Shepherd.** In 11:17, it was the worthless shepherd who was to be struck; now it is the Good Shepherd (cf. 12:10) whose death was designed by God from before the foundation of the world (cf. Is. 53:10; Acts 2:23; 1 Pet. 1:18-20). **sheep...scattered.** *See notes on Matt. 26:31; Mark 14:27,* where Jesus applies this prophecy to the disciples who defected from Him after His arrest (Matt. 26:56; Mark 14:50), including Peter's denial (Matt. 26:33-35,69-75). **the little ones.** The same as the "poor of the flock" (11:7). The reference is to the remnant of believers, among the Jews, who were faithful to the Messiah after His crucifixion. Turning God's hand "against" them could mean they would suffer persecution, which they did (cf. John 15:18,20; 16:2; James 1:1), or it could be translated "upon" and refer to God's protection of the faithful.

8 And it shall come to pass in all the land,"
Says the LORD,
"*That* [o]two-thirds in it shall be cut off *and* die,
[p]But *one*-third shall be left in it:
9 I will bring the *one*-third [q]through the fire,
Will [r]refine them as silver is refined,
And test them as gold is tested.
[s]They will call on My name,
And I will answer them.
[t]I will say, 'This *is* My people';
And each one will say, 'The LORD *is* my God.' "

The Day of the LORD

14 Behold, [a]the day of the LORD is coming,
And your [1]spoil will be divided in your midst.
2 For [b]I will gather all the nations to battle against Jerusalem;
The city shall be taken,
The houses [2]rifled,
And the women ravished.
Half of the city shall go into captivity,
But the remnant of the people shall not be cut off from the city.
3 Then the LORD will go forth
And fight against those nations,
As He fights in the day of battle.
4 And in that day His feet will stand
[c]on the Mount of Olives,
Which faces Jerusalem on the east.
And the Mount of Olives shall be split in two,
From east to west,
[d]*Making* a very large valley;
Half of the mountain shall move toward the north
And half of it toward the south.

5 Then you shall flee *through* My mountain valley,
For the mountain valley shall reach to Azal.
Yes, you shall flee
As you fled from the [e]earthquake
In the days of Uzziah king of Judah.

[f]Thus the LORD my God will come,
And [g]all the saints with [3]You.

6 It shall come to pass in that day
That there will be no light;

8 [o]Is. 6:13; Ezek. 5:2, 4, 12 [p][Rom. 11:5]
9 [q]Is. 48:10; Ezek. 20:38; Mal. 3:3 [r]1 Pet. 1:6, 7 [s]Ps. 50:15; Zeph. 3:9; [Zech. 12:10] [t]Jer. 30:22; Hos. 2:23

CHAPTER 14

1 [a][Is. 13:6, 9; Joel 2:1; Mal. 4:1] [1]*plunder* or *booty*
2 [b]Joel 3:2; Zech. 12:2, 3 [2]Or *plundered*
4 [c]Ezek. 11:23; Acts 1:9-12 [d]Joel 3:12
5 [e]Is. 29:6; Amos 1:1 [f][Ps. 96:13]; Is. 66:15, 16; Matt. 24:30, 31; 25:31; Jude 14 [g]Joel 3:11 [3]Or *you*; LXX, Tg., Vg. *Him*

13:8 two-thirds...*one*-third. Only a portion of the people of Israel will remain faithful to Christ and be alive in the end. The spiritual survivors will be the remnant who look upon Christ in repentance at His return (cf. 12:10–13:1), which will include those who make up the 144,000 (cf. Rev. 7:4). These will be the sheep of the sheep-goat judgment after Christ's return who enter the kingdom alive (cf. Is. 35:10; Jer. 30:11; Matt. 25:31-46).

13:9 each one. From the midst of their fiery refinement, the elect remnant of Israel will see Jesus Christ, their Messiah and call on Him as their Savior and Lord. Israel will thus be saved and restored to covenant relationship with the Lord.

14:1-21 Chapter 14 is an amplification of 13:8,9. Prior to Israel's national conversion (cf. 12:10–13:1), the Jews will make a pact with a false messiah (cf. Dan. 9:27), known as the foolish shepherd (cf. 11:15-17) or Antichrist. In the middle of that 7-year covenant, Antichrist will break his treaty with Israel and require the worship of him alone (Dan. 9:24-27; Matt. 24:15; 2 Thess. 2:3,4). When Israel refuses, the armies of the world will gather to do battle, climaxing in a great siege of Jerusalem and the Battle of Armageddon (Rev. 19). Following the Lord's victory at that battle (cf. Rev. 19:11-16), will come the full restoration of Israel as anticipated in Hos. 14:4-7; Joel 3:18-21; Amos 9:13-15; Mic. 4:1-3; Zeph. 3:14-20.

14:1 the day of the LORD is coming. The "Day of the Lord" is a technical term for God's wrath unleashed against sinners. Here, Zechariah is looking at the Day of the Lord when His wrath is unleashed against the whole world of sinners, which results in the establishment of the Lord's millennial reign on earth. *See note on Is. 2:12* and Introduction to Joel: Historical and Theological Themes. **spoil...divided in your midst.** Jerusalem will be so overcome by the enemy that the spoil will be leisurely divided in the midst of the city, illustrating how completely Jerusalem will be overthrown. This atrocity then triggers the wrath of God against the world in the Day of the Lord.

14:2 I will gather all the nations. God Himself will gather the nations, using them to purge, refine, and judge (cf. Rev. 16:13,14,16). Their presence results in an unprecedented time of national calamity. This is the climax of "the time of Jacob's trouble" (Jer. 30:5-7).

14:3,4 His feet will stand on the Mount of Olives. To prevent the eradication of His remnant, the Lord will personally intervene to fight against the gathered nations. Just as He fought for His people in the past, so He will do so in the future as the ultimate Warrior-King. Jesus will literally return to the Mt. of Olives, located E of the Kidron Valley, just as the angels announced at His ascension (cf. Acts 1:11). When He does, there will be a tremendous topographical upheaval (perhaps an earthquake), a phenomenon not uncommon when God announces His coming in judgment (cf. Mic. 1:2-4; Nah. 1:5; Rev. 16:18-21).

14:4 the Mount of Olives shall be split in two. A valley running E and W will be created as the mountain is pulled northward and southward (cf. Mic. 1:2-4; Nah. 1:5; Rev. 16:18,19).

14:5 Azal. It is best understood as a place E of Jerusalem, marking the eastern end of the newly created valley. Though exact identification is unknown, it is possibly the Valley of Jehoshaphat or Valley of Decision (cf. Joel 3:12,14) which will be for judgment of the nations and for the escape of the half who were not captured (v. 2). **all the saints with You.** This term could refer to angels, Jewish believers or Gentile Christians together (cf. Rev. 19:14).

14:6,7 As these Jews are fleeing through this newly created valley, the lights in the world will go out (cf. Is. 13:9,10; 24:23; Joel 2:10; 3:14-16; Matt. 24:29,30; Rev. 6:12-14) and be replaced by the light of Christ's glory (cf. Is. 60:19,20). The reaction of people is given in Rev. 6:15-17. Only the Lord knows the fullness of the plan for that day—when the lights go out and are lit again in the millennial kingdom (cf. Is. 30:26; Mal. 4:2).

The [4]lights will diminish.
7 It shall be one day
[h]Which is known to the LORD—
Neither day nor night.
But at [i]evening time it shall happen
That it will be light.

8 And in that day it shall be
That living [j]waters shall flow from
Jerusalem,
Half of them toward [5]the eastern
sea
And half of them toward [6]the
western sea;
In both summer and winter it shall
occur.
9 And the LORD shall be [k]King over
all the earth.
In that day it shall be—
[l]"The LORD *is* one,"
And His name one.

10 All the land shall be turned into a
plain from Geba to Rimmon south of Jerusalem. [7]*Jerusalem* shall be raised up and
[m]inhabited in her place from Benjamin's
Gate to the place of the First Gate and the
Corner Gate, [n]and *from* the Tower of Hananel to the king's winepresses.

11 *The people* shall dwell in it;
And [o]no longer shall there be utter
destruction,
[p]But Jerusalem shall be safely
inhabited.

6 [4]Lit. *glorious ones*
7 [h]Matt. 24:36 [i]Is. 30:26
8 [j]Ezek. 47:1-12; Joel 3:18; [John 7:38; Rev. 22:1, 2] [5]The Dead Sea [6]The Mediterranean Sea
9 [k][Jer. 23:5, 6; Rev. 11:15] [l][Eph. 4:5, 6]; Deut. 6:4
10 [m]Jer. 30:18; Zech. 12:6 [n]Neh. 3:1; Jer. 31:38 [7]Lit. *She*
11 [o]Jer. 31:40 [p]Jer. 23:6; Ezek. 34:25-28; Hos. 2:18
12 [8]Lit. *decay*
13 [q]1 Sam. 14:15, 20 [r]Judg. 7:22; 2 Chr. 20:23; Ezek. 38:21
14 [s]Ezek. 39:10, 17
15 [t]Zech. 14:12

12 And this shall be the plague with
which the LORD will strike all the people
who fought against Jerusalem:

Their flesh shall [8]dissolve while
they stand on their feet,
Their eyes shall dissolve in their
sockets,
And their tongues shall dissolve in
their mouths.
13 It shall come to pass in that day
That [q]a great panic from the LORD
will be among them.
Everyone will seize the hand of his
neighbor,
And raise [r]his hand against his
neighbor's hand;
14 Judah also will fight at Jerusalem.
[s]And the wealth of all the
surrounding nations
Shall be gathered together:
Gold, silver, and apparel in great
abundance.

15 [t]Such also shall be the plague
On the horse *and* the mule,
On the camel and the donkey,
And on all the cattle that will be in
those camps.
So *shall* this plague *be*.

The Nations Worship the King

16 And it shall come to pass *that* every-

14:8 The highest elevation of the temple mount in Jerusalem is more than 300 ft. lower than the Mt. of Olives, but the topographical alterations described in vv. 4,10 will allow the spring to flow towards the Dead Sea (E) and the Mediterranean Sea (W) (*see notes on Ezek. 47:1-12*). It will not dry up in summer, as most Palestinian streams do, but will flow all year, making the desert "blossom as the rose" (Is. 35:1).

14:9 LORD *is* one...His name one. Cf. Rev. 11:15. There will be only one religion in the entire world during the millennial reign of Christ. Ruling with a rod of iron (cf. Rev. 19:15), Christ will have done away with all false religions spawned by Satan. This will be the ultimate fulfillment of the Abrahamic Covenant providing a Jewish people, the nation of Israel, and the land given to Abraham; the Davidic Covenant which promised a king from the tribe of Judah and the line of David; and the New Covenant which held out the hope of spiritual redemption for Jew and Gentile. All of this will be fulfilled in and by the Lord Jesus Christ.

14:10 All the land...into a plain. The term "plain" pictures the Jordan Valley, extending from Mt. Hermon (elevation 9,100 ft.) to the Gulf of Aqabah. Here the entire land, from Geba 6 mi. to the N to Rimmon in the S, would be leveled to become like the well-watered and fertile lowlands of the Jordan Valley (cf. Gen. 13:10), causing Jerusalem to be exalted above like a solitaire diamond on a ring. Jerusalem, having been rebuilt according to these dimensions, will be exalted in both place and purpose, the prominent royal city containing the temple of God and the throne of Jesus Christ (cf. Ezek. 40–48). The locations of these landmarks would be the equivalent of meaning "all Jerusalem, E to W and N to S."

14:11 safely inhabited. Jerusalem, the city of peace, has been fought over more frequently than any other city on earth, and prayed for over the millennia (Ps. 122:6-9). As promised by God (2 Sam. 7:10-17; Ps. 2:6; Ezek. 37:24-28; Joel 3:16-17), she will know permanent righteousness and with it peace, rest, and safety.

14:12-15 The prophet, one final time, cycles back over the judgment that precedes the kingdom. God will strike the heathen forces gathered against Israel (vv. 1-3) with a supernatural plague similar to His judgment of the Assyrian army (Is. 37:36), causing a panic so great that they begin to attack one another (cf. Judg. 7:22; 1 Sam. 14:15-20; 2 Chr. 20:23), aiding in the escape of the half (cf. vv. 2,5). God will enable His people to fight (cf. Is. 11:13,14). Then He will send a widespread plague that even extends to their animals, preventing their use for military endeavors or escape. This depicts the thwarting of their efforts as God ultimately destroys them by the Messiah (Rev. 19:11-16).

14:16-19 This very important passage reveals that some Gentiles will go into the millennial kingdom alive along with the redeemed Jews. A converted remnant from those heathen nations will make annual pilgrimages to Jerusalem to worship the Lord and to celebrate the Feast of Tabernacles during the Millennium. Commemorating the time when God "tabernacled" with Israel in the wilderness, the feast represented the last of the 3 major pilgrimage festivals (Lev. 23:34-36), marked the final harvest of the year's crops, and provided a time of rejoicing. In the Millennium, it will celebrate Messiah's presence again dwelling among His people and the joyful restoration of Israel, including the ingathering of the nations. Those who refuse to go will experience drought and plague. Tragically, as the thousand years go on, there will be many people from all over the world who will reject

one who is left of all the nations which
came against Jerusalem shall [u]go up from
year to year to [v]worship the King, the
LORD of hosts, and to keep [w]the Feast of
Tabernacles. 17 [x]And it shall be *that*
whichever of the families of the earth do
not come up to Jerusalem to worship the
King, the LORD of hosts, on them there will
be no rain. 18 If the family of [y]Egypt will
not come up and enter in, [z]they *shall have*
no *rain;* they shall receive the plague with
which the LORD strikes the nations who do
not come up to keep the Feast of Tabernacles. 19 This shall be the [9]punishment of
Egypt and the punishment of all the nations that do not come up to keep the Feast
of Tabernacles.
20 In that day [a]"HOLINESS TO THE
LORD" shall be *engraved* on the bells of the
horses. The [b]pots in the LORD's house shall
be like the bowls before the altar. 21 Yes,
[1]every pot in Jerusalem and Judah shall be
holiness to the LORD of hosts. Everyone
who sacrifices shall come and take them
and cook in them. In that day there shall no
longer be a [c]Canaanite [d]in the house of the
LORD of hosts.

16 [u] [Is. 2:2, 3; 60:6-9; 66:18-21; Mic. 4:1, 2] [v] Is. 27:13
16 [w] Lev. 23:34-44; Neh. 8:14; Hos. 12:9; John 7:2
17 [x] Is. 60:12
18 [y] Is. 19:21 [z] Deut. 11:10
19 [9] Lit. *sin*
20 [a] Ex. 28:36; 39:30; Is. 23:18; Jer. 2:3 [b] Ezek. 46:20
21 [c] Is. 35:8; Ezek. 44:9; Joel 3:17; Rev. 21:27; 22:15 [d] [Eph. 2:19-22]

[1] *Or on every pot . . . shall be engraved "HOLINESS TO THE LORD OF HOSTS"*

Christ as Savior and King, joining in a final war against Him, only to be destroyed and cast into hell forever (cf. Rev. 20:7-15).

14:16 Feast of Tabernacles. The historical background can be found in Lev. 23:33-36; Num. 29:12-38; Deut. 16:13-17. In addition to the Feast of Tabernacles, two other feasts will be celebrated in the Millennium, i.e., 1) Feast of the New Year (Ezek. 45:18-20) and 2) Passover (Ezek. 45:21-25). These feasts are no more efficacious than were the feasts of the Mosaic era or the Lord's Supper in the church age. They all provided a symbolic anticipation or remembrance of Christ's unique and once-for-all sacrifice at Calvary.

14:17 no rain. Drought is a dreaded punishment (cf. 1 Kin. 17:1-7; 2 Chr. 7:13,14; James 5:17,18) since it deprives the people of life-sustaining water.

14:20-21 Just as the High-Priest, whose turban was engraved with the phrase "HOLINESS TO THE LORD," was set apart for the service of the Lord (cf. Zech. 3:5; also Ex. 28:36; 39:30), so even mundane and ordinary things like the bells that decorate horses and common pots and pans will be as holy as the High-Priest and the altar bowls used in sacrifices. There will be no need for distinctions between holy and secular. Everything will be set apart to the service of the Lord in the Messiah's glorious kingdom.

14:21 Canaanite. This identification is used as a figure for the morally and spiritually unclean persons who will be excluded from entering the millennial temple. Before Israel conquered the Promised Land, the vile Canaanites inhabited it; thus the term became proverbial in Israel for a morally degenerate, ceremonial unclean person.

The Book of
MALACHI

Title

The title is derived from the prophecy's author, Malachi. With this last work in the Minor Prophets, God closes the OT canon historically and prophetically.

Author and Date

Some have suggested that the book was written anonymously, noting that the name, meaning "my messenger" or "the LORD's messenger," could be a title rather than a proper name. It is pointed out that the name occurs nowhere else in the OT, nor is any background material provided about the author. However, since all other prophetic books have historically identified their author in the introductory heading, this suggests that Malachi was indeed the name of the last OT writing prophet in Israel. Jewish tradition identifies him as a member of the Great Synagogue that collected and preserved the Scriptures.

Looking solely at internal evidence, the date of the prophecy points to the late fifth century B.C., most likely during Nehemiah's return to Persia ca. 433–424 B.C. (cf. Neh. 5:14; 13:6). Sacrifices were being made at the second temple (1:7-10; 3:8), which was finished in 516 B.C. (cf. Ezra 6:13-15). Many years had passed since then as the priests had increasingly become complacent and corrupt (1:6–2:9). Malachi's reference to "governor" (1:8) speaks of the time of Persian dominance in Judah when Nehemiah was revisiting Persia (Neh. 13:6), while his emphasis on the law (4:4) coincides with a similar focus by Ezra and Nehemiah (cf. Ezra 7:14,25,26; Neh. 8:18). They shared other concerns as well, such as marriages to foreign wives (2:11-15; cf. Ezra 9,10; Neh. 13:23-27), withholding of tithes (3:8-10; cf. Neh. 13:10-14), and social injustice (3:5; cf. Neh. 5:1-13). Nehemiah came to Jerusalem in 445 B.C. to rebuild the wall, and returned to Persia in 433 B.C. He later returned to Israel (ca. 424 B.C.) to deal with the sins Malachi described (Neh. 13:6). So it is likely that Malachi was written during the period of Nehemiah's absence, almost a century after Haggai and Zechariah began to prophesy. Similar to Rev. 2,3, in which Christ writes what He thinks about the conditions of the churches, here God writes through Malachi to impress upon Israel His thoughts about the nation.

Background and Setting

Only 50,000 exiles had returned to Judah from Babylon (538–536 B.C.). The temple had been rebuilt under the leadership of Zerubbabel (516 B.C.) and the sacrificial system renewed. Ezra had returned in 458 B.C., followed by Nehemiah in 445 B.C. After being back in the land of Palestine for only a century, the ritual of the Jews' religious routine led to hard-heartedness toward God's great love for them and to widespread departure from His law by both people and priest. Malachi rebuked and condemned these abuses, forcefully indicting the people and calling them to repentance. When Nehemiah returned from Persia the second time (ca. 424 B.C.), he vigorously rebuked them for these abuses in the temple and priesthood, for the violation of the Sabbath rest, and for the unlawful divorce of their Jewish wives so they could marry Gentile women (cf. Neh. 13).

As over two millennia of OT history since Abraham concluded, none of the glorious promises of the Abrahamic, Davidic, and New Covenants had been fulfilled in their ultimate sense. Although there had been a few high points in Israel's history, e.g., Joshua, David, and Josiah, the Jews had seemingly lost all opportunity to receive God's favor since less than 100 years after returning from captivity, they had already sunk to a depth of sin that exceeded the former iniquities which brought on the Assyrian and Babylonian deportations. Beyond this, the long anticipated Messiah had not arrived and did not seem to be in sight.

So, Malachi wrote the capstone prophecy of the OT in which he delivered God's message of judgment on Israel for their continuing sin and God's promise that one day in the future, when the Jews would repent, Messiah would be revealed and God's covenant promises would be fulfilled. There were over 400 years of divine silence, with only Malachi's words ringing condemnation in their ears, before another prophet arrived with a message from God. That was John the Baptist preaching, "Repent, for the Kingdom of heaven is at hand!" (Matt. 3:2). Messiah had come.

Historical and Theological Themes

The Lord repeatedly referred to His covenant with Israel (cf. 2:4,5,8,10,14; 3:1), reminding them, from His opening words, of their unfaithfulness to His love/marriage relationship with them (cf. 1:2-5). God's love for His people pervades the book. Apparently the promises by the former prophets of the coming Messiah who would bring final deliverance and age-long blessings, and the encouragement from the recent promises (ca. 500 B.C.) of Haggai and Zechariah, had only made the people and their leaders more resolute in their complacency. They thought that this love relationship could be maintained by formal ritual alone, no matter how they lived. In a penetrating rebuke of both priests (1:6–2:9) and people (2:10-16), the prophet reminds them that the Lord's coming, which they were seeking (3:1), would be in judgment to refine, purify, and purge (3:2,3). The Lord not only wanted outward compliance to the law, but an inward acceptance as well (cf. Matt. 23:23). The prophet assaults the corruption, wickedness, and false security by directing his judgments at their hypocrisy, infidelity, compromise, divorce, false worship, and arrogance.

Malachi set forth his prophecy in the form of a dispute, employing the question-and-answer method. The Lord's accusations against His people were frequently met by cynical questions from the people (1:2,6,7; 2:17; 3:7,8,13). At other times, the prophet presented himself as God's advocate in a lawsuit, posing rhetorical questions to the people based on their defiant criticisms (1:6,8,9; 2:10,15; 3:2).

Malachi indicted the priests and the people on at least 6 counts of willful sin: 1) repudiating God's love (1:2-5); 2) refusing God His due honor (1:6–2:9); 3) rejecting God's faithfulness (2:10-16); 4) redefining God's righteousness (2:17–3:5); 5) robbing God's riches (3:6-12); and 6) reviling God's grace (3:13-15). There are 3 interludes in which Malachi rendered God's judgment: 1) to the priests (2:1-9); 2) to the nation (3:1-6); and 3) to the remnant (3:16–4:6).

Interpretive Challenges

The meaning of Elijah being sent "before the coming of the great and dreadful day of the LORD" (4:5) has been debated. Was this fulfilled in John the Baptist or is it yet future? Will Elijah be reincarnated? It seems best to view Malachi's prophecy as a reference to John the Baptist and not to a literally-returned Elijah. Not only did the angel announce that John the Baptist would "go before Him in the spirit and power of Elijah" (Luke 1:17), but John the Baptist himself said he was not Elijah (John 1:21). Thus John was like Elijah, internally in "spirit and power" and externally in rugged independence and nonconformity. If the Jews would receive the Messiah, then he would be the Elijah spoken of (cf. Matt. 11:14; 17:9-13); if they refused the King, then another Elijah-like prophet would be sent in the future, perhaps as one of the two witnesses (cf. Rev. 11:1-19).

Outline

- I. The Denunciation of Israel's Sins (1:1–2:16)
  - A. Reminder of God's Love for Israel (1:1-5)
  - B. Rebuke of the Priests (1:6–2:9)
    - 1. Contempt for God's altar (1:6-14)
    - 2. Contempt for God's glory (2:1-3)
    - 3. Contempt for God's law (2:4-9)
  - C. Rebuke of the People (2:10-16)
- II. The Declaration of Israel's Judgment and Blessing (2:17–4:6)
  - A. Coming of a Messenger (2:17–3:5)
  - B. Challenge to Repent (3:6-12)
  - C. Criticism by Israel Against the Lord (3:13-15)
  - D. Consolation to the Faithful Remnant (3:16–4:6)

1 The [1]burden of the word of the LORD to
Israel [2]by Malachi.

Israel Beloved of God

2 "I[a] have loved you," says the LORD.
"Yet you say, 'In what way have You
loved us?'
Was not Esau Jacob's brother?"
Says the LORD.
"Yet [b]Jacob I have loved;
3 But Esau I have hated,
And [c]laid waste his mountains and
his heritage
For the jackals of the wilderness."

4 Even though Edom has said,
"We have been impoverished,
But we will return and build the
desolate places,"

Thus says the LORD of hosts:

"They may build, but I will [d]throw
down;
They shall be called the Territory of
Wickedness,
And the people against whom the
LORD will have indignation
forever.
5 Your eyes shall see,

CHAPTER 1

1 [1] *oracle, prophecy* [2] Lit. *by the hand of*
2 [a] Deut. 4:37; 7:8; 23:5; Is. 41:8, 9; [Jer. 31:3]; John 15:12 [b] Rom. 9:13
3 [c] Jer. 49:18; Ezek. 35:9, 15
4 [d] Jer. 49:16-18
5 [e] Ps. 35:27; Mic. 5:4
6 [f] [Ex. 20:12]; Prov. 30:11, 17; [Matt. 15:4-8; Eph. 6:2, 3] [g] [Is. 63:16; 64:8]; Jer. 31:9; Luke 6:46 [h] Mal. 2:14
7 [i] Deut. 15:21 [j] Ezek. 41:22 [3] Or *to be despised*
8 [k] Lev. 22:22; Deut. 15:19-23

And you shall say,
[e]'The LORD is magnified beyond the
border of Israel.'

Polluted Offerings

6 "A son [f]honors *his* father,
And a servant *his* master.
[g]If then I am the Father,
Where *is* My honor?
And if I *am* a Master,
Where *is* My reverence?
Says the LORD of hosts
To you priests who despise My
name.
[h]Yet you say, 'In what way have we
despised Your name?'

7 "You offer [i]defiled food on My altar,
But say,
'In what way have we defiled You?'
By saying,
[j]'The table of the LORD is
[3]contemptible.'
8 And [k]when you offer the blind as a
sacrifice,
Is it not evil?
And when you offer the lame and
sick,
Is it not evil?
Offer it then to your governor!

1:1–2:16 In the first of two major sections (cf. 2:17; 4:6), Malachi delivered God's message which denounced sin among the people of Israel.

1:1 burden. This term refers to the heavy sentence pronounced by the prophet. *See notes on Is. 13:1; Nah. 1:1; Hab. 1:1; Zech. 9:1; 12:1.*

1:2 I have loved you. The great privilege of Israel as God's beloved people is forcefully presented by comparing the nation with Edom. In response to the affirmation of the Lord's love for them, the people, looking only at what they had lost since the captivity and how feeble their nation was, incredulously expressed doubt about God's love and insolently challenged it. Nevertheless, God reaffirmed His love to them, recalling His covenant choice of Jacob over Esau, father of the Edomites (cf. Gen. 25:23). In this closing book of the OT, God's electing love toward Israel, sovereign, undeserved, and persistent (cf. Rom. 9:13), is boldly and explicitly reiterated by the Lord Himself and illustrated by His choice of Jacob and his offspring. Unconditionally, and completely apart from any consideration of human merit, God elected Jacob and his descendants to become His heirs of promise (cf. Rom. 9:6-29). No one should conclude that God does not love His people because He afflicted them, but rather He loves them because He elected them.

1:3 Esau I have hated. While Genesis mentions no divine hatred toward Esau, Obadiah's prophecy over a 1,000 years later (see Obad. 1-21) indicated that the Lord's hatred was against Esau's idolatrous descendants. In the same way, the Lord's love for Jacob refers to his descendants who were His sovereignly elected people through whom the world's Redeemer would come. Nor does the love/hate language signify a comparative love in which He loved Jacob more and Esau less. Rather, the context here speaks of love as "choosing for intimate fellowship" and hate as "not choosing for intimate fellowship" in the realm of redemption. *See notes on Rom. 9:6-13.* **laid waste his mountains...heritage.** A reference to Edom's (later called Idumea) destruction, first by Nebuchadnezzar and later by neighboring people, e.g., Egypt, Ammon, and Moab, as well as at the hands of the Nabateans. See Introduction to Obadiah: Background and Setting; Historical and Theological Themes.

1:4,5 Though the Edomites would attempt to rebuild their ruins, God would negate their efforts. Israel, on the other hand, is restored; and though complete restoration has been delayed, it will come and the nation will bear witness to God's gracious rulership, both within as well as beyond her borders (cf. Gen. 12:3; Mal. 1:11).

1:6–2:9 Affirming the unconditional love of the Lord (vv. 2-5) did not absolve guilt, thus Malachi delivered an opening indictment against the priests, the nation's spiritual leaders, pointing out how they were showing contempt for God's sacrifices (vv. 6-14), His glory (2:1-3), and His law (2:4-9).

1:6 priests. He addressed the priests first because they should be leaders in righteous devotion to God, but were foremost in despising His name, though their question was tantamount to a denial of their wicked attitude toward God (cf. Luke 6:46).

1:7 defiled food. That the reference here is to animal sacrifices is evident from v. 8. The priests were offering ceremonially unclean or blemished (cf. v. 13) sacrifices, strictly forbidden by the Lord (cf. Lev. 22:20-25; Deut. 15:21), and again hypocritically questioning such an indictment. They had only contempt for the Lord as indicated by the offerings brought to the Lord of "blind," "lame" and "sick" animals (v. 8). **table of the LORD.** This refers to the altar for sacrifices (cf. Ezek. 41:22).

1:8 Offer it then to your governor! The priests had the audacity to offer God what their governor, as a form of taxation, would never have accepted from them. They were more fearful of the governor's rejection than of God's. This would have been during the time that Nehemiah was back in Persia (cf. Neh. 3:6) when he would have relinquished the office for some time.

Would he be pleased with you?
Would he [l]accept[4] you favorably?"
Says the LORD of hosts.

9 "But now entreat God's favor,
That He may be gracious to us.
[m]*While* this is being *done* by your hands,
Will He accept you favorably?"
Says the LORD of hosts.

10 "Who *is there* even among you who would shut the doors,
[n]So that you would not kindle fire *on* My altar in vain?
I have no pleasure in you,"
Says the LORD of hosts,
[o]"Nor will I accept an offering from your hands.

11 For [p]from the rising of the sun, even to its going down,
My name *shall be* great [q]among the Gentiles;
[r]In every place [s]incense *shall be* offered to My name,
And a pure offering;
[t]For My name shall be great among the nations,"
Says the LORD of hosts.

12 "But you profane it,
In that you say,
[u]'The table of the [5]LORD is defiled;
And its fruit, its food, *is* contemptible.'

13 You also say,
'Oh, what a [v]weariness!'
And you sneer at it,"
Says the LORD of hosts.
"And you bring the stolen, the lame, and the sick;
Thus you bring an offering!
[w]Should I accept this from your hand?"
Says the LORD.

14 "But cursed *be* [x]the deceiver

8 [l][Job 42:8] [4]Lit. *lift up your face*
9 [m]Hos. 13:9
10 [n]1 Cor. 9:13 [o]Is. 1:11
11 [p]Is. 59:19 [q]Is. 60:3, 5
[r]1 Tim. 2:8 [s]Rev. 8:3 [t]Is. 66:18, 19
12 [u]Mal. 1:7 [5]So with Bg.; MT *Lord*
13 [v]Is. 43:22 [w]Lev. 22:20
14 [x]Mal. 1:8

1:9 The invitation to repent is best taken as irony. How could they expect God to extend His grace when they were insulting Him with unacceptable sacrifices?

1:10 shut the doors. God, speaking in the first person, desired for someone to shut the temple doors, thereby preventing the useless, insincere presentation of sacrifices (cf. Is. 1:11-15). It would be better to stop all sacrifices than to offer insincere offerings.

1:11 from the rising of the sun…going down. The phrase is a way of referring to the whole earth (cf. Pss. 50:1; 103:12; Is. 45:6; 59:19; Zech. 8:7), as the subsequent phrase, "In every place," indicates (cf. 1:5). Although no indication is given as to the time when such worship of God will fill the earth, this cannot be a reference to any historic Jewish worship outside the borders of Israel. Malachi's zeal for Israel's sacrifices, coupled with his negative attitude toward foreigners and their gods (vv. 2-5; 2:11), points to the millennial era, when they will worship in the rebuilt temple and incense plus offerings will be present (cf. Ezek. 40–48). At that time, and not until that time, the Lord will receive pure worship throughout the world and His name will be honored everywhere (cf. Is. 2:24; 19:19-21; 24:14-16; 45:22-24; 66:18-21; Mic. 4:1-3; Zech. 8:20-23; 14:16-19).

1:12,13 The reproof of vv. 7,8 is repeated. The exacting requirements of the sacrifices wearied the priests. They did not literally say the Lord's table (the place of offerings) is contemptible, but they virtually said so by refusing to lead the people to reverence and to offer the Lord their best; thus their attitude and actions were profaning the altar and insulting to the Lord (cf. Is. 43:22-24; Mic. 6:3), so He rejected their offerings.

Old Testament Names for God

1.	Elohim, "God," i.e., His power and might	Gen. 1:1; Ps. 19:1
2.	El-Elyon, "The most high God"	Gen. 14:17-20; Is. 14:13,14
3.	El-Olam, "The everlasting God"	Is. 40:28-31
4.	El-Roi, "The strong one who sees"	Gen. 16:12
5.	El-Shaddai, "God Almighty"	Gen. 17:1; Ps. 91:1
6.	Adonai, "Lord," i.e., the Lordship of God	Mal. 1:6
7.	Jehovah (Yahweh), "The LORD," i.e., God's eternal nature	Gen. 2:4
8.	Jehovah-Jireh, "The LORD will provide"	Gen. 22:13,14
9.	Jehovah-Maccaddeshem, "The LORD your sanctifier"	Ex. 31:13
10.	Jehova-Nissi, "The LORD our banner"	Ex. 17:15
11.	Jehovah-Rapha, "The LORD our healer"	Ex. 16:26
12.	Jehovah-Rohi, "The LORD my shepherd"	Ps. 23:1
13.	Jehovah-Sabbaoth, "The LORD of Hosts"	Is. 6:1-3
14.	Jehovah-Shalom, "The LORD is peace"	Judg. 6:24
15.	Jehovah-Shammah, "The LORD who is present"	Ezek. 48:35
16.	Jehovah-Tsidkenu, "The LORD our righteousness"	Jer. 23:6

Who has in his flock a male,
And takes a vow,
But sacrifices to the Lord [y]what is blemished—
For [z]I *am* a great King,"
Says the LORD of hosts,
"And My name *is to be* feared among the nations.

Corrupt Priests

2 "And now, O [a]priests, this commandment is for you.
2 [b]If you will not hear,
And if you will not take *it* to heart,
To give glory to My name,"
Says the LORD of hosts,
"I will send a curse upon you,
And I will curse your blessings.
Yes, I have cursed them [c]already,
Because you do not take *it* to heart.

3 "Behold, I will rebuke your descendants
And spread [d]refuse on your faces,
The refuse of your solemn feasts;
And *one* will [e]take you away [1]with it.
4 Then you shall know that I have sent this commandment to you,
That My covenant with Levi may continue,"
Says the LORD of hosts.
5 "My[f] covenant was with him, *one* of life and peace,
And I gave them to him [g]*that he might* fear *Me;*
So he feared Me
And was reverent before My name.
6 [h]The[2] law of truth was in his mouth,
And [3]injustice was not found on his lips.
He walked with Me in peace and equity,
And [i]turned many away from iniquity.

7 "For[j] the lips of a priest should keep knowledge,
And *people* should seek the law from his mouth;
[k]For he is the messenger of the LORD of hosts.
8 But you have departed from the way;
You [l]have caused many to stumble at the law.
[m]You have corrupted the covenant of Levi,"
Says the LORD of hosts.
9 "Therefore [n]I also have made you contemptible and base
Before all the people,
Because you have not kept My ways
But have shown [o]partiality in the law."

Treachery of Infidelity

10 [p]Have we not all one Father?
[q]Has not one God created us?

14 [y]Lev. 22:18-20 [z]Ps. 47:2

CHAPTER 2

1 [a]Mal. 1:6
2 [b][Lev. 26:14, 15; Deut. 28:15] [c]Mal. 3:9
3 [d]Ex. 29:14 [e]1 Kin. 14:10 [1]Lit. *to it*
5 [f]Num. 25:12; Ezek. 34:25 [g]Deut. 33:9
6 [h]Deut. 33:10 [i]Jer. 23:22; [James 5:20] [2]Or *True instruction* [3]Or *unrighteousness*
7 [j]Num. 27:21; Deut. 17:8-11; Jer. 18:18 [k][Gal. 4:14]
8 [l]Jer. 18:15 [m]Num. 25:12, 13; Neh. 13:29; Ezek. 44:10
9 [n]1 Sam. 2:30 [o]Deut. 1:17; Mic. 3:11; 1 Tim. 5:21
10 [p]Jer. 31:9; 1 Cor. 8:6; [Eph. 4:6] [q]Job 31:15

1:14 what is blemished. Instead of the unblemished male animal (cf. Lev. 22:19), which was considered more valuable and which he had vowed to voluntarily give, the offerer suddenly substituted a blemished female. The fact that it was voluntary makes it that much more incongruous (cf. Acts 5:1-5). **a great King.** If such presentations are unacceptable to their governor (v. 8), how much more to the King of the universe? (cf. Ps. 48:2; Matt. 5:35).

2:2 I will send a curse. Failing to render glory to God would result in a curse being sent upon them. This is a fundamental OT theme: blessing for obedience, cursing for disobedience (cf. 1:14; Deut. 27:15-26; 28:15-68). **your blessings.** These were not restricted to material blessings only (cf. Num. 18:21) but referred to all the benefits of God's gracious hand (cf. v. 5), including the blessings pronounced by the priests over the people (cf. Num. 6:23-27).

2:3 refuse. This very graphic language shows how God viewed unfaithful priests as worthy of the most unthinkable disgrace. As the internal waste of the sacrificial animal was normally carried outside the camp and burned (cf. Ex. 29:14; Lev. 4:11,12; 8:17; 16:27), so the priests would be discarded and suffer humiliation and loss of office. The Lord's purpose in such a warning was to shake them out of their complacency.

2:4,5 My covenant with Levi. The relationship of God to the priesthood was clearly set forth in the Levitic covenant (Num. 3:44-48; 18:8-24; Deut. 33:8-11). The covenant was one of mutual responsibility, in which God expected reverence for Himself in exchange for life and peace for the priests. Verbally similar to the covenant made with Phinehas relating to the lineage of the High-Priest (cf. Num. 25:10-13), this covenant was made with Aaron of Levi's line and his descendants. The Jewish priests of Malachi's day had deceived themselves by claiming the privileges of the covenant, while neglecting the conditions of it, as if God was bound to bless them even while they rejected the obligation to serve Him.

2:4 Then you shall know. The priests will know the price of disobedience by bitter experience with the consequences.

2:6 Aaron, unlike the priests of Malachi's time, feared and reverenced God. Aaron also fulfilled this responsibility and lived the godliness he taught (Lev. 8,9). *See note on vv. 4,5.*

2:7 The priests were the messengers of God in Israel. Not only were they to represent the people to God, but they were also responsible to represent God to the people by teaching the law of Moses to the nation (cf. Lev. 10:9-11; Deut. 33:10; Ezra 7:10; Hos. 4:6).

2:8,9 The priests of Malachi's day had made a radical departure from God's standard, originally given to Levi, causing others to stumble by their bad example and false interpretation of the law. Consequently, the worst shame and degradation fell upon them (cf. v. 3; Neh. 13:29).

2:10-16 Israel's spiritual leaders committed grievous sins (1:6–2:9), leading the people to do the same. They too were violating the requirements of God's law by profaning the institution of the Levitical priesthood, marrying foreign wives (vv. 10-12), and divorcing the wives of their youth (vv. 13-16).

2:10 one Father. Though God is Father of all through creation (cf. Acts 17:29; Eph. 3:14,15), the primary focus is directed to God as the

Why do we deal treacherously
with one another
By profaning the covenant of the
fathers?
11 Judah has dealt treacherously,
And an abomination has been
committed in Israel and in
Jerusalem,
For Judah has [r]profaned
The LORD's holy *institution* which
He loves:
He has married the daughter of a
foreign god.
12 May the LORD cut off from the
tents of Jacob
The man who does this, being
[4]awake and aware,
Yet [s]who brings an offering to the
LORD of hosts!

13 And this is the second thing you do:
You cover the altar of the LORD
with tears,
With weeping and crying;
So He does not regard the offering
anymore,
Nor receive *it* with goodwill from
your hands.

14 Yet you say, "For what reason?"
Because the LORD has been witness
Between you and [t]the wife of your
youth,
With whom you have dealt
treacherously;
[u]Yet she is your companion
And your wife by covenant.
15 But [v]did He not make *them* one,
Having a remnant of the Spirit?
And why one?
He seeks [w]godly offspring.
Therefore take heed to your spirit,
And let none deal treacherously
with the wife of his youth.

16 "For [x]the LORD God of Israel says
That He hates divorce,
For it covers one's garment with
violence,"
Says the LORD of hosts.
"Therefore take heed to your spirit,
That you do not deal treacherously."

17 [y]You have wearied the LORD with
your words;
Yet you say,

11 [r] Ezra 9:1, 2; Neh. 13:23 **12** [s] Neh. 13:29 [4] Talmud, Vg. *teacher and student*

14 [t] Prov. 5:18; Jer. 9:2; Mal. 3:5 [u] Prov. 2:17 **15** [v] Gen. 2:24; Matt. 19:4, 5 [w] Ezra 9:2; [1 Cor. 7:14] **16** [x] Deut. 24:1; [Matt. 5:31; 19:6-8] **17** [y] Is. 43:22, 24

Father of Israel as His covenant people (see "Father" in 1:6, where this indictment began; also cf. Jer. 2:27).

2:10,11 deal treacherously. This key phrase (vv. 10,11,14,15,16) refers to the violation of God's will by divorcing Jewish wives and marrying foreign women. God is the Father who gave life to Israel (cf. Is. 43:1; 60:21), yet they had, through intermarriage with idol worshipers, introduced division by violating the covenant He made with their fathers to insure the maintenance of a separated people (cf. Ex. 19:5; 24:8; 34:14-16; Lev. 20:24,26; Deut. 7:1-4).

2:11 married the daughter of a foreign god. A worshiper of an idol was considered to be its child (Jer. 2:27). The prophets often mixed the ideas of adultery and idolatry or physical and spiritual adultery. Unless they became true proselytes to Judaism, pagan women led their husbands into idolatry and thereby contaminated Israelite worship (cf. Judg. 3:5-7). Those Jews who married them profaned God's temple and the covenant community. Solomon's violation of this law had opened the door for idolatry to enter Judah (1 Kin. 11:1-6). Both Ezra (Ezra 9:2-15) and Nehemiah (Neh. 13:23-29) faced this sinful problem.

2:12 cut off. This common term was generally used for death. Their adulterous actions of divorce and intermarriage disqualified them from participation in the rights and privileges of the community of Israel, so their offerings to God would be rejected. **awake and aware.** A proverbial expression referring to two classes of people, "the active watcher" who is "awake" to reality and "the passive hearer" whom he makes "aware." This proverb apparently came from nomadic people who had guards around their tents to stay awake and make others aware of danger. This signified judgment so that everyone who sins in this gross, idolatrous way would be exterminated.

2:13 cover the altar...with tears. Weeping and wailing would achieve nothing because sin had shut the door of access to God. They had violated their marriage vows and the separation from idols as God required. This double disloyalty made their offerings a hypocritical mockery. Since lay people had no access to the altars but the priests did, it was clearly their guilt which was foremost, and their hypocrisy so unacceptable to God.

2:14 your wife by covenant. The prophet accentuated the iniquity by mentioning the legally binding nature of the marriage contract, a covenant made before God as witness (cf. Gen. 31:50; Prov. 2:17). Wives were married young, sometimes before 15 years of age (cf. Prov. 5:18; Is. 54:6).

2:15 Noting God's original institution of marriage (Gen. 2:24), in which He made two into one, Malachi reminded them that God provided only one woman for one man. Though He had the life-giving power of the Spirit, and could have made Adam a number of wives, He created only one—to raise up a "godly offspring. Polygamy, divorce, and marriage to idolatrous women are destructive to obtaining the godly remnant in the line of the promised Messiah. Only when both parents remain faithful to their marriage vows can the children be given the security which provides the basis for godly living. Because this foundational divine institution of marriage was being threatened, Malachi urged that no husband act in a treacherous way toward his wife. For polygamy *see note on 1 Kin. 11:1-6*.

2:16 He hates divorce. *See notes on Matt. 5:32; 19:3-12; 1 Cor. 7.* The Lord emphasized what He had been saying by this emphatic declaration. In fact, God sees this unwarranted divorce as a gross act of sin which, like blood splattered from a murder victim on the killer, leaves evidence of the evil deed. For discussion of divorce, which God actually commanded the Jews to do by separating from these idolatrous wives, *see notes on Ezra 10:10-19* and the Ezra Introduction: Interpretive Challenges. Though God hates divorce, there are times when it is the lesser of the evils and would prevent a future and even greater spiritual catastrophe. *See notes on Matt. 5:32; 19:3-12; 1 Cor. 7:10-16.*

2:17–4:6 The denunciation of Israel's sins was followed by a declaration of the judgment on the unrepentant and subsequent blessing on the faithful remnant. Verse 17 is the introduction to the rest of the book. These faithless, disobedient priests and people had worn out God's patience by their skepticism and self-justification, so judgment is on the way.

2:17 wearied the LORD. Disillusionment followed the rebuilding of the temple. The presence of God had not come to the new temple.

"In what way have we wearied
Him?"
In that you say,
[z]"Everyone who does evil
Is good in the sight of the LORD,
And He delights in them,"
Or, "Where *is* the God of justice?"

The Coming Messenger

3 "Behold, [a]I send My messenger,
And he will [b]prepare the way
before Me.
And the Lord, whom you seek,
Will suddenly come to His temple,
[c]Even the Messenger of the
covenant,
In whom you delight.
Behold, [d]He is coming,"
Says the LORD of hosts.

2 "But who can endure [e]the day of
His coming?
And [f]who can stand when He
appears?
For [g]He *is* like a refiner's fire
And like launderers' soap.
3 [h]He will sit as a refiner and a
purifier of silver;
He will purify the sons of Levi,
And [1]purge them as gold and
silver,
That they may [i]offer to the LORD
An offering in righteousness.

4 "Then [j]the offering of Judah and
Jerusalem
Will be [2]pleasant to the LORD,
As in the days of old,
As in former years.
5 And I will come near you for
judgment;
I will be a swift witness
Against sorcerers,
Against adulterers,
[k]Against perjurers,
Against those who [l]exploit wage
earners and [m]widows and
orphans,
And against those who turn away
an alien—
Because they do not fear Me,"
Says the LORD of hosts.

6 "For I *am* the LORD, [n]I do not
change;

17 [z] Is. 5:20; Zeph. 1:12

CHAPTER 3

1 [a] Matt. 11:10; Mark 1:2; Luke 1:76; 7:27; John 1:23; 2:14, 15 [b] [Is. 40:3] [c] Is. 63:9 [d] Hab. 2:7
2 [e] Jer. 10:10; Joel 2:11; Nah. 1:6; [Mal. 4:1] [f] Is. 33:14; Ezek. 22:14; Rev. 6:17 [g] Is. 4:4; Zech. 13:9; [Matt. 3:10-12; 1 Cor. 3:13-15]
3 [h] Is. 1:25; Dan. 12:10; Zech. 13:9 [i] [1 Pet. 2:5] [1] Or *refine*
4 [j] Mal. 1:11 [2] *pleasing*
5 [k] Lev. 19:12; Zech. 5:4; [James 5:12] [l] Lev. 19:13; James 5:4 [m] Ex. 22:22
6 [n] [Num. 23:19; Rom. 11:29; James 1:17]

They began to live in indifference to God. Calloused and lacking in spiritual discernment, the people persisted in cynical expressions of innocence. They had rejected all intention of taking right and wrong seriously. So deeply gripped by complacent self-righteousness, they had the gall to insolently question the Lord, implying that He seemed to favor the wicked and was unconcerned about the righteous. The prophet faced them with imminent judgment, telling them God was coming, but to refine and purify (cf. 3:1,5).

3:1 My messenger. It was a custom of the Near Eastern kings to send messengers before them to remove obstacles to their visit. Employing a wordplay on the name of Malachi, ("the LORD's messenger"), the Lord Himself announced He was sending one who would "prepare the way before Me." This is "the voice of one crying in the wilderness" (Is. 40:3) and the Elijah of 4:5 who comes before the Lord. The NT clearly identifies him as John the Baptist (cf. Matt. 3:3; 11:10,14; 17:12ff.; Mark 1:2; Luke 1:17; 7:26,27; John 1:23). **Will suddenly come.** To come "suddenly" does not mean immediately, but instantaneously and unannounced. It usually refers to a calamitous event (cf. Is. 47:11; 48:3; Jer. 4:20, etc.). When all the preparations are completed, the Lord will come, not to Zerubbabel's temple, nor in partial fulfillment to Herod's temple (*see notes on John 2:13-25*), but finally to that millennial temple which Ezekiel describes in Ezek. 40–48. The unexpected coming of Christ, partially fulfilled at His first advent, will be accomplished in full at His second coming (cf. Matt. 24:40-42). **Messenger of the covenant.** Probably not the messenger just mentioned. Rather, because this Messenger "will come to His temple," it is most likely a reference to the Lord Himself, the One who has the authority to reward or judge His people on the basis of their faithfulness to His covenant with them. The title may reflect earlier OT references to His "angel," which is lit. "messenger" (cf. Ex. 23:20-23; 32:34; Is. 63:9). **In whom you delight.** This is likely sarcastic. These sinful people were not delighting in God then, nor would they when He came in judgment on their hypocritical worship and cleansed the temple (cf. John 2:13-25). All the ungodly will be destroyed at His return (cf. Rev. 19:11ff.).

3:2 refiner's fire...launderers' soap. Instead of bringing rewards, His coming is likened to two purifying agents—fire to burn off dross and alkali to whiten—an indication of the true condition of their hearts. The fire will burn off the dross of iniquity; the soap will wash out the stain of sin. His coming will be one in which He removes all impurities. No one will escape this cleansing. Importantly, He will come purifying and cleansing, but not necessarily destroying (cf. Is. 1:25; 48:10; Jer. 6:29,30; Ezek. 22:17-22).

3:3 purify the sons of Levi. Since the Levitical priests were instrumental in leading the nation astray and a new group of pure priests was required for the work of the millennial temple (cf. Ezek. 44–45:8), the cleansing of the nation would begin with them (cf. Ezek. 9:6). Then they can "offer to the LORD" what is righteous as called for in the millennial sacrifices (cf. Ezek. 45:9–46:24). **offering in righteousness.** Given from cleansed hearts in a right condition before God, their offerings will be "in righteousness." These millennial sacrifices will be a memorial for the redeemed nation of Israel, commemorating Christ's sacrifice at Calvary. *See notes on Ezek. 44–46.*

3:4 the days of old. Only after the priesthood is purged and when the people are cleansed, will they be able to offer what pleases the Lord as in the days of Solomon (2 Chr. 7:8-10); Hezekiah (2 Chr. 30:26); Josiah (2 Chr. 35:18); and Ezra (Neh. 8:7).

3:5 What is a refining process for the remnant of repentant Jews who acknowledge their Messiah (cf. Zech. 12–14; Rom. 11:25-27), preparing them to enter the kingdom and worship in the millennial temple, will be for others utter destruction. All the iniquitous behavior in this verse are evidence that these are people who "do not fear God." In 2:17, they asked a question, and here is the answer, "I will come near for judgment." Occult practices were clearly forbidden (cf. Ex. 22:18; Deut. 18:10-12), but continued into NT times (cf. Acts 8:9). Adultery also violated God's law (2:16), as did perjury (cf. Ex. 20:16; Lev. 19:12; Deut. 19:16-20), extortion, and oppression.

3:6-12 These verses form a parenthesis between two messages concerning God's justice and judgment. What the Jews have labeled

[o]Therefore you are not consumed,
O sons of Jacob.
7 Yet from the days of [p]your fathers
You have gone away from My
ordinances
And have not kept *them.*
[q]Return to Me, and I will return to
you,"
Says the LORD of hosts.
[r]"But you said,
'In what way shall we return?'

Do Not Rob God

8 "Will a man rob God?
Yet you have robbed Me!
But you say,
'In what way have we robbed You?'
[s]In tithes and offerings.
9 You are cursed with a curse,
For you have robbed Me,
Even this whole nation.
10 [t]Bring all the tithes into the
[u]storehouse,
That there may be food in My
house,
And try Me now in this,"
Says the LORD of hosts,
"If I will not open for you the
[v]windows of heaven
And [w]pour out for you *such* blessing
That *there will* not *be room* enough
to receive it.

6 [o] [Lam. 3:22]
7 [p] Acts 7:51 [q] Zech. 1:3 [r] Mal. 1:6
8 [s] Neh. 13:10-12
10 [t] Prov. 3:9, 10 [u] 1 Chr. 26:20 [v] Gen. 7:11 [w] 2 Chr. 31:10

11 "And I will rebuke [x]the devourer
for your sakes,
So that he will not destroy the fruit
of your ground,
Nor shall the vine fail to bear fruit
for you in the field,"
Says the LORD of hosts;
12 And all nations will call you
blessed,
For you will be [y]a delightful land,"
Says the LORD of hosts.

The People Complain Harshly

13 "Your[z] words have been [3]harsh
against Me,"
Says the LORD,
"Yet you say,
'What have we spoken against
You?'
14 [a]You have said,
'It is useless to serve God;
What profit *is it* that we have kept
His ordinance,
And that we have walked as
mourners
Before the LORD of hosts?
15 So now [b]we call the proud blessed,
For those who do wickedness are
[4]raised up;
They even [c]tempt God and go
free.' "

11 [x] Amos 4:9
12 [y] Dan. 8:9
13 [z] Mal. 2:17 [3] Lit. *strong*
14 [a] Job 21:14
15 [b] Ps. 73:12 [c] Ps. 95:9 [4] Lit. *built*

as God's injustice is not God's being unrighteous or unfair, but his being mercifully patient. A genuine call of repentance is then issued (v. 7) and the fruit of it described (v. 10).

3:6,7 Contrary to God's having become unjust and thus not acting on behalf of Israel, in light of their history of rebellion, Israel's existence was due only to the Lord's unchanging character and unswerving commitment to His covenant promise with the patriarchs (cf. Num. 23:19; 1 Sam. 15:29; James 1:17 in general; Jer. 31:35-37; 33:14-22 in particular). They may experience God's goodness again, and be blessed—if they repent. In view of the Lord's coming to refine and purify, Malachi presents a powerful challenge to repent (cf. Zech. 1:3). Yet, apparently unwilling to admit the sins on their part needing repentance (also cf. v. 8b), the invitation to return is met with another cynical query, asking how they can return when, from their perspective, they haven't left—God has. The truth was, God hasn't changed and neither have they; He was as righteous as ever and they as unrighteous.

3:8-12 In answer to their query about how they have deviated from God's way and need to return, the prophet picked an illustration of their spiritual defection that is very visible and undeniable. The Lord pointed out that they had not brought the required tithes and offerings, those used to fund the theocracy by sustaining the Levites (cf. Lev. 27:30-33; Num. 18:8-28; Deut. 12:18; Neh. 13:10), the natural religious festivals (Deut. 12:6-17; 14:22-27), and the poor (Deut. 14:28, 29). But in not paying their taxes, and so robbing God, they had robbed themselves, for God had withheld His blessing. On believers' responsibility to pay taxes, *see notes on Matt. 22:21; Rom. 13:1-7.* On NT freewill giving, *see 1 Cor. 16:1,2; 2 Cor. 8,9.*

3:8,9 you have robbed Me! Here was a glaring, widespread sin; they had stolen from God what was rightfully His by divine law.

3:10-12 try Me. Contrary to the normal biblical pattern, the people were invited to put God to the test (cf. Is. 7:11,12; 1 Kin. 18:20-46). If they would honor Him by reversing their robbery and in a show of true repentance bring what He required, He would shower them with excessive abundance (cf. Prov. 11:24,25), protect them from locusts ("the devourer"), and they would be the delight of the nations (cf. Is. 62:4). *See notes on Luke 6:38; 2 Cor. 9:6-11.*

3:10 all the tithes. *See note on vv. 8-12.* When tithes were unpaid, the priests were deprived and had to give up their ministry and to begin farming. The nation's religious life was hindered and the poor and strangers suffered (cf. Neh. 13:10-11). But, the real iniquity was that such disobedience was robbing God, who was the true King of the theocracy of Israel. **storehouse.** A room in the temple to store the tithes of crops and animals brought by the people (cf. 2 Chr. 31:11; Neh. 10:38,39; 12:44; 13:12). This was the temple treasury. One of Nehemiah's tasks was to insure that the supplies needed for support of the temple ministry did not fail as it had during his absence (cf. Neh. 13:10-13).

3:13 These sinful priests and people had not just questioned God (2:17), violated God's covenant (2:11), disobeyed His laws (2:9), defiled His altar (1:7,12) and despised His name (1:6), but had openly spoken against Him. In spite of what was promised (vv. 10-12), the people complained that obedience to God's law brought no rewards (v. 14). Only the proud and wicked prospered, they said (v. 15).

3:14 walked as mourners. The people pretended to grieve for their sins, walking around in sackcloth or even with blackened faces to convey apparent sorrow (cf. Is. 58:5; Joel 2:13; Matt. 6:16-18), then complained that all that religious activity was useless.

3:15 tempt God. The proud and wicked, with apparent impunity, put God to the test by seeing how far they could go in doing evil (cf.

A Book of Remembrance

16 Then those [d]who feared the LORD
[e]spoke to one another,
And the LORD listened and heard
them;
So [f]a book of remembrance was
written before Him
For those who fear the LORD
And who [5]meditate on His
name.

17 "They[g] shall be Mine," says the
LORD of hosts,
"On the day that I make them My
[h]jewels.[6]
And [i]I will spare them
As a man spares his own son who
serves him."
18 [j]Then you shall again discern
Between the righteous and the
wicked,
Between one who serves God
And one who does not serve Him.

The Great Day of God

4 "For behold, [a]the day is coming,
Burning like an oven,
And all [b]the proud, yes, all who do
wickedly will be [c]stubble.
And the day which is coming shall
burn them up,"
Says the LORD of hosts,
"That will [d]leave them neither root
nor branch.
2 But to you who [e]fear My name
The [f]Sun of Righteousness shall
arise
With healing in His wings;
And you shall go out
And grow fat like stall-fed
calves.
3 [g]You shall trample the wicked,
For they shall be ashes under the
soles of your feet
On the day that I do *this,*"
Says the LORD of hosts.

4 "Remember the [h]Law of Moses, My
servant,
Which I commanded him in Horeb
for all Israel,
With [i]*the* statutes and
judgments.
5 Behold, I will send you [j]Elijah the
prophet

16 [d] Ps. 66:16 [e] Heb. 3:13 [f] Ps. 56:8 [5] Or *esteem*
17 [g] Ex. 19:5; Deut. 7:6; Is. 43:21; [1 Pet. 2:9] [h] Is. 62:3 [i] Ps. 103:13 [6] Lit. *special treasure*
18 [j] [Ps. 58:11]

CHAPTER 4

1 [a] Ps. 21:9; [Nah. 1:5, 6; Mal. 3:2, 3; 2 Pet. 3:7] [b] Mal. 3:18 [c] Is. 5:24; Obad. 18 [d] Amos 2:9
2 [e] Mal. 3:16 [f] Matt. 4:16; Luke 1:78; Acts 10:43; 2 Cor. 4:6; Eph. 5:14
3 [g] Mic. 7:10
4 [h] Ex. 20:3 [i] Deut. 4:10
5 [j] [Matt. 11:14; 17:10-13; Mark 9:11-13; Luke 1:17]; John 1:21

Ps. 73:2-14). In v. 10, God invited His people to see how far He would go in blessing.

3:16–4:6 Malachi ended with an encouraging word for the faithful remnant.

3:16 book of remembrance. In the hearts of the true and righteous worshipers who loved and served God in Israel, all the talk of judgment produced fear that they, too, might be swept away when God's wrath came. To encourage the godly remnant, Malachi noted how the Lord had not forgotten those "who fear the Lord and who meditate on His name." The book may be a reference to the "book of life" in which the names of God's children are recorded (e.g., Ex. 32:32-34; Neh. 13:14; Ps. 69:28; Dan. 12:1). The Persians had a custom of recording in a book all acts of a person that should be rewarded in the future (e.g., Esth. 6:1,2). The psalmist knew of such a book as well (Ps. 56:8).

3:17 Mine...My jewels. "Mine" is emphatic in the Hebrew. The godly remnant will belong to Him and will be His special treasure (cf. same word in Ex. 19:5; Deut. 7:6; 14:2; 26:18; Ps. 135:4). In the midst of judgment, He will spare them (cf. Ps. 103:13).

3:18 The distinction between the godly and ungodly will be evident for all when the righteous Lord is present, ruling from the throne of David in Jerusalem.

4:1 the day is coming. The first 3 verses continue the thought of the closing verses of the previous chapter, elaborating on God's punishment of the wicked and His deliverance of the godly (cf. 3:1-5). This eschatological reference to the Day of the Lord (cf. Is. 13:6; Joel 2:11,31; Zeph. 1:14) is injected 4 times into the prophet's final words (3:17; 4:1,3,5). It anticipated the return of the Lord Jesus in judgment (cf. Rev. 19:11-21). **Burning like an oven.** Adding to the imagery of a refining fire (3:2), Malachi spoke of God's judgment as a destructive fire that swiftly and totally consumes with excessive heat (cf. with the proud of 3:15). The destruction of the roots, normally protected by their subsurface location, provide a vivid, proverbial picture of its totality. All who refuse to repent will be cast in to the fire of hell (cf. Rev. 20:11-15).

4:2 Sun of Righteousness. While the wicked will be devoured by the heat of His wrath; those who fear Him will feel His warmth with healing in His "rays" or "beams" (cf. Is. 30:26; 60:1,3). The reference is to the Messiah; He is "the Lord our Righteousness" (Ps. 84:11; Jer. 23:5,6; 1 Cor. 1:30). **healing.** The reference should not be limited to the physical recovery from the harm done by the wicked (cf. 3:5). This sickness is inextricably linked with sin, with healing coming only through the suffering of the Servant (cf. Ps. 103:3; Is. 53:5; 57:18,19; 1 Pet. 2:24). **like stall-fed calves.** Calves, when confined to a stall for extended periods of time, leap for sheer joy when turned loose into the sunlight. The picture is one of a joyful, vigorous, and carefree life.

4:3 ashes under...your feet. The destruction of the wicked is appreciated by those who suffered at their hand. Ashes were often poured on foot trails to provide a more solid pathway during wet weather. Here the wicked are compared to ashes, which the righteous will tread down as a result of the fire of God's judgment (cf. v. 1). The prophet desires, as should all believers, that there be far-reaching repentance, and if not, destruction of the impenitent is inescapable.

4:4 Both the law and the prophets play a part in preparing for the arrival of the Day of the Lord. First, the people were to remember what was given at Sinai (Horeb), the law of Moses primarily focusing on the obligations to obedience at the time of entering into that covenant (Ex. 24:1ff.; Josh. 8:32; 23:6; 1 Kin. 2:3).

4:5 Elijah. The mention of Elijah was to announce the Messiah's arrival (see Introduction: Interpretive Challenges). John the Baptist was a type of Elijah at Christ's first advent (cf. Luke 1:17). Moses and Elijah appeared together at the Mt. of Transfiguration (cf. Matt. 17:14) and may be the two witnesses in the Great Tribulation (cf. Rev. 11:1-3). Most likely, this will be an Elijah-like person, as John the Baptist was Elijah-like (*see note on 3:1*). In that day, his task will be to preach reconciliation to God so that souls can believe and be spared God's curse. He will be effective (v. 6).

[k]Before the coming of the great and
dreadful day of the LORD.
6 And he will turn
The hearts of the fathers to the
children,
And the hearts of the children to
their fathers,
Lest I come and [l]strike the earth
with [m]a curse."

5 [k]Joel 2:31
6 [l]Zech. 14:12
[m]Zech. 5:3

4:6 turn…hearts. The very opposite of what occurred at Christ's first coming (cf. Matt. 10:34-36) anticipates a general societal repentance (cf. Matt. 25:31-46; Rev. 7:9-17; 20:4-6), so that complete destruction might be averted. The earth will be restored to Edenic wonder, the curse reversed, the kingdom established with Messiah reigning, and the righteous Jews and Gentiles entering it. **curse.** Not the normal word for curse, this word refers to the practice of devoting things or persons irrevocably to God, often by total destruction. Cities of Canaan were put under the "curse," and thus the people were to be exterminated (cf. Deut. 13:12-18; 20:16ff.). Its use here suggests that God would make a whole burnt offering of the earth if there was not a repentant remnant.

Roman Control of Palestine

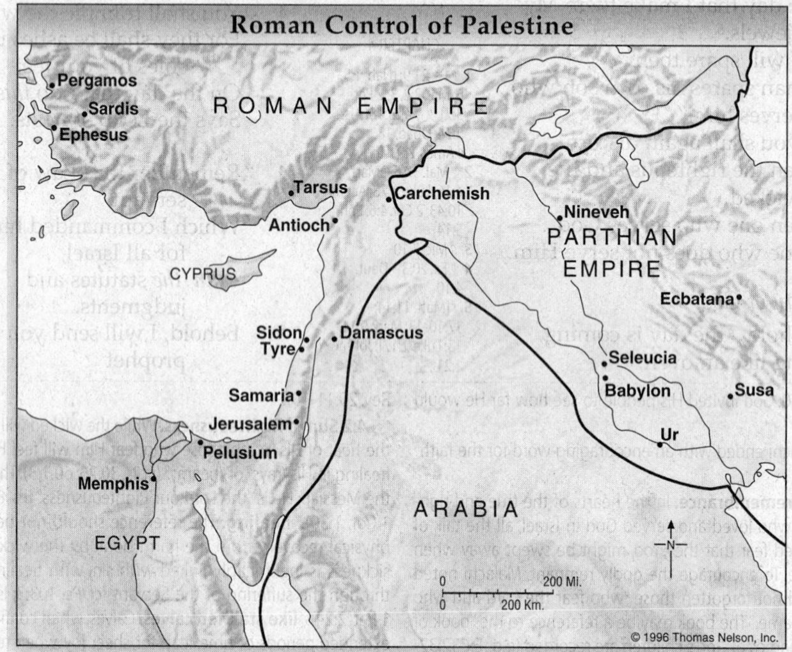

Introduction to the
INTERTESTAMENTAL PERIOD

Over 400 years separated the final events (Neh. 13:4-30) and final prophecy (Mal. 1:1–4:6) recorded in the Old Testament from the beginning actions (Luke 1:5-25) narrated in the New Testament (ca. 424–26 B.C.). Because there was no prophetic word from God during this time, this period is sometimes called "the four hundred silent years." However, the history of these years followed the pattern predicted in Daniel (Dan. 2:24,45; 7:1-28; 8:1-27; 11:1-35) with exact precision. Though the voice of God was silent, the hand of God was actively directing the course of events during these centuries.

Jewish History

As predicted by Daniel, control of the land of Israel passed from the empire of Medo-Persia to Greece and then to Rome (Dan. 2:39,40; 7:5-7). For about 200 years, the Persian Empire ruled the Jews (539–332 B.C.). The Persians allowed the Jews to return, rebuild, and worship at the temple in Jerusalem (2 Chr. 36:22,23; Ezra 1:1-4). For about 100 years after the close of the Old Testament canon, Judea continued to be a Persian territory under the governor of Syria with the High-Priest exercising a measure of civil authority. The Jews were allowed to observe their religious tenets without any official governmental interference.

Between 334 B.C. and 331 B.C., Alexander the Great defeated the Persian king, Darius III, in 3 decisive battles that gave him control of the lands of the Persian Empire. The land of Israel thus passed into Greek control in 332 B.C. (Dan. 8:5-7,20,21; 11:3). Alexander permitted the Jews in Judea to observe their laws and granted them an exemption from taxes during their sabbatical years. However, Alexander sought to bring Greek culture, called "Hellenism," to the lands he had conquered. He wished to create a world united by Greek language and thinking. This policy, carried on by Alexander's successors, was as dangerous to the religion of Israel as the cult of Baal had been, because the Greek way of life was attractive, sophisticated, and humanly appealing, but utterly ungodly.

Upon Alexander's death in 323 B.C., a struggle ensued among his generals as his empire was divided (Dan. 8:22; 11:4). Ptolemy I Sater, founder of the Ptolemies of Egypt, took control of Israel, even though an agreement in 301 B.C. assigned it to Seleucus I Nicator, founder of the Seleucids of Syria. This caused continuing contention between the Seleucid and Ptolemaic dynasties (Dan. 11:5). The Ptolemies ruled Judea from 301 B.C. to 198 B.C. (Dan. 11:6-12). Under the Ptolemies, the Jews had comparative religious freedom in a setting of economic oppression.

In 198 B.C., Antiochus III the Great defeated Ptolemy V Epiphanes and took control of Palestine (Dan. 11:13-16). Judea was under Seleucid rule until 143 B.C. (Dan. 11:17-35). Early Seleucid toleration of Jewish religious practices came to an end in the reign of Antiochus IV Epiphanes (175–164 B.C.). Antiochus desecrated and plundered the temple of Jerusalem in 170 B.C. In 167 B.C., Antiochus ordered Hellenization in Palestine and forbade the Jews from keeping their laws, observing the Sabbath, keeping festivals, offering sacrifices, and circumcising their children. Copies of the

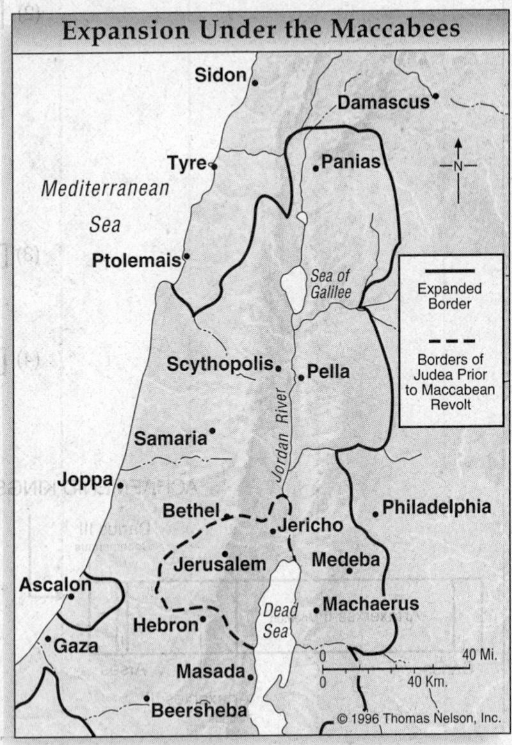

Chronology of the Intertestamental Period

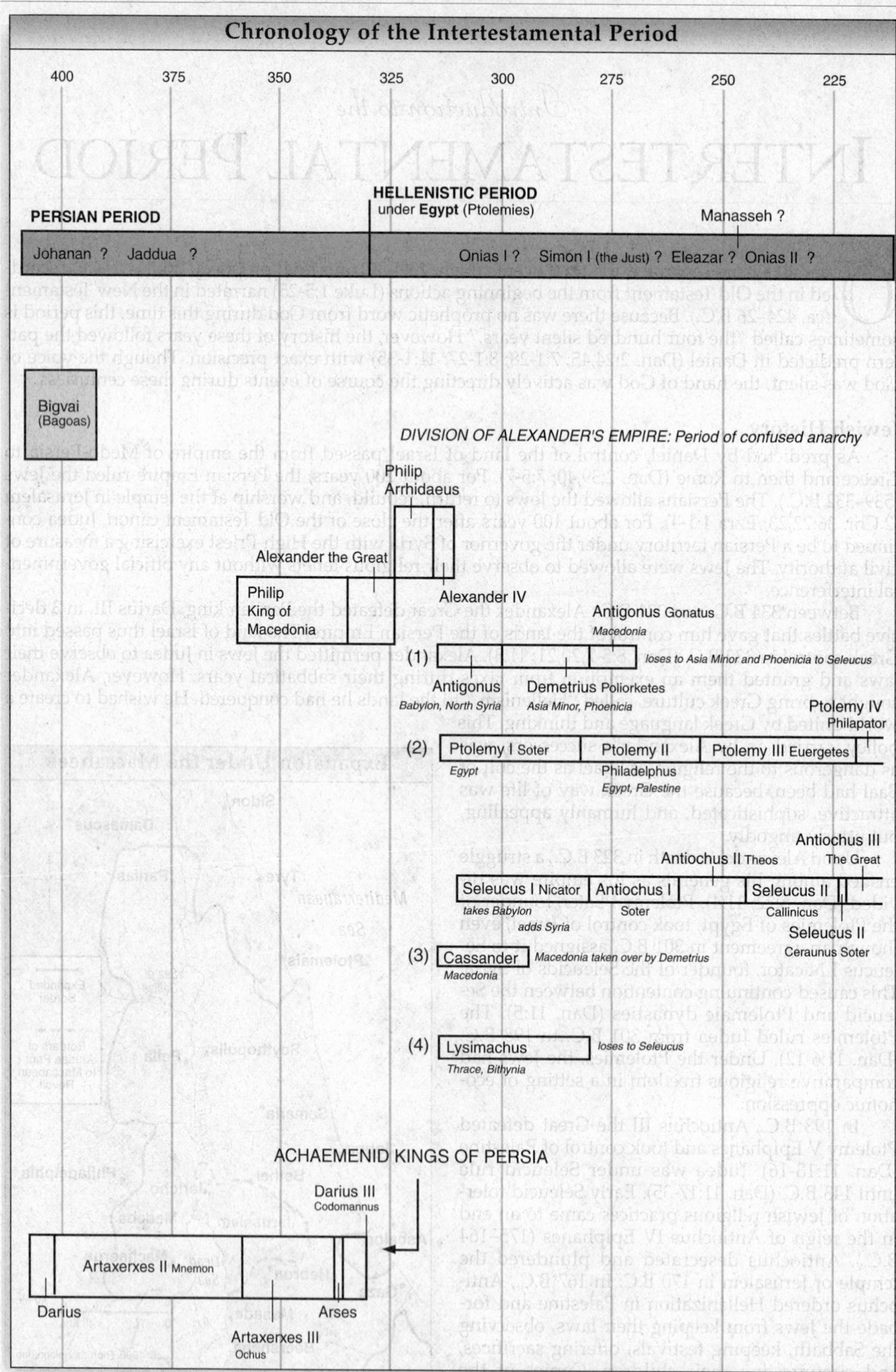
400
375
350
325
300
275
250
225
PERSIAN PERIOD
HELLENISTIC PERIOD
under Egypt (Ptolemies)
Manasseh ?
Johanan ? Jaddua ?
Onias I ? Simon I (the Just) ? Eleazar ? Onias II ?
Bigvai (Bagoas)
DIVISION OF ALEXANDER'S EMPIRE: Period of confused anarchy
Philip Arrhidaeus
Alexander the Great
Philip King of Macedonia
Alexander IV
Antigonus Gonatus
Macedonia
(1)
loses to Asia Minor and Phoenicia to Seleucus
Antigonus
Babylon, North Syria
Demetrius Poliorketes
Asia Minor, Phoenicia
Ptolemy IV
Philapator
(2)
Ptolemy I Soter
Egypt
Ptolemy II
Philadelphus
Egypt, Palestine
Ptolemy III Euergetes
Antiochus III
The Great
Antiochus II Theos
Seleucus I Nicator
takes Babylon
adds Syria
Antiochus I
Soter
Seleucus II
Callinicus
Seleucus II
Ceraunus Soter
(3)
Cassander
Macedonia
Macedonia taken over by Demetrius
(4)
Lysimachus
Thrace, Bithynia
loses to Seleucus
ACHAEMENID KINGS OF PERSIA
Darius III
Codomannus
Artaxerxes II Mnemon
Darius
Arses
Artaxerxes III
Ochus

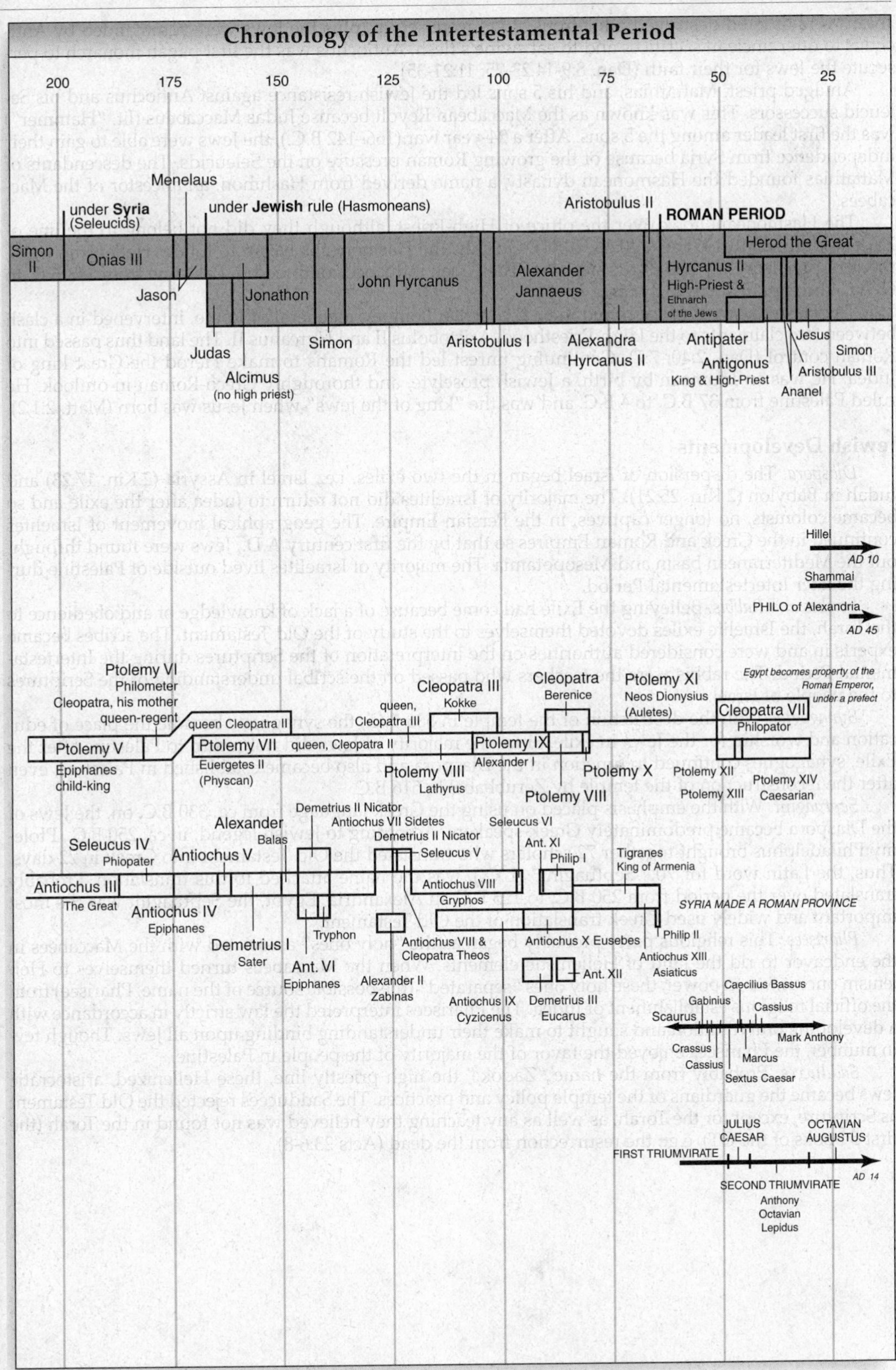

Chronology of the Intertestamental Period
200
175
150
125
100
75
50
25
Menelaus
under Syria (Seleucids)
under Jewish rule (Hasmoneans)
Aristobulus II
ROMAN PERIOD
Simon II
Onias III
Herod the Great
Jason
Jonathon
John Hyrcanus
Alexander Jannaeus
Hyrcanus II High-Priest & Ethnarch of the Jews
Judas
Simon
Aristobulus I
Alexandra
Hyrcanus II
Antipater
Antigonus King & High-Priest
Jesus
Simon
Aristobulus III
Ananel
Alcimus (no high priest)
Hillel
AD 10
Shammai
PHILO of Alexandria
AD 45
Ptolemy VI Philometer
Cleopatra, his mother queen-regent
Cleopatra III Kokke
Cleopatra Berenice
Ptolemy XI Neos Dionysius (Auletes)
Egypt becomes property of the Roman Emperor, under a prefect
queen Cleopatra II
queen, Cleopatra III
Cleopatra VII Philopator
Ptolemy V Epiphanes child-king
Ptolemy VII Euergetes II (Physcan)
queen, Cleopatra II
Ptolemy IX Alexander I
Ptolemy VIII Lathyrus
Ptolemy X
Ptolemy VIII
Ptolemy XII
Ptolemy XIII
Ptolemy XIV Caesarian
Demetrius II Nicator
Antiochus VII Sidetes
Demetrius II Nicator
Seleucus V
Alexander Balas
Seleucus VI
Ant. XI
Seleucus IV Phiopater
Antiochus V
Tigranes King of Armenia
Philip I
Antiochus III The Great
Antiochus VIII Gryphos
Antiochus IV Epiphanes
SYRIA MADE A ROMAN PROVINCE
Tryphon
Demetrius I Sater
Antiochus VIII & Cleopatra Theos
Antiochus X Eusebes
Philip II
Antiochus XIII Asiaticus
Ant. VI Epiphanes
Alexander II Zabinas
Ant. XII
Antiochus IX Cyzicenus
Demetrius III Eucarus
Caecilius Bassus
Gabinius
Cassius
Scaurus
Mark Anthony
Crassus
Cassius
Marcus
Sextus Caesar
JULIUS CAESAR
OCTAVIAN AUGUSTUS
FIRST TRIUMVIRATE
AD 14
SECOND TRIUMVIRATE
Anthony
Octavian
Lepidus

Torah were ordered destroyed, idolatrous altars were set up, plus the Jews were commanded by Antiochus to offer unclean sacrifices and to eat swine's flesh. Antiochus was the first pagan monarch to persecute the Jews for their faith (Dan. 8:9-14,23-25; 11:21-35).

An aged priest, Mattathias, and his 5 sons led the Jewish resistance against Antiochus and his Seleucid successors. This was known as the Maccabean Revolt because Judas Maccabeus (lit. "Hammer") was the first leader among the 5 sons. After a 24-year war (166–142 B.C.), the Jews were able to gain their independence from Syria because of the growing Roman pressure on the Seleucids. The descendants of Mattathias founded the Hasmonean dynasty, a name derived from Hashmon, an ancestor of the Maccabees.

The Hasmoneans took over the office of High-Priest, although they did not belong to the line of Zadok (Num. 25:10-13; Ezek. 40:46; 48:11). Quickly, the Hasmoneans began to follow Hellenistic ways, the very practices they had at first resisted. The Greek influence continued in Palestine from 142 B.C. to 63 B.C. through this native dynasty.

The Hasmonean dynasty ended in 63 B.C. when Pompey, a general of Rome, intervened in a clash between two claimants to the High-Priesthood, Aristobulus II and Hyrcanus II. The land thus passed into Roman control (Dan. 2:40; 7:7). Continuing unrest led the Romans to make Herod the Great king of Judea. He was an Idumean by birth, a Jewish proselyte, and thoroughly Greco-Roman in outlook. He ruled Palestine from 37 B.C. to 4 B.C. and was the "king of the Jews" when Jesus was born (Matt. 2:1,2).

Jewish Developments

Diaspora. The dispersion of Israel began in the two exiles, i.e., Israel in Assyria (2 Kin. 17:23) and Judah in Babylon (2 Kin. 25:21). The majority of Israelites did not return to Judea after the exile and so became colonists, no longer captives, in the Persian Empire. The geographical movement of Israelites continued in the Greek and Roman Empires so that by the first century A.D., Jews were found throughout the Mediterranean basin and Mesopotamia. The majority of Israelites lived outside of Palestine during the later Intertestamental Period.

Scribes and Rabbis. Believing the Exile had come because of a lack of knowledge of and obedience to the Torah, the Israelite exiles devoted themselves to the study of the Old Testament. The scribes became experts in and were considered authorities on the interpretation of the Scriptures during the Intertestamental Period. The rabbis were the teachers who passed on the scribal understanding of the Scriptures to the people of Israel.

Synagogue. With the destruction of the temple in 586 B.C., the synagogue became the place of education and worship for the Jews in exile. Since the majority of Jews did not return to Palestine after the Exile, synagogues continued to function in the Diaspora and also became established in Palestine, even after the reconstruction of the temple by Zerubbabel in 516 B.C.

Septuagint. With the emphasis placed on using the Greek language from ca. 330 B.C. on, the Jews of the Diaspora became predominately Greek-speakers. According to Jewish legend, in ca. 250 B.C., Ptolemy Philadelphus brought together 72 scholars who translated the Old Testament into Greek in 72 days. Thus, the Latin word for 70, "Septuagint" (LXX), was the name attached to this translation. Probably translated over the period from 250 B.C. to 125 B.C. in Alexandria, Egypt, the Septuagint was the most important and widely used Greek translation of the Old Testament.

Pharisees. This religious party probably began as the "holy ones" associated with the Maccabees in the endeavor to rid the land of Hellenistic elements. When the Maccabees turned themselves to Hellenism once it was in power, these holy ones "separated" (the possible source of the name, Pharisee) from the official religious establishment of Judea. The Pharisees interpreted the law strictly in accordance with a developing oral tradition and sought to make their understanding binding upon all Jews. Though few in number, the Pharisees enjoyed the favor of the majority of the people in Palestine.

Sadducees. Probably from the name "Zadok," the high priestly line, these Hellenized, aristocratic Jews became the guardians of the temple policy and practices. The Sadducees rejected the Old Testament as Scripture, except for the Torah, as well as any teaching they believed was not found in the Torah (the first 5 books of the OT), e.g., the resurrection from the dead (Acts 23:6-8).

The NEW TESTAMENT

Introduction to the

GOSPELS

The English word "gospel" derives from the Anglo-Saxon word *godspell,* which can mean either "a story about God," or "a good story." The latter meaning is in harmony with the Greek word translated "gospel," *euangellion,* which means "good news." In secular Greek, *euangellion* referred to a good report about an important event. The 4 gospels are the good news about the most significant events in all of history—the life, sacrificial death, and resurrection of Jesus of Nazareth.

The gospels are not biographies in the modern sense of the word, since they do not intend to present a complete life of Jesus (cf. John 20:30; 21:25). Apart from the birth narratives, they give little information about the first 30 years of Jesus' life. While Jesus' public ministry lasted over 3 years, the gospels focus much of their attention on the last week of His life (cf. John 12-20). Though they are completely accurate historically, and present important biographical details of Jesus' life, the primary purposes of the gospels are theological and apologetic (John 20:31). They provide authoritative answers to questions about Jesus' life and ministry, and they strengthen believers' assurance regarding the reality of their faith (Luke 1:4).

Although many spurious gospels were written, the church from earliest times has accepted only Matthew, Mark, Luke, and John as inspired Scripture. While each gospel has its unique perspective (see the discussion of the "Synoptic Problem" in the Introduction to Mark: Interpretive Challenges), Matthew, Mark, and Luke, when compared to John, share a common point of view. Because of that, they are known as the synoptic (from a Greek word meaning "to see together," or "to share a common point of view") gospels. Matthew, Mark, and Luke, for example, focus on Christ's Galilean ministry, while John focuses on His ministry in Judea. The synoptic gospels contain numerous parables, while John records none. John and the synoptic gospels record only two common events (Jesus' walking on the water, and the feeding of the 5,000) prior to Passion Week. These differences between John and the synoptic gospels, however, are not contradictory, but complementary.

As already noted, each gospel writer wrote from a unique perspective, for a different audience. As a result, each gospel contains distinctive elements. Taken together, the 4 gospels form a complete testimony about Jesus Christ.

Matthew wrote primarily to a Jewish audience, presenting Jesus of Nazareth as Israel's long-awaited Messiah and rightful King. His genealogy, unlike Luke's, focuses on Jesus' royal descent from Israel's greatest king, David. Interspersed throughout Matthew are OT quotes presenting various aspects of Jesus' life and ministry as the fulfillment of OT messianic prophecy. Matthew alone uses the phrase "kingdom of heaven," avoiding the parallel phrase "kingdom of God" because of the unbiblical connotations it had in first-century Jewish thought. Matthew wrote his gospel, then, to strengthen the faith of Jewish Christians, and it provides a useful apologetic tool for Jewish evangelism.

Mark targeted a Gentile audience, especially a Roman one (see Introduction to Mark: Background and Setting). Mark is the gospel of action; the frequent use of "immediately" and "then" keeps his narrative moving rapidly along. Jesus appears in Mark as the Servant (cf. Mark 10:45) who came to suffer for the sins of many. Mark's fast-paced approach would especially appeal to the practical, action-oriented Romans.

Luke addressed a broader Gentile audience. As an educated Greek (see Introduction to Luke: Author and Date), Luke wrote using the most sophisticated literary Greek of any NT writer. He was a careful researcher (Luke 1:1-4) and an accurate historian. Luke portrays Jesus as the Son of Man (a title appearing 26 times), the answer to the needs and hopes of the human race, who came to seek and save lost sinners (Luke 9:56; 19:10).

John, the last gospel written, emphasizes the deity of Jesus Christ (e.g., 5:18; 8:58; 10:30-33; 14:9). John wrote to strengthen the faith of believers and to appeal to unbelievers to come to faith in Christ. The apostle clearly stated his purpose for writing in 20:31: ". . . these are written that you may believe that Jesus is the Christ, the Son of God, and that believing you may have life in His name."

Taken together, the 4 gospels weave a complete portrait of the God-Man, Jesus of Nazareth. In Him were blended perfect humanity and deity, making Him the only sacrifice for the sins of the world, and the worthy Lord of those who believe.

The Roman Empire in the New Testament Era

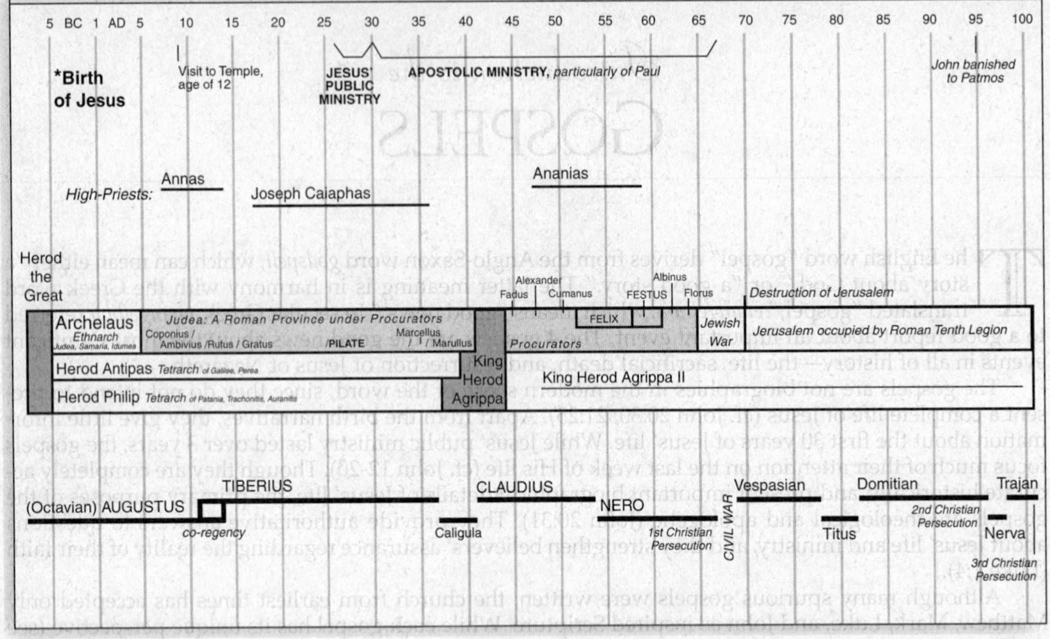

5 BC 1 AD 5 10 15 20 25 30 35 40 45 50 55 60 65 70 75 80 85 90 95 100
*Birth of Jesus
Visit to Temple, age of 12
JESUS' PUBLIC MINISTRY
APOSTOLIC MINISTRY, particularly of Paul
John banished to Patmos
High-Priests:
Annas
Joseph Caiaphas
Ananias
Herod the Great
Alexander
Fadus
Cumanus
Albinus
FESTUS
Florus
Destruction of Jerusalem
Archelaus
Ethnarch
Judea, Samaria, Idumea
Judea: A Roman Province under Procurators
Coponius / Ambivius /Rufus / Gratus
/PILATE
Marcellus / / Marullus
King Herod Agrippa
Procurators
FELIX
Jewish War
Jerusalem occupied by Roman Tenth Legion
Herod Antipas Tetrarch of Galilee, Perea
King Herod Agrippa II
Herod Philip Tetrarch of Patania, Trachonitis, Auranitis
TIBERIUS
CLAUDIUS
Vespasian
Domitian
Trajan
(Octavian) AUGUSTUS
NERO
co-regency
Caligula
1st Christian Persecution
CIVIL WAR
Titus
2nd Christian Persecution
Nerva
3rd Christian Persecution

The Ministries of the Apostles

30 32 34 36 38 40 42 43 44 46 48 50 52 54 56 58 60 62 64 66
First Missionary Journey
Second Missionary Journey
Third Missionary Journey
First Roman Imprisonment
Paul in Damascus and Arabia
"after three years"
18 mo. Corinth
2 yr. 3 mo. Ephesus
Final travels
Paul in Tarsus
Paul in Antioch
"fourteen years after"
Crucifixion Resurrection Pentecost
Martyrdom of Stephen & Conversion of Paul
Paul's first visit to Jerusalem
Martyrdom of James
Famine relief visit to Jerusalem
Jerusalem Council
Arrest in Jerusalem
Caesarean Imprisonment
Voyage to Rome
Release from Imprisonment
Martyrdom of Peter and Paul

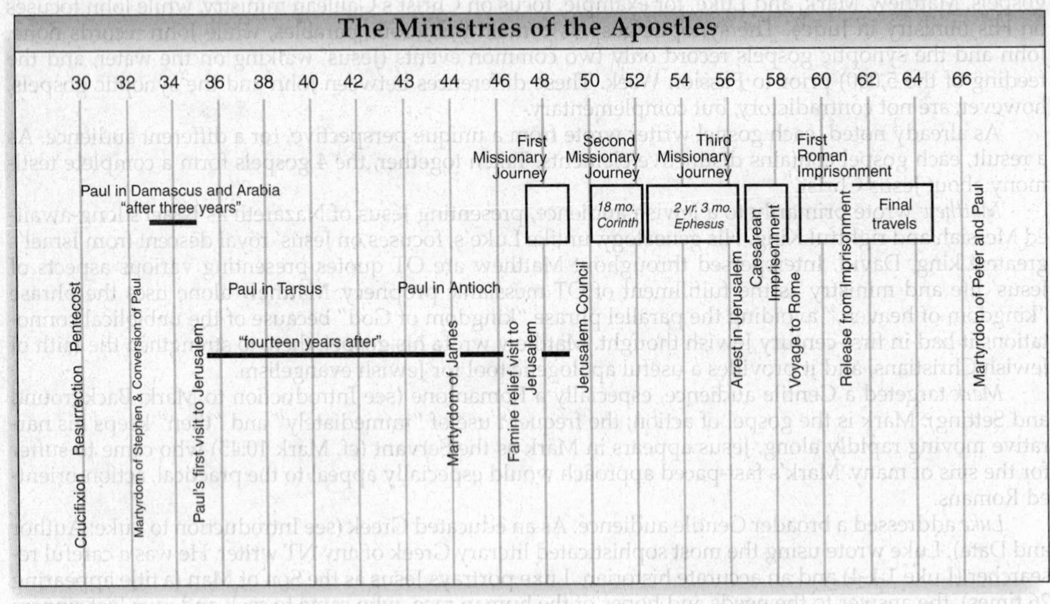

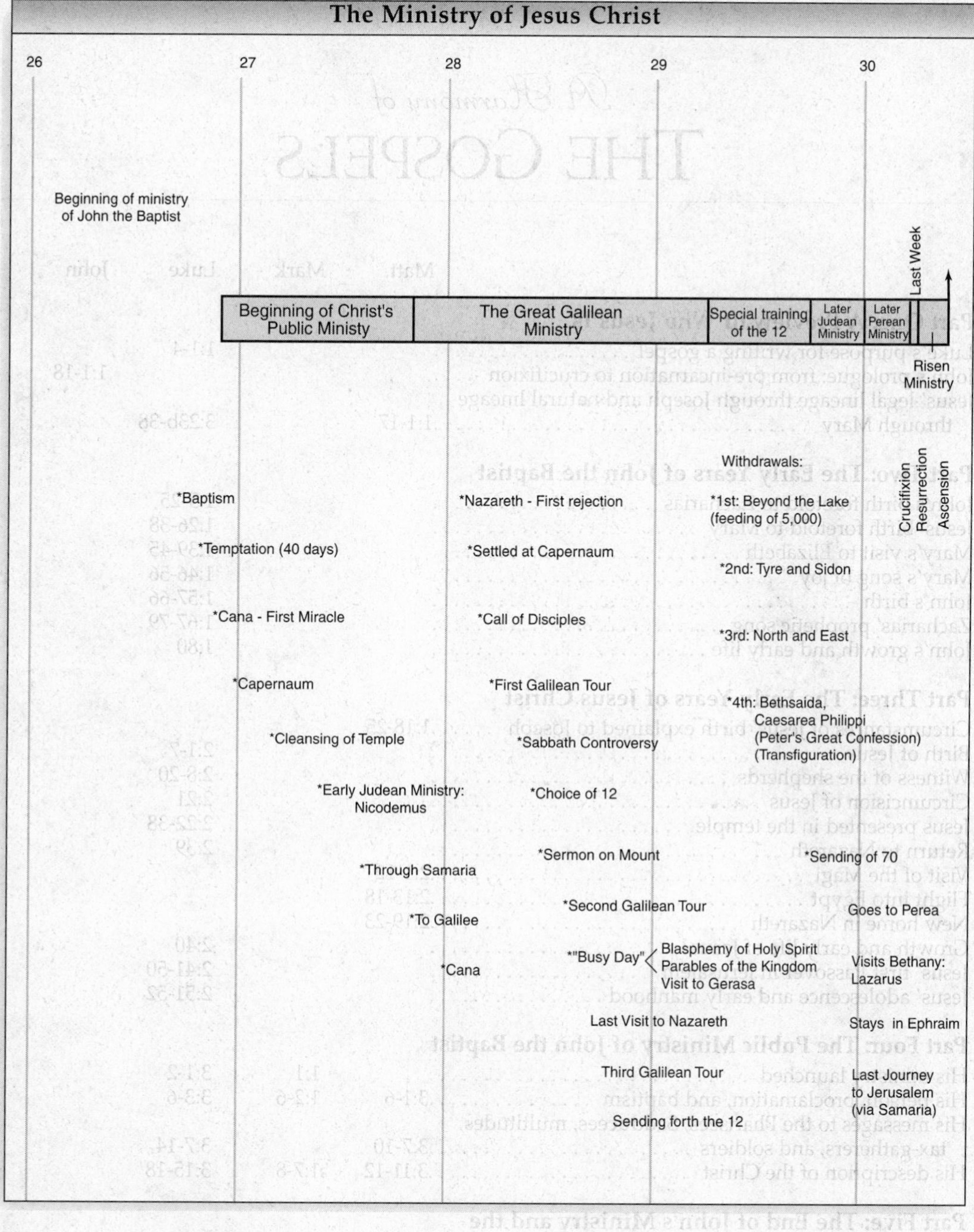
The Ministry of Jesus Christ
26
27
28
29
30
Beginning of ministry of John the Baptist
Last Week
Beginning of Christ's Public Ministy
The Great Galilean Ministry
Special training of the 12
Later Judean Ministry
Later Perean Ministry
Risen Ministry
Withdrawals:
Crucifixion
Resurrection
Ascension
*Baptism
*Temptation (40 days)
*Cana - First Miracle
*Capernaum
*Cleansing of Temple
*Early Judean Ministry: Nicodemus
*Through Samaria
*To Galilee
*Cana
*Nazareth - First rejection
*Settled at Capernaum
*Call of Disciples
*First Galilean Tour
*Sabbath Controversy
*Choice of 12
*Sermon on Mount
*Second Galilean Tour
*"Busy Day"
Blasphemy of Holy Spirit
Parables of the Kingdom
Visit to Gerasa
Last Visit to Nazareth
Third Galilean Tour
Sending forth the 12
*1st: Beyond the Lake (feeding of 5,000)
*2nd: Tyre and Sidon
*3rd: North and East
*4th: Bethsaida, Caesarea Philippi (Peter's Great Confession) (Transfiguration)
*Sending of 70
Goes to Perea
Visits Bethany: Lazarus
Stays in Ephraim
Last Journey to Jerusalem (via Samaria)

A Harmony of THE GOSPELS

	Matt.	Mark	Luke	John
Part One: A Preview of Who Jesus Is				
Luke's purpose for writing a gospel			1:1-4	
John's prologue: from pre-incarnation to crucifixion				1:1-18
Jesus' legal lineage through Joseph and natural lineage through Mary	1:1-17		3:23b-38	
Part Two: The Early Years of John the Baptist				
John's birth foretold to Zacharias			1:5-25	
Jesus' birth foretold to Mary			1:26-38	
Mary's visit to Elizabeth			1:39-45	
Mary's song of joy			1:46-56	
John's birth			1:57-66	
Zacharias' prophetic song			1:67-79	
John's growth and early life			1:80	
Part Three: The Early Years of Jesus Christ				
Circumstances of Jesus' birth explained to Joseph	1:18-25			
Birth of Jesus			2:1-7	
Witness of the shepherds			2:8-20	
Circumcision of Jesus			2:21	
Jesus presented in the temple			2:22-38	
Return to Nazareth			2:39	
Visit of the Magi	2:1-12			
Flight into Egypt	2:13-18			
New home in Nazareth	2:19-23			
Growth and early life of Jesus			2:40	
Jesus' first Passover in Jerusalem			2:41-50	
Jesus' adolescence and early manhood			2:51-52	
Part Four: The Public Ministry of John the Baptist				
His ministry launched		1:1	3:1-2	
His person, proclamation, and baptism	3:1-6	1:2-6	3:3-6	
His messages to the Pharisees, Sadducees, multitudes, tax-gatherers, and soldiers	3:7-10		3:7-14	
His description of the Christ	3:11-12	1:7-8	3:15-18	
Part Five: The End of John's Ministry and the Beginning of Christ's (largely in Judea)				
Jesus' baptism by John	3:13-17	1:9-11	3:21-23a	
Jesus' temptation in the wilderness	4:1-11	1:12-13	4:1-13	
John's self-indentification to the priests and Levites				1:19-28
John's identification of Jesus as the Son of God				1:29-34
Jesus' first followers				1:35-51
First miracle, water becomes wine				2:1-11
Visit at Capernaum with His disciples				2:12
First cleansing of the temple at the Passover				2:13-22
An early response to Jesus' miracle				2:23-25

	Matt.	Mark	Luke	John
Nicodemus' interview with Jesus				3:1-21
John superseded by Jesus				3:22-36
Jesus' departure from Judea	4:12	1:14a	3:19-20; 4:14a	4:1-4
Discussion with a Samaritan woman				4:5-26
Challenge of a spiritual harvest				4:27-38
Evangelization of Sychar				4:39-42
Arrival in Galilee				4:43-45
Part Six: The Ministry of Christ in Galilee				
OPPOSITION AT HOME AND A NEW HEADQUARTERS				
Nature of the Galilean ministry	4:17	1:14b-15	4:14b-15	
Child at Capernaum healed by Jesus while at Cana				4:46-54
Ministry and rejection at Nazareth			4:16-31	
Move to Capernaum	4:13-16			
DISCIPLES CALLED AND MINISTRY THROUGHOUT GALILEE				
First call of the four	4:18-22	1:16-20		
Teaching in the synagogue of Capernaum authenticated by healing a demoniac		1:21-28	4:31b-37	
Peter's mother-in-law and others healed	8:14-17	1:29-34	4:38-41	
Tour of Galilee with Simon and others	4:23-24	1:35-39	4:42-44	
Second call of the four			5:1-11	
Cleansing of a leper followed by much publicity	8:2-4	1:40-45	5:12-16	
Forgiving and healing of a paralytic	9:1-8	2:1-12	5:17-26	
Call of Matthew	9:9	2:13-14	5:27-28	
Banquet at Matthew's house	9:10-13	2:15-17	5:29-32	
Changed conditions with the Messiah present explained by three illustrations	9:14-17	2:18-22	5:33-39	
SABBATH CONTROVERSIES AND WITHDRAWAL				
A lame man healed in Jerusalem on the Sabbath				5:1-9
Effort to kill Jesus for breaking the Sabbath and saying He was equal with God				5:10-18
Discourse demonstrating the Son's equality with the Father				5:19-47
Controversy over disciples' picking grain on the Sabbath	12:1-8	2:23-28	6:1-5	
Healing of a man's withered hand on the Sabbath	12:9-14	3:1-6	6:6-11	
Withdrawal to the Sea of Galilee with a great multitude from many places	12:15-21; 4:25	3:7-12		
APPOINTMENT OF THE TWELVE AND SERMON ON THE MOUNT				
Twelve apostles named		3:13-19	6:12-16	
Setting of the Sermon	5:1-2		6:17-19	
Blessings of those who inherit the kingdom and woes to those who do not	5:3-12		6:20-26	
Responsibility while awaiting the kingdom	5:13-16			
Law, righteousness, and the kingdom	5:17-20			
Six contrasts in interpreting the law	5:21-48		6:27-30, 32-36	
Three hypocritical practices to be avoided	6:1-18			
Three prohibitions against avarice, harsh judgement, and unwise exposure of sacred things	6:19–7:6		6:37-42	
Application and conclusion	7:7-27		6:31,43-49	
Reaction of the multitudes	7:28-29			
GROWING FAME AND EMPHASIS ON REPENTANCE				
A certain centurion's faith and the healing of his servant	8:1,5-13		7:1-10	
A widow's son raised at Nain			7:11-17	
John the Baptist's relationship to the kingdom	11:2-19		7:18-35	
Woes upon Chorazin and Bethsaida for failure to repent	11:20-30			

	Matt.	Mark	Luke	John
Christ's feet annointed by a sinful, but contrite, woman			7:36-50	
FIRST PUBLIC REJECTION BY JEWISH LEADERS				
A tour with the twelve and other followers			8:1-3	
Blasphemous accusation by the scribes and Pharisees	12:22-37	3:20-30		
Request for a sign refused	12:38-45			
Announcement of new spiritual ties	12:46-50	3:31-35	8:19-21	
PARABOLIC MYSTERIES ABOUT THE KINGDOM				
To the Crowds by the Sea				
The setting of the parables	13:1-3a	4:1-2	8:4	
The parable of the soils	13:3b-23	4:3-25	8:5-18	
The parable of the seed's spontaneous growth		4:26-29		
The parable of the tares	13:24-30			
The parable of the mustard tree	13:31-32	4:30-32		
The parable of the leavened loaf	13:33-35	4:33-34		
To the Disciples in the House				
The parable of the tares explained	13:36-43			
The parable of the hidden treasure	13:44			
The parable of the pearl of great price	13:45-46			
The parable of the dragnet	13:47-50			
The parable of the householder	13:51-52			
CONTINUING OPPOSITION				
Departure across the sea and calming the storm	13:53; 8:18,23-27	4:35-41	8:22-25	
Healing the Gerasene demoniacs and resultant opposition	8:28-34	5:1-20	8:26-39	
Return to Galilee, healing of woman who touched Christ's garment, and raising of Jairus' daughter	9:18-26	5:21-43	8:40-56	
Three miracles of healing and another blasphemous accusation	9:27-34			
Final visit to unbelieving Nazareth	13:54-58	6:1-6a		
FINAL GALILEAN CAMPAIGN				
Shortage of workers	9:35-38	6:6b		
Commissioning of the twelve	10:1-42	6:7-11	9:1-5	
Workers sent out	11:1	6:12-13	9:6	
Antipas' mistaken identification of Jesus	14:1-2	6:14-16	9:7-9	
Earlier imprisonment and beheading of John the Baptist	14:3-12	6:17-29		
Return of the workers		6:30	9:10a	

Part Seven: The Ministry of Christ Around Galilee

	Matt.	Mark	Luke	John
LESSON ON THE BREAD OF LIFE				
Withdrawal from Galilee	14:13-14	6:31-34	9:10b-11	6:1-3
Feeding the 5,000	14:15-21	6:35-44	9:12-17	6:4-13
A premature attempt to make Jesus king blocked	14:22-23	6:45-46		6:14-15
Walking on the water during a storm at sea	14:24-33	6:47-52		6:16-21
Healings at Gennesaret	14:34-36	6:53-56		
Discourse on the true bread of life				6:22-59
Defection among the disciples				6:60-71
LESSON ON THE LEAVEN OF THE PHARISEES, SADDUCESS, AND HERODIANS				
Conflict over the tradition of ceremonial defilement	15:1-20	7:1-23		7:1
Ministry to a believing Gentile woman in Tyre and Sidon	15:21-28	7:24-30		
Healings in Decapolis	15:29-31	7:31-37		
Feeding the 4,000 in Decapolis	15:32-38	8:1-9		
Return to Galilee and encounter with the Pharisees and Sadducees	15:39–16:4	8:10-12		
Warning about the error of the Pharisees, Sadducees, and Herodians	16:5-12	8:13-21		
Healing a blind man at Bethsaida		8:22-26		

	Matt.	Mark	Luke	John
LESSON OF MESSIAHSHIP LEARNED AND CONFIRMED				
Peter's identification of Jesus as the Christ, and first prophecy of the church	16:13-20	8:27-30	9:18-21	
First direct prediction of the rejection, crucifixion, and resurrection	16:21-26	8:31-37	9:22-25	
Coming of the Son of Man and judgment	16:27-28	8:38–9:1	9:26-27	
Transfiguration of Jesus	17:1-8	9:2-8	9:28-36a	
Command to keep transfiguration a secret	17:9	9:9-10	9:36b	
Elijah, John the Baptist, and the Son of Man's coming	17:10-13	9:11-13		
LESSONS ON RESPONSIBILITY TO OTHERS				
Healing of the demoniac boy, and faithfulessness rebuked	17:14-20, [21]	9:14-29	9:37-43a	
Second prediction of the resurrection	17:22-23	9:30-32	9:43b-45	
Payment of the temple tax	17:24-27			
Rivalry over greatness dispelled	18:1-5	9:33-37	9:46-48	
Warning against causing believers to stumble	18:6-14	9:38-50	9:49-50	
Treatment and forgiveness of a sinning brother	18:15-35			
JOURNEY TO JERUSALEM FOR THE FEAST OF TABERNACLES (BOOTHS)				
Ridicule by the Lord's half-brothers				7:2-9
Journey through Samaria			9:51-56	7:10
Complete commitment required of followers	8:19-22		9:57-62	

Part Eight: The Later Judean Ministry of Christ

	Matt.	Mark	Luke	John
TEACHINGS AT THE FEAST OF TABERNACLES (BOOTHS)				
Mixed reaction to Jesus' teaching and miracles				7:11-31
Frustrated attempt to arrest Jesus				7:32-52
[Jesus' forgiveness of an adulteress]				[7:53–8:11]
Conflict over Jesus' claim to be the light of the world				8:12-20
Invitation to believe in Jesus				8:21-30
Relationship to Abraham, and attempted stoning				8:31-59
PRIVATE LESSONS ON LOVING SERVICE AND PRAYER				
Commissioning of the seventy			10:1-16	
Return of the seventy			10:17-24	
Story of the good Samaritan			10:25-37	
Jesus' visit with Mary and Martha			10:38-42	
Lesson on how to pray and parable of the importunate friend			11:1-13	
SECOND DEBATE WITH THE SCRIBES AND PHARISEES				
A third blasphemous accusation and a second debate			11:14-36	
Woes against the scribes and Pharisees while eating with a Pharisee			11:37-54	
Warning the disciples about hypocrisy			12:1-12	
Warning about greed and trust in wealth			12:13-34	
Warning against being unprepared for the Son of Man's coming			12:35-48	
Warning about the coming division			12:49-53	
Warning against failing to discern the present time			12:54-59	
Two alternatives: repent or perish			13:1-9	
Opposition from a synagogue official for healing a woman on the Sabbath			13:10-21	
TEACHING AT THE FEAST OF DEDICATION				
Healing of a man born blind				9:1-7
Reaction of the blind man's neighbors				9:8-12
Examination and excommunication of the blind man by the Pharisees				9:13-34
Jesus' identification of Himself to the blind man				9:35-38

	Matt.	Mark	Luke	John
Spiritual blindness of the Pharisees				9:39-41
Allegory of the Good Shepherd and the thief				10:1-18
Further division among the Jews				10:19-21
Another attempt to stone or arrest Jesus for blasphemy				10:22-39
Part Nine: The Ministry of Christ in and around Perea				
PRINCIPLES OF DISCIPLESHIP				
From Jerusalem to Perea				10:40-42
Question about salvation and entering the kingdom			13:22-30	
Anticipation of His coming death and lament over Jerusalem			13:31-35	
Healing of a man with dropsy while eating with a Pharisaic leader on the Sabbath			14:1-24	
Cost of discipleship			14:25-35	
Parables in defense of associations with sinners			15:1-32	
Parable to teach the proper use of money			16:1-13	
Story to teach the danger of wealth			16:14-31	
Four lessons on discipleship			17:1-10	
RAISING OF LAZARUS AND A BRIEF TOUR THROUGH SAMARIA AND GALILEE				
Sickness and death of Lazarus				11:1-16
Lazarus raised from the dead				11:17-44
Decision of the Sanhedrin to put Jesus to death				11:45-54
Healing of ten lepers while passing through Samaria and Galilee			17:11-21	
Instructions regarding the Son of Man's coming			17:22-37	
TEACHING WHILE ON FINAL JOURNEY TO JERUSALEM				
Two parables on prayer: the importunate widow and the Pharisee and the publican			18:1-14	
Conflict with the Pharisaic teaching on divorce	19:1-12	10:1-12		
Example of little children in relation to the kingdom	19:13-15	10:13-16	18:15-17	
Riches and the kingdom	19:16-30	10:17-31	18:18-30	
Parable of the landowner's sovereignty	20:1-16			
Third prediction of the resurrection	20:17-19	10:32-34	18:31-34	
Warning against ambitious pride	20:20-28	10:35-45		
Healing of blind Bartimaeus and his companion	20:29-34	10:46-52	18:35-43	
Salvation of Zacchaeus			19:1-10	
Parable to teach responsibility while the kingdom is delayed			19:11-28	
Part Ten: The Formal Presentation of Christ to Israel and the Resulting Conflict				
TRIUMPHAL ENTRY AND THE FIG TREE				
Arrival at Bethany				11:55–12:1
Mary's anointing of Jesus for burial	26:6-13	14:3-9		12:2-11
Triumphal entry into Jerusalem	21:1-11, 14-17	11:1-11	19:29-44	12:12-19
Cursing of the fig tree having leaves but no figs	21:18-19a	11:12-14		
Second cleansing of the temple	21:12-13	11:15-18	19:45-48	
Request of some Greeks and necessity of the Son of Man's being lifted up				12:20-36a
Departure from the unbelieving multitude and Jesus' response				12:36b-50
Withered fig tree and the lesson on faith	21:19b-22	11:19-25,[26]		
OFFICIAL CHALLENGE OF CHRIST'S AUTHORITY				
A question by the chief priests, scribes, and elders	21:23-27	11:27-33	20:1-8	

	Matt.	Mark	Luke	John
Faithful discharge of responsibility taught by 3 parables	21:28–22:14	12:1-12	20:9-19	
A question by the Pharisees and Herodians	22:15-22	12:13-17	20:20-26	
A question by the Sadducees	22:23-33	12:18-27	20:27-40	
A question by a Pharisee scribe	22:34-40	12:28-34		
CHRIST'S RESPONSE TO HIS ENEMIES' CHALLENGES				
Christ's relationship to David as Son and Lord	22:41-46	12:35-37	20:41-44	
Seven woes against the scribes and Pharisees	23:1-36	12:38-40	20:45-47	
Lament over Jerusalem	23:37-39			
A poor widow's gift of all she had		12:41-44	21:1-4	
Part Eleven: Prophecies in Preparation for the Death of Christ				
THE OLIVET DISCOURSE: PROPHECIES ABOUT THE TEMPLE AND THE RETURN OF CHRIST				
Setting of the discourse	24:1-3	13:1-4	21:5-7	
Beginning of birth pangs	24:4-14	13:5-13	21:8-19	
Abomination of desolation and subsequent distress	24:15-28	13:14-23	21:20-24	
Coming of the Son of Man	24:29-31	13:24-27	21:25-27	
Signs of nearness, but unknown time	24:32-41	13:28-32	21:28-33	
Five parables to teach watchfulness and faithfulness	24:42–25:30	13:33-37	21:34-36	
Judgment at the Son of Man's coming	25:31-46			
ARRANGEMENTS FOR BETRAYAL				
Plot by the Sanhedrin to arrest and kill Jesus	26:1-5	14:1-2	21:37–22:2	
Judas' agreement to betray Jesus	26:14-16	14:10-11	22:3-6	
THE LAST SUPPER				
Preparation for the Passover meal	26:17-19	14:12-16	22:7-13	
Beginning of the Passover meal	26:20	14:17	22:14-16	
Washing the disciples' feet				13:1-20
Indentification of the betrayer	26:21-25	14:18-21	22:21-23	13:21-30
Dissension among the disciples over greatness			22:24-30	
First prediction of Peter's denial			22:31-38	13:31-38
Conclusion of the meal and the Lord's Supper instituted (1 Cor. 11:23-26)	26:26-29	14:22-25	22:17-20	
DISCOURSE AND PRAYERS FROM THE UPPER ROOM TO GETHSEMANE				
Questions about His destination, the Father, and the Holy Spirit answered				14:1-31
The Vine and the branches				15:1-17
Opposition from the world				15:18–16:4
Coming and ministry of the Spirit				16:5-15
Prediction of joy over His resurrection				16:16-22
Promise of answered prayer and peace				16:23-33
Jesus' prayer for His disciples and all who will believe				17:1-26
Second prediction of Peter's denial	16:30-35	14:26-31	22:39-40a	18:1
Jesus' 3 agonizing prayers in Gethsemane	26:36-46	14:32-42	22:40b-46	
Part Twelve: The Death of Christ				
BETRAYAL AND ARREST				
Jesus betrayed, arrested, and forsaken	26:47-56	14:43-52	22:47-53	18:2-12
TRIAL				
First Jewish phase, before Anna				18:13-24
Second Jewish phase, before Caiaphas and the Sanhedrin	26:57-68	14:53-65	22:54	
Peter's denials	26:69-75	14:66-72	22:55-65	18:25-27
Third Jewish phase, before the Sanhedrin	27:1	15:1a	22:66-71	

	Matt.	Mark	Luke	John
Remorse and suicide of Judas Iscariot (Acts 1:18-19)	27:3-10			
First Roman phase, before Pilate	27:2,11-14	15:1b-5	23:1-5	18:28-38
Second Roman phase, before Herod Antipas			23:6-12	
Third Roman phase, before Pilate	27:15-26	15:6-15	23:13-25	18:39–19:16
CRUCIFIXION				
Mockery by the Roman soldiers	27:27-30	15:16-19		
Journey to Golgotha	27:31-34	15:20-23	23:26-33a	19:17
First 3 hours of crucifixion	27:35-44	15:24-32	23:33b-43	19:18-27
Last 3 hours of crucifixion	27:45-50	15:33-37	23:44-45a, 46	19:28-30
Witnesses of Jesus' death	27:51-56	15:38-41	23:45b, 47-49	
BURIAL				
Certification of death and procurement of the body	27:57-58	15:42-45	23:50-52	19:31-38
Jesus' body placed in a tomb	27:59-60	15:46	23:53-54	19:39-42
Tomb watched by the women and guarded by the soldiers	27:61-66	15:47	23:55-56	

Part Thirteen: The Resurrection and Ascension of Christ

	Matt.	Mark	Luke	John
THE EMPTY TOMB				
The tomb visited by the women	28:1	16:1		
The stone rolled away	28:2-4			
The tomb found to be empty by the women	28:5-8	16:2-8	24:1-8	20:1
The tomb found the be empty by Peter and John			24:9-11, [12]	20:2-10
THE POST-RESURRECTION APPEARANCES				
Appearance to Mary Magdalene		[16:9-11]		20:11-18
Appearance to the other women	28:9-10			
Report of the soldiers to the Jewish authorities	28:11-15			
Appearance to two disciples traveling to Emmaus		[16:12-13]	24:13-32	
Report of the two disciples to the rest (1 Cor. 15:5a)			24:33-35	
Appearance to the 10 assembled disciples		[16:14]	24:36-43	20:19-25
Appearance to the 11 assembled disciples (1 Cor. 15:5b)				20:26-31
Appearance to the 7 disciples while fishing				21:1-25
Appearance to the 11 in Galilee (1 Cor. 15:6)	28:16-20	[16:15-18]		
Appearance to James, His brother (1 Cor. 15:7)				
Appearance to the disciples in Jerusalem (Acts 1:3-8)			24:44-49	
THE ASCENSION				
Christ's parting blessing and departure (Acts 1:9-12)		[16:19-20]	24:50-53	

A Brief Overview of Christ's Life

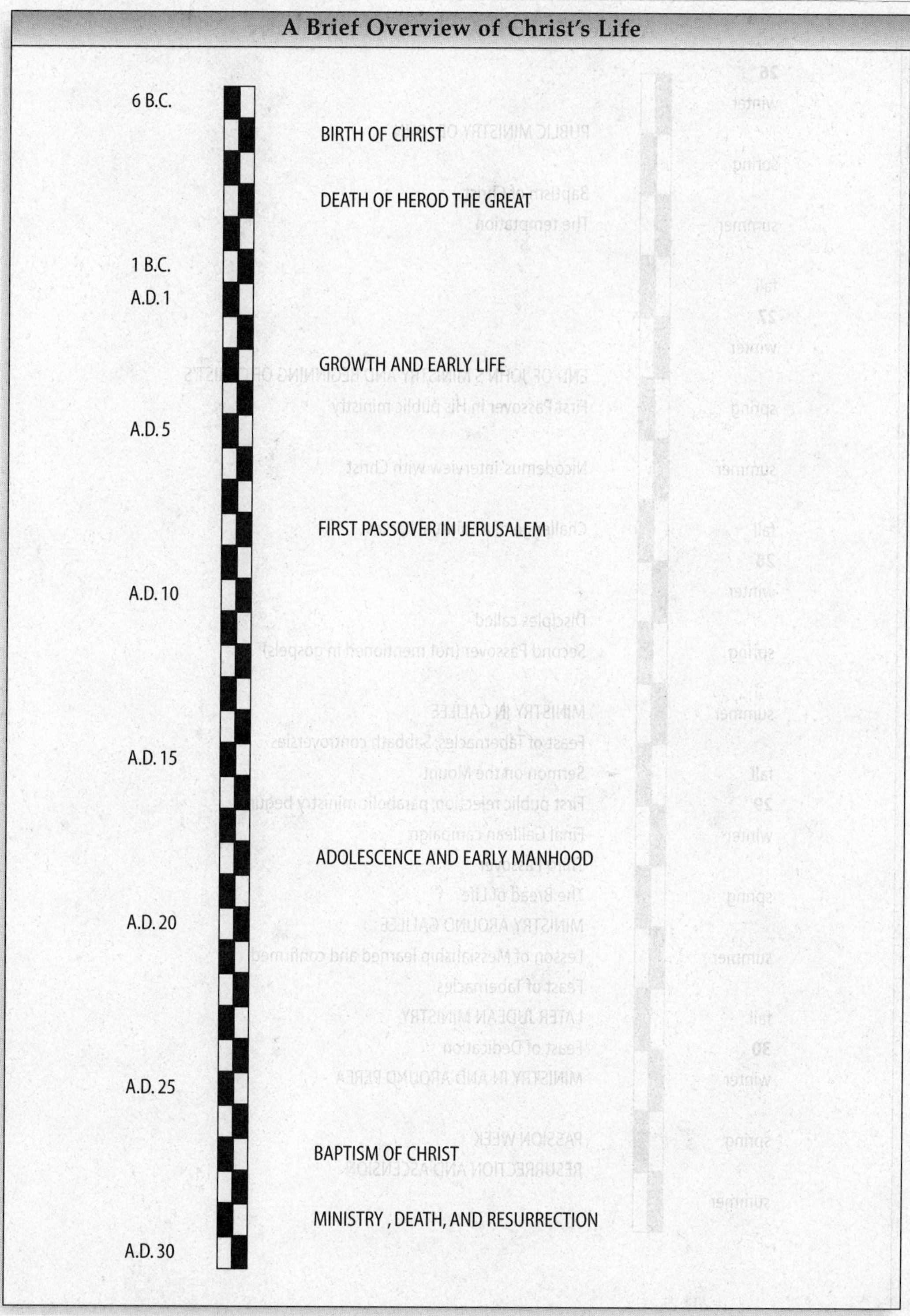

A Brief Overview of Christ's Ministry

26	
winter	
	PUBLIC MINISTRY OF JOHN
spring	
	Baptism of Christ
summer	The temptation
fall	
27	
winter	
	END OF JOHN'S MINISTRY AND BEGINNING OF CHRIST'S
spring	First Passover in His public ministry
summer	Nicodemus' interview with Christ
fall	Challenge of a spiritual harvest
28	
winter	
	Disciples called
spring	Second Passover (not mentioned in gospels)
summer	MINISTRY IN GALILEE
	Feast of Tabernacles; Sabbath controversies
fall	Sermon on the Mount
29	First public rejection; parabolic ministry begun
winter	Final Galilean campaign
	Third Passover
spring	The Bread of Life
	MINISTRY AROUND GALILEE
summer	Lesson of Messiahship learned and confirmed
	Feast of Tabernacles
fall	LATER JUDEAN MINISTRY
30	Feast of Dedication
winter	MINISTRY IN AND AROUND PEREA
spring	PASSION WEEK
	RESURRECTION AND ASCENSION
summer	

The Passovers of Christ's Ministry

A.D. 27	First Passover of Christ's ministry
A.D. 28	Second Passover of Christ's ministry
A.D. 29	Third Passover of Christ's ministry
A.D. 30	Crucifixion of Christ

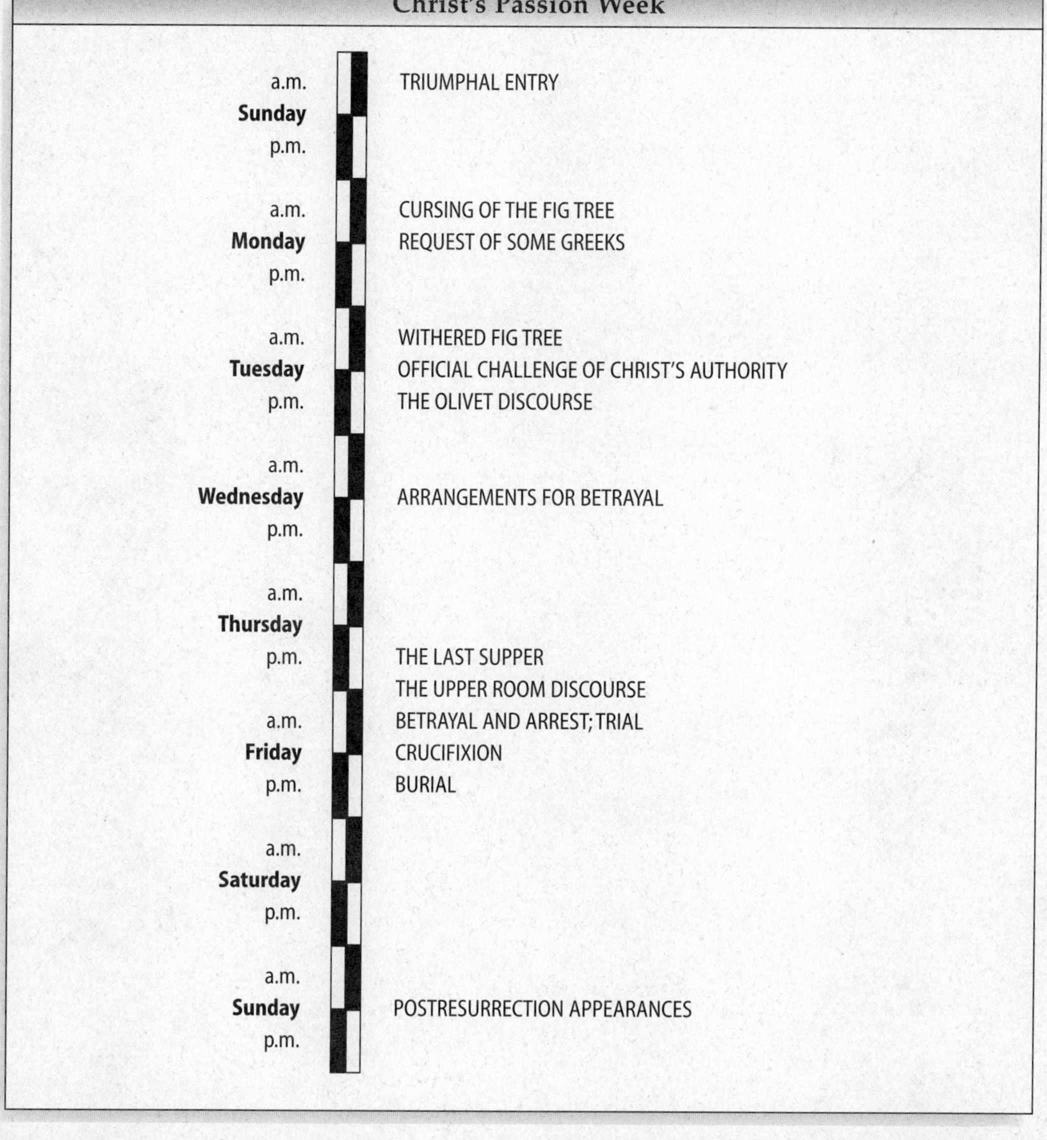

Christ's Passion Week
a.m.
Sunday
p.m.
TRIUMPHAL ENTRY
a.m.
Monday
p.m.
CURSING OF THE FIG TREE
REQUEST OF SOME GREEKS
a.m.
Tuesday
p.m.
WITHERED FIG TREE
OFFICIAL CHALLENGE OF CHRIST'S AUTHORITY
THE OLIVET DISCOURSE
a.m.
Wednesday
p.m.
ARRANGEMENTS FOR BETRAYAL
a.m.
Thursday
p.m.
THE LAST SUPPER
THE UPPER ROOM DISCOURSE
a.m.
Friday
p.m.
BETRAYAL AND ARREST; TRIAL
CRUCIFIXION
BURIAL
a.m.
Saturday
p.m.
a.m.
Sunday
p.m.
POSTRESURRECTION APPEARANCES

The Gospel According to
MATTHEW

Title

Matthew, meaning "gift of the Lord," was the other name of Levi (9:9), the tax collector who left everything to follow Christ (Luke 5:27,28). Matthew was one of the 12 apostles (10:3; Mark 3:18; Luke 6:15; Acts 1:13). In his own list of the 12, he explicitly calls himself a "tax collector" (10:3). Nowhere else in Scripture is the name Matthew associated with "tax collector"; the other evangelists always employ his former name, Levi, when speaking of his sinful past. This is evidence of humility on Matthew's part. As with the other 3 gospels, this work is known by the name of its author.

Author and Date

The canonicity and Matthean authorship of this gospel were unchallenged in the early church. Eusebius (ca. A.D. 265–339) quotes Origen (ca. A.D. 185–254):

> Among the four Gospels, which are the only indisputable ones in the Church of God under heaven, I have learned by tradition that the first was written by Matthew, who was once a publican, but afterwards an apostle of Jesus Christ, and it was prepared for the converts from Judaism (*Ecclesiastical History,* 6:25).

It is clear that this gospel was written at a relatively early date—prior to the destruction of the temple in A.D. 70. Some scholars have proposed a date as early as A.D. 50. For a further discussion of some of the issues related to the authorship and dating of this gospel, especially "The Synoptic Problem," see Introduction to Mark: Interpretive Challenges.

Background and Setting

The Jewish flavor of Matthew's gospel is remarkable. This is evident even in the opening genealogy, which Matthew traces back only as far as Abraham. In contrast, Luke, aiming to show Christ as the Redeemer of humanity, goes all the way back to Adam. Matthew's purpose is somewhat narrower: to demonstrate that Christ is the King and Messiah of Israel. This gospel quotes more than 60 times from OT prophetic passages, emphasizing how Christ is the fulfillment of all those promises.

The probability that Matthew's audience was predominantly Jewish is further evident from several facts: Matthew usually cites Jewish custom without explaining it, in contrast to the other gospels (cf. Mark 7:3; John 19:40). He constantly refers to Christ as "the Son of David" (1:1; 9:27; 12:23; 15:22; 20:30; 21:9,15; 22:42,45). Matthew even guards Jewish sensibilities regarding the name of God, referring to "the kingdom of heaven" where the other evangelists speak of "the kingdom of God." All the book's major themes are rooted in the OT and set in light of Israel's messianic expectations.

Matthew's use of Greek may suggest that he was writing as a Palestinian Jew to Hellenistic Jews elsewhere. He wrote as an eyewitness of many of the events he described, giving firsthand testimony about the words and works of Jesus of Nazareth.

His purpose is clear: to demonstrate that Jesus is the Jewish nation's long-awaited Messiah. His voluminous quoting of the OT is specifically designed to show the tie between the Messiah of promise and the Christ of history. This purpose is never out of focus for Matthew, and he even adduces many incidental details from the OT prophecies as proofs of Jesus' messianic claims (e.g., 2:17,18; 4:13-15; 13:35; 21:4,5; 27:9,10).

Historical and Theological Themes

Since Matthew is concerned with setting forth Jesus as Messiah, the King of the Jews, an interest in the OT kingdom promises runs throughout this gospel. Matthew's signature phrase "the kingdom of heaven" occurs 32 times in this book (and nowhere else in all of Scripture).

The opening genealogy is designed to document Christ's credentials as Israel's king, and the rest of the book completes this theme. Matthew shows that Christ is the heir of the kingly line. He demonstrates that He is the fulfillment of dozens of OT prophecies regarding the king who would come. He offers evidence after evidence to establish Christ's kingly prerogative. All other historical and theological themes in the book revolve around this one.

Matthew records 5 major discourses: the Sermon on the Mount (chaps. 5–7); the commissioning of the apostles (chap. 10); the parables about the kingdom (chap. 13); a discourse about the childlikeness of the believer (chap. 18); and the discourse on His second coming (chaps. 24,25). Each discourse ends with a variation of this phrase: "when Jesus had ended these sayings" (7:28; 11:1; 13:53; 19:1; 26:1). That becomes a motif signaling a new narrative portion. A long opening section (chaps. 1–4) and a short conclusion (28:16-20), bracket the rest of the gospel, which naturally divides into 5 sections, each with a discourse and a narrative section. Some have seen a parallel between these 5 sections and the 5 books of Moses in the OT.

The conflict between Christ and Pharisaism is another common theme in Matthew's gospel. But Matthew is keen to show the error of the Pharisees for the benefit of his Jewish audience—not for personal or self-aggrandizing reasons. Matthew omits, for example, the parable of the Pharisee and the tax collector, even though that parable would have put him in a favorable light.

Matthew also mentions the Sadducees more than any of the other gospels. Both Pharisees and Sadducees are regularly portrayed negatively, and held up as warning beacons. Their doctrine is a leaven that must be avoided (16:11,12). Although these groups were doctrinally at odds with one another, they were united in their hatred of Christ. To Matthew, they epitomized all in Israel who rejected Christ as King.

The rejection of Israel's Messiah is another constant theme in this gospel. In no other gospel are the attacks against Jesus portrayed as strongly as here. From the flight into Egypt to the scene at the cross, Matthew paints a more vivid portrayal of Christ's rejection than any of the other evangelists. In Matthew's account of the crucifixion, for example, no thief repents, and no friends or loved ones are seen at the foot of the cross. In His death, He is forsaken even by God (27:46). The shadow of rejection is never lifted from the story.

Yet Matthew portrays Him as a victorious King who will one day return "on the clouds of heaven with power and great glory" (24:30).

Interpretive Challenges

As noted above, Matthew groups his narrative material around 5 great discourses. He makes no attempt to follow a strict chronology, and a comparison of the gospels reveals that Matthew freely places things out of order. He is dealing with themes and broad concepts, not laying out a timeline.

The prophetic passages present a particular interpretive challenge. Jesus' Olivet discourse, for example, contains some details that evoke images of the violent destruction of Jerusalem in A.D. 70 Jesus' words in 24:34 have led some to conclude that all these things were fulfilled—albeit not literally—in the Roman conquest of that era. This is the view known as "preterism." But this is a serious interpretive blunder, forcing the interpreter to read into these passages spiritualized, allegorical meanings unwarranted by normal exegetical methods. The grammatical-historical hermeneutical approach to these passages is the approach to follow, and it yields a consistently futuristic interpretation of crucial prophecies.

For a discussion of the Synoptic Problem, see Introduction to Mark: Interpretive Challenges.

Outline

- I. (Prologue) The King's Advent (1:1–4:25)
  - A. His Birth (1:1–2:23)
    1. His ancestry (1:1-17)
    2. His arrival (1:18-25)
    3. His adoration (2:1-12)
    4. His adversaries (2:13-23)
  - B. His Entry into Public Ministry (3:1–4:25)
    1. His forerunner (3:1-12)
    2. His baptism (3:13-17)
    3. His temptation (4:1-11)
    4. His earliest ministry (4:12-25)
- II. The King's Authority (5:1–9:38)
  - A. Discourse 1: The Sermon on the Mount (5:1–7:29)
    1. Righteousness and happiness (5:1-12)
    2. Righteousness and discipleship (5:13-16)
    3. Righteousness and the Scriptures (5:17-20)
    4. Righteousness and morality (5:21-48)
    5. Righteousness and practical religion (6:1-18)
    6. Righteousness and mundane things (6:19-34)
    7. Righteousness and human relations (7:1-12)
    8. Righteousness and salvation (7:13-29)

- B. Narrative 1: The Authenticating Miracles (8:1–9:38)
  1. A leper cleansed (8:1-4)
  2. The centurion's servant healed (8:5-13)
  3. Peter's mother-in-law healed (8:14,15)
  4. Multitudes healed (8:16-22)
  5. The winds and sea rebuked (8:23-27)
  6. Two demoniacs delivered (8:28-34)
  7. A paralytic pardoned and healed (9:1-8)
  8. A tax collector called (9:9-13)
  9. A question answered (9:14-17)
  10. A girl raised from the dead (9:18-26)
  11. Two blind men given sight (9:27-31)
  12. A mute speaks (9:32-34)
  13. Multitudes viewed with compassion (9:35-38)

III. The King's Agenda (10:1–12:50)

- A. Discourse 2: The Commissioning of the Twelve (10:1-42)
  1. The Master's men (10:1-4)
  2. The sending of the disciples (10:5-23)
  3. Hallmarks of discipleship (10:24-42)
- B. Narrative 2: The Mission of the King (11:1–12:50)
  1. Jesus' identity affirmed for John's disciples (11:1-19)
  2. Woes pronounced on the impenitent (11:20-24)
  3. Rest offered to the weary (11:25-30)
  4. Lordship asserted over the Sabbath (12:1-13)
  5. Opposition fomented by the Jewish leaders (12:14-45)
  6. Eternal relationships defined by spiritual ancestry (12:46-50)

IV. The King's Adversaries (13:1–17:27)

- A. Discourse 3: The Kingdom Parables (13:1-52)
  1. The soils (13:1-23)
  2. The wheat and tares (13:24-30,34-43)
  3. The mustard seed (13:31,32)
  4. The leaven (13:33)
  5. The hidden treasure (13:44)
  6. The pearl of great price (13:45,46)
  7. The dragnet (13:47-50)
  8. The householder (13:51,52)
- B. Narrative 3: The Kingdom Conflict (13:53–17:27)
  1. Nazareth rejects the King (13:53-58)
  2. Herod murders John the Baptist (14:1-12)
  3. Jesus feeds the 5,000 (14:13-21)
  4. Jesus walks on water (14:22-33)
  5. Multitudes seek healing (14:34-36)
  6. The Scribes and Pharisees challenge Jesus (15:1-20)
  7. A Syro-phoenician woman believes (15:21-28)
  8. Jesus heals multitudes (15:29-31)
  9. Jesus feeds the 4,000 (15:32-39)
  10. The Pharisees and Sadducees seek a sign (16:1-12)
  11. Peter confesses Christ (16:13-20)
  12. Jesus predicts His death (16:21-28)
  13. Jesus reveals His glory (17:1-13)
  14. Jesus heals a child (17:14-21)
  15. Jesus foretells His betrayal (17:22,23)
  16. Jesus pays the temple tax (17:24-27)

V. The King's Administration (18:1–23:39)

- A. Discourse 4: The Childlikeness of the Believer (18:1-35)
  1. A call for childlike faith (18:1-6)
  2. A warning against offenses (18:7-9)
  3. A parable about a lost sheep (18:10-14)

4. A pattern for church discipline (18:15-20)
5. A lesson about forgiveness (18:21-35)

B. Narrative 4: The Jerusalem Ministry (19:1–23:39)
1. Some kingly lessons (19:1–20:28)
   a. On divorce (19:1-10)
   b. On celibacy (19:11,12)
   c. On children (19:13-15)
   d. On surrender (19:16-22)
   e. On who may be saved (19:23-30)
   f. On equality in the kingdom (20:1-16)
   g. On His death (20:17-19)
   h. On true greatness (20:20-28)
2. Some kingly deeds (20:29–21:27)
   a. He heals two blind men (20:29-34)
   b. He receives adoration (21:1-11)
   c. He cleanses the temple (21:12-17)
   d. He curses a fig tree (21:18-22)
   e. He answers a challenge (21:23-27)
3. Some kingly parables (21:28–22:14)
   a. The two sons (21:28-32)
   b. The wicked vinedressers (21:33-46)
   c. The wedding feast (22:1-14)
4. Some kingly answers (22:15-46)
   a. The Herodians: on paying taxes (22:15-22)
   b. The Sadducees: on the resurrection (22:23-33)
   c. The Scribes: on the first and great commandment (22:34-40)
   d. The Pharisees: on David's greater Son (22:41-46)
5. Some kingly pronouncements (23:1-39)
   a. Woe to the scribes and Pharisees (23:1-36)
   b. Woe to Jerusalem (23:37-39)

VI. The King's Atonement (24:1–28:15)

A. Discourse 5: The Olivet Discourse (24:1–25:46)
1. The destruction of the temple (24:1,2)
2. The signs of the times (24:3-31)
3. The parable of the fig tree (24:32-35)
4. The lesson of Noah (24:36-44)
5. The parable of the two servants (24:45-51)
6. The parable of the ten virgins (25:1-13)
7. The parable of the talents (25:14-30)
8. The judgment of the nations (25:31-46)

B. Narrative 5: The Crucifixion and Resurrection (26:1–28:15)
1. The plot to kill the King (26:1-5)
2. Mary's anointing (26:6-13)
3. Judas' betrayal (26:14-16)
4. The Passover (26:17-30)
5. The prophecy of Peter's denial (26:31-35)
6. Jesus' agony (26:36-46)
7. Jesus' arrest (26:47-56)
8. The trial before the Sanhedrin (26:57-68)
9. Peter's denial (26:69-75)
10. Judas' suicide (27:1-10)
11. The trial before Pilate (27:11-26)
12. The soldiers' mocking (27:27-31)
13. The crucifixion (27:32-56)
14. The burial (27:57-66)
15. The resurrection (28:1-15)

VII. (Epilogue) The King's Assignment (28:16-20)

Genealogy of Christ
Ruth 4:18-22; 1 Chr. 1:34, 2:1-15; Luke 3:31-34

1 The book of the [a]genealogy[1] of Jesus
Christ, [b]the Son of David, [c]the Son of
Abraham:
2 [d]Abraham begot Isaac, [e]Isaac begot Jacob, and Jacob begot [f]Judah and his brothers. 3 [g]Judah begot Perez and Zerah by
Tamar, [h]Perez begot Hezron, and Hezron
begot Ram. 4 Ram begot Amminadab, Amminadab begot Nahshon, and Nahshon
begot Salmon. 5 Salmon begot [i]Boaz by
Rahab, Boaz begot Obed by Ruth, Obed
begot Jesse, 6 and [j]Jesse begot David the
king.
[k]David the king begot Solomon by her
[2]*who had been the wife* of Uriah. 7 [l]Solomon
begot Rehoboam, Rehoboam begot [m]Abi-
jah, and Abijah begot [3]Asa. 8 Asa begot
[n]Jehoshaphat, Jehoshaphat begot Joram,
and Joram begot [o]Uzziah. 9 Uzziah begot
Jotham, Jotham begot [p]Ahaz, and Ahaz
begot Hezekiah. 10 [q]Hezekiah begot Manasseh, Manasseh begot [4]Amon, and
Amon begot [r]Josiah. 11 [s]Josiah begot [5]Jeco-
niah and his brothers about the time they
were [t]carried away to Babylon.
12 And after they were brought to Babylon, [u]Jeconiah begot Shealtiel, and Shealtiel begot [v]Zerubbabel. 13 Zerubbabel begot
Abiud, Abiud begot Eliakim, and Eliakim
begot Azor. 14 Azor begot Zadok, Zadok
begot Achim, and Achim begot Eliud. 15 Eliud begot Eleazar, Eleazar begot Matthan,
and Matthan begot Jacob. 16 And Jacob
begot Joseph the husband of [w]Mary, of
whom was born Jesus who is called Christ.
17 So all the generations from Abraham
to David *are* fourteen generations, from
David until the captivity in Babylon *are*
fourteen generations, and from the captivity in Babylon until the Christ *are* fourteen
generations.

Birth of Christ

18 Now the [x]birth of Jesus Christ was as
follows: After His mother Mary was betrothed to Joseph, before they came together, she was found with child [y]of the Holy
Spirit. 19 Then Joseph her husband, being
[6]a just *man*, and not wanting [z]to make her

CHAPTER 1

1 [a]Luke 3:23 [b]2 Sam. 7:12-16; Ps. 132:11; Is. 9:6; 11:1; Jer. 23:5; [Matt. 1:18; Luke 3:23, 31]; John 7:42; Acts 2:30; [Rom. 1:3]; Rev. 22:16 [c]Gen. 12:3; 22:18; [Gal. 3:16] [1]Lit. *generation* **2** [d]Gen. 21:2, 12 [e]Gen. 25:26; 28:14 [f]Gen. 29:35 **3** [g]Gen. 38:27; 49:10 [h]Ruth 4:18-22; 1 Chr. 2:1-15; Matt. 1:3-6 **5** [i]Ruth 2:1; 4:1-13 **6** [j]1 Sam. 16:1; Is. 11:1, 10 [k]2 Sam. 7:12; 12:24; Is. 9:7 [2]Words in italic type have been added for clarity. They are not found in the original Greek. **7** [l]1 Kin. 11:43; 1 Chr. 3:10 [m]2 Chr. 11:20 [3]NU *Asaph* **8** [n]1 Chr. 3:10 [o]2 Kin. 15:13 **9** [p]2 Kin. 15:38 **10** [q]2 Kin. 20:21 [r]1 Kin. 13:2 [4]NU *Amos* **11** [s]1 Chr. 3:15, 16 [t]2 Kin. 24:14-16; Jer. 27:20; Matt. 1:17 [5]Or *Coniah* or *Jehoiachin* **12** [u]1 Chr. 3:17 [v]Ezra 3:2; Neh. 12:1; Hag. 1:1 **16** [w]Matt. 13:55; Mark 6:3 **18** [x]Matt. 12:46; Luke 1:27 [y]Is. 7:14; 49:5; Luke 1:35 **19** [z]Deut. 24:1; John 8:4, 5 [6]*an upright*

1:1 book of the genealogy of Jesus Christ. This phrase is viewed by some as Matthew's title for the entire gospel. The Gr. phrase translated "book of the genealogy" is exactly the same phrase used in Gen. 5:1 in the LXX. **Jesus Christ.** The Hebrew *Jeshua* means "the Lord is Salvation." *Christos* means "anointed one" and is the exact equivalent of the Heb. word for "Messiah" (Dan. 9:25). **Son of David.** A messianic title used as such in only the synoptic gospels (*see notes on 22:42,45*). **Son of Abraham.** Takes His royal lineage all the way back to the nation's inception in the Abrahamic Covenant (Gen. 12:1-3).

1:2 For a comparison of this genealogy and the one given by Luke, *see note on Luke 3:23-38.*

1:3 Tamar. It is unusual for women to be named in genealogies. Matthew names 5: "Tamar" was a Canaanite woman who posed as a prostitute to seduce Judah (Gen. 38:13-30). "Rahab" (v. 5) was a Gentile and a prostitute (Josh. 2:1). "Ruth" (v. 5) was a Moabite woman (Ruth 1:3) and thus her offspring were forbidden to enter the assembly of the Lord for 10 generations (Deut. 23:3). "Bathsheba" ("Uriah's wife," v. 6) committed adultery with David (2 Sam. 11). And "Mary" (v. 16) bore the stigma of pregnancy outside of wedlock. Each of these women is an object lesson about the workings of divine grace.

1:5,6 Salmon begot Boaz by Rahab...and Jesse begot David the king. This is not an exhaustive genealogy. Several additional generations must have elapsed between Rahab (in Joshua's time) and David (v. 6)—nearly 4 centuries later. Matthew's genealogy (like most of the biblical ones) sometimes skips over several generations between well known characters in order to abbreviate the listing.

1:8 Joram begot Uzziah. Cf. 1 Chr. 3:10-12. Matthew skips over Ahaziah, Joash, and Amaziah, going directly from Joram to Uzziah (Azariah)—using a kind of genealogical shorthand. He seems to do this intentionally in order to make a symmetrical 3-fold division in v. 17.

1:11 Josiah begot Jeconiah. Again, Matthew skips a generation between Josiah and Jeconiah (cf. 1 Chr. 3:14-16). Jeconiah is also called Jehoiachin (2 Kin. 24:6; 2 Chr. 36:8) and sometimes Coniah (Jer. 22:24). Jeconiah's presence in this genealogy presents an interesting dilemma. A curse on him forbade any of his descendants from the throne of David forever (Jer. 22:30). Since Jesus was heir through Joseph to the royal line of descent, but not an actual son of Joseph and thus not a physical descendant through this line, the curse bypassed him.

1:12 Shealtiel begot Zerubbabel. See 1 Chr. 3:17-19, where Zerubbabel is said to be the offspring of Pedaiah, Shealtiel's brother. Elsewhere in the OT, Zerubbabel is always called the son of Shealtiel. (e.g., Hag. 1:1; Ezra 3:2; Neh. 12:1). Possibly Shealtiel adopted his nephew (*see note on Hag. 2:23*). Zerubbabel is the last character in Matthew's list who appears in any of the OT genealogies.

1:16 Joseph the husband of Mary, of whom was born Jesus. This is the only entry in the entire genealogy where the word "begot" is not used—including those where whole generations were skipped. The pronoun "whom" is sing., referring to Mary alone. The unusual way in which this final entry is phrased underscores the fact that Jesus was not Joseph's literal offspring. The genealogy nonetheless establishes His claim to the throne of David as Joseph's legal heir.

1:17 fourteen generations. The significance of the number 14 is not clear, but Matthew's attention to numbers—a distinctly Hebrew characteristic—is evident throughout the gospel. The systematic ordering may be an aid for memorization. Note that Matthew counts Jeconiah in both the third and fourth groups, representing both the last generation before the Babylonian captivity and the first generation after.

1:18 betrothed. Jewish betrothal was as binding as modern marriage. A divorce was necessary to terminate the betrothal (v. 19) and the betrothed couple were regarded legally as husband and wife (v. 19)—although physical union had not yet taken place. *See note on Luke 2:5.* **with child of the Holy Spirit.** See vv. 20,23; Luke 1:26-35.

1:19 Joseph...being a just *man*...was minded to put her away secretly. Stoning was the legal prescription for this sort of adultery (Deut. 22:23,24). Joseph's righteousness meant he was also merciful; thus he did not intend to make Mary "a public example." The

a public example, was minded to put her
away secretly. 20 But while he thought
about these things, behold, an angel of the
Lord appeared to him in a dream, saying,
"Joseph, son of David, do not be afraid to
take to you Mary your wife, [a]for that
which is [7]conceived in her is of the Holy
Spirit. 21 [b]And she will bring forth a Son,
and you shall call His name [8]JESUS, [c]for He
will save His people from their sins."
22 So all this was done that it might be
fulfilled which was spoken by the Lord
through the prophet, saying: 23 [d]*"Behold,*[9]
the virgin shall be with child, and bear a
Son, and they shall call His name Immanu-
el," which is translated, "God with us."
24 Then Joseph, being aroused from
sleep, did as the angel of the Lord commanded him and took to him his wife,
25 and [1]did not know her till she had
brought forth [e]her[2] firstborn Son. And he
called His name JESUS.

Visit of Wise Men

2 Now after [a]Jesus was born in Bethlehem of Judea in the days of Herod the
king, behold, [1]wise men [b]from the East
came to Jerusalem, 2 saying, [c]"Where is He
who has been born King of the Jews? For
we have seen [d]His star in the East and
have come to worship Him."
3 When Herod the king heard *this,* he
was troubled, and all Jerusalem with him.
4 And when he had gathered all [e]the chief
priests and [f]scribes of the people together,
[g]he inquired of them where the Christ was
to be born.
5 So they said to him, "In Bethlehem of
Judea, for thus it is written by the prophet:

6 *'But[h] you, Bethlehem, in the land of Judah,*
Are not the least among the rulers of Judah;
For out of you shall come a Ruler
[i]*Who will shepherd My people Israel.'"*

7 Then Herod, when he had secretly
called the [2]wise men, determined from
them what time the [j]star appeared. 8 And
he sent them to Bethlehem and said, "Go
and search carefully for the young Child,
and when you have found *Him,* bring back

20 [a] Luke 1:35 [7] Lit. *begotten*
21 [b] [Is. 7:14; 9:6, 7]; Luke 1:31; 2:21 [c] Luke 2:11; John 1:29; [Acts 4:12; 5:31; 13:23, 38; Rom. 5:18, 19; Col. 1:20-23] [8] Lit. *Savior*
23 [d] Is. 7:14 [9] Words in oblique type in the New Testament are quoted from the Old Testament.
25 [e] Ex. 13:2; Luke 2:7, 21 [1] Kept her a virgin [2] NU *a Son*

CHAPTER 2

1 [a] Mic. 5:2; Luke 2:4-7 [b] Gen. 25:6; 1 Kin. 4:30 [1] Gr. *magoi*
2 [c] Luke 2:11 [d] [Num. 24:17; Is. 60:3]
4 [e] 2 Chr. 36:14 [f] 2 Chr. 34:13 [g] Mal. 2:7
6 [h] Mic. 5:2; John 7:42 [i] Gen. 49:10; [Rev. 2:27]
7 [j] Num. 24:17 [2] Gr. *magoi*

phrase "a just man" is a Hebraism suggesting that he was a true believer in God who had thereby been declared righteous, and who carefully obeyed the law (see Gen. 6:9). To "put her away" would be to obtain a legal divorce (19:8, 9; Deut. 24:1), which according to the Jewish custom was necessary in order to dissolve a betrothal (*see note on v. 18*).

1:20 an angel of the Lord. This is one of only a few such angelic visitations in the NT, most of which are associated with Christ's birth. For others, see 28:2; Acts 5:19; 8:26; 10:3; 12:7-10; 27:23; Rev. 1:1. **in a dream.** As if to underscore the supernatural character of Christ's advent, Matthew's narrative of the event describes 5 such revelatory dreams: v. 20; 2:12, 13, 19, 22. Here the angel told Joseph he was to take Mary into his own home.

1:21 JESUS. See v. 25; Luke 1:31. The name actually means "Savior" (*see note on v. 1*).

1:22 that it might be fulfilled. Matthew points out fulfillments of OT prophecies no less than a dozen times (cf. 2:15, 17, 23; 4:14; 8:17; 12:17; 13:14, 35; 21:4; 26:54-56; 27:9, 35). He quotes from the OT more than 60 times, more frequently than any other NT writer, except Paul in Romans.

1:23 *virgin.* Scholars sometimes dispute whether the Hebrew term in Is. 7:14 means "virgin" or "maiden." Matthew is quoting here from the LXX which uses the unambiguous Gr. term for "virgin" (*see note on Is. 7:14*). Thus Matthew, writing under the Spirit's inspiration, ends all doubt about the meaning of the word in Is. 7:14. ***Immanuel.*** Cf. Is. 8:8, 10.

1:24 took to him his wife. *See note on Luke 2:5.*

1:25 know her. A euphemism for sexual intercourse. See Gen. 4:1, 17, 25; 38:26; Judg. 11:39.

2:1 Bethlehem. A small village on the southern outskirts of Jerusalem. Hebrew scholars in Jesus' day clearly expected Bethlehem to be the birthplace of the Messiah (cf. Mic. 5:2; John 7:42). **in the days of Herod the king.** This refers to Herod the Great, the first of several important rulers from the Herodian dynasty who are named in Scripture. This Herod, founder of the famous line, ruled from 37–4 B.C. He is thought to have been Idumean, a descendant of the Edomites, offspring of Esau. Herod was ruthless and cunning. He loved opulence and grand building projects, and many of the most magnificent ruins that can be seen in modern Israel date back to the days of Herod the Great. His most famous project was the rebuilding of the temple at Jerusalem (*see note on 24:1*). That project alone took several decades and was not completed until long after Herod's death (cf. John 2:20). *See note on v. 22.* **wise men from the East.** The number of wise men is not given. The traditional notion that there were 3 stems from the number of gifts they brought. These were not kings, but Magi, magicians or astrologers—possibly Zoroastrian wise men from Persia whose knowledge of the Hebrew Scriptures could be traced back to the time of Daniel (cf. Dan. 5:11).

2:2 saying. This present participle conveys the idea of continuous action. It suggests they went around the city questioning everyone they met. **star.** This could not have been a supernova or a conjunction of planets, as some modern theories suggest, because of the way the star moved and settled over one place (cf. v. 9). It is more likely a supernatural reality similar to the Shekinah that guided the Israelites in the days of Moses (Ex. 13:21).

2:4 chief priests. These were the temple hierarchy. They were mostly Sadducees (*see note on 3:7*). **scribes.** Primarily Pharisees, i.e., authorities on Jewish law. Sometimes they are referred to as "lawyers" (*see note on Luke 10:25*). They were professional scholars whose specialty was explaining the application of the law. They knew exactly where the Messiah was to be born (v. 5), but lacked the faith to accompany the Magi to the place where He was.

2:6 This ancient prophecy from Mic. 5:2 was written in the eighth century B.C. The original prophecy, not quoted in full by Matthew, declared the deity of Israel's Messiah: "Out of you shall come forth to Me the One to be Ruler in Israel, whose goings forth *are* from of old, from everlasting." ***a Ruler who will shepherd My people Israel.*** This portion of Matthew's quote actually seems to be a reference to God's words to Saul when Israel's kingdom was originally established (2 Sam. 5:2; 1 Chr. 11:2). The Gr. word for "ruler" evokes the image of strong, even stern, leadership. "Shepherd" emphasizes tender care. Christ's rule involves both (cf. Rev. 12:5).

word to me, that I may come and worship
Him also."
9 When they heard the king, they departed; and behold, the star which they
had seen in the East went before them, till
it came and stood over where the young
Child was. 10 When they saw the star, they
rejoiced with exceedingly great joy. 11 And
when they had come into the house, they
saw the young Child with Mary His mother, and fell down and worshiped Him. And
when they had opened their treasures,
[k]they presented gifts to Him: gold, frankincense, and myrrh.
12 Then, being divinely warned [l]in a
dream that they should not return to
Herod, they departed for their own country another way.

Flight into Egypt

13 Now when they had departed, behold, an angel of the Lord appeared to Joseph in a dream, saying, "Arise, take the
young Child and His mother, flee to Egypt,
and stay there until I bring you word; for
Herod will seek the young Child to destroy Him."
14 When he arose, he took the young
Child and His mother by night and departed for Egypt, 15 and was there until the
death of Herod, that it might be fulfilled
which was spoken by the Lord through the
prophet, saying, [m]*"Out of Egypt I called
My Son."*

Herod Kills the Children

16 Then Herod, when he saw that he was
deceived by the wise men, was exceedingly angry; and he sent forth and put to
death all the male children who were in
Bethlehem and in all its districts, from two
years old and under, according to the time
which he had determined from the wise
men. 17 Then was fulfilled what was spoken by Jeremiah the prophet, saying:

18 *"A[n] voice was heard in Ramah,*
Lamentation, weeping, and great mourning,
Rachel weeping for her children,

11 [k]Ps. 72:10; Is. 60:6
12 [l][Job 33:15, 16]; Matt. 1:20
15 [m]Num. 24:8; Hos. 11:1
18 [n]Jer. 31:15

2:8 that I may come and worship Him. Herod actually wanted to kill the Child (vv. 13-18), whom he saw as a potential threat to his throne.

2:11 into the house. By the time the wise men arrived, Mary and Joseph were situated in a house, not a stable (cf. Luke 2:7). **the young Child with Mary His mother.** Whenever Matthew mentions Mary in connection with her Child, Christ is always given first place (cf. vv. 13,14,20,21). **gold, frankincense, and myrrh.** Gifts suitable for a king (cf. Is. 60:6). The fact that Gentiles would offer such worship had prophetic significance as well (Ps. 72:10).

2:12,13 in a dream. *See note on 1:20.*

2:15 the death of Herod. Recent scholarship sets this date at 4 B.C. It is probable that the stay in Egypt was very brief—perhaps no more than a few weeks. ***Out of Egypt.*** This quotation is from Hos. 11:1 (*see note there*), which speaks of God's leading Israel out of Egypt in the Exodus. Matthew suggests that Israel's sojourn in Egypt was a pictorial prophecy, rather than a specific verbal one such as v. 6; cf. 1:23. These are called "types" and all are always fulfilled in Christ, and identified clearly by the NT writers. Another example of a type is found in John 3:14. *See note on v. 17.*

2:16 put to death all the male children. Herod's act is all the more heinous in light of his full knowledge that the Lord's Anointed One was the target of his murderous plot.

2:17 fulfilled. *See note on v. 15.* Again, this prophecy is in the form

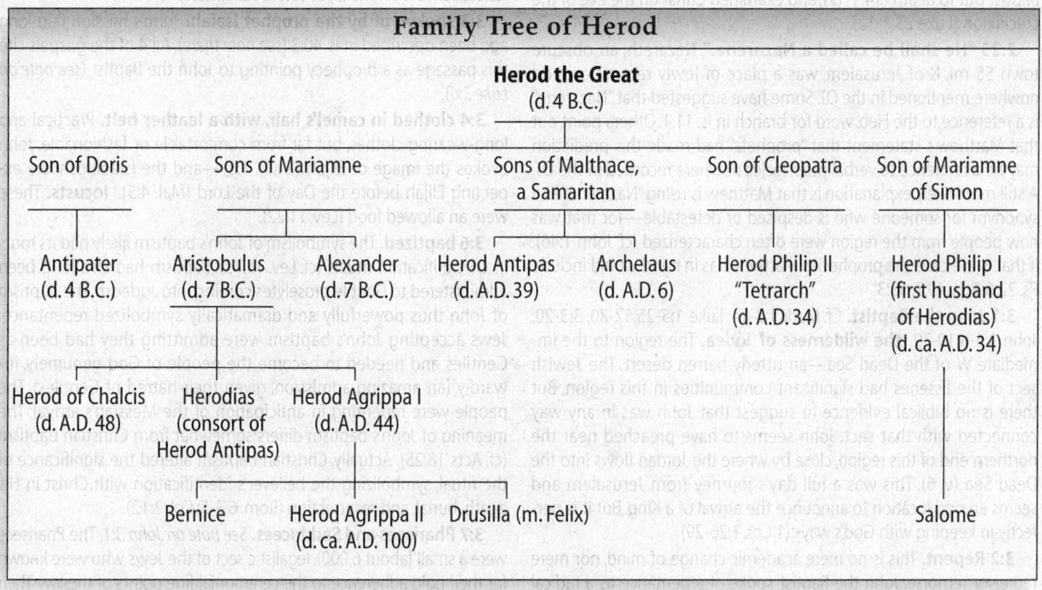

Refusing to be comforted,
Because they are no more."

Jesus Returns to Nazareth—Luke 2:39

19 Now when Herod was dead, behold,
an angel of the Lord appeared in a dream
to Joseph in Egypt, 20 [o]saying, "Arise, take
the young Child and His mother, and go to
the land of Israel, for those who [p]sought
the young Child's life are dead." 21 Then
he arose, took the young Child and His
mother, and came into the land of Israel.
22 But when he heard that Archelaus
was reigning over Judea instead of his father Herod, he was afraid to go there. And
being warned by God in a [q]dream, he
turned aside [r]into the region of Galilee.
23 And he came and dwelt in a city called
[s]Nazareth, that it might be fulfilled [t]which
was spoken by the prophets, "He shall be
called a Nazarene."

The Person of John the Baptist
Mark 1:2-6; Luke 3:3-6

3 In those days [a]John the Baptist came
preaching [b]in the wilderness of Judea,
2 and saying, "Repent, for [c]the kingdom of
heaven is at hand!" 3 For this is he who was
spoken of by the prophet Isaiah, saying:

[d]*"The voice of one crying in the*
wilderness:
[e]*'Prepare the way of the* LORD*;*
Make His paths straight.'"

4 Now [f]John himself was clothed in
camel's hair, with a leather belt around his
waist; and his food was [g]locusts and [h]wild
honey. 5 [i]Then Jerusalem, all Judea, and all
the region around the Jordan went out to
him 6 [j]and were baptized by him in the Jordan, confessing their sins.

The Preaching of John the Baptist
Mark 1:7-9; Luke 3:7-9, 16, 17

7 But when he saw many of the Pharisees and Sadducees coming to his baptism,
he said to them, [k]"Brood of vipers! Who
warned you to flee from [l]the wrath to
come? 8 Therefore bear fruits worthy of repentance, 9 and do not think to say to

20 [o] Luke 2:39 [p] Matt. 2:16
22 [q] Matt. 2:12, 13, 19 [r] Matt. 3:13; Luke 2:39
23 [s] Luke 1:26; 2:39; John 1:45, 46 [t] Judg. 13:5

CHAPTER 3

1 [a] Matt. 3:1-12; Mark 1:3-8; Luke 3:2-17; John 1:6-8, 19-28 [b] Josh. 14:10
2 [c] Dan. 2:44; Mal. 4:6; Matt. 4:17; Mark 1:15; Luke 1:17; 10:9; 11:20; 21:31
3 [d] Is. 40:3; Luke 3:4; John 1:23 [e] Luke 1:76
4 [f] 2 Kin. 1:8; Zech. 13:4; Matt. 11:8; Mark 1:6 [g] Lev. 11:22 [h] 1 Sam. 14:25, 26
5 [i] Mark 1:5
6 [j] Acts 19:4, 18
7 [k] Matt. 12:34; Luke 3:7-9 [l] [Rom. 5:9; 1 Thess. 1:10]

of a type. Verse 18 quotes Jer. 31:15 (*see note there*), which speaks of all Israel's mourning at the time of the Babylonian captivity (ca. 586 B.C.). That wailing prefigured the wailing over Herod's massacre.

2:19 in a dream. *See note on 1:20.*

2:22 Archelaus. Herod's kingdom was divided 3 ways and given to his sons: Archelaus ruled Judea, Samaria, and Idumea; Herod Philip II ruled the regions N of Galilee (Luke 3:1); and Herod Antipas ruled Galilee and Perea (Luke 3:1). History records that Archelaus was so brutal and ineffective that he was deposed by Rome after a short reign and replaced with a governor appointed by Rome. Pontius Pilate was the fifth governor of Judea. Herod Antipas is the main Herod in the gospel accounts. He was the one who had John the Baptist put to death (14:1-12), and examined Christ on the eve of the crucifixion (Luke 23:7-12).

2:23 "He shall be called a Nazarene." Nazareth, an obscure town 55 mi. N of Jerusalem, was a place of lowly reputation, and nowhere mentioned in the OT. Some have suggested that "Nazarene" is a reference to the Heb. word for branch in Is. 11:1. Others point out that Matthew's statement that "prophets" had made this prediction may be a reference to verbal prophecies nowhere recorded in the OT. A still more likely explanation is that Matthew is using "Nazarene" as a synonym for someone who is despised or detestable—for that was how people from the region were often characterized (cf. John 1:46). If that is the case, the prophecies Matthew has in mind would include Ps. 22:6-8; Is. 49:7; 53:3.

3:1 John the Baptist. Cf. Mark 1:2-14; Luke 1:5-25,57-80; 3:3-20; John 1:6-8,19-39. **the wilderness of Judea.** The region to the immediate W of the Dead Sea—an utterly barren desert. The Jewish sect of the Essenes had significant communities in this region. But there is no biblical evidence to suggest that John was in any way connected with that sect. John seems to have preached near the northern end of this region, close by where the Jordan flows into the Dead Sea (v. 6). This was a full day's journey from Jerusalem and seems an odd location to announce the arrival of a King. But it is perfectly in keeping with God's ways (1 Cor. 1:26-29).

3:2 Repent. This is no mere academic change of mind, nor mere regret or remorse. John the Baptist spoke of repentance as a radical turning from sin that inevitably became manifest in the fruit of righteousness (v. 8). Jesus' first sermon began with the same imperative (4:17). For a discussion of the nature of repentance, *see notes on 2 Cor. 7:8-11.* **the kingdom of heaven.** This is an expression unique to Matthew's gospel. Matthew uses the word "heaven" as a euphemism for God's name—to accommodate his Jewish readers' sensitivities (cf. 23:22). Throughout the rest of Scripture, the kingdom is called "the kingdom of God." Both expressions refer to the sphere of God's dominion over those who belong to Him. The kingdom is now manifest in heaven's spiritual rule over the hearts of believers (Luke 17:21); and one day will be established in a literal earthly kingdom (Rev. 20:4-6). **is at hand.** In one sense the kingdom is a present reality, but in its fullest sense it awaits a yet-future fulfillment.

3:3 spoken of by the prophet Isaiah. John's mission had long ago been described in Is. 40:3 (*see note there*). All 4 of the gospels cite this passage as a prophecy pointing to John the Baptist (*see note on Luke 3:6*).

3:4 clothed in camel's hair, with a leather belt. Practical and long-wearing clothes, but far from comfortable or fashionable. John evokes the image of Elijah (2 Kin. 1:8)—and the Israelites were expecting Elijah before the Day of the Lord (Mal. 4:5). **locusts.** These were an allowed food (Lev. 11:22).

3:6 baptized. The symbolism of John's baptism likely had its roots in OT purification rituals (cf. Lev. 15:13). Baptism had also long been administered to Gentile proselytes coming into Judaism. The baptism of John thus powerfully and dramatically symbolized repentance. Jews accepting John's baptism were admitting they had been as Gentiles and needed to become the people of God genuinely, inwardly (an amazing admission, given their hatred of Gentiles). The people were repenting in anticipation of the Messiah's arrival. The meaning of John's baptism differs somewhat from Christian baptism (cf. Acts 18:25). Actually, Christian baptism altered the significance of the ritual, symbolizing the believer's identification with Christ in His death, burial, and resurrection (Rom. 6:3-5; Col. 2:12).

3:7 Pharisees and Sadducees. *See note on John 3:1.* The Pharisees were a small (about 6,000), legalistic sect of the Jews who were known for their rigid adherence to the ceremonial fine points of the law. Their

yourselves, [m]'We have Abraham as *our* father.' For I say to you that God is able to
raise up children to Abraham from these
stones. 10 And even now the ax is laid to
the root of the trees. [n]Therefore every tree
which does not bear good fruit is cut down
and thrown into the fire. 11 [o]I indeed baptize you with water unto repentance, but
He who is coming after me is mightier
than I, whose sandals I am not worthy to
carry. [p]He will baptize you with the Holy
Spirit [1]and fire. 12 [q]His winnowing fan *is*
in His hand, and He will thoroughly clean
out His threshing floor, and gather His
wheat into the barn; but He will [r]burn up
the chaff with unquenchable fire."

Baptism of Jesus
Mark 1:9-11; Luke 3:21-23

13 [s]Then Jesus came [t]from Galilee to
John at the Jordan to be baptized by him.
14 And John *tried to* prevent Him, saying,
"I need to be baptized by You, and are You
coming to me?"
15 But Jesus answered and said to him,
"Permit *it to be so* now, for thus it is fitting
for us to fulfill all righteousness." Then he
allowed Him.
16 [u]When He had been baptized, Jesus
came up immediately from the water; and
behold, the heavens were opened to Him,
and [2]He saw [v]the Spirit of God descending
like a dove and alighting upon Him.
17 [w]And suddenly a voice *came* from heav-
en, saying, [x]"This is My beloved Son, in
whom I am well pleased."

First Temptation
Mark 1:12, 13; Luke 4:1-4

4 Then [a]Jesus was led up by [b]the Spirit
into the wilderness to be tempted by
the devil. 2 And when He had fasted forty
days and forty nights, afterward He was
hungry. 3 Now when the tempter came to
Him, he said, "If You are the Son of God,

9 [m] John 8:33; Acts 13:26; [Rom. 4:1, 11, 16; Gal. 3:29] **10** [n] [Ps. 92:12-14]; Matt. 7:19; Luke 13:7, 9; [John 15:6] **11** [o] Mark 1:4, 8; Luke 3:16; John 1:26; Acts 1:5 [p] [Is. 4:4; John 20:22; Acts 2:3, 4; 1 Cor. 12:13] [1] M omits *and fire* **12** [q] Mal. 3:3 [r] Mal. 4:1; Matt. 13:30 **13** [s] Matt. 3:13-17; Mark 1:9-11; Luke 3:21, 22; John 1:31-34 [t] Matt. 2:22 **16** [u] Mark 1:10 [v] [Is. 11:2]; Luke 3:22; John 1:32; Acts 7:56 [2] Or *he* **17** [w] John 12:28 [x] Ps. 2:7; Is. 42:1; Mark 1:11; Luke 1:35; 9:35; Col. 1:13

CHAPTER 4

1 [a] Matt. 4:1-11; Mark 1:12; Luke 4:1 [b] Ezek. 3:14; Acts 8:39

name means "separated ones." Jesus' interaction with the Pharisees was usually adversarial. He rebuked them for using human tradition to nullify Scripture (15:3-9), and especially for rank hypocrisy (15:7,8; 22:18; 23:13,23,25,29; Luke 12:1). The Sadducees were known for their denial of things supernatural. They denied the resurrection of the dead (22:23) and the existence of angels (Acts 23:8). Unlike the Pharisees, they rejected human tradition and scorned legalism. They accepted only the Pentateuch as authoritative. They tended to be wealthy, aristocratic members of the priestly tribe, and in the days of Herod their sect controlled the temple (*see note on 2:4*), though they were fewer in number than the Pharisees. Pharisees and Sadducees had little in common. Pharisees were ritualists; Sadducees were rationalists. Pharisees were legalists; Sadducees were liberals. Pharisees were separatists; Sadducees were compromisers and political opportunists. Yet they united together in their opposition to Christ (22:15,16,23,34,35). John publicly addressed them as deadly snakes. **the wrath to come.** *See note on Luke 3:7.* John's preaching echoed the familiar OT theme of promised wrath in the Day of the Lord (e.g., Ezek. 7:19; Zeph. 1:18; see Introduction to Joel: Historical and Theological Themes). This must have been a particularly stinging rebuke to the Jewish leaders, who imagined that divine wrath was reserved only for non-Jews.

3:8 fruits worthy of repentance. *See note on v. 2.* Repentance itself is not a work, but works are its inevitable fruit. Repentance and faith are inextricably linked in Scripture. Repentance means turning from one's sin, and faith is turning to God (cf. 1 Thess. 1:9). They are like opposite sides of the same coin. That is why both are linked to conversion (Mark 1:15; Acts 3:19; 20:21). Note that the works John demanded to see were "fruits" of repentance. But repentance itself is no more a "work" than faith is (*see note on 2 Tim. 2:25*).

3:9 Abraham as *our* father. See John 8:39-44. They believed that merely being descendants of Abraham, members of God's chosen race, made them spiritually secure. But Abraham's real descendants are those who share his faith (cf. Rom. 4:16). And "only those who are of faith are sons of Abraham" (Gal. 3:7,29). *See note on Luke 3:8.*

3:10 the ax is laid to the root. Irreversible judgment was imminent (*see note on 11:3*).

3:11 Three types of baptism are referred to here: 1) **with water unto repentance.** John's baptism symbolized cleansing (*see note on v. 6*); 2) **with the Holy Spirit.** All believers in Christ are Spirit-baptized (1 Cor. 12:13); and 3) **with...fire.** Because fire is used throughout this context as a means of judgment (vv. 10,12), this must speak of a baptism of judgment upon the unrepentant.

3:12 winnowing fan. A tool for tossing grain into the wind so that the chaff is blown away.

3:14 John *tried to* prevent Him. John's baptism symbolized repentance, and John saw this as inappropriate for the One he knew was the spotless Lamb of God (cf. John 1:29).

3:15 it is fitting for us to fulfill all righteousness. Christ was here identifying Himself with sinners. He will ultimately bear their sins; His perfect righteousness will be imputed to them (2 Cor. 5:21). This act of baptism was a necessary part of the righteousness He secured for sinners. This first public event of His ministry is also rich in meaning: 1) it pictured His death and resurrection (cf. Luke 12:50); 2) it therefore prefigured the significance of Christian baptism (*see note on v. 6*); 3) it marked His first public identification with those whose sins he would bear (Is. 53:11; 1 Pet. 3:18); and 4) it was a public affirmation of His messiahship by testimony directly from heaven (*see note on v. 17*).

3:16,17 Jesus...the Spirit of God...a voice *came from* heaven. Here all 3 Persons of the Trinity are clearly delineated. *See note on Luke 3:22.* The Father's command to hear His Son and the Spirit's vindication and empowerment (*see note on 12:31*) officially inaugurated Christ's ministry.

3:17 My beloved Son, in whom I am well pleased. This heavenly pronouncement combines language from Ps. 2:7 and Is. 42:1—prophecies that would have been well known to those with messianic expectations. Cf. 17:5; Mark 1:11; 9:7; Luke 3:22; 9:35.

4:1 led up by the Spirit...to be tempted by the devil. God Himself is never the agent of temptation (James 1:13), but here—as in the book of Job—God uses even satanic tempting to serve His sovereign purposes. Christ was tempted in all points (Heb. 4:15; 1 John 2:16); Satan tempted Him with "the lust of the flesh" (vv. 2,3); "the lust of the eyes" (vv. 8,9); and "the pride of life" (vv. 5,6).

4:2 forty days and forty nights. Similarly, Moses was without food or drink on Sinai for "forty days and forty nights" (Deut. 9:9), and Elijah also fasted that long (1 Kin. 19:8). *See note on 12:40.*

4:3 If You are the Son of God. The conditional "if" carries the meaning of "since" in this context. There was no doubt in Satan's mind who Jesus was; but Satan's design was to get Him to violate the plan of God and employ the divine power that He had set aside in His humiliation (cf. Phil. 2:7).

command that these stones become
bread."
4 But He answered and said, "It is written, [c] *'Man shall not live by bread alone,*
but by every word that proceeds from the
mouth of God.'"

Second Temptation—Luke 4:9-12

5 Then the devil took Him up [d] into the
holy city, set Him on the pinnacle of the
temple, 6 and said to Him, "If You are the
Son of God, throw Yourself down. For it is
written:

> [e] *'He shall give His angels charge*
> *over you,'*

and,

> [f] *'In their hands they shall bear you*
> *up,*
> *Lest you dash your foot against a*
> *stone.'"*

7 Jesus said to him, "It is written again,
[g] *'You shall not* [1] *tempt the* L*ORD your*
God.'"

Third Temptation
Mark 1:13; Luke 4:5-8, 13

8 Again, the devil took Him up on an exceedingly high mountain, and [h] showed
Him all the kingdoms of the world and
their glory. 9 And he said to Him, "All

4 [c] Deut. 8:3
5 [d] Neh. 11:1, 18; Dan. 9:24; Matt. 27:53
6 [e] Ps. 91:11 [f] Ps. 91:12
7 [g] Deut. 6:16 [1] *test*
8 [h] [Matt. 16:26; 1 John 2:15-17]
10 [i] Deut. 6:13; 10:20; Josh. 24:14 [2] M *Get behind Me*
11 [j] [James 4:7] [k] Matt. 26:53; Luke 22:43; [Heb. 1:14]
12 [l] Matt. 14:3; Mark 1:14; Luke 3:20; John 4:43
15 [m] Is. 9:1, 2
16 [n] Is. 42:7; Luke 2:32
17 [o] Mark 1:14, 15 [p] Matt. 3:2; 10:7 [3] *has drawn near*

these things I will give You if You will fall
down and worship me."
10 Then Jesus said to him, [2] "Away with
you, Satan! For it is written, [i] *'You shall*
worship the L*ORD your God, and Him only*
you shall serve.'"
11 Then the devil [j] left Him, and behold,
[k] angels came and ministered to Him.

Jesus Begins His Ministry
Mark 1:14, 15; Luke 4:14, 31

12 [l] Now when Jesus heard that John had
been put in prison, He departed to Galilee.
13 And leaving Nazareth, He came and
dwelt in Capernaum, which is by the sea,
in the regions of Zebulun and Naphtali,
14 that it might be fulfilled which was spoken by Isaiah the prophet, saying:

> 15 *"The* [m] *land of Zebulun and the land*
> *of Naphtali,*
> *By the way of the sea, beyond the*
> *Jordan,*
> *Galilee of the Gentiles:*
> 16 [n] *The people who sat in darkness*
> *have seen a great light,*
> *And upon those who sat in the*
> *region and shadow of death*
> *Light has dawned."*

17 [o] From that time Jesus began to preach
and to say, [p] "Repent, for the kingdom of
heaven [3] is at hand."

4:4 It is written. All 3 of Jesus' replies to the Devil were taken from Deuteronomy. This one, from Deut. 8:3, states that God allowed Israel to hunger, so that He might feed them with manna and teach them to trust Him to provide for them. So the verse is directly applicable to Jesus' circumstances and a fitting reply to Satan's temptation. ***every word that proceeds from the mouth of God.*** A more important source of sustenance than food, it nurtures our spiritual needs in a way that benefits us eternally, rather than merely providing temporal relief from physical hunger.

4:5 pinnacle of the temple. This was probably a roof with a portico at the SE corner of the temple complex, where a massive retaining wall reached from a level well above the temple mount, deep into the Kidron Valley. According to the Jewish historian Josephus, this was a drop of nearly 450 ft.

4:6 For it is written...*Lest you dash your foot against a stone.* Note that Satan also quoted Scripture (Ps. 91:11,12)—but utterly twisted its meaning, employing a passage about *trusting* God to justify *testing* Him.

4:7 It is written again. Christ replied with another verse from Israel's wilderness experience (Deut. 6:16)—recalling the experience at Massah, where the grumbling Israelites put the Lord to the test, angrily demanding that Moses produce water where there was none (Ex. 17:2-7).

4:9 I will give You. Satan is the "ruler of this world" (John 12:31; 14:30; 16:11), and the "god of this age" (2 Cor. 4:4). The whole world lies in his power (1 John 5:19). This is illustrated in Dan. 10:13 (*see note there*), where demonic power controlled the kingdom of Persia, so that a demon is called the Prince of Persia.

4:10 For it is written. Here Christ was citing and paraphrasing Deut. 6:13,14. Again, these relate to the Israelites' wilderness experiences. Christ, like them, was led into the wilderness to be tested (cf. Deut. 8:2). Unlike them, He withstood every aspect of the test.

4:11 angels came and ministered to Him. Psalm 91:11,12—the verse Satan tried to twist—was thus fulfilled in God's way, and in God's perfect timing.

4:12 John had been put in prison. John was imprisoned for his bold rebuke of Herod Antipas. See 14:3,4.

4:13 leaving Nazareth. Some time elapsed between vv. 12 and 13. Jesus' stay in Nazareth ended abruptly when He was violently rejected by the people of Nazareth, who tried to murder Him (see Luke 4:16-30). **Capernaum.** He settled in this important town on the trade route at the N end of the Sea of Galilee. Capernaum was the home of Peter and Andrew (v. 18), James and John (v. 21), and Matthew (9:9). A comparison of the gospels reveals that Christ had already ministered extensively in Capernaum (*see note on Luke 4:23*).

4:15 *Galilee of the Gentiles.* This name was used even in Isaiah's time because Galilee lay on the route through which all Gentiles passed in and out of Israel. In Jesus' time, the region of Galilee had become an important center of Roman occupation. The prophecy cited by Matthew is from Is. 9:1,2. See Is. 42:6,7.

4:17 From that time Jesus began to preach. This marks the beginning of His public ministry. Note that His message was an exact echo of what John the Baptist preached. **Repent, for the kingdom of heaven is at hand.** *See note on 3:2.* The opening word of this first sermon sets the tone for Jesus' entire earthly ministry (cf. Luke 5:32). Repentance was a constant motif in all His public preaching. And in

Jesus Calls His First Disciples
Mark 1:16-20

18 [q]And Jesus, walking by the Sea of Galilee, saw two brothers, Simon [r]called Peter,
and Andrew his brother, casting a net into
the sea; for they were fishermen. 19 Then
He said to them, "Follow Me, and [s]I will
make you fishers of men." 20 [t]They immediately left *their* nets and followed Him.
21 [u]Going on from there, He saw two
other brothers, James *the son* of Zebedee,
and John his brother, in the boat with Zebedee their father, mending their nets. He
called them, 22 and immediately they left
the boat and their father, and followed Him.

Jesus Ministers in Galilee
Mark 1:39; Luke 4:44

23 And Jesus went about all Galilee,
[v]teaching in their synagogues, preaching
[w]the gospel of the kingdom, [x]and healing
all kinds of sickness and all kinds of disease
among the people. 24 Then [4]His fame went
throughout all Syria; and they [y]brought to
Him all sick people who were afflicted with
various diseases and torments, and those
who were demon-possessed, epileptics,
and paralytics; and He healed them.
25 [z]Great multitudes followed Him—from
Galilee, and *from* [5]Decapolis, Jerusalem,
Judea, and beyond the Jordan.

The Beatitudes—Luke 6:20-26

5 And seeing the multitudes, [a]He went
up on a mountain, and when He was
seated His disciples came to Him. 2 Then
He opened His mouth and [b]taught them,
saying:

3 "Blessed [c]*are* the poor in spirit,
For theirs is the kingdom of heaven.
4 [d]Blessed *are* those who mourn,
For they shall be comforted.
5 [e]Blessed *are* the meek,
For [f]they shall inherit the [1]earth.
6 Blessed *are* those who [g]hunger and thirst for righteousness,
[h]For they shall be filled.

18 [q] Matt. 4:18-22; Mark 1:16-20; Luke 5:2-11; John 1:40-42 [r] Matt. 10:2; 16:18; John 1:40-42
19 [s] Luke 5:10
20 [t] Matt. 19:27; Mark 10:28
21 [u] Mark 1:19
23 [v] Ps. 22:22; Matt. 9:35; Mark 1:21; 6:2; 10:1; Luke 4:15; 6:6; 13:10; John 6:59; 18:20 [w] [Matt. 24:14]; Mark 1:14; Luke 4:43; 8:1; 16:16 [x] Mark 1:34; Luke 4:40; 7:21; Acts 10:38
24 [y] Mark 1:32, 33; Luke 4:40 [4] Lit. *the report of Him*
25 [z] Matt. 5:1; 8:1, 18; Mark 3:7, 8 [5] Lit. *Ten Cities*

CHAPTER 5

1 [a] Matt. 14:23; 15:29; 17:1; Mark 3:13; Luke 6:17; 9:28; John 6:3, 15
2 [b] [Matt. 7:29]; Mark 10:1; 12:35; John 8:2
3 [c] Prov. 16:19; Is. 66:2; Luke 6:20-23
4 [d] Is. 61:2, 3; Luke 6:21; [John 16:20]; Acts 16:34; [2 Cor. 1:7]; Rev. 21:4
5 [e] Ps. 37:11; Is. 29:19 [f] [Rom. 4:13] [1] Or *land*
6 [g] Luke 1:53; Acts 2:4 [h] [Is. 55:1; 65:13; John 4:14; 6:48; 7:37]

His closing charge to the apostles, He commanded them to preach repentance as well (Luke 24:47).

4:18 two brothers. Jesus had encountered Peter and Andrew before, near Bethabara, in the Jordan region, where Andrew (and perhaps Peter as well) had become a disciple of John the Baptist (John 1:35-42). They left John to follow Jesus for a time before returning to fishing in Capernaum. Perhaps they had returned to Capernaum during Jesus' earlier ministry here (*see note on Luke 4:23*). Here He called them to follow Him in long-term discipleship.

4:21 James *the son* of Zebedee. This James is easy to distinguish from the other men named James in the NT, because he is never mentioned in Scripture apart from his brother John. His martyrdom by Herod Agrippa I marked the beginning of a time of severe persecution in the early church (Acts 12:2). For information on others named James, *see note on 10:2*; Introduction to James: Author and Date.

4:23 teaching…preaching…healing. The 3 main aspects of Christ's public ministry.

4:24 Syria. The area immediately NE of Galilee.

4:25 Decapolis. A confederation of 10 Hellenized cities S of Galilee and mostly E of the Jordan. The league of cities was formed shortly after Pompey's invasion of Palestine (ca. 64 B.C.) to preserve Gr. culture in the Semitic region. These cities were naturally Gentile strongholds.

5:1–7:29 The Sermon on the Mount introduces a series of 5 important discourses recorded in Matthew (see Introduction: Historical and Theological Themes). This sermon is a masterful exposition of the law and a potent assault on Pharisaic legalism, closing with a call to true faith and salvation (7:13-29). Christ expounded the full meaning of the law, showing that its demands were humanly impossible (cf. 5:48). This is the proper use of the law with respect to salvation: It closes off every possible avenue of human merit and leaves sinners dependent on nothing but divine grace for salvation (cf. Rom. 3:19,20; Gal. 3:23,24). Christ plumbed the depth of the law, showing that its true demands went far beyond the surface meaning of the words (5:28,39,44) and set a standard that is higher than the most diligent students of the law had heretofore realized (5:20). *See note on Luke 6:17-49.*

5:1 was seated. This was the normal posture for rabbis while teaching (cf. 13:1,2; 26:55; Mark 4:1; 9:35; Luke 5:3; John 6:3; 8:2). *See note on Luke 4:20.*

5:3 Blessed. The word lit. means "happy, fortunate, blissful." Here it speaks of more than a surface emotion. Jesus was describing the divinely-bestowed well-being that belongs only to the faithful. The Beatitudes demonstrate that the way to heavenly blessedness is antithetical to the worldly path normally followed in pursuit of happiness. The worldly idea is that happiness is found in riches, merriment, abundance, leisure, and such things. The real truth is the very opposite. The Beatitudes give Jesus' description of the character of true faith. **poor in spirit.** The opposite of self-sufficiency. This speaks of the deep humility of recognizing one's utter spiritual bankruptcy apart from God. It describes those who are acutely conscious of their own lostness and hopelessness apart from divine grace (cf. 9:12; Luke 18:13). *See note on 19:17.* **theirs is the kingdom of heaven.** *See note on 3:2.* Notice that the truth of salvation by grace is clearly presupposed in this opening verse of the Sermon on the Mount. Jesus was teaching that the kingdom is a gracious gift to those who sense their own poverty of spirit.

5:4 those who mourn. This speaks of mourning over sin, the godly sorrow that produces repentance leading to salvation without regret (2 Cor. 7:10). The "comfort" is the comfort of forgiveness and salvation (cf. Is. 40:1,2).

5:5 the meek. Meekness is the opposite of being out of control. It is not weakness, but supreme self-control empowered by the Spirit (cf. Gal. 5:23). The fact that "the meek shall inherit the earth" is quoted from Ps. 37:11. *See notes on vv. 9-11.*

5:6 hunger and thirst for righteousness. This is the opposite of the self-righteousness of the Pharisees. It speaks of those who seek God's righteousness rather than attempting to establish a righteousness of their own (Rom. 10:3; Phil. 3:9). What they seek will fill them, i.e., it will satisfy their hunger and thirst for a right relationship with God.

7 Blessed *are* the merciful,
[i]For they shall obtain mercy.
8 [j]Blessed *are* the pure in heart,
For [k]they shall see God.
9 Blessed *are* the peacemakers,
For they shall be called sons of
God.
10 [l]Blessed are those who are
persecuted for righteousness'
sake,
For theirs is the kingdom of
heaven.

11 [m]"Blessed are you when they revile and
persecute you, and say all kinds of [n]evil
against you falsely for My sake. 12 [o]Rejoice
and be exceedingly glad, for great *is* your
reward in heaven, for [p]so they persecuted
the prophets who were before you.

The Similitudes

13 "You are the salt of the earth; [q]but if the
salt loses its flavor, how shall it be seasoned?
It is then good for nothing but to be thrown
out and trampled underfoot by men.
14 [r]"You are the light of the world. A city
that is set on a hill cannot be hidden.

7 [i]Ps. 41:1; Mark 11:25
8 [j]Ps. 15:2; 24:4; Heb. 12:14 [k]Acts 7:55, 56; 1 Cor. 13:12
10 [l][2 Cor. 4:17]; 1 Pet. 3:14
11 [m]Luke 6:22 [n]1 Pet. 4:14
12 [o]Luke 6:23; Acts 5:41; 1 Pet. 4:13, 14 [p]2 Chr. 36:16; Neh. 9:26; Matt. 23:37; Acts 7:52; 1 Thess. 2:15; Heb. 11:35-37; James 5:10
13 [q]Mark 9:50; Luke 14:34
14 [r][Prov. 4:18; John 8:12]; Phil. 2:15
15 [s]Mark 4:21; Luke 8:16; Phil. 2:15
16 [t]1 Pet. 2:12 [u][John 15:8]; 1 Cor. 14:25
17 [v]Rom. 10:4
18 [w]Matt. 24:35; Luke 16:17 [2]Gr. *iota*, Heb. *yod*, the smallest letter [3]The smallest stroke in a Heb. letter
19 [x][James 2:10]
20 [y][Rom. 10:3]

15 Nor do they [s]light a lamp and put it
under a basket, but on a lampstand, and it
gives light to all *who are* in the house. 16 Let
your light so shine before men, [t]that they
may see your good works and [u]glorify
your Father in heaven.

Jesus Fulfills the Law

17 [v]"Do not think that I came to destroy
the Law or the Prophets. I did not come to
destroy but to fulfill. 18 For assuredly, I say
to you, [w]till heaven and earth pass away,
one [2]jot or one [3]tittle will by no means
pass from the law till all is fulfilled.
19 [x]Whoever therefore breaks one of the
least of these commandments, and teaches
men so, shall be called least in the kingdom of heaven; but whoever does and
teaches *them,* he shall be called great in the
kingdom of heaven. 20 For I say to you,
that unless your righteousness exceeds
[y]*the righteousness* of the scribes and Pharisees, you will by no means enter the kingdom of heaven.

Murder

21 "You have heard that it was said to

5:7 they shall obtain mercy. The converse is also true. Cf. James 2:13.

5:8 see God. Not only with the perception of faith, but in the glory of heaven. Cf. Heb. 12:14; Rev. 22:3,4.

5:9 peacemakers. See vv. 44,45 for more on this quality.

5:10 persecuted. Cf. James 5:10,11; 1 Pet. 4:12-14. *See note on Luke 6:22.*

5:13 if the salt loses its flavor, how shall it be seasoned? Salt is both a preservative and a flavor enhancer. No doubt its use as a preservative is what Jesus had mostly in view here. Pure salt cannot lose its flavor or effectiveness, but the salt that is common in the Dead Sea area is contaminated with gypsum and other minerals and may have a flat taste or be ineffective as a preservative. Such mineral salts were useful for little more than keeping footpaths free of vegetation.

5:16 light so shine. A godly life gives convincing testimony of the saving power of God. That brings Him glory. Cf. 1 Pet. 2:12.

5:17 Do not think that I came to destroy the Law or the Prophets. We are not to think that Jesus' teaching in the verses that follow was meant to alter, abrogate, or replace the moral content of the OT law. He was neither giving a new law nor modifying the old, but rather explaining the true significance of the moral content of Moses' law and the rest of the OT. "The Law and the Prophets" speaks of the entirety of the OT Scriptures, not the rabbinical interpretations of them. **fulfill.** This speaks of fulfillment in the same sense that prophecy is fulfilled. Christ was indicating that He is the fulfillment of the law in all its aspects. He fulfilled the moral law by keeping it perfectly. He fulfilled the ceremonial law by being the embodiment of everything the law's types and symbols pointed to. And he fulfilled the judicial law by personifying God's perfect justice (cf. 12:18,20).

5:18 till heaven and earth pass away...till all is fulfilled. Here Christ was emphasizing both the inspiration and the enduring authority of all Scripture. He was specifically affirming the utter inerrancy and absolute authority of the OT as the Word of God—down to the least jot and tittle. Again (*see note on v. 17*), this suggests that the NT should not be seen as supplanting and abrogating the OT, but as fulfilling and explicating it. For example, all the ceremonial requirements of the Mosaic law were fulfilled in Christ and are no longer to be observed by Christians (Col. 2:16,17). Yet not one jot or tittle is thereby erased; the underlying truths of those Scriptures remain—and in fact the mysteries behind them are now revealed in the brighter light of the gospel. They have not passed from the law is the sense Jesus means here. **one jot or one tittle.** A "jot" refers to the smallest Heb. letter, the *yohd,* which is a meager stroke of the pen, like an accent mark or an apostrophe. The "tittle" is a tiny extension on a Heb. letter, like the serif in modern typefaces.

5:19 shall be called least...shall be called great. Any violation of God's law makes one least in the kingdom, which is equal to being outside the kingdom and under condemnation (cf. Gal. 3:10-12). The one who keeps God's law is great, which is equal to being in the kingdom and in God's salvation. In chap. 13, the parables of the tares (13:24-30) and the dragnet (13:47-50) indicate that in the visible, external kingdom of those who identify with God there will be true and false people (cf. 7:21-27). The "least" refers to those who will be judged and cast out (13:30,41,42,49,50) while the "great" shall be included and rewarded (v. 43).

5:20 unless your righteousness exceeds *the righteousness* of the scribes and Pharisees. On the one hand, Jesus was calling His disciples to a deeper, more radical holiness than that of the Pharisees. Pharisaism had a tendency to soften the law's demands by focusing only on external obedience. In the verses that follow, Jesus unpacks the full moral significance of the law, and shows that the righteousness the law calls for actually involves an internal conformity to the spirit of the law, rather than mere external compliance to the letter. **will by no means enter the kingdom of heaven.** On the other hand, this sets up an impossible barrier to works-salvation. Scripture teaches repeatedly that sinners are capable of nothing but a flawed and imperfect righteousness (e.g., Is. 64:6). Therefore the only righteousness by which sinners may be justified is the perfect righteousness of God that is imputed to those who believe (Gen. 15:6; Rom. 4:5).

5:21,22 You have heard.... But I say to you. See vv. 27,31,33,

those [4]of old, [z]*'You shall not murder,* and
whoever murders will be in danger of the
judgment.' 22 But I say to you that [a]who-
ever is angry with his brother [5]without a
cause shall be in danger of the judgment.
And whoever says to his brother, [b]'Raca!'[6]
shall be in danger of the council. But whoever says, [7]'You fool!' shall be in danger of
[8]hell fire. 23 Therefore [c]if you bring your
gift to the altar, and there remember that
your brother has something against you,
24 [d]leave your gift there before the altar,
and go your way. First be reconciled to
your brother, and then come and offer
your gift. 25 [e]Agree with your adversary
quickly, [f]while you are on the way with
him, lest your adversary deliver you to the
judge, the judge hand you over to the officer, and you be thrown into prison. 26 Assuredly, I say to you, you will by no means
get out of there till you have paid the last
penny.

Adultery

27 "You have heard that it was said [9]to
those of old, [g]*'You shall not commit adultery.'* 28 But I say to you that whoever
[h]looks at a woman to lust for her has already committed adultery with her in his
heart. 29 [i]If your right eye causes you to
[1]sin, [j]pluck it out and cast *it* from you; for
it is more profitable for you that one of
your members perish, than for your whole
body to be cast into hell. 30 And if your
right hand causes you to [2]sin, cut it off
and cast *it* from you; for it is more profitable for you that one of your members perish, than for your whole body to be cast
into hell.

Divorce

31 "Furthermore it has been said, [k]'Whoever divorces his wife, let him give her a
certificate of divorce.' 32 But I say to you
that [l]whoever divorces his wife for any
reason except [3]sexual immorality causes
her to commit adultery; and whoever marries a woman who is divorced commits
adultery.

Oaths

33 "Again you have heard that [m]it was
said to those of [4]old, [n]'You shall not swear
falsely, but [o]shall perform your oaths to the
Lord.' 34 But I say to you, [p]do not swear at
all: neither by heaven, for it is [q]God's
throne; 35 nor by the earth, for it is His
footstool; nor by Jerusalem, for it is the city
of [r]the great King. 36 Nor shall you swear
by your head, because you cannot make
one hair white or black. 37 [s]But let [5]your
'Yes' be 'Yes,' and your 'No,' 'No.' For
whatever is more than these is from the
evil one.

21 [z] Ex. 20:13; Deut. 5:17 [4] *in ancient times*
22 [a] [1 John 3:15] [b] [James 2:20; 3:6] [5] NU omits *without a cause* [6] Lit., in Aram., *Empty head* [7] Gr. *More* [8] Gr. *Gehenna*
23 [c] Matt. 8:4
24 [d] [Job 42:8; 1 Tim. 2:8; 1 Pet. 3:7]
25 [e] [Prov. 25:8]; Luke 12:58, 59 [f] [Ps. 32:6; Is. 55:6]
27 [g] Ex. 20:14; Deut. 5:18 [9] NU, M omit *to those of old*
28 [h] 2 Sam. 11:2-5; Job 31:1; Prov. 6:25; [Matt. 15:19; James 1:14, 15]
29 [i] Mark 9:43 [j] [Col. 3:5] [1] Lit. *stumble* or *offend*
30 [2] Lit. *stumble* or *offend*
31 [k] Deut. 24:1; [Jer. 3:1]; Mark 10:2
32 [l] [Matt. 19:9; Mark 10:11; Luke 16:18; Rom. 7:3]; 1 Cor. 7:11 [3] Or *fornication*
33 [m] Matt. 23:16 [n] [Ex. 20:7]; Lev. 19:12; Num. 30:2 [o] Deut. 23:23 [4] *ancient times*
34 [p] Matt. 23:16; James 5:12 [q] Is. 66:1
35 [r] Ps. 48:2; [Matt. 5:2, 19; 6:10]
37 [s] [Col. 4:6]; James 5:12 [5] Lit. *your word be yes yes*

38,43. The quotes are from Ex. 20:13; Deut. 5:17. Jesus was not altering the terms of the law in any of these passages. Rather, He was correcting what they had "heard"—the rabbinical understanding of the law (*see note on v. 38*).

5:22 Raca! Lit. "Empty-headed!" Jesus suggested here that the verbal abuse stems from the same sinful motives (anger and hatred) that ultimately lead to murder. The internal attitude is what the law actually prohibits, and therefore an abusive insult carries the same kind of moral guilt as an act of murder. **hell.** A reference to the Hinnom Valley, SW of Jerusalem. Ahaz and Manasseh permitted human sacrifices there during their reigns (2 Chr. 28:3; 33:6), and therefore it was called "The Valley of Slaughter" (Jer. 19:6). In Jesus' day, it was a garbage dump where fires burned continually and was thus an apt symbol of eternal fire.

5:25 Agree...quickly. Jesus calls for reconciliation to be sought eagerly, aggressively, quickly—even if it involves self-sacrifice. It is better to be wronged than to allow a dispute between brethren to be a cause for dishonoring Christ (1 Cor. 6:7). **adversary.** This speaks of one's opponent in a law case. **prison.** Debtor's prison, where the person could work to earn back what he had defrauded.

5:27 Quoted from Ex. 20:14; Deut. 5:18.

5:29 pluck it out and cast *it* from you. Jesus was not advocating self-mutilation (for this would not in fact cure lust, which is actually a problem of the heart). He was using this graphic hyperbole to demonstrate the seriousness of sins of lust and evil desire. The point is that it would be "more profitable" (v. 30) to lose a member of one's own body than to bear the eternal consequences of the guilt from such a sin. Sin must be dealt with drastically because of its deadly effects.

5:31 it has been said. *See note on Deut. 24:1-4.* The rabbis had taken liberty with what Scripture actually said. They referred to Deut. 24:1-4 as if it were given merely to regulate the paperwork when one sought divorce (*see note on 19:7*). Thus, they had wrongly concluded that men could divorce their wives for anything that displeased them, as long as they gave "a certificate of divorce." But Moses provided this as a concession to protect the woman who was divorced (*see notes on 19:7-9*), not to justify or legalize divorce under all circumstances.

5:32 except sexual immorality. *See note on 19:9.* Divorce was allowed in cases of adultery. Luke 16:18 must be understood in the light of this verse. **causes her to commit adultery.** The assumption is that divorced people will remarry. If the divorce was not for sexual immorality any remarriage is adultery, because God does not acknowledge the divorce. For more on divorce, *see note on 1 Cor. 7:15.*

5:33 You shall not swear falsely. This expresses teaching from Lev. 19:12; Num. 30:2; Deut. 23:21,23.

5:34 do not swear at all. Cf. James 5:12. This should not be taken as a universal condemnation of oaths in all circumstances. God Himself confirmed a promise with an oath (Heb. 6:13-18; cf. Acts 2:30). Christ Himself spoke under oath (26:63,64). And the law prescribed oaths in certain circumstances (e.g., Num. 5:19,21; 30:2,3). What Christ is forbidding here is the flippant, profane, or careless use of oaths in everyday speech. In that culture, such oaths were often employed for deceptive purposes. To make the person being victimized believe the truth was being told, the Jews would swear by "heaven," "earth," "Jerusalem," or their own "heads" (vv. 34-36), not by God, hoping to avoid divine judgment for their lie. But it all was in God's creation, so it drew Him in and produced guilt before Him, exactly as if the oath were made in His name. Jesus suggested that all our speech should be as if we were under an oath to tell the truth (v. 37).

Retaliation

38 "You have heard that it was said, [t]*'An
eye for an eye and a tooth for a tooth.'*
39 [u]But I tell you not to resist an evil person. [v]But whoever slaps you on your right
cheek, turn the other to him also. **40** If anyone wants to sue you and take away your
tunic, let him have *your* cloak also. **41** And
whoever [w]compels you to go one mile, go
with him two. **42** Give to him who asks
you, and [x]from him who wants to borrow
from you do not turn away.

Love—Luke 6:27, 32

43 "You have heard that it was said,
[y]*'You shall love your neighbor* [z]and hate
your enemy.' **44** [6]But I say to you, [a]love
your enemies, bless those who curse you,
[b]do good to those who hate you, and pray
[c]for those who spitefully use you and persecute you, **45** that you may be sons of your
Father in heaven; for [d]He makes His sun
rise on the evil and on the good, and sends
rain on the just and on the unjust. **46** [e]For if
you love those who love you, what reward
have you? Do not even the tax collectors
do the same? **47** And if you greet your
[7]brethren only, what do you do more *than
others?* Do not even the [8]tax collectors do
so? **48** [f]Therefore you shall be perfect, just
[g]as your Father in heaven is perfect.

38 [t]Ex. 21:24; Lev. 24:20; Deut. 19:21
39 [u][Prov. 20:22]; Luke 6:29; [Rom. 12:17; 1 Cor. 6:7; 1 Pet. 3:9] [v]Is. 50:6; Lam. 3:30
41 [w]Matt. 27:32
42 [x]Deut. 15:7-11; Luke 6:30-34; 1 Tim. 6:18
43 [y]Lev. 19:18 [z]Deut. 23:3-6; Ps. 41:10
44 [a]Luke 6:27; Rom. 12:14 [b][Rom. 12:20] [c]Luke 23:34; Acts 7:60; 1 Cor. 4:12; 1 Pet. 2:23 [6]NU *But I say to you, love your enemies and pray for those who persecute you*
45 [d]Job 25:3; Ps. 65:9-13; Luke 12:16, 17; Acts 14:17
46 [e]Luke 6:32
47 [7]M *friends* [8]NU *Gentiles*
48 [f]Gen. 17:1; Lev. 11:44; 19:2; Luke 6:36; [Col. 1:28; 4:12]; James 1:4; 1 Pet. 1:15 [g]Eph. 5:1

CHAPTER 6

2 [a]Rom. 12:8
4 [b]Luke 14:12-14 [1]NU omits *openly*
5 [2]*pretenders*
6 [c]2 Kin. 4:33 [3]NU omits *openly*
7 [d]Eccl. 5:2 [e]1 Kin. 18:26

Charitable Deeds

6 "Take heed that you do not do your
charitable deeds before men, to be seen
by them. Otherwise you have no reward
from your Father in heaven. **2** Therefore,
[a]when you do a charitable deed, do not
sound a trumpet before you as the hypocrites do in the synagogues and in the
streets, that they may have glory from
men. Assuredly, I say to you, they have
their reward. **3** But when you do a charitable deed, do not let your left hand know
what your right hand is doing, **4** that your
charitable deed may be in secret; and your
Father who sees in secret [b]will Himself reward you [1]openly.

Prayer—Luke 11:2-4

5 "And when you pray, you shall not be
like the [2]hypocrites. For they love to pray
standing in the synagogues and on the corners of the streets, that they may be seen by
men. Assuredly, I say to you, they have
their reward. **6** But you, when you pray, [c]go
into your room, and when you have shut
your door, pray to your Father who *is* in the
secret *place;* and your Father who sees in secret will reward you [3]openly. **7** And when
you pray, [d]do not use vain repetitions as
the heathen *do.* [e]For they think that they
will be heard for their many words.

5:38 ***An eye for an eye.*** The law did establish this standard as a principle for limiting retribution to that which was just (Ex. 21:24; Lev. 24:20; Deut. 19:21). Its design was to insure that the punishment in civil cases fit the crime. It was never meant to sanction acts of personal retaliation. So again (*see notes on vv. 17,18*) Jesus made no alteration to the true meaning of the law. He was merely explaining and affirming the law's true meaning.

5:39 not to resist an evil person. Like v. 38, this deals only with matters of personal retaliation, not criminal offenses or acts of military aggression. Jesus applied this principle of non-retaliation to affronts against one's dignity (v. 39), lawsuits to gain one's personal assets (v. 40), infringements on one's liberty (v. 41), and violations of property rights (v. 42). He was calling for a full surrender of all personal rights.

5:41 compels. The word speaks of coercion or force. The NT picture of this is when Roman soldiers "compelled" Simon the Cyrene to carry Jesus' cross (27:32).

5:43 ***love your neighbor*** **and hate your enemy.** The first half of this is found in Moses' law (Lev. 19:18). The second part was found in how the scribes and Pharisees explained and applied that OT command. Jesus' application was exactly the opposite, resulting in a much higher standard: Love for one's neighbors should extend even to those neighbors who are enemies (v. 44). Again, this was no innovation, since even the OT taught that God's people should do good to their enemies (Prov. 25:21).

5:44,45 love your enemies...that you may be sons of your Father. This plainly teaches that God's love extends even to His enemies. This universal love of God is manifest in blessings which God bestows on all indiscriminately. Theologians refer to this as common grace. This must be distinguished from the everlasting love God has for the elect (Jer. 31:3), but it is a sincere goodwill nonetheless (cf. Ps. 145:9).

5:46 tax collectors. Disloyal Israelites hired by the Romans to tax other Jews for personal profit. They became symbols for the worst kind of people. Cf. 9:10,11; 11:19; 18:17; 21:31; Mark 2:14-16; Luke 5:30; 7:25,29,34; 18:11-13. Matthew had been one of them (*see notes on 9:9; Mark 2:15*).

5:48 you shall be perfect. Christ sets an unattainable standard. This sums up what the law itself demanded (James 2:10). Though this standard is impossible to meet, God could not lower it without compromising His own perfection. He who is perfect could not set an imperfect standard of righteousness. The marvelous truth of the gospel is that Christ has met this standard on our behalf (*see note on 2 Cor. 5:21*).

6:1-18 Here Christ expands the thought of 5:20, showing how the Pharisees' righteousness was deficient by exposing their hypocrisy in the matters of "charitable deeds" (vv. 1-4); "prayer" (vv. 5-15); and "fasting" (vv. 16-18). All of these acts are supposed to be worship rendered to God, never displays of self-righteousness to gain the admiration of others.

6:2 hypocrites. This word had its origins in Gr. theater, describing a character who wore a mask. The term, as used in the NT, normally described an unregenerate person who was self-deceived. **they have their reward.** Cf. vv. 5,16. Their reward is that they were seen by men, nothing more. God does not reward hypocrisy, but He does punish it (cf. 23:13-23).

6:4 sees in secret. Cf. vv. 6,18; Jer. 17:10; Heb. 4:13. God is omniscient.

6:7 vain repetitions. Prayers are not to be merely recited, nor are our words to be repeated thoughtlessly, or as if they were automatic formulas. But this is not a prohibition against importunity (*see notes on Luke 11:1-8*).

8 "Therefore do not be like them. For
your Father [f]knows the things you have
need of before you ask Him. 9 In this
[g]manner, therefore, pray:

[h]Our Father in heaven,
Hallowed be Your [i]name.
10 Your kingdom come.
[j]Your will be done
On earth [k]as *it is* in heaven.
11 Give us this day our [l]daily bread.
12 And [m]forgive us our debts,
As we forgive our debtors.
13 [n]And do not lead us into temptation,
But [o]deliver us from the evil one.
[4]For Yours is the kingdom and the
power and the glory forever.
Amen.

14 [p]"For if you forgive men their trespasses, your heavenly Father will also forgive you. 15 But [q]if you do not forgive men
their trespasses, neither will your Father
forgive your trespasses.

Fasting

16 "Moreover, [r]when you fast, do not be
like the [5]hypocrites, with a sad countenance. For they disfigure their faces that
they may appear to men to be fasting. Assuredly, I say to you, they have their reward. 17 But you, when you fast, [s]anoint
your head and wash your face, 18 so that
you do not appear to men to be fasting, but
to your Father who *is* in the secret *place;*
and your Father who sees in secret will reward you [6]openly.

Wealth—Luke 11:34-36; 12:22-34

19 [t]"Do not lay up for yourselves treasures on earth, where moth and rust destroy and where thieves break in and steal;
20 [u]but lay up for yourselves treasures in
heaven, where neither moth nor rust destroys and where thieves do not break in
and steal. 21 For where your treasure is,
there your heart will be also.

22 [v]"The lamp of the body is the eye. If
therefore your eye is [7]good, your whole
body will be full of light. 23 But if your eye
is [8]bad, your whole body will be full of
darkness. If therefore the light that is in you
is darkness, how great *is* that darkness!

24 [w]"No one can serve two masters; for
either he will hate the one and love the
other, or else he will be loyal to the one and
despise the other. [x]You cannot serve God
and [9]mammon.

25 "Therefore I say to you, [y]do not worry
about your life, what you will eat or what
you will drink; nor about your body, what
you will put on. Is not life more than food
and the body more than clothing? 26 [z]Look
at the birds of the air, for they neither sow
nor reap nor gather into barns; yet your
heavenly Father feeds them. Are you not of

8 [f] [Rom. 8:26, 27]
9 [g] Matt. 6:9-13; Luke 11:2-4; [John 16:24; Eph. 6:18; Jude 20] [h] [Matt. 5:9, 16] [i] Mal. 1:11
10 [j] Matt. 26:42; Luke 22:42; Acts 21:14 [k] Ps. 103:20
11 [l] [Job 23:12]; Prov. 30:8; Is. 33:16; Luke 11:3
12 [m] [Matt. 18:21, 22]
13 [n] [Matt. 26:41; 1 Cor. 10:31; 2 Pet. 2:9; Rev. 3:10] [o] John 17:15; [2 Thess. 3:3]; 2 Tim. 4:18; [1 John 5:18] [4] NU omits the rest of v. 13.
14 [p] [Matt. 7:2]; Mark 11:25; [Eph. 4:32; Col. 3:13]
15 [q] Matt. 18:35; James 2:13
16 [r] Is. 58:3-7; Luke 18:12 [5] *pretenders*
17 [s] Ruth 3:3; 2 Sam. 12:20; Dan. 10:3
18 [6] NU, M omit *openly*
19 [t] Prov. 23:4; [1 Tim. 6:17; Heb. 13:5]; James 5:1
20 [u] Matt. 19:21; Luke 12:33; 18:22; 1 Tim. 6:19; 1 Pet. 1:4
22 [v] Luke 11:34, 35 [7] Clear, or healthy
23 [8] Evil, or unhealthy
24 [w] Luke 16:9, 11, 13 [x] [Gal. 1:10; 1 Tim. 6:17; James 4:4; 1 John 2:15] [9] Lit., in Aram., *riches*

25 [y] [Ps. 55:22]; Luke 12:22; [Phil. 4:6; 1 Pet. 5:7] **26** [z] Job 38:41; Ps. 147:9; Matt. 10:29; Luke 12:24

6:9 In this manner. Cf. Luke 11:2-4. The prayer is a model, not merely a liturgy. It is notable for its brevity, simplicity, and comprehensiveness. Of the 6 petitions, 3 are directed to God (vv. 9,10) and 3 toward human needs (vv. 11-13).

6:10 Your will be done. All prayer, first of all, willingly submits to God's purposes, plans, and glory. *See note on 26:39.*

6:12 forgive us our debts. The parallel passage (Luke 11:4) uses a word that means "sins," so that in context, spiritual debts are intended. Sinners are debtors to God for their violations of His laws (*see notes on 18:23-27*). This request is the heart of the prayer; it is what Jesus stressed in the words that immediately follow the prayer (vv. 14,15; cf. Mark 11:25).

6:13 do not lead us into temptation. Cf. Luke 22:40. God does not tempt men (James 1:13), but He will subject them to trials that may expose them to Satan's assaults, as in the case of Job and Peter (Luke 22:31,32). This petition reflects the believing one's desire to avoid the dangers of sin altogether. God knows what one's need is before one asks (v. 8), and He promises that no one will be subjected to testing beyond what can be endured. He also promises a way of escape—often through endurance (1 Cor. 10:13). But still, the proper attitude for the believer is the one expressed in this petition.

6:15 neither will your Father forgive your trespasses. This is not to suggest that God will withdraw justification from those who have already received the free pardon He extends to all believers. Forgiveness in that sense—a permanent and complete acquittal from the guilt and ultimate penalty of sin—belongs to all who are in Christ (cf. John 5:24; Rom. 8:1; Eph. 1:7). Yet, Scripture also teaches that God chastens His children who disobey (Heb. 12:5-7). Believers are to confess their sins in order to obtain a day-to-day cleansing (1 John 1:9). This sort of forgiveness is a simple washing from the worldly defilements of sin; not a repeat of the wholesale cleansing from sin's corruption that comes with justification. It is like a washing of the feet rather than a bath (cf. John 13:10). Forgiveness in this latter sense is what God threatens to withhold from Christians who refuse to forgive others (cf. 18:23-35).

6:16,17 when you fast. This indicates that fasting is assumed to be a normal part of one's spiritual life (cf. 1 Cor. 7:5). Fasting is associated with sadness (9:14,15), prayer (17:21), charity (Is. 58:3-6), and seeking the Lord's will (Acts 13:2,3; 14:23).

6:20 treasures. Don't amass earthly wealth. He commends the use of financial assets for purposes which are heavenly and eternal. *See notes on Luke 16:1-9.*

6:22,23 This is an argument from the lesser to the greater. The analogy is simple. If your eye is bad, no light can come in and you are left with darkness because of that malady. How much worse when the problem is not merely related to external perception, but an internal corruption of one's whole nature, so that the darkness actually emanates from within and affects one's whole being. He was indicting them for their superficial earthly religion that left their hearts dark. *See note on Luke 11:34.*

6:24 mammon. Earthly, material treasures, especially money. *See note on Luke 16:13.*

6:26 your heavenly Father feeds them. Obviously this in no way advocates a sinful kind of idleness (Prov. 19:15). Birds are not idle, either. But it is God who provides them with food to eat.

more value than they? 27 Which of you by
worrying can add one [1]cubit to his [2]stature?
28 "So why do you worry about cloth-
ing? Consider the lilies of the field, how
they grow: they neither toil nor spin;
29 and yet I say to you that even Solomon
in all his glory was not [3]arrayed like one of
these. 30 Now if God so clothes the grass of
the field, which today is, and tomorrow is
thrown into the oven, *will He* not much
more *clothe* you, O you of little faith?
31 "Therefore do not worry, saying, 'What
shall we eat?' or 'What shall we drink?' or
'What shall we wear?' 32 For after all these
things the Gentiles seek. For your heavenly
Father knows that you need all these things.
33 But [a]seek first the kingdom of God and
His righteousness, and all these things shall
be added to you. 34 Therefore do not worry
about tomorrow, for tomorrow will worry
about its own things. Sufficient for the day
is its own trouble.

Judging—Luke 6:37-42

7 "Judge[1] [a]not, that you be not judged.
2 For with what [2]judgment you judge,
you will be judged; [b]and with the measure
you use, it will be measured back to you.
3 [c]And why do you look at the speck in
your brother's eye, but do not consider the
plank in your own eye? 4 Or how can you
say to your brother, 'Let me remove the
speck from your eye'; and look, a plank *is*
in your own eye? 5 Hypocrite! First remove the plank from your own eye, and
then you will see clearly to remove the
speck from your brother's eye.
6 [d]"Do not give what is holy to the dogs;
nor cast your pearls before swine, lest they
trample them under their feet, and turn
and tear you in pieces.

"Ask, and It Will Be Given"—Luke 11:9-13

7 [e]"Ask, and it will be given to you; seek,
and you will find; knock, and it will be
opened to you. 8 For [f]everyone who asks receives, and he who seeks finds, and to him
who knocks it will be opened. 9 [g]Or what
man is there among you who, if his son asks
for bread, will give him a stone? 10 Or if he
asks for a fish, will he give him a serpent?
11 If you then, [h]being evil, know how to
give good gifts to your children, how much
more will your Father who is in heaven give
good things to those who ask Him!

Golden Rule—Luke 6:31

12 Therefore, [i]whatever you want men
to do to you, do also to them, for [j]this is the
Law and the Prophets.

Two Ways of Life

13 [k]"Enter by the narrow gate; for wide
is the gate and broad *is* the way that leads
to destruction, and there are many who go
in by it. 14 [3]Because narrow *is* the gate and
[4]difficult *is* the way which leads to life, and
there are few who find it.

27 [1] About 18 inches [2] *height*
29 [3] *dressed*
33 [a] 1 Kin. 3:13; Luke 12:31; [1 Tim. 4:8]

CHAPTER 7

1 [a] Matt. 7:1-5; Luke 6:37; Rom. 14:3; [1 Cor. 4:3, 4] [1] Condemn
2 [b] Mark 4:24; Luke 6:38 [2] Condemnation
3 [c] Luke 6:41
6 [d] Prov. 9:7, 8; Acts 13:45
7 [e] [Matt. 21:22; Mark 11:24]; Luke 11:9-13; 18:1-8; [John 15:7; James 1:5, 6; 1 John 3:22]
8 [f] Prov. 8:17; Jer. 29:12
9 [g] Luke 11:11
11 [h] Gen. 6:5; 8:21; Ps. 84:11; Is. 63:7; [Rom. 8:32; James 1:17]; 1 John 3:1
12 [i] Luke 6:31 [j] Matt. 22:40; Rom. 13:8; Gal. 5:14; [1 Tim. 1:5]
13 [k] Luke 13:24
14 [3] NU, M *How narrow . . . !* [4] *confined*

6:27 add one cubit to his stature. The Gr. phrase may also refer to adding time to one's lifespan.

6:29 Solomon in all his glory. The glory and pageantry of Solomon's kingdom was famous worldwide. Cf. 2 Chr. 9.

6:30 you of little faith. Cf. 8:26; 14:31; 16:8; 17:20. This was the Lord's recurring rebuke of the weak disciples.

6:32 Gentiles. I.e., those outside the people of promise and outside the blessing of God. Cf. Eph. 4:17-19.

6:33 kingdom of God. This is the same as kingdom of heaven. *See note on 3:2.* It refers to the sphere of salvation. He was urging them to seek salvation—and with it would come the full care and provision of God. Cf. Rom. 8:32; Phil. 4:19; 1 Pet. 5:7.

7:1 Judge not. As the context reveals, this does not prohibit all types of judging (v. 16). There is a righteous kind of judgment we are supposed to exercise with careful discernment (John 7:24). Censorious, hypocritical, self-righteous, or other kinds of unfair judgments are forbidden; but in order to fulfill the commandments that follow, it is necessary to discern dogs and swine (v. 6) from one's own brethren (vv. 3-5).

7:6 Do not give what is holy to the dogs. This principle is why Jesus Himself did not do miracles for unbelievers (13:58). This is to be done in respect for what is holy, not merely out of contempt for the dogs and swine. Nothing here contradicts the principle of 5:44. That verse governs personal dealings with one's enemies (*see note there*); this principle governs how one handles the gospel in the face of those who hate the truth.

7:11 you . . . being evil. Jesus presupposes the doctrine of human depravity (*see note on Romans 1:18–3:20*). **how much more.** If earthly fathers give what their sons need (vv. 9,10), will not God give to His sons what they ask (vv. 7,8)? *See note on James 1:17.*

7:12 do also to them. Versions of the "Golden Rule" existed before Christ, in the rabbinic writings and even in Hinduism and Buddhism. All of them cast the rule as a negative command, such as Rabbi Hillel's version, "What is hateful to yourself do not to someone else." Jesus made it a positive command, enriching its meaning and underscoring that this one imperative aptly summarizes the whole gist of the ethical principles contained in the Law and the Prophets.

7:13-29 This closing section of the Sermon on the Mount is a gospel application. Here are two gates, two ways, two destinations, and two groups of people (vv. 13,14); two kinds of trees and two kinds of fruit (vv. 17-20); two groups at the judgment (vv. 21-23); and two kinds of builders, building on two kinds of foundations (vv. 24-28). Christ is drawing the line as clearly as possible between the way that leads to destruction and the way which leads to life.

7:13,14 Both the narrow gate and the wide gate are assumed to provide the entrance to God's kingdom. Two ways are offered to people. The narrow gate is by faith, only through Christ, constricted and precise. It represents true salvation in God's way that leads to life eternal. The wide gate includes all religions of works and self-righteousness, with no single way (cf. Acts 4:12), but leads to hell, not heaven.

7:14 difficult *is* the way. Christ continually emphasized the difficulty of following Him (10:38; 16:24,25; John 15:18,19; 16:1-3; cf. Acts 14:22). Salvation is by grace alone, but is not easy. It calls for knowledge of the truth, repentance, submission to Christ as Lord, and a willingness to obey His will and Word. *See notes on 19:16-28.*

False and True Teaching—Luke 6:43-45

15 [l]"Beware of false prophets, [m]who
come to you in sheep's clothing, but inwardly they are ravenous wolves. 16 [n]You
will know them by their fruits. [o]Do men
gather grapes from thornbushes or figs
from thistles? 17 Even so, [p]every good tree
bears good fruit, but a bad tree bears bad
fruit. 18 A good tree cannot bear bad fruit,
nor *can* a bad tree bear good fruit. 19 [q]Every
tree that does not bear good fruit is cut
down and thrown into the fire. 20 Therefore
by their fruits you will know them.

True Way into the Kingdom—Luke 6:46

21 "Not everyone who says to Me,
[r]'Lord, Lord,' shall enter the kingdom of
heaven, but he who [s]does the will of My
Father in heaven. 22 Many will say to Me in
that day, 'Lord, Lord, have we [t]not prophesied in Your name, cast out demons in
Your name, and done many wonders in
Your name?' 23 And [u]then I will declare to
them, 'I never knew you; [v]depart from Me,
you who practice lawlessness!'

Parable of the Two Builders—Luke 6:47-49

24 "Therefore [w]whoever hears these sayings of Mine, and does them, I will liken
him to a wise man who built his house on
the rock: 25 and the rain descended, the
floods came, and the winds blew and beat
on that house; and it did not fall, for it was
founded on the rock.
26 "But everyone who hears these sayings of Mine, and does not do them, will be

15 [l] Deut. 13:3; Jer. 23:16; Ezek. 22:28; Mark 13:22; [Luke 6:26]; Rom. 16:17; Eph. 5:6; [Col. 2:8; 2 Pet. 2:1; 1 John 4:1-3] [m] Mic. 3:5
16 [n] Matt. 7:20; 12:33; Luke 6:44; James 3:12 [o] Luke 6:43
17 [p] Jer. 11:19; Matt. 12:33
19 [q] Matt. 3:10; Luke 3:9; [John 15:2, 6]
21 [r] Hos. 8:2; Matt. 25:11; Luke 6:46; Acts 19:13 [s] Rom. 2:13; James 1:22
22 [t] Num. 24:4
23 [u] Matt. 25:12; Luke 13:25; [2 Tim. 2:19] [v] Ps. 5:5; 6:8; [Matt. 25:41]; Luke 13:27
24 [w] Matt. 7:24-27; Luke 6:47-49
28 [x] Matt. 13:54; Mark 1:22; 6:2; Luke 4:32; John 7:46
29 [y] [John 7:46]

CHAPTER 8

2 [a] Matt. 8:2-4; Mark 1:40-45; Luke 5:12-14 [b] Matt. 2:11; 9:18; 15:25; John 9:38; Acts 10:25
3 [c] Matt. 11:5; Luke 4:27
4 [d] Matt. 9:30; Mark 5:43; Luke 4:41; 8:56; 9:21 [e] Lev. 14:3, 4, 10; Mark 1:44; Luke 5:14 [f] Lev. 14:4-32; Deut. 24:8
5 [g] Luke 7:1-3 [h] Matt. 27:54; Acts 10:1

like a foolish man who built his house on
the sand: 27 and the rain descended, the
floods came, and the winds blew and beat
on that house; and it fell. And great was its
fall."

Response to the Sermon

28 And so it was, when Jesus had ended
these sayings, that [x]the people were astonished at His teaching, 29 [y]for He taught
them as one having authority, and not as
the scribes.

The Leper Is Cleansed
Mark 1:40-44; Luke 5:12-14

8 When He had come down from the
mountain, great multitudes followed
Him. 2 [a]And behold, a leper came and
[b]worshiped Him, saying, "Lord, if You are
willing, You can make me clean."
3 Then Jesus put out *His* hand and
touched him, saying, "I am willing; be
cleansed." Immediately his leprosy [c]was
cleansed.
4 And Jesus said to him, [d]"See that you
tell no one; but go your way, show yourself
to the priest, and offer the gift that [e]Moses
[f]commanded, as a testimony to them."

The Centurion's Servant Is Healed
Luke 7:1-10

5 [g]Now when Jesus had entered Capernaum, a [h]centurion came to Him,
pleading with Him, 6 saying, "Lord, my
servant is lying at home paralyzed, dreadfully tormented."

7:15 false prophets. These deceive not by disguising themselves as sheep, but by impersonating true shepherds. They promote the wide gate and the wide way. **sheep's clothing.** This may refer to the woolen attire that was the characteristic garb of a shepherd.

7:16 You will know them by their fruits. *See note on 3:8.* False doctrine cannot restrain the flesh, so false prophets manifest wickedness. Cf. 2 Pet. 2:12-22.

7:21 Not everyone who says…but he who does. The barrenness of this sort of faith demonstrates its real character (cf. v. 20)—the faith that says but does not do is really unbelief. Jesus was not suggesting that works are meritorious for salvation, but that true faith will not fail to produce the fruit of good works. This is precisely the point of James 1:22-25; 2:26.

7:22 have we not prophesied…cast out demons…and done many wonders. Note that far from being totally devoid of works of any kind, these people were claiming to have done some remarkable signs and wonders. In fact, their whole confidence was in these works—further proof that these works, spectacular as they might have appeared, could not have been authentic. No one so bereft of genuine faith could possibly produce true good works. A bad tree cannot bear good fruit (v. 18).

7:23 lawlessness. All sin is lawlessness (1 John 3:4), i.e., rebellion against the law of God (cf. 13:41).

7:24-28 The house represents a religious life; the rain represents divine judgment. Only the one built on the foundation of obedience to God's Word stands, which calls for repentance, rejection of salvation by works, and trust in God's grace to save through His merciful provision. *See notes on James 1:22-25.*

7:29 not as the scribes. The scribes quoted others to establish the authority of their teachings; Jesus was His own authority (28:18). This matter of authority was a major issue between Jesus and the Jews, who felt their authority challenged. *See note on 21:23.* Cf. Mark 1:22; 11:28-33; Luke 4:32; 20:2-8; John 12:49,50; 14:10.

8:1 down from the mountain. Cf. 5:1.

8:2 if You are willing. He had no doubt about Christ's power, only His will (cf. Mark 1:40-45).

8:4 tell no one. Publicity over such miracles might hinder Christ's mission and divert public attention from His message. Mark records that this is precisely what happened. In this man's exuberance over the miracle, he disobeyed; as a result, Christ had to move His ministry away from the city and into the desert regions (Mark 1:45). **the gift that Moses commanded.** A sacrifice of two birds, one of which was killed and the other set free (Lev. 14:4-7). **as a testimony to them.** I.e., the priests.

8:5 Capernaum. *See note on 4:13.* **centurion.** A Roman military officer who commanded (cf. v. 9) 100 men. Luke indicates that the centurion appealed to Jesus through intermediaries (Luke 7:3-6)—because of his own sense of unworthiness (v. 8; cf. Luke 7:7). Matthew makes no mention of the intermediaries.

7 And Jesus said to him, "I will come
and heal him."
8 The centurion answered and said,
"Lord, [i]I am not worthy that You should
come under my roof. But only [j]speak a
word, and my servant will be healed. 9 For
I also am a man under authority, having
soldiers under me. And I say to this *one*,
'Go,' and he goes; and to another, 'Come,'
and he comes; and to my servant, 'Do this,'
and he does *it*."
10 When Jesus heard *it*, He marveled,
and said to those who followed, "Assuredly, I say to you, I have not found such
great faith, not even in Israel! 11 And I say
to you that [k]many will come from east and
west, and sit down with Abraham, Isaac,
and Jacob in the kingdom of heaven. 12 But
[l]the sons of the kingdom [m]will be cast out
into outer darkness. There will be weeping
and gnashing of teeth." 13 Then Jesus said
to the centurion, "Go your way; and as you
have believed, *so* let it be done for you."
And his servant was healed that same hour.

Peter's Mother-in-Law Is Healed
Mark 1:29-34; Luke 4:38-41

14 [n]Now when Jesus had come into Peter's house, He saw [o]his wife's mother
lying sick with a fever. 15 So He touched
her hand, and the fever left her. And she
arose and served [1]them.

8 [i] Luke 15:19,21 [j] Ps. 107:20
11 [k] [Gen. 12:3; Is. 2:2, 3; 11:10]; Mal. 1:11; Luke 13:29; [Acts 10:45; 11:18; 14:27; Rom. 15:9-13; Eph. 3:6]
12 [l] [Matt. 21:43] [m] Matt. 13:42, 50; 22:13; 24:51; 25:30; Luke 13:28; 2 Pet. 2:17; Jude 13
14 [n] Matt. 8:14-16; Mark 1:29-31; Luke 4:38,39 [o] 1 Cor. 9:5
15 [1] NU, M *Him*
16 [p] Mark 1:32-34; Luke 4:40,41
17 [q] Is. 53:4; 1 Pet. 2:24
19 [r] Matt. 8:19-22; Luke 9:57,58
21 [s] Luke 9:59,60 [t] 1 Kin. 19:20
24 [u] Mark 4:37; Luke 8:23-25

16 [p]When evening had come, they
brought to Him many who were demon-
possessed. And He cast out the spirits with
a word, and healed all who were sick,
17 that it might be fulfilled which was spoken by Isaiah the prophet, saying:

[q]"He Himself took our infirmities
And bore our sicknesses."

Demands of Discipleship—Luke 9:57-62

18 And when Jesus saw great multitudes
about Him, He gave a command to depart
to the other side. 19 [r]Then a certain scribe
came and said to Him, "Teacher, I will follow You wherever You go."
20 And Jesus said to him, "Foxes have
holes and birds of the air *have* nests, but the
Son of Man has nowhere to lay *His* head."
21 [s]Then another of His disciples said to
Him, "Lord, [t]let me first go and bury my
father."
22 But Jesus said to him, "Follow Me,
and let the dead bury their own dead."

The Sea Is Stilled
Mark 4:35-41; Luke 8:22-25

23 Now when He got into a boat, His disciples followed Him. 24 [u]And suddenly a
great tempest arose on the sea, so that the
boat was covered with the waves. But He
was asleep. 25 Then His disciples came to

8:8 I am not worthy that You should come under my roof. Jewish tradition held that a person who entered a Gentile's house was ceremonially defiled (cf. John 18:28). The centurion, undoubtedly familiar with this law, felt unworthy of having Jesus suffer such an inconvenience for his sake. He also had faith enough to know that Christ could heal by merely speaking a word (*see note on v. 10*).

8:10 I have not found such great faith, not even in Israel! This centurion understood Jesus' absolute authority (vv. 8,9). Even some of Jesus' own disciples did not see things so clearly (cf. v. 26).

8:11 many...from east and west. Gentiles, in the kingdom with Abraham, will enjoy salvation and the blessing of God (cf. Is. 49:8-12; 59:19; Mal. 1:11; Luke 13:28,29).

8:12 sons of the kingdom. The Hebrew nation, physical heirs of Abraham. **will be cast out.** This was exactly opposite to the rabbinical understanding, which suggested that the kingdom would feature a great feast in the company of Abraham and the Messiah—open to Jews only. **weeping and gnashing.** *See note on 22:13.* Cf. 24:51; 25:30; Luke 13:28. This expression describes the eternal agonies of those in hell.

8:13 as you have believed. Sometimes faith was involved in the Lord's healings (in this case not by the one being healed, as in 9:2; 15:28); other times it was not a factor (vv. 14-16; Luke 22:51).

8:16 demon-possessed. This means "demonized," or under the internal control of a demon. All of the cases of demonization dealt with by Christ involved the actual indwelling of demons who utterly controlled the bodies of their victims, even to the point of speaking through them (Mark 5:5-9), causing derangement (John 10:20), violence (Luke 8:29), or rendering them mute (Mark 9:17-22).

8:17 spoken by Isaiah the prophet. *See note on healing and the atonement at Is. 53:4,5.* Matthew was citing that passage here. Christ bore both the guilt and the curse of sin (cf. Gal. 3:13). Both physical healing and ultimate victory over death are guaranteed by Christ's atoning work, but these will not be fully realized until the very end (1 Cor. 15:26).

8:18 the other side. The eastern shore of the lake.

8:19 a certain scribe. As a scribe, this man was breaking with his fellow scribes by publicly declaring his willingness to follow Jesus. Nonetheless, Jesus evidently knew that he had not counted the cost in terms of suffering and inconvenience.

8:20 Son of Man. *See notes on Mark 2:10; John 1:51.* This is the name Jesus used for Himself more than any other. It is used 83 times in the gospels, always by Jesus Himself. It was a messianic title (Dan. 7:13,14), with an obvious reference to the humanity and the humility of Christ. Yet, it also speaks of His everlasting glory, as Dan. 7:13,14 shows (cf. 24:27; Acts 7:56).

8:21 let me first go and bury my father. This does not mean that the man's father was already dead. The phrase, "I must bury my father" was a common figure of speech meaning, "Let me wait until I receive my inheritance."

8:22 let the dead bury their own dead. Let the world (the spiritually dead) take care of mundane things.

8:24 suddenly a great tempest arose. The Sea of Galilee is more than 690 ft. below sea level. To the N, Mt. Hermon rises 9,200 ft., and from May to Oct. strong winds often sweep through the narrow surrounding gorges into this valley, causing extremely sudden and violent storms. **He was asleep.** Just before the disciples saw one of the most awesome displays of His deity, they were given a touching picture of His humanity. He was so weary that not even the violent tossing of the boat awakened Him—even though the disciples feared they would drown (v. 25).

Him and awoke Him, saying, "Lord, save
us! We are perishing!"
26 But He said to them, "Why are you
fearful, O you of little faith?" Then [v]He
arose and rebuked the winds and the sea,
and there was a great calm. 27 So the men
marveled, saying, [2]"Who can this be, that
even the winds and the sea obey Him?"

Demons Are Cast into Swine
Mark 5:1-17; Luke 8:26-37

28 [w]When He had come to the other side,
to the country of the [3]Gergesenes, there
met Him two demon-possessed *men,* coming out of the tombs, exceedingly fierce, so
that no one could pass that way. 29 And
suddenly they cried out, saying, "What
have we to do with You, Jesus, You Son of
God? Have You come here to torment us
before the time?"
30 Now a good way off from them there
was a herd of many swine feeding. 31 So
the demons begged Him, saying, "If You
cast us out, [4]permit us to go away into the
herd of swine."
32 And He said to them, "Go." So when
they had come out, they went into the herd
of swine. And suddenly the whole herd of
swine ran violently down the steep place
into the sea, and perished in the water.
33 Then those who kept *them* fled; and
they went away into the city and told
everything, including what *had happened* to
the demon-possessed *men.* 34 And behold,
the whole city came out to meet Jesus. And
when they saw Him, [x]they begged *Him* to
depart from their region.

The Paralytic Is Forgiven
Mark 2:1-12; Luke 5:17-26

9 So He got into a boat, crossed over,
[a]and came to His own city. 2 [b]Then behold, they brought to Him a paralytic lying
on a bed. [c]When Jesus saw their faith, He
said to the paralytic, "Son, be of good
cheer; your sins are forgiven you."
3 And at once some of the scribes said
within themselves, "This Man blasphemes!"
4 But Jesus, [d]knowing their thoughts,
said, "Why do you think evil in your
hearts? 5 For which is easier, to say, *'Your*
sins are forgiven you,' or to say, 'Arise and
walk'? 6 But that you may know that the
Son of Man has power on earth to forgive
sins"—then He said to the paralytic, "Arise,
take up your bed, and go to your house."
7 And he arose and departed to his house.
8 Now when the multitudes saw *it,* they
[e]marveled[1] and glorified God, who had
given such power to men.

Matthew Is Called
Mark 2:14; Luke 5:27, 28

9 [f]As Jesus passed on from there, He saw
a man named Matthew sitting at the tax office. And He said to him, "Follow Me." So
he arose and followed Him.

26 [v]Ps. 65:7; 89:9; 107:29
27 [2]Lit. *What sort of man is this*
28 [w]Mark 5:1-4; Luke 8:26-33 [3]NU *Gadarenes*
31 [4]NU *send us into*
34 [x]Deut. 5:25; 1 Kin. 17:18; Amos 7:12; Luke 5:8; Acts 16:39

CHAPTER 9

1 [a]Matt. 4:13; 11:23; Mark 5:21
2 [b]Mark 2:3-12; Luke 5:18-26 [c]Matt. 8:10
4 [d]Ps. 139:2; Matt. 12:25; Mark 12:15; Luke 5:22; 6:8; 9:47; 11:17
8 [e]Matt. 8:27; John 7:15 [1]NU *were afraid*
9 [f]Mark 2:14; Luke 5:27

8:26 you of little faith. *See note on 6:30.* **calm.** Cf. Pss. 65:7; 89:9.

8:27 the winds and the sea obey Him. This was convincing proof of His deity (cf. Pss. 29:3,4; 89:9; 93:4; 107:25-29).

8:28 country of the Gergesenes. Some texts say "Gadarenes" (cf. Mark 5:1; Luke 8:26). This refers to a small town on the lake opposite Tiberius, perhaps where the modern village of Khersa (Kursi) is located. Some ancient tombs are there, and the shoreline descends steeply into the water, exactly matching the description of the terrain in this account. **two demon-possessed *men*.** Mark 5:2 and Luke 8:27 mention only one of the men. Evidently one was more dominant than the other.

8:29 to torment us before the time. Evidently, even the demons not only recognized the deity of Jesus, but also knew there was a divinely-appointed time for their judgment and He would be their judge. Their eschatology was factually correct, but it is one thing to know the truth, and quite another thing to love it (cf. James 2:19).

8:30 herd of many swine. Mark 5:13 adds that there were 2,000 in this herd. Such a large herd of unclean animals suggests that Gentiles dominated the region. It also suggests that the number of demons was large (cf. Mark 5:9).

8:31 the demons begged Him. Luke 8:31 relates they pleaded not to be sent into the abyss, meaning the pit, the underworld, the prison of bound demons who disobeyed (*see notes on 2 Pet. 2:4; Jude 6*). They knew Jesus had the power and authority to send them there if He desired.

8:34 begged *Him* to depart. Perhaps they were concerned with the financial impact from the loss of the pigs. More likely, they were all ungodly people frightened to be in the presence of such spiritual power (cf. Mark 5:14,15).

9:1 His own city. Capernaum (*see note on 4:13*). Jesus had left there to get away from the crowds for a time (8:18).

9:2 your sins are forgiven. The fact that the man was brought on a bed indicates that his paralysis was severe. Jesus' words of forgiveness may indicate that the paralysis was a direct consequence of the man's own sin. Cf. John 9:1-3; *see notes on Luke 5:20-26.*

9:3 This Man blasphemes! This would be a true judgment about anyone but God incarnate, for only the One who has been sinned against has the prerogative to forgive. Jesus' words to the man were therefore an unequivocal claim of divine authority.

9:4 knowing their thoughts. Cf. 12:25; John 2:24. Though the Lord Jesus humbled Himself (Phil. 2:4-8) and set aside the independent use of His divine prerogatives in incarnation (John 5:30), He was still fully God and, therefore, omniscient. See Mark 13:32; Luke 2:52.

9:5 which is easier. It is certainly easier to claim the power to pronounce absolution from sin than to demonstrate the power to heal. Christ actually proved His power to forgive by instantly healing the man of his paralysis. If He could do the apparently harder, He could also do what seemed easier. The actual forgiving of the sins was in reality the more difficult task, however, because it ultimately required Him to sacrifice His life.

9:9 sitting at the tax office. Matthew's own humility is seen here. He did not disguise his past or make any excuse for it. Whereas Mark 2:14 and Luke 5:27 employ his former name, Levi, Matthew himself used the name by which he was known after becoming a disciple (cf. Mark 3:18; Luke 6:15). Tax collectors were among the most despised persons in this society. The money they collected was often

The Disciples Eat with Sinners
Mark 2:15-17; Luke 5:29-32

10 [g]Now it happened, as Jesus sat at the
table in the house, *that* behold, many tax
collectors and sinners came and sat down
with Him and His disciples. 11 And when
the Pharisees saw *it,* they said to His disciples, "Why does your Teacher eat with [h]tax
collectors and [i]sinners?"
12 When Jesus heard *that,* He said to
them, "Those who are well have no need of
a physician, but those who are sick. 13 But
go and learn what *this* means: [j]*'I desire*
mercy and not sacrifice.' For I did not
come to call the righteous, [k]but sinners, [2]to
repentance."

The Disciples Do Not Fast
Mark 2:18-22; Luke 5:33-39

14 Then the disciples of John came to
Him, saying, [l]"Why do we and the Pharisees fast [3]often, but Your disciples do not
fast?"
15 And Jesus said to them, "Can [m]the
[4]friends of the bridegroom mourn as long
as the bridegroom is with them? But the
days will come when the bridegroom will
be taken away from them, and [n]then they
will fast. 16 No one puts a piece of unshrunk cloth on an old garment; for [5]the
patch pulls away from the garment, and
the tear is made worse. 17 Nor do they put
new wine into old wineskins, or else the
wineskins [6]break, the wine is spilled, and
the wineskins are ruined. But they put new
wine into new wineskins, and both are preserved."

Life Is Restored—Mark 5:21-43; Luke 8:40-56

18 [o]While He spoke these things to them,
behold, a ruler came and worshiped Him,
saying, "My daughter has just died, but
come and lay Your hand on her and she
will live." 19 So Jesus arose and followed
him, and so *did* His [p]disciples.
20 [q]And suddenly, a woman who had a
flow of blood for twelve years came from
behind and [r]touched the hem of His garment. 21 For she said to herself, "If only I
may touch His garment, I shall be made
well." 22 But Jesus turned around, and
when He saw her He said, "Be of good
cheer, daughter; [s]your faith has made you
well." And the woman was made well
from that hour.
23 [t]When Jesus came into the ruler's
house, and saw [u]the flute players and the
noisy crowd wailing, 24 He said to them,
[v]"Make room, for the girl is not dead, but
sleeping." And they ridiculed Him. 25 But
when the crowd was put outside, He went
in and [w]took her by the hand, and the girl

10 [g] Mark 2:15; Luke 5:29
11 [h] Matt. 11:19; Mark 2:16; Luke 5:30; 15:2 [i] [Gal. 2:15]
13 [j] Hos. 6:6; [Mic. 6:6-8]; Matt. 12:7 [k] Mark 2:17; Luke 5:32; 1 Tim. 1:15 [2] NU omits *to repentance*
14 [l] Mark 2:18; Luke 5:33-35; 18:12 [3] NU brackets *often* as disputed.
15 [m] John 3:29 [n] Acts 13:2, 3; 14:23 [4] Lit. *sons of the bridechamber*
16 [5] Lit. *that which is put on*
17 [6] *burst*
18 [o] Mark 5:22-43; Luke 8:41-56
19 [p] Matt. 10:2-4
20 [q] Mark 5:25; Luke 8:43 [r] Num. 15:38; Deut. 22:12; Matt. 14:36; 23:5; Mark 6:56
22 [s] Matt. 9:29; 15:28; Mark 5:34; 10:52; Luke 7:50; 8:48; 17:19; 18:42
23 [t] Mark 5:38; Luke 8:51 [u] 2 Chr. 35:25; Jer. 9:17; 16:6; Ezek. 24:17
24 [v] John 11:3; Acts 20:10
25 [w] Matt. 8:3, 15; Mark 1:31

---

partly extorted for personal gain (cf. Luke 19:8) and partly a tax for Rome, which made them not only thieves, but also traitors to the Jewish nation (*see notes on 5:46; Mark 2:15*).

9:11 tax collectors. *See note on 5:46,47.*

9:12 well...sick. The Pharisees thought they were well—religiously pure and whole. The outcasts knew they were not. Salvation can't come to the self-righteous.

9:13 go and learn what *this* means. This phrase was commonly used as a rebuke for those who did not know something they should have known. The verse Jesus cites is Hos. 6:6 (cf. 1 Sam. 15:22; Mic. 6:6-8), which emphasizes the absolute priority of the law's moral standards over the ceremonial requirements. The Pharisees tended to focus on the outward, ritual, and ceremonial aspects of God's law—to the neglect of its inward, eternal, and moral precepts. In doing so, they became harsh, judgmental, and self-righteously scornful of others. Jesus repeated this same criticism in 12:7.

9:14 disciples of John. Luke implies that the Pharisees asked this question (*see note on Luke 5:33*; cf. Mark 2:18-20). Evidently, some Pharisees were still present when John's disciples came. Both groups together may have asked this question. **the Pharisees fast often.** Cf. Luke 18:12.

9:15 then they will fast. *See note on 6:17.* Using the analogy of a wedding party, Jesus answered that as long as Christ was present with them there was too much joy for fasting, which was connected to seasons of sorrow and intense prayer.

9:16 unshrunk cloth on an old garment. That new cloth does not work on old material is analogous to trying to patch New Covenant truth onto old Mosaic ceremonial forms.

9:17 new wine into old wineskins. Animal skins were used for fermentation of wine because of their elasticity. As the wine fermented, pressure built up, stretching the wineskin. A previously stretched skin lacked elasticity and would rupture, ruining both wine and wineskin. Jesus used this as an illustration to teach that the forms of old rituals, such as the ceremonial fastings practiced by the Pharisees and John's disciples, were not fit for the new wine of the New Covenant era (cf. Col. 2:17). In both analogies (vv. 16,17), the Lord was saying that what the Pharisees did in fasting or any other ritual had no part with the gospel.

9:18 ruler. Jairus (Mark 5:22; Luke 8:41) was a ruler of the synagogue.

9:20 a flow of blood for twelve years. This woman's affliction not only was serious physically but also left her permanently unclean for ceremonial reasons (cf. Lev. 15:25-27). This meant she would have been shunned by all, including her own family, and excluded from both synagogue and temple. **the hem of His garment.** Cf. 14:36. Probably one of the tassels that were sown to the corners of a garment in order to remind the wearer to obey God's commandments (Num. 15:38-40; Deut. 22:12).

9:22 made you well. Lit. "saved you."

9:23 flute players and the noisy crowd. Typical fixtures at a time of mourning in that culture (cf. 2 Chr. 35:25). The crowd at a funeral usually included professional mourners, women whose task it was to wail plaintively, while reciting the name of the departed one, as well as any other loved ones who had died recently. The result was a noisy, chaotic din.

9:24 sleeping. Jesus was not saying that her death was a misdiagnosis. This was a prophecy that she would live again. He made a similar comment about Lazarus' death (John 11:11)—and then had to explain to the disciples that he was speaking metaphorically (John 11:14). Sleep is a designation for death in the NT (cf. 1 Cor. 11:30; 15:51; 1 Thess. 5:10). **they ridiculed Him.** How quickly their paid act of mourning turned to derision!

arose. 26 And the [x]report of this went out
into all that land.

Sight Is Restored

27 When Jesus departed from there, [y]two
blind men followed Him, crying out and
saying, [z]"Son of David, have mercy on
us!"
28 And when He had come into the
house, the blind men came to Him. And Jesus said to them, "Do you believe that I am
able to do this?"
They said to Him, "Yes, Lord."
29 Then He touched their eyes, saying,
"According to your faith let it be to you."
30 And their eyes were opened. And Jesus
sternly warned them, saying, [a]"See *that* no
one knows *it*." 31 [b]But when they had departed, they [7]spread the news about Him
in all that [8]country.

Speech Is Restored

32 [c]As they went out, behold, they
brought to Him a man, mute and demon-
possessed. 33 And when the demon was
cast out, the mute spoke. And the multitudes marveled, saying, "It was never seen
like this in Israel!"
34 But the Pharisees said, [d]"He casts out
demons by the ruler of the demons."

The Need for Delegation of Power

35 Then Jesus went about all the cities and
villages, [e]teaching in their synagogues,
preaching the gospel of the kingdom, and
healing every sickness and every disease
[9]among the people. 36 [f]But when He saw the
multitudes, He was moved with compassion for them, because they were [1]weary
and scattered, [g]like sheep having no shepherd. 37 Then He said to His disciples, [h]"The
harvest truly *is* plentiful, but the laborers *are*
few. 38 [i]Therefore pray the Lord of the harvest to send out laborers into His harvest."

The Twelve Apostles Are Sent

Mark 6:7; Luke 9:1

10 And [a]when He had called His
twelve disciples to *Him*, He gave
them power *over* unclean spirits, to cast
them out, and to heal all kinds of sickness
and all kinds of disease. 2 Now the names
of the twelve apostles are these: first, Simon, [b]who is called Peter, and Andrew his
brother; James the *son* of Zebedee, and John
his brother; 3 Philip and Bartholomew;
Thomas and Matthew the tax collector;
James the *son* of Alphaeus, and [1]Lebbaeus,
whose surname was Thaddaeus; 4 [c]Simon
the [2]Cananite, and Judas [d]Iscariot, who
also betrayed Him.

26 [x] Matt. 4:24; Mark 1:28, 45; Luke 4:14, 37; 5:15; 7:17
27 [y] Matt. 20:29-34 [z] Matt. 15:22; Mark 10:47; Luke 18:38, 39
30 [a] Matt. 8:4; Luke 5:14
31 [b] Mark 7:36 [7] Lit. *made Him known* [8] Lit. *land*
32 [c] Matt. 12:22, 24; Luke 11:14
34 [d] Matt. 12:24; Mark 3:22; Luke 11:15; John 7:20
35 [e] Matt. 4:23 [9] NU omits *among the people*
36 [f] Mark 6:34 [g] Num. 27:17; 1 Kin. 22:17; Ezek. 34:5; Zech. 10:2; Mark 6:34 [1] NU, M *harassed*
37 [h] Luke 10:2; John 4:35
38 [i] [Matt. 28:19, 20; Eph. 4:11, 12]; 2 Thess. 3:1

CHAPTER 10

1 [a] Mark 3:13; Luke 6:13
2 [b] John 1:42
3 [1] NU omits *Lebbaeus, whose surname was*
4 [c] Luke 6:15; Acts 1:13 [d] Matt. 26:14; Luke 22:3; John 13:2, 26 [2] NU *Cananaean*

9:27 Son of David. Cf. 1:1; 12:23; 21:9,15. A messianic title (*see note on 1:1*). See 20:29-34 for a remarkably similar, but separate, account.

9:29 According to your faith. *See note on 8:13.*

9:30 See *that* no one knows. *See note on 8:4.*

9:34 the ruler of the demons. The Pharisees had seen enough of Jesus' power to know it was God's power. But, in their willful unbelief, they said His was the power of Satan. *See note on 12:24*; cf. 25:41; Mark 3:22; Luke 11:15.

9:35 every sickness and every disease. Jesus banished illness in an unprecedented healing display, giving impressive evidence of His deity, and making the Jews' rejection all the more heinous. *See note on 12:15.*

9:36 He was moved with compassion. Here the humanity of Christ allowed expression of His attitude toward sinners in terms of human passion. He was "moved" with compassion. Whereas God, who is immutable, is not subject to the rise and fall and change of emotions (Num. 23:19), Christ, who was fully human with all the faculties of humanity, was on occasion moved to literal tears over the plight of sinners (Luke 19:41; *see note on Luke 13:34*). God Himself expressed similar compassion through the prophets (Ex. 33:19; Ps. 86:15; Jer. 9:1; 13:17; 14:17). **they were weary and scattered.** The people's spiritual needs were even more desperate than the need for physical healing. Meeting that need would require more laborers (v. 37).

9:37 harvest. Cf. Luke 10:1,2. The Lord spoke of the spiritual harvest of souls for salvation.

9:38 Therefore pray. Jesus affirmed the fact that believers' prayers participate in the fulfillment of God's plans.

10:1,2 disciples…apostles. "Disciple" means "student," one who is being taught by another. "Apostles" refers to qualified representatives who are sent on a mission. The two terms emphasize different aspects of their calling.

10:1 He gave them power. *See note on 2 Cor. 12:12.* Jesus delegated His power to the apostles to show clearly that He and His kingdom were sovereign over the physical and spiritual realms, the effects of sin, and the efforts of Satan. This was an unheard of display of power, never before seen in all redemptive history, to announce Messiah's arrival and authenticate Him plus His apostles who preached His gospel. This power was a preview of the power Christ will exhibit in His earthly kingdom, when Satan will be bound (Rev. 20) and the curse on physical life curtailed (Is. 65:20-25).

10:2 the names of the twelve apostles. The 12 are always listed in a similar order (cf. Mark 3:16-19; Luke 6:13-16; Acts 1:13). Peter is always named first. The list contains 3 groups of 4. The 3 subgroups are always listed in the same order, and the first name in each subgroup is always the same, though there is some variation in the order within the subgroups—but Judas Iscariot is always named last. **Peter…Andrew…James…and John.** The first subgroup of 4 are the most familiar to us. These two sets of brothers, all fishermen, represent an inner circle of disciples often seen closest to Jesus (*see note on 17:1*). **James the *son* of Alphaeus.** There are 4 men in the NT named James: 1) the Apostle James, brother of John (*see note on 4:21*); 2) the disciple mentioned here, also called "James the Less" (Mark 15:40); 3) James, father of Judas (not Iscariot, Luke 6:16); and 4) James, the Lord's half-brother (Gal. 1:19; Mark 6:3), who wrote the epistle that bears the name. He also played a leading role in the early Jerusalem Church (Acts 12:17; 15:13; Gal. 1:19).

10:3 Lebbaeus, whose surname was Thaddaeus. Elsewhere he is called Judas, son of James (Luke 6:16; Acts 1:13).

10:4 Simon the Cananite. The better manuscripts read "Cananaean"—a term for the party of the Zealots, a group determined to overthrow Roman domination in Palestine. Acts 1:13 refers to him as "Simon the Zealot." Simon was probably a member of the Zealot party before coming to Christ. *See note on Mark 3:18.*

The Twelve Apostles Are Instructed
Mark 6:8-13; Luke 9:2-6, 12:2-10

5 These twelve Jesus sent out and commanded them, saying: [e]"Do not go into the
way of the Gentiles, and do not enter a city
of [f]the Samaritans. 6 [g]But go rather to the
[h]lost sheep of the house of Israel. 7 [i]And as
you go, preach, saying, [j]'The kingdom of
heaven [3]is at hand.' 8 Heal the sick,
[4]cleanse the lepers, [5]raise the dead, cast
out demons. [k]Freely you have received,
freely give. 9 [l]Provide neither gold nor silver nor [m]copper in your money belts,
10 nor bag for *your* journey, nor two tunics,
nor sandals, nor staffs; [n]for a worker is
worthy of his food.

11 [o]"Now whatever city or town you
enter, inquire who in it is worthy, and stay
there till you go out. 12 And when you go
into a household, greet it. 13 [p]If the household is worthy, let your peace come upon
it. [q]But if it is not worthy, let your peace return to you. 14 [r]And whoever will not receive you nor hear your words, when you
depart from that house or city, [s]shake off
the dust from your feet. 15 Assuredly, I say
to you, [t]it will be more tolerable for the
land of Sodom and Gomorrah in the day of
judgment than for that city!

16 [u]"Behold, I send you out as sheep in
the midst of wolves. [v]Therefore be wise as
serpents and [w]harmless[6] as doves. 17 But
beware of men, for [x]they will deliver you
up to councils and [y]scourge you in their
synagogues. 18 [z]You will be brought before
governors and kings for My sake, as a testimony to them and to the Gentiles. 19 [a]But
when they deliver you up, do not worry
about how or what you should speak. For
[b]it will be given to you in that hour what
you should speak; 20 [c]for it is not you who
speak, but the Spirit of your Father who
speaks in you.

21 [d]"Now brother will deliver up brother to death, and a father *his* child; and children will rise up against parents and cause
them to be put to death. 22 And [e]you will
be hated by all for My name's sake. [f]But he
who endures to the end will be saved.
23 [g]When they persecute you in this city,
flee to another. For assuredly, I say to you,
you will not have [h]gone through the cities
of Israel [i]before the Son of Man comes.

24 [j]"A disciple is not above *his* teacher,
nor a servant above his master. 25 It is
enough for a disciple that he be like his
teacher, and a servant like his master. If
[k]they have called the master of the house
[7]Beelzebub, how much more *will they call*
those of his household! 26 Therefore do not

5 [e] Matt. 4:15 [f] 2 Kin. 17:24; Luke 9:52; 10:33; 17:16; John 4:9
6 [g] Matt. 15:24; Acts 13:46 [h] Is. 53:6; Jer. 50:6
7 [i] Luke 9:2 [j] Matt. 3:2; Luke 10:9 [3] *has drawn near*
8 [k] [Acts 8:18] [4] NU *raise the dead, cleanse the lepers* [5] M omits *raise the dead*
9 [l] 1 Sam. 9:7; Mark 6:8 [m] Mark 6:8
10 [n] Luke 10:7; [1 Cor. 9:4-14]; 1 Tim. 5:18
11 [o] Luke 10:8
13 [p] Luke 10:5 [q] Ps. 35:13
14 [r] Mark 6:11; Luke 9:5 [s] Neh. 5:13; Luke 10:10, 11; Acts 13:51
15 [t] Matt. 11:22, 24
16 [u] Luke 10:3 [v] 2 Cor. 12:16; Eph. 5:15; Col. 4:5 [w] [Phil. 2:14-16] [6] *innocent*
17 [x] Matt. 23:34; Mark 13:9; Luke 12:11 [y] Acts 5:40; 22:19; 26:11
18 [z] Acts 12:1; 2 Tim. 4:16
19 [a] Mark 13:11; Luke 12:11, 12; 21:14, 15 [b] Ex. 4:12; Jer. 1:7
20 [c] 2 Sam. 23:2; [2 Tim. 4:17]
21 [d] Mic. 7:6; Luke 21:16
22 [e] Matt. 24:9; Luke 21:17; John 15:18 [f] [Dan. 12:12]; Matt. 24:13; Mark 13:13 **23** [g] Matt. 2:13; Acts 8:1 [h] [Matt. 24:14; Mark 13:10] [i] Matt. 16:28 **24** [j] Luke 6:40; John 15:20 **25** [k] Mark 3:22; Luke 11:15, 18, 19; John 8:48, 52 [7] NU, M *Beelzebul;* a Philistine deity, 2 Kin. 1:2, 3

10:5–11:1 This is the second of 5 major discourses recorded in Matthew (see Introduction: Historical and Theological Themes).

10:5 Do not go into the way of the Gentiles. Christ did not forbid the disciples to preach to Gentiles or Samaritans if they encountered them on the way, but they were to take the message first to the covenant people, in the regions nearby (cf. Rom. 1:16).

10:6 lost sheep of the house of Israel. Cf. 15:24; Jer. 50:6. Jesus narrowed this priority even more when He said the gospel was only for those who knew they were spiritually sick (9:13) and needed a physician (Luke 5:31,32).

10:7 at hand. *See note on 3:2.*

10:8 Freely you have received, freely give. Jesus was giving them great power, to heal the sick and raise the dead. If they sold these gifts for money, they could have made quite a fortune. But that would have obscured the message of grace Christ sent them to preach. So he forbade them to charge money for their ministry. Yet they were permitted to accept support to meet their basic needs, for a workman is worthy of such support (v. 10).

10:9,10 *See note on Luke 9:3.* The restrictions on what they were to carry were unique for this mission. See Luke 22:36 where, on a later mission, Christ gave completely different instructions. The point here was to teach them to trust the Lord to supply their needs through the generosity of the people to whom they ministered, and to teach those who received the blessing of their ministry to support the servants of Christ. Cf. 1 Tim. 5:18.

10:13 peace. This is equivalent to the Heb. "shalom" and refers to prosperity, well being, or blessing.

10:14 hear your words. The priority was to preach that the King had come and His kingdom was near. The message was the main thing. The signs and wonders were to authenticate it. **shake off the dust from your feet.** It was common for Jews to shake the dust off their feet—as an expression of disdain—when returning from Gentile regions. Paul and Barnabas also did this when expelled from Antioch (Acts 13:51). This was a visible protest, signifying that they regarded the place as no better than a pagan land.

10:15 Sodom and Gomorrah. Those cities and the entire surrounding region were judged without warning, and with the utmost severity. *See notes on Gen. 19:1-29.*

10:16 wolves. Used to describe false prophets who persecute the true ones and seek to destroy the Church (cf. 7:15; Luke 10:3; Acts 20:29). *See note on Luke 10:3.*

10:17 deliver you up. This is a technical word, in this context, used for handing over a prisoner for punishment. Persecution of believers has often been the official policy of governments. Such persecutions give opportunity for testifying to the truth of the gospel. Cf. John 16:1-4; 2 Tim. 4:16.

10:19 do not worry. *See note on Luke 12:11.*

10:21-23 These verses clearly have an eschatological significance that goes beyond the disciples' immediate mission. The persecutions he describes seem to belong to the tribulation period that precedes Christ's second coming, alluded to in v. 23.

10:22 he who endures…end. *See note on 24:13.*

10:24 not above. If the Teacher (Christ) suffers, so will His pupils. If they attack the Master (Christ) with blasphemies, so will they curse the servants. This was the promise of persecution. Cf. John 15:20.

10:25 Beelzebub. The Philistine deity associated with satanic idolatry. The name came to be used for Satan, the prince of demons (*see notes on 2 Kin. 1:2; Luke 11:15*).

fear them. [l]For there is nothing covered
that will not be revealed, and hidden that
will not be known.
27 "Whatever I tell you in the dark,
[m]speak in the light; and what you hear in
the ear, preach on the housetops. 28 [n]And
do not fear those who kill the body but
cannot kill the soul. But rather [o]fear Him
who is able to destroy both soul and body
in [8]hell. 29 Are not two [p]sparrows sold for
a [9]copper coin? And not one of them falls
to the ground apart from your Father's
will. 30 [q]But the very hairs of your head are
all numbered. 31 Do not fear therefore; you
are of more value than many sparrows.
32 [r]"Therefore whoever confesses Me
before men, [s]him I will also confess before
My Father who is in heaven. 33 [t]But whoever denies Me before men, him I will also
deny before My Father who is in heaven.
34 [u]"Do not think that I came to bring
peace on earth. I did not come to bring
peace but a sword. 35 For I have come to
[v]*'set[1] a man against his father, a daughter*
against her mother, and a daughter-in-law
against her mother-in-law'; 36 and [w]*'a*
man's enemies will be those of his own
household.' 37 [x]He who loves father or
mother more than Me is not worthy of Me.
And he who loves son or daughter more
than Me is not worthy of Me. 38 [y]And he
who does not take his cross and follow
after Me is not worthy of Me. 39 [z]He who
finds his life will lose it, and he who loses
his life for My sake will find it.
40 [a]"He who receives you receives Me,
and he who receives Me receives Him who
sent Me. 41 [b]He who receives a prophet in
the name of a prophet shall receive a
prophet's reward. And he who receives a
righteous man in the name of a righteous
man shall receive a righteous man's reward. 42 [c]And whoever gives one of these
little ones only a cup of cold *water* in the
name of a disciple, assuredly, I say to you,
he shall by no means lose his reward."

11 Now it came to pass, when Jesus
finished commanding His twelve
disciples, that He departed from there to
[a]teach and to preach in their cities.

Rejection of John the Baptist—Luke 7:19-30

2 [b]And when John had heard [c]in prison
about the works of Christ, he [1]sent two of
his disciples 3 and said to Him, "Are You
[d]the Coming One, or do we look for another?"
4 Jesus answered and said to them, "Go
and tell John the things which you hear
and see: 5 [e]*The* blind see and *the* lame walk;
the lepers are cleansed and *the* deaf hear;
the dead are raised up and [f]*the* poor have

26 [l]Mark 4:22; Luke 8:17; 12:2, 3; [1 Cor. 4:5] **27** [m]Luke 12:3; Acts 5:20 **28** [n]Luke 12:4; [1 Pet. 3:14] [o]Is. 8:13; Matt. 5:22; Luke 12:5 [8]Gr. *Gehenna* **29** [p]Luke 12:6, 7 [9]Gr. *assarion,* a coin worth about 1/16 of a denarius **30** [q]1 Sam. 14:45; 2 Sam. 14:11; 1 Kin. 1:52; Luke 21:18; Acts 27:34 **32** [r]Ps. 119:46; Luke 12:8; [Rom. 10:9] [s][Rev. 3:5] **33** [t][Mark 8:38; Luke 9:26]; 2 Tim. 2:12 **34** [u][Luke 12:49] **35** [v]Mic. 7:6; Matt. 10:21; Luke 12:53 [1]*alienate a man from* **36** [w]Ps. 41:9; 55:13; John 13:18 **37** [x]Deut. 33:9; Luke 14:26 **38** [y][Matt. 16:24; Mark 8:34; Luke 9:23; 14:27] **39** [z]Matt. 16:25; Mark 8:35; Luke 9:24; 17:33; John 12:25

40 [a]Mark 9:37; Luke 9:48; John 12:44; Gal. 4:14 **41** [b]1 Kin. 17:10; 2 Kin. 4:8 **42** [c][Matt. 25:40]; Mark 9:41; Heb. 6:10
CHAPTER 11

1 [a]Matt. 9:35; Luke 23:5 **2** [b]Luke 7:18-35 [c]Matt. 4:12; 14:3; Mark 6:17; Luke 9:7 [1]NU *sent by his* **3** [d]Gen. 49:10; Num. 24:17; Deut. 18:15, 18; Dan. 9:24; John 6:14 **5** [e]Is. 29:18; 35:4-6; John 2:23 [f]Ps. 22:26; Is. 61:1; Luke 4:18; James 2:5

10:28 fear Him. God is the one who destroys in hell. Cf. Luke 12:5. Persecutors can only harm the body.

10:29 apart from your Father's will. Not merely "without His knowledge"; Jesus was teaching that God providentially controls the timing and circumstances of such insignificant events as the death of a sparrow. Even the number of hairs on our heads is controlled by His sovereign will (v. 30). In other words, divine providence governs even the smallest details and even the most mundane matters. These are very powerful affirmations of the sovereignty of God.

10:32 confesses Me. The person who acknowledges Christ as Lord in life or in death, if necessary, is the one whom the Lord will acknowledge before God as His own. *See notes on 13:20; 2 Tim. 2:10-13.*

10:33 *See note on Luke 12:9.*

10:34 not...peace but a sword. Though the ultimate end of the gospel is peace with God (John 14:27; Rom. 8:6), the immediate result of the gospel is frequently conflict. Conversion to Christ can result in strained family relationships (vv. 35,36), persecution, and even martyrdom. Following Christ presupposes a willingness to endure such hardships (vv. 32,33,37-39). Though He is called "Prince of Peace" (Is. 9:6), Christ will have no one deluded into thinking that He calls believers to a life devoid of all conflict.

10:35,36 Quoted from Mic. 7:6.

10:38 take his cross. Here is Jesus' first mention of the word "cross" to His disciples (*see note on 16:21*). To them it would have evoked a picture of a violent, degrading death (*see note on 27:31*). He was demanding total commitment from them—even unto physical death—and making this call to full surrender a part of the message they were to proclaim to others. This same call to life-or-death devotion to Christ is repeated in 16:24; Mark 8:34; Luke 9:23; 14:27. For those who come to Christ with self-renouncing faith, there will be true and eternal life (v. 39).

10:40 He who receives you receives Me. Christ lives in His people. They also come in His name as His ambassadors (2 Cor. 5:20). Therefore, how they are treated is how He is treated (cf. 18:5; 25:45; Luke 9:48).

10:41 in the name of a prophet...in the name of a righteous man. This expands on the principle of v. 40. To welcome Christ's emissaries is tantamount to welcoming Him (cf. 25:40).

10:42 little ones. Believers. *See notes on 18:3-10; 25:40.*

11:1 in their cities. I.e., in Galilee. Meanwhile, the disciples were also ministering in the Jewish towns in and around Galilee (10:5,6).

11:3 Are You the Coming One, or do we look for another? John the Baptist had introduced Christ as One who would bring a fierce judgment and "burn up the chaff with unquenchable fire" (3:12). He was understandably confused by the turn of events: he was imprisoned, and Christ was carrying on a ministry of healing, not judgment, in Galilee, far from Jerusalem, the city of the King—and not finding a completely warm reception there (cf. 8:34). John wondered if he had misunderstood Jesus' agenda. It would be wrong to interpret this as a wavering of his faith (v. 7).

11:4 tell John. He sent John's disciples back as eyewitnesses of many miracles. Evidently He performed these miracles in their presence just so that they could report back to John that they had personally seen proof that He was indeed the Messiah (cf. Is. 29:18,19; 35:5-10). Note, however, that he offered no further explanation to John, knowing exactly how strong John's faith was (cf. 1 Cor. 10:13).

the gospel preached to them. 6 And
blessed is he who is not [g]offended because
of Me.”
7 [h]As they departed, Jesus began to say
to the multitudes concerning John: “What
did you go out into the wilderness to see?
[i]A reed shaken by the wind? 8 But what
did you go out to see? A man clothed in
soft garments? Indeed, those who wear
soft *clothing* are in kings’ houses. 9 But
what did you go out to see? A prophet?
Yes, I say to you, [j]and more than a prophet.
10 For this is *he* of whom it is written:

[k]‘Behold, I send My messenger
before Your face,
Who will prepare Your way before
You.’

11 “Assuredly, I say to you, among those
born of women there has not risen one
greater than John the Baptist; but he who is
least in the kingdom of heaven is greater
than he. 12 [l]And from the days of John the
Baptist until now the kingdom of heaven
suffers violence, and the violent take it by
force. 13 [m]For all the prophets and the law
prophesied until John. 14 And if you are
willing to receive *it*, he is [n]Elijah who is to
come. 15 [o]He who has ears to hear, let him
hear!

Rejection by Jesus’ Generation
Luke 7:31-35

16 [p]“But to what shall I liken this generation? It is like children sitting in the marketplaces and calling to their companions,
17 and saying:

‘We played the flute for you,
And you did not dance;
We mourned to you,
And you did not [2]lament.’

18 For John came neither eating nor drinking, and they say, ‘He has a demon.’ 19 The
Son of Man came eating and drinking, and
they say, ‘Look, a glutton and a [3]winebib-
ber, [q]a friend of tax collectors and sinners!’
[r]But wisdom is justified by her [4]children.”

Rejection of Chorazin, Bethsaida, and Capernaum—Luke 10:12-15

20 [s]Then He began to rebuke the cities in
which most of His mighty works had been
done, because they did not repent: 21 “Woe
to you, Chorazin! Woe to you, Bethsaida!
For if the mighty works which were done
in you had been done in Tyre and Sidon,
they would have repented long ago [t]in
sackcloth and ashes. 22 But I say to you, [u]it
will be more tolerable for Tyre and Sidon
in the day of judgment than for you.
23 And you, Capernaum, [v]who[5] are exalted to heaven, will be brought down to
Hades; for if the mighty works which were
done in you had been done in Sodom, it
would have remained until this day. 24 But
I say to you [w]that it shall be more tolerable
for the land of Sodom in the day of judgment than for you.”

Invitation to Come to Jesus

25 [x]At that time Jesus answered and
said, “I thank You, Father, Lord of heaven
and earth, that [y]You have hidden these
things from *the* wise and prudent [z]and

6 [g] Is. 8:14, 15; [Rom. 9:32]; 1 Pet. 2:8
7 [h] Luke 7:24 [i] [Eph. 4:14]
9 [j] Matt. 14:5; 21:26; Luke 1:76; 20:6
10 [k] Mal. 3:1; Mark 1:2; Luke 1:76
12 [l] Luke 16:16
13 [m] Mal. 4:4-6
14 [n] Mal. 4:5; Matt. 17:10-13; Mark 9:11-13; Luke 1:17; John 1:21
15 [o] Matt. 13:9; Luke 8:8; Rev. 2:7, 11, 17, 29; 3:6, 13
16 [p] Luke 7:31
17 [2] Lit. *beat your breast*
19 [q] Matt. 9:10 [r] Luke 7:35; John 2:1-11 [3] *wine drinker* [4] NU *works*
20 [s] Luke 10:13-15, 18
21 [t] Jon. 3:6-8
22 [u] Matt. 10:15; 11:24
23 [v] Is. 14:13; Lam. 2:1; Ezek. 26:20; 31:14; 32:18, 24 [5] NU *will you be exalted to heaven? No, you will be*
24 [w] Matt. 10:15
25 [x] Luke 10:21, 22 [y] Ps. 8:2; 1 Cor. 1:19; [2 Cor. 3:14] [z] Matt. 16:17

11:10 Quoted from Mal. 3:1.

11:11 least...is greater than he. John was greater than the OT prophets because he actually saw with his eyes and personally participated in the fulfillment of what they only prophesied (vv. 10,13; cf. 1 Pet. 1:10,11). But all believers after the cross are greater still, because they participate in the full understanding and experience of something John merely foresaw in shadowy form—the actual atoning work of Christ.

11:12 the kingdom of heaven suffers violence. From the time he began his preaching ministry, John the Baptist evoked a strong reaction. Having been imprisoned already, John ultimately fell victim to Herod’s savagery. But the kingdom can never be subdued or opposed by human violence. Notice that where Matthew says, “the violent take it by force,” Luke has, “everyone is pressing into it” (Luke 16:16). So the sense of this verse may be rendered this way: “The kingdom presses ahead relentlessly, and only the relentless press their way into it.” Thus again Christ is magnifying the difficulty of entering the kingdom (*see notes on 7:13,14*).

11:14 he is Elijah. I.e., he is the fulfillment of Mal. 4:5,6 (see 17:12,13). The Jews were aware that Elijah had not died (cf. 2 Kin. 2:11). This does not suggest that John was Elijah returned. In fact, John himself denied that he was Elijah (John 1:21); yet he came in the spirit and power of Elijah (Luke 1:17). If they had believed, John would have been the fulfillment of the Elijah prophecies. *See notes on Mark 9:13; Rev. 11:5,6.*

11:16 like children. *See note on Luke 7:32.*

11:19 eating and drinking. *See note on Luke 7:34.*

11:21 Woe to you, Chorazin!...Bethsaida! Both were cities very close to Capernaum, near the northern shore of the Sea of Galilee. **Tyre...Sidon.** Phoenician cities on the shore of the Mediterranean. The prophecy about the destruction of Tyre and Sidon in Ezek. 26–28 was fulfilled in precise detail.

11:22,24 more tolerable. This indicates that there will be degrees of punishment in hell for the ungodly (*see notes on 10:15; Mark 6:11; Luke 12:47,48; Heb. 10:29*).

11:23 Capernaum...exalted...brought down. Capernaum, chosen by Jesus to be His headquarters, faced an even greater condemnation. Curiously, there is no record that the people of that city ever mocked or ridiculed Jesus, ran Him out of town, or threatened His life. Yet the sin of that city—indifference to Christ—was worse than Sodom’s gross wickedness (cf. 10:15).

11:25 wise and prudent...babes. There is sarcasm in these words as the Jewish leaders are ironically identified as wise and prudent and the followers of Christ as the infants (cf. 18:3-10)—yet God has revealed to those followers the truth of the Messiah and His gospel. Cf. 13:10-17.

have revealed them to babes. 26 Even so,
Father, for so it seemed good in Your sight.
27 [a]All things have been delivered to Me
by My Father, and no one knows the Son
except the Father. [b]Nor does anyone know
the Father except the Son, and *the one* to
whom the Son wills to reveal *Him.* 28 Come
to [c]Me, all *you* who labor and are heavy
laden, and I will give you rest. 29 Take My
yoke upon you [d]and learn from Me, for I
am [6]gentle and [e]lowly in heart, [f]and you
will find rest for your souls. 30 [g]For My
yoke *is* easy and My burden is light."

Controversy over Sabbath-Labor
Mark 2:23-28; Luke 6:1-5

12 At that time [a]Jesus went through
the grainfields on the Sabbath. And
His disciples were hungry, and began to
[b]pluck heads of grain and to eat. 2 And
when the Pharisees saw *it,* they said to
Him, "Look, Your disciples are doing what
is not lawful to do on the Sabbath!"
3 But He said to them, "Have you not
read [c]what David did when he was hungry, he and those who were with him:
4 how he entered the house of God and ate
[d]the showbread which was not lawful for
him to eat, nor for those who were with
him, [e]but only for the priests? 5 Or have
you not read in the [f]law that on the Sabbath the priests in the temple [1]profane the
Sabbath, and are blameless? 6 Yet I say to
you that in this place there is [g]*One* greater
than the temple. 7 But if you had known
what *this* means, [h]*'I desire mercy and not*
sacrifice,' you would not have condemned
the guiltless. 8 For the Son of Man is Lord
[2]even of the Sabbath."

Controversy over Sabbath-Healing
Mark 3:1-5; Luke 6:6-10

9 [i]Now when He had departed from
there, He went into their synagogue.
10 And behold, there was a man who had a
withered hand. And they asked Him, saying, [j]"Is it lawful to heal on the Sabbath?"—that they might accuse Him.
11 Then He said to them, "What man is
there among you who has one sheep, and if
it falls into a pit on the Sabbath, will not lay
hold of it and lift *it* out? 12 Of how much
more value then is a man than a sheep?
Therefore it is lawful to do good on the Sabbath." 13 Then He said to the man, "Stretch
out your hand." And he stretched *it* out,
and it was restored as whole as the other.

Pharisees Plan to Destroy Christ
Mark 3:6-12; Luke 6:11

14 Then [k]the Pharisees went out and plotted against Him, how they might destroy
Him.
15 But when Jesus knew *it,* [l]He withdrew from there. [m]And great [3]multitudes

27 [a]Matt. 28:18; Luke 10:22; John 3:35; 13:3; 1 Cor. 15:27 [b]John 1:18; 6:46; 10:15
28 [c][John 6:35-37]
29 [d][John 13:15]; Eph. 4:2; [Phil. 2:5; 1 Pet. 2:21; 1 John 2:6] [e]Zech. 9:9; [Phil. 2:7, 8] [f]Jer. 6:16 [6]*meek*
30 [g][1 John 5:3]

CHAPTER 12

1 [a]Mark 2:23; Luke 6:1-5 [b]Deut. 23:25
3 [c]Ex. 31:15; 35:2; 1 Sam. 21:6
4 [d]Ex. 25:30; Lev. 24:5 [e]Ex. 29:32; Lev. 8:31; 24:9
5 [f]Num. 28:9; [John 7:22] [1]*desecrate*
6 [g][2 Chr. 6:18; Is. 66:1, 2; Mal. 3:1]; Matt. 12:41, 42
7 [h][1 Sam. 15:22; Hos. 6:6; Mic. 6:6-8]; Matt. 9:13
8 [2]NU, M omit *even*
9 [i]Mark 3:1-6; Luke 6:6-11
10 [j]Luke 13:14; 14:3; John 9:16
14 [k]Ps. 2:2; Matt. 27:1; Mark 3:6; [Luke 6:11]; John 5:18; 10:39; 11:53
15 [l]Matt. 10:23; Mark 3:7 [m]Matt. 19:2 [3]NU brackets *multitudes* as disputed.

11:26 it seemed good in Your sight. Cf. Luke 10:21,22. This is a powerful affirmation of the sovereignty of God over all the affairs of men; and in the verse that follows, Christ claimed that the task of executing the divine will had been committed to Him—a claim that would be utterly blasphemous if Jesus were anything less than sovereign God Himself.

11:28-30 Come to Me, all *you* who labor and are heavy laden. There is an echo of the first beatitude (5:3) in this passage. Note that this is an open invitation to all who hear—but phrased in such a way that the only ones who will respond to the invitation are those who are burdened by their own spiritual bankruptcy and the weight of trying to save themselves by keeping the law. The stubbornness of humanity's sinful rebellion is such that without a sovereignly-bestowed spiritual awakening, all sinners refuse to acknowledge the depth of their spiritual poverty. That is why, as Jesus says in v. 27, our salvation is the sovereign work of God. But the truth of divine election in v. 27 is not incompatible with the free offer to all in vv. 28-30.

11:29 you will find rest. I.e., from the endless, fruitless effort to save oneself by the works of the law (cf. Heb. 4:1-3,6,9-11). This speaks of a permanent respite in the grace of God which is apart from works (v. 30).

12:2 not lawful to do on the Sabbath. Actually, no law prohibited the plucking of grain in order to eat on the Sabbath. Gleaning handfuls of grain from a neighbor's field to satisfy one's immediate hunger was explicitly permitted (Deut. 23:25). What was prohibited was labor for the sake of profit. Thus a farmer could not harvest for profit on the Sabbath, but an individual could glean enough grain to eat.

12:3 He said. Jesus' answer in vv. 3-8 points out that the Sabbath laws do not restrict deeds of necessity (vv. 3,4); service to God (vv. 5,6); or acts of mercy (vv. 7,8). He reaffirmed that the Sabbath was made for man's benefit and God's glory. It was never intended to be a yoke of bondage to the people of God (Mark 2:27). *See note on Luke 6:9.*

12:4 the showbread. The consecrated bread of the Presence, 12 loaves baked fresh each Sabbath, which was usually eaten by the priests only (Lev. 24:5-9). God was not offended by David's act, done to satisfy a legitimate need when his men were weak with hunger (1 Sam. 21:4-6). *See notes on Mark 2:26; Luke 6:30.*

12:5 profane the Sabbath, and are blameless. I.e., the priests have to do their work on the Sabbath, proving that some aspects of the Sabbath restrictions are not inviolable moral absolutes, but rather precepts pertaining to the ceremonial features of the law.

12:6 greater than the temple. This was a straightforward claim of deity. The Lord Jesus was God incarnate—God dwelling in human flesh—far superior to a building which God merely visited.

12:7 *mercy and not sacrifice.* Quoted from Hos. 6:6. *See note on 9:13.*

12:8 the Son of Man is Lord even of the Sabbath. Christ has the prerogative to rule over not only their man-made sabbatarian rules, but also over the Sabbath itself—which was designed for worshiping God. Again, this was an inescapable claim of deity—and as such it prompted the Pharisees' violent outrage (v. 14).

12:10 Is it lawful to heal on the Sabbath? Jewish tradition prohibited the practice of medicine on the Sabbath, except in life-threatening situations. But no actual law in the OT forbade the giving of medicine, healing, or any other acts of mercy on the Sabbath. It is always lawful to do good.

followed Him, and He healed them all.
16 Yet He [n]warned them not to make Him
known, 17 that it might be fulfilled which
was spoken by Isaiah the prophet, saying:

18 *"Behold![o] My Servant whom I have*
chosen,
My Beloved [p] in whom My soul is
well pleased!
I will put My Spirit upon Him,
And He will declare justice to the
Gentiles.
19 *He will not quarrel nor cry out,*
Nor will anyone hear His voice in
the streets.
20 *A bruised reed He will not break,*
And smoking flax He will not
quench,
Till He sends forth justice to
victory;
21 *And in His name Gentiles will*
trust."

Pharisees Blaspheme the Holy Spirit
Mark 3:22-27; Luke 11: 17-23

22 [q]Then one was brought to Him who
was demon-possessed, blind and mute;
and He healed him, so that the [4]blind and
mute man both spoke and saw. 23 And all
the multitudes were amazed and said,
"Could this be the [r]Son of David?"
24 [s]Now when the Pharisees heard *it*
they said, "This *fellow* does not cast out
demons except by [5]Beelzebub, the ruler of
the demons."

25 But Jesus [t]knew their thoughts, and
said to them: "Every kingdom divided
against itself is brought to desolation, and
every city or house divided against itself
will not stand. 26 If Satan casts out Satan,
he is divided against himself. How then
will his kingdom stand? 27 And if I cast out
demons by Beelzebub, by whom do your
sons cast *them* out? Therefore they shall be
your judges. 28 But if I cast out demons by
the Spirit of God, [u]surely the kingdom of
God has come upon you. 29 [v]Or how can
one enter a strong man's house and plunder his goods, unless he first binds the
strong man? And then he will plunder his
house. 30 He who is not with Me is against
Me, and he who does not gather with Me
scatters abroad.

Pharisees Commit the Unpardonable Sin
Mark 3:28, 29

31 "Therefore I say to you, [w]every sin
and blasphemy will be forgiven men, [x]but
the blasphemy *against* the Spirit will not be
forgiven men. 32 Anyone who [y]speaks a
word against the Son of Man, [z]it will be
forgiven him; but whoever speaks against
the Holy Spirit, it will not be forgiven him,
either in this age or in the *age* to come.
33 "Either make the tree good and [a]its
fruit good, or else make the tree bad and its
fruit bad; for a tree is known by *its* fruit.
34 [b]Brood[6] of vipers! How can you, being
evil, speak good things? [c]For out of the
abundance of the heart the mouth speaks.

16 [n] Matt. 8:4; 9:30; 17:9
18 [o] Is. 42:1-4; 49:3 [p] Matt. 3:17; 17:5
22 [q] Matt. 9:32; [Mark 3:11]; Luke 11:14, 15 [4] NU omits *blind and*
23 [r] Matt. 9:27; 21:9
24 [s] Matt. 9:34; Mark 3:22; Luke 11:15 [5] NU, M *Beelzebul*, a Philistine deity
25 [t] Matt. 9:4; John 2:25; Rev. 2:23
28 [u] [Dan. 2:44; 7:14; Luke 1:33]; 11:20; [17:20, 21; 1 John 3:8]
29 [v] Is. 49:24; [Luke 11:21-23]
31 [w] Mark 3:28-30; Luke 12:10; [Heb. 6:4-6; 10:26, 29; 1 John 5:16] [x] Acts 7:51
32 [y] Matt. 11:19; 13:55; John 7:12, 52 [z] 1 Tim. 1:13
33 [a] Matt. 7:16-18; Luke 6:43, 44; [John 15:4-7]
34 [b] Matt. 3:7; 23:33; Luke 3:7 [c] 1 Sam. 24:13; Is. 32:6; [Matt. 15:18]; Luke 6:45; Eph. 4:29; [James 3:2-12] [6] *Offspring*

12:15 healed them all. *See note on 9:35.* In all of OT history there was never a time or a person who exhibited such extensive healing power. Physical healings were very rare in the OT. Christ chose to display His deity by healing, raising the dead, and liberating people from demons. That not only showed the Messiah's power over the physical and spiritual realms, but also demonstrated the compassion of God toward those affected by sin. *See note on John 11:35.*

12:16 warned them not to make Him known. *See note on 8:4.* Here Christ seems concerned about the potential zealotry of those who would try to press Him into the conquering-hero mold that the rabbinical experts had made out of messianic prophecy (*see note on v. 18*).

12:18 *Behold! My Servant.* Verses 18-21 are quoted from Is. 42:1-4, to demonstrate that (contrary to the typical first-century rabbinical expectations) the Messiah would not arrive with political agendas, military campaigns, and great fanfare, but with gentleness and meekness—declaring righteousness even "to the Gentiles."

12:19 *not quarrel nor cry out.* The Messiah would not try to stir up a revolution or force His way into power.

12:20 *bruised reed…smoking flax.* The reed was used by shepherds to fashion a small musical instrument. Once cracked or worn, it was useless. A smoldering wick was also useless for giving light. These represent people who are deemed useless by the world. Christ's work was to restore and rekindle such people, not to "break" them or "quench" them. This speaks of His tender compassion toward the lowliest of the lost. He came not to gather the strong for a revolution, but to show mercy to the weak. Cf. 1 Cor. 1:26-29.

12:23 Son of David. *See note on 1:1.*

12:24 Beelzebub. *See note on 10:25.* After all the displays of Jesus' deity, the Pharisees declared that He was from Satan—exactly opposite the truth, and they knew it (*see note on v. 31*; cf. 9:34; Mark 3:22; Luke 11:15).

12:28 kingdom of God has come. That was precisely true. The King was in their midst, displaying His sovereign power. He showed it by demonstrating His ability to bind Satan and his demons (v. 29).

12:31 the blasphemy *against* the Spirit. The sin He was confronting was the Pharisees' deliberate rejection of that which they knew to be of God (cf. John 11:48; Acts 4:16). They could not deny the realty of what the Holy Spirit had done through Him, so they attributed to Satan a work that they knew was of God (v. 24; Mark 3:22).

12:32 it will be forgiven him. Someone never exposed to Christ's divine power and presence might reject Him in ignorance and be forgiven—assuming the unbelief gives way to genuine repentance. Even a Pharisee such as Saul of Tarsus could be forgiven for speaking "against the Son of Man" or persecuting His followers—because his unbelief stemmed from ignorance (1 Tim. 1:13). But those who know His claims are true and reject Him anyway sin "against the Holy Spirit"—because it is the Holy Spirit who testifies of Christ and makes His truth known to us (John 15:26; 16:14,15). No forgiveness was possible for these Pharisees who witnessed His miracles firsthand, knew the truth of His claims, and still blasphemed the Holy Spirit—because they had already rejected the fullest possible revelation. *See notes on Heb. 6:4-6; 10:29.*

35 A good man out of the good treasure [7]of
his heart brings forth good things, and an
evil man out of the evil treasure brings forth
evil things. 36 But I say to you that for every
idle word men may speak, they will give account of it in the day of judgment. 37 For by
your words you will be justified, and by
your words you will be condemned."

Pharisees Demand a Sign
Luke 11:24-26, 29-32

38 [d]Then some of the scribes and Pharisees answered, saying, "Teacher, we want
to see a sign from You."
39 But He answered and said to them,
"An evil and [e]adulterous generation seeks
after a sign, and no sign will be given to it
except the sign of the prophet Jonah. 40 [f]For
as Jonah was three days and three nights in
the belly of the great fish, so will the Son of
Man be three days and three nights in the
heart of the earth. 41 [g]The men of Nineveh
will rise up in the judgment with this generation and [h]condemn it, [i]because they repented at the preaching of Jonah; and indeed a greater than Jonah *is* here. 42 [j]The
queen of the South will rise up in the judgment with this generation and condemn it,
for she came from the ends of the earth to
hear the wisdom of Solomon; and indeed a
greater than Solomon *is* here.
43 [k]"When an unclean spirit goes out of

35 [7] NU, M omit *of his heart*
38 [d] Matt. 16:1; Mark 8:11; Luke 11:16; John 2:18; 1 Cor. 1:22
39 [e] Is. 57:3; Matt. 16:4; Mark 8:38; [Luke 11:29-32]; John 4:48
40 [f] Jon. 1:17; Luke 24:46; Acts 10:40; 1 Cor. 15:4
41 [g] Jon. 3:5; Luke 11:32 [h] Jer. 3:11; Ezek. 16:51; [Rom. 2:27] [i] Jon. 3:5
42 [j] 1 Kin. 10:1-13; 2 Chr. 9:1; Luke 11:31
43 [k] Luke 11:24-26 [l] [Job 1:7; 1 Pet. 5:8]
45 [m] Mark 5:9; Luke 11:26; [Heb. 6:4-8; 10:26; 2 Pet. 2:20-22]
46 [n] Mark 3:31-35; Luke 8:19-21 [o] Matt. 13:55; Mark 6:3; John 2:12; 7:3, 5; Acts 1:14; 1 Cor. 9:5; Gal. 1:19
47 [p] Matt. 13:55, 56; John 2:12; Acts 1:14
49 [q] John 20:17; [Rom. 8:29]
50 [r] John 15:14; [Gal. 5:6; 6:15; Col. 3:11; Heb. 2:11]

CHAPTER 13

1 [a] Matt. 13:1-15; Mark 4:1-12; Luke 8:4-10
2 [b] Luke 8:4

a man, [l]he goes through dry places, seeking rest, and finds none. 44 Then he says, 'I
will return to my house from which I
came.' And when he comes, he finds *it*
empty, swept, and put in order. 45 Then he
goes and takes with him seven other spirits more wicked than himself, and they
enter and dwell there; [m]and the last *state* of
that man is worse than the first. So shall it
also be with this wicked generation."

Jesus and the True Brethren—Mark 3:31-35

46 While He was still talking to the multitudes, [n]behold, His mother and [o]brothers
stood outside, seeking to speak with Him.
47 Then one said to Him, "Look, [p]Your
mother and Your brothers are standing
outside, seeking to speak with You."
48 But He answered and said to the one
who told Him, "Who is My mother and
who are My brothers?" 49 And He
stretched out His hand toward His disciples and said, "Here are My mother and
My [q]brothers! 50 For [r]whoever does the
will of My Father in heaven is My brother
and sister and mother."

Parable of the Soils
Mark 4:1-20; Luke 8:4-15

13 On the same day Jesus went out of
the house [a]and sat by the sea.
2 [b]And great multitudes were gathered to-

12:36 every idle word. The most seemingly insignificant sin—even a slip of the tongue—carries the full potential of all hell's evil (cf. James 3:6). No infraction against God's holiness is therefore a trifling thing, and each person will ultimately give account of every such indiscretion. There is no truer indication of a bad tree than the bad fruit of speech (vv. 33,35). The poisonous snakes were known by their poisonous mouths revealing evil hearts (v. 34; cf. Luke 6:45). Every person is judged by his words, because they reveal the state of his heart.

12:38 we want to see a sign from You. They were hoping for a sign of astronomical proportions (Luke 11:16). Instead, he gives them a "sign" from Scripture. *See notes on 16:1; 21:21.*

12:39 An evil and adulterous generation. This speaks of spiritual adultery—unfaithfulness to God (cf. Jer. 5:7,8).

12:40 three days and three nights. Quoted from Jon. 1:17. This sort of expression was a common way of underscoring the prophetic significance of a period of time. An expression like "forty days and forty nights" (*see note on 4:2*) may in some cases simply refer to a period of time longer than a month. "Three days and three nights" was an emphatic way of saying "three days," and by Jewish reckoning this would be an apt way of expressing a period of time that includes parts of 3 days. Thus, if Christ was crucified on a Friday, and His resurrection occurred on the first day of the week, by Hebrew reckoning this would qualify as 3 days and 3 nights. All sorts of elaborate schemes have been devised to suggest that Christ might have died on a Wednesday or Thursday, just to accommodate the extreme literal meaning of these words. But the original meaning would not have required that sort of wooden interpretation. *See note on Luke 13:32.*

12:41 men of Nineveh...repented. *See Jon. 3:5-10.* The revival in Nineveh under Jonah's preaching was one of the most extraordinary spiritual revivals the world has ever seen. Some have suggested that the repentance of the Ninevites stopped short of saving faith, because the city reverted within one generation to its old pagan ways (cf. Nah. 3:7,8). From Jesus' words here, however, it is clear that the revival under Jonah represented authentic saving conversions. Only eternity will reveal how many souls from that one generation were swept into the kingdom as a result of the revival.

12:42 queen of the South. See 1 Kin. 10:1-13. The queen of Sheba came to see Solomon's glory (*see note on 6:29*) and in the process encountered the glory of Solomon's God (1 Kin. 10:9).

12:45 the last *state* of that man is worse than the first. The problem is that the evil spirit found the house "empty" (v. 44). This is the description of someone who attempts moral reform without ever being indwelt by the Holy Spirit. Reform apart from regeneration is never effective and eventually reverts back to pre-reform behavior.

12:46 brothers. These are actual siblings (half-brothers) of Jesus. Matthew explicitly connects them with Mary, indicating that they were not cousins or Joseph's sons from a previous marriage, as some of the church fathers imagined. They are mentioned in all the gospels (Mark 3:31; Luke 8:19-21; John 7:3-5). Matthew and Mark give the names of 4 of Jesus' brothers, and mention that He had sisters as well (13:55; Mark 6:3).

12:48,49 He was not repudiating His earthly family (cf. John 19:26,27). Rather, He was emphasizing the supremacy and eternality of spiritual relationships (cf. 10:37). After all, even His own family needed Him as Savior (cf. John 7:5).

12:50 does the will of My Father. This is not salvation by works. Doing the will of God is the evidence of salvation by grace. *See notes on 7:21-27.*

13:1-52 This is the third of 5 discourses featured in Matthew (see Introduction: Historical and Theological Themes).

gether to Him, so that [c]He got into a boat
and sat; and the whole multitude stood on
the shore.
3 Then He spoke many things to them in
parables, saying: [d]"Behold, a sower went
out to sow. 4 And as he sowed, some *seed*
fell by the wayside; and the birds came and
devoured them. 5 Some fell on stony
places, where they did not have much
earth; and they immediately sprang up because they had no depth of earth. 6 But
when the sun was up they were scorched,
and because they had no root they withered away. 7 And some fell among thorns,
and the thorns sprang up and choked
them. 8 But others fell on good ground and
yielded a crop: some [e]a hundredfold, some
sixty, some thirty. 9 [f]He who has ears to
hear, let him hear!"
10 And the disciples came and said to
Him, "Why do You speak to them in parables?"
11 He answered and said to them, "Because [g]it has been given to you to know the
[1]mysteries of the kingdom of heaven, but
to them it has not been given. 12 [h]For whoever has, to him more will be given, and he
will have abundance; but whoever does
not have, even what he has will be taken
away from him. 13 Therefore I speak to
them in parables, because seeing they do
not see, and hearing they do not hear, nor
do they understand. 14 And in them the
prophecy of Isaiah is fulfilled, which says:

2 [c] Luke 5:3
3 [d] Luke 8:5
8 [e] Gen. 26:12; Matt. 13:23
9 [f] Matt. 11:15; Mark 4:9; Rev. 2:7, 11, 17, 29; 3:6, 13, 22
11 [g] [Matt. 11:25; 16:17]; Mark 4:10, 11; [John 6:65; 1 Cor. 2:10; Col. 1:27; 1 John 2:20, 27] [1] *secret* or *hidden truths*
12 [h] Matt. 25:29; Mark 4:25; Luke 8:18; 19:26
14 [i] Is. 6:9, 10; Ezek. 12:2; Mark 4:12; Luke 8:10; John 12:40; Acts 28:26, 27; Rom. 11:8; [2 Cor. 3:14, 15] [j] [John 3:36]
15 [k] Ps. 119:70; Zech. 7:11; 2 Tim. 4:4; Heb. 5:11 [l] Luke 19:42 [m] Acts 28:26, 27 [2] NU, M *would*
16 [n] [Prov. 20:12; Matt. 16:17]; Luke 10:23, 24; [John 20:29]
17 [o] John 8:56; Heb. 11:13; 1 Pet. 1:10, 11
18 [p] Mark 4:13-20; Luke 8:11-15
19 [q] Matt. 4:23
20 [r] Is. 58:2; Ezek. 33:31, 32; John 5:35
21 [s] [Acts 14:22] [t] Matt. 11:6; 2 Tim. 1:15
22 [u] Matt. 19:23; Mark 10:23; Luke 18:24; 1 Tim. 6:9; 2 Tim. 4:10 [v] Jer. 4:3

[i]'Hearing you will hear and shall
not understand,
And seeing you will see and not
[j]perceive;
15 *For the hearts of this people have*
grown dull.
Their ears [k]are hard of hearing,
And their eyes they have [l]closed,
Lest they should see with their eyes
and hear with their ears,
Lest they should understand with
their hearts and turn,
So that I [2]should [m]heal them.'

16 But [n]blessed *are* your eyes for they see,
and your ears for they hear; 17 for assuredly, I say to you [o]that many prophets and
righteous *men* desired to see what you see,
and did not see *it*, and to hear what you
hear, and did not hear *it*.
18 [p]"Therefore hear the parable of the
sower: 19 When anyone hears the word [q]of
the kingdom, and does not understand *it*,
then the wicked *one* comes and snatches
away what was sown in his heart. This is he
who received seed by the wayside. 20 But
he who received the seed on stony places,
this is he who hears the word and immediately [r]receives it with joy; 21 yet he has no
root in himself, but endures only for a
while. For when [s]tribulation or persecution
arises because of the word, immediately
[t]he stumbles. 22 Now [u]he who received
seed [v]among the thorns is he who hears the

13:3 parables. Parables were a common form of teaching in Judaism. The Gr. term for "parable" appears 45 times in the LXX. A parable is a long analogy, often cast in the form of a story. Before this point in His ministry, Jesus had employed many graphic analogies (cf. 5:13-16), but their meaning was fairly clear in the context of His teaching. Parables required more explanation (cf. v. 36) and Jesus employed them to obscure the truth from unbelievers while making it clearer to His disciples (vv. 11,12). For the remainder of His Galilean ministry, He did not speak to the multitudes except in parables (v. 34). Jesus' veiling the truth from unbelievers this way was both an act of judgment and an act of mercy. It was "judgment" because it kept them in the darkness that they loved (cf. John 3:19), but it was "mercy" because they had already rejected the light, so any exposure to more truth would only increase their condemnation. *See note on v. 13.*

13:4 wayside. The fields were bordered by paths beaten hard by foot traffic and baking sun.

13:5 stony places. Very shallow soil atop a layer of bedrock. From the top it looks fertile, but there is no depth to sustain a root system or reach water (v. 21).

13:7 thorns. Weeds, the roots of which were still in the ground after plowing had been done.

13:11 it has been given to you. Here Jesus clearly affirms that the ability to comprehend spiritual truth is a gracious gift of God, sovereignly bestowed on the elect (v. 11). The reprobate ones, on the other hand, are passed over. They reap the natural consequence of their own unbelief and rebellion—spiritual blindness (v. 13). **the mysteries of the kingdom of heaven.** "Mysteries" are those truths which have been hidden from all ages in the past and revealed in the NT. *See notes on 1 Cor. 2:7; 4:1; Eph. 3:4,5.* Many specific doctrines of the NT are identified as "mysteries" (e.g., Rom. 11:25; 1 Cor. 15:51; Eph. 5:32; 6:19; Col. 1:26,27; 2 Thess. 2:7; 1 Tim. 3:9,16).

13:13 because seeing they do not see. Here Matthew seems to suggest that their own unbelief is the cause of their spiritual blindness. Luke 8:10, however, emphasizes God's initiative in obscuring the truth from these unbelievers ("to the rest it is given in parables, [so] that 'Seeing they may not see, And hearing they may not understand'"—cf. Is. 6:9). Both things are true, of course. Yet we are not to think that God blinds them because He somehow delights in their destruction (cf. Ezek. 33:11; *see note on 23:37*). This judicial blinding may be viewed as an act of mercy, lest their condemnation be increased (*see note on v. 3*).

13:14,15 Quoted from Is. 6:9,10 (*see notes there*).

13:17 many...desired to see. Cf. John 8:56; 1 Pet. 1:9-12.

13:19 word of the kingdom. The message of how to enter God's kingdom, the sphere of salvation, i.e., the gospel (cf. "word of reconciliation" in 2 Cor. 5:19). **wicked *one*.** Satan. Cf. 1 John 5:19. The gospel never penetrates these souls, so it disappears from the surface of their understanding—seen as the enemy snatching it away.

13:20 stony places. Some people make an emotional, superficial commitment to salvation in Christ, but it is not real. They remain interested only until there is a sacrificial price to pay, and then abandon Christ. *See note on 1 John 2:19.*

13:22 who received seed among the thorns. These make superficial commitments without a true repentance. They can't break with the love of money and the world (James 4:4; 1 John 2:15-17; *see notes on 19:16-22*).

The Parables of Jesus

Parable	Matthew	Mark	Luke
1. Lamp Under a Basket	5:14-16	4:21,22	8:16,17; 11:33-36
2. A Wise Man Builds on Rock and a Foolish Man Builds on Sand	7:24-27		6:47-49
3. Unshrunk (New) Cloth on an Old Garment	9:16	2:21	5:36
4. New Wine in Old Wineskins	9:17	2:22	5:37,38
5. The Sower	13:3-23	4:2-20	8:4-15
6. The Tares (Weeds)	13:24-30		
7. The Mustard Seed	13:31,32	4:30-32	13:18,19
8. The Leaven	13:33		13:20,21
9. The Hidden Treasure	13:44		
10. The Pearl of Great Price	13:45,46		
11. The Dragnet	13:47-50		
12. The Lost Sheep	18:12-14		15:3-7
13. The Unforgiving Servant	18:23-35		
14. The Workers in the Vineyard	20:1-16		
15. The Two Sons	21:28-32		
16. The Wicked Vinedressers	21:33-45	12:1-12	20:9-19
17. The Wedding Feast	22:2-14		
18. The Fig Tree	24:32-44	13:28-32	21:29-33
19. The Wise and Foolish Virgins	25:1-13		
20. The Talents	25:14-30		
21. The Growing Seed		4:26-29	
22. The Absent Householder		13:33-37	
23. The Creditor and Two Debtors			7:41-43
24. The Good Samaritan			10:30-37
25. A Friend in Need			11:5-13
26. The Rich Fool			12:16-21
27. The Watchful Servants			12:35-40
28. The Faithful Servant and the Evil Servant			12:42-48
29. The Barren Fig Tree			13:6-9
30. The Great Supper			14:16-24
31. Building a Tower and a King Making War			14:25-35
32. The Lost Coin			15:8-10
33. The Lost Son			15:11-32
34. The Unjust Steward			16:1-13
35. The Rich Man and Lazarus			16:19-31
36. Unprofitable Servants			17:7-10
37. The Persistent Widow			18:1-8
38. The Pharisee and the Tax Collector			18:9-14
39. The Minas (Pounds)			19:11-27

word, and the cares of this world and the
deceitfulness of riches choke the word, and
he becomes unfruitful. **23** But he who received seed on the good ground is he who
hears the word and understands *it,* who indeed bears [w]fruit and produces: some a
hundredfold, some sixty, some thirty."

Parable of the Wheat and Tares

24 Another parable He put forth to them,
saying: "The kingdom of heaven is like a
man who sowed good seed in his field;
25 but while men slept, his enemy came
and sowed tares among the wheat and
went his way. **26** But when the grain had
sprouted and produced a crop, then the
tares also appeared. **27** So the servants of
the owner came and said to him, 'Sir, did
you not sow good seed in your field? How
then does it have tares?' **28** He said to
them, 'An enemy has done this.' The servants said to him, 'Do you want us then to
go and gather them up?' **29** But he said,
'No, lest while you gather up the tares you
also uproot the wheat with them. **30** Let
both grow together until the harvest, and
at the time of harvest I will say to the
reapers, "First gather together the tares
and bind them in bundles to burn them,
but [x]gather the wheat into my barn." ' "

Parable of the Mustard Seed
Mark 4:30-32; Luke 13:18, 19

31 Another parable He put forth to them,
saying: [y]"The kingdom of heaven is like a
mustard seed, which a man took and
sowed in his field, **32** which indeed is the
least of all the seeds; but when it is grown
it is greater than the herbs and becomes a
[z]tree, so that the birds of the air come and
nest in its branches."

Parable of the Leaven—Luke 13:20, 21

33 [a]Another parable He spoke to them:
"The kingdom of heaven is like leaven,
which a woman took and hid in three
[3]measures of meal till [b]it was all leavened."
34 [c]All these things Jesus spoke to the
multitude in parables; and without a parable He did not speak to them, **35** that it
might be fulfilled which was spoken by the
prophet, saying:

[d]*"I will open My mouth in parables;*
[e]*I will utter things kept secret from*
the foundation of the world."

Parable of the Tares Explained

36 Then Jesus sent the multitude away
and went into the house. And His disciples
came to Him, saying, "Explain to us the
parable of the tares of the field."
37 He answered and said to them: "He
who sows the good seed is the Son of Man.
38 [f]The field is the world, the good seeds are
the sons of the kingdom, but the tares are
[g]the sons of the wicked *one.* **39** The enemy
who sowed them is the devil, [h]the harvest is
the end of the age, and the reapers are the
angels. **40** Therefore as the tares are gathered and burned in the fire, so it will be at
the end of this age. **41** The Son of Man will
send out His angels, [i]and they will gather
out of His kingdom all things that offend,
and those who practice lawlessness, **42** [j]and
will cast them into the furnace of fire.
[k]There will be wailing and gnashing of
teeth. **43** [l]Then the righteous will shine forth
as the sun in the kingdom of their Father.
[m]He who has ears to hear, let him hear!

Parable of the Hidden Treasure

44 "Again, the kingdom of heaven is like

23 [w] [John 15:5]; Phil. 1:11; Col. 1:6
30 [x] Matt. 3:12
31 [y] [Is. 2:2, 3; Mic. 4:1]; Mark 4:30; Luke 13:18, 19
32 [z] Ps. 104:12; Ezek. 17:22-24; 31:3-9; Dan. 4:12

33 [a] Luke 13:20, 21 [b] [1 Cor. 5:6; Gal. 5:9] [3] Gr. *sata,* same as a Heb. *seah;* approximately 2 pecks in all
34 [c] Mark 4:33, 34; John 10:6; 16:25
35 [d] Ps. 78:2 [e] Rom. 16:25, 26; 1 Cor. 2:7; Eph. 3:9; Col. 1:26
38 [f] Matt. 24:14; 28:19; Mark 16:15; Luke 24:47; Rom. 10:18; Col. 1:6 [g] Gen. 3:15; John 8:44; Acts 13:10
39 [h] Joel 3:13; Rev. 14:15
41 [i] Matt. 18:7; 2 Pet. 2:1, 2
42 [j] Matt. 3:12; Rev. 19:20; 20:10 [k] Matt. 8:12; 13:50
43 [l] [Dan. 12:3; 1 Cor. 15:42, 43, 58] [m] Matt. 13:9

13:23 the good ground. As there were 3 soils with no fruit, thus no salvation, there are 3 kinds of good soil with fruit. Not all believers are equally fruitful, but all are fruitful (cf. 7:16; John 15:8).

13:25 tares. Probably darnel, a type of weed that can hardly be distinguished from wheat until the head matures. In an agricultural setting, sowing darnel in someone else's wheat field was a way for enemies to destroy someone's livelihood catastrophically. It pictures Satan's efforts to devastate the church by mingling his children with God's, in some cases making it impossible for believers to discern the true from the false. The parable is explained in vv. 36-43.

13:32 a tree, so that the birds of the air come and nest in its branches. Palestinian mustard plants are large shrubs, sometimes up to 15 ft. high—certainly large enough for birds to lodge in. This is undoubtedly a reference to several OT passages, including Ezek. 17:23; 31:6; Dan. 4:21—passages which prophesied the inclusion of Gentiles in the kingdom.

13:33 The kingdom of heaven is like leaven. Here the kingdom is pictured as yeast, multiplying quietly and permeating all that it contacts. The lesson is the same as the parable of the mustard seed. Some interpreters suggest that since leaven is nearly always a symbol of evil in Scripture (*see note on Mark 8:15*) it must carry that connotation here as well. They make the leaven some evil influence inside the kingdom. But that twists Jesus actual words and violates the context, in which Jesus is repeatedly describing that kingdom itself as the pervading influence.

13:34 without a parable He did not speak to them. For the rest of His Galilean ministry all Jesus' public teaching consisted only of parables.

13:35 spoken by the prophet. The "prophet" in this case was the psalmist. See Ps. 78:2.

13:37 He who sows. The true sower of salvation seed is the Lord Himself. He alone can give the power in the heart to transform. He is the One who saves sinners, even through the preaching and witnessing of believers (Rom. 10:14).

13:43 shine forth as the sun. Cf. Dan. 12:3. Believers already shine in that they possess the Spirit of Christ and the glorious message of the gospel (5:16; 2 Cor. 4:3-7). We will shine even more in the glory of Christ's kingdom and eternal heaven (Rom. 8:16-23; Phil. 3:20,21; Rev. 19:7-9).

13:44-46 These two parables have identical meanings. Both pic-

treasure hidden in a field, which a man
found and hid; and for joy over it he goes
and [n]sells all that he has and [o]buys that
field.

Parable of the Pearl of Great Price

45 "Again, the kingdom of heaven is like
a merchant seeking beautiful pearls,
46 who, when he had found [p]one pearl of
great price, went and sold all that he had
and bought it.

Parable of the Dragnet

47 "Again, the kingdom of heaven is like
a dragnet that was cast into the sea and
[q]gathered some of every kind, 48 which,
when it was full, they drew to shore; and
they sat down and gathered the good into
vessels, but threw the bad away. 49 So it
will be at the end of the age. The angels
will come forth, [r]separate the wicked from
among the just, 50 and cast them into the
furnace of fire. There will be wailing and
gnashing of teeth."

Parable of the Householder

51 [4]Jesus said to them, "Have you understood all these things?"
They said to Him, "Yes, [5]Lord."
52 Then He said to them, "Therefore
every [6]scribe instructed [7]concerning the
kingdom of heaven is like a householder
who brings out of his treasure [s]*things* new
and old."
53 Now it came to pass, when Jesus had
finished these parables, that He departed
from there.

44 [n] Phil. 3:7, 8 [o] [Is. 55:1; Rev. 3:18]
46 [p] Prov. 2:4; 3:14, 15; 8:10, 19
47 [q] Matt. 22:9, 10
49 [r] Matt. 25:32
51 [4] NU omits *Jesus said to them* [5] NU omits *Lord*
52 [s] Song 7:13 [6] A scholar of the Old Testament [7] Or *for*
54 [t] Ps. 22:22; Matt. 2:23; Mark 6:1; Luke 4:16; John 7:15
55 [u] Is. 49:7; Mark 6:3; [Luke 3:23]; John 6:42 [v] Matt. 12:46 [w] Mark 15:40 [8] NU *Joseph*
57 [x] Matt. 11:6; Mark 6:3, 4 [y] Luke 4:24; John 4:44
58 [z] Mark 6:5, 6; John 5:44, 46, 47

CHAPTER 14

1 [a] Mark 6:14-29; Luke 9:7-9
3 [b] Matt. 4:12; Mark 6:17; Luke 3:19, 20
4 [c] Lev. 18:16; 20:21
5 [d] Matt. 21:26; Luke 20:6

Rejection at Nazareth—Mark 6:1-6

54 [t]When He had come to His own country, He taught them in their synagogue, so
that they were astonished and said,
"Where did this *Man* get this wisdom and
these mighty works? 55 [u]Is this not the
carpenter's son? Is not His mother called
Mary? And [v]His brothers [w]James, [8]Joses,
Simon, and Judas? 56 And His sisters, are
they not all with us? Where then did this
Man get all these things?" 57 So they [x]were
offended at Him.
But Jesus said to them, [y]"A prophet is
not without honor except in his own country and in his own house." 58 Now [z]He did
not do many mighty works there because
of their unbelief.

Present Response to Jesus
Mark 6:14-16; Luke 9:7-9

14 At that time [a]Herod the tetrarch
heard the report about Jesus 2 and
said to his servants, "This is John the Baptist; he is risen from the dead, and therefore these powers are at work in him."

Recount of the Murder of John the Baptist
Mark 6:17-29

3 [b]For Herod had laid hold of John and
bound him, and put *him* in prison for the
sake of Herodias, his brother Philip's wife.
4 Because John had said to him, [c]"It is not
lawful for you to have her." 5 And although he wanted to put him to death, he
feared the multitude, [d]because they counted him as a prophet.
6 But when Herod's birthday was celebrated, the daughter of Herodias danced

ture salvation as something hidden from most people (*see note on v. 11*), but so valuable that people who have it revealed to them are willing to give up all they have to possess it.

13:47 dragnet. Some fishing was done with a large weighted net dragged along the bottom of the lake. When pulled in, it contained an assortment that had to be separated. In a similar way the visible kingdom, the sphere of those who claim to be believers, is full of both good and bad and will be sorted in the judgment.

13:49 angels. They serve God in judgment (cf. v. 41; 2 Thess. 1:7-10).

13:52 brings out of his treasure *things* new and old. The disciples were not to spurn the old for the sake of the new. Rather the new insights they gleaned from Jesus' parables were to be understood in light of the old truths, and vice versa.

13:54 His own country. I.e., Nazareth.

13:55 His brothers. *See note on 12:46.* The fact that Joseph does not actually appear in any of these accounts suggests that he was no longer living.

13:57 A prophet...in his own country. This is an ancient proverb paralleling the modern saying, "familiarity breeds contempt." They knew Jesus too well as a boy and a young man from their own town—and they concluded that He was nothing special. Verse 58 gives the sad result (cf. Mark 6:4).

13:58 He did not do many mighty works there. *See note on Mark 6:5.*

14:1-12 The record of the murder of John the Baptist is also in Mark 6:14-29; cf. Luke 9:7-9.

14:1 Herod. *See note on 2:22.* This was Herod Antipas, ruler of Galilee. **tetrarch.** One of 4 rulers of a divided region. After the death of Herod the Great, Palestine had been divided among his sons. Elsewhere, Matthew refers to Herod as "King" (v. 9), because that was the title by which he was known among the Galileans.

14:3 Herodias, his brother Philip's wife. Herodias was the daughter of Aristobulus, another son of Herod the Great; so when she married Philip, she was marrying her own father's brother. What precipitated the arrest of John the Baptist was that Herod Antipas (another of Herodias' uncles) talked Herodias into leaving her husband (his brother) in order to marry him (Mark 6:17)—thus compounding the incest, as well as violating Lev. 18:16. John was outraged that a ruler in Israel would commit such a sin openly, so he rebuked Herod severely (v. 4). For this, he was imprisoned and later killed (Mark 6:14-29).

14:6 the daughter of Herodias. Salome, daughter of Herodias and Philip. According to Josephus, the Jewish historian, she married yet another son (her own father's brother and her mother's uncle) of Herod the Great, thus further tangling the web of incest in that family.

before them and pleased Herod. 7 Therefore he promised with an oath to give her
whatever she might ask.
8 So she, having been prompted by her
mother, said, "Give me John the Baptist's
head here on a platter."
9 And the king was sorry; nevertheless,
because of the oaths and because of those
who sat with him, he commanded *it* to be
given to *her.* 10 So he sent and had John beheaded in prison. 11 And his head was
brought on a platter and given to the girl,
and she brought *it* to her mother. 12 Then
his disciples came and took away the body
and buried it, and went and told Jesus.

Jesus Feeds 5,000

Mark 6:31-44; Luke 9:11-17; John 6:1-13

13 [e]When Jesus heard *it,* He departed
from there by boat to a deserted place by
Himself. But when the multitudes heard it,
they followed Him on foot from the cities.
14 And when Jesus went out He saw a
great multitude; and He [f]was moved with
compassion for them, and healed their
sick. 15 [g]When it was evening, His disciples came to Him, saying, "This is a deserted place, and the hour is already late.
Send the multitudes away, that they may
go into the villages and buy themselves
food."
16 But Jesus said to them, "They do not
need to go away. You give them something
to eat."
17 And they said to Him, "We have here
only five loaves and two fish."
18 He said, "Bring them here to Me."
19 Then He commanded the multitudes to
sit down on the grass. And He took the five
loaves and the two fish, and looking up to
heaven, [h]He blessed and broke and gave
the loaves to the disciples; and the disciples gave to the multitudes. 20 So they all
ate and were filled, and they took up
twelve baskets full of the fragments that
remained. 21 Now those who had eaten
were about five thousand men, besides
women and children.

Jesus Walks on Water

Mark 6:45-52; John 6:14-21

22 Immediately Jesus [1]made His disciples get into the boat and go before Him to
the other side, while He sent the multitudes away. 23 [i]And when He had sent the
multitudes away, He went up on the
mountain by Himself to pray. [j]Now when
evening came, He was alone there. 24 But
the boat was now [2]in the middle of the sea,
tossed by the waves, for the wind was contrary.
25 Now in the fourth watch of the night
Jesus went to them, walking on the sea.
26 And when the disciples saw Him [k]walk-
ing on the sea, they were troubled, saying,
"It is a ghost!" And they cried out for fear.
27 But immediately Jesus spoke to them,
saying, [3]"Be of good [l]cheer! [4]It is I; do not
be afraid."
28 And Peter answered Him and said,
"Lord, if it is You, command me to come to
You on the water."
29 So He said, "Come." And when Peter
had come down out of the boat, he walked
on the water to go to Jesus. 30 But when he
saw [5]that the wind *was* boisterous, he was
afraid; and beginning to sink he cried out,
saying, "Lord, save me!"
31 And immediately Jesus stretched out
His hand and caught him, and said to him,
"O you of [m]little faith, why did you
doubt?" 32 And when they got into the
boat, the wind ceased.
33 Then those who were in the boat
[6]came and worshiped Him, saying, "Truly
[n]You are the Son of God."

Jesus Heals Many—Mark 6:53-56

34 [o]When they had crossed over, they
came [7]to the land of Gennesaret. 35 And
when the men of that place recognized
Him, they sent out into all that surrounding region, brought to Him all who were
sick, 36 and begged Him that they might
only [p]touch the hem of His garment. And
[q]as many as touched *it* were made perfectly well.

13 [e] Matt. 10:23; 12:15; Mark 6:32-44; Luke 9:10-17; John 6:1, 2
14 [f] Matt. 9:36; Mark 6:34
15 [g] Mark 6:35; Luke 9:12
19 [h] 1 Sam. 9:13; Matt. 15:36; 26:26; Mark 6:41; 8:7; 14:22; Luke 24:30; Acts 27:35; [Rom. 14:6]

22 [1] *invited, strongly urged*
23 [i] Mark 6:46; Luke 9:28; John 6:15 [j] John 6:16
24 [2] NU *many furlongs away from the land*
26 [k] Job 9:8
27 [l] Acts 23:11; 27:22, 25, 36 [3] *Take courage* [4] Lit. *I am*
30 [5] NU brackets *that* and *boisterous* as disputed.
31 [m] Matt. 6:30; 8:26
33 [n] Ps. 2:7; Matt. 16:16; 26:63; Mark 1:1; Luke 4:41; John 1:49; 6:69; 11:27; Acts 8:37; Rom. 1:4 [6] NU omits *came and*
34 [o] Mark 6:53; Luke 5:1 [7] NU *to land at*
36 [p] [Mark 5:24-34] [q] Matt. 9:20; Mark 3:10; [Luke 6:19]; Acts 19:12

14:8 prompted by her mother. *See note on v. 6.*

14:9 because of the oaths. A promise made with a certain oath was considered sacred and inviolable (*see note on 5:34*)—especially when made by a ruling monarch. Herod was widely known for his duplicity, so it was not honesty that he was concerned about, but rather the appearance of things. He did not want to be embarrassed in front of his dinner guests.

14:12 buried it. In a cave (Mark 6:29).

14:13 multitudes...followed Him on foot. They traveled great distances over land to reach the secluded spot where He had come by boat.

14:14 moved with compassion. *See note on 9:36.*

14:16 give them something to eat. Jesus knew they did not have enough food to feed the crowd. He wanted the disciples to state it plainly so the record would be clear that a miracle by His power occurred (vv. 17,18). See 16:9,10.

14:24 tossed by the waves. *See notes on 8:24,27.*

14:25 fourth watch. 3:00–6:00 a.m.

14:33 You are the Son of God. Cf. 27:43,54.

14:34 Gennesaret. A town on the NW shore of the Sea of Galilee.

14:36 the hem of His garment. *See note on 9:20.*

Debate over Tradition—Mark 7:1-23

15 Then [a]the scribes and Pharisees
who were from Jerusalem came to
Jesus, saying, 2 [b]"Why do Your disciples
transgress the tradition of the elders? For
they do not wash their hands when they
eat bread."
3 He answered and said to them, "Why
do you also transgress the commandment
of God because of your tradition? 4 For
God commanded, saying, [c]*'Honor your fa-*
ther and your mother'; and, [d]*'He who*
curses father or mother, let him be put to
death.' 5 But you say, 'Whoever says to his
father or mother, [e]"Whatever profit you
might have received from me *is* a gift *to*
God"— 6 then he need not honor his father
[1]or mother.' Thus you have made the
[2]commandment of God of no effect by
your tradition. 7 [f]Hypocrites! Well did Isaiah prophesy about you, saying:

8 *'These[g] people [3] draw near to Me*
with their mouth,
And honor Me with their lips,
But their heart is far from Me.
9 *And in vain they worship Me,*
[h]*Teaching as doctrines the*
commandments of men.'"

10 [i]When He had called the multitude to
Himself, He said to them, "Hear and understand: 11 [j]Not what goes into the mouth
defiles a man; but what comes out of the
mouth, this defiles a man."
12 Then His disciples came and said to
Him, "Do You know that the Pharisees
were offended when they heard this saying?"
13 But He answered and said, [k]"Every
plant which My heavenly Father has not
planted will be uprooted. 14 Let them
alone. [l]They are blind leaders of the blind.
And if the blind leads the blind, both will
fall into a ditch."
15 [m]Then Peter answered and said to
Him, "Explain this parable to us."
16 So Jesus said, [n]"Are you also still
without understanding? 17 Do you not yet
understand that [o]whatever enters the
mouth goes into the stomach and is eliminated? 18 But [p]those things which proceed
out of the mouth come from the heart, and
they defile a man. 19 [q]For out of the heart
proceed evil thoughts, murders, adulteries,
fornications, thefts, false witness, blasphemies. 20 These are *the things* which defile a man, but to eat with unwashed hands
does not defile a man."

Jesus Heals the Gentile Woman's Daughter
Mark 7:24-30

21 [r]Then Jesus went out from there and
departed to the region of Tyre and Sidon.
22 And behold, a woman of Canaan came
from that region and cried out to Him, saying, "Have mercy on me, O Lord, [s]Son of
David! My daughter is severely demon-
possessed."
23 But He answered her not a word.
And His disciples came and urged Him,
saying, "Send her away, for she cries out
after us."
24 But He answered and said, [t]"I was not
sent except to the lost sheep of the house of
Israel."
25 Then she came and worshiped Him,
saying, "Lord, help me!"
26 But He answered and said, "It is not
good to take the children's bread and
throw *it* to the little [u]dogs."
27 And she said, "Yes, Lord, yet even the
little dogs eat the crumbs which fall from
their masters' table."

CHAPTER 15

1 [a]Mark 7:1; John 1:19; Acts 25:7
2 [b]Mark 7:5
4 [c]Ex. 20:1, 12; Lev. 19:3; [Deut. 5:16]; Prov. 23:22; [Eph. 6:2, 3] [d]Ex. 21:17; Lev. 20:9; Deut. 27:16; Prov. 20:20; 30:17
5 [e]Mark 7:11, 12
6 [1]NU omits *or mother* [2]NU *word*
7 [f]Mark 7:6
8 [g]Ps. 78:36; Is. 29:13; Ezek. 33:31 [3]NU omits *draw near to Me with their mouth, And*
9 [h]Is. 29:13; [Col. 2:18-22]; Titus 1:14
10 [i]Mark 7:14
11 [j][Acts 10:15; Rom. 14:14, 17, 20; 1 Tim. 4:4; Titus 1:15]
13 [k][Is. 60:21; 61:3; John 15:2; 1 Cor. 3:12, 13]
14 [l]Is. 9:16; Mal. 2:8; Matt. 23:16, 24; Luke 6:39; Rom. 2:19
15 [m]Mark 7:17
16 [n]Matt. 16:9; Mark 7:18
17 [o][1 Cor. 6:13]
18 [p][Matt. 12:34]; Mark 7:20; [James 3:6]
19 [q]Gen. 6:5; 8:21; Prov. 6:14; Jer. 17:9; Mark 7:21; [Rom. 1:29-32; Gal. 5:19-21]
21 [r]Mark 7:24-30
22 [s]Matt. 1:1; 22:41, 42
24 [t]Matt. 10:5, 6; [Rom. 15:8]
26 [u]Matt. 7:6; Phil. 3:2

15:2 tradition of the elders. This was a body of extrabiblical law that had existed only in oral form and only since the time of the Babylonian captivity. Later it was committed to writing in the *Mishna* near the end of the second century. The law of Moses contained no commandment about washing one's hands before eating—except for priests who were required to wash before eating holy offerings (Lev. 22:6,7).

15:3 transgress. The nature of this sin is identified in vv. 4-6 as dishonoring one's parents in a cleverly devised way. The commandments of God were clear (quoted from Ex. 20:12; 21:17; Deut. 5:16); but to circumvent them, some people claimed they could not financially assist their parents because they had dedicated a certain sum of money to God, who was greater than their parents. The rabbis had approved this exception to the commandments of Moses and thus in effect nullified God's law (v. 6).

15:6 you have made the commandment of God of no effect by your tradition. *See note on Mark 7:13.*

15:8,9 Quoted from Is. 29:13.

15:11 what comes out of the mouth, this defiles a man. People might defile themselves ceremonially (under the Old Covenant) by eating something unclean, but they would defile themselves morally by saying something sinful (cf. James 3:6). Here Jesus clearly distinguished between the law's ceremonial requirements and its inviolable moral standard. Ceremonial defilement could be dealt with through ceremonial means. But moral defilement corrupts a person's soul.

15:14 Let them alone. This severe judgment is a form God's wrath. It signifies abandonment by God and is described as "giving them over" in Rom. 1:18-32 (*see notes there*). Cf. Hos. 4:17.

15:15 this parable. I.e., v. 11. The "parable" is not at all hard to understand, but it was hard for even the disciples to accept. Years later, Peter still found it hard to accept that all foods are clean (Acts 10:14).

15:22 Son of David. *See note on 1:1.*

15:24 lost sheep of the house of Israel. *See note on 10:6.*

15:26 the children's bread. The lost sheep of the house of Israel must be fed before the "little dogs" (*see note on 10:5*). Christ employed a word here that speaks of a family pet. His words with this woman are not to be understood as harsh or unfeeling. In fact, He was tenderly drawing from her an expression of her faith in v. 27.

28 Then Jesus answered and said to her,
“O woman, [v]great *is* your faith! Let it be to
you as you desire.” And her daughter was
healed from that very hour.

Jesus Heals Many—Mark 7:31-37

29 [w]Jesus departed from there, [x]skirted
the Sea of Galilee, and went up on the
mountain and sat down there. 30 [y]Then
great multitudes came to Him, having
with them *the* lame, blind, mute, [4]maimed,
and many others; and they laid them down
at Jesus’ [z]feet, and He healed them. 31 So
the multitude marveled when they saw *the*
mute speaking, *the* [5]maimed made whole,
the lame walking, and *the* blind seeing; and
they [a]glorified the God of Israel.

Jesus Feeds 4,000—Mark 8:1-10

32 [b]Now Jesus called His disciples to
Himself and said, “I have compassion on
the multitude, because they have now continued with Me three days and have nothing to eat. And I do not want to send them
away hungry, lest they faint on the way.”
33 [c]Then His disciples said to Him,
“Where could we get enough bread in the
wilderness to fill such a great multitude?”
34 Jesus said to them, “How many loaves
do you have?”
And they said, “Seven, and a few little
fish.”
35 So He commanded the multitude to
sit down on the ground. 36 And [d]He took
the seven loaves and the fish and [e]gave
thanks, broke *them* and gave *them* to His
disciples; and the disciples *gave* to the multitude. 37 So they all ate and were filled,
and they took up seven large baskets full
of the fragments that were left. 38 Now
those who ate were four thousand men,
besides women and children. 39 [f]And He
sent away the multitude, got into the boat,
and came to the region of [6]Magdala.

Debate over a Sign from Heaven
Mark 8:11, 12

16 Then the [a]Pharisees and Sadducees
came, and testing Him asked that
He would show them a sign from heaven.
2 He answered and said to them, “When it
is evening you say, ‘*It will be* fair weather,
for the sky is red’; 3 and in the morning, ‘*It*
will be foul weather today, for the sky is red
and threatening.’ [1]Hypocrites! You know
how to discern the face of the sky, but you
cannot *discern* the signs of the times. 4 [b]A
wicked and adulterous generation seeks
after a sign, and no sign shall be given to it
except the sign of [2]the prophet Jonah.”
And He left them and departed.

Withdrawal of Jesus—Mark 8:13-21

5 Now [c]when His disciples had come to
the other side, they had forgotten to take
bread. 6 Then Jesus said to them, [d]“Take
heed and beware of the [3]leaven of the
Pharisees and the Sadducees.”
7 And they reasoned among themselves,
saying, “*It is* because we have taken no
bread.”
8 But Jesus, being aware of *it*, said to
them, “O you of little faith, why do you
reason among yourselves because you
[4]have brought no bread? 9 [e]Do you not yet
understand, or remember the five loaves of
the five thousand and how many baskets
you took up? 10 [f]Nor the seven loaves of
the four thousand and how many large
baskets you took up? 11 How is it you do
not understand that I did not speak to you
concerning bread?—*but* to beware of the
[5]leaven of the Pharisees and Sadducees.”
12 Then they understood that He did not
tell *them* to beware of the leaven of bread,
but of the [6]doctrine of the Pharisees and
Sadducees.

28 [v] Luke 7:9
29 [w] Matt. 15:29-31; Mark 7:31-37 [x] Matt. 4:18
30 [y] Is. 35:5, 6; Matt. 11:5; Luke 7:22 [z] Mark 7:25; Luke 7:38; 8:41; 10:39 [4] *crippled*
31 [a] Luke 5:25, 26; 19:37, 38 [5] *crippled*
32 [b] Mark 8:1-10
33 [c] 2 Kin. 4:43
36 [d] Matt. 14:19; 26:27; Luke 22:17, 19; John 6:11, 23; Acts 27:35; [Rom. 14:6] [e] 1 Sam. 9:13; Luke 22:19
39 [f] Mark 8:10 [6] NU *Magadan*

CHAPTER 16

1 [a] Matt. 12:38; Mark 8:11; Luke 11:16; 12:54-56; 1 Cor. 1:22
3 [1] NU omits *Hypocrites*
4 [b] Prov. 30:12; Matt. 12:39; Luke 11:29; 24:46 [2] NU omits *the prophet*
5 [c] Mark 8:14
6 [d] Mark 8:15; Luke 12:1 [3] *yeast*
8 [4] NU *have no bread*
9 [e] Matt. 14:15-21; Mark 6:30-44; Luke 9:10-17; John 6:1-14
10 [f] Matt. 15:32-38; Mark 8:1-9
11 [5] *yeast*
12 [6] *teaching*

15:29 skirted the Sea of Galilee. He actually traveled N from Tyre to Sidon and then cut a wide path around the eastern shore of Galilee to the Decapolis (Mark 7:31), a primarily Gentile region. He may have taken this route to avoid the territory ruled by Herod Antipas (cf. 14:1,2). The events that follow must have occurred in the Decapolis (*see note on 4:25*).

15:33 Where could we get enough bread. No wonder our Lord called them men of little faith (8:26; 14:31; 16:8; 17:20), when they asked a question like that in the light of the recent feeding of the 5,000 (14:13-21).

15:34 *See note on 14:16.* Again the Lord had them confess for the record how little food they had in comparison to the size of the crowd. This made clear that the feeding was miraculous evidence of His deity.

15:38 four thousand. Christ ended His ministry in Galilee with the feeding of the 5,000 (14:13-21). Here, He ended His ministry in the Gentile regions by feeding the 4,000. He later would end His Jerusalem ministry with a meal in the upper room with His disciples.

16:1 a sign from heaven. *See note on 12:38.* This time Jesus rebuked them for being so concerned with heavenly signs that they could not even interpret the signs of the times all around them. Then He referred them to the same sign He gave them before, the sign of the prophet Jonah (v. 4; cf. 12:39).

16:2,3 As primitive as their method of predicting the weather was, their ability to discern spiritual matters was worse. They had the long-promised and long-awaited Messiah in their midst and refused to acknowledge Him.

16:6 the leaven of the Pharisees and the Sadducees. When Jesus warned of this dangerous influence, the disciples thought He was talking about bread. Again, He reminded them of the fact that the Lord provided plenty of bread, so they didn't need the bread the Pharisees were offering. How soon they forgot the miracles. *See note on 13:33.*

16:12 the doctrine of the Pharisees and Sadducees. Here the

Revelation of the Person of the King
Mark 8:27-30; Luke 9:18-21

13 When Jesus came into the region of
Caesarea Philippi, He asked His disciples,
saying, [g]"Who do men say that I, the Son
of Man, am?"
14 So they said, [h]"Some *say* John the Baptist, some Elijah, and others Jeremiah or
[i]one of the prophets."
15 He said to them, "But who do [j]you
say that I am?"
16 Simon Peter answered and said, [k]"You
are the Christ, the Son of the living God."
17 Jesus answered and said to him,
"Blessed are you, Simon Bar-Jonah, [l]for
flesh and blood has not revealed *this* to
you, but [m]My Father who is in heaven.

Revelation of the Church

18 And I also say to you that [n]you are Peter, and [o]on this rock I will build My
church, and [p]the gates of Hades shall not
[7]prevail against it. 19 [q]And I will give you
the keys of the kingdom of heaven, and
whatever you bind on earth [8]will be
bound in heaven, and whatever you loose
on earth will be loosed in heaven."
20 [r]Then He commanded His disciples
that they should tell no one that He was Jesus the Christ.

Revelation of Jesus' Death
Mark 8:31-33; Luke 9:22

21 From that time Jesus began [s]to show
to His disciples that He must go to Jerusalem, and suffer many things from the elders and chief priests and scribes, and be
killed, and be raised the third day.
22 Then Peter took Him aside and began
to rebuke Him, saying, [9]"Far be it from
You, Lord; this shall not happen to You!"
23 But He turned and said to Peter, "Get
behind Me, [t]Satan! [u]You are [1]an offense to
Me, for you are not mindful of the things of
God, but the things of men."

13 [g] Mark 8:27; Luke 9:18
14 [h] Matt. 14:2; Luke 9:7-9 [i] Matt. 21:11
15 [j] John 6:67
16 [k] Matt. 14:33; Mark 8:29; Luke 9:20; John 6:69; 11:27; Acts 8:37; 9:20; Heb. 1:2, 5; 1 John 4:15
17 [l] [Eph. 2:8] [m] [Matt. 11:27; 1 Cor. 2:10]; Gal. 1:16
18 [n] John 1:42 [o] Acts 2:41; [Eph. 2:20; Rev. 21:14] [p] Job 33:17; Ps. 9:13; 107:18; Is. 38:10 [7] *be victorious*
19 [q] Matt. 18:18; John 20:23 [8] Or *will have been bound . . . will have been loosed*
20 [r] Matt. 17:9; Mark 8:30; Luke 9:21
21 [s] Matt. 20:17; Mark 8:31; 9:31; Luke 9:22; 18:31; 24:46; John 2:19
22 [9] Lit. *Merciful to You* (May God be merciful)
23 [t] Matt. 4:10 [u] [Rom. 8:7] [1] *a stumbling block*

leaven of the Pharisees is their "doctrine." In Luke 12:1 it is their "hypocrisy." The two things are inextricably linked. The most sinister influence of the Jewish leaders was a pragmatic doctrine that made room for hypocrisy. They were too concerned with externals and ceremonies and the way things appeared, and not concerned enough with matters of the heart. Jesus rebuked them for their hypocrisy again and again. *See note on 23:25.*

16:13 Caesarea Philippi. A district about 25 mi. N of Galilee, at the base of Mt. Hermon. This was different from the city of Caesarea built by Herod the Great on the Mediterranean coast.

16:16 the living God. An OT name for Jehovah (e.g., Deut. 5:26; Josh. 3:10; 1 Sam. 17:26,36; 2 Kin. 19:4,16; Pss. 42:2; 84:2; Dan. 6:26; Hos. 1:10) as contrasted with the dead, dumb idols (Jer. 10:8; 18:15; 1 Cor. 12:2).

16:17 flesh and blood has not revealed *this* to you. Christ's messianic claims had always been subtle allusions to OT prophecies, combined with miraculous works that substantiated those claims. Never before had He explicitly taught Peter and the apostles the fullness of His identity. God the Father had opened Peter's eyes to the full significance of those claims, and revealed to him who Jesus really was. In other words, God had opened Peter's heart to this deeper knowledge of Christ by faith. Peter was not merely expressing an academic opinion about the identity of Christ; this was a confession of Peter's personal faith, made possible by a divinely-regenerated heart.

16:18 on this rock. The word for "Peter," *Petros,* means a small stone (John 1:42). Jesus used a play on words here with *petra* which means a foundation boulder (cf. 7:24,25). Since the NT makes it abundantly clear that Christ is both the foundation (Acts 4:11,12; 1 Cor. 3:11) and the head (Eph. 5:23) of the church, it is a mistake to think that here He is giving either of those roles to Peter. There is a sense in which the apostles played a foundational role in the building of the church (Eph. 2:20), but the role of primacy is reserved for Christ alone, not assigned to Peter. So Jesus' words here are best interpreted as a simple play on words in that a boulder-like truth came from the mouth of one who was called a small stone. Peter himself explains the imagery in his first epistle: the church is built of "living stones" (1 Pet. 2:5) who, like Peter, confess that Jesus is the Christ, the Son of the living God. And Christ Himself is the "chief cornerstone" (1 Pet. 2:6,7). **church.** Matthew is the only gospel where this term is found (see also 18:17). Christ called it "My church," emphasizing that He alone is its Architect, Builder, Owner, and Lord. The Gr. word for church means "called out ones." While God had since the beginning of redemptive history been gathering the redeemed by grace, the unique church He promised to build began at Pentecost with the coming of the Holy Spirit, by whom the Lord baptized believers into His body—which is the church (*see notes on Acts 2:1-4; 1 Cor. 12:12,13*). **the gates of Hades.** Hades is the place of punishment for the spirits of dead unbelievers. The point of entry for such is death. This, then, is a Jewish phrase referring to death. Even death, the ultimate weapon of Satan (cf. Heb. 2:14,15), has no power to stop the church. The blood of martyrs, in fact, has sped the growth of the church in size and spiritual power.

16:19 the keys of the kingdom of heaven. These represent authority, and here Christ gives Peter (and by extension all other believers) authority to declare what was bound or loosed in heaven. This echoed the promise of John 20:23, where Christ gave the disciples authority to forgive or retain the sins of people. All this must be understood in the context of 18:15-17, where Christ laid out specific instructions for dealing with sin in the church (*see note on 18:15*). The sum of it all means that any duly constituted body of believers, acting in accord with God's Word, has the authority to declare if someone is forgiven or unforgiven. The church's authority is not to determine these things, but to declare the judgment of heaven based on the principles of the Word. When they make such judgments on the basis of God's Word, they can be sure heaven is in accord. In other words, whatever they "bind" or "loose" on earth is already "bound" or "loosed" in heaven. When the church says the unrepentant person is bound in sin, the church is saying what God says about that person. When the church acknowledges that a repentant person has been loosed from that sin, God agrees.

16:20 tell no one. *See notes on 8:4; 12:16.*

16:21 From that time. This marks the beginning of a new emphasis in Matthew's account. He turns his attention from Jesus' public ministry, to His private instructions for the disciples, which took on a new, somber tone. The disciples had confessed their faith in Him as Messiah. From then on, He began to prepare them for His death. *See note on 20:19.*

16:23 Get behind Me, Satan! The harshness of this rebuke contrasts sharply with Christ's words of commendation in vv. 17-19. Jesus suggested that Peter was being a mouthpiece for Satan. Jesus' death

Revelation of Jesus' Reward
Mark 8:34-37; Luke 9:23-25

24 [v]Then Jesus said to His disciples, "If
anyone desires to come after Me, let him
deny himself, and take up his cross, and
[w]follow Me. 25 For [x]whoever desires to
save his life will lose it, but whoever loses
his life for My sake will find it. 26 For
what [y]profit is it to a man if he gains the
whole world, and loses his own soul? Or
[z]what will a man give in exchange for his
soul?

The Prophecy of the Second Coming
Mark 8:38–9:1; Luke 9:26, 27

27 For [a]the Son of Man will come in the
glory of His Father [b]with His angels, [c]and
then He will reward each according to his
works. 28 Assuredly, I say to you, [d]there
are some standing here who shall not taste
death till they see the Son of Man coming
in His kingdom."

The Transfiguration
Mark 9:2-13; Luke 9:28-36; 2 Pet. 1:17, 18

17 Now [a]after six days Jesus took Peter, James, and John his brother, led
them up on a high mountain by themselves; 2 and He was transfigured before
them. His face shone like the sun, and His
clothes became as white as the light. 3 And
behold, Moses and Elijah appeared to
them, talking with Him. 4 Then Peter answered and said to Jesus, "Lord, it is good
for us to be here; if You wish, [1]let us make
here three tabernacles: one for You, one for
Moses, and one for Elijah."
5 [b]While he was still speaking, behold, a
bright cloud overshadowed them; and
suddenly a voice came out of the cloud,
saying, [c]"This is My beloved Son, [d]in
whom I am well pleased. [e]Hear Him!"
6 [f]And when the disciples heard *it*, they
fell on their faces and were greatly afraid.
7 But Jesus came and [g]touched them and
said, "Arise, and do not be afraid." 8 When
they had lifted up their eyes, they saw no
one but Jesus only.
9 Now as they came down from the
mountain, Jesus commanded them, saying, "Tell the vision to no one until the Son
of Man is risen from the dead."
10 And His disciples asked Him, saying,
[h]"Why then do the scribes say that Elijah
must come first?"
11 Jesus answered and said to them, "Indeed, Elijah is coming [2]first and will [i]re-
store all things. 12 [j]But I say to you that Elijah has come already, and they [k]did not
know him but did to him whatever they
wished. Likewise [l]the Son of Man is also
about to suffer at their hands." 13 [m]Then
the disciples understood that He spoke to
them of John the Baptist.

Instruction About Faith
Mark 9:14-29; Luke 9:37-42

14 [n]And when they had come to the mul-

24 [v]Mark 8:34; Luke 9:23; [Acts 14:22; 2 Cor. 4:10, 11; 1 Thess. 3:3; 2 Tim. 3:12] [w][1 Pet. 2:21]
25 [x]Luke 17:33; John 12:25
26 [y]Luke 12:20, 21 [z]Ps. 49:7, 8
27 [a]Matt. 26:64; Mark 8:38; Luke 9:26 [b][Dan. 7:10]; Zech. 14:5 [c]Job 34:11; Ps. 62:12; Prov. 24:12; Rom. 2:6; 2 Cor. 5:10; 1 Pet. 1:17; Rev. 2:23
28 [d]Mark 9:1; Luke 9:27; Acts 7:55, 56; Rev. 19:11

CHAPTER 17

1 [a]Matt. 17:1-8; Mark 9:2-8; Luke 9:28-36
4 [1]NU *I will make*
5 [b]2 Pet. 1:17 [c]Ps. 2:7; Matt. 3:17; Mark 1:11; Luke 1:35; 3:22; [John 12:28-30] [d]Is. 42:1; Matt. 3:17; 12:18; 2 Pet. 1:17 [e][Deut. 18:15, 19; Acts 3:22, 23]
6 [f]2 Pet. 1:18
7 [g]Dan. 8:18
10 [h]Mal. 4:5; Matt. 11:14; 16:14; Mark 9:11
11 [i][Mal. 4:6]; Luke 1:17 [2]NU omits *first*
12 [j]Matt. 11:14; Mark 9:12, 13 [k]Matt. 14:3, 10 [l]Matt. 16:21
13 [m]Matt. 11:14
14 [n]Matt. 17:14-19; Mark 9:14-28; Luke 9:37-42

was part of God's sovereign plan (Acts 2:23; 4:27,28). "It pleased the Lord to bruise Him" (Is. 53:10). Christ had come with the express purpose of dying as an atonement for sin (John 12:27). And those who would thwart His mission were doing Satan's work.

16:24 take up his cross. *See note on 10:38.*

16:26 exchange. At the judgment when he faces the disastrous hell of remorse and suffering for his lost soul, with what will he buy it back from perdition? Nothing.

16:27 will come...will reward. There is coming a time of rewards in the future for believers (1 Cor. 4:5; 2 Cor. 5:8-10; Rev. 22:12). Here, however, the Lord was concerned with the reward of the ungodly—final and eternal judgment (Rom. 2:5-11; 2 Thess. 1:6-10).

16:28 some standing. In all 3 of the synoptic gospels, this promise is made immediately prior to the Transfiguration (Mark 9:1-8; Luke 9:27-36). Furthermore the word for "kingdom" can be translated "royal splendor." Therefore, it seems most natural to interpret this promise as a reference to the Transfiguration, which "some" of the disciples—Peter, James, and John, would witness only 6 days later (*see note on 17:1*).

17:1 after six days. The precise reference to the amount of time elapsed is unusual for Matthew. It seems he is carefully drawing the connection between Jesus' promise in 16:28 and the event that immediately follows. Mark agrees on the figure of 6 days (Mark 9:2), but Luke, probably counting the day of Peter's confession and the day of Christ's Transfiguration separately at the start and end of this time period, says it was "about eight days" (Luke 9:28). **Peter, James, and John.** These 3, in the inner circle closest to Christ (*see note on 10:2*), are often seen alone together with Jesus (26:37; Mark 5:37; 13:3).

17:2 transfigured. Christ underwent a dramatic change in appearance, so the disciples could behold Him in His glory.

17:3 Moses and Elijah. Representing the law and the prophets respectively, both of which had foretold Christ's death, and that is what Luke says the 3 of them were discussing (Luke 9:31).

17:4 three tabernacles. This is undoubtedly a reference to the booths that were used to celebrate the Feast of Tabernacles, when the Israelites dwelt in booths for 7 days (Lev. 23:34-42). Peter was expressing a wish to stay in that place.

17:5 Hear Him! Peter erred in placing Moses and Elijah on the same level as Christ. Christ was the very one to whom Elijah and Moses had pointed. The voice of the Father (v. 5) interrupted while Peter "was still speaking." The words were the same as those spoken from heaven at Christ's baptism (3:17).

17:6 fell on their faces. A common response to the realization that the Holy God of the universe is present. Cf. Is. 6:5; Ezek. 1:28; Rev. 1:17.

17:9 Tell the vision to no one. *See notes on 8:4 and 12:16.*

17:10 Why...Elijah must come first? Because it was so prophesied by Mal. 4:5,6. *See note on 11:14.*

17:12 Elijah has come already. *See note on 11:14.* The Jewish leaders had failed to recognize John the Baptist (though the disciples did, v. 13). John came in the spirit and power of Elijah—and the Jewish leaders had killed him. The Messiah was "about to suffer" similarly.

17:17 O faithless and perverse generation. Verse 20 indicates that the Lord was referring to the disciples and their weak faith (*see note on 15:33*).

titude, a man came to Him, kneeling down
to Him and saying, 15 "Lord, have mercy
on my son, for he is [3]an epileptic and suffers severely; for he often falls into the fire
and often into the water. 16 So I brought
him to Your disciples, but they could not
cure him."
17 Then Jesus answered and said, "O
[4]faithless and [o]perverse generation, how
long shall I be with you? How long shall I
bear with you? Bring him here to Me."
18 And Jesus [p]rebuked the demon, and it
came out of him; and the child was cured
from that very hour.
19 Then the disciples came to Jesus privately and said, "Why could we not cast it
out?"
20 So Jesus said to them, "Because of
your [5]unbelief; for assuredly, I say to you,
[q]if you have faith as a mustard seed, you
will say to this mountain, 'Move from here
to there,' and it will move; and nothing
will be impossible for you. 21 [6]However,
this kind does not go out except by prayer
and fasting."

Instruction About Jesus' Death
Mark 9:30-32; Luke 9:43-45

22 [r]Now while they were [7]staying in
Galilee, Jesus said to them, "The Son of
Man is about to be betrayed into the hands
of men, 23 and they will kill Him, and the
third day He will be raised up." And they
were exceedingly [s]sorrowful.

Instruction About Taxes

24 [t]When they had come to [8]Caperna-
um, those who received the [9]*temple* tax
came to Peter and said, "Does your
Teacher not pay the *temple* tax?"
25 He said, "Yes."
And when he had come into the house,
Jesus anticipated him, saying, "What do
you think, Simon? From whom do the
kings of the earth take customs or taxes,
from their sons or from [u]strangers?"
26 Peter said to Him, "From strangers."
Jesus said to him, "Then the sons are
free. 27 Nevertheless, lest we offend them,
go to the sea, cast in a hook, and take the
fish that comes up first. And when you
have opened its mouth, you will find a
[1]piece of money; take that and give it to
them for Me and you."

Instruction About Humility
Mark 9:33-37; Luke 9:46-48

18 At [a]that time the disciples came to
Jesus, saying, "Who then is greatest
in the kingdom of heaven?"
2 Then Jesus called a little [b]child to Him,
set him in the midst of them, 3 and said,
"Assuredly, I say to you, [c]unless you are
converted and become as little children,
you will by no means enter the kingdom of
heaven. 4 [d]Therefore whoever humbles
himself as this little child is the greatest in
the kingdom of heaven. 5 [e]Whoever receives one little child like this in My name
receives Me.

Punishment of Offenders—Mark 9:42-48

6 [f]"Whoever causes one of these little
ones who believe in Me to sin, it would be
better for him if a millstone were hung
around his neck, and he were drowned in
the depth of the sea. 7 Woe to the world be-

15 [3] Lit. *moonstruck*
17 [o] Deut. 32:5; Phil. 2:15 [4] *unbelieving*
18 [p] Luke 4:41
20 [q] Matt. 21:21; Mark 11:23; Luke 17:6; [1 Cor. 12:9] [5] NU *little faith*
21 [6] NU omits v. 21.
22 [r] Matt. 16:21; 26:57; Mark 8:31; Luke 9:22, 44; John 18:12 [7] NU *gathering together*
23 [s] Matt. 26:22; 27:50; Luke 23:46; 24:46; John 16:6; 19:30; Acts 10:40
24 [t] Mark 9:33 [8] NU *Capharnaum,* here and elsewhere [9] Lit. *double drachma*
25 [u] [Is. 60:10-17]
27 [1] Gr. *stater,* the exact temple tax for two

CHAPTER 18

1 [a] Mark 9:33-37; Luke 9:46-48; 22:24-27
2 [b] Matt. 19:14; Mark 10:14; Luke 18:14-17
3 [c] Ps. 131:2; Matt. 19:14; Mark 10:15; Luke 18:16; [1 Cor. 14:20; 1 Pet. 2:2]
4 [d] [Matt. 20:27; 23:11]
5 [e] [Matt. 10:42]; Luke 9:48
6 [f] Mark 9:42; Luke 17:2; [1 Cor. 8:12]

17:19 "Why could we not cast it out?" When Christ sent the disciples out (10:6-8), He explicitly commissioned them to do these kinds of miracles. Less than a year later, they failed where they had once succeeded. Christ's explanation for their failure was that their faith was deficient (v. 20). The deficiency did not consist in a lack of confidence; they were surprised that they could not cast out this demon. The problem probably lay in a failure to make God—rather than their own gifts—the object of their confidence (*see note on v. 20*).

17:20 faith as a mustard seed. True faith, by Christ's definition, always involves surrender to the will of God. What He was teaching here is nothing like positive-thinking psychology. He was saying that both the source and the object of all genuine faith—even the weak, mustard-seed variety—is God. And "with God nothing will be impossible" (Luke 1:37). *See also note on 21:21.* **nothing will be impossible.** Here, Christ assumes the qualifying thought that is explicitly added by 1 John 5:14: what we ask for must be "according to His will."

17:21 except by prayer and fasting. Again, this suggests that the underlying problem was the disciples' failure to make God the object of their faith (*see notes on vv. 19,20*). But this verse is not found in the best manuscripts.

17:22 about to be betrayed. By Judas Iscariot. *See notes on 26:47,50.*

17:24 the *temple* tax. A half-shekel tax (equivalent to about two days' wages) collected annually from every male over 20, for the upkeep of the temple (Ex. 30:13,14; 2 Chr. 24:9). As kings did not tax their own sons, technically, Jesus, as God's son, was exempt from the tax (v. 26). But to avoid offense, He paid on behalf of Himself and Peter (v. 27). Cf. Rom. 13:1-7; Tit. 3:1; 1 Pet. 2:13-17.

18:1-35 This is the fourth of 5 discourses around which Matthew frames his narrative (see Introduction: Historical and Theological Themes). This section's theme is the childlikeness of the believer.

18:3 become as little children. This is how Jesus characterized conversion. Like the Beatitudes, it pictures faith as the simple, helpless, trusting dependence of those who have no resources of their own. Like children, they have no achievements and no accomplishments to offer or commend themselves with.

18:5 Whoever receives. *See note on 10:41.* **one little child like this.** This speaks not of literal children, but children in the sense described in vv. 3,4 (those who have humbled themselves like children), i.e., true believers (v. 6). *See notes on 10:42; 19:14.*

18:6 millstone. A stone used for grinding grain. Lit. "the millstone of an ass"—a stone so large it took a donkey to turn it. Gentiles used this form of execution, and therefore it was particularly repulsive to the Jews.

18:7 Woe to the world. It is expected that those in the world will cause Christians to be offended, stumble and sin, and they will be

cause of [1]offenses! For [g]offenses must
come, but [h]woe to that man by whom the
offense comes!
8 [i]"If your hand or foot causes you to sin,
cut it off and cast *it* from you. It is better for
you to enter into life lame or maimed,
rather than having two hands or two feet,
to be cast into the everlasting fire. 9 And if
your eye causes you to sin, pluck it out and
cast *it* from you. It is better for you to enter
into life with one eye, rather than having
two eyes, to be cast into [2]hell fire.
10 "Take heed that you do not despise
one of these little ones, for I say to you that
in heaven [j]their angels always [k]see the face
of My Father who is in heaven. 11 [l]For[3] the
Son of Man has come to save that which
was lost.

Parable of the Lost Sheep—Luke 15:4-7

12 [m]"What do you think? If a man has a
hundred sheep, and one of them goes
astray, does he not leave the ninety-nine
and go to the mountains to seek the one
that is straying? 13 And if he should find it,
assuredly, I say to you, he rejoices more
over that *sheep* than over the ninety-nine
that did not go astray. 14 Even so it is not
the [n]will of your Father who is in heaven
that one of these little ones should perish.

The Offended Brother

15 "Moreover [o]if your brother sins
against you, go and tell him his fault be-

7 [g]Luke 17:1; [1 Cor. 11:19]; 1 Tim. 4:1 [h]Matt. 26:24; 27:4, 5 [1]*enticements to sin*
8 [i]Matt. 5:29, 30; Mark 9:43, 45
9 [2]Gr. *Gehenna*
10 [j][Ps. 34:7]; Zech. 13:7; [Heb. 1:14] [k]Esth. 1:14; Luke 1:19; Acts 12:15; [Rev. 8:2]
11 [l]Luke 9:56; John 3:17 [3]NU omits v. 11.
12 [m]Matt. 18:12-14; Luke 15:4-7
14 [n][1 Tim. 2:4]
15 [o]Lev. 19:17; [Luke 17:3, 4; Gal. 6:1]; 2 Thess. 3:15; [James 5:19] [p][James 5:20]; 1 Pet. 3:1
16 [q]Deut. 17:6; 19:15; John 8:17; 2 Cor. 13:1; 1 Tim. 5:19; Heb. 10:28
17 [r]Rom. 16:17; 1 Cor. 5:9; [2 Thess. 3:6, 14; 2 John 10]
18 [s]Matt. 16:19; [John 20:22, 23; 1 Cor. 5:4]
19 [t][1 Cor. 1:10] [u][1 John 3:22; 5:14] [4]NU, M *Again, assuredly, I say*
20 [v]Acts 20:7; 1 Cor. 14:26
21 [w]Luke 17:4
22 [x][Matt. 6:14; Mark 11:25]; Col. 3:13
25 [y]Ex. 21:2; Lev. 25:39; 2 Kin. 4:1; Neh. 5:5, 8

tween you and him alone. If he hears you,
[p]you have gained your brother. 16 But if he
will not hear, take with you one or two
more, that [q]'*by the mouth of two or three
witnesses every word may be established.*'
17 And if he refuses to hear them, tell *it* to
the church. But if he refuses even to hear
the church, let him be to you like a [r]hea-
then and a tax collector.
18 "Assuredly, I say to you, [s]whatever
you bind on earth will be bound in heaven,
and whatever you loose on earth will be
loosed in heaven.
19 [t]"Again[4] I say to you that if two of
you agree on earth concerning anything
that they ask, [u]it will be done for them by
My Father in heaven. 20 For where two or
three are gathered [v]together in My name, I
am there in the midst of them."

Instruction About Forgiveness

21 Then Peter came to Him and said,
"Lord, how often shall my brother sin
against me, and I forgive him? [w]Up to
seven times?"
22 Jesus said to him, "I do not say to you,
[x]up to seven times, but up to seventy times
seven. 23 Therefore the kingdom of heaven
is like a certain king who wanted to settle
accounts with his servants. 24 And when
he had begun to settle accounts, one was
brought to him who owed him ten thousand talents. 25 But as he was not able to
pay, his master commanded [y]that he be

---

judged for it. But it should not be that fellow believers lead others into sin, directly or indirectly. One would be better off dead. Cf. Rom. 14:13,19,21; 15:2; 1 Cor. 8:13.

18:8,9 cut it off…pluck it out. *See note on 5:29.*

18:10 do not despise. I.e., spurn or belittle another believer by treating him or her unkindly or indifferently. **their angels.** This does not suggest that each believer has a personal guardian angel. Rather, the pronoun is collective and refers to the fact that believers are served by angels in general. These angels are pictured "always" watching the face of God so as to hear His command to them to help a believer when needed. It is extremely serious to treat any fellow believer with contempt since God and the holy angels are so concerned for their well-being.

18:14 perish. The word here can (and does in this context) refer to spiritual devastation rather than utter eternal destruction. This does not suggest that God's children ever could perish in the ultimate sense (cf. John 10:28).

18:15 The prescription for church discipline in vv. 15-17 must be read in light of the parable of the lost sheep in vv. 12-14. The goal of this process is restoration. If successful, "you have gained your brother." Step 1 is to "tell him his fault" privately.

18:16 if he will not hear. I.e., if he remains impenitent, follow step 2: "take with you one or two more," to fulfill the principle of Deut. 19:15.

18:17 tell *it* to the church. If he still refuses to repent, step 3 requires that the matter be reported to the whole assembly (v. 17)—so that all may lovingly pursue the sinning brother's reconciliation. But failing that, step 4 means that the offender must be excommunicated, regarded by the church as "a heathen and a tax collector" (*see note on 5:46*). The idea is not merely to punish the offender, or to shun him completely, but to remove him as a detrimental influence from the fellowship of the church, and henceforth to regard him as an evangelistic prospect rather than as a brother. Ultimately, the sin for which he is excommunicated is a hard-hearted impenitence.

18:18 bind on earth…bound in heaven. *See note on 16:19.*

18:19 if two of you agree on earth. This promise applies to the issue of discipline discussed in vv. 15-17. The "two of you" spoken of here harks back to the two or three witnesses involved in step two of the discipline process (*see note on v. 15*).

18:20 two or three. Jewish tradition requires at least 10 men (a *minyan*) to constitute a synagogue or even hold public prayer. Here, Christ promised to be present in the midst of an even smaller flock—"two or three witnesses" gathered in His name for the purpose of discipline (*see note on v. 15*).

18:21 Up to seven times. Peter thought he was being magnanimous. The rabbis, citing several verses from Amos (1:3,6,9,11,13) taught that since God forgave Israel's enemies only 3 times, it was presumptuous and unnecessary to forgive anyone more than 3 times.

18:22 seventy times seven. Innumerable times. *See note on Luke 17:4.*

18:23 servants. Due to the large amounts of money involved, it is likely these "servants" would have been provincial governors who owed the king the money from taxation.

18:24 ten thousand talents. This represents an incomprehensible amount of money. The talent was the largest denomination of

sold, with his wife and children and all
that he had, and that payment be made.
26 The servant therefore fell down before
him, saying, 'Master, have patience with
me, and I will pay you all.' 27 Then the
master of that servant was moved with
compassion, released him, and forgave
him the debt.

28 "But that servant went out and found
one of his fellow servants who owed him a
hundred denarii; and he laid hands on him
and took *him* by the throat, saying, 'Pay me
what you owe!' 29 So his fellow servant fell
down [5]at his feet and begged him, saying,
'Have patience with me, and I will pay you
[6]all.' 30 And he would not, but went and
threw him into prison till he should pay
the debt. 31 So when his fellow servants
saw what had been done, they were very
grieved, and came and told their master all
that had been done. 32 Then his master,
after he had called him, said to him, 'You
wicked servant! I forgave you [z]all that debt
because you begged me. 33 Should you not
also have had compassion on your fellow
servant, just as I had pity on you?' 34 And
his master was angry, and delivered him to
the torturers until he should pay all that
was due to him.

35 [a]"So My heavenly Father also will do
to you if each of you, from his heart, does
not forgive his brother [7]his trespasses."

29 [5] NU omits *at his feet* [6] NU, M omit *all*
32 [z] Luke 7:41-43
35 [a] Prov. 21:13; Matt. 6:12; Mark 11:26; James 2:13 [7] NU omits *his trespasses*

CHAPTER 19

1 [a] Matt. 19:1-9; Mark 10:1-12; John 10:40
2 [b] Matt. 12:15
4 [c] Gen. 1:27; 5:2; [Mal. 2:15] [1] NU *created*
5 [d] Gen. 2:24; Mark 10:5-9; Eph. 5:31 [e] [1 Cor. 6:16; 7:2]
7 [f] Deut. 24:1-4; Matt. 5:31
8 [g] Heb. 3:15 [h] Mal. 2:16
9 [i] [Matt. 5:32]; Mark 10:11; Luke 16:18; 1 Cor. 7:10 [2] Or *fornication*

Instruction About Divorce
Mark 10:1-16; Luke 18:15-17

19 Now it came to pass, [a]when Jesus
had finished these sayings, *that* He
departed from Galilee and came to the region of Judea beyond the Jordan. 2 [b]And
great multitudes followed Him, and He
healed them there.

3 The Pharisees also came to Him, testing
Him, and saying to Him, "Is it lawful for a
man to divorce his wife for *just* any reason?"

4 And He answered and said to them,
"Have you not read that He who [1]made
them at the beginning [c]*'made them male
and female,'* 5 and said, [d]*'For this reason a
man shall leave his father and mother and
be joined to his wife, and* [e]*the two shall become one flesh'*? 6 So then, they are no
longer two but one flesh. Therefore what
God has joined together, let not man separate."

7 They said to Him, [f]"Why then did Moses command to give a certificate of divorce, and to put her away?"

8 He said to them, "Moses, because of
the [g]hardness of your hearts, permitted
you to divorce your [h]wives, but from the
beginning it was not so. 9 [i]And I say to
you, whoever divorces his wife, except for
[2]sexual immorality, and marries another,
commits adultery; and whoever marries
her who is divorced commits adultery."

currency, and "ten thousand" in common parlance signified an infinite number.

18:25 that he be sold. A way to recover some of this loss was for the king to sell the family members into slavery.

18:27 forgave him. Picturing the generous, compassionate forgiveness of God to a pleading sinner who owes him an unpayable debt. Cf. Col. 2:14.

18:28 a hundred denarii. About 3 months' wages. This was not a negligible amount by normal standards, but it was a pittance in comparison to what the servant had been forgiven.

18:29 Have patience...I will pay you all. Cf. v. 26. The forgiven man heard the same pleading he had given before his master, but was utterly without compassion (v. 30).

18:31 fellow servants...grieved. A lack of forgiveness is offensive to fellow believers. Most of all it offends God, who chastens His unforgiving children severely (vv. 32-34). *See notes on v. 34*; cf. 6:15.

18:34 his master was angry. Because He is holy and just, God is always angry at sin, including the sins of His children (cf. Heb. 12:5-11). **torturers.** Not executioners. This pictures severe discipline, not final condemnation. **all that was due to him.** The original debt was unpayable and the man still without resources. So it seems unlikely that the slave was saddled once again with the same debt he had already been forgiven. Rather, what he now owed his master would be exacted in chastening by his master until he was willing to forgive others.

19:1 the region of Judea beyond the Jordan. Perea was the name of the region just E of the Jordan River. It was not technically part of Judea, but the territory ruled by Herod the Great had included both regions, and it was commonly referred to this way. Christ's ministry in Perea lasted only a few months. It was from here that He would make His final journey to Jerusalem just prior to the Passion Week (20:17-19).

19:3 Is it lawful. A hotly-debated difference of opinion existed between the Rabbis Shammai and Hillel (both near-contemporaries of Christ). The Shammaites interpreted the law rigidly, and permitted a man to divorce his wife only if she was guilty of sexual immorality. **for *just* any reason.** The Hillelites took a wholly pragmatic approach, and permitted a man to divorce his wife indiscriminately.

19:4 Quoted from Gen. 1:27; 5:2. Jesus' challenge to the Pharisees echoed the question raised by Mal. 2:15: "But did He not make *them* one...?" (cf. v. 6).

19:5 Quoted from Gen. 2:24 (*see note there*).

19:7 Why then did Moses command to give a certificate of divorce. The Pharisees misrepresented Deut. 24:1-4. It was not a "command" for divorce, but a limitation on remarriage in the event of a divorce. While recognizing the legitimacy of divorce when a man "has found some uncleanness" (Deut. 24:1) in his wife (sexual sin, by Jesus' interpretation in v. 9), Moses did not "command" divorce. *See note on Deut. 24:1-4.*

19:8 Moses...permitted you to divorce. The stress is certainly on the word "permitted." Thus Jesus clearly sides with the Shammai school of interpretation (*see note on v. 3*). **because of the hardness of your hearts.** The phrase underscores the truth that divorce is only a last-resort response to hard-hearted sexual immorality (v. 9).

19:9 sexual immorality. This is a term that encompasses all sorts of sexual sins. Both here and in 5:32, Jesus includes this "exception clause," clearly permitting the innocent party in such a divorce to remarry without incurring the stigma of one who "commits adultery." *See notes on 5:31,32.*

10 His disciples said to Him, [j]"If such is
the case of the man with *his* wife, it is better not to marry."
11 But He said to them, [k]"All cannot accept this saying, but only *those* to whom it
has been given: 12 For there are [3]eunuchs
who were born thus from *their* mother's
womb, and [l]there are eunuchs who were
made eunuchs by men, and there are eunuchs who have made themselves eunuchs
for the kingdom of heaven's sake. He who
is able to accept *it*, let him accept *it*."
13 [m]Then little children were brought to
Him that He might put *His* hands on them
and pray, but the disciples rebuked them.
14 But Jesus said, "Let the little children
come to Me, and do not forbid them; for
[n]of such is the kingdom of heaven."
15 And He laid *His* hands on them and departed from there.

Rich Young Ruler

Mark 10:17-27; Luke 18:18-27

16 [o]Now behold, one came and said to
Him, [p]"Good[4] Teacher, what good thing
shall I do that I may have eternal life?"
17 So He said to him, [5]"Why do you call
Me good? [6]No one *is* [q]good but One, *that*
is, God. But if you want to enter into life,
[r]keep the commandments."
18 He said to Him, "Which ones?"
Jesus said, [s]"*'You shall not murder,'*
'You shall not commit adultery,' 'You shall
not steal,' 'You shall not bear false wit-
ness,' 19 [t]*'Honor your father and your*
mother,' and, [u]*'You shall love your neigh-*
bor as yourself.'"
20 The young man said to Him, "All
these things I have [v]kept [7]from my youth.
What do I still lack?"
21 Jesus said to him, "If you want to be
perfect, [w]go, sell what you have and give
to the poor, and you will have treasure in
heaven; and come, follow Me."
22 But when the young man heard that
saying, he went away sorrowful, for he
had great possessions.
23 Then Jesus said to His disciples, "Assuredly, I say to you that [x]it is hard for a
rich man to enter the kingdom of heaven.
24 And again I say to you, it is easier for a
camel to go through the eye of a needle
than for a rich man to enter the kingdom of
God."

10 [j] [Prov. 21:19]
11 [k] [1 Cor. 7:2, 7, 9, 17]
12 [l] [1 Cor. 7:32] [3] Emasculated men
13 [m] Matt. 20:31; Mark 10:13; Luke 18:15
14 [n] Matt. 18:3, 4; Mark 10:15; Luke 18:17; [1 Cor. 14:20; 1 Pet. 2:2]
16 [o] Matt. 19:16-29; Mark 10:17-30; Luke 18:18-30 [p] Luke 10:25 [4] NU omits *Good*
17 [q] Ps. 25:8; 34:8; Nah. 1:7; [Rom. 2:4] [5] NU *Why do you ask Me about what is good?* [6] NU *There is One who is good. But* [r] Lev. 18:5; Deut. 4:40; 6:17; 7:11; 11:22; 28:9; Neh. 9:29; Ezek. 20:21; [Gal. 3:10]
18 [s] Ex. 20:13-16; Deut. 5:17-20
19 [t] Ex. 20:12-16; Deut. 5:16-20; Matt. 15:4 [u] Lev. 19:18; Matt. 22:39; [Rom. 13:9; Gal. 5:14; James 2:8]
20 [v] [Phil. 3:6, 7] [7] NU omits *from my youth*
21 [w] Matt. 6:20; Luke 12:33; Acts 2:45; 4:34, 35; 1 Tim. 6:18, 19
23 [x] [Matt. 13:22]; Mark 10:24; 1 Cor. 1:26; [1 Tim. 6:9]

19:10 it is better not to marry. The disciples correctly understood the binding nature of marriage, and that Jesus was setting a very high standard, permitting divorce only in the most extreme of circumstances.

19:12 let him accept *it*. Since all cannot handle it (v. 11), Christ is not enjoining celibacy here. Rather, He makes it entirely a matter of personal choice—except for those who are physically unable to marry, either through natural causes or because of the violence of other men. Still others may find there are pragmatic reasons not to marry for the good of the kingdom (*see notes on 1 Cor. 7:7-9*). But in no way did Christ suggest that celibacy is superior to marriage (cf. Gen. 2:18; 1 Tim. 4:3).

19:14 of such. These children were too young to have exercised personal faith. See Luke 18:15, where Luke refers to them as "infants." Therefore, it is all the more significant that Christ used them as an illustration of those who make up "the kingdom of heaven" (cf. 18:1-4). Mark 10:16 also says He "blessed them." God often shows a special mercy to those who because of age or mental deficiency are incapable of either faith or willful unbelief (cf. Jon. 4:11). They are called "innocents" in Jer. 19:4. This does not mean they are free from the inherited guilt and moral corruption of Adam's sin (*see notes on Rom. 5:12-19*), but rather that they are not culpable in the same sense as those whose sins are premeditated and deliberate. Jesus' words here suggest that God's mercy is graciously extended to infants so that those who die are sovereignly regenerated and granted entrance into the kingdom—not because they are deserving of heaven, but because God in His grace chooses to redeem them. *See notes on 2 Sam. 12:23; Mark 10:14.*

19:16 Good Teacher. This is not necessarily a recognition of Christ's deity. The young man simply meant that Christ was righteous and a teacher from God who apparently had eternal life and might know how he could get it.

19:17 Why do you call Me good? No one *is* good but One. Jesus was not disclaiming His own deity, but rather teaching the young man that all but God are sinners. This young man's most serious spiritual defect was his reluctance to confess his own utter spiritual bankruptcy. *See note on 5:3*; cf. Luke 18:11. **if you want to enter into life, keep the commandments.** This, of course, is law, not gospel. Before showing him the way to life, Jesus wanted to impress on the young man both the high standard required by God and the absolute futility of seeking salvation by his own merit. This should have elicited a response about the impossibility of keeping the law perfectly (like the disciples' response in v. 25), but instead the young man confidently declared that he qualified for heaven under those terms.

19:18,19 These are 5 of the 6 commandments that make up the second table of the Ten Commandments—all dealing with human relationships (cf. Ex. 20:12-16; Deut. 5:16-20). *See note on 22:40.* Christ omitted the tenth commandment, which deals with covetousness, and added Lev. 19:18, the summation of the second half of the Decalogue. Cf. Rom. 13:1-10.

19:20 I have kept. The self-righteous young man would not admit to his own sin. *See note on 9:13.*

19:21 go, sell what you have and give to the poor. Again, Jesus was not setting forth terms for salvation, but rather exposing the young man's true heart. His refusal to obey here revealed two things: 1) he was not blameless as far as the law was concerned, because he was guilty of loving himself and his possessions more than his neighbors (cf. v. 19); and 2) he lacked true faith, which involves a willingness to surrender all at Christ's bidding (16:24). Jesus was not teaching salvation by philanthropy; but He was demanding that this young man give Him first place. The young man failed the test (v. 22). **come, follow Me.** This was the answer to the young man's question in v. 16. It was a call to faith. It is likely that the young man never even heard or contemplated it, though, because his own love of his possessions was such a stumbling block that he had already rejected Jesus' claim to lordship over his life. Thus he walked away in unbelief.

19:24 camel...eye of a needle. I.e., it is impossible. Jesus was underscoring the impossibility of anyone's being saved by merit.

25 When His disciples heard *it*, they were greatly astonished, saying, "Who then can be saved?"

26 But Jesus looked at *them* and said to them, "With men this is impossible, but [y]with God all things are possible."

The Apostles' Reward
Mark 10:28-30; Luke 18:28-30

27 Then Peter answered and said to Him, "See, [z]we have left all and followed You. Therefore what shall we have?"

28 So Jesus said to them, "Assuredly I say to you, that in the regeneration, when the Son of Man sits on the throne of His glory, [a]you who have followed Me will also sit on twelve thrones, judging the twelve tribes of Israel. 29 [b]And everyone who has left houses or brothers or sisters or father or mother [8]or wife or children or [9]lands, for My name's sake, shall receive a hundredfold, and inherit eternal life. 30 [c]But many *who are* first will be last, and the last first.

Parable of the Laborers—Mark 10:31

20

"For the kingdom of heaven is like a landowner who went out early in the morning to hire laborers for his vineyard. 2 Now when he had agreed with the laborers for a denarius a day, he sent them into his vineyard. 3 And he went out about the third hour and saw others standing idle in the marketplace, 4 and said to them, 'You also go into the vineyard, and whatever is right I will give you.' So they went. 5 Again he went out about the sixth and the ninth hour, and did likewise. 6 And about the eleventh hour he went out and found others standing [1]idle, and said to them, 'Why have you been standing here idle all day?' 7 They said to him, 'Because no one hired us.' He said to them, 'You also go into the vineyard, [2]and whatever is right you will receive.'

8 "So when evening had come, the owner of the vineyard said to his steward, 'Call the laborers and give them *their* wages, beginning with the last to the first.' 9 And when those came who *were hired* about the eleventh hour, they each received a denarius. 10 But when the first came, they supposed that they would receive more; and they likewise received each a denarius. 11 And when they had received *it*, they [3]complained against the landowner, 12 saying, 'These last *men* have worked *only* one hour, and you made them equal to us who have borne the burden and the heat of the day.' 13 But he answered one of them and said, 'Friend, I am doing you no wrong. Did you not agree with me for a denarius? 14 Take *what is* yours and go your way. I wish to give to this last man *the same* as to you. 15 [a]Is it not lawful for me to do what I wish with my own things? Or [b]is your eye evil because I am good?' 16 [c]So the last will be first, and the first last. [d]For[4] many are called, but few chosen."

26 [y] Gen. 18:14; Num. 11:23; Job 42:2; Is. 59:1; Jer. 32:17; Zech. 8:6; Luke 1:37
27 [z] Deut. 33:9; Matt. 4:20; Luke 5:11
28 [a] Matt. 20:21; Luke 22:28-30; [1 Cor. 6:2; Rev. 2:26]
29 [b] [Matt. 6:33]; Mark 10:29, 30; Luke 18:29, 30 [8] NU omits *or wife* [9] Lit. *fields*
30 [c] [Matt. 20:16; 21:31, 32]; Mark 10:31; Luke 13:30

CHAPTER 20

6 [1] NU omits *idle*
7 [2] NU omits the rest of v. 7.
11 [3] *grumbled*
15 [a] [Rom. 9:20, 21] [b] Deut. 15:9; Prov. 23:6; [Matt. 6:23]; Mark 7:22
16 [c] Matt. 19:30; Mark 10:31; Luke 13:30 [d] Matt. 22:14 [4] NU omits the rest of v. 16.

Since wealth was deemed proof of God's approval, and those who had it could give more alms, it was commonly thought that rich people were the most likely candidates for heaven (*see note on Mark 10:25*). Jesus destroyed that notion, and along with it, the notion that anyone can merit enough divine favor to gain entrance into heaven. *See note on v. 25.*

19:25 Who then can be saved? This was the right question to ask; it showed that they got Jesus' message (*see note on v. 17*). Salvation is possible only through divine grace (v. 26). *See notes on Rom. 3:9-20; Gal. 3:10-13; Phil. 3:4-9.*

19:27 we have left all and followed You. Peter points out that they had already done what Christ demanded of the rich young ruler (v. 21). They had embarked on the life of faith with Christ. Note that Jesus did not rebuke Peter for his expectation of reward (cf. Rev. 22:12).

19:28 regeneration. Here the term does not carry its normal theological meaning of personal regeneration (cf. Titus 3:5). Instead, Jesus was speaking of "the times of restoration of all things, which God has spoken by the mouth of all His holy prophets since the world began" (Acts 3:21). This is a reference to the earthly kingdom described in Rev. 20:1-15, when believers will "sit on…thrones" with Christ (Rev. 3:21). **judging.** Governing. Cf. 1 Cor. 6:2,3.

19:30 first will be last, and the last first. This statement means that everyone ends up the same, a truth that is explained by the parable that follows (*see note on 20:16*).

20:1 hire laborers. This was typical during harvest. Day laborers stood in the market place from dawn, hoping to be hired for the day's work. The work day began at 6:00 a.m. and went to 6:00 p.m.

20:2 a denarius a day. A fair wage for a full day's labor (*see note on 22:19*).

20:3 third hour. 9:00 a.m. They were standing idle because no one had hired them (v. 7).

20:4 whatever is right. So eager to work, these men did not even negotiate a specific wage.

20:6 eleventh hour. I.e., 5:00 p.m. Desperate for work, they had waited nearly "all day." They would take whatever they could get.

20:8 last to the first. This is the clue that opens the parable (*see note on v. 16*).

20:13 I am doing you no wrong. Everyone received a full day's wage, to their shock (vv. 9-11). The man was acting graciously to those whom he overpaid. This was no slight against those whom he paid a full wage for a full day's work. That was precisely what they agreed to in the beginning. But it was his privilege to extend the same generosity to all (v. 15; cf. Rom. 9:15).

20:16 the last will be first, and the first last. In other words, everyone finishes in a dead heat. No matter how long each of the workers worked, they each received a full day's wage. Similarly, the thief on the cross will enjoy the full blessings of heaven alongside those who have labored their whole lives for Christ. Such is the grace of God (*see note on 19:30*).

Instruction About Jesus' Death
Mark 10:32-34; Luke 18:31-34

17 [e]Now Jesus, going up to Jerusalem,
took the twelve disciples aside on the road
and said to them, 18 [f]"Behold, we are going
up to Jerusalem, and the Son of Man will
be betrayed to the chief priests and to the
scribes; and they will condemn Him to
death, 19 [g]and deliver Him to the Gentiles
to [h]mock and to [i]scourge and to [j]crucify.
And the third day He will [k]rise again."

Instruction About Ambition
Mark 10:35-45

20 [l]Then the mother of [m]Zebedee's sons
came to Him with her sons, kneeling down
and asking something from Him.
21 And He said to her, "What do you
wish?"

She said to Him, "Grant that these two
sons of mine [n]may sit, one on Your right
hand and the other on the left, in Your
kingdom."
22 But Jesus answered and said, "You do
not know what you ask. Are you able to
drink [o]the cup that I am about to drink,
[5]and be baptized with [p]the baptism that I
am baptized with?"

They said to Him, "We are able."
23 So He said to them, [q]"You will indeed
drink My cup, [6]and be baptized with the
baptism that I am baptized with; but to sit
on My right hand and on My left is not
Mine to give, but *it is for those* for whom it
is prepared by My Father."
24 [r]And when the ten heard *it,* they were
greatly displeased with the two brothers.
25 But Jesus called them to *Himself* and
said, "You know that the rulers of the Gentiles lord it over them, and those who are
great exercise authority over them. 26 Yet
[s]it shall not be so among you; but [t]who-
ever desires to become great among you,
let him be your servant. 27 [u]And whoever
desires to be first among you, let him be
your slave— 28 [v]just as the [w]Son of Man
did not come to be served, [x]but to serve,
and [y]to give His life a ransom [z]for many."

The Blind Men Recognize the King
Mark 10:46-52; Luke 18:35-43

29 [a]Now as they went out of Jericho, a
great multitude followed Him. 30 And behold, [b]two blind men sitting by the road,
when they heard that Jesus was passing by,
cried out, saying, "Have mercy on us, O
Lord, [c]Son of David!"
31 Then the multitude [d]warned them

17 [e] Matt. 20:17-19; Mark 10:32-34; Luke 18:31-33; John 12:12 **18** [f] Matt. 16:21; 26:47-57; Mark 14:42, 64; John 18:5; 19:7 **19** [g] Matt. 27:2; Mark 15:1, 16; Luke 23:1; John 18:28; Acts 3:13 [h] Matt. 26:67, 68; 27:29, 41; Mark 15:20, 31 [i] Matt. 27:26; Mark 15:15; John 19:1 [j] Matt. 27:35; Luke 23:33; Acts 3:13-15 [k] Matt. 28:5, 6; Mark 16:6, 9; Luke 24:5-8, 46; Acts 10:40; 1 Cor. 15:4 **20** [l] Mark 10:35-45 [m] Matt. 4:21; 10:2 **21** [n] [Matt. 19:28] **22** [o] Is. 51:17, 22; Jer. 49:12; Matt. 26:39, 42; Mark 14:36; Luke 22:42; John 18:11 [p] Luke 12:50 [5] NU omits *and be baptized with the baptism that I am baptized with* **23** [q] [Acts 12:2; Rom. 8:17; 2 Cor. 1:7; Rev. 1:9] [6] NU omits *and be baptized with the baptism that I am baptized with* **24** [r] Mark 10:41; Luke 22:24, 25 **26** [s] [1 Pet. 5:3] [t] Matt. 23:11; Mark 9:35; 10:43; Luke 22:26

27 [u] [Matt. 18:4] **28** [v] John 13:4 [w] [Matt. 26:28; John 13:13; 2 Cor. 8:9; Phil. 2:6, 7; 1 Tim. 2:5, 6; Titus 2:14; Heb. 9:28; Rev. 1:5] [x] Luke 22:27; John 13:14 [y] [Is. 53:10, 11; Dan. 9:24, 26; John 11:51, 52; 1 Pet. 1:18, 19] [z] [Rom. 5:15, 19; Heb. 9:28] **29** [a] Mark 10:46-52; Luke 18:35-43 **30** [b] Matt. 9:27 [c] [2 Sam. 7:14-17; Ps. 89:3-5, 19-37; Is. 11:10-12; Ezek. 37:21-25]; Matt. 1:1; Luke 1:31, 32; [Acts 15:14-17] **31** [d] Matt. 19:13

20:17 going up to Jerusalem. Thus began his final journey to the cross.

20:19 crucify. This was the third time Jesus told the disciples of His death (*see note on 16:21*; cf. 17:22,23)—plus 3 of the disciples had overheard Jesus discussing His death with Moses and Elijah at the Transfiguration (Luke 9:31). This time, however, He added more details.

20:20 mother of Zebedee's sons. Mark 10:35 says James and John themselves raised the question of v. 21. There is no contradiction. It is possible either that the 3 of them asked together, or perhaps even more likely that they had discussed it among themselves beforehand, and each posed the question to Jesus privately.

20:21 Grant...these two sons of mine. Probably playing off the words of Jesus in 19:28, James and John had enlisted their mother to convey their proud, self-seeking request to Jesus. This was a recurring matter among the disciples (cf. 18:1,4; 23:11; Mark 9:34, Luke 9:46; 22:24,26), right up to the table at the Last Supper.

20:22 You do not know what you ask. The greatest glory goes to those who suffer the most for Christ. **the cup that I am about to drink.** The cup of God's wrath (*see notes on 26:39; Mark 14:36; Luke 22:42; John 18:11*). **the baptism that I am baptized with.** This refers to the immersion of the Lord into suffering (cf. Luke 12:50). However, the phrases referring to baptism here and in v. 23 do not appear in the best manuscripts.

20:23 You will indeed. James was beheaded (Acts 12:2) and John tortured and exiled to Patmos (Rev. 1:9) for the sake of Christ. **for whom it is prepared.** God alone has chosen.

20:24 were greatly displeased. Jealous displeasure, no doubt. They all would have petitioned Jesus for the exalted, favored positions, given the opportunity. *See note on v. 21.*

20:25-28 In this rich text, the Lord was teaching the disciples that the style of greatness and leadership for believers is different. The Gentile leaders dominate in dictatorial fashion, using carnal power and authority. Believers are to do the opposite—they lead by being servants and giving themselves away for others, as Jesus did.

20:28 to give His life a ransom for many. The word translated "for" means "in the place of," underscoring the substitutionary nature of Christ's sacrifice. A "ransom" is a price paid to redeem a slave or a prisoner. Redemption does not involve a price paid to Satan. Rather, the ransom is offered to God—to satisfy His justice and wrath against sin. The price paid was Christ's own life—as a blood atonement (cf. Lev. 17:11; Heb. 9:22). This, then, is the meaning of the cross: Christ subjected Himself to the divine punishment against sin on our behalf (cf. Is. 53:4,5; *see note on 2 Cor. 5:21*). Suffering the brunt of divine wrath in the place of sinners was the "cup" He spoke of having to drink, and the baptism He was preparing to undergo (v. 22).

20:29 out of Jericho. *See note on v. 30.*

20:30 two blind men. Mark 10:46 and Luke 18:35 mention only one blind man, and both say this encounter took place as Christ was approaching Jericho rather than when He was leaving (v. 29). The difficulties are fairly simple to reconcile: there were two blind men, but Bartimaeus (Mark 10:46) was the spokesman of the two and was, therefore, the sole focus of both Luke's and Mark's accounts (*see note on 8:28*). It is also a fact that there were two Jerichos—one the mound of the ancient city (the ruins of which may still be seen today), and the other, the inhabited city of Jericho, close by. Jesus may have been going "out of" old Jericho and entering new Jericho. Or it may also be that the events are telescoped for us, so that Christ first encountered the blind men on His way into the city, but the healing took place as he was departing. **Son of David.** *See note on 1:1.*

that they should be quiet; but they cried
out all the more, saying, "Have mercy on
us, O Lord, Son of David!"
32 So Jesus stood still and called them,
and said, "What do you want Me to do for
you?"
33 They said to Him, "Lord, that our eyes
may be opened." 34 So Jesus had [e]compas-
sion and touched their eyes. And immediately their eyes received sight, and they
followed Him.

The Triumphal Entry
Mark 11:1-10; Luke 19:29-38; John 12:12-15

21 Now [a]when they drew near Jerusalem, and came to [1]Bethphage, at
[b]the Mount of Olives, then Jesus sent two
disciples, 2 saying to them, "Go into the
village opposite you, and immediately you
will find a donkey tied, and a colt with her.
Loose *them* and bring *them* to Me. 3 And if
anyone says anything to you, you shall say,
'The Lord has need of them,' and immediately he will send them."
4 [2]All this was done that it might be fulfilled which was spoken by the prophet,
saying:

5 *"Tell[c] the daughter of Zion,*
'Behold, your King is coming to you,
Lowly, and sitting on a donkey,
A colt, the foal of a donkey.' "

6 [d]So the disciples went and did as Jesus
commanded them. 7 They brought the
donkey and the colt, [e]laid their clothes on
them, [3]and set *Him* on them. 8 And a very
great multitude spread their clothes on the
road; [f]others cut down branches from the
trees and spread *them* on the road. 9 Then
the multitudes who went before and those
who followed cried out, saying:

"Hosanna to the Son of David!
[g]*'Blessed is He who comes in the*
name of the LORD!'
Hosanna in the highest!"

10 [h]And when He had come into Jerusalem, all the city was moved, saying, "Who
is this?"
11 So the multitudes said, "This is Jesus,
[i]the prophet from Nazareth of Galilee."

The Cleansing of the Temple
Mark 11:15-17; Luke 19:45, 46

12 [j]Then Jesus went into the temple [4]of
God and drove out all those who bought
and sold in the temple, and overturned the
tables of the [k]money changers and the
seats of those who sold doves. 13 And He
said to them, "It is written, [l]*'My house*
shall be called a house of prayer,' but you
have made it a [m]*'den of thieves.'* "
14 Then *the* blind and *the* lame came to
Him in the temple, and He healed them.
15 But when the chief priests and scribes
saw the wonderful things that He did, and
the children crying out in the temple and
saying, "Hosanna to the [n]Son of David!"

34 [e] Matt. 9:36; 14:14; 15:32; 18:27

CHAPTER 21

1 [a] Mark 11:1-10; Luke 19:29-38 [b] [Zech. 14:4] [1] M *Bethsphage*
4 [2] NU omits *All*
5 [c] Is. 62:11; Zech. 9:9; John 12:15
6 [d] Mark 11:4
7 [e] 2 Kin. 9:13 [3] NU *and He sat*
8 [f] Lev. 23:40; John 12:13
9 [g] Ps. 118:26; Matt. 23:39
10 [h] John 2:13, 15
11 [i] [Deut. 18:15, 18]; Matt. 2:23; 16:14; Luke 4:16-29; John 6:14; 7:40; 9:17; [Acts 3:22, 23]
12 [j] Mal. 3:1; Mark 11:15-18; Luke 19:45-47; John 2:13-16 [k] Deut. 14:25 [4] NU omits *of God*
13 [l] Is. 56:7 [m] Jer. 7:11
15 [n] Matt. 1:1; John 7:42

21:1 Bethphage. A small town near Bethany, on the SE slope of the Mt. of Olives. It is mentioned nowhere else in Scripture except in connection with Christ's triumphal entry (Mark 11:1; Luke 19:29).

21:3 if anyone says anything to you. Mark recorded that this was in fact exactly what happened (Mark 11:5,6). Having just arrived in Bethphage (v. 1), Jesus would have had no opportunity to make arrangements for the use of these animals. Yet He knew precisely the location of the animals and the disposition of the owners. Such detailed foreknowledge reveals His divine omniscience.

21:5 A colt, the foal of a donkey. An exact quotation from Zech. 9:9 (cf. Is. 62:11). The precise fulfillment of this messianic prophecy would not have escaped the Jewish multitudes, who responded with titles and accolades fit only for the Messiah (*see note on v. 9*).

21:7 the donkey and the colt. Matthew is the only gospel writer who mentions the mare donkey. But all mention the young age of the donkey (John 12:14), or state that no man had ever sat on him (Mark 11:2; Luke 19:30). The mare was brought along, possibly to induce the colt to cooperate. **set *Him* on them.** I.e., on the clothes. Christ rode on the young colt (Mark 11:7).

21:8 spread their clothes on the road. Spreading one's garments on the street was an ancient act of homage reserved for high royalty (cf. 2 Kin. 9:13), suggesting that they recognized His claim to be King of the Jews.

21:9 Hosanna. This transliterates the Heb. expression which is translated "Save now" in Ps. 118:25. ***Blessed is He.*** This is an exact quotation from v. 26 of the same psalm. This, along with the messianic title "Son of David," make it clear that the crowd was acknowledging Christ's messianic claim (*see note on 1:1*). The date of this entry was Sunday, 9 Nisan, A.D. 30, exactly 483 years after the decree of Artaxerxes mentioned in Dan. 9:24-26 (*see notes there*).

21:12 drove out. This was the second time Jesus had cleansed the temple. John 2:14-16 describes a similar incident at the beginning of Christ's public ministry. There are distinct differences in the two incidents. In the first cleansing, temple officials confronted Christ immediately afterward (*see note on v. 23*; cf. John 2:18); none of the accounts of this second cleansing mention any such confrontation. Instead, the synoptics all describe how Jesus addressed all present (v. 13) and even made the incident an occasion for public teaching (Mark 11:17; Luke 19:46,47). **those who bought and sold.** He regarded both merchants and customers guilty of desecrating the temple. Items being bought and sold included "doves" and other animals for sacrifice (cf. John 2:14). **money changers.** Currency-exchange agents, present in droves, were needed because Roman coins and other forms of currency were deemed unacceptable for temple offerings. Evidently, both merchants and money changers were charging such excessive rates that the temple marketplace took on the atmosphere of a thieves' den (v. 13). This kind of commerce took place in the court of the Gentiles, a large area covering several acres on the temple mount.

21:13 It is written. Jesus conflates two OT prophecies, Is. 56:7 ("My house shall be called a house of prayer for all nations") and Jer. 7:11 ("Has this house, which is called by My name, become a den of thieves in your eyes?").

21:15 children. Lit. "boys." The crowd in Jerusalem for the

they were [s]indignant 16 and said to Him,
"Do You hear what these are saying?"
And Jesus said to them, "Yes. Have you
never read,

[o]'*Out of the mouth of babes and*
nursing infants
You have perfected praise'?"

17 Then He left them and [p]went out of
the city to Bethany, and He lodged there.

Cursing of the Fig Tree
Mark 11:11-14, 20-24

18 [q]Now in the morning, as He returned
to the city, He was hungry. 19 [r]And seeing
a fig tree by the road, He came to it and
found nothing on it but leaves, and said to
it, "Let no fruit grow on you ever again."
Immediately the fig tree withered away.
20 [s]And when the disciples saw *it*, they
marveled, saying, "How did the fig tree
wither away so soon?"
21 So Jesus answered and said to them,
"Assuredly, I say to you, [t]if you have faith
and [u]do not doubt, you will not only do
what was done to the fig tree, [v]but also if
you say to this mountain, 'Be removed and
be cast into the sea,' it will be done. 22 And
[w]whatever things you ask in prayer, believing, you will receive."

Question of Jesus' Authority
Mark 11:27-33; Luke 20:1-18

23 [x]Now when He came into the temple,
the chief priests and the elders of the people confronted Him as He was teaching,
and [y]said, "By what authority are You
doing these things? And who gave You
this authority?"
24 But Jesus answered and said to them,
"I also will ask you one thing, which if you
tell Me, I likewise will tell you by what authority I do these things: 25 The [z]baptism
of [a]John—where was it from? From heav-
en or from men?"
And they reasoned among themselves,
saying, "If we say, 'From heaven,' He will
say to us, 'Why then did you not believe
him?' 26 But if we say, 'From men,' we
[b]fear the multitude, [c]for all count John as a
prophet." 27 So they answered Jesus and
said, "We do not know."
And He said to them, "Neither will I tell
you by what authority I do these things.

Parable of the Two Sons

28 "But what do you think? A man had
two sons, and he came to the first and said,
'Son, go, work today in my [d]vineyard.'
29 He answered and said, 'I will not,' but
afterward he regretted it and went. 30 Then
he came to the second and said likewise.
And he answered and said, 'I *go*, sir,' but
he did not go. 31 Which of the two did the
will of *his* father?"
They said to Him, "The first."
Jesus said to them, [e]"Assuredly, I say to
you that tax collectors and harlots enter the
kingdom of God before you. 32 For [f]John

15 [s]*angry*
16 [o]Ps. 8:2; Matt. 11:25
17 [p]Matt. 26:6; Mark 11:1, 11, 12; 14:3; Luke 19:29; 24:50; John 11:1, 18; 12:1
18 [q]Mark 11:12-14, 20-24
19 [r]Mark 11:13
20 [s]Mark 11:20
21 [t]Matt. 17:20 [u]James 1:6 [v]1 Cor. 13:2
22 [w]Matt. 7:7-11; Mark 11:24; Luke 11:9; [John 15:7; James 5:16; 1 John 3:22; 5:14]
23 [x]Mark 11:27-33; Luke 20:1-8 [y]Ex. 2:14; Acts 4:7; 7:27
25 [z][John 1:29-34] [a]John 1:15-28
26 [b]Matt. 14:5; 21:46; Luke 20:6 [c]Matt. 14:5; Mark 6:20
28 [d]Matt. 20:1; 21:33
31 [e]Luke 7:29, 37-50
32 [f]Luke 3:1-12; 7:29

Passover would have included a large number of 12-year-olds preparing for *bar mitzvah,* who were there to celebrate their first Passover, just as Jesus Himself had done (*see note on Luke 2:42*).

21:16 Yes. Have you never read. Jesus' reply to the "indignant" chief priests and scribes amounted to an inescapable assertion of His deity. He quoted from Ps. 8:2, which speaks of "praise" offered to God. By employing that verse in defense of the worship God had ordained "out of the mouth of babes" on His behalf, He was claiming the right to receive worship as God.

21:19 Immediately. This is a relative term; the tree may have died at once, but Mark 11:14,20 (*see note there*) suggested that the withering was not visible until the following day. Jesus' cursing of the tree was a purposeful divine object lesson, not an impetuous act of frustration. The fig tree is often employed in Scripture as a symbol of Israel (Hos. 9:10; Joel 1:7)—and the barren fig tree often symbolizes divine judgment on Israel because of her spiritual fruitlessness (*see note on 3:8*) despite an abundance of spiritual advantages (Jer. 8:13; Joel 1:12). Jesus' act therefore illustrates God's judgment against earthly Israel for shameful fruitlessness, exemplified in the rejection of their Messiah. One of Christ's parables taught a similar lesson (Luke 13:6-9).

21:21 if you have faith and do not doubt. This presupposes that the thing requested is actually God's will (*see note on 17:20*)—for only God-given faith is so doubt-free (cf. Mark 9:24). **it will be done.** A miracle on such a cosmic scale was precisely what the scribes and Pharisees wanted Christ to do, but He always declined (*see note on 12:38*). Here, He was speaking figuratively about the immeasurable power of God, unleashed in the lives of those with true faith.

21:23 these things. I.e., both His public teaching and miracles. They may have also had in mind His act of cleansing the temple on the day before (*see note on v. 12*). **who gave You this authority?** They were forced to acknowledge that He had some source of indisputable authority. His miracles were too obvious and too numerous to be fraudulent. Even His teaching was with such force and clarity that it was obvious to all that there was authority in His words (*see note on 7:29*).

21:25 The baptism of John—where was it from? Jesus caught the Jewish leaders in their own trap. They had no doubt hoped that He would answer by asserting that His authority came directly from God (as He had many times before—cf. John 5:19-23; 10:18). They then accused Him of blasphemy and used the charge as an excuse to kill Him—as they had also attempted to do before (John 5:18; 10:31-33). Here, however, He asked a question that placed them in an impossible dilemma, because John was widely revered by the people. They could not affirm John's ministry without condemning themselves. And if they denied John's legitimacy, they feared the response of the people (v. 26). In effect, Jesus exposed their own lack of any authority to examine Him. *See note on Luke 20:5.*

21:31 Which of the two did the will of *his* father? Jesus forced them to testify against themselves. The point of the parable was that doing is more important than saying (cf. 7:21-27; James 1:22). They had to acknowledge this, yet in doing so they condemned themselves. The idea that repentant tax collectors and harlots would enter the kingdom before outwardly religious hypocrites was a recurring theme in His ministry (*see note on 5:20*), and this infuriated the Jewish leaders.

came to you in the way of righteousness,
and you did not believe him; [g]but tax collectors and harlots believed him; and when
you saw *it*, you did not afterward [6]relent
and believe him.

Parable of the Landowner
Mark 12:1-12; Luke 20:9-19

33 "Hear another parable: There was a
certain landowner [h]who planted a vineyard and set a hedge around it, dug a
winepress in it and built a tower. And he
leased it to vinedressers and [i]went into a
far country. 34 Now when vintage-time
drew near, he sent his servants to the vinedressers, that they might receive its fruit.
35 [j]And the vinedressers took his servants,
beat one, killed one, and stoned another.
36 Again he sent other servants, more than
the first, and they did likewise to them.
37 Then last of all he sent his [k]son to them,
saying, 'They will respect my son.' 38 But
when the vinedressers saw the son, they
said among themselves, [l]'This is the heir.
[m]Come, let us kill him and seize his inheritance.' 39 [n]So they took him and cast *him*
out of the vineyard and killed *him*.
40 "Therefore, when the owner of the
vineyard comes, what will he do to those
vinedressers?"
41 [o]They said to Him, [p]"He will destroy
those wicked men miserably, [q]and lease
his vineyard to other vinedressers who
will [7]render to him the fruits in their seasons."
42 Jesus said to them, "Have you never
read in the Scriptures:

[r]'The stone which the builders rejected
Has become the chief cornerstone.
This was the LORD's doing,
And it is marvelous in our eyes'?

43 "Therefore I say to you, [s]the kingdom
of God will be taken from you and given to
a nation bearing the fruits of it. 44 And
[t]whoever falls on this stone will be broken;
but on whomever it falls, [u]it will grind him
to powder."
45 Now when the chief priests and
Pharisees heard His parables, they [8]per-
ceived that He was speaking of them.
46 But when they sought to lay hands on
Him, they [v]feared the multitudes, because
[w]they took Him for a prophet.

Parable of the Marriage Feast

22 And Jesus answered [a]and spoke to
them again by parables and said:
2 "The kingdom of heaven is like a certain
king who arranged a marriage for his son,
3 and sent out his servants to call those
who were invited to the wedding; and they
were not willing to come. 4 Again, he sent
out other servants, saying, 'Tell those who

32 [g] Luke 3:12, 13 [6] *regret it*
33 [h] Ps. 80:9; Mark 12:1-12; Luke 20:9-19 [i] Matt. 25:14
35 [j] 2 Chr. 24:21; 36:16; [Matt. 23:34, 37; Acts 7:52; 1 Thess. 2:15]; Heb. 11:36, 37
37 [k] [John 3:16]
38 [l] [Ps. 2:8; Heb. 1:2] [m] [Ps. 2:2]; John 11:53; Acts 4:27
39 [n] [Matt. 26:50]; Mark 14:46; Luke 22:54; John 18:12; [Acts 2:23]
41 [o] Luke 20:16 [p] [Luke 21:24] [q] [Matt. 8:11; Acts 13:46; Rom. 9; 10] [7] *give*
42 [r] Ps. 118:22, 23; Is. 28:16; Mark 12:10; Luke 20:17; Acts 4:11; [Rom. 9:33]; Eph. 2:20; [1 Pet. 2:6, 7]
43 [s] [Matt. 8:12]; Acts 13:46
44 [t] Is. 8:14, 15; Zech. 12:3; Luke 20:18; [Rom. 9:33]; 1 Pet. 2:8 [u] [Is. 60:12; Dan. 2:44]
45 [8] *knew*
46 [v] Matt. 21:26; Mark 11:18, 32 [w] Matt. 21:11; Luke 7:16; John 7:40

CHAPTER 22
1 [a] Luke 14:16; [Rev. 19:7-9]

21:32 the way of righteousness. I.e., the repentance and faith that results in the imputation of God's righteousness (*see note on Rom. 3:21*). **tax collectors and harlots.** *See notes on 5:46; 9:9; Mark 2:15.* The pariahs of Jewish society, most publicly despised by the chief priests and elders, had found salvation while the self-righteous leaders had not. Cf. Rom. 10:3.

21:33 a vineyard...a winepress. See Is. 5:2. Jesus was clearly alluding to this OT passage, which would have been familiar to the Jewish leaders. The "vineyard" is a common symbol for the Jewish nation in Scripture. Here the landowner, representing God, developed the vineyard with great care, then leased it to vinedressers, representing the Jewish leaders.

21:34 his servants. I.e., the OT prophets.

21:35 beat one, killed one, and stoned another. Matthew often blends and simplifies details (*see notes on v. 19; 8:28; 20:30*). From Mark's account we learn that in Jesus' telling of this story, 3 different servants came individually. The tenants "beat" the first one, "stoned" the second, and "killed" the third (Mark 12:2-5). This corresponds to the Jewish rulers' treatment of many of the OT prophets (1 Kin. 22:24; 2 Chr. 24:20,21; 36:15,16; Neh. 9:26; Jer. 2:30).

21:37 my son. This person represents the Lord Jesus Christ, whom they killed (vv. 38,39) and thereby incurred divine judgement (v. 41).

21:41 lease *his* vineyard to other vinedressers. Again the Jewish leaders pronounced their own judgment (*see note on v. 31*). Their verdict against the evil vinedressers was also Christ's judgment against them (v. 43). The kingdom and all the spiritual advantages given to Israel would now be given to "other vinedressers," symbolizing the Church (v. 43), which consists primarily of Gentiles (cf. Rom. 11:11).

21:42 *The stone...rejected.* This refers to His crucifixion; and the restoration of "the chief cornerstone" anticipates His resurrection. ***the chief cornerstone.*** To the superficial eye, this quotation from Ps. 118:22,23 is irrelevant to the parable that precedes it. But it is taken from a messianic psalm. Jesus cited it to suggest that the Son who was killed and thrown out of the vineyard was also "the chief cornerstone" in God's redemptive plan.

21:43 a nation bearing the fruits of it. The church. *See note on v. 41.* Peter spoke of the church as "a holy nation" (1 Pet. 2:9).

21:44 this stone. Christ is "a stone of stumbling and a rock of offense" to unbelievers (Is. 8:14; 1 Pet. 2:9). And the prophet Daniel pictured Him as a great stone "cut out of the mountain without hands," which falls on the kingdoms of the world and crushes them (Dan. 2:44,45). Whether a ceramic vessel "falls on" a rock, or the rock "falls" on the vessel, the result is the same. The saying suggests that both enmity and apathy are wrong responses to Christ, and those guilty of either are in danger of judgment.

21:45 they perceived that He was speaking of them. By evoking so much familiar messianic imagery (vv. 42-44), Christ made His meaning inescapable to the chief priests and Pharisees.

22:2 like a certain king who arranged a marriage. Jesus told a similar, but different, parable in Luke 14:16-23. Here, the banquet was a wedding feast for the king's own son, making the apathy (v. 5) and rejection (v. 6) of those invited much more of a personal slight against the king. Also, here they actually mistreated and killed the king's messengers—an unthinkable affront to the king's goodness.

22:4 Again, he sent out other servants. This illustrates God's patience and forbearance with those who deliberately spurn Him. He continues to extend the invitation even after His goodness has been ignored or rebuffed.

are invited, "See, I have prepared my dinner; [b]my oxen and fatted cattle *are* killed,
and all things *are* ready. Come to the wedding." ' 5 But they made light of it and
went their ways, one to his own farm, another to his business. 6 And the rest seized
his servants, treated *them* [1]spitefully, and
killed *them.* 7 But when the king heard
about it, he was furious. And he sent out
[c]his armies, destroyed those murderers,
and burned up their city. 8 Then he said to
his servants, 'The wedding is ready, but
those who were invited were not [d]worthy.
9 Therefore go into the highways, and as
many as you find, invite to the wedding.'
10 So those servants went out into the highways and [e]gathered together all whom
they found, both bad and good. And the
wedding *hall* was filled with guests.
11 "But when the king came in to see the
guests, he saw a man there [f]who did not
have on a wedding garment. 12 So he said
to him, 'Friend, how did you come in here
without a wedding garment?' And he was
[g]speechless. 13 Then the king said to the
servants, 'Bind him hand and foot, [2]take
him away, and cast *him* [h]into outer darkness; there will be weeping and gnashing
of teeth.'
14 [i]"For many are called, but few *are* chosen."

Conflict with Pharisees and Herodians

Mark 12:13-17; Luke 20:20-26

15 [j]Then the Pharisees went and plotted
how they might entangle Him in *His* talk.
16 And they sent to Him their disciples
with the [k]Herodians, saying, "Teacher, we
know that You are true, and teach the way
of God in truth; nor do You care about anyone, for You do not [3]regard the person of
men. 17 Tell us, therefore, what do You
think? Is it lawful to pay taxes to Caesar, or
not?"
18 But Jesus [4]perceived their wickedness, and said, "Why do you test Me, *you*
hypocrites? 19 Show Me the tax money."
So they brought Him a denarius.
20 And He said to them, "Whose image
and inscription *is* this?"

4 [b] Prov. 9:2
6 [1] *insolently*
7 [c] [Dan. 9:26]
8 [d] Matt. 10:11
10 [e] Matt. 13:38, 47, 48; [Acts 28:28]
11 [f] [2 Cor. 5:3; Eph. 4:24; Col. 3:10, 12; Rev. 3:4; 16:15; 19:8]
12 [g] [Rom. 3:19]
13 [h] Matt. 8:12; 25:30; Luke 13:28 [2] NU omits *take him away, and*
14 [i] Matt. 20:16
15 [j] Mark 12:13-17; Luke 20:20-26
16 [k] Mark 3:6; 8:15; 12:13 [3] Lit. *look at the face of*
18 [4] *knew*

22:7 he was furious. His vast patience finally exhausted, He judges them. **burned up their city.** The judgment Jesus described anticipated the destruction of Jerusalem in A.D. 70. Even the massive stone temple was destroyed by fire and reduced to rubble in that conflagration. *See notes on 23:36; 24:2; Luke 19:43.*

22:9 as many as you find, invite to the wedding. This illustrates the free offer of the gospel, which is extended to all indiscriminately (cf. Rev. 22:17).

22:11 a wedding garment. All without exception were invited to the banquet, so this man is not to be viewed as a common party-crasher. In fact, all the guests were rounded up hastily from "the highways" and therefore none could be expected to come with proper attire. That means the wedding garments were supplied by the king himself. So this man's lack of a proper garment indicates he had purposely rejected the king's own gracious provision. His affront to the king was actually a greater insult than those who refused to come at all, because he committed his impertinence in the very presence of the king. The imagery seems to represent those who identify with the kingdom externally, profess to be Christians, belong to the church in a visible sense—yet spurn the garment of righteousness Christ offers (cf. Is. 61:10) by seeking to establish a righteousness of their own (cf. Rom. 10:3; Phil. 3:8,9). Ashamed to admit their own spiritual poverty (*see note on 5:3*), they refuse the better garment the King graciously offers—and thus they are guilty of a horrible sin against His goodness.

22:12 And he was speechless. I.e., he had no excuse.

22:13 outer darkness. This would describe the darkness farthest from the light, i.e., outer darkness. **weeping and gnashing of teeth.** This speaks of inconsolable grief and unremitting torment. Jesus commonly used the phrases in this verse to describe hell (cf. 13:42,50; 24:51).

22:14 many are called, but few *are* chosen. The call spoken of here is sometimes referred to as the "general call" (or the "external" call)—a summons to repentance and faith that is inherent in the gospel message. This call extends to all who hear the gospel. "Many" hear it; "few" respond (see the many-few comparison in 7:13,14). Those who respond are the "chosen," the elect. In the Pauline writings, the word "call" usually refers to God's irresistible calling extended to the elect alone (Rom. 8:30)—known as the "effectual call" (or the "internal" call). The effectual call is the supernatural drawing of God which Jesus speaks of in John 6:44. Here a general call is in view, and this call extends to all who hear the gospel—this call is the great "whosoever will" of the gospel (cf. Rev. 22:17). Here, then, is the proper balance between human responsibility and divine sovereignty: the "called" who reject the invitation do so willingly, and therefore their exclusion from the kingdom is perfectly just. The "chosen" enter the kingdom only because of the grace of God in choosing and drawing them.

22:16 Herodians. A party of the Jews who supported the Roman-backed Herodian dynasty. The Herodians were not a religious party, like the Pharisees, but a political party, probably consisting largely of Sadducees (including the rulers of the temple). By contrast, the Pharisees hated Roman rule and the Herodian influence. The fact that these groups would conspire together to entrap Jesus reveals how seriously both groups viewed Him as a threat. Herod himself wanted Jesus dead (Luke 13:31), and the Pharisees were already plotting to kill Him as well (John 11:53). So they joined efforts to seek their common goal.

22:17 Is it lawful to pay taxes to Caesar, or not? At issue was the poll tax, an annual fee of one denarius (*see note on v. 19*) per person. Such "taxes" were part of the heavy taxation Rome assessed. Since these funds were used to finance the occupying armies, all Roman taxes were hated by the people. But the poll tax was the most hated of all because it suggested that Rome owned even the people, while they viewed themselves and their nation as possessions of God. It was therefore significant that they questioned Christ about the poll tax in particular. If He answered no to their question, the Herodians would charge Him with treason against Rome. If He said yes, the Pharisees would accuse Him of disloyalty to the Jewish nation, and He would lose the support of the multitudes.

22:19 denarius. *See note on Mark 12:16.* A silver coin, the value of a day's wage for a Roman soldier. The coins were minted under the emperor's authority since only he could issue gold or silver coins. The "denarius" of Jesus' day was minted by Tiberius. One side bore an image of his face; the other featured an engraving of him sitting on his throne in priestly robes. The Jews considered such images idolatry, forbidden by the second commandment (Ex. 20:4), which made this tax and these coins doubly offensive.

21 They said to Him, "Caesar's."
And He said to them, [l]"Render[5] therefore to Caesar the things that are [m]Cae-
sar's, and to God the things that are
[n]God's." 22 When they had heard *these*
words, they marveled, and left Him and
went their way.

Conflict with Sadducees
Mark 12:18-27; Luke 20:27-40

23 [o]The same day the Sadducees, [p]who
say there is no resurrection, came to Him
and asked Him, 24 saying: "Teacher, [q]Mo-
ses said that if a man dies, having no children, his brother shall marry his wife and
raise up offspring for his brother. 25 Now
there were with us seven brothers. The first
died after he had married, and having no
offspring, left his wife to his brother.
26 Likewise the second also, and the third,
even to the seventh. 27 Last of all the
woman died also. 28 Therefore, in the resurrection, whose wife of the seven will she
be? For they all had her."
29 Jesus answered and said to them,
"You are [6]mistaken, [r]not knowing the
Scriptures nor the power of God. 30 For in
the resurrection they neither marry nor are
given in marriage, but [s]are like angels [7]of
God in heaven. 31 But concerning the resurrection of the dead, have you not read
what was spoken to you by God, saying,
32 [t]*'I am the God of Abraham, the God of*
Isaac, and the God of Jacob'? God is not
the God of the dead, but of the living."
33 And when the multitudes heard *this,*
[u]they were astonished at His teaching.

The Greatest Commandment
Mark 12:28-34

34 [v]But when the Pharisees heard that
He had silenced the Sadducees, they gathered together. 35 Then one of them, [w]a
lawyer, asked *Him a question,* testing Him,
and saying, 36 "Teacher, which *is* the great
commandment in the law?"
37 Jesus said to him, [x]" *'You shall love*
the LORD your God with all your heart,
with all your soul, and with all your mind.'
38 This is *the* first and great commandment.
39 And *the* second *is* like it: [y]*'You shall love*
your neighbor as yourself.' 40 [z]On these
two commandments hang all the Law and
the Prophets."

The Son of David
Mark 12:35-37; Luke 20:41-44

41 [a]While the Pharisees were gathered
together, Jesus asked them, 42 saying,
"What do you think about the Christ?
Whose Son is He?"
They said to Him, *"The* [b]*Son* of David."
43 He said to them, "How then does David in the Spirit call Him *'Lord,'* saying:

44 *'The*[c] *LORD said to my Lord,*
" Sit at My right hand,

21 [l]Matt. 17:25 [m][Rom. 13:1-7; 1 Pet. 2:13-15] [n][1 Cor. 3:23; 6:19, 20; 12:27] [5]*Pay*
23 [o]Mark 12:18-27; Luke 20:27-40 [p]Acts 23:8
24 [q]Deut. 25:5
29 [r]John 20:9 [6]*deceived*
30 [s][1 John 3:2] [7]NU omits *of God*
32 [t]Gen. 17:7; 26:24; 28:21; Ex. 3:6, 15; Mark 12:26; Luke 20:37; Acts 7:32; [Heb. 11:16]
33 [u]Matt. 7:28
34 [v]Mark 12:28-31; Luke 10:25-37
35 [w]Luke 7:30; 10:25; 11:45, 46, 52; 14:3; Titus 3:13
37 [x]Deut. 6:5; 10:12; 30:6
39 [y]Lev. 19:18; Matt. 19:19; Mark 12:31; Luke 10:27; [Rom. 13:9; Gal. 5:14; James 2:8]
40 [z][Matt. 7:12; Rom. 13:10; 1 Tim. 1:5]
41 [a]Mark 12:35-37; Luke 20:41-44
42 [b]Matt. 1:1; 21:9
44 [c]Ps. 110:1; [Matt. 26:64]; Mark 16:19; Acts 2:34; 1 Cor. 15:25; Heb. 1:13; 10:13

22:21 Caesar's...God's. Caesar's image is stamped on the coin; God's image is stamped on the person (Gen 1:26,27). The Christian must "render" obedience to Caesar in Caesar's realm (Rom. 13:1-7; 1 Pet. 2:13-17), but "the things that are God's" are things that do not belong to Caesar and should be given only to God. Christ thus acknowledged Caesar's right to assess and collect taxes, and He made it the duty of Christians to pay them. But He did not suggest (as some suppose) that Caesar had sole or ultimate authority in the social or political realms. Ultimately, all things are God's (Rom. 11:36; 2 Cor. 5:18; Rev. 4:11)—including the realm in which Caesar or any other earthly ruler exercises authority.

22:23 no resurrection. *See note on 3:7.*

22:24 his brother shall marry his wife. This refers to the law of levirate marriage, found in Deut. 25:5-10 (*see note there*). This was a provision to ensure that family lines were kept intact and widows were cared for.

22:30 like angels of God in heaven. The Sadducees did not believe in angels (*see note on 3:7*)—so here Jesus was exposing another of their false beliefs. Angels are deathless creatures who do not propagate and therefore have no need for marriage. "In the resurrection," the saints will have those same characteristics.

22:32 not the God of the dead. Jesus' argument (taken from the Pentateuch, because the Sadducees recognized only Moses' authority—*see note on 3:7*) was based on the emphatic present tense "I AM" of Ex. 3:6. This subtle but effective argument utterly silenced the Sadducees (v. 34). *See note on Mark 12:26.*

22:35 a lawyer. A scribe whose specialty was interpreting the law. *See notes on 2:4; Luke 10:25.*

22:36 *See note on Mark 12:28.*

22:37 *heart...soul...mind.* Mark 12:30 adds "strength." The quote is from Deut. 6:5, part of the *shema,* (Heb. for "hear"—Deut. 6:4). That verse says "heart...soul...strength." Some LXX manuscripts added "mind." The use of the various terms is not meant to delineate distinct human faculties, but to underscore the completeness of the kind of love that is called for.

22:39 *love your neighbor as yourself.* This is a quotation from Lev. 19:18. Contrary to some contemporary interpretations, it is not a mandate for self-love. Rather, it contains in different words the same very idea as the Golden Rule (*see note on 7:12*). It prompts believers to measure their love for others by what they wish for themselves.

22:40 all the Law and the Prophets. I.e., the whole OT. Thus Jesus subsumes man's whole moral duty under two categories: love for God, and love for one's neighbors. These same two categories differentiate the first 4 commandments of the Decalogue from the final 6.

22:42 What do you think. A phrase often used by Christ to introduce a question designed to test someone (v. 17; 17:25; 18:12; 21:28; 26:66). Here, the Pharisees, Herodians, Sadducees, and scribes had all put Him to the test. He also had a test for them. ***The Son of David.*** *See note on 1:1.* "Son of David" was the most common messianic title in the usage of Jesus' day. Their answer reflected their conviction that the Messiah would be no more than a man, and Jesus' reply was another assertion of His deity. *See note on v. 45.*

22:43 in the Spirit. I.e., under the inspiration of the Holy Spirit (cf. Mark 12:36).

22:44 Quoted from Ps. 110:1.

Till I make Your enemies Your
footstool"'?

45 If David then calls Him *'Lord,'* how is
He his Son?" 46 [d]And no one was able to
answer Him a word, [e]nor from that day on
did anyone dare question Him anymore.

Jesus Characterizes the Pharisees
Mark 12:38-40; Luke 20:45-47

23 Then Jesus spoke to the multitudes
and to His disciples, 2 saying: [a]"The
scribes and the Pharisees sit in Moses' seat.
3 Therefore whatever they tell you [1]to observe, *that* observe and do, but do not do
according to their works; for [b]they say, and
do not do. 4 [c]For they bind heavy burdens,
hard to bear, and lay *them* on men's shoulders; but they *themselves* will not move
them with one of their fingers. 5 But all
their works they do to [d]be seen by men.
They make their phylacteries broad and enlarge the borders of their garments. 6 [e]They
love the [2]best places at feasts, the best seats
in the synagogues, 7 greetings in the marketplaces, and to be called by men, 'Rabbi,
Rabbi.' 8 [f]But you, do not be called 'Rabbi';
for One is your [3]Teacher, [4]the Christ, and
you are all brethren. 9 Do not call anyone
on earth your father; [g]for One is your Father, He who is in heaven. 10 And do not be
called teachers; for One is your Teacher, the
Christ. 11 But [h]he who is greatest among
you shall be your servant. 12 [i]And whoever
exalts himself will be [5]humbled, and he
who humbles himself will be [6]exalted.

Jesus Condemns the Pharisees

13 "But [j]woe to you, scribes and Pharisees, hypocrites! For you shut up the kingdom of heaven against men; for you neither go in yourselves, nor do you allow
those who are entering to go in. 14 [7]Woe to
you, scribes and Pharisees, hypocrites!
[k]For you devour widows' houses, and for
a pretense make long prayers. Therefore
you will receive greater condemnation.
15 "Woe to you, scribes and Pharisees,
hypocrites! For you travel land and sea to
win one proselyte, and when he is won,
you make him twice as much a son of [8]hell
as yourselves.
16 "Woe to you, [l]blind guides, who say,
[m]'Whoever swears by the temple, it is
nothing; but whoever swears by the gold
of the temple, he is obliged *to perform it.'*
17 Fools and blind! For which is greater,
the gold [n]or the temple that [9]sanctifies the
gold? 18 And, 'Whoever swears by the
altar, it is nothing; but whoever swears by
the gift that is on it, he is obliged *to perform*
it.' 19 Fools and blind! For which is greater,
the gift [o]or the altar that sanctifies the gift?

46 [d] Luke 14:6 [e] Mark 12:34; Luke 20:40

CHAPTER 23

2 [a] Deut. 33:3; Ezra 7:6, 25; Neh. 8:4, 8; [Mal. 2:7]; Mark 12:38; Luke 20:45
3 [b] [Rom. 2:19] [1] NU omits *to observe*
4 [c] [Matt. 11:29, 30]; Luke 11:46; Acts 15:10; Rom. 2:17-24; [Gal. 5:1; 6:13; Col. 2:16, 17]
5 [d] [Matt. 6:1-6, 16-18]
6 [e] Mark 12:38, 39; Luke 11:43; 20:46; 3 John 9 [2] Or *place of honor*
8 [f] [2 Cor. 1:24; James 3:1; 1 Pet. 5:3] [3] *Leader* [4] NU omits *the Christ*
9 [g] [Mal. 1:6]; Matt. 5:16, 48; 6:1, 9, 14, 26, 32; 7:11
11 [h] Matt. 20:26, 27
12 [i] Job 22:29; Prov. 15:33; 29:23; Luke 14:11; 18:14; James 4:6; 1 Pet. 5:5 [5] *put down* [6] *lifted up*
13 [j] Luke 11:52
14 [k] Mark 12:40; Luke 20:47; [2 Tim. 3:6; Titus 1:10, 11] [7] NU omits v. 14.
15 [8] Gr. *Gehenna*
16 [l] Matt. 15:14; 23:24 [m] [Matt. 5:33, 34]
17 [n] Ex. 30:29 [9] NU *sanctified* **19** [o] Ex. 29:37

22:45 David then calls Him *'Lord.'* David would not have addressed a merely human descendant as "Lord." Here Jesus was not disputing whether "Son of David" was an appropriate title for the Messiah; after all, the title is based on what is revealed about the Messiah in the OT (Is. 11:1; Jer. 23:5) and it is used as a messianic title in 1:1 (*see note there*). But Jesus was pointing out that the title "son of David" did not begin to sum up all that is true about the Messiah who is also "son of God" (Luke 22:70). The inescapable implication is that Jesus was declaring His deity.

23:2 Moses' seat. The expression is equivalent to a university's "chair of philosophy." To "sit in Moses' seat" was to have the highest authority to instruct people in the law. The expression here may be translated, "[they] have seated themselves in Moses' seat"—stressing the fact that this was an imaginary authority they claimed for themselves. There was a legitimate sense in which the priests and Levites had authority to decide matters of the law (Deut. 17:9), but the scribes and Pharisees had gone beyond any legitimate authority and were adding human tradition to the Word of God (15:3-9). For that Jesus condemned them (vv. 8-36).

23:3 observe and do. I.e., insofar as it accords with the Word of God. The Pharisees were prone to bind "heavy burdens" (v. 4) of extra-biblical traditions and put them on others' shoulders. Jesus explicitly condemned that sort of legalism.

23:5 phylacteries. Leather boxes containing a parchment on which is written in 4 columns Ex. 13:1-10; 11-16; Deut. 6:4-9; 11:13-21. These are worn by men during prayer—one on the middle of the forehead and one on the left arm just above the elbow. The use of phylacteries was based on an overly literal interpretation of passages like Ex. 13:9,10; Deut. 6:8. Evidently the Pharisees would broaden the leather straps by which the phylacteries were bound to their arms and foreheads, in order to make the phylacteries more prominent. **the borders of their garments.** I.e., the tassels. Jesus Himself wore them (*see note on 9:20*), so it was not the tassels themselves that He condemned, only the mentality that would lengthen the tassels to make it appear that one was especially spiritual.

23:8-10 Rabbi...father...teachers. Here Jesus condemns pride and pretense, not titles per se. Paul repeatedly speaks of "teachers" in the church, and even refers to himself as the Corinthians' "father" (1 Cor. 4:15). Obviously, this does not forbid the showing of respect, either (cf. 1 Thess. 5:11,12; 1 Tim. 5:1). Christ is merely forbidding the use of such names as spiritual titles, or in an ostentatious sense that accords undue spiritual authority to a human being, as if he were the source of truth rather than God.

23:13 nor do you allow. The Pharisees, having shunned God's righteousness, were seeking to establish a righteousness of their own (Rom. 10:3)—and teaching others to do so as well. Their legalism and self-righteousness effectively obscured the narrow gate by which the kingdom must be entered (*see notes 7:13,14*).

23:14 This verse does not appear in the earliest available manuscripts of Matthew, but does appear in Mark. *See notes on Mark 12:40.*

23:15 proselyte. A Gentile convert to Judaism. *See Acts 6:5.* **a son of hell.** I.e., someone whose eternal destination is hell.

23:16 it is nothing. This was an arbitrary distinction the Pharisees had made, which gave them a sanctimonious justification for lying with impunity. If someone swore "by the temple" (or the altar, v. 18; or heaven, v. 22), his oath was not considered binding, but if he swore "by the gold of the temple," he could not break his word without being subject to the penalties of Jewish law. Our Lord makes it clear that swearing by those things is tantamount to swearing by God Himself. *See note on 5:34.*

20 Therefore he who [1]swears by the altar,
swears by it and by all things on it. 21 He
who swears by the temple, swears by it
and by [p]Him who [2]dwells in it. 22 And he
who swears by heaven, swears by [q]the
throne of God and by Him who sits on it.
23 "Woe to you, scribes and Pharisees,
hypocrites! [r]For you pay tithe of mint and
anise and cummin, and [s]have neglected
the weightier *matters* of the law: justice and
mercy and faith. These you ought to have
done, without leaving the others undone.
24 Blind guides, who strain out a gnat and
swallow a camel!
25 "Woe to you, scribes and Pharisees,
hypocrites! [t]For you cleanse the outside of
the cup and dish, but inside they are full of
extortion and [3]self-indulgence. 26 Blind
Pharisee, first cleanse the inside of the cup
and dish, that the outside of them may be
clean also.
27 "Woe to you, scribes and Pharisees,
hypocrites! [u]For you are like whitewashed
tombs which indeed appear beautiful outwardly, but inside are full of dead *men's*
bones and all uncleanness. 28 Even so you
also outwardly appear righteous to men,
but inside you are full of hypocrisy and
lawlessness.
29 [v]"Woe to you, scribes and Pharisees,
hypocrites! Because you build the tombs of
the prophets and [4]adorn the monuments
of the righteous, 30 and say, 'If we had
lived in the days of our fathers, we would
not have been partakers with them in the
blood of the prophets.'
31 "Therefore you are witnesses against
yourselves that [w]you are sons of those who
murdered the prophets. 32 [x]Fill up, then, the
measure of your fathers' *guilt.* 33 Serpents,
[y]brood[5] of vipers! How can you escape the
condemnation of hell? 34 [z]Therefore, indeed, I send you prophets, wise men, and
scribes: [a]*some* of them you will kill and crucify, and [b]*some* of them you will scourge in
your synagogues and persecute from city to
city, 35 [c]that on you may come all the righteous blood shed on the earth, [d]from the
blood of righteous Abel to [e]the blood of
Zechariah, son of Berechiah, whom you
murdered between the temple and the altar.
36 Assuredly, I say to you, all these things
will come upon this generation.

Jesus Laments over Jerusalem

37 [f]"O Jerusalem, Jerusalem, the one who
kills the prophets [g]and stones those who are
sent to her! How often [h]I wanted to gather
your children together, as a hen gathers her
chicks [i]under *her* wings, but you were not

20 [1] Swears an oath
21 [p] 1 Kin. 8:13; 2 Chr. 6:2; Ps. 26:8; 132:14 [2] M *dwelt*
22 [q] Ps. 11:4; Is. 66:1; Matt. 5:34; Acts 7:49
23 [r] Matt. 23:13; Luke 11:42; 18:12 [s] [1 Sam. 15:22; Hos. 6:6; Mic. 6:8]; Matt. 9:13; 12:7
25 [t] Mark 7:4; Luke 11:39 [3] M *unrighteousness*
27 [u] Luke 11:44; Acts 23:3
29 [v] Luke 11:47, 48 [4] *decorate*
31 [w] Matt. 23:34, 37; [Acts 7:51, 52]; 1 Thess. 2:15
32 [x] Gen. 15:16; [1 Thess. 2:16]
33 [y] Matt. 3:7; 12:34; Luke 3:7 [5] *offspring*
34 [z] Matt. 21:34, 35; Luke 11:49 [a] John 16:2; Acts 7:54-60; 22:19 [b] Matt. 10:17; Acts 5:40; 2 Cor. 11:24, 25
35 [c] Rev. 18:24 [d] Gen. 4:8; Heb. 11:4; 1 John 3:12 [e] 2 Chr. 24:20, 21
37 [f] Luke 13:34, 35 [g] 2 Chr. 24:20, 21; 36:15, 16; Neh. 9:26; Matt. 21:35, 36 [h] Deut. 32:11, 12; Matt. 11:28-30 [i] Ps. 17:8; 91:4; Is. 49:5

23:23 tithe of mint and anise and cummin. Garden herbs, not really the kind of farm produce that the tithe was designed to cover (Lev. 27:30). But the Pharisees fastidiously weighed out a tenth of every herb, perhaps even counting individual anise seeds. Jesus' point, however, was not to condemn their observance of the law's fine points. The problem was that they "neglected the weightier *matters*" of justice and mercy and faith—the moral principles underlying all the laws. They were satisfied with their focus on the incidentals and externals but willfully resisted the spiritual meaning of the law. He told them they should have concentrated on those larger issues "without leaving the others undone."

23:24 strain out a gnat and swallow a camel. Some Pharisees would strain their beverages through a fine cloth to make sure they did not inadvertently swallow a gnat—the smallest of unclean animals (Lev. 11:23). The camel was the largest of all the unclean animals (Lev. 11:4).

23:25 you cleanse the outside. The Pharisees' focus on external issues lay at the heart of their error. Who would want to drink from a cup that had been washed on the outside but was still filthy inside? Yet the Pharisees lived their lives as if external appearance were more important than internal reality. That was the very essence of their hypocrisy, and Jesus rebuked them for it repeatedly (*see notes on 5:20; 16:12*).

23:27 whitewashed tombs. Tombs were regularly whitewashed to make them stand out. Accidentally touching or stepping on a grave caused ceremonial uncleanness (Num. 19:16). A freshly whitewashed tomb would be brilliantly white and clean-looking—and sometimes spectacularly ornate. But the inside was full of defilement and decay. Contrast Jesus' words here and in Luke 11:44.

23:30 we would not have been partakers. A ridiculous claim to self-righteousness when they were already plotting the murder of the Messiah (cf. John 11:47-53).

23:34 prophets, wise men, and scribes. I.e., the disciples, as well as the prophets, evangelists, and pastors who followed them (cf. Eph. 4:11).

23:35 Abel...Zechariah. The first and last OT martyrs, respectively. **son of Berechiah.** (Zech. 1:1). The OT does not record how he died. However, the death of another Zechariah, son of Jehoiada, is recorded in 2 Chr. 24:20,21. He was stoned in the court of the temple, exactly as Jesus describes here. All the best manuscripts of Matthew contain the phrase "Zechariah, son of Berechiah" (though it does not appear in Luke 11:51). Some have suggested that the Zechariah in 2 Chr. 24 was actually a grandson of Jehoiada, and that his father's name was also Berechiah. But there is no difficulty if we simply take Jesus' words at face value and accept His infallible testimony that Zechariah the prophet was martyred between the temple and the altar, in a way very similar to how the earlier Zechariah was killed.

23:36 this generation. Historically, this was the generation that experienced the utter destruction of Jerusalem and the burning of the temple in A.D. 70. Jesus' lament over Jerusalem and His removal of the blessing of God from the temple (vv. 37,38) strongly suggest that the sacking of Jerusalem in A.D. 70 was the judgment He was speaking about. *See notes on 22:7; 24:2; Luke 19:43.*

23:37 I wanted...but you were not willing! God is utterly sovereign and therefore fully capable of bringing to pass whatever He desires (cf. Is. 46:10)—including the salvation of whomever He chooses (Eph. 1:4,5). Yet, He sometimes expresses a wish for that which He does not sovereignly bring to pass (cf. Gen. 6:6; Deut. 5:29; Ps. 81:13; Is. 48:18). Such expressions in no way suggest a limitation on the sovereignty of God or imply any actual change in Him (Num. 23:19). But these statements do reveal essential aspects of the divine character: He is full of compassion, sincerely good to all, desirous of good, not evil—and therefore not delighting in the destruction of the wicked (Ezek. 18:32; 33:11). While affirming God's sovereignty, one must understand His

willing! 38 See! Your house is left to you desolate; 39 for I say to you, you shall see Me no
more till you say, [j]*'Blessed is He who comes
in the name of the LORD!'"*

The Temple to Be Destroyed
Mark 13:1, 2; Luke 21:5, 6

24 Then [a]Jesus went out and departed
from the temple, and His disciples
came up to show Him the buildings of the
temple. 2 And Jesus said to them, "Do you
not see all these things? Assuredly, I say to
you, [b]not *one* stone shall be left here upon
another, that shall not be thrown down."

The Disciples' Two Questions
Mark 13:3, 4; Luke 21:7

3 Now as He sat on the Mount of Olives,
[c]the disciples came to Him privately, saying, [d]"Tell us, when will these things be?
And what *will be* the sign of Your coming,
and of the end of the age?"

The Tribulation—Mark 13:5-23; Luke 21:5-24

4 And Jesus answered and said to them:
[e]"Take heed that no one deceives you.
5 For [f]many will come in My name, saying,
'I am the Christ,' [g]and will deceive many.
6 And you will hear of [h]wars and rumors
of wars. See that you are not troubled; for
[1]all *these things* must come to pass, but the
end is not yet. 7 For [i]nation will rise
against nation, and kingdom against kingdom. And there will be [j]famines, [2]pesti-
lences, and earthquakes in various places.
8 All these *are* the beginning of sorrows.
9 [k]"Then they will deliver you up to
tribulation and kill you, and you will be
hated by all nations for My name's sake.
10 And then many will be offended, will
betray one another, and will hate one another. 11 Then [l]many false prophets will
rise up and [m]deceive many. 12 And be-

39 [j]Ps. 118:26; Matt. 21:9

CHAPTER 24

1 [a]Mark 13:1; Luke 21:5-36
2 [b]1 Kin. 9:7; Mic. 3:12; Luke 19:44
3 [c]Mark 13:3 [d][Matt. 24:27, 37, 39; Luke 17:20-37; 1 Thess. 5:1-3]
4 [e]Eph. 5:6; [Col. 2:8, 18; 2 Thess. 2:3; 1 John 4:1-3]
5 [f]Jer. 14:14; John 5:43; Acts 5:36; [1 John 2:18; 4:3] [g]Matt. 24:11
6 [h][Rev. 6:2-4] [1]NU omits *all*
7 [i]2 Chr. 15:6; Is. 19:2; Hag. 2:22; Zech. 14:13 [j]Acts 11:28; Rev. 6:5, 6 [2]NU omits *pestilences*
9 [k]Matt. 10:17; Luke 21:12; [John 16:2]; Acts 4:2, 3; Rev. 2:10
11 [l]Acts 20:29; 2 Pet. 2:1; Rev. 13:11; 19:20 [m][1 Tim. 4:1]

pleas for the repentance of the reprobate as well meant appeals—and His goodness toward the wicked as a genuine mercy designed to provoke them to repentance (Rom. 2:4). The emotion displayed by Christ here (and in all similar passages, such as Luke 19:41) is obviously a deep, sincere passion. All Christ's feelings must be in perfect harmony with the divine will (cf. John 8:29)—and therefore these lamentations should not be thought of as mere exhibitions of His humanity.

23:38 Your house is left to you desolate. A few days earlier, Christ had referred to the temple as His Father's "house" (21:13). But the blessing and glory of God were being removed from Israel (see 1 Sam. 4:21). When Christ "departed from the temple" (24:1), the glory of God went with Him. Ezekiel 11:23 described Ezekiel's vision of the departure of the Shekinah glory in His day. The glory left the temple and stood on the Mt. of Olives, (*see notes on 24:3; Luke 19:29*) exactly the same route Christ followed here (cf. 24:3).

23:39 you shall see Me no more. Christ's public teaching ministry was over. He withdrew from national Israel until the time yet future when they will recognize Him as Messiah (Rom. 11:23-26). Then Christ quoted from Ps. 118:26.

24:1–25:46 This is the last of the 5 discourses Matthew features (see Introduction: Historical and Theological Themes). It is known as the Olivet Discourse, and it contains some of the most important prophetic material in all of Scripture.

24:1 the buildings of the temple. This temple was begun by Herod the Great in 20 B.C. (*see note on 2:1*) and was still under construction when the Romans destroyed it in A.D. 70 (*see note on v. 2*). At the time of Jesus' ministry, the temple was one of the most impressive structures in the world, made of massive blocks of stone bedecked with gold ornamentation. Some of the stones in the temple complex measured 40x12x12 ft. and were expertly quarried to fit perfectly against one another. The temple buildings were made of gleaming white marble, and the whole eastern wall of the large main structure was covered with gold plates that reflected the morning sun, making a spectacle that was visible for miles. The entire temple mount had been enlarged by Herod's engineers, by means of large retaining walls and vaulted chambers on the S side and SE corner. By this means the large courtyard area atop the temple mount was effectively doubled. The whole temple complex was magnificent by any standard. The disciples' conversation here may have been prompted by Jesus' words in 23:38. They were undoubtedly wondering how a site so spectacular could be left "desolate."

24:2 not *one* stone shall be left here. These words were literally fulfilled in A.D. 70. Titus, the Roman general, built large wooden scaffolds around the walls of the temple buildings, piled them high with wood and other flammable items, and set them ablaze. The heat from the fires was so intense that the stones crumbled. The rubble was then sifted to retrieve the melted gold, and the remaining ruins were "thrown down" into the Kidron Valley. *See notes on 22:7; Luke 19:43.*

24:3 Mount of Olives. The hill directly opposite the temple, across the Kidron Valley to the E (*see note on Luke 19:29*). This spot affords the best panoramic view of Jerusalem. At the base of this mountain is Gethsemane (*see note on 26:36*). **what *will be* the sign of Your coming.** Luke 19:11 records that the disciples still "thought the kingdom of God would appear immediately." The destruction of the temple (v. 2) did not fit the eschatological scheme they envisioned, so they asked for clarification. Jesus addressed their questions in reverse order, describing the prophetic sign of His coming (actually a series of signs) in vv. 4-35 and then addressing their question about the timing of these events beginning in v. 36. When they asked about His coming (Gr., *parousia;* lit. "presence"), they did not envision a second coming in the far-off future. They were speaking of His coming in triumph as Messiah, an event which they no doubt anticipated would occur presently. Even if they were conscious of His approaching death, which he had plainly prophesied to them on repeated occasions (*see note on 20:19*), they could not have anticipated His ascension to heaven and the long intervening church age. However, when Jesus used the term *parousia* in His discourse, He used it in the technical sense as a reference to His second coming.

24:6 but the end is not yet. False prophets, as well as wars and rumors of wars, characterize the whole of the present age, but will escalate toward the end (cf. 2 Tim. 3:13).

24:8 sorrows. The word means "birth pangs." Famines, earthquakes, and conflicts have always characterized life in a fallen world; but by calling these things "the beginning" of labor pains, He indicated that things will get notably and remarkably worse at the end of the era as these unique tribulations signal the soon arrival of Messiah to judge sinful humanity and set up His millennial kingdom. Cf. 1 Thess. 5:3; Rev. 6:1-17; 8:1–9:21; 16:1-21; *see note on v. 14.*

24:9 deliver you up. *See note on 10:17.*

24:10 many will be offended. Lit. "caused to stumble"—suggesting professing believers who fall away—and even turn against "one another" in shocking acts of spiritual treachery. Those who fall

cause lawlessness will abound, the love of
many will grow [n]cold. **13** [o]But he who endures to the end shall be saved. **14** And this
[p]gospel of the kingdom [q]will be preached
in all the world as a witness to all the nations, and then the end will come.
15 [r]"Therefore when you see the [s]*'abomination of desolation,'* spoken of by Daniel
the prophet, standing in the holy place"
[t](whoever reads, let him understand),
16 "then let those who are in Judea flee to
the mountains. **17** Let him who is on the
housetop not go down to take anything
out of his house. **18** And let him who is in
the field not go back to get his clothes.
19 But [u]woe to those who are pregnant and
to those who are nursing babies in those
days! **20** And pray that your flight may not
be in winter or on the Sabbath. **21** For [v]then
there will be great tribulation, such as has
not been since the beginning of the world
until this time, no, nor ever shall be. **22** And
unless those days were shortened, no flesh

12 [n][2 Thess. 2:3; 2 Tim. 3:1-3] **13** [o]Matt. 10:22; Mark 13:13 **14** [p]Matt. 4:23 [q]Rom. 10:18; Col. 1:6, 23 **15** [r]Mark 13:14; Luke 21:20; [John 11:48]; Acts 6:13; 21:28 [s]Dan. 9:27; 11:31; 12:11 [t]Dan. 9:23 **19** [u]Luke 23:29 **21** [v]Dan. 9:26 **22** [w]Is. 65:8, 9; [Zech. 14:2] [3]*chosen ones'* **23** [x]Mark 13:21; Luke 17:23 **24** [y]Deut. 13:1; John 4:48; [2 Thess. 2:9]; Rev. 13:13 [z][John 6:37; Rom. 8:28; 2 Tim. 2:19] **27** [a]Luke 17:24 **28** [b]Job 39:30; Ezek. 39:17; Hab. 1:8; Luke 17:37 **29** [c][Dan. 7:11] [d]Is. 13:10; 24:23; Ezek. 32:7; Joel 2:10, 31; 3:15; Amos 5:20; 8:9; Zeph. 1:15; Matt. 24:29-35; Acts 2:20; Rev. 6:12-17; 8:12

would be saved; [w]but for the [3]elect's sake
those days will be shortened.
23 [x]"Then if anyone says to you, 'Look,
here *is* the Christ!' or 'There!' do not believe
it. **24** For [y]false christs and false prophets
will rise and show great signs and wonders
to deceive, [z]if possible, even the elect.
25 See, I have told you beforehand.
26 "Therefore if they say to you, 'Look,
He is in the desert!' do not go out; *or* 'Look,
He is in the inner rooms!' do not believe *it.*

The Second Coming
Mark 13:24-27; Luke 21:25-28

27 [a]For as the lightning comes from the east
and flashes to the west, so also will the
coming of the Son of Man be. **28** [b]For wherever the carcass is, there the eagles will be
gathered together.
29 [c]"Immediately after the tribulation of
those days [d]the sun will be darkened, and
the moon will not give its light; the stars
will fall from heaven, and the powers of

away in such a manner give evidence that they never were true believers at all (*see note on v. 13*).

24:13 endures to the end...be saved. Cf. 10:22. The ones who persevere are the same ones who are saved—not the ones whose love grows cold (v. 12). This does not suggest that our perseverance secures our salvation. Scripture everywhere teaches precisely the opposite: God, as part of His saving work, secures our perseverance. True believers are "are kept by the power of God through faith for salvation" (1 Pet. 1:5). The guarantee of our perseverance is built into the New Covenant promise. God says: "I will put My fear in their hearts so that they will not depart from Me" (Jer. 32:40). Those who do fall away from Christ give conclusive proof that they were never truly believers to begin with (1 John 2:19). To say that God secures our perseverance is not to say that we are passive in the process, however. He keeps us "through faith" (1 Pet. 1:5)—our faith. Scripture sometimes calls us to hold fast to our faith (Heb. 10:23; Rev. 3:11) or warns us against falling away (Heb. 10:26-29). Such admonitions do not negate the many promises that true believers will persevere (John 10:28,29; Rom. 8:38,39; 1 Cor. 1:8,9; Phil. 1:6). Rather, the warnings and pleas are among the means God uses to secure our perseverance in the faith. Notice that the warnings and the promises often appear side by side. For example, when Jude urges believers, "keep yourselves in the love of God" (Jude 21), he immediately points them to God, "who is able to keep you from stumbling" (Jude 24).

24:14 preached in all the world. Despite all the tribulations that would come—the deception of false teachers, the wars, persecutions, natural disasters, defections from Christ, and all the obstacles to the spread of the gospel—the message ultimately penetrates every part of the globe. God is never without a witness, and He will proclaim the gospel from heaven itself if necessary (cf. Rev. 14:6). **and then the end will come.** "The end" refers to the final, excruciating birth pangs (*see note on v. 8*). This is how Christ characterizes the time of Great Tribulation described in the verses that follow.

24:15 *abomination of desolation.* *See notes on Daniel 9:27; 11:31.* This phrase originally referred to the desecration of the temple by Antiochus Epiphanes, king of Syria in the second century B.C. Antiochus invaded Jerusalem in 168 B.C., made the altar into a shrine to Zeus, and even sacrificed pigs on it. However, Jesus clearly was looking toward a yet-future "abomination of desolation." Some suggest that this prophecy was fulfilled in A.D. 70 when Titus invaded Jerusalem and destroyed the temple (*see note on v. 2*). However, the Apostle Paul saw a still-future fulfillment (2 Thess. 2:3,4), as did John (Rev. 13:14,15)—when the Antichrist sets up an image in the temple during the future tribulation. Christ's words here therefore look beyond the events of A.D. 70 to a time of even greater global cataclysm that will immediately precede His coming (cf. vv. 29-31).

24:16 the mountains. Probably a reference to the region SE of Jerusalem, particularly the Dead Sea area, where there are many caves and places of refuge. David hid from Saul in this area (1 Sam. 23:29). This would also include the hills of Moab and Edom.

24:21 great tribulation. The words "has not been" and "nor ever shall be"—along with the description that follows—identify this as the yet-future time in which God's wrath shall be poured out upon the earth (*see note on Rev. 7:14*). Jesus' descriptions of the cataclysms that follow closely resemble the outpouring of divine wrath described in the bowl judgments of Rev. 16 and His subsequent appearing in Rev. 19 (*see note on v. 30*).

24:22 those days will be shortened. If the afflictions of this time were to continue, "no flesh would be saved," i.e., no one would survive. But "for the elect's sake" (so that redeemed people do not suffer more than they can bear) the time is "shortened"—i.e., held short of total destruction. Both Dan. 7:25 and Rev. 12:14 (*see notes there*) suggest that the actual length of time the Beast will be permitted to terrorize the world is fixed at 3 ½ years.

24:24 to deceive, if possible, even the elect. This clearly implies that such deception is not possible (John 10:4,5).

24:26 do not believe *it*. No one should consider the claims of self-styled messiahs because all of them are false. When Christ returns, no one will miss it (vv. 27,28).

24:28 the eagles will be gathered together. The location of a carcass is visible from great distances because of the circling carrion birds overhead (cf. Job 39:27-30). Similarly, Christ's return will be clearly evident to all near and far. The same point is made by the lightning in v. 27. The eagle-carcass imagery here also speaks of the judgment that will accompany His return (Rev. 19:21).

24:29 the sun will be darkened. Such phenomena are a common feature of Day of the Lord prophecy (see Is. 13:9,10; Ezek. 32:7,8; Joel 2:10,31; 3:15; Amos 8:9). The ultimate fulfillment of these prophe-

the heavens will be shaken. **30** [e]Then the
sign of the Son of Man will appear in heav-
en, [f]and then all the tribes of the earth will
mourn, and they will see the Son of Man
coming on the clouds of heaven with
power and great glory. **31** [g]And He will
send His angels with a great sound of a
trumpet, and they will gather together His
[4]elect from the four winds, from one end of
heaven to the other.

Parable of the Fig Tree
Mark 13:28-31; Luke 21:29-33

32 "Now learn [h]this parable from the fig
tree: When its branch has already become
tender and puts forth leaves, you know
that summer *is* near. **33** So you also, when
you see all these things, know [i]that [5]it is
near—at the doors! **34** Assuredly, I say to
you, [j]this generation will by no means pass
away till all these things take place.
35 [k]Heaven and earth will pass away, but
My words will by no means pass away.

Illustration of the Days of Noah
Mark 13:32-37; Luke 21:34-36

36 [l]"But of that day and hour no one
knows, not even the angels of [6]heaven,
[m]but My Father only. **37** But as the days of
Noah *were,* so also will the coming of the
Son of Man be. **38** [n]For as in the days before the flood, they were eating and drinking, marrying and giving in marriage,
until the day that Noah entered the ark,
39 and did not know until the flood came
and took them all away, so also will the
coming of the Son of Man be. **40** [o]Then two
men will be in the field: one will be taken
and the other left. **41** Two *women will be*
grinding at the mill: one will be taken and
the other left. **42** [p]Watch therefore, for you
do not know what [7]hour your Lord is
coming. **43** [q]But know this, that if the master of the house had known what [8]hour
the thief would come, he would have
watched and not allowed his house to be
broken into. **44** [r]Therefore you also be
ready, for the Son of Man is coming at an
hour you do not expect.

Illustration of the Two Servants
Luke 12:41-48

45 [s]"Who then is a faithful and wise servant, whom his master made ruler over his
household, to give them food [9]in due season? **46** [t]Blessed *is* that servant whom his
master, when he comes, will find so doing.
47 Assuredly, I say to you that [u]he will
make him ruler over all his goods. **48** But if
that evil servant says in his heart, 'My master [v]is delaying [1]his coming,' **49** and begins to beat *his* fellow servants, and to eat
and drink with the drunkards, **50** the master of that servant will come on a day when
he is not looking for *him* and at an hour
that he is [w]not aware of, **51** and will cut
him in two and appoint *him* his portion

30 [e][Dan. 7:13, 14; Matt. 16:27; 24:3, 37, 39] [f]Zech. 12:12
31 [g]Ex. 19:16; Deut. 30:4; Is. 27:13; Zech. 9:14; [1 Cor. 15:52; 1 Thess. 4:16]; Heb. 12:19; Rev. 8:2; 11:15 [4]*chosen ones*
32 [h]Luke 21:29
33 [i][James 5:9; Rev. 3:20] [5]*Or He*
34 [j][Matt. 10:23; 16:28; 23:36]
35 [k]Ps. 102:25, 26; Is. 51:6; Mark 13:31; Luke 21:33; [1 Pet. 1:23-25; 2 Pet. 3:10]
36 [l]Mark 13:32; Acts 1:7; 1 Thess. 5:2; 2 Pet. 3:10 [m]Zech. 14:7 [6]NU adds *nor the Son*
38 [n][Gen. 6:3-5]; Luke 17:26; [1 Pet. 3:20]
40 [o]Luke 17:34
42 [p]Matt. 25:13; Luke 21:36; 1 Thess. 5:6 [7]NU *day*
43 [q]Luke 12:39; 1 Thess. 5:2; Rev. 3:3 [8]Lit. *watch of the night*
44 [r]Luke 12:35-40; [1 Thess. 5:6]
45 [s]Luke 12:42-46; [Acts 20:28] [9]*at the right time*
46 [t]Rev. 16:15
47 [u]Matt. 25:21, 23; Luke 22:29
48 [v][2 Pet. 3:4-9] [1]NU omits *his coming*
50 [w]Mark 13:32

cies takes place during the time of the Beast's reign (Rev. 6:12,13; 8:12).

24:30 the sign of the Son of Man. I.e., the Son of Man Himself is the sign. The events described here precisely parallel the description in Dan. 7:13; Rev. 19:11-21. **all the tribes of the earth will mourn.** I.e., over their own rebellion. Israel in particular will mourn over their rejection of the Messiah (cf. Zech 12:10-12).

24:31 from one end of heaven to the other. All the "elect" from heaven and earth are gathered and assembled before Christ. This is the culmination of world history, ushering in the millennial reign of Christ (cf. Rev. 20:4).

24:32 parable from the fig tree. When the fig branch "puts forth leaves," only a short time remains until summer. Likewise, when the final labor pains begin (*see note on v. 14*), Christ's return "is near; it is at the doors!" (v. 33).

24:34 this generation. This cannot refer to the generation living at that time of Christ, for "all these things"—the abomination of desolation (v. 15), the persecutions and judgments (vv. 17-22), the false prophets (vv. 23-26), the signs in the heavens (vv. 27-29), Christ's final return (v. 30), and the gathering of the elect (v. 31)—did not "take place" in their lifetime. It seems best to interpret Christ's words as a reference to the generation alive at the time when those final hard labor pains begin (*see note on v. 14*). This would fit with the lesson of the fig tree, which stresses the short span of time in which these things will occur (*see note on v. 32*).

24:35 Heaven and earth will pass away. Cf. Is. 24:18-20. *See notes on 2 Pet. 3:10-13.*

24:36 day and hour. *See note on Mark 13:32.* The disciples wanted to fix the precise time, but this was not for them to know (Acts 1:7). Christ's emphasis instead is on faithfulness, watchfulness, stewardship, expectancy, and preparedness. These are the lessons He taught in the parables that immediately follow.

24:37 as the days of Noah *were.* Jesus' emphasis here is not so much on the extreme wickedness of Noah's day (Gen. 6:5), but on the people's preoccupation with mundane matters of everyday life ("eating and drinking, marrying and giving in marriage"—v. 38), when judgment fell suddenly. They had received warnings, in the form of Noah's preaching (2 Pet. 2:5)—and the ark itself, which was a testimony to the judgment that was to come. But they were unconcerned about such matters and therefore were swept away unexpectedly in the midst of their daily activities.

24:40,41 one will be taken. I.e., taken in judgment (cf. v. 39) just as in Noah's day ("took them"; v. 39). This is clearly not a reference to the catching away of believers described in 1 Thess. 4:16,17.

24:43 the thief. As no one knows what hour the thief will come, no one knows the hour of the Lord's return or the Day of the Lord that accompanies His coming (cf. 1 Thess. 5:2; 2 Pet. 3:10). But the believer is to be ready at all times.

24:44 at an hour you do not expect. The parables that follow teach Christ's followers to be ready in case He comes sooner than anticipated (vv. 43-51); and also to be prepared in case He delays longer than expected (25:1-13).

24:45-51 The evil servant represents an unbeliever who refuses to take seriously the promise of Christ's return (cf. 2 Pet. 3:4). Though he is an unbeliever (as demonstrated by his punishment—*see note on 22:13*), he is nonetheless accountable to Christ for the stewardship

with the hypocrites. [x]There shall be weeping and gnashing of teeth.

Parable of the Ten Virgins

25 "Then the kingdom of heaven shall
be likened to ten virgins who took
their lamps and went out to meet [a]the
bridegroom. 2 [b]Now five of them were
wise, and five *were* foolish. 3 Those who
were foolish took their lamps and took no
oil with them, 4 but the wise took oil in
their vessels with their lamps. 5 But while
the bridegroom was delayed, [c]they all
slumbered and slept.
6 "And at midnight [d]a cry was *heard:* 'Behold, the bridegroom [1]is coming; go out to
meet him!' 7 Then all those virgins arose
and [e]trimmed their lamps. 8 And the foolish said to the wise, 'Give us *some* of your
oil, for our lamps are going out.' 9 But the
wise answered, saying, '*No,* lest there
should not be enough for us and you; but
go rather to those who sell, and buy for
yourselves.' 10 And while they went to
buy, the bridegroom came, and those who
were ready went in with him to the wedding; and [f]the door was shut.
11 "Afterward the other virgins came
also, saying, [g]'Lord, Lord, open to us!'
12 But he answered and said, 'Assuredly, I
say to you, [h]I do not know you.'
13 [i]"Watch therefore, for you [j]know neither the day nor the hour [2]in which the
Son of Man is coming.

Parable of the Talents

14 [k]"For *the kingdom of heaven is* [l]like a
man traveling to a far country, *who* called
his own servants and delivered his goods
to them. 15 And to one he gave five talents,
to another two, and to another one, [m]to
each according to his own ability; and immediately he went on a journey. 16 Then he
who had received the five talents went and
traded with them, and made another five
talents. 17 And likewise he who *had received*
two gained two more also. 18 But he who
had received one went and dug in the
ground, and hid his lord's money. 19 After
a long time the lord of those servants came
and settled accounts with them.
20 "So he who had received five talents
came and brought five other talents, saying, 'Lord, you delivered to me five talents;
look, I have gained five more talents besides them.' 21 His lord said to him, 'Well
done, good and faithful servant; you were
[n]faithful over a few things, [o]I will make
you ruler over many things. Enter into [p]the
joy of your lord.' 22 He also who had received two talents came and said, 'Lord,
you delivered to me two talents; look, I
have gained two more talents besides
them.' 23 His lord said to him, [q]'Well *done,*
good and faithful servant; you have been
faithful over a few things, I will make you
ruler over many things. Enter into [r]the joy
of your lord.'
24 "Then he who had received the one
talent came and said, 'Lord, I knew you to
be a hard man, reaping where you have
not sown, and gathering where you have
not scattered seed. 25 And I was afraid, and
went and hid your talent in the ground.
Look, *there* you have *what is* yours.'
26 "But his lord answered and said to
him, 'You [s]wicked and lazy servant, you
knew that I reap where I have not sown,
and gather where I have not scattered seed.
27 So you ought to have deposited my

51 [x] Matt. 8:12; 25:30

CHAPTER 25

1 [a] [Eph. 5:29, 30; Rev. 19:7; 21:2, 9]
2 [b] Matt. 13:47; 22:10
5 [c] 1 Thess. 5:6
6 [d] [Matt. 24:31; 1 Thess. 4:16] [1] NU omits *is coming*
7 [e] Luke 12:35
10 [f] [Matt. 7:21]; Luke 13:25
11 [g] [Matt. 7:21-23; Luke 13:25-30]
12 [h] [Ps. 5:5; Hab. 1:13; John 9:31]
13 [i] Mark 13:35; [Luke 21:36]; 1 Thess. 5:6 [j] Matt. 24:36, 42 [2] NU omits the rest of v. 13.
14 [k] Luke 19:12-27 [l] Matt. 21:33
15 [m] [Rom. 12:6; 1 Cor. 12:7, 11, 29; Eph. 4:11]
21 [n] [Luke 16:10; 1 Cor. 4:2; 2 Tim. 4:7, 8] [o] [Matt. 24:47; 25:34, 46; Luke 12:44; 22:29, 30; Rev. 3:21; 21:7] [p] [2 Tim. 2:12; Heb. 12:2; 1 Pet. 1:8]
23 [q] Matt. 24:45, 47; 25:21 [r] [Ps. 16:11; John 15:10, 11]
26 [s] Matt. 18:32; Luke 19:22

of his time. Jesus was teaching that every person in the world holds his life, natural abilities, wealth, and possessions in trust from God and must give account of how these things are used.

24:51 weeping and gnashing of teeth. *See note on 22:13.*

25:1-13 The parable of the 10 virgins is given to underscore the importance of being ready for Christ's return in any event—even if He delays longer than expected. For when He does return, there will be no second chances for the unprepared (vv. 11,12).

25:1 ten virgins. I.e., bridesmaids. The wedding would begin at the bride's house when the bridegroom arrived to observe the wedding ritual. Then a procession would follow as the bridegroom took the bride to his house for the completion of festivities. For a night wedding, "lamps," which were actually torches, were needed for the procession.

25:14-30 The parable of the talents illustrates the tragedy of wasted opportunity. The man who goes on the journey represents Christ, and the servants represent professing believers given different levels of responsibility. Faithfulness is what he demands of them (*see note on v. 23*), but the parable suggests that all who are faithful will be fruitful to some degree. The fruitless person is unmasked as a hypocrite and utterly destroyed (v. 30).

25:15 talents. A talent was a measure of weight, not a specific coin, so that a talent of gold was more valuable than a talent of silver. A talent of silver (the word translated "money" in v. 18 is lit. silver) was a considerable sum of money. The modern meaning of the word "talent," denoting a natural ability, stems from the fact that this parable is erroneously applied to the stewardship of one's natural gifts.

25:23 the joy of your lord. Both the man with 5 talents and the man with two received exactly the same reward, indicating that the reward is based on faithfulness, not results.

25:24 a hard man. His characterization of the master maligns the man as a cruel and ruthless opportunist, "reaping and gathering" what he had no right to claim as his own. This slothful servant does not represent a genuine believer, for it is obvious that this man had no true knowledge of the master.

25:26 you knew that I reap where I have not sown. In repeating the servant's charge against him, the master was not acknowledging that it was true. He was allowing the man's own words to condemn him. If the servant really believed the master to be the kind of man he portrayed, that was all the more reason for him not to be slothful. His accusation against the master—even if it had been true—did not justify his own laziness.

money with the bankers, and at my coming
I would have received back my own with
interest. 28 So take the talent from him, and
give *it* to him who has ten talents.
29 [t]'For to everyone who has, more will
be given, and he will have abundance; but
from him who does not have, even what he
has will be taken away. 30 And cast the unprofitable servant [u]into the outer darkness.
[v]There will be weeping and [w]gnashing of
teeth.'

Judgement of the Gentiles

31 [x]"When the Son of Man comes in His
glory, and all the [3]holy angels with Him,
then He will sit on the throne of His glory.
32 [y]All the nations will be gathered before
Him, and [z]He will separate them one from
another, as a shepherd divides *his* sheep
from the goats. 33 And He will set the
[a]sheep on His right hand, but the goats on
the left. 34 Then the King will say to those
on His right hand, 'Come, you blessed of
My Father, [b]inherit the kingdom [c]prepared
for you from the foundation of the world:
35 [d]for I was hungry and you gave Me
food; I was thirsty and you gave Me drink;
[e]I was a stranger and you took Me in; 36 I
was [f]naked and you clothed Me; I was sick
and you visited Me; [g]I was in prison and
you came to Me.'
37 "Then the righteous will answer Him,
saying, 'Lord, when did we see You hungry
and feed *You,* or thirsty and give *You* drink?
38 When did we see You a stranger and take
You in, or naked and clothe *You?* 39 Or
when did we see You sick, or in prison, and
come to You?' 40 And the King will answer
and say to them, 'Assuredly, I say to you,
[h]inasmuch as you did *it* to one of the least
of these My brethren, you did *it* to Me.'
41 "Then He will also say to those on the
left hand, [i]'Depart from Me, you cursed,
[j]into the everlasting fire prepared for [k]the
devil and his angels: 42 for I was hungry
and you gave Me no food; I was thirsty
and you gave Me no drink; 43 I was a
stranger and you did not take Me in, naked
and you did not clothe Me, sick and in
prison and you did not visit Me.'
44 "Then they also will answer [4]Him,
saying, 'Lord, when did we see You hungry or thirsty or a stranger or naked or sick
or in prison, and did not minister to You?'
45 Then He will answer them, saying, 'Assuredly, I say to you, [l]inasmuch as you did
not do *it* to one of the least of these, you
did not do *it* to Me.' 46 And [m]these will go
away into everlasting punishment, but the
righteous into eternal life."

The Religious Leaders Plot to Kill Jesus
Mark 14:1, 2; Luke 22:1, 2

26 Now it came to pass, when Jesus
had finished all these sayings, *that*
He said to His disciples, 2 [a]"You know that

29 [t] Matt. 13:12; Mark 4:25; Luke 8:18; [John 15:2]
30 [u] Matt. 8:12; 22:13; [Luke 13:28] [v] Matt. 7:23; 8:12; 24:51 [w] Ps. 112:10
31 [x] [Zech. 14:5]; Matt. 16:27; Mark 8:38; Acts 1:11; [1 Thess. 4:16]; 2 Thess. 1:7; [Jude 14]; Rev. 1:7 [3] NU omits *holy*
32 [y] [Rom. 14:10; 2 Cor. 5:10; Rev. 20:12] [z] Ezek. 20:38
33 [a] Ps. 79:13; 100:3; [John 10:11, 27, 28]
34 [b] [Rom. 8:17; 1 Pet. 1:4, 9; Rev. 21:7] [c] Matt. 20:23; Mark 10:40; 1 Cor. 2:9; Heb. 11:16
35 [d] Is. 58:7; Ezek. 18:7, 16; [James 1:27; 2:15, 16] [e] Job 31:32; [Heb. 13:2]; 3 John 5
36 [f] Is. 58:7; Ezek. 18:7, 16; [James 2:15, 16] [g] 2 Tim. 1:16
40 [h] Prov. 14:31; Matt. 10:42; Mark 9:41; Heb. 6:10
41 [i] Ps. 6:8; Matt. 7:23; Luke 13:27 [j] Matt. 13:40, 42 [k] [2 Pet. 2:4]; Jude 6
44 [4] NU, M omit *Him*
45 [l] Prov. 14:31; Zech. 2:8; Acts 9:5
46 [m] [Dan. 12:2; John 5:29; Acts 24:15; Rom. 2:7]

CHAPTER 26 2 [a] Matt. 27:35; Mark 14:1, 2; Luke 22:1, 2; John 13:1; 19:18

25:29 to everyone who has, more will be given. See 13:12. The recipients of divine grace inherit immeasurable blessings in addition to eternal life and the favor of God (cf. Rom. 8:32). But those who despise the riches of God's goodness, forbearance, and longsuffering (Rom. 2:4), burying them in the ground and clinging instead to the paltry and transient goods of this world, will ultimately lose everything they have (cf. 6:19; John 12:25).

25:30 outer darkness...weeping and gnashing of teeth. *See note on 22:13.*

25:31 He will sit on the throne of His glory. This speaks of the earthly reign of Christ described in Rev. 20:4-6. The judgment described here in vv. 32-46 is different from the Great White Throne judgment of Rev. 20:11-15. This judgment precedes Christ's millennial reign, and the subjects seem to be only those who are alive at His coming. This is sometimes referred to as the judgment of the nations, but His verdicts address individuals in the nations, not the nations as a whole (cf. v. 46).

25:32,33 sheep. I.e., believers (10:16; Ps. 79:13; Ezek. 34). They are given the place at "His right hand"—the place of favor. **goats.** These represent unbelievers, consigned to the place of dishonor and rejection.

25:34 prepared for you. This terminology underscores that their salvation is a gracious gift of God, not something merited by the deeds described in vv. 35,36. Before "the foundation of the world," they were chosen by God and ordained to be holy (Eph. 1:4)—predestined to be conformed to Christ's image (Rom. 8:29). So the good deeds commended in vv. 35,36 are the fruit, not the root of their salvation. The deeds are not the basis for their entrance into the kingdom, but merely manifestations of God's grace in their lives. They are the objective criteria for judgment, because they are the evidence of saving faith (cf. James 2:14-26).

25:40 the least of these My brethren. This refers in particular to other disciples. Some would apply this to national Israel; others to needy people in general. But here Christ is specifically commending "those on His right" (v. 34) for the way they received His emissaries. *See note on 18:5.*

25:46 everlasting punishment...eternal life. The same Gr. word is used in both instances. The punishment of the wicked is as never-ending as the bliss of the righteous. The wicked are not given a second chance, nor are they annihilated. The punishment of the wicked dead is described throughout Scripture as "everlasting fire" (v. 41); "unquenchable fire" (3:12); "shame and everlasting contempt" (Dan. 12:2); a place where "their worm does not die, and the fire is not quenched" (Mark 9:44-49); a place of "torments" and "flame" (Luke 16:23,24); "everlasting destruction" (2 Thess. 1:9); a place of torment with "fire and brimstone" where "the smoke of their torment ascends forever and ever" (Rev. 14:10,11); and a "lake of fire and brimstone" where the wicked are "tormented day and night forever and ever" (Rev. 20:10). Here Jesus indicates that the punishment itself is everlasting—not merely the smoke and flames. The wicked are forever subject to the fury and the wrath of God. They consciously suffer shame and contempt and the assaults of an accusing conscience—along with the fiery wrath of an offended deity—for all of eternity. Even hell will acknowledge the perfect justice of God (Ps. 76:10); those who are there will know that their punishment is just and that they alone are to blame (cf. Deut. 32:3-5).

after two days is the Passover, and the Son
of Man will be delivered up to be crucified."
3 [b]Then the chief priests, [1]the scribes,
and the elders of the people assembled at
the palace of the high priest, who was
called Caiaphas, 4 and [c]plotted to take Jesus by [2]trickery and kill *Him.* 5 But they
said, "Not during the feast, lest there be an
uproar among the [d]people."

3 [b] Ps. 2:2; John 11:47; Acts 4:25 [1] NU omits *the scribes*
4 [c] John 11:47; Acts 4:25-28 [2] *deception*
5 [d] Matt. 21:26
6 [e] Matt. 8:2; Mark 14:3-9; Luke 7:37-39; John 11:1, 2; 12:1-8
8 [f] John 12:4

Mary Anoints Jesus for Burial
Mark 14:3-9; John 12:2-8

6 And when Jesus was in [e]Bethany at the
house of Simon the leper, 7 a woman came
to Him having an alabaster flask of very
costly fragrant oil, and she poured *it* on His
head as He sat *at the table.* 8 [f]But when His
disciples saw *it,* they were indignant, saying, "Why this waste? 9 For this fragrant oil

26:2 Passover. This was God's chosen time for Christ to die. He was the antitype to which the Passover Lamb had always referred. Christ had always avoided His enemies' plots to kill Him (Luke 4:29,30; John 5:18; 10:39), but now it was His time (*see note on v. 5*). The true Lamb of God would take away the sin of the world (John 1:29).

26:3 Caiaphas. Caiaphas served as High-Priest from A.D. 18 to 36, an unusually long tenure for anyone in that role. His longevity suggests he had a close relationship with both Rome and the Herodian dynasty. He was son-in-law to his predecessor, Annas (John 18:13; *see note on Luke 3:2*). He controlled the temple and no doubt personally profited from the corrupt merchandising that was taking place there (*see note on 21:12*). His enmity against Jesus seems intensely personal and especially malevolent; every time he appears in Scripture, he is seeking Jesus' destruction.

26:5 Not during the feast. The Jewish leaders, who had been eager to kill him for so long, decided to postpone their plot until a more politically opportune time. But they could not; God's chosen time had come (*see notes on vv. 2,18,54*).

26:6 Simon the leper. Simon is mentioned nowhere else in Scripture. He was almost certainly someone whom Jesus had healed of leprosy, for lepers were deemed unclean and therefore not permitted to socialize or even live in cities. *See note on Lev. 13:2* for a discussion on leprosy.

26:7 an alabaster flask of very costly fragrant oil. Mark sets the value at "more than three hundred denarii" (*see note on Mark 14:5*), nearly a year's wages—very costly indeed. Even the expensive flask was broken (Mark 14:3), making the act that much more costly. "Alabaster" was a fine variety of marble, quarried in Egypt, which could be carved into delicate containers for storing costly perfumes. John tells us this woman was Mary, sister of Martha and Lazarus (John 12:3), thus Martha and Mary were evidently serving the meal for Simon the leper. Matthew and Mark mention that she anointed his head. John adds that she anointed His feet and wiped them with her hair. A similar act of worship is related in Luke 7:36-38, but the differences in timing, location, and other details make it clear that the two occasions were different.

26:8 they were indignant. John says Judas was the spokesman who voiced the complaint, and that he did it for hypocritical reasons (John 12:4-6). Evidently the other disciples, being undiscerning, were quick to voice sympathy with Judas' protest.

Christ's Trials, Crucifixion, and Resurrection

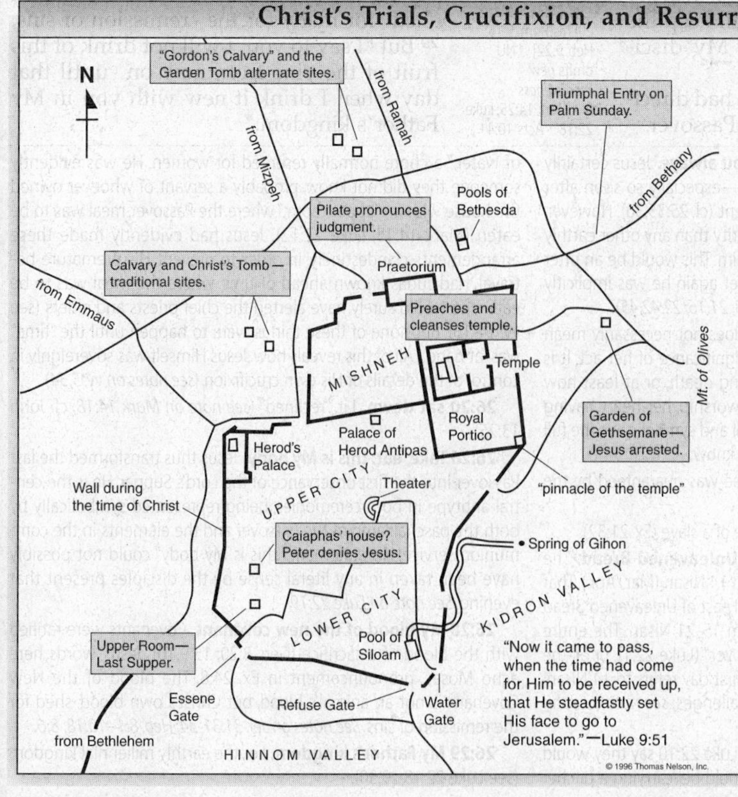

The events of Passion Week occurred in the city of Jerusalem, beginning with Jesus' Triumphal Entry on Palm Sunday. The accompanying map details the chronology of events. However, after His resurrection, Jesus appeared to His disciples and over five hundred other believers throughout the entire regions of Judea and Galilee.

might have been sold for much and given
to *the* poor."
10 But when Jesus was aware of *it,* He
said to them, "Why do you trouble the
woman? For she has done a good work for
Me. 11 [g]For you have the poor with you always, but [h]Me you do not have always.
12 For in pouring this fragrant oil on My
body, she did *it* for My [i]burial. 13 Assuredly, I say to you, wherever this gospel
is preached in the whole world, what this
woman has done will also be told as a
memorial to her."

Judas Agrees to Betray Jesus
Mark 14:10, 11; Luke 22:3-6

14 [j]Then one of the twelve, called [k]Judas
Iscariot, went to the chief priests 15 and
said, [l]"What are you willing to give me if I
deliver Him to you?" And they counted out
to him thirty pieces of silver. 16 So from that
time he sought opportunity to betray Him.

The Passover Is Prepared
Mark 14:12-16; Luke 22:7-13

17 [m]Now on the first *day of the Feast* of
Unleavened Bread the disciples came to Jesus, saying to Him, "Where do You want
us to prepare for You to eat the Passover?"
18 And He said, "Go into the city to a
certain man, and say to him, 'The Teacher
says, [n]"My time is at hand; I will keep the
Passover at your house with My disciples." ' "
19 So the disciples did as Jesus had directed them; and they prepared the Passover.

The Passover Is Celebrated
Mark 14:17-21; Luke 22:14, 21-23; John 13:21, 22

20 [o]When evening had come, He sat
down with the twelve. 21 Now as they
were eating, He said, "Assuredly, I say to
you, one of you will [p]betray Me."
22 And they were exceedingly sorrowful, and each of them began to say to Him,
"Lord, is it I?"
23 He answered and said, [q]"He who
dipped *his* hand with Me in the dish will
betray Me. 24 The Son of Man indeed goes
just [r]as it is written of Him, but [s]woe to
that man by whom the Son of Man is betrayed! [t]It would have been good for that
man if he had not been born."
25 Then Judas, who was betraying Him,
answered and said, "Rabbi, is it I?"
He said to him, "You have said it."

The Lord's Supper Is Instituted
Mark 14:22-25; Luke 22:19, 20; 1 Cor. 11:23-26

26 [u]And as they were eating, [v]Jesus took
bread, [3]blessed and broke *it,* and gave *it* to
the disciples and said, "Take, eat; [w]this is
My body."
27 Then He took the cup, and gave
thanks, and gave *it* to them, saying,
[x]"Drink from it, all of you. 28 For [y]this is
My blood [z]of the [4]new covenant, which is
shed [a]for many for the [5]remission of sins.
29 But [b]I say to you, I will not drink of this
fruit of the vine from now on [c]until that
day when I drink it new with you in My
Father's kingdom."

11 [g] [Deut. 15:11; Mark 14:7]; John 12:8 [h] [Matt. 18:20; 28:20; John 13:33; 14:19; 16:5, 28; 17:11]
12 [i] Matt. 27:60; Luke 23:53; John 19:38-42
14 [j] Mark 14:10, 11; Luke 22:3-6; John 13:2, 30 [k] Matt. 10:4
15 [l] Ex. 21:32; Zech. 11:12; Matt. 27:3
17 [m] Ex. 12:6, 18-20
18 [n] Luke 9:51; John 12:23; 13:1; 17:1
20 [o] Mark 14:17-21; Luke 22:14; John 13:21
21 [p] Matt. 26:46; Mark 14:42; Luke 22:21-23; John 6:70, 71; 13:21
23 [q] Ps. 41:9; Luke 22:21; John 13:18
24 [r] Ps. 22; Dan. 9:26; Mark 9:12; Luke 24:25, 26, 46; Acts 17:2, 3; 26:22, 23; 1 Cor. 15:3 [s] Matt. 27:3-5; Luke 17:1; Acts 1:16-20 [t] John 17:12; Acts 1:25
26 [u] Mark 14:22-25; Luke 22:17-20 [v] 1 Cor. 11:23-25 [w] [1 Pet. 2:24] [3] M *gave thanks for*
27 [x] Mark 14:23
28 [y] [Ex. 24:8; Lev. 17:11; Heb. 9:20] [z] Jer. 31:31 [a] Matt. 20:28; [Rom. 5:15; Heb. 9:22] [4] NU omits *new* [5] *forgiveness*
29 [b] Mark 14:25; Luke 22:18 [c] Acts 10:41

26:11 For you have the poor with you always. Jesus certainly was not disparaging ministry to the poor—especially so soon after the lesson of the sheep and goats judgment (cf. 25:35,36). However, He revealed here that there is a higher priority than any other earthly ministry, and that is worship rendered to Him. This would be an utter blasphemy for anyone less than God, so yet again he was implicitly affirming His deity (*see notes on 8:27; 12:6,8; 21:16; 22:42,45*).

26:12 she did *it* for My burial. This does not necessarily mean that Mary was consciously aware of the significance of her act. It is doubtful that she knew of His approaching death, or at least how close it was. But this was an act of pure worship, her heart having been moved by God to perform a sacrificial and symbolic act, the full significance of which she probably did not know.

26:13 a memorial to her. This promise was guaranteed by the inclusion of this story in the NT.

26:15 thirty pieces of silver. The price of a slave (Ex. 21:32).

26:17 the first *day of the Feast* of Unleavened Bread. The Passover lambs were killed (Mark 14:12) on 14 Nisan (Mar./Apr.). That evening, the Passover meal was eaten. The Feast of Unleavened Bread followed immediately after Passover, from 15-21 Nisan. The entire time was often referred to either as "Passover" (Luke 22:1), or as the Feast of Unleavened Bread. Therefore the first day refers to 14 Nisan. See Introduction to John: Interpretive Challenges; *see note on John 19:14.*

26:18 a certain man. Mark 14:13 and Luke 22:10 say they would be able to identify the man because he would be "carrying a pitcher of water," a chore normally reserved for women. He was evidently someone they did not know, probably a servant of whoever owned the house with an "upper room," where the Passover meal was to be eaten (Mark 14:15; Luke 22:12). Jesus had evidently made these arrangements clandestinely, in order to prevent His premature betrayal. Had Judas known ahead of time where the meal was to be eaten, he would surely have alerted the chief priests and elders (see vv. 14-16). But none of these things were to happen until the "time" was "at hand." All of this reveals how Jesus Himself was sovereignly in control of the details of His own crucifixion (*see notes on vv. 5,54*).

26:20 sat down. Lit. "reclined" (*see note on Mark 14:18*; cf. John 13:25).

26:26 Take, eat; this is My body. Jesus thus transformed the last Passover into the first observance of the Lord's Supper. He is the central antitype in both ceremonies, being represented symbolically by both the paschal lamb of the Passover and the elements in the communion service. His statement, "this is My body" could not possibly have been taken in any literal sense by the disciples present that evening. *See note on Luke 22:19.*

26:28 My blood of the new covenant. Covenants were ratified with the blood of a sacrifice (Gen. 8:20; 15:9,10). Jesus' words here echo Moses' pronouncement in Ex. 24:8. The blood of the New Covenant is not an animal's blood, but Christ's own blood, shed for the remission of sins. *See notes on Jer. 31:31-34; Heb. 8:1–10:18; 8:6.*

26:29 My Father's kingdom. I.e., the earthly millennial kingdom (see Luke 22:18,29,30).

Peter's Denial Is Predicted
Mark 14:26-31; Luke 22:34, 39; John 13:37, 38

30 [d]And when they had sung a hymn,
they went out to the Mount of Olives.
31 Then Jesus said to them, [e]"All of you
will [f]be [6]made to stumble because of Me
this night, for it is written:

[g]'I will strike the Shepherd,
And the sheep of the flock will be
scattered.'

32 But after I have been raised, [h]I will go
before you to Galilee."
33 Peter answered and said to Him,
"Even if all are [7]made to stumble because
of You, I will never be made to stumble."
34 Jesus said to him, [i]"Assuredly, I say to
you that this night, before the rooster
crows, you will deny Me three times."
35 Peter said to Him, "Even if I have to
die with You, I will not deny You!"
And so said all the disciples.

Jesus' Three Prayers
Mark 14:32-42; Luke 22:40-46

36 [j]Then Jesus came with them to a place
called Gethsemane, and said to the disciples, "Sit here while I go and pray over
there." 37 And He took with Him Peter and
[k]the two sons of Zebedee, and He began
to be sorrowful and deeply distressed.
38 Then He said to them, [l]"My soul is exceedingly sorrowful, even to death. Stay
here and watch with Me."
39 He went a little farther and fell on His
face, and [m]prayed, saying, [n]"O My Father,
if it is possible, [o]let this cup pass from Me;
nevertheless, [p]not as I will, but as You
will."
40 Then He came to the disciples and
found them sleeping, and said to Peter,
"What! Could you not watch with Me one
hour? 41 [q]Watch and pray, lest you enter
into temptation. [r]The spirit indeed *is* willing, but the flesh *is* weak."
42 Again, a second time, He went away
and prayed, saying, "O My Father, [8]if this
cup cannot pass away from Me unless I
drink it, Your will be done." 43 And He
came and found them asleep again, for
their eyes were heavy.
44 So He left them, went away again,
and prayed the third time, saying the same
words. 45 Then He came to His disciples
and said to them, "Are *you* still sleeping
and resting? Behold, the hour [9]is at hand,
and the Son of Man is being [s]betrayed into
the hands of sinners. 46 Rise, let us be
going. See, My betrayer is at hand."

Jesus' Betrayal and Arrest
Mark 14:43-52; Luke 22:47-53; John 18:1-11

47 And [t]while He was still speaking, behold, Judas, one of the twelve, with a great
multitude with swords and clubs, came
from the chief priests and elders of the
people.
48 Now His betrayer had given them a
sign, saying, "Whomever I kiss, He is the
One; seize Him." 49 Immediately he went
up to Jesus and said, "Greetings, Rabbi!"
[u]and kissed Him.

30 [d] Mark 14:26-31; Luke 22:31-34
31 [e] Matt. 26:56; Mark 14:27; John 16:32 [f] [Matt. 11:6] [g] Zech. 13:7 [6] *caused to take offense at Me*
32 [h] Matt. 28:7, 10, 16; Mark 14:28; 16:7; John 21:1
33 [7] *caused to take offense at You*
34 [i] Matt. 26:74, 75; Mark 14:30; Luke 22:34; John 13:38
36 [j] Mark 14:32-35; Luke 22:39, 40; John 18:1
37 [k] Matt. 4:21; 17:1; Mark 5:37
38 [l] John 12:27
39 [m] Mark 14:36; Luke 22:42; [Heb. 5:7-9] [n] John 12:27 [o] Matt. 20:22 [p] Ps. 40:8; Is. 50:5; John 5:30; 6:38; Phil. 2:8
41 [q] Mark 13:33; 14:38; Luke 22:40, 46; [Eph. 6:18] [r] Ps. 103:14-16; [Rom. 7:15; 8:23; Gal. 5:17]
42 [8] NU *if this may not pass away unless*
45 [s] Matt. 17:22, 23; 20:18, 19 [9] *has drawn near*
47 [t] Mark 14:43-50; Luke 22:47-53; John 18:3-11; Acts 1:16
49 [u] 2 Sam. 20:9; [Prov. 27:6]

26:30 sung a hymn. Probably Ps. 118. The Talmud designated Pss. 113-118 as the Hallel (praise psalms) of Egypt. These psalms were sung at Passover (*see notes on Pss. 113–118*).

26:31 stumble. See v. 56. The Gr. word is the same word Jesus used for "offended" in 24:10, describing the falling away and spiritual treachery that would occur in the last days. Here, however, Jesus spoke of something less than full and final apostasy. In a moment of fleshly fear they disowned Christ (v. 34), but He prayed that their faith would not fail (Luke 22:32; John 17:9-11), and that prayer was answered. The verse Jesus quotes here is Zech. 13:7 (*see note there*).

26:32 I will go before you to Galilee. *See note on 28:7.*

26:34 before the rooster crows. Mark adds "twice." The rooster would begin crowing about 3:00 a.m. (cf. Mark 13:35). Though Peter and all the disciples insisted that they would never deny Christ (vv. 33,35), they were only a few hours away from fulfilling this prophecy (vv. 74,75; Mark 14:66-72).

26:36 Gethsemane. Lit. "oil press." This was a frequent meeting place for Christ and His disciples (John 18:2), just across the Kidron Valley from Jerusalem (John 18:1). A garden of ancient olive trees is there to this day. Judas' familiarity with Jesus' patterns enabled him to find Jesus there—even though Christ had not previously announced His intentions.

26:38 sorrowful, even to death. His anguish had nothing to do with fear of men or the physical torments of the cross. He was sorrowful because within hours the full cup of divine fury against sin would be His to drink (*see note on v. 39*).

26:39 this cup. Cf. v. 42. A cup is often the symbol of divine wrath against sin in the OT (Is. 51:17,22; Jer. 25:15-17,27-29; Lam. 4:21,22; Ezek. 23:31-34; Hab. 2:16). The next day Christ would "bear the sins of many" (Heb. 9:28)—and the fullness of divine wrath would fall on Him (Is. 53:10,11; 2 Cor. 5:21). This was the price of the sin He bore, and He paid it in full. His cry of anguish in 27:46 reflects the extreme bitterness of the cup of wrath He was given. **not as I will, but as You *will.*** This implies no conflict between the Persons of the Godhead. Rather, it graphically reveals how Christ in His humanity voluntarily surrendered His will to the will of the Father in all things—precisely so that there would be no conflict between the divine will and His desires. See John 4:34; 6:38; 8:29; Phil. 2:8. *See note on John 5:30.*

26:41 the flesh *is* weak. The tenderness of this plea is touching. Christ Himself was well acquainted with the feeling of human infirmities (Heb. 4:15)—yet without sin. At that very moment He was locked in a struggle against human passions which, while not sinful in themselves, must be subjugated to the divine will if sin was to be avoided. *See note on v. 39.*

26:47 Judas, one of the twelve. See v. 14. All 4 evangelists refer to Judas this way (Mark 14:10,43; Luke 22:47; John 6:71). Only once (John 20:24) is another disciple so described. The gospel writers seem to use the expression to underscore the insidiousness of Judas' crime—especially here, in the midst of the betrayal.

26:48,49 *See note on Mark 14:44,45.*

50 But Jesus said to him, [v]"Friend, why
have you come?"
Then they came and laid hands on Jesus
and took Him. 51 And suddenly, [w]one of
those *who were* with Jesus stretched out *his*
hand and drew his sword, struck the servant of the high priest, and cut off his ear.
52 But Jesus said to him, "Put your
sword in its place, [x]for all who take the
sword will [1]perish by the sword. 53 Or do
you think that I cannot now pray to My Father, and He will provide Me with [y]more
than twelve legions of angels? 54 How then
could the Scriptures be fulfilled, [z]that it
must happen thus?"
55 In that hour Jesus said to the multitudes, "Have you come out, as against a
robber, with swords and clubs to take Me?
I sat daily with you, teaching in the temple,
and you did not seize Me. 56 But all this
was done that the [a]Scriptures of the
prophets might be fulfilled."
Then [b]all the disciples forsook Him and
fled.

Two False Witnesses
Mark 14:53-65; Luke 22:54, 55, 63-65; John 18:12, 18, 24

57 [c]And those who had laid hold of Jesus
led *Him* away to Caiaphas the high priest,
where the scribes and the elders were assembled. 58 But [d]Peter followed Him at a
distance to the high priest's courtyard.
And he went in and sat with the servants
to see the end.
59 Now the chief priests, [2]the elders, and
all the council sought [e]false testimony
against Jesus to put Him to death, 60 [3]but
found none. Even though [f]many false witnesses came forward, they found none. But
at last [g]two [4]false witnesses came forward
61 and said, "This *fellow* said, [h]'I am able to
destroy the temple of God and to build it
in three days.' "
62 [i]And the high priest arose and said to
Him, "Do You answer nothing? What *is it*
these men testify against You?" 63 But [j]Je-
sus kept silent. And the high priest answered and said to Him, [k]"I put You under
oath by the living God: Tell us if You are
the Christ, the Son of God!"
64 Jesus said to him, "*It is as* you said.
Nevertheless, I say to you, [l]hereafter you
will see the Son of Man [m]sitting at the right
hand of the Power, and coming on the
clouds of heaven."
65 [n]Then the high priest tore his clothes,
saying, "He has spoken blasphemy! What
further need do we have of witnesses?
Look, now you have heard His [o]blas-
phemy! 66 What do you think?"

50 [v]Ps. 41:9; 55:13 **51** [w]Mark 14:47; Luke 22:50; John 18:10 **52** [x]Gen. 9:6; Rev. 13:10 [1]M *die* **53** [y]2 Kin. 6:17; Dan. 7:10 **54** [z]Is. 50:6; 53:2-11; Luke 24:25-27, 44-46; John 19:28; Acts 13:29; 17:3; 26:23 **56** [a]Lam. 4:20 [b]Zech. 13:7; Matt. 26:31; Mark 14:27; John 18:15 **57** [c]Matt. 17:22; Mark 14:53-65; Luke 22:54; John 18:12, 19-24 **58** [d]John 18:15, 16

59 [e]Ex. 20:16; Ps. 35:11 [2]NU omits *the elders* **60** [f]Ps. 27:12; 35:11; Mark 14:55; Acts 6:13 [g]Deut. 19:15 [3]NU *but found none, even though many false witnesses came forward.* [4]NU omits *false witnesses* **61** [h]Matt. 27:40; Mark 14:58; 15:29; John 2:19; Acts 6:14 **62** [i]Mark 14:60 **63** [j]Ps. 38:13, 14; Is. 53:7; Matt. 27:12, 14; Acts 8:32 [k]Lev. 5:1; 1 Sam. 14:24, 26; Luke 22:67-71

64 [l]Dan. 7:13; Matt. 16:27; 24:30; 25:31; Luke 21:27; [John 1:51; Rom. 14:10; 1 Thess. 4:16]; Rev. 1:7 [m]Ps. 110:1; [Acts 7:55] **65** [n]2 Kin. 18:37 [o]John 10:30-36

26:50 Friend. Not the usual Gr. word for "friend," but another word meaning "comrade."

26:51 one of those. John identifies the swordsman as Peter and the victim as Malchus (John 18:10). Clearly, Peter was not aiming for the ear, but for the head. Only Luke mentions that Jesus healed Malchus' ear (*see note on Luke 22:51*).

26:52 perish by the sword. Peter's action was vigilantism. No matter how unjust the arrest of Jesus, Peter had no right to take the law into his own hands in order to stop it. Jesus' reply was a restatement of the Gen. 9:6 principle: "Whoever sheds man's blood, by man his blood shall be shed," an affirmation that capital punishment is an appropriate penalty for murder.

26:53 more than twelve legions. A Roman legion was composed of 6,000 soldiers, so this would represent more than 72,000 angels. In 2 Kin. 19:35 a single angel killed more than 185,000 men in a single night, so this many angels would make a formidable army. *See note on Luke 2:13.*

26:54 Scriptures be fulfilled. God Himself had foreordained the very minutest details of how Jesus would die (Acts 2:23; 4:27,28). Dying was Christ's consummate act of submission to the Father's will (*see note on v. 39*). Jesus Himself was in absolute control (John 10:17,18). Yet it was not Jesus alone, but everyone around Him—His enemies included—who fulfilled precisely the details of the OT prophecies. These events display His divine sovereignty. *See notes on v. 2; 1:22; 5:18; 27:50.*

26:57 Caiaphas the high priest. *See note on v. 3.* From John 18:13, we learn that Christ was taken first to Annas (former High-Priest and father-in-law to Caiaphas). He then was sent bound to Caiaphas' house (John 18:24). The conspiracy was well planned, so that "the scribes and the elders" (the Sanhedrin, *see note on v. 59*) were already "assembled" at Caiaphas' house and ready to try Jesus. The time was sometime between midnight and the first rooster's crowing (v. 74). Such a hearing was illegal on several counts: criminal trials were not to be held at night (*see note on 27:1*); and trials in capital cases could only be held at the temple and only in public. *See note on 27:2* for a fuller chronology of the events leading up to the crucifixion.

26:59 the council. *See note on John 3:1.* The great Sanhedrin was the Supreme Court of Israel, consisting of 71 members, presided over by the High-Priest. They met daily in the temple to hold court, except on the Sabbath and other holy days. Technically, they did not have the power to administer capital punishment (John 18:31), but in the case of Stephen, for example, this was no deterrent to his stoning (cf. Acts 6:12-14; 7:58-60). Roman governors evidently sometimes ignored such incidents as a matter of political expediency. In Jesus' case, the men who were trying Him were the same ones who had conspired against Him (cf. John 11:47-50).

26:60 they found none. Even though many were willing to perjure themselves, the Sanhedrin could not find a charge that had enough credibility to indict Jesus. Evidently the "false witnesses" could not agree between themselves.

26:61 destroy the temple of God. See John 2:19-21. The witnesses' account was a distortion of Jesus' meaning. Mark 14:58 gives a fuller account of their testimony.

26:63 under oath. *See note on 5:34.* Caiaphas was trying to break Jesus' silence (v. 62). The oath was supposed to make Him legally obligated to reply. Jesus' answer (v. 64) implies acceptance of the oath.

26:64 The imagery was taken from Ps. 110:1 and Dan. 7:13.

26:65 the high priest tore his clothes. Normally this was an expression of deep grief (2 Kin. 19:1; Job 1:20; Jer. 36:24). The High-Priest was forbidden to tear his clothes (Lev. 10:6; 21:10)—but the Talmud

They answered and said, [p]"He is deserving of death."
67 [q]Then they spat in His face and beat
Him; and [r]others struck *Him* with [5]the
palms of their hands, 68 saying, [s]"Prophesy to us, Christ! Who is the one who
struck You?"

Three Denials of Peter
Mark 14:66-72; Luke 22:55-62; John 18:15-18, 25-27

69 [t]Now Peter sat outside in the courtyard. And a servant girl came to him, saying, "You also were with Jesus of Galilee."
70 But he denied it before *them* all, saying, "I do not know what you are saying."
71 And when he had gone out to the
gateway, another *girl* saw him and said to
those *who were* there, "This *fellow* also was
with Jesus of Nazareth."
72 But again he denied with an oath, "I
do not know the Man!"
73 And a little later those who stood by
came up and said to Peter, "Surely you also
are *one* of them, for your [u]speech betrays
you."
74 Then [v]he began to [6]curse and [7]swear,
saying, "I do not know the Man!"
Immediately a rooster crowed. 75 And
Peter remembered the word of Jesus who
had said to him, [w]"Before the rooster
crows, you will deny Me three times." So
he went out and wept bitterly.

Jesus Is Delivered to Pilate
Mark 15:1; Luke 22:66; 23:1; John 18:28

27 When morning came, [a]all the chief
priests and elders of the people
plotted against Jesus to put Him to death.
2 And when they had bound Him, they led
Him away and [b]delivered Him to [1]Pontius
Pilate the governor.

Judas Repents—Acts 1:18, 19

3 [c]Then Judas, His betrayer, seeing that
He had been condemned, was remorseful
and brought back the thirty [d]pieces of silver to the chief priests and elders, 4 saying,
"I have sinned by betraying innocent
blood."
And they said, "What *is that* to us? You
see *to it!*"
5 Then he threw down the pieces of silver in the temple and [e]departed, and went
and hanged himself.
6 But the chief priests took the silver
pieces and said, "It is not lawful to put
them into the treasury, because they are the
price of blood." 7 And they consulted together and bought with them the potter's
field, to bury strangers in. 8 Therefore that
field has been called [f]the Field of Blood to
this day.
9 Then was fulfilled what was spoken by
Jeremiah the prophet, saying, [g]*"And they*
took the thirty pieces of silver, the value of
Him who was priced, whom they of the
children of Israel priced, 10 *and* [h]*gave*
them for the potter's field, as the LORD *di-*
rected me."

Jesus Is Examined
Mark 15:2-5; Luke 23:2-5; John 18:29-38

11 Now Jesus stood before the governor.
[i]And the governor asked Him, saying,
"Are You the King of the Jews?"
Jesus said to him, [j]*"It is as* you say."
12 And while He was being accused by the
chief priests and elders, [k]He answered
nothing.
13 Then Pilate said to Him, [l]"Do You not

66 [p] Lev. 24:16; Matt. 20:18; John 19:7
67 [q] Job 16:10; Is. 50:6; 53:3; Lam. 3:30; Matt. 27:30 [r] Mic. 5:1; Luke 22:63-65; John 19:3 [5] Or *rods,*
68 [s] Mark 14:65; Luke 22:64
69 [t] Mark 14:66-72; Luke 22:55-62; John 18:16-18, 25-27
73 [u] Mark 14:70; Luke 22:59; John 18:26
74 [v] Matt. 26:34; Mark 14:71; Luke 22:34; John 13:38 [6] *call down curses* [7] Swear oaths
75 [w] Matt. 26:34; Luke 22:61; John 13:38

CHAPTER 27

1 [a] Ps. 2:2; Mark 15:1; Luke 22:66; 23:1; John 18:28
2 [b] Matt. 20:19; Luke 18:32; Acts 3:13 [1] NU omits *Pontius*
3 [c] Matt. 26:14 [d] Matt. 26:15
5 [e] 2 Sam. 17:23; Matt. 18:7; 26:24; John 17:12; Acts 1:18
8 [f] Acts 1:19
9 [g] Zech. 11:12
10 [h] Jer. 32:6-9; Zech. 11:12, 13
11 [i] Mark 15:2-5; Luke 23:2, 3; John 18:29-38 [j] John 18:37; 1 Tim. 6:13
12 [k] Ps. 38:13, 14; Matt. 26:63; John 19:9
13 [l] Matt. 26:62; John 19:10

made an exception for High-Priests who witnessed a blasphemy. But Caiaphas' supposed grief was as phony as the charge of blasphemy against Jesus; he was gloating over having found something to base his charges on (v. 67).

26:74 he began to curse and swear. I.e., calling on God as His witness, he declared, "I do not know the Man!" and pronounced a curse of death on himself at God's hand if his words were untrue. All 4 gospels record Peter's betrayal. Cf. vv. 31-35.

26:75 And Peter remembered. Luke 22:61 records that Jesus made eye contact with Peter at this very moment, which must have magnified Peter's already unbearable sense of shame. "He went out"—evidently departing from Caiaphas' house—"and wept bitterly." The true Peter is seen not in his denial but in his repentance. This account reminds us of not only our own weakness, but also the richness of divine grace (see also John 21:15-19).

27:1 When morning came. The Sanhedrin waited until daybreak to render their official verdict (cf. 26:66), possibly a token nod to the rule against criminal trials at night (*see note on 26:57*).

27:2 delivered Him...Pilate. Jesus had two trials, one Jewish and religious, the other Roman and secular. Rome reserved the right of execution in capital cases (*see note on 26:59*), so Jesus had to be handed over to the Roman authorities for execution of the death sentence. Pilate's headquarters were in Caesarea, on the Mediterranean coast, but he was in Jerusalem for the Passover celebrations, so he oversaw the trial (*see note on Mark 15:1*). Christ was brought before Pilate (vv. 2-14), then was sent to Herod for yet another hearing (Luke 23:6-12), then returned to Pilate for the final hearing and pronouncing of sentence (vv. 15-26).

27:3 remorseful. Judas felt the sting of his own guilt, but this was not genuine repentance. There is a godly sorrow that leads to repentance, but Judas' remorse was of a different kind, as demonstrated by his suicide (v. 5). Cf. 2 Cor. 7:10.

27:5 hanged himself. *See note on Acts 1:18.*

27:9 spoken by Jeremiah. Actually the statement paraphrases Zech. 11:12,13. But the Hebrew canon was divided into 3 sections, Law, Writings, and Prophets (cf. Luke 24:44). Jeremiah came first in the order of prophetic books, so the Prophets were sometimes collectively referred to by his name.

27:11 *It is as* you say. These words were probably spoken immediately after the dialogue John 18:34-36 reports.

hear how many things they testify against
You?" 14 But He answered him not one
word, so that the governor marveled
greatly.

Barabbas Is Freed
Mark 15:6-14; Luke 23:17-23; John 18:39, 40

15 [m]Now at the feast the governor was
accustomed to releasing to the multitude
one prisoner whom they wished. 16 And at
that time they had a notorious prisoner
called [2]Barabbas. 17 Therefore, when they
had gathered together, Pilate said to them,
"Whom do you want me to release to you?
Barabbas, or Jesus who is called Christ?"
18 For he knew that they had handed Him
over because of [n]envy.

19 While he was sitting on the judgment
seat, his wife sent to him, saying, "Have
nothing to do with that just Man, for I have
suffered many things today in a dream because of Him."

20 [o]But the chief priests and elders persuaded the multitudes that they should
ask for Barabbas and destroy Jesus. 21 The
governor answered and said to them,
"Which of the two do you want me to release to you?"

They said, [p]"Barabbas!"

22 Pilate said to them, "What then shall I
do with Jesus who is called Christ?"

They all said to him, "Let Him be crucified!"

23 Then the governor said, [q]"Why, what
evil has He done?"

But they cried out all the more, saying,
"Let Him be crucified!"

24 When Pilate saw that he could not
prevail at all, but rather *that* a [3]tumult was
rising, he [r]took water and washed *his*
hands before the multitude, saying, "I am
innocent of the blood of this [4]just Person.
You see *to it*."

25 And all the people answered and said,
[s]"His blood *be* on us and on our children."

Jesus Is Scourged
Mark 15:15-17; Luke 23:24, 25; John 19:16

26 Then he released Barabbas to them;
and when [t]he had [5]scourged Jesus, he delivered *Him* to be crucified.

27 [u]Then the soldiers of the governor
took Jesus into the [6]Praetorium and gathered the whole [7]garrison around Him.
28 And they [v]stripped Him and [w]put a
scarlet robe on Him.

Jesus Is Lead to Golgotha
Mark 15:18-22; Luke 23:26-33; John 19:17

29 [x]When they had [8]twisted a crown of
thorns, they put *it* on His head, and a reed
in His right hand. And they bowed the
knee before Him and mocked Him, saying,
"Hail, King of the Jews!" 30 Then [y]they
spat on Him, and took the reed and struck
Him on the head. 31 And when they had
mocked Him, they took the robe off Him,
put His *own* clothes on Him, [z]and led Him
away to be crucified.

32 [a]Now as they came out, [b]they found a
man of Cyrene, Simon by name. Him they

15 [m] Mark 15:6-15; Luke 23:17-25; John 18:39–19:16
16 [2] NU *Jesus Barabbas*
18 [n] Matt. 21:38; [John 15:22-25]
20 [o] Mark 15:11; Luke 23:18; John 18:40; Acts 3:14
21 [p] Acts 3:14
23 [q] Acts 3:13
24 [r] Deut. 21:6-8 [3] *an uproar* [4] NU omits *just*
25 [s] Deut. 19:10; Josh. 2:19; 2 Sam. 1:16; 1 Kin. 2:32; Acts 5:28
26 [t] [Is. 50:6; 53:5]; Matt. 20:19; Mark 15:15; Luke 23:16, 24, 25; John 19:1, 16 [5] *flogged* with a Roman scourge
27 [u] Mark 15:16-20; John 19:2 [6] The governor's headquarters [7] *cohort*
28 [v] Mark 15:17; John 19:2 [w] Luke 23:11
29 [x] Ps. 69:19; Is. 53:3; Matt. 20:19; Mark 10:34; Luke 18:32 [8] Lit. *woven*
30 [y] Is. 50:6; 52:14; Mic. 5:1; Matt. 26:67; Mark 10:34; 14:65; 15:19
31 [z] Is. 53:7; Matt. 20:19
32 [a] 1 Kin. 21:13; Acts 7:58; Heb. 13:12 [b] Mark 15:21; Luke 23:26; John 19:17

27:25 His blood *be* on us. The Jews accepted the blame for the execution of Jesus and did not hold the Romans responsible. Cf. 21:38,39.

27:26 scourged. The whip used for scourging consisted of several strands of leather attached to a wooden handle. Each strand had a bit of metal or bone attached to the end. The victim was bound to a post by the wrists, high over his head, so that the flesh of the back would be taut. An expert at wielding the scourge could literally tear the flesh from the back, lacerating muscles, and sometimes even exposing the kidneys or other internal organs. Scourging alone was fatal in some cases.

27:27 Praetorium. Pilate's residence in Jerusalem. It was probably located in the Antonia Fortress, adjacent to the NW corner of the temple. "The soldiers of the governor" were part of a "garrison"—about 600 soldiers—assigned to serve the governor (Pilate) during his stay in Jerusalem.

27:28 scarlet robe. Mark 15:17 and John 19:2 say "purple," suggesting that the robe may have been something between royal purple, and "scarlet," the closest thing they could find to the traditional garb of royalty. The word for "robe" refers to a military cloak undoubtedly belonging to one of the soldiers.

27:29 a reed in His right hand. To imitate a scepter they purposely chose something flimsy-looking.

27:30 they spat on Him. See Is. 50:6. **struck Him on the head.** A reed long enough to make a mock scepter would be firm enough to be extremely painful, about like a broom handle. John 19:3 says they hit him with their fists as well.

27:31 to be crucified. Crucifixion was a form of punishment that had been passed down to the Romans from the Persians, Phoenicians, and Carthaginians. Roman crucifixion was a lingering doom—by design. Roman executioners had perfected the art of slow torture while keeping the victim alive. Some victims even lingered until they were eaten alive by birds of prey or wild beasts. Most hung on the cross for days before dying of exhaustion, dehydration, traumatic fever, or—most likely—suffocation. When the legs would no longer support the weight of the body, the diaphragm was constricted in a way that made breathing impossible. That is why breaking the legs would hasten death (John 19:31-33), but this was unnecessary in Jesus' case. The hands were usually nailed through the wrists, and the feet through the instep or the Achilles tendon (sometimes using one nail for both feet). None of these wounds would be fatal, but their pain would become unbearable as the hours dragged on. The most notable feature of crucifixion was the stigma of disgrace that was attached to it (Gal. 3:13; 5:11; Heb. 12:2). One indignity was the humiliation of carrying one's own cross, which might weigh as much as 200 pounds. Normally a quaternion, 4 soldiers, would escort the prisoner through the crowds to the place of crucifixion. A placard bearing the indictment would be hung around the person's neck.

27:32 Cyrene. A city in N Africa. Evidently the scourging had so weakened Jesus that He was unable to carry the cross. This is another touching picture of His humanity, beset with all human weaknesses except sin (Heb 4:15).

compelled to bear His cross. **33** [c]And when
they had come to a place called Golgotha,
that is to say, Place of a Skull, **34** [d]they gave
Him [9]sour wine mingled with gall to
drink. But when He had tasted *it*, He
would not drink.

Jesus Is Crucified
Mark 15:23-32; Luke 23:33-43; John 19:18-24

35 [e]Then they crucified Him, and divided His garments, casting lots, [1]that it
might be fulfilled which was spoken by the
prophet:

> [f]*"They divided My garments among*
> *them,*
> *And for My clothing they cast lots."*

36 [g]Sitting down, they kept watch over
Him there. **37** And they [h]put up over His
head the accusation written against Him:

THIS IS JESUS THE KING OF THE JEWS.

38 [i]Then two robbers were crucified with
Him, one on the right and another on the
left.
39 And [j]those who passed by blasphemed
Him, wagging their heads **40** and saying,
[k]"You who destroy the temple and build *it*
in three days, save Yourself! [l]If You are the
Son of God, come down from the cross."
41 Likewise the chief priests also, mocking with the [2]scribes and elders, said,
42 "He [m]saved others; Himself He cannot
save. [3]If He is the King of Israel, let Him
now come down from the cross, and we
will believe [4]Him. **43** [n]He trusted in God;
let Him deliver Him now if He will have
Him; for He said, 'I am the Son of God.' "
44 [o]Even the robbers who were crucified
with Him reviled Him with the same thing.

Jesus Dies
Mark 15:33-37; Luke 2:44-46; John 19:28-30

45 [p]Now from the sixth hour until the
ninth hour there was darkness over all the
land. **46** And about the ninth hour [q]Jesus
cried out with a loud voice, saying, "Eli,
Eli, lama sabachthani?" that is, [r]*"My God,*
My God, why have You forsaken Me?"
47 Some of those who stood there, when
they heard *that*, said, "This Man is calling
for Elijah!" **48** Immediately one of them ran
and took a sponge, [s]filled *it* with sour wine
and put *it* on a reed, and offered it to Him
to drink.
49 The rest said, "Let Him alone; let us
see if Elijah will come to save Him."
50 And Jesus [t]cried out again with a loud
voice, and [u]yielded up His spirit.

Signs Accompanying Jesus' Death
Mark 15:38-41; Luke 23:45, 47-49

51 Then, behold, [v]the veil of the temple
was torn in two from top to bottom; and
the earth quaked, and the rocks were split,
52 and the graves were opened; and many
bodies of the saints who had fallen asleep

33 [c] Mark 15:22-32; Luke 23:33-43; John 19:17
34 [d] Ps. 69:21; Matt. 27:48 [9] NU omits *sour*
35 [e] Mark 15:24; Luke 23:34; John 19:24 [f] Ps. 22:18 [1] NU, M omit the rest of v. 35.
36 [g] Ps. 22:17; Matt. 27:54
37 [h] Mark 15:26; Luke 23:38; John 19:19
38 [i] Is. 53:9, 12; Mark 15:27; Luke 23:32, 33; John 19:18
39 [j] Job 16:4; Ps. 22:7; 109:25; Lam. 2:15; Mark 15:29; Luke 23:35
40 [k] Matt. 26:61; John 2:19 [l] Matt. 26:63
41 [2] M *scribes, the Pharisees, and the elders*
42 [m] [Matt. 18:11; John 3:14, 15]
[3] NU omits *If* [4] NU, M *in Him*
43 [n] Ps. 22:8
44 [o] Mark 15:32; Luke 23:39-43
45 [p] Amos 8:9; Mark 15:33-41; Luke 23:44-49
46 [q] [Heb. 5:7] [r] Ps. 22:1
48 [s] Ps. 69:21; Mark 15:36; Luke 23:36; John 19:29
50 [t] Mark 15:37; Luke 23:46; John 19:30 [u] Dan. 9:26; Zech. 11:10, 11; Matt. 17:23; [John 10:18; 1 Cor. 15:3]
51 [v] Ex. 26:31; 2 Chr. 3:14; Zech. 11:10; Mark 15:38; Luke 23:45; Heb. 9:3

27:33 Place of a Skull. "Golgotha" may have been a skull-shaped hill, or it may have been so named because as a place of crucifixion, it accumulated skulls. None of the gospels mention a hill. Luke 23:33 uses the name "Calvary," from the Lat., *calvaria*, "skull."

27:34 wine mingled with gall. "Gall" simply refers to something bitter. Mark 15:23 identifies it as myrrh, a narcotic. The Jews had a custom, based on Prov. 31:6, of administering a pain-deadening medication mixed with wine to victims of crucifixion, in order to deaden the pain. Tasting what it was, Christ, though thirsty, "would not drink," lest it dull His senses before He completed His work. The lessening of physical pain would probably not have diminished the efficacy of His atoning work (*see notes on 26:38,39*). But He needed His full mental faculties for the hours yet to come. It was necessary for Him to be awake and fully conscious, for example, to minister to the dying thief (Luke 23:43).

27:35 divided His garments. The garments of the victim were the customary spoils of the executioners. John 19:23,24 gives a fuller account. This action was foretold in Ps. 22:18.

27:37 the accusation. For a reconciliation of the differences between the various accounts of this inscription, *see note on Luke 23:38* (cf. Mark 15:26). The fact that the placard was placed "over His head" suggests that this cross was in the familiar shape with an upright protruding above the transom, and not the T-shaped cross that was also sometimes used.

27:38 robbers. This word denotes a rebel and brigand who plunders as he steals. Mere thieves were not usually crucified. These were probably cohorts of Barabbas.

27:40 destroy the temple and build *it* in three days. See 26:61. They had missed His point. "He was speaking of the temple of His body" (John 2:21). He would not "come down from the cross," but it was not because He was powerless to do so (John 10:18). The proof that He was the Son of God came "in three days" (*see note on 12:40*), when He returned with "the temple" (i.e., His body) rebuilt.

27:42 we will believe Him. *See notes on 12:38; 16:1.*

27:45 from the sixth hour until the ninth hour. From noon until 3:00 p.m. The crucifixion began at 9:00 a.m. (*see notes on Mark 15:25; Luke 23:44*).

27:46 Eli, Eli, lama sabachthani. "Eli" is Heb.; the rest Aram. (Mark 15:34 gives the entire wail in Aramaic.) This cry is a fulfillment of Psalm 22:1, one of many striking parallels between that psalm and the specific events of the crucifixion (*see notes on Ps. 22*). Christ at that moment was experiencing the abandonment and despair that resulted from the outpouring of divine wrath on Him as sin-bearer (*see note on 26:39*).

27:50 yielded up His spirit. A voluntary act. See John 10:18. *See note on 26:54.*

27:51 the veil of the temple. I.e., the curtain that blocked the entrance to the Most Holy Place (Ex. 26:33; Heb. 9:3). The tearing of the veil signified that the way into God's presence was now open to all through a new and living way (Heb. 10:19-22). The fact that it tore "from top to bottom" showed that no man had split the veil. God did it.

27:52 bodies of the saints...were raised. Matthew alone mentions this miracle. Nothing more is said about these people, which

were raised; 53 and coming out of the
graves after His resurrection, they went
into the holy city and appeared to many.
54 [w]So when the centurion and those
with him, who were guarding Jesus, saw
the earthquake and the things that had
happened, they feared greatly, saying,
[x]"Truly this was the Son of God!"
55 And many women [y]who followed Jesus from Galilee, ministering to Him, were
there looking on from afar, 56 [z]among
whom were Mary Magdalene, Mary the
mother of James and [5]Joses, and the mother of Zebedee's sons.

Jesus Is Buried
Mark 15:42-47; Luke 23:50-55; John 19:38-42

57 Now [a]when evening had come, there
came a rich man from Arimathea, named
Joseph, who himself had also become a
disciple of Jesus. 58 This man went to Pilate
and asked for the body of Jesus. Then Pilate commanded the body to be given to
him. 59 When Joseph had taken the body,
he wrapped it in a clean linen cloth, 60 and
[b]laid it in his new tomb which he had
hewn out of the rock; and he rolled a large
stone against the door of the tomb, and departed. 61 And Mary Magdalene was there,
and the other Mary, sitting [6]opposite the
tomb.
62 On the next day, which followed the
Day of Preparation, the chief priests and
Pharisees gathered together to Pilate,
63 saying, "Sir, we remember, while He was
still alive, how that deceiver said, [c]'After
three days I will rise.' 64 Therefore command that the tomb be made secure until
the third day, lest His disciples come [7]by
night and steal Him *away,* and say to the
people, 'He has risen from the dead.' So the
last deception will be worse than the first."
65 Pilate said to them, "You have a
guard; go your way, make *it* as secure as
you know how." 66 So they went and made
the tomb secure, [d]sealing the stone and setting the guard.

The Empty Tomb
Mark 16:1-8; Luke 24:1-11

28 Now [a]after the Sabbath, as the first
day of the week began to dawn,
Mary Magdalene [b]and the other Mary
came to see the tomb. 2 And behold, there
was a great earthquake; for [c]an angel of the
Lord descended from heaven, and came
and rolled back the stone [1]from the door,
and sat on it. 3 [d]His countenance was like
lightning, and his clothing as white as
snow. 4 And the guards shook for fear of
him, and became like [e]dead *men.*
5 But the angel answered and said to the
women, "Do not be afraid, for I know that
you seek Jesus who was crucified. 6 He is
not here; for He is risen, [f]as He said. Come,
see the place where the Lord lay. 7 And go
quickly and tell His disciples that He is
risen from the dead, and indeed [g]He is
going before you into Galilee; there you
will see Him. Behold, I have told you."

54 [w]Mark 15:39; Luke 23:47 [x]Matt. 14:33
55 [y]Mark 15:41; Luke 8:2, 3
56 [z]Matt. 28:1; Mark 15:40, 47; 16:9; Luke 8:2; John 19:25; 20:1, 18 [5]NU *Joseph*
57 [a]Mark 15:42-47; Luke 23:50-56; John 19:38-42
60 [b]Is. 53:9; Matt. 26:12
61 [6]*in front of*
63 [c]Matt. 16:21; 17:23; 20:19; 26:61; Mark 8:31; 10:34; Luke 9:22; 13:33; 24:6, 7; John 2:19
64 [7]NU omits *by night*
66 [d]Dan. 6:17

CHAPTER 28

1 [a]Mark 16:1-8; Luke 24:1-10; John 20:1-8 [b]Matt. 27:56, 61
2 [c]Mark 16:5; Luke 24:4; John 20:12 [1]NU omits *from the door*
3 [d]Dan. 7:9; 10:6; Mark 9:3; John 20:12; Acts 1:10
4 [e]Rev. 1:17
6 [f]Hos. 6:2; Ps. 16:10; 49:15; Matt. 12:40; 16:21; 17:23; 20:19
7 [g]Matt. 26:32; 28:10, 16; Mark 16:7

would be unlikely if they remained on earth for long. Evidently, these people were given glorified bodies; they appeared "to many" (v. 53), enough to establish the reality of the miracle; and then they no doubt ascended to glory—a kind of foretaste of 1 Thess. 4:16.

27:54 the centurion. *See note on 8:5.* **those with him.** These were probably men under his charge. Mark 15:39 says the centurion was the one who uttered the words of confession, but he evidently spoke for his men as well. Their "fear" speaks of an awareness of their sin, and the word "truly" suggests a certainty and conviction that bespeaks genuine faith. These men represent an answer to Jesus' prayer in Luke 23:34. Their response contrasts sharply with the mocking taunts of vv. 39-44.

27:56 Mary Magdalene. She had been delivered from 7 demons (Luke 8:2); the other "Mary" ("wife of Clopas," John 19:25—a variant of Alphaeus) was the mother of the apostle known as "James the Less" (Mark 15:40; *see note on 10:2*). **the mother of Zebedee's sons.** Salome (Mark 15:40), mother of James and John. From John 19:26, we learn that Mary, the mother of Jesus, was also present at the cross—possibly standing apart from these 3, who were "looking on from afar" (v. 55), as if they could not bear to watch His sufferings, but neither could they bear to leave Him.

27:57 Joseph. Mark 15:43 and Luke 23:50,51 identify him as a member of the Sanhedrin (*see note on 26:59*), though Luke says "he had not consented to their decision and deed" in condemning Christ. Joseph and Nicodemus (John 19:39), both being prominent Jewish leaders, buried Christ in Joseph's own "new tomb" (v. 60), thus fulfilling exactly the prophecy of Is. 53:9. **Arimathea.** A town about 20 mi. NW of Jerusalem.

27:62 the next day. The Sabbath. **the Day of Preparation.** This was on Friday.

28:1 as the first *day* of the week began to dawn. Sabbath officially ended with sundown on Saturday. At that time the women could purchase and prepare spices (Luke 24:1). The event described here occurred the next morning, at dawn on Sunday, the first day of the week. **other Mary.** The mother of James the Less (*see note on 27:56*).

28:2 a great earthquake. The second earthquake associated with Christ's death (27:51). This one may have been confined to the immediate area around the grave, when "an angel" supernaturally "rolled back the stone from the door"—not to let Jesus out, for if He could rise from the dead, He would need no help escaping an earthly tomb, but to let the women and the apostles in (v. 6).

28:4 became like dead *men.* This suggests that they were not merely paralyzed with fear, but completely unconscious, totally traumatized by what they had seen. The word translated "shook" has the same root as the word for "earthquake" in v. 2. The sudden appearance of this angel, at the same time the women arrived, was their first clue that anything extraordinary was happening.

28:6 Come, see the place where the Lord lay. *See note on Luke 24:4* for the order of these events as gleaned from all 4 gospels.

28:7 there you will see Him. See vv. 10,16; 26:32; John 21:1-14. This does not mean they would not see Him until then. He was seen

[8] So they went out quickly from the
tomb with fear and great joy, and ran to
bring His disciples word.

The Appearance of Jesus to the Women

[9] And [2]as they went to tell His disciples,
behold, [h]Jesus met them, saying, "Rejoice!" So they came and held Him by the
feet and worshiped Him. [10] Then Jesus
said to them, "Do not be afraid. Go *and* tell
[i]My brethren to go to Galilee, and there
they will see Me."

The Bribery of the Soldiers

[11] Now while they were going, behold,
some of the guard came into the city and
reported to the chief priests all the things
that had happened. [12] When they had assembled with the elders and consulted together, they gave a large sum of money to
the soldiers, [13] saying, "Tell them, 'His disciples came at night and stole Him *away*
while we slept.' [14] And if this comes to the
governor's ears, we will appease him and
make you secure." [15] So they took the
money and did as they were instructed;
and this saying is commonly reported
among the Jews until this day.

The Appearance of Jesus to the Disciples

[16] Then the eleven disciples went away
into Galilee, to the mountain [j]which Jesus
had appointed for them. [17] When they saw
Him, they worshiped Him; but some
[k]doubted.

The Great Commission

[18] And Jesus came and spoke to them,
saying, [l]"All authority has been given to
Me in heaven and on earth. [19] [m]Go [3]there-
fore and [n]make disciples of all the nations,
baptizing them in the name of the Father
and of the Son and of the Holy Spirit,
[20] [o]teaching them to observe all things that
I have commanded you; and lo, I am [p]with
you always, *even* to the end of the age."
[4]Amen.

9 [h] Mark 16:9; John 20:14 [2] NU omits *as they went to tell His disciples*
10 [i] Ps. 22:22; John 20:17; Rom. 8:29; [Heb. 2:11]
16 [j] Matt. 26:32; 28:7, 10; Mark 14:28; 15:41; 16:7
17 [k] John 20:24-29
18 [l] [Dan. 7:13, 14]; Matt. 11:27; Luke 1:32; 10:22; John 3:35; Acts 2:36; Rom. 14:9; 1 Cor. 15:27; [Eph. 1:10, 21]; Phil. 2:9, 10; [Heb. 1:2]; 1 Pet. 3:22
19 [m] Mark 16:15 [n] Is. 52:10; Luke 24:47; [Acts 2:38, 39]; Rom. 10:18; Col. 1:23 [3] M omits *therefore*
20 [o] [Acts 2:42] [p] [Acts 4:31; 18:10; 23:11] [4] NU omits *Amen.*

by the apostles several times before they saw Him in Galilee (Luke 24:15,34,36; John 20:19,26). But His supreme post-resurrection appearance was in Galilee, where "He was seen by over five hundred brethren at once" (1 Cor. 15:6). *See note on v. 16.*

28:9 Jesus met them. For a summary of Christ's post-resurrection appearances, *see note on Luke 24:34.*

28:10 My brethren. I.e., the disciples.

28:11 reported to the chief priests. The Jewish leaders' determination to cover up what had occurred reveals the obstinacy of unbelief in the face of evidence (Luke 16:31).

28:12 a large sum of money. Lit. "silver" (cf. 26:15). The bribery was necessary because the soldiers' story, if true, could cost them their lives—since they were charged with guard duty under Pilate's personal orders (27:65). The Jewish leaders also promised to cover for the soldiers if the false story they spread leaked back to Pilate (v. 14).

28:13 while we slept. The story was obviously bogus, and not a very good cover-up. They could not possibly know what had happened while they were asleep.

28:16 the eleven disciples. This does not mean that only the 11 were present. The fact that some there "doubted" (v. 17) strongly suggests that more than the 11 were present. It is likely that Christ arranged this meeting in Galilee because that was where most of His followers were. This seems the most likely location for the massive gathering of disciples Paul describes in 1 Cor. 15:6 (*see note on v. 7*).

28:17 but some doubted. That simple phrase is one of countless testimonies to the integrity of Scripture. The transparent honesty of a statement like this shows that Matthew was not attempting to exclude or cover up facts that might lessen the perfection of such a glorious moment.

28:18 All authority. See 11:27; John 3:35. Absolute sovereign authority—lordship over all—is handed to Christ, "in heaven and on earth." This is clear proof of His deity. The time of His humiliation was at an end, and God had exalted Him above all (Phil. 2:9-11).

28:19 therefore. I.e., on the basis of His authority, the disciples were sent to "make disciples of all nations." The sweeping scope of their commission is consummate with His unlimited authority. **in the name of the Father…Son and…Holy Spirit.** The formula is a strong affirmation of trinitarianism.

28:20 teaching them to observe all things that I have commanded you. The kind of evangelism called for in this commission does not end with the conversion of the unbeliever. **I am with you.** There's a touching echo of the beginning of Matthew's gospel here. Immanuel (1:23) "which is translated, 'God with us'"—remains "with" us "even to the end of the age"—i.e., until He returns bodily to judge the world and establish His earthly kingdom.

The Gospel According to

MARK

Title

Mark, for whom this gospel is named, was a close companion of the Apostle Peter and a recurring character in the book of Acts, where he is known as "John whose surname was Mark" (Acts 12:12,25; 15:37,39). It was to John Mark's mother's home in Jerusalem that Peter went when released from prison (Acts 12:12).

John Mark was a cousin of Barnabas (Col. 4:10), who accompanied Paul and Barnabas on Paul's first missionary journey (Acts 12:25; 13:5). But he deserted them along the way in Perga and returned to Jerusalem (Acts 13:13). When Barnabas wanted Paul to take John Mark on the second missionary journey, Paul refused. The friction which resulted between Paul and Barnabas led to their separation (Acts 15:38-40).

But John Mark's earlier vacillation evidently gave way to great strength and maturity, and in time he proved himself even to the Apostle Paul. When Paul wrote the Colossians, he instructed them that if John Mark came, they were to welcome him (Col. 4:10). Paul even listed Mark as a fellow worker (Philem. 24). Later, Paul told Timothy to "Get Mark and bring him with you, for he is useful to me for ministry" (2 Tim. 4:11).

John Mark's restoration to useful ministry may have been, in part, due to the ministry of Peter. Peter's close relationship with Mark is evident from his description of him as "Mark my son" (1 Pet. 5:13). Peter, of course, was no stranger to failure himself, and his influence on the younger man was no doubt instrumental in helping him out of the instability of his youth and into the strength and maturity he would need for the work to which God had called him.

Author and Date

Unlike the epistles, the gospels do not name their authors. The early church fathers, however, unanimously affirm that Mark wrote this second gospel. Papias, bishop of Hieropolis, writing about A.D. 140, noted:

> And the presbyter [the Apostle John] said this: Mark having become the interpreter of Peter, wrote down accurately whatsoever he remembered. It was not, however, in exact order that he related the sayings or deeds of Christ. For he neither heard the Lord nor accompanied Him. But afterwards, as I said, he accompanied Peter, who accommodated his instructions to the necessities [of his hearers], but with no intention of giving a regular narrative of the Lord's sayings. Wherefore Mark made no mistake in thus writing some things as he remembered them. For of one thing he took especial care, not to omit anything he had heard, and not to put anything fictitious into the statements. [*From the Exposition of the Oracles of the Lord* (6)]

Justin Martyr, writing about A.D. 150, referred to the Gospel of Mark as "the memoirs of Peter," and suggested that Mark committed his gospel to writing while in Italy. This agrees with the uniform voice of early tradition, which regarded this gospel as having been written in Rome, for the benefit of Roman Christians. Irenaeus, writing about A.D. 185, called Mark "the disciple and interpreter of Peter," and recorded that the second gospel consisted of what Peter preached about Christ. The testimony of the church fathers differs as to whether this gospel was written before or after Peter's death (ca. A.D. 67–68).

Evangelical scholars have suggested dates for the writing of Mark's gospel ranging from A.D. 50 to 70. A date before the destruction of Jerusalem and the temple in A.D. 70 is required by the comment of Jesus in 13:2. Luke's gospel was clearly written before Acts (Acts 1:1-3). The date of the writing of Acts can probably be fixed at about A.D. 63, because that is shortly after the narrative ends (see Introduction to Acts: Author and Date). It is therefore likely, though not certain, that Mark was written at an early date, probably sometime in the 50s.

Background and Setting

Whereas Matthew was written to a Jewish audience, Mark seems to have targeted Roman believers, particularly Gentiles. When employing Aramaic terms, Mark translated them for his readers (3:17; 5:41;

7:11,34; 10:46; 14:36; 15:22,34). On the other hand, in some places he used Latin expressions instead of their Greek equivalents (5:9; 6:27; 12:15,42; 15:16,39). He also reckoned time according to the Roman system (6:48; 13:35) and carefully explained Jewish customs (7:3,4; 14:12; 15:42). Mark omitted Jewish elements, such as the genealogies found in Matthew and Luke. This gospel also makes fewer references to the OT, and includes less material that would be of particular interest to Jewish readers—such as that which is critical of the Pharisees and Sadducees (Sadducees are mentioned only once, in 12:18). When mentioning Simon the Cyrene (15:21), Mark identifies him as the father of Rufus, a prominent member of the church at Rome (Rom. 16:13). All of this supports the traditional view that Mark was written for a Gentile audience initially at Rome.

Historical and Theological Themes

Mark presents Jesus as the suffering Servant of the Lord (10:45). His focus is on the deeds of Jesus more than His teaching, particularly emphasizing service and sacrifice. Mark omits the lengthy discourses found in the other gospels, often relating only brief excerpts to give the gist of Jesus' teaching. Mark also omits any account of Jesus' ancestry and birth, beginning where Jesus' public ministry began, with His baptism by John in the wilderness.

Mark demonstrated the humanity of Christ more clearly than any of the other evangelists, emphasizing Christ's human emotions (1:41; 3:5; 6:34; 8:12; 9:36;), His human limitations (4:38; 11:12; 13:32), and other small details that highlight the human side of the Son of God (e.g., 7:33,34; 8:12; 9:36; 10:13-16).

Interpretive Challenges

Three significant questions confront the interpreter of Mark: 1) What is the relationship of Mark to Luke and Matthew? (*see below, "The Synoptic Problem"*); 2) How should one interpret the eschatological passages? (*see notes on chaps. 4,13*); and 3) Were the last 12 verses of chap. 16 originally part of Mark's gospel? (*see note on 16:9-20*).

The Synoptic Problem

Even a cursory reading of Matthew, Mark, and Luke reveals both striking similarities (cf. 2:3-12; Matt. 9:2-8; Luke 5:18-26) and significant differences, as each views the life, ministry, and teaching of Jesus. The question of how to explain those similarities and differences is known as the "Synoptic Problem" (*syn* means "together"; *optic* means "seeing").

The modern solution—even among evangelicals—has been to assume that some form of literary dependence exists between the synoptic gospels. The most commonly accepted theory to explain such an alleged literary dependence is known as the "Two-Source" theory. According to that hypothesis, Mark was the first gospel written, and Matthew and Luke then used Mark as a source in writing their gospels. Proponents of this view imagine a non-existent, second source, labeled Q (from the German word *Quelle*, "source"), and argue that this allegedly is the source of the material in Matthew and Luke that does not appear in Mark. They advance several lines of evidence to support their scenario.

First, most of Mark is paralleled in Matthew and Luke. Since it is much shorter than Matthew and Luke, the latter must be expansions of Mark. Second, the 3 gospels follow the same general chronological outline, but when either Matthew or Luke departs from Mark's chronology, the other agrees with Mark. Put another way, Matthew and Luke do not both depart from Mark's chronology in the same places. That, it is argued, shows that Matthew and Luke used Mark for their historical framework. Third, in passages common to all 3 gospels, Matthew's and Luke's wording seldom agrees when it differs from Mark's. Proponents of the "Two-Source" theory see that as confirmation that Matthew and Luke used Mark's gospel as a source.

But those arguments do not prove that Matthew and Luke used Mark's gospel as a source. In fact, the weight of evidence is strongly against such a theory:

1) The nearly unanimous testimony of the church until the nineteenth century was that Matthew was the first gospel written. Such an impressive body of evidence cannot be ignored.

2) Why would Matthew, an apostle and eyewitness to the events of Christ's life, depend on Mark (who was not an eyewitness)—even for the account of his own conversion?

3) A significant statistical analysis of the synoptic gospels has revealed that the parallels between them are far less extensive and the differences more significant than is commonly acknowledged. The differences, in particular, argue against literary dependence between the gospel writers.

4) Since the gospels record actual historical events, it would be surprising if they did not follow the same general historical sequence. For example, the fact that 3 books on American history all had the Revolutionary War, the Civil War, World War I, World War II, the Vietnam War, and the Gulf War in the same chronological order would not prove that the authors had read each others' books. General agreement in content does not prove literary dependency.

5) The passages in which Matthew and Luke agree against Mark (see argument 3 in favor of the

"Two-Source" theory) amount to about one-sixth of Matthew and one-sixth of Luke. If they used Mark's gospel as a source, there is no satisfactory explanation for why Matthew and Luke would so often both change Mark's wording in the same way.

6) The "Two-Source" theory cannot account for the important section in Mark's gospel (6:45–8:26) which Luke omits. That omission suggests Luke had not seen Mark's gospel when he wrote.

7) There is no historical or manuscript evidence that the *Q* document ever existed; it is purely a fabrication of modern skepticism and a way to possibly deny the verbal inspiration of the gospels.

8) Any theory of literary dependence between the gospel writers overlooks the significance of their personal contacts with each other. Mark and Luke were both companions of Paul (cf. Philem. 24); the early church (including Matthew) met for a time in the home of Mark's mother (Acts 12:12); and Luke could easily have met Matthew during Paul's two-year imprisonment at Caesarea (*see note on Acts 27:1*). Such contacts make theories of mutual literary dependence unnecessary.

The simplest solution to the Synoptic Problem is that no such problem exists! Because critics cannot prove literary dependence between the gospel writers, there is no need to explain it. The traditional view that the gospel writers were inspired by God and wrote independently of each other—except that all 3 were moved by the same Holy Spirit (2 Pet. 1:20)—remains the only plausible view.

As the reader compares the various viewpoints in the gospels, it becomes clear how well they harmonize and lead to a more complete picture of the whole event or message. The accounts are not contradictory, but complementary, revealing a fuller understanding when brought together. Apparent difficulties are dealt with in the notes of each gospel.

Outline

- I. Prologue: In the Wilderness (1:1-13)
  - A. John's Message (1:1-8)
  - B. Jesus' Baptism (1:9-11)
  - C. Jesus' Temptation (1:12,13)
- II. Beginning His Ministry: In Galilee and the Surrounding Regions (1:14–7:23)
  - A. He Announces His Message (1:14,15)
  - B. He Calls His Disciples (1:16-20)
  - C. He Ministers in Capernaum (1:21-34)
  - D. He Reaches Out to Galilee (1:35-45)
  - E. He Defends His Ministry (2:1–3:6)
  - F. He Ministers to Multitudes (3:7-12)
  - G. He Commissions the Twelve (3:13-19)
  - H. He Rebukes the Scribes and Pharisees (3:20-30)
  - I. He Identifies His Spiritual Family (3:31-35)
  - J. He Preaches in Parables (4:1-34)
    - 1. The sower (4:1-9)
    - 2. The reason for parables (4:10-12)
    - 3. The parable of the sower explained (4:13-20)
    - 4. The lamp (4:21-25)
    - 5. The seed (4:26-29)
    - 6. The mustard seed (4:30-34)
  - K. He Demonstrates His Power (4:35–5:43)
    - 1. Calming the waves (4:35-41)
    - 2. Casting out demons (5:1-20)
    - 3. Healing the sick (5:21-34)
    - 4. Raising the dead (5:35-43)
  - L. He Returns to His Hometown (6:1-6)
  - M. He Sends out His Disciples (6:7-13)
  - N. He Gains a Powerful Enemy (6:14-29)
  - O. He Regroups with the Disciples (6:30-32)
  - P. He Feeds the Five Thousand (6:33-44)
  - Q. He Walks on Water (6:45-52)
  - R. He Heals Many People (6:53-56)
  - S. He Answers the Pharisees (7:1-23)

- III. Broadening His Ministry: In Various Gentile Regions (7:24–9:50)
  - A. Tyre and Sidon: He Delivers a Gentile Woman's Daughter (7:24-30)
  - B. Decapolis: He Heals a Deaf-Mute (7:31-37)
  - C. The Eastern Shore of Galilee: He Feeds the Four Thousand (8:1-9)
  - D. Dalmanutha: He Disputes with the Pharisees (8:10-12)
  - E. The Other Side of the Lake: He Rebukes the Disciples (8:13-21)
  - F. Bethsaida: He Heals a Blind Man (8:22-26)
  - G. Caesarea Philippi and Capernaum: He Instructs the Disciples (8:27–9:50)
    - 1. Peter confesses Jesus as Christ (8:27-30)
    - 2. He predicts His death (8:31-33)
    - 3. He explains the cost of discipleship (8:34-38)
    - 4. He reveals His glory (9:1-10)
    - 5. He clarifies Elijah's role (9:11-13)
    - 6. He casts out a stubborn spirit (9:14-29)
    - 7. He again predicts His death and resurrection (9:30-32)
    - 8. He defines kingdom greatness (9:33-37)
    - 9. He identifies true spiritual fruit (9:38-41)
    - 10. He warns would-be stumbling blocks (9:42-50)
- IV. Concluding His Ministry: The Road to Jerusalem (10:1-52)
  - A. He Teaches on Divorce (10:1-12)
  - B. He Blesses the Children (10:13-16)
  - C. He Confronts the Rich Young Ruler (10:17-27)
  - D. He Confirms the Disciples' Rewards (10:28-31)
  - E. He Prepares the Disciples for His Death (10:32-34)
  - F. He Challenges the Disciples to Humble Service (10:35-45)
  - G. He Heals a Blind Man (10:46-52)
- V. Consummating His Ministry: Jerusalem (11:1–16:20)
  - A. Triumphal Entry (11:1-11)
  - B. Purification (11:12-19)
    - 1. Cursing the fig tree (11:12-14)
    - 2. Cleansing the temple (11:15-19)
  - C. Teaching in Public and in Private (11:20–13:37)
    - 1. Publicly: in the temple (11:20–12:44)
      - a. Prelude: the lesson of the cursed fig tree (11:20-26)
      - b. Concerning His authority (11:27-33)
      - c. Concerning His rejection (12:1-12)
      - d. Concerning paying taxes (12:13-17)
      - e. Concerning the resurrection (12:18-27)
      - f. Concerning the greatest commandment (12:28-34)
      - g. Concerning the Messiah's true sonship (12:35-37)
      - h. Concerning the scribes (12:38-40)
      - i. Concerning true giving (12:41-44)
    - 2. Privately: on the Mount of Olives (13:1-37)
      - a. The disciples' question about the end times (13:1)
      - b. The Lord's answer (13:2-37)
  - D. Arrangements for Betrayal (14:1,2,10,11)
  - E. Anointing, the Last Supper, Betrayal, Arrest, Trial [Jewish Phase] (14:3-9; 12-72)
    - 1. The anointing: Bethany (14:3-9)
    - 2. The Last Supper: Jerusalem (14:12-31)
    - 3. The prayer: Gethsemane (14:32-42)
    - 4. The betrayal: Gethsemane (14:43-52)
    - 5. The Jewish trial: Caiaphas' house (14:53-72)
  - F. Trial (Roman Phase), Crucifixion (15:1-41)
    - 1. The Roman trial: Pilate's Praetorium (15:1-15)
    - 2. The crucifixion: Golgotha (15:16-41)
  - G. Burial in Joseph of Arimathea's Tomb (15:42-47)
  - H. Resurrection (16:1-8)
  - I. Postscript (16:9-20)

The Forerunner of the Servant
Matt. 3:1-11; Luke 3:3-16; John 1:19-34

1 The [a]beginning of the gospel of Jesus
Christ, [b]the Son of God. 2 As it is written in [1]the Prophets:

[c]*"Behold, I send My messenger*
before Your face,
Who will prepare Your way
before You."
3 *"The[d] voice of one crying in the*
wilderness:
'Prepare the way of the LORD;
Make His paths straight.' "

4 [e]John came baptizing in the wilderness
and preaching a baptism of repentance
[2]for the remission of sins. 5 [f]Then all the
land of Judea, and those from Jerusalem,
went out to him and were all baptized by
him in the Jordan River, confessing their
sins.
6 Now John was [g]clothed with camel's
hair and with a leather belt around his
waist, and he ate locusts and wild honey.
7 And he preached, saying, [h]"There comes
One after me who is mightier than I, whose
sandal strap I am not worthy to stoop
down and loose. 8 [i]I indeed baptized you
with water, but He will baptize you [j]with
the Holy Spirit."

The Baptism of the Servant
Matt. 3:13-17; Luke 3:21-23

9 [k]It came to pass in those days *that* Jesus
came from Nazareth of Galilee, and was

CHAPTER 1
1 [a] Matt. 1:1; 3:1; Luke 3:22 [b] Ps. 2:7; Matt. 14:33; Luke 1:35
2 [c] Mal. 3:1; Matt. 11:10; Luke 7:27 [1] NU *Isaiah the prophet*
3 [d] Is. 40:3; Matt. 3:3; Luke 3:4; John 1:23
4 [e] Mal. 4:6; Matt. 3:1; Luke 3:3 [2] Or *because of forgiveness*
5 [f] Matt. 3:5
6 [g] Matt. 3:4
7 [h] Matt. 3:11; John 1:27; Acts 13:25
8 [i] Acts 1:5; 11:16 [j] Is. 44:3; John 20:22; [Acts 2:4; 10:45, 46; 1 Cor. 12:13]
9 [k] Matt. 3:13-17; Luke 3:21, 22

1:1 The beginning…the Son of God. This is best viewed as Mark's title for his gospel. The historical record of the gospel message began with John the Baptist (cf. Matt. 11:12; Luke 16:16; Acts 1:22; 10:37; 13:24). **gospel.** The good news about the life, death, and resurrection of Jesus Christ, of which the 4 gospels are written records (see Introduction to the Gospels). **Jesus Christ.** "Jesus" is the Gr. form of the Heb. name *Joshua* ("the LORD is salvation"); "Christ" ("anointed one") is the Gr. equivalent of the Heb. word *Messiah.* "Jesus" is the Lord's human name (cf. Matt. 1:21; Luke 1:31); "Christ" signifies His office as ruler of God's coming kingdom (Dan. 9:25,26). **Son of God.** An affirmation of Jesus' deity, stressing His unique relationship to the Father (cf. 3:11; 5:7; 9:7; 13:32; 15:39; *see note on John 1:34*).

1:2 it is written. A phrase commonly used in the NT to introduce OT quotes (cf. 7:6; 9:13; 14:21,27; Matt. 2:5; 4:4,6,7; Luke 2:23; 3:4; John 6:45; 12:14; Acts 1:20; 7:42; Rom. 3:4; 8:36; 1 Cor. 1:31; 9:9; 2 Cor. 8:14; 9:9; Gal. 3:10; 4:22; Heb. 10:7; 1 Pet. 1:16). **in the Prophets.** The better Gr. manuscripts read "Isaiah the prophet." Mark's quote is actually from two OT passages (Mal. 3:1; Is. 40:3), which probably explains the reading "the Prophets" found in some manuscripts. The gospels all introduce John the Baptist's ministry by quoting Is. 40:3 (cf. Matt. 3:3; Luke 3:4; John 1:23). ***My messenger.*** John was the divinely-promised messenger, sent to prepare the way for the Messiah. In ancient times, a king's envoys would travel ahead of him, making sure the roads were safe and fit for him to travel on, as well as announcing his arrival.

1:4 John. A common Jewish name in NT times, it is the Gr. equivalent of the Heb. name "Johanan" (cf. 2 Kin. 25:23; 1 Chr. 3:15; Jer. 40:8), meaning "the LORD is gracious." John's name was given by the angel Gabriel to his father Zacharias, during his time of priestly service in the temple (Luke 1:13). His mother, Elizabeth, also a descendant of Aaron (Luke 1:5), was a relative of Mary the mother of Jesus (Luke 1:36). As the last OT prophet and the divinely ordained forerunner of the Messiah (*see note on v. 2*), John was the culmination of OT history and prophecy (Luke 16:16) as well as the beginning of the historical record of the gospel of Jesus Christ. Not surprisingly, Jesus designated John as the greatest man who had lived until his time (Matt. 11:11). **baptizing.** Being the distinctive mark of John's ministry, his baptism differed from the ritual Jewish washings in that it was a one-time act. The Jews performed a similar one-time washing of Gentile proselytes, symbolizing their embracing of the true faith. That Jews would participate in such a rite was a startling admission that they, although members of God's covenant people, needed to come to God through repentance and faith just like Gentiles. **in the wilderness.** The desolate, arid region between Jerusalem and the Dead Sea (*see note on Matt. 3:1*). **baptism of repentance.** A baptism resulting from true repentance. John's ministry was to call Israel to repentance in preparation for the coming of Messiah. Baptism did not produce repentance, but was its result (cf. Matt. 3:7,8). Far more than a mere change of mind or remorse, repentance involves a turning from sin to God (cf. 1 Thess. 1:9), which results in righteous living. Genuine repentance is a work of God in the human heart (Acts 11:18). For a discussion of the nature of repentance, *see notes on 2 Cor. 7:9-12.* **for the remission of sins.** John's rite of baptism did not produce forgiveness of sin (*see notes on Acts 2:38; 22:16*); it was only the outward confession and illustration of the true repentance that results in forgiveness (cf. Luke 24:47; Acts 3:19; 5:31; 2 Cor. 7:10).

1:5 all the land of Judea, and those from Jerusalem. After centuries without a prophetic voice in Israel (Malachi had prophesied more than 400 years earlier), John's ministry generated an intense amount of interest. **Judea.** The southernmost division of Palestine (Samaria and Galilee being the others) in Jesus' day. It extended from about Bethel in the N to Beersheba in the S, and from the Mediterranean Sea in the W to the Dead Sea and Jordan River in the E. Included within Judea was the city of Jerusalem. **Jordan River.** Palestine's major river, flowing through the Jordan Rift Valley from Lake Hula (drained in modern times), N of the Sea of Galilee, S to the Dead Sea. According to tradition, John began his baptizing ministry at the fords near Jericho. **confessing.** To confess one's sins, as they were being baptized, is to agree with God about them. John baptized no one who did not confess and repent of his sins.

1:6 camel's hair…leather belt. The traditional clothes of a wilderness dweller which were sturdy, but neither fashionable nor comfortable. John's clothing would have reminded his audience of Elijah (cf. 2 Kin. 1:8), whom they expected to come before Messiah (Mal. 4:5; cf. Matt. 17:10-13). **locusts and wild honey.** The OT dietary regulations permitted the eating of "locusts" (Lev. 11:21,22). "Wild honey" could often be found in the wilderness (Deut. 32:13; 1 Sam. 14:25-27). John's austere diet was in keeping with his status as a lifelong Nazirite (cf. Luke 1:15; for Nazirite, *see notes on Num. 6:2-13*)

1:7 preached. Better translated "proclaimed," John was Jesus' herald, sent to announce His coming (*see note on v. 4*). **whose sandal strap I am not worthy to stoop down and loose.** The most menial task a slave could perform. John vividly expressed his humility.

1:8 baptize you with the Holy Spirit. This takes place when a person comes to faith in Christ (*see notes on Acts 1:5; 8:16,17; 1 Cor. 12:13*).

1:9 in those days. At some unspecified time during John's baptizing ministry at the Jordan. **Nazareth.** An obscure village (not mentioned in the OT, or by Josephus, or in the Talmud) about 70 mi. N of Jerusalem, that did not enjoy a favorable reputation (cf. John 1:46). Jesus had apparently been living there before His public appearance

The Miracles of Jesus

	Miracle	Matthew	Mark	Luke	John
1.	Cleansing a Leper	8:2	1:40	5:12	
2.	Healing a Centurion's Servant (of paralysis)	8:5		7:1	
3.	Healing Peter's Mother-in-Law	8:14	1:30	4:38	
4.	Healing the Sick at Evening	8:16	1:32	4:40	
5.	Stilling the Storm	8:23	4:35	8:22	
6.	Demons Entering a Herd of Swine	8:28	5:1	8:26	
7.	Healing a Paralytic	9:2	2:3	5:18	
8.	Raising the Ruler's Daughter	9:18,23	5:22,35	8:40,49	
9.	Healing the Hemorrhaging Woman	9:20	5:25	8:43	
10.	Healing Two Blind Men	9:27			
11.	Curing a Demon-Possessed, Mute Man	9:32			
12.	Healing a Man's Withered Hand	12:9	3:1	6:6	
13.	Curing a Demon-Possessed, Blind and Mute Man	12:22		11:14	
14.	Feeding the Five Thousand	14:13	6:30	9:10	6:1
15.	Walking on the Sea	14:25	6:48		6:19
16.	Healing the Gentile Woman's Daughter	15:21	7:24		
17.	Feeding the Four Thousand	15:32	8:1		
18.	Healing the Epileptic Boy	17:14	9:17	9:38	
19.	Temple Tax in the Fish's Mouth	17:24			
20.	Healing Two Blind Man	20:30	10:46	18:35	
21.	Withering the Fig Tree	21:18	11:12		
22.	Casting Out an Unclean Spirit		1:23	4:33	
23.	Healing a Deaf-Mute		7:31		
24.	Healing a Blind Man at Bethsaida		8:22		
25.	Escape from the Hostile Multitude			4:30	
26.	Catch of Fish			5:1	
27.	Raising of a Widow's Son at Nain			7:11	
28.	Healing the Infirm, Bent Woman			13:11	
29.	Healing the Man with Dropsy			14:1	
30.	Cleansing the Ten Lepers			17:11	
31.	Restoring a Servant's Ear			22:51	
32.	Turning Water into Wine				2:1
33.	Healing the Nobleman's Son (of fever)				4:46
34.	Healing an Infirm Man at Bethesda				5:1
35.	Healing the Man Born Blind				9:1
36.	Raising of Lazarus				11:43
37.	Second Catch of Fish				21:1

baptized by John in the Jordan. 10 [l]And
immediately, coming up [3]from the water,
He saw the heavens [4]parting and the Spirit [m]descending upon Him like a dove.
11 Then a voice came from heaven, [n]"You
are My beloved Son, in whom I am well
pleased."

The Tempation of the Servant
Matt. 4:1-11; Luke 4:1-13

12 [o]Immediately the Spirit [5]drove Him
into the wilderness. 13 And He was there
in the wilderness forty days, tempted by
Satan, and was with the wild beasts; [p]and
the angels ministered to Him.

The Work of the Servant
Matt. 4:12-17; Luke 4:14, 15

14 [q]Now after John was put in prison, Jesus came to Galilee, [r]preaching the gospel
[6]of the kingdom of God, 15 and saying,
[s]"The time is fulfilled, and [t]the kingdom of
God [7]is at hand. Repent, and believe in the
gospel."

The First Disciples Are Called
Matt. 4:18-22

16 [u]And as He walked by the Sea of Galilee, He saw Simon and Andrew his brother casting a net into the sea; for they were
fishermen. 17 Then Jesus said to them,
"Follow Me, and I will make you become
[v]fishers of men." 18 [w]They immediately
left their nets and followed Him.
19 When He had gone a little farther
from there, He saw James the *son* of Zebedee, and John his brother, who also *were* in
the boat mending their nets. 20 And immediately He called them, and they left their
father Zebedee in the boat with the hired
servants, and went after Him.

10 [l] Ezek. 1:1; Matt. 3:16; John 1:32 [m] Is. 11:2; 61:1; Acts 10:38 [3] NU *out of* [4] *torn open*
11 [n] [Ps. 2:7]; Is. 42:1; Matt. 3:17; 12:18; Mark 9:7; Luke 3:22
12 [o] Matt. 4:1-11; Luke 4:1-13 [5] *sent Him out*
13 [p] Matt. 4:10, 11
14 [q] Matt. 4:12 [r] Matt. 4:23 [6] NU omits *of the kingdom*
15 [s] Dan. 9:25; [Gal. 4:4; Eph. 1:10; 1 Tim. 2:6]; Titus 1:3 [t] Matt. 3:2; 4:17; [Acts 20:21] [7] *has drawn near*
16 [u] Matt. 4:18-22; Luke 5:2-11; John 1:40-42
17 [v] Matt. 13:47, 48
18 [w] Matt. 19:27; [Luke 14:26]

to Israel. **baptized by John.** Over John's objections (cf. Matt. 3:14), who saw no need for the sinless Lamb of God (John 1:29) to participate in a baptism of repentance (*see notes on vv. 4,5;* for an explanation of why Jesus was baptized, *see note on Matt. 3:15*).

1:10 immediately. In keeping with his fast-paced narrative style (see Introduction to the Gospels), Mark used this adverb more than the other 3 gospel writers combined. This first occurrence sets the stage for the audible and visible signs that followed Jesus' baptism. **the Spirit descending upon Him like a dove.** This was most likely symbolic of Jesus' empowerment for ministry (Is. 61:1). *See note on Matt. 3:16.*

1:11 The Father's pronouncement would have reminded the audience of the messianic prophecies of Ps. 2:7; Is. 42:1.

1:12 Immediately. *See note on v. 10.* Jesus' temptation came right after His baptism. **the Spirit drove Him.** Compelled by the Spirit, Jesus confronted Satan and took the first step toward overthrowing his evil kingdom (cf. 1 John 3:8). Though God tempts no one (James 1:13), He sometimes sovereignly permits Satan to tempt His people (e.g., Job; Luke 22:31,32). **the wilderness.** The exact location of Jesus' encounter with Satan is unknown. It most likely would have been the same wilderness where John lived and ministered (*see note on v. 4*), the desolate region farther S, or the arid Arabian desert across the Jordan.

1:13 forty days. Perhaps reminiscent of Israel's 40 years of wandering in the wilderness (Num. 14:33; 32:13). Matthew and Luke add that Jesus went without food during this time. Moses (twice, Deut. 9:9,18) and Elijah (1 Kin. 19:8) also fasted for that length of time. **Satan.** From a Heb. word meaning "adversary." Since He had no fallen nature, Jesus' temptation was not an internal emotional or psychological struggle, but an external attack by a personal being. **wild beasts.** A detail unique to Mark's account, stressing Jesus' loneliness and complete isolation from other people. **angels ministered to Him.** Cf. Ps. 91:11,12. The tense of this Gr. verb, "to minister," suggests the angels ministered to Jesus throughout His temptation.

1:14 John was put in prison. He was incarcerated for rebuking Herod Antipas over his incestuous marriage to his niece, Herodias (*see notes on 6:17-29*). **Jesus came to Galilee.** From Judea (Matt. 4:12; Luke 4:13; John 4:3). Mark, along with Matthew and Luke, passes directly from the temptation to the beginning of the Galilean ministry, skipping Jesus' intervening ministry in Judea (John 2:13–4:4). Galilee was the northernmost region of Palestine, and the most heavily populated. **the gospel...of God.** The good news of salvation both about God and from Him (*see note on Rom. 1:1*; cf. Rom. 15:16; 1 Thess. 2:2,8,9; 1 Tim. 1:11; 1 Pet. 4:17).

1:15 The time is fulfilled. Not time in a chronological sense, but the time for decisive action on God's part. With the arrival of the King, a new era in God's dealings with men had come. *See note on Gal. 4:4.* **the kingdom of God.** God's sovereign rule over the sphere of salvation; at present in the hearts of His people (Luke 17:21), and in the future, in a literal, earthly kingdom (Rev. 20:4-6). **at hand.** Because the King was present. **Repent, and believe.** Repentance (*see note on v. 4*) and faith (*see note on Rom. 1:16*) are man's required response to God's gracious offer of salvation (cf. Acts 20:21).

1:16 Sea of Galilee. Also known as the Sea of Chinnereth (Num. 34:11), the Lake of Gennesaret (Luke 5:1), and the Sea of Tiberias (John 6:1). A large, freshwater lake about 13 mi. long and 7 mi. wide, and about 690 ft. below sea level (making it the lowest body of fresh water on earth), the Sea of Galilee was home to a thriving fishing industry. **Simon and Andrew.** The first of two sets of brothers Jesus called to follow him. Like James and John, they were fishermen. Since Andrew had been a follower of John the Baptist (John 1:40), it is possible that Peter had been as well. They had evidently returned to their fishing business after John's arrest (*see note on v. 14*). They had already met and spent time with Jesus (*see note on Matt. 4:18*), but were here called to follow Him permanently. **net.** A rope forming a circle about 9 ft. in diameter with a net attached. It could be thrown by hand into the water, then hauled in by means of the length of weighted rope attached to it.

1:17 Follow Me. Used frequently in the gospels in reference to discipleship (2:14; 8:34; 10:21; Matt. 4:19; 8:22; 9:9; 10:38; 16:24; 19:21; Luke 9:23,59,61; 18:22; John 1:43; 10:27; 12:26). **fishers of men.** Evangelism was the primary purpose for which Jesus called the apostles, and it remains the central mission for His people (cf. Matt. 28:19,20; Acts 1:8).

1:18 followed Him. I.e., became His permanent disciples (*see note on v. 16*).

1:19 James...John. The second set of fishermen brothers called by Jesus (*see note on v. 16*). Their mother and Jesus' mother may have been sisters (cf. 15:40; Matt. 27:55,56 with John 19:25). If so, they were Jesus' cousins.

1:20 hired servants. This indicates that Zebedee's fishing business was a prosperous one and that he was a man of importance (cf. John 18:15).

Demons Are Cast Out—Luke 4:31-37

21 [x]Then they went into Capernaum,
and immediately on the Sabbath He entered the [y]synagogue and taught. 22 [z]And
they were astonished at His teaching, for
He taught them as one having authority,
and not as the scribes.
23 Now there was a man in their synagogue with an [a]unclean spirit. And he
cried out, 24 saying, "Let *us* alone! [b]What
have we to do with You, Jesus of Nazareth? Did You come to destroy us? I
[c]know who You are—the [d]Holy One of
God!"
25 But Jesus [e]rebuked him, saying, [8]"Be
quiet, and come out of him!" 26 And when
the unclean spirit [f]had convulsed him and
cried out with a loud voice, he came out of
him. 27 Then they were all amazed, so that
they questioned among themselves, saying, [9]"What is this? What new [1]doctrine *is*
this? For with authority He commands
even the unclean spirits, and they obey
Him." 28 And immediately His [g]fame
spread throughout all the region around
Galilee.

21 [x]Matt. 4:13; Luke 4:31-37 [y]Ps. 22:22; Matt. 4:23; Luke 4:16; 13:10
22 [z]Matt. 7:28, 29; 13:54
23 [a][Matt. 12:43]; Mark 5:2; 7:25; Luke 4:33
24 [b]Matt. 8:28, 29; Mark 5:7, 8; Luke 8:28 [c]Mark 3:11; Luke 4:41; James 2:19 [d]Ps. 16:10
25 [e][Luke 4:39] [8]Lit. *Be muzzled*
26 [f]Mark 9:20
27 [9]NU *What is this? A new doctrine with authority! He* [1]*teaching*
28 [g]Matt. 4:24; 9:31
29 [h]Matt. 8:14, 15; Luke 4:38, 39
32 [i]Matt. 8:16, 17; Luke 4:40, 41
34 [j]Matt. 9:33; Luke 13:32 [k]Mark 3:12; Luke 4:41; Acts 16:17, 18
35 [l]Luke 4:42, 43 [m]Matt. 26:39, 44; Mark 6:46; Luke 5:16; 6:12; 9:28, 29; Heb. 5:7 [2]*deserted*
37 [n]Matt. 4:25; John 3:26; 12:19 [o][Heb. 11:6]

Peter's Mother-in-Law Is Healed
Matt. 8:14, 15; Luke 4:38, 39

29 [h]Now as soon as they had come out of
the synagogue, they entered the house of
Simon and Andrew, with James and John.
30 But Simon's wife's mother lay sick with
a fever, and they told Him about her at
once. 31 So He came and took her by the
hand and lifted her up, and immediately
the fever left her. And she served them.

Many Healings
Matt. 8:16, 17, 4:23; Luke 4:40-44

32 [i]At evening, when the sun had set,
they brought to Him all who were sick and
those who were demon-possessed. 33 And
the whole city was gathered together at the
door. 34 Then He healed many who were
sick with various diseases, and [j]cast out
many demons; and He [k]did not allow the
demons to speak, because they knew Him.
35 Now [l]in the morning, having risen a
long while before daylight, He went out
and departed to a [2]solitary place; and there
He [m]prayed. 36 And Simon and those *who
were* with Him searched for Him. 37 When
they found Him, they said to Him, [n]"Everyone [o]is looking for You."

1:21 Capernaum. A prosperous fishing village on the NW shore of the Sea of Galilee, Capernaum was a more important city than Nazareth; it contained a Roman garrison and was located on a major road. Jesus made the city his headquarters (cf. 2:1) after his rejection at Nazareth (Matt. 4:13; Luke 4:16-31). **synagogue.** The place where Jewish people gathered for worship ("synagogue" is a transliteration of a Gr. word meaning "to gather together"). Synagogues originated in the Babylonian captivity after the 586 B.C. destruction of the temple by Nebuchadnezzar. They served as places of worship and instruction. Jesus frequently taught in the synagogues (cf. v. 39; 3:1; 6:2), as did Paul (cf. Acts 13:5; 14:1; 17:1). **taught.** Mark frequently mentions Jesus' teaching ministry (cf. 2:13; 4:1,2; 6:2,6,34; 10:1; 11:17; 12:35; 14:49).

1:22 authority. Jesus' authoritative teaching, as the spoken Word of God, was in sharp contrast to that of the scribes (experts in the OT Scriptures), who based their authority largely on that of other rabbis. Jesus' direct, personal, and forceful teaching was so foreign to their experience that those who heard Him were "astonished" (cf. Titus 2:15).

1:23 man...cried out. Satan and his demon hosts opposed Jesus' work throughout His ministry, culminating in the cross. Jesus always triumphed over their futile efforts (cf. Col. 2:15), convincingly demonstrating His ultimate victory by His resurrection. **unclean spirit.** I.e., morally impure. The term is used interchangeably in the NT with "demon." *See note on 5:2.*

1:24 What have we to do with You. Or, possibly, "Why do you interfere with us?" The demon was acutely aware that he and Jesus belonged to two radically different kingdoms, and thus had nothing in common. That the demon used the plural pronoun "we" indicates he spoke for all the demons. **Nazareth.** *See note on v. 9.* **the Holy One of God.** Cf. Ps. 16:10; Dan. 9:24; Luke 4:34; Acts 2:27; 3:14; 4:27; Rev. 3:7. Amazingly, the demon affirmed Jesus' sinlessness and deity—truths which many in Israel denied, and still deny.

1:25 Be quiet. Jesus wanted no testimony to the truth from the demonic realm to fuel charges that he was in league with Satan (cf. 3:22; Acts 16:16-18).

1:27 with authority. *See note on v. 22.* Jesus had absolute authority in His actions as well as His words (Matt. 28:18).

1:29 the house of Simon and Andrew. Originally from Bethsaida (John 1:44), the two brothers had moved to Capernaum when Jesus established his headquarters there (*see note on v. 21*). **James and John.** Only Mark mentions their presence at the healing of Peter's mother-in-law.

1:30 Simon's wife's mother. Paul also affirmed that Peter was married (1 Cor. 9:5). That his mother-in-law was living with Peter and his wife may indicate that her husband was dead. **a fever.** That she was too ill to get out of bed, coupled with Luke's description of her fever as a "high fever" (Luke 4:38), suggests her illness was serious, even life-threatening.

1:32 when the sun had set. Marking the close of the Sabbath and the easing of the restrictions associated with it. Specifically, rabbinic law prohibited carrying any burdens (such as stretchers) on the Sabbath. **they brought.** The report of Jesus' healing of the demon-possessed man in the synagogue and Peter's mother-in-law created a sensation in Capernaum and aroused the hopes of other sufferers.

1:34 did not allow the demons to speak. *See notes on v. 25; 3:11,12.* **they knew Him.** The demons' theology is absolutely orthodox (James 2:19); but though they know the truth, they reject it and God, who is its source.

1:36 Simon and those *who were* with Him. The first instance in the gospels of Peter's assuming of leadership. Those with Peter are not revealed, though Andrew, James, and John were likely among them.

1:37 Finding Jesus after a diligent search (v. 36), Peter and the others excitedly implored Him to return to Capernaum and capitalize on the excitement generated by the previous night's healings.

38 But He said to them, [p]"Let us go into
the next towns, that I may preach there
also, because [q]for this purpose I have come
forth."
39 [r]And He was preaching in their synagogues throughout all Galilee, and [s]cast-
ing out demons.

A Leper Is Cleansed
Matt. 8:1-4; Luke 5:12-16

40 [t]Now a leper came to Him, imploring
Him, kneeling down to Him and saying to
Him, "If You are willing, You can make me
clean."
41 Then Jesus, moved with [u]compassion,
stretched out *His* hand and touched him,
and said to him, "I am willing; be
cleansed." 42 As soon as He had spoken,
[v]immediately the leprosy left him, and he
was cleansed. 43 And He strictly warned
him and sent him away at once, 44 and said
to him, "See that you say nothing to anyone; but go your way, show yourself to the
priest, and offer for your cleansing those
things [w]which Moses commanded, as a
testimony to them."
45 [x]However, he went out and began to
proclaim *it* freely, and to spread the matter,
so that Jesus could no longer openly enter
the city, but was outside in deserted places;
[y]and they came to Him from every direction.

A Paralytic Is Healed
Matt. 9:1-8; Luke 5:17-26

2 And again [a]He entered Capernaum
after *some* days, and it was heard that
He was in the house. 2 [1]Immediately many
gathered together, so that there was no
longer room to receive *them,* not even near
the door. And He preached the word to
them. 3 Then they came to Him, bringing a
[b]paralytic who was carried by four *men.*
4 And when they could not come near Him
because of the crowd, they uncovered the
roof where He was. So when they had broken through, they let down the bed on
which the paralytic was lying.
5 When Jesus saw their faith, He said to
the paralytic, "Son, your sins are forgiven
you."
6 And some of the scribes were sitting
there and reasoning in their hearts, 7 "Why
does this *Man* speak blasphemies like this?
[c]Who can forgive sins but God alone?"
8 But immediately, when Jesus perceived

38 [p] Luke 4:43 [q] [Is. 61:1, 2; Mark 10:45; John 16:28; 17:4, 8]
39 [r] Ps. 22:22; Matt. 4:23; 9:35; Mark 1:21; 3:1; Luke 4:44 [s] Mark 5:8, 13; 7:29, 30
40 [t] Matt. 8:2-4; Luke 5:12-14
41 [u] Luke 7:13
42 [v] Matt. 15:28; Mark 5:29
44 [w] Lev. 14:1-32
45 [x] Matt. 28:15; Luke 5:15
[y] Mark 2:2, 13; 3:7; Luke 5:17; John 6:2

CHAPTER 2

1 [a] Matt. 9:1
2 [1] NU omits *Immediately*
3 [b] Matt. 4:24; 8:6; Acts 8:7; 9:33
7 [c] Job 14:4; Is. 43:25; Dan. 9:9

1:39 throughout all Galilee. Mark's terse statement summarizes a preaching tour that must have lasted for weeks, or even months (cf. Matt. 4:23,24).

1:40-45 Mark relates one of Jesus' many healings during the Galilean ministry summarized in v. 39. The leper's healing emphasizes Jesus' miraculous power over disease, since leprosy was one of the most dreaded diseases of antiquity.

1:40 leper. Lepers were considered ceremonially unclean, and were outcasts from society (Lev. 13:11). While the OT term for leprosy included other skin diseases (*see note on Lev. 13:2*), this man may have actually had true leprosy (Hansen's Disease), or else his cure would not have created such a sensation (v. 45).

1:41 compassion. Only Mark records Jesus' emotional reaction to the leper's desperate plight. The Gr. word appears only in the synoptic gospels and (apart from parables) is used only in reference to Jesus. **touched him.** Unlike rabbis, who avoided lepers lest they become ceremonially defiled, Jesus expressed His compassion with a physical gesture.

1:44 say nothing to anyone. The ensuing publicity would hinder Jesus' ability to minister (as in fact happened, cf. v. 45) and divert attention away from His message. Cf. 3:12; 5:43; 7:36; *see note on Matt. 8:4.* **go your way, show yourself to the priest.** The "priest" was the one on duty at the temple. Jesus commanded the healed leper to observe the OT regulations concerning cleansed lepers (Lev. 14:1-32). Until the required offerings had been made, the man remained ceremonially unclean. **a testimony to them.** The priest's acceptance of the man's offering would be public affirmation of his cure and cleansing.

1:45 proclaim *it* freely. Only Mark records the cleansed leper's disobedience, although Luke hints at it (Luke 5:15). **no longer openly enter the city.** The result of the leper's disobedience was that Jesus could no longer enter a city without being mobbed by those seeking to be cured of diseases. Jesus' ministry of teaching in that area thus came to a halt. **deserted places.** Jesus kept to the relatively uninhabited regions to allow the excitement over his cure of the leper to die down. Luke also notes that He used His time in the wilderness for prayer (Luke 5:16).

2:1 He was in the house. This is better translated, "He was at home." This was likely Peter's home, where Jesus had taken up temporary residence (cf. Matt. 4:13).

2:2 the word. The good news of the gospel, that salvation is by grace alone, through faith alone, for the forgiveness of sins.

2:3 a paralytic. Since he was lying on a bed, the man's paralysis was severe—perhaps he was a quadriplegic.

2:4 they uncovered the roof. Most homes in Palestine had flat roofs used for relaxation in the cool of the day and for sleeping on hot nights. And there was usually an external stairway that extended to the roof. Often, as here, the roof was made of slabs of burnt or dried clay that were placed on supporting beams which stretched from wall to wall. The builder then spread a uniform coat of fresh, wet clay over those slabs of hardened clay to serve as a seal against the rain. The paralytic's friends took him up to the top of such a house and dug out the top coat of clay, removing several of the slabs until they made enough room to lower him down into Jesus' presence. **the paralytic.** *See note on v. 3.*

2:5 When Jesus saw their faith. The aggressive, persistent effort of the paralytic's friends was visible evidence of their faith in Christ to heal. **"Son, your sins are forgiven you."** Many Jews in that day believed that all disease and affliction was a direct result of one's sins. This paralytic may have believed that as well; thus he would have welcomed forgiveness of his sins before healing. The Gr. verb for "are forgiven" refers to sending or driving away (cf. Ps. 103:12; Jer. 31:34; Mic. 7:19). Thus Jesus dismissed the man's sin and freed him from the guilt of it (*see note on Matt. 9:2*).

2:6 the scribes. *See note on Matt. 2:4*; cf. 1:22.

2:7 this *Man*...blasphemies. The scribes were correct in saying that only God can forgive sins (cf. Is. 43:25), but incorrect in saying Jesus blasphemed. They refused to recognize Jesus' power as coming from God, much less that He Himself was God.

in His spirit that they reasoned thus within themselves, He said to them, "Why do
you reason about these things in your
hearts? 9 [d]Which is easier, to say to the paralytic, '*Your* sins are forgiven you,' or to
say, 'Arise, take up your bed and walk'?
10 But that you may know that the Son of
Man has [2]power on earth to forgive
sins"—He said to the paralytic, 11 "I say to
you, arise, take up your bed, and go to
your house." 12 Immediately he arose, took
up the bed, and went out in the presence of
them all, so that all were amazed and [e]glo-
rified God, saying, "We never saw *anything*
like this!"

Call of Matthew—Matt. 9:9-13; Luke 5:27-32

13 [f]Then He went out again by the sea;
and all the multitude came to Him, and He
taught them. 14 [g]As He passed by, He saw
Levi the *son* of Alphaeus sitting at the tax
office. And He said to him, [h]"Follow Me."
So he arose and [i]followed Him.

15 [j]Now it happened, as He was dining
in *Levi's* house, that many tax collectors and

9 [d] Matt. 9:5
10 [2] *authority*
12 [e] Matt. 15:31; [Phil. 2:11]
13 [f] Matt. 9:9
14 [g] Matt. 9:9-13; Luke 5:27-32 [h] Matt. 4:19; 8:22; 19:21; John 1:43; 12:26; 21:22 [i] Luke 18:28
15 [j] Matt. 9:10

2:8 in His spirit. This can also be translated, "by His spirit." This is not the Holy Spirit, but the omniscient mind of the Savior.

2:9 Which is easier. It is much easier to say, "Your sins are forgiven you." No human can prove that such a thing actually occurred since it is invisible. Commanding a paralytic to walk would be more difficult to say convincingly, however, because the actions of the paralytic would immediately verify the effect of the command (*see note on Matt. 9:5*).

2:10 But that you may know. Jesus' power to heal the paralytic's physical infirmities proved the veracity of His claim and power to forgive sins. **Son of Man.** Jesus used this term for Himself to emphasize His humiliation (*see notes on 14:62; Matt. 8:20*). It appears 14 times in Mark (v. 10,28; 8:31,38; 9:9,12,31; 10:33,45; 13:26; 14:21,41,62).

2:14 Levi the *son* of Alphaeus. One of the 12, more commonly known as Matthew (see Introduction to Matthew: Title). **tax office.** Matthew was a publican, a tax collector, a despised profession in Palestine because such men were viewed as traitors. Publicans were Jews who had bought tax franchises from the Roman government. Any amount they collected over what Rome required they were allowed to keep. Thus many publicans became wealthy at the expense of their own people (*see notes on Matt. 5:46; 9:9*). **he arose and followed Him.** This simple action of Matthew signified his conversion. Because his response was so immediate, it is likely Matthew was already convicted of his sin and recognized his need of forgiveness.

2:15 dining. This can also be translated, "reclining at table," a common posture for eating when guests were present. According to Luke 5:29, this was a feast that Matthew gave in Jesus' honor. **tax collectors.** There were two categories of tax collectors: 1) *gabbai* collected general taxes on land and property, and on income, referred to as poll or registration taxes; 2) *mokhes* collected a wide variety of use

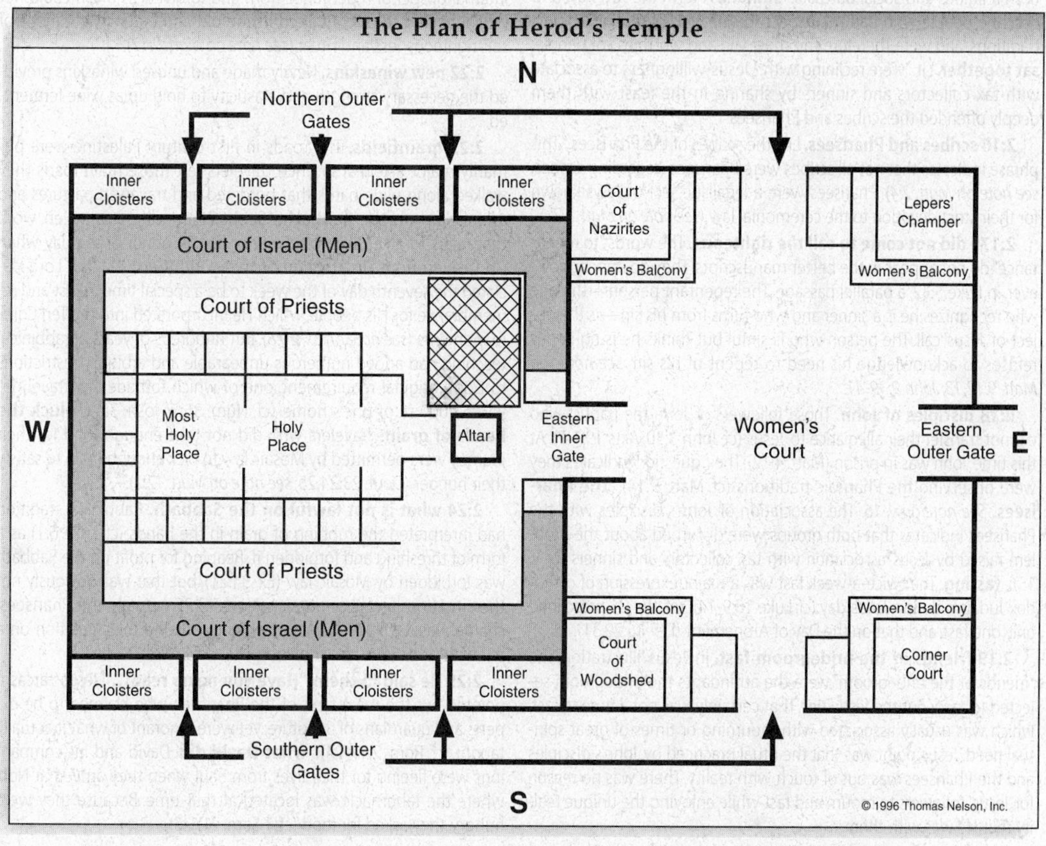

sinners also sat together with Jesus and His
disciples; for there were many, and they followed Him. 16 And when the scribes [3]and
Pharisees saw Him eating with the tax collectors and sinners, they said to His disciples, "How *is it* that He eats and drinks
with tax collectors and sinners?"
17 When Jesus heard *it,* He said to them,
[k]"Those who are well have no need of a
physician, but those who are sick. I did not
come to call *the* righteous, but sinners, [4]to
repentance."

Parable of Cloth and Wineskins
Matt. 9:14-17; Luke 5:33-39

18 [l]The disciples of John and of the
Pharisees were fasting. Then they came
and said to Him, "Why do the disciples of
John and of the Pharisees fast, but Your
disciples do not fast?"
19 And Jesus said to them, "Can the
[5]friends of the bridegroom fast while the
bridegroom is with them? As long as they
have the bridegroom with them they cannot fast. 20 But the days will come when
the bridegroom will be [m]taken away from
them, and then they will fast in those days.
21 No one sews a piece of unshrunk cloth
on an old garment; or else the new piece
pulls away from the old, and the tear is
made worse. 22 And no one puts new wine
into old wineskins; or else the new wine
bursts the wineskins, the wine is spilled,
and the wineskins are ruined. But new
wine must be put into new wineskins."

Controversy over Sabbath-Work
Matt. 12:1-8; Luke 6:1-5

23 [n]Now it happened that He went
through the grainfields on the Sabbath;
and as they went His disciples began [o]to
pluck the heads of grain. 24 And the Pharisees said to Him, "Look, why do they do
what is [p]not lawful on the Sabbath?"
25 But He said to them, "Have you never
read [q]what David did when he was in

16 [3] NU *of the*
17 [k] Matt. 9:12, 13; 18:11; Luke 5:31, 32; 19:10 [4] NU omits *to repentance*
18 [l] Matt. 9:14-17; Luke 5:33-38
19 [5] Lit. *sons of the bridechamber*
20 [m] Acts 1:9; 13:2, 3; 14:23
23 [n] Matt. 12:1-8; Luke 6:1-5 [o] Deut. 23:25
24 [p] Ex. 20:10; 31:15
25 [q] 1 Sam. 21:1-6

taxes, similar to our import duties, business license fees, and toll fees. There were two categories of *mokhes:* great *mokhes* hired others to collect taxes for them; small *mokhes* did their own assessing and collecting. Matthew was a small *mokhe.* It is likely representatives of both classes attended Matthew's feast. All of them were considered both religious and social outcasts. **sinners.** A term the Jews used to describe people who had no respect for the Mosaic law or rabbinic traditions, and were therefore the most vile and worthless of people. **sat together.** Lit. "were reclining with." Jesus' willingness to associate with tax collectors and sinners by sharing in the feast with them deeply offended the scribes and Pharisees.

2:16 scribes and Pharisees. Lit. "the scribes of the Pharisees." This phrase indicates that not all scribes were Pharisees (regarding scribes, *see note on Matt. 2:4*). Pharisees were a legalistic sect of Jews known for their strict devotion to the ceremonial law (*see note on Matt. 3:7*).

2:17 I did not come to call *the* righteous. The words "to repentance" do not appear in the better manuscripts. They do appear, however, in Luke 5:32, a parallel passage. The repentant person—the one who recognizes he is a sinner and who turns from his sin—is the object of Jesus' call. The person who is sinful but thinks he is righteous refuses to acknowledge his need to repent of his sin. *See notes on Matt. 9:12,13; John 9:39-41.*

2:18 disciples of John. Those followers of John the Baptist who did not transfer their allegiance to Jesus (cf. John 3:30; Acts 19:1-7). At this time John was in prison (Matt. 4:12). Their question indicates they were observing the Pharisaic traditions (cf. Matt. 9:14). **the Pharisees.** *See note on v. 16.* The association of John's disciples with the Pharisees indicates that both groups were disturbed about the problem raised by Jesus' association with tax collectors and sinners (cf. v. 15). **fasting.** The twice-a-week fast was a major expression of orthodox Judaism during Jesus' day (cf. Luke 18:9-14). Yet, the OT prescribed only one fast, and that on the Day of Atonement (Lev. 16:29,31).

2:19 friends of the bridegroom fast. In Jesus' illustration, the "friends of the bridegroom" were the attendants the bridegroom selected to carry out the festivities. That certainly was not a time to fast, which was usually associated with mourning or times of great spiritual need. Jesus' point was that the ritual practiced by John's disciples and the Pharisees was out of touch with reality. There was no reason for Jesus' followers to mourn and fast while enjoying the unique reality that He was with them.

2:20 taken away from them. This refers to a sudden removal or being snatched away violently—an obvious reference to Jesus' capture and crucifixion. **then they will fast.** An appropriate time for mourning was to be at the crucifixion of Jesus.

2:21,22 Jesus offered two parables to illustrate that his new and internal gospel of repentance from and forgiveness of sin could not be connected to or contained in the old and external traditions of self-righteousness and ritual (*see note on Matt. 9:17*).

2:22 new wineskins. Newly made and unused wineskins provided the necessary strength and elasticity to hold up as wine fermented.

2:23 grainfields. The roads in first-century Palestine were primarily major arteries; so once travelers left those main roads they walked along wide paths that bordered and traversed pastures and grainfields. **on the Sabbath.** "Sabbath" transliterates a Heb. word that refers to a ceasing of activity or rest. In honor of the day when God rested from His creation of the world (Gen. 2:3), the Lord declared the seventh day of the week to be a special time of rest and remembrance for His people, which He incorporated into the Ten Commandments (*see note on Ex. 20:8*). But hundreds of years of rabbinical teaching had added numerous unbearable and arbitrary restrictions to God's original requirement, one of which forbade any travel beyond 3,000 ft. of one's home (cf. Num. 35:5; Josh. 3:4). **pluck the heads of grain.** Travelers who did not take enough food for their journey were permitted by Mosaic law to pick enough grain to satisfy their hunger (Deut. 23:24,25; *see note on Matt. 12:2*).

2:24 what is not lawful on the Sabbath. Rabbinical tradition had interpreted the rubbing of grain in the hands (cf. Luke 6:1) as a form of threshing and forbidden it. Reaping for profit on the Sabbath was forbidden by Mosaic law (Ex. 34:21), but that was obviously not the situation here (*see note on Matt. 12:2*). Actually the Pharisees' charge was itself sinful since they were holding their tradition on a par with God's Word (*see notes on Matt. 15:2-9*).

2:25 He said to them, "Have you never read…" Jesus' sarcasm pointed out the main fault of the Pharisees, who claimed to be experts and guardians of Scripture, yet were ignorant of what it actually taught (cf. Rom. 2:17-24). **what David did.** David and his companions were fleeing for their lives from Saul when they arrived at Nob, where the tabernacle was located at that time. Because they were hungry, they asked for food (cf. 1 Sam. 21:1-6).

need and hungry, he and those with him:
26 how he went into the house of God *in the*
days of Abiathar the high priest, and ate the
showbread, [r]which is not lawful to eat except for the priests, and also gave some to
those who were with him?"
27 And He said to them, "The Sabbath
was made for man, and not man for the
[s]Sabbath. 28 Therefore [t]the Son of Man is
also Lord of the Sabbath."

Controversy over Sabbath-Healing
Matt 12:9-13; Luke 6:6-10

3 And [a]He entered the synagogue again,
and a man was there who had a withered hand. 2 So they [b]watched Him closely,
whether He would [c]heal him on the Sabbath, so that they might [1]accuse Him.
3 And He said to the man who had the
withered hand, [2]"Step forward." 4 Then
He said to them, "Is it lawful on the Sabbath to do good or to do evil, to save life or
to kill?" But they kept silent. 5 And when
He had looked around at them with anger,
being grieved by the [d]hardness of their
hearts, He said to the man, "Stretch out
your hand." And he stretched *it* out, and
his hand was restored [3]as whole as the
other.

Pharisees Counsel to Destroy Jesus
Matt. 12:14-16; Luke 6:11

6 [e]Then the Pharisees went out and immediately plotted with [f]the Herodians against
Him, how they might destroy Him.
7 But Jesus withdrew with His disciples
to the sea. And a great multitude from Galilee followed Him, [g]and from Judea 8 and
Jerusalem and Idumea and beyond the Jordan; and those from Tyre and Sidon, a
great multitude, when they heard how
[h]many things He was doing, came to Him.
9 So He told His disciples that a small boat
should be kept ready for Him because of
the multitude, lest they should crush Him.
10 For He healed [i]many, so that as many as

26 [r]Ex. 29:32, 33; Lev. 24:5-9
27 [s]Gen. 2:3; Ex. 23:12; Deut. 5:14; Neh. 9:14; Ezek. 20:12
28 [t]Matt. 12:8

CHAPTER 3

1 [a]Matt. 12:9-14; Luke 6:6-11
2 [b][Ps. 37:32]; Luke 14:1; 20:20 [c]Luke 13:14 [1]*bring charges against*
3 [2]Lit. *Arise into the midst*
5 [d]Zech. 7:12 [3]NU omits *as whole as the other*
6 [e]Ps. 2:2; Mark 12:13 [f]Matt. 22:16
7 [g]Matt. 4:25; Luke 6:17
8 [h]Mark 5:19
10 [i]Mark 5:29, 34; Luke 7:21

2:26 *in the days* of Abiathar the high priest. The phrase "in the days" can mean "during the lifetime." According to 1 Sam. 21:1, Ahimelech was the priest who gave the bread to David. Abiathar was Ahimelech's son, who later was the High-Priest during David's reign. Since Ahimelech died shortly after this incident (cf. 1 Sam. 22:19,20), it is likely that Mark simply added this designation to identify the well known companion of David who later became the High-Priest, along with Zadok (2 Sam. 15:35). **the showbread.** Twelve loaves of unleavened bread (representing the 12 tribes of Israel) were placed on the table in the sanctuary and at the end of the week replaced with fresh ones. The old loaves were to be eaten only by the priests. While it was not normally lawful for David and his companions to eat this showbread, neither did God want them to starve, so nowhere does Scripture condemn them for eating (*see note on Matt. 12:4*).

2:27 The Sabbath was made for man. God instituted the Sabbath to benefit man by giving him a day to rest from his labors and to be a blessing to him. The Pharisees turned it into a burden and made man a slave to their myriad of man-made regulations.

2:28 also Lord of the Sabbath. Jesus claimed He was greater than the Sabbath, and thus was God. Based on that authority, Jesus could in fact reject the Pharisaic regulations concerning the Sabbath and restore God's original intention for Sabbath observance to be a blessing not a burden.

3:1-6 This is the last of the 5 conflict episodes which began in 2:1 (2:1-11; 13-17; 18-22; 23-28), and as such it gives a sense of climax to the growing antagonism between Jesus and the Jewish leaders. In this encounter, Jesus gave the Pharisees a living illustration of scriptural Sabbath observance and His sovereign authority over both man and the Sabbath.

3:1 synagogue. The Jews' local places of assembly and worship (*see note on 1:21*). **withered hand.** This describes a condition of paralysis or deformity from an accident, a disease, or a congenital defect.

3:2 accuse. The Pharisees were not open to learning from Jesus, but only looked for an opportunity to charge Him with a violation of the Sabbath, an accusation they could bring before the Sanhedrin.

3:4 Jesus countered the Pharisees with a question that elevated the issue at hand from a legal to a moral problem. **Is it lawful.** A reference to the Mosaic law. Jesus was forcing the Pharisees to examine their tradition regarding the Sabbath to see if it was consistent with God's OT law. **to do good...evil, to save...kill.** Christ used a device common in the Middle East—He framed the issue in terms of clear-cut extremes. The obvious implication is that failure to do good or save a life was wrong and not in keeping with God's original intention for the Sabbath (*see notes on 2:27; Matt. 12:10*). **But they kept silent.** The Pharisees refused to answer Jesus' question, and by so doing implied that their Sabbath views and practices were false.

3:5 anger. Definite displeasure with human sin reveals a healthy, moral nature. Jesus' reaction was consistent with His divine nature and proved that He is the righteous Son of God. This kind of holy indignation with sinful attitudes and practices was to be more fully demonstrated when Jesus cleansed the temple (cf. 11:15-18; Matt. 21:12,13; Luke 19:45-48). **hardness of their hearts.** This phrase refers to an inability to understand because of a rebellious attitude (Ps. 95:8; Heb. 3:8,15). The Pharisees' hearts were becoming more and more obstinate and unresponsive to the truth (cf. 16:14; Rom. 9:18).

3:6 the Pharisees...plotted. They absolutely refused to be persuaded by anything Jesus said and did (cf. John 3:19), but were instead determined to kill Him. The Gr. word for "plotted" (lit. "counseled together") includes the notion of carrying out a decision already made—the Pharisees were simply discussing how to implement theirs. **Herodians.** This secular political party, which took its name from Herod Antipas and was strong in its support for Rome, opposed the Pharisees on nearly every issue, but were willing to join forces with them because both desperately wanted to destroy Jesus. *See note on Matt. 22:16.*

3:8 In spite of His conflicts with the Pharisees, Jesus remained very popular with the ordinary people. Mark is the only gospel writer who at this point in Jesus' ministry noted that the masses came from all parts of Palestine to see and hear Him. **Idumea.** An area SE of Judea, mentioned only here in the NT and populated by many Edomites (originally descendants of Esau, *see note on Gen. 36:43*). By this time it had become mostly Jewish in population and was considered a part of Judea. **beyond the Jordan.** The region E of the Jordan River, also called Perea, and ruled by Herod Antipas. Its population contained a large number of Jews. **Tyre and Sidon.** Two Phoenician cities on the Mediterranean coast, N of Galilee. Phoenicia as a whole was often designated by these cities (cf. Jer. 47:4; Joel 3:4; Matt. 11:21; Acts 12:20).

had afflictions pressed about Him to
[j]touch Him. 11 [k]And the unclean spirits,
whenever they saw Him, fell down before
Him and cried out, saying, [l]"You are the
Son of God." 12 But [m]He sternly warned
them that they should not make Him
known.

Selection of the Twelve—Luke 6:12-16

13 [n]And He went up on the mountain
and called to *Him* those He Himself wanted. And they came to Him. 14 Then He appointed twelve, [4]that they might be with
Him and that He might send them out to
preach, 15 and to have [5]power [6]to heal
sicknesses and to cast out demons: 16 [7]Si-
mon, [o]to whom He gave the name Peter;
17 James the *son* of Zebedee and John the
brother of James, to whom He gave the
name Boanerges, that is, "Sons of Thunder"; 18 Andrew, Philip, Bartholomew,
Matthew, Thomas, James the *son* of Alphaeus, Thaddaeus, Simon the Cananite;
19 and Judas Iscariot, who also betrayed
Him. And they went into a house.

10 [j] Matt. 9:21; 14:36; Mark 6:56; 8:22
11 [k] Mark 1:23, 24; Luke 4:41 [l] Matt. 8:29; 14:33; Mark 1:1; 5:7; Luke 8:28
12 [m] Matt. 12:16; Mark 1:25, 34
13 [n] Matt. 10:1; Mark 6:7; Luke 9:1
14 [4] NU adds *whom He also named apostles*
15 [5] *authority* [6] NU omits *to heal sicknesses and*
16 [o] Matt. 16:18; John 1:42 [7] NU *and He appointed the twelve: Simon . . .*
20 [p] Mark 6:31
21 [q] Ps. 69:8; Matt. 13:55; Mark 6:3; John 2:12 [r] John 7:5; 10:20; Acts 26:24; [2 Cor. 5:13]
22 [s] Matt. 9:34; 10:25; Luke 11:15; John 7:20; 8:48, 52; 10:20 [t] [John 12:31; 14:30; 16:11; Eph. 2:2]
23 [u] Matt. 12:25-29; Luke 11:17-22
27 [v] [Is. 49:24, 25]; Matt. 12:29

Opposition of His Friends

20 Then the multitude came together
again, [p]so that they could not so much as
eat bread. 21 But when His [q]own people
heard *about this,* they went out to lay hold
of Him, [r]for they said, "He is out of His
mind."

Scribes Commit the Unpardonable Sin
Matt. 12:24-32; Luke 11:17-23

22 And the scribes who came down from
Jerusalem said, [s]"He has Beelzebub," and,
"By the [t]ruler of the demons He casts out
demons."
23 [u]So He called them to *Himself* and
said to them in parables: "How can Satan
cast out Satan? 24 If a kingdom is divided
against itself, that kingdom cannot stand.
25 And if a house is divided against itself,
that house cannot stand. 26 And if Satan
has risen up against himself, and is divided, he cannot stand, but has an end. 27 [v]No
one can enter a strong man's house and
plunder his goods, unless he first binds the
strong man. And then he will plunder his
house.

3:10 afflictions. Lit. "a whip, a lash," sometimes translated "plagues," or "scourges." This metaphorically describes various painful, agonizing, physical ailments and illnesses.

3:11 unclean spirits. This refers to demons (*see note on 1:23*; cf. Luke 4:41). **whenever they saw Him.** The tense of the Gr. verb means there were many times when demons looked at Jesus and contemplated the truth of His character and identity. **"You are the Son of God."** Cf. 1:24. The demons unhesitatingly affirmed the uniqueness of Jesus' nature, which Mark saw as clear proof of Jesus' deity.

3:12 warned...not make Him known. Jesus always rebuked demons for their testimonies about Him. He wanted His teaching and actions, not the impure words of demons, to proclaim who He was (*see note on 1:25*; cf. Acts 16:16-18).

3:13 called...those He Himself wanted. The Gr. verb "called" stresses that Jesus acted in His own sovereign interest when He chose the 12 disciples (cf. John 15:16).

3:14 appointed twelve. Christ, by an explicit act of His will, formed a distinct group of 12 men who were among His followers (*see note on Matt. 10:1*). This new group constituted the foundation of His church (cf. Eph. 2:20).

3:15 have power. This word is sometimes rendered "authority." Along with the main task of preaching, Jesus gave the 12 the right to expel demons (cf. Luke 9:1).

3:16-19 A list of the 12 (*see notes on Matt. 10:2-4*).

3:16 Peter. From this point on (except in 14:37), Mark uses this name for Simon, though this is not when the designation was first given (cf. John 1:42), nor does it mark the complete replacement of the name Simon (cf. Acts 15:14). The name means "stone," and describes Peter's character and activities, namely his position as a foundation rock in the building of the church (cf. Matt. 16:18; Eph. 2:20).

3:17 "Sons of Thunder." Mark defines the Aram. term "Boanerges" for his Gentile readers. This name for the two brothers probably referred to their intense, outspoken personalities (cf. 9:38; Luke 9:54).

3:18 Thaddaeus. The only name that is not the same in all the NT lists of the 12 (cf. Matt. 10:2-4; Luke 6:14-16; Acts 1:13). Matthew calls him Lebbaeus, with Thaddaeus as a surname (Matt. 10:3); Luke and Acts call him "Judas *the son* of James"; and John 14:22 refers to him as "Judas (not Iscariot)." **the Cananite.** This does not indicate that this Simon was a native of Cana. Rather, the word is derived from the Aram. which means "to be zealous" and was used for those who were zealous for the law. Luke uses the word transliterated from the Gr. term that meant "the Zealot" (Luke 6:15; *see note on Matt. 10:4*).

3:19 Iscariot. This Heb. term means "man of Kerioth," as in Kerioth-Hezron, S of Hebron (Josh. 15:25). **went into a house.** A clearer translation is "went home," which would refer to Jesus' return to Capernaum (cf. 2:1). Verse divisions of the text are also misleading here; the phrase should be included with v. 20 and actually start the new paragraph.

3:21 His own people. In Gr., this expression was used in various ways to describe someone's friends or close associates. In the strictest sense, it meant family, which is probably the best understanding here. **lay hold of Him.** Mark used this same term elsewhere to mean the arrest of a person (6:17; 12:12; 14:1,44,46,51). Jesus' relatives evidently heard the report of v. 20 and came to Capernaum to restrain Him from His many activities and bring Him under their care and control, all supposedly for His own good. **out of His mind.** Jesus' family could only explain His unconventional lifestyle, with its willingness for others always to impose on Him, by saying He was irrational or had lost His mind.

3:22 scribes. Jewish scholars, also called lawyers, (mostly Pharisees) who were experts on the law and its application (*see note on Matt. 2:4*). **Beelzebub.** Satan (*see note on Luke 11:15*).

3:23 parables. Jesus answered the scribes by making an analogy between well known facts and the truths He expounded (*see note on Matt. 13:3*).

3:26 has an end. An expression used only in Mark which refers to Satan's ultimate doom as head of the demonic world system. *See notes on Rev. 20:1-10.*

3:27 enter a strong man's house and plunder his goods. One must be stronger than Satan in order to enter his domain ("strong man's house"), bind him (restrain his action), and free ("plunder") people ("his goods") from his control. Only Jesus had such power over the devil. Cf. Rom. 16:20; Heb. 2:14,15.

28 [w]"Assuredly, I say to you, all sins will
be forgiven the sons of men, and whatever
blasphemies they may utter; 29 but he who
blasphemes against the Holy Spirit never
has forgiveness, but is subject to eternal
condemnation"— 30 because they [x]said,
"He has an unclean spirit."

New Relationships Are Defined
Matt. 12:46-50; Luke 8:19-21

31 [y]Then His brothers and His mother
came, and standing outside they sent to
Him, calling Him. 32 And a multitude was
sitting around Him; and they said to Him,
"Look, Your mother and Your brothers
[8]are outside seeking You."
33 But He answered them, saying, "Who
is My mother, or My brothers?" 34 And He
looked around in a circle at those who sat
about Him, and said, "Here are My mother and My brothers! 35 For whoever does
the [z]will of God is My brother and My sister and mother."

Parable of the Soils
Matt. 13:1-23; Luke 8:4-15

4 And [a]again He began to teach by the
sea. And a great multitude was gathered to Him, so that He got into a boat and
sat *in it* on the sea; and the whole multitude was on the land facing the sea. 2 Then
He taught them many things by parables,
[b]and said to them in His teaching:

28 [w] Matt. 12:31, 32; Luke 12:10; [1 John 5:16]
30 [x] Matt. 9:34; John 7:20; 8:48, 52; 10:20
31 [y] Matt. 12:46-50; Luke 8:19-21
32 [8] NU, M add *and Your sisters*
35 [z] Eph. 6:6; Heb. 10:36; 1 Pet. 4:2; [1 John 2:17]

CHAPTER 4

1 [a] Matt. 13:1-15; Luke 8:4-10
2 [b] Mark 12:38
4 [1] NU, M omit *of the air*
7 [2] Lit. *fruit*
9 [3] NU, M omit *to them*
10 [c] Matt. 13:10; Luke 8:9
11 [d] [Matt. 11:25; 1 Cor. 2:10-16; 2 Cor. 4:6] [e] [1 Cor. 5:12, 13; Col. 4:5; 1 Thess. 4:12; 1 Tim. 3:7] [4] *secret* or *hidden truths*
12 [f] Is. 6:9, 10; 43:8; Jer. 5:21; Ezek. 12:2; Matt. 13:14; Luke 8:10; John 12:40; Rom. 11:8

3 "Listen! Behold, a sower went out to
sow. 4 And it happened, as he sowed, *that*
some *seed* fell by the wayside; and the
birds [1]of the air came and devoured it.
5 Some fell on stony ground, where it did
not have much earth; and immediately it
sprang up because it had no depth of
earth. 6 But when the sun was up it was
scorched, and because it had no root it
withered away. 7 And some *seed* fell
among thorns; and the thorns grew up
and choked it, and it yielded no [2]crop.
8 But other *seed* fell on good ground and
yielded a crop that sprang up, increased
and produced: some thirtyfold, some
sixty, and some a hundred."
9 And He said [3]to them, "He who has
ears to hear, let him hear!"
10 [c]But when He was alone, those
around Him with the twelve asked Him
about the parable. 11 And He said to them,
"To you it has been given to [d]know the
[4]mystery of the kingdom of God; but to
[e]those who are outside, all things come in
parables, 12 so that

[f]'*Seeing they may see and not*
perceive,
And hearing they may hear and
not understand;
Lest they should turn,
And their sins be forgiven them.'"

3:28 Assuredly, I say to you. Mark's first use of this expression, which occurs throughout the gospels, was employed as a formula that always introduced truthful and authoritative words from Jesus (cf. 6:11; 8:12; 9:1, 41; 10:15, 29; 11:23; 12:43; 13:30; 14:9, 18, 25, 30).

3:29 he who blasphemes...never has forgiveness. Whenever someone deliberately and disrespectfully slanders the person and ministry of the Holy Spirit in pointing to the Lordship and redemption of Jesus Christ, he completely negates and forfeits any possibility of present or future forgiveness of sins (*see note on Matt. 12:31*), because he has wholly rejected the only basis of God's salvation.

3:31 His brothers and His mother. Jesus' earthly family (*see notes on v. 21; Matt. 12:46*). The narrative that left off at v. 21 resumes here.

3:35 Jesus made a decisive and comprehensive statement on true Christian discipleship. Such discipleship involves a spiritual relationship that transcends the physical family and is open to all who are empowered by the Spirit of God to come to Christ in repentance and faith and enabled to live a life of obedience to God's Word.

4:1 sat. The typical rabbinical position for teaching; and more practically, Jesus may have sat because of the rocking of the boat in the water.

4:2 parables. A common method of teaching in Judaism, which Jesus employed to conceal the truth from unbelievers while explaining it to His disciples (cf. v. 11; *see note on Matt. 13:3*).

4:3-8 This parable depicts the teaching of the gospel throughout the world and the various responses of people to it. Some will reject it; some will accept it for a brief time but then fall away; yet some will believe and will lead others to believe.

4:4 wayside. Either a road near a field's edge or a path that traversed a field, both of which were hard surfaces due to constant foot traffic.

4:5 stony ground. Beds of solid rock, usually limestone, lying under the surface of good soil. They are a little too deep for the plow to reach, and too shallow to allow a plant to reach water and develop a decent root system in the small amount of soil that covers them.

4:7 thorns. Tough, thistle-bearing weeds that use up the available space, light, and water which good plants need.

4:8 increased...a hundred. An average ratio of harvested grain to what had been sown was 8 to 1, with a 10 to 1 ratio considered exceptional. The yields Jesus refers to are like an unbelievable harvest.

4:9 "He who has ears to hear, let him hear!" On the surface, this is a call for the listener to be attentive and discern the meaning of His analogy. Yet more than human understanding is necessary to interpret the parable—only those who have been redeemed will have the true meaning explained to them by the divine Teacher.

4:11 mystery...parables. A "mystery" in the NT refers to something previously hidden and unknown but revealed in the NT (*see notes on 1 Cor. 2:7; Eph. 3:4-6*). In context, the subject of the mystery is the kingdom of heaven (*see note on Matt. 3:2*), which Jesus communicates in the form of parables. Thus the mystery is revealed to those who believe, yet it remains concealed to those who reject Christ and His gospel (*see note on Matt. 13:11*). **to those who are outside.** Those who are not followers of Christ.

4:12 so that. *See note on Matt. 13:13.* Unlike Matthew, which specifically quotes Is. 6:9,10, Mark quotes Jesus as giving the substance of what Isaiah wrote in that text. ***Lest they should turn.*** The implication is that unbelievers do not want to turn from sin (*see notes on Matt. 13:3,13*).

13 And He said to them, "Do you not understand this parable? How then will you
understand all the parables? 14 [g]The sower
sows the word. 15 And these are the ones
by the wayside where the word is sown.
When they hear, Satan comes immediately
and takes away the word that was sown in
their hearts. 16 These likewise are the ones
sown on stony ground who, when they
hear the word, immediately receive it with
gladness; 17 and they have no root in themselves, and so endure only for a time. Afterward, when tribulation or persecution
arises for the word's sake, immediately
they stumble. 18 Now these are the ones
sown among thorns; *they are* the ones who
hear the word, 19 and the [h]cares of this
world, [i]the deceitfulness of riches, and the
desires for other things entering in choke
the word, and it becomes unfruitful. 20 But
these are the ones sown on good ground,
those who hear the word, [5]accept *it,* and
bear [j]fruit: some thirtyfold, some sixty, and
some a hundred."

Parable of the Lamp—Luke 8:16-18

21 [k]Also He said to them, "Is a lamp
brought to be put under a basket or under
a bed? Is it not to be set on a lampstand?
22 [l]For there is nothing hidden which will
not be revealed, nor has anything been kept
secret but that it should come to light. 23 [m]If
anyone has ears to hear, let him hear."
24 Then He said to them, "Take heed
what you hear. [n]With the same measure
you use, it will be measured to you; and to
you who hear, more will be given. 25 [o]For
whoever has, to him more will be given;
but whoever does not have, even what he
has will be taken away from him."

Parable of the Growing Seed

26 And He said, [p]"The kingdom of God
is as if a man should [6]scatter seed on the
ground, 27 and should sleep by night and
rise by day, and the seed should sprout
and [q]grow, he himself does not know how.
28 For the earth [r]yields crops by itself: first
the blade, then the head, after that the full
grain in the head. 29 But when the grain
ripens, immediately [s]he puts in the sickle,
because the harvest has come."

Parable of the Mustard Seed
Matt. 13:31-35

30 Then He said, [t]"To what shall we
liken the kingdom of God? Or with what
parable shall we picture it? 31 *It is* like a

14 [g] Matt. 13:18-23; Luke 8:11-15
19 [h] Luke 21:34 [i] Prov. 23:5; Eccl. 5:13; Luke 18:24; 1 Tim. 6:9, 10, 17
20 [j] [John 15:2, 5; Rom. 7:4] [5] *receive*
21 [k] Matt. 5:15; Luke 8:16; 11:33
22 [l] Eccl. 12:14; Matt. 10:26, 27; Luke 12:3; [1 Cor. 4:5]
23 [m] Matt. 11:15; 13:9, 43; Mark 4:9; Luke 8:8; 14:35; Rev. 3:6, 13, 22; 13:9
24 [n] Matt. 7:2; Luke 6:38; 2 Cor. 9:6
25 [o] Matt. 13:12; 25:29; Luke 8:18; 19:26
26 [p] [Matt. 13:24-30, 36-43]; Luke 8:1 [6] *sow*
27 [q] [2 Cor. 3:18; 2 Pet. 3:18]
28 [r] [John 12:24]
29 [s] [Mark 13:30, 39]; Rev. 14:15
30 [t] Matt. 13:31, 32; Luke 13:18, 19; [Acts 2:41; 4:4; 5:14; 19:20]

4:13 all the parables. Understanding the parable of the sower was to be key in the disciples' ability to discern the meaning of Jesus' other parables of the kingdom (vv. 21-34).

4:14-20 Jesus' explanation of the parable of the sower, who is in fact Jesus Himself (cf. Matt. 13:37) and anyone who proclaims the gospel.

4:14 the word. Luke 8:11 says it is the "word of God," and Matt. 13:19 calls it the "word of the kingdom." It is the salvation gospel (*see note on Matt. 13:19*).

4:16 receive it with gladness. An enthusiastic, emotional, yet superficial response to the gospel that does not take into account the cost involved.

4:17 no root. Because the person's heart is hard, like the stony ground (*see note on v. 5*), the gospel never takes root in the individual's soul and never transforms his life—there is only a temporary, surface change. **tribulation or persecution.** Not the routine difficulties and troubles of life, but specifically the suffering, trials, and persecutions which result from one's association with God's Word. **stumble.** The Gr. word also means, "to fall" or "to cause offense," and from which comes the Eng. word "scandalize." All those meanings are appropriate since the superficial believer is offended, stumbles, and falls away when his faith is put to the test (cf. John 8:31; 1 John 2:19).

4:19 cares of this world. Lit. "the distractions of the age." A preoccupation with the temporal issues of this present age blinds a person to any serious consideration of the gospel (cf. James 4:4; 1 John 2:15,16). **deceitfulness of riches.** Not only can money and material possessions not satisfy the desires of the heart or bring the lasting happiness they deceptively promise, but they also blind those who pursue them to eternal, spiritual concerns (1 Tim. 6:9,10).

4:20 hear...accept...bear fruit. Three Gr. present participles mark continuing action. Believers, in contrast to unbelievers, hear God's Word because God allows them to hear it. They "accept" it—they understand and obey it because God opens their mind and heart and transforms their lives. The result is that they produce spiritual fruit.

4:21 lamp. This refers to a very small clay bowl made with a spout to hold a wick and containing a few ounces of oil that served as the fuel. **a lampstand.** In common homes, this was simply a shelf protruding from the wall. Wealthier homes might have separate, ornate stands (cf. Rev. 1:12).

4:22 there is nothing hidden...revealed. The purpose in keeping something hidden is so that one day it can be revealed. Jesus' teaching was never intended to be just for an inner circle of followers. It would be the responsibility of the disciples to communicate the gospel of the kingdom to the world at large (cf. Matt. 28:19,20).

4:24 With the same measure. The spiritual results which the disciples realized were to be based on the amount of effort they put forth; they would reap as they had sown. **more will be given.** The one who has learned spiritual truth and applied it diligently will receive even more truth to faithfully apply.

4:26-29 This parable is recorded only by Mark and complements the parable of the sower by explaining in more depth the results of spiritual growth accomplished in good soil.

4:26 kingdom of God. *See note on 1:15.*

4:29 he puts in the sickle, because the harvest has come. When the grain is ripe, the sower of the seed must harvest the crop. There are two possible interpretations of this unexplained parable. It could be referring to the entire scope of the kingdom, from the time Jesus sowed the gospel message until the final harvest in the future. His disciples would continue the work of presenting the gospel that would eventually yield a harvest. The better interpretation pictures the gospel working in lives. After the gospel is presented, the Word of God works in the individual heart, sometimes slowly, until the time when God reaps the harvest in that individual and saves him.

4:30-32 This parable of the mustard seed pictures the kingdom of God beginning with a small influence and then becoming worldwide in its scope.

mustard seed which, when it is sown on
the ground, is smaller than all the seeds on
earth; 32 but when it is sown, it grows up
and becomes greater than all herbs, and
shoots out large branches, so that the birds
of the air may nest under its shade."
33 [u]And with many such parables He
spoke the word to them as they were able
to hear *it.* 34 But without a parable He did
not speak to them. And when they were
alone, [v]He explained all things to His disciples.

The Sea Is Stilled

Matt. 8:23-27; Luke 8:22-25

35 [w]On the same day, when evening had
come, He said to them, "Let us cross over
to the other side." 36 Now when they had
left the multitude, they took Him along in
the boat as He was. And other little boats
were also with Him. 37 And a great windstorm arose, and the waves beat into the
boat, so that it was already filling. 38 But
He was in the stern, asleep on a pillow.
And they awoke Him and said to Him,
[x]"Teacher, [y]do You not care that we are
perishing?"
39 Then He arose and [z]rebuked the
wind, and said to the sea, [a]"Peace,[7] be
still!" And the wind ceased and there was
a great calm. 40 But He said to them, "Why
are you so fearful? [b]How[8] *is it* that you
have no faith?" 41 And they feared exceedingly, and said to one another, "Who can
this be, that even the wind and the sea
obey Him!"

Demons Are Cast into Swine

Matt. 8:28-34; Luke 8:26-39

5 Then [a]they came to the other side of
the sea, to the country of the [1]Gada-
renes. 2 And when He had come out of the
boat, immediately there met Him out of
the tombs a man with an [b]unclean spirit,
3 who had *his* dwelling among the tombs;
and no one could bind [2]him, not even with
chains, 4 because he had often been bound
with shackles and chains. And the chains
had been pulled apart by him, and the
shackles broken in pieces; neither could

33 [u]Matt. 13:34, 35; [John 16:12]
34 [v]Luke 24:27, 45
35 [w]Matt. 8:18, 23-27; Luke 8:22, 25
38 [x][Matt. 23:8-10] [y]Ps. 44:23
39 [z]Mark 9:25; Luke 4:39 [a]Ps. 65:7; 89:9; 93:4; 104:6, 7; Matt. 8:26; Luke 8:24 [7]Lit. *Be quiet*
40 [b]Matt. 14:31, 32; Luke 8:25 [8]NU *Have you still no faith?*

CHAPTER 5

1 [a]Matt. 8:28-34; Luke 8:26-37 [1]NU *Gerasenes*
2 [b]Mark 1:23; 7:25; [Rev. 16:13, 14]
3 [2]NU adds *anymore*

4:31 a mustard seed. A reference to the common black mustard plant. The leaves were used as a vegetable and the seed as a condiment. It also had medicinal benefits. **smaller than all.** The mustard seed is not the smallest of all seeds in existence, but it was in comparison to all the other seeds the Jews sowed in Palestine.

4:32 herbs. Refers to garden vegetables grown specifically for eating. **birds of the air.** While not a tree in the truest sense of the word, the mustard shrub has been known to grow as large as 15 ft. high and to have the properties of a tree, such as having branches large enough for birds to nest in. The tree represents the sphere of salvation, which would grow so large that it would provide shelter, protection, and benefit to people (*see note on Matt. 13:32*). Even unbelievers have been blessed by association with the gospel and the power of God in salvation. Christians have been a benediction to the world. *See note on 1 Cor. 7:14.*

4:33,34 This conclusion to Mark's account of Jesus' parables highlights Mark's recording only representative samples of all the parables Jesus taught.

4:34 But without a parable He did not speak to them. On that particular day, Jesus spoke to the larger crowd only in parables. This method of teaching left unbelievers with riddles and kept them from being forced to believe or disbelieve Him—they could make no decision to follow Him since they did not understand what He taught.

4:35-41 This account demonstrates Jesus' unlimited power over the natural world.

4:35 the other side. Jesus and His disciples were on the western shore of the Sea of Galilee. To escape the crowds for a brief respite, Jesus wanted to go to the eastern shore, which had no large cities and therefore fewer people.

4:37 great windstorm. Wind is a common occurrence on that lake, about 690 ft. below sea level and surrounded by hills. The Gr. word can also mean "whirlwind." In this case, it was a storm so severe that it took on the properties of a hurricane (*see note on Matt. 8:24*). The disciples, used to being on the lake in the wind, thought this storm would drown them (v. 38).

4:38 He was…asleep. Jesus was so exhausted from a full day of healing and preaching, even that storm could not wake Him up (*see note on Matt. 8:24*).

4:39 "Peace, be still!" Lit. "be silent, be muzzled" (*see note on 1:25*). Storms normally subside gradually, but when the Creator gave the order, the natural elements of this storm ceased immediately.

4:41 they feared exceedingly. This was not fear of being harmed by the storm, but a reverence for the supernatural power Jesus had just displayed. The only thing more terrifying than having a storm outside the boat was having God in the boat! **Who can this be.** This statement betrayed the disciples' wonder at the true identity of Jesus.

5:1 the other side of the sea. The eastern shore of the Sea of Galilee (cf. Luke 8:26). **the country of the Gadarenes.** The preferred reading in Mark is "Gerasenes" rather than "Gadarenes." It most likely refers to the small town of Gersa (or Khersa, Kursi; *see note on Matt. 8:28*) which was located midway on the eastern shore. "Country of" refers to the general region that included Gersa and was under the jurisdiction of the city of Gadara, which was located some 6 mi. SE of the Sea of Galilee; this was probably why Luke referred to the region as the country of the Gaderenes (Luke 8:26,37).

5:2 out of the tombs a man. Mark mentions only one of the demon-possessed men, who was probably the more prominent of the two (cf. Matt. 8:28). The "tombs"—common dwelling places for the demented of that day—were burial chambers carved out of rock hillsides on the outskirts of town. If the man and his possible companion were Jews, for whom touching dead bodies was a great defilement, living in such an area was an added torment. **unclean spirit.** This refers to the demon who was controlling the man. Such spirits in themselves were morally filthy and caused much harm for those whom they possessed (*see notes on 1:32-34*; cf. Luke 4:33,36; 7:21; 8:2).

5:3 no one could bind him. Multiple negatives are used in the Gr. text to emphasize the man's tremendous strength.

5:4 shackles and chains. "Shackles" (probably metal or perhaps, in part, cord or rope) were used to restrain the feet and "chains" were metal restraints for the rest of the body.

anyone tame him. 5 And always, night and
day, he was in the mountains and in the
tombs, crying out and cutting himself with
stones.

6 When he saw Jesus from afar, he ran
and worshiped Him. 7 And he cried out
with a loud voice and said, "What have I to
do with You, Jesus, Son of the Most High
God? I [c]implore[3] You by God that You do
not torment me."

8 For He said to him, [d]"Come out of the
man, unclean spirit!" 9 Then He asked him,
"What *is* your name?"

And he answered, saying, "My name *is*
Legion; for we are many." 10 Also he
begged Him earnestly that He would not
send them out of the country.

11 Now a large herd of [e]swine was feeding there near the mountains. 12 So all the
demons begged Him, saying, "Send us to
the swine, that we may enter them."
13 And [4]at once Jesus gave them permission. Then the unclean spirits went out and
entered the swine (there were about two
thousand); and the herd ran violently
down the steep place into the sea, and
drowned in the sea.

14 So those who fed the swine fled, and
they told *it* in the city and in the country.
And they went out to see what it was that
had happened. 15 Then they came to Jesus,
and saw the one *who had been* [f]demon-pos-
sessed and had the legion, [g]sitting and
[h]clothed and in his right mind. And they
were afraid. 16 And those who saw it told
them how it happened to him *who had been*
demon-possessed, and about the swine.
17 Then [i]they began to plead with Him to
depart from their region.

18 And when He got into the boat, [j]he
who had been demon-possessed begged
Him that he might be with Him. 19 However, Jesus did not permit him, but said to
him, "Go home to your friends, and tell
them what great things the Lord has done
for you, and how He has had compassion
on you." 20 And he departed and began to
[k]proclaim in [5]Decapolis all that Jesus had
done for him; and all [l]marveled.

Jairus Pleads for His Daughter
Matt. 9:18, 19; Luke 8:41, 42

21 [m]Now when Jesus had crossed over
again by boat to the other side, a great multitude gathered to Him; and He was by the
sea. 22 [n]And behold, one of the rulers of
the synagogue came, Jairus by name. And
when he saw Him, he fell at His feet 23 and
begged Him earnestly, saying, "My little
daughter lies at the point of death. Come

7 [c] Matt. 26:63; Mark 1:24; Acts 19:13 [3] *adjure*
8 [d] Mark 1:25; 9:25; [Acts 16:18]
11 [e] Lev. 11:7, 8; Deut. 14:8; Luke 15:15, 16
13 [4] NU *He gave*
15 [f] Matt. 4:24; 8:16; Mark 1:32 [g] Luke 10:39 [h] [Is. 61:10]
17 [i] Matt. 8:34; Acts 16:39
18 [j] Luke 8:38, 39
20 [k] Ex. 15:2; Ps. 66:16 [l] Matt. 9:8, 33; John 5:20; 7:21; Acts 3:12; 4:13 [5] Lit. *Ten Cities*
21 [m] Matt. 9:1; Luke 8:40
22 [n] Matt. 9:18-26; Luke 8:41-56; Acts 13:15

5:5 crying out and cutting himself with stones. "Crying out" describes a continual unearthly scream uttered with intense emotion. The "stones" likely were rocks made of flint with sharp, jagged edges.

5:7 What have I to do with You. A common expression of protest (*see note on 1:24*). **Son of the Most High God.** The demons knew that Jesus was deity, the God-Man. "Most High God" was an ancient title used by both Jews and Gentiles to identify the one, true, and living God of Israel and distinguish Him from all false idol gods (cf. Gen. 14:18-20; Num. 24:16; Deut. 32:8; Pss. 18:13; 21:7; Is. 14:14; Dan. 3:26; Luke 1:32; Heb. 7:1). **I implore You...do not torment me.** *See note on Matt. 8:29.* Mark adds "I implore you," which shows the demon tried to have Jesus soften the severity of his inevitable fate. Cf. James 2:19.

5:9 "What *is* your name?" Most likely, Jesus asked this in view of the demon's appeal not to be tormented. However, He did not need to know the demon's name in order to expel him. Rather, Jesus posed the question to bring the reality and complexity of this case into the open. **Legion.** A Lat. term, by then common to Jews and Greeks, that defined a Roman military unit of 6,000 infantrymen. Such a name denotes that the man was controlled by an extremely large number of militant evil spirits, a truth reiterated by the expression "for we are many."

5:10 he begged. The demon understood that Jesus had all power over him and addressed Him with an intense desire that his request be granted. **not send them out of the country.** *See note on v. 1.* The demons wanted to remain in the same area where they had been exercising their evil powers.

5:11 swine. Pigs were unclean animals to the Jews, so the people tending this herd were either Gentiles or Jews unconcerned about the law (*see note on Matt. 8:30*).

5:13 Jesus gave them permission. According to His sovereign purposes Jesus allowed the demons to enter the pigs and destroy them—the text offers no other explanation (cf. Deut. 29:29; Rom. 9:20). By doing this, Jesus gave the man a graphic, visible, and powerful lesson on the immensity of the evil from which he had been delivered.

5:15 sitting. The man's restful condition was a strong contrast with his former restless, agitated state. **in his right mind.** He was no longer under the frenzied, screaming control of the demons.

5:16 those who saw it told...about the swine. "Those" may refer to both the 12 and the men who tended the pigs. They wanted people to know what had happened to the man and the pigs, and the relationship between the two events.

5:17 plead with Him to depart from their region. The residents of the region became frightened and resentful toward Jesus because of what had happened. They may have been concerned about the disruption of their normal routine and the loss of property, and they wanted Jesus and His powers to leave the area so no more such financial losses would occur. More compelling, however, was the reality that they were ungodly people frightened by Christ's display of spiritual power (*see note on Matt. 8:34*).

5:19 tell them...the Lord has done. Jesus was referring to Himself as God who controlled both the natural and the supernatural worlds (cf. Luke 8:39).

5:20 Decapolis. A league of 10 Greek-influenced (Hellenized) cities E of the Jordan River (*see note on Matt. 4:25*).

5:21 the other side. Jesus and the disciples returned to the NW shore of the Sea of Galilee.

5:22 rulers of the synagogue. They presided over the elders of local synagogues. Those elder groups, made up of lay officials, were in charge of arranging the services and overseeing other synagogue affairs.

and [o]lay Your hands on her, that she may
be healed, and she will live." 24 So *Jesus*
went with him, and a great multitude followed Him and thronged Him.

A Woman with Issue Is Healed
Matt. 9:20-22; Luke 8:43-48

25 Now a certain woman [p]had a flow of
blood for twelve years, 26 and had suffered
many things from many physicians. She
had spent all that she had and was no better, but rather grew worse. 27 When she
heard about Jesus, she came behind *Him* in
the crowd and [q]touched His garment.
28 For she said, "If only I may touch His
clothes, I shall be made well."
29 Immediately the fountain of her blood
was dried up, and she felt in *her* body that
she was healed of the [6]affliction. 30 And
Jesus, immediately knowing in Himself
that [r]power had gone out of Him, turned
around in the crowd and said, "Who
touched My clothes?"
31 But His disciples said to Him, "You
see the multitude thronging You, and You
say, 'Who touched Me?' "
32 And He looked around to see her who
had done this thing. 33 But the woman,
[s]fearing and trembling, knowing what had
happened to her, came and fell down before Him and told Him the whole truth.
34 And He said to her, "Daughter, [t]your
faith has made you well. [u]Go in peace, and
be healed of your affliction."

Jairus's Daughter Is Healed
Matt. 9:23-26; Luke 8:49-56

35 [v]While He was still speaking, *some*
came from the ruler of the synagogue's
house who said, "Your daughter is dead.
Why trouble the Teacher any further?"
36 As soon as Jesus heard the word that
was spoken, He said to the ruler of the synagogue, "Do not be afraid; only [w]believe."
37 And He permitted no one to follow Him
except Peter, James, and John the brother
of James. 38 Then He came to the house of
the ruler of the synagogue, and saw [7]a tumult and those who [x]wept and wailed
loudly. 39 When He came in, He said to
them, "Why make this commotion and
weep? The child is not dead, but [y]sleep-
ing."
40 And they ridiculed Him. [z]But when
He had put them all outside, He took the
father and the mother of the child, and
those *who were* with Him, and entered
where the child was lying. 41 Then He took
the child by the hand, and said to her,
"Talitha, cumi," which is translated, "Little

23 [o] Matt. 8:15; Mark 6:5; 7:32; 8:23, 25; 16:18; Luke 4:40; Acts 9:17; 28:8
25 [p] Lev. 15:19, 25; Matt. 9:20
27 [q] Matt. 14:35, 36; Mark 3:10; 6:56
29 [6] *suffering*
30 [r] Luke 6:19; 8:46
33 [s] [Ps. 89:7]
34 [t] Matt. 9:22; Mark 10:52; Acts 14:9 [u] 1 Sam. 1:17; 20:42; 2 Kin. 5:19; Luke 7:50; 8:48; Acts 16:36; [James 2:16]
35 [v] Luke 8:49
36 [w] [Mark 9:23; John 11:40]
38 [x] Mark 16:10; Acts 9:39 [7] *an uproar*
39 [y] John 11:4, 11
40 [z] Acts 9:40

5:25 flow of blood. Denotes a chronic internal hemorrhage, perhaps from a tumor or other disease (*see note on Matt. 9:20*).

5:26 suffered many things from many physicians. In NT times, it was common practice in difficult medical cases for people to consult many different doctors and receive a variety of treatments. The supposed cures were often conflicting, abusive, and many times made the ailment worse, not better. (Luke, the physician, in Luke 8:43 suggested the woman was not helped because her condition was incurable.)

5:28 If only I may touch His clothes. The woman's faith in Jesus' healing powers was so great that she believed even indirect contact with Him through His garments (*see note on Matt. 9:20*) would be enough to produce a cure.

5:29 fountain of her blood. The source of her bleeding, with the analogy being to the origin of a spring.

5:30 power had gone out of Him. Christ's "power," His inherent ability to minister and work supernaturally, proceeded from Him under the conscious control of His sovereign will. **"Who touched My clothes?"** Jesus asked this question, not out of ignorance, but so He might draw the woman out of the crowd and allow her to praise God for what had happened.

5:34 your faith has made you well. Jesus' public statement concerning the woman's faith (expressed in vv. 28,33) and its results. The form of the Gr. verb translated "has made you well," which can also be rendered "has made you whole," indicates that her healing was complete. It is the same Gr. word often translated "to save" (*see note on Matt. 9:22*) and is the normal NT word for saving from sin, which strongly suggests that the woman's faith also led to spiritual salvation.

5:36 only believe. The verb is a command for present, continuous action urging Jairus to maintain the faith he had initially demonstrated in coming to Jesus. Christ knew there was no other proper response to Jairus' helpless situation, and He was confident of faith's outcome (cf. Luke 8:50).

5:37 Peter, James, and John. This is the first time Mark gives special status to these 3 disciples. Scripture never explains why these men were sometimes allowed to witness things that the other disciples were excluded from (cf. 9:2; 14:33), but the trio did constitute an inner circle within the 12. Even the Gr. grammar implies this inner grouping by placing their 3 names under one definite article.

5:38 wept and wailed. In that culture, a sure sign that a death had occurred. Because burial followed soon after death, it was the people's only opportunity to mourn publicly. The wailing was especially loud and mostly from paid mourners (*see note on Matt. 9:23*).

5:39 not dead, but sleeping. With this figurative expression, Jesus meant that the girl was not dead in the normal sense, because her condition was temporary and would be reversed (*see note on Matt. 9:24*; cf. John 11:11-14; Acts 7:60; 13:36; 1 Cor. 11:30; 15:6,18, 20,51; 1 Thess. 4:13,14).

5:40 ridiculed. This could more literally be translated, "laughed Him to scorn," or "were laughing in His face." They understood Jesus' words literally and thought they were absurd, so "ridiculed" most likely refers to repeated bursts of laughter aimed at humiliating the Lord. This reaction, although shallow and irreverent, indicates the people were convinced of the irreversible nature of the girl's death and underscores the reality of the miracle Jesus was about to do. **put them all outside.** This was an emphatic, forceful expulsion which showed Christ's authority and was done because the disbelieving mourners had disqualified themselves from witnessing the girl's resurrection.

5:41 "Talitha, cumi." Mark is the only gospel writer who recorded Jesus' original Aram. words. "Talitha" is a feminine form of "lamb," or "youth." "Cumi" is an imperative meaning "arise." As in other such instances, Jesus addressed the person of the one being raised, not just the dead body (cf. Luke 7:14; John 11:43).

girl, I say to you, arise." 42 Immediately the
girl arose and walked, for she was twelve
years *of age*. And they were [a]overcome
with great amazement. 43 But [b]He commanded them strictly that no one should
know it, and said that *something* should be
given her to eat.

Jesus Is Rejected at Nazareth
Matt. 13:54-58

6 Then [a]He went out from there and
came to His own country, and His disciples followed Him. 2 And when the Sabbath had come, He began to teach in the
synagogue. And many hearing *Him* were
[b]astonished, saying, [c]"Where *did* this Man
get these things? And what wisdom *is* this
which is given to Him, that such mighty
works are performed by His hands! 3 Is this
not the carpenter, the Son of Mary, and
[d]brother of James, Joses, Judas, and Simon?

42 [a]Mark 1:27; 7:37
43 [b][Matt. 8:4; 12:16-19; 17:9]; Mark 3:12

CHAPTER 6

1 [a]Matt. 13:54; Luke 4:16
2 [b]Matt. 7:28; Luke 4:32; Acts 4:13 [c]John 6:42
3 [d]Matt. 12:46; Gal. 1:19 [e][Matt. 11:6]
4 [f]Matt. 13:57; Luke 4:24; John 4:44
5 [g]Gen. 19:22; 32:25; Matt. 13:58; [Mark 9:23]
6 [h]Is. 59:16; Matt. 17:17, 20; [Heb. 3:18, 19; 4:2] [i]Matt. 9:35; Luke 13:22; Acts 10:38; Eph. 2:17
7 [j]Matt. 10:1; 28:19, 20; Mark 3:13, 14; Luke 9:1 [k][Eccl. 4:9, 10]
9 [l][Eph. 6:15]

And are not His sisters here with us?" So
they [e]were offended at Him.
4 But Jesus said to them, [f]"A prophet is
not without honor except in his own country, among his own relatives, and in his
own house." 5 [g]Now He could do no
mighty work there, except that He laid His
hands on a few sick people and healed
them. 6 And [h]He marveled because of their
unbelief. [i]Then He went about the villages
in a circuit, teaching.

Twelve Are Sent to Serve
Matt. 10:1-42; Luke 9:1-6

7 [j]And He called the twelve to *Himself*,
and began to send them out [k]two *by* two,
and gave them power over unclean spirits.
8 He commanded them to take nothing for
the journey except a staff—no bag, no bread,
no copper in *their* money belts— 9 but [l]to
wear sandals, and not to put on two tunics.

5:43 no one should know it. Knowledge of the miracle could not be completely withheld, but Christ did not want news of it to spread until after He had left the area, because He knew such news might cause His many Jewish opponents in Galilee to seek Him out and kill Him prematurely. He also wanted to be known for bringing the gospel, not as simply a miracle-worker. Jesus was no doubt concerned that the girl and her parents not be made the center of undue curiosity and sensationalism.

6:1 His own country. Nazareth, Jesus' hometown (*see note on Matt. 2:23*). **His disciples.** This was not a private, family visit for Jesus, but a time for ministry.

6:2 Sabbath. *See note on 2:23.* This implies that no public teaching was done until the Sabbath. **teach in the synagogue.** *See note on 1:21.* **astonished.** The same word as used in 1:22 (*see note there*); however, here the people's initial reaction gave way to skepticism and a critical attitude toward Jesus.

6:3 carpenter. The people of Nazareth still thought of Jesus as one who carried on his father's trade (cf. Matt. 13:55) as a craftsman who worked in wood and other hard materials (e.g., stones, bricks). The common earthly position of Jesus and His family caused the townspeople to stumble—they refused to see Him as higher than themselves and found it impossible to accept Him as the Son of God and Messiah. **Son of Mary.** Only here is Jesus called this. The normal Jewish practice was to identify a son by his father's (Joseph's) name. Perhaps that was not done here because Joseph was already dead, or because Christ's audience were recalling the rumors concerning Jesus' illegitimate birth (cf. John 8:41; 9:29)—a man was called the son of his mother if his father was unknown—and were purposely insulting Him with this title as a reference to illegitimacy. **brother of James, Joses, Judas, and Simon.** *See note on Matt. 12:46.* These were actual half-brothers of Jesus. "James" was later the leader in the Jerusalem church (cf. Acts 12:17; 15:13; 21:18; 1 Cor. 15:7; Gal. 1:19; 2:9,12) and wrote the epistle of James. "Judas" (Heb. name "Judah") wrote the epistle of Jude. Nothing more is known of the other two. **His sisters.** Actual half-sisters whose names are never given in the NT. Nothing is known of them, not even if they became believers as the other family members did. **they were offended at Him.** The Eng. term "scandalize" comes from the Gr. verb translated "were offended," which essentially means "to stumble," or "become ensnared," and fall into a sin (*see note on 4:17*). The residents of Nazareth were deeply offended at Jesus' posturing Himself as some great teacher because of His ordinary background, His limited formal education, and His lack of an officially-sanctioned religious position.

6:4 *See note on Matt. 13:57.* Jesus called Himself a prophet, in accord with one of His roles (cf. v. 15; 8:28; Matt. 21:11,46; Luke 7:16; 24:19; John 6:14; 7:40; 9:17). **own house.** His own family (cf. John 7:5; Acts 1:14).

6:5 He could do no mighty work there. Cf. Matt. 13:58. This is not to suggest that His power was somehow diminished by their unbelief. It may suggest that because of their unbelief people were not coming to Him for healing or miracles the way they did in Capernaum and Jerusalem. Or, more importantly it may signify that Christ limited His ministry both as an act of mercy, so that the exposure to greater light would not result in a worse hardening that would only subject them to greater condemnation, and a judgment on their unbelief. He had the power to do more miracles, but not the will, because they rejected Him. Miracles belonged among those who were ready to believe.

6:6 He marveled because of their unbelief. "Marveled" means Jesus was completely astonished and amazed at Nazareth's reaction to Him, His teaching, and His miracles. He was not surprised at the fact of the people's unbelief, but at how they could reject Him while claiming to know all about Him. Faith should have been the response in that town in Galilee, the region where Christ did so many miracles and so much teaching. **villages in a circuit.** The outcome of Jesus' visit to Nazareth was that He left there and made a teaching tour of other places in Galilee, concluding near where He started (cf. Matt. 9:35).

6:7 the twelve. *See notes on 3:16-19; Matt. 10:2-4.* The 12 disciples were by then a divinely-commissioned, recognized group. **send them out.** The form of this Gr. verb indicates that Jesus individually commissioned each pair to go out as His representatives. **two *by* two.** This was a prudent practice (cf. Eccl. 4:9-12) employed by Jewish alms collectors, by John the Baptist (Luke 7:19), by Jesus on other occasions (11:1; 14:13; Luke 10:1), and by the early church (Acts 13:2,3; 15:39-41; 19:22). The practice gave the disciples mutual help and encouragement and met the legal requirement for an authentic testimony (Deut. 19:15). **unclean spirits.** *See notes on 1:23; 5:2.*

6:8 a staff. The walking stick, a universal companion of travelers in those days, which also provided potential protection from criminals and wild animals. **no bag.** They were not to carry the usual leather traveling bag or food sack.

6:9 to wear sandals. Ordinary footwear consisting of leather or wood soles bound on by straps around the ankle and instep. "Sandals" were necessary protection for the feet in view of the hot, rough terrain of Palestine. **not to put on two tunics.** "Tunics" were stan-

10 [m]Also He said to them, "In whatever
place you enter a house, stay there till you
depart from that place. 11 [n]And [1]whoever
will not receive you nor hear you, when
you depart from there, [o]shake off the dust
under your feet as a testimony against
them. [2]Assuredly, I say to you, it will be
more tolerable for Sodom and Gomorrah
in the day of judgment than for that city!"
12 So they went out and preached that
people should repent. 13 And they cast out
many demons, [p]and anointed with oil
many who were sick, and healed *them.*

John the Baptist Is Murdered
Matt. 14:1-12; Luke 9:7-9

14 [q]Now King Herod heard *of Him,* for His
name had become well known. And he said,
"John the Baptist is risen from the dead, and
therefore [r]these powers are at work in him."
15 [s]Others said, "It is Elijah."
And others said, "It is [3]the Prophet, [t]or
like one of the prophets."
16 [u]But when Herod heard, he said,
"This is John, whom I beheaded; he has
been raised from the dead!" 17 For Herod
himself had sent and laid hold of John, and
bound him in prison for the sake of Herodias, his brother Philip's wife; for he had
married her. 18 Because John had said to
Herod, [v]"It is not lawful for you to have
your brother's wife."
19 Therefore Herodias [4]held it against
him and wanted to kill him, but she could
not; 20 for Herod [w]feared John, knowing
that he *was* a just and holy man, and he
protected him. And when he heard him, he
[5]did many things, and heard him gladly.
21 [x]Then an opportune day came when
Herod [y]on his birthday gave a feast for his
nobles, the high officers, and the chief *men*
of Galilee. 22 And when Herodias' daughter herself came in and danced, and
pleased Herod and those who sat with him,
the king said to the girl, "Ask me whatever
you want, and I will give *it* to you." 23 He
also swore to her, [z]"Whatever you ask me,
I will give you, up to half my kingdom."

10 [m] Matt. 10:11; Luke 9:4; 10:7,8
11 [n] Matt. 10:14; Luke 10:10 [o] Acts 13:51; 18:6 [1] NU *whatever place* [2] NU omits the rest of v. 11.
13 [p] [James 5:14]
14 [q] Matt. 14:1-12; Mark 6:14-16; Luke 9:7-9 [r] Luke 19:37
15 [s] Matt. 16:14; Mark 8:28; Luke 9:19 [t] Matt. 21:11 [3] NU, M *a prophet, like one*
16 [u] Matt. 14:2; Luke 3:19
18 [v] Lev. 18:16; 20:21
19 [4] *held a grudge*
20 [w] Matt. 14:5; 21:26 [5] NU *was very perplexed, yet*
21 [x] Matt. 14:6 [y] Gen. 40:20
23 [z] Esth. 5:3, 6; 7:2

dard garments of clothing. Men of comparative wealth would wear two, but Jesus wanted the disciples to identify with common people and travel with just minimum clothing.

6:10 The disciples were to carefully select where they stayed (cf. Matt. 10:11), but once there, the sole focus was to be on ministry. Contentment with their first host and his accommodations would be a testimony to others while the disciples ministered (cf. 1 Tim. 6:6).

6:11 shake off the dust. A symbolic act that signified complete renunciation of further fellowship with those who rejected them (*see note on Matt. 10:14*). When the disciples made this gesture, it would show that the people had rejected Jesus and the gospel, and were hence rejected by the disciples and by the Lord. **more tolerable for Sodom and Gomorrah.** People who reject Christ's gracious, saving gospel will face a fate worse than those pagans killed by divine judgment on the two OT cities (*see notes on Gen. 19:24; Matt. 10:15*).

6:12,13 preached...cast out many demons. Cf. v. 7. They were heralds of the gospel and had repeated success in expelling evil spirits from people. This demonstrated Christ's power over the supernatural world and confirmed His claim to being God.

6:12 repent. *See notes on 1:15; Matt. 3:2.*

6:13 anointed with oil...sick. In Jesus' day olive oil was often used medicinally (cf. Luke 10:34). But here it represented the power and presence of the Holy Spirit and was used symbolically in relation to supernatural healing (cf. Is. 11:2; Zech. 4:1-6; Matt. 25:2-4; Rev. 1:4,12). As a well known healing agent, the oil was an appropriate, tangible medium the people could identify with as the disciples ministered to the sick among them.

6:14 King Herod heard. *See note on Matt. 14:1.* The context indicates Herod heard some exciting news centering on Jesus and resulting from the disciples' recent preaching and miracle working in Galilee. **John the Baptist.** The forerunner of Christ (*see notes on 1:4-7; Matt. 3:1,4,6*).

6:15 "It is Elijah." This identification of Jesus, which probably had been discussed repeatedly among the Jews, was based on the Jewish expectation that the prophet Elijah would return prior to Messiah's coming (*see notes on Mal. 4:5; Matt. 11:14; Luke 1:17*). **the Prophet... one of the prophets.** Some saw Jesus as the fulfillment of Deut. 18:15, the messianic prophecy that looked to the One who, like Moses, would lead His people. Others were willing to identify Jesus only as a great prophet, or one who was resuming the suspended line of OT prophets. These and the other opinions, although misplaced, show that the people still thought Jesus was special or somehow supernatural.

6:16 John...has been raised from the dead! By this excited, guilt-laden confession, Herod showed that he could not forget the evil he had done in beheading John the Baptist and that his conscience had led him to the eerie fear that John was back from the dead (cf. Matt. 14:1,2; Luke 9:7-9).

6:17 John...bound him in prison. Herod kept him fettered while imprisoned, probably at Machaerus, near the NE shore of the Dead Sea. Herod's intention was to protect John from the plots of Herodias (cf. v. 20). **Herodias.** Herod's niece, the daughter of his half-brother Aristobulus. **Philip's.** Herod Philip II, another half-brother to Herod Antipas (the Herod in this passage). Therefore, Philip was also an uncle to Herodias (*see note on Matt. 14:3*).

6:18 John had said...It is not lawful. The tense of the Gr. verb and Mark's wording imply that John had repeatedly rebuked Herod Antipas in private confrontation that his marriage to Herodias was contrary to Mosaic law (*see note on Matt. 14:3*; cf. Matt. 3:7-10).

6:20 he did many things. The preferred reading is "he was very perplexed," which indicates that Herod's interaction with John left him in great internal conflict—a moral struggle between his lust for Herodias and the prodding of his guilty conscience.

6:21 nobles. This term may also be translated "lords," or "great ones." These were men who held high civil offices under Herod. **high officers.** High-ranking military officials (Gr., *chiliarchs*) who each commanded 1,000 men. **chief *men* of Galilee.** The key social leaders of the region.

6:22 Herodias' daughter. Salome, her daughter by Philip (*see note on Matt. 14:6*). **danced.** Refers to a solo dance with highly suggestive hand and body movements, comparable to a modern striptease. It was unusual and almost unprecedented that Salome would have performed in this way before Herod's guests (cf. Esth. 1:11,12).

6:23 up to half my kingdom. This was an exaggeration designed to enhance his previous statement of generosity. As a Roman tetrarch, Herod actually had no "kingdom" to give.

24 So she went out and said to her mother, "What shall I ask?"
And she said, "The head of John the
Baptist!"
25 Immediately she came in with haste to
the king and asked, saying, "I want you to
give me at once the head of John the Baptist on a platter."
26 [a]And the king was exceedingly sorry;
yet, because of the oaths and because of
those who sat with him, he did not want to
refuse her. 27 Immediately the king sent an
executioner and commanded his head to
be brought. And he went and beheaded
him in prison, 28 brought his head on a
platter, and gave it to the girl; and the girl
gave it to her mother. 29 When his disciples
heard *of it*, they came and [b]took away his
corpse and laid it in a tomb.

Twelve Return—Luke 9:10

30 [c]Then the apostles gathered to Jesus
and told Him all things, both what they had
done and what they had taught. 31 [d]And He
said to them, "Come aside by yourselves to
a deserted place and rest a while." For
[e]there were many coming and going, and
they did not even have time to eat.

Five Thousand Are Fed
Matt. 14:13-21; Luke 9:11-17; John 6:1-14

32 [f]So they departed to a deserted place in
the boat by themselves.
33 But [6]the multitudes saw them departing, and many [g]knew Him and ran there
on foot from all the cities. They arrived before them and came together to Him.
34 [h]And Jesus, when He came out, saw a
great multitude and was moved with compassion for them, because they were like
[i]sheep not having a shepherd. So [j]He
began to teach them many things.
35 [k]When the day was now far spent, His
disciples came to Him and said, "This is a
deserted place, and already the hour *is*
late. 36 Send them away, that they may go
into the surrounding country and villages
and buy themselves [7]bread; for they have
nothing to eat."
37 But He answered and said to them,
"You give them something to eat."
And they said to Him, [l]"Shall we go and
buy two hundred denarii worth of bread
and give them *something* to eat?"
38 But He said to them, "How many
loaves do you have? Go and see."
And when they found out they said,
[m]"Five, and two fish."
39 Then He [n]commanded them to make
them all sit down in groups on the green
grass. 40 So they sat down in ranks, in hundreds and in fifties. 41 And when He had
taken the five loaves and the two fish, He
[o]looked up to heaven, [p]blessed and broke
the loaves, and gave *them* to His disciples
to set before them; and the two fish He divided among *them* all. 42 So they all ate and
were filled. 43 And they took up twelve
baskets full of fragments and of the fish.
44 Now those who had eaten the loaves
were [8]about five thousand men.

26 [a] Matt. 14:9
29 [b] 1 Kin. 13:29, 30; Matt. 27:58-61; Acts 8:2
30 [c] Luke 9:10
31 [d] Matt. 14:13 [e] Mark 3:20
32 [f] Matt. 14:13-21; Luke 9:10-17; John 6:5-13
33 [g] [Col. 1:6] [6] NU, M *they*
34 [h] Matt. 9:36; 14:14; [Heb. 5:2] [i] Num. 27:17; 1 Kin. 22:17; 2 Chr. 18:16; Zech. 10:2 [j] [Is. 48:17; 61:1-3]; Luke 9:11
35 [k] Matt. 14:15; Luke 9:12
36 [7] NU *something to eat* and omits the rest of v. 36.
37 [l] Num. 11:13, 22; 2 Kin. 4:43
38 [m] Matt. 14:17; Luke 9:13; John 6:9
39 [n] Matt. 15:35; Mark 8:6
41 [o] John 11:41, 42 [p] 1 Sam. 9:13; Matt. 15:36; 26:26; Mark 8:7; Luke 24:30
44 [8] NU, M omit *about*

6:26 because of the oaths. Herod, as a monarch, felt bound because oaths were considered sacred and unbreakable (*see notes on Matt. 5:34; 14:9*).

6:27 executioner. Originally meant spy or scout, but came to describe a staff member of a Roman tribune. They served as couriers and bodyguards as well as executioners. Herod had adopted the custom of surrounding himself with such men.

6:31 by yourselves. Jesus' invitation for a retreat into the desert was restricted to the 12. He knew they needed rest and privacy after their tiring ministry expedition and the continuing press of the people.

6:32 departed…in the boat by themselves. The disciples obeyed Jesus' proposal, departing from His headquarters in Capernaum using the same boat as in 5:2.

6:33 ran there on foot. The direction (toward the NE shore of the lake) and speed of the boat, along with the immediate lack of other available boats, caused the crowd to follow by land. **arrived before them.** Contained only in Mark's account, this does not necessarily mean everyone arrived before the boat, because the land distance was probably 8 mi., twice as far as the 4 mi. the boat had to travel. Rather, those young and eager in the crowd were able to outrun both the rest and the boat (probably because it encountered no wind or a contrary wind) and actually arrive at the shore before the boat (cf. Matt. 14:13,14; Luke 9:11; John 6:3,5).

6:34 was moved with compassion. *See note on Matt. 9:36.* **sheep not having a shepherd.** An OT picture (cf. Num. 27:17; 1 Kin. 22:17; 2 Chr. 18:16; Ezek. 34:5) used to describe the people as helpless and starving, lacking in spiritual guidance and protection, and exposed to the perils of sin and spiritual destruction.

6:37 two hundred denarii. A single denarius (*see note on Matt. 22:19*) was equivalent to a day's pay for the day laborer (cf. Matt. 20:2). "Two hundred" would therefore equal 8 months' wages and be quite beyond the disciples' (or any average person's) means.

6:38 loaves. Lit. "bread-cakes," or "rolls."

6:39 green grass. This detail indicates it was the spring rainy season, before the hot summer would have turned the grass dry and brown.

6:40 in hundreds and in fifties. A symmetrical seating arrangement, possibly 50 semi-circles of 100 people each, with the semi-circles one behind the other in ranks. Such an arrangement was familiar to the Jews during their festivals, and it made food distribution more convenient.

6:41 looked up to heaven. A typical prayer posture for Jesus (cf. 7:34; Luke 24:35; John 11:41; 17:1). Heaven was universally regarded as the Father's dwelling place (Matt. 6:9).

6:42 all ate and were filled. The hunger of everyone in the crowd was completely satisfied (cf. John 6:11).

6:43 twelve baskets full. The "baskets," apparently the same ones used to bring the food, were small wicker containers like the ones the Jews used to carry food.

6:44 five thousand men. The Gr. word for "men" means strictly males, so the numerical estimate did not include women and chil-

Jesus Walks on Water
Matt. 14:22-23; John 6:15-21

45 [q]Immediately He [9]made His disciples get into the boat and go before Him
to the other side, to Bethsaida, while He
sent the multitude away. 46 And when He
had sent them away, He [r]departed to the
mountain to pray. 47 Now when evening
came, the boat was in the middle of the
sea; and He *was* alone on the land. 48 Then
He saw them straining at rowing, for the
wind was against them. Now about the
fourth watch of the night He came to
them, walking on the sea, and [s]would
have passed them by. 49 And when they
saw Him walking on the sea, they supposed it was a [t]ghost, and cried out; 50 for
they all saw Him and were troubled. But
immediately He talked with them and
said to them, [u]"Be [1] of good cheer! It is I;
do not be [v]afraid." 51 Then He went up
into the boat to them, and the wind
[w]ceased. And they were greatly [x]amazed
in themselves beyond measure, and marveled. 52 For [y]they had not understood
about the loaves, because their [z]heart was
hardened.

45 [q] Matt. 14:22-32; John 6:15-21 [9] *invited, strongly urged*
46 [r] Mark 1:35; Luke 5:16
48 [s] Luke 24:28
49 [t] Matt. 14:26; Luke 24:37
50 [u] Matt. 9:2; John 16:33 [v] Is. 41:10 [1] *Take courage*
51 [w] Ps. 107:29 [x] Mark 1:27; 2:12; 5:42; 7:37
52 [y] Matt. 16:9-11; Mark 8:17, 18 [z] Is. 63:17; Mark 3:5; 16:14
53 [a] Matt. 14:34-36; John 6:24, 25
54 [2] Lit. *they*
56 [b] Matt. 9:20; Mark 5:27, 28; [Acts 19:12] [c] Num. 15:38, 39

CHAPTER 7

1 [a] Matt. 15:1-20
2 [b] Matt. 15:20 [1] NU omits *when* [2] NU omits *they found fault*
3 [c] Mark 7:5, 8, 9, 13; Gal. 1:14; 1 Pet. 1:18 [3] Lit. *with the fist*

Jesus Heals at Gennesaret—Matt. 14:34-36

53 [a]When they had crossed over, they
came to the land of Gennesaret and anchored there. 54 And when they came out
of the boat, immediately [2]the people recognized Him, 55 ran through that whole
surrounding region, and began to carry
about on beds those who were sick to
wherever they heard He was. 56 Wherever
He entered, into villages, cities, or the
country, they laid the sick in the marketplaces, and begged Him that [b]they might
just touch the [c]hem of His garment. And as
many as touched Him were made well.

Pharisees and Defilement—Matt. 15:1-20

7 Then [a]the Pharisees and some of the
scribes came together to Him, having
come from Jerusalem. 2 Now [1]when they
saw some of His disciples eat bread with
defiled, that is, with [b]unwashed hands,
[2]they found fault. 3 For the Pharisees and
all the Jews do not eat unless they wash
their hands [3]in a special way, holding the
[c]tradition of the elders. 4 *When they come*
from the marketplace, they do not eat unless they wash. And there are many other
things which they have received and hold,

dren (cf. Matt. 14:21). The women and children were traditionally seated separately from the men for meals. When everyone was added, there could have been at least 20,000.

6:45 the boat. *See note on v. 32.* **go before Him.** The implication is that Jesus was to rejoin the disciples later. **Bethsaida.** A town on the W side of the Sea of Galilee and S of Capernaum (cf. Matt. 11:21).

6:46 the mountain. The entire E side of the Sea of Galilee is mountainous with steep slopes leading up to a plateau. Up one of the slopes was a good place to pray, away from the crowd (cf. John 6:15).

6:47 middle of the sea. Normally in traveling across the northern end of the lake they would have been within one or two mi. of shore. But on that occasion, the wind had carried the boat several mi. S, closer to the center of the lake (cf. Matt. 14:24).

6:48 fourth watch. 3:00 a.m. to 6:00 a.m. **walking on the sea.** The verb's tense depicts a steady progress, unhindered by the waves. **would have passed them by.** The more literal rendering, "desired to come alongside of," indicates Jesus' intention here. He wanted to test the disciples' faith, so He deliberately changed course and came parallel to the boat to see if they would recognize Him and His supernatural powers and invite Him aboard.

6:49 a ghost. An apparition or imaginary creature. The Gr. term gives us the English "phantom." Because of the impossibility of such an act and their fatigue and fear in the stormy conditions, the 12, even though each one saw Him, did not at first believe the figure was actually Jesus.

6:50 Be of good cheer! This command, always linked in the gospels to a situation of fear and apprehension (cf. 10:49; Matt. 9:2, 22; 14:27; Luke 8:48; John 16:33; Acts 23:11), urged the disciples to have a continuing attitude of courage. **It is I.** Lit. "I AM." This statement clearly identified the figure as the Lord Jesus, not some phantom. It also echoed the OT self-revelation of God (cf. Ex. 3:14).

6:52 they had not understood about the loaves. An explanation of the disciples' overwhelming astonishment at what had just happened. Because they misunderstood the real significance of that afternoon's miracle, they could not grasp Jesus' supernatural character as displayed in His power over the lake. **their heart was hardened.** Cf. 8:17. The disciples' minds were impenetrable, so that they could not perceive what Christ was saying (cf. 4:11, 12). This phrase conveys or alludes to rebellion, not just ignorance (*see note on 3:5*).

6:53 Gennesaret. *See note on Matt. 14:34.*

6:56 marketplaces. Open spaces, usually just inside city walls or near city centers, where people congregated for various business and social purposes. Here the term might indicate its original meaning of any place where people generally assembled. The people brought the sick to such locations because Jesus was more likely to pass by. **His garment.** *See note on 5:28.*

7:1 Pharisees...come from Jerusalem. This delegation of leading representatives of Judaism came from Jerusalem probably at the request of the Galilean Pharisees. **scribes.** *See notes on 3:22; Matt. 2:4.*

7:2 defiled. The disciples of Jesus were being accused of eating with hands that had not been ceremonially cleansed, and thus had not been separated from the defilement associated with their having touched anything profane.

7:3 wash. This washing had nothing to do with cleaning dirty hands but with a ceremonial rinsing. The ceremony involved someone pouring water out of a jar onto another's hands, whose fingers must be pointing up. As long as the water dripped off at the wrist, the person could proceed to the next step. He then had water poured over both hands with the fingers pointing down. Then each hand was to be rubbed with the fist of the other hand. **tradition of the elders.** This body of extrabiblical laws and interpretations of Scripture had in actuality supplanted Scripture as the highest religious authority in Judaism (*see note on Matt. 15:2*).

7:4 marketplace. *See note on 6:56.* **couches.** This word does not appear in the better manuscripts.

like the washing of cups, pitchers, copper
vessels, and couches.
5 [d]Then the Pharisees and scribes asked
Him, "Why do Your disciples not walk according to the tradition of the elders, but
eat bread with unwashed hands?"
6 He answered and said to them, "Well
did Isaiah prophesy of you [e]hypocrites, as
it is written:

> [f]*'This people honors Me with their*
> *lips,*
> *But their heart is far from Me.*
> 7 *And in vain they worship Me,*
> *Teaching as doctrines the*
> *commandments of men.'*

8 For laying aside the commandment of
God, you hold the tradition of men—[4]the
washing of pitchers and cups, and many
other such things you do."
9 He said to them, "*All too* well [g]you [5]re-
ject the commandment of God, that you
may keep your tradition. 10 For Moses
said, [h]*'Honor your father and your moth-*
er'; and, [i]*'He who curses father or mother,*
let him be put to death.' 11 But you say, 'If
a man says to his father or mother, [j]"Whatever profit you might have received from
me *is* Corban"—' (that is, a gift *to God*),
12 then you no longer let him do anything
for his father or his mother, 13 making the
word of God of no effect through your tradition which you have handed down. And
many such things you do."
14 [k]When He had called all the multitude to *Himself*, He said to them, "Hear
Me, everyone, and [l]understand: 15 There is
nothing that enters a man from outside
which can defile him; but the things which
come out of him, those are the things that
[m]defile a man. 16 [n]If[6] anyone has ears to
hear, let him hear!"
17 [o]When He had entered a house away
from the crowd, His disciples asked Him
concerning the parable. 18 So He said to
them, [p]"Are you thus without understanding also? Do you not perceive that whatever enters a man from outside cannot defile
him, 19 because it does not enter his heart
but his stomach, and is eliminated, [7]*thus*
purifying all foods?" 20 And He said,
[q]"What comes out of a man, that defiles a
man. 21 [r]For from within, out of the heart
of men, [s]proceed evil thoughts, [t]adulteries,
[u]fornications, murders, 22 thefts, [v]covet-
ousness, wickedness, [w]deceit, [x]lewdness,
an evil eye, [y]blasphemy, [z]pride, foolishness. 23 All these evil things come from
within and defile a man."

Syro-Phoenician's Daughter Is Healed
Matt. 15:21-28

24 [a]From there He arose and went to the
region of Tyre [8]and Sidon. And He entered
a house and wanted no one to know *it*, but
He could not be [b]hidden. 25 For a woman

5 [d]Matt. 15:2
6 [e]Matt. 23:13-29 [f]Is. 29:13
8 [4]NU omits the rest of v. 8.
9 [g]Prov. 1:25; Is. 24:5; Jer. 7:23, 24 [5]*set aside*
10 [h]Ex. 20:12; Deut. 5:16; Matt. 15:4 [i]Ex. 21:17; Lev. 20:9; Prov. 20:20
11 [j]Matt. 15:5; 23:18
14 [k]Matt. 15:10 [l]Matt. 16:9, 11, 12
15 [m]Is. 59:3; [Heb. 12:15]
16 [n]Matt. 11:15 [6]NU omits v. 16.
17 [o]Matt. 15:15
18 [p][Is. 28:9-11; 1 Cor. 3:2; Heb. 5:11-14]
19 [7]NU sets off the final phrase as Mark's comment that Jesus has declared all foods clean.
20 [q]Ps. 39:1; [Matt. 12:34-37; James 3:6]
21 [r]Gen. 6:5; 8:21; Prov. 6:18; Jer. 17:9; Matt. 15:19 [s][Gal. 5:19-21] [t]2 Pet. 2:14 [u]1 Thess. 4:3
22 [v]Luke 12:15 [w]Rom. 1:28, 29 [x]1 Pet. 4:3 [y]Rev. 2:9 [z]1 John 2:16
24 [a]Matt. 15:21 [b]Mark 2:1, 2 [8]NU omits *and Sidon*

7:5 Why do Your disciples not. The Pharisees and scribes went to the disciples' Master for an explanation of the disciples' allegedly disgraceful conduct. In reality they were accusing Jesus of teaching His disciples to disobey the traditions of the elders. **unwashed hands.** *See note on v. 3.*

7:6 did Isaiah prophesy. Isaiah 29:13 is quoted almost word for word from the Gr. translation of the OT (LXX). Isaiah's prophecy perfectly fit the actions of the Pharisees and scribes (*see note on Is. 29:13*). **hypocrites.** Spiritual phonies (*see note on Matt. 6:2*). They followed the traditions of men because such teaching required only mechanical and thoughtless conformity without a pure heart.

7:8 commandment of God...tradition of men. Jesus first accused them of abandoning all the commandments contained in God's Word. Then He charged them with substituting God's standard with a humanly designed standard. *See note on Matt. 15:2.*

7:10 Moses said. Quoted from Ex. 20:12 (the fifth commandment) and Ex. 21:17. Both refer specifically to the duty of honoring one's parents, which includes treating them with respect, love, reverence, dignity, and assisting them financially. The second quotation indicates how seriously God regards this obligation.

7:11 Corban. A Heb. term meaning, "given to God." It refers to any gift or sacrifice of money or goods an individual vowed to dedicate specifically to God. As a result of such dedication, the money or goods could be used only for sacred purposes.

7:13 making the word of God of no effect through your tradition. "Making...of no effect" means, "to deprive of authority" or "to cancel." The "tradition" in question allowed any individual to call all his possessions "Corban" (*see note on v. 11*). If a son became angry with his parents, he could declare his money and property "Corban." Since Scripture teaches that any vow made to God could not be violated (Num. 30:2), his possessions could not be used for anything but service to God and not as a resource of financial assistance for his parents. But Jesus condemned this practice by showing that the Pharisees and scribes were guilty of canceling out God's Word (and His command to honor one's parents) through their tradition.

7:16 This verse does not occur in the best manuscripts.

7:18 defile him. *See note on v. 2.*

7:19 Since food is merely physical, no one who eats it will defile his heart or inner person, which is spiritual. Physical pollution, no matter how corrupt, cannot cause spiritual or moral pollution. Neither can external ceremonies and rituals cleanse a person spiritually. ***thus* purifying all foods.** By overturning the tradition of hand washing, Jesus in effect removed the restrictions regarding dietary laws. This comment by Mark had the advantage of hindsight as he looked back on the event, and was no doubt influenced by Peter's (see Introduction: Author and Date) own experience in Joppa (*see note on Acts 10:15*).

7:20 What comes out of a man. A person's defiled heart is expressed in both what he says and what he does (*see note on Matt. 15:11*; cf. 12:34-37). **defiles.** *See note on v. 2.*

7:21 fornications. Lit. illicit sexual activity.

7:22 lewdness. Lit. unrestrained, shameless behavior. **an evil eye.** A Heb. expression referring to envy and jealousy (Deut. 28:54; Prov. 23:6; Matt. 20:15).

7:24 Tyre...Sidon. *See note on 3:8.* **wanted no one to know.** Jesus did not seek a public ministry in the area. It is likely He wanted time to rest from the pressure of the Jewish leaders and an opportu-

whose young daughter had an unclean
spirit heard about Him, and she came and
[c]fell at His feet. 26 The woman was a
[9]Greek, a [1]Syro-Phoenician by birth, and
she kept [2]asking Him to cast the demon
out of her daughter. 27 But Jesus said to
her, "Let the children be filled first, for it is
not good to take the children's bread and
throw *it* to the little dogs."

28 And she answered and said to Him,
"Yes, Lord, yet even the little dogs under
the table eat from the children's crumbs."

29 Then He said to her, "For this saying
go your way; the demon has gone out of
your daughter."

30 And when she had come to her house,
she found the demon gone out, and her
daughter lying on the bed.

Deaf and Mute Man Is Healed

31 [d]Again, departing from the region of
Tyre and Sidon, He came through the
midst of the region of Decapolis to the Sea
of Galilee. 32 Then [e]they brought to Him
one who was deaf and had an impediment
in his speech, and they begged Him to put
His hand on him. 33 And He took him
aside from the multitude, and put His fingers in his ears, and [f]He spat and touched
his tongue. 34 Then, [g]looking up to heaven,
[h]He sighed, and said to him, "Ephphatha,"
that is, "Be opened."

25 [c]Mark 5:22; John 11:32; Rev. 1:17
26 [9]*Gentile* [1]A Syrian of Phoenicia [2]*begging*
31 [d]Matt. 15:29; Mark 15:37; Luke 23:46; 24:46; Acts 10:40; 1 Cor. 15:4
32 [e]Matt. 9:32; Luke 11:14
33 [f]Mark 8:23; John 9:6
34 [g]Mark 6:41; John 11:41; 17:1 [h]John 11:33, 38

35 [i]Is. 35:5, 6 [3]Lit. *bond*
36 [j]Mark 5:43
37 [k]Mark 6:51; 10:26 [l]Matt. 12:22

CHAPTER 8

1 [a]Matt. 15:32-39; Mark 6:34-44; Luke 9:12
2 [b]Matt. 9:36; 14:14; Mark 1:41; 6:34
5 [c]Matt. 15:34; Mark 6:38; John 6:9

35 [i]Immediately his ears were opened,
and the [3]impediment of his tongue was
loosed, and he spoke plainly. 36 Then [j]He
commanded them that they should tell no
one; but the more He commanded them,
the more widely they proclaimed *it*. 37 And
they were [k]astonished beyond measure,
saying, "He has done all things well. He
[l]makes both the deaf to hear and the mute
to speak."

Four Thousand Are Fed—Matt. 15:32-38

8 In those days, [a]the multitude being
very great and having nothing to eat,
Jesus called His disciples *to Him* and said
to them, 2 "I have [b]compassion on the multitude, because they have now continued
with Me three days and have nothing to
eat. 3 And if I send them away hungry to
their own houses, they will faint on the
way; for some of them have come from
afar."

4 Then His disciples answered Him,
"How can one satisfy these people with
bread here in the wilderness?"

5 [c]He asked them, "How many loaves
do you have?"

And they said, "Seven."

6 So He commanded the multitude to sit
down on the ground. And He took the
seven loaves and gave thanks, broke *them*
and gave *them* to His disciples to set before

nity to further prepare the disciples for His coming crucifixion and their ministry.

7:25 unclean spirit. A demon (*see note on 1:23*; cf. Matt. 15:22).

7:26 Greek. A non-Jew in both her language and religion (*see note on Rom. 1:14*). **Syro-Phoenician.** The region of Phoenicia at that time was part of the province of Syria. Matthew 15:22 adds that she was a descendant of the Canaanites.

7:27 first. The illustration Jesus gave was in essence a test of the woman's faith. Jesus' "first" responsibility was to preach the gospel to the children of Israel (cf. Rom. 1:16; 15:8). But that also implied there would come a time when Gentiles would be the recipients of God's blessings. **the children's bread and throw *it* to the little dogs.** "The children's bread" refers to God's blessings offered to the Jews. This picture indicates that the "little dogs" (Gentiles) had a place in the household of God, but not the prominent one (*see note on Matt. 15:26*). **little dogs.** The diminutive form suggests that this reference is to dogs that were kept as pets. Jesus was referring to the Gentiles, but He did not use the derisive term the Jews usually employed for them that described mangy, vicious mongrels.

7:28 Yes, Lord. Indicative of the woman's humble faith and worshipful attitude. She knew she was sinful and undeserving of any of God's blessing. Her response was characterized by a complete absence of pride and self-reliance, which Jesus answered by granting her request (vv. 29,30).

7:31 departing from the region of Tyre and Sidon...Sea of Galilee. Jesus traveled 20 mi. N from Tyre and passed through Sidon, which was deep into Gentile territory. From there He went E, crossed the Jordan, and traveled S along the eastern shore of the Sea of Galilee. **Decapolis.** *See note on 5:20.*

7:33 put His fingers in his ears. Because the man could not hear, Jesus used His own form of sign language to tell him that He was about to heal the man's deafness. **He spat and touched his tongue.** Also a form of sign language in which Jesus offered the man hope for a restored speech.

7:34 "Ephphatha." An Aram. word that Mark immediately defines.

7:36 tell no one. Although Jesus ministered to Gentiles as the need arose, His intention was not to have a public ministry among them. *See note on 1:44.*

8:1-10 While all 4 gospels record the feeding of the 5,000, only Matthew (15:32-38) and Mark record the feeding of the 4,000.

8:1 the multitude being very great. Probably because of the widespread report of Jesus' healing of the deaf and mute man (7:36).

8:2 I have compassion. Only here and in the parallel passage (Matt. 15:32) did Jesus use this word of Himself. When he fed the 5,000, Jesus expressed "compassion" for the people's lost spiritual condition (6:34); here, He expressed "compassion" for people's physical needs (cf. Matt. 6:8,32). Jesus could empathize with their hunger, having experienced it Himself (Matt. 4:2). **continued with Me three days.** This reflects the crowd's eagerness to hear Jesus' teaching and experience His healings (cf. Matt. 15:30). That they were with Him for that time before the miraculous feeding distinguishes this event from the earlier feeding of the 5,000, in which the crowd gathered, ate, and dispersed in one day (Matt. 14:14,15,22,23).

8:4 How can one satisfy these people with bread. Some find the disciples' question incredible in light of the earlier feeding of the 5,000. But it was consistent with their spiritual dullness and lack of understanding (cf. vv. 14-21; 6:52). **in the wilderness.** The Decapolis (*see note on 5:20*) region was not as heavily populated as Galilee.

8:5 loaves. Flat cakes of bread which could easily be broken into smaller pieces.

them; and they set *them* before the multitude. 7 They also had a few small fish; and
[d]having blessed them, He said to set them
also before *them.* 8 So they ate and were
filled, and they took up seven large baskets
of leftover fragments. 9 Now those who
had eaten were about four thousand. And
He sent them away, 10 [e]immediately got
into the boat with His disciples, and came
to the region of Dalmanutha.

Pharisees Seek a Sign—Matt. 15:39–16:4

11 [f]Then the Pharisees came out and
began to dispute with Him, seeking from
Him a sign from heaven, testing Him.
12 But He [g]sighed deeply in His spirit, and
said, "Why does this generation seek a
sign? Assuredly, I say to you, [h]no sign shall
be given to this generation."
13 And He left them, and getting into the
boat again, departed to the other side.

Disciples Do Not Understand
Matt. 16:5-12

14 [i]Now [1]the disciples had forgotten to
take bread, and they did not have more
than one loaf with them in the boat.
15 [j]Then He charged them, saying, "Take
heed, beware of the [2]leaven of the Pharisees and the leaven of Herod."
16 And they reasoned among themselves,
saying, "*It is* because we have no bread."
17 But Jesus, being aware of *it,* said to
them, "Why do you reason because you
have no bread? [k]Do you not yet perceive
nor understand? Is your heart [3]still hardened? 18 Having eyes, do you not see? And
having ears, do you not hear? And do you
not remember? 19 [l]When I broke the five
loaves for the five thousand, how many
baskets full of fragments did you take up?"
They said to Him, "Twelve."
20 "Also, [m]when I broke the seven for
the four thousand, how many large baskets full of fragments did you take up?"
And they said, "Seven."
21 So He said to them, "How *is it* [n]you
do not understand?"

A Blind Man Is Healed

22 Then He came to Bethsaida; and they
brought a [o]blind man to Him, and begged
Him to [p]touch him. 23 So He took the blind
man by the hand and led him out of the
town. And when [q]He had spit on his eyes
and put His hands on him, He asked him if
he saw anything.
24 And he looked up and said, "I see
men like trees, walking."
25 Then He put *His* hands on his eyes
again and made him look up. And he was
restored and saw everyone clearly. 26 Then
He sent him away to his house, saying,
[4]"Neither go into the town, [r]nor tell anyone in the town."

7 [d] Matt. 14:19; Mark 6:41
10 [e] Matt. 15:39
11 [f] Matt. 12:38; 16:1; Luke 11:16; John 2:18; 6:30; 1 Cor. 1:22
12 [g] Mark 7:34 [h] Matt. 12:39
14 [i] Matt. 16:5 [1] NU, M *they*
15 [j] Matt. 16:6; Luke 12:1 [2] *yeast*
17 [k] Mark 6:52; 16:14 [3] NU omits *still*
19 [l] Matt. 14:20; Mark 6:43; Luke 9:17; John 6:13
20 [m] Matt. 15:37
21 [n] [Mark 6:52]
22 [o] Matt. 9:27; John 9:1 [p] Luke 18:15
23 [q] Mark 7:33
26 [r] Matt. 8:4; Mark 5:43; 7:36 [4] NU *"Do not even go into the town."*

8:8 seven large baskets. Not the same baskets mentioned in the feeding of the 5,000 (6:43). Those were small baskets, commonly used by the Jewish people to hold one or two meals when traveling. The word here refers to large baskets (large enough to hold a man, Acts 9:25) used by Gentiles. What was done with the leftover food is not mentioned. It was likely given back to the people to sustain them on their trip home, since the disciples evidently did not take it with them (cf. v. 14).

8:9 four thousand. The number of the men only, not including the women and children (Matt. 15:38). This could indicate at least 16,000 people.

8:10 Dalmanutha. This location is not mentioned in any secular literature and only mentioned here in the NT. The location is unknown, but clearly in the region near Magdala (cf. Matt. 15:39 margin, where Magadan is the preferred reading). Recent archeological work in the area, when the water level of Galilee was at an all-time low, revealed several heretofore unknown anchorages. One small harbor has been found between Magadala and Capernaum which may be Dalmanutha.

8:11 Pharisees. *See notes on 2:16; Matt. 3:7.* **sign from heaven.** The skeptical Pharisees demanded further miraculous proof of Jesus' messianic claims. Not content with the countless miracles He had performed on earth, they demanded some sort of astronomical miracle. Having already given them more than enough proof, Jesus refused to accommodate their spiritual blindness. The supreme sign verifying His claim to be Son of God and Messiah was to be His resurrection (Matt. 16:39,40).

8:13 the other side. To the NE shore, where Bethsaida was located (v. 22).

8:15 leaven of the Pharisees and...Herod. "Leaven" in the NT is an illustration of influence (*see note on Matt. 13:33*) and most often symbolizes the evil influence of sin. The "leaven" of the Pharisees included both their false teaching (Matt. 16:12) and their hypocritical behavior (Luke 12:1); the "leaven" of Herod Antipas was his immoral, corrupt conduct (cf. 6:17-29). The Pharisees and the Herodians were allied against Christ (3:6).

8:17 Why do you reason...no bread? Jesus' question rebuked the disciples for completely missing His point (*see note on v. 15*). He was concerned with spiritual truth, not mundane physical matters. **heart still hardened.** I.e., they were rebellious, spiritually insensitive, and unable to understand spiritual truth (*see notes on 3:5; 6:52*).

8:18-20 Jesus' 5 questions further rebuked the disciples for their hardness of heart, and also reminded them of His ability to provide anything they might lack.

8:21 "How *is it* you do not understand?" An appeal based on the questions He had just asked. Matthew's parallel account reveals that the disciples finally understood His point (Matt. 16:12).

8:22-26 The second of Jesus' two miracles recorded only in Mark (cf. 7:31-37). It is also the first of two healings of blind men recorded in Mark (cf. 10:46-52).

8:22 Bethsaida. *See note on 6:45.*

8:23 spit on his eyes. This action and Jesus' touching his eyes with His hands (v. 25) were apparently meant to reassure the blind man (who would naturally depend on his other senses, such as touch) that Jesus would heal his eyes (cf. 7:33; John 9:6).

8:26 Neither go into the town. Jesus led the blind man out of town before healing him (v. 23), probably to avoid publicity and the mob scene that would otherwise result. Unlike others in the past (cf. 1:45; 7:36), he apparently obeyed.

Peter's Confession of Christ
Matt. 16:13-23; Luke 9:18-22

27 [s]Now Jesus and His disciples went
out to the towns of Caesarea Philippi; and
on the road He asked His disciples, saying
to them, "Who do men say that I am?"
28 So they answered, [t]"John the Baptist;
but some *say,* [u]Elijah; and others, one of
the prophets."
29 He said to them, "But who do you say
that I am?"
Peter answered and said to Him, [v]"You
are the Christ."
30 [w]Then He strictly warned them that
they should tell no one about Him.
31 And [x]He began to teach them that the
Son of Man must suffer many things, and
be [y]rejected by the elders and chief priests
and scribes, and be [z]killed, and after three
days rise again. 32 He spoke this word
openly. Then Peter took Him aside and
began to rebuke Him. 33 But when He had
turned around and looked at His disciples,
He [a]rebuked Peter, saying, "Get behind
Me, Satan! For you are not [5]mindful of the
things of God, but the things of men."

27 [s] Matt. 16:13-16; Luke 9:18-20
28 [t] Matt. 14:2 [u] Mark 6:14, 15; Luke 9:7, 8
29 [v] John 1:41; 4:42; 6:69; 11:27; Acts 2:36; 8:37; 9:20
30 [w] Matt. 8:4; 16:20; Luke 9:21
31 [x] [Is. 53:3-11]; Matt. 16:21; 20:19; Luke 18:31-33; 1 Pet. 1:11 [y] Mark 10:33 [z] Mark 9:31; 10:34
33 [a] Mark 16:14; [Rev. 3:19] [5] *setting your mind on*
34 [b] [Matt. 10:38]; Luke 14:27
35 [c] Matt. 10:39; Luke 17:33; John 12:25
38 [d] Matt. 10:33; Luke 9:26; 12:9 [e] Rom. 1:16; 2 Tim. 1:8, 9; 2:12

CHAPTER 9

1 [a] Matt. 16:28; Mark 13:26; Luke 9:27; Acts 7:55, 56; Rev. 20:4 [b] [Matt. 24:30] [1] *having come*

Cost of Discipleship
Matt. 16:24-27; Luke 9:22-26

34 When He had called the people to
Himself, with His disciples also, He said to
them, [b]"Whoever desires to come after Me,
let him deny himself, and take up his cross,
and follow Me. 35 For [c]whoever desires to
save his life will lose it, but whoever loses
his life for My sake and the gospel's will
save it. 36 For what will it profit a man if he
gains the whole world, and loses his own
soul? 37 Or what will a man give in exchange for his soul? 38 [d]For whoever [e]is
ashamed of Me and My words in this adulterous and sinful generation, of him the
Son of Man also will be ashamed when He
comes in the glory of His Father with the
holy angels."

The Transfuguration
Matt. 16-28–17:3; Luke 9:27-36

9 And He said to them, [a]"Assuredly,
I say to you that there are some standing here who will not taste death till they
see [b]the kingdom of God [1]present with
power."

8:27 Caesarea Philippi. A city about 25 mi. N of Bethsaida near Mt. Hermon, not to be confused with the Caesarea located on the Mediterranean coast about 60 mi. NW of Jerusalem.

8:28 Elijah. *See notes on 6:15; Mal. 4:5; Matt. 11:14; Luke 1:17.*

8:29 "But who do you say that I am?" After they reported the prevailing erroneous views about Jesus (v. 28), He asked the disciples to give their own evaluation of who He was. The answer every person gives to this question will determine his or her eternal destiny. **"You are the Christ."** Peter unhesitatingly replied on behalf of the 12 (cf. Matt. 14:28; 15:15; 17:4; 19:27; 26:33; John 6:68; 13:36), clearly and unequivocally affirming that they believed Jesus to be the Messiah.

8:30 tell no one. Jesus' messianic mission cannot be understood apart from the cross, which the disciples did not yet understand (cf. vv. 31-33; 9:30-32). For them to have proclaimed Jesus as Messiah at this point would have only furthered the misunderstanding that the Messiah was to be a political-military deliverer. The fallout was that the Jewish people, desperate to be rid of the yoke of Rome, would seek to make Jesus king by force (John 6:15; cf. 12:12-19).

8:31–10:52 In this section, as they traveled to Jerusalem, Jesus prepared the disciples for His death.

8:31 Son of Man. *See note on 2:10.* **must suffer many things.** Jesus' sufferings and death were inevitable because they were divinely ordained (Acts 2:22,23; 4:13-15), though, humanly speaking, caused by His rejection from the Jewish leaders. *See notes on Ps. 118:22,23; Is. 53:3;* cf. 12:10; Matt. 21:42. **elders.** *See note on 7:3.* **chief priests.** Members of the Sanhedrin and representatives of the 24 orders of ordinary priests (cf. Luke 1:8). **scribes.** Experts in the OT law (*see note on Matt. 2:4*). **after three days.** In keeping with the sign of Jonah (Matt. 12:40). **rise again.** Jesus always mentioned His resurrection in connection with His death (cf. 9:31; 10:34; Matt. 16:21; 17:23; 20:19; Luke 9:22; 18:33), making it all the more incomprehensible that the disciples were so slow to understand.

8:32 He spoke…openly. I.e., not in parables or allusions (cf. John 16:29). **Peter…began to rebuke Him.** The disciples still could not comprehend a dying Messiah (*see note on v. 30*). Peter, as usual (*see note on v. 29*) expressed the thoughts of the rest of the 12 (cf. v. 33). His brash outburst expressed not only presumption and misunderstanding, but also deep love for Jesus.

8:33 Get behind Me, Satan! In a startling turnaround, Peter, who had just been praised for being God's spokesman (Matt. 16:17-19), was then condemned as Satan's mouthpiece. Yet Jesus' sacrificial death was God's plan (Acts 2:22,23; 4:27,28) and whoever opposed it was, wittingly or not, advocating Satan's work.

8:34 deny himself. No one who is unwilling to deny himself can legitimately claim to be a disciple of Jesus Christ. **take up his cross.** This reveals the extent of self-denial—to the point of death, if necessary. The extent of desperation on the part of the penitent sinner who is aware he can't save himself reaches the place where nothing is held back (cf. Matt. 19:21,22). **and follow Me.** *See notes on 1:17; Matt. 10:38.*

8:35 loses his life…will save it. This paradoxical saying reveals an important spiritual truth: those who pursue a life of ease, comfort, and acceptance by the world will not find eternal life. On the other hand, those who give up their lives (*see note on v. 34*) for the sake of Christ and the gospel will find it. Cf. John 12:25.

8:36,37 soul. The real person, who will live forever in heaven or hell. To have all that the world has to offer yet not have Christ is to be eternally bankrupt; all the world's goods will not compensate for losing one's soul eternally. *See note on Matt. 16:26.*

8:38 ashamed of Me and My words. Those who reject the demands of discipleship prove themselves to be ashamed of Jesus Christ and the truth He taught, thus not redeemed from sin at all. **Son of Man.** *See note on 2:10.* **when He comes.** Mark's first reference to Jesus' second coming, an event later described in detail in the Olivet Discourse (13:1-37).

9:1 Assuredly, I say to you. A solemn statement appearing only in the gospels and always spoken by Jesus. It introduces topics of utmost significance (*see note on 3:28*). **not taste death till they see the kingdom.** The event Jesus had in mind has been variously interpreted as His resurrection and ascension, the coming of the Spirit at Pentecost, the spread of Christianity, or the destruction of Jerusalem in A.D. 70. The most accurate interpretation, however, is to connect

2 [c]Now after six days Jesus took Peter,
James, and John, and led them up on a
high mountain apart by themselves; and
He was transfigured before them. 3 His
clothes became shining, exceedingly
[d]white, like snow, such as no launderer on
earth can whiten them. 4 And Elijah appeared to them with Moses, and they were
talking with Jesus. 5 Then Peter answered
and said to Jesus, "Rabbi, it is good for us
to be here; and let us make three tabernacles: one for You, one for Moses, and one
for Elijah"— 6 because he did not know
what to say, for they were greatly afraid.
7 And a [e]cloud came and overshadowed
them; and a voice came out of the cloud,
saying, "This is [f]My beloved Son. [g]Hear
Him!" 8 Suddenly, when they had looked
around, they saw no one anymore, but
only Jesus with themselves.
9 [h]Now as they came down from the
mountain, He commanded them that they
should tell no one the things they had seen,
till the Son of Man had risen from the
dead. 10 So they kept this word to themselves, questioning [i]what the rising from
the dead meant.
11 And they asked Him, saying, "Why do
the scribes say [j]that Elijah must come first?"
12 Then He answered and told them,
"Indeed, Elijah is coming first and restores
all things. And [k]how is it written concerning the Son of Man, that He must suffer
many things and [l]be treated with contempt? 13 But I say to you that [m]Elijah has
also come, and they did to him whatever
they wished, as it is written of him."

Demon-Possessed Son Is Delivered
Matt. 17:14-21; Luke 9:37-42

14 [n]And when He came to the disciples,
He saw a great multitude around them,

2 [c] Matt. 17:1-8; Luke 9:28-36
3 [d] Dan. 7:9; Matt. 28:3
7 [e] Ex. 40:34; 1 Kin. 8:10; Acts 1:9; Rev. 1:7 [f] Ps. 2:7; [Is. 42:1]; Matt. 3:17; Mark 1:11; Luke 1:35; 3:22; 2 Pet. 1:17 [g] Acts 3:22
9 [h] Matt. 17:9-13; Mark 16:6; Luke 24:6, 7, 46
10 [i] John 2:19-22
11 [j] Mal. 4:5; Matt. 17:10
12 [k] Ps. 22:6; Is. 53:3; Dan. 9:26 [l] Luke 23:11; Phil. 2:7
13 [m] Mal. 4:5; Matt. 11:14; 17:12; Luke 1:17
14 [n] Matt. 17:14-19; Luke 9:37-42

Christ's promise with the Transfiguration in the context (vv. 2-8), which provided a foretaste of His second coming glory. That all 3 synoptic gospels place this promise immediately before the Transfiguration supports this view, as does the fact that "kingdom" can refer to royal splendor.

9:2 after six days. Matthew and Mark place the Transfiguration "six days" after Jesus' promise (v. 1); Luke, no doubt including the day the promise was made and the day of the Transfiguration itself, describes the interval as "about eight days" (Luke 9:28). **Peter, James, and John.** *See note on 5:37.* As the inner circle of Jesus' disciples, these 3 were sometimes allowed to witness events that the other disciples were not (cf. 14:33). **a high mountain.** Most likely Mt. Hermon (about 9,200 ft. above sea level), the highest mountain in the vicinity of Caesarea Philippi (cf. 8:27). **transfigured.** From a Gr. word meaning "to change in form," or "to be transformed." In some inexplicable way, Jesus manifested some of His divine glory to the 3 disciples (cf. 2 Pet. 1:16).

9:3 shining, exceedingly white. The divine glory emanating from Jesus made even his clothing radiate brilliant white light. Light is often associated with God's visible presence (cf. Ps. 104:2; Dan. 7:9; 1 Tim. 6:16; Rev. 1:14; 21:23).

9:4 Elijah...with Moses. Symbolic of the Prophets and the Law, the two great divisions of the OT. The order, "Elijah," then "Moses," is unique to Mark (who reverses the order in v. 5). **talking with Jesus.** The subject was His coming death (Luke 9:31).

9:5 Rabbi. Lit. "my master." A title of esteem and honor given by the Jews to respected teachers. In the NT, it is also used of John the Baptist (John 3:26). **let us make three tabernacles.** So as to make the 3 illustrious figures' stay permanent. It is also possible that Peter's suggestion reflected his belief that the millennial kingdom was about to be inaugurated (cf. Zech. 14:16).

9:7 a cloud...overshadowed them. This is the glory cloud, Shekinah, which throughout the OT was symbolic of God's presence (*see note on Rev. 1:7*; cf. Ex. 13:21; 33:18-23; 40:34,35; Num. 9:15; 14:14; Deut. 9:33). **a voice came out of the cloud.** The Father's voice from the cloud cut off Peter's fumbling words (Matt. 17:5; Luke 9:34). **This is My beloved Son.** The Father repeated the affirmation of His love for the Son first given at Jesus' baptism (1:11). The parallel accounts of the Transfiguration (Matt. 17:5; Luke 9:35) also record these words, as does Peter (2 Pet. 1:17). **Hear Him!** Jesus, the One to whom the Law and Prophets pointed (cf. Deut. 18:15), is the One whom the disciples are to listen to and obey (cf. Heb. 1:1,2).

9:9 commanded them...tell no one. *See note on 8:30.* **till the Son of man had risen from the dead.** This looks to the time when the true nature of Jesus' messianic mission became evident to all, that He came to conquer sin and death, not the Romans. **Son of Man.** *See note on 2:10.*

9:10 questioning what the rising from the dead meant. Like most of the Jewish people (the Sadducees being notable exceptions), the disciples believed in a future resurrection (cf. John 11:24). What confused them was Jesus' implication that His own resurrection was imminent, and thus so was His death. The disciples' confusion provides further evidence that they still did not understand Jesus' messianic mission (*see notes on v. 9; 8:30*).

9:11 Elijah must come first. Cf. 8:28,29. The scribes' teaching in this case was not based on rabbinical tradition, but on the OT (Mal. 3:1; 4:5). Malachi's prediction was well known among the Jews of Jesus' day, and the disciples were no doubt trying to figure out how to harmonize it with the appearance of Elijah they had just witnessed. The scribes and Pharisees also no doubt argued that Jesus could not be the Messiah based on the fact that Elijah had not yet appeared. Confused, the 3 disciples asked Jesus for His interpretation.

9:12 Elijah is coming first. Jesus affirmed the correctness of the scribal interpretation of Mal. 3:1; 4:5, which must have puzzled the disciples even more. **Son of Man.** *See note on 2:10.* **suffer...be treated with contempt.** Jesus pointed out that the prophecies about Elijah in no way precluded the suffering and death of Messiah, for that, too, was predicted in the OT (e.g., Pss. 22; 69:20,21; Is. 53; *see note on Rom. 1:2*).

9:13 Elijah has also come. Jesus directly addressed the disciples' question: the prophecies of Elijah's coming had been fulfilled in John the Baptist. Though certainly not a reincarnation of Elijah (cf. John 1:21), John came in the "spirit and power of Elijah," and would have fulfilled prophecies if they had believed (*see notes on Matt. 11:14; Luke 1:17*). Because they did reject both John the Baptist and Jesus, there will be another who will come in the spirit and power of Elijah before the second coming of Christ (*see notes on Matt. 11:14; Rev. 11:5,6*). **they did to him.** The Jewish leaders rejected John the Baptist (Matt. 21:25; Luke 7:33), and Herod killed him (6:17-29). **as it is written of him.** No specific OT prophecies predicted that Messiah's forerunner would die. Therefore, this statement is best understood as having been fulfilled typically. The fate intended for Elijah (1 Kin. 19:1,2) had befallen the Baptist. *See notes on Matt. 11:11-14.*

9:14 the disciples. The 9 who had remained behind.

and scribes disputing with them. 15 Immediately, when they saw Him, all the people
were greatly amazed, and running to *Him*,
greeted Him. 16 And He asked the scribes,
"What are you discussing with them?"
17 Then [o]one of the crowd answered
and said, "Teacher, I brought You my son,
who has a mute spirit. 18 And wherever it
seizes him, it throws him down; he foams
at the mouth, gnashes his teeth, and becomes rigid. So I spoke to Your disciples,
that they should cast it out, but they could
not."
19 He answered him and said, "O [p]faith-
less[2] generation, how long shall I be with
you? How long shall I [3]bear with you?
Bring him to Me." 20 Then they brought
him to Him. And [q]when he saw Him, immediately the spirit convulsed him, and he
fell on the ground and wallowed, foaming
at the mouth.
21 So He asked his father, "How long has
this been happening to him?"
And he said, "From childhood. 22 And
often he has thrown him both into the fire
and into the water to destroy him. But if
You can do anything, have compassion on
us and help us."
23 Jesus said to him, [r]"If[4] you can believe, all things *are* possible to him who believes."
24 Immediately the father of the child
cried out and said with tears, "Lord, I believe; [s]help my unbelief!"

17 [o] Matt. 17:14; Luke 9:38 **19** [p] John 4:48 [2] *unbelieving* [3] *put up with* **20** [q] Mark 1:26; Luke 9:42 **23** [r] Matt. 17:20; Mark 11:23; Luke 17:6; John 11:40 [4] NU *"'If You can!' All things* **24** [s] Luke 17:5

25 [t] Mark 1:25 **28** [u] Matt. 17:19 **29** [v] [James 5:16] [5] NU omits *and fasting* **31** [w] Matt. 17:22; Luke 9:44 [x] Matt. 16:21; 27:50; Luke 18:33; 23:46; Acts 2:23 [y] Matt. 20:19; Luke 24:46; Acts 10:40; 1 Cor. 15:4 **32** [z] Luke 2:50; 18:34; John 12:16 **33** [a] Matt. 18:1-5; Mark 14:53, 64; Luke 9:46-48; 22:24; John 18:12; 19:7 [6] *discussed*

25 When Jesus saw that the people came
running together, He [t]rebuked the unclean
spirit, saying to it, "Deaf and dumb spirit,
I command you, come out of him and enter
him no more!" 26 Then *the spirit* cried out,
convulsed him greatly, and came out of
him. And he became as one dead, so that
many said, "He is dead." 27 But Jesus took
him by the hand and lifted him up, and he
arose.
28 [u]And when He had come into the
house, His disciples asked Him privately,
"Why could we not cast it out?"
29 So He said to them, "This kind can
come out by nothing but [v]prayer [5]and fasting."

Jesus Foretells His Death
Matt. 17:22, 23; Luke 9:43-45

30 Then they departed from there and
passed through Galilee, and He did not
want anyone to know *it*. 31 [w]For He taught
His disciples and said to them, "The Son of
Man is being betrayed into the hands of
men, and they will [x]kill Him. And after He
is killed, He will [y]rise the third day." 32 But
they [z]did not understand this saying, and
were afraid to ask Him.

Attitude of Servanthood
Matt. 18:1-5; Luke 9:46-50

33 [a]Then He came to Capernaum. And
when He was in the house He asked them,
"What was it you [6]disputed among your-

9:17 has a mute spirit. The boy had a demonically-induced inability to speak, a detail found only in Mark's account.

9:18 they could not. The disciples' failure is surprising, in light of the power granted them by Jesus (3:15; 6:13).

9:19 O faithless generation. Cf. Ps. 95:10. The word "generation" indicates that Jesus' exasperation was not merely with the father, or the 9 disciples, but also with the unbelieving scribes, who were no doubt gloating over the disciples' failure (cf. v. 14), and with unbelieving Israel in general.

9:22 to destroy him. This demon was an especially violent and dangerous one. Open fires and unfenced bodies of water were common in first-century Palestine, providing ample opportunity for the demon's attempts to destroy the child. The father's statement added to the pathos of the situation. The boy himself was probably disfigured from burn scars, and possibly further ostracized because of them. His situation also created a hardship for his family, who would have had to watch the boy constantly to protect him from harm.

9:23 all things *are* possible. The oldest manuscripts omit "believe," thus making the phrase "If you can" a question or exclamation on Jesus' part. The issue was not His lack of power but the father's lack of faith. Though Jesus often healed apart from the faith of those involved, here He chose to emphasize the power of faith (cf. Matt. 17:20; Luke 17:6). Jesus healed multitudes, but many, if not most, did not believe in Him. Cf. Luke 17:15-19.

9:24 I believe; help my unbelief! Admitting the imperfection of his faith, mixed as it was with doubt, the desperate father pleaded with Jesus to help him to have the greater faith the Lord demanded of him.

9:25 the people came running. Noting the growing crowd, Jesus acted without further delay, perhaps to spare the boy and his anguished father any further embarrassment. Also, the Lord did not perform miracles to satisfy thrill seekers (cf. 8:11; Luke 23:8,9). **I command you.** Jesus' absolute authority over demons is well attested in the NT (e.g., 1:32-34; 5:1-13; Luke 4:33-35). His healings demonstrated His deity by power over the natural world. His authority over demons demonstrated His deity by power over the supernatural world.

9:29 This kind. Some demons are more powerful and obstinate, and thus more resistant to being cast out, than others (cf. Matt. 12:45). *See notes on Dan. 10:10-21.* **nothing but prayer.** Perhaps overconfident from their earlier successes (cf. 6:13), the disciples became enamored of their own gifts and neglected to draw on divine power. **fasting.** The earliest manuscripts omit this word.

9:30 passed through Galilee. Leaving the region around Caesarea Philippi, Jesus and the disciples began the journey to Jerusalem that would result in His crucifixion several months later. Their immediate destination was Capernaum (v. 33). **did not want anyone to know.** Jesus continued to seek seclusion so He could prepare the disciples for His death (cf. 7:24).

9:31 Son of Man. *See note on 2:10.*

9:31,32 Jesus continued His teaching about His upcoming death and resurrection—a subject the disciples still did not understand (*see notes on v. 10; 8:30-33*).

9:33 Capernaum. *See note on 1:21.* **the house.** The use of the definite article suggests this to be the house Jesus habitually stayed in when in Capernaum. Whether it was Peter's house (cf. 1:29) or someone else's is not known.

selves on the road?" 34 But they kept silent,
for on the road they had [b]disputed among
themselves who *would be the* [c]greatest.
35 And He sat down, called the twelve, and
said to them, [d]"If anyone desires to be first,
he shall be last of all and servant of all."
36 Then [e]He took a little child and set him
in the midst of them. And when He had
taken him in His arms, He said to them,
37 "Whoever receives one of these little
children in My name receives Me; and
[f]whoever receives Me, receives not Me but
Him who sent Me."
38 [g]Now John answered Him, saying,
"Teacher, we saw someone who does not
follow us casting out demons in Your
name, and we forbade him because he
does not follow us."
39 But Jesus said, "Do not forbid him,
[h]for no one who works a miracle in My
name can soon afterward speak evil of Me.
40 For [i]he who is not against [7]us is on [8]our
side. 41 [j]For whoever gives you a cup of
water to drink in My name, because you
belong to Christ, assuredly, I say to you, he
will by no means lose his reward.

Warning About Hell—Matt. 18:6-9

42 [k]"But whoever causes one of these little ones who believe in Me [9]to stumble, it
would be better for him if a millstone were
hung around his neck, and he were thrown
into the sea. 43 [l]If your hand causes you to
sin, cut it off. It is better for you to enter
into life [1]maimed, rather than having two
hands, to go to [2]hell, into the fire that shall
never be quenched— 44 [3]where

> [m]'*Their worm does not die*
> *And the fire is not quenched.*'

45 And if your foot causes you to sin, cut it
off. It is better for you to enter life lame,
rather than having two feet, to be cast into
[4]hell, [5]into the fire that shall never be
quenched— 46 where

> [n]'*Their worm does not die*
> *And the fire is not quenched.*'

47 And if your eye causes you to sin, pluck it
out. It is better for you to enter the kingdom
of God with one eye, rather than having two
eyes, to be cast into [6]hell fire— 48 where

> [o]'*Their worm does not die*
> *And the* [p]*fire is not quenched.*'

49 "For everyone will be [q]seasoned with

34 [b][Prov. 13:10]; Mark 15:20, 31 [c]Matt. 18:4; [Mark 9:50]; 14:65; 15:15, 37; Luke 22:24; 23:46; 24:46
35 [d]Matt. 20:26, 27; 23:11; Mark 10:43, 44; Luke 22:26, 27
36 [e]Mark 10:13-16
37 [f]Matt. 10:40; Luke 10:16; John 13:20
38 [g]Num. 11:27-29; Luke 9:49
39 [h]1 Cor. 12:3
40 [i][Matt. 12:30]; Luke 11:23 [7]M *you* [8]M *your*
41 [j]Matt. 10:42
42 [k]Matt. 18:6; Luke 17:1, 2; [1 Cor. 8:12]
[9]To fall into sin
43 [l][Deut. 13:6]; Matt. 5:29, 30; 18:8, 9 [1]*crippled* [2]Gr. *Gehenna*
44 [m]Is. 66:24 [3]NU omits v. 44.
45 [4]Gr. *Gehenna* [5]NU omits the rest of v. 45 and all of v. 46.
46 [n]Is. 66:24
47 [6]Gr. *Gehenna*
48 [o]Is. 66:24 [p]Jer. 7:20; [Rev. 21:8]
49 [q][Matt. 3:11]

9:34 they kept silent. Convicted and embarrassed, the disciples were speechless. **who *would be the* greatest.** A dispute possibly triggered by the privilege granted Peter, James, and John to witness the Transfiguration. The disciples' quarrel highlights their failure to apply Jesus' explicit teaching on humility (e.g., Matt. 5:3), and the example of His own suffering and death (vv. 31,32; 8:30-33). It also prompted them to ask Jesus to settle the issue, which He did—though not as they had expected.

9:35 sat down. Rabbis usually sat down to teach (cf. Matt. 15:29; Luke 4:20; 5:3; John 8:2). **If anyone desires to be first.** As the disciples undeniably did (v. 34; cf. 10:35-37). **last of all and servant of all.** The disciples' concept of greatness and leadership, drawn from their culture, needed to be completely reversed. Not those who lord their position over others are great in God's kingdom, but those who humbly serve others (cf. 10:31,43-45; Matt. 19:30–20:16; 23:11,12; Luke 13:30; 14:8-11; 18:14; 22:24-27).

9:36 a little child. The Gr. word indicates an infant or toddler. If the house they were in was Peter's (*see note on v. 33*), this may have been one of his children. The child became in Jesus' masterful teaching an example of believers who have humbled themselves and become like trusting children.

9:37 Whoever receives one of these little children in My name. Not actual children, but true believers—those who have humbled themselves like little children (*see note on v. 36*).

9:38 John answered. The only recorded instance in the synoptic gospels in which he alone speaks. In light of Jesus' rebuke (vv. 35-37), John's conscience troubled him about an earlier incident he had been involved in. It is clear that the unnamed exorcist was not a fraud because he actually was casting out demons. He was apparently a true believer in Jesus; John and the others opposed him because he was not openly and officially allied with Jesus, as they were.

9:39,40 Jesus ordered them not to hinder the exorcist, making the logical point that someone sincerely acting in His name would not soon turn against Him. There is no neutral ground regarding Jesus Christ; those "who [are] not against [Him are] on [His] side," but by the same token, "He who is not with Me is against Me, and he who does not gather with Me scatters abroad" (Matt. 12:30).

9:41 because you belong to Christ. Jesus considered acts of kindness done to His followers to have been done to Him (cf. Matt. 25:37-40). **assuredly, I say to you.** *See note on 3:28.* **his reward.** That is, his unique place and service in the eternal kingdom.

9:42 whoever causes...to stumble. The word translated "to stumble" lit. means "to cause to fall." To entice, trap, or lead a believer into sin is a very serious matter. **little ones who believe in Me.** *See note on v. 37.* **millstone.** This refers to a large, upper millstone so heavy that it had to be turned by a donkey (*see note on Matt. 18:6*). Even such a horrifying death (a Gentile form of execution) is preferable to leading a Christian into sin.

9:43 cut it off. *See note on Matt. 5:29.* Jesus' words are to be taken figuratively; no amount of self-mutilation can deal with sin, which is an issue of the heart. The Lord is emphasizing the seriousness of sin and the need to do whatever is necessary to deal with it. **life.** The contrast of "life" with "hell" indicates that Jesus was referring to eternal life. **hell.** The Gr. word refers to the Valley of Hinnom near Jerusalem, a garbage dump where fires constantly burned, furnishing a graphic symbol of eternal torment (*see note on Matt. 5:22*). **the fire that shall never be quenched.** *See note on Matt. 25:46.* That the punishment of hell lasts for eternity is the unmistakable teaching of Scripture (cf. Dan. 12:2; Matt. 25:41; 2 Thess. 1:9; Rev. 14:10,11; 20:10).

9:46,48. The better Gr. manuscripts omit these verses, which merely repeat the quote from Is. 66:24 found in v. 44.

9:47 kingdom of God. *See note on 1:15.*

9:49 The meaning of this difficult verse seems to be that believers are purified through suffering and persecution. The link between salt and fire seems to lie in the OT sacrifices, which were accompanied by salt (Lev. 2:13).

fire, [r]and[7] every sacrifice will be seasoned
with salt. 50 [s]Salt *is* good, but if the salt
loses its flavor, how will you season it?
[t]Have salt in yourselves, and [u]have peace
with one another."

Marriage and Divorce—Matt. 19:1-9

10 Then [a]He arose from there and
came to the region of Judea by the
other side of the Jordan. And multitudes
gathered to Him again, and as He was
accustomed, He taught them again.
2 [b]The Pharisees came and asked Him,
"Is it lawful for a man to divorce *his* wife?"
testing Him.
3 And He answered and said to them,
"What did Moses command you?"
4 They said, [c]"Moses permitted *a man* to
write a certificate of divorce, and to dismiss *her*."
5 And Jesus answered and said to them,
"Because of the hardness of your heart he
wrote you this [1]precept. 6 But from the
beginning of the creation, God [d]*'made*
them male and female.' 7 [e]*'For this reason*
a man shall leave his father and mother
and be joined to his wife, 8 *and the two*
shall become one flesh'; so then they are
no longer two, but one flesh. 9 Therefore
what God has joined together, let not man
separate."
10 In the house His disciples also asked
Him again about the same *matter.* 11 So He
said to them, [f]"Whoever divorces his wife
and marries another commits adultery
against her. 12 And if a woman divorces
her husband and marries another, she
commits adultery."

Children and the Kingdom
Matt. 19:13-15; Luke 18:15-17

13 [g]Then they brought little children to
Him, that He might touch them; but the
disciples rebuked those who brought *them.*
14 But when Jesus saw *it,* He was greatly
displeased and said to them, "Let the little
children come to Me, and do not forbid
them; for [h]of such is the kingdom of God.

49 [r]Lev. 2:13; Ezek. 43:24 [7]NU omits the rest of v. 49.
50 [s]Matt. 5:13; Luke 14:34 [t][Eph. 4:29]; Col. 4:6 [u]Rom. 12:18; 14:19; 2 Cor. 13:11; 1 Thess. 5:13; Heb. 12:14

CHAPTER 10

1 [a]Matt. 19:1-9; John 10:40; 11:7
2 [b]Matt. 19:3
4 [c]Deut. 24:1-4; Matt. 5:31; 19:7
5 [1]*command*
6 [d]Gen. 1:27; 5:2
7 [e]Gen. 2:24; [1 Cor. 6:16]; Eph. 5:31
11 [f]Ex. 20:14; [Matt. 5:32; 19:9]; Luke 16:18; [Rom. 7:3]; 1 Cor. 7:10, 11
13 [g]Matt. 19:13-15; Luke 18:15-17
14 [h][1 Cor. 14:20; 1 Pet. 2:2]

9:50 Salt *is* good. Salt was an essential item in first-century Palestine. In a hot climate, without refrigeration, salt was the practical means of preserving food. **Have salt in yourselves.** The work of the Word (Col. 3:16) and the Spirit (Gal. 5:22,23) produce godly character, enabling a person to act as a preservative in society. Cf. Matt. 5:13. **have peace with one another.** Cf. Matt. 5:9; Rom. 12:18; 2 Cor. 13:11; 1 Thess. 5:13; James 3:18.

10:1 other side of the Jordan. This region was known as Perea. Jesus was to minister there until leaving for Jerusalem shortly before Passion Week (*see note on Matt. 19:1*). **Jordan.** *See note on 1:5.*

10:2 Pharisees. *See note on 2:16.* **came and asked Him...testing Him.** The Pharisees hoped to publicly discredit Jesus' ministry. The resulting loss of popularity, they hoped, would make it easier for them to destroy Him. Also, Perea (*see note on v. 1*) was ruled by Herod Antipas—who had imprisoned John the Baptist for his views on divorce and remarriage (6:17,18). The Pharisees no doubt hoped a similar fate would befall Jesus. **Is it lawful...to divorce.** The Pharisees attempted to entrap Jesus with a volatile issue in first-century Judaism: divorce. There were two schools of thought, one allowing divorce for virtually any reason, the other denying divorce except on grounds of adultery (*see note on Matt. 19:3*). The Pharisees undoubtedly expected Jesus to take one side, in which case He would lose the support of the other faction.

10:3 "What did Moses command you?" Jesus set the proper ground rules for the discussion. The issue was not rabbinical interpretations, but the teaching of Scripture.

10:4 permitted. The Mosaic law, as the Pharisees were forced to concede, nowhere commanded divorce. The passage in question, Deut. 24:1-4, recognized the reality of divorce and sought to protect the wife's rights and reputation and also regulated remarriage. **certificate of divorce.** In this document, the husband was required to state the reason for the divorce, thus protecting the wife's reputation (if she were, in fact, innocent of wrongdoing). It also served as her formal release from the marriage, and affirmed her right to remarry (assuming she was not guilty of immorality). The liberal wing of the Pharisees had misconstrued Deut. 24 to be teaching that divorce was "permitted" for any cause whatsoever (citing as legitimate grounds such trivial events as the wife's ruining dinner or the husband's simply finding a more desirable woman), providing the proper legal paperwork was done. They thus magnified a detail, mentioned merely in passing, into the main emphasis of the passage.

10:5 the hardness of your heart. *See notes on 3:5; 6:52.* This refers to the flagrant, unrepentant pursuit of sexual immorality—divorce was to be a last resort in dealing with such hard-heartedness. The Pharisees mistook God's gracious provision in permitting divorce (under certain circumstances) for His ordaining of it.

10:6 from the beginning. Divorce formed no part of God's original plan for marriage, which was that one man be married to one woman for life (Gen. 2:24). ***male and female.*** Lit. "a male and a female," Adam and Eve. Mark quoted from Gen. 1:27; 5:2.

10:7,8 Jesus took the issue beyond mere rabbinical quibbling over the technicalities of divorce to God's design for marriage. The passage Christ quotes (Gen. 2:24) presents 3 reasons for the inviolability of marriage: 1) God created only two humans (*see note on v. 6*), not a group of males and females who could configure as they pleased or switch partners as it suited them; 2) the word translated "be joined" lit. means "to glue," thus reflecting the strength of the marriage bond; 3) in God's eyes a married couple is "one flesh," forming an indivisible union, manifesting that oneness in a child.

10:9 Therefore what God has joined together. Jesus added a fourth reason for the inviolability of marriage (*see note on vv. 7,8*): God ordains marriages and thus they are not to be broken by man.

10:11,12 Remarriage after a divorce—except for legitimate biblical grounds—proliferates adultery. The innocent party—one whose spouse has committed prolonged, hard-hearted, unrepentant adultery—may remarry without being guilty of adultery, as may a believer whose unbelieving spouse has chosen to leave the marriage (*see note on 1 Cor. 7:15*).

10:13 little children. *See note on 9:36.* **that He might touch them.** I.e., lay His hands on them and pray for them (Matt. 19:13). Jewish parents commonly sought the blessing of prominent rabbis for their children.

10:14 do not forbid them. Jesus rebuked the disciples for their attempt to prevent the children from seeing Him (v. 13). They were not the ones to decide who had access to Jesus (cf. Matt. 15:23). **of such is the kingdom of God.** Most, if not all, of these children would have been too young to exercise personal faith. Jesus' words imply

15 Assuredly, I say to you, [i]whoever does
not receive the kingdom of God as a little
child will [j]by no means enter it." 16 And
He took them up in His arms, laid *His*
hands on them, and blessed them.

Rich Young Ruler
Matt. 19:16-22; Luke 18:18-23

17 [k]Now as He was going out on the
road, one came running, knelt before Him,
and asked Him, "Good Teacher, what shall
I [l]do that I may inherit eternal life?"
18 So Jesus said to him, "Why do you call
Me good? No one *is* good but One, *that is,*
[m]God. 19 You know the commandments:
[n]*'Do not commit adultery,' 'Do not mur-*
der,' 'Do not steal,' 'Do not bear false wit-
ness,' 'Do not defraud,' *'Honor your father*
and your mother.' "
20 And he answered and said to Him,
"Teacher, all these things I have [o]kept from
my youth."
21 Then Jesus, looking at him, loved him,

15 [i] Matt. 18:3, 4; 19:14; Luke 18:17 [j] Luke 13:28
17 [k] Matt. 19:16-30; Luke 18:18-30 [l] John 6:28; Acts 2:37
18 [m] 1 Sam. 2:2
19 [n] Ex. 20:12-16; Deut. 5:16-20; [Rom. 13:9; James 2:10, 11]
20 [o] Phil. 3:6
21 [p] [Luke 12:33; 16:9] [q] Matt. 6:19, 20; 19:21 [r] [Mark 8:34]
23 [s] Matt. 19:23; [Mark 4:19]; Luke 18:24
24 [t] Job 31:24; Ps. 52:7; 62:10; [Prov. 11:28; 1 Tim. 6:17] [2] NU omits *for those who trust in riches*
25 [u] [Matt. 13:22; 19:24]

and said to him, "One thing you lack: Go
your way, [p]sell whatever you have and
give to the poor, and you will have [q]trea-
sure in heaven; and come, [r]take up the
cross, and follow Me."
22 But he was sad at this word, and went
away sorrowful, for he had great possessions.

Difficulty of Riches
Matt. 19:23-26; Luke 18:24-27

23 [s]Then Jesus looked around and said
to His disciples, "How hard it is for those
who have riches to enter the kingdom of
God!" 24 And the disciples were astonished at His words. But Jesus answered
again and said to them, "Children, how
hard it is [2]for those [t]who trust in riches to
enter the kingdom of God! 25 It is easier for
a camel to go through the eye of a needle
than for a [u]rich man to enter the kingdom
of God."
26 And they were greatly astonished,

that God graciously extends salvation to those too young or too mentally impaired to exercise faith (*see note on Matt. 19:14*). **kingdom of God.** *See note on 1:15.*

10:15 Assuredly, I say to you. *See note on 3:28.* **as a little child.** With humble, trusting dependence, and the recognition of having achieved nothing of value or virtue.

10:16 blessed them. *See note on v. 13.*

10:17 one. The other synoptic gospels reveal that he was young (Matt. 19:20), and a "ruler," probably in the synagogue (Luke 18:18). He was also wealthy (v. 22). **what shall I do.** Steeped in the legalism of his day, the young man naturally thought in terms of some religious deed that would guarantee him eternal life. His lack of understanding about the true nature of salvation, however, does not mean he was insincere. **eternal life.** More than just eternal existence, it is a different quality of life. Eternal life is in Christ alone (*see notes on John 3:15,16*; cf. John 10:28; 17:2,3; Rom. 6:23; 1 John 5:11,13,20). Those who possess it have "passed from death to life" (John 5:24; 1 John 3:14; cf. Eph. 2:1-3); they have died to sin and are alive to God (Rom. 6:11); they have the very life of Christ in them (2 Cor. 4:11; Gal. 2:20); and enjoy a relationship with Jesus Christ that will never end (John 17:3).

10:18 Why do you call Me good? Jesus challenged the ruler to think through the implications of ascribing to Him the title "good." Since only God is intrinsically good, was he prepared to acknowledge Jesus' deity? By this query Jesus did not deny His deity; on the contrary, He affirmed it.

10:19 Quoted from Ex. 20:12-16. **Do not defraud.** This was not the wording of any of the Ten Commandments, and unique to Mark's account. It seems to be a paraphrase for the command against coveting.

10:20 all these things I have kept. His answer was no doubt sincere, but superficial and untrue. He, like Paul (Phil. 3:6), may have been blameless in terms of external actions, but not in terms of internal attitudes and motives (cf. Matt. 5:21-48).

10:21 Jesus...loved him. I.e., felt great compassion for this sincere truth-seeker who was so hopelessly lost. God does love the unsaved (*see notes on Matt. 5:43-48*). **sell whatever you have.** Jesus was not making either philanthropy or poverty a requirement for salvation, but exposing the young man's heart. He was not blameless, as he maintained (v. 20), since he loved his possessions more than his neighbors (cf. Lev. 19:18). More importantly, he refused to obey Christ's direct command, choosing to serve riches instead of God (Matt. 6:24). The issue was to determine whether he would submit to the Lordship of Christ no matter what He asked of him. So, as he would not acknowledge his sin and repent, neither would he submit to the Sovereign Savior. Such unwillingness on both counts kept him from the eternal life he sought. **treasure in heaven.** Salvation and all its benefits, given by the Father who dwells there, both in this life and the life to come (cf. Matt. 13:44-46). **take up the cross.** *See notes on 8:34-38.*

10:22 went away sorrowful. It was purely a worldly disappointment based on the fact that he didn't receive the eternal life he sought because the price of sacrifice was too high. He loved his wealth (cf. 8:36,37).

10:23 How hard it is for those who have riches. *See note on v. 27.* "Hard" in this context means impossible (cf. v. 25). "Riches" tend to breed self-sufficiency and a false sense of security, leading those who have them to imagine they do not need divine resources (see Luke 16:13; contra. Luke 19:2; cf. 1 Tim. 6:9,17,18).

10:24 astonished. *See note on v. 26.*

10:25 camel...eye of a needle. The Persians expressed impossibility by saying it would be easier to put an elephant through the eye of a needle. This was a Jewish colloquial adaptation of that expression denoting impossibility (the largest animal in Palestine was a camel). Many improbable interpretations have arisen that attempt to soften this phrase, e.g., that "needle" referred to a tiny gate in the Jerusalem city wall that camels could enter only with difficulty (but there is no evidence that such a gate ever existed, and if it had, any sensible camel driver would have simply found a larger gate); or that a copyist's error resulted in *kamelos* (camel) being substituted for *kamilos* (a large rope or cable) (but a large rope could no more go through the eye of a needle than a camel could, and it is extremely unlikely that the text of all 3 synoptic gospels would have been changed in exactly the same way). Jesus' use of this illustration was to explicitly say that salvation by human effort is impossible; it is wholly by God's grace. The Jews believed that with alms a man purchased salvation (as recorded in the Talmud), so the more wealth one had, the more alms he could give, the more sacrifices and offerings he could offer, thus purchasing redemption. The disciples' question (v. 26) makes it clear that they understood what Jesus meant—that not even the rich could buy salvation. *See note on Matt. 19:24.*

saying among themselves, "Who then can
be saved?"
27 But Jesus looked at them and said,
"With men *it is* impossible, but not [v]with
God; for with God all things are possible."

Eternal Reward
Matt. 19:27-30; Luke 18:28-30

28 [w]Then Peter began to say to Him,
"See, we have left all and followed You."
29 So Jesus answered and said, "Assuredly,
I say to you, there is no one who
has left house or brothers or sisters or father
or mother [3]or wife or children or
[4]lands, for My sake and the gospel's,
30 [x]who shall not receive a hundredfold
now in this time—houses and brothers and
sisters and mothers and children and
lands, with [y]persecutions—and in the age
to come, eternal life. 31 [z]But many *who are*
first will be last, and the last first."

Coming Crucifixion
Matt. 20:17-19; Luke 18:31-34

32 [a]Now they were on the road, going up
to Jerusalem, and Jesus was going before
them; and they were amazed. And as they
followed they were afraid. [b]Then He took
the twelve aside again and began to tell
them the things that would happen to Him:
33 "Behold, we are going up to Jerusalem,
and the Son of Man will be betrayed to the
chief priests and to the scribes; and they will
condemn Him to death and deliver Him to
the Gentiles; 34 and they will mock Him,
and [5]scourge Him, and spit on Him, and kill
Him. And the third day He will rise again."

"Whoever Desires to Become Great"
Matt. 20:20-28

35 [c]Then James and John, the sons of
Zebedee, came to Him, saying, "Teacher, we
want You to do for us whatever we ask."
36 And He said to them, "What do you
want Me to do for you?"
37 They said to Him, "Grant us that we
may sit, one on Your right hand and the
other on Your left, in Your glory."
38 But Jesus said to them, "You do not
know what you ask. Are you able to drink
the [d]cup that I drink, and be baptized with
the [e]baptism that I am baptized with?"
39 They said to Him, "We are able."
So Jesus said to them, [f]"You will indeed
drink the cup that I drink, and with the
baptism I am baptized with you will be
baptized; 40 but to sit on My right hand
and on My left is not Mine to give, but *it is*
for those [g]for whom it is prepared."
41 [h]And when the ten heard *it*, they

27 [v] Job 42:2; Jer. 32:17; Matt. 19:26; Luke 1:37
28 [w] Matt. 19:27; Luke 18:28
29 [3] NU omits *or wife* [4] Lit. *fields*
30 [x] 2 Chr. 25:9; Luke 18:29, 30 [y] 1 Thess. 3:3; 2 Tim. 3:12; [1 Pet. 4:12, 13]
31 [z] Matt. 19:30; 20:16; Luke 13:30
32 [a] Matt. 20:17-19; Luke 18:31-33 [b] Mark 8:31; 9:31; Luke 9:22; 18:31
34 [5] *flog Him* with a Roman scourge
35 [c] [James 4:3]
38 [d] Matt. 26:39, 42; Mark 14:36; Luke 22:42; John 18:11 [e] Luke 12:50
39 [f] Matt. 10:17, 18, 21, 22; 24:9; John 16:33; Acts 12:2; Rev. 1:9
40 [g] [Matt. 25:34; John 17:2, 6, 24; Rom. 8:30; Heb. 11:16]
41 [h] Matt. 20:24

10:26 "Who then can be saved?" Jesus' teaching ran counter to the prevailing rabbinical teaching, which gave the wealthy a clear advantage for salvation. Jesus' emphatic teaching that even the rich could not be saved by their own efforts left the bewildered disciples wondering what chance the poor stood. *See notes on Rom. 3:9-20; Gal. 3:10-13; Phil. 3:4-9.*

10:27 With men *it is* impossible, but not with God. It is impossible for anyone to be saved by his own efforts (*see note on v. 25*) since salvation is entirely a gracious, sovereign work of God. *See notes on Rom. 3:21-28; 8:28-30; Gal. 3:6-9; 26-29.*

10:28 we have left all. Peter noted that the 12 had done what the Lord had asked the rich young ruler to do (cf. v. 21) and had come to Him on His terms. Would that self-abandoning faith, Peter asked, qualify them for a place in the kingdom?

10:29 Assuredly, I say to you. *See note on 3:28.*

10:30 in this time…the age to come. Following Jesus brings rewards in this present age and when Messiah's glorious kingdom comes. **with persecutions.** Great trials often accompany great blessings (*see notes on Rom. 8:17; Phil. 1:29; 2 Tim. 3:12*). **eternal life.** *See note on v. 17.*

10:31 Believers will share equally in the blessings of heaven—a truth illustrated by the parable of Matt. 19:30–20:16 (*see notes there*).

10:32 going up to Jerusalem. From Perea (*see note on v. 1*), via Jericho (v. 46). This is the first mention of Jerusalem as Jesus' destination. Because of the elevation of Jerusalem (about 2,550 ft. above sea level), travelers always spoke of going up to the city, regardless of where in Israel they started. **amazed.** At Jesus' resolute determination to go to Jerusalem (cf. Luke 9:51) despite the cruel death that awaited Him there (cf. vv. 32-34). **they followed.** The Gr. syntax makes it clear that this was a group distinct from the 12, probably pilgrims en route to Jerusalem for Passover. They were afraid because they realized something significant was about to happen that they did not understand. **the twelve.** *See note on 3:14.*

10:32-34 The third and last prediction of His death and resurrection that Jesus made to the 12 is given (cf. 8:31; 9:31). This is also the most detailed of the 3 predictions, specifically mentioning that He would be mocked (15:17-20; Luke 23:11,35-39), scourged (15:15), and spat upon (14:65; 15:19).

10:35-45 This incident reveals yet again the disciples' failure to grasp Jesus' teaching on humility (*see notes on 9:34; Matt. 20:21*). Ignoring the Lord's repeated instruction that He was going to Jerusalem to die (*see note on vv. 32-34*), the disciples still thought the physical manifestation of the kingdom was about to appear and were busy maneuvering for the places of prominence in it (cf. Matt. 18:1).

10:35 James and John, the sons of Zebedee. *See note on 1:19.* Matthew reveals that their mother accompanied them and spoke first (Matt. 20:20,21), after which James and John reiterated her request. If she was Jesus' aunt, the 3 undoubtedly hoped to capitalize on the family ties.

10:37 sit…on Your right…Your left. In the places of highest prominence and honor beside the throne. **in Your glory.** In the glorious majesty of His kingdom (cf. Matt. 20:21).

10:38 the cup…the baptism. Endure suffering and sin-bearing death as Jesus would (cf. vv. 32-34; *see note on Matt. 20:22*).

10:39 James and John would suffer like their Master (cf. Acts 12:2; Rev. 1:9), but that in itself would not earn them the honors they desired.

10:40 not Mine to give. Honors in the kingdom are bestowed not on the basis of selfish ambition, but of divine sovereign will.

10:41 the ten…began to be greatly displeased. Not righteous indignation, since they, too, had been guilty in the past of such self-serving conduct (9:33,34) and would be so in the future (Luke 22:24). The rest of the disciples resented James and John for their attempt to gain an advantage over the others in pursuing the honor they all wanted.

began to be greatly displeased with James
and John. 42 But Jesus called them to *Himself* and said to them, [i]"You know that
those who are considered rulers over the
Gentiles lord it over them, and their great
ones exercise authority over them. 43 [j]Yet it
shall not be so among you; but whoever
desires to become great among you shall
be your servant. 44 And whoever of you
desires to be first shall be slave of all. 45 For
even [k]the Son of Man did not come to be
served, but to serve, and [l]to give His life a
ransom for many."

Blind Bartimaeus Is Healed
Matt. 20:29-34; Luke 18:35-43

46 [m]Now they came to Jericho. As He
went out of Jericho with His disciples and
a great multitude, blind Bartimaeus, the
son of Timaeus, sat by the road begging.
47 And when he heard that it was Jesus of
Nazareth, he began to cry out and say, "Jesus, [n]Son of David, [o]have mercy on me!"
48 Then many warned him to be quiet;
but he cried out all the more, "Son of David, have mercy on me!"

49 So Jesus stood still and commanded
him to be called.

Then they called the blind man, saying
to him, "Be of good cheer. Rise, He is calling you."

50 And throwing aside his garment, he
rose and came to Jesus.

51 So Jesus answered and said to him,
"What do you want Me to do for you?"

The blind man said to Him, [6]"Rabboni,
that I may receive my sight."

52 Then Jesus said to him, "Go your way;
[p]your faith has [7]made you well." And immediately he received his sight and followed Jesus on the road.

The Triumphal Entry
Matt. 21:1-11; Luke 19:29-40

11 Now [a]when they drew near Jerusalem, to [1]Bethphage and Bethany, at
the Mount of Olives, He sent two of His
disciples; 2 and He said to them, "Go into
the village opposite you; and as soon as
you have entered it you will find a colt
tied, on which no one has sat. Loose it and
bring *it*. 3 And if anyone says to you, 'Why

42 [i]Luke 22:25
43 [j]Matt. 20:26, 28; Mark 9:35; Luke 9:48
45 [k]Luke 22:27; John 13:14; [Phil. 2:7, 8] [l]Matt. 20:28; [2 Cor. 5:21; 1 Tim. 2:5, 6; Titus 2:14]
46 [m]Matt. 20:29-34; Luke 18:35-43
47 [n]Jer. 23:5; Matt. 22:42; Rom. 1:3, 4; Rev. 22:16 [o]Matt. 15:22; Luke 17:13
51 [6]Lit. *My Great One*
52 [p]Matt. 9:22; Mark 5:34 [7]Lit. *saved you*

CHAPTER 11

1 [a]Matt. 21:1-9; Luke 19:29; John 2:13 [1]M *Bethsphage*

10:42 lord it over them...exercise authority. These parallel phrases convey the sense of autocratic, domineering authority.

10:43 not be so among you. There is no place in the church for domineering leaders (cf. 9:35; Matt. 23:8-12; 1 Pet. 5:3-6; 3 John 9,10).

10:45 Son of Man. *See note on 2:10.* **did not come to be served.** Jesus was the supreme example of servant leadership (cf. John 13:13-15). The King of Kings, and Lord of Lords (Rev. 19:16) relinquished His privileges (Phil. 2:5-8) and gave His life as a selfless sacrifice in serving others. **ransom for many.** *See note on Matt. 20:28.* "Ransom" refers to the price paid to free a slave or a prisoner; "for" means "in place of." Christ's substitutionary death on behalf of those who would put their faith in Him is the most glorious, blessed truth in all of Scripture (cf. Rom. 8:1-3; 1 Cor. 6:20; Gal. 3:13; 4:5; Eph. 1:7; Titus 2:14; 1 Pet. 1:18,19). The ransom was not paid to Satan, as some erroneous theories of the atonement teach. Satan is presented in Scripture as a foe to be defeated, not a ruler to be placated. The ransom price was paid to God to satisfy His justice and holy wrath against sin. In paying it, Christ "bore our sins in His own body on the [cross]" (1 Pet. 2:24). *See notes on 2 Cor. 5:21.*

10:46-52 The second of two healings of blind men recorded in Mark (cf. 8:22-26).

10:46 Jericho. A city located about 15 mi. NE of Jerusalem and 5 mi. from the Jordan River. The route from Perea to Jerusalem passed through it. This is the only recorded visit of Jesus to Jericho. **As He went out.** Mark and Matthew state that the healing took place as Jesus was leaving Jericho, Luke as He was entering the city. Mark and Matthew may be referring to the ancient walled city, just N of the NT city, while Luke refers to NT Jericho. Or Luke's words may simply mean Jesus was in the vicinity of Jericho when the healing took place. *See note on Matt. 20:30.* **blind...begging.** Matthew notes that there were two blind beggars, whereas Mark and Luke focus on the more vocal of them (cf. Matt. 8:28 with 5:2; Luke 8:27). Since they were unable to work, blind people commonly made their living by begging (cf. John 9:8). These men had staked out a good site on the main road to Jerusalem. **son of Timaeus.** The translation of "Bartimaeus"; the Aram. prefix "bar" means "son of."

10:47 Nazareth. *See note on 1:9.* **Son of David.** A common messianic title, used as such only in the synoptic gospels (*see note on Matt. 1:1*).

10:49 Jesus...commanded him to be called. Thus implicitly rebuking those trying to silence him (v. 48).

10:51 Rabboni. An intensified form of "rabbi" (*see note on 9:5*).

10:52 your faith has made you well. Lit. "saved you." Bartimaeus' physical and spiritual eyes were likely opened at the same time. The outward healing reflected the inner wellness of salvation.

11:1-11 This passage, traditionally called Jesus' triumphal entry (more accurately, it was Jesus' coronation as the true King), was His last major public appearance before His crucifixion. The importance of this event is indicated by the fact that this is only the second time all 4 gospels include the same event (cf. Matt. 21:1-11; Luke 19:29-44; John 12:12-19).

11:1 drew near Jerusalem. A general transition statement marking the end of the narrative in chap. 10. It also indicates the beginning of the final phase of Christ's 3-year ministry. **Bethphage.** A small town just E of Jerusalem whose name lit. means "house of unripe figs" (*see note on Matt. 21:1*). **Bethany.** The hometown of Mary, Martha, and Lazarus (John 11:1) on the eastern slope of the Mt. of Olives, two mi. E of Jerusalem. **Mount of Olives.** This mountain stood between Bethany and Jerusalem (*see note on Matt. 24:3*).

11:2 the village opposite you. Most likely Bethphage. "Opposite" implies that it was somewhat off the main road. **colt.** According to usage of this word in Gr. papyri (ordinary written documents dating from NT times that were made of papyrus reed), this was most likely a young donkey—a definition also in harmony with other Scripture usage (*see note on Matt. 21:5*; cf. Gen. 49:11; Judg. 10:4; 12:14; Zech. 9:9). **no one has sat.** The Jews regarded animals that had never been ridden as especially suited for holy purposes (cf. Num. 19:2; Deut. 21:3; 1 Sam. 6:7).

11:3 if anyone says to you. Because of its very nature, Jesus anticipated the disciples' action would be challenged (v. 5). **Lord.** Even though he does not use "Lord" with this meaning in the rest of his

are you doing this?' say, 'The Lord has
need of it,' and immediately he will send it
here."
4 So they went their way, and found [2]the
colt tied by the door outside on the street,
and they loosed it. 5 But some of those who
stood there said to them, "What are you
doing, loosing the colt?"
6 And they spoke to them just as Jesus
had commanded. So they let them go.
7 Then they brought the colt to Jesus and
threw their clothes on it, and He sat on it.
8 [b]And many spread their clothes on the
road, and others cut down leafy branches
from the trees and spread *them* on the road.
9 Then those who went before and those
who followed cried out, saying:

"Hosanna!
[c]'*Blessed is He who comes in the name of the* LORD!'
10 Blessed *is* the kingdom of our father David
That comes [3]in the name of the Lord!
[d]Hosanna in the highest!"

4 [2]NU, M *a*
8 [b]Matt. 21:8
9 [c]Ps. 118:25, 26; Matt. 21:9
10 [d]Ps. 148:1 [3]NU omits *in the name of the Lord*

11 [e]And Jesus went into Jerusalem and into
the temple. So when He had looked
around at all things, as the hour was already late, He went out to Bethany with
the twelve.

A Fig Tree Is Cursed—Matt. 21:18, 19

12 [f]Now the next day, when they had
come out from Bethany, He was hungry.
13 [g]And seeing from afar a fig tree having
leaves, He went to see if perhaps He would
find something on it. When He came to it,
He found nothing but leaves, for it was not
the season for figs. 14 In response Jesus
said to it, "Let no one eat fruit from you
ever again."
And His disciples heard *it*.

The Temple Is Cleansed
Matt. 21:12, 13; Luke 19:45, 46

15 [h]So they came to Jerusalem. Then Jesus went into the temple and began to
drive out those who bought and sold in the
temple, and overturned the tables of the
money changers and the seats of those

11 [e]Matt. 21:12
12 [f]Matt. 21:18-22
13 [g]Matt. 21:19
15 [h]Mal. 3:1; Matt. 21:12-16; Luke 19:45-47; John 2:13-16

gospel, Mark was referring to Jesus. In Luke and John this appears often as a name for Jesus. People in the area knew Christ and the disciples well and the owner would have understood the reference.

11:8 spread their clothes. Such action was part of the ancient practice of welcoming a new king (*see note on Matt. 21:8*). **branches.** Palm branches which symbolized joy and salvation and pictured future royal tribute to Christ (Rev. 7:9). The crowd was greatly excited and filled with praise for the Messiah who taught with such authority, healed the sick, and raised the dead (Lazarus; cf. John 12:12-18).

11:9 Hosanna. Originally a Heb. prayer meaning "save now." On that occasion it probably served simply as an acclamation of welcome. ***Blessed is He who comes.*** *See note on Matt. 21:9.* This phrase is part (Ps. 118:26) of the Hallel (the Heb. word for "praise"), comprised of Pss. 113–118, which was sung at all the Jewish religious festivals, most notably at the Passover. "He who comes" was not an OT messianic title, but definitely had come to carry such implications for the Jews (cf. Matt. 11:3; Luke 7:19; John 3:31; 6:14; 11:27; Heb. 10:37).

11:10 the kingdom of our father David. This tribute, recorded only by Mark, acknowledges Jesus as bringing in the messianic kingdom promised to David's Son. The crowd paraphrased the quote from Ps. 118:26 (v. 9) in anticipation that Jesus was fulfilling prophecy by bringing in the kingdom.

11:11 temple. Not a reference limited to the inner, sacred sanctuary, but the entire area of courts and buildings. **looked around at all things.** A description distinctive to Mark, quite possibly based on one of Peter's eyewitness memories. Christ acted as one who had the authority to inspect temple conditions, and His observation missed nothing. **He went out to Bethany.** Nearby "Bethany" was a relatively safe place to avoid sudden, premature arrest by the Jewish leaders.

11:12 the next day. Matthew 21:18 says this was "in the morning," probably before 6:00 a.m. **Bethany.** *See note on v. 1.*

11:13 fig tree having leaves. Fig trees were common as a source of food. Three years were required from planting until fruit bearing. After that, a tree could be harvested twice a year, usually yielding much fruit. The figs normally grew with the leaves. This tree had leaves but, strangely, no fruit. That this tree was along the side of the road (cf. Matt. 21:19), implies it was public property. It was also apparently in good soil because its foliage was ahead of season and ahead of the surrounding fig trees. The abundance of leaves held out promise that the tree might also be ahead of schedule with its fruit. **not the season for figs.** The next normal fig season was in June, more than a month away. This phrase, unique to Mark, emphasizes the unusual nature of this fig tree.

11:14 "Let no one eat fruit from you ever again." Jesus' direct address to the tree personified it and condemned it for not providing what its appearance promised. This incident was not the acting out of the parable of the fig tree (Luke 13:6-9), which was a warning against spiritual fruitlessness. Here, Jesus cursed the tree for its misleading appearance that suggested great productivity without providing it. It should have been full of fruit, but was barren. The fig tree was frequently an OT type of the Jewish nation (Hos. 9:10; Nah. 3:12; Zech. 3:10), and in this instance Jesus used the tree by the road as a divine object lesson concerning Israel's spiritual hypocrisy and fruitlessness (*see note on Matt. 21:19*; cf. Is. 5:1-7).

11:15-19 *See note on Matt. 21:12.* Although Jesus had cleansed the temple 3 years earlier (John 2:14-16), it had become more corrupt and profane than ever and thus He was compelled to again offer clear testimony to God's holiness and to His judgment against spiritual desecration and false religion. Even as God sent His prophets repeatedly throughout the OT to warn His people of their sin and idolatry, Christ never stopped declaring God's will to a rebellious people, no matter how often they rejected it. With this temple cleansing, Jesus showed vividly that He was on a divine mission as the Son of God.

11:15 temple. *See note on v. 11.* The large Court of the Gentiles was the setting for the events that followed. **bought and sold.** Animals were needed by the Jews for their sacrificial temple offerings, and it was more convenient for the worshipers to buy them there rather than bring the animals from a distance and risk that they would not pass the High-Priest's inspection. The sellers either belonged to the High-Priestly hierarchy or paid a large fee to temple authorities for the privilege of selling. Whichever was the case, the High-Priest's family benefited monetarily. **money changers.** They were in the court to exchange Greek and Roman coins for Jewish or Tyrian coins which pilgrims (every Jewish male 20 and older) had to use for

who sold [i]doves. 16 And He would not
allow anyone to carry wares through the
temple. 17 Then He taught, saying to them,
"Is it not written, [j]*'My house shall be
called a house of prayer for all nations'*?
But you have made it a [k]*'den of thieves.'*"
18 And [l]the scribes and chief priests
heard it and sought how they might destroy Him; for they feared Him, because
[m]all the people were astonished at His
teaching. 19 When evening had come, He
went out of the city.

15 [i] Lev. 14:22
17 [j] Is. 56:7 [k] Jer. 7:11
18 [l] Ps. 2:2; Matt. 21:45, 46; Luke 19:47 [m] Matt. 7:28; Mark 1:22; 6:2; Luke 4:32
20 [n] Matt. 21:19-22
23 [o] Matt. 17:20; 21:21; Luke 17:6

Power of Faith—Matt. 21:20-22

20 [n]Now in the morning, as they passed
by, they saw the fig tree dried up from the
roots. 21 And Peter, remembering, said to
Him, "Rabbi, look! The fig tree which You
cursed has withered away."
22 So Jesus answered and said to them,
"Have faith in God. 23 For [o]assuredly, I say
to you, whoever says to this mountain, 'Be
removed and be cast into the sea,' and does
not doubt in his heart, but believes that
those things he says will be done, he will
have whatever he says. 24 Therefore I say
to you, [p]whatever things you ask when
you pray, believe that you receive *them,*
and you will have *them.*

Necessity of Forgiveness

25 "And whenever you stand praying,
[q]if you have anything against anyone, forgive him, that your Father in heaven may
also forgive you your trespasses. 26 [4]But [r]if
you do not forgive, neither will your Father in heaven forgive your trespasses."

Question of Authority
Matt. 21:23-27; Luke 20:1-8

27 Then they came again to Jerusalem.
[s]And as He was walking in the temple, the

24 [p] Matt. 7:7; Luke 11:9; [John 14:13; 15:7; 16:24; James 1:5, 6]
25 [q] Matt. 6:14; 18:23-35; Eph. 4:32; [Col. 3:13]
26 [r] Matt. 6:15; 18:35 [4] NU omits v. 26.
27 [s] Matt. 21:23-27; Luke 20:1-8

---

the annual half-shekel payment for temple religious services (*see note on Matt. 21:12*). A fee as high as 10 or 12 percent was assessed for this exchange service. **those who sold doves.** These birds were so often used for sacrifice that Mark makes separate mention of their sellers. Doves were the normal offering of the poor (Lev. 5:7) and were also required for other purposes (Lev. 12:6; 14:22; 15:14,29).

11:16 not allow anyone to carry wares. Jesus did not want people to continue the practice of using the court as a shortcut through which to carry utensils and containers with merchandise to other parts of Jerusalem because such a practice revealed great irreverence for the temple—and ultimately for God Himself.

11:17 Jesus defended Himself by appealing to Scripture (*see note on Matt. 21:13*) after His actions had caused a crowd to gather. ***a house of prayer for all nations.*** The true purpose for God's temple. Only Mark includes "for all nations" from Isaiah's text (56:7), probably because he was mainly addressing Gentiles. The Court of the Gentiles was the only part of the temple they were permitted to use for prayer and worship of God, and the Jews had frustrated that worship by turning it into a place of greedy business. ***a 'den of thieves.'*** Using Jeremiah's phrase (Jer. 7:11), Jesus described the religious leaders as robbers who found refuge in the temple, comparable to how highwaymen took refuge in caves with other robbers. The temple had become a place where God's people, instead of being able to worship undisturbed, were extorted and their extortioners were protected.

11:18 scribes and chief priests. Here Mark uses this combination for the first time. These men were among those who comprised the principle leadership in the Sanhedrin (*see notes on Matt. 2:4; 26:59*). **sought how they might destroy Him.** *See note on 3:6.* The leaders had continuing discussions on how to kill Jesus. **astonished at His teaching.** *See note on 1:22.*

11:19 went out of the city. Jesus' practice during the first 3 days of Passion Week was not to leave Jerusalem until sunset, when the crowds dispersed and the city gates were about to be closed.

11:20 in the morning. *See note on v. 12.* **dried up from the roots.** The tree blight that prevented fruit (v. 14) had spread upward through the tree and killed it. Matthew described the event in a more compact fashion, but his account still allows the same time frame as Mark's (*see note on Matt. 21:19*).

11:21 Rabbi. *See note on 9:5.*

11:22 Have faith in God. A gentle rebuke for the disciples' lack of faith in the power of His word. Such faith believes in God's revealed truth, His power, and seeks to do His will (cf. 1 John 5:14; *see note on Matt. 21:21*).

11:23 this mountain...into the sea. This expression was related to a common metaphor of that day, "rooter up of mountains," which was used in Jewish literature of great rabbis and spiritual leaders who could solve difficult problems and seemingly do the impossible. Obviously, Jesus did not literally uproot mountains; in fact, He refused to do such spectacular miracles for the unbelieving Jewish leaders (*see note on Matt. 12:38*). Jesus' point is that if believers sincerely trust in God and truly realize the unlimited power that is available through such faith in Him, they will see His mighty powers at work (cf. John 14:13,14; *see note on Matt. 21:21*).

11:24 whatever things you ask when you pray. This places no limits on a believer's prayers, as long as they are according to God's will and purpose (*see note on Matt. 17:20*). This therefore means that man's faith and prayer are not inconsistent with God's sovereignty. And it is not the believer's responsibility to figure out how that can be true, but simply to be faithful and obedient to the clear teaching on prayer, as Jesus gives it in this passage. God's will is being unfolded through all of redemptive history, by means of the prayers of His people—as His saving purpose is coming to pass through the faith of those who hear the gospel and repent. Cf. James 5:16.

11:25 stand praying. The traditional Jewish prayer posture (cf. 1 Sam. 1:26; 1 Kin. 8:14,22; Neh. 9:4; Matt. 6:5; Luke 18:11,13). Kneeling or lying with one's face on the ground were used during extraordinary circumstances or for extremely urgent requests (cf. 1 Kin. 8:54; Ezra 9:5; Dan. 6:10; Matt. 26:39; Acts 7:60). **anything against anyone.** An all-inclusive statement that includes both sins and simple dislikes, which cause the believer to hold something against another person. "Anyone" incorporates believers and unbelievers. **forgive.** Jesus states the believer's ongoing duty to have a forgiving attitude. Successful prayer requires forgiveness as well as faith. *See notes on Matt. 5:22-24; Eph. 4:32.*

11:26 *See notes on Matt. 6:14,15; 18:21-35.* This is the only occurrence in Mark of "trespasses," a term that denotes a falling aside or departing from the path of truth and uprightness.

11:27 temple. Again this was the Court of the Gentiles; this time more specifically Solomon's porch or the royal porch on the S side of the court (cf. v. 11; John 10:23; Acts 5:12). **chief priests.** *See note on Matt. 2:4.* The group that met Jesus might well have included Caiaphas and Annas, who served concurrently for several years (Luke 3:2). Because of the importance of this confrontation, the captain of the temple, the second highest official, may also have been present.

chief priests, the scribes, and the elders
came to Him. 28 And they said to Him, "By
what [t]authority are You doing these
things? And who gave You this authority
to do these things?"
29 But Jesus answered and said to them,
"I also will ask you one question; then answer Me, and I will tell you by what authority I do these things: 30 The [u]baptism
of John—was it from heaven or from men?
Answer Me."
31 And they reasoned among themselves, saying, "If we say, 'From heaven,'
He will say, 'Why then did you not believe
him?' 32 But if we say, 'From men' "—they
feared the people, for [v]all counted John to
have been a prophet indeed. 33 So they
answered and said to Jesus, "We do not
know."
And Jesus answered and said to them,
"Neither will I tell you by what authority I
do these things."

Parable of the Vineyard Owner
Matt. 21:33-46; Luke 20:9-19

12 Then [a]He began to speak to them in
parables: "A man planted a vineyard
and set a hedge around *it*, dug *a place for* the
wine vat and built a tower. And he leased it
to [1]vinedressers and went into a far country. 2 Now at vintage-time he sent a servant
to the vinedressers, that he might receive
some of the fruit of the vineyard from the
vinedressers. 3 And they took *him* and beat
him and sent *him* away empty-handed.
4 Again he sent them another servant, [2]and
at him they threw stones, wounded *him* in
the head, and sent *him* away shamefully
treated. 5 And again he sent another, and
him they killed; and many others, [b]beating
some and killing some. 6 Therefore still having one son, his beloved, he also sent him to
them last, saying, 'They will respect my
son.' 7 But those [3]vinedressers said among
themselves, 'This is the heir. Come, let us
kill him, and the inheritance will be ours.'
8 So they took him and [c]killed *him* and cast
him out of the vineyard.
9 "Therefore what will the owner of the
vineyard do? He will come and destroy the
vinedressers, and give the vineyard to others. 10 Have you not even read this Scripture:

[d]'*The stone which the builders*
rejected

28 [t]John 5:27
30 [u][Mark 1:4, 5, 8]; Luke 7:29, 30
32 [v]Matt. 3:5; 14:5; Mark 6:20

CHAPTER 12
1 [a]Matt. 21:33-46; Luke 20:9-19

[1] *tenant farmers*
4 [2]NU omits *and at him they threw stones*
5 [b]2 Chr. 36:16
7 [3]*tenant farmers*
8 [c][Acts 2:23]
10 [d]Ps. 118:22, 23

11:28 By what authority. The leaders wanted to know what credentials Jesus—an untrained, unrecognized, seemingly self-appointed rabbi—claimed that would authorize Him to do what He was doing. They had recovered from the initial shock of the previous day's events, and had become aggressive in demanding an explanation (*see note on Matt. 21:23*; cf. John 2:18). **these things.** Primarily a reference to His actions in cleansing the temple. But the undefined, vague nature of this expression leaves open the inclusion of everything Jesus had been doing and teaching during His public ministry.

11:30 baptism of John. *See notes on 1:4; Matt. 21:25.* Jesus put them on the defensive and made their evaluation of John's authority a test case for their evaluation of His own authority. **was it from heaven or from men?** Jesus gave the Jewish leaders only those two alternatives in judging the source of John's authority, and by implication, His own authority. Christ was in effect forcing the men to carry out their roles as religious guides for the people and to go on record with an evaluation of both John's and His ministries (*see note on Matt. 21:25*). **Answer Me.** This challenge by Jesus is only in Mark's account. It implies that the Jews did not have the courage to answer His question honestly.

12:1-12 Jesus taught this parable to confront the chief priests and elders and reveal their hypocritical character.

12:1 them. The chief priests, scribes, and elders (cf. 11:27). **parables.** *See notes on 4:2,11.* **vineyard.** A common sight in that region. The hillsides of Palestine were covered with grape vineyards, the backbone of the economy. Here it is a symbol for Israel (cf. Ps. 80:8-16; Is. 5:1-7; Jer. 2:21). Jesus uses Is. 5:1,2 as the basis for this imagery (*see note on Matt. 21:33*). **a hedge.** Lit. "a fence." It may have been a stone wall or a hedge of briars built for protection. **wine vat.** Located under the winepress. The grapes were squeezed in the press and the juice ran through a trough into this lower basin, where it could be collected into wineskins or jars. **tower.** This structure had a 3-fold purpose: 1) it served as a lookout post; 2) it provided shelter for the workers; and 3) it was used for storage of seed and tools. **leased it to vinedressers.** Jesus added to the picture from Is. 5:1,2. The owner makes an agreement with men he believes are reliable caretakers, who are to pay a certain percentage of the proceeds to him as rent. The rest of the profit belonged to them for their work in cultivating the crop. The "vinedressers" represent the Jewish leaders.

12:2 vintage-time. Better translated, "harvesttime." This usually occurred for the first time in the fifth year after the initial planting (cf. Lev. 19:23-25). **servant.** All the servants in the parable represent the OT prophets.

12:6 son, his beloved. The son represents Jesus Christ (*see note on Matt. 21:37*).

12:7 the inheritance will be ours. The vinedressers were greedy; because they wanted the entire harvest and the vineyard for themselves and would stop at nothing to achieve that end, they plotted to kill the owner's son. Because Jesus had achieved such a following, the Jewish leaders believed the only way to maintain their position and power over the people was to kill Him (cf. John 11:48).

12:9 destroy the vinedressers. The owner of the vineyard will execute the vinedressers, thus serving as a prophecy of the destruction of Jerusalem (A.D. 70) and the nation of Israel. According to Matthew, this verdict was echoed by the chief priests, scribes, and elders (*see note on Matt. 21:41*). **give the vineyard to others.** This was fulfilled in the establishment of Christ's church and its leaders, who were mostly Gentiles.

12:10,11 This messianic prophecy is a quotation of Ps. 118:22,23 from the LXX. Jesus continued His teaching in the form of a parable, but here His kingdom is seen as a building instead of a vineyard. The point is that the rejected son and the rejected stone represent Christ.

12:10 *The stone which the builders rejected.* Builders typically rejected stones until they found one perfectly straight in lines that could serve as the cornerstone, which was critical to the symmetry and stability of the building. In Jesus' metaphor, He Himself is the stone the builders (the Jewish religious leaders) rejected (crucified).

Has become the chief cornerstone.
11 *This was the LORD's doing,*
And it is marvelous in our eyes'?"

12 [e]And they sought to lay hands on Him,
but feared the multitude, for they knew He
had spoken the parable against them. So
they left Him and went away.

Question of Taxes
Matt. 22:15-22; Luke 20:20-26

13 [f]Then they sent to Him some of the
Pharisees and the Herodians, to catch Him
in *His* words. 14 When they had come, they
said to Him, "Teacher, we know that You
are true, and [4]care about no one; for You
do not [5]regard the person of men, but
teach the [g]way of God in truth. Is it lawful
to pay taxes to Caesar, or not? 15 Shall we
pay, or shall we not pay?"

But He, knowing their [h]hypocrisy, said
to them, "Why do you test Me? Bring Me a
denarius that I may see *it.*" 16 So they
brought *it.*

And He said to them, "Whose image
and inscription *is* this?" They said to Him,
"Caesar's."

17 And Jesus answered and said to them,
[6]"Render to Caesar the things that are
Caesar's, and to [i]God the things that are
God's."

And they marveled at Him.

Question of the Resurrection
Matt. 22:23-33; Luke 20:27-40

18 [j]Then *some* Sadducees, [k]who say
there is no resurrection, came to Him; and
they asked Him, saying: 19 "Teacher, [l]Mo-
ses wrote to us that if a man's brother
dies, and leaves *his* wife behind, and
leaves no children, his brother should
take his wife and raise up offspring for his
brother. 20 Now there were seven brothers. The first took a wife; and dying, he
left no offspring. 21 And the second took
her, and he died; nor did he leave any offspring. And the third likewise. 22 So the
seven had her and left no offspring. Last
of all the woman died also. 23 Therefore,
in the resurrection, when they rise, whose
wife will she be? For all seven had her as
wife."

24 Jesus answered and said to them,
"Are you not therefore [7]mistaken, because
you do not know the Scriptures nor the
power of God? 25 For when they rise from

12 [e] Matt. 21:45,46; Mark 11:18; John 7:25,30,44
13 [f] Matt. 22:15-22; Luke 20:20-26
14 [g] Acts 18:26 [4] Court no man's favor [5] Lit. *look at the face of men*
15 [h] Matt. 23:28; Luke 12:1
17 [i] [Eccl. 5:4,5] [6] *Pay*
18 [j] Matt. 22:23-33; Luke 20:27-38 [k] Acts 23:8
19 [l] Deut. 25:5
24 [7] Or *deceived*

But the resurrected Christ is the cornerstone (cf. Acts 4:10-12; 1 Pet. 2:6,7; *see note on Matt. 21:42*).

12:12 against them. The chief priests, scribes, and elders were completely aware that Christ was condemning their actions, but it only aroused their hatred, not their repentance.

12:13-17 The second of a series of questions that the Jewish religious leaders hoped would trap Jesus into declaring Himself an insurrectionist (cf. 11:28). This one concerns the controversial issue of paying taxes to Rome.

12:13 Pharisees and the Herodians. Matthew indicates that disciples of the Pharisees accompanied the Herodians. The Pharisees may have hoped that Jesus would not recognize them and be caught off-guard by their seemingly sincere question. The Herodians were a political party of Jews who backed Herod Antipas, who in turn was but a puppet of Rome (*see note on Matt. 22:16*).

12:14 regard the person of men. This speaks of impartiality, or showing no favoritism. While this was flattery on the part of the Pharisees and Herodians, it was nonetheless true that Jesus would not be swayed by a person's power, prestige, or position. **taxes to Caesar.** The Gr. word for "taxes" was borrowed from the Lat. word that gives us the Eng. "census." The Romans counted all the citizens and made each one pay an annual poll tax of one denarius (*see note on Matt. 22:17*).

12:15 hypocrisy. The Pharisees and Herodians, using feigned interest in His teaching, attempted to hide their true intention to trap Jesus. But He perceived their true motives (cf. John 2:25). **Why do you test Me?** Jesus' response exposed the true motive of the Pharisees and Herodians and revealed their hypocrisy. **denarius.** This small silver coin, minted by the Roman emperor, was the equivalent of a day's wage for a common laborer or soldier (*see note on Matt. 22:19*).

12:16 image. On one side of the denarius was likely the image of the current emperor, Tiberius, though at that time it could have also been Augustus, since both coins were in circulation. Tiberius is most likely because the response was "Caesar's," indicating the current ruler rather than the past one. **inscription.** If the coin was minted by Tiberius, it would have read, "Tiberius Caesar Augustus, the son of the Divine Augustus" on one side and "Chief Priest" on the other. *See note on Matt. 22:19.*

12:17 Render to Caesar. The Gr. word for "render" means, "to pay or give back," which implies a debt. All who lived within the realm of Caesar were obligated to return to him the tax that was owed him. It was not optional. Thus Jesus declared that all citizens are under divine obligation to pay taxes to whatever government is over them (cf. Rom. 13:1-7; 1 Pet. 2:13-17; *see note on Matt. 22:21*).

12:18 Sadducees. The most wealthy, influential, and aristocratic of all the Jewish sects. All the High-Priests, chief priests, and the majority of the Sanhedrin (*see note on Matt. 26:59*) were Sadducees. They ignored the oral law, traditions, and scribal laws of the Pharisees, viewing only the Pentateuch as authoritative (*see note on Matt. 3:7*). **who say there is no resurrection.** The most distinctive aspect of the Sadducees' theology, which they adopted because of their allegiance to the Pentateuch and their belief that Moses did not teach a literal resurrection from the dead. With such a disregard for the future, the Sadducees lived for the moment and whatever profit they could make. Since they controlled the temple businesses, they were extremely upset when Jesus cleansed the temple of the money changers because He cut into their profits (11:15-18)—the reason they also wanted to discredit Jesus in front of the people.

12:19 The Sadducees were summarizing Deut. 25:5,6, which refers to the custom of a levirate marriage (marriage to a dead husband's brother). God placed it in the law of Moses to preserve tribal names, families, and inheritances (*see note on Matt. 22:24*). **Moses wrote.** The Sadducees appealed to Moses because they were fully aware of Jesus' high regard for Scripture, and therefore believed He would not contest the validity of the levirate marriage.

12:24 the power of God. Their ignorance of the Scriptures extended to their lack of understanding regarding the miracles God performed throughout the OT. Such knowledge would have enabled them to believe in God's power to raise the dead.

the dead, they neither marry nor are given
in marriage, but [m]are like angels in heaven.
26 But concerning the dead, that they [n]rise,
have you not read in the book of Moses, in
the *burning* bush *passage,* how God spoke to
him, saying, [o]*'I am the God of Abraham, the
God of Isaac, and the God of Jacob'*? 27 He is
not the God of the dead, but the God of the
living. You are therefore greatly [8]mistaken."

Question of the Greatest Commandment
Matt. 22:34-40

28 [p]Then one of the scribes came, and
having heard them reasoning together,
[9]perceiving that He had answered them
well, asked Him, "Which is the [1]first commandment of all?"

29 Jesus answered him, "The [2]first of all
the commandments *is:* [q]*'Hear, O Israel, the
LORD our God, the LORD is one.* 30 *And you
shall* [r]*love the LORD your God with all
your heart, with all your soul, with all your
mind, and with all your strength.'* [3]This *is*
the first commandment. 31 And the second, like *it, is* this: [s]*'You shall love your
neighbor as yourself.'* There is no other
commandment greater than [t]these."

32 So the scribe said to Him, "Well *said,*
Teacher. You have spoken the truth, for
there is one God, [u]and there is no other but
He. 33 And to love Him with all the heart,
with all the understanding, [4]with all the
soul, and with all the strength, and to love
one's neighbor as oneself, [v]is more than all
the whole burnt offerings and sacrifices."

34 Now when Jesus saw that he answered wisely, He said to him, "You are
not far from the kingdom of God."

[w]But after that no one dared question
Him.

Jesus Questions the Leaders
Matt. 22:41-45; Luke 20:41-44

35 [x]Then Jesus answered and said, while
He taught in the temple, "How *is it* that the
scribes say that the Christ is the Son of David? 36 For David himself said [y]by the
Holy Spirit:

[z]*'The LORD said to my Lord,*
"Sit at My right hand,

25 [m] [1 Cor. 15:42, 49, 52]
26 [n] [John 5:25, 28, 29]; Acts 26:8; Rom. 4:17; [Rev. 20:12, 13] [o] Ex. 3:6, 15
27 [8] Or *deceived*
28 [p] Matt. 22:34-40; Luke 10:25-28; 20:39 [9] NU *seeing* [1] *foremost*
29 [q] Deut. 6:4, 5; Is. 44:8; 45:22; 46:9; 1 Cor. 8:6 [2] *foremost*
30 [r] [Deut. 10:12; 30:6]; Luke 10:27 [3] NU omits the rest of v. 30.
31 [s] Lev. 19:18; Matt. 22:39; Gal. 5:14; James 2:8 [t] [Rom. 13:9]
32 [u] Deut. 4:39; Is. 45:6, 14; 46:9; [John 1:14, 17; 14:6]
33 [v] [1 Sam. 15:22; Hos. 6:6; Mic. 6:6-8; Matt. 9:13; 12:7] [4] NU omits *with all the soul*
34 [w] Matt. 22:46
35 [x] Matt. 22:41-46; Luke 20:41-44
36 [y] 2 Sam. 23:2 [z] Ps. 110:1

12:25 neither marry. Marriage was designed by God for companionship and the perpetuation of the human race on the earth. Jesus was emphasizing the fact that in heaven there will be no exclusive or sexual relationships. Believers will experience an entirely new existence in which they will have perfect spiritual relationships with everyone else. **like angels.** Believers will be like angels in that they will be spiritual, eternal beings who will not die (cf. 1 Cor. 15:39-44,48,49; *see note on Matt. 22:30*).

12:26 book of Moses. The Pentateuch—the first 5 books of the OT. Jesus appealed to the only Scriptures the Sadducees held as completely authoritative. **the *burning* bush *passage.*** A reference to Ex. 3:1–4:17 where God first appeared to Moses at the bush. **how God spoke to him, saying, *'I am.'*** By keying on the emphatic present tense of Ex. 3:6, "I *am* the God of Abraham, the God of Isaac, and the God of Jacob," Jesus was underscoring the personal and perpetual covenantal relationship God established with the 3 patriarchs. Even though all 3 were dead when God spoke to Moses, God was still their God just as much as when they were alive on earth—and more so in that they were experiencing eternal fellowship with Him in heaven (*see note on Matt. 22:32*).

12:27 You are...greatly mistaken. Jesus accused the Sadducees of making a complete error in teaching that there is no resurrection.

12:28 scribes. *See note on 1:22.* **Which is the first commandment.** The rabbis had determined that there were 613 commandments contained in the Pentateuch, one for each letter of the Ten Commandments. Of the 613 commandments, 248 were seen as affirmative and 365 as negative. Those laws were also divided into heavy and light categories, with the heavy laws being more binding than the light ones. The scribes and rabbis, however, had been unable to agree on which were heavy and which were light. This orientation to the law led the Pharisees to think Jesus had devised His own theory. So the Pharisees asked this particular question to get Jesus to incriminate Himself by revealing His unorthodox and unilateral beliefs.

12:29 *Hear, O Israel.* By quoting the first part of the Shema (Deut. 6:4,5), which is Heb. for "hear," Jesus confirmed the practice of every pious Jew who recited the entire Shema (Num. 15:37-41; Deut. 6:4-9; 11:13-21) every morning and evening.

12:30 *love the LORD.* Taken from Deut. 10:12; 30:6, Jesus used God's own word from the Pentateuch to answer the question, indicating the orthodox nature of His theology. *See note on Matt. 22:37.*

12:31 the second. Jesus took the Pharisees' question one step further by identifying the second greatest commandment because it was critical to an understanding of the complete duty of love. This commandment, also from the books of Moses (Lev. 19:18) is of the same nature and character as the first. Genuine love for God is followed in importance by a genuine love for people (*see note on Matt. 22:39*). ***neighbor.*** Cf. Luke 10:29-37.

12:32,33 the scribe said. The scribe's response reveals he understood OT teaching that moral concerns took precedence over ceremonial practices (cf. 1 Sam. 15:22; Is. 1:11-15; Hos. 6:6; Mic. 6:6-8).

12:33 burnt offerings. Sacrifices that were completely consumed on the altar (cf. Lev. 1:1-17; 6:8-13).

12:34 not far from the kingdom. Jesus both complimented and challenged the scribe. Jesus acknowledged the scribe's insight regarding the importance of love. Yet by stating that the scribe was "not far" from the kingdom He emphasized that he was not in the kingdom. He understood the requirements of love, he needed only to love and obey the One who alone could grant him entrance to the kingdom.

12:35 Jesus' question exposed the Jewish religious leaders' ineptness as teachers and their ignorance of what the OT taught regarding the true nature of the Messiah. **temple.** *See note on 11:11.* **Christ.** This is a translation of the OT Heb. word "Messiah," which means "anointed one" and refers to the King whom God had promised. **Son of David.** The common messianic title that was standard scribal teaching. The religious leaders were convinced that the Messiah would be no more than a man, thus they deemed such a title appropriate (*see notes on 10:47; Matt. 22:42*).

12:36 David himself said by the Holy Spirit. David used his own words, yet he wrote under the inspiration of the Holy Spirit (cf. 2 Sam. 73:2). ***The LORD said to my Lord.*** In this quote from the Heb. text (Ps. 110:1), the first word for "LORD" is *Yahweh,* which is God's covenant name. The second word for "Lord" is a different word that

Till I make Your enemies Your
footstool."'

37 Therefore David himself calls Him
'Lord'; how is He *then* his [a]Son?"
And the common people heard Him
gladly.

Jesus Condemns the Leaders
Matt. 23:1-14; Luke 20:45–21:4

38 Then [b]He said to them in His teaching, [c]"Beware of the scribes, who desire to
go around in long robes, [d]*love* greetings in
the marketplaces, 39 the [e]best seats in the
synagogues, and the best places at feasts,
40 [f]who devour widows' houses, and [5]for a
pretense make long prayers. These will receive greater condemnation."
41 [g]Now Jesus sat opposite the treasury
and saw how the people put money [h]into
the treasury. And many *who were* rich put
in much. 42 Then one poor widow came
and threw in two [6]mites, which make a
[7]quadrans. 43 So He called His disciples to
Himself and said to them, "Assuredly, I say
to you that [i]this poor widow has put in
more than all those who have given to the
treasury; 44 for they all put in out of their
abundance, but she out of her poverty put
in all that she had, [j]her whole livelihood."

Questions from the Disciples
Matt. 24:1-3; Luke 21:5-7

13 Then [a]as He went out of the temple,
one of His disciples said to Him,
"Teacher, see what manner of stones and
what buildings *are here!*"
2 And Jesus answered and said to him,
"Do you see these great buildings? [b]Not
one stone shall be left upon another, that
shall not be thrown down."
3 Now as He sat on the Mount of Olives
opposite the temple, [c]Peter, [d]James, [e]John,
and [f]Andrew asked Him privately, 4 [g]"Tell
us, when will these things be? And what
will be the sign when all these things will
be fulfilled?"

37 [a][Acts 2:29-31] **38** [b]Mark 4:2 [c]Matt. 23:1-7; Luke 20:45-47 [d]Matt. 23:7; Luke 11:43 **39** [e]Luke 14:7 **40** [f]Matt. 23:14 [5]*for appearance' sake* **41** [g]Luke 21:1-4 [h]2 Kin. 12:9 **42** [6]Gr. *lepta*, very small copper coins [7]A Roman coin **43** [i][2 Cor. 8:12] **44** [j]Deut. 24:6; [1 John 3:17]

CHAPTER 13

1 [a]Matt. 24:1; Luke 21:5-36 **2** [b]Luke 19:44 **3** [c]Matt. 16:18; Mark 1:16 [d]Mark 1:19 [e]Mark 1:19 [f]John 1:40 **4** [g]Matt. 24:3; Luke 21:7

---

the Jews used as a title for God. Here David pictures God speaking to the Messiah, whom David calls his Lord. The religious leaders of Jesus' day recognized this psalm as messianic.

12:37 David himself calls Him *'Lord.'* Jesus interpreted Ps. 110:1 for the Pharisees. David would not have called one of his descendants "Lord." Thus the Messiah is more than the "Son of David"—He is also the "Son of God." Jesus was proclaiming the Messiah's deity, and thus His own (cf. Rom. 1:3; 2 Tim. 2:8; *see note on Matt. 22:45*). **common people.** The multitude of people who observed this confrontation between Jesus and the religious leaders.

12:38 Beware. This means "to see" or "to watch." It carries the idea of guarding against the evil influence of the scribes. **long robes.** A long, flowing cloak that essentially trumpeted the wearer as a devout and noted scholar. **greetings.** Accolades for those holding titles of honor.

12:39 best seats in the synagogues. The bench in the synagogue nearest the chest where the sacred scrolls were housed—an area reserved for leaders and people of renown (*see note on James 2:3*).

12:40 devour widows' houses. Jesus exposed the greedy, unscrupulous practice of the scribes. Scribes often served as estate planners for widows, which gave them the opportunity to convince distraught widows that they would be serving God by supporting the temple or the scribe's own holy work. In either case, the scribe benefited monetarily and effectively robbed the widow of her husband's legacy to her. **long prayers.** The Pharisees attempted to flaunt their piety by praying for long periods. Their motive was not devotion to God, but a desire to be revered by the people.

12:41 treasury. This refers to the 13 trumpet-shaped receptacles on the walls in the court of the women where offerings and donations to the temple were placed.

12:42 two mites. A "mite" was a small copper coin, which was the smallest denomination in use. It was worth about an eighth of a cent. **a quadrans.** For the benefit of his Roman audience (see Introduction: Background and Setting), Mark related the "mite" to this smallest denomination of Roman coinage. A "quadrans" was equal to 1/64 of a denarius, and a denarius was the equivalent of a day's wage.

12:43 Assuredly, I say to you. *See note on 3:28.*

12:44 her whole livelihood. This could be translated, "all she had to live on." That meant she would not be able to eat until she earned more. The widow exemplified true sacrificial giving.

13:1-37 This great sermon by Jesus is commonly known as the Olivet Discourse because Jesus delivered it on the Mt. of Olives just E of the temple across the Kidron Valley. Jesus' prediction of the coming destruction of the temple prompted a question from the disciples about the character of the end times. The remainder of the passage (vv. 5-37) is His response to their question as He describes His second coming at the end of the present age.

13:1 what manner of stones and what buildings. *See note on Matt. 24:1.* This unidentified disciple was admiring the magnificence and beauty of the temple and the surrounding buildings and was encouraging a like response from Jesus. It is likely that he could not comprehend how such an awesome structure could be left "desolate" (cf. Matt. 23:38).

13:2 Jesus answered. In response to the disciple's admiration, Jesus again predicted that the temple would be destroyed. About 40 years later, in A.D. 70, the Romans ransacked Jerusalem, killed a million Jews, and demolished the temple. **Not *one* stone.** The only stones left undisturbed were huge foundation stones that were not actually a part of the temple edifice but formed footings for the retaining wall under the entire temple mount. These can be viewed today in the "Rabbi's Tunnel" which runs N-S along the western wall. It is a portion of the western side of the retaining wall that today is called the Wailing Wall. More of that retaining wall, including the steps used to ascend and descend from the temple mount have also been uncovered on the southern side.

13:3 Mount of Olives. *See note on 11:1.* **Peter, James, John, and Andrew asked Him privately.** These 4 disciples were asking on behalf of all the 12.

13:4 The disciples were speculating that Jesus would imminently usher in the kingdom, so they asked a twofold question: 1) When would the temple be destroyed and the kingdom begin? and 2) What event would herald the beginning of the kingdom? **when will these things be?** "When" implies immediacy. The disciples thought that Jesus was about to usher in the kingdom of God at any time (cf. Luke 19:11), at least by the end of the Passover season. "These things" refers to the desolation and destruction of the temple (cf. Matt. 23:38; 24:2) **the sign.** The disciples probably expected some miraculous

The Tribulation
Matt. 24:4-26; Luke 21:8-24

5 And Jesus, answering them, began to
say: [h]"Take heed that no one deceives
you. 6 For many will come in My name,
saying, 'I am *He,*' and will deceive many.
7 But when you hear of wars and rumors
of wars, do not be troubled; for *such*
things must happen, but the end *is* not
yet. 8 For nation will rise against nation,
and [i]kingdom against kingdom. And
there will be earthquakes in various
places, and there will be famines [1]and
troubles. [j]These *are* the beginnings of
[2]sorrows.
9 "But [k]watch out for yourselves, for
they will deliver you up to councils, and
you will be beaten in the synagogues.
You will [3]be brought before rulers and
kings for My sake, for a testimony to
them. 10 And [l]the gospel must first be
preached to all the nations. 11 [m]But when
they arrest *you* and deliver you up, do not
worry beforehand, [4]or premeditate what
you will speak. But whatever is given
you in that hour, speak that; for it is not
you who speak, [n]but the Holy Spirit.
12 Now [o]brother will betray brother to
death, and a father *his* child; and children
will rise up against parents and cause
them to be put to death. 13 [p]And you will
be hated by all for My name's sake. But
[q]he who [5]endures to the end shall be
saved.
14 [r]"So when you see the [s]*'abomination*
of desolation,' [6]spoken of by Daniel the
prophet, standing where it ought not" (let
the reader understand), "then [t]let those
who are in Judea flee to the mountains.
15 Let him who is on the housetop not go
down into the house, nor enter to take anything out of his house. 16 And let him who
is in the field not go back to get his clothes.

5 [h] Jer. 29:8; Eph. 5:6; [Col. 2:8]; 1 Thess. 2:3; 2 Thess. 2:3
8 [i] Hag. 2:22 [j] Matt. 24:8 [1] NU omits *and troubles* [2] Lit. *birth pangs*
9 [k] Matt. 10:17, 18; 24:9; Acts 12:4; [Rev. 2:10] [3] NU, M *stand*
10 [l] Matt. 24:14
11 [m] Matt. 10:19-22; Luke 12:11; 21:12-17 [n] Acts 2:4; 4:8, 31 [4] NU omits *or premeditate*
12 [o] Mic. 7:6; Matt. 10:21; 24:10; Luke 21:16
13 [p] Matt. 24:9; Luke 21:17; John 15:21 [q] Dan. 12:12; Matt. 10:22; 24:13; [Rev. 2:10] [5] *bears patiently*
14 [r] Matt. 24:15 [s] Dan. 9:27; 11:31; 12:11 [t] Luke 21:21 [6] NU omits *spoken of by Daniel the prophet*

occurrence—such as complete darkness, brilliant light, or an angel from heaven—to announce the coming millennial kingdom (*see note on Matt. 24:3*). All of those things will occur at that time (*see notes on vv. 24-27*).

13:5 Take heed. This Gr. word lit. means, "to see," but was often used as it is here with the idea of "keep your eyes open," or "beware."

13:6 'I am *He.*' Many false prophets will come forward claiming to be messiahs and deliverers, offering themselves as the solution to the world's problems. Some will even claim to be Christ Himself. The number of false christs will increase as the end nears (cf. 24:23,24).

13:7 the end. The consummation of the present age (*see note on Matt. 24:6*).

13:8 the beginnings of sorrows. The Gr. word for "sorrows" means "birth pangs." The Lord was referring to the pain a woman experiences in childbirth. Birth pains signal the end of pregnancy—they are infrequent at first and gradually increase just before the child is born. Likewise, the signs of vv. 6-8 will be infrequent, relatively speaking, in the beginning and will escalate to massive and tragic proportions just prior to Christ's second coming (cf. 1 Thess. 5:3; *see note on Matt. 24:8*).

13:9 councils. The Gr. word is lit. "sanhedrins." These were local, Jewish courts attached to the synagogues which tried charges of heresy and normal infractions of the law. The historian Josephus says that each city's council was composed of 7 judges (*Antiquities*, 4.8.14), and the *Mishnah* records that there were 23 judges in every city with more than 100 Jewish men ("Sanhedrin" I.6). These "councils" were like smaller versions of the great Sanhedrin that convened in Jerusalem (*see note on Matt. 26:59*). **beaten.** These local councils usually administered 39 stripes so as not to violate Deut. 25:2,3. The recipient of the punishment was stripped bare to the waist. He received 13 lashings to his chest and 26 to his back (*see note on 2 Cor. 11:24*). **in the synagogues.** The "synagogues" were the places for Jewish assembly and worship. When the "councils" convened, they typically met in the "synagogue."

13:10 first be preached to all the nations. Before the end (*see note on v. 7*), there will be a worldwide proclamation of the gospel. This may even refer to the occasion when an angel will supernaturally proclaim the gospel throughout the world before God pours out His judgment at the end of the Tribulation (Rev. 14:6-8; *see note on Matt. 24:14*).

13:11 what you will speak. Although the persecution will be terrifying, Christians are not to be anxious in anticipation of those events. **for it is not you who speak.** Rather than being fearful, believers can remain calm and depend on the Holy Spirit, who will give them the appropriate and effective words to say in defense of their faith in Christ. *See note on Luke 12:11.*

13:13 endures to the end shall be saved. *See note on Matt. 24:13.* This endurance does not produce salvation; it is Spirit-empowered perseverance and proof of the reality of salvation in the one who endures. Christ will eventually deliver such believers out of the present evil system into God's eternal kingdom (cf. Matt. 10:22).

13:14 the *'abomination of desolation.'* This first referred to the desecration of the temple by Antiochus Epiphanes, the king of Syria, in the second century B.C. when he sacrificed a pig on the temple altar. That event was similar in character to what Jesus refers to here, i.e., the Antichrist's ultimate desecration when he sets up an image of himself in the temple during the tribulation (*see notes on Dan. 9:27; 11:31; Matt. 24:15; 2 Thess. 2:4*). **standing where it ought not.** Matthew 24:15 indicates the location as the "holy place." On the only other occasion where this phrase from Matthew appears in the NT, it clearly refers to the temple (Acts 21:8). This specifically implies that the temple will be rebuilt in the future and that the daily sacrificial system will be reinstated. "Standing" indicates that the abomination of desolation will be continuous, actually lasting for 3 ½ years (Dan. 12:11; cf. Rev. 12:6). **(let the reader understand).** This indicates that Jesus was not issuing these warnings to the disciples or to others of their generation who would not experience this event, but to believers in the end time. Those who will read these truths will be prepared and "understand" the trials they are enduring. **flee to the mountains.** The Gr. word for "flee" is related to the Eng. word "fugitive," a person who is on the run to escape danger. Jesus warns those who live in Judea to escape the holocaust by taking refuge in the mountains (*see note on Matt. 24:16*).

13:15 into the house. So urgent will be the need to flee that if a person happens to be on the roof of his house (*see note on 2:4*) when he hears the news, he is to run down the outside stairway and leave town without going inside his house to retrieve any belongings.

13:16 clothes. The Gr. word refers to the outer cloak. Jesus warns those working in the fields not to take the time to retrieve their cloaks that may be at home or some distance away at the entrance to the field.

17 [u]But woe to those who are pregnant and
to those who are nursing babies in those
days! 18 And pray that your flight may not
be in winter. 19 [v]For *in* those days there
will be tribulation, such as has not been
since the beginning of the creation which
God created until this time, nor ever shall
be. 20 And unless the Lord had shortened
those days, no flesh would be saved; but
for the elect's sake, whom He chose, He
shortened the days.

21 [w]"Then if anyone says to you, 'Look,
here *is* the Christ!' or, 'Look, *He is* there!' do
not believe it. 22 For false christs and false
prophets will rise and show signs and
[x]wonders to deceive, if possible, even the
[7]elect. 23 But [y]take heed; see, I have told
you all things beforehand.

The Second Coming
Matt. 24:29-31; Luke 21:25-28

24 [z]"But in those days, after that tribulation, the sun will be darkened, and the
moon will not give its light; 25 the stars of
heaven will fall, and the powers in the
heavens will be [a]shaken. 26 [b]Then they will
see the Son of Man coming in the clouds
with great power and glory. 27 And then
He will send His angels, and gather together His [8]elect from the four winds, from
the farthest part of earth to the farthest
part of heaven.

Parable of the Fig Tree—Matt. 24:32-35

28 [c]"Now learn this parable from the fig
tree: When its branch has already become
tender, and puts forth leaves, you know
that summer is near. 29 So you also, when
you see these things happening, know that
[9]it is near—at the doors! 30 Assuredly, I say
to you, this generation will by no means
pass away till all these things take place.
31 Heaven and earth will pass away, but
[d]My words will by no means pass away.

17 [u] Luke 21:23
19 [v] Dan. 9:26; 12:1; Joel 2:2; Matt. 24:21; Mark 10:6
21 [w] Matt. 24:23; Luke 17:23; 21:8
22 [x] Deut. 13:1-3; Rev. 13:13, 14 [7] *chosen ones*
23 [y] John 16:1-4; [2 Pet. 3:17]
24 [z] Zeph. 1:15; Matt. 24:29
25 [a] Is. 13:10; 34:4; Heb. 12:26; Rev. 6:13
26 [b] [Dan. 7:13, 14; Matt. 16:27; 24:30]; Mark 14:62; Acts 1:11; [1 Thess. 4:16; 2 Thess. 1:7, 10]; Rev. 1:7
27 [8] *chosen ones*
28 [c] Matt. 24:32; Luke 21:29
29 [9] *Or He*
31 [d] Is. 40:8; [2 Pet. 3:7, 10, 12]

13:17 pregnant and…nursing babies. Jesus certainly felt compassion for those women who will be hindered from fleeing quickly because they carry children. But He may have been warning them about atrocities that could include unborn children being slashed in the wombs and tiny infants being crushed (cf. Hos. 13:16).

13:18 in winter. This refers to the rainy season in Palestine, when streams could become impassable and it would be difficult to glean food from barren fields.

13:19 tribulation, such as has not been. This reveals that the tribulation Jesus was referring to is in the future and that it will be the greatest that has ever occurred. It will be of long duration and characterized by severe pressure and continual anguish. This is the Great Tribulation at the end of the age (cf. Rev. 7:14; *see note on Matt. 24:21*).

13:20 shortened. Lit. "mutilated" or "amputated." Jesus was referring to the determination of God to cut short or limit the period of time to only 3 ½ years (cf. Dan. 7:25; Rev. 12:14; *see note on Matt. 24:22*). **the elect's sake.** The "elect" could refer to the nation of Israel (cf. Is. 45:4), or those who become Christians during the Tribulation (Rev. 17:14). In either case, God cuts short the days for their benefit.

13:21 'Look, here *is* the Christ!' Satan will cause false christs to appear in an attempt to deceive the elect into leaving their places of refuge. False teachers will claim that Christ is in their midst or is back in Jerusalem or elsewhere in Judea.

13:22 signs and wonders. Satanic inspired pseudo-miracles employed to support their claims to be the true Christ (cf. 2 Thess. 2:9).

13:23 take heed. Jesus issues a prophetic warning to be on guard. He has told the elect refugees of the future all that they need to know to avoid being misled and deceived by Satan's emissaries.

13:24 in those days, after that tribulation. "Those days" describes the events of vv. 6-23 and, thus, "that tribulation" refers to the Great Tribulation Jesus just spoke of. This also means that what He was about to describe (vv. 24-27) will occur immediately at the end of the future tribulation period (cf. Matt. 24:29). **the sun will be darkened.** The sun will go black as the universe begins to disintegrate prior to the return of Christ (*see notes on Matt. 24:29; Acts 2:20; Rev. 6:12*).

13:25 stars of heaven will fall. Heavenly bodies will careen at random through space (cf. Rev. 6:13,14; 8:10-13; 16:8,17-20). **powers in the heavens.** All the forces of energy that hold everything in space constant, and which Christ controls, He will allow to become random and chaotic (cf. Is. 13:6-16; 34:1-5; 2 Pet. 3:10-12).

13:26 Son of Man. *See note on 2:10.* **coming in the clouds with great power and glory.** Jesus will return to earth in the same manner in which He left it (cf. Acts 1:9-11; cf. Dan. 7:13,14; Rev. 1:7). The psalmist said that God uses "clouds" as His chariot (Ps. 104:3), and Is. 19:1 pictures the Lord riding on a cloud. Although these "clouds" could be natural, they more likely describe the supernatural "glory cloud" that represented God's presence in OT Israel (*see note on Rev. 1:7*). While Christ possesses "great power and glory," His return will be accompanied with visible manifestations of that power and glory (cf. Rev. 6:15-17; 11:15-19; 16:17-21; 19:11-16)—He will redeem the elect, restore the devastated earth, and establish His rule on earth.

13:27 angels. A number of angels return with Christ (cf. 8:38; Matt. 16:27; *see following note*). **gather…His elect.** Angels are God's gatherers—they gather unbelievers for judgment (Matt. 13:41,49, 50), and they gather the elect for glory. The "elect" will include the 144,000 Jewish witnesses (*see note on Rev. 7:4*), their converts (Rev. 7:9), and the converts of the angelic preachers (*see note on Rev. 14:6*). They will also include the OT saints, gathered out of their graves and united with their redeemed spirits (Dan. 12:1-3). **from the four winds.** A colloquial expression meaning "from everywhere," and similar to the expression "from the four corners of the world." None of the elect on earth or in heaven will miss entering the kingdom.

13:28 this parable. *See note on 4:2.* **fig tree.** *See note on 11:13.*

13:29 Just as the fig tree's buds turning into leaves was a sign of the nearness of summer, the events Jesus described as birth pains (vv. 6-23) are to be a clear indication of the return of Christ (*see note on Matt. 24:32*). **these things.** The events of vv. 6-23. **it is.** Luke 21:31 refers to "it" as the kingdom of God. That is consistent with the question the disciples initially asked Jesus (v. 4), which was about the signs that would herald the establishment of the kingdom.

13:30 Assuredly, I say to you. *See note on 3:28.* **this generation.** The generation of people living during the end times that witnesses the signs and events leading to the return of Christ (*see note on Matt. 24:34*).

13:31 Heaven and earth will pass away. The universe as we know it will be dramatically altered after the thousand-year reign of Christ (*see notes on 2 Pet. 3:10-13*). **My words will by no means pass away.** It is impossible for God's Word to be negated, destroyed, or altered in any way (cf. Ps. 19:9; Matt. 5:18; Luke 16:17; John 10:35).

Exhortation to Watch
Matt. 24:36-51; Luke 21:34-36

32 "But of that day and hour [e]no one
knows, not even the angels in heaven, nor
the Son, but only the [f]Father. 33 [g]Take heed,
watch and pray; for you do not know when
the time is. 34 [h]*It is* like a man going to a far
country, who left his house and gave [i]au-
thority to his servants, and to each his work,
and commanded the doorkeeper to watch.
35 [j]Watch therefore, for you do not know
when the master of the house is coming—in
the evening, at midnight, at the crowing of
the rooster, or in the morning— 36 lest, coming suddenly, he find you sleeping. 37 And
what I say to you, I say to all: Watch!"

Leaders Plot to Kill Jesus
Matt. 26:1-5; Luke 22:1, 2

14 After [a]two days it was the Passover
and [b]*the Feast* of Unleavened Bread.
And the chief priests and the scribes
sought how they might take Him by [1]trick-
ery and put *Him* to death. 2 But they said,
"Not during the feast, lest there be an uproar of the people."

Mary Anoints Jesus
Matt. 26:6-13; John 12:2-8

3 [c]And being in Bethany at the house of
Simon the leper, as He sat at the table, a
woman came having an alabaster flask of
very costly [2]oil of spikenard. Then she
broke the flask and poured *it* on His head.
4 But there were some who were indignant
among themselves, and said, "Why was
this fragrant oil wasted? 5 For it might
have been sold for more than three hundred [d]denarii and given to the poor." And
they [e]criticized[3] her sharply.
6 But Jesus said, "Let her alone. Why do
you trouble her? She has done a good

32 [e]Matt. 25:13 [f]Matt. 24:36; Acts 1:7
33 [g]Matt. 24:42; 25:13; Luke 12:40; 21:34; [Rom. 13:11]; 1 Thess. 5:6; 1 Pet. 4:7
34 [h]Matt. 24:45; 25:14 [i][Matt. 16:19]
35 [j]Matt. 24:42, 44

CHAPTER 14

1 [a]Matt. 26:2-5; Luke 22:1, 2; John 11:55; 13:1 [b]Ex. 12:1-27; Mark 14:12

[1]deception
3 [c]Matt. 26:6; Luke 7:37; John 12:1, 3 [2]Perfume of pure nard
5 [d]Matt. 18:28; Mark 12:15 [e]Matt. 20:11; John 6:61 [3]scolded

13:32 that day and hour. The exact day and time of Christ's return (*see note on Matt. 24:36*). **no one knows.** The time of Christ's return will not be revealed in advance to any man. At this time, it was known only to God the Father. **angels.** While all the angelic beings enjoy intimacy with God, hover around His throne to do His bidding (Is. 26:2-7), and continually behold Him (Matt. 18:10), they have no knowledge of the time of Christ's return. **nor the Son.** When Jesus spoke these words to the disciples, even He had no knowledge of the date and time of His return. Although Jesus was fully God (John 1:1,14), when He became a man, He voluntarily restricted the use of certain divine attributes (Phil. 2:6-8). He did not manifest them unless directed by the Father (John 4:34; 5:30; 6:38). He demonstrated His omniscience on several occasions (cf. John 2:25; 3:13), but He voluntarily restricted that omniscience to only those things God wanted Him to know during the days of His humanity (John 15:15). Such was the case regarding the knowledge of the date and time of His return. After He was resurrected, Jesus resumed His full divine knowledge (cf. Matt. 28:18; Acts 1:7).

13:33 watch and pray. Christ sounded a warning for believers to be on guard (*see note on v. 5*) in two practical ways: 1) "watch" is a call to stay awake and be alert, looking for approaching danger; and 2) "pray" emphasizes the believer's constant need for divine assistance in this endeavor. Even believers do not have in themselves sufficient resources to be alert to spiritual dangers that can so easily surprise them.

13:34 doorkeeper. In Jesus' day, this individual guarded the outer gate of the house, so as to be ready to let the returning master in upon his arrival. All Christ's disciples are to be like doorkeepers, always remaining alert and vigilant for their Master's return.

13:35 in the evening...or in the morning. The normal expressions designating the 4 three-hour watches of the night from 6:00 p.m. to 6:00 a.m. Their names identify the ends of the three-hour periods rather than the periods' beginnings.

14:1 After two days. In the context of Matt. 26:2, Jesus predicted His crucifixion was to take place in "two days," which would be Friday since when He was speaking it was Wednesday evening. Mark's time line here is the same as Matthew's (*see note on Matt. 26:2*). **the Passover.** Friday of Passover which would have begun on Thursday at sunset. The Passover commemorated the "passing over" of the homes of the Israelites by the angel of death, who killed the firstborn of Egypt (Ex. 12:1–13:16). The Passover began on the 14th day of Nisan (the first month of the Jewish calendar) with the slaying of the Passover lamb, and continued into the early hours of the 15th (*see notes on Ex. 12:6; Matt. 26:2*). ***Feast* of Unleavened Bread.** This feast commemorated the departure of the Israelites from Egypt (Ex. 23:15). It began immediately after the Passover and lasted from Nisan 15–21. Unleavened bread refers to the type of bread the Israelites were to take with them in their escape which represented the absence of the leaven of sin in their lives and household (*see notes on Ex. 12:14; Lev. 23:6-8*). **chief priests.** *See note on 8:31.* **scribes.** *See note on Matt. 2:4.*

14:2 Not during the feast. Because the Passover had to be celebrated in Jerusalem, the city would have been overflowing—perhaps as many as two million people were there. Since many would have been from Galilee—an area where Jesus had many followers—and the religious leaders did not want to start a riot, they determined to wait until after the Passover season when the crowds would be diminished (*see note on Matt. 26:5*).

14:3-9 The incident recorded here had occurred the previous Saturday (cf. John 12:1). It is Mark's account of the anointing of Jesus by Mary in preparation for His crucifixion (cf. Matt. 26:6-13; John 12:2-8).

14:3 Bethany. *See note on 11:1.* **Simon the leper.** This man is mentioned in the NT only in connection with this narrative. Since a leper was an outcast in Jewish society, he was probably miraculously cleansed of His leprosy by Jesus, and may have planned this meal for Jesus in gratitude (*see notes on Lev. 13; Matt. 26:6*). **a woman.** John 12:3 identifies her as Mary, the sister of Martha and Lazarus, who were also present at this meal. **alabaster flask.** This long-necked bottle was made out of a special variety of marble, a material which proved to be the best container for preserving expensive perfumes and oils (*see note on Matt. 26:7*). **spikenard.** This actually represents two words in the Gr. that could be translated "pure nard." The oil was derived from the nard plant, which was native to India. That it was pure meant it was genuine and unadulterated, which is what made it so costly. **broke the flask.** She may have simply broken the neck of the bottle so that she could pour out the contents more quickly, an expression of her sincere and total devotion to the Lord.

14:4 some who were indignant. John 12:4,5 says that Judas was the instigator, and Matt. 26:8 indicates that all the disciples, following Judas' lead, were angry with Mary's waste of a very valuable commodity.

14:5 three hundred denarii. Since a denarius was a day's wage for a common laborer, it represented almost a year's work for such a person. **given to the poor.** While 11 of the disciples would have agreed to this use of the money, the fact is the poor may never have seen it. Since Judas was in reality a thief masquerading as the treasurer of the 12, he could have embezzled all of it (John 12:6).

work for Me. 7 [f]For you have the poor with
you always, and whenever you wish you
may do them good; [g]but Me you do not
have always. 8 She has done what she
could. She has come beforehand to anoint
My body for burial. 9 Assuredly, I say to
you, wherever this gospel is [h]preached in
the whole world, what this woman has
done will also be told as a memorial to
her."

Judas Plans to Betray Jesus

Matt. 26:14; Luke 22:3-6

10 [i]Then Judas Iscariot, one of the
twelve, went to the chief priests to betray
Him to them. 11 And when they heard *it,*
they were glad, and promised to give him
money. So he sought how he might conveniently betray Him.

The Passover Is Prepared

Matt. 26:17-19; Luke 22:7-13

12 [j]Now on the first day of Unleavened
Bread, when they [4]killed the Passover
lamb, His disciples said to Him, "Where do
You want us to go and prepare, that You
may eat the Passover?"

13 And He sent out two of His disciples
and said to them, "Go into the city, and a
man will meet you carrying a pitcher of
water; follow him. 14 Wherever he goes in,
say to the master of the house, 'The Teacher
says, "Where is the guest room in which I
may eat the Passover with My disciples?" '
15 Then he will show you a large upper
room, furnished *and* prepared; there make
ready for us."

16 So His disciples went out, and came
into the city, and found it just as He had
said to them; and they prepared the
Passover.

The Passover Is Celebrated

Matt. 26:20-25; Luke 22:14-16; John 13:21-30

17 [k]In the evening He came with the
twelve. 18 Now as they sat and ate, Jesus
said, "Assuredly, I say to you, [l]one of you
who eats with Me will betray Me."

19 And they began to be sorrowful, and

7 [f]Deut. 15:11; Matt. 26:11; John 12:8 [g][John 7:33; 8:21; 14:2, 12; 16:10, 17, 28]
9 [h]Matt. 28:19, 20; Mark 16:15; Luke 24:47
10 [i]Ps. 41:9; 55:12-14; Matt. 10:2-4
12 [j]Ex. 12:8; Matt. 26:17-19; Luke 22:7-13 [4]*sacrificed*
17 [k]Matt. 26:20-24; Luke 22:14, 21-23
18 [l]Ps. 41:9; Matt. 26:46; Mark 14:42; John 6:70, 71; 13:18

14:7 you have the poor with you always. Opportunities to minister to the poor are "always" available, but Jesus would be in their presence for only a limited time. This was not a time for meeting the needs of the poor and the sick—it was a time for sacrificial worship of the One who would soon suffer and be crucified (*see note on Matt. 26:11; cf. 2:19*).

14:8 anoint My body for burial. Mary did so probably without ever realizing what she was doing. Her anointing of Jesus became a symbol that anticipated His death and burial (*see note on Matt. 26:12*).

14:9 Assuredly, I say to you. *See note on 3:28.* **gospel.** *See note on 1:1.*

14:10 Judas Iscariot. Standing in sharp contrast to the love and devotion of Mary was the hatred and treachery of Judas. This disciple, who is understandably referred to last in the lists of the 12, was the son of Simon, who was also called "Iscariot." The name "Iscariot" means "man of Kerioth," which was a small town in Judea about 23 mi. S of Jerusalem (cf. 3:19). Thus Judas was not a Galilean like the other disciples. It is clear that Judas never had any spiritual interest in Jesus—he was attracted to Him because he expected Jesus to become a powerful religious and political leader. He saw great potential for power, wealth, and prestige through his association with Him. But Jesus knew what Judas was like from the start, and that is why He chose him as one of the 12. He was the one who would betray Him so that the Scripture and God's plan of salvation would be fulfilled (Pss. 41:9; 55:12-15,20,21; Zech. 11:12,13; John 6:64,70,71; 13:18; 17:12). **the twelve.** *See note on 3:14.* **chief priests.** *See note on 8:31.*

14:11 money. Matthew says the amount Judas agreed to as blood money was 30 pieces of silver (*see note on Matt. 26:15*). **sought how he might conveniently.** "Sought" is better translated "began to seek." "Conveniently" means that Judas was looking for a suitable occasion to carry out his evil plan, which would be when Jesus was away from the crowds (Luke 22:6).

14:12 Unleavened Bread. Passover and the Feast of Unleavened Bread were so closely associated that both terms were used interchangeably to refer to the 8-day celebration that began with the Passover. Although Unleavened Bread is used here, Mark's clear intention is the preparation for Passover (*see notes on v. 1; Matt. 26:17*). **killed the Passover *lamb.*** The lambs were killed on 14 Nisan at twilight (Ex. 12:6), a Heb. term meaning, "between the two evenings," or between 3:00 and 5:00 p.m. After the lamb was slaughtered and some of its blood sprinkled on the altar, the lamb was taken home, roasted whole, and eaten in the evening meal with unleavened bread, bitter herbs, *charoseth* (a paste made of crushed apples, dates, pomegranates, and nuts, into which they dipped bread), and wine.

14:13 two of His disciples. Peter and John (Luke 22:8). Only two people were allowed to accompany a lamb to the sacrifice. **man...carrying a pitcher of water.** This is the only way that Jesus identified the man. But he stood out because it was uncommon for a man to carry a pitcher of water—women usually performed that chore (*see note on Matt. 26:18*).

14:14 guest room. The word is translated "inn" in Luke 2:7. It typically referred to a place where a traveler could spend the night—a place of lodging or a guest room in someone's home, as was the case here (cf. Matt. 26:18).

14:15 large upper room. This indicates the room was located upstairs, and may have been a roof chamber built on top of the house. **make ready.** Peter and John were to prepare the Passover meal for Jesus and the other disciples.

14:17 In the evening. The Passover meal was to be eaten at night after sunset, but had to be completed before midnight (Ex. 12:8-14). **with the twelve.** Peter and John may have rejoined Jesus and the other disciples and led them to the upper room. This may also be a general reference to the 12, meaning that Jesus came with the other 10 disciples to meet Peter and John.

14:18 sat and ate. The order of the Passover meal was: 1) drinking a cup of red wine mixed with water (cf. Luke 22:17); 2) the ceremonial washing of hands symbolizing the need for spiritual and moral cleansing; 3) eating the bitter herbs, symbolic of the bondage in Egypt; 4) drinking the second cup of wine, at which time the head of the household explained the meaning of Passover; 5) singing of the Hallel (Pss. 113–118)—at this point they sang the first two; 6) the lamb was brought out, and the head of the household distributed pieces of it with the unleavened bread; 7) drinking the third cup of wine (*see notes on 1 Cor. 10:16*).

to say to Him one by one, *"Is it I?"* [5]And
another *said*, *"Is it I?"*
20 He answered and said to them, *"It is*
one of the twelve, who dips with Me in the
dish. 21 [m]The Son of Man indeed goes just
as it is written of Him, but woe to that man
by whom the Son of Man is betrayed! It
would have been good for that man if he
had never been born."

The Lord's Supper Is Instituted
Matt. 26:26-29; Luke 22:17-23

22 [n]And as they were eating, Jesus took
bread, blessed and broke *it*, and gave *it* to
them and said, "Take, [6]eat; this is My
[o]body."
23 Then He took the cup, and when He
had given thanks He gave *it* to them, and
they all drank from it. 24 And He said to
them, "This is My blood of the [7]new
covenant, which is shed for many. 25 Assuredly, I say to you, I will no longer
drink of the fruit of the vine until that day
when I drink it new in the kingdom of
God."

19 [5] NU omits the rest of v. 19.
21 [m] Matt. 26:24; Luke 22:22; Acts 1:16-20
22 [n] Matt. 26:26-29; Luke 22:17-20; 1 Cor. 11:23-25 [o] [1 Pet. 2:24] [6] NU omits *eat*
24 [7] NU omits *new*
26 [p] Matt. 26:30 [8] Or *hymns*
27 [q] Matt. 26:31-35; Mark 14:50; John 16:32 [r] [Is. 53:5, 10]; Zech. 13:7 [9] NU omits *because of Me this night*
28 [s] Matt. 28:16; Mark 16:7; John 21:1
29 [t] Matt. 26:33, 34; Luke 22:33, 34; John 13:37, 38 [1] *fall away*
32 [u] Matt. 26:36-46; Luke 22:40-46; John 18:1

Jesus Predicts Peter's Denial
Matt. 26:30-35; Luke 22:31-39; John 13:36-38

26 [p]And when they had sung [8]a hymn,
they went out to the Mount of Olives.
27 [q]Then Jesus said to them, "All of you
will be made to stumble [9]because of Me
this night, for it is written:

[r]'I will strike the Shepherd,
And the sheep will be scattered.'

28 "But [s]after I have been raised, I will
go before you to Galilee."
29 [t]Peter said to Him, "Even if all are
made to [1]stumble, yet I *will* not *be*."
30 Jesus said to him, "Assuredly, I say to
you that today, *even* this night, before the
rooster crows twice, you will deny Me
three times."
31 But he spoke more vehemently, "If I
have to die with You, I will not deny You!"
And they all said likewise.

Jesus Prays in Gethsemane
Matt. 26:36-46; Luke 22:39-46

32 [u]Then they came to a place which was

14:20 dips with Me in the dish. There were likely several dishes around the table—Judas was probably one of several sitting near Jesus and thus would have dipped in the same bowl with Him.

14:21 Son of Man. *See note on 2:10.* **as it is written.** Jesus was no victim—His betrayal by Judas was prophesied in the OT (Ps. 22; Is. 53), and was part of God's predetermined plan to provide salvation (Acts 2:23). **good...if he had never been born.** Cf. John 8:21-24; 16:8-11. This is because the terror Judas would experience in hell would be so great. The severest punishment is reserved for Judas and others like him (Heb. 10:29). This is one of the strongest statements in Scripture on human responsibility for believing in Jesus Christ, coupled with the consequences of such unbelief.

14:22-25 At this point in the narrative, it appears that Judas had gone (John 13:23-30) and Jesus was alone with the faithful 11 disciples (*see note on Luke 22:21*). Then it was that He transformed the Passover of the Old Covenant into the Lord's Supper of the New Covenant, creating a new memorial feast to remember God's deliverance from sin.

14:22 as they were eating. There is no indication from any of the gospel accounts as to which part of the meal they were eating, but it is likely that this occurred just prior to eating the roasted lamb or concurrently with it. It is significant that Jesus established the truth of New Covenant while in the midst of eating the Passover. **this is My body.** Jesus gave new meaning to eating the bread. The unleavened bread symbolized the severing of the Israelites from the old life in Egypt. It represented a separation from worldliness, sin, and false religion and the beginning of a new life of holiness and godliness. From then on in the Lord's Supper, the bread would symbolize Christ's body, which He sacrificed for the salvation of men (*see note on Matt. 26:26*).

14:23 the cup. The third cup of wine in the ceremony (*see note on 1 Cor. 10:16*).

14:24 My blood of the new covenant. The shedding of blood in a sacrifice was always God's requirement in establishing any covenant (cf. Gen. 8:20; 15:10; Ex. 24:5-8). Here, Christ's blood needed to be shed for the remission of sins (Heb. 9:22; 1 Pet. 1:19; *see note on Matt. 26:28*). **for many.** This lit. means "for the benefit of many." The "many" are all who believe, both Jew and Gentile. *See note on 10:45*; cf. Matt. 20:28.

14:25 Assuredly, I say to you. *See note on 3:28.* **I will no longer drink.** Jesus declared that this would be the last Passover, and that He would not even drink wine with them again, since this was His last meal. Until the inauguration of the millennial kingdom, believers are to share this memorial meal (*see notes on 1 Cor. 11:23-34*). **drink it new.** This served as an assurance to them of Jesus' return and His establishment of His earthly, millennial kingdom. It possibly implies that the communion service will continue to be observed in the millennial kingdom, as a memorial to the cross. It more probably indicates that Jesus would not have another Passover with them until the kingdom (*see notes on Ezek. 45:18-25; 45:21-24*). It is also true that in the kingdom, commemorative sacrifices from the Old Covenant will be restored (Ezek. 43–45) which will have meaning never understood before the cross of Christ to which they pointed. **kingdom of God.** The earthly millennial kingdom is in view.

14:26 sung a hymn. Probably Ps. 118, the last psalm of the traditional Hallel sung at Passover (*see note on Matt. 26:30*). **Mount of Olives.** *See note on 11:1.*

14:27 made to stumble. *See note on 4:17; Matt. 26:31.* This can be translated, "fall away," and it refers to the disciples' temporary falling away from their loyalty to Jesus. **it is written.** Quoted from Zech. 13:7.

14:28 to Galilee. Jesus' promise to meet the disciples in His post-resurrection form (cf. 16:7; Matt. 28:16,17; *see note on Matt. 28:7*).

14:30 Assuredly, I say to you. *See note on 3:28.* **before the rooster crows twice.** In Jewish reckoning of time, "cock crow" was the third watch of the night, ending at 3:00 a.m., which was when roosters typically began to crow (*see note on 13:35*). Mark, alone of the gospels, indicates that the cock crowed two times (v. 72; *see note on Matt. 26:34*).

14:32 Gethsemane. The name means "oil press," and referred to a garden filled with olive trees on a slope of the Mt. of Olives. Jesus frequented this spot with the disciples when He wanted to get away from the crowds to pray (cf. John 18:12; *see note on Matt. 26:36*).

named Gethsemane; and He said to His
disciples, "Sit here while I pray." 33 And
He [v]took Peter, James, and John with Him,
and He began to be troubled and deeply
distressed. 34 Then He said to them, [w]"My
soul is exceedingly sorrowful, *even* to
death. Stay here and watch."
35 He went a little farther, and fell on the
ground, and prayed that if it were possible,
the hour might pass from Him. 36 And He
said, [x]"Abba, Father, [y]all things *are* possible for You. Take this cup away from Me;
[z]nevertheless, not what I will, but what
You *will*."
37 Then He came and found them sleeping, and said to Peter, "Simon, are you
sleeping? Could you not watch one hour?
38 [a]Watch and pray, lest you enter into
temptation. [b]The spirit indeed *is* willing,
but the flesh *is* weak."
39 Again He went away and prayed, and
spoke the same words. 40 And when He returned, He found them asleep again, for
their eyes were heavy; and they did not
know what to answer Him.
41 Then He came the third time and said
to them, "Are you still sleeping and resting? It is enough! [c]The hour has come; behold, the Son of Man is being betrayed into
the hands of sinners. 42 [d]Rise, let us be
going. See, My betrayer is at hand."

Judas Bretrays Jesus
Matt. 26:47-56; Luke 22:47-53; John 18:1-11

43 [e]And immediately, while He was still
speaking, Judas, one of the twelve, with a
great multitude with swords and clubs,
came from the chief priests and the scribes
and the elders. 44 Now His betrayer had
given them a signal, saying, "Whomever I
[f]kiss, He is the One; seize Him and lead
Him away safely."
45 As soon as he had come, immediately

33 [v]Mark 5:37; 9:2; 13:3
34 [w]Is. 53:3, 4; Matt. 26:38; John 12:27
36 [x]Rom. 8:15; Gal. 4:6 [y][Heb. 5:7] [z]Is. 50:5; John 5:30; 6:38
38 [a]Luke 21:36 [b][Rom. 7:18, 21-24; Gal. 5:17]
41 [c]John 13:1; 17:1
42 [d]Matt. 26:46; Mark 14:18; Luke 9:44; John 13:21; 18:1, 2
43 [e]Ps. 3:1; Matt. 26:47-56; Luke 22:47-53; John 18:3-11
44 [f][Prov. 27:6]

14:33 Peter, James, and John. *See note on 5:37.* Jesus likely had them accompany Him into the garden because they were the leaders of the 12 and had to learn an important lesson to pass on to the others (vv. 34-42). **troubled.** The Gr. word refers to a feeling of terrified amazement. In the face of the dreadful prospect of bearing God's full fury against sin, Jesus was in the grip of terror (*see note on Matt. 26:38*).

14:34 *even* to death. Jesus' sorrow was so severe that it threatened to cause His death at that moment. It is possible for a person to die from sheer anguish (cf. Luke 22:44; *see note on Matt. 26:38*).

14:35 if...possible. Jesus was not asking God if He had the power to let the cup pass from Him, but if it were possible in God's plan. Christ was to soon partake of this cup in the cross as God's only sacrifice for sin (cf. Acts 4:12). **the hour.** The time of His sacrificial death as decreed by God. It included everything from the betrayal (v. 41) to Jesus' trials, the mockery, and His crucifixion.

14:36 Abba. An endearing, intimate Aram. term that is essentially equivalent to the Eng. word "Daddy" (cf. Rom. 8:15; Gal. 4:6). **all things *are* possible.** Jesus knew that it was in the scope of God's power and omniscience to provide an alternate plan of salvation, if He desired (*see note on v. 35*). **cup.** This was the cup of divine wrath referred to in the OT (Ps. 75:8; Is. 51:17; Jer. 49:12). Christ was to endure the fury of God over sin, Satan, the power of death, and the guilt of iniquity (*see notes on Matt. 26:39; Luke 22:42; John 18:11*). **not what I will, but what You *will*.** This reveals Jesus' total resolution and resignation to do the will of God. He came into the world to do God's will, and that remained His commitment while here (*see notes on Matt. 26:39; John 6:38-40*).

14:37 Simon. Jesus' use of "Simon" may have implied that Peter was not living up to the significance and meaning of his new name, "Peter" (*see note on Matt. 16:18*). **one hour.** This suggests that Jesus had spent an hour praying, a duration in which Peter had been unable to stay awake.

14:38 Watch. This Gr. word means "to keep alert." Jesus was encouraging Peter, James, and John to discern when they were under spiritual attack. They were not to let their self-confidence lull them to sleep spiritually. **the flesh *is* weak.** Because willing spirits are still attached to unredeemed flesh, believers are not always able to practice the righteousness they desire to do (cf. Rom. 7:15-23; *see note on Matt. 26:41*).

14:41 Are you still sleeping and resting? The 3 disciples remained indifferent not only to the needs of Christ at that moment, but their need of strength and watchfulness for the impending temptation that all 11 would face. The disciples needed to learn that spiritual victory goes to those who are alert in prayer and depend on God, and that self-confidence and spiritual unpreparedness lead to spiritual disaster. **Son of Man.** *See note on 2:10.*

14:43 Judas, one of the twelve. *See notes on 3:19; Matt. 26:47.* All the gospel writers refer to him this way (vv. 10,20; Matt. 26:14,47; Luke 22:47; John 6:71); and in so doing, they display remarkable restraint in describing and evaluating Judas. Especially in this context, such a simple description actually heightens the evil of his crime more than any series of derogatory epithets or negative criticisms could do. It also points out the precise fulfillment of Jesus' announcement in vv. 18-20. **a great multitude with swords and clubs.** This "multitude" was a carefully selected group whose sole purpose was arresting Jesus so He could be put to death. A cohort (600 men at full strength) of Roman soldiers (John 18:3,12) was in this crowd because the Jewish leaders (cf. Luke 22:52) who organized the throng needed permission from Rome to carry out the death penalty and feared the crowds. The "swords" were the regular small hand weapons of the Romans, and the wood "clubs" were ordinary weapons carried by the Jewish temple police. **chief priests...scribes...elders.** Although 3 distinct sections of the Sanhedrin (as indicated by the Gr. definite article with each), they were acting in unity. These Jewish leaders had evidently for some time (*see notes on 3:6; 11:18*) hoped to accuse Jesus of rebellion against Rome. Then, His execution could be blamed on the Romans and the leaders could escape potential reprisals from those Jews who admired Jesus. The Sanhedrin likely had hurried to Pontius Pilate, the Roman governor, to ask immediate use of his soldiers; or perhaps acted on a prearranged agreement for troop use on short notice. Whatever the case, the leaders procured the assistance of the Roman military from Fort Antonia in Jerusalem.

14:44 kiss. In addition to being a special act of respect and affection, this kind of kiss was a sign of homage in Middle East culture. Out of the varieties of this kiss (on the feet, on the back of the hand, on the palm, on the hem of the garment), Judas chose the embrace and the kiss on the cheek—the one that showed the closest love and affection, normally reserved for one with whom a person had a close, intimate relationship (such as a pupil for his teacher). Judas could not have chosen a more despicable way to identify Jesus, because he perverted its usual meaning so treacherously and hypocritically.

he went up to Him and said to Him,
"Rabbi, Rabbi!" and kissed Him.
46 Then they laid their hands on Him and
took Him. 47 And one of those who stood
by drew his sword and struck the servant
of the high priest, and cut off his ear.
48 [g]Then Jesus answered and said to
them, "Have you come out, as against a
robber, with swords and clubs to take Me?
49 I was daily with you in the temple
[h]teaching, and you did not seize Me. But
[i]the Scriptures must be fulfilled."
50 [j]Then they all forsook Him and fled.
51 Now a certain young man followed
Him, having a linen cloth thrown around
his naked *body.* And the young men laid
hold of him, 52 and he left the linen cloth
and fled from them naked.

The Sanhedrin Tries Jesus

Matt. 26:57-68; Luke 22:54, 55, 63-65; John 18:12, 18, 24

53 [k]And they led Jesus away to the high
priest; and with him were [l]assembled all
the [m]chief priests, the elders, and the
scribes. 54 But [n]Peter followed Him at a
distance, right into the courtyard of the
high priest. And he sat with the servants
and warmed himself at the fire.
55 [o]Now the chief priests and all the
council sought testimony against Jesus to
put Him to death, but found none. 56 For
many bore [p]false witness against Him, but
their testimonies [2]did not agree.
57 Then some rose up and bore false witness against Him, saying, 58 "We heard
Him say, [q]'I will destroy this temple made
with hands, and within three days I will
build another made without hands.' "
59 But not even then did their testimony
agree.
60 [r]And the high priest stood up in the
midst and asked Jesus, saying, "Do You
answer nothing? What *is it* these men testify against You?" 61 But [s]He kept silent and
answered nothing.

48 [g] Matt. 26:55; Luke 22:52
49 [h] Matt. 21:23 [i] Ps. 22:6; Is. 53:7; Luke 22:37; 24:44
50 [j] Ps. 88:8; Zech. 13:7; Matt. 26:31; Mark 14:27
53 [k] Matt. 26:57-68; Mark 10:33; Luke 22:54; John 18:12, 13, 19-24
[l] Mark 15:1 [m] Matt. 16:21; 27:12; Luke 9:22; 23:23; John 7:32; 18:3; 19:6
54 [n] John 18:15
55 [o] Matt. 26:59
56 [p] Ex. 20:16; Ps. 27:12; 35:11; Prov. 6:16-19; 19:5 [2] *were not consistent*
58 [q] Matt. 26:61; Mark 15:29; John 2:19; [2 Cor. 5:1]
60 [r] Matt. 26:62; Mark 15:3-5
61 [s] Is. 53:7; John 19:9; Acts 8:32; [1 Pet. 2:23]

14:45 Rabbi. "My master" (*see note on 9:5*). **kissed Him.** "Kissed" is an intensified form of the verb for "kiss" in v. 44, and it denotes a fervent, continuous expression of affection (cf. Luke 7:38,45; 15:20; Acts 20:37). It was with intensity that Judas pretended to love Christ. The act was likely prolonged enough so the crowd had time to identify Jesus.

14:47 one of those who stood by. Simon Peter (John 18:10), one of the two disciples who brought a weapon (Luke 22:38). Mark and the other synoptic writers do not identify Peter explicitly, perhaps because they wrote earlier than John, during the time when Peter would still have been in danger of Jewish revenge. **the servant of the high priest.** Malchus (John 18:10). He was neither a soldier nor temple policeman, but rather was a high-ranking personal slave of Caiaphas, the High-Priest, probably sent along to observe Judas and report on the events of the evening.

14:48 as against a robber. Jesus expressed a righteous resentment toward the crowd's actions and attitudes. "Robber" was normally a highwayman or armed bandit who would resist arrest. The setting which the crowd orchestrated was completely inconsistent with His well known ministry as a religious teacher.

14:49 temple. *See note on 11:11.* This was the most public place in Jerusalem. **the Scriptures must be fulfilled.** Entirely apart from the crowd's sinful intentions against Jesus, God was sovereignly using it to fulfill prophecy (cf. Is. 53:7-9,12) and accomplish His gracious purposes (*see note on Matt. 26:54*).

14:50 forsook Him. The disciples found no comfort in Jesus' reference to Scripture, but instead their faith in Him collapsed as they realized He would not resist arrest and that they also might be captured.

14:51 certain young man. This perhaps was Mark himself. If the mob under Judas' guidance had first gone to Mark's mother's house in search of Jesus—possibly where the last Passover was observed by Jesus and the 12—Mark could have heard the noise, suspected what was happening, and hurried to follow the multitude. **a linen cloth.** Either a loose-fitting linen sleeping garment or a sheet Mark had hastily wrapped around himself after being roused from bed.

14:52 fled...naked. Mark escaped capture and ran, but in so doing his covering came off or was pulled off, and he left with nothing at all on, or nothing more than undergarments.

14:53–15:15 Mark's account of Jesus' trials, like that of all the gospels, makes it clear that Christ was tried in two general phases: first, before the religious authorities (the Jewish Sanhedrin), and second, before the secular political authorities (Rome, represented by governor Pontius Pilate). Each of these phases had 3 parts: preliminary interrogation, formal arraignment, and formal sentencing. Mark, like the other gospel writers, did not include a comprehensive account of all the details and stages. A complete picture requires the material from all 4 gospels being combined.

14:53 high priest. Caiaphas, the leader of the Sanhedrin (*see notes on Matt. 26:3,57*; cf. John 18:24). He was the official High-Priest in A.D. 18–36. **all the chief priests, the elders, and the scribes.** *See note on v. 43.* The entire Sanhedrin, the whole hierarchy, was out in force.

14:54 courtyard of the high priest. A quadrangle in the center of the High-Priest's residence.

14:55 council. The Sanhedrin (*see note on Matt. 26:59*).

14:56 Because Jesus was innocent, the Jewish leaders could not convict Him except by relying on perjured testimony and perverted justice. The Jews were intent on doing whatever was necessary, even if they had to violate every biblical and rabbinical rule. **many bore false witness against Him.** There was no lack of people to come forward at the Sanhedrin's invitation to consciously present false, lying testimony. **did not agree.** The testimonies were grossly inconsistent. The law, however, required exact agreement between two witnesses (Deut. 17:6; 19:15).

14:57,58 false witness. The witnesses maliciously garbled and misrepresented Jesus' statements. Quite possibly they blended His figurative statement regarding His death and resurrection in John 2:19-22 with His prediction of a literal destruction of the temple in 13:2. Their charge claimed He was disloyal to the present order of religion and worship (by replacing the current temple), and that He was blaspheming God (by saying He would so quickly rebuild the temple without hands).

14:58 I will destroy this temple made with hands. This refers to the material sanctuary in Jerusalem. Jesus boldly made this assertion in front of the temple the Jews revered, but His words were not fully understood (*see previous note and notes on John 2:19,20*).

14:60 Caiaphas attempted to salvage the tense situation when the continued false charges were failing to establish a case or elicit a response from the Lord. The High-Priest could not understand how Jesus could remain silent and not offer any defense.

14:61 kept silent. The silence of innocence, integrity, and faith in

[t]Again the high priest asked Him, saying to Him, "Are You the Christ, the Son of
the Blessed?"
62 Jesus said, "I am. [u]And you will see
the Son of Man sitting at the right hand of
the Power, and coming with the clouds of
heaven."
63 Then the high priest tore his clothes
and said, "What further need do we have
of witnesses? **64** You have heard the [v]blas-
phemy! What do you think?"
And they all condemned Him to be deserving of [w]death.
65 Then some began to [x]spit on Him,
and to blindfold Him, and to beat Him,
and to say to Him, "Prophesy!" And the officers [3]struck Him with the palms of their
hands.

Peter Denies Jesus
Matt. 26:69-75; Luke 22:55-62;
John 18:15-18, 25-27

66 [y]Now as Peter was below in the courtyard, one of the servant girls of the high
priest came. **67** And when she saw Peter
warming himself, she looked at him and
said, "You also were with [z]Jesus of Nazareth."
68 But he denied it, saying, "I neither
know nor understand what you are saying." And he went out on the porch, and a
rooster crowed.
69 [a]And the servant girl saw him again,
and began to say to those who stood by,
"This is one of them." **70** But he denied it
again.
[b]And a little later those who stood by
said to Peter again, "Surely you are *one* of
them; [c]for you are a Galilean, [4]and your
[5]speech shows *it*."
71 Then he began to curse and swear, "I
do not know this Man of whom you speak!"
72 [d]A second time *the* rooster crowed.
Then Peter called to mind the word that Jesus had said to him, "Before the rooster
crows twice, you will deny Me three
times." And when he thought about it, he
wept.

Pilate Tries Jesus
Matt. 27:1, 2, 11-23; Luke 23:1-5, 13-23;
John 18:28–19:15

15 Immediately, [a]in the morning, the
chief priests held a consultation
with the elders and scribes and the whole
council; and they bound Jesus, led *Him*

61 [t]Matt. 26:63; Luke 22:67-71
62 [u]Matt. 24:30; 26:64; Luke 22:69
64 [v]John 10:33, 36 [w]Matt. 20:18; Mark 10:33; John 19:7
65 [x]Job 16:10; Is. 50:6; 52:14; Lam. 3:30; Mark 10:34; Luke 18:32 [3]NU *received Him with slaps*
66 [y]Matt. 26:58, 69-75; Luke 22:55-62; John 18:16-18, 25-27
67 [z]Mark 10:47; John 1:45; Acts 10:38
69 [a]Matt. 26:71; Luke 22:58; John 18:25
70 [b]Matt. 26:73; Luke 22:59; John 18:26 [c]Acts 2:7 [4]NU omits the rest of v. 70. [5]*accent*
72 [d]Matt. 26:75; Mark 14:30; Luke 22:34; John 13:38

CHAPTER 15
1 [a]Ps. 2:2; Matt. 27:1; Luke 22:66; 23:1; John 18:28; Acts 3:13; 4:26

God. An answer by Jesus would have given all the false testimonies and illegal proceedings an appearance of legitimacy. **Christ.** This term refers to Jesus' claim to be the promised Messiah (*see note on Matt. 1:1*). **Son of the Blessed.** This refers to Jesus claim to deity. This is the only NT use of the expression, and it is an example of Jewish wording that avoided using God's name (*see note on John 8:58*). Jesus' acceptance of messiahship and deity (cf. Luke 4:18-21; John 4:25,26; 5:17,18; 8:58) had always brought vigorous opposition from the Jewish leaders (John 5:19-47; 8:16-19; 10:29-39). Clearly, the High-Priest was asking this question in hopes that Jesus would affirm it and open Himself to the formal charge of blasphemy.

14:62 I am. An explicit, unambiguous declaration that Jesus was and is both the Messiah and the Son of God. **Son of Man.** *See notes on 2:10; Matt. 8:20.* Jesus used this commonly acknowledged messianic title of Himself more than 80 times in the gospels, here in a reference to Ps. 110:1 and Dan. 7:13 (cf. Rev. 1:13; 14:14). **right hand of the Power.** Cf. 10:37; Acts 2:33; 7:55; Heb. 2:9; Rev. 12:5. Jesus' glorified position is next to the throne of God (the "Power" is another reference to God). **clouds.** *See note on 13:26*; cf. Matt. 24:30; 26:64; Luke 21:27; Acts 1:9-11; Rev. 1:7; 14:14.

14:63 tore his clothes. A ceremonial, and in this case contrived, display of grief and indignation over the presumed dishonoring of God's name by Jesus (cf. Gen 37:29; Lev. 10:6; Job 1:20; Acts 14:13,19: *see note on Matt. 26:65*). **further need…of witnesses.** A rhetorical question that expressed relief that the tense and embarrassing situation was finally over. Because Jesus had allegedly incriminated Himself in the eyes of the Sanhedrin, they would not need to summon any more lying witnesses.

14:64 blasphemy. *See note on 2:7*; cf. 3:29. Strictly speaking, Jesus' words were not "blasphemy," or defiant irreverence of God (Lev. 24:10-23), but Caiaphas regarded them as such because Jesus claimed for Himself equal power and prerogative with God.

14:65 spit on Him…beat Him. For the Jews, to "spit" in another's face was the grossest, most hateful form of personal insult (cf. Num. 12:14; Deut. 25:9). Their brutal cruelty reached a climax and revealed the great depravity of their hearts when they "beat Him," or hit Him with clenched fists. **"Prophesy!"** They jeeringly and disrespectfully ordered Jesus to use the prophetic powers He claimed to have—even in the frivolous manner of telling them who struck Him (Matt. 26:68).

14:66 below. The apartments around it were higher than the courtyard itself. **one of the servant girls.** Female slave, or maid, in the household of the High-Priest. She might have been the same gate keeper (cf. John 18:15,16) who admitted Peter, and who being curious and suspicious of him, wanted a closer look.

14:67 of Nazareth. Their reference to Jesus' hometown communicates a feeling of contempt, in keeping with the views of the Jewish leaders and the poor reputation Nazareth generally had (cf. John 1:46).

14:68 the porch. Used only here in the NT, this term denotes "the forecourt," or "entryway," a covered archway of the courtyard, opening onto the street. **a rooster crowed.** This reference brings to mind Jesus' prediction in v. 30 (*see note there*) and Matt. 26:34. Amid all the accusations being hurled at him, Peter either did not hear the rooster's crowing, or failed to realize its significance. When the rooster crowed the second time, Jesus looked at Peter (Luke 22:61), triggering Peter's memory and bringing conviction of his denials (cf. v. 72).

14:70 Galilean. Frequently used as a derisive label by people in Jerusalem toward their northern neighbors. It strongly suggested that natives of Galilee were deemed unsophisticated and uneducated (cf. Acts 4:13).

15:1 Immediately, in the morning. At daybreak, probably between 5:00 and 6:00 a.m. Having illegally decided Jesus' guilt during the night (14:53-65; John 18:13-24), the Sanhedrin formally convened after daybreak to pronounce a sentence. **chief priests.** *See note on Matt. 2:4.* **a consultation.** This meeting is described in Luke 22:66-71. It amounted to little more than reiterating the charges earlier made against Jesus and affirming His guilty verdict. **elders and scribes.** *See notes on 14:43, Matt. 2:4.* **the whole council.** The entire

away, and [b]delivered *Him* to Pilate. 2 [c]Then
Pilate asked Him, "Are You the King of the
Jews?"
He answered and said to him, "*It is as*
you say."
3 And the chief priests accused Him of
many things, but He [d]answered nothing.
4 [e]Then Pilate asked Him again, saying,
"Do You answer nothing? See how many
things [1]they testify against You!" 5 [f]But Jesus still answered nothing, so that Pilate
marveled.
6 Now [g]at the feast he was accustomed
to releasing one prisoner to them, whomever they requested. 7 And there was one
named Barabbas, *who was* chained with his
fellow rebels; they had committed murder
in the rebellion. 8 Then the multitude, [2]cry-
ing aloud, began to ask *him to do* just as he
had always done for them. 9 But Pilate answered them, saying, "Do you want me to
release to you the King of the Jews?" 10 For
he knew that the chief priests had handed
Him over because of envy.
11 But [h]the chief priests stirred up the
crowd, so that he should rather release
Barabbas to them. 12 Pilate answered and
said to them again, "What then do you
want me to do *with Him* whom you call the
[i]King of the Jews?"
13 So they cried out again, "Crucify
Him!"
14 Then Pilate said to them, "Why, [j]what
evil has He done?"
But they cried out all the more, "Crucify
Him!"

Jesus Is Beaten

Matt. 27:26-34; Luke 23:24-32; John 19:16-22

15 [k]So Pilate, wanting to gratify the
crowd, released Barabbas to them; and he
delivered Jesus, after he had scourged
Him, to be [l]crucified.
16 [m]Then the soldiers led Him away into
the hall called [3]Praetorium, and they called
together the whole garrison. 17 And they
clothed Him with purple; and they twisted a
crown of thorns, put it on His *head*, 18 and
began to salute Him, "Hail, King of the
Jews!" 19 Then they [n]struck Him on the
head with a reed and spat on Him; and bowing the knee, they worshiped Him. 20 And
when they had [o]mocked Him, they took the
purple off Him, put His own clothes on
Him, and led Him out to crucify Him.
21 [p]Then they compelled a certain man,
Simon a Cyrenian, the father of Alexander

1 [b] Luke 18:32; Acts 3:13
2 [c] Matt. 27:11-14; Luke 23:2, 3; John 18:29-38
3 [d] Is. 53:7; John 19:9; Acts 8:32
4 [e] Matt. 27:13 [1] NU *of which they accuse You*
5 [f] Ps. 38:13, 14; Is. 53:7; John 19:9
6 [g] Matt. 27:15-26; Luke 23:18-25; John 18:39–19:16
8 [2] NU *going up*
11 [h] Matt. 27:20; Acts 3:14
12 [i] Ps. 2:6; [Is. 9:7]; Jer. 23:5; 33:15; Mic. 5:2
14 [j] Is. 53:9; John 8:46; 1 Pet. 2:21-23
15 [k] Is. 50:6; Matt. 27:26; Mark 10:34; John 19:1, 16 [l] [Is. 53:8]
16 [m] Matt. 27:27-31 [3] The governor's headquarters
19 [n] [Is. 50:6; 52:14; 53:5]; Mic. 5:1; Mark 14:65
20 [o] Ps. 35:16; 69:19; Is. 53:3; Matt. 20:19; Mark 10:34; Luke 22:63; 23:11
21 [p] Matt. 27:32; Luke 23:26

Sanhedrin (*see notes on 14:43,53; Matt. 26:59*). **Pilate.** Roman procurator (governor) of Judea from A.D. 26–36. His official residence was at Caesarea, but he was in Jerusalem for Passover.

15:2 Pilate asked. John records (John 18:30) that the Jewish leaders demanded that Pilate simply agree to the death sentence they had already pronounced on Jesus (14:64). Pilate refused, and the Jewish leaders then presented their false charges against Jesus (Luke 23:2). Having heard those charges, Pilate then questioned Him. **"Are You the King of the Jews?"** The only charge Pilate took seriously was that Jesus claimed to be a king, thus making Him guilty of rebellion against Rome. Pilate's question reveals that he had already been informed of this charge (Luke 23:2). ***"It is as* you say."** Jesus' answer acknowledged that He was the rightful king of Israel, but implied that Pilate's concept of what that meant differed from His (cf. John 18:34-37).

15:3 many things. Cf. Luke 23:2,5.

15:4 "Do You answer nothing?" Pilate was amazed at Jesus' silence, since accused prisoners predictably and vehemently denied the charges against them. Jesus may have remained silent in fulfillment of prophecy (Is. 42:1,2; 53:7), because Pilate had already pronounced him innocent (Luke 23:4; John 18:38), or both.

15:6 at the feast. The Passover. **accustomed to.** Ancient secular sources indicate that Roman governors occasionally granted amnesty at the request of their subjects. Assuming that the people would ask for their king (whom they had so acknowledged earlier in the week; 11:1-10) to be freed, Pilate undoubtedly saw this annual custom as the way out of his dilemma regarding Jesus.

15:7 Barabbas. A robber (John 18:40) and murderer (Luke 23:18,19) in some way involved as an anti-Roman insurrectionist. Whether his involvement was motivated by political conviction or personal greed is not known. It is impossible to identify the specific insurrection in question, but such uprisings were common in Jesus' day and were precursors of the wholesale revolt of A.D. 66–70.

15:10 because of envy. Pilate realized that the Jewish authorities had not handed Jesus over to him out of loyalty to Rome. He saw through their deceit to the underlying reason—their jealousy over Jesus' popularity with the people.

15:13 Crucify. *See note on v. 15.*

15:15 scourged. With a whip (known as a *flagellum*) consisting of a wooden handle to which metal-tipped leather thongs were attached. Being scourged with a *flagellum* was a fearful ordeal, ripping the flesh down to the bone, causing severe bleeding. It was a beating from which prisoners often died. **crucified.** *See note on Matt. 27:31.* Crucifixion, the common Roman method of execution for slaves and foreigners, was described by the Roman writer Cicero as "the cruelest and most hideous punishment possible."

15:16 Praetorium. The governor's official residence in Jerusalem, probably located in the Fortress Antonia complex. **whole garrison.** The Roman cohort, consisting of 600 men, was stationed in Jerusalem. All the soldiers who were not on duty at that time gathered to mock Jesus.

15:17 clothed Him with purple...crown of thorns. "Purple" was the color traditionally worn by royalty; the "crown of thorns" was in mockery of a royal crown. The callous soldiers decided to hold a mock coronation of Jesus as king of the Jews.

15:18 "Hail, King of the Jews!" The greeting was a parody of that given to Caesar.

15:19 a reed. An imitation of a royal scepter.

15:21 Condemned prisoners were required to carry the heavy crossbeam of their cross to the execution site. Exhausted from a sleepless night and severely wounded and weakened by His scourging, Jesus was unable to continue. The Roman guards conscripted, Simon, apparently at random, to carry Jesus' crossbeam the rest of the way. Simon, from the North African city of Cyrene, was on his way into Jerusalem. The identification of him as "the father of Alexander and Rufus" (cf. Rom. 16:13) is evidence of Mark's connection with the church at Rome (see Introduction: Background and Setting).

and Rufus, as he was coming out of the
country and passing by, to bear His cross.
22 [q]And they brought Him to the place
Golgotha, which is translated, Place of a
Skull. 23 [r]Then they gave Him wine mingled with myrrh to drink, but He did not
take *it*.

Jesus Is Crucified

Matt. 27:35-56; Luke 23:33-49; John 19:18, 23-30

24 And when they crucified Him, [s]they
divided His garments, casting lots for
them to determine what every man should
take.
25 Now [t]it was the third hour, and they
crucified Him. 26 And [u]the inscription of
His [4]accusation was written above:

THE KING OF THE JEWS.

27 [v]With Him they also crucified two robbers, one on His right and the other on His
left. 28 [5]So the Scripture was fulfilled
which says, [w]*"And He was numbered
with the transgressors."*
29 And [x]those who passed by blasphemed Him, [y]wagging their heads and
saying, "Aha! [z]*You* who destroy the temple
and build *it* in three days, 30 save Yourself,
and come down from the cross!"
31 Likewise the chief priests also, [a]mock-
ing among themselves with the scribes,
said, "He saved [b]others; Himself He cannot save. 32 Let the Christ, the King of Israel, descend now from the cross, that we
may see and [6]believe."
Even [c]those who were crucified with
Him reviled Him.
33 Now [d]when the sixth hour had come,
there was darkness over the whole land
until the ninth hour. 34 And at the ninth
hour Jesus cried out with a loud voice, saying, "Eloi, Eloi, lama sabachthani?" which
is translated, [e]*"My God, My God, why
have You forsaken Me?"*
35 Some of those who stood by, when
they heard *that*, said, "Look, He is calling
for Elijah!" 36 Then [f]someone ran and filled
a sponge full of sour wine, put *it* on a reed,
and [g]offered *it* to Him to drink, saying,
"Let Him alone; let us see if Elijah will
come to take Him down."

22 [q] Matt. 27:33-44; Luke 23:33-43; John 19:17-24; Heb. 13:12
23 [r] Ps. 69:21; Matt. 27:34
24 [s] Ps. 22:18; Luke 23:34; John 19:23
25 [t] Matt. 27:45; Luke 23:44; John 19:14
26 [u] Matt. 27:37; John 19:19 [4] *crime*
27 [v] Is. 53:9, 12; Matt. 27:38; Luke 22:37
28 [w] Is. 53:12; Luke 22:37 [5] NU omits v. 28.
29 [x] Ps. 22:6, 7; 69:7
[y] Ps. 109:25 [z] Mark 14:58; John 2:19-21
31 [a] Luke 18:32 [b] Luke 7:14, 15; John 11:43, 44
32 [c] Amos 8:9; Matt. 27:44; Luke 23:39 [6] M *believe Him*
33 [d] Matt. 27:45-56; Luke 23:44-49
34 [e] Ps. 22:1; Matt. 27:46
36 [f] Matt. 27:48; John 19:29 [g] Ps. 69:21

15:22 Golgotha…Place of a Skull. "Golgotha" is an Aram. word meaning "skull," which Mark translated for his readers (see Introduction: Background and Setting). Although the exact site is unknown, today two locations in Jerusalem are considered as possibilities: 1) Gordon's Calvary (named for the man who discovered it in modern times) to the N; and 2) the traditional site to the W at the Church of the Holy Sepulchre, a tradition dating to the fourth century.

15:23 wine mingled with myrrh. To temporarily deaden the pain (*see note on Matt. 27:34*), the Romans allowed this drink to be administered to victims of crucifixion, probably not out of compassion, but to keep them from struggling while being crucified.

15:24 crucified. *See note on v. 15.* None of the gospel accounts give a detailed description of the actual crucifixion process. **divided His garments.** This was in fulfillment of Ps. 22:18. The executioners customarily divided the victim's clothes among themselves.

15:25 third hour. The crucifixion occurred at 9:00 a.m. based on the Jewish method of reckoning time. John notes that it was "about the sixth hour" when Pilate sentenced Jesus to be crucified (John 19:14). John apparently used the Roman method of reckoning time, which counted the hours from midnight. Thus John's "sixth hour" would have been about 6:00 a.m.

15:26 inscription of His accusation. The crime for which a condemned man was executed was written on a wooden board, which was fastened to the cross above his head. Jesus' inscription was written in Aram., Heb., and Gr.(John 19:20). *See note on Matt. 27:37.* **THE KING OF THE JEWS.** Since Pilate had repeatedly declared Jesus to be innocent of any crime (Luke 23:4,14,15,22), he ordered this inscription written for Him. Whether Pilate's intent was probably neither to mock or honor Jesus, he certainly intended it as an affront to the Jewish authorities, who had given him so much trouble. When the outraged Jewish leaders demanded the wording be changed, Pilate bluntly refused (*see note on John 19:22*). A comparison of all 4 gospel accounts reveals that the full inscription read THIS IS JESUS OF NAZARETH, THE KING OF THE JEWS. *See note on Luke 23:38.*

15:27 two robbers. They were probably involved with Barabbas in the rebellion (*see note on v. 7*), since robbery itself was not a capital offense under Roman law.

15:28 By placing Jesus' cross between the two robbers (v. 27), Pilate may have intended to further insult the Jews, implying that their king was nothing but a common criminal. God intended it, however, as a fulfillment of prophecy (cf. Is. 53:12).

15:29 wagging their heads. A gesture of contempt and derision (cf. 2 Kin. 19:21; Pss. 22:7; 44:14; 109:25; Jer. 18:16; Lam. 2:15). ***You* who destroy the temple and build *it* in three days.** The passersby repeated the false charge made during Jesus' trial before Caiaphas (14:58). The charge was a misunderstanding of Jesus' words in John 2:19-21.

15:32 Christ. *See note on 1:1.* **descend…from the cross.** A final demand for a miracle by the unbelieving Jewish authorities (cf. 8:11). Their claim that they would then see and believe was false, since they later refused to believe the even greater miracle of Christ's resurrection. **those who were crucified with Him.** The two robbers joined in the reviling of Jesus, though one later repented (Luke 23:40-43).

15:33 sixth hour. Noon, by Jewish reckoning, at the half-way point of Jesus' 6 hours on the cross (*see note on v. 25*). **darkness.** A mark of divine judgment (cf. Is. 5:30; 13:10,11; Joel 2:1,2; Amos 5:20; Zeph. 1:14,15; Matt. 8:12; 22:13; 25:30). The geographical extent of the darkness is not known, although the writings of the church fathers hint that it extended beyond Palestine. **ninth hour.** I.e., 3:00 p.m.

15:34 Eloi…sabachthani. The Aram. words of Ps. 22:1. Matthew, who also recorded this cry, gave the Heb. words (Matt. 27:46). ***why have You forsaken Me?*** Jesus felt keenly His abandonment by the Father, resulting from God's wrath being poured out on Him as the substitute for sinners (*see notes on 2 Cor. 5:21*).

15:35 Elijah. Further mockery which in effect meant, "Let the forerunner come and save this so-called Messiah" (*see note on Luke 1:17*).

15:36 sour wine. Cheap wine commonly consumed by soldiers and workers. It may have been an act of mercy, or merely intended to prolong His suffering. **a reed.** A hyssop branch (John 18:29).

37 [h]And Jesus cried out with a loud
voice, and breathed His last.
38 Then [i]the veil of the temple was torn
in two from top to bottom. 39 So [j]when the
centurion, who stood opposite Him, saw
that [7]He cried out like this and breathed
His last, he said, "Truly this Man was the
Son of God!"
40 [k]There were also women looking on
[l]from afar, among whom were Mary
Magdalene, Mary the mother of James the
Less and of Joses, and Salome, 41 who also
[m]followed Him and ministered to Him
when He was in Galilee, and many other
women who came up with Him to Jerusalem.

Jesus Is Buried
Matt. 27:57-61; Luke 23:50-55; John 19:38-42

42 [n]Now when evening had come, because it was the Preparation Day, that is,
the day before the Sabbath, 43 Joseph of Arimathea, a prominent council member,
who [o]was himself waiting for the kingdom
of God, coming and taking courage, went
in to Pilate and asked for the body of Jesus.
44 Pilate marveled that He was already
dead; and summoning the centurion, he
asked him if He had been dead for some
time. 45 So when he found out from the
centurion, he granted the body to Joseph.
46 [p]Then he bought fine linen, took Him
down, and wrapped Him in the linen. And
he laid Him in a tomb which had been
hewn out of the rock, and rolled a stone
against the door of the tomb. 47 And Mary
Magdalene and Mary *the mother* of Joses
observed where He was laid.

The Resurrection of Jesus
Matt. 28:1-8; Luke 24:1-9

16 Now [a]when the Sabbath was past,
Mary Magdalene, Mary *the mother*
of James, and Salome [b]bought spices, that
they might come and anoint Him. 2 [c]Very
early in the morning, on the first *day* of the

37 [h] Dan. 9:26; Zech. 11:10, 11; Matt. 27:50; Mark 8:31; Luke 23:46; John 19:30
38 [i] Ex. 26:31-33; Matt. 27:51; Luke 23:45
39 [j] Matt. 27:54; Luke 23:47 [7] NU *He thus breathed His last*
40 [k] Matt. 27:55; Luke 23:49; John 19:25 [l] Ps. 38:11
41 [m] Luke 8:2, 3
42 [n] Matt. 27:57-61; Luke 23:50-56; John 19:38-42
43 [o] Matt. 27:57; Luke 2:25, 38; 23:51; John 19:38
46 [p] Is. 53:9; Matt. 27:59, 60; Luke 23:53; John 19:40

CHAPTER 16

1 [a] Matt. 28:1-8; Luke 24:1-10; John 20:1-8 [b] Luke 23:56; John 19:39
2 [c] Luke 24:1; John 20:1

15:37 cried out with a loud voice. Demonstrating amazing strength in light of the intense suffering He had endured, His shout reveals that His life did not slowly ebb away, but that He voluntarily gave it up (John 10:17,18). For the words of Christ's cry, see Luke 23:46.

15:38 the veil of the temple was torn in two. The massive curtain separating the Holy of Holies from the rest of the sanctuary (Ex. 26:31-33; 40:20,21; Lev. 16:2; Heb. 9:3). Its rending signified that the way into God's presence was open by the death of His Son.

15:39 centurion. The Roman officer in charge of the crucifixion. Centurions, considered the backbone of the Roman army, commanded 100 soldiers. **saw that He cried out like this.** The centurion had seen many crucified victims die, but none like Jesus. The strength He possessed at His death, as evidenced by His loud cry (v. 37), was unheard of for a victim of crucifixion. That, coupled with the earthquake that coincided with Christ's death (Matt. 27:51-54) convinced the centurion that Jesus "truly…was the Son of God." According to tradition, this man actually became a believer (*see note on Matt. 27:54*).

15:40 Some of these women had earlier been at the foot of the cross (John 19:25-27). By then, unable to watch Jesus' suffering at such close range, they were "looking on from afar." Their sympathetic loyalty was in sharp contrast to the disciples who, except for John, were nowhere to be found. **Mary Magdalene.** She was from the village of Magdala, on the W shore of the Sea of Galilee, hence her name. Luke notes that Jesus had cast 7 demons out of her (Luke 8:2). She is usually named first when the women who followed Jesus are listed, which may suggest that she was their leader. **Mary the mother of James the Less and of Joses.** She is distinguished from the other Marys by the name of her sons. "James the Less," (called "James the son of Alphaeus" in Matt. 10:2) was one of the 12. **Salome.** The wife of Zebedee (Matt. 27:56), and the mother of James and John (*see note on 10:35*).

15:41 many other women. They had been with Jesus since the days of His Galilean ministry, traveling with Him and the disciples, caring for their needs (cf. Luke 8:2,3).

15:42 Preparation Day. Friday, the day before the Sabbath (Saturday).

15:43 Joseph of Arimathea. "Arimathea," known in the OT as Ramah, or Ramathaim-zophim (the birthplace of Samuel, 1 Sam. 1:1,19; 2:11), was located about 15 mi. NW of Jerusalem. Joseph was a prominent member of the "council" (or the Sanhedrin, *see note on 14:43*), who had opposed Jesus' condemnation (Luke 23:51). **kingdom of God.** *See note on 1:15.* **coming and taking courage.** Pilate would not likely have been pleased to see a member of the Sanhedrin, after that group had forced him to crucify an innocent man. Further, Joseph's public identification with Jesus would enrage the other members of the Sanhedrin. **asked for the body of Jesus.** Though prisoners sentenced to death forfeited the right to burial under Roman law, their bodies were usually granted to relatives who asked for them, but Jesus' mother was emotionally exhausted from the ordeal. There is no evidence that His brothers and sisters were in Jerusalem, and His closest friends, the disciples, had fled (except for John, who had Mary to take care of; John 19:26,27). In the absence of those closest to Jesus, Joseph courageously asked Pilate for Jesus' body.

15:44 Pilate marveled. Victims of crucifixion often lingered for days, hence Pilate's surprise that Jesus was dead after only 6 hours. Before granting Jesus' body to Joseph, Pilate checked with the "centurion" in charge of the crucifixion (*see note on v. 39*) to verify that Jesus was really dead.

15:45 he granted the body to Joseph. Having received confirmation from the centurion that Jesus was dead, Pilate granted Jesus' body to Joseph. By that act, the Romans officially pronounced Jesus dead.

15:46 wrapped Him in the linen. The Jews did not embalm corpses, but wrapped them in perfumed burial cloths (*see note on 16:1*). Nicodemus, another prominent member of the Sanhedrin (cf. John 7:50), assisted Joseph in caring for the body of Jesus (John 19:39,40). These men, who had kept their allegiance to Jesus secret during His lifetime, then came forward publicly to bury Him, while the disciples, who had openly followed Jesus, hid (John 20:19). **tomb…hewn out of the rock.** This "tomb" was located near Golgotha (John 19:42). Matthew adds that it was Joseph's own (Matt. 27:60), while Luke and John note that no one as yet had been buried in it (Luke 23:53; John 19:41).

16:1 Sabbath was past. The Sabbath officially ended at sundown on Saturday, after which the women were able to purchase spices. **Mary Magdalene, Mary *the mother* of James, and Salome.** *See note on Matt. 27:56.* John adds that Mary the mother of Jesus was there (John 19:26), and Luke mentions that Joanna and other women were also there (Luke 24:10; cf. 15:41). **spices.** The women bought more spices in addition to those prepared earlier (cf. Luke 23:56; John 19:39,40). **anoint.** Unlike the Egyptians, the Jewish

week, they came to the tomb when the sun
had risen. 3 And they said among themselves, "Who will roll away the stone from
the door of the tomb for us?" 4 But when
they looked up, they saw that the stone
had been rolled away—for it was very
large. 5 [d]And entering the tomb, they saw
a young man clothed in a long white robe
sitting on the right side; and they were
alarmed.
6 [e]But he said to them, "Do not be
alarmed. You seek Jesus of Nazareth, who
was crucified. He is risen! He is not here.
See the place where they laid Him. 7 But
go, tell His disciples—and Peter—that He
is going [1]before you into Galilee; there you
will see Him, [f]as He said to you."
8 So they went out [2]quickly and fled
from the tomb, for they trembled and were
amazed. [g]And they said nothing to anyone, for they were afraid.

The Appearances of Jesus
Luke 24:13-48; John 20:1-10

9 [3]Now when *He* rose early on the first
day of the week, He appeared first to Mary
Magdalene, [h]out of whom He had cast
seven demons. 10 [i]She went and told those
who had been with Him, as they mourned
and wept. 11 [j]And when they heard that
He was alive and had been seen by her,
they did not believe.
12 After that, He appeared in another
form [k]to two of them as they walked and
went into the country. 13 And they went
and told *it* to the rest, *but* they did not believe them either.
14 [l]Later He appeared to the eleven as

5 [d]Luke 24:3; John 20:11,12
6 [e]Ps. 16:10; 49:15; Hos. 6:2; Matt. 28:6; Mark 9:31; Luke 24:6
7 [f]Matt. 26:32; 28:16, 17; Mark 14:28
[1]*ahead of*
8 [g]Matt. 28:8 [2]NU, M omit *quickly*
9 [h]Luke 8:2 [3]Vv. 9-20 are bracketed in NU as not in the original text. They are lacking in Codex Sinaiticus and Codex Vaticanus, although nearly all other mss. of Mark contain them.
10 [i]Luke 24:10
11 [j]Matt. 28:17; Luke 24:11,41; John 20:25
12 [k]Luke 24:13-35
14 [l]Luke 24:36; John 20:19,26; 1 Cor. 15:5

people did not embalm their dead. Anointing was an act of love, to offset the stench of a decaying body. That the women came to anoint Jesus' body on the third day after His burial showed that they, like the disciples, were not expecting Him to rise from the dead (cf. 8:31; 9:31; 10:34).

16:2 when the sun had risen. John 20:1 says that Mary Magdalene arrived at the tomb while it was still dark. She may have gone on ahead of the other women, or the whole party may have set out together while it was still dark and arrived at the tomb after sunrise.

16:3 Who will roll away the stone. Only Mark records this discussion on the way to the tomb. The women realized they had no men with them to move the heavy stone (v. 4) away from the entrance to the tomb. Since they had last visited the tomb on Friday evening, they did not know it had been sealed and a guard posted, which took place on Saturday (Matt. 27:62-66).

16:4 the stone had been rolled away. This was not to let Jesus out, but to let the witnesses in. The earthquake when the angel rolled away the stone (Matt. 28:2) may have affected only the area around the tomb, since the women apparently did not feel it.

16:5 entering the tomb. The outer chamber, separated from the burial chamber by a small doorway. **young man clothed in a long white robe.** The angel, having rolled away the stone (Matt. 28:2), had then entered the burial chamber. Luke records that there were two angels in the tomb; Matthew and Mark focus on the one who spoke (for similar instances, *see note on 10:46*).

16:6 Jesus of Nazareth, who was crucified. Better, "the Nazarene" (*see note on Matt. 2:23*). The inspired account leaves no doubt about who had been in the tomb. The idea of some unbelievers that the women went to the wrong tomb is ludicrous. **He is risen!** Christ's resurrection is one of the central truths of the Christian faith (1 Cor. 15:4) and the only plausible explanation for the empty tomb. Even the Jewish leaders did not deny the reality of the empty tomb, but concocted the story that the disciples had stolen Jesus' body (Matt. 28:11-15). The idea that the fearful (John 19:19), doubting (vv. 11,13; Luke 24:10,11) disciples somehow overpowered the Roman guard detachment and stole Jesus' body is absurd. That they did it while the guards were asleep is even more preposterous. Surely, in moving the heavy stone from the mouth of the tomb, the disciples would have awakened at least one of the soldiers. And in any case, how could the guards have known what happened while they were asleep? Many other theories have been sinfully invented over the centuries to explain away the empty tomb, all of them equally futile.

16:7 and Peter. Peter was not singled out as the leader of the disciples, but to be reassured that, despite his denials of Christ, he was still one of them. **He is going before you into Galilee…as He said.** *See note on 14:28.* The disciples' lack of faith made them slow to act on these words; they did not leave for Galilee (Matt. 28:7,16) until after Jesus repeatedly appeared to them in Jerusalem (cf. Luke 24:13-32; John 20:19-31).

16:8 afraid. They were overwhelmed by the frightening appearance of the angel and the awesome mystery of the Resurrection.

16:9-20 The external evidence strongly suggests these verses were not originally part of Mark's gospel. While the majority of Gr. manuscripts contain these verses, the earliest and most reliable do not. A shorter ending also existed, but it is not included in the text. Further, some that include the passage note that it was missing from older Gr. manuscripts, while others have scribal marks indicating the passage was considered spurious. The fourth-century church fathers Eusebius and Jerome noted that almost all Gr. manuscripts available to them lacked vv. 9-20. The internal evidence from this passage also weighs heavily against Mark's authorship. The transition between vv. 8 and 9 is abrupt and awkward. The Gr. particle translated "now" that begins v. 9 implies continuity with the preceding narrative. What follows, however, does not continue the story of the women referred to in v. 8, but describes Christ's appearance to Mary Magdalene (cf. John 20:11-18). The masculine participle in v. 9 expects "he" as its antecedent, yet the subject of v. 8 is the women. Although she had just been mentioned 3 times (v. 1; 15:40,47), v. 9 introduces Mary Magdalene as if for the first time. Further, if Mark wrote v. 9, it is strange that he would only now note that Jesus had cast 7 demons out of her. The angel spoke of Jesus' appearing to His followers in Galilee, yet the appearances described in vv. 9-20 are all in the Jerusalem area. Finally, the presence in these verses of a significant number of Gr. words used nowhere else in Mark argues that Mark did not write them. Verses 9-20 represent an early (they were known to the second-century fathers Irenaeus, Tatian, and, possibly, Justin Martyr) attempt to complete Mark's gospel. While for the most part summarizing truths taught elsewhere in Scripture, vv. 9-20 should always be compared with the rest of Scripture, and no doctrines should be formulated based solely on them. Since, in spite of all these considerations of the likely unreliability of this section, it is possible to be wrong on the issue, and thus, it is good to consider the meaning of this passage and leave it in the text, just as with John 7:53–8:11.

16:9 *He* rose early on the first *day* of the week. That is, early Sunday morning. **Mary Magdalene.** *See note on 15:40.*

16:12,13 This incident is related in Luke 24:13-32.

16:14 the eleven. The 12 minus Judas, who had committed

they sat at the table; and He rebuked their
unbelief and hardness of heart, because
they did not believe those who had seen
Him after He had risen. 15 [m]And He said to
them, "Go into all the world [n]and preach
the gospel to every creature. 16 [o]He who
believes and is baptized will be saved; [p]but
he who does not believe will be condemned. 17 And these [q]signs will follow
those who [4]believe: [r]In My name they will
cast out demons; [s]they will speak with
new tongues; 18 [t]they[5] will take up serpents; and if they drink anything deadly, it
will by no means hurt them; [u]they will lay
hands on the sick, and they will recover."

15 [m] Matt. 28:19; [John 15:16; Acts 1:8]; Col. 1:6 [n] [Col. 1:23]
16 [o] [John 3:18, 36; Acts 2:38; 16:30, 31; Rom. 10:8-10] [p] [John 12:48]
17 [q] Acts 5:12 [r] Mark 9:38; Luke 10:17; Acts 5:16; 8:7; 16:18; 19:12 [s] [Acts 2:4; 1 Cor. 12:10] [4] *have believed*
18 [t] [Luke 10:19]; Acts 28:3-6 [u] [Acts 5:15]; James 5:14 [5] NU *and in their hands they will*

The Ascension of Jesus
Luke 24:49-53; Acts 1:9

19 So then, [v]after the Lord had spoken to
them, He was [w]received up into heaven,
and [x]sat down at the right hand of God.
20 And they went out and preached everywhere, the Lord working with *them* [y]and
confirming the word through the accompanying signs. Amen.

19 [v] Acts 1:2, 3 [w] Ps. 68:18; Luke 9:51; 24:51; John 6:62; 20:17; Acts 1:2,9-11; [1 Tim. 3:16; Rev. 4:2] [x] [Ps. 110:1]; Luke 22:69; [Acts 7:55]; 1 Pet. 3:22 20 [y] Acts 5:12; [1 Cor. 2:4, 5; Heb. 2:4]

suicide (Matt. 27:3-10). **unbelief and hardness of heart.** In not believing the witnesses of the resurrection (vv. 12,13; cf. Luke 24:10, 11).

16:15,16 Similar to Matthew's account of the Great Commission, with the added contrast of those who have been baptized (believers) with those who refuse to believe and are condemned. Even if v. 16 is a genuine part of Mark's gospel, it does not teach that baptism saves, since the lost are condemned for unbelief, not for not being baptized (*see note on Acts 2:38*).

16:17,18 These signs were promised to the apostolic community (Matt. 10:1; 2 Cor. 12:12), not all believers in all ages (cf. 1 Cor. 12:29,30). All (with the exception of drinking poison) were experienced by some in the apostolic church and reported in Scripture (e.g., Acts 28:5), but not afterward (cf. v. 20).

16:19 right hand of God. The place of honor Jesus assumed after His ascension (*see note on Acts 2:33*).

16:20 confirming the word through…signs. *See notes on Acts 2:22; 2 Cor. 12:12; Heb. 2:4.*

The Gospel According to

LUKE

Title

As with the other 3 gospels, the title is derived from the author's name. According to tradition, Luke was a Gentile. The Apostle Paul seems to confirm this, distinguishing Luke from those who were "of the circumcision" (Col. 4:11,14). That would make Luke the only Gentile to pen any books of Scripture. He is responsible for a significant portion of the NT, having written both this gospel and the book of Acts (see Author and Date).

Very little is known about Luke. He almost never included personal details about himself, and nothing definite is known about his background or his conversion. Both Eusebius and Jerome identified him as a native of Antioch (which may explain why so much of the book of Acts centers on Antioch—cf. Acts 11:19-27; 13:1-3; 14:26; 15:22,23,30-35; 18:22,23). Luke was a frequent companion of the Apostle Paul, at least from the time of Paul's Macedonian vision (Acts 16:9,10) right up to the time of Paul's martyrdom (2 Tim. 4:11).

The Apostle Paul referred to Luke as a physician (Col. 4:14). Luke's interest in medical phenomena is evident in the high profile he gave to Jesus' healing ministry (e.g., 4:38-40; 5:15-25; 6:17-19; 7:11-15; 8:43-47,49-56; 9:2,6,11; 13:11-13; 14:2-4; 17:12-14; 22:50,51). In Luke's day, physicians did not have a unique vocabulary of technical terminology; so when Luke discusses healings and other medical issues, his language is not markedly different from that of the other gospel writers.

Author and Date

The Gospel of Luke and the book of Acts clearly were written by the same individual (cf. 1:1-4; Acts 1:1). Although he never identified himself by name, it is clear from his use of "we" in many sections of Acts that he was a close companion of the Apostle Paul (Acts 16:10-17; 20:5-15; 21:1-18; 27:1–28:16). Luke is the only person, among the colleagues Paul mentions in his own epistles (Col. 4:14; 2 Tim. 4:11; Philem. 24), who fits the profile of the author of these books. That accords perfectly with the earliest tradition of the church which unanimously attributed this gospel to Luke.

Luke and Acts appear to have been written at about the same time—Luke first, then Acts. Combined, they make a 2-volume work addressed to "Theophilus" (1:3; Acts 1:1; see Background and Setting) giving a sweeping history of the founding of Christianity, from the birth of Christ to Paul's imprisonment under house arrest in Rome (Acts 28:30,31).

The book of Acts ends with Paul still in Rome, which leads to the conclusion that Luke wrote these books from Rome during Paul's imprisonment there (ca. A.D. 60–62). Luke records Jesus' prophecy of the destruction of Jerusalem in A.D. 70 (19:42-44; 21:20-24) but makes no mention of the fulfillment of that prophecy, either here or in Acts. Luke made it a point to record such prophetic fulfillments (cf. Acts 11:28), so it is extremely unlikely he wrote these books after the Roman invasion of Jerusalem. Acts also includes no mention of the great persecution that began under Nero in A.D. 64. In addition, many scholars set the date of James' martyrdom at A.D. 62, and if that was before Luke completed his history, he certainly would have mentioned it. So, the most likely date for this gospel is A.D. 60 or 61.

Background and Setting

Luke dedicated his works to "most excellent Theophilus" (lit. "lover of God"—1:3; cf. Acts 1:1). This designation, which may be a nickname or a pseudonym, is accompanied by a formal address ("most excellent")—possibly signifying that "Theophilus" was a well known Roman dignitary, perhaps one of those who had turned to Christ in "Caesar's household" (Phil. 4:22).

It is almost certain, however, that Luke envisioned a much broader audience for his work than this one man. The dedications at the outset of Luke and Acts are like the formal dedication in a modern book. They are not like the address of an epistle.

Luke expressly stated that his knowledge of the events recorded in his gospel came from the reports of those who were eyewitnesses (1:1,2)—strongly implying that he himself was not an eyewitness. It is clear from his prologue that his aim was to give an ordered account of the events of Jesus' life, but this does not mean he always followed a strict chronological order in all instances (e.g., *see note on 3:20*).

By acknowledging that he had compiled his account from various extant sources (*see note on 1:1*),

Luke was not disclaiming divine inspiration for his work. The process of inspiration never bypasses or overrides the personalities, vocabularies, and styles of the human authors of Scripture. The unique traits of the human authors are always indelibly stamped on all the books of Scripture. Luke's research is no exception to this rule. The research itself was orchestrated by divine Providence. And in his writing, Luke was moved by the Spirit of God (2 Pet. 1:21). Therefore, his account is infallibly true (*see note on 1:3*).

Historical and Theological Themes

Luke's style is that of a scholarly, well-read author (*see note on 1:1-4*). He wrote as a meticulous historian, often giving details that helped identify the historical context of the events he described (1:5; 2:1,2; 3:1,2; 13:1-4).

His account of the nativity is the fullest in all the gospel records—and (like the rest of Luke's work) more polished in its literary style. He included in the birth narrative a series of praise psalms (1:46-55; 1:68-79; 2:14; 2:29-32; 34,35). He alone reported the unusual circumstances surrounding the birth of John the Baptist, the annunciation to Mary, the manger, the shepherds, and Simeon and Anna (2:25-38).

A running theme in Luke's gospel is Jesus' compassion for Gentiles, Samaritans, women, children, tax collectors, sinners, and others often regarded as outcasts in Israel. Every time he mentions a tax collector (3:12; 5:27; 7:29; 15:1; 18:10-13; 19:2), it is in a positive sense. Yet, Luke did not ignore the salvation of those who were rich and respectable—e.g., 23:50-53. From the outset of Jesus' public ministry (4:18) to the Lord's final words on the cross (23:40-43), Luke underscored this theme of Christ's ministry to the pariahs of society. Again and again he showed how the Great Physician ministered to those most aware of their need (cf. 5:31,32; 15:4-7; 31,32; 19:10).

The high profile Luke accords to women is particularly significant. From the nativity account, where Mary, Elizabeth, and Anna are given prominence (chaps. 1; 2), to the events of resurrection morning, where women again are major characters (24:1,10), Luke emphasized the central role of women in the life and ministry of our Lord (e.g., 7:12-15,37-50; 8:2,3,43-48; 10:38-42; 13:11-13; 21:2-4; 23:27-29,49,55,56).

Several other recurring themes form threads through Luke's gospel. Examples of these are human fear in the presence of God (*see note on 1:12*); forgiveness (3:3; 5:20-25; 6:37; 7:41-50; 11:4; 12:10; 17:3,4; 23:34; 24:47); joy (*see note on 1:14*); wonder at the mysteries of divine truth (*see note on 2:18*); the role of the Holy Spirit (1:15,35,41,67; 2:25-27; 3:16,22; 4:1,14,18; 10:21; 11:13; 12:10,12); the temple in Jerusalem (1:9-22; 2:27-38,46-49; 4:9-13; 18:10-14; 19:45-48; 20:1–21:6; 21:37,38; 24:53); and Jesus' prayers (*see note on 6:12*).

Starting with 9:51, Luke devoted 10 chapters of his narrative to a travelogue of Jesus' final journey to Jerusalem. Much of the material in this section is unique to Luke. This is the heart of Luke's gospel, and it features a theme Luke stressed throughout: Jesus' relentless progression toward the cross. This was the very purpose for which Christ had come to earth (cf. 9:22,23; 17:25; 18:31-33; 24:25,26,46), and He would not be deterred. The saving of sinners was His whole mission (19:10).

Interpretive Challenges

Luke, like Mark, and in contrast to Matthew, appears to target a Gentile readership (for a discussion of the Synoptic Problem, see Introduction to Mark: Interpretive Challenges). He identified locations that would have been familiar to all Jews (e.g., 4:31; 23:51; 24:13), suggesting that his audience went beyond those who already had knowledge of Palestinian geography. He usually preferred Greek terminology over Hebraisms (e.g., "Calvary" instead of "Golgotha" in 23:33). The other gospels all use occasional Semitic terms such as "Abba" (Mark 14:36), "rabbi" (Matt. 23:7,8; John 1:38,49), and "hosanna" (Matt. 21:9; Mark 11:9,10; John 12:13)—but Luke either omitted them or used Greek equivalents.

Luke quoted the OT more sparingly than Matthew, and when citing OT passages, he nearly always employed the LXX, a Greek translation of the Hebrew Scriptures. Furthermore, most of Luke's OT citations are allusions rather than direct quotations, and many of them appear in Jesus' words rather than Luke's narration (2:23,24; 3:4-6; 4:4,8,10-12,18,19; 7:27; 10:27; 18:20; 19:46; 20:17,18,37,42,43; 22:37).

Luke, more than any of the other gospel writers, highlighted the universal scope of the gospel invitation. He portrayed Jesus as the Son of Man, rejected by Israel, and then offered to the world. As noted above (see Historical and Theological Themes), Luke repeatedly related accounts of Gentiles, Samaritans, and other outcasts who found grace in Jesus' eyes. This emphasis is precisely what we would expect from a close companion of the "apostle of the Gentiles" (Rom. 11:13).

Yet some critics have claimed to see a wide gap between Luke's theology and that of Paul. It is true that Luke's gospel is practically devoid of terminology that is uniquely Pauline. Luke wrote with his own style. Yet the underlying theology is perfectly in harmony with that of the apostle's. The centerpiece of Paul's doctrine was justification by faith (*see note on Rom. 3:24*). Luke also highlighted and illustrated justification by faith in many of the incidents and parables he related, chiefly the account of the Pharisee and the publican (18:9-14); the familiar story of the Prodigal Son (15:11-32); the incident at Simon's house (7:36-50); and the salvation of Zacchaeus (19:1-10).

Outline

- I. The Prelude to Christ's Ministry (1:1–4:13)
  - A. Preamble (1:1-4)
  - B. The Birth of Jesus (1:5–2:38)
    - 1. The annunciation to Zacharias (1:5-25)
    - 2. The annunciation to Mary (1:26-38)
    - 3. The visitation (1:39-45)
    - 4. The Magnificat (1:46-56)
    - 5. The birth of the forerunner (1:57-80)
    - 6. The nativity (2:1-38)
  - C. The Boyhood of Jesus (2:39-52)
    - 1. In Nazareth (2:39,40)
    - 2. In the temple (2:41-50)
    - 3. In His family (2:51,52)
  - D. The Baptism of Jesus (3:1–4:13)
    - 1. The preaching of John the Baptist (3:1-20)
    - 2. The testimony of heaven (3:21,22)
    - 3. The genealogy of the Son of Man (3:23-38)
    - 4. The temptation of the Son of God (4:1-13)
- II. The Ministry in Galilee (4:14–9:50)
  - A. The Commencement of His Ministry (4:14-44)
    - 1. Nazareth (4:14-30)
    - 2. Capernaum (4:31-42)
      - a. A demon cast out (4:31-37)
      - b. Multitudes healed (4:38-42)
    - 3. The cities of Galilee (4:43,44)
  - B. The Calling of His Disciples (5:1–6:16)
    - 1. Four fishermen (5:1-26)
      - a. Fishing for men (5:1-11)
      - b. Healing infirmities (5:12-16)
      - c. Pardoning sins (5:17-26)
    - 2. Levi (5:27–6:11)
      - a. The gospel: not for the righteous, but for sinners (5:27-32)
      - b. The wineskins: not old, but new (5:33-39)
      - c. The Sabbath: not for bondage, but for doing good (6:1-11)
    - 3. The twelve (6:12-16)
  - C. The Continuation of His Work (6:17–9:50)
    - 1. Preaching on the plateau (6:17-49)
      - a. Beatitudes (6:17-23)
      - b. Woes (6:24-26)
      - c. Commandments (6:27-49)
    - 2. Ministering in the cities (7:1–8:25)
      - a. He heals a centurion's servant (7:1-10)
      - b. He raises a widow's son (7:11-17)
      - c. He encourages John the Baptist's disciples (7:18-35)
      - d. He forgives a sinful woman (7:36-50)
      - e. He gathers loving disciples (8:1-3)
      - f. He teaches the multitudes with parables (8:4-21)
      - g. He stills the winds and waves (8:22-25)
    - 3. Traveling in Galilee (8:26–9:50)
      - a. He delivers a demoniac (8:26-39)
      - b. He heals a woman (8:40-48)

- c. He raises a girl (8:49-56)
- d. He sends out the Twelve (9:1-6)
- e. He confounds Herod (9:7-9)
- f. He feeds the multitude (9:10-17)
- g. He predicts His crucifixion (9:18-26)
- h. He unveils His glory (9:27-36)
- i. He casts out an unclean spirit (9:37-42)
- j. He instructs His disciples (9:43-50)

III. The Journey to Jerusalem (9:51–19:27)
- A. Samaria (9:51–10:37)
  1. A village turns Him away (9:51-56)
  2. He turns away the half-hearted (9:57-62)
  3. He sends out the seventy (10:1-24)
  4. He gives the parable of the Good Samaritan (10:25-37)
- B. Bethany and Judea (10:38–13:35)
  1. Mary and Martha (10:38-42)
  2. The Lord's prayer (11:1-4)
  3. The importance of importunity (11:5-13)
  4. The impossibility of neutrality (11:14-36)
  5. Woes upon Pharisees and lawyers (11:37-54)
  6. Lessons along the way (12:1-59)
     - a. Against hypocrisy (12:1-12)
     - b. Against worldly materialism (12:13-21)
     - c. Against worry (12:22-34)
     - d. Against unfaithfulness (12:35-48)
     - e. Against love of ease (12:49-53)
     - f. Against unpreparedness (12:54-56)
     - g. Against division (12:57-59)
  7. Questions answered (13:1-30)
     - a. About the justice of God (13:1-9)
     - b. About the Sabbath (13:10-17)
     - c. About the kingdom (13:18-21)
     - d. About the few who are saved (13:22-30)
  8. Christ's lament (13:31-35)
- C. Perea (14:1–19:27)
  1. Guest of a Pharisee (14:1-24)
     - a. He tests them about the Sabbath (14:1-6)
     - b. He teaches them about humility (14:7-14)
     - c. He tells them about the heavenly banquet (14:15-24)
  2. Teacher of multitudes (14:25–18:34)
     - a. The cost of discipleship (14:25-35)
     - b. The parable of the lost sheep (15:1-7)
     - c. The parable of the lost coin (15:8-10)
     - d. The parable of the lost son (15:11-32)
     - e. The parable of the unjust steward (16:1-18)
     - f. The rich man and Lazarus (16:19-31)
     - g. A lesson about forgiveness (17:1-4)
     - h. A lesson about faithfulness (17:5-10)
     - i. A lesson about thankfulness (17:11-19)
     - j. A lesson about readiness (17:20-37)
     - k. The parable of the persistent widow (18:1-8)
     - l. The parable of the Pharisee and the publican (18:9-14)

- m. A lesson about childlikeness (18:15-17)
- n. A lesson about commitment (18:18-30)
- o. A lesson about the plan of redemption (18:31-34)

3. Friend of sinners (18:35–19:10)
   - a. He opens blind eyes (18:35-43)
   - b. He seeks and saves the lost (19:1-10)
4. Judge of all the earth (19:11-27)
   - a. The end of a long journey (19:11)
   - b. The parable of the minas (19:12-27)

IV. The Passion Week (19:28–23:56)

- A. Sunday (19:28-44)
  1. The triumphal entry (19:28-40)
  2. Christ weeps over the city (19:41-44)
- B. Monday (19:45-48)
  1. He cleanses the temple (19:45,46)
  2. He teaches the Passover crowds (19:47,48)
- C. Tuesday (20:1–21:38)
  1. He contends with the Jewish rulers (20:1-8)
  2. He teaches the Passover crowds (20:9–21:38)
     - a. The parable of the wicked vinedressers (20:9-19)
     - b. An answer to the Pharisees about paying taxes (20:20-26)
     - c. An answer to the Sadducees about the resurrection (20:27-40)
     - d. A question for the scribes about messianic prophecy (20:41-47)
     - e. The lesson of the widow's mites (21:1-4)
     - f. A prophecy about the destruction of Jerusalem (21:5-24)
     - g. Some signs of the times (21:25-38)
- D. Wednesday (22:1-6)
  1. The plot against Jesus (22:1,2)
  2. Judas joins the conspiracy (22:3-6)
- E. Thursday (22:7-53)
  1. Preparation for Passover (22:7-13)
  2. The Lord's Supper (22:14-38)
     - a. The New Covenant instituted (22:14-22)
     - b. Disputes among the disciples (22:23-30)
     - c. Peter's denial predicted (22:31-34)
     - d. God's provision promised (22:35-38)
  3. The agony in the garden (22:39-46)
  4. Jesus' arrest (22:47-53)
- F. Friday (22:54–23:55)
  1. Peter's denial (22:54-62)
  2. Jesus mocked and beaten (22:63-65)
  3. The trial before the Sanhedrin (22:66-71)
  4. The trial before Pilate (23:1-25)
     - a. The indictment (23:1-5)
     - b. The hearing before Herod (23:6-12)
     - c. Pilate's verdict (23:13-25)
  5. The crucifixion (23:26-49)
  6. The burial (23:50-55)
- G. The Sabbath (23:56)

V. The Consummation of Christ's Ministry (24:1-53)

- A. The Resurrection (24:1-12)
- B. The Road to Emmaus (24:13-45)
- C. The Ascension (24:46-53)

The Purpose and Method of Luke's Gospel

1 Inasmuch as many have taken in hand
to set in order a narrative of those
[a]things which [1]have been fulfilled among
us, 2 just as those who [b]from the beginning
were [c]eyewitnesses and ministers of the
word [d]delivered them to us, 3 it seemed
good to me also, having [2]had perfect understanding of all things from the very
first, to write to you an orderly account,
[e]most excellent Theophilus, 4 [f]that you
may know the certainty of those things in
which you were instructed.

Zacharias Ministers in the Temple

5 There was [g]in the days of Herod, the
king of Judea, a certain priest named Zacharias, [h]of the division of [i]Abijah. His [j]wife
was of the daughters of Aaron, and her
name *was* Elizabeth. 6 And they were both
righteous before God, walking in all the
commandments and ordinances of the
Lord blameless. 7 But they had no child,
because Elizabeth was barren, and they
were both well advanced in years.
8 So it was, that while he was serving as
priest before God in the order of his division, 9 according to the custom of the
priesthood, [3]his lot fell [k]to burn incense
when he went into the temple of the Lord.
10 [l]And the whole multitude of the people
was praying outside at the hour of incense.

An Angel Announces the Birth of John the Baptist

11 Then an angel of the Lord appeared to
him, standing on the right side of [m]the
altar of incense. 12 And when Zacharias

CHAPTER 1

1 [a]John 20:31 [1]*Or are most surely believed*
2 [b]Mark 1:1; John 15:27; Acts 1:21,22 [c]Acts 1:2 [d]Acts 1:3; 10:39; Heb. 2:3; 1 Pet. 5:1; 2 Pet. 1:16; 1 John 1:1
3 [e]Acts 1:1 [2]*Lit. accurately followed*
4 [f][John 20:31]
5 [g]Matt. 2:1 [h]1 Chr. 24:1,10 [i]Neh. 12:4 [j]Lev. 21:13,14
9 [k]Ex. 30:7,8; 1 Chr. 23:13; 2 Chr. 29:11 [3]*he was chosen by lot*
10 [l]Lev. 16:17
11 [m]Ex. 30:1

1:1-4 These 4 verses make a single sentence, written in the polished style of a Gr. literary classic. It was common for Gr. historical works to begin with such a prologue. After this formal prologue, however, Luke shifted into a simpler style of narrative, probably patterned after the familiar style of the LXX.

1:1 many. Although Luke wrote direct divine revelation inspired by the Holy Spirit, he acknowledged the works of others (*see note on v. 2*) who had set down in writing events from Christ's life. All those sources have been long lost, except for the inspired gospels. Since Matthew and Mark were most likely written before Luke, it has been suggested that either one or both of those may have been among Luke's sources when he did his research. It is also known that he was personally acquainted with many firsthand witnesses to the events of Christ's life. And it is possible that some of his sources were word-of-mouth reports. About 60 percent of the material in Mark is repeated in Luke, and Luke seems to follow Mark's order of events closely (see Introduction to Mark: Interpretive Challenges, the Synoptic Problem). **to set in order.** Luke proposed to narrate the ministry of Christ in an authoritative, logical, and factual order (though not always strictly chronological—v. 3). **those things which have been fulfilled.** I.e., the OT messianic promises fulfilled in Christ. **among us.** I.e., in our generation. This phrase does not mean Luke was personally an eyewitness to the life of Christ (*see note on v. 2.*).

1:2 eyewitnesses and ministers of the word. Luke's primary sources were the apostles themselves, who delivered facts about Jesus' life and teaching—both orally and by means of recorded memoirs in written documents made available to Luke. In any case, Luke made no pretense of being an eyewitness himself, but explained that these were facts supported by careful research (*see note on v. 3*).

1:3 having had perfect understanding. Lit. "having traced out carefully." Luke's gospel was the result of painstaking investigation. Luke, more than anyone else in the early church, had the abilities and the opportunity to consult with eyewitnesses of Jesus' ministry and consolidate their accounts. He spent more than two years during Paul's imprisonment at Caesarea (Acts 24:26,27), during which time he would have been able to meet and interview many of the apostles and other eyewitnesses of Jesus' ministry. We know, for example, that he met Philip (Acts 21:8), who was undoubtedly one of Luke's sources. In his travels through Asia Minor, he may also have encountered the Apostle John. Joanna, wife of Herod's steward, is mentioned only in Luke's gospel (*see note on 8:3*; cf. 24:10), so she must have been a personal acquaintance of his. Luke also related details about Herod's dealings with Christ not found in the other gospels (13:31-33; 23:7-12). No doubt it was from Joanna (or someone in a similar position) that Luke learned those facts. However, his understanding was perfect because of the divine revelation he received from the Holy Spirit (1 Tim. 3:16,17; 2 Pet. 1:19-21). **from the very first.** This could mean from the beginning of Christ's earthly life. However, the word can mean "from above" (John 3:31; 19:11; James 3:15). "From the beginning" in v. 2 uses a different Gr. word, *archē*—so it is best to understand that Luke was saying he used earthly sources for his material, but was given heavenly guidance as he did his research and writing. It is clear that he regarded his account as authoritative (*see note on v. 4*). **an orderly account.** Luke's account is predominantly ordered chronologically, but he does not follow such an arrangement slavishly. **most excellent.** This was a title used to address governors (Acts 23:26; 24:3; 26:25). This sort of language was reserved for the highest dignitaries, suggesting that "Theophilus" was a such a person.

1:4 certainty. Note the implicit claim of authority. Though Luke drew from other sources (v. 3), he regarded the reliability and authority of his gospel as superior to uninspired sources. **instructed.** Theophilus had been schooled in the apostolic tradition, possibly even by the Apostle Paul himself. Yet the written Scripture by means of this gospel sealed the certainty of what he had heard.

1:5 Herod. Herod the Great. *See note on Matt. 2:1.* **Zacharias.** Lit. "Jehovah has remembered." **the division of Abijah.** The temple priesthood was organized into 24 divisions, with each division serving twice a year for (1 Chr. 24:4-19); Abijah's was the 8th division (1 Chr. 24:10). **daughters of Aaron.** I.e., both husband and wife were from the priestly tribe.

1:6 both righteous before God. I.e., they were believers, justified in God's sight. There is a clear echo of Pauline theology in this expression. See Introduction: Interpretive Challenges.

1:7 barren...well advanced in years. This was seen by many as a sign of divine disfavor. *See note on v. 25.*

1:8 in the order of his division. I.e., his division was on duty for one of their two annual stints (*see note on v. 5*).

1:9 his lot fell to burn incense. A high honor (Ex. 30:7,8; 2 Chr. 29:11). Because of the large number of priests, most would never be chosen for such a duty, and no one was permitted to serve in this capacity twice. Zacharias no doubt regarded this as the supreme moment in a lifetime of priestly service. The incense was kept burning perpetually, just in front of the veil that divided the holy place from the most holy place. The lone priest would offer the incense every morning and every evening, while the rest of the priests and worshipers stood outside the holy place in prayer (v. 10).

saw *him*, [n]he was troubled, and fear fell
upon him.
13 But the angel said to him, "Do not be
afraid, Zacharias, for your prayer is
heard; and your wife Elizabeth will bear
you a son, and [o]you shall call his name
John. 14 And you will have joy and gladness, and [p]many will rejoice at his birth.
15 For he will be [q]great in the sight of the
Lord, and [r]shall drink neither wine nor
strong drink. He will also be filled with
the Holy Spirit, [s]even from his mother's
womb. 16 And he will turn many of the
children of Israel to the Lord their God.
17 [t]He will also go before Him in the spirit and power of Elijah, *'to turn the hearts of the fathers to the children,'* and the
disobedient to the wisdom of the just, to
make ready a people prepared for the
Lord."

12 [n] Judg. 6:22; Dan. 10:8; Luke 2:9; Acts 10:4; Rev. 1:17
13 [o] Luke 1:57, 60, 63
14 [p] Luke 1:58
15 [q] [Luke 7:24-28] [r] Num. 6:3; Judg. 13:4; Matt. 11:18 [s] Jer. 1:5; Gal. 1:15
17 [t] Mal. 4:5, 6; Matt. 3:2; 11:14; Mark 1:4; 9:12

1:12 fear. The normal response—and an appropriate one (12:5)—when someone is confronted by a divine visitation or a mighty work of God (Judg. 6:22; 13:22; Mark 16:5; *see note on Rev. 1:17*). Luke seems especially to take note of this; he often reports fear in the presence of God and His works (cf. vv. 30,65; 2:9,10; 5:10,26; 7:16; 8:25,37,50; 9:34,45; 23:40).

1:13 your prayer. Probably a prayer for children to be in his home (*see note on v. 7*; cf. v. 25). **John.** Lit. "Jehovah has shown grace."

1:14 joy and gladness. The hallmarks of the messianic kingdom (Is. 25:9; Pss. 14:7; 48:11). The motif of joy runs through Luke's gospel (cf. vv. 44,47,58; 2:10; 6:23; 8:13; 10:17-21; 13:17; 15:5-10,22-32; 19:6,37; 24:52).

1:15 neither wine nor strong drink. This was a key element of the Nazirite vow (Num. 6:1-21) and would probably have been understood as such by Zacharias. Usually such a vow was temporary, but Samson (Judg. 16:17) and Samuel (1 Sam. 1:11) were subject to it from birth. The language here is reminiscent of the angel's instructions to Samson's parents (Judg. 13:4-7). However, no mention is made here of any restriction on the cutting of John's hair. Luke may have simply omitted that detail to avoid weighing his Gentile audience down with the details of Jewish law. **even from his mother's womb.** Reminiscent of Jeremiah (Jer. 1:5). This illustrates God's sovereignty in salvation.

1:17 in the spirit and power of Elijah. Elijah, like John the Baptist, was known for his bold, uncompromising stand for the Word of God—even in the face of a ruthless monarch (cf. 1 Kin. 18:17-24; Mark 6:15). The final two verses of the OT (Mal. 4:5,6) had promised the return of Elijah before the Day of the Lord. *See notes on Matt. 3:4; 11:14; Mark 9:11,12.* ***to turn the hearts.*** Quoted from Mal. 4:6, showing that John the Baptist fulfilled that prophecy. **make ready.** Possibly an allusion to Is. 40:3-5 (*see notes on 3:4; Matt. 3:3*).

New Testament Women

Mary, the virgin mother of Jesus, has a place of honor among the women of the New Testament. She is an enduring example of faith, humility, and service (Luke 1:26-56). Other notable women of the New Testament include the following:

Name	Description	Biblical Reference
Anna	Recognized Jesus as the long-awaited Messiah	Luke 2:36-38
Bernice	Sister of Agrippa before whom Paul made his defense	Acts 25:13
Candace	A queen of Ethiopia	Acts 8:27
Chloe	Woman who knew of divisions in the church at Corinth	1 Cor. 1:11
Claudia	Christian of Rome	2 Tim. 4:21
Damaris	Woman of Athens converted under Paul's ministry	Acts 17:34
Dorcas (Tabitha)	Christian in Joppa who was raised from the dead by Peter	Acts 9:36-41
Drusilla	Wife of Felix, governor of Judea	Acts 24:24
Elizabeth	Mother of John the Baptist	Luke 1:5,13
Eunice	Mother of Timothy	2 Tim. 1:5
Herodias	Queen who demanded the execution of John the Baptist	Matt. 14:3-10
Joanna	Provided for the material needs of Jesus	Luke 8:3
Lois	Grandmother of Timothy	2 Tim. 1:5
Lydia	Converted under Paul's ministry in Philippi	Acts 16:14
Martha and Mary	Sisters of Lazarus; friends of Jesus	Luke 10:38-42
Mary Magdalene	Woman from whom Jesus cast out demons	Matt. 27:56-61; Mark 16:9
Phoebe	A servant, perhaps a deaconess, in the church at Cenchrea	Rom. 16:1,2
Priscilla	Wife of Aquila; laborer with Paul at Corinth and Ephesus	Acts 18:2,18,19
Salome	Mother of Jesus' disciples James and John	Matt. 20:20-24
Sapphira	Held back goods from the early Christian community	Acts 5:1
Susanna	Provided for the material needs of Jesus	Luke 8:3

Zacharias Is Unable to Speak

18 And Zacharias said to the angel,
[u]"How shall I know this? For I am an old
man, and my wife is well advanced in
years."
19 And the angel answered and said to
him, "I am [v]Gabriel, who stands in the
presence of God, and was sent to speak to
you and bring you [4]these glad [w]tidings.
20 But behold, [x]you will be mute and not
able to speak until the day these things
take place, because you did not believe my
words which will be fulfilled in their own
time."
21 And the people waited for Zacharias,
and marveled that he lingered so long in
the temple. 22 But when he came out, he
could not speak to them; and they perceived that he had seen a vision in the temple, for he beckoned to them and remained
speechless.
23 So it was, as soon as [y]the days of his
service were completed, that he departed
to his own house. 24 Now after those days
his wife Elizabeth conceived; and she hid
herself five months, saying, 25 "Thus the
Lord has dealt with me, in the days when
He looked on *me,* to [z]take away my reproach among people."

Gabriel Announces Christ's Birth

26 Now in the sixth month the angel Gabriel was sent by God to a city of Galilee
named Nazareth, 27 to a virgin [a]betrothed
to a man whose name was Joseph, of the
house of David. The virgin's name *was*
Mary. 28 And having come in, the angel
said to her, [b]"Rejoice, highly favored *one,*
[c]the Lord *is* with you; [5]blessed *are* you
among women!"
29 But [6]when she saw *him,* [d]she was
troubled at his saying, and considered
what manner of greeting this was. 30 Then
the angel said to her, "Do not be afraid,
Mary, for you have found [e]favor with God.
31 [f]And behold, you will conceive in your
womb and bring forth a Son, and [g]shall
call His name JESUS. 32 He will be great,
[h]and will be called the Son of the Highest;
and [i]the Lord God will give Him the
[j]throne of His [k]father David. 33 [l]And He
will reign over the house of Jacob forever,
and of His kingdom there will be no end."

Mary Miraculously Conceives

34 Then Mary said to the angel, "How
can this be, since I [7]do not know a man?"
35 And the angel answered and said to
her, [m]"*The* Holy Spirit will come upon you,
and the power of the Highest will overshadow you; therefore, also, that Holy One

18 [u]Gen. 17:17
19 [v]Dan. 8:16; [Matt. 18:10]; Heb. 1:4 [w]Luke 2:10 [4]*this good news*
20 [x]Ezek. 3:26; 24:27
23 [y]2 Kin. 11:5; 1 Chr. 9:25
25 [z]Gen. 30:23; Is. 4:1; 54:1,4
27 [a]Matt. 1:18; Luke 2:4,5
28 [b]Dan. 9:23 [c]Judg. 6:12 [5]NU omits *blessed are you among women*
29 [d]Luke 1:12 [6]NU omits *when she saw him*
30 [e]Luke 2:52
31 [f]Is. 7:14; Matt. 1:21,25; Gal. 4:4 [g]Luke 2:21; [Phil. 2:9-11]
32 [h]Matt. 3:17; 17:5; Mark 5:7; Luke 1:35, 76; 6:35; Acts 7:48 [i]2 Sam. 7:12, 13, 16; Ps. 132:11; [Is. 9:6, 7; 16:5; Jer. 23:5] [j]2 Sam. 7:14-17; Acts 2:33; 7:55 [k]Matt. 1:1
33 [l][Dan. 2:44; Obad. 21; Mic. 4:7]; John 12:34; [Heb. 1:8]; 2 Pet. 1:11
34 [7]Am a virgin
35 [m]Matt. 1:20

1:18 "How shall I know this?" Abraham also asked for a sign under similar circumstances (Gen. 15:8). The sign given Zacharias was also a mild rebuke for doubting (v. 20).

1:19 Gabriel. Lit. "strong man of God." Gabriel also appears in Dan. 8:16; 9:21 (*see notes there*). He is one of only two holy angels whose names are given in Scripture, the other being Michael (Dan. 10:13,21; Jude 9; Rev. 12:7).

1:21 marveled that he lingered so long. Zacharias was only supposed to offer incense, then come out to pronounce the familiar blessing of Num. 6:23-27 on the people who were waiting in the temple court. The conversation with the angel would have taken additional time.

1:23 the days of his service. A week. *See note on v. 5.* **to his own house.** In the hill country of Judea (v. 39).

1:24 hid herself. Probably an act of devotion out of deep gratitude to the Lord.

1:25 my reproach. Childlessness carried a reproach in a culture where blessings were tied to birthrights and family lines. Barrenness could occasionally be a sign of divine disfavor (Lev. 20:20,21), but it was not always so (cf. Gen. 30:23; 1 Sam. 1:5-10). Still, it carried a social stigma that could be humiliating.

1:26 in the sixth month. I.e., Elizabeth's sixth month of pregnancy. **Nazareth.** *See note on Matt. 2:23.*

1:27 a virgin. The importance of the virgin birth cannot be overstated. A right view of the incarnation hinges on the truth that Jesus was virgin-born. Both Luke and Matthew expressly state that Mary was a virgin when Jesus was conceived (*see note on Matt. 1:23*). The Holy Spirit wrought the conception through supernatural means (*see notes on v. 35; Matt. 1:18*). The nature of Christ's conception testifies of both His deity and His sinlessness. **betrothed.** *See notes on Matt. 1:18,19.*

1:28 highly favored. Lit. "full of grace"—a term used of all believers in Eph. 1:6, where it is translated "accepted." This portrays Mary as a recipient, not a dispenser, of divine grace.

1:30 Do not be afraid. The same thing Gabriel had said to Zacharias (v. 13). *See note on v. 12.*

1:31 JESUS. *See notes on Matt. 1:1,21.*

1:32 He will be great. This same promise was made of John the Baptist. However, the subsequent title is what set Jesus apart: **the Son of the Highest.** Cf. v. 76, where John the Baptist is called "the prophet of the Highest." The Gr. term Luke uses for "Highest" is the one employed in the LXX to translate the Heb., "The Most High God." Since a son bears his father's qualities, calling a person someone else's "son" was a way of signifying equality. Here the angel was telling Mary that her Son would be equal to the Most High God. **His father David.** *See note on Matt. 9:27.* Jesus was David's physical descendant through Mary's line. David's "throne" was emblematic of the messianic kingdom (cf. 2 Sam. 7:13-16; Ps. 89:26-29).

1:33 over the house of Jacob forever. This emphasizes both the Jewish character of the millennial kingdom and the eternal permanence of Christ's rule over all. *See notes on Is. 9:7; Dan. 2:44.*

1:34 I do not know a man. I.e., conjugally. Mary understood that the angel was speaking of an immediate conception, and she and Joseph were still in the midst of the long betrothal, or engagement period (*see note on Matt. 1:18*), before the actual marriage and consummation. Her question was borne out of wonder, not doubt, nor disbelief, so the angel did not rebuke her as he had Zacharias (v. 20).

1:35 *The* Holy Spirit will come upon you. This was a creative act of the Holy Spirit, not the sort of divine-human cohabitation sometimes seen in pagan mythology.

who is to be born will be called [n]the Son of
God. 36 Now indeed, Elizabeth your relative has also conceived a son in her old
age; and this is now the sixth month for her
who was called barren. 37 For [o]with God
nothing will be impossible."
38 Then Mary said, "Behold the maidservant of the Lord! Let it be to me according
to your word." And the angel departed
from her.

Mary Visits Elizabeth

39 Now Mary arose in those days and
went into the hill country with haste, [p]to a
city of Judah, 40 and entered the house of
Zacharias and greeted Elizabeth. 41 And it
happened, when Elizabeth heard the greeting of Mary, that the babe leaped in her
womb; and Elizabeth was [q]filled with the
Holy Spirit. 42 Then she spoke out with a
loud voice and said, [r]"Blessed *are* you
among women, and blessed *is* the fruit of
your womb! 43 But why *is* this *granted* to
me, that the mother of my Lord should
come to me? 44 For indeed, as soon as the
voice of your greeting sounded in my ears,
the babe leaped in my womb for joy.
45 [s]Blessed *is* she who [8]believed, for there
will be a fulfillment of those things which
were told her from the Lord."
46 And Mary said:

[t]"My soul [9]magnifies the Lord,
47 And my spirit has [u]rejoiced in
[v]God my Savior.
48 For [w]He has regarded the lowly
state of His maidservant;
For behold, henceforth [x]all
generations will call me
blessed.
49 For He who is mighty [y]has done
great things for me,
And [z]holy *is* His name.
50 And [a]His mercy *is* on those who
fear Him
From generation to generation.
51 [b]He has shown strength with His
arm;
[c]He has scattered *the* proud in the
imagination of their hearts.
52 [d]He has put down the mighty from
their thrones,
And exalted *the* lowly.
53 He has [e]filled *the* hungry with
good things,
And *the* rich He has sent away
empty.
54 He has helped His [f]servant Israel,
[g]In remembrance of *His* mercy,
55 [h]As He spoke to our [i]fathers,
To Abraham and to his [j]seed
forever."

56 And Mary remained with her about
three months, and returned to her house.

35 [n]Ps. 2:7; Matt. 3:17; 14:33; 17:5; Mark 1:1; John 1:34; 20:31; Acts 8:37; [Rom. 1:1-4; Heb. 1:2, 8]
37 [o]Gen. 18:14; Jer. 32:17; Matt. 19:26; Mark 10:27; Rom. 4:21
39 [p]Josh. 21:9
41 [q]Acts 6:3
42 [r]Judg. 5:24
45 [s]John 20:29 [8]Or *believed that there*
46 [t]1 Sam. 2:1-10; Ps. 34:2, 3; Hab. 3:18 [9]Declares the greatness of
47 [u]Ps. 35:9; Hab. 3:18 [v]1 Tim. 1:1; 2:3; Titus 1:3; 2:10; 3:4; Jude 25
48 [w]1 Sam. 1:11; Ps. 138:6 [x]Luke 11:27
49 [y]Ps. 71:19; 126:2, 3 [z]Ps. 111:9; Rev. 4:8
50 [a]Gen. 17:7; Ex. 20:6; 34:6, 7; Ps. 103:17
51 [b]Ps. 98:1; 118:15; Is. 40:10 [c]Ps. 33:10; [1 Pet. 5:5]
52 [d]1 Sam. 2:7, 8
53 [e][Matt. 5:6]
54 [f]Is. 41:8 [g]Ps. 98:3; [Jer. 31:3]
55 [h]Gen. 17:19; Ps. 132:11; [Gal. 3:16] [i][Rom. 11:28] [j]Gen. 17:7

1:36 Elizabeth your relative. It seems most reasonable to regard the genealogy of 3:23-28 as Mary's (*see note on 3:23*). This would make her a direct descendant of David (*see note on v. 32*). Yet, Elizabeth was a descendant of Aaron (*see note on v. 5*). Therefore, Mary must have been related to Elizabeth through her mother, who would have been of Aaronic descent. Thus, Mary was a descendant of David through her father.

1:38 Let it be to me according to your word. Mary was in an extremely embarrassing and difficult position. Betrothed to Joseph, she faced the stigma of unwed motherhood. Joseph would obviously have known that the child was not his. She knew she would be accused of adultery—an offense punishable by stoning (Deut. 22:13-21; cf. John 8:3-5). Yet she willingly and graciously submitted to the will of God.

1:41 filled with the Holy Spirit. I.e., controlled by the Holy Spirit, who undoubtedly guided Elizabeth's remarkable expression of praise. *See notes on vv. 43,44,67.*

1:43 the mother of my Lord. This expression is not in praise of Mary, but in praise of the Child whom she bore. It was a profound expression of Elizabeth's confidence that Mary's Child would be the long-hoped-for Messiah—the one whom even David called "Lord" (cf. 20:44). Elizabeth's grasp of the situation was extraordinary, considering the aura of mystery that overshadowed all these events (cf. 2:19). She greeted Mary not with skepticism but with joy. She understood the response of the child in her own womb. And she seemed to comprehend the immense importance of the Child who Mary was carrying. All of this must be attributed to the illuminating work of the Spirit (v. 41).

1:44 the babe leaped in my womb for joy. The infant, like his mother, was Spirit-filled (cf. vv. 15,41). His response, like that of Elizabeth, was supernaturally prompted by the Spirit of God (*see note on v. 41*).

1:46-55 Mary's *Magnificat* (the first word in the Latin translation; *see notes on vv. 68-79; 2:29-32*) is filled with OT allusions and quotations. It reveals that Mary's heart and mind were saturated with the Word of God. It contains repeated echoes of Hannah's prayers, e.g., 1 Sam. 1:11; 2:1-10. These verses also contain numerous allusions to the law, the psalms, and the prophets. The entire passage is a point-by-point reciting of the covenant promises of God.

1:47 my Savior. Mary referred to God as "Savior," indicating both that she recognized her own need of a Savior, and that she knew the true God as her Savior. Nothing here or anywhere else in Scripture indicates Mary thought of herself as "immaculate" (free from the taint of original sin). Quite the opposite is true; she employed language typical of someone whose only hope for salvation is divine grace. Nothing in this passage lends support to the notion that Mary herself ought to be an object of adoration. *See notes on vv. 46-55.*

1:48 lowly state. The quality of Mary that shines most clearly through this passage is a deep sense of humility. **maidservant.** I.e., a female slave.

1:56 about three months. Mary arrived in the sixth month of Elizabeth's pregnancy (v. 26), so she evidently stayed until John the Baptist was born. **her house.** At this point Mary was still betrothed to Joseph, not yet living in his house (cf. Matt. 1:24).

Elizabeth Gives Birth to John

57 Now Elizabeth's full time came for
her to be delivered, and she brought forth
a son. 58 When her neighbors and relatives
heard how the Lord had shown great
mercy to her, they [k]rejoiced with her.

59 So it was, [l]on the eighth day, that they
came to circumcise the child; and they
would have called him by the name of his
father, Zacharias. 60 His mother answered
and said, [m]"No; he shall be called John."

61 But they said to her, "There is no one
among your relatives who is called by this
name." 62 So they made signs to his father—what he would have him called.

63 And he asked for a writing tablet, and
wrote, saying, "His name is John." So they
all marveled. 64 Immediately his mouth
was opened and his tongue *loosed,* and he
spoke, praising God. 65 Then fear came on
all who dwelt around them; and all these
sayings were discussed throughout all the
hill country of Judea. 66 And all those who
heard *them* [n]kept *them* in their hearts, saying, "What kind of child will this be?" And
[o]the hand of the Lord was with him.

Zacharias Prophesies of John's Ministry

67 Now his father Zacharias [p]was filled
with the Holy Spirit, and prophesied, saying:

68 "Blessed [q]*is* the Lord God of Israel,
For [r]He has visited and redeemed
His people,
69 [s]And has raised up a horn of
salvation for us
In the house of His servant David,
70 [t]As He spoke by the mouth of His
holy prophets,
Who *have been* [u]since the world
began,
71 That we should be saved from our
enemies
And from the hand of all who hate
us,
72 [v]To perform the mercy *promised* to
our fathers
And to remember His holy
covenant,
73 [w]The oath which He swore to our
father Abraham:
74 To grant us that we,
Being delivered from the hand of
our enemies,
Might [x]serve Him without fear,
75 [y]In holiness and righteousness
before Him all the days of our
life.

76 "And you, child, will be called the
[z]prophet of the Highest;
For [a]you will go before the face of
the Lord to prepare His ways,
77 To give [b]knowledge of salvation to
His people
By the remission of their sins,
78 Through the tender mercy of our
God,
With which the [1]Dayspring from
on high [2]has visited us;
79 [c]To give light to those who sit in
darkness and the shadow of
death,
To [d]guide our feet into the way of
peace."

80 So [e]the child grew and became strong
in spirit, and [f]was in the deserts till the day
of his manifestation to Israel.

58 [k][Rom. 12:15]
59 [l]Gen. 17:12; Lev. 12:3; Luke 2:21; Phil. 3:5
60 [m]Luke 1:13, 63
66 [n]Luke 2:19 [o]Gen. 39:2; Acts 11:21
67 [p]Joel 2:28
68 [q]1 Kin. 1:48; Ps. 106:48 [r]Ex. 3:16
69 [s]2 Sam. 22:3; Ps. 132:17; Ezek. 29:21
70 [t]Jer. 23:5; Rom. 1:2
[u]Acts 3:21
72 [v]Lev. 26:42
73 [w]Gen. 12:3; 22:16-18; [Heb. 6:13]
74 [x][Rom. 6:18; Heb. 9:14]
75 [y]Jer. 32:39; [Eph. 4:24; 2 Thess. 2:13]
76 [z]Matt. 3:3; 11:9; Mark 3:2, 3; Luke 3:4; John 1:23 [a]Is. 40:3; Mal. 3:1; Matt. 11:10
77 [b][Jer. 31:34; Mark 1:4]; Luke 3:3
78 [1]Lit. *Dawn;* the Messiah [2]NU *shall visit*
79 [c]Is. 9:2; Matt. 4:16; [Acts 26:18; 2 Cor. 4:6; Eph. 5:14] [d][John 10:4; 14:27; 16:33]
80 [e]Luke 2:40 [f]Matt. 3:1

1:59 the eighth day. In accord with God's commandment (Gen. 17:12; Lev. 12:1-3; cf. Phil. 3:5), it had become customary to name a child at circumcision. The ritual brought together family and friends, who in this case, pressured the parents to give the baby "the name of his father"—probably intending this as a gesture of respect to Zacharias.

1:60 No. Elizabeth had learned from Zacharias in writing (v. 63), of everything Gabriel had said to him.

1:62 made signs to his father. The priests conducting the circumcision ceremony appear to have assumed that since he could not speak he was also deaf.

1:65 fear. *See note on v. 12.* **all the hill country of Judea.** I.e., Jerusalem and the surrounding area. John the Baptist's reputation began to spread from the time of his birth (v. 66).

1:67 filled with the Holy Spirit. *See note on v. 41.* In every case where someone was Spirit-filled in Luke's nativity account, the result was Spirit-directed worship. Cf. Eph. 5:18-20.

1:68-79 This passage is known as the *Benedictus* (the first word of v. 68 in the Latin translation; *see notes on vv. 46-55; 2:29-32*). Like Mary's Magnificat, it is liberally sprinkled with OT quotations and allusions. When Zacharias was struck mute in the temple (v. 20), he was supposed to deliver a benediction (*see note on v. 21*). So it is fitting that when his speech was restored, the first words out of his mouth were this inspired benediction.

1:69 horn of salvation. A common expression in the OT (2 Sam. 22:3; Ps. 18:2; cf. 1 Sam. 2:1). The horn is a symbol of strength (Deut. 33:17). These words were clearly not meant to exalt John the Baptist. Since both Zacharias and Elizabeth were Levites (*see note on v. 5*), the One raised up "In the house of…David" could not be John, but spoke of Someone greater than he (John 1:26,27). Verses 76-79 speak of John's role.

1:72 His holy covenant. I.e., the Abrahamic Covenant (v. 73), with its promise of salvation by grace. *See note on Gen. 12:1-3.*

1:76 the prophet of the Highest. *See note on v. 32.*

1:77 the remission of their sins. Forgiveness of sins is the heart of salvation. God saves sinner from separation from Him and from eternal hell only by atoning for and forgiving their sins. *See notes on Rom. 4:6-8; 2 Cor. 5:19; Eph. 1:7; Heb. 9:22.*

1:78 Dayspring. A messianic reference (cf. Is. 9:2; 60:1-3; Mal. 4:2; 2 Pet. 1:19; Rev. 22:16).

1:80 was in the deserts. Several groups of ascetics inhabited the wilderness regions E of Jerusalem. One was the famous Qumran

Christ Is Born

2 And it came to pass in those days *that* a
decree went out from Caesar Augustus
that all the world should be registered.
2 [a]This census first took place while Quirinius was governing Syria. 3 So all went to
be registered, everyone to his own city.
4 Joseph also went up from Galilee, out
of the city of Nazareth, into Judea, to [b]the
city of David, which is called Bethlehem,
[c]because he was of the house and lineage
of David, 5 to be registered with Mary, [d]his
betrothed [1]wife, who was with child. 6 So
it was, that while they were there, the days
were completed for her to be delivered.
7 And [e]she brought forth her firstborn Son,
and wrapped Him in swaddling cloths,
and laid Him in a [2]manger, because there
was no room for them in the inn.

The Angels Announce Jesus to the Shepherds

8 Now there were in the same country
shepherds living out in the fields, keeping
watch over their flock by night. 9 And [3]be-
hold, an angel of the Lord stood before
them, and the glory of the Lord shone
around them, [f]and they were greatly
afraid. 10 Then the angel said to them,
[g]"Do not be afraid, for behold, I bring you

CHAPTER 2
2 [a] Dan. 9:25; Acts 5:37
4 [b] 1 Sam. 16:1; Mic. 5:2 [c] Matt. 1:16
5 [d] [Matt. 1:18] [1] NU omits *wife*
7 [e] Matt. 1:25; Luke 1:31 [2] *feed trough*
9 [f] Luke 1:12 [3] NU omits *behold*
10 [g] Luke 1:13, 30

community, source of the Dead Sea Scrolls. John's parents, already old when he was born, might have given him over to the care of someone with ties to such a community. In a similar way, Hannah consecrated Samuel to the Lord by entrusting him to Eli (1 Sam. 1:22-28). However, there is nothing concrete in Scripture to suggest that John was part of any such group. On the contrary, he is painted as a solitary figure, in the spirit of Elijah. *See note on v. 17.*

2:1 Caesar Augustus. Caius Octavius, grand-nephew, adopted son, and primary heir to Julius Caesar. Before and after Julius' death in 44 B.C., the Roman government was constantly torn by power struggles. Octavius ascended to undisputed supremacy in 31 B.C. by defeating his last remaining rival, Antony, in a military battle at Actium. In 29 B.C., the Roman senate declared Octavius Rome's first emperor. Two years later they honored him with the title "Augustus" ("exalted one"—a term signifying religious veneration). Rome's republican government was effectively abolished, and Augustus was given supreme military power. He reigned until his death at age 76 (A.D. 14). Under his rule, the Roman Empire dominated the Mediterranean region, ushering in a period of great prosperity and relative peace (the *Pax Romana*). He ordered "all the world" (i.e., the world of the Roman Empire) to be "registered." This was not merely a one-time census; the decree actually established a cycle of enrollments that were to occur every 14 years. Palestine had previously been excluded from the Roman census, because Jews were exempt from serving in the Roman army, and the census was designed primarily to register young men for military service (as well as account for all Roman citizens). This new, universal census was ostensibly to number each nation by family and tribe (hence Joseph, a Judean, had to return to his ancestral home to register—*see note on v. 3*). Property and income values were not recorded in this registration. But soon the names and population statistics gathered in this census were used for the levying of poll taxes (*see note on Matt. 22:17*), and the Jews came to regard the census itself as a distasteful symbol of Roman oppression. *See note on v. 2.*

2:2 Quirinius was governing Syria. Fixing a precise date for this census is problematic. Publius Sulpicius Quirinius is known to have governed Syria during A.D. 6–9. A well known census was taken in Palestine in A.D. 6. Josephus records that it sparked a violent Jewish revolt (mentioned by Luke, quoting Gamaliel, in Acts 5:37). Quirinius was responsible for administering that census, and he also played a major role in quelling the subsequent rebellion. However, that cannot be the census Luke has in mind here, because it occurred about a decade after the death of Herod (*see note on Matt. 2:1*)—much too late to fit Luke's chronology (cf. 1:5). In light of Luke's meticulous care as a historian, it would be unreasonable to charge him with such an obvious anachronism. Indeed, archeology has vindicated Luke. A fragment of stone discovered at Tivoli (near Rome) in A.D. 1764 contains an inscription in honor of a Roman official who, it states, was twice governor of Syria and Phoenicia during the reign of Augustus. The name of the official is not on the fragment, but among his accomplishments are listed details that, as far as is known, can fit no one other than Quirinius. Thus, he must have served as governor in Syria twice. He was probably military governor at the same time that history records Varus was civil governor there. With regard to the dating of the census, some ancient records found in Egypt mention a worldwide census ordered in 8 B.C. That date is not without problems, either. It is generally thought by scholars that 6 B.C. is the earliest possible date for Christ's birth. Evidently, the census was ordered by Caesar Augustus in 8 B.C. but was not actually carried out in Palestine until 2–4 years later, perhaps because of political difficulties between Rome and Herod. Therefore, the precise year of Christ's birth cannot be known with certainty, but it was probably no earlier than 6 B.C. and certainly no later than 4 B.C. Luke's readers, familiar with the political history of that era, would no doubt have been able to discern a very precise date from the information he gave.

2:3 own city. I.e., the place of tribal origin.

2:4 Nazareth...Bethlehem. Both Joseph and Mary were descendants of David and therefore went to their tribal home in Judea to be registered. This was a difficult trek of more than 70 mi. through mountainous terrain—a particularly grueling journey for Mary, on the verge of delivery. Perhaps she and Joseph were conscious that a birth in Bethlehem would fulfill the prophecy in Mic. 5:2.

2:5 betrothed. *See note on Matt. 1:18.* Matthew 1:24 indicates that when the angel told Joseph about Mary's pregnancy, he "took to him his wife"—i.e., he took her into his home. But they did not consummate their marriage until after the birth of Jesus (Matt. 1:25). Therefore, technically, they were still betrothed.

2:7 firstborn. Mary had other children subsequent to this. *See note on Matt. 12:46.* **swaddling cloths.** Strips of cloth used to bind a baby tightly. It kept the baby from injuring sensitive facial skin and eyes with its own (often sharp) fingernails, and was believed to strengthen the limbs. This is still the custom in some Eastern cultures. The absence of swaddling cloths was a sign of poverty or lack of parental care (Ezek. 16:4). **manger.** A feeding trough for animals. This is the source of the notion that Christ was born in a stable, something nowhere stated in Scripture. Ancient tradition held that He was born in a cave (possibly one used as a shelter for animals). But no actual description of the location is given. **no room for them in the inn.** Possibly because many were returning to this ancient town to register in the census.

2:8 shepherds. Bethlehem was nearby Jerusalem, and many of the sheep used in the temple sacrifices came from there. The surrounding hills were prime grazing land, and shepherds worked in the area day and night, all year round. Therefore it is not possible to draw any conclusion about the time of year by the fact that shepherds were living out in the fields.

2:10 Do not be afraid. *See note on 1:12*; cf. 1:65.

good tidings of great joy [h]which will be to
all people. 11 [i]For there is born to you this
day in the city of David [j]a Savior, [k]who is
Christ the Lord. 12 And this *will be* the sign
to you: You will find a Babe wrapped in
swaddling cloths, lying in a [4]manger."
13 [l]And suddenly there was with the
angel a multitude of the heavenly host
praising God and saying:

14 "Glory[m] to God in the highest,
And on earth [n]peace, [o]goodwill[5]
toward men!"

The Shepherds Visit Jesus

15 So it was, when the angels had gone
away from them into heaven, that the
shepherds said to one another, "Let us now
go to Bethlehem and see this thing that has
come to pass, which the Lord has made
known to us." 16 And they came with haste
and found Mary and Joseph, and the Babe
lying in a manger. 17 Now when they had
seen *Him,* they made [6]widely known the
saying which was told them concerning
this Child. 18 And all those who heard *it*
marveled at those things which were told
them by the shepherds. 19 [p]But Mary kept
all these things and pondered *them* in her
heart. 20 Then the shepherds returned, glorifying and [q]praising God for all the things
that they had heard and seen, as it was told
them.

10 [h] Gen. 12:3; Is. 49:6; [Matt. 28:19; Mark 1:15; Col. 1:23]
11 [i] Is. 9:6 [j] Matt. 1:21; John 4:42; [Acts 5:31] [k] Matt. 1:16; 16:16, 20; John 11:27; Acts 2:36; Phil. 2:11
12 [4] *feed trough*
13 [l] Gen. 28:12; Ps. 103:20; 148:2; Dan. 7:10; [Heb. 1:14]; Rev. 5:11
14 [m] Matt. 21:9; Luke 19:38; Eph. 1:6 [n] Is. 57:19; [Rom. 5:1]; Eph. 2:17; [Col. 1:20] [o] [John 3:16; Eph. 2:4, 7; 2 Thess. 2:16; 1 John 4:9] [5] NU *toward men of goodwill*
17 [6] NU omits *widely*
19 [p] Gen. 37:11; Luke 1:66
20 [q] Luke 19:37
21 [r] Gen. 17:12; Lev. 12:3 [s] [Matt. 1:21] [t] Luke 1:31 [7] NU *for His circumcision*
22 [u] Lev. 12:2-8
23 [v] Ex. 13:12; 22:29; Lev. 27:26; Deut. 18:4; Neh. 10:36 [w] Ex. 13:2, 12, 15; Num. 3:13; 8:17
24 [x] Lev. 12:2, 8
25 [y] Is. 40:1; Mark 15:43; Luke 2:38; 23:51
26 [z] Ps. 89:48; [John 8:51; Heb. 11:5]
27 [a] Matt. 4:1
29 [b] Gen. 46:30; [Phil. 1:23]

Christ Is Circumcised

21 [r]And when eight days were completed [7]for the circumcision of the Child, His
name was called [s]JESUS, the name given by
the angel [t]before He was conceived in the
womb.
22 Now when [u]the days of her purification according to the law of Moses were
completed, they brought Him to Jerusalem
to present *Him* to the Lord 23 [v](as it is written in the law of the Lord, [w]*"Every male
who opens the womb shall be called holy
to the LORD"*), 24 and to offer a sacrifice according to what is said in the law of the
Lord, [x]*"A pair of turtledoves or two young
pigeons."*

Simeon's Prophecy

25 And behold, there was a man in Jerusalem whose name was Simeon, and this
man was just and devout, [y]waiting for the
Consolation of Israel, and the Holy Spirit
was upon him. 26 And it had been revealed
to him by the Holy Spirit that he would not
[z]see death before he had seen the Lord's
Christ. 27 So he came [a]by the Spirit into the
temple. And when the parents brought in
the Child Jesus, to do for Him according to
the custom of the law, 28 he took Him up in
his arms and blessed God and said:

29 "Lord, [b]now You are letting Your
servant depart in peace,
According to Your word;

2:11 city of David. I.e., Bethlehem, the town where David was born—not the City of David, which was on the southern slope of Mt. Zion (cf. 2 Sam. 5:7-9). **a Savior.** This is one of only two places in the gospels where Christ is referred to as "Savior"—the other being John 4:42, where the men of Sychar confessed Him as "Savior of the world." **Christ.** "Christ" is the Gr. equivalent of "Messiah" (*see note on Matt. 1:1*). **Lord.** The Gr. word can mean "master"—but it is also the word used to translate the covenant name of God. Here (and in most of its NT occurrences), it is used in the latter sense, as a title of deity.

2:13 host. A term used to describe an army encampment. Christ also used military imagery to describe the angels in Matt. 26:53 (*see note there*). Revelation 5:11 suggests that the number of the angelic host may be too large for the human mind to fathom. Note that here the heavenly army brought a message of peace and goodwill (v. 14).

2:14 the highest. I.e., heaven. **peace.** This is not to be taken as a universal declaration of peace toward all humanity. Rather, peace with God is a corollary of justification (*see note on Rom. 5:1*). **goodwill toward men.** Note the marginal rendering. The Gr. word for "goodwill" is also used in 10:21. The verb form of the same word is used in 3:22; 12:32. In each case, it refers to God's sovereign good pleasure. So a better rendering here might be "peace toward men on whom God's sovereign pleasure rests." God's peace is not a reward for those who have good will, but a gracious gift to those who are the objects of His good will.

2:18 all those who heard *it* marveled. Wonderment at the mysteries of Christ's words and works is one of the threads that runs through Luke's gospel. Cf. vv. 19,33,47,48; 1:21,63; 4:22,36; 5:9; 8:25; 9:43-45; 11:14; 20:26; 24:12,41. *See note on v. 20.*

2:20 praising God. Luke often reports this response. Cf. v. 28; 1:64; 5:25,26; 7:16; 13:13; 17:15-18; 18:43; 19:37-40; 23:47; 24:52,53.

2:21 eight days. *See note on 1:59.*

2:22 her purification. A woman who bore a son was ceremonially unclean for 40 days (twice that if she bore a daughter—Lev. 12:2-5). After that she was to offer a yearling lamb and a dove or pigeon (Lev. 12:6). If poor, she could offer two doves or pigeons (Lev. 12:8). Mary's offering indicates that she and Joseph were poor (v. 24). **to Jerusalem.** A journey of about 6 mi. from Bethlehem. **to present *Him* to the Lord.** The dedication of the firstborn son was also required by Moses' law (v. 23, cf. Ex. 13:2,12-15).

2:24 *A pair of turtledoves.* *See note on v. 22.* Quoted from Lev. 12:8.

2:25 Simeon. He is mentioned nowhere else in Scripture. **the Consolation of Israel.** A messianic title, evidently derived from verses like Is. 25:9; 40:1,2; 66:1-11.

2:26 it had been revealed to him. It is significant that with messianic expectation running so high (cf. 3:15), and with the many OT prophecies that spoke of His coming, still only a handful of people realized the significance of Christ's birth. Most of them, including Simeon, received some angelic message or other special revelation to make the fulfillment of the OT prophecies clear.

2:29-32 Simeon's psalm is known as the *Nunc Dimittis,* from the first two words of the Latin translation (*see notes on 1:46-55; 1:68-79*). It is the fourth of 5 psalms of praise Luke included in his birth narrative (see Introduction: Historical and Theological Themes). It is a touching expression of Simeon's extraordinary faith.

30 For my eyes [c]have seen Your
salvation
31 Which You have prepared before
the face of all peoples,
32 [d]A light to *bring* revelation to the
Gentiles,
And the glory of Your people
Israel."

33 [8]And Joseph and His mother marveled at those things which were spoken of
Him. 34 Then Simeon blessed them, and
said to Mary His mother, "Behold, this
Child is destined for the [e]fall and rising of
many in Israel, and for [f]a sign which will be
spoken against 35 (yes, [g]a sword will pierce
through your own soul also), that the
thoughts of many hearts may be revealed."

Anna's Testimony

36 Now there was one, Anna, a prophetess, the daughter of Phanuel, of the tribe of
[h]Asher. She was of a great age, and had
lived with a husband seven years from her
virginity; 37 and this woman *was* a widow
[9]of about eighty-four years, who did not
depart from the temple, but served *God*
with fastings and prayers [i]night and day.
38 And coming in that instant she gave
thanks to [1]the Lord, and spoke of Him to
all those who [j]looked for redemption in Jerusalem.

Jesus Returns to Nazareth—Matt. 2:19-23

39 So when they had performed all
things according to the law of the Lord,
they returned to Galilee, to their *own* city,
Nazareth. 40 [k]And the Child grew and became strong [2]in spirit, filled with wisdom;
and the grace of God was upon Him.

Jesus Celebrates the Passover

41 His parents went to [l]Jerusalem
[m]every year at the Feast of the Passover.
42 And when He was twelve years old,
they went up to Jerusalem according to the
[n]custom of the feast. 43 When they had finished the [o]days, as they returned, the Boy
Jesus lingered behind in Jerusalem. And
[3]Joseph and His mother did not know *it;*
44 but supposing Him to have been in the
company, they went a day's journey, and
sought Him among *their* relatives and acquaintances. 45 So when they did not find
Him, they returned to Jerusalem, seeking
Him. 46 Now so it was *that* after three days
they found Him in the temple, sitting in
the midst of the teachers, both listening to

30 [c]Ps. 119:166, 174; [Is. 52:10; Luke 3:6]
32 [d]Is. 9:2; 42:6; 49:6; 60:1-3; Matt. 4:16; Acts 10:45; 13:47; 28:28; [Rom. 9:24; Gal. 3:14]
33 [8]NU *And His father and mother*
34 [e]Is. 8:14; Hos. 14:9; Matt. 21:44; [Rom. 9:32]; 1 Cor. 1:23; [2 Cor. 2:16; 1 Pet. 2:7, 8] [f]Matt. 28:12-15; Acts 4:2; 17:32; 28:22; [1 Pet. 2:12; 4:14]
35 [g]Ps. 42:10; John 19:25
36 [h]Josh. 19:24
37 [i]Acts 26:7; 1 Tim. 5:5 [9]NU *until she was eighty-four*
38 [j]Lam. 3:25, 26; Mark 15:43; Luke 24:21 [1]NU *God*
40 [k]Luke 1:80; 2:52; [1 Cor. 1:24, 30] [2]NU omits *in spirit*
41 [l]John 4:20 [m]Ex. 23:15, 17; 34:23; Deut. 16:1, 16; Luke 22:15
42 [n]Ex. 23:14, 15
43 [o]Ex. 12:15 [3]NU *His parents*

2:30 Your salvation. I.e., the One who would redeem His people from their sins.

2:31 all peoples. I.e., all nations, tongues, and tribes (cf. Rev. 7:9)—both Israel and the Gentiles (v. 32).

2:34 fall and rising of many in Israel. To those who reject Him, He is a stone of stumbling (1 Pet. 2:8); those who receive Him are raised up (Eph. 2:6). Cf. Is. 8:14,15; Hos. 14:9; 1 Cor. 1:23,24. **spoken against.** This was synecdoche. Simeon mentioned only the verbal insults hurled at Christ, but the expression actually embraced more than that—Israel's rejection, and hatred, and crucifixion of the Messiah. *See note on v. 35.*

2:35 a sword. This was undoubtedly a reference to the personal grief Mary would endure when she watched her own Son die in agony (John 19:25). **that the thoughts of many hearts may be revealed.** The rejection of the Messiah (*see note on v. 34*) would reveal the appalling truth about the apostate state of the Jews.

2:36 a prophetess. This refers to a woman who spoke God's Word. She was a teacher of the OT, not a source of revelation. The OT mentions only 3 women who prophesied: Miriam (Ex. 15:20); Deborah (Judg. 4:4); Huldah (2 Kin. 22:14; 2 Chr. 34:22). One other, the "prophetess" Noadiah, was evidently a false prophet, grouped by Nehemiah with his enemies. Isaiah 8:3 refers to the prophet's wife as a "prophetess"—but there is no evidence Isaiah's wife prophesied. Perhaps she is so-called because the child she bore was given a name that was prophetic (Is. 8:3,4). This use of the title for Isaiah's wife also shows that the title does not necessarily indicate an ongoing revelatory prophetic ministry. Rabbinical tradition also regarded Sarah, Hannah, Abigail, and Esther as prophetesses (apparently to make an even 7 with Miriam, Deborah, and Huldah). In the NT, the daughters of Philip prophesied (*see note on Acts 21:9*).

2:37 a widow of about eighty-four years. This probably means she was an 84-year-old widow, not that she had been widowed that long, since if she had been widowed 84 years after a 7-year marriage (v. 35), she would have been at least 104 years old. **not depart from the temple.** She evidently had her living quarters on the temple grounds. There would have been several such dwelling places for priests in the outer court, and Anna must have been allowed to live there permanently because of her unusual status as a prophetess.

2:39 they returned to Galilee. Luke omitted the visit of the Magi and the flight into Egypt (Matt. 2:1-18). The theme of early rejection, so prominent in Matthew (see Introduction to Matthew: Historical and Theological Themes), was not where Luke focused his attention.

2:41 Feast of the Passover. *See note on Ex. 23:14-19.* Passover was a one-day feast, followed immediately by the week-long Feast of Unleavened Bread (*see note on Matt. 26:17*).

2:42 when He was twelve years old. *Bar mitzvah* (when a Jewish boy became a "son of the commandment") was at age 13, so most boys celebrated their first feast at age 12, in preparation for that rite of passage into adulthood. *See note on Matt. 21:15.*

2:43 Jesus lingered. In stark contrast to the apocryphal gospels' spurious tales of youthful miracles and supernatural exploits, this lone biblical insight into the youth of Jesus portrays Him as a typical boy in a typical family. His lingering was neither mischievous nor disobedient; it was owing to a simple mistaken presumption on His parents' part (v. 44) that He was left behind.

2:44 in the company. Obviously Joseph and Mary were traveling with a large caravan of friends and relatives from Nazareth. No doubt hundreds of people from their community went together to the feast. Men and women in such a group might have been separated by some distance, and it appears each parent thought He was with the other.

2:46 three days. This probably does not mean they searched Jerusalem for 3 days. They apparently realized He was missing at the end of a full day's travel. That required another full day's journey back to Jerusalem, and the better part of another day was spent seeking Him. **listening to them and asking them questions.** He was utterly respectful, taking the role of the student. But even at that young age, His questions showed a wisdom that put the teachers to shame.

them and asking them questions. 47 And
[p]all who heard Him were astonished at His
understanding and answers. 48 So when
they saw Him, they were amazed; and His
mother said to Him, "Son, why have You
done this to us? Look, Your father and I
have sought You anxiously."
49 And He said to them, "Why did you
seek Me? Did you not know that I must be
[q]about [r]My Father's business?" 50 But
[s]they did not understand the statement
which He spoke to them.

Jesus Grows in Wisdom

51 Then He went down with them and
came to Nazareth, and was [4]subject to
them, but His mother [t]kept all these things
in her heart. 52 And Jesus [u]increased in
wisdom and stature, [v]and in favor with
God and men.

The Ministry of John the Baptist
Matt. 3:1-12; Mark 1:2-8; John 1:19-31

3 Now in the fifteenth year of the reign of
Tiberius Caesar, [a]Pontius Pilate being
governor of Judea, Herod being tetrarch of
Galilee, his brother Philip tetrarch of Iturea
and the region of Trachonitis, and Lysanias
tetrarch of Abilene, 2 [1]while [b]Annas and
Caiaphas were high priests, the word of
God came to [c]John the son of Zacharias in
the wilderness. 3 [d]And he went into all the
region around the Jordan, preaching a baptism of repentance [e]for the remission of
sins, 4 as it is written in the book of the
words of Isaiah the prophet, saying:

[f]"The voice of one crying in the
wilderness:
'Prepare the way of the LORD;
Make His paths straight.
5 *Every valley shall be filled*
And every mountain and hill
brought low;
The crooked places shall be made
straight
And the rough ways smooth;
6 *And [g]all flesh shall see the*
salvation of God.' "

7 Then he said to the multitudes that
came out to be baptized by him, [h]"Brood[2]

47 [p]Matt. 7:28; 13:54; 22:33; Mark 1:22; 6:2; 11:18; Luke 4:32; John 7:15
49 [q]John 9:4 [r][Mark 1:22; Luke 4:22, 32; John 4:34; 5:17, 36]
50 [s]Mark 9:32; Luke 9:45; 18:34; John 7:15, 46
51 [t]Dan. 7:28 [4]*obedient*
52 [u][Is. 11:2, 3; Col. 2:2, 3] [v]1 Sam. 2:26; [Prov. 3:1-4]

CHAPTER 3

1 [a]Matt. 27:2
2 [b]John 11:49; 18:13; Acts 4:6 [c]Luke 1:13 [1]NU, M *in the high priesthood of Annas and Caiaphas*
3 [d]Matt. 3:1; Mark 1:4 [e]Luke 1:77
4 [f]Is. 40:3-5; Matt. 3:3; Mark 1:3
6 [g]Ps. 98:2; Is. 52:10; Luke 2:10; [Rom. 10:8-18]
7 [h]Matt. 3:7; 12:34; 23:33 [2]*Offspring*

2:48 why have You done this to us? Mary's words convey a tone of exasperation and rebuke—normal for any mother under such circumstances, but misplaced in this case. He was not hiding from them or defying their authority. In fact, He had done precisely what any child should do under such circumstances (being left by His parents)—He went to a safe, public place, in the presence of trusted adults, where His parents could be expected to come looking for Him (v. 49). **Your father.** I.e., Joseph, who was legally His father.

2:49 My Father's business. Contrasting with Mary's "your father" in v. 48. His reply was in no sense insolent, but reveals a genuine amazement that they did not know where to look for Him. This also reveals that even at so young an age, He had a clear consciousness of His identity and mission.

2:51 was subject. His relationship with His Heavenly Father did not override or nullify His duty to His earthly parents. His obedience to the fifth commandment was an essential part of the perfect legal obedience He rendered on our behalf (Heb. 4:4; 5:8,9). He had to fulfill all righteousness (*see note on Matt. 3:15*).

2:52 And Jesus increased. Jesus did not cease being God or divest Himself of divine attributes in order to become man. Rather, He took on a human nature (an addition, not a subtraction), and submitted the use of His divine attributes to the will of the Father (John 5:19,30; 8:28; Phil. 2:5-8). Therefore, there were times when His omniscience was on display (Matt. 9:4; John 2:24,25; 4:17,18; 11:11-14; 16:30) and other times when it was veiled by His humanity in accordance with the Father's will (Mark 13:32). Christ was therefore subject to the normal process of human growth, intellectually, physically, spiritually, and socially. *See note on Mark 13:32.*

3:1 fifteenth year of the reign of Tiberius. Because of the way Tiberius came to power, this date is hard to fix precisely. When the Roman Senate declared Augustus emperor (*see note on 2:1*), they did so on condition that his power would end with his death, rather than passing to his heirs. The idea was that the senate, rather than the emperor himself, was to choose the heir to the throne. However, Augustus circumvented that difficulty by appointing a co-regent, on whom he planned gradually to confer the imperial powers. When he outlived his first choice for successor, Augustus next selected his son-in-law, Tiberius, whom he adopted and made his heir in A.D. 4 (Augustus disliked Tiberius but hoped to pass power to his grandsons through him). Tiberius was made co-regent in A.D. 11, then automatically became sole ruler at the death of Augustus on Aug. 19, A.D. 14. If Luke's chronology is dated from Tiberius' appointment to the co-regency, the 15th year would be A.D. 25 or 26. If Luke was reckoning from the death of Augustus, this date would fall between Aug. 19, A.D. 28 and Aug. 18, A.D. 29. One other fact complicates the setting of a precise date: the Jews reckoned a ruler's term from the Jewish New Year following accession, so if Luke was using the Jewish system, the actual dates could be slightly later. **Pontius Pilate...Herod...Philip.** *See note on Matt. 2:22.* **Lysanias.** Ruler of the area NW of Damascus. History is virtually silent about him.

3:2 Annas and Caiaphas were high priests. *See note on Acts 4:6.* According to Josephus, Annas served as High-Priest A.D. 6–15, when he was deposed by Roman officials. He nonetheless retained *de facto* power, as seen in the fact that his successors included 5 of his sons and Caiaphas, a son-in-law (*see note on Matt. 26:3*). Caiaphas was the actual High-Priest during the time Luke describes, but Annas still controlled the office. This is seen clearly in the fact that Christ was taken to Annas first after His arrest, then to Caiaphas (*see note on Matt. 26:57*). **wilderness.** *See note on Matt. 3:1.*

3:3 baptism of repentance. *See note on Matt. 3:6.* **for the remission of sins.** I.e., to symbolize and testify of the forgiveness already received upon repentance (*see note on Acts 2:38*).

3:4 *Make His paths straight.* Quoted from Is. 40:3-5 (*see notes there*). A monarch traveling in wilderness regions would have a crew of workmen go ahead to make sure the road was clear of debris, obstructions, potholes, and other hazards that made the journey difficult. In a spiritual sense, John was calling the people of Israel to prepare their hearts for the coming of their Messiah.

3:6 *all flesh.* I.e., Gentiles as well as Jews (*see note on 2:31*). All 4 gospels quote Is. 40:3 (Matt. 3:3; Mark 1:3; John 1:23). Only Luke adds vv. 5,6—thus using a familiar text from Isaiah to stress his theme of the universal scope of the gospel (see Introduction: Interpretive Challenges).

of vipers! Who warned you to flee from the
wrath to come? 8 Therefore bear fruits
[i]worthy of repentance, and do not begin to
say to yourselves, 'We have Abraham as
our father.' For I say to you that God is able
to raise up children to Abraham from these
stones. 9 And even now the ax is laid to the
root of the trees. Therefore [j]every tree
which does not bear good fruit is cut down
and thrown into the fire."
10 So the people asked him, saying,
[k]"What shall we do then?"
11 He answered and said to them, [l]"He
who has two tunics, let him give to him
who has none; and he who has food, [m]let
him do likewise."
12 Then [n]tax collectors also came to be
baptized, and said to him, "Teacher, what
shall we do?"
13 And he said to them, [o]"Collect no
more than what is appointed for you."
14 Likewise the soldiers asked him, saying,
"And what shall we do?"
So he said to them, "Do not [3]intimidate
anyone [p]or accuse falsely, and be content
with your wages."
15 Now as the people were in expectation,
and all reasoned in their hearts about John,
whether he was the Christ *or* not, 16 John
answered, saying to all, [q]"I indeed baptize
you with water; but One mightier than I is
coming, whose sandal strap I am not worthy
to loose. He will [r]baptize you with the
Holy Spirit and fire. 17 His winnowing fan
is in His hand, and He will thoroughly clean
out His threshing floor, and [s]gather the
wheat into His barn; but the chaff He will
burn with unquenchable fire."
18 And with many other exhortations he
preached to the people. 19 [t]But Herod the
tetrarch, being rebuked by him concerning
Herodias, his [4]brother Philip's wife, and
for all the evils which Herod had done,
20 also added this, above all, that he shut
John up in prison.

The Baptism of Christ

Matt. 3:13-17; Mark 1:9-11; John 1:32-34

21 When all the people were baptized, [u]it
came to pass that Jesus also was baptized;
and while He prayed, the heaven was
opened. 22 And the Holy Spirit descended
in bodily form like a dove upon Him, and
a voice came from heaven which said,
"You are My beloved Son; in You I am
[v]well pleased."

The Genealogy of Christ Through Mary

Gen. 5:1-32; 11:10-26; Ruth 4:18-22; 1 Chr. 1:1-4, 24-27, 34; 2:1-15; Matt. 1:2-6

23 Now Jesus Himself began *His ministry*
at [w]about thirty years of age, being (as was
supposed) [x]*the* son of Joseph, *the son* of Heli,
24 *the son* of Matthat, *the son* of Levi, *the son*

8 [i] [2 Cor. 7:9-11]
9 [j] Matt. 7:19; Luke 13:6-9
10 [k] Luke 3:12, 14; [Acts 2:37, 38; 16:30, 31]
11 [l] Luke 11:41; 2 Cor. 8:14; James 2:15, 16; [1 John 3:17; 4:20] [m] Is. 58:7; [1 Tim. 6:17, 18]
12 [n] Matt. 21:32; Luke 7:29
13 [o] Luke 19:8
14 [p] Ex. 20:16; 23:1; Lev. 19:11 [3] Lit. *shake down* for money
16 [q] Matt. 3:11, 12; Mark 1:7, 8 [r] John 7:39; 20:22; Acts 2:1-4
17 [s] Mic. 4:12; Matt. 13:24-30
19 [t] Matt. 14:3; Mark 6:17 [4] NU *brother's wife*
21 [u] Matt. 3:13-17; John 1:32
22 [v] Ps. 2:7; [Is. 42:1]; Matt. 3:17; 17:5; Mark 1:11; Luke 1:35; 9:35; 2 Pet. 1:17
23 [w] [Num. 4:3, 35, 39, 43, 47] [x] Matt. 13:55; John 6:42

3:7 the wrath to come. Possibly a reference to the coming destruction of Jerusalem. But this certainly also looks beyond any earthly calamity to the eschatological outpouring of divine wrath in the Day of the Lord, and especially the final judgment, where divine wrath will be the just fruit of all the unrepentant (cf. Rom. 1:18; 1 Thess. 1:10; Heb. 10:27). *See note on Matt. 3:7.*

3:8 children to Abraham. Abraham's true children are not merely physical descendants, but those who follow his faith, believing God's Word the way he did (Rom. 4:11-16; 9:8; Gal. 3:7). To trust one's physical ancestry is to shift the focus of faith away from God Himself—and that is spiritually fatal (cf. John 8:39-44). **stones.** Cf. 19:40. The imagery may echo OT verses such as Ezek. 11:19; 36:26; God can sovereignly turn a heart of stone into a believing heart. He can raise up children to Abraham from inanimate objects if he chooses—or even from stony-hearted Gentiles (cf. Gal. 3:29).

3:9 ax...to the root. *See note on Matt. 3:10.*

3:11 two tunics. Shirt-like garments. Only one could be worn at a time. John was still stressing the imminence of the coming judgment. This was not a time to hoard one's surplus goods.

3:12 tax collectors. *See note on Matt. 5:46.*

3:14 soldiers. No doubt these were members of the occupying Roman army, hated by the Jewish people for their brutality and paganism. Perhaps these particular soldiers were assigned to enforce the will of the tax collectors (v. 12). The fact that such people responded to John's preaching reveals the powerful influence his ministry had—especially on the outcasts of society (cf. Matt. 21:31,32). **Do not intimidate anyone.** Here and in v. 13, John demanded integrity and high character in the practical matters of everyday life, not a monastic lifestyle or a mystical asceticism. Cf. James 1:27.

3:16 baptize. *See note on Matt. 3:11.* **sandal strap.** Unfastening the sandal strap was the lowliest slave's task, preliminary to washing the feet (*see note on John 13:5*).

3:17 fan. *See note on Matt. 3:12.*

3:19 rebuked...concerning Herodias. *See note on Matt. 14:3.*

3:20 shut John up in prison. This event actually occurred much later during Jesus' ministry (John 3:22-24; Matt. 14:1-12). But Luke organized his material on John the Baptist topically rather than chronologically (see Introduction: Background and Setting).

3:21 baptized. *See note on Matt. 3:15.* **while He prayed.** Luke alone notes that Jesus was praying. Prayer is one of Luke's themes (see Introduction: Historical and Theological Themes).

3:22 Holy Spirit. *See note on Matt. 3:16,17.* All 3 persons of the Trinity are distinguishable in this verse, a strong proof against the heresy of modalism, which suggests that God is one Person who manifests Himself in 3 distinct modes, one at a time. **in bodily form.** I.e., physical and visible to all (cf. Matt. 3:16; John 1:32). **like a dove.** A picture of gentleness (Matt. 10:16). **My beloved Son.** *See note on Matt. 3:17.*

3:23-38 Luke's genealogy moves backward, from Jesus to Adam; Matthew's moves forward, from Abraham to Joseph. Luke's entire section from Joseph to David differs starkly from that given by Matthew. The two genealogies are easily reconciled if Luke's is seen as Mary's genealogy, and Matthew's version represents Joseph's. Thus the royal line is passed through Jesus' legal father, and His physical descent from David is established by Mary's lineage. Luke, unlike Matthew (*see note on Matt. 1:3*), includes no women in his genealogy—even Mary herself. Joseph was "the son of Heli" by marriage (Heli having no sons of his own), and thus is named here in v. 23 as the representative of Mary's generation. Moses himself established precedent for this sort of substitution in Num. 27:1-11; 36:1-12. The men listed from Heli (v. 23) to Rhesa (v. 27) are found nowhere else in Scripture. Zerubbabel

of Melchi, *the son* of Janna, *the son* of Joseph,
25 *the son* of Mattathiah, *the son* of Amos, *the*
son of Nahum, *the son* of Esli, *the son* of Nag-
gai, 26 *the son* of Maath, *the son* of Mattathiah,
the son of Semei, *the son* of Joseph, *the son* of
Judah, 27 *the son* of Joannas, *the son* of Rhesa,
the son of [y]Zerubbabel, *the son* of Shealtiel,
the son of Neri, 28 *the son* of Melchi, *the son* of
Addi, *the son* of Cosam, *the son* of Elmodam,
the son of Er, 29 *the son* of Jose, *the son* of Eliezer, *the son* of Jorim, *the son* of Matthat, *the*
son of Levi, 30 *the son* of Simeon, *the son* of Judah, *the son* of Joseph, *the son* of Jonan, *the*
son of Eliakim, 31 *the son* of Melea, *the son* of
Menan, *the son* of Mattathah, *the son* of [z]Na-
than, [a]*the son* of David, 32 [b]*the son* of Jesse,
the son of Obed, *the son* of Boaz, *the son* of
Salmon, *the son* of Nahshon, 33 *the son* of
Amminadab, *the son* of Ram, *the son* of Hezron, *the son* of Perez, *the son* of Judah, 34 *the*
son of Jacob, *the son* of Isaac, *the son* of Abraham, [c]*the son* of Terah, *the son* of Nahor, 35 *the*
son of Serug, *the son* of Reu, *the son* of Peleg,
the son of Eber, *the son* of Shelah, 36 [d]*the son* of
Cainan, *the son* of [e]Arphaxad, [f]*the son* of
Shem, *the son* of Noah, *the son* of Lamech,
37 *the son* of Methuselah, *the son* of Enoch, *the*
son of Jared, *the son* of Mahalalel, *the son* of
Cainan, 38 *the son* of Enosh, *the son* of Seth,
the son of Adam, [g]*the son* of God.

The Temptation of Christ
Matt. 4:1-11; Mark 1:12, 13

4 Then [a]Jesus, being filled with the Holy
Spirit, returned from the Jordan and
[b]was led by the Spirit [1]into the wilderness,
2 being [2]tempted for forty days by the
devil. And [c]in those days He ate nothing,
and afterward, when they had ended, He
was hungry.
3 And the devil said to Him, "If You are
[d]the Son of God, command this stone to
become bread."
4 But Jesus answered him, saying, "It is
written, [e]'*Man shall not live by bread*
alone, [3]*but by every word of God.*' "
5 [4]Then the devil, taking Him up on a
high mountain, showed Him all the kingdoms of the world in a moment of time.
6 And the devil said to Him, "All this authority I will give You, and their glory; for
[f]this has been delivered to me, and I give it
to whomever I wish. 7 Therefore, if You
will worship before me, all will be Yours."
8 And Jesus answered and said to him,
[5]"Get behind Me, Satan! [6]For it is written,
[g]'*You shall worship the* LORD *your God,*
and Him only you shall serve.' "
9 [h]Then he brought Him to Jerusalem, set
Him on the pinnacle of the temple, and said
to Him, "If You are the Son of God, throw
Yourself down from here. 10 For it is written:
[i]'*He shall give His angels charge*
over you,
To keep you,'
11 and,
[j]'*In their hands they shall bear you*
up,
Lest you dash your foot against a
stone.' "
12 And Jesus answered and said to him,
"It has been said, [k]'*You shall not* [7]*tempt*
the LORD *your God.*' "
13 Now when the devil had ended every
[8]temptation, he departed from Him [l]until
an opportune time.

Acceptance Throughout Galilee
Matt. 4:12; Mark 1:14

14 [m]Then Jesus returned [n]in the power of
the Spirit to [o]Galilee, and [p]news of Him
went out through all the surrounding region. 15 And He [q]taught in their synagogues, [r]being glorified by all.

27 [y]Ezra 2:2; 3:8
31 [z]Zech. 12:12 [a]2 Sam. 5:14; 7:12; 1 Chr. 3:5; 17:11; Is. 9:7; Jer. 23:5
32 [b]Ruth 4:18-22; 1 Chr. 2:10-12; Is. 11:1, 10
34 [c]Gen. 11:24, 26-30; 12:3; Num. 24:17; 1 Chr. 1:24-27
36 [d]Gen. 11:12 [e]Gen. 10:22, 24; 11:10-13; 1 Chr. 1:17, 18 [f]Gen. 5:6-32; 9:27; 11:10
38 [g]Gen. 5:1, 2

CHAPTER 4

1 [a][Is. 11:2; 61:1]; Matt. 4:1-11; Mark 1:12, 13 [b]Ezek. 3:12; Luke 2:27 [1]NU *in*
2 [c]Ex. 34:28; 1 Kin. 19:8 [2]*tested*
3 [d]Mark 3:11; John 20:31
4 [e]Deut. 8:3 [3]NU omits *but by every word of God*
5 [4]NU *And taking Him up, he showed Him*
6 [f][John 12:31; 14:30; Rev. 13:2, 7]
8 [g]Deut. 6:13; 10:20; Matt. 4:10 [5]NU omits *Get behind Me, Satan* [6]NU, M omit *For*
9 [h]Matt. 4:5-7
10 [i]Ps. 91:11
11 [j]Ps. 91:12
12 [k]Deut. 6:16 [7]*test*
13 [l][John 14:30; Heb. 4:15; James 4:7] [8]*testing*
14 [m]Matt. 4:12 [n]John 4:43 [o]Acts 10:37 [p]Matt. 4:24
15 [q]Ps. 22:22; Matt. 4:23 [r]Is. 52:13

and Shealtiel (v. 27) are the only two names here that correspond to names in Matthew's genealogy between David and Jesus. For an explanation *see notes on Hag. 2:23; Matt. 1:12.*

3:23 about thirty years of age. Luke was probably not fixing an exact age. Rather, this was an approximation, 30 being a customary age for entering into the office of prophet (Ezek. 1:1); priest (Num. 4:3,35,39,43,47), or king (Gen. 41:46; 2 Sam. 5:4). **as was supposed.** Luke had already established the fact of the virgin birth (1:34,35); here he made clear once again that Joseph was not Jesus' true father.

4:1 led by the Spirit. *See note on Matt. 4:1.*

4:2 tempted for forty days. Evidently the temptation of Christ encompassed the full 40 days of His fast (*see note on Matt. 4:2*). Both Matthew and Luke give a condensed recounting of only 3 specific temptations. Luke reverses the order of the last two temptations in Matthew's account. Luke occasionally ordered material logically, rather than chronologically (see Introduction: Background and Setting; see note on 1:3). Luke may have had some purpose for doing so here—perhaps to end his account of Jesus' temptation at the temple in Jerusalem (cf. v. 9), a very important location in Luke's narrative (see Introduction: Historical and Theological Themes).

4:3-13 *See notes on Matt. 4:3-10.*

4:4 Jesus quoted Deut. 8:3.

4:8 Jesus quoted Deut. 6:13.

4:10,11 Satan quoted Ps. 91:11,12.

4:12 Jesus quoted Deut. 6:16.

4:13 until an opportune time. Satan's temptations did not end here for Christ, but persisted throughout His ministry (cf. Heb. 4:15), and culminated in Gethsemane (22:39-46).

4:14 returned…to Galilee. The synoptic gospels are largely silent about Jesus' ministry between His baptism and His return to Galilee, but John recorded a fairly extensive ministry in Jerusalem and Judea (John 2:12–4:1). Because of this, news of Him quickly spread.

4:15 synagogues. *See note on Mark 1:21.*

Rejection at Nazareth

16 So He came to [s]Nazareth, where He
had been brought up. And as His custom
was, [t]He went into the synagogue on the
Sabbath day, and stood up to read. 17 And
He was handed the book of the prophet
Isaiah. And when He had opened the book,
He found the place where it was written:

18 *"The[u] Spirit of the LORD is upon Me,*
Because He has anointed Me
To preach the gospel to the poor;
He has sent Me [9] to heal the
brokenhearted,
To proclaim liberty to the captives
And recovery of sight to the blind,
To [v] set at liberty those who are
[1] oppressed;
19 *To proclaim the acceptable year of*
the LORD."

20 Then He closed the book, and gave *it*
back to the attendant and sat down. And
the eyes of all who were in the synagogue
were fixed on Him. 21 And He began to say
to them, "Today this Scripture is [w]fulfilled
in your hearing." 22 So all bore witness to
Him, and [x]marveled at the gracious words
which proceeded out of His mouth. And
they said, [y]"Is this not Joseph's son?"
23 He said to them, "You will surely say
this proverb to Me, 'Physician, heal yourself! Whatever we have heard done in [z]Ca-
pernaum,[2] do also here in [a]Your country.' "

16 [s] Matt. 2:23; 13:54; Mark 6:1 [t] Mark 1:21; John 18:20; Acts 13:14-16; 17:2
18 [u] Is. 49:8, 9; 61:1, 2; Matt. 11:5; 12:18; John 3:34 [v] [Dan. 9:24] [9] NU omits *to heal the brokenhearted* [1] *downtrodden*
21 [w] Matt. 1:22, 23; Acts 13:29
22 [x] [Ps. 45:2]; Matt. 13:54; Mark 6:2; Luke 2:47; [John 1:14, 17] [y] John 6:42
23 [z] Matt. 4:13; 11:23 [a] Matt. 13:54; Mark 6:1 [2] NU *Capharnaum,* here and elsewhere
24 [b] Matt. 13:57; Mark 6:4; John 4:44
25 [c] 1 Kin. 17:9; James 5:17
26 [3] Gr. *Sarepta*
27 [d] 2 Kin. 5:1-14
28 [e] Luke 6:11 [4] *rage*
29 [f] Luke 17:25; John 8:37; 10:31
30 [g] John 8:59; 10:39
31 [h] Is. 9:1; Matt. 4:13; Mark 1:21
32 [i] Matt. 7:28, 29 [j] Luke 4:36; [John 6:63; 7:46; 8:26, 28, 38, 47; 12:49, 50]
33 [k] Mark 1:23
34 [l] Luke 4:41 [m] Ps. 16:10; Is. 49:7; Dan. 9:24; Luke 1:35

24 Then He said, "Assuredly, I say to you,
no [b]prophet is accepted in his own country.
25 But I tell you truly, [c]many widows were
in Israel in the days of Elijah, when the
heaven was shut up three years and six
months, and there was a great famine
throughout all the land; 26 but to none of
them was Elijah sent except to [3]Zarephath,
in the region of Sidon, to a woman *who was* a
widow. 27 [d]And many lepers were in Israel
in the time of Elisha the prophet, and none
of them was cleansed except Naaman the
Syrian."
28 So all those in the synagogue, when
they heard these things, were [e]filled with
[4]wrath, 29 [f]and rose up and thrust Him out
of the city; and they led Him to the brow of
the hill on which their city was built, that
they might throw Him down over the cliff.
30 Then [g]passing through the midst of
them, He went His way.

Demons Are Cast Out—Mark 1:21-28

31 Then [h]He went down to Capernaum,
a city of Galilee, and was teaching them on
the Sabbaths. 32 And they were [i]astonished
at His teaching, [j]for His word was with authority. 33 [k]Now in the synagogue there
was a man who had a spirit of an unclean
demon. And he cried out with a loud
voice, 34 saying, "Let us alone! What have
we to do with You, Jesus of Nazareth? Did
You come to destroy us? [l]I know who You
are—[m]the Holy One of God!"

4:16 He came to Nazareth. Luke acknowledged in v. 23 (*see note there*) that Christ had already ministered in Capernaum. Yet Luke purposely situated this episode at the beginning of his account of Christ's public ministry. Here is an example of Luke's ordering things logically rather than chronologically (see Introduction: Background and Setting; see note on 1:3). **as His custom was.** Nazareth was his hometown, so He would have been well known to all who regularly attended this synagogue.

4:18 *He has anointed Me.* I.e., the Spirit Himself was the anointing (vv. 1,14).

4:19 *the acceptable year of the LORD.* Or, "the year of the Lord's favor." The passage Christ read was Is. 61:1,2. He stopped in the middle of v. 2. The rest of the verse prophesies judgment in the day of God's vengeance. Since that part of the verse pertains to the second advent, He did not read it.

4:20 sat down. It was customary for a teacher to stand respectfully during the reading of the Scriptures (v. 16), and sit humbly to teach. *See note on Matt. 5:1.*

4:21 this Scripture is fulfilled. This was an unambiguous claim that He was the Messiah who fulfilled the prophecy. They correctly understood His meaning but could not accept such lofty claims from One whom they knew so well as the carpenter's son (v. 22; cf. Matt. 13:55).

4:23 Capernaum. Obviously Christ had already gained a reputation for His miraculous works in Capernaum. Scripture gives few details about that first year of public ministry. Most of what we know about those months is found in John's gospel, and it suggests Christ ministered mostly in Judea. However, John 2:12 mentions a brief visit to Capernaum, with no other details. John 4:46-54 describes how while Christ was at Cana, He healed a nobleman's son who lay sick in Capernaum. We also know that Christ had already gathered some of His disciples, who were men from the N shore of the Sea of Galilee (John 1:35-42; *see note on Matt. 4:18*). He might have visited there more than once during that first year of ministry. In any case, He had been there long enough to do miracles, and His fame had spread throughout Galilee (cf. v. 14).

4:25-27 Both the widow of Zarephath (1 Kin. 17:8-24) and Naaman the Syrian (2 Kin. 5) were Gentiles. Both lived during times of widespread unbelief in Israel. Jesus' point was that God bypassed all the widows and lepers in Israel, yet showed grace to two Gentiles. God's concern for Gentiles and outcasts is one of the thematic threads that runs through Luke's gospel (see Introduction: Historical and Theological Themes).

4:28 filled with wrath. This is Luke's first mention of hostile opposition to Christ's ministry. What seems to have sparked the Nazarenes' fury was Christ's suggestion that divine grace might be withheld from them yet extended to Gentiles.

4:30 passing through the midst of them. The implication is that this was a miraculous escape—the first of several similar incidents in which He escaped a premature death at the hands of a mob (cf. John 7:30; 8:59; 10:39).

4:32 authority. *See note on Matt. 7:29.*

4:33 demon. *See note on Matt. 8:16.*

4:34 Holy One of God. Demons always recognized Christ immediately (cf. v. 41; 8:28; Matt. 8:29; Mark 1:24; 3:11; 5:7)

35 But Jesus rebuked him, saying, [5]"Be
quiet, and come out of him!" And when
the demon had thrown him in *their* midst,
it came out of him and did not hurt him.
36 Then they were all amazed and spoke
among themselves, saying, "What a word
this *is!* For with authority and power He
commands the unclean spirits, and they
come out." 37 And the report about Him
went out into every place in the surrounding region.

Peter's Mother-in-Law Healed
Matt. 8:14, 15; Mark 1:29-31

38 [n]Now He arose from the synagogue
and entered Simon's house. But Simon's
wife's mother was [6]sick with a high fever,
and they [o]made request of Him concerning
her. 39 So He stood over her and [p]rebuked
the fever, and it left her. And immediately
she arose and served them.

Jesus Ministers Throughout Galilee
Matt. 4:23-25; 8:16, 17; Mark 1:32-39

40 [q]When the sun was setting, all those
who had any that were sick with various
diseases brought them to Him; and He laid
His hands on every one of them and
healed them. 41 [r]And demons also came
out of many, crying out and saying, [s]"You
are [7]the Christ, the Son of God!"
And He, [t]rebuking *them,* did not allow
them to [8]speak, for they knew that He was
the Christ.
42 [u]Now when it was day, He departed
and went into a deserted place. And the
crowd sought Him and came to Him, and
tried to keep Him from leaving them;
43 but He said to them, "I must [v]preach the
kingdom of God to the other cities also, because for this purpose I have been sent."
44 [w]And He was preaching in the synagogues of [9]Galilee.

35 [5] Lit. *Be muzzled*
38 [n] Matt. 8:14, 15; Mark 1:29-31 [o] Mark 5:23 [6] *afflicted with*
39 [p] Luke 8:24
40 [q] Matt. 8:16, 17; Mark 1:32-34
41 [r] Mark 1:34; 3:11; Acts 8:7 [s] Mark 8:29 [t] Mark 1:25, 34; 3:11; Luke 4:34, 35 [7] NU omits *the Christ* [8] Or *say that they knew*
42 [u] Mark 1:35-38; Luke 9:10
43 [v] Mark 1:14; [John 9:4]
44 [w] Matt. 4:23; 9:35; Mark 1:39 [9] NU *Judea*

CHAPTER 5

1 [a] Matt. 4:18-22; Mark 1:16-20; John 1:40-42 [b] Acts 13:44
3 [c] John 8:2
4 [d] John 21:6
5 [e] John 21:3 [f] Ps. 33:9
8 [g] 2 Sam. 6:9; 1 Kin. 17:18
9 [h] Mark 5:42; 10:24, 26
10 [i] Matt. 4:19; Mark 1:17
11 [j] Matt. 4:20; 19:27; [Mark 1:18; 8:34, 35; Luke 9:59-62]; John 12:26 [1] *left behind*
12 [k] Matt. 8:2-4; Mark 1:40-44 [l] Lev. 13:14 [2] *begged*

The First Disciples Are Called

5 So[a] it was, as the multitude pressed
about Him to [b]hear the word of God,
that He stood by the Lake of Gennesaret,
2 and saw two boats standing by the lake;
but the fishermen had gone from them and
were washing *their* nets. 3 Then He got into
one of the boats, which was Simon's, and
asked him to put out a little from the land.
And He [c]sat down and taught the multitudes from the boat.
4 When He had stopped speaking, He
said to Simon, [d]"Launch out into the deep
and let down your nets for a catch."
5 But Simon answered and said to Him,
"Master, we have toiled all night and
caught [e]nothing; nevertheless [f]at Your
word I will let down the net." 6 And when
they had done this, they caught a great
number of fish, and their net was breaking.
7 So they signaled to *their* partners in the
other boat to come and help them. And
they came and filled both the boats, so that
they began to sink. 8 When Simon Peter
saw *it,* he fell down at Jesus' knees, saying,
[g]"Depart from me, for I am a sinful man,
O Lord!"
9 For he and all who were with him were
[h]astonished at the catch of fish which they
had taken; 10 and so also *were* James and
John, the sons of Zebedee, who were partners with Simon. And Jesus said to Simon,
"Do not be afraid. [i]From now on you will
catch men." 11 So when they had brought
their boats to land, [j]they [1]forsook all and
followed Him.

A Leper Is Cleansed
Matt. 8:2-4; Mark 1:40-45

12 [k]And it happened when He was in a
certain city, that behold, a man who was
full of [l]leprosy saw Jesus; and he fell on *his*
face and [2]implored Him, saying, "Lord, if
You are willing, You can make me clean."

4:38 Simon's wife's mother. Peter was married (cf. 1 Cor. 9:5), though no details about his wife are given anywhere in Scripture. **a high fever.** Matthew 8:14,15 and Mark 1:30,31 also report this miracle. But only Luke, the physician, remarks that the fever was "high," and makes note of the means Jesus used to heal her (v. 39).

4:40 the sun was setting. Signifying the end of the Sabbath. As soon as they were free to travel, the multitudes came.

4:41 "You are the Christ, the Son of God!" *See note on v. 34.*

4:43 kingdom of God. This term, so prominent throughout the remainder of Luke's gospel, is introduced here for the first time. *See note on Matt. 3:2.*

5:1 Lake of Gennesaret. I.e., the Sea of Galilee, sometimes also called the Sea of Tiberius (John 6:1; 21:1). It is actually a large freshwater lake, over 690 ft. below sea level, and serves as the main source of water and commerce for the Galilee region.

5:2 washing *their* nets. Having fished all night with nothing to show for their labor (cf. v. 5), they were drying and mending their nets for another night's work.

5:3 He sat. *See notes on 4:20; Matt. 5:1.*

5:4 let down your nets. Normally, the fish that were netted in shallow water at night would migrate during the daylight hours to waters too deep to reach easily with nets, which is why Peter fished at night. Peter no doubt thought Jesus' directive made no sense, but he obeyed anyway, and was rewarded for his obedience. (v. 6).

5:8 Depart from me. The remarkable catch of fish was clearly a miracle, astonishing to all the fishermen in Capernaum (v. 9). Peter immediately realized he was in the presence of the Holy One exercising His divine power, and he was stricken with shame over his own sin. Cf. Ex. 20:19; 33:20; Judg. 13:22; Job 42:5,6. *See note on Is. 6:5.*

5:11 forsook all and followed Him. *See note on Matt. 4:18.* Luke gave more detail than Matthew, but they were describing the same incident.

5:12 full of leprosy. Luke's emphasis suggests this was an extremely serious case of leprosy. *See note on Mark 1:40.*

13 Then He put out *His* hand and
touched him, saying, "I am willing; be
cleansed." [m]Immediately the leprosy left
him. 14 [n]And He charged him to tell no
one, "But go and show yourself to the
priest, and make an offering for your
cleansing, as a testimony to them, [o]just as
Moses commanded."
15 However, [p]the report went around
concerning Him all the more; and [q]great
multitudes came together to hear, and to
be healed by Him of their infirmities.

A Paralytic Is Healed
Matt. 9:1-8; Mark 2:1-12

16 [r]So He Himself *often* withdrew into the
wilderness and [s]prayed.
17 Now it happened on a certain day, as
He was teaching, that there were Pharisees
and teachers of the law sitting by, who had
come out of every town of Galilee, Judea,
and Jerusalem. And the power of the Lord
was *present* [3]to heal them. 18 [t]Then behold,
men brought on a bed a man who was paralyzed, whom they sought to bring in and
lay before Him. 19 And when they could
not find how they might bring him in, because of the crowd, they went up on the
housetop and let him down with *his* bed
through the tiling into the midst [u]before
Jesus.
20 When He saw their faith, He said to
him, "Man, your sins are forgiven you."
21 [v]And the scribes and the Pharisees
began to reason, saying, "Who is this who
speaks blasphemies? [w]Who can forgive
sins but God alone?"
22 But when Jesus [x]perceived their
thoughts, He answered and said to them,
"Why are you reasoning in your hearts?
23 Which is easier, to say, 'Your sins are forgiven you,' or to say, 'Rise up and walk'?
24 But that you may know that the Son of
Man has power on earth to forgive sins"—
He said to the man who was paralyzed, [y]"I
say to you, arise, take up your bed, and go
to your house."
25 Immediately he rose up before them,
took up what he had been lying on, and
departed to his own house, [z]glorifying
God. 26 And they were all amazed, and
they [a]glorified God and were filled with
fear, saying, "We have seen strange things
today!"

Matthew Is Called—Matt. 9:9; Mark 2:13, 14

27 [b]After these things He went out and
saw a tax collector named Levi, sitting at
the tax office. And He said to him, [c]"Follow Me." 28 So he left all, rose up, and [d]fol-
lowed Him.

Jesus Eats with Sinners
Matt. 9:10-13; Mark 2:15-17

29 [e]Then Levi gave Him a great feast in
his own house. And [f]there were a great
number of tax collectors and others who
sat down with them. 30 [4]And their scribes
and the Pharisees [5]complained against His
disciples, saying, [g]"Why do You eat and
drink with tax collectors and sinners?"
31 Jesus answered and said to them,
"Those who are well have no need of a
physician, but those who are sick. 32 [h]I
have not come to call *the* righteous, but sinners, to repentance."

13 [m]Matt. 20:34; Luke 8:44; John 5:9
14 [n]Matt. 8:4; Luke 17:14 [o]Lev. 13:1-3; 14:2-32
15 [p]Mark 1:45 [q]Matt. 4:25; Mark 3:7; John 6:2
16 [r]Luke 9:10 [s]Matt. 14:23; Mark 1:35; Luke 6:12; 9:18; 11:1
17 [3]NU *with Him to heal*
18 [t]Matt. 9:2-8; Mark 2:3-12
19 [u]Matt. 15:30
21 [v]Matt. 9:3; 26:65; Mark 2:6, 7; John 10:33 [w]Ps. 32:5; 130:4; Is. 43:25
22 [x]Luke 9:47; John 2:25
24 [y]Mark 2:11; 5:41; Luke 7:14
25 [z]Luke 17:15, 18; Acts 3:8
26 [a]Luke 1:65; 7:16
27 [b]Matt. 9:9-17; Mark 2:13-22 [c][Mark 8:34]; Luke 9:59; John 12:26; 21:19, 22
28 [d]Matt. 4:22; 19:27; Mark 10:28
29 [e]Matt. 9:9, 10; Mark 2:15 [f]Luke 15:1
30 [g]Matt. 11:19; Luke 15:2; Acts 23:9 [4]NU *But the Pharisees and their scribes* [5]*grumbled*
32 [h]Matt. 9:13; 1 Tim. 1:15

5:13 Immediately. One of the characteristics of Jesus' healings was immediate and total wholeness. Cf. 17:14; Matt. 8:13; Mark 5:29; John 5:9.

5:14 tell no one. *See note on Matt. 8:4.* **show yourself to the priest.** I.e., in accordance with the law governing leprosy (Lev. 13:1-46).

5:17 Pharisees. *See note on Matt. 3:7.* **teachers of the law.** I.e., scribes. *See note on Matt. 2:4.* These Jewish leaders came from as far away as Jerusalem. His reputation had spread, and already the scribes and Pharisees were watching Him critically.

5:19 through the tiling. This appears to have been a wealthy person's home, built in the Greco-Roman style, with roof tiles which, when removed, gave access to lower the man between the roof beams. The extreme measures they took to lay this man before Jesus indicates that the crowds following Him were very large. With the press of people around Jesus, it would have been impossible for men carrying a paralytic to get close enough to Him, even if they waited until He left the house.

5:20 your sins are forgiven. Christ ignored the paralysis and addressed the man's greater need first. *See note on Matt. 9:2.* In doing so He asserted a prerogative that was God's alone (v. 21; cf. 7:49). His subsequent healing of the man's paralysis was proof that He had the authority to forgive sins as well.

5:21 blasphemies. Their assessment would have been correct if He were not God incarnate. *See note on Matt. 9:3.*

5:22 perceived. I.e., by means of His omniscience. Cf. Matt. 9:4; John 5:24,25.

5:23 Which is easier. *See note on Matt. 9:5.*

5:24 that you may know. His ability to heal anyone and everyone at will—totally and immediately (v. 25)—was incontrovertible proof of His deity. As God, He had all authority to forgive sins. This was a decisive moment and should have ended once and for all the Pharisees' opposition. Instead, they began to try to discredit Him by charging him with violating their Sabbath rules (*see notes on 6:2-11*).

5:26 strange things. The response is curiously non-committal—not void of wonder and amazement, but utterly void of true faith.

5:27 Levi. Matthew's name prior to his conversion. *See notes on Matt. 9:9,11.*

5:28 left all. Cf. v. 11; 9:59-62. This implies an irreversible action.

5:29 a great number of tax collectors. Levi's immediate response was to introduce his former comrades to Christ.

5:30 eat and drink. Consorting with outcasts on any level—even merely speaking to them—was bad enough. Eating and drinking with them implied a level of friendship that was abhorrent to the Pharisees (cf. 7:34; 15:2; 19:7).

5:31 who are well. I.e., those who think they are whole don't seek healing. *See note on Matt. 9:12.*

Jesus Teaches About Fasting
Matt. 9:14, 15; Mark 2:18-20

33 Then they said to Him, [i]"Why[6] do the
disciples of John fast often and make
prayers, and likewise those of the Pharisees, but Yours eat and drink?"
34 And He said to them, "Can you make
the friends of the bridegroom fast while
the [j]bridegroom is with them? 35 But the
days will come when the bridegroom will
be taken away from them; then they will
fast in those days."

Parable of the Cloth and Wineskins
Matt. 9:16, 17; Mark 2:21, 22

36 [k]Then He spoke a parable to them:
"No one [7]puts a piece from a new garment on an old one; otherwise the new
makes a tear, and also the piece that was
taken out of the new does not match the
old. 37 And no one puts new wine into
old wineskins; or else the new wine will
burst the wineskins and be spilled, and
the wineskins will be ruined. 38 But new
wine must be put into new wineskins,
[8]and both are preserved. 39 And no one,
having drunk old *wine*, [9]immediately desires new; for he says, 'The old is [1]bet-
ter.' "

Jesus Works on the Sabbath
Matt. 12:1-8; Mark 2:23-28

6 Now [a]it happened [1]on the second Sabbath after the first that He went
through the grainfields. And His disciples
plucked the heads of grain and ate *them*,
rubbing *them* in *their* hands. 2 And some of
the Pharisees said to them, "Why are you
doing [b]what is not lawful to do on the Sabbath?"
3 But Jesus answering them said, "Have
you not even read this, [c]what David did
when he was hungry, he and those who
were with him: 4 how he went into the
house of God, took and ate the showbread, and also gave some to those with
him, [d]which is not lawful for any but the
priests to eat?" 5 And He said to them,
"The Son of Man is also Lord of the Sabbath."

Jesus Heals on the Sabbath
Matt. 12:9-14; Mark 3:1-6

6 [e]Now it happened on another Sabbath, also, that He entered the synagogue
and taught. And a man was there whose
right hand was withered. 7 So the scribes
and Pharisees watched Him closely,
whether He would [f]heal on the Sabbath,
that they might find an [g]accusation
against Him. 8 But He [h]knew their
thoughts, and said to the man who had
the withered hand, "Arise and stand
here." And he arose and stood. 9 Then Jesus said to them, "I will ask you one thing:
[i]Is it lawful on the Sabbath to do good or
to do evil, to save life or [2]to destroy?"
10 And when He had looked around at
them all, He said to [3]the man, "Stretch out
your hand." And he did so, and his hand
was restored [4]as whole as the other. 11 But
they were filled with rage, and discussed
with one another what they might do to
Jesus.

33 [i] Matt. 9:14; Mark 2:18; Luke 7:33 [6] NU omits *Why do,* making the verse a statement
34 [j] John 3:29
36 [k] Matt. 9:16, 17; Mark 2:21, 22 [7] NU *tears a piece from a new garment and puts it on an old one*
38 [8] NU omits *and both are preserved*
39 [9] NU omits *immediately* [1] NU *good*

CHAPTER 6

1 [a] Matt. 12:1-8; Mark 2:23-28 [1] NU *on a Sabbath that He went*
2 [b] Ex. 20:10
3 [c] 1 Sam. 21:6
4 [d] Lev. 24:9
6 [e] Matt. 12:9-14; Mark 3:1-6; Luke 13:14; 14:3; John 9:16
7 [f] Luke 13:14; 14:1-6 [g] Luke 20:20
8 [h] Matt. 9:4; John 2:24, 25
9 [i] John 7:23 [2] M *to kill*
10 [3] NU, M *him* [4] NU omits *as whole as the other*

5:33 fast often. Jesus did fast on at least one occasion (Matt. 4:2)—but privately, in accordance with His own teaching (cf. Matt. 6:16-18). The law also prescribed a fast on the Day of Atonement (Lev. 16:29-31; 23:27)—but all other fasts were supposed to be voluntary, for specific reasons such as penitence and earnest prayer. The fact that these Pharisees raised this question shows that they thought of fasting as a public exercise to display one's own spirituality. Yet, the OT also rebuked hypocritical fasting (Is. 58:3-6). *See notes on Matt. 6:17; 9:15.*

5:36-38 *See notes on Matt. 9:16,17.*

5:39 'The old is better.' Those who had acquired a taste for Old Covenant ceremonies and Pharisaic traditions were loath to give them up for the new wine of Jesus' teaching. Luke alone adds this saying.

6:2 not lawful. *See note on Matt. 12:2.*

6:3 Have you not…read. A rebuke, suggesting that they were culpable for their ignorance of so basic a truth (cf. Matt. 12:5; 19:4; 21:16,42; 22:31;). **what David did.** *See notes on 1 Sam. 21:1-6.*

6:4 the showbread. *See note on Matt. 12:4.*

6:5 Lord of the Sabbath. *See note on Matt. 12:8.*

6:7 whether He would heal on the Sabbath. The scribes and Pharisees spotted the man with the withered hand (v. 6) and, with Christ present, they immediately knew that this would be an occasion for the man's healing. In stark contrast to all other so-called healers, Christ was not selective. He healed all who came to Him (v. 19; cf. 4:40; Matt. 8:16).

6:8 knew their thoughts. Cf. 5:22. *See note on Matt. 9:4.* **stand here.** Jesus purposely did this miracle openly, before all, as if to demonstrate His contempt for the Pharisees' man-made regulations.

6:9 to do good. The Sabbath laws forbade labor for profit, frivolous diversions, and things extraneous to worship. Activity per se was not unlawful. Good works were especially appropriate on the Sabbath—particularly deeds of charity, mercy, and worship. Works necessary for the preservation of life were also permitted. To corrupt the Sabbath to forbid such works was a perversion of God's design. *See notes on Matt. 12:2,3.* **to do evil.** Refusal to do good is tantamount to doing evil (James 4:17).

6:10 looked around at them. I.e., giving them a chance to respond to the question of v. 9. Evidently no one did.

6:11 filled with rage. A curious response in the face of so glorious a miracle. Such irrational hatred was their response to having been publicly humiliated—something they hated worse than anything (cf. Matt. 23:6,7). They were unable to answer His reasoning (vv. 9,10). And furthermore, by healing the man only with a command, He had performed no actual "work" that they could charge Him with. Desperately seeking a reason to accuse Him (v. 7), they could find none. Their response was blind fury.

Selection of the Twelve Apostles
Mark 3:13-19

12 Now it came to pass in those days that
He went out to the mountain to pray, and
continued all night in [j]prayer to God.
13 And when it was day, He called His disciples to *Himself;* [k]and from them He chose
[l]twelve whom He also named apostles:
14 Simon, [m]whom He also named Peter,
and Andrew his brother; James and John;
Philip and Bartholomew; 15 Matthew and
Thomas; James the *son* of Alphaeus, and Simon called the Zealot; 16 Judas [n]*the son* of
James, and [o]Judas Iscariot who also became a traitor.

17 And He came down with them and
stood on a level place with a crowd of His
disciples [p]and a great multitude of people
from all Judea and Jerusalem, and from the
seacoast of Tyre and Sidon, who came to
hear Him and be healed of their diseases,
18 as well as those who were tormented
with unclean spirits. And they were
healed. 19 And the whole multitude
[q]sought to [r]touch Him, for [s]power went
out from Him and healed *them* all.

The Beatitudes—Matt. 5:1-12

20 Then He lifted up His eyes toward
His disciples, and said:

[t]"Blessed *are you* poor,
For yours is the kingdom of God.
21 [u]Blessed *are you* who hunger now,
For you shall be [v]filled.[5]
[w]Blessed *are you* who weep now,
For you shall [x]laugh.
22 [y]Blessed are you when men hate you,
And when they [z]exclude you,
And revile *you,* and cast out your name as evil,
For the Son of Man's sake.
23 [a]Rejoice in that day and leap for joy!
For indeed your reward *is* great in heaven,
For [b]in like manner their fathers did to the prophets.

24 "But[c] woe to you [d]who are rich,
For [e]you have received your consolation.
25 [f]Woe to you who are full,
For you shall hunger.
[g]Woe to you who laugh now,
For you shall mourn and [h]weep.
26 [i]Woe [6]to you when [7]all men speak well of you,
For so did their fathers to the false prophets.

Rules of Kingdom Life
Matt. 5:39-48; 7:1, 2, 12

27 [j]"But I say to you who hear: Love
your enemies, do good to those who hate
you, 28 [k]bless those who curse you, and
[l]pray for those who spitefully use you.
29 [m]To him who strikes you on the *one*
cheek, offer the other also. [n]And from him
who takes away your cloak, do not withhold *your* tunic either. 30 [o]Give to everyone
who asks of you. And from him who takes

12 [j] Matt. 14:23; Mark 1:35; Luke 5:16; 9:18; 11:1
13 [k] John 6:70 [l] Matt. 10:1
14 [m] John 1:42
16 [n] Jude 1 [o] Luke 22:3-6
17 [p] Matt. 4:25; Mark 3:7, 8
19 [q] Matt. 9:21; 14:36; Mark 3:10 [r] Mark 5:27, 28; Luke 8:44-47 [s] Mark 5:30; Luke 8:46
20 [t] Matt. 5:3-12; [11:5]; Luke 6:20-23; [James 2:5]
21 [u] Is. 55:1; 65:13; Matt. 5:6 [v] [Rev. 7:16] [w] [Is. 61:3; Rev. 7:17] [x] Ps. 126:5 [5] *satisfied*
22 [y] Matt. 5:11; 1 Pet. 2:19; 3:14; 4:14 [z] [John 16:2]
23 [a] Matt. 5:12; Acts 5:41; [Col. 1:24]; James 1:2 [b] Acts 7:51
24 [c] Amos 6:1; Luke 12:21; James 5:1-6 [d] Luke 12:21 [e] Matt. 6:2, 5, 16; Luke 16:25
25 [f] [Is. 65:13] [g] [Prov. 14:13] [h] James 4:9
26 [i] [John 15:19; 1 John 4:5] [6] NU, M omit *to you* [7] M omits *all*
27 [j] Ex. 23:4; Prov. 25:21; Matt. 5:44; Rom. 12:20
28 [k] Rom. 12:14 [l] Luke 23:24; Acts 7:60
29 [m] Matt. 5:39-42 [n] [1 Cor. 6:7]
30 [o] Deut. 15:7, 8; Prov. 3:27; 21:26; Matt. 5:42

6:12 continued all night in prayer. Luke frequently shows Jesus praying—and particularly before major events in His ministry. Cf. 3:21; 5:16; 9:18,28,29; 11:1; 22:32,40-46.

6:13 He called His disciples. *See notes on Matt. 10:1-4.* Christ had many disciples. At one point He sent 70 out in pairs to proclaim the gospel (10:1). But on this occasion, He chose 12 and specifically commissioned them as apostles, i.e., "sent ones," with a special authority to deliver His message on His behalf (cf. Acts 1:21,22).

6:17-49 The Sermon on the Plateau. The similarity to the Sermon on the Mount (*see notes on Matt. 5:1–7:29*) is remarkable. It is possible, of course, that Jesus simply preached the same sermon on more than one occasion. (It is evident that He often used the same material more than once—e.g., 12:58,59; cf. Matt. 5:25,26.) It appears more likely, however, that these are variant accounts of the same event. Luke's version is abbreviated somewhat, because he omitted sections from the sermon that are uniquely Jewish (particularly Christ's exposition of the law). Aside from that, the two sermons follow exactly the same flow of thought, beginning with the Beatitudes and ending with the parable about building on the rock. Differences in wording between the two accounts are undoubtedly owing to the fact that the sermon was originally delivered in Aramaic. Luke and Matthew translate into Gr. with slight variances. Of course, both translations are equally inspired and authoritative.

6:17 a level place. Elsewhere it says "on a mountain" (5:1). These harmonize easily if Luke is referring to a either a plateau or a level place on the mountainside. Indeed, there is such a place at the site near Capernaum where tradition says this sermon was delivered. **Tyre and Sidon.** *See notes on Matt. 11:21; Mark 3:8.*

6:18 unclean spirits. Another name for demons, used 10 times in the gospels.

6:19 power went out from Him. Cf. 8:45,46; *see note on Mark 5:30.*

6:20-25 Luke's account of the Beatitudes is abbreviated (cf. Matt. 5:3-12). He lists only 4, and balances them with 4 parallel woes.

6:20 *you* poor. Christ's concern for the poor and outcasts is one of Luke's favorite themes (see Introduction: Historical and Theological Themes). Luke used a personal pronoun ("you") where Matt. 5:3 employed a definite article ("the"); Luke was underscoring the tender, personal sense of Christ's words. A comparison of the two passages reveals that Christ was dealing with something more significant than mere material poverty and wealth, however. The poverty spoken of here refers primarily to a sense of one's own spiritual impoverishment.

6:21 *you* who hunger. No mere craving for food, but a hunger and thirst for righteousness (*see note on Matt. 5:6*).

6:22 For the Son of Man's sake. Persecution per se is not something to be sought. But when evil is spoken against a Christian falsely and for Christ's sake (Matt. 5:11), such persecution carries with it the blessing of God.

6:29 offer the other also. *See notes on Matt. 5:39.*

away your goods do not ask *them* back.
31 [p]And just as you want men to do to you,
you also do to them likewise.
32 [q]"But if you love those who love you,
what credit is that to you? For even sinners
love those who love them. 33 And if you do
good to those who do good to you, what
credit is that to you? For even sinners do
the same. 34 [r]And if you lend *to those* from
whom you hope to receive back, what
credit is that to you? For even sinners lend
to sinners to receive as much back. 35 But
[s]love your enemies, [t]do good, and [u]lend,
[8]hoping for nothing in return; and your reward will be great, and [v]you will be sons
of the Most High. For He is kind to the unthankful and evil. 36 [w]Therefore be merciful, just as your Father also is merciful.
37 [x]"Judge not, and you shall not be
judged. Condemn not, and you shall not
be condemned. [y]Forgive, and you will be
forgiven. 38 [z]Give, and it will be given to
you: good measure, pressed down, shaken
together, and running over will be put into
your [a]bosom. For [b]with the same measure
that you use, it will be measured back to
you."

Parable of the Blind Leading the Blind
Matt. 7:3-5, 16-18

39 And He spoke a parable to them:
[c]"Can the blind lead the blind? Will they
not both fall into the ditch? 40 [d]A disciple is
not above his teacher, but everyone who is
perfectly trained will be like his teacher.
41 [e]And why do you look at the speck in
your brother's eye, but do not perceive the
plank in your own eye? 42 Or how can you
say to your brother, 'Brother, let me remove the speck that *is* in your eye,' when
you yourself do not see the plank that *is* in
your own eye? Hypocrite! First remove the
plank from your own eye, and then you
will see clearly to remove the speck that is
in your brother's eye.

31 [p] Matt. 7:12
32 [q] Matt. 5:46
34 [r] Matt. 5:42
35 [s] [Rom. 13:10] [t] Heb. 13:16 [u] Lev. 25:35-37; Ps. 37:26 [v] Matt. 5:46 [8] *expecting*
36 [w] Matt. 5:48; Eph. 4:32
37 [x] Matt. 7:1-5; Rom. 14:4; [1 Cor. 4:5] [y] Matt. 18:21-35
38 [z] [Prov. 19:17; 28:27] [a] Ps. 79:12; Is. 65:6, 7; Jer. 32:18 [b] Matt. 7:2; Mark 4:24; James 2:13
39 [c] Matt. 15:14; 23:16; Rom. 2:19
40 [d] Matt. 10:24; [John 13:16; 15:20]
41 [e] Matt. 7:3

43 [f]"For a good tree does not bear bad
fruit, nor does a bad tree bear good fruit.
44 For [g]every tree is known by its own
fruit. For *men* do not gather figs from
thorns, nor do they gather grapes from a
bramble bush. 45 [h]A good man out of the
good treasure of his heart brings forth
good; and an evil man out of the evil [9]trea-
sure of his heart brings forth evil. For out
[i]of the abundance of the heart his mouth
speaks.

Parable of the Two Foundations
Matt. 7:21-27

46 [j]"But why do you call Me 'Lord,
Lord,' and not do the things which I say?
47 [k]Whoever comes to Me, and hears My
sayings and does them, I will show you
whom he is like: 48 He is like a man building a house, who dug deep and laid the
foundation on the rock. And when the
flood arose, the stream beat vehemently
against that house, and could not shake it,
for it was [1]founded on the rock. 49 But he
who heard and did nothing is like a man
who built a house on the earth without a
foundation, against which the stream beat
vehemently; and immediately it [2]fell. And
the ruin of that house was great."

A Centurion's Servant Is Healed
Matt. 8:5-13

7 Now when He concluded all His sayings in the hearing of the people, He
[a]entered Capernaum. 2 And a certain centurion's servant, who was dear to him, was
sick and ready to die. 3 So when he heard
about Jesus, he sent elders of the Jews to
Him, pleading with Him to come and heal
his servant. 4 And when they came to Jesus, they begged Him earnestly, saying
that the one for whom He should do this
was deserving, 5 "for he loves our nation,
and has built us a synagogue."
6 Then Jesus went with them. And when

43 [f] Matt. 7:16-18, 20
44 [g] Matt. 12:33
45 [h] Matt. 12:35 [i] Prov. 15:2, 28; 16:23; 18:21; Matt. 12:34 [9] NU omits *treasure of his heart*
46 [j] Mal. 1:6; Matt. 7:21; 25:11; Luke 13:25
47 [k] Matt. 7:24-27; [John 14:21]; James 1:22-25
48 [1] NU *well built*
49 [2] NU *collapsed*

CHAPTER 7

1 [a] Matt. 8:5-13

6:31 *See note on Matt. 7:12.*

6:35 sons of the Most High. I.e., God's children should bear the indelible stamp of His moral character. Since He is loving, gracious, and generous—even to those who are His enemies—we should be like Him. *See note on Matt. 5:44,45*; cf. Eph. 5:1,2.

6:37 Judge not. This forbids hypocrisy and a condemning spirit rising from self-righteousness. It does not condemn true discernment. *See note on Matt. 7:1.* **you will be forgiven.** *See note on Matt. 6:15.*

6:38 put into your bosom. I.e., poured into your lap. A long robe was used to carry the overflow of grain. Cf. Ps. 79:12; Is. 65:6; Jer. 32:18.

6:41 speck...plank. The humor of the imagery was no doubt intentional. Christ often employed hyperbole to paint comical images (cf. 18:25; Matt. 23:24).

6:46 you call Me 'Lord, Lord.' It is not sufficient to give lip service to Christ's lordship. Genuine faith produces obedience. A tree is known by its fruits (v. 44). *See notes on Matt. 7:21-23.*

6:47-49 *See note on Matt. 7:24-28.*

7:2 centurion's servant. *See note on Matt. 8:5.* The centurion's tender concern for a lowly slave was contrary to the reputation Roman army officers had acquired in Israel. Yet, this is one of 3 centurions featured in the NT who gave evidence of genuine faith (*see note on Matt. 27:54*; cf. Acts 10).

7:3 elders of the Jews. Matthew 8:5-13 does not mention that the centurion appealed to Jesus through these intermediaries. It is a measure of the respect this man had in the community that Jewish elders would be willing to bring his cause to Jesus. He loved the Jewish nation and was somehow personally responsible for the building of the local synagogue (v. 5). He obviously was being drawn to Christ by God Himself (cf. John 6:44,65). Like all men under conviction, he deeply sensed his own unworthiness (*see note on 5:8*), and that is why he used intermediaries rather than speaking to Jesus personally (vv. 6,7).

He was already not far from the house, the
centurion sent friends to Him, saying to
Him, "Lord, do not trouble Yourself, for I
am not worthy that You should enter
under my roof. 7 Therefore I did not even
think myself worthy to come to You. But
[b]say the word, and my servant will be
healed. 8 For I also am a man placed under
[c]authority, having soldiers under me. And
I say to one, 'Go,' and he goes; and to another, 'Come,' and he comes; and to my
servant, 'Do this,' and he does *it*."
9 When Jesus heard these things, He
marveled at him, and turned around and
said to the crowd that followed Him, "I say
to you, I have not found such great faith,
not even in Israel!" 10 And those who were
sent, returning to the house, found the servant well [1]who had been sick.

A Widow's Son Is Raised

11 Now it happened, the day after, *that*
He went into a city called Nain; and many
of His disciples went with Him, and a
large crowd. 12 And when He came near
the gate of the city, behold, a dead man
was being carried out, the only son of his
mother; and she was a widow. And a large
crowd from the city was with her. 13 When
the Lord saw her, He had [d]compassion on
her and said to her, [e]"Do not weep."
14 Then He came and touched the open
coffin, and those who carried *him* stood
still. And He said, "Young man, I say to
you, [f]arise." 15 So he who was dead [g]sat up
and began to speak. And He [h]presented
him to his mother.
16 [i]Then fear [2]came upon all, and they
[j]glorified God, saying, [k]"A great prophet
has risen up among us"; and, [l]"God has
visited His people."

John's Question's Are Answered
Matt. 11:2-6

17 And this report about Him went
throughout all Judea and all the surrounding region.
18 [m]Then the disciples of John reported
to him concerning all these things. 19 And
John, calling two of his disciples to *him*,
sent *them* to [3]Jesus, saying, "Are You [n]the
Coming One, or [4]do we look for another?"
20 When the men had come to Him, they
said, "John the Baptist has sent us to You,
saying, 'Are You the Coming One, or do
we look for another?' " 21 And that very
hour He cured many of [5]infirmities, afflictions, and evil spirits; and to many blind
He gave sight.
22 [o]Jesus answered and said to them,
"Go and tell John the things you have seen
and heard: [p]that *the* blind [q]see, *the* lame
[r]walk, *the* lepers are [s]cleansed, *the* deaf
[t]hear, *the* dead are raised, [u]*the* poor have
the gospel preached to them. 23 And
blessed is *he* who is not [6]offended because
of Me."

Jesus Praises John—Matt. 11:7-15

24 [v]When the messengers of John had
departed, He began to speak to the multitudes concerning John: "What did you go
out into the wilderness to see? A reed shak-
en by the wind? 25 But what did you go out
to see? A man clothed in soft garments? Indeed those who are gorgeously appareled
and live in luxury are in kings' courts.
26 But what did you go out to see? A
prophet? Yes, I say to you, and more than a
prophet. 27 This is *he* of whom it is written:

[w]'Behold, I send My messenger
before Your face,
Who will prepare Your way before
You.'

28 For I say to you, among those born of
women there is [7]not a [x]greater prophet
than John the Baptist; but he who is least in
the kingdom of God is greater than he."

7 [b] Ps. 33:9; 107:20
8 [c] [Mark 13:34]
10 [1] NU omits *who had been sick*
13 [d] Lam. 3:32; John 11:35; [Heb. 4:15] [e] Luke 8:52
14 [f] Mark 5:41; Luke 8:54; John 11:43; Acts 9:40; [Rom. 4:17]
15 [g] Matt. 11:5; Luke 8:55; John 11:44 [h] 1 Kin. 17:23; 2 Kin. 4:36
16 [i] Luke 1:65 [j] Luke 5:26 [k] Luke 24:19; John 4:19; 6:14; 9:17 [l] Luke 1:68 [2] *seized them all*

18 [m] Matt. 11:2-19
19 [n] [Mic. 5:2; Zech. 9:9; Mal. 3:1-3] [3] NU *the Lord* [4] *should we expect*
21 [5] *illnesses*
22 [o] Matt. 11:4 [p] Is. 35:5 [q] John 9:7 [r] Matt. 15:31 [s] Luke 17:12-14 [t] Mark 7:37 [u] [Is. 61:1-3; Luke 4:18]
23 [6] *caused to stumble*
24 [v] Matt. 11:7
27 [w] Is. 40:3; Mal. 3:1; Matt. 11:10; Mark 1:2
28 [x] [Luke 1:15] [7] NU *none greater than John;*

7:6 not worthy. *See note on Matt. 8:8.*

7:11 Nain. A small town SE of Nazareth.

7:12 only son. *See note on 9:38.*

7:14 touched the open coffin. A ceremonially defiling act, normally. Jesus graphically illustrated how impervious He was to such defilements. When he touched the coffin, its defilement did not taint Him; rather, His power immediately dispelled the presence of all death and defilement (*see notes on v. 39; 8:44*). This was the first of 3 times Jesus raised people from the dead (cf. 8:49-56; John 11). Verse 22 implies that Christ also raised others who are not specifically mentioned.

7:18 the disciples of John. John the Baptist evidently kept apprised of Christ's ministry—even after his imprisonment—through disciples who acted as messengers for him. Cf. Acts 19:1-7.

7:19 Are You the Coming One. John was not the sort of man who vacillated (v. 24). We are not to think that his faith was failing or that he had lost confidence in Christ. But with so many unexpected turns of events—John in prison, Christ encountering unbelief and hostility—John wanted reassurance from Christ himself. That is precisely what Jesus gave him (vv. 22,23). *See notes on Matt. 11:3-11.*

7:22 Go and tell John. Verses 22,23 are quoted from Is. 35:5,6; 61:1. These were messianic promises. (Is. 61:1 is from the same passage Jesus read in the Nazareth synagogue—*see note on 4:19.*) John's disciples were to report that Jesus was doing precisely what Scripture foretold of the Messiah (v. 21)—even though the scheme of prophetic fulfillment was not unfolding quite the way John the Baptist had envisioned it.

***7:23 he* who is not offended.** This was not meant as a rebuke for John the Baptist, but as encouragement for him (cf. v. 28).

7:27 Quoted from Mal. 3:1.

7:28 *See note on Matt. 11:11.*

29 And when all the people heard *Him*,
even the tax collectors [8]justified God,
[y]having been baptized with the baptism of
John. 30 But the Pharisees and [9]lawyers rejected [z]the will of God for themselves, not
having been baptized by him.

Jesus Criticizes His Generation
Matt. 11:16-19

31 [1]And the Lord said, [a]"To what then
shall I liken the men of this generation, and
what are they like? 32 They are like children sitting in the marketplace and calling
to one another, saying:

'We played the flute for you,
　And you did not dance;
We mourned to you,
　And you did not weep.'

33 For [b]John the Baptist came [c]neither eating bread nor drinking wine, and you say,
'He has a demon.' 34 The Son of Man has
come [d]eating and drinking, and you say,
'Look, a glutton and a [2]winebibber, a
friend of tax collectors and sinners!' 35 [e]But
wisdom is justified by all her children."

A Woman Anoints Jesus' Feet

36 [f]Then one of the Pharisees asked Him
to eat with him. And He went to the Pharisee's house, and sat down to eat. 37 And
behold, a woman in the city who was a sinner, when she knew that *Jesus* sat at the
table in the Pharisee's house, brought an
alabaster flask of fragrant oil, 38 and stood
at His feet behind *Him* weeping; and she
began to wash His feet with her tears, and
wiped *them* with the hair of her head; and
she kissed His feet and anointed *them* with
the fragrant oil. 39 Now when the Pharisee
who had invited Him saw *this*, he spoke to
himself, saying, [g]"This Man, if He were a
prophet, would know who and what manner of woman *this is* who is touching Him,
for she is a sinner."

The Parable of the Two Debtors

40 And Jesus answered and said to him,
"Simon, I have something to say to you."
So he said, "Teacher, say it."
41 "There was a certain creditor who had
two debtors. One owed five hundred [h]de-
narii, and the other fifty. 42 And when they
had nothing with which to repay, he freely
forgave them both. Tell Me, therefore,
which of them will love him more?"
43 Simon answered and said, "I suppose
the *one* whom he forgave more."
And He said to him, "You have rightly
judged." 44 Then He turned to the woman
and said to Simon, "Do you see this
woman? I entered your house; you gave
Me no [i]water for My feet, but she has
washed My feet with her tears and wiped
them with the hair of her head. 45 You gave

29 [y] Matt. 3:5; Luke 3:12 [8] *declared the righteousness of*
30 [z] Acts 20:27 [9] *the experts in the law*
31 [a] Matt. 11:16 [1] NU, M omit *And the Lord said*
33 [b] Matt. 3:1 [c] [Matt. 3:4]; Luke 1:15
34 [d] Luke 15:2 [2] An excessive drinker
35 [e] Matt. 11:19
36 [f] Matt. 26:6; Mark 14:3; John 11:2
39 [g] Luke 15:2
41 [h] Matt. 18:28; Mark 6:37
44 [i] Gen. 18:4; 19:2; 43:24; Judg. 19:21; 1 Tim. 5:10

7:29 justified God. The common people and the outcast tax collectors who heard John the Baptist's preaching acknowledged that what he required by way of repentance was from God and was righteous.

7:30 lawyers. *See note on 10:25.* **rejected the will of God.** John's call to repentance was an expression of the will of God. By refusing repentance, they rejected not just John the Baptist, but also God Himself.

7:32 like children. Christ used strong derision to rebuke the Pharisees. He suggested they were behaving childishly, determined not to be pleased, whether invited to "dance" (a reference to Christ's joyous style of ministry, "eating and drinking" with sinners—v. 34), or urged to "weep" (a reference to John the Baptist's call to repentance, and John's more austere manner of ministry—v. 33).

7:34 eating and drinking. I.e., living an ordinary life. This passage explains why John's style of ministry differed so dramatically from Jesus' approach, although their message was the same (*see note on Matt. 4:17*). The different methods took away all the Pharisees' excuses. The very thing they had professed to want to see in Jesus—rigid abstinence and a Spartan lifestyle—was what characterized the ministry of John the Baptist, yet they had already rejected him, too. The real problem lay in the corruption of their own hearts, but they would not acknowledge that. **friend of…sinners.** *See notes on 5:30-33; 15:2.*

7:35 wisdom is justified by all her children. I.e., true wisdom is vindicated by its consequences—what it produces. Cf. James 2:14-17.

7:36 one of the Pharisees. His name was Simon (v. 40). He does not appear to have been sympathetic to Jesus (cf. vv. 44-46). Undoubtedly his motive was either to entrap Jesus, or to find some reason to accuse Him (cf. 6:7).

7:37 an alabaster flask. *See note on Matt. 26:7.* This is similar in many ways to the events described in Matt. 26:6-13; Mark 14:3-9; John 12:2-8, but it is clearly a different incident. That took place in Bethany, near Jerusalem, during the Passion Week. In the anointing at Bethany it was Mary, sister of Martha and Lazarus, who anointed Jesus. This incident takes place in Galilee and involves "a woman…who was a sinner"—i.e., a prostitute. There is no reason to identify this woman with Mary Magdalene, as some have done (*see note on 8:2*).

7:38 stood at His feet behind *Him*. He was reclining at a low table, as was the custom. It would have been shocking to all for a woman of such low reputation to come to a Pharisee's house. Such dinners involving dignitaries were often open to spectators—but no one would have expected a prostitute to attend. Her coming took great courage, and reveals the desperation with which she sought forgiveness. Her "weeping" was an expression of deep repentance.

7:39 what manner of woman. The Pharisees showed nothing but contempt for sinners. Simon was convinced that if Jesus knew her character, He would have sent her away, for her touching Him was presumed to convey ceremonial uncleanness. *See notes on v. 14; 8:44.*

7:40 Jesus answered. Jesus knew Simon's thoughts (cf. 5:22; *see note on Matt. 9:4*)—demonstrating to Simon that He was indeed a Prophet.

7:41 denarii. Each denarius was worth a day's labor (*see note on Matt. 22:19*), so this was a large sum—about two years' full wages.

7:44 no water for My feet. A glaring oversight. Washing a guest's feet was an essential formality (*see note on John 13:4,5*). Not to offer a guest water for the washing of feet was tantamount to an insult—like it would be in modern Western culture if one did not offer to take a guest's coat.

Me no [j]kiss, but this woman has not ceased
to kiss My feet since the time I came in.
46 [k]You did not anoint My head with oil,
but this woman has anointed My feet with
fragrant oil. 47 [l]Therefore I say to you, her
sins, *which are* many, are forgiven, for she
loved much. But to whom little is forgiven,
the same loves little."
48 Then He said to her, [m]"Your sins are
forgiven."
49 And those who sat at the table with
Him began to say to themselves, [n]"Who is
this who even forgives sins?"
50 Then He said to the woman, [o]"Your
faith has saved you. Go in peace."

Certain Women Minister to Christ

8 Now it came to pass, afterward, that He
went through every city and village,
preaching and [1]bringing the glad tidings of
the kingdom of God. And the twelve *were*
with Him, 2 and [a]certain women who had
been healed of evil spirits and [2]infirmi-
ties—Mary called Magdalene, [b]out of
whom had come seven demons, 3 and Joanna the wife of Chuza, Herod's steward,
and Susanna, and many others who provided for [3]Him from their [4]substance.

The Parable of the Soils
Matt. 13:1-23; Mark 4:1-20

4 [c]And when a great multitude had
gathered, and they had come to Him from
every city, He spoke by a parable: 5 "A
sower went out to sow his seed. And as he
sowed, some fell by the wayside; and it
was trampled down, and the birds of the
air devoured it. 6 Some fell on rock; and as
soon as it sprang up, it withered away because it lacked moisture. 7 And some fell
among thorns, and the thorns sprang up
with it and choked it. 8 But others fell on
good ground, sprang up, and yielded [5]a
crop a hundredfold." When He had said
these things He cried, [d]"He who has ears
to hear, let him hear!"
9 [e]Then His disciples asked Him, saying,
"What does this parable mean?"
10 And He said, "To you it has been
given to know the [6]mysteries of the kingdom of God, but to the rest *it is given* in
parables, that

[f]'Seeing they may not see,
And hearing they may not
understand.'

11 [g]"Now the parable is this: The seed is
the [h]word of God. 12 Those by the wayside
are the ones who hear; then the devil
comes and takes away the word out of
their hearts, lest they should believe and
be saved. 13 But the ones on the rock *are*
those who, when they hear, receive the
word with joy; and these have no root,
who believe for a while and in time of
[7]temptation fall away. 14 Now the ones *that*
fell among thorns are those who, when
they have heard, go out and are choked
with cares, [i]riches, and pleasures of life,
and bring no fruit to maturity. 15 But the

45 [j]Rom. 16:16
46 [k]2 Sam. 12:20; Ps. 23:5; Eccl. 9:8; Dan. 10:3
47 [l][1 Tim. 1:14]
48 [m]Matt. 9:2; Mark 2:5
49 [n]Matt. 9:3; [Mark 2:7]; Luke 5:21
50 [o]Matt. 9:22; Mark 5:34; 10:52; Luke 8:48; 18:42

CHAPTER 8

1 [1]*proclaiming the good news*
2 [a]Matt. 27:55; Mark 15:40, 41; Luke 23:49, 55 [b]Matt. 27:56; Mark 16:9 [2]*sicknesses*
3 [3]NU, M *them* [4]*possessions*
4 [c]Matt. 13:2-9; Mark 4:1-9
8 [d]Matt. 11:15; Mark 7:16; Luke 14:35; Rev. 2:7, 11, 17, 29; 3:6, 13, 22; 13:9 [5]Lit. *fruit*
9 [e]Matt. 13:10-23; Mark 4:10-20
10 [f]Is. 6:9; Matt. 13:14; Acts 28:26 [6]*secret or hidden truths*
11 [g]Matt. 13:18; Mark 4:14; [1 Pet. 1:23] [h]Luke 5:1; 11:28
13 [7]*testing*
14 [i]Matt. 19:23; 1 Tim. 6:9, 10

7:47 for she loved much. This is not to suggest that she was forgiven because she loved much. The parable (vv. 41-43) pictured a forgiveness that was unconditional, and love was the result. Therefore to make the woman's love the reason for her forgiveness would be to distort the lesson Jesus is teaching here. "For" here has the sense of "wherefore." And her faith (v. 50), not the act of anointing Jesus' feet, was the instrument by which she laid hold of His forgiveness.

7:49 forgives sins. *See notes on 5:20,21; Matt. 9:1-3; Mark 2:7.*

7:50 Your faith has saved you. Not all whom Jesus healed were saved, but those who exhibited true faith were (cf. 17:19; 18:42; Matt. 9:22; *see note on Mark 5:34*).

8:2 certain women. Rabbis normally did not have women as disciples. **Mary called Magdalene.** Her name probably derives from the Galilean town of Magdala. Some believe she is the woman described in 7:37-50, but it seems highly unlikely that Luke would introduce her here by name for the first time if she were the main figure in the account he just completed. Also, while it is clear that she had suffered at the hands of "demons," there is no reason whatsoever to think that she had ever been a prostitute.

8:3 Joanna. This woman is also mentioned in 24:10, but nowhere else in Scripture. It is possible that she was a source for some of the details Luke recounts about Herod (cf. 23:8,12). *See note on 1:3.* **Susanna.** Aside from this reference, she is nowhere mentioned in Scripture. She is probably someone Luke knew personally. **from their substance.** It was a Jewish custom for disciples to support rabbis in this way. Cf. 10:7; 1 Cor. 9:4-11; Gal 6:6; 1 Tim. 5:17,18.

8:4 spoke by a parable. This marked a significant turning point in Jesus' ministry. *See notes on Matt. 13:3,34.*

8:5 to sow his seed. Seed was sown by hand over plowed soil. In throwing seed toward the edges of a field, the sower would naturally throw some that landed or was blown onto the hard beaten path on the edges of the field, where it could not penetrate the soil and grow (*see notes on Matt. 13:4,19*). This could refer to the hard, obstinate Jewish leaders.

8:6 on rock. I.e., very shallow soil with a layer of rock lying just below the surface. *See notes on Matt. 13:5,20.* This could refer to the fickle mob that followed Jesus only for His miracles.

8:7 thorns. *See notes on Matt. 13:7,22.* This could refer to the materialists to whom earthly wealth was more important than spiritual riches.

8:8 a hundredfold. Luke simplified the parable. Matthew 13:8 and Mark 4:8 described 3 levels of fruitfulness. "Hundredfold" simply speaks of inconceivable abundance (cf. Gen. 26:12). **He who has ears.** All 3 of the synoptics include this admonition with the parable of the sower (cf. Matt. 13:9, Mark 4:9). Jesus often said this to stress particularly important statements cast in mysterious language (cf. 14:35; Matt. 11:15; 13:43; Mark 4:23).

8:10 mysteries. *See notes on Matt. 13:11,13.* ***Seeing they may not see.*** This quotation from Is. 6:9 describes God's act of judicially blinding unbelievers.

8:13 who believe for a while. I.e., with a nominal, non-saving faith. *See note on Matt. 13:20.*

ones *that* fell on the good ground are those
who, having heard the word with a noble
and good heart, keep *it* and bear fruit with
[j]patience.[8]

Parable of the Lamp—Mark 4:21-25

16 [k]"No one, when he has lit a lamp, covers it with a vessel or puts *it* under a bed,
but sets *it* on a lampstand, that those who
enter may see the [l]light. 17 [m]For nothing is
secret that will not be [n]revealed, nor *anything* hidden that will not be known and
come to light. 18 Therefore take heed how
you hear. [o]For whoever has, to him *more*
will be given; and whoever does not have,
even what he [9]seems to [p]have will be
taken from him."

Christ's True Brethren
Matt. 12:46-50; Mark 3:31-35

19 [q]Then His mother and brothers came
to Him, and could not approach Him because of the crowd. 20 And it was told Him
by some, who said, "Your mother and Your
brothers are standing outside, desiring to
see You."
21 But He answered and said to them,
"My mother and My brothers are these
who hear the word of God and do it."

The Storm Is Stilled
Matt. 8:23-27; Mark 4:35-41

22 [r]Now it happened, on a certain day,
that He got into a boat with His disciples.
And He said to them, "Let us cross over to
the other side of the lake." And they
launched out. 23 But as they sailed He fell
asleep. And a windstorm came down on
the lake, and they were filling *with water,*
and were in [1]jeopardy. 24 And they came
to Him and awoke Him, saying, "Master,
Master, we are perishing!"
Then He arose and rebuked the wind
and the raging of the water. And they
ceased, and there was a calm. 25 But He
said to them, [s]"Where is your faith?"
And they were afraid, and marveled,
saying to one another, [t]"Who can this be?

15 [j] [Rom. 2:7; Heb. 10:36-39; James 5:7, 8] [8] *endurance*
16 [k] Matt. 5:15; Mark 4:21; Luke 11:33 [l] Matt. 5:14
17 [m] Matt. 10:26; Luke 12:2; [1 Cor. 4:5] [n] [Eccl. 12:14; 2 Cor. 5:10]
18 [o] Matt. 25:29 [p] Matt. 13:12 [9] *thinks that he has*
19 [q] Ps. 69:8; Matt. 12:46-50; Mark 3:31-35
22 [r] Matt. 8:23-27; Mark 4:36-41
23 [1] *danger*
25 [s] Luke 9:41 [t] Luke 4:36; 5:26
26 [u] Matt. 8:28-34; Mark 5:1-17 [2] NU *Gerasenes*
27 [3] NU *and for a long time wore no clothes*
28 [v] Mark 1:26; 9:26 [w] Mark 1:23, 24 [x] Luke 4:41
31 [y] Rom. 10:7; [Rev. 20:1, 3]
32 [z] Lev. 11:7; Deut. 14:8
35 [a] [Matt. 11:28] [b] Matt. 28:9; Mark 7:25; Luke 10:39; 17:16; John 11:32 [c] [2 Tim. 1:7]
36 [4] *delivered*
37 [d] Matt. 8:34 [e] Mark 1:24; Luke 4:34 [f] Job 21:14; Acts 16:39 [5] NU *Gerasenes*

For He commands even the winds and
water, and they obey Him!"

Demons Are Cast into Swine
Matt. 8:28-34; Mark 5:1-20

26 [u]Then they sailed to the country of the
[2]Gadarenes, which is opposite Galilee.
27 And when He stepped out on the land,
there met Him a certain man from the city
who had demons [3]for a long time. And he
wore no clothes, nor did he live in a house
but in the tombs. 28 When he saw Jesus, he
[v]cried out, fell down before Him, and with
a loud voice said, [w]"What have I to do
with [x]You, Jesus, Son of the Most High
God? I beg You, do not torment me!" 29 For
He had commanded the unclean spirit to
come out of the man. For it had often
seized him, and he was kept under guard,
bound with chains and shackles; and he
broke the bonds and was driven by the
demon into the wilderness.
30 Jesus asked him, saying, "What is
your name?"
And he said, "Legion," because many
demons had entered him. 31 And they
begged Him that He would not command
them to go out [y]into the abyss.
32 Now a herd of many [z]swine was feeding there on the mountain. So they begged
Him that He would permit them to enter
them. And He permitted them. 33 Then the
demons went out of the man and entered
the swine, and the herd ran violently down
the steep place into the lake and drowned.
34 When those who fed *them* saw what
had happened, they fled and told *it* in the
city and in the country. 35 Then they went
out to see what had happened, and came
to Jesus, and found the man from whom
the demons had departed, [a]sitting at the
[b]feet of Jesus, clothed and in his [c]right
mind. And they were afraid. 36 They also
who had seen *it* told them by what means
he who had been demon-possessed was
[4]healed. 37 [d]Then the whole multitude of
the surrounding region of the [5]Gadarenes
[e]asked Him to [f]depart from them, for they

8:15 heard...keep...bear fruit. This constitutes evidence of true salvation. "Heard" is a reference to understanding and believing (John 8:31,47). "Keep" refers to ongoing obedience (11:28; *see note on John 14:21-24*). "Fruit" is good works (Matt. 7:16-20; James 2:14-26).

8:16 under a bed. The fact that Christ taught mysteries in parables was not to suggest that His message was meant for elite disciples or that it should be kept secret. A lamp is not lit to be hidden, but must put on a lampstand, where its light will reach furthest. Still, only those with eyes to see will see it.

8:17 nothing is secret that will not be revealed. All truth will be manifest in the judgment. Cf. 12:2,3; 1 Cor. 4:5; 1 Tim. 5:24,25. God's ultimate purpose is not to hide the truth, but to make it known.

8:18 take heed how you hear. One's response to the light in this life is crucial, because at the throne of judgment there will be no opportunity to embrace truth that was formerly spurned (Rev. 20:11-15). Those who scorn the light of the gospel now will have all light removed from them in eternity. Cf. 19:26; Matt. 25:29.

8:19 brothers. *See notes on Matt. 12:46-49.*

8:20,21 *See notes on Mark 3:31,35.*

8:22-25 *See notes on Matt. 8:24-27.*

8:26-38 *See notes on Matt. 8:28-34.*

8:27 a certain man. Matthew reveals there were actually two men. Only one did the talking. *See note on Matt. 8:28.*

8:30 Legion. *See notes on Matt. 8:30; Mark 5:9.*

8:31 the abyss. *See note on Matt. 8:31.*

were seized with great [g]fear. And He got
into the boat and returned.
38 Now [h]the man from whom the
demons had departed begged Him that he
might be with Him. But Jesus sent him
away, saying, 39 "Return to your own
house, and tell what great things God has
done for you." And he went his way and
proclaimed throughout the whole city
what great things Jesus had done for him.
40 So it was, when Jesus returned, that
the multitude welcomed Him, for they
were all waiting for Him.

A Woman Is Healed
Matt. 9:18-22; Mark 5:21-34

41 [i]And behold, there came a man named
Jairus, and he was a ruler of the synagogue. And he fell down at Jesus' feet and
begged Him to come to his house, 42 for he
had an only daughter about twelve years
of age, and she [j]was dying.
But as He went, the multitudes thronged
Him. 43 [k]Now a woman, having a [l]flow of
blood for twelve years, who had spent all
her livelihood on physicians and could not
be healed by any, 44 came from behind and
[m]touched the border of His garment. And
immediately her flow of blood stopped.
45 And Jesus said, "Who touched Me?"
When all denied it, Peter [6]and those
with him said, "Master, the multitudes
throng and press You, [7]and You say, 'Who
touched Me?' "
46 But Jesus said, "Somebody touched
Me, for I perceived [n]power going out from
Me." 47 Now when the woman saw that
she was not hidden, she came trembling;
and falling down before Him, she declared
to Him in the presence of all the people the
reason she had touched Him and how she
was healed immediately.
48 And He said to her, "Daughter, [8]be of
good cheer; [o]your faith has made you well.
[p]Go in peace."

Jairus's Daughter Is Raised
Matt. 9:23-26; Mark 5:35-43

49 [q]While He was still speaking, someone came from the ruler of the synagogue's
house, saying to him, "Your daughter is
dead. Do not trouble the [9]Teacher."
50 But when Jesus heard *it,* He answered
him, saying, "Do not be afraid; [r]only believe, and she will be made well." 51 When
He came into the house, He permitted no
one to go [1]in except [2]Peter, James, and
John, and the father and mother of the girl.
52 Now all wept and mourned for her; but
He said, [s]"Do not weep; she is not dead,
[t]but sleeping." 53 And they ridiculed Him,
knowing that she was dead.
54 But He [3]put them all outside, took her
by the hand and called, saying, "Little girl,
[u]arise." 55 Then her spirit returned, and she
arose immediately. And He commanded
that she be given *something* to eat. 56 And her
parents were astonished, but [v]He charged
them to tell no one what had happened.

Twelve Are Sent to Preach
Matt. 10:1-14; 14:1-14; Mark 6:7-16, 30-34

9 Then [a]He called His twelve disciples
together and [b]gave them power and
authority over all demons, and to cure diseases. 2 [c]He sent them to preach the kingdom of God and to heal the sick. 3 [d]And He
said to them, "Take nothing for the journey,
neither staffs nor bag nor bread nor money;
and do not have two tunics apiece.
4 [e]"Whatever house you enter, stay
there, and from there depart. 5 [f]And whoever will not receive you, when you go out
of that city, [g]shake off the very dust from
your feet as a testimony against them."
6 [h]So they departed and went through
the towns, preaching the gospel and healing everywhere.
7 [i]Now Herod the tetrarch heard of all
that was done by Him; and he was perplexed, because it was said by some that
John had risen from the dead, 8 and by

37 [g]Luke 5:26
38 [h]Mark 5:18-20
41 [i]Matt. 9:18-26; Mark 5:22-43
42 [j]Luke 7:2
43 [k]Matt. 9:20 [l]Luke 15:19-22
44 [m]Mark 6:56; Luke 5:13
45 [6]NU omits *and those with him* [7]NU omits the rest of v. 45.
46 [n]Mark 5:30; Luke 6:19
48 [o]Mark 5:34; Luke 7:50 [p]John 8:11 [8]NU omits *be of good cheer*
49 [q]Mark 5:35 [9]NU adds *anymore*
50 [r][Mark 11:22-24]
51 [1]NU adds *with Him* [2]NU, M *Peter, John, and James*
52 [s]Luke 7:13 [t][John 11:11, 13]
54 [u]Luke 7:14; John 11:43 [3]NU omits *put them all outside*
56 [v]Matt. 8:4; 9:30; Mark 5:43

CHAPTER 9

1 [a]Matt. 10:1, 2; Mark 3:13; 6:7 [b]Mark 16:17, 18; [John 14:12]
2 [c]Matt. 10:7, 8; Mark 6:12; Luke 10:1, 9
3 [d]Matt. 10:9-15; Mark 6:8-11; Luke 10:4-12; 22:35
4 [e]Matt. 10:11; Mark 6:10
5 [f]Matt. 10:14 [g]Luke 10:11; Acts 13:51
6 [h]Mark 6:12; Luke 8:1
7 [i]Matt. 14:1, 2; Mark 6:14

8:41 a ruler of the synagogue. *See note on 13:14.* Jesus had once cast a demon out of a man in Jairus' synagogue (4:33-37).

8:42 only daughter. *See note on 9:38.* **thronged.** Lit. "choked," i.e., they almost crushed Him.

8:43 a flow of blood. *See note on Matt. 9:20.*

8:44 came from behind and touched. Because of her affliction, she would normally render anyone she touched unclean. The effect here was precisely the opposite. *See notes on 7:14,39.* **border.** *See note on Matt. 9:20.*

8:46 power going out from Me. *See note on Mark 5:30.*

8:50 only believe. Though not all Jesus' healings required faith (cf. 22:51), at times He required it.

8:51 Peter, James, and John. *See notes on 9:28; Matt. 10:2; 17:1.*

8:52 she is not dead. *See notes on Matt. 9:23,24.*

8:56 tell no one. *See note on Matt. 8:4.*

9:1-6 *See notes on Matt. 10:1-42.*

9:3 Take nothing. Slight differences between Matthew, Mark, and Luke have troubled some. Matthew 10:9,10 and this text say the disciples were not to take staffs (*see notes there*); but Mark 6:8 prohibited everything "except a staff." Mark 6:9 also instructed them to "wear sandals"; but in Matt. 10:10 sandals were included in the things they were not to carry. Actually, however, what Matt. 10:10 and this verse prohibited was the packing of extra staffs and sandals. The disciples were not to be carrying baggage for the journey, but merely to go with the clothes on their backs.

9:7 Herod the tetrarch. *See note on Matt. 14:1.* News of Christ reached to the highest levels of government. **John had risen from the dead.** Of course, this was not true, but Herod himself nonetheless seemed gripped by guilty fear (cf. Mark 6:16).

some that Elijah had appeared, and by others that one of the old prophets had risen
again. 9 Herod said, "John I have beheaded, but who is this of whom I hear such
things?" [j]So he sought to see Him.
10 [k]And the apostles, when they had returned, told Him all that they had done.
[l]Then He took them and went aside privately into a deserted place belonging to
the city called Bethsaida. 11 But when the
multitudes knew *it,* they followed Him;
and He received them and spoke to them
about the kingdom of God, and healed
those who had need of healing.

Five Thousand Are Fed
Matt. 14:15-21; Mark 6:35-44; John 6:1-14

12 [m]When the day began to wear away, the
twelve came and said to Him, "Send the
multitude away, that they may go into the
surrounding towns and country, and lodge
and get provisions; for we are in a deserted place here."
13 But He said to them, "You give them
something to eat."
And they said, "We have no more than
five loaves and two fish, unless we go and
buy food for all these people." 14 For there
were about five thousand men.
Then He said to His disciples, "Make
them sit down in groups of fifty." 15 And
they did so, and made them all sit down.
16 Then He took the five loaves and the
two fish, and looking up to heaven, He
[n]blessed and broke *them,* and gave *them* to
the disciples to set before the multitude.
17 So they all ate and were [1]filled, and
twelve baskets of the leftover fragments
were taken up by them.

9 [j] Luke 23:8
10 [k] Mark 6:30 [l] Matt. 14:13
12 [m] Matt. 14:15; Mark 6:35; John 6:1, 5
16 [n] Luke 22:19; 24:30
17 [1] *satisfied*
18 [o] Matt. 16:13-16; Mark 8:27-29
19 [p] Matt. 14:2
20 [q] Matt. 16:16; John 6:68, 69
21 [r] Matt. 8:4; 16:20; Mark 8:30
22 [s] Matt. 16:21; 17:22; Luke 18:31-33; 23:46; 24:46
23 [t] Matt. 10:38; 16:24; Mark 8:34; Luke 14:27 [2] M omits *daily*
24 [u] Matt. 10:39; Luke 17:33; [John 12:25]
25 [v] Matt. 16:26; Mark 8:36; [Luke 16:19-31]; Acts 1:18, 25
26 [w] [Rom. 1:16] [x] Matt. 10:33; Mark 8:38; Luke 12:9; 2 Tim. 2:12
27 [y] Matt. 16:28; Mark 9:1; Acts 7:55, 56; Rev. 20:4
28 [z] Matt. 17:1-8; Mark 9:2-8

Peter's Confession of Faith
Matt. 16:13-21; Mark 8:27-31

18 [o]And it happened, as He was alone
praying, *that* His disciples joined Him, and
He asked them, saying, "Who do the
crowds say that I am?"
19 So they answered and said, [p]"John the
Baptist, but some *say* Elijah; and others *say*
that one of the old prophets has risen again."
20 He said to them, "But who do you say
that I am?"
[q]Peter answered and said, "The Christ of
God."
21 [r]And He strictly warned and commanded them to tell this to no one, 22 saying, [s]"The Son of Man must suffer many
things, and be rejected by the elders and
chief priests and scribes, and be killed, and
be raised the third day."

True Cost of Discipleship
Matt. 16:24-27; Mark 9:34-38

23 [t]Then He said to *them* all, "If anyone
desires to come after Me, let him deny himself, and take up his cross [2]daily, and follow Me. 24 [u]For whoever desires to save his
life will lose it, but whoever loses his life for
My sake will save it. 25 [v]For what profit is it
to a man if he gains the whole world, and is
himself destroyed or lost? 26 [w]For whoever
is ashamed of Me and My words, of him
the Son of Man will be [x]ashamed when He
comes in His *own* glory, and *in His* Father's,
and of the holy angels.

The Transfiguration
Matt. 16:28–17:9; Mark 9:1-9; 2 Pet. 1:17, 18

27 [y]But I tell you truly, there are some
standing here who shall not taste death till
they see the kingdom of God."
28 [z]Now it came to pass, about eight days

9:8 Elijah. *See note on 1:17.*

9:9 he sought to see Him. Only Luke gives this detail. *See notes on 1:3; 8:3.*

9:10 into a deserted place. They were trying to get some rest and a break from the crowds. Cf. Mark 6:31,32. **Bethsaida.** *See note on Matt. 11:21.* Bethsaida is on the N shore of Galilee, where the Jordan River enters the lake. Peter, Philip, and Andrew had all grown up there (John 1:44).

9:12-17 Aside from the resurrection, the feeding of the 5,000 is the only miracle of Jesus recorded in all 4 gospels (cf. Matt. 14:15-21; Mark 6:35-44; John 6:4-13).

9:14 about five thousand men. Counting women and children, the actual size of the crowd may have been closer to 20,000.

9:17 baskets. *See notes on Mark 6:43; 8:8.*

9:18-21 *See notes on Matt. 16:13-20.*

9:19 John the Baptist…Elijah…one of the old prophets. Cf. vv. 7,8. Such rumors were apparently quite common. *See notes on 1:17; Matt. 11:14; Mark 9:13; Rev. 11:5,6.*

9:20 "The Christ of God." I.e., the Messiah promised in the OT (Dan. 9:25,26). *See note on Matt. 16:16.*

9:21 tell this to no one. *See notes on Matt. 8:4; 12:16.*

9:22 The Son of Man must suffer. This pronouncement signified a great turning point in Jesus' ministry. *See note on Matt. 16:21.*

9:23 cross. *See note on Matt. 10:38.* Self-denial was a common thread in Christ's teaching to his disciples (cf. 14:26,27; Matt. 10:38; 16:24; Mark 8:34; John 12:24-26). The kind of self-denial He sought was not a reclusive asceticism (*see note on 7:34*), but a willingness to obey His commandments, serve one another, and suffer—perhaps even die—for His sake.

9:24 whoever loses his life for My sake. Aside from the command "follow Me," this saying is repeated more times in the gospels than any other saying of Christ. Cf. 17:33; Matt. 10:39; 16:25; Mark 8:35; John 12:25. *See note on 14:11.*

9:26 whoever is ashamed of Me. I.e., unbelievers. Cf. Matt. 10:33; Rom. 9:33; 10:11; 2 Tim. 2:12. *See note on 12:9.*

9:27 see the kingdom. *See note on Matt. 16:28.*

9:28 about eight days. A common expression signifying about a week (cf. John 20:26). *See note on Matt. 17:1.* **after these sayings.**

after these sayings, that He took Peter,
John, and James and went up on the mountain to pray. 29 As He prayed, the appearance of His face was altered, and His robe
became white *and* glistening. 30 And behold,
two men talked with Him, who were [a]Mo-
ses and [b]Elijah, 31 who appeared in glory
and spoke of His [3]decease which He was
about to accomplish at Jerusalem. 32 But
Peter and those with him [c]were heavy with
sleep; and when they were fully awake,
they saw His glory and the two men who
stood with Him. 33 Then it happened, as
they were parting from Him, *that* Peter said
to Jesus, "Master, it is good for us to be
here; and let us make three [4]tabernacles:
one for You, one for Moses, and one for Elijah"—not knowing what he said.
34 While he was saying this, a cloud came
and overshadowed them; and they were
fearful as they entered the [d]cloud. 35 And a
voice came out of the cloud, saying, [e]"This is
[5]My beloved Son. [f]Hear Him!" 36 When the
voice had ceased, Jesus was found alone.
[g]But they kept quiet, and told no one in
those days any of the things they had seen.

Demoniac Son Is Healed
Matt. 17:14-18; Mark 9:14-27

37 [h]Now it happened on the next day,
when they had come down from the
mountain, that a great multitude met Him.
38 Suddenly a man from the multitude
cried out, saying, "Teacher, I implore You,
look on my son, for he is my only child.
39 And behold, a spirit seizes him, and he
suddenly cries out; it convulses him so that
he foams *at the mouth;* and it departs from
him with great difficulty, bruising him.
40 So I implored Your disciples to cast it
out, but they could not."
41 Then Jesus answered and said, "O
[6]faithless and perverse generation, how
long shall I be with you and [7]bear with
you? Bring your son here." 42 And as he
was still coming, the demon threw him
down and convulsed *him.* Then Jesus rebuked the unclean spirit, healed the child,
and gave him back to his father.

Christ Prophesies His Coming Death
Matt. 17:22, 23; Mark 9:30-32

43 And they were all amazed at the
majesty of God.
But while everyone marveled at all the
things which Jesus did, He said to His disciples, 44 [i]"Let these words sink down into
your ears, for the Son of Man is about to be
betrayed into the hands of men." 45 [j]But
they did not understand this saying, and it
was hidden from them so that they did not
perceive it; and they were afraid to ask
Him about this saying.

True Greatness—Matt. 18:1-5; Mark 9:33-40

46 [k]Then a dispute arose among them as
to which of them would be greatest.
47 And Jesus, [l]perceiving the thought of
their heart, took a [m]little child and set him
by Him, 48 and said to them, [n]"Whoever
receives this little child in My name receives Me; and [o]whoever receives Me [p]re-
ceives Him who sent Me. [q]For he who is
least among you all will be great."

30 [a] Heb. 11:23-29 [b] 2 Kin. 2:1-11
31 [3] Death, lit. *departure*
32 [c] Dan. 8:18; 10:9; Matt. 26:40, 43; Mark 14:40
33 [4] *tents*
34 [d] Ex. 13:21; Acts 1:9
35 [e] Ps. 2:7; [Is. 42:1; Matt. 3:17; 12:18]; Mark 1:11; Luke 3:22 [f] Acts 3:22 [5] NU *My Son, the Chosen One*
36 [g] Matt. 17:9; Mark 9:9
37 [h] Matt. 17:14-18; Mark 9:14-27
41 [6] *unbelieving* [7] *put up with*
44 [i] Matt. 17:22; Mark 10:33; 14:53; Luke 22:54; John 18:12
45 [j] Mark 9:32; Luke 2:50; 18:34
46 [k] Matt. 18:1-5; Mark 9:33-37; Luke 22:24
47 [l] Matt. 9:4; John 2:24, 25 [m] Luke 18:17
48 [n] Matt. 18:5 [o] Matt. 10:40; Mark 9:37; John 12:44 [p] John 13:20 [q] [Matt. 23:11, 12]; 1 Cor. 15:9; Eph. 3:8

This expression ties the promise of seeing the kingdom (v. 27) to the events that follow (*see note on Matt. 16:28*). **Peter, John, and James.** These 3 alone were permitted to witness the raising of Jairus' daughter (8:51), the Transfiguration (cf. Matt. 17:1), and Christ's agony in the garden (Mark 14:33). **the mountain.** The traditional site, Mt. Tabor, is unlikely. Jesus and the disciples had been in "the region of Caesarea Philippi" (Matt. 16:13), and Tabor is nowhere near there. Besides, Tabor had evidently been the site of pagan worship (Hos. 5:1), and in Jesus' day, an army garrison had their fortress at the top. The actual location of the Transfiguration is nowhere identified, but Mt. Hermon (7,000 ft higher than Tabor, and closer to Caesarea Philippi) is believed by many to be the place.

9:29 As He prayed. *See note on 3:21.* As at His baptism, while He was praying, the Father's voice came from heaven (cf. Introduction: Historical and Theological Themes). **glistening.** Lit. "emitting light." This word is used only here in the NT. It suggests a brilliant flashing light, similar to lightning.

9:30 Moses and Elijah. *See note on Matt. 17:3.*

9:31 His decease. Peter uses the same term to speak of his own death (2 Pet. 1:15). Only Luke mentions the subject matter of their conversation and the fact that Peter, James, and John had fallen asleep (v. 32). Cf. 22:45.

9:32 saw His glory. Cf. Ex. 33:18-23.

9:33 three tabernacles. *See note on Matt. 17:4.*

9:34 the cloud. Matthew 17:5 says "a bright cloud," i.e., enveloping the glory of God—similar to the pillar of cloud that led the Israelites in the OT (Ex. 14:19,20). The brightness of this cloud and the sleepiness of the disciples (v. 32) suggests that this event may have occurred at night.

9:35 This is My beloved Son. *See note on Matt. 3:17.*

9:38 my only child. Cf. 7:12; 8:42. The son of the widow of Nain was her only child; and Jairus' daughter was his only child. Luke alone mentions these details.

9:39 a spirit seizes him. This was no mere case of epilepsy; it was plainly demon possession. There's no reason to think Luke, a physician, was merely accommodating the understanding of his readers. Besides, Jesus healed the boy by rebuking the demon (v. 42; cf. Mark 9:25).

9:40 they could not. *See notes on Matt. 17:19-21.*

9:41 faithless and perverse generation. *See note on Matt. 17:17.*

9:44 about to be betrayed. *See note on Matt. 17:22.*

9:45 hidden from them. I.e., in accord with God's sovereign design. Cf. 24:45.

9:46 be greatest. *See note on Matt. 20:21.*

9:48 Whoever receives this little child. *See note on Matt. 18:5.* **he who is least...will be great.** The way to preeminence in Christ's kingdom is by sacrifice and self-denial. *See note on v. 23.*

49 [r]Now John answered and said, "Master, we saw someone casting out demons in
Your name, and we forbade him because
he does not follow with us."
50 But Jesus said to him, "Do not forbid
him, for [s]he who is not against [8]us is on
[9]our side."

Samaria Rejects Christ

51 Now it came to pass, when the time
had come for [t]Him to be received up, that
He steadfastly set His face to go to Jerusalem, 52 and sent messengers before His face.
And as they went, they entered a village of
the Samaritans, to prepare for Him. 53 But
[u]they did not receive Him, because His face
was *set* for the journey to Jerusalem. 54 And
when His disciples [v]James and John saw
this, they said, "Lord, do You want us to
command fire to come down from heaven
and consume them, [1]just as [w]Elijah did?"
55 But He turned and rebuked them,
[2]and said, "You do not know what manner
of [x]spirit you are of. 56 [3]For [y]the Son of
Man did not come to destroy men's lives
but to save *them.*" And they went to another village.

49 [r] Mark 9:38-40
50 [s] Matt. 12:30; Luke 11:23 [8] NU *you* [9] NU *your*
51 [t] Is. 50:7; Mark 16:19; Acts 1:2
53 [u] John 4:4,9
54 [v] Mark 3:17 [w] 2 Kin. 1:10,12 [1] NU omits *just as Elijah did*
55 [x] [Rom. 8:15; 2 Tim. 1:7] [2] NU omits the rest of v. 55.
56 [y] Luke 19:10; John 3:17; 12:47 [3] NU omits *For the Son of Man did not come to destroy men's lives but to save them.*
57 [z] Matt. 8:19-22
58 [a] Luke 2:7; 8:23
59 [b] Matt. 8:21,22
61 [c] 1 Kin. 19:20
62 [d] 2 Tim. 4:10

CHAPTER 10

1 [a] Matt. 10:1; Mark 6:7 [1] NU *seventy-two others*
2 [b] Matt. 9:37, 38; John 4:35

True Cost of Discipleship—Matt. 8:18-22

57 [z]Now it happened as they journeyed
on the road, *that* someone said to Him,
"Lord, I will follow You wherever You go."
58 And Jesus said to him, "Foxes have
holes and birds of the air *have* nests, but the
Son of Man [a]has nowhere to lay *His* head."
59 [b]Then He said to another, "Follow Me."
But he said, "Lord, let me first go and
bury my father."
60 Jesus said to him, "Let the dead bury
their own dead, but you go and preach the
kingdom of God."
61 And another also said, "Lord, [c]I will
follow You, but let me first go *and* bid them
farewell who are at my house."
62 But Jesus said to him, "No one, having put his hand to the plow, and looking
back, is [d]fit for the kingdom of God."

Mission of the Seventy

10 After these things the Lord appointed [1]seventy others also, and [a]sent
them two by two before His face into every
city and place where He Himself was
about to go. 2 Then He said to them, [b]"The
harvest truly *is* great, but the laborers *are*

9:49 because he does not follow with us. It is ironic that John, who came to be known as "the apostle of love," would be the one to raise this objection (*see note on v. 54*). John came to see that only legitimate tests of another person's ministry are the test of doctrine (1 John 4:1-3; 2 John 7-11) and the test of fruit (1 John 2:4-6,29; 3:4-12; 4:5,20; cf. Matt. 7:16). This man would have passed both tests, but John was inclined to reject him because of his group affiliation. That is the error of sectarianism.

9:50 he who is not against us is on our side. Contrast this with 11:23. There is no middle ground and no neutrality. Here Christ gave a test of outward conduct to use for measuring others. In 11:23, He gave a test of the inward life that is to be applied to oneself.

9:51 steadfastly set His face to go to Jerusalem. This begins a major section of Luke's gospel. From here to 19:27, Christ's face was set toward Jerusalem (*see note on v. 53*), and Luke's narrative is a travelogue of that long journey to the cross. This was a dramatic turning point in Christ's ministry. After this, Galilee was no longer His base of operation. Although 17:11-37 describes a return visit to Galilee, Luke included everything between this point and that short Galilean sojourn as part of the journey to Jerusalem. We know from a comparison of the gospels that, during this period of Christ's ministry, He made short visits to Jerusalem to celebrate feasts (*see notes on 13:22; 17:11*). Nonetheless, those brief visits were only interludes in this period of ministry that would culminate in a final journey to Jerusalem for the purpose of dying there. Thus Luke underscored this turning point in Christ's ministry more dramatically than any of the other gospels, by showing Christ's determination to complete His mission of going to the cross. *See note on 12:50.*

9:52 Samaritans. These people were descendants of Jewish mixed marriages from the days of captivity. They were rivals of the Jewish nation and had devised their own worship, a hybrid of Judaism and paganism, with a temple of their own on Mt. Gerizim. They were considered unclean by the Jews and were so hated that most Jewish travelers from Galilee to Judah took the longer route E of the Jordan to avoid traveling through Samaria. *See note on John 4:4.*

9:53 because His face was *set* for...Jerusalem. Traveling to Jerusalem for worship implied rejection of the temple on Mt. Gerizim and a contempt for Samaritan worship (*see note on v. 52*). This was a strong point of contention between Jews and Samaritans (cf. John 4:20-22).

9:54 James and John. Jesus nicknamed these brothers "Boanerges"—Sons of Thunder (Mark 3:17)—a fitting title, apparently. This was John's second sin against charity in such a short time (*see note on v. 49*). It is interesting to note that several years later, the Apostle John journeyed through Samaria once again with Peter, this time preaching the gospel in Samaritan villages (Acts 8:25).

9:55 rebuked them. Christ's response to the Samaritans exemplifies the attitude the church ought to have with regard to all forms of religious persecution. The Samaritans' worship was pagan at heart, plainly wrong (*see note on John 4:22*). Compounding that was their intolerance. Yet, the Lord would not retaliate with force against them. Nor did He even revile them verbally. He had come to save, not to destroy, and so His response was grace rather than destructive fury. Nonetheless, Christ's words of disapproval here must not be taken as condemnation of Elijah's actions in 1 Kin. 18:38-40 or 2 Kin. 1:10-12. Elijah was commissioned to a special ministry as prophet in a theocracy, and it was his God-ordained task to confront an evil monarch (Ahab) who was attempting to usurp God's authority. Elijah was specifically authorized to measure out the reprisal of God's wrath. Elijah acted with an authority comparable to that of modern civil authorities (cf. Rom. 13:4)—not in a capacity that parallels that of ministers of the gospel.

9:59,60 *See notes on Matt. 8:21,22.*

9:62 looking back. A plowman looking back cuts a crooked furrow.

10:1 seventy others. The commissioning of the 70 is recorded only in Luke. Moses also appointed 70 elders as his representatives (Num. 11:16,24-26). The 12 disciples had been sent into Galilee (9:1-6); the 70 were sent into every city and place where He was about to go—i.e., into Judea, and possibly Perea (*see note on Matt. 19:1*). **two by two.** As the 12 had been sent (Mark 6:7; cf. Eccl. 4:9,11; Acts 13:2; 15:27,39,40; 19:22; Rev. 11:3).

few; therefore [c]pray the Lord of the harvest
to send out laborers into His harvest. 3 Go
your way; [d]behold, I send you out as
lambs among wolves. 4 [e]Carry neither
money bag, knapsack, nor sandals; and
[f]greet no one along the road. 5 [g]But whatever house you enter, first say, 'Peace to
this house.' 6 And if a son of peace is there,
your peace will rest on it; if not, it will return to you. 7 [h]And remain in the same
house, [i]eating and drinking such things as
they give, for [j]the laborer is worthy of his
wages. Do not go from house to house.
8 Whatever city you enter, and they receive
you, eat such things as are set before you.
9 [k]And heal the sick there, and say to them,
[l]'The kingdom of God has come near to
you.' 10 But whatever city you enter, and
they do not receive you, go out into its
streets and say, 11 [m]'The very dust of your
city which clings to [2]us we wipe off
against you. Nevertheless know this, that
the kingdom of God has come near you.'
12 [3]But I say to you that [n]it will be more
tolerable in that Day for Sodom than for
that city.

13 [o]"Woe to you, Chorazin! Woe to you,
Bethsaida! [p]For if the mighty works which
were done in you had been done in Tyre
and Sidon, they would have repented long
ago, sitting in sackcloth and ashes. 14 But it
will be more tolerable for Tyre and Sidon at
the judgment than for you. 15 [q]And you,
Capernaum, [4]who are [r]exalted to heaven,
[s]will be brought down to Hades. 16 [t]He
who hears you hears Me, [u]he who rejects
you rejects Me, and [v]he who rejects Me rejects Him who sent Me."

2 [c][1 Cor. 3:9]; 2 Thess. 3:1
3 [d]Matt. 10:16
4 [e]Matt. 10:9-14; Mark 6:8-11; Luke 9:3-5 [f]2 Kin. 4:29
5 [g]1 Sam. 25:6; Matt. 10:12
7 [h]Matt. 10:11 [i]1 Cor. 10:27 [j][Matt. 10:10]; 1 Cor. 9:4-8; 1 Tim. 5:18
9 [k]Mark 3:15 [l]Matt. 3:2; 10:7; Luke 10:11
11 [m]Matt. 10:14; Mark 6:11; Luke 9:5; Acts 13:51 [2]NU *our feet*
12 [n]Gen. 19:24-28; Lam. 4:6; Matt. 10:15; 11:24; Mark 6:11 [3]NU, M omit *But*
13 [o]Matt. 11:21-23 [p]Ezek. 3:6
15 [q]Matt. 11:23 [r]Gen. 11:4; Deut. 1:28; Is. 14:13-15; Jer. 51:53 [s]Ezek. 26:20 [4]NU *will you be exalted to heaven? You will be thrust down to Hades!*
16 [t]Matt. 10:40; Mark 9:37; John 13:20; Gal. 4:14 [u][John 12:48]; 1 Thess. 4:8 [v]John 5:23

Return of the Seventy

17 Then [w]the [5]seventy returned with joy,
saying, "Lord, even the demons are subject
to us in Your name."
18 And He said to them, [x]"I saw Satan
fall like lightning from heaven. 19 Behold,
[y]I give you the authority to trample on serpents and scorpions, and over all the
power of the enemy, and nothing shall by
any means hurt you. 20 Nevertheless do
not rejoice in this, that the spirits are subject to you, but [6]rather rejoice because
[z]your names are written in heaven."
21 [a]In that hour Jesus rejoiced in the
Spirit and said, "I thank You, Father, Lord
of heaven and earth, that You have hidden
these things from *the* wise and prudent
and revealed them to babes. Even so, Father, for so it seemed good in Your sight.
22 [b]All[7] things have been delivered to Me
by My Father, and [c]no one knows who the
Son is except the Father, and who the Father is except the Son, and *the one* to whom
the Son wills to reveal *Him*."
23 Then He turned to *His* disciples and
said privately, [d]"Blessed *are* the eyes which
see the things you see; 24 for I tell you [e]that
many prophets and kings have desired to see
what you see, and have not seen *it*, and to
hear what you hear, and have not heard *it*."

How to Inherit Eternal Life

25 And behold, a certain [8]lawyer stood
up and tested Him, saying, [f]"Teacher, what
shall I do to inherit eternal life?"

17 [w]Luke 10:1 [5]NU *seventy-two*
18 [x]John 12:31; Rev. 9:1; 12:8, 9
19 [y]Ps. 91:13; Mark 16:18; Acts 28:5
20 [z][Ex. 32:32, 33]; Ps. 69:28; Is. 4:3; Dan. 12:1; Phil. 4:3; Heb. 12:23; Rev. 13:8 [6]NU, M omit *rather*
21 [a]Matt. 11:25-27
22 [b]Matt. 28:18; John 3:35; 5:27; 17:2 [c][John 1:18; 6:44, 46] [7]M *And turning to the disciples He said, "All*
23 [d]Matt. 13:16, 17
24 [e]1 Pet. 1:10, 11
25 [f]Matt. 19:16-19; 22:35 [8]*expert in the law*

10:3 lambs among wolves. I.e., they would face hostility (cf. Ezek. 2:3-6; John 15:20) and spiritual danger (cf. Matt. 7:15; John 10:12).

10:4 neither money bag, knapsack, nor sandals. I.e., travel without luggage. This does not mean they would be barefoot. *See note on 9:3.* **greet no one.** A greeting in that culture was an elaborate ceremony, involving many formalities, perhaps even a meal, and long delays (*see note on 11:43*). A person on an extremely urgent mission could be excused from such formalities without being thought rude. Everything in Jesus' instructions speaks of the shortness of time and the great urgency of the task.

10:7 Do not go from house to house. I.e., for lodging (*see note on Mark 6:10*). They were to establish headquarters in a village and not waste time moving around or seeking more comfortable housing.

10:11,12 *See notes on Matt. 10:14,15.*

10:13-15 *See notes on Matt. 11:21,23.*

10:16 These words elevate the office of a faithful minister of Christ, and magnify the guilt and the condemnation of those who reject the message.

10:17 returned with joy. How long the mission lasted is not recorded. It may have been several weeks. The 70 probably did not return all at once, but this dialogue appears to have occurred after they had all reassembled.

10:18 I saw Satan fall. In this context, it appears Jesus' meaning was, "Don't be so surprised that the demons are subject to you; I saw their commander cast out of heaven, so it is no wonder if his minions are cast out on earth. After all, I am the source of the authority that makes them subject to you" (v. 19). He may also have intended a subtle reminder and warning against pride—the reason for Satan's fall (cf. 1 Tim. 3:6). For discussions of Satan's fall, *see notes on Is. 14:12-14; Ezek. 28:12-15.*

10:19 serpents and scorpions. Cf. Ps. 91:13; Ezek. 2:6. These appear to be figurative terms for demonic powers (cf. Rom. 16:20).

10:20 do not rejoice in this. Rather than being so enthralled with extraordinary manifestations such as power over demons and the ability to work miracles, they should have realized that the greatest wonder of all is the reality of salvation—the whole point of the gospel message and the central issue to which all the miracles pointed. **because your names are written in heaven.** Cf. Phil. 4:3; Heb. 12:23; Rev. 21:27. By contrast, unbelievers are "written in the earth" (Jer. 17:13).

10:21,22 *See notes on Matt. 11:25,26.*

10:25 lawyer. I.e., a scribe who was supposedly an expert in the law of God. Aside from one usage of this word in Matt. 22:35 (*see note there*), Luke is the only one of the gospel writers who uses it (11:45,46). **what shall I do to inherit eternal life?** The same question is raised by several inquirers (18:18-23; Matt. 19:16-22; John 3:1-15).

26 He said to him, "What is written in the law? What is your reading *of it?*"

27 So he answered and said, [g]" 'You shall love the LORD your God with all your heart, with all your soul, with all your strength, and with all your mind,' and [h]'your neighbor as yourself.' "

28 And He said to him, "You have answered rightly; do this and [i]you will live."

Parable of the Good Samaritan

29 But he, wanting to [j]justify himself, said to Jesus, "And who is my neighbor?"

30 Then Jesus answered and said: "A certain *man* went down from Jerusalem to Jericho, and fell among [9]thieves, who stripped him of his clothing, wounded *him,* and departed, leaving *him* half dead. 31 Now by chance a certain priest came down that road. And when he saw him, [k]he passed by on the other side. 32 Likewise a Levite, when he arrived at the place, came and looked, and passed by on the other side. 33 But a certain [l]Samaritan, as he journeyed, came where he was. And when he saw him, he had [m]compassion. 34 So he went to *him* and bandaged his wounds, pouring on oil and wine; and he set him on his own animal, brought him to an inn, and took care of him. 35 On the next day, [1]when he departed, he took out two [n]denarii, gave *them* to the innkeeper, and said to him, 'Take care of him; and whatever more you spend, when I come again, I will repay you.' 36 So which of these three do you think was neighbor to him who fell among the thieves?"

37 And he said, "He who showed mercy on him."

Then Jesus said to him, [o]"Go and do likewise."

Mary and Martha Are Contrasted

38 Now it happened as they went that He entered a certain village; and a certain woman named [p]Martha welcomed Him into her house. 39 And she had a sister called Mary, [q]who also [r]sat at [2]Jesus' feet and heard His word. 40 But Martha was distracted with much serving, and she approached Him and said, "Lord, do You not care that my sister has left me to serve alone? Therefore tell her to help me."

41 And [3]Jesus answered and said to her, "Martha, Martha, you are worried and troubled about many things. 42 But [s]one thing is needed, and Mary has chosen that good part, which will not be taken away from her."

The Lord's Prayer—Matt. 6:9-13

11 Now it came to pass, as He was praying in a certain place, when He ceased, *that* one of His disciples said to Him, "Lord, teach us to pray, as John also taught his disciples."

27 [g] Deut. 6:5 [h] Lev. 19:18; Matt. 19:19
28 [i] Lev. 18:5; Neh. 9:29; Ezek. 20:11, 13, 21; Matt. 19:17; Rom. 10:5
29 [j] Luke 16:15
30 [9] *robbers*
31 [k] Ps. 38:11
33 [l] John 4:9 [m] Luke 15:20
35 [n] Matt. 20:2 [1] NU omits *when he departed*
37 [o] Prov. 14:21; [Matt. 9:13; 12:7]
38 [p] John 11:1; 12:2, 3
39 [q] [1 Cor. 7:32-40] [r] Luke 8:35; Acts 22:3 [2] NU *the Lord's*
41 [3] NU *the Lord*
42 [s] [Ps. 27:4; John 6:27]

10:27 he answered. The lawyer summed up the requirements of the law (Lev. 19:18; Deut. 6:5) exactly as Christ did on another occasion (*see notes on Matt. 22:37-40*).

10:28 do this and you will live. Cf. Ex. 20:11; Lev. 18:5; Ezek. 20:11. "Do and live" is the promise of the law. But since no sinner can obey perfectly, the impossible demands of the law are meant to drive us to seek divine mercy (Gal. 3:10-13,22-25). This man should have responded with a confession of his own guilt, rather than self-justification (v. 29).

10:29 wanting to justify himself. This reveals the man's self-righteous character. **who is my neighbor?** The prevailing opinion among scribes and Pharisees was that one's neighbors were the righteous alone. According to them, the wicked—including rank sinners (such as tax collectors and prostitutes), Gentiles, and especially Samaritans—were to be hated because they were the enemies of God. They cited Ps. 139:21,22 to justify their position. As that passage suggests, hatred of evil is the natural corollary of loving righteousness. But the truly righteous person's "hatred" for sinners is not a malevolent enmity. It is a righteous abhorrence of all that is base and corrupt—not a spiteful, personal loathing of individuals. Godly hatred is marked by a broken-hearted grieving over the condition of the sinner. And as Jesus taught here and elsewhere (6:27-36; Matt. 5:44-48), it is also tempered by a genuine love. The Pharisees had elevated hostility toward the wicked to the status of a virtue, in effect nullifying the second Great Commandment. Jesus' answer to this lawyer demolished the pharisaical excuse for hating one's enemies.

10:30 down from Jerusalem to Jericho. A rocky, winding, treacherous descent of about 3,300 feet in 17 miles. That stretch of road was notorious for being beset with thieves and danger.

10:32 Levite. These were from the tribe of Levi, but not descendants of Aaron. They assisted the priests in the work of the temple.

10:33 Samaritan. For a Samaritan to travel this road was unusual. The Samaritan himself was risking not only the thieves, but also the hostility of other travelers.

10:34 oil and wine. Probably carried by most travelers in small amounts as a kind of first-aid kit. The wine was antiseptic; the oil soothing and healing.

10:35 two denarii. I.e., two days' wages (*see notes on Matt. 20:2; 22:19*). Probably more than enough to permit the man to stay until he recovered.

10:36 neighbor to him. Jesus reversed the lawyer's original question (v. 29). The lawyer assumed it was up to others to prove themselves neighbor to him (*see note on v. 29*). Jesus' reply makes it clear that each has a responsibility to be a neighbor—especially to those who are in need.

10:38 a certain village. Bethany, two mi. E of the temple in Jerusalem, on the E slope of the Mt. of Olives. This was the home of Mary, Martha, and Lazarus (cf. John 11:1).

10:40 distracted. Lit. "dragging all around." The expression implies that Martha was in a tumult. **with much serving.** Martha was evidently fussing about with details that were unnecessarily elaborate.

10:42 one thing...good part. Jesus was not speaking of the number of dishes to be served. The one thing necessary was exemplified by Mary, i.e, an attitude of worship and meditation, listening with an open mind and heart to Jesus' words.

11:1 Lord, teach us to pray. Rabbis often composed prayers for their disciples to recite. Having seen Jesus pray many times, they knew of His love for prayer, and they knew prayer was not just the reciting of words (*see note on Matt. 6:7*).

2 So He said to them, "When you pray,
say:

[a]Our [1] Father [2]in heaven,
Hallowed be Your name.
Your kingdom come.
[3]Your will be done
On earth as *it is* in heaven.
3 Give us day by day our daily
bread.
4 And [b]forgive us our sins,
For we also forgive everyone who
is indebted to us.
And do not lead us into
temptation,
[4]But deliver us from the evil one."

Parable of the Persistent Friend

5 And He said to them, "Which of you
shall have a friend, and go to him at midnight and say to him, 'Friend, lend me
three loaves; 6 for a friend of mine has
come to me on his journey, and I have
nothing to set before him'; 7 and he will answer from within and say, 'Do not trouble
me; the door is now shut, and my children
are with me in bed; I cannot rise and give
to you'? 8 I say to you, [c]though he will not
rise and give to him because he is his
friend, yet because of his persistence he
will rise and give him as many as he needs.
9 [d]"So I say to you, ask, and it will be
given to you; [e]seek, and you will find;
knock, and it will be opened to you. 10 For
everyone who asks receives, and he who
seeks finds, and to him who knocks it will
be opened.

Parable of the Good Father—Matt. 7:7-11

11 [f]If a son asks for [5]bread from any father
among you, will he give him a stone? Or if
he asks for a fish, will he give him a serpent
instead of a fish? 12 Or if he asks for an egg,
will he offer him a scorpion? 13 If you then,
being evil, know how to give [g]good gifts to
your children, how much more will *your*
heavenly Father give the Holy Spirit to
those who ask Him!"

Christ Heals the Demoniac

14 [h]And He was casting out a demon,
and it was mute. So it was, when the
demon had gone out, that the mute spoke;
and the multitudes marveled.

Christ's Power Not from Satan
Matt. 12:25-30, 43-45; Mark 3:22-27

15 But some of them said, [i]"He casts out
demons by [6]Beelzebub, the ruler of the
demons."
16 Others, testing *Him,* [j]sought from Him
a sign from heaven. 17 [k]But [l]He, knowing
their thoughts, said to them: "Every kingdom divided against itself is brought to desolation, and a house *divided* against a house
falls. 18 If Satan also is divided against himself, how will his kingdom stand? Because
you say I cast out demons by Beelzebub.
19 And if I cast out demons by Beelzebub,
by whom do your sons cast *them* out?
Therefore they will be your judges. 20 But if
I cast out demons [m]with the finger of God,
surely the kingdom of God has come upon
you. 21 [n]When a strong man, fully armed,

CHAPTER 11
2 [a] Matt. 6:9-13 [1] NU omits *Our* [2] NU omits *in heaven* [3] NU omits the rest of v. 2.
4 [b] [Eph. 4:32] [4] NU omits *But deliver us from the evil one*
8 [c] [Luke 18:1-5]
9 [d] Ps. 50:14, 15; Jer. 33:3; [Matt. 7:7; 21:22; Mark 11:24; John 15:7; James 1:5, 6; 1 John 3:22; 5:14, 15] [e] Is. 55:6
11 [f] Matt. 7:9 [5] NU omits *bread from any father among you, will he give him a stone? Or if he asks for*
13 [g] James 1:17
14 [h] Matt. 9:32-34; 12:22, 24
15 [i] Matt. 9:34; 12:24 [6] NU, M *Beelzebul*
16 [j] Matt. 12:38; 16:1; Mark 8:11
17 [k] Matt. 12:25-29; Mark 3:23-27 [l] Matt. 9:4; John 2:25
20 [m] Ex. 8:19
21 [n] Matt. 12:29; Mark 3:27

11:2 Our Father in heaven. Virtually the same prayer was given as a model on two separate occasions by Christ, first in the Sermon on the Mount (*see notes on Matt. 6:9-13*), and then here, in response to a direct question. That accounts for minor variations between the two versions. **Your name.** God's name represents all His character and attributes. Cf. Pss. 8:1,9; 9:10; 22:21; 53:9; 115:1.

11:4 sins. *See note on Matt. 6:12.*

11:7 my children are with me in bed. The one-room houses that were common in Palestine had a common sleeping area shared by the whole family. If one person arose and lit a lamp to get bread, all would be awakened.

11:8 persistence. The word can even mean "impudence." It conveys the ideas of urgency, audacity, earnestness, boldness, and relentlessness—like the persistent asking of a desperate beggar.

11:13 being evil. I.e., by nature. *See note on Matt. 7:11.*

11:14 it was mute. I.e., the demon. **the mute spoke.** I.e., the man.

11:15 Beelzebub. Originally this referred to Baal-Zebul ("Baal, the prince"), chief god of the Philistine city of Ekron; the Israelites disdainfully referred to him as Baal-Zebub ("Lord of Flies"). *See note on 2 Kin. 1:2.*

11:16 a sign from heaven. I.e., a miraculous work of cosmological proportions, like the rearranging of the constellations, or something far greater than the casting out of a demon, which they had just witnessed. *See note on Matt. 12:38.*

11:17 knowing their thoughts. Jesus was God with full omniscience if He used it (*see notes on 2:52; John 2:24,25; Mark 13:32*). **kingdom divided against itself.** This may have been a subtle jab at the Jewish nation, a kingdom divided in the time of Jeroboam, and still marked by various kinds of bitter internal strife and factionalism, right up to the destruction of Jerusalem in A.D. 70.

11:19 by whom do your sons cast *them* out? There were Jewish exorcists who claimed power to cast out demons (Acts 19:13-15). Jesus' point was that if such exorcisms could be done via satanic power, the Pharisaical exorcists must be suspect as well. And in fact, the evidence in Acts 19 suggests that the sons of Sceva were charlatans who employed fraud and trickery to fabricate phony exorcisms. **your judges.** I.e., witnesses against you. This seems to suggest that the fraudulent exorcisms (which had their approval) stood as a testimony against the Pharisees themselves, who disapproved of Christ's genuine exorcisms.

11:20 with the finger of God. In Ex. 8:19 the phony magicians of Egypt were forced to confess that Moses' miracles were genuine works of God, not mere trickery such as they had performed. Here Jesus made a similar comparison between His exorcisms and the work of the Jewish exorcists. **the kingdom of God has come.** *See note on Matt. 12:28.*

11:21 a strong man. I.e., Satan.

guards his own palace, his goods are in
peace. 22 But [o]when a stronger than he
comes upon him and overcomes him, he
takes from him all his armor in which
he trusted, and divides his [7]spoils. 23 [p]He
who is not with Me is against Me, and he
who does not gather with Me scatters.

24 [q]"When an unclean spirit goes out of a
man, he goes through dry places, seeking
rest; and finding none, he says, 'I will return
to my house from which I came.' 25 And
when he comes, he finds *it* swept and put in
order. 26 Then he goes and takes with *him*
seven other spirits more wicked than himself, and they enter and dwell there; and [r]the
last *state* of that man is worse than the first."

27 And it happened, as He spoke these
things, that a certain woman from the
crowd raised her voice and said to Him,
[s]"Blessed *is* the womb that bore You, and
the breasts which nursed You!"

28 But He said, [t]"More than that, blessed
are those who hear the word of God and
keep it!"

Christ's Only Sign Is Jonah
Matt. 12:39-42

29 [u]And while the crowds were thickly
gathered together, He began to say, "This is
an evil generation. It seeks a [v]sign, and no
sign will be given to it except the sign of Jonah [8]the prophet. 30 For as [w]Jonah became
a sign to the Ninevites, so also the Son of
Man will be to this generation. 31 [x]The
queen of the South will rise up in the judgment with the men of this generation and
condemn them, for she came from the ends
of the earth to hear the wisdom of Solomon; and indeed a [y]greater than Solomon
is here. 32 The men of Nineveh will rise up
in the judgment with this generation and
condemn it, for [z]they repented at the
preaching of Jonah; and indeed a greater
than Jonah *is* here.

Parable of the Lighted Lamp

33 [a]"No one, when he has lit a lamp, puts
it in a secret place or under a [b]basket, but
on a lampstand, that those who come in
may see the light. 34 [c]The lamp of the body
is the eye. Therefore, when your eye is
[9]good, your whole body also is full of
light. But when *your eye* is [1]bad, your body
also *is* full of darkness. 35 Therefore take
heed that the light which is in you is not
darkness. 36 If then your whole body *is* full
of light, having no part dark, *the* whole
body will be full of light, as when the bright
shining of a lamp gives you light."

"Woes" on the Pharisees

37 And as He spoke, a certain Pharisee
asked Him to dine with him. So He went in
and sat down to eat. 38 [d]When the Pharisee
saw *it*, he marveled that He had not first
washed before dinner.

39 [e]Then the Lord said to him, "Now you
Pharisees make the outside of the cup and
dish clean, but [f]your inward part is full of
[2]greed and wickedness. 40 Foolish ones!
Did not [g]He who made the outside make
the inside also? 41 [h]But rather give alms of
[3]such things as you have; then indeed all
things are clean to you.

22 [o][Is. 53:12; Col. 2:15] [7]*plunder*
23 [p]Matt. 12:30; Mark 9:40
24 [q]Matt. 12:43-45; Mark 1:27; 3:11; 5:13; Acts 5:16; 8:7
26 [r]John 5:14; [Heb. 6:4-6; 10:26; 2 Pet. 2:20]
27 [s]Luke 1:28, 48
28 [t]Ps. 1:1, 2; 112:1; 119:1, 2; Is. 48:17, 18; [Matt. 7:21; Luke 8:21]; James 1:25
29 [u]Matt. 12:38-42 [v]1 Cor. 1:22 [8]NU omits *the prophet*
30 [w]Jon. 1:17; 2:10; 3:3-10; Luke 24:46; Acts 10:40; 1 Cor. 15:4
31 [x]1 Kin. 10:1-9; 2 Chr. 9:1-8 [y][Is. 9:6; Rom. 9:5]
32 [z]Jon. 3:5
33 [a]Matt. 5:15; Mark 4:21; Luke 8:16 [b]Matt. 5:15
34 [c]Matt. 6:22, 23 [9]Clear, or healthy [1]Evil, or unhealthy
38 [d]Matt. 15:2; Mark 7:2, 3
39 [e]Matt. 23:25 [f]Gen. 6:5; Titus 1:15 [2]Lit. *eager grasping* or *robbery*
40 [g]Gen. 1:26, 27
41 [h]Is. 58:7; Dan. 4:27; [Luke 12:33; 16:9] [3]Or *what is inside*

11:22 a stronger than he. I.e., Christ. **divides his spoils.** Probably a reference to Is. 53:12. When a demon is defeated by the power of Christ, the soul vacated by the power of darkness is taken over by Christ. Cf. vv. 24-26.

11:23 He who is not with Me is against Me. *See note on 9:50.*

11:24 unclean spirit goes out. Christ was characterizing the work of the phony exorcists (*see note on v. 19*). What appears to be a true exorcism is merely a temporary respite, after which the demon returns with 7 others (v. 26).

11:26 worse than the first. *See note on Matt. 12:45.*

11:28 More than that. This has the sense of, "Yes, but rather. . . ." While not denying the blessedness of Mary, Christ did not countenance any tendency to elevate Mary as an object of veneration. Mary's relationship to Him as His physical mother did not confer on her any greater honor than the blessedness of those who hear and obey the word of God. *See note on 1:47.*

11:29 It seeks a sign. *See note on v. 16.* Jesus always declined to give signs on demand. Evidences were not the means by which He appealed to unbelievers. *See note on 16:31.*

11:30 Jonah became a sign. I.e., a sign of judgment to come. Jonah's emergence from the fish's belly pictured Christ's resurrection. Jesus clearly regarded Jonah's account as historically accurate. *See notes on Matt. 12:39,40.*

11:31,32 *See notes on Matt. 12:41,42.*

11:33 *See note on 8:16.*

11:34 The lamp of the body. This is a different metaphor from the one in v. 33. There the lamp speaks of the Word of God; here the eye is the "lamp"—i.e., the source of light—for the body. *See note on Matt. 6:22,23.* **when *your eye* is bad.** The problem was their perception, not a lack of light. They did not need a sign; they needed hearts to believe the great display of divine power they had already seen.

11:38 He had not first washed. The Pharisee was concerned with ceremony, not hygiene. The Gr. word for "washed" refers to a ceremonial ablution. Nothing in the law commanded such washings, but the Pharisees practiced them, believing the ritual cleansed them of any accidental ceremonial defilement. *See notes on Mark 7:2,3.*

11:39 full of greed and wickedness. I.e., they were preoccupied with external ceremonies but overlooked the more important issue of internal morality. *See note on Matt. 23:25.*

11:40 Foolish ones! I.e., persons who lack understanding. This was the truth and not the sort of coarse name-calling Christ forbade in Matt. 5:22.

11:41 alms of such things as you have. Lit. "Give that which is within as your alms." This contrasts inner virtues with external ceremonies. Alms are to be given not for show, but as an expression of a faithful heart (cf. Matt. 6:1-4)—and the true almsgiving is not the external act, but one's attitude before God.

42 [i]"But woe to you Pharisees! For you
tithe the mint and rue and all manner of herbs,
and [j]pass by justice and the [k]love of God.
These you ought to have done, without
leaving the others undone. 43 [l]Woe to you
Pharisees! For you love the [4]best seats in
the synagogues and greetings in the marketplaces. 44 [m]Woe to you, [5]scribes and
Pharisees, hypocrites! [n]For you are like
graves which are not seen, and the men
who walk over *them* are not aware *of them*."

"Woes" on the Lawyers

45 Then one of the lawyers answered
and said to Him, "Teacher, by saying these
things You reproach us also."
46 And He said, "Woe to you also,
lawyers! [o]For you load men with burdens
hard to bear, and you yourselves do not
touch the burdens with one of your fingers.
47 [p]Woe to you! For you build the tombs of
the prophets, and your fathers killed them.
48 In fact, you bear witness that you approve the deeds of your fathers; for they indeed killed them, and you build their
tombs. 49 Therefore the wisdom of God
also said, [q]'I will send them prophets and
apostles, and *some* of them they will kill
and persecute,' 50 that the blood of all the
prophets which was shed from the foundation of the world may be required of this
generation, 51 [r]from the blood of Abel to
[s]the blood of Zechariah who perished between the altar and the temple. Yes, I say to
you, it shall be required of this generation.
52 [t]"Woe to you lawyers! For you have
taken away the key of knowledge. You did
not enter in yourselves, and those who
were entering in you hindered."
53 [6]And as He said these things to them,
the scribes and the Pharisees began to assail *Him* vehemently, and to cross-examine
Him about many things, 54 lying in wait
for Him, [7]and [u]seeking to catch Him in
something He might say, [8]that they might
accuse Him.

Christ Warns About Hypocrisy
Matt. 10:26-33

12 In [a]the meantime, when an innumerable multitude of people had
gathered together, so that they trampled
one another, He began to say to His disciples first *of all*, [b]"Beware of the [1]leaven of
the Pharisees, which is hypocrisy. 2 [c]For
there is nothing covered that will not be revealed, nor hidden that will not be known.
3 Therefore whatever you have spoken in
the dark will be heard in the light, and
what you have spoken in the ear in inner
rooms will be proclaimed on the housetops.
4 [d]"And I say to you, [e]My friends, do not
be afraid of those who kill the body, and
after that have no more that they can do.
5 But I will show you whom you should
fear: Fear Him who, after He has killed,
has power to cast into hell; yes, I say to
you, [f]fear Him!
6 "Are not five sparrows sold for two
[2]copper coins? And [g]not one of them is
forgotten before God. 7 But the very hairs
of your head are all numbered. Do not fear
therefore; you are of more value than
many sparrows.
8 [h]"Also I say to you, whoever confesses
Me [i]before men, him the Son of Man also
will confess before the angels of God. 9 But
he who [j]denies Me before men will be denied before the angels of God.

42 [i]Matt. 23:23 [j][Mic. 6:7, 8] [k]John 5:42
43 [l]Matt. 23:6; Mark 12:38, 39; Luke 14:7; 20:46 [4]*Or places of honor*
44 [m]Matt. 23:27 [n]Ps. 5:9 [5]NU omits *scribes and Pharisees, hypocrites*
46 [o]Matt. 23:4
47 [p]Matt. 23:29; Acts 7:52
49 [q]Prov. 1:20; Matt. 23:34
51 [r]Gen. 4:8; 2 Chr. 36:16 [s]2 Chr. 24:20, 21
52 [t]Matt. 23:13
53 [6]NU *And when He left there*
54 [u]Mark 12:13 [7]NU omits *and seeking* [8]NU omits *that they might accuse Him*

CHAPTER 12

1 [a]Matt. 16:6; Mark 8:15 [b]Matt. 16:12; Luke 11:39 [1]*yeast*
2 [c]Matt. 10:26; Mark 4:22; Luke 8:17; [1 Cor. 4:5]
4 [d]Is. 51:7, 8, 12, 13; Jer. 1:8; Matt. 10:28 [e][John 15:13-15]
5 [f]Ps. 119:120
6 [g]Matt. 6:26 [2]Gr. *assarion,* a coin worth about 1/16 of a denarius
8 [h]1 Sam. 2:30; Matt. 10:32; [Mark 8:38; Rom. 10:9; 2 Tim. 2:12; 1 John 2:23]
[i]Ps. 119:46
9 [j]Matt. 10:33; [Mark 8:38; 2 Tim. 2:12]

11:42 tithe. *See note on Matt. 23:23.*

11:43 greetings. These were ostentatious ceremonies that were more or less elaborate depending on the rank of the person being greeted.

11:44 graves which are not seen. Hidden sources of defilement. They had carefully concealed their own inward corruption, but it still was a source of defilement. *See note on Matt. 23:27.*

11:45 lawyers. I.e., scribes. *See note on 10:25.*

11:46 burdens. *See note on Matt. 23:3.*

11:47 you build the tombs of the prophets. They thought they were honoring those prophets, but in reality they had more in common with those who killed the prophets (v. 48). *See note on Matt. 23:30.*

11:49 the wisdom of God also said. There is no OT source for this quotation. Christ is prophetically announcing the coming judgment of God, not quoting a previously written source, but giving them a direct warning from God.

11:49-51 *See notes on Matt. 23:34-36.*

11:52 the key of knowledge. They had locked up the truth of the Scriptures and thrown away the key by imposing their faulty interpretations and human traditions on God's Word. *See note on Matt. 23:13.*

11:54 to catch. The same word is used in Gr. literature for the hunting of animals.

12:1 innumerable. The Gr. word is the same from which we get the word "myriads." **leaven.** *See notes on Matt. 16:12; Mark 8:15.*

12:2,3 *See notes on 8:17; Mark 4:22.*

12:5 Fear Him. *See note on Matt. 10:28.*

12:6 two copper coins. Gr., *assariōn,* a Roman coin equal to a 16th of a denarius. One assarius would be less than an hour's wage. **not one of them is forgotten before God.** Divine providence governs even the most inconsequential details of God's creation. He cares for all that He created, regardless of how insignificant. *See note on Matt. 10:29.*

12:8 before the angels of God. I.e., in the day of judgment. Cf. Matt. 25:31-34; Jude 24. *See note on Matt. 10:32.*

12:9 he who denies Me before men. This describes a soul-damning denial of Christ—not the sort of temporary wavering Peter was guilty of (22:56-62)—but the sin of those who through fear, shame, neglect, delay, or love of the world reject all evidence and revelation and decline to confess Christ as Savior and King, until it is too late.

10 "And [k]anyone who speaks a word
against the Son of Man, it will be forgiv-
en him; but to him who blasphemes
against the Holy Spirit, it will not be forgiven.
11 [l]"Now when they bring you to the
synagogues and magistrates and authorities, do not worry about how or what you
should answer, or what you should say.
12 For the Holy Spirit will [m]teach you in
that very hour what you ought to say."

Parable of the Rich Fool

13 Then one from the crowd said to Him,
"Teacher, tell my brother to divide the inheritance with me."
14 But He said to him, [n]"Man, who made
Me a judge or an arbitrator over you?"
15 And He said to them, [o]"Take heed and
beware of [3]covetousness, for one's life
does not consist in the abundance of the
things he possesses."
16 Then He spoke a parable to them, saying: "The ground of a certain rich man
yielded plentifully. 17 And he thought
within himself, saying, 'What shall I do,
since I have no room to store my crops?'
18 So he said, 'I will do this: I will pull
down my barns and build greater, and
there I will store all my crops and my
goods. 19 And I will say to my soul, [p]"Soul,
you have many goods laid up for many
years; take your ease; [q]eat, drink, *and* be
merry." ' 20 But God said to him, 'Fool!
This night [r]your soul will be required of
you; [s]then whose will those things be
which you have provided?'
21 "So *is* he who lays up treasure for
himself, [t]and is not rich toward God."

Seek the Kingdom of God—Matt. 6:25-33

22 Then He said to His disciples, "Therefore I say to you, [u]do not worry about
your life, what you will eat; nor about the
body, what you will put on. 23 Life is more
than food, and the body *is more* than clothing. 24 Consider the ravens, for they neither sow nor reap, which have neither
storehouse nor barn; and [v]God feeds
them. Of how much more value are you
than the birds? 25 And which of you by
worrying can add one cubit to his stature?
26 If you then are not able to do *the* least,
why [4]are you anxious for the rest? 27 Consider the lilies, how they grow: they neither toil nor spin; and yet I say to you,
even [w]Solomon in all his glory was not
[5]arrayed like one of these. 28 If then God
so clothes the grass, which today is in the
field and tomorrow is thrown into the
oven, how much more *will He clothe* you,
O *you* of [x]little faith?
29 "And do not seek what you should
eat or what you should drink, nor have
an anxious mind. 30 For all these things
the nations of the world seek after, and
your Father [y]knows that you need these
things. 31 [z]But seek [6]the kingdom of God,
and all these things shall be added to
you.
32 "Do not fear, little flock, for [a]it is your
Father's good pleasure to give you the
kingdom. 33 [b]Sell what you have and give
[c]alms; [d]provide yourselves money bags
which do not grow old, a treasure in the
heavens that does not fail, where no thief
approaches nor moth destroys. 34 For
where your treasure is, there your heart
will be also.

10 [k] [Matt. 12:31, 32; Mark 3:28; 1 John 5:16]
11 [l] Matt. 6:25; 10:19; Mark 13:11
12 [m] [John 14:26]
14 [n] [John 18:36]
15 [o] [1 Tim. 6:6-10] [3] NU *all covetousness*
19 [p] Eccl. 11:9; 1 Cor. 15:32; James 5:5 [q] [Eccl. 2:24; 3:13; 5:18; 8:15]
20 [r] Job 27:8; Ps. 52:7; [James 4:14] [s] Ps. 39:6; Jer. 17:11
21 [t] [Matt. 6:20; Luke 12:33; 1 Tim. 6:18, 19; James 2:5; 5:1-5]
22 [u] Matt. 6:25-33
24 [v] Job 38:41; Ps. 147:9
26 [4] *do you worry*
27 [w] 1 Kin. 10:4-7; 2 Chr. 9:3-6 [5] *clothed*
28 [x] Matt. 6:30; 8:26; 14:31; 16:8
30 [y] Matt. 6:31, 32
31 [z] Matt. 6:33 [6] NU *His kingdom, and these things*
32 [a] [Dan. 7:18, 27]; Zech. 13:7; [Matt. 11:25, 26; Luke 22:29, 30]
33 [b] Matt. 19:21; Acts 2:45; 4:34 [c] Luke 11:41 [d] Matt. 6:20; Luke 16:9; [1 Tim. 6:19]

12:10 blasphemes against the Holy Spirit. *See notes on Matt. 12:31,32.* This was not a sin of ignorance, but a deliberate, willful, settled hostility toward Christ—exemplified by the Pharisees in Matt. 12, who attributed to Satan the work of Christ (cf. 11:15).

12:11 do not worry. I.e., do not be anxious. This does not suggest that ministers and teachers should forego preparation in their normal spiritual duties. To cite this passage and others like it (21:12-15; Matt. 10:19) to justify the neglect of study and meditation is to twist the meaning of Scripture. This verse is meant as a comfort for those under life-threatening persecution, not an excuse for laziness in ministry. The exact same expression is used in v. 22, speaking of concern for one's material necessities. In neither context was Jesus condemning legitimate toil and preparation. He was promising the Holy Spirit's aid for times of persecution when there can be no preparation. *See note on Mark 13:11.*

12:13 tell my brother to divide the inheritance. "The right of the firstborn" was a double portion of the inheritance (Deut. 21:17). Perhaps this man wanted an equal share. In any case, Jesus seemed unconcerned about the implied injustice, and refused the man's request to arbitrate the family dispute.

12:14 who made Me a judge? One of Christ's roles is that of Judge of all the earth (John 5:22), but He did not come to be an arbiter of petty earthly disputes. Settling an inheritance dispute was a matter for civil authorities.

12:22-31 *See notes on Matt. 6:26-33.*

12:22 do not worry. *See note on v. 11.*

12:32 good pleasure. *See note on 2:14.* Christ stressed the Father's tender care over His little flock as an antidote to anxiety (vv. 22-30).

12:33 Sell what you have and give alms. Those who amassed earthly possessions, falsely thinking their security lay in material resources (vv. 16-20), needed to lay up treasure in heaven instead. *See note on Matt. 6:20.* Believers in the early church did sell their goods to meet the basic needs of poorer brethren (Acts 2:44,45; 4:32-37). But this commandment is not to be twisted into an absolute prohibition of all earthly possessions. In fact, Peter's words to Ananias in Acts 5:4 make it clear that the selling of one's possessions was optional. **money bags which do not grow old.** These purses that do not wear out (so as to lose the money) are defined as "treasure in the heavens that does not fail." The surest place to put one's money is in such a purse—in heaven, where it is safe from thieves and decay as well.

12:34 your heart will be also. Where one puts his money reveals the priorities of his heart. Cf. 16:1-13; Matt 6:21.

Parable of the Expectant Steward

35 [e]"Let your waist be girded and [f]your
lamps burning; 36 and you yourselves be
like men who wait for their master, when
he will return from the wedding, that
when he comes and knocks they may open
to him immediately. 37 [g]Blessed *are* those
servants whom the master, when he
comes, will find watching. Assuredly, I say
to you that he will gird himself and have
them sit down *to eat,* and will come and
serve them. 38 And if he should come in
the second watch, or come in the third
watch, and find *them* so, blessed are those
servants. 39 [h]But know this, that if the master of the house had known what hour the
thief would come, he would [7]have
watched and not allowed his house to be
broken into. 40 [i]Therefore you also be
ready, for the Son of Man is coming at an
hour you do not expect."

Parable of the Faithful Steward
Matt. 24:45-51

41 Then Peter said to Him, "Lord, do You
speak this parable *only* to us, or to all *people?"*
42 And the Lord said, [j]"Who then is that
faithful and wise steward, whom *his* master will make ruler over his household, to
give *them their* portion of food [8]in due season? 43 Blessed *is* that servant whom his
master will find so doing when he comes.
44 [k]Truly, I say to you that he will make
him ruler over all that he has. 45 [l]But if that
servant says in his heart, 'My master is
delaying his coming,' and begins to beat
the male and female servants, and to eat
and drink and be drunk, 46 the master of
that servant will come on a [m]day when he
is not looking for *him,* and at an hour when
he is not aware, and will cut him in two
and appoint *him* his portion with the unbelievers. 47 And [n]that servant who [o]knew
his master's will, and did not prepare *himself* or do according to his will, shall be
beaten with many *stripes.* 48 [p]But he who
did not know, yet committed things deserving of stripes, shall be beaten with few.
For everyone to whom much is given, from
him much will be required; and to whom
much has been committed, of him they
will ask the more.

Christ Warns of the Costs of Discipleship

49 [q]"I came to send fire on the earth, and
how I wish it were already kindled! 50 But
[r]I have a baptism to be baptized with, and
how distressed I am till it is [s]accomplished!
51 [t]Do *you* suppose that I came to give
peace on earth? I tell you, not at all, [u]but
rather division. 52 [v]For from now on five in
one house will be divided: three against
two, and two against three. 53 [w]Father will
be divided against son and son against father, mother against daughter and daughter against mother, mother-in-law against
her daughter-in-law and daughter-in-law
against her mother-in-law."

Christ Warns of Not Discerning the Times

54 Then He also said to the multitudes,
[x]"Whenever *you see* a cloud rising out of
the west, immediately you say, 'A shower
is coming'; and so it is. 55 And when you
see the [y]south wind blow, you say, 'There
will be hot weather'; and there is. 56 Hypocrites! You can discern the face of the sky
and of the earth, but how *is it* you do not
discern [z]this time?

35 [e] [Eph. 6:14; 1 Pet. 1:13] [f] [Matt. 25:1-13]
37 [g] Matt. 24:46
39 [h] Matt. 24:43; 1 Thess. 5:2; [2 Pet. 3:10]; Rev. 3:3; 16:15 [7] NU *not have allowed*
40 [i] Matt. 24:44; 25:13; Mark 13:33; [Luke 21:34, 36]; 1 Thess. 5:6; [2 Pet. 3:12]
42 [j] Matt. 24:45, 46; 25:21; [1 Cor. 4:2] [8] *at the right time*
44 [k] Matt. 24:47; 25:21; [Rev. 3:21]
45 [l] Matt. 24:48; 2 Pet. 3:3, 4
46 [m] 1 Thess. 5:3
47 [n] Num. 15:30; Deut. 25:2; [John 9:41; 15:22; Acts 17:30] [o] [James 4:17]
48 [p] [Lev. 5:17]; Num. 15:29; [1 Tim. 1:13]
49 [q] Luke 12:51
50 [r] Matt. 20:18, 22, 23; Mark 10:38 [s] John 12:27; 19:30
51 [t] Matt. 10:34-36 [u] Mic. 7:6; John 7:43; 9:16; 10:19; Acts 14:4
52 [v] Matt. 10:35; Mark 13:12
53 [w] Matt. 10:21, 36
54 [x] Matt. 16:2, 3
55 [y] Job 37:17
56 [z] Luke 19:41-44

12:35 girded. Speaks of preparedness. Long, flowing robes would be tucked into the belt to allow freedom to work. Cf. Ex. 12:11; 1 Pet. 1:13.

12:36 when he will return. The servants were responsible to meet him with burning torches.

12:37 watching. The key here is readiness at all times for Christ's return. *See notes on Matt. 25:1-13.* **gird himself.** I.e., he will take the servant's role and wait on them. This remarkable statement pictures Christ, at His return, ministering as a servant to believers.

12:38 second watch. 9:00 p.m. to midnight. **third.** Midnight to 3:00 a.m.

12:40 an hour you do not expect. Cf. 21:34; Matt. 24:36,42-44; 1 Thess. 5:2-4; 2 Pet. 3:10; Rev. 3:3; 16:15.

12:42 Christ did not directly answer Peter's question (v. 41), but implied that these truths apply to all believers—most of all those to whom much has been committed (v. 48). **steward.** *See note on 16:1.*

12:43 Blessed *is* that servant. The faithful steward pictures the genuine believer, who manages well the spiritual riches God has put in his care for the benefit of others, and the careful management of the master's estate. Faithful expression of the duty of such spiritual stewardship will result in honor and reward (v. 44).

12:45 to beat the...servants. This wicked steward's unfaithfulness and cruel behavior illustrates the evil of an unbelieving heart.

12:46 cut him in two. I.e., utterly destroy him. This speaks of the severity of final judgment of unbelievers.

12:47,48 The degree of punishment is commensurate with the extent to which the unfaithful behavior was willful. Note that ignorance is nonetheless no excuse (v. 48). That there will be varying degrees of punishment in hell is clearly taught in Matt. 10:15; 11:22,24; Mark 6:11 and Heb. 10:29 (*see notes there*).

12:49 fire. I.e., judgment. *See note on Matt. 3:11.* For the connection between fire and judgment, see Is. 66:15; Joel 2:30; Amos 1:7,10-14; 2:2,5; Mal. 3:2,5; 1 Cor. 3:13; 2 Thess. 1:7,8.

12:50 a baptism. A baptism of suffering. Christ was referring to His death. Christian baptism symbolizes identification with Him in death, burial, and resurrection. **distressed.** *See note on Matt. 26:38.* **till it is accomplished.** Though distressed about His coming passion, it was nonetheless the work He came to do, and He set His face steadfastly to accomplish it (*see note on 9:51*; cf. John 12:23-27).

12:51 not at all. *See note on Matt. 10:34.*

12:54-56 *See note on Matt. 16:2,3.*

57 "Yes, and why, even of yourselves, do
you not judge what is right? 58 [a]When you
go with your adversary to the magistrate,
make every effort [b]along the way to settle
with him, lest he drag you to the judge, the
judge deliver you to the officer, and the officer throw you into prison. 59 I tell you,
you shall not depart from there till you
have paid the very last mite."

Christ Teaches on Repentance

13 There were present at that season
some who told Him about the Galileans whose blood Pilate had [1]mingled
with their sacrifices. 2 And Jesus answered
and said to them, "Do you suppose that
these Galileans were worse sinners than all
other Galileans, because they suffered such
things? 3 I tell you, no; but unless you repent you will all likewise perish. 4 Or those
eighteen on whom the tower in Siloam fell
and killed them, do you think that they
were worse sinners than all *other* men who
dwelt in Jerusalem? 5 I tell you, no; but unless you repent you will all likewise perish."
6 He also spoke this parable: [a]"A certain
man had a fig tree planted in his vineyard,
and he came seeking fruit on it and found
none. 7 Then he said to the keeper of his
vineyard, 'Look, for three years I have
come seeking fruit on this fig tree and find
none. Cut it down; why does it [2]use up the
ground?' 8 But he answered and said to
him, 'Sir, let it alone this year also, until I
dig around it and fertilize *it*. 9 [3]And if it
bears fruit, *well*. But if not, after that you
can [b]cut it down.' "

Christ Heals the Crippled Woman

10 Now He was teaching in one of the
synagogues on the Sabbath. 11 And behold, there was a woman who had a spirit
of infirmity eighteen years, and was bent
over and could in no way [4]raise *herself* up.
12 But when Jesus saw her, He called *her* to
Him and said to her, "Woman, you are
loosed from your [c]infirmity." 13 [d]And He
laid *His* hands on her, and immediately she
was made straight, and glorified God.
14 But the ruler of the synagogue answered with indignation, because Jesus
had [e]healed on the Sabbath; and he said to
the crowd, [f]"There are six days on which
men ought to work; therefore come and be
healed on them, and [g]not on the Sabbath
day."
15 The Lord then answered him and
said, [5]"Hypocrite! [h]Does not each one of
you on the Sabbath loose his ox or donkey
from the stall, and lead *it* away to water it?

58 [a] Prov. 25:8; Matt. 5:25, 26 [b] [Ps. 32:6; Is. 55:6]

CHAPTER 13

1 [1] *mixed*
6 [a] Is. 5:2; Matt. 21:19
7 [2] *waste*
9 [b] [John 15:2] [3] NU *And if it bears fruit after that, well. But if not, you can*
11 [4] *straighten up*
12 [c] Luke 7:21; 8:2
13 [d] Mark 16:18; Acts 9:17
14 [e] [Luke 6:6-11; 14:1-6]; John 5:16 [f] Ex. 20:9; 23:12 [g] Matt. 12:10; Mark 3:2; Luke 6:7; 14:3
15 [h] [Matt. 7:5; 23:13]; Luke 14:5 [5] NU, M *Hypocrites*

12:58 make every effort along the way. *See note on Matt. 5:25.*

12:59 mite. *See notes on 21:2; Mark 12:42.*

13:1 Galileans whose blood Pilate had mingled with their sacrifices. This incident is in keeping with what was known about the character of Pilate. Evidently, some worshipers from Galilee were condemned by Rome—perhaps because they were seditious zealots (*see note on Matt. 10:4*)—and were sought out and killed in the temple by Roman authorities while in the process of offering a sacrifice. Such a killing would have been the grossest sort of blasphemy. Incidents like this inflamed the Jews' hatred of Rome and finally led to rebellion, and the destruction of Jerusalem in A.D. 70.

13:2 worse sinners. It was the belief of many that disaster and sudden death always signified divine displeasure over particular sins (cf. Job 4:7). Those who suffered in uncommon ways were therefore assumed to be guilty of some more severe immorality (cf. John 9:2).

13:3 unless you repent. Jesus did not deny the connection between catastrophe and human evil, for all such afflictions ultimately stem from the curse of humanity's fallenness (Gen. 3:17-19). Furthermore, specific calamities may indeed be the fruit of certain iniquities (Prov. 24:16). But Christ challenged the people's notion that they were morally superior to those who suffered in such catastrophes. He called all to repent, for all were in danger of sudden destruction. No one is guaranteed time to prepare for death, so now is the time for repentance for all (cf. 2 Cor. 6:2). **you will all likewise perish.** These words prophetically warned of the approaching judgment of Israel, which culminated in the catastrophic destruction of Jerusalem in AD 70. Thousands in Jerusalem were killed by the Romans. *See note on Matt. 23:36.*

13:4 Siloam. An area at the S end of the lower city of Jerusalem, where there was a well known pool (cf. John 9:7,11). Evidently one of the towers guarding the aqueduct collapsed, perhaps while under construction, killing some people. Again, the question in the minds of people was regarding the connection between calamity and iniquity ("worse sinners"). Jesus responded by saying that such a calamity was not God's way to single out an especially evil group for death, but as a means of warning to all sinners. Calamitous judgment was eventually coming to all if they did not repent.

13:6 fig tree. Often used as a symbol for Israel (*see notes on Matt. 21:19; Mark 11:14*). In this case, however, the parable's lesson about fruitlessness applies equally to the whole nation, and to each individual soul.

13:8 let it alone this year. This illustrates both the intercession of Christ and the extreme patience and graciousness of the Father.

13:10 synagogues. *See note on Mark 1:21.* **the Sabbath.** The Pharisees' Sabbath traditions were the issue that most frequently provoked controversy in Jesus' ministry. Cf. 6:5-11; 14:1-5; Matt. 12:2-10; Mark 2:23–3:4.

13:11 had a spirit of infirmity. This suggests that her physical ailment, which left her unable to stand erect, was caused by an evil spirit. However, Christ did not have to confront and drive out a demon, but simply declared her loosed (v. 12), so her case appears somewhat different from other cases of demonic possession He often encountered (cf. 11:14; *see note on v. 16*).

13:12 He called *her* to *Him*. The healing was unsolicited; He took the initiative (cf. 7:12-14). Furthermore, no special faith was required on her part or anyone else's. Jesus sometimes called for faith, but not always (cf. 8:48; Mark 5:34).

13:14 ruler. An eminent layman whose responsibilities included conducting meetings, caring for the building, and supervising the teaching in the synagogue (cf. 8:41; Matt. 9:18; Mark 5:38).

13:15 loose his ox. Nothing in Scripture forbade either the watering of an ox or the healing of the sick (*see notes on 6:9; Matt. 12:2,3,10*). Their Sabbath traditions actually placed a higher value on animals than on people in distress—and therefore corrupted the whole purpose of the Sabbath (Mark 2:27).

16 So ought not this woman, [i]being a
daughter of Abraham, whom Satan has
bound—think of it—for eighteen years, be
loosed from this bond on the Sabbath?"
17 And when He said these things, all His
adversaries were put to shame; and all the
multitude rejoiced for all the glorious
things that were [j]done by Him.

Parable of the Mustard Seed
Matt. 13:31, 32; Mark 4:30-32

18 [k]Then He said, "What is the kingdom
of God like? And to what shall I compare
it? 19 It is like a mustard seed, which a man
took and put in his garden; and it grew
and became a [6]large tree, and the birds of
the air nested in its branches."

Parable of the Leaven—Matt. 13:33-35

20 And again He said, "To what shall I
liken the kingdom of God? 21 It is like
[7]leaven, which a woman took and hid in
three [l]measures [8] of meal till it was all leavened."

The Way into the Kingdom

22 [m]And He went through the cities and
villages, teaching, and journeying toward
Jerusalem. 23 Then one said to Him, "Lord,
are there [n]few who are saved?"
And He said to them, 24 [o]"Strive to
enter through the narrow gate, for [p]many,
I say to you, will seek to enter and will not
be able. 25 [q]When once the Master of the
house has risen up and [r]shut the door, and
you begin to stand outside and knock at
the door, saying, [s]'Lord, Lord, open for
us,' and He will answer and say to you, [t]'I
do not know you, where you are from,'
26 then you will begin to say, 'We ate and
drank in Your presence, and You taught in
our streets.' 27 [u]But He will say, 'I tell you
I do not know you, where you are from.
[v]Depart from Me, all you workers of iniquity.' 28 [w]There will be weeping and
gnashing of teeth, [x]when you see Abraham and Isaac and Jacob and all the
prophets in the kingdom of God, and
yourselves thrust out. 29 They will come
from the east and the west, from the north
and the south, and sit down in the kingdom of God. 30 [y]And indeed there are last
who will be first, and there are first who
will be last."

Christ Mourns over Jerusalem

31 [9]On that very day some Pharisees
came, saying to Him, "Get out and depart
from here, for Herod wants to kill You."
32 And He said to them, "Go, tell that

16 [i] Luke 19:9
17 [j] Mark 5:19, 20
18 [k] Matt. 13:31, 32; Mark 4:30-32
19 [6] NU omits *large*
21 [l] Matt. 13:33 [7] *yeast* [8] Gr. *sata*, same as Heb. *seah*; approximately 2 pecks in all
22 [m] Matt. 9:35; Mark 6:6
23 [n] [Matt. 7:14; 20:16]
24 [o] [Matt. 7:13] [p] [John 7:34; 8:21; 13:33; Rom. 9:31]
25 [q] [Ps. 32:6]; Is. 55:6 [r] Matt. 25:10; Rev. 22:11 [s] Luke 6:46 [t] Matt. 7:23; 25:12
27 [u] [Matt. 7:23; 25:41] [v] Ps. 6:8; [Matt. 25:41]; Titus 1:16
28 [w] Matt. 8:12; 13:42; 24:51 [x] Matt. 8:11
30 [y] [Matt. 19:30; 20:16]; Mark 10:31
31 [9] NU *In that very hour*

13:16 a daughter of Abraham. She was a Jewess. **whom Satan has bound.** Job's physical ailments and other disasters were also inflicted by Satan, with divine permission. This woman had apparently been permitted to suffer, not because of any evil she had done, but so that the glory of God might be manifest in her (cf. John 9:3).

13:19,21 *See notes on Matt. 13:32,33.*

13:22 through the cities and villages. Luke's geographical points of reference are often vague; the readers he had in mind were probably largely unfamiliar with Palestinian geography anyway. Matthew 19:1; Mark 10:1; and John 10:40 all say that Christ moved His ministry to the region E of the Jordan, known as Perea. That move probably took place at about this point in Luke's narrative. Therefore the cities and villages He traveled through may have included places in both Judea and Perea. **journeying toward Jerusalem.** During His ministry in Judea to Perea, Christ actually went to Jerusalem on more than one occasion—at least once for the Feast of Tabernacles (John 7:11–8:59), another time for the Feast of Dedication (John 9:1–10:39), and another time when He raised Lazarus. Luke's focus was on Christ's constant progression toward His final trek to Jerusalem for the express purpose of dying there—and he therefore described all Christ's traveling as one long trek toward Jerusalem. *See notes on 9:51; 17:11.*

13:23 are there few who are saved? That question may have been prompted by a number of factors. The great multitudes that had once followed Christ were subsiding to a faithful few (cf. John 6:66). Great crowds still came to hear (14:25), but committed followers were increasingly scarce. Moreover, Christ's messages often seemed designed to discourage the half-hearted (*see note on 14:33*). And He himself had stated that the way is so narrow that few find it (Matt. 7:14). This contradicted the Jewish belief that all Jews, except for tax collectors and other notorious sinners, would be saved. Christ's reply once again underscored the difficulty of entering at the narrow gate. After the resurrection, only 120 disciples gathered in the upper room in Jerusalem (Acts 1:15), and only about 500 in Galilee (1 Cor. 15:6; *see notes on 24:34; Matt. 28:16*).

13:24 Strive. This signifies a great struggle against conflict. Christ was not suggesting that anyone could *merit* heaven by striving for it. No matter how rigorously they labored, sinners could never save themselves. Salvation is solely by grace, not by works (Eph. 2:8,9). But entering the narrow gate is nonetheless difficult because of its cost in terms of human pride, because of the sinner's natural love for sin, and because of the world's and Satan's opposition to the truth. *See notes on 16:16; Matt. 11:12.* **many...will seek to enter.** I.e., at the judgment, when many will protest that they deserve entrance into heaven (cf. Matt. 7:21-23).

13:25 I do not know you. Cf. Matt. 7:23; 25:12. Clearly, no relationship ever existed, though they had deluded themselves into thinking they knew the owner of the house (v. 26). Despite their protests, he repeated his denial emphatically in v. 27.

13:28 weeping and gnashing of teeth. *See note on Matt. 22:13.*

13:29 They will come. By including people from the 4 corners of the earth, Jesus made it clear that even Gentiles would be invited to the heavenly banquet table. This was contrary to prevailing rabbinical thought, but perfectly consistent with the OT Scriptures (Ps. 107:3; Is. 66:18,19; Mal. 1:11). *See notes on 2:31; Mark 13:27.*

13:30 last...first...first...last. *See note on Matt. 20:16.* In this context the saying seems to contrast Jews ("the first") and Gentiles ("the last"). *See note on 14:11.*

13:31 depart from here. Herod Antipas ruled Galilee and Perea (*see note on Matt. 2:22*). Christ was probably either approaching Perea or ministering there already (*see note on v. 22*). The Pharisees—no friends of Herod themselves—may have warned Christ because they hoped the threat of violence from Herod would either silence Him—or drive Him back to Judea, where the Sanhedrin would have jurisdiction over Him.

fox, 'Behold, I cast out demons and perform cures today and tomorrow, and the
third *day* [z]I shall be [1]perfected.' **33** Nevertheless I must journey today, tomorrow,
and the *day* following; for it cannot be that
a prophet should perish outside of Jerusalem.

34 [a]"O Jerusalem, Jerusalem, the one
who kills the prophets and stones those
who are sent to her! How often I wanted to
gather your children together, as a hen
gathers her brood under *her* wings, but you
were not willing! **35** See! [b]Your house is left
to you desolate; and [2]assuredly, I say to
you, you shall not see Me until *the time*
comes when you say, [c]*'Blessed is He who
comes in the name of the LORD!'* "

Instruction on the Sabbath

14 Now it happened, as He went into
the house of one of the rulers of the
Pharisees to eat bread on the Sabbath, that
they watched Him closely. **2** And behold,
there was a certain man before Him who
had dropsy. **3** And Jesus, answering, spoke
to the lawyers and Pharisees, saying, [a]"Is it
lawful to heal on the [1]Sabbath?"
4 But they kept silent. And He took *him*
and healed him, and let him go. **5** Then He
answered them, saying, [b]"Which of you,
having a [2]donkey or an ox that has fallen
into a pit, will not immediately pull him
out on the Sabbath day?" **6** And they could
not answer Him regarding these things.

Parable of the Ambitious Guest

7 So He told a parable to those who were
invited, when He noted how they chose
the best places, saying to them: **8** "When
you are invited by anyone to a wedding
feast, do not sit down in the best place, lest
one more honorable than you be invited by
him; **9** and he who invited you and him
come and say to you, 'Give place to this
man,' and then you begin with shame to
take the lowest place. **10** [c]But when you are
invited, go and sit down in the lowest
place, so that when he who invited you
comes he may say to you, 'Friend, go up
higher.' Then you will have glory in the
presence of those who sit at the table with
you. **11** [d]For whoever exalts himself will be
[3]humbled, and he who humbles himself
will be exalted."

12 Then He also said to him who invited
Him, "When you give a dinner or a supper,

32 [z] Luke 24:46; Acts 10:40; 1 Cor. 15:4; [Heb. 2:10; 5:9; 7:28] [1] Resurrected
34 [a] Matt. 23:37-39; 2 Chr. 24:20, 21; 36:15, 16
35 [b] Lev. 26:31, 32; Ps. 69:25; Is. 1:7; Jer. 22:5; Dan. 9:27; Mic. 3:12 [c] Ps. 118:26; Matt. 21:9; Mark 11:10; Luke 19:38; John 12:13 [2] NU, M omit *assuredly*

CHAPTER 14

3 [a] Matt. 12:10 [1] NU adds *or not*
5 [b] [Ex. 23:5; Deut. 22:4]; Luke 13:15 [2] NU, M *son*
10 [c] Prov. 25:6, 7
11 [d] Job 22:29; Ps. 18:27; Prov. 29:23; Matt. 23:12; Luke 18:14; James 4:6; [1 Pet. 5:5] [3] *put down*

13:32 that fox. Some have suggested that Jesus' use of this expression is hard to reconcile with Ex. 22:28; Eccl. 10:20; and Acts 23:5. However, those verses apply to everyday discourse. Prophets, speaking as mouthpieces of God, and with divine authority, were often commissioned to rebuke leaders publicly (cf. Is. 1:23; Ezek. 22:27; Hos. 7:3-7; Zeph. 3:3). Since Jesus spoke with perfect divine authority, He had every right to speak of Herod in such terms. Rabbinical writings often used "the fox" to signify someone who was both crafty and worthless. The Pharisees, who trembled at Herod's power, must have been astonished at Christ's boldness. **today and tomorrow, and the third *day*.** This expression signified only that Christ was on His own divine timetable; it was not meant to lay out a literal 3-day schedule. Expressions like this were common in Semitic usage, and seldom were employed in a literal sense to specify precise intervals of time. *See note on Matt. 12:40.* **be perfected.** I.e., by death, in the finishing of His work. Cf. Heb. 2:10; John 17:4,5; 19:30. Herod was threatening to kill Him, but no one could kill Christ before His time (John 10:17,18).

13:33 it cannot be. Not all prophets who were martyred died in Jerusalem, of course. John the Baptist, for example, was beheaded by Herod, probably at Herod's palace in Tiberias. This saying was probably a familiar proverb, like the adage in 4:24; Matt. 13:57. The statement is full of irony, noting that most of the OT prophets were martyred at the hands of the Jewish people, not by foreign enemies. Luke's inclusion of this saying underscores his theme in this section of His gospel—Jesus' relentless journey to Jerusalem for the purpose of dying (*see note on 9:51*).

13:34 O Jerusalem, Jerusalem. There is great tenderness in these words, as seen in the imagery of a hen with chickens. This outpouring of divine compassion foreshadows His weeping over the city as He approached it for the final time (19:41). Clearly, these are deep and sincere emotions (*see note on Matt. 9:36*). **I wanted...but you were not willing.** Lit. "I willed, but you willed not." Christ's repeated expressions of grief over the plight of Jerusalem do not diminish the reality of His absolute sovereignty over all that happens. Nor should the truth of divine sovereignty be used to depreciate the sincerity of His compassion. *See note on Matt. 23:37.*

13:35 This account of Luke's clearly falls at an earlier point in Christ's ministry than the parallel account in Matt. 23:37-39, which took place in the temple during Christ's final days in Jerusalem. The wording of the two laments is nonetheless virtually identical. Here Christ delivers prophetically the same message He would later pronounce as a final judgment. ***Blessed.*** Quotation from Ps. 118:26.

14:1 Sabbath. *See note on 13:10.* Luke shows Christ healing on the Sabbath more frequently than any of the other gospels. Christ seems to have favored the Sabbath as a day for doing acts of mercy. **watched Him closely.** Evidently the Pharisee had less than honorable motives for inviting Him to a meal.

14:2 dropsy. A condition where fluid is retained in the tissues and cavities of the body—often caused by kidney or liver ailments, including cancer.

14:3 lawyers. I.e., scribes. *See note on 10:25.* **Is it lawful.** He had repeatedly defended Sabbath healings, and His arguments consistently silenced the nay-sayers (cf. 6:9,10; 13:14-17). Here and in 6:9, He questioned the scribes about the legality of healing on the Sabbath beforehand—and still they could give no cogent reasons why they believed healing was a violation of Sabbath laws (cf. v. 6).

14:5 a donkey or an ox. Cf. 13:15; Matt. 12:11,12. Common humanitarianism (not to mention economic necessity) taught them that it was right to show mercy to animals on the Sabbath. Should not the same principles be applied in showing mercy to suffering people?

14:7 best places. I.e., the best seats at the table. Cf. 11:43; Matt. 23:6.

14:11 whoever exalts himself will be humbled. Jesus favored this sort of paradoxical play on words (cf. 9:24; 13:30 17:33; 18:14; Matt. 23:11,12). This comment made the point of vv. 8-10 clear. The point of this whole lesson closely parallels Prov. 25:6,7.

do not ask your friends, your brothers,
your relatives, nor rich neighbors, lest they
also invite you back, and you be repaid.
13 But when you give a feast, invite [e]*the*
poor, *the* [4]maimed, *the* lame, *the* blind.
14 And you will be [f]blessed, because they
cannot repay you; for you shall be repaid
at the resurrection of the just."

Parable of the Great Supper

15 Now when one of those who sat at the
table with Him heard these things, he said
to Him, [g]"Blessed *is* he who shall eat
[5]bread in the kingdom of God!"

16 [h]Then He said to him, "A certain man
gave a great supper and invited many,
17 and [i]sent his servant at supper time to
say to those who were invited, 'Come, for
all things are now ready.' 18 But they all
with one *accord* began to make excuses.
The first said to him, 'I have bought a piece
of ground, and I must go and see it. I ask
you to have me excused.' 19 And another
said, 'I have bought five yoke of oxen, and
I am going to test them. I ask you to have
me excused.' 20 Still another said, 'I have
married a wife, and therefore I cannot
come.' 21 So that servant came and report-

13 [e] Neh. 8:10, 12 [4] *crippled*
14 [f] [Matt. 25:34-40]
15 [g] Rev. 19:9 [5] M *dinner*
16 [h] Matt. 22:2-14
17 [i] Prov. 9:2, 5
21 [6] *crippled*
24 [j] [Matt. 21:43; 22:8; Acts 13:46]
26 [k] Deut. 13:6; 33:9; Matt. 10:37 [l] Rom. 9:13 [m] Rev. 12:11
27 [n] Matt. 16:24; Mark 8:34; Luke 9:23; [2 Tim. 3:12]
28 [o] Prov. 24:27

ed these things to his master. Then the
master of the house, being angry, said to
his servant, 'Go out quickly into the streets
and lanes of the city, and bring in here *the*
poor and *the* [6]maimed and *the* lame and *the*
blind.' 22 And the servant said, 'Master, it
is done as you commanded, and still there
is room.' 23 Then the master said to the servant, 'Go out into the highways and
hedges, and compel *them* to come in, that
my house may be filled. 24 For I say to you
[j]that none of those men who were invited
shall taste my supper.' "

Christ Teaches on Discipleship

25 Now great multitudes went with Him.
And He turned and said to them, 26 [k]"If
anyone comes to Me [l]and does not hate his
father and mother, wife and children,
brothers and sisters, [m]yes, and his own life
also, he cannot be My disciple. 27 And
[n]whoever does not bear his cross and come
after Me cannot be My disciple. 28 For
[o]which of you, intending to build a tower,
does not sit down first and count the cost,
whether he has *enough* to finish *it*— 29 lest,
after he has laid the foundation, and is not
able to finish, all who see *it* begin to mock

14:12 do not ask your friends, your brothers. Clearly this is not to be taken as an absolute prohibition against inviting friends or relatives to a meal. Christ employed similar hyperbole in v. 26. Such language is common in Semitic discourse and is used for emphasis. His point here is that inviting one's friends and relatives cannot be classified as a spiritual act of true charity. It may also be a rebuke against those prone to reserve their hospitality for "rich neighbors" who they know will feel obligated to return the favor. Cf. Deut. 14:28,29.

14:14 repaid at the resurrection. I.e., with treasure in heaven (cf. 18:22).

14:15 he who shall eat bread in the kingdom. The man probably held the common view that only Jews would be invited to the heavenly feast (*see note on Matt. 8:12*). Perhaps this was an idle or pious saying, made without much serious reflection. Christ replied with a parable that pictures the inclusion of Gentiles.

14:16 a great supper. This parable, similar in many ways to the one in Matt. 22:2-14, and making the same point, is nonetheless distinct. That parable was told on a different occasion, and some key details differ. **invited many.** Apparently no one declined the invitation. The man evidently had every reason to expect that all who were invited would attend.

14:17 those who are invited. Guests for a wedding, which could last a full week, were preinvited and given a general idea of the time. When all the many preparations were finally ready, the preinvited guests were notified that the event would commence. The preinvited guests refer to the people of Israel, who by the OT had been told to be ready for the arrival of the Messiah.

14:18 excuses. All the excuses smack of insincerity. One does not purchase property without seeing it first. And since the purchase was already complete, there was no urgency. The land would still be there after the banquet. Likewise (v. 19), one does not purchase oxen without first testing them. The man who had recently married (v. 20) was excused from business travel, or serving in the military (Deut. 24:5), but there was no legitimate reason for newlyweds to avoid such a social engagement.

14:21 *the* poor and *the* maimed and *the* lame and *the* blind. I.e., people the Pharisees tended to regard as unclean or unworthy. The religious leaders condemned Jesus for His associations with prostitutes and tax collectors (cf. 5:29,30; 15:1; Matt. 9:10,11; 11:19; 21:31,32; Mark 2:15,16).

14:22 still there is room. God is more willing to save sinners than sinners are to be saved.

14:23 into the highways and hedges. This evidently represents the Gentile regions. **compel *them* to come in.** I.e., not by force or violence, but by earnest persuasion.

14:24 none of those men who were invited. I.e., those who refused. Having spurned the invitation, Israel was shut out of the banquet. The master's judgment against them was to seal their own decision. Most of them were killed by divine judgment at the hands of the Romans in A.D. 70. *See notes on Matt. 22:7; 23:36; 24:2.*

14:25 great multitudes. Christ's aim was not to gather appreciative crowds, but to make true disciples (*see note on 13:23*). He never adapted His message to majority preferences, but always plainly declared the high cost of discipleship. Here He made several bold demands that would discourage the half-hearted.

14:26 hate. A similar statement in Matt. 10:37 is the key to understanding this difficult command. The "hatred" called for here is actually a lesser love. Jesus was calling His disciples to cultivate such a devotion to Him that their attachment to everything else—including their own lives—would seem like hatred by comparison. See 16:13; Gen. 29:30,31 for similar usages of the word "hate."

14:27 bear his cross. I.e., willingly. This parallels the idea of hating one's own life in v. 26. *See notes on 9:23; Matt. 10:38*; cf. Mark 8:34.

14:28 count the cost. The multitudes were positive but uncommitted. Far from making it easy for them to respond positively, He set the cost of discipleship as high as possible (vv. 26,27,33)—and encouraged them to do a careful inventory before declaring their willingness to follow. Cf. 9:57-62.

him, 30 saying, 'This man began to build and was not able to finish.' 31 Or what king, going to make war against another king, does not sit down first and consider whether he is able with ten thousand to meet him who comes against him with twenty thousand? 32 Or else, while the other is still a great way off, he sends a delegation and asks conditions of peace. 33 So likewise, whoever of you [p]does not forsake all that he has cannot be My disciple.

34 [q]"Salt *is* good; but if the salt has lost its flavor, how shall it be seasoned? 35 It is neither fit for the land nor for the [7]dunghill, *but* men throw it out. He who has ears to hear, let him hear!"

Parable of the Lost Sheep—Matt. 18:12-14

15 Then [a]all the tax collectors and the sinners drew near to Him to hear Him. 2 And the Pharisees and scribes complained, saying, "This Man [1]receives sinners [b]and eats with them." 3 So He spoke this parable to them, saying:

4 [c]"What man of you, having a hundred sheep, if he loses one of them, does not leave the ninety-nine in the wilderness, and go after the one which is lost until he finds it? 5 And when he has found *it*, he lays *it* on his shoulders, rejoicing. 6 And when he comes home, he calls together *his* friends and neighbors, saying to them, [d]'Rejoice with me, for I have found my sheep [e]which was lost!' 7 I say to you that likewise there will be more joy in heaven over one sinner who repents [f]than over ninety-nine [2]just persons who [g]need no repentance.

Parable of the Lost Coin

8 "Or what woman, having ten silver [3]coins, if she loses one coin, does not light a lamp, sweep the house, and search carefully until she finds *it?* 9 And when she has found *it*, she calls *her* friends and neighbors together, saying, 'Rejoice with me, for I have found the piece which I lost!' 10 Likewise, I say to you, there is joy in the presence of the angels of God over one sinner who repents."

Parable of the Lost Son

11 Then He said: "A certain man had two sons. 12 And the younger of them said to *his* father, 'Father, give me the portion of goods that falls *to me.*' So he divided to them [h]*his* livelihood. 13 And not many days after, the younger son gathered all together, journeyed to a far country, and there wasted his possessions with [4]prodigal living. 14 But when he had spent all,

33 [p] Matt. 19:27
34 [q] Matt. 5:13; [Mark 9:50]
35 [7] *rubbish heap*

CHAPTER 15

1 [a] [Matt. 9:10-13]
2 [b] Acts 11:3; Gal. 2:12 [1] *welcomes*
4 [c] Matt. 18:12-14; 1 Pet. 2:25
6 [d] [Rom. 12:15] [e] [Luke 19:10; 1 Pet. 2:10, 25]
7 [f] [Luke 5:32] [g] [Mark 2:17] [2] *upright*
8 [3] Gr. *drachma*, a valuable coin often worn in a ten-piece garland by married women
12 [h] Mark 12:44
13 [4] *wasteful*

14:33 forsake all. Only those willing to carefully assess the cost (vv. 28-32) and invest all they had in His kingdom were worthy to enter. This speaks of something far more than mere abandonment of one's material possessions; it is an absolute, unconditional surrender. His disciples were permitted to retain no privileges and make no demands. They were to safeguard no cherished sins; treasure no earthly possessions; and cling to no secret self-indulgences. Their commitment to Him must be without reservation. *See notes on 9:23-26.*

14:34 Salt *is* good. *See notes on Matt. 5:13; Mark 9:50.* Christ employed this same imagery on at least 3 different occasions in His ministry.

15:1 the tax collectors and the sinners. *See notes on 14:21; Matt. 5:46; 21:32.* Despite the difficulties of Christ's message (14:25-35), the outcasts of society were drawn to Him, while the religious leaders grew more and more determined to kill Him. Cf. 1 Cor. 1:26-29.

15:2 complained. Lit. "murmured greatly"—i.e., through the crowds. Their complaining prompted 3 parables designed to illustrate the joy of God over the repentance of sinners. **This Man receives sinners.** This phrase is the key to the trilogy of parables that follow. Christ was not ashamed to be known as a "friend of tax collectors and sinners" (7:34).

15:4 go after the one which is lost. The first two parables both picture God as taking the initiative in seeking sinners. The rabbis taught that God would receive sinners who sought His forgiveness earnestly enough, but here God is the One seeking the sinner (*see note on 19:10*). The shepherd in the Middle East was responsible for every sheep. He was obligated to his master to see that none was lost, killed, or injured (cf. Matt. 18:11-14).

15:5 lays *it* on his shoulders. The picture of a loving shepherd. Cf. John 10:11; Ps. 24:1. **rejoicing.** Joy over the return of the lost is the most prominent feature in all 3 parables (vv. 7, 10, 32).

15:7 joy in heaven. A reference to the joy of God Himself. There was complaining on earth, among the Pharisees (v. 2); but there was great joy with God and among the angels (v. 10). **persons who need no repentance.** I.e., those who think themselves righteous (cf. 5:32; 16:15; 18:9).

15:8 silver coins. The drachma was a Greek coin roughly equivalent in value to the Roman denarius (*see note on Matt. 22:19*). **light a lamp.** The typical one-room house had no windows. **sweep the house.** This illustrates the thoroughness of the search.

15:11,12 The parable of the prodigal son is the most familiar and beloved of all Christ's parables. It is one of the longest and most detailed parables. And unlike most parables, it has more than one lesson. The prodigal is an example of sound repentance. The elder brother illustrates the wickedness of the Pharisees' self-righteousness, prejudice, and indifference toward repenting sinners. And the father pictures God, eager to forgive, and longing for the return of the sinner. The main feature, however, as in the other two parables in this chapter, is the joy of God, the celebrations that fill heaven when a sinner repents.

15:12 give me the portion of goods that falls *to me*. A shocking request, tantamount to saying he wished his father were dead. He was not entitled to any inheritance while his father still lived. Yet the father graciously fulfilled the request, giving him his full portion, which would have been one-third of the entire estate—because the right of the firstborn (Deut. 21:17) gave the elder brother a double portion. This act pictures all sinners (related to God the Father by creation), who waste their potential privileges and refuse any relationship with Him, choosing instead a life of sinful self-indulgence.

15:13 gathered all together. The prodigal son evidently took his share in liquid assets, and left, abandoning his father, and heading into a life of iniquity. **prodigal living.** Not merely wasteful extravagance, but also wanton immorality (v. 30). The Gr. word for "prodigal" means "dissolute" and conveys the idea of an utterly debauched lifestyle.

there arose a severe famine in that land,
and he began to be in want. 15 Then he
went and joined himself to a citizen of that
country, and he sent him into his fields to
feed swine. 16 And he would gladly have
filled his stomach with the [5]pods that the
swine ate, and no one gave him *anything*.
17 "But when he came to himself, he
said, 'How many of my father's hired servants have bread enough and to spare, and
I perish with hunger! 18 I will arise and go
to my father, and will say to him, "Father,
[i]I have sinned against heaven and before
you, 19 and I am no longer worthy to be
called your son. Make me like one of your
hired servants." '
20 "And he arose and came to his father.
But [j]when he was still a great way off, his father saw him and had compassion, and ran
and fell on his neck and kissed him. 21 And
the son said to him, 'Father, I have sinned
against heaven [k]and in your sight, and am
no longer worthy to be called your son.'
22 "But the father said to his servants,
[6]'Bring out the best robe and put *it* on him,
and put a ring on his hand and sandals on
his feet. 23 And bring the fatted calf here
and kill *it*, and let us eat and be merry;
24 [l]for this my son was dead and is alive
again; he was lost and is found.' And they
began to be merry.
25 "Now his older son was in the field.
And as he came and drew near to the
house, he heard music and dancing. 26 So
he called one of the servants and asked
what these things meant. 27 And he said to
him, 'Your brother has come, and because
he has received him safe and sound, your
father has killed the fatted calf.'
28 "But he was angry and would not go
in. Therefore his father came out and
pleaded with him. 29 So he answered and
said to *his* father, 'Lo, these many years I
have been serving you; I never transgressed your commandment at any time;
and yet you never gave me a young goat,
that I might make merry with my friends.
30 But as soon as this son of yours came,
who has devoured your livelihood with
harlots, you killed the fatted calf for him.'
31 "And he said to him, 'Son, you are always with me, and all that I have is yours.
32 It was right that we should make merry
and be glad, [m]for your brother was dead

16 [5] *carob pods*
18 [i] Ex. 9:27; 10:16; Num. 22:34; Josh. 7:20; 1 Sam. 15:24, 30; 26:21; 2 Sam. 12:13; 24:10, 17; Ps. 51:4; Matt. 27:4
20 [j] [Jer. 3:12]; Matt. 9:36; [Acts 2:39; Eph. 2:13, 17]
21 [k] Ps. 51:4
22 [6] NU *Quickly bring*
24 [l] Matt. 8:22; Luke 9:60; 15:32; Rom. 11:15; [Eph. 2:1, 5; 5:14; Col. 2:13; 1 Tim. 5:6]
32 [m] Luke 15:24

15:15 to feed swine. This was the worst sort of degradation imaginable for Jesus' Jewish audience; swine were the worst sort of unclean animals.

15:16 would gladly have filled his stomach with the pods. I.e., Carob pods, used to feed swine but virtually undigestible for humans. In other words, the only reason he did not eat the same food as the swine is that he could not. **no one gave him *anything*.** He could not even eke out a living by begging. His situation could hardly have been more desperate. Thus he symbolizes the estranged sinner who is helpless in despair.

15:17 came to himself. I.e., came to his senses. When his incessant sinning had left him utterly bankrupt and hungry, he was able to think more clearly. In that condition, he was a candidate for salvation (*see notes on Matt. 5:3-6*).

15:18 will say to him. He carefully contemplated what he would say and counted the cost of his repentance (v. 19). **sinned against heaven.** A euphemism, meaning he had sinned against God. He not only realized the futility of his situation, but he also understood the gravity of his transgressions against the father.

15:20 his father saw him. Clearly, the father had been waiting and looking for his son's return. **ran.** The father's eagerness and joy at his son's return is unmistakable. This is the magnificent attribute of God that sets Him apart from all the false gods invented by men and demons. He is not indifferent or hostile, but a Savior by nature, longing to see sinners repent and rejoicing when they do. *See notes on 1 Tim. 2:4; 4:10.* From Gen. 3:8 to Rev. 22:17, from the fall to the consummation, God has been and will be seeking to save sinners, and rejoicing each time one repents and is converted.

15:21 Note that the son did not get to finish his rehearsed words of repentance before the father interrupted to grant forgiveness. This pictures God's eagerness to forgive.

15:22 the father said. Without a single word of rebuke, for the past, the father pours out his love for the son, and expresses his joy that what was lost had been found. Each of the father's gifts said something unique about his acceptance of the son: **robe.** Reserved for the guest of honor. **ring.** A symbol of authority. **sandals.** These were not usually worn by slaves, and therefore signified his full restoration to sonship.

15:23 the fatted calf. Reserved only for the most special of occasions—a sacrifice or a feast of great celebration. All this (vv. 22,23) symbolizes the lavishness of salvation's blessings (cf. Eph. 1:3; 2:4-7).

15:25 older son. He symbolizes the Pharisee, the hypocritical religious person, who stays close to the place of the Father (the temple) but has no sense of sin, no real love for the Father (so as to share in His joy), and no interest in repenting sinners.

15:28 he was angry. This parallels the complaining done by the scribes and Pharisees (v. 2).

15:29 I never transgressed your commandment at any time. Unlikely, given the boy's obvious contempt for his father, shown by his refusal to participate in the father's great joy. This statement reveals the telltale problem with all religious hypocrites. They will not recognize their sin and repent (*see notes on Matt. 9:12,13; 19:16-20*). The elder son's comment reeks of the same spirit as the words of the Pharisee in 18:11. **you never gave me a young goat.** All those years of service to the father appear to have been motivated too much by concern what he could get for himself. This son's self-righteous behavior was more socially acceptable than the younger brother's debauchery, but it was equally dishonoring to the father—and called for repentance.

15:30 this son of yours. An expression of deep contempt (cf. "this tax collector" in 18:11). He could not bring himself to refer to him as "my brother."

15:31 all that I have is yours. The inheritance had already been distributed (v. 12). Everything the father had was literally in the elder son's possession. Yet the elder son was begrudging even the love the father showed to the prodigal son. The Pharisees and scribes had easy access to all the riches of God's truth. They spent their lives dealing with Scripture and public worship—but they never really possessed any of the treasures enjoyed by the repentant sinner.

15:32 It was right that we should make merry. This summarizes the point of all 3 parables. **your brother.** *See note on v. 30.*

and is alive again, and was lost and is
found.' "

Parable of the Unjust Servant

16 He also said to His disciples: "There
was a certain rich man who had a
steward, and an accusation was brought to
him that this man was [1]wasting his goods.
2 So he called him and said to him, 'What
is this I hear about you? Give an [a]account
of your stewardship, for you can no longer
be steward.'
3 "Then the steward said within himself,
'What shall I do? For my master is taking
the stewardship away from me. I cannot
dig; I am ashamed to beg. 4 I have resolved
what to do, that when I am put out of the
stewardship, they may receive me into
their houses.'
5 "So he called every one of his master's
debtors to *him,* and said to the first, 'How
much do you owe my master?' 6 And he
said, 'A hundred [2]measures of oil.' So he
said to him, 'Take your bill, and sit down
quickly and write fifty.' 7 Then he said to another, 'And how much do you owe?' So he
said, 'A hundred [3]measures of wheat.' And
he said to him, 'Take your bill, and write
eighty.' 8 So the master commended the unjust steward because he had dealt shrewdly.
For the sons of this world are more shrewd
in their generation than [b]the sons of light.
9 "And I say to you, [c]make friends for
yourselves by unrighteous [4]mammon, that
when [5]you fail, they may receive you into
an everlasting home. 10 [d]He who *is* faithful
in *what is* least is faithful also in much; and
he who is unjust in *what is* least is unjust
also in much. 11 Therefore if you have not
been faithful in the unrighteous mammon,
who will commit to your trust the true *riches?* 12 And if you have not been faithful in
what is another man's, who will give you
what is your [e]own?
13 [f]"No servant can serve two masters;
for either he will hate the one and love the
other, or else he will be loyal to the one and
despise the other. You cannot serve God
and mammon."

Christ Warns the Pharisees

14 Now the Pharisees, [g]who were lovers
of money, also heard all these things, and
they [6]derided Him. 15 And He said to
them, "You are those who [h]justify yourselves [i]before men, but [j]God knows your

CHAPTER 16
1 [1] *squandering*
2 [a] [Rom. 14:12; 2 Cor. 5:10; 1 Pet. 4:5, 6]
6 [2] Gr. *batos,* same as Heb. *bath;* 8 or 9 gallons each
7 [3] Gr. *koros,* same as Heb. *kor;* 10 or 12 bushels each
8 [b] [John 12:36; Eph. 5:8]; 1 Thess. 5:5
9 [c] Dan. 4:27; [Matt. 6:19; 19:21]; Luke 11:41; [1 Tim. 6:17-19] [4] Lit., in Aram., *wealth* [5] NU *it fails*
10 [d] Matt. 25:21; Luke 19:17
12 [e] [1 Pet. 1:3, 4]
13 [f] Matt. 6:24; Gal. 1:10
14 [g] Matt. 23:14 [6] Lit. *turned up their nose at*
15 [h] Luke 10:29 [i] [Matt. 6:2, 5, 16] [j] 1 Chr. 28:9; 2 Chr. 6:30; Ps. 7:9; Prov. 15:11; Jer. 17:10

16:1 steward. A steward was a trusted servant, usually someone born in the household, who was chief of the management and distribution of household provisions. He provided food for all the other servants, thus managing his master's resources for the well being of others. He acted as an agent for his master, with full authority to transact business in the master's name. **was wasting his goods.** His prodigality is a thread that ties this parable to the preceding one. Like the younger son in the earlier parable, this steward was guilty of wasting the resources available to him. Unlike the prodigal, however, he had enough sense to make sure that his wastefulness did not leave him friendless and unprovided for in the future.

16:2 you can no longer be steward. By announcing his intention to fire the man, the owner acted unwisely, and it cost him even more. Evidently he thought the man guilty of incompetence, rather than fraud. That would explain his reaction in v. 8.

16:3 I cannot dig. I.e., he did not consider himself fit for physical labor.

16:4 resolved what to do. Cleverly, he arranged to give large discounts to his master's debtors, which they would eagerly agree to pay. **receive me into their houses.** By reducing their debts to his master, he gained their indebtedness to him. They would thus be obligated to take him into their homes when he was put out of his master's home.

16:6 quickly. This was a secret transaction, unauthorized by the master. The borrower was guilty of deliberate complicity in the man's fraud.

16:8 the master commended the unjust steward. Outwitted, he applauded the man's cunning. His admiration for the evil steward's criminal genius shows that he, too, was a wicked man. It is the natural tendency of fallen hearts to admire a villain's craftiness (Ps. 49:18). Note that all the characters in this parable are unjust, unscrupulous, and corrupt. **more shrewd.** I.e., most unbelievers are wiser in the ways of the world than some believers ("sons of light," cf. John 12:36; Eph. 5:18) are toward the things of God.

16:9 unrighteous mammon. I.e., money. The unjust steward used his master's money to buy earthly friends; believers are to use their Master's money in a way that will accrue friends for eternity—by investing in the kingdom gospel that brings sinners to salvation, so that when they arrive in heaven ("an everlasting home"), those sinners will be there to welcome them. Christ did not commend the man's dishonesty; He pointedly called him "unjust" (v. 8). He only used him as an illustration to show that even the most wicked sons of this world are shrewd enough to provide for themselves against coming evil. Believers ought to be more shrewd, because they are concerned with eternal matters, not just earthly ones. Cf. 12:33; Matt. 6:19-21.

16:10 He who *is* faithful. Probably a common proverb. Cf. 19:17; Matt. 25:21.

16:11 true *riches.* Faithful use of one's earthly wealth is the repeatedly tied to the accumulation of treasure in heaven (cf. 12:33; 18:22; Matt. 16:19-21).

16:12 what is another man's. Lit. "what is another's"—referring to God, and the believer's stewardship of His money, which believers only manage as stewards.

16:13 You cannot serve God and mammon. Many of the Pharisees taught that devotion to money and devotion to God were perfectly compatible (v. 14). This went hand-in-hand with the commonly-held notion that earthly riches signified divine blessing. Rich people were therefore regarded as God's favorites (*see note on Matt. 19:24*). While not condemning wealth per se, Christ denounced both love of wealth and devotion to mammon. On the love of money, *see notes on 1 Tim. 6:9, 10, 17-19.*

16:15 justify yourselves. The Pharisees' belief was that their own goodness was what justified them (cf. Rom. 10:3). This is the very definition of "self-righteousness." But, as Jesus suggested, their righteousness was flawed, being an external veneer only. That might be enough to justify them before men, but not before God, because He knew their hearts. He repeatedly exposed their habit of seeking the approval of people (cf. Matt. 6:2, 5, 16; 23:28).

hearts. For [k]what is highly esteemed
among men is an abomination in the sight
of God.
16 [l]"The law and the prophets *were* until
John. Since that time the kingdom of God
has been preached, and everyone is pressing into it. 17 [m]And it is easier for heaven
and earth to pass away than for one [7]tittle
of the law to fail.

Christ Teaches on Divorce

18 [n]"Whoever divorces his wife and
marries another commits adultery; and
whoever marries her who is divorced from
her husband commits adultery.

Parable of the Rich Man and Lazarus

19 "There was a certain rich man who
was clothed in purple and fine linen and
[8]fared sumptuously every day. 20 But there
was a certain beggar named Lazarus, full
of sores, who was laid at his gate, 21 desiring to be fed with [9]the crumbs which fell
from the rich man's table. Moreover the
dogs came and licked his sores. 22 So it was
that the beggar died, and was carried by
the angels to [o]Abraham's bosom. The rich
man also died and was buried. 23 And
being in torments in Hades, he lifted up his
eyes and saw Abraham afar off, and Lazarus in his bosom.
24 "Then he cried and said, 'Father Abraham, have mercy on me, and send Lazarus
that he may dip the tip of his finger in
water and [p]cool my tongue; for I [q]am tormented in this flame.' 25 But Abraham
said, 'Son, [r]remember that in your lifetime
you received your good things, and likewise Lazarus evil things; but now he is
comforted and you are tormented. 26 And
besides all this, between us and you there
is a great gulf fixed, so that those who
want to pass from here to you cannot, nor
can those from there pass to us.'
27 "Then he said, 'I beg you therefore, father, that you would send him to my father's house, 28 for I have five brothers,
that he may testify to them, lest they also
come to this place of torment.' 29 Abraham
said to him, [s]'They have Moses and the
prophets; let them hear them.' 30 And he
said, 'No, father Abraham; but if one goes

15 [k] 1 Sam. 16:7; Ps. 10:3; Prov. 6:16-19; 16:5
16 [l] Matt. 3:1-12; 4:17; 11:12, 13; Luke 7:29
17 [m] Ps. 102:26, 27; Is. 40:8; 51:6; Matt. 5:18; 1 Pet. 1:25 [7] The smallest stroke in a Heb. letter
18 [n] Matt. 5:32; 19:9; Mark 10:11; 1 Cor. 7:10, 11
19 [8] *lived in luxury*
21 [9] NU *what fell*
22 [o] Matt. 8:11
24 [p] Zech. 14:12 [q] [Is. 66:24; Mark 9:42-48]
25 [r] Job 21:13; Luke 6:24; James 5:5
29 [s] Is. 8:20; 34:16; [John 5:39, 45]; Acts 15:21; 17:11; [2 Tim. 3:15]

16:16 until John. John the Baptist's ministry marked the turning point of redemptive history. Prior to that, the great truths of Christ and His kingdom were veiled in the types and shadows of the law, and promised in the writings of the prophets (cf. 1 Pet. 1:10-12). But John the Baptist introduced the King Himself (*see note on Matt. 11:11*). The Pharisees, who thought of themselves as experts in the law and the prophets, missed the significance of the very One to whom the law and the prophets pointed. **everyone is pressing into it.** Cf. Jer. 29:13. While the Pharisees were busy opposing Christ, sinners were entering his kingdom in droves. The language of this expression speaks of violent force—probably signifying the zeal with which sinners were seeking with all of their heart to enter the kingdom (*see notes on 13:24; Is. 55:6,7; Matt. 11:12*).

16:17 than for one tittle of the law to fail. Lest anyone think the statement in v. 16 meant He was declaring the law and the prophets annulled, He added this (*see note on Matt. 5:18*). The great moral principles of the law, the eternal truths contained in the law's types and symbols, and the promises recorded by the prophets all remain in force and are not abrogated by the kingdom message.

16:18 commits adultery. I.e., if the divorce had no legitimate grounds. Luke gave an abbreviated record of Jesus' teaching on divorce, stressing only the main issue. Matthew's fuller account makes it clear that He permitted divorce in cases where one's spouse was guilty of adultery. *See notes on Matt. 5:31,32; 19:3-9.* This countered the rabbis' doctrine, which permitted men to divorce their wives easily, and for almost any cause (Matt. 19:3).

16:20 Lazarus. Clearly not the Lazarus in John 11 (who died at a later time). This beggar was the only character in any of Jesus' parables ever given a name. Some therefore have speculated that this was no imaginary tale, but an actual incident that really took place. Either way, Christ employs it in the same fashion as all His parables, to teach a lesson, in this case for the benefit of the Pharisees. The rich man in the parable is sometimes called *Dives,* after the Latin word for "rich."

16:21 The mention of table scraps, sores, and dogs all made this poor man appear odious in the eyes of the Pharisees. They were inclined to see all such things as proof of divine disfavor. They would have viewed such a person as not only unclean, but also despised by God.

16:22 Abraham's bosom. This same expression (found only here in Scripture) was used in the Talmud as a figure for heaven. The idea was that Lazarus was given a place of high honor, reclining next to Abraham at the heavenly banquet.

16:23 in Hades. The suggestion that a rich man would be excluded from heaven would have scandalized the Pharisees (*see note on Matt. 19:24*); especially galling was the idea that a beggar who ate scraps from his table was granted the place of honor next to Abraham. "Hades" was the Gr. term for the abode of the dead. In the LXX, it was used to translate the Heb. *Sheol,* which referred to the realm of the dead in general, without necessarily distinguishing between righteous or unrighteous souls. However, in NT usage, "Hades" always refers to the place of the wicked prior to final judgment in hell. The imagery Jesus used fit the erroneous common rabbinical idea that Sheol had two parts, one for the souls of the righteous and the other for the souls of the wicked—separated by an impassable gulf. But there is no reason to suppose, as some do, that "Abraham's bosom" spoke of a temporary prison for the souls of OT saints, who were brought to heaven only after He had actually atoned for their sins. Scripture consistently teaches that the spirits of the righteous dead go immediately into the presence of God (cf. 23:43; 2 Cor. 5:8; Phil. 1:23). And the presence of Moses and Elijah on the Mount of Transfiguration (9:30) belies the notion that they were confined in a compartment of Sheol until Christ finished His work.

16:24 I am tormented. Christ pictured Hades as a place where the unspeakable torment of hell had already begun. Among the miseries featured here are unquenchable flame (*see note on Matt. 25:46*); an accusing conscience fed by undying memories of lost opportunity (v. 25); and permanent, irreversible separation from God and everything good (v. 26).

16:27 send him to my father's house. The rich man retained a condescending attitude toward Lazarus even in hell, repeatedly asking Abraham to "send" Lazarus to wait on him (cf. v. 24). The flames of hell do not atone for sin or purge hardened sinners from their depravity (cf. Rev. 22:11).

16:29 They have Moses and the prophets. I.e., the OT Scriptures.

to them from the dead, they will repent.'
31 But he said to him, [t]'If they do not hear
Moses and the prophets, [u]neither will they
be persuaded though one rise from the
dead.' "

Christ Teaches on Offenses

17 Then He said to the disciples, [a]"It is
impossible that no [1]offenses should
come, but [b]woe *to him* through whom they
do come! 2 It would be better for him if a
millstone were hung around his neck, and
he were thrown into the sea, than that he
should [2]offend one of these little ones.
3 Take heed to yourselves. [c]If your brother
sins [3]against you, [d]rebuke him; and if he
repents, forgive him. 4 And if he sins
against you seven times in a day, and
seven times in a day returns [4]to you, saying, 'I repent,' you shall forgive him."
5 And the apostles said to the Lord, "Increase our faith."
6 [e]So the Lord said, "If you have faith as
a mustard seed, you can say to this mulberry tree, 'Be pulled up by the roots and
be planted in the sea,' and it would obey
you. 7 And which of you, having a servant
plowing or tending sheep, will say to him
when he has come in from the field, 'Come
at once and sit down to eat'? 8 But will he
not rather say to him, 'Prepare something
for my supper, and gird yourself [f]and
serve me till I have eaten and drunk, and
afterward you will eat and drink'? 9 Does
he thank that servant because he did the
things that were commanded [5]him? I think
not. 10 So likewise you, when you have
done all those things which you are commanded, say, 'We are [g]unprofitable servants. We have done what was our duty to
do.' "

Christ Cleanses Ten Lepers

11 Now it happened [h]as He went to Jerusalem that He passed through the midst of
Samaria and Galilee. 12 Then as He entered
a certain village, there met Him ten men
who were lepers, [i]who stood afar off.
13 And they lifted up *their* voices and said,
"Jesus, Master, have mercy on us!"
14 So when He saw *them,* He said to
them, [j]"Go, show yourselves to the
priests." And so it was that as they went,
they were cleansed.
15 And one of them, when he saw that he
was healed, returned, and with a loud
voice [k]glorified God, 16 and fell down on
his face at His feet, giving Him thanks. And
he was a [l]Samaritan.
17 So Jesus answered and said, "Were
there not ten cleansed? But where *are* the
nine? 18 Were there not any found who re-

31 [t][John 5:46] [u]John 12:10, 11

CHAPTER 17

1 [a][1 Cor. 11:19] [b]Matt. 18:6, 7; 26:24; Mark 9:42; [2 Thess. 1:6]; Jude 11 [1]*stumbling blocks*
2 [2]*cause one of these little ones to stumble*
3 [c][Matt. 18:15, 21] [d]Lev. 19:17; [Prov. 17:10; Gal. 6:1; James 5:19, 20] [3]NU omits *against you*
4 [4]M omits *to you*
6 [e]Matt. 17:20; 21:21; [Mark 9:23; 11:23]; Luke 13:19
8 [f][Luke 12:37]
9 [5]NU omits the rest of v. 9; M omits *him*
10 [g]Job 22:3; 35:7; Ps. 16:2; Matt. 25:30; Rom. 3:12; 11:35; [1 Cor. 9:16, 17]; Philem. 11
11 [h]Luke 9:51, 52; John 4:4
12 [i]Lev. 13:46; Num. 5:2
14 [j]Lev. 13:1-59; 14:1-32; Matt. 8:4; Luke 5:14
15 [k]Luke 5:25; 18:43
16 [l]2 Kin. 17:24; Luke 9:52, 53; John 4:9

16:31 neither will they be persuaded. This speaks powerfully of the singular sufficiency of Scripture to overcome unbelief. The gospel itself is the power of God unto salvation (Rom. 1:16). Since unbelief is at heart a moral, rather than an intellectual, problem, no amount of evidences will ever turn unbelief to faith. But the revealed Word of God has inherent power to do so (cf. John 6:63; Heb. 4:12; James 1:18; 1 Pet. 1:23).

17:1 offenses. Lit. "snares." *See note on Matt. 18:7.*

17:2 a millstone. Lit. "the millstone of a donkey." *See note on Matt. 18:6.* **little ones.** Believers; God's children who are under His care. *See note on Matt. 18:5.*

17:3 rebuke him. It is the Christian's duty to deal straightforwardly with a brother or sister in sin. *See note on Matt. 18:15.*

17:4 seven times in a day. I.e., no matter how many times he sins and repents. *See notes on Matt 18:21,22.* The number 7 was not to set a limit on the number of times to forgive (cf. Ps. 119:164), but precisely the opposite. Christ meant that forgiveness should be granted unendingly (cf. Eph. 4:32; Col. 3:13).

17:5 "Increase our faith." Lit. "Give us more faith." They felt inadequate in the face of the high standard He set for them.

17:6 faith as a mustard seed. *See note on Matt. 17:20.*

17:7-10 The point of this parable was that a servant should expect no special reward for doing what was his duty in the first place. The demanding standards Christ set (vv. 1-4) may have seemed too high to the disciples, but they represented only the minimal duties for a servant of Christ. Those who obey are not to think their obedience is meritorious.

17:10 unprofitable servants. I.e., not worthy of any special honor.

17:11 as He went to Jerusalem...through...Samaria and Galilee. Luke did not explain the reason for such a circuitous route, but a comparison of the gospels yields several clues. It appears that time elapsed between v. 10 and v. 11. The raising of Lazarus at Bethany, near Jerusalem (John 11) appears to fit into this timeframe. John 11:54 states that after raising Lazarus, to avoid the authorities who were seeking to kill Him, Christ went to "a city called Ephraim"—N of Jerusalem near the border of Samaria. From there he apparently traveled N through Samaria and Galilee one more time, possibly to join friends and family from Galilee who would be making a pilgrimage to Jerusalem for the Passover. From there He would have traveled S by the conventional route, which would have brought Him through Jericho (18:35) to Jerusalem. *See notes on 9:51; 13:22.*

17:12 lepers. These men were ceremonially defiled and forced to live outside the village (Lev. 13:46; Num. 5:2,3). They were legally required to stand at a distance, and thus their communication with Christ was by shouting. For a description of leprosy, *see note on Lev. 13:2.*

17:13 have mercy on us. Cf. 16:24; 18:38,39; Matt. 9:27; 15:22; 17:15; 20:31; Mark 10:47,48. This was a common plea from those desiring healing.

17:14 show yourselves to the priests. I.e., to be declared clean (Lev. 13:2,3; 14:2-32). **as they went.** The healing was sudden and immediately visible, but occurred after they obeyed His command.

17:15 one of them...returned. His response was reminiscent of the conduct of Naaman (2 Kin. 5:15). The others, eager to be declared clean so that they could return to normal life in society, evidently continued on to the priest, forgetting to give thanks.

17:16 he was a Samaritan. Jesus' sending the lepers to show themselves to the priest suggests that they were Jewish. This Samaritan had been permitted to associate with them when all were ceremonially unclean, but in their healing, they did not share his deep gratitude.

turned to give glory to God except this foreigner?" 19 [m]And He said to him, "Arise, go
your way. Your faith has made you well."

Christ Teaches on the Second Coming

20 Now when He was asked by the
Pharisees when the kingdom of God
would come, He answered them and said,
"The kingdom of God does not come with
observation; 21 [n]nor will they say, [6]'See
here!' or 'See there!' For indeed, [o]the kingdom of God is [7]within you."

22 Then He said to the disciples, [p]"The
days will come when you will desire to see
one of the days of the Son of Man, and you
will not see *it*. 23 [q]And they will say to you,
[8]'Look here!' or 'Look there!' Do not go
after *them* or follow *them*. 24 [r]For as the
lightning that flashes out of one *part* under
heaven shines to the other *part* under heav-
en, so also the Son of Man will be in His
day. 25 [s]But first He must suffer many
things and be [t]rejected by this generation.
26 [u]And as it [v]was in the [w]days of [x]Noah,
so it will be also in the days of the Son of
Man: 27 They ate, they drank, they married
wives, they were given in marriage, until
the [y]day that Noah entered the ark, and
the flood came and [z]destroyed them all.
28 [a]Likewise as it was also in the days of
Lot: They ate, they drank, they bought,
they sold, they planted, they built; 29 but
on [b]the day that Lot went out of Sodom it
rained fire and brimstone from heaven and
destroyed *them* all. 30 Even so will it be in
the day when the Son of Man [c]is revealed.

31 "In that day, he [d]who is on the housetop, and his [9]goods *are* in the house, let
him not come down to take them away.
And likewise the one who is in the field, let
him not turn back. 32 [e]Remember Lot's
wife. 33 [f]Whoever seeks to save his life will
lose it, and whoever loses his life will preserve it. 34 [g]I tell you, in that night there
will be two [1]*men* in one bed: the one will be
taken and the other will be left. 35 [h]Two
women will be grinding together: the one
will be taken and the other left. 36 [2]Two
men will be in the field: the one will be
taken and the other left."

37 And they answered and said to Him,
[i]"Where, Lord?"

So He said to them, "Wherever the
body is, there the eagles will be gathered
together."

Parable of the Woman and the Judge

18 Then He spoke a parable to them,
that men [a]always ought to pray and
not lose heart, 2 saying: "There was in a
certain city a judge who did not fear God
nor [1]regard man. 3 Now there was a

19 [m]Matt. 9:22; Mark 5:34; 10:52; Luke 7:50; 8:48; 18:42
21 [n]Luke 17:23 [o][Rom. 14:17] [6]NU reverses *here* and *there* [7]*in your midst*
22 [p]Matt. 9:15; Mark 2:20; Luke 5:35; [John 17:12]
23 [q]Matt. 24:23; Mark 13:21; [Luke 21:8] [8]NU reverses *here* and *there*
24 [r]Matt. 24:27
25 [s]Matt. 26:67; 27:29-31; Mark 8:31; 9:31; 10:33 [t]Luke 9:22
26 [u]Matt. 24:37-39 [v][Gen. 6:5-7] [w][Gen. 6:8-13] [x]1 Pet. 3:20
27 [y]Gen. 7:1-16 [z]Gen. 7:19-23
28 [a]Gen. 19
29 [b]Gen. 19:16, 24, 29; 2 Pet. 2:6, 7
30 [c][Matt. 16:27]; 1 Cor. 1:7; [Col. 3:4; 2 Thess. 1:7]; 1 Pet. 1:7; 4:13; 1 John 2:28
31 [d]Matt. 24:17, 18; Mark 13:15 [9]*possessions*
32 [e]Gen. 19:26
33 [f]Matt. 10:39; 16:25; Mark 8:35; Luke 9:24; John 12:25

34 [g]Matt. 24:40, 41; [1 Thess. 4:17] [1]Or *people* 35 [h]Matt. 24:40, 41
36 [2]NU, M omit v. 36. 37 [i]Job 39:30; Matt. 24:28
CHAPTER 18 1 [a]Luke 11:5-10; Rom. 12:12; [Eph. 6:18]; Col. 4:2; 1 Thess. 5:17 2 [1]*respect*

17:18 this foreigner. Evidently Jesus did not view Samaritans as anything more or less than other Gentiles. *See note on John 4:4.*

17:19 made you well. Lit. "saved you" (cf. Matt. 9:22; *see note on Mark 5:34*).

17:20 when the kingdom of God would come. They may have asked the question mockingly, having already concluded that He was not the Messiah. **does not come with observation.** The Pharisees believed that the Messiah's triumph would be immediate. They were looking for Him to come, overthrow Rome, and set up the millennial kingdom. Christ's program was altogether different. He was inaugurating an era in which the kingdom would be manifest in the rule of God in men's hearts through faith in the Savior (v. 21; cf. Rom. 14:17). That kingdom was neither confined to a particular geographical location nor visible to human eyes. It would come quietly, invisibly, and without the normal pomp and splendor associated with the arrival of a king. Jesus did not suggest that the OT promises of an earthly kingdom were hereby nullified. Rather, that earthly, visible manifestation of the kingdom is yet to come (Rev. 20:1-6).

17:21 within you. I.e., within people's hearts. The pronoun could hardly refer to the Pharisees in general.

17:22 The days will come. This introduces a brief discourse that has some similarities to the Olivet Discourse of Matt. 24,25. **you will desire to see one of the days of the Son of Man.** I.e., desire to have Him physically present. This suggests a longing for His return to set things right (cf. Rev. 6:9-11; 22:20).

17:23,24 *See notes on Matt. 24:26,27.*

17:25 must suffer. I.e., because it was the sovereign plan of God for Him to die as a substitute for sinners. Cf. 9:22; 18:31-33; 24:25,26; Matt. 16:21; Mark 8:31.

17:26,27 *See note on Matt. 24:37,38.*

17:28 in the days of Lot. I.e., judgment came suddenly, destroying people in the midst of their everyday activities (Gen 19:24,25). None of the things Jesus cited with regard to Noah's day or Lot's day were inherently sinful. But people were so absorbed in the things of this life that they were utterly unprepared when the time of judgment came.

17:31 housetop. The typical house had a flat roof with an external stairway. The danger would be so great that those on the roofs should flee, without going into the house to retrieve anything.

17:32 Lot's wife was destroyed on the very threshold of deliverance. Her attachment to Sodom was so powerful that she delayed and looked back; she was overwhelmed by oncoming judgment, just before reaching the place of safety (Gen. 19:26).

17:33 *See note on 14:11.*

17:34-36 *See note on Matt 24:40,41.*

17:37 *See note on Matt. 24:28.*

18:1 always...pray. A common theme in Paul's epistles (see Introduction: Interpretive Challenges). Cf. Rom. 1:9; 12:12; Eph. 6:18; 1 Thess. 5:17; 2 Thess. 1:11. **not lose heart.** I.e., in light of the afflictions and hardships of life, and the evidence of approaching judgment (described in the preceding discourse).

18:2 did not fear God nor regard man. This man was thoroughly wicked. Christ described him as "unjust" (v. 6)—like the steward in 16:8. The judge is not given as a symbol of God, but rather in contrast to Him. If such an unjust man would respond to persistent pleas, would not God, who is not only just, but also loving and merciful, do so more readily?

widow in that city; and she came to him,
saying, [2]'Get justice for me from my adversary.' 4 And he would not for a while;
but afterward he said within himself,
'Though I do not fear God nor regard man,
5 [b]yet because this widow troubles me I
will [3]avenge her, lest by her continual
coming she weary me.' "
6 Then the Lord said, "Hear what the
unjust judge said. 7 And [c]shall God not
avenge His own elect who cry out day and
night to Him, though He bears long with
them? 8 I tell you [d]that He will avenge
them speedily. Nevertheless, when the Son
of Man comes, will He really find faith on
the earth?"

Parable of the Pharisee and the Tax Collector

9 Also He spoke this parable to some
[e]who trusted in themselves that they were
righteous, and despised others: 10 "Two
men went up to the temple to pray, one a
Pharisee and the other a tax collector.
11 The Pharisee [f]stood and prayed thus
with himself, [g]'God, I thank You that I am
not like other men—extortioners, unjust,
adulterers, or even as this tax collector.
12 I fast twice a week; I give tithes of all
that I possess.' 13 And the tax collector,
standing afar off, would not so much as
raise *his* eyes to heaven, but beat his
breast, saying, 'God, be merciful to me a
sinner!' 14 I tell you, this man went down
to his house justified *rather* than the other;
[h]for everyone who exalts himself will be
[4]humbled, and he who humbles himself
will be exalted."

3 [2] *Avenge me on*
5 [b] Luke 11:8
[3] *vindicate*
7 [c] Rev. 6:10
8 [d] Heb. 10:37; [2 Pet. 3:8, 9]
9 [e] Prov. 30:12; Luke 10:29; 16:15
11 [f] Ps. 135:2 [g] Is. 1:15; 58:2; Rev. 3:17
14 [h] Job 22:29; Matt. 23:12; Luke 14:11; [James 4:6; 1 Pet. 5:5] [4] *put down*

Christ Blesses the Children
Matt. 19:13-15; Mark 10:13-16

15 [i]Then they also brought infants to
Him that He might touch them; but when
the disciples saw *it*, they rebuked them.
16 But Jesus called them to *Him* and said,
"Let the little children come to Me, and do
not forbid them; for [j]of such is the kingdom of God. 17 [k]Assuredly, I say to you,
whoever does not receive the kingdom of
God as a little child will by no means enter
it."

Rich Young Ruler
Matt. 19:16-26; Mark 10:17-27

18 [l]Now a certain ruler asked Him, saying, "Good Teacher, what shall I do to inherit eternal life?"
19 So Jesus said to him, "Why do you call
Me good? No one *is* good but [m]One, *that is*,
God. 20 You know the commandments:
[n]*'Do not commit adultery,' 'Do not mur-*
der,' 'Do not steal,' 'Do not bear false wit-
ness,' [o]*'Honor your father and your moth-*
er.' "
21 And he said, "All [p]these things I have
kept from my youth."
22 So when Jesus heard these things, He
said to him, "You still lack one thing. [q]Sell
all that you have and distribute to the poor,
and you will have treasure in heaven; and
come, follow Me."
23 But when he heard this, he became
very sorrowful, for he was very rich.
24 And when Jesus saw that he became
very sorrowful, He said, [r]"How hard it is
for those who have riches to enter the kingdom of God! 25 For it is easier for a camel

15 [i] Matt. 19:13-15; Mark 10:13-16
16 [j] Matt. 18:3; 1 Cor. 14:20; 1 Pet. 2:2
17 [k] Matt. 18:3; 19:14; Mark 10:15
18 [l] Matt. 19:16-29; Mark 10:17-30
19 [m] Ps. 86:5; 119:68
20 [n] Ex. 20:12-16; Deut. 5:16-20; Mark 10:19; Rom. 13:9
[o] Eph. 6:2; Col. 3:20
21 [p] Phil. 3:6
22 [q] Matt. 6:19, 20; 19:21; [1 Tim. 6:19]
24 [r] Prov. 11:28; Matt. 19:23; Mark 10:23

18:5 weary me. Lit. "hit under the eye." What the judge would not do out of compassion for the widow or reverence for God, he would do out of sheer frustration with her incessant pleading.

18:6 Hear what the unjust judge said. I.e., listen to the point of the story, namely, that God, who always does right and is filled with compassion for believers who suffer, will certainly respond to His beloved ones who cry for His help (v. 7).

18:8 speedily. He may delay long, but He does so for good reason (cf. 2 Pet. 3:8,9) and when He acts, His vengeance is swift. **will He really find faith.** This suggests that when He returns, the true faith will be comparatively rare—as in the days of Noah (17:26), when only 8 souls were saved. The period before His return will be marked by persecution, apostasy, and unbelief (Matt. 24:9-13,24).

18:9 This parable is rich with truth about the doctrine of justification by faith. It illustrates perfectly how a sinner who is utterly devoid of personal righteousness may be declared righteous before God instantaneously through an act of repentant faith. The parable is addressed to Pharisees who trusted their own righteousness (vv. 10,11). Such confidence in one's inherent righteousness is a damning hope (cf. Rom. 10:3; Phil 3:9), because human righteousness—even the righteousness of the most fastidious Pharisee—falls short of the divine standard (Matt. 5:48). Scripture consistently teaches that sinners are justified when God's perfect righteousness is imputed to their account (cf. Gen. 15:6; Rom. 4:4,5; 2 Cor. 5:21; Phil. 3:4-9)—and it was only on that basis that this tax collector (or anyone else) could be saved.

18:12 fast twice a week. I.e., more than is required by any biblical standard (*see note on 5:33*). By exalting his own works, the Pharisee revealed that his entire hope lay in his not being as bad as someone else. He utterly lacked any sense of his own unworthiness and sin. Cf. vv. 18-21; Matt. 19:17-20. *See notes on 17:7-10.*

18:13 The tax collector's humility is notable in everything about his posture and behavior. Here was a man who had been made to face the reality of his own sin, and his only response was abject humility and repentance. He contrasts with the Pharisee in virtually every detail. **God, be merciful.** He had no hope but the mercy of God. This is the point to which the law aims to bring every sinner (cf. Rom. 3:19,20; 7:13; Gal 3:22-24).

18:14 justified. I.e., reckoned righteous before God by means of an imputed righteousness (*see note on v. 9*).

18:17 as a little child. *See note on Matt. 18:3.*

18:18-30 *See notes on Matt. 19:16-29; Mark 10:17-30.*

18:20 Quoted from Ex. 20:12-16; Deut. 5:16-20.

to go through the eye of a needle than for a
rich man to enter the kingdom of God."
26 And those who heard it said, "Who
then can be saved?"
27 But He said, [s]"The things which are impossible with men are possible with God."

Christ Will Reward Sacrifice
Matt. 19:27-29; Mark 10:28-30

28 [t]Then Peter said, "See, we have left
[5]all and followed You."
29 So He said to them, "Assuredly, I say
to you, [u]there is no one who has left house
or parents or brothers or wife or children,
for the sake of the kingdom of God,
30 [v]who shall not receive many times more
in this present time, and in the age to come
eternal life."

Christ Foretells His Death and Resurrection
Matt. 20:17-19; Mark 10:32-34

31 [w]Then He took the twelve aside and
said to them, "Behold, we are going up to
Jerusalem, and all things [x]that are written
by the prophets concerning the Son of
Man will be [6]accomplished. 32 For [y]He
will be delivered to the Gentiles and will
be mocked and insulted and spit upon.
33 They will scourge *Him* and kill Him.
And the third day He will rise again."
34 [z]But they understood none of these
things; this saying was hidden from them,
and they did not know the things which
were spoken.

Christ Heals Bartimaeus
Matt. 20:29-34; Mark 10:46-52

35 [a]Then it happened, as He was coming
near Jericho, that a certain blind man sat by
the road begging. 36 And hearing a multitude passing by, he asked what it meant.
37 So they told him that Jesus of Nazareth
was passing by. 38 And he cried out, saying,
"Jesus, [b]Son of David, have mercy on me!"
39 Then those who went before warned
him that he should be quiet; but he cried
out all the more, "Son of David, have
mercy on me!"
40 So Jesus stood still and commanded
him to be brought to Him. And when he
had come near, He asked him, 41 saying,
"What do you want Me to do for you?"
He said, "Lord, that I may receive my
sight."
42 Then Jesus said to him, "Receive your
sight; [c]your faith has made you well."
43 And immediately he received his sight,
and followed Him, [d]glorifying God. And
all the people, when they saw *it*, gave
praise to God.

Christ Abides with Zacchaeus

19 Then *Jesus* entered and passed
through [a]Jericho. 2 Now behold,
there was a man named Zacchaeus who
was a chief tax collector, and he was rich.
3 And he sought to [b]see who Jesus was, but
could not because of the crowd, for he was
of short stature. 4 So he ran ahead and
climbed up into a sycamore tree to see
Him, for He was going to pass that *way*.
5 And when Jesus came to the place, He
looked up [1]and saw him, and said to him,
"Zacchaeus, [2]make haste and come down,
for today I must stay at your house." 6 So
he [3]made haste and came down, and received Him joyfully. 7 But when they saw

27 [s] Job 42:2; Jer. 32:17; Zech. 8:6; Matt. 19:26; Luke 1:37
28 [t] Matt. 19:27 [5] NU *our own*
29 [u] Deut. 33:9
30 [v] Job 42:10
31 [w] Matt. 16:21; 17:22; 20:17; Mark 10:32; Luke 9:51 [x] Ps. 22; [Is. 53] [6] *fulfilled*
32 [y] Matt. 26:67; 27:2, 29, 41; Mark 14:65; 15:1, 19, 20, 31; Luke 23:1; John 18:28; Acts 3:13
34 [z] Mark 9:32; Luke 2:50; 9:45; [John 10:6; 12:16]
35 [a] Matt. 20:29-34; Mark 10:46-52
38 [b] Matt. 9:27
42 [c] Luke 17:19
43 [d] Luke 5:26; Acts 4:21; 11:18

CHAPTER 19

1 [a] Josh. 6:26; 1 Kin. 16:34
3 [b] John 12:21
5 [1] NU omits *and saw him* [2] *hurry*
6 [3] *hurried*

18:31 all things that are written by the prophets. E.g., Pss. 22; 69; Is. 53; Dan. 9:26; Zech. 13:7.

18:32 delivered to the Gentiles. Each prophecy of His death (cf. 9:22,44; 12:50; 13:32,33; 17:25) was more explicit than the last. This is His first mention of being turned over to the Gentiles.

18:33 He will rise again. Christ had predicted His resurrection on the third day before (9:22). But the disciples missed the import of these words, and when He actually did rise, they were surprised by it (24:6).

18:34 they did not know. The whole matter of Christ's death and resurrection was not grasped by the 12. The reason may have been that they were enamored with other ideas about the Messiah and how His earthly rule would operate (cf. Matt. 16:22; 17:10; Acts 1:6).

18:35 Jericho. *See note on Mark 10:46.* **blind man.** There were actually two blind men. One probably spoke for both of them. *See note on Matt. 20:30.*

18:38 Son of David. An affirmation that he recognized Jesus as Messiah and King. *See note on Matt. 9:27.*

18:42 made you well. Lit. "saved you" (cf. Matt. 9:22; *see note on Mark 5:34*).

19:2 chief tax collector. *See note on Matt. 5:46.* Zacchaeus probably oversaw a large tax district, and had other tax collectors working for him. Jericho alone was a prosperous trading center, so it is certain that Zacchaeus was a wealthy man. It is striking to note that only a chapter earlier, Luke recorded the account of the rich young ruler, and Jesus' statement about "how hard it is for those who have riches to enter the kingdom of God" (18:24). Here Jesus demonstrates that with God, nothing is impossible (cf. 18:27).

19:3 the crowd. Christ was probably traveling with a large entourage of pilgrims to the Passover in Jerusalem. But "the crowd" apparently refers to people in Jericho who lined the street to see Him pass through. They had undoubtedly heard about the recent raising of Lazarus in Bethany, less than 15 mi. away (John 11). That, combined with His fame as a healer and teacher, stirred the entire city when word arrived that He was coming.

19:4 sycamore tree. A sturdy tree with low, spreading branches. A small person could get out on a limb and hang over the road. This was an undignified position for someone of Zacchaeus' rank, but he was desperate to see Christ.

19:5 I must stay at your house. This was worded as a mandate, not a request. It is the only place in all the gospels where Jesus invited Himself to be someone's guest (cf. Is. 65:1).

19:6 joyfully. Such a despicable sinner as a typical tax collector

it, they all [4]complained, saying, [c]"He has
gone to be a guest with a man who is a sinner."
8 Then Zacchaeus stood and said to the
Lord, "Look, Lord, I give half of my goods
to the [d]poor; and if I have taken anything
from anyone by [e]false accusation, [f]I restore
fourfold."
9 And Jesus said to him, "Today salvation has come to this house, because [g]he
also is [h]a son of Abraham; 10 [i]for the Son of
Man has come to seek and to save that
which was lost."

Christ Gives the Parable of the Ten Minas

11 Now as they heard these things, He
spoke another parable, because He was near
Jerusalem and because [j]they thought the
kingdom of God would appear immediately. 12 [k]Therefore He said: "A certain nobleman went into a far country to receive for
himself a kingdom and to return. 13 So he
called ten of his servants, delivered to them
ten [5]minas, and said to them, 'Do business
till I come.' 14 [l]But his citizens hated him,
and sent a delegation after him, saying, 'We
will not have this *man* to reign over us.'
15 "And so it was that when he returned,
having received the kingdom, he then
commanded these servants, to whom he
had given the money, to be called to him,
that he might know how much every man
had gained by trading. 16 Then came the
first, saying, 'Master, your mina has
earned ten minas.' 17 And he said to him,
[m]'Well *done,* good servant; because you
were [n]faithful in a very little, have authority over ten cities.' 18 And the second came,
saying, 'Master, your mina has earned five
minas.' 19 Likewise he said to him, 'You
also be over five cities.'
20 "Then another came, saying, 'Master,
here is your mina, which I have kept put
away in a handkerchief. 21 [o]For I feared
you, because you are [6]an austere man. You
collect what you did not deposit, and reap
what you did not sow.' 22 And he said to
him, [p]'Out of your own mouth I will judge
you, *you* wicked servant. [q]You knew that I

7 [c] Matt. 9:11; Luke 5:30; 15:2 [4] *grumbled*
8 [d] [Ps. 41:1] [e] Luke 3:14 [f] Ex. 22:1; Lev. 6:5; Num. 5:7; 1 Sam. 12:3; 2 Sam. 12:6
9 [g] Luke 3:8; 13:16; [Rom. 4:16; Gal. 3:7] [h] [Luke 13:16]
10 [i] Matt. 18:11; [Luke 5:32; Rom. 5:8]
11 [j] Acts 1:6
12 [k] Matt. 25:14-30; Mark 13:34
13 [5] Gr. *mna*, same as Heb. *minah*, each worth about three months' salary
14 [l] [John 1:11]
17 [m] Matt. 25:21, 23 [n] Luke 16:10
21 [o] Matt. 25:24 [6] *a severe*
22 [p] 2 Sam. 1:16; Job 15:6; [Matt. 12:37] [q] Matt. 25:26

(*see note on Matt. 5:46*) might have been distressed at the prospect of a visit from the perfect, sinless Son of God. But Zacchaeus' heart was prepared.

19:7 they all complained. Both the religious elite and the common people hated Zacchaeus. They did not understand, and in their blind pride refused to see, what possible righteous purpose Jesus had in visiting such a notorious sinner. But He had come to seek and to save the lost (v. 10). *See note on 15:2.*

19:8 I restore fourfold. Zacchaeus' willingness to make restitution was proof that his conversion was genuine. It was the fruit, not the condition, of his salvation. The law required a penalty of one-fifth as restitution for money acquired by fraud (Lev. 6:5; Num. 5:6,7), so Zacchaeus was doing more than was required. The law required 4-fold restitution only when an animal was stolen and killed (Ex. 22:1). If the animal was found alive, only two-fold restitution was required (Ex. 22:4). But Zacchaeus judged his own crime severely, acknowledging that he was as guilty as the lowest common robber. Since much of his wealth had probably been acquired fraudulently, this was a costly commitment. On top of that, he gave half his goods to the poor. But Zacchaeus had just found incomprehensible spiritual riches and did not mind the loss of material wealth (*see notes on 14:28; Matt. 13:44-46*). He stands in stark contrast with the rich young ruler in 18:18-24.

19:9 a son of Abraham. A Jew by race for whom Christ came as Savior (cf. Matt. 1:21; 10:6; 15:24; John 4:22).

19:10 the Son of Man. *See note on Matt. 8:20.* **to seek and to save that which was lost.** The main theme of Luke's gospel. Cf. 5:31,32; 15:4-7,32; *see notes on 1 Tim. 2:4; 4:10.*

19:11 they thought. The disciples still mistakenly assumed that Christ would establish his kingdom on earth at Jerusalem (*see note on 17:20*).

19:12 a far country. Kings in Roman provinces like Galilee and Perea actually went to Rome to receive their kingdoms. The entire Herodian dynasty was dependent on Rome for ruling power, and Herod the Great himself had gone to Rome to be given his kingdom. This parable illustrates Christ, who would soon depart to receive His kingdom, and will one day return to rule. It is similar to the parable of the talents (Matt. 25:14-30) but there are significant differences (*see note on v. 13*). That parable was told during the Olivet Discourse (*see note on Matt. 24:1–25:46*); this one was told on the road from Jericho up to Jerusalem (cf. v. 28).

19:13 minas. A Gr. measure of money (*see note on 15:8*), equal to slightly more than 3 month's salary. The mina was one-sixtieth of a talent, meaning that the 10 servants in this parable had been given a considerably smaller sum to account for than any of the 3 servants in the parable of the talents (Matt. 25:14-30).

19:14 sent a delegation after him. This was precisely what had happened to Archelaus (*see note on Matt. 2:22*), son of Herod the Great, when he went to Rome to be made tetrarch of Judea. A delegation of Jews traveled to Rome with a protest to Caesar Augustus (*see note on 2:1*). He refused their complaint and made Archelaus king anyway. Archelaus subsequently built his palace in Jericho, not far from where Jesus told this parable. Archelaus' rule was so inept and despotic that Rome quickly replaced him with a succession of procurators, of whom Pontius Pilate was the fifth. With this parable Jesus warned that the Jews were about to do the same thing, in a spiritual sense, to their true Messiah.

19:15-27 *See notes on Matt. 25:14-30.*

19:15 when he returned. This pictured Christ's return to earth. The full manifestation of His kingdom on earth awaits that time. *See note on 17:20.*

19:17 faithful in a very little. *See note on v. 13.* Those with relatively small gifts and opportunities are just as responsible to use them faithfully as those who are given much more. **over ten cities.** The reward is incomparably greater than the 10 minas warranted. Note also that the rewards were apportioned according to the servants' diligence: the one who gained 10 minas was given 10 cities, the one who gained 5 minas, 5 cities (v. 19), and so on.

19:21 I feared you. A craven fear, not borne out of love or reverence, but tainted with contempt for the master (*see note on Matt. 25:24*). Had he had any true regard for the master, a righteous "fear" would have provoked diligence rather than sloth.

19:22 You knew. *See note on Matt. 25:26.* This did not suggest that what the man "knew" about the master was true. However, even the knowledge he claimed to have was enough to condemn him. Thus will it be with the wicked in the day of judgment.

was an austere man, collecting what I did
not deposit and reaping what I did not
sow. 23 Why then did you not put my
money in the bank, that at my coming I
might have collected it with interest?'
24 "And he said to those who stood by,
'Take the mina from him, and give *it* to him
who has ten minas.' 25 (But they said to
him, 'Master, he has ten minas.') 26 'For I
say to you, [r]that to everyone who has will
be given; and from him who does not
have, even what he has will be taken away
from him. 27 But bring here those enemies
of mine, who did not want me to reign
over them, and slay *them* before me.' "

The Triumphal Entry
Matt. 21:1-9; Mark 11:1-10; John 12:12-19

28 When He had said this, [s]He went on
ahead, going up to Jerusalem. 29 [t]And it
came to pass, when He drew near to
[7]Bethphage and [u]Bethany, at the mountain
called [v]Olivet, *that* He sent two of His disciples, 30 saying, "Go into the village opposite *you*, where as you enter you will find a
colt tied, on which no one has ever sat.
Loose it and bring *it here.* 31 And if anyone
asks you, 'Why are you loosing *it?*' thus
you shall say to him, 'Because the Lord has
need of it.' "
32 So those who were sent went their
way and found *it* just [w]as He had said to
them. 33 But as they were loosing the colt,
the owners of it said to them, "Why are
you loosing the colt?"
34 And they said, "The Lord has need of
him." 35 Then they brought him to Jesus.
[x]And they threw their own clothes on the
colt, and they set Jesus on him. 36 And as
He went, *many* spread their clothes on the
road.
37 Then, as He was now drawing near
the descent of the Mount of Olives, the
whole multitude of the disciples began to
[y]rejoice and praise God with a loud voice
for all the mighty works they had seen,
38 saying:

[z]" *'Blessed is the King who comes in*
the name of the LORD!'
[a]Peace in heaven and glory in the
highest!"

39 And some of the Pharisees called to
Him from the crowd, "Teacher, rebuke
Your disciples."
40 But He answered and said to them, "I
tell you that if these should keep silent,
[b]the stones would immediately cry out."
41 Now as He drew near, He saw the city
and [c]wept over it, 42 saying, "If you had
known, even you, especially in this [d]your
day, the things *that* [e]*make* for your [f]peace!
But now they are hidden from your eyes.
43 For days will come upon you when your
enemies will [g]build an embankment
around you, surround you and close you
in on every side, 44 [h]and level you, and
your children within you, to the ground;
and [i]they will not leave in you one stone

26 [r]Matt. 13:12; 25:29; Mark 4:25; Luke 8:18
28 [s]Mark 10:32
29 [t]Matt. 21:1; Mark 11:1 [u]Matt. 26:6; John 12:1 [v]John 8:1; Acts 1:12 [7]M *Bethsphage*
32 [w]Luke 22:13
35 [x]2 Kin. 9:13; Matt. 21:7; Mark 11:7
37 [y]Luke 13:17; 18:43
38 [z]Ps. 118:26; Luke 13:35 [a]Luke 2:14; [Eph. 2:14]
40 [b]Hab. 2:11
41 [c]Is. 53:3; John 11:35
42 [d]Ps. 95:7, 8; Heb. 3:13 [e][Luke 1:77-79; Acts 10:36] [f][Rom. 5:1]
43 [g]Is. 29:3, 4; Jer. 6:3, 6; Luke 21:20
44 [h]1 Kin. 9:7, 8; Mic. 3:12 [i]Matt. 24:2; Mark 13:2; Luke 21:6

19:26 *See note on Matt. 25:29.*

19:27 those enemies of mine. These illustrated the Jews who actively opposed him. **slay *them* before me.** This spoke of harsh, violent judgment and may be a reference to the destruction of Jerusalem (*see note on Matt. 24:2*).

19:28 up to Jerusalem. The road from Jericho to Jerusalem was a steep ascent, rising some 4,000 feet in about 20 miles. This represented the last leg of the long journey that began in 9:51 (*see note there*).

19:29 Bethphage. *See note on Matt. 21:1.* **Bethany.** Jesus often stayed there during His visits to Jerusalem. *See note on 10:38.* **mountain called Olivet.** The main peak of a ridge running N to S, located E of the Kidron Valley adjacent to the temple. Olivet derived its name from the dense olive groves that once covered it. *See note on Matt. 24:3.*

19:30-36 *See notes on Matt. 21:1-8; Mark 11:1-8.*

19:30 colt. The other gospels say this was a donkey colt (cf. Zech. 9:9), and Matt. reveals that the mare was brought along as well (*see note on Matt. 21:6*). **which no one has ever sat.** *See note on Mark 11:2.*

19:36 spread their clothes. *See notes on Matt. 21:8; Mark 11:8.* Luke omits the cutting of palm branches mentioned by Matthew and Mark.

19:37 the whole multitude of the disciples. Doubtless many in the crowd were not true disciples. **mighty works.** John 12:17,18 specifically mentions that news of the raising of Lazarus had provoked many in the crowd to come to see Him.

19:38 *Blessed is the King.* Quoting Ps. 118:26, they hailed Jesus as Messiah. *See note on Matt. 21:9.* **Peace in heaven.** Only Luke reported this phrase. It is reminiscent of the angels' message in 2:14.

19:39 rebuke Your disciples. The Pharisees were offended by people offering Him such worshipful praise. They wanted Him to stop them.

19:40 the stones would immediately cry out. This was a strong claim of deity, and perhaps a reference to the words of Hab. 2:11. Scripture often speaks of inanimate nature praising God. Cf. Pss. 96:11; 98:7-9; 114:7; Is. 55:12. Cf. also the words of John the Baptist in Matt. 3:9; note the fulfillment of Jesus' words in Matt. 27:51.

19:41,42 Only Luke recorded the weeping of Jesus over the city of Jerusalem. Christ grieved over Jerusalem on at least two other occasions (13:34; Matt. 23:37). The timing of this lament may seem incongruous with the triumphal entry, but it reveals that Jesus knew the true superficiality of the peoples' hearts, and His mood was anything but giddy as He rode into the city. The same crowd would soon cry for his death (23:21).

19:43 surround you and close you in. Cf. 21:20. This is precisely the method used by Titus when he laid siege to Jerusalem in A.D. 70. He surrounded the city on Apr. 9, cutting off all supplies, and trapping thousands of people who had been in Jerusalem for the Passover and Feast of Unleavened Bread (just completed). The Romans systematically built embankments around the city, gradually starving the city's inhabitants. The Romans held the city in this manner through the summer, defeating various sections of the city one by one. The final overthrow of the city occurred in early Sep.

19:44 and level you. This was literally fulfilled. The Romans utter-

upon another, [j]because you did not know
the time of your visitation."

Cleansing the Temple
Matt. 21:12, 13; Mark 11:15-17

45 [k]Then He went into the temple and
began to drive out those who [8]bought and
sold in it, 46 saying to them, "It is written,
[l]'*My house* [9]*is a house of prayer,*' but you
have made it a [m]'*den of thieves.*'"
47 And He [n]was teaching daily in the
temple. But [o]the chief priests, the scribes,
and the leaders of the people sought to destroy Him, 48 and were unable to do anything; for all the people were very attentive
to [p]hear Him.

Religious Leaders Question Christ's
Authority—Matt. 21:23-27; Mark 11:27-33

20 Now [a]it happened on one of those
days, as He taught the people in the
temple and preached the gospel, *that* the
chief priests and the scribes, together with
the elders, confronted *Him* 2 and spoke to
Him, saying, "Tell us, [b]by what authority
are You doing these things? Or who is he
who gave You this authority?"
3 But He answered and said to them, "I
also will ask you one thing, and answer
Me: 4 The [c]baptism of John—was it from
heaven or from men?"
5 And they reasoned among themselves,
saying, "If we say, 'From heaven,' He will
say, 'Why [1]then did you not believe him?'

44 [j][Dan. 9:24; Luke 1:68, 78; 1 Pet. 2:12]
45 [k]Mal. 3:1; Matt. 21:12, 13; Mark 11:11, 15-17; John 2:13-16 [8]NU *were selling, saying*
46 [l]Is. 56:7 [m]Jer. 7:11 [9]NU *shall be*
47 [n]Luke 21:37; 22:53 [o]Mark 11:18; Luke 20:19; John 7:19; 8:37
48 [p]Luke 21:38

CHAPTER 20

1 [a]Matt. 21:23-27; Mark 11:27-33
2 [b]Acts 4:7; 7:27
4 [c]John 1:26, 31
5 [1]NU, M omit *then*
6 [d]Matt. 14:5; 21:26; Mark 6:20; Luke 7:24-30
9 [e]Ps. 80:8; Matt. 21:33-46; Mark 12:1-12 [2]*tenant farmers*
10 [f]2 Kin. 17:13, 14; 2 Chr. 36:15, 16; [Acts 7:52; 1 Thess. 2:15] [3]Lit. *the season*
14 [g][Heb. 1:1-3] [h]Matt. 27:21-23 [i]John 11:47, 48
15 [j]Luke 23:33; Acts 2:22, 23; 3:15
16 [k][John 1:11-13]; Rom. 11:1, 11; 1 Cor. 6:15; Gal. 2:17; 3:21; 6:14

6 But if we say, 'From men,' all the people
will stone us, [d]for they are persuaded that
John was a prophet." 7 So they answered
that they did not know where *it was* from.
8 And Jesus said to them, "Neither will I
tell you by what authority I do these
things."

Parable of the Vineyard Owner
Matt. 21:33-44; Mark 12:1-11

9 Then He began to tell the people this
parable: [e]"A certain man planted a vineyard, leased it to [2]vinedressers, and went
into a far country for a long time. 10 Now
at [3]vintage-time he [f]sent a servant to the
vinedressers, that they might give him
some of the fruit of the vineyard. But the
vinedressers beat him and sent *him* away
empty-handed. 11 Again he sent another
servant; and they beat him also, treated
him shamefully, and sent *him* away empty-
handed. 12 And again he sent a third; and
they wounded him also and cast *him* out.
13 "Then the owner of the vineyard said,
'What shall I do? I will send my beloved
son. Probably they will respect *him* when
they see him.' 14 But when the vinedressers
saw him, they reasoned among themselves,
saying, 'This is the [g]heir. Come, [h]let us kill
him, that the inheritance may be [i]ours.'
15 So they cast him out of the vineyard and
[j]killed *him*. Therefore what will the owner
of the vineyard do to them? 16 He will
come and destroy those vinedressers and
give the vineyard to [k]others."

ly demolished the city, temple, residences, and people. Men, women, and children were brutally slaughtered by the tens of thousands. The few survivors were carried off to become victims of the Roman circus games and gladiatorial bouts. **because you did not know the time of your visitation.** I.e., Jerusalem's utter destruction was divine judgment for their failure to recognize and embrace their Messiah when He visited them (cf. 20:13-16; John 1:10,11).

19:45,46 This was the second time Jesus had driven the sellers out of the temple, and is a different incident from the one described in John 2:14-16. He quotes from Is. 56:7. *See note on Matt. 21:12.*

19:47 chief priests. *See note on Matt. 2:4.* The rulers of the temple. **scribes.** Mostly Pharisees, experts in the law and traditions. **leaders of the people.** Prominent Jewish laymen with influence in temple affairs. By bringing His ministry to the temple, Christ had walked into the very heart of the opposition against Him. **sought to destroy Him.** I.e., kill Him (cf. 22:2; Matt. 26:3,4; John 5:16-18; 7:1,19,25).

20:1 one of those days. Probably Tuesday of Passion Week. The triumphal entry was on Sunday, and the cleansing of the temple on Monday. The events in this chapter best fit Tuesday in the chronology of that week. This chapter features a series of carefully coordinated attacks on Christ by the Jewish leaders. **chief priests...scribes...elders.** *See note on 19:47.* Each of these groups played a unique role in the various attacks that follow. Each was also represented in the Sanhedrin, the Jewish council (*see note on Matt. 26:59*)—suggesting that the council had met to orchestrate the attack against Him. Their attacks came in the form of a series of questions designed to entrap Him (*see notes on vv. 2,22,33*).

20:2-8 *See notes on Matt. 21:23,25.*

20:2 This was the first in a series of questions designed to entrap Him. This question was raised by the chief priests, scribes, and elders—evidently representatives of the Sanhedrin. *See notes on vv. 22,33.*

20:5 'Why then did you not believe him?' John had clearly testified that Jesus was the Messiah. If John was a prophet whose words were true, they ought to believe His testimony about Christ. On the other hand, it would have been political folly for the Pharisees to attack the legitimacy of John the Baptist or deny his authority as a prophet of God. John was enormously popular with the people, and a martyr at the hands of the despised Herod. For the Pharisees to question John's authority was to attack a national hero, and they knew better than that. So they pleaded ignorance (v. 6).

20:8 Neither will I tell you. Jesus exposed the hypocrisy of the question, unmasking their evil motives. He wasted no truth on them (cf. Matt. 7:6).

20:9-19 *See notes on Matt. 21:33-45; Mark 12:1-12.*

20:9 the people. Luke alone noted the parable was addressed to all the people, not just the Jewish leaders.

20:13 beloved son. Both Luke and Mark recorded this expression, which makes clear that the son in the parable is an illustration of Christ (*see note on Matt. 21:37*).

20:16 destroy those vinedressers. This probably pictures the destruction of Jerusalem (*see note on 19:43*). **give the vineyard to others.** *See note on 21:24.* **Certainly not!** Only Luke recorded this hostile reaction from the crowd. The response suggests that they grasped the meaning of the parable.

And when they heard *it* they said, "Certainly not!"
17 Then He looked at them and said,
"What then is this that is written:

[l]'*The stone which the builders*
rejected
Has become the chief
cornerstone'?

18 Whoever falls on that stone will be [m]bro-
ken; but [n]on whomever it falls, it will
grind him to powder."

Herodians Question Tribute Money
Matt. 21:45, 46; 22:15-22; Mark 12:12-17

19 And the chief priests and the scribes
that very hour sought to lay hands on
Him, but they [4]feared the people—for they
knew He had spoken this parable against
them.
20 [o]So they watched *Him*, and sent spies
who pretended to be righteous, that they
might seize on His words, in order to deliver Him to the power and the authority
of the governor.
21 Then they asked Him, saying,
[p]"Teacher, we know that You say and teach
rightly, and You do not show personal favoritism, but teach the way of God in
truth: 22 Is it lawful for us to pay taxes to
Caesar or not?"
23 But He perceived their craftiness, and
said to them, [5]"Why do you test Me?
24 Show Me a denarius. Whose image and
inscription does it have?"
They answered and said, "Caesar's."
25 And He said to them, [q]"Render[6]
therefore to Caesar the things that are Caesar's, and to God the things that are
God's."
26 But they could not catch Him in His
words in the presence of the people. And
they marveled at His answer and kept
silent.

Sadducees Question Resurrection
Matt. 22:23-32; Mark 12:18-27

27 [r]Then some of the Sadducees, [s]who
deny that there is a resurrection, came to
Him and asked Him, 28 saying: "Teacher,
Moses wrote to us *that* if a man's brother
dies, having a wife, and he dies without
children, his brother should take his wife
and raise up offspring for his brother.
29 Now there were seven brothers. And the
first took a wife, and died without children. 30 And the second [7]took her as wife,
and he died childless. 31 Then the third
took her, and in like manner the seven
[8]also; and they left no children, and died.
32 Last of all the woman died also.
33 Therefore, in the resurrection, whose
wife does she become? For all seven had
her as wife."
34 Jesus answered and said to them,
"The sons of this age marry and are given
in marriage. 35 But those who are [t]counted
worthy to attain that age, and the resurrection from the dead, neither marry nor are
given in marriage; 36 nor can they die anymore, for [u]they are equal to the angels and
are sons of God, [v]being sons of the resurrection. 37 But even Moses showed in the
burning bush *passage* that the dead are
raised, when he called the Lord [w]'*the God*
of Abraham, the God of Isaac, and the God
of Jacob.' 38 For He is not the God of the
dead but of the living, for [x]all live to Him."

17 [l]Ps. 118:22; Matt. 21:42; 1 Pet. 2:7, 8
18 [m]Is. 8:14, 15 [n][Dan. 2:34, 35, 44, 45]; Matt. 21:44
19 [4]M *were afraid—for*
20 [o]Matt. 22:15
21 [p]Matt. 22:16; Mark 12:14
23 [5]NU omits *Why do you test Me?*
25 [q]Matt. 17:24-27; Rom. 13:7; [1 Pet. 2:13-17] [6]*Pay*
27 [r]Matt. 22:23-33; Mark 12:18-27 [s]Acts 23:6, 8
30 [7]NU omits the rest of v. 30.
31 [8]NU, M *also left no children*
35 [t]Phil. 3:11
36 [u][1 Cor. 15:42, 49, 52; 1 John 3:2] [v]Rom. 8:23
37 [w]Ex. 3:1-6, 15; Acts 7:30-32
38 [x][Rom. 6:10, 11; 14:8, 9; Heb. 11:16]

20:17 Quoted from Ps. 118:22.

20:18 Whoever falls...on whomever it falls. *See note on Matt. 21:44.* The expression was a quotation from Is. 8:13-15, which speaks of Jehovah. Like so many other OT passages applied to Christ, it proves that He was Jehovah incarnate.

20:20 spies. The fact that the Jewish leaders resorted to such tactics is a measure of their desperation. They could not find any legitimate reason to accuse Him (cf. 6:7; 11:53,54; Matt. 22:15; 26:59,60). **the governor.** I.e., Pilate, who was in town for the coming Passover and Feast of Unleavened Bread (*see note on Matt. 27:2*).

20:21-26 *See notes on Matt. 22:16-22; Mark 12:13-17.*

20:22 This was the second in a series of questions designed to entrap Him. This question was raised by the Pharisees and Herodians (Mark 12:13). *See notes on vv. 2,33.*

20:24 Whose image. The image on the denarius was one of the main reasons the Jews chafed at the poll tax. They claimed it was a violation of the commandment against graven images, and since Caesar pretended to a position tantamount to deity, the paying of the tax was unlawful worship—and in the minds of many, tantamount to gross idolatry. *See notes on Matt. 22:19; Mark 12:16.*

20:25 Render therefore to Caesar. Christ thus recognized that all citizens have duties to the secular state, as well as duties to God—and He recognized a legitimate distinction between the two (*see notes on Matt. 22:21; Mark 12:17*).

20:27-38 *See notes on Matt. 22:23-32; Mark 12:18-27.*

20:27 Sadducees. *See note on Matt. 3:7.*

20:28 his brother should take his wife. According to the law of levirate marriage outlined in Deut. 25:5 (*see note on Matt. 22:24*).

20:33 This was the third in a series of questions designed to entrap Him. This question was raised by the Sadducees (v. 27). *See notes on vv. 2,22.* Matthew 22:34-40 and Mark 12:28-34 recorded one last question raised by a scribe. Luke omitted it from his record.

20:36 equal to the angels. I.e., like the angels in that they do not procreate (*see note on Matt. 22:30*).

20:37 the *burning* bush *passage*. Ex. 3:1–4:17. In that passage God identified Himself to Moses as the God of Abraham, Isaac, and Jacob—using the present tense. He didn't say He *was* their God, but "I AM" their God, indicating that their existence had not ended with their deaths.

20:38 all live to Him. Only Luke records this phrase. All people—whether departed from their earthly bodies or not—are still living, and will live forever. No one is annihilated in death (cf. John 5:28-30).

Christ Questions the Scribes
Matt. 22:41–23:14; Mark 12:35-40

39 Then some of the scribes answered
and said, "Teacher, You have spoken well."
40 But after that they dared not question
Him anymore.
41 And He said to them, [y]"How can they
say that the Christ is the Son of David?
42 Now David himself said in the Book of
Psalms:

[z]'The LORD said to my Lord,
"Sit at My right hand,
43 *Till I make Your enemies Your*
footstool." '

44 Therefore David calls Him *'Lord'*; [a]how
is He then his Son?"
45 [b]Then, in the hearing of all the people,
He said to His disciples, 46 [c]"Beware of the
scribes, who desire to go around in long
robes, [d]love greetings in the marketplaces,
the best seats in the synagogues, and the
best places at feasts, 47 [e]who devour widows' houses, and for a [f]pretense make long
prayers. These will receive greater condemnation."

Christ Teaches on the Widow's Mites
Mark 12:41-44

21 And He looked up [a]and saw the
rich putting their gifts into the treasury, 2 and He saw also a certain [b]poor
widow putting in two [c]mites.[1] 3 So He
said, "Truly I say to you [d]that this poor
widow has put in more than all; 4 for all
these out of their abundance have put in
offerings [2]for God, but she out of her
poverty put in [e]all the livelihood that she
had."

The Disciples' Two Questions
Matt. 24:1-3; Mark 13:1-4

5 [f]Then, as some spoke of the temple,
how it was [3]adorned with beautiful stones
and donations, He said, 6 "These things
which you see—the days will come in
which [g]not *one* stone shall be left upon another that shall not be thrown down."
7 So they asked Him, saying, "Teacher,
but when will these things be? And what
sign *will there be* when these things are
about to take place?"

Signs of Christ's Coming
Matt. 24:4-13; Mark 13:5-13

8 And He said: [h]"Take heed that you not
be deceived. For many will come in My
name, saying, 'I am *He*,' and, 'The time has
drawn near.' [4]Therefore do not [5]go after
them. 9 But when you hear of [i]wars and
commotions, do not be terrified; for these
things must come to pass first, but the end
will not come immediately."
10 [j]Then He said to them, "Nation will
rise against nation, and kingdom against
kingdom. 11 And there will be great [k]earth-
quakes in various places, and famines and
pestilences; and there will be fearful sights
and great signs from heaven. 12 [l]But before
all these things, they will lay their hands
on you and persecute *you*, delivering *you*
up to the synagogues and [m]prisons. [n]You
will be brought before kings and rulers
[o]for My name's sake. 13 But [p]it will turn
out for you as an occasion for testimony.
14 [q]Therefore settle *it* in your hearts not to
meditate beforehand on what you will [6]an-
swer; 15 for I will give you a mouth and
wisdom [r]which all your adversaries will
not be able to contradict or [7]resist. 16 [s]You

41 [y] Matt. 22:41-46; Mark 12:35-37
42 [z] Ps. 110:1; Acts 2:34, 35
44 [a] Acts 13:22, 23; Rom. 1:3; 9:4, 5
45 [b] Matt. 23:1-7; Mark 12:38-40
46 [c] Matt. 23:5 [d] Luke 11:43; 14:7
47 [e] Matt. 23:14 [f] [Matt. 6:5, 6]

CHAPTER 21

1 [a] Mark 12:41-44
2 [b] [2 Cor. 6:10] [c] Mark 12:42 [1] Gr. *lepta*, very small copper coins
3 [d] [2 Cor. 8:12]
4 [e] [2 Cor. 8:12] [2] NU omits *for God*
5 [f] Matt. 24:1; Mark 13:1 [3] *decorated*
6 [g] Is. 64:10, 11; Lam. 2:6-9; Mic. 3:12; Luke 19:41-44
8 [h] Matt. 24:4; Mark 13:5; Eph. 5:6; 2 Thess. 2:3; [1 John 4:1] [4] NU omits *Therefore* [5] *follow*
9 [i] Rev. 6:4
10 [j] Matt. 24:7
11 [k] Rev. 6:12
12 [l] Mark 13:9; John 16:2; [Rev. 2:10] [m] Acts 4:3; 5:18; 12:4; 16:24 [n] Acts 25:23 [o] 1 Pet. 2:13
13 [p] [Phil. 1:12-14, 28; 2 Thess. 1:5]
14 [q] Matt. 10:19; Mark 13:11; Luke 12:11 [6] *say in defense*
15 [r] Acts 6:10 [7] *withstand*
16 [s] Mic. 7:6; Mark 13:12

20:39 "Teacher, You have spoken well." Christ had given a powerful argument for the resurrection of the dead, and on that subject, the Pharisees agreed with Him against the Sadducees. This scribe, in spite of his hatred for Christ, was pleased with the answer He had given.

20:40 they dared not question Him. The more questions He answered the clearer it became that His understanding and authority were vastly superior to that of the scribes and Pharisees. Cf. Matt. 22:46; Mark 12:34.

20:41-44 After the Jewish leaders gave up questioning Him, Christ turned the tables and posed a question to them. *See notes on Matt. 22:42-45; Mark 12:35-37.*

20:42 Quoted from Ps. 110:1.

20:45-47 *See notes on Mark 12:38-40.*

21:1 the treasury. Thirteen chests with funnel-shaped openings stood in the court of the women. Each was labeled for a specific use, and donations were given accordingly.

21:2 poor widow. The Gr. expression signifies extreme poverty. This woman was desperately poor, and more fit to be a recipient of charity than a donor. **mites.** The smallest copper coins in use in Palestine, worth about one-eighth of a cent, but representing all this woman had to live on (v. 4). *See note on Mark 12:42.*

21:3 has put in more. I.e., more in proportion to her means, and therefore more in the sight of God.

21:4 out of their abundance. There was nothing sacrificial about their giving.

21:5 beautiful stones. *See notes on Matt. 24:1; Mark 13:1.* **donations.** Wealthy people gave gifts of gold sculpture, golden plaques, and other treasures to the temple. Herod had donated a golden vine with clusters of golden grapes nearly 6 feet tall. The gifts were displayed on the walls and suspended in the portico. They constituted an unimaginable collection of wealth. All of these riches were looted by the Romans when the temple was destroyed (v. 6).

21:6-17 *See notes on Matt. 24:2-10; Mark 13:2-11.*

21:8 do not go after them. Cf. 17:23. *See note on Matt. 24:26.*

21:9 the end. *See notes on Matt. 24:6, 14.*

21:11 signs from heaven. The cross references in Matt. 24:7 and Mark 13:8 omit this phrase. Cf. v. 25. *See note on Mark 13:25.*

21:13 an occasion for testimony. Trials are always opportunities (James 1:2-4), and persecution is often an opportunity to magnify one's testimony.

21:14 not to meditate beforehand. *See note on 12:11.*

will be betrayed even by parents and
brothers, relatives and friends; and they
will put [t]*some* of you to death. 17 And [u]you
will be hated by all for My name's sake.
18 [v]But not a hair of your head shall be lost.
19 By your patience possess your souls.

Destruction of Jerusalem
Matt. 24:15-21; Mark 13:14-19

20 [w]"But when you see Jerusalem surrounded by armies, then know that its desolation is near. 21 Then let those who are in
Judea flee to the mountains, let those who
are in the midst of her depart, and let not
those who are in the country enter her. 22 For
these are the days of vengeance, that [x]all
things which are written may be fulfilled.
23 [y]But woe to those who are pregnant and
to those who are nursing babies in those
days! For there will be great distress in the
land and wrath upon this people. 24 And
they will fall by the edge of the sword, and
be led away captive into all nations. And Jerusalem will be trampled by Gentiles [z]until
the times of the Gentiles are fulfilled.

The Second Coming
Matt. 24:29-31; Mark 13:24-27

25 [a]"And there will be signs in the sun,
in the moon, and in the stars; and on the
earth distress of nations, with perplexity,
the sea and the waves roaring; 26 men's
hearts failing them from fear and the expectation of those things which are coming
on the earth, [b]for the powers of the heavens will be shaken. 27 Then they will see
the Son of Man [c]coming in a cloud with
power and great glory. 28 Now when these
things begin to happen, look up and lift up
your heads, because [d]your redemption
draws near."

Parable of the Fig Tree
Matt. 24:32-35; Mark 13:28-31

29 [e]Then He spoke to them a parable:
"Look at the fig tree, and all the trees.
30 When they are already budding, you see
and know for yourselves that summer is
now near. 31 So you also, when you see
these things happening, know that the
kingdom of God is near. 32 Assuredly, I say
to you, this generation will by no means
pass away till all things take place.
33 [f]Heaven and earth will pass away, but
My [g]words will by no means pass away.

Warning to Watch for His Coming
Matt. 24:36-44; Mark 13:32-37

34 "But [h]take heed to yourselves, lest
your hearts be weighed down with [8]ca-
rousing, drunkenness, and [i]cares of this
life, and that Day come on you unexpectedly. 35 For [j]it will come as a snare on all
those who dwell on the face of the whole
earth. 36 [k]Watch therefore, and [l]pray always that you may [9]be counted [m]worthy
to escape all these things that will come to
pass, and [n]to stand before the Son of Man."
37 [o]And in the daytime He was teaching
in the temple, but [p]at night He went out
and stayed on the mountain called Olivet.
38 Then early in the morning all the people
came to Him in the temple to hear Him.

Judas Agrees to Betray Christ
Matt. 26:1-5, 14-16; Mark 14:1, 2, 10, 11

22 Now [a]the Feast of Unleavened
Bread drew near, which is called
Passover. 2 And [b]the chief priests and the

16 [t]Acts 7:59; 12:2
17 [u]Matt. 10:22
18 [v]Matt. 10:30; Luke 12:7
20 [w]Matt. 24:15; Mark 13:14
22 [x]Is. 63:4; [Dan. 9:24-27]; Hos. 9:7; [Zech. 11:1]
23 [y]Matt. 24:19
24 [z][Dan. 9:27; 12:7]
25 [a]Is. 13:9, 10, 13; Matt. 24:29; Mark 13:24; [2 Pet. 3:10-12]
26 [b]Matt. 24:29
27 [c]Dan. 7:13; [Matt. 16:27; 24:30; 26:64]; Mark 13:26; Rev. 1:7; 14:14
28 [d][Rom. 8:19, 23]
29 [e]Matt. 24:32; Mark 13:28
33 [f]Is. 51:6; Matt. 24:35; Heb. 1:10, 11; [2 Pet. 3:7, 10, 12] [g]Is. 40:8; Luke 16:17; 1 Pet. 1:24, 25
34 [h]Matt. 24:42-44; Mark 4:19; Luke 12:40, 45; Rom. 13:13; 1 Thess. 5:6; 1 Pet. 4:7 [i]Luke 8:14 [8]*dissipation*
35 [j]1 Thess. 5:2; [2 Pet. 3:10]; Rev. 3:3; 16:15
36 [k]Matt. 24:42; 25:13; Mark 13:33; Luke 12:40 [l]Luke 18:1; [Eph. 6:18]; Col. 4:2; 1 Thess. 5:17 [m]Luke 20:35 [n]Ps. 1:5; [Eph. 6:13] [9]NU *have strength to*
37 [o]John 8:1, 2 [p]Luke 22:39

CHAPTER 22

1 [a]Matt. 26:2-5; Mark 14:1, 2
2 [b]Ps. 2:2; John 11:47; Acts 4:27

21:18 not a hair. Cf. v. 16. This was not a promise for the preservation of their physical lives, but a guarantee that they would suffer no eternal loss. God Himself sovereignly preserves His own. *See notes on John 10:28,29.*

21:19 The true sense of this verse seems to be, "By endurance you shall obtain salvation," referring to the final aspect of salvation, namely, glorification. *See note on Matt. 24:13.*

21:20 Jerusalem surrounded by armies. *See note on 19:43.* A comparison with Matt. 24:15,16 and Mark 13:14 suggests that this sign is closely associated with "the abomination of desolation" (*see notes on Matt. 24:15; Dan. 9:27; 11:31*). This sign of Jerusalem under siege was previewed in A.D. 70, but awaits its fulfillment in the future.

21:21 the mountains. *See notes on Matt. 24:16; Mark 13:14.*

21:22 vengeance. I.e., God's righteous retribution against sin.

21:23 pregnant...nursing. *See note on Mark 13:17.*

21:24 the times of the Gentiles. This expression is unique to Luke. It identifies the era from Israel's captivity (ca. 586 B.C. to Babylon; cf. 2 Kin. 25) to her restoration in the kingdom (Rev. 20:1-6). It has been a time during which, in accord with God's purpose, Gentiles have dominated or threatened Jerusalem. The era has also been marked by vast spiritual privileges for the Gentile nations (cf. Is. 66:12; Mal. 1:11; Matt. 24:14; Mark 13:10).

21:25 there will be signs. The celestial signs and wonders described here immediately precede the return of Christ. *See note on Matt. 24:29.*

21:27 coming. Quoted from Dan. 7:13. *See notes on Matt. 24:30,31; Mark 13:26,27.* Cf. 2 Thess. 1:7-10; Rev. 19:11-16.

21:28 lift up your heads. The dreadful tribulations and signs that mark the last days are a cause of great expectation, joy, and triumph for the true believer. **redemption.** I.e., the final fullness of redemption, when the redeemed are reunited with Christ forever.

21:29-33 *See notes on Matt. 24:32-36; Mark 13:29-32.*

21:34 that Day. I.e., the day of His return. *See note on Matt. 24:37.* When Christ mentions His return, he invariably enjoins watchfulness (cf. 12:37-40; Matt. 25:13; Mark 13:33-37).

21:36 pray always. *See note on 18:1.* **that you may be counted worthy.** Older manuscripts say "that you may have strength."

21:37 in the daytime. I.e., during the days of that final week in Jerusalem.

22:1 which is called Passover. *See note on Matt. 26:17.* Passover was a single day, followed immediately by the Feast of the Unleav-

scribes sought how they might kill Him,
for they feared the people.
3 [c]Then Satan entered Judas, surnamed
Iscariot, who was numbered among the
[d]twelve. 4 So he went his way and conferred with the chief priests and captains,
how he might betray Him to them. 5 And
they were glad, and [e]agreed to give him
money. 6 So he promised and sought opportunity to [f]betray Him to them in the absence of the multitude.

The Upper Room Is Prepared
Matt. 26:17-19; Mark 14:12-16

7 [g]Then came the Day of Unleavened
Bread, when the Passover must be [1]killed.
8 And He sent Peter and John, saying, "Go
and prepare the Passover for us, that we
may eat."
9 So they said to Him, "Where do You
want us to prepare?"
10 And He said to them, "Behold, when
you have entered the city, a man will meet
you carrying a pitcher of water; follow him
into the house which he enters. 11 Then
you shall say to the master of the house,
'The Teacher says to you, "Where is the
guest room where I may eat the Passover
with My disciples?"' 12 Then he will show
you a large, furnished upper room; there
make ready."
13 So they went and [h]found it just as He
had said to them, and they prepared the
Passover.

The Passover Is Celebrated
Matt. 26:20, 29; Mark 14:17, 25

14 [i]When the hour had come, He sat
down, and the [2]twelve apostles with Him.
15 Then He said to them, "With *fervent* desire I have desired to eat this Passover with
you before I suffer; 16 for I say to you, I will
no longer eat of it [j]until it is fulfilled in the
kingdom of God."
17 Then He took the cup, and gave
thanks, and said, "Take this and divide *it*
among yourselves; 18 for [k]I say to you, [3]I
will not drink of the fruit of the vine until
the kingdom of God comes."

The Lord's Supper Is Instituted
Matt. 26:26-28; Mark 14:22-24

19 [l]And He took bread, gave thanks and
broke *it*, and gave *it* to them, saying, "This
is My [m]body which is given for you; [n]do
this in remembrance of Me."

3 [c] Matt. 26:14-16; Mark 14:10, 11; John 13:2, 27 [d] Matt. 10:2-4 **5** [e] Zech. 11:12 **6** [f] Ps. 41:9 **7** [g] Matt. 26:17-19; Mark 14:12-16 [1] Sacrificed **13** [h] Luke 19:32 **14** [i] Matt. 26:20; Mark 14:17 [2] NU omits *twelve* **16** [j] Luke 14:15; [Acts 10:41; Rev. 19:9] **18** [k] Matt. 26:29; Mark 14:25 [3] NU adds *from now on* **19** [l] Matt. 26:26; Mark 14:22 [m] [1 Pet. 2:24] [n] 1 Cor. 11:23-26

ened Bread (Lev. 23:5,6). The whole season could be referred to by either name (cf. v. 7).

22:2 chief priests and the scribes. *See notes on 19:47; 20:1.* **for they feared the people.** They were therefore plotting secretly, hoping to eliminate Him after the Passover season, when Jerusalem would not be filled with so many people (cf. v. 6; Matt. 26:4,5; Mark 14:1,2). But these events occurred according to God's timetable, not theirs (*see note on Matt. 26:2*).

22:3 Satan entered. I.e., Judas was possessed by Satan himself. Satan evidently gained direct control over Judas on two occasions—once just before Judas arranged his betrayal with the chief priests, and again during the Last Supper (John 13:27), immediately before the betrayal was actually carried out.

22:4 captains. I.e., the temple guard, a security force consisting of Levites.

22:5 agreed to give him money. Matthew 26:15 says 30 pieces of silver, the price of a slave (Ex. 21:32).

22:7 the Day of Unleavened Bread. I.e., the first day of the feast season (*see note on Matt. 26:17*). The people from Galilee celebrated the Passover on Thursday evening (see Introduction to John: Interpretive Challenges) so the lambs were killed in the afternoon of that day. The disciples and Jesus ate the Passover meal that evening, after sundown, (when Passover officially began). Judeans would follow this same sequence one day later on Friday.

22:8 Peter and John. Identified only by Luke. **Go and prepare.** This was no small task. They had to take the paschal lamb to be sacrificed, and make preparations for a meal for 13 (v. 14). But preliminary arrangements for the meal had apparently been made personally by Jesus Himself, and the owner of the upper room was taking care of many of those details for them. *See note on Matt. 26:18.*

22:10 a man...carrying...water. Probably part of his work to prepare for the meal. Normally carrying water was woman's work, so a man carrying a pitcher would stand out. It is unlikely that the water pitcher was any sort of prearranged signal. Christ's knowledge of what the man would be doing at the precise moment the disciples arrived appears to be a manifestation of His divine omniscience.

22:12 a large, furnished upper room. One of many such rooms for rent in Jerusalem that were maintained for the express purpose of providing pilgrims a place to celebrate feasts. The furnishings undoubtedly included a large banquet table and everything necessary to prepare and serve a meal.

22:14 the hour had come. I.e., sundown, marking the official beginning of Passover (*see note on v. 7*). **sat down.** I.e., reclined.

22:15 With *fervent* desire. Cf. John 13:1. He wanted to prepare them for what was coming.

22:16 fulfilled. Christ's death on the following day fulfilled the symbolism of the Passover meal. Passover was both a memorial of the deliverance from Egypt, and a prophetic type of the sacrifice of Christ.

22:17 Then He took the cup. Luke mentions two cups (cf. v. 20). The Passover seder involved the sharing of 4 cups of diluted red wine. This cup was the first of the 4 (the cup of thanksgiving) and was preliminary to the institution of the Lord's Supper (*see note on 1 Cor. 10:16*). It represented the end of His time of eating and drinking with the disciples, particularly partaking of the Passover (v. 18; cf. 5:34,35; Matt. 9:15; 26:29; *see note on Mark 14:25*).

22:19 This is My body. I.e., it represented His body (cf. the words of 8:11, "The seed is the word of God"—and also v. 20). Such metaphorical language was a typical Hebraism. No eucharistic miracle of transubstantiation was implied, nor could the disciples have missed the symbolic intent of His statement, for His actual body—yet unbroken—was before their very eyes. *See note on Matt. 26:26.* **do this.** Thus He established the observance as an ordinance for worship (*see notes on 1 Cor. 11:23-26*). **remembrance of Me.** Passover had looked forward to the sacrifice of Christ; He transformed the seder into an altogether different ceremony, which looks back in remembrance at His atoning death.

20 Likewise He also *took* the cup after
supper, saying, [o]"This cup *is* the new
covenant in My blood, which is shed for
you.

Christ Predicts His Betrayer
Matt. 26:21-25; Mark 14:18-21; John 13:21-26

21 [p]But behold, the hand of My betrayer *is*
with Me on the table. 22 [q]And truly the Son
of Man goes [r]as it has been determined,
but woe to that man by whom He is betrayed!"
23 [s]Then they began to question among
themselves, which of them it was who
would do this thing.

The Disciples Argue over Who Is the Greatest

24 [t]Now there was also a dispute among
them, as to which of them should be considered the greatest. 25 [u]And He said to
them, "The kings of the Gentiles exercise
lordship over them, and those who exercise authority over them are called 'benefactors.' 26 [v]But not so *among* you; on the
contrary, [w]he who is greatest among you,
let him be as the younger, and he who governs as he who serves. 27 [x]For who *is*
greater, he who sits at the table, or he who
serves? *Is* it not he who sits at the table? Yet
[y]I am among you as the One who serves.
28 "But you are those who have continued with Me in [z]My trials. 29 And [a]I bestow upon you a kingdom, just as My Father bestowed *one* upon Me, 30 that [b]you
may eat and drink at My table in My kingdom, [c]and sit on thrones judging the
twelve tribes of Israel."

Christ Predicts Peter's Denial
Matt. 26:31-35; Mark 14:27-31; John 13:36-38

31 [4]And the Lord said, "Simon, Simon!
Indeed, [d]Satan has asked for you, that he
may [e]sift *you* as wheat. 32 But [f]I have
prayed for you, that your faith should not
fail; and when you have returned to *Me*,
[g]strengthen your brethren."
33 But he said to Him, "Lord, I am ready
to go with You, both to prison and to
death."
34 [h]Then He said, "I tell you, Peter, the
rooster shall not crow this day before you
will deny three times that you know Me."

20 [o] 1 Cor. 10:16
21 [p] Ps. 41:9; Matt. 26:21, 23; Mark 14:18; Luke 22:48; John 13:21, 26, 27
22 [q] Matt. 26:24 [r] John 17:12; Acts 2:23
23 [s] Matt. 26:22; John 13:22, 25
24 [t] Mark 9:34; Luke 9:46-48
25 [u] [Matt. 20:25-28]; Mark 10:42-45
26 [v] Matt. 20:26; [1 Pet. 5:3] [w] Luke 9:48
27 [x] [Luke 12:37] [y] Matt. 20:28; John 13:13, 14; Phil. 2:7
28 [z] [Heb. 2:18; 4:15]
29 [a] Matt. 24:47
30 [b] [Matt. 8:11; Rev. 19:9] [c] Ps. 49:14; [Matt. 19:28; 1 Cor. 6:2; Rev. 3:21]
31 [d] 1 Pet. 5:8 [e] Amos 9:9 [4] NU omits *And the Lord said*
32 [f] [John 17:9, 11, 15] [g] John 21:15-17; Acts 1:15; 2:14; 2 Pet. 1:10-15
34 [h] Matt. 26:33-35; Mark 14:29-31; Luke 22:61; John 13:37, 38

22:20 *took* the cup. This is the third (the cup of blessing) of the 4 cups in the Passover celebration (*see note on 1 Cor. 10:16*). **after supper.** Cf. 1 Cor. 11:25. These two verses are virtually identical in form. Paul stated that he had received his information about this event from the Lord Himself (1 Cor. 11:23). **This cup *is* the new covenant.** Clearly, the cup only represented the New Covenant (*see note on v. 19*).

22:21 the hand of My betrayer *is* with Me. Luke recounted the details of the Lord's Supper topically, not chronologically (see Introduction: Background and Setting; see *note on 1:3*). Matthew and Mark placed Jesus' warning about the betrayer prior to the giving of the bread and cup; Luke put it afterward. Only John 13:30 records Judas' departure, but John says nothing about the bread and cup. So it is difficult to tell by comparison whether Judas left before or after the institution of the Lord's Supper. But Luke's words here seem to imply that Judas actually shared in that event. If so, his presence at that table makes his hypocrisy and crime all the more despicable (cf. 1 Cor. 11:27-30).

22:22 as it has been determined. Every detail of the crucifixion of Christ was under the sovereign control of God and in accord with His eternal purposes. Cf. Acts 2:23; 4:26-28. **but woe.** The fact that Judas' betrayal was part of God's plan does not free him from the guilt of a crime he entered into willfully. God's sovereignty is never a legitimate excuse for human guilt.

22:24 a dispute. Cf. 9:46; Matt. 20:20-24. This dispute may have prompted the episode where Christ washed their feet (John 13:1-20). It reveals how large an issue this was in the minds of the disciples, and how far they were from grasping all that He had taught them.

22:25 'benefactors.' Cf. Matt. 20:25. This title was used by the heathen rulers of both Egypt and Syria, though it was rarely a fitting description. The intent was to portray themselves as champions of their people, but it had a very condescending ring to it—especially when so many "benefactors" were actually ruthless tyrants.

22:26 he who serves. Cf. Matt. 20:26-28. This is an apparent reference to the washing of their feet (*see note on v. 24*). Christ Himself had modeled such servitude throughout His ministry (v. 27; cf. Phil. 2:5-8).

22:28 My trials. Christ's entire life and ministry were filled with temptations (4:1-13); hardships (9:58); sorrows (19:41); and agonies (v. 44)—not to mention the sufferings of the cross which He knew were yet to come.

22:29 I bestow upon you a kingdom. Christ confirmed the disciples' expectation of an earthly kingdom yet to come. It would not come in the timing or the manner that they hoped, but He affirmed the promise that such a kingdom would indeed be established, and that they would have a principal role in it (v. 30; cf. Matt. 19:28).

22:30 judging the twelve tribes of Israel. The language identifies this as a millennial promise. *See note on Rev. 20:4.*

22:31 Simon, Simon. The repetition of the name (cf. 10:41; Acts 9:4) implied an earnest and somber tone of warning. Christ Himself had given Simon the name Peter (6:14), but here He reverted to his old name, perhaps to intensify His rebuke about Peter's fleshly overconfidence. The context also suggests that Peter may have been one of the more vocal participants in the dispute of v. 24. **Satan has asked for you.** Though addressed specifically to Peter, this warning embraced the other disciples as well. The pronoun "you" is plural in the Gr. text. **sift *you* as wheat.** The imagery is apt. It suggests that such trials, though unsettling and undesirable, have a necessary refining effect.

22:32 I have prayed for you. The pronoun "you" is singular (*see note on v. 31*). Although it is clear that He prayed for all of them (John 17:6-19), He personally assured Peter of His prayers and of Peter's ultimate victory, even encouraging Peter to be an encourager to the others. **that your faith should not fail.** Peter himself failed miserably, but his faith was never overthrown (cf. John 21:18,19).

22:34 you will deny. This prediction of Peter's denial evidently took place in the upper room (cf. John 13:38). Matthew 26:34 and Mark 14:30 record a second, nearly identical incident, which took place on the Mt. of Olives on the way to Gethsemane (cf. Matt. 26:30; Mark 14:26).

Christ Predicts Coming Conflict

35 [i]And He said to them, "When I sent
you without money bag, knapsack, and
sandals, did you lack anything?"
So they said, "Nothing."
36 Then He said to them, "But now, he
who has a money bag, let him take *it*, and
likewise a knapsack; and he who has no
sword, let him sell his garment and buy one.
37 For I say to you that this which is written
must still be [5]accomplished in Me: [j]'*And He
was numbered with the transgressors.*' For
the things concerning Me have an end."
38 So they said, "Lord, look, here *are* two
swords."
And He said to them, "It is enough."

Christ Prays in Gethsemane
Matt. 26:36-46; Mark 14:32-42; John 18:1

39 [k]Coming out, [l]He went to the Mount
of Olives, as He was accustomed, and His
disciples also followed Him. 40 [m]When He
came to the place, He said to them, "Pray
that you may not enter into temptation."
41 [n]And He was withdrawn from them
about a stone's throw, and He knelt down
and prayed, 42 saying, "Father, if it is Your
will, take this cup away from Me; nevertheless [o]not My will, but Yours, be done."
43 [6]Then [p]an angel appeared to Him from
heaven, strengthening Him. 44 [q]And being
in agony, He prayed more earnestly. Then
His sweat became like great drops of blood
falling down to the ground.
45 When He rose up from prayer, and
had come to His disciples, He found them
sleeping from sorrow. 46 Then He said to
them, "Why [r]do you sleep? Rise and [s]pray,
lest you enter into temptation."

Judas Betrays Christ
Matt. 26:47-56; Mark 14:43-50; John 18:2-11

47 And while He was still speaking, [t]be-
hold, a multitude; and he who was called
[u]Judas, one of the twelve, went before
them and drew near to Jesus to kiss Him.
48 But Jesus said to him, "Judas, are you
betraying the Son of Man with a [v]kiss?"
49 When those around Him saw what
was going to happen, they said to Him,
"Lord, shall we strike with the sword?"
50 And [w]one of them struck the servant of
the high priest and cut off his right ear.
51 But Jesus answered and said, "Permit
even this." And He touched his ear and
healed him.

35 [i] Matt. 10:9; Mark 6:8; Luke 9:3; 10:4
37 [j] Is. 53:12; Matt. 27:38; Mark 15:28; Luke 22:32 [5] *fulfilled*
39 [k] Matt. 26:36; John 18:1 [l] Luke 21:37
40 [m] Matt. 26:36-46; Mark 14:32-42
41 [n] Matt. 26:39; Mark 14:35; [Luke 18:11-14]
42 [o] Is. 50:5; John 4:34; 5:30; 6:38; 8:29
43 [p] Matt. 4:11 [6] NU brackets vv. 43 and 44 as not in the original text.
44 [q] John 12:27; [Heb. 5:7]
46 [r] Luke 9:32 [s] 1 Chr. 16:11; Luke 22:40; [Eph. 6:18]; 1 Thess. 5:17
47 [t] Matt. 26:47-56; Mark 14:43-50; John 18:3-11 [u] Ps. 41:9; Matt. 20:18; Luke 9:44; 22:21; Acts 1:16, 17
48 [v] [Prov. 27:6]
50 [w] Matt. 26:51

22:35 When I sent you. Cf. 9:3; 10:4.

22:36 But now. When Christ sent them out before, He had sovereignly arranged for their needs to be met. Henceforth they were to use normal means to provide for their own support and protection. The money bag, knapsack, and sword were figurative expressions for such means (the sword being emblematic of protection, not aggression). But they mistakenly took His words literally (v. 38).

22:37 Quoted from Is. 53:12.

22:38 two swords. These were short, dagger-like instruments—more like knives than swords. There was nothing unusual about the carrying of such weapons in that culture. They had many practical uses besides violence against other people. **"It is enough."** I.e., enough of such talk (cf. v. 51).

22:39 Mount of Olives. *See notes on 19:29; Matt. 24:3.* **His disciples also followed Him.** Matthew 26:36,37 and Mark 14:32,33 give more details. He left most of the disciples at the entrance to Gethsemane, and took Peter, James, and John inside with Him to pray.

22:40 the place. Gethsemane. *See notes on Matt. 26:36; Mark 14:32.* **Pray.** He had already warned them—and Peter in particular—that an egregious trial was imminent (v. 31). Sadly, that warning, as well as His imploring them to pray, went unheeded.

22:41 about a stone's throw. I.e., within earshot. His prayer was partly for their benefit (cf. John 11:41,42).

22:42 this cup. I.e., the cup of divine wrath (cf. Is. 51:17,22; Jer. 25:15-17,27-29; Lam. 4:21,22; Ezek. 23:31-34; Hab. 2:16). **not My will.** Cf. Matt. 26:39; John 4:34; 5:30; 6:38; 8:29. This does not imply that there was any conflict between the will of the Father and the will of the Son. It was a perfectly normal expression of His humanity that He shrank from the cup of divine wrath (*see note on Matt. 26:39*). But even though the cup was abhorrent to Him, He willingly took it, because it was the will of the Father. In this prayer He was consciously, deliberately, and voluntarily subjugating all His human desires to the Father's perfect will. Thus there was neither conflict between Father and Son, nor between the deity of Christ and His human desires.

22:43,44 The facts in these verses are related only by Luke, the physician.

22:44 like great drops of blood. This suggests a dangerous condition known as *hematidrosis*, the effusion of blood in one's perspiration. It can be caused by extreme anguish or physical strain. Subcutaneous capillaries dilate and burst, mingling blood with sweat. Christ Himself stated that His distress had brought Him to the threshold of death (*see notes on Matt. 26:38; Mark 14:34*; cf. Heb 12:3,4).

22:45 sleeping from sorrow. Cf. 9:32. The emotional strain was wearing on the disciples as well as Christ. Their response, however, was to capitulate to fleshly cravings. Thus they gratified their immediate desire for sleep, rather than staying awake to pray for strength, as Christ had commanded them (v. 40). All the reasons for their subsequent failure are found in their behavior in the garden.

22:46 Rise and pray. A tender appeal to the disciples, who in their weakness were disobeying Him at a critical moment. He may have been summoning them to a standing posture, to help overcome their drowsiness. Matthew 26:43 and Mark 14:40 reveal that he again found them sleeping at least one more time.

22:47 a multitude. These were heavily armed representatives of the Sanhedrin (Matt. 26:47; Mark 14:43), accompanied by a Roman cohort with lanterns, torches, and weapons (John 18:3). **kiss.** A typical greeting, but this was the prearranged signal by which Judas would identify Christ for the soldiers (cf. Matt. 26:48,49; *see note on Mark 14:44*).

22:50 cut off his right ear. All 4 gospels record this incident. Only John reveals that the swordsman was Peter and the victim was named Malchus (John 18:10). And only Luke, the physician, records the subsequent healing (v. 51).

22:51 "Permit even this." I.e., the betrayal and arrest (cf. John 18:11). All was proceeding according to the divine timetable (*see note on v. 22*). **touched his ear and healed him.** This is the only instance in all of Scripture where Christ healed a fresh wound. The miracle is also unique in that Christ healed an enemy, unasked, and without any

52 [x]Then Jesus said to the chief priests,
captains of the temple, and the elders
who had come to Him, "Have you come
out, as against a [y]robber, with swords
and clubs? 53 When I was with you daily
in the [z]temple, you did not try to seize
Me. But this is your [a]hour, and the power
of darkness."

Peter Denies Christ
Matt 26:57, 58, 69-75; Mark 14:53, 54, 66-72; John 18:15-18, 25-27

54 [b]Having arrested Him, they led *Him*
and brought Him into the high priest's
house. [c]But Peter followed at a distance.
55 [d]Now when they had kindled a fire in
the midst of the courtyard and sat down
together, Peter sat among them. 56 And a
certain servant girl, seeing him as he sat by
the fire, looked intently at him and said,
"This man was also with Him."
57 But he denied [7]Him, saying, "Woman,
I do not know Him."
58 [e]And after a little while another saw
him and said, "You also are of them."
But Peter said, "Man, I am not!"
59 [f]Then after about an hour had passed,
another confidently affirmed, saying,
"Surely this *fellow* also was with Him, for
he is a [g]Galilean."
60 But Peter said, "Man, I do not know
what you are saying!"
Immediately, while he was still speaking, [8]the rooster crowed. 61 And the Lord
turned and looked at Peter. Then [h]Peter remembered the word of the Lord, how He
had said to him, [i]"Before the rooster
[9]crows, you will deny Me three times."
62 So Peter went out and wept bitterly.

Christ Is Beaten
Matt. 26:67, 68; Mark 14:65

63 [j]Now the men who held Jesus
mocked Him and [k]beat Him. 64 [1]And having blindfolded Him, they [l]struck Him on
the face and asked Him, saying, "Prophesy! Who is the one who struck You?"
65 And many other things they blasphemously spoke against Him.

The Sanhedrin Tries Christ
Matt. 27:1; Mark 15:1

66 [m]As soon as it was day, [n]the elders of
the people, both chief priests and scribes,
came together and led Him into their
council, saying, 67 [o]"If You are the Christ,
tell us."
But He said to them, "If I tell you, you
will [p]by no means believe. 68 And if I [2]also
ask *you*, you will by no means answer [3]Me
or let *Me* go. 69 [q]Hereafter the Son of Man
will sit on the right hand of the power of
God."
70 Then they all said, "Are You then the
Son of God?"
So He said to them, [r]"You *rightly* say
that I am."

52 x Matt. 26:55 y Luke 23:32
53 z Luke 19:47, 48 a [John 12:27]
54 b Is. 53:7, 8; Matt. 26:57; Mark 14:53; Luke 9:44; Acts 8:32 c Matt. 26:58; Mark 14:54; John 18:15
55 d Matt. 26:69-75; Mark 14:66-72; John 18:15, 17, 18
57 7 NU *it*
58 e Matt. 26:71; Mark 14:69; John 18:25
59 f Matt. 26:73; Mark 14:70; John 18:26 g Acts 1:11; 2:7
60 8 NU, M *a rooster*
61 h Matt. 26:75; Mark 14:72 i Matt. 26:34, 75; Mark 14:30; Luke 22:34; John 13:38 9 NU adds *today*
63 j Ps. 69:1, 4, 7-9; Matt. 26:67, 68; Mark 14:65; John 18:22 k Job 16:10; Is. 50:6; Lam. 3:30
64 l Zech. 13:7 1 NU *And having blindfolded Him, they asked Him*
66 m Matt. 27:1; Mark 15:1 n Ps. 2:2; Acts 4:26
67 o Matt. 26:63-66; Mark 14:61-63; Luke 22:67-71; John 18:19-21 p Luke 20:5-7
68 2 NU omits *also* 3 NU omits the rest of v. 68. **69** q [Ps. 110:1; Matt. 26:64; Mark 14:62; 16:19]; Acts 2:33; 7:55; Eph. 1:20; Col. 3:1; Heb. 1:3; 8:1 **70** r Matt. 26:64; 27:11; Mark 14:62; Luke 1:35

evidence of faith in the recipient. It is also remarkable that such a dramatic miracle had no effect whatsoever on the hearts of those men. Neither had the explosive power of Jesus' words, which knocked them to the ground (John 18:6). They carried on with the arrest as if nothing peculiar had happened (v. 54).

22:53 this is your hour. I.e., nighttime, the hour of darkness. They had not the courage to confront Him in the presence of the crowds at the temple, where He had openly taught each day. Their skulking tactics betrayed the truth about their hearts. Nighttime was a fitting hour for the servants of the power of darkness (Satan) to be afoot (cf. John 3:20,21; Eph. 5:8,12-15; 1 Thess. 5:5-7).

22:54 the high priest's house. I.e., Caiaphas' house. *See note on Matt 26:57.* **Peter followed at a distance.** All 4 gospels record this fact. John indicates that another disciple—presumably himself—also followed (John 18:15).

22:56 a certain servant girl. All 4 gospels mention her. She appears to have been the doorkeeper of Annas' house (cf. Matt. 26:69; Mark 14:66; John 18:17).

22:57 But he denied Him. John 18:13-18 says this first denial took place while Jesus was being examined by Annas, father-in-law to Caiaphas (*see note on 3:2*). Both accounts mention a fire in the courtyard (v. 55; John 18:18) so it may be that the houses of Annas and Caiaphas shared a common courtyard. Only John mentions the examination by Annas, so the other gospels describe Peter's 3-fold denial as an incident that took place in the porch and courtyard of Caiaphas' house.

22:58 another saw him. "Another" is a masculine pronoun in the Gr., indicating a man. Mark 14:69 says this second challenge to Peter came from the same servant girl who first recognized him (v. 56). The supposed discrepancy is easily reconciled when it is remembered that Peter was among several bystanders, and many of them questioned him at once (Matt. 26:73). He responded with his second denial.

22:59 he is a Galilean. They knew because of his accent (Matt. 26:73).

22:61 the Lord turned and looked at Peter. Luke alone records that Jesus made eye contact with Peter. The verb used suggests an intent, fixed look. The fact that He could see Peter suggests that the men holding Jesus had already brought Him into the courtyard to beat Him (v. 63). **Peter remembered.** *See note on Matt. 26:75; Mark 14:72.*

22:63 mocked Him and beat Him. Luke includes no details about Caiaphas' first interrogation of Jesus, recorded in Matt. 26:59-68; Mark 14:55-65. The beating described here evidently took place after that first examination, before the Sanhedrin could assemble for its official hearing (v. 66).

22:66 As soon as it was day. Criminal trials were not deemed legal if held at night, so the Sanhedrin dutifully waited until daybreak to render the verdict they had already agreed on anyway (cf. Matt. 26:66; Mark 14:64).

22:67 If You are the Christ. The Sanhedrin subjected Him to the same set of questions He had been asked in the nighttime trial, and the answers He gave were substantially the same (cf. vv. 67-71; Matt. 26:63-66; Mark 14:61-64).

71 [s]And they said, "What further testimony do we need? For we have heard it
ourselves from His own mouth."

Pilate Tries Christ
Matt. 27:2, 11-14; Mark 15:1-5; John 18:28-38

23 Then [a]the whole multitude of
them arose and led Him to [b]Pilate.
2 And they began to [c]accuse Him, saying,
"We found this *fellow* [d]perverting [1]the nation, and [e]forbidding to pay taxes to Caesar, saying [f]that He Himself is Christ, a
King."
3 [g]Then Pilate asked Him, saying, "Are
You the King of the Jews?"
He answered him and said, "*It is as* you
say."
4 So Pilate said to the chief priests and
the crowd, [h]"I find no fault in this Man."
5 But they were the more fierce, saying,
"He stirs up the people, teaching throughout all Judea, beginning from [i]Galilee to
this place."
6 When Pilate heard [2]of Galilee, he
asked if the Man were a Galilean. 7 And as
soon as he knew that He belonged to
[j]Herod's jurisdiction, he sent Him to
Herod, who was also in Jerusalem at that
time.

Herod Tries Christ

8 Now when Herod saw Jesus, [k]he was exceedingly glad; for he had desired for a
long *time* to see Him, because [l]he had
heard many things about Him, and he
hoped to see some miracle done by Him.
9 Then he questioned Him with many
words, but He answered him [m]nothing.
10 And the chief priests and scribes stood
and vehemently accused Him. 11 [n]Then
Herod, with his [3]men of war, treated Him
with contempt and mocked *Him,* arrayed
Him in a gorgeous robe, and sent Him
back to Pilate. 12 That very day [o]Pilate and
Herod became friends with each other, for
previously they had been at enmity with
each other.

Pilate Tries Christ Again
Matt. 27:15-26; Mark 15:6-15;
John 18:39–19:16

13 [p]Then Pilate, when he had called together the chief priests, the rulers, and the
people, 14 said to them, [q]"You have
brought this Man to me, as one who mis-
leads the people. And indeed, [r]having examined *Him* in your presence, I have
found no fault in this Man concerning
those things of which you accuse Him;
15 no, neither did Herod, for [4]I sent you
back to him; and indeed nothing deserving
of death has been done by Him. 16 [s]I will
therefore chastise Him and release *Him*"
17 [t](for [5]it was necessary for him to release
one to them at the feast).
18 And [u]they all cried out at once, saying, "Away with this *Man,* and release to
us Barabbas"— 19 who had been thrown
into prison for a certain rebellion made in
the city, and for murder.

71 [s]Matt. 26:65; Mark 14:63; John 19:7

CHAPTER 23

1 [a]Matt. 27:2; Mark 15:1; Luke 18:32; John 18:28 [b]Luke 3:1; 13:1
2 [c]Acts 24:2 [d]Acts 17:7 [e]Matt. 17:27; Mark 12:17 [f]John 19:12 [1]NU *our*
3 [g]Matt. 27:11; 1 Tim. 6:13
4 [h]Matt. 27:19; [1 Pet. 2:22]
5 [i]John 7:41
6 [2]NU omits *of Galilee*
7 [j]Matt. 14:1; Mark 6:14; Luke 3:1; 9:7; 13:31
8 [k]Luke 9:9 [l]Matt. 14:1; Mark 6:14
9 [m]Is. 53:7; Matt. 27:12, 14; Mark 15:5; John 19:9
11 [n]Is. 53:3 [3]*troops*
12 [o]Acts 4:26, 27
13 [p]Matt. 27:23; Mark 15:14; John 18:38
14 [q]Luke 23:1, 2 [r]Luke 23:4
15 [4]NU *he sent Him back to us*
16 [s]Matt. 27:26; Mark 15:15; Luke 23:22; John 19:1; Acts 16:37
17 [t]Matt. 27:15; Mark 15:6; John 18:39 [5]NU omits v. 17.
18 [u]Is. 53:3; Acts 3:13-15

23:1 the whole multitude of them. I.e., the entire Sanhedrin, some 70 men. At least one member of the council, Joseph of Arimathea, dissented from the decision to condemn Christ (vv. 50-52). **led Him to Pilate.** *See note on Matt. 27:2.*

23:2 forbidding to pay taxes to Caesar. This was a deliberate lie. Members of the Sanhedrin had publicly questioned Jesus on this very issue (hoping to discredit Him before the Jews), and He expressly upheld Caesar's right to demand taxes (20:20-25). **saying that He...is Christ, a King.** This was innuendo, implying that He was seditious against Rome—another untrue charge.

23:3 *It is as* you say. John 18:33-37 gives a fuller account of Jesus' reply to this question.

23:4 no fault. Despite the Jewish leaders' desperate attempts to accuse Him, Pilate was satisfied that Jesus was no insurrectionist, but the ferocity of the people made him afraid to exonerate Jesus. He was relieved to hear that Jesus was a Galilean, because that gave him an excuse to send Him to Herod (vv. 5,6).

23:7 Herod's jurisdiction. *See note on 13:31.* **sent Him to Herod.** Herod had come to Jerusalem for the feasts, and Pilate seized the opportunity to free himself from a political dilemma by sending Jesus to his rival. *See note on v. 12.*

23:8 desired...to see Him. Herod's interest in Christ was fueled by the fact that Christ reminded him of his late nemesis, John the Baptist (cf. 9:7-9). At one time Herod had apparently threatened to kill Jesus (13:31-33), but with Christ in Judea rather than Galilee and Perea (where Herod ruled), the king's concern seems to have been nothing more than an eager curiosity.

23:9 answered him nothing. It is significant that in all Jesus' various interrogations, Herod was the only one to whom He refused to speak. Cf. Matt. 7:6. Herod had summarily rejected the truth when he heard it from John the Baptist, so it would have been pointless for Jesus to answer him. Cf. Is. 53:7; Pss. 38:13,14; 39:1,2,9; 1 Pet. 2:23.

23:11 men of war. I.e., his security force. **treated Him with contempt.** Herod made Christ and the charges against Him as an occasion for a joke for Pilate's amusement (v. 12). **a gorgeous robe.** Probably not the same robe mentioned in Matt. 27:28, which was a military cloak. This was an elegant king's garment, probably one that Herod was prepared to discard.

23:12 friends. Based on their common unjust and cowardly treatment of Jesus.

23:13 called together. Pilate intended to declare Christ not guilty (v. 14), and it was his intention to make the verdict as public as possible. He undoubtedly expected that it would put an end to the whole matter.

23:14,15 Pilate and Herod concurred in the verdict (cf. 1 Tim. 6:13).

23:16 I will...chastise Him. Cf. v. 22. Though Pilate found Him innocent of any wrongdoing, he was prepared to scourge Him merely to pacify the Jews. But even that punishment, severe as it was (*see note on Matt. 27:26*), could not quench their thirst for His blood.

23:17 it was necessary. I.e., because it was a longstanding Jewish custom (John 18:39), traditionally honored by the Romans.

23:18 Barabbas. *See note on Mark 15:7.*

20 Pilate, therefore, wishing to release Jesus, again called out to them. 21 But they
shouted, saying, "Crucify *Him,* crucify
Him!"
22 Then he said to them the third time,
"Why, what evil has He done? I have
found no reason for death in Him. I will
therefore chastise Him and let *Him* go."
23 But they were insistent, demanding
with loud voices that He be crucified. And
the voices of these men [6]and of the chief
priests prevailed. 24 So [v]Pilate gave sentence that it should be as they requested.
25 [w]And he released [7]to them the one they
requested, who for rebellion and murder
had been thrown into prison; but he delivered Jesus to their will.

Christ Is Crucified
Matt. 27:31-56; Mark 15:20-41; John 19:16-30

26 [x]Now as they led Him away, they laid
hold of a certain man, Simon a Cyrenian,
who was coming from the country, and on
him they laid the cross that he might bear
it after Jesus.
27 And a great multitude of the people
followed Him, and women who also
mourned and lamented Him. 28 But Jesus,
turning to them, said, "Daughters of Jerusalem, do not weep for Me, but weep for
yourselves and for your children. 29 [y]For
indeed the days are coming in which they
will say, 'Blessed *are* the barren, wombs
that never bore, and breasts which never
nursed!' 30 Then they will begin [z]'*to say to
the mountains, "Fall on us!" and to the
hills, "Cover us!"*' 31 [a]For if they do these
things in the green wood, what will be
done in the dry?"
32 [b]There were also two others, criminals, led with Him to be put to death.
33 And [c]when they had come to the place
called Calvary, there they crucified Him,
and the criminals, one on the right hand
and the other on the left. 34 [8]Then Jesus
said, "Father, [d]forgive them, for [e]they do
not know what they do."
And [f]they divided His garments and
cast lots. 35 And [g]the people stood looking
on. But even the [h]rulers with them
sneered, saying, "He saved others; let Him
save Himself if He is the Christ, the chosen
of God."
36 The soldiers also mocked Him, coming and offering Him [i]sour wine, 37 and
saying, "If You are the King of the Jews,
save Yourself."
38 [j]And an inscription also was [9]written
over Him in letters of Greek, Latin, and
Hebrew:

THIS IS THE KING OF THE JEWS.

39 [k]Then one of the criminals who were

23 [6]NU omits *and of the chief priests*
24 [v]Matt. 27:26; Mark 15:15; John 19:16
25 [w]Is. 53:8 [7]NU, M omit *to them*
26 [x]Matt. 27:32; Mark 15:21; John 19:17
29 [y]Matt. 24:19; Luke 21:23
30 [z]Is. 2:19; Hos. 10:8; Rev. 6:16, 17; 9:6
31 [a][Prov. 11:31; Jer. 25:29]; Ezek. 20:47; 21:3, 4; 1 Pet. 4:17
32 [b]Is. 53:9, 12; Matt. 27:38; Mark 15:27; John 19:18
33 [c]Ps. 22:16-18; Matt. 27:33-44; Mark 15:22-32; John 19:17-24
34 [d]Ps. 109:4; [Matt. 5:44]; Acts 7:60; 1 Cor. 4:12 [e]Acts 3:17 [f]Ps. 22:18; Matt. 27:35; Mark 15:24; John 19:23 [8]NU brackets the first sentence as a later addition.
35 [g]Ps. 22:17; [Zech. 12:10] [h]Ps. 22:8; Matt. 27:39; Mark 15:29
36 [i]Ps. 69:21
38 [j]Matt. 27:37; Mark 15:26; John 19:19 [9]NU omits *written* and *in letters of Greek, Latin, and Hebrew*
39 [k]Matt. 27:44; Mark 15:32

23:21 Crucify *Him*. Crucifixion was the most painful and disgraceful form of execution the Romans employed. *See note on Matt. 27:31.*

23:22 the third time. Pilate repeatedly gave powerful testimony to the innocence of Christ (vv. 4,14,15). In doing so, he not only condemned the Jews, who demanded Jesus' death, but also himself, because he handed the Savior over without cause.

23:24 Pilate gave sentence. Pilate's response reveals his lack of principle. His desire to please the Jews for political reasons (to save himself from Rome's displeasure) ultimately overcame his desire to set Jesus free (cf. v. 20). John 8:39–19:16 gives a much more detailed account of Pilate's decision to hand Jesus over.

23:26 Simon a Cyrenian. All 3 synoptic gospels mention Simon. *See notes on Matt. 27:32; Mark 15:21.*

23:28 Daughters of Jerusalem. There is nothing to suggest that these women were Christ's disciples. They may have been professional mourners, obligatory at Jewish funerals (*see note on Matt. 9:23*), and probably present at high-profile executions as well. **weep for yourselves.** Christ's reply to them was a prophetic warning. Only Luke recorded this incident.

23:29 Blessed *are* the barren. I.e., a time is coming when those who have no children to mourn will be considered blessed.

23:30 *to say.* Quoted from Hos. 10:8. Cf. Rev. 6:16,17; 9:6.

23:31 green wood...dry. This was probably a common proverb. Jesus' meaning seems to be this: If the Romans would perpetrate such atrocities on Jesus (the "green wood"—young, strong, and a source of life), what would they do to the Jewish nation (the "dry wood"—old, barren, and ripe for judgment)?

23:32 two others, criminals. *See notes on Matt. 27:38; Mark 15:27.*

23:33 Calvary. The Latin equivalent of *Golgotha. See notes on Matt. 27:33; Mark 15:22.* **crucified.** *See note on Matt. 27:31.*

23:34 forgive them. I.e., His tormentors, both Jews and Romans (cf. Acts 7:60). Some of the fruit of this prayer can be in the salvation of thousands of people in Jerusalem at Pentecost (Acts 2:41). **they do not know what they do.** I.e., they were not aware of the full scope of their wickedness. They did not recognize Him as the true Messiah (Acts 13:27,28). They were blind to the light of divine truth, "For if they had understood it, they would not have crucified the Lord of glory" (1 Cor. 2:8). Still, their ignorance certainly did not mean that they deserved forgiveness; rather, their spiritual blindness itself was a manifestation of their guilt (John 3:19). But Christ's prayer while they were in the very act of mocking Him is an expression of the boundless compassion of divine grace. **cast lots.** *See notes on Matt. 27:35; Mark 15:24.*

23:35 sneered. Cf. Ps. 22:6,7,16-18.

22:36 sour wine. Cf. Ps. 69:21; *see note on Matt. 27:34.*

23:38 an inscription. All 4 gospel writers mentioned the inscription, but each reported a slightly different variation. Both Luke and John (19:20) said that the inscription was written in Greek, Latin, and Hebrew, so the varying reports in the gospels may simply reflect variant ways the inscription was translated on the placard itself. It is even more likely that all 4 evangelists simply reported the substance of the inscription elliptically, with each one omitting different parts of the full inscription. All 4 concurred with Mark that the inscription said THE KING OF THE JEWS (Matt. 27:37; Mark 15:26; John 19:19). Luke added "THIS IS" at the beginning, and Matthew started with "THIS IS JESUS." John's version began, "JESUS OF NAZARETH." Putting them all together, the full inscription would read "THIS IS JESUS OF NAZARETH, THE KING OF THE JEWS."

23:39 one of the criminals. Matthew 27:44 and Mark 15:32 report that both criminals were mocking Christ along with the crowd.

hanged blasphemed Him, saying, [1]"If You
are the Christ, save Yourself and us."
40 But the other, answering, rebuked
him, saying, "Do you not even fear God,
seeing you are under the same condemnation? 41 And we indeed justly, for we receive the due reward of our deeds; but this
Man has done [l]nothing wrong." 42 Then he
said [2]to Jesus, "Lord, remember me when
You come into Your kingdom."
43 And Jesus said to him, "Assuredly, I
say to you, today you will be with Me in
[m]Paradise."
44 [n]Now it [3]was about the sixth hour,
and there was darkness over all the earth
until the ninth hour. 45 Then the sun was
[4]darkened, and [o]the veil of the temple was
torn in [5]two. 46 And when Jesus had cried
out with a loud voice, He said, "Father,
[p]*'into Your hands I commit My spirit.'* "
[q]Having said this, He breathed His last.
47 [r]So when the centurion saw what had
happened, he glorified God, saying, "Certainly this was a righteous Man!"
48 And the whole crowd who came together to that sight, seeing what had been
done, beat their breasts and returned.
49 [s]But all His acquaintances, and the
women who followed Him from Galilee,
stood at a distance, watching these things.

Christ Is Buried

Matt. 27:57-61; Mark 15:42-47; John 19:38-42

50 [t]Now behold, *there was* a man named
Joseph, a council member, a good and just
man. 51 He had not consented to their decision and deed. *He was* from Arimathea, a
city of the Jews, [u]who[6] himself was also
waiting for the kingdom of God. 52 This
man went to Pilate and asked for the body
of Jesus. 53 [v]Then he took it down,
wrapped it in linen, and laid it in a tomb
that was hewn out of the rock, where no
one had ever lain before. 54 That day was
[w]the Preparation, and the Sabbath drew
near.
55 And the women [x]who had come with
Him from Galilee followed after, and [y]they
observed the tomb and how His body was
laid.

In the Grave

56 Then they returned and [z]prepared
spices and fragrant oils. And they rested

39 [1] NU *Are You not the Christ? Save* 41 [l] [2 Cor. 5:21; Heb. 7:26; 1 Pet. 2:21-24] 42 [2] NU *"Jesus, remember me* 43 [m] [2 Cor. 12:4; Eph. 4:8-10; Rev. 2:7] 44 [n] Amos 8:9; Matt. 27:45-56; Mark 15:33-41 [3] NU adds *already* 45 [o] Ex. 26:31-33; Zech. 11:10; Matt. 27:51; Mark 15:38; [Heb. 9:3; 10:19, 20] [4] NU *obscured* [5] *the middle* 46 [p] Ps. 31:5; 1 Pet. 2:23 [q] Dan. 9:26; Zech. 11:10, 11; Matt. 27:50; Mark 15:37; Luke 9:22; 18:33; John 19:30 47 [r] Matt. 27:54; Mark 15:39 49 [s] Ps. 38:11; Matt. 27:55; Mark 15:40; John 16:20-22; 19:25 50 [t] Matt. 27:57-61; Mark 15:42-47; John 19:38-42 51 [u] Mark 15:43; Luke 2:25, 38 [6] NU *who was waiting*

53 [v] Is. 53:9; Matt. 27:59; Mark 15:46 54 [w] Matt. 27:62; Mark 15:42 55 [x] Luke 8:2 [y] Mark 15:47 56 [z] Mark 16:1; Luke 24:1

As the hours wore on, however, this criminal's conscience was smitten, and he repented. When the impenitent thief resumed his mocking (v. 39), this thief rebuked him and refused to participate again.

23:41 this Man has done nothing wrong. Cf. vv. 4,15,22. Even the thief testified of His innocence.

23:42 Lord, remember me. The penitent thief's prayer reflected his belief that the soul lives on after death; that Christ had a right to rule over a kingdom of the souls of men; and that He would soon enter that kingdom despite His impending death. His request to be remembered was a plea for mercy, which also reveals that the thief understood he had no hope but divine grace, and that the dispensing of that grace lay in Jesus' power. All of this demonstrates true faith on the part of the dying thief, and Christ graciously affirmed the man's salvation (v. 43).

23:43 Paradise. The only other places this word is used in the NT are 2 Cor. 12:4 and Rev. 2:7. The word suggests a garden (it is the word used of Eden in the LXX), but in all 3 NT uses it speaks of heaven.

23:44 sixth hour...until the ninth hour. From noon to 3:00 p.m. Luke was using the Jewish method of reckoning time. *See notes on Matt. 27:45; Mark 15:25.* **darkness.** *See note on Mark 15:33.* This could not have been caused by an eclipse, because the Jews used a lunar calendar, and Passover always fell on the full moon, making a solar eclipse out of the question. This was a supernatural darkness.

23:45 the veil. *See note on Matt. 27:51.*

23:46 *into Your hands.* This quotes Ps. 31:5, and the manner of His death accords with John 10:18. Normally victims of crucifixion died much slower deaths. He, being in control, simply yielded up His soul (John 10:18; 19:30), committing it to God. Thus He "offered Himself without spot to God" (Heb. 9:14).

23:47 the centurion. *See note on Matt. 27:54.* **a righteous Man.** Matthew 27:54 and Mark 15:39 say the centurion stated, "This [man] was the Son of God." Luke may be giving an equivalent expression; or, more likely, the centurion said both things.

23:48 beat their breasts. Luke alone records this expression of remorse and anguish (cf. 18:13).

23:49 the women...from Galilee. Matthew 27:56 and Mark 15:40,41 (*see notes there*) report that this included Mary Magdalene (*see note on 8:2*); Mary, mother of James (the less) and Joses; Salome, mother of James and John, and many others. The same women were present at His burial (v. 55; Matt. 27:61; Mark 15:47) and His resurrection (24:1; Matt. 28:1; Mark 16:1)—so they were eyewitnesses to all the crucial events of the gospel (cf. 1 Cor. 15:3,4).

23:50 Joseph. *See notes on Matt. 27:57; Mark 15:43; John 19:38.* All 4 evangelists mentioned him; Mark and Luke identified him as a member of the Sanhedrin; only Luke noted that he dissented from the council's verdict against Jesus (v. 51).

23:51 waiting for the kingdom of God. I.e., he believed Jesus' claims. John 19:38 refers to him as a secret disciple.

23:53 a tomb...hewn out of the rock. Joseph, a wealthy man, undoubtedly had the tomb built for his own family. It had remained unused. Christ's burial there was a wonderful fulfillment of Is. 53:9.

23:54 the Preparation. I.e., Friday, the day before the Sabbath.

23:55 observed...how His body was laid. According to John 19:39, Nicodemus brought a hundred pounds of spices and aloes (probably obtained while Joseph was negotiating with Pilate for Jesus' body), and he and Joseph wrapped the body with linen and the spices. These women, from Galilee, were probably unfamiliar with Joseph and Nicodemus, who were Judeans. After all, both men were associated with the Jewish leaders who orchestrated the conspiracy against Jesus (v. 50; John 3:1). So the women were determined to prepare Jesus' body for burial themselves. So they returned (i.e., went to their homes) to prepare their own spices and perfumes (v. 56). They had to have Jesus' body placed in the tomb before sunset, when the Sabbath began, so they were not able to finish preparing the body. Mark 16:1 says they purchased more spices "when the Sabbath was past," i.e., after sundown Saturday. Then they returned Sunday morning with the spices (24:1), expecting to finish the task that had been interrupted by the Sabbath.

on the Sabbath [a]according to the commandment.

The Resurrection
Matt. 28:1-8; Mark 16:1-8; John 20:1-10

24 Now [a]on the first *day* of the week,
very early in the morning, they, [1]and
certain *other women* with them, came to the
tomb [b]bringing the spices which they had
prepared. 2 [c]But they found the stone rolled
away from the tomb. 3 [d]Then they went in
and did not find the body of the Lord Jesus.
4 And it happened, as they were [2]greatly
perplexed about this, that [e]behold, two men
stood by them in shining garments. 5 Then,
as they were afraid and bowed *their* faces to
the earth, they said to them, "Why do you
seek the living among the dead? 6 He is not
here, but is risen! [f]Remember how He
spoke to you when He was still in Galilee,
7 saying, 'The Son of Man must be [g]deliv-
ered into the hands of sinful men, and be
crucified, and the third day rise again.' "
8 And [h]they remembered His words.
9 [i]Then they returned from the tomb and
told all these things to the eleven and to all
the rest. 10 It was Mary Magdalene, [j]Jo-
anna, Mary *the mother* of James, and the
other *women* with them, who told these
things to the apostles. 11 [k]And their words
seemed to them like [3]idle tales, and they
did not believe them. 12 [l]But Peter arose
and ran to the tomb; and stooping down,
he saw the linen cloths [4]lying by themselves; and he departed, marveling to himself at what had happened.

Christ Appears on the Road to Emmaus
Mark 16:12, 13

13 [m]Now behold, two of them were traveling that same day to a village called Emmaus, which was [5]seven miles from Jerusalem. 14 And they talked together of all
these things which had happened. 15 So it
was, while they conversed and reasoned,
that [n]Jesus Himself drew near and went
with them. 16 But [o]their eyes were restrained, so that they did not know Him.
17 And He said to them, "What kind of
conversation *is* this that you have with one
another as you [6]walk and are sad?"
18 Then the one [p]whose name was Cleopas answered and said to Him, "Are You
the only stranger in Jerusalem, and have
You not known the things which happened
there in these days?"
19 And He said to them, "What things?"
So they said to Him, "The things concerning Jesus of Nazareth, [q]who was a
Prophet [r]mighty in deed and word before
God and all the people, 20 [s]and how the
chief priests and our rulers delivered Him
to be condemned to death, and crucified
Him. 21 But we were hoping [t]that it was
He who was going to redeem Israel. Indeed, besides all this, today is the third day

56 [a]Ex. 20:10; Deut. 5:14

CHAPTER 24

1 [a]Matt. 28:1-8; Mark 16:1-8; John 20:1-8 [b]Luke 23:56 [1]NU omits *and certain other women with them*
2 [c]Matt. 28:2; Mark 16:4
3 [d]Mark 16:5
4 [e]John 20:12; Acts 1:10 [2]NU omits *greatly*
6 [f]Matt. 16:21; Mark 8:31; Luke 9:22
7 [g]Hos. 6:1, 2; Luke 9:44; 11:29, 30; 18:31-33
8 [h]Luke 9:22, 44; John 2:19-22
9 [i]Matt. 28:8; Mark 16:10
10 [j]Luke 8:3
11 [k]Luke 24:25 [3]*nonsense*
12 [l]John 20:3-6 [4]NU omits *lying*
13 [m]Mark 16:12 [5]Lit. *60 stadia*
15 [n][Matt. 18:20]
16 [o]John 20:14; 21:4
17 [6]NU *walk? And they stood still, looking sad.*
18 [p]John 19:25
19 [q]Matt. 21:11; Luke 7:16; John 3:2; Acts 2:22 [r]Acts 7:22
20 [s]Luke 23:1; Acts 13:27, 28
21 [t]Luke 1:68; 2:38; [Acts 1:6]

24:1 bringing the spices. *See note on 23:55.* The women were not expecting to find Jesus risen from the dead; their only plan was to finish anointing His body for burial. *See note on Mark 16:1.*

24:2 the stone rolled away. Matthew 28:2-4 records that an earthquake occurred and an angel rolled the stone away. The Roman guards fainted with fear. Mark, Luke, and John make no mention of the guards, so it appears they fled when they awoke to find the empty tomb. The women must have arrived shortly after.

24:4 two men. These were angels. Only Luke mentioned them both (*see note on Mark 16:5*). Mark was concerned only with the one who spoke for the duo. Such minor differences in the gospel accounts are all reconcilable. Here's a summary of the events of the resurrection, assembled from all 4 evangelists' accounts: Finding the stone rolled away, the women entered the tomb, but found it empty (v. 3). While they were still in the tomb, the angels suddenly appeared (v. 4; Mark 16:5). The angel who spoke reminded them of Jesus' promises (vv. 6-8), then sent them to find Peter and the disciples to report that Jesus was risen (Matt. 28:7,8; Mark 16:7,8). The women did as they were told (vv. 9-11). The disciples were skeptical at first (v. 11), but ran to where the tomb was, John arriving first (John 20:4), but Peter actually entering the tomb first (John 20:6). They saw the linen wrappings intact but empty, proof that Jesus was risen (v. 12; John 20:6-8). They left immediately (v. 12; John 20:10). Meanwhile, Mary Magdalene returned to the tomb, and was standing outside weeping when Christ suddenly appeared to her (John 20:11-18). That was His first appearance (Mark 16:9). Sometime soon after that, He met the other women on the road and appeared to them as well (Matt. 28:9,10). Later that day he appeared to two of the disciples on the road to Emmaus (vv. 13-32), and to Peter (v. 34). For a chronological listing of all His post-resurrection appearances, *see note on v. 34.*

24:6 how He spoke to you...in Galilee. *See notes on 9:22; 18:31-33.*

24:9 all the rest. I.e., other disciples, mostly from Galilee, who were in Jerusalem for the Passover.

24:10 Mary Magdalene. *See note on 8:2.* She was the first to see Jesus alive (Mark 16:9; John 20:11-18). *See note on v. 4.* **Joanna.** Her husband was Herod's steward. *See note on 8:3.* **Mary *the mother* of James.** *See note on Matt. 27:56.* **the other *women*.** They are never explicitly identified (cf. 23:49,55).

24:11 idle tales. I.e., nonsense.

24:12 Peter...ran. John ran with Peter, but reached the tomb first (John 20:4). **linen cloths.** I.e., the empty shell of wrappings that had contained the body.

24:13 two of them. These evidently were not any of the 11 disciples. According to v. 18, one was named Cleopas. **Emmaus.** Mentioned nowhere else in Scripture. Its exact location is not known, but tradition says it is a town known as Kubeibeh, 7 mi. NW of Jerusalem.

24:16 their eyes were restrained. I.e., they were kept by God from recognizing him.

24:18 Are You the only stranger in Jerusalem. The crucifixion of Jesus was already such a well known event around Jerusalem that they were shocked that He seemed not to know about it.

24:21 But we were hoping. They had been looking for an immediate earthly kingdom. With Jesus crucified, they were probably struggling with doubt about whether He was the Messiah who would reign. But they still regarded Him as a true prophet (v. 19). **the third day.**

since these things happened. 22 Yes, and
[u]certain women of our company, who arrived at the tomb early, astonished us.
23 When they did not find His body, they
came saying that they had also seen a vision of angels who said He was alive.
24 And [v]certain of those *who were* with us
went to the tomb and found *it* just as the
women had said; but Him they did not
see."

25 Then He said to them, "O foolish
ones, and slow of heart to believe in all that
the prophets have spoken! 26 [w]Ought not
the Christ to have suffered these things
and to enter into His [x]glory?" 27 And beginning at [y]Moses and [z]all the Prophets,
He [7]expounded to them in all the Scriptures the things concerning Himself.

28 Then they drew near to the village
where they were going, and [a]He [8]indi-
cated that He would have gone farther.
29 But [b]they constrained Him, saying,
[c]"Abide with us, for it is toward evening,
and the day is far spent." And He went in
to stay with them.

30 Now it came to pass, as [d]He sat at the
table with them, that He took bread,
blessed and broke *it*, and gave it to them.
31 Then their eyes were opened and they

22 [u] Matt. 28:8; Mark 16:10; Luke 24:9, 10
24 [v] Luke 24:12
26 [w] Acts 17:2, 3; [Heb. 2:9, 10] [x] [1 Pet. 1:10-12]
27 [y] [Gen. 3:15; 12:3; Num. 21:9; Deut. 18:15]; John 5:46 [z] [Ps. 16:9, 10; 22; 132:11; Is. 7:14; 9:6; Jer. 23:5; 33:14, 15; Ezek. 34:23; 37:25; Dan. 9:24]; Mic. 7:20; [Mal. 3:1; 4:2]; John 1:45; 5:39; [Rom. 1:1-6] [7] *explained*
28 [a] Gen. 32:26; 42:7; Mark 6:48 [8] *acted as if*
29 [b] Gen. 19:2, 3; Acts 16:15 [c] [John 14:23]
30 [d] Matt. 14:19; Mark 8:6; Luke 9:16
34 [e] 1 Cor. 15:5
35 [9] *recognized*
36 [f] Mark 16:14; John 20:19; 1 Cor. 15:5
37 [g] Matt. 14:26; Mark 6:49
39 [h] John 20:20, 27; 1 John 1:1 [i] [1 Cor. 15:50]
40 [1] Some printed New Testaments omit v. 40. It is found in nearly all Gr. mss.

knew Him; and He vanished from their
sight.

32 And they said to one another, "Did
not our heart burn within us while He
talked with us on the road, and while He
opened the Scriptures to us?"

The Proof of His Resurrection
Mark 16:4; John 20:19-23; 1 Cor. 15:5

33 So they rose up that very hour and returned to Jerusalem, and found the eleven
and those *who were* with them gathered together, 34 saying, "The Lord is risen indeed, and [e]has appeared to Simon!"
35 And they told about the things *that had
happened* on the road, and how He was
[9]known to them in the breaking of bread.

36 [f]Now as they said these things, Jesus
Himself stood in the midst of them, and
said to them, "Peace to you." 37 But they
were terrified and frightened, and supposed they had seen [g]a spirit. 38 And He
said to them, "Why are you troubled? And
why do doubts arise in your hearts? 39 Behold My hands and My feet, that it is I Myself. [h]Handle Me and see, for a [i]spirit does
not have flesh and bones as you see I
have."

40 [1]When He had said this, He showed

There may have been a glimmer of hope in these words. They had heard rumors of His resurrection already (vv. 22-24). Perhaps Cleopas recalled the Lord's promises of 9:22; 18:33. More likely, however, it seems this was his way of expressing surprise that this Stranger did not yet know the news everyone else in Jerusalem had been discussing for the past 3 days.

24:24 certain of those *who were* with us. I.e., Peter and John (*see note on v. 12*). **but Him they did not see.** This was true. Evidently Cleopas and his companion had not heard about the appearance to Mary Magdalene (*see note on v. 4*).

24:26 Ought not. I.e., "Was it not necessary?" OT prophesies spoke often of a suffering servant of Jehovah (*see note on v. 27*).

24:27 Moses and all the Prophets. Verse 44 gives the 3-fold division; this expression is merely a shortened way to say the same thing. **in all the Scriptures.** In the inscrutable wisdom of divine providence, the substance of Christ's exposition of the OT messianic prophecies was not recorded. But the gist of what He expounded would have undoubtedly included an explanation of the OT sacrificial system, which was full of types and symbols that spoke of His sufferings and death. He also would have pointed them to the major prophetic passages which spoke of the crucifixion, such as Pss. 16:9-11; 22; 69; Is. 52:14–53:12; Zech. 12:10; 13:7. And He would have pointed out the true meaning of passages like Gen. 3:15; Num. 21:6-9; Ps. 16:10; Jer. 23:5,6; Dan. 9:26—and a host of other key messianic prophecies, particularly those that spoke of His death and resurrection.

24:30 took bread. A simple expression, meaning to share a meal (v. 35).

24:31 their eyes were opened. I.e., by God. They had been sovereignly kept from recognizing Him until this point (cf. v. 16). His resurrection body was glorified, and altered from its previous appearance (see John's description in Rev. 1:13-16), and this surely explains why even Mary did not recognize Him at first (cf. John 20:14-16). But in this case, God actively intervened to keep them from recognizing Him until it was time for Him to depart. **He vanished from their sight.** His resurrection body, though real and tangible (John 20:27)—and even capable of ingesting earthly food (vv. 42,43)—nonetheless possessed certain properties that indicate it was glorified, altered in a mysterious way (cf. 1 Cor. 15:35-54; Phil. 3:21). Christ could appear and disappear bodily, as seen in this text. His body could pass through solid objects—such as the grave clothes (*see note on v. 12*), or the walls and doors of a closed room (John 20:19,26). He could apparently travel great distances in a moment, for by the time these disciples returned to Jerusalem, Christ had already appeared to Peter (v. 34). The fact that He ascended into heaven bodily demonstrated that His resurrection body was already fit for heaven. Yet it was His body, the same one that was missing from the tomb, even retaining identifying features such as the nail-wounds (John 20:25-27). He was no ghost or phantom.

24:34 appeared to Simon. Cf. 1 Cor. 15:5-8. Scripture describes at least 10 distinct appearances of Christ between the resurrection and ascension. He appeared to: 1) Mary Magdalene at the tomb (Mark 16:9; John 20:11-18); 2) to the women on the road (Matt. 28:9,10); 3) to the disciples on the road to Emmaus (vv. 13-32); 4) to Peter (v. 34); 5) to 10 of the 11 disciples, Thomas being absent (vv. 36-43; Mark 16:14; John 20:19-25); 6) to the 11 disciples (with Thomas present) 8 days later (John 20:26-31); 7) to 7 disciples by the shore of the Sea of Galilee (John 21:1-25); 8) to more than 500 disciples, probably on a mountain in Galilee (1 Cor. 15:6; *see note on Matt. 28:16*); 9) to James (1 Cor. 15:7); and 10) to the apostles when He ascended into heaven (Acts 1:3-11). After His ascension, He appeared to Paul (1 Cor. 15:8). The next time He appears it will be in glory (Matt. 24:30).

24:36 Jesus Himself stood in the midst of them. The doors were closed and locked (John 20:19). *See note on v. 31.*

24:39 Behold My hands and My feet. He was showing them the nail wounds to prove it was really Him. Cf. John 20:27.

them His hands and His feet. 41 But while
they still did not believe [j]for joy, and marveled, He said to them, [k]"Have you any
food here?" 42 So they gave Him a piece of
a broiled fish [2]and some honeycomb.
43 [l]And He took *it* and ate in their presence.

The Great Commission—Acts 1:3-8

44 Then He said to them, [m]"These *are* the
words which I spoke to you while I was
still with you, that all things must be fulfilled which were written in the Law of
Moses and *the* Prophets and *the* Psalms
concerning Me." 45 And [n]He opened their
understanding, that they might comprehend the Scriptures.

46 Then He said to them, [o]"Thus it is written, [3]and thus it was necessary for the Christ
to suffer and to rise from the dead the third
day, 47 and that repentance and [p]remission
of sins should be preached in His name [q]to
all nations, beginning at Jerusalem. 48 And
[r]you are witnesses of these things.

The Ascension—Mark 16:19; Acts 1:9

49 [s]Behold, I send the Promise of My Father upon you; but tarry in the city [4]of Jerusalem until you are endued with power
from on high."

50 And He led them out [t]as far as Bethany, and He lifted up His hands and blessed
them. 51 [u]Now it came to pass, while He
blessed them, that He was parted from
them and carried up into heaven. 52 [v]And
they worshiped Him, and returned to Jerusalem with great joy, 53 and were continually [w]in the temple [5]praising and blessing
God. [6]Amen.

41 [j]Gen. 45:26 [k]John 21:5
42 [2]NU omits *and some honeycomb*
43 [l]Acts 10:39-41
44 [m]Matt. 16:21; 17:22; 20:18; Mark 8:31; Luke 9:22; 18:31
45 [n]Acts 16:14; 1 John 5:20
46 [o]Ps. 22; Hos. 6:2; Luke 11:29, 30; Acts 17:3 [3]NU *that the Christ should suffer and rise*
47 [p]Dan. 9:24; Acts 5:31; 10:43; 13:38; 26:18 [q][Ps. 22:27; Jer. 31:34; Mic. 4:2]
48 [r][Acts 1:8]; 1 Pet. 5:1
49 [s]Is. 44:3; Joel 2:28; Acts 2:4 [4]NU omits *of Jerusalem*
50 [t]Matt. 21:17; Acts 1:12 51 [u]Ps. 68:18; 110:1; Mark 16:19; Acts 1:9-11 52 [v]Matt. 28:9 53 [w]Acts 2:46 [5]NU omits *praising and* [6]NU omits *Amen.*

24:41-43 *See note on v. 31.* Cf. Acts 10:41.

24:44 the Law of Moses and *the* Prophets and *the* Psalms. I.e., the whole OT. *See note on v. 27.*

24:45 opened their understanding. He undoubtedly taught them from the OT, as He had on the road to Emmaus (*see note on v. 27*). But the gist of the expression also seems to convey a supernatural opening of their minds to receive the truths He unfolded. Whereas their understanding was once dull (9:45), they finally saw clearly (cf. Ps. 119:18; Is. 29:18,19; 2 Cor. 3:14-16).

24:46-53 This section contains several ideas that are echoed in the opening of Acts, including Christ's suffering and resurrection (v. 46; Acts 1:3); the message of repentance and remission of sins (v. 47; Acts 2:38); the disciples as His witnesses (v. 48; Acts 1:8); the Promise of the Father (v. 49; Acts 1:4); tarrying in Jerusalem (v. 49; Acts 1:4) and the beginning of gospel outreach there (v. 47; Acts 1:8); power from on high (v. 49; Acts 1:8); Christ's ascension (v. 51; Acts 1:9-11); the disciples' return to Jerusalem (v. 52; Acts 1:12); and their meeting in the temple (v. 53; Acts 2:46).

24:46 it is written. I.e., in the OT. *See note on v. 27.*

24:47 This was the Great Commission (cf. Matt. 28:19,20; Mark 16:15).

24:49 the Promise of My Father. I.e., the Holy Spirit (John 14:26; 15:26; cf. Joel 2:28,29; Acts 2:1-4).

24:50 Bethany. *See notes on 19:29; Mark 11:1.*

24:51 carried up into heaven. I.e., visibly. Before when the resurrected Christ left them, He simply vanished (v. 31). This time they saw Him ascend. Cf. Acts 1:9-11.

24:52 they worshiped Him. I.e., a formal act of worship. Now that He had opened their understanding (*see note on v. 45*), they perceived the full truth of His deity, unclouded by the darkness of confusion or doubt. Cf. Matt. 28:9; John 20:28; contra. Matt. 28:17.

24:53 in the temple. This became the first meeting-place of the church (Acts 2:46; 5:21,42). There were rooms around the porticoes of the outer court available for such meetings.

The Gospel According to

JOHN

Title

The title of the fourth gospel continues the pattern of the other gospels, being identified originally as "According to John." Like the others, "The Gospel" was added later.

Author and Date

Although the author's name does not appear in the gospel, early church tradition strongly and consistently identified him as the Apostle John. The early church father Irenaeus (ca. A.D. 130–200) was a disciple of Polycarp (ca. A.D. 70–160), who was a disciple of the Apostle John, and he testified on Polycarp's authority that John wrote the gospel during his residence at Ephesus in Asia Minor when he was advanced in age (*Against Heresies* 2.22.5; 3.1.1). Subsequent to Irenaeus, all the church fathers assumed John to be the gospel's author. Clement of Alexandria (ca. A.D. 150–215) wrote that John, aware of the facts set forth in the other gospels and being moved by the Holy Spirit, composed a "spiritual gospel" (see Eusebius' *Ecclesiastical History* 6.14.7).

Reinforcing early church tradition are significant internal characteristics of the gospel. While the synoptic gospels (Matthew, Mark, Luke) identify the Apostle John by name approximately 20 times (including parallels), he is not directly mentioned by name in the Gospel of John. Instead, the author prefers to identify himself as the disciple "whom Jesus loved" (13:23; 19:26; 20:2; 21:7,20). The absence of any mention of John's name directly is remarkable when one considers the important part played by other named disciples in this gospel. Yet, the recurring designation of himself as the disciple "whom Jesus loved," a deliberate avoidance by John of his personal name, reflects his humility and celebrates his relation to his Lord Jesus. No mention of his name was necessary since his original readers clearly understood that he was the gospel's author. Also, through a process of elimination based primarily on analyzing the material in chaps. 20,21, this disciple "whom Jesus loved" narrows down to the Apostle John (e.g., 21:24; cf. 21:2). Since the gospel's author is exacting in mentioning the names of other characters in the book, if the author had been someone other than John the apostle, he would not have omitted John's name.

The gospel's anonymity strongly reinforces the arguments favoring John's authorship, for only someone of his well known and preeminent authority as an apostle would be able to write a gospel that differed so markedly in form and substance from the other gospels and have it receive unanimous acceptance in the early church. In contrast, apocryphal gospels produced from the mid-second century onward were falsely ascribed to apostles or other famous persons closely associated with Jesus, yet universally rejected by the church.

John and James, his older brother (Acts 12:2), were known as "the sons of Zebedee" (Matt. 10:2-4), and Jesus gave them the name "Sons of Thunder" (Mark 3:17). John was an apostle (Luke 6:12-16) and one of the 3 most intimate associates of Jesus (along with Peter and James—cf. Matt. 17:1; 26:37), being an eyewitness to and participant in Jesus' earthly ministry (1 John 1:1-4). After Christ's ascension, John became a "pillar" in the Jerusalem church (Gal. 2:9). He ministered with Peter (Acts 3:1; 4:13; 8:14) until he went to Ephesus (tradition says before the destruction of Jerusalem), from where he wrote this gospel and from where the Romans exiled him to Patmos (Rev. 1:9). Besides the gospel that bears his name, John also authored 1-3 John and the Book of Revelation (Rev. 1:1).

Because the writings of some church fathers indicate that John was actively writing in his old age and that he was already aware of the synoptic gospels, many date the gospel sometime after their composition, but prior to John's writing of 1-3 John or Revelation. John wrote his gospel ca. A.D. 80–90, about 50 years after he witnessed Jesus' earthly ministry.

Background and Setting

Strategic to John's background and setting is the fact that according to tradition John was aware of the synoptic gospels. Apparently, he wrote his gospel in order to make a unique contribution to the record of the Lord's life ("a spiritual gospel") and, in part, to be supplementary as well as complementary to Matthew, Mark, and Luke.

The gospel's unique characteristics reinforce this purpose: First, John supplied a large amount of unique material not recorded in the other gospels. Second, he often supplied information that helps the understanding of the events in the synoptics. For example, while the synoptics begin with Jesus' ministry in Galilee, they imply that Jesus had a ministry prior to that (e.g., Matt. 4:12; Mark 1:14). John supplies the answer with information on Jesus' prior ministry in Judea (chap. 3) and Samaria (chap. 4). In Mark 6:45, after the feeding of the 5,000, Jesus compelled his disciples to cross the Sea of Galilee to Bethsaida. John recorded the reason. The people were about to make Jesus king because of His miraculous multiplying of food, and He was avoiding their ill-motivated efforts (6:26). Third, John is the most theological of the gospels, containing, for example, a heavily theological prologue (1:1-18), larger amounts of didactic and discourse material in proportion to narrative (e.g., 3:13-17), and the largest amount of teaching on the Holy Spirit (e.g., 14:16,17,26; 16:7-14). Although John was aware of the synoptics and fashioned his gospel with them in mind, he did not depend upon them for information. Rather, under the inspiration of the Holy Spirit, he utilized his own memory as an eyewitness in composing the gospel (1:14; 19:35; 21:24).

John's gospel is the only one of the 4 that contains a precise statement regarding the author's purpose (20:30,31). He declares, "these are written that you may believe that Jesus is the Christ, the Son of God, and that believing you may have life in His name" (20:31). The primary purposes, therefore, are two-fold: evangelistic and apologetic. Reinforcing the evangelistic purpose is the fact that the word "believe" occurs approximately 100 times in the gospel (the synoptics use the term less than half as much). John composed his gospel to provide reasons for saving faith in his readers and, as a result, to assure them that they would receive the divine gift of eternal life (1:12).

The apologetic purpose is closely related to the evangelistic purpose. John wrote to convince his readers of Jesus' true identity as the incarnate God-Man whose divine and human natures were perfectly united into one person who was the prophesied Christ ("Messiah") and Savior of the world (e.g., 1:41; 3:16; 4:25,26; 8:58). He organized his whole gospel around 8 "signs" or proofs that reinforce Jesus' true identity leading to faith. The first half of his work centers around 7 miraculous signs selected to reveal Christ's person and engender belief: 1) water made into wine (2:1-11); 2) the healing of the royal official's son (4:46-54); 3) the healing of the lame man (5:1-18); 4) the feeding of multitude (6:1-15); 5) walking on water (6:16-21); 6) healing of the blind man (9:1-41); and 7) the raising of Lazarus (11:1-57). The eighth sign is the miraculous catch of fish (21:6-11) after Jesus' resurrection.

Historical and Theological Themes

In accordance with John's evangelistic and apologetic purposes, the overall message of the gospel is found in 20:31: "Jesus is the Christ, the Son of God." The book, therefore, centers on the person and work of Christ. Three predominant words ("signs," "believe," and "life") in 20:30,31 receive constant reemphasis throughout the gospel to enforce the theme of salvation in Him, which is first set forth in the prologue (1:1-18; cf. 1 John 1:1-4) and re-expressed throughout the gospel in varying ways (e.g., 6:35,48; 8:12; 10:7,9; 10:11-14; 11:25; 14:6; 17:3). In addition, John provides the record of how men responded to Jesus Christ and the salvation that He offered. Summing up, the gospel focuses on: 1) Jesus as the Word, the Messiah, and Son of God; 2) who brings the gift of salvation to mankind; 3) who either accept or reject the offer.

John also presents certain contrastive sub-themes that reinforce his main theme. He uses dualism (life and death, light and darkness, love and hate, from above and from below) to convey vital information about the person and work of Christ and the need to believe in Him (e.g., 1:4,5,12,13; 3:16-21; 12:44-46; 15:17-20).

There are also 7 emphatic "I AM" statements which identify Jesus as God and Messiah (6:35; 8:12; 10:7,9; 10:11,14; 11:25; 14:6; 15:1,5).

Interpretive Challenges

Because John composed his record in a clear and simple style, one might tend to underestimate the depth of this gospel. Since John's gospel is a "spiritual" gospel (see Authorship and Date), the truths he conveys are profound. The reader must prayerfully and meticulously explore the book, in order to discover the vast richness of the spiritual treasures that the apostle, under the guidance of the Holy Spirit (14:26; 16:13), has lovingly deposited in his gospel.

The chronological reckoning between John's gospel and the synoptics presents a challenge, especially in relation to the time of the Last Supper (13:2). While the synoptics portray the disciples and the Lord at the Last Supper as eating the Passover meal on Thursday evening (Nisan 14) and Jesus being crucified on Friday, John's gospel states that the Jews did not enter into the Praetorium "lest they should be defiled, but that they might eat the Passover" (18:28). So, the disciples had eaten the Passover on Thursday evening, but the Jews had not. In fact, John (19:14) states that Jesus' trial and crucifixion were on the day of Preparation for the Passover and not after the eating of the Passover, so that with the trial and crucifixion on Friday Christ was actually sacrificed at the same time the Passover lambs were being slain (19:14). The question is, "Why did the disciples eat the Passover meal on Thursday?"

The answer lies in a difference among the Jews in the way they reckoned the beginning and ending of days. From Josephus, the Mishna, and other ancient Jewish sources we learn that the Jews in northern Palestine calculated days from sunrise to sunrise. That area included the region of Galilee, where Jesus and all the disciples, except Judas, had grown up. Apparently most, if not all, of the Pharisees used that system of reckoning. But Jews in the southern part, which centered in Jerusalem, calculated days from sunset to sunset. Because all the priests necessarily lived in or near Jerusalem, as did most of the Sadducees, those groups followed the southern scheme.

That variation doubtlessly caused confusion at times, but it also had some practical benefits. During Passover time, for instance, it allowed for the feast to be celebrated legitimately on two adjoining days, thereby permitting the temple sacrifices to be made over a total period of four hours rather than two. That separation of days may also have had the effect of reducing both regional and religious clashes between the two groups.

On that basis the seeming contradictions in the gospel accounts are easily explained. Being Galileans, Jesus and the disciples considered Passover day to have started at sunrise on Thursday and to end at sunrise on Friday. The Jewish leaders who arrested and tried Jesus, being mostly priests and Sadducees, considered Passover day to begin at sunset on Thursday and end at sunset on Friday. By that variation, predetermined by God's sovereign provision, Jesus could thereby legitimately celebrate the last Passover meal with His disciples and yet still be sacrificed on Passover day.

Once again one can see how God sovereignly and marvelously provides for the precise fulfillment of His redemptive plan. Jesus was anything but a victim of men's wicked schemes, much less of blind circumstance. Every word He spoke and every action He took were divinely directed and secured. Even the words and actions by others against Him were divinely controlled. See, e.g., 11:49-52; 19:11.

Outline

I. The Incarnation of the Son of God (1:1-18)
   A. His Eternality (1:1,2)
   B. His Pre-incarnate Work (1:3-5)
   C. His Forerunner (1:6-8)
   D. His Rejection (1:9-11)
   E. His Reception (1:12,13)
   F. His Deity (1:14-18)
II. The Presentation of the Son of God (1:19–4:54)
   A. Presentation by John the Baptist (1:19-34)
      1. To the religious leaders (1:19-28)
      2. At Christ's baptism (1:29-34)
   B. Presentation to John's Disciples (1:35-51)
      1. Andrew and Peter (1:35-42)
      2. Philip and Nathanael (1:43-51)
   C. Presentation in Galilee (2:1-12)
      1. First sign: water to wine (2:1-10)
      2. Disciples believe (2:11,12)
   D. Presentation in Judea (2:13–3:36)
      1. Cleansing the temple (2:13-25)
      2. Teaching Nicodemus (3:1-21)
      3. Preaching by John the Baptist (3:22-36)
   E. Presentation in Samaria (4:1-42)
      1. Witness to the Samaritan woman (4:1-26)
      2. Witness to the disciples (4:27-38)
      3. Witness to the Samaritans (4:39-42)

F. Presentation in Galilee (4:43-54)
  1. Reception by the Galileans (4:43-45)
  2. Second sign: healing the nobleman's son (4:46-54)

III. The Opposition to the Son of God (5:1–12:50)
  A. Opposition at the Feast in Jerusalem (5:1-47)
    1. Third sign: healing the paralytic (5:1-9)
    2. Rejection by the Jews (5:10-47)
  B. Opposition During Passover (6:1-71)
    1. Fourth sign: feeding the 5,000 (6:1-14)
    2. Fifth sign: walking on water (6:15-21)
    3. Bread of Life discourse (6:22-71)
  C. Opposition at the Feast of Tabernacles (7:1–10:21)
  D. Opposition at the Feast of Dedication (10:22-42)
  E. Opposition at Bethany (11:1–12:11)
    1. Seventh sign: raising of Lazarus (11:1-44)
    2. Pharisees plot to kill Christ (11:45-57)
    3. Mary anointing Christ (12:1-11)
  F. Opposition in Jerusalem (12:12-50)
    1. The triumphal entry (12:12-22)
    2. The discourse on faith and rejection (12:23-50)

IV. The Preparation of the Disciples by the Son of God (13:1–17:26)
  A. In the Upper Room (13:1–14:31)
    1. Washing feet (13:1-20)
    2. Announcing the betrayal (13:21-30)
    3. Discourse on Christ's departure (13:31–14:31)
  B. On the Way to the Garden (15:1–17:26)
    1. Instructing the disciples (15:1–16:33)
    2. Interceding with the Father (17:1-26)

V. The Execution of the Son of God (18:1–19:37)
  A. The Rejection of Christ (18:1–19:16)
    1. His arrest (18:1-11)
    2. His trials (18:12–19:16)
  B. The Crucifixion of Christ (19:17-37)

VI. The Resurrection of the Son of God (19:38–21:23)
  A. The Burial of Christ (19:38-42)
  B. The Resurrection of Christ (20:1-10)
  C. The Appearances of Christ (20:11–21:23)
    1. To Mary Magdalene (20:11-18)
    2. To the disciples without Thomas (20:19-25)
    3. To the disciples with Thomas (20:26-29)
    4. Statement of purpose for the Gospel (20:30,31)
    5. To the disciples (21:1-14)
    6. To Peter (21:15-23)

VII. Conclusion (21:24,25)

The Deity of Christ

1 In the beginning [a]was the Word, and
the [b]Word was [c]with God, and the
Word was [d]God. 2 [e]He was in the beginning with God.

The Preincarnate Work of Christ

3 [f]All things were made through Him, and
without Him nothing was made that was
made. 4 [g]In Him was life, and [h]the life was
the light of men. 5 And [i]the light shines in
the darkness, and the darkness did not
[1]comprehend it.

The Forerunner of Christ

6 There was a [j]man sent from God,
whose name *was* John. 7 This man came for
a [k]witness, to bear witness of the Light,

CHAPTER 1

1 [a] Gen. 1:1; [Col. 1:17]; 1 John 1:1 [b] [John 1:14]; Rev. 19:13 [c] [John 17:5; 1 John 1:2] [d] [1 John 5:20]
2 [e] Gen. 1:1
3 [f] Ps. 33:6; [Eph. 3:9; Col. 1:16, 17; Heb. 1:2]
4 [g] [1 John 5:11] [h] John 8:12; 9:5; 12:46
5 [i] [John 3:19] [1] Or *overcome* 6 [j] Mal. 3:1; Matt. 3:1-17; Mark 1:1-11; Luke 3:1-22 7 [k] John 3:25-36; 5:33-35

1:1-18 These verses constitute the prologue which introduces many of the major themes that John will treat, especially the main theme that "Jesus is the Christ, the Son of God" (vv. 12-14,18; cf. 20:31). Several key words repeated throughout the gospel (e.g., life, light, witness, glory) appear here. The remainder of the gospel develops the theme of the prologue as to how the eternal "Word" of God, Jesus the Messiah and Son of God, became flesh and ministered among men so that all who believe in Him would be saved. Although John wrote the prologue with the simplest vocabulary in the NT, the truths which the prologue conveys are the most profound. Six basic truths about Christ as the Son of God are featured in the prologue: 1) the eternal Christ (vv. 1-3); 2) the incarnate Christ (vv. 4,5); 3) the forerunner of Christ (vv. 6-8); 4) the unrecognized Christ (vv. 9-11); 5) the omnipotent Christ (vv. 12,13); and 6) the glorious Christ (vv. 14-18).

1:1 In the beginning. In contrast to 1 John 1:1 where John used a similar phrase ("from the beginning") to refer to the starting point of Jesus' ministry and gospel preaching, this phrase parallels Gen. 1:1 where the same phrase is used. John used the phrase in an absolute sense to refer to the beginning of the time-space-material universe. **was.** The verb highlights the eternal pre-existence of the Word, i.e., Jesus Christ. Before the universe began, the Second Person of the Trinity always existed; i.e., He always was (cf. 8:58). This word is used in contrast with the verb "was made" (or "were made") in v. 3 which indicate a beginning in time. Because of John's theme that Jesus Christ is the eternal God, the Second Person of the Trinity, he did not include a genealogy as Matthew and Luke did. While in terms of Jesus' humanity, He had a human genealogy; in terms of His deity, He has no genealogy. **the Word.** John borrowed the use of the term "Word" not only from the vocabulary of the OT but also from Gr. philosophy, in which the term was essentially impersonal, signifying the rational principle of "divine reason," "mind," or even "wisdom." John, however, imbued the term entirely with OT and Christian meaning (e.g., Gen. 1:3 where God's Word brought the world into being; Pss. 33:6; 107:20; Prov. 8:27 where God's Word is His powerful self-expression in creation, wisdom, revelation, and salvation) and made it refer to a person, i.e., Jesus Christ. Greek philosophical usage, therefore, is not the exclusive background of John's thought. Strategically, the term "Word" serves as a bridge-word to reach not only Jews but also the unsaved Greeks. John chose this concept because both Jews and Greeks were familiar with it. **the Word was with God.** The Word, as the Second Person of the Trinity, was in intimate fellowship with God the Father throughout all eternity. Yet, although the Word enjoyed the splendors of heaven and eternity with the Father (Is. 6:1-13; cf. 12:41; 17:5), He willingly gave up His heavenly status, taking the form of a man, and became subject to the death of the cross (*see notes on Phil. 2:6-8*). **was God.** The Gr. construction emphasizes that the Word had all the essence or attributes of deity, i.e., Jesus the Messiah was fully God (cf. Col. 2:9). Even in His incarnation when He emptied Himself, He did not cease to be God but took on a genuine human nature/body and voluntarily refrained from the independent exercise of the attributes of deity.

1:3 All things were made through Him. Jesus Christ was God the Father's agent involved in creating everything in the universe (Col. 1:16,17; Heb. 1:2).

1:4,5 life…light…darkness. John introduces the reader to contrastive themes that occur throughout the gospel. "Life" and "light" are qualities of the Word that are shared not only among the Godhead (5:26) but also by those who respond to the gospel message regarding Jesus Christ (8:12; 9:5; 10:28; 11:25; 14:6). John uses the word "life" about 36 times in his gospel, far more than any other NT book. It refers not only in a broad sense to physical and temporal life that the Son imparted to the created world through His involvement as the agent of creation (v. 3), but especially to spiritual and eternal life imparted as a gift through belief in Him (3:15; 17:3; Eph. 2:5). In Scripture "light" and "darkness" are very familiar symbols. Intellectually, "light" refers to biblical truth while "darkness" refers to error or falsehood (cf. Ps. 119:105; Prov. 6:23). Morally, "light" refers to holiness or purity (1 John 1:5) while "darkness" refers to sin or wrongdoing (3:19; 12:35,46; Rom. 13:11-14; 1 Thess. 5:4-7; 1 John 1:6; 2:8-11). "Darkness" has special significance in relationship to Satan (and his demonic cohorts) who rules the present spiritually dark world (1 John 5:19) as the "prince of the power of the air" promoting spiritual darkness and rebellion against God (Eph. 2:2). John uses the term "darkness" 14 times (8 in the gospel and 6 in 1 John) out of its 17 occurrences in the NT, making it almost an exclusive Johannine word. In John, "light" and "life" have their special significance in relationship to the Jesus Christ, the Word (v. 9; 9:5; 1 John 1:5-7; 5:12,20).

1:5 comprehend. The better meaning of this term in context is "overcome." Darkness is not able to overcome or conquer the light. Just as a single candle can overcome a room filled with darkness, so also the powers of darkness are overcome by the person and work of the Son through His death on the cross (cf. 19:11a).

1:6 sent from God. As forerunner to Jesus, John was to bear witness to Him as the Messiah and Son of God. With John's ministry, the "400 silent years" between the end of the OT and the beginning of the NT period, during which God had given no revelation, ended. **John.** The name "John" always refers to John the Baptist in this gospel, never to the Apostle John. The writer of this gospel calls him merely "John" without using the phrase "the Baptist," unlike the other gospels which use the additional description to identify him (Matt. 3:1; Mark 1:4; Luke 7:20). Moreover, John the apostle (or, son of Zebedee) never identified himself directly by name in the gospel even though he was one of the 3 most intimate associates of Jesus (Matt. 17:1). Such silence argues strongly that John the apostle authored the gospel and that his readers knew full well that he composed the gospel that bears his name. For more on John the Baptist, cf. Matt. 3:1-6; Mark 1:2-6; Luke 1:5-25,57-80.

1:7 witness…bear witness. The terms "witness" or "bear witness" receive special attention in this gospel, reflecting the courtroom language of the OT where the truth of a matter was to be established on the basis of multiple witnesses (8:17,18; cf. Deut. 17:6; 19:15). Not only did John the Baptist witness regarding Jesus as Messiah and Son of God (vv. 19-34; 3:27-30; 5:35), but there were other witnesses: 1) the Samaritan woman (4:29); 2) the works of Jesus (10:25); 3) the Father (5:32-37); 4) the OT (5:39,40); 5) the crowd (12:17); and 6) the Holy Spirit (15:26,27). **that all through him might believe.** "Him" refers not to Christ but to John as the agent who witnessed to Christ. The purpose of his testimony was to produce faith in Jesus Christ as the Savior of the world.

that all through him might [l]believe. **8** He
was not that Light, but *was sent* to bear witness of that [m]Light.

The Rejection of Christ

9 [n]That [2]was the true Light which gives
light to every man coming into the world.
10 He was in the world, and the world
was made through Him, and [o]the world
did not know Him. **11** [p]He came to His
[3]own, and His [4]own did not receive Him.

The Acceptance of Christ

12 But [q]as many as received Him, to
them He gave the [5]right to become children of God, to those who believe in His
name: **13** [r]who were born, not of blood, nor
of the will of the flesh, nor of the will of
man, but of God.

The Incarnation of Christ

14 [s]And the Word [t]became [u]flesh and
dwelt among us, and [v]we beheld His glory,
the glory as of the only begotten of the Father, [w]full of grace and truth.

7 [l] [John 3:16]
8 [m] Is. 9:2; 49:6
9 [n] Is. 49:6 [2] Or *That was the true Light which, coming into the world, gives light to every man.*
10 [o] Acts 13:27; 1 Cor. 8:6; Col. 1:16; Heb. 1:2
11 [p] Is. 53:3; [Luke 19:14] [3] His own things or domain [4] His own people
12 [q] [John 11:52]; Gal. 3:26 [5] *authority*
13 [r] [John 3:5]; James 1:18; [1 Pet. 1:23; 1 John 2:29; 3:9]
14 [s] Matt. 1:16; Rev. 19:13 [t] Rom. 1:3; Gal. 4:4; Phil. 2:7; 1 Tim. 3:16; Heb. 2:14; 1 John 1:1; 4:2; 2 John 7 [u] Heb. 2:11 [v] Is. 40:5; 2 Pet. 1:16-18 [w] [John 8:32; 14:6; 18:37]; Col. 1:19

1:8 He was not that Light. While John the Baptist was the agent of belief, Jesus Christ is the object of belief. Although John's person and ministry were vitally important (Matt. 11:11), he was merely the forerunner who announced the coming of the Messiah. Many years after John's ministry and death, some still failed to understand John's subordinate role to Jesus (Acts 19:1-3).

1:9 the true Light...coming into the world. The marginal note is the preferred translation. The words "coming into the world" would be better grammatically if attached to "light" rather than "every man" and thus translated "the true Light coming into the world gives light to every man." This highlights the incarnation of Jesus Christ (v. 14; 3:16). **which gives light to every man.** Through God's sovereign power, every man has enough light to be responsible. God has planted His knowledge in man through general revelation in creation and conscience. The result of general revelation, however, does not produce salvation but either leads to the complete light of Jesus Christ or produces condemnation in those who reject such "light" (*see notes on Rom. 1:19,20; 2:12-16*). The coming of Jesus Christ was the fulfillment and embodiment of the light that God had placed inside the heart of man. **the world.** The basic sense of this Gr. word meaning "an ornament" is illustrated by the word "cosmetic" (1 Pet. 3:3). While the NT uses it a total of 185 times, John had a particular fondness for this term, using it 78 times in his gospel, 24 times in 1-3 John and 3 times in Revelation. John gives it several shades of meaning: 1) the physical created universe (v. 9; cf. v. 3; 21:24,25); 2) humanity in general (3:16; 6:32,51; 12:19); and 3) the invisible spiritual system of evil dominated by Satan and all that it offers in opposition to God, His Word, and His people (3:19; 4:42; 7:7; 14:17,22,27,30; 15:18,19; 16:8,20, 33; 17:6,9,14; cf. 1 Cor. 1:21; 2 Cor. 4:4; 2 Pet. 1:4; 1 John 5:19). The latter concept is the significant new use that the term acquires in the NT and that predominates in John. Thus, in the majority of times that John uses the word, it has decidedly negative overtones.

1:11 His own...His own. The first usage of "His own" most likely refers to the world of mankind in general, while the second refers to the Jewish nation. As Creator, the world belongs to the Word as His property but the world did not even recognize Him due to spiritual blindness (cf. also v. 10). John used the second occurrence of "His own" in a narrower sense to refer to refer to Jesus' own physical lineage, the Jews. Although they possessed the Scriptures that testified of His person and coming, they still did not accept Him (Is. 65:2,3; Jer. 7:25). This theme of Jewish rejection of their promised Messiah receives special attention in John's gospel (12:37-41).

1:12,13 These verses stand in contrast to vv. 10,11. John softens the sweeping rejection of Messiah by stressing a believing remnant. This previews the book since the first 12 chapters stress the rejection of Christ, while chaps. 13–21 focus on the believing remnant who received Him.

1:12 as many as received Him...to those who believe in His name. The second phrase describes the first. To receive Him who is the Word of God means to acknowledge His claims, place one's faith in Him, and thereby yield allegiance to Him. **gave.** The term emphasizes the grace of God involved in the gift of salvation (cf. Eph. 2:8-10). **the right.** Those who receive Jesus, the Word, receive full authority to claim the exalted title of "God's children." **His name.** Denotes the character of the person himself. *See notes on 14:13,14.*

1:13 of God. The divine side of salvation: ultimately it is not a man's will that produces salvation but God's will (cf. 3:6-8; Titus 3:5; 1 John 2:29).

1:14 the Word became flesh. While Christ as God was uncreated and eternal (*see notes on v. 1*), the word "became" emphasizes Christ's taking on humanity (cf. Heb. 1:1-3; 2:14-18). This reality is surely the most profound ever because it indicates that the Infinite became finite; the Eternal was conformed to time; the Invisible became visible; the supernatural One reduced Himself to the natural. In the incarnation, however, the Word did not cease to be God but became God in human flesh, i.e., undiminished deity in human form as a man (1 Tim. 3:16). **dwelt.** Meaning "to pitch a tabernacle," or "live in a tent." The term recalls to mind the OT tabernacle where God met with Israel before the temple was constructed (Ex. 25:8). It was called the "tabernacle of meeting" (Ex. 33:7; "tabernacle of witness"—LXX) where "the LORD spoke to Moses face to face, as a man speaks to his friend" (Ex. 33:11). In the NT, God chose to dwell among His people in a far more personal way through becoming a man. In the OT, when the tabernacle was completed, God's Shekinah presence filled the entire structure (Ex. 40:34; cf. 1 Kin. 8:10). When the Word became flesh, the glorious presence of deity was embodied in Him (cf. Col. 2:9). **we beheld His glory.** Although His deity may have been veiled in human flesh, glimpses exist in the gospels of His divine majesty. The disciples saw glimpses of His glory on the Mount of Transfiguration (Matt. 17:1-8). The reference to Christ's glory, however, was not only visible but also spiritual. They saw Him display the attributes or characteristics of God (grace, goodness, mercy, wisdom, truth, etc.; cf. Ex. 33:18-23). **the glory as of...Father.** Jesus as God displayed the same essential glory as the Father. They are one in essential nature (cf. 5:17-30; 8:19; 10:30). **only begotten.** The term "only begotten" is a mistranslation of the Gr. word. The word does not come from the term meaning "beget" but instead has the idea of "the only beloved one." It, therefore, has the idea of singular uniqueness, of being beloved like no other. By this word, John emphasized the exclusive character of the relationship between the Father and the Son in the Godhead (cf. 3:16,18; 1 John 4:9). It does not connote origin but rather unique prominence; e.g., it was used of Isaac (Heb. 11:17) who was Abraham's second son (Ishmael being the first; cf. Gen. 16:15 with Gen. 21:2,3). **full of grace and truth.** John probably had Ex. 33,34 in mind. On that occasion, Moses requested that God display His glory to him. The Lord replied to Moses that He would make all His "goodness" pass before him, and then as He passed by God declared "The LORD...merciful and gracious, longsuffering, and abounding in goodness and truth" (Ex. 33:18,19; 34:5-7). These attributes of God's glory emphasize the goodness of God's character, espe-

15 [x]John bore witness of Him and cried
out, saying, "This was He of whom I said,
[y]'He who comes after me [6]is preferred before me, [z]for He was before me.' "
16 [7]And of His [a]fullness we have all received, and grace for grace. 17 For [b]the law
was given through Moses, *but* [c]grace and
[d]truth came through Jesus Christ. 18 [e]No
one has seen God at any time. [f]The only
begotten [8]Son, who is in the bosom of the
Father, He has declared *Him.*

John's Witness to the Priests and Levites
Matt. 3:1-12; Mark 1:2-8; Luke 3:3-16

19 Now this is [g]the testimony of John,
when the Jews sent priests and Levites
from Jerusalem to ask him, "Who are
you?"
20 [h]He confessed, and did not deny, but
confessed, "I am not the Christ."
21 And they asked him, "What then? Are
you Elijah?"
He said, "I am not."
"Are you [i]the Prophet?"
And he answered, "No."
22 Then they said to him, "Who are you,
that we may give an answer to those who
sent us? What do you say about yourself?"
23 He said: [j]"I *am*

[k]'The voice of one crying in the
wilderness:
"Make straight the way of the
LORD,"'

as the prophet Isaiah said."
24 Now those who were sent were from
the Pharisees. 25 And they asked him, saying, "Why then do you baptize if you are
not the Christ, nor Elijah, nor the
Prophet?"
26 John answered them, saying, [l]"I baptize with water, [m]but there stands One
among you whom you do not know. 27 [n]It

15 [x] Mal. 3:1; John 3:32 [y] [Matt. 3:11] [z] [Col. 1:17] [6] *ranks higher than I*
16 [a] [Eph. 1:23; 3:19; 4:13; Col. 1:19; 2:9] [7] NU *For*
17 [b] [Ex. 20:1] [c] John 1:14; [Rom. 5:21; 6:14] [d] [John 8:32; 14:6; 18:37]
18 [e] Ex. 33:20; Matt. 11:27; 1 Tim. 6:16 [f] Ps. 2:7; John 3:16, 18; 1 John 4:9 [8] NU *God*
19 [g] John 5:33
20 [h] Luke 3:15; John 3:28; Acts 13:25
21 [i] Deut. 18:15, 18; Matt. 21:11; John 6:14; 7:40
23 [j] Matt. 3:3 [k] Is. 40:3; Mal. 3:1
26 [l] Matt. 3:11; [Mark 1:8; Luke 3:16; Acts 1:5] [m] Mal. 3:1; John 4:10; 8:19; 9:30; Acts 13:27
27 [n] [John 3:31]; Acts 19:4; [Col. 1:17]

cially in relationship to salvation. Jesus as Yahweh of the OT (8:58; "I AM") displayed the same divine attributes when he tabernacled among men in the NT era (Col. 2:9).

1:15 John the Baptist's testimony corroborates John the apostle's statement regarding the eternality of the Incarnate Word (cf. v. 14).

1:16 grace for grace. This phrase emphasizes the superabundance of grace that has been displayed by God toward mankind, especially believers (Eph. 1:5-8; 2:7).

1:17,18 Corroborating the truth of v. 14, these verses draw a closing contrast to the prologue. The law, given by Moses, was not a display of God's grace but God's demand for holiness. God designed the law as a means to demonstrate the unrighteousness of man in order to show the need for a Savior, Jesus Christ (Rom. 3:19,20; Gal. 3:10-14,21-26). Furthermore, the law revealed only a part of truth and was preparatory in nature. The reality or full truth toward which the law pointed came through the person of Jesus Christ.

1:18 who is in the bosom of the Father. This term denotes the mutual intimacy, love and knowledge existing in the Godhead (13:23; Luke 16:22,23). **declared.** Theologians derived the term "exegesis" or "to interpret" from this word. John meant that all that Jesus is and does interprets and explains who God is and what He does (14:8-10).

1:19-37 In these verses, John presented the first of many witnesses to prove that Jesus is the Messiah and Son of God, thus reinforcing his main theme (20:30,31). The testimony of John the Baptist was given on 3 different days to 3 different groups (cf. vv. 29,35,36). Each time, he spoke of Christ in a different way and emphasized distinct aspects regarding Him. The events in these verses took place in A.D. 26/27, just a few months after John's baptism of Jesus (cf. Matt. 3:13-17; Luke 3:21,22).

1:19 John. John, born into a priestly family, belonged to the tribe of Levi (Luke 1:5). He began his ministry in the Jordan Valley when he was approximately 29 or 30 years old and boldly proclaimed the need for spiritual repentance and preparation for the coming of the Messiah. He was the cousin of Jesus Christ and served as His prophetic forerunner (Matt. 3:3; Luke 1:5-25,36). **the Jews...from Jerusalem.** This may refer to the Sanhedrin, the main governing body of the Jewish nation. The Sanhedrin was controlled by the family of the High-Priest, and thus the envoys would naturally be priests and Levites who would be interested in John's ministry, both his message and his baptism.

1:20 "I am not the Christ." Some thought that John was the Messiah (Luke 3:15-17). **Christ.** The term "Christ" is the Gr. equivalent of the Heb. term for "Messiah."

1:21 "...Are you Elijah?" Malachi 4:5 (*see note there*) promises that the prophet Elijah will return before Messiah establishes His earthly kingdom. If John was the forerunner of Messiah was he Elijah, they asked? The angel announcing John's birth said that John would go before Jesus "in the spirit and power of Elijah" (Luke 1:17), thus indicating that someone other than literal Elijah could fulfill the prophecy. God sent John who was like Elijah, i.e., one who had the same type of ministry, the same power and similar personality (2 Kin. 1:8; cf. Matt. 3:4). If they had received Jesus as Messiah, John would have fulfilled that prophecy (*see notes on Matt. 11:14; Mark 9:13; Luke 1:17; Rev. 11:5,6*). **"Are you the Prophet?"** This is a reference to Deut. 18:15-18 which predicted God would raise up a great prophet like Moses who would function as His voice. While some in John's time interpreted this prophecy as referring to another forerunner of Messiah, the NT (Acts 3:22,23; 7:37) applies the passage to Jesus.

1:23 John quoted and applied Is. 40:3 to himself (cf. Matt. 3:3; Mark 1:3; Luke 3:4). In the original context of Is. 40:3, the prophet heard a voice calling for the leveling of a path through the eastern desert so that the God of Israel could lead His people home from Babylonian exile. This call was a prophetic picture that foreshadowed the final and greatest return of Israel to their God from spiritual darkness and alienation through the spiritual redemption accomplished by the Messiah (cf. Rom. 11:25-27). In humility, John compared himself to a voice rather than a person, thus focusing the attention exclusively upon Christ (cf. Luke 17:10).

1:25 baptize. Since John had identified himself as a mere voice (v. 24), the question arose as to his authority for baptizing. The OT associated the coming of Messiah, with repentance and spiritual cleansing (Ezek. 36,37; Zech. 13:1). John focused attention on his position as forerunner of Messiah, who used traditional proselyte baptism as a symbol of the need to recognize those Jews who were outside God's saving covenant like Gentiles. They too needed spiritual cleansing and preparation (repentance—Matt. 3:11; Mark 1:4; Luke 3:7,8) for Messiah's advent. *See notes on Matt. 3:6,11,16,17* for an explanation of the significance of John's baptism.

1:27 John the Baptist's words here continue a theme of the preeminence of Messiah in the prologue (vv. 6-8,15) and demonstrate extraordinary humility. Each time John had opportunity to focus on himself in these encounters, he instead shifted the focus onto Messiah.

is He who, coming after me, [9]is preferred
before me, whose sandal strap I am not
worthy to loose."
28 These things were done [o]in [1]Bethaba-
ra beyond the Jordan, where John was baptizing.

John's Witness at Christ's Baptism
Matt. 3:13-17; Mark 1:9-11; Luke 3:21, 22

29 The next day John saw Jesus coming
toward him, and said, "Behold! [p]The Lamb
of God [q]who takes away the sin of the
world! 30 This is He of whom I said, 'After
me comes a Man who [2]is preferred before
me, for He was before me.' 31 I did not
know Him; but that He should be revealed
to Israel, [r]therefore I came baptizing with
water."
32 [s]And John bore witness, saying, "I saw
the Spirit descending from heaven like a
dove, and He remained upon Him. 33 I did
not know Him, but He who sent me to baptize with water said to me, 'Upon whom
you see the Spirit descending, and remaining on Him, [t]this is He who baptizes with
the Holy Spirit.' 34 And I have seen and testified that this is the [u]Son of God."

Andrew and Peter Follow Christ

35 Again, the next day, John stood with
two of his disciples. 36 And looking at Jesus as He walked, he said, [v]"Behold the
Lamb of God!"
37 The two disciples heard him speak,
and they [w]followed Jesus. 38 Then Jesus
turned, and seeing them following, said to
them, "What do you seek?"
They said to Him, "Rabbi" (which is to
say, when translated, Teacher), "where are
You staying?"
39 He said to them, "Come and see."
They came and saw where He was staying,
and remained with Him that day (now it
was about the tenth hour).
40 One of the two who heard John *speak,*
and followed Him, was [x]Andrew, Simon
Peter's brother. 41 He first found his own
brother Simon, and said to him, "We have

27 [9] *ranks higher than I*
28 [o] Judg. 7:24 [1] NU, M *Bethany*
29 [p] [Ex. 12:3]; Acts 8:32; [1 Pet. 1:19]; Rev. 5:6-14 [q] [Is. 53:11; 1 Cor. 15:3; Gal. 1:4; 1 Pet. 2:24; 1 John 2:2; Rev. 1:5]
30 [2] *ranks higher than I*
31 [r] Mal. 3:1; Matt. 3:6
32 [s] Is. 42:1; 61:1; Matt. 3:16; Mark 1:10; Luke 3:22
33 [t] Matt. 3:11; Mark 1:8; Luke 3:16; Acts 1:5
34 [u] Ps. 2:7; Luke 1:35; John 11:27
36 [v] John 1:29
37 [w] Matt. 4:20, 22
40 [x] Matt. 4:18; Mark 1:29; 13:3; John 6:8; 12:22

John went so far as to state that he, unlike a slave that was required to remove his master's shoes, was not even worthy of performing this action in relationship to Messiah.

1:28 Bethabara. This word has been substituted for "Bethany" which is in the original text because some feel that John incorrectly identified Bethany as the place of these events. The solution is that two Bethany's existed, i.e., one near Jerusalem where Mary, Martha, and Lazarus lived (11:1) and one "beyond the Jordan" near the region of Galilee. Since John took great pains to identify the other Bethany's close proximity to Jerusalem, he most likely was referring here to that other town with the same name.

1:29-34 This portion deals with John's witness to a second group of Jews on the second day (see vv. 19-28 for the first group and day) regarding Jesus. This section forms something of a bridge. It continues the theme of John the Baptist's witness but also introduces a lengthy list of titles applied to Jesus: Lamb of God (vv. 29,36), Rabbi (vv. 38,49), Messiah/Christ (v. 41), Son of God (vv. 34,49), King of Israel (v. 49), Son of Man (v. 51) and "Him of whom Moses in the law, and also the prophets, wrote" (v. 45).

1:29 The next day. This phrase probably refers to the day after John's response to the Jerusalem delegation. It also initiates a sequence of days (v. 43; 2:1) that culminated in the miracle at Cana (2:1-11). **The Lamb of God.** The use of a lamb for sacrifice was very familiar to Jews. A lamb was used as a sacrifice during Passover (Ex. 12:1-36); a lamb was led to the slaughter in the prophecies of Isaiah (Is. 53:7); a lamb was offered in the daily sacrifices of Israel (Lev. 14:12-21; cf. Heb. 10:5-7). John the Baptist used this expression as a reference to the ultimate sacrifice of Jesus on the cross to atone for the sins of the world, a theme which John the apostle carries throughout his writings (19:36; cf. Rev. 5:1-6; 7:17; 17:14) and that appears in other NT writings (e.g., 1 Pet. 1:19). **sin of the world.** *See note on v. 9*; cf. 3:16; 6:33,51. In this context "world" has the connotation of humanity in general, not specifically every person. The use of the singular "sin" in conjunction with "of the world" indicates that Jesus' sacrifice for sin potentially reaches all human beings without distinction (cf. 1 John 2:2). John makes clear, however, that its efficacious effect is only for those who receive Christ (vv. 11,12). For discussion of the relation of Christ's death to the world, *see note on 2 Cor. 5:19*.

1:31 I did not know Him. Although John was Jesus' cousin, he did not know Jesus as the "Coming One" or "Messiah" (v. 30).

1:32 the Spirit descending. God had previously communicated to John that this sign was to indicate the promised Messiah (v. 33), so when John witnessed this act, he was able to identify the Messiah as Jesus (cf. Matt. 3:16; Mark 1:10; Luke 3:22).

1:34 the Son of God. Although, in a limited sense, believers can be called "sons of God" (e.g., v. 12; Matt. 5:9; Rom. 8:14), John uses this phrase with the full force as a title that points to the unique oneness and intimacy that Jesus sustains to the Father as "Son." The term carries the idea of the deity of Jesus as Messiah (v. 49; 5:16-30; cf. 2 Sam. 7:14; Ps. 2:7; *see notes on Heb. 1:1-9*).

1:35-51 This portion deals with John's witness to a third group, i.e., some of John's disciples, on the third day (see vv. 19-28; 29-34 for the first and second groups) regarding Jesus. Consistent with John's humility (v. 27), he focuses the attention of his own disciples onto Jesus (v. 37).

1:37 they followed Jesus. Although the verb "follow" usually means "to follow as a disciple" in the writing of the apostle (v. 43; 8:12; 12:26; 21:19,20,22), it may also have a neutral sense (11:31). The "following" here does not necessarily mean that they became permanent disciples at this time. The implication may be that they went after Jesus to examine Him more closely because of John's testimony. This event constituted a preliminary exposure of John the Baptist's disciples to Jesus (e.g., Andrew; 1:40). They eventually dedicated their lives to Him as true disciples and apostles when Jesus called them to permanent service after these events (Matt. 4:18-22; 9:9; Mark 1:16-20). At this point in the narrative, John the Baptist fades from the scene and the attention focuses upon the ministry of Christ.

1:39 the tenth hour. The Jews divided the daylight period of the day into 12 hours (starting at sunrise, approximately 6:00 a.m.). This would make the time about 4:00 p.m. John mentions the precise time most likely to emphasize that he was the other disciple of John the Baptist who was with Andrew (v. 40). As an eyewitness to these events occurring on 3 successive days, John's first meeting with Jesus was so life-changing that he remembered the exact hour when he first met the Lord.

found the [3]Messiah" (which is translated,
the Christ). **42** And he brought him to Jesus.
Now when Jesus looked at him, He said,
"You are Simon the son of [4]Jonah. [y]You
shall be called Cephas" (which is translated, [5]A Stone).

Philip and Nathanael Follow Christ

43 The following day Jesus wanted to go
to Galilee, and He found [z]Philip and said to
him, "Follow Me." **44** Now [a]Philip was from
Bethsaida, the city of Andrew and Peter.
45 Philip found [b]Nathanael and said to him,
"We have found Him of whom [c]Moses in
the law, and also the [d]prophets, wrote—Jesus [e]of Nazareth, the [f]son of Joseph."
46 And Nathanael said to him, [g]"Can
anything good come out of Nazareth?"
Philip said to him, "Come and see."

47 Jesus saw Nathanael coming toward
Him, and said of him, "Behold, [h]an Israelite indeed, in whom is no deceit!"
48 Nathanael said to Him, "How do You
know me?"
Jesus answered and said to him, "Before
Philip called you, when you were under
the fig tree, I saw you."
49 Nathanael answered and said to Him,
"Rabbi, [i]You are the Son of God! You are
[j]the King of Israel!"
50 Jesus answered and said to him, "Because I said to you, 'I saw you under the
fig tree,' do you believe? You will see
greater things than these." **51** And He said
to him, "Most assuredly, I say to you,
[k]hereafter[6] you shall see heaven open, and
the angels of God ascending and descending upon the Son of Man."

41 [3] Lit. *Anointed One*
42 [y] Matt. 16:18 [4] NU *John* [5] Gr. *Petros,* usually translated *Peter*
43 [z] Matt. 10:3; John 6:5; 12:21, 22; 14:8, 9
44 [a] John 12:21
45 [b] John 21:2 [c] [Gen. 3:15; Deut. 18:18]; Luke 24:27 [d] [Is. 4:2; 7:14; 9:6; Mic. 5:2; Zech. 6:12]; Luke 24:27 [e] [Matt. 2:23]; Luke 2:4 [f] Luke 3:23
46 [g] John 7:41, 42, 52
47 [h] Ps. 32:2; 73:1
49 [i] Ps. 2:7; Matt. 14:33; Luke 1:35 [j] Matt. 21:5
51 [k] Gen. 28:12; [Luke 2:9, 13]; Acts 1:10; 7:55, 56 [6] NU omits *hereafter*

1:41 Messiah. The term "Messiah" is a transliteration of a Heb. or Aram. verbal adjective that means "Anointed One." It comes from a verb that means "to anoint" someone as an action involved in consecrating that person to a particular office or function. While the term at first applied to the king of Israel ("the Lord's anointed"—1 Sam. 16:6), the High-Priest ("the anointed priest," Lev. 4:3) and, in one passage, the patriarchs ("my anointed ones," Ps. 105:15), the term eventually came to point above all to the prophesied "Coming One" or "Messiah" in His role as prophet, priest, and king. The term "Christ," a Gr. word (verbal adjective) that comes from a verb meaning "to anoint," is used in translating the Heb. term, so that the terms "Messiah" or "Christ" are titles and not personal names of Jesus.

1:42 when Jesus looked at him. Jesus knows hearts thoroughly (vv. 43-51) and not only sees into them (vv. 47,48) but also transforms a person into what He wants him to become. **You shall be called Cephas.** Up to this time, Peter had been known as "Simon son of Jonah" (the name "Jonah" in Aram. means "John"; cf. 21:15-17; Matt. 16:17). The term "Cephas" means "rock" in Aram. which is translated "Peter" in Greek. Jesus' assignment of the name "Cephas" or "Peter" to Simon occurred at the outset of His ministry (cf. Matt. 16:18; Mark 3:16). The statement not only is predictive of what Peter would be called but also declarative of how Jesus would transform his character and use him in relationship to the foundation of the church (cf. 21:18,19; Matt. 16:16-18; Acts 2:14–4:32).

1:43-51 This section introduces the fourth day since the beginning of John the Baptist's witness (cf. vv. 19,29,35).

1:44 Bethsaida, the city of Andrew and Peter. While Mark 1:21,29 locates Peter's house in Capernaum, John relates that he was from Bethsaida. Resolution centers in the fact that Peter (and Andrew) most likely grew up in Bethsaida and later relocated to Capernaum in the same way that Jesus was consistently identified with his hometown of Nazareth, though he lived elsewhere later (Matt. 2:23; 4:13; Mark 1:9; Luke 1:26).

1:45 Him of whom Moses in the law, and also the prophets, wrote. This phrase encapsulates the stance of John's whole gospel: Jesus is the fulfillment of OT Scripture (cf. v. 21; 5:39; Deut. 18:15-19; Luke 24:44,47; Acts 10:43; 18:28; 26:22,23; Rom. 1:2; 1 Cor. 15:3; 1 Pet. 1:10,11; Rev. 19:10).

1:46 "Can anything good come out of Nazareth?" Nathanael was from Cana (21:2), another town in Galilee. While Galileans were despised by Judeans, Galileans themselves despised people from Nazareth. In light of 7:52, Nathanael's scorn may have centered in the fact that Nazareth was an insignificant village without seeming prophetic importance (cf., however, Matt. 2:23). Later, some would contemptuously refer to Christians as the "sect of the Nazarenes" (Acts 24:5).

1:47 no deceit. Jesus' point was that Nathanael's bluntness revealed that he was an Israelite without duplicitous motives who was willing to examine for himself the claims being made about Jesus. The term reveals an honest seeking heart. The reference here may be an allusion to Gen. 27:35 where Jacob, in contrast to the sincere Nathanael, was known for his trickery. The meaning may be that the employment of trickery characterized not only Jacob but also his descendants. In Jesus' mind, an honest and sincere Israelite had become an exception rather than the rule (cf. 2:23-25).

1:48 I saw you. A brief glimpse of Jesus' supernatural knowledge. Not only was Jesus' brief summary of Nathanael accurate (v. 47), but He also revealed information that could only be known by Nathanael himself. Perhaps Nathanael had some significant or outstanding experience of communion with God at the location, and he was able to recognize Jesus' allusion to it. At any rate, Jesus had knowledge of this event not available to men.

1:49 the Son of God!...the King of Israel! Jesus' display of supernatural knowledge and Philip's witness removed Nathanael's doubts, so John added the witness of Nathanael to this section. The use of "the" with "Son of God" most likely indicates that the expression is to be understood as bearing its full significance (cf. v. 34; 11:27). For Nathanael, here was One who could not be described merely in human terms.

1:51 Most assuredly. Cf. 5:19,24,25. A phrase used frequently for emphasizing the importance and truth of the coming statement. **heaven open, and the angels of God ascending and descending.** In light of the context of v. 47, this verse most likely refers to Gen. 28:12 where Jacob dreamed about a ladder from heaven. Jesus' point to Nathanael was that just like Jacob experienced supernatural or heaven-sent revelation, Nathanael and the other disciples would experience supernatural communication confirming who Jesus was. Moreover, the term "Son of Man" replaced the ladder in Jacob's dream, signifying that Jesus was the means of access between God and man. **Son of Man.** *See note on Matt. 8:20.* This is Jesus' favorite self-designation, for it was mostly spoken by Jesus who used it over 80 times. In the NT, it refers only to Jesus and appears mostly in the gospels (cf. Acts 7:56). In the fourth gospel, the expression occurs 13 times and is most commonly associated with the themes of crucifixion and suffering (3:14; 8:28) and revelation (6:27,53) but also with eschatological authority (5:27; 9:39). While the term at times may refer merely to a human being or as a substitute for "I" (6:27; cf. 6:20), it especially takes on an eschatological significance referring to Dan. 7:13,14 where the "Son of Man" or Messiah comes in glory to receive the kingdom from the "Ancient of Days" (i.e., the Father).

Christ Changes Water to Wine

2 On the third day there was a [a]wedding
in [b]Cana of Galilee, and the [c]mother of
Jesus was there. 2 Now both Jesus and His
disciples were invited to the wedding.
3 And when they ran out of wine, the
mother of Jesus said to Him, "They have
no wine."

4 Jesus said to her, [d]"Woman, [e]what does
your concern have to do with Me? [f]My
hour has not yet come."

5 His mother said to the servants,
"Whatever He says to you, do *it*."

6 Now there were set there six waterpots
of stone, [g]according to the manner of purification of the Jews, containing twenty or
thirty gallons apiece. 7 Jesus said to them,
"Fill the waterpots with water." And they
filled them up to the brim. 8 And He said
to them, "Draw *some* out now, and take *it*
to the master of the feast." And they took
it. 9 When the master of the feast had tasted [h]the water that was made wine, and did
not know where it came from (but the servants who had drawn the water knew), the
master of the feast called the bridegroom.
10 And he said to him, "Every man at the
beginning sets out the good wine, and
when the *guests* have well drunk, then the
inferior. You have kept the good wine until
now!"

The Disciples Believe

11 This [i]beginning of signs Jesus did in
Cana of Galilee, [j]and [1]manifested His
glory; and His disciples believed in Him.

12 After this He went down to [k]Caperna-
um, He, His mother, [l]His brothers, and His
disciples; and they did not stay there many
days.

Christ Cleanses the Temple

13 [m]Now the Passover of the Jews was at

CHAPTER 2

1 [a] [Heb. 13:4] [b] John 4:46 [c] John 19:25
4 [d] John 19:26 [e] 2 Sam. 16:10 [f] John 7:6, 8, 30; 8:20
6 [g] Matt. 15:2; [Mark 7:3; Luke 11:39]; John 3:25
9 [h] John 4:46
11 [i] John 4:54 [j] [John 1:14] [1] *revealed*
12 [k] Matt. 4:13; John 4:46 [l] Matt. 12:46; 13:55
13 [m] Ex. 12:14; Deut. 16:1-6; John 5:1; 6:4; 11:55

2:1-11 John relates the first great sign performed by Jesus to demonstrate His deity, the turning of water into wine. Only God can create from nothing. John identifies 8 miracles in his gospel that constitute "signs" or confirmation of whom Jesus is. Each of the 8 miracles were different; no two were alike (cf. v. 11).

2:1 On the third day. This phrase has reference to the last narrated event, i.e., the calling of Philip and Nathanael (1:43). **wedding.** Such a wedding celebration in Palestine could last for a week. Financial responsibility lay with the groom (vv. 9,10). To run out of wine for the guests would have been an embarrassment to the groom and may have even opened him to a potential lawsuit from the relatives of the bride. **Cana of Galilee.** Cana was the home of Nathanael (21:2). Its exact location is unknown. A probable location is Khirbet Qana, a village now in ruins approximately 9 mi. N of Nazareth.

2:2 both Jesus and His disciples were invited. The fact that Jesus, His mother, and His disciples all attended the wedding suggests that the wedding may have been for a relative or close family friend. The disciples that accompanied Him are the 5 mentioned in chap. 1: Andrew, Simon Peter, Philip, Nathanael, and the unnamed disciple (1:35) who was surely John, who also witnessed this miracle. **wine.** The wine served was subject to fermentation. In the ancient world, however, to quench thirst without inducing drunkenness, wine was diluted with water to between one-third and one-tenth of its strength. Due to the climate and circumstances, even "new wine" fermented quickly and had an inebriating effect if not mixed (Acts 2:13). Because of a lack of water purification process, wine mixed with water was also safer to drink than water alone. While the Bible condemns drunkenness, it does not necessarily condemn the consumption of wine (Ps. 104:15; Prov. 20:1; *see notes on Eph. 5:18*).

2:4 Woman. The term is not necessarily impolite, but it does have the effect of distancing Jesus from His mother and her request. Perhaps, it has the equivalent of "ma'am." **what does your concern have to do with Me?** The expression, common in Semitic idiom (Judg. 11:12; 2 Sam. 16:10), always distances the two parties, the speaker's tone conveying some degree of reproach. Jesus' tone was not rude, but abrupt. The phrase asks what is shared in common between the parties. The thrust of Jesus' comment was that He had entered into the purpose for His mission on earth, so that He subordinated all activities to the fulfillment of that mission. Mary had to recognize Him not so much as a son that she raised but as the promised Messiah and Son of God. Cf. Mark 3:31-35. **My hour has not yet come.** The phrase constantly refers to Jesus' death and exaltation (7:30; 8:20; 12:23,27; 13:1; 17:1). He was on a divine schedule decreed by God before the foundation of the world. Since the prophets characterized the messianic age as a time when wine would flow liberally (Jer. 31:12; Hos. 14:7; Amos 9:13,14), Jesus was likely referring to the fact that the necessity of the cross must come before the blessings of the millennial age.

2:6 purification of the Jews. The 6 water jars were made of stone because stone was more impervious than earthenware and did not contract uncleanness. Also, this made them more suitable to ceremonial washing (cf. Mark 7:3,4).

2:11 signs. John used the word "sign" here to refer to significant displays of power that pointed beyond themselves to the deeper divine realities that could be perceived by the eyes of faith. By this word, John emphasized that miracles were not merely displays of power but had a significance beyond the mere act themselves.

2:12-25 John used this section where Jesus cleansed the temple in righteous indignation to reinforce his main theme that He was the promised Messiah and Son of God. In this section, he highlighted 3 attributes of Jesus that confirm His deity: 1) His passion for reverence (vv. 13-17); 2) His power of resurrection (vv. 18-22); and 3) His perception of reality (vv. 23-25).

2:12 After this. The phrase "after this" (or similar wording such as "after these things") is a frequent connective between narratives in this gospel (e.g., 3:22; 5:1,14; 6:1; 7:1; 11:7,11; 19:28,38). John placed this verse here as a transition to explain Jesus' movement from Cana in Galilee to Capernaum and eventual arrival at Jerusalem for the Passover celebration. Capernaum was on the NW shore of Galilee about 16 mi. NE of Cana.

2:13-17 The first way John demonstrated Christ's deity in the narrative of the temple cleansing was to show His passion for reverence. God alone exercises the right to regulate His worship.

2:13 Passover of the Jews. This is the first of 3 Passovers which John mentions (v. 13; 6:4; 11:55). Jews selected the lamb on the tenth of the month, and celebrated Passover on the 14th day of the lunar month of Nisan (full moon at the end of Mar. or beginning of Apr.). They slaughtered the lamb between 3:00 and 6:00 p.m. on the night of the feast. Passover commemorates the deliverance of the Jews from slavery in Egypt when the angel of death "passed over" Jewish homes in Egypt whose "doorposts" were sprinkled with blood (Ex. 12:23-27). **Jesus went up to Jerusalem.** Jesus' journeying to Jerusalem for the Passover was a standard annual procedure for

hand, and Jesus went up to Jerusalem.
14 [n]And He found in the temple those who
sold oxen and sheep and doves, and the
money changers [2]doing business. 15 When
He had made a whip of cords, He drove
them all out of the temple, with the sheep
and the oxen, and poured out the changers' money and overturned the tables.
16 And He said to those who sold doves,
"Take these things away! Do not make
[o]My Father's house a house of merchandise!" 17 Then His disciples remembered
that it was written, [p]*"Zeal for Your house*
[3]*has eaten Me up."*
18 So the Jews answered and said to
Him, [q]"What sign do You show to us, since
You do these things?"
19 Jesus answered and said to them,

14 [n] Mal. 3:1; Matt. 21:12; Mark 11:15, 17; Luke 19:45 [2] Lit. *sitting*
16 [o] Luke 2:49
17 [p] Ps. 69:9 [3] NU, M *will eat*
18 [q] Matt. 12:38; John 6:30

every devout Jewish male over 12 years old (Ex. 23:14-17). Jewish pilgrims crowded into Jerusalem for this greatest of Jewish feasts.

2:14 those who sold...the money changers. During the celebration of Passover, worshipers came from all over Israel and the Roman Empire to Jerusalem. Because many traveled large distances, it was inconvenient to bring their sacrificial animals with them. Opportunistic merchants, seeing a chance to provide a service and probably eyeing considerable profit during this time, set up areas in the outer courts of the temple in order for travelers to buy animals. The money changers were needed because the temple tax, paid annually by every conscientious Jewish male 20 years of age or older (Ex. 30:13,14; Matt. 17:24-27), had to be in Jewish or Tyrian coinage (because of its high purity of silver). Those coming from foreign lands would need to exchange their money into the proper coinage for the tax. The money changers charged a high fee for the exchange. With such a large group of travelers and because of the seasonal nature of the celebration, both the animal dealers and money exchangers exploited the situation for monetary gain ("den of thieves"; Matt. 21:13). Religion had become crass and materialistic.

2:15 As John recorded this cleansing of the temple at the beginning of Jesus' ministry, the synoptic gospels record a temple cleansing at the end of Jesus' ministry during the final Passover week before Jesus' crucifixion (Matt. 21:12-17; Mark 11:15-18; Luke 19:45,46). The historical circumstances and literary contexts of the two temple cleansings differ so widely that attempts to equate the two are unsuccessful. Furthermore, that two cleansings occurred is entirely consistent with overall context of Jesus' ministry, for the Jewish nation as a whole never recognized Jesus' authority as Messiah (Matt. 23:37-39). Instead, they rejected His message as well as His person, making such repeated cleansing of the temple highly probable (as well as necessary). **drove them all out of the temple.** When the holiness of God and His worship was at stake, Jesus took fast and furious action. The "all" indicates that He drove not only men out but also animals. Yet, although His physical action was forceful, it was not cruel. The moderation of His actions is seen in the fact that no riotous uproar occurred; otherwise the specially large contingent of Roman troops in Jerusalem at that time because of the Passover crowds, stationed in the Antonia Fortress overlooking the temple, would have swiftly reacted. Although the primary reference is to the actions of the Messiah in the millennial kingdom, Jesus' actions in cleansing the temple was an initial fulfillment of Mal. 3:1-3 (and Zech. 14:20,21) that speak of Messiah's purifying the religious worship of His people.

2:16 Do not make. The force of the Gr. imperative should better be translated "stop making," indicating Jesus' demand that they stop their current practice. God's holiness demands holiness in worship. **My Father's.** John gave a subtle hint of Jesus' divine Sonship as well as His messiahship with the recording of this phrase (see 5:17,18). **house a house of merchandise.** Jesus may have intended a play on words. The word "merchandise" pictures a trading house filled with wares.

2:17 Quoted from Ps. 69:9 to indicate that Jesus would not tolerate irreverence toward God. When David wrote this psalm, he was being persecuted because of his zeal toward God's house and his defense of God's honor. The disciples were afraid that Jesus' actions would precipitate the same type of persecution. Paul quotes the latter half of Ps. 69:9 (*"The reproaches of those who reproached You fell on Me"*) in Rom. 15:3, clearly indicating the messianic nature that the psalm had for the early church.

2:18-22 The second way John demonstrated Christ's deity in the account of the temple cleansing was to show His power over death through resurrection. Only God has this right.

2:18 the Jews. Most likely the temple authorities or representatives of the Sanhedrin (cf. 1:19). **sign.** The Jews demanded that Jesus show some type of miraculous sign that would indicate His authority for the actions that He had just taken in regulating the activities of the temple. Their demand of a sign reveals that they had not grasped the significance of Jesus' rebuke that centered in their need for proper attitudes and holiness in worship. Such an action itself constituted a "sign" of Jesus' person and authority. Moreover, they were requesting from Jesus a crass display of miracles on demand, further displaying their unbelief.

2:19 At his trial, the authorities charged Jesus (Mark 14:29,58) with making a threatening statement against the temple, revealing that they did not understand Jesus' response here. Once again John's gospel supplements the other gospels at this point by indicating that Jesus enigmatically referred to His resurrection. As with His usage of parables, Jesus' cryptic statement most likely was designed to reveal the truth to His disciples but conceal its meaning from unbelievers who questioned Him (Matt. 13:10,11). Only after His resurrection, however, did the disciples understand the real significance of this statement (v. 22; cf. Matt. 12:40). Importantly, through the death and resurrection of Christ, temple worship in Jerusalem was destroyed (cf. 4:21) and reinstituted in the hearts of those who were built into a spiritual temple called the church (Eph. 2:19-22).

The Seven Signs

Turns water into wine (John 2:1-12)	Jesus is the source of life.
Heals a nobleman's son (John 4:46-54)	Jesus is master over distance.
Heals a lame man at the pool of Bethesda (John 5:1-17)	Jesus is master over time.
Feeds 5,000 (John 6:1-14)	Jesus is the bread of life.
Walks on water, stills a storm (John 6:15-21)	Jesus is master over nature.
Heals a man blind from birth (John 9:1-41)	Jesus is the light of the world.
Raises Lazarus from the dead (John 11:17-45)	Jesus has power over death.

[r]"Destroy this temple, and in three days I
will raise it up."
20 Then the Jews said, "It has taken
forty-six years to build this temple, and
will You raise it up in three days?"
21 But He was speaking [s]of the temple of
His body. 22 Therefore, when He had risen
from the dead, [t]His disciples remembered
that He had said this [4]to them; and they
believed the Scripture and the word which
Jesus had said.
23 Now when He was in Jerusalem at the
Passover, during the feast, many believed in
His name when they saw the [u]signs which
He did. 24 But Jesus did not commit Himself to them, because He [v]knew all *men*,
25 and had no need that anyone should testify of man, for [w]He knew what was in man.

19 [r] Matt. 26:61; 27:40; [Mark 14:58; 15:29]; Luke 24:46; Acts 6:14; 10:40; 1 Cor. 15:4
21 [s] [1 Cor. 3:16; 6:19; 2 Cor. 6:16; Col. 2:9; Heb. 8:2]
22 [t] Luke 24:8; John 2:17; 12:16; 14:26 [4] NU, M omit *to them*
23 [u] [John 5:36; Acts 2:22]
24 [v] Matt. 9:4; John 16:30; Rev. 2:23
25 [w] 1 Sam. 16:7; 1 Chr. 28:9; Matt. 9:4; [Mark 2:8]; John 6:64; 16:30; Acts 1:24; Rev. 2:23

Christ Witnesses to Nicodemus

3 There was a man of the Pharisees
named Nicodemus, a ruler of the Jews.
2 [a]This man came to Jesus by night and
said to Him, "Rabbi, we know that You are
a teacher come from God; for [b]no one can
do these signs that You do unless [c]God is
with him."
3 Jesus answered and said to him, "Most
assuredly, I say to you, [d]unless one is born
[1]again, he cannot see the kingdom of God."

CHAPTER 3 2 [a] John 7:50; 19:39 [b] John 9:16, 33; Acts 2:22 [c] [Acts 10:38] 3 [d] [John 1:13; Gal. 6:15; Titus 3:5; James 1:18; 1 Pet. 1:23; 1 John 3:9] [1] Or *from above*

2:20 forty-six years to build this temple. This was not a reference to the Solomonic temple, since it had been destroyed during the Babylonian conquest in 586 B.C. When the captives returned from Babylon, Zerubbabel and Joshua began rebuilding the temple (Ezra 1–4). Encouraged by the prophets Haggai and Zechariah (Ezra 5:1–6:18), the Jews completed the work in 516 B.C. In 20/19 B.C. Herod the Great began a reconstruction and expansion. Workers completed the main part of the project in 10 years, but other parts were still being constructed even at the time Jesus cleansed the temple. Interestingly, the finishing touches on the whole enterprise were still being made at its destruction by the Romans along with Jerusalem in A.D. 70. The famous "Wailing Wall" is built on part of the Herodian temple foundation.

2:23-25 The third way John demonstrated Christ's deity in the account of the temple cleansing was to show His perception of reality. Only God truly knows the hearts of men.

2:23,24 many believed in His name.... But Jesus did not commit Himself. John based these two phrases on the same Gr. verb for "believe." This verse subtly reveals the true nature of belief from a biblical standpoint. Because of what they knew of Jesus from His miraculous signs many came to believe in Him. However, Jesus made it His habit not to wholeheartedly "entrust" or "commit" Himself to them because He knew their hearts. Verse 24 indicates that Jesus looked for genuine conversion rather than enthusiasm for the spectacular. The latter verse also leaves a subtle doubt as to the genuineness of the conversion of some (cf. 8:31,32). This emphatic contrast between vv. 23,24 in terms of type of trust, therefore, reveals that "belief into His name" involved much more than intellectual assent. It called for whole-hearted commitment of one's life as Jesus' disciple (cf. Matt. 10:37; 16:24-26).

3:1-21 The story of Jesus and Nicodemus reinforces John's themes that Jesus is the Messiah and Son of God (apologetic) and that he came to offer salvation to men (evangelistic). John 2:23,24 actually serves as the introduction to Nicodemus' story, since chap. 3 constitutes tangible evidence of Jesus' ability to know men's hearts and thereby also demonstrates Jesus' deity. Jesus also presented God's plan of salvation to Nicodemus, showing that He was God's messenger, whose redemptive work brings about the promised salvation to His people (v. 14). The chapter may be divided into two sections: 1) Jesus' dialogue with Nicodemus (vv. 1-10); and 2) Jesus' discourse on God's plan of salvation (vv. 11-21).

3:1-10 This section on Jesus' dialogue with Nicodemus may be divided into 3 sections: 1) Nicodemus' inquiry of Jesus (vv. 1-3); 2) Jesus' insight into Nicodemus (vv. 4-8); and 3) Jesus' indictment of Nicodemus (vv. 9,10).

3:1 Pharisees. *See note on Matt. 3:7.* The word "Pharisee" most likely comes from a Heb. word meaning "to separate" and therefore probably means "separated ones." They were not separatists in the sense of isolationists but in the puritanical sense, i.e., they were highly zealous for ritual and religious purity according to the Mosaic law as well as their own traditions that they added to the OT legislation. Although their origin is unknown, they seem to have arisen as an offshoot from the "Hasidim" or "pious ones" during the Maccabean era. They were generally from the Jewish middle class and mostly consisted of laity (business men) rather than priests or Levites. They represented the orthodox core of Judaism and very strongly influenced the common people of Israel. According to Josephus, 6,000 existed at the time of Herod the Great. Jesus condemned them for their hyper-concentration on externalizing religion (rules and regulations) rather than inward spiritual transformation (vv. 3,7). **Nicodemus.** Although Nicodemus was a Pharisee, his name was Gr. in origin and means "victor over the people." He was a prominent Pharisee and member of the Sanhedrin ("a ruler of the Jews"). Nothing is known about his family background. He eventually came to believe in Jesus (7:50-52), risking His own life and reputation by helping to give Jesus' body a decent burial (19:38-42). **a ruler of the Jews.** This is a reference to the Sanhedrin (*see note on Matt. 26:59*), the main ruling body of the Jews in Palestine. It was the Jewish "supreme court" or ruling council of the time and arose most likely during the Persian period. In NT times, the Sanhedrin was composed of the High-Priest (president), chief priests, elders (family heads), and scribes for a total of 71 people. The method of appointment was both hereditary and political. It executed both civil and criminal jurisdiction according to Jewish law. However, capital punishment cases required the sanction of the Roman procurator (18:30-32). After A.D. 70 and the destruction of Jerusalem, the Sanhedrin was abolished and replaced by the Beth Din (court of Judgment) that was composed of scribes whose decisions had only moral and religious authority.

3:2 came to Jesus by night. While some have thought that Nicodemus' visit at night was somehow figurative of the spiritual darkness of his heart (cf. 1:5; 9:4; 11:10; 13:30) or that he decided to come at this time because he could take more time with Jesus and be unhurried in conversation, perhaps the most logical explanation lies in the fact that, as a ruler of the Jews, Nicodemus was afraid of the implications of associating openly in conversation with Jesus. He chose night in order to have a clandestine meeting with Jesus rather than risk disfavor with his fellow Pharisees among whom Jesus was generally unpopular.

3:3 born again. The phrase lit. means "born from above." Jesus answered a question that Nicodemus does not even ask. He read Nicodemus' heart and came to the very core of his problem, i.e., the need for spiritual transformation or regeneration produced by the Holy Spirit. New birth is an act of God whereby eternal life is imparted to the believer (2 Cor. 5:17; Titus 3:5; 1 Pet. 1:3; 1 John 2:29; 3:9; 4:7; 5:1,4,18). Chapter 1:12,13 indicates that "born again" also carries the idea "to become children of God" through trust in the name of the incarnate Word. **cannot see the kingdom of God.** In context, this is

4 Nicodemus said to Him, "How can a
man be born when he is old? Can he enter
a second time into his mother's womb and
be born?"
5 Jesus answered, "Most assuredly, I say
to you, [e]unless one is born of water and the
Spirit, he cannot enter the kingdom of
God. 6 That which is born of the flesh is
[f]flesh, and that which is born of the Spirit
is spirit. 7 Do not marvel that I said to you,
'You must be born again.' 8 [g]The wind
blows where it wishes, and you hear the
sound of it, but cannot tell where it comes
from and where it goes. So is everyone
who is born of the Spirit."
9 Nicodemus answered and said to Him,
[h]"How can these things be?"
10 Jesus answered and said to him, "Are
you the teacher of Israel, and do not know
these things? 11 [i]Most assuredly, I say to
you, We speak what We know and testify
what We have seen, and [j]you do not receive
Our witness. 12 If I have told you earthly
things and you do not believe, how will you
believe if I tell you heavenly things? 13 [k]No
one has ascended to heaven but He who
came down from heaven, *that is,* the Son of
Man [2]who is in heaven. 14 [l]And as Moses
lifted up the serpent in the wilderness, even
so [m]must the Son of Man be lifted up, 15 that
whoever [n]believes in Him should [3]not perish but [o]have eternal life. 16 [p]For God so
loved the world that He gave His only begotten [q]Son, that whoever believes in Him
should not perish but have everlasting life.
17 [r]For God did not send His Son into the
world to condemn the world, but that the
world through Him might be saved.

5 [e] Mark 16:16; [Acts 2:38]
6 [f] John 1:13; 1 Cor. 15:50
8 [g] Ps. 135:7; Eccl. 11:5; Ezek. 37:9; 1 Cor. 2:11
9 [h] John 6:52,60
11 [i] [Matt. 11:27] [j] John 3:32; 8:14
13 [k] Deut. 30:12; Prov. 30:4; Acts 2:34; Rom. 10:6; 1 Cor. 15:47; Eph. 4:9 [2] NU omits *who is in heaven*
14 [l] Num. 21:9 [m] Matt. 27:35; Mark 15:24; Luke 23:33; John 8:28; 12:34; 19:18
15 [n] John 6:47 [o] John 3:36 [3] NU omits *not perish but*
16 [p] Rom. 5:8; Eph. 2:4; 2 Thess. 2:16; [1 John 4:9, 10; Rev. 1:5] [q] [Is. 9:6]
17 [r] Matt. 1:21; Luke 9:56; 1 John 4:14

primarily a reference to participation in the millennial kingdom at the end of the age, fervently anticipated by the Pharisees and other Jews. Since the Pharisees were supernaturalists, they naturally and eagerly expected the coming of the prophesied resurrection of the saints and institution of the messianic kingdom (Is. 11:1-16; Dan. 12:2). Their problem was that they thought that mere physical lineage and keeping of religious externals qualified them for entrance into the kingdom rather than the needed spiritual transformation which Jesus emphasized (cf. 8:33-39; Gal. 6:15). The coming of the kingdom at the end of the age can be described as the "regeneration" of the world (Matt. 19:28) but regeneration of the individual is required before the end of the world in order to enter the kingdom.

3:4 Nicodemus' response regarding physical birth indicated that he had no idea what Jesus meant and was incredulous at what he was hearing.

3:5 born of water and the Spirit. Jesus referred not to literal water here but to the need for "cleansing" (e.g., Ezek. 36:24-27). When water is used figuratively in the OT, it habitually refers to renewal or spiritual cleansing, especially when used in conjunction with "spirit" (Num. 19:17-19; Ps. 51:9,10; Is. 32:15; 44:3-5; 55:1-3; Jer. 2:13; Joel 2:28,29). Thus, Jesus made reference to the spiritual washing or purification of the soul, accomplished by the Holy Spirit through the Word of God at the moment of salvation (cf. Eph. 5:26; Titus 3:5), required for belonging to His kingdom.

3:8 The wind blows where it wishes. Jesus' point was that just as the wind cannot be controlled or understood by human beings but its effects can be witnessed, so also it is with the Holy Spirit. He cannot be controlled or understood, but the proof of His work is apparent. Where the Spirit works, there is undeniable and unmistakable evidence.

3:10 the teacher. The use of the definite article "the" indicates that Nicodemus was a renowned master-teacher in the nation of Israel, an established religious authority *par excellence.* He enjoyed a high standing among the rabbis or teachers of his day. Jesus' reply emphasized the spiritual bankruptcy of the nation at that time, since even one of the greatest of Jewish teachers did not recognize this teaching on spiritual cleansing and transformation based clearly in the OT (cf. v. 5). The net effect is to show that externals of religion may have a deadening effect on one's spiritual perception.

3:11-21 The focus of these verses turns away from Nicodemus and centers on Jesus' discourse regarding the true meaning of salvation. The key word in these verses is "believe," used 7 times. The new birth must be appropriated by an act of faith. While vv. 1-10 center on the divine initiative in salvation, vv. 11-21 emphasize the human reaction to the work of God in regeneration. In vv. 11-21, the section may be divided into 3 parts: 1) the problem of unbelief (vv. 11,12); 2) the answer to unbelief (vv. 13-17); and 3) the results of unbelief (vv. 18-21).

3:11,12 Jesus focused on the idea that unbelief is the cause of ignorance. At heart, Nicodemus' failure to understand Jesus' words centered not so much in his intellect but in his failure to believe Jesus' witness.

3:11 you do not receive Our witness. The plural "you" here refers back to the "we" of v. 2, where Nicodemus was speaking as a representative of his nation Israel ("we know"). Jesus replied in v. 11 with "you" indicting that Nicodemus' unbelief was typical of the nation as a collective whole.

3:13 No one has ascended to heaven. This verse contradicts other religious systems' claims to special revelation from God. Jesus insisted that no one has ascended to heaven in such a way as to return and talk about heavenly things (cf. 2 Cor. 12:1-4). Only He had His permanent abode in heaven prior to His incarnation and, therefore, only He has the true knowledge regarding heavenly wisdom (cf. Prov. 30:4).

3:14 so must the Son of Man be lifted up. Cf. 8:28; 12:32,34; 18:31,32. This is a veiled prediction of Jesus' death on the cross. Jesus referred to the story of Num. 21:5-9 where the Israelite people who looked at the serpent lifted up by Moses were healed. The point of this illustration or analogy is in the "lifted up." Just as Moses lifted up the snake on the pole so that all who looked upon it might live physically, those who look to Christ, who was "lifted up" on the cross for the sins of the world, will live spiritually and eternally.

3:15 eternal life. This is the first of 10 references to "eternal life" in John's gospel. The same Gr. word is translated 8 times as "everlasting life." The two expressions appear in the NT nearly 50 times. Eternal life refers not only to eternal quantity but divine quality of life. It means lit. "life of the age to come" and refers therefore to resurrection and heavenly existence in perfect glory and holiness. This life for believers in the Lord Jesus is experienced before heaven is reached. This "eternal life" is in essence nothing less than participation in the eternal life of the Living Word, Jesus Christ. It is the life of God in every believer, yet not fully manifest until the resurrection (Rom. 8:19-23; Phil. 3:20,21).

3:16 For God so loved the world. The Son's mission is bound up in the supreme love of God for the evil, sinful "world" of humanity (cf. 6:32,51; 12:47; *see note on 1:9*; *see note on Matt. 5:44,45*) that is in rebellion against Him. The word "so" emphasizes the intensity or greatness of His love. The Father gave His unique and beloved Son to die on behalf of sinful men (*see note on 2 Cor. 5:21*). **everlasting life.** *See note on v. 15*; cf. 17:3; 1 John 5:20.

18 [s]"He who believes in Him is not condemned; but he who does not believe is
condemned already, because he has not believed in the name of the only begotten Son
of God. 19 And this is the condemnation,
[t]that the light has come into the world, and
men loved darkness rather than light, because their deeds were evil. 20 For [u]every-
one practicing evil hates the light and does
not come to the light, lest his deeds should
be exposed. 21 But he who does the truth
comes to the light, that his deeds may be
clearly seen, that they have been [v]done in
God."

John the Baptist Witnesses Concerning Christ

22 After these things Jesus and His disciples came into the land of Judea, and there
He remained with them [w]and baptized.
23 Now John also was baptizing in Aenon
near [x]Salim, because there was much
water there. [y]And they came and were
baptized. 24 For [z]John had not yet been
thrown into prison.
25 Then there arose a dispute between
some of John's disciples and the Jews about
purification. 26 And they came to John and
said to him, "Rabbi, He who was with you
beyond the Jordan, [a]to whom you have
testified—behold, He is baptizing, and all
[b]are coming to Him!"
27 John answered and said, [c]"A man
can receive nothing unless it has been
given to him from heaven. 28 You yourselves bear me witness, that I said, [d]'I am
not the Christ,' but, [e]'I have been sent before Him.' 29 [f]He who has the bride is the
bridegroom; but [g]the friend of the bridegroom, who stands and hears him, rejoices greatly because of the bridegroom's
voice. Therefore this joy of mine is fulfilled. 30 [h]He must increase, but I *must* decrease. 31 [i]He who comes from above [j]is
above all; [k]he who is of the earth is earthly and speaks of the earth. [l]He who
comes from heaven is above all. 32 And

18 [s] John 5:24; 6:40, 47; 20:31; Rom. 8:1
19 [t] [John 1:4, 9-11]
20 [u] Job 24:13; Eph. 5:11, 13
21 [v] [John 15:4, 5]; 1 Cor. 15:10
22 [w] John 4:1, 2
23 [x] 1 Sam. 9:4 [y] Matt. 3:5, 6
24 [z] Matt. 4:12; 14:3; Mark 6:17; Luke 3:20
26 [a] John 1:7, 15, 27, 34 [b] Mark 2:2; 3:10; 5:24; Luke 8:19
27 [c] [Rom. 12:5-8]; 1 Cor. 3:5, 6; 4:7; Heb. 5:4; [James 1:17; 1 Pet. 4:10, 11]
28 [d] John 1:19-27 [e] Mal. 3:1; Mark 1:2; [Luke 1:17]
29 [f] Matt. 22:2; [2 Cor. 11:2; Eph. 5:25, 27]; Rev. 21:9 [g] Song 5:1
30 [h] [Is. 9:7]
31 [i] John 3:13; 8:23 [j] Matt. 28:18; John 1:15, 27; 13:13; Rom. 9:5; [Col. 1:17, 18] [k] 1 Cor. 15:47 [l] John 6:33; 1 Cor. 15:47; Eph. 1:21; Phil. 2:9

3:18 believed in the name. This phrase (lit. "to believe into the name") means more than mere intellectual assent to the claims of the gospel. It includes trust and commitment to Christ as Lord and Savior which results in receiving a new nature (v. 7) which produces a change in heart and obedience to the Lord (*see notes on 2:23-25*).

3:22-36 This section constitutes John the Baptist's last testimony in this gospel regarding Christ. As his ministry faded away, Jesus' ministry moved to the forefront. In spite of the fact that John the Baptist received widespread fame in Israel and was generally accepted by the common people of the land as well as those who were social outcasts, his testimony regarding Jesus was rejected, especially by the leaders of Israel (cf. Matt. 3:5-10; Luke 7:29).

3:22 into the land of Judea. While the previous episode with Nicodemus took place in Jerusalem (2:23), which was part of Judea, the phrase here means that Jesus went out into the rural areas of that region. **baptized.** Chapter 4:22 specifically says that Jesus did not personally baptize but that His disciples carried on this work.

3:23 Aenon near Salim. The exact location of this reference is disputed. The phrase may refer to either Salim near Shechem or Salim that is 6 mi. S of Beth Shean. Both are in the region of Samaria. Aenon is a transliterated Heb. word meaning "springs," and both of these possible sights have plenty of water ("much water there").

3:24 John had not yet been thrown into prison. This provides another indication that John supplemented the synoptic gospels by providing additional information that helps further understanding of the movements of John the Baptist and Jesus (see Introduction). In Matthew and Mark, Christ's temptation is followed by John's imprisonment. With this phrase, John the apostle fills in the slot between Jesus' baptism and temptation and the Baptist's imprisonment.

3:25 there arose a dispute. The dispute probably concerned the relation of the baptismal ministries of John and Jesus to the Jews' purification practices alluded to in 2:6. The real underlying impetus, however, centered in the concern of John's disciples that Jesus was in competition with him.

3:25-36 This section may be divided into 3 parts which highlight the significance of what was occurring in relationship to John's and Jesus' ministry: 1) John the Baptist constituted the end of the old age (vv. 25-29); 2) the transition to Jesus' ministry (v. 30); and 3) Jesus' ministry as constituting the beginning of the new age (vv. 31-36). Instead of jealousy, John exhibited humble faithfulness to the superiority of Jesus' person and ministry.

3:26 all are coming to Him. The potential conflict between John and Jesus was heightened by the fact that both were engaged in ministry in close proximity to one another. Because baptism is mentioned in v. 22, Jesus may have been close to Jericho near the fords of the Jordan, while John was a short distance N baptizing at Aenon. John's followers were especially disturbed by the fact that so many were flocking to Jesus whereas formerly they had come to John.

3:27 given to him from heaven. This verse emphasizes God's sovereign authority in granting ministry opportunity (cf. 1 Cor. 4:7; 15:10).

3:29 bridegroom...friend of bridegroom. John conveyed his understanding of his own role through the use of a parable. The "friend of the bridegroom" was the ancient equivalent of the best man who organized the details and presided over the Judean wedding (Galilean weddings were somewhat different). This friend found his greatest joy in watching the ceremony proceed without problems. Most likely, John was also alluding to OT passages where faithful Israel is depicted as the bride of the Lord (Is. 62:4,5; Jer. 2:2; Hos. 2:16-20).

3:31-36 In these verses, John the Baptist gave 5 reasons for Christ's superiority to him: 1) Christ had a heavenly origin (v. 21); 2) Christ knew what was true by firsthand experience (v. 32); 3) Christ's testimony always agreed with God (v. 33); 4) Christ experienced the Holy Spirit in an unlimited manner (v. 34); and 5) Christ was supreme because the Father sovereignly had granted that status to Him (v. 35).

3:31,32 above all. These verses bring together several of the themes from the entire chapter. From the immediate context, John explained why Jesus the incarnate word must become greater, i.e., he alone is "from above" (heavenly origin) and therefore "above all." The Gr. term "above all" recalls v. 3 where the new birth "from above" can only be experienced by faith in the One who is "from above." In contrast, all others are "of the earth" signifying finitude and limitation. In the immediate context, John the Baptist had to become less (v. 30) because he was "of the earth" and belonged to the earth. Although he called for repentance and baptism, John could not reveal heaven's counsel like Jesus, the God-Man.

[m]what He has seen and heard, that He testifies; and no one receives His testimony.
33 He who has received His testimony [n]has
certified that God is true. **34** [o]For He whom
God has sent speaks the words of God, for
God does not give the Spirit [p]by measure.
35 [q]The Father loves the Son, and has given
all things into His hand. **36** [r]He who believes in the Son has everlasting life; and he
who does not believe the Son shall not see
life, but the [s]wrath of God abides on him."

Christ Witnesses to the Woman at the Well

4 Therefore, when the Lord knew that
the Pharisees had heard that Jesus
made and [a]baptized more disciples than
John **2** (though Jesus Himself did not baptize, but His disciples), **3** He left Judea and
departed again to Galilee. **4** But He needed
to go through Samaria.
5 So He came to a city of Samaria which
is called Sychar, near the plot of ground
that [b]Jacob [c]gave to his son Joseph. **6** Now
Jacob's well was there. Jesus therefore,
being wearied from *His* journey, sat thus
by the well. It was about the sixth hour.
7 A woman of Samaria came to draw
water. Jesus said to her, "Give Me a drink."
8 For His disciples had gone away into the
city to buy food.
9 Then the woman of Samaria said to
Him, "How is it that You, being a Jew, ask

32 [m] Is. 53:1, 3; John 3:11; 15:15 **33** [n] Rom. 3:4; 1 John 5:10 **34** [o] Deut. 18:18; John 7:16 [p] John 1:16 **35** [q] Matt. 11:27; Luke 10:22; John 5:20; [Heb. 2:8] **36** [r] John 3:16, 17; 6:47; Rom. 1:17; 1 John 5:10 [s] Rom. 1:18; Eph. 5:6; 1 Thess. 1:10

CHAPTER 4

1 [a] John 3:22, 26; 1 Cor. 1:17 **5** [b] Gen. 33:19; Josh. 24:32 [c] Gen. 48:22; Josh. 4:12

3:34 the Spirit by measure. God gave the Spirit to the Son without limits (1:32,33; Is. 11:2; 42:1; 61:1).

3:36 This constitutes a fitting climax to the chapter. John the Baptist laid out two alternatives, genuine faith and defiant disobedience, thereby bringing to the forefront the threat of looming judgment. As John faded from the forefront, he offered an invitation to faith in the Son and clearly expressed the ultimate consequence of failure to believe, i.e., "the wrath of God."

4:1-26 The story of the Samaritan woman reinforces John's main theme that Jesus is the Messiah and Son of God. The thrust of these verses is not so much her conversion but that Jesus is Messiah (v. 26). While her conversion is clearly implied, the apostle's focus centers on Jesus' declaration foretold in the Scriptures (v. 25). Important also is the fact that this chapter demonstrates Jesus' love and understanding of people. His love for mankind involved no boundaries, for He lovingly and compassionately reached out to a woman who was a social outcast. In contrast to the limitations of human love, Christ exhibits the character of divine love that is indiscriminate and all-encompassing (3:16).

4:3 He left Judea. John the Baptist and Jesus had official scrutiny focused on them because of their distinctive message regarding repentance and the kingdom. Most likely, Jesus wanted to avoid any possible trouble with John's disciples who were troubled with His growing popularity and, since the Pharisees were also focusing on His growing influence, Jesus decided to leave Judea and travel N in order to avoid any conflict.

4:4 He needed to go through. Several roads led from Judea to Galilee: one near the seacoast; another through the region of Perea; and one through the heart of Samaria. Even with the strong antipathy between Jews and Samaritans, the Jewish historian Josephus relates that the custom of Judeans at the time of the great festivals was to travel through the country of the Samaritans because it was the shorter route. Although the verb "needed" may possibly refer to the fact that Jesus wanted to save time and needless steps, because of the gospel's emphasis on the Lord's consciousness of fulfilling His Father's plan (2:4; 7:30; 8:20; 12:23; 13:1; 14:31), the apostle may have been highlighting divine, spiritual necessity, i.e., Jesus had an appointment with divine destiny in meeting the Samaritan woman, to whom He would reveal His messiahship. **Samaria.** When the nation of Israel split politically after Solomon's rule, King Omri named the capital of the northern kingdom of Israel "Samaria" (1 Kin. 16:24). The name eventually referred to the entire district and sometimes to the entire northern kingdom, which had been taken captive (capital, Samaria) by Assyria in 722 B.C. (2 Kin. 17:1-6). While Assyria led most of the populace of the 10 northern tribes away (into the region which today is northern Iraq), it left a sizable population of Jews in the northern Samaritan region and transported many non-Jews into Samaria. These groups intermingled to form a mixed race through intermarriage. Eventually tension developed between the Jews who returned from captivity and the Samaritans. The Samaritans withdrew from the worship of Yahweh at Jerusalem and established their worship at Mt. Gerizim in Samaria (vv. 20-22). Samaritans regarded only the Pentateuch as authoritative. As a result of this history, Jews repudiated Samaritans and considered them heretical. Intense ethnic and cultural tensions raged historically between the two groups so that both avoided contact as much as possible (v. 9; Ezra 4:1-24; Neh. 4:1-6; Luke 10:25-37). *See note on 2 Kin. 17:24.*

4:5 Sychar. This town is probably identified with the modern village of Askar on the shoulder of Mt. Ebal, opposite Mt. Gerizim. A continuous line of tradition identifies Jacob's well as lying about a half mile S of Askar.

4:5,6 These verses refer back to Gen. 48:22 where Jacob bequeathed a section of land to Joseph which he had purchased from the "children of Hamor" (cf. Gen. 33:19). When the Jews returned from Egypt, they buried Joseph's bones in that land at Shechem. This area became the inheritance of Joseph's descendants. The precise location of "Jacob's well" has been set by a firm tradition among Jews, Samaritans, Muslims, and Christians and lies today in the shadow of the crypt of an unfinished Orthodox church. The term used here for "well" denotes a running spring, while in vv. 11,12 John used another term for "well" that means "cistern" or "dug-out-well" indicating that the well was both dug out and fed by an underground spring. This spring is still active today.

4:6 wearied from *His* journey. Since the Word became flesh (1:14), He also suffered from physical limitations in His humanity (Heb. 2:10-14). **the sixth hour.** If John used the Jewish reckoning of time, calculated from sunrise at about 6:00 a.m., the time was about noon. If John used Roman time, which started reckoning from 12:00 p.m., the time would be about 6:00 p.m.

4:7 A woman of Samaria came to draw water. Women generally came in groups to collect water, either earlier or later in the day to avoid the sun's heat. If the Samaritan woman alone came at 12:00 p.m. (*see note on v. 6*), this may indicate that her public shame (vv. 16-19) caused her to be isolated from other women. **"Give Me a drink."** For a Jewish man to speak to a woman in public, let alone to ask from her, a Samaritan, a drink was a definite breach of rigid social custom as well as a marked departure from the social animosity that existed between the two groups. Further, a "rabbi" and religious leader did not hold conversations with women of ill-repute (v. 18).

4:8 to buy food. This verse indicates that since Jesus and his disciples were willing to purchase food from Samaritans, they did not follow some the self-imposed regulations of stricter Jews, who would have been unwilling to eat food handled by outcast Samaritans.

a drink from me, a Samaritan woman?"
For [d]Jews have no dealings with [e]Samari-
tans.
10 Jesus answered and said to her, "If
you knew the [f]gift of God, and who it is
who says to you, 'Give Me a drink,' you
would have asked Him, and He would
have given you [g]living water."
11 The woman said to Him, "Sir, You
have nothing to draw with, and the well is
deep. Where then do You get that living
water? 12 Are You greater than our father
Jacob, who gave us the well, and drank
from it himself, as well as his sons and his
livestock?"
13 Jesus answered and said to her,
"Whoever drinks of this water will thirst
again, 14 but [h]whoever drinks of the water
that I shall give him will never thirst. But
the water that I shall give him [i]will become
in him a fountain of water springing up
into everlasting life."
15 [j]The woman said to Him, "Sir, give
me this water, that I may not thirst, nor
come here to draw."
16 Jesus said to her, "Go, call your husband, and come here."
17 The woman answered and said, "I
have no husband."
Jesus said to her, "You have well said, 'I
have no husband,' 18 for you have had five
husbands, and the one whom you now
have is not your husband; in that you
spoke truly."
19 The woman said to Him, "Sir, [k]I perceive that You are a prophet. 20 Our fathers
worshiped on [l]this mountain, and you
Jews say that in [m]Jerusalem is the place
where one ought to worship."
21 Jesus said to her, "Woman, believe
Me, the hour is coming [n]when you will
neither on this mountain, nor in Jerusalem,
worship the Father. 22 You worship [o]what
you do not know; we know what we worship, for [p]salvation is of the Jews. 23 But
the hour is coming, and now is, when the
true worshipers will [q]worship the Father
in [r]spirit [s]and truth; for the Father is seeking such to worship Him. 24 [t]God *is* Spirit,
and those who worship Him must worship
in spirit and truth."

9 [d]Acts 10:28 [e]2 Kin. 17:24; Matt. 10:5, 6; Luke 9:52; 10:33; 17:16; John 8:48
10 [f][Rom. 5:15] [g]Is. 12:3; 44:3; Jer. 2:13; Zech. 13:1; 14:8; John 7:38
14 [h][John 6:35, 58] [i]John 7:37, 38
15 [j]John 6:34, 35; 17:2, 3; [Rom. 6:23; 1 John 5:20]
19 [k]Matt. 21:11; Luke 7:16, 39; 24:19; John 6:14; 7:40; 9:17
20 [l]Gen. 12:6-8; 33:18, 20; Judg. 9:7 [m]Deut. 12:5, 11; 1 Kin. 9:3; 2 Chr. 7:12; Ps. 122:1-9
21 [n][Mal. 1:11]; 1 Tim. 2:8
22 [o][2 Kin. 17:28-41] [p][Is. 2:3; Luke 24:47; Rom. 3:1; 9:4, 5]
23 [q]Matt. 18:20; [Heb. 13:10-14] [r]Phil. 3:3 [s][John 1:17]
24 [t]2 Cor. 3:17

4:10 living water. The OT is the background for this term, which has important metaphorical significance. In Jer. 2:13, Yahweh decries the disobedient Jews for rejecting Him, the "fountain of living waters." The OT prophets looked forward to a time when "living waters shall flow from Jerusalem" (Zech. 14:8; Ezek. 47:9). The OT metaphor spoke of the knowledge of God and His grace which provides cleansing, spiritual life, and the transforming power of the Holy Spirit (cf. Is. 1:16-18; 12:3; 44:3; Ezek. 36:25-27). John applies these themes to Jesus Christ as the living water which is symbolic of eternal life mediated by the Holy Spirit from Him (cf. v. 14; 6:35; 7:37-39). Jesus used the woman's need for physical water to sustain life in this arid region in order to serve as an object lesson for her need for spiritual transformation.

4:15 The woman, like Nicodemus (3:4), did not realize that Jesus was talking about her spiritual needs. Instead, in her mind, she wanted such water in order to avoid her frequent trips to Jacob's well.

4:16 call your husband. Since the woman failed to understand the nature of the living water He offered (v. 15), Jesus abruptly turned the dialogue to focus sharply on her real spiritual need for conversion and cleansing from sin. His intimate knowledge of her morally depraved life not only indicated His supernatural ability, but also focused on her spiritual condition.

4:18 not your husband. She was living conjugally with a man whom Jesus said was not her husband. By such an explicit statement, our Lord rejected the notion that when two people live together it constitutes marriage. Biblically, marriage is always restricted to a public, formal, official, and recognized covenant.

4:19 You are a prophet. His knowledge of her life indicated He had supernatural inspiration.

4:20 on this mountain. Both Jews and Samaritans recognized that God had commanded their forefathers to identify a special place for worshiping Him (Deut. 12:5). The Jews, recognizing the entire Hebrew canon, chose Jerusalem (2 Sam. 7:5-13; 2 Chr. 6:6). The Samaritans, recognizing only the Pentateuch, noted that the first place Abraham built an altar to God was at Shechem (Gen. 12:6,7), which was overlooked by Mt. Gerizim, where the Israelites had shouted the blessings promised by God before they entered the Promised Land (Deut. 11:29,30). As a result, they chose Mt. Gerizim for the place of their temple.

4:21 neither on this mountain, nor in Jerusalem. There was no reason to debate locations, since both places would be obsolete soon and neither would have any role to play in the lives of those who genuinely worship God. Jerusalem would even be destroyed with its temple (A.D. 70).

4:22 you do not know. The Samaritans did not know God. They did not have the full revelation of Him, and thus could not worship in truth. The Jews did have the full revelation of God in the OT; thus they knew the God they worshiped, because salvation's truth came first to them (*see note on Luke 19:9*) and through them to the world (cf. Rom. 3:2; 9:4,5).

4:23 hour. This refers to Jesus' death, resurrection, and ascension to God, having completed redemption. **true worshipers.** Jesus' point is that in light of His coming as Messiah and Savior, worshipers will be identified, not by a particular shrine or location, but by their worship of the Father through the Son. With Christ's coming, previous distinctions between true and false worshipers based on locations disappeared. True worshipers are all those everywhere who worship God through the Son, from the heart (cf. Phil. 3:3).

4:24 God *is* Spirit. This verse represents the classical statement on the nature of God as Spirit. The phrase means that God is invisible (Col. 1:15; 1 Tim. 1:17; Heb. 11:27) as opposed to the physical or material nature of man (1:18; 3:6). The word order of this phrase puts an emphasis on "Spirit," and the statement is essentially emphatic. Man could never comprehend the invisible God unless He revealed Himself, as He did in Scripture and the Incarnation. **must worship.** Jesus is not speaking of a desirable element in worship but that which is absolutely necessary. **in spirit and truth.** The word "spirit" does not refer to the Holy Spirit but to the human spirit. Jesus' point here is that a person must worship not simply by external conformity to religious rituals and places (outwardly) but inwardly ("in spirit") with the proper heart attitude. The reference to "truth" refers to worship of God consistent with the revealed Scripture and centered on the "Word made flesh" who ultimately revealed His Father (14:6).

25 The woman said to Him, "I know that
Messiah [u]is coming" (who is called Christ).
"When He comes, [v]He will tell us all
things."
26 Jesus said to her, [w]"I who speak to
you am *He.*"

Christ Witnesses to the Disciples

27 And at this *point* His disciples came,
and they marveled that He talked with a
woman; yet no one said, "What do You
seek?" or, "Why are You talking with her?"
28 The woman then left her waterpot,
went her way into the city, and said to the
men, 29 "Come, see a Man [x]who told me all
things that I ever did. Could this be the
Christ?" 30 Then they went out of the city
and came to Him.
31 In the meantime His disciples urged
Him, saying, "Rabbi, eat."
32 But He said to them, "I have food to
eat of which you do not know."
33 Therefore the disciples said to one another, "Has anyone brought Him *anything*
to eat?"
34 Jesus said to them, [y]"My food is to do
the will of Him who sent Me, and to [z]finish
His work. 35 Do you not say, 'There are still
four months and *then* comes [a]the harvest'?
Behold, I say to you, lift up your eyes and
look at the fields, [b]for they are already
white for harvest! 36 [c]And he who reaps receives wages, and gathers fruit for eternal
life, that [d]both he who sows and he who
reaps may rejoice together. 37 For in this the
saying is true: [e]'One sows and another
reaps.' 38 I sent you to reap that for which
you have not labored; [f]others have labored,
and you have entered into their labors."

Christ Witnesses to the Samaritans

39 And many of the Samaritans of that
city believed in Him [g]because of the word
of the woman who testified, "He told me
all that I *ever* did." 40 So when the Samaritans had come to Him, they urged Him to
stay with them; and He stayed there two
days. 41 And many more believed because
of His own [h]word.
42 Then they said to the woman, "Now
we believe, not because of what you said,
for [i]we ourselves have heard *Him* and we
know that this is indeed [1]the Christ, the
Savior of the world."

Christ Is Received by the Galileans

43 Now after the two days He departed
from there and went to Galilee. 44 For [j]Jesus

25 [u] Deut. 18:15 [v] John 4:29, 39
26 [w] Dan. 9:25; Matt. 26:63, 64; Mark 14:61, 62
29 [x] John 4:25
34 [y] Ps. 40:7, 8; Heb. 10:9 [z] Job 23:12; [John 6:38; 17:4; 19:30]
35 [a] Gen. 8:22 [b] Matt. 9:37; Luke 10:2
36 [c] Dan. 12:3; Rom. 6:22 [d] 1 Thess. 2:19
37 [e] 1 Cor. 3:5-9
38 [f] Jer. 44:4; [1 Pet. 1:12]
39 [g] John 4:29
41 [h] Luke 4:32; [John 6:63]
42 [i] John 17:8; 1 John 4:14 [1] NU omits *the Christ*
44 [j] Matt. 13:57; Mark 6:4; Luke 4:24

4:25 Messiah. The Samaritans also anticipated Messiah's coming.

4:26 I who speak to you am *He*. Jesus forthrightly declared Himself to be Messiah, though His habit was to avoid such declarations to His own Jewish people who had such crassly political and militaristic views regarding Messiah (cf. 10:24; Mark 9:41). The "He" in this translation is not in the original Gr. for Jesus lit. said "I who speak to you am." The usage of "I am" is reminiscent of 8:58 (*see notes there*). This claim constitutes the main point of the story regarding the Samaritan woman.

4:27-42 These verses reinforce Jesus' acknowledgment that He was Messiah by offering proof for His claim. John gave 5 genuine, but subtle, proofs that Jesus was truly Messiah and Son of God which reinforced his main theme of 20:31: 1) proof from His immediate control of everything (v. 27); 2) proof from His impact on the woman (vv. 28-30); 3) proof from His intimacy with the Father (vv. 31-34); 4) proof from His insight into men's souls (vv. 35-38); and 5) proof from His impression on the Samaritans (vv. 39-42).

4:27 at this *point*. Had the disciples arrived earlier, they would have interrupted and destroyed the conversation, and if they had arrived any later, she would have gone and they would not have heard His declaration of messiahship. This feature subtly reveals Jesus' divine control over the situation that was occurring.

4:28-31 to the men. Jesus had such an impact on the woman that she was eager to share the news among the townspeople whom she had previously avoided because of her reputation. Her witness and candor regarding her own life so impressed them that they came to see Jesus for themselves.

4:32,33 I have food. Just like the Samaritan woman's misunderstanding of Jesus words regarding literal water (v. 15), Jesus' own disciples thought only of literal food. John commonly used such misunderstanding to advance the argument of his gospel (e.g., 2:20; 3:3).

4:34 My food is to do the will of Him who sent Me. Most likely Jesus echoed Deut. 8:3 where Moses stated, "man shall not live by bread alone; but man lives by every *word* that proceeds from the mouth of the LORD" (cf. Matt. 4:4; Luke 4:4). When He talked with the Samaritan woman, Jesus was performing the will of the Father and thereby received greater sustenance and satisfaction than any mere physical food could offer Him (5:23,24; 8:29; 17:4). Obedience to and dependence upon God's will summed up Jesus' whole life (Eph. 5:17). God's will for Him to finish is explained in 6:38-40 (*see notes there*).

4:35 four months and *then* comes the harvest. The event probably happened in Dec. or Jan. which was 4 months before the normal spring harvest (mid-Apr.). Crops were planted in Nov., and by Dec. or Jan. the grain would be sprouting up in vibrant green color. Jesus used the fact that they were surrounded by crops growing in the field and waiting to be harvested as an object lesson to illustrate His urgency about reaching the lost which the "harvest" symbolized. Jesus points out the Samaritan woman and people of Sychar ("lift up your eyes") who were at that moment coming upon the scene (v. 30) looking like a ripened "harvest" that urgently need to be "gathered," i.e., evangelized. **already white for harvest.** Their white clothing seen above the growing grain may have looked like white heads on the stalks, an indication of readiness for harvest. Jesus knew the hearts of all (2:24), so was able to state their readiness for salvation (cf. vv. 39-41).

4:36-38 The Lord's call to His disciples to do the work of evangelism contains promises of reward ("wages"), fruit that brings eternal joy (v. 36), and the mutual partnership of shared privilege (vv. 37,38).

4:42 Savior of the world. This phrase occurs also in 1 John 4:14. The verse constitutes the climax to the story of the woman of Samaria. The Samaritans themselves became another in a series of witnesses in John's gospel that demonstrated the identity of Jesus as the Messiah and Son of God. This episode represents the first instance of cross-cultural evangelism (Acts 1:8).

4:43-54 The episode of Jesus' healing of the official's son constitutes the second major "sign" of 8 which John used to reinforce Jesus'

Himself testified that a prophet has no
honor in his own country. 45 So when He
came to Galilee, the Galileans received Him,
[k]having seen all the things He did in Jerusalem at the feast; [l]for they also had gone to
the feast.

Christ Heals the Nobleman's Son

46 So Jesus came again to Cana of Galilee
[m]where He had made the water wine. And
there was a certain [2]nobleman whose son
was sick at Capernaum. 47 When he heard
that Jesus had come out of Judea into Galilee, he went to Him and implored Him to
come down and heal his son, for he was at
the point of death. 48 Then Jesus said to
him, [n]"Unless you *people* see signs and
wonders, you will by no means believe."
49 The nobleman said to Him, "Sir, come
down before my child dies!"
50 Jesus said to him, "Go your way; your
son lives." So the man believed the word
that Jesus spoke to him, and he went his
way. 51 And as he was now going down,
his servants met him and told *him,* saying,
"Your son lives!"
52 Then he inquired of them the hour
when he got better. And they said to him,
"Yesterday at the seventh hour the fever
left him." 53 So the father knew that *it was*
at the same hour in which Jesus said to
him, "Your son lives." And he himself believed, and his whole household.
54 This again *is* the second sign Jesus did
when He had come out of Judea into Galilee.

Christ Heals the Paralytic Man

5 After [a]this there was a feast of the Jews,
and Jesus [b]went up to Jerusalem. 2 Now
there is in Jerusalem [c]by the Sheep *Gate* a
pool, which is called in Hebrew, [1]Bethesda,

45 [k] John 2:13,23; 3:2 [l] Deut. 16:16
46 [m] John 2:1,11 [2] *royal official*
48 [n] John 6:30; Rom. 15:19; 1 Cor. 1:22; 2 Cor. 12:12; [2 Thess. 2:9]; Heb. 2:4

CHAPTER 5

1 [a] Lev. 23:2; Deut. 16:16 [b] John 2:13
2 [c] Neh. 3:1,32; 12:39 [1] NU *Bethzatha*

true identity for producing belief in his readers (v. 54). In this episode, Jesus chided the official's unbelief in needing a miraculous sign in order to trust in Christ (v. 48). While some believe that this story is the same as the healing of the centurion's son (Matt. 8:5-13; Luke 7:2-10), sufficient differences exist to demonstrate that it is different from the synoptic account; e.g., 1) no evidence exists that the official's son was a Gentile; 2) the official's son, not his servant, was healed; and 3) Jesus was far more negative regarding the official's faith (v. 48) than the centurion's (Matt. 8:9). One may divide this section into 3 parts: 1) Jesus contemplating unbelief (vv. 43-45); 2) Jesus confronting unbelief (vv. 46-49); and 3) Jesus conquering unbelief (vv. 50-54).

4:43 went to Galilee. After two days in Samaria, Jesus traveled to Galilee resuming the trip that began in v. 3.

4:44 prophet has no honor in his own country. This proverb (also in Matt. 13:57; Mark 6:4) contrasts the believing response of the Samaritans (v. 39) with the characteristic unbelief of Jesus' own people in Galilee (and Judea) whose reticent faith depended so much on Jesus' performance of miracles (v. 48). While in Samaria, Jesus had enjoyed his first unqualified and unopposed success. His own people's hearts were not open to Him, but exhibited reluctance and hardness.

4:45 the Galileans received Him. The apostle may have meant these words as irony especially in light of the surrounding context of vv. 44,48. The reception was likely that of curiosity seekers whose appetite centered more on seeing miracles than believing in Jesus as Messiah—as it had been at "the feast" (*see notes on 2:23-25*).

4:46 Cana of Galilee. The deep irony of the statement in v. 45 increases with the fact that Jesus had only recently performed a miracle in Cana at the wedding. Instead of responding in belief, the people wanted more (*see note on v. 48*). The basis of their welcome was extremely crass. **nobleman.** The Gr. terms means "royal official" and most likely designated someone officially attached to the service of King Herod Antipas, Tetrarch of Galilee from 4 B.C. to A.D. 39. **sick at Capernaum.** Capernaum was approximately 16 mi. NE of Cana.

4:47 implored Him. The language here indicates that he repeatedly begged Jesus to heal his son. His approach to Jesus was out of desperation, but he had little appreciation of who Jesus was. In light of v. 46, apparently the nobleman's motivation centered in Jesus' reputation as a miracle worker rather than as Messiah.

4:48 Unless you *people* see signs and wonders. The "you" is plural. Jesus addresses these words to the Galileans as a whole and not just to the nobleman (*see notes on vv. 45-56*). The response of the Galileans was fundamentally flawed because it disregarded the person of Christ and centered in the need for a constant display of miraculous signs. Such an attitude represents the deepest state of unbelief.

4:50 your son lives. Jesus met the demands of Galilean unbelief by healing the official's son, revealing not only His sympathy, but His marvelous graciousness in spite of such a faithless demand for miracles.

4:52 the seventh hour. About 1:00 p.m., reckoning from sunrise. *See note on v. 6.*

4:53 at the same hour. The time when the official's son improved corresponded precisely with the time that he had spoken with Jesus. This served to strengthen the nobleman's faith and, as a result, the "whole household" believed.

5:1–7:52 This section evidences the shift from reservation and hesitation about Jesus as Messiah (3:26; 4:1-3) to outright rejection (7:52). The opposition started with controversy regarding Jesus' healing on the Sabbath (vv. 1-18), intensified in chap. 6 with many of His disciples abandoning Him (6:66), and finally hardened in chap. 7 into official opposition against Him with the religious authorities' unsuccessful attempt to arrest Him (7:20-52). Accordingly, the theme of this section is the rejection of Jesus as Messiah.

5:1-18 Although opposition to Jesus smoldered beneath the surface (e.g., 2:13-20), the story of Jesus' healing at the Pool of Bethesda highlights the beginning of open hostility toward Him in Jerusalem in the southern parts of Palestine. The passage may be divided into 3 parts: 1) the miracle performed (vv. 1-9); 2) the Master persecuted (vv. 10-16); and 3) the murder planned (vv. 16-18).

5:1 feast of the Jews. John repeatedly tied his narrative to various Jewish feasts, (2:13—Passover; 6:4—Passover; 7:2—Tabernacles; 10:22—Hanukkah or Feast of Dedication; and 11:55—Passover), but this reference is the only instance when he did not identify the particular feast occurring at the time.

5:2 Sheep *Gate.* Most likely this is a reference to the gate identified in Neh. 3:1,32; 12:39. It was a small opening in the N wall of the city, just W of the NE corner. **there is…a pool.** Some have suggested that John wrote his gospel before the destruction of Jerusalem in A.D. 70, because his usage of "is" here implies that the pool still existed. However, John frequently used what is known as a "historical present" to refer to past events, so this argument carries little weight. For more on the date of writing, see Introduction: Author and Date. **Bethesda.** "Bethesda" is the Gr. transliteration of a Heb. (or Aram.) name meaning "house of outpouring."

having five porches. 3 In these lay a great
multitude of sick people, blind, lame, [2]par-
alyzed, [3]waiting for the moving of the
water. 4 For an angel went down at a certain time into the pool and stirred up the
water; then whoever stepped in first, after
the stirring of the water, was made well of
whatever disease he had. 5 Now a certain
man was there who had an infirmity thirty-eight years. 6 When Jesus saw him lying
there, and knew that he already had been
in that condition a long time, He said to him,
"Do you want to be made well?"
7 The sick man answered Him, "Sir, I
have no man to put me into the pool when
the water is stirred up; but while I am coming, another steps down before me."
8 Jesus said to him, [d]"Rise, take up your
bed and walk." 9 And immediately the
man was made well, took up his bed, and
walked.

Christ Heals on the Sabbath

And [e]that day was the Sabbath. 10 The
Jews therefore said to him who was cured,
"It is the Sabbath; [f]it is not lawful for you
to carry your bed."
11 He answered them, "He who made
me well said to me, 'Take up your bed and
walk.' "
12 Then they asked him, "Who is the
Man who said to you, 'Take up your bed
and walk'?" 13 But the one who was
[g]healed did not know who it was, for Jesus
had withdrawn, a multitude being in *that*
place. 14 Afterward Jesus found him in the
temple, and said to him, "See, you have
been made well. [h]Sin no more, lest a worse
thing come upon you."
15 The man departed and told the Jews
that it was Jesus who had made him well.
16 For this reason the Jews [i]persecuted
Jesus, [4]and sought to kill Him, because He
had done these things on the Sabbath.

Equality with God in Nature

17 But Jesus answered them, [j]"My Father

3 [2] *withered* [3] NU omits the rest of v. 3 and all of v. 4.
8 [d] Matt. 9:6; Mark 2:11; Luke 5:24
9 [e] John 9:14
10 [f] Ex. 20:10; Neh. 13:19; Jer. 17:21, 22; Matt. 12:2; Mark 2:24; Luke 6:2
13 [g] Luke 13:14; 22:51
14 [h] Matt. 12:45; [Mark 2:5]; John 8:11
16 [i] Luke 4:29; John 8:37; 10:39 [4] NU omits *and sought to kill Him*
17 [j] [John 9:4; 17:4]

5:3a lay. It was a custom at that time for people with infirmities to gather at this pool. Intermittent springs may have fed the pool and caused the disturbance of the water (v. 7). Some ancient witnesses indicate that the waters of the pool were red with minerals, and thus thought to have medicinal value.

5:3b,4 The statement in the latter half of v. 3, "waiting for the moving of the water," along with v. 4 are not original to the gospel. The earliest and best Gr. manuscripts, as well as the early versions, exclude the reading. The presence of words or expressions unfamiliar to John's writings also militate against its inclusion.

5:5 thirty-eight years. John included this figure to emphasize the gravity of the debilitating disease that afflicted the individual. Since his sickness had been witnessed by many people for almost 4 decades, when Jesus cured him everyone knew the genuineness of the healing (cf. v. 9).

5:6 knew. The word implies supernatural knowledge of the man's situation (1:47,48; 4:17). Jesus picked the man out from among many sick people. The sovereign initiative was His, and no reason is given as to His choice.

5:8 Rise, take...walk. In the same way that He spoke the world into being at creation, (Gen. 1:3), Jesus' spoken words had the power to cure (cf. 1:3; 8:58; Gen. 1:1; Col. 1:16; Heb. 1:2). **bed.** The "bed" or "mat" was normally made of straw and was light enough so that it could be carried on the shoulder of a well person who assisted the infirm (cf. Mark 2:1).

5:9 took up his bed, and walked. This phrase emphasizes the completeness of the cure (cf. v. 5).

5:10,11 The OT had forbidden work on the Sabbath but did not stipulate what "work" was specifically indicated (Ex. 20:8-11). The assumption in Scripture seems to be that "work" was one's customary employment, but rabbinical opinion had developed oral tradition beyond the OT which stipulated 39 activities forbidden (Mishnah *Shabbath* 7:2; 10:5), including carrying anything from one domain to another. Thus, the man had broken oral tradition, not OT law (*see notes on v. 16*).

5:10 it is not lawful. The phrase reveals that the Judaism during Jesus' time had degenerated into pious hypocrisy. Such hypocrisy especially enraged the Lord Jesus (cf. Matt. 22,23), who used this incident to set up a confrontation with Jewish hyper-legalism and identified the need for national repentance.

5:14 Sin no more, lest a worse thing come upon you. The basic thrust of Jesus' comments here indicate that sin has its inevitable consequences (cf. Gal 6:7,8). Although Scripture makes clear that not all disease is a consequence of sin (cf. 9:1-3; Luke 13:1-5), illness at times may be directly tied into one's moral turpitude (cf. 1 Cor. 11:29,30; James 5:15). Jesus may specifically have chosen this man in order to highlight this point.

5:16 persecuted. The verb tense means that the Jews repeatedly persecuted Jesus, i.e., continued hostile activity. This was not an isolated incident of their hatred toward Him because of His healings on the Sabbath (cf. Mark 3:1-6). **on the Sabbath.** Jesus did not break God's law since in it there was no prohibition of doing good on that day (Mark 2:27). However, Jesus disregarded the oral law of the Jews that had developed, i.e., "the traditions of men" (cf. also Matt. 15:1-9). Most likely, Jesus deliberately practiced such healing on the Sabbath to provoke a confrontation with their religious hypocrisy that blinded them to the true worship of God (see vv. 17-47 for the main reason for Jesus' confrontation; *see notes on vv. 10,11*).

5:17-47 These verses reveal the ultimate reason Jesus confronted the Jews' religious hypocrisy, i.e., the opportunity to declare who He was. This section is Christ's own personal statement of His deity. As such, it is one of the greatest Christological discourses in Scripture. Herein Jesus makes 5 claims to equality with God: 1) He is equal with God in His person (vv. 17,18); 2) He is equal with God in His works (vv. 19,20); 3) He is equal with God in His power and sovereignty (v. 21); 4) He is equal with God in His judgment (v. 22); and 5) He is equal with God in His honor (v. 23).

5:17 Jesus' point is that whether he broke the Sabbath or not, God was working continuously and, since Jesus Himself worked continuously, He also must be God. Furthermore, God does not need a day of rest for He never wearies (Is. 40:28). For Jesus' self-defense to be valid, the same factors that apply to God must also apply to Him. Jesus is Lord of the Sabbath (Matt. 12:8)! Interestingly, even the rabbis admitted that God's work had not ceased after the Sabbath because He sustains the universe.

has been working until now, and I have
been working."
18 Therefore the Jews [k]sought all the
more to kill Him, because He not only
broke the Sabbath, but also said that God
was His Father, [l]making Himself equal
with God.

Equality with God in Power

19 Then Jesus answered and said to them,
"Most assuredly, I say to you, [m]the Son can
do nothing of Himself, but what He sees
the Father do; for whatever He does, the
Son also does in like manner. 20 For [n]the
Father loves the Son, and [o]shows Him all
things that He Himself does; and He will
show Him greater works than these, that
you may marvel. 21 For as the Father raises
the dead and gives life to *them,* [p]even so
the Son gives life to whom He will.

Equality with God in Authority

22 For the Father judges no one, but [q]has
committed all judgment to the Son, 23 that
all should honor the Son just as they honor
the Father. [r]He who does not honor the
Son does not honor the Father who sent
Him.

24 "Most assuredly, I say to you, [s]he
who hears My word and believes in Him
who sent Me has everlasting life, and shall
not come into judgment, [t]but has passed
from death into life. 25 Most assuredly, I
say to you, the hour is coming, and now is,
when [u]the dead will hear the voice of the
Son of God; and those who hear will live.
26 For [v]as the Father has life in Himself, so
He has granted the Son to have [w]life in
Himself, 27 and [x]has given Him authority
to execute judgment also, [y]because He is
the Son of Man. 28 Do not marvel at this;
for the hour is coming in which all who
are in the graves will [z]hear His voice
29 [a]and come forth—[b]those who have
done good, to the resurrection of life, and
those who have done evil, to the resurrection of condemnation. 30 [c]I can of Myself
do nothing. As I hear, I judge; and My
judgment is righteous, because [d]I do not
seek My own will but the will of the Father who sent Me.

Witness of John the Baptist

31 [e]"If I bear witness of Myself, My witness is not [5]true. 32 [f]There is another who
bears witness of Me, and I know that the

18 [k] John 7:1, 19 [l] John 10:30; Phil. 2:6
19 [m] Matt. 26:39; John 5:30; 6:38; 8:28; 12:49; 14:10
20 [n] Matt. 3:17; John 3:35; 2 Pet. 1:17 [o] [Matt. 11:27]
21 [p] Luke 7:14; 8:54; [John 11:25]
22 [q] Matt. 11:27; 28:18; [John 3:35; 17:2; Acts 17:31; 1 Pet. 4:5]
23 [r] Luke 10:16; 1 John 2:23
24 [s] John 3:16, 18; 6:47 [t] [1 John 3:14]
25 [u] [Eph. 2:1, 5; Col. 2:13]
26 [v] Ps. 36:9 [w] [John 1:4; 14:6]; 1 Cor. 15:45
27 [x] John 9:39; [Acts 10:42; 17:31] [y] Dan. 7:13
28 [z] [1 Thess. 4:15-17]
29 [a] Is. 26:19; [1 Cor. 15:52] [b] Dan. 12:2; Matt. 25:46; Acts 24:15
30 [c] John 5:19 [d] Matt. 26:39; John 4:34; 6:38
31 [e] John 8:14; Rev. 3:14 [5] *valid* as testimony
32 [f] [Matt. 3:17; John 8:18; 1 John 5:6]

5:18 This verse confirms that the Jews instantly grasped the implications of His remarks that He was God (*see notes on v. 17*).

5:19 Most assuredly. Cf. vv. 24,25; 1:51. This is an emphatic way of saying "I'm telling you the truth." In response to Jewish hostility at the implications of His assertions of equality with God, Jesus became even more fearless, forceful, and emphatic. Jesus essentially tied His activities of healing on the Sabbath directly to the Father. The Son never took independent action that set Him against the Father because the Son only did those things that were coincident with and co-extensive with all that the Father does. Jesus thus implied that the only One who could do what the Father does must be as great as the Father.

5:20 greater works. This refers to the powerful work of raising the dead. God has that power (cf. 1 Kin. 17:17-24; 2 Kin. 4:32-37; 5:7) and so does the Lord Jesus (vv. 21-29; 11:25-44; 14:19; 20:1-18).

5:23 honor the Son. This verse gives the reason that God entrusted all judgment to the Son (v. 22), i.e., so that all men should honor the Son just as they honor the Father. This verse goes far beyond making Jesus a mere ambassador who is acting in the name of a monarch, but gives Him full and complete equality with the Father (cf. Phil. 2:9-11). **honor the Father.** Jesus turned the tables on the Jewish accusation against Him of blasphemy. Instead, Jesus affirmed that the only way anyone can honor the Father is through receiving the Son. Therefore, the Jews were the ones who actually blasphemed the Father by rejection of His Son.

5:24 passed from death into life. This develops the truth of v. 21, that Jesus gives life to whomever He desires. The people who receive that life are here identified as those who hear the Word and believe in the Father and the Son. They are the people who have eternal life and never will be condemned (Rom. 8:1; Col. 1:13).

5:25-29 The theme of these verses is resurrection. Jesus related that all men, saved and unsaved, will be literally and physically resurrected from the dead. However, only the saved experience a spiritual ("born again"), as well as physical resurrection unto eternal life. The unsaved will be resurrected unto judgment and eternal punishment through separation from God (i.e., the second death; cf. Rev. 20:6,14; 21:8). These verses also constitute proof of the deity of Jesus Christ since the Son has resurrection power (vv. 25,26), and the Father has granted Him the status of Judge of all mankind (v. 27). In the light of other Scripture, it is clear that Jesus speaks generally about resurrection, but not about one, general resurrection (*see notes on Dan. 12:2; 1 Cor. 15:23; 1 Thess. 4:16*).

5:25 hour is coming, and now is. Cf. 4:23. This phrase reveals an already/not yet tension regarding the resurrection. Those who are born again are already "spiritually" resurrected ("now is"; Eph. 2:1; Col. 2:13), and yet a future physical resurrection still awaits them ("hour is coming"; 1 Cor. 15:35-54; Phil. 3:20,21).

5:26 He has granted the Son. The Son from all eternity had the right to grant life (1:4). The distinction involves Jesus' deity versus His incarnation. In becoming a man, Jesus voluntarily set aside the independent exercise of His divine attributes and prerogatives (Phil. 2:6-11). Jesus here affirmed that even in His humanity, the Father granted Him "life-giving" power, i.e., the power of resurrection (*see note on v. 20*).

5:27 authority. Cf. 17:2; *see note on Matt. 28:18.*

5:29 those who have done good . . . evil. Jesus was not teaching justification by works (see 6:29). In the context, the "good" is believing on the Son so as to receive a new nature that produces good works (3:21; James 2:14-20), while the "evil" done is to reject the Son (the unsaved) and hate the light which has the result of evil deeds (3:18,19). In essence, works merely evidence one's nature as saved or unsaved (*see notes on Rom. 2:5-10*), but human works never determine one's salvation.

5:30 the will of the Father. In summarizing all He has said from v. 19 on about His equality with God, Jesus claimed that the judgment He exercised was because everything He did was dependent upon the Father's word and will (cf. vv. 19,20).

5:32-47 The background of these verses is Deut. 17:6; 19:15

witness which He witnesses of Me is true.
33 You have sent to John, [g]and he has borne
witness to the truth. 34 Yet I do not receive
testimony from man, but I say these things
that you may be saved. 35 He was the
burning and [h]shining lamp, and [i]you were
willing for a time to rejoice in his light.

Witness of the Works of Christ

36 But [j]I have a greater witness than John's;
for [k]the works which the Father has given
Me to finish—the very [l]works that I do—
bear witness of Me, that the Father has sent
Me.

Witness of the Father

37 And the Father Himself, who sent Me,
[m]has testified of Me. You have neither
heard His voice at any time, [n]nor seen His
form. 38 But you do not have His word
abiding in you, because whom He sent,
Him you do not believe.

Witness of the Scriptures

39 [o]You search the Scriptures, for in them
you think you have eternal life; and [p]these
are they which testify of Me. 40 [q]But you
are not willing to come to Me that you may
have life.
41 [r]"I do not receive honor from men.
42 But I know you, that you do not have
the love of God in you. 43 I have come in
My Father's name, and you do not receive
Me; if another comes in his own name,
him you will receive. 44 [s]How can you believe, who receive honor from one another, and do not seek [t]the honor that *comes*
from the only God? 45 Do not think that I
shall accuse you to the Father; [u]there is
one who accuses you—Moses, in whom
you trust. 46 For if you believed Moses,
you would believe Me; [v]for he wrote
about Me. 47 But if you [w]do not believe
his writings, how will you believe My
words?"

Christ Feeds 5,000
Matt. 14:13-21; Mark 6:31-44; Luke 9:11-17

6 After [a]these things Jesus went over the
Sea of Galilee, which is *the Sea* of [b]Ti-
berias. 2 Then a great multitude followed
Him, because they saw His signs which He
performed on those who were [c]diseased.[1]
3 And Jesus went up on the mountain, and
there He sat with His disciples.
4 [d]Now the Passover, a feast of the Jews,
was near. 5 [e]Then Jesus lifted up *His* eyes,
and seeing a great multitude coming toward Him, He said to [f]Philip, "Where shall
we buy bread, that these may eat?" 6 But
this He said to test him, for He Himself
knew what He would do.

33 [g][John 1:15, 19, 27, 32]
35 [h]2 Sam. 21:17; 2 Pet. 1:19 [i]Matt. 13:20; Mark 6:20
36 [j]1 John 5:9 [k]John 3:2; 10:25; 17:4 [l]John 9:16; 10:38
37 [m]Matt. 3:17; John 6:27; 8:18 [n]Deut. 4:12; John 1:18; 1 Tim. 1:17; 1 John 4:12
39 [o]Is. 8:20; 34:16; Luke 16:29; Acts 17:11 [p]Deut. 18:15, 18; Luke 24:27
40 [q][John 1:11; 3:19]
41 [r]John 5:44; 7:18; 1 Thess. 2:6
44 [s]John 12:43 [t][Rom. 2:29]
45 [u]Rom. 2:12
46 [v][Gen. 3:15]; Deut. 18:15, 18; John 1:45; Acts 26:22
47 [w]Luke 16:29, 31

CHAPTER 6

1 [a]Matt. 14:13; Mark 6:32; Luke 9:10, 12 [b]John 6:23; 21:1
2 [c]Matt. 4:23; 8:16; 9:35; 14:36; 15:30; 19:2 [1]*sick*
4 [d]Lev. 23:5, 7; Deut. 16:1; John 2:13
5 [e]Matt. 14:14; Mark 6:35; Luke 9:12 [f]John 1:43

where witnesses were to establish the truthfulness of a matter (*see note on 1:7*). Jesus Himself emphasized the familiar theme of witnesses who testify to the identity of the Son: 1) John the Baptist (vv. 32-35); 2) Jesus' works (vv. 35,36); 3) the Father (vv. 37,38); and 4) the OT Scriptures (vv. 39-47).

5:36 the very works that I do. Cf. 10:25. The miracles of Jesus were witness to His deity and messiahship. Such miracles are the major signs recorded by John in this gospel, so as to fulfill His purpose in 20:30,31 (see Introduction: Historical and Theological Themes).

5:37 Father…has testified. Cf. Matt. 3:17; Mark 1:11; Luke 3:22.

5:39 You search. Although the verb "search" could also be understood as a command (i.e., "Search the Scriptures!") most prefer this translation as an indicative. The verb implies diligent scrutiny in investigating the Scriptures to find "eternal life." However, Jesus points out that with all their fastidious effort, they miserably failed in their understanding of the true way to eternal life through the Son of God (*see notes on Matt. 19:16-25*; cf. 14:6; 2 Tim. 3:15). **testify of Me.** Cf. v. 45. Christ is the main theme of Scripture. *See note on 1:45.*

5:40 not willing. They searched for eternal life, but were not willing to trust its only source (cf. v. 24; 1:11; 3:19).

5:41 honor from men. If Jesus agreed to be the kind of Messiah the Jews wanted, providing miracles and food along with political and military power, He would receive honor from them. But He sought only to please God (vv. 19ff.).

5:43 him you will receive. The Jewish historian, Josephus, records that a string of messianic pretenders arose in the years before A.D. 70. This verse contrasts the Jewish rejection of their true Messiah because they did not love or know God (v. 42), with their willing acceptance of charlatans.

5:46 Moses…for he wrote about Me. Jesus does not mention any specific passage in the 5 books of Moses although there are many (e.g., Deut. 18:15; cf. 1:21; 4:19; 6:14; 7:40,52).

6:1-14 The story of the feeding of the 5,000 is the fourth sign John employed to demonstrate that Jesus is the Messiah and Son of God. It is the only miracle recorded in all 4 gospels (Matt. 14:13-23; Mark 6:30-46; Luke 9:10-17). Since John most likely wrote to supplement and provide additional information not recorded in the synoptics (see Introduction: Background and Setting), his recording of this miracle emphasized its strategic importance in two ways: 1) it demonstrated the creative power of Christ more clearly than any other miracle, and 2) it decisively supported John's purposes of demonstrating the deity of Jesus Christ while also serving to set the stage for Jesus' discourse on the "bread of life" (vv. 22-40). Interestingly, both creative miracles of Jesus, the water into wine (2:1-10) and the multiplying of bread (vv. 1-14) speak of the main elements in the Lord's supper or communion (v. 53).

6:1 After these things. A large gap of time may exist between chaps. 5 and 6. If the feast in 5:1 is Tabernacles, then at least 6 months passed (Oct. to Apr.). If the feast of 5:1 is Passover, then a year passed between these chapters. **the Sea of Galilee.** Chapter 6 is very close to the same structure as chap. 5 since both occur around a Jewish feast and both lead to a discourse of Jesus' deity. While chap. 5 takes place in the S around Judea and Jerusalem, chap. 6 takes place in the N around Galilee. The result of both chapters is the same: He is rejected not only in the southern but also in the northern regions. *See note on 21:1.*

6:2 they saw His signs. The crowds followed not out of belief but out of curiosity concerning the miracles that He performed (v. 26). However, in spite of the crowd's crass motivations, Jesus, having compassion on them, healed their sick and fed them (cf. Matt. 13:14; Mark 6:34).

7 Philip answered Him, [g]"Two hundred
denarii worth of bread is not sufficient for
them, that every one of them may have a
little."
8 One of His disciples, [h]Andrew, Simon
Peter's brother, said to Him, 9 "There is a
lad here who has five barley loaves and
two small fish, [i]but what are they among
so many?"
10 Then Jesus said, "Make the people sit
down." Now there was much grass in the
place. So the men sat down, in number
about five thousand. 11 And Jesus took
the loaves, and when He had given
thanks He distributed *them* [2]to the disciples, and the disciples to those sitting
down; and likewise of the fish, as much as
they wanted. 12 So when they were filled,
He said to His disciples, "Gather up the
fragments that remain, so that nothing is
lost." 13 Therefore they gathered *them* up,
and filled twelve baskets with the fragments of the five barley loaves which
were left over by those who had eaten.
14 Then those men, when they had seen
the sign that Jesus did, said, "This is truly
[j]the Prophet who is to come into the
world."

7 [g] Num. 11:21, 22
8 [h] John 1:40
9 [i] 2 Kin. 4:43
11 [2] NU omits *to the disciples, and the disciples*
14 [j] Gen. 49:10; Deut. 18:15, 18; John 1:21; 7:40; Acts 3:22; 7:37

Christ Walks on the Water
Matt. 14:22-33; Mark 6:45-52

15 Therefore when Jesus perceived that
they were about to come and take Him by
force to make Him [k]king, He departed
again to the mountain by Himself alone.
16 [l]Now when evening came, His disciples went down to the sea, 17 got into the
boat, and went over the sea toward Capernaum. And it was already dark, and Jesus had not come to them. 18 Then the sea
arose because a great wind was blowing.
19 So when they had rowed about [3]three or
four miles, they saw Jesus walking on the
sea and drawing near the boat; and they
were [m]afraid. 20 But He said to them, [n]"It
is I; do not be afraid." 21 Then they willingly received Him into the boat, and immediately the boat was at the land where
they were going.

"I Am the Bread of Life"

22 On the following day, when the people
who were standing on the other side of the
sea saw that there was no other boat there,
except [4]that one [5]which His disciples had
entered, and that Jesus had not entered the
boat with His disciples, but His disciples
had gone away alone— 23 however, other

15 [k] [John 18:36]
16 [l] Matt. 14:23; Mark 6:47
19 [m] Matt. 17:6 [3] Lit. *25 or 30 stadia*
20 [n] Is. 43:1, 2
22 [4] NU omits *that* [5] NU omits *which His disciples had entered*

6:7 Two hundred denarii. Since one denarius was a day's pay for a common laborer, 200 denarii would be approximately 8 months' wages. The crowd, however, was so large that such a significant amount was still inadequate to feed them.

6:10 five thousand. The number of men was 5,000, not including women and children, who probably brought the total up to 20,000.

6:14 the Prophet. The crowd referred to "the Prophet" of Deut. 18:15. Sadly, these comments, coming right after Jesus healed and fed them, indicate that the people desired a Messiah who met their physical, rather than spiritual, needs. Apparently, no recognition existed for the need of spiritual repentance and preparation for the kingdom (Matt. 4:17). They wanted an earthly, political Messiah to meet all their needs and to deliver them from Roman oppression. Their reaction typifies many who want a "Christ" that makes no demands of them (cf. Matt. 10:34-39; 16:24-26), but of whom they can make their selfish personal requests.

6:15 take Him by force to make Him king. John supplemented the information in Matthew and Mark by indicating that the reason Jesus dismissed the disciples and withdrew from the crowd into a mountain alone was because of His supernatural knowledge of their intention to make Him king in light of His healing and feeding of them. The crowd, incited by mob enthusiasm, was ready to proceed with crassly political intentions that would have jeopardized God's will.

6:16-21 The story of Jesus' walking on the water constituted the fifth sign in John's gospel designed to demonstrate the writer's purpose that Jesus is the Messiah and Son of God (20:30,31). The miracle demonstrates Jesus' deity by His sovereignty over the laws of nature.

6:17 toward Capernaum. Matthew 14:22 and Mark 6:45 indicate that as soon as Jesus had fed the multitudes, he immediately dismissed His disciples to travel W toward Capernaum (vv. 16,17).

6:18 a great wind was blowing. The Sea of Galilee is almost 700 ft. below sea level. Cooler air from the northern mountains and southeastern tablelands rushes down into the lake and displaces the warm moist air, causing violent churning of the water.

6:19,20 Jesus walking on the sea. The synoptics reveal that in fear and the darkness, they thought He was a ghost (Matt. 14:26; Mark 6:49). The Son of God, who made the world, was in control of its forces and, in this case, He suspended the law of gravity. The act was not frivolous on Jesus' part, for it constituted a dramatic object lesson to the disciples of Jesus' true identity as the sovereign Lord of all creation (cf. 1:3).

6:21 immediately the boat was at the land. This wording indicates that another miracle occurred besides walking on the water, i.e., the boat miraculously and instantly arrived at its precise destination as soon as Jesus stepped into the boat.

6:22-58 Jesus' famous discourse on the bread of life. The key theme is v. 35, i.e., "I am the bread of Life," which is the first of 7 emphatic "I AM" statements of Jesus in this gospel (8:12; 10:7,9; 10:11,14; 11:25; 14:6; 15:1,5). This analogy of Jesus as "the bread" of life reinforces John's theme of Jesus as the Messiah and Son of God (20:30,31). Although John records Jesus' miracles to establish His deity, he moves quickly to Jesus' discourse on the spiritual realities of His person in order to define correctly who Jesus Christ was, i.e., not merely a wonder-worker but the Son of God who came to save mankind from sin (3:16). This discourse took place in the synagogue at Capernaum (v. 59).

6:22,23 These verses indicate that the crowds who witnessed Jesus' healings and His feeding of the multitudes were still at the original sight of these miracles (E of the Lake) and, out of heightened curiosity, desired to find Jesus once again. Other boats loaded with people from Tiberias (on the NW shore of the lake) also heard of the miracles and sought Him out.

boats came from Tiberias, near the place
where they ate bread after the Lord had
given thanks— 24 when the people therefore saw that Jesus was not there, nor His
disciples, they also got into boats and came
to Capernaum, [o]seeking Jesus. 25 And
when they found Him on the other side of
the sea, they said to Him, "Rabbi, when did
You come here?"
26 Jesus answered them and said, "Most
assuredly, I say to you, you seek Me, not
because you saw the signs, but because
you ate of the loaves and were filled.
27 [p]Do not labor for the food which perishes, but [q]for the food which endures to everlasting life, which the Son of Man will give
you, [r]because God the Father has set His
seal on Him."
28 Then they said to Him, "What shall we
do, that we may work the works of God?"
29 Jesus answered and said to them,
[s]"This is the work of God, that you believe
in Him whom He sent."
30 Therefore they said to Him, [t]"What
sign will You perform then, that we may
see it and believe You? What work will You
do? 31 [u]Our fathers ate the manna in the
desert; as it is written, [v]*'He gave them*
bread from heaven to eat.' "
32 Then Jesus said to them, "Most assuredly, I say to you, Moses did not give
you the bread from heaven, but [w]My Father gives you the true bread from heaven.
33 For the bread of God is He who comes
down from heaven and gives life to the
world."
34 [x]Then they said to Him, "Lord, give
us this bread always."
35 And Jesus said to them, [y]"I am the
bread of life. [z]He who comes to Me shall
never hunger, and he who believes in Me
shall never [a]thirst. 36 [b]But I said to you that
you have seen Me and yet [c]do not believe.
37 [d]All that the Father gives Me will come
to Me, and [e]the one who comes to Me I will
[6]by no means cast out. 38 For I have come

24 [o]Mark 1:37; Luke 4:42
27 [p]Matt. 6:19 [q]John 4:14; [Eph. 2:8, 9] [r]Ps. 2:7; Is. 42:1; Matt. 3:17; 17:5; Mark 1:11; 9:7; Luke 3:22; 9:35; John 5:37; Acts 2:22; 2 Pet. 1:17
29 [s]1 Thess. 1:3; James 2:22; [1 John 3:23]; Rev. 2:26
30 [t]Matt. 12:38; 16:1; Mark 8:11; 1 Cor. 1:22
31 [u]Ex. 16:15; Num. 11:7; 1 Cor. 10:3 [v]Ex. 16:4, 15; Neh. 9:15; Ps. 78:24
32 [w]John 3:13, 16
34 [x]John 4:15
35 [y]John 6:48, 58 [z]John 4:14; 7:37; Rev. 7:16 [a]Is. 55:1, 2
36 [b]John 6:26, 64; 15:24 [c]John 10:26
37 [d]John 6:45 [e][Matt. 24:24; John 10:28, 29]; 2 Tim. 2:19; 1 John 2:19
[6] *certainly not*

6:26 because you ate. This phrase emphasizes Jesus' point that the crowds which followed Him were motivated by superficial desires of food rather than any understanding of the true spiritual significance of Jesus' person and mission (8:14-21; Mark 6:52).

6:27 food which perishes. Jesus rebuked the crowd for purely materialistic notions of the messianic kingdom (cf. v. 26; 4:15). Although Messiah's kingdom would be literal and physical someday, the people failed to see the overriding spiritual character and blessing of "everlasting life" given immediately to those who believe the witness of God to His Son. **food which endures to everlasting life.** The continuing discourse indicates that this was a reference to Jesus Himself (v. 35).

6:28 works of God. They thought Jesus was saying that God required them to do some works to earn everlasting life, which they thought they would be able to do.

6:29 the work of God, that you believe. The crowd misunderstood Jesus' prohibition in v. 27 ("Do not labor") which prompted Jesus to remind them that an exclusive focus on material blessings is wrong. The only work God desired was faith or trust in Jesus as Messiah and Son of God (cf. Mal. 3:1). The "work" that God requires is to believe in His Son (cf. 5:24).

6:30 What sign will You perform. The question demonstrated the obtuseness, the spiritual blindness of the crowd, and their shallow, selfish curiosity. The feeding of 20,000 (v. 10) was a sufficient enough sign to demonstrate Christ's deity (cf. Luke 16:31).

6:31 Our fathers ate the manna. The crowd's logic appeared to be that Jesus' miraculous feeding was a small miracle compared to what Moses did. In order for them to believe in Him, they would need to see Him feed the nation of Israel on the same scale that God did when He sent manna and fed the entire nation of Israel during their wilderness wanderings for 40 years (Ex. 16:11-36). They were demanding that Jesus outdo Moses if they were to believe in Him. He quoted from Ps. 78:24.

6:32 true bread from heaven. The manna God gave was temporary and perished and was only a meager shadow of what God offered them in the true bread, Jesus Christ, who gives spiritual and eternal life to mankind ("world").

6:33 bread of God. This phrase is synonymous with the phrase "bread of heaven" (v. 32).

6:34 "Lord, give us this bread always." This statement once again demonstrated the blindness of the crowd, for they were thinking of some physical bread and failed to understand the spiritual implication that Jesus was that "bread" (cf. 4:15).

6:35 I am the bread of life. The obtuseness in v. 34 prompted Jesus to speak very plainly that He was referring to Himself.

6:37 All that the Father gives Me will come to Me. This verse emphasizes the sovereign will of God in the selection of those who come to come to Him for salvation (cf. vv. 44,65; 17:6,12,24). The Father has predestined those who would be saved (*see notes on Rom. 8:29,30; Eph. 1:3-6; 1 Pet. 1:2*). The absolute sovereignty of God is the basis of Jesus' confidence in the success of His mission (*see note on v. 40*; cf. Phil. 1:6). The security of salvation rests in the sovereignty of God, for God is the guarantee that "all" He has chosen will come to Him for salvation. The idea of "gives me" is that every person chosen by God and drawn by God (v. 44) must be seen as a gift of the Father's love to the Son. The Son receives each "love gift" (v. 37), holds on to each (v. 39), and will raise each to eternal glory (vv. 39,40). No one chosen will be lost (*see notes on Rom. 8:31-39*). This saving purpose is the Father's will which the Son will not fail to do perfectly (v. 38; cf. 4:34; 10:28,29; 17:6,12,24).

The "I AM" Statements

Twenty-three times in all we find our Lord's meaningful "I AM" (*ego eimi*, Gr.) in the Greek text of this gospel (4:26; 6:20,35,41,48,51; 8:12,18,24,28,58; 10:7,9,11,14; 11:25; 13:19; 14:6; 15:1,5; 18:5,6,8). In several of these, He joins His "I AM" with seven tremendous metaphors which are expressive of His saving relationship toward the world.

"I AM the Bread of life" (6:35,41,48,51).

"I AM the Light of the world" (8:12).

"I AM the Door of the sheep" (10:7,9).

"I AM the Good Shepherd" (10:11,14).

"I AM the Resurrection and the Life" (11:25).

"I AM the Way, the Truth, and the Life" (14:6).

"I AM the true Vine" (15:1,5).

down from heaven, [f]not to do My own
will, [g]but the will of Him who sent Me.
39 This is the will of the Father who sent
Me, [h]that of all He has given Me I should
lose nothing, but should raise it up at the
last day. 40 And this is the will of Him who
sent Me, [i]that everyone who sees the Son
and believes in Him may have everlasting
life; and I will raise him up at the last day."
41 The Jews then [7]complained about
Him, because He said, "I am the bread
which came down from heaven." 42 And
they said, [j]"Is not this Jesus, the son of Joseph, whose father and mother we know?
How is it then that He says, 'I have come
down from heaven'?"
43 Jesus therefore answered and said to
them, [8]"Do not murmur among yourselves.
44 [k]No one can come to Me unless the Father who sent Me [l]draws him; and I will
raise him up at the last day. 45 It is written in
the prophets, [m]'*And they shall all be taught*
by God.' [n]Therefore everyone who [9]has
heard and learned from the Father comes to
Me. 46 [o]Not that anyone has seen the Father,
[p]except He who is from God; He has seen
the Father. 47 Most assuredly, I say to you,
[q]he who believes [1]in Me has everlasting life.
48 [r]I am the bread of life. 49 [s]Your fathers ate
the manna in the wilderness, and are dead.
50 [t]This is the bread which comes down
from heaven, that one may eat of it and not
die. 51 I am the living bread [u]which came
down from heaven. If anyone eats of this
bread, he will live forever; and [v]the bread
that I shall give is My flesh, which I shall
give for the life of the world."
52 The Jews therefore [w]quarreled among
themselves, saying, "How can this Man
give us *His* flesh to eat?"
53 Then Jesus said to them, "Most assuredly, I say to you, unless [x]you eat the

38 [f]Matt. 26:39; John 5:30 [g]John 4:34
39 [h]John 10:28; 17:12; 18:9
40 [i]John 3:15, 16; 4:14; 6:27, 47, 54
41 [7]*grumbled*
42 [j]Matt. 13:55; Mark 6:3; Luke 4:22
43 [8]*Stop grumbling*
44 [k]Song 1:4 [l][Eph. 2:8, 9; Phil. 1:29; 2:12, 13]
45 [m]Is. 54:13; Jer. 31:34; Mic. 4:2; [Heb. 8:10]
[n]John 6:37 [9]*M hears and has learned*
46 [o]John 1:18 [p]Matt. 11:27; [Luke 10:22]; John 7:29
47 [q][John 3:16, 18] [1]NU omits *in Me*
48 [r]John 6:33, 35; [Gal. 2:20; Col. 3:3, 4]
49 [s]John 6:31, 58 **50** [t]John 6:51, 58 **51** [u]John 3:13 [v]Heb. 10:5
52 [w]John 7:43; 9:16; 10:19 **53** [x]Matt. 26:26

6:40 everyone who sees the Son and believes in Him. This verse emphasizes human responsibility in salvation. Although God is sovereign, He works through faith, so that a man must believe in Jesus as the Messiah and Son of God who alone offers the only way of salvation (cf. 14:6). However, even faith is a gift of God (Rom. 12:3; Eph. 2:8,9). Intellectually harmonizing the sovereignty of God and the responsibility of man is impossible humanly, but perfectly resolved in the infinite mind of God.

6:41-50 This section constitutes the beginning of the crowd's reaction to Jesus' discourse on the bread of life and may be divided into 3 sections: 1) the murmuring reaction of the crowd (vv. 41,42); 2) Jesus' rebuke of the crowd for their reaction (vv. 43-46); and 3) Jesus' reiteration of His message to the crowd (vv. 47-51).

6:41 The Jews. In this gospel, the term "Jews" is often associated with hostility toward Christ. It is used ironically to indicate the incongruity of their rising hostility toward their Messiah. Since they hardened their hearts, God judicially hardened their hearts also (cf. 12:37-40; Is. 6:10; 53:1; Matt. 13:10-15). In the tribulation, Israel will turn to Jesus as their true Messiah and be saved (Rom. 11:25-27; Rev. 1:7; 7:1-8; cf. Zech. 12:10-14). **complained.** The reaction of the synagogue crowds to Jesus' statements was the same as the Jews in the wilderness who murmured against God both before and after the manna was given to them (Ex. 16:2,8,9; Num. 11:4-6). **because He said, "I am the bread...from heaven."** The Jews' anger centered in two things: 1) that Jesus said He was the bread and 2) that He came down from heaven. Both the Jews in Jerusalem (5:18) and the Galileans reacted negatively when Jesus placed Himself equal with God.

6:42 whose father and mother we know. On the human level, they knew Jesus as a fellow Galilean. These words are reminiscent of Jesus' words in 4:44, "a prophet has no honor in his own country." Their hostility sprang from the root of unbelief. Jesus' death was impending because hostility had resulted everywhere He went.

6:44 draws him. Cf. v. 65. The combination of v. 37a and v. 44 indicate that the divine drawing activity which Jesus referred to cannot be reduced to what theologians call "prevenient grace," i.e., that somehow the power to come to Christ is allegedly dispensed to all of mankind, thus enabling everyone to accept or reject the gospel according to their own will alone. Scripture indicates that no "free will" exists in man's nature, for man is enslaved to sin (total depravity) and unable to believe apart from God's empowerment (Rom. 3:1-19; Eph. 2:1-3; 2 Cor. 4:4; 2 Tim. 1:9). While "whosoever will" may come to the Father, only those whom the Father gives the ability to will toward Him will actually come to Him. The drawing here is selective and efficacious (producing the desired effect) upon those whom God has sovereignly chosen for salvation, i.e., those whom God has chosen will believe because God has sovereignly determined that result from eternity past (Eph. 1:9-11).

6:45 Jesus paraphrased Is. 54:13 to support the point that if someone comes to faith and repentance to God, it is because they have been "taught," and hence drawn, by God. The "drawing" and "learning" are just different aspects of God's sovereign direction in the person's life. Those taught by God to grasp the truth are also drawn by God the Father to embrace the Son.

6:49,50 Jesus contrasted the earthly and heavenly bread. The manna that was given in the wilderness, although sent from heaven to help sustain the Israelites for their physical needs, could not impart eternal life nor meet their spiritual needs as could the "bread of life" (v. 48) that came down from heaven in the person of Jesus the Messiah. The proof of this contrast centers in the irrefutable fact that all the fathers died who ate the wilderness manna.

6:51-59 This section may be divided into 3 divisions: 1) Jesus' pronouncement (v. 51); 2) the crowd's perplexity (v. 52); and 3) Jesus' promises (vv. 53-59).

6:51 This pronouncement exactly reiterates vv. 33,35,47,48. **My flesh, which I shall give for the life of the world.** Jesus refers here prophetically to His impending sacrifice upon the cross (cf. 2 Cor. 5:21; 1 Pet. 2:24). Jesus voluntarily laid down His life for evil, sinful mankind (10:18; 1 John 2:2).

6:52 quarreled. Once again the perplexity of the Jews indicates that they failed to understand the spiritual truth behind Jesus' illustration. Every time Jesus had given them a veiled saying or physical illustration, the Jews failed to see its spiritual significance (e.g., 3:4; 4:15). The Mosaic law prohibited the drinking of blood or the eating of meat with blood still in it (Lev. 17:10-14; Deut. 12:16; Acts 15:29). The Jews, unable to go beyond the mere physical perspective, were perplexed and angered.

6:53-58 eat...drink. Jesus' point was an analogy that has spiritual, rather than literal, significance: just as eating and drinking are necessary for physical life, so also is belief in His sacrificial death on the cross necessary for eternal life. The eating of His flesh and drinking of His blood metaphorically symbolize the need for accepting Jesus' cross work. For the Jews, however, a crucified Messiah was unthinkable

flesh of the Son of Man and drink His
blood, you have no life in you. 54 [y]Who-
ever eats My flesh and drinks My blood
has eternal life, and I will raise him up at
the last day. 55 For My flesh is [2]food indeed, and My blood is [3]drink indeed.
56 He who eats My flesh and drinks My
blood [z]abides in Me, and I in him. 57 As the
living Father sent Me, and I live because of
the Father, so he who feeds on Me will live
because of Me. 58 [a]This is the bread which
came down from heaven—not [b]as your fathers ate the manna, and are dead. He who
eats this bread will live forever."

59 These things He said in the synagogue as He taught in Capernaum.

Rejection by Many Followers

60 [c]Therefore many of His disciples,
when they heard *this*, said, "This is a [4]hard
saying; who can understand it?"
61 When Jesus knew in Himself that His
disciples [5]complained about this, He said to
them, "Does this [6]offend you? 62 [d]*What*
then if you should see the Son of Man ascend where He was before? 63 [e]It is the Spirit who gives life; the [f]flesh profits nothing.
The [g]words that I speak to you are spirit,
and *they* are life. 64 But [h]there are some of
you who do not believe." For [i]Jesus knew
from the beginning who they were who did
not believe, and who would betray Him.
65 And He said, "Therefore [j]I have said to
you that no one can come to Me unless it
has been granted to him by My Father."
66 [k]From that *time* many of His disciples
went [7]back and walked with Him no more.

Confession by Peter

67 Then Jesus said to the twelve, "Do you
also want to go away?"
68 But Simon Peter answered Him,
"Lord, to whom shall we go? You have [l]the
words of eternal life. 69 [m]Also we have
come to believe and know that You are the
[8]Christ, the Son of the living God."
70 Jesus answered them, [n]"Did I not
choose you, the twelve, [o]and one of you is
a devil?" 71 He spoke of [p]Judas Iscariot, *the
son* of Simon, for it was he who would [q]be-
tray Him, being one of the twelve.

Christ's Brothers Do Not Believe

7 After these things Jesus walked in Galilee; for He did not want to walk in
Judea, [a]because the [1]Jews sought to kill

54 [y] John 4:14; 6:27, 40
55 [2] NU *true food* [3] NU *true drink*
56 [z] [1 John 3:24; 4:15, 16]
58 [a] John 6:49-51 [b] Ex. 16:14-35
60 [c] Matt. 11:6; John 6:66 [4] *difficult*
61 [5] *grumbled* [6] *make you stumble*
62 [d] Mark 16:19; John 3:13; Acts 1:9; 2:32, 33; Eph. 4:8
63 [e] Gen. 2:7; 2 Cor. 3:6 [f] John 3:6 [g] [John 6:68; 14:24]
64 [h] John 6:36 [i] John 2:24, 25; 13:11
65 [j] John 6:37, 44, 45
66 [k] Luke 9:62; John 6:60 [7] Or *away*; lit. *to the back*
68 [l] Acts 5:20
69 [m] Matt. 16:16; Mark 8:29; Luke 9:20; John 1:49; 11:27 [8] NU *Holy One of God.*
70 [n] Luke 6:13 [o] [John 13:27]
71 [p] John 12:4; 13:2, 26 [q] Matt. 26:14-16

CHAPTER 7

1 [a] Matt. 21:38; 26:4; John 5:18; 7:19, 25; 8:37, 40 [1] The ruling authorities

(cf. Acts 17:1-3). Once again, the Jews, in their willful and judicial blindness, could not see the real spiritual significance and truth behind Jesus' statements. Moreover, Jesus' reference here to eating and drinking was not referring to the ordinance of communion for two significant reasons: 1) communion had not been instituted yet, and 2) if Jesus was referring to communion, then the passage would teach that anyone partaking of communion would receive eternal life.

6:60-71 These verses constitute the reaction of Jesus' disciples to His sermon on the "bread of life." As with the crowds' response in Jerusalem (chap. 5) and in Galilee (chap. 6), the response of many of His disciples was unbelief and rejection of Him. John lists two groups and their reactions: 1) the false disciples' reaction of unbelief (vv. 60-66), and 2) the true disciples' reaction of belief (vv. 67-71). After this sermon, only a small nucleus of disciples remained (v. 67).

6:61 His disciples complained. Many of Jesus' disciples had the same reaction as the Jews in v. 41 and of the first generation of Israelites to manna, i.e., they murmured (Ex. 16:2).

6:64 Jesus knew. Reminiscent of Jesus' words in 2:23-25, Jesus knew the hearts of men, including those disciples who followed Him. He supernaturally knew that many did not believe in Him as Messiah and Son of God so He did not entrust Himself to them. These false disciples were simply attracted to the physical phenomena (e.g., miracles and food), and failed to understand the true significance of Jesus' teaching (v. 61).

6:65 I have said. *See notes on vv. 37,44.* Although men and women are commanded to believe and will be held accountable for unbelief, genuine faith is never exclusively a matter of human decision. Once again, in the face of unbelief, Jesus reiterated God's sovereignty involved in selection for salvation.

6:66 disciples...walked with Him no more. The language indicates that the abandonment was decisive and final (cf. 1 Pet. 2:6-8; 1 John 2:19).

6:69 we have come to believe. Peter's words were somewhat pretentious in that he implied that the true disciples somehow had superior insight and, as a result, came to belief through that insight.

6:70 Did I not choose you, the twelve. In response to Peter's words that the disciples had come to believe in Jesus, He reminds them that He sovereignly chose them (vv. 37,44,65). Jesus would not allow even a whisper of human pretension in God's sovereign selection. **a devil.** The word "devil" means "slanderer" or "false accuser." The idea perhaps is better rendered "one of you is *the* devil." This meaning is clear from 13:2,27; Mark 8:33; Luke 22:3. The supreme adversary of God so operates behind failing human beings that his malice becomes theirs (cf. Matt. 16:23). Jesus supernaturally knew the source and identified it precisely. This clearly fixes the character of Judas, not as a well intentioned but misguided man trying to force Jesus to exert His power and set up His kingdom (as some suggest), but as a tool of Satan doing unmitigated wickedness (*see notes on 13:21-30*).

6:71 Iscariot. The word most likely is from a Heb. word meaning "man of Kerioth," the name of a village in Judah. As with the other 3 gospels, as soon as he was named, he became identified as the betrayer.

7:1–8:59 The main thrust of this section can be summarized as "high intensity hatred" since the smoldering dislike of Jesus in chaps. 5,6 erupted into a blazing inferno. The culmination of this hatred occurs in 11:45-57 where the Jewish authorities plot to kill the Son of God, culminating ultimately in His crucifixion. Both chapters deal with Jesus at the Feast of Tabernacles in Jerusalem. Especially noteworthy is the fact that two major themes associated with Tabernacles, i.e., water and light, come to prominence in these two chapters (vv. 37-39; 8:12). At the next Passover following this celebration of Tabernacles, Jesus was crucified. The central truth that dominates this whole passage is that Jesus was on a divine timetable. His life was not random, but operated according to God's sovereign and perfect timing and direction.

7:1-13 This section has two parts: 1) Jesus' avoidance of the wrong time in God's sovereign plan (vv. 1-9), and 2) Jesus' perfect obedience to the right time in God's sovereign plan (vv. 10-13).

Him. 2 [b]Now the Jews' Feast of Tabernacles was at hand. 3 [c]His brothers therefore
said to Him, "Depart from here and go into
Judea, that Your disciples also may see the
works that You are doing. 4 For no one
does anything in secret while he himself
seeks to be known openly. If You do these
things, show Yourself to the world." 5 For
[d]even His [e]brothers did not believe in
Him.

6 Then Jesus said to them, [f]"My time has
not yet come, but your time is always
ready. 7 [g]The world cannot hate you, but it
hates Me [h]because I testify of it that its
works are evil. 8 You go up to this feast. I
am not [2]yet going up to this feast, [i]for My
time has not yet fully come." 9 When He
had said these things to them, He remained in Galilee.

Christ Secretly Goes to the Feast

10 But when His brothers had gone up,
then He also went up to the feast, not
openly, but as it were in secret. 11 Then [j]the
Jews sought Him at the feast, and said,
"Where is He?" 12 And [k]there was much
complaining among the people concerning
Him. [l]Some said, "He is good"; others
said, "No, on the contrary, He deceives the
people." 13 However, no one spoke openly
of Him [m]for fear of the Jews.

Christ's Authority from the Father

14 Now about the middle of the feast

2 [b] Lev. 23:34; Deut. 16:13-15; Neh. 8:14, 18; Zech. 14:16-19
3 [c] Matt. 12:46; Mark 3:21; John 7:5, 10; Acts 1:14
5 [d] Ps. 69:8; Mic. 7:6 [e] Matt. 12:46; 13:55; Mark 3:21; John 7:3, 10
6 [f] John 2:4; 8:20
7 [g] [John 15:19] [h] John 3:19
8 [i] John 8:20 [2] NU omits *yet*
11 [j] John 11:56
12 [k] John 9:16; 10:19 [l] Matt. 21:46; Luke 7:16; John 6:14; 7:40
13 [m] [John 9:22; 12:42; 19:38]

7:1 After these things. A 7 month gap most likely took place between chaps. 6 and 7. While chap. 6 occurred around Passover (6:4—Apr.), chap. 7 occurs at the Feast of Tabernacles (Oct.). John wrote nothing about those months since his purpose was not to present an exhaustive chronology of Christ's life but to portray Him as the Messiah and Son of God and show how men reacted to Him. **walked in Galilee.** Chapter 6 indicates Jesus spent two days with the multitude of 20,000 people (6:22), but He spent 7 months teaching His 12 disciples who believed in Him. This phrase subtly highlights the great importance of discipleship, for Jesus concentrated great lengths of time upon training His future spiritual leaders.

7:2 Feast of Tabernacles. *See note on 5:1.* The Feast of Tabernacles was associated in the OT with the ingathering of the harvest of grapes and olives (Ex. 23:16; Lev. 23:33-36,39-43; Deut. 16:13-15), while grain was reaped between Apr. and June. The feast occurred for 7 days from the 15th to the 21st of Tishri (Sep.-Oct.). According to Josephus, this feast was the most popular of the 3 principle Jewish feasts (Passover, Pentecost, and Tabernacles). People living in rural areas built makeshift structures of light branches and leaves to live in for the week (hence, "booths" or "tabernacles"; cf. Lev. 23:42) while town dwellers put up similar structures on their flat roofs or in their courtyards. The feast was known for water-drawing and lamp-lighting rites to which Jesus makes reference ("If anyone thirsts, let him come to Me and drink"—vv. 37,38 and "I am the light of the world"—8:12).

7:3 His brothers. Matthew 13:55 lists Jesus' brothers as "James, Joses, Simon, and Judas." James authored the NT epistle that bears his name and became the leader of the Jerusalem church and Judas (or, Jude) wrote the epistle that also bears his name. Because of Jesus' virgin birth, they were only the half-brothers of Jesus since Mary, not Joseph, was Jesus' only human parent (cf. Matt. 1:16,18,23; Luke 1:35).

7:4 to be known openly.... show Yourself to the world. Jesus' brothers wanted Him to put on a display of His miracles. Although the text does not clearly state their motivation, perhaps they made the request for two reasons: 1) they wanted to see the miracles for themselves to determine their genuineness, and 2) they may have had similar crass political motives as the people, namely that He would become their social and political Messiah. Jerusalem's acceptance of Him was to be the acid test for them as to whether His own family would believe in Him as Messiah.

7:5 As with the crowds in Jerusalem and Galilee, even His own brothers did not believe in Him at first. They did not become His followers until after the resurrection (Acts 1:14; 1 Cor. 15:7).

7:6 My time has not yet come. This recalls the response to Jesus' mother at the wedding in Cana (see 2:4). It also reveals the first reason why Jesus would not go to the feast: it was not in God's perfect timing. The sentence reveals Jesus' complete dependence and commitment to the Father's sovereign timetable for His life (cf. 8:20; Acts 1:7; 17:26). Furthermore, Jesus never committed Himself to being motivated by unbelief, even that of His own half-brothers. **your time is always ready.** Because Jesus' brothers did not believe in Him, they were of the world and therefore, knew nothing of God or His purposes. Because of unbelief, they did not listen to His word, did not recognize God's schedule, and could not perceive the incarnate Word before them. As a result, any time would do for them, preferably that moment.

7:7 The world cannot hate you. The world cannot hate Jesus' brothers because they belonged to the world and the world loves its own (cf. 15:18,19). The evil world system and all who reject the Word and Son of God lie in the control of the evil one himself (1 John 5:19). **I testify of it that its works are evil.** A true born-again believer who is living a life for God's glory should experience the hatred and antagonism of the world (cf. 15:18-25; 16:1-3; 2 Tim. 3:12).

7:8 My time has not yet fully come. This reveals the second reason why Jesus would not go to the feast in Jerusalem. The Jews could not kill Him before God's perfect timing and plan was ready (cf. Gal. 4:4). Jesus' commitment to God's timetable would not permit any deviance from what God had decreed.

7:10 in secret. The assumption is that the Father had directed Jesus to permit Him to go to Jerusalem. Jesus left Galilee for the last time before the cross. The secrecy of His journey indicates His maximum discretion which was the complete opposite of what His brothers had demanded of Him (cf. v. 4).

7:11 the Jews sought Him. The contrast between the phrase "the Jews" in this verse and "the people" in v. 12 indicate that the term "Jews" designates the hostile Jewish authorities in Judea who were headquartered in Jerusalem. The search for Jesus was certainly hostile in intent.

7:12,13 complaining among the people. The crowds, made up of Judeans, Galileans, and Diaspora (scattered) Jews, expressed various opinions regarding Christ. The spectrum ranged from superficial acceptance ("He is good") to cynical rejection ("he deceives the people"). The Jewish Talmud reveals that the latter view of deception became the predominant opinion of many Jews (Babylonian Talmud *Sanhedrin* 43a).

7:14-24 The increasing hostility to Jesus did not prevent His teaching ministry. Instead, Jesus relentlessly set forth His claims regarding His identity and mission. In the midst of the Feast of Tabernacles, when Jews from all over Israel had migrated into Jerusalem, Jesus once again began to teach. In this section, Jesus set forth the justification of His ministry and taught with authority as God's Son. In this passage, 5 reasons are set forth as to why Jesus' claims regarding Himself are true: 1) His supernatural knowledge originated from the

Jesus went up into the temple and [n]taught.
15 [o]And the Jews marveled, saying, "How
does this Man know letters, having never
studied?"
16 [3]Jesus answered them and said, [p]"My
doctrine is not Mine, but His who sent Me.
17 [q]If anyone wills to do His will, he shall
know concerning the doctrine, whether it
is from God or *whether* I speak on My own
authority. 18 [r]He who speaks from himself
seeks his own glory; but He who [s]seeks the
glory of the One who sent Him is true, and
[t]no unrighteousness is in Him. 19 [u]Did not
Moses give you the law, yet none of you
keeps the law? [v]Why do you seek to kill
Me?"
20 The people answered and said, [w]"You
have a demon. Who is seeking to kill You?"
21 Jesus answered and said to them, "I
did one work, and you all marvel. 22 [x]Mo-
ses therefore gave you circumcision (not
that it is from Moses, [y]but from the fathers),
and you circumcise a man on the Sabbath.
23 If a man receives circumcision on the Sabbath, so that the law of Moses should not be
broken, are you angry with Me because [z]I
made a man completely well on the Sabbath? 24 [a]Do not judge according to appearance, but judge with righteous judgment."

Christ's Origin from the Father

25 Now some of them from Jerusalem
said, "Is this not He whom they seek to
[b]kill? 26 But look! He speaks boldly, and
they say nothing to Him. [c]Do the rulers
know indeed that this is [4]truly the Christ?
27 [d]However, we know where this Man is
from; but when the Christ comes, no one
knows where He is from."

14 [n] Ps. 22:22; Matt. 4:23; 5:2; 7:29; Mark 6:34; Luke 4:15; 5:3; John 8:2
15 [o] Matt. 13:54; Mark 6:2; [Luke 4:22]; Acts 2:7
16 [p] Deut. 18:15, 18, 19; John 3:11 [3] NU, M *So Jesus*
17 [q] Ps. 25:9, 14; Prov. 3:32; Dan. 12:10; John 3:21; 8:43
18 [r] John 5:41 [s] John 8:50 [t] John 8:46; [2 Cor. 5:21; Heb. 4:15; 7:26; 1 Pet. 1:19; 2:22]
19 [u] Ex. 24:3; Deut. 33:4; Acts 7:38 [v] Matt. 12:14
20 [w] John 8:48, 52
22 [x] Lev. 12:3 [y] Gen. 17:9-14; Acts 7:8
23 [z] John 5:8, 9, 16
24 [a] Deut. 1:16; Prov. 24:23; John 8:15; James 2:1
25 [b] Matt. 21:38; 26:4; Luke 22:2; John 5:18; 8:37, 40 **26** [c] John 7:48 [4] NU omits *truly* **27** [d] Matt. 13:55; Mark 6:3; Luke 4:22

Father Himself (vv. 15,16); 2) His teaching and knowledge could be confirmed by testing (v. 17); 3) His actions demonstrated His selflessness (v. 18); 4) His impact on the world was startling (vv. 19,20); and 5) His deeds demonstrated His identity as the Son of God (vv. 21-24).

7:14 middle of the feast. Jesus may have waited until the middle of the feast in order to prevent a premature "triumphal entry" that some may have forced upon Him for political motivations. **into the temple and taught.** Jesus taught according to the custom of the teachers or rabbis of His day. Prominent rabbis would enter the temple environs and expound on the OT to crowds who sat around them.

7:15 marveled. Jesus' knowledge of Scripture was supernatural. The people were amazed that someone who had never studied at any great rabbinical centers or under any great rabbis could display such profound mastery of Scripture. Both the content and manner of Jesus' teachings were qualitatively different than any other teacher.

7:16 His who sent Me. The qualitative difference of Jesus' teaching was found in its source, i.e., the Father gave it to Him (8:26,40, 46,47; 12:49,50). It originated from God the Father Himself, in contrast to rabbis who received it from man (Gal. 1:12). While rabbis merely relied on the authority of others (a long chain of human tradition), Jesus' authority centered in Himself (cf. Matt. 7:28,29; Acts 4:13).

7:17 If anyone wills to do His will, he shall know. Those who are fundamentally committed to doing God's will will be guided by Him in the affirmation of His truth. God's truth is self-authenticating through the teaching ministry of the Holy Spirit (cf. 16:13; 1 John 2:20,27).

7:18 He who seeks the glory of the One who sent Him. While other saviors and messiahs acted for their own selfish interests, thereby revealing their falseness, Jesus Christ as God's Son came solely to glorify the Father and accomplish the Father's will (2 Cor. 2:17; Phil. 2:5-11; Heb. 10:7).

7:19,20 kill Me. If Jesus were another religious fake, the world never would have reacted in such hatred. Since the evil world system loves its own, its hatred toward Him demonstrates that He came from God (15:18,19).

7:21 one work. The context makes clear (vv. 22,23) that Jesus had reference to the healing of the paralytic that evoked the beginning of persecution against Him by the Jewish authorities because it took place on the Sabbath (see 5:1-16).

7:22 but from the fathers. The patriarchal period during the time of Abraham when God instituted the sign of circumcision (Gen. 17:10-12), which was later included as part of the Mosaic covenant at Sinai (Ex. 4:26; 12:44,45). This observation not only depreciated the Jewish esteem for Moses, but even more importantly showed that this rite was antecedent to the Mosaic law and took precedence over it (Gal. 3:17). Furthermore, circumcision antedates the Sabbath law also.

7:23 on the Sabbath. The law required that circumcision occur on the eighth day (Lev. 12:1-3). If a child was born on the Sabbath, then the eighth day would fall again on the subsequent Sabbath, when the Jews would circumcise the child. Jesus' point was that the Jews broke their own Sabbath law with the circumcision of the child. Their hypocrisy is evident. **I made a man completely well.** Jesus used an argument of the lesser to the greater. If ceremonial cleansing of one part of the body is permitted on the Sabbath through the act of circumcision (the less), how much more so should the actual healing of the entire body be permitted on the Sabbath (the greater).

7:24 with righteous judgment. While Jesus forbade harsh, censorious judgment that self-righteous legalism promotes (Matt. 7:1), He demanded the exercise of moral and theological discernment.

7:25-36 In this section, John once again reiterated the claims of Jesus to His identity as the Messiah and Son of God. He focused on His divine origin and citizenship. While some believed in Him at this time (v. 31), the religious leaders became even more angry at Him and nefariously planned to seize Him (v. 32). Jesus confronted the people with 3 dilemmas recorded in these verses: 1) the problem of dense confusion (vv. 25-29); 2) the problem of divided conviction (vv. 30-32); and 3) the problem of delayed conversion (vv. 33-36). These 3 problems left Jerusalem in a state of utter despair.

7:26 He speaks boldly. What surprised the masses was that in spite of the ominous threat from the religious authorities (vv. 20,32), Jesus boldly proclaimed His identity. **Do the rulers know.** The question indicates the crowds and the rulers were in great confusion and uncertainty as to who Jesus was and what to do about Him. They did not really have any firm convictions regarding Jesus' identity, for their question reveals their doubt and unbelief. They were also perplexed at the religious leaders' failure to arrest and silence Him if He really were a fraud. Such dense confusion caused the crowd to wonder if the religious authorities in private concluded that He was indeed the Christ. Mass confusion among all groups reigned regarding Jesus. **Christ.** *See notes on 1:20,41.*

7:27 no one knows where He is from. Only information regarding Messiah's birthplace was revealed in Scripture (Mic. 5:2; Matt. 2:5,6). Beyond that, a tradition had developed in Jewish circles that Messiah would appear suddenly to the people, based on a misinter-

28 Then Jesus cried out, as He taught in
the temple, saying, [e]"You both know Me,
and you know where I am from; and [f]I
have not come of Myself, but He who sent
Me [g]is true, [h]whom you do not know.
29 [5]But [i]I know Him, for I am from Him,
and He sent Me."
30 Therefore [j]they sought to take Him;
but [k]no one laid a hand on Him, because
His hour had not yet come. 31 And [l]many
of the people believed in Him, and said,
"When the Christ comes, will He do more
signs than these which this *Man* has
done?"

Christ's Departure to the Father

32 The Pharisees heard the crowd murmuring these things concerning Him, and
the Pharisees and the chief priests sent officers to take Him. 33 Then Jesus said [6]to
them, [m]"I shall be with you a little while
longer, and *then* I [n]go to Him who sent Me.
34 You [o]will seek Me and not find *Me*, and
where I am you [p]cannot come."
35 Then the Jews said among themselves, "Where does He intend to go that
we shall not find Him? Does He intend to
go to [q]the Dispersion among the Greeks
and teach the Greeks? 36 What is this thing
that He said, 'You will seek Me and not
find Me, and where I am you cannot
come'?"

Christ Reveals the "Living Water"

37 [r]On the last day, that great *day* of the
feast, Jesus stood and cried out, saying,
[s]"If anyone thirsts, let him come to Me
and drink. 38 [t]He who believes in Me, as
the Scripture has said, [u]out of his heart
will flow rivers of living water." 39 [v]But

28 [e] John 8:14 [f] John 5:43 [g] Rom. 3:4 [h] John 1:18; 8:55 **29** [i] Matt. 11:27; John 8:55; 17:25 [5] NU, M omit *But* **30** [j] Mark 11:18 [k] Matt. 21:46; John 7:32, 44; 8:20; 10:39 **31** [l] Matt. 12:23 **33** [m] John 13:33 [n] [Mark 16:19; Luke 24:51; Acts 1:9; Heb. 9:24; 1 Pet. 3:22] [6] NU, M omit *to them* **34** [o] Hos. 5:6 [p] [Matt. 5:20; 1 Cor. 6:9; 15:50; Rev. 21:27] **35** [q] Ps. 147:2; [Is. 11:12; 56:8; Zeph. 3:10]; James 1:1; 1 Pet. 1:1 **37** [r] Lev. 23:36; Num. 29:35; Neh. 8:18 [s] [Is. 55:1] **38** [t] Deut. 18:15 [u] Is. 12:3; 43:20; 44:3; 55:1; [John 6:35]; Rev. 21:6; 22:17 **39** [v] Is. 44:3; [Joel 2:28]; John 1:33

pretation of Is. 53:8 and Mal. 3:1. In light of this, the meaning of this phrase most likely is that the identity of the Messiah would be wholly unknown until He suddenly appeared in Israel and accomplished Israel's redemption. In contrast, Jesus had lived His life in Nazareth and was known (at least superficially) to the people (v. 28).

7:28 cried out. Jesus gave the greatest publicity to this important teaching by voicing it loudly (cf. v. 37; 1:15; 12:44). **You both know Me, and you know where I am from.** These words stand in antithesis with 8:19 where Jesus told His enemies that they neither knew Him nor the Father, thus indicating a deep irony and sarcasm on Jesus' part here. Jesus' point is that contrary to what they thought, they really had no true understanding of who He was. They knew him in the earthly sense, but not in the spiritual sense, because they didn't know God either. **whom you do not know.** Although they thought that they were acutely perceptive and spiritually oriented, their rejection of Jesus revealed their spiritual bankruptcy (Rom. 2:17-19).

7:30 His hour had not yet come. This reveals the reason why they could not seize Him, i.e., God's sovereign timetable and plan for Jesus would not allow it.

7:31 many...believed. Divided conviction existed among the people regarding Jesus. While some wanted to seize Him, a small remnant of genuine believers existed among the crowds. The question here anticipates a negative answer, i.e., the Messiah could do no greater kinds of miracles than those Jesus had done.

7:32 Pharisees and the chief priests. *See note on 3:1.* The Pharisees and chief priests historically did not have harmonious relationships with each other. Most of the chief priests were Sadducees, who were political and religious opponents to the Pharisees. John repeatedly links these two groups in his gospel (see also v. 45; 11:47,57; 18:3) in order to emphasize that their cooperation stemmed from their mutual hatred of Jesus. Both were alarmed at the faith of those indicated in v. 31 and, in order to avoid any veneration of Jesus as Messiah, attempted unsuccessfully to arrest Him (v. 30). **officers.** Temple guards who functioned as a kind of police force composed of Levites who were in charge of maintaining order in the temple environs. They could also be used by the Sanhedrin in areas outside the temple environs in religious disputes that did not affect Roman policy.

7:34 where I am you cannot come. Jesus referred here to His return to His heavenly origin with His Father after His crucifixion and resurrection (see 17:15).

7:35,36 John again highlights the ignorance of the Jews regarding Jesus' words. The words were spoken to mock Jesus.

7:35 teach the Greeks. The phrase "teach the Greeks" probably had reference to Jewish proselytes, i.e., Gentiles. John may have been citing this phrase with ironic force since the gospel eventually went to the Gentiles because of Jewish blindness and rejection of their Messiah. *See notes on Rom. 11:7-11.*

7:37-52 This section catalogues the different reactions of people to Jesus' claims. These reactions have become universal patterns for reactions to Him through the ages. This section may be divided into the claim of Christ (vv. 37-39) and the reactions to Christ (vv. 40-52). The reactions may be subdivided into 5 sections: 1) the reaction of the convinced (vv. 40-41a); 2) the reaction of the contrary (vv. 41b-42); 3) the reaction of the hostile (vv. 43,44); 4) the rejection of the confused (vv. 45,46); and 5) the reaction of the religious authorities (vv. 47-52).

7:37 On the last day. This suggests that this occasion occurred on a different day than the controversy in vv. 11-36. **If anyone thirsts.** A tradition grew up in the few centuries before Jesus that on the 7 days of the Feast of Tabernacles, a golden container filled with water from the pool of Siloam was carried in procession by the High-Priest back to the temple. As the procession came to the Watergate on the S side of the inner temple court, 3 trumpet blasts were made to mark the joy of the occasion and the people recited Is. 12:3, "With joy you will draw water from the wells of salvation." At the temple, while onlookers watched, the priests would march around the altar with the water container while the temple choir sang the Hallel (Pss. 113–118). The water was offered in sacrifice to God at the time of the morning sacrifice. The use of the water symbolized the blessing of adequate rainfall for crops. Jesus used this event as an object lesson and opportunity to make a very public invitation on the last day of the feast for His people to accept Him as the living water. His words recall Is. 55:1. **thirsts...come...drink.** These 3 words summarize the gospel invitation. A recognition of need leads to an approach to the source of provision, followed by receiving what is needed. The thirsty, needy soul feels the craving to come to the Savior and drink, i.e., receive the salvation that He offers.

7:38 living water. The water-pouring rite was also associated within Jewish tradition as a foreshadowing of the eschatological rivers of living water foreseen in Ezek. 47:1-9 and Zech. 13:1. The significance of Jesus' invitation centers in the fact that He was the fulfillment of all the Feast of Tabernacles anticipated, i.e., He was the One who provided the living water that gives eternal life to man (cf. 4:10,11).

this He spoke concerning the Spirit, whom
those [7]believing in Him would receive; for
the [8]Holy Spirit was not yet *given,* because
Jesus was not yet [w]glorified.

Israel Is Divided over Christ

40 Therefore [9]many from the crowd,
when they heard this saying, said, "Truly
this is [x]the Prophet." **41** Others said, "This
is [y]the Christ."
But some said, "Will the Christ come out
of Galilee? **42** [z]Has not the Scripture said
that the Christ comes from the seed of David and from the town of Bethlehem,
[a]where David was?" **43** So [b]there was a
division among the people because of
Him. **44** Now [c]some of them wanted to
take Him, but no one laid hands on Him.

The Sanhedrin Is Confused over Christ

45 Then the officers came to the chief
priests and Pharisees, who said to them,
"Why have you not brought Him?"
46 The officers answered, [d]"No man ever
spoke like this Man!"
47 Then the Pharisees answered them,
"Are you also deceived? **48** Have any of the
rulers or the Pharisees believed in Him?
49 But this crowd that does not know the
law is accursed."
50 Nicodemus [e](he who came to [1]Jesus
[2]by night, being one of them) said to them,
51 [f]"Does our law judge a man before it
hears him and knows what he is doing?"
52 They answered and said to him, "Are
you also from Galilee? Search and look, for
[g]no prophet [3]has arisen out of Galilee."

A Woman Is Caught in Adultery

53 [4]And everyone went to his *own* house.
8 But Jesus went to the Mount of Olives.
2 Now [1]early in the morning He
came again into the temple, and all the people came to Him; and He sat down and
[a]taught them. **3** Then the scribes and Pharisees brought to Him a woman caught in
adultery. And when they had set her in the
midst, **4** they said to Him, "Teacher, [2]this
woman was caught in [b]adultery, in the very
act. **5** [c]Now [3]Moses, in the law, commanded us [4]that such should be stoned. But
what do You [5]say?" **6** This they said, testing
Him, that they [d]might have *something* of
which to accuse Him. But Jesus stooped
down and wrote on the ground with *His*
finger, [6]as though He did not hear.
7 So when they continued asking Him,
He [7]raised Himself up and said to them,
[e]"He who is without sin among you, let
him throw a stone at her first." **8** And again

39 [w]John 12:16; 13:31; 17:5 [7]NU *who believed* [8]NU omits *Holy*
40 [x]Deut. 18:15, 18 [9]NU *some*
41 [y]John 4:42; 6:69
42 [z]Ps. 132:11; Jer. 23:5; Mic. 5:2; Matt. 2:5; [Luke 2:4] [a]1 Sam. 16:1, 4
43 [b]John 7:12
44 [c]John 7:30
46 [d]Matt. 13:54, 56; Luke 4:22
50 [e]John 3:1, 2; 19:39 [1]Lit. *Him* [2]NU *before*
51 [f]Deut. 1:16, 17; 19:15
52 [g][Is. 9:1, 2]; Matt. 4:15 [3]NU *is to rise*
53 [4]NU brackets 7:53 through 8:11 as not in the original text. They are present in over 900 mss. of John.

CHAPTER 8

2 [a]John 8:20; 18:20 [1]M *very early*
4 [b]Ex. 20:14; [Matt. 5:27; 19:9; Rom. 7:3] [2]M *we found this woman*
5 [c]Lev. 20:10; Deut. 22:22-24 [3]M *in our law Moses commanded* [4]NU, M *to stone such* [5]M adds *about her*
6 [d]Matt. 22:15 [6]NU, M omit *as though He did not hear*
7 [e]Deut. 17:7; [Rom. 2:1] [7]M *He looked up*

7:39 He spoke concerning the Spirit. The impartation of the Holy Spirit is the source of spiritual and eternal life. *See note on 16:7.*

7:41 out of Galilee. This betrays the people's great ignorance, because Jesus was born in Bethlehem of Judea not Galilee (Mic. 5:2 cf. Matt. 2:6; Luke 2:4). They did not even bother to investigate His true birthplace, showing their lack of interest in messianic credentials.

7:43 division. See Matt. 10:34-36; Luke 12:51-53.

7:44 *See notes on vv. 8,30.*

7:45 the officers. The officers failed in their attempt to arrest Jesus when they were confronted with His person and powerful teaching. Since they were religiously trained, Jesus' words struck at their very heart. For their identity, *see notes on v. 32.*

7:47,48 The Pharisees mocked the officers, not on professional (as police officers) but religious grounds (as Levites). In essence, they accused them of being seduced by a deceiver (i.e., Jesus) in contrast to the Pharisees themselves who arrogantly and self-righteously felt that in their wisdom and knowledge no one could ever deceive them.

7:49 crowd. The Pharisees condescendingly labeled the people as a "crowd." The rabbis viewed the common people (or, people of the land) as ignorant and impious in contrast to themselves. This ignorance was not only because of their ignorance of Scripture, but especially the common people's failure to follow the Pharisees' oral traditions. **accursed.** The people were considered damned because they did not belong to the elite group nor follow their beliefs regarding the law.

7:50-52 Nicodemus' (see 3:10) mind had not closed regarding Christ's claims, so that while not defending Jesus directly, he did raise a procedural point in Jesus' favor.

7:51 Does our law judge. No explicit OT text can be cited that makes Nicodemus' point. Most likely he referred to rabbinical traditions contained in their oral law.

7:52 no prophet has arisen out of Galilee. The real ignorance lay with the arrogant Pharisees who did not carefully search out the facts as to where Jesus was actually born. While they accused the crowds of ignorance, they too were really as ignorant (v. 42). Furthermore, the prophets Jonah and Nahum did come from Galilee.

7:53–8:11 This section dealing with the adulteress most likely was not a part of the original contents of John. It has been incorporated into various manuscripts at different places in the gospel (e.g., after vv. 36,44,52, or 21:25), while one manuscript places it after Luke 21:38. External manuscript evidence representing a great variety of textual traditions is decidedly against its inclusion, for the earliest and best manuscripts exclude it. Many manuscripts mark the passage to indicate doubt as to its inclusion. Significant early versions exclude it. No Gr. church father comments on the passage until the twelfth century. The vocabulary and style of the section also are different from the rest of the gospel, and the section interrupts the sequence of v. 52 with 8:12ff. Many, however, do think that it has all the earmarks of historical veracity, perhaps being a piece of oral tradition that circulated in parts of the western church, so that a few comments are in order. In spite of all these considerations of the likely unreliability of this section, it is possible to be wrong on the issue, and thus it is good to consider the meaning of this passage and leave it in the text, just as with Mark 16:9-20.

8:6 testing Him...to accuse Him. If Jesus rejected the law of Moses (Lev. 20:10; Deut. 22:22), His credibility would be gone. If He held to Mosaic law, His reputation for compassion and forgiveness would have been questioned.

8:7 He who is without sin. This directly refers to Deut. 13:9; 17:7, where the witnesses of a crime are to start the execution. Only those who were not guilty of the same sin could participate.

He stooped down and wrote on the
ground. 9 Then those who heard *it,* [f]being[8]
convicted by *their* conscience, went out one
by one, beginning with the oldest *even* to
the last. And Jesus was left alone, and the
woman standing in the midst. 10 When Jesus had raised Himself up [9]and saw no
one but the woman, He said to her,
"Woman, where are those accusers [1]of
yours? Has no one condemned you?"
11 She said, "No one, Lord."
And Jesus said to her, [g]"Neither do I
condemn you; go [2]and [h]sin no more."

"I Am the Light of the World"

12 Then Jesus spoke to them again, saying, [i]"I am the light of the world. He who
[j]follows Me shall not walk in darkness, but
have the light of life."
13 The Pharisees therefore said to Him,
[k]"You bear witness of Yourself; Your witness is not [3]true."
14 Jesus answered and said to them,
"Even if I bear witness of Myself, My witness is true, for I know where I came from
and where I am going; but [l]you do not
know where I come from and where I am
going. 15 [m]You judge according to the
flesh; [n]I judge no one. 16 And yet if I do
judge, My judgment is true; for [o]I am not
alone, but I *am* with the Father who sent
Me. 17 [p]It is also written in your law that
the testimony of two men is true. 18 I am
One who bears witness of Myself, and
[q]the Father who sent Me bears witness of
Me."
19 Then they said to Him, "Where is
Your Father?"
Jesus answered, [r]"You know neither
Me nor My Father. [s]If you had known
Me, you would have known My Father
also."
20 These words Jesus spoke in [t]the treasury, as He taught in the temple; and [u]no
one laid hands on Him, for [v]His hour had
not yet come.
21 Then Jesus said to them again, "I am
going away, and [w]you will seek Me, and
[x]will die in your sin. Where I go you cannot come."
22 So the Jews said, "Will He kill Himself, because He says, 'Where I go you cannot come'?"

9 [f]Rom. 2:22 [8]NU, M omit *being convicted by their conscience*
10 [9]NU omits *and saw no one but the woman;* M *He saw her and said,* [1]NU, M omit *of yours*
11 [g][Luke 9:56; 12:14; John 3:17] [h][John 5:14] [2]NU, M add *from now on*
12 [i]Is. 9:2; Mal. 4:2; John 1:4; 9:5; 12:35; [2 Tim. 1:10] [j]1 Thess. 5:5
13 [k]John 5:31 [3]*valid as testimony*
14 [l]John 7:28; 9:29
15 [m]1 Sam. 16:7; John 7:24 [n][John 3:17; 12:47; 18:36]
16 [o]John 16:32
17 [p]Deut. 17:6; 19:15; Matt. 18:16; 2 Cor. 13:1; Heb. 10:28
18 [q]John 5:37; 1 John 5:9
19 [r]John 16:3 [s]John 14:7
20 [t]Mark 12:41, 43; Luke 21:1 [u]John 2:4; 7:30 [v]John 7:8
21 [w]John 7:34; 13:33 [x]John 8:24

8:8 Cf. v. 6. This seems to have been a delaying device, giving them time to think.

8:11 sin no more. Actually, "Leave your life of sin" (cf. 3:17; 12:47; Matt. 9:1-8; Mark 2:13-17).

8:12-21 Excluding the story of the adulterous woman in 7:53–8:11, this verse attaches itself well to 7:52. The word "again" indicates that Jesus spoke once more to the people at this same Feast of Tabernacles (see 7:2,10). While Jesus first used the water-drawing rite (7:37-39) as a metaphor to portray the ultimate spiritual truth of Himself as Messiah who fulfills all that the feast anticipated, He then turned to another rite that traditionally occurred at the feast: the lighting ceremony. During Tabernacles, 4 large lamps in the temple's court of women were lit and an exuberant nightly celebration took place under their light with people dancing through the night and holding burning torches in their hands while singing songs and praises. The levitical orchestras also played. Jesus took this opportunity of the lighting celebration to portray another spiritual analogy for the people: "I am the light of the world."

8:12 I am the light of the world. This is the second "I AM" statement (see 6:35). John has already used the "light" metaphor for Jesus (1:4). Jesus' metaphor here is steeped in OT allusions (Ex. 13:21,22; 14:19-25; Pss. 27:1; 119:105; Prov. 6:23; Ezek. 1:4,13,26-28; Hab. 3:3,4). The phrase highlights Jesus' role as Messiah and Son of God (Ps. 27:1; Mal. 4:2). The OT indicates that the coming age of Messiah would be a time when the Lord would be a light for His people (Is. 60:19-22; cf. Rev. 21:23,24) as well as for the whole earth (Is. 42:6; 49:6). Zechariah 14:5b-8 has an emphasis on God as the light of the world who gives living waters to His people. This latter passage probably formed the liturgical readings for the Feast of Tabernacles. For further significance of Jesus as the "light," *see notes on 1:4,5; 1 John 1:5.* **He who follows Me.** The word "follows" conveys the idea of someone who gives himself completely to the person followed. No half-hearted followers exist in Jesus' mind (cf. Matt. 8:18-22; 10:38,39). A veiled reference exists here to the Jews, following the pillar of cloud and fire that led them during the Exodus (Ex. 13:21).

8:13 You bear witness of Yourself. The Jews mockingly brought up Jesus' own words from 5:31. However, Jesus' words there and here are reconciled by the fact that OT law required not one but multiple witnesses to establish the truth of a matter (Deut. 17:6). Jesus was not alone in His witness that pointed to Him as Messiah, for many had already testified concerning this truth (*see note on 1:7*).

8:14-18 These verses give 3 reasons why Jesus' witness was true: 1) Jesus knew His origin and destiny while the Jews were ignorant even of basic spiritual truths, making their judgment limited and superficial (vv. 14,15); 2) the intimate union of the Son with the Father guaranteed the truth of the Son's witness (v. 16); and 3) the Father and Son witnessed harmoniously together regarding the identity of the Son (vv. 17,18).

8:17 written in your law. *See Deut. 17:6; 19:15 and notes on 1:7.*

8:19 "Where is your Father?" The Jews, as was their habit (e.g., 3:4; 4:11; 6:52), once again thought merely on human terms in asking about Jesus' paternity.

8:21-30 Jesus revealed the consequence of the rejection of Him as Messiah and Son of God, i.e., spiritual death (v. 24; cf. Heb. 10:26-31). These verses reveal 4 ways that ensure someone will die in their sins and, as a result, experience spiritual death: 1) being self-righteous (vv. 20-22); 2) being earthbound (vv. 23,24); 3) being unbelieving (v. 24); and 4) being willfully ignorant (vv. 25-29). The Jews who rejected Jesus displayed all 4 of these characteristics.

8:21 Jesus repeated His message of 7:33,34 but with more ominous overtones regarding the consequences of rejecting Him. **I am going away.** By means of His impending death, resurrection, and ascension to the Father.

8:22 Will He kill Himself. The Jews spoke either in confusion (*see notes on 7:34,35*) or, perhaps more likely, in mockery of Christ. Jewish tradition condemned suicide as a particularly heinous sin that resulted in permanent banishment to the worst part of Hades (Josephus, *Jewish Wars* iii.viii.5 [iii.375]). God did deliver Him to be killed (Acts 2:23); thus, as God, He gave up His own life (10:18).

23 And He said to them, [y]"You are from
beneath; I am from above. [z]You are of this
world; I am not of this world. 24 [a]Therefore
I said to you that you will die in your sins;
[b]for if you do not believe that I am *He,* you
will die in your sins."
25 Then they said to Him, "Who are You?"
And Jesus said to them, "Just what I
[c]have been saying to you from the beginning. 26 I have many things to say and to
judge concerning you, but [d]He who sent
Me is true; and [e]I speak to the world those
things which I heard from Him."
27 They did not understand that He
spoke to them of the Father.
28 Then Jesus said to them, "When you
[f]lift[4] up the Son of Man, [g]then you will
know that I am *He,* and [h]*that* I do nothing
of Myself; but [i]as My Father taught Me, I
speak these things. 29 And [j]He who sent
Me is with Me. [k]The Father has not left Me
alone, [l]for I always do those things that
please Him." 30 As He spoke these words,
[m]many believed in Him.

23 [y] John 3:31 [z] John 15:19; 17:16; 1 John 4:5
24 [a] John 8:21 [b] [Mark 16:16]
25 [c] John 4:26
26 [d] John 7:28 [e] John 3:32; 15:15
28 [f] Matt. 27:35; Mark 15:24; Luke 23:33; John 3:14; 12:32; 19:18 [g] [Rom. 1:4] [h] John 5:19, 30 [i] Deut. 18:15, 18, 19; John 3:11 [4] Crucify
29 [j] John 14:10 [k] John 8:16; 16:32 [l] John 4:34; 5:30; 6:38
30 [m] John 7:31; 10:42; 11:45
31 [n] [John 14:15, 23]
32 [o] [John 1:14, 17; 14:6] [p] [Rom. 6:14, 18, 22; James 1:25; 2:12]
33 [q] Lev. 25:42; [Matt. 3:9]; Luke 3:8

31 Then Jesus said to those Jews who believed Him, "If you [n]abide in My word,
you are My disciples indeed. 32 And you
shall know the [o]truth, and [p]the truth shall
make you free."
33 They answered Him, [q]"We are Abraham's descendants, and have never been
in bondage to anyone. How *can* You say,
'You will be made free'?"
34 Jesus answered them, "Most assuredly, I say to you, [r]whoever commits sin is a
slave of sin. 35 And [s]a slave does not abide
in the house forever, *but* a son abides forever. 36 [t]Therefore if the Son makes you
free, you shall be free indeed.
37 "I know that you are Abraham's descendants, but [u]you seek to kill Me, because My word has no place in you. 38 [v]I
speak what I have seen with My Father,
and you do what you have [5]seen with
your father."

34 [r] Prov. 5:22; Rom. 6:16; 2 Pet. 2:19 35 [s] Gen. 21:10; Gal. 4:30
36 [t] [Rom. 8:2; 2 Cor. 3:17]; Gal. 5:1 37 [u] John 7:19 38 [v] [John 3:32; 5:19, 30; 14:10, 24] [5] NU *heard from*

8:23 You are from beneath. The contrast here is between the realm of God and that of the fallen, sinful world (i.e.,"from beneath"). The world in this context is the invisible spiritual system of evil dominated by Satan and all that it offers in opposition to God, His Word, and His people (*see notes on 1:9; 1 John 5:19*). Jesus declared that His opponents' true kinship was with Satan and his realm. By this domination, they were spiritually blinded (see 2 Cor. 4:4; Eph. 2:1-3).

8:24 if you do not believe. Jesus emphasized that the fatal, unforgivable, and eternal sin is failure to believe in Him as Messiah and Son of God. In truth, all other sins can be forgiven if this one is repented of. *See notes on 16:8,9.* **I am *He.*** *"He"* is not part of the original statement. Jesus' words were not constructed normally but were influenced by OT Heb. usage. It is an absolute usage meaning "I AM" and has immense theological significance. The reference may be to both Ex. 3:14 where the Lord declared His name as "I AM" and to Is. 40–55 where the phrase "I am" occurs repeatedly (especially 43:10,13,25; 46:4; 48:12). In this, Jesus referred to Himself as the God (Yahweh—the LORD) of the OT, and directly claimed full deity for Himself, prompting the Jews' question of v. 25. *See note on v. 58.*

8:25 "Who are You?" The Jews were willfully ignorant because chaps. 1–8 demonstrate that multiple witnesses testified to Jesus' identity, and Jesus Himself in words and actions persistently proved throughout His ministry on earth that He was the Son of God and Messiah. **from the beginning.** The start of Jesus' ministry among the Jews.

8:28 When you lift up the Son of Man. Jesus' impending crucifixion. **you will know that I am *He.*** Having refused to accept Him by faith and having nailed Him to the cross, they would one day awaken to the terrifying realization that this One whom they despised was the One whom they should have worshiped (cf. Phil. 2:9-11; Rev. 1:7). Many Jews believed on Christ after His death and ascension, realizing that the One whom they rejected was truly the Messiah (Acts 2:36,37,41).

8:31-36 These verses are a pivotal passage in understanding genuine salvation and true discipleship. John emphasized these realities by stressing truth and freedom. The focus in the passage is upon those who were exercising the beginnings of faith in Jesus as Messiah and Son of God. Jesus desired them to move on in their faith. Saving faith is not fickle but firm and settled. Such maturity expresses itself in full commitment to the truth in Jesus Christ resulting in genuine freedom. The passage has 3 features: 1) the progress of freedom (vv. 31,32); 2) the pretense of freedom (vv. 33,34); and 3) the promise of freedom (vv. 35,36).

8:31 who believed Him. The first step in the progress toward true discipleship is belief in Jesus Christ as Messiah and Son of God. **If you abide in My word, you are My disciples indeed.** This reveals the second step in the progress toward true discipleship. Perseverance in obedience to Scripture (cf. Matt. 28:19,20) is the fruit or evidence of genuine faith (see Eph. 2:10). The word "abide" means to habitually abide in Jesus words. A genuine believer holds fast, obeys, and practices Jesus' teaching. The one who continues in His teaching has both the Father and the Son (2 John 9; cf. Heb. 3:14; Rev. 2:26). Real disciples are both learners (the basic meaning of the word) and faithful followers.

8:32 the truth. "Truth" here has reference not only to the facts surrounding Jesus as the Messiah and Son of God but also to the teaching that He brought. A genuinely saved and obedient follower of the Lord Jesus will know divine truth and both freedom from sin (v. 34) and the search for reality. This divine truth comes not merely by intellectual assent (1 Cor. 2:14) but saving commitment to Christ (cf. Titus 1:1,2).

8:33 never been in bondage to anyone. Because the Jews had often been in political subjection to many nations (Egypt, Assyria, Babylon, Greece, Syria, and Rome), they must have been referring to their inward sense of freedom.

8:34 Most assuredly. *See note on 1:51.* **whoever commits sin.** The kind of slavery that Jesus had in mind was not physical slavery but slavery to sin (cf. Rom. 6:17,18). The idea of "commits sin" means to practice sin habitually (1 John 3:4,8,9). The ultimate bondage is not political or economic enslavement but spiritual bondage to sin and rebellion against God. Thus, this also explains why Jesus would not let Himself be reduced to merely a political Messiah (6:14,15).

8:35,36 The notion of slavery in v. 34 moves to the status of slaves. While the Jews thought of themselves only as free sons of Abraham, in reality, they were slaves of sin. The genuine son in the context is Christ Himself, who sets the slaves free from sin. Those whom Jesus Christ liberates from the tyranny of sin and the bondage of legalism are really free (Rom. 8:2; Gal. 5:1).

39 They answered and said to Him,
[w]"Abraham is our father."
Jesus said to them, [x]"If you were Abraham's children, you would do the works of
Abraham. 40 [y]But now you seek to kill Me,
a Man who has told you the truth [z]which I
heard from God. Abraham did not do this.
41 You do the deeds of your father."
Then they said to Him, "We were not
born of fornication; [a]we have one Father—
God."
42 Jesus said to them, [b]"If God were your
Father, you would love Me, for [c]I proceeded forth and came from God; [d]nor have I
come of Myself, but He sent Me. 43 [e]Why
do you not understand My speech? Because you are not able to listen to My
word. 44 [f]You are of *your* father the devil,
and the [g]desires of your father you want to
[h]do. He was a murderer from the beginning, and [i]does not stand in the truth, because there is no truth in him. When he
speaks a lie, he speaks from his own *resources*, for he is a liar and the father of it.
45 But because I tell the truth, you do not
believe Me. 46 Which of you convicts Me of
sin? And if I tell the truth, why do you not
believe Me? 47 [j]He who is of God hears
God's words; therefore you do not hear,
because you are not of God."

48 Then the Jews answered and said to
Him, "Do we not say rightly that You are a
Samaritan and [k]have a demon?"
49 Jesus answered, "I do not have a
demon; but I honor My Father, and [l]you
dishonor Me. 50 And [m]I do not seek My
own glory; there is One who seeks and
judges. 51 Most assuredly, I say to you, [n]if
anyone keeps My word he shall never see
death."
52 Then the Jews said to Him, "Now we
know that You [o]have a demon! [p]Abraham
is dead, and the prophets; and You say, 'If
anyone keeps My word he shall never taste
death.' 53 Are You greater than our father
Abraham, who is dead? And the prophets
are dead. [q]Who do You make Yourself out
to be?"
54 Jesus answered, [r]"If I honor Myself,
My honor is nothing. [s]It is My Father who
honors Me, of whom you say that He is
[6]your God. 55 Yet [t]you have not known
Him, but I know Him. And if I say, 'I do
not know Him,' I shall be a liar like you;
but I do know Him and [u]keep His word.
56 Your father Abraham [v]rejoiced to see
My day, [w]and he saw *it* and was glad."
57 Then the Jews said to Him, "You are
not yet fifty years old, and have You seen
Abraham?"

39 [w] Matt. 3:9; John 8:37 [x] [Rom. 2:28; Gal. 3:7, 29]
40 [y] John 8:37 [z] John 8:26
41 [a] Deut. 32:6; Is. 63:16; Mal. 1:6
42 [b] 1 John 5:1 [c] John 16:27; 17:8, 25 [d] John 5:43; Gal. 4:4
43 [e] [John 7:17]
44 [f] Matt. 13:38; 1 John 3:8 [g] 1 John 2:16, 17 [h] [1 John 3:8-10, 15] [i] [Jude 6]
47 [j] Luke 8:15; John 10:26; 1 John 4:6
48 [k] John 7:20; 10:20
49 [l] John 5:41
50 [m] John 5:41; 7:18; [Phil. 2:6-8]
51 [n] John 5:24; 11:26
52 [o] John 7:20; 10:20 [p] Zech. 1:5; Heb. 11:13
53 [q] John 10:33; 19:7
54 [r] John 5:31, 32 [s] John 5:41; Acts 3:13 [6] NU, M *our*
55 [t] John 7:28, 29 [u] [John 15:10]
56 [v] Luke 10:24 [w] Matt. 13:17; Heb. 11:13

8:39 If you were Abraham's children. The construction of this phrase indicates that Jesus was denying that mere physical lineage was sufficient for salvation (see Phil. 3:4-9). The sense would be "if you were Abraham's children, but you are not, then you would act like Abraham did." Just as children, inherit genetic characteristics from their parents, so also those who are truly Abraham's offspring will act like Abraham, i.e., imitate Abraham's faith and obedience (see Rom. 4:16; Gal. 3:6-9; Heb. 11:8-19; James 2:21-24). **works of Abraham.** Abraham's faith was demonstrated through his obedience to God (James 2:21-24). Jesus' point was that the conduct of the unbelieving Jews was diametrically opposed by the conduct of Abraham, who lived a life of obedience to all that God had commanded. Their conduct toward Jesus demonstrated that their real father was Satan (vv. 41,44).

8:41 We were not born of fornication. The Jews may well have been referring to the controversy surrounding Jesus' birth. The Jews knew the story about Mary's betrothal and that Joseph was not Jesus' real father; thus they implied that Jesus' birth was illegitimate (see Matt. 1:18-25; Luke 1:26-38).

8:42 If God were your Father, you would love Me. The construction here (as in v. 39) denies that God is truly their Father. Although the OT calls Israel His "firstborn son" (Ex. 4:22) and affirms that God is Israel's father by creation and separation (Jer. 31:9), the unbelief of the Jews toward Jesus demonstrated that God was not their Father spiritually. Jesus stressed that the explicit criterion verifying the claim to be a child of God is love for His Son, Jesus. Since God is love, those who love His Son also demonstrate His nature (1 John 4:7-11; 5:1).

8:44 *your* father the devil. Sonship is predicated on conduct. A son will manifest his father's characteristics (cf. Eph. 5:1,2). Since the Jews exhibited the patterns of Satan in their hostility toward Jesus and their failure to believe in Him as Messiah, their paternity was the exact opposite of their claims, i.e., they belonged to Satan. **He was a murderer from the beginning.** Jesus' words refer to the fall when Satan tempted Adam and Eve and successfully killed their spiritual life (Gen. 2:17; 3:17-24; Rom. 5:12; Heb. 2:14). Some think that the reference may also refer to Cain's murder of Abel (Gen. 4:1-9; 1 John 3:12).

8:46 convicts Me of sin. Although the Jews argued that Jesus was guilty of sin (5:18), the sense here is that the perfect holiness of Christ was demonstrated, not by the Jews' silence at Jesus' question here, but by the assurance of His direct consciousness of the purity of His whole life. Only a perfectly holy One who has the closest and most intimate communion with the Father could speak such words. The Jews could martial no convincing evidence that could convict Him of sin in the heavenly court.

8:48 You are a Samaritan. Since the Jews could not attack Jesus' personal life and conduct (v. 46), they tried an *ad hominem* attack of personal abuse toward Him. The reference to Jesus as a "Samaritan" probably centers in the fact that the Samaritans, like Jesus, questioned the Jews' exclusive right to be called Abraham's children (see vv. 33,39).

8:51 never see death. Heeding Jesus' teaching and following Him results in eternal life (6:63,68). Physical death cannot extinguish such life (see 5:24; 6:40,47; 11:25,26).

8:52 Abraham is dead. Jesus' assertion that anyone who keeps His word will never die (v. 51) prompted the Jews to offer a retort that once again revealed their thinking on strictly a literal and earthly level (see 3:4; 4:15).

8:56 Hebrews 11:13 indicates that Abraham saw Christ's day ("having seen them afar off"; *see note there*). Abraham particularly saw in the continuing seed of Isaac the beginning of God's fulfilling the covenant (Gen. 12:1-3; 15:1-21; 17:1-8; cf. 22:8) that would culminate in Christ.

58 Jesus said to them, "Most assuredly, I
say to you, [x]before Abraham was, [y]I AM."
59 Then [z]they took up stones to throw at
Him; but Jesus hid Himself and went out
of the temple, [a]going[7] through the midst of
them, and so passed by.

Christ Heals the Blind Man

9 Now as *Jesus* passed by, He saw a man
who was blind from birth. 2 And His
disciples asked Him, saying, "Rabbi, [a]who
sinned, this man or his parents, that he was
born blind?"
3 Jesus answered, "Neither this man nor
his parents sinned, [b]but that the works of
God should be revealed in him. 4 [c]I[1] must
work the works of Him who sent Me while
it is [d]day; *the* night is coming when no one
can work. 5 As long as I am in the world, [e]I
am the light of the world."
6 When He had said these things, [f]He
spat on the ground and made clay with the
saliva; and He anointed the eyes of the
blind man with the clay. 7 And He said to
him, "Go, wash [g]in the pool of Siloam"

58 [x] Mic. 5:2; John 17:5; Heb. 7:3; Rev. 22:13 [y] Ex. 3:14; Is. 43:13; John 17:5, 24; Col. 1:17; Rev. 1:8
59 [z] John 10:31; 11:8 [a] Luke 4:30; John 10:39 [7] NU omits the rest of v. 59.

CHAPTER 9

2 [a] Luke 13:2; John 9:34; Acts 28:4
3 [b] John 11:4
4 [c] [John 4:34; 5:19, 36; 17:4] [d] John 11:9, 10; 12:35; Gal. 6:10 [1] NU *We*
5 [e] [John 1:5, 9; 3:19; 8:12; 12:35, 46]
6 [f] Mark 7:33; 8:23
7 [g] Neh. 3:15; Is. 8:6; Luke 13:4; John 9:11 [h] 2 Kin. 5:14
8 [2] NU *a beggar*
9 [3] NU *"No, but he is like him."*
11 [i] John 9:6, 7 [4] NU omits *the pool of*

(which is translated, Sent). So [h]he went
and washed, and came back seeing.
8 Therefore the neighbors and those who
previously had seen that he was [2]blind
said, "Is not this he who sat and begged?"
9 Some said, "This is he." Others *said,*
[3]"He is like him."
He said, "I am *he.*"
10 Therefore they said to him, "How
were your eyes opened?"
11 He answered and said, [i]"A Man
called Jesus made clay and anointed my
eyes and said to me, 'Go to [4]the pool of Siloam and wash.' So I went and washed,
and I received sight."
12 Then they said to him, "Where is He?"
He said, "I do not know."
13 They brought him who formerly was
blind to the Pharisees. 14 Now it was a Sabbath when Jesus made the clay and opened
his eyes. 15 Then the Pharisees also asked
him again how he had received his sight.
He said to them, "He put clay on my eyes,
and I washed, and I see."
16 Therefore some of the Pharisees said,

8:58 Most assuredly. *See note on 1:51.* **I AM.** *See note on 6:22-58.* Here Jesus declared Himself to be Yahweh, i.e., the Lord of the OT. Basic to the expression are such passages as Ex. 3:14; Deut. 32:39; Is. 41:4; 43:10 where God declared Himself to be the eternally pre-existent God who revealed Himself in the OT to the Jews. *See also notes on vv. 24,28.*

8:59 they took up stones. The Jews understood Jesus' claim and followed Lev. 24:16, which indicates that any man who falsely claims to be God should be stoned. **hid Himself...going through the midst of them.** Jesus repeatedly escaped arrest and death because His hour had not yet come (*see notes on 7:30,44; 18:6*). The verse most likely indicates escape by miraculous means.

9:1-13 Jesus performed a miracle by recreating the eyes of a man who was born with congenital blindness (v. 1). Four features highlight this healing: 1) the problem that precipitated the healing (v. 1); 2) the purpose for the man's being born blind (vv. 2-5); 3) the power that healed him (vv. 6,7); and 4) the perplexity of the people who saw the healing (vv. 8-13).

9:2 who sinned. While sin may be a cause of suffering, as clearly indicated in Scripture (see 5:14; Num. 12; 1 Cor. 11:30; James 5:15), it is not always the case necessarily (see Job; 2 Cor. 12:7; Gal. 4:13). The disciples assumed, like most Palestinians of their day, that sin was the primary, if not exclusive, cause of all suffering. In this instance, however, Jesus made it clear that personal sin was not the reason for the blindness (see v. 3).

9:3 Jesus did not deny the general connection between sin and suffering, but refuted the idea that personal acts of sin were the direct cause. God's sovereignty and purposes play a part in such matters, as is clear from Job 1,2.

9:4 while it is day. Jesus meant as long as He was still on earth with His disciples. The phrase does not mean that Jesus somehow stopped being the light of the world once He ascended but that the light shone most brightly among men when He was on the earth doing the Father's will (cf. 8:12). ***the* night is coming.** *See notes on 1:4,5; 1 John 1:5-7.* The darkness has special reference to the period when Jesus was taken from His disciples during His crucifixion (v. 5).

9:5 I am the light of the world. *See note on 8:12*; cf. 1:5,9; 3:19; 12:35,46. Not only was Jesus spiritually the light of the world, but He would also provide the means of physical light for this blind man.

9:6 made clay with the saliva. As He had done when He originally made human beings out of the dust of the ground (Gen. 2:7), Jesus may have used the clay to fashion a new pair of eyes.

9:7 wash in the pool of Siloam. The term "Siloam" is Heb. for "Sent." The pool of Siloam was SE of Jerusalem. Its water source was through a channel (Hezekiah's tunnel) that carried water to it from the spring of Gihon in the Kidron Valley. It may be identified with the "lower pool" or "old pool" mentioned in Is. 22:9,11. Water for the water-pouring rites at the Feast of Tabernacles was drawn from this pool (*see notes on 7:37-39*).

9:8,9 In ancient times, such severe physical deformities like congenital blindness sentenced a person to begging as the only means of support (see Acts 3:1-7). The drastic change in the healed man caused many to faithlessly believe that he was not the person born blind.

9:13-34 This section in the story of the healing of the blind man reveals some key characteristics of willful unbelief: 1) unbelief sets false standards; 2) unbelief always wants more evidence but never has enough; 3) unbelief does biased research on a purely subjective basis; 4) unbelief rejects the facts; and 5) unbelief is self-centered. John included this section on the dialogue of the Pharisees with the blind man most likely for two reasons: 1) the dialogue carefully demonstrates the character of willful and fixed unbelief, and 2) the story confirms the first great schism between the synagogue and Christ's new followers. The blind man was the first known person thrown out of the synagogue because He chose to follow Christ (see 16:1-3).

9:13 They. This has reference to the blind man's "neighbors and those who previously had seen that he was blind" (v. 8). **to the Pharisees.** The people brought the blind man to the Pharisees most likely because the miracle had happened on the Sabbath (v. 14), and they were aware that the Pharisees reacted negatively to those who violated the Sabbath (cf. 5:1-15). The people also wanted advice from their local synagogue and religious leaders.

"This Man is not from God, because He
does not [5]keep the Sabbath."
Others said, [j]"How can a man who is a
sinner do such signs?" And [k]there was a
division among them.
17 They said to the blind man again,
"What do you say about Him because He
opened your eyes?"
He said, [l]"He is a prophet."
18 But the Jews did not believe concerning him, that he had been blind and received his sight, until they called the parents of him who had received his sight.
19 And they asked them, saying, "Is this
your son, who you say was born blind?
How then does he now see?"
20 His parents answered them and said,
"We know that this is our son, and that he
was born blind; 21 but by what means he
now sees we do not know, or who opened
his eyes we do not know. He is of age; ask
him. He will speak for himself." 22 His parents said these *things* because [m]they feared
the Jews, for the Jews had agreed already
that if anyone confessed *that* He *was* Christ,
he [n]would be put out of the synagogue.
23 Therefore his parents said, "He is of age;
ask him."
24 So they again called the man who was
blind, and said to him, [o]"Give God the
glory! [p]We know that this Man is a sinner."
25 He answered and said, "Whether He
is a sinner *or not* I do not know. One thing
I know: that though I was blind, now I
see."
26 Then they said to him again, "What
did He do to you? How did He open your
eyes?"
27 He answered them, "I told you already, and you did not listen. Why do you
want to hear *it* again? Do you also want to
become His disciples?"
28 Then they reviled him and said, "You
are His disciple, but we are Moses' disciples. 29 We know that God [q]spoke to [r]Mo-
ses; *as for* this *fellow,* [s]we do not know
where He is from."
30 The man answered and said to them,
[t]"Why, this is a marvelous thing, that you
do not know where He is from; yet He has
opened my eyes! 31 Now we know that
[u]God does not hear sinners; but if anyone
is a worshiper of God and does His will,
He hears him. 32 Since the world began it
has been unheard of that anyone opened
the eyes of one who was born blind. 33 [v]If
this Man were not from God, He could do
nothing."
34 They answered and said to him,
[w]"You were completely born in sins, and
are you teaching us?" And they [6]cast him
out.
35 Jesus heard that they had cast him
out; and when He had [x]found him, He said
to him, "Do you [y]believe in [z]the Son of
[7]God?"

16 [j]John 3:2; 9:33 [k]John 7:12, 43; 10:19 [5]*observe*
17 [l][John 4:19; 6:14]
22 [m]John 7:13; 12:42; 19:38; Acts 5:13 [n]John 16:2
24 [o]Josh. 7:19; 1 Sam. 6:5; Ezra 10:11; Rev. 11:13 [p]John 9:16
29 [q]Ex. 19:19, 20; 33:11; 34:29; Num. 12:6-8 [r][John 5:45-47] [s]John 7:27, 28; 8:14
30 [t]John 3:10
31 [u]Job 27:9; 35:12; Ps. 18:41; Prov. 1:28; 15:29; 28:9; Is. 1:15; Jer. 11:11; 14:12; Ezek. 8:18; Mic. 3:4; Zech. 7:13; [James 5:16]
33 [v]John 3:2; 9:16
34 [w]Ps. 51:5; John 9:2 [6]Excommunicated him
35 [x]John 5:14 [y]John 1:7; 16:31 [z]Matt. 14:33; 16:16; Mark 1:1; John 10:36; 1 John 5:13 [7]NU *Man*

9:16 not from God. The reasoning may have been that since Jesus violated their interpretation of the Sabbath law, He could not be the promised Prophet of God (Deut. 13:1-5). **a division.** Earlier the crowds were divided in opinion regarding Jesus (7:40-43); here the authorities also became divided.

9:17 He is a prophet. While the blind man saw clearly that Jesus was more than a mere man, the sighted but obstinate Pharisees were spiritually blind to that truth (see v. 39). Blindness in the Bible is a metaphor for spiritual darkness, i.e., inability to discern God or His truth (2 Cor. 4:3-6; Col. 1:12-14).

9:18 called the parents. While neighbors may have been mistaken as to the man's identity, the parents would know if this was their own son. The authorities considered the witness of the healed man worthless.

9:24 Give God the glory! This means that the authorities wanted the man to own up and admit the truth that Jesus was a sinner because He violated their traditions and threatened their influence (cf. Josh. 7:19). **We know that this Man is a sinner.** Enough unanimity existed among the religious authorities to conclude that Jesus was a sinner (cf. 8:46). Because of this already predetermined opinion, they refused to accept any of the testimony that a miracle had actually taken place.

9:27 In order to forcefully emphasize their hypocrisy, the healed man resorted to biting sarcasm when he suggested they desired to be Jesus' disciples.

9:28 You are His disciple, but we are Moses'. At this point, the meeting degenerated into a shouting match of insults. The healed man's wit had exposed the bias of his inquisitors. As far as the authorities were concerned, the conflict between Jesus and Moses was irreconcilable. If the healed man defended Jesus, then such defense could only mean that he was Jesus' disciple.

9:30 The healed man demonstrated more spiritual insight and common sense than all of the religious authorities combined who sat in judgment of Jesus and him. His penetrating wit focused in on their intractable unbelief. His logic was that such an extraordinary miracle could only indicate that Jesus was from God, for the Jews believed that God responds in proportion to the righteousness of the one praying (see Job 27:9; 35:13; Pss. 66:18; 109:7; Prov. 15:29; Is. 1:15; cf. 14:13,14; 16:23-27; 1 John 3:21,22). The greatness of the miracle could only indicate that Jesus was actually from God.

9:34 are you teaching us. The Pharisees were incensed with the man, and their anger prevented them from seeing the penetrating insight that the uneducated healed man had demonstrated. The phrase also revealed their ignorance of Scripture, for the OT indicated that the coming messianic age would be evidenced by restoration of sight to the blind (Is. 29:18; 35:5; 42:7; cf. Matt. 11:4,5; Luke 4:18,19).

9:35-41 While vv. 1-34 dealt with Jesus' restoration of physical sight in the blind man, vv. 35-41 featured Jesus bringing spiritual "sight" to him.

9:35 Do you believe. Jesus invited the man to put his trust in Him as the One who revealed God to man. Jesus placed great emphasis on public acknowledgment of who He was and confession of faith in Him (Matt. 10:32; Luke 12:8). **Son of God.** As in the marginal note, this should be Son of Man (cf. 1:51; 3:13,14; 5:27; 6:27,53,62; 8:28).

36 He answered and said, "Who is He,
Lord, that I may believe in Him?"
37 And Jesus said to him, "You have both
seen Him and [a]it is He who is talking with
you."
38 Then he said, "Lord, I believe!" And
he [b]worshiped Him.
39 And Jesus said, [c]"For judgment I have
come into this world, [d]that those who do
not see may see, and that those who see
may be made blind."
40 Then *some* of the Pharisees who were
with Him heard these words, [e]and said to
Him, "Are we blind also?"
41 Jesus said to them, [f]"If you were
blind, you would have no sin; but now you
say, 'We see.' Therefore your sin remains.

"I Am the Good Shepherd"

10 "Most assuredly, I say to you, he
who does not enter the sheepfold
by the door, but climbs up some other way,
the same is a thief and a robber. 2 But he
who enters by the door is the shepherd of
the sheep. 3 To him the doorkeeper opens,
and the sheep hear his voice; and he calls
his own sheep by [a]name and leads them
out. 4 And when he brings out his own
sheep, he goes before them; and the sheep
follow him, for they know his voice. 5 Yet
they will by no means follow a [b]stranger,
but will flee from him, for they do not
know the voice of strangers." 6 Jesus used
this illustration, but they did not understand the things which He spoke to them.
7 Then Jesus said to them again, "Most
assuredly, I say to you, I am the door of the
sheep. 8 All who *ever* came [1]before Me are
thieves and robbers, but the sheep did not
hear them. 9 [c]I am the door. If anyone enters by Me, he will be saved, and will go in
and out and find pasture. 10 The thief does
not come except to steal, and to kill, and to
destroy. I have come that they may have
life, and that they may have *it* more abundantly.

37 [a] John 4:26
38 [b] Matt. 8:2
39 [c] [John 3:17; 5:22, 27; 12:47] [d] Matt. 13:13; 15:14
40 [e] [Rom. 2:19]
41 [f] John 15:22, 24

CHAPTER 10

3 [a] John 20:16
5 [b] [2 Cor. 11:13-15]
8 [1] M omits *before Me*
9 [c] [John 14:6; Eph. 2:18]

9:36 Lord. The word here should be understood not as an indication that He understood Jesus' deity but as meaning "sir." See also v. 38. Since the blind man had never seen Jesus (v. 7) nor met Him since he went to wash in the pool, he did not recognize Jesus at first as the One who healed him.

9:39 For judgment. Not that His purpose was to condemn, but rather to save (12:47; Luke 19:10); saving some, nevertheless, involves condemning others (*see notes on 3:16-21*). The last part of this verse is taken from Is. 6:10; 42:19 (cf. Mark 4:12). **those who do not see.** Those people who know they are in spiritual darkness. **those who see.** Refers in an ironic way to those who think they are in the light, but are not (cf. Mark 2:17; Luke 5:31).

9:40 "Are we blind also?" Apparently Jesus found (v. 35) the man in a public place, where the Pharisees were present listening.

9:41 your sin remains. Jesus had particular reference to the sin of unbelief and rejection of Him as Messiah and Son of God. If they knew their lostness and darkness and cried out for spiritual light, they would no longer be guilty of the sin of unbelief in Christ. But satisfied that their darkness was light, and continuing in rejection of Christ, their sin remained. *See note on Matt. 6:22,23.*

10:1-39 Jesus' discourse on Himself as the "Good Shepherd" flowed directly from chap. 9, as Jesus continued to talk to the very same people. The problem of chap. 9 was that Israel was led by false shepherds who drew them astray from the true knowledge and kingdom of Messiah (9:39-41). In chap. 10, Jesus declared Himself to be the "Good Shepherd" who was appointed by His Father as Savior and King, in contrast to the false shepherds of Israel who were self-appointed and self-righteous (Ps. 23:1; Is. 40:11; Jer. 3:15; cf. Is. 56:9-12; Jer. 23:1-4; 25:32-38; Ezek. 34:1-31; Zech. 11:16).

10:1 sheepfold. Jesus spoke in vv. 1-30 using a sustained metaphor based on first century sheep ranching. The sheep were kept in a pen, which had a gate through which the sheep entered and left. The shepherd engaged a "doorkeeper" (v. 3) or "hireling" (v. 12) as an undershepherd to guard the gate. The shepherd entered through that gate. He whose interest was stealing or wounding the sheep would chose another way to attempt entrance. The words of Ezek. 34 most likely form the background to Jesus' teaching since God decried the false shepherds of Israel (i.e., the spiritual leaders of the nation) for not caring properly for the flock of Israel (i.e., the nation). The gospels themselves contain extensive sheep/shepherd imagery (see Matt. 9:36; Mark 6:34; 14:27; Luke 15:1-7).

10:3 the doorkeeper. The doorkeeper was a hired undershepherd who recognized the true shepherd of the flock, opened the gate for Him, assisted the shepherd in caring for the flock, and especially guarded them at night. **the sheep hear his voice.** Near Eastern shepherds stand at different locations outside the sheep pen, sounding out their own unique calls which their sheep recognize. As a result, the sheep gather around the shepherd. **he calls his own sheep by name.** This shepherd goes even further by calling each sheep by its own special name (see 3 John 15). Jesus' point is that He comes to the fold of Israel and calls out His own sheep individually to come into His own messianic fold. The assumption is that they are already in some way His sheep even before He calls them by name (see vv. 25-27; 6:37,39,44,64,65; 17:6,9,24; 18:9).

10:4,5 Unlike Western shepherds who drive the sheep from the side or behind, often using sheep dogs, Near Eastern shepherds lead their flocks, their voice calling them to move on. This draws a remarkable picture of the master/disciple relationship. NT spiritual leadership is always by example, i.e., a call to imitate conduct (cf. 1 Tim. 4:12; 1 Pet. 5:1-3).

10:6 illustration. The word here is best translated "illustration" or "figure of speech" and conveys the idea that something cryptic or enigmatic is intended in it. It occurs again in 16:25,29 but not in the synoptics. Having given the illustration (vv. 1-5), Jesus then began to draw salient spiritual truth from it.

10:7-10 I am the door. This is the third of 7 "I AM" statements of Jesus (see 6:35; 8:12). Here, He changes the metaphor slightly. While in vv. 1-5 He was the shepherd, here He is the gate. While in vv. 1-5, the shepherd led the sheep out of the pen, here He is the entrance to the pen (v. 9) that leads to proper pasture. This section echoes Jesus' words in 14:6 that He is the only way to the Father. His point is that He serves as the sole means to approach the Father and partake of God's promised salvation. As some Near Eastern shepherds slept in the gateway to guard the sheep, Jesus here pictures Himself as the gate.

10:9,10 These two verses are a proverbial way of insisting that belief in Jesus as the Messiah and Son of God is the only way of being "saved" from sin and hell and receiving eternal life. Only Jesus Christ is the one true source for the knowledge of God and the one basis for spiritual security.

11 [d]"I am the good shepherd. The good
shepherd gives His life for the sheep.
12 But a [2]hireling, *he who is* not the shepherd, one who does not own the sheep,
sees the wolf coming and [e]leaves the sheep
and flees; and the wolf catches the sheep
and scatters them. **13** The hireling flees because he is a hireling and does not care
about the sheep. **14** I am the good shepherd; and [f]I know My *sheep,* and [g]am
known by My own. **15** [h]As the Father
knows Me, even so I know the Father; [i]and
I lay down My life for the sheep. **16** And
[j]other sheep I have which are not of this
fold; them also I must bring, and they will
hear My voice; [k]and there will be one flock
and one shepherd.

17 "Therefore My Father [l]loves Me, [m]be-
cause I lay down My life that I may take it
again. **18** No one takes it from Me, but I lay
it down of Myself. I [n]have power to lay it
down, and I have power to take it again.
[o]This command I have received from My
Father."

19 Therefore [p]there was a division again
among the Jews because of these sayings.
20 And many of them said, [q]"He has a
demon and is [3]mad. Why do you listen to
Him?"

21 Others said, "These are not the words
of one who has a demon. [r]Can a demon
[s]open the eyes of the blind?"

The Opposition at the Feast of Dedication in Jerusalem

22 Now it was the Feast of Dedication in
Jerusalem, and it was winter. **23** And Jesus
walked in the temple, [t]in Solomon's porch.
24 Then the Jews surrounded Him and said
to Him, "How long do You keep us in
[4]doubt? If You are the Christ, tell us plainly."

25 Jesus answered them, "I told you, and
you do not believe. [u]The works that I do in
My Father's name, they [v]bear witness of
Me. **26** But [w]you do not believe, because
you are not of My sheep, [5]as I said to you.
27 [x]My sheep hear My voice, and I know
them, and they follow Me. **28** And I give
them eternal life, and they shall never perish; neither shall anyone snatch them out
of My hand. **29** [y]My Father, [z]who has given
them to Me, is greater than all; and no one
is able to snatch *them* out of My Father's
hand. **30** [a]I and *My* Father are one."

11 [d] Gen. 49:24; Is. 40:11; Ezek. 34:23; [Heb. 13:20]; 1 Pet. 2:25; 5:4; Rev. 7:17 **12** [e] Zech. 11:16, 17 [2] *hired man* **14** [f] Is. 40:11; Nah. 1:7; Zech. 13:7; John 6:64; 2 Tim. 2:19 [g] 2 Tim. 1:12 **15** [h] Matt. 11:27 [i] Matt. 27:50; Mark 15:37; Luke 23:46; [John 15:13; 19:30]; 1 John 3:16 **16** [j] Is. 42:6; 56:8; Acts 10:45; 11:18; 13:46 [k] Ezek. 37:22; John 11:52; 17:20; Eph. 2:13-18; 1 Pet. 2:25 **17** [l] John 5:20 [m] [Is. 53:7, 8, 12; Heb. 2:9] **18** [n] Matt. 26:53; [John 2:19; 5:26] [o] [John 6:38; 14:31; 17:4; Acts 2:24, 32] **19** [p] John 7:43; 9:16 **20** [q] John 7:20 [3] *insane*

21 [r] [Ex. 4:11] [s] John 9:6, 7, 32, 33 **23** [t] Acts 3:11; 5:12 **24** [4] Suspense

25 [u] John 5:36; 10:38 [v] Matt. 11:4; John 2:11; 20:30 **26** [w] [John 8:47] [5] NU omits *as I said to you* **27** [x] John 10:4, 14 **29** [y] John 14:28 [z] [John 17:2, 6, 12, 24] **30** [a] John 17:11, 21-24

10:11-18 Jesus picked up another expression from vv. 1-5, i.e., He is the "good shepherd" in contrast to the present evil leadership of Israel (9:40,41). This is the fourth of 7 "I AM" statements of Jesus (see vv. 7,9; 6:35; 8:12). The term "good" has the idea of "noble" and stands in contrast to the "hireling" who cares only for self-interest.

10:11 gives His life for the sheep. This is a reference to Jesus' substitutionary death for sinners on the cross. Cf. v. 15; 6:51; 11:50,51; 17:19; 18:14.

10:12 sees the wolf coming...flees. The hireling (or, hired hand) likely represents religious leaders who perform their duty in good times but who never display sacrificial care for the sheep in times of danger. They stand in contrast to Jesus, who laid down His life for His flock (see 15:13).

10:16 not of this fold. This refers to Gentiles who will respond to His voice and become a part of the church (cf. Rom. 1:16). Jesus' death was not only for Jews (*see notes on vv. 1-3*), but also non-Jews whom He will make into one new body, the church (*see notes on 11:51,52*; cf. Eph. 2:11-22).

10:17,18 take it again. Jesus repeated this phrase twice in these two verses indicating that His sacrificial death was not the end. His resurrection followed in demonstration of His messiahship and deity (Rom. 1:4). His death and resurrection resulted in His ultimate glorification (12:23; 17:5) and the outpouring of the Holy Spirit (7:37-39; cf. Acts 2:16-39).

10:19-21 The Jews once again had a mixed reaction to Jesus' words (see 7:12,13). While some charged Him with demon possession (see 7:20; 8:48; cf. Matt. 12:22-32), others concluded His works and words were a demonstration of God's sanction upon Him.

10:22 Feast of Dedication. The Jewish celebration of Hanukkah, which celebrates the Israelite victory over the Syrian leader Antiochus Epiphanes, who persecuted Israel. In ca. 170 B.C. he conquered Jerusalem and desecrated the Jewish temple by setting up a pagan altar to displace the altar of God. Under the leadership of an old priest named Mattathias (his family name was called the Hasmoneans), the Jews fought guerrilla warfare (known as the Maccabean Revolt—166–142 B.C.) against Syria and freed the temple and the land from Syrian dominance until 63 B.C. when Rome (Pompey) took control of Palestine. It was in 164 B.C. on 25 Kislev (Dec. approximately), that the Jews liberated the temple and rededicated it. The celebration is also known as the "Feast of Lights" because of the lighting of lamps and candles in Jewish homes to commemorate the event. **it was winter.** John indicated by this phrase that the cold weather drove Jesus to walk on the eastern side of the temple in the sheltered area of Solomon's porch, which after the resurrection became the regular gathering place of Christians where they would proclaim the gospel (see Acts 3:11; 5:12).

10:24 tell us plainly. In light of the context of vv. 31-39, the Jews were not seeking merely for clarity and understanding regarding who Jesus was, but rather wanted Him to declare openly that He was Messiah in order to justify attacking Him.

10:26,27 This clearly indicates that God has chosen His sheep and it is they who believe and follow (*see notes on vv. 3,16*; cf. 6:37-40,44,65).

10:28,29 The security of Jesus' sheep rests with Him as the good shepherd, who has the power to keep them safe. Neither thieves and robbers (vv. 1,8) nor the wolf (v. 12) can harm them. Verse 29 makes clear that the Father ultimately stands behind the sheep's security, for no one is able to steal from God, who is in sovereign control of all things (Col. 3:3). *See notes on Rom. 8:31-39.* No stronger passage in the OT or NT exists for the absolute, eternal security of every true Christian.

10:30 I and *My* Father are one. Both Father and Son are committed to the perfect protection and preservation of Jesus' sheep. The sentence, stressing the united purpose and action of both in the security and safety of the flock, presupposes unity of nature and essence (see 5:17-23; 17:22).

31 Then [b]the Jews took up stones again
to stone Him. 32 Jesus answered them,
"Many good works I have shown you from
My Father. For which of those works do
you stone Me?"
33 The Jews answered Him, saying, "For
a good work we do not stone You, but for
[c]blasphemy, and because You, being a
Man, [d]make Yourself God."
34 Jesus answered them, "Is it not written in your law, [e]*'I said, "You are gods"'*?
35 If He called them gods, [f]to whom the
word of God came (and the Scripture [g]can-
not be broken), 36 do you say of Him
[h]whom the Father sanctified and [i]sent into
the world, 'You are blaspheming,' [j]because
I said, 'I am [k]the Son of God'? 37 [l]If I do not
do the works of My Father, do not believe
Me; 38 but if I do, though you do not believe Me, [m]believe the works, that you may
know and [6]believe [n]that the Father *is* in
Me, and I in Him." 39 [o]Therefore they
sought again to seize Him, but He escaped
out of their hand.
40 And He went away again beyond the
Jordan to the place [p]where John was baptizing at first, and there He stayed. 41 Then
many came to Him and said, "John performed no sign, [q]but all the things that
John spoke about this Man were true."
42 And many believed in Him there.

Christ Raises Lazarus

11 Now a certain *man* was sick, Lazarus of Bethany, the town of [a]Mary
and her sister Martha. 2 [b]It was *that* Mary
who anointed the Lord with fragrant oil
and wiped His feet with her hair, whose
brother Lazarus was sick. 3 Therefore the
sisters sent to Him, saying, "Lord, behold,
he whom You love is sick."
4 When Jesus heard *that,* He said, "This

31 [b] John 8:59
33 [c] Matt. 9:3 [d] John 5:18
34 [e] Ps. 82:6
35 [f] Matt. 5:17, 18 [g] 1 Pet. 1:25
36 [h] John 6:27 [i] John 3:17 [j] John 5:17, 18 [k] Luke 1:35
37 [l] John 10:25; 15:24
38 [m] John 5:36 [n] John 14:10, 11 [6] NU *understand*
39 [o] John 7:30, 44
40 [p] John 1:28
41 [q] [John 1:29, 36; 3:28-36; 5:33]

CHAPTER 11

1 [a] Luke 10:38, 39; John 11:5, 19
2 [b] Matt. 26:7

10:31 For the third time John records that the Jews attempted to stone Jesus (see 5:18; 8:59). Jesus' assertion (v. 30) that He was One with the Father affirmed His claim to deity and caused the Jews to seek His execution (v. 33). Although the OT permitted stoning in certain instances (e.g., Lev. 24:16), the Romans reserved the right of capital punishment for themselves (18:31). Nevertheless, out-of-control Jews attempted a mob action in lieu of legal proceedings (see Acts 7:54-60).

10:33 make Yourself God. There was no doubt in the minds of those Jews that Jesus was claiming to be God (cf. 5:18).

10:34-36 Quoted from Ps. 82:6 where God calls some unjust judges "gods" and pronounces calamity against them. Jesus' argument is that this psalm proves that the word "god" can be legitimately used to refer to others than God Himself. His reasoning is that if there are others whom God can address as "god" or "sons of the Most High," why then should the Jews object to Jesus' statement that He is "the Son of God" (v. 36)?

10:35 Scripture cannot be broken. An affirmation of the absolute accuracy and authority of Scripture (*see notes on Matt. 5:17-19*).

10:38 believe the works. Jesus did not expect to be believed merely on His own assertions. Since He did the same things that the Father does (*see notes on 5:19*), His enemies should consider this in their evaluation of Him. The implication is, however, that they were so ignorant of God that they could not recognize the works of the Father or the One whom the Father sent (see also 14:10,11).

10:40 He went away again beyond the Jordan. Because of the increasing hostility (see v. 39), Jesus went from the region of Judea into the unpopulated area across the Jordan. **to the place where John was baptizing at first.** Cf. Matt. 3:1-6; Mark 1:2-6; Luke 3:3-6. This is probably a reference to either Perea or Batanea, the general area in the tetrarchy of Philip in the E and NE of the Sea of Galilee. The statement is ironic, since the area where John first began became the last area in which Jesus stayed before He left for Jerusalem and crucifixion. The people remembered John's testimony to Christ and affirmed their faith in Him (vv. 41,42).

11:1–12:50 The previous passage (10:40-42) marked the end of John's treatment of Jesus' public ministry. At that point, He began to move into seclusion and minister to His own disciples and those who loved Him as He prepared to face death. Israel had her day of opportunity; the sun was setting and the night was coming. These two chapters form the transition to chaps. 13–21 which record the passion of Christ, i.e., the events surrounding the cross.

11:1-57 As chap. 11 begins, Jesus stands in the shadow of facing the cross. The little time that He had in the area beyond the Jordan came to an end. John picked up the story after He moved back into the area of Jerusalem and His death on the cross was only a few days away. In those last few days before His death, the scene in John's gospel changes from hatred and rejection (10:39) to an unmistakable and blessed witness of the glory of Christ. All the rejection and hatred could not dim His glory as displayed through the resurrection of Lazarus. That miracle evidences His glory in 3 ways: 1) it pointed to His deity; 2) it strengthened the faith of the disciples; and 3) it led directly to the cross (12:23). The chapter can be divided as follows: 1) the preparation for the miracle (vv. 1-16); 2) the arrival of Jesus (vv. 17-37); 3) the miracle itself (vv. 38-44); and 4) the results of the miracle (vv. 45-57).

11:1 Lazarus. The resurrection of Lazarus is the climactic and most dramatic sign in this gospel, and the capstone of His public ministry. Six miracles have already been presented (water into wine [2:1-11], healing of the nobleman's son [4:46-54], restoring the impotent man [5:1-15], multiplying the loaves and fishes [6:1-14], walking on the water [6:15-21], and curing the man born blind [9:1-12]). Lazarus' resurrection is more potent than all those and even more monumental than the raising of the widow's son in Nain (Luke 7:11-16) or Jairus' daughter (Luke 8:40-56) because those two resurrections occurred immediately after death. Lazarus was raised after 4 days of being in the grave with the process of decomposition already having started (v. 39). **Bethany.** This Bethany is different from the other "Bethany beyond the Jordan" in 1:28 (*see note there*). It lies on the E side of the Mt. of Olives about two mi. from Jerusalem (v. 18) along the road leading toward Jericho. **Mary...Martha.** This is the first mention of this family in John. John related the story of Mary's anointing of Jesus in 12:1-8, but this reference may indicate that the original readers were already familiar with the event. Cf. Luke 10:38-42.

11:3 sent to Him. Since Jesus was in the Transjordan and Lazarus was near Jerusalem, the message to Jesus would most likely have taken one whole day to reach Him. Surely by omniscience, Jesus already knew of Lazarus' condition (see v. 6; 1:47). He may have died before the messenger reached Jesus, since he was dead 4 days (v. 17) when Jesus arrived, after a two day delay (v. 6) and a one day journey. **he whom You love.** This phrase is a touching hint at the close friendship that Jesus had with Lazarus. Cf. 13:1.

sickness is not unto death, but for the glory
of God, that the Son of God may be glorified through it."
5 Now Jesus loved Martha and her sister
and Lazarus. 6 So, when He heard that he
was sick, [c]He stayed two more days in the
place where He was. 7 Then after this He
said to *the* disciples, "Let us go to Judea
again."
8 *The* disciples said to Him, "Rabbi, lately the Jews sought to [d]stone You, and are
You going there again?"
9 Jesus answered, "Are there not twelve
hours in the day? [e]If anyone walks in the
day, he does not stumble, because he sees
the [f]light of this world. 10 But [g]if one walks
in the night, he stumbles, because the light
is not in him." 11 These things He said, and
after that He said to them, "Our friend
Lazarus [h]sleeps, but I go that I may wake
him up."
12 Then His disciples said, "Lord, if he
sleeps he will get well." 13 However, Jesus
spoke of his death, but they thought that
He was speaking about taking rest in sleep.
14 Then Jesus said to them plainly, "Lazarus is dead. 15 And I am glad for your sakes
that I was not there, that you may believe.
Nevertheless let us go to him."

6 [c] John 10:40
8 [d] John 8:59; 10:31
9 [e] Luke 13:33; John 9:4; 12:35 [f] Is. 9:2
10 [g] John 12:35
11 [h] Deut. 31:16; [Dan. 12:2]; Matt. 9:24; Acts 7:60; [1 Cor. 15:18, 51]
16 [i] Matt. 10:3; Mark 3:18; Luke 6:15; John 14:5; 20:26-28; Acts 1:13
18 [1] Lit. *15 stadia*
22 [j] [John 9:31; 11:41]
24 [k] [Luke 14:14; John 5:29]
25 [l] John 5:21; 6:39, 40, 44; [Rev. 1:18] [m] John 3:16, 36; 1 John 5:10 [n] 1 Cor. 15:22; [Heb. 9:27]
27 [o] Matt. 16:16; Luke 2:11; John 4:42; 6:14, 69

16 Then [i]Thomas, who is called the Twin,
said to his fellow disciples, "Let us also go,
that we may die with Him."
17 So when Jesus came, He found that he
had already been in the tomb four days.
18 Now Bethany was near Jerusalem, about
[1]two miles away. 19 And many of the Jews
had joined the women around Martha and
Mary, to comfort them concerning their
brother.
20 Now Martha, as soon as she heard
that Jesus was coming, went and met Him,
but Mary was sitting in the house. 21 Now
Martha said to Jesus, "Lord, if You had
been here, my brother would not have
died. 22 But even now I know that [j]what-
ever You ask of God, God will give You."
23 Jesus said to her, "Your brother will
rise again."
24 Martha said to Him, [k]"I know that he
will rise again in the resurrection at the last
day."
25 Jesus said to her, "I am [l]the resurrection and the life. [m]He who believes in Me,
though he may [n]die, he shall live. 26 And
whoever lives and believes in Me shall
never die. Do you believe this?"
27 She said to Him, "Yes, Lord, [o]I believe

11:4 the Son of God may be glorified. This phrase reveals the real purpose behind Lazarus' sickness, i.e., not death, but that the Son of God might be glorified through his resurrection (cf. v. 4; *see notes on 9:3*).

11:6 He stayed two more days. The decision to delay coming did not bring about Lazarus' death, since Jesus already supernaturally knew His plight. Most likely by the time the messenger arrived to inform Jesus, Lazarus was already dead. The delay was because He loved the family (v. 5) and that love would be clear as He greatly strengthened their faith by raising Lazarus from the dead. The delay also ensured that Lazarus had been dead long enough that no one could misinterpret the miracle as a fraud or mere resuscitation.

11:7,8 The disciples realized that the animosity toward Jesus was so great that His return could result in His death because of the murderous Jews (cf. 8:59; 10:31).

11:9,10 During the light of the sun, most people did their work safely. When darkness came, they stopped. The proverbial saying, however, had a deeper meaning. As long as the Son performed His Father's will (i.e., during the daylight period of His ministry when He is able to work), He was safe. The time would soon come (nighttime) when, by God's design, His earthly work would end and He would "stumble" in death. Jesus was stressing that as long as He was on earth doing God's will, even at this late time in His ministry, He would safely complete God's purposes.

11:11-13 sleeps. A euphemistic term used in the NT to refer to death, particularly with reference to believers who will be physically raised to eternal life (cf. 1 Cor. 11:30; 15:51; 1 Thess. 4:13).

11:14,15 The resurrection of Lazarus was designed to strengthen His disciples' faith in Him as the Messiah and Son of God in the face of the strong Jewish rejection of Him.

11:16 Thomas' words reflect loyal devotion and, at the same time, pessimism over the fact that they would probably all die. His fears were not unrealistic in the face of bitter hostility toward Jesus, and had not the Lord protected them in the garden (18:1-11), they may also have been arrested and executed. Cf. 20:24-29.

11:17 in the tomb. The term "tomb" means a stone sepulcher. In Palestine such a grave was common. Either a cave or rock area would be hewn out, the floor inside leveled and graded to make a shallow descent. Shelves were cut out or constructed inside the area in order to bury additional family members. A rock was rolled in front to prevent wild animals or grave robbers from entering (see also v. 38). The evangelist made special mention of the fourth day (*see note on v. 3*) in order to stress the magnitude of the miracle, for the Jews did not embalm and by then the body would have been in a state of rapid decomposition.

11:18,19 The implication of these verses is that the family was rather prominent. The mention of the Jews also heightens the reader's awareness of the great risk that Jesus took in coming so close to Jerusalem, which was seething with the leaders' hatred for Him.

11:21 if You had been here. Cf. v. 32. Not a rebuke of Jesus but a testimony of her trust in His healing power.

11:22 whatever You ask of God. Based on her statement in v. 39, she was not saying she believed Jesus could raise Lazarus from the dead, but that she knew He had a special relationship to God so that His prayers could bring some good from this sad event.

11:25,26 This is the fifth in a series of 7 great "I AM" statements of Jesus (see 6:35; 8:12; 10:7,9; 10:11,14). With this statement, Jesus moved Mary from an abstract belief in the resurrection that will take place "at the last day" (cf. 5:28,29) to a personalized trust in Him who alone can raise the dead. No resurrection or eternal life exists outside of the Son of God. Time ("at the last day") is no barrier to the One who has the power of resurrection and life (1:4) for He can give life at any time.

11:27 She said to Him. Her confession is representative of the very reason John wrote this inspired gospel (cf. 20:30,31). See Peter's confession in Matt. 16:16.

that You are the Christ, the Son of God,
who is to come into the world."
28 And when she had said these things,
she went her way and secretly called Mary
her sister, saying, "The Teacher has come
and is calling for you." 29 As soon as she
heard *that,* she arose quickly and came to
Him. 30 Now Jesus had not yet come into
the town, but [2]was in the place where Martha met Him. 31 [p]Then the Jews who were
with her in the house, and comforting her,
when they saw that Mary rose up quickly
and went out, followed her, [3]saying, "She
is going to the tomb to weep there."
32 Then, when Mary came where Jesus
was, and saw Him, she [q]fell down at His
feet, saying to Him, [r]"Lord, if You had been
here, my brother would not have died."
33 Therefore, when Jesus saw her weeping, and the Jews who came with her
weeping, He groaned in the spirit and was
troubled. 34 And He said, "Where have
you laid him?"
They said to Him, "Lord, come and see."
35 [s]Jesus wept. 36 Then the Jews said,
"See how He loved him!"
37 And some of them said, "Could not
this Man, [t]who opened the eyes of the
blind, also have kept this man from dying?"
38 Then Jesus, again groaning in Himself, came to the tomb. It was a cave, and a
[u]stone lay against it. 39 Jesus said, "Take
away the stone."

30 [2] NU *was still*
31 [p] John 11:19, 33 [3] NU *supposing that she was going*
32 [q] Mark 5:22; 7:25; Rev. 1:17 [r] John 11:21
35 [s] Luke 19:41
37 [t] John 9:6, 7
38 [u] Matt. 27:60, 66; Mark 15:46; Luke 24:2; John 20:1
40 [v] [John 11:4, 23]
41 [4] NU omits *from the place where the dead man was lying*
42 [w] John 12:30; 17:21
44 [x] John 19:40 [y] John 20:7
45 [z] John 2:23; 10:42; 12:11, 18
46 [a] John 5:15
47 [b] Ps. 2:2; Matt. 26:3; Mark 14:1; Luke 22:2 [c] John 12:19; Acts 4:16

Martha, the sister of him who was dead,
said to Him, "Lord, by this time there is a
stench, for he has been *dead* four days."
40 Jesus said to her, "Did I not say to you
that if you would believe you would [v]see
the glory of God?" 41 Then they took away
the stone [4]*from the place* where the dead
man was lying. And Jesus lifted up *His*
eyes and said, "Father, I thank You that
You have heard Me. 42 And I know that
You always hear Me, but [w]because of the
people who are standing by I said *this,* that
they may believe that You sent Me."
43 Now when He had said these things, He
cried with a loud voice, "Lazarus, come
forth!" 44 And he who had died came out
bound hand and foot with [x]graveclothes,
and [y]his face was wrapped with a cloth. Jesus said to them, "Loose him, and let him
go."

The Pharisees Plan to Kill Christ

45 Then many of the Jews who had come
to Mary, [z]and had seen the things Jesus
did, believed in Him. 46 But some of them
went away to the Pharisees and [a]told them
the things Jesus did. 47 [b]Then the chief
priests and the Pharisees gathered a council and said, [c]"What shall we do? For this
Man works many signs. 48 If we let Him
alone like this, everyone will believe in
Him, and the Romans will come and take
away both our place and nation."

11:32 *See note on v. 21.*

11:33 the Jews who came with her weeping. According to Jewish oral tradition, the funeral custom indicated that even a poor family must hire at least two flute players and a professional wailing woman to mourn the dead. Because the family may have been well-to-do, a rather large group appears present. **He groaned in the spirit and was troubled.** The phrase here does not mean merely that Jesus was deeply touched or moved with sympathy at the sight. The Gr. term "groaned" always suggests anger, outrage, or emotional indignation (see v. 38; cf. Matt. 9:30; Mark 1:43; 14:5). Most likely Jesus was angered at the emotional grief of the people because it implicitly revealed unbelief in the resurrection and the temporary nature of death. The group was acting like pagans who had no hope (1 Thess. 4:13). While grief is understandable, the group was acting in despair, thus indicating a tacit denial of the resurrection and the Scripture that promised it. Jesus may also have been angered because He was indignant at the pain and sorrow in death that sin brought into the human condition.

11:35 Jesus wept. The Gr. word here has the connotation of silently bursting into tears in contrast to the loud lament of the group (see v. 33). His tears here were not generated out of mourning, since He was to raise Lazarus, but out of grief for a fallen world entangled in sin-caused sorrow and death. He was "a Man of sorrows and acquainted with grief" (3:16; Is. 53:3).

11:39 stench. Although Jews used aromatic spices, their custom was not to embalm the body but to use the spices to counteract the repulsive odors from decomposition. They would wrap the body in linen cloth, adding spice in the layers and folds. The Jews did not wrap the body tightly like Egyptian mummies, but rather loosely with the head wrapped separately. This is indicated by the fact that Lazarus could move out of the tomb before he was unwrapped (v. 44; cf. 20:7).

11:41,42 Jesus' prayer was not really a petition, but thanksgiving to the Father. The reason for the miracle was to authenticate His claims to be the Messiah and Son of God.

11:43 This was a preview of the power to be fully displayed in the final resurrection when all the dead hear the voice of the Son of God and live (5:25,28,29).

11:45,46 Jesus' teaching and actions often divided the Jews (e.g., 6:14,15; 7:10-13; 45-52). While some believed (cf. v. 40), others, apparently with malicious intent, informed the Pharisees of Jesus' action.

11:47 gathered a council. Alerted by the Pharisees, a Sanhedrin committee consisting of chief priests (former High-Priests and members of High-Priestly families) and Pharisees, called the Sanhedrin to session. The Pharisees could not by themselves take any judicial action against Jesus. Though subject to Roman control, the Sanhedrin was the highest judicial body in Israel and exercised judicial, legislative, and executive powers at that time. In Jesus' day, the 70 members of the Sanhedrin were dominated by the chief priests, and virtually all the priests were Sadducees. The Pharisees constituted an influential minority. While the Pharisees and Sadducees were often in conflict, their mutual hatred of Jesus united them into action.

11:48 the Romans will come. The Jews were not willing to believe in Jesus as the Son of God even though Lazarus had been raised. They feared that escalating messianic expectations could start a movement against Roman oppression and occupation that would cause the Romans to come and take away all their rights and freedoms.

49 And one of them, [d]Caiaphas, being
high priest that year, said to them, "You
know nothing at all, 50 [e]nor do you consider that it is expedient for [5]us that one
man should die for the people, and not
that the whole nation should perish."
51 Now this he did not say on his own *authority;* but being high priest that year he
prophesied that Jesus would die for the
nation, 52 and [f]not for that nation only, but
[g]also that He would gather together in one
the children of God who were scattered
abroad.
53 Then, from that day on, they plotted
to [h]put Him to death. 54 [i]Therefore Jesus
no longer walked openly among the
Jews, but went from there into the country near the wilderness, to a city called
[j]Ephraim, and there remained with His
disciples.
55 [k]And the Passover of the Jews was
near, and many went from the country up
to Jerusalem before the Passover, to [l]purify
themselves. 56 [m]Then they sought Jesus,
and spoke among themselves as they
stood in the temple, "What do you think—
that He will not come to the feast?" 57 Now
both the chief priests and the Pharisees
had given a command, that if anyone
knew where He was, he should report *it,*
that they might [n]seize Him.

Mary Anoints Christ
Matt. 26:6-12; Mark 14:3-9

12 Then, six days before the Passover,
Jesus came to Bethany, [a]where
Lazarus was [1]who had been dead, whom
He had raised from the dead. 2 [b]There they
made Him a supper; and Martha served,
but Lazarus was one of those who sat at
the table with Him. 3 Then [c]Mary took a
pound of very costly oil of [d]spikenard,
anointed the feet of Jesus, and wiped His
feet with her hair. And the house was filled
with the fragrance of the oil.
4 But one of His disciples, [e]Judas Iscariot, Simon's *son,* who would betray Him,
said, 5 "Why was this fragrant oil not sold
for [2]three hundred denarii and given to
the poor?" 6 This he said, not that he cared
for the poor, but because he was a thief,
and [f]had the money box; and he used to
take what was put in it.
7 But Jesus said, "Let her alone; [3]she has

49 [d] Matt. 26:3; Luke 3:2; John 18:14; Acts 4:6
50 [e] John 18:14 [5] NU *you*
52 [f] Is. 49:6; Acts 10:45; 11:18; 13:46; [1 John 2:2] [g] Ps. 22:27; John 10:16; [Eph. 2:14-17]
53 [h] Matt. 26:4; Luke 6:11; 19:47; 22:2; John 5:16
54 [i] John 4:1, 3; 7:1 [j] 2 Chr. 13:19
55 [k] Matt. 26:1; Mark 14:1; Luke 22:1; John 2:13; 5:1; 6:4 [l] Num. 9:10, 13; 31:19, 20; 2 Chr. 30:17; Luke 2:22
56 [m] John 7:11
57 [n] Matt. 26:14-16

CHAPTER 12
1 [a] Matt. 21:17; John 11:1, 43 [1] NU omits *who had been dead*
2 [b] Matt. 26:6; Mark 14:3; Luke 10:38-41
3 [c] Luke 10:38, 39; John 11:2 [d] Song 1:12
4 [e] John 13:26
5 [2] About one year's wages for a worker
6 [f] John 13:29
7 [3] NU *that she may keep*

11:49 Caiaphas. Caiaphas became High-Priest ca. A.D. 18, being appointed by the Roman prefect, Valerius Gratus. His father-in-law was Annas who had previously functioned in that same position from ca. A.D. 7–14 and who exercised great influence over the office even after his tenure (see 18:12-14). Caiaphas remained in office until A.D. 36 when, along with Pontius Pilate, he was removed by the Romans. He took a leading part in the trial and condemnation of Jesus. In his court or palace, the chief priests (Sadducees) and Pharisees assembled "and plotted to take Jesus by trickery and kill *Him*" (see Matt. 26:3,4).

11:50 one man should die for the people. He only meant that Jesus should be executed in order to spare their own positions and nation from Roman reprisals, but Caiaphas unwittingly used sacrificial, substitutionary language and prophesied the death of Christ for sinners. Cf. 2 Cor. 5:21; 1 Pet. 2:24.

11:51 he prophesied. Caiaphas did not realize the implications of what he spoke. While he uttered blasphemy against Christ, God parodied his statement into truth (cf. Ps. 76:10). The responsibility for the wicked meaning of his words belonged to Caiaphas, but God's providence directed the choice of words so as to express the heart of God's glorious plan of salvation (Acts 4:27,28). He actually was used by God as a prophet because he was the High-Priest and originally the High-Priest was the means of God's will being revealed (2 Sam. 15:27).

11:52 gather together in one the children of God. In context, this had reference to believing Jews of the dispersion who would be gathered together in the Promised Land to share the kingdom of God (Is. 43:5; Ezek. 34:12). In a wider sense, this also anticipated the Gentile mission (see 12:32). As a result of Christ's sacrificial death and resurrection, both Jew and Gentile have been made into one group, the church (Eph. 2:11-18).

11:53 from that day on. The phrase indicates that their course of action toward Jesus was then fixed. It remained only to accomplish it. Notice that Jesus was not arrested to be tried. He had already been judged guilty of blasphemy. The trial was a mere formality for a sentence already passed (Mark 14:1,2).

11:54 Ephraim. This probably refers to the OT city of Ephron (see 2 Chr. 13:19). Its modern village name is Et-Taiyibeh, and it is located 4 mi. NE of Bethel and about 12 mi. from Jerusalem. The location was far enough away for temporary safety until the time of Passover (v. 55).

11:55 Passover. This is the third Passover mentioned in John (see 2:13; 6:4) and the last in Jesus' earthly ministry at which His sacrificial death occurred. For the chronology of the Passover Week, see Introduction to Luke: Outline.

11:56 they sought Jesus. The Jews who filled Jerusalem for Passover were wondering if Jesus would show Himself at this time and were actively seeking to find Him. The plot of the chief priests and Pharisees (see v. 47; 7:12) was known widely enough to peak their curiosity as to whether Jesus would dare show Himself in Jerusalem.

11:57 if anyone knew. The plotters ensured that the whole city was filled with potential informants.

12:1-50 This chapter focuses on the reactions of love and hate, belief and rejection toward Christ, leading to the cross.

12:1 six days before the Passover. This most likely was the previous Saturday with Passover coming 6 days later on Thursday evening through sunset Friday. See Introduction: Interpretive Challenges.

12:3 a pound of very costly oil of spikenard. The term used for "pound" actually indicates a weight around three-fourths of a pound (approximately 12 ounces). "Spikenard" was an oil extracted from the root of a plant grown in India. **anointed the feet of Jesus.** Since those who were eating reclined at the table, their feet extended away from it making it possible for Mary to anoint the feet of Jesus. The act symbolized Mary's humble devotion and love for Him.

12:5 three hundred denarii. Since one denarius was a day's wage given to common laborers, 300 was equivalent to a year's wages (no money was earned on the Sabbath or other holy days).

12:6 a thief. Judas' altruism was really a front for his own personal avarice. Because he was the apostolic band's treasurer, he was able to secretly pilfer the group treasury for his own desires.

kept this for the day of My burial. 8 For
[g]the poor you have with you always, but
Me you do not have always."
9 Now a great many of the Jews knew
that He was there; and they came, not for
Jesus' sake only, but that they might also
see Lazarus, [h]whom He had raised from
the dead. 10 [i]But the chief priests plotted to
put Lazarus to death also, 11 [j]because on
account of him many of the Jews went
away and believed in Jesus.

The Triumphal Entry
Matt. 21:1-9; Mark 11:1-10; Luke 19:29-38

12 [k]The next day a great multitude that
had come to the feast, when they heard
that Jesus was coming to Jerusalem, 13 took
branches of palm trees and went out to
meet Him, and cried out:

"Hosanna!
[l]'*Blessed is He who comes in the*
name of the LORD!'
The King of Israel!"

14 [m]Then Jesus, when He had found a
young donkey, sat on it; as it is written:

15 "*Fear*[n] *not, daughter of Zion;*
Behold, your King is coming,
Sitting on a donkey's colt."

16 [o]His disciples did not understand
these things at first; [p]but when Jesus was
glorified, [q]then they remembered that
these things were written about Him and
that they had done these things to Him.
17 Therefore the people, who were with
Him when He called Lazarus out of his
tomb and raised him from the dead, bore
witness. 18 [r]For this reason the people also
met Him, because they heard that He had
done this sign. 19 The Pharisees therefore
said among themselves, [s]"You see that you
are accomplishing nothing. Look, the
world has gone after Him!"
20 Now there [t]were certain Greeks
among those [u]who came up to worship at
the feast. 21 Then they came to Philip, [v]who
was from Bethsaida of Galilee, and asked
him, saying, "Sir, we wish to see Jesus."
22 Philip came and told Andrew, and in
turn Andrew and Philip told Jesus.

The Messiah Teaches

23 But Jesus answered them, saying,
[w]"The hour has come that the Son of Man
should be glorified. 24 Most assuredly, I

8 [g] Deut. 15:11; Matt. 26:11; Mark 14:7; John 17:11
9 [h] John 11:43, 44
10 [i] Luke 16:31
11 [j] John 11:45; 12:18
12 [k] Matt. 21:4-9; Mark 11:7-10; Luke 19:35-38
13 [l] Ps. 118:25, 26
14 [m] Matt. 21:7
15 [n] Is. 40:9; Zech. 9:9
16 [o] Luke 18:34 [p] John 7:39; 12:23 [q] [John 14:26]
18 [r] John 12:11
19 [s] John 11:47, 48
20 [t] Mark 7:26; Acts 17:4 [u] 1 Kin. 8:41, 42; Acts 8:27
21 [v] John 1:43, 44; 14:8-11
23 [w] Matt. 26:18, 45; John 13:32; Acts 3:13

12:7 kept this for the day of My burial. Mary performed this act to signal her devotion but, as in the case of Caiaphas (11:49-52), her act revealed more than she realized at the time. During the first century, lavish sums were spent on funerals, which included costly perfumes to cover the smell of decay (*see note on 11:39*).

12:8 This does not mean that alms should not be distributed to the poor (Deut. 15:11) but was a reminder that, while the poor would remain, Jesus would not always be with them. See Matt. 26:11; Mark 14:7.

12:11 went away and believed. This phrase signaled both a conscious, deliberate move away from the religion of the authorities and a move toward genuine faith in Jesus as Messiah and Son of God.

12:12-19 This section marks Jesus' triumphal entry into Jerusalem referred to as Palm Sunday. It is one of the few incidents in Jesus' life reported in all 4 gospels (Matt. 21:1-11; Mark 11:1-11; Luke 19:29-38). By this action, He presented Himself officially to the nation as the Messiah and Son of God. The Sanhedrin and other Jewish leaders wanted him dead but did not want Him killed during the Passover time because they feared stirring up the multitudes with whom He was popular (Matt. 26:5; Mark 14:2; Luke 22:2). Jesus entered the city, however, on His own time and forced the whole issue in order that it might happen exactly on the Passover day when the lambs were being sacrificed. As the Scripture says, "Christ, our Passover, was sacrificed for us" (1 Cor. 5:7; 1 Pet. 1:19). In God's perfect timing (see 7:30; 8:20), at the precise time foreordained from eternity, He presented Himself to die (v. 23; 10:17,18; 17:1; 19:10,11; cf. Acts 2:23; 4:27,28; Gal. 4:4).

12:12 The next day. Sunday, the day after Jesus' visit to Bethany (*see note on v. 1*).

12:13 took branches of palm trees. The supply of date palms was plentiful; they still grow in Jerusalem today. From about two centuries earlier, the waving of palm branches had become a national, if not nationalistic, symbol, which signaled the fervent hope that a messianic liberator was arriving on the scene (6:14,15). **Hosanna!** The term "hosanna" is a transliteration of a Heb. word that means "give salvation now." It was a term of acclamation or praise occurring in Ps. 118:26 which was familiar to every Jew, since that psalm was part of the Hallel (Pss. 113–118) sung each morning by the temple choir during the Feast of Tabernacles (7:37) and associated with the Feast of Dedication (10:22) and especially the Passover. After shouting out the "Hosanna," the crowds shouted Ps. 118:26; significantly, the original context of Ps. 118 may well have been the pronouncement of blessing upon a Davidic king. Jewish commentaries on the psalm have understood the verse to bear messianic implications. "He who comes in the name of the LORD" refers to Messiah, especially in context with the phrase, "The King of Israel," though that messianic title is not from Ps. 118.

12:14,15 The synoptic gospels give more information here regarding Jesus' selection of a donkey (see Matt. 21:1-9; Mark 11:1-10; Luke 19:29-38). They convey the fact that Jesus deliberately planned to present Himself to the nation in this manner as a conscious fulfillment of the messianic prophecy of Zech. 9:9 (quoted here). The words, "Fear not," are not found in the Zechariah passage but were added from Is. 40:9. Only after His ascension did the disciples grasp the meaning of the triumphal entry (cf. 14:26).

12:19 the world has gone after Him. "The world" means the people in general, as opposed to everyone in particular. Clearly, most people in the world did not even know of Him at that time, and many in Israel did not believe in Him. Often, "world" is used in this general sense (v. 47; 1:29; 3:17; 4:42; 14:22; 17:9,21).

12:20,21 Most likely Gentile proselytes to Judaism who had come up for the Passover and who, in their desire to see Jesus, stood in direct antithesis to the attitude of the national leaders who desired to kill Him. At the very moment when the Jewish authorities virulently plotted to kill Him, Gentiles began to desire His attention.

12:23 hour. Refers to the time of Jesus' death, resurrection, and exaltation (v. 27; 13:1; 17:1). Up to this point, Jesus' hour had always been future (2:4; 4:21,23; 7:30; 8:20). **Son of Man.** *See note on 1:51.*

say to you, [x]unless a grain of wheat falls
into the ground and dies, it remains alone;
but if it dies, it produces much [4]grain.
25 [y]He who loves his life will lose it, and he
who hates his life in this world will keep it
for eternal life. 26 If anyone serves Me, let
him [z]follow Me; and [a]where I am, there
My servant will be also. If anyone serves
Me, him *My* Father will honor.
27 [b]"Now My soul is troubled, and what
shall I say? 'Father, save Me from this
hour'? [c]But for this purpose I came to this
hour. 28 Father, glorify Your name."
[d]Then a voice came from heaven, *saying,*
"I have both glorified *it* and will glorify *it*
again."
29 Therefore the people who stood by
and heard *it* said that it had thundered.
Others said, "An angel has spoken to
Him."
30 Jesus answered and said, [e]"This voice
did not come because of Me, but for your
sake. 31 Now is the judgment of this world;
now [f]the ruler of this world will be cast
out. 32 And I, [g]if I am [5]lifted up from the
earth, will draw [h]all *peoples* to Myself."
33 [i]This He said, signifying by what death
He would die.
34 The people answered Him, [j]"We have
heard from the law that the Christ remains
forever; and how *can* You say, 'The Son of
Man must be lifted up'? Who is this Son of
Man?"
35 Then Jesus said to them, "A little
while longer [k]the light is with you. [l]Walk
while you have the light, lest darkness
overtake you; [m]he who walks in darkness
does not know where he is going. 36 While
you have the light, believe in the light, that
you may become [n]sons of light." These
things Jesus spoke, and departed, and
[o]was hidden from them.
37 But although He had done so many
[p]signs before them, they did not believe in
Him, 38 that the word of Isaiah the prophet
might be fulfilled, which he spoke:

> [q]*"Lord, who has believed our report?*
> *And to whom has the arm of the*
> *LORD been revealed?"*

39 Therefore they could not believe, because Isaiah said again:

> 40 *"He[r] has blinded their eyes and*
> *hardened their hearts,*
> [s]*Lest they should see with their*
> *eyes,*
> *Lest they should understand with*
> *their hearts and turn,*
> *So that I should heal them."*

41 [t]These things Isaiah said [6]when he saw
His glory and spoke of Him.
42 Nevertheless even among the rulers
many believed in Him, but [u]because of the
Pharisees they did not confess *Him,* lest
they should be put out of the synagogue;
43 [v]for they loved the praise of men more
than the praise of God.

24 [x][Rom. 14:9]; 1 Cor. 15:36 [4]Lit. *fruit*
25 [y]Matt. 10:39; Mark 8:35; Luke 9:24
26 [z][Matt. 16:24] [a]John 14:3; 17:24; [1 Thess. 4:17]
27 [b][Matt. 26:38, 39]; Mark 14:34; Luke 12:50; John 11:33 [c]Luke 22:53; John 18:37
28 [d]Matt. 3:17; 17:5; Mark 1:11; 9:7; Luke 3:22; 9:35
30 [e]John 11:42
31 [f]Matt. 12:29; Luke 10:18; [Acts 26:18; 2 Cor. 4:4]
32 [g]John 3:14; 8:28 [h][Rom. 5:18; Heb. 2:9] [5]Crucified
33 [i]John 18:32; 21:19
34 [j]Ps. 89:36, 37; Is. 9:6, 7; Mic. 4:7
35 [k][John 1:9; 7:33; 8:12] [l]Jer. 13:16; [Gal. 6:10]; Eph. 5:8
[m]John 11:10; [1 John 2:9-11]
36 [n]Luke 16:8; John 8:12 [o]John 8:59
37 [p]John 11:47
38 [q]Is. 53:1; Rom. 10:16
40 [r]Is. 6:9, 10 [s]Matt. 13:14
41 [t]Is. 6:1 [6]NU *because*
42 [u]John 7:13; 9:22
43 [v]John 5:41, 44

12:24 As the sown kernel dies to bring forth a rich harvest, so also the death of the Son of God will result in the salvation of many.

12:25,26 Not only is the principle of death applicable to Jesus (see v. 24) but it is also applicable to His followers. They, too, as His disciples may have to lose their life in service and witness for Him (see Matt. 10:37-39; 16:24,25).

12:27 My soul is troubled. The term used here is strong and signifies horror, anxiety, and agitation. Jesus' contemplation of taking on the wrath of God for the sins of the world caused revulsion in the sinless Savior (cf. 2 Cor. 5:21).

12:28 glorify Your name. This request embodied the principle that Jesus lived by and would die by. See 7:18; 8:29,50. **I have…and will glorify.** The Father answered the Son in an audible voice. This is only one of 3 instances during Jesus' ministry when this took place (cf. Matt. 3:17—His baptism; 17:5—His transfiguration).

12:31 the ruler of this world. A reference to Satan (see 14:30; 16:11; cf. Matt. 4:8,9; Luke 4:6,7; 2 Cor. 4:4; Eph. 2:2; 6:12). Although the cross might have appeared to signal Satan's victory over God, in reality it marked Satan's defeat (cf. Rom. 16:20; Heb. 2:14).

12:32 lifted up from the earth. This refers to His crucifixion (v. 33; 18:32). *See note on 3:14.*

12:34 remains forever. The term "law" was used broadly enough to include not only the 5 books of Moses but also the whole of the OT (see Rom. 10:4). Perhaps they had in mind Is. 9:7 which promised that Messiah's kingdom would last forever, or Ezek. 37:25 where God promised that the final David would be Israel's prince forever (see also Ps. 89:35-37).

12:35,36 Jesus said to them. A final invitation from Jesus was recorded by John to focus on his theme of believing in the Messiah and Son of God (see 20:30,31).

12:37-40 In these verses, John gave the Scriptural explanation for such large-scale, catastrophic unbelief on the part of the Jewish nation. The explanation was that the unbelief was not only foreseen in Scripture but necessitated by it. In v. 38, John quotes Is. 53:1 and in v. 40 he quotes Is. 6:10 (see Rom. 10:16), both of which stress the sovereign plan of God in His judicial hardening of Israel (cf. Paul's argument in Rom. 9–11). Although God predestined such judgment, it was not apart from human responsibility and culpability (see 8:24).

12:41 Isaiah…saw His glory and spoke of Him. This is a reference to Isaiah 6:1 (*see notes there*). John unambiguously ties Jesus to God or Yahweh of the OT (*see note on 8:58*). Therefore, since v. 41 refers to Jesus, it makes Him the author of the judicial hardening of Israel. That fits His role as Judge (see 5:22,23,27,30; 9:39).

12:42,43 The indictment of vv. 37-41 is followed by the exceptions of vv. 42,43 (see 1:10,11 vs. 1:12,13). While the people seemed to trust Jesus with much more candor and fervency, the leaders of Israel who believed in Him demonstrated inadequate, irresolute, even spurious faith (*see notes on 2:23-25; 6:60; 8:30,31*). The faith of the latter was so weak that they refused to take any position that would threaten their position in the synagogue. This is one of the saddest statements about spiritual leadership, for they preferred the praises of men above the praises of God in their refusal to publicly acknowledge Jesus as Messiah and Son of God.

44 Then Jesus cried out and said, [w]"He
who believes in Me, [x]believes not in Me [y]but
in Him who sent Me. **45** And [z]he who sees
Me sees Him who sent Me. **46** [a]I have come
as a light into the world, that whoever believes in Me should not abide in darkness.
47 And if anyone hears My words and does
not [7]believe, [b]I do not judge him; for [c]I did
not come to judge the world but to save the
world. **48** [d]He who rejects Me, and does not
receive My words, has that which judges
him—[e]the word that I have spoken will
judge him in the last day. **49** For [f]I have not
spoken on My own *authority;* but the Father
who sent Me gave Me a command, [g]what I
should say and what I should speak. **50** And
I know that His command is everlasting life.
Therefore, whatever I speak, just as the Father has told Me, so I [h]speak."

Christ Washes the Disciples' Feet

13 Now [a]before the Feast of the Passover, when Jesus knew that [b]His
hour had come that He should depart from
this world to the Father, having loved His
own who were in the world, He [c]loved
them to the end.
2 And [1]supper being ended, [d]the devil
having already put it into the heart of Judas Iscariot, Simon's *son,* to betray Him,
3 Jesus, knowing [e]that the Father had
given all things into His hands, and that
He [f]had come from God and [g]was going to
God, **4** [h]rose from supper and laid aside
His garments, took a towel and girded
Himself. **5** After that, He poured water into
a basin and began to wash the disciples'
feet, and to wipe *them* with the towel with
which He was girded. **6** Then He came to
Simon Peter. And *Peter* said to Him,
[i]"Lord, are You washing my feet?"
7 Jesus answered and said to him, "What
I am doing you [j]do not understand now,
[k]but you will know after this."
8 Peter said to Him, "You shall never
wash my feet!"
Jesus answered him, [l]"If I do not wash
you, you have no part with Me."
9 Simon Peter said to Him, "Lord, not my
feet only, but also *my* hands and *my* head!"
10 Jesus said to him, "He who is bathed
needs only to wash *his* feet, but is completely clean; and [m]you are clean, but not
all of you." **11** For [n]He knew who would
betray Him; therefore He said, "You are
not all clean."
12 So when He had washed their feet,
taken His garments, and sat down again,
He said to them, "Do you [2]know what I
have done to you? **13** [o]You call Me Teacher
and Lord, and you say well, for *so* I am.
14 [p]If I then, *your* Lord and Teacher, have
washed your feet, [q]you also ought to wash
one another's feet. **15** For [r]I have given you
an example, that you should do as I have

44 [w] Mark 9:37 [x] [John 3:16, 18, 36; 11:25, 26] [y] [John 5:24]
45 [z] [John 14:9]
46 [a] John 1:4, 5; 8:12; 12:35, 36
47 [b] John 5:45 [c] John 3:17 [7] NU *keep them*
48 [d] [Luke 10:16] [e] Deut. 18:18, 19; [John 5:45; 8:47]
49 [f] John 8:38 [g] Deut. 18:18
50 [h] John 5:19; 8:28

CHAPTER 13

1 [a] Matt. 26:2 [b] John 12:23; 17:1 [c] John 15:9
2 [d] Luke 22:3 [1] NU *during supper*
3 [e] Matt. 11:27; [John 5:20-23; 17:2]; Acts 2:36; 1 Cor. 15:27; [Heb. 2:8] [f] John 8:42; 16:28 [g] John 17:11; 20:17
4 [h] [Luke 22:27; Phil. 2:7, 8]
6 [i] Matt. 3:14
7 [j] John 12:16; 16:12 [k] John 13:19
8 [l] [Ps. 51:2, 7; Ezek. 36:25; Acts 22:16; 1 Cor. 6:11; Eph. 5:26; Titus 3:5; Heb. 10:22]
10 [m] [John 15:3; Eph. 5:26]
11 [n] John 6:64; 18:4
12 [2] *understand*
13 [o] Matt. 23:8, 10; Luke 6:46; [1 Cor. 8:6; 12:3]; Eph. 6:9; [Phil. 2:11]
14 [p] Luke 22:27 [q] [Rom. 12:10; Gal. 6:1, 2; 1 Pet. 5:5]
15 [r] Matt. 11:29; Phil. 2:5; [1 Pet. 2:21-24]; 1 John 2:6

13:1–17:16 In these remaining chapters before His crucifixion, the record looks at Jesus' devoting Himself to His own disciples. While chaps. 1–12 center on the rejection of Jesus by the nation (cf. 1:11), chaps. 13–17 center on those who did receive Him (see 1:12). Beginning in chap. 13, Jesus moved completely away from public ministry to private ministry with those who had received Him. Chapters 13–17 were spoken by Jesus as a farewell on the night of His betrayal and arrest to communicate His coming legacy to His followers (chaps. 13–16) and pray for them (chap. 17). The cross was only one day away.

13:1 to the end. Meaning "to perfection" with perfect love. God loves the world (3:16), and sinners (3:16; Matt. 5:44,45; Titus 3:4) with compassion and common grace, but loves His own with perfect, saving, eternal love.

13:2 supper. Passover on Thursday night after sunset. See Introduction: Interpretive Challenges. **the devil...the heart of Judas.** This does not exonerate Judas, because his wicked heart desired exactly what the devil desired, the death of Jesus. The devil and Judas were in accord.

13:3 going to God. He faced the betrayal, agony, and death because He knew He would be exalted to the Father afterward, where He would receive the glory and fellowship He had eternally enjoyed within the Trinity (see 17:4,5). This was the "joy set before Him" that enabled Him to "endure the cross" (Heb. 12:2).

13:4,5 The dusty and dirty conditions of the region necessitated the need for footwashing. Although the disciples most likely would have been happy to wash Jesus' feet, they could not conceive of washing each other's feet. This was because in the society of the time footwashing was reserved for the lowliest of menial servants. Peers did not wash one another's feet, except very rarely and as a mark of great love. Luke points out (22:24) that they were arguing about who was the greatest of them, so that none was willing to stoop to wash feet. When Jesus moved to wash their feet, they were shocked. His actions serve also as symbolic of spiritual cleansing (vv. 6-9) and a model of Christian humility (vv. 12-17). Through this action Jesus taught the lesson of selfless service that was supremely exemplified by His death on the cross.

13:6-10 These proceedings embarrassed all of the disciples. While others remained silent, Peter, perhaps on behalf of others (see Matt. 16:13-23), spoke up in indignation that Jesus would stoop so low as to wash his feet. He failed to see beyond the humble service itself to the symbolism of spiritual cleansing involved (v. 7; cf. 1 John 1:7-9). Jesus' response made the real point of His actions clear: Unless the Lamb of God cleanses a person's sin (i.e., as portrayed in the symbolism of washing), one can have no part with Him.

13:10 needs only to wash *his* feet. The cleansing that Christ does at salvation never needs to be repeated—atonement is complete at that point. But all who have been cleansed by God's gracious justification need constant washing in the experiential sense as they battle sin in the flesh. Believers are justified and granted imputed righteousness (Phil. 3:8,9), but still need sanctification and personal righteousness (Phil. 3:12-14).

13:11,12 not all clean. This verse refers to Judas (6:70), who was soon to lead the mob to capture Jesus (18:3).

13:15 an example. The word used here suggests both "example" and "pattern" (Heb. 4:11; 8:5; 9:25; James 5:10; 2 Pet. 2:6). Jesus' purpose in this action was to establish the model of loving humility.

done to you. 16 [s]Most assuredly, I say to
you, a servant is not greater than his master; nor is he who is sent greater than he
who sent him. 17 [t]If you know these things,
blessed are you if you do them.
18 "I do not speak concerning all of you.
I know whom I have chosen; but that the
[u]Scripture may be fulfilled, [v]*'He who eats*
[3]bread with Me has lifted up his heel
against Me.' 19 [w]Now I tell you before it
comes, that when it does come to pass, you
may believe that I am *He.* 20 [x]Most assuredly, I say to you, he who receives
whomever I send receives Me; and he who
receives Me receives Him who sent Me."

Christ Announces Judas, the Betrayer
Matt. 26:21, 22; Mark 14:18, 19; Luke 22:21-23

21 [y]When Jesus had said these things,
[z]He was troubled in spirit, and testified
and said, "Most assuredly, I say to you,
[a]one of you will betray Me." 22 Then the
disciples looked at one another, perplexed
about whom He spoke.
23 Now [b]there was [4]leaning on Jesus'
bosom one of His disciples, whom Jesus
loved. 24 Simon Peter therefore motioned
to him to ask who it was of whom He
spoke.
25 Then, leaning [5]back on Jesus' breast,
he said to Him, "Lord, who is it?"
26 Jesus answered, "It is he to whom I
shall give a piece of bread when I have
dipped *it.*" And having dipped the bread,
He gave *it* to [c]Judas Iscariot, *the son* of Simon. 27 [d]Now after the piece of bread, Satan
entered him. Then Jesus said to him, "What
you do, do quickly." 28 But no one at the
table knew for what reason He said this to
him. 29 For some thought, because [e]Judas
had the money box, that Jesus had said to
him, "Buy *those things* we need for the
feast," or that he should give something to
the poor.
30 Having received the piece of bread, he
then went out immediately. And it was
night.

Christ Announces His Departure

31 So, when he had gone out, Jesus said,
[f]"Now the Son of Man is glorified, and
[g]God is glorified in Him. 32 If God is glorified in Him, God will also glorify Him in
Himself, and [h]glorify Him immediately.
33 Little children, I shall be with you a [i]lit-
tle while longer. You will seek Me; [j]and as
I said to the Jews, 'Where I am going, you
cannot come,' so now I say to you. 34 [k]A
new commandment I give to you, that you
love one another; as I have loved you, that
you also love one another. 35 [l]By this all
will know that you are My disciples, if you
have love for one another."

Christ Foretells Peter's Denial
Matt. 26:34, 35; Mark 14:30, 31; Luke 22:33, 34

36 Simon Peter said to Him, "Lord,
where are You going?"
Jesus answered him, "Where I [m]am
going you cannot follow Me now, but [n]you
shall follow Me afterward."

16 [s] Matt. 10:24; [Luke 6:40]; John 15:20
17 [t] Matt. 7:24; Luke 11:28; [James 1:25]
18 [u] John 15:25; 17:12 [v] Ps. 41:9; Matt. 26:23 [3] NU *My bread has*
19 [w] John 14:29; 16:4
20 [x] Matt. 10:40; Mark 9:37; Luke 9:48; 10:16; Gal. 4:14
21 [y] Matt. 26:21; Mark 14:18; Luke 22:21 [z] John 12:27 [a] Ps. 41:9; Matt. 26:46; Mark 14:42; Luke 22:48; John 6:64; 18:5; Acts 1:17; 1 John 2:19
23 [b] John 19:26; 20:2; 21:7,20 [4] *reclining*
25 [5] NU, M add *thus*
26 [c] Matt. 10:4; John 6:70,71; 12:4; Acts 1:16
27 [d] Luke 22:3
29 [e] John 12:6
31 [f] John 12:23; Acts 3:13 [g] [John 14:13; 17:4; 1 Pet. 4:11]
32 [h] John 12:23
33 [i] John 12:35; 14:19; 16:16-19 [j] Mark 16:19; [John 7:34; 8:21]; Acts 1:9
34 [k] Lev. 19:18; Eph. 5:2; 1 Thess. 4:9; James 2:8; 1 Pet. 1:22; 1 John 2:7
35 [l] 1 John 2:5
36 [m] John 13:33; 14:2; 16:5 [n] John 21:17; 2 Pet. 1:14

13:17 blessed are you if you do them. Joy is always tied to obedience to God's revealed Word (see 15:14).

13:18 whom I have chosen. A reference to the 12 disciples whom the Lord had selected (see 15:16), whom the Lord knew perfectly, including Judas, who was chosen that the prophecy of Ps. 41:9 would be fulfilled.

13:21 troubled. For the meaning of this word, *see note on 12:27.*

13:23 one of His disciples, whom Jesus loved. This is the first reference to John the apostle, the author of the gospel (see Introduction: Author and Date). He specifically mentioned Himself at the cross (19:26,27), at the empty tomb (20:2-9), by the Sea of Tiberias (21:1,20-23), and in the next to last verse where He is referenced as the author of the gospel (21:24).

13:26 He gave *it* to Judas Iscariot. The host at a feast (whose role was filled by Jesus) would dip into a common bowl and pull out a particularly tasty bit and pass it to a guest as a special mark of honor or friendship. Because Jesus passed it so easily to Judas, it has been suggested that He was seated near the Lord in a place of honor. Jesus was demonstrating a final gesture of His love for Judas even though he would betray Him.

13:27 Satan entered him. Judas was personally possessed by Satan himself in his betrayal of Jesus. *See note on v. 2.*

13:30 it was night. Although this was a historical reminiscence of John, the phrase may also be imbued with profound theological implications. It was the hour for Judas to be handed over completely to the power of darkness (Satan; cf. Luke 22:53).

13:31-33 glorified. With Judas gone, the final events were set in motion. Rather than looking at the agony of the cross, Jesus looked past the cross, anticipating the glory that He would have with the Father when it was over (see 17:4,5; Heb. 12:2).

13:33 as I said to the Jews. That statement is recorded in 8:21.

13:34,35 Having announced His departure and having insisted that His disciples could not come with Him, Jesus began to lay out what He expected of them after His leaving. Love is to serve as the distinguishing characteristic of discipleship (v. 35; cf. 1 John 2:7-11; 3:10-12; 4:7-10,20,21).

13:34 A new commandment...as I have loved you. The commandment to love was not new. Deuteronomy 6:5 commanded love for God and Lev. 19:18 commanded loving one's neighbor as oneself (cf. Matt. 22:34-40; Rom. 13:8-10; Gal. 5:14; James 2:8). However, Jesus' command regarding love presented a distinctly new standard for two reasons: 1) it was sacrificial love modeled after His love ("as I loved you"; cf. 15:13), and 2) it is produced through the New Covenant by the transforming power of the Holy Spirit (cf. Jer. 31:29-34; Ezek. 36:24-26; Gal. 5:22).

13:36 you cannot follow. His work was nearly finished, theirs was just beginning (Matt. 28:16-20; Mark 16:15; Luke 24:47). Particularly, Peter had a work to do (*see notes on 21:15-19*). Only Jesus, as the sinless sacrifice for the trespasses of the world, could go to the cross and die (1 Pet. 2:22-24). Also, only He could be glorified in the presence of the Father with the glory that He possessed before His incarnation (see 12:41; 17:1-5).

37 Peter said to Him, "Lord, why can I
not follow You now? I will [o]lay down my
life for Your sake."
38 Jesus answered him, "Will you lay
down your life for My sake? Most assuredly, I say to you, the rooster shall not [p]crow
till you have denied Me three times.

Christ Comforts His Disciples

14 "Let [a]not your heart be troubled; you
believe in God, believe also in Me.
2 In My Father's house are many [1]mansions;
if *it were* not *so*, [2]I would have told you. [b]I go
to prepare a place for you. 3 And if I go and
prepare a place for you, [c]I will come again
and receive you to Myself; that [d]where I am,
there you may be also. 4 And where I go you
know, and the way you know."

Christ Answers Thomas

5 [e]Thomas said to Him, "Lord, we do not
know where You are going, and how can
we know the way?"
6 Jesus said to him, "I am [f]the way, [g]the
truth, and [h]the life. [i]No one comes to the
Father [j]except through Me.
7 [k]"If you had known Me, you would
have known My Father also; and from now
on you know Him and have seen Him."

Christ Answers Philip

8 Philip said to Him, "Lord, show us the
Father, and it is sufficient for us."
9 Jesus said to him, "Have I been with
you so long, and yet you have not known
Me, Philip? [l]He who has seen Me has seen
the Father; so how can you say, 'Show us
the Father'? 10 Do you not believe that [m]I
am in the Father, and the Father in Me?
The words that I speak to you [n]I do not
speak on My own *authority;* but the Father
who dwells in Me does the works. 11 Believe Me that I *am* in the Father and the Father in Me, [o]or else believe Me for the sake
of the works themselves.
12 [p]"Most assuredly, I say to you, he who
believes in Me, the works that I do he will do
also; and greater *works* than these he will do,
because I go to My Father. 13 [q]And whatever you ask in My name, that I will do, that
the Father may be [r]glorified in the Son. 14 If
you [3]ask anything in My name, I will do *it*.

37 [o]Matt. 26:33-35; Mark 14:29-31; Luke 22:33,34
38 [p]Matt. 26:74; Mark 14:30; Luke 22:61; John 18:25-27

CHAPTER 14

1 [a][John 14:27; 16:22,24]
2 [b]Matt. 25:34; John 13:33,36; Heb. 11:16 [1]Lit. *dwellings* [2]NU *would I have told you that I go* or *I would have told you; for I go*
3 [c][Acts 1:11] [d][John 12:26; 1 Thess. 4:17]
5 [e]Matt. 10:3; John 11:16; 20:24-29; 21:2
6 [f][John 10:9; Rom. 5:2; Eph. 2:18; Heb. 9:8; 10:19,20] [g][John 1:14,17; 8:32; 18:37] [h][John 11:25] [i]1 Tim. 2:5 [j][John 10:7-9; Acts 4:12]
7 [k]John 8:19
9 [l]John 12:45; Col. 1:15; Heb. 1:3
10 [m]John 10:38; 14:11,20 [n]Deut. 18:18; John 5:19; 14:24
11 [o]John 5:36; 10:38 12 [p]Matt. 21:21; Mark 16:17; Luke 10:17
13 [q]Matt. 7:7; [Mark 11:24]; Luke 11:9; John 15:16; 16:23, 24; [James 1:5-7; 1 John 3:22] [r]John 13:31 14 [3]NU *ask Me*

13:38 See 18:25-27; cf. Matt. 26:71-75; Mark 14:69-72; Luke 22:54-62.

14:1-31 This whole chapter centers in the promise that Christ is the One who gives the believer comfort, not only in His future return but also in the present with the ministry of the Holy Spirit (v. 26). The scene continues to be the upper room where the disciples had gathered with Jesus before He was arrested. Judas had been dismissed (13:30) and Jesus had begun His valedictory address to the remaining 11. The world of the disciples was about to be shattered; they would be bewildered, confused, and ridden with anxiety because of the events that would soon transpire. Anticipating their devastation, Jesus spoke to comfort their hearts.

14:1 Instead of the disciples lending support to Jesus in the hours before His cross, He had to support them spiritually as well as emotionally. This reveals His heart of serving love (cf. Matt. 20:26-28). **troubled.** Faith in Him can stop the heart from being agitated. *See note on 12:27.*

14:2 mansions. Lit. dwelling places, rooms, or even apartments (in modern terms). All are in the large "Father's house."

14:2,3 I go to prepare. His departure would be for their advantage since He was going away to prepare a heavenly home for them and will return to take them so that they may be with Him. This is one of the passages that refers to the rapture of the saints at the end of the age when Christ returns. The features in this description do not describe Christ coming to earth with His saints to establish His kingdom (Rev. 19:11-15), but taking believers from earth to live in heaven. Since no judgment on the unsaved is described here, this is not the event of His return in glory and power to destroy the wicked (cf. Matt. 13:36-43; 47-50). Rather, this describes His coming to gather His own who are alive and raise the bodies of those who have died to take them all to heaven. This rapture event is also described in 1 Cor. 15:51-54; 1 Thess. 4:13-18. After being raptured, the church will celebrate the marriage supper (Rev. 19:7-10), be rewarded (1 Cor. 3:10-15; 4:5; 2 Cor. 5:9,10), and later return to earth with Christ when He comes again to set up His kingdom (Rev. 19:11–20:6).

14:6 This is the sixth "I AM" statement of Jesus in John (see 6:35; 8:12; 10:7,9; 10:11,14; 11:25; 15:1,5). In response to Thomas' query (v. 4), Jesus declared that He is the way to God because He is the truth of God (1:14) and the life of God (1:4; 3:15; 11:25). In this verse, the exclusiveness of Jesus as the only approach to the Father is emphatic. Only one way, not many ways, exist to God, i.e., Jesus Christ (10:7-9; cf. Matt. 7:13,14; Luke 13:24; Acts 4:12).

14:7-11 from now on you know Him. They know God because they had come to know Christ in His ministry and soon in His death and resurrection. To know Him is to know God. This constant emphasis on Jesus as God incarnate is unmistakably clear in this gospel (v. 11; 1:1-3,14,17,18; 5:10-23,26; 8:58; 9:35; 10:30,38; 12:41; 17:1-5; 20:28).

14:12 greater *works* than these he will do. Jesus did not mean greater works in power, but in extent. They would become witnesses to all the world through the power of the indwelling and infilling of the Holy Spirit (Acts 1:8) and would bring many to salvation because of the Comforter dwelling in them. The focus is on spiritual rather than physical miracles. The book of Acts constitutes the beginning historical record of the impact that the Spirit-empowered disciples had on the world (cf. Acts 17:6). **because I go to My Father.** The only way Jesus' disciples would be able to be used to do those greater works was through the power of the Holy Spirit and He could not be sent as the Comforter until Jesus returned to the Father (v. 26; 7:39).

14:13,14 In their hour of loss at the departure of Jesus, He comforted them with the means that would provide them with the necessary resources to accomplish their task without His immediate presence which they had come to depend upon. To ask in Jesus' "name" does not mean to tack such an expression on the end of a prayer as a mere formula. It means: 1) the believer's prayer should be for His purposes and kingdom and not selfish reasons; 2) the believer's prayer should be on the basis of His merits and not any personal merit or worthiness; and 3) the believer's prayer should be in pursuit of His glory alone. *See notes on 16:26-28;* on the disciples' prayer, *see notes on Matt. 6:9,10.*

15 [s]"If you love Me, [4]keep My commandments. 16 And I will pray the Father, and [t]He will give you another [5]Helper, that He may abide with you forever— 17 [u]the Spirit of truth, [v]whom the world cannot receive, because it neither sees Him nor knows Him; but you know Him, for He dwells with you [w]and will be in you. 18 [x]I will not leave you orphans; [y]I will come to you.

19 "A little while longer and the world will see Me no more, but [z]you will see Me. [a]Because I live, you will live also. 20 At that day you will know that [b]I *am* in My Father, and you in Me, and I in you. 21 [c]He who has My commandments and keeps them, it is he who loves Me. And he who loves Me will be loved by My Father, and I will love him and [6]manifest Myself to him."

Christ Answers Judas

22 [d]Judas (not Iscariot) said to Him, "Lord, how is it that You will manifest Yourself to us, and not to the world?"

23 Jesus answered and said to him, "If anyone loves Me, he will keep My word; and My Father will love him, [e]and We will come to him and make Our home with him. 24 He who does not love Me does not keep My words; and [f]the word which you hear is not Mine but the Father's who sent Me.

25 "These things I have spoken to you while being present with you. 26 But [g]the [7]Helper, the Holy Spirit, whom the Father will [h]send in My name, [i]He will teach you all things, and bring to your [j]remembrance all things that I said to you. 27 [k]Peace I leave with you, My peace I give to you; not as the world gives do I give to you. Let not your heart be troubled, neither let it be afraid. 28 You have heard Me [l]say to you, 'I am going away and coming *back* to you.' If you loved Me, you would rejoice because [8]I said, [m]'I am going to the Father,' for [n]My Father is greater than I.

29 "And [o]now I have told you before it comes, that when it does come to pass, you

15 [s]1 John 5:3 [4]NU *you will keep* **16** [t][John 15:26; 20:22]; Acts 2:4, 33; Rom. 8:15 [5]*Comforter,* Gr. *Parakletos* **17** [u][John 15:26; 16:13; 1 John 4:6; 5:7] [v][1 Cor. 2:14] [w][1 John 2:27] **18** [x][Matt. 28:20] [y][John 14:3, 28] **19** [z]John 16:16, 22 [a][Rom. 5:10; 1 Cor. 15:20; 2 Cor. 4:10] **20** [b]John 10:38; 14:11 **21** [c]1 John 2:5 [6]*reveal* **22** [d]Luke 6:16; Acts 1:13 **23** [e]2 Cor. 6:16; Eph. 3:17; [1 John 2:24]; Rev. 3:20; 21:3 **24** [f]John 5:19 **26** [g]Luke 24:49 [h]John 15:26 [i]1 Cor. 2:13 [j]John 2:22; 12:16; 1 John 2:20 [7]*Comforter,* Gr. *Parakletos*

27 [k]Luke 1:79; [John 16:33; 20:19; Phil. 4:7]; Col. 3:15 **28** [l]John 14:3, 18 [m]John 16:16 [n][John 5:18; Phil. 2:6] [8]NU omits *I said* **29** [o]John 13:19

14:15-31 In these verses, Jesus promises believers comfort from 5 supernatural blessings that the world does not enjoy: 1) a supernatural Helper (vv. 15-17); 2) a supernatural life (vv. 18,19); 3) a supernatural union (vv. 20-25), 4) a supernatural Teacher (v. 26); and 5) a supernatural peace (vv. 27-31). The key to all of this is v. 15 which relates that these supernatural promises are for those who love Jesus Christ; whose love is evidenced by obedience.

14:15 If you love Me, keep My commandments. Cf. vv. 21-24. Love for Christ is inseparable from obedience (see Luke 6:46; 1 John 5:2,3). "My commandments" are not only Jesus' ethical commandments in context (vv. 23,24), but the entire revelation from the Father (see 3:31,32; 12:47-49; 17:6).

14:16 pray the Father. The priestly and intercessory work of Christ began with the request that the Father send the Holy Spirit to indwell in the people of faith (7:39; 15:26; 16:7; *see note on 20:22*; cf. Acts 1:8; 2:4,33). **another.** The Gr. word specifically means another of the same kind, i.e., someone like Jesus Himself who will take His place and do His work. The Spirit of Christ is the Third Person of the Trinity, having the same essence of deity as Jesus and as perfectly one with Him as He is with the Father. **Helper.** The Gr. term here lit. means "one called alongside to help" and has the idea of someone who encourages and exhorts (*see note on 16:7*). "Abiding" has to do with His permanent residence in believers (Rom. 8:9; 1 Cor. 6:19,20; 12:13).

14:17 Spirit of truth. He is the Spirit of truth in that He is the source of truth and communicates the truth to His own (v. 26; 16:12-15). Apart from Him, men cannot know God's truth (1 Cor. 2:12-16; 1 John 2:20,27). **dwells with you and will be in you.** This indicates some distinction between the ministry of the Holy Spirit to believers before and after Pentecost. While clearly the Holy Spirit has been with all who have ever believed throughout redemptive history as the source of truth, faith, and life, Jesus is saying something new is coming in His ministry. John 7:37-39 indicates this unique ministry would be like "rivers of living water." Acts 19:1-7 introduces some Old Covenant believers who had not received the Holy Spirit in this unique fullness and intimacy. Cf. Acts 1:8; 2:1-4; 1 Cor. 12:11-13.

14:18 orphans. In this veiled reference to His death, He promised not to leave them alone (Rom. 8:9).

14:18,19 I will come to you…you will see Me. First, He was referring to His resurrection, after which they would see Him (20:19-29). There is no record that any unbelievers saw Him after He rose (see 1 Cor. 15:1-9). In another sense, this has reference to the mystery of the Trinity. Through the coming and indwelling of the Holy Spirit at Pentecost, Jesus would be back with His children (16:16; cf. Matt. 28:20; Rom. 8:9; 1 John 4:13).

14:19 you will live also. Because of His resurrection and by the indwelling life of the Spirit of Christ, believers possess eternal life (see Rom. 6:1-11; Col. 3:1-4).

14:20 At that day. This refers to His resurrection when He returns to them alive.

14:21-24 Once again, Jesus emphasized the need for the habitual practice of obedience to His commands as evidence of the believer's love for Him and the Father (*see note on v. 15*). This is consistent with the teaching of James 2:14-26 that true saving faith is manifest by works produced by God in the transforming, regenerating power of the Spirit. Those works are expressions of the love which the Spirit pours into the believer's heart (Rom. 5:5; Gal. 5:22).

14:26 will teach you all things. The Holy Spirit energized the hearts and minds of the apostles in their ministry, helping them to produce the NT Scripture. The disciples had failed to understand many things about Jesus and what He taught; but because of this supernatural work, they came to an inerrant and accurate understanding of the Lord and His work, and recorded it in the gospels and the rest of the NT Scriptures (2 Tim. 3:16; 2 Pet. 1:20,21). *See note on 16:7.*

14:27 Peace I leave…not as the world gives. The word "peace" reflects the Heb. "Shalom," which became a greeting to His disciples after the resurrection (20:19-26). At the individual level this peace, unknown to the unsaved, secures composure in difficult trouble (cf. v. 1), dissolves fear (Phil. 4:7), and rules in the hearts of God's people to maintain harmony (Col. 3:15). The greatest reality of this peace will be in the messianic kingdom (Num. 6:26; Ps. 29:11; Is. 9:6,7; 52:7; 54:13; 57:19; Ezek. 37:26; Hag. 2:9; cf. Acts 10:36; Rom. 1:7; 5:1; 14:17).

14:28 greater than I. He was not admitting inferiority to the Father (after claiming equality repeatedly, *see note on vv. 7-11*), but was saying that if the disciples loved Him, they would not be reluctant to

may believe. 30 I will no longer talk much
with you, [p]for the ruler of this world is
coming, and he has [q]nothing in Me. 31 But
that the world may know that I love the
Father, and [r]as the Father gave Me commandment, so I do. Arise, let us go from
here.

The Relationship of Believers to Christ

15 "I am the true vine, and My Father is
the vinedresser. 2 [a]Every branch in
Me that does not bear fruit He [1]takes away;
and every *branch* that bears fruit He prunes,
that it may bear [b]more fruit. 3 [c]You are already clean because of the word which I
have spoken to you. 4 [d]Abide in Me, and I
in you. As the branch cannot bear fruit of itself, unless it abides in the vine, neither can
you, unless you abide in Me.
5 "I am the vine, you *are* the branches.
He who abides in Me, and I in him, bears
much [e]fruit; for without Me you can do
[f]nothing. 6 If anyone does not abide in Me,
[g]he is cast out as a branch and is withered;
and they gather them and throw *them* into
the fire, and they are burned. 7 If you abide
in Me, and My words [h]abide in you, [i]you[2]
will ask what you desire, and it shall be
done for you. 8 [j]By this My Father is glorified, that you bear much fruit; [k]so you will
be My disciples.
9 "As the Father [l]loved Me, I also have
loved you; abide in My love. 10 [m]If you
keep My commandments, you will abide
in My love, just as I have kept My Father's
commandments and abide in His love.
11 "These things I have spoken to you,
that My joy may remain in you, and [n]*that*
your joy may be full.

The Relationship of Believers to Each Other

12 [o]This is My [p]commandment, that you
love one another as I have loved you.
13 [q]Greater love has no one than this, than
to lay down one's life for his friends.

30 [p] [John 12:31] [q] [John 8:46; 2 Cor. 5:21; Heb. 4:15; 1 Pet. 1:19; 2:22]
31 [r] Is. 50:5; John 10:18; Phil. 2:8

CHAPTER 15

2 [a] Matt. 15:13 [b] [Matt. 13:12] [1] Or *lifts up*
3 [c] [John 13:10; 17:17]; Eph. 5:26
4 [d] John 17:23; Eph. 3:17; [Col. 1:23]
5 [e] Hos. 14:8; [Gal. 5:22, 23] [f] 2 Cor. 3:5
6 [g] Matt. 3:10
7 [h] 1 John 2:14 [i] John 14:13; 16:23 [2] NU omits *you will*
8 [j] Ps. 22:23; [Matt. 5:16]; John 13:31; 17:4; [Phil. 1:11]; 1 Pet. 4:11 [k] John 8:31
9 [l] John 5:20; 17:26 10 [m] John 14:15 11 [n] [John 16:24]; 1 John 1:4 12 [o] John 13:34; 1 John 3:11 [p] Rom. 12:9 13 [q] Eph. 5:2; 1 John 3:16

let Him go to the Father because He was returning to the realm where He belonged and to the full glory He gave up (17:5). He was going back to share equal glory with the Father which would be greater than what He had experienced in His incarnation. He will in no way be inferior in that glory, because His humiliation was over.

14:30 the ruler of this world. Judas was only a tool of the "prince" who rules the system of darkness—Satan (6:70; 13:21,27). **nothing in Me.** The Heb. idiom means that Satan had nothing on Jesus, could make no claim on Him, nor charge Him with any sin. Therefore, Satan could not hold Him in death. Christ would triumph and destroy Satan (Heb. 2:14). His death was no sign that Satan won, but that God's will was being done. (v. 31).

15:1-17 Through this extended metaphor of the vine and branches, Jesus set forth the basis of Christian living. Jesus used the imagery of agricultural life at the time; i.e., vines and vine crops (see also Matt. 20:1-16; 21:23-41; Mark 12:1-9; Luke 13:6-9; 20:9-16). In the OT, the vine is used commonly as a symbol for Israel, (Ps. 80:9-16; Is. 5:1-7; 27:2-6; Jer. 2:21:12:10; Ezek. 15:1-8; 17:1-21; 19:10-14; Hos. 10:1,2). He specifically identified Himself as the "true vine" and the Father as the "vinedresser" or caretaker of the vine. The vine has two types of branches: 1) branches that bear fruit (vv. 2,8), and 2) branches that do not (vv. 2,6). The branches that bear fruit are genuine believers. Though in immediate context the focus is upon the 11 faithful disciples, the imagery also encompasses all believers down through the ages. The branches that do not bear fruit are those who profess to believe, but their lack of fruit indicates genuine salvation has never taken place and they have no life from the vine. Especially in the immediate context, Judas was in view, but the imagery extends from him to all those who make a profession of faith in Christ but do not actually possess salvation. The image of non-fruit-bearing branches being burned pictures eschatological judgment and eternal rejection (see Ezek. 15:6-8).

15:1 I am the true vine. This is the last of 7 claims to deity in the form of "I AM" statements by Jesus in the gospel of John (see 6:35; 8:12; 10:7,9; 10:11,14; 11:25; 14:6).

15:2 He takes away. The picture is of the vinedresser (i.e., the Father) getting rid of dead wood so that the living, fruit bearing branches may be sharply distinguished. This is a picture of apostate Christians who never genuinely believed and will be taken away in judgment (v. 6; Matt. 7:16; Eph. 2:10); the transforming life of Christ has never pulsated within them (8:31,32; cf. Matt. 13:18-23; 24:12; Heb. 3:14-19; 6:4-8; 10:27-31; 1 John 2:19; 2 John 9). **He prunes.** God removes all things in the believer's life that would hinder fruit-bearing, i.e., he chastises to cut away sin and hindrances that would drain spiritual life just as the farmer removes anything on the branches that keep them from bearing maximum fruit (Heb. 12:3-11).

15:4-6 Abide in Me. The word "abide" means to remain or stay around. The "remaining" is evidence that salvation has already taken place (1 John 2:19) and not vice versa. The fruit or evidence of salvation is continuance in service to Him and in His teaching (8:31; 1 John 2:24; Col. 1:23). The abiding believer is the only legitimate believer. Abiding and believing actually are addressing the same issue of genuine salvation (Heb. 3:6-19). For a discussion of the perseverance of the saints, *see note on Matt. 24:13.*

15:6 The imagery here is one of destruction (cf. Matt. 3:10-12; 5:22; 13:40-42,50; 25:41; Mark 9:43-49; Luke 3:17; 2 Thess. 1:7-9; Rev. 20:10-15). It pictures the judgment awaiting all those who were never saved.

15:7-10 True believers obey the Lord's commands, submitting to His Word (14:21,23). Because of their commitment to God's Word, they are devoted to His will, thus their prayers are fruitful (14:13,14), which puts God's glory on display as He answers.

15:9,10 abide in My love. Cf. Jude 21. This is not emotional or mystical, but defined in v. 10 as obedience. Jesus set the model by His perfect obedience to the Father, which we are to use as the pattern for our obedience to Him.

15:11 your joy may be full. Just as Jesus maintained that His obedience to the Father was the basis of His joy, so also the believers who are obedient to His commandments will experience the same joy (17:13; cf. 16:24).

15:12 Cf. 13:34,35. *See notes on 1 John 2:7-11.*

15:13 This is a reference to the supreme evidence and expression of Jesus' love (v. 12), His sacrificial death upon the cross. Christians are called to exemplify the same kind of sacrificial giving toward one another, even if such sacrifice involves the laying down of one's own life in imitation of Christ's example (cf. 1 John 3:16).

14 [r]You are My friends if you do whatever I
command you. 15 No longer do I call you
servants, for a servant does not know what
his master is doing; but I have called you
friends, [s]for all things that I heard from My
Father I have made known to you. 16 [t]You
did not choose Me, but I chose you and
[u]appointed you that you should go and
bear fruit, and *that* your fruit should remain, that whatever you ask the Father [v]in
My name He may give you. 17 These things
I command you, that you love one another.

The Relationship of Believers to the World

18 [w]"If the world hates you, you know
that it hated Me before *it hated* you. 19 [x]If
you were of the world, the world would
love its own. Yet [y]because you are not of
the world, but I chose you out of the world,
therefore the world hates you. 20 Remember the word that I said to you, [z]'A servant
is not greater than his master.' If they persecuted Me, they will also persecute you.
[a]If they kept My word, they will keep
yours also. 21 But [b]all these things they will
do to you for My name's sake, because they
do not know Him who sent Me. 22 [c]If I had
not come and spoken to them, they would
have no sin, [d]but now they have no excuse
for their sin. 23 [e]He who hates Me hates My
Father also. 24 If I had not done among
them [f]the works which no one else did,
they would have no sin; but now they have
[g]seen and also hated both Me and My Father. 25 But *this happened* that the word
might be fulfilled which is written in their
law, [h]*'They hated Me without a cause.'*

The Promise of the Holy Spirit

26 [i]"But when the [3]Helper comes, whom
I shall send to you from the Father, the
Spirit of truth who proceeds from the Father, [j]He will testify of Me. 27 And [k]you
also will bear witness, because [l]you have
been with Me from the beginning.

16 "These things I have spoken to you,
that you [a]should not be made to
stumble. 2 [b]They will put you out of the
synagogues; yes, the time is coming [c]that
whoever kills you will think that he offers

14 [r][Matt. 12:50; 28:20]; John 14:15, 21; Acts 10:42; 1 John 3:23, 24
15 [s]Gen. 18:17
16 [t]John 6:70; 13:18; 15:19; 1 John 4:10 [u][Matt. 28:19; Mark 16:15; Col. 1:6] [v]John 14:13; 16:23, 24
18 [w]John 7:7; 1 John 3:13
19 [x]1 John 4:5 [y]John 17:14
20 [z]Matt. 10:24; John 13:16 [a]Ezek. 3:7
21 [b]Matt. 10:22; 24:9; [1 Pet. 4:14]; Rev. 2:3
22 [c]John 9:41; 15:24 [d][Rom. 1:20; James 4:17]
23 [e]1 John 2:23
24 [f]John 3:2 [g]John 14:9
25 [h]Ps. 35:19; 69:4; 109:3-5
26 [i]Luke 24:49; [John 14:17]; Acts 2:4, 33 [j]1 John 5:6 [3]*Comforter*, Gr. *Parakletos*
27 [k]Luke 24:48; 1 Pet. 5:1; 2 Pet. 1:16 [l]Matt. 3:14; Luke 1:2; 1 John 1:1
CHAPTER 16 1 [a]Matt. 11:6 2 [b]John 9:22 [c]Acts 8:1

15:14,15 friends. Just as Abraham was called the "friend of God" (2 Chr. 20:7; James 2:23) because he enjoyed extraordinary access to the mind of God through God's revelation to him which he believed, so also those who follow Christ are privileged with extraordinary revelation through the Messiah and Son of God and, believing, become "friends" of God also. It was for His "friends" that the Lord laid down His life (v. 13; 10:11,15,17).

15:16 I chose you. Cf. v. 19. In case any pretense might exist among the disciples in terms of spiritual pride because of the privileges they enjoyed, Jesus made it clear that such privilege rested not in their own merit, but on His sovereign choice of them. God chose Israel (Is. 45:4; Amos 3:2), but not for any merit (Deut. 7:7; 9:4-6). God elected angels to be forever holy (1 Tim. 5:21). He elected believers to salvation apart from any merit (Matt. 24:24,31; *see notes on Rom. 8:29-33; Eph. 1:3-6; Col. 3:12; Titus 1:1; 1 Pet. 1:2*). **bear fruit.** One purpose of God's sovereign election is that the disciples who have been blessed with such revelation and understanding should produce spiritual fruit. The NT describes fruit as godly attitudes (Gal. 5:22,23), righteous behavior (Phil. 1:11), praise (Heb. 13:15), and especially leading others to faith in Jesus as Messiah and Son of God (Rom. 1:13-16).

15:18,19 Since Satan is the one who dominates the evil world system in rebellion against God (14:30), the result is that the world hates not only Jesus, but those who follow Him (2 Tim. 3:12). Hatred toward Jesus means also hatred toward the Father who sent Him (v. 23).

15:20 servant...master. That axiom, spoken also in 13:16, reflects the obvious truth that led Jesus to inform His disciples. They could expect to be treated like He was treated because those who hated Him don't know God (v. 21) and would hate them also; and conversely, those who listened with faith to Him, would hear them also.

15:22-24 they would have no sin. He did not mean that if He had not come, they would have been sinless. But His coming incited the severest and most deadly sin, that of rejecting and rebelling against God and His truth. It was the decisive sin of rejection, the deliberate and fatal choice of darkness over light and death over life of which He spoke. He had done so many miracles and spoken innumerable words to prove He was Messiah and Son of God, but they were belligerent in their love of sin and rejection of the Savior. *See Heb. 4:2-5; 6:4-6; 10:29-31.*

15:25 Jesus quotes Pss. 35:19; 69:4. The logic here is that if David, a mere man, could have been hated in such a terrible manner by the enemies of God, how much more would the wicked hate David's perfect, divine Son who was the promised king that would confront sin and reign forever over His kingdom of righteousness (see 2 Sam 7:16).

15:26,27 when the Helper comes. Again, Jesus promised to send the Holy Spirit (7:39; 14:16,17,26; 16:7,13,14). This time He emphasized the Spirit's help for witnessing—proclaiming the gospel. *See note on 16:7.*

16:1-15 Jesus continued the thoughts of 15:18-25 regarding the world's hatred of His disciples and its opposition to the testimony of the Holy Spirit regarding Him as Messiah and Son of God. In this section, He specified in greater detail how the Spirit confronts the world, i.e., not only does He testify about Jesus but He convicts men of sin. Through conviction of sin and testimony of the gospel, the Spirit turns the hostile hearts of men away from rebellion against God into belief regarding Jesus as Savior and Lord. This section may be divided into 4 parts: 1) the killing of the disciples by the world (vv. 1-4); 2) the comforting of the disciples by the Lord (vv. 5-7); 3) the conviction of men by the Holy Spirit (vv. 8-12); and 4) the guidance of the believer into all truth by the Holy Spirit (vv. 13-15).

16:1 These things. This is what He had just said in 15:18-25. **stumble.** The connotation of this word has the idea of setting a trap. The hatred of the world was such that it would seek to trap and destroy the disciples in an effort to prevent their witness to Jesus as Messiah and Son of God. Jesus did not want them to be caught unaware (v. 4).

16:2 he offers God service. Paul, before he was saved, personified this attitude as he persecuted the church thinking that he was doing service for God (Acts 22:4,5; 26:9-11; Gal. 1:13-17; Phil. 3:6; 1 Tim. 1:12-17). After Paul's conversion, the persecutor became the persecuted because of the hatred of the world (2 Cor. 11:22-27; cf. Stephen in Acts 7:54–8:3).

God service. 3 And [d]these things they will
do [1]to you because they have not known
the Father nor Me. 4 But these things I have
told you, that when [2]the time comes, you
may remember that I told you of them.
“And these things I did not say to you at
the beginning, because I was with you.
5 “But now I [e]go away to Him who sent
Me, and none of you asks Me, ‘Where are
You going?’ 6 But because I have said these
things to you, [f]sorrow has filled your
heart. 7 Nevertheless I tell you the truth. It
is to your advantage that I go away; for if I
do not go away, the Helper will not come
to you; but [g]if I depart, I will send Him to
you. 8 And when He has [h]come, He will
convict the world of sin, and of righteousness, and of judgment: 9 [i]of sin, because
they do not believe in Me; 10 [j]of righteousness, [k]because I go to My Father and you
see Me no more; 11 [l]of judgment, because
[m]the ruler of this world is judged.
12 “I still have many things to say to you,
[n]but you cannot bear *them* now. 13 However, when He, [o]the Spirit of truth, has
come, [p]He will guide you into all truth; for
He will not speak on His own *authority,* but
whatever He hears He will speak; and He
will tell you things to come. 14 [q]He will
glorify Me, for He will take of what is Mine
and declare *it* to you. 15 [r]All things that the
Father has are Mine. Therefore I said that
He [3]will take of Mine and declare *it* to you.

The Prediction of Christ's Death and Resurrection

16 “A [s]little while, and you will not see
Me; and again a little while, and you will
see Me, [t]because I go to the Father.”
17 Then *some* of His disciples said among
themselves, “What is this that He says to
us, ‘A little while, and you will not see Me;
and again a little while, and you will see
Me’; and, ‘because I go to the Father’?”
18 They said therefore, “What is this that
He says, ‘A little while’? We do not [4]know
what He is saying.”
19 Now Jesus knew that they desired to
ask Him, and He said to them, “Are you inquiring among yourselves about what I
said, ‘A little while, and you will not see
Me; and again a little while, and you will
see Me’? 20 Most assuredly, I say to you that
you will weep and [u]lament, but the world
will rejoice; and you will be sorrowful, but
your sorrow will be turned into [v]joy. 21 [w]A

3 [d]John 8:19; 15:21; Acts 13:27; Rom. 10:2 [1]NU, M omit *to you*
4 [2]NU *their*
5 [e]John 7:33; 13:33; 14:28; 17:11
6 [f]Matt. 17:23; [John 16:20, 22]
7 [g]Acts 2:33
8 [h]Acts 1:8; 2:1-4, 37
9 [i]Acts 2:22
10 [j]Acts 2:32 [k]John 5:32
11 [l]Acts 26:18 [m][Luke 10:18]
12 [n]Mark 4:33
13 [o][John 14:17] [p]John 14:26; Acts 11:28; Rev. 1:19
14 [q]John 15:26
15 [r]Matt. 11:27; John 3:35 [3]NU, M *takes of Mine and will declare*
16 [s]John 7:33; 12:35; 13:33; 14:19; 19:40-42; 20:19 [t]John 13:3
18 [4]*understand*
20 [u]Mark 16:10; Luke 23:48; 24:17 [v]Luke 24:32, 41
21 [w]Gen. 3:16; Is. 13:8; 26:17; 42:14; 1 Thess. 5:3

16:4 I was with you. He didn't need to warn them because He was there to protect them.

16:5 none of you asks. Earlier they had done so (13:36; 14:5), but they were then so absorbed in their own sorrow and confusion as to lose interest in where He was going. They were apparently consumed with what would happen to them (v. 6).

16:7 the Helper will not come. Again, the promise of the Holy Spirit being sent is given to comfort the disciples. *See note on 15:26,27.* The first emphasis was on His life-giving power (7:37-39). The next featured His indwelling presence (14:16,17). The next marked His teaching ministry (14:26). His ministry of empowering for witness is marked in 15:26.

16:8 when He has come. The coming of the Holy Spirit at Pentecost was approximately 40 or more days away at this point (see Acts 2:1-13). **convict.** This word has two meanings: 1) the judicial act of conviction with a view toward sentencing (i.e., a courtroom term—conviction of sin) or 2) the act of convincing. Here the second idea is best, since the purpose of the Holy Spirit is not condemnation but conviction of the need for the Savior. The Son does the judgment, with the Father (5:22,27,30). In v. 14, it is said that He will reveal the glories of Christ to His people. He will also inspire the writing of the NT, guiding the apostles to write it (v. 13), and He will reveal "things to come," through the NT prophecies (v. 13).

16:9 sin. The singular indicates that a specific sin is in view; i.e., that of not believing in Jesus as Messiah and Son of God. This is the only sin, ultimately, that damns people to hell (*see note on 8:24*). Though all men are depraved, cursed by their violation of God's law and sinful by nature, what ultimately damns them to hell is their unwillingness to believe in the Lord Jesus Christ as Savior (cf. 8:24).

16:10 righteousness. The Holy Spirit's purpose here is to shatter the pretensions of self-righteousness (hypocrisy), exposing the darkness of the heart (3:19-21; 7:7; 15:22,24). While Jesus was on the earth, He performed this task especially toward the shallowness and emptiness of Judaism that had degenerated into legalistic modes without life-giving reality (e.g., 2:13-22; 5:10-16; 7:24; Is. 64:5,6). With Jesus gone to the Father, the Holy Spirit continues His convicting role.

16:11 judgment. The judgment here in context is that of the world under Satan's control. Its judgments are blind, faulty, and evil as evidenced in their verdict on Christ. The world can't make righteous judgments (7:24), but the Spirit of Christ does (8:16). All Satan's adjudications are lies (8:44-47), so the Spirit convicts men of their false judgment of Christ. Satan, the ruler of the world (14:30; Eph. 2:1-3) who, as the god of this world, has perverted the world's judgment and turned people from believing in Jesus as the Messiah and Son of God (2 Cor. 4:4), was defeated at the cross. While Christ's death looked like Satan's greatest victory, it actually was Satan's destruction (cf. Col. 2:15; Heb. 2:14,15; Rev. 20:10). The Spirit will lead sinners to true judgment.

16:13 all truth. This verse, like 14:26, points to the supernatural revelation of all truth by which God has revealed Himself in Christ (vv. 14,15), particularly. This is the subject of the inspired NT writings. *See note on v. 7.*

16:14 He will glorify Me. This is really the same as v. 13, in that all NT truth revealed by God centers in Christ (Heb. 1:1,2). Christ was the theme of the OT, as the NT claims (1:45; 5:37; Luke 24:27,44; Acts 10:43; 18:28; Rom. 1:1,2; 1 Cor. 15:3; 1 Pet. 1:10,11; Rev. 19:10).

16:16-19 Jesus was referring to His ascension ("you will not see Me") and the coming of the Holy Spirit ("you will see Me"), emphatically claiming that the Spirit and He are one (Rom. 8:9; Phil. 1:19; 1 Pet. 1:11; Rev. 19:10). Christ dwells in believers through the Holy Spirit—in that sense they see Him. *See notes on 14:16-18.*

16:20 sorrow will be turned into joy. The very event that made the hateful realm of mankind ("world") rejoice and cause grief to Jesus' disciples, will be the same event that will lead to the world's sorrow and the believer's joy. The disciples would soon realize the marvelous nature of God's gift of salvation and the Spirit through what He accomplished, and the blessing of answered prayer (v. 24). Acts records the coming of the Holy Spirit and the power and joy (Acts 2:4-47; 13:52) of the early church.

woman, when she is in labor, has sorrow
because her hour has come; but as soon as
she has given birth to the child, she no
longer remembers the anguish, for joy that
a human being has been born into the
world. 22 Therefore you now have sorrow;
but I will see you again and [x]your heart
will rejoice, and your joy no one will take
from you.
23 "And in that day you will ask Me
nothing. [y]Most assuredly, I say to you,
whatever you ask the Father in My name
He will give you. 24 Until now you have
asked nothing in My name. Ask, and you
will receive, [z]that your joy may be [a]full.
25 "These things I have spoken to you in
figurative language; but the time is coming
when I will no longer speak to you in figurative language, but I will tell you [b]plainly
about the Father. 26 In that day you will ask
in My name, and I do not say to you that I
shall pray the Father for you; 27 [c]for the Father Himself loves you, because you have
loved Me, and [d]have believed that I came
forth from God. 28 [e]I came forth from the Father and have come into the world. Again, I
leave the world and go to the Father."
29 His disciples said to Him, "See, now
You are speaking plainly, and using no figure of speech! 30 Now we are sure that [f]You
know all things, and have no need that
anyone should question You. By this [g]we
believe that You came forth from God."
31 Jesus answered them, "Do you now
believe? 32 [h]Indeed the hour is coming,
yes, has now come, that you will be scattered, [i]each to his [5]own, and will leave Me
alone. And [j]yet I am not alone, because the
Father is with Me. 33 These things I have
spoken to you, that [k]in Me you may have
peace. [l]In the world you [6]will have tribulation; but be of good cheer, [m]I have overcome the world."

Christ Prays for Himself

17 Jesus spoke these words, lifted up
His eyes to heaven, and said: "Father, [a]the hour has come. Glorify Your Son,
that Your Son also may glorify You, 2 [b]as
You have given Him authority over all
flesh, that He [1]should give eternal life to as
many [c]as You have given Him. 3 And [d]this

22 [x] Luke 24:41; John 14:1, 27; 20:20; Acts 2:46; 13:52; 1 Pet. 1:8
23 [y] Matt. 7:7; [John 14:13; 15:16]
24 [z] John 17:13 [a] John 15:11
25 [b] John 7:13
27 [c] [John 14:21, 23] [d] John 3:13
28 [e] John 13:1, 3; 16:5, 10, 17
30 [f] John 21:17 [g] John 17:8
32 [h] Zech. 13:7; Matt. 26:31, 56; Mark 14:27, 50; Acts 8:1 [i] John 20:10 [j] John 8:29 [5] *own things* or *place*
33 [k] [Is. 9:6; Rom. 5:1; Eph. 2:14] [l] 2 Tim. 3:12 [m] Rom. 8:37; [1 John 4:4] [6] NU, M omit *will*

CHAPTER 17

1 [a] John 12:23
2 [b] Dan. 7:14; Matt. 11:27; John 3:35; [Phil. 2:10; Heb. 2:8] [1] M *shall*

16:22 I will see you. After the resurrection, Jesus did see His disciples (20:19-29; 21:1-23; cf. 1 Cor. 15:1-8). Beyond that brief time of personal fellowship (Acts 1:1-3), He would be with them permanently in His Spirit (*see notes on vv. 16-19; 14:16-19*).

16:23 in that day. This is a reference to Pentecost when the Holy Spirit came (Acts 2:1-13) and sorrow turned to joy. This is a reference also to the "last days" which were inaugurated after His resurrection and the Spirit's coming (Acts 2:17; 2 Tim. 3:1; Heb. 1:2; James 5:3; 2 Pet. 3:3; 1 John 2:18). **you will ask Me nothing.** After His departure and sending of the Spirit, believers will no longer ask Him since He is not present. Instead, they will ask the Father in His name (*see notes on vv. 26-28; 14:13,14*).

16:24 joy may be full. In this case, the believer's joy will be related to answered prayer and a full supply of heavenly blessing for everything consistent with the purpose of the Lord in one's life. *See note on 15:11.*

16:25 in figurative language. The word means "veiled, pointed statement" that is pregnant with meaning, i.e., something that is obscure. What seemed hard to understand for the disciples during the life of Jesus would become clear after His death, resurrection, and the coming of the Holy Spirit (see vv. 13,14; 14:26; 15:26,27). They would actually understand the ministry of Christ better than they had while they were with Him, as the Spirit inspired them to write the gospels and epistles and ministered in and through them.

16:26-28 I do not say. Christ was clarifying what He meant by praying in His name. He did not mean asking Him to ask the Father, as if the Father was indifferent to believers, but not to His Son. On the contrary, the Father loves Christ's own. In fact, the Father sent the Son to redeem them and then return. Asking in Jesus' name means simply asking on the basis of His merit, His righteousness, and for whatever would honor and glorify Him so as to build His kingdom.

16:33 in Me you may have peace. *See note on 14:27.* **tribulation.** This word often refers to eschatological woes (Mark 13:9; Rom. 2:9) and to persecution of believers because of their testimony for Christ (cf. 15:18–16:4; Acts 11:19; Eph. 3:13). **overcome.** The fundamental ground for endurance in persecution is the victory of Jesus over the world (12:31; 1 Cor. 15:57). Through His impending death, He rendered the world's opposition null and void. While the world continues to attack His people, such attacks fall harmlessly, for Christ's victory has already accomplished a smashing defeat of the whole evil rebellious system. *See notes on Rom. 8:35-39.*

17:1-26 Although Matt. 6:9-13 and Luke 11:2-4 have become known popularly as the "Lord's Prayer," that prayer was actually a prayer taught to the disciples by Jesus as a pattern for their prayers. The prayer recorded here is truly the Lord's Prayer, exhibiting the face to face communion the Son had with the Father. Very little is recorded of the content of Jesus' frequent prayers to the Father (Matt. 14:23; Luke 5:16), so this prayer reveals some of the precious content of the Son's communion and intercession with Him. This chapter is a transitional chapter, marking the end of Jesus' earthly ministry and the beginning of His intercessory ministry for believers (Heb. 7:25). In many respects, the prayer is a summary of John's entire gospel. Its principle themes include: 1) Jesus' obedience to His Father; 2) the glorification of His Father through his death and exaltation; 3) the revelation of God in Jesus Christ; 4) the choosing of the disciples out of the world; 5) their mission to the world; 6) their unity modeled on the unity of the Father and Son; and 7) the believer's final destiny in the presence of the Father and Son. The chapter divides into three parts: 1) Jesus' prayer for Himself (vv. 1-5); 2) Jesus' prayer for the apostles (vv. 6-19); and 3) Jesus' prayer for all NT believers who will form the church (vv. 20-26).

17:1 the hour has come. The time of His death. *See note on 12:23.* **Glorify Your Son.** The very event that would glorify the Son was His death. By it, He has received the adoration, worship, and love of millions whose sins He bore. He accepted this path to glory, knowing that by it He would be exalted to the Father. The goal is that the Father may be glorified for His redemptive plan in the Son. So He sought by His own glory the glory of His Father (13:31,32).

17:2 authority over all flesh. Cf. 5:27; *see note on Matt. 28:18.* **as many as You have given Him.** A reference to God's choosing of those who will come to Christ (*see notes on 6:37,44*). The biblical doctrine of election or predestination is presented throughout the NT (15:16,19; Acts 13:48; Rom. 8:29-33; Eph. 1:3-6; 1 Thess. 2:13; Titus 1:1; 1 Pet. 1:2).

is eternal life, that they may know You,
[e]the only true God, and Jesus Christ
[f]whom You have sent. **4** [g]I have glorified
You on the earth. [h]I have finished the work
[i]which You have given Me to do. **5** And
now, O Father, glorify Me together [2]with
Yourself, with the glory [j]which I had with
You before the world was.

Christ Prays for His Disciples

6 [k]"I have [3]manifested Your name to the
men [l]whom You have given Me out of the
world. [m]They were Yours, You gave them
to Me, and they have kept Your word.
7 Now they have known that all things
which You have given Me are from You.
8 For I have given to them the words
[n]which You have given Me; and they have
received *them,* [o]and have known surely
that I came forth from You; and they have
believed that [p]You sent Me.
9 "I pray for them. [q]I do not pray for the
world but for those whom You have given
Me, for they are Yours. **10** And all Mine are
Yours, and [r]Yours are Mine, and I am glorified in them. **11** [s]Now I am no longer in the
world, but these are in the world, and I come
to You. Holy Father, [t]keep[4] through Your
name those whom You have given Me, that
they may be one [u]as We *are.* **12** While I was
with them [5]in the world, [v]I kept them in
[6]Your name. Those whom You gave Me I
have kept; and [w]none of them is [7]lost [x]ex-
cept the son of [8]perdition, [y]that the Scripture might be fulfilled. **13** But now I come to
You, and these things I speak in the world,
that they may have My joy fulfilled in themselves. **14** I have given them Your word; [z]and
the world has hated them because they are
not of the world, [a]just as I am not of the
world. **15** I do not pray that You should take
them out of the world, but [b]that You should
keep them from the evil one. **16** They are not
of the world, just as I am not of the world.
17 [c]Sanctify[9] them by Your truth. [d]Your
word is truth. **18** [e]As You sent Me into the
world, I also have sent them into the world.
19 And [f]for their sakes I sanctify Myself, that
they also may be sanctified by the truth.

Christ Prays for All Believers

20 "I do not pray for these alone, but also
for those who [1]will believe in Me through
their word; **21** [g]that they all may be one, as
[h]You, Father, *are* in Me, and I in You; that

2 [c]John 6:37, 39; 17:6, 9, 24 **3** [d][Is. 53:11]; Jer. 9:23, 24 [e]1 Cor. 8:4; 1 Thess. 1:9 [f]John 3:34 **4** [g]John 13:31 [h][Dan. 9:24]; John 4:34; 19:30 [i]Is. 49:3; 50:5; John 14:31 **5** [j]Prov. 8:22–30; John 1:1, 2; Phil. 2:6; Col. 1:15; Heb. 1:3 [2]Lit. *alongside* **6** [k]Ps. 22:22 [l]John 6:37 [m]Ezek. 18:4; Rom. 14:8 [3]*revealed* **8** [n]John 8:28 [o]John 8:42; 16:27, 30 [p]Deut. 18:15, 18 **9** [q][1 John 5:19] **10** [r]John 16:15 **11** [s][Mark 16:19; Luke 24:51]; John 13:1; [Acts 1:9; Heb. 4:14; 9:24; 1 Pet. 3:22] [t][1 Pet. 1:5]; Jude 1 [u]John 10:30 [4]NU, M *keep them through Your name which You have given Me* **12** [v]Heb. 2:13 [w][John 6:39; 18:9]; 1 John 2:19 [x]Matt. 27:4, 5; John 6:70; Acts 1:16-20 [y]Ps. 41:9; 109:8; John 13:18; Acts 1:20 [5]NU omits *in the world* [6]NU *Your name which You gave Me. And I guarded them;* (or *it;*) [7]*destroyed* [8]*destruction* **14** [z]Matt. 24:9; Luke 6:22; 21:17; John 15:19; 1 John 3:13 [a]John 8:23 **15** [b]Matt. 6:13; Gal. 1:4; 2 Thess. 3:3; [2 Tim. 4:18]; 2 Pet. 2:9; 1 John 5:18 **17** [c][Acts 15:9; Eph. 5:26; 1 Pet. 1:22] [d]Ps. 119:9, 142, 151 [9]*Set them apart* **18** [e]John 4:38; 20:21 **19** [f]1 Cor. 1:2; 1 Thess. 4:7; [Heb. 10:10] **20** [1]NU, M omit *will* **21** [g][John 10:16; Rom. 12:5; Gal. 3:28]; Eph. 4:4, 6

17:3 eternal life. *See notes on 3:15,16; 5:24;* cf. 1 John 5:20.

17:5 glorify Me together with Yourself. Having completed His work (v. 4), Jesus looked past the cross and asked to be returned to the glory that He shared with the Father before the world began (*see notes on 1:1; 8:58; 12:41*). The actual completion of bearing judgment wrath for sinners was declared by Christ in the cry, "It is finished" (19:30).

17:6-10 They were Yours. This phrase sums up all of Jesus' ministry, including the cross that was just hours away. Again, the Son emphasized that those who believed in Him were given by the Father (*see note on v. 2*). "They were Yours" (cf. v. 9) is a potent assertion that before conversion, they belonged to God (cf. 6:37). That is true because of God's election. They were chosen before the foundation of the world (Eph. 1:4), when their names were written in the Lamb's book of life (Rev. 17:8). Cf. Acts 18:10, where God says He has many people in Corinth who belong to Him but are not yet saved. *See notes on 10:1-5,16.*

17:8 they have believed. The Son of God affirmed the genuine saving faith of His disciples.

17:11 I am no longer in the world. So sure was His death and departure back to the Father that Jesus treated His departure as an already accomplished fact. He prayed here for His disciples because they would have to face the world's temptation and hatred without His immediate presence and protection (15:18–16:4). Based on the eternal nature of immutable God ("name"), He prayed for the eternal security of those who believed. He prayed that as the Trinity experiences eternal unity, so may believers. See Rom. 8:31-39.

17:12 I kept them in Your name. Jesus protected them and kept them safe from the world as He said in 6:37-40,44. One illustration of that can be seen in 18:1-11. Believers are secure forever because they are held by Christ and by God. *See notes on 10:28,29.* **son of perdition.** This identifies Judas by pointing to his destiny, i.e., eternal damnation (Matt. 7:13; Acts 8:20; Rom. 9:22; Phil. 1:28; 3:19; 1 Tim. 6:9; Heb. 10:39; 2 Pet. 2:1; 3:7; Rev. 17:8,11). The defection of Judas was not a failure on Jesus part, but was foreseen and foreordained in Scripture (Pss. 41:9; 109:8; cf. 13:18).

17:15 keep them from the evil one. The reference here refers to protection from Satan and all the wicked forces following him (Matt. 6:13; 1 John 2:13,14; 3:12; 5:18,19). Though Jesus' sacrifice on the cross was the defeat of Satan, he is still loose and orchestrating his evil system against believers. He seeks to destroy believers (1 Pet. 5:8), as with Job and Peter (Luke 22:31,32), and in general (Eph. 6:12), but God is their strong protector (12:31; 16:11; cf. Ps. 27:1-3; 2 Cor. 4:4; Jude 24,25).

17:17 Sanctify. This verb also occurs in John's gospel at v. 19; 10:36. The idea of sanctification is the setting apart of something for a particular use. Accordingly, believers are set apart for God and His purposes alone so that the believer does only what God wants and hates all that God hates (Lev. 11:44,45; 1 Peter 1:16). Sanctification is accomplished by means of the truth, which is the revelation that the Son gave regarding all that the Father commanded Him to communicate and is now contained in the Scriptures left by the apostles. Cf. Eph. 5:26; 2 Thess. 2:13; James 1:21; 1 Pet. 1:22,23.

17:19 I sanctify Myself. Meaning only that He was totally set apart for the Father's will (cf. 4:34; 5:19; 6:38; 7:16; 9:4). He did that in order that believers might be set apart to God by the truth He brought.

17:21 they all may be one. The basis of this unity centers in adherence to the revelation the Father mediated to His first disciples through His Son. Believers are also to be united in the common belief of the truth that was received in the Word of God (Phil. 2:2). This is not still a wish, but it became a reality when the Spirit came (cf. Acts 2:4; 1 Cor. 12:13). It is not experiential unity, but the unity of common eternal life shared by all who believe the truth, and it results in the one body of Christ all sharing His life. *See notes on Eph. 4:4-6.*

they also may be one in Us, that the world
may believe that You sent Me. 22 And the
[i]glory which You gave Me I have given
them, [j]that they may be one just as We are
one: 23 I in them, and You in Me; [k]that they
may be made perfect in one, and that the
world may know that You have sent Me,
and have loved them as You have loved Me.
24 [l]"Father, I desire that they also whom
You gave Me may be with Me where I am,
that they may behold My glory which You
have given Me; [m]for You loved Me before
the foundation of the world. 25 O righteous
Father! [n]The world has not known You,
but [o]I have known You; and [p]these have
known that You sent Me. 26 [q]And I have
declared to them Your name, and will declare *it,* that the love [r]with which You
loved Me may be in them, and I in them."

The Arrest of Christ
Matt. 26:47-56; Mark 14:43-52; Luke 22:47-53

18 When Jesus had spoken these words,
[a]He went out with His disciples over
[b]the Brook Kidron, where there was a garden, which He and His disciples entered.

21 [h]John 10:38; 17:11, 23
22 [i]John 14:20; 1 John 1:3 [j][2 Cor. 3:18]
23 [k][Col. 3:14]
24 [l][John 12:26; 14:3; 1 Thess. 4:17] [m]Matt. 25:34; John 17:5
25 [n]John 15:21 [o]John 7:29; 8:55; 10:15 [p]John 3:17; 17:3, 8, 18, 21, 23
26 [q]Ex. 34:5-7; John 17:6 [r]John 15:9; [Eph. 3:17-19]

CHAPTER 18
1 [a]Matt. 26:30, 36; Mark 14:26, 32; Luke 22:39 [b]2 Sam. 15:23; 1 Kin. 2:37; 15:13; 2 Kin. 23:4, 6, 12; 2 Chr. 15:16; 29:16; 30:14; Jer. 31:40
2 [c]Luke 21:37; 22:39
3 [d]Matt. 26:47-56; Mark 14:43-50; Luke 22:47-53; Acts 1:16
4 [e]John 6:64; 13:1, 3; 19:28

2 And Judas, who betrayed Him, also knew
the place; [c]for Jesus often met there with
His disciples. 3 [d]Then Judas, having received a detachment *of troops,* and officers
from the chief priests and Pharisees, came
there with lanterns, torches, and weapons.
4 Jesus therefore, [e]knowing all things that
would come upon Him, went forward and
said to them, "Whom are you seeking?"
5 They answered Him, [f]"Jesus [1]of Nazareth."
Jesus said to them, "I am *He.*" And Judas, who [g]betrayed Him, also stood with
them. 6 Now when He said to them, "I am
He," they drew back and fell to the ground.
7 Then He asked them again, "Whom
are you seeking?"
And they said, "Jesus of Nazareth."
8 Jesus answered, "I have told you that I
am *He.* Therefore, if you seek Me, let these
go their way," 9 that the saying might be
fulfilled which He spoke, [h]"Of those
whom You gave Me I have lost none."
10 [i]Then Simon Peter, having a sword,

5 [f]Matt. 21:11; Mark 1:24; 14:67; 16:6; Luke 18:37; 24:19 [g]Ps. 41:9; Matt. 20:18; 26:21; John 13:21 [1]Lit. *the Nazarene* 9 [h][John 6:39; 17:12]

17:22 the glory which You gave Me. This refers to the believer's participation in all of the attributes and essence of God through the indwelling presence of the Holy Spirit (v. 10; cf. Col. 1:27; 2 Pet. 1:4), as v. 23 makes clear ("I in them").

17:23 made perfect in one. The idea here is that they may be brought together in the same spiritual life around the truth that saves. That prayer was answered by the reality of 1 Cor. 12:12,13; Eph. 2:14-22.

17:24 be with Me. This will be in heaven, where one can see the full glory that is His (cf. v. 5). Someday believers will not only see His glory, but share it (Phil. 3:20,21; 1 John 3:2). Until then, we participate in it spiritually (2 Cor. 3:18).

17:25,26 This summarizes the prayer of this chapter and promises the continuing indwelling Christ and His love. Cf. Rom. 5:5.

18:1-40 The events of Jesus' arrest and trial receive emphasis in this chapter. Since John's purpose was to present Jesus as the Messiah and Son of God, he produced evidence to substantiate this purpose throughout his account of Jesus' passion. Through all of the debasing, shameful acts that were directed toward Jesus, John skillfully shows that these events, rather than detracting from His person and mission, actually constitute decisive evidence confirming who He was and the reason for which He came (1:29; cf. 2 Cor. 5:21).

18:1 He went out. Jesus' supreme courage is seen in His determination to go to the cross, where His purity and sinlessness would be violated as He bore the wrath of God for the sins of the world (3:16; *see note on 12:27*). The time of "the power of darkness" had come (Luke 22:53; *see notes on 1:5; 9:4; 13:30*). **Brook Kidron.** "Brook" signifies that it was an intermittent stream that was dry most of the year but became a torrent during seasonal rains. This stream ran through the Kidron Valley between the temple mount on the E of Jerusalem and the Mt. of Olives further to the E. **a garden.** On the slopes of the Mt. of Olives, named for ever present olive groves, were many gardens. Matthew 26:36 and Mark 14:32 call this particular garden "Gethsemane," which means "oil press." **entered.** The wording here suggests a walled enclosure around the garden.

18:3 a detachment *of troops,* and officers from the chief priests and Pharisees. The term "detachment of troops" refers to a cohort of Roman troops. A full auxiliary cohort had the potential strength of 1,000 men (i.e., 760 foot soldiers and 240 cavalry led by a *chiliarch* or "leader of a thousand"). Usually, however, in practice a cohort normally numbered 600 men, but could sometimes refer to as little as 200 (i.e., a "maniple"). Roman auxiliary troops were usually stationed at Caesarea, but during feast days they were garrisoned in the Antonia Fortress, on the NW perimeter of the temple complex (in order to ensure against mob violence or rebellion because of the large population that filled Jerusalem). The second group designated as "officers" refers to temple police who were the primary arresting officers since Jesus' destination after the arrest was to be brought before the High-Priest (vv. 12-14). They came ready for resistance from Jesus and His followers ("weapons").

18:4 knowing all things. John, in a matter-of-fact way, states that Jesus was omniscient, thus God.

18:4-8 "Whom are you seeking?" By twice asking that question (vv. 4,7), to which they replied, "Jesus of Nazareth" (vv. 5,7), Jesus was forcing them to acknowledge that they had no authority to take His disciples. In fact, He demanded that they let the disciples go (v. 8). The force of His demand was established by the power of His words. When He spoke, "I am *He*" (v. 6), a designation He had used before to declare Himself God (8:28,58; cf. 6:35; 8:12; 10:7,9,11,14; 11:25; 14:6; 15:1,5), they were jolted backward and to the ground (v. 6). This power display and the authoritative demand not to take the disciples was of immense significance, as the next verse indicates.

18:9 I have lost none. Jesus was saying that He protected the disciples from being arrested, so He would not lose any of them, thus fulfilling the promises He made earlier (6:39,40,44; 10:28; 17:12). He knew that being arrested and perhaps imprisoned or executed was more than they could bear, and it could shatter their faith. So He made sure it did not happen. All believers are weak and vulnerable if not protected by the Lord. But He will never let them be tempted beyond what they can bear (1 Cor. 10:13), as evidenced here. Believers are eternally secure, not in their own strength, but by the gracious and constant protection of the Savior (cf. Rom. 8:35-39).

drew it and struck the high priest's servant, and cut off his right ear. The servant's
name was Malchus.
11 So Jesus said to Peter, "Put your
sword into the sheath. Shall I not drink [j]the
cup which My Father has given Me?"

First Jewish Trial Before Annas
Matt. 26:69, 70; Mark 14:66-68; Luke 22:55-57

12 Then the detachment *of troops* and the
captain and the officers of the Jews arrested Jesus and bound Him. 13 And [k]they led
Him away to [l]Annas first, for he was the
father-in-law of [m]Caiaphas who was high
priest that year. 14 [n]Now it was Caiaphas
who advised the Jews that it was [2]expedi-
ent that one man should die for the people.
15 [o]And Simon Peter followed Jesus, and
so *did* [p]another[3] disciple. Now that disciple was known to the high priest, and
went with Jesus into the courtyard of the
high priest. 16 [q]But Peter stood at the door
outside. Then the other disciple, who was
known to the high priest, went out and
spoke to her who kept the door, and
brought Peter in. 17 Then the servant girl
who kept the door said to Peter, "You are
not also *one* of this Man's disciples, are
you?"
He said, "I am [r]not."
18 Now the servants and officers who
had made a fire of coals stood there, for it
was cold, and they warmed themselves.
And Peter stood with them and warmed
himself.
19 The high priest then asked Jesus
about His disciples and His doctrine.
20 Jesus answered him, [s]"I spoke openly
to the world. I always taught [t]in synagogues and [u]in the temple, where [4]the
Jews always meet, and in secret I have said
nothing. 21 Why do you ask Me? Ask
[v]those who have heard Me what I said to
them. Indeed they know what I said."
22 And when He had said these things,
one of the officers who stood by [w]struck[5]
Jesus with the palm of his hand, saying,
"Do You answer the high priest like that?"
23 Jesus answered him, "If I have spoken
evil, bear witness of the evil; but if well,
why do you strike Me?"

Second Jewish Trial Before Caiaphas
Matt. 26:57-68, 73-75; Mark 14:53-65, 70-72;
Luke 22:59-65

24 [x]Then Annas sent Him bound to [y]Ca-
iaphas the high priest.
25 Now Simon Peter stood and warmed
himself. [z]Therefore they said to him, "You
are not also *one* of His disciples, are you?"
He denied *it* and said, "I am not!"
26 One of the servants of the high priest,
a relative *of him* whose ear Peter cut off,
said, "Did I not see you in the garden with
Him?" 27 Peter then denied again; and
[a]immediately a rooster crowed.

10 [i]Matt. 26:51; Mark 14:47; Luke 22:49, 50
11 [j]Matt. 20:22; 26:39; Mark 14:36; Luke 22:42
13 [k]Matt. 26:57 [l]Luke 3:2; John 18:24; Acts 4:6 [m]Matt. 26:3; John 11:49, 51
14 [n]John 11:50 [2]*advantageous*
15 [o]Matt. 26:58; Mark 14:54; Luke 22:54 [p]John 20:2-5 [3]M *the other*
16 [q]Matt. 26:69; Mark 14:66-68; Luke 22:55-57
17 [r]Matt. 26:34
20 [s]Matt. 26:55; Luke 4:15; John 8:26 [t]John 6:59 [u]Mark 14:49; John 7:14, 28 [4]NU *all the Jews meet*
21 [v]Mark 12:37
22 [w]Job 16:10; Is. 50:6; Jer. 20:2; Lam. 3:30; Acts 23:2 [5]Lit. *gave Jesus a slap*,
24 [x]Matt. 26:57; Luke 3:2; Acts 4:6 [y]John 11:49
25 [z]Matt. 26:71-75; Mark 14:69-72; Luke 22:58-62
27 [a]Matt. 26:74; Mark 14:72; Luke 22:60; John 13:38

18:10 Simon Peter. He surely aimed for Malchus' head, ready to start the battle in defense of His Lord, but his was an ignorant love and courage. Christ healed his ear (Luke 22:51).

18:11 drink the cup. Peter's impetuous bravery in v. 10 was not only misguided, but exhibited failure to understand the centrality of the death that Jesus came to die. The "cup" in the OT is associated with suffering and especially judgment, i.e., the cup of God's wrath (Ps. 75:8; Is. 51:17,22; Jer. 25:15; Ezek. 23:31-34; *see notes on Matt. 26:39; Mark 14:36; Luke 22:42*; cf. Rev. 14:10; 16:19).

18:13 Annas first. Annas held the High-Priesthood office from A.D. 6–15 when Valerius Gratus, Pilate's predecessor, removed him from office. In spite of this, Annas continued to wield influence over the office, most likely because He was still regarded as the true High-Priest and also because no fewer than 5 of his sons, and his son-in-law Caiaphas, held the office at one time or another. Two trials occurred: one Jewish and one Roman. The Jewish phase began with the informal examination by Annas (vv. 12-14,19-23), probably giving time for the members of the Sanhedrin to hurriedly gather together. A session before the Sanhedrin was next (Matt. 26:57-68) at which consensus was reached to send Jesus to Pilate (Matt. 27:1,2). The Roman phase began with a first examination before Pilate (vv. 28-38a; Matt. 27:11-14) and then Herod Antipas ("that fox"—Luke 13:32) interrogated Him (Luke 23:6-12). Lastly, Jesus appeared again before Pilate (vv. 38b–19:16; Matt. 27:15-31).

18:13,14 Caiaphas. *See notes on 11:49.* The examination under Caiaphas was not reported by John (see Matt. 26:57-68).

18:15 another disciple...that disciple. Traditionally this person has been identified with the "beloved disciple" (13:23,24), i.e., John the apostle who authored this gospel, but he never mentioned his own name (see Introduction: Author and Date).

18:16-18 Peter. Here is the record of the first of Peter's predicted 3 denials (*see note on 18:25-27*).

18:16 known to the high priest. Apparently, John was more than just an acquaintance, because the term for "known" can mean a friend (Luke 2:44). The fact that he mentioned Nicodemus (3:1) and Joseph (19:38) may indicate his knowledge of other prominent Jews.

18:19 At the core of their concern was Jesus' claim that He was the Son of God (19:7). In a formal Jewish hearing, to question the defendant may have been illegal because a case had to rest on the weight of the testimony of witnesses (*see note on 1:7*). If this was an informal interrogation before the High-Priest emeritus and not before the Sanhedrin, Annas may have thought that He was not bound by such rules. Jesus, however, knew the law and demanded that witnesses be called (vv. 20,21). An official knew Jesus was rebuking Annas and retaliated (v. 22).

18:23 In essence, Jesus was asking for a fair trial, while His opponents, who had already decided on the sentence (see 11:47-57), had no intention of providing one.

18:24 Annas recognized that he was not getting anywhere with Jesus and sent Him to Caiaphas because, if Jesus was to be brought before Pilate for execution, the legal accusation must be brought by the current reigning High-Priest (i.e., Caiaphas) in his capacity as chairman of the Sanhedrin (*see also note on v. 13*).

18:25-27 Simon Peter. Here was the final fulfillment of Jesus' prediction that Peter would deny Him 3 times (cf. Matt. 26:34).

First Roman Trial Before Pilate
Matt. 27:2, 11-14; Mark 15:1-5; Luke 23:1-5

28 [b]Then they led Jesus from Caiaphas to
the Praetorium, and it was early morning.
[c]But they themselves did not go into the
[6]Praetorium, lest they should be defiled,
but that they might eat the Passover. 29 [d]Pi-
late then went out to them and said, "What
accusation do you bring against this
Man?"
30 They answered and said to him, "If
He were not [7]an evildoer, we would not
have delivered Him up to you."
31 Then Pilate said to them, "You take
Him and judge Him according to your
law."
Therefore the Jews said to him, "It is not
lawful for us to put anyone to death,"
32 [e]that the saying of Jesus might be fulfilled which He spoke, [f]signifying by what
death He would die.
33 [g]Then Pilate entered the [8]Praetorium
again, called Jesus, and said to Him, "Are
You the King of the Jews?"
34 Jesus answered him, "Are you speaking for yourself about this, or did others
tell you this concerning Me?"
35 Pilate answered, "Am I a Jew? Your
own nation and the chief priests have delivered You to me. What have You done?"
36 [h]Jesus answered, [i]"My kingdom is
not of this world. If My kingdom were of
this world, My servants would fight, so
that I should not be delivered to the Jews;
but now My kingdom is not from here."
37 Pilate therefore said to Him, "Are You
a king then?"
Jesus answered, "You say *rightly* that I
am a king. For this cause I was born, and
for this cause I have come into the world,
[j]that I should bear [k]witness to the truth.
Everyone who [l]is of the truth [m]hears My
voice."
38 Pilate said to Him, "What is truth?"
And when he had said this, he went out
again to the Jews, and said to them, [n]"I
find no fault in Him at all.

Second Roman Trial Before Pilate
Matt. 27:15-31; Mark 15:6-20; Luke 23:13-25

39 [o]"But you have a custom that I should
release someone to you at the Passover. Do
you therefore want me to release to you the
King of the Jews?"
40 [p]Then they all cried again, saying,
"Not this Man, but Barabbas!" [q]Now Barabbas was a robber.

28 [b] Matt. 27:2; Mark 15:1; Luke 23:1; Acts 3:13 [c] John 11:55; Acts 10:28; 11:3 [6] The governor's headquarters
29 [d] Matt. 27:11-14; Mark 15:2-5; Luke 23:2, 3
30 [7] *a criminal*
32 [e] Matt. 20:17-19; 26:2; Mark 10:33; Luke 18:32 [f] John 3:14; 8:28; 12:32, 33
33 [g] Matt. 27:11 [8] The governor's headquarters
36 [h] 1 Tim. 6:13 [i] [Dan. 2:44; 7:14]; Luke 12:14; John 6:15; 8:15
37 [j] [Matt. 5:17; 20:28; Luke 4:43; 12:49; 19:10; John 3:17; 9:39; 10:10; 12:47] [k] Is. 55:4; Rev. 1:5 [l] [John 14:6] [m] John 8:47; 10:27; [1 John 3:19; 4:6]
38 [n] Is. 53:9; Matt. 27:24; Luke 23:4; John 19:4, 6; 1 Pet. 2:22-24
39 [o] Matt. 27:15-26; Mark 15:6-15; Luke 23:17-25
40 [p] Is. 53:3; Acts 3:14 [q] Luke 23:19

18:28–19:16 This section deals with Jesus' trial before Pilate. Although Pilate appears in every scene here, Jesus Himself and the nature of His kingdom occupy center stage.

18:28 Praetorium. The headquarters of the commanding officer of the Roman military camp or the headquarters of the Roman military governor (i.e., Pilate). Pilate's normal headquarters was in Caesarea, in the palace that Herod the Great had built for himself. However, Pilate and his predecessors made it a point to be in Jerusalem during the feasts in order to quell any riots. Jerusalem became his *praetorium* or headquarters. **early morning.** The word is ambiguous. Most likely, it refers to around 6:00 a.m. since many Roman officials began their day very early and finished by 10:00 or 11:00 a.m. **lest they should be defiled.** Jewish oral law gives evidence that a Jew who entered the dwelling places of Gentiles became ceremonially unclean. Their remaining outside in the colonnade avoided that pollution. John loads this statement with great irony by noting the chief priests' scrupulousness in the matter of ceremonial cleansing, when all the time they were incurring incomparably greater moral defilement by their proceedings against Jesus.

18:29 What accusation. This question formally opened the Roman civil phase of proceedings against Jesus (in contrast to the religious phase before the Jews in v. 24). The fact that Roman troops were used at the arrest (*see note on v. 3*) proves that the Jewish authorities communicated something about this case to Pilate in advance. Although they most likely had expected Pilate to confirm their judgment against Jesus and order His death sentence, Pilate ordered instead a fresh hearing in his presence.

18:31 It is not lawful. When Rome took over Judea and began direct rule through a prefect in A.D. 6, capital jurisdiction (i.e., the right to execute) was taken away from the Jews and given to the Roman governor. Capital punishment was the most jealously guarded of all the attributes in Roman provincial administration.

18:32 the saying of Jesus...fulfilled. Jesus had said that He would die by being "lifted up" (3:14; 8:28; 12:32,33). If the Jews had executed Him it would have been by throwing Him down and stoning Him. But God providentially controlled all the political procedures to assure that when sentence was finally passed, He would be crucified by the Romans and not stoned by the Jews, as was Stephen (Acts 7:59). The Jews may have preferred this form of execution based on Deut. 21:23.

18:34 others. Again (cf. vv. 20,21), Jesus demanded witnesses.

18:36 My kingdom is not of this world. By this phrase, Jesus meant that His kingdom is not connected to earthly political and national entities, nor does it have its origin in the evil world system that is in rebellion against God. If His kingdom was of this world, He would have fought. The kingships of this world preserve themselves by fighting with force. Messiah's kingdom does not originate in the efforts of man but with the Son of Man forcefully and decisively conquering sin in the lives of His people and someday conquering the evil world system at His second coming when He establishes the earthly form of His kingdom. His kingdom was no threat to the national identity of Israel or the political and military identity of Rome. It exists in the spiritual dimension until the end of the age (Rev. 11:15).

18:38 "What is truth?" In response to Jesus' mention of "truth" in v. 37, Pilate responded rhetorically with cynicism, convinced that no answer existed to the question. The retort proved that he was not among those whom the Father had given to the Son ("Everyone who is of the truth hears My voice"—v. 37; *see notes on 10:1-5*). **no fault.** Cf. 19:4. John made it clear that Jesus was not guilty of any sin or crime, thus exhibiting the severe injustice and guilt of both the Jews and Romans who executed Him.

18:40 Now Barabbas was a robber. The word "robber" means "one who seizes plunder" and may depict not only a robber but a terrorist or guerrilla fighter who participated in bloody insurrection (see Mark 15:7).

19

So then [a]Pilate took Jesus and
scourged *Him.* 2 And the soldiers
twisted a crown of thorns and put *it* on
His head, and they put on Him a purple
robe. 3 [1]Then they said, "Hail, King of the
Jews!" And they [b]struck Him with their
hands.
4 Pilate then went out again, and said to
them, "Behold, I am bringing Him out to
you, [c]that you may know that I find no
fault in Him."
5 Then Jesus came out, wearing the
crown of thorns and the purple robe. And
Pilate said to them, "Behold the Man!"
6 [d]Therefore, when the chief priests and
officers saw Him, they cried out, saying,
"Crucify *Him,* crucify *Him!*"
Pilate said to them, "You take Him and
crucify *Him,* for I find no fault in Him."
7 The Jews answered him, [e]"We have a
law, and according to [2]our law He ought to
die, because [f]He made Himself the Son of
God."
8 Therefore, when Pilate heard that saying, he was the more afraid, 9 and went
again into the Praetorium, and said to Jesus, "Where are You from?" [g]But Jesus
gave him no answer.
10 Then Pilate said to Him, "Are You not
speaking to me? Do You not know that I
have [3]power to crucify You, and [3]power to
release You?"
11 Jesus answered, [h]"You could have no
power at all against Me unless it had been
given you from above. Therefore [i]the one
who delivered Me to you has the greater
sin."
12 From then on Pilate sought to release
Him, but the Jews cried out, saying, "If you
let this Man go, you are not Caesar's
friend. [j]Whoever makes himself a king
speaks against Caesar."
13 [k]When Pilate therefore heard that saying, he brought Jesus out and sat down in
the judgment seat in a place that is called
The Pavement, but in Hebrew, Gabbatha.
14 Now [l]it was the Preparation Day of the

CHAPTER 19

1 [a] Matt. 20:19; 27:26; Mark 15:15; Luke 18:33
3 [b] Is. 50:6 [1] NU *And they came up to Him and said*
4 [c] Is. 53:9; John 18:33, 38; 1 Pet. 2:22-24
6 [d] Acts 3:13
7 [e] Lev. 24:16 [f] Matt. 26:63-66; John 5:18; 10:33 [2] NU *the law*
9 [g] Is. 53:7; Matt. 27:12, 14; Luke 23:9
10 [3] *authority*
11 [h] [Luke 22:53]; John 7:30 [i] John 3:27; Rom. 13:1
12 [j] Luke 23:2; John 18:33; Acts 17:7
13 [k] Deut. 1:17; 1 Sam. 15:24; Prov. 29:25; Is. 51:12; Acts 4:19
14 [l] Matt. 27:62; John 19:31, 42

19:1 scourged. Pilate appears to have flogged Jesus as a strategy to set Him free (see vv. 4-6). He was hoping that the Jews would be appeased by this action and that sympathy for Jesus' suffering would result in their desire that He be released (see Luke 23:13-16). Scourging was a horribly cruel act in which the victim was stripped, tied to a post and beaten by several torturers, i.e., soldiers who alternated when exhausted. For victims who were not Roman citizens, the preferred instrument was a short wooden handle to which several leather thongs were attached. Each leather thong had pieces of bones or metal on the end. The beatings were so savage that sometimes victims died. The body could be torn or lacerated to such an extent that muscles, veins or bones were exposed. Such flogging often preceded execution in order to weaken and dehumanize the victim (Is. 53:5). Apparently, however, Pilate intended this to create sympathy for Jesus.

19:2 crown of thorns. This "crown" was made from the long spikes (up to 12 inches) of a date palm formed into an imitation of the radiating crowns which oriental kings wore. The long thorns would have cut deeply into Jesus' head, adding to the pain and bleeding. **purple robe.** The color represented royalty. The robe probably was a military cloak flung around Jesus' shoulders, intended to mock His claim to be King of the Jews.

19:4 I find no fault in Him. *See note on 18:38.*

19:5 "Behold the Man!" Pilate dramatically presented Jesus after His torturous treatment by the soldiers. Jesus would have been swollen, bruised, and bleeding. Pilate displayed Jesus as a beaten and pathetic figure hoping to gain the people's choice of Jesus for release. Pilate's phrase is filled with sarcasm since He was attempting to impress upon the Jewish authorities that Jesus was not the dangerous man that they had made Him out to be.

19:6 You take Him and crucify *Him*. The pronouns "you" and "Him" have an emphatic force indicating Pilate's disgust and indignation at the Jews for their callousness toward Jesus.

19:7 We have a law. This probably refers to Lev. 24:16: "whoever blasphemes the name of the LORD shall surely be put to death." The charge of blasphemy (5:18; 8:58,59; 10:33,36) was central in Jesus' trial before Caiaphas (see Matt. 26:57-68).

19:8 more afraid. Many Roman officials were deeply superstitious. While Jews interpreted Jesus' claims as messianic, to the Greco-Roman person, the title "Son of God" would place Jesus in the category of "divine men" who were gifted with supernatural powers. Pilate was afraid because he had just whipped and tortured someone who, in his mind, could bring down a curse or vengeance upon him.

19:9 "Where are You from?" He was concerned about Jesus' origins. His superstitious mind was wondering with just what kind of person was he dealing.

19:11 Jesus' statement here indicates that even the worst evil cannot escape the sovereignty of God. Pilate had no real control (vv. 10,11), yet still stood as a responsible moral agent for his actions. When confronted with opposition and evil, Jesus often found solace in the sovereignty of His Father (e.g., 6:43,44,65; 10:18,28,29). **the one who delivered Me to you has the greater sin.** This could refer either to Judas or Caiaphas. Since Caiaphas took such an active part in the plot against Jesus (11:49-53) and presided over the Sanhedrin, the reference may center on him (18:30,35). The critical point is not the identity of the person but guilt because of the deliberate, high-handed, and coldly calculated act of handing Jesus over to Pilate, after having seen and heard the overwhelming evidence that He was Messiah and Son of God. Pilate had not been exposed to that. *See notes on 9:41; 15:22-24; Heb. 10:26-31.*

19:12 not Caesar's friend. This statement by the Jews was loaded with irony, for the Jews' hatred of Rome certainly indicated they too were no friends of Caesar. But they knew Pilate feared Tiberius Caesar (the Roman emperor at the time of Jesus' crucifixion) since he had a highly suspicious personality and exacted ruthless punishment. Pilate had already created upheaval in Palestine by several foolish acts that had infuriated the Jews, and so was under the scrutiny of Rome to see if his ineptness continued. The Jews were intimidating him by threatening another upheaval that could spell the end of his power in Palestine, if he did not execute Jesus.

19:13 the judgment seat. Pilate capitulated under pressure (v. 12) and prepared to render judgment on the original charge of sedition against Rome. This "judgment seat" was the place Pilate sat to render the official verdict. The seat was placed on an area paved with stones known as the "Pavement." The irony is that Pilate rendered judgment on the One whom the Father Himself entrusted with all judgment (5:22) and who would render a just condemnation of Pilate.

19:14 Preparation Day of the Passover. Since this refers to the day before the Passover when preparation for the Passover was done,

Passover, and about the sixth hour. And he
said to the Jews, "Behold your King!"
15 But they cried out, "Away with *Him*,
away with *Him!* Crucify Him!"
Pilate said to them, "Shall I crucify your
King?"
The chief priests answered, [m]"We have
no king but Caesar!"
16 [n]Then he delivered Him to them to be
crucified. Then they took Jesus [4]and led
Him away.

The Crucifixion of Christ

Matt. 27:32-38, 48, 50; Mark 15:21-26, 36, 37; Luke 23:26-33, 38, 46

17 [o]And He, bearing His cross, [p]went out
to a place called *the Place* of a Skull, which
is called in Hebrew, Golgotha, 18 where
they crucified Him, and [q]two others with
Him, one on either side, and Jesus in the
center. 19 [r]Now Pilate wrote a title and put
it on the cross. And the writing was:

JESUS OF NAZARETH, THE KING OF THE JEWS.

20 Then many of the Jews read this title, for
the place where Jesus was crucified was
near the city; and it was written in Hebrew,
Greek, *and* Latin.
21 Therefore the chief priests of the Jews
said to Pilate, "Do not write, 'The King of
the Jews,' but, 'He said, "I am the King of
the Jews."' "
22 Pilate answered, "What I have written, I have written."
23 [s]Then the soldiers, when they had
crucified Jesus, took His garments and
made four parts, to each soldier a part, and
also the tunic. Now the tunic was without
seam, woven from the top in one piece.
24 They said therefore among themselves,
"Let us not tear it, but cast lots for it, whose
it shall be," that the Scripture might be fulfilled which says:

[t]*"They divided My garments among them,*
And for My clothing they cast lots."

Therefore the soldiers did these things.
25 [u]Now there stood by the cross of Jesus
His mother, and His mother's sister, Mary
the *wife* of [v]Clopas, and Mary Magdalene.
26 When Jesus therefore saw His mother,
and [w]the disciple whom He loved standing

15 [m] [Gen. 49:10] **16** [n] Matt. 27:26, 31; Mark 15:15; Luke 23:24 [4] NU omits *and led Him away* **17** [o] Matt. 27:31, 33; Mark 15:21, 22; Luke 23:26, 33 [p] Num. 15:36; Heb. 13:12 **18** [q] Ps. 22:16-18; Is. 53:12; Matt. 20:19; 26:2 **19** [r] Matt. 27:37; Mark 15:26; Luke 23:38
23 [s] Matt. 27:35; Mark 15:24; Luke 23:34 **24** [t] Ps. 22:18 **25** [u] Matt. 27:55; Mark 15:40; Luke 2:35; 23:49 [v] Luke 24:18 **26** [w] John 13:23; 20:2; 21:7, 20, 24

John presents Jesus as being sent to execution about the time Passover lambs were being slaughtered. For the chronology of the week, see Introduction: Interpretive Challenges. **about the sixth hour.** John is here reckoning time by the Roman method of the day beginning at midnight. *See note on Mark 15:25.* **"Behold your King!"** That was Pilate's mockery—that such a brutalized and helpless man was a fitting king for them. This mockery continued in the placard on the cross (vv. 19-22).

19:17 bearing His cross. This refers to the cross-member, the horizontal bar. The condemned man carried it on his shoulders to the place of execution. Jesus carried his cross as far as the city gate, but due to the effects of the previous brutal beating, someone else had to eventually carry it for Him, i.e., Simon of Cyrene (Matt. 27:32; Mark 15:21; Luke 23:26). **Golgatha.** This term is an Eng. transliteration of the Gr. which, in turn, is a translation of the Aram. word meaning "skull." The place probably derived its name from its appearance. The precise location of the site today is uncertain.

19:18 crucified Him. Jesus was made to lie on the ground while his arms were stretched out and nailed to the horizontal beam that he carried. The beam was then hoisted up, along with the victim, and fastened to the vertical beam. His feet were nailed to the vertical beam to which sometimes was attached a piece of wood that served as a kind of seat that partially supported the weight of the body. The latter, however, was designed to prolong and increase the agony, not relieve it. Having been stripped naked and beaten, Jesus could hang in the hot sun for hours if not days. To breathe, it was necessary to push with the legs and pull with the arms, creating excruciating pain. Terrible muscle spasms wracked the entire body; but since collapse meant asphyxiation, the struggle for life continued (*see note on Matt. 27:31*). **two others.** Matthew (27:38) and Luke (23:33) use the same word for these two as John used for Barabbas, i.e., guerrilla fighters. *See note on 18:40.*

19:19-22 wrote a title. The custom in such executions was to place a placard or tablet around the neck of the victim as he made his way to execution. The tablet would then be nailed to the victim's cross (see Matt. 27:37; Mark 15:26; Luke 23:38). Pilate used this opportunity for mocking revenge on the Jews who had so intimidated him into this execution (*see note on v. 12*).

19:23 His garments...and also the tunic. By custom, the clothes of the condemned person were the property of the executioners. The division of the garments suggests that the execution squad was made up of 4 soldiers (cf. Acts 12:4). The tunic was worn next to the skin. The plural "garments" probably refers to other clothes, including an outer garment, belt, sandals, and head covering.

19:24 John cites Ps. 22:18. In the psalm, David, beset by physical distress and mockery by his opponents, used the symbolism of the common practice in an execution scene in which the executioner divided the victim's clothes to portray the depth of his trouble. It is notable that David precisely described a form of execution that he had never seen. The passage was typologically prophetic of Jesus, David's heir to the messianic throne (see Matt. 27:46; Mark 15:34).

19:25 Although the exact number of women mentioned here is questioned, John probably refers to 4 women rather than 3, i.e., two by name and two without naming them: 1) "His mother" (Mary); 2) "His mother's sister" (probably Salome [Mark 15:40] the sister of Mary and mother of James and John, the sons of Zebedee [Matt. 27:56,57; Mark 15:40]); 3) "Mary the *wife* of Cleopas" (the mother of James the younger and Joses—Matt. 27:56); and 4) Mary Magdalene ("Magdalene" signifies "Magdala" a village on the W shore of Galilee, 2 or 3 mi. N of Tiberias). Mary Magdalene figures prominently in the resurrection account (see 20:1-18; cf. Luke 8:2,3 where Jesus healed her from demon possession).

19:26 the disciple whom He loved. This is a reference to John (*see note on 13:23*; cf. Introduction: Author and Date). Jesus, as firstborn and breadwinner of the family before He started His ministry, did not give the responsibility to His brothers because they were not sympathetic to His ministry nor did they believe in Him (7:3-5) and they likely were not present at the time (i.e., their home was in Capernaum—see 2:12).

by, He said to His mother, [x]"Woman, behold your son!" 27 Then He said to the disciple, "Behold your mother!" And from
that hour that disciple took her [y]to his own
home.
28 After this, Jesus, [5]knowing that all
things were now accomplished, [z]that the
Scripture might be fulfilled, said, "I thirst!"
29 Now a vessel full of sour wine was sitting
there; and [a]they filled a sponge with sour
wine, put *it* on hyssop, and put *it* to His
mouth. 30 So when Jesus had received the
sour wine, He said, [b]"It is finished!" And
bowing His head, He gave up His spirit.
31 [c]Therefore, because it was the Preparation *Day,* [d]that the bodies should not remain on the cross on the Sabbath (for that
Sabbath was a [e]high day), the Jews asked
Pilate that their legs might be broken, and
that they might be taken away. 32 Then the
soldiers came and broke the legs of the first
and of the other who was crucified with
Him. 33 But when they came to Jesus and
saw that He was already dead, they did
not break His legs. 34 But one of the soldiers pierced His side with a spear, and immediately [f]blood and water came out.
35 And he who has seen has testified, and
his testimony is [g]true; and he knows that
he is telling the truth, so that you may [h]be-
lieve. 36 For these things were done that
the Scripture should be fulfilled, [i]*"Not one
of His bones shall be broken."* 37 And
again another Scripture says, [j]*"They shall
look on Him whom they pierced."*

The Burial of Christ
Matt. 27:57-60; Mark 15:42-46; Luke 23:50-54

38 [k]After this, Joseph of Arimathea,
being a disciple of Jesus, but secretly, [l]for
fear of the Jews, asked Pilate that he might
take away the body of Jesus; and Pilate
gave *him* permission. So he came and took
the body of Jesus. 39 And [m]Nicodemus,
who at first came to Jesus by night, also
came, bringing a mixture of [n]myrrh and
aloes, about a hundred pounds. 40 Then
they took the body of Jesus, and [o]bound it
in strips of linen with the spices, as the custom of the Jews is to bury. 41 Now in the
place where He was crucified there was a
garden, and in the garden a new tomb in

26 [x]John 2:4
27 [y]Luke 18:28; John 1:11; 16:32; Acts 21:6
28 [z]Ps. 22:15 [5]M *seeing*
29 [a]Ps. 69:21; Matt. 27:48, 50; Mark 15:36; Luke 23:36
30 [b]Dan. 9:26; Zech. 11:10, 11; John 17:4
31 [c]Matt. 27:62; Mark 15:42; Luke 23:54 [d]Deut. 21:23; Josh. 8:29; 10:26 [e]Ex. 12:16; Lev. 23:6, 7
34 [f][1 John 5:6, 8]
35 [g]John 21:24 [h][John 20:31]
36 [i][Ex. 12:46; Num. 9:12]; Ps. 34:20
37 [j]Ps. 22:16, 17; Zech. 12:10; 13:6; Rev. 1:7
38 [k]Matt. 27:57-61; Mark 15:42-47; Luke 23:50-56 [l][John 7:13; 9:22; 12:42]
39 [m]John 3:1, 2; 7:50 [n]Ps. 45:8; Prov. 7:17; Song 4:14; Matt. 2:11
40 [o]Luke 24:12; John 20:5, 7; Acts 5:6

19:29 The drink here is not to be confused with the "wine mixed with myrrh" offered to Him on the way to the cross (Matt. 27:34) intended to help deaden pain. The purpose of this drink (cf. Mark 15:36) was to prolong life and increase the torture and pain. It was a cheap, sour wine used by soldiers. The use of this word recalls Ps. 69:21 where the same noun occurs in the LXX. Hyssop is a little plant that is ideal for sprinkling (see Ex. 12:22).

19:30 "It is finished!" The verb here carries the idea of fulfilling one's task and, in religious contexts, has the idea of fulfilling one's religious obligations (see 17:4). The entire work of redemption had been brought to completion. The single Gr. word here (translated "it is finished") has been found in the papyri being placed on receipts for taxes meaning "paid in full" (see Col. 3:13,14). **He gave up His spirit.** The sentence signaled that Jesus "handed over" His spirit as an act of His will. No one took his life from Him, for He voluntarily and willingly gave it up (see 10:17,18).

19:31 Preparation *Day.* This refers to Friday, the day before or "the preparation" day for the Sabbath. See Introduction: Interpretive Challenges. **should not remain on the cross on the Sabbath.** The normal Roman practice was to leave crucified men and women on the cross until they died (and this could take days) and then leave their rotting bodies hanging there to be devoured by vultures. The Mosaic law insisted that anyone being impaled (usually after execution) should not remain there overnight (Deut. 21:22,23). Such a person was under God's curse, and to leave him exposed would be to desecrate the land in their minds. **their legs might be broken.** In order to hasten death for certain reasons, soldiers would smash the legs of the victim with an iron mallet. Not only did this action induce shock and additional loss of blood, but it prevented the victim from pushing with his legs to keep breathing (*see note on v. 18.*), and thus the victim died due to asphyxiation.

19:34 The soldier's stabbing of Jesus' side caused significant penetration because of the sudden flow of blood and water. Either the spear pierced Jesus' heart or the chest cavity was pierced at the bottom. In either event, John mentioned the outflow of "blood and water" to emphasize that Jesus was unquestionably dead.

19:35 he who has seen. This has reference to John the apostle who was an eyewitness of these events (v. 26; 13:23; 20:2; 21:7,20; cf. 1 John 1:1-4).

19:36,37 John quoted from either Ex. 12:46 or Num. 9:12, both of which specify that no bone of the Passover lamb may be broken. Since the NT portrays Jesus as the Passover Lamb that takes away the sins of the world (1:29; cf. 1 Cor. 5:7; 1 Pet. 1:19), these verses have special typologically prophetic significance for Him. The quote in v. 37 comes from Zech. 12:10, which indicates God Himself was pierced when His representative, the Shepherd (Zech. 13:7; cf. Zech. 11:4,8,9,15-17) was pierced. The anguish and contrition of the Jews in the Zechariah passage, because of their wounding of God's Shepherd, is typologically prophetic of the time of the coming of the Son of God, Messiah, when at His return, Israel shall mourn for the rejection and killing of their King (cf. Rev. 1:7).

19:38 Joseph of Arimathea. This man appears in all 4 gospels, only in connection with Jesus' burial. The synoptics relate that he was a member of the Sanhedrin (Matt. 27:57), he was rich (Matt. 27:57), and he was looking for the kingdom of God (Luke 23:51). John treated the idea of secret disciples negatively (see 12:42,43) but since Joseph publicly risked his reputation and even his life in asking for the body of Jesus, John pictured him in a more positive light.

19:39 Nicodemus. *See notes on 3:1-10.* **about a hundred pounds.** An inaccurate understanding of the term used in the original, this mixture of spices weighed closer to 65 pounds. Myrrh was a very fragrant gummy resin, which the Jews turned into a powdered form and mixed with aloes, a powder from the aromatic sandalwood. The Jews did not embalm but did this procedure to stifle the smell of putrefaction (*see note on 11:39*).

19:40 strips...spices. The spices most likely were laid on the entire length of the strips of linen which were then wound around Jesus' body. More spices were laid under the body and perhaps packed around it. The sticky resin would help the cloth adhere.

19:41,42 garden...new tomb. Only John relates that the tomb was near the place where Jesus was crucified. Since the Sabbath, when all work had to cease, was nearly upon them (6:00 p.m., sunset),

which no one had yet been laid. 42 So
[p]there they laid Jesus, [q]because of the Jews'
Preparation *Day*, for the tomb was nearby.

The Resurrection of Christ
Matt. 28:1-8; Mark 16:1-8; Luke 24:1-12

20 Now the [a]first *day* of the week Mary
Magdalene went to the tomb early,
while it was still dark, and saw *that* the
[b]stone had been taken away from the
tomb. 2 Then she ran and came to Simon
Peter, and to the [c]other disciple, [d]whom Jesus loved, and said to them, "They have
taken away the Lord out of the tomb, and
we do not know where they have laid
Him."
3 [e]Peter therefore went out, and the
other disciple, and were going to the tomb.
4 So they both ran together, and the other
disciple outran Peter and came to the tomb
first. 5 And he, stooping down and looking
in, saw [f]the linen cloths lying *there;* yet he
did not go in. 6 Then Simon Peter came,
following him, and went into the tomb;
and he saw the linen cloths lying *there,*
7 and [g]the [1]handkerchief that had been
around His head, not lying with the linen
cloths, but folded together in a place by itself. 8 Then the [h]other disciple, who came
to the tomb first, went in also; and he saw
and believed. 9 For as yet they did not
[2]know the [i]Scripture, that He must rise
again from the dead. 10 Then the disciples
went away again to their own homes.

Christ Appears to Mary Magdalene

11 [j]But Mary stood outside by the tomb
weeping, and as she wept she stooped
down *and looked* into the tomb. 12 And she
saw two angels in white sitting, one at the
head and the other at the feet, where the
body of Jesus had lain. 13 Then they said to
her, "Woman, why are you weeping?"
She said to them, "Because they have
taken away my Lord, and I do not know
where they have laid Him."
14 [k]Now when she had said this, she
turned around and saw Jesus standing
there, and [l]did not know that it was Jesus.
15 Jesus said to her, "Woman, why are you
weeping? Whom are you seeking?"
She, supposing Him to be the gardener,

42 [p]Is. 53:9; Matt. 26:12; Mark 14:8 [q]John 19:14, 31

CHAPTER 20

1 [a]Matt. 28:1-8; Mark 16:1-8; Luke 24:1-10; Acts 20:7; 1 Cor. 16:2 [b]Matt. 27:60, 66; 28:2; Mark 15:46; 16:4; Luke 24:2; John 11:38
2 [c]John 21:23, 24 [d]John 13:23; 19:26; 21:7, 20, 24
3 [e]Luke 24:12
5 [f]John 19:40
7 [g]John 11:44 [1]face cloth
8 [h]John 21:23, 24
9 [i]Ps. 16:10; Acts 2:25, 31; 13:34, 35 [2]understand
11 [j]Mark 16:5
14 [k]Matt. 28:9; Mark 16:9 [l][Luke 24:16, 31]; John 21:4

the nearness of the tomb was helpful. John does not mention that Joseph of Arimathea rolled a stone across the tomb's mouth or that Mary Madgdalene and Mary the mother of Joses saw where He was laid (Matt. 27:58-61). For the time of the Lord's death and burial, *see notes on Matt. 27:45,57-61.*

20:1-31 This chapter records the appearances of Jesus to His own followers: 1) the appearance to Mary Magdalene (vv. 1-18); 2) the appearance to the 10 disciples (vv. 19-23); and 3) the appearance to Thomas (vv. 24-29). Jesus did not appear to unbelievers (see 14:19; 16:16,22) because the evidence of His resurrection would not have convinced them as the miracles had not (Luke 16:31). The god of this world had blinded them and prevented their belief (2 Cor. 4:4). Jesus, therefore, appears exclusively to His own in order to confirm their faith in the living Christ. Such appearances were so profound that they transformed the disciples from cowardly men hiding in fear to bold witnesses for Jesus (e.g., Peter; see 18:27; cf. Acts 2:14-39). Once again John's purpose in recording these resurrection appearances was to demonstrate that Jesus' physical and bodily resurrection was the crowning proof that He truly is the Messiah and Son of God who laid down His life for His own (10:17,18; 15:13; cf. Rom. 1:4).

20:1 first *day* of the week. A reference to Sunday. From then on, believers set aside Sunday to meet and remember the marvelous resurrection of the Lord (see Acts 20:7; 1 Cor. 16:2). It became known as the Lord's Day (Rev. 1:10). *See notes on Luke 24:4,34.* **Mary Magdalene went to the tomb early, while it was still dark.** Perhaps the reason why Jesus first appeared to Mary Magdalene was to demonstrate grace by His personal, loving faithfulness to someone who formerly had a sordid past; but clearly also because she loved Him so dearly and deeply, that she appeared before anyone else at the tomb. Her purpose in coming was to finish the preparation of Jesus' body for burial by bringing more spices to anoint the corpse (Luke 24:1).

20:2 other disciple, whom Jesus loved. This is the author John. **They have taken.** Though Jesus had predicted His resurrection numerous times, it was more than she could believe at that point. It would take His showing Himself alive to them by many "infallible proofs" (Acts 1:3) for them to believe.

20:5-7 saw the linen cloths lying *there.* A contrast existed between the resurrection of Lazarus (11:44) and that of Jesus. While Lazarus came forth from the grave wearing his graveclothes, Jesus' body, though physical and material, was glorified and was now able to pass through the graveclothes much in the same way that He later appeared in the locked room (see vv. 19,20; cf. Phil. 3:21). **linen cloths...handkerchief.** The state of those items indicates no struggle, no hurried unwrapping of the body by grave robbers, who wouldn't unwrap the body anyway, since transporting it elsewhere would be easier and more pleasant if it was left in its wrapped and spiced condition. All appearances indicated that no one had taken the body, but that it had moved through the cloth and left it behind in the tomb.

20:8 the other disciple. John saw the graveclothes and was convinced by them that He had risen.

20:9 did not know the Scripture. Neither Peter nor John understood that Scripture said Jesus would rise (Ps. 16:10). This is evident by the reports of Luke (24:25-27,32,44-47). Jesus had foretold His resurrection (2:17; Matt. 16:21; Mark 8:31; 9:31; Luke 9:22), but they would not accept it (Matt. 16:22; Luke 9:44,45). By the time John wrote this gospel, the church had developed an understanding of the OT prediction of Messiah's resurrection (cf. "as yet").

20:11-13 weeping. Mary's sense of grief and loss may have driven her back to the tomb. She apparently had not crossed paths with Peter or John and thus did not know of Jesus' resurrection (see v. 9).

20:12 two angels. Luke (24:4) describes both. Matthew (28:2,3) and Mark (16:5) report only one. John's reason for the mention of angels is to demonstrate that no grave robbers took the body. This was an operation of the power of God.

20:14 did not know that it was Jesus. The reason for Mary's failure to recognize Jesus is uncertain. She may not have recognized Him because her tears blurred her eyes (v. 11). Possibly also, the vivid memories of Jesus' bruised and broken body were still etched in her mind, and Jesus' resurrection appearance was so dramatically different that she failed to recognize Him. Perhaps, however, like the disciples on the road to Emmaus, she was supernaturally prevented from recognizing Him until He chose for her to do so (see Luke 24:16).

said to Him, "Sir, if You have carried Him
away, tell me where You have laid Him,
and I will take Him away."
16 Jesus said to her, [m]"Mary!"
She turned and said to [3]Him, "Rabboni!" (which is to say, Teacher).
17 Jesus said to her, "Do not cling to Me,
for I have not yet [n]ascended to My Father;
but go to [o]My brethren and say to them, [p]'I
am ascending to My Father and your Father, and *to* [q]My God and your God.'"
18 [r]Mary Magdalene came and told the
[4]disciples that she had seen the Lord, and
that He had spoken these things to her.

Christ Appears to the Disciples (Thomas Absent)—Mark 16:14; Luke 24:36-43

19 [s]Then, the same day at evening, being
the first *day* of the week, when the doors
were shut where the disciples were [5]as-
sembled, for [t]fear of the Jews, Jesus came
and stood in the midst, and said to them,
[u]"Peace *be* with you." 20 When He had said
this, He [v]showed them *His* hands and His
side. [w]Then the disciples were glad when
they saw the Lord.
21 So Jesus said to them again, "Peace to
you! [x]As the Father has sent Me, I also
send you." 22 And when He had said this,
He breathed on *them,* and said to them,
"Receive the Holy Spirit. 23 [y]If you forgive
the sins of any, they are forgiven them; if

16 [m] John 10:3 [3] NU adds *in Hebrew*
17 [n] Mark 16:19; Luke 24:5; Acts 1:9; 2:34-36; Eph. 4:8-10; Heb. 4:14 [o] Ps. 22:22; Matt. 18:10; Rom. 8:29; Heb. 2:11 [p] John 16:28; 17:11 [q] Eph. 1:17
18 [r] Matt. 28:10; Luke 24:10,23 [4] NU *disciples, "I have seen the Lord,"*
19 [s] Mark 16:14; Luke 24:36; John 14:27; 1 Cor. 15:5 [t] John 9:22; 19:38 [u] John 14:27; 16:33; Eph. 2:17 [5] NU omits *assembled*
20 [v] Acts 1:3 [w] John 16:20,22
21 [x] [Matt. 28:18-20]; John 17:18, 19; [2 Tim. 2:2]; Heb. 3:1
23 [y] Matt. 16:19; 18:18

you retain the *sins* of any, they are retained."
24 Now Thomas, [z]called the Twin, one of
the twelve, was not with them when Jesus
came. 25 The other disciples therefore said
to him, "We have seen the Lord."
So he said to them, "Unless I see in His
hands the print of the nails, and put my
finger into the print of the nails, and put
my hand into His side, I will not believe."

Christ Appears to the Disciples (Thomas Present)—1 Cor. 15:5

26 And after eight days His disciples
were again inside, and Thomas with them.
Jesus came, the doors being shut, and
stood in the midst, and said, "Peace to
you!" 27 Then He said to Thomas, "Reach
your finger here, and look at My hands;
and [a]reach your hand *here,* and put *it* into
My side. Do not be [b]unbelieving, but believing."
28 And Thomas answered and said to
Him, "My Lord and my God!"
29 Jesus said to him, [6]"Thomas, because
you have seen Me, you have believed.
[c]Blessed *are* those who have not seen and
yet have believed."

The Purpose of John's Gospel

30 And [d]truly Jesus did many other signs
in the presence of His disciples, which are

24 [z] John 11:16
27 [a] Ps. 22:16; Zech. 12:10; 13:6; 1 John 1:1 [b] Mark 16:14
29 [c] 2 Cor. 5:7; 1 Pet. 1:8 [6] NU, M omit *Thomas*
30 [d] John 21:25

20:16 "Mary!" Whatever the reason for her failure to recognize Jesus, the moment He spoke the single word, "Mary," she immediately recognized Him. This is reminiscent of Jesus' words "My sheep hear My voice, and I know them, and they follow Me" (10:27; cf. 10:3,4).

20:17 Do not cling to Me, for I have not yet ascended. Mary was expressing a desire to hold on to His physical presence for fear that she would once again lose Him. Jesus' reference to His ascension signifies that He would only be temporarily with them and though she desperately wanted Him to stay, He could not. Jesus was with them only for 40 more days and then He ascended (Acts 1:3-11). After He went to the Father, He sent the Holy Spirit ("The Helper") so that they would not feel abandoned (*see note on 14:18,19*). **My brethren.** Disciples have been called "servants" or "friends" (15:15), but not "brothers," until here. Because of Jesus' work on the cross in place of the sinner, this new relationship to Christ was made possible (Rom. 8:14-17; Gal. 3:26,27; Eph. 1:5; Heb. 2:10-13).

20:19 the same day. *See note on v. 1.* **the doors were shut.** The Gr. word indicates the doors were locked for fear of the Jews. Since the authorities had executed their leader, they reasonably expected that Jesus' fate could be their own. **Peace *be* with you.** *See notes on 14:27; 16:33.* Jesus' greeting complements His "It is finished," for His work on the cross accomplished peace between God and His people (Rom. 5:1; Eph. 2:14-17).

20:20 Jesus proved that He who appeared to them was the same One who was crucified (cf. Luke 24:39).

20:21 This commission builds on 17:18. See Matt. 28:19,20.

20:22 Since the disciples did not actually receive the Holy Spirit until the day of Pentecost, some 40 days in the future (Acts 1:8; 2:1-3), this statement must be understood as a pledge on Christ's part that the Holy Spirit would be coming.

20:23 *See notes on Matt. 16:19; 18:18.* This verse does not give authority to Christians to forgive sins. Jesus was saying that the believer can boldly declare the certainty of a sinner's forgiveness by the Father because of the work of His Son if that sinner has repented and believed the gospel. The believer with certainty can also tell those who do not respond to the message of God's forgiveness through faith in Christ that their sins, as a result, are not forgiven.

20:24-26 Thomas has already been portrayed as loyal but pessimistic. Jesus did not rebuke Thomas for His failure, but instead compassionately offered him proof of His resurrection. Jesus lovingly met him at the point of His weakness (2 Tim. 2:13). Thomas' actions indicated that Jesus had to convince the disciples rather forcefully of His resurrection, i.e., they were not gullible people predisposed to believing in resurrection. The point is they would not have fabricated it or hallucinated it, since they were so reluctant to believe even with the evidence they could see.

20:28 "My Lord and my God!" With these words, Thomas declared His firm belief in the resurrection and, therefore, the deity of Jesus the Messiah and Son of God (Titus 2:13). This is the greatest confession a person can make. Thomas' confession functions as the fitting capstone of John's purpose in writing (see vv. 30,31).

20:29 Jesus foresaw the time when such tangible evidence as Thomas received would not be available. When Jesus ascended permanently to the Father, all those who believe would do so without the benefit of seeing the resurrected Lord. Jesus pronounced a special blessing on those who believe without having Thomas' privilege (1 Peter 1:8,9).

20:30,31 These verses constitute the goal and purpose for which John wrote the gospel (see Introduction: Background and Setting).

not written in this book; 31 [e]but these are
written that [f]you may believe that Jesus [g]is
the Christ, the Son of God, [h]and that believing you may have life in His name.

Christ Appears to the Seven Disciples

21 After these things Jesus showed
Himself again to the disciples at the
[a]Sea of Tiberias, and in this way He
showed *Himself*: 2 Simon Peter, [b]Thomas
called the Twin, [c]Nathanael of [d]Cana in
Galilee, [e]the *sons* of Zebedee, and two others of His disciples were together. 3 Simon
Peter said to them, "I am going fishing."
They said to him, "We are going with
you also." They went out and [1]immedi-
ately got into the boat, and that night they
caught nothing. 4 But when the morning
had now come, Jesus stood on the shore;
yet the disciples [f]did not know that it was
Jesus. 5 Then [g]Jesus said to them, "Children, have you any food?"
They answered Him, "No."
6 And He said to them, [h]"Cast the net on
the right side of the boat, and you will find
some." So they cast, and now they were not
able to draw it in because of the multitude
of fish.
7 Therefore [i]that disciple whom Jesus
loved said to Peter, "It is the Lord!" Now
when Simon Peter heard that it was the
Lord, he put on *his* outer garment (for he
had removed it), and plunged into the sea.
8 But the other disciples came in the little
boat (for they were not far from land, but
about two hundred cubits), dragging the
net with fish. 9 Then, as soon as they had
come to land, they saw a fire of coals there,
and fish laid on it, and bread. 10 Jesus said
to them, "Bring some of the fish which you
have just caught."
11 Simon Peter went up and dragged the
net to land, full of large fish, one hundred
and fifty-three; and although there were so
many, the net was not broken. 12 Jesus said
to them, [j]"Come *and* eat breakfast." Yet
none of the disciples dared ask Him, "Who
are You?"—knowing that it was the Lord.
13 Jesus then came and took the bread and
gave it to them, and likewise the fish.
14 This *is* now [k]the third time Jesus
showed Himself to His disciples after He
was raised from the dead.

Christ Speaks to Peter

15 So when they had eaten breakfast, Jesus said to Simon Peter, "Simon, *son* of [2]Jo-
nah, do you love Me more than these?"

31 [e] Luke 1:4 [f] John 19:35; 1 John 5:13 [g] Luke 2:11; 1 John 5:1 [h] John 3:15, 16; 5:24; [1 Pet. 1:8, 9]

CHAPTER 21

1 [a] Matt. 26:32; Mark 14:28; John 6:1
2 [b] John 20:24 [c] John 1:45-51 [d] John 2:1 [e] Matt. 4:21; Mark 1:19; Luke 5:10
3 [1] NU omits *immediately*
4 [f] Luke 24:16; John 20:14
5 [g] Luke 24:41
6 [h] Luke 5:4, 6, 7
7 [i] John 13:23; 20:2
12 [j] Acts 10:41
14 [k] John 20:19, 26
15 [2] NU *John*

21:1-25 The epilogue or appendix of John's gospel. While 20:30,31 constitute the conclusion of the body of the fourth gospel, the information here at the end of his work provides a balance to his prologue in 1:1-18. The epilogue essentially ties up 5 loose ends that were unanswered in chap. 20. 1) Will Jesus no longer directly provide for His own (cf. 20:17)? This question is answered in vv. 1-14. 2) What happened to Peter? Peter had denied Christ 3 times and fled. The last time Peter was seen was in 20:6-8 where both he and John saw the empty tomb but only John believed (20:8). This question is answered in vv. 15-17. 3) What about the future of the disciples now that they are without their Master? This question is answered in vv. 18,19. 4) Was John going to die? Jesus answers this question in vv. 20-23. 5) Why weren't other things that Jesus did recorded by John? John gives the answer to that in vv. 24,25.

21:1 Sea of Tiberias. An alternate name for the Sea of Galilee, found only in John (see 6:1).

21:2 Simon Peter. In all lists of the apostles, he is named first, indicating his general leadership of the group (e.g., Matt. 10:2).

21:3 "I am going fishing." The most reasonable explanation for Peter and the others to go to Galilee in order to fish was that they went in obedience to the Lord's command to meet Him in Galilee (Matt. 28:16). Peter and the others occupied themselves with fishing, which was their former livelihood, while they awaited Jesus' appearance.

21:4 This could be another instance in which the Lord kept His disciples from recognizing Him (20:14,15; cf. Luke 24:16).

21:7 that disciple whom Jesus loved. John immediately recognized that the stranger was the risen Lord, for only He had such supernatural knowledge and power (v. 6). Peter impulsively jumped in and headed to see the Lord.

21:8 two hundred cubits. Approximately 300 ft. from the shore.

21:9 fish...and bread. Apparently, the Lord created this breakfast as He had created food for the multitudes (6:1-13).

21:11 one hundred and fifty-three. John's recording of the precise number reinforces the fact that he was an eyewitness author of the events he recorded (1 John 1:1-4). Jesus' action here in providing the fish also indicated that He would still provide for His disciples' needs (see Phil. 4:19; Matt. 6:25-33).

21:14 the third time. The reference to the "third time" refers only to the appearances reported in John's gospel, i.e., the first being in 20:19-23 and the second in 20:26-29.

21:15-17 The meaning of this section hinges upon the usage of two synonyms for love. In terms of interpretation, when two synonyms are placed in close proximity in context, a difference in meaning, however slight, is emphasized. When Jesus asked Peter if he loved Him, He used a word for love that signified total commitment. Peter responded with a word for love that signified his love for Jesus, but not necessarily His total commitment. This was not because he was reluctant to express that greater love, but because he had been disobedient and denied the Lord in the past. He was, perhaps, now reluctant to make a claim of supreme devotion when, in the past, his life did not support such a claim. Jesus pressed home to Peter the need for unswerving devotion by repeatedly asking Peter if He loved Him supremely. The essential message here is that Jesus demands total commitment from His followers. Their love for Him must place Him above their love for all else. Jesus confronted Peter with love because He wanted Peter to lead the apostles (Matt. 16:18), but in order for Peter to be an effective shepherd, his overwhelming drive must exemplify supreme love for his Lord.

21:15 more than these. This probably refers to the fish (v. 11) representing Peter's profession as a fisherman, for he had gone back to it while waiting for Jesus (see v. 3). Jesus wanted Peter to love Him so supremely as to forsake all that he was familiar with and be exclusively devoted to being a fisher of men (Matt. 4:19). The phrase may

He said to Him, "Yes, Lord; You know
that I [3]love You."
He said to him, [l]"Feed My lambs."
16 He said to him again a second time,
"Simon, *son* of [4]Jonah, do you love Me?"
He said to Him, "Yes, Lord; You know
that I [5]love You."
[m]He said to him, "Tend My [n]sheep."
17 He said to him the third time, "Simon,
son of [6]Jonah, do you [7]love Me?" Peter was
grieved because He said to him the third
time, "Do you [7]love Me?"
And he said to Him, "Lord, [o]You know
all things; You know that I [7]love You."
Jesus said to him, "Feed My sheep.
18 [p]Most assuredly, I say to you, when you
were younger, you girded yourself and
walked where you wished; but when you
are old, you will stretch out your hands,
and another will gird you and carry *you*
where you do not wish." 19 This He spoke,
signifying [q]by what death he would glorify God. And when He had spoken this, He
said to him, [r]"Follow Me."

15 [l] Acts 20:28; 1 Tim. 4:6; 1 Pet. 5:2 [3] *have affection for*
16 [m] Matt. 2:6; Acts 20:28; Heb. 13:20; 1 Pet. 2:25; 5:2, 4 [n] Ps. 79:13; Matt. 10:16; 15:24; 25:33; 26:31 [4] NU *John* [5] *have affection for*
17 [o] John 2:24, 25; 16:30 [6] NU *John* [7] *have affection for*
18 [p] John 13:36; Acts 12:3, 4
19 [q] 2 Pet. 1:13, 14 [r] [Matt. 4:19; 16:24]; John 21:22
20 [s] John 13:23; 20:2 [t] John 13:25
22 [u] [Matt. 16:27, 28; 25:31; 1 Cor. 4:5; 11:26; Rev. 2:25; 3:11; 22:7, 20] [8] *desire*
24 [v] John 19:35; 3 John 12
25 [w] John 20:30 [x] Amos 7:10

20 Then Peter, turning around, saw the
disciple [s]whom Jesus loved following,
[t]who also had leaned on His breast at the
supper, and said, "Lord, who is the one who
betrays You?" 21 Peter, seeing him, said to
Jesus, "But Lord, what *about* this man?"
22 Jesus said to him, "If I [8]will that he remain [u]till I come, what *is that* to you? You
follow Me."
23 Then this saying went out among the
brethren that this disciple would not die.
Yet Jesus did not say to him that he would
not die, but, "If I will that he remain till I
come, what *is that* to you?"

The Conclusion of John's Gospel

24 This is the disciple who [v]testifies of
these things, and wrote these things; and
we know that his testimony is true.
25 [w]And there are also many other
things that Jesus did, which if they were
written one by one, [x]I suppose that even
the world itself could not contain the
books that would be written. Amen.

refer to the other disciples, since Peter had claimed he would be more devoted than all the others (Matt. 26:33). **"Feed My lambs."** The word "feed" conveys the idea of being devoted to the Lord's service as an undershepherd who cares for His flock (see 1 Pet. 5:1-4). The word has the idea of constantly feeding and nourishing the sheep. This served as a reminder that the primary duty of the messenger of Jesus Christ is to teach the Word of God (2 Tim. 4:2). Acts 1–13 records Peter's obedience to this commission.

21:17 Peter was grieved. The third time Jesus asked Peter, He used Peter's word for love that signified something less than total devotion, questioning even that level of love Peter thought he was safe in claiming (*see note on vv. 15-17*). The lessons driven home to Peter grieved his heart, so that he sought for a proper understanding of his heart, not by what he said or had done, but based on the Lord's omniscience (cf. 2:24,25).

21:18,19 A prophecy of Peter's martyrdom. Jesus' call of devotion to Him would also mean that Peter's devotion would entail his own death (Matt. 10:37-39). Whenever any Christian follows Christ, he must be prepared to suffer and die (Matt. 16:24-26). Peter lived 3 decades serving the Lord and anticipating the death that was before him (2 Pet. 1:12-15), but he wrote that such suffering and death for the Lord brings praise to God (1 Pet. 4:14-16). Church tradition records that Peter suffered martyrdom under Nero (ca. A.D. 67–68), being crucified upside down, because he refused to be crucified like his Lord.

21:20-22 Jesus' prophecy regarding Peter's martyrdom prompted Peter to ask what would happen to John ("the disciple whom Jesus loved"—see 13:23). He may have asked this because of his deep concern for John's future, since he was an intimate friend. Jesus' reply, "You follow Me," signified that his primary concern must not be John but his continued devotion to the Lord and His service, i.e., Christ's service must be his all-consuming passion and nothing must detract from it.

21:22,23 till I come. Jesus' hypothetical statement for emphasis was that, if John lived until His second coming, it was none of Peter's concern. He needed to live his own life in faithfulness, not compare it with any other.

21:24 the disciple who testifies. John is a personal witness of the truth of the events that he recorded. The "we" most likely is an editorial device referring only to John (see 1:14; 1 John 1:1-4; 3 John 12), or it may include the collective witness of his apostolic colleagues.

21:25 John explained that he had been selective rather than exhaustive in His testimony. Although selective, the truth revealed in John's gospel is sufficient to bring anyone to faith in the Messiah and Son of God (14:26; 16:13).

THE ACTS
of the Apostles

Title

As the second book Luke addressed to Theophilus (see Luke 1:3), Acts may originally have had no title. The Greek manuscripts title it "Acts," and many add "of the Apostles." The Greek word translated "Acts" (*praxeis*) was often used to describe the achievements of great men. Acts does feature the notable figures in the early years of the church, especially Peter (chaps. 1–12) and Paul (chaps. 13–28). But the book could more properly be called "The Acts of the Holy Spirit through the Apostles," since His sovereign, superintending work was far more significant than that of any man. It was the Spirit's directing, controlling, and empowering ministry that strengthened the church and caused it to grow in numbers, spiritual power, and influence.

Author and Date

Since Luke's gospel was the first book addressed to Theophilus (Luke 1:3), it is logical to conclude that Luke is also the author of Acts, although he is not named in either book. The writings of the early church Fathers such as Irenaeus, Clement of Alexandria, Tertullian, Origen, Eusebius, and Jerome affirm Luke's authorship, and so does the Muratorian Canon (ca. A.D. 170). Because he is a relatively obscure figure, mentioned only 3 times in the NT (Col. 4:14; 2 Tim. 4:11, Philem. 24), it is unlikely that anyone would have forged a work to make it appear to be Luke's. A forger surely would have attributed his work to a more prominent person.

Luke was Paul's close friend, traveling companion, and personal physician (Col. 4:14). He was a careful researcher (Luke 1:1-4) and an accurate historian, displaying an intimate knowledge of Roman laws and customs, as well as the geography of Palestine, Asia Minor, and Italy. In writing Acts, Luke drew on written sources (15:23-29; 23:26-30), and also no doubt interviewed key figures, such as Peter, John, and others in the Jerusalem church. Paul's two-year imprisonment at Caesarea (24:27) gave Luke ample opportunity to interview Philip and his daughters (who were considered important sources of information on the early days of the church). Finally, Luke's frequent use of the first person plural pronouns "we" and "us"(16:10-17; 20:5–21:18; 27:1–28:16) reveals that he was an eyewitness to many of the events recorded in Acts.

Some believe Luke wrote Acts after the fall of Jerusalem (A.D. 70; his death was probably in the mid-eighties). It is more likely, however, that he wrote much earlier, before the end of Paul's first Roman imprisonment (ca. A.D. 60–62). That date is the most natural explanation for the abrupt ending of Acts—which leaves Paul awaiting trial before Caesar. Surely Luke, who devoted more than half of Acts to Paul's ministry, would have given the outcome of that trial, and described Paul's subsequent ministry, second imprisonment (cf. 2 Tim. 4:11), and death, if those events had happened before he wrote Acts. Luke's silence about such notable events as the martyrdom of James, head of the Jerusalem church (A.D. 62 according to the Jewish historian Josephus), the persecution under Nero (A.D. 64), and the fall of Jerusalem (A.D. 70) also suggests he wrote Acts before those events transpired.

Background and Setting

As Luke makes clear in the prologue to his gospel, he wrote to give Theophilus (and the others who would read his work) a "narrative of those things" (Luke 1:1) which Jesus had accomplished during His earthly ministry. Accordingly, Luke wrote in his gospel "an orderly account" (Luke 1:3) of those momentous events. Acts continues that record, noting what Jesus accomplished through the early church. Beginning with Jesus' ascension, through the birth of the church on the Day of Pentecost, to Paul's preaching at Rome, Acts chronicles the spread of the gospel and the growth of the church (cf. 1:15; 2:41,47; 4:4; 5:14; 6:7; 9:31; 12:24; 13:49; 16:5; 19:20). It also records the mounting opposition to the gospel (cf. 2:13; 4:1-22; 5:17-42; 6:9–8:4; 12:1-5; 13:6-12,45-50; 14:2-6,19,20; 16:19-24; 17:5-9; 19:23-41; 21:27-36; 23:12-21; 28:24).

Theophilus, whose name means "lover of God," is unknown to history apart from his mention in Luke and Acts. Whether he was a believer whom Luke was instructing, or a pagan whom Luke sought to convert is not known. Luke's address of him as "most excellent Theophilus" (Luke 1:3) suggests he was a Roman official of some importance (cf. 24:3; 26:25).

Historical and Theological Themes

As the first work of church history ever penned, Acts records the initial response to the Great Commission (Matt. 28:19,20). It provides information on the first 3 decades of the church's existence—material found nowhere else in the NT. Though not primarily a doctrinal work, Acts nonetheless emphasizes that Jesus of Nazareth was Israel's long-awaited Messiah, shows that the gospel is offered to all men (not merely the Jewish people), and stresses the work of the Holy Spirit (mentioned more than 50 times). Acts also makes frequent use of the OT: e.g., 2:17-21 (Joel 2:28-32); 2:25-28 (Ps. 16:8-11); 2:35 (Ps. 110:1); 4:11 (Ps. 118:22); 4:25,26 (Ps. 2:1,2); 7:49,50 (Is. 66:1,2); 8:32,33 (Is. 53:7,8); 28:26,27 (Is. 6:9,10).

Acts abounds with transitions: from the ministry of Jesus to that of the apostles; from the Old Covenant to the New Covenant; from Israel as God's witness nation to the church (composed of both Jews and Gentiles) as God's witness people. The book of Hebrews sets forth the theology of the transition from the Old Covenant to the New; Acts depicts the New Covenant's practical outworking in the life of the church.

Interpretive Challenges

Because Acts is primarily a historical narrative, not a theological treatise like Romans or Hebrews, it contains relatively few interpretive challenges. Those that exist mainly concern the book's transitional nature (see Historical and Theological Themes) and involve the role of signs and wonders. Those issues are addressed in the notes to the relevant passages (e.g., 2:1-47; 15:1-29).

Outline

Prologue (1:1-8)

I. The Witness to Jerusalem (1:9–8:3)
   - A. The Anticipation of the Church (1:9-26)
   - B. The Founding of the Church (2:1-47)
   - C. The Growth of the Church (3:1–8:3)
     1. Apostles: Preaching, healing, and enduring persecution (3:1–5:42)
     2. Deacons: Praying, teaching, and enduring persecution (6:1–8:3)

II. The Witness to Judea and Samaria (8:4–12:25)
   - A. The Gospel to the Samaritans (8:4-25)
   - B. The Conversion of a Gentile (8:26-40)
   - C. The Conversion of Saul (9:1-31)
   - D. The Gospel to Judea (9:32-43)
   - E. The Gospel to the Gentiles (10:1–11:30)
   - F. The Persecution by Herod (12:1-25)

III. The Witness to the Ends of the Earth (13:1–28:31)
   - A. Paul's First Missionary Journey (13:1–14:28)
   - B. The Jerusalem Council (15:1-35)
   - C. Paul's Second Missionary Journey (15:36–18:22)
   - D. Paul's Third Missionary Journey (18:23–21:16)
   - E. Paul's Jerusalem and Caesarean Trials (21:17–26:32)
   - F. Paul's Journey to Rome (27:1–28:31)

Prologue

1 The former account I made, O
[a]Theophilus, of all that Jesus began
both to do and teach, 2 [b]until the day in
which [1]He was taken up, after He through
the Holy Spirit [c]had given commandments
to the apostles whom He had chosen, 3 [d]to
whom He also presented Himself alive
after His suffering by many [2]infallible
proofs, being seen by them during forty
days and speaking of the things pertaining
to the kingdom of God.

The Holy Spirit Promised

4 [e]And being assembled together with
them, He commanded them not to depart
from Jerusalem, but to wait for the Promise
of the Father, "which," *He said,* "you have
[f]heard from Me; 5 [g]for John truly baptized
with water, [h]but you shall be baptized
with the Holy Spirit not many days from
now." 6 Therefore, when they had come together, they asked Him, saying, "Lord, will
You at this time restore the kingdom to Israel?" 7 And He said to them, [i]"It is not for
you to [j]know times or seasons which the
Father has put in His own authority. 8 [k]But
you shall receive power [l]when the Holy
Spirit has come upon you; and [m]you shall
be [3]witnesses to Me in Jerusalem, and in
all Judea and [n]Samaria, and to the [o]end of
the earth."

Jesus Ascends to Heaven

9 [p]Now when He had spoken these
things, while they watched, [q]He was taken
up, and a cloud received Him out of their
sight. 10 And while they looked steadfastly
toward heaven as He went up, behold, two
men stood by them [r]in white apparel,
11 who also said, "Men of Galilee, why do
you stand gazing up into heaven? This
same Jesus, who was taken up from you

CHAPTER 1

1 [a]Luke 1:3
2 [b]Mark 16:19; Acts 1:9, 11, 22 [c]Matt. 28:19; Mark 16:15; John 20:21; Acts 10:42 [1]He ascended into heaven.
3 [d]Matt. 28:17; Mark 16:12, 14; Luke 24:34, 36; John 20:19, 26; 21:1, 14; 1 Cor. 15:5-7 [2]*unmistakable*
4 [e]Luke 24:49 [f][John 14:16, 17, 26; 15:26]; Acts 2:33
5 [g]Matt. 3:11; Mark 1:8; Luke 3:16; John 1:33; Acts 11:16 [h][Joel 2:28]
7 [i]1 Thess. 5:1 [j]Matt. 24:36; Mark 13:32
8 [k][Acts 2:1, 4] [l]Luke 24:49 [m]Luke 24:48; John 15:27 [n]Acts 8:1, 5, 14 [o]Matt. 28:19; Mark 16:15; Rom. 10:18; Col. 1:23; [Rev. 14:6] [3]NU *My witnesses*
9 [p]Luke 24:50, 51 [q]Ps. 68:18; 110:1; Mark 16:19; Luke 23:43; John 20:17; Acts 1:2; [Heb. 4:14; 9:24; 1 Pet. 3:22] 10 [r]Matt. 28:3; Mark 16:5; Luke 24:4; John 20:12; Acts 10:3, 30

1:1 former account. The Gospel of Luke (Luke 1:1-4; see Introduction: Background and Setting). That account chronicled the life and teaching of Jesus, through His death, resurrection, and ascension (Luke 24:51). **Theophilus.** The original recipient of this book. *See note on Luke 1:3.* **all that Jesus began both to do and teach.** Jesus taught the disciples by word and deed the truth necessary to carry on His work. On the cross, He finished the work of redemption, but He had only started the proclamation of its glories.

1:2 taken up. Christ's ascension to the Father (cf. Luke 24:51). Luke uses this term 3 other times (vv. 9,11,22) to describe the end of the Lord's earthly ministry (cf. John 6:62; 13:1,3; 16:28; 17:13; 20:17). **through the Holy Spirit had given commandments.** The Spirit was the source and power of Jesus' earthly ministry (cf. Matt. 4:1; 12:18; Mark 1:12; Luke 3:22; 4:1,14,18) and of the apostles' service (cf. Luke 24:49; John 14:16,17; 16:7). "Commandments" are authoritative NT truths, revealed to the apostles (cf. John 14:26; 16:13-15). **He had chosen.** The Lord sovereignly chose the apostles for salvation and service (cf. John 6:70; 15:16).

1:3 presented Himself...by many infallible proofs. Cf. John 20:30; 1 Cor. 15:5-8. To give the apostles confidence to present His message, Jesus entered a locked room (John 20:19), showed His crucifixion wounds (Luke 24:39), and ate and drank with the disciples (Luke 24:41-43). **forty days.** The time period between Jesus' death and ascension during which He appeared at intervals to the apostles and others (1 Cor. 15:5-8) and provided convincing evidence of His resurrection. **kingdom of God.** Cf. 8:12; 14:22; 19:8; 20:25; 28:23,31. Here this expression refers to the sphere of salvation, the gracious domain of divine rule over believers' hearts (*see notes on 1 Cor. 6:9; Eph. 5:5*; cf. 17:7; Col. 1:13,14; Rev. 11:15; 12:10). This was the dominant theme during Christ's earthly ministry (cf. Matt. 4:23; 9:35; Mark 1:15; Luke 4:43; 9:2; John 3:3-21).

1:4 being assembled together with *them*. An alternative reading, "eating with them," is preferred (cf. 10:41; Luke 24:42,43). The fact that Jesus ate provides additional proof of His bodily resurrection. **wait for the Promise of the Father.** Jesus repeatedly promised that God would send them His Spirit (Luke 11:13; 24:49; John 7:39; 14:16,26; 15:26; 16:7; *see note on John 20:22*).

1:5 John...baptized with water. *See notes on 2:38; John 1:33.* **baptized with the Holy Spirit.** The apostles had to wait until the Day of Pentecost, but since then all believers are baptized with the Holy Spirit at salvation (*see note on 1 Cor. 12:13*; cf. Rom. 8:9; 1 Cor. 6:19,20; Titus 3:5,6). **not many days from now.** God's promise was fulfilled just 10 days later.

1:6 restore the kingdom to Israel. The apostles still believed the earthly form of the kingdom of Messiah would soon be re-established (cf. Luke 19:11; 24:21). They also knew that Ezek. 36 and Joel 2 connected the coming of the kingdom with the outpouring of the Spirit whom Jesus had promised.

1:7 This verse shows that the apostles' expectation of a literal, earthly kingdom mirrored what Christ taught and what the OT predicted. Otherwise, He would have corrected them about such a crucial aspect of His teaching. **times or seasons.** These two words refer to features, eras, and events that will be part of His earthly kingdom reign, which will begin at the second coming (Matt. 25:21-34). The exact time of His return, however, remains unrevealed (Mark 13:32; cf. Deut. 29:29).

1:8 The apostles' mission of spreading the gospel was the major reason the Holy Spirit empowered them. This event dramatically altered world history, and the gospel message eventually reached all parts of the earth (Matt. 28:19,20). **receive power.** The apostles had already experienced the Holy Spirit's saving, guiding, teaching, and miracle-working power. Soon they would receive His indwelling presence and a new dimension of power for witness (*see notes on 2:4; 1 Cor. 6:19,20; Eph. 3:16,20*). **witnesses.** People who tell the truth about Jesus Christ (cf. John 14:26; 1 Pet. 3:15). The Gr. word means "one who dies for his faith" because that was commonly the price of witnessing. **Judea.** The region in which Jerusalem was located. **Samaria.** The region immediately to the N of Judea (*see note on 8:5*).

1:9 taken up. *See note on v. 2.* God the Father took Jesus, in His resurrection body, from this world to His rightful place at the Father's right hand (Luke 24:51; cf. 2:33; John 17:1-6). **a cloud.** A visible reminder that God's glory was present as the apostles watched the ascension. For some of them, this was not the first time they had witnessed divine glory (Mark 9:26); neither will it be the last time clouds accompany Jesus (Mark 13:26; 14:62; *see note on Rev. 1:7*).

1:10 two men...in white apparel. Two angels in the form of men (cf. Gen. 18:2; Josh. 5:13-15; Mark 16:5).

1:11 Men of Galilee. All the apostles were from Galilee except for

into heaven, [s]will so come in like manner
as you saw Him go into heaven."

The Upper Room Prayer Meeting

12 [t]Then they returned to Jerusalem
from the mount called Olivet, which is
near Jerusalem, a Sabbath day's journey.
13 And when they had entered, they went
up [u]into the upper room where they were
staying: [v]Peter, James, John, and Andrew;
Philip and Thomas; Bartholomew and
Matthew; James *the son* of Alphaeus and
[w]Simon the Zealot; and [x]Judas *the son* of
James. 14 [y]These all continued with one
[4]accord in prayer [5]and supplication, with
[z]the women and Mary the mother of Jesus,
and with [a]His brothers.

Matthias Chosen

15 And in those days Peter stood up in
the midst of the [6]disciples (altogether the
number [b]of names was about a hundred
and twenty), and said, 16 "Men *and*
brethren, this Scripture had to be fulfilled,
[c]which the Holy Spirit spoke before by the
mouth of David concerning Judas, [d]who
became a guide to those who arrested Jesus; 17 for [e]he was numbered with us and
obtained a part in [f]this ministry."

18 [g](Now this man purchased a field
with [h]the [7]wages of iniquity; and falling
headlong, he burst open in the middle and
all his [8]entrails gushed out. 19 And it
became known to all those dwelling in Jerusalem; so that field is called in their own
language, Akel Dama, that is, Field of
Blood.)

20 "For it is written in the Book of
Psalms:

> [i]'*Let his dwelling place be*
> [9]*desolate,*
> *And let no one live in it';*

and,

> [j]'*Let another take his* [1]*office.*'

21 "Therefore, of these men who have accompanied us all the time that the Lord Jesus went in and out among us, 22 beginning from the baptism of John to that day

11 [s]Dan. 7:13; Mark 13:26; Luke 21:27; [John 14:3]; 2 Thess. 1:10; Rev. 1:7
12 [t]Luke 24:52
13 [u]Mark 14:15; Luke 22:12; Acts 9:37, 39; 20:8 [v]Matt. 10:2-4 [w]Luke 6:15 [x]Jude 1
14 [y]Acts 2:1, 46 [z]Luke 23:49, 55 [a]Matt. 13:55 [4]*purpose or mind* [5]NU omits *and supplication*
15 [b]Luke 22:32; Rev. 3:4 [6]NU *brethren*
16 [c]Ps. 41:9 [d]Matt. 26:47; Mark 14:43; Luke 22:47; John 18:3
17 [e]Matt. 10:4 [f]Acts 1:25
18 [g]Matt. 27:3-10 [h]Matt. 18:7; 26:14, 15, 24; Mark 14:21; Luke 22:22; John 17:12 [7]*reward of unrighteousness* [8]*intestines*
20 [i]Ps. 69:25 [j]Ps. 109:8 [9]*deserted* [1]Gr. *episkopen,* position of overseer

Judas, who had killed himself by this time (cf. v. 18). **in like manner.** Christ one day will return to earth (to the Mt. of Olives), in the same way He ascended (with clouds), to set up His kingdom (cf. Dan. 7:13; Zech. 14:4; Matt. 24:30; 26:64; Rev. 1:7; 14:14).

1:12 mount called Olivet. Located across the Kidron Valley, E of Jerusalem, this large hill rising about 200 ft. higher in elevation than the city, was the site from which Jesus ascended into heaven (Luke 24:50,51). **Sabbath day's journey.** One-half of a mi. (about 2,000 cubits), the farthest distance a faithful Jew could travel on the Sabbath to accommodate the prohibition of Ex. 16:29. This measurement was derived from tradition based on Israel's encampments in the wilderness. The tents farthest out on the camp's perimeter were 2,000 cubits from the center tabernacle—the longest distance anyone had to walk to reach the tabernacle on the Sabbath (Josh. 3:4; cf. Num. 35:5).

1:13 upper room. Where the Last Supper may have been celebrated (Mark 14:15) and where Jesus had appeared to the apostles after His resurrection. **Bartholomew.** *See note on Matt. 10:3.* This disciple is also called Nathanael (John 1:45-49; 21:2). **James *the son* of Alphaeus.** *See note on Matt. 10:2.* The same person as James the younger, also called "the Less" to distinguish him from James, the brother of John (Mark 15:40). **Zealot.** *See note on Matt. 10:4.* **Judas *the son* of James.** The preferred rendering is "the brother of." *See note on Matt. 10:3.* He was also known as Thaddaeus (Mark 3:18).

1:14 continued...in prayer. The pattern of praying in the name of Jesus started at this time (cf. John 14:13,14). **with the women.** Doubtless they included Mary Magdalene, Mary the wife of Clopas, the sisters Mary and Martha, and Salome. Some of the apostles' wives also may have been present (cf. 1 Cor. 9:5). **Mary the mother of Jesus.** *See note on Luke 1:27,28.* Mary's name does not appear again in the NT. **brothers.** Jesus' half-brothers, named in Mark 6:3 as James, Joses, Judas, and Simon. James was the leader of the Jerusalem church (12:17; 15:13-22) and author of the epistle that bears his name. Judas (Jude) wrote the epistle of Jude. At this time they were new believers in Jesus as God, Savior, and Lord, whereas only 8 months earlier John had mentioned their unbelief (John 7:5). Their conversions are not recorded in the NT, but James may have been saved following a post-resurrection appearance by Jesus (1 Cor. 15:7).

1:15 in those days. Some unspecified time during the believers' 10 days of prayer and fellowship between the ascension and Pentecost. **Peter.** *See note on Matt. 10:2.* The acknowledged leader of the apostles took charge.

1:16 Men *and* brethren. The 120 believers who were gathered (v. 15). **this Scripture had to be fulfilled.** The two OT passages Peter quotes in v. 20 are Pss. 69:25; 109:8. When God gives prophecies, they will come to pass (cf. Ps. 115:3; Is. 46:10; 55:11). **the Holy Spirit...by the mouth of David.** Scripture contains no clearer description of divine inspiration. God spoke through David's mouth, actually referring to his writing (*see note on 2 Pet. 1:21*).

1:17 obtained a part in this ministry. Judas Iscariot was a member of the 12, but was never truly saved which is why he was called "the son of perdition" (John 17:12). *See Matt. 26:24; John 6:64,70,71;* cf. 2:23; Luke 22:22.

1:18 this man purchased a field. Because the field was bought with the money the Jewish leaders paid Judas to betray Jesus, which he returned to them (Matt. 27:3-10), Luke refers to Judas as if he was the buyer (cf. Zech. 11:12,13). **wages of iniquity.** The 30 pieces of silver paid to Judas. **falling headlong.** Apparently the tree on which Judas chose to hang himself (Matt. 27:5) overlooked a cliff. Likely, the rope or branch broke (or the knot slipped) and his body was shattered on the rocks below.

1:19 Akel Dama...Field of Blood. This is the Aram. name of the field bought by the Jewish leaders. Traditionally, the field is located S of Jerusalem in the Valley of Hinnom, where that valley crosses the Kidron Valley. The soil there was good for making pottery, thus Matthew identifies it as "the potter's field" (Matt. 27:7,10; *see notes on v. 18*).

1:20 it is written. *See note on v. 16.* Peter used the most compelling proof, Scripture, to reassure the believers that Judas' defection and the choice of his replacement were both in God's purpose (cf. Ps. 55:12-15).

1:21 went in and out among us. The first requirement for Judas' successor was that he had participated in Jesus' earthly ministry.

when [k]He was taken up from us, one of
these must [l]become a witness with us of
His resurrection."
23 And they proposed two: Joseph called
[m]Barsabas, who was surnamed Justus, and
Matthias. 24 And they prayed and said,
"You, O Lord, [n]who know the hearts of all,
show which of these two You have chosen
25 [o]to take part in this ministry and apostleship from which Judas by transgression
fell, that he might go to his own place."
26 And they cast their lots, and the lot fell
on Matthias. And he was numbered with
the eleven apostles.

Coming of the Holy Spirit

2 When [a]the Day of Pentecost had fully
come, [b]they were all [1]with one accord
in one place. 2 And suddenly there came a
sound from heaven, as of a rushing mighty
wind, and [c]it filled the whole house where
they were sitting. 3 Then there appeared to

22 [k] Acts 1:9 [l] Acts 1:8; 2:32
23 [m] Acts 15:22
24 [n] 1 Sam. 16:7; Jer. 17:10; Acts 1:2
25 [o] Acts 1:17

CHAPTER 2

1 [a] Lev. 23:15; Deut. 16:9; Acts 20:16; 1 Cor. 16:8 [b] Acts 1:14 [1] NU *together*
2 [c] Acts 4:31

1:22 baptism of John. Jesus' baptism by John the Baptist (Matt. 3:13-17; Mark 1:9-11; Luke 3:21-23). **a witness with us of His resurrection.** A second requirement for Judas' successor was that he had to have seen the resurrected Christ. The resurrection was central to apostolic preaching (cf. 2:24,32; 3:15; 5:30; 10:40; 13:30-37).

1:23 Barsabas...Justus. Barsabas means "son of the Sabbath." Justus ("the righteous") was Joseph's Lat. name. Many Jews in the Roman Empire had equivalent Gentile names. **Matthias.** The name means "gift of God." The ancient historian Eusebius claims Matthias was among the 70 of Luke 10:1.

1:24 You have chosen. Judas' successor was sovereignly determined (*see notes on v. 20*).

1:25 his own place. Judas chose his own fate of hell by rejecting Christ. It is not unfair to say that Judas and all others who go to hell belong there (cf. John 6:70).

1:26 cast their lots. A common OT method of determining God's will (cf. Lev. 16:8-10; Josh. 7:14; Prov. 18:18; *see note on Prov. 16:33*). This is the last biblical mention of lots—the coming of the Spirit made them unnecessary.

2:1 Day of Pentecost. "Pentecost" means "fiftieth" and refers to the Feast of Weeks (Ex. 34:22,23) or Harvest (Lev. 23:16), which was celebrated 50 days after Passover in May/June (Lev. 23:15-22). It was one of 3 annual feasts for which the nation was to come to Jerusalem (*see notes on Ex. 23:14-19*). At Pentecost, an offering of firstfruits was made (Lev. 23:20). The Holy Spirit came on this day as the firstfruits of the believer's inheritance (cf. 2 Cor. 5:5; Eph. 1:11,14). Those gathered into the church then were also the firstfruits of the full harvest of all believers to come after. **in one place.** The upper room mentioned in 1:13.

2:2 a sound...as...mighty wind. Luke's simile described God's action of sending the Holy Spirit. Wind is frequently used in Scripture as a picture of the Spirit (cf. Ezek. 37:9,10; John 3:8).

Ministries of the Holy Spirit

• Baptismal Medium	1 Cor. 12:13
• Calls to Ministry	Acts 13:2-4
• Channel of Divine Revelation	2 Sam. 23:2; Neh. 9:30; Zech. 7:12; John 14:17
• Empowers	Ex. 31:1,2; Judg. 13:25; Acts 1:8
• Fills	Luke 4:1; Acts 2:4; Eph. 5:18
• Guarantees	2 Cor. 1:22; 5:5; Eph. 1:14
• Guards	2 Tim. 1:14
• Helps	John 14:16,26; 15:26; 16:7
• Illuminates	1 Cor. 2:10-13
• Indwells	Rom. 8:9-11; 1 Cor. 3:16; 6:19
• Intercedes	Rom. 8:26,27
• Produces fruit	Gal. 5:22,23
• Provides Spiritual Character	Gal. 5:16,18,25
• Regenerates	John 3:5,6,8
• Restrains/Convicts of Sin	Gen. 6:3; John 16:8-10; Acts 7:51
• Sanctifies	Rom. 15:16; 1 Cor. 6:11; 2 Thess. 2:13
• Seals	2 Cor. 1:22; Eph. 1:14; 4:30
• Selects Overseers	Acts 20:28
• Source of Fellowship	2 Cor. 13:14; Phil. 2:1
• Source of Liberty	2 Cor. 3:17,18
• Source of Power	Eph. 3:16
• Source of Unity	Eph. 4:3,4
• Source of Spiritual Gifts	1 Cor. 12:4-11
• Teaches	John 14:26; Acts 15:28; 1 John 2:20,27

them [2]divided tongues, as of fire, and *one*
sat upon each of them. 4 And [d]they were
all filled with the Holy Spirit and began [e]to
speak with other tongues, as the Spirit
gave them utterance.

The Crowd's Response

5 And there were dwelling in Jerusalem
Jews, [f]devout men, from every nation
under heaven. 6 And when this sound occurred, the [g]multitude came together, and
were confused, because everyone heard
them speak in his own language. 7 Then
they were all amazed and marveled, saying to one another, "Look, are not all these
who speak [h]Galileans? 8 And how *is it that*
we hear, each in our own [3]language in
which we were born? 9 Parthians and
Medes and Elamites, those dwelling in
Mesopotamia, Judea and [i]Cappadocia,
Pontus and Asia, 10 Phrygia and Pamphylia, Egypt and the parts of Libya adjoining Cyrene, visitors from Rome, both
Jews and proselytes, 11 Cretans and
[4]Arabs—we hear them speaking in our
own tongues the wonderful works of
God." 12 So they were all amazed and perplexed, saying to one another, "Whatever
could this mean?"
13 Others mocking said, "They are full of
new wine."

Peter's Sermon

14 But Peter, standing up with the
eleven, raised his voice and said to them,
"Men of Judea and all who dwell in Jerusalem, let this be known to you, and heed my
words. 15 For these are not drunk, as you
suppose, [j]since it is *only* [5]the third hour of
the day. 16 But this is what was spoken by
the prophet Joel:

17 *'And[k] it shall come to pass in the*
last days, says God,

3 [2] *Or tongues as of fire, distributed and resting on each*
4 [d] Matt. 3:11; 5:6; 10:20; Luke 3:16; John 14:16; 16:7-15; Acts 1:5 [e] Mark 16:17; Acts 10:46; 19:6; [1 Cor. 12:10, 28, 30; 13:1]
5 [f] Luke 2:25; Acts 8:2
6 [g] Acts 4:32
7 [h] Matt. 26:73; Acts 1:11
8 [3] *dialect*
9 [i] 1 Pet. 1:1
11 [4] *Arabians*
15 [j] 1 Thess. 5:7 [5] 9 A.M.
17 [k] Is. 44:3; Ezek. 11:19; Joel 2:28-32; [Zech. 12:10; John 7:38]

2:3 The disciples could not comprehend the significance of the Spirit's arrival without the Lord sovereignly illustrating what was occurring with a visible phenomenon. **tongues, as of fire.** Just as the sound, like wind, was symbolic, these were not literal flames of fire but supernatural indicators, like fire, that God had sent the Holy Spirit upon each believer. In Scripture, fire often denoted the divine presence (cf. Ex. 3:2-6). God's use of a fire-like appearance here parallels what He did with the dove when Jesus was baptized (Matt. 3:11; Luke 3:16).

2:4 all. The apostles and the 120. Cf. Joel 2:28-32. **filled with the Holy Spirit.** In contrast to the baptism with the Spirit, which is the one-time act by which God places believers into His body (*see notes on 1 Cor. 12:13*), the filling is a repeated reality of Spirit-controlled behavior that God commands believers to maintain (*see notes on Eph. 5:18*). Peter and many others in Acts 2 were filled with the Spirit again (e.g., 4:8,31; 6:5; 7:55) and so spoke boldly the Word of God. The fullness of the Spirit affects all areas of life, not just speaking boldly (cf. Eph. 5:19-33). **with other tongues.** Known languages (*see notes on v. 6; 1 Cor. 14:1-25*), not ecstatic utterances. These languages given by the Spirit were a sign of judgment to unbelieving Israel (*see notes on 1 Cor. 14:21,22*). They also showed that from then on God's people would come from all nations, and marked the transition from Israel to the church. Tongues speaking occurs only twice more in Acts (10:46; 19:6).

2:5 Jews, devout men. Hebrew males who made the pilgrimage to Jerusalem. They were expected to celebrate Pentecost (*see note on v. 1*) in Jerusalem, as part of observing the Jewish religious calendar. *See note on Ex. 23:14-19.*

2:6 this sound. The noise like gusty wind (v. 2), not the sound of the various languages. **speak in his own language.** As the believers were speaking, each pilgrim in the crowd recognized the language or dialect from his own country.

2:7 Galileans. Inhabitants of the mostly rural area of northern Israel around the Sea of Galilee. Galilean Jews spoke with a distinct regional accent and were considered to be unsophisticated and uneducated by the southern Judean Jews. When Galileans were seen to be speaking so many different languages, the Judean Jews were astonished.

2:9-11 The listing of specific countries and ethnic groups proves again that these utterances were known human languages.

2:9 Parthians. They lived in what is modern Iran. **Medes.** In Daniel's time, they ruled with the Persians, but had settled in Parthia. **Elamites.** They were from the southwestern part of the Parthian Empire. **Mesopotamia.** This means "between the rivers" (the Tigris and Euphrates). Many Jews still lived there, descendants of those who were in captivity and who never returned to Palestine (cf. 2 Chr. 36:22,23). **Judea.** All the region once controlled by David and Solomon, including Syria.

2:9,10 Cappadocia, Pontus and Asia, Phrygia and Pamphylia. All were districts in Asia Minor, in what is now Turkey.

2:10 Egypt. Many Jews lived there, especially in the city of Alexandria. The nation then covered the same general area as modern Egypt. **Libya adjoining Cyrene.** These districts were W of Egypt, along the North African coast. **Rome.** The capital of the Empire had a sizeable Jewish population, dating from the second century B.C. **proselytes.** Gentile converts to Judaism. Jews in Rome were especially active in seeking such converts.

2:11 Cretans. Residents of the island of Crete, off the southern coast of Greece. **Arabs.** Jews who lived S of Damascus, among the Nabatean Arabs (cf. Gal. 1:17). **we hear them speaking.** *See note on v. 6.* **wonderful works of God.** The Christians were quoting from the OT what God had done for His people (cf. Ex. 15:11; Pss. 40:5; 77:11; 96:3; 107:21). Such praises were often heard in Jerusalem during festival times.

2:13 new wine. A drink that could have made one drunk.

2:14-40 After the Holy Spirit's arrival, the first major event of church history was Peter's sermon, which led to 3,000 conversions and established the church (vv. 41-47).

2:14 with the eleven. This number of the apostles included the newly-appointed Matthias, who replaced Judas Iscariot (*see notes on 1:23,24*).

2:15 the third hour. Calculated in Jewish fashion from sunrise, this was 9:00 a.m.

2:16-21 See Introduction to Joel: Interpretive Challenges; *see notes on Joel 2:28-32.* Joel's prophecy will not be completely fulfilled until the millennial kingdom and the final judgment. But Peter, by using it, shows that Pentecost was a pre-fulfillment, a taste of what will happen in the millennial kingdom when the Spirit is poured out on all flesh (cf. 10:45).

2:17 *last days.* This phrase refers to the present era of redemptive

[l]That I will pour out of My Spirit
on all flesh;
Your sons and [m]your daughters
shall prophesy,
Your young men shall see visions,
Your old men shall dream dreams.
18 *And on My menservants and on*
My maidservants
I will pour out My Spirit in those
days;
[n]And they shall prophesy.
19 *[o]I will show wonders in heaven*
above
And signs in the earth beneath:
Blood and fire and vapor of smoke.
20 *[p]The sun shall be turned into*
darkness,
And the moon into blood,
Before the coming of the great and
awesome day of the LORD.
21 *And it shall come to pass*
That [q]whoever calls on the name of
the LORD
Shall be saved.'

22 "Men of Israel, hear these words: Jesus
of Nazareth, a Man attested by God to you
[r]by miracles, wonders, and signs which
God did through Him in your midst, as
you yourselves also know— 23 Him, [s]being
delivered by the determined purpose and
foreknowledge of God, [t]you [6]have taken
by lawless hands, have crucified, and put
to death; 24 [u]whom God raised up, having
[7]loosed the [8]pains of death, because it was
not possible that He should be held by it.
25 For David says concerning Him:

[v]'I foresaw the LORD always before
my face,
For He is at my right hand, that I
may not be shaken.
26 *Therefore my heart rejoiced, and*
my tongue was glad;
Moreover my flesh also will rest in
hope.
27 *For You will not leave my soul in*
Hades,
Nor will You allow Your Holy One
to see [w]corruption.
28 *You have made known to me the*
ways of life;
You will make me full of joy in
Your presence.'

29 "Men *and* brethren, let *me* speak freely
to you [x]of the patriarch David, that he is
both dead and buried, and his tomb is with
us to this day. 30 Therefore, being a prophet,
[y]and knowing that God had sworn with an

17 [l]Acts 10:45 [m]Acts 21:9
18 [n]Acts 21:4,9; 1 Cor. 12:10
19 [o]Joel 2:30
20 [p]Is. 13:10; Ezek. 32:7; Matt. 24:29; Mark 13:24, 25; Luke 21:25; Rev. 6:12
21 [q]Rom. 10:13
22 [r]Is. 50:5; John 3:2; 5:6; Acts 10:38
23 [s]Matt. 26:4; Luke 22:22; Acts 3:18; 4:28; [1 Pet. 1:20]
[t]Acts 5:30 [6]NU omits *have taken*
24 [u][Rom. 8:11; 1 Cor. 6:14; 2 Cor. 4:14; Eph. 1:20; Col. 2:12]; 1 Thess. 1:10; Heb. 13:20 [7]*destroyed* or *abolished* [8]Lit. *birth pangs*
25 [v]Ps. 16:8-11
27 [w]Acts 13:30-37
29 [x]Acts 13:36
30 [y]2 Sam. 7:12; Ps. 132:11; Luke 1:32; Rom. 1:3; 2 Tim. 2:8

history from the first coming of Christ (Heb. 1:2; 1 Pet. 1:20; 1 John 2:18) to His return. ***My Spirit.*** *See notes on 1:2,5,8.*

2:17,18 *all flesh.* This indicates all people will receive the Holy Spirit, because everyone who enters the millennial kingdom will be redeemed (cf. Matt. 24:29–25:46; Rev. 20:4-6).

2:17 *visions...dreams.* Dreams (Gen. 20:3; Dan. 7:1) and visions (Gen. 15:1; Rev. 9:17) were some of God's most memorable means of revelation since they were pictorial in nature. While they were not limited to believers (e.g., Abimelech, Gen. 20:3 and Pharaoh, Gen. 41:1-8), they were primarily reserved for prophets and apostles (cf. Num. 12:6). While frequent in the OT, they were rare in the NT. In Acts, all of God's visions were given to either Peter (chaps. 10,11) or Paul (chaps. 9,18; cf. 2 Cor. 12:1). Most frequently they were used to reveal apocalyptic imagery (cf. Ezek., Dan., Zech., Rev.). They were not considered normal in biblical times, nor should they be so now. The time will come, however, when God will use visions and dreams during the Tribulation period as predicted by Joel 2:28-32.

2:18 prophesy. The proclamation of God's truth will be pervasive in the millennial kingdom.

2:19 *wonders...signs.* Cf. 4:30; 5:12; 14:3; 15:12. "Wonders" is the amazement people experience when witnessing supernatural works (miracles). "Signs" point to the power of God behind miracles—marvels have no value unless they point to God and His truth. Such works were often done by the Holy Spirit through the apostles (5:12-16) and their associates (6:8) to authenticate them as the messengers of God's truth. Cf. 2 Cor. 12:12; Heb. 2:3,4. ***Blood...fire...vapor of smoke.*** These phenomena are all connected with events surrounding Christ's second coming and signal the establishment of the earthly kingdom: blood (Rev. 6:8; 8:7,8; 9:15; 14:20; 16:3); fire (Rev. 8:5,7,8,10); and smoke (Rev. 9:2,3,17,18; 18:9,18).

2:20 *sun...darkness...moon into blood.* Cf. Matt. 24:29,30; *see note on Rev. 6:12.* ***day of the LORD.*** See Introduction to Joel: Interpretive Challenges; *see note on 1 Thess. 5:2.* This Day of the Lord will come with the return of Jesus Christ (cf. 2 Thess. 2:2; Rev. 19:11-15).

2:21 *whoever calls.* Up to that hour of judgment and wrath, any who turn to Christ as Lord and Savior will be saved (*see notes on Rom. 10:10-13*).

2:22-36 Here is the main body of Peter's sermon, in which he presented and defended Jesus Christ as Israel's Messiah.

2:22 Jesus of Nazareth. The humble name that often identified the Lord during His earthly ministry (Matt. 21:11; Mark 10:47; Luke 24:19; John 18:5). **attested...by miracles, wonders, and signs.** By a variety of supernatural means and works, God validated Jesus as the Messiah (cf. Matt. 11:1-6; Luke 7:20-23; John 3:2; 5:17-20; 8:28; Phil. 2:9; *see notes on 1:3; 2:19*).

2:23 by the determined purpose and foreknowledge of God. From eternity past (2 Tim. 1:9; Rev. 13:8) God predetermined that Jesus would die an atoning death as part of the His pre-ordained plan (4:27,28; 13:27-29). **lawless hands, have crucified.** An indictment against "men of Israel" (v. 22), those unbelieving Jews who instigated Jesus' death, which was carried out by the Romans. That the crucifixion was predetermined by God does not absolve the guilt of those who caused it.

2:24 not possible. Because of His divine power (John 11:25; Heb. 2:14) and God's promise and purpose (Luke 24:46; John 2:18-22; 1 Cor. 15:16-26), death could not keep Jesus in the grave.

2:25-28 David says. The Lord was speaking of His resurrection prophetically through David (*see notes on Ps. 16:8-11*).

2:27 *Hades.* Cf. v. 31; *see note on Luke 16:23.* The NT equivalent of the OT grave or "sheol." Though sometimes it identifies hell (Matt. 11:23), here it refers to the general place of the dead.

2:29 his tomb is with us. A reminder to the Jews that David's body had never been raised, so he could not be the fulfillment of the prophecy of Ps. 16.

oath to him that of the fruit of his body, [g]according to the flesh, He would raise up the Christ to sit on his throne, **31** he, foreseeing this, spoke concerning the resurrection of the Christ, [z]that His soul was not left in Hades, nor did His flesh see corruption. **32** [a]This Jesus God has raised up, [b]of which we are all witnesses. **33** Therefore [c]being exalted [1]to [d]the right hand of God, and [e]having received from the Father the promise of the Holy Spirit, He [f]poured out this which you now see and hear.

34 "For David did not ascend into the heavens, but he says himself:

> [g]'The LORD said to my Lord,
> " Sit at My right hand,
> **35** Till I make Your enemies Your footstool." '

36 "Therefore let all the house of Israel know assuredly that God has made this Jesus, whom you crucified, both Lord and Christ."

30 [g] NU *He would seat one on his throne,*
31 [z] Ps. 16:10; Is. 50:8; 53:10
32 [a] Acts 2:24 [b] Acts 1:8; 3:15
33 [c] Ps. 68:18; [Acts 5:31]; Phil. 2:9 [d] Ps. 110:1; Mark 16:19; [Heb. 10:12] [e] Luke 24:49; [John 14:26] [f] Matt. 3:11; 5:6; Luke 3:16; 22:69; John 14:16; 16:7-15; Acts 2:1-11, 17; 10:45; Eph. 4:8 [1] *Possibly by*
34 [g] Ps. 68:18; 110:1; Matt. 22:44; Luke 23:43; John 20:17; 1 Cor. 15:25; Eph. 1:20; Heb. 1:13
37 [h] [Zech. 12:10]; Luke 3:10, 12, 14; John 16:8
38 [i] Luke 24:47 [2] *forgiveness*
39 [j] Joel 2:28, 32 [k] Acts 11:15, 18; Eph. 2:13
40 [3] *crooked*

37 Now when they heard *this,* [h]they were cut to the heart, and said to Peter and the rest of the apostles, "Men *and* brethren, what shall we do?"

38 Then Peter said to them, [i]"Repent, and let every one of you be baptized in the name of Jesus Christ for the [2]remission of sins; and you shall receive the gift of the Holy Spirit. **39** For the promise is to you and [j]to your children, and [k]to all who are afar off, as many as the Lord our God will call."

A Vital Church Grows

40 And with many other words he testified and exhorted them, saying, "Be saved from this [3]perverse generation." **41** Then those who [4]gladly received his word were baptized; and that day about three thousand souls were added *to them.* **42** [l]And they continued steadfastly in the apostles' [5]doctrine and fellowship, in the breaking of

41 [4] NU omits *gladly* **42** [l] Acts 1:14; Rom. 12:12; Eph. 6:18; Col. 4:2; Heb. 10:25 [5] *teaching*

2:30-32 Peter exposits the meaning of Ps. 16 as referring not to David, but to Jesus Christ. He would be raised to reign (v. 30; cf. Pss. 2:1-9; 89:3; 138:11).

2:30 being a prophet. Peter quoted Ps. 132:11. As God's spokesman, David knew that God would keep His oath (2 Sam. 7:11-16) and Christ would come.

2:31 Peter quoted Ps. 16:10.

2:32 God has raised up. Cf. v. 24; 10:40; 17:31; 1 Cor. 6:14; Eph. 1:20. That He did so attests to His approval of Christ's work on the cross. **we are all witnesses.** The early preachers preached the resurrection (3:15,26; 4:10; 5:30; 10:40; 13:30,33,34,37; 17:31).

2:33 After Jesus was risen and ascended, God's promise to send the Holy Spirit was fulfilled (cf. John 7:39; Gal. 3:14) and manifest that day. **exalted to the right hand of God.** *See note on 7:55.*

2:34 *The LORD said to my Lord.* Peter quoted another psalm (Ps. 110:1) concerning the exaltation of Messiah by ascension to the right hand of God, and reminds the reader that it was not fulfilled by David (as bodily resurrection had not yet been; *see note on v. 29*), but by Jesus Christ (v. 36). Peter had been an eyewitness to that ascension (1:9-11).

2:36 Peter summarizes his sermon with a powerful statement of certainty: The OT prophecies of resurrection and exaltation provide evidence that overwhelmingly points to the crucified Jesus as the Messiah. **both Lord and Christ.** Jesus is God as well as anointed Messiah (cf. Rom. 1:4; 10:9; 1 Cor. 12:3; Phil. 2:9,11).

2:37 cut to the heart. The Gr. word for "cut" means "pierce" or "stab," and thus denotes something sudden and unexpected. In grief, remorse, and intense spiritual conviction, Peter's listeners were stunned by his indictment that they had killed their Messiah.

2:38 Repent. This refers to a change of mind and purpose that turns an individual from sin to God (1 Thess. 1:9). Such change involves more than fearing the consequences of God's judgment. Genuine repentance knows that the evil of sin must be forsaken and the person and work of Christ totally and singularly embraced. Peter exhorted his hearers to repent, otherwise they would not experience true conversion (*see note on Matt. 3:2;* cf. 3:19; 5:31; 8:22; 11:18; 17:30; 20:21; 26:20; Matt. 4:17). **be baptized.** This Gr. word lit. means "be dipped or immersed" in water. Peter was obeying Christ's command from Matt. 28:19 and urging the people who repented and turned to the Lord Christ for salvation to identify, through the waters of baptism, with His death, burial, and resurrection (cf. 19:5; Rom. 6:3,4; 1 Cor. 12:13; Gal. 3:27; *see notes on Matt. 3:2*). This is the first time the apostles publicly enjoined people to obey that ceremony. Prior to this, many Jews had experienced the baptism of John the Baptist, (*see notes on Matt. 3:1-3*) and were also familiar with the baptism of Gentile converts to Judaism (proselytes). **in the name of Jesus Christ.** For the new believer, it was a crucial but costly identification to accept. **for the remission of sins.** This might better be translated "because of the remission of sins." Baptism does not produce forgiveness and cleansing from sin. *See notes on 1 Pet. 3:20,21.* The reality of forgiveness precedes the rite of baptism (v. 41). Genuine repentance brings from God the forgiveness (remission) of sins (cf. Eph. 1:7), and because of that the new believer was to be baptized. Baptism, however, was to be the ever-present act of obedience, so that it became synonymous with salvation. Thus to say one was baptized for forgiveness was the same as saying one was saved. *See note on "one baptism" in Eph. 4:5.* Every believer enjoys the complete remission of sins (Matt. 26:28; Luke 24:47; Eph. 1:7; Col. 2:13; 1 John 2:12). **the gift of the Holy Spirit.** *See notes on 1:5,8.*

2:39 the promise. *See note on 1:4.* **all who are afar off.** Gentiles, who would also share in the blessings of salvation (cf. Eph. 2:11-13). **as many as the Lord our God will call.** Salvation is ultimately from the Lord. *See note on Rom. 3:24.*

2:41 those who...received his word were baptized. *See note on v. 38.* **three thousand.** Peter's use of a specific number suggests records were kept of conversions and baptisms (*see note on v. 38*). Archeological work on the S side of the temple mount has uncovered numerous Jewish *mikvahs,* large baptistry-like facilities where Jewish worshipers would immerse themselves in ritual purification before entering the temple. More than enough existed to facilitate the large number of baptisms in a short amount of time.

2:42 apostles' doctrine. The foundational content for the believer's spiritual growth and maturity was the Scripture, God's revealed truth, which the apostles received (*see notes on John 14:26; 15:26,27; 16:13*) and taught faithfully. *See notes on 2 Pet. 1:19-21; 3:1,2,16.* **fellowship.** Lit. "partnership," or "sharing." Because Christians become

bread, and in prayers. 43 Then fear came
upon every soul, and [m]many wonders and
signs were done through the apostles.
44 Now all who believed were together, and
[n]had all things in common, 45 and [6]sold
their possessions and goods, and [o]divided[7]
them among all, as anyone had need.
46 [p]So continuing daily with one accord
[q]in the temple, and [r]breaking bread from
house to house, they ate their food with
gladness and simplicity of heart, 47 praising God and having favor with all the people. And [s]the Lord added [8]to the church
daily those who were being saved.

A Lame Man Healed

3 Now Peter and John went up together
[a]to the temple at the hour of prayer,
[b]the ninth *hour.* 2 And [c]a certain man lame
from his mother's womb was carried,
whom they laid daily at the gate of the
temple which is called Beautiful, [d]to [1]ask
alms from those who entered the temple;
3 who, seeing Peter and John about to go
into the temple, asked for alms. 4 And fixing his eyes on him, with John, Peter said,
"Look at us." 5 So he gave them his attention, expecting to receive something from
them. 6 Then Peter said, "Silver and gold I
do not have, but what I do have I give you:
[e]In the name of Jesus Christ of Nazareth,
rise up and walk." 7 And he took him by
the right hand and lifted *him* up, and immediately his feet and ankle bones received strength. 8 So he, [f]leaping up, stood
and walked and entered the temple with
them—walking, leaping, and praising
God. 9 [g]And all the people saw him walking and praising God. 10 Then they knew
that it was he who [h]sat begging alms at the
Beautiful Gate of the temple; and they
were filled with wonder and amazement at
what had happened to him.

Preaching in Solomon's Portico

11 Now as the lame man who was healed
held on to Peter and John, all the people ran
together to them in the porch [i]which is
called Solomon's, greatly amazed. 12 So
when Peter saw *it,* he responded to the people: "Men of Israel, why do you marvel at
this? Or why look so intently at us, as
though by our own power or godliness we
had made this man walk? 13 [j]The God of
Abraham, Isaac, and Jacob, the God of our
fathers, [k]glorified His Servant Jesus, whom
you [l]delivered up and [m]denied in the presence of Pilate, when he was determined to
let *Him* go. 14 But you denied [n]the Holy One
[o]and the Just, and [p]asked for a murderer to

43 [m] Mark 16:17; Acts 2:22
44 [n] Acts 4:32, 34, 37; 5:2
45 [o] Is. 58:7 [6] *would sell* [7] *distributed*
46 [p] Acts 1:14 [q] Luke 24:53 [r] Luke 24:30; Acts 2:42; 20:7; [1 Cor. 10:16]
47 [s] Acts 5:14 [8] NU omits *to the church*

CHAPTER 3

1 [a] Acts 2:46 [b] Ps. 55:17; Matt. 27:45; Acts 10:30
2 [c] Acts 14:8 [d] John 9:8; Acts 3:10 [1] Beg
6 [e] Acts 4:10
8 [f] Is. 35:6
9 [g] Acts 4:16, 21
10 [h] John 9:8; Acts 3:2
11 [i] John 10:23; Acts 5:12
13 [j] John 5:30 [k] Is. 49:3; John 7:39; 12:23; 13:31 [l] Matt. 27:2 [m] Matt. 27:20; Mark 15:11; Luke 23:18; John 18:40; Acts 13:28
14 [n] Ps. 16:10; Mark 1:24; Luke 1:35 [o] Acts 7:52; 2 Cor. 5:21 [p] John 18:40

partners with Jesus Christ and all other believers (1 John 1:3), it is their spiritual duty to stimulate one another to righteousness and obedience (cf. Rom. 12:10; 13:8; 15:5; Gal. 5:13; Eph. 4:2,25; 5:21; Col. 3:9; 1 Thess. 4:9; Heb. 3:13; 10:24,25; 1 Pet. 4:9,10). **breaking of bread.** A reference to the Lord's Table, or Communion, which is mandatory for all Christians to observe (cf. 1 Cor. 11:24-29). **prayers.** Of individual believers and the church corporately (see 1:14,24; 4:24-31; cf. John 14:13,14).

2:43 wonders and signs. *See note on v. 19.* In the NT, the ability to perform miracles was limited to the apostles and their close colleagues (e.g., Philip in 8:13; cf. 2 Cor. 12:12; Heb. 2:3,4). These produced awe and respect for divine power.

2:44 all things in common. See 4:32. This phrase conveys not that the early Christians lived in a commune or pooled and redistributed everything equally, but that they held their own possessions lightly, ready to use them at any moment for someone else, as needs arose.

2:45 sold their possessions. This indicates that they had not pooled their resources (*see note on v. 44*) but sold their own possessions to provide money for those of the church in need (cf. v. 46; 4:34-37; 2 Cor. 8:13,14).

2:46 daily...in the temple. Believers went to the temple to praise God (v. 47), observe the daily hours of prayer (cf. 3:1), and witness to the gospel (v. 47; 5:42). **breaking bread from house to house.** This has reference to the daily means that believers shared with one another. **gladness and simplicity of heart.** The Jerusalem church was joyful because its single focus was on Jesus Christ. *See notes on 2 Cor. 11:3; Phil. 3:13,14.*

2:47 the Lord added. Cf. v. 39; 5:14. *See note on Matt. 16:18.* Salvation is God's sovereign work.

3:1 hour of prayer, the ninth *hour*. 3:00 p.m. The Jews had 3 daily times of prayer (Ps. 55:17); the other two were 9:00 a.m. (third hour) and 12:00 noon (sixth hour).

3:2 gate of the temple...called Beautiful. A large and ornate gate inside the temple mount on the eastern side, separating the Court of the Gentiles from the Court of the Women. **alms.** A charitable donation of money.

3:3 into the temple. Beggars considered the temple the best site to operate because the daily throngs came to impress God with their pious good works, including offerings at the temple treasury.

3:10 Beautiful Gate. *See note on v. 2.*

3:11 porch...Solomon's. A portico surrounding the temple's Court of the Gentiles. This was also where Jesus had taught about the Good Shepherd (John 10:23). Cf. Is. 35:6.

3:13 The God of Abraham, Isaac, and Jacob. A description of God familiar to Peter's Jewish audience (cf. Ex. 3:6,15; 1 Kin. 18:36; 1 Chr. 29:18; 2 Chr. 30:6; Matt. 22:32). He used this formula, which stressed God's covenant faithfulness, to demonstrate that he declared the same God and Messiah whom the prophets had proclaimed. **His Servant Jesus.** Peter depicted Jesus as God's personal representative. This is an unusual NT title for Jesus, used only 4 other places (v. 26; 4:27,30; Matt. 12:18), but a more familiar OT name for Messiah (Is. 42:1-4,19; 49:5-7; *see notes on 52:13–53:12*; cf. Matt. 20:28; John 6:38; 8:28; 13:1-7). **Pilate...determined to let *Him* go.** Pontius Pilate, the Roman governor at Jesus' trial, came from a national tradition that strongly supported justice (cf. 16:37,38; 22:25-29; 25:16). He knew Jesus' crucifixion would be unjust and therefore declared Him innocent 6 times (Luke 23:4,14,15,22; John 18:38; 19:4,6) and repeatedly sought to release Him (Luke 23:13-22; *see notes on John 19:12,13*).

3:14 the Holy One. Cf. Ps. 10:10; Luke 4:34; John 6:69. **the Just.** Cf. 1 John 2:1. **murderer.** Barabbas (Matt. 27:16-21; Mark 15:11; Luke 23:18; John 18:40).

be granted to you, **15** and killed the [2]Prince
of life, [q]whom God raised from the dead,
[r]of which we are witnesses. **16** [s]And His
name, through faith in His name, has made
this man strong, whom you see and know.
Yes, the faith which *comes* through Him has
given him this perfect soundness in the
presence of you all.

17 "Yet now, brethren, I know that [t]you
did *it* in ignorance, as *did* also your rulers.
18 But [u]those things which God foretold
[v]by the mouth of all His prophets, that the
Christ would suffer, He has thus fulfilled.
19 [w]Repent therefore and be converted,
that your sins may be blotted out, so that
times of refreshing may come from the
presence of the Lord, **20** and that He may
send [3]Jesus Christ, who was [4]preached to
you before, **21** [x]whom heaven must receive
until the times of [y]restoration of all things,
[z]which God has spoken by the mouth of all
His holy prophets since [5]the world began.
22 For Moses truly said to the fathers, [a]*'The*
LORD your God will raise up for you a
Prophet like me from your brethren. Him
you shall hear in all things, whatever He
says to you. **23** *And it shall be that every*
soul who will not hear that Prophet shall
be utterly destroyed from among the peo-
ple.' **24** Yes, and [b]all the prophets, from
Samuel and those who follow, as many as
have spoken, have also [6]foretold these
days. **25** [c]You are sons of the prophets, and
of the covenant which God made with our
fathers, saying to Abraham, [d]*'And in your*
seed all the families of the earth shall be
blessed.' **26** To you [e]first, God, having
raised up His Servant Jesus, sent Him to
bless you, [f]in turning away every one *of*
you from your iniquities."

Peter and John Arrested

4 Now as they spoke to the people, the
priests, the captain of the temple, and
the [a]Sadducees came upon them, **2** being
greatly disturbed that they taught the people and preached in Jesus the resurrection
from the dead. **3** And they laid hands on
them, and put *them* in custody until the
next day, for it was already evening.
4 However, many of those who heard the
word believed; and the number of the men
came to be about five thousand.

Addressing the Sanhedrin

5 And it came to pass, on the next day,
that their rulers, elders, and scribes, **6** as
well as [b]Annas the high priest, Caiaphas,

15 [q] Acts 2:24 [r] Acts 2:32 [2] Or *Originator*
16 [s] Matt. 9:22; Acts 4:10; 14:9
17 [t] Luke 23:34; John 16:3; [Acts 13:27; 17:30]; 1 Cor. 2:8; 1 Tim. 1:13
18 [u] Luke 24:44; Acts 26:22 [v] Ps. 22; Is. 50:6; 53:5; Dan. 9:26; Hos. 6:1; Zech. 13:6; 1 Pet. 1:10
19 [w] [Acts 2:38; 26:20]
20 [3] NU, M *Christ Jesus* [4] NU, M *ordained for you before*
21 [x] Acts 1:11 [y] Matt. 17:11; [Rom. 8:21] [z] Luke 1:70 [5] Or *time*
22 [a] Deut. 18:15, 18, 19; Acts 7:37
24 [b] 2 Sam. 7:12; Luke 24:25 [6] NU, M *proclaimed*
25 [c] Acts 2:39; [Rom. 9:4, 8; Gal. 3:26] [d] Gen. 12:3; 18:18; 22:18; 26:4; 28:14
26 [e] Matt. 15:24; John 4:22; Acts 13:46; [Rom. 1:16; 2:9] [f] Is. 42:1; Matt. 1:21

CHAPTER 4
1 [a] Matt. 22:23
6 [b] Luke 3:2; John 11:49; 18:13

3:15 killed...God raised...we are witnesses. Peter's confident and forceful declaration (cf. 1 Cor. 15:3-7) was a clear defense of and provided further evidence for Christ's resurrection. Peter's claim was undeniable; the Jews never showed any evidence, such as Jesus' corpse, to disprove it. **Prince of life.** The Gr. word for "prince" means originator, pioneer, or beginner of something. Both Heb. 2:10 and 12:2 translate it "author." It describes Jesus as the Divine Originator of life (cf. Ps. 36:9; Heb. 2:10; 12:2; 1 John 5:11,20).

3:18 foretold by the mouth of all His prophets. Cf. Gen. 3:15; Ps. 22; Is. 53; Zech. 12:10.

3:19-21 times of refreshing...times of restoration of all things. "Times" means epoch, era, or season. Two descriptions are given to the coming era of the millennial kingdom. This is clear because they bracket the reference to Jesus Christ being sent from God to bring those times. Peter points to Christ's earthly reign (*see notes on 1:7*; cf. Rom. 11:26). The period will be marked by all kinds of blessings and renewal (cf. Is. 11:6-10; 35:1-10; Ezek. 34:26; 44:3; Joel 2:26; Matt. 19:28; Rev. 19:1-10).

3:19 Repent...be converted. *See notes on 2:38; Matt. 3:2.* "Converted" is a frequent NT word that relates to sinners turning to God (9:35; 14:15; 26:18,20; Luke 1:16,17; 2 Cor. 3:16; 1 Pet. 2:25). **your sins...blotted out.** Cf. Ps. 51:9; Is. 43:25; 44:22. "Blotted out" compares forgiveness to the complete wiping away of ink from the surface of a document (Col. 2:14).

3:22 Quoted from Deut. 18:15. Moses was revered by the Jews as their first and greatest prophet, and the Jews viewed the prophet "like him" to refer to the Messiah.

3:23 Quoted from Deut. 18:19; cf. Lev. 23:29. Peter's audience was in the precarious position of losing covenant blessings by rejecting the Messiah.

3:24 prophets, from Samuel. Samuel was called a prophet in the OT (1 Sam. 3:20). Although he did not directly prophesy about Christ, he did anoint David as king and speak of his kingdom (1 Sam. 13:14; 15:28; 16:13; 28:17), and the promises David received were and will be fulfilled in Christ (cf. 2 Sam. 7:10-16).

3:25 *in your seed.* Quoted from Gen. 22:18; 26:4. Jesus Christ was the ultimate fulfillment of the Abrahamic Covenant and its blessings (Gal. 3:16), which are still available to the Jews.

3:26 God...raised up. *See note on 2:32.* **His Servant.** *See note on v. 13.*

4:1 priests. The office of priest in the OT began with Aaron and his sons (Lev. 8). They became the human intermediaries between holy God and sinful humanity. They were characterized by 3 qualities: 1) they were chosen and set apart for priestly service by God; 2) they were to be holy in character; and 3) they were the only ones allowed to come near to God on behalf of the people with the High-Priest being the chief go-between on the Day of Atonement (Lev. 16). Cf. Num. 16:5. **the captain of the temple.** Chief of the temple police force (composed of Levites) and second-ranking official to the High-Priest. The Romans had delegated the temple-policing responsibility to the Jews. **Sadducees.** *See notes on 23:8; Matt. 3:7.*

4:2 preached in Jesus the resurrection. This part of the apostles' message was the most objectionable to the Jewish leaders. They had executed Christ as a blasphemer and now Peter and John were proclaiming His resurrection.

4:3 already evening. The Jews detained Peter and John overnight in jail because Jewish law did not permit trials at night. It had been too late to convene the Sanhedrin (*see note on v. 15*) that afternoon, so the apostles would face a hearing the next day before that council.

4:4 five thousand. The cumulative total of men in the Jerusalem church by this time, not the number of those converted after Peter's latest message.

4:5 rulers, elders, and scribes. These positions made up the Jewish ruling body, the Sanhedrin (*see note on v. 15*).

4:6 Annas...Caiaphas. *See notes on John 18:13.* Even though

John, and Alexander, and as many as were
of the family of the high priest, were gathered together at Jerusalem. 7 And when
they had set them in the midst, they asked,
[c]"By what power or by what name have
you done this?"
8 [d]Then Peter, filled with the Holy Spirit,
said to them, "Rulers of the people and elders of Israel: 9 If we this day are judged for
a good deed *done* to a helpless man, by
what means he has been made well, 10 let it
be known to you all, and to all the people
of Israel, [e]that by the name of Jesus Christ
of Nazareth, whom you crucified, [f]whom
God raised from the dead, by Him this man
stands here before you whole. 11 This is the
[g]*'stone which was rejected by you builders,*
which has become the chief cornerstone.'
12 [h]Nor is there salvation in any other, for
there is no other name under heaven given
among men by which we must be saved."

7 [c]Ex. 2:14; Matt. 21:23; Acts 7:27
8 [d]Luke 12:11, 12
10 [e]Acts 2:22; 3:6, 16 [f]Acts 2:24
11 [g]Ps. 118:22; Is. 28:16; Matt. 21:42
12 [h]Is. 42:1, 6, 7; 53:11; Dan. 9:24; [Matt. 1:21; John 14:6; Acts 10:43; 1 Tim. 2:5, 6]
13 [i]Matt. 11:25; [1 Cor. 1:27]
14 [j]Acts 3:11
16 [k]John 11:47 [l]Acts 3:7-10 [1]*remarkable sign* [2]*well known*
18 [m]Acts 5:28, 40

The Name of Jesus Forbidden

13 Now when they saw the boldness of
Peter and John, [i]and perceived that they
were uneducated and untrained men, they
marveled. And they realized that they had
been with Jesus. 14 And seeing the man
who had been healed [j]standing with them,
they could say nothing against it. 15 But
when they had commanded them to go
aside out of the council, they conferred
among themselves, 16 saying, [k]"What shall
we do to these men? For, indeed, that a
[1]notable miracle has been done through
them *is* [l]evident[2] to all who dwell in Jerusalem, and we cannot deny *it.* 17 But so
that it spreads no further among the people, let us severely threaten them, that
from now on they speak to no man in this
name."
18 [m]So they called them and commanded them not to speak at all nor teach in the

Annas (A.D. 6–15) had been replaced and Caiaphas was now High-Priest (A.D. 18–36), he retained his title and wielded great influence. **John...Alexander.** Their identities are uncertain. "John" could be an alternate reading for "Jonathan," who was one of Annas' sons and replaced Caiaphas as High-Priest in A.D. 36.

4:8-12 Peter put the Sanhedrin on trial by preaching the gospel to those same men who condemned Jesus Christ and made themselves enemies of God.

4:8 filled with the Holy Spirit. *See note on 2:4.* Because Peter was under the control of the Spirit, he was able to face persecution and preach the gospel with power (cf. Luke 12:11,12). **Rulers...elders.** *See note on v. 5.*

4:11 *rejected...the chief cornerstone.* Quoted from Ps. 118:22 (*see note*); cf. Eph. 2:19-22; 1 Pet. 2:4-8.

4:12 no other name. This refers to the exclusivism of salvation by faith in Jesus Christ. There are only two religious paths: the broad way of works salvation leading to eternal death, and the narrow way of faith in Jesus, leading to eternal life (Matt. 7:13,14; cf. John 10:7,8; 14:6). Sadly, the Sanhedrin and its followers were on the first path.

4:13 uneducated and untrained men. Peter and John were not educated in the rabbinical schools and had no formal training in OT theology.

4:15-17 It would be risky to punish the two apostles when they had broken no laws and had performed a miracle that captured the entire city's attention. But the Sanhedrin believed it had to stop the preaching of the incriminating truth that its members had executed the Messiah.

4:15 council. The Sanhedrin, the Jews' national ruling body and supreme court. It had 71 members, including the High-Priest (*see note on v. 5*).

Major Sermons in Acts

Sermon	Theme	Reference
Peter to crowds at Pentecost	Peter's explanation of the meaning of Pentecost	Acts 2:14-40
Peter to crowds at the temple	The Jewish people should repent for crucifying the Messiah	Acts 3:12-26
Peter to the Sanhedrin	Testimony that a helpless man was healed by the power of Jesus	Acts 4:5-12
Stephen to the Sanhedrin	Stephen's rehearsal of Jewish history, accusing the Jews of killing the Messiah	Acts 7:2-53
Peter to Gentiles	Gentiles can be saved in the same manner as Jews	Acts 10:28-47
Peter to church at Jerusalem	Peter's testimony of his experiences at Joppa and a defense of his ministry to the Gentiles	Acts 11:4-18
Paul to synagogue at Antioch	Jesus was the Messiah in fulfillment of Old Testament prophecies	Acts 13:16-41
Peter to Jerusalem Council	Salvation by grace available to all	Acts 15:7-11
James to Jerusalem Council	Gentile converts do not require circumcision	Acts 15:13-21
Paul to Ephesian elders	Remain faithful in spite of false teachers and persecution	Acts 20:17-35
Paul to crowd at Jerusalem	Paul's statement of his conversion and his mission to the Gentiles	Acts 22:1-21
Paul to Sanhedrin	Paul's defense, declaring himself a Pharisee and a Roman citizen	Acts 23:1-6
Paul to King Agrippa	Paul's statement of his conversion and his zeal for the gospel	Acts 26:2-23
Paul to Jewish leaders at Rome	Paul's statement about his Jewish heritage	Acts 28:17-20

name of Jesus. 19 But Peter and John answered and said to them, [n]"Whether it is
right in the sight of God to listen to you
more than to God, you judge. 20 [o]For we
cannot but speak the things which [p]we
have seen and heard." 21 So when they had
further threatened them, they let them go,
finding no way of punishing them, [q]be-
cause of the people, since they all [r]glorified
God for [s]what had been done. 22 For the
man was over forty years old on whom
this miracle of healing had been performed.

Prayer for Boldness

23 And being let go, [t]they went to their
own *companions* and reported all that the
chief priests and elders had said to them.
24 So when they heard that, they raised
their voice to God with one accord and
said: "Lord, [u]You *are* God, who made
heaven and earth and the sea, and all that
is in them, 25 who [3]by the mouth of Your
servant David have said:

[v]'Why did the nations rage,
And the people plot vain things?
26 *The kings of the earth took their*
stand,
And the rulers were gathered
together
Against the LORD and against His
Christ.'

27 "For [w]truly against [x]Your holy Servant Jesus, [y]whom You anointed, both
Herod and Pontius Pilate, with the Gentiles and the people of Israel, were gathered together 28 [z]to do whatever Your
hand and Your purpose determined before
to be done. 29 Now, Lord, look on their
threats, and grant to Your servants [a]that
with all boldness they may speak Your
word, 30 by stretching out Your hand to
heal, [b]and that signs and wonders may be
done [c]through the name of [d]Your holy Servant Jesus."

31 And when they had prayed, [e]the
place where they were assembled together
was shaken; and they were all filled with
the Holy Spirit, [f]and they spoke the word
of God with boldness.

Sharing in All Things

32 Now the multitude of those who believed [g]were of one heart and one soul;
[h]neither did anyone say that any of the
things he possessed was his own, but they
had all things in common. 33 And with
[i]great power the apostles gave [j]witness to
the resurrection of the Lord Jesus. And
[k]great grace was upon them all. 34 Nor was
there anyone among them who lacked; [l]for
all who were possessors of lands or houses
sold them, and brought the proceeds of the
things that were sold, 35 [m]and laid *them* at
the apostles' feet; [n]and they distributed to
each as anyone had need.

36 And [4]Joses, who was also named
Barnabas by the apostles (which is translated Son of [5]Encouragement), a Levite of
the country of Cyprus, 37 [o]having land,
sold *it*, and brought the money and laid *it*
at the apostles' feet.

19 [n] Acts 5:29
20 [o] Acts 1:8; 2:32 [p] Acts 22:15; [1 John 1:1, 3]
21 [q] Matt. 21:26; Luke 20:6, 19; 22:2; Acts 5:26 [r] Matt. 15:31 [s] Acts 3:7, 8
23 [t] Acts 2:44-46; 12:12
24 [u] Ex. 20:11; 2 Kin. 19:15; Neh. 9:6; Ps. 146:6
25 [v] Ps. 2:1, 2 [3] NU *through the Holy Spirit, by the mouth of our father, Your servant David,*
27 [w] Matt. 26:3; Luke 22:2; 23:1, 8 [x] [Luke 1:35] [y] Luke 4:18; John 10:36
28 [z] Acts 2:23; 3:18
29 [a] Acts 4:13, 31; 9:27; 13:46; 14:3; 19:8; 26:26; Eph. 6:19
30 [b] Acts 2:43; 5:12 [c] Acts 3:6, 16 [d] Acts 4:27
31 [e] Matt. 5:6; Acts 2:2, 4; 16:26 [f] Acts 4:29
32 [g] Acts 5:12; Rom. 15:5, 6; 2 Cor. 13:11; Phil. 1:27; 2:2; 1 Pet. 3:8 [h] Acts 2:44
33 [i] [Acts 1:8] [j] Acts 1:22 [k] Rom. 6:15
34 [l] [Matt. 19:21]; Acts 2:45
35 [m] Acts 4:37; 5:2 [n] Acts 2:45; 6:1
36 [4] NU *Joseph* [5] Or *Consolation*
37 [o] Acts 4:34, 35; 5:1, 2

4:19 to listen to you more than to God. Christians should obey governmental authority (Rom. 13:1-7; 1 Pet. 2:13-17), but when government decrees are clearly contrary to God's Word, God must be obeyed (cf. Ex. 1:15-17; Dan. 6:4-10).

4:23 chief priests. A small group within the Sanhedrin (*see note on v. 15*), composed of former High-Priests and members of influential priestly families (*see note on Matt. 2:4*). **elders.** *See note on v. 5.*

4:24-30 Peter and John's experience did not frighten or discourage the other disciples, but exhilarated them. They took confidence in God's sovereign control of all events, even their sufferings. Furthermore, they were comforted that the opposition whom they were facing was foreseen in the OT (vv. 25,26).

4:24 Lord. The Gr. word is an uncommon NT title for God that means "absolute master" (Luke 2:29; 2 Tim. 2:21; 2 Pet. 2:1; Jude 4; Rev. 6:10), which represented the disciples' recognition of God's sovereignty.

4:25 by the mouth of Your servant David. *See note on 1:16.* In the events of recent days, the disciples saw a fulfillment of Ps. 2:1,2 which they quoted.

4:28 Your hand and Your purpose. God has written all of history according to His eternal plan. The crucifixion of Jesus was no exception (*see note on 2:23*; cf. Rom. 8:29,30; 1 Cor. 2:7; Eph. 1:5-11).

4:30 signs and wonders. *See note on 2:19.* **holy Servant.** *See note on 3:13.*

4:31 was shaken. As on Pentecost, a physical phenomenon indicated the presence of the Holy Spirit (*see notes on 2:2,3*). **filled with the Holy Spirit.** *See notes on v. 8; 2:4.*

4:32-35 all things in common. *See notes on 2:44-46.* Believers understood that all they had belonged to God, and therefore when a brother or sister had a need those who could meet it were obligated to do so (cf. James 2:15,16; 1 John 3:17). The method was to give the money to the apostles who would distribute it (vv. 35,37).

4:33 witness to the resurrection. *See note on 1:22.* **great grace.** This means "favor" and carries a twofold meaning here: 1) favor from the people outside the church. Because of the believers' love and unity, the common people were impressed (cf. 2:47); and 2) favor from God who was granting blessing.

4:36 Joses...Barnabas...a Levite. Luke introduces Barnabas as a role model from among those who donated property proceeds. Barnabas was a member of the priestly tribe of the Levites and a native of the island of Cyprus. He becomes an associate of Paul and a prominent figure later in the book (cf. 9:26,27; 11:22-24,30; chaps. 13–15). **Cyprus.** The third largest island in the Mediterranean after Sicily and Sardinia, located some 60 mi. W off the Syrian coast (*see note on 13:4*).

4:37 having land, sold *it*. The OT prohibited Levites from owning property in Israel (Num. 18:20,24; Deut. 10:9), but that law was apparently no longer in force. It is also possible that the land was in Cyprus.

Lying to the Holy Spirit

5 But a certain man named Ananias,
with Sapphira his wife, sold a possession. 2 And he kept back *part* of the proceeds, his wife also being aware *of it*, and
brought a certain part and laid *it* at the
apostles' feet. 3 [a]But Peter said, "Ananias,
why has [b]Satan filled your heart to lie to
the Holy Spirit and keep back *part* of the
price of the land for yourself? 4 While it remained, was it not your own? And after it
was sold, was it not in your own control?
Why have you conceived this thing in your
heart? You have not lied to men but to
God."

5 Then Ananias, hearing these words,
[c]fell down and breathed his last. So great
fear came upon all those who heard these
things. 6 And the young men arose and
[d]wrapped him up, carried *him* out, and
buried *him*.

7 Now it was about three hours later
when his wife came in, not knowing what
had happened. 8 And Peter answered her,
"Tell me whether you sold the land for so
much?"

She said, "Yes, for so much."

9 Then Peter said to her, "How is it that
you have agreed together [e]to test the Spirit of the Lord? Look, the feet of those who
have buried your husband *are* at the door,
and they will carry you out." 10 [f]Then immediately she fell down at his feet and
breathed her last. And the young men
came in and found her dead, and carrying
her out, buried *her* by her husband. 11 [g]So
great fear came upon all the church and
upon all who heard these things.

Continuing Power in the Church

12 And [h]through the hands of the apostles many signs and wonders were done
among the people. [i]And they were all with
one accord in Solomon's Porch. 13 Yet
[j]none of the rest dared join them, [k]but the
people esteemed them highly. 14 And believers were increasingly added to the
Lord, multitudes of both men and women,
15 so that they brought the sick out into the
streets and laid *them* on beds and couches,
[l]that at least the shadow of Peter passing
by might fall on some of them. 16 Also a
multitude gathered from the surrounding
cities to Jerusalem, bringing [m]sick people
and those who were tormented by unclean
spirits, and they were all healed.

Imprisoned Apostles Freed

17 [n]Then the high priest rose up, and all
those who *were* with him (which is the sect
of the Sadducees), and they were filled
with [1]indignation, 18 [o]and laid their hands
on the apostles and put them in the common prison. 19 But at night [p]an angel of the
Lord opened the prison doors and brought
them out, and said, 20 "Go, stand in the

CHAPTER 5
3 [a] Num. 30:2; Deut. 23:21; Eccl. 5:4 [b] Matt. 4:10; Luke 22:3; John 13:2,27
5 [c] Ezek. 11:13; Acts 5:10,11
6 [d] John 19:40
9 [e] Matt. 4:7; Acts 5:3,4
10 [f] Ezek. 11:13; Acts 5:5
11 [g] Acts 2:43; 5:5; 19:17
12 [h] Acts 2:43; 4:30; 6:8; 14:3; 15:12; [Rom. 15:19]; 2 Cor. 12:12; Heb. 2:4 [i] Acts 3:11; 4:32
13 [j] John 9:22 [k] Acts 2:47; 4:21
15 [l] Matt. 9:21; 14:36; Acts 19:12
16 [m] Mark 16:17, 18; [John 14:12]
17 [n] Matt. 3:7; Acts 4:1, 2, 6 [1] *jealousy*
18 [o] Luke 21:12; Acts 4:3; 16:37
19 [p] Matt. 1:20, 24; 2:13, 19; 28:2; Luke 1:11; 2:9; Acts 12:7; 16:26

5:1 Ananias…Sapphira. These are two classic examples of hypocrisy among Christians who faked their spirituality to impress others (cf. Matt. 6:1-6,16-18; 15:7; 23:13-36). They were "in the congregation of those who believed" (4:32) and were involved with the Holy Spirit (v. 3), but remained hypocrites.

5:2 he kept back *part* of the proceeds. This was not a sin in and of itself. However, they had promised, perhaps publicly, that they were giving the full amount received to the Lord. Their outward sin was lying about how much they were giving to the church, but the deeper, more devastating sin was their spiritual hypocrisy based on selfishness.

5:3 Satan filled your heart. Ananias and Sapphira were satanically inspired in contrast to Barnabas' Spirit-filled gesture (4:37).

5:3,4 lie to the Holy Spirit. Ananias must have promised the Lord he would give the whole amount. He lied to the ever-present Holy Spirit in him (1 Cor. 6:19,20) and in the church (Eph. 2:21,22).

5:5 great fear. *See v. 11.* They were afraid about the seriousness of hypocrisy and sin in the church. The people learned that death can be the consequence of sin (see 1 Cor. 11:30-32; 1 John 5:16). That fear extended beyond those present to all who heard about the divine judgment (v. 11). Cf. 1 Pet. 3:10; 4:17.

5:6-10 The Jews did not embalm, but customarily buried the dead the same day, especially someone who died by divine judgment (see Deut. 21:22,23).

5:9 test the Spirit of the Lord. Sapphira had gone too far in presuming upon God's forbearance. The folly of such blatant human presumption had to be shown as a sin, hence the ultimate divine chastening that followed.

5:11 church. This is the first use of "church" in Acts, although it is the most common word used to describe the assembly of those who had believed (cf. 4:32).

5:12 signs and wonders. *See note on 2:19.* **Solomon's Porch.** *See note on 3:11.*

5:13 none…dared join them. *See note on v. 5.* These unbelievers had respect for the followers of Jesus, but feared the deadly potential of joining the church.

5:14 believers…both men and women. While the unbelievers stayed away due to fear of the consequence of sin, there were multitudes who heard the gospel witness, gladly believed, and joined the church.

5:15 shadow of Peter. The people truly believed he had divine healing power and that it might even extend to them through his shadow (cf. 3:1-10). But Scripture does not say Peter's shadow ever healed anyone; in fact, the healing power of God through him seemed to go far beyond his shadow (v. 16, "multitude…all were healed"). This outpouring of healing was an answer to the prayer in 4:29,30.

5:16 unclean spirits. Cf. Matt. 10:1; 12:43-45; Mark 1:23-27; 5:1-13; 6:7; 9:25; Luke 4:36; 8:29; 9:42. They are demons, fallen angels (Rev. 12:3) who are so designated because of their vile wickedness. They frequently live inside unbelievers, particularly those who vent their wicked nature.

5:17 high priest. *See note on 4:6.* Here the title could refer to Annas (cf. 4:6) or Caiaphas. **Sadducees.** *See notes on 23:8; Matt. 3:7.*

5:18 the common prison. The public jail.

5:19 an angel of the Lord. This person should not be confused with "the Angel of the Lord" in the OT (*see note on Ex. 3:2*).

temple and speak to the people [q]all the
words of this life."
21 And when they heard *that,* they entered the temple early in the morning and
taught. [r]But the high priest and those with
him came and called the [2]council together,
with all the [3]elders of the children of Israel,
and sent to the prison to have them
brought.

Apostles on Trial Again

22 But when the officers came and did
not find them in the prison, they returned
and reported, 23 saying, "Indeed we found
the prison shut securely, and the guards
standing [4]outside before the doors; but
when we opened them, we found no one
inside!" 24 Now when [5]the high priest, [s]the
captain of the temple, and the chief priests
heard these things, they wondered what
the outcome would be. 25 So one came and
told them, [6]saying, "Look, the men whom
you put in prison are standing in the temple and teaching the people!"
26 Then the captain went with the officers and brought them without violence,
[t]for they feared the people, lest they
should be stoned. 27 And when they had
brought them, they set *them* before the
council. And the high priest asked them,
28 saying, [u]"Did we not strictly command
you not to teach in this name? And look,
you have filled Jerusalem with your doctrine, [v]and intend to bring this Man's
[w]blood on us!"
29 But Peter and the *other* apostles answered and said: [x]"We ought to obey God
rather than men. 30 [y]The God of our fathers raised up Jesus whom you murdered
by [z]hanging on a tree. 31 [a]Him God has exalted to His right hand *to be* [b]Prince and
[c]Savior, [d]to give repentance to Israel and
forgiveness of sins. 32 And [e]we are His witnesses to these things, and *so* also *is* the
Holy Spirit [f]whom God has given to those
who obey Him."

Gamaliel's Advice

33 When they heard *this,* they were [g]fu-
rious[7] and plotted to kill them. 34 Then
one in the council stood up, a Pharisee
named [h]Gamaliel, a teacher of the law
held in respect by all the people, and commanded them to put the apostles outside
for a little while. 35 And he said to them:
"Men of Israel, [8]take heed to yourselves
what you intend to do regarding these
men. 36 For some time ago Theudas rose
up, claiming to be somebody. A number of
men, about four hundred, [9]joined him. He
was slain, and all who obeyed him were
scattered and came to nothing. 37 After
this man, Judas of Galilee rose up in the
days of the census, and drew away many
people after him. He also perished, and all
who obeyed him were dispersed. 38 And
now I say to you, keep away from these
men and let them alone; for if this plan or
this work is of men, it will come to nothing; 39 [i]but if it is of God, you cannot overthrow it—lest you even be found [j]to fight
against God."
40 And they agreed with him, and when
they had [k]called for the apostles [l]and beat-
en *them,* they commanded that they
should not speak in the name of Jesus, and
let them go. 41 So they departed from the
presence of the council, [m]rejoicing that
they were counted worthy to suffer shame
for [1]His name. 42 And daily [n]in the temple, and in every house, [o]they did not
cease teaching and preaching Jesus *as* the
Christ.

20 [q] [John 6:63, 68; 17:3; 1 John 5:11]
21 [r] Acts 4:5, 6 [2] Sanhedrin [3] *council of elders* or *senate*
23 [4] NU, M omit *outside*
24 [s] Luke 22:4; Acts 4:1; 5:26 [5] NU omits *the high priest*
25 [6] NU, M omit *saying*
26 [t] Matt. 21:26
28 [u] Acts 4:17, 18 [v] Acts 2:23, 36 [w] Matt. 23:35
29 [x] Acts 4:19
30 [y] Acts 3:13, 15 [z] Acts 10:39; 13:29; [Gal. 3:13; 1 Pet. 2:24]
31 [a] Mark 16:19; [Acts 2:33, 36; Phil. 2:9–11] [b] Acts 3:15; Rev. 1:5 [c] Matt. 1:21 [d] Luke 24:47; [Eph. 1:7; Col. 1:14]
32 [e] John 15:26, 27; Acts 15:28; Rom. 8:16; Heb. 2:4 [f] Acts 2:4; 10:44
33 [g] Acts 2:37; 7:54 [7] *cut to the quick*
34 [h] Acts 22:3
35 [8] *be careful*
36 [9] *followed*
39 [i] Luke 21:15; 1 Cor. 1:25 [j] Acts 7:51; 9:5
40 [k] Acts 4:18 [l] Matt. 10:17; Mark 13:9; Acts 16:22, 23; 21:32; 2 Cor. 11:25
41 [m] Matt. 5:10–12; Rom. 5:3; 2 Cor. 12:10; Heb. 10:34; [James 1:2; 1 Pet. 4:13–16] [1] NU *the name;* M *the name of Jesus*
42 [n] Acts 2:46 [o] Acts 4:20, 29

5:20 the words of this life. The gospel (cf. Phil. 2:16; 1 John 1:1–4). Jesus Christ came into this world to provide abundant and eternal life to spiritually dead people (cf. John 1:4; 11:25; 1 John 5:20).

5:28 doctrine. The gospel of Jesus Christ (*see notes on 2:14–40; 4:12, 13*). **this Man's blood on us.** The Sanhedrin had apparently forgotten the brash statement its supporters had made before Pilate that the responsibility for Jesus' death should be on them and their children (Matt. 27:25).

5:29 obey God rather than men. *See note on 4:19.*

5:30 hanging on a tree. Cf. Deut. 21:23; Gal. 3:13.

5:31 Him God has exalted to His right hand. *See notes on 1:9; Mark 6:19; Phil. 2:9–11.* **Prince.** *See note on 3:15.* **repentance to Israel.** Salvation for the Jews. Salvation demands repentance (cf. 2:38; 3:19; 17:30; 20:21; 26:20). For the nature of repentance, *see notes on 2 Cor. 7:9–12.*

5:32 *so* also *is* the Holy Spirit. Every believer receives the Spirit the moment one is saved by obeying the gospel (*see note on 2:4;* cf. Rom. 8:9; 1 Cor. 6:19, 20).

5:34 Gamaliel. Like his grandfather, the prominent rabbi Hillel, Gamaliel the most noted rabbi of his time, led the liberal faction of the Pharisees. His most famous student was the Apostle Paul (22:3).

5:36 Theudas. An otherwise unknown individual who led a revolt in Judea in the early years of the first century, not to be confused with a later Theudas cited in Josephus as a revolutionary.

5:37 Judas of Galilee rose up. The founder of the Zealots who led another revolt in Palestine early in the first century. Zealots, a party of Jews who were fanatical nationalists, believed that radical action was required to overthrow the Roman power in Palestine. They even sought to take up arms against Rome. **days of the census.** One ordered by Quirinius, governor of Syria, in A.D. 6–7 (cf. Luke 2:2).

5:38,39 Members of the Sanhedrin heeded Gamaliel's words concerning the apostles. But, based on his knowledge of Scripture, Gamaliel should have been more decisive and less pragmatic about accepting Jesus as the risen Messiah.

5:40 beaten *them*. The apostles were unjustly flogged, probably with 39 lashes, the standard number given to avoid exceeding the OT legal limit of 40 (cf. Deut. 25:3).

Seven Chosen to Serve

6 Now in those days, [a]when *the number*
of the disciples was multiplying, there
arose a complaint against the Hebrews by
the [b]Hellenists,[1] because their widows
were neglected [c]in the daily distribution.
2 Then the twelve summoned the multitude of the disciples and said, [d]"It is not
desirable that we should leave the word
of God and serve tables. 3 Therefore,
brethren, [e]seek out from among you seven
men of *good* reputation, full of the Holy
Spirit and wisdom, whom we may appoint over this [f]business; 4 but we [g]will
give ourselves continually to prayer and
to the ministry of the word."
5 And the saying pleased the whole multitude. And they chose Stephen, [h]a man full
of faith and the Holy Spirit, and [i]Philip,
Prochorus, Nicanor, Timon, Parmenas, and
[j]Nicolas, a proselyte from Antioch, 6 whom
they set before the apostles; and [k]when
they had prayed, [l]they laid hands on them.
7 Then [m]the word of God spread, and
the number of the disciples multiplied
greatly in Jerusalem, and a great many [n]of
the priests were obedient to the faith.

Stephen Accused of Blasphemy

8 And Stephen, full of [2]faith and power,
did great [o]wonders and signs among the
people. 9 Then there arose some from what
is called the Synagogue of the Freedmen
(Cyrenians, Alexandrians, and those from
Cilicia and Asia), disputing with Stephen.
10 And [p]they were not able to resist the
wisdom and the Spirit by which he spoke.
11 [q]Then they secretly induced men to say,
"We have heard him speak blasphemous
words against Moses and God." 12 And
they stirred up the people, the elders, and
the scribes; and they came upon *him*,
seized him, and brought *him* to the council.
13 They also set up false witnesses who
said, "This man does not cease to speak
[3]blasphemous words against this holy
place and the law; 14 [r]for we have heard
him say that this Jesus of Nazareth will destroy this place and change the customs

CHAPTER 6

1 [a] Acts 2:41; 4:4 [b] Acts 9:29; 11:20 [c] Acts 4:35; 11:29 [1] Greek-speaking Jews
2 [d] Ex. 18:17
3 [e] Deut. 1:13; 1 Tim. 3:7 [f] Phil. 1:1; 1 Tim. 3:8-13
4 [g] Acts 2:42
5 [h] Acts 6:3; 11:24 [i] Acts 8:5, 26; 21:8 [j] Rev. 2:6, 15
6 [k] Acts 1:24 [l] Num. 8:10; 27:18; Deut. 34:9; [Mark 5:23; Acts 8:17; 9:17; 13:3; 19:6; 1 Tim. 4:14; 2 Tim. 1:6]; Heb. 6:2
7 [m] Acts 12:24; Col. 1:6 [n] John 12:42
8 [o] Acts 2:43; 5:12; 8:15; 14:3 [2] NU *grace*
10 [p] Ex. 4:12; Is. 54:17; Luke 21:15
11 [q] 1 Kin. 21:10, 13; Matt. 26:59, 60
13 [3] NU omits *blasphemous*
14 [r] Acts 10:38; 25:8

6:1 multiplying. *See note on 4:4.* The figure could have reached over 20,000 men and women. **Hebrews…Hellenists.** "Hebrews" were the native Jewish population of Palestine; "Hellenists" were Jews from the Diaspora. The Hellenists' absorption of aspects of Gr. culture made them suspect to the Palestinian Jews. **widows were neglected.** The Hellenists believed their widows were not receiving an adequate share of the food the church provided for their care (cf. 1 Tim. 5:3-16).

6:2 serve tables The word translated "tables" can refer to tables used in monetary matters (cf. Matt. 21:12; Mark 11:15; John 2:15), as well as those used for serving meals. To be involved either in financial matters or in serving meals would take the 12 away from their first priority (*see note on v. 4*).

6:3 seven men. These were not deacons in terms of the later church office (1 Tim. 3:8-13), although they performed some of the same duties. Stephen and Philip (the only ones of the 7 mentioned elsewhere in Scripture) clearly were evangelists, not deacons. Acts later mentions elders (14:23; 20:17), but not deacons. It seems, therefore, that a permanent order of deacons was not established at that time. **full of the Holy Spirit.** Cf. v. 5; *see notes on 2:4.*

6:4 Prayer and the ministry of the Word (cf. v. 2) define the highest priorities of church leaders.

6:5 The 7 men chosen by the church all had Gr. names, implying they were all Hellenists. The church, in a display of love and unity, may have chosen them to rectify the apparent imbalance involving the Hellenistic widows. **they chose Stephen…Nicolas.** For Stephen's ministry, see 6:9–7:60. His martyrdom became the catalyst for the spread of the gospel beyond Palestine (8:1-4; 11:19). Philip also played a key role in the spread of the gospel (cf. 8:4-24,26-40). Nothing certain is known of the other 5. According to some early traditions, Prochorus became the Apostle John's amanuensis when he wrote his gospel and Nicholas was a Gentile convert to Judaism from Antioch.

6:6 prayed…laid hands on them. This expression was used of Jesus when He healed (Mark 6:5; Luke 4:40; 13:13; cf. 28:8) and sometimes indicated being taken prisoner (5:18; Mark 14:46). In the OT, offerers of sacrifices laid their hands on the animal as an expression of identification (Lev. 8:14,18,22; Heb. 6:2). But in the symbolic sense, it signified the affirmation, support, and identification with someone and his ministry. *See 1 Tim. 4:14; 5:22; 2 Tim. 1:6*; cf. Num. 27:23.

6:7 One of Luke's periodic statements summarizing the growth of the church and the spread of the gospel (cf. 2:41,47; 4:4; 5:14; 9:31; 12:24; 13:49; 16:5; 19:20). **great many of the priests.** The conversion of large numbers of priests may account for the vicious opposition that arose against Stephen. **were obedient to the faith.** *See note on Rom. 1:5.*

6:8 wonders and signs. *See note on 2:19.*

6:9 It seems that this verse describes 3 synagogues: the Synagogue of the Freedmen, a second composed of Cyrenians and Alexandrians, and a third composed of those from Cilicia and Asia. Cultural and linguistic differences among the 3 groups make it unlikely they all attended the same synagogue. **Synagogue.** These were meeting places which began in the intertestamental period where the dispersed Jews (usually Hellenists), who did not have temple access, could meet in their community to worship and read the OT. *See note on Mark 1:21.* **Freedmen.** Descendants of Jewish slaves captured by Pompeii (63 B.C.) and taken to Rome. They were later freed and formed a Jewish community there. **Cyrenians.** Men from Cyrene, a city in North Africa. Simon, the man conscripted to carry Jesus' cross, was a native of Cyrene (Luke 23:26). **Alexandrians.** Alexandria, another major North African city, was located near the mouth of the Nile River. The powerful preacher Apollos was from Alexandria (*see note on 18:24*). **Cilicia and Asia.** Roman provinces in Asia Minor (modern Turkey). Since Paul's hometown (Tarsus) was located in Cilicia, he probably attended this synagogue. **disputing with Stephen.** The word translated "disputing" signifies a formal debate. They no doubt focused on such themes as the death and resurrection of Jesus, and the OT evidence that He was the Messiah.

6:11 blasphemous words against Moses and God. Unable to prevail over Stephen in open debate, his enemies resorted to deceit and conspiracy. As with Jesus (Matt. 26:59-61), they secretly recruited false witnesses to spread lies about Stephen. The charges were serious, since blasphemy was punishable by death (Lev. 24:16).

6:14 Jesus of Nazareth will destroy this place. Another lie, since Jesus' words (John 2:19) referred to His own body (John 2:21).

which Moses delivered to us." 15 And all
who sat in the council, looking steadfastly
at him, saw his face as the face of an angel.

Stephen's Address: The Call of Abraham

7 Then the high priest said, "Are these
things so?"
2 And he said, [a]"Brethren and fathers,
listen: The [b]God of glory appeared to our
father Abraham when he was in
Mesopotamia, before he dwelt in [c]Haran,
3 and said to him, [d]*'Get out of your country and from your relatives, and come to a
land that I will show you.'* 4 Then [e]he came
out of the land of the Chaldeans and dwelt
in Haran. And from there, when his father
was [f]dead, He moved him to this land in
which you now dwell. 5 And *God* gave him
no inheritance in it, not even *enough* to set
his foot on. But even when *Abraham* had no
child, [g]He promised to give it to him for a
possession, and to his descendants after
him. 6 But God spoke in this way: [h]that his
descendants would dwell in a foreign
land, and that they would bring them into
[i]bondage and oppress *them* four hundred
years. 7 [j]*'And the nation to whom they
will be in bondage I will* [k]*judge,'* said God,
[l]*'and after that they shall come out and
serve Me in this place.'* 8 [m]Then He gave
him the covenant of circumcision; [n]and so
Abraham begot Isaac and circumcised him
on the eighth day; [o]and Isaac *begot* Jacob,
and [p]Jacob *begot* the twelve patriarchs.

The Patriarchs in Egypt

9 [q]"And the patriarchs, becoming envious, [r]sold Joseph into Egypt. [s]But God was
with him 10 and delivered him out of all his
troubles, [t]and gave him favor and wisdom
in the presence of Pharaoh, king of Egypt;
and he made him governor over Egypt and
all his house. 11 [u]Now a famine and great
[1]trouble came over all the land of Egypt
and Canaan, and our fathers found no sustenance. 12 [v]But when Jacob heard that
there was grain in Egypt, he sent out our fathers first. 13 And the [w]second *time* Joseph
was made known to his brothers, and Joseph's family became known to the Pharaoh. 14 [x]Then Joseph sent and called his father Jacob and [y]all his relatives to *him,*
[2]seventy-five people. 15 [z]So Jacob went
down to Egypt; [a]and he died, he and our
fathers. 16 And [b]they were carried back to
Shechem and laid in [c]the tomb that Abraham bought for a sum of money from the
sons of Hamor, *the father* of Shechem.

God Delivers Israel by Moses

17 "But when [d]the time of the promise
drew near which God had sworn to Abraham, [e]the people grew and multiplied in
Egypt 18 till another king [f]arose who did
not know Joseph. 19 This man dealt treach-

CHAPTER 7
2 [a] Acts 22:1 [b] Ps. 29:3; 1 Cor. 2:8 [c] Gen. 11:31, 32
3 [d] Gen. 12:1
4 [e] Gen. 11:31; 15:7; Heb. 11:8-10 [f] Gen. 11:32
5 [g] Gen. 12:7; 13:15; 15:3, 18; 17:8; 26:3
6 [h] Gen. 15:13, 14, 16; 47:11, 12 [i] Ex. 1:8-14; 12:40, 41; Gal. 3:17
7 [j] Gen. 15:14 [k] Ex. 14:13-31 [l] Ex. 3:12; Josh. 3:1-17
8 [m] Gen. 17:9-14 [n] Gen. 21:1-5 [o] Gen. 25:21-26 [p] Gen. 29:31–30:24; 35:18, 22-26
9 [q] Gen. 37:4, 11, 28; Ps. 105:17 [r] Gen. 37:28 [s] Gen. 39:2, 21, 23
10 [t] Gen. 41:38-44
11 [u] Gen. 41:54; 42:5 [1] *affliction*
12 [v] Gen. 42:1, 2
13 [w] Gen. 45:4, 16
14 [x] Gen. 45:9, 27 [y] Gen. 46:26, 27; Deut. 10:22 [2] Or *seventy,* Ex. 1:5
15 [z] Gen. 46:1-7 [a] Gen. 49:33; Ex. 1:6
16 [b] Gen. 50:13; Ex. 13:19; Josh. 24:32 [c] Gen. 23:16
17 [d] Gen. 15:13; Ex. 2:23-25; Acts 7:6, 7 [e] Ex. 1:7-9; Ps. 105:24, 25
18 [f] Ex. 1:8

6:15 face of an angel. Pure, calm, unruffled composure, reflecting the presence of God (cf. Ex. 34:29-35).

7:1 high priest. *See note on 4:6.* Probably Caiaphas (*see note on John 18:13*), who remained in office until A.D. 36. **Are these things so?** In modern legal terminology, "How do you plead?"

7:2-53 Stephen's response does not seem to answer the High-Priest's question. Instead, he gave a masterful, detailed defense of the Christian faith from the OT and concluded by condemning the Jewish leaders for rejecting Jesus.

7:2 The God of glory. A title used only here and in Ps. 29:3. God's glory is the sum of His attributes (*see notes on Ex. 33:18,19*). **Abraham...Mesopotamia, before he dwelt in Haran.** Genesis 12:1-4 refers to the repeat of this call after Abraham had settled in Haran (ca. 500 mi. NW of Ur). Evidently, God had originally called Abraham while he was living in Ur (cf. Gen. 15:7; Neh. 9:7), then repeated that call at Haran (*see notes on Gen. 11:31–12:1-3*).

7:3 Quoted from Gen. 12:1.

7:4 land of the Chaldeans. Where Abraham's original home city of Ur was located (Gen. 11:28,31; 15:7; Neh. 9:7). **when his father was dead.** At first glance, Gen. 11:26,32 and 12:4 seem to indicate that Terah lived for 60 years after Abraham's departure from Haran. Terah was 70 when his first son was born (Gen. 11:26); Abraham was 75 when he left Haran (Gen. 12:4; Terah would have been 145); and Terah lived to be 205 (Gen. 11:32). The best solution to this apparent difficulty is that Abraham was not Terah's firstborn son, but was mentioned first (Gen. 11:26) because he was most prominent. Abraham, then, would have been born when Terah was 130.

7:5 Quoted from Gen. 17:8; 48:4.

7:6 four hundred years. This is taken directly from Gen. 15:13,14 where God Himself rounded off the exact length of Israel's sojourn in Egypt (430 years, Ex. 12:40).

7:7 Quoted from Ex. 3:12.

7:8 covenant of circumcision. Circumcision was the sign of the Abrahamic Covenant (*see notes on Gen. 17:11*). **twelve patriarchs.** The 12 sons of Jacob, who became the heads of the 12 tribes of Israel (Gen. 35:22-26).

7:13 second *time*. Joseph revealed himself to his brothers on their second trip to Egypt to buy grain (Gen. 43:1-3; 45:1-3).

7:14 Jacob and all his relatives...seventy-five people. Genesis 46:26,27; Ex. 1:5; Deut. 10:22 give the figure as 70. However the LXX (the Gr. translation of the OT, which as a Hellenist Stephen would have used) in Gen. 46:27 reads "seventy-five." The additional 5 people were Joseph's descendants born in Egypt. *See notes on Gen. 46:26,27.*

7:16 they were...laid in the tomb. "They" refers to Joseph (Josh. 24:32) and his brothers, but not Jacob, who was buried in Abraham's tomb at Machpelah (Gen. 50:13). **the tomb that Abraham bought...of Shechem.** Joshua 24:32 states that Jacob bought this tomb, although Abraham had earlier built an altar at Shechem (Gen. 12:6,7), and probably purchased the land on which he built it. Abraham did not settle there, however, and the land apparently reverted to the people of Hamor. Jacob then repurchased it from Shechem (Gen. 33:18-20), much like Isaac repurchased the well at Beersheba (Gen. 26:28-31) that Abraham had originally bought (Gen. 21:27-30). It is clear that Joseph was buried at Shechem as he requested (Gen. 50:25; Ex. 13:19; Josh. 24:32). The OT does not record when Joseph's brothers were buried, but Stephen reveals it was in Shechem.

7:18 king...did not know Joseph. *See note on Ex. 1:8.*

erously with our people, and oppressed
our forefathers, [g]making them expose their
babies, so that they might not live. 20 [h]At
this time Moses was born, and [i]was well
pleasing to God; and he was brought up in
his father's house for three months. 21 But
[j]when he was set out, [k]Pharaoh's daughter
took him away and brought him up as her
own son. 22 And Moses was learned in all
the wisdom of the Egyptians, and was
[l]mighty in words and deeds.
23 [m]"Now when he was forty years old, it
came into his heart to visit his brethren, the
children of Israel. 24 And seeing one of *them*
suffer wrong, he defended and avenged
him who was oppressed, and struck down
the Egyptian. 25 For he supposed that his
brethren would have understood that God
would deliver them by his hand, but they
did not understand. 26 And the next day he
appeared to two of them as they were fighting, and *tried to* reconcile them, saying,
'Men, you are brethren; why do you wrong
one another?' 27 But he who did his neighbor wrong pushed him away, saying,
[n]*'Who made you a ruler and a judge over*
us? 28 Do you want to kill me as you did the
Egyptian yesterday?' 29 [o]Then, at this saying, Moses fled and became a dweller in the
land of Midian, where he [p]had two sons.
30 [q]"And when forty years had passed,
an Angel [3]of the Lord appeared to him in a
flame of fire in a bush, in the wilderness of
Mount Sinai. 31 When Moses saw *it,* he
marveled at the sight; and as he drew near
to observe, the voice of the Lord came to
him, 32 *saying,* [r]*'I am the God of your fa-*
thers—the God of Abraham, the God of
Isaac, and the God of Jacob.' And Moses
trembled and dared not look. 33 [s]*'Then the*
LORD said to him, "Take your sandals off
your feet, for the place where you stand is
holy ground. 34 I have surely [t]seen the op-
pression of My people who are in Egypt; I
have heard their groaning and have come
down to deliver them. And now come, I
will [u]send you to Egypt." '
35 "This Moses whom they rejected, saying, [v]*'Who made you a ruler and a judge?'*
is the one God sent *to be* a ruler and a deliverer [w]by the hand of the Angel who appeared to him in the bush. 36 [x]He brought
them out, after he had [y]shown wonders
and signs in the land of Egypt, [z]and in the
Red Sea, [a]and in the wilderness forty years.

Israel Rebels Against God

37 "This is that Moses who said to the
children of Israel, [b]*'The LORD your God*
will raise up for you a Prophet like me
from your brethren. [c]Him[4] you shall hear.'
38 [d]"This is he who was in the [5]congre-
gation in the wilderness with [e]the Angel
who spoke to him on Mount Sinai, and
with our fathers, [f]the one who received the
living [g]oracles[6] to give to us, 39 whom our
fathers [h]would not obey, but rejected. And
in their hearts they turned back to Egypt,
40 [i]saying to Aaron, *'Make us gods to go*
before us; as for *this Moses who brought us*
out of the land of Egypt, we do not know
what has become of him.' 41 [j]And they
made a calf in those days, offered sacrifices
to the idol, and [k]rejoiced in the works of
their own hands. 42 Then [l]God turned and
gave them up to worship [m]the host of

19 [g]Ex. 1:22
20 [h]Ex. 2:1, 2 [i]Heb. 11:23
21 [j]Ex. 2:3, 4 [k]Ex. 2:5-10
22 [l]Luke 24:19
23 [m]Ex. 2:11, 12; Heb. 11:24-26
27 [n]Ex. 2:14; Luke 12:14; Acts 7:35
29 [o]Heb. 11:27 [p]Ex. 2:15, 21, 22; 4:20; 18:3
30 [q]Ex. 3:1-10; Is. 63:9 [3]NU omits *of the Lord*
32 [r]Ex. 3:6, 15; [Matt. 22:32]; Heb. 11:16
33 [s]Ex. 3:5, 7, 8, 10
34 [t]Ex. 2:24, 25 [u]Ps. 105:26
35 [v]Ex. 2:14; Acts 7:27 [w]Ex. 14:21
36 [x]Ex. 12:41; 33:1; Deut. 6:21, 23; Heb. 8:9 [y]Ex. 7:8, 9; Deut. 6:22; Ps. 105:27; John 4:48 [z]Ex. 14:21 [a]Ex. 16:1, 35; Num. 14:33; Ps. 95:8-10; Acts 7:42; 13:18; Heb. 3:8
37 [b]Deut. 18:15, 18, 19; Acts 3:22 [c]Matt. 17:5 [4]NU, M omit *Him you shall hear*
38 [d]Ex. 19:3 [e]Is. 63:9; Gal. 3:19; Heb. 2:2 [f]Ex. 21:1; Deut. 5:27; John 1:17 [g]Rom. 3:2; Heb. 5:12; 1 Pet. 4:11 [5]Gr. *ekklesia, assembly or church* [6]*sayings*
39 [h]Ps. 95:8-11
40 [i]Ex. 32:1, 23
41 [j]Ex. 32:2-4; Deut. 9:16; Ps. 106:19 [k]Ex. 32:6, 18, 19
42 [l]Ps. 81:12; [2 Thess. 2:11] [m]Deut. 4:19; 2 Kin. 21:3

7:19 expose their babies. Only the male babies (Ex. 1:15-22).

7:20,21 Moses...was set out. In God's providence, however, he was rescued by Pharaoh's daughter. *See notes on Ex. 2:5-10.*

7:23 he was forty years old. Moses' life may be divided into three 40 year periods. The first 40 years encompassed his birth and life in Pharaoh's court; the second his exile in Midian (vv. 29,30); and the third revolved around the events of the Exodus and the years of Israel's wilderness wandering (v. 36).

7:27,28 Cf. v. 35. Quoted from Ex. 2:14.

7:29 fled...Midian. Because he feared Pharaoh would learn of his killing of the Egyptian (v. 28) and view him as the leader of a Jewish rebellion. **two sons.** Gershom (Ex. 2:22), and Eliezer (Ex. 18:4).

7:30 Angel of the Lord. *See note on Ex. 3:2.* **Mount Sinai.** *See notes on Ex. 19:3-10.*

7:32 Quoted from Ex. 3:6,15.

7:33 Quoted from Ex. 3:5.

7:34 Quoted from Ex. 3:7,8.

7:35 *Who made you.* Quoted from Ex. 2:14. **This Moses...sent *to be* a ruler and a deliverer.** Thus began Israel's long history of rejecting her God-sent deliverers (cf. Matt. 21:33-46; 23:37). **Angel.** The Angel of the Lord (v. 30). *See note on Ex. 3:2.*

7:36 wonders and signs. The 10 plagues in Egypt, and the miracles during the wilderness wandering (e.g., the parting of the Red Sea, Ex. 14:1-31; the miraculous provision of water at Rephidim, Ex. 17:1-7; and the destruction of Korah, Dathan, and Abiram, Num. 16:1-40). *See note on 2:19.*

7:37 *Prophet like me.* Quoted from Deut. 18:15, this refers to the Messiah (cf. John 1:21,25; 6:14; 7:40).

7:38 the congregation in the wilderness. Israel (cf. Ex. 12:3,6,19,47; 16:1,2,9,10; 17:1; 35:1; Lev. 4:13; 16:5; Num. 1:2; 8:9; 13:26; 14:2; Josh. 18:1). **the Angel...on Mount Sinai.** Most likely this is the Angel of the Lord (vv. 30,35) who was assisted by a multitude of angels (cf. Deut. 33:3; Gal. 3:19; Heb. 2:2). *See note on v. 53.* **the living oracles.** The law given to Moses by God through the Angel of the Lord and a whole host of angels (cf. Heb. 4:12; 1 Pet. 1:23).

7:39 would not obey. Israel rejected Moses' leadership and longed to return to slavery in Egypt (cf. Num. 11:5).

7:40 *Make us gods.* A man-made representation of the true God (Ex. 32:1-5) which was forbidden (Ex. 20:4). Quoted from Ex. 32:1,23.

7:41 a calf. *See note on Ex. 32:4.*

7:42 God...gave them up. Quoted from Amos 5:25-27. Judicially abandoning the people to their sin and idolatry (cf. Hos. 4:17; *see notes on Rom. 1:24,26,28*). **the host of heaven.** Israel's idolatrous worship of the sun, moon, and stars began in the wilderness and lasted through the Babylonian captivity (cf. Deut. 4:19; 17:3; 2 Kin. 17:16; 21:3-5; 23:4; 2 Chr. 33:3,5; Jer. 8:2; 19:13; Zeph. 1:5).

heaven, as it is written in the book of the
Prophets:

[n]'Did you offer Me slaughtered
animals and sacrifices during
forty years in the wilderness,
O house of Israel?
43 *You also took up the tabernacle of*
Moloch,
And the star of your god
Remphan,
Images which you made to
worship;
And [o]I will carry you away beyond
Babylon.'

God's True Tabernacle

44 "Our fathers had the tabernacle of
witness in the wilderness, as He appointed, instructing Moses [p]to make it according to the pattern that he had seen,
45 [q]which our fathers, having received it in
turn, also brought with Joshua into the
land possessed by the Gentiles, [r]whom
God drove out before the face of our fathers until the [s]days of David, 46 [t]who
found favor before God and [u]asked to find
a dwelling for the God of Jacob. 47 [v]But
Solomon built Him a house.
48 "However, [w]the Most High does not
dwell in temples made with hands, as the
prophet says:

49 *'Heaven[x] is My throne,*
And earth is My footstool.
What house will you build for Me?
says the LORD,
Or what is the place of My rest?
50 *Has My hand not [y]made all these*
things?'

Israel Resists the Holy Spirit

51 "*You* [z]stiff-necked[7] and [a]uncircum-
cised in heart and ears! You always resist
the Holy Spirit; as your fathers *did,* so *do*
you. 52 [b]Which of the prophets did your fathers not persecute? And they killed those
who foretold the coming of [c]the Just One,
of whom you now have become the be-
trayers and murderers, 53 [d]who have received the law by the direction of angels
and have not kept *it.*"

Stephen the Martyr

54 [e]When they heard these things they
were [8]cut to the heart, and they gnashed at
him with *their* teeth. 55 But he, [f]being full of
the Holy Spirit, gazed into heaven and saw
the [g]glory of God, and Jesus standing at the
right hand of God, 56 and said, "Look! [h]I
see the heavens opened and the [i]Son of
Man standing at the right hand of God!"
57 Then they cried out with a loud voice,
stopped their ears, and ran at him with one
accord; 58 and they cast *him* out of the city
and stoned *him.* And [j]the witnesses laid
down their clothes at the feet of a young
man named Saul. 59 And they stoned
Stephen as he was calling on *God* and saying, "Lord Jesus, [k]receive my spirit."
60 Then he knelt down and cried out with
a loud voice, [l]"Lord, do not charge them
with this sin." And when he had said this,
he fell asleep.

42 [n]Amos 5:25-27
43 [o]2 Chr. 36:11-21; Jer. 25:9-12
44 [p]Ex. 25:40; [Heb. 8:5]
45 [q]Deut. 32:49; Josh. 3:14; 18:1; 23:9 [r]Neh. 9:24; Ps. 44:2 [s]2 Sam. 6:2-15
46 [t]2 Sam. 7:1-13; 1 Kin. 8:17 [u]1 Chr. 22:7; Ps. 132:4, 5
47 [v]1 Kin. 6:1-38; 8:20, 21; 2 Chr. 3:1-17
48 [w]1 Kin. 8:27; 2 Chr. 2:6; Acts 17:24
49 [x]Is. 66:1, 2; Matt. 5:34
50 [y]Ps. 102:25
51 [z]Ex. 32:9; Is. 6:10 [a]Lev. 26:41 [7]*stubborn*
52 [b]2 Chr. 36:16; Matt. 21:35; 23:35; 1 Thess. 2:15 [c]Acts 3:14; 22:14; 1 John 2:1
53 [d]Ex. 20:1; Deut. 33:2; Acts 7:38; Gal. 3:19; Heb. 2:2
54 [e]Acts 5:33 [8]*furious*
55 [f]Matt. 5:8; 16:28; Mark 9:1; Luke 9:27; Acts 6:5 [g][Ex. 24:17]
56 [h]Matt. 3:16 [i]Dan. 7:13
58 [j]Acts 22:20
59 [k]Ps. 31:5
60 [l]Matt. 5:44; Luke 23:34

7:43 *Babylon.* Amos wrote Damascus (Amos 5:27), while Stephen said Babylon. Amos was prophesying the captivity of the northern kingdom in Assyria, a deportation beyond Damascus. Later the southern kingdom was taken captive to Babylon. Stephen, inspired to do so, extended the prophecy to embrace the judgment on the whole nation summarizing their idolatrous history and its results.

7:44-50 To counter the false charge that he blasphemed the temple (6:13,14), Stephen recounted its history to show his respect for it.

7:44 tabernacle of witness. The predecessor of the temple (Ex. 25:8,9,40).

7:48 Most High. A common OT title for God (cf. Gen. 14:18-20,22; Num. 24:16; Deut. 32:8; 2 Sam. 22:14; Pss. 7:17; 9:2; 18:13; 21:7; 73:11; 87:5; 91:1; 107:11; Is. 14:14; Lam. 3:35,38; Dan. 4:17,24,25,32,34; 7:25).

7:49,50 Quoted from Is. 66:1,2. Stephen's point is that God is greater than the temple, and thus the Jewish leaders were guilty of blaspheming by confining God to it.

7:51-53 The climax of Stephen's sermon indicted the Jewish leaders for rejecting God in the same way that their ancestors had rejected Him in the OT.

7:51 stiff-necked. Obstinate, like their fathers (Ex. 32:9; 33:5). **uncircumcised in heart and ears!** Thus as unclean before God as the uncircumcised Gentiles (*see notes on Deut. 10:16; Jer. 4:4; Rom. 2:28,29*). **resist the Holy Spirit.** By rejecting the Spirit's messengers and their message. Cf. Jesus' sermon in Matt. 23:13-39.

7:52 the Just One. *See note on 3:14.*

7:53 law by the direction of angels. See Deut. 33:2; Gal. 3:19; Heb. 2:2. Scripture does not delineate their precise role in the giving of the law, but clearly states the fact of their presence.

7:54 gnashed...with *their* teeth. In anger and frustration (cf. Pss. 35:16; 37:12; Matt. 8:11,12; 13:41,42,50; 22:13; 24:51; 25:30; Luke 13:28).

7:55 full of the Holy Spirit. *See note on 2:4.* **the glory of God.** Isaiah (Is. 6:1-3), Ezekiel (Ezek. 1:26-28), Paul (2 Cor. 12:2-4), and John (Rev. 1:10) also received visions of God's glory in heaven. **standing at the right hand of God.** Jesus is frequently so depicted (2:34; cf. Matt. 22:44; 26:64; Luke 22:69; Eph. 1:20; Col. 3:1; Heb. 1:3; 8:1; 10:11,12; 12:2).

7:56 Son of Man. *See note on Dan. 7:13,14.*

7:58 laid down their clothes...Saul. Paul's first appearance in Scripture. That he was near enough to the action to be holding the clothes of Stephen's killers reflects his deep involvement in the sordid affair (*see note on 8:1*).

7:59 stoned. This was the punishment prescribed in the law for blasphemy (Lev. 24:16); however, this was not a formal execution but an act of mob violence.

7:60 do not charge them with this sin. As had Jesus before him (Luke 23:34), Stephen prayed for God to forgive his killers. **he fell asleep.** A common NT euphemism for the death of believers (cf. John 11:11-14; 1 Cor. 11:30; 15:20,51; 1 Thess. 4:14; 5:10).

Saul Persecutes the Church

8 Now Saul was consenting to his death.
At that time a great persecution
arose against the church which was at Jerusalem; and [a]they were all scattered
throughout the regions of Judea and Samaria, except the apostles. 2 And devout
men carried Stephen *to his burial,* and
[b]made great lamentation over him.
3 As for Saul, [c]he made havoc of the
church, entering every house, and dragging off men and women, committing *them*
to prison.

Christ Is Preached in Samaria

4 Therefore [d]those who were scattered
went everywhere preaching the word.
5 Then [e]Philip went down to [1]the city of Samaria and preached Christ to them. 6 And
the multitudes with one accord heeded the
things spoken by Philip, hearing and seeing
the miracles which he did. 7 For [f]unclean
spirits, crying with a loud voice, came out
of many who were possessed; and many
who were paralyzed and lame were healed.
8 And there was great joy in that city.

The Sorcerer's Profession of Faith

9 But there was a certain man called Simon, who previously [g]practiced [2]sorcery
in the city and [h]astonished the [3]people of
Samaria, claiming that he was someone
great, 10 to whom they all gave heed, from
the least to the greatest, saying, "This man
is the great power of God." 11 And they
heeded him because he had astonished
them with his [4]sorceries for a long time.
12 But when they believed Philip as he
preached the things [i]concerning the kingdom of God and the name of Jesus Christ,
both men and women were baptized.
13 Then Simon himself also believed; and
when he was baptized he continued with
Philip, and was amazed, seeing the miracles and signs which were done.

The Sorcerer's Sin

14 Now when the [j]apostles who were at
Jerusalem heard that Samaria had received
the word of God, they sent Peter and John
to them, 15 who, when they had come
down, prayed for them [k]that they might
receive the Holy Spirit. 16 For [l]as yet He
had fallen upon none of them. [m]They had
only been baptized in [n]the name of the
Lord Jesus. 17 Then [o]they laid hands on
them, and they received the Holy Spirit.
18 And when Simon saw that through

CHAPTER 8
1 [a] John 16:2; Acts 8:4; 11:19
2 [b] Gen. 23:2
3 [c] Acts 7:58; 1 Cor. 15:9; Gal. 1:13; Phil. 3:6; 1 Tim. 1:13
4 [d] Matt. 10:23
5 [e] Acts 6:5; 8:26, 30 [1] Or *a*
7 [f] Mark 16:17
9 [g] Acts 8:11; 13:6 [h] Acts 5:36 [2] *magic* [3] Or *nation*
11 [4] *magic arts*
12 [i] Acts 1:3; 8:4
14 [j] Acts 5:12, 29, 40
15 [k] Acts 2:38; 19:2
16 [l] Acts 19:2 [m] Matt. 28:19; Acts 2:38 [n] Acts 10:48; 19:5
17 [o] Acts 6:6; 19:6; Heb. 6:2

8:1 consenting. Paul's murderous hatred of all believers was manifested here in his attitude toward Stephen (1 Tim. 1:13-15). **scattered.** Led by a Jew named Saul of Tarsus, the persecution scattered the Jerusalem fellowship and led to the first missionary outreach of the church. Not all members of the Jerusalem church were forced to flee; the Hellenists, because Stephen was likely one, bore the brunt of the persecution (cf. 11:19,20). **except the apostles.** They remained because of their devotion to Christ, to care for those at Jerusalem, and to continue evangelizing the region (cf. 9:26,27).

8:2 devout men. Probably pious Jews (cf. 2:5; Luke 2:25) who publicly protested Stephen's death.

8:3 he made havoc of the church. "Made havoc" was used in extrabiblical writings to refer to the destruction of a city or mangling by a wild animal.

8:4 went everywhere. This Gr. word is used frequently in Acts for missionary efforts (v. 40; 9:32; 13:6; 14:24; 15:3,41; 16:6; 18:23; 19:1,21; 20:2).

8:5 Philip. Cf. 6:5. The first missionary named in Scripture and the first to be given the title "evangelist" (21:8). **the city of Samaria.** The ancient capital of the northern kingdom of Israel, which eventually fell to the Assyrians (722 B.C.) after over 200 years of idolatry and rebellion against God. After resettling many of the people in other lands, the Assyrians located Gentiles from other areas into the region, resulting in a mix of Jews and Gentiles who became known as Samaritans (*see notes on John 4:9,20*).

8:7 unclean spirits. *See note on 5:16.*

8:9 sorcery. Magic which originally referred to the practices of the Medo-Persians: a mixture of science and superstition, including astrology, divination, and the occult (*see notes on Deut. 18:9-12; Rev. 9:21*).

8:10,11 the great power of God. Simon claimed to be united to God. The early church Fathers claimed he was one of the founders of Gnosticism, which asserted there were a series of divine emanations reaching up to God. They were called "Powers," and the people believed he was at the top of the ladder.

8:13 Simon...believed. His belief was motivated by purely selfish reasons and could never be considered genuine. Cf. John 2:23,24. He saw it as an external act useful to gain the power he believed Philip possessed. By following Philip, he also was able to maintain contact with his former audience.

8:15 receive the Holy Spirit. *See note on 2:4.*

8:16 as yet...upon none of them. This verse does not support the false notion that Christians receive the Holy Spirit subsequent to salvation. This was a transitional period in which confirmation by the apostles was necessary to verify the inclusion of a new group of people into the church. Because of the animosity that existed between Jews and Samaritans, it was essential for the Samaritans to receive the Spirit, in the presence of the leaders of the Jerusalem church, for the purpose of maintaining a unified church. The delay also revealed the Samaritans' need to come under apostolic authority. The same transitional event occurred when the Gentiles were added to the church (11:44-46; cf. 15:6-12; 19:6).

8:17 laid hands on them. This signified apostolic affirmation and solidarity. *See note on 6:6.* **received the Holy Spirit.** That this actually occurred likely demonstrated that believers also spoke in tongues here, just as those who received the Spirit did on the Day of Pentecost (*see note on 2:4*), as the Gentiles did when they received the Spirit (10:46), and as those followers of John did (19:6). As Samaritans, Gentiles, and believers from the Old Covenant were added to the church, the unity of the church was established. No longer could one nation (Israel) be God's witness people, but the church made up of Jews, Gentiles, half-breed Samaritans, and OT saints who became NT believers (19:1-7). To demonstrate the unity, it was imperative that there be some replication in each instance of what had occurred at Pentecost with the believing Jews, such as the presence of the apostles and the coming of the Spirit manifestly indicated through speaking in the languages of Pentecost (2:5-12).

the laying on of the apostles' hands the
Holy Spirit was given, he offered them
money, 19 saying, "Give me this power
also, that anyone on whom I lay hands
may receive the Holy Spirit."
20 But Peter said to him, "Your money
perish with you, because [p]you thought that
[q]the gift of God could be purchased with
money! 21 You have neither part nor portion
in this matter, for your [r]heart is not right in
the sight of God. 22 Repent therefore of this
your wickedness, and pray God [s]if perhaps
the thought of your heart may be forgiven
you. 23 For I see that you are [t]poisoned by
bitterness and bound by iniquity."
24 Then Simon answered and said,
[u]"Pray to the Lord for me, that none of the
things which you have spoken may come
upon me."
25 So when they had testified and
preached the word of the Lord, they returned to Jerusalem, preaching the gospel
in many villages of the Samaritans.

Christ Is Preached to an Ethiopian

26 Now an angel of the Lord spoke to
[v]Philip, saying, "Arise and go toward the
south along the road which goes down
from Jerusalem to Gaza." This is [5]desert.
27 So he arose and went. And behold, [w]a
man of Ethiopia, a eunuch of great authority under Candace the queen of the Ethiopians, who had charge of all her treasury,
and [x]had come to Jerusalem to worship,
28 was returning. And sitting in his chariot,
he was reading Isaiah the prophet. 29 Then
the Spirit said to Philip, "Go near and
overtake this chariot."
30 So Philip ran to him, and heard him
reading the prophet Isaiah, and said, "Do
you understand what you are reading?"
31 And he said, "How can I, unless
someone guides me?" And he asked Philip
to come up and sit with him. 32 The place
in the Scripture which he read was this:

[y]"He was led as a sheep to the
slaughter;
And as a lamb before its shearer is
silent,
[z]So He opened not His mouth.
33 *In His humiliation His [a]justice was*
taken away,
And who will declare His
generation?
For His life is [b]taken from the
earth."

34 So the eunuch answered Philip and
said, "I ask you, of whom does the prophet
say this, of himself or of some other man?"
35 Then Philip opened his mouth, [c]and beginning at this Scripture, preached Jesus to
him. 36 Now as they went down the road,
they came to some water. And the eunuch
said, "See, *here is* water. [d]What hinders me
from being baptized?"
37 [6]Then Philip said, [e]"If you believe
with all your heart, you may."
And he answered and said, [f]"I believe
that Jesus Christ is the Son of God."
38 So he commanded the chariot to stand
still. And both Philip and the eunuch went
down into the water, and he baptized him.
39 Now when they came up out of the
water, [g]the Spirit of the Lord caught Philip
away, so that the eunuch saw him no more;
and he went on his way rejoicing. 40 But
Philip was found at [7]Azotus. And passing
through, he preached in all the cities till he
came to [h]Caesarea.

The Damascus Road: Saul Converted

9 Then [a]Saul, still breathing threats and
murder against the disciples of the
Lord, went to the high priest 2 and asked

20 [p] 2 Kin. 5:16; Is. 55:1; Dan. 5:17; [Matt. 10:8] [q] [Acts 2:38; 10:45; 11:17]
21 [r] Jer. 17:9
22 [s] Dan. 4:27; 2 Tim. 2:25
23 [t] Heb. 12:15
24 [u] Gen. 20:7, 17; Ex. 8:8; Num. 21:7; 1 Kin. 13:6; Job 42:8; James 5:16
26 [v] Acts 6:5 [5] Or *a deserted place*
27 [w] Ps. 68:31; 87:4; Is. 56:3; Zeph. 3:10 [x] 1 Kin. 8:41, 42; John 12:20
32 [y] Is. 53:7, 8 [z] Matt. 26:62, 63; 27:12, 14; John 19:9
33 [a] Luke 23:1-25 [b] Luke 23:33-46
35 [c] Luke 24:27; Acts 17:2; 18:28; 28:23
36 [d] Acts 10:47; 16:33
37 [e] Matt. 28:19; [Mark 16:16; Rom. 10:9, 10] [f] Matt. 16:16; John 6:69; 9:35, 38; 11:27 [6] NU, M omit v. 37. It is found in Western texts, including the Latin tradition.
39 [g] 1 Kin. 18:12; 2 Kin. 2:16; Ezek. 3:12, 14; 2 Cor. 12:2
40 [h] Acts 21:8 [7] Same as Heb. *Ashdod*

CHAPTER 9

1 [a] Acts 7:57; 8:1, 3; 26:10, 11; Gal. 1:13; 1 Tim. 1:13

8:22-24 Although he was certainly fearful, he was unwilling to repent and seek forgiveness, wanting only to escape the consequences of his sin.

8:26 Gaza. One of 5 chief cities of the Philistines. The original city was destroyed in the first century B.C. and a new city was built near the coast.

8:27 Ethiopia. In those days, a large kingdom located S of Egypt. **eunuch.** This can refer to one who had been emasculated or generally, to a government official. It is likely he was both since Luke refers to him as a eunuch and as one who held a position of authority in the queen's court—that of treasurer, much like a Minister of Finance or Secretary of the Treasury. As a physical eunuch, he would have been denied access to the temple (Deut. 23:1) and the opportunity to become a full proselyte to Judaism. **Candace.** Probably not a name, but an official title (like Pharaoh or Caesar) given to the queen mothers in that land.

8:28 reading Isaiah. He knew the importance of seeking God through the Scripture (Luke 24:25-27; John 5:39,46; Rom. 10:12-15).

8:32,33 The place…he read. Isaiah 53:7,8.

8:34 whom does the prophet say…? His confusion was understandable. Even the Jewish religious experts were divided on the meaning of this passage. Some believed the slaughtered sheep represented Israel, others thought Isaiah was referring to himself, and others thought the Messiah was Isaiah's subject.

8:37 This verse is not found in the oldest and most reliable manuscripts.

8:39 caught Philip away. Elijah (1 Kin. 18:12; 2 Kin. 2:16) and Ezekiel (Ezek. 3:12,14; 8:3) were also snatched away in a miraculous fashion. This was a powerful confirmation to the caravan that Philip was God's representative.

8:40 Azotus. The first-century name for the ancient Philistine city of Ashdod, located 20 mi. N of Gaza. **Caesarea.** Where Philip and his family probably lived (21:9; *see note on 9:30*).

9:1 Saul. See Introduction to Romans: Author and Date. The Apostle Paul was originally named Saul, after the first king of Israel. He was born a Jew, studied in Jerusalem under Gamaliel (22:3), and became a Pharisee (23:6). He was also a Roman citizen, a right he inherited from

[b]letters from him to the synagogues of Damascus, so that if he found any who were
of the Way, whether men or women, he
might bring them bound to Jerusalem.
3 [c]As he journeyed he came near Damascus, and suddenly a light shone around
him from heaven. 4 Then he fell to the
ground, and heard a voice saying to him,
"Saul, Saul, [d]why are you persecuting
Me?"
5 And he said, "Who are You, Lord?"
Then the Lord said, "I am Jesus, whom
you are persecuting. [1]It *is* hard for you to
kick against the goads."
6 So he, trembling and astonished, said,
"Lord, what do You want me to do?"
Then the Lord *said* to him, "Arise and go
into the city, and you will be told what you
must do."
7 And [e]the men who journeyed with him
stood speechless, hearing a voice but seeing no one. 8 Then Saul arose from the
ground, and when his eyes were opened
he saw no one. But they led him by the
hand and brought *him* into Damascus.
9 And he was three days without sight,
and neither ate nor drank.

Ananias Baptizes Saul

10 Now there was a certain disciple at
Damascus [f]named Ananias; and to him the
Lord said in a vision, "Ananias."
And he said, "Here I am, Lord."
11 So the Lord *said* to him, "Arise and go
to the street called Straight, and inquire at
the house of Judas for *one* called Saul [g]of
Tarsus, for behold, he is praying. 12 And in
a vision he has seen a man named Ananias
coming in and putting *his* hand on him, so
that he might receive his sight."
13 Then Ananias answered, "Lord, I
have heard from many about this man,
[h]how much [2]harm he has done to Your
saints in Jerusalem. 14 And here he has authority from the chief priests to bind all
[i]who call on Your name."
15 But the Lord said to him, "Go, for [j]he
is a chosen vessel of Mine to bear My name
before [k]Gentiles, [l]kings, and the [m]chil-
dren[3] of Israel. 16 For [n]I will show him
how many things he must suffer for My
[o]name's sake."
17 [p]And Ananias went his way and entered the house; and [q]laying his hands on
him he said, "Brother Saul, the Lord [4]Jesus,
who appeared to you on the road as you
came, has sent me that you may receive
your sight and [r]be filled with the Holy
Spirit." 18 Immediately there fell from his
eyes *something* like scales, and he received
his sight at once; and he arose and was
baptized.
19 So when he had received food, he was
strengthened. [s]Then Saul spent some days
with the disciples at Damascus.

Saul Preaches Christ

20 Immediately he preached [5]the Christ
in the synagogues, that He is the Son of
God.

2 [b]Acts 22:5
3 [c]Acts 22:6; 26:12, 13; 1 Cor. 15:8
4 [d][Matt. 25:40]
5 [1]NU, M omit the rest of v. 5 and begin v. 6 with *But arise and go*
7 [e]Dan. 10:7; John 12:29; [Acts 22:9; 26:13]
10 [f]Acts 22:12
11 [g]Acts 21:39; 22:3
13 [h]Acts 9:1 [2]*bad things*
14 [i]Acts 7:59; 9:2, 21; 1 Cor. 1:2; 2 Tim. 2:22
15 [j]Acts 13:2; 22:21; Rom. 1:1; 1 Cor. 15:10; Gal. 1:15; Eph. 3:7, 8; 1 Tim. 2:7; 2 Tim. 1:11 [k]Rom. 1:5; 11:13; Gal. 2:7, 8 [l]Acts 25:22, 23; 26:1 [m]Acts 21:40; Rom. 1:16; 9:1-5 [3]Lit. *sons*
16 [n]Acts 20:23; 2 Cor. 11:23-28; 12:7-10; Gal. 6:17; Phil. 1:29, 30 [o]2 Cor. 4:11
17 [p]Acts 22:12, 13 [q]Acts 8:17 [r]Acts 2:4; 4:31; 8:17; 13:52 [4]M omits *Jesus*
19 [s]Acts 26:20
20 [5]NU *Jesus*

his father (22:8). Verses 1-19 record the external facts of his conversion (see also 22:1-22; 26:9-20). Philippians 3:1-14 records the internal spiritual conversion (*see notes there*). **threats and murder.** See 1 Tim. 1:12,13; 1 Cor. 15:9.

9:2 Damascus. An ancient city, the capital of Syria, located 60 mi. inland from the Mediterranean and ca. 160 mi. NE of Jerusalem. Apparently, it had a large population of Jews, including Hellenist believers who fled Jerusalem to avoid persecution (8:2). **who were of the Way.** This description of Christianity, derived from Jesus' description of Himself (John 14:6), appears several times in Acts (19:9,23; 22:4; 24:14,22). This is an appropriate title because Christianity is the way of God (18:26), the way into the Holy Place (Heb. 10:19,20), and the way of truth (John 14:6; 2 Pet. 2:2).

9:3-6 This was the first of 6 visions to be seen by Paul in Acts (cf. 16:9,10; 18:9,10; 22:17,18; 23:11; 27:23,24).

9:3 a light...from heaven. The appearance of Jesus Christ in glory (cf. 22:6; 26:13), visible only to Saul (26:9).

9:4 why are you persecuting Me? An inseparable union exists between Christ and His followers. Saul's persecution represented a direct attack on Christ. Cf. Matt. 18:5,6.

9:5 goads. Sticks for prodding cattle (26:14).

9:10 Ananias. One of the leaders of the Damascus church, and therefore, one of Saul's targets (cf. 22:12).

9:11 street called Straight. This street, which runs through Damascus from the E gate to the W, still exists and is called Darb el-Mustaqim. **Tarsus.** The birthplace of Paul and a key city in the Roman province of Cilicia, located on the banks of the Cydnus River near the border of Asia Minor and Syria. It served as both a commercial and educational center. The wharves on the Cydnus were crowded with commerce, while its university ranked with those of Athens and Alexandria as the finest in the Roman world.

9:15 chosen vessel. Lit. "a vessel of election." There was perfect continuity between Paul's salvation and his service; God chose him to convey His grace to all men (Gal. 1:1; cf. 1 Tim. 2:7; 2 Tim. 1:11). Paul used this same word 4 times (Rom. 9:21,23; 2 Cor. 4:7; 2 Tim. 2:21). **before Gentiles, kings, and the children of Israel.** Paul began his ministry preaching to Jews (13:14; 14:1; 17:1,10; 18:4; 19:8), but his primary calling was to Gentiles (Rom. 11:13; 15:16). God also called him to minister to kings such as Agrippa (25:23–26:32) and likely Caesar (cf. 25:10-12; 2 Tim. 4:16,17).

9:17 laying his hands on him. *See note on 6:6.* **be filled with the Holy Spirit.** *See note on 2:4.* The Spirit had already been active in Paul's life: convicting him of sin (John 16:9), convincing him of the Lordship of Christ (1 Cor. 12:3), transforming him (Titus 3:5), and indwelling him permanently (1 Cor. 12:13). He was then filled with the Spirit and empowered for service (cf. 2:4,14; 4:8,31; 6:5,8; *see also note on Eph. 5:16*). Saul received the Spirit without any apostles present because he was a Jew (the inclusion of Jews in the church had already been established at Pentecost) and because he was an apostle in his own right because Christ personally chose him and commissioned him for service (Rom. 1:1).

9:20 He is the Son of God. The content of Paul's message was that Jesus Christ is God (*see notes on Heb. 1:4,5*).

21 Then all who heard were amazed, and
said, [t]"Is this not he who destroyed those
who called on this name in Jerusalem, and
has come here for that purpose, so that he
might bring them bound to the chief
priests?"
22 But Saul increased all the more in
strength, [u]and confounded the Jews who
dwelt in Damascus, proving that this *Jesus*
is the Christ.

Saul Escapes Death

23 Now after many days were past, [v]the
Jews plotted to kill him. 24 [w]But their plot
became known to Saul. And they watched
the gates day and night, to kill him.
25 Then the disciples took him by night
and [x]let *him* down through the wall in a
large basket.

Saul at Jerusalem

26 And [y]when Saul had come to Jerusalem, he tried to join the disciples; but they
were all afraid of him, and did not believe
that he was a disciple. 27 [z]But Barnabas
took him and brought *him* to the apostles.
And he declared to them how he had seen
the Lord on the road, and that He had spoken to him, [a]and how he had preached
boldly at Damascus in the name of Jesus.
28 So [b]he was with them at Jerusalem,
coming in and going out. 29 And he spoke
boldly in the name of the Lord Jesus and
disputed against the [c]Hellenists,[6] [d]but
they attempted to kill him. 30 When the
brethren found out, they brought him
down to Caesarea and sent him out to Tarsus.

The Church Prospers

31 [e]Then the [7]churches throughout all
Judea, Galilee, and Samaria had peace and
were [f]edified.[8] And walking in the [g]fear of
the Lord and in the [h]comfort of the Holy
Spirit, they were [i]multiplied.

Aeneas Healed

32 Now it came to pass, as Peter went
[j]through all *parts of the country,* that he also
came down to the saints who dwelt in
Lydda. 33 There he found a certain man
named Aeneas, who had been bedridden
eight years and was paralyzed. 34 And Peter said to him, "Aeneas, [k]Jesus the Christ
heals you. Arise and make your bed."
Then he arose immediately. 35 So all who
dwelt at Lydda and [l]Sharon saw him and
[m]turned to the Lord.

Dorcas Restored to Life

36 At Joppa there was a certain disciple
named [9]Tabitha, which is translated [1]Dor-
cas. This woman was full [n]of good works
and charitable deeds which she did. 37 But
it happened in those days that she became
sick and died. When they had washed her,
they laid *her* in [o]an upper room. 38 And
since Lydda was near Joppa, and the disciples had heard that Peter was there, they
sent two men to him, imploring *him* not to
delay in coming to them. 39 Then Peter
arose and went with them. When he had
come, they brought *him* to the upper room.
And all the widows stood by him weeping,
showing the tunics and garments which
Dorcas had made while she was with them.
40 But Peter [p]put them all out, and [q]knelt
down and prayed. And turning to the body
he [r]said, "Tabitha, arise." And she opened
her eyes, and when she saw Peter she sat
up. 41 Then he gave her *his* hand and lifted
her up; and when he had called the saints
and widows, he presented her alive. 42 And
it became known throughout all Joppa,

21 [t]Acts 8:3; 9:13; Gal. 1:13, 23
22 [u]Acts 18:28
23 [v]Acts 23:12; 2 Cor. 11:26
24 [w]2 Cor. 11:32
25 [x]Josh. 2:15; 1 Sam. 19:12
26 [y]Acts 22:17-20; 26:20; Gal. 1:17, 18
27 [z]Acts 4:36; 13:2 [a]Acts 9:20, 22
28 [b]Gal. 1:18
29 [c]Acts 6:1; 11:20 [d]Acts 9:23; 2 Cor. 11:26 [6]Greek-speaking Jews
31 [e]Acts 5:11; 8:1; 16:5 [7]NU *church . . . was* [f][Eph. 4:16, 29] [g]Ps. 34:9 [h]John 14:16 [i]Acts 16:5 [8]*built up*
32 [j]Acts 8:14
34 [k][Acts 3:6, 16; 4:10]
35 [l]1 Chr. 5:16; 27:29; Is. 33:9; 35:2; 65:10 [m]Acts 11:21; 15:19
36 [n]1 Tim. 2:10; Titus 3:8 [9]Lit., in Aram., *Gazelle* [1]Lit., in Gr., *Gazelle*
37 [o]Acts 1:13; 9:39
40 [p]Matt. 9:25 [q]Luke 22:41; Acts 7:60 [r]Mark 5:41, 42; John 11:43

9:23 after many days were past. A period of 3 years, in which he ministered in Nabtean Arabia, an area encompassing Damascus S to the Sinai peninsula (*see notes on Gal. 1:17,18*).

9:24 gates. Damascus was a walled city, thus the gates were the only conventional means of escape.

9:25 let *him* down…in a large basket. "Basket" was a large woven hamper suitable for hay, straw, or bales of wool.

9:27 Barnabas. *See note on 4:36.*

9:29 Hellenists. The same group Stephen debated (*see note on 6:1*).

9:30 Caesarea. Cf. 8:40. An important port city on the Mediterranean located 30 mi. N of Joppa. As the capital of the Roman province of Judea and the home of the Roman procurator, it served as the headquarters of a large Roman garrison. **sent him out to Tarsus.** Paul disappeared from prominent ministry for several years, although he possibly founded some churches around Syria and Cilicia (15:23; Gal. 1:21).

9:31 the churches…had peace and were edified. Paul's conversion and political changes contributed to the rest. A stricter Roman governor and the expansion of Herod Agrippa's authority restricted the persecution.

9:32 Lydda. Lod in the OT. Located about 10 mi. SE of Joppa, it was a hub servicing roads from Egypt to Syria and from Joppa to Jerusalem.

9:33 Aeneas. Use of "certain man" to describe him means he was an unbeliever (cf. v. 36). His paralysis was incurable by the limited medical knowledge of that day.

9:35 Sharon. The plain surrounding Lydda and Joppa and extending N to Caesarea.

9:36 Joppa. A seacoast town today known as Jaffa, S of Tel Aviv. **Tabitha.** She was more commonly known by her Gr. name, "Dorcas." Both names mean "gazelle."

9:37 upper room. This arrangement was similar to that of the upstairs room in 1:13; 2:1. While it was customary to bury a body immediately, the believers in Joppa had another plan.

9:38 near Joppa. 10 mi. SE.

9:39 tunics…garments. Close fitting undergarments and long outer robes.

[s]and many believed on the Lord. **43** So it
was that he stayed many days in Joppa
with [t]Simon, a tanner.

Cornelius Sends a Delegation

10 There was a certain man in [a]Cae-
sarea called Cornelius, a centurion
of what was called the Italian [1]Regiment,
2 [b]a devout *man* and one who [c]feared God
with all his household, who gave [2]alms
generously to the people, and prayed to
God always. **3** About [3]the ninth hour of the
day [d]he saw clearly in a vision an angel of
God coming in and saying to him, "Cornelius!"
4 And when he observed him, he was
afraid, and said, "What is it, lord?"
So he said to him, "Your prayers and
your alms have come up for a memorial
before God. **5** Now [e]send men to Joppa,
and send for Simon whose surname is Peter. **6** He is lodging with [f]Simon, a tanner,
whose house is by the sea. [g]He[4] will tell
you what you must do." **7** And when the
angel who spoke to him had departed,
Cornelius called two of his household servants and a devout soldier from among
those who waited on him continually. **8** So
when he had explained all *these* things to
them, he sent them to Joppa.

Peter's Vision

9 The next day, as they went on their
journey and drew near the city, [h]Peter
went up on the housetop to pray, about
[5]the sixth hour. **10** Then he became very
hungry and wanted to eat; but while they
made ready, he fell into a trance **11** and
[i]saw heaven opened and an object like a
great sheet bound at the four corners, descending to him and let down to the earth.
12 In it were all kinds of four-footed animals of the earth, wild beasts, creeping
things, and birds of the air. **13** And a voice
came to him, "Rise, Peter; kill and eat."
14 But Peter said, "Not so, Lord! [j]For I
have never eaten anything common or unclean."
15 And a voice *spoke* to him again the second time, [k]"What God has [6]cleansed you
must not call common." **16** This was done
three times. And the object was taken up
into heaven again.

Summoned to Caesarea

17 Now while Peter [7]wondered within
himself what this vision which he had seen
meant, behold, the men who had been sent
from Cornelius had made inquiry for Simon's house, and stood before the gate.
18 And they called and asked whether Simon, whose surname was Peter, was lodging there.
19 While Peter thought about the vision,
[l]the Spirit said to him, "Behold, three men
are seeking you. **20** [m]Arise therefore, go
down and go with them, doubting nothing; for I have sent them."
21 Then Peter went down to the men
[8]who had been sent to him from Cornelius,
and said, "Yes, I am he whom you seek.
For what reason have you come?"
22 And they said, "Cornelius *the* centurion, a just man, one who fears God and
[n]has a good reputation among all the nation of the Jews, was divinely instructed by
a holy angel to summon you to his house,
and to hear words from you." **23** Then he
invited them in and lodged *them*.
On the next day Peter went away with
them, [o]and some brethren from Joppa accompanied him.

42 [s]John 11:45
43 [t]Acts 10:6

CHAPTER 10

1 [a]Acts 8:40; 23:23 [1]*Cohort*
2 [b]Acts 8:2; 9:22; 22:12 [c][Acts 10:22, 35; 13:16, 26] [2]*charitable gifts*
3 [d]Acts 10:30; 11:13 [3]3 P.M.
5 [e]Acts 11:13, 14
6 [f]Acts 9:43 [g]Acts 11:14 [4]NU, M omit the rest of v. 6.
9 [h]Acts 10:9-32; 11:5-14 [5]Noon
11 [i]Ezek. 1:1; Matt. 3:16; Acts 7:56; Rev. 4:1; 19:11
14 [j]Lev. 11:4; 20:25; Deut. 14:3, 7; Ezek. 4:14
15 [k][Matt. 15:11; Mark 7:19]; Acts 10:28; [Rom. 14:14]; 1 Cor. 10:25; [1 Tim. 4:4; Titus 1:15] [6]Declared clean
17 [7]*was perplexed*
19 [l]Acts 11:12
20 [m]Acts 15:7-9
21 [8]NU, M omit *who had been sent to him from Cornelius*
22 [n]Acts 22:12
23 [o]Acts 10:45; 11:12

9:43 Simon, a tanner. Cf. 10:5,6. Peter breaks down a cultural barrier by staying with a tanner, an occupation despised by Jewish society because the tanner dealt with the skins of dead animals. The local synagogue probably shunned Simon.

10:1 a centurion. One of 60 officers in a Roman legion, each of whom commanded 100 men (*see note on Matt. 8:5*). **Italian Regiment.** Or "Italian Cohort." Ten cohorts of 600 men each made up a legion.

10:2 feared God. A technical term used by Jews to refer to Gentiles who had abandoned their pagan religion in favor of worshiping Jehovah God. Such a person, while following the ethics of the OT, had not become a full proselyte to Judaism through circumcision. Cornelius was to receive the saving knowledge of God in Christ (*see note on Rom. 1:20*).

10:3 About the ninth hour. 3:00 p.m. (*see note on 3:1*).

10:4 memorial. A remembrance. Cornelius' prayers, devotion, faith, and goodness were like a fragrant offering rising up to God.

10:7 devout soldier. *See note on vv. 1,2.*

10:9 housetop to pray. All kinds of worship occurred on the flat roofs of Jewish homes (2 Kin. 23:12; Jer. 19:13; 32:29). **sixth hour.** 12:00 noon.

10:12 all kinds of four-footed animals. Both clean and unclean animals. To keep the Israelites separate from their idolatrous neighbors, God set specific dietary restrictions regarding the consumption of such animals (cf. Lev. 11:25,26).

10:13 kill and eat. With the coming of the New Covenant and the calling of the church, God ended the dietary restrictions (cf. Mark 7:19).

10:14 common or unclean. Unholy or defiled.

10:15 God has cleansed. More than just abolishing the OT dietary restrictions, God made unity possible in the church of both Jews, symbolized by the clean animals, and Gentiles, symbolized by the unclean animals, through the comprehensive sacrificial death of Christ (*see note on Eph. 2:14*).

10:22 instructed by a holy angel. Cf. vv. 3-6.

10:23 invited them in. Self-respecting Jews did not invite any Gentiles into their home, especially soldiers of the hated Roman army. **some brethren.** Six Jewish believers (11:12), identified as "those of the circumcision" in v. 45.

Peter Meets Cornelius

24 And the following day they entered Caesarea. Now Cornelius was waiting for them, and had called together his relatives and close friends. 25 As Peter was coming in, Cornelius met him and fell down at his feet and worshiped *him.* 26 But Peter lifted him up, saying, [p]"Stand up; I myself am also a man." 27 And as he talked with him, he went in and found many who had come together. 28 Then he said to them, "You know how [q]unlawful it is for a Jewish man to keep company with or go to one of another nation. But [r]God has shown me that I should not call any man common or unclean. 29 Therefore I came without objection as soon as I was sent for. I ask, then, for what reason have you sent for me?"

30 So Cornelius said, [9]"Four days ago I was fasting until this hour; and at the ninth hour I prayed in my house, and behold, [s]a man stood before me [t]in bright clothing, 31 and said, 'Cornelius, [u]your prayer has been heard, and [v]your [1]alms are remembered in the sight of God. 32 Send therefore to Joppa and call Simon here, whose surname is Peter. He is lodging in the house of Simon, a tanner, by the sea. [2]When he comes, he will speak to you.' 33 So I sent to you immediately, and you have done well to come. Now therefore, we are all present before God, to hear all the things commanded you by God."

Preaching to Cornelius' Household

34 Then Peter opened *his* mouth and said: [w]"In truth I perceive that God shows no partiality. 35 But [x]in every nation whoever fears Him and works righteousness is [y]accepted by Him. 36 The word which *God* sent to the [3]children of Israel, [z]preaching peace through Jesus Christ—[a]He is Lord of all— 37 that word you know, which was proclaimed throughout all Judea, and [b]began from Galilee after the baptism which John preached: 38 how [c]God anointed Jesus of Nazareth with the Holy Spirit and with power, who [d]went about doing good and healing all who were oppressed by the devil, [e]for God was with Him. 39 And we are [f]witnesses of all things which He did both in the land of the Jews and in Jerusalem, whom [4]they [g]killed by hanging on a tree. 40 Him [h]God raised up on the third day, and showed Him openly, 41 [i]not to all the people, but to witnesses chosen before by God, *even* to us [j]who ate and drank with Him after He arose from the dead. 42 And [k]He commanded us to preach to the people, and to testify [l]that it is He who was ordained by God *to be* Judge [m]of the living and the dead. 43 [n]To Him all the prophets witness that, through His name, [o]whoever believes in Him will receive [p]remission[5] of sins."

The Holy Spirit Falls on the Gentiles

44 While Peter was still speaking these words, [q]the Holy Spirit fell upon all those who heard the word. 45 [r]And [6]those of the circumcision who believed were astonished, as many as came with Peter, [s]because the gift of the Holy Spirit had been poured out on the Gentiles also. 46 For they heard them speak with tongues and magnify God.

Then Peter answered, 47 "Can anyone forbid water, that these should not be baptized who have received the Holy Spirit [t]just as we *have?*" 48 [u]And he commanded them to be baptized [v]in the name of the Lord. Then they asked him to stay a few days.

Peter Defends God's Grace

11 Now the apostles and brethren who were in Judea heard that the Gentiles had also received the word of God. 2 And when Peter came up to Jerusalem, [a]those of the circumcision contended with him, 3 saying, [b]"You went in to uncircumcised men [c]and ate with them!"

26 [p] Acts 14:14, 15; Rev. 19:10; 22:8
28 [q] John 4:9; 18:28; Acts 11:3; Gal. 2:12 [r] [Acts 10:14, 35; 15:8, 9]
30 [s] Acts 1:10 [t] Matt. 28:3; Mark 16:5 [9] NU *Four days ago to this hour, at the ninth hour*
31 [u] Dan. 10:12 [v] Heb. 6:10 [1] *charitable gifts*
32 [2] NU omits the rest of v. 32.
34 [w] Deut. 10:17; 2 Chr. 19:7; Rom. 2:11; Gal. 2:6; Eph. 6:9
35 [x] Acts 15:9; [1 Cor. 12; 13; Eph. 2:13] [y] Ps. 15:1, 2
36 [z] Is. 57:19; Eph. 2:14; [Col. 1:20] [a] Matt. 28:18; Acts 2:36; Rom. 10:12; 1 Cor. 15:27 [3] Lit. *sons*
37 [b] Luke 4:14
38 [c] Is. 61:1-3; Luke 4:18 [d] Matt. 4:23 [e] John 3:2; 8:29
39 [f] Acts 1:8 [g] Acts 2:23 [4] NU, M *they also*
40 [h] Hos. 6:2; Matt. 12:39, 40; 16:4; 20:19; John 2:19-21; Acts 2:24
41 [i] [John 14:17, 19, 22; 15:27] [j] Luke 24:30, 41-43
42 [k] Matt. 28:19 [l] John 5:22, 27; Acts 17:31 [m] Rom. 14:9; 2 Tim. 4:1; 1 Pet. 4:5
43 [n] [Is. 42:1; 53:11; 61:1]; Jer. 31:34; Dan. 9:24; Hos. 6:1-3; Mic. 7:18; Zech. 13:1; Mal. 4:2 [o] [John 3:16, 18; Acts 26:18]; Rom. 10:11; Gal. 3:22 [p] Acts 13:38, 39 [5] *forgiveness*
44 [q] Acts 4:31
45 [r] Acts 10:23 [s] Is. 42:1, 6; 49:6; Luke 2:32; John 11:52; Acts 11:18 [6] The Jews
47 [t] Acts 2:4; 10:44; 11:17; 15:8
48 [u] 1 Cor. 1:14-17 [v] Acts 2:38; 8:16; 19:5 CHAPTER 11 **2** [a] Acts 10:45 **3** [b] Matt. 9:11; Acts 10:28 [c] Gal. 2:12

10:26 I myself am also a man. Cf. 14:11-15; Rev. 22:8,9. Only the triune God deserves our worship.

10:28 unlawful. Lit. "breaking a taboo." Peter followed the Jewish standards and traditions his whole life. His comments reveal his acceptance of a new standard in which Jews no longer were to consider Gentiles profane.

10:34 God shows no partiality. Taught in both the OT (Deut. 10:17; 2 Chr. 19:7; Job 34:19) and NT (Rom. 2:11; 3:29,30; James 2:1). The reality of this truth was taking on new dimensions for Peter.

10:35 accepted. This Gr. word means "marked by a favorable manifestation of the divine pleasure."

10:36 preaching peace. Christ, by paying the price of sin through His sacrificial death, established peace between man and God (*see note on Rom. 5:1-11*).

10:37 the baptism which John preached. Cf. 1:22; 13:24; 18:25; 19:34; *see notes on Matt. 3:2-12.*

10:38 how God anointed Jesus. Cf. 4:27. The beginning of Jesus' earthly ministry (cf. Matt. 3:13-17; Luke 3:21,22).

10:41 to witnesses chosen. Jesus became visible after His resurrection only to believers (cf. 1 Cor. 15:5-8).

10:43 believes in Him. The means of salvation—faith in Christ alone (*see note on Rom. 1:16*; cf. John 3:14-17; 6:69; Rom. 10:11; Gal. 3:22; Eph. 2:8,9).

10:44 the Holy Spirit fell. *See notes on 2:4; 8:17.*

10:45 the circumcision. Cf. 11:2. Jewish Christians (*see note on v. 23*).

10:46 tongues. *See notes on 2:4; 8:17.*

11:3 ate with them! The Jewish believers were outraged over such a blatant breach of Jewish custom. It was difficult for them to conceive that Jesus could be equally Lord of Gentile believers.

4 But Peter explained *it* to them [d]in order
from the beginning, saying: 5 [e]"I was in the
city of Joppa praying; and in a trance I saw
a vision, an object descending like a great
sheet, let down from heaven by four corners; and it came to me. 6 When I observed
it intently and considered, I saw four-footed animals of the earth, wild beasts, creeping things, and birds of the air. 7 And I
heard a voice saying to me, 'Rise, Peter; kill
and eat.' 8 But I said, 'Not so, Lord! For
nothing common or unclean has at any
time entered my mouth.' 9 But the voice
answered me again from heaven, 'What
God has cleansed you must not call common.' 10 Now this was done three times,
and all were drawn up again into heaven.
11 At that very moment, three men stood
before the house where I was, having been
sent to me from Caesarea. 12 Then [f]the
Spirit told me to go with them, doubting
nothing. Moreover [g]these six brethren accompanied me, and we entered the man's
house. 13 [h]And he told us how he had seen
an angel standing in his house, who said to
him, 'Send men to Joppa, and call for Simon whose surname is Peter, 14 who will
tell you words by which you and all your
household will be saved.' 15 And as I
began to speak, the Holy Spirit fell upon
them, [i]as upon us at the beginning. 16 Then
I remembered the word of the Lord, how
He said, [j]'John indeed baptized with
water, but [k]you shall be baptized with the
Holy Spirit.' 17 [l]If therefore God gave them
the same gift as *He gave* us when we believed on the Lord Jesus Christ, [m]who was
I that I could withstand God?"
18 When they heard these things they became silent; and they glorified God, saying, [n]"Then God has also granted to the
Gentiles repentance to life."

Barnabas and Saul at Antioch

19 [o]Now those who were scattered after
the persecution that arose over Stephen
traveled as far as Phoenicia, Cyprus, and
Antioch, preaching the word to no one but
the Jews only. 20 But some of them were
men from Cyprus and Cyrene, who, when
they had come to Antioch, spoke to [p]the
Hellenists, preaching the Lord Jesus.
21 And [q]the hand of the Lord was with
them, and a great number believed and
[r]turned to the Lord.
22 Then news of these things came to the
ears of the church in Jerusalem, and they
sent out [s]Barnabas to go as far as Antioch.
23 When he came and had seen the grace of
God, he was glad, and [t]encouraged them
all that with purpose of heart they should
continue with the Lord. 24 For he was a
good man, [u]full of the Holy Spirit and of
faith. [v]And a great many people were
added to the Lord.
25 Then Barnabas departed for [w]Tarsus
to seek Saul. 26 And when he had found
him, he brought him to Antioch. So it was
that for a whole year they assembled with
the church and taught a great many people. And the disciples were first called
Christians in Antioch.

Relief to Judea

27 And in these days [x]prophets came
from Jerusalem to Antioch. 28 Then one of
them, named [y]Agabus, stood up and
showed by the Spirit that there was going
to be a great famine throughout all the
world, which also happened in the days of
[z]Claudius Caesar. 29 Then the disciples,

4 [d]Luke 1:3
5 [e]Acts 10:9
12 [f][John 16:13]; Acts 10:19; 15:7 [g]Acts 10:23
13 [h]Acts 10:30
15 [i]Acts 2:1-4; 15:7-9
16 [j]Matt. 3:11; Mark 1:8; John 1:26, 33; Acts 1:5; 19:4 [k]Is. 44:3
17 [l][Acts 15:8, 9] [m]Acts 10:47
18 [n]Is. 42:1, 6; 49:6; Luke 2:32; John 11:52; Rom. 10:12, 13; 15:9, 16
19 [o]Acts 8:1, 4
20 [p]Acts 6:1; 9:29
21 [q]Luke 1:66; Acts 2:47 [r]Acts 9:35; 14:1
22 [s]Acts 4:36; 9:27
23 [t]Acts 13:43; 14:22
24 [u]Acts 6:5 [v]Acts 5:14; 11:21
25 [w]Acts 9:11, 30
27 [x]Acts 2:17; 13:1; 15:32; 21:9; 1 Cor. 12:28; Eph. 4:11
28 [y]John 16:13; Acts 21:10 [z]Acts 18:2

11:4-14 Cf. 10:1-23,28-33.

11:14 your household. All who were under Cornelius' authority and care, who could comprehend the gospel and believe (cf. 16:15,31). This does not include infants.

11:15 at the beginning. God attested to the reality of Gentile salvation with the same phenomenon that occurred at Pentecost (*see note on 8:17*).

11:16 baptized with the Holy Spirit. *See note on 1:5.*

11:18 God has also granted to the Gentiles repentance to life. One of the most shocking admissions in Jewish history, but an event that the OT had prophesied (Is. 42:1,6; 49:6; *see note on 2:38*).

11:19 *See notes on 8:1-3.* **Phoenicia.** The coastal region directly N of Judea, containing the trading ports of Tyre and Sidon. **Cyprus.** *See note on 4:36.* **Antioch.** Located some 200 mi. N of Sidon, Antioch was a major pagan metropolis, the third largest in the Roman Empire, behind Rome and Alexandria.

11:20 men from Cyprus and Cyrene. *See notes on 6:9; 13:4.* **Hellenists.** Cf. 6:1; 9:29. The preferred reading is "Greeks," or Greek-speaking non-Jews (*see note on 6:1*).

11:21 hand of the Lord. This refers to God's power expressed in judgment (cf. Ex. 9:33; Deut. 2:15; Josh. 4:24; 1 Sam. 5:6; 7:13) and in blessing (Ezra 7:9; 8:18; Neh. 2:8,18). Here, it refers to blessing.

11:22 Barnabas. *See note on 4:36.* Since he was a Cypriot Jew, he came from a similar background to the founders of the Antioch church.

11:25 Tarsus. *See note on 9:11.* **to seek Saul.** This was to be no easy task. Several years had elapsed since Saul fled Jerusalem (9:30). Apparently, he had been disinherited and forced to leave his home due to his new allegiance to Christianity (Phil. 3:8).

11:26 Christians. A term of derision meaning "of the party of Christ." Cf. 26:28; 1 Pet. 4:16.

11:27 prophets. Preachers of the NT (cf. 1 Cor. 14:32; Eph. 2:20; *see notes on 13:1; 21:9; Eph. 4:11*).

11:28 Agabus. One of the Jerusalem prophets who years later played an important part in Paul's ministry (21:10,11). **a great famine.** Several ancient writers (Tacitus [*Annals* XI.43], Josephus [*Antiquities* XX.ii.5], and Suetonius [*Claudius* 18]) affirm the occurrence of great famines in Israel ca. A.D. 45–46. **all the world.** The famine reached beyond the region of Palestine. **Claudius Caesar.** Emperor of Rome (A.D. 41–54).

each according to his ability, determined to send [a]relief to the brethren dwelling in Judea. **30** [b]This they also did, and sent it to the elders by the hands of Barnabas and Saul.

Herod's Violence to the Church

12 Now about that time Herod the king stretched out *his* hand to harass some from the church. **2** Then he killed James [a]the brother of John with the sword. **3** And because he saw that it pleased the Jews, he proceeded further to seize Peter also. Now it was *during* [b]the Days of Unleavened Bread. **4** So [c]when he had arrested him, he put *him* in prison, and delivered *him* to four [1]squads of soldiers to keep him, intending to bring him before the people after Passover.

Peter Freed from Prison

5 Peter was therefore kept in prison, but [2]constant prayer was offered to God for him by the church. **6** And when Herod was about to bring him out, that night Peter was sleeping, bound with two chains between two soldiers; and the guards before the door were [3]keeping the prison. **7** Now behold, [d]an angel of the Lord stood by *him*, and a light shone in the prison; and he struck Peter on the side and raised him up, saying, "Arise quickly!" And his chains fell off *his* hands. **8** Then the angel said to him, "Gird yourself and tie on your sandals"; and so he did. And he said to him, "Put on your garment and follow me." **9** So he went out and followed him, and [e]did not know that what was done by the angel was real, but thought [f]he was seeing a vision.

10 When they were past the first and the second guard posts, they came to the iron gate that leads to the city, [g]which opened to them of its own accord; and they went out and went down one street, and immediately the angel departed from him.

11 And when Peter had come to himself, he said, "Now I know for certain that [h]the Lord has sent His angel, and [i]has delivered me from the hand of Herod and *from* all the expectation of the Jewish people."

12 So, when he had considered *this,* [j]he came to the house of Mary, the mother of [k]John whose surname was Mark, where many were gathered together [l]praying. **13** And as Peter knocked at the door of the gate, a girl named Rhoda came to answer. **14** When she recognized Peter's voice, because of *her* gladness she did not open the gate, but ran in and announced that Peter stood before the gate. **15** But they said to her, "You are beside yourself!" Yet she kept insisting that it was so. So they said, [m]"It is his angel."

16 Now Peter continued knocking; and when they opened *the door* and saw him, they were astonished. **17** But [n]motioning to them with his hand to keep silent, he declared to them how the Lord had brought him out of the prison. And he said, "Go, tell these things to James and to the brethren." And he departed and went to another place.

18 Then, as soon as it was day, there was no small [4]stir among the soldiers about what had become of Peter. **19** But when Herod had searched for him and not found him, he examined the guards and commanded that *they* should be put to death.

And he went down from Judea to Caesarea, and stayed *there.*

29 [a] Rom. 15:26; 1 Cor. 16:1; 2 Cor. 9:1
30 [b] Acts 12:25

CHAPTER 12

2 [a] Matt. 4:21; 20:23
3 [b] Ex. 12:15; 23:15; Acts 20:6
4 [c] John 21:18 [1] Gr. *tetrads,* squads of four
5 [2] NU *constantly* or *earnestly*
6 [3] *guarding*
7 [d] Acts 5:19
9 [e] Ps. 126:1 [f] Acts 10:3, 17; 11:5
10 [g] Acts 5:19; 16:26
11 [h] [Ps. 34:7]; Dan. 3:28; 6:22; [Heb. 1:14] [i] Job 5:19; [Ps. 33:18, 19; 34:22; 41:2]; 2 Cor. 1:10; [2 Pet. 2:9]
12 [j] Acts 4:23 [k] Acts 13:5, 13; 15:37; 2 Tim. 4:11; Philem. 24; 1 Pet. 5:13 [l] Acts 12:5
15 [m] Gen. 48:16; [Matt. 18:10]
17 [n] Acts 13:16; 19:33; 21:40
18 [4] *disturbance*

11:30 elders. This is the first mention of the men who were pastor-overseers of the churches (15:4,6,22,23; 16:4; 21:18); i.e., a plurality of godly men responsible to lead the church (*see notes on 1 Tim. 3:1-7; Titus 1:5-9*). They soon began to occupy the leading role in the churches, transitioning from the apostles and prophets, who were foundational (cf. Eph. 2:20; 4:11).

12:1 Herod the king. Herod Agrippa I reigned from A.D. 37–44 and was the grandson of Herod the Great. He ran up numerous debts in Rome and fled to Palestine. Imprisoned by Emperor Tiberius after some careless comments, he eventually was released following Tiberius' death, and was made ruler of northern Palestine, to which Judea and Samaria were added in A.D. 41. As a hedge against his shaky relationship with Rome, he curried favor with the Jews by persecuting Christians.

12:2 James. The first of the apostles to be martyred (*see note on Matt. 10:2*). **with the sword.** The manner of his execution indicates James was accused of leading people to follow false gods (cf. Deut. 13:12-15). ***during* the Days of Unleavened Bread.** The weekly feast following Passover (*see notes on Ex. 23:14-19; Matt. 26:17*).

12:4 four squads. Each squad contained four soldiers and rotated the watch on Peter. At all times two guards were chained to him in his cell, while the other two stood guard outside the cell door (v. 6).

12:12 Mary. Mark is called the cousin of Barnabas in Col. 4:10, so she was his aunt. **John...Mark.** Cousin of Barnabas (Col. 4:10), acquaintance of Peter in his youth (1 Pet. 5:13), he accompanied Barnabas and Paul to Antioch (v. 25) and later to Cyprus (13:4,5). He deserted them at Perga (13:13) and Paul refused to take him on his second missionary journey because of that desertion (15:36-41). He accompanied Barnabas to Cyprus (15:39). He disappeared until he was seen with Paul at Rome as an accepted companion and co-worker (Col. 4:10; Philem. 24). During Paul's second imprisonment at Rome, Paul sought John Mark's presence as useful to him (2 Tim. 4:11). He wrote the second gospel that bears his name, being enriched in his task by the aid of Peter (1 Pet. 5:13).

12:15,16 his angel. According to Jewish superstition, each person had his own guardian angel who could assume that person's form.

12:17 James. The Lord's brother, now head of the Jerusalem church (see Introduction to James; *see note on 15:13*). **he departed.** Except for a brief appearance in chap. 15, Peter fades from the scene as the rest of Acts revolves around Paul and his ministry.

12:19 Herod. *See note on v. 1.* **put to death.** According to Justinian's *Code* (ix. 4:4), a guard who allowed a prisoner to escape would suffer the same fatal penalty that awaited the prisoner. **Caesarea.** *See note on 9:30.*

Herod's Violent Death

20 Now Herod had been very angry with
the people of [o]Tyre and Sidon; but they
came to him with one accord, and having
made Blastus [5]the king's personal aide
their friend, they asked for peace, because
[p]their country was [6]supplied with food by
the king's *country*.
21 So on a set day Herod, arrayed in
royal apparel, sat on his throne and gave
an oration to them. 22 And the people kept
shouting, "The voice of a god and not of a
man!" 23 Then immediately an angel of the
Lord [q]struck him, because [r]he did not give
glory to God. And he was eaten by worms
and [7]died.
24 But [s]the word of God grew and multiplied.

Barnabas and Saul Appointed

25 And [t]Barnabas and Saul returned
[8]from Jerusalem when they had [u]fulfilled
their ministry, and they also [v]took with
them [w]John whose surname was Mark.
13 Now [a]in the church that was at Antioch there were certain prophets
and teachers: [b]Barnabas, Simeon who was
called Niger, [c]Lucius of Cyrene, Manaen
who had been brought up with Herod the
tetrarch, and Saul. 2 As they ministered to
the Lord and fasted, the Holy Spirit said,
[d]"Now separate to Me Barnabas and Saul
for the work [e]to which I have called
them." 3 Then, [f]having fasted and prayed,
and laid hands on them, they sent *them*
away.

Preaching in Cyprus

4 So, being sent out by the Holy Spirit,
they went down to Seleucia, and from
there they sailed to [g]Cyprus. 5 And when
they arrived in Salamis, [h]they preached
the word of God in the synagogues of the
Jews. They also had [i]John as *their* assistant.
6 Now when they had gone through
[1]the island to Paphos, they found [j]a certain sorcerer, a false prophet, a Jew whose
name *was* Bar-Jesus, 7 who was with the
proconsul, Sergius Paulus, an intelligent
man. This man called for Barnabas and
Saul and sought to hear the word of God.
8 But [k]Elymas the sorcerer (for so his name

20 [o]Matt. 11:21 [p]1 Kin. 5:11; Ezra 3:7; Ezek. 27:17 [5]*who was in charge of the king's bedchamber* [6]Lit. *nourished*
23 [q]1 Sam. 25:38; 2 Sam. 24:16, 17; 2 Kin. 19:35; Acts 5:19 [r]Ps. 115:1 [7]*breathed his last*
24 [s]Is. 55:11; Acts 6:7; 19:20
25 [t]Acts 11:30 [u]Acts 11:30 [v]Acts 13:5, 13 [w]Acts 12:12; 15:37 [8]NU, M *to*

CHAPTER 13

1 [a]Acts 14:26 [b]Acts 11:22 [c]Rom. 16:21
2 [d]Num. 8:14; Acts 9:15; 22:21; Rom. 1:1; Gal. 1:15; 2:9 [e]Matt. 9:38; Acts 14:26; Rom. 10:15; Eph. 3:7, 8; 1 Tim. 2:7; 2 Tim. 1:11; Heb. 5:4
3 [f]Matt. 9:15; Mark 2:20; Luke 5:35; Acts 6:6
4 [g]Acts 4:36
5 [h][Acts 13:46] [i]Acts 12:25; 15:37

6 [j]Acts 8:9 [1]NU *the whole island* 8 [k]Ex. 7:11; 2 Tim. 3:8

12:20 Herod. *See note on v. 1.* **Tyre and Sidon.** Two port cities N of Caesarea, in a region call Phoenicia. Mutual interdependence existed between these cities and Galilee, although Tyre and Sidon were more dependent on Galilee (*see note on Mark 3:8*). **Blastus.** The king's treasurer acted as an intermediary between Herod and the representatives of Tyre and Sidon.

12:21 So on a set day. A feast in honor of Herod's patron, the Roman emperor Claudius. **arrayed in royal apparel.** According to Josephus, he wore a garment made of silver.

12:23 did not give glory to God. The crime for which Herod was executed by God (A.D. 44), who will eventually condemn and execute all who are guilty of this crime (Rom. 1:18-23).

12:23 eaten by worms. According to Josephus, Herod endured terrible pain for 5 days before he died.

12:25 had fulfilled *their* ministry. After Herod's death, they delivered the famine relief to the Jerusalem church (11:30). **John...Mark.** *See note on v. 12.*

13:1 Chapter 13 marks a turning point in Acts. The first 12 chapters focus on Peter; the remaining chapters revolve around Paul. With Peter, the emphasis is the Jewish church in Jerusalem and Judea; with Paul, the focus is the spread of the Gentile church throughout the Roman world, which began at the church in Antioch. **prophets.** These had a significant role in the apostolic church (*see notes on 1 Cor. 12:28; Eph. 2:20*). They were preachers of God's Word and were responsible in the early years of the church to instruct local congregations. On some occasions, they received new revelation that was of a practical nature (cf. 11:28; 21:10), a function that ended with the cessation of the temporary sign gifts. Their office was also replaced by pastor-teachers and evangelists (*see note on Eph. 4:11*). **Barnabas.** *See note on 4:36.* **Simeon...called Niger.** "Niger" means "black." He may have been a dark-skinned man, an African, or both. No direct evidence exists to equate him with Simon of Cyrene (Mark 15:21). **Lucius of Cyrene.** Not the Lucius of Rom. 16:21, or Luke, the physician and author of Acts. **who had been brought up with.** Can be translated "foster-brother." Manean was reared in Herod the Great's household. **Herod the tetrarch.** Herod Antipas, the Herod of the gospels (*see note on Matt. 14:1*).

13:2 ministered. This is from a Gr. word which in Scripture describes priestly service. Serving in leadership in the church is an act of worship to God, and consists of offering spiritual sacrifices to Him, including prayer, oversight of the flock, plus preaching and teaching the Word. **fasted.** This is often connected with vigilant, passionate prayer (cf. Neh. 1:4; Ps. 35:13; Dan. 9:3; Matt. 17:21; Luke 2:37), and includes either a loss of desire for food or the purposeful setting aside of eating to concentrate on spiritual issues (*see note on Matt. 6:16,17*).

13:3 laid hands on them. *See note on 6:6.*

13:4 Seleucia. This city served as the port for Antioch, some 16 mi. away at the mouth of the Orontes River. **Cyprus.** *See note on 4:36.* Saul and Barnabas chose to begin their missionary outreach there because it was Barnabas' home, which was only a two-day journey from Antioch, and had a large Jewish population.

13:5 arrived in Salamis. The chief port and commercial center of Cyprus. **synagogues.** *See note on 6:9.* Paul established the custom of preaching to the Jews first whenever he entered a new city (cf. v. 14,42; 14:1; 17:1,10,17; 18:4,19,26; 19:8) because he had an open door, as a Jew, to speak and introduce the gospel. Also, if he preached to Gentiles first, the Jews would never have listened to him. **John as *their* assistant.** *See note on 12:12.*

13:6 Paphos. The capital of Cyprus and thus the seat of the Roman government. It also was a great center for the worship of Aphrodite (Venus), and thus a hotbed for all kinds of immorality. **a certain sorcerer...a Jew.** "Sorcerer" is better translated "magician." Originally it carried no evil connotation, but later was used to describe all kinds of practitioners and dabblers in the occult. This particular magician put his knowledge to evil use (*see note on 8:9*).

13:7 the proconsul. A Roman official who served as provincial governor (cf. 18:12).

13:8 Elymas. The Gr. name of Bar-Jesus, a transliteration of the Arab. word for magician.

is translated) [2]withstood them, seeking to
turn the proconsul away from the faith.
9 Then Saul, who also *is called* Paul, [l]filled
with the Holy Spirit, looked intently at
him 10 and said, "O full of all deceit and
all fraud, [m]*you* son of the devil, *you* enemy
of all righteousness, will you not cease
perverting the straight ways of the Lord?
11 And now, indeed, [n]the hand of the Lord
is upon you, and you shall be blind, not
seeing the sun for a time."

And immediately a dark mist fell on
him, and he went around seeking someone
to lead him by the hand. 12 Then the proconsul believed, when he saw what had
been done, being astonished at the teaching of the Lord.

At Antioch in Pisidia

13 Now when Paul and his party set sail
from Paphos, they came to Perga in Pamphylia; and [o]John, departing from them,
returned to Jerusalem. 14 But when they
departed from Perga, they came to Antioch
in Pisidia, and [p]went into the synagogue
on the Sabbath day and sat down. 15 And
[q]after the reading of the Law and the
Prophets, the rulers of the synagogue sent
to them, saying, "Men *and* brethren, if you
have [r]any word of [3]exhortation for the
people, say on."

16 Then Paul stood up, and motioning
with *his* hand said, "Men of Israel, and
[s]you who fear God, listen: 17 The God of
this people [4]Israel [t]chose our fathers, and
exalted the people [u]when they dwelt as
strangers in the land of Egypt, and with
[5]an uplifted arm He [v]brought them out of
it. 18 Now [w]for a time of about forty years
He put up with their ways in the wilderness. 19 And when He had destroyed
[x]seven nations in the land of Canaan, [y]He
distributed their land to them by allotment.

20 "After that [z]He gave *them* judges for
about four hundred and fifty years, [a]until
Samuel the prophet. 21 [b]And afterward
they asked for a king; so God gave them
[c]Saul the son of Kish, a man of the tribe of
Benjamin, for forty years. 22 And [d]when
He had removed him, [e]He raised up for
them David as king, to whom also He
gave testimony and said, [f]*'I have found
David* the *son* of Jesse, [g]*a man after My
own heart,* who will do all My will.'
23 [h]From this man's seed, according [i]to *the*
promise, God raised up for Israel [j]a [6] Savior—Jesus— 24 [k]after John had first
preached, before His coming, the baptism
of repentance to all the people of Israel.
25 And as John was finishing his course,
he said, [l]'Who do you think I am? I am not
He. But behold, [m]there comes One after
me, the sandals of whose feet I am not
worthy to loose.'

26 "Men *and* brethren, sons of the [7]fam-
ily of Abraham, and [n]those among you
who fear God, [o]to you the [8]word of this
salvation has been sent. 27 For those who
dwell in Jerusalem, and their rulers, [p]be-
cause they did not know Him, nor even the
voices of the Prophets which are read
every Sabbath, have fulfilled *them* in condemning *Him.* 28 [q]And though they found
no cause for death *in Him,* they asked Pilate that He should be put to death.
29 [r]Now when they had fulfilled all that
was written concerning Him, [s]they took
Him down from the tree and laid *Him* in a

8 [2] *opposed*
9 [l] Acts 2:4; 4:8
10 [m] Matt. 13:38; John 8:44; [1 John 3:8]
11 [n] Ex. 9:3; 1 Sam. 5:6; Job 19:21; Ps. 32:4; Heb. 10:31
13 [o] Acts 15:38
14 [p] Acts 16:13
15 [q] Luke 4:16 [r] Heb. 13:22
[3] *encouragement*
16 [s] Acts 10:35
17 [t] Ex. 6:1, 6; 13:14, 16; Deut. 7:6-8
[u] Acts 7:17 [v] Ex. 14:8
[4] M omits *Israel*
[5] Mighty power
18 [w] Ex. 16:35; Num. 14:34; Acts 7:36
19 [x] Deut. 7:1 [y] Josh. 14:1, 2; 19:51; Ps. 78:55
20 [z] Judg. 2:16; 1 Sam. 4:18; 7:15 [a] 1 Sam. 3:20; Acts 3:24
21 [b] 1 Sam. 8:5
[c] 1 Sam. 10:20-24
22 [d] 1 Sam. 15:23, 26, 28 [e] 1 Sam. 16:1, 12, 13 [f] Ps. 89:20
[g] 1 Sam. 13:14
23 [h] Is. 11:1 [i] Ps. 132:11 [j] [Matt. 1:21]
[6] M *salvation, after*
24 [k] Matt. 3:1; [Luke 3:3]
25 [l] Matt. 3:11; Mark 1:7; Luke 3:16
[m] John 1:20, 27
26 [n] Ps. 66:16 [o] Matt. 10:6 [7] *stock*
[8] *message*
27 [p] Luke 23:34
28 [q] Matt. 27:22, 23; Mark 15:13, 14; Luke 23:21-23; John 19:15; Acts 3:14; [2 Cor. 5:21; Heb. 4:15]; 1 Pet. 2:22
29 [r] Luke 18:31
[s] Matt. 27:57-61; Mark 15:42-47; Luke 23:50-56; John 19:38-42

13:9 Saul...called Paul. Paul's Hebrew and Roman names.

13:13 came to Perga in Pamphylia. Perga was a major city in the Roman province of Pamphylia, in Asia Minor—some 200 mi. N across the Mediterranean from Cyprus. **John, departing from them.** Whatever reason John Mark gave for leaving, Paul didn't accept it (15:38). While his desertion did not hamper the mission, it did later create dissension between Paul and Barnabas (15:36-40). This was finally resolved (cf. Col. 4:10; 2 Tim. 4:11). *See note on 12:12.*

13:14 Antioch in Pisidia. Not to be confused with Antioch in Syria, the location of the first Gentile church. This Antioch was located in the mountains of Asia Minor (modern Turkey).

13:15 reading of the Law and the Prophets. The reading of the Scriptures. This occupied the third part in the liturgy of the synagogue, after the recitation of the *shema* (Deut. 6:4) and further prayers, but before the teaching, which was usually based on what had been read from the Scriptures. **rulers of the synagogue.** Those who had general oversight of the synagogue (*see note on 6:9*), including designating who would read from the Scriptures.

13:16 who fear God. *See note on 10:2.*

13:19 seven nations. *See note on Deut. 7:1.* **by allotment.** A better reading would be, "as an inheritance."

13:20 about four hundred and fifty years. Four hundred years of captivity in Egypt, 40 years wandering in the wilderness, and about 10 years from the crossing of the Jordan to the division of the Land (Josh. 14:1-5). **Samuel the prophet.** The last judge who anointed the first king, Saul (see Introduction to 1 Samuel; *see note on 3:24*).

13:21 Saul. *See note on 1 Sam. 9:2.*

13:22 *a man after My own heart.* *See note on 1 Sam. 13:14.* Some would question the reality of this designation for David since he proved to be such a sinner at times (cf. 1 Sam. 11:1-4; 12:9; 21:10–22:1). No man after God's own heart is perfect; yet he will recognize sin and repent of it, as did David (cf. Pss. 32,38,51). Paul quoted from 1 Sam. 13:14 and Ps. 89:20.

13:23 according to *the* promise. OT prophecy points to Messiah as a descendant of David (cf. 2 Sam. 7:12-16; Ps. 132:11; Is. 11:10; Jer. 23:5). Jesus is the fulfillment of the OT prophecies of the coming Messiah (Matt. 1:1,20,21; Rom. 1:3; 2 Tim. 2:8).

13:24 baptism of repentance. Cf. 1:22; 10:37.

13:26 who fear God. *See note on 10:2.*

13:27 rulers. The supposed experts in the OT, including the scribes, Pharisees, Sadducees, and priests.

13:28 Pilate. *See notes on 3:13; Matt. 27:2.*

tomb. 30 [t]But God raised Him from the
dead. 31 [u]He was seen for many days by
those who came up with Him from Galilee
to Jerusalem, who are His witnesses to the
people. 32 And we declare to you glad tidings—[v]that promise which was made to
the fathers. 33 God has fulfilled this for us
their children, in that He has raised up Jesus. As it is also written in the second
Psalm:

[w]'You are My Son,
Today I have begotten You.'

34 And that He raised Him from the dead,
no more to return to [9]corruption, He has
spoken thus:

[x]'I will give you the sure [1]mercies of
David.'

35 Therefore He also says in another *Psalm:*

[y]'You will not allow Your Holy One
to see corruption.'

36 "For David, after he had served [2]his
own generation by the will of God, [z]fell
asleep, was buried with his fathers, and
[3]saw corruption; 37 but He whom God
raised up [4]saw no corruption. 38 Therefore
let it be known to you, brethren, that
[a]through this Man is preached to you the
forgiveness of sins; 39 and [b]by Him everyone who believes is justified from all
things from which you could not be justified by the law of Moses. 40 Beware therefore, lest what has been spoken in the
prophets come upon you:

41 *'Behold, [c]you despisers,*
Marvel and perish!
For I work a work in your days,
A work which you will by no
means believe,
Though one were to declare it to
you.'"

Blessing and Conflict at Antioch

42 [5]So when the Jews went out of the
synagogue, the Gentiles begged that these
words might be preached to them the next
Sabbath. 43 Now when the congregation
had broken up, many of the Jews and devout proselytes followed Paul and Barnabas, who, speaking to them, [d]persuaded
them to continue in [e]the grace of God.

44 On the next Sabbath almost the whole
city came together to hear the word of
God. 45 But when the Jews saw the multitudes, they were filled with envy; and contradicting and blaspheming, they [f]op-
posed the things spoken by Paul. 46 Then
Paul and Barnabas grew bold and said,
[g]"It was necessary that the word of God
should be spoken to you first; but [h]since
you reject it, and judge yourselves unworthy of everlasting life, behold, [i]we turn to
the Gentiles. 47 For so the Lord has commanded us:

[j]'I have set you as a light to the
Gentiles,
That you should be for salvation to
the ends of the earth.'"

48 Now when the Gentiles heard this,
they were glad and glorified the word of
the Lord. [k]And as many as had been appointed to eternal life believed.

49 And the word of the Lord was being
spread throughout all the region. 50 But the

30 [t]Ps. 16:10, 11; Hos. 6:2; Matt. 12:39, 40; 28:6
31 [u]Matt. 28:16; Acts 1:3, 11; 1 Cor. 15:5-8
32 [v][Gen. 3:15]
33 [w]Ps. 2:7; Heb. 1:5
34 [x]Is. 55:3 [9]*the state of decay* [1]*blessings*
35 [y]Ps. 16:10; Acts 2:27
36 [z]Acts 2:29 [2]*in his* [3]*underwent decay*
37 [4]*underwent no decay*
38 [a]Jer. 31:34
39 [b][Is. 53:11; John 3:16]
41 [c]Hab. 1:5
42 [5]*Or And when they went out of the synagogue of the Jews;* NU *And when they went out of the synagogue, they begged*
43 [d]Acts 11:23 [e]Titus 2:11; Heb. 12:15; 1 Pet. 5:12
45 [f]Acts 18:6; 1 Pet. 4:4; Jude 10
46 [g]Matt. 10:6; Acts 3:26; Rom. 1:16 [h]Ex. 32:10; Deut. 32:21; Is. 55:5; Matt. 21:43; Rom. 10:19 [i]Acts 18:6
47 [j]Is. 42:6; 49:6; Luke 2:32
48 [k][Acts 2:47]

13:29,30 tree…tomb…God raised. The OT predicted the crucifixion of Christ on a cross (Ps. 22; Num. 34), at the time when this particular form of execution was not used. His burial in a "tomb" was also prophesied (Is. 53:9), yet victims of crucifixions were commonly tossed into mass graves. The climax of Paul's message was the resurrection of Christ, the ultimate proof that Jesus is the Messiah, and the fulfillment of 3 specific prophecies (*see notes on vv. 33-35*).

13:31 witnesses. More than 500 (cf. 1 Cor. 15:5-8).

13:33 Quoted from Ps. 2:7.

13:34 Quoted from Is. 55:3.

13:35 Quoted from Ps. 16:10; *see note on 2:27.*

13:39 justified from. This is better translated "freed from." **you could not be justified by the law of Moses.** Keeping the law of Moses did not free anyone from their sins (cf. Rom. 3:28; 1 Cor. 1:30; Gal. 2:16; 3:11; Phil. 3:9). But the atoning death of Jesus completely satisfied the demands of God's law, making forgiveness of all sins available to all who believe (Gal. 3:16; Col. 2:13,14). Only the forgiveness Christ offers can free people from their sins (Rom. 3:20,22).

13:41 Quoted from Hab. 1:5.

13:43 devout proselytes. Full converts to Judaism who had been circumcised. **continue in the grace of God.** Those who are truly saved persevere and validate the reality of their salvation by continuing in the grace of God (cf. John 8:31; 15:1-6; Col. 1:21-23; 1 John 2:19). With such encouragement, Paul and Barnabas hoped to prevent those who were intellectually convinced of the truths of the gospel, yet had stopped short of saving faith, from reverting to legalism rather than embracing Christ completely.

13:46 to you first. God offered the plan of salvation to the Jews first (Matt. 10:5,6; 15:24; Luke 24:47; Rom. 1:16). Although the thrust of Paul's ministry was to Gentiles, he had a desire to see Jews saved (Rom. 9:1-5; 10:1), preaching to them first in many cities (*see note on v. 5*). **we turn to the Gentiles.** Because the Jews rejected the gospel. But God never planned salvation as an exclusive possession of the Jews (Is. 42:1,6; 49:6).

13:47 Quoted from Is. 49:6.

13:48 appointed to eternal life. One of Scripture's clearest statements on the sovereignty of God in salvation. God chooses man for salvation, not the opposite (John 6:65; Eph. 1:4; Col. 3:12; 2 Thess. 2:13). Faith itself is a gift from God (Eph. 2:8,9).

Jews stirred up the devout and prominent
women and the chief men of the city,
[l]raised up persecution against Paul and
Barnabas, and expelled them from their region. 51 [m]But they shook off the dust from
their feet against them, and came to Iconium. 52 And the disciples [n]were filled with
joy and [o]with the Holy Spirit.

At Iconium

14 Now it happened in Iconium that
they went together to the synagogue of the Jews, and so spoke that a
great multitude both of the Jews and of the
[a]Greeks believed. 2 But the unbelieving
Jews stirred up the Gentiles and [1]poisoned
their [2]minds against the brethren. 3 Therefore they stayed there a long time, speaking boldly in the Lord, [b]who was bearing
witness to the word of His grace, granting
signs and [c]wonders to be done by their
hands.

4 But the multitude of the city was [d]di-
vided: part sided with the Jews, and part
with the [e]apostles. 5 And when a violent
attempt was made by both the Gentiles
and Jews, with their rulers, [f]to abuse and
stone them, 6 they became aware of it and
[g]fled to Lystra and Derbe, cities of Lycaonia, and to the surrounding region. 7 And
they were preaching the gospel there.

Idolatry at Lystra

8 [h]And in Lystra a certain man without
strength in his feet was sitting, a cripple
from his mother's womb, who had never
walked. 9 *This* man heard Paul speaking.
[3]Paul, observing him intently and seeing
that he had faith to be healed, 10 said with
a loud voice, [i]"Stand up straight on your
feet!" And he leaped and walked. 11 Now
when the people saw what Paul had done,
they raised their voices, saying in the Lycaonian *language*, [j]"The gods have come
down to us in the likeness of men!" 12 And
Barnabas they called [4]Zeus, and Paul,
[5]Hermes, because he was the chief speaker. 13 Then the priest of Zeus, whose temple was in front of their city, brought oxen
and garlands to the gates, [k]intending to
sacrifice with the multitudes.

14 But when the apostles Barnabas and
Paul heard this, [l]they tore their clothes and
ran in among the multitude, crying out
15 and saying, "Men, [m]why are you doing
these things? [n]We also are men with the
same nature as you, and preach to you that
you should turn from [o]these useless things
[p]to the living God, [q]who made the heaven,
the earth, the sea, and all things that are in
them, 16 [r]who in bygone generations allowed all nations to walk in their own
ways. 17 [s]Nevertheless He did not leave
Himself without witness, in that He did
good, [t]gave us rain from heaven and fruitful seasons, filling our hearts with [u]food
and gladness." 18 And with these sayings
they could scarcely restrain the multitudes
from sacrificing to them.

50 [l] Acts 7:52; 2 Tim. 3:11
51 [m] Matt. 10:14; Mark 6:11; [Luke 9:5]
52 [n] Matt. 5:12; John 16:22 [o] Acts 2:4; 4:8, 31; 13:9

CHAPTER 14

1 [a] John 7:35; Acts 18:4; Rom. 1:14, 16; 1 Cor. 1:22
2 [1] *embittered* [2] Lit. *souls*
3 [b] Mark 16:20; Acts 4:29; 20:32; Heb. 2:4 [c] Acts 5:12
4 [d] Luke 12:51 [e] Acts 13:2, 3
5 [f] 2 Tim. 3:11
6 [g] Matt. 10:23
8 [h] Acts 3:2
9 [3] Lit. *Who*
10 [i] [Is. 35:6]
11 [j] Acts 8:10; 28:6
12 [4] *Jupiter* [5] *Mercury*
13 [k] Dan. 2:46
14 [l] Num. 14:6; Matt. 26:65; Mark 14:63
15 [m] Acts 10:26 [n] James 5:17 [o] 1 Sam. 12:21; Jer. 8:19; 14:22; Amos 2:4; 1 Cor. 8:4 [p] 1 Thess. 1:9 [q] Gen. 1:1; Ex. 20:11; Ps. 146:6; Acts 4:24; 17:24; Rev. 14:7
16 [r] Ps. 81:12; Mic. 4:5; 1 Pet. 4:3
17 [s] Acts 17:24-27; Rom. 1:19, 20 [t] Lev. 26:4; Deut. 11:14; [Matt. 5:45] [u] Ps. 145:16

13:51 shook off the dust from their feet. The Jews' antagonism toward Gentiles extended to their unwillingness to even bring Gentile dust into Israel. The symbolism of Paul and Barnabas' act is clear that they considered the Jews at Antioch no better than heathen. There could have been no stronger condemnation.

13:52 filled…with the Holy Spirit. *See notes on 2:4; Eph. 5:18.*

14:1 Iconium. A cultural melting pot of native Phrygians, Greeks, Jews, and Roman colonists, located 80 mi. SE of Pisidian Antioch.

14:3 granting signs and wonders. *See notes on 2:19.* Acts of such divine power confirmed that Paul and Barnabas spoke for God.

14:4 apostles. *See notes on Rom. 1:1; Eph. 4:11.* Barnabas was not an apostle in the same sense as Paul and the 12 since he was not an eyewitness of the resurrected Christ nor had he been called by Him. It is best to translate "apostles" here as "messengers" (cf. 2 Cor. 8:23; Phil. 2:25). The verb means "to send." The 12 and Paul were "apostles of Christ," (2 Cor. 11:13; 1 Thess. 2:6), while Barnabas and others were "apostles of the churches" (2 Cor. 8:23).

14:5 stone them. This proves that their Jewish opponents were the instigators, since stoning was a Jewish form of execution, usually for blasphemy.

14:6 Lystra and Derbe, cities of Lycaonia. Lycaonia was a district in the Roman province of Galatia. Lystra was about 18 mi. from Iconium, and was the home of Lois, Eunice, and Timothy (16:1; 2 Tim. 1:5). Luke mentions no synagogue in connection with Lystra, and since Paul began his ministry there by preaching to a crowd, it likely had a small Jewish population. Derbe was about 40 mi. SE of Lystra.

14:11-13 The strange reaction by the people of Lystra to the healing had its roots in local folklore. According to tradition, the gods Zeus and Hermes visited Lystra incognito, asking for food and lodging. All turned them away except for a peasant named Philemon and his wife, Baucis. The gods took vengeance by drowning everyone in a flood. But they turned the lowly cottage of Philemon and Baucis into a temple, where they were to serve as priest and priestess. Not wanting to repeat their ancestors' mistake, the people of Lystra believed Barnabas to be Zeus and Paul to be Hermes.

14:11 Lycaonian *language*. Paul and Barnabas were unable to understand the intentions of the people.

14:13 priest of Zeus. It was his job to lead the people in worship of the two men they believed to be gods.

14:14 tore their clothes. A Jewish expression of horror and revulsion at blasphemy (*see note on Matt. 26:65*).

14:15-17 *See note on 17:23,24.* Because the crowd at Lystra was pagan and had no knowledge of the OT, Paul adjusted his message to fit the audience. Instead of proclaiming the God of Abraham, Isaac, and Jacob, he appealed to the universal and rational knowledge of the One who created the world (cf. 17:22-26; Jon. 1:9).

14:15 useless things. An appropriate description of idolatry and all false religions.

14:16 allowed all nations. The path that they all have walked is described in Rom. 1:18-32.

14:17 did not leave Himself without witness. God's providence and His creative power testify to man's reason of His existence (Rom. 1:18-20), as does man's own conscience, which contains His moral law (Rom. 2:13-15).

Stoning, Escape to Derbe

19 [v]Then Jews from Antioch and Iconium came there; and having persuaded
the multitudes, [w]they stoned Paul *and*
dragged *him* out of the city, supposing him
to be [x]dead. 20 However, when the disciples gathered around him, he rose up and
went into the city. And the next day he departed with Barnabas to Derbe.

Strengthening the Converts

21 And when they had preached the
gospel to that city [y]and made many disciples, they returned to Lystra, Iconium, and
Antioch, 22 strengthening the souls of the
disciples, [z]exhorting *them* to continue in
the faith, and *saying,* [a]"We must through
many tribulations enter the kingdom of
God." 23 So when they had [b]appointed elders in every church, and prayed with fasting, they commended them to the Lord in
whom they had believed. 24 And after they
had passed through Pisidia, they came to
Pamphylia. 25 Now when they had
preached the word in Perga, they went
down to Attalia. 26 From there they sailed
to Antioch, where they had been commended to the grace of God for the work
which they had completed.
27 Now when they had come and gathered the church together, [c]they reported all
that God had done with them, and that He
had [d]opened the door of faith to the Gentiles. 28 So they stayed there a long time
with the disciples.

19 [v] Acts 13:45, 50; 14:2-5; 1 Thess. 2:14 [w] Acts 14:5; 2 Cor. 11:25; 2 Tim. 3:11 [x] [2 Cor. 12:1-4]
21 [y] Matt. 28:19
22 [z] Acts 11:23 [a] Matt. 10:38; Luke 22:28; [Rom. 8:17; 2 Tim. 2:12; 3:12]
23 [b] Matt. 9:15; Mark 2:20; Luke 5:35; 2 Cor. 8:19; Titus 1:5
27 [c] Acts 15:4, 12 [d] 1 Cor. 16:9; 2 Cor. 2:12; Col. 4:3; Rev. 3:8

CHAPTER 15

1 [a] Gal. 2:12 [b] John 7:22; Acts 15:5; Gal. 5:2; Phil. 3:2; [Col. 2:8, 11, 16]
2 [c] Gal. 2:1
3 [d] Acts 20:38; 21:5; Rom. 15:24; 1 Cor. 16:6, 11; 2 Cor. 1:16; Titus 3:13; 3 John 6 [e] Acts 14:27; 15:4, 12
7 [f] Acts 10:20
8 [g] 1 Chr. 28:9; Acts 1:24 [h] Acts 2:4; 10:44, 47 [1] bore witness to

Conflict over Circumcision

15 And [a]certain *men* came down from
Judea and taught the brethren,
[b]"Unless you are circumcised according to
the custom of Moses, you cannot be
saved." 2 Therefore, when Paul and Barnabas had no small dissension and dispute
with them, they determined that [c]Paul and
Barnabas and certain others of them
should go up to Jerusalem, to the apostles
and elders, about this question.
3 So, [d]being sent on their way by the
church, they passed through Phoenicia
and Samaria, [e]describing the conversion of
the Gentiles; and they caused great joy to
all the brethren. 4 And when they had
come to Jerusalem, they were received by
the church and the apostles and the elders;
and they reported all things that God had
done with them. 5 But some of the sect of
the Pharisees who believed rose up, saying, "It is necessary to circumcise them,
and to command *them* to keep the law of
Moses."

The Jerusalem Council

6 Now the apostles and elders came together to consider this matter. 7 And when
there had been much dispute, Peter rose
up and said to them: [f]"Men and brethren,
you know that a good while ago God
chose among us, that by my mouth the
Gentiles should hear the word of the
gospel and believe. 8 So God, [g]who knows
the heart, [1]acknowledged them by [h]giving
them the Holy Spirit, just as *He did* to us,

14:19 they stoned Paul…supposing him to be dead. Paul did not die from the stoning as some claim, who link it to his third-heaven experience in 2 Cor. 12. "Supposing" usually means "to suppose something that is not true." The main NT use of this word argues that the crowd's supposition was incorrect and that Paul was not dead. Another argument in favor of this position is that if Paul was resurrected, why didn't Luke mention it? Also, the dates of Paul's third-heaven experience and the time of the stoning do not reconcile.

14:20 Derbe. *See note on v. 6.*

14:22 kingdom of God. *See note on 1:3.*

14:23 appointed elders. *See note on 11:30.*

14:24 Pisidia. A mountainous and rugged region that offered no opportunities for evangelism. **Pamphylia.** *See note on 13:13.*

14:25 Perga. *See note on 13:13.*

14:26 From there. Thus ended Paul's first missionary journey. **Antioch.** *See note on 11:19.*

14:28 a long time. About one year.

15:1-30 Throughout its history, the church's leaders have met to settle doctrinal issues. Historians point to 7 ecumenical councils in the church's early history, especially the Councils of Nicea (A.D. 325) and Chalcedon (A.D. 451). Yet the most important council was the first one—the Jerusalem Council—because it established the answer to the most vital doctrinal question of all: "What must a person do to be saved?" The apostles and elders defied efforts to impose legalism and ritualism as necessary prerequisites for salvation. They forever affirmed that salvation is totally by grace through faith in Christ alone.

15:1 certain *men*. Judaizers—false teachers who were self-appointed guardians of legalism, teaching a doctrine of salvation by works. **from Judea.** *See note on 1:8.* **Unless you are circumcised…you cannot be saved.** Cf. v. 24. The heresy propagated by the Judaizers. *See notes on Gen. 17:10-12.*

15:2 up to Jerusalem. *See note on 18:22.* **elders.** Leaders of the Jerusalem church (*see note on 11:30*).

15:4 Paul and Barnabas and others went into great detail to report the many works God was accomplishing through their efforts. No doubt they provided sufficient evidence to verify the genuineness of the Gentiles' salvation (cf. 10:44-48; 11:17,18).

15:7 Peter rose up. Peter gave the first of 3 speeches at the Council that amount to one of the strongest defenses of salvation by grace through faith alone contained in Scripture. Peter began his defense by reviewing how God saved Gentiles in the early days of the church without a requirement of circumcision, law keeping, or ritual—referring to the salvation of Cornelius and his household (10:44-48; 11:17,18). If God did not require any additional qualifications for salvation, neither should the legalists. **by my mouth.** *See 10:1-48.*

15:8 giving them the Holy Spirit. The Judaizers could have argued that Cornelius and the others could not have been saved because they did not meet the legalistic requirements. To thwart that potential argument, Peter reiterates that God gave them the Holy Spirit, thus proving the genuineness of their salvation (*see note on 2:4*).

9 [i]and made no distinction between us and
them, [j]purifying their hearts by faith.
10 Now therefore, why do you test God [k]by
putting a yoke on the neck of the disciples
which neither our fathers nor we were able
to bear? 11 But [l]we believe that through the
grace of the Lord Jesus [2]Christ we shall be
saved in the same manner as they."

12 Then all the multitude kept silent and
listened to Barnabas and Paul declaring
how many miracles and wonders God had
[m]worked through them among the Gentiles. 13 And after they had [3]become silent,
[n]James answered, saying, "Men *and*
brethren, listen to me: 14 [o]Simon has declared how God at the first visited the Gentiles to take out of them a people for His
name. 15 And with this the words of the
prophets agree, just as it is written:

16 *'After[p] this I will return*
And will rebuild the tabernacle of
David, which has fallen down;
I will rebuild its ruins,
And I will set it up;
17 *So that the rest of mankind may*
seek the LORD,
Even all the Gentiles who are
called by My name,
Says the [4]LORD who does all these
things.'

18 [5]"Known to God from eternity are all
His works. 19 Therefore [q]I judge that we
should not trouble those from among the
Gentiles who [r]are turning to God, 20 but
that we [s]write to them to abstain [t]from
things polluted by idols, [u]*from* [6]sexual immorality, [v]*from* things strangled, and *from*
blood. 21 For Moses has had throughout
many generations those who preach him
in every city, [w]being read in the synagogues every Sabbath."

The Jerusalem Decree

22 Then it pleased the apostles and elders, with the whole church, to send chosen men of their own company to Antioch
with Paul and Barnabas, *namely,* Judas
who was also named [x]Barsabas,[7] and Silas,
leading men among the brethren.
23 They wrote this *letter* by them:

The apostles, the elders, and the
brethren,

To the brethren who are of the
Gentiles in Antioch, Syria, and
Cilicia:

Greetings.

24 Since we have heard that [y]some
who went out from us have
troubled you with words,
[z]unsettling your souls, [8]saying,

9 [i] Rom. 10:12 [j] Acts 10:15,28
10 [k] Matt. 23:4; Gal. 5:1
11 [l] Rom. 3:4; 5:15; 2 Cor. 13:14; [Eph. 2:5-8; Titus 2:11] [2] NU, M omit *Christ*
12 [m] Acts 14:27; 15:3,4
13 [n] Acts 12:17 [3] *stopped speaking*
14 [o] Acts 15:7; 2 Pet. 1:1
16 [p] Amos 9:11,12
17 [4] NU LORD, *who makes these things*
18 [5] NU (continuing v. 17) *known from eternity (of old).'*
19 [q] Acts 15:28; 21:25 [r] 1 Thess. 1:9
20 [s] Acts 21:25 [t] Gen. 35:2; Ex. 20:3,23; Ezek. 20:30; [1 Cor. 8:1; 10:20,28]; Rev. 2:14 [u] [1 Cor. 6:9]; Gal. 5:19; Eph. 5:3; Col. 3:5; 1 Thess. 4:3; 1 Pet. 4:3 [v] Gen. 9:4; Lev. 3:17; Deut. 12:16; 1 Sam. 14:33 [6] Or *fornication*
21 [w] Acts 13:15,27; 2 Cor. 3:14
22 [x] Acts 1:23 [7] NU, M *Barsabbas*
24 [y] Acts 15:1; Gal. 2:4; 5:12; Titus 1:10, 11 [z] Gal. 1:7; 5:10 [8] NU omits *saying, "You must be circumcised and keep the law"*

15:10 a yoke. A description of the law and the legalism of the scribes and Pharisees (Matt. 23:4; cf. Luke 11:46). The legalists expected the Gentiles to carry a load they themselves were unwilling to bear.

15:11 through the grace of the Lord Jesus Christ. A resounding affirmation of salvation by grace through faith alone (*see notes on Rom. 3:24,25*).

15:12 Barnabas and Paul. They delivered the second speech in which they recounted the work of God on their just completed first missionary journey among Gentiles. **miracles and wonders.** *See note on 2:19.*

15:13 James answered. He delivers the third speech in defense of salvation by faith alone by relating how God's future plans for Gentile salvation agree with His current work.

15:14 people for His name. *See notes on chaps. 10,11.* Cf. Mal. 2:2,5; 3 John 7.

15:15-17 James quotes Amos' prophecy (9:11,12) of the millennial kingdom to prove that Gentile salvation was not contrary to God's plan for Israel. In fact, in the kingdom God's messengers will announce salvation to the Gentiles (Zech. 8:20-23).

15:17 *Gentiles...called by My name.* James' point is that Amos makes no mention of Gentiles becoming Jewish proselytes. If Gentiles can be saved without becoming Jews in the kingdom, there is no need for Gentiles to become proselytes in the present age.

15:19 we should not trouble. The Gr. word for "trouble" means "to throw something in the path of someone to annoy them." The decision of the Jerusalem Council, after considering all the evidence, was that keeping the law and observing rituals were not requirements for salvation. The Judaizers were to cease troubling and annoying the Gentiles.

15:20 James and the other leaders did not want the Gentiles to revel in their freedom in Christ, which could cause the Jewish believers to follow that same liberty and violate their consciences. So James proposed that the Gentiles abstain from 4 pagan, idolatrous practices that were violations of the law of Moses so as not to offend Jews. **things polluted by idols.** Food offered to pagan gods and then sold in temple butcher shops. Because idolatry was so repulsive to Jews and forbidden by God (cf. Ex. 20:3; 34:17; Deut. 5:7), they would avoid anything to do with idols, including meat offered to idols (cf. 1 Cor. 8:1-13). **sexual immorality.** Sexual sins in general, but particularly the orgies associated with the worship of pagan gods. The Gentiles were to avoid being offensive to Jewish sensibilities in their marriages and any relationship with the opposite sex. **things strangled, and *from* blood.** Dietary restrictions (Gen. 9:4; Lev. 3:17; 7:26; 17:12-14; 19:26; Deut. 12:16,23; 15:23; 1 Sam. 14:34; Ezek. 33:25).

15:22 Judas. Nothing more is known about him except that he was a prophet (v. 32). **Silas.** *See note on v. 40.* Also known as Silvanus, he accompanied Paul on his second missionary journey (v. 40; 16:19,25,29; 17:4,10,14,15; 18:5) and later was Peter's amanuensis (scribe) for his first epistle (1 Pet. 5:12).

15:23 in Antioch, Syria, and Cilicia. Antioch was the capital of Syria and Cilicia, which was administered as a single Roman district. The churches in Cilicia were probably founded by Paul when he went there after fleeing Jerusalem (9:30).

15:24 troubled...unsettling. "Troubled" is a different Gr. word from the one in v. 19, meaning "to deeply upset," "to deeply disturb," "to perplex," or "to create fear." The Gr. word for "unsettling" was used in extrabiblical writings to speak of someone going bankrupt. To-

"You must be circumcised and keep
the law"—to whom we gave no
such commandment— 25 it seemed
good to us, being assembled with
one [9]accord, to send chosen men to
you with our beloved Barnabas
and Paul, 26 [a]men who have risked
their lives for the name of our Lord
Jesus Christ. 27 We have therefore
sent Judas and Silas, who will also
report the same things by word of
mouth. 28 For it seemed good to
the Holy Spirit, and to us, to lay
upon you no greater burden than
these necessary things: 29 [b]that you
abstain from things offered to
idols, [c]from blood, from things
strangled, and from [d]sexual [1]
immorality. If you keep yourselves
from these, you will do well.

Farewell.

Continuing Ministry in Syria

30 So when they were sent off, they came
to Antioch; and when they had gathered
the multitude together, they delivered the
letter. 31 When they had read it, they rejoiced over its encouragement. 32 Now
Judas and Silas, themselves being
[e]prophets also, [f]exhorted and strengthened the brethren with many words.
33 And after they had stayed *there* for a
time, they were [g]sent back with greetings
from the brethren to [2]the apostles.
34 [3]However, it seemed good to Silas to
remain there. 35 [h]Paul and Barnabas also remained in Antioch, teaching and preaching
the word of the Lord, with many others also.

25 [9] *purpose* or *mind*
26 [a] Acts 13:50; 14:19; 1 Cor. 15:30; 2 Cor. 11:23-26
29 [b] Acts 15:20; 21:25; Rev. 2:14, 20 [c] Lev. 17:14 [d] 1 Cor. 5:1; 6:18; 7:2; Col. 3:5; 1 Thess. 4:3 [1] Or *fornication*
32 [e] Acts 11:27; 1 Cor. 12:28; Eph. 4:11; Rev. 18:20 [f] Acts 14:22; 18:23
33 [g] Mark 5:34; Acts 16:36; 1 Cor. 16:11; Heb. 11:31 [2] NU *those who had sent them*
34 [3] NU, M omit v. 34.
35 [h] Acts 13:1
37 [i] Acts 12:12, 25; Col. 4:10; 2 Tim. 4:11; Philem. 24 [4] *resolved*
38 [j] Acts 13:13
39 [k] Acts 4:36; 13:4
40 [l] Acts 11:23; 14:26 [5] *committed*
41 [m] Acts 16:5

CHAPTER 16

1 [a] Acts 14:6 [b] Acts 19:22; Rom. 16:21; 1 Cor. 4:17; 16:10; Phil. 1:1; 2:19; 1 Thess. 3:2; 2 Tim. 1:2 [c] 2 Tim. 1:5; 3:15
3 [d] [1 Cor. 9:20; Gal. 2:3; 5:2]
4 [e] Acts 15:19-21 [f] Acts 15:28, 29
5 [g] Acts 2:47; 15:41

Division over John Mark

36 Then after some days Paul said to
Barnabas, "Let us now go back and visit
our brethren in every city where we have
preached the word of the Lord, *and see* how
they are doing." 37 Now Barnabas [4]was
determined to take with them [i]John called
Mark. 38 But Paul insisted that they should
not take with them [j]the one who had departed from them in Pamphylia, and had
not gone with them to the work. 39 Then
the contention became so sharp that they
parted from one another. And so Barnabas
took Mark and sailed to [k]Cyprus; 40 but
Paul chose Silas and departed, [l]being
[5]commended by the brethren to the grace
of God. 41 And he went through Syria and
Cilicia, [m]strengthening the churches.

Timothy Joins Paul and Silas

16 Then he came to [a]Derbe and Lystra.
And behold, a certain disciple was
there, [b]named Timothy, [c]*the* son of a certain Jewish woman who believed, but his
father *was* Greek. 2 He was well spoken of
by the brethren who were at Lystra and
Iconium. 3 Paul wanted to have him go on
with him. And he [d]took *him* and circumcised him because of the Jews who were in
that region, for they all knew that his father was Greek. 4 And as they went
through the cities, they delivered to them
the [e]decrees to keep, [f]which were determined by the apostles and elders at Jerusalem. 5 [g]So the churches were strengthened in the faith, and increased in number
daily.

gether these words aptly describe the chaos caused by the Judaizers. **circumcised.** Cf. v. 1; *see notes on Gen. 17:10-12.*

15:26 risked their lives. On the first missionary journey they faced persecution (13:50) and Paul was nearly killed (14:19,20).

15:29 *See notes on v. 20.*

15:34 This verse is not in the best manuscripts.

15:36 *see* how they are doing. In addition to proclaiming the gospel, Paul also recognized his responsibility to mature the new believers in their faith (Matt. 28:19,20; Eph. 4:12,13; Phil. 1:8; Col. 1:28; 1 Thess. 2:17). So he planned his second missionary journey to retrace his first one.

15:37,38 John called Mark. *See note on 12:12; 13:13.*

15:39 contention...parted. This was not an amicable parting—they were in sharp disagreement regarding John Mark. The weight of the evidence favors Paul's decision, especially since he was an apostle of Jesus Christ. That alone should have caused Barnabas to submit to his authority. But they eventually did reconcile (1 Cor. 9:6). **Cyprus.** *See note on 13:4.*

15:40 Silas. He was perfectly suited to be Paul's companion, since he was a prophet and could proclaim and teach the Word. Being a Jew gave him access to the synagogues (*see note on 6:9*). Because he was a Roman citizen (16:37), he enjoyed the same benefits and protection as Paul. His status as a respected leader in the Jerusalem fellowship helped to reinforce Paul's teaching that Gentile salvation was by grace alone through faith alone (*see note on v. 22*).

15:41 Syria and Cilicia. Paul visited congregations he had most likely founded before his connection with the Antioch church (Gal. 1:21). The circumcision question had been raised there also.

16:1 Derbe and Lystra. *See note on 14:6.* **a certain disciple...Timothy.** A young man (late teens or early 20s) of high regard, a "true child in the faith" (1 Tim. 1:2; cf. 2 Tim. 1:2), who eventually became Paul's right-hand man (1 Cor. 4:17; 1 Thess. 3:2; Phil. 2:19; see Introduction to 1 Timothy). In essence, he became John Mark's replacement. After being commissioned by the elders of the local church (1 Tim. 4:14; 2 Tim. 1:6), he joined Paul and Silas. **his father *was* Greek.** The grammar likely suggests his father was dead. By being both Jew and Gentile, Timothy had access to both cultures—an indispensable asset for missionary service.

16:3 circumcised him. This was done to aid his acceptance by the Jews and provide full access to the synagogues (*see note on 6:9*) he would be visiting with Paul and Silas. If Timothy had not been circumcised, the Jews could have assumed he had renounced his Jewish heritage and had chosen to live as a Gentile.

16:4 the decrees. The determinations of the Jerusalem Council (*see notes on 15:23-29*).

The Macedonian Call

6 Now when they had gone through
Phrygia and the region of [h]Galatia, they
were forbidden by the Holy Spirit to preach
the word in [1]Asia. 7 After they had come to
Mysia, they tried to go into Bithynia, but the
[2]Spirit did not permit them. 8 So passing by
Mysia, they [i]came down to Troas. 9 And a
vision appeared to Paul in the night. A [j]man
of Macedonia stood and pleaded with him,
saying, "Come over to Macedonia and help
us." 10 Now after he had seen the vision,
immediately we sought to go [k]to Macedonia, concluding that the Lord had called us
to preach the gospel to them.

Lydia Baptized at Philippi

11 Therefore, sailing from Troas, we ran a
straight course to Samothrace, and the next
day came to Neapolis, 12 and from there to
[l]Philippi, which is the [3]foremost city of
that part of Macedonia, a colony. And we
were staying in that city for some days.
13 And on the Sabbath day we went out of
the city to the riverside, where prayer was
customarily made; and we sat down and
spoke to the women who met *there*. 14 Now
a certain woman named Lydia heard *us*.
She was a seller of purple from the city of
[m]Thyatira, who worshiped God. [n]The
Lord opened her heart to heed the things
spoken by Paul. 15 And when she and her
household were baptized, she begged *us*,
saying, "If you have judged me to be faithful to the Lord, come to my house and
stay." So [o]she persuaded us.

Paul and Silas Imprisoned

16 Now it happened, as we went to
prayer, that a certain slave girl [p]possessed
with a spirit of divination met us, who
brought her masters [q]much profit by fortune-telling. 17 This girl followed Paul and
us, and cried out, saying, "These men are
the servants of the Most High God, who
proclaim to us the way of salvation."
18 And this she did for many days.
But Paul, [r]greatly [4]annoyed, turned and
said to the spirit, "I command you in the
name of Jesus Christ to come out of her."
[s]And he came out that very hour. 19 But
[t]when her masters saw that their hope of
profit was gone, they seized Paul and Silas
and [u]dragged *them* into the marketplace to
the authorities.
20 And they brought them to the magistrates, and said, "These men, being Jews,
[v]exceedingly trouble our city; 21 and they

6 [h] Acts 18:23; Gal. 1:1, 2 [1] The Roman province of Asia
7 [2] NU adds *of Jesus*
8 [i] Acts 16:11; 20:5; 2 Cor. 2:12; 2 Tim. 4:13
9 [j] Acts 10:30
10 [k] 2 Cor. 2:13
12 [l] Acts 20:6; Phil. 1:1; 1 Thess. 2:2 [3] Lit. *first*
14 [m] Rev. 1:11; 2:18, 24 [n] Luke 24:45
15 [o] Gen. 19:3; 33:11; Judg. 19:21; Luke 24:29; [Heb. 13:2]
16 [p] Lev. 19:31; 20:6, 27; Deut. 18:11; 1 Sam. 28:3, 7; 2 Kin. 21:6; 1 Chr. 10:13; Is. 8:19 [q] Acts 19:24
18 [r] Mark 1:25, 34 [s] Mark 16:17 [4] *distressed*
19 [t] Acts 16:16; 19:25, 26 [u] Matt. 10:18
20 [v] 1 Kin. 18:17; Acts 17:8

16:6 Holy Spirit…Asia. Paul was not allowed to fulfill his intention to minister in Asia Minor (modern Turkey) and to such cities as Ephesus, Smyrna, Philadelphia, Laodicea, Colosse, Sardis, Pergamos, and Thyatira.

16:7,8 Mysia…Troas. The NW part of the province of Asia Minor.

16:7 Bithynia. A separate Roman province NE of Mysia. **the Spirit did not permit them.** Once the Holy Spirit had providentially stopped their travel N, they had nowhere else to go but Troas, a seaport on the Aegean Sea.

16:9,10 This was the second of 6 visions received by the apostle (cf. 9:3-6; 18:9,10; 22:17,18; 23:11; 27:23,24).

16:9 Macedonia. The region located across the Aegean Sea on the mainland of Greece. The cities of Philippi and Thessalonica were located there. Most significantly, going there was to take the gospel from Asia into Europe.

16:10 we. A change from the third person pronoun to the second person indicates that Luke joined up with Paul, Silas, and Timothy (see Introduction: Author and Date).

16:11 Samothrace. An island in the Aegean Sea about halfway between Asia Minor and the Greek mainland. They stayed there overnight to avoid the hazards associated with sailing in the dark. **Neapolis.** The port city for Philippi.

16:12 Philippi. See Introduction to Philippians. Located 10 mi. inland from Neapolis, Philippi was named for Philip II of Macedon (the father of Alexander the Great). **a colony.** Philippi became a Roman colony in 31 B.C., so it carried the right of freedom (it was self-governing and independent of the provincial government), the right of exemption from tax, and the right of holding land in full ownership.

16:13 to the riverside. Evidently, the Jewish community did not have the minimum of 10 Jewish men who were heads of households required to form a synagogue. In such cases, a place of prayer under the open sky and near a river or sea was adopted as a meeting place. Most likely this spot was located where the road leading out of the city crossed the Gangites River. **women who met *there*.** In further evidence of the small number of Jewish men, it was women who met to pray, read from the OT law, and discuss what they read.

16:14 Lydia…from the city of Thyatira. Her home city was located in the Roman province of Lydia, thus the name "Lydia" was probably associated with her place of origin. **seller of purple.** "Purple" fabrics. Because purple dye was extremely expensive, purple garments were usually worn by royalty and the wealthy. As a result, Lydia's business turned a nice profit, which enabled her to have a house large enough to accommodate the missionary team (v. 15) and the new church at Philippi (v. 40). **who worshiped God.** Like Cornelius, she believed in the God of Israel but had not become a full proselyte (cf. 10:2). **The Lord opened her heart.** This is another proof of the sovereignty of God in salvation (*see note on 13:48*).

16:15 household. *See note on 11:14.* Cf. v. 31.

16:16 a spirit of divination. Lit. "a python spirit." That expression comes from Gr. mythology; Python was a snake that guarded the oracle at Delphi. Essentially, this girl was a medium in contact with demons who could supposedly predict the future. *See note on Deut. 18:9-12.*

16:17 the Most High God. El Elyon, the Absolutely Sovereign God, is an OT title (used about 50 times) for the God of Israel (see Gen. 14:18-22; Ps. 78:35; Dan. 5:18).

16:18 I command you in the name of Jesus Christ. The demon left the girl in obedience to Paul's command and his apostolic authority. The ability to cast out demons was a special ability of Christ's apostles (Mark 3:15; 2 Cor. 12:12).

16:20 Jews…trouble our city. Anti-Semitism was alive even then. The Emperor Claudius issued an order around that time expelling the Jews from Rome (18:2). This may explain why they apprehended only Paul and Silas, since Luke was a Gentile and Timothy half-Gentile.

teach customs which are not lawful for us,
being Romans, to receive or observe."
22 Then the multitude rose up together
against them; and the magistrates tore off
their clothes [w]and commanded *them* to be
beaten with rods. 23 And when they had
laid many stripes on them, they threw *them*
into prison, commanding the jailer to keep
them securely. 24 Having received such a
charge, he put them into the inner prison
and fastened their feet in the stocks.

The Philippian Jailer Saved

25 But at midnight Paul and Silas were
praying and singing hymns to God, and
the prisoners were listening to them.
26 [x]Suddenly there was a great earthquake,
so that the foundations of the prison were
shaken; and immediately [y]all the doors
were opened and everyone's chains were
loosed. 27 And the keeper of the prison,
awaking from sleep and seeing the prison
doors open, supposing the prisoners had
fled, drew his sword and was about to kill
himself. 28 But Paul called with a loud
voice, saying, "Do yourself no harm, for
we are all here."
29 Then he called for a light, ran in, and
fell down trembling before Paul and Silas.
30 And he brought them out and said,
[z]"Sirs, what must I do to be saved?"
31 So they said, [a]"Believe on the Lord Jesus Christ, and you will be saved, you and
your household." 32 Then they spoke the
word of the Lord to him and to all who
were in his house. 33 And he took them the
same hour of the night and washed *their*
stripes. And immediately he and all his
family were baptized. 34 Now when he
had brought them into his house, [b]he set
food before them; and he rejoiced, having
believed in God with all his household.

Paul Refuses to Depart Secretly

35 And when it was day, the magistrates
sent the [5]officers, saying, "Let those men
go."
36 So the keeper of the prison reported
these words to Paul, saying, "The magistrates have sent to let you go. Now therefore depart, and go in peace."
37 But Paul said to them, "They have
beaten us openly, uncondemned [c]Romans,
and have thrown *us* into prison. And now
do they put us out secretly? No indeed! Let
them come themselves and get us out."
38 And the officers told these words to
the magistrates, and they were afraid
when they heard that they were Romans.
39 Then they came and pleaded with them
and brought *them* out, and [d]asked *them* to
depart from the city. 40 So they went out of
the prison [e]and entered *the house of* Lydia;
and when they had seen the brethren, they
encouraged them and departed.

Preaching Christ at Thessalonica

17 Now when they had passed
through Amphipolis and Apollonia,
they came to [a]Thessalonica, where there
was a synagogue of the Jews. 2 Then Paul,
as his custom was, [b]went in to them, and
for three Sabbaths [c]reasoned with them
from the Scriptures, 3 explaining and
demonstrating [d]that the Christ had to suffer and rise again from the dead, and *saying,* "This Jesus whom I preach to you is
the Christ." 4 [e]And some of them were per-

22 [w]2 Cor. 6:5; 11:23, 25; 1 Thess. 2:2
26 [x]Acts 4:31 [y]Acts 5:19; 12:7, 10
30 [z]Luke 3:10; Acts 2:37; 9:6; 22:10
31 [a][John 3:16, 36; 6:47; Acts 13:38, 39; Rom. 10:9-11; 1 John 5:10]
34 [b]Matt. 5:4; Luke 5:29; 19:6
35 [5]*lictors,* lit. *rod bearers*
37 [c]Acts 22:25-29
39 [d]Matt. 8:34
40 [e]Acts 16:14

CHAPTER 17

1 [a]Acts 17:11, 13; 20:4; 27:2; Phil. 4:16; 1 Thess. 1:1; 2 Thess. 1:1; 2 Tim. 4:10
2 [b]Luke 4:16; Acts 9:20; 13:5, 14; 14:1; 16:13; 19:8 [c]1 Thess. 2:1-16
3 [d]Luke 24:26, 46; Acts 18:5, 28; Gal. 3:1
4 [e]Acts 28:24

16:21 teach customs…not lawful for us…Romans. It was technically true that Roman citizens were not to engage in any foreign religion that had not been sanctioned by the state. But it was a false charge that they were creating chaos.

16:22 magistrates. Every Roman colony had two of these men serving as judges. In this case, they did not uphold Roman justice: They did not investigate the charges, conduct a proper hearing, or give Paul and Silas the chance to defend themselves. **beaten.** This was an illegal punishment since they had not been convicted of any crime. The officers (v. 35) under the command of the magistrates administered the beating with rods tied together in a bundle. Paul received the same punishment on two other occasions (2 Cor. 11:25).

16:24 inner prison…in the stocks. The most secure part of the prison. The jailer took further precautions by putting their feet "in the stocks." This particular security measure was designed to produce painful cramping so the prisoner's legs were spread as far apart as possible.

16:27 prison doors open…about to kill himself. Instead of waiting to face humiliation and a painful execution. A Roman soldier, who let a prisoner escape, paid for his negligence with his life (12:19; 27:42).

16:31 Believe on the Lord Jesus Christ. One must believe He is who He claimed to be (John 20:31) and believe in what He did (1 Cor. 15:3,4; *see note on Rom. 1:16*). **you and your household.** All of his family, servants, and guests who could comprehend the gospel and believe heard the gospel and believed (*see note on 11:14*). This does not include infants. Cf. v. 15.

16:37 Romans. To inflict corporal punishment on a Roman citizen was a serious crime, and made more so since Paul and Barnabas did not receive a trial. As a result, the magistrates faced the possibility of being removed from office, and having Philippi's privileges as a Roman colony revoked (*see note on v. 12*).

17:1 Amphipolis and Apollonia…Thessalonica. SW from Philippi along the Egnatian Way. "Amphipolis" was about 30 mi. from Philippi, and "Apollonia" another 30 mi. beyond. The narrative indicates that the travelers stopped only for the night in those cities. Forty mi. beyond "Apollonia" was "Thessalonica," the capital city of Macedonia with a population of 200,000. It was a major port city and an important commercial center. **synagogue.** *See note on 13:5.* Luke refers to a synagogue only in Thessalonica, which may explain why Paul and his companions did not stay in the other two cities.

17:2 as his custom was. Paul began his ministry in each town with the Jews (*see note on 13:5*). **three Sabbaths.** The length of his initial public ministry. The actual amount of time spent in Thessalonica would have been longer, extending perhaps to 4–6 months.

suaded; and a great multitude of the devout Greeks, and not a few of the leading
women, joined Paul and [f]Silas.

Assault on Jason's House

5 But the Jews [1]who were not persuaded, [2]becoming [g]envious, took some of the
evil men from the marketplace, and gathering a mob, set all the city in an uproar
and attacked the house of [h]Jason, and
sought to bring them out to the people.
6 But when they did not find them, they
dragged Jason and some brethren to the
rulers of the city, crying out, [i]"These who
have turned the world upside down have
come here too. 7 Jason has [3]harbored them,
and these are all acting contrary to the decrees of Caesar, [j]saying there is another
king—Jesus." 8 And they troubled the
crowd and the rulers of the city when they
heard these things. 9 So when they had
taken security from Jason and the rest, they
let them go.

Ministering at Berea

10 Then [k]the brethren immediately sent
Paul and Silas away by night to Berea.
When they arrived, they went into the synagogue of the Jews. 11 These were more
[4]fair-minded than those in Thessalonica, in
that they received the word with all readiness, and [l]searched the Scriptures daily *to
find out* whether these things were so.
12 Therefore many of them believed, and
also not a few of the Greeks, prominent
women as well as men. 13 But when the
Jews from Thessalonica learned that the
word of God was preached by Paul at
Berea, they came there also and stirred up
the crowds. 14 [m]Then immediately the
brethren sent Paul away, to go to the sea;

4 [f]Acts 15:22, 27, 32, 40
5 [g]Acts 13:45 [h]Acts 17:6, 7, 9; Rom. 16:21 [1]NU omits *who were not persuaded* [2]M omits *becoming envious*
6 [i][Acts 16:20]
7 [j]Luke 23:2; John 19:12; 1 Pet. 2:13 [3]*welcomed*
10 [k]Acts 9:25; 17:14
11 [l]Is. 34:16; Luke 16:29; John 5:39 [4]Lit. *noble*
14 [m]Matt. 10:23
15 [n]Acts 18:5
16 [o]2 Pet. 2:8 [5]*full of idols*
18 [p]1 Cor. 15:12 [6]NU, M add *also* [7]Lit. *seed picker,* an idler who makes a living picking up scraps
19 [8]Lit. *Hill of Ares,* or *Mars' Hill*
22 [9]Lit. *Hill of Ares,* or *Mars' Hill*

but both Silas and Timothy remained
there. 15 So those who conducted Paul
brought him to Athens; and [n]receiving a
command for Silas and Timothy to come to
him with all speed, they departed.

The Philosophers at Athens

16 Now while Paul waited for them at
Athens, [o]his spirit was provoked within him
when he saw that the city was [5]given over to
idols. 17 Therefore he reasoned in the synagogue with the Jews and with the *Gentile*
worshipers, and in the marketplace daily
with those who happened to be there.
18 [6]Then certain Epicurean and Stoic philosophers encountered him. And some said,
"What does this [7]babbler want to say?"
Others said, "He seems to be a proclaimer
of foreign gods," because he preached to
them [p]Jesus and the resurrection.
19 And they took him and brought him to
the [8]Areopagus, saying, "May we know
what this new doctrine *is* of which you
speak? 20 For you are bringing some strange
things to our ears. Therefore we want to
know what these things mean." 21 For all
the Athenians and the foreigners who were
there spent their time in nothing else but either to tell or to hear some new thing.

Addressing the Areopagus

22 Then Paul stood in the midst of the
[9]Areopagus and said, "Men of Athens, I
perceive that in all things you are very religious; 23 for as I was passing through and
considering the objects of your worship, I
even found an altar with this inscription:

TO THE UNKNOWN GOD.

Therefore, the One whom you worship

17:5 the house of Jason. The mob assumed Paul, Silas, and Timothy were staying there. Nothing is known of Jason except that he was probably Jewish, since Jason was a name adopted by many of the dispersed Jews.

17:7 contrary to the decrees of Caesar. One of the most serious crimes in the Roman Empire was to acknowledge allegiance to any king but Caesar (cf. John 19:15).

17:9 taken security. A pledge or bond, which would be forfeited by Jason should Paul and his companions cause more trouble. As a result, they had no choice but to leave Thessalonica.

17:10 Berea. An important town that was not on a main route. **synagogue.** *See note on 13:5.*

17:15 Athens. The cultural center of Greece. At its zenith, Athens was home to the most renowned philosophers in history, including Socrates, Plato, and Aristotle, who was arguably the most influential philosopher of all. Two other significant philosophers taught there: Epicurus, founder of Epicureanism, and Zeno, founder of Stoicism—two of the dominant philosophies in that day (*see note on v. 18*).

17:16 given over to idols. Athens was also the religious center of Greece—virtually every deity known to man could be worshiped there. Paul viewed Athens as a city of lost humanity, all doomed to a Christless eternity because of rampant pagan idolatry.

17:17 synagogue. *See note on 13:5.*

17:18 Epicurean and Stoic philosophers. Epicurean philosophy taught that the chief end of man was the avoidance of pain. Epicureans were materialists—they did not deny the existence of God, but they believed He did not become involved with the affairs of men. When a person died, they believed his body and soul disintegrated. Stoic philosophy taught self-mastery—that the goal in life was to reach a place of indifference to pleasure or pain. **babbler.** Lit. "seed picker." Some of the philosophers viewed Paul as an amateur philosopher—one who had no ideas of his own but only picked among prevailing philosophies and constructed one with no depth.

17:19 The Areopagus. A court named for the hill on which it once met. Paul was not being formally tried; only being asked to defend his teaching.

17:22 religious. Lit. "in fear of Gods."

17:23,24 TO THE UNKNOWN GOD. The Athenians were supernaturalists—they believed in supernatural powers that intervened in

without knowing, Him I proclaim to you:
24 [q]God, who made the world and everything in it, since He is [r]Lord of heaven and
earth, [s]does not dwell in temples made
with hands. 25 Nor is He worshiped with
men's hands, as though He needed anything, since He [t]gives to all life, breath, and
all things. 26 And He has made from one
[1]blood every nation of men to dwell on all
the face of the earth, and has determined
their preappointed times and [u]the boundaries of their dwellings, 27 [v]so that they
should seek the Lord, in the hope that they
might grope for Him and find Him,
[w]though He is not far from each one of us;
28 for [x]in Him we live and move and have
our being, [y]as also some of your own poets
have said, 'For we are also His offspring.'
29 Therefore, since we are the offspring of
God, [z]we ought not to think that the Divine Nature is like gold or silver or stone,
something shaped by art and man's devising. 30 Truly, [a]these times of ignorance God
overlooked, but [b]now commands all men
everywhere to repent, 31 because He has
appointed a day on which [c]He will judge
the world in righteousness by the Man
whom He has ordained. He has given assurance of this to all by [d]raising Him from
the dead."
32 And when they heard of the resurrection of the dead, some mocked, while others said, "We will hear you again on this
matter." 33 So Paul departed from among
them. 34 However, some men joined him
and believed, among them Dionysius the
Areopagite, a woman named Damaris, and
others with them.

24 [q] Is. 42:5; Acts 14:15 [r] Deut. 10:14; Ps. 115:16; Matt. 11:25 [s] 1 Kin. 8:27; Acts 7:48-50
25 [t] Gen. 2:7; Is. 42:5; Dan. 5:23
26 [u] Deut. 32:8; Job 12:23; Dan. 4:35 [1] NU omits *blood*
27 [v] [Rom. 1:20] [w] Deut. 4:7; Ps. 139:7, 10; Jer. 23:23, 24; [Acts 14:17]
28 [x] [Col. 1:17; Heb. 1:3] [y] Titus 1:12
29 [z] Ps. 115:4-7; Is. 40:18, 19; Rom. 1:23
30 [a] Acts 14:16; [Rom. 3:25] [b] Luke 24:47; Acts 26:20; [Titus 2:11, 12]; 1 Pet. 1:14; 4:3
31 [c] Ps. 9:8; 96:13; 98:9; John 5:22, 27; Acts 10:42; Rom. 2:16
[d] Acts 2:24

Ministering at Corinth

18 After these things Paul departed
from Athens and went to Corinth.
2 And he found a certain Jew named [a]Aq-
uila, born in Pontus, who had recently
come from Italy with his wife Priscilla (because Claudius had commanded all the
Jews to depart from Rome); and he came to
them. 3 So, because he was of the same
trade, he stayed with them [b]and worked;
for by occupation they were tentmakers.
4 [c]And he reasoned in the synagogue
every Sabbath, and persuaded both Jews
and Greeks.
5 [d]When Silas and Timothy had come
from Macedonia, Paul was [e]compelled [1]by

CHAPTER 18

2 [a] Rom. 16:3; 1 Cor. 16:19; 2 Tim. 4:19
3 [b] Acts 20:34; 1 Cor. 4:12; 9:14; 2 Cor. 11:7; 12:13; 1 Thess. 2:9; 4:11; 2 Thess. 3:8
4 [c] Acts 17:2
5 [d] Acts 17:14, 15 [e] Acts 18:28 [1] Or *in his spirit* or *in the Spirit*

the course of natural laws. They at least acknowledged the existence of someone beyond their ability to understand who had made all things. Paul thus had the opportunity to introduce them to the Creator-God who could be known (Deut. 4:35; 1 Kin. 8:43; 1 Chr. 28:9; Ps. 9:10; Jer. 9:24; 24:7; 31:34; John 17:3). When evangelizing pagans, Paul started from creation, the general revelation of God (cf. 14:15-17). When evangelizing Jews, he started from the OT (vv. 10-13).

17:24 God, who made the world. This teaching flatly contradicted both the Epicureans, who believed matter was eternal and therefore had no creator, and the Stoics, who as pantheists believed God was part of everything and could not have created Himself. Paul's teaching finds its support throughout Scripture (Gen. 1:1; Ps. 146:5,6; Is. 40:28; 45:18; Jer. 10:12; 32:17; Jon. 1:9; Zech. 12:1; Eph. 3:9; Col. 1:16; Rev. 4:11; 10:6).

17:26 one blood. All men are equal in God's sight since all came from one man, Adam. This teaching was a blow to the national pride of the Greeks, who believed all non-Greeks were barbarians (*see note on Rom. 1:14*). **determined their preappointed times.** God sovereignly controls the rise and fall of nations and empires (cf. Dan. 2:36-45; Luke 21:24). **the boundaries of their dwellings.** God is responsible for establishing nations as to their racial identity and their specific geographical locations (Deut. 32:8) and determining the extent of their conquests (cf. Is. 10:12-15).

17:27 seek the Lord. God's objective for man in revealing Himself as the creator, ruler, and controller of the world. Men have no excuse for not knowing about God because He has revealed Himself in man's conscience and in the physical world (*see notes on Rom. 1:19,20; 2:15*).

17:28 in Him we live and move and have our being. A quote from the Cretan poet Epimendes.

17:29 the offspring of God. A quote from Aratus, who came from Paul's home region of Cilicia. **not...like gold or silver.** If man is the offspring of God, as the Greek poet suggested, it is foolish to think that God could be nothing more than a man-made idol. Such reasoning points out the absurdity of idolatry (cf. Is. 44:9-20).

17:30 times of ignorance God overlooked. *See note on Rom. 3:25.*

17:31 Man whom He has ordained. Jesus Christ (John 5:22-27).

17:32 resurrection of the dead. Gr. philosophy did not believe in bodily resurrection.

17:34 the Areopagite. A member of the Areopagus court (*see note on v. 19*).

18:1 Corinth. See Introduction to 1 Corinthians. The leading political and commercial center in Greece. It was located at a strategic point on the isthmus of Corinth, which connected the Peloponnesian peninsula with the rest of Greece. Virtually all traffic between northern and southern Greece had to pass through the city. Because Corinth was a trade center and host to all sorts of travelers, it had an unsettled population that was extremely debauched. It also housed the temple of Aphrodite, the goddess of love. One thousand temple priestesses, who were ritual prostitutes, came each evening into the city to practice their trade.

18:2 Aquila...Priscilla. This husband and wife team were to become Paul's close friends who even risked their lives for him (Rom. 16:3,4). The remaining 5 times they are mentioned in Scripture, Priscilla is listed first, which could imply she had a higher social rank than Aquila or that she was the more prominent of the two in the church. They probably were Christians when Paul met them, having come from Rome where a church already existed (Rom. 1:7,8). **Claudius.** *See note on 11:28.* **commanded all the Jews to depart from Rome.** The decree that forced Priscilla and Aquila to leave Rome ca. A.D. 49 (*see note on 16:20*).

18:3 tentmakers. This could also refer to leatherworkers.

18:4 synagogue. *See note on 13:5.* **Greeks.** Gentile God-fearers in the synagogue (*see note on 10:2*).

18:5 Silas and Timothy had come from Macedonia. As Paul desired, Silas and Timothy joined him in Athens (17:15). From there he sent Timothy back to Thessalonica (1 Thess. 3:1-6). Paul evidently sent Silas somewhere in Macedonia, possibly Philippi (cf. Phil. 4:15; 2 Cor. 11:9), since he returned to Corinth from that province.

the Spirit, and testified to the Jews *that* Jesus *is* the Christ. 6 But [f]when they opposed
him and blasphemed, [g]he shook *his* garments and said to them, [h]"Your blood *be*
upon your *own* heads; [i]I *am* clean. [j]From
now on I will go to the Gentiles." 7 And he
departed from there and entered the house
of a certain *man* named [2]Justus, *one* who
worshiped God, whose house was next
door to the synagogue. 8 [k]Then Crispus,
the ruler of the synagogue, believed on the
Lord with all his household. And many of
the Corinthians, hearing, believed and
were baptized.
9 Now [l]the Lord spoke to Paul in the
night by a vision, "Do not be afraid, but
speak, and do not keep silent; 10 [m]for I am
with you, and no one will attack you to
hurt you; for I have many people in this
city." 11 And he continued *there* a year and
six months, teaching the word of God
among them.
12 When Gallio was proconsul of Achaia,
the Jews with one accord rose up against
Paul and brought him to the [3]judgment
seat, 13 saying, "This *fellow* persuades men
to worship God contrary to the law."
14 And when Paul was about to open *his*
mouth, Gallio said to the Jews, "If it were a
matter of wrongdoing or wicked crimes, O
Jews, there would be reason why I should
bear with you. 15 But if it is a [n]question of
words and names and your own law, look *to*
it yourselves; for I do not want to be a judge
of such *matters*." 16 And he drove them from
the judgment seat. 17 Then [4]all the Greeks
took [o]Sosthenes, the ruler of the synagogue,
and beat *him* before the judgment seat. But
Gallio took no notice of these things.

Paul Returns to Antioch

18 So Paul still remained [5]a good while.
Then he took leave of the brethren and
sailed for Syria, and Priscilla and Aquila
were with him. [p]He had *his* hair cut off at
[q]Cenchrea, for he had taken a vow. 19 And
he came to Ephesus, and left them there;
but he himself entered the synagogue and
reasoned with the Jews. 20 When they
asked *him* to stay a longer time with them,
he did not consent, 21 but took leave of
them, saying, [r]"I[6] must by all means keep
this coming feast in Jerusalem; but I will
return again to you, [s]God willing." And he
sailed from Ephesus.
22 And when he had landed at [t]Caesa-
rea, and [7]gone up and greeted the church,
he went down to Antioch. 23 After he had

6 [f] Acts 13:45 [g] Neh. 5:13; Matt. 10:14; Acts 13:51 [h] Lev. 20:9, 11, 12; 2 Sam. 1:16; 1 Kin. 2:33; Ezek. 18:13; 33:4, 6, 8; Matt. 27:25; Acts 20:26 [i] [Ezek. 3:18, 19] [j] Acts 13:46-48; 28:28
7 [2] NU *Titius Justus*
8 [k] 1 Cor. 1:14
9 [l] Acts 23:11
10 [m] Jer. 1:18, 19
12 [3] Gr. *bema*
15 [n] Acts 23:29; 25:19
17 [o] 1 Cor. 1:1 [4] NU *they all*
18 [p] Num. 6:2, 5, 9, 18; Acts 21:24 [q] Rom. 16:1 [5] Lit. *many days*
21 [r] Acts 19:21; 20:16 [s] 1 Cor. 4:19; Heb. 6:3; James 4:15 [6] NU omits *I must by all means keep this coming feast in Jerusalem*
22 [t] Acts 8:40 [7] To Jerusalem

18:6 Your blood *be* upon your *own* heads. Paul held his opponents completely responsible for blaspheming Christ and rejecting his message (cf. Josh. 2:19; 2 Sam. 1:16; 1 Kin. 2:37; Ezek. 18:13; 33:4; Matt. 27:25).

18:7 house of...Justus. A Gentile who showed interest in the God of Israel and was associated with the synagogue next door. His name indicates he was a Roman, and since Romans usually had 3 names, his may have been Gaius Titius Justus, meaning he was the same Gaius mentioned in Rom. 16:23 and 1 Cor. 1:14. ***one* who worshiped God.** *See note on 16:14.*

18:8 Crispus, the ruler of the synagogue. The conversion of this respected leader must have sent shock waves throughout the Jewish community (*see note on 6:9*). **all his household.** *See note on 11:14.*

18:9,10 This was the third of 6 visions given to Paul (cf. 9:3-6; 16:9,10; 22:17,18; 23:11; 27:23,24).

18:10 I have many people in this city. God had appointed a number of people in Corinth for salvation, who had not yet heard the gospel (cf. 13:48; Rom. 10:13-15). The effect of Paul's preaching would be to bring the elect to faith (Titus 1:1).

18:11 a year and six months. Paul's longest stay in any city, except Ephesus (20:31) and Rome (28:30).

18:12 When Gallio was proconsul of Achaia. From July, A.D. 51 to June, A.D. 52. **judgment seat.** A large, raised stone platform in the marketplace, situated in front of the residence of the proconsul, where he would try public cases.

18:13 contrary to the law. While Judaism was not an official religion, it was officially tolerated in the Roman world, and Christianity was viewed as a sect of Judaism. The Jews in Corinth claimed that Paul's teaching was external to Judaism, and therefore should be banned. Had Gallio ruled in the Jews' favor, Christianity could have been outlawed throughout the Empire.

18:14-16 Gallio was no fool and saw through the Jews' plan. He refused to get caught up in what he viewed as an internal squabble within Judaism. In essence, he rendered what would be called a summary judgment—he officially ruled that no crime had been committed, that the dispute was over semantics, and threw the case out.

18:17 Sosthenes...beat *him*. The Greeks had reasons for being hostile to Sosthenes; they were venting general hostility toward Jews on him, or they may have been angry with his unsuccessful attempt, as leader of the Jews, at prosecuting the case against Paul. Since he was the ruler of the synagogue, he would have presented the case to Gallio. Later, he converted to Christ (1 Cor. 1:1).

18:18 Priscilla and Aquila. *See note on v. 2.* That they could accompany Paul means there was sufficient leadership in Corinth, with men such as Gaius, Sosthenes, Stephanas, and Crispus. **He had *his* hair cut off...he had taken a vow.** To show God his gratitude for helping him through a difficult time in Corinth, he took a Nazirite vow—a special pledge of separation and devotion to God (cf. Num. 6:2-5,13-21). The vow generally lasted a specific period of time, although Samson (Judg. 13:5), Samuel (1 Sam. 1:11), and John the Baptist (Luke 1:15) were Nazirites for life. In Paul's day, if someone made the vow while away from Jerusalem, at the termination of his vow he would shave his head, as Paul did, and afterwards present the shorn hair at the temple within 30 days. **Cenchrea.** The eastern port of Corinth.

18:19 Ephesus. The most important city in Asia Minor (see Introduction to Ephesians). **left them there.** Priscilla and Aquila remained in Ephesus to establish their business. Apparently they lived in Ephesus for several years—a church met in their home (1 Cor. 16:19)—before they returned to Rome (16:3-5). **synagogue.** *See note on 13:5.*

18:22 gone up...went down to Antioch. Although Luke does not mention it in detail, his description of the geography indicates Paul went to Jerusalem to greet the church. Because Jerusalem was elevated over the surrounding region, travelers had to go "up" to get there and "down" to any other place. Paul also had to return to

spent some time *there,* he departed and
went over the region of [u]Galatia and
Phrygia [8]in order, [v]strengthening all the
disciples.

Ministry of Apollos

24 [w]Now a certain Jew named Apollos,
born at Alexandria, an eloquent man *and*
mighty in the Scriptures, came to Ephesus.
25 This man had been instructed in the
way of the Lord; and being [x]fervent in
spirit, he spoke and taught accurately the
things of the Lord, [y]though he knew only
the baptism of John. 26 So he began to
speak boldly in the synagogue. When
Aquila and Priscilla heard him, they took
him aside and explained to him the way of
God more accurately. 27 And when he desired to cross to Achaia, the brethren
wrote, exhorting the disciples to receive
him; and when he arrived, [z]he greatly
helped those who had believed through
grace; 28 for he vigorously refuted the
Jews publicly, [a]showing from the Scriptures that Jesus is the Christ.

23 [u] Gal. 1:2 [v] Acts 14:22; 15:32, 41
[8] *successively*
24 [w] Acts 19:1; 1 Cor. 1:12; 3:4; 16:12; Titus 3:13
25 [x] Rom. 12:11
[y] [Matt. 3:1-11; Mark 1:7, 8; Luke 3:16, 17; 7:29; John 1:26, 33]; Acts 19:3
27 [z] 1 Cor. 3:6
28 [a] Acts 9:22; 17:3; 18:5

CHAPTER 19

1 [a] 1 Cor. 1:12; 3:5, 6; Titus 3:13 [b] Acts 18:23
2 [c] 1 Sam. 3:7; Acts 8:16
3 [d] Luke 7:29; Acts 18:25
4 [e] Matt. 3:11; Mark 1:4, 7, 8; Luke 3:16; [John 1:15, 26, 27]; Acts 13:24
5 [f] Matt. 28:19; Acts 8:12, 16; 10:48
6 [g] Acts 6:6; 8:17
[h] Mark 16:17; Acts 2:4; 10:46
8 [i] Acts 17:2; 18:4

Paul at Ephesus

19 And it happened, while [a]Apollos
was at Corinth, that Paul, having
passed through [b]the upper regions, came
to Ephesus. And finding some disciples
2 he said to them, "Did you receive the
Holy Spirit when you believed?"
So they said to him, [c]"We have not so
much as heard whether there is a Holy
Spirit."
3 And he said to them, "Into what then
were you baptized?"
So they said, [d]"Into John's baptism."
4 Then Paul said, [e]"John indeed baptized with a baptism of repentance, saying
to the people that they should believe on
Him who would come after him, that is, on
Christ Jesus."
5 When they heard *this,* they were baptized [f]in the name of the Lord Jesus. 6 And
when Paul had [g]laid hands on them, the
Holy Spirit came upon them, and [h]they
spoke with tongues and prophesied.
7 Now the men were about twelve in all.
8 [i]And he went into the synagogue and

Jerusalem so he could fulfill his vow. This ended the second missionary journey.

18:23 some time *there.* Possibly from the summer of A.D. 52 to the spring of A.D. 53. **Galatia and Phrygia.** *See note on 16:6.* Paul's return to those regions marked the beginning of his third missionary journey.

18:24 Apollos. An OT saint and follower of John the Baptist (v. 25). After further instruction by Aquila and Priscilla (v. 26), he became a powerful Christian preacher. His ministry profoundly influenced the Corinthians (cf. 1 Cor. 1:12). **Alexandria.** An important city in Egypt located near the mouth of the Nile. In the first century, it had a large Jewish population. Thus Apollos, though born outside of Israel, was reared in a Jewish cultural setting. **mighty in the Scriptures.** Used only here, this phrase refers to Apollos' knowledge of the OT Scriptures. That knowledge, combined with his eloquence, allowed him to crush his Jewish opponents in debate (v. 28).

18:25 the way of the Lord. This did not include the Christian faith (cf. v. 26). The OT uses the phrase to describe the spiritual and moral standards God required His people to observe (Gen. 18:19; Judg. 2:22; 1 Sam. 12:23; 2 Sam. 22:22; 2 Kin. 21:22; 2 Chr. 17:6; Pss. 18:21; 25:8,9; 138:5; Prov. 10:29; Jer. 5:4,5; Ezek. 18:25,29; 33:17,20; Hos. 14:9). **baptism of John.** Despite his knowledge of the OT, Apollos did not fully understand Christian truth. John's baptism was to prepare Israel for the Messiah's arrival (cf. Luke 1:16,17; *see notes on 2:38; Matt. 3:6*). Apollos accepted that message, even acknowledging that Jesus of Nazareth was Israel's Messiah. He did not, however, understand such basic Christian truths as the significance of Christ's death and resurrection, the ministry of the Holy Spirit, and the church as God's new witness people. He was a redeemed OT believer (v. 24).

18:26 the way of God more accurately. Aquila and Priscilla completed Apollos' training in divine truth by instructing him in the fullness of the Christian faith.

18:27 Achaia. *See note on v. 12.* Apollos planned to cross from Asia Minor (modern Turkey) to Corinth on the Greek mainland (19:1). **the brethren wrote.** Such letters of commendation were common in the early church (cf. Rom 16:1,2; 1 Cor. 16:10; 2 Cor. 3:1,2; Col. 4:10). The Ephesian Christians wrote to inform their Corinthian brethren that Apollos was now a fully informed Christian.

18:28 the Christ. The Messiah of Israel.

19:1 the upper regions. The area of Asia Minor N of Ephesus, where Luke left Paul before the interlude describing Apollos' ministry (18:23). By going through that area, Paul took the direct route to Ephesus, not the more common trade route. **Ephesus.** See Introduction to Ephesians. **some disciples.** They were of John the Baptist (v. 3); hence OT seekers. That they did not yet fully understand the Christian faith is evident from their reply to Paul's question (v. 2). The word "disciple" means "learner," or "follower," and does not always refer to Christians (cf. Matt. 9:14; 11:2; Mark 2:18; Luke 5:33; 7:18,19; 11:1; John 1:35; 6:66). Followers of John the Baptist, like this group, existed into the second century.

19:2 "Did you receive the Holy Spirit when you believed?" The question reflects Paul's uncertainty about their spiritual status. Since all Christians receive the Holy Spirit at the moment of salvation (*see notes on Rom. 8:9; 1 Cor. 12:13*), their answer revealed they were not yet fully Christians. They had not yet received Christian baptism (having been baptized only "into John's baptism") which further evidenced that they were not Christians (*see note on 2:38*).

19:4 baptism of repentance...believe on...Christ Jesus. These disciples did not realize Jesus of Nazareth was the One to whom John's baptism pointed. Paul gave them instruction not on how to receive the Spirit, but about Jesus Christ.

19:5 baptized in the name of the Lord Jesus. They believed Paul's presentation of the gospel and came to saving faith in the Lord Jesus Christ (cf. 2:41). Although required of all Christians, baptism does not save (*see note on 2:38*).

19:6 Paul...laid hands on them. This signified their inclusion into the church (*see note on 8:17*). Apostles were also present when the church was born (chap. 2), and when the Samaritans (chap. 8) and Gentiles (chap. 10) were included. In each case, God's purpose was to emphasize the unity of the church. **spoke with tongues and prophesied.** This served as proof that they were part of the church (*see note on 8:17*). They also needed tangible evidence that the Holy Spirit now indwelt them, since they had not heard that He had come (v. 2).

19:8 synagogue. *See note on 13:5.* **three months.** Paul's longest

spoke boldly for three months, reasoning
and persuading [j]concerning the things of
the kingdom of God. 9 But [k]when some
were hardened and did not believe, but
spoke evil [l]of the Way before the multitude, he departed from them and withdrew the disciples, reasoning daily in the
school of Tyrannus. 10 And [m]this continued for two years, so that all who dwelt in
Asia heard the word of the Lord Jesus,
both Jews and Greeks.

Miracles Glorify Christ

11 Now [n]God worked unusual miracles
by the hands of Paul, 12 [o]so that even
handkerchiefs or aprons were brought
from his body to the sick, and the diseases left them and the evil spirits went
out of them. 13 [p]Then some of the itinerant Jewish exorcists [q]took it upon themselves to call the name of the Lord Jesus
over those who had evil spirits, saying,
[1]"We [2]exorcise you by the Jesus whom
Paul [r]preaches." 14 Also there were seven
sons of Sceva, a Jewish chief priest, who
did so.
15 And the evil spirit answered and said,
"Jesus I know, and Paul I know; but who
are you?"

8 [j] Acts 1:3; 28:23
9 [k] 2 Tim. 1:15; 2 Pet. 2:2; Jude 10 [l] Acts 9:2; 19:23; 22:4; 24:14
10 [m] Acts 19:8; 20:31
11 [n] Mark 16:20; Acts 14:3
12 [o] 2 Kin. 4:29; Acts 5:15
13 [p] Matt. 12:27; Luke 11:19 [q] Mark 9:38; Luke 9:49 [r] 1 Cor. 1:23; 2:2 [1] NU *I* [2] *adjure,* solemnly command
16 [3] M *and they overpowered them* [4] NU *both of them*
17 [s] Luke 1:65; 7:16; Acts 2:43; 5:5, 11
18 [t] Matt. 3:6
20 [u] Acts 6:7; 12:24
21 [v] Rom. 15:25; Gal. 2:1 [w] Acts 20:22; 2 Cor. 1:16 [x] Acts 20:1; 1 Cor. 16:5 [y] Acts 18:21; 23:11; Rom. 1:13; 15:22-29
22 [z] 1 Tim. 1:2 [a] Rom. 16:23; 2 Tim. 4:20
23 [b] 2 Cor. 1:8 [c] Acts 9:2

16 Then the man in whom the evil spirit
was leaped on them, [3]overpowered them,
and prevailed against [4]them, so that they
fled out of that house naked and wounded.
17 This became known both to all Jews and
Greeks dwelling in Ephesus; and [s]fear fell
on them all, and the name of the Lord Jesus
was magnified. 18 And many who had believed came [t]confessing and telling their
deeds. 19 Also, many of those who had
practiced magic brought their books together and burned *them* in the sight of all.
And they counted up the value of them,
and *it* totaled fifty thousand *pieces* of silver.
20 [u]So the word of the Lord grew mightily
and prevailed.

The Riot at Ephesus

21 [v]When these things were accomplished, Paul [w]purposed in the Spirit,
when he had passed through [x]Macedonia
and Achaia, to go to Jerusalem, saying,
"After I have been there, [y]I must also see
Rome." 22 So he sent into Macedonia two
of those who ministered to him, [z]Timothy
and [a]Erastus, but he himself stayed in Asia
for a time.
23 And [b]about that time there arose a
great commotion about [c]the Way. 24 For a

stay in any synagogue, with the possible exception of the one at Corinth. **kingdom of God.** *See note on 1:3.*

19:9 hardened. The Gr. word always refers to defiance against God (Rom. 9:18; Heb. 3:8,13,15; 4:7). Truth rejected leads to a hardened heart, causing the life-giving message of salvation to become "the aroma of death *leading* to death" (2 Cor. 2:16). **the Way.** *See note on 9:2.* **the school of Tyrannus.** Tyrannus was either the owner of the lecture hall, or a philosopher who taught there. If the latter, his name, which means "our tyrant," may have been a nickname given him by his students. Paul used the hall during the afternoon break (from about 11:00 a.m. to 4:00 p.m.), when it would otherwise be unoccupied.

19:10 two years. The length of time Paul taught in the school of Tyrannus, not the total length of his ministry at Ephesus (cf. 20:31). **all...in Asia heard.** Though Paul probably never left Ephesus, his converts (cf. 2 Tim. 2:2) spread the gospel throughout the province of Asia Minor (modern Turkey). This two-year period saw the founding of the churches at Colosse and Hierapolis, and possibly some of the 7 churches mentioned in Rev. 2,3, beyond the one at Ephesus.

19:11 unusual miracles. These confirmed that Paul was God's messenger, since there was no completed NT to use to determine the truth of his message (cf. 2 Cor. 12:12; Heb. 2:3,4).

19:12 handkerchiefs...aprons. The headbands and outer clothing Paul wore while making tents. The belief that mystical power could be so transmitted was widespread in the ancient world, e.g., believing that Peter's shadow could heal (cf. 5:15; Matt. 9:21).

19:13 itinerant Jewish exorcists. Simon Magus (8:9-25) and Bar-Jesus (13:6-12) were other possible examples of such charlatans (cf. Matt. 12:27). In contrast to the absolute authority exercised by Jesus and the apostles over demons, those exorcists sought to expel the demons by attempting to call on a more potent spirit being—in this case the Lord Jesus.

19:14 Sceva, a Jewish chief priest. Since there is no record of a Jewish High-Priest by that name, he probably assumed that title falsely to impress people.

19:15 Jesus...Paul I know. Recognizing that the exorcists had no authority over him (unlike Jesus and Paul), the demon rejected their attempt to expel him from his victim. This confirms that the power to cast out demons belonged to Jesus and the apostles and no one else. Even the demons give testimony to that.

19:16 Cf. Mark 5:1-4.

19:19 books. Of secret magical spells. Burning them proved the genuineness of the magicians' repentance (*see note on 2:38*); having destroyed these books, they could not easily resume their practices. **fifty thousand *pieces* of silver.** Fifty thousand days' wages for a common laborer—an astonishing sum of money given to indicate how widespread the practice of magic was in Ephesus.

19:21 purposed in the Spirit. Probably his own spirit, not the Holy Spirit (contra. the NKJV translation). **Macedonia and Achaia.** *See notes on 16:9; 18:12.* Located on the Greek mainland, these provinces were in the opposite direction from Jerusalem. Paul, however, took this roundabout route to collect an offering for the needy in the Jerusalem church (Rom. 15:25-27; 1 Cor. 16:1-4; 2 Cor. 8,9). **I must also see Rome.** Paul had not visited the Imperial capital, but because of the strategic importance of the church there, he could stay away no longer. In addition, Paul intended to use Rome as a jumping off point for ministry in the strategic region of Spain (Rom. 15:22-24). This simple declaration marked a turning point in Acts; from this point on, Rome became Paul's goal. He would ultimately arrive there as a Roman prisoner (28:16).

19:22 Timothy and Erastus. For Timothy, *see note on 16:1.* Nothing more is known of Erastus; though the name appears two other times in Scripture (Rom. 16:23; 2 Tim. 4:20), he cannot with certainty be identified with either one. Paul sent these two ahead of him to assist in his collection of the offering.

19:23 the Way. *See note on 9:2.*

certain man named Demetrius, a silversmith, who made silver shrines of [5]Diana,
brought [d]no small profit to the craftsmen.
25 He called them together with the workers
of similar occupation, and said: "Men, you
know that we have our prosperity by this
trade. 26 Moreover you see and hear that
not only at Ephesus, but throughout almost
all Asia, this Paul has persuaded and turned
away many people, saying that [e]they are
not gods which are made with hands. 27 So
not only is this trade of ours in danger of
falling into disrepute, but also the temple of
the great goddess Diana may be despised
and [6]her magnificence destroyed, whom all
Asia and the world worship."

28 Now when they heard *this,* they were
full of wrath and cried out, saying, "Great
is Diana of the Ephesians!" 29 So the whole
city was filled with confusion, and rushed
into the theater with one accord, having
seized [f]Gaius and [g]Aristarchus, Macedonians, Paul's travel companions. 30 And
when Paul wanted to go in to the people,
the disciples would not allow him. 31 Then
some of the [7]officials of Asia, who were his
friends, sent to him pleading that he
would not venture into the theater.
32 Some therefore cried one thing and
some another, for the assembly was confused, and most of them did not know why
they had come together. 33 And they drew
Alexander out of the multitude, the Jews
putting him forward. And [h]Alexander
[i]motioned with his hand, and wanted to
make his defense to the people. 34 But
when they found out that he was a Jew, all
with one voice cried out for about two
hours, "Great *is* Diana of the Ephesians!"

35 And when the city clerk had quieted
the crowd, he said: "Men of Ephesus, what
man is there who does not know that the
city of the Ephesians is temple guardian of
the great goddess [8]Diana, and of the *image*
which fell down from [9]Zeus? 36 Therefore,
since these things cannot be denied, you
ought to be quiet and do nothing rashly.
37 For you have brought these men here
who are neither robbers of temples nor blasphemers of [1]your goddess. 38 Therefore, if
Demetrius and his fellow craftsmen have a
[2]case against anyone, the courts are open
and there are proconsuls. Let them bring
charges against one another. 39 But if you
have any other inquiry to make, it shall be
determined in the lawful assembly. 40 For
we are in danger of being [3]called in question
for today's uproar, there being no reason
which we may give to account for this disorderly gathering." 41 And when he had said
these things, he dismissed the assembly.

Journeys in Greece

20 After the uproar had ceased, Paul
called the disciples to *himself,* embraced *them,* and [a]departed to go to Macedonia. 2 Now when he had gone over that
region and encouraged them with many

24 [d]Acts 16:16, 19 [5]Gr. *Artemis*
26 [e]Deut. 4:28; Ps. 115:4; Is. 44:10-20; Jer. 10:3; Acts 17:29; 1 Cor. 8:4; 10:19; Rev. 9:20
27 [6]NU *she be deposed from her magnificence*
29 [f]Acts 20:4; Rom. 16:23; 1 Cor. 1:14; 3 John 1 [g]Acts 20:4; 27:2; Col. 4:10; Philem. 24
31 [7]*Asiarchs, rulers of Asia,* the province
33 [h]1 Tim. 1:20; 2 Tim. 4:14
[i]Acts 12:17
35 [8]Gr. *Artemis* [9]*heaven*
37 [1]NU *our*
38 [2]Lit. *matter*
40 [3]Or *charged with rebellion concerning today*

CHAPTER 20
1 [a]1 Cor. 16:5; 1 Tim. 1:3

19:24 Demetrius, a silversmith. Probably not the individual commended by John (3 John 12), since the name was a common one. **silver shrines.** These were of the goddess Diana (Artemis). These shrines were used as household idols, and in the worship at the temple of Diana. **Diana.** She was also known as "Artemis." Worship of her, centered at the great temple of Diana at Ephesus (one of the Seven Wonders of the Ancient World), was widespread throughout the Roman Empire. It is likely that the riot described in this passage took place during the annual spring festival held in her honor at Ephesus. **brought no small profit.** This statement suggests Demetrius may have been the head of the silversmiths' guild—which would explain his taking the lead in opposing the Christian preachers.

19:27 Demetrius cleverly played upon his hearers' fears of financial ruin, religious zeal, and concern for their city's prestige. The Christian preachers, he argued, threatened the continued prosperity of Ephesus. His audience's violent reaction shows they took the threat seriously (v. 28).

19:29 Gaius and Aristarchus. These men are described as Macedonians, though 20:4 lists Gaius' hometown as Derbe, a city in Galatia. Possibly the Gaius of 20:4 was a different person.

19:31 officials of Asia. Known by the title "Asiarchs," these members of the aristocracy were dedicated to promoting Roman interests. Though only one Asiarch ruled at a time, they bore the title for life. That such powerful, influential men were Paul's friends shows that they did not regard him or his message as criminal. Hence, there was no legitimate cause for the riot.

19:32 assembly. The frenzied mob gathered in the theater. Though Paul courageously sought to address them, the Asiarchs (along with the Ephesian Christians, v. 30) begged him to stay away (v. 31). They feared both for the apostle's safety, and that his presence would exacerbate the already explosive situation.

19:33 Alexander. Probably not the false teacher later active at Ephesus (1 Tim. 1:20), or the individual who opposed Paul at Rome (2 Tim. 4:14), since the name was common. He was either a Christian Jew or a spokesman for Ephesus' Jewish community. Either way, the Jews' motive for putting him forward was the same—to disassociate themselves from the Christians and avoid a massacre of the Jews. **make his defense.** Either of the Christians, or the Jews, depending on which group he represented.

19:34 a Jew. Whatever the Jews intended by putting Alexander forward backfired; the crowd shouted him down, and in a mindless display of religious frenzy, chanted the name of their goddess for two hours.

19:35 city clerk. In modern terms, he was Ephesus' mayor. He was the liaison between the town council and the Roman authorities—who would hold him personally responsible for the riot. ***image* which fell...Zeus.** This probably refers to a meteorite, since meteorites were incorporated with the worship of Diana.

19:38-40 The city clerk (v. 35) correctly blamed the crowd for the riot, noting that they should have followed proper judicial procedure and gone to the courts and proconsuls if they had any complaints, so as not to incur serious consequences from Rome.

20:1 departed. Paul left on his trip to Jerusalem via Greece (*see note on 19:21*). ***Macedonia.*** *See note on 16:9.*

20:2 he had gone over that region. Macedonia and Achaia (*see note on 19:21*).

words, he came to [b]Greece **3** and stayed
three months. And [c]when the Jews plotted
against him as he was about to sail to Syria,
he decided to return through Macedonia.
4 And Sopater of Berea accompanied him to
Asia—also [d]Aristarchus and Secundus of
the Thessalonians, and [e]Gaius of Derbe,
and [f]Timothy, and [g]Tychicus and [h]Trophi-
mus of Asia. **5** These men, going ahead,
waited for us at [i]Troas. **6** But we sailed away
from Philippi after [j]the Days of Unleavened
Bread, and in five days joined them [k]at
Troas, where we stayed seven days.

Ministering at Troas

7 Now on [l]the first *day* of the week, when
the disciples came together [m]to break
bread, Paul, ready to depart the next day,
spoke to them and continued his message
until midnight. **8** There were many lamps
[n]in the upper room where [1]they were gathered together. **9** And in a window sat a certain young man named Eutychus, who was
sinking into a deep sleep. He was overcome by sleep; and as Paul continued
speaking, he fell down from the third story
and was taken up dead. **10** But Paul went
down, [o]fell on him, and embracing *him*
said, [p]"Do not trouble yourselves, for his
life is in him." **11** Now when he had come
up, had broken bread and eaten, and talked
a long while, even till daybreak, he departed. **12** And they brought the young man in
alive, and they were not a little comforted.

From Troas to Miletus

13 Then we went ahead to the ship and
sailed to Assos, there intending to take
Paul on board; for so he had [2]given orders,
intending himself to go on foot. **14** And
when he met us at Assos, we took him on
board and came to Mitylene. **15** We sailed
from there, and the next *day* came opposite
Chios. The following *day* we arrived at
Samos and stayed at Trogyllium. The next
day we came to Miletus. **16** For Paul had
decided to sail past Ephesus, so that he
would not have to spend time in Asia; for

2 [b] Acts 17:15; 18:1
3 [c] Acts 9:23; 23:12; 25:3; 2 Cor. 11:26
4 [d] Acts 19:29; Col. 4:10 [e] Acts 19:29 [f] Acts 16:1 [g] Eph. 6:21; Col. 4:7; 2 Tim. 4:12; Titus 3:12 [h] Acts 21:29; 2 Tim. 4:20
5 [i] 2 Cor. 2:12; 2 Tim. 4:13
6 [j] Ex. 12:14, 15 [k] Acts 16:8; 2 Cor. 2:12; 2 Tim. 4:13
7 [l] 1 Cor. 16:2; Rev. 1:10 [m] Acts 2:42, 46; 20:11; 1 Cor. 10:16
8 [n] Acts 1:13 [1] NU, M *we*
10 [o] 1 Kin. 17:21; 2 Kin. 4:34 [p] Matt. 9:23, 24; Mark 5:39
13 [2] *arranged it*

20:3 three months. Most or all of it were likely spent in Corinth. **Jews plotted against him.** See 9:20,23; 13:45; 14:2,19; 17:5-9,13; 18:6,12,13; 19:9; 21:27-36; 23:12-15. Tragically, most of the opposition to Paul's ministry stemmed from his fellow countrymen (cf. 2 Cor. 11:26). The Jewish community of Corinth hated Paul because of its humiliating debacle before Gallio (18:12-17), and the stunning conversions of two of its most prominent leaders, Crispus (18:8), and Sosthenes (18:17; 1 Cor. 1:1). Luke does not record the details of the Jews' plot, but it undoubtedly involved murdering Paul during the voyage to Palestine. The apostle would have been an easy target on a small ship packed with Jewish pilgrims. Because of that danger, Paul canceled his plans to sail from Greece to Syria. Instead, he decided to go N into Macedonia, cross the Aegean Sea to Asia Minor, and catch another ship from there. That delay cost Paul his opportunity to reach Palestine in time for Passover; but he hurried to be there in time for Pentecost (v. 16).

20:4 Sopater of Berea...Trophimus of Asia. Paul's traveling companions came from the various provinces in which he had ministered. These men were likely the official representatives of their churches, chosen to accompany Paul as he took the offering to Jerusalem (*see note on 19:21*; cf. 1 Cor. 16:3,4).

20:5 for us. The first person plural pronoun reveals that Luke rejoined Paul in Philippi (v. 6). Being a Gentile, he was able to remain there to minister after Paul and Silas were forced to leave (16:20, 39,40). This verse begins the second of the three "we passages" in which Luke accompanied Paul on his travels (see Introduction: Author and Date). **Troas.** *See note on 16:7,8.*

20:6 from Philippi. Paul, along with Luke, and possibly Titus, crossed the Aegean Sea from Philippi to Troas. That crossing, due to unfavorable winds, took 5 days; Paul's earlier crossing from Troas to Neapolis (Philippi's port) had taken only two days (16:11). In Troas, they were reunited with the rest of their party. **Days of Unleavened Bread.** I.e., Passover (Ex. 12:17).

20:7 first *day* of the week. Sunday, the day the church gathered for worship, because it was the day of Christ's resurrection. Cf. Matt. 28:1; Mark 16:2,9; Luke 24:1; John 20:1,19; 1 Cor. 16:2. The writings of the early church Fathers confirm that the church continued to meet on Sunday after the close of the NT period. Scripture does not require Christians to observe the Saturday Sabbath: 1) the Sabbath was the sign of the Mosaic Covenant (Ex. 31:16,17; Neh. 9:14; Ezek. 20:12), whereas Christians are under the New Covenant (2 Cor. 3; Heb. 8); 2) there is no NT command to keep the Sabbath; 3) the first command to keep the Sabbath was not until the time of Moses (Ex. 20:8); 4) the Jerusalem Council (chap. 15) did not order Gentile believers to keep the Sabbath; 5) Paul never cautioned Christians about breaking the Sabbath; and 6) the NT explicitly teaches that Sabbath keeping was not a requirement (*see notes on Rom. 14:5; Gal. 4:10,11; Col. 2:16,17*). **to break bread.** The common meal associated with the communion service (1 Cor. 11:20-22).

20:8 lamps. The fumes given off by these oil-burning lamps help explain why Eutychus fell asleep (v. 9). **upper room.** *See note on 1:13.* The early church met in homes (Rom. 16:5; 1 Cor. 16:19; Col. 4:15; Philem. 2); the first church buildings date from the third century.

20:9 young man. The Gr. word suggests he was between 7 and 14 years old. His youth, the fumes from the lamps, and the lateness of the hour (v. 7) gradually overcame his resistance. He dozed off, fell out of the open window, and was killed.

20:10 his life is in him. This does not mean that he had not died, but that his life had been restored. As a physician, Luke knew whether someone had died, as he plainly states (v. 9) was the case with Eutychus.

20:13 Assos. Located 20 mi. S of Troas, across the neck of a small peninsula. **on foot.** Because the ship had to sail around the peninsula, Paul could have arrived in Assos not long after it did. Paul presumably chose to walk to Assos so he could continue to teach the believers from Troas who accompanied him.

20:14 Mitylene. Chief city of the island of Lesbos, S of Assos.

20:15 Chios. An island off the coast of Asia Minor, S of Lesbos. Chios was the birthplace of the Greek poet Homer. **Samos.** An island off the coast near Ephesus. The famed mathematician Pythagoras was born on Samos. **Trogyllium.** A promontory jutting into the Aegean Sea between Samos and Miletus. Whether the ship actually stopped there is unclear, since many Gr. manuscripts do not mention Trogyllium. **Miletus.** A city in Asia Minor, about 30 mi. S of Ephesus.

20:16 decided to sail past Ephesus. Still trying to reach Jerusalem before Pentecost (50 days after Passover), Paul decided to have the elders (i.e., pastors, overseers) of the Ephesian church meet him in Miletus.

[q]he was hurrying [r]to be at Jerusalem, if
possible, on [s]the Day of Pentecost.

The Ephesian Elders Exhorted

17 From Miletus he sent to Ephesus and
called for the elders of the church. 18 And
when they had come to him, he said to
them: "You know, [t]from the first day that
I came to Asia, in what manner I always
lived among you, 19 serving the Lord with
all humility, with many tears and trials
which happened to me [u]by the plotting of
the Jews; 20 how [v]I kept back nothing that
was helpful, but proclaimed it to you, and
taught you publicly and from house to
house, 21 [w]testifying to Jews, and also to
Greeks, [x]repentance toward God and
faith toward our Lord Jesus Christ. 22 And
see, now [y]I go bound in the spirit to Jerusalem, not knowing the things that will
happen to me there, 23 except that [z]the
Holy Spirit testifies in every city, saying
that chains and tribulations await me.
24 [3]But [a]none of these things move me;
nor do I count my life dear to myself, [b]so
that I may finish my [4]race with joy, [c]and
the ministry [d]which I received from the
Lord Jesus, to testify to the gospel of the
grace of God.
25 "And indeed, now I know that you
all, among whom I have gone preaching
the kingdom of God, will see my face no
more. 26 Therefore I testify to you this day
that I *am* [e]innocent[5] of the blood of all *men.*
27 For I have not [6]shunned to declare to
you [f]the whole counsel of God. 28 [g]There-
fore take heed to yourselves and to all the
flock, among which the Holy Spirit [h]has
made you overseers, to shepherd the
church [7]of God [i]which He purchased [j]with
His own blood. 29 For I know this, that
after my departure [k]savage wolves will
come in among you, not sparing the flock.
30 Also [l]from among yourselves men will
rise up, speaking [8]perverse things, to draw
away the disciples after themselves.
31 Therefore watch, and remember that
[m]for three years I did not cease to warn
everyone night and day with tears.
32 "So now, brethren, I commend you to
God and [n]to the word of His grace, which
is able [o]to build you up and give you [p]an
inheritance among all those who are sanc-

16 [q] Acts 18:21; 19:21; 21:4 [r] Acts 24:17 [s] Acts 2:1; 1 Cor. 16:8
18 [t] Acts 18:19; 19:1, 10; 20:4, 16
19 [u] Acts 20:3
20 [v] Acts 20:27
21 [w] Acts 18:5; 19:10 [x] Mark 1:15
22 [y] Acts 19:21
23 [z] Acts 21:4, 11
24 [a] Acts 21:13 [b] Acts 13:25; 2 Tim. 4:7 [c] Acts 1:17 [d] Gal. 1:1 [3] NU *But I do not count my life of any value or dear to myself* [4] *course*
26 [e] Acts 18:6; 2 Cor. 7:2 [5] Lit. *clean*
27 [f] Luke 7:30; John 15:15; Eph. 1:11 [6] *avoided declaring*
28 [g] Luke 12:32; John 21:15-17; Acts 20:29; [1 Tim. 4:16]; 1 Pet. 5:2 [h] 1 Cor. 12:28 [i] Eph. 1:7, 14; Col. 1:14; Titus 2:14; Heb. 9:12; [1 Pet. 1:19]; Rev. 5:9 [j] Heb. 9:14 [7] M *of the Lord and God*
29 [k] Ezek. 22:27; Matt. 7:15
30 [l] 1 Tim. 1:20; 2 Tim. 1:15 [8] *misleading*
31 [m] Acts 19:8, 10; 24:17
32 [n] Heb. 13:9 [o] Acts 9:31 [p] Acts 26:18; Eph. 1:14, 18; 5:5; Col. 1:12; 3:24; [Heb. 9:15; 1 Pet. 1:4]

20:19 with many tears. Paul wept because of: 1) those who did not know Christ (cf. Rom. 9:2,3); 2) struggling, immature believers (2 Cor. 2:4); and 3) the threat of false teachers (v. 29,30). **plotting of the Jews.** See 2 Cor. 11:24,26. Ironically, it was the plot of the Jews at Corinth that allowed the Ephesian elders this opportunity to spend time with Paul (*see note on v. 3*).

20:20 publicly and from house to house. Paul taught in the synagogue (19:8; *see note on 6:9*) and the school of Tyrannus (19:10). He reinforced that public teaching with practical instruction of individuals and households.

20:21 repentance. An essential element of the gospel (*see notes on 2:38*; cf. 26:20; Matt. 4:17; Luke 3:8; 5:32; 24:47).

20:22 bound in the spirit. Paul's deep sense of duty toward the Master who had redeemed him and called him to service drove him onward despite the threat of danger and hardship (v. 23).

20:23 Holy Spirit testifies. Paul knew he faced persecution in Jerusalem (cf. Rom. 15:31), though he would not know the details until he heard Agabus' prophecy (21:10,11).

20:24 my race...the ministry...received from the Lord Jesus. Cf. 2 Tim. 4:7. **gospel of the grace of God.** An apt description, since salvation is solely by God's grace (Eph. 2:8,9; Titus 2:11).

20:25 you all...will see my face no more. Aware that he faced severe opposition in Jerusalem, Paul did not anticipate ever returning to Asia Minor. Though he may have done so after his release from his first Roman imprisonment, he could not at this time have foreseen that possibility. **kingdom of God.** *See note on 1:3.*

20:26 innocent of the blood. Cf. Ezek. 33:7-9; James 3:1.

20:27 whole counsel of God. The entire plan and purpose of God for man's salvation in all its fullness: divine truths of creation, election, redemption, justification, adoption, conversion, sanctification, holy living, and glorification. Paul strongly condemned those who adulterate the truth of Scripture (2 Cor. 2:17; 2 Tim. 4:3,4; cf. Rev. 22:18,19).

20:28-30 A timely warning, proven true by later events at Ephesus (1 Tim. 1:3-7,19,20; 6:20,21; Rev. 2:2). False teachers were already plaguing the churches of Galatia (Gal. 1:6) and the Corinthian church (2 Cor. 11:4).

20:28 take heed to yourselves. Paul repeated this call to self-examination to Timothy when his young son in the faith served as pastor of the Ephesian congregation (1 Tim. 4:16; 2 Tim. 2:20,21). **overseers.** These are the same as elders and pastors (*see note on 1 Tim. 3:1*). The word stresses the leaders' responsibility to watch over and protect their congregations—an appropriate usage in the context of a warning against false teachers. Church rule, which minimizes the biblical authority of elders in favor of a cultural, democratic process, is foreign to the NT (cf. 1 Thess. 5:12,13; Heb. 13:17). **with His own blood.** *See note on 1 Pet. 1:18.* Paul believed so strongly in the unity of God the Father and the Lord Jesus Christ that he could speak of Christ's death as shedding the blood of God—who has no body (John 4:24; cf. Luke 24:39) and hence no blood.

20:29 savage wolves. Borrowed from Jesus (Matt. 7:15; 10:16), this metaphor stresses the extreme danger false teachers pose to the church.

20:30 from among yourselves. Even more deadly than attacks from outside the church are the defections of those (especially leaders) within the church (1 Tim. 1:20; 2 Tim. 1:15; 2:17; cf. Jude 3,4,10-13). **perverse things.** The Gr. word means "distorted," or "twisted." False teachers twist God's Word for their own evil ends (13:10; 2 Pet. 3:16).

20:31 three years. The total length of Paul's Ephesian ministry, including the two years he taught in the school of Tyrannus (19:10).

20:32 word of His grace. The Scriptures, the record of God's gracious dealings with mankind. **build you up.** The Bible is the source of spiritual growth (1 Thess. 2:13; 2 Tim. 3:16,17; 1 Pet. 2:2) for all Christians. And since the church is "the pillar and ground of the truth" (1 Tim. 3:15), its leaders must be familiar with that truth. **inheritance.** *See note on 1 Pet. 1:4.*

tified. 33 I have coveted no one's silver or
gold or apparel. 34 [9]Yes, you yourselves
know [q]that these hands have provided for
my necessities, and for those who were
with me. 35 I have shown you in every
way, [r]by laboring like this, that you must
support the weak. And remember the
words of the Lord Jesus, that He said, 'It is
more blessed to give than to receive.' "
36 And when he had said these things,
he knelt down and prayed with them all.
37 Then they all [s]wept [1]freely, and [t]fell on
Paul's neck and kissed him, 38 sorrowing
most of all for the words which he spoke,
that they would see his face no more. And
they accompanied him to the ship.

Warnings on the Journey to Jerusalem

21 Now it came to pass, that when we
had departed from them and set sail,
running a straight course we came to Cos,
the following *day* to Rhodes, and from there
to Patara. 2 And finding a ship sailing over
to Phoenicia, we went aboard and set sail.
3 When we had sighted Cyprus, we passed
it on the left, sailed to Syria, and landed at
Tyre; for there the ship was to unload her
cargo. 4 And finding [1]disciples, we stayed
there seven days. [a]They told Paul through
the Spirit not to go up to Jerusalem. 5 When
we had come to the end of those days, we
departed and went on our way; and they all
accompanied us, with wives and children,
till *we were* out of the city. And [b]we knelt
down on the shore and prayed. 6 When we
had taken our leave of one another, we
boarded the ship, and they returned [c]home.
7 And when we had finished *our* voyage
from Tyre, we came to Ptolemais, greeted
the brethren, and stayed with them one
day. 8 On the next *day* we [2]who were Paul's
companions departed and came to [d]Caesa-
rea, and entered the house of Philip [e]the
evangelist, [f]who was *one* of the seven, and
stayed with him. 9 Now this man had four
virgin daughters [g]who prophesied. 10 And
as we stayed many days, a certain prophet
named [h]Agabus came down from Judea.
11 When he had come to us, he took Paul's
belt, bound his *own* hands and feet, and
said, "Thus says the Holy Spirit, [i]'So shall
the Jews at Jerusalem bind the man who
owns this belt, and deliver *him* into the
hands of the Gentiles.' "

34 [q] Acts 18:3; 1 Cor. 4:12; 1 Thess. 2:9; 2 Thess. 3:8 [9] NU, M omit *Yes*
35 [r] Rom. 15:1; 1 Cor. 9:12; 2 Cor. 11:9, 12; Eph. 4:28; 1 Thess. 4:11; 2 Thess. 3:8
37 [s] Acts 21:13 [t] Gen. 45:14 [1] Lit. *much*

CHAPTER 21

4 [a] [Acts 20:23; 21:12] [1] NU *the disciples*
5 [b] Luke 22:41; Acts 9:40; 20:36
6 [c] John 1:11
8 [d] Acts 8:40; 21:16 [e] Acts 8:5, 26, 40; Eph. 4:11; 2 Tim. 4:5 [f] Acts 6:5 [2] NU omits *who were Paul's companions*
9 [g] Joel 2:28; Acts 2:17
10 [h] Acts 11:28
11 [i] Acts 20:23; 21:33; 22:25

20:33 coveted. Love of money is a hallmark of false teachers (cf. Is. 56:11; Jer. 6:13; 8:10; Mic. 3:11; Titus 1:11; 2 Pet. 2:3), but did not characterize Paul's ministry. *See note on 1 Tim. 6:3,5.*

20:34 these hands...provided for my necessities. Paul had the right to earn his living from the gospel (1 Cor. 9:3-14) and sometimes accepted support (2 Cor. 11:8,9; Phil. 4:10-19). Yet, he often worked to support himself so he could "present the gospel of Christ without charge" (1 Cor. 9:18).

20:35 support the weak. Cf. 1 Cor. 4:12; 1 Thess. 2:9; 2 Thess. 3:8,9. **the words of the Lord Jesus.** This is the only direct quote from Jesus' earthly ministry recorded outside the gospels. The Bible does not record all the words or deeds of Jesus (John 21:25).

20:37 fell on Paul's neck. A common biblical way of expressing extreme emotion and affection (cf. Gen. 33:4; 45:14; 46:29).

21:1 departed. Lit. means "to tear away." It reiterates the difficulty of Paul's parting from the Ephesian elders (20:37,38). **straight course...to Cos.** The chief city of the island of Cos. **Rhodes.** An island SE of Cos; also the name of its capital city. Its harbor was home to the great statue known as the Colossus of Rhodes, one of the 7 Wonders of the Ancient World. **Patara.** A busy port city in the extreme southern portion of Asia Minor. Paul and the others had now rounded the southwestern corner of Asia Minor. Each of the ports they stopped in represented one day's sailing; the ship did not sail at night.

21:2 finding a ship...Phoenicia. Realizing he would never reach Jerusalem in time for Pentecost if he continued to hug the coast, Paul decided to risk sailing directly across the Mediterranean Sea to Tyre (v. 3). The ship they embarked on would have been considerably larger than the small coastal vessels on which they had been sailing. The ship that later took Paul on his ill-fated voyage to Rome held 276 people (27:37); this one was probably of comparable size.

21:3 Cyprus. *See note on 11:19.* **Tyre.** *See note on 12:20*; cf. Josh. 19:29; Matt. 11:21. The voyage across the Mediterranean from Patara to Tyre normally took 5 days.

21:4 disciples. The church in Tyre had been founded by some of those who fled Jerusalem after Stephen's martyrdom (11:19)—a persecution Paul himself had spearheaded. **told Paul...not to go.** This was not a command from the Spirit for Paul not to go to Jerusalem. Rather, the Spirit had revealed to the believers at Tyre that Paul would face suffering in Jerusalem. Understandably, they tried (as his friends shortly would, v. 12) to dissuade him from going there. Paul's mission to Jerusalem had been given him by the Lord Jesus (20:24); the Spirit would never command him to abandon it.

21:7 Ptolemais. Old Testament Acco (Judg. 1:31), located 25 mi. S of Tyre.

21:8 Paul's companions. This phrase is omitted by the better Gr. manuscripts. As is clear from v. 11, Paul accompanied his companions to Caesarea. **Caesarea.** *See note on 8:40.* **Philip the evangelist.** *See note on 6:5.* No one else in Scripture is called an evangelist, though Paul commanded Timothy to do the work of an evangelist (2 Tim. 4:5). Once enemies, Philip and Paul were now fellow preachers of God's gospel of grace. **the seven.** *See note on 6:3.*

21:9 virgin daughters. That they were virgins may indicate that they had been called by God for special ministry (cf. 1 Cor. 7:34). The early church regarded these women as important sources of information on the early years of the church (see Introduction: Author and Date). **prophesied.** Luke does not reveal the nature of their prophesy. They may have had an ongoing prophetic ministry, or prophesied only once. Since women are not to be preachers or teachers in the church (1 Cor. 14:34-36; 1 Tim. 2:11,12), they probably ministered to individuals. For an explanation of NT prophets *see notes on 11:27; 1 Cor. 12:28; Eph 4:11.*

21:10 prophet named Agabus. *See note on 11:28.* **down from Judea.** Although it was located in Judea, the Jews considered Caesarea, seat of the Roman government, to be a foreign city (*see note on 18:22*).

21:11 belt. Old Testament prophets sometimes acted out their prophecies (cf. 1 Kin. 11:29-39; Is. 20:2-6; Jer. 13:1-11; Ezek. 4,5). Agabus' action foreshadowed Paul's arrest and imprisonment by the Romans. **hands of the Gentiles.** Though falsely accused by the Jews (vv. 27,28), Paul was arrested and imprisoned by the Romans (vv. 31-33).

12 Now when we heard these things,
both we and those from that place pleaded
with him not to go up to Jerusalem.
13 Then Paul answered, [j]"What do you
mean by weeping and breaking my heart?
For I am ready not only to be bound, but
also to die at Jerusalem for the name of the
Lord Jesus."
14 So when he would not be persuaded,
we ceased, saying, [k]"The will of the Lord
be done."

Paul Urged to Make Peace

15 And after those days we [3]packed and
went up to Jerusalem. 16 Also some of the
disciples from Caesarea went with us and
brought with them a certain Mnason of
Cyprus, an early disciple, with whom we
were to lodge.
17 [l]And when we had come to Jerusalem, the brethren received us gladly. 18 On
the following *day* Paul went in with us to
[m]James, and all the elders were present.
19 When he had greeted them, [n]he told in
detail those things which God had done
among the Gentiles [o]through his ministry.
20 And when they heard *it,* they glorified
the Lord. And they said to him, "You see,
brother, how many myriads of Jews there
are who have believed, and they are all
[p]zealous for the law; 21 but they have been
informed about you that you teach all the
Jews who are among the Gentiles to forsake Moses, saying that they ought not to
circumcise *their* children nor to walk according to the customs. 22 [4]What then? The
assembly must certainly meet, for they will
hear that you have come. 23 Therefore do
what we tell you: We have four men who
have taken a vow. 24 Take them and be purified with them, and pay their expenses so
that they may [q]shave *their* heads, and that
all may know that those things of which
they were informed concerning you are
nothing, but *that* you yourself also walk orderly and keep the law. 25 But concerning
the Gentiles who believe, [r]we have written
and decided [5]that they should observe no
such thing, except that they should keep
themselves from *things* offered to idols,
from blood, from things strangled, and
from [6]sexual immorality."

Arrested in the Temple

26 Then Paul took the men, and the next
day, having been purified with them, [s]en-
tered the temple [t]to announce the [7]expira-
tion of the days of purification, at which

13 [j] Acts 20:24, 37
14 [k] Matt. 6:10; 26:42; Luke 11:2; 22:42
15 [3] *made preparations*
17 [l] Acts 15:4
18 [m] Acts 15:13; Gal. 1:19; 2:9
19 [n] Acts 15:4, 12; Rom. 15:18, 19 [o] Acts 1:17; 20:24; 1 Tim. 2:7
20 [p] Acts 15:1; 22:3; [Rom. 10:2]; Gal. 1:14
22 [4] NU *What then is to be done? They will certainly hear*
24 [q] Num. 6:2, 13, 18; Acts 18:18
25 [r] Acts 15:19, 20, 29 [5] NU omits *that they should observe no such thing, except* [6] *fornication*
26 [s] John 11:55; Acts 21:24; 24:18 [t] Num. 6:13; Acts 24:18 [7] *completion*

21:12 we and those from that place. Both Paul's friends (Luke and the others traveling with him) and the Caesarean Christians.

21:13 for the name. Baptism (*see note on 2:38*; cf. 8:16; 10:48; 19:5), healing (3:6,16; 4:10), signs and wonders (4:30), and preaching (4:18; 5:40; 8:12), were all done in the name of the Lord Jesus. His name represents all that He is.

21:14 will of the Lord be done. A confident expression of trust that God's will is best (cf. 1 Sam. 3:18; Matt. 6:10; Luke 22:42; James 4:13-15).

21:15 up to Jerusalem. Jerusalem was SE of Caesarea, located on a plateau so travelers were always said to go up to it (cf. 11:2; 15:2; 18:22; Mark 10:32; Luke 2:22; John 2:13; Gal. 1:17,18).

21:16 Mnason. His Gr. name may mean he was a Hellenistic Jew. If so, Paul and his Gentile companions may have chosen to stay with him because of his acquaintance with Gr. culture. That would have made him more comfortable in housing a party of Gentiles than the Palestinian Jews would have been. **early disciple.** Possibly one of those saved on the Day of Pentecost. If so, Mnason could have been another source of historical information for Luke.

21:17 come to Jerusalem. Presumably in time to celebrate Pentecost, as Paul had planned (20:16). **the brethren received us gladly.** This was because of the much-needed offering they brought. Also, and more importantly, the Jerusalem believers rejoiced because the Gentile converts with Paul provided visible evidence of God's work of salvation in the Roman world. This initial, unofficial reception may have taken place at Mnason's house.

21:18 James. The brother of Jesus and head of the Jerusalem church (*see note on 12:17*), not James, the brother of John, who had been executed by Herod (12:2). **all the elders.** The mention of elders indicates that the apostles, often away on evangelistic work, had turned over rule of the Jerusalem church to them. Some have speculated that there were 70 elders, paralleling the Sanhedrin. Given the large size of the Jerusalem church, there probably were at least that many. God had decreed that after the apostles were gone, the church was to be ruled by elders (cf. 14:30; 20:17; 1 Tim. 5:17; Titus 1:5; James 5:14; 1 Pet. 5:1,5).

21:19 told in detail. Paul's official report of his missionary work did not involve meaningless generalities; he related specific incidents from his journeys (cf. 11:4). As always (cf. 14:27; 15:4,12), Paul gave all credit and glory for his accomplishments to God.

21:20 zealous for the law. Some Jewish believers continued to observe the ceremonial aspects of the Mosaic law. Unlike the Judaizers (*see note on 15:1*), they did not view the law as a means of salvation.

21:21 to forsake Moses. The Judaizers were spreading false reports that Paul was teaching Jewish believers to forsake their heritage. That Paul had not abandoned Jewish customs is evident from his circumcision of Timothy (16:1-3) and his own taking of a Nazirite vow (18:18).

21:23 taken a vow. A Nazirite vow, symbolizing total devotion to God (*see notes on 18:18; Num. 6:1-21*).

21:24 be purified. Having just returned from an extended stay in Gentile lands, Paul was considered ceremonially unclean. He therefore needed to undergo ritual purification before participating (as their sponsor) in the ceremony marking the end of the 4 men's vows. **pay their expenses.** For the temple ceremony in which the 4 would shave their heads, and the sacrifices associated with the Nazirite vow. Paying those expenses for another was considered an act of piety, and by so doing, Paul would give further proof that he had not forsaken his Jewish heritage. **shave *their* heads.** A practice commonly associated with a Nazirite vow (Num. 6:18).

21:25 *See note on 15:19.* James made it clear that what he was asking Paul to do by no means changed the decision of the Jerusalem Council regarding Gentiles. Since Paul was Jewish, that decision did not apply to him.

21:26 having been purified. *See note on v. 24.*

time an offering should be made for each
one of them.
27 Now when the seven days were almost ended, [u]the Jews from Asia, seeing
him in the temple, stirred up the whole
crowd and [v]laid hands on him, 28 crying
out, "Men of Israel, help! This is the man
[w]who teaches all *men* everywhere against
the people, the law, and this place; and furthermore he also brought Greeks into the
temple and has defiled this holy place."
29 (For they had [8]previously seen [x]Trophi-
mus the Ephesian with him in the city,
whom they supposed that Paul had
brought into the temple.)
30 And [y]all the city was disturbed; and
the people ran together, seized Paul, and
dragged him out of the temple; and immediately the doors were shut. 31 Now as
they were [z]seeking to kill him, news came
to the commander of the [9]garrison that all
Jerusalem was in an uproar. 32 [a]He immediately took soldiers and centurions, and
ran down to them. And when they saw the
commander and the soldiers, they stopped
beating Paul. 33 Then the [b]commander
came near and took him, and [c]commanded
him to be bound with two chains; and he
asked who he was and what he had done.

27 [u] Acts 20:19; 24:18 [v] Acts 26:21
28 [w] [Matt. 24:15]; Acts 6:13; 24:6
29 [x] Acts 20:4 [8] M omits *previously*
30 [y] 2 Kin. 11:15; Acts 16:19; 26:21
31 [z] 2 Cor. 11:23 [9] *cohort*
32 [a] Acts 23:27; 24:7
33 [b] Acts 24:7 [c] Acts 20:23; 21:11; Eph. 6:20; 2 Tim. 1:16; 2:9
36 [d] Luke 23:18; John 19:15; Acts 22:22
38 [e] Acts 5:36
39 [f] Acts 9:11; 22:3; 2 Cor. 11:22; Phil. 3:4-6 [1] *insignificant*
40 [g] Acts 12:17 [h] John 5:2; Acts 22:2

34 And some among the multitude cried
one thing and some another.
So when he could not ascertain the truth
because of the tumult, he commanded him
to be taken into the barracks. 35 When he
reached the stairs, he had to be carried by
the soldiers because of the violence of the
mob. 36 For the multitude of the people followed after, crying out, [d]"Away with
him!"

Addressing the Jerusalem Mob

37 Then as Paul was about to be led into
the barracks, he said to the commander,
"May I speak to you?"
He replied, "Can you speak Greek?
38 [e]Are you not the Egyptian who some
time ago stirred up a rebellion and led the
four thousand assassins out into the
wilderness?"
39 But Paul said, [f]"I am a Jew from Tarsus, in Cilicia, a citizen of no [1]mean city;
and I implore you, permit me to speak to
the people."
40 So when he had given him permission, Paul stood on the stairs and [g]mo-
tioned with his hand to the people. And
when there was a great silence, he spoke to
them in the [h]Hebrew language, saying,

21:27 seven days. The length of the purification process (*see note on v. 24*). Paul had to appear at the temple on the third and seventh days. The incident that follows took place on the seventh day, when the process was almost completed. **Jews from Asia.** Probably from Ephesus, since they recognized Trophimus as a Gentile (v. 29). They were in Jerusalem celebrating the Feast of Pentecost.

21:28 the people, the law, and this place. Paul's enemies leveled 3 false charges against him. They claimed that he taught Jews to forsake their heritage—the same lie told by the Judaizers (*see note on v. 21*). The second charge, that Paul opposed the law, was a very dangerous one, albeit false, in this setting. Originally, Pentecost was a celebration of the firstfruits of the harvest. But by this time, it had become a celebration of Moses' receiving the law on Mt. Sinai. Thus, the Jewish people were especially zealous for the law during this feast. The third charge, of blaspheming or defiling the temple, had helped bring about the deaths of Jesus (Mark 14:57,58) and Stephen (6:13). All 3 charges were, of course, totally false. **brought Greeks into the temple.** The Asian Jews accused Paul of having brought Trophimus past the Court of the Gentiles into the part of the temple which Gentiles were forbidden. Such a charge was absurd, for it would have entailed Paul's risking his friend's life (the Romans had granted the Jews permission to execute any Gentile who so defiled the temple).

21:30 doors were shut. This was done by the temple guards, since Paul's death on the temple grounds would defile the temple (cf. 2 Kin. 11:15). They made no effort, however, to rescue the apostle from the crowd, which was intent on beating him to death.

21:31 commander. The tribune (Claudias Lysias, 23:26) commanding the Roman cohort based in Jerusalem. He was the highest ranking Roman official stationed in Jerusalem (the governor's official residence was in Caesarea, *see note on 8:40*). **the garrison.** The 1,000 man Roman occupation force. Their headquarters was Fort Antonia, located on a precipice overlooking the temple complex. From that vantage point, Roman sentries spotted the riot and informed their commander.

21:32 soldiers and centurions. The use of the plural "centurions" suggests Lysias took at least 200 soldiers with him, since each centurion commanded 100 men.

21:33 two chains. Assuming Paul to be guilty of something (since the Jews were so enraged at him), Lysias arrested him. The tribune thought he knew who Paul was (v. 38).

21:34 barracks. In Fort Antonia, overlooking the temple grounds.

21:36 "Away with him!" Or, "Kill him" (cf. 22:22; Luke 23:18; John 19:15).

21:37 "Can you speak Greek?" Paul's use of the language of educated people startled Lysias, who assumed his prisoner was an uncultured criminal.

21:38 the Egyptian...stirred up a rebellion. Lysias' question revealed who he (wrongly) assumed Paul was. The Egyptian was a false prophet who, several years earlier, had promised to drive out the Romans. Before he could do so, however, his forces were attacked and routed by Roman troops led by governor Felix. Though several hundred of his followers were killed or captured, he managed to escape. Lysias assumed he had returned and been captured by the crowd. **assassins.** Called "sicarii," they were a terrorist group whose Jewish nationalism led them to murder Romans and Jews perceived as sympathetic to Rome. Since they often used the cover of a crowd to stab their victims, Lysias assumed the mob had caught one of their leaders in the act.

21:39 Tarsus. *See note on 9:11.* Tarsus was an important cultural city, with a university rivaling those at Athens and Alexandria.

22 "Brethren[a] and fathers, hear my defense before you now." 2 And when
they heard that he spoke to them in the
[b]Hebrew language, they kept all the more
silent.
Then he said: 3 [c]"I am indeed a Jew, born
in Tarsus of Cilicia, but brought up in this
city [d]at the feet of [e]Gamaliel, taught [f]ac-
cording to the strictness of our fathers' law,
and [g]was zealous toward God [h]as you all
are today. 4 [i]I persecuted this Way to the
death, binding and delivering into prisons
both men and women, 5 as also the high
priest bears me witness, and [j]all the council
of the elders, [k]from whom I also received
letters to the brethren, and went to Damascus [l]to bring in chains even those who were
there to Jerusalem to be punished.
6 "Now [m]it happened, as I journeyed
and came near Damascus at about noon,
suddenly a great light from heaven shone
around me. 7 And I fell to the ground and
heard a voice saying to me, 'Saul, Saul,
why are you persecuting Me?' 8 So I answered, 'Who are You, Lord?' And He said
to me, 'I am Jesus of Nazareth, whom you
are persecuting.'
9 "And [n]those who were with me indeed
saw the light [1]and were afraid, but they did
not hear the voice of Him who spoke to me.
10 So I said, 'What shall I do, Lord?' And
the Lord said to me, 'Arise and go into Damascus, and there you will be told all
things which are appointed for you to do.'
11 And since I could not see for the glory of
that light, being led by the hand of those
who were with me, I came into Damascus.
12 "Then [o]a certain Ananias, a devout
man according to the law, [p]having a good
testimony with all the [q]Jews who dwelt
there, 13 came to me; and he stood and said
to me, 'Brother Saul, receive your sight.'
And at that same hour I looked up at him.
14 Then he said, [r]'The God of our fathers
[s]has chosen you that you should [t]know His
will, and [u]see the Just One, [v]and hear the
voice of His mouth. 15 [w]For you will be His
witness to all men of [x]what you have seen
and heard. 16 And now why are you waiting? Arise and be baptized, [y]and wash away
your sins, [z]calling on the name of the Lord.'
17 "Now [a]it happened, when I returned to
Jerusalem and was praying in the temple,
that I was in a trance 18 and [b]saw Him saying to me, [c]'Make haste and get out of Jerusalem quickly, for they will not receive your
testimony concerning Me.' 19 So I said,
'Lord, [d]they know that in every synagogue I
imprisoned and [e]beat those who believe on
You. 20 [f]And when the blood of Your martyr
Stephen was shed, I also was standing by
[g]consenting [2]to his death, and guarding the
clothes of those who were killing him.'
21 Then He said to me, 'Depart, [h]for I will
send you far from here to the Gentiles.' "

CHAPTER 22
1 [a] Acts 7:2
2 [b] Acts 21:40
3 [c] Acts 21:39; 2 Cor. 11:22 [d] Deut. 33:3 [e] Acts 5:34 [f] Acts 23:6; 26:5; Phil. 3:6 [g] Acts 21:20; Gal. 1:14 [h] [Rom. 10:2]
4 [i] Acts 8:3; 26:9-11; Phil. 3:6; 1 Tim. 1:13
5 [j] Acts 23:14; 24:1; 25:15 [k] Luke 22:66; Acts 4:5; 1 Tim. 4:14 [l] Acts 9:2
6 [m] Acts 9:3; 26:12, 13
9 [n] Dan. 10:7; Acts 9:7 [1] NU omits *and were afraid*
12 [o] Acts 9:17 [p] Acts 10:22 [q] 1 Tim. 3:7
14 [r] Acts 3:13; 5:30 [s] Acts 9:15; 26:16; Gal. 1:15 [t] Acts 3:14; 7:52 [u] Acts 9:17; 26:16; 1 Cor. 9:1; 15:8 [v] 1 Cor. 11:23; Gal. 1:12
15 [w] Acts 23:11 [x] Acts 4:20; 26:16
16 [y] Acts 2:38; 1 Cor. 6:11; [Eph. 5:26]; Heb. 10:22 [z] Acts 9:14; Rom. 10:13
17 [a] Acts 9:26; 26:20; 2 Cor. 12:2
18 [b] Acts 22:14 [c] Matt. 10:14
19 [d] Acts 8:3; 22:4 [e] Matt. 10:17; Acts 26:11
20 [f] Acts 7:54–8:1 [g] Luke 11:48 [2] NU omits *to his death*
21 [h] Acts 9:15; Rom. 1:5; 11:13; Gal. 2:7, 8; Eph. 3:7, 8; 1 Tim. 2:7; 2 Tim. 1:11

22:1-22 Paul's first of 6 defenses (cf. 22:30–23:10; 24:10-21; 25:1-12; 26:1-29; 28:17-29).

22:2 Hebrew language. Aramaic, the language commonly spoken in Palestine (cf. 2 Kin. 18:26; Is. 36:11). *See note on 21:37.*

22:3 I am indeed a Jew. A response to the false charges raised by the Asian Jews (*see note on 21:21*). **born in Tarsus.** *See note on 21:39.* **Cilicia.** *See note on 6:9.* Tarsus was the chief city of Cilicia. **brought up in this city.** Paul was born among the Hellenistic Jews of the Diaspora, but had been brought up in Jerusalem. **Gamaliel.** *See note on 5:34.* That Paul had studied under the most celebrated rabbi of that day was further evidence that the charges against him were absurd. **fathers' law.** As a student of Gamaliel, Paul received extensive training both in the OT law, and in the rabbinic traditions. Also, though he did not mention it to the crowd, he also had been a Pharisee. In light of all that, the charge that Paul opposed the law (*see note on 21:21*) was ridiculous.

22:4 I persecuted this Way. *See note on 9:2.* As the leading persecutor of the Christian church after Stephen's martyrdom (cf. Gal. 1:13), Paul's zeal for his Jewish heritage far outstripped that of his hearers.

22:5 council of the elders. The Sanhedrin (*see notes on 4:15; Matt. 26:59*).

22:6-16 The second of 3 NT accounts of Paul's conversion (cf. 9:1-19; 26:12-18).

22:6 about noon. Paul's reference to the time of day emphasizes how bright the light from heaven really was. It outshone the sun at its peak.

22:7,8 Cf. 9:4,5.

22:9 did not hear the voice. This is no contradiction with 9:7. Since Jesus spoke only to Paul, only he understood the Lord's words. His companions heard the sound, but could not make out the words (cf. John 12:29).

22:11 glory of that light. Paul's companions saw the light, but only he saw the Lord Jesus Christ (v. 14; 9:7,17,27; 26:16; 1 Cor. 9:1; 15:8).

22:12 Ananias. *See note on 9:10.* His testimony as a respected member of Damascus' Jewish community would carry weight with Paul's hostile audience.

22:14 the Just One. A title given to the Messiah (cf. 3:14; 7:52; Is. 53:11).

22:15 His witness. Paul never wavered in his claim to have seen the risen, glorified Christ on the Damascus road (*see note on v. 11*).

22:16 wash away your sins. Grammatically this phrase, "calling on the name of the Lord," precedes "arise and be baptized." Salvation comes from calling on the name of the Lord (Rom. 10:9,10,13), not from being baptized (*see note on 2:38*).

22:17 when I returned to Jerusalem. After a brief ministry in Damascus (9:20-25) and 3 years in Nabatean Arabia (Gal. 1:17,18). **a trance.** Paul was carried beyond his senses into the supernatural realm to receive revelation from Jesus Christ. The experience was unique to the apostles, since only Peter (10:10; 11:5) and John (Rev. 1:10) had similar revelations. This was the fourth of 6 visions received by Paul in Acts (cf. 9:3-6; 16:9,10; 18:9,10; 23:11; 27:23,24).

22:20 martyr. *See notes on 6:5; 7:54-60.* **consenting.** See 8:1.

22:21-23 Paul's insistence that the Lord had sent him to minister to the despised Gentiles was too much for the crowd. They viewed the teaching that Gentiles could be saved without first becoming

Paul's Roman Citizenship

22 And they listened to him until this
word, and *then* they raised their voices and
said, [i]"Away with such a *fellow* from the
earth, for [j]he is not fit to live!" 23 Then, as
they cried out and [3]tore off *their* clothes
and threw dust into the air, 24 the commander ordered him to be brought into the
barracks, and said that he should be examined under scourging, so that he might
know why they shouted so against him.
25 And as they bound him with thongs,
Paul said to the centurion who stood by,
[k]"Is it lawful for you to scourge a man who
is a Roman, and uncondemned?"
26 When the centurion heard *that*, he
went and told the commander, saying,
"Take care what you do, for this man is a
Roman."
27 Then the commander came and said
to him, "Tell me, are you a Roman?"
He said, "Yes."
28 The commander answered, "With a
large sum I obtained this citizenship."
And Paul said, "But I was born *a citizen*."
29 Then immediately those who were
about to examine him withdrew from him;
and the commander was also afraid after
he found out that he was a Roman, and because he had bound him.

The Sanhedrin Divided

30 The next day, because he wanted to
know for certain why he was accused by
the Jews, he released him from *his* bonds,
and commanded the chief priests and all
their council to appear, and brought Paul
down and set him before them.

23 Then Paul, looking earnestly at the
council, said, "Men *and* brethren, [a]I
have lived in all good conscience before
God until this day." 2 And the high priest
Ananias commanded those who stood by
him [b]to strike him on the mouth. 3 Then
Paul said to him, "God will strike you, *you*
whitewashed wall! For you sit to judge me
according to the law, and [c]do you command me to be struck contrary to the law?"
4 And those who stood by said, "Do you
revile God's high priest?"
5 Then Paul said, [d]"I did not know,
brethren, that he was the high priest; for it
is written, [e]*'You shall not speak evil of a
ruler of your people.'* "
6 But when Paul perceived that one part
were Sadducees and the other Pharisees,

22 [i] Acts 21:36; 1 Thess. 2:16 [j] Acts 25:24
23 [3] Lit. *threw*
25 [k] Acts 16:37

CHAPTER 23

1 [a] Acts 24:16; 1 Cor. 4:4; 2 Cor. 1:12; 4:2; 2 Tim. 1:3; Heb. 13:18
2 [b] 1 Kin. 22:24; Jer. 20:2; John 18:22
3 [c] Lev. 19:35; Deut. 25:1, 2; John 7:51
5 [d] Lev. 5:17, 18 [e] Ex. 22:28; Eccl. 10:20; 2 Pet. 2:10

Jewish proselytes (thus granting them equal status with the Jewish people before God) as intolerable blasphemy.

22:23 tore off *their* clothes. They did this in preparation to stone Paul, in horror at his "blasphemy" (*see note on 14:14*) or in uncontrollable rage—or, most likely, for all 3 reasons. Their passions inflamed by racial pride, the members of the crowd lost any semblance of self control. **threw dust.** A sign of intense emotion (cf. 2 Sam. 16:13; Job 2:12; Rev. 18:19).

22:24 the commander ordered him to be brought into the barracks. Lysias realized he would have to interrogate Paul privately. He ordered his soldiers to bring the prisoner into Fort Antonia, away from the angry mob. **that he should be examined under scourging.** A brutal Roman interrogation method. Prisoners frequently died after being flogged with the Roman *flagellum* (metal-tipped leather thongs attached to a wooden handle).

22:25 bound him. This was done in preparation for his examination by scourging. Stretching Paul taut would magnify the effects of the *flagellum* on his body. **centurion.** *See notes on 10:1; Matt. 8:5.* There would have been 10 centurions in the 1,000 man Roman garrison in Jerusalem. **who is a Roman.** Roman citizens were exempted (by the Valerian and Porcian laws) from such brutal methods of interrogation. Paul now exerted his rights as a Roman citizen. His claim would not have been questioned, because the penalty for falsely claiming Roman citizenship was death.

22:26 "Take care…this man is a Roman." The centurion informed his commander of Paul's citizenship, cautioning him against an act that could have ended Lysias' military career—or even cost him his life.

22:28 With a large sum. Roman citizenship was officially not for sale, but could sometimes be obtained by bribing corrupt officials.

22:30–23:10 Paul's second of 6 defenses (cf. vv. 1-21; 24:10-21; 25:1-12; 26:1-29; 28:17-29).

22:30 chief priests and all their council. He convened an unofficial meeting of the Sanhedrin (*see notes on 4:15,23*).

23:1 the council. The Sanhedrin (*see notes on 4:15; Matt. 26:59*). **good conscience.** *See note on 2 Cor. 1:12*; cf. 24:16; 2 Tim. 1:3.

23:2 high priest Ananias. Not the Annas of the gospels (*see note on Luke 3:2*), this man was one of Israel's cruelest and most corrupt High-Priests (*see note on 4:6*). His pro-Roman policies alienated him from the Jewish people, who murdered him at the outset of the revolt against Rome (A.D. 66). **commanded…to strike him.** An illegal act in keeping with Ananias' brutal character. The verb translated "strike" is used of the mob's beating of Paul (21:32) and the Roman soldiers' beating of Jesus (Matt. 27:30). It was no mere slap on the face, but a vicious blow.

23:3 whitewashed wall. Cf. Ezek. 13:10-16; Matt. 23:27. **contrary to the law.** Outraged by the High-Priest's flagrant violation of Jewish law, Paul flared up in anger. When Jesus was similarly struck in violation of the law, He reacted by calmly asking the reason for the blow (John 18:23). Paul's reaction was wrong, as he would shortly admit (v. 5). Although an evil man, Ananias still held a God-ordained office, and was to be granted the respect that position demanded.

23:4 revile. Those standing near Paul were appalled by his harsh rebuke of the High-Priest. "Revile" is the same word used in John 9:28 to describe the Jewish leaders' insulting remarks to the blind man whom Jesus had healed. Peter used it to speak of the abuse Jesus endured (1 Pet. 2:23).

23:5 I did not know. Some believe this to be another manifestation of Paul's eye problems (cf. Gal. 4:15); or that Paul was so angry that he forgot to whom he was speaking; or that he was being sarcastic, since Ananias was not acting like a High-Priest should. The simplest explanation is to take Paul's words at face value. He had been gone from Jerusalem for many years and would not likely have recognized Ananias by sight. That this was an informal gathering of the Sanhedrin (*see note on 22:30*) would have meant the High-Priest would not have been wearing his official garments. **it is written.** Quoted from Ex. 22:28.

23:6 Ananias' haughty attitude and illegal act convinced Paul he would not receive a fair hearing before the Sanhedrin. Accordingly, he

he cried out in the council, "Men *and*
brethren, [f]I am a Pharisee, the son of a
Pharisee; [g]concerning the hope and resurrection of the dead I am being judged!"
7 And when he had said this, a dissension arose between the Pharisees and the
Sadducees; and the assembly was divided.
8 [h]For Sadducees say that there is no resurrection—and no angel or spirit; but the
Pharisees confess both. 9 Then there arose
a loud outcry. And the scribes of the Pharisees' party arose and protested, saying,
[i]"We find no evil in this man; [1]but [j]if a
spirit or an angel has spoken to him, [k]let us
not fight against God."
10 Now when there arose a great dissension, the commander, fearing lest Paul
might be pulled to pieces by them, commanded the soldiers to go down and take
him by force from among them, and bring
him into the barracks.

The Plot Against Paul

11 But [l]the following night the Lord
stood by him and said, [2]"Be of good cheer,
Paul; for as you have testified for Me in
[m]Jerusalem, so you must also bear witness
at [n]Rome."
12 And when it was day, [o]some of the
Jews banded together and bound themselves under an oath, saying that they
would neither eat nor drink till they had
[p]killed Paul. 13 Now there were more than
forty who had formed this conspiracy.
14 They came to the chief priests and [q]el-
ders, and said, "We have bound ourselves
under a great oath that we will eat nothing
until we have killed Paul. 15 Now you,
therefore, together with the council, suggest to the commander that he be brought
down to you [3]tomorrow, as though you
were going to make further inquiries concerning him; but we are ready to kill him
before he comes near."
16 So when Paul's sister's son heard of
their ambush, he went and entered the barracks and told Paul. 17 Then Paul called one
of the centurions to *him* and said, "Take this
young man to the commander, for he has
something to tell him." 18 So he took him
and brought *him* to the commander and
said, "Paul the prisoner called me to *him*
and asked *me* to bring this young man to
you. He has something to say to you."
19 Then the commander took him by the
hand, went aside, and asked privately,
"What is it that you have to tell me?"
20 And he said, [r]"The Jews have agreed
to ask that you bring Paul down to the
council tomorrow, as though they were
going to inquire more fully about him.
21 But do not yield to them, for more than
forty of them lie in wait for him, men who
have bound themselves by an oath that
they will neither eat nor drink till they
have killed him; and now they are ready,
waiting for the promise from you."
22 So the commander let the young man
depart, and commanded *him*, "Tell no one
that you have revealed these things to me."

Sent to Felix

23 And he called for two centurions, saying, "Prepare two hundred soldiers, seven-

6 [f]Acts 26:5; Phil. 3:5 [g]Acts 24:15, 21; 26:6; 28:20
8 [h]Matt. 22:23; Mark 12:18; Luke 20:27
9 [i]Acts 25:25; 26:31 [j]John 12:29; Acts 22:6, 7, 17, 18 [k]Acts 5:39 [1]NU *what if a spirit or an angel has spoken to him?* omitting the last clause
11 [l]Acts 18:9; 27:23, 24 [m]Acts 21:18, 19; 22:1-21 [n]Acts 28:16, 17, 23 [2]*Take courage*
12 [o]Acts 23:21, 30; 25:3 [p]Acts 9:23, 24; 25:3; 26:21; 27:42; 1 Thess. 2:15
14 [q]Acts 4:5, 23; 6:12; 22:5; 24:1; 25:15
15 [3]NU omits *tomorrow*
20 [r]Acts 23:12

decided on a bold step. As a Pharisee, and possibly a former member of the Sanhedrin (*see note on 26:10*), Paul was well aware of the tensions between the Sanhedrin's two factions. He appealed to the Pharisees for support, reminding them that he himself was a Pharisee, and appealing to the major theological difference between them and the Sadducees (*see note on v. 7*). Paul thus created a split between the Sanhedrin's factions. **Sadducees…Pharisees.** *See note on Matt. 3:7.* **council.** *See note on 4:15.*

23:7 a dissension arose. There were major social, political, and theological differences between the Sadducees and Pharisees. By raising the issue of the resurrection, Paul appealed to the Pharisees for support on perhaps the most important theological difference (*see note on v. 8*). Since the resurrection of Jesus Christ is also the central theme of Christianity, this was no cynical ploy on Paul's part to divide the Sanhedrin over a trivial point of theology.

23:8 Sadducees…Pharisees. The Sadducees accepted only the Pentateuch as divinely inspired Scripture. Since they claimed (wrongly, cf. Matt. 22:23-33) that the Pentateuch did not teach that there would be a resurrection, they rejected it. The Pharisees, however, believed in the resurrection and afterlife. Their beliefs were thus closer to Christianity than those of the Sadducees. Significantly, the Scripture records the conversion of Pharisees (15:5; John 3:1), but not of Sadducees.

23:9 scribes of the Pharisees' party. So intense was their theological disagreement with the Sadducees that they were willing to defend Paul—even though he was a leader of the hated sect of the Christians (cf. 24:5).

23:11 the Lord stood by him. The fifth of 6 visions Paul received in Acts (cf. 9:3-6; 16:9,10; 18:9,10; 22:17,18; 27:23,24), all coming at crucial points in his ministry. **bear witness at Rome.** Jesus encouraged Paul by telling him that his desire (Rom. 1:9-11; 15:23) to visit Rome would be granted.

23:12 bound themselves under an oath. Lit. they "anathematized" themselves (cf. Gal. 1:8,9), thus invoking divine judgment if they failed (cf. 1 Sam. 14:44; 2 Sam. 3:35; 19:13; 1 Kin. 2:23; 2 Kin. 6:31).

23:14 chief priests and elders. *See notes on 4:23; Matt. 16:21.* Being Sadducees, they would be more inclined to help the conspirators. Significantly excluded are the scribes who, being mostly Pharisees, had already shown their willingness to defend Paul (v. 9).

23:16 Paul's sister's son. The only clear reference in Scripture to Paul's family (for other possible references see Rom. 16:7,11,21). Why he was in Jerusalem, away from the family home in Tarsus is not known. Nor is it evident why he would want to warn his uncle, since Paul's family possibly disinherited him when he became a Christian (Phil. 3:8). **entered the barracks and told Paul.** Since Paul was not under arrest, but merely in protective custody, he was able to receive visitors.

23:17 centurions. *See note on 22:25.*

ty horsemen, and two hundred spearmen
to go to [s]Caesarea at the third hour of the
night; 24 and provide mounts to set Paul
on, and bring *him* safely to Felix the governor." 25 He wrote a letter in the following
manner:

26 Claudius Lysias,

To the most excellent governor
Felix:

Greetings.

27 [t]This man was seized by the Jews
and was about to be killed by
them. Coming with the troops I
rescued him, having learned that
he was a Roman. 28 [u]And when I
wanted to know the reason they
accused him, I brought him before
their council. 29 I found out that he
was accused [v]concerning questions
of their law, [w]but had nothing
charged against him deserving of
death or chains. 30 And [x]when it
was told me that [4]the Jews lay in
wait for the man, I sent him
immediately to you, and [y]also
commanded his accusers to state
before you the charges against him.

Farewell.

31 Then the soldiers, as they were commanded, took Paul and brought *him* by
night to Antipatris. 32 The next day they
left the horsemen to go on with him, and
returned to the barracks. 33 When they
came to [z]Caesarea and had delivered the
[a]letter to the governor, they also presented
Paul to him. 34 And when the governor
had read *it,* he asked what province he was
from. And when he understood that *he was*
from [b]Cilicia, 35 he said, [c]"I will hear you
when your accusers also have come." And
he commanded him to be kept in [d]Herod's
[5]Praetorium.

Accused of Sedition

24 Now after [a]five days [b]Ananias the
high priest came down with the elders and a certain orator *named* Tertullus.
These gave evidence to the governor
against Paul.

2 And when he was called upon, Tertullus began his accusation, saying: "Seeing that through you we enjoy great peace,
and [1]prosperity is being brought to this
nation by your foresight, 3 we accept *it* always and in all places, most noble Felix,
with all thankfulness. 4 Nevertheless, not
to be tedious to you any further, I beg you
to hear, by your [2]courtesy, a few words
from us. 5 [c]For we have found this man a
plague, a creator of dissension among all
the Jews throughout the world, and a

23 [s]Acts 8:40; 23:33
27 [t]Acts 21:30, 33; 24:7
28 [u]Acts 22:30
29 [v]Acts 18:15; 25:19 [w]Acts 25:25; 26:31
30 [x]Acts 23:20 [y]Acts 24:8; 25:6 [4]NU *there would be a plot against the man*
33 [z]Acts 8:40 [a]Acts 23:26-30
34 [b]Acts 6:9; 21:39
35 [c]Acts 24:1, 10; 25:16 [d]Matt. 27:27 [5]Headquarters

CHAPTER 24

1 [a]Acts 21:27 [b]Acts 23:2, 30, 35; 25:2
2 [1]Or *reforms are*
4 [2]*graciousness*
5 [c]Luke 23:2; Acts 6:13; 16:20; 17:6; 21:28; 1 Pet. 2:12, 15

23:23,24 To foil the conspirators' plot, avoid a potentially explosive confrontation with the Jews, and save Paul's life, Lysias realized he had to get the apostle out of Jerusalem and to his superior, Governor Felix in Caesarea.

23:23 soldiers…horsemen…spearmen. The "soldiers" were legionnaires, the elite soldiers of the Roman army; the "horsemen" were from the garrison's cavalry detachment; and the "spearmen," or javelin throwers, were soldiers less heavily armed than the legionnaires. Lysias sent almost half of his 1,000 man garrison, showing how seriously he viewed the plot against Paul. **third hour of the night.** 9:00 p.m.

23:26 governor Felix. *See note on 24:3.*

23:27 having learned that he was a Roman. Actually, Lysias did not find this out until after he arrested Paul (22:25,26). Lysias sought to portray himself in the best possible light before the governor. For that reason, he also neglected to mention his order to have Paul scourged (22:24), and his mistaken assumption that he was the notorious Egyptian assassin (21:38).

23:29 questions of their law. Lysias' failure to mention any crimes against Roman law was tantamount to declaring Paul innocent.

23:30 to state before you the charges. The plot against Paul's life rendered any further hearings at Jerusalem unsafe, thus requiring Lysias to burden Felix with the case.

23:31 Antipatris. A Roman military post about 40 mi. from Jerusalem. Travelers from Jerusalem to Caesarea often rested there. To get there from Jerusalem in one night (v. 32) would have been an exhausting forced march for the foot soldiers.

23:32 horsemen. Since there was much less danger of ambush in the largely Gentile region of Samaria, the foot soldiers were no longer needed.

23:33 Caesarea. *See note on 8:40.*

23:34 what province he was from. Felix needed to determine whether he had jurisdiction to hear Paul's case. **from Cilicia.** Judea and Cilicia were at that time both under the legate of Syria, so Felix had the authority to hear his case.

23:35 Herod's Praetorium. Felix's official residence in Caesarea.

24:1 after five days. A very short period of time for the Jewish leaders to put their case together, hire an attorney ("orator"), and make the trip to Caesarea. Perhaps they feared Felix would dismiss the case against Paul if they did not pursue it rapidly. **Ananias the high priest.** *See note on 23:2.* **elders.** Important leaders of the Sanhedrin (*see note on 4:5*). **Tertullus.** Possibly a Roman, but more likely a Hellenistic Jew (cf. v. 6).

24:3 Felix. Governor of Judea from A.D. 52 to 59. Felix was a former slave whose brother (a favorite of Emperor Claudius) had obtained for him the position as governor. He was not highly regarded by the influential Romans of his day and accomplished little during his term as governor. He defeated the Egyptian and his followers (*see note on 21:38*), but his brutality angered the Jews and led to his ouster as governor by Emperor Nero two years after Paul's hearing (v. 27).

24:5-7 Having dispensed with the obligatory flattery of Felix, Tertullus set forth the specific charges against Paul. They included sedition (a violation of Roman law), sectarianism (a violation of Jewish law), and sacrilege (a violation of God's law).

24:5 a plague. This statement, while reflecting the Sanhedrin's hatred of the apostle and Christianity, was not a specific charge of wrongdoing. **a creator of dissension.** The first and (in a Roman court) most serious charge leveled against Paul: sedition (rebellion). The Romans did not tolerate those who incited rebellion (as the Jews

ringleader of the sect of the Nazarenes.
6 [d]He even tried to profane the temple,
and we seized him, [3]and wanted [e]to judge
him according to our law. 7 [f]But the commander Lysias came by and with great violence took *him* out of our hands, 8 [g]com-
manding his accusers to come to you. By
examining him yourself you may ascertain all these things of which we accuse
him." 9 And the Jews also [4]assented,
maintaining that these things were so.

The Defense Before Felix

10 Then Paul, after the governor had
nodded to him to speak, answered: "Inasmuch as I know that you have been for
many years a judge of this nation, I do the
more cheerfully answer for myself, 11 because you may ascertain that it is no more
than twelve days since I went up to Jerusalem [h]to worship. 12 [i]And they neither
found me in the temple disputing with
anyone nor inciting the crowd, either in the
synagogues or in the city. 13 Nor can they
prove the things of which they now accuse
me. 14 But this I confess to you, that according to [j]the Way which they call a sect,
so I worship the [k]God of my fathers, be-

6 [d] Acts 21:28 [e] John 18:31 [3] NU ends the sentence here and omits the rest of v. 6, all of v. 7, and the first clause of v. 8.
7 [f] Acts 21:33; 23:10
8 [g] Acts 23:30
9 [4] NU, M *joined the attack*
11 [h] Acts 21:15, 18, 26, 27; 24:17
12 [i] Acts 25:8; 28:17
14 [j] Amos 8:14; Acts 9:2; 24:22 [k] 2 Tim. 1:3 [l] Acts 26:22; 28:23
15 [m] Acts 23:6; 26:6, 7; 28:20 [n] [Dan. 12:2; John 5:28, 29; 11:24] [5] NU omits *of the dead*
16 [o] Acts 23:1
17 [p] Acts 11:29, 30; Rom. 15:25-28; 1 Cor. 16:1-4; 2 Cor. 8:1-4; 9:1, 2, 12; Gal. 2:10
18 [q] Acts 21:27; 26:21 [r] Acts 21:26
19 [s] [Acts 23:30; 25:16]
20 [6] NU, M *what wrongdoing they found*
21 [t] [Acts 23:6; 24:15; 28:20]
22 [u] Acts 9:2; 18:26; 19:9, 23; 22:4 [v] Acts 23:26; 24:7

lieving all things which are written in [l]the
Law and in the Prophets. 15 [m]I have hope
in God, which they themselves also accept,
[n]that there will be a resurrection [5]of *the*
dead, both of *the* just and *the* unjust.
16 [o]This *being* so, I myself always strive to
have a conscience without offense toward
God and men.
17 "Now after many years [p]I came to
bring alms and offerings to my nation,
18 [q]in the midst of which some Jews from
Asia found me [r]purified in the temple, neither with a mob nor with tumult. 19 [s]They
ought to have been here before you to object if they had anything against me. 20 Or
else let those who are *here* themselves say
[6]if they found any wrongdoing in me
while I stood before the council, 21 unless *it*
is for this one statement which I cried out,
standing among them, [t]'Concerning the
resurrection of the dead I am being judged
by you this day.'"

Felix Procrastinates

22 But when Felix heard these things,
having more accurate knowledge of *the*
[u]Way, he adjourned the proceedings and
said, "When [v]Lysias the commander

present would learn a few years later in A.D. 66). Had the Jewish leaders been able to substantiate this charge, Paul would have faced severe punishment, possibly even execution. Tertullus carefully avoided naming any specific incidents, since Felix could then have transferred Paul's case to the governor in whose jurisdiction the incident took place. The Jews wanted Paul tried before a governor over whom they had some influence. **ringleader...sect of the Nazarenes.** The second charge brought against Paul was sectarianism (heresy). Tertullus' contemptuous reference to Christianity as "the sect of the Nazarenes" (cf. 6:14; John 1:46; 7:41,52) was intended to portray Paul as the leader of a messianic sect posing a danger to Rome.

24:6 tried to profane the temple. The third accusation leveled against Paul was sacrilege, blasphemy against God. The Jewish leaders, through their spokesman, repeated the false charges of the Asian Jews (21:28). Trying to whitewash the angry crowd's savage beating of Paul, they claimed (falsely) to have arrested him.

24:6-8a He even...to you. Many ancient manuscripts omit this passage, raising the question of who Tertullus was urging Felix to examine. If the passage is omitted, Tertullus would be asking Felix to examine Paul; but the apostle would merely have denied Tertullus' false accusations. If the passage is genuine, Tertullus would be falsely accusing Lysias of overstepping his authority by meddling in a proper Jewish legal proceeding. He would then be claiming that an examination of Lysias would confirm the Jewish leaders' false interpretation of the events. That would help explain Felix's decision to adjourn the hearing until he sent for Lysias (v. 22).

24:7,8a Another falsehood, intended to shift the blame for the incident. Actually, it was the Jewish mob that was guilty of violence; Lysias put a stop to the riot and rescued Paul.

24:10-21 Paul's third of 6 defenses (cf. 22:1-21; 22:30–23:10; 25:1-12; 26:1-29; 28:17-19).

24:10 many years a judge. Both as governor, and before that during his service under the governor of Samaria. Unlike Tertullus, Paul was not flattering Felix, but reminding him of his acquaintance with Jewish laws, customs, and beliefs. Felix was thus bound to give a just verdict.

24:11 twelve days. Five of which had been spent at Caesarea waiting for his accusers to arrive (v. 1). Several of the remaining 7 had been taken up with his purification rites (*see notes on 21:24,27*). Paul's point was that, even if he had wanted to, he had not had the time to incite a revolt.

24:14 the Way. *See note on 9:2.* **the Law and in the Prophets.** The "Law and the Prophets" refers to the OT (see Matt. 7:12). The Sadducees rejected much of the OT (*see note on 23:8*), while both they and the Pharisees rejected the OT's witness to Jesus Christ (cf. Luke 24:27,44; John 1:45; 5:39,46). In contrast, Paul viewed the entire OT as the inspired Word of God, and believed everything it taught.

24:15 hope in God. The great hope of the Jewish people was the resurrection (Job 19:25-27; Is. 26:19; Dan. 12:2). It was Paul, not the skeptical Sadducees, who stood in the mainstream of traditional Jewish theology.

24:16 conscience without offense. *See note on 23:1.*

24:17 alms and offerings. The only reference in Acts to the delivery of the offering Paul had been collecting for the poor saints in Jerusalem (*see note on 19:21*). Far from seeking to stir up strife, Paul had gone to Jerusalem on a humanitarian mission.

24:18 Jews from Asia. *See note on 21:27.* **purified.** *See note on 21:24.*

24:21 Concerning the resurrection of the dead. Belief in the resurrection was not a crime under either Jewish or Roman law. Nor was Paul responsible for the longstanding feud between the Sadducees and Pharisees that erupted into open dissension when he made his statement.

24:22 having more accurate knowledge of *the* Way. Probably from his wife Drusilla, who was Jewish (25:24). **adjourned the proceedings.** The witnesses to Paul's alleged crime (the Jews from Asia) had failed to show up for the hearing. Nor could the Jewish leaders prove him guilty of a crime. The only verdict Felix could ren-

comes down, I will make a decision on
your case." 23 So he commanded the centurion to keep Paul and to let *him* have liberty, and [w]told him not to forbid any of his
friends to provide for or visit him.
24 And after some days, when Felix
came with his wife Drusilla, who was Jewish, he sent for Paul and heard him concerning the [x]faith in Christ. 25 Now as he
reasoned about righteousness, self-control,
and the judgment to come, Felix was afraid
and answered, "Go away for now; when I
have a convenient time I will call for you."
26 Meanwhile he also hoped that [y]money
would be given him by Paul, [7]that he
might release him. Therefore he sent for
him more often and conversed with him.
27 But after two years Porcius Festus
succeeded Felix; and Felix, [z]wanting to do
the Jews a favor, left Paul bound.

Paul Appeals to Caesar

25 Now when Festus had come to the
province, after three days he went
up from [a]Caesarea to Jerusalem. 2 [b]Then
the [1]high priest and the chief men of the
Jews informed him against Paul; and they
petitioned him, 3 asking a favor against
him, that he would summon him to Jerusalem—[c]while *they* lay in ambush along the
road to kill him. 4 But Festus answered that
Paul should be kept at Caesarea, and that
he himself was going *there* shortly.
5 "Therefore," he said, "let those who have
authority among you go down with *me*
and accuse this man, to see [d]if there is any
fault in him."
6 And when he had remained among
them more than ten days, he went down to
Caesarea. And the next day, sitting on the
judgment seat, he commanded Paul to be
brought. 7 When he had come, the Jews
who had come down from Jerusalem stood
about [e]and laid many serious complaints
against Paul, which they could not prove,
8 while he answered for himself, [f]"Neither
against the law of the Jews, nor against the
temple, nor against Caesar have I offended
in anything at all."
9 But Festus, [g]wanting to do the Jews a
favor, answered Paul and said, [h]"Are you
willing to go up to Jerusalem and there be
judged before me concerning these
things?"
10 So Paul said, "I stand at Caesar's
judgment seat, where I ought to be judged.
To the Jews I have done no wrong, as you
very well know. 11 [i]For if I am an offender,
or have committed anything deserving of
death, I do not object to dying; but if there
is nothing in these things of which these
men accuse me, no one can deliver me to
them. [j]I appeal to Caesar."
12 Then Festus, when he had conferred

23 [w] Acts 23:16; 27:3; 28:16
24 [x] [John 3:15; 5:24; 11:25; 12:46; 20:31; Rom. 10:9]
26 [y] Ex. 23:8 [7] NU omits *that he might release him*
27 [z] Ex. 23:2; Acts 12:3; 23:35; 25:9, 14

CHAPTER 25

1 [a] Acts 8:40; 25:4, 6, 13
2 [b] Acts 24:1; 25:15 [1] NU *chief priests*
3 [c] Acts 23:12, 15
5 [d] Acts 18:14; 25:18
7 [e] Mark 15:3; Luke 23:2, 10; Acts 24:5, 13
8 [f] Acts 6:13; 24:12; 28:17
9 [g] Acts 12:2; 24:27 [h] Acts 25:20
11 [i] Acts 18:14; 23:29; 25:25; 26:31 [j] Acts 26:32; 28:19

der consistent with Roman law was not guilty, which would infuriate the Jews, and possibly lead to further trouble. Since as governor, Felix's primary responsibility was to maintain order, he decided the best decision was no decision, and adjourned the proceedings on the pretext of needing further information from Lysias. **commander comes down.** Lysias' written report had already stated that the dispute involved questions of Jewish law (23:29), and that Paul was not guilty of any crime (23:29). It is difficult to see what more he could have added, and there is no evidence that Felix ever summoned him.

24:24 Drusilla. The youngest daughter of Agrippa I (*see note on 12:1*), and Felix's third wife. Felix, struck by her beauty, had lured her away from her husband. At the time of Paul's hearing, she was not yet 20 years old.

24:25 righteousness, self-control, and the judgment. God demands "righteousness" of all men, because of His holy nature (Matt. 5:48; 1 Pet. 1:15,16). For men and women to conform to that absolute standard requires "self-control." The result of failing to exhibit self-control and to conform oneself to God's righteous standard is (apart from salvation) "judgment." **Felix was afraid.** Living with a woman he had lured away from her husband, Felix obviously lacked "righteousness" and "self-control." The realization that he faced "judgment" alarmed him, and he hastily dismissed Paul. **when I have a convenient time.** The moment of conviction passed, and Felix foolishly passed up his opportunity to repent (cf. 2 Cor. 6:2).

24:26 money would be given him by Paul. Roman law prohibited the taking of bribes, which was nonetheless commonplace.

24:27 Porcius Festus succeeded Felix. *See note on v. 3.* Festus was a member of the Roman nobility, unlike the former slave, Felix. Little is known of his brief tenure as governor (he died two years after assuming office), but the Jewish historian Josephus described him as better than either his predecessor or his successor. **do the Jews a favor.** He did this since Jewish complaints to Rome about his brutality eventually led to his ouster from office. He had brutally suppressed a riot in Caesarea and infuriated the Jews who managed to complain to Rome and have him replaced. Emperor Nero recalled him to Rome where he would have faced severe punishment if his influential brother, Pallas, had not interceded for him.

25:1-12 Paul's fourth of 6 defenses (cf. 22:1-21; 22:30–23:10; 24:10-21; 26:1-29; 28:17-29).

25:1 after three days…Caesarea to Jerusalem. To acquaint himself with the situation in his new province.

25:3 ambush. A second ambush plot. This time, however, the members of the Sanhedrin were not accomplices (cf. 23:14,15), but the plotters.

25:4 Festus. *See note on 24:27.* **Caesarea.** *See note on 8:40.* As the headquarters of Roman government in Judea, Caesarea was the proper place for Paul, a Roman citizen, to be tried.

25:6 the judgment seat. This signified that this hearing was an official Roman trial (see vv. 10,17; 18:12; Matt. 27:19; John 19:13).

25:9 wanting to do the Jews a favor. Cf. 24:27.

25:10 Caesar's judgment seat. Festus' compromise gave the Jewish leaders all that they hoped for; they intended to murder Paul before he got to Jerusalem. The apostle therefore rejected Festus' attempt at compromise and reminded the governor that he was standing at Caesar's judgment seat where, as a Roman citizen, he had every right to be judged.

25:11 I appeal to Caesar. He declared his right as a Roman citizen to have a trial in Rome.

with the council, answered, "You have appealed to Caesar? To Caesar you shall go!"

Paul Before Agrippa

13 And after some days King Agrippa
and Bernice came to Caesarea to greet Festus. 14 When they had been there many
days, Festus laid Paul's case before the
king, saying: [k]"There is a certain man left a
prisoner by Felix, 15 [l]about whom the chief
priests and the elders of the Jews informed
me, when I was in Jerusalem, asking for a
judgment against him. 16 [m]To them I answered, 'It is not the custom of the Romans
to deliver any man [2]to destruction before
the accused meets the accusers face to face,
and has opportunity to answer for himself
concerning the charge against him.'
17 Therefore when they had come together,
[n]without any delay, the next day I sat on
the judgment seat and commanded the
man to be brought in. 18 When the accusers
stood up, they brought no accusation
against him of such things as I [3]supposed,
19 [o]but had some questions against him
about their own religion and about a certain Jesus, who had died, whom Paul affirmed to be alive. 20 And because I was
uncertain of such questions, I asked
whether he was willing to go to Jerusalem
and there be judged concerning these matters. 21 But when Paul [p]appealed to be reserved for the decision of Augustus, I commanded him to be kept till I could send
him to Caesar."
22 Then [q]Agrippa said to Festus, "I also
would like to hear the man myself."

"Tomorrow," he said, "you shall hear
him."
23 So the next day, when Agrippa and
Bernice had come with great [4]pomp, and
had entered the auditorium with the
commanders and the prominent men of
the city, at Festus' command [r]Paul was
brought in. 24 And Festus said: "King
Agrippa and all the men who are here
present with us, you see this man about
whom [s]the whole assembly of the Jews petitioned me, both at Jerusalem and here,
crying out that he was [t]not fit to live any
longer. 25 But when I found that [u]he had
committed nothing deserving of death,
[v]and that he himself had appealed to Augustus, I decided to send him. 26 I have
nothing certain to write to my lord concerning him. Therefore I have brought him
out before you, and especially before you,
King Agrippa, so that after the examination has taken place I may have something
to write. 27 For it seems to me unreasonable to send a prisoner and not to specify
the charges against him."

Paul's Early Life

26 Then Agrippa said to Paul, "You are
permitted to speak for yourself."
So Paul stretched out his hand and answered for himself: 2 "I think myself
[a]happy, King Agrippa, because today I
shall answer [b]for myself before you concerning all the things of which I am [c]ac-
cused by the Jews, 3 especially because you
are expert in all customs and questions

14 [k]Acts 24:27
15 [l]Acts 24:1; 25:2, 3
16 [m]Acts 25:4, 5 [2]NU omits *to destruction,* although it is implied
17 [n]Matt. 27:19; Acts 25:6, 10
18 [3]*suspected*
19 [o]Acts 18:14, 15; 23:29
21 [p]Acts 25:11, 12
22 [q]Acts 9:15
23 [r]Acts 9:15 [4]*pageantry*
24 [s]Acts 25:2, 3, 7 [t]Acts 21:36; 22:22
25 [u]Acts 23:9, 29; 26:31 [v]Acts 25:11, 12

CHAPTER 26

2 [a][1 Pet. 3:14; 4:14] [b][1 Pet. 3:15, 16] [c]Acts 21:28; 24:5, 6

25:12 the council. Festus' advisers. **To Caesar you shall go!** By granting the appeal, the governor removed himself from the case and transferred it to the emperor.

25:13 King Agrippa. Herod Agrippa II, son of the Herod who killed James and imprisoned Peter (*see note on 12:1*). He was the last of the Herods, who play a prominent role in NT history. His great-uncle, Herod Antipas, was the Herod of the gospels (Mark 6:14-29; Luke 3:1; 13:31-33; 23:7-12), while his great-grandfather, Herod the Great, ruled at the time Jesus was born (Matt. 2:1-19; Luke 1:5). Though not the ruler of Judea, Agrippa was well versed in Jewish affairs (cf. 26:3). **Bernice.** Not Agrippa's wife, but his consort and sister. (Their sister, Drusilla, was married to the former governor, Felix). Their incestuous relationship was the talk of Rome, where Agrippa grew up. Bernice for a while became the mistress of Emperor Vespasian, then of his son, Titus, but always returned to her brother.

25:19 religion. Such charges did not belong in a Roman court (cf. 18:12-16).

25:20 I was uncertain of such questions. Festus, a pagan Roman and new in Judea, could not be expected to understand the theological differences between Christians and Jews.

25:21 Augustus...Caesar. "Augustus," meaning "revered" or "worshiped one," was a title commonly applied to the emperor. The "Caesar" ruling at this time was the infamous Nero.

25:22 I also would like to hear. The Gr. verb tense implies Herod had been wanting to hear Paul for a long time. As an expert on Jewish affairs (cf. 26:3), he relished hearing Christianity's leading spokesman in person.

25:23 Agrippa and Bernice. The two are inseparable in Luke's account (cf. v. 13; 26:30); she is a constant reminder of Agrippa's scandalous private life (*see note on v. 13*). **commanders.** The 5 tribunes commanding the 5 cohorts stationed in Caesarea (*see note on 10:1*). **prominent men.** The civic leaders of the city.

25:25 Augustus. *See note on v. 21.*

25:26 I have nothing certain. Since Festus did not understand the nature of the charges against Paul, he did not know what to write in his official report to Nero. For a provincial governor to send a prisoner to the emperor with no clear charges against him was foolish, if not dangerous. **especially before you, King Agrippa.** Festus hoped Herod's expertise in Jewish affairs (26:3) would enable him to make sense of the charges against Paul.

26:1-29 Paul's fifth of 6 defenses (cf. 22:1-21; 22:30–23:10; 24:10-21; 25:1-12; 28:17-19).

26:1 permitted to speak. Since no one was there to accuse Paul, Herod permitted him to speak in his defense. **stretched out his hand.** A common gesture at the beginning of a speech (cf. 12:17; 13:16; 19:33).

26:3 expert in all customs and questions...with the Jews. *See note on 25:26.* Paul's main purpose was not to defend himself but to convert Agrippa and the others (vv. 28,29).

which have to do with the Jews. Therefore I beg you to hear me patiently.

4 "My manner of life from my youth, which was spent from the beginning among my own nation at Jerusalem, all the Jews know. 5 They knew me from the first, if they were willing to testify, that according to [d]the strictest sect of our religion I lived a Pharisee. 6 [e]And now I stand and am judged for the hope of [f]the promise made by God to our fathers. 7 To this *promise* [g]our twelve tribes, earnestly serving *God* [h]night and day, [i]hope to attain. For this hope's sake, King Agrippa, I am accused by the Jews. 8 Why should it be thought incredible by you that God raises the dead?

9 [j]"Indeed, I myself thought I must do many things [1]contrary to the name of [k]Jesus of Nazareth. 10 [l]This I also did in Jerusalem, and many of the saints I shut up in prison, having received authority [m]from the chief priests; and when they were put to death, I cast my vote against *them.* 11 [n]And I punished them often in every synagogue and compelled *them* to blaspheme; and being exceedingly enraged against them, I persecuted *them* even to foreign cities.

Paul Recounts His Conversion

12 [o]"While thus occupied, as I journeyed to Damascus with authority and commission from the chief priests, 13 at midday, O king, along the road I saw a light from heaven, brighter than the sun, shining around me and those who journeyed with me. 14 And when we all had fallen to the ground, I heard a voice speaking to me and saying in the Hebrew language, 'Saul, Saul, why are you persecuting Me? *It is* hard for you to kick against the goads.' 15 So I said, 'Who are You, Lord?' And He said, 'I am Jesus, whom you are persecuting. 16 But rise and stand on your feet; for I have appeared to you for this purpose, [p]to make you a minister and a witness both of the things which you have seen and of the things which I will yet reveal to you. 17 I will [2]deliver you from the *Jewish* people, as well as *from* the Gentiles, [q]to whom I [3]now send you, 18 [r]to open their eyes, *in order* [s]to turn *them* from darkness to light, and *from* the power of Satan to God, [t]that they may receive forgiveness of sins and [u]an inheritance among those who are [v]sanctified[4] by faith in Me.'

Paul's Post-Conversion Life

19 "Therefore, King Agrippa, I was not disobedient to the heavenly vision, 20 but [w]declared first to those in Damascus and in Jerusalem, and throughout all the region of Judea, and *then* to the Gentiles, that they should repent, turn to God, and do [x]works befitting repentance. 21 For these reasons the Jews seized me in the temple and tried to kill *me.* 22 Therefore, having obtained help from God, to this day I stand, witnessing both to small and great, saying no other things than those [y]which the prophets and [z]Moses said would come— 23 [a]that the Christ would suffer, [b]that He

5 [d] [Acts 22:3; 23:6; 24:15, 21]; Phil. 3:5
6 [e] Acts 23:6 [f] [Gen. 3:15; 22:18; 26:4; 49:10; Deut. 18:15; 2 Sam. 7:12; Ps. 132:11; Is. 4:2; 7:14; 9:6; 40:10; Jer. 23:5; 33:14-16; Ezek. 34:23; 37:24; Dan. 9:24]; Acts 13:32; Rom. 15:8; [Titus 2:13]
7 [g] James 1:1 [h] Luke 2:37; 1 Thess. 3:10; 1 Tim. 5:5 [i] Phil. 3:11
9 [j] John 16:2; 1 Cor. 15:9; 1 Tim. 1:12, 13 [k] Acts 2:22; 10:38 [1] *against*
10 [l] Acts 8:1-3; 9:13; Gal. 1:13 [m] Acts 9:14
11 [n] Matt. 10:17; Acts 22:19
12 [o] Acts 9:3-8; 22:6-11; 26:12-18
16 [p] Acts 22:15; Eph. 3:6-8
17 [q] Acts 22:21 [2] *rescue* [3] NU, M omit *now*
18 [r] Is. 35:5; 42:7, 16; Luke 1:79; [John 8:12; 2 Cor. 4:4]; Eph. 1:18; 1 Thess. 5:5 [s] 2 Cor. 6:14; Eph. 4:18; 5:8; [Col. 1:13]; 1 Pet. 2:9 [t] Luke 1:77 [u] Eph. 1:11; Col. 1:12 [v] Acts 20:32 [4] *set apart*
20 [w] Acts 9:19, 20, 22; 11:26 [x] Matt. 3:8; Luke 3:8
22 [y] Luke 24:27; Acts 24:14; 28:23; Rom. 3:21 [z] John 5:46
23 [a] Luke 24:26 [b] 1 Cor. 15:20, 23; Col. 1:18; Rev. 1:5

26:5 lived a Pharisee. *See note on Matt. 3:7*; cf. Phil. 3:5.

26:6 the hope of the promise. The coming of the Messiah and His kingdom (cf. 1:6; 3:22-24; 13:23-33; Gen. 3:15; Is. 7:14; 9:6; Dan. 7:14; Mic. 5:2; Titus 2:13; 1 Pet. 1:11,12).

26:7 twelve tribes. A common NT designation for Israel (cf. Matt. 19:28; James 1:1; Rev. 21:12). The 10 northern tribes were not lost. Representatives from each intermingled with the two southern tribes before and after the Exile—a process that had begun during the reigns of Hezekiah (2 Chr. 30:1-11) and Josiah (2 Chr. 34:1-9).

26:8 Paul found it inconceivable that he should be condemned for believing in the resurrection—the great hope of the Jewish people (*see note on 24:15*).

26:10 saints. Christian believers (1 Cor. 1:2). **I cast my vote.** Lit. "I threw my pebble"—a reference to the ancient custom of recording votes by means of colored pebbles. This verse may also indicate that Paul had once been a member of the Sanhedrin.

26:11 compelled *them* to blaspheme. To renounce their faith in Jesus Christ.

26:12-14 The third NT account of Paul's conversion (*see notes on 9:1-19; 22:6-21*).

26:16 things which I will yet reveal to you. See 18:9,10; 22:17-21; 23:11; 2 Cor. 12:1-7; Gal. 1:11,12.

26:17 Gentiles to whom I now send you. Paul's commissioning as the apostle to the Gentiles (Rom. 11:13; 1 Tim. 2:7).

26:18 to open their eyes. Unbelievers are blinded to spiritual truth by Satan (2 Cor. 4:4; 6:14; cf. Matt. 15:14). **from darkness to light.** Since unbelievers are in the darkness of their spiritual blindness, the Bible often uses light to picture salvation (v. 23; 13:47; Matt. 4:16; John 1:4,5,7-9; 3:19-21; 8:12; 9:5; 12:36; 2 Cor. 4:4; 6:14; Eph. 5:8,14; Col. 1:12,13; 1 Thess. 5:5; 1 Pet. 2:9; 1 John 1:7; 2:8-10). **forgiveness of sins.** This is the most significant result of salvation (*see note on 2:38*; cf. 3:19; 5:31; 10:43; 13:38; Matt. 1:21; 26:28; Luke 1:77; 24:47; 1 Cor. 15:3; Gal. 1:4; Col. 1:14; Heb. 8:12; 9:28; 10:12; 1 Pet. 2:24; 3:18; 1 John 2:1,2; 3:5; 4:10; Rev. 1:5). **an inheritance.** The blessings believers will enjoy throughout eternity in heaven (cf. 20:32; Eph. 1:11,14,18; Col. 1:12; 3:24; Heb. 9:15). **sanctified by faith.** The Bible plainly and repeatedly teaches that salvation comes solely through faith apart from human works (13:39; 15:9; 16:31; John 3:14-17; 6:69; Rom. 3:21-28; 4:5; 5:1; 9:30; 10:9-11; Gal. 2:16; 3:11,24; Eph. 2:8,9; Phil. 3:9).

26:20 works befitting repentance. Genuine repentance is inseparably linked to a changed lifestyle (*see note on 2:38; Matt. 3:8; James 2:18*).

26:21 the Jews...tried to kill *me*. *See 21:27-32.* The true reason in contrast to the lies of the Jewish leaders (24:6).

26:22 the prophets and Moses. *See note on 24:14.* The term "Moses" is used interchangeably with "law," since he was the author of the Pentateuch, the 5 books of law.

26:23 Christ would suffer...rise from the dead. Messiah's suffering (Ps. 22; Is. 53) and resurrection (Ps. 16:10; cf. 13:30-37), the central themes of Paul's preaching, are clearly taught in the OT.

would be the first to rise from the dead,
and [c]would proclaim light to the *Jewish*
people and to the Gentiles."

Agrippa Parries Paul's Challenge

24 Now as he thus made his defense,
Festus said with a loud voice, "Paul, [d]you
are beside yourself! Much learning is driving you mad!"
25 But he said, "I am not [5]mad, most noble
Festus, but speak the words of truth and reason. 26 For the king, before whom I also
speak freely, [e]knows these things; for I am
convinced that none of these things escapes
his attention, since this thing was not done
in a corner. 27 King Agrippa, do you believe
the prophets? I know that you do believe."
28 Then Agrippa said to Paul, "You almost persuade me to become a Christian."
29 And Paul said, [f]"I would to God that
not only you, but also all who hear me
today, might become both almost and altogether such as I am, except for these chains."
30 When he had said these things, the
king stood up, as well as the governor and
Bernice and those who sat with them;
31 and when they had gone aside, they
talked among themselves, saying, [g]"This
man is doing nothing deserving of death
or chains."
32 Then Agrippa said to Festus, "This
man might have been set [h]free [i]if he had
not appealed to Caesar."

23 [c] Is. 42:6; 49:6; Luke 2:32; 2 Cor. 4:4
24 [d] 2 Kin. 9:11; John 10:20; [1 Cor. 1:23; 2:13, 14; 4:10]
25 [5] *out of my mind*
26 [e] Acts 26:3
29 [f] 1 Cor. 7:7
31 [g] Acts 23:9, 29; 25:25
32 [h] Acts 28:18 [i] Acts 25:11

The Voyage to Rome Begins

27 And when [a]it was decided that we
should sail to Italy, they delivered
Paul and some other prisoners to *one*
named Julius, a centurion of the Augustan
Regiment. 2 So, entering a ship of Adramyttium, we put to sea, meaning to sail
along the coasts of Asia. [b]Aristarchus, a
Macedonian of Thessalonica, was with us.
3 And the next *day* we landed at Sidon.
And Julius [c]treated Paul kindly and gave
him liberty to go to his friends and receive
care. 4 When we had put to sea from there,
we sailed under *the shelter of* Cyprus, because the winds were contrary. 5 And
when we had sailed over the sea which is
off Cilicia and Pamphylia, we came to
Myra, *a city* of Lycia. 6 There the centurion
found [d]an Alexandrian ship sailing to Italy,
and he put us on board.
7 When we had sailed slowly many
days, and arrived with difficulty off
Cnidus, the wind not permitting us to proceed, we sailed under *the shelter of* [e]Crete
off Salmone. 8 Passing it with difficulty, we
came to a place called Fair Havens, near
the city *of* Lasea.

Paul's Warning Ignored

9 Now when much time had been spent,
and sailing was now dangerous [f]because
[1]the Fast was already over, Paul advised

CHAPTER 27

1 [a] Acts 25:12, 25
2 [b] Acts 19:29
3 [c] Acts 24:23; 28:16
6 [d] Acts 28:11
7 [e] Acts 2:11; 27:12, 21; Titus 1:5, 12
9 [f] Lev. 16:29-31; 23:27-29; Num. 29:7 [1] The Day of Atonement, late September or early October

26:24 you are beside yourself! Festus was astonished that a learned scholar like Paul could actually believe that the dead would live again—something no intelligent Roman would accept. Unable to contain himself, he interrupted the proceedings, shouting that Paul's tremendous learning had driven him insane (cf. Mark 3:21; John 8:48,52; 10:20).

26:26 not done in a corner. The death of Jesus and the Christians' claim that He rose from the dead were common knowledge in Palestine.

26:27 do you believe the prophets? Paul's shrewd question put Herod in a dilemma. If he affirmed his belief in the prophets, he would also have to admit that what they taught about Jesus' death and resurrection was true—an admission that would make him appear foolish before his Roman friends. Yet to deny the prophets would outrage his Jewish subjects.

26:28 You almost persuade me. A better translation is "Do you think you can convince me to become a Christian in such a short time?" Recognizing his dilemma, Agrippa parried Paul's question with one of his own.

26:30-32 The hearing over, Agrippa and Festus met privately to discuss Paul's case. Both agreed that he was innocent of any crime and could be set free, had he not appealed to Caesar.

27:1 we. The use of the pronoun "we" marks the return of Paul's close friend Luke, who has been absent since 21:18. He had likely been living near Caesarea so he could care for Paul during his imprisonment. Now he rejoined the apostle for the journey to Rome. **centurion of the Augustan Regiment.** A cohort (regiment) of that name was stationed in Palestine during the reign of Agrippa II (*see note on 25:13*). Julius may have been on detached duty, performing such tasks as escorting important prisoners.

27:2 Adramyttium. A city on the NW coast of Asia Minor (modern Turkey) near Troas, where the centurion planned to find a ship sailing to Italy. **we put to sea.** From Caesarea the ship sailed 70 mi. N to Sidon. **Aristarchus...with us.** He had been seized by the crowd during the riot at Ephesus (19:29), while accompanying Paul to Jerusalem with the offering (20:4). Aristarchus would be with Paul during the apostle's first Roman imprisonment (Col. 4:10).

27:3 landed at Sidon. *See note on 12:20.* The Christians there ministered to Paul—possibly by providing him with provisions for his trip.

27:4 sailed under *the shelter of* Cyprus. They kept to the lee side of the island (passing between it and the mainland), seeking shelter from the strong winds.

27:5 off Cilicia and Pamphylia. *See notes on 2:10; 6:9.* **Myra...Lycia.** One of the main ports of the imperial grain fleet, whose ships brought Egyptian grain to Italy.

27:6 Alexandrian ship. Part of the imperial grain fleet.

27:7 Cnidus. Located on a peninsula in extreme SW Asia Minor, this port also served ships of the imperial grain fleet. Having reached Cnidus, the ship could not sail farther W due to the strong headwinds. It was forced to turn S and head for the island of Crete. ***the shelter of* Crete.** This large island off the SW coast of Asia Minor provided some relief from the strong NW winds buffeting the ship. **Salmone.** A promontory on Crete's NE coast.

27:8 Fair Havens...Lasea. The ship fought its way around the SE corner of Crete, finally reaching the shelter of the bay known as Fair Havens.

27:9 the Fast was already over. *See note on Zech. 7:3*; cf. Lev. 23:26-32. Travel in the open sea was dangerous from mid-Sept. to

them, 10 saying, "Men, I perceive that this
voyage will end with disaster and much
loss, not only of the cargo and ship, but
also our lives." 11 Nevertheless the centurion was more persuaded by the helmsman
and the owner of the ship than by the
things spoken by Paul. 12 And because the
harbor was not suitable to winter in, the
majority advised to set sail from there also,
if by any means they could reach Phoenix,
a harbor of Crete opening toward the
southwest and northwest, *and* winter *there.*

In the Tempest

13 When the south wind blew softly,
supposing that they had obtained *their* desire, putting out to sea, they sailed close by
Crete. 14 But not long after, a tempestuous
head wind arose, called [2]Euroclydon. 15 So
when the ship was caught, and could not
head into the wind, we let *her* [3]drive.
16 And running under *the shelter of* an island called [4]Clauda, we secured the skiff
with difficulty. 17 When they had taken it
on board, they used cables to undergird
the ship; and fearing lest they should run
aground on the [5]Syrtis *Sands,* they struck
sail and so were driven. 18 And because we
were exceedingly tempest-tossed, the next
day they lightened the ship. 19 On the third
day [g]we threw the ship's tackle overboard
with our own hands. 20 Now when neither
sun nor stars appeared for many days, and
no small tempest beat on *us,* all hope that
we would be saved was finally given up.
21 But after long abstinence from food,
then Paul stood in the midst of them and
said, "Men, you should have listened to
me, and not have sailed from Crete and incurred this disaster and loss. 22 And now I
urge you to take [6]heart, for there will be no
loss of life among you, but only of the ship.
23 [h]For there stood by me this night an
angel of the God to whom I belong and
[i]whom I serve, 24 saying, 'Do not be afraid,
Paul; you must be brought before Caesar;
and indeed God has granted you all those
who sail with you.' 25 Therefore take heart,
men, [j]for I believe God that it will be just
as it was told me. 26 However, [k]we must
run aground on a certain island."

27 Now when the fourteenth night had
come, as we were driven up and down in
the Adriatic *Sea,* about midnight the sailors
sensed that they were drawing near some
land. 28 And they took soundings and
found *it* to be twenty fathoms; and when
they had gone a little farther, they took
soundings again and found *it* to be fifteen
fathoms. 29 Then, fearing lest we should
run aground on the rocks, they dropped
four anchors from the stern, and [7]prayed
for day to come. 30 And as the sailors were
seeking to escape from the ship, when they
had let down the skiff into the sea, under
pretense of putting out anchors from the
prow, 31 Paul said to the centurion and
the soldiers, "Unless these men stay in the
ship, you cannot be saved." 32 Then the
soldiers cut away the ropes of the skiff and
let it fall off.

33 And as day was about to dawn, Paul
implored *them* all to take food, saying, "To-

14 [2] A southeast wind that stirs up broad waves; NU *Euraquilon*, a northeaster
15 [3] *be driven*
16 [4] NU *Cauda*
17 [5] M *Syrtes*
19 [g] Jon. 1:5
22 [6] *courage*
23 [h] Acts 18:9; 23:11; 2 Tim. 4:17 [i] Dan. 6:16; Rom. 1:9; 2 Tim. 1:3
25 [j] Luke 1:45; Rom. 4:20, 21; 2 Tim. 1:12
26 [k] Acts 28:1
29 [7] Or *wished*

---

mid-Nov., after which it ceased altogether until Feb. Since the Fast (the Day of Atonement) of late Sept. or early Oct. was past, further travel was already extremely hazardous.

27:10 end with disaster. Because of the lateness of the season, and the difficulties they had already experienced, Paul wisely counseled them to spend the winter at Fair Havens.

27:11 centurion. *See note on 10:1.* Because the ship was part of the Imperial grain fleet (*see note on v. 5*) Julius, not the helmsman nor the ship's owner, was the ranking official on board. **helmsman.** The ship's pilot, or captain.

27:12 not suitable to winter in. The professional sailors deemed Fair Havens an unsuitable location to wait out the winter (*see note on v. 9*). **Phoenix.** Located 40 mi. from Fair Havens with a harbor that provided better shelter from the winter storms.

27:14 Euroclydon. *Euraquilon* is the preferred reading (see marginal note), from the Gr. word *euros* ("east wind") and the Lat. word *aquilo* ("north wind"). It is a strong, dangerous windstorm greatly feared by those who sailed the Mediterranean.

27:16 Clauda. An island 23 mi. SW of Crete. **secured the skiff.** Taking advantage of Clauda's shelter, the sailors began to rig the ship for the storm by hauling the ship's dinghy on board.

27:17 used cables to undergird the ship. A procedure known as frapping. The cables, wrapped around the hull and winched tight, helped the ship endure the battering of the wind and waves. **Syrtis.** A region of sandbars and shoals off the coast of Africa, much feared as a graveyard of ships. **struck sail.** This phrase could best be translated "let down the sea anchor." The sailors undoubtedly did both, since putting out an anchor with the sails up would be self-defeating.

27:18 lightened the ship. Throwing all unnecessary gear and cargo overboard would lighten the ship, enabling it to ride more easily over the waves.

27:23,24 The last of 6 visions Paul received as recorded by Luke (cf. 9:3-6; 16:9,10; 18:9,10; 22:17,18; 23:11).

27:24 brought before Caesar. The angel reaffirmed the promise Jesus Himself had earlier made to Paul (23:11).

27:27 fourteenth night. Since they sailed from Fair Havens (v. 13). **Adriatic *Sea*.** The central Mediterranean Sea, not the present Adriatic Sea located between Italy and Croatia. The modern Adriatic was known in Paul's day as the Gulf of Adria. **sensed.** The sailors probably heard the sound of waves breaking on a shore.

27:28 took soundings. With a weight attached to a length of rope they measured the depth of the sea. **twenty fathoms…fifteen fathoms.** 120 feet…90 feet. The decreasing depth of the water confirmed the ship was approaching land.

27:29 dropped four anchors from the stern. An attempt to hold the ship in place and keep the bow pointed toward the shore.

27:30 skiff. The same dinghy hauled aboard earlier (v. 16). **putting out anchors from the prow.** This would have been for additional stability (cf. v. 29).

day is the fourteenth day you have waited
and continued without food, and eaten
nothing. 34 Therefore I urge you to take
nourishment, for this is for your survival,
[l]since not a hair will fall from the head of
any of you." 35 And when he had said
these things, he took bread and [m]gave
thanks to God in the presence of them all;
and when he had broken *it* he began to eat.
36 Then they were all encouraged, and also
took food themselves. 37 And in all we
were two hundred and seventy-six [n]per-
sons on the ship. 38 So when they had
eaten enough, they lightened the ship and
threw out the wheat into the sea.

Shipwrecked on Malta

39 When it was day, they did not recognize the land; but they observed a bay with
a beach, onto which they planned to run
the ship if possible. 40 And they [8]let go the
anchors and left *them* in the sea, meanwhile loosing the rudder ropes; and they
hoisted the mainsail to the wind and made
for shore. 41 But striking [9]a place where
two seas met, [o]they ran the ship aground;
and the prow stuck fast and remained immovable, but the stern was being broken
up by the violence of the waves.
42 And the soldiers' plan was to kill the
prisoners, lest any of them should swim
away and escape. 43 But the centurion,
wanting to save Paul, kept them from *their*
purpose, and commanded that those who
could swim should jump *overboard* first and
get to land, 44 and the rest, some on boards
and some on *parts* of the ship. And so it was
[p]that they all escaped safely to land.

Paul's Ministry on Malta

28 Now when they had escaped, they
then found out that [a]the island was
called Malta. 2 And the [b]natives[1] showed
us unusual kindness; for they kindled a fire
and made us all welcome, because of the
rain that was falling and because of the
cold. 3 But when Paul had gathered a bundle of sticks and laid *them* on the fire, a
viper came out because of the heat, and fastened on his hand. 4 So when the natives
saw the creature hanging from his hand,
they said to one another, "No doubt this
man is a murderer, whom, though he has
escaped the sea, yet justice does not allow
to live." 5 But he shook off the creature into
the fire and [c]suffered no harm. 6 However,
they were expecting that he would swell up
or suddenly fall down dead. But after they
had looked for a long time and saw no
harm come to him, they changed their
minds and [d]said that he was a god.
7 In that region there was an estate of the
[2]leading citizen of the island, whose name
was Publius, who received us and entertained us courteously for three days. 8 And
it happened that the father of Publius lay
sick of a fever and dysentery. Paul went in
to him and [e]prayed, and [f]he laid his hands
on him and healed him. 9 So when this was
done, the rest of those on the island who
had diseases also came and were healed.
10 They also honored us in many [g]ways;
and when we departed, they provided
such things as were [h]necessary.

Arrival at Rome

11 After three months we sailed in [i]an
Alexandrian ship whose figurehead was
the [3]Twin Brothers, which had wintered at
the island. 12 And landing at Syracuse, we
stayed three days. 13 From there we circled
round and reached Rhegium. And after
one day the south wind blew; and the next
day we came to Puteoli, 14 where we found
[j]brethren, and were invited to stay with
them seven days. And so we went toward

34 [l] 1 Kin. 1:52; [Matt. 10:30; Luke 12:7; 21:18]
35 [m] 1 Sam. 9:13; Matt. 15:36; Mark 8:6; John 6:11; [1 Tim. 4:3, 4]
37 [n] Acts 2:41; 7:14; Rom. 13:1; 1 Pet. 3:20
40 [8] *cast off*
41 [o] 2 Cor. 11:25 [9] A reef
44 [p] Acts 27:22, 31

CHAPTER 28

1 [a] Acts 27:26
2 [b] Acts 28:4; Rom. 1:14; 1 Cor. 14:11; Col. 3:11 [1] Lit. *barbarians*
5 [c] Mark 16:18; Luke 10:19
6 [d] Acts 12:22; 14:11
7 [2] Magistrate
8 [e] Acts 9:40; [James 5:14, 15] [f] Matt. 9:18; Mark 5:23; 6:5; 7:32; 16:18; Luke 4:40; Acts 19:11, 12; [1 Cor. 12:9, 28]
10 [g] Matt. 15:6; 1 Tim. 5:17 [h] [Phil. 4:19]
11 [i] Acts 27:6 [3] Gr. *Dioskouroi,* Zeus's sons Castor and Pollux
14 [j] Rom. 1:8

27:33 without food. Because of seasickness and the difficulty of preparing and preserving food, the passengers and crew had eaten little or nothing in the two weeks since they left Fair Havens.

27:34 not a hair will fall. A common Jewish saying (1 Sam. 14:45; 2 Sam. 14:11; 1 Kin. 1:52; Luke 21:18) denoting absolute protection.

27:37 two hundred and seventy-six persons on the ship. As an ocean-going vessel, this ship was considerably larger than the smaller vessel Paul sailed in from Caesarea to Lycia.

27:38 lightened the ship. *See note on v. 18.*

27:41 a place where two seas met. A sandbar or reef short of the shore.

27:42 the soldiers' plan was to kill the prisoners. Knowing they could face punishment or death if their prisoners escaped (cf. 12:19; 16:27).

28:1 Malta. An island, 17 mi. long and 9 mi. wide, about 60 mi. S of Sicily. None of the sailors had previously been to the bay (known today as St. Paul's Bay) where they were shipwrecked.

28:3 a viper. A venomous snake. Cf. Mark 16:18.

28:6 said that he was a god. *See 14:11,12.*

28:7 leading citizen. The Gr. phrase indicates Publius was the Roman governor of Malta.

28:8 sick of a fever and dysentery. The gastric fever (caused by a microbe found in goat's milk) that was common on Malta. Dysentery, often the result of poor sanitation, was widespread in the ancient world.

28:11 After three months. Since sea travel was dangerous during this period (*see note on 27:9*). **Alexandrian ship.** Probably another in the imperial grain fleet (*see notes on 27:5,6*). **Twin Brothers.** Castor and Pollux, Zeus' sons according to Gr. mythology, were believed to protect sailors.

28:12 Syracuse. An important city on the island of Sicily. Tradition holds that Paul established a church during the ship's 3-day stopover there.

28:13 Rhegium. A harbor on the southern tip of the Italian mainland. There the ship waited one day for a favorable wind to permit it to sail through the Straits of Messina (separating Sicily from the Italian mainland). **Puteoli.** Modern Pozzuoli, located on the Bay of

Rome. 15 And from there, when the
brethren heard about us, they came to
meet us as far as Appii Forum and Three
Inns. When Paul saw them, he thanked
God and took courage.
16 Now when we came to Rome, the centurion delivered the prisoners to the captain of the guard; but [k]Paul was permitted
to dwell by himself with the soldier who
guarded him.

Paul's Ministry at Rome

17 And it came to pass after three days
that Paul called the leaders of the Jews together. So when they had come together,
he said to them: "Men *and* brethren,
[l]though I have done nothing against our
people or the customs of our fathers, yet [m]I
was delivered as a prisoner from Jerusalem
into the hands of the Romans, 18 who,
[n]when they had examined me, wanted to
let *me* go, because there was no cause for
putting me to death. 19 But when the [4]Jews
spoke against *it,* [o]I was compelled to appeal to Caesar, not that I had anything of
which to accuse my nation. 20 For this reason therefore I have called for you, to see
you and speak with *you,* because [p]for the
hope of Israel I am bound with [q]this
chain."
21 Then they said to him, "We neither received letters from Judea concerning you,
nor have any of the brethren who came reported or spoken any evil of you. 22 But we
desire to hear from you what you think; for
concerning this sect, we know that [r]it is
spoken against everywhere."
23 So when they had appointed him a
day, many came to him at *his* lodging, [s]to
whom he explained and solemnly testified
of the kingdom of God, persuading them
concerning Jesus [t]from both the Law of
Moses and the Prophets, from morning till
evening. 24 And [u]some were persuaded by
the things which were spoken, and some
disbelieved. 25 So when they did not agree
among themselves, they departed after
Paul had said one word: "The Holy Spirit
spoke rightly through Isaiah the prophet to
[5]our fathers, 26 saying,

[v]*'Go to this people and say:*
"Hearing you will hear, and shall
not understand;
And seeing you will see, and not
perceive;
27 *For the hearts of this people have*
grown dull.
Their ears are hard of hearing,
And their eyes they have closed,
Lest they should see with their eyes
and hear with their ears,
Lest they should understand with
their hearts and turn,
So that I should heal them."'

28 "Therefore let it be known to you that
the salvation of God has been sent [w]to the
Gentiles, and they will hear it!" 29 [6]And
when he had said these words, the Jews
departed and had a great dispute among
themselves.
30 Then Paul dwelt two whole years in
his own rented house, and received all
who came to him, 31 [x]preaching the kingdom of God and teaching the things which
concern the Lord Jesus Christ with all confidence, no one forbidding him.

16 [k]Acts 23:11; 24:25; 27:3 **17** [l]Acts 23:29; 24:12, 13; 26:31 [m]Acts 21:33 **18** [n]Acts 22:24; 24:10; 25:8; 26:32 **19** [o]Acts 25:11, 21, 25 [4]The ruling authorities **20** [p]Acts 26:6, 7 [q]Acts 26:29; Eph. 3:1; 4:1; 6:20; 2 Tim. 1:8, 16; Philem. 10, 13 **22** [r]Luke 2:34; Acts 24:5, 14; [1 Pet. 2:12; 3:16; 4:14, 16] **23** [s]Luke 24:27; [Acts 17:3; 19:8] [t]Acts 26:6, 22 **24** [u]Acts 14:4; 19:9 **25** [5]NU *your* **26** [v]Is. 6:9, 10; Jer. 5:21; Ezek. 12:2; Matt. 13:14, 15; Mark 4:12; Luke 8:10; John 12:40, 41; Rom. 11:8 **28** [w]Is. 42:1, 6; 49:6; Matt. 21:41; Luke 2:32; Rom. 11:11 **29** [6]NU omits v. 29. **31** [x]Acts 4:31; Eph. 6:19

Naples near Pompeii. Rome's main port and the most important one in Italy, Puteoli was also the main port for the Egyptian grain fleet (*see note on 27:5*).

28:14 Rome. Almost as a footnote, Luke mentions the party's arrival in the Imperial capital—Paul's longtime goal (*see note on 19:21*).

28:15 Appii Forum. A market town 43 mi. S of Rome on the Appian Way. **Three Inns.** A rest stop on the Appian Way, about 30 mi. S of Rome.

28:16 centurion delivered the prisoners to the captain of the guard. Many Gr. manuscripts omit this phrase. If part of the original text, it indicates either that Julius delivered the prisoners to his commanding officer, or to the commander of the Praetorian Guard. **dwell by himself...guarded.** Possibly through Julius' intervention, Paul was allowed to live under guard in his own rented quarters (cf. v. 30).

28:17-29 Paul's sixth and final defense recorded in Acts (cf. 22:1-21; 22:30–23:10; 24:10-21; 25:1-12; 26:1-29).

28:17 leaders of the Jews. The most prominent men from Rome's synagogues (*see note on 6:9*). **the customs of our fathers.** Paul began by denying that he was guilty of any infraction against the Jewish people or their traditions (cf. 22:3; 24:14; 26:4,5).

28:19 appeal to Caesar. *See note on 25:11.*

28:20 the hope of Israel. *See notes on 24:15; 26:6.*

28:23 kingdom of God. *See note on 1:3.* **persuading them...Law of Moses...Prophets.** Paul's method of Jewish evangelism throughout Acts was to prove from the OT that Jesus was the Messiah (cf. 13:16-41).

28:26,27 Quoted from Is. 6:9,10 (*see note there*).

28:28 salvation of God has been sent to the Gentiles. See 11:18; 13:46,47; 14:27; 15:14-17; 18:6.

28:29 Many ancient manuscripts omit this verse.

28:30,31 The best explanation for this rather abrupt ending to the book is that Luke wrote Acts before Paul's release from his first Roman imprisonment (see Introduction: Author and Date).

28:31 with all confidence, no one forbidding him. Helped by his loyal fellow workers (cf. Col. 4:10; Philem. 24), Paul evangelized Rome (cf. Phil. 1:13; 4:22).

The Epistle of Paul to the
ROMANS

Title

This epistle's name comes from its original recipients: the members of the church in Rome, the capital of the Roman Empire (1:7).

Author and Date

No one disputes that the apostle Paul wrote Romans. Like his namesake, Israel's first king (Saul was Paul's Hebrew name; Paul his Greek name), Paul was from the tribe of Benjamin (Phil. 3:5). He was also a Roman citizen (Acts 16:37; 22:25). Paul was born about the time of Christ's birth, in Tarsus (Acts 9:11), an important city (Acts 21:39) in the Roman province of Cilicia, located in Asia Minor (modern Turkey). He spent much of his early life in Jerusalem as a student of the celebrated rabbi Gamaliel (Acts 22:3). Like his father before him, Paul was a Pharisee (Acts 23:6), a member of the strictest Jewish sect (cf. Phil. 3:5).

Miraculously converted while on his way to Damascus (ca. A.D. 33–34) to arrest Christians in that city, Paul immediately began proclaiming the gospel message (Acts 9:20). After narrowly escaping from Damascus with his life (Acts 9:23-25; 2 Cor. 11:32,33), Paul spent 3 years in Nabatean Arabia, south and east of the Dead Sea (Gal. 1:17,18). During that time, he received much of his doctrine as direct revelation from the Lord (Gal. 1:11,12).

More than any other individual, Paul was responsible for the spread of Christianity throughout the Roman Empire. He made 3 missionary journeys through much of the Mediterranean world, tirelessly preaching the gospel he had once sought to destroy (Acts 26:9). After he returned to Jerusalem bearing an offering for the needy in the church there, he was falsely accused by some Jews (Acts 21:27-29), savagely beaten by an angry mob (Acts 21:30,31), and arrested by the Romans. Though two Roman governors, Felix and Festus, as well as Herod Agrippa, did not find him guilty of any crime, pressure from the Jewish leaders kept Paul in Roman custody. After two years, the apostle exercised his right as a Roman citizen and appealed his case to Caesar. After a harrowing trip (Acts 27,28), including a violent, two-week storm at sea that culminated in a shipwreck, Paul reached Rome. Eventually released for a brief period of ministry, he was arrested again and suffered martyrdom at Rome in ca. A.D. 65-67 (cf. 2 Tim. 4:6).

Though physically unimpressive (cf. 2 Cor. 10:10; Gal. 4:14), Paul possessed an inner strength granted him through the Holy Spirit's power (Phil. 4:13). The grace of God proved sufficient to provide for his every need (2 Cor. 12:9,10), enabling this noble servant of Christ to successfully finish his spiritual race (2 Tim. 4:7).

Paul wrote Romans from Corinth, as the references to Phoebe (Rom. 16:1, Cenchrea was Corinth's port), Gaius (Rom. 16:23), and Erastus (Rom. 16:23)—all of whom were associated with Corinth—indicate. The apostle wrote the letter toward the close of his third missionary journey (most likely in A.D. 56), as he prepared to leave for Palestine with an offering for the poor believers in the Jerusalem church (Rom. 15:25). Phoebe was given the great responsibility of delivering this letter to the Roman believers (16:1,2).

Background and Setting

Rome was the capital and most important city of the Roman Empire. It was founded in 753 B.C., but is not mentioned in Scripture until NT times. Rome is located along the banks of the Tiber River, about 15 miles from the Mediterranean Sea. Until an artificial harbor was built at nearby Ostia, Rome's main harbor was Puteoli, some 150 miles away (*see note on Acts 28:13*). In Paul's day, the city had a population of over one million people, many of whom were slaves. Rome boasted magnificent buildings, such as the Emperor's palace, the Circus Maximus, and the Forum, but its beauty was marred by the slums in which so many lived. According to tradition, Paul was martyred outside Rome on the Ostian Way during Nero's reign (A.D. 54–68).

Some of those converted on the Day of Pentecost probably founded the church at Rome (cf. Acts 2:10). Paul had long sought to visit the Roman church, but had been prevented from doing so (1:13). In God's providence, Paul's inability to visit Rome gave the world this inspired masterpiece of gospel doctrine.

Paul's primary purpose in writing Romans was to teach the great truths of the gospel of grace to be-

First Century Rome

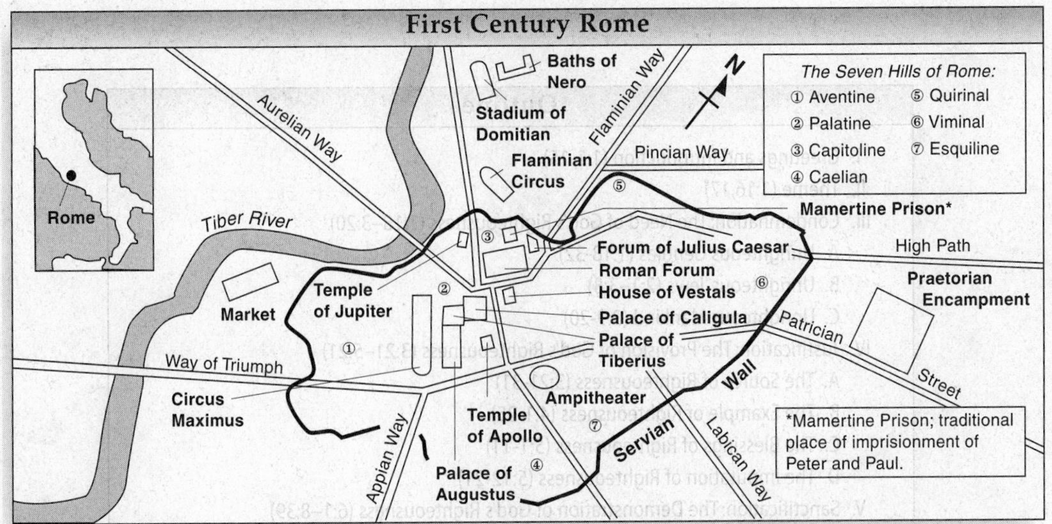

lievers who had never received apostolic instruction. The letter also introduced him to a church where he was personally unknown, but hoped to visit soon for several important reasons: to edify the believers (1:11); to preach the gospel (1:15); and to get to know the Roman Christians, so they could encourage him (1:12; 15:32), better pray for him (15:30), and help him with his planned ministry in Spain (15:28).

Unlike some of Paul's other epistles (e.g., 1, 2 Cor., Gal.), his purpose for writing was not to correct aberrant theology or rebuke ungodly living. The Roman church was doctrinally sound, but, like all churches, it was in need of the rich doctrinal and practical instruction this letter provides.

Historical and Theological Themes

Since Romans is primarily a work of doctrine, it contains little historical material. Paul does use such familiar OT figures as Abraham (chap. 4), David (4:6-8), Adam (5:12-21), Sarah (9:9), Rebekah (9:10), Jacob and Esau (9:10-13), and Pharaoh (9:17) as illustrations. He also recounts some of Israel's history (chaps. 9–11). Chapter 16 provides insightful glimpses into the nature and character of the first-century church and its members.

The overarching theme of Romans is the righteousness that comes from God: the glorious truth that God justifies guilty, condemned sinners by grace alone through faith in Christ alone. Chapters 1–11 present the theological truths of that doctrine, while chaps. 12–16 detail its practical outworking in the lives of individual believers and the life of the whole church. Some specific theological topics include principles of spiritual leadership (1:8-15); God's wrath against sinful mankind (1:18-32); principles of divine judgment (2:1-16); the universality of sin (3:9-20); an exposition and defense of justification by faith alone (3:21–4:25); the security of salvation (5:1-11); the transference of Adam's sin (5:12-21); sanctification (chaps. 6–8); sovereign election (chap. 9); God's plan for Israel (chap. 11); spiritual gifts and practical godliness (chap. 12); the believer's responsibility to human government (chap. 13); and principles of Christian liberty (14:1–15:12).

Interpretive Challenges

As the preeminent doctrinal work in the NT, Romans naturally contains a number of difficult passages. Paul's discussion of the perpetuation of Adam's sin (5:12-21) is one of the deepest, most profound theological passages in all of Scripture. The nature of mankind's union with Adam, and how his sin was transferred to the human race has always been the subject of intense debate. Bible students also disagree on whether 7:7-25 describes Paul's experience as a believer or unbeliever, or is a literary device not intended to be autobiographical at all. The closely related doctrines of election (8:28-30) and the sovereignty of God (9:6-29) have confused many believers. Others question whether chaps. 9–11 teach that God has a future plan for the nation of Israel. Some have ignored Paul's teaching on the believer's obedience to human government (13:1-7) in the name of Christian activism, while others have used it to defend slavish obedience to totalitarian regimes.

All of these and more interpretive challenges are addressed in the notes to the respective passages.

Outline

I. Greetings and Introduction (1:1-15)

II. Theme (1:16,17)

III. Condemnation: The Need of God's Righteousness (1:18–3:20)

- A. Unrighteous Gentiles (1:18-32)
- B. Unrighteous Jews (2:1–3:8)
- C. Unrighteous Mankind (3:9-20)

IV. Justification: The Provision of God's Righteousness (3:21–5:21)

- A. The Source of Righteousness (3:21-31)
- B. The Example of Righteousness (4:1-25)
- C. The Blessings of Righteousness (5:1-11)
- D. The Imputation of Righteousness (5:12-21)

V. Sanctification: The Demonstration of God's Righteousness (6:1–8:39)

VI. Restoration: Israel's Reception of God's Righteousness (9:1–11:36)

VII. Application: The Behavior of God's Righteousness (12:1–15:13)

VIII. Conclusion, Greetings, and Benediction (15:14–16:27)

Greeting

1 Paul, a bondservant of Jesus Christ,
[a]called *to be* an apostle, [b]separated to
the gospel of God 2 [c]which He promised
before [d]through His prophets in the Holy
Scriptures, 3 concerning His Son Jesus
Christ our Lord, who [1]was [e]born of the
seed of David according to the flesh, 4 *and*
[f]declared *to be* the Son of God with power
according [g]to the Spirit of holiness, by the
resurrection from the dead. 5 Through
Him [h]we have received grace and apostleship for [i]obedience to the faith among all
nations [j]for His name, 6 among whom you
also are the called of Jesus Christ;

7 To all who are in Rome, beloved of
God, [k]called *to be* saints:

[l]Grace to you and peace from God our
Father and the Lord Jesus Christ.

Desire to Visit Rome

8 First, [m]I thank my God through Jesus

CHAPTER 1

1 [a] 1 Cor. 1:1; 9:1; 15:9; 2 Cor. 1:1; 1 Tim. 1:11 [b] Acts 9:15; 13:2; [Gal. 1:15]
2 [c] Acts 26:6 [d] Gal. 3:8
3 [e] 2 Sam. 7:12; 1 Chr. 17:11; Is. 9:7; Jer. 23:5; Gal. 4:4 [1] *came*
4 [f] Ps. 2:7; Acts 9:20; 13:33; Heb. 1:2 [g] Ps. 16:10; [Heb. 9:14]
5 [h] Eph. 3:8 [i] Acts 6:7; Rom. 16:26
[j] Acts 9:15
7 [k] Acts 9:13; Rom. 8:28; 1 Cor. 1:2, 24 [l] Num. 6:25; 1 Cor. 1:3; 2 Cor. 1:2; Gal. 1:3; Eph. 1:2; Phil. 1:2; Col. 1:2; 1 Thess. 1:1; 2 Thess. 1:2
8 [m] 1 Cor. 1:4; Eph. 1:15; Phil. 1:3; Col. 1:3; 1 Thess. 1:2; 2:13

1:1 Paul. See Introduction: Author and Date. **bondservant.** *Doulos,* the common NT word for servant. Although in Gr. culture it is most often referred to the involuntary, permanent service of a slave, Paul elevates this word by using it in its Heb. sense to describe a servant who willingly commits himself to serve a master he loves and respects (Ex. 21:5,6; Gal. 1:10; Titus 1:1; cf. Gen. 26:24; Num. 12:7; 2 Sam. 7:5; Is. 53:11). **apostle.** The Gr. word means "one who is sent." In the NT, it primarily refers to the 12 men Christ chose to accompany Him (Mark 3:13-19) and Matthaias, whom the other apostles chose to replace Judas (Acts 1:15-26). Christ gave them power to confirm their apostleship with miracles (Matt. 10:1; 2 Cor. 12:12), and authority to speak as His proxies—every NT book was written either by an apostle or under his auspices (cf. John 14:26). Their teaching is the foundation of the church (Eph. 2:20). Christ Himself selected Paul for this position (Acts 9:15; 22:14; 26:16; cf. Gal. 1:1) and trained him to fulfill this ministry (Gal. 1:12,16). **gospel of God.** Used in its verb and noun forms some 60 times in this epistle, the Gr. word for this phrase means "good news" (see Mark 1:1). Rome incorporated it into its emperor worship. The town herald used this word to begin important favorable announcements about the emperor—such as the birth of a son. But Paul's good news is not from the emperor but "of God"; it originated with Him. Its message that God will forgive sins, deliver from sin's power, and give eternal hope (1:16; cf. 1 Cor. 15:1-4) comes not only as a gracious offer, but also as a command to be obeyed (10:16). Paul was consumed with this message (1 Cor. 9:23).

1:2 which He promised before. Paul's Jewish antagonists accused him of preaching a revolutionary new message unrelated to Judaism (Acts 21:28). But the OT is replete with prophecies concerning Christ and the gospel (1 Pet. 1:10-12; cf. Matt. 5:17; Heb. 1:1). **His prophets.** All the writers of the OT. The "Law and the Prophets" constitute all the OT (Acts 24:14). But the law—or the Pentateuch—was written by Moses, whom Scripture also calls a prophet (Deut. 18:15). **Holy Scriptures.** While the rabbinical writings popular in the first century—and often studied more diligently than Scripture itself—may not have taught the gospel of God, the divinely inspired OT certainly did (cf. Luke 24:25,27,32; John 5:39; Acts 3:18; 7:52; 10:43; 13:32; 26:22,23; *see note on Gen. 3:15*). The prophets spoke clearly of a New Covenant (Jer. 31:31-34; Ezek. 36:25-27; cf. Heb. 8:6-13) and of the Messiah whose sacrifice would make it possible (Is. 9:6,7; 53:1-12).

1:3 born. Jesus was conceived in a virgin's womb by the Holy Spirit (Luke 1:35; cf. Is. 7:14), and was delivered normally. This word emphasizes that He is an actual historical figure. Many well known ancient writers, including the Roman historian Tacitus (*Annals* 15.44), the familiar Jewish historian Josephus (*Antiquities,* 2.18.3), and Pliny the Younger (*Letters* 10.96,97) verify Jesus' historicity. **seed of David.** The OT had prophesied that Messiah would be in the lineage of David (2 Sam. 7:12,13; Ps. 89:3,4,19,24; Is. 11:1-5; Jer. 23:5,6). Both Mary, Jesus' mother (Luke 3:23,31), and Joseph, his legal father (Matt. 1:6,16; Luke 1:27), were descendants of David. John makes believing that Christ has come in the flesh a crucial test of orthodoxy (1 John 4:2,3). Because He is fully human—as well as fully God—He can serve as man's substitute (John 1:29; 2 Cor. 5:21) and as a sympathetic High-Priest (Heb. 4:15,16).

1:4 declared. The Gr. word, from which the English word "horizon" comes, means "to distinguish." Just as the horizon serves as a clear demarcation line, dividing earth and sky, the resurrection of Jesus Christ clearly divides Him from the rest of humanity, providing irrefutable evidence that He is the Son of God (*see note on 10:9*). **Son of God.** This title, used nearly 30 times in the gospels, identifies Jesus Christ as the same in essence as God. *See notes on John 1:34,49; 10:36; 11:27; 19:7.* (cf. Heb. 1:5; 2 Sam. 7:14). The resurrection clearly declared that Jesus was deity, the expression of God Himself in human form. While He was eternally the Son in anticipation of His incarnation, it was when He entered the world in incarnation that He was declared to all the world as the Son of God and took on the role of submission to the Father (*See notes on Ps. 2:7; Heb. 1:5,6*). **Spirit of holiness.** In His incarnation, Christ voluntarily submitted Himself to do the will of the Father only through the direction, agency, and power of the Holy Spirit (Matt. 3:16; Luke 4:1; John 3:34; *see note on Acts 1:2*). **resurrection from the dead.** His victory over death was the supreme demonstration and most conclusive evidence that He is God the Son (*see note on 10:9*; cf. Acts 13:29-33; 1 Cor. 15:14-17).

1:5 grace. The unmerited favor which God shows guilty sinners. This is the book's first reference to the most crucial part of the gospel message: salvation is a gift from God wholly separate from any human effort or achievement (3:24,27; 4:1-5; 5:20,21; *see note on Eph. 2:8,9*). **apostleship.** Although the term "apostle" refers to the 12 in a unique way (*see note on 1:1*), in a broader and less official sense it can describe anyone whom God has sent with the message of salvation (cf. Acts 14:14; Rom. 16:7; Heb. 3:1). **obedience to the faith.** True saving faith always produces obedience and submission to the Lordship of Jesus Christ (16:19,26; cf. 10:9,10; cf. Matt. 7:13,14,22-27; James 2:17-20).

1:6 called. *See note on 1:7.* Always in the NT epistles the "call" of God refers to God's effectual call of elect sinners to salvation (cf. 8:28-30), rather than the general call to all men to believe (cf. Matt. 20:16).

1:7 Rome. See Introduction: Background and Setting. **beloved of God, called...saints.** The Gr. text records these as 3 separate privileges: 1) God has set His love on His own (5:5; 8:35; Eph. 1:6; 2:4,5; 1 John 3:1); 2) He has extended to them not only the general, external invitation to believe the gospel (Is. 45:22; 55:6; Ezek. 33:11; Matt. 11:28; John 7:37; Rev. 22:17), but His effectual calling—or His drawing to Himself all those He has chosen for salvation (8:30; 2 Thess. 2:13,14; 2 Tim. 1:9; *see note on John 6:44*); and 3) God has set believers apart from sin unto Himself, so that they are holy ones (1 Cor. 3:16,17; 1 Pet. 2:5,9). **Grace...peace.** Paul's standard greeting (1 Cor. 1:3; 2 Cor. 1:2; Gal. 1:3; Eph. 1:2; Phil. 1:2; Col. 1:2; 1 Thess. 1:1; 2 Thess. 1:2; 1 Tim. 1:2; 2 Tim. 1:2; Titus 1:4; Philem. 3).

1:8 I thank my God. In every letter Paul wrote, he expressed his gratitude for those who would receive it (e.g., 1 Cor. 1:4), except in his letter to the Galatians, whose defection from the true gospel caused

Christ for you all, that [n]your faith is spoken of throughout the whole world. 9 For
[o]God is my witness, [p]whom I serve [2]with
my spirit in the gospel of His Son, that
[q]without ceasing I make mention of you always in my prayers, 10 making request if,
by some means, now at last I may find a
way in the will of God to come to you.
11 For I long to see you, that [r]I may impart
to you some spiritual gift, so that you may
be established— 12 that is, that I may be
encouraged together with you by [s]the mutual faith both of you and me.
13 Now I do not want you to be unaware, brethren, that I often planned to
come to you (but [t]was hindered until
now), that I might have some [u]fruit
among you also, just as among the other
Gentiles. 14 I am a debtor both to Greeks
and to barbarians, both to wise and to unwise. 15 So, as much as is in me, *I am* ready
to preach the gospel to you who are in
Rome also.

The Just Live by Faith

16 For [v]I am not ashamed of the gospel
[3]of Christ, for [w]it is the power of God to
salvation for everyone who believes, [x]for
the Jew first and also for the Greek. 17 For
[y]in it the righteousness of God is revealed

7 [n] Acts 28:22; Rom. 16:19
9 [o] Rom. 9:1 [p] Acts 27:23 [q] 1 Thess. 3:10 [2] Or *in*
11 [r] Rom. 15:29
12 [s] Titus 1:4
13 [t] [1 Thess. 2:18] [u] Phil. 4:17
16 [v] Ps. 40:9, 10 [w] 1 Cor. 1:18, 24 [x] Luke 2:30; Acts 3:26; Rom. 2:9 [3] NU omits *of Christ*
17 [y] Rom. 3:21; 9:30; Phil. 3:9

him to dispense with any opening commendations (Gal. 1:6-12). **your faith.** The genuineness of their salvation. The testimony of the church in Rome was so strong that in A.D. 49 the emperor Claudius expelled all the Jews because of the influence of "Chrestus," which was undoubtedly a reference to Christ (cf. Acts 18:2). **throughout the whole world.** As the center of the Roman Empire and the inhabited world, whatever happened in Rome became known universally.

1:9 serve with my spirit. In the NT, this Gr. word for "serve" always refers to religious service, and is sometimes translated "worship." Paul had seen the shallow, hypocritical religion of the Pharisees and the superstitious hedonism of pagan idolatry. His spiritual service (*see note on 12:1*), however, did not result from abject fear or legal obligation, but was genuine and sincere (cf. Phil. 3:3; 2 Tim. 1:3; 2:22). **in my prayers.** Paul frequently recorded the content of his requests (Eph. 3:14-19; Phil. 1:9-11; Col. 1:9-11; 2 Thess. 1:11,12) and urged his readers to join him in prayer (15:30-32; 1 Thess. 5:17; Eph. 6:18).

1:10 will of God. God's sovereign orchestration of Paul's circumstances (cf. Matt. 6:10; Acts 21:11-14; James 4:13,14).

1:11 spiritual gift. The Gr. word translated "gift" is *charisma*, which means a "gift of grace"—a spiritual enablement whose source is the Spirit of God. Romans uses this same term to describe: 1) Christ Himself (5:15,16); 2) general blessings from God (11:29; cf. 1 Tim. 6:17); and 3) specific spiritual gifts given to members of the body to minister to the whole (12:6-8; cf. 1 Cor. 12:1-31; 1 Pet. 4:10,11). Paul probably intends to encompass all 3.

1:12 mutual. A glimpse of Paul's genuine humility (cf. 1 Pet. 5:3,4).

1:13 fruit. Scripture catalogs 3 kinds of spiritual fruit: 1) spiritual attitudes that characterize a Spirit-led believer (Gal. 5:22,23); 2) righteous actions (6:22; Phil. 4:16,17; Heb. 13:15); and 3) new converts (16:5). In this context, Paul is probably referring to the third one—a desire that was eventually realized during his imprisonment in Rome (Phil. 4:22). **among the other Gentiles.** This implies the church in Rome consisted primarily of non-Jews.

1:14 debtor. He had an obligation to God (cf. 1 Cor. 9:16-17) to fulfill His divine mandate to minister to Gentiles (1:5; Acts 9:15). **Greeks.** People of many different nationalities who had embraced the Gr. language, culture, and education. They were the sophisticated elite of Paul's day. Because of their deep interest in Greek philosophy, they were considered "wise." Because of this prevalence of Greek culture, Paul sometimes used this word to describe all Gentiles (cf. 3:9). **barbarians.** A derisive term coined by the Greeks for all who had not been trained in Gr. language and culture. When someone spoke in another language, it sounded to the Greeks like "bar-bar-bar," or unintelligible chatter. Although in the narrowest sense "barbarian" referred to the uncultured, uneducated masses, it was often used to describe all non-Greeks—the unwise of the world. Paul's point is that God is no respecter of persons—the gospel must reach both the world's elite and its outcasts (cf. John 4:4-42; James 2:1-9).

1:15 gospel. *See note on 1:1.*

1:16,17 These two verses crystallize the thesis of the entire book—the gospel of Jesus Christ—which Paul will unfold and explain in the following chapters.

1:16 I am not ashamed. He had been imprisoned in Philippi (Acts 16:23,24), chased out of Thessalonica (Acts 17:10), smuggled out of Berea (Acts 17:14), laughed at in Athens (Acts 17:32), regarded as a fool in Corinth (1 Cor. 1:18,23), and stoned in Galatia (Acts 14:19), but Paul remained eager to preach the gospel in Rome—the seat of contemporary political power and pagan religion. Neither ridicule, criticism, nor physical persecution could curb his boldness. *See notes on 2 Cor. 4:5-18; 11:23-28; 12:9,10.* **power.** The Eng. word "dynamite" comes from this Gr. word. Although the message may sound foolish to some (1 Cor. 1:18), the gospel is effective because it carries with it the omnipotence of God (cf. Ex. 15:6; Deut. 32:39; Job 9:4; Pss. 33:8,9; 89:13; 106: 8,9; Is. 26:4; 43:13; Jer. 10:12; 27:5; Matt. 28:18; Rom. 9:21). Only God's power is able to overcome man's sinful nature and give him new life (5:6; 8:3; John 1:12; 1 Cor. 1:18,23-25; 2:1-4; 4:20; 1 Pet. 1:23). **salvation.** Used 5 times in Romans (the verb form occurs 8 times), this key word basically means "deliverance" or "rescue." The power of the gospel delivers people from lostness (Matt. 18:11), from the wrath of God (Rom. 5:9), from willful spiritual ignorance (Hos. 4:6; 2 Thess. 1:8), from evil self-indulgence (Luke 14:26), and from the darkness of false religion (Col. 1:13; 1 Pet. 2:9). It rescues them from the ultimate penalty of their sin, i.e., eternal separation from God and eternal punishment (*see note on Rev. 20:6*). **believes.** To trust, rely on, or have faith in. When used of salvation, this word usually occurs in the present tense ("is believing") which stresses that faith is not simply a one-time event, but an ongoing condition. True saving faith is supernatural, a gracious gift of God that He produces in the heart (*see note on Eph. 2:8*) and is the only means by which a person can appropriate true righteousness (cf. 3:22,25; 4:5,13,20; 5:1; *see notes on 4:1-25*). Saving faith consists of 3 elements: 1) mental: the mind understands the gospel and the truth about Christ (10:14-17); 2) emotional: one embraces the truthfulness of those facts with sorrow over sin and joy over God's mercy and grace (6:17; 15:13); and 3) volitional: the sinner submits his will to Christ and trusts in Him alone as the only hope of salvation (*see note on 10:9*). Genuine faith will always produce authentic obedience (*see note on 4:3; cf. John 8:31; 14:23,24*). **Jew first.** God chose Israel to be His witness nation (Ex. 19:6) and gave her distinct privileges (3:2; 9:4,5). Christ's ministry was first to Israel (Matt. 15:24), and it was through Israel that salvation was to come to the world (John 4:22; cf. 13:46). **Greek.** *See note on 1:14.*

1:17 righteousness of God. Better translated, "righteousness from God." A major theme of the book, appearing over 30 times in one form or another, righteousness is the state or condition of perfectly conforming to God's perfect law and holy character. Other terms from the same Gr. root also occur some 30 times and are usual-

from faith to faith; as it is written, [z]*"The
just shall live by faith."*

God's Wrath on Unrighteousness

18 [a]For the wrath of God is revealed
from heaven against all ungodliness and
[b]unrighteousness of men, who [4]suppress
the truth in unrighteousness, 19 because
[c]what may be known of God is [5]manifest
[6]in them, for [d]God has shown *it* to them.
20 For since the creation of the world [e]His
invisible *attributes* are clearly seen, being
understood by the things that are made,
even His eternal power and [7]Godhead, so
that they are without excuse, 21 because,
although they knew God, they did not glorify *Him* as God, nor were thankful, but
[f]became futile in their thoughts, and their
foolish hearts were darkened. 22 [g]Profess-
ing to be wise, they became fools, 23 and
changed the glory of the [h]incorruptible
[i]God into an image made like [8]corruptible

17 [z] Hab. 2:4; Gal. 3:11; Heb. 10:38
18 [a] [Acts 17:30] [b] Rom. 6:13; 2 Thess. 2:10; 2 Pet. 2:13; 1 John 5:17 [4] *hold down*
19 [c] [Acts 14:17; 17:24] [d] [John 1:9] [5] *evident* [6] *among*
20 [e] Job 12:7-9; Ps. 19:1-6; Jer. 5:22 [7] *divine nature, deity*
21 [f] 2 Kin. 17:15; Jer. 2:5; Eph. 4:17
22 [g] Jer. 10:14; [1 Cor. 1:20] 23 [h] 1 Tim. 1:17; 6:15, 16 [i] Deut. 4:16-18; Ps. 106:20; Jer. 2:11; Acts 17:29 [8] *perishable*

ly translated "justified," "justification" or similarly. Only God is inherently righteous (Deut. 32:4; Job 9:2; Pss. 11:7; 116:5; John 17:25; Rom. 3:10; 1 John 2:1; Rev. 16:5), and man falls woefully short of the divine standard of moral perfection (3:23; Matt. 5:48). But the gospel reveals that on the basis of faith—and faith alone—God will impute His righteousness to ungodly sinners (*see notes on 3:21-24; 4:5; 2 Cor. 5:21; Phil. 3:8,9*). **from faith to faith.** This may be a parallel expression to "everyone who believes" (1:16), as if Paul were singling out the faith of each individual believer—from one person's faith to another's faith to another's and so on. Or perhaps Paul's point is that the righteousness from God is completely on the basis of faith from beginning to end. **as it is written.** *See note on Hab. 2:4.* ***The just shall live by faith.*** Paul intends to prove that it has always been God's way to justify sinners by grace on the basis of faith alone. God established Abraham as a pattern of faith (4:22-25; Gal. 3:6,7) and thus calls him the father of all who believe (4:11,16). Elsewhere, Paul uses this same phrase to argue that no one has ever been declared righteous before God except by faith alone (Gal. 3:11) and that true faith will demonstrate itself in action (Phil. 2:12,13). This expression emphasizes that true faith is not a single event, but a way of life—it endures. That endurance is called the perseverance of the saints (cf. Col. 1:22,23; Heb. 3:12-14). One central theme of the story of Job is that no matter what Satan does, saving faith cannot be destroyed. *See notes on 8:31-39.*

1:18-3:20 After introducing the righteousness which comes from God (1:17), a theme he develops at length (3:21-5:21), Paul presents the overwhelming evidence of man's sinfulness, underscoring how desperately he needs this righteousness that only God can provide. He presents God's case against the irreligious, immoral pagan (1:18-32; the Gentiles) the religious, outwardly moral person (2:1-3:8; the Jews); and concludes by showing that all men alike deserve God's judgment (3:9-20).

1:18 wrath of God. This is not an impulsive outburst of anger aimed capriciously at people whom God does not like. It is the settled, determined response of a righteous God against sin (cf. Pss. 2:5,12; 45:7; 75:8; 76:6,7; 78:49-51; 90:7-9; Is. 51:17; Jer. 25:15,16; John 3:36; Rom. 9:22; Eph. 5:6; Col. 3:5,6). **is revealed.** More accurately, "is constantly revealed." The word essentially means "to uncover, make visible, or make known." God reveals His wrath in two ways: 1) indirectly, through the natural consequences of violating His universal moral law, and 2) directly through His personal intervention (the OT record—from the sentence passed on Adam and Eve to the worldwide flood, from the fire and brimstone that leveled Sodom to the Babylonian captivity—clearly displays this kind of intervention). The most graphic revelation of God's holy wrath and hatred against sin was when He poured out divine judgment on His Son on the cross. God has various kinds of wrath: 1) eternal wrath, which is hell; 2) eschatological wrath, which is the final Day of the Lord; 3) cataclysmic wrath like the flood and the destruction of Sodom and Gomorrah; 4) consequential wrath, which is the principle of sowing and reaping; and 5) the wrath of abandonment, which is removing restraint and letting people go to their sins (for examples of this wrath, *see notes on Ps. 81:11,12; Prov. 1:23-31; Hos. 4:17*). Here, it is that fifth form, God's abandoning the wicked continually through history to pursue their sin and its consequences (vv. 24-32). **ungodliness.** This indicates a lack of reverence for, devotion to, and worship of the true God—a defective relationship with Him (cf. Jude 14,15). **unrighteousness.** This refers to the result of ungodliness: a lack of conformity in thought, word, and deed to the character and law of God (*see note on 1:17*). **suppress the truth.** Although the evidence from conscience (1:19; 2:14), creation (1:20), and God's Word is irrefutable, men choose to resist and oppose God's truth by holding fast to their sin (cf. Ps. 14:1; John 3:19,20).

1:19 is manifest in them. God has sovereignly planted evidence of His existence in the very nature of man by reason and moral law (1:20,21,28,32; 2:15).

1:20 invisible *attributes*. This refers specifically to the two mentioned in this verse. **by the things that are made.** The creation delivers a clear, unmistakable message about God's person (cf. Pss. 19:1-8; 94:9; Acts 14:15-17; 17:23-28). **His eternal power.** The Creator, who made all that we see around us and constantly sustains it, must be a being of awesome power. **Godhead.** That is, His divine nature, particularly His faithfulness (Gen. 8:21,22), kindness, and graciousness (Acts 14:17). **they are without excuse.** God holds all men responsible for their refusal to acknowledge what He has shown them of Himself in His creation. Even those who have never had an opportunity to hear the gospel have received a clear witness about the existence and character of God—and have suppressed it. If a person will respond to the revelation he has, even if it is solely natural revelation, God will provide some means for that person to hear the gospel (cf. Acts 8:26-39; 10:1-48; 17:27).

1:21 knew God. Man is conscious of God's existence, power, and divine nature through general revelation (vv. 19,20). **they did not glorify *Him*.** Man's chief end is to glorify God (Lev. 10:3; 1 Chr. 16:24-29; Ps. 148; Rom. 15:5,6), and Scripture constantly demands it (Ps. 29:1,2; 1 Cor. 10:31; Rev. 4:11). To glorify Him is to honor Him, to acknowledge His attributes, and to praise Him for His perfections (cf. Ex. 34:5-7). It is to recognize His glory and extol Him for it. Failing to give Him glory is man's greatest affront to his Creator (Acts 12:22,23). **nor were thankful.** They refused to acknowledge that every good thing they enjoyed came from God (Matt. 5:45; Acts 14:15-17; 1 Tim. 6:17; James 1:17). **futile.** Man's search for meaning and purpose will produce only vain, meaningless conclusions. **hearts were darkened.** When man rejects the truth, the darkness of spiritual falsehood replaces it (cf. John 3:19,20).

1:22 Professing to be wise, they became fools. Man rationalizes his sin and proves his utter foolishness by devising and believing his own philosophies about God, the universe, and himself (cf. Pss. 14:1; 53:1).

1:23 changed the glory...into an image. They substitute the worship of idols for the worship of the true God. Historians report that many ancient cultures did not originally have idols. For example, Persia (Herodotus; *The Histories,* 1:31), Rome (Varro in Augustine; *The City of God,* 4:31), even Greece and Egypt (Lucian; *The Syrian Goddess,* 34) had no idolatry at their founding. The fourth-century A.D. historian Eusebius reported that the oldest civilizations had no idols. The

man—and birds and four-footed animals
and creeping things.
24 [j]Therefore God also gave them up to
uncleanness, in the lusts of their hearts, [k]to
dishonor their bodies [l]among themselves,
25 who exchanged [m]the truth of God [n]for
the lie, and worshiped and served the creature rather than the Creator, who is blessed
forever. Amen.
26 For this reason God gave them up to
[o]vile passions. For even their [9]women exchanged the natural use for what is against
nature. 27 Likewise also the [1]men, leaving
the natural use of the [2]woman, burned in
their lust for one another, [1]men with [1]men
committing what is shameful, and receiving in themselves the penalty of their error
which was due.
28 And even as they did not like to retain
God in *their* knowledge, God gave them
over to a debased mind, to do those things
[p]which are not fitting; 29 being filled with
all unrighteousness, [3]sexual immorality,
wickedness, [4]covetousness, [5]malicious-
ness; full of envy, murder, strife, deceit,
evil-mindedness; *they are* whisperers,
30 backbiters, haters of God, violent,
proud, boasters, inventors of evil things,
disobedient to parents, 31 [6]undiscerning,
untrustworthy, unloving, [7]unforgiving,
unmerciful; 32 who, [q]knowing the righteous judgment of God, that those who
practice such things [r]are deserving of
death, not only do the same but also [s]ap-
prove of those who practice them.

God's Righteous Judgment

2 Therefore you are [a]inexcusable, O
man, whoever you are who judge, [b]for
in whatever you judge another you condemn yourself; for you who judge practice
the same things. 2 But we know that the
judgment of God is according to truth
against those who practice such things.
3 And do you think this, O man, you who
judge those practicing such things, and
doing the same, that you will escape the
judgment of God? 4 Or do you despise [c]the
riches of His goodness, [d]forbearance, and
[e]longsuffering, [f]not knowing that the
goodness of God leads you to repentance?

24 [j]Ps. 81:12; Acts 7:42; Eph. 4:18, 19 [k]1 Cor. 6:18 [l]Lev. 18:22
25 [m]1 Thess. 1:9 [n]Is. 44:20; Jer. 10:14; 13:25; 16:19
26 [o]Lev. 18:22; Eph. 5:12 [9]Lit. *females*
27 [1]Lit. *males* [2]Lit. *female*
28 [p]Eph. 5:4
29 [3]NU omits *sexual immorality* [4]*greed* [5]*malice*
31 [6]*without understanding* [7]NU omits *unforgiving*
32 [q][Rom. 2:2] [r][Rom. 6:21] [s][Ps. 50:18]; Hos. 7:3

CHAPTER 2

1 [a][Rom. 1:20] [b]2 Sam. 12:5-7; [Matt. 7:1-5; Luke 6:37]; John 8:9; Rom. 14:22
4 [c]Rom. 9:23; 11:33; [2 Cor. 8:2; Eph. 1:7, 18; 2:7; Phil. 4:19; Col. 1:27; 2:2; Titus 3:6] [d][Rom. 3:25] [e]Ex. 34:6; [Rom. 9:22; 1 Tim. 1:16]; 1 Pet. 3:20 [f]Is. 30:18; [2 Pet. 3:9, 15]

earliest biblical record of idolatry was among Abram's family in Ur (Josh. 24:2). The first commandment forbids it (Ex. 20:3-5), and the prophets continually ridiculed those who foolishly practiced it (Is. 44:9-17; cf. 2 Kin. 17:13-16). Although the false gods which men worship do not exist, demons often impersonate them (1 Cor. 10:20).

1:24-32 This section describes the downward spiral of the wrath of abandonment (*see note on v. 18*) in the life of man when God abandons him. Paul shows the essence (vv. 24,25), the expression (vv. 26,27), and the extent (vv. 28-32) of man's sinfulness.

1:24 God also gave them up. This is a judicial term in Gr., used for lording over a prisoner to his sentence. When men consistently abandon God, He will abandon them (cf. Judg. 10:13; 2 Chr. 15:2; 24:20; Ps. 81:11,12; Hos. 4:17; Matt. 15:14; Acts 7:38-42; 14:16). He accomplishes this 1) indirectly and immediately, by removing His restraint and allowing their sin to run its inevitable course, and 2) directly and eventually, by specific acts of divine judgment and punishment. **uncleanness.** A general term often used of decaying matter, like the contents of a grave. It speaks here of sexual immorality (2 Cor. 12:21; cf. Gal. 5:19-23; Eph. 5:3; 1 Thess. 4:7), which begins in the heart and moves to the shame of the body.

1:25 the lie. A denial of God's existence and His right to be obeyed and glorified (vv. 19-21; Is. 44:20; Jer. 13:25; cf. John 8:44).

1:26 God gave them up. *See notes on vv. 18,24.* **vile passions.** Identified in vv. 26,27 as homosexuality, a sin roundly condemned in Scripture (Gen. 19; Lev. 18:22; 1 Cor. 6:9-11; cf. Gal. 5:19-21; Eph. 5:3-5; 1 Tim. 1:9,10; Jude 7). **women.** Rather than the normal Gr. term for women, this is a general word for female. Paul mentions women first to show the extent of debauchery under the wrath of abandonment, because in most cultures women are the last to be affected by moral collapse.

1:27 receiving in themselves the penalty. Here the law of sowing and reaping (Gal. 6:7,8) takes effect, as Paul refers to the self-destructive nature of this sin, of which AIDS is one frightening evidence.

1:28 God gave them over. *See notes on 1:18,24.* **debased.** This translates a Gr. word that means "not passing the test." It was often used to describe useless, worthless metals, discarded because they contained too much impurity. God has tested man's minds and found them worthless and useless (cf. Jer. 6:30).

1:32 knowing. Not ignorance, but blatant rebellion (*see note on 2:15*).

2:1-16 Having demonstrated the sinfulness of the immoral pagan (1:18-32), Paul presents his case against the religious moralist—Jew or Gentile—by cataloging 6 principles that govern God's judgment: 1) knowledge (v. 1); 2) truth (vv. 2,3); 3) guilt (vv. 4,5); 4) deeds (vv. 6-10); 5) impartiality (vv. 11-15); and 6) motive (v. 16).

2:1 inexcusable...you...who judge. Both Jews (Paul's primary audience here; cf. v. 17) and moral Gentiles who think they are exempt from God's judgment because they have not indulged in the immoral excesses described in chap. 1, are tragically mistaken. They have more knowledge than the immoral pagan (3:2; 9:4) and thus a greater accountability (cf. Heb. 10:26-29; James 3:1). **condemn yourself.** If someone has sufficient knowledge to judge others, he condemns himself, because he shows he has the knowledge to evaluate his own condition. **practice the same things.** In their condemnation of others they have excused and overlooked their own sins. Self-righteousness exists because of two deadly errors: 1) minimizing God's moral standard usually by emphasizing externals; and 2) underestimating the depth of one's own sinfulness (cf. Matt. 5:20-22,27,28; 7:1-3; 15:1-3; Luke 18:21).

2:2 according to truth. The meaning is "right." Whatever God does is by nature right (cf. 3:4; 9:14; Pss. 9:4,8; 96:13; 145:17; Is. 45:19).

2:3 *See note on v. 1.*

2:4 despise. Lit. "to think down on," thus to underestimate someone's or something's value, and even to treat with contempt. **goodness.** This refers to "common grace," the benefits God bestows on all men (cf. Matt. 5:45; Acts 14:15-17). **forbearance.** This word, which means "to hold back," was sometimes used of a truce between warring parties. Rather than destroying every person the moment he or she sins, God graciously holds back His judgment (cf. 3:25). He saves sinners in a physical and temporal way from what they deserve (*see note on 1 Tim. 4:10*), to show them His saving character, that they might come to Him and receive salvation that is spiritual and eternal. **longsuffering.** This word indicates the duration for which God dem-

5 But in accordance with your hardness
and your [1]impenitent heart [g]you are [2]trea-
suring up for yourself wrath in the day of
wrath and revelation of the righteous judgment of God, 6 who [h]*"will render to each
one according to his deeds"*: 7 eternal life
to those who by patient continuance in
doing good seek for glory, honor, and immortality; 8 but to those who are self-seeking and [i]do not obey the truth, but obey
unrighteousness—indignation and wrath,
9 tribulation and anguish, on every soul of
man who does evil, of the Jew [j]first and
also of the [3]Greek; 10 [k]but glory, honor, and
peace to everyone who works what is
good, to the Jew first and also to the Greek.
11 For [l]there is no partiality with God.
12 For as many as have sinned without
law will also perish without law, and as
many as have sinned in the law will be
judged by the law 13 (for [m]not the hearers
of the law *are* just in the sight of God, but
the doers of the law will be justified; 14 for
when Gentiles, who do not have the law,
by nature do the things in the law, these,
although not having the law, are a law to
themselves, 15 who show the [n]work of the
law written in their hearts, their [o]con-
science also bearing witness, and between
themselves *their* thoughts accusing or else
excusing *them*) 16 [p]in the day when God
will judge the secrets of men [q]by Jesus
Christ, [r]according to my gospel.

The Jews Guilty as the Gentiles

17 [4]Indeed [s]you are called a Jew, and

5 [g][Deut. 32:34]; Prov. 1:18; James 5:3 [1]*unrepentant* [2]*storing*
6 [h][Job 34:11]; Ps. 62:12; Prov. 24:12; Jer. 17:10; [2 Cor. 5:10; Rev. 20:12, 13]
8 [i]Job 24:13; [2 Thess. 1:8]
9 [j]Amos 3:2; Luke 12:47; Acts 3:26; Rom. 1:16; 1 Pet. 4:17 [3]*Gentile*
10 [k]Rom. 2:7; Heb. 2:7; [1 Pet. 1:7]
11 [l]Deut. 10:17; [Job 34:19]; Acts 10:34; [Eph. 6:9]
13 [m]Matt. 7:21, 22; John 13:17; [James 1:22, 25; 1 John 3:7]
15 [n]1 Cor. 5:1 [o]Acts 24:25
16 [p]Eccl. 12:14; [Matt. 25:31]; Rev. 20:12 [q]John 5:22; Acts 10:42; 17:31; Rom. 3:6; 14:10 [r]1 Tim. 1:11
17 [s][Matt. 3:9]; John 8:33 [4]NU *But if*

onstrates His goodness and forbearance—for long periods of time (cf. 2 Pet. 2:5). Together these 3 words speak of God's common grace—the way He demonstrates His grace to all mankind (cf. Job 12:10; Pss. 119:68; 145:9). **repentance.** The act of turning from sin to Christ for forgiveness and salvation. *See notes on 2 Cor. 7:9-11.*

2:5 hardness. The Eng. word "sclerosis" (as in arteriosclerosis, a hardening of the arteries) comes from this Gr. word. But here the danger is not physical, but spiritual hardness (Ezek. 36:26; Matt. 19:8; Mark 3:5; 6:52; 8:17; John 12:40; Heb. 3:8,15; 4:7). **impenitent heart.** A refusal to repent (cf. v. 4) and accept God's pardon of sin through Jesus Christ. **treasuring up...wrath.** To reject God's offer of forgiveness and cling to one's sin is to accumulate more of God's wrath and earn a severer judgment (*see notes on Heb. 10:26-30; Rev. 20:12*). **day of wrath and...judgment.** Refers to the final judgment of wicked men that comes at the Great White Throne at the end of the Millennium (*see notes on Rev. 20:11-15*).

2:6-10 *See notes on 2:1-16.* Although Scripture everywhere teaches that salvation is not on the basis of works (*see notes on 4:1-4; Eph. 2:8,9*), it consistently teaches that God's judgment is always on the basis of a man's deeds (Is. 3:10,11; Jer. 17:10; John 5:28,29; 1 Cor. 3:8; 2 Cor. 5:10; Gal. 6:7-9; cf. Rom. 14:12). Paul describes the deeds of two distinct groups: the redeemed (vv. 7,10) and the unredeemed (vv. 8,9). The deeds of the redeemed are not the basis of their salvation but the evidence of it. They are not perfect and are prone to sin, but there is undeniable evidence of righteousness in their lives (*see notes on James 2:14-20,26*).

2:7 eternal life. Not simply in duration, because even unbelievers will live forever (2 Thess. 1:9; Rev. 14:9-11), but also in quality (*see note on John 17:3*). Eternal life is a kind of life, the holy life of the eternal God given to believers.

2:8 self-seeking. This word may have originally been used to describe a hireling or mercenary; someone who does what he does for money regardless of how his actions affect others. **wrath.** *See note on 1:18.*

2:9 the Jew first. Just as the Jews were given the first opportunity to hear and respond to the gospel (1:16), they will be first to receive God's judgment if they refuse (cf. Amos 3:2). Israel will receive severer punishment because she was given greater light and blessing (see 9:3,4).

2:11 partiality. Lit. "to receive a face," that is, to give consideration to someone simply because of his position, wealth, influence, popularity, or appearance. Because it is God's nature to be just, it is impossible for Him to be anything but impartial (Acts 10:34; Gal. 2:6; Eph. 6:7,8; Col. 3:25; 1 Pet. 1:17).

2:12 sinned without law. The Gentiles who never had the opportunity to know God's moral law (Ex. 20:1ff.) will be judged on their disobedience in relationship to their limited knowledge (*see notes on 1:19,20*). **judged by the law.** The Jews and many Gentiles who had access to God's moral law will be accountable for their greater knowledge (cf. Matt. 11:20-23; Heb. 6:4-6; 10:26-31).

2:13 will be justified. *See note on 3:24;* cf. James 2:20-26.

2:14 by nature do...the law. Without knowing the written law of God, people in pagan society generally value and attempt to practice its most basic tenets. This is normal for cultures instinctively (*see note on v. 15*) to value justice, honesty, compassion, and goodness toward others, reflecting the divine law written in the heart. **law to themselves.** Their practice of some good deeds and their aversion to some evil ones demonstrate an innate knowledge of God's law—a knowledge that will actually witness against them on the day of judgment.

2:15 work of the law. Probably best understood as "the same works the Mosaic law prescribes." **conscience.** Lit. "with knowledge." That instinctive sense of right and wrong that produces guilt when violated. In addition to an innate awareness of God's law, men have a warning system that activates when they choose to ignore or disobey that law. Paul urges believers not to violate their own consciences or cause others to (13:5; 1 Cor. 8:7,12; 10:25,29; 2 Cor. 5:11; cf. 9:1; Acts 23:1; 24:16), because repeatedly ignoring the conscience's warnings desensitizes it and eventually silences it (1 Tim. 4:2). See 2 Cor. 1:12; 4:2.

2:16 the day. *See note on 2:5.* **secrets.** This primarily refers to the motives that lie behind men's actions (1 Chr. 28:9; Ps. 139:1-3; Jer. 17:10; Matt. 6:4,6,18; cf. Luke 8:17; Heb. 4:12). **by Jesus Christ.** *See note on John 5:23.* **my gospel.** Not his own personal message, but the divinely-revealed message of Jesus Christ (*see note on 1:1*), which is "good news" in light of the bad news of judgment.

2:17-29 Having shown that outwardly moral people—Jew and Gentiles alike—will stand condemned by God's judgment, Paul turns his argument exclusively to the Jews, God's covenant people. Neither their heritage (v. 17a), their knowledge (vv. 17b-24), nor their ceremonies, specifically circumcision (vv. 25-29), will protect them from God's righteous judgment.

2:17 Jew. Previously called Hebrews and Israelites, by the first century "Jew" had become the most common name for the descendants of Abraham through Isaac. "Jew" comes from "Judah," (meaning "praise"), one of the 12 tribes and the designation for the southern half of Solomon's kingdom after his death. From the time of the Babylonian captivity, the whole race bore this title. Their great heritage, however, (cf. Gen. 12:3) became a source of pride and complacency

[t]rest[5] on the law, [u]and make your boast in
God, 18 and [v]know *His* will, and [w]approve
the things that are excellent, being instructed out of the law, 19 and [x]are confident that
you yourself are a guide to the blind, a
light to those who are in darkness, 20 an instructor of the foolish, a teacher of babes,
[y]having the form of knowledge and truth
in the law. 21 [z]You, therefore, who teach
another, do you not teach yourself? You
who preach that a man should not steal, do
you steal? 22 You who say, "Do not commit
adultery," do you commit adultery? You
who abhor idols, [a]do you rob temples?
23 You who [b]make your boast in the law,
do you dishonor God through breaking
the law? 24 For [c]*"the name of God is* [d]*blasphemed among the Gentiles because of
you,"* as it is written.

Circumcision of No Avail

25 [e]For circumcision is indeed profitable
if you keep the law; but if you are a breaker of the law, your circumcision has become
uncircumcision. 26 Therefore, [f]if an uncircumcised man keeps the righteous requirements of the law, will not his uncircumcision be counted as circumcision? 27 And
will not the physically uncircumcised, if he
fulfills the law, [g]judge you who, *even* with
your [6]written *code* and circumcision, *are* a
transgressor of the law? 28 For [h]he is not a
Jew who *is one* outwardly, nor *is* circumcision that which *is* outward in the flesh;
29 but *he is* a Jew [i]who *is one* inwardly; and
[j]circumcision *is that* of the heart, [k]in the
Spirit, not in the letter; [l]whose [7]praise *is* not
from men but from God.

God's Judgment Defended

3 What advantage then has the Jew, or
what *is* the profit of circumcision?
2 Much in every way! Chiefly because [a]to
them were committed the [1]oracles of God.
3 For what if [b]some did not believe? [c]Will
their unbelief make the faithfulness of God
without effect? 4 [d]Certainly not! Indeed, let
[e]God be [2]true but [f]every man a liar. As it is
written:

> [g]*"That You may be justified in Your*
> *words,*
> *And may overcome when You are*
> *judged."*

5 But if our unrighteousness demonstrates the righteousness of God, what
shall we say? *Is* God unjust who inflicts

17 [t]Mic. 3:11; John 5:45; Rom. 2:23; 9:4 [u]Is. 48:1, 2 [5]*rely*
18 [v]Deut. 4:8 [w]Phil. 1:10
19 [x]Matt. 15:14; John 9:34
20 [y][2 Tim. 3:5]
21 [z]Ps. 50:16; Matt. 23:3
22 [a]Mal. 3:8
23 [b]Mic. 3:11; John 5:45; Rom. 2:17; 9:4
24 [c]Ezek. 16:27 [d]2 Sam. 12:14; Is. 52:5; Ezek. 36:22
25 [e]Gen. 17:10-14; [Gal. 5:3]
26 [f][Acts 10:34]
27 [g]Matt. 12:41
[6]Lit. *letter*
28 [h][Matt. 3:9]; John 8:39; Rom. 2:17; 9:6; [Gal. 6:15]
29 [i][1 Pet. 3:4] [j]Phil. 3:3; Col. 2:11 [k]Deut. 30:6; Rom. 2:27; 7:6; [2 Cor. 3:6] [l]John 5:44; 12:43; [1 Cor. 4:5; 2 Cor. 10:18]; 1 Thess. 2:4 [7]A play on words—*Jew* is literally *praise.*

CHAPTER 3

2 [a]Deut. 4:5-8; Ps. 147:19; Rom. 9:4 [1]*sayings,* Scriptures
3 [b]Rom. 10:16; Heb. 4:2 [c]Num. 23:19; [2 Tim. 2:13] 4 [d]Job 40:8 [e][John 3:33] [f]Ps. 62:9 [g]Ps. 51:4 [2]Found true

(cf. Jon. 4:2; Mic. 3:11,12; Matt. 3:7-9; John 8:31-34,40-59), which led to judgment instead of "praise."

2:19,20 the blind…babes. Because they possessed the law, the Jews were confident that they were spiritually superior teachers: guides to blind pagans (cf. Matt. 23:24-28), light (cf. Is. 42:6), wise in God's ways, and able to teach babes (probably a reference to Gentile proselytes to Judaism).

2:21,23 A series of questions designed to contrast most Jews' practice with what they knew and taught (cf. Ps. 50:16-20; Matt. 23:3,4; James 3:1).

2:22 do you rob temples? May refer to fraudulently skimming funds from money given to the temple or withholding part of their temple tax or offerings (cf. Mal. 3:8-10). More likely, however, it refers to the common practice—in direct violation of God's command (Deut. 7:25)—of looting pagan temples and selling the idols and vessels for personal profit (cf. Acts 19:37) under the pretext of religion.

2:24 it is written. Quoted from Is. 52:5.

2:25 circumcision. *See note on Gen. 17:11.* **profitable.** As an act of obedience and a reminder of their covenant relationship to God (*see notes on Gen. 17:10-14*). **uncircumcision.** A Jew who continually transgressed God's law had no more of a saving relationship to God than an uncircumcised Gentile. The outward symbol was nothing without the inner reality.

2:26 counted as circumcision. God will regard the believing Gentile as favorably as a circumcised, believing Jew.

2:27 A Gentile's humble obedience to the law should serve as a stern rebuke to a Jew who, in spite of his great advantages, lives in disobedience.

2:28 outwardly. This refers to physical descendants of Abraham who have been properly circumcised (cf. 9:6; Matt. 3:9).

2:29 *he is* a Jew. A true child of God; the true spiritual seed of Abraham. (See 4:16; cf. Gal. 3:29). **circumcision *is that* of the heart.** The outward rite is of value only when it reflects the inner reality of a heart separated from sin unto God. Cf. Deut. 10:16; 30:6. **Spirit…letter.** Salvation results from the work of God's Spirit in the heart, not mere external efforts to conform to his law.

3:2 oracles. This Gr. word is *logion,* a diminutive form of the common NT word *logos,* which is normally translated "word." These are important sayings or messages, especially supernatural ones. Here Paul uses the word to encompass the entire OT—the Jews received the very words of the true God (Deut. 4:1,2; 6:1,2; cf. Mark 12:24; Luke 16:29; John 5:39). The Jews had a great advantage in having the OT, because it contained the truth about salvation (2 Tim. 3:15) and about the gospel in its basic form (Gal. 3:8). When Paul said "preach the Word" (2 Tim. 4:2), he meant the "oracles of God" (1 Pet. 4:11) recorded in Scripture.

3:3,4 Paul anticipated that Jewish readers would disagree with his statements that God has not guaranteed to fulfill His promises to every physical descendant of Abraham. They would argue that such teaching nullifies all the promises God made to the Jews in the OT. But his answer reflects both the explicit and implicit teaching of the OT; before any Jew, regardless of the purity of his lineage, can inherit the promises, he must come to repentance and faith (cf. 9:6,7; Is. 55:6,7).

3:3 the faithfulness of God. God will fulfill all the promises He made to the nation, even if individual Jews are not able to receive them because of their unbelief.

3:4 every man a liar. If all mankind were to agree that God had been unfaithful to His promises, it would only prove that all are liars and God is true. Cf. Titus 1:1. **it is written.** This is quoted from Ps. 51:4.

3:5-8 Paul anticipates and answers the objection that his teaching actually impugned the very holiness and purity of God's character (*see note on 3:3,4*).

3:5 demonstrates the righteousness of God. *See note on 1:17.* By contrast, like a jeweler who displays a diamond on black velvet to

wrath? [h](I speak as a man.) 6 Certainly not!
For then [i]how will God judge the world?
7 For if the truth of God has increased
through my lie to His glory, why am I also
still judged as a sinner? 8 And *why* not *say,*
[j]"Let us do evil that good may come"?—as
we are slanderously reported and as some
affirm that we say. Their [3]condemnation is
just.

All Have Sinned

9 What then? Are we better *than they?*
Not at all. For we have previously charged
both Jews and Greeks that [k]they are all
under sin.
10 As it is written:

[l]"There is none righteous, no, not
one;
11 *There is none who understands;*
There is none who seeks after God.
12 *They have all turned aside;*
They have together become
unprofitable;
There is none who does good, no,
not one."
13 *"Their[m] throat is an open [4]tomb;*
With their tongues they have
practiced deceit";
[n]"The poison of asps is under their
lips";
14 *"Whose[o] mouth is full of cursing*
and bitterness."
15 *"Their[p] feet are swift to shed blood;*
16 *Destruction and misery are in their*
ways;
17 *And the way of peace they have*
not known."
18 *"There[q] is no fear of God before*
their eyes."

19 Now we know that whatever [r]the law
says, it says to those who are under the
law, that [s]every mouth may be stopped,
and all the world may become [5]guilty before God. 20 Therefore [t]by the deeds of the
law no flesh will be justified in His sight,
for by the law *is* the knowledge of sin.

5 [h] Rom. 6:19; 1 Cor. 9:8; 15:32; Gal. 3:15
6 [i] [Gen. 18:25]
8 [j] Rom. 5:20 [3] Lit. *judgment*
9 [k] Rom. 3:19, 23; 11:32; Gal. 3:22
10 [l] Ps. 14:1-3; 53:1-3; Eccl. 7:20
13 [m] Ps. 5:9 [n] Ps. 140:3 [4] *grave*
14 [o] Ps. 10:7
15 [p] Prov. 1:16; Is. 59:7, 8
18 [q] Ps. 36:1
19 [r] John 10:34 [s] Job 5:16; Ps. 107:42 [5] *accountable*
20 [t] Ps. 143:2; [Acts 13:39; Gal. 2:16]

make the stone appear even more beautiful. **(I speak as a man).** He is simply paraphrasing the weak, unbiblical logic of his opponents—the product of their natural, unregenerate minds.

3:6 judge. A major theme of Scripture (Gen. 18:25; Pss. 50:6; 58:11; 94:2), here it probably refers to the great future day of judgment (*see note on 2:5*). Paul's point is that if God condoned sin, He would have no equitable, righteous basis for judgment.

3:8 slanderously reported. Tragically, the apostle's gospel message of salvation by grace through faith alone had been perverted by his opponents who argued it provided not only a license to sin, but outright encouragement to do so (5:20; 6:1,2).

3:9-20 Paul concludes his indictment of mankind with this summary: Jew and Gentile alike stand guilty before God (*see note on 1:18–3:20*).

3:9 Are we better? "We" probably refers to the Christians in Rome who will receive this letter. Christians do not have an intrinsically superior nature to all those Paul has shown to stand under God's condemnation. **Greeks.** *See note on 1:14.* **under sin.** Completely enslaved and dominated by sin.

3:10-17 Paul strings together a series of OT quotations that indict the character (vv. 10-12), conversation (vv. 13,14), and conduct (vv. 15-17) of all men. Nine times he uses words such as "none" and "all" to show the universality of human sin and rebellion.

3:10-12 This is quoted from Pss. 14:1-3; 53:1-3.

3:10 As it is written. The common introduction to OT quotations (cf. 1:17; 2:24; 3:4; Matt. 4:4,6,7,10). The tense of the Gr. verb stresses continuity and permanence, and implies its divine authority. ***none righteous.*** Man is universally evil (cf. Ps. 14:1; *see notes on 1:17*).

3:11 *none...understands.* Man is unable to comprehend the truth of God or grasp His standard of righteousness (*see Pss. 14:2; 53:3*; cf. 1 Cor. 2:14). Sadly, his spiritual ignorance does not result from a lack of opportunity (1:19,20; 2:15), but is an expression of his depravity and rebellion (Eph. 4:18). ***none...seeks.*** See Ps. 14:2. This verse clearly implies that the world's false religions are fallen man's attempts to escape the true God—not to seek Him. Man's natural tendency is to seek his own interests (cf. Phil. 2:21), but his only hope is for God to seek him (John 6:37,44). It is only as a result of God's work in the heart that anyone seeks Him (Ps. 16:8; Matt. 6:33).

3:12 *turned aside.* See Ps. 14:3. This word basically means "to lean in the wrong direction." It was used to describe a soldier's running the wrong way, or deserting. All men are inclined to leave God's way and pursue their own (cf. Is. 53:6). ***none who does good.*** *See note on v. 10.*

3:13 *open tomb.* See Ps. 5:9. Tombs were sealed not only to show respect for the deceased, but to hide the sight and stench of the body's decay. As an unsealed tomb allows those who pass to see and smell what is inside, the unregenerate man's open throat—that is, the foul words that come from it—reveal the decay of his heart (cf. Prov. 10:31,32; 15:2,28; Jer. 17:9; Matt. 12:34,35; 15:18; James 3:1-12). ***asps.*** See Ps. 140:3; cf. Matt. 3:7; 12:34.

3:14 *cursing.* This is quoted from Ps. 10:7. It refers to wanting the worst for someone and publicly expressing that desire in caustic, derisive language. ***bitterness.*** The open, public expression of emotional hostility against one's enemy (cf. Ps. 64:3,4).

3:15-17 This is quoted from Is. 59:7,8.

3:16 *Destruction and misery.* Man damages and destroys everything he touches, leaving a trail of pain and suffering in his wake.

3:17 *way of peace.* Not the lack of an inner sense of peace, but man's tendency toward strife and conflict, whether between individuals or nations (cf. Jer. 6:14).

3:18 *fear of God.* See Ps. 36:1. Man's true spiritual condition is nowhere more clearly seen than in the absence of a proper submission to and reverence for God. Biblical fear for God consists of : 1) awe of His greatness and glory, and 2) dread of the results of violating that holy nature (*see note on Prov. 1:7*; cf. Prov. 9:10; 16:6; Acts 5:1-11; 1 Cor. 11:30).

3:19 those...under the law. Every unredeemed human being. Jews received the written law through Moses (3:2), and Gentiles have the works of the law written on their hearts (2:15), so that both groups are accountable to God. **every mouth...stopped...guilty.** There is no defense against the guilty verdict God pronounces on the entire human race.

3:20 deeds of the law. Doing perfectly what God's moral law requires is impossible, so that every person is cursed by that inability (*see notes on Gal. 3:10,13*). **justified.** *See note on 3:24.* **by the law *is* the knowledge of sin.** The law makes sin known, but can't save. *See note on 7:7.*

God's Righteousness Through Faith

21 But now [u]the righteousness of God
apart from the law is revealed, [v]being witnessed by the Law [w]and the Prophets,
22 even the righteousness of God, through
faith in Jesus Christ, to all [6]and on all who
believe. For [x]there is no difference; 23 for
[y]all have sinned and fall short of the glory
of God, 24 being justified [7]freely [z]by His
grace [a]through the redemption that is in
Christ Jesus, 25 whom God set forth [b]*as* a
[8]propitiation [c]by His blood, through faith,
to demonstrate His righteousness, because
in His forbearance God had passed over
[d]the sins that were previously committed,
26 to demonstrate at the present time His
righteousness, that He might be just and
the justifier of the one who has faith in
Jesus.

Boasting Excluded

27 [e]Where *is* boasting then? It is excluded. By what law? Of works? No, but by the
law of faith. 28 Therefore we conclude
[f]that a man is [9]justified by faith apart from
the deeds of the law. 29 Or *is He* the God of
the Jews only? *Is He* not also the God of
the Gentiles? Yes, of the Gentiles also,
30 since [g]*there is* one God who will justify
the circumcised by faith and the uncircumcised through faith. 31 Do we then
make void the law through faith? Certainly not! On the contrary, we establish the
law.

21 [u]Acts 15:11 [v]John 5:46 [w]1 Pet. 1:10
22 [x]Rom. 10:12; [Gal. 3:28; Col. 3:11] [6]NU omits *and on all*
23 [y]Gal. 3:22
24 [z]Rom. 4:4, 16; [Eph. 2:8; Titus 3:5, 7] [a][Matt. 20:28; Eph. 1:7; Col. 1:14; 1 Tim. 2:6; Heb. 9:12, 15; 1 Pet. 1:18, 19] [7]*without any cost*
25 [b]Lev. 16:15 [c]Col. 1:20 [d]Acts 14:16; 17:30; [Rom. 2:4] [8]*mercy seat*
27 [e]Rom. 2:17, 23; [1 Cor. 1:29]; Eph. 2:9
28 [f]Gal. 2:16 [9]*declared righteous*
30 [g]Rom. 10:12; [Gal. 3:8, 20]

3:21–5:21 Having conclusively proved the universal sinfulness of man and his need for righteousness (1:18–3:20), Paul develops the theme he introduced in 1:17, i.e., God has graciously provided a righteousness that comes from Him on the basis of faith alone (3:21–5:21).

3:21 But now. Not a reference to time, but a change in the flow of the apostle's argument. Having shown the impossibility of gaining righteousness by human effort, he turns to explain the righteousness that God Himself has provided. **righteousness.** *See note on 1:17.* This righteousness is unique: 1) God is its source (Is. 45:8); 2) it fulfills both the penalty and precept of God's law. Christ's death as a substitute pays the penalty exacted on those who failed to keep God's law, and His perfect obedience to every requirement of God's law fulfills God's demand for comprehensive righteousness (2 Cor. 5:21; 1 Pet. 2:24; cf. Heb. 9:28); and 3) because God's righteousness is eternal (Ps. 119:142; Is. 51:8; Dan. 9:24), the one who receives it from Him enjoys it forever. **apart from the law.** Entirely apart from obedience to any law (4:15; Gal. 2:16; 3:10,11; 5:1,2,6; Eph. 2:8,9; cf. Phil. 3:9; 2 Tim. 1:9; Titus 3:5). **witnessed by the Law and the Prophets.** *See note on 1:2.*

3:22 through faith...all...who believe. *See note on 1:16.*

3:22,23 there is no difference...glory of God. A parenthetical comment explaining that God can bestow His righteousness on all who believe, Jew or Gentile, because all men—without distinction—fail miserably to live up to the divine standard.

3:23 all have sinned. Paul has already made this case (1:18–3:20).

3:24 justified. This verb, and related words from the same Gr. root (e.g., justification), occur some 30 times in Romans and are concentrated in 2:13–5:1. This legal or forensic term comes from the Gr. word for "righteous" and means "to declare righteous." This verdict includes: pardon from the guilt and penalty of sin, and the imputation of Christ's righteousness to the believer's account, which provides for the positive righteousness man needs to be accepted by God. God declares a sinner righteous solely on the basis of the merits of Christ's righteousness. God imputed a believer's sin to Christ's account in His sacrificial death (Is. 53:4,5; 1 Pet. 2:24), and He imputes Christ's perfect obedience to God's law to Christians (cf. 5:19; 1 Cor. 1:30; *see notes on 2 Cor. 5:21; Phil. 3:9*). The sinner receives this gift of God's grace by faith alone (3:22,25; *see notes on 4:1-25*). Sanctification, the work of God by which He makes righteous those whom He has already justified, is distinct from justification but without exception, always follows it (8:30). **freely by His grace.** Justification is a gracious gift God extends to the repentant, believing sinner, wholly apart from human merit or work (*see note on 1:5*). **redemption.** The imagery behind this Gr. word comes from the ancient slave market. It meant paying the necessary ransom to obtain the prisoner or slave's release. The only adequate payment to redeem sinners from sin's slavery and its deserved punishment was "in Christ Jesus" (1 Tim. 2:6; 1 Pet. 1:18,19), and was paid to God to satisfy His justice.

3:25 whom God set forth. This great sacrifice was not accomplished in secret, but God publicly displayed His Son on Calvary for all to see. **propitiation.** Crucial to the significance of Christ's sacrifice, this word carries the idea of appeasement or satisfaction—in this case Christ's violent death satisfied the offended holiness and wrath of God against those for whom Christ died (Is. 53:11; Col. 2:11-14). The Heb. equivalent of this word was used to describe the mercy seat—the cover to the ark of the covenant—where the High-Priest sprinkled the blood of the slaughtered animal on the Day of Atonement to make atonement for the sins of the people. In pagan religions, it is the worshiper not the god who is responsible to appease the wrath of the offended deity. But in reality, man is incapable of satisfying God's justice apart from Christ, except by spending eternity in hell. Cf. 1 John 2:2. **through faith.** *See note on 1:16.* **forbearance.** *See note on 2:4.* **passed over the sins.** This means neither indifference nor remission. God's justice demands that every sin and sinner be punished. God would have been just, when Adam and Eve sinned, to destroy them, and with them, the entire human race. But in His goodness and forbearance (see 2:4), He withheld His judgment for a certain period of time (cf. Ps. 78:38,39; Acts 17:30,31; 2 Pet. 3:9).

3:26 to demonstrate...His righteousness. Through the incarnation, sinless life, and substitutionary death of Christ. **just and the justifier.** The wisdom of God's plan allowed Him to punish Jesus in the place of sinners and thereby justify those who are guilty without compromising His justice.

3:27 Where *is* boasting then? Cf. 4:1,2; 1 Cor. 1:26-29.

3:28 justified by faith. *See note on v. 24.* Although the word "alone" does not appear in the Gr. text, that is Paul's clear meaning (cf. 4:3-5; *see note on James 2:24*). **deeds of the law.** *See note on v. 20.*

3:29 God of the Gentiles. There is only one true God (cf. 1 Cor. 8:5,6).

3:31 Knowing he would be accused of antinomianism (being against the law) for arguing that a man was justified apart from keeping the law, Paul introduced here the defense he later developed in chaps. 6,7. **through faith...we establish the law.** Salvation by grace through faith does not denigrate the law, but underscores its true importance: 1) by providing a payment for the penalty of death, which the law required for failing to keep it; 2) by fulfilling the law's original purpose, which is to serve as a tutor to show mankind's utter inability to obey God's righteous demands and to drive people to Christ (Gal. 3:24); and 3) by giving believers the capacity to obey it (8:3,4).

Abraham Justified by Faith

4 What then shall we say that [a]Abraham
our [b]father[1] has found according to the
flesh? 2 For if Abraham was [c]justified by
works, he has *something* to boast about, but
not before God. 3 For what does the Scripture say? [d]*"Abraham believed God, and it
was [2] accounted to him for righteousness."*
4 Now [e]to him who works, the wages are
not counted [3]as grace but [3]as debt.

David Celebrates the Same Truth

5 But to him who [f]does not work but believes on Him who justifies [g]the ungodly,
his faith is accounted for righteousness,
6 just as David also [h]describes the blessedness of the man to whom God imputes
righteousness apart from works:

7 *"Blessed[i] are those whose lawless*
deeds are forgiven,
And whose sins are covered;
8 *Blessed is the man to whom the*
LORD shall not impute sin."

Abraham Justified Before Circumcision

9 *Does* this blessedness then *come* upon
the circumcised *only,* or upon the uncircumcised also? For we say that faith was
accounted to Abraham for righteousness.
10 How then was it accounted? While he
was circumcised, or uncircumcised? Not
while circumcised, but while uncircumcised. 11 And [j]he received the sign of circumcision, a seal of the righteousness of
the faith which *he had while still* uncircumcised, that [k]he might be the father of all
those who believe, though they are uncircumcised, that righteousness might be imputed to them also, 12 and the father of circumcision to those who not only *are* of the
circumcision, but who also walk in the
steps of the faith which our father [l]Abra-
ham *had while still* uncircumcised.

The Promise Granted Through Faith

13 For the promise that he would be the
[m]heir of the world *was* not to Abraham or
to his seed through the law, but through

CHAPTER 4

1 [a] Gen. 11:27–25:9; Is. 51:2; [Matt. 3:9]; John 8:33 [b] [Luke 3:8]; John 8:53; James 2:21 [1] Or *(fore)father according to the flesh has found?*
2 [c] Rom. 3:20, 27
3 [d] Gen. 15:6; Rom. 4:9, 22; Gal. 3:6; James 2:23 [2] *imputed, credited, reckoned, counted*
4 [e] Rom. 11:6 [3] *according to*
5 [f] [Gal. 2:16; Eph. 2:8, 9] [g] Josh. 24:2
6 [h] Ps. 32:1, 2
7 [i] Ps. 32:1, 2
11 [j] Gen. 17:10 [k] Luke 19:9; Rom. 4:16
12 [l] Rom. 4:18-22
13 [m] Gen. 17:4-6; 22:17

4:1 Abraham our father. Paul uses the model of Abraham to prove justification by faith alone because the Jews held him up as the supreme example of a righteous man (John 8:39), and because it clearly showed that Judaism with its works-righteousness had deviated from the faith of the Jews' patriarchal ancestors. In a spiritual sense, Abraham was the forerunner of the primarily Gentile church in Rome as well (*see notes on 1:13; 4:11,16;* cf. Gal. 3:6,7).

4:2 justified by works. Declared righteous on the basis of human effort (*see note on 3:24*). **boast.** If Abraham's own works had been the basis of his justification, he would have had every right to boast in God's presence. That makes the hypothetical premise of v. 2 unthinkable (Eph. 2:8,9; 1 Cor. 1:29).

4:3 A quotation of Gen. 15:6, one of the clearest statements in all Scripture about justification (*see note on 3:24*). ***believed.*** Abraham was a man of faith (*see note on 1:16;* cf. 4:18-21; Gal. 3:6,7,9; Heb. 11:8-10). But faith is not a meritorious work. It is never the ground of justification—it is simply the channel through which it is received and it, too, is a gift. *See note on Eph. 2:8.* ***accounted.*** Cf. vv. 5,9,10,22. Also translated "imputed" (vv. 6,8,11,23,24). Used in both financial and legal settings, this Gr. word, which occurs 9 times in chap. 4 alone, means to take something that belongs to someone and credit to another's account. It is a one-sided transaction—Abraham did nothing to accumulate it; God simply credited it to him. God took His own righteousness and credited it to Abraham as if it were actually his. This God did because Abraham believed in Him (*see note on Gen. 15:6*). ***righteousness.*** *See notes on 1:17; 3:21.*

4:4,5 Broadening his argument from Abraham to all men, the apostle here makes it clear that the forensic act of declaring a man righteous is completely apart from any kind of human work. If salvation were on the basis of one's own effort, God would owe salvation as a debt—but salvation is always a sovereignly given gift of God's grace (3:24; Eph. 2:8,9) to those who believe (cf. 1:16). Since faith is contrasted with work, faith must mean the end of any attempt to earn God's favor through personal merit.

4:5 justifies the ungodly. Only those who relinquish all claims to goodness and acknowledge they are ungodly are candidates for justification (cf. Luke 5:32). **accounted.** *See note on v. 3.*

4:6-8 Paul turns for support of his argument to Ps. 32:1,2, a penitential psalm written by David after his adultery with Bathsheba and his murder of her husband (2 Sam. 11). In spite of the enormity of his sin and the utter absence of personal merit, David knew the blessing of imputed righteousness.

4:9-12 Paul anticipated what his Jewish readers would be thinking: If Abraham was justified by his faith alone, why did God command him and his descendants to be circumcised? His response not only answers those concerned with circumcision, but the millions who still cling to some other kind of religious ceremony or activity as their basis for righteousness. *See notes on Gen. 15:6.*

4:9 circumcised. This refers to Jews (*see notes on Gen. 17:10-14;* cf. Acts 15:19-29; Rom. 2:25-29; 4:11; Gal. 5:1-4; 6:12; Phil. 3:2-5). **uncircumcised.** All Gentiles (*see notes on 2:25-29*).

4:10 Not while...but while uncircumcised. The chronology of Genesis proves Paul's case. Abraham was 86 when Ishmael was born (Gen. 16:16), and Abraham was 99 when he was circumcised. But God declared him righteous before Ishmael had even been conceived (Gen. 15:6; 16:2-4)—at least 14 years before Abraham's circumcision.

4:11,12 the father of all those who believe. Racially, Abraham is the father of all Jews (circumcised); spiritually, he is the father of both believing Jews (v. 12) and believing Gentiles (uncircumcised; v. 11). Cf. 4:16; Gal. 3:29.

4:11 sign. This indicates man's need for spiritual cleansing (cf. 2:28,29; Jer. 4:3,4; 9:24-26) and of the covenant relationship between God and His people (*see note on Gen. 17:11*). **seal.** An outward demonstration of the righteousness God had credited to him by faith.

4:13-15 Just as Abraham was not justified by the rite of circumcision (vv. 9-12), neither was he justified by keeping the Mosaic law (vv. 13-15).

4:13 promise...heir of the world. This refers to Christ and is the essence of the covenant God made with Abraham and his descendants (*see notes on Gen. 12:3; 15:5; 18:18; 22:18*). The final provision of that covenant was that through Abraham's seed all the world would be blessed (Gen. 12:3). Paul argues that "the seed" refers specifically to Christ and that this promise really constituted the gospel (Gal. 3:8,16; cf. John 8:56). All believers, by being in Christ, become heirs of the promise (Gal. 3:29; cf. 1 Cor. 3:21-23). **not...through the law.** That is,

the righteousness of faith. 14 For [n]if those
who are of the law *are* heirs, faith is made
void and the promise made of no effect,
15 because [o]the law brings about wrath; for
where there is no law *there is* no transgression.
16 Therefore *it is* of faith that *it might be*
[p]according to grace, [q]so that the promise
might be [4]sure to all the seed, not only to
those who are of the law, but also to those
who are of the faith of Abraham, [r]who is
the father of us all 17 (as it is written, [s]*"I
have made you a father of many nations"*)
in the presence of Him whom he believed—God, [t]who gives life to the dead
and calls those [u]things which do not exist
as though they did; 18 who, contrary to
hope, in hope believed, so that he became
the father of many nations, according to
what was spoken, [v]*"So shall your descendants be."* 19 And not being weak in faith,
[w]he did not consider his own body, already dead (since he was about a hundred
years old), [x]and the deadness of Sarah's
womb. 20 He did not waver at the promise
of God through unbelief, but was strengthened in faith, giving glory to God, 21 and
being fully convinced that what He had
promised [y]He was also able to perform.
22 And therefore [z]*"it was accounted to him
for righteousness."*
23 Now [a]it was not written for his sake
alone that it was imputed to him, 24 but
also for us. It shall be imputed to us who
believe [b]in Him who raised up Jesus our
Lord from the dead, 25 [c]who was delivered
up because of our offenses, and [d]was
raised because of our justification.

Faith Triumphs in Trouble

5 Therefore, [a]having been justified by
faith, [1]we have [b]peace with God
through our Lord Jesus Christ, 2 [c]through
whom also we have access by faith into
this grace [d]in which we stand, and [e]rejoice
in hope of the glory of God. 3 And not only

14 [n]Gal. 3:18
15 [o]Rom. 3:20
16 [p][Rom. 3:24] [q][Gal. 3:22] [r]Is. 51:2 [4]*certain*
17 [s]Gen. 17:5 [t][Rom. 8:11] [u]Rom. 9:26
18 [v]Gen. 15:5
19 [w]Gen. 17:17 [x]Heb. 11:11
21 [y]Gen. 18:14; [Ps. 115:3; Luke 1:37; Heb. 11:19]
22 [z]Gen. 15:6
23 [a]Rom. 15:4; 1 Cor. 10:6
24 [b]Acts 2:24
25 [c]Is. 53:4, 5; [Rom. 5:6, 8; 8:32; Gal. 2:20; Eph. 5:2; Heb. 9:28] [d][Rom. 5:18; 1 Cor. 15:17; 2 Cor. 5:15]

CHAPTER 5

1 [a]Is. 32:17; John 16:33 [b][Is. 53:5]; Acts 10:36; [Eph. 2:14] [1]Some ancient mss. *let us have*
2 [c][John 10:9; Eph. 2:18; 3:12; Heb. 10:19; 1 Pet. 3:18] [d]1 Cor. 15:1 [e]Heb. 3:6

not as a result of Abraham's keeping the law. **righteousness of faith.** Righteousness received from God by faith (*see note on 1:17*).

4:14 those who are of the law. If only those who perfectly keep the law—an impossibility—receive the promise, faith has no value. **promise...of no effect.** Making a promise contingent on an impossible condition nullifies the promise (*see note on v. 13*).

4:15 law brings about wrath. By exposing man's sinfulness (cf. 7:7-11; Gal. 3:19,24).

4:16 of faith. Justification is through faith alone (*see notes on 1:16,17 and 3:24*). **according to grace.** But the power of justification is God's great grace (*see note on 1:5*), not man's faith. **promise.** *See note on v. 13.* **those who are of the law.** Believing Jews. **those who are of the faith of Abraham.** Believing Gentiles. **father of us all.** *See note on v. 11.*

4:17 as it is written. Quoted from Gen. 17:5. **gives life to the dead.** Abraham had experienced this firsthand (Heb. 11:11,12; cf. Rom. 4:19). **calls those things which do not exist as though they did.** This is another reference to the forensic nature of justification. God can declare believing sinners to be righteous even though they are not, by imputing His righteousness to them, just as God made or declared Jesus "sin" and punished Him, though He was not a sinner. Those whom He justifies, He will conform to the image of His Son (8:29,30).

4:18-25 Having shown that justification is through faith not works (vv. 1-8), and that it is by grace, not the keeping of law (vv. 9-17), Paul now concludes by showing that it results from divine power, not human effort (vv. 18-25).

4:18 contrary to hope. From the human perspective, it seemed impossible (cf. v. 19). Cf. Gen. 17:5. **what was spoken.** Quoted from Gen. 15:5.

4:19 weak in faith. When doubt erodes one's confidence in God's Word. **the deadness of Sarah's womb.** She was only 10 years younger than Abraham (Gen. 17:17), 90 years old (well past childbearing age) when they received the promise of Isaac.

4:20 the promise. Of the birth of a son (Gen. 15:4; 17:16; 18:10). **giving glory to God.** Believing God affirms His existence and character and thus gives Him glory (cf. Heb. 11:6; 1 John 5:10).

4:22 therefore. Because of his genuine faith (see Gen. 15:6).

4:23 not...for his sake alone. All Scripture has universal application (cf. 15:4; 2 Tim. 3:16,17), and Abraham's experience is no exception. If Abraham was justified by faith, then all others are justified on the same basis.

4:25 A paraphrase of the LXX (Gr. translation of the OT) rendering of Is. 53:12. Perhaps these words were adapted to and quoted from an early Christian confession or hymn. **delivered up.** I.e., crucified. **because of our justification.** The resurrection provided proof that God had accepted the sacrifice of His Son and would be able to be just and yet justify the ungodly.

5:1-11 Paul completed his case that God justifies sinners on the basis of faith alone, and he turned his pen to counter the notion that although believers receive salvation by faith, they will preserve it by good works. He argues that they are bound eternally to Jesus Christ, preserved by His power and not by human effort (cf. Is. 11:5; Ps. 36:5; Lam. 3:23; Eph. 1:18-20; 2 Tim. 2:13; Heb. 10:23). For the Christian, the evidences of that eternal tie are: 1) his peace with God (v. 1); 2) his standing in grace (v. 2a); 3) his hope of glory (vv. 2b-5a); 4) his receiving of divine love (vv. 5b-8); 5) his certain escape of divine wrath (vv. 9,10); and 6) his joy in the Lord (v. 11).

5:1 having been justified. The Gr. construction—and its Eng. translation—underscores that justification is a one-time legal declaration with continuing results (*see note on 3:24*), not an ongoing process. **peace with God.** Not a subjective, internal sense of calm and serenity, but an external, objective reality. God has declared Himself to be at war with every human being because of man's sinful rebellion against Him and His laws (v. 10; cf. 1:18; 8:7; Ex. 22:24; Deut. 32:21,22; Ps. 7:11; John 3:36; Eph. 5:6). But the first great result of justification is that the sinner's war with God is ended forever (Col. 1:21,22). Scripture refers to the end of this conflict as a person's being reconciled to God (vv. 10,11; 2 Cor. 5:18-20).

5:2 access. Used only twice elsewhere in the NT (Eph. 2:18; 3:12), this word always refers to the believer's access to God through Jesus Christ. What was unthinkable to the OT Jew (cf. Ex. 19:9,20,21; 28:35) is now available to all who come (Jer. 32: 38,40; Heb. 4:16; 10:19-22; cf. Matt. 27:51). **stand.** This refers to the permanent, secure position believers enjoy in God's grace (cf. v. 10; 8:31-34; John 6:37; Phil. 1:6; 2 Tim. 1:12; Jude 24). **hope of the glory of God.** Unlike the Eng. word "hope," the NT word contains no uncertainty; it speaks of something that is certain, but not yet realized. The believer's ultimate destiny is to

that, but [f]we also glory in tribulations,
[g]knowing that tribulation produces [2]per-
severance; 4 [h]and perseverance, [3]charac-
ter; and character, hope. 5 [i]Now hope does
not disappoint, [j]because the love of God
has been poured out in our hearts by the
Holy Spirit who was given to us.

Christ in Our Place

6 For when we were still without
strength, [4]in due time [k]Christ died for the
ungodly. 7 For scarcely for a righteous man
will one die; yet perhaps for a good man
someone would even dare to die. 8 But
[l]God demonstrates His own love toward
us, in that while we were still sinners,
Christ died for us. 9 Much more then, having now been justified [m]by His blood, we
shall be saved [n]from wrath through Him.

3 [f] Matt. 5:11, 12; [John 16:33; Acts 5:41; 2 Cor. 12:9]; James 1:2 [g] James 1:3 [2] *endurance*
4 [h] Phil. 2:22; [James 1:12] [3] *approved character*
5 [i] Phil. 1:20 [j] 2 Cor. 1:22; Eph. 1:13
6 [k] Is. 53:5; [Rom. 4:25; 5:8; 8:32; Gal. 2:20; Eph. 5:2] [4] *at the right time*
8 [l] [John 3:16; 15:13; Rom. 8:39]
9 [m] Eph. 2:13; [1 John 1:7] [n] Rom. 1:18; 1 Thess. 1:10

10 [o] [Rom. 8:32] [p] Rom. 11:28; 2 Cor. 5:18; [Eph. 2:5, 6]; Col. 1:21 [q] John 14:19
11 [r] [Gal. 4:9]
12 [s] Gen. 2:17; 3:6, 19;

10 For [o]if when we were enemies [p]we were
reconciled to God through the death of His
Son, much more, having been reconciled,
we shall be saved [q]by His life. 11 And not
only *that,* but we also [r]rejoice in God
through our Lord Jesus Christ, through
whom we have now received the reconciliation.

Death in Adam, Life in Christ

12 Therefore, just as [s]through one man
sin entered the world, and [t]death through
sin, and thus death spread to all men, because all sinned— 13 (For until the law sin
was in the world, but [u]sin is not imputed
when there is no law. 14 Nevertheless
death reigned from Adam to Moses, even
over those who had not sinned according

[Rom. 5:15-17; 1 Cor. 15:21] [t] Gen. 2:17 13 [u] 1 John 3:4

share in the very glory of God (8:29,30; John 17:22; 2 Cor. 3:18; Phil. 3:20,21; 1 John 3:1,2), and that hope will be realized because Christ Himself secures it (1 Tim. 1:1). Without the clear and certain promises of the Word of God, the believer would have no basis for hope (15:4; Ps. 119:81,114; Eph. 2:12; cf. Jer. 14:8).

5:3 tribulations. A word used for pressure, like that of a press squeezing the fluid from olives or grapes. Here they are not the normal pressures of living (cf. 8:35), but the inevitable troubles that come to followers of Christ because of their relationship with Him (Matt. 5:10-12; John 15:20; 2 Cor. 4:17; 1 Thess. 3:3; 2 Tim. 3:12; 1 Pet. 4:19). Such difficulties produce rich spiritual benefits (vv. 3,4). **perseverance.** Sometimes translated "patience," this word refers to endurance, the ability to remain under tremendous weight and pressure without succumbing (15:5; Col. 1:22,23; 2 Thess. 1:4; Rev. 14:12).

5:4 character. A better translation is "proven character." The Gr. word simply means "proof." It was used of testing metals to determine their purity. Here the proof is Christian character (cf. James 1:12). Christians can glory in tribulations because of what those troubles produce.

5:5 love of God…poured out. God's love for us (cf. v. 8) has been lavishly poured out to the point of overflowing within our hearts. Paul moves from the objective aspects of our security in Christ to the internal, more subjective. God has implanted within our hearts evidence that we belong to Him in that we love the One who first loved us (1 Cor. 16:22; cf. Gal. 5:22; Eph. 3:14-19; 1 John 4:7-10). **Spirit who was given.** A marvelous testimony to God's love for us (8:9,14,16,17; John 7:38,39; 1 Cor. 6:19,20; 12:13; Eph. 1:18).

5:6 without strength. Lit. "helpless." Unregenerate sinners are spiritually dead and incapable of doing anything to help themselves (John 6:44; Eph. 2:1). **in due time.** At the moment God had chosen (cf. Gal. 4:4). **Christ died for the ungodly.** God's love for His own is unwavering because it is not based on how lovable we are, but on the constancy of His own character; God's supreme act of love came when we were at our most undesirable (cf. Matt. 5:46).

5:7 righteous man…good man. As uncommon as such a sacrifice is, Paul's point is that we were neither of these persons—yet Christ sacrificed Himself for us.

5:9 Much more. What Paul is about to say is even more amazing and wonderful. **justified.** *See note on 3:24.* **by His blood.** Through His violent, substitutionary death. References to the blood of the Savior include the reality that He bled in His death (a necessity to fulfill the OT imagery of sacrifice), but are not limited to the fluid itself. NT writers also use the term "blood" as a graphic way to describe violent death (see Matt. 23:30,35; 27:4-8,24,25; John 6:53-56; Acts 5:28; 20:26). References to the Savior's blood are not simply pointing to the fluid, but at His death and entire atoning work (cf. 3:25; Eph. 1:7; 2:13; Col. 1:14,20; Heb. 9:12; 10:19; 13:12; 1 Pet. 1:2,19; 1 John 1:7; Rev. 1:5). **wrath.** *See note on 1:18.* Christ bore the full fury of God's wrath in the believing sinner's place, and there is none left for him (see 8:1; 1 Thess. 1:10; 5:9).

5:10 saved by His life. When we were God's enemies, Christ was able by His death to reconcile us to God. Certainly now that we are God's children, the Savior can keep us by His living power.

5:11 reconciliation. This is between God and sinners. *See notes on 2 Cor. 5:18-20.*

5:12-21 In one of the most enigmatic passages in the entire book, Paul sets out to show how one man's death can provide salvation for many. To prove his point, he uses Adam to establish the principle that it is possible for one man's actions to inexorably affect many other people.

5:12 just as…sin entered. Not a particular sin, but the inherent propensity to sin entered the human realm; men became sinners by nature. Adam passed to all his descendants the inherent sinful nature he possessed because of his first disobedience. That nature is present from the moment of conception (Ps. 51:5), making it impossible for man to live in a way that pleases God. Satan, the father of sin (1 John 3:8), first brought temptation to Adam and Eve (Gen. 3:1-7). **through one man.** When Adam sinned, all mankind sinned in his loins (v. 18; cf. Heb. 7:7-10). Since his sin transformed his inner nature and brought spiritual death and depravity, that sinful nature would be passed on seminally to his posterity as well (Ps. 51:5). **death.** Adam was not originally subject to death, but through his sin it became a grim certainty for him and his posterity. Death has 3 distinct manifestations: 1) spiritual death or separation from God (cf. Eph. 1:1,2; 4:18); 2) physical death (Heb. 9:27); and 3) eternal death (also called the second death), which includes not only eternal separation from God, but eternal torment in the lake of fire (Rev. 20:11-15). **because all sinned.** Because all humanity existed in the loins of Adam, and have through procreation inherited his fallenness and depravity, it can be said that all sinned in him. Therefore, humans are not sinners because they sin, but rather they sin because they are sinners.

5:13 sin is not imputed. *See notes on Acts 17:3; 2 Cor. 5:19.* Though all men were regarded as sinners (v. 12), because there was no explicit list of commands, there was no strict accounting of their specific points of violation. **when there is no law.** The period from Adam to Moses, when God had not yet given the Mosaic law.

5:14 Nevertheless death reigned. But even without the law, death was universal. All men from Adam to Moses were subject to death, not because of their sinful acts against the Mosaic law (which they did not yet have), but because of their own inherited sinful

to the likeness of the transgression of
Adam, [v]who is a type of Him who was to
come. 15 But the free gift *is* not like the [5]of-
fense. For if by the one man's offense many
died, much more the grace of God and the
gift by the grace of the one Man, Jesus
Christ, abounded [w]to many. 16 And the gift
is not like *that which came* through the one
who sinned. For the judgment *which came*
from one *offense resulted* in condemnation,
but the free gift *which came* from many [6]of-
fenses *resulted* in justification. 17 For if by
the one man's [7]offense death reigned
through the one, much more those who receive abundance of grace and of the gift of
righteousness will reign in life through the
One, Jesus Christ.)
18 Therefore, as through [8]one man's offense *judgment* came to all men, resulting
in condemnation, even so through [x]one[9]
Man's righteous act *the free gift came* [y]to all
men, resulting in justification of life. 19 For
as by one man's disobedience many were
made sinners, so also by [z]one Man's obedience many will be made righteous.
20 Moreover [a]the law entered that the offense might abound. But where sin
abounded, grace [b]abounded much more,
21 so that as sin reigned in death, even so
grace might reign through righteousness
to eternal life through Jesus Christ our
Lord.

14 [v][1 Cor. 15:21, 22]
15 [w][Is. 53:11]
[5] *trespass* or *false step*
16 [6] *trespasses*
17 [7] *trespass*
18 [x][1 Cor. 15:21, 45]
[8] Or *one trespass*
[9] Or *one righteous act*
[y] Matt. 1:21; [John 12:32]
19 [z] Is. 53:11, 12; [Phil. 2:8]
20 [a] John 15:22
[b] Luke 7:47; Rom. 6:1; 1 Tim. 1:14

CHAPTER 6

1 [a] Rom. 3:8; 6:15
2 [b] [Rom. 6:11; 7:4, 6; Gal. 2:19; Col. 2:20; 3:3]; 1 Pet. 2:24
3 [c] Acts 2:38; 8:16; 19:5; [Gal. 3:27]; Col. 2:12 [d] [1 Cor. 15:29]

Dead to Sin, Alive to God

6 What shall we say then? [a]Shall we continue in sin that grace may abound?
2 Certainly not! How shall we who [b]died to
sin live any longer in it? 3 Or do you not
know that [c]as many of us as were baptized
into Christ Jesus [d]were baptized into His

nature. **not sinned...likeness...of Adam.** Those who had no specific revelation as did Adam (Gen. 2:16,17) or those who had the Mosaic law (cf. v. 13), but nevertheless sinned against the holiness of God, i.e., those who "sinned without law" (2:12). **a type of Him...to come.** Both Adam and Christ were similar in that their acts affected many others. This phrase serves as transition from the apostle's discussion of the transference of Adam's sin to the crediting of Christ's righteousness.

5:15-21 In this passage Paul explores the contrasts between the condemning act of Adam and the redemptive act of Christ. They were different in their effectiveness (v. 15), their extent (v. 16), their efficacy (v. 17), their essence (vv. 18,19), and their energy (vv. 20,21).

5:15 many died. Paul uses the word "many" with two distinct meanings in v. 15, just as he will the word "all" in v. 18. He has already established that all men, without exception, bear the guilt of sin and are therefore subject to death (*see notes on v. 12*). So the "many" who die must refer to all Adam's descendants. **much more.** Christ's one act of redemption was immeasurably greater than Adam's one act of condemnation.

5:16 the gift. Salvation by grace. **the judgment...from one *offense*.** *See notes on 5:12.* **condemnation.** The divine guilty verdict; the opposite of justification. **many offenses.** Adam brought upon all men the condemnation for only one offense—his willful act of disobedience. Christ, however, delivers the elect from the condemnation of many offenses. **justification.** *See note on 3:24.*

5:17 death reigned. Adam's sin brought universal death—exactly opposite the result he expected and Satan had promised: "You will be like God" (Gen. 3:5). Christ's sacrifice brought salvation to those who believe. **gift of righteousness.** *See notes on 1:17 and 3:24*; see also 2 Cor. 5:21; Phil. 3:8,9. **will reign in life.** Unlike Adam's act, Christ's act has—and will—accomplish exactly what He intended (cf. Phil. 1:6), i.e., spiritual life (cf. Eph. 2:5).

5:18,19 Summaries of the analogy of Adam and Christ.

5:18 condemnation. *See note on v. 16.* **one Man's righteous act.** Not a reference to a single event, but generally to Christ's obedience (cf. v. 19; Luke 2:49; John 4:34; 5:30; 6:38), culminating in the greatest demonstration of that obedience, death on a cross (Phil. 2:8). ***free gift*...to all men.** This cannot mean that all men will be saved; salvation is only for those who exercise faith in Jesus Christ (cf. 1:16,17; 3:22,28; 4:5,13). Rather, like the word "many" in v. 15, Paul is using "all" with two different meanings for the sake of parallelism, a common practice in the Heb. OT.

5:19 made righteous. This expression probably refers to one's legal status before God and not an actual change in character, since Paul is contrasting justification and condemnation throughout this passage, and he has not yet introduced the doctrine of sanctification (chaps. 6–8) which deals with the actual transformation of the sinner as a result of redemption.

5:20 the law entered. Cf. Gal. 3:19. Although the Mosaic law is not flawed (7:12), its presence caused man's sin to increase (cf. 7:8-11). Thus it made men more aware of their own sinfulness and inability to keep God's perfect standard (7:7; Gal. 3:21,22), and it served as a tutor to drive them to Christ (Gal. 3:24).

5:21 This is the final summary of the analogy of Adam and Christ.

6:1-8:39 Paul moves from demonstrating the doctrine of justification, which is God's declaring the believing sinner righteous (3:20–5:21), to demonstrating the practical ramifications of salvation on those who have been justified. He specifically discusses the doctrine of sanctification, which is God's producing actual righteousness in the believer (6:1–8:39).

6:1-10 He begins his lesson on sanctification by arguing that in spite of their past, all whom God has justified will experience personal holiness (cf. 1 Cor. 6:9-11a; 1 Tim. 1:12,13).

6:1 Shall we continue in sin. Because of his past Pharisaic experience, Paul was able to anticipate the major objections of his critics. He had already alluded to this criticism, that by preaching a justification based solely on the free grace of God, he was encouraging people to sin (cf. 3:5,6,8).

6:2 Certainly not! Lit. "may it never be!" Used 14 times in Paul's epistles (10 in Romans: 3:4,6,31; 6:2,15; 7:7,13; 9:14; 11:1,11), this expression is the strongest Gr. idiom for repudiating a statement, and it contains a sense of outrage that anyone would ever think the statement was true. **we...died to sin.** Not a reference to the believer's ongoing daily struggle with sin, but to a one-time event completed in the past. Because we are "in Christ" (6:11; 8:1), and He died in our place (5:6-8), we are counted dead with Him. This is the fundamental premise of chap. 6, and Paul spends the remainder of the chapter explaining and supporting it.

6:3 baptized into Christ Jesus. This does not refer to water baptism. Paul is actually using the word "baptized" in a metaphorical sense, as we might in saying someone was immersed in his work, or underwent his baptism of fire when experiencing some trouble. All Christians have, by placing saving faith in Him, been spiritually immersed into the person Christ, that is, united and identified with Him (cf. 1 Cor. 6:17; 10:2; Gal. 3:27; 1 Pet. 3:21; 1 John 1:3; *see note on Acts 2:38*). Certainly water baptism pictures this reality, which is the purpose—to show the transformation of the justified. **into His death.**

death? 4 Therefore we were [e]buried with
Him through baptism into death, that [f]just
as Christ was raised from the dead by [g]the
glory of the Father, [h]even so we also
should walk in newness of life.
5 [i]For if we have been united together in
the likeness of His death, certainly we also
shall be *in the likeness* of *His* resurrection,
6 knowing this, that [j]our old man was crucified with *Him,* that [k]the body of sin
might be [1]done away with, that we should
no longer be slaves of sin. 7 For [l]he who
has died has been [2]freed from sin. 8 Now
[m]if we died with Christ, we believe that we
shall also live with Him, 9 knowing that
[n]Christ, having been raised from the dead,
dies no more. Death no longer has dominion over Him. 10 For *the death* that He died,
[o]He died to sin once for all; but *the life* that
He lives, [p]He lives to God. 11 Likewise you
also, [3]reckon yourselves to be [q]dead indeed to sin, but [r]alive to God in Christ Jesus our Lord.
12 [s]Therefore do not let sin reign in your
mortal body, that you should obey it in its
lusts. 13 And do not present your [t]mem-
bers *as* [4]instruments of unrighteousness to
sin, but [u]present yourselves to God as
being alive from the dead, and your members *as* [4]instruments of righteousness to
God. 14 For [v]sin shall not have dominion
over you, for you are not under law but
under grace.

From Slaves of Sin to Slaves of God

15 What then? Shall we sin [w]because we

4 [e] Col. 2:12 [f] 1 Cor. 6:14 [g] John 2:11 [h] Rom. 7:6; [2 Cor. 5:17; Gal. 6:15; Eph. 4:23; Col. 3:10]
5 [i] 2 Cor. 4:10; Phil. 3:10; Col. 2:12; 3:1
6 [j] Gal. 2:20; 5:24; 6:14 [k] Col. 2:11 [1] *rendered inoperative*
7 [l] 1 Pet. 4:1 [2] *cleared*
8 [m] Rom. 6:4; 2 Cor. 4:10; 2 Tim. 2:11
9 [n] Rev. 1:18
10 [o] Heb. 9:27 [p] Luke 20:38
11 [q] [Rom. 6:2; 7:4, 6] [r] [Gal. 2:19; Col. 2:20; 3:3]; 1 Pet. 2:24 [3] *consider*
12 [s] Ps. 19:13
13 [t] Rom. 6:16, 19; 7:5; Col. 3:5; James 4:1 [u] Rom. 12:1; 2 Cor. 5:14; 1 Pet. 2:24; 4:2 [4] *Or weapons*
14 [v] [Rom. 7:4, 6; 8:2; Gal. 5:18]
15 [w] 1 Cor. 9:21

This means that immersion or identification is specifically with Christ's death and resurrection, as the apostle will explain (see 6:4-7).

6:4 buried with Him. Since we are united by faith with Him, as baptism symbolizes, His death and burial become ours. **newness of life.** This is true if, in Christ, we died and were buried with Him, we have also been united with Him in His resurrection. There is a new quality and character to our lives, a new principle of life. This speaks of the believer's regeneration (cf. Ezek. 36:26; 2 Cor. 5:17; Gal. 6:15; Eph. 4:24). Whereas sin describes the old life, righteousness describes the new.

6:6 our old man. A believer's unregenerate self. The Gr. word for "old" does not refer to something old in years but to something that is worn out and useless. Our old self died with Christ, and the life we now enjoy is a new divinely-given life that is the life of Christ Himself (cf. Gal. 2:20). We have been removed from the unregenerate self's presence and control, so we should not follow the remaining memories of its old sinful ways as if we were still under its evil influence (*see notes on Eph. 4:20-24; Gal. 5:24; Col. 3:9,10*). **body of sin.** Essentially synonymous with "our old man." Paul uses the terms "body" and "flesh" to refer to sinful propensities that are intertwined with physical weaknesses and pleasures (e.g., 8:10,11,13,23). Although the old self is dead, sin retains a foothold in our temporal flesh or our unredeemed humanness, with its corrupted desires (7:14-24). The believer does not have two competing natures, the old and the new; but one new nature that is still incarcerated in unredeemed flesh (*see note on v. 12*). But the term "flesh" is not equivalent to the physical body, which can be an instrument of holiness (v. 19; 12:1; 1 Cor. 6:20). **done away.** Rendered powerless or inoperative.

6:7 has died. Through his union with Christ (*see note on v. 3*). **freed from sin.** No longer under its domination and control.

6:8 we shall also live with Him. The context suggests that Paul means not only that believers will live in the presence of Christ for eternity, but also that all who have died with Christ, which is true of all believers, will live a life here that is fully consistent with His holiness.

6:9 dominion. Mastery, control, or domination. Cf. vv. 11,12.

6:10 He died to sin. Christ died to sin in two senses: 1) in regard to sin's penalty—He met its legal demands upon the sinner; and 2) in regard to sin's power—forever breaking its power over those who belong to Him. And His death will never need repeating (Heb. 7:26,27; 9:12,28; 10:10; cf. 1 Pet. 3:18). Paul's point is that believers have died to sin in the same way. **He lives to God.** For God's glory.

6:11-14 Paul addresses the logical conclusion of his readers: If the old self is dead, why is there continually a struggle with sin and how can the new self become dominant (see also 7:1-25)? His exhortation is contained in 2 key words: "reckon" (vv. 11b,12) and "present" (vv. 13,14).

6:11 Likewise. This implies the importance of his readers knowing what he just explained. Without that foundation, what he is about to teach will not make sense. Scripture always identifies knowledge as the foundation for one's practice (cf. Col. 3:10). **reckon.** While it simply means to count or number something, it was often used metaphorically to refer to having an absolute, unreserved confidence in what one's mind knows to be true—the kind of heartfelt confidence that affects his actions and decisions. Paul is not referring to mind games in which we trick ourselves into thinking a certain way. Rather he is urging us to embrace by faith what God has revealed to be true. **dead...to sin.** See vv. 2-7. **in Christ.** Paul's favorite expression of our union with Christ. This is its first occurrence in Romans (cf. Eph. 1:3-14).

6:12 mortal body. The only remaining repository where sin finds the believer vulnerable. The brain and its thinking processes are part of the body and thus tempt our souls with its sinful lusts (*see note on v. 6*; cf. 8:22,23; 1 Cor. 15:53; 1 Pet. 2:9-11).

6:13 present. Refers to a decision of the will. Before sin can have power over a believer, it must first pass through his will (cf. Phil. 2:12,13). **your members.** The parts of the physical body, the headquarters from which sin operates in the believer (7:18,22-25; cf. 12:1; 1 Cor. 9:27). **instruments of unrighteousness.** Tools for accomplishing that which violates God's holy will and law.

6:14 sin shall not have dominion. Sin must be able to exercise control in our bodies or Paul's admonition becomes unnecessary (v. 13). But sin does not have to reign there; so the apostle expresses his confidence that those who are Christ's will not allow it to. **not under law but under grace.** This does not mean God has abrogated His moral law (3:31; cf. Matt. 5:17-19). The law is good, holy, and righteous (7:12; cf. 1 Tim. 1:8), but it cannot be kept, so it curses. Since it cannot assist anyone to keep God's moral standard (cf. 7:7-11), it can only show the standard and thus rebuke and condemn those who fail to keep it. But the believer is no longer under the law as a condition of acceptance with God—an impossible condition to meet and one designed only to show man his sinfulness (*see notes on 3:19,20*; cf. Gal. 3:10-13)—but under grace, which enables him to truly fulfill the law's righteous requirements (7:6; 8:3,4). Chapter 7 is Paul's complete commentary on this crucial expression.

6:15-23 This section continues Paul's discussion of sanctification by reminding his readers of their past slavery to sin and their new slavery to righteousness. He wants them to live in submission to their new master, Jesus Christ, and not to be entangled again with the sins that characterized their old life, sins which no longer have any claim over them.

6:15 Shall we sin. Cf. 3:5,6,8; 6:1. **not under law but under grace.** *See note on v. 14.*

are not under law but under grace? Certainly not! 16 Do you not know that [x]to
whom you present yourselves slaves to
obey, you are that one's slaves whom you
obey, whether of sin *leading* to death, or of
obedience *leading* to righteousness? 17 But
God be thanked that *though* you were
slaves of sin, yet you obeyed from the
heart [y]that form of doctrine to which you
were [5]delivered. 18 And [z]having been set
free from sin, you became slaves of righteousness. 19 I speak in human *terms* because of the weakness of your flesh. For
just as you presented your members *as*
slaves of uncleanness, and of lawlessness
leading to *more* lawlessness, so now present
your members *as* slaves *of* righteousness
[6]for holiness.
20 For when you were [a]slaves of sin, you
were free in regard to righteousness.
21 [b]What fruit did you have then in the
things of which you are now ashamed? For
[c]the end of those things *is* death. 22 But
now [d]having been set free from sin, and
having become slaves of God, you have
your fruit [7]to holiness, and the end, everlasting life. 23 For [e]the wages of sin *is*
death, but [f]the [8]gift of God *is* eternal life in
Christ Jesus our Lord.

Freed from the Law

7 Or do you not know, brethren (for I
speak to those who know the law), that
the law [1]has dominion over a man as long
as he lives? 2 For [a]the woman who has a
husband is bound by the law to *her* husband as long as he lives. But if the husband
dies, she is released from the law of *her*
husband. 3 So then [b]if, while *her* husband
lives, she marries another man, she will be
called an adulteress; but if her husband
dies, she is free from that law, so that she is
no adulteress, though she has married another man. 4 Therefore, my brethren, you
also have become [c]dead to the law through
the body of Christ, that you may be married to another—to Him who was raised
from the dead, that we should [d]bear fruit
to God. 5 For when we were in the flesh,
the sinful passions which were aroused by

16 [x]Prov. 5:22; [Matt. 6:24]; John 8:34; 2 Pet. 2:19
17 [y]2 Tim. 1:13 [5]*entrusted*
18 [z]John 8:32; Rom. 6:22; 8:2; 1 Cor. 7:22; Gal. 5:1; 1 Pet. 2:16
19 [6]*unto sanctification*
20 [a]John 8:34
21 [b]Jer. 12:13; Ezek. 16:63; Rom. 7:5 [c]Rom. 1:32; Gal. 6:8
22 [d][John 8:32]; Rom. 6:18; 8:2
[7]*unto sanctification*
23 [e]Gen. 2:17 [f]Rom. 2:7; 1 Pet. 1:4 [8]*free gift*

CHAPTER 7

1 [1]*rules*
2 [a]1 Cor. 7:39
3 [b][Matt. 5:32]
4 [c]Rom. 8:2; Gal. 2:19; 5:18; [Col. 2:14] [d]Gal. 5:22

6:17 form of doctrine...delivered. In the Gk. "form" is a word for a mold such as a craftsman would use to cast molten metal. Paul's point is that God pours His new children into the mold of divine truth (12:2; cf. Titus 2:1). New believers have an innate and compelling desire to know and obey God's Word (1 Pet. 2:2).

6:18 having been set free. *See note on v. 2.* **slaves of righteousness.** See v. 16.

6:19 human *terms*...weakness of your flesh. Paul's use of the master/slave analogy was an accommodation to their humanness and their difficulty in grasping divine truth. **your members.** *See note on v. 13.* ***more* lawlessness.** Like a vicious animal, sin's appetite only grows when it is fed (Gen. 4:7).

6:21 fruit. Or benefit.

6:22 set free from sin. *See note on v. 2.* **holiness.** The benefit of being slaves to God is sanctification, the outcome of which is eternal life.

6:23 This verse describes two inexorable absolutes: 1) spiritual death is the paycheck for every man's slavery to sin; and 2) eternal life is a free gift God gives undeserving sinners who believe in His Son (cf. Eph. 2:8,9).

7:1–8:4 Knowing that his readers—especially Jewish ones—would have many questions about how the law relates to their faith in Christ, Paul sets out to explain that relationship (he refers to the law 27 times in this passage). In a detailed explanation of what it means not to be under law, but under grace (6:14,15), Paul teaches that: 1) the law can no longer condemn a believer (7:1-6); 2) it convicts unbelievers (and believers) of sin (7:7-13); 3) it cannot deliver a believer from sin (7:14-25); and 4) believers who walk in the power of the Spirit can fulfill the law (8:1-4).

7:1 know the law. Lit. "those who know law." Although Paul intends to include God's written law, he is not referring to any specific law code, but to a principle that is true of all law—Greek, Roman, Jewish, or biblical. **dominion.** I.e., jurisdiction. No matter how serious a criminal's offenses may be, he is no longer subject to prosecution and punishment after he dies.

7:2,3 These two verses are not a complex allegory, but a simple analogy, using marriage law to illustrate the point Paul just made about law's jurisdiction (v. 1). This passage is not teaching that only the death of a spouse frees a Christian to remarry; it is not teaching about divorce and remarriage at all. Both Christ and Paul have fully addressed those issues elsewhere (cf. Matt. 5:31,32; 19:3-12; 1 Cor. 7:10-15).

7:3 The law that governs a married woman's actions no longer has any jurisdiction over her once her husband dies. Widows are free to marry again, and Paul even encourages younger ones to remarry as long as their potential mate is a believer (1 Cor. 7:39; 1 Tim. 5:14). Even the illegitimately divorced can marry again (*see notes on 1 Cor. 7:8,9*).

7:4 Therefore. The logical conclusion or application of Paul's brief argument (vv. 1-3) follows. **become dead.** The Gr. construction of this verb emphasizes two important points: 1) this death happened at a point in time, with results that are complete and final; and 2) someone else—in this case God Himself—initiated this death (lit. "you were made to die"). In response to faith in His Son, God makes the believing sinner forever dead to the condemnation and penalty of the law (cf. 8:1). **through the body of Christ.** Because, as the substitute for sinners, He suffered the penalty of death that the law demanded. **be married to another.** Just as the widow in Paul's analogy (vv. 2,3) was freed to remarry, the believer has been freed from his hostile relationship to a law that condemned him, and can, therefore, be remarried—this time to Christ (cf. 2 Cor. 11:5; Eph. 5:24-27). **fruit.** A transformed life that manifests new attitudes (Gal. 5:22,23) and actions (John 15:1,2; Phil. 1:11; cf. 2 Cor. 5:21; Gal. 2:19,20; Eph. 2:10; *see note on 1:13*).

7:5 flesh. Scripture uses this term in a non-moral sense to describe man's physical being (John 1:14), and in a morally evil sense to describe man's unredeemed humanness (*see notes on 6:6; Rom. 8; Gal. 5; Eph. 2*), i.e., that remnant of the old man which will remain with each believer until each receives his or her glorified body (8:23). "In the flesh" here describes a person who is able to operate only in the sphere of fallen mankind—an unredeemed, unregenerate person (8:9). Although the believer can manifest some of the deeds of the flesh, he can never again be "in the flesh." **sinful passions.** The overwhelming impulses to think and do evil, which characterize those who are "in the flesh" (Eph. 2:3). **aroused by the law.** The unbeliever's rebellious nature is awakened when restrictions are placed on him and makes him want to do the very things the law forbids (*see*

the law [e]were at work in our members [f]to
bear fruit to death. 6 But now we have been
delivered from the law, having died to
what we were held by, so that we should
serve [g]in the newness of the Spirit and not
in the oldness of the letter.

Sin's Advantage in the Law

7 What shall we say then? *Is* the law sin?
Certainly not! On the contrary, [h]I would
not have known sin except through the
law. For I would not have known covetousness unless the law had said, [i]*"You
shall not covet."* 8 But [j]sin, taking opportunity by the commandment, produced in
me all *manner of evil* desire. For [k]apart from
the law sin *was* dead. 9 I was alive once
without the law, but when the commandment came, sin revived and I died. 10 And
the commandment, [l]which *was* to *bring*
life, I found to *bring* death. 11 For sin, taking occasion by the commandment, deceived me, and by it killed *me*. 12 Therefore
[m]the law *is* holy, and the commandment
holy and just and good.

Law Cannot Save from Sin

13 Has then what is good become death
to me? Certainly not! But sin, that it might
appear sin, was producing death in me
through what is good, so that sin through
the commandment might become exceedingly sinful. 14 For we know that the law is
spiritual, but I am carnal, [n]sold under sin.

5 [e] Rom. 6:13 [f] Rom. 6:21; Gal. 5:19; James 1:15
6 [g] Rom. 2:29; 2 Cor. 3:6
7 [h] Rom. 3:20 [i] Ex. 20:17; Deut. 5:21; Acts 20:33
8 [j] Rom. 4:15 [k] 1 Cor. 15:56
10 [l] Lev. 18:5; Ezek. 20:11, 13, 21; Luke 10:28; Rom. 10:5; 2 Cor. 3:7; Gal. 3:12
12 [m] Ps. 19:8
14 [n] 1 Kin. 21:20, 25; 2 Kin. 17:17; Rom. 6:16

note on v. 8; cf. 1:32). **our members.** *See note on 6:13.* **fruit to death.** The sinful passions at work in unbelievers produce a harvest of eternal death (*see note on 5:12*; cf. Gal. 6:7,8).

7:6 delivered from the law. Not freedom to do what God's law forbids (6:1,15; 8:4; cf. 3:31), but freedom from the spiritual liabilities and penalties of God's law (*see note on v. 4*; cf. Gal. 3:13). Because we died in Christ when He died (*see note on 6:2*), the law with its condemnation and penalties no longer has jurisdiction over us (vv. 1-3). **serve.** This is the verb form of the word for "bondservant" (*see note on 1:1*), but here it is parallel to being slaves of righteousness (cf. 6:22), emphasizing that this service is not voluntary. Not only is the believer able to do what is right, he will do what is right. **the newness of the Spirit.** A new state of mind which the Spirit produces, characterized by a new desire and ability to keep the law of God (*see note on 8:4*). **oldness of the letter.** The external, written law code that produced only hostility and condemnation.

7:7 *Is* the law sin? Paul wanted to make certain his readers did not conclude (from vv. 4-6) that the law itself was evil (cf. v. 12). **I would not have known sin.** The law reveals the divine standard, and as believers compare themselves against that standard, they can accurately identify sin, which is the failure to meet the standard. Paul uses the personal pronoun "I" throughout the rest of the chapter, using his own experience as an example of what is true of unredeemed mankind (vv. 7-12) and true of Christians (vv. 13-25). ***covet.*** Quoted from Ex. 20:17; Deut. 5:21.

7:8 opportunity by the commandment. The word "opportunity" describes a starting point or base of operations for an expedition. Sin uses the specific requirements of the law as a base of operation from which to launch its evil work. Confronted by God's law, the sinner's rebellious nature finds the forbidden thing more attractive, not because it is inherently attractive, but because it furnishes an opportunity to assert one's self-will. **sin *was* dead.** Not lifeless or nonexistent (*see notes on 5:12,13*), but dormant. When the law comes, sin becomes fully active and overwhelms the sinner.

7:9 without the law. Not ignorance of or lack of concern for the law (cf. Phil. 3:6), but a purely external, imperfect conception of it. **when the commandment came.** When he began to understand the true requirements of God's moral law at some point prior to his conversion. **sin revived.** He realized his true condition as a desperately wicked sinner (cf. 1 Tim. 1:15). **I died.** He realized his deadness, spiritually; that all his religious credentials and accomplishments were rubbish (Phil. 3:7,8).

7:10 *was* to *bring* life. Theoretically, perfect obedience to the law could bring eternal life, and with it happiness and holiness. But no one except Christ has—or could—ever fully obey it (2 Cor. 5:21; *see note on 10:5*).

7:11 sin...deceived me. By leading him to expect life from his keeping of the law, when what he found was death (v. 10); and by convincing him that he is acceptable to God because of his own merit and good works.

7:12 The fact that the law reveals, arouses, and condemns sin, bringing death to the sinner, does not mean that the law is evil (cf. v. 7). Rather the law is a perfect reflection of God's holy character (cf. vv. 14,16,22; Ps. 19:7-11) and the standard for believers to please Him.

7:13 Has then what is good become death. Sin is the cause of spiritual death, not the good law. **sin...might become...sinful.** An awareness of the true nature of sin and its deadly character, which brings the sinner to see his need of salvation—the very purpose God intended the law to serve (Gal. 3:19-22).

7:14-25 Some interpret this chronicle of Paul's inner conflict as describing his life before Christ. They point out that Paul describes the person as "sold under sin" (v. 14); as having "nothing good" in him (v. 18); and as a "wretched man" trapped in a "body of death" (v. 24). Those descriptions seem to contradict the way Paul describes the believer in chap. 6 (cf. vv. 2,6,7,11,17,18,22). However, it is correct to understand Paul here to be speaking about a believer. This person desires to obey God's law and hates his sin (vv. 15,19,21); he is humble, recognizing that nothing good dwells in his humanness (v. 18); he sees sin in himself, but not as all that is there (vv. 17,20-22); and he serves Jesus Christ with his mind (v. 25). Paul has already established that none of those attitudes ever describe the unsaved (cf. 1:18-21,32; 3:10-20). Paul's use of present tense verbs in vv. 14-25 strongly supports the idea that he is describing his life currently as a Christian. For those reasons, it seems certain that chap. 7 describes a believer. However, of those who agree that this is a believer, there is still disagreement. Some see a carnal, fleshly Christian; others a legalistic Christian, frustrated by his feeble attempts in his own power to please God by keeping the Mosaic law. But the personal pronoun "I" refers to the apostle Paul, a standard of spiritual health and maturity. So, in vv. 14-25 Paul must be describing all Christians—even the most spiritual and mature—who, when they honestly evaluate themselves against the righteous standard of God's law, realize how far short they fall. He does so in a series of 4 laments (vv. 14-17,18-20,21-23,24,25).

7:14 the law is spiritual. I.e., it reflects God's holy character. **carnal.** Lit. "of flesh." This means earthbound, mortal, and still incarcerated in unredeemed humanness. Paul does not say he is still "in the flesh" (*see note on 7:5*), but the flesh is in him. **sold under sin.** Sin no longer controls the whole man (as with an unbeliever; cf. 6:6), but it does hold captive the believer's members, or his fleshly body (v. 23; cf. v. 18). Sin contaminates him and frustrates his inner desire to obey the will of God.

15 For what I am doing, I do not understand. [o]For what I will to do, that I do not
practice; but what I hate, that I do. 16 If,
then, I do what I will not to do, I agree with
the law that *it is* good. 17 But now, *it is* no
longer I who do it, but sin that dwells in
me. 18 For I know that [p]in me (that is, in
my flesh) nothing good dwells; for to will
is present with me, but *how* to perform
what is good I do not find. 19 For the good
that I will *to do,* I do not do; but the evil I
will not *to do,* that I practice. 20 Now if I do
what I will not *to do,* it is no longer I who
do it, but sin that dwells in me.
21 I find then a law, that evil is present
with me, the one who wills to do good.
22 For I [q]delight in the law of God according to [r]the inward man. 23 But [s]I see another law in [t]my members, warring
against the law of my mind, and bringing
me into captivity to the law of sin which is
in my members. 24 O wretched man that I
am! Who will deliver me [u]from this body
of death? 25 [v]I thank God—through Jesus
Christ our Lord!
So then, with the mind I myself serve the
law of God, but with the flesh the law of
sin.

Free from Indwelling Sin

8 *There is* therefore now no condemnation to those who are in Christ Jesus,
[a]who [1] do not walk according to the flesh,
but according to the Spirit. 2 For [b]the law
of [c]the Spirit of life in Christ Jesus has
made me free from [d]the law of sin and

15 [o] Rom. 7:19; [Gal. 5:17]
18 [p] [Gen. 6:5; 8:21]
22 [q] Ps. 1:2 [r] [2 Cor. 4:16; Eph. 3:16; 1 Pet. 3:4]
23 [s] Rom. 6:19; [Gal. 5:17]; James 4:1; 1 Pet. 2:11 [t] Rom. 6:13, 19
24 [u] [Rom. 8:11; 1 Cor. 15:51, 52; 1 Thess. 4:14-17]
25 [v] 1 Cor. 15:57

CHAPTER 8

1 [a] Gal. 5:16 [1] NU omits the rest of v. 1.
2 [b] Rom. 6:18, 22 [c] [1 Cor. 15:45] [d] Rom. 7:24, 25

7:15 understand. This refers to knowledge that goes beyond the factual and includes the idea of an intimate relationship (cf. Gal. 4:9). By extension, this word was sometimes used to express approving or accepting (cf. 1 Cor. 8:3). That is its sense here, i.e., Paul found himself doing things he did not approve of.

7:16 I agree with the law that *it is* good. Paul's new nature defends the divine standard—the perfectly righteous law is not responsible for his sin (v. 12). His new self longs to honor the law and keep it perfectly (v. 22).

7:17 no longer I who do it. The Gr. adverb for "no longer" signifies a complete and permanent change. Paul's new inner self (*see note on 6:6*), the new "I," no longer approved of the sin that was still residing in his flesh, like his old self did (cf. v. 22; Gal. 2:20), but rather, strongly disapproved. Many have misconstrued Paul's comments as abdicating personal responsibility for his sin by embracing a form of Greek dualism (which would later spawn Gnosticism; see Introduction to 1 John). Dualism taught that the body is evil and the spirit is good, so its adherents sinned with impunity by claiming they were not responsible; their sin was entirely the product of their physical bodies, while their spirits remained untouched and unsullied. But the apostle has already acknowledged personal guilt for his sin (v. 14; cf. 1 John 1:10). **sin that dwells in me.** His sin does not flow out of his new redeemed innermost self ("I"), but from his unredeemed humanness, his flesh "in me" (Gal. 5:17).

7:18 in me...nothing good dwells. The flesh serves as a base camp from which sin operates in the Christian's life. It is not sinful inherently (*see note 6:6*), but because of its fallenness, it is still subject to sin and is thoroughly contaminated. **my flesh.** The part of the believer's present being that remains unredeemed (*see notes on 6:6,12; 7:5*).

7:20 no longer I who do it, but sin. *See note on v. 17.*

7:21 law. Not a reference to God's law, but to an inviolable spiritual principle.

7:22 I delight in the law of God. The believer's justified, new inner self no longer sides with sin, but joyfully agrees with the law of God against sin (Pss. 1:2; 119:14,47,77,105,140; cf. 2 Cor. 4:16; Eph. 3:16).

7:23 another law. A corresponding spiritual principle to the one in v. 21. But this principle, which Paul identifies as "the law of sin," operates in the members of his body—that is, his unredeemed and still sinful humanness (*see note on 6:6*)—waging war against his desire to obey God's law. **law of my mind.** Equivalent to the new inner self (2 Cor. 5:17; *see notes on 6:6*), which longs to obey the law of God (*see notes on vv. 21,22*). Paul is not saying his mind is spiritual and his body is inherently evil (*see note on v. 17*).

7:24 wretched man. In frustration and grief, Paul laments his sin (cf. Pss. 38:14; 130:1-5). A believer perceives his own sinfulness in direct proportion to how clearly he sees the holiness of God and perfection of His law. **deliver.** This word means "to rescue from danger" and was used of a soldier pulling his wounded comrade from the battlefield. Paul longed to be rescued from his sinful flesh (cf. 8:23). **body of death.** The believer's unredeemed humanness, which has its base of operation in the body (*see notes on 6:6,12; 7:5*). Tradition says that an ancient tribe near Tarsus tied the corpse of a murder victim to its murderer, allowing its spreading decay to slowly infect and execute the murderer—perhaps that is the image Paul has in mind.

7:25 The first half of this verse answers the question Paul just raised (v. 24)—he is certain that Christ will eventually rescue him when He returns (cf. 8:18,23; 1 Cor. 15:52,53,56,57; 2 Cor. 5:4). The second half summarizes the two sides of the struggle Paul has described (vv. 14-24). **with the mind.** *See note on v. 23.* **I myself.** Paul's new redeemed self (*see note on 6:6*). **the flesh.** *See notes on 6:6,12; 7:5.* **law of sin.** *See note on v. 23.*

8:1 therefore. The result or consequence of the truth just taught. Normally it marks the conclusion of the verses immediately preceding it. But here it introduces the staggering results of Paul's teaching in the first 7 chapters: that justification is by faith alone on the basis of God's overwhelming grace. **no condemnation.** Occurring only 3 times in the NT, all in Romans (cf. 5:16,18), "condemnation" is used exclusively in judicial settings as the opposite of justification. It refers to a verdict of guilty and the penalty that verdict demands. No sin a believer can commit—past, present, or future—can be held against him, since the penalty was paid by Christ and righteousness was imputed to the believer. And no sin will ever reverse this divine legal decision (*see note on v. 33*). **those...in Christ Jesus.** I.e., every true Christian; to be in Christ means to be united with Him (*see notes on 6:2,11*; cf. 6:1-11; 1 Cor. 12:13,27; 15:22). **walk according to the flesh...the Spirit.** This phrase is not found here in the earliest manuscripts but only at the end of v. 4, perhaps indicating an inadvertent copyist insertion.

8:2-30 The Spirit, who was mentioned only once in chaps. 1–7 (cf. 1:4), is referred to nearly 20 times in chap. 8. He frees us from sin and death (vv. 2,3); enables us to fulfill God's law (v. 4); changes our nature and grants us strength for victory over our unredeemed flesh (vv. 5-13); confirms our adoption as God's children (vv. 14-16); and guarantees our ultimate glory (vv. 17-30).

8:2 The word "for" introduces the reason there is no condemnation for the believer, the Spirit has replaced the law that produced only sin and death (7:5,13) with a new, simple law that produces life: the law of faith (3:27), or the message of the gospel. **the law of the Spirit of life.** Synonymous with the gospel, the law of faith. **the law of sin and death.** The law of God. Although it is good, holy, and righ-

death. 3 For [e]what the law could not do in
that it was weak through the flesh, [f]God
did by sending His own Son in the likeness
of sinful flesh, on account of sin: He condemned sin in the flesh, 4 that the righteous requirement of the law might be fulfilled in us who [g]do not walk according to
the flesh but according to the Spirit. 5 For
[h]those who live according to the flesh set
their minds on the things of the flesh, but
those *who live* according to the Spirit, [i]the
things of the Spirit. 6 For [j]to be [2]carnally
minded *is* death, but to be spiritually
minded *is* life and peace. 7 Because [k]the
[3]carnal mind *is* enmity against God; for it
is not subject to the law of God, [l]nor indeed can be. 8 So then, those who are in the
flesh cannot please God.
9 But you are not in the flesh but in the
Spirit, if indeed the Spirit of God dwells in
you. Now if anyone does not have the
Spirit of Christ, he is not His. 10 And if
Christ *is* in you, the body *is* dead because
of sin, but the Spirit *is* life because of righteousness. 11 But if the Spirit of [m]Him who
raised Jesus from the dead dwells in you,
[n]He who raised Christ from the dead will
also give life to your mortal bodies
[4]through His Spirit who dwells in you.

Sonship Through the Spirit

12 [o]Therefore, brethren, we are debtors—
not to the flesh, to live according to the
flesh. 13 For [p]if you live according to the
flesh you will die; but if by the Spirit you
[q]put to death the deeds of the body, you
will live. 14 For [r]as many as are led by the
Spirit of God, these are sons of God. 15 For

3 [e] Acts 13:39; [Heb. 7:18] [f] [2 Cor. 5:21; Gal. 3:13]
4 [g] [Rom. 6:4; 2 Cor. 5:7]; Gal. 5:16, 25; Eph. 4:1; 5:2, 15; [1 John 1:7; 2:6]
5 [h] John 3:6 [i] [Gal. 5:22-25]
6 [j] Gal. 6:8 [2] *fleshly*
7 [k] James 4:4 [l] 1 Cor. 2:14 [3] *fleshly*
11 [m] Acts 2:24; Rom. 6:4 [n] 1 Cor. 6:14 [4] Or *because of*
12 [o] [Rom. 6:7, 14]
13 [p] Gal. 6:8 [q] Eph. 4:22; [Col. 3:5-10]
14 [r] [Gal. 5:18]

teous (7:12), because of the weakness of the flesh (*see notes on 7:7-11; 8:3*), it can produce only sin and death (7:5,13).

8:3 what the law could not do. Deliver sinners from its penalty (Acts 13:38,39; Gal. 3:10) or make them righteous (Gal. 3:21). **weak...the flesh.** Because of the sinful corruption of unregenerate men, the law was powerless to produce righteousness (Gal. 3:21). **His own Son.** *See notes on Ps. 2:7; Gal. 4:4; Phil. 2:6,7; Heb. 1:1-5.* **in the likeness of sinful flesh.** Although in His incarnation Christ became fully man (*see note on 1:3*), He took only the outward appearance of sinful flesh, because He was completely without sin (Heb. 4:15). **condemned sin in the flesh.** God's condemnation against sin was fully poured out on the sinless flesh of Christ (Is. 53:4-8; cf. Phil. 2:7).

8:4 righteous requirement of the law. The thoughts, words, and deeds which the moral law of God demands. The ceremonial aspect of the Mosaic law has been set aside (Col. 2:14-17), and the basic responsibility for the civil aspect, which shows the application of the moral law in a community, has been transferred to human government (13:1-7). The moral law finds its basis in the character of God and is presented in outline form in the Ten Commandments; its most condensed form is in Jesus' commands to love God and to love one's neighbor as one's self. It has never been abrogated, but finds its authority in the New Covenant. Every unbeliever is still under its requirement of perfection and its condemnation, until he comes to Christ (Gal. 3:23-25) and every believer still finds in it the standard for behavior. **fulfilled.** Although the believer is no longer in bondage to the moral law's condemnation and penalty (7:6), the law still reflects the moral character of God and His will for His creatures. But what the external, written code was unable to accomplish, the Spirit is able to do by writing the law on our hearts (Jer. 31:33,34) and giving us the power to obey it. **not walk according to the flesh but...the Spirit.** Not an admonition, but a statement of fact that applies to all believers. "Walk" refers to a lifestyle, the habits of living and thinking that characterize a person's life (cf. Luke 1:6; Eph. 4:17; 1 John 1:7). Since every true Christian is indwelt by the Spirit (v. 9), every Christian will manifest the fruit He produces in their life (Gal. 5:22,23).

8:5 those who live...the flesh. All unbelievers (*see note on v. 4*). **set their minds.** This Gr. verb refers to a basic orientation of the mind—a mindset that includes one's affections, mental processes, and will (cf. Phil. 2:2,5; 3:15,19; Col. 3:2). Paul's point is that unbelievers' basic disposition is to satisfy the cravings of their unredeemed flesh (Phil. 3:19; 2 Pet. 2:10). **those *who live*...the Spirit.** All believers (*see note on v. 4*).

8:6 carnally minded. In the Gr. "minded" is a noun form of the verb in v. 5. "Carnally" means "of flesh." This is a simple spiritual equation: The person with the mind set on the flesh is spiritually dead (cf. 1 Cor. 2:14; Eph. 2:1). **spiritually minded.** This describes every Christian. The person with his mind set on the things of the Spirit is very much spiritually alive and at peace with God (*see note on 5:1*; cf. Eph. 2:5).

8:7 enmity against God. The unbeliever's problem is much deeper than acts of disobedience, which are merely outward manifestations of inner fleshly compulsions. His basic inclinations and orientation toward gratifying himself—however outwardly religious or moral he may appear—are directly hostile to God. Even the good deeds unbelievers perform are not truly a fulfillment of God's law, because they are produced by the flesh, for selfish reasons, and from a heart that is in rebellion (*see note on 5:1*).

8:8 in the flesh. *See note on 7:5.*

8:9 dwells. Refers to being in one's own home. The Spirit of God makes His home in every person who trusts in Jesus Christ. Cf. 1 Cor. 6:19,20; 12:13. When there is no evidence of His presence by the fruit He produces (Gal. 5:22,23), a person has no legitimate claim to Christ as Savior and Lord.

8:10 the body *is* dead because of sin. The body is unredeemed and dead in sin (*see notes on 6:6,12; 7:5*; cf. 8:11,23). **the Spirit *is* life because of righteousness.** It is best to translate the word "spirit" as the person's spirit, not the Holy Spirit. Paul is saying that if God's Spirit indwells you (v. 9), the human spirit is alive (cf. Eph. 2:5) and can manifest true righteousness (cf. v. 4).

8:11 your mortal bodies. *See note on 6:12*; cf. 8:23.

8:12 the flesh. Our unredeemed humanness—that complex of sinful passions that sin generates through its one remaining domain, our bodies (*see notes on 6:6,12; 7:5*).

8:13 put to death the deeds of the body. Paul's first instruction concerning what his readers must do in the struggle with sin destroys several false views of how believers are made holy: 1) that in a crisis-moment we are immediately made perfect; 2) that we must "let God" take over while we remain idle; and 3) that some turning-point decision will propel us to a higher level of holiness. Rather, the apostle says the Spirit provides us with the energy and power to continually and gradually be killing our sins, a process never completed in this life. The means the Spirit uses to accomplish this process is our faithful obedience to the simple commands of Scripture (*see notes on Eph. 5:18; Col. 3:16*; cf. 13:14; Pss. 1:2; 119:11; Luke 22:40; John 17:17; 1 Cor. 6:18; 9:25-27; 1 Pet. 2:11).

8:14 led by the Spirit. Believers are not led through subjective, mental impressions or promptings to provide direction in making life's decisions—something Scripture nowhere teaches. Instead, God's Spirit objectively leads His children sometimes through the orchestration of

[s]you did not receive the spirit of bondage
again [t]to fear, but you received the [u]Spirit
of adoption by whom we cry out, [v]"Abba,[5]
Father." 16 [w]The Spirit Himself bears witness with our spirit that we are children of
God, 17 and if children, then [x]heirs—heirs
of God and joint heirs with Christ, [y]if indeed we suffer with *Him,* that we may also
be glorified together.

From Suffering to Glory

18 For I consider that [z]the sufferings of
this present time are not worthy *to be com-*
pared with the glory which shall be revealed in us. 19 For [a]the earnest expectation of the creation eagerly waits for the
revealing of the sons of God. 20 For [b]the
creation was subjected to futility, not willingly, but because of Him who subjected *it*
in hope; 21 because the creation itself also
will be delivered from the bondage of [6]cor-
ruption into the glorious [c]liberty of the
children of God. 22 For we know that the
whole creation [d]groans and labors with
birth pangs together until now. 23 Not only
that, but we also who have [e]the firstfruits
of the Spirit, [f]even we ourselves groan
[g]within ourselves, eagerly waiting for the
adoption, the [h]redemption of our body.
24 For we were saved in this hope, but
[i]hope that is seen is not hope; for why does
one still hope for what he sees? 25 But if we
hope for what we do not see, we eagerly
wait for *it* with perseverance.

26 Likewise the Spirit also helps in our
weaknesses. For [j]we do not know what we
should pray for as we ought, but [k]the Spirit Himself makes intercession [7]for us with
groanings which cannot be uttered.
27 Now [l]He who searches the hearts knows
what the mind of the Spirit *is,* because He
makes intercession for the saints [m]accord-
ing to *the will of* God.

28 And we know that all things work together for good to those who love God, to
those [n]who are the called according to *His*

15 [s] [1 Cor. 2:12]; Heb. 2:15 [t] 2 Tim. 1:7 [u] [Is. 56:5] [v] Mark 14:36; Gal. 4:6 [5] Lit., in Aram., *Father*
16 [w] Eph. 1:13
17 [x] Acts 26:18 [y] Phil. 1:29
18 [z] 2 Cor. 4:17; [1 Pet. 1:6; 4:13]
19 [a] [2 Pet. 3:13]
20 [b] Gen. 3:17-19
21 [c] [2 Cor. 3:17]; Gal. 5:1, 13 [6] *decay*
22 [d] Jer. 12:4, 11
23 [e] 2 Cor. 5:5; Eph. 1:14 [f] 2 Cor. 5:2, 4 [g] [Luke 20:36] [h] Luke 21:28; Eph. 1:14; 4:30; [Phil. 3:20, 21]
24 [i] Rom. 4:18; 2 Cor. 5:7; Heb. 11:1
26 [j] Matt. 20:22; 2 Cor. 12:8 [k] John 14:16; Rom. 8:15; Eph. 6:18 [7] NU omits *for us*
27 [l] 1 Chr. 28:9 [m] 1 John 5:14
28 [n] 2 Tim. 1:9

circumstances (Acts 16:7) but primarily through: 1) illumination, divinely clarifying Scripture to make it understandable to our sinful, finite minds (Luke 24:44,45; 1 Cor. 2:14-16; Eph. 1:17-19; cf. Eph. 3:16-19; Col. 1:9); and 2) sanctification, divinely enabling us to obey Scripture (Gal. 5:16,17; 5:25). **sons of God.** When a person experiences the Spirit's leading in those ways, he gains assurance that God has adopted him into His family (*see notes on 8:15-17; 1 John 3:2;* for other tests of true faith see Introduction to 1 John: Historical and Theological Themes).

8:15 spirit of bondage...to fear. Because of their life of sin, unregenerate people are slaves to their fear of death (Heb. 2:14,15), and to their fear of final punishment (1 John 4:18). **Spirit of adoption.** Not primarily a reference to the transaction by which God adopts us (*see notes on Eph. 1:5; Gal. 4:5-7*), but to a Spirit-produced awareness of the rich reality that God has made us His children, and, therefore, that we can come before Him without fear or hesitation as our beloved Father. It includes the confidence that we are truly sons of God. **Abba.** An informal, Aram. term for Father that conveys a sense of intimacy. Like the Eng. terms "Daddy" or "Papa," it connotes tenderness, dependence, and a relationship free of fear or anxiety (cf. Mark 14:36).

8:16 bears witness with our spirit. In Roman culture, for an adoption to be legally binding, 7 reputable witnesses had to be present, attesting to its validity. God's Holy Spirit confirms the validity of our adoption, not by some inner, mystical voice, but by the fruit He produces in us (Gal. 5:22,23) and the power He provides for spiritual service (Acts 1:8).

8:17 heirs. Every believer has been made an heir of God, our Father (Matt. 25:34; Gal. 3:29; Eph. 1:11; Col. 1:12; 3:24; Heb. 6:12; 9:15; 1 Pet. 1:4). We will inherit eternal salvation (Titus 3:7), God Himself (Lam. 3:24; cf. Ps. 73:25; Rev. 21:3), glory (5:2), and everything in the universe (Heb. 1:2). Unlike the Jewish practice of the primacy of the firstborn son, under Roman law the inheritance was divided equally between the children, where the law more carefully protected possessions that had been inherited. **joint heirs.** God has appointed His Son to be heir of all things (Heb. 1:2). Every adopted child will receive by divine grace the full inheritance Christ receives by divine right (cf. Matt. 25:21; John 17:22; 2 Cor. 8:9). **if...we suffer with *Him*.** Proof of the believer's ultimate glory is that he suffers—whether it comes as mockery, ridicule, or physical persecution—because of His Lord (Matt. 5:10-12; John 15:18-21; 2 Cor. 4:17; 2 Tim. 3:12).

8:18 glory...revealed in us. This looks forward to the resurrection of the body (v. 23) and the subsequent complete Christlikeness which is the believer's eternal glory. See Phil. 3:20,21; Col. 3:4; 1 John 3:2.

8:19 the creation. This includes everything in the physical universe except human beings, whom he contrasts with this term (vv. 22,23). All creation is personified to be, as it were, longing for transformation from the curse and its effects. **the revealing.** Lit. "an uncovering," or "an unveiling." When Christ returns, God's children will share His glory. *See note on v. 18.*

8:20 futility. This refers to the inability to achieve a goal or purpose. Because of man's sin, God cursed the physical universe (Gen. 3:17-19), and now, no part of creation entirely fulfills God's original purpose.

8:21 delivered. Cf. 2 Pet. 3:10; Rev. 21:4,5.

8:23 firstfruits of the Spirit. Just as the first pieces of produce to appear on a tree provide hope of a future harvest, the fruit which the Spirit produces in us now (Gal. 5:22,23) provides hope that we will one day be like Christ. **groan.** With grief over our remaining sinfulness (7:24; cf. Ps. 38:4,9,10). **adoption.** The process that began with God's choice (Eph. 1:5) and included our actually becoming His children at salvation (Gal. 4:5-7) will culminate with our glorification—the full realization of our inheritance (see vv. 29,30). **redemption of our body.** Not the physical body only, but all of man's remaining fallenness (*see notes on 6:6,12; 7:5;* cf. 1 Cor. 15:35-44; Phil. 3:20,21; 2 Pet. 1:3,4; 1 John 3:2).

8:24 hope. *See note on 5:2.*

8:26 Likewise. As the creation (v. 22) and believers (v. 23) both groan for ultimate restoration, the Spirit does as well. **groanings which cannot be uttered.** Divine articulations within the Trinity that cannot be expressed in words, but carry profound appeals for the welfare of every believer (cf. 1 Cor. 2:11). This word of the Holy Spirit parallels the high priestly work of intercession by the Lord Jesus on behalf of believers (see Heb. 2:17,18; 4:14-16; 7:24-26).

8:27 the mind of the Spirit. No words are necessary because the Father understands and agrees with what the Spirit thinks. *See note on Jude 20.*

8:28 The best manuscript evidence records this verse as, "we know that God causes all things...." **good.** In His providence, God orchestrates every event in life—even suffering, temptation, and sin—to accomplish both our temporal and eternal benefit (cf. Deut. 8:15,16). **called.** Cf. v. 30; *see note on 1:7.* As always, in the NT epistles, this call is God's effectual calling of His elect that brings them to salvation.

purpose. 29 For whom [o]He foreknew, [p]He
also predestined [q]*to be* conformed to the
image of His Son, [r]that He might be the
firstborn among many brethren. 30 Moreover whom He predestined, these He also
[s]called; whom He called, these He also
[t]justified; and whom He justified, these He
also [u]glorified.

God's Everlasting Love

31 What then shall we say to these things?
[v]If God *is* for us, who *can be* against us?
32 [w]He who did not spare His own Son, but
[x]delivered Him up for us all, how shall He
not with Him also freely give us all things?
33 Who shall bring a charge against God's
elect? [y]*It is* God who justifies. 34 [z]Who *is* he
who condemns? *It is* Christ who died, and
furthermore is also risen, [a]who is even at the
right hand of God, [b]who also makes intercession for us. 35 Who shall separate us from
the love of Christ? *Shall* tribulation, or distress, or persecution, or famine, or nakedness, or peril, or sword? 36 As it is written:

[c]*"For Your sake we are killed all day*
long;
We are accounted as sheep for the
slaughter."

37 [d]Yet in all these things we are more
than conquerors through Him who loved
us. 38 For I am persuaded that neither
death nor life, nor angels nor [e]principali-
ties nor powers, nor things present nor
things to come, 39 nor height nor depth,
nor any other created thing, shall be able to
separate us from the love of God which is
in Christ Jesus our Lord.

Israel's Rejection of Christ

9 I [a]tell the truth in Christ, I am not lying,
my conscience also bearing me witness
in the Holy Spirit, 2 [b]that I have great sorrow and continual grief in my heart. 3 For [c]I
could wish that I myself were accursed from
Christ for my brethren, my [1]countrymen

29 [o] 2 Tim. 2:19 [p] Rom. 9:23; 1 Cor. 2:7; Eph. 1:5, 11 [q] [2 Cor. 3:18] [r] [Col. 1:15, 18]; Heb. 1:6
30 [s] Rom. 8:28; 9:24; 1 Cor. 1:9; Gal. 1:6, 15; 5:8; Eph. 1:11; 3:11; 2 Thess. 2:14; [Heb. 9:15; 1 Pet. 2:9; 3:9] [t] 1 Cor. 6:11; [Gal. 2:16] [u] John 17:22; Rom. 8:21
31 [v] Num. 14:9
32 [w] Rom. 5:6, 10 [x] [Rom. 4:25]
33 [y] Is. 50:8, 9; Rev. 12:10
34 [z] John 3:18 [a] Mark 16:19; Col. 3:1; Heb. 1:3 [b] Heb. 7:25; 9:24
36 [c] Ps. 44:22; Acts 20:24; 1 Cor. 4:9; 15:30; [2 Cor. 1:9; 4:10; 6:9; 11:23]
37 [d] John 16:33; 1 Cor. 15:57; 2 Cor. 2:14; 1 John 5:4
38 [e] [1 Cor. 15:24; Eph. 1:21; 1 Pet. 3:22]

CHAPTER 9 1 [a] 2 Cor. 1:23 2 [b] Rom. 10:1 3 [c] Ex. 32:32 [1] Or *relatives*

8:29 foreknew. Not a reference simply to God's omniscience—that in eternity past He knew who would come to Christ. Rather, it speaks of a predetermined choice to set His love on us and established an intimate relationship—or His election (cf. Acts 2:23—an inviolable rule of Gr. grammar, called the Granville Sharp rule, equates "predestinated" and "foreknowledge;" *see notes on 1 Pet. 1:1,2,* and cf. with 1:20—the term must be interpreted the same in both verses). *See notes on election in 9:10-24.* **predestined.** Lit. "to mark out, appoint, or determine beforehand." Those God chooses, He destines for His chosen end—that is, likeness to His Son (*see notes on Eph. 1:4,5,11*). **conformed to the image of His Son.** The goal of God's predestined purpose for His own is that they would be made like Jesus Christ. This is the "prize of the upward call" (Phil. 3:14); cf. Eph. 4:13; Col. 1:28; Phil. 3:20,21; 1 John 3:2). **firstborn.** The preeminent one, the only one who is the rightful heir (cf. Ps. 89:27; Col. 1:15-18; Rev. 1:5). Jesus Christ is the most notable one among those who have become "brethren" by being made like Him.

8:30 predestined. *See note on v. 29.* **called.** *See note on 1:7.* **justified.** *See note on 3:24.* **glorified.** Paul uses the past tense for a future event to stress its certainty (cf. vv. 18,21; 2 Tim. 2:10).

8:31-39 Paul closes his teaching about the believer's security in Christ with a crescendo of questions and answers for the concerns his readers might still have. The result is an almost poetic expression of praise for God's grace in bringing salvation to completion for all who are chosen and believe—a hymn of security.

8:31 If God *is* for us. The Gr. construction is better translated "Since God is for us."

8:32 Paul's point is: Would God do less for His children than He did for His enemies? **freely give.** This word means "to bestow out of grace." Paul often uses it to denote forgiveness (2 Cor. 2:7,10; 12:13; Col. 2:13; 3:13) and may intend that here. **all things.** Referring either to every sin the believer commits (if "freely give" is translated "forgiveness") or to whatever is necessary to complete the purpose He had in choosing us (vv. 29,30; cf. Phil. 1:6)

8:33,34 The setting of these verses is the divine courtroom.

8:33 God's elect. *See notes on vv. 29,30.* ***It is* God who justifies.** *See note on 3:24.* Who can successfully accuse someone whom God has declared righteous?

8:34 condemns. To declare guilty and sentence to punishment. There are 4 reasons the believer can never be found guilty: 1) Christ's death; 2) His resurrection; 3) His exalted position; and 4) His continual intercession for them. **intercession.** Cf. Is. 53:12; Heb. 7:25.

8:35-39 This list of experiences and persons that can't separate the believer from God's love in Christ was not just theory to Paul. It was rather personal testimony from one who had personally survived assaults from these entities and emerged triumphant.

8:35 the love of Christ. Not our love for Christ, but His love for us (John 13:1), specifically here as He demonstrated it in salvation (1 John 4:9,10). **tribulation.** *See note on 5:3.* Here the word probably refers to the kind of adversity common to all men. **distress.** This refers to being strictly confined in a narrow, difficult place or being helplessly hemmed in by one's circumstances. **persecution.** Suffering inflicted on us by men because of our relationship with Christ (Matt. 5:10-12).

8:36 This is a quotation from the LXX (the ancient Gr. translation of the Heb. OT) of Ps. 44:22.

8:37 more than conquerors. A compound Gr. word, which means to over-conquer, to conquer completely, without any real threat to personal life or health.

8:38 principalities. Fallen angels or demons (cf. Eph. 6:12; Col. 2:15; Jude 6). **powers.** The plural form of this common word for "power" is used to refer to either miracles or to persons in positions of authority.

8:39 nor height nor depth. Common astronomical terms used to refer to the high and low points of a star's path; nothing in life's path, from beginning to end, can separate us from Christ's love. Possibly, Paul may intend to describe all of space from top to bottom. **nor any other created thing.** In case anything or anyone might be left out, this covers everything but the Creator Himself. **the love of God.** Cf. 5:5-11.

9:1 conscience. *See note on 2:15.* **in the Holy Spirit.** Only when the Spirit controls the conscience can it be trusted—but it remains imperfect and its warnings must always be evaluated against the Word of God (cf. 1 Cor. 4:3-5).

9:3 accursed. The Gr. word is *anathema,* which means "to devote to destruction in eternal hell" (cf. 1 Cor. 12:3; 16:22; Gal. 1:8,9). Although Paul understood the exchange he was suggesting was im-

according to the flesh, **4** who are Israelites,
[d]to whom *pertain* the adoption, [e]the glory,
[f]the covenants, [g]the giving of the law, [h]the
service *of God,* and [i]the promises; **5** [j]of
whom *are* the fathers and from [k]whom, according to the flesh, Christ *came,* [l]who is
over all, *the* eternally blessed God. Amen.

Israel's Rejection and God's Purpose

6 [m]But it is not that the word of God has
taken no effect. For [n]they *are* not all Israel
who *are* of Israel, **7** [o]nor *are they* all children
because they are the seed of Abraham; but,
[p]*"In Isaac your seed shall be called."* **8** That
is, those who *are* the children of the flesh,
these *are* not the children of God; but [q]the
children of the promise are counted as the
seed. **9** For this *is* the word of promise: [r]*"At
this time I will come and Sarah shall have
a son."*

10 And not only *this,* but when [s]Rebecca
also had conceived by one man, *even* by
our father Isaac **11** (for *the children* not yet
being born, nor having done any good or
evil, that the purpose of God according to
election might stand, not of works but of
[t]Him who calls), **12** it was said to her,
[u]*"The older shall serve the younger."* **13** As
it is written, [v]*"Jacob I have loved, but Esau
I have hated."*

Israel's Rejection and God's Justice

14 What shall we say then? [w]*Is there* unrighteousness with God? Certainly not!
15 For He says to Moses, [x]*"I will have
mercy on whomever I will have mercy,
and I will have compassion on whomever
I will have compassion."* **16** So then *it is*
not of him who wills, nor of him who
runs, but of God who shows mercy. **17** For

4 [d]Ex. 4:22; [Rom. 8:15] [e]1 Sam. 4:21 [f]Gen. 17:2; Deut. 29:14; Luke 1:72; Acts 3:25 [g]Deut. 4:13; Ps. 147:19 [h]Heb. 9:1, 6 [i][Acts 2:39; 13:32; Eph. 2:12]
5 [j]Deut. 10:15 [k][Luke 1:34, 35; 3:23] [l]Jer. 23:6
6 [m]Num. 23:19 [n][John 8:39; Gal. 6:16]
7 [o][John 8:33, 39; Gal. 4:23] [p]Gen. 21:12; Heb. 11:18
8 [q]Gal. 4:28
9 [r]Gen. 18:10, 14; Heb. 11:11
10 [s]Gen. 25:21
11 [t][Rom. 4:17; 8:28]
12 [u]Gen. 25:23
13 [v]Mal. 1:2, 3
14 [w]Deut. 32:4
15 [x]Ex. 33:19

possible (8:38,39; John 10:28), it was still the sincere expression of his deep love for his fellow Jews (cf. Ex. 32:32).

9:4 Israelites. The descendants of Abraham through Jacob, whose name God changed to Israel (Gen. 32:28). **adoption.** Not in the sense of providing salvation to every person born a Jew (*see notes on 8:15-23*; cf. 9:6), but sovereignly selecting an entire nation to receive His special calling, covenant, and blessing and to serve as His witness nation (Ex. 4:22;19:6; Hos. 11:1; cf. Is. 46:3,4). **glory.** The glory cloud (Shekinah) that pictured God's presence in the OT (Ex. 16:10; 24:16,17; 29:42,43; Lev. 9:23). His glory was supremely present in the Holy of Holies in both the tabernacle and the temple, which served as the throne room of Yahweh, Israel's King (Ex. 25:22; 40:34; 1 Kin. 8:11). **covenants.** *See note on Gen. 9:16.* A covenant is a legally binding promise, agreement, or contract. Three times in the NT the word "covenants" is used in the plural (Gal. 4:24; Eph. 2:12). All but one of God's covenants with man are eternal and unilateral—that is, God promised to accomplish something based on His own character and not on the response or actions of the promised beneficiary. The 6 biblical covenants include: 1) the covenant with Noah (Gen. 9:8-17); 2) the covenant with Abraham (Gen. 12:1-3; *see note on 4:13*); 3) the covenant of law given through Moses at Sinai (Ex. 19-31; cf. Deut. 29,30); 4) the priestly covenant (Num. 25:10-13); 5) the covenant of an eternal kingdom through David's greatest Son (2 Sam. 7:8-16); and 6) the New Covenant (Jer. 31:31-34; Ezek. 37:26; cf. Heb. 8:6-13). All but the Mosaic Covenant are eternal and unilateral. It is neither, since Israel's sin abrogated it and it has been replaced by the New Covenant (cf. Heb. 8:7-13). **service.** Better translated "temple service," this refers to the entire sacrificial and ceremonial system that God revealed through Moses (cf. Ex. 29:43-46). **promises.** Probably this refers to the promised Messiah, who would come out of Israel, bringing eternal life and an eternal kingdom (cf. Acts 2:39; 13:32-34; 26:6; Gal. 3:16,21).

9:5 fathers. The patriarchs Abraham, Isaac, and Jacob, through whom the promises of the Messiah were fulfilled. **Christ...*the* eternally blessed God.** This is not intended primarily as a benediction, but as an affirmation of the sovereignty and deity of Christ.

9:6 word of God. This refers specifically to the privileges and promises God had revealed to Israel (v. 4; cf. Is. 55:11; Jer. 32:42). **not all Israel who *are* of Israel.** Not all the physical descendants of Abraham are true heirs of the promise (*see notes on 2:28,29*).

9:7 To illustrate the truth of v. 6, Paul reminds his readers that even the racial and national promises made to Abraham were not made to every physical descendant of his, but only to those who came through Isaac. Cf. Gen. 21:12. **children.** Only Isaac's descendants could truly be called the children of Abraham, the inheritors of those racial and national promises (Gen. 17:19-21).

9:8 children of the flesh. Abraham's other children by Hagar and Keturah were not chosen to receive the national promises made to him. **children of God.** Paul's point is that just as not all of Abraham's descendants belonged to the physical people of God—or national Israel—not all of those who are true children of Abraham through Isaac are the true spiritual people of God and enjoy the promises made to Abraham's spiritual children (4:6,11; cf. 11:3,4).

9:9 Quoted from Gen. 18:10.

9:11 *the children.* The twins Jacob and Esau. **done any good or evil.** God's choice of Jacob, instead of Esau, to continue the physical line was not based on his personal merit or demerit. **the purpose of God according to election.** Rather, God's choice of Jacob resides solely in His own sovereign plan, a perfect example of election unto salvation. God has chosen some Jews—and some Gentiles—but not all, for salvation. **not of works but of Him who calls.** The fact that God made His choice of Jacob before the boys were born and apart from personal merit demonstrates that election unto spiritual life is unrelated to any human effort, and is based only on the prerogative of God who makes His selection (*see note on 8:29*; cf. 1 Cor. 1:9).

9:12 Quoted from Gen. 25:23.

9:13 *Jacob I have loved, but Esau I have hated.* Quoted from Mal. 1:2,3. Actual emotional hatred for Esau and his offspring is not the point here. Malachi, who wrote this declaration more than 1,500 years after their death, was looking back at these two men—and by extension the nations (Israel and Edom) that came from their loins. God chose one for divine blessing and protection, and the other He left to divine judgment.

9:14 *Is there* unrighteousness with God? Paul once again anticipates his readers' objection to Paul's theology: If God were to choose some people for salvation and pass over others apart from their merits or actions that would make God arbitrary and unfair (cf. Gen. 18:25; Pss. 7:9; 48:10; 71:19; 119:137,142; Jer. 9:23,24).

9:15 Quoted from Ex. 33:19. In response to the accusation that such a teaching about God's sovereign election is inconsistent with His fairness, Paul cites this text from the OT that clearly indicates that God is absolutely sovereign and does elect who will be saved without violating His other attributes. He determines who receives mercy.

9:16 *it.* God's gracious choice of certain people unto eternal life (*see note on 8:29*). **who wills.** Salvation is not initiated by human choice—even faith is a gift of God (*see note on 1:16*; cf. John 6:37; Eph. 2:8,9). **who runs.** Salvation is not merited by human effort (*see notes on v. 11*).

[y]the Scripture says to the Pharaoh, [z]"For
this very purpose I have raised you up,
that I may show My power in you, and
that My name may be declared in all the
earth." 18 Therefore He has mercy on
whom He wills, and whom He wills He
[a]hardens.

19 You will say to me then, "Why does
He still find fault? For [b]who has resisted
His will?" 20 But indeed, O man, who are
you to reply against God? [c]Will the thing
formed say to him who formed *it*, "Why
have you made me like this?" 21 Does not
the [d]potter have power over the clay, from
the same lump to make [e]one vessel for
honor and another for dishonor?

22 *What* if God, wanting to show *His*
wrath and to make His power known, endured with much longsuffering [f]the vessels of wrath [g]prepared for destruction,
23 and that He might make known [h]the
riches of His glory on the vessels of mercy,
which He had [i]prepared beforehand for
glory, 24 *even* us whom He [j]called, [k]not of
the Jews only, but also of the Gentiles?
25 As He says also in Hosea:

[l]"I will call them My people, who
were not My people,
And her beloved, who was not
beloved."
26 *"And[m] it shall come to pass in the*
place where it was said to
them,
'You are not My people,'
There they shall be called sons of
the living God."

27 Isaiah also cries out concerning Israel:

[n]"Though the number of the children
of Israel be as the sand of the
sea,
[o]The remnant will be saved.
28 *For [2]He will finish the work and*
cut it short in righteousness,
[p]Because the LORD will make a short
work upon the earth."

29 And as Isaiah said before:

[q]"Unless the LORD of [3]Sabaoth had
left us a seed,

17 [y]Gal. 3:8 [z]Ex. 9:16
18 [a]Ex. 4:21; Deut. 2:30; Josh. 11:20; John 12:40; Rom. 11:7,25
19 [b]2 Chr. 20:6; Job 9:12; Dan. 4:35
20 [c]Is. 29:16; Jer. 18:6; Rom. 9:22; 2 Tim. 2:20
21 [d]Prov. 16:4 [e]2 Tim. 2:20
22 [f][1 Thess. 5:9] [g]Prov. 16:4; [1 Pet. 2:8]
23 [h][Col. 1:27] [i][Rom. 8:28-30]
24 [j][Rom. 8:28] [k]Is. 42:6, 7; 49:6; Luke 2:32; Rom. 3:29
25 [l]Hos. 2:23; 1 Pet. 2:10
26 [m]Hos. 1:10
27 [n]Is. 10:22, 23 [o]Rom. 11:5
28 [p]Is. 10:23; 28:22 [2]NU *the LORD will finish the work and cut it short upon the earth*
29 [q]Is. 1:9 [3]Lit., in Heb., *Hosts*

9:17 Quoted from Ex. 9:16. This again (as v. 15) is an OT quote to prove that God does sovereignly choose who will serve His purposes and how. ***raised you up.*** Refers to bringing forward or lifting up and was often used to describe the rise of leaders and countries to positions of prominence (cf. Hab. 1:6; Zech. 11:16). Undoubtedly, Pharaoh thought his position and actions were of his own free choice to accomplish his own purposes, but in reality he was there to serve God's purpose. ***My name.*** The sum of the character of God (cf. Ex. 34:5-7).

9:18 The mighty act of God in freeing Israel from the hand of Pharaoh demonstrated two corollary truths. Both Moses and Pharaoh were wicked sinners, even murderers, and were equally worthy of God's wrath and eternal punishment. But Moses received mercy while Pharaoh received God's judgment, because that was God's sovereign will (cf. 11:7; Josh. 11:18-20; 1 Thess. 5:9; 2 Pet. 2:12). **hardens.** The Gr. word literally means to make something hard, but is often used figuratively to refer to making stubborn or obstinate. Ten times Exodus refers to God's hardening Pharaoh's heart (e.g., 4:21; 7:3,13), and other times to Pharaoh's hardening his own heart (e.g., 8:32; 9:34). This does not mean that God actively created unbelief or some other evil in Pharaoh's heart (cf. James 1:13), but rather that He withdrew all the divine influences that ordinarily acted as a restraint to sin and allowed Pharaoh's wicked heart to pursue its sin unabated (cf. 1:24,26,28).

9:19 Why does He still find fault? The objection is: How can God blame anyone for sin and unbelief when He has sovereignly determined that person's destiny?

9:20 O man, who are you to reply against God? The nature of Paul's reply makes it clear that he is not addressing those with honest questions about this difficult doctrine, but those who seek to use it to excuse their own sin and unbelief.

9:20,21 Using the familiar OT analogy of the potter (cf. Is. 64:6-8; Jer. 18:3-16), Paul argues that it is as irrational, and far more arrogant, for men to question God's choice of certain sinners for salvation, as for a piece of pottery to question the purposes of the potter.

9:22,23 These verses are not intended to identify the origin of evil or explain fully why God has allowed it, but they do provide 3 reasons He has permitted its presence and contamination: 1) to demonstrate His wrath; 2) to make His power known; and 3) to put the riches of His glorious mercy on display. No one is treated unfairly: Some receive the justice they earn and deserve (6:23), others graciously receive mercy.

9:22 *What if.* This introduces a statement of fact in the form of a rhetorical question. **wanting.** The Gr. word speaks of divine intention, not passive resignation. **endured.** God could justly destroy sinners the first time they sin. But He patiently endures their rebellion rather than giving them what every sin immediately deserves: eternal punishment. *See note on 2:4.* **vessels of wrath.** Continuing the analogy of a potter, Paul refers to those whom God has not chosen for salvation, but rather allowed to incur the just penalty for their sin—God's wrath (*see note on 1:18*). **prepared for destruction.** By their own rejection of Him. God does not make men sinful, but He leaves them in the sin they have chosen (*see note on v. 18*).

9:23 glory. The greatness of His character, seen especially in the grace, mercy, compassion, and forgiveness He grants sinners in Christ. **vessels of mercy.** Those He has chosen for salvation. **He had prepared beforehand.** Refers to divine election (*see note on v. 29*).

9:25-33 Paul finishes his argument that Israel's unbelief is not inconsistent with God's plan of redemption by using the OT to show that her unbelief reflects exactly what the prophets recorded (8:25-29), and that it is consistent with God's prerequisite of faith (vv. 30-33).

9:25,26 Paul quotes Hos. 1:9,10; 2:23. Hosea spoke of the ultimate restoration of Israel to God, but Paul's emphasis is that restoration necessarily implies her present alienation from God. Therefore, Israel's unbelief is consistent with the OT revelation.

9:27,28 See Is. 10:22,23. Isaiah prophesied that the southern kingdom of Judah would be conquered and scattered—temporarily rejected by God—because of her unbelief. Paul's point is that the scattering Isaiah described was only a preview of Israel's rejection of the Messiah and her subsequent destruction and scattering.

9:29 See Is. 1:9. Again, only a remnant of Israel will survive God's wrath, solely because of His mercy. ***LORD of Sabaoth.*** Cf. James 5:4. This OT title for God is translated "Lord of hosts" and refers to His all-encompassing sovereignty.

[r] *We would have become like Sodom,*
And we would have been made
like Gomorrah."

Present Condition of Israel

30 What shall we say then? [s]That Gentiles, who did not pursue righteousness,
have attained to righteousness, [t]even the
righteousness of faith; **31** but Israel, [u]pur-
suing the law of righteousness, [v]has not attained to the law [4]of righteousness.
32 Why? Because *they did* not *seek it* by
faith, but as it were, [5]by the works of the
law. For [w]they stumbled at that stumbling
stone. **33** As it is written:

[x]*"Behold, I lay in Zion a stumbling*
stone and rock of offense,
And [y] *whoever believes on Him*
will not be put to shame."

Israel Needs the Gospel

10 Brethren, my heart's desire and
prayer to God for [1]Israel is that they
may be saved. **2** For I bear them witness
[a]that they have a zeal for God, but not according to knowledge. **3** For they being ignorant of [b]God's righteousness, and seeking to establish their own [c]righteousness,
have not submitted to the righteousness of
God. **4** For [d]Christ *is* the end of the law for
righteousness to everyone who believes.

5 For Moses writes about the righteousness which is of the law, [e]*"The man who*
does those things shall live by them." **6** But
the righteousness of faith speaks in this
way, [f]*"Do not say in your heart, 'Who will*
ascend into heaven?' " (that is, to bring
Christ down *from above*) **7** or, [g]*" 'Who will*
descend into the abyss?' " (that is, to bring
Christ up from the dead). **8** But what does
it say? [h]*"The word is near you, in your*
mouth and in your heart" (that is, the word
of faith which we preach): **9** that [i]if you
confess with your mouth the Lord Jesus
and believe in your heart that God has
raised Him from the dead, you will be
saved. **10** For with the heart one believes
unto righteousness, and with the mouth
confession is made unto salvation. **11** For
the Scripture says, [j]*"Whoever believes on*

29 [r] Deut. 29:23; Is. 13:19; Jer. 49:18; 50:40; Amos 4:11
30 [s] Rom. 4:11 [t] Rom. 1:17; 3:21; 10:6; [Gal. 2:16; 3:24; Phil. 3:9]; Heb. 11:7
31 [u] [Rom. 10:2-4] [v] [Gal. 5:4] [4] NU omits *of righteousness*
32 [w] [Luke 2:34; 1 Cor. 1:23] [5] NU *by works,* omitting *of the law*
33 [x] [Ps. 118:22]; Is. 8:14; 28:16; [Matt. 21:42; 1 Pet. 2:6-8] [y] Rom. 5:5; 10:11

CHAPTER 10

1 [1] NU *them*
2 [a] Acts 21:20; Gal. 1:14
3 [b] [Rom. 1:17] [c] [Phil. 3:9]
4 [d] Matt. 5:17; [Rom. 7:1-4; Gal. 3:24; 4:5]
5 [e] Lev. 18:5; Neh. 9:29; Ezek. 20:11, 13, 21; Rom. 7:10; Gal. 3:12
6 [f] Deut. 30:12-14
7 [g] Deut. 30:13
8 [h] Deut. 30:14
9 [i] Matt. 10:32; Luke 12:8; Acts 8:37; Rom. 14:9; [1 Cor. 12:3]; Phil. 2:11
11 [j] Is. 28:16; Jer. 17:7; Rom. 9:33

9:30-32 Paul concludes the lesson on God's divine choice by reminding his readers that although God chooses some to receive His mercy, those who receive His judgment do so not because of something God has done to them, but because of their own unwillingness to believe the gospel (cf. 1 Thess. 2:10). Sinners are condemned for their personal sins, the supreme one being rejection of God and Christ (cf. 2:2-6,9,12; John 8:21-24; 16:8-11).

9:30 righteousness of faith. Righteousness which comes from God on the basis of faith (*see note on 1:17*).

9:31 the law of righteousness. Righteousness earned by keeping the law (cf. 3:20; *see note on 8:3*).

9:32 not...by faith. *See notes on 3:21-24.* **works of the law.** By doing everything the law prescribed (cf. Gal. 2:16; 3:2,5,10).

9:33 See Is. 8:14 and 28:16. Long before His coming, the OT prophets had predicted that Israel would reject her Messiah, illustrating again that her unbelief is perfectly consistent with the Scripture.

10:1 prayer to God for Israel. Paul's calling as an apostle to the Gentiles (11:13; Acts 9:15) did not diminish his continual entreaties to God (cf. 1 Tim. 2:1-3) for Israel to be saved (cf. 1:16; John 4:22; Acts 1:8), or his own evangelistic efforts toward Jews

10:2 zeal for God. Demonstrated by legalistic conformity to the law and fierce opposition to Judaism's opponents (Acts 22:3; 26:4,5; Gal. 1:13,14; Phil. 3:5,6).

10:3 ignorant of God's righteousness. Ignorant both of God's inherent righteousness revealed in the law and the rest of the OT (which should have shown the Jews their own unrighteousness) and of the righteousness which comes from Him on the basis of faith (*see note on 1:17*). **their own righteousness.** Based on their conformity to God's law and often to the less demanding standards of their own traditions (Mark 7:1-13).

10:4 Christ *is* the end of the law. Although the Gr. word translated "end" can mean either "fulfillment" or "termination," this is not a reference to Christ's having perfectly fulfilled the law through His teaching (Matt. 5:17,18) or through His sinless life (2 Cor. 5:21). Instead, as the second half of the verse shows, Paul means that belief in Christ as Lord and Savior ends the sinner's futile quest for righteousness through his imperfect attempts to save himself by efforts to obey the law (cf. 3:20-22; Is. 64:6; Col. 2:13,14).

10:5 the righteousness which is of the law. A righteous standing before God on the basis of obedience to the law. ***The man who does those things shall live by them.*** Quoted from Lev. 18:5. To hope for a righteousness based on obedience to the law requires perfect conformity in every detail (Gal. 3:10; James 2:10; cf. Deut. 27:26)—an utter impossibility.

10:6,7 Paul speaks of the righteousness based on faith as if it were a person and puts in its mouth a quotation from Deut. 30:12,13. His point is that the righteousness of faith does not require some impossible odyssey through the universe to find Christ.

10:8 *The word is near you.* Quoted from Deut. 30:14. The journey of vv. 6,7 is unnecessary because God has clearly revealed the way of salvation: It is by faith. **word of faith.** The message of faith is the way to God.

10:9 confess...the Lord Jesus. Not a simple acknowledgment that He is God and the Lord of the universe, since even demons acknowledge that to be true (James 2:19). This is the deep personal conviction, without reservation, that Jesus is that person's own master or sovereign. This phrase includes repenting from sin, trusting in Jesus for salvation, and submitting to Him as Lord. This is the volitional element of faith (*see note on 1:16*). **believe in your heart.** *See note on 1:16.* **God has raised Him from the dead.** Christ's resurrection was the supreme validation of His ministry (cf. John 2:18-21). Belief in it is necessary for salvation because it proved that Christ is who He claimed to be and that the Father had accepted His sacrifice in the place of sinners (4:24; cf. Acts 13:32,33; 1 Pet. 1:3,4). Without the resurrection, there is no salvation (1 Cor. 15:14-17). *See note on 1:4.* **will be saved.** *See note on 1:16.*

10:10 confession. This Gr. word basically means to say the same thing, or to be in agreement with someone. The person who confesses Jesus as Lord (v. 9), agrees with the Father's declaration that Jesus is Savior and Lord.

10:11 Quoted from Is. 28:16 and 49:23. This quotation not only demonstrates that salvation by grace through faith alone has always

Him will not be put to shame." 12 For
[k]there is no distinction between Jew and
Greek, for [l]the same Lord over all [m]is rich
to all who call upon Him. 13 For [n]*"who-*
ever calls [o] *on the name of the LORD shall be*
saved."

Israel Rejects the Gospel

14 How then shall they call on Him in
whom they have not believed? And how
shall they believe in Him of whom they
have not heard? And how shall they hear
[p]without a preacher? 15 And how shall
they preach unless they are sent? As it is
written:

[q]*"How beautiful are the feet of those*
who [2]*preach the gospel of*
peace,
Who bring glad tidings of good
things!"

16 But they have not all obeyed the
gospel. For Isaiah says, [r]*"LORD, who has*
believed our report?" 17 So then faith
comes by hearing, and hearing by the
word of God.
18 But I say, have they not heard? Yes indeed:

[s]*"Their sound has gone out to all the*
earth,
[t]*And their words to the ends of the*
world."

19 But I say, did Israel not know? First
Moses says:

[u]*"I will provoke you to jealousy by*
those who are not a nation,
I will move you to anger by a
[v]*foolish nation."*

20 But Isaiah is very bold and says:

[w]*"I was found by those who did not*
seek Me;
I was made manifest to those who
did not ask for Me."

21 But to Israel he says:

[x]*"All day long I have stretched out*
My hands
To a disobedient and contrary
people."

Israel's Rejection Not Total

11 I say then, [a]has God cast away His
people? [b]Certainly not! For [c]I also
am an Israelite, of the seed of Abraham, *of*
the tribe of Benjamin. 2 God has not cast
away His people whom [d]He foreknew. Or
do you not know what the Scripture says
of Elijah, how he pleads with God against
Israel, saying, 3 [e]*"LORD, they have killed*
Your prophets and torn down Your altars,
and I alone am left, and they seek my
life"? 4 But what does the divine response

12 [k]Acts 15:9; Rom. 3:22, 29; Gal. 3:28 [l]Acts 10:36; 1 Tim. 2:5 [m]Eph. 1:7
13 [n]Joel 2:32; Acts 2:21 [o]Acts 9:14
14 [p]Acts 8:31; Titus 1:3
15 [q]Is. 52:7; Nah. 1:15 [2]NU omits *preach the gospel of peace, Who*
16 [r]Is. 53:1; John 12:38
18 [s]Ps. 19:4; Matt. 24:14; Mark 16:15; Rom. 1:8; Col. 1:6, 23; 1 Thess. 1:8 [t]1 Kin. 18:10; Matt. 4:8
19 [u]Deut. 32:21; Rom. 11:11 [v]Titus 3:3
20 [w]Is. 65:1; Rom. 9:30
21 [x]Is. 65:2

CHAPTER 11

1 [a]Ps. 94:14; Jer. 46:28 [b]1 Sam. 12:22; Jer. 31:37 [c]2 Cor. 11:22; Phil. 3:5
2 [d][Rom. 8:29]
3 [e]1 Kin. 19:10, 14

been God's salvation plan, but that no one—including Gentiles—was ever to be excluded (1:16; 3:21,22; 2 Pet. 3:9; see also Jon. 3:5).

10:12 there is no distinction. Cf. 3:22,23; Gal. 3:28,29; Eph. 2:11-13; 3:4-6.

10:13 Paul quoted Joel (2:32) to further emphasize that salvation is available for people of all nations and races. ***calls on the name.*** This familiar OT expression (e.g., Pss. 79:5,6; 105:1; 116:4,5) does not refer to some desperate cry to just any deity but to the one true God as He has revealed Himself—a revelation which now includes recognition of Jesus as Lord (v. 9) and of the One who raised up Jesus from the dead (v. 9).

10:14,15 Paul's main point in this series of rhetorical questions is that a clear presentation of the gospel message must precede true saving faith. True faith always has content—the revealed Word of God. Salvation comes to those who hear and believe the facts of the gospel.

10:15 beautiful…feet of those who preach the gospel. Quoted from Is. 52:7. It is the message of good news which those feet carry that is so welcome.

10:16 obeyed the gospel. The good news is not only a gracious offer but a command to believe and repent (1:4-6; 2:8; 6:17; Acts 6:7; 2 Thess. 1:7,8; Heb. 5:9). ***believed our report.*** Quoted from Is. 53:1. The report Isaiah described was of the substitutionary death of Christ (53:5)—the good news of the gospel.

10:17 faith…by hearing. *See note on vv. 14,15.* **the word of God.** The preferred rendering is "the word of Christ," which means "the message about Christ"—the gospel (cf. Matt. 28:19,20; Acts 20:21).

10:18 Paul cited this quotation from the LXX (the Gr. translation of the Heb. OT) version of Ps. 19:4 to show that even David understood that God's revelation of Himself has reached the entire earth (cf. 1:18-20; Jer. 29:13; Matt. 24:14; John 1:9; Col. 1:5,6).

10:19-21 Israel was ignorant of the salvation truth contained in her own Scriptures, including that the gospel would reach the Gentiles, as promised in Deut. 32:21; Is. 65:1,2.

10:19 *those who are not a nation.* The Gentiles, who are not a part of Israel, God's special, chosen nation.

10:20,21 Quoted from Is. 65:1,2.

10:21 *disobedient.* Lit. "to contradict," or "to speak against." As throughout her history, Israel once again had contradicted the Word of God—this time it was the truth of the gospel (cf. Matt. 21:33-41; Luke 14:21-24).

11:1-36 In this section Paul answers the question that logically arises from 10:19-21: "Is God's setting aside of Israel for rejecting Christ permanent?" At stake is whether God can be trusted to keep His unconditional promises to that nation (cf. Jer. 33:19-26).

11:1 cast away. To thrust away from oneself. The form of the question in the Gr. text expects a negative answer. Despite Israel's disobedience (9:1-13; 10:14-21), God has not rejected His people (cf. 1 Sam. 12:22; 1 Kin. 6:13; Pss. 89:31-37; 94:14; Is. 49:15; 54:1-10; Jer. 33:19-26). **Certainly not!** The strongest form of negation in Gr. (*see note on 6:2*).

11:2 whom He foreknew. *See note on 8:29.* Israel's disobedience does not nullify God's predetermined love relationship with her. **Elijah.** *See note on 1 Kin. 17:1.*

11:3 Quoted from 1 Kin. 19:10.

say to him? [f]"I have reserved for Myself
seven thousand men who have not bowed
the knee to Baal." **5** [g]Even so then, at this
present time there is a remnant according
to the election of grace. **6** And [h]if by grace,
then *it is* no longer of works; otherwise
grace is no longer grace. [1]But if *it is* of
works, it is no longer grace; otherwise
work is no longer work.
7 What then? [i]Israel has not obtained
what it seeks; but the elect have obtained
it, and the rest were [j]blinded. **8** Just as it is
written:

[k]*"God has given them a spirit of*
stupor,
[l]*Eyes that they should not see*
And ears that they should not hear,
To this very day."

9 And David says:

[m]*"Let their table become a snare and*
a trap,
A stumbling block and a
recompense to them.
10 *Let their eyes be darkened, so that*
they do not see,
And bow down their back always."

Israel's Rejection Not Final

11 I say then, have they stumbled that
they should fall? Certainly not! But
[n]through their [2]fall, to provoke them to
[o]jealousy, salvation *has come* to the Gentiles. **12** Now if their [3]fall *is* riches for the
world, and their failure riches for the Gentiles, how much more their fullness!
13 For I speak to you Gentiles; inasmuch
as [p]I am an apostle to the Gentiles, I magnify my ministry, **14** if by any means I may
provoke to jealousy *those who are* my flesh
and [q]save some of them. **15** For if their
being cast away *is* the reconciling of the
world, what *will* their acceptance *be* [r]but
life from the dead?
16 For if [s]the firstfruit *is* holy, the lump *is*
also *holy;* and if the root *is* holy, so *are* the
branches. **17** And if [t]some of the branches
were broken off, [u]and you, being a wild
olive tree, were grafted in among them,

4 [f]1 Kin. 19:18
5 [g]2 Kin. 19:4; Rom. 9:27
6 [h]Rom. 4:4 [1]NU omits the rest of v. 6.
7 [i]Rom. 9:31 [j]Mark 6:52; Rom. 9:18; 11:25; 2 Cor. 3:14
8 [k]Is. 29:10, 13 [l]Deut. 29:3, 4; Is. 6:9; Matt. 13:13, 14; John 12:40; Acts 28:26, 27
9 [m]Ps. 69:22, 23
11 [n]Is. 42:6, 7; Acts 28:28 [o]Deut. 32:21; Acts 13:46; Rom. 10:19 [2]*trespass*
12 [3]*trespass*
13 [p]Acts 9:15; 22:21; Gal. 1:16; 2:7-9; Eph. 3:8
14 [q]1 Cor. 9:22; 1 Tim. 4:16; James 5:20
15 [r][Is. 26:16-19]
16 [s]Lev. 23:10; [James 1:18]
17 [t]Jer. 11:16; [John 15:2] [u]Acts 2:39; [Eph. 2:12]

11:4 Quoted from 1 Kin. 19:18. ***Baal.*** *See note on 1 Kin. 16:31,32;* cf. Num. 22:41.

11:5 a remnant. Although the nation had rejected Jesus, thousands of individual Jews had come to faith in Him (cf. Acts 2:41; 4:4; 6:1). **election of grace.** God did not choose this remnant because of its foreseen faith, good works, spiritual worthiness, or racial descent, but solely because of His grace (cf. Deut. 7:7,8; Eph. 2:8,9; 2 Tim. 1:9).

11:6 grace...no longer of works. Human effort and God's grace are mutually exclusive ways to salvation (cf. 3:21-31; 4:1-11; 9:11; Gal. 2:16,21; 3:11,12,18; Titus 3:5).

11:7 Israel...what it seeks. In spite of their intense religious zeal, the Jews of Paul's day had failed to obtain God's righteousness (9:31,32; 10:2,3). **the elect.** Those whom God graciously had chosen in turn sought and found His righteousness (*see notes on 9:30; 10:4*). **were blinded.** By a judicial act of God (cf. Ex. 4:21; 7:3; 9:12; 10:20,27; 11:10; 14:4,8,17; Deut. 2:30; John 12:40), in response to their hardened hearts (cf. Ex. 8:15,32; 9:34; 10:1; 2 Chr. 36:13; Ps. 95:8; Prov. 28:14; Matt. 19:8; Mark 3:5; Eph. 4:18; Heb. 3:8,15; 4:7).

11:8-10 These OT quotes both illustrate God's judicial hardening of unbelieving Israel, and show that what Paul is teaching is not in violation of or inconsistent with the OT.

11:8 it is written. *See note on 3:10.* The first line was quoted from Is. 29:10 and the last lines are adapted from Deut. 29:4.

11:9 Adapted from Ps. 69:22,23. A person's "table" was thought to be a place of safety, but the table of the ungodly is a trap. Many people trust in the very things that damn them.

11:11 stumbled...fall. The form of Paul's question (*see note on v. 1*) and his strong response confirms that Israel's blindness, hardening, and apostasy are not irreversible. **their fall.** Israel's rejection of Jesus Christ. **provoke...to jealousy.** God intends to use His offer of salvation to the despised Gentiles (*see note on Acts 22:21-23*) to draw the nation back to Him (vv. 25-27). **salvation...to the Gentiles.** Something the OT had long prophesied (cf. Gen. 12:3; Is. 49:6; Matt. 8:11,12; 21:43; 22:1-14; Acts 13:46,47; 28:25-28).

11:12 riches for the world. The rich truths of salvation (Gen. 12:3; Is. 49:6; cf. 2 Cor. 8:9). **their failure.** To acknowledge Jesus of Nazareth as their Messiah and be God's witness nation resulted in the Gentile church being given that privilege. **their fullness.** Their future spiritual renewal (Rev. 7:4,9; cf. Zech. 8:23; 12:10; 13:1; 14:9,11,16). Israel's "fall" and "failure" is temporary (vv. 25-27).

11:13 apostle to the Gentiles. See Acts 18:6; 22:21; 26:17,18; Eph. 3:8; 1 Tim. 2:7.

11:14 provoke to jealousy. *See note on v. 11.* **my flesh.** His fellow Israelites (*see note on 9:3*).

11:15 their being cast away... reconciling of the world...acceptance. *See notes on v. 12.* **life from the dead.** Not bodily resurrection, but the passing from spiritual death to spiritual life (John 5:24). This phrase also describes the future spiritual rebirth of Israel (cf. vv. 25-27; Zech. 12:10; 13:1).

11:16 firstfruit. The first portion of the harvest, which was to be given to the Lord (Ex. 23:19; 34:26; Lev. 2:12; 23:10; Num. 15:19-21; 18:12,13; Deut. 18:4). **the lump *is* also *holy.*** Because the firstfruit offering represented the entire portion, the entire piece of dough could be said to be holy, set apart to God (cf. Ex. 31:15; Lev. 27:14,30,32; Josh. 6:19). **root.** The patriarchs Abraham, Isaac, and Jacob. *See note on 4:13.* **branches.** The patriarchs' descendants: the nation of Israel.

11:17-24 In this section, Paul sternly warns the Gentiles against pride and arrogance (cf. vv. 18,20) because of Israel's rejection and their being grafted in.

11:17 branches were broken off. See Jer. 5:10; 11:16,17; Matt. 21:43. Some, but not all, of the branches of Israel (*see note on v. 16*) were removed; God always preserved a believing remnant (cf. vv. 3,4). **a wild olive tree...grafted in.** Olives were an important crop in the ancient world. Although trees often lived for hundreds of years, individual branches eventually stopped producing olives. When that happened, branches from younger trees were grafted in to restore productivity. Paul's point is that the old, unproductive branches (Israel) were broken off and branches from a wild olive tree (Gentiles) were grafted in. **the root and fatness.** Once grafted in, Gentiles partake of the richness of God's covenant blessings as the spiritual heirs of Abraham (*see note on 4:11; Gal. 3:29*). **the olive tree.** The place of divine blessing; God's covenant of salvation made with Abraham (Gen. 12:1-3; 15:1-21; 17:1-27).

and with them became a partaker of the
root and [4]fatness of the olive tree, 18 [v]do
not boast against the branches. But if you
do boast, *remember that* you do not support
the root, but the root supports you.
19 You will say then, "Branches were
broken off that I might be grafted in."
20 Well *said.* Because of [w]unbelief they
were broken off, and you stand by faith.
Do not be haughty, but fear. 21 For if God
did not spare the natural branches, He may
not spare you either. 22 Therefore consider
the goodness and severity of God: on those
who fell, severity; but toward you, [5]good-
ness, [x]if you continue in *His* goodness.
Otherwise [y]you also will be cut off. 23 And
they also, [z]if they do not continue in unbelief, will be grafted in, for God is able to
graft them in again. 24 For if you were cut
out of the olive tree which is wild by nature, and were grafted contrary to nature
into a cultivated olive tree, how much
more will these, who *are* natural *branches,*
be grafted into their own olive tree?
25 For I do not desire, brethren, that you
should be ignorant of this mystery, lest you
should be [a]wise in your own [6]opinion, that
[b]blindness in part has happened to Israel
[c]until the fullness of the Gentiles has come
in. 26 And so all Israel will be [7]saved, as it
is written:

[d]"The Deliverer will come out of Zion,
And He will turn away
ungodliness from Jacob;
27 *For [e]this is My covenant with them,*
When I take away their sins."

28 Concerning the gospel *they are* enemies for your sake, but concerning the election *they are* [f]beloved for the sake of the fathers. 29 For the gifts and the calling of God
are [g]irrevocable. 30 For as you [h]were once
disobedient to God, yet have now obtained
mercy through their disobedience, 31 even
so these also have now been disobedient,
that through the mercy shown you they
also may obtain mercy. 32 For God has
[8]committed them [i]all to disobedience, that
He might have mercy on all.

17 [4] *richness*
18 [v] [1 Cor. 10:12]
20 [w] Heb. 3:19
22 [x] 1 Cor. 15:2; Heb. 3:6, 14 [y] [John 15:2] [5] NU adds *of God*
23 [z] [2 Cor. 3:16]
25 [a] Rom. 12:16 [b] 2 Cor. 3:14 [c] Luke 21:24; John 10:16; Rom. 11:12 [6] *estimation*
26 [d] Ps. 14:7; Is. 59:20, 21 [7] *Or delivered*
27 [e] Is. 27:9; Heb. 8:12
28 [f] Deut. 7:8; 10:15; Rom. 9:5
29 [g] Num. 23:19
30 [h] [Eph. 2:2]
32 [i] Rom. 3:9; [Gal. 3:22] [8] *shut them all up in*

11:18 do not boast. There is no place in the church for spiritual pride, still less for anti-Semitism—we are the spiritual offspring of Abraham (4:11,16; Gal. 3:29). **branches.** The unbelieving Jews who had been broken off. **the root supports you.** Gentiles are not the source of blessing, but have been grafted into the covenant of salvation that God made with Abraham (cf. Gal. 3:6-9,13,14).

11:19 Branches. *See note on v. 17.* **grafted in.** *See note on v. 18.*

11:20 unbelief...faith. Branches were broken off and others grafted in based solely on the issue of faith, not race, ethnicity, social or intellectual background, or external morality. Salvation is ever and always by faith alone (cf. 1:16,17; Eph. 2:8,9). **fear.** See 1 Cor. 10:12; 2 Cor. 13:5. God will judge the apostate church (cf. Rev. 2:15,16; 3:16) just as surely as He judged apostate Israel.

11:21 If Israel (the "natural branches") was not spared despite being God's covenant nation, why should Gentiles, strangers to God's covenants (Eph. 2:11,12; *see note on 9:4*), expect to be spared if they sin against the truth of the gospel?

11:22 consider the goodness and severity. All of God's attributes work in harmony; there is no conflict between His goodness and love, and His justice and wrath. Those who accept His gracious offer of salvation experience His goodness (2:4); those who reject it experience His severity (2:5). **those who fell.** The unbelieving Jews described in vv. 12-21. "Fell" translates a Gr. word meaning "to fall so as to be completely ruined." Those who reject God's offer of salvation bring upon themselves utter spiritual ruin. **if you continue.** Genuine saving faith always perseveres (cf. John 8:31; 15:5,6; Col. 1:22,23; Heb. 3:12-14; 4:11; 1 John 2:19). **cut off.** From the same Gr. root word translated "severity" earlier in the verse. God will deal swiftly and severely with those who reject Him.

11:23,24 In the future, Israel will repent of unbelief and embrace the Messiah (Zech. 12:10). In the terms of Paul's analogy, God will at that time gladly graft the (believing) Jewish people back into the olive tree of His covenant blessings because it was theirs originally (9:4)—unlike the wild branches (the Gentiles, cf. Eph. 2:11,12).

11:25 mystery. This word is used to refer to NT truth previously not revealed (*see notes on 1 Cor. 2:7; Eph. 3:3-6*). This mystery has two components: 1) Israel has experienced a partial spiritual hardening, and 2) that hardening will last only for a divinely specified period of time. *See note on 16:25.* **wise in your own opinion.** Another warning to the Gentiles against spiritual pride and arrogance (*see notes on vv. 17-24*). **blindness in part.** The nation's blindness does not extend to every individual Jew. Through all of history God has always preserved a believing remnant (*see notes on vv. 5,17*). **until the fullness of the Gentiles has come in.** "Until" refers to a specific point in time; "fullness" refers to completion; "has come in" translates a Gr. verb often used to speak of coming to salvation (cf. Matt. 5:20; Mark 9:43,45,47; John 3:5; Acts 14:22). Israel's spiritual hardening (which began with rejecting Jesus as Messiah) will last until the complete number of elect Gentiles has come to salvation.

11:26,27a Quoted from Is. 59:20,21.

11:26 all Israel. All the elect Jewish people alive at the end of the Tribulation, not the believing remnant of Jews within the church during this church age (*see notes on vv. 5,17*). Since the remnant has already embraced the truth of the gospel (*see note on v. 25*), it could not be in view here, since it no longer needs the salvation this verse promises. ***The Deliverer will come out of Zion.*** See Pss. 14:7; 53:6; Is. 46:13. The Lord Jesus Christ's millennial rule will be associated with Mt. Zion (Ps. 110:2). ***Zion.*** *See note on 9:33.*

11:27 *covenant.* The Abrahamic Covenant (Gen. 12:1-3; Is. 59:21). ***When I take away their sins.*** Quoted from Is. 27:9. A necessary prerequisite for Israel's salvation (cf. Ezek. 36:25-29; Heb. 8:12).

11:28 gospel...enemies. Israel's temporary situation during her time of spiritual hardening (*see note on v. 25*). **concerning the election.** From the perspective of God's eternal choice, Israel will always be His covenant people (*see note on v. 1*). **the sake of the fathers.** The patriarchs (Abraham, Isaac, and Jacob), recipients of the Abrahamic Covenant (Ex. 2:24; Lev. 26:4; 2 Kin. 13:23).

11:29 the gifts...*are* irrevocable. *See note on v. 1.* God's sovereign election of Israel, like that of individual believers, is unconditional and unchangeable, because it is rooted in His immutable nature and expressed in the unilateral, eternal Abrahamic Covenant (*see note on 9:4*).

11:30,31 God will extend His grace to unbelieving Israel, just as He did to unbelieving Gentiles (cf. Rom. 5:8). Salvation, whether of Jews or Gentiles, flows from God's mercy (cf. 1 Tim. 1:12-14).

11:32 Though not the author of sin (Ps. 5:4; Hab. 1:13; James 1:13),

33 Oh, the depth of the riches both of the
wisdom and knowledge of God! How unsearchable *are* His judgments and His
ways past finding out!

34 *"For who has known the* [j] *mind of*
the LORD?
Or [k] *who has become His*
counselor?"
35 *"Or* [l] *who has first given to Him*
And it shall be repaid to him?"

36 For [m] of Him and through Him and to
Him *are* all things, [n] to whom *be* glory forever. Amen.

Living Sacrifices to God

12 I [a] beseech[1] you therefore, brethren,
by the mercies of God, that you
present your bodies [b] a living sacrifice,
holy, acceptable to God, *which is* your [2] reasonable service. 2 And [c] do not be conformed to this world, but [d] be transformed
by the renewing of your mind, that you
may [e] prove what *is* that good and acceptable and perfect will of God.

Serve God with Spiritual Gifts

3 For I say, [f] through the grace given to
me, to everyone who is among you, [g] not to
think *of himself* more highly than he ought
to think, but to think soberly, as God has
dealt [h] to each one a measure of faith. 4 For
[i] as we have many members in one body,
but all the members do not have the same
function, 5 so [j] we, *being* many, are one
body in Christ, and individually members
of one another. 6 Having then gifts differ-

34 [j] Is. 40:13; Jer. 23:18; 1 Cor. 2:16 [k] Job 36:22
35 [l] Job 41:11
36 [m] [1 Cor. 8:6; 11:12]; Col. 1:16; Heb. 2:10 [n] Heb. 13:21

CHAPTER 12

1 [a] 1 Cor. 1:10; 2 Cor. 10:1-4 [b] Phil. 4:18; Heb. 10:18, 20 [1] *urge* [2] *rational*
2 [c] Matt. 13:22; Gal. 1:4; 1 John 2:15 [d] Eph. 4:23; [Titus 3:5] [e] [1 Thess. 4:3]
3 [f] Rom. 1:5; 15:15; 1 Cor. 3:10; 15:10; Gal. 2:9; Eph. 3:7 [g] Prov. 25:27 [h] [Eph. 4:7]
4 [i] 1 Cor. 12:12-14; [Eph. 4:4, 16]
5 [j] [1 Cor. 10:17]; Gal. 3:28

God allowed man to pursue his sinful inclinations so that He could receive glory by demonstrating His grace and mercy to disobedient sinners (cf. Eph. 2:2; 5:6).

11:33-36 The majesty, grandeur, and wisdom of God's plan revealed in vv. 1-32 caused Paul to burst out in praise. This doxology is a fitting response not only to God's future plans for Israel (chaps. 9–11), but to Paul's entire discussion of justification by faith (chaps. 1–11).

11:33 wisdom. See Ps. 104:24; Dan. 2:20; Eph. 3:10; Rev. 7:12. **knowledge.** God's omniscience (cf. 1 Sam. 2:3; 1 Kin. 8:39; Ps. 44:21; 147:5). **judgments.** God's purposes or decrees, which are beyond human understanding (cf. Ps. 36:6). **ways.** The methods God chooses to accomplish His purposes (cf. Job 5:9; 9:10; 26:14).

11:34 Quoted from Is. 40:13.

11:35 Quoted from Job 41:11.

11:36 See 1 Cor. 8:6; 15:28; Eph. 1:23; 4:6; Heb. 2:10. God is the source, the sustainer, and the rightful end of everything that exists.

12:1–16:27 In these final 5 chapters, Paul explains in great detail how believers are to practically live out the rich theological truths of chaps. 1–11. God has graciously given believers so much, that Paul exhorts them to respond in grateful obedience.

12:1 beseech. This Gr. word comes from a root which means "to call alongside to help." Jesus used a related word, often translated "comforter," in reference to the Holy Spirit (John 14:16,26; 15:26; 16:7). This family of words later came to connote exhorting, encouraging, or counseling. Paul was speaking as a counselor to his readers, but his counsel carried the full weight of his apostleship. **therefore.** This refers to the last refrain of his doxology of praise in 11:36. Since all things are for His glory, we must respond by offering ourselves for that purpose. **mercies of God.** The gracious, extravagant, divine graces Paul expounded in the first 11 chapters, including God's love (1:7; cf. 5:5; 8:35,39), grace (1:6,7; 3:24; 5:2,20,21; 6:15), righteousness (1:17; 3:21,22; 4:5,6,22-24; 5:17,19), and the gift of faith (1:5,17; 3:22,26; 4:5,13; 5:1; 10:17; 12:3). **present your bodies a living sacrifice.** Under the Old Covenant, God accepted the sacrifices of dead animals. But because of Christ's ultimate sacrifice, the OT sacrifices are no longer of any effect (Heb. 9:11,12). For those in Christ, the only acceptable worship is to offer themselves completely to the Lord. Under God's control, the believer's yet-unredeemed body (*see note on 6:6,12; 7:5*; cf. 8:11,23) can and must be yielded to Him as an instrument of righteousness (6:12,13; cf. 8:11-13). **reasonable service.** "Reasonable" is from the Gr. for "logic." In light of all the spiritual riches believers enjoy solely as the fruit of God's mercies (Rom. 11:33,36), it logically follows that they owe God their highest form of service. Understood here is the idea of priestly, spiritual service, which was such an integral part of OT worship.

12:2 do not be conformed. "Conformed" refers to assuming an outward expression that does not reflect what is really inside, a kind of masquerade or act. The word's form implies that Paul's readers were already allowing this to happen and must stop. **this world.** Better translated, "age," which refers to the system of beliefs, values—or the spirit of the age—at any time current in the world. This sum of contemporary thinking and values forms the moral atmosphere of our world and is always dominated by Satan (cf. 2 Cor. 4:4). **transformed.** The Gr. word, from which the Eng. word "metamorphosis" comes, connotes a change in outward appearance. Matthew uses the same word to describe the Transfiguration (Matt. 17:2). Just as Christ briefly and in a limited way displayed outwardly His inner, divine nature and glory at the Transfiguration, Christians should outwardly manifest their inner, redeemed natures, not once, however, but daily (cf. 2 Cor. 3:18; Eph. 5:18). **renewing of your mind.** That kind of transformation can occur only as the Holy Spirit changes our thinking through consistent study and meditation of Scripture (Ps. 119:11; cf. Col. 1:28; 3:10,16; Phil. 4:8). The renewed mind is one saturated with and controlled by the Word of God. **good...acceptable...perfect.** Holy living of which God approves. These words borrow from OT sacrificial language and describe a life that is morally and spiritually spotless, just as the sacrificial animals were to be (cf. Lev. 22:19-25).

12:3 grace. The divine, undeserved favor that called Paul to be an apostle and gave him spiritual authority (Rom. 1:1-5; cf. 1 Cor. 3:10; Gal. 2:9) and also produced sincere humility (1 Tim. 1:12-14). **soberly.** The exercise of sound judgment, which will lead believers to recognize that in themselves they are nothing (cf. 1 Pet. 5:5), and will yield the fruit of humility (cf. 3 John 9). **measure of faith.** The correct proportion of the spiritual gift—or supernatural endowment and ability—the Holy Spirit gives each believer (*see note on 1 Pet. 4:10,11*) so he may fulfill his role in the body of Christ (1 Cor. 12:7,11). "Faith" is not saving faith, but rather faithful stewardship, the kind and quantity required to use one's own particular gift (cf. 1 Cor. 12:7,11). Every believer receives the exact gift and resources he needs to fulfill his role in the body of Christ.

12:4-8 One of two NT passages (cf. 1 Cor. 12:12-14) listing the general categories of spiritual gifts. The emphasis in each list is not on believers' identifying their gift perfectly, but on faithfully using the unique enablement God has given each. The fact that the two lists differ clearly implies the gifts are like a palette of basic colors, from which God selects to blend a unique hue for each disciple's life (*see notes on vv.6-8; 1 Cor. 12:12-14*).

12:4 many members...one body. Just as in the natural body, God has sovereignly given the body of Christ a unified diversity (*see note on 1 Cor. 12:14-20*).

ing according to the grace that is [k]given to
us, *let us use them:* if prophecy, *let us* [l]*proph-*
esy in proportion to our faith; **7** or ministry,
let us use it in *our* ministering; [m]he who
teaches, in teaching; **8** [n]he who exhorts, in
exhortation; [o]he who gives, with liberality;
[p]he who leads, with diligence; he who
shows mercy, [q]with cheerfulness.

Behave Like a Christian

9 [r]*Let* love *be* without hypocrisy. [s]Abhor
what is evil. Cling to what is good. **10** [t]*Be*
kindly affectionate to one another with
brotherly love, [u]in honor giving preference
to one another; **11** not lagging in diligence,
fervent in spirit, serving the Lord; **12** [v]re-
joicing in hope, [w]patient[3] in tribulation,
[x]continuing steadfastly in prayer; **13** [y]dis-
tributing to the needs of the saints, [z]given[4]
to hospitality.

14 [a]Bless those who persecute you; bless
and do not curse. **15** [b]Rejoice with those
who rejoice, and weep with those who
weep. **16** [c]Be of the same mind toward one
another. [d]Do not set your mind on high

6 [k][John 3:27] [l]Acts 11:27
7 [m]Eph. 4:11
8 [n]Acts 15:32 [o][Matt. 6:1-3] [p][Acts 20:28] [q]2 Cor. 9:7
9 [r]2 Cor. 6:6; 1 Tim. 1:5 [s]Ps. 34:14
10 [t]John 13:34; 1 Thess. 4:9; Heb. 13:1; 2 Pet. 1:7 [u]Rom. 13:7; Phil. 2:3; [1 Pet. 2:17]
12 [v]Luke 10:20 [w]Luke 21:19 [x]Luke 18:1 [3]*persevering*
13 [y]1 Cor. 16:1; Heb. 13:16; 1 Pet. 4:9 [z]Matt. 25:35; 1 Tim. 3:2 [4]Lit. *pursuing*
14 [a][Matt. 5:44]; Luke 6:28; 1 Cor. 4:12
15 [b][1 Cor. 12:26]
16 [c]Rom. 15:5; 2 Cor. 13:11; [Phil. 2:2; 4:2]; 1 Pet. 3:8 [d]Jer. 45:5

12:5 in Christ. *See notes on 8:1; Eph. 1:3-14.*

12:6 gifts. *See note on 12:3.* **according to the grace...given.** Undeserved and unmerited (*see note on v. 3*). The gift itself (1 Cor. 12:4), the specific way in which it is used (1 Cor. 12:5), and the spiritual results (1 Cor. 12:6) are all sovereignly chosen by the Spirit completely apart from personal merit (1 Cor. 12:11). **prophecy.** *See note on 1 Cor. 12:10.* This Gr. word means "speaking forth" and does not necessarily include prediction of the future or any other mystical or supernatural aspects. Although some prophets in Acts did make predictions of future events (11:27,28; 21:10,11), others made no predictions but spoke the truth of God to encourage and strengthen their hearers (15:32; cf. vv. 22-31). The evidence does suggest, however, that in the first century, before the NT was complete and the sign gifts had ceased (*see notes on 1 Cor. 13:8*; cf. 2 Cor. 12:12; Heb. 2:3,4), this word may have had both non-revelatory and revelatory facets. In its non-revelatory sense, the word "prophecy" simply identifies the skill of public proclamation of the Word of God (*see notes on 1 Cor. 14:3,24,25; 1 Pet. 4:11*). **in proportion to our faith.** Lit. "the faith," or the full revealed message or body of Christian faith (Jude 3; cf. 2 Tim. 4:2). The preacher must be careful to preach the same message the apostles delivered. Or, it could also refer to the believer's personal understanding and insight regarding the gospel (*see note on v. 3*).

12:7 ministry. From the same Gr. word as "deacon," "deaconess" come from, it refers to those who serve. This gift, similar to the gift of helps (1 Cor. 12:28), has broad application to include every kind of practical help (cf. Acts 20:35; 1 Cor. 12:28). **teaching.** The ability to interpret, clarify, systematize, and explain God's truth clearly (cf. Acts 18:24,25; 2 Tim. 2:2). Pastors must have the gift of teaching (1 Tim. 3:2; Titus 1:9; cf. 1 Tim. 4:16), but many mature, qualified laymen also have this gift. This differs from preaching (prophecy), not in content, but in the unique skill for public proclamation (*see note on v. 6*).

12:8 exhortation. The gift which enables a believer to effectively call others to obey and follow God's truth (*see note on v. 1*). It may be used negatively to admonish and correct regarding sin (2 Tim. 4:2), or positively, to encourage, comfort, and strengthen struggling believers (cf. 2 Cor. 1:3-5; Heb. 10:24,25). **gives.** This denotes the sacrificial sharing and giving of one's resources and self to meet the needs of others (cf. 2 Cor. 8:3-5,9; 11; Eph. 4:28). **liberality.** Simplicity, single-mindedness, and openhearted generosity. The believer who gives with a proper attitude does not do so for thanks and personal recognition, but to glorify God (cf. Matt. 6:2; Acts 2:44,45; 4:37-5:11; 2 Cor. 8:2-5). **leads.** Lit. "standing before." Paul calls this gift "administrations" (1 Cor. 12:28), a word that means "to guide" and is used of the person who steers a ship (Acts 27:11; Rev. 18:17). In the NT, this word is used to describe only leadership in the home (1 Tim. 3:4,5,12) and the church (1 Cor. 12:28; 1 Tim. 5:17; cf. Acts 27:11; Rev. 18:17). Again, the church's leaders must exercise this gift, but it is certainly not limited to them. **shows mercy.** One who actively shows sympathy and sensitivity to those in suffering and sorrow, and who has both the willingness and the resources to help lessen their afflictions. Frequently, this gift accompanies the gift of exhortation. **cheerfulness.** This attitude is crucial to ensure that the gift of mercy becomes a genuine help, not a discouraging commiseration with those who are suffering (cf. Prov. 14:21,31; Luke 4:18,19).

12:9-21 This passage provides a comprehensive and mandatory list of traits that characterize the Spirit-filled life (cf. John 15:8; Eph. 2:10). Paul presents these characteristics under 4 categories: 1) personal duties (v. 9); 2) family duties (vv. 10-13); 3) duties to others (vv. 14-16); and 4) duties to those who consider us enemies (vv. 17-21).

12:9 love. The supreme NT virtue, which centers completely on the needs and welfare of the one loved and does whatever necessary to meet those needs (cf. Matt. 22:37-39; Gal. 5:22; 1 Pet. 4:8; 1 John 4:16; *see notes on 1 Cor. 13*). **hypocrisy.** *See note on Matt. 6:2.* Christian love is to be shown purely and sincerely, without self-centeredness or guile.

12:10 kindly affectionate...with brotherly love. To be devoted to other Christians with a family sort of love, not based on personal attraction or desirability (cf. 1 Thess. 4:9). This quality is the primary way the world can recognize us as followers of Christ (John 13:35; cf. 1 John 3:10,17-19). **in honor giving preference.** To show genuine appreciation and admiration for fellow believers by putting them first (Phil. 2:3).

12:11 Whatever is worth doing in the Christian life is valuable enough to be done with enthusiasm and care (John 9:4; Gal. 6:10; Heb. 6:10,11: cf. Eccl. 9:10; 2 Thess. 3:13). Sloth and indifference not only prevent good, but allow evil to prosper (Prov. 18:9; Eph. 5:15,16). **fervent in spirit.** Lit. "to boil in spirit." This phrase suggests having plenty of heat to produce adequate, productive energy, but not so much heat that one goes out of control (cf. Acts 18:25; 1 Cor. 9:26; Gal. 6:9).

12:12 rejoicing in hope. Of Christ's return and our ultimate redemption (*see notes on 5:2; 8:19*; cf. Matt. 25:21; 1 Cor. 15:58; 2 Tim. 4:8). **patient.** Perseverance (*see note on 5:3*). **tribulation.** *See note on 5:3.* **continuing steadfastly in prayer.** Cf. Acts 2:42; 1 Thess. 5:17; 1 Tim. 2:8.

12:13 distributing. From a Gr. word that means commonality, partnership, or mutual sharing, which is often translated "fellowship," and "communion" (Acts 2:42,44; cf. 4:32; 1 Tim. 6:17,18). **given to hospitality.** Lit. "pursuing the love of strangers" (Heb. 13:2)—not merely entertaining one's friends. In NT times, travel was dangerous and inns were evil, scarce, and expensive. So the early believers often opened their homes to travelers, especially to fellow believers (2 Tim. 1:16-18; 3 John 5-8; cf. Luke 14:12-14; 1 Pet. 4:9). Church leaders should be role models of this virtue (Titus 1:8).

12:14 Bless those who persecute you. Treat enemies as if they were your friends (Luke 6:27-33; cf. Matt. 5:44; Luke 23:34; Acts 7:60; 1 Pet. 2:21-23).

12:15 Rejoice...weep. To be glad in the blessings, honor, and welfare of others—no matter what one's own situation (cf. 1 Cor. 12:26; 2 Cor. 2:3), and to be sensitive or compassionate to the hardships and sorrows of others (Col. 3:12; James 5:11; cf. Luke 19:41-44; John 11:35).

12:16 same mind toward one another. To be impartial (*see*

things, but associate with the humble. Do
not be wise in your own opinion.
17 [e]Repay no one evil for evil. [f]Have[5] regard for good things in the sight of all men.
18 If it is possible, as much as depends on
you, [g]live peaceably with all men. 19 Beloved, [h]do not avenge yourselves, but
rather give place to wrath; for it is written,
[i]*"Vengeance is Mine, I will repay,"* says
the Lord. 20 Therefore

[j]*"If your enemy is hungry, feed him;*
If he is thirsty, give him a drink;
For in so doing you will heap coals
of fire on his head."

21 Do not be overcome by evil, but [k]over-
come evil with good.

Submit to Government

13 Let every soul be [a]subject to the
governing authorities. For there is
no authority except from God, and the authorities that exist are appointed by God.
2 Therefore whoever resists [b]the authority
resists the ordinance of God, and those
who resist will [1]bring judgment on themselves. 3 For rulers are not a terror to good
works, but to evil. Do you want to be unafraid of the authority? [c]Do what is good,
and you will have praise from the same.
4 For he is God's minister to you for good.
But if you do evil, be afraid; for he does not
bear the sword in vain; for he is God's minister, an avenger to *execute* wrath on him
who practices evil. 5 Therefore [d]*you* must
be subject, not only because of wrath [e]but
also for conscience' sake. 6 For because of
this you also pay taxes, for they are God's
ministers attending continually to this
very thing. 7 [f]Render therefore to all their
due: taxes to whom taxes *are due,* customs
to whom customs, fear to whom fear,
honor to whom honor.

Love Your Neighbor

8 Owe no one anything except to love
one another, for [g]he who loves another has

17 [e] [Matt. 5:39]; 1 Pet. 3:9 [f] 2 Cor. 8:21 [5] Or *Provide good*
18 [g] Heb. 12:14
19 [h] Lev. 19:18 [i] Deut. 32:35; Ps. 94:1; 1 Thess. 4:6; Heb. 10:30
20 [j] 2 Kin. 6:22; Prov. 25:21, 22; [Matt. 5:44]; Luke 6:27
21 [k] [Rom. 12:1, 2]

CHAPTER 13
1 [a] Titus 3:1; 1 Pet. 2:13
2 [b] [Titus 3:1] [1] Lit. *receive*
3 [c] 1 Pet. 2:14
5 [d] Eccl. 8:2 [e] Acts 24:16; [1 Pet. 2:13, 19]
7 [f] Matt. 22:21; Mark 12:17; Luke 20:25
8 [g] [Matt. 7:12; 22:39; John 13:34; Rom. 13:10; Gal. 5:13, 14; 1 Tim. 1:5; James 2:8]

notes on 2:11; James 2:1-4,9; cf. Acts 10:34; 1 Tim. 5:21; 1 Pet. 1:17). **set your mind...high things.** To be haughty with self-seeking pride (cf. Phil. 2:3). **wise in your own opinion.** Christians are not to have conceit or feelings of superiority toward fellow believers (cf. 1:22).

12:17 Repay no one evil for evil. The OT law of "eye for eye, tooth for tooth" was never intended to be applied by individuals in the OT or NT; but it was a standard for the collective society to use to enforce good conduct among people (1 Thess. 5:15; *see note on Ex. 21:23,24;* cf. Lev. 24:20; Deut. 19:21; 1 Pet. 3:8,9). **regard for good things.** Christians are to respect what is intrinsically proper and honest. "Good" also carries the idea of visibly and obviously having the right behavior when they are around others, especially unbelievers.

12:18 If it is possible. Although we should do everything possible to be at peace with others, it will not always come, because it also depends on others' attitudes and responses.

12:19 wrath. Of God (*see note on 1:18*). ***Vengeance.*** Divine retribution as quoted from Deut. 32:35.

12:20 *heap coals of fire on his head.* Refers to an ancient Egyptian custom in which a person who wanted to show public contrition carried a pan of burning coals on his head. The coals represented the burning pain of his shame and guilt. When believers lovingly help their enemies, it should bring shame to such people for their hate and animosity (cf. Prov. 25:21,22).

13:1 be subject. This Gr. word was used of a soldier's absolute obedience to his superior officer. Scripture makes one exception to this command: when obedience to civil authority would require disobedience to God's Word (Ex. 1:17; Dan. 3:16-18; 6:7,10; *see notes on Acts 4:19,20; 5:28,29*). **governing authorities.** Every position of civil authority without regard to competency, morality, reasonableness, or any other caveat (1 Thess. 4:11,12; 1 Tim. 2:1,2; Titus 3:1,2). **there is no authority except from God.** Since He alone is the sovereign ruler of the universe (Pss. 62:11; 103:19; 1 Tim. 6:15), He has instituted 4 authorities on earth: 1) the government over all citizens; 2) the church over all believers; 3) the parents over all children; and 4) the masters over all employees. **appointed.** Human government's authority derives from and is defined by God. He instituted human government to reward good and to restrain sin in an evil, fallen world.

13:2 resists the ordinance of God. Since all government is God-ordained, disobedience is rebellion against God. **judgment.** Not God's judgment, but punishment from the government for breaking the law (*see note on v. 4*).

13:3 not a terror to good works, but to evil. Even the most wicked, godless governments act as a deterrent to crime. **Do what is good...have praise.** Peaceful, law-abiding citizens need not fear the authorities. Few governments will harm those who obey their laws. In fact, governments usually commend such people.

13:4 God's minister...for good. By helping restrain evil and protecting life and property. Paul took advantage of his government's role in promoting what is good when he exercised his rights as a Roman citizen to obtain justice (Acts 16:37; 22:25,29; 25:11). **bear the sword.** This symbolizes the government's right to inflict punishment on wrongdoers—especially capital punishment (Gen. 9:6; cf. Matt. 26:52; Acts 25:11). **to *execute* wrath.** Not God's wrath, but the punishment inflicted by the civil authorities.

13:5 be subject. *See note on v. 1.* **because of...conscience' sake.** Out of a sense of obligation to God and to keep a clear conscience before Him (*see note on 2 Cor. 1:12*), not merely to avoid punishment from the civil authorities.

13:6 because of this. Because God ordained human government and demands submission to it (vv. 1-5). **taxes.** The Gr. word referred specifically to taxes paid by individuals, particularly those living in a conquered nation to their foreign rulers—which makes the tax even more onerous. That tax was usually a combined income and property tax. In this context, however, Paul uses the term in the broadest possible sense to speak of all kinds of taxes. Jesus explicitly taught that taxes are to be paid—even to the pagan Roman government (Matt. 22:17-21). He also set an example by willingly paying the temple tax (Matt. 17:24-27).

13:7 Render...to all their due. "Render" translates a Gr. word signifying the payment of something owed—not a voluntary contribution—and is reinforced by the word "due." The apostle reiterates that paying taxes is mandatory (*see note on v. 6*). **customs.** Tolls or taxes on goods. **fear...honor.** God demands that we show sincere respect and an attitude of genuine high esteem for all public officials.

13:8 Owe no one anything. Not a prohibition against borrowing money, which Scripture permits and regulates (cf. Ex. 22:25; Lev. 25:35-

fulfilled the law. **9** For the commandments,
[h]*"You shall not commit adultery," "You*
shall not murder," "You shall not steal,"
[2]*"You shall not bear false witness," "You*
shall not covet," and if *there is* any other
commandment, are *all* summed up in this
saying, namely, [i]*"You shall love your*
neighbor as yourself." **10** Love does no
harm to a neighbor; therefore [j]love *is* the
fulfillment of the law.

Put on Christ

11 And *do* this, knowing the time, that
now *it is* high time [k]to awake out of sleep;
for now our salvation *is* nearer than when
we *first* believed. **12** The night is far spent,
the day is at hand. [l]Therefore let us cast off
the works of darkness, and [m]let us put on
the armor of light. **13** [n]Let us walk [3]prop-
erly, as in the day, [o]not in revelry and
drunkenness, [p]not in lewdness and lust,
[q]not in strife and envy. **14** But [r]put on the
Lord Jesus Christ, and [s]make no provision
for the flesh, to *fulfill its* lusts.

The Law of Liberty

14 Receive[a] one who is weak in the
faith, *but* not to disputes over doubtful things. **2** For one believes he [b]may eat all
things, but he who is weak eats *only* vegetables. **3** Let not him who eats despise him

9 [h] Ex. 20:13-17; Deut. 5:17-21; Matt. 19:18 [i] Lev. 19:18; Mark 12:31; James 2:8 [2] NU omits *"You shall not bear false witness,"*
10 [j] [Matt. 7:12; 22:39, 40; John 13:34]; Rom. 13:8; Gal. 5:14; James 2:8
11 [k] Mark 13:37; [1 Cor. 15:34; Eph. 5:14]; 1 Thess. 5:6
12 [l] Eph. 5:11 [m] [2 Cor. 6:7; 10:4; Eph. 6:11, 13; 1 Thess. 5:8]
13 [n] Phil. 4:8 [o] Prov. 23:20 [p] [1 Cor. 6:9] [q] James 3:14 [3] *decently*
14 [r] Job 29:14; Gal. 3:27; [Eph. 4:24; Col. 3:10, 12] [s] [Gal. 5:16]; 1 Pet. 2:11 CHAPTER 14 **1** [a] [Rom. 14:2; 15:1; 1 Cor. 8:9; 9:22]
2 [b] 1 Cor. 10:25; [Titus 1:15]

37; Deut. 15:7-9; Neh. 5:7; Pss. 15:5; 37:21,26; Ezek. 22:12; Matt. 5:42; Luke 6:34). Paul's point is that all our financial obligations must be paid when they are due. *See notes on Deut. 23:19,20; 24:10-13.* **love one another.** Believers are commanded to love not only other Christians (John 13:34,35; 1 Cor. 14:1; Phil. 1:9; Col. 3:14; 1 Thess. 4:9; 1 Tim. 2:15; Heb. 6:10; 1 Pet. 1:22; 4:8; 1 John 2:10; 3:23; 4:7,21), but also non-Christians (Matt. 5:44; Luke 6:27,35; cf. Luke 6:28,34; Rom. 12:14,20; Gal. 6:10; 1 Thess. 5:15). **fulfilled the law.** *See note on 13:10.*

13:9 To demonstrate that love fulfills the law, Paul cites 4 of the Ten Commandments dealing with human relations and ties them in with an overarching OT command. He quotes Ex. 20:13-15,17 (cf. Deut. 5:17-19,21). **summed up…*love your neighbor as yourself.*** This command, quoting Lev. 19:18, encompasses all of God's laws concerning human relationships (Matt. 22:39); if we truly love our neighbor (anyone with whom we have contact, cf. Luke 10:25-37), we will only do what is in his best interest (13:10).

13:10 love *is* the fulfillment of the law. If we treat others with the same care that we have for ourselves, we will not violate any of God's laws regarding interpersonal relationships (Matt. 7:12; James 2:8).

13:11 time. The Gr. word views time not in terms of chronology, but as a period, era, or age (cf. 3:26; Matt. 16:3; Mark 1:15; Luke 21:8; Acts 1:7; 3:19; Rev. 1:3). **sleep.** Spiritual apathy and lethargy, i.e. unresponsiveness to the things of God. **our salvation.** Not our justification, but the final feature of our redemption, glorification (*see note on 8:23*). ***is* nearer.** We will be glorified when Jesus returns (*see note on 8:23*), which draws closer with each passing day. The Bible frequently uses the return of Jesus Christ to motivate believers to holy living (2 Cor. 5:10; Titus 2:11-13; Heb. 10:24,25; James 5:7,8; 1 Pet. 4:7-11; 2 Pet. 3:11-14).

13:12 night. Of man's depravity and Satan's dominion (cf. 1 Thess. 5:4,5). **day.** Of Christ's return and reign (cf. 1 Thess. 5:2-4). **cast off.** In light of Christ's imminent return, Paul exhorts believers to repent of and forsake their sins (2 Pet. 3:14; 1 John 2:28; cf. Eph. 4:22; Col. 3:8-10; Heb. 12:1,14; James 1:21; 1 Pet. 2:1; 4:1-3). **the armor of light.** The protection that practical righteousness provides (cf. Eph. 6:11-17).

13:13 Let us walk properly. By living a life pleasing to God, manifesting in our outward behavior the inner reality of a redeemed life (cf. 6:4; 8:4; Luke 1:6; Gal. 5:16; 25; Eph. 2:10; 4:1,17; 5:2,8,15; Phil. 1:27; 3:16,17; Col. 1:10; 2:6; 1 Thess. 2:12; 4:1,12; 1 Pet. 2:12; 1 John 2:6; 2 John 4,6). **revelry.** Wild parties, sexual orgies, brawls, riots (cf. Gal. 5:21; 1 Pet. 4:3). **lewdness and lust.** Sexual immorality (cf. 1 Cor. 6:18; Eph. 5:3; Col. 3:5; 1 Thess. 4:3; 2 Tim. 2:22). **strife and envy.** Closely associated iniquities (cf. 1 Cor. 3:3; 2 Cor. 12:20; Gal. 5:20; Phil. 1:15; 1 Tim. 6:4), since the former is often the result of the latter.

13:14 But put on the Lord Jesus Christ. This phrase summarizes sanctification, the continuing spiritual process in which those who have been saved by faith are transformed into His image and likeness (cf. 2 Cor. 3:18; Gal. 4:19; Phil. 3:13,14; Col. 2:7; 1 John 3:2,3). The image Paul uses to describe that process is taking off and putting on clothing, which is symbolic of thoughts and behavior. *See notes on Eph. 4:20-24.* **no provision.** This word has the basic meaning of planning ahead or forethought. Most sinful behavior results from wrong ideas and lustful desires we allow to linger in our minds (cf. James 1:14,15). **the flesh.** *See note on 7:5.* ***its* lusts.** See Gal. 5:17; Eph. 2:3.

14:1-12 The diversity of the church displays Christ's power to bring together dissimilar people in genuine unity. Yet Satan often works on man's unredeemed flesh to create division and threaten that unity. The threat to unity Paul addresses in this passage arises when mature (strong) believers—both Jews and Gentiles—conflict with immature (weak) believers. The strong Jewish believers understood their freedom in Christ and realized the ceremonial requirements of the Mosaic law were no longer binding. The mature Gentiles understood that idols are not gods and, therefore, that they could eat meat that had been offered to them. But in both cases the weaker brothers' consciences were troubled, and they were even tempted to violate their consciences (a bad thing to train oneself to do), become more legalistic under the feelings of guilt, or even to sin. Knowing that the mature Jews and Gentiles would be able to understand these struggles, Paul addresses most of his comments to them.

14:1 Receive. The Gr. word refers to personal and willing acceptance of another. **weak in the faith.** This characterizes those believers who are unable to let go of the religious ceremonies and rituals of their past. The weak Jewish believer had difficulty abandoning the rites and prohibitions of the Old Covenant; he felt compelled to adhere to dietary laws, observe the Sabbath, and offer sacrifices in the temple. The weak Gentile believer had been steeped in pagan idolatry and its rituals; he felt that any contact with anything remotely related to his past, including eating meat that had been offered to a pagan deity and then sold in the marketplace, tainted him with sin. Both had very sensitive consciences in these areas, and were not yet mature enough to be free of those convictions. Cf. 1 Cor. 8:1-13. **disputes over doubtful things.** Better translated, "for the purpose of passing judgment on his opinions (or scruples)." The mature believer should not sit in judgment on the sincere but underdeveloped thoughts that govern the weak believer's conduct.

14:2 one believes. The strong believer, whose mature faith allows him to exercise his freedom in Christ by eating the inexpensive meat sold at the pagan meat markets—inexpensive because a worshiper had first offered it as a sacrifice to a pagan deity (*see notes on 1 Cor. 8:1-13*). ***only* vegetables.** The strict diet weak Jewish and Gentile believers ate to avoid eating meat that was unclean or may have been sacrificed to idols.

who does not eat, and [c]let not him who
does not eat judge him who eats; for God
has received him. 4 [d]Who are you to judge
another's servant? To his own master he
stands or falls. Indeed, he will be made to
stand, for God is able to make him stand.

5 [e]One person esteems *one* day above another; another esteems every day *alike.* Let
each be fully convinced in his own mind.
6 He who [f]observes the day, observes *it* to
the Lord; [1]and he who does not observe the
day, to the Lord he does not observe *it.* He
who eats, eats to the Lord, for [g]he gives God
thanks; and he who does not eat, to the
Lord he does not eat, and gives God thanks.
7 For [h]none of us lives to himself, and no
one dies to himself. 8 For if we [i]live, we live
to the Lord; and if we die, we die to the
Lord. Therefore, whether we live or die, we
are the Lord's. 9 For [j]to this end Christ died
[2]and rose and lived again, that He might be
[k]Lord of both the dead and the living. 10 But
why do you judge your brother? Or why do
you show contempt for your brother? For

3 [c][Rom. 14:10, 13; Col. 2:16]
4 [d] Rom. 9:20; James 4:11, 12
5 [e] Gal. 4:10
6 [f] Gal. 4:10 [g] Matt. 14:19; 15:36; [1 Cor. 10:31; 1 Tim. 4:3] [1] NU omits the rest of this sentence.
7 [h] [1 Cor. 6:19; Gal. 2:20]; 1 Thess. 5:10; [1 Pet. 4:2]
8 [i] 2 Cor. 5:14, 15
9 [j] 2 Cor. 5:15 [k] Acts 10:36 [2] NU omits *and rose*
10 [l] Rom. 2:16; 2 Cor. 5:10 [3] NU *God*
11 [m] Is. 45:23; [Phil. 2:10, 11]
12 [n] Matt. 12:36; 16:27; [Gal. 6:5]; 1 Pet. 4:5
13 [o] 1 Cor. 8:9 [4] *any longer*
14 [p] 1 Cor. 10:25
15 [q] Rom. 14:20; 1 Cor. 8:11
16 [r] [Rom. 12:17]
17 [s] 1 Cor. 8:8

[l]we shall all stand before the judgment seat
of [3]Christ. 11 For it is written:

[m]"As I live, says the LORD,
Every knee shall bow to Me,
And every tongue shall confess to
God."

12 So then [n]each of us shall give account
of himself to God. 13 Therefore let us not
judge one another [4]anymore, but rather resolve this, [o]not to put a stumbling block or
a cause to fall in *our* brother's way.

The Law of Love

14 I know and am convinced by the Lord
Jesus [p]that *there is* nothing unclean of itself;
but to him who considers anything to be
unclean, to him *it is* unclean. 15 Yet if your
brother is grieved because of *your* food,
you are no longer walking in love. [q]Do not
destroy with your food the one for whom
Christ died. 16 [r]Therefore do not let your
good be spoken of as evil; 17 [s]for the king-

14:3 despise...judge. "Despise" indicates a contempt for someone as worthless, who deserves only disdain and abhorrence. "Judge" is equally strong and means "to condemn." Paul uses them synonymously: The strong hold the weak in contempt as legalistic and self-righteous; the weak judge the strong to be irresponsible at best and perhaps depraved.

14:4 To his own master he stands or falls. How Christ evaluates each believer is what matters, and His judgment does not take into account religious tradition or personal preference (cf. 8:33,34; 1 Cor. 4:3-5).

14:5 esteems *one* day. Though it was no longer required by God, the weak Jewish believer felt compelled to observe the Sabbath and other special days associated with Judaism (cf. Gal. 4:9,10; *see notes on Col. 2:16,17*). On the other hand, the weak Gentile wanted to separate himself from the special days of festivities associated with his former paganism because of its immorality and idolatry. **esteems every day *alike.*** The mature believers were unaffected by those concerns. **Let each be fully convinced.** Each Christian must follow the dictates of his own conscience in matters not specifically commanded or prohibited in Scripture. Since conscience is a God-given mechanism to warn, and responds to the highest standard of moral law in the mind (2:14,15), it is not sensible to train yourself to ignore it. Rather, respond to its compunctions and as you mature, by learning more, your mind will not alert it to those things which are not essential.

14:6 The strong believer eats whatever he pleases and thanks the Lord. The weak brother eats according to his ceremonial diet and thanks the Lord that he made a sacrifice on His behalf. In either case, the believer thanks the Lord, so the motive is the same. **to the Lord.** Whether weak or strong, the motive behind a believer's decisions about issues of conscience must be to please the Lord.

14:7 lives to himself...dies to himself. The focus of Christian living is never oneself—everything we do should be to please our sovereign Lord (cf. 1 Cor. 6:20; 10:31).

14:9 Lord of both the dead and the living. Christ died not only to free us from sin, but to enslave us to Himself (6:22); to establish Himself as Sovereign over the saints in His presence and those still on earth (cf. Phil. 2:11; 1 Tim. 6:15; Rev. 17:14; 19:16).

14:10 judge...show contempt. *See note on v. 3.* **your brother.** A fellow believer in Christ. **the judgment seat of Christ.** The preferred rendering is "the judgment seat of God" (*see notes on 1 Cor. 3:13-15*). Every believer will give an account of himself, and the Lord will judge the decisions he made—including those concerning issues of conscience. That verdict is the only one that matters (*see notes on 1 Cor. 4:1-5; 2 Cor. 5:9,10*).

14:11 it is written. Paul quotes Is. 45:23; 49:18 (cf. Phil. 2:10,11).

14:13 judge. *See note on v. 3.* **but rather resolve.** The same Gr. word translated "judge" (14:3,10,13) is here translated "resolve." In vv. 3,10,13a the meaning is negative: to condemn. In v. 13b, the meaning is positive: to determine or make a careful decision. The point of Paul's play on words is that instead of passing judgment on their brothers, they should use their best judgment to help fellow believers. **stumbling block.** Anything a believer does—even though Scripture may permit it—that causes another to fall into sin (1 Cor. 8:9).

14:14 I know and am convinced by the Lord Jesus. This truth was not the product of his own thinking or the teaching of others, but of divine revelation (cf. Gal. 1:12). *See note on 1 Cor. 7:12.* **nothing unclean of itself.** *See note on Acts 10:15*; cf. Mark 7:15; 1 Tim. 4:3-5; Titus 1:15). **unclean.** The Gr. word originally meant "common" but came to mean "impure" or "evil" (*see note on Acts 10:14*). **to him who considers...to him *it is* unclean.** If a believer is convinced a certain behavior is sin—even if his assessment is wrong—he should never do it. If he does, he will violate his conscience, experience guilt (cf. 1 Cor. 8:4-7; *see note on 2:15*), and perhaps be driven back into deeper legalism instead of moving toward freedom (*see note on v. 5*).

14:15 grieved. The Gr. word refers to causing pain or distress. A weak believer may be hurt when he sees a brother do something he believes is sinful. But still worse, the strong believer may cause his weaker brother to violate his own conscience (cf. 1 Cor. 8:8-13). **love.** *See notes on 1 Cor. 13:1-13.* Love will ensure that the strong Christian is sensitive and understanding of his brother's weaknesses (1 Cor. 8:8-13). **destroy.** This refers to complete devastation. In the NT, it is often used to indicate eternal damnation (Matt. 10:28; Luke 13:3; John 3:16; Rom. 2:12). In this context, however, it refers to a serious devastation of one's spiritual growth (cf. Matt. 18:3,6,14). **the one for whom Christ died.** Any Christian (cf. 1 Cor. 8:11).

14:16 your good. The rightful exercise of one's Christian liberty (cf. 1 Cor. 10:23-32). **spoken of as evil.** To blaspheme. When unbelievers see a strong Christian abusing his freedom in Christ and harm-

dom of God is not eating and drinking, but
righteousness and [t]peace and joy in the
Holy Spirit. **18** For he who serves Christ in
[5]these things [u]*is* acceptable to God and approved by men.
19 [v]Therefore let us pursue the things
which make for peace and the things by
which [w]one may [6]edify another. **20** [x]Do not
destroy the work of God for the sake of
food. [y]All things indeed *are* pure, [z]but *it is*
evil for the man who eats with [7]offense. **21** *It*
is good neither to eat [a]meat nor drink wine
nor *do anything* by which your brother
stumbles [8]or is offended or is made weak.
22 [9]Do you have faith? Have *it* to yourself
before God. [b]Happy *is* he who does not condemn himself in what he approves. **23** But
he who doubts is condemned if he eats, because *he does* not *eat* from faith; for [c]what-
ever *is* not from faith is [1]sin.

Bearing Others' Burdens

15 We [a]then who are strong ought to
bear with the [1]scruples of the weak,
and not to please ourselves. **2** [b]Let each of
us please *his* neighbor for *his* good, leading
to [2]edification. **3** [c]For even Christ did not
please Himself; but as it is written, [d]*"The*
reproaches of those who reproached You
fell on Me." **4** For [e]whatever things were
written before were written for our learning, that we through the [3]patience and
comfort of the Scriptures might have hope.
5 [f]Now may the God of patience and comfort grant you to be like-minded toward
one another, according to Christ Jesus,
6 that you may [g]with one mind *and* one
mouth glorify the God and Father of our
Lord Jesus Christ.

Glorify God Together

7 Therefore [h]receive one another, just [i]as
Christ also received [4]us, to the glory of
God. **8** Now I say that [j]Jesus Christ has be-

17 [t][Rom. 8:6]
18 [u]2 Cor. 8:21; Phil. 4:8; 1 Pet. 2:12 [5]NU *this thing*
19 [v]Ps. 34:14; Rom. 12:18; 1 Cor. 7:15; 2 Tim. 2:22; Heb. 12:14 [w]1 Cor. 14:12; 1 Thess. 5:11 [6]*build up*
20 [x]Rom. 14:15 [y]Acts 10:15 [z]1 Cor. 8:9-12 [7]A feeling of giving offense
21 [a]1 Cor. 8:13 [8]NU omits the rest of v. 21.
22 [b][1 John 3:21] [9]NU *The faith which you have—have*
23 [c]Titus 1:15 [1]M puts Rom. 16:25-27 here.

CHAPTER 15

1 [a]Rom. 14:1; [Gal. 6:1, 2]; 1 Thess. 5:14 [1]*weaknesses*
2 [b]1 Cor. 9:22; 10:24, 33; 2 Cor. 13:9 [2]*building up*
3 [c]Matt. 26:39; [Phil. 2:5-8] [d]Ps. 69:9
4 [e]Rom. 4:23, 24; 1 Cor. 10:11; 2 Tim. 3:16, 17 [3]*perseverance*
5 [f]1 Cor. 1:10; Phil. 1:27
6 [g]Acts 4:24
7 [h]Rom. 14:1, 3 [i]Rom. 5:2 [4]NU, M *you*
8 [j]Matt. 15:24; Acts 3:26

ing a weaker brother, they will conclude that Christianity is filled with unloving people, which reflects badly on God's reputation (cf. 2:24).

14:17 kingdom of God. The sphere of salvation where God rules in the hearts of those He has saved (*see notes on Acts 1:3; 1 Cor. 6:9*). **eating and drinking.** Non-essentials and external observances. **righteousness.** Holy, obedient living (cf. Eph. 6:14; Phil. 1:11). **peace.** The loving tranquillity, produced by the Spirit, that should characterize believers' relationships with God and each other (Gal. 5:22). **joy in the Holy Spirit.** Another part of the Spirit's fruit, this describes an abiding attitude of praise and thanksgiving regardless of circumstances, which flows from one's confidence in God's sovereignty (Gal. 5:22; 1 Thess. 1:6).

14:18 approved by men. This refers to approving something after a careful examination, like a jeweler inspecting a stone to determine its quality and value. Christians are under the microscope of a skeptical world that is assessing how they live with and treat each other (cf. John 13:35; Phil. 2:15).

14:20 work of God. A fellow Christian who has been redeemed by the efforts of the Father, Son, and Holy Spirit, not his own (cf. v. 15; Eph. 2:10). **All things...pure.** The discretionary liberties which God has given to believers and are good in themselves (cf. vv. 14,16). **who eats with offense.** One who uses those God-given liberties carelessly and selfishly, offending his weaker brother.

14:21 stumbles. *See note on v. 13.* **offended...made weak.** This phrase does not appear in the better manuscripts.

14:22,23 The strongest Christian can bring harm to himself in the area of Christian liberty by denouncing or belittling the freedom God has given him (Gal. 5:1), or by carelessly flaunting his liberty without regard for how that might affect others (cf. 1 Cor. 10:23-32).

14:22 Have *it* to yourself before God. This is better translated, "have as your own conviction before God." Paul urges the strong believer to understand his liberty, enjoy it, and keep it between God and himself. **what he approves.** The strong believer maintains a healthy conscience because he does not give a weak believer a cause to stumble.

14:23 who doubts is condemned. When the weak brother violates his conscience, he sins. **whatever *is* not from faith.** The thoughts and actions that our conscience condemns.

15:1 We...who are strong. *See notes on 14:1-12.* **to bear.** The word means "to pick up and carry a weight." It is used of carrying a pitcher of water (Mark 14:13), of carrying a man (Acts 21:35), and figuratively of bearing an obligation (Acts 15:10). The strong are not to simply tolerate the weaknesses of their weaker brothers; they are to help the weak shoulder their burdens by showing loving and practical consideration for them (Gal. 6:2; cf. 1 Cor. 9:19-22; Phil. 2:2-4). **scruples.** Better translated, "weaknesses." **weak.** *See note on 14:1.*

15:2 edification. To build up and strengthen. This is essentially the same appeal Paul made earlier (14:19), only with the additional qualification of self-sacrifice (1 Cor. 10:23,24; cf. Phil. 2:2-5).

15:3 Christ did not please Himself. His ultimate purpose was to please God and accomplish His will (John 4:34; 5:30; 6:38; 8:25,27-29; Phil. 2:6-8). **it is written.** Quoted from Ps. 69:9. ***The reproaches...fell on Me.*** "Reproaches" refers to slander, false accusations, and insults. Men hate God, and they manifested that same hate toward the One He sent to reveal Himself (cf. John 1:10,11,18).

15:4 things...written before. The divinely revealed OT. **written for our learning.** Although Christians live under the New Covenant and are not under the authority of the Old Covenant, God's moral law has not changed and all Scripture is of spiritual benefit (1 Cor. 10:6,10,11; 2 Pet. 1:20,21). Paul's description of the benefits of Scripture certainly includes the NT, but speaks primarily about "the sacred writings"—or the OT (2 Tim. 3:15-17). **patience.** *See note on 5:3.* **comfort.** Lit. "encouragement." The Word of God not only informs believers how to endure, but it also encourages them in the process. **hope.** *See note on 5:2.* Without the clear and certain promises of the Word of God, the believer has no basis for hope (cf. Ps. 119:81,114; Eph. 2:12; Jer. 14:8).

15:5 to be like-minded toward one another. Paul urges the strong and the weak (*see notes on 14:1-12*), despite their differing views on these non-essential issues, to pursue loving, spiritual harmony in regard to matters on which the Bible is silent.

15:6 with one mind *and* one mouth. Our unity should be both real (one mind) and apparent (one mouth). But the consummate purpose of unity is not to please other believers but to glorify God. **God and Father.** This expression emphasizes the deity of Christ. Jesus is not an adopted son of God; He is of the same essential being and nature as God. This is such an important connection that it appears frequently in the NT (2 Cor. 1:3; 11:31; Eph. 1:3; Col. 1:3; 1 Pet. 1:3).

come a [5]servant to the circumcision for the
truth of God, [k]to confirm the promises
made to the fathers, 9 and [l]that the Gentiles
might glorify God for *His* mercy, as it is
written:

[m]"For this reason I will confess to
You among the Gentiles,
And sing to Your name."

10 And again he says:

[n]"Rejoice, O Gentiles, with His
people!"

11 And again:

[o]"Praise the LORD, all you Gentiles!
Laud Him, all you peoples!"

12 And again, Isaiah says:

[p]"There shall be a root of Jesse;
And He who shall rise to reign
over the Gentiles,
In Him the Gentiles shall hope."

13 Now may the God of hope fill you
with all [q]joy and peace in believing, that
you may abound in hope by the power of
the Holy Spirit.

From Jerusalem to Illyricum

14 Now [r]I myself am confident concerning you, my brethren, that you also are full
of goodness, [s]filled with all knowledge,
able also to admonish [6]one another.
15 Nevertheless, brethren, I have written
more boldly to you on *some* points, as reminding you, [t]because of the grace given
to me by God, 16 that [u]I might be a minister of Jesus Christ to the Gentiles, ministering the gospel of God, that the [v]offering
[7]of the Gentiles might be acceptable, sanctified by the Holy Spirit. 17 Therefore I
have reason to glory in Christ Jesus [w]in the
things *which pertain* to God. 18 For I will not
dare to speak of any of those things [x]which
Christ has not accomplished through me,
in word and deed, [y]to make the Gentiles
obedient— 19 [z]in mighty signs and wonders, by the power of the Spirit of God, so
that from Jerusalem and round about to Illyricum I have fully preached the gospel of
Christ. 20 And so I have made it my aim to
preach the gospel, not where Christ was

8 [k][Rom. 4:16]; 2 Cor. 1:20 [5]*minister*
9 [l]John 10:16 [m]2 Sam. 22:50; Ps. 18:49
10 [n]Deut. 32:43
11 [o]Ps. 117:1
12 [p]Is. 11:1, 10
13 [q]Rom. 12:12; 14:17
14 [r]2 Pet. 1:12 [s]1 Cor. 1:5; 8:1, 7, 10 [6]M *others*
15 [t]Rom. 1:5; 12:3
16 [u]Acts 9:15; Rom. 11:13 [v][Is. 66:20] [7]Consisting of
17 [w]Heb. 2:17; 5:1
18 [x]Acts 15:12; 21:19; 2 Cor. 3:5; Gal. 2:8 [y]Rom. 1:5
19 [z]Acts 19:11

15:7 receive. *See note on 14:1.* **as Christ...received us.** If the perfect, sinless Son of God was willing to bring sinners into God's family, how much more should forgiven believers be willing to warmly embrace and accept each other in spite of their disagreements over issues of conscience (Matt. 10:24; 11:29; Eph. 4:32–5:2).

15:8 a servant to the circumcision. Jesus was born a Jew (*see note on Matt. 1:1*), and as a child, He was circumcised and identified physically with the sign of the covenant (*see notes on 4:11; Gen. 17:10-14*). **promises *made* to the fathers.** The covenant with Abraham that God reiterated to both Isaac and Jacob (*see note on 4:13*).

15:9-12 To show that God's plan has always been to bring Jew and Gentile alike into His kingdom and to soften the prejudice of Christian Jews against their Gentile brothers, Paul quotes from the Law, the Prophets, and twice from the Psalms—all the recognized divisions of the OT—proving God's plan from their own Scriptures.

15:9 that the Gentiles might glorify God for *His* mercy. Because He extended His grace and mercy to a people outside the covenant (*see notes on 10:11-21; 11:11-18*). **it is written.** Quoted from 2 Sam. 22:50; Ps. 18:49. The psalmist sings praise to God among the nations, which alludes to Gentile salvation.

15:10 Quoted from Deut. 32:43.

15:11 Quoted from Ps. 117:1. ***Laud.*** Praise.

15:12 Quoted from Is. 11:10. ***root of Jesse.*** A way of referring to Jesus as the descendant of David, and thus of David's father Jesse (*see note on Rev. 5:5*).

15:13 God of hope. God is the source of eternal hope, life, and salvation, and He is the object of hope for every believer (*see note on 5:2*). **by the power of the Holy Spirit.** The believer's hope comes through the Scripture (cf. 15:4; Eph. 1:13,14), which was written and is applied to every believing heart by the Holy Spirit.

15:14-22 Not wanting to jeopardize his relationship with the believers in Rome by seeming to be insensitive, presumptuous, or unloving, Paul sets out to explain how he could write such a forthright letter to a church he did not found and had never visited.

15:14 goodness. High moral character. The believers in Rome hated evil and loved righteousness, attitudes their lives clearly displayed. **knowledge.** Refers to deep, intimate knowledge indicating that the Roman believers were doctrinally sound (Col. 2:2,3), illustrating the fact that truth and virtue are inseparable (cf. 1 Tim. 1:19). **admonish.** To encourage, warn, or advise—a comprehensive term for preaching (1 Cor. 14:3) and personal counseling (*see note on 12:1*). Every believer is responsible to encourage and strengthen other believers with God's Word and is divinely equipped to do so (2 Tim. 3:16).

15:15 as reminding you. In spite of their spiritual strength, these Christians needed to be reminded of truths they already knew but could easily neglect or even forget (cf. 1 Tim. 4:6; 2 Tim. 2:8-14; Titus 3:1).

15:16 minister. "Minister" was a general Gr. term used of public officials. But in the NT it is used most often of those who serve God in some form of public worship (e.g., Phil. 2:17; Heb. 1:7,14; 8:1,2,6), including that of a priest (Luke 1:23). **to the Gentiles.** Although Paul's practice was always to present the gospel to the Jews first in every city he visited (*see note on Acts 13:5*), his primary apostolic calling was to the Gentiles (11:13; Acts 9:15). **the offering.** Having referred to himself as a minister, a word with priestly overtones, Paul explains that his priestly ministry is to present to God an offering of a multitude of Gentile converts.

15:17 glory. Lit. "to boast. Paul never boasted in his accomplishments as an apostle, but only in what Christ had accomplished through him (1 Cor. 1:27-29,31; 2 Cor. 10:13-17; 12:5,9; Gal. 6:14; 1 Tim. 1:12-16).

15:19 signs and wonders. *See notes on Acts 2:19; 2 Cor. 12:12.* God used them to authenticate true preaching and teaching. **to Illyricum.** The region that roughly corresponds to the former European country of Yugoslavia. From Jerusalem to Illyricum was a span of some 1,400 miles.

15:20 gospel. *See note on 1:1.* **another man's foundation.** Paul's goal was to reach those who had never heard the gospel—the primary function of a NT evangelist (Eph. 4:11). But for pastor-

named, [a]lest I should build on another
man's foundation, 21 but as it is written:

[b]*"To whom He was not announced,*
they shall see;
And those who have not heard
shall understand."

Plan to Visit Rome

22 For this reason [c]I also have been much
hindered from coming to you. 23 But now
no longer having a place in these parts,
and [d]having a great desire these many
years to come to you, 24 whenever I journey to Spain, [8]I shall come to you. For I
hope to see you on my journey, [e]and to be
helped on my way there by you, if first I
may [f]enjoy your *company* for a while.
25 But now [g]I am going to Jerusalem to
[9]minister to the saints. 26 For [h]it pleased
those from Macedonia and Achaia to make
a certain contribution for the poor among
the saints who are in Jerusalem. 27 It
pleased them indeed, and they are their
debtors. For [i]if the Gentiles have been partakers of their spiritual things, [j]their duty
is also to minister to them in material
things. 28 Therefore, when I have performed this and have sealed to them [k]this
fruit, I shall go by way of you to Spain.
29 [l]But I know that when I come to you, I
shall come in the fullness of the blessing
[1]of the gospel of Christ.
30 Now I beg you, brethren, through the
Lord Jesus Christ, and [m]through the love
of the Spirit, [n]that you strive together with
me in prayers to God for me, 31 [o]that I may
be delivered from those in Judea who [2]do
not believe, and that [p]my service for Jerusalem may be acceptable to the saints,
32 [q]that I may come to you with joy [r]by the
will of God, and may [s]be refreshed together with you. 33 Now [t]the God of peace *be*
with you all. Amen.

Sister Phoebe Commended

16 I commend to you Phoebe our sister, who is a servant of the church in
[a]Cenchrea, 2 [b]that you may receive her in

20 [a] 1 Cor. 3:10; [2 Cor. 10:13, 15, 16]
21 [b] Is. 52:15
22 [c] Rom. 1:13; 1 Thess. 2:17, 18
23 [d] Acts 19:21; 23:11; Rom. 1:10, 11
24 [e] Acts 15:3 [f] Rom. 1:12 [8] NU omits *I shall come to you* and joins *Spain* with the next sentence.
25 [g] Acts 19:21 [9] *serve*
26 [h] 1 Cor. 16:1; 2 Cor. 8:1-15
27 [i] Rom. 11:17 [j] 1 Cor. 9:11
28 [k] Phil. 4:17
29 [l] [Rom. 1:11] [1] NU omits *of the gospel*
30 [m] Phil. 2:1 [n] 2 Cor. 1:11; Col. 4:12
31 [o] 2 Tim. 3:11; 4:17 [p] 2 Cor. 8:4 [2] *are disobedient*
32 [q] Rom. 1:10 [r] Acts 18:21 [s] 1 Cor. 16:18
33 [t] Rom. 16:20; 1 Cor. 14:33; 2 Cor. 13:11; Phil. 4:9; [1 Thess. 5:23]; 2 Thess. 3:16; Heb. 13:20

CHAPTER 16 1 [a] Acts 18:18 2 [b] Phil. 2:29

teachers, building on the foundation laid by such an evangelist is the crucial part of their ministry (cf. 1 Cor. 3:6).

15:21 it is written. Quoted from Is. 52:15; *see note on 3:10.* The OT quotation refers primarily to Christ's second coming, but in its broader application it refers to the process of evangelism that began in Paul's day and continues throughout church history until Christ returns.

15:22 hindered from coming. The form of this Gr. verb indicates an ongoing problem, and that something external created the hindrance. Paul was providentially being prevented by God from going to Rome (cf. Acts 16:7).

15:23,24 Careful and sensible planning does not demonstrate a lack of trust in God's providence. But plans must always be subject to the Lord's control and alteration—just as Paul's were (cf. Prov. 16:9).

15:23 no longer having a place. Paul believed he had covered the region with the gospel sufficiently and could move on to other areas. **a great desire...to come to you.** *See 1:10-13.*

15:24 Spain. The city and region referred to in the OT as Tarshish (1 Kin. 10:22; Jon. 1:3), located on the far western end of the European continent. It had become a major center of commerce and culture, made accessible by the vast network of Roman roads. Its most famous ancient son was Seneca, the philosopher and statesman who tutored Nero and served as prime minister of the Empire. **helped on my way there by you.** Paul hoped the church at Rome would supply him with an escort and supplies to make the journey to Spain.

15:25 minister. *See note on Acts 6:2.*

15:26 Macedonia and Achaia. *See notes on Acts 16:9; 18:12.* Paul ministered in these regions during his first and second missionary journeys. **contribution.** The Gr. word carries the basic idea of sharing and is usually translated "fellowship" or "communion." The context indicates that here it is the sharing of a financial gift to help support the poor in Jerusalem (1 Cor. 16:1; 2 Cor. 8:2-4; Gal. 2:9,10).

15:27 their spiritual things. The "things" were gospel truths first preached to the Gentile believers by the Jewish apostles, prophets, teachers, and evangelists.

15:28 this fruit. The financial gift for the Jerusalem church; the fruit of their genuine love and gratitude. **Spain.** *See note on 15:24.*

15:30 the love of the Spirit. This phrase occurs only here in Scripture and refers to Paul's love for the Holy Spirit, not the Spirit's love for him (cf. Ps. 143:10).

15:30,31 prayers...that I may be delivered. Many Jews in Judea rejected the gospel and were prepared to attack Paul when he returned. Aware of the trouble that awaited him (Acts 20:22-24), he wanted the Roman Christians to pray for his deliverance only so he could complete the ministry the Lord had given him. Their prayers were answered in that he met with success in Jerusalem (Acts 21:17,19,20) and was delivered from death, but not imprisonment (Acts 21:10,11; 23:11).

15:31 may be acceptable. Paul wanted the Jewish Christians in Jerusalem to receive the financial gift from the Gentiles with loving gratitude, recognizing it as a gesture of brotherly love and kindness.

15:32 the will of God. *See note on 1:10.* **refreshed together with you.** Paul eventually found the joy and rest he was looking for (Acts 28:15).

15:33 the God of peace. Just as He is the God of hope (*see note on v. 13*), God is also the source of true peace (cf. Eph. 2:11-14; Phil. 4:7).

16:1-27 This chapter, which has almost no explicit teaching and contains several lists of mostly unknown people, is the most extensive and intimate expression of Paul's love and affection for other believers and co-workers found anywhere in his NT letters. It also provides insights into the lives of ordinary first-century Christians and gives an inside look at the nature and character of the early church.

16:1 Phoebe. Means "bright and radiant," which aptly fits Paul's brief description of her personality and Christian character. **servant.** The term from which we get "deacon" and "deaconess" (*see notes on 1 Tim. 3:10,11,13*). In the early church, women servants cared for sick believers, the poor, strangers, and those in prison. They instructed the women and children (cf. Titus 2:3-5). Whether Phoebe had an official title or not, she had the great responsibility of delivering this letter to the Roman church. When they had served faithfully and become widowed and destitute, such women were to be cared for by the church (*see notes on 1 Tim. 5:3-16*). **Cenchrea.** A neighboring port city of Corinth, where Paul wrote Romans. The church in Cenchrea was probably planted by the Corinthian church.

the Lord [c] in a manner worthy of the saints,
and assist her in whatever business she has
need of you; for indeed she has been a
helper of many and of myself also.

Greeting Roman Saints

3 Greet [d] Priscilla and Aquila, my fellow
workers in Christ Jesus, 4 who risked their
own necks for my life, to whom not only I
give thanks, but also all the churches of the
Gentiles. 5 Likewise *greet* [e] the church that
is in their house.
Greet my beloved Epaenetus, who is
[f] the firstfruits of [1] Achaia to Christ. 6 Greet
Mary, who labored much for us. 7 Greet
Andronicus and Junia, my countrymen
and my fellow prisoners, who are of note
among the [g] apostles, who also [h] were in
Christ before me.
8 Greet Amplias, my beloved in the
Lord. 9 Greet Urbanus, our fellow worker
in Christ, and Stachys, my beloved.
10 Greet Apelles, approved in Christ. Greet
those who are of the *household* of Aristobulus. 11 Greet Herodion, my [2] countryman.
Greet those who are of the *household* of
Narcissus who are in the Lord.
12 Greet Tryphena and Tryphosa, who
have labored in the Lord. Greet the
beloved Persis, who labored much in the
Lord. 13 Greet Rufus, [i] chosen in the Lord,
and his mother and mine. 14 Greet
Asyncritus, Phlegon, Hermas, Patrobas,
Hermes, and the brethren who are with
them. 15 Greet Philologus and Julia, Ne-
reus and his sister, and Olympas, and all
the saints who are with them.
16 [j] Greet one another with a holy kiss.
[3] The churches of Christ greet you.

Avoid Divisive Persons

17 Now I urge you, brethren, note those
[k] who cause divisions and offenses, contrary to the doctrine which you learned,
and [l] avoid them. 18 For those who are such
do not serve our Lord [4] Jesus Christ, but
[m] their own belly, and [n] by smooth words
and flattering speech deceive the hearts of
the simple. 19 For [o] your obedience has become known to all. Therefore I am glad on
your behalf; but I want you to be [p] wise in

2 [c] Phil. 1:27
3 [d] Acts 18:2, 18, 26; 1 Cor. 16:19; 2 Tim. 4:19
5 [e] 1 Cor. 16:19; Col. 4:15; Philem. 2 [f] 1 Cor. 16:15 [1] NU *Asia*
7 [g] Acts 1:13, 26 [h] Rom. 8:11; 16:3, 9, 10; 2 Cor. 5:17; 12:2; Gal. 1:22
11 [2] Or *relative*
13 [i] 2 John 1
16 [j] 1 Cor. 16:20; 2 Cor. 13:12; 1 Thess. 5:26; 1 Pet. 5:14 [3] NU *All the churches*
17 [k] [Acts 15:1] [l] [1 Cor. 5:9]
18 [m] Phil. 3:19 [n] Col. 2:4; 2 Pet. 2:3 [4] NU, M omit *Jesus*
19 [o] Rom. 1:8 [p] Jer. 4:22; Matt. 10:16; 1 Cor. 14:20

16:3 Priscilla and Aquila. *See notes on Acts 18:1-3.*

16:4 risked their own necks for my life. Probably at Corinth or Ephesus, but the details are not known.

16:5 Epaenetus. Probably saved through Paul's preaching and lovingly discipled by the apostle. **firstfruits.** *See note on 1:13.* He was the first convert in Asia Minor (modern Turkey), which in the best manuscripts replaces the word "Achaia."

16:6 Mary, who labored much for us. "Labored much" connotes hard work to the point of exhaustion. The context suggests she might have ministered in the church at Rome since its founding and been mentioned to Paul by others (possibly Priscilla and Aquila). But nothing more is known of her.

16:7 Andronicus and Junia. Perhaps a married couple, since "Junia" can be a woman's name. **fellow prisoners.** Probably a reference to their actually sharing the same cell or adjacent cells at some point. **of note among the apostles.** Their ministry with Paul, and perhaps with Peter and some of the other apostles in Jerusalem before Paul was converted, was well known and appreciated by the apostles.

16:8 Amplias. A common name among the emperor's household slaves at that time; he may have been one of those in "Caesar's household" (Phil. 4:22).

16:9 Stachys. An uncommon Gr. name meaning "ear of corn." He was obviously close to Paul, but the details are unknown.

16:10 Aristobulus. Since Paul does not greet him personally, he was probably not a believer, although some relatives and household servants apparently were. One noted biblical scholar believes that he was the brother of Herod Agrippa I and the grandson of Herod the Great.

16:11 Herodion. Related to the Herod family, and so perhaps associated with the household of Aristobulus. **my countryman.** The preferred reading is "my kinsman," indicating that he may have been one of Paul's Jewish relatives. **Narcissus.** *See note on 16:10.* Some scholars believe that this was the Emperor Claudius' secretary. If so, two households within the palace had Christians in them (cf. Phil. 4:22).

16:12 Tryphena and Tryphosa. Possibly twin sisters, whose names mean "delicate" and "dainty." **Persis.** Named after her native Persia; since her work is spoken of in the past tense, she was probably older than the other two women in this verse.

16:13 Rufus. Biblical scholars generally agree that he was one of the sons of Simon of Cyrene, the man enlisted to carry Jesus' cross (cf. Mark 15:21) and was likely saved through that contact with Christ. Mark wrote his gospel in Rome, possibly after the letter to Rome was written, and circulated. Paul would not have mentioned Rufus if that name were not well known to the church in Rome. **chosen in the Lord.** Elected to salvation. Some translations render "chosen" as "choice," which indicates he was widely known as an extraordinary believer because of his great love and service. **his mother and mine.** Rufus was not Paul's natural brother. Rather, Rufus' mother, the wife of Simon of Cyrene, at some time had cared for Paul during his ministry travels.

16:14,15 "Brethren" in this context, probably refers to both men and women, which indicates that these names represent the outstanding leaders of two of the assemblies in Rome.

16:16 holy kiss. Kissing of friends on the forehead, cheek, or beard was common in the OT. The Jews in the NT church carried on the practice, and it became especially precious to new believers, who were often outcasts from their own families because of their faith, because of the spiritual kinship it signified.

16:17-20 Paul considered it necessary to insert into his greetings of love this caution against harmful teachings and practices that undermine the truth of Christianity and are its greatest threat. Genuine love will be ready to forgive evil, but it will not condone or ignore it. Those such as Paul, who truly love other believers who are dear to them, will warn them about sin and harm (cf. 1 Cor. 13:6).

16:17 divisions and offenses. Doctrinal falsehood and unrighteous practices (cf. Matt. 24:24; Acts 20:27-32; Gal. 1:6-8; Eph. 4:14).

16:18 belly. Driven by self-interest and self-gratification, often seen in their pretentious, extravagant, and immoral lifestyles (cf. Phil. 3:18,19; 2 Tim. 3:7,8; 2 Pet. 1:20–2:3,10-19; Jude 12,13). **simple.** The unsuspecting or naive person (cf. 2 Cor. 11:13-15).

16:19 become known. *See note on 1:8.*

what is good, and [5]simple concerning evil.
20 And [q]the God of peace [r]will crush Satan
under your feet shortly.

[s]The grace of our Lord Jesus Christ *be*
with you. Amen.

Greetings from Paul's Friends

21 [t]Timothy, my fellow worker, and [u]Lu-
cius, [v]Jason, and [w]Sosipater, my countrymen, greet you.

22 I, Tertius, who wrote *this* epistle, greet
you in the Lord.

23 [x]Gaius, my host and *the host* of the
whole church, greets you. [y]Erastus, the
treasurer of the city, greets you, and Quartus, a brother. 24 [z]The[6] grace of our Lord
Jesus Christ *be* with you all. Amen.

Benediction

25 [7]Now [a]to Him who is able to establish
you [b]according to my gospel and the
preaching of Jesus Christ, [c]according to the
revelation of the mystery [d]kept secret since
the world began 26 but [e]now made manifest, and by the prophetic Scriptures made
known to all nations, according to the commandment of the everlasting God, for
[f]obedience to the faith— 27 to [g]God, alone
wise, *be* glory through Jesus Christ forever.
Amen.

19 [5]*innocent* **20** [q]Rom. 15:33 [r]Gen. 3:15 [s]1 Cor. 16:23; 2 Cor. 13:14; Gal. 6:18; Phil. 4:23; 1 Thess. 5:28; 2 Thess. 3:18; Rev. 22:21 **21** [t]Acts 16:1; Heb. 13:23 [u]Acts 13:1 [v]Acts 17:5 [w]Acts 20:4 **23** [x]1 Cor. 1:14 [y]Acts 19:22; 2 Tim. 4:20 **24** [z]1 Thess. 5:28 [6]NU omits v. 24. **25** [a][Eph. 3:20; Jude 24] [b]Rom. 2:16 [c]Matt. 13:35; Rom. 11:25; 1 Cor. 2:1,7; 4:1; Eph. 1:9 [d]Col. 1:26; 2:2; 4:3; [1 Tim. 3:16] [7]M puts Rom. 16:25-27 after Rom. 14:23. **26** [e]Eph. 1:9 [f][Acts 6:7]; Rom. 1:5 **27** [g]Jude 25

16:20 God of peace. See 15:33; Heb. 13:20. **will crush Satan.** *See note on Gen. 3:15.* **shortly.** "Soon, speedily, quickly" (Acts 12:7; 22:18; cf. Rev. 22:7,12,20). **grace of our Lord Jesus Christ.** *See note on 1:7.*

16:21 Lucius. Either 1) a native of Cyrene, one of the prophets and teachers in Antioch who participated in Paul and Barnabas' commissioning (Acts 13:1-3) or 2) another form of "Luke," the author of the Gospel of Luke and the book of Acts. **Jason.** One of the first converts in Thessalonica, who evidently let Paul stay in his home for a short time before Paul and Silas were sent to Berea (*see notes on Acts 17:5-10*). **Sosipater.** A longer form of "Sopater" (Acts 20:4-6), a Berean (cf. Acts 17:10-12) who joined other believers in meeting Paul at Troas after the apostle left Ephesus. **my countrymen.** *See note on v. 11.*

16:22 Tertius. Paul's secretary, who wrote this letter as Paul dictated it, inserts a personal greeting.

16:23 Gaius. One of Paul's converts at Corinth (cf. 1 Cor. 1:14). His full name was most likely "Gaius Titius Justus" (Acts 18:7). **the whole church.** The congregation that met in Gaius' house. **Erastus.** A common name in NT times, but probably not the same man referred to in Acts 19:22 or 2 Tim. 4:20. **treasurer.** In Corinth. This was a prominent position with political clout. **Quartus.** May have been a physical brother of Erastus, but more likely just the final brother in Christ listed here.

16:24 This verse is not found in the earliest Gr. manuscripts of Romans which is understandable in view of the longer, more explicit benediction that follows.

16:25-27 The letter concludes with a beautiful doxology that praises God for His work through Jesus Christ and thereby summarizes the major themes in Romans (*see notes on 11:33-36*; cf. Matt. 6:13; Luke 19:37,38; Eph. 3:20,21; Heb. 13:20,21; Rev. 5:9,10).

16:25 my gospel. *See notes on 1:1; 2:16*; cf. Gal. 1:11; 2:2. **preaching of Jesus Christ.** Synonymous with the gospel, it was Paul's supreme life commitment (*see notes on 10:14,15,17*; cf. 1 Cor. 1:23,24; 2 Cor. 4:5,6). **the mystery.** *See note on 11:25.* In the NT, this word does not have its modern connotation. Instead, it refers to something hidden in former times but now made known (1 Cor. 4:1; Eph. 5:32; 6:19; Col. 1:25,26; 2 Thess. 2:7,8; 1 Tim. 3:9,16). The NT's most common mystery is that God would provide salvation for Gentiles as well as Jews (Eph. 3:3-9).

16:26 prophetic Scriptures made known. God had told Israel that He would not only call her to righteousness, but appoint her as a light (of the gospel) to the nations (*see notes on Is. 42:6; 49:6; 1 Pet. 1:10,11*; cf. Gen. 12:3; Ex. 19:6; Is. 49:22; 53:11; 60:3-5; Jer. 31:31,33).

16:27 to God...*be* glory. It was through the Father that the gospel was ultimately revealed, therefore He deserves all the credit, praise, and worship.

The First Epistle of Paul to the CORINTHIANS

Title

The letter is named for the city of Corinth, where the church to whom it was written was located. With the exception of personal epistles addressed to Timothy, Titus, and Philemon, all Paul's letters bear the name of the city where the church addressed existed.

Author and Date

As indicated in the first verse, the epistle was written by the Apostle Paul, whose authorship cannot be seriously questioned. Pauline authorship has been universally accepted by the church since the first century, when 1 Corinthians was penned. Internally, the apostle claimed to have written the epistle (1:1,13; 3:4-6; 4:15; 16:21). Externally, this correspondence has been acknowledged as genuine since A.D. 95 by Clement of Rome, who was writing to the Corinthian church. Other early Christian leaders who authenticated Paul as author include Ignatius (ca. A.D. 110), Polycarp (ca. A.D. 135), and Tertullian (ca. A.D. 200).

This epistle was most likely written in the first half of A.D. 55 from Ephesus (16:8,9,19) while Paul was on his third missionary journey. The apostle intended to remain on at Ephesus to complete his 3 year stay (Acts 20:31) until Pentecost (May/June) A.D. 55 (16:8). Then he hoped to winter (A.D. 55–56) at Corinth (16:6; Acts 20:2). His departure for Corinth was anticipated even as he wrote (4:19; 11:34; 16:8).

Background and Setting

The city of Corinth was located in southern Greece, in what was the Roman province of Achaia, ca. 45 mi. W from Athens. This lower part, the Peloponnesus, is connected to the rest of Greece by a 4-mile-wide isthmus, which is bounded on the E by the Saronic Gulf and on the W by the Gulf of Corinth. Corinth is near the middle of the isthmus and is prominently situated on a high plateau. For many centuries, all N-S land traffic in that area had to pass through or near this ancient city. Since travel by sea around the Peloponnesus involved a 250 mile voyage that was dangerous and obviously time consuming, most captains carried their ships on skids or rollers across the isthmus directly past Corinth. Corinth understandably prospered as a major trade city, not only for most of Greece but for much of the Mediterranean area, including North Africa, Italy, and Asia Minor. A canal across the isthmus was begun by the emperor Nero during the first century A.D., but was not completed until near the end of the nineteenth century.

The Isthmian games, one of the two most famous athletic events of that day (the other being the Olympian games), was hosted by Corinth, causing more people-traffic. Even by the pagan standards of its own culture, Corinth became so morally corrupt that its very name became synonymous with debauchery and moral depravity. To "corinthianize" came to represent gross immorality and drunken debauchery. In 6:9,10, Paul lists some of the specific sins for which the city was noted and which formerly had characterized many believers in the church there. Tragically, some of the worst sins were still found among some church members. One of those sins, incest, was condemned even by most pagan Gentiles (5:1).

Like most ancient Greek cities, Corinth had an acropolis (lit. "a high city"), which rose 2,000 feet and was used both for defense and for worship. The most prominent edifice on the acropolis was a temple to Aphrodite, the Greek goddess of love. Some 1,000 priestesses, who were "religious" prostitutes, lived and worked there and came down into the city in the evening to offer their services to male citizens and foreign visitors.

The church in Corinth was founded by Paul on his second missionary journey (Acts 18:1ff.). As usual, his ministry began in the synagogue, where he was assisted by two Jewish believers, Priscilla and Aquila, with whom he lived for a while and who were fellow tradesmen. Soon after, Silas and Timothy joined them and Paul began preaching even more intensely in the synagogue. When most of the Jews resisted the gospel, he left the synagogue, but not before Crispus, the leader of the synagogue, his family, and many other Corinthians were converted (Acts 18:5-8).

After ministering in Corinth for over a year and a half (Acts 18:11), Paul was brought before a

Roman tribunal by some of the Jewish leaders. Because the charges were strictly religious and not civil, the proconsul, Gallio, dismissed the case. Shortly thereafter, Paul took Priscilla and Aquila with him to Ephesus. From there he returned to Israel (vv. 18-22).

Unable to fully break with the culture from which it came, the church at Corinth was exceptionally factional, showing its carnality and immaturity. After the gifted Apollos had ministered in the church for some time, a group of his admirers established a clique and had little to do with the rest of the church. Another group developed that was loyal to Paul, another claimed special allegiance to Peter (Cephas), and still another to Christ alone (see 1:10-13; 3:1-9).

The most serious problem of the Corinthian church was worldliness, an unwillingness to divorce the culture around them. Most of the believers could not consistently separate themselves from their old, selfish, immoral, and pagan ways. It became necessary for Paul to write to correct this, as well as to command the faithful Christians not only to break fellowship with the disobedient and unrepentant members, but to put those members out of the church (5:9-13).

Before he wrote this inspired letter, Paul had written the church other correspondence (see 5:9), which was also corrective in nature. Because a copy of that letter has never been discovered, it has been referred to as "the lost epistle." There was another non-canonical letter after 1 Corinthians, usually called "the severe letter" (2 Cor. 2:4).

Historical and Theological Themes

Although the major thrust of this epistle is corrective of behavior rather than of doctrine, Paul gives seminal teaching on many doctrines that directly relate to the matters of sin and righteousness. In one way or another, wrong living always stems from wrong belief. Sexual sins for example, including divorce, are inevitably related to disobeying God's plan for marriage and the family (7:1-40). Proper worship is determined by such things as recognition of God's holy character (3:17), the spiritual identity of the church (12:12-27) and pure partaking of the Lord's Supper (11:17-34). It is not possible for the church to be edified faithfully and effectively unless believers understand and exercise their spiritual gifts (12:1–14:40). The importance of the doctrine of the resurrection, of course, cannot be overestimated because if there is no resurrection of the dead, then Christ is not risen. And if Christ is not risen, then preaching is empty and so is faith (15:13,14).

In addition to those themes, Paul deals briefly with God's judgment of believers, the right understanding of which will produce right motives for godly living (see 3:13-15). The right understanding of idols and of false gods, in general, was to help the immature Corinthians think maturely about such things as eating meat that had been sacrificed to idols (8:1–11:1). The right understanding and expression of genuine, godly love was mandatory to right use of the gifts and even to right knowledge about all the things of God (13:1-13).

So Paul deals with the cross, divine wisdom and human wisdom, the work of the Spirit in illumination, carnality, eternal rewards, the transformation of salvation, sanctification, the nature of Christ, union with Him, the divine role for women, marriage and divorce, Spirit baptism, indwelling and gifting, the unity of the church in one body, the theology of love, and the doctrine of resurrection. All these establish foundational truth for godly behavior.

Interpretive Challenges

By far the most controversial issue for interpretation is that of the sign gifts discussed in chaps. 12–14, particularly the gifts of miracles and tongues-speaking. Many believe that all the gifts are permanent, so that the gift of speaking in tongues will cease (13:8) only at the time the gifts of prophecy and of knowledge cease, namely, when that which is perfect has come (v. 10). Those who maintain that tongues and miracles are still valid spiritual gifts in the church today believe they should be exercised with the same power they were in NT times by the apostles. Others believe the miraculous sign gifts have ceased. This controversy will be resolved in the appropriate notes on chaps. 12–14.

The issue of divorce is a troubling one for many. Chapter 7 addresses the subject, but calls for careful interpretation to yield consistent biblical doctrine on the matter.

Advocates of universalism, the idea that all men will eventually be saved, use 15:22 in support of that view, claiming that, just as every human being died spiritually because of Adam's sin, they will all be saved through Christ's righteousness. The note on that verse will confront the challenge of such universalists.

From that same chapter, the obscure phrase "baptized for the dead" (v. 29) is used to defend the notion that a dead person can be saved by being baptized vicariously through a living Christian. There have been over 40 suggested explanations for this baptism. As the notes will point out, regardless of how that particular verse is interpreted, the falsehood of dead people having the opportunity to be saved is proven by many other texts that are indisputably clear.

A much less serious issue concerns the meaning of 6:4, which pertains to Christians taking other Christians to court before unbelievers. The resolution of that problem lies primarily in being obedient to a verse which is unambiguous.

Outline

- I. Introduction: The Calling and Benefits of Sainthood (1:1-9)
- II. Disunity in the Church (1:10–4:21)
  - A. The Need for Unity (1:10–3:23)
  - B. The Need for Servanthood (4:1-21)
- III. Immorality in the Church (5:1–6:20)
- IV. Marriage in the Church (7:1-40)
- V. Liberty in the Church (8:1–11:1)
- VI. Worship in the Church (11:2–14:40)
  - A. Roles of Men and Women in the Church (11:2-16)
  - B. The Lord's Supper (11:17-34)
  - C. Spiritual Gifts (12:1–14:40)
- VII. The Hope of the Church: Resurrection (15:1-58)
- VIII. A Charge to the Church (16:1-24)
  - A. Stewardship (16:1-4)
  - B. Personal Plans and Greetings (16:5-24)

Greeting

1 Paul, [a]called *to be* an apostle of Jesus
Christ [b]through the will of God, and
[c]Sosthenes *our* brother,

2 To the church of God which is at
Corinth, to those who [d]are [1]sanctified in
Christ Jesus, [e]called *to be* saints, with all
who in every place call on the name of Jesus Christ [f]our Lord, [g]both theirs and ours:

3 [h]Grace to you and peace from God our
Father and the Lord Jesus Christ.

Spiritual Gifts at Corinth

4 [i]I thank my God always concerning
you for the grace of God which was given
to you by Christ Jesus, 5 that you were enriched in everything by Him [j]in all [2]utter-
ance and all knowledge, 6 even as [k]the testimony of Christ was confirmed [3]in you,
7 so that you come short in no gift, eagerly
[l]waiting for the revelation of our Lord Jesus Christ, 8 [m]who will also confirm you to
the end, [n]*that you may be* blameless in the
day of our Lord Jesus Christ. 9 [o]God *is*
faithful, by whom you were called into
[p]the fellowship of His Son, Jesus Christ our
Lord.

Sectarianism Is Sin

10 Now I plead with you, brethren, by
the name of our Lord Jesus Christ, [q]that
you all [4]speak the same thing, and *that*
there be no [5]divisions among you, but *that*
you be perfectly joined together in the
same mind and in the same judgment.
11 For it has been declared to me concerning you, my brethren, by those of Chloe's
household, that there are [6]contentions

CHAPTER 1

1 [a]Rom. 1:1 [b]2 Cor. 1:1 [c]Acts 18:17
2 [d][Acts 15:9] [e]Rom. 1:7; Eph. 4:1; 1 Thess. 2:12 [f][1 Cor. 8:6] [g][Rom. 3:22] [1]*set apart*
3 [h]Rom. 1:7
4 [i]Rom. 1:8
5 [j][1 Cor. 12:8] [2]*speech*
6 [k]2 Thess. 1:10; 1 Tim. 2:6; 2 Tim. 1:8; Rev. 1:2 [3]Or *among*
7 [l]Luke 17:30; Rom. 8:19, 23; Phil. 3:20; Titus 2:13; [2 Pet. 3:12]
8 [m]1 Thess. 3:13; 5:23 [n]Phil. 1:6; Col. 1:22; 2:7
9 [o]Deut. 7:9; Is. 49:7; 1 Cor. 10:13; 2 Cor. 1:18; 1 Thess. 5:24; 2 Thess. 3:3 [p][John 15:4]

10 [q]2 Cor. 13:11; 1 Pet. 3:8 [4]Have a uniform testimony [5]*schisms* or *dissensions* **11** [6]*quarrels*

1:1 apostle. Lit. "a sent one." Paul establishes his authority as an emissary of the Lord Jesus by God's appointment (9:1; 15:8; cf. Acts 9:3-6,17; 22:11-15), made especially necessary because so much of the message of this epistle is corrective (2:1-7). *See notes on Rom. 1:1; Eph. 4:11.* Since he was delegated by God to speak and write, resisting him was resisting God. **Sosthenes.** Probably Paul's secretary, a former leader of the Corinthian synagogue who had become a brother in Christ. On one occasion, he was beaten for bringing Paul before the civil court at Corinth (Acts 18:12-17).

1:2 saints. Not referring to a specially pious or revered person canonized by an ecclesiastical body, but a reference to everyone who by salvation has been sanctified, that is, set apart from sin in Christ Jesus (cf. Gal. 1:6; Eph. 4:1,4; Col. 3:15-17; 1 Tim. 6:12; Heb. 10:10,14; 1 Pet. 2:9,21; 3:9; 2 Pet. 1:3; Jude 1).

1:3 Grace to you and peace. A greeting Paul used in all his letters. The basic meaning of "grace" is favor; "peace" is a result of God's saving grace (John 14:27; Phil. 4:7).

1:4 grace of God...given. This looks at the past, i.e., their salvation, when God justified them by undeserved and unrepayable love and mercy, forgiving their sin through the work of His Son.

1:5 enriched in everything by Him. In the present, the believer has everything the Lord has to give and therefore everything he needs (see 3:21; Eph. 1:3; Col. 2:10; 2 Pet. 1:3). The two particular blessings spoken of here are related to presenting the truth of God's Word. **utterance.** In regard to speaking for God (cf. Acts 4:29,31; Eph. 6:19; 2 Tim. 2:15; 1 Pet. 3:15), believers are able to speak when God wants them to because of His enablement. Prayer reaches out for that ability (cf. Acts 4:29,31; Eph. 6:19), and diligence in study of God's Word aids it (2 Tim. 2:15; 1 Pet. 3:15). **all knowledge.** God provides believers with all the knowledge they need in order to speak effectively for Him (cf. 2:9; Matt. 11:15; 2 Cor. 4:6; Col. 1:9,10).

1:6 testimony of Christ...confirmed in you. This is a reference to the moment of salvation when the gospel was heard and believed and settled in the heart. At that moment, the enabling of v. 4 took place, because one became a recipient of the grace of God.

1:7 come short in no gift. "Gift" in Gr. is specifically "a gift of grace." While the blessings of speech and knowledge were primarily for evangelizing the lost, the spiritual gifts (chaps. 12–14) edify the church. Because these gifts are given to each believer (12:11,12) without regard for maturity or spirituality, the Corinthians, though sinful, had them in full. **the revelation.** Paul looks to the blessing of future grace. At the Lord's second coming, His full glory, honor, and majesty will be revealed in blazing splendor (Rev. 4:11; 5:12; 17:14), at which time all true believers will be fixed solidly forever as holy and without sin in full resurrected glory and purity to live in heaven with God forever. See Eph. 5:25-27; 2 Cor. 11:2.

1:8 the day of our Lord Jesus Christ. Cf. 5:5; 2 Cor. 1:14. This refers to the coming of the Lord for His church, the rapture (John 14:1-3; 1 Thess. 4:13-18; Rev. 3:10). This is to be distinguished from the Day of the Lord (1 Thess. 5:2,4; 2 Thess. 2:2), a term referring to judgment on the ungodly (see Introduction to Joel: Historical and Theological Themes).

1:9 God *is* faithful. Because of God's sovereign and unchangeable promise, believers are assured of this grace—past, present, and future—and will remain saved, assured of future glory at Christ's appearing (Eph. 5:26,27). **by whom you were called.** This call, as always in the epistles of the NT, refers to an effectual call that saves (*see note on Rom. 8:30*). God who calls to salvation and heaven will be faithful to give the grace needed to fulfill that call. **the fellowship of His Son.** *See notes on 1 John 1:3-7.*

1:10 speak the same thing. Paul is emphasizing the unity of doctrine in the local assembly of believers, not the spiritual unity of His universal church. Doctrinal unity, clearly and completely based on Scripture, must be the foundation of all church life (cf. John 17:11,21-23; Acts 2:46,47). Both weak commitment to doctrine and commitment to disunity of doctrine will severely weaken a church and destroy the true unity. In its place, there can be only shallow sentimentalism or superficial harmony. **joined together.** The basic idea is that of putting back together something that was broken or separated so it is no longer divided. The term is used in both the NT and in classical Gr. to speak of mending such things as nets, broken bones or utensils, torn garments, and dislocated joints. Cf. Rom. 16:17; Phil. 1:27. **same mind...same judgment.** Cf. Phil 3:15,16. The demand is for unity internally in their individual minds and externally in decisions made among themselves—unified in truth by beliefs, convictions, standards, and in behavior by applied principles of living (Acts 4:32; Eph. 4:3). The only source of such unity is God's Word which establishes the standard of truth on which true unity rests.

1:11-13 Cf. 3:4-8.

1:11 Chloe's *household.* Probably a prominent person in the Corinthian church who had written or come to visit Paul in Ephesus to tell him of the factions in the church. It is not known whether Chloe was a man or a woman.

among you. 12 Now I say this, that [r]each of
you says, "I am of Paul," or "I am of [s]Apol-
los," or "I am of [t]Cephas," or "I am of
Christ." 13 [u]Is Christ divided? Was Paul
crucified for you? Or were you baptized in
the name of Paul?
14 I thank God that I baptized [v]none of
you except [w]Crispus and [x]Gaius, 15 lest
anyone should say that I had baptized in
my own name. 16 Yes, I also baptized the
household of [y]Stephanas. Besides, I do not
know whether I baptized any other. 17 For
Christ did not send me to baptize, but to
preach the gospel, [z]not with wisdom of
words, lest the cross of Christ should be
made of no effect.

Christ the Power and Wisdom of God

18 For the [7]message of the cross is [a]fool-
ishness to [b]those who are perishing, but to
us [c]who are being saved it is the [d]power of
God. 19 For it is written:

[e]"I will destroy the wisdom of the
wise,
And bring to nothing the
understanding of the
prudent."

20 [f]Where *is* the wise? Where *is* the
scribe? Where *is* the [8]disputer of this age?
[g]Has not God made foolish the wisdom of
this world? 21 For since, in the [h]wisdom of
God, the world through wisdom did not
know God, it pleased God through the
foolishness of the message preached to
save those who believe. 22 For [i]Jews request a sign, and Greeks seek after wisdom; 23 but we preach Christ crucified, [j]to
the Jews a [9]stumbling block and to the
[1]Greeks [k]foolishness, 24 but to those who
are called, both Jews and Greeks, Christ
[l]the power of God and [m]the wisdom of
God. 25 Because the foolishness of God is
wiser than men, and the weakness of God
is stronger than men.

Glory Only in the Lord

26 For [2]you see your calling, brethren,
[n]that not many wise according to the flesh,

12 [r] Matt. 3:8-10; 1 Cor. 3:4 [s] Acts 18:24; 1 Cor. 3:22 [t] John 1:42; 1 Cor. 3:22; 9:5; 15:5
13 [u] 2 Cor. 11:4
14 [v] John 4:2 [w] Acts 18:8 [x] Rom. 16:23
16 [y] 1 Cor. 16:15, 17
17 [z] [1 Cor. 2:1, 4, 13]
18 [a] 1 Cor. 2:14 [b] 2 Cor. 2:15 [c] [1 Cor. 15:2] [d] Rom. 1:16; 1 Cor. 1:24 [7] Lit. *word*
19 [e] Is. 29:14
20 [f] Is. 19:12; 33:18 [g] Job 12:17; Matt. 13:22; 1 Cor. 2:6, 8; 3:18, 19 [8] *debater*
21 [h] Dan. 2:20; [Rom. 11:33]
22 [i] Matt. 12:38; Mark 8:11; John 2:18; 4:48
23 [j] Is. 8:14; Luke 2:34; John 6:60; Gal. 5:11; [1 Pet. 2:8] [k] [1 Cor. 2:14] [9] Gr. *skandalon, offense* [1] NU *Gentiles*
24 [l] [Rom. 1:4] [m] Col. 2:3
26 [n] John 7:48 [2] *consider*

1:12 Apollos. *See notes on 16:12; Acts 18:24-28.* **Cephas.** The Apostle Peter.

1:13 Is Christ divided? No human leader, not even an apostle, should be given the loyalty that belongs only to the Lord. Such elevation of leaders leads only to contention, disputes, and a divided church. Christ is not divided and neither is His body, the church. Paul depreciates his worth in comparison to the Lord Jesus. For passages on unity, see 12:12,13; Rom. 12:5; Eph. 4:4-6.

1:14 Crispus. The leader of the synagogue in Corinth who was converted under Paul's preaching (Acts 18:8). His conversion led to that of many others. **Gaius.** Since Romans was written from Corinth, this man was probably the host referred to in Rom. 16:23.

1:16 Stephanas. Nothing is known of this family.

1:17 This verse does not mean that people should not be baptized (cf. Acts 2:38), but that God did not send Paul to start a private cult of people personally baptized by him. See Acts 26:16-18. He was called to preach the gospel and bring people to oneness in Christ, not baptize a faction around himself.

1:18 message of the cross. God's total revelation, i.e., the gospel in all its fullness, which centers in the incarnation and crucifixion of Christ (2:2); the entire divine plan and provision for the redemption of sinners, which is the theme of all Scripture, is in view. **foolishness.** Translates the word from which "moron" is derived. **perishing... being saved.** Every person is either in the process of salvation (though not completed until the redemption of the body; see Rom. 8:23; 13:11) or the process of destruction. One's response to the cross of Christ determines which. To the Christ-rejectors who are in the process of being destroyed (cf. Eph. 2:1,2) the gospel is nonsense. To those who are believers it is powerful wisdom.

1:19 it is written. Quoted from Is. 29:14 (*see note there*) to emphasize that man's wisdom will be destroyed. Isaiah's prophecy will have its ultimate fulfillment in the last days when Christ sets up His kingdom (cf. Rev. 17:14) and all of human wisdom dies.

1:20 Where *is* the wise? Paul paraphrased Is. 19:12, where the prophet was referring to the wise men of Egypt who promised, but never produced wisdom. Human wisdom always proves to be unreliable and impermanent (cf. v. 17; Prov. 14:12; Is. 29:14; Jer. 8:9; Rom. 1:18-23). **scribe.** Probably Paul has in mind the Assyrians, who sent scribes along with their soldiers to record the booty taken in battle. God saw to it they had nothing to record (Is. 33:18). **disputer.** This was a Gr. word with no OT counterpart, identifying those who were adept at arguing philosophy.

1:21 in the wisdom of God. God wisely established that men could not come to know Him by human wisdom. That would exalt man, so God designed to save helpless sinners through the preaching of a message that was so simple the "worldly wise" deemed it nonsense. Cf. Rom 1:18-23. **who believe.** From the human side, salvation requires and comes only through faith. Cf. John 1:12; Rom. 10:8-17.

1:22 a sign. Unbelieving Jews still wanted supernatural signs (Matt. 12:38-44), yet they refused to accept the most glorious of all the supernatural sign-works of God, namely providing salvation through a virgin-born, crucified, and risen Messiah. In fact, the sign was a stumbling block to them (cf. Rom. 9:31-33). **wisdom.** Gentiles wanted proof by means of human reason, through ideas they could set forth, discuss, and debate. Like the Athenian philosophers, they were not sincere, with no interest in divine truth, but merely wanting to argue intellectual novelty (Acts 17:21).

1:23 Christ crucified. The only true sign and the only true wisdom. This alone was the message Paul would preach (2:2) because it alone had the power to save all who believed.

1:24,25 called. *See note on v. 9.* To all the "called," the message of the cross, which seems so pointless and irrelevant to man's proud, natural mind, actually exhibits God's greatest power and greatest wisdom.

1:26-28 God disdained human wisdom, not only by disallowing it as a means to knowing Him, but also by choosing to save the lowly. He does not call to salvation many whom the world would call wise, mighty, and noble (cf. Matt. 11:25; 18:3,4). God's wisdom is revealed to the foolish, weak, and common, i.e., those considered nothing by the elite, who trust in Jesus Christ as Savior and Lord. God clearly received all the credit and the glory for causing such lowly ones to know Him and the eternal truths of His heavenly kingdom. No saved sinner can boast that he has achieved salvation by his intellect (v. 29).

not many mighty, not many [3]noble, *are*
called. 27 But [o]God has chosen the foolish
things of the world to put to shame the
wise, and God has chosen the weak things
of the world to put to shame the things
which are mighty; 28 and the [4]base things
of the world and the things which are despised God has chosen, and the things
which are not, to bring to nothing the
things that are, 29 that no flesh should
glory in His presence. 30 But of Him you
are in Christ Jesus, who became for us wisdom from God—and [p]righteousness and
sanctification and redemption— 31 that, as
it is written, [q]*"He who glories, let him*
glory in the LORD."

Christ Crucified

2 And I, brethren, when I came to you,
did not come with excellence of speech
or of wisdom declaring to you the [1]testi-
mony of God. 2 For I determined not to
know anything among you [a]except Jesus
Christ and Him crucified. 3 [b]I was with
you [c]in weakness, in fear, and in much
trembling. 4 And my speech and my
preaching [d]*were* not with persuasive words
of [2]human wisdom, [e]but in demonstration
of the Spirit and of power, 5 that your faith
should not be in the wisdom of men but in
the [f]power of God.

26 [3] *well-born*
27 [o] Ps. 8:2; Matt. 11:25
28 [4] *insignificant* or *lowly*
30 [p] Jer. 23:5; 33:16; [2 Cor. 5:21; Phil. 3:9]
31 [q] Jer. 9:23, 24; 2 Cor. 10:17

CHAPTER 2

1 [1] NU *mystery*
2 [a] 1 Cor. 1:23; Gal. 6:14
3 [b] Acts 18:1 [c] [2 Cor. 4:7]
4 [d] 2 Pet. 1:16 [e] Rom. 15:19; 1 Cor. 4:20 [2] NU omits *human*
5 [f] Rom. 1:16; 1 Thess. 1:5
7 [3] *predetermined*
8 [g] Luke 23:34 [h] Matt. 27:33-50
9 [i] [Is. 64:4; 65:17]
10 [j] Matt. 11:25; 13:11; 16:17; [Gal. 1:12; Eph. 3:3, 5]
11 [k] Job 32:8; Eccl. 12:7; [1 Cor. 6:20; James 2:26] [l] Rom. 11:33
12 [m] [Rom. 8:15]

Spiritual Wisdom

6 However, we speak wisdom among
those who are mature, yet not the wisdom
of this age, nor of the rulers of this age,
who are coming to nothing. 7 But we speak
the wisdom of God in a mystery, the hidden *wisdom* which God [3]ordained before
the ages for our glory, 8 which none of the
rulers of this age knew; for [g]had they
known, they would not have [h]crucified the
Lord of glory.
9 But as it is written:

> [i]*"Eye has not seen, nor ear heard,*
> *Nor have entered into the heart of man*
> *The things which God has prepared for those who love Him."*

10 But [j]God has revealed *them* to us
through His Spirit. For the Spirit searches
all things, yes, the deep things of God.
11 For what man knows the things of a
man except the [k]spirit of the man which is
in him? [l]Even so no one knows the things
of God except the Spirit of God. 12 Now we
have received, not the spirit of the world,
but [m]the Spirit who is from God, that we
might know the things that have been
freely given to us by God.
13 These things we also speak, not in

1:30,31 The redeemed not only are given salvation by God's wisdom rather than by their own, but are also graciously given ("by His doing") a measure of His divine wisdom, as well as imputed righteousness (Rom. 4:5; 2 Cor. 5:21), sanctification from sin (Eph. 2:10), and redemption by God (Eph 1:14; 1 Pet. 1:18,19) in order that, above all else, the Lord will be glorified (cf. Gal. 6:4).

1:31 Quoted from Jer. 9:24.

2:1 excellence of speech or of wisdom. *See notes on 1:20-22.*

2:2 crucified. Though Paul expounded the whole counsel of God to the church (Acts 20:27) and taught the Corinthians the Word of God (Acts 18:11), the focus of his preaching and teaching to unbelievers was Jesus Christ, who paid the penalty for sin on the cross (Acts 20:20; 2 Cor. 4:2; 2 Tim. 4:1,2). Until someone understands and believes the gospel, there is nothing more to say to them. The preaching of the cross (1:18) was so dominant in the early church that believers were accused of worshiping a dead man.

2:3 weakness…fear…trembling. Paul came to Corinth after being beaten and imprisoned in Philippi, run out of Thessalonica and Berea, and scoffed at in Athens (Acts 16:22-24; 17:10,13,14,32), so he may have been physically weak. But in that weakness, he was most powerful (see vv. 4,5; 2 Cor. 12:9,10) There were no theatrics or techniques to manipulate people's response. His fear and shaking was because of the seriousness of his mission.

2:6 mature. Paul uses this word to refer to genuine believers who have been saved by Christ, as in Heb. 6:1; 10:14. **rulers.** Those in authority. *See notes on 1:19,20.* **this age.** All periods of human history until the Lord returns.

2:7 mystery. This term does not refer to something puzzling, but to truth known to God before time, that He has kept secret until the appropriate time for Him to reveal it. *See notes on Matt. 13:11; Eph. 3:4,5.* **for our glory.** The truth God established before time and revealed in the NT wisdom of the gospel is the truth that God will save and glorify sinners. *See notes on Eph. 3:8-12.*

2:8 had they known. The crucifixion is proof that the rulers/Jewish religious leaders lacked wisdom. Cf. 1 Tim. 1:12,13.

2:9 These words from Is. 64:4, often incorrectly thought to refer to the wonders of heaven, refer rather to the wisdom God has prepared for believers. God's truth is not discoverable by eye or ear (objective, empirical evidence), nor is it discovered by the mind (subjective, rational conclusions).

2:10-16 The wisdom that saves, which man's wisdom can't know, is revealed to us by God. He makes it known by revelation, inspiration, and illumination. Revelation (vv. 10,11) and inspiration (vv. 12,13) were given to those who wrote the Bible; illumination (vv. 14-16) is given to all believers who seek to know and understand that divinely written truth. In each case, the Holy Spirit is the divine agent doing the work (cf. 2 Pet. 1:21).

2:10 God has revealed *them*. By the Holy Spirit, God disclosed His saving truth (cf. Matt. 11:25; 13:10-13). The Spirit alone was qualified because He knows all that God knows, Himself being God. **to us.** As with the "we's" in vv. 6,7 and vv. 12,13, Paul is, first of all, speaking of himself (as in John 14:26; 15:26,27; *see notes there*), and, in a sense, of believers who have been given the Word as recorded by the apostles and their associates who wrote the NT.

2:12 we have received. The "we" and "us" refer to the apostles and other writers of the Word of God. The means was inspiration (*see notes on 2 Tim. 3:16; 2 Pet. 1:20,21*), by which God freely gave the gift of His Word. It was this process of inspiration that turned the spiritual thoughts into spiritual words (v. 13) to give life (cf. Matt. 4:4).

words which man's wisdom teaches but
which the [4]Holy Spirit teaches, comparing
spiritual things with spiritual. 14 [n]But the
natural man does not receive the things of
the Spirit of God, for they are foolishness
to him; nor can he know *them*, because
they are spiritually discerned. 15 But he
who is spiritual judges all things, yet he
himself is *rightly* judged by no one. 16 For
[o]*"who has known the mind of the LORD*
that he may instruct Him?" [p]But we have
the mind of Christ.

Sectarianism Is Carnal

3 And I, brethren, could not speak to you
as to spiritual *people* but as to carnal, as
to [a]babes in Christ. 2 I fed you with [b]milk
and not with solid food; [c]for until now you
were not able *to receive it*, and even now
you are still not able; 3 for you are still carnal. For where *there are* envy, strife, and
divisions among you, are you not carnal
and [1]behaving like *mere* men? 4 For when
one says, "I am of Paul," and another, "I *am*
of Apollos," are you not carnal?

13 [4] NU omits *Holy*
14 [n] Matt. 16:23
16 [o] Job 15:8; Is. 40:13; Rom. 11:34 [p] [John 15:15]

CHAPTER 3

1 [a] 1 Cor. 2:6; Eph. 4:14; Heb. 5:13
2 [b] Heb. 5:12; 1 Pet. 2:2 [c] John 16:12
3 [1] Lit. *walking according to man*
5 [d] Rom. 15:16; 2 Cor. 3:3, 6; 4:1; 5:18; 6:4; Eph. 3:7; Col. 1:25; 1 Tim. 1:12
6 [e] Acts 18:4; 1 Cor. 4:15; 9:1; 15:1; 2 Cor. 10:14 [f] Acts 18:24-27; 1 Cor. 1:12 [g] [2 Cor. 3:5]
7 [h] 2 Cor. 12:11; [Gal. 6:3]
8 [i] Ps. 62:12; Rom. 2:6
9 [j] Mark 16:20; Acts 15:4; 2 Cor. 6:1 [k] [1 Cor. 3:16; Eph. 2:20-22]; Col. 2:7; Heb. 3:3, 4; [1 Pet. 2:5]
10 [l] Rom. 1:5 [m] 1 Cor. 4:15
11 [n] Is. 28:16; Matt. 16:18; 2 Cor. 11:4 [o] Eph. 2:20; 1 Pet. 2:4

Watering, Working, Warning

5 Who then is Paul, and who *is* Apollos,
but [d]ministers through whom you believed, as the Lord gave to each one? 6 [e]I
planted, [f]Apollos watered, [g]but God gave
the increase. 7 So then [h]neither he who
plants is anything, nor he who waters, but
God who gives the increase. 8 Now he who
plants and he who waters are one, [i]and
each one will receive his own reward according to his own labor.

9 For [j]we are God's fellow workers; you
are God's field, *you are* [k]God's building.
10 [l]According to the grace of God which
was given to me, as a wise master builder
I have laid [m]the foundation, and another
builds on it. But let each one take heed
how he builds on it. 11 For no other foundation can anyone lay than [n]that which is
laid, [o]which is Jesus Christ. 12 Now if anyone builds on this foundation *with* gold,
silver, precious stones, wood, hay, straw,
13 each one's work will become clear; for
the Day [p]will declare it, because [q]it will be
revealed by fire; and the fire will test each

13 [p] 1 Pet. 1:7 [q] Mal. 3:1-3; Luke 2:35

2:14 natural man. This refers to the unconverted, who lack supernatural life and wisdom. **spiritually discerned.** Through illumination of the Word, the Holy Spirit provides His saints the capacity to discern divine truth (see Ps. 119:18), which the spiritually dead are unable to comprehend (cf. John 5:37-39; *see notes on 1 John 2:20,27*). The doctrine of illumination does not mean we know everything (cf. Deut. 29:29), that we do not need teachers (cf. Eph. 4:11,12), or that understanding does not require hard work (cf. 2 Tim. 2:15).

2:15 judged by no one. Obviously, unbelievers are able to recognize Christians' faults and shortcomings; but they are not able to evaluate their true nature as spiritual people who have been transformed into children of God (cf. 1 John 3:2).

2:16 the mind of Christ. Quoted from Is. 40:13. The same word is translated "understanding" in 14:14,15,19. Believers are allowed, by the Word and the Spirit, to know the thoughts of their Lord. Cf. Luke 24:45.

3:1 The cause of problems in the church was more than external, worldly influence. It was also internal carnality. The pressures of the world were combined with the weakness of the flesh. **carnal.** Although Corinthian believers were no longer "natural," they were not "spiritual" (fully controlled by the Holy Spirit). In fact, they were "carnal" (controlled by the fallen flesh). Though all believers have the Holy Spirit (cf. Rom. 8:9) they still battle the fallen flesh (*see notes on Rom. 7:14-25; 8:23*). **babes in Christ.** The carnality of those believers was indicative of their immaturity. They had no excuse for not being mature, since Paul implied that he should have been able to write to them as mature, in light of all he had taught them (v. 2). *See notes on Heb. 5:12-14; 1 Pet. 2:1,2.*

3:2 milk. Not a reference to certain doctrines, but to the more easily digestible truths of doctrine that were given to new believers. **solid food.** The deeper features of the doctrines of Scripture. The difference is not in kind of truth, but degree of depth. Spiritual immaturity makes one unable to receive the richest truths.

3:3 envy, strife. Carnality produces the attitude of envy, a severe form of selfishness, which produces the action of strife and the subsequent divisions. ***mere* men.** Apart from the will of the Spirit, hence carnal, not spiritual.

3:4 Paul...Apollos. Factionalism was the divisive product of carnality. Cf. 1:11-13.

3:5-7 Who then is Paul...Apollos. A humble, but accurate assessment of the roles that ministers play. **the Lord gave...God gave...God who gives.** It is the Lord alone who can give the faith to the spiritually ignorant and dead. Salvation is God's work of grace to whom He chooses to give it (*see notes on Rom. 9:15-19; Eph. 2:8,9*).

3:8 are one. All the human instruments God uses to produce salvation life are equally considered and rewarded for their willingness to be used by God. But all the glory goes to Him, who alone saves. Because of that, the silly favoritism of v. 4; 1:12 is condemned. *See notes on Matt. 20:1-16.*

3:9 we. Paul, Apollos, Peter, and all ministers are equal workers in the field, but the spiritual life from that field is entirely by God's grace and power. **God's building.** Paul shifts the imagery from agricultural to construction (vv. 10-17).

3:10 master builder...foundation. The Gr. word is the root for architect, but contained the idea of builder as well as designer. Paul's specialty was designing and building spiritual foundations (cf. Rom. 15:20). He was used by God to establish the groundwork for churches in Asia Minor, Macedonia, and Greece. Others (e.g., Timothy, Apollos) built the churches up from his foundations. That God used him in that way was all of grace (cf. v. 7; 15:20; Rom. 15:18; Eph. 3:7,8; Col. 1:29). **each one.** This primarily refers to evangelists and pastor-teachers.

3:11 no other foundation. Paul did not design the foundation, he only laid it down by preaching Christ. Cf. 1 Pet. 2:6-8.

3:12 if anyone builds. This is, first of all, in reference to the evangelists and pastors (v. 9), and then to all believers who are called to build the church through faithful ministry. **gold, silver, precious stones.** His quality materials represent dedicated, spiritual service to build the church. **wood, hay, straw.** Inferior materials implying shallow activity with no eternal value. They do not refer to activities that are evil (*see note on v. 13*).

one's work, of what sort it is. 14 If anyone's work which he has built on *it* endures, he will receive a reward. 15 If anyone's work is burned, he will suffer loss;
but he himself will be saved, yet so as
through fire.
16 [r]Do you not know that you are the
temple of God and *that* the Spirit of God
dwells in you? 17 If anyone [2]defiles the
temple of God, God will destroy him. For
the temple of God is holy, which *temple*
you are.

Avoid Worldly Wisdom

18 [s]Let no one deceive himself. If anyone
among you seems to be wise in this age, let
him become a fool that he may become
wise. 19 For the wisdom of this world is
foolishness with God. For it is written,
[t]*"He catches the wise in their own crafti-*
ness"; 20 and again, [u]*"The LORD knows the*
thoughts of the wise, that they are futile."
21 Therefore let no one boast in men. For
[v]all things are yours: 22 whether Paul or
Apollos or Cephas, or the world or life or
death, or things present or things to
come—all are yours. 23 And [w]you *are*
Christ's, and Christ *is* God's.

Stewards of the Mysteries of God

4 Let a man so consider us, as [a]servants
of Christ [b]and stewards of the mysteries of God. 2 Moreover it is required in
stewards that one be found faithful. 3 But
with me it is a very small thing that I
should be judged by you or by a human
[1]court. In fact, I do not even judge myself.
4 For I know of nothing against myself, yet
I am not justified by this; but He who
judges me is the Lord. 5 [c]Therefore judge
nothing before the time, until the Lord
comes, who will both bring to [d]light the
hidden things of darkness and [e]reveal the
[2]counsels of the hearts. [f]Then each one's
praise will come from God.

16 [r] Rom. 8:9; 1 Cor. 6:19; 2 Cor. 6:16; Eph. 2:21
17 [2] *destroys*
18 [s] Prov. 3:7
19 [t] Job 5:13
20 [u] Ps. 94:11
21 [v] [2 Cor. 4:5]
23 [w] [Rom. 14:8]; 1 Cor. 15:23; 2 Cor. 10:7; [Gal. 3:29]

CHAPTER 4
1 [a] Matt. 24:45; Rom. 13:6; 2 Cor. 3:6; Col. 1:25 [b] Luke 12:42; 1 Cor. 9:17; Titus 1:7; 1 Pet. 4:10
3 [1] Lit. *day*
5 [c] Matt. 7:1; Rom. 2:1; [Rev. 20:12] [d] Matt. 10:26 [e] 1 Cor. 3:13 [f] Rom. 2:29; 1 Cor. 3:8; [2 Cor. 5:10] [2] *motives*

3:13 the Day. Refers to the time of the Judgment Seat of Christ (*see notes on 2 Cor. 5:10*). **revealed by fire.** The fire of God's discerning judgment (cf. Job 23;10; Zech. 13:9; 1 Pet. 1:17,18; Rev. 3:18). Second Corinthians 5:10 indicates that the wood, hay, and straw are "worthless" things that don't stand the test of judgment fire (*see note there*; cf. Col. 2:18).

3:14 endures. All that which has been accomplished in His power and for His glory will survive (cf. Matt. 25:21,23; 2 Cor. 5:9; Phil. 3:13,14; 1 Thess. 2:19,20; 2 Tim. 4:7,8; James 1:12; 1 Pet. 5:4; Rev. 22:12). **reward.** Cf. Rev. 22:12. This is not a judgment for sin. Christ has paid that price (Rom. 8:1), so that no believer will ever be judged for sin. This is only to determine eternal reward (cf. 4:5, "each one's praise").

3:15 be saved. No matter how much is worthless, no believer will forfeit salvation.

3:16,17 Here is a severe warning to any who would try to interfere with or destroy the building of the church on the foundation of Christ. *See notes on Matt. 18:6,7.*

3:18,19a deceive himself. *See notes on 1:18-25.* Those who defile the church and think they can succeed in destroying it by their human wisdom, would be far better to reject that wisdom and accept the foolishness of Christ's cross.

3:19b,20 With quotations from Job 5:13 and Ps. 94:11, Paul reinforces his point from 1:18-25 by reminding them that human wisdom which cannot save, also cannot either build a church or prevent its growth.

3:21 boast in men. Cf. v. 4; 1:12. Paul, Apollos, and all others receive no credit for the building of the church. **all things are yours.** All believers share equally in God's most important and valuable provisions and glories; human boasting, therefore, is ludicrous as well as sinful.

3:22 the world. Although the universe is now in Satan's grip, it is still the God-given and God-made possession of Christians (2 Cor. 4:15; 1 John 5:19). In the millennial kingdom and throughout eternity, however, believers will possess both the recreated and eternal earth in an infinitely more complete and rich way (Matt. 5:5; Rev. 21). **life.** Spiritual, eternal life (cf. John 14:23; cf. 2 Pet. 1:3,4). **death.** Spiritual and eternal death (15:54-57; Phil. 1:21-24). **things present.** Everything the believer has or experiences in this life (cf. Rom. 8:37-39). **things to come.** All the blessings of heaven. Cf. 1 Pet. 1:3,4. **all are yours.** In Christ, all good and holy things are for believers' blessing and for God's glory. Cf. Eph. 1:3; 2 Pet. 1:3.

3:23 Christ's...God's. Knowing that believers belong to Christ and therefore to each other is the greatest incentive for unity in the church (6:17; John 9:9,10,21-23; Phil. 2:1-4).

4:1 so consider us. Paul wanted everyone to view him and his fellow ministers only as the humble messengers God ordained them to be (cf. 3:9,22). **servants.** Paul expresses his humility by using a word lit. meaning "under rowers," referring to the lowest, most menial, and most despised galley slaves, who rowed on the bottom tier of a ship (9:16; see Luke 1:2; Acts 20:19). **stewards.** Paul defines his responsibilities as an apostle by using a word originally referring to a person entrusted with and responsible for his master's entire household: e.g., buildings, fields, finances, food, other servants, and sometimes even children of the owner. Cf. 1 Pet. 4:10. **mysteries of God.** "Mystery" is used in the NT to refer to divine revelation previously hidden. *See notes on 2:7; Matt. 13:11; Eph. 3:4,5.* Here the word is used in its broadest sense as God's full revealed truth in the NT (Acts 20:20,21,27; 2 Tim. 2:15; 3:16). It was all that truth which Paul had to oversee and dispense as God's servant and steward.

4:2 faithful. The most essential quality of a servant or steward is obedient loyalty to his master (v. 17; 7:25; cf. Matt. 24:45-51; Col. 1:7; 4:7).

4:3 human court. Paul is not being arrogant or saying that he is above fellow ministers, other Christians, or even certain unbelievers. He is saying that a human verdict on his life is not the one that matters, even if it was his own.

4:4 nothing against myself. Paul was not aware of any unconfessed or habitual sin in his own life, but his limited understanding assumed that his was not the final verdict (*see note on 2 Cor. 1:12*). **not justified by this.** Paul's own sincere evaluation of his life did not acquit him of all failures to be faithful. **the Lord.** He is the ultimate and only qualified Judge of any man's obedience and faithfulness (2 Tim. 2:15). *See notes on 2 Cor. 5:9,10.*

4:5 hidden things of darkness...counsels of the hearts. These refer to the inner motives, thoughts, and attitudes which only God can know. Since final rewards will be based, not just on outward service, but on inward devotion (cf. 10:31), only God can give the praise each deserves. *See notes on 3:12-14.*

Fools for Christ's Sake

6 Now these things, brethren, I have figuratively transferred to myself and Apollos for your sakes, that you may learn in us
not to think beyond what is written, that
none of you may be [3]puffed up on behalf
of one against the other. 7 For who [4]makes
you differ *from another?* And [g]what do you
have that you did not receive? Now if you
did indeed receive *it,* why do you boast as
if you had not received *it?*
8 You are already full! [h]You are already
rich! You have reigned as kings without
us—and indeed I could wish you did
reign, that we also might reign with you!
9 For I think that God has displayed us, the
apostles, last, as men condemned to death;
for we have been made a [i]spectacle[5] to the
world, both to angels and to men. 10 We *are*
[j]fools for Christ's sake, but you *are* wise in
Christ! [k]We *are* weak, but you *are* strong!
You *are* distinguished, but we *are* dishonored! 11 To the present hour we both
hunger and thirst, and we are poorly
clothed, and beaten, and homeless. 12 [l]And
we labor, working with our own hands.
[m]Being reviled, we bless; being persecuted,
we endure; 13 being defamed, we [6]entreat.
[n]We have been made as the filth of the
world, the offscouring of all things until
now.

Paul's Paternal Care

14 I do not write these things to shame
you, but [o]as my beloved children I warn *you.*
15 For though you might have ten thousand
instructors in Christ, yet *you do* not *have*
many fathers; for [p]in Christ Jesus I have begotten you through the gospel. 16 Therefore
I urge you, [q]imitate me. 17 For this reason I
have sent [r]Timothy to you, [s]who is my
beloved and faithful son in the Lord, who
will [t]remind you of my ways in Christ, as I
[u]teach everywhere [v]in every church.
18 [w]Now some are [7]puffed up, as though
I were not coming to you. 19 [x]But I will come
to you shortly, [y]if the Lord wills, and I will
know, not the word of those who are puffed
up, but the power. 20 For [z]the kingdom of
God *is* not in word but in [a]power. 21 What

6 [3] *arrogant*
7 [g] John 3:27; Rom. 12:3, 6; 1 Pet. 4:10 [4] *distinguishes you*
8 [h] Rev. 3:17
9 [i] Heb. 10:33 [5] Lit. *theater*
10 [j] Acts 17:18; 26:24; 1 Cor. 1:18 [k] 1 Cor. 2:3; 2 Cor. 13:9
12 [l] Acts 18:3; 20:34 [m] Matt. 5:44
13 [n] Lam. 3:45 [6] *exhort, encourage*
14 [o] 2 Cor. 6:13; 12:14; 1 Thess. 2:11; 1 John 2:1; 3 John 4
15 [p] Num. 11:12; Acts 18:11; 1 Cor. 3:8; Gal. 4:19; Philem. 10
16 [q] [1 Cor. 11:1]; Phil. 3:17; 4:9; [1 Thess. 1:6]; 2 Thess. 3:9
17 [r] Acts 19:22; Phil. 2:19 [s] 1 Cor. 4:14; 1 Tim. 1:2, 18; 2 Tim. 1:2 [t] 1 Cor. 11:2 [u] 1 Cor. 7:17; Titus 1:5 [v] 1 Cor. 14:33
18 [w] 1 Cor. 5:2 [7] *arrogant*
19 [x] Acts 19:21; 20:2; 1 Cor. 11:34; 16:5, 7-9; 2 Cor. 1:15 [y] Acts 18:21; Heb. 6:3; James 4:15
20 [z] 1 Thess. 1:5
20 [a] 1 Cor. 2:4

4:6 these things. Paul is referring to the analogies he used to depict those who minister for the Lord, including himself and Apollos: farmers (3:6-9), builders (3:10-15), and servant-stewards (vv. 1-5). **your sakes.** Paul's humility, expressed in light of God's judgment on the greatest apostles and preachers, was useful to teach believers not to exalt any of them (cf. Gen. 18:27; 32:10; Ex. 3:11; Judg. 6:15; Matt. 3:14; Luke 5:8; John 1:26,27; Acts 20:19; 2 Cor. 3:5; Eph. 3:8). **what is written.** God's faithful servants are to be treated with respect only within the bounds of what is scriptural (1 Thess. 5:12; 1 Tim. 5:17; Heb. 13:7,17). **puffed up.** Pride and arrogance were great problems in the Corinthian church (see vv. 18,19; 5:2; 8:1; 13:4; 2 Cor. 12:20).

4:7 boast. Pride is deception, since everything a person possesses is from God's providential hand (cf. 1 Chr. 29:11-16; Job 1:21; James 1:17).

4:8 full...rich...reigned. In a severe rebuke, Paul heaps on false praise, sarcastically suggesting that those Corinthians who were self-satisfied had already achieved spiritual greatness. They were similar to the Laodiceans (see Rev. 3:17). Cf. Phil 3:12; 2 Tim. 4:8; James 1:12; 1 Pet. 5:4. **reign.** Yet, Paul genuinely wished it really were the coronation time of the Millennium, so that they all might share in the glory of the Lord.

4:9 last. The imagery is of condemned prisoners brought into a Roman arena to fight and die; the last ones brought out for slaughter were the grand finale. In His sovereign wisdom and for His ultimate glory, God chose to display the apostles figuratively before men and angels during the present age as just such worthless and condemned spectacles (cf. Matt. 19:28). Like doomed gladiators, they were ridiculed, spit on, imprisoned, and beaten; yet, God glorified His name through them as He used them to build His kingdom.

4:10 fools...wise. Again using sarcasm, this time on himself as if mimicking the attitude of the proud Corinthians toward him, Paul rebukes them (cf. Acts 17:18).

4:11-13 The apostles and early preachers lived at the lowest levels of society. While the Corinthians believers thought they were kings (v. 8), the apostle knew he was a suffering slave (cf. 2 Cor. 1:8,9; 4:8-12; 6:4-10; 11:23-28).

4:12 our own hands. The apostles did manual labor which Greeks, including some in the church at Corinth, considered beneath their dignity and suitable only for slaves. But Paul was not resentful about any necessary labor needed to support gospel preaching (cf. Acts 18:3; 20:34; 2 Cor. 11:23-28; 1 Thess. 2:9; 2 Thess. 3:8; 2 Tim. 3:12).

4:13 filth...offscouring. The scum and dregs scraped from a dirty dish or garbage pot, figuratively used of the lowest, most degraded criminals who were often sacrificed in pagan ceremonies. Not in God's sight, but in the world's, Paul and his fellow preachers were so designated. What a rebuke of the proud, carnal Corinthians who saw themselves at the top, while the humble apostle considered himself at the bottom.

4:14 beloved children. Despite their carnal, even sometimes hateful immaturity, Paul always looked on the Corinthian believers with affection (cf. 2 Cor. 12:14,15; Gal. 4:19; Phil. 1:23-27; 3 John 4). **warn.** Lit. "put in mind," with the purpose of admonishing and reproving, presupposing that something is wrong and should be corrected (cf. Matt. 18:15-20; Acts 20:31; 1 Thess. 2:7-12; 5:14).

4:15 ten thousand instructors. The terms actually say "countless tutors," referring by hyperbole to an unlimited number of moral guardians used with children. Only Paul was their spiritual father; hence, no one cared like him.

4:16 imitate me. See 11:1. A bold, but justified exhortation. Spiritual leaders must set an example of Christlikeness to follow (cf. 1 Tim. 4:12; Heb. 13:7)

4:17 Timothy. He had been so faithfully discipled by Paul that he could be sent in the great apostle's place with confidence that he would perfectly represent him. Cf. 2 Tim. 2:2; 3:10-14. **I teach.** Referring to doctrine, not advice. By his own instruction and example, Timothy would reinforce the eternal truths Paul had taught him.

4:18,19 puffed up. They were arrogant, thinking they would never have to face Paul again. But, if God allowed, he was planning to see them soon. He would not let their proud sinning go unchallenged, for their own sake as well as the gospel's (cf. Heb. 12:6). The reality of how much real spiritual power they had would become clear in that confrontation.

4:20 word...power. Spiritual character is measured not by the impressiveness of words, but in the power of the life (cf. Matt. 7:21-23).

do you want? [b]Shall I come to you with a
rod, or in love and a spirit of gentleness?

Immorality Defiles the Church

5 It is actually reported *that there is* sexual immorality among you, and such
sexual immorality as is not even [1]named
among the Gentiles—that a man has his
father's [a]wife! **2** [b]And you are [2]puffed up,
and have not rather [c]mourned, that he
who has done this deed might be taken
away from among you. **3** [d]For I indeed, as
absent in body but present in spirit, have
already judged (as though I were present)
him who has so done this deed. **4** In the
[e]name of our Lord Jesus Christ, when you
are gathered together, along with my spirit, [f]with the power of our Lord Jesus
Christ, **5** [g]deliver such a one to [h]Satan for
the destruction of the flesh, that his spirit
may be saved in the day of the Lord
[3]Jesus.
6 [i]Your glorying *is* not good. Do you not
know that [j]a little leaven leavens the
whole lump? **7** Therefore [4]purge out the
old leaven, that you may be a new lump,
since you truly are unleavened. For indeed
[k]Christ, our [l]Passover, was sacrificed [5]for
us. **8** Therefore [m]let us keep the feast, [n]not
with old leaven, nor [o]with the leaven of
malice and wickedness, but with the unleavened *bread* of sincerity and truth.

Immorality Must Be Judged

9 I wrote to you in my epistle [p]not to
[6]keep company with sexually immoral
people. **10** Yet *I* certainly *did* not *mean* with
the sexually immoral people of this world,
or with the covetous, or extortioners, or
idolaters, since then you would need to go
[q]out of the world. **11** But now I have written to you not to keep company [r]with anyone named a brother, who is sexually immoral, or covetous, or an idolater, or a
reviler, or a drunkard, or an extortioner—
[s]not even to eat with such a person.
12 For what *have* I *to do* with judging those
also who are outside? Do you not judge
those who are inside? **13** But those who are
outside God judges. Therefore [t]*"put away
from yourselves the evil person."*

21 [b]2 Cor. 10:2

CHAPTER 5

1 [a]Lev. 18:6-8; Deut. 22:30; 27:20 [1]NU omits *named*
2 [b]1 Cor. 4:18 [c]2 Cor. 7:7-10 [2]*arrogant*
3 [d]Col. 2:5; 1 Thess. 2:17
4 [e][Matt. 18:20] [f][Matt. 16:19; John 20:23]; 2 Cor. 12:9
5 [g]Ps. 109:6; Prov. 23:14; Luke 22:31; 1 Tim. 1:20 [h][Acts 26:18] [3]NU omits *Jesus*
6 [i]1 Cor. 3:21 [j]Hos. 7:4; Matt. 16:6, 12; Gal. 5:9; 2 Tim. 2:17
7 [4]*clean out* [k]Is. 53:7 [l]John 19:14 [5]NU omits *for us*
8 [m]Ex. 12:15 [n]Deut. 16:3 [o]Matt. 16:6
9 [p]2 Cor. 6:14; Eph. 5:11; 2 Thess. 3:6 [6]*associate*
10 [q]John 17:15
11 [r]Matt. 18:17 [s]Gal. 2:12
13 [t]Deut. 13:5; 17:7, 12; 19:19; 21:21; 22:21, 24; 24:7; 1 Cor. 5:2

4:21 rod. Spiritual leaders need to use the rod of correction if people persist in sin. The pattern for that correction is illustrated and explained in 5:1-13; cf. Matt. 18:15-18.

5:1 sexual immorality. This sin was so vile that even the church's pagan neighbors were doubtless scandalized by it. The Corinthians had rationalized or minimized this sin which was common knowledge, even though Paul had written them before about it (v. 9). The Gr. for "immorality" is the root of the Eng. word "pornography." **his father's wife.** The man's stepmother, with whom having sexual relations bore the same sinful stigma as if between him and his natural mother. Incest was punishable by death in the OT (Lev. 18:7,8,29; cf. Deut. 22:30) and was both uncommon ("not even named") and illegal under Roman law.

5:2 puffed up. So arrogant and carnal as to excuse even that extreme wickedness. **taken away.** Excommunicated as in v. 7 (see Matt 18:15-17; Eph. 5:3,11; 2 Thess. 3:6).

5:3 already judged. Paul had passed judgment on the sinner, and the church also needed to.

5:4 name of our Lord. Consistent with His holy person and will. **gathered together.** This action is to be done when the church meets publicly (*see notes on Matt. 18:15-18*). **power.** Authority is in view. Action against unrepentant sinning in the church carries the weight of the Lord's authority.

5:5 deliver...to Satan. "Deliver" is a strong term, used of judicial sentencing. This is equal to excommunicating the professed believer. It amounts to putting that person out of the blessing of Christian worship and fellowship by thrusting him into Satan's realm, the world system. *See note on 1 Tim. 1:20.* **the destruction of the flesh.** This refers to divine chastening for sin that can result in illness and even death. *See notes on 11:29-32*; cf. Acts 5:1-11. **spirit...saved.** The unrepentant person may suffer greatly under God's judgment, but will not be an evil influence in the church; and he will more likely be saved under that judgment than if tolerated and accepted in the church. **day of the Lord Jesus.** This is the time when the Lord returns with His rewards for His people. *See note on 1:8.*

5:6 glorying. Better, "boasting." It was not good because their proud sense of satisfaction blinded them to their duty in regard to blatant sin that devastated the church. **leaven.** *See note on Mark 8:15.* In Scripture, it is used to represent influence, in most cases evil influence, although in Matt. 13:33 it refers to the good influence of the kingdom of heaven (cf. Ex. 13:3,7). **whole lump.** When tolerated, sin will permeate and corrupt the whole local church.

5:7 Christ, our Passover. Just as unleavened bread symbolized being freed from Egypt by the Passover (Ex. 12:15-17), so the church is to be unleavened, since it has been separated from the dominion of sin and death by the perfect Passover Lamb, the Lord Jesus Christ. The church is, therefore, to remove everything sinful in order to be separate from the old life, including the influence of sinful church members.

5:8 keep the feast. In contrast to the OT Passover feast celebrated annually, believers constantly celebrate the "feast" of the new Passover—Jesus Christ. As the Jews who celebrate Passover do so with unleavened bread, so believers celebrate their continual Passover with unleavened lives.

5:9 my epistle. A previous letter that Paul had written the church at Corinth instructed them to disassociate with the immoral (cf. v. 11; 2 Thess. 3:6-15).

5:10 people of this world. Evidently, the church had misinterpreted the advice in that letter and had stopped having contact with the unsaved in the world, while continuing to tolerate the sin of those in the church, which was even more dangerous to the fellowship. See John 17:15,18. God intends us to be in the world as witnesses (cf. Matt. 5:13-16; Acts 1:8; Phil. 2:15).

5:11 named a brother. Paul clarifies his intention in the earlier letter. He expected them to disassociate with all who said they were brothers, but had a consistent pattern of sin. **not even to eat.** The meal was a sign of acceptance and fellowship in those days. See 2 Thess. 3:6,14.

5:12,13 outside. Paul never intended himself or the church to be judges of unbelievers outside the church, but to judge those inside (cf. 1 Pet. 4:17). Those on the outside are for God to judge and believers to evangelize. Those who sin on the inside, the church is to put out. Verse 13 is quoted from Deut. 17:7.

Do Not Sue the Brethren

6 Dare any of you, having a matter
against another, go to law before the
unrighteous, and not before the [a]saints?
2 Do you not know that [b]the saints will
judge the world? And if the world will be
judged by you, are you unworthy to judge
the smallest matters? 3 Do you not know
that we shall [c]judge angels? How much
more, things that pertain to this life? 4 If
then you have [1]judgments concerning
things pertaining to this life, do you appoint those who are least esteemed by the
church to judge? 5 I say this to your shame.
Is it so, that there is not a wise man among
you, not even one, who will be able to
judge between his brethren? 6 But brother
goes to law against brother, and that before
unbelievers!

7 Now therefore, it is already an utter
failure for you that you go to law against
one another. [d]Why do you not rather accept wrong? Why do you not rather *let*
yourselves be cheated? 8 No, you yourselves do wrong and cheat, and *you do*
these things *to your* brethren! 9 Do you
not know that the unrighteous will not
inherit the kingdom of God? Do not be
deceived. [e]Neither fornicators, nor idolaters, nor adulterers, nor [2]homosexuals,
nor [3]sodomites, 10 nor thieves, nor covetous, nor drunkards, nor revilers, nor
extortioners will inherit the kingdom of
God. 11 And such were [f]some of you.
[g]But you were washed, but you were
[4]sanctified, but you were justified in the
name of the Lord Jesus and by the Spirit
of our God.

CHAPTER 6

1 [a] Dan. 7:22; Matt. 19:28
2 [b] Ps. 49:14
3 [c] 2 Pet. 2:4
4 [1] *courts*
7 [d] [Prov. 20:22]
9 [e] Acts 20:32; [1 Cor. 15:50]; Gal. 5:21; Eph. 5:5; 1 Tim. 1:9 [2] *catamites*, those submitting to homosexuals [3] *male homosexuals*
11 [f] [1 Cor. 12:2; Col. 3:5-7; Titus 3:3-7] [g] Heb. 10:22 [4] *set apart*

6:1 Dare. Suing another believer in a secular law court is a daring act of disobedience because of its implications related to all sin—the displeasure of God. **a matter against another.** The phrase in Gr. was commonly used of a lawsuit ("go to law"). **unrighteous.** This does not refer to their moral character, but to their unsaved spiritual condition. **before the saints.** Believers are to settle all issues between themselves within the church.

6:2 judge the world. Because Christians will assist Christ to judge the world in the millennial kingdom (Rev. 2:26,27; 3:21; cf. Dan. 7:22), they are more than qualified with the truth, the Spirit, the gifts, and the resources they presently have in Him to settle small matters that come up among themselves in this present life.

6:3 judge angels. The Gr. word can mean "rule or govern." Since the Lord Himself will judge fallen angels (2 Pet. 2:4; Jude 6), it is likely this means we will have some rule in eternity over holy angels. Since angels are "ministering spirits" to serve the saints (Heb. 1:14), it seems reasonable that they will serve us in glory.

6:4 This is a difficult verse to translate, as suggested by the widely varying Eng. renderings. But the basic meaning is clear: when Christians have earthly quarrels and disputes among themselves, it is inconceivable that they would turn to those least qualified (unbelievers) to resolve the matter. The most legally untrained believers, who know the Word of God and are obedient to the Spirit, are far more competent to settle disagreements between believers than the most experienced unbeliever, void of God's truth and Spirit.

6:5,6 shame. Such conduct as suing a fellow believer is not only a sinful shame (v. 5), but a complete failure to act obediently and righteously. Christians who take fellow Christians to court suffer moral defeat and spiritual loss even before the case is heard, and they become subject to divine chastening (cf. Heb. 12:3ff.).

6:7 Why...not...accept wrong? The implied answer is because of the shameful sin (v. 5) and the moral defeat (v. 8) that result from selfishness, a willingness to discredit God, His wisdom, power, and sovereign purpose, and to harm the church and the testimony of Christ's gospel. **cheated.** Christians have no right to insist on legal recourse in a public court. It is far better to trust God's sovereign purposes in trouble and lose financially, than to be disobedient and suffer spiritually (*see notes on Matt. 5:39,40; 18:21-35*).

6:8 you yourselves do wrong and cheat. He is referring to those who sue their brothers in Christ being as guilty of the same misconduct they are suing to rectify.

6:9,10 This catalog of sins, though not exhaustive, represents the major types of moral sin that characterize the unsaved.

6:9 not inherit the kingdom. The kingdom is the spiritual sphere of salvation where God rules as king over all who belong to Him by faith (*see notes on Matt. 5:3,10*). All believers are in that spiritual kingdom, yet are waiting to enter into the full inheritance of it in the age to come. People who are characterized by these iniquities are not saved (v. 10). *See notes on 1 John 3:9,10.* While believers can and do commit these sins, they do not characterize them as an unbroken life pattern. When they do, it demonstrates that the person is not in God's kingdom. True believers who do sin, resent that sin and seek to gain the victory over it (cf. Rom. 7:14-25). **fornicators.** All who indulge in sexual immorality, but particularly unmarried persons. **idolaters.** Those who worship any false god or follow any false religious system. **adulterers.** Married persons who indulge in sexual acts outside their marriage. **homosexuals...sodomites.** These terms refer to those who exchange and corrupt normal male-female sexual roles and relations. Transvestism, sex changes, and other gender perversions are included (cf. Gen. 1:27; Deut. 22:5). Sodomites are so-called because the sin of male-male sex dominated the city of Sodom (Gen. 18:20; 19:4,5). This sinful perversion is condemned always, in any form, by Scripture (cf. Lev. 18:22; 20:13; Rom. 1:26,27; 1 Tim. 1:10).

6:10 thieves...covetous. Both are guilty of the same basic sin of greed. Those who are covetous desire what belongs to others; thieves actually take it. **revilers.** People who try to destroy others with words. **extortioners.** Swindlers and embezzlers who steal indirectly, taking unfair advantage of others for their own financial gain.

6:11 some of you. Though not all Christians have been guilty of all those particular sins, every Christian is equally an ex-sinner, since Christ came to save sinners (cf. Matt. 9:13; Rom. 5:20). Some who used to have those patterns of sinful life were falling into those old sins again, and needed reminding that if they went all the way back to live as they used to, they were not going to inherit eternal salvation, because it would indicate that they never were saved (cf. 2 Cor. 5:17). **washed.** Refers to new life, through spiritual cleansing and regeneration (cf. John 3:3-8; 2 Cor. 5:17; Eph. 2:10; Titus 3:5). **sanctified.** This results in new behavior, which a transformed life always produces. Sin's total domination is broken and replaced by a new pattern of obedience and holiness. Though not perfection, this is a new direction (see Rom. 6:17,18,22). **justified.** This refers to a new standing before God, in which the Christian is clothed in Christ's righteousness. In His death, the believer's sins were put to His account and He suffered for them, so that His righteousness might be put to an account, so that we might be blessed for it (Rom. 3:26; 4:22-25; 2 Cor. 5:21; Phil. 3:8,9; 1 Pet. 3:18). **by the Spirit.** The Holy Spirit is the agent of salvation's transformation (cf. John 3:3-5).

Glorify God in Body and Spirit

12 [h]All things are lawful for me, but all
things are not [5]helpful. All things are lawful for me, but I will not be brought under
the power of [6]any. 13 [i]Foods for the stomach and the stomach for foods, but God
will destroy both it and them. Now the
body *is* not for [j]sexual immorality but [k]for
the Lord, [l]and the Lord for the body.
14 And [m]God both raised up the Lord and
will also raise us up [n]by His power.
15 Do you not know that [o]your bodies are
members of Christ? Shall I then take the
members of Christ and make *them* members
of a harlot? Certainly not! 16 Or do you not
know that he who is joined to a harlot is one
body *with her?* For [p]*"the two,"* He says,
"shall become one flesh." 17 [q]But he who is
joined to the Lord is one spirit *with Him.*
18 [r]Flee sexual immorality. Every sin
that a man does is outside the body, but he
who commits sexual immorality sins
[s]against his own body. 19 Or [t]do you not
know that your body is the temple of the
Holy Spirit *who is* in you, whom you have
from God, [u]and you are not your own?
20 For [v]you were bought at a price; therefore glorify God in your body [7]and in your
spirit, which are God's.

Principles of Marriage

7 Now concerning the things of which
you wrote to me:
[a]*It is* good for a man not to touch a
woman. 2 Nevertheless, because of sexual
immorality, let each man have his own
wife, and let each woman have her own

12 [h] 1 Cor. 10:23 [5] *profitable* [6] Or *anything* 13 [i] Matt. 15:17; [Rom. 14:17]; Col. 2:22 [j] 1 Cor. 5:1; Gal. 5:19; Eph. 5:3; Col. 3:5; 1 Thess. 4:3 [k] 1 Thess. 4:3 [l] [Eph. 5:23] 14 [m] Rom. 6:5, 8; 2 Cor. 4:14 [n] Eph. 1:19 15 [o] Rom. 12:5; 1 Cor. 6:13; 12:27; Eph. 5:30 16 [p] Gen. 2:24; Matt. 19:5; Mark 10:8; Eph. 5:31 17 [q] [John 17:21-23; Rom. 8:9-11]; 1 Cor. 6:15; [Gal. 2:20]; Eph. 4:4 18 [r] Rom. 6:12; 1 Cor. 6:9; 2 Cor. 12:21; Eph. 5:3; Col. 3:5; Heb. 13:4 [s] Rom. 1:24; 1 Thess. 4:4

19 [t] John 2:21; 1 Cor. 3:16; 2 Cor. 6:16 [u] Rom. 14:7 20 [v] Acts 20:28; 1 Cor. 7:23; Gal. 3:13; 1 Pet. 1:18; 2 Pet. 2:1; Rev. 5:9 [7] NU omits the rest of v. 20. CHAPTER 7 1 [a] 1 Cor. 7:8, 26

6:12-20 As one who is washed, sanctified, and justified eternally by God's grace, the believer is set free (cf. Rom. 8:21,33; Gal. 5:1,13). The Corinthians had done with that freedom just what Paul had warned the Galatians not to do: "Do not *use* your liberty as an opportunity for the flesh" (Gal. 5:13). So in this section, Paul exposed the error in the Corinthian Christians' rationalization that they were free to sin, because it was covered by God's grace.

6:12 All things are lawful...not helpful. That may have been a Corinthian slogan. It was true that no matter what sins a believer commits, God forgives (Eph. 1:7), but not everything they did was profitable or beneficial. The price of abusing freedom and grace was very high. Sin always produces loss. **power.** Sin has power. The word means "mastered" (cf. Rom. 6:14), and no sin is more enslaving than sexual sin. While it can never be the unbroken pattern of a true believer's life, it can be the recurring habit that saps joy, peace, usefulness and brings divine chastening and even church discipline (cf. 5:1ff.). *See notes on 1 Thess. 4:3-5.* Sexual sin controls, so the believer must never allow sin to have that control, but must master it in the Lord's strength (*see note on 9:27*). Paul categorically rejects the ungodly notion that freedom in Christ gives license to sin (cf. Rom. 7:6; 8:13,21).

6:13 Foods...stomach. Perhaps this was a popular proverb to celebrate the idea that sex is purely biological, like eating. The influence of philosophical dualism may have contributed to this idea since it made only the body evil; therefore, what one did physically was not preventable and thus inconsequential. Because the relationship between these two is purely biological and temporal, the Corinthians, like many of their pagan friends, probably used that analogy to justify sexual immorality. **the body...the Lord.** Paul rejects the convenient justifying analogy. Bodies and food are temporal relations that will perish.

6:14 Cf. Acts 2:32; Eph. 1:19. Bodies of believers and the Lord have an eternal relationship that will never perish. He is referring to the believer's body to be changed, raised, glorified, and made heavenly. See 15:35-54; cf. Phil. 3:20,21.

6:15 members. The believer's body is not only for the Lord here and now (v. 14) but is of the Lord, a part of His body, the church (Eph. 1:22,23). The Christian's body is a spiritual temple in which the Spirit of Christ lives (12:3; John 7:38,39; 20:22; Acts 1:8; Rom. 8:9; 2 Cor. 6:16); therefore, when a believer commits a sexual sin, it involves Christ with a harlot. All sexual sin is harlotry. **Certainly not!** These words translate the strongest Gr. negative—"may it never be so."

6:16 *one flesh.* Paul supports his point in the previous verse by appealing to the truth of Gen. 2:24 that defines the sexual union between a man and a woman as "one flesh." When a person is joined to a harlot, it is a one flesh experience; therefore Christ spiritually is joined to that harlot.

6:17 one spirit *with Him.* Further strengthening the point, Paul affirms that all sex outside of marriage is sin; but illicit relationships by believers are especially reprehensible because they profane Jesus Christ with whom believers are one (John 14:18-23; 15:4,7; 17:20-23; Rom. 12:5). This argument should make such sin unthinkable.

6:18 Every sin...is outside. There is a sense in which sexual sin destroys a person like no other, because it is so intimate and entangling, corrupting on the deepest human level. But Paul is probably alluding to venereal disease, prevalent and devastating in his day and today. No sin has greater potential to destroy the body, something a believer should avoid because of the reality given in vv. 19,20.

6:19 not your own. A Christian's body belongs to the Lord (v. 13), is a member of Christ (v. 15), and is the Holy Spirit's temple. *See notes on Rom. 12:1,2.* Every act of fornication, adultery, or any other sin is committed by the believer in the sanctuary, the Holy of Holies, where God dwells. In the OT, the High-Priest only went in there once a year, and only after extensive cleansing, lest he be killed (Lev. 16).

6:20 a price. The precious blood of Christ (*see notes on 1 Pet. 1:18,19*). **glorify God.** The Christian's supreme purpose (10:31).

7:1–11:34 This section comprises Paul's answers to practical questions about which the Corinthians had written him (7:1) in a letter probably delivered by Stephanas, Fortunatus, and Achaicus (16:17). The first of those questions had to do with marriage, an area of trouble due to the moral corruption of the culture which tolerated fornication, adultery, homosexuality, polygamy, and concubinage.

7:1-7 Some had the notion that because of all the sexual sin and marital confusion, it would be better to be single, even more spiritual to be celibate. This could lead some falsely pious people to advocate divorce in order to be single. These verses elevate singleness, as long as it is celibate, but they in no way teach that marriage is either wrong or inferior.

7:1 touch a woman. This is a Jewish euphemism for sexual intercourse (see, e.g., Gen. 20:6; Ruth 2:9; Prov. 6:29). Paul is saying that it is good not to have sex, that is, to be single and celibate. It is not, however, the only good or even better than marriage (cf. Gen. 1:28; 2:18).

7:2 sexual immorality. There is a great danger of sexual sin when single (cf. Matt. 19:12). Marriage is God's only provision for sexual fulfillment. Marriage should not be reduced simply to that, however. Paul has a much higher view and articulates it in Eph. 5:22,23. He is, here, stressing the issue of sexual sin for people who are single.

husband. 3 [b]Let the husband render to his
wife the affection due her, and likewise
also the wife to her husband. 4 The wife
does not have authority over her own
body, but the husband *does*. And likewise
the husband does not have authority over
his own body, but the wife *does*. 5 [c]Do not
deprive one another except with consent
for a time, that you may give yourselves to
fasting and prayer; and come together
again so that [d]Satan does not tempt you
because of your lack of self-control. 6 But I
say this as a concession, [e]not as a commandment. 7 For [f]I wish that all men were
even as I myself. But each one has his own
gift from God, one in this manner and another in that.

8 But I say to the unmarried and to the
widows: [g]It is good for them if they remain
even as I am; 9 but [h]if they cannot exercise
self-control, let them marry. For it is better
to marry than to burn *with passion*.

3 [b] Ex. 21:10
5 [c] Joel 2:16
[d] 1 Thess. 3:5
6 [e] 2 Cor. 8:8
7 [f] Acts 26:29
8 [g] 1 Cor. 7:1, 26
9 [h] 1 Tim. 5:14
10 [i] Mark 10:6-10
[j] Mal. 2:14; [Matt. 5:32]
14 [k] Ezra 9:2; Mal. 2:15
15 [l] Rom. 12:18

Keep Your Marriage Vows

10 Now to the married I command, *yet*
not I but the [i]Lord: [j]A wife is not to depart
from *her* husband. 11 But even if she does
depart, let her remain unmarried or be reconciled to *her* husband. And a husband is
not to divorce *his* wife.

12 But to the rest I, not the Lord, say: If
any brother has a wife who does not believe, and she is willing to live with him,
let him not divorce her. 13 And a woman
who has a husband who does not believe,
if he is willing to live with her, let her not
divorce him. 14 For the unbelieving husband is sanctified by the wife, and the
unbelieving wife is sanctified by the husband; otherwise [k]your children would be
unclean, but now they are holy. 15 But if
the unbeliever departs, let him depart; a
brother or a sister is not under bondage in
such *cases*. But God has called us [l]to peace.

7:3 render...affection due. Married believers are not to sexually deprive their spouses. While celibacy is right for the single, it is wrong for the married. The practice of deprivation may have been most common when a believer had an unsaved spouse (for more on unsaved spouses, *see notes on vv. 10-17*).

7:4 authority. By the marriage covenant, each partner is given the right over the spouse's body for the satisfaction of the other.

7:5 deprive. Lit. "stop depriving each other!" This command may indicate that this kind of deprivation was going on among believers, perhaps reacting to the gross sexual sins of their past and wanting to leave all that behind. Husbands and wives may abstain temporarily from sexual activity, but only when they mutually agree to do so for intercession, as a part of their fasting. **come together again.** Sexual intercourse is to be soon renewed after the spiritual interruption. **so that Satan does not tempt.** Cf. 1 Thess. 3:5. After the agreed-upon "time" of abstinence, sexual desires intensify and a spouse becomes more vulnerable to sinful desire. *See notes on Matt. 4:1-11; 2 Cor. 2:11.*

7:6 concession. A better translation of the Gr. would be "awareness" or "to have a mutual opinion." Paul was very aware of the God-ordained advantages of both singleness and marriage, and was not commanding marriage because of the temptation of singleness. Spirituality is not connected at all to marital status, though marriage is God's good gift (see 1 Pet. 3:7, "the grace of life").

7:7 as I myself. As a single person, Paul recognized the special freedom and independence he had to serve Christ (*see notes on vv. 32-34*). But he did not expect all believers to be single, nor all who were single to stay that way, nor all who were married to act celibate as if they were single. **gift from God.** Both singleness and marriage are God's gracious gifts.

7:8 unmarried...widows. "Unmarried" is a term used 4 times in the NT, and only in 1 Corinthians (cf. vv. 11,32,34). This verse makes it clear that the unmarried and widows are distinct. Verse 11 identifies the divorced as the "unmarried" to be distinguished from "widows" (vv. 39,40; single by death) and virgins (vv. 25,28; never married). Each use of "unmarried," then, refers to those formerly married, presently single, but not widowed. They are the divorced. It is likely these people who were formerly married wanted to know if they, as Christians, could or should remarry. **as I am.** Paul was possibly a widower, and could here affirm his former marriage by identifying with the unmarried and widows. His first suggestion is that they stay single because of its freedoms in serving the Lord (vv. 25-27,32-34). *See notes on Anna in Luke 2:36-38.*

7:9 let them marry. The Gr. tense indicates a command, since a person can't live a happy life and serve the Lord effectively if dominated by unfulfilled sexual passion—especially in that Corinthian society.

7:10 not I but the Lord. What Paul writes to these believers was already made clear by Jesus during His earthly ministry (Matt. 5:31,32; 19:5-8; cf. Gen. 2:24; Mal. 2:16). **depart.** This word is used as a synonym for divorce, as indicated by the parallel use of the word "divorce," in v. 11. Apparently, some Christians felt they should divorce their unsaved spouses, to live celibately or marry a believer.

7:11 remain unmarried. If a Christian divorces another Christian except for adultery (*see notes on Matt. 5:31,32; 19:8,9*), neither partner is free to marry another person. They should reconcile, or at least remain unmarried.

7:12 to the rest. Those not covered by the instruction of vv. 10,11. **I...say.** Not a denial of inspiration or an indication that Paul is giving human opinion, but simply a way of saying that Jesus had not spoken on this and God had not previously given revelation on the matter, as Paul was then writing.

7:12,13 Some believers must have felt that being married to an unbeliever was somehow defiling. However, just the opposite is true (v. 14).

7:14 sanctified. This does not refer to salvation; otherwise the spouse would not be spoken of as unbelieving. The sanctification is matrimonial and familial, not personal or spiritual, and means that the unsaved partner is set apart for temporal blessing because the other belongs to God. One Christian in a marriage brings grace that spills over on the spouse—even possibly leading them to salvation. **children...are holy.** The Christian need not separate from an unbeliever because of fear that the unbelieving spouse may defile the children. God promises the opposite. They would be unclean if both parents were unsaved, but the presence of one believing parent exposes the children to blessing and brings them protection. The presence of even one Christian parent will protect children from undue spiritual harm and they will receive many blessings, and often that includes salvation.

7:15 let him depart. A term referring to divorce (cf. vv. 10,11). When an unbelieving spouse cannot tolerate the partner's faith and wants a divorce, it is best to let that happen in order to preserve peace in the family (cf. Rom. 12:18). The bond of marriage is broken only by death (Rom. 7:2), adultery (Matt. 19:9), or an unbeliever's leaving. **not**

16 For how do you know, O wife, whether
you will [m]save *your* husband? Or how do
you know, O husband, whether you will
save *your* wife?

Live as You Are Called

17 But as God has distributed to each
one, as the Lord has called each one, so let
him walk. And [n]so I [1]ordain in all the
churches. 18 Was anyone called while circumcised? Let him not become uncircumcised. Was anyone called while uncircumcised? [o]Let him not be circumcised.
19 [p]Circumcision is nothing and uncircumcision is nothing, but [q]keeping the commandments of God *is what matters.* 20 Let
each one remain in the same calling in
which he was called. 21 Were you called
while a slave? Do not be concerned about it;
but if you can be made free, rather use *it.*
22 For he who is called in the Lord *while* a
slave is [r]the Lord's freedman. Likewise he
who is called *while* free is [s]Christ's slave.
23 [t]You were bought at a price; do not become slaves of men. 24 Brethren, let each
one remain with [u]God in that *state* in
which he was called.

To the Unmarried and Widows

25 Now concerning virgins: [v]I have no
commandment from the Lord; yet I give
judgment as one [w]whom the Lord in His
mercy *has made* [x]trustworthy. 26 I suppose
therefore that this is good because of the
present distress—[y]that *it is* good for a man
to remain as he is: 27 Are you bound to a
wife? Do not seek to be loosed. Are you
loosed from a wife? Do not seek a wife.
28 But even if you do marry, you have not
sinned; and if a virgin marries, she has not
sinned. Nevertheless such will have trouble in the flesh, but I would spare you.
29 But [z]this I say, brethren, the time *is*
short, so that from now on even those who

16 [m] Rom. 11:14; 1 Pet. 3:1
17 [n] 1 Cor. 4:17 [1] *direct*
18 [o] Acts 15:1
19 [p] [Rom. 2:27, 29; Gal. 3:28; 5:6; 6:15; Col. 3:11] [q] [John 15:14]
22 [r] [John 8:36]; Rom. 6:18; Philem. 16
[s] [1 Cor. 9:21; Gal. 5:13]; Eph. 6:6; Col. 3:24; 1 Pet. 2:16
23 [t] Lev. 25:42; 1 Cor. 6:20; 1 Pet. 1:18, 19; Rev. 5:9
24 [u] [Eph. 6:5-8; Col. 3:22-24]
25 [v] 2 Cor. 8:8 [w] 2 Cor. 4:1; 1 Tim. 1:13, 16 [x] 1 Tim. 1:12
26 [y] 1 Cor. 7:1, 8
29 [z] [Rom. 13:11]; 1 Cor. 7:31; 1 Pet. 4:7; [2 Pet. 3:8, 9]

under bondage. When the bond is broken in any of those ways, a Christian is free to marry another believer. Throughout Scripture, whenever legitimate divorce occurs, remarriage is assumed. When divorce is permitted, so is remarriage. By implication, the permission for a widow to remarry (vv. 39,40; Rom. 7:3) because the "bond" is broken, extends to this case where there is no more "bondage."

7:16 Some may have been reluctant to let go of their unsaved spouse, who wanted out and was creating discord in the home—thinking they could evangelize the spouse by hanging on for the purpose of seeing that one converted. Paul says there are no such assurances and it is better to divorce and be at peace (v. 15), if the unsaved partner wants to end the marriage that way.

7:17-24 Discontent was prevalent among these new believers in the Corinthian church. As noted up to this point (vv. 1-16), some wanted to change their marital status, some were slaves who wanted to be free, and some used their freedom in Christ to rationalize sinning. In a general response to that, this passage plainly repeats the basic principle that Christians should willingly accept the marital condition and social situations into which God has placed them and be content to serve Him there until He leads them elsewhere.

7:17 For the first of 3 times (vv. 20,24), Paul states the principle of contentment which is required of all Christians.

7:18 called. As always in the epistles, this term refers to God's effectual call that saves (*see note on Rom. 8:30*). **circumcised...uncircumcised.** With Judaizers demanding all Gentile believers in Christ to be circumcised (Gal. 5:1-6), and with some Christian Jews wanting to disassociate with Judaism and thus having a surgery to become circumcised (as addressed in rabbinic literature), Paul needed to clarify the issue by saying that neither was necessary. Figuratively, the idea is that when a Jew became a Christian, he was not to give up his racial and cultural identity in order to appear like a Gentile. Likewise, a Gentile was not to become culturally like a Jew (v. 19). Culture, social order, external ceremony have no bearing on spiritual life. What matters is faith and obedience.

7:21 *while* a slave. Paul was not approving all slavery, but is teaching that a person who is a slave is still able to obey and honor Christ (Eph. 6:5-8; Col. 3:23; 1 Tim. 6:1,2). **Do not be concerned about.** In modern society, this seems an insensitive command to those who wrongly assume that freedom is some God-given right, rather than a preferable option.

7:22 the Lord's freedman. In the ways that truly count, no man is freer than a Christian. No bondage is as terrible as that of sin, from which Christ frees the believer. **Christ's slave.** Those who are not slaves, but free in the social sense, are in the spiritual sense made slaves of Christ in salvation (Rom. 6:22).

7:23 price. The blood of Christ (6:20; 1 Pet. 1:19). **slaves of men.** This refers to sinful slavery, i.e., becoming slaves to the ways of men, the ways of the world, and of the flesh. This is the slavery about which to be concerned.

7:25-40 Having already established that both marriage and singleness are good and right before the Lord (vv. 1-9), and for the person who has the gift of singleness (v. 7), that state has many practical advantages, Paul continued to answer the questions about which the Corinthians had written him (*see note on v. 1*). Paul gives 6 reasons for never marrying, in relationship to the downside of marriage, but remaining single (virgins): 1) pressure from the system (vv. 25-27); 2) problems of the flesh (v. 28); 3) passing of the world (vv. 29-31); 4) preoccupations of marriage (vv. 32-35); 5) promises from fathers (vv. 36-38); and 6) permanency of marriage (vv. 39,40).

7:25 I have no commandment. *See note on v. 12.* The conviction given here is not a command, but is thoroughly dependable and sound advice to remain a virgin, which is counsel included by the inspiration of the Spirit from a trustworthy man.

7:26 present distress. An unspecified, current calamity. Perhaps Paul anticipated the imminent Roman persecutions which began within 10 years after this epistle was written. **remain as he is.** Persecution is difficult enough for a single person to endure, but problems and pain are multiplied for those who are married, especially if they have children.

7:27 The benefits of singleness notwithstanding, married people must remain married. **loosed.** Divorce is in view.

7:28 marry, you have not sinned. Marriage is a fully legitimate and godly option for both the divorced (on biblical grounds; *see note on v. 15*) and virgins. **trouble in the flesh.** "Trouble" means lit. "pressed together, or under pressure." Marriage can involve conflicts, demands, difficulties, and adjustments that singleness does not, because it presses two fallen people into intimate life that leads to inevitable "trouble." The troubles of singleness may be exceeded by the conflicts of marriage.

7:29 time *is* short. Human life is brief (cf. James 4:14; 1 Pet. 1:24).

have wives should be as though they had
none, 30 those who weep as though they
did not weep, those who rejoice as though
they did not rejoice, those who buy as
though they did not possess, 31 and those
who use this world as not [a]misusing *it.* For
[b]the form of this world is passing away.
32 But I want you to be without [2]care.
[c]He who is unmarried [3]cares for the things
of the Lord—how he may please the Lord.
33 But he who is married cares about the
things of the world—how he may please
his wife. 34 There is a difference between a
wife and a virgin. The unmarried woman
[d]cares about the things of the Lord, that
she may be holy both in body and in spirit. But she who is married cares about the
things of the world—how she may please
her husband. 35 And this I say for your
own profit, not that I may put a leash on
you, but for what is proper, and that you
may serve the Lord without distraction.
36 But if any man thinks he is behaving
improperly toward his [4]virgin, if she is
past the flower of youth, and thus it must
be, let him do what he wishes. He does not
sin; let them marry. 37 Nevertheless he
who stands steadfast in his heart, having
no necessity, but has power over his own
will, and has so determined in his heart
that he will keep his [5]virgin, does well.
38 [e]So then he who gives [6]*her* in marriage
does well, but he who does not give *her* in
marriage does better.
39 [f]A wife is bound by law as long as her
husband lives; but if her husband dies, she
is at liberty to be married to whom she
wishes, [g]only in the Lord. 40 But she is
happier if she remains as she is, [h]according
to my judgment—and [i]I think I also have
the Spirit of God.

Be Sensitive to Conscience

8 Now [a]concerning things offered to
idols: We know that we all have
[b]knowledge. [c]Knowledge [1]puffs up, but
love [2]edifies. 2 And [d]if anyone thinks that
he knows anything, he knows nothing yet
as he ought to know. 3 But if anyone loves
God, this one is known by Him.

31 [a] 1 Cor. 9:18 [b] Ps. 39:6; 1 Cor. 7:29; James 1:10; 4:14; 1 Pet. 1:24; 4:7; [1 John 2:17]
32 [c] 1 Tim. 5:5 [2] *concern* [3] *is concerned about*
34 [d] Luke 10:40
36 [4] *Or virgin daughter*
37 [5] *Or virgin daughter*
38 [e] Heb. 13:4 [6] NU *his own virgin*
39 [f] Rom. 7:2 [g] 2 Cor. 6:14
40 [h] 1 Cor. 7:6, 25 [i] 1 Thess. 4:8

CHAPTER 8

1 [a] Acts 15:20; 1 Cor. 8:4, 7, 10 [b] Rom. 14:14 [c] Rom. 14:3 [1] *makes arrogant* [2] *builds up*
2 [d] [1 Cor. 13:8–12]; Gal. 6:3; [1 Tim. 6:4]

as though they had none. This does not teach that marriage is no longer binding or treated with seriousness (cf. Eph. 5:22-38; Col. 3:18,19), nor should there be any physical deprivation (vv. 3-5); but Paul is teaching that marriage should not at all reduce one's devotion to the Lord and service to Him (cf. Col. 3:2). He means to keep the eternal priority (see v. 31).

7:30 The mature Christian does not get so swept up in the emotion of this life, so as to lose motivation, hope, and purpose.

7:31 use…not misusing. This refers to the normal commercial materialism and pleasures that govern in the world. Believers are not to be swept up in earthly enterprises so that heavenly matters become secondary. **form.** This refers to a manner of life, a fashion, or way of doing things.

7:32,33 be without care. A single person is free from concern about the earthly needs of a spouse and therefore potentially better able to set himself apart exclusively for the Lord's work.

7:33 things of the world. These are earthly matters connected to the passing system (v. 31).

7:33,34 how he may please *his* wife…husband. Here is a basic and expected principle for a good marriage—each seeking to please the other.

7:34 The first part of this verse is preferably rendered in some manuscripts, "and his interests are divided. And the woman who is unmarried and the virgin…." This is important because it distinguishes clearly between the "unmarried" and "virgins," who, therefore, can't be the same. "Virgins" are single people never married, while "unmarried" must be single by divorce. Widows is the term for those made single by death (*see note on v. 8*).

7:35 Marriage does not prevent great devotion to the Lord, but it brings more potential matters to interfere with it. Singleness has fewer hindrances, though not guaranteed greater spiritual virtue. **distraction.** *See notes on vv. 26,29,33.*

7:36 his virgin. That is, a man's daughter. Apparently in Corinth some of the fathers intending devotion to the Lord, had dedicated their young daughters to the Lord as permanent virgins. **past the flower of youth.** Fully matured as a woman capable of child-bearing. **it must be.** When daughters became of marriageable age and insisted on being married, their fathers were free to break the vow and let them marry.

7:37 no necessity. This means the father who has kept his daughter a virgin and is not under constraint by the daughter to change his mind, does well to fulfill his desire for her to be singularly devoted to the Lord (v. 34). As with those who remain single (v. 28), the choice was not between right and wrong.

7:39 bound by law. God's law designed marriage for life (cf. Gen 2:24; Mal. 2:16; Rom. 7:1-3). It is so permanent that the disciples thought it may be better not to marry (*see note on Matt. 19:10*). **only in the Lord.** That is, free to marry a believer only. This is true for all believers who marry or remarry (see 2 Cor. 6:14-16).

7:40 I also have the Spirit. Perhaps with a touch of sarcasm, Paul affirmed that this sound advice was given by the Holy Spirit.

8:1–11:1 Paul addresses liberty in the church (*see notes on Rom. 14*).

8:1 things offered to idols. The Greeks and Romans were polytheistic (worshiping many gods) and polydemonistic (believing in many evil spirits). They believed that evil spirits would try to invade human beings by attaching themselves to food before it was eaten, and that the spirits could be removed only by the food's being sacrificed to a god. The sacrifice was meant not only to gain favor with the god, but also to cleanse the meat from demonic contamination. Such decontaminated meat was offered to the gods as a sacrifice. That which was not burned on the altar was served at wicked pagan feasts. What was left was sold in the market. After conversion, believers resented eating such food bought out of idol markets, because it reminded sensitive Gentile believers of their previous pagan lives and the demonic worship. **we all have knowledge.** Paul and mature believers knew better than to be bothered by such food offered once to idols and then sold in the marketplace. They knew the deities didn't exist and that evil spirits did not contaminate the food. *See note on 1 Tim. 4:3.* **love edifies.** Knowledge mingled with love prevents a believer from exercising freedoms that offend weaker believers and, rather, builds the others up in truth and wisdom (cf. 13:1-4).

8:2,3 Love is the proof of knowing God. Cf. 1 John 4:19–5:1.

8:4 Paul states his agreement with the well taught believers who knew idols were nothing, so food offered to idols was not defiled.

4 Therefore concerning the eating of
things offered to idols, we know that [e]an
idol *is* nothing in the world, [f]and that *there*
is no other God but one. 5 For even if there
are [g]so-called gods, whether in heaven or
on earth (as there are many gods and many
lords), 6 yet [h]for us *there is* one God, the Father, [i]of whom *are* all things, and we for
Him; and [j]one Lord Jesus Christ, [k]through
whom *are* all things, and [l]through whom
we *live*.
7 However, *there is* not in everyone that
knowledge; for some, [m]with consciousness
of the idol, until now eat *it* as a thing offered to an idol; and their conscience,
being weak, is [n]defiled. 8 But [o]food does
not commend us to God; for neither if we
eat are we the better, nor if we do not eat
are we the worse.
9 But [p]beware lest somehow this liberty
of yours become [q]a [3]stumbling block to
those who are weak. 10 For if anyone sees
you who have knowledge eating in an
idol's temple, will not [r]the conscience of
him who is weak be emboldened to eat
those things offered to idols? 11 And [s]be-
cause of your knowledge shall the weak
brother perish, for whom Christ died?
12 But [t]when you thus sin against the
brethren, and wound their weak conscience, you sin against Christ. 13 Therefore, [u]if food makes my brother stumble, I
will never again eat meat, lest I make my
brother stumble.

4 [e]Is. 41:24 [f]Deut. 4:35, 39; 6:4; 1 Cor. 8:6
5 [g][John 10:34]
6 [h]Mal. 2:10; Eph. 4:6 [i]Acts 17:28 [j]John 13:13; 1 Cor. 1:2; Eph. 4:5; [1 Tim. 2:5] [k]John 1:3; [Col. 1:16, 17]; Heb. 1:2 [l]Rom. 5:11; Rev. 4:11; 5:9, 10
7 [m][1 Cor. 10:28] [n]Rom. 14:14, 22
8 [o][Rom. 14:17]
9 [p]Gal. 5:13 [q]Rom. 14:13, 21; 1 Cor. 10:28 [3]*cause of offense*
10 [r]1 Cor. 10:28
11 [s]Rom. 14:15, 20
12 [t]Matt. 25:40
13 [u]Rom. 14:21; 1 Cor. 10:32; 2 Cor. 6:3; 11:29

CHAPTER 9

1 [a]Acts 9:15; 2 Cor. 12:12 [b]Acts 9:3, 17; 18:9; 22:14, 18; 23:11; 1 Cor. 15:8 [c]1 Cor. 3:6; 4:15
2 [d]2 Cor. 12:12 [1]*certification*
4 [e]1 Cor. 9:14; [1 Thess. 2:6, 9]; 2 Thess. 3:8 [2]*authority*
5 [f]Matt. 13:55 [g]Matt. 8:14; John 1:42 [3]Lit. *a sister, a wife*
6 [h]Acts 4:36; [2 Thess. 3:8]
7 [i]2 Cor. 10:4; 1 Tim. 1:18; 2 Tim. 2:3 [j]Deut. 20:6; Prov. 27:18; 1 Cor. 3:6, 8 [k]John 21:15
9 [l]Deut. 25:4; 1 Tim. 5:18

A Pattern of Self-Denial

9 Am [a]I not an apostle? Am I not free?
[b]Have I not seen Jesus Christ our
Lord? [c]Are you not my work in the Lord?
2 If I am not an apostle to others, yet doubtless I am to you. For you are [d]the [1]seal of
my apostleship in the Lord.
3 My defense to those who examine me
is this: 4 [e]Do we have no [2]right to eat and
drink? 5 Do we have no right to take along
[3]a believing wife, as *do* also the other
apostles, [f]the brothers of the Lord, and
[g]Cephas? 6 Or *is it* only Barnabas and I
[h]*who* have no right to refrain from working? 7 Who ever [i]goes to war at his own
expense? Who [j]plants a vineyard and does
not eat of its fruit? Or who [k]tends a flock
and does not drink of the milk of the
flock?
8 Do I say these things as a *mere* man? Or
does not the law say the same also? 9 For it
is written in the law of Moses, [l]*"You shall*
not muzzle an ox while it treads out the
grain." Is it oxen God is concerned about?
10 Or does He say *it* altogether for our
sakes? For our sakes, no doubt, *this* is written, that [m]he who plows should plow in
hope, and he who threshes in hope should
be partaker of his hope. 11 [n]If we have
sown spiritual things for you, *is it* a great
thing if we reap your material things? 12 If
others are partakers of *this* right over you,
are we not even more?

10 [m]2 Tim. 2:6 11 [n]Rom. 15:27; 1 Cor. 9:14

8:5 so-called gods. Some were outright fakes and some were manifestations of demons, but none were truly gods (Ps. 115:4-7; Acts 19:26).

8:6 one God, the Father...one Lord Jesus Christ. A powerful and clear affirmation of the essential equality of God the Father and God the Son (cf. Eph. 4:4-6).

8:7 conscience...is defiled. The consciences of some newer converts were still accusing them strongly with regard to allowing them to eat idol food without feeling spiritually corrupted and guilty. They still imagined that idols were real and evil. A defiled conscience is one that has been violated, bringing fear, shame, and guilt. *See notes on Rom. 14:20-23.*

8:8 commend us to God. The idea is of bringing us nearer to God or making us approved by Him. Food is spiritually neutral.

8:9-11 stumbling block. Some believers would be caused to fall back into old sins by getting involved with foods offered to idols.

8:11 perish. This is better translated "ruined," with the idea of "come to sin." *See note on Matt. 18:14.* **for whom Christ died.** Christ died for all who believe, actually bearing the penalty for their sin and fully satisfying the wrath of God.

8:12 you sin against Christ. A strong warning that causing a brother or sister in Christ to stumble is more than simply an offense against that person; it is a serious offense against the Lord Himself (*see notes on Matt. 18:6-14*).

8:13 *See notes on Rom. 14:14,15,19-21.*

9:1,2 In chap. 8, Paul set out the limits of Christian liberty. In this chapter he sets forth how he followed them in his own life. In vv. 1-18, he discusses his right to be financially supported by those to whom he ministers. In vv. 19-27, he explains how he would give up all rights to win people to Christ. All of these questions are rhetorical, the "yes" answer to each being assumed.

9:2 seal of my apostleship. The existence of the church in Corinth was evidence of Paul's apostolic authenticity.

9:3 examine. Using this Gr. legal term for a preliminary investigation required before a decision was reached in a case, Paul sets out to defend his rights.

9:4 right to eat and drink. Cf. Gal. 6:6; 1 Tim. 5:17,18. He was entitled to be married (v. 5) and to receive financial support from those to whom he ministered.

9:5 Cephas. Peter, who was married (cf. Mark 1:29-31).

9:6 working. With sarcasm, Paul, a tentmaker (Acts 18:3), let the Corinthians know that he and Barnabas had as much right as others to receive full financial support from their work. Except for help from a few churches (e.g., Phil. 4:15,16), they paid their own expenses not because of obligation or necessity, but voluntarily.

9:7 Who plants a vineyard. Cf. 2 Tim. 2:6.

9:9 law. The Scripture, as quoted from Deut. 25:4.

9:10 for our sakes. As in agriculture, men should earn their living from their labor.

9:11 material things. Financial support. *See note on 1 Tim. 5:17.* Cf. 2 Cor. 8:1-5.

9:12 others are partakers. Apparently, the church had financially

[o]Nevertheless we have not used this
right, but endure all things [p]lest we hinder
the gospel of Christ. 13 [q]Do you not know
that those who minister the holy things eat
of the things of the [r]temple, and those who
serve at the altar partake of *the offerings of*
the altar? 14 Even so [s]the Lord has commanded [t]that those who preach the gospel
should live from the gospel.
15 But [u]I have used none of these things,
nor have I written these things that it
should be done so to me; for [v]it *would be* better for me to die than that anyone should
make my boasting void. 16 For if I preach
the gospel, I have nothing to boast of, for
[w]necessity is laid upon me; yes, woe is me if
I do not preach the gospel! 17 For if I do this
willingly, [x]I have a reward; but if against
my will, [y]I have been entrusted with a stewardship. 18 What is my reward then? That
[z]when I preach the gospel, I may present
the gospel [4]of Christ without charge, that I
[a]may not abuse my authority in the gospel.

Serving All Men

19 For though I am [b]free from all *men*, [c]I
have made myself a servant to all, [d]that I
might win the more; 20 and [e]to the Jews I
became as a Jew, that I might win Jews; to
those *who are* under the law, as under the
[5]law, that I might win those *who are* under
the law; 21 [f]to [g]those *who are* without law,
as without law [h](not being without [6]law toward God, but under [7]law toward Christ),
that I might win those *who are* without law;
22 [i]to the weak I became [8]as weak, that I
might win the weak. [j]I have become all
things to all *men*, [k]that I might by all means
save some. 23 Now this I do for the gospel's
sake, that I may be partaker of it with *you*.

Striving for a Crown

24 Do you not know that those who run
in a race all run, but one receives the prize?
[l]Run in such a way that you may [9]obtain
it. 25 And everyone who competes *for the
prize* [1]is temperate in all things. Now they
do it to obtain a perishable crown, but we
for [m]an imperishable *crown*. 26 Therefore I
run thus: [n]not with uncertainty. Thus I

12 [o][Acts 18:3; 20:33]; 1 Cor. 9:15, 18 [p]2 Cor. 11:12 **13** [q]Lev. 6:16, 26; 7:6, 31 [r]Num. 18:8-31; Deut. 18:1 **14** [s]Matt. 10:10; Luke 10:7, 8; 1 Tim. 5:18 [t]Rom. 10:15 **15** [u]Acts 18:3; 20:33; 1 Cor. 9:12, 18 [v]2 Cor. 11:10 **16** [w]Acts 9:15; [Rom. 1:14] **17** [x]John 4:36; 1 Cor. 3:8, 14; 9:18 [y]1 Cor. 4:1; Gal. 2:7; Eph. 3:2; Col. 1:25 **18** [z]1 Cor. 10:33 [a]1 Cor. 7:31; 9:12 [4]NU omits *of Christ* **19** [b]1 Cor. 9:1 [c]2 Cor. 4:5; Gal. 5:13 [d]Matt. 18:15; 1 Pet. 3:1 **20** [e]Acts 16:3; 21:23-26; Rom. 11:14 [5]NU adds *though not being myself under the law* **21** [f][Gal. 2:3; 3:2] [g][Rom. 2:12, 14] [h][1 Cor. 7:22; Gal. 6:2] [6]NU *God's law* [7]NU *Christ's law* **22** [i]Rom. 14:1; 15:1; 2 Cor. 11:29 [j]1 Cor. 10:33 [k]Rom. 11:14 [8]NU omits *as* **24** [l]Gal. 2:2; 2 Tim. 4:7; Heb. 12:1 [9]*win* **25** [m]2 Tim. 4:8; James 1:12; [1 Pet. 5:4; Rev. 2:10; 3:11] [1]*exercises self-control* **26** [n]2 Tim. 2:5

supported other ministers. **endure.** False teachers sought money. Paul wanted to be certain he was not classed with them, so he endured not accepting support, so as not to offend. Cf. Acts 20:34; 2 Thess. 3:8.

9:13 partake of *the offerings*. OT priests were supported by the tithes of crops and animals, as well as of financial gifts (Num. 18:8-24; cf. Gen. 14:18-21).

9:14 live from the gospel. This refers to earning a living by preaching the good news.

9:15 none of these things. The 6 reasons given in vv. 1-14 that indicate his right to financial support. **nor have I written.** He was not underhandedly hoping that, despite his protest, the Corinthians would feel obligated to pay him (2 Cor. 11:8,9; cf. 1 Thess. 2:9; 2 Thess. 3:8; 1 Pet. 5:2). **better...to die.** He preferred death to having anyone think he ministered with a financial motive. See Acts 20:33-35; 1 Pet. 5:2. **make my boasting void.** The term "boast" refers to that in which one glories or to the basis of one's glorying, and carries the idea of rejoicing. It is a statement of sincere joy, not pride (cf. 1:31; Rom 15:17). He was genuinely overjoyed for the privilege of serving the Lord and did not want material support to rob him of it in any way.

9:16 nothing to boast of. That is to say, his boast (cf. v. 15) was not personal. He was not proud as if it were his gospel; nor was he proud about the way he preached it, as if it were his ability. **necessity.** Paul did not preach from personal pride, but from divine compulsion. He had no other choice, because God had sovereignly set him apart for service (see Acts 9:3-6,15; 26:13-19; Gal. 1:15; Col. 1:25; cf. Jer. 1:5; 20:9; Luke 1:13-17). **woe.** God's severest chastening is reserved for unfaithful ministers (Heb. 13:17; James 3:1).

9:17 against my will. This does not indicate that Paul was unwilling to obey but that his will had no part in the call itself. Since it was God's sovereign choice and call, he received not a "reward," but a "stewardship" (a valuable responsibility or duty to be carefully managed).

9:18 my reward. Not money, but the privilege of preaching the gospel without support, was Paul's reward, so that he set aside his liberty ("right").

9:19 a servant. By choice, he set aside his right to be supported, and thus "enslaved" himself to self-support, in order to remove a potential offense and win more people to Jesus Christ (cf. Prov. 11:30).

9:20 became as a Jew. Within the limits of God's Word and his Christian conscience, he would be as culturally and socially Jewish as necessary when witnessing to Jews (cf. Rom. 9:3; 10:1; 11:14). He was not bound to ceremonies and traditions of Judaism. All legal restraints had been removed, but there was the constraint of love (cf. Rom. 9:3; 10:1; 11:14). For examples of this identification with customs of the Jews, *see notes on Acts 16:3; 18:18; 21:20-26.*

9:21 those...without law. Gentiles. Paul was not suggesting the violating of God's moral law, but, as he explained, not being lawless toward God, but abiding by the law of Jesus Christ (cf. James 1:25; 2:8,12).

9:22 weak. He stooped to make the gospel clear at the lower level of comprehension, which Paul no doubt had done often while dealing with the Corinthians themselves (cf. 2:1-5). **all things...all means.** Within the bounds of God's Word, he would not offend the Jew, Gentile, or those weak in understanding. Not changing Scripture or compromising the truth, he would condescend in ways that could lead to salvation.

9:24-27 Liberty cannot be limited without self-control, since the flesh resists limits as its freedom. Here, Paul speaks of his personal self-control.

9:24 race. The Greeks enjoyed two great athletic events, the Olympic games and the Isthmian games, and because the Isthmian events were held in Corinth, believers there were quite familiar with this analogy of running to win.

9:25 temperate. Self-control is crucial to victory. **crown.** A wreath of greenery given to the winner of the race. Cf. 2 Tim. 4-8; 1 Pet. 1:4.

9:26 not with uncertainty. Four times he has mentioned his goal of winning people to salvation (vv. 19,22). **beats the air.** Paul changes the metaphor to boxing to illustrate the point that he was no shadow boxer, just waving his arms without effect (cf. 1 Tim. 1:18).

fight: not as *one who* beats the air. 27 [o]But I
discipline my body and [p]bring *it* into subjection, lest, when I have preached to others, I myself should become [q]disqualified.

Old Testament Examples

10 Moreover, brethren, I do not want
you to be unaware that all our fathers were under [a]the cloud, all passed
through [b]the sea, 2 all were baptized into
Moses in the cloud and in the sea, 3 all ate
the same [c]spiritual food, 4 and all drank
the same [d]spiritual drink. For they drank
of that spiritual Rock that followed them,
and that Rock was Christ. 5 But with most
of them God was not well pleased, for *their
bodies* [e]were scattered in the wilderness.

6 Now these things became our examples, to the intent that we should not lust
after evil things as [f]they also lusted.
7 [g]And do not become idolaters as *were*
some of them. As it is written, [h]*"The people sat down to eat and drink, and rose up
to play."* 8 [i]Nor let us commit sexual immorality, as [j]some of them did, and [k]in one
day twenty-three thousand fell; 9 nor let us
[1]tempt Christ, as [l]some of them also
tempted, and [m]were destroyed by serpents; 10 nor complain, as [n]some of them
also complained, and [o]were destroyed by
[p]the destroyer. 11 Now [2]all these things
happened to them as examples, and [q]they
were written for our [3]admonition, [r]upon
whom the ends of the ages have come.

12 Therefore [s]let him who thinks he
stands take heed lest he fall. 13 No temptation has overtaken you except such as is
common to man; but [t]God *is* faithful, [u]who
will not allow you to be tempted beyond
what you are able, but with the temptation
will also make the way of escape, that you
may be able to [4]bear *it*.

Flee from Idolatry

14 Therefore, my beloved, [v]flee from
idolatry. 15 I speak as to [w]wise men; judge
for yourselves what I say. 16 [x]The cup of
blessing which we bless, is it not the

27 [o] [Rom. 8:13] [p] [Rom. 6:18] [q] Jer. 6:30; 2 Cor. 13:5

CHAPTER 10

1 [a] Ex. 13:21, 22; Ps. 105:39 [b] Ex. 14:21, 22, 29; Neh. 9:11; Ps. 66:6
3 [c] Ex. 16:4, 15, 35; Deut. 8:3; Neh. 9:15, 20; Ps. 78:24; John 6:31
4 [d] Ex. 17:5-7; Num. 20:11; Ps. 78:15
5 [e] Num. 14:29, 37; 26:65; Heb. 3:17; Jude 5
6 [f] Num. 11:4, 34; Ps. 106:14
7 [g] Ex. 32:4; 1 Cor. 5:11; 10:14 [h] Ex. 32:6; 1 Cor. 15:32
8 [i] Rev. 2:14 [j] Num. 25:1-9 [k] Ps. 106:29
9 [l] Ex. 17:2, 7 [m] Num. 21:6-9 [1] *test*
10 [n] Ex. 16:2 [o] Num. 14:37 [p] Ex. 12:23; 2 Sam. 24:16; 1 Chr. 21:15; Heb. 11:28
11 [q] Rom. 15:4 [r] Phil. 4:5 [2] NU omits *all*

[3] *instruction* **12** [s] Rom. 11:20 **13** [t] 1 Cor. 1:9 [u] Ps. 125:3 [4] *endure*
14 [v] 2 Cor. 6:17 **15** [w] 1 Cor. 8:1 **16** [x] Matt. 26:26-28; Mark 14:23; Luke 22:20; 1 Cor. 11:25

9:27 discipline. From a term lit. meaning to hit under the eye. He knocked out the bodily impulses to keep them from preventing him from his mission of winning souls to Christ. **disqualified.** Another metaphor from the athletic games. A contestant who failed to meet basic training requirements could not participate at all, much less have an opportunity to win. Paul may be especially referring to such fleshly sins that disqualify a man from preaching and leading the church, particularly being blameless and above reproach in the sexual area, since such sin is a disqualification (*see notes on Ps. 101:6; Prov. 6:33; 1 Tim. 3:2; Titus 1:6*).

10:1-13 Ancient Israel's 40-year journey between Egypt and Canaan (Ex. 13:21; 14:16; 16:15; 17:6) is a sobering illustration of the misuse of freedom and the dangers of overconfidence. The Israelites misused their new-found freedom, fell into idolatry, immorality, and rebelliousness, disqualifying themselves from receiving the Lord's blessing.

10:1 Moreover...unaware. This transition leads from the lack of self-discipline and subsequent disqualification spoken of in 9:27 to an illustration of it in ancient Israel. **all our fathers.** Paul is referring to ancient Israel, of whom he was a descendant. In particular, he asked his readers to remember what had happened to Israel in the wilderness, because of freedom without self-control. **under the cloud.** Guided by God's presence as a cloud by day and column of fire at night (see Ex. 13:21). **through the sea.** The Red Sea, which opened for Israel to pass through and closed to drown the Egyptian army (see Ex. 14:26-31).

10:2 baptized. Israel was immersed, not in the sea, but "into Moses," indicating their oneness, or solidarity, with him as their leader.

10:3,4 spiritual food...drink. Actual food provided by the spiritual power of God. See Ex. 16:15; 17:6.

10:4 that spiritual Rock. The Jews had a legend that the actual rock Moses struck followed them throughout their wilderness wanderings, providing water for them. Paul says they have a Rock providing all they need, but it is Christ. Rock (*petra*) refers to a massive cliff, not simply a large stone or boulder, signifying the pre-incarnate Messiah (Christ), who protected and sustained His people. Cf. Matt. 16:18.

10:5 not well pleased. This is an understatement. Because of Israel's extreme disobedience, God allowed only two of the men who had originally left Egypt (Joshua and Caleb) to enter the Promised Land; all the others died in the wilderness, including Moses and Aaron who were disqualified from entering the Land (Num. 20:8-12,24).

10:6 our examples. They died in the wilderness because of their failure of self-discipline and consequent indulgence of every desire (*see note on 9:27*). Four major sins characterized them: idolatry (v. 7); sexual immorality (v. 8); testing God (v. 9); and complaining (v. 10).

10:7 idolaters. The Israelites were barely out of Egypt when they fell into idol worship. Exodus 32 records the story (v. 6 is quoted here). Some 3,000 were executed for instigating an immoral orgy at Sinai (Ex. 32:28). See Ex. 20:3; Ezek. 14:3; 1 John 5:21; Rev. 22:9. ***play.*** A euphemism for the gross sexual relations which followed the excessive feasting.

10:8 twenty-three thousand. Having just quoted from Ex. 32 in v. 7, this very likely also refers to the incident in Ex. 32, not to the incident at Shittim in Num. 25 (contra. marginal ref.). Apparently 3,000 were killed by the Levites (Ex. 32:28) and 20,000 died in the plague (Ex. 32:35).

10:9 tempt Christ. Numbers 21 records this story of the people questioning the goodness and plan of the One carrying them through the wilderness, the Protector and Provider, the spiritual Rock, Christ pre-incarnate (*see note on v. 4*). **serpents.** See Num. 21:6; cf. 11:30.

10:10 destroyer. This incident is recorded in Num. 16:3-41. The same angel had slain the firstborn of the Egyptians (Ex. 12:23), the 70,000 men because of David's census (2 Sam. 24:15,16), and the entire Assyrian army that was besieging Jerusalem (2 Chr. 32:21).

10:11 the ends of the ages. The time of Messiah; the last days of redemptive history before the messianic kingdom. See Heb. 9:26; 1 John 2:18.

10:12 Cf. Prov. 16:18. The Bible is filled with examples of overconfidence (see Esth. 3–5; Is. 37:36-38; Luke 22:33,34,54-62; Rev. 3:1-3,17).

10:13 temptation. *See notes on James 1:13-15*; cf. Matt. 6:13. **common to man.** One Gr. word meaning "that which is human."

10:16 cup of blessing. The proper name given to the third cup during the Passover Feast. At the last Passover with the disciples, Jesus

[5]communion of the blood of Christ? [y]The
bread which we break, is it not the communion of the body of Christ? 17 For [z]we,
though many, are one bread *and* one body;
for we all partake of that one bread.
18 Observe [a]Israel [b]after the flesh: [c]Are
not those who eat of the sacrifices [6]par-
takers of the altar? 19 What am I saying
then? [d]That an idol is anything, or what is
offered to idols is anything? 20 Rather, that
the things which the Gentiles [e]sacrifice
[f]they sacrifice to demons and not to God,
and I do not want you to have fellowship
with demons. 21 [g]You cannot drink the cup
of the Lord and [h]the cup of demons; you
cannot partake of the [i]Lord's table and of
the table of demons. 22 Or do we [j]provoke
the Lord to jealousy? [k]Are we stronger
than He?

All to the Glory of God

23 All things are lawful [7]for me, but not
all things are [l]helpful; all things are lawful
[7]for me, but not all things [8]edify. 24 Let no
one seek his own, but each one [m]the
other's *well-being.*
25 [n]Eat whatever is sold in the meat market, asking no questions for conscience'
sake; 26 for [o]"*the earth is the* LORD's, *and
all its fullness.*"
27 If any of those who do not believe invites you *to dinner,* and you desire to go,
[p]eat whatever is set before you, asking no
question for conscience' sake. 28 But if anyone says to you, "This was offered to
idols," do not eat it [q]for the sake of the one
who told you, and for conscience' sake;
[9]for [r]"*the earth is the* LORD's, *and all its
fullness.*" 29 "Conscience," I say, not your
own, but that of the other. For [s]why is my
liberty judged by another *man's* conscience? 30 But if I partake with thanks,
why am I evil spoken of for *the food* [t]over
which I give thanks?
31 [u]Therefore, whether you eat or drink,
or whatever you do, do all to the glory of
God. 32 [v]Give no offense, either to the Jews
or to the Greeks or to the church of God,
33 just [w]as I also please all *men* in all *things,*
not seeking my own profit, but the *profit* of
many, that they may be saved.

11 Imitate[a] me, just as I also *imitate*
Christ.

Head Coverings

2 Now I praise you, brethren, that you remember me in all things and keep the traditions just as I delivered *them* to you. 3 But

16 [y]Matt. 26:26; Luke 22:19; Acts 2:42; 1 Cor. 11:23 [5]*fellowship* or *sharing*
17 [z]Rom. 12:5; 1 Cor. 12:12, 27; Eph. 4:4, 16; Col. 3:15
18 [a]Rom. 4:12 [b]Rom. 4:1 [c]Lev. 3:3; 7:6, 14; Deut. 12:17 [6]*fellowshippers* or *sharers*
19 [d]1 Cor. 8:4
20 [e]Lev. 17:7 [f]Deut. 32:17; Ps. 106:37; Gal. 4:8; Rev. 9:20
21 [g]2 Cor. 6:15, 16 [h]Deut. 32:38 [i][1 Cor. 11:23-29]
22 [j]Deut. 32:21 [k]Ezek. 22:14
23 [l]1 Cor. 6:12 [7]NU omits *for me* [8]*build up*
24 [m]Phil. 2:4
25 [n][1 Tim. 4:4]
26 [o]Ex. 19:5; Ps. 24:1; 50:12; 1 Tim. 4:4
27 [p]Luke 10:7, 8
28 [q][1 Cor. 8:7, 10, 12] [r]Deut. 10:14; Ps. 24:1 [9]NU omits the rest of v. 28.
29 [s]Rom. 14:16; [1 Cor. 9:19]
30 [t]Rom. 14:6
31 [u]Col. 3:17; 1 Pet. 4:11
32 [v]Rom. 14:13
33 [w]Rom. 15:2; 1 Cor. 9:22; [Gal. 1:10] CHAPTER 11 **1** [a]Eph. 5:1

used the third cup as the symbol of His blood shed for sin. That cup became the one used to institute the Lord's Supper. He set the cup apart as a token of salvation blessing before passing it to the 12 (*see notes on Luke 22:17,20*). **communion.** Means "to have in common, to participate and have partnership with." The same Gr. word is used in 1:9; 2 Cor. 8:4; Phil. 2:1; 3:10. Commemorating the Lord's Supper was a regular and cherished practice in the early church, by which believers remembered their Savior's death and celebrated their common salvation and eternal life which reflected their perfect spiritual oneness. **the blood of Christ.** A vivid phrase used to represent Christ's sacrificial death and full atoning work. *See note on Rom. 5:9.* See Acts 20:28; Rom. 3:25; Eph. 1:7; 2:13; Col. 1:20; 1 Pet. 1:19; 1 John 1:7; Rev. 1:5; 5:9. **the bread.** This symbolized our Lord's body as the cup symbolized His blood. Both point to His death as a sacrifice for the salvation of men.

10:17 are one bread. This refers to the bread of communion as the symbol of Christ's body given for all who believe. Since we all partake of that body, we are one. *See note on 6:17.*

10:18 Observe Israel. In the OT sacrifices, the offering was in behalf of all who ate (see Lev. 7:15-18). By such action, the people were identifying with the offering and affirming their devotion to God to whom it was offered. Paul was, by this, implying how any sacrifice made to an idol (see vv. 7,14) was identifying with and participating with that idol. It is completely inconsistent for believers to participate in any such worship (v. 21).

10:19,20 Idols and the things sacrificed to them have no spiritual nature or power in themselves (cf. 8:4,8), but they do represent the demonic. If pagan worshipers believe an idol was a god, demons act out the part of the imagined god (cf. 2 Thess. 2:9-11). There is not a true god in the idol, but there is a satanic spiritual force (cf. Deut. 32:17; Ps. 106:37).

10:22 jealousy. God tolerates no competition and will not allow idolatry to go unpunished. (Deut. 32:21; Jer. 25:6,9; Rev. 21:8; cf. 11:30).

10:23-30 Paul gives 4 principles for Christian liberty: 1) edification over gratification (v. 23); 2) others over self (v. 24); 3) liberty over legalism (vv. 25-27); and 4) condescension over condemnation (vv. 28-30).

10:23 *See note on 6:12.* **edify.** To build up in Christian doctrine (cf. 8:1; 14:3,4,26; Acts 20:32; 2 Cor. 12:19; Eph. 4:12; 2 Tim. 3:16,17).

10:24 *See notes on Phil. 2:3,4.*

10:25,26 Quoting Ps. 24:1, Paul declares that believers, though not participating in idol ceremonies (*see notes on vv. 18-20*), should not hesitate to buy meat once used in such ceremonies and eat it without guilt (*see note on 1 Tim. 4:4,5*).

10:27 eat whatever. So as not to offend the unbeliever.

10:28,29 Even if you are the guest of an unbeliever and don't want to offend him, it is better to offend the unbeliever and not eat for the sake of the weaker Christian who would be offended to eat, since love to other believers is the strongest witness we have (John 13:34,35).

10:29 my liberty judged by another. Offending a weaker brother with one's freedom will cause the offended person to condemn us.

10:30 We can't truly offer thanks to God for some food by which we cause another believer to stumble.

10:31 glory. Christian liberty, as well as the most common behavior, is to be conducted to the honor of God. Cf. Ezek. 36:23.

10:32 Those 3 groups cover all humanity. We are to be careful to offend none.

10:33 please all *men*. *See notes on 9:19-23.*

11:1 Imitate. *See notes on 4:16; Eph. 5:1; Phil. 3:17; 4:9.*

11:2 traditions. In the strict sense used here, a synonym for God's Word (cf. 2 Thess. 2:15). The NT sometimes uses the word in a negative way, referring to man-made ideas or practices, especially those that conflict with Scripture (cf. Matt. 15:2-6; Gal. 1:14; Col. 2:8).

I want you to know that [b]the head of every
man is Christ, [c]the head of woman *is* man,
and [d]the head of Christ *is* God. 4 Every man
praying or [e]prophesying, having *his* head
covered, dishonors his head. 5 But every
woman who prays or prophesies with *her*
head uncovered dishonors her head, for
that is one and the same as if her head were
[f]shaved. 6 For if a woman is not covered, let
her also be shorn. But if it is [g]shameful for
a woman to be shorn or shaved, let her be
covered. 7 For a man indeed ought not to
cover *his* head, since [h]he is the image and
glory of God; but woman is the glory of
man. 8 For man is not from woman, but
woman [i]from man. 9 Nor was man created
for the woman, but woman [j]for the man.
10 For this reason the woman ought to have
a symbol of authority on *her* head, because of
the angels. 11 Nevertheless, [k]neither *is* man
independent of woman, nor woman independent of man, in the Lord. 12 For as
woman *came* from man, even so man also
comes through woman; but all things are
from God.

13 Judge among yourselves. Is it proper
for a woman to pray to God with her head
uncovered? 14 Does not even nature itself
teach you that if a man has long hair, it is a
dishonor to him? 15 But if a woman has
long hair, it is a glory to her; for *her* hair is
given [l]to her for a covering. 16 But [l]if anyone seems to be contentious, we have no
such custom, [m]nor *do* the churches of God.

Conduct at the Lord's Supper

17 Now in giving these instructions I do
not praise *you,* since you come together not

3 [b] Eph. 1:22; 4:15; 5:23; Col. 1:18; 2:19 [c] Gen. 3:16; [Eph. 5:23] [d] John 14:28
4 [e] 1 Cor. 12:10
5 [f] Deut. 21:12
6 [g] Num. 5:18
7 [h] Gen. 1:26, 27; 5:1; 9:6; James 3:9
8 [i] Gen. 2:21-23; 1 Tim. 2:13
9 [j] Gen. 2:18
11 [k] [Gal. 3:28]
15 [1] M omits *to her*
16 [l] 1 Tim. 6:4 [m] 1 Cor. 7:17

11:3-15 There is no distinction between men and women as far as personal worth, intellect, or spirituality are concerned (cf. Gal. 3:28). That women function uniquely in God's order, however, submitting to men's authority, Paul affirms by several points: 1) the pattern in the Godhead (v. 3); 2) the divine design of male and female (v. 7); 3) the order of creation (v. 8); 4) the purpose of woman in regard to man (v. 9); 5) the concern of the angels (v. 10); and 6) the characteristics of natural physiology (vv. 13-15).

11:3 Christ. Christ is the head of the church as its Savior and Lord (cf. Eph. 1:22,23; 4:15; Col. 1:18). He is also the Lord over every unbeliever (cf. Matt. 28:18; Heb. 2:8). Someday all will acknowledge His authority (cf. Phil. 2:10,11). **man.** Men have authority over women in the basic order of creation (cf. vv. 8,9; cf. Is. 3:12; Eph. 5:22-33). *See notes on 1 Tim. 2:11-15.* **God.** Christ has never been in any way inferior in essence to the Father (John 10:30; 17:21-24), but in His incarnation He willingly submitted Himself to the Father's will in humble obedience (3:23; 15:24-28; cf. John 4:34; 5:30; 6:38).

11:4 covered, dishonors. Lit. "having down from head," is probably a reference to men wearing a head covering, which seems to have been a local custom. Jews began wearing head coverings during the fourth century A.D., although some may already have been wearing them in NT times. Apparently, Corinthian men were doing the same, and Paul informs them that it is a disgrace. Paul is not stating a universal law from God, but acknowledging a local custom, which did reflect divine principle. In that society, a man's uncovered head was a sign of his authority over women, who were to have their heads covered. For a man to cover his head was to suggest a reversal of proper roles.

11:5 woman who prays or prophesies. Paul makes clear directives that women are not to lead or speak in the services of the church (cf. 14:34; 1 Tim. 2:12), but they may pray and proclaim the truth to unbelievers, as well as teaching children and other women (cf. 1 Tim. 5:16; Titus 2:3,4). *See note on Acts 21:9.* Wherever and whenever women do pray and proclaim the Word appropriately, they must do so maintaining a proper distinction from men. **uncovered.** In the culture of Corinth, a woman's covered head while ministering or worshiping was a symbol to signify a subordinate relationship to her husband. The apostle is not laying down an absolute law for women to wear veils or coverings in all churches for all time, but is declaring that the symbols of the divinely-established male and female roles are to be genuinely honored in every culture. As in the case of meat offered to idols (chaps. 8,9), there is nothing spiritual about wearing or not wearing a covering. But manifesting rebellion against God's order was wrong. **dishonors her head.** "Head" may refer to her own self being disgraced by refusing to conform to recognized symbols of submission, or to her husband, who is disgraced by her behavior.

11:6 shameful...to be shorn. In that day only a prostitute or a feminist would shave her head. If a Christian woman rejected the covering that symbolized her submission in that culture, she might as well have shaved her head—the shame was similar.

11:7 image and glory of God. Though men and women were both created in God's image (Gen. 1:27), it is man who bears the glory of God uniquely by his role. Like God, he is given a sphere of sovereignty as the earthly sovereign over God's created order. *See notes on Gen. 3:16,17.*

11:7,8 woman is the glory of man. As man carries authority delegated to him by God, so woman carries authority delegated to her by God through her husband. Man came from God; woman came from man (cf. Gen. 2:9-23; 1 Tim. 2:11-13).

11:9 See Gen. 2:18-23.

11:10 angels. Women are to be submissive by wearing the symbol of authority so as not to offend these most holy and submissive creatures who watch the church (cf. Matt. 18:10; Eph. 3:9,10), who were present (Job 38:4,7) at creation, when God designed the order of authority for men and women.

11:11,12 All believers, male and female, are equal in the Lord and complementary in the Lord's work. Their roles are different in function and relationships, not in spirituality or importance (cf. Gal. 3:28). *See note on 1 Tim. 2:15.*

11:13 Is it proper. Aside from apostolic command, Paul asked, in effect, "Isn't it self-evident that women should not be uncovered?"

11:14,15 nature. The term can convey the idea of basic human awareness, i.e., the innate sense of what is normal and right. The male hormone, testosterone, speeds up the loss of hair in men. Estrogen causes women's hair to grow longer and for longer time. Women are rarely bald, no matter how old. This physiology is reflected in most cultures in the custom of longer hair on women. God has given her hair as a covering to show tenderness, softness, and beauty.

11:16 no such custom. Neither the Lord, the apostles, nor the churches would allow female rebellion. Women were to maintain their distinctively feminine hairdos; and when custom dictated, they should wear a covering.

11:17-34 The early church love feasts (cf. Jude 12) usually closed with observance of the Lord's Supper. The worldly, carnal church at Corinth had turned those sacred meals into gluttonous, drunken revelries (v. 17; cf. 2 Pet. 2:13). Beyond that, wealthy believers brought ample food and drink for themselves but refused to share, letting their poorer brethren go away hungry (v. 21).

for the better but for the worse. 18 For first
of all, when you come together as a church,
[n]I hear that there are divisions among you,
and in part I believe it. 19 For [o]there must
also be factions among you, [p]that those
who are approved may be [2]recognized
among you. 20 Therefore when you come
together in one place, it is not to eat the
Lord's Supper. 21 For in eating, each one
takes his own supper ahead of *others;* and
one is hungry and [q]another is drunk.
22 What! Do you not have houses to eat
and drink in? Or do you despise [r]the
church of God and [s]shame [3]those who
have nothing? What shall I say to you?
Shall I praise you in this? I do not praise
you.

Institution of the Lord's Supper

23 For [t]I received from the Lord that
which I also delivered to you: [u]that the
Lord Jesus on the *same* night in which He
was betrayed took bread; 24 and when He
had given thanks, He broke *it* and said,
[4]"Take, eat; this is My body which is [5]bro-
ken for you; do this in remembrance of
Me." 25 In the same manner *He* also *took*
the cup after supper, saying, "This cup is
the new covenant in My blood. This do, as
often as you drink *it,* in remembrance of
Me."

26 For as often as you eat this bread and
drink this cup, you proclaim the Lord's
death [v]till He comes.

Examine Yourself

27 Therefore whoever eats [w]this bread or
drinks *this* cup of the Lord in an unworthy
manner will be guilty of the body and
[6]blood of the Lord. 28 But [x]let a man examine himself, and so let him eat of the bread
and drink of the cup. 29 For he who eats and
drinks [7]in an unworthy manner eats and
drinks judgment to himself, not discerning
the [8]Lord's body. 30 For this reason many *are*
weak and sick among you, and many
[9]sleep. 31 For [y]if we would judge ourselves,
we would not be judged. 32 But when we are
judged, [z]we are chastened by the Lord, that
we may not be condemned with the world.
33 Therefore, my brethren, when you
[a]come together to eat, wait for one another.
34 But if anyone is hungry, let him eat at
home, lest you come together for judgment.
And the rest I will set in order when I come.

Spiritual Gifts: Unity in Diversity

12 Now [a]concerning spiritual *gifts,*
brethren, I do not want you to be ignorant: 2 You know [b]that[1] you were

18 [n] 1 Cor. 1:10-12; 3:3
19 [o] Matt. 18:7; Luke 17:1; 1 Tim. 4:1; 2 Pet. 2:1 [p] [Deut. 13:3]; Luke 2:35; 1 John 2:19 [2] Lit. *manifest, evident*
21 [q] 2 Pet. 2:13; Jude 12
22 [r] 1 Cor. 10:32 [s] James 2:6 [3] The poor
23 [t] 1 Cor. 15:3; Gal. 1:12; Col. 3:24 [u] Matt. 26:26-28; Mark 14:22-24; Luke 22:17-20; 1 Cor. 10:16
24 [4] NU omits *Take, eat* [5] NU omits *broken*
26 [v] John 14:3; [Acts 1:11]
27 [w] [John 6:51] [6] NU, M *the blood*
28 [x] Matt. 26:22; 2 Cor. 13:5; Gal. 6:4
29 [7] NU omits *in an unworthy manner* [8] NU omits *Lord's*
30 [9] Are dead
31 [y] [Ps. 32:5; 1 John 1:9]
32 [z] 2 Sam. 7:14; Ps. 94:12; [Heb. 12:5-10; Rev. 3:19]
33 [a] 1 Cor. 14:26

CHAPTER 12 1 [a] 1 Cor. 12:4; 14:1, 37 2 [b] 1 Cor. 6:11; Eph. 2:11; 1 Pet. 4:3 [1] NU, M *that when*

11:17 worse. A comparative Gr. word which refers to moral evil.

11:18 divisions. The church was torn by dissension (see 1:10-17; 3:1-3).

11:19 approved…recognized. Factions revealed who passed the test of spiritual genuineness and purity (cf. 1 Thess. 2:4).

11:20 it is not to eat the Lord's Supper. The love feast and communion celebration had become so perverted that it was a sinful, selfish mockery. They could not legitimately say it was devoted to the Lord, since it was not honoring to Him.

11:21,22 If they intended to selfishly indulge themselves, they might as well have stayed at home.

11:23-26 While the information was not new to the Corinthians, because Paul had previously "delivered" it, it is an important reminder. This description of Christ's final supper with his disciples is one of the most beautiful in all of Scripture, yet it was given in the midst of a strong rebuke of carnal selfishness. If this letter was written before any of the gospels (see Matt. 26:26-30; Mark 14:22-26; Luke 22:17-20; John 13:2), as most conservative scholars believe, then Paul's instruction was the first biblical record of the institution of the Lord's Supper—given directly from the Lord and not through his reading of any other apostles (cf. Gal. 1:10-12).

11:24 broken. There is weak manuscript evidence for this word being included. See John 19:33,36.

11:25 new covenant in My blood. The Old Covenant was practiced repeatedly by the blood of animals offered by men; but the New Covenant has been ratified once and for all by the death of Christ (cf. Heb. 9:28). **in remembrance of Me.** Jesus transformed the third cup of the Passover into the cup of remembrance of His offering (*see note on 10:16*).

11:26 The gospel is presented through the service of communion as the elements are explained. They point to His physical incarnation, sacrificial death, resurrection, and coming kingdom.

11:27,29 in an unworthy manner. I.e., ritualistically, indifferently, with an unrepentant heart, a spirit of bitterness, or any other ungodly attitude.

11:27 guilty. To come to the Lord's Table clinging to one's sin does not only dishonor the ceremony, but it also dishonors His body and blood, treating lightly the gracious sacrifice of Christ for us. It is necessary to set all sin before the Lord (v. 28), then partake, so as not to mock the sacrifice for sin, by holding on to it.

11:29 judgment. I.e., chastisement. **not discerning the Lord's body.** When believers do not properly judge the holiness of the celebration of Communion, they treat with indifference the Lord Himself—His life, suffering, and death (cf. Acts 7:52; Heb. 6:6; 10:29).

11:30 sleep. I.e., are dead. *See note on 15:18.* The offense was so serious that God put the worst offenders to death, an extreme but effective form of church purification (cf. Luke 13:1-5; Acts 5:1-11; 1 John 5:16).

11:32 Believers are kept from being consigned to hell, not only by divine decree, but by divine intervention. The Lord chastens to drive His people back to righteous behavior and even sends death to some in the church (v. 30) to remove them before they could be condemned (cf. Jude 24).

11:34 There is no point in gathering together to sin and be chastened.

12:1–14:40 This section focuses on spiritual gifts in the church, dealing with a vital, but controversial subject. The false religion situation in Corinth caused counterfeit spiritual manifestations that had to be confronted. The church was being informed on this subject by Paul and its behavior would be regulated by the truth and the Spirit.

12:1 spiritual *gifts.* The NKJV translators italicized *"gifts"* to indi-

Gentiles, carried away to these [c]dumb[2]
idols, however you were led. **3** Therefore I
make known to you that no one speaking
by the Spirit of God calls Jesus [3]accursed,
and [d]no one can say that Jesus is Lord except by the Holy Spirit.
4 [e]There are [4]diversities of gifts, but [f]the
same Spirit. **5** [g]There are differences of
ministries, but the same Lord. **6** And there
are diversities of activities, but it is the
same God [h]who works [5]all in all. **7** But the
manifestation of the Spirit is given to each
one for the profit *of all:* **8** for to one is given
[i]the word of wisdom through the Spirit, to
another [j]the word of knowledge through
the same Spirit, **9** [k]to another faith by the
same Spirit, to another [l]gifts of healings by

2 [c] Ps. 115:5; Is. 46:7; Jer. 10:5; Hab. 2:18 [2] *mute, silent*
3 [d] Matt. 16:17 [3] Gr. *anathema*
4 [e] Rom. 12:3-8; 1 Cor. 12:11; Eph. 4:4, 11; Heb. 2:4 [f] Eph. 4:4 [4] *allotments* or *various kinds*
5 [g] Rom. 12:6
6 [h] 1 Cor. 15:28; Eph. 1:23; 4:6 [5] *all things in*
8 [i] 1 Cor. 2:6, 7; 2 Cor. 1:12 [j] Rom. 15:14; [1 Cor. 2:11, 16]; 2 Cor. 8:7
9 [k] Matt. 17:19; [1 Cor. 13:2]; 2 Cor. 4:13 [l] Matt. 10:1; Mark 3:15; 16:18; James 5:14

cate that the word is not in the original but is implied by the context (cf. vv. 4,9,28,30,31; 14:1). The Gr. lit. means "pertaining to the Spirit," referring to that which has spiritual qualities or characteristics or is under some form of spiritual control. Spiritual gifts are divine enablements for ministry that the Holy Spirit gives in some measure to all believers and that are to be completely under His control and used for the building of the church to Christ's glory (*see notes on Rom. 12:4-8*). These had to be distinguished from the mystical experiences called "ecstasy" (supernatural, sensuous communion with a deity) and "enthusiasm" (divination, dreams, revelations, visions) that were found in the pagan religions of Corinth.

12:2 Gentiles. That is, non-Christian pagans (1 Thess. 4:5; 1 Pet. 2:12). **carried away.** Incredibly, some church members were mimicking certain dramatic and bizarre practices of the mystery religions in which they had been formerly involved. The practice of ecstasy, considered to be the highest expression of religious experience, involved supposed supernatural interaction with a deity, induced through frenzied hypnotic chants and ceremonies. The practice frequently included drunkenness (cf. Eph. 5:18) and sexual orgies, to which the devotees willfully yielded themselves to be led into gross sin.

12:3 accursed. This is the most severe kind of condemnation. Some of the Corinthians were fleshly and given over to ecstasies that were controlled by demons. In that condition, they actually claimed to be prophesying or teaching in the Spirit while demonically blaspheming the name of the Lord whom they were supposed to be worshiping. They had been judging the use of gifts on the basis of experience and not content. Satan always assaults the person of Christ. It is possible that the curser of Christ was a Gentile claiming to be a Christian, but holding to a philosophy that all matter was evil, including the human Jesus (i.e., pre-gnosticism). They might have said that the Christ spirit left the human Jesus before His death, and therefore Jesus died a cursed death as a mere man. **Jesus is Lord.** Cf. Acts 2:36; Rom. 10:9,10; Eph. 1:20,21; Phil. 2:9-11. The validity of any speaking exercise is determined by the truthfulness of it. If the speaker affirms the lordship of Jesus, it is the truth from the Holy Spirit. What a person believes and says about Jesus Christ is the test of whether he speaks from the Holy Spirit. He always leads people to Christ's lordship (cf. 2:8-14; John 15:26; 1 John 5:6-8).

12:4 gifts. These categories of giftedness are not natural talents, skills, or abilities, such as are possessed by believers and unbelievers alike. They are sovereignly and supernaturally bestowed by the Holy Spirit on all believers (vv. 7,11), enabling them to spiritually edify each other effectively and thus honor the Lord. The varieties of gifts fall into two general types, speaking and serving (see vv. 8-10; cf. Rom. 12:6-8; 1 Pet. 4:10,11). The speaking, or verbal, gifts (prophecy, knowledge, wisdom, teaching, and exhortation) and the serving, nonverbal gifts (leadership, helps, giving, mercy, faith, and discernment) are all permanent gifts that will operate throughout the church age. Their purpose is to edify the church and glorify God. The list here and in Rom. 12:3-8 is best seen as representative of categories of giftedness which the Holy Spirit draws from to give each believer whatever kind or combination of kinds He chooses (v. 11). Some believers may be gifted categorically similar to others but are personally unique as the Spirit suits each grace gift to the individual. Miracles, healing, languages, and the interpretation of languages were temporary sign gifts limited to the apostolic age and have, therefore, ceased. Their purpose was to authenticate the apostles and their message as the true Word of God, until God's written Word was completed and became self-authenticating. *See notes on vv. 9,10.*

12:5,6 differences of ministries...diversities of activities. The Lord gives believers unique ministry arenas in which to fulfill their giftedness, and provides varieties of power to energize and accomplish them (cf. Rom. 12:6).

12:7 manifestation of the Spirit. No matter what the gift, ministry, or effect, all spiritual gifts are from the Holy Spirit. They make Him known, understood, and evident in the church and in the world, by spiritually profiting all who receive their ministry.

12:8 the word of wisdom. "Word" indicates a speaking gift (*see note on v. 4*; cf. 1 Pet. 4:11). In the NT, "wisdom" is most often used of the ability to understand God's Word and His will, and to skillfully apply that understanding to life (cf. Matt. 11:19; 13:54; Mark 6:2; Luke 7:35; Acts 6:10; James 1:5; 3:13,17; 2 Pet. 3:15). **the word of knowledge.** This gift may have been revelatory in the first century, but it is today the ability to understand and speak God's truth, with insight into the mysteries of His Word, that cannot be known apart from God's revelation (Rom. 16:25; Eph. 3:3; Col. 1:26; 2:2; 4:3; cf. 13:2). Knowledge majors on grasping the meaning of the truth; wisdom emphasizes the practical conviction and conduct that applies it.

12:9 faith. Distinct from saving faith or persevering faith, both of which all believers possess, this gift is exercised in persistent prayer and endurance in intercession, along with a strong trust in God in the midst of difficult circumstances (cf. Matt. 17:20). **healings.** A temporary sign gift used by Christ (Matt. 8:16,17), the apostles (Matt. 10:1), the seventy (Luke 10:1), and a few associates of the apostles, such as Philip (Acts 8:5-7). This ability was identified as a gift belonging to the apostles (cf. 2 Cor. 12:12). Although Christians today do not have the gift of healings, God certainly still hears and answers the faithful prayers of His children (see James 5:13-16). Some people feel that healing should be common and expected in every era, but this is not the case. Physical healings are very rare throughout the OT record. Only a few are recorded. There was never a time before the coming of Christ when healings were common. Only in His lifetime and that of His apostles was there a veritable explosion of healing. This was due to the unique need to accredit the Messiah and to authenticate the first miracles of the gospel. Jesus and His apostles temporarily banished disease from Palestine, but that was the most monumental era of redemptive history and called for such authentication. To normalize healing would be to normalize the arrival of the Savior. This gift belonged to the sign gifts for that era only. The gift of healings were never used solely for bringing people physical health. Paul was sick but never healed himself or asked another human to heal him. His friend Epaphroditus was near death (Phil. 2:27), and Paul did not heal him. God intervened. When Timothy was sick, Paul did not heal him, but told him to take some wine (1 Tim. 5:23). Paul left Trophimus "sick at Miletus" (2 Tim. 4:20). Healings were not the everyday norm in Paul's ministry, but did occur when he entered a new region, e.g., Malta, where the gospel and its preacher needed authentication (see Acts 28:8,9). That healing was the first mention of healing since the

[6]the same Spirit, 10 [m]to another the working of miracles, to another [n]prophecy, to
another [o]discerning of spirits, to another
[p]*different* kinds of tongues, to another the
interpretation of tongues. 11 But one and
the same Spirit works all these things, [q]dis-
tributing to each one individually [r]as He
wills.

Unity and Diversity in One Body

12 For [s]as the body is one and has many
members, but all the members of that one
body, being many, are one body, [t]so also *is*
Christ. 13 For [u]by one Spirit we were all
baptized into one body—[v]whether Jews or
Greeks, whether slaves or free—and [w]have
all been made to drink [7]into one Spirit.
14 For in fact the body is not one member
but many.
15 If the foot should say, "Because I am
not a hand, I am not of the body," is it
therefore not of the body? 16 And if the ear
should say, "Because I am not an eye, I am
not of the body," is it therefore not of the
body? 17 If the whole body *were* an eye,
where *would be* the hearing? If the whole

9 [6]NU *one*
10 [m]Mark 16:17 [n]Rom. 12:6 [o]1 John 4:1 [p]Acts 2:4-11
11 [q]Rom. 12:6; 2 Cor. 10:13 [r][John 3:8]
12 [s]Rom. 12:4,5; 1 Cor. 10:17; Eph. 4:4 [t][Gal. 3:16]
13 [u][Rom. 6:5] [v]Rom. 3:22; Gal. 3:28; [Eph. 2:13-18]; Col. 3:11 [w][John 7:37-39] [7]NU omits *into*

lame man was healed in Lystra (Acts 14:9) in connection with the arrival of Paul and the gospel there. Prior to that, the nearest healing was by Peter in Acts 9:34, and the resurrection of Tabitha in 9:41, so that people would believe the gospel Peter preached (9:42).

12:10 miracles. This temporary sign gift was for the working of divine acts contrary to nature, so that there was no explanation for the action except that it was by the power of God. This, too, was to authenticate Christ and the apostolic preachers of the gospel. John 2:11 notes that Jesus did His first miracle at Cana to "manifest His glory," not enhance the party (cf. John's purpose for recording the miracles of Jesus in this gospel, 20:30,31). Acts 2:22 affirms that Jesus did miracles to "attest" that God was working through Him, so that people would believe in Him as Lord and Savior. Jesus performed miracles and healed only for the 3 years of His ministry, not at all in the 30 years before. His miracles began when His ministry began. Though Jesus did miracles related to nature (made wine, created food, walked on water with Peter, ascended), no apostle ever is reported to have done a miracle in the natural realm. What miracle did the apostles do? The answer is in the word "miracles," meaning "power," and is frequently connected to casting out demons (Luke 4:36; 6:18; 9:42). It is precisely that power that the Lord gave the disciples (Luke 9:1; 10:17-19; cf. Acts 6:8; 8:7; 13:6-12). *See notes on Acts 19:14-16.* **prophecy.** The meaning is simply that of "speaking forth," or "proclaiming publicly" to which the connotation of prediction was added sometime in the Middle Ages. Since the completion of Scripture, prophecy has not been a means of new revelation, but is limited to proclaiming what has already been revealed in the written Word. Even the biblical prophets were preachers, proclaimers of God's truth both by revelation and reiteration. Old Testament prophets like Isaiah, Jeremiah, and Ezekiel spent lifetimes proclaiming God's Word. Only a comparatively small amount of what they preached is recorded in the Bible as God's direct revelation. They must have continually repeated and re-emphasized those truths, as preachers today repeat, explain, and re-emphasize the Word of God in Scripture. The best definition for this gift is given in 14:3. The importance of this gift is given in 14:1,39. Its supremacy to other gifts, especially tongues, is the theme of chap. 14. *See notes on 1 Thess. 5:20; Rev. 19:10.* **discerning of spirits.** Satan is the great deceiver (John 8:44) and his demons counterfeit God's message and work. Christians with the gift of discernment have the God-given ability to recognize lying spirits and to identify deceptive and erroneous doctrine (cf. Acts 17:11; 1 John 4:1). Paul illustrated the use of this gift in Acts 16:16-18, as Peter had exercised it in Acts 5:3. When it was not being exercised in the Corinthian church, grave distortion of the truth occurred (see v. 3; 14:29). Though its operation has changed since apostolic times, because of the completion of Scripture, it is still essential to have people in the church who are discerning. They are the guardians, the watchmen who protect the church from demonic lies, false doctrines, perverted cults, and fleshly elements. As it requires diligent study of the Word to exercise gifts of knowledge, wisdom, preaching, and teaching, so it does with discernment. *See notes on 1 Thess. 5:20-22; Acts 17:11.* **tongues...interpretation.** These temporary sign gifts, using the normal words for speaking a foreign language and translating it, like the others (miracles, healings) were for the authentication of the truth and those who preached it. This true gift was clearly identified in Acts 2:5-12 as languages, which validated the gospel as divine. They were, however, because of their counterfeit in the culture, disproportionately exalted and seriously abused in Corinth. Here, Paul identified them, but throughout chap. 14 he discussed them in detail. *See notes on 14:1-29.*

12:11 one and the same Spirit. While stressing the diversity of gifts (vv. 4-11), Paul also stressed the singular source in the Spirit (cf. vv. 4,5,6,8,9.) This is the fifth mention, in this chapter, of the source of gifts being the Holy Spirit. It emphasizes that gifts are not something to seek, but to be received from the Spirit "as He wills." It is He alone who "works" or energizes (v. 6) all gifts as He chooses.

12:12 body...members. Paul used the human body as an analogy (cf. 10:17) for the unity of the church in Christ. From this point on to v. 27, he used "body" 18 times (cf. Rom. 12:5; Eph. 1:23; 2:16; 4:4,12,16; Col. 1:18).

12:13 baptized. The church, the spiritual body of Christ, is formed as believers are immersed by Christ with the Holy Spirit. Christ is the baptizer (*see note on Matt. 3:11*) who immerses each believer with the Spirit into unity with all other believers. Paul is not writing of water baptism. That outward sign depicts the believer's union with Christ in His death and resurrection (*see notes on Rom. 6:3-5*). Similarly, all believers are also immersed into the body of Christ by means of the Holy Spirit. Paul's point is to emphasize the unity of believers. There cannot be any believer who has not been Spirit-baptized, nor can there be more than one Spirit baptism or the whole point of unity in the body of Christ is convoluted. Believers have all been Spirit-baptized and thus are all in one body. *See notes on Eph. 4:4-6.* This is not an experience to seek, but a reality to acknowledge. *See also notes on Acts 8:17; 10:44,45; 11:15-17.* **drink into one Spirit.** At salvation, all believers not only become full members of Christ's body, the church, but the Holy Spirit is placed within each of them (Rom. 8:9; cf. 6:19; Col. 2:10; 2 Pet. 1:3,4). There is no need (or divine provision) for any such thing as a second blessing, a triumphalistic experience of a deeper life, or a formula for instantly increased spirituality (cf. John 3:34). Christ's salvation provision is perfect and He calls only for obedience and trust in what has already been given (Heb. 10:14).

12:14-20 By his illustration of how every part of a human body is essential to the function of that body, Paul showed that unity is an indispensable need of the church; but divinely-provided diversity within that unity is also necessary. His words additionally implied that some selfish members were discontent with their gifts, wanting the gifts they had not been given (v. 11). With that attitude, they in effect questioned God's wisdom and implied He had made a mistake in assignments (cf. v. 3; Rom. 9:20,21). In seeking showy abilities and power, they also became vulnerable to carnal, demonically counterfeited gifts.

were hearing, where *would be* the smelling?
18 But now [x]God has set the members,
each one of them, in the body [y]just as He
pleased. **19** And if they *were* all one member, where *would* the body *be?*
20 But now indeed *there are* many members, yet one body. **21** And the eye cannot
say to the hand, "I have no need of you";
nor again the head to the feet, "I have no
need of you." **22** No, much rather, those
members of the body which seem to be
weaker are necessary. **23** And those *members* of the body which we think to be less
honorable, on these we bestow greater
honor; and our unpresentable *parts* have
greater modesty, **24** but our presentable
parts have no need. But God composed
the body, having given greater honor to
that *part* which lacks it, **25** that there
should be no [8]schism in the body, but *that*
the members should have the same care
for one another. **26** And if one member
suffers, all the members suffer with *it;* or
if one member is honored, all the members rejoice with *it.*
27 Now [z]you are the body of Christ, and
[a]members individually. **28** And [b]God has
appointed these in the church: first [c]apos-
tles, second [d]prophets, third teachers, after
that [e]miracles, then [f]gifts of healings,
[g]helps, [h]administrations, varieties of
tongues. **29** *Are* all apostles? *Are* all
prophets? *Are* all teachers? *Are* all workers
of miracles? **30** Do all have gifts of healings? Do all speak with tongues? Do all interpret? **31** But [i]earnestly desire the [9]best
gifts. And yet I show you a more excellent
way.

The Greatest Gift

13 Though I speak with the tongues of
men and of angels, but have not
love, I have become sounding brass or a
clanging cymbal. **2** And though I have *the*

18 [x] 1 Cor. 12:28 [y] Rom. 12:3
25 [8] *division*
27 [z] Rom. 12:5; Eph. 1:23; 4:12; 5:23, 30; Col. 1:24 [a] Eph. 5:30
28 [b] Eph. 4:11 [c] [Eph. 2:20; 3:5] [d] Acts 13:1; Rom. 12:6 [e] 1 Cor. 12:10, 29; Gal. 3:5 [f] Mark 16:18; 1 Cor. 12:9, 30 [g] Num. 11:17 [h] Rom. 12:8; 1 Tim. 5:17; Heb. 13:17, 24
31 [i] 1 Cor. 14:1, 39 [9] NU *greater*

12:18 Here again, as in v. 11, Paul dealt with the foolish and carnal Corinthians who were discontent with what had been given them sovereignly for the edification of the church and the glory of its Lord. *See note on v. 31.*

12:21 no need. While some in Corinth were bemoaning the fact that they did not have the showy gifts (*see note on vv. 14-20*), those who did were belittling those with the more quiet and less prominent gifts. The "eye" and the "head," which are highly visible and the focus of all who engage each other, represent the people with public gifts. They so overestimated their own importance that they disdained those whom they perceived as less gifted and less significant. They were apparently indifferent ("I have no need") and self-sufficient.

12:22-24 Paul's answer to the pride of the more visibly gifted was to engage his analogy again and remind them that the more fragile and less lovely, in fact, ugly parts of the body which are not publicly "presentable" (v. 24) are given the greater respect for their necessity. He spoke of the internal organs.

12:25 God has designed visible, public gifts to have a crucial place, but equally designed and more vital to life are the hidden gifts, thus maintaining the perspective of unity—all are essential to the working of the body of Christ.

12:26,27 This is a call to mutual love and concern in the fellowship of believers (cf. Phil. 2:1-4) which maintains the unity that honors the Lord. There is one body in which all function, yet never do they lose their personal identity and the essential necessity of ministry as God has designed them to do it.

12:28-30 God has appointed. Again emphasizing the sovereignty of God (cf. vv. 7,11,18), Paul illustrates the individuality and unity of the body by a repeat of the representative categories of ministries, callings, and giftedness.

12:28 apostles...prophets. *See notes on Eph. 4:11.* Their purpose was: 1) to lay the foundation of the church (Eph. 2:20); 2) to receive and declare the revelation of God's Word (Acts 11:28; 21:10,11; Eph. 3:5); and 3) to give confirmation of that Word through signs, wonders, and miracles (2 Cor. 12:12; cf. Acts 8:6,7; Heb. 2:3,4). "Apostles" refers, primarily, to those 12 chosen by our Lord plus Paul and Matthias (Acts 1:26). *See note on Rom. 1:1.* In a secondary sense, others served as messengers of the church: Barnabas (Acts 14:14) Silas and Timothy (1 Thess. 2:6) and others (Rom. 16:7; 2 Cor. 8:23; Phil. 2:25). Apostles of Christ were the source of the church's doctrine (Acts 2:42); apostles of the church (2 Cor. 8:23) were its early leaders. "Prophets" were specially gifted men in the local churches, who preached God's Word (Acts 11:21-28; 13:1). Any message preached by a prophet had to be judged by the word of the apostles (*see note on 14:36,37*). **teachers.** Could be the same as pastor-teachers (*see note on Eph. 4:11*), but probably should be broadened to include all who are gifted for teaching in the church, whether they have the office of pastor or not. **miracles...healings...tongues.** *See notes on vv. 9,10.* **helps, administration.** These less public gifts are mingled with the more public manifestations of the Spirit to show their vital necessity (v. 22). "Helps" is an ability for service; in fact, the gift of ministry ("service") in Rom. 12:7 is in the same category. "Administration" is leadership. The word comes from the Gr., meaning "to pilot a ship" (Acts 27:11) and speaks of one who can lead ministries of the church efficiently and effectively.

12:29,30 Each of these rhetorical queries expects a "no" answer. The body of Christ is diverse and God sovereignly designs it that way.

12:31 earnestly desire. In context, this could not mean that believers should desire the more prominent gifts, when the whole chapter has just been confronting the fact that they have sinfully been doing just that. Desiring a gift for selfish reasons is wrong, since they are sovereignly given by God as He wills (vv. 7,11,18,28). Therefore, this must be rendered not as an imperative (command), but, as the verb form allows, as an indicative (statement of fact), "You are desiring the showy gifts, wrongly." The real imperative is to stop doing that and learn the "more excellent way," the way of love, which Paul will explain in chap. 13.

13:1-13 Spiritual gifts were present in Corinth (1:7); right doctrine was even in place (11:2); but love was absent. This led to the quarrels and exhibitions of selfishness and pride that plagued the church—notably in the area of spiritual gifts (*see notes on 12:14-31*). Instead of selfishly and jealously desiring showy gifts which they don't have, believers should pursue the greatest thing of all—love for each other. This chapter is considered by many the greatest literary passage ever penned by Paul. It is central to his earnestly dealing with spiritual gifts (chaps. 12–14), because after discussing the endowment of gifts (chap. 12) and before presenting the function of gifts (chap. 14), he addresses the attitude necessary in all ministry in the church (chap. 13).

13:1 tongues of men. Cf. 12:10,28; 14:4-33. That this gift was actual languages is established in Acts 2:4-12 (*see notes there*), affirmed in this text by Paul's calling it "of men"—clearly a reference to human

gift of [a]prophecy, and understand all mysteries and all knowledge, and though I
have all faith, [b]so that I could remove
mountains, but have not love, I am nothing. 3 And [c]though I bestow all my goods
to feed *the poor,* and though I give my body
[1]to be burned, but have not love, it profits
me nothing.
4 [d]Love suffers long *and* is [e]kind; love
[f]does not envy; love does not parade itself,
is not [2]puffed up; 5 does not behave rudely, [g]does not seek its own, is not provoked,
[3]thinks no evil; 6 [h]does not rejoice in iniquity, but [i]rejoices in the truth; 7 [j]bears all
things, believes all things, hopes all things,
endures all things.
8 Love never fails. But whether *there are*
prophecies, they will fail; whether *there are*
tongues, they will cease; whether *there is*
knowledge, it will vanish away. 9 [k]For we
know in part and we prophesy in part.
10 But when that which is [4]perfect has come,
then that which is in part will be done away.
11 When I was a child, I spoke as a child,
I understood as a child, I thought as a
child; but when I became a man, I put
away childish things. 12 For [l]now we see in
a mirror, dimly, but then [m]face to face.
Now I know in part, but then I shall know
just as I also am known.
13 And now abide faith, hope, love,
these three; but the greatest of these *is* love.

CHAPTER 13

2 [a] Matt. 7:22; 1 Cor. 12:8-10, 28; 14:1 [b] Matt. 17:20; 21:21; Mark 11:23; Luke 17:6
3 [c] Matt. 6:1, 2 [1] NU *so I may boast*
4 [d] Prov. 10:12; 17:9; 1 Thess. 5:14; [1 Pet. 4:8] [e] Eph. 4:32 [f] Gal. 5:26 [2] *arrogant*
5 [g] 1 Cor. 10:24; Phil. 2:4 [3] *keeps no accounts of evil*
6 [h] Ps. 10:3; Rom. 1:32 [i] 2 John 4; 3 John 3
7 [j] Rom. 15:1; Gal. 6:2; 2 Tim. 2:24
9 [k] 1 Cor. 8:2; 13:12
10 [4] *complete*
12 [l] [2 Cor. 3:18; 5:7]; Phil. 3:12; James 1:23 [m] Gen. 32:30; Num. 12:8; Matt. 18:10; [1 John 3:2]

language. This was the gift which the Corinthians prized so highly, abused so greatly, and counterfeited so disastrously. God gave the ability to speak in a language not known to the speaker, as a sign with limited function (*see notes on 14:1-33*). **tongues...of angels.** The apostle was writing in general hypothetical terms. There is no biblical teaching of any special angelic language that people could learn to speak. **love.** Self-giving love that is more concerned with giving than receiving (John 3:16; cf. 14:1; Matt. 5:44,45; John 13:1,34,35; 15:9; Rom. 5:10; Eph. 2:4-7; Phil. 2:2; Col. 3:14; Heb. 10:24). The word was not admired and thus seldom used in ancient Gr. literature, but it is common in the NT. Without love, no matter how linguistically gifted one is to speak his own language, other languages, or even (hypothetically) the speech of angels, his speech is noise only. In NT times, rites honoring the pagan deities Cybele, Bacchus, and Dionysius included ecstatic noises accompanied by gongs, cymbals, and trumpets. Unless the speech of the Corinthians was done in love, it was no better than the gibberish of pagan ritual.

13:2 *the gift of* prophecy. *See notes on 12:10.* In 14:1-5, Paul speaks of this gift as the most essential one because it brings God's truth to people. Even this gift must be ministered in love (cf. Eph. 4:15). **understand all mysteries and all knowledge.** This encompasses gifts of wisdom, knowledge, and discernment (*see notes on 12:8,10*), which are to be exercised in love (see Phil. 1:9). **all faith.** *See note on Matt. 17:20.* This refers to the gift of faith (enduring, believing prayer; *see note on 12:9*), which is useless without selfless love for the church.

13:3 burned. The practice of burning Christians at the stake did not begin until some years later, but it was clearly understood to be an extremely horrible death. Neither volunteering for giving up all your possessions or being burned would produce any spiritual benefit if not done out of love for the body of Christ.

13:4-7 In the previous comments (vv. 1-3), the focus is on the emptiness produced when love is absent from ministry. In these verses, the fullness of love is described, in each case by what love does. Love is action, not abstraction. Positively, love is patient with people and gracious to them with generosity. Negatively, love never envies, or brags, or is arrogant, since that is the opposite of selfless service to others. Never rude or overbearing, love never wants its own way, is not irritated or angered in personal offense, and finds no pleasure in someone else's sin, even the sin of an enemy. On the positive side again, love is devoted to truth in everything. With regard to "all things" within God's righteous and gracious will, love protects, believes, hopes, and endures what others reject.

13:8-10 never fails. This refers to love's lastingness or permanence as a divine quality. Love outlasts all failures (cf. 1 Pet. 4:8; 1 John 4:16). Paul strengthens his point on the permanence of love by comparing it to the spiritual gifts which the Corinthians so highly prized: prophecy, knowledge, and languages, all of which will have an end. There may be a distinction made on how prophecy and knowledge come to an end, and how the gift of languages does. This is indicated by the Gr. verb forms used. In the case of prophecy and knowledge, they are both said to "be abolished" (in both cases the verb indicates that something will put an end to those two functions. Verses 9,10 indicate that what will abolish knowledge and prophecy is "that which is perfect." When that occurs, those gifts will be rendered inoperative. The "perfect" is not the completion of Scripture, since there is still the operation of those two gifts and will be in the future kingdom (cf. Joel 2:28; Acts 2:17; Rev. 11:3). The Scriptures do not allow us to see "face to face" or have perfect knowledge as God does (v. 12). The "perfect" is not the rapture of the church or the second coming of Christ, since the kingdom to follow these events will have an abundance of preachers and teachers (cf. Is. 29:18; 32:3,4; Joel 2:28; Rev. 11:3). The perfect must be the eternal state, when we in glory see God face to face (Rev. 22:4) and have full knowledge in the eternal new heavens and new earth. Just as a child grows to full understanding, believers will come to perfect knowledge and no such gifts will be necessary.

On the other hand, Paul uses a different word for the end of the gift of languages, thus indicating it will "cease" by itself, as it did at the end of the apostolic age. It will not end by the coming of the "perfect," for it will already have ceased. The uniqueness of the gift of languages and its interpretations was, as all sign gifts, to authenticate the message and messages of the gospel before the NT was completed (Heb. 2:3,4). "Tongues" was also limited by being a judicial sign from the God of Israel's judgment (*see note on 14:21*; cf. Is. 28:11,12). "Tongues" were also not a sign to believers, but unbelievers (*see note on 14:22*), specifically those unbelieving Jews. Tongues also ceased because there was no need to verify the true messages from God once the Scripture was given. It became the standard by which all are to be deemed true. "Tongues" was a means of edification in a way far inferior to preaching and teaching (*see notes on 14:5,12,13,27,28*). In fact, chap. 14 was designed to show the Corinthians, so preoccupied with tongues, that it was an inferior means of communication (vv. 1-12), an inferior means of praise (vv. 13-19), and an inferior means of evangelism (vv. 20-25). Prophecy was and is, far superior (vv. 1,3-6,24,29,31,39). That tongues have ceased should be clear from their absence from any other books in the NT, except Acts. Tongues ceased to be an issue of record or practice in the early church, as the Scripture was being written. That tongues has ceased should be clear also from its absence through church history since the first century, appearing only sporadically and then only in questionable groups. A more detailed discussion is given in the notes on chap. 14.

13:13 love. The objects of faith and hope will be fulfilled and perfectly realized in heaven, but love, the God-like virtue, is everlasting (cf. 1 John 4:8). Heaven will be the place for the expression of nothing but perfect love toward God and each other.

Prophecy and Tongues

14 Pursue love, and [a]desire spiritual
gifts, [b]but especially that you may
prophesy. 2 For he who [c]speaks in a tongue
does not speak to men but to God, for no
one understands *him;* however, in the spirit he speaks mysteries. 3 But he who
prophesies speaks [d]edification and [e]exhor-
tation and comfort to men. 4 He who
speaks in a tongue edifies himself, but he
who prophesies edifies the church. 5 I wish
you all spoke with tongues, but even more
that you prophesied; [1]for he who prophesies *is* greater than he who speaks with
tongues, unless indeed he interprets, that
the church may receive edification.

CHAPTER 14

1 [a] 1 Cor. 12:31; 14:39 [b] Num. 11:25, 29
2 [c] Acts 2:4; 10:46
3 [d] Rom. 14:19; 15:2; 2 Cor. 10:8; 12:19; Eph. 4:12, 29 [e] 1 Tim. 4:13; 2 Tim. 4:2; Titus 1:9; 2:15; Heb. 3:13; 10:25
5 [1] NU *and*
6 [f] 1 Cor. 14:26; Eph. 1:17

Tongues Must Be Interpreted

6 But now, brethren, if I come to you
speaking with tongues, what shall I profit
you unless I speak to you either by [f]revela-
tion, by knowledge, by prophesying, or by
teaching? 7 Even things without life,
whether flute or harp, when they make a
sound, unless they make a distinction in
the sounds, how will it be known what is
piped or played? 8 For if the trumpet
makes an uncertain sound, who will prepare for battle? 9 So likewise you, unless
you utter by the tongue words easy to understand, how will it be known what is
spoken? For you will be speaking into the
air. 10 There are, it may be, so many kinds

14:1 Pursue love. A command for every believer. Because lovelessness was a root spiritual problem in the Corinthian church, the godly love just described should have been sought after by them with particular determination and diligence. **desire spiritual *gifts.*** Love does not preclude the use of these enablements. Since Paul has addressed not desiring showy gifts (12:31) and not elevating one over the other (12:14-25), some might think it best to set them all aside for unity's sake. Spiritual gifts, on the other hand, are sovereignly bestowed by God on each believer and necessary for the building of the church (12:1-10). Desire for them, in this context, is in reference to their use collectively and faithfully in His service—not a personal yearning to have an admired gift that one did not possess. As a congregation, the Corinthians should be wanting the full expression of all the gifts to be exercised. "You" is plural, emphasizing the corporate desire of the church. **especially...prophesy.** This spiritual gift was desirable in the life of the church to serve in a way that tongues cannot, namely, by edifying the entire church (v. 5).

14:2-39 Although it is not indicated consistently in some translations, the distinction between the singular *tongue* and the plural *tongues* is foundational to the proper interpretation of this chapter. Paul seems to use the singular to distinguish the counterfeit gift of pagan gibberish and the plural to indicate the genuine gift of a foreign language (*see note on v. 2*). It was perhaps in recognition of that, that the King James Version (KJV) translators added consistently the word "unknown" before every singular form (see vv. 2,4,13,14,19,27). The implications of that distinction will be noted as appropriate. Against the backdrop of carnality and counterfeit ecstatic speech learned from the experience of the pagans, Paul covers 3 basic issues with regard to speaking in languages by the gift of the Holy Spirit: 1) its position, inferior to prophecy (vv. 1-19); 2) its purpose, a sign to unbelievers not believers (vv. 20-25); and 3) its procedure, systematic, limited, and orderly (vv. 26-40).

14:2 he who speaks in a tongue. This is singular (*see previous note*; cf. vv. 4,13,14,19,27), indicating that it refers to the false gibberish of the counterfeit pagan ecstatic speech. The singular is used because gibberish can't be plural; there are not various kinds of non-language. There are, however, various languages; hence when speaking of the true gift of language, Paul uses the plural to make the distinction (vv. 6,18,22,23,29). The only exception is in vv. 27,28 (*see note there*), where it refers to a single person speaking a single genuine language. **no one understands *him;*...in the spirit he speaks mysteries.** The carnal Corinthians using the counterfeit ecstatic speech of paganism were not interested in being understood, but in making a dramatic display. The spirit by which they spoke was not the Holy Spirit, but their own human spirit or some demon; and the mysteries they declared were the type associated with the pagan mystery religions, which was espoused to be the depths that only the initiated few were privileged to know and understand. Those mysteries were totally unlike the ones mentioned in Scripture (e.g., Matt. 13:11; Eph. 3:9), which are divine revelations of truths previously hidden (*see notes on 12:7; Eph. 3:3-6*). **does not speak to men but to God.** This is better translated, "to a god." The Gr. text has no definite article (see similar translation in Acts 17:23, "an unknown god"). Their gibberish was worship of pagan deities. The Bible records no incident of any believer ever speaking to God in any other than normal human language.

14:3 prophesies. In dramatic contrast to the bedlam of counterfeit tongues was the gift of genuine prophesy or preaching of the truth (*see note on 12:10*). It produced the building up in truth, the encouragement to obedience, and the comfort in trouble that God desired for His church. Spiritual gifts are always for the benefit of others, never self.

14:4 a tongue. Again (as in v. 2), Paul uses the singular to refer to the pagan counterfeit gibberish and sarcastically (cf. v. 16; 4:8-10 for other sarcasm) marks its selfishness as some kind of self-edification. This illicit building up of self comes from pride-induced emotion which only produces more pride. **edifies the church.** *See note on 12:7.*

14:5 all spoke with tongues...that you prophesied. Here the plural, "tongues," appears as Paul was referring to the real gift of languages (*see note on v. 2*). Obviously this was not Paul's true desire, even for the true gift, since the very idea was impossible and contrary to God's sovereign distribution of gifts (12:11,30). He was simply suggesting hypothetically that, if they insisted on clamoring after gifts they did not possess, they at least should seek the one that was more enduring and more valuable for the church. The only purpose tongues renders to the church is when it is interpreted (the normal Gr. word for translation). Wherever God gave the gift of languages, He also gave the gift for translation, so that the sign would also be edifying. Never was the gift to be used without such translation (v. 28), so that the church would always be edified.

14:6 if I come to you...what shall I profit? Even an apostle who spoke in tongues did not spiritually benefit a congregation unless, through interpretation, his utterance was clarified so that the revelation and knowledge could be understandably preached and taught. Any private use of this gift is excluded for several reasons: 1) it is a sign to unbelievers (v. 22); 2) it must have a translator to have any meaning, even to the speaker (v. 2); and 3) it must edify the church (v. 6).

14:7-9 Here, Paul illustrates his previous point about the uselessness of even the true gift apart from translation for the church to understand. If even inanimate musical instruments are expected to make sensible sounds, how much more should human speech make sense, especially when it deals with the things of God? *See note on v. 23.*

of languages in the world, and none of
them *is* without [2]significance. 11 Therefore,
if I do not know the meaning of the language, I shall be a [3]foreigner to him who
speaks, and he who speaks *will be* a foreigner to me. 12 Even so you, since you are
[4]zealous for spiritual *gifts, let it be* for the
[5]edification of the church *that* you seek to
excel.
13 Therefore let him who speaks in a
tongue pray that he may [g]interpret. 14 For
if I pray in a tongue, my spirit prays, but
my understanding is unfruitful. 15 What is
the conclusion then? I will pray with the
spirit, and I will also pray with the understanding. [h]I will sing with the spirit, and I
will also sing [i]with the understanding.
16 Otherwise, if you bless with the spirit,
how will he who occupies the place of the
uninformed say "Amen" [j]at your giving of
thanks, since he does not understand what
you say? 17 For you indeed give thanks
well, but the other is not edified.

10 [2]*meaning*
11 [3]Lit. *barbarian*
12 [4]*eager* [5]*building up*
13 [g]1 Cor. 12:10
15 [h]Eph. 5:19; Col. 3:16 [i]Ps. 47:7
16 [j]Deut. 27:15-26; 1 Chr. 16:36; Neh. 5:13; 8:6; Ps. 106:48; Jer. 11:5; 28:6; 1 Cor. 11:24; Rev. 5:14; 7:12

20 [k]Ps. 131:2; [Matt. 11:25; 18:3; 19:14]; Rom. 16:19; 1 Cor. 3:1; Eph. 4:14; Heb. 5:12, 13 [l][Matt. 18:3; 1 Pet. 2:2]
21 [m]John 10:34; 1 Cor. 14:34 [n]Is. 28:11, 12
22 [o]Mark 16:17

18 I thank my God I speak with tongues
more than you all; 19 yet in the church I
would rather speak five words with my
understanding, that I may teach others
also, than ten thousand words in a
tongue.

Tongues a Sign to Unbelievers

20 Brethren, [k]do not be children in understanding; however, in malice [l]be babes,
but in understanding be mature.
21 [m]In the law it is written:

[n]*"With men of other tongues and other lips*
I will speak to this people;
And yet, for all that, they will not hear Me,"

says the Lord.
22 Therefore tongues are for a [o]sign, not
to those who believe but to unbelievers;
but prophesying is not for unbelievers but

14:10,11 Paul simply points up the obvious: the purpose of *every* language is to communicate, not to impress and certainly not to confuse, as the Corinthians had been doing with their counterfeits. That was clearly the point in the first instance of tongues: Each heard the apostles speak in his own language (Acts 2:6, cf. v. 8). This section makes an undeniable case for the fact that the true gift of tongues was never some unintelligible gibberish, but was human language that was to be translated (v. 13).

14:12 Again Paul returned to the issue of edification, central to all gifts (12:7).

14:14-17 Paul continued to speak sarcastically (cf. v. 16; 4:8-10) about counterfeit tongues, so he used the singular "tongue" (*see note on vv. 2-39*), which refers to the fake gift. He was speaking hypothetically to illustrate the foolishness and pointlessness of speaking in ecstatic gibberish. The speaker could not understand, and what virtue is there in praying to God or praising God without understanding? No one can "Amen" such nonsense.

14:16 uninformed. From the Gr. word meaning ignorant or unlearned.

14:18 I speak with tongues more than you all. Paul emphasized that by writing all of this, he was not condemning genuine tongues (plural); nor, as some may have thought to accuse him, was he envious of a gift he did not possess. At that point, he stopped speaking hypothetically about counterfeit tongue-speaking. He actually had more occasions to use the true gift than all of them (though we have no record of a specific instance). He knew the true gift and had used it properly. It is interesting, however, that the NT makes no mention of Paul's actually exercising that gift. Nor does Paul in his own writings make mention of a *specific* use of it by *any* Christian.

14:19 teach others. This is the general principle that summarizes what he has been saying, i.e., teaching others is the important matter and that requires understanding.

14:20-25 This very important passage deals with the primary purpose of the gift of languages. Paul has clearly indicated that such speaking was not something for all believers to do, since it was dispensed sovereignly like all other gifts (12:11); nor was it connected to the baptism with the Holy Spirit which all believers receive (12:13); nor was it some superior sign of spirituality, but rather an inferior gift (v. 5). Because of all that, and the corruption of the real gift by the Corinthians, the apostle gives the principles for its proper and limited operation as a sign.

14:20 in malice be babes, but in understanding be mature. Most of the Corinthian believers were the opposite of what Paul here admonished. They were extremely experienced in evil, but greatly lacking in wisdom. Yet mature understanding was especially essential for proper comprehension and use of the gift of tongues, because the conspicuous and fascinating nature of that gift made it so attractive to the flesh. He was asking his readers to put aside emotion and experience, along with the desires of the flesh and pride, to think carefully about the purpose of tongues.

14:21 it is written. In a freely rendered quotation from Is. 28:11,12, Paul explains that centuries earlier the Lord had predicted that one day He would use men of other tongues, that is, foreigners speaking unknown languages, as a sign to *unbelieving Israel,* who "will not hear Me." These "other tongues" are what they knew as the gift of languages, given solely as a sign to unbelieving Israel. That sign was 3-fold: cursing, blessing, and authority. To emphasize the cursing, Paul quoted Isaiah's words of warning to Judah of the judgment from Assyria (*see note on Is. 28:11,12*). The leaders thought his words were too simple and rejected him. The time would come, the prophet said, when they would hear Assyrian, a language they could not understand, indicating judgment. Jeremiah spoke similarly of the Babylonians who were also to come and destroy Judah (cf. Jer. 5:15). When the apostles spoke at Pentecost in all those foreign languages (Acts 2:3-12), the Jews should have known that the judgment prophesied and historically fulfilled first by the Assyrians and then by the Babylonian captivity was about to fall on them again for their rejection of Christ, including the destruction of Jerusalem (A.D. 70) as it had happened in 586 B.C. under Babylonian power.

14:22 Therefore tongues are for a sign, not to those who believe but to unbelievers. Explaining further, he says explicitly that all tongues are for the sake of unbelievers. In other words, that gift has no purpose in the church when everyone present is a believer. And once the sign served its purpose to pronounce judgment or cursing on Israel, and the judgment fell, the purpose ceased along with the sign gift. The blessing of that sign was that God would build a new nation of Jews and Gentiles to be his people (Gal. 3:28), to make Israel jealous and someday repent (see Rom. 11:11,12,25-27). The sign was thus repeated when Gentiles were included in the

for those who believe. **23** Therefore if the
whole church comes together in one place,
and all speak with tongues, and there
come in *those who are* uninformed or unbelievers, [p]will they not say that you are [6]out
of your mind? **24** But if all prophesy, and
an unbeliever or an uninformed person
comes in, he is convinced by all, he is convicted by all. **25** [7]And thus the secrets of his
heart are revealed; and so, falling down on
his face, he will worship God and report
[q]that God is truly among you.

Order in Church Meetings

26 How is it then, brethren? Whenever
you come together, each of you has a
psalm, [r]has a teaching, has a tongue, has a
revelation, has an interpretation. [s]Let all
things be done for [8]edification. **27** If anyone speaks in a tongue, *let there be* two or at
the most three, *each* in turn, and let one in-

23 [p] Acts 2:13 [6] *insane*
25 [q] Is. 45:14; Dan. 2:47; Zech. 8:23; Acts 4:13 [7] NU omits *And thus*
26 [r] 1 Cor. 12:8-10; 14:6 [s] 1 Cor. 12:7; [2 Cor. 12:19] [8] *building up*
29 [t] 1 Cor. 12:10
30 [u] [1 Thess. 5:19, 20]
32 [v] 1 John 4:1
33 [w] 1 Cor. 11:16 [9] *disorder*
34 [x] 1 Tim. 2:11; 1 Pet. 3:1 [y] Gen. 3:16 [1] NU omits *your*

terpret. **28** But if there is no interpreter, let
him keep silent in church, and let him
speak to himself and to God. **29** Let two or
three prophets speak, and [t]let the others
judge. **30** But if *anything* is revealed to another who sits by, [u]let the first keep silent.
31 For you can all prophesy one by one,
that all may learn and all may be encouraged. **32** And [v]the spirits of the prophets
are subject to the prophets. **33** For God is
not *the author* of [9]confusion but of peace,
[w]as in all the churches of the saints.

34 [x]Let [1]your women keep silent in the
churches, for they are not permitted to
speak; but *they are* to be submissive, as the
[y]law also says. **35** And if they want to learn
something, let them ask their own husbands at home; for it is shameful for
women to speak in church.

36 Or did the word of God come *original-*
ly from you? Or *was it* you only that it

---

church (Acts 10:44-46). The sign also gave authority to those who preached both the judgment and blessing (2 Cor. 12:12), including Paul (v. 18). **but prophesying is…for those who believe.** In the completely opposite way, the gift of prophesying benefits only believers, who are able, by their new natures and the indwelling Holy Spirit, to understand spiritual truth (cf. 2:14; 1 John 2:20,27).

14:23 Therefore if…all speak with tongues. As Paul explains in more detail later (vv. 27,28), even for unbelievers, even when the gift of tongues was exercised in its proper time in history, when it was dominant and uncontrolled in the church, bedlam ensued and the gospel was disgraced and discredited. **out of your mind.** The Gr. word means to be in an uncontrolled frenzy. When the real gift was used in Acts 2, there was no madness, and everyone understood in his own language (v. 11). In Corinth, there was charismatic chaos.

14:24,25 But if all prophesy. This means to publicly proclaim the Word of God (*see note on 2:10*). "All" does not mean all at once (see v. 31), but rather means that hypothetically if the cacophony of all the Corinthians could be replaced by all of them preaching the Word, the effect on unbelievers would be amazingly powerful, the gospel would be honored, and souls would be converted to worshiping God.

14:26-40 In this last section on the topic of tongues, the stress is on how they were to be systematically limited for use in the church in an orderly way. For the sake of hypothetical discussion, it is noteworthy that even if one granted that the gift was still in use today, the modern movement would be totally discredited as illegitimate by its failure to follow the clear, controlling commands in these verses.

14:26 each of you has. It seems that chaos and lack of order was rampant in that assembly (v. 33). It is interesting that no elders or pastors are mentioned, and the prophets were not even exercising control (see vv. 29,32,37). Everyone was participating with whatever expression they desired "whenever" they desired. **a psalm.** The reading or singing of an OT psalm. **a teaching.** This probably refers to a doctrine or subject of special interest (v. 33). **a tongue.** In the singular, this refers to the counterfeit. *See note on vv. 2-39.* **a revelation.** Some supposed word from God, whether spurious or genuine. **an interpretation.** This refers to that of a tongue's message. **for edification.** This was Paul's way of calling a halt to the chaos. Edification is the goal, (cf. vv. 3-5,12,17,26,31) and the Corinthian chaos could not realize it (cf. 1 Thess. 5:11; Rom. 15:2,3).

14:27,28 These verses provide regulations for the exercise of the gift: 1) only two or three persons in a service; 2) only speaking in turn, one at a time; and 3) only with an interpreter. Without those conditions, one was to meditate and pray silently.

14:29-31 Since Paul's pastoral epistles (1, 2 Tim.; Titus) do not mention prophets, it seems evident that this unique office had ceased to function in the church even before the end of the apostolic age. When Paul wrote the Corinthians, however, prophets were still central to the work of that church (cf. Acts 13:1). Here he gave 4 regulations for their preaching: 1) only two or three were to speak; 2) the other prophets were to judge what was said; 3) if while one was speaking, God gave a revelation, the speaker was to defer to the one hearing from God; and 4) each prophet was to speak in turn. *See notes on Eph. 2:20; 4:11.*

14:32 Not only were the prophets to judge others with discernment, but they were also to have control over themselves. God does not desire out-of-spirit or out-of-mind experiences. Those who received and proclaimed the truth were to have clear minds. There was nothing bizarre, ecstatic, trance-like, or wild about receiving and preaching God's Word, as with demonic experiences.

14:33 confusion. Here is the key to the whole chapter. The church at worship before God should reflect His character and nature because He is a God of peace and harmony, order and clarity, not strife and confusion (cf. Rom. 15:33; 2 Thess. 3:16; Heb. 13:20). **as in all the churches.** This phrase does not belong in v. 33, but at the beginning of v. 34, as a logical introduction to a universal principle for churches.

14:34,35 women keep silent in the churches. The principle of women not speaking in church services is universal; this applies to all the churches, not just locally, geographically, or culturally. The context in this verse concerns prophecy, but includes the general theme of the chapter, i.e., tongues. Rather than leading, they are to be submissive as God's Word makes clear (*see notes on 11:3-15; Gen. 3:16; 1 Tim. 2:11-15*). It is not coincidental that many modern churches that have tongues-speaking and claim gifts of healings and miracles also permit women to lead worship, preach, and teach. Women may be gifted teachers, but they are not permitted by God "to speak" in churches. In fact, for them to do so is "shameful," meaning "disgraceful." Apparently, certain women were out of order in disruptively asking questions publicly in the chaotic services.

14:36,37 Paul knew that the Corinthians would react to all these firm regulations that would end the free-for-all in their services. The prophets, tongues-speakers, and women may all have been resistant to words, so he anticipated that resistance by sarcastically challenging those who put themselves above his word, and thus, above Scripture by either ignoring it or interpreting it to fit their predisposed

reached? 37 [z]If anyone thinks himself to be
a prophet or spiritual, let him acknowledge that the things which I write to you
are the commandments of the Lord. 38 But
[2]if anyone is ignorant, let him be ignorant.
39 Therefore, brethren, [a]desire earnestly
to prophesy, and do not forbid to speak
with tongues. 40 [b]Let all things be done decently and in order.

The Risen Christ, Faith's Reality

15 Moreover, brethren, I declare to you
the gospel [a]which I preached to
you, which also you received and [b]in
which you stand, 2 [c]by which also you are
saved, if you hold fast that word which I
preached to you—unless [d]you believed in
vain.
3 For [e]I delivered to you first of all that
[f]which I also received: that Christ died for
our sins [g]according to the Scriptures,
4 and that He was buried, and that He rose
again the third day [h]according to the
Scriptures, 5 [i]and that He was seen by
[1]Cephas, then [j]by the twelve. 6 After that

37 [z] 2 Cor. 10:7; [1 John 4:6]
38 [2] NU *if anyone does not recognize this, he is not recognized.*
39 [a] 1 Cor. 12:31; 1 Thess. 5:20
40 [b] 1 Cor. 14:33

CHAPTER 15

1 [a] Rom. 2:16; [Gal. 1:11] [b] [Rom. 5:2; 11:20; 2 Cor. 1:24]
2 [c] Rom. 1:16; 1 Cor. 1:21 [d] Gal. 3:4
3 [e] 1 Cor. 11:2, 23 [f] [Gal. 1:12] [g] Ps. 22:15; Is. 53:5-12; Acts 3:18; 1 Pet. 1:11
4 [h] Gen. 1:9-13; 2 Kin. 20:8; Ps. 16:9-11; 68:18; 110:1; Is. 53:10; Hos. 6:2; Jon. 1:17; 2:10; Matt. 12:39, 40; Mark 8:31; Luke 11:29, 30; 24:26; John 2:19-21; Acts 2:25
5 [i] Luke 24:34 [j] Matt. 28:17 [1] Peter

ideas. If anyone was genuinely a prophet or had the true spiritual gift of tongues, he or she would submit to the principles God had revealed through the apostle.

14:36 did the word of God come...from you? *See notes on 1 Thess. 2:13; 2 Tim. 3:15-17; 2 Pet. 1:19-21.*

14:38 ignorant. That is, anyone who does not recognize the authority of Paul's teaching should himself not be recognized as a legitimate servant gifted by God.

14:39 do not forbid...tongues. Legitimate languages were limited in purpose and in duration, but as long as it was still active in the early church, it was not to be hindered. But prophecy was the most desirable gift to be exercised because of its ability to edify, exhort, and comfort with the truth (v. 3).

14:40 *See notes on v. 33.*

15:1-58 This chapter is the most extensive treatment of resurrection in the Bible. Both the resurrection of Jesus Christ as recorded in the gospels and the resurrection of believers as promised in the gospels are here explained.

15:1-11 To begin his teachings about the resurrection of believers, Paul reviewed the evidences for Jesus' resurrection: 1) the church (vv. 1,2); 2) the Scriptures (vv. 3,4); 3) the eyewitnesses (vv. 5-7); 4) the apostle himself (vv. 8-10); and 5) the common message (v. 11).

15:1,2 preached...received...stand. This was not a new message. They had heard of the resurrection, believed in it, and had been saved by it.

15:2 unless you believed in vain. By this qualifying statement, Paul recognized and called to their attention that some may have had a shallow, non-saving faith (*see notes on Matt. 7:13,14,22-27; 13:24-30,34-43,47-50; 25:1-30*). Some believed only as the demons believed (James 2:19), i.e., they were convinced the gospel was true, but had no love for God, Christ, and righteousness. True believers "hold fast" to the gospel (cf. John 8:31; 2 Cor. 13:5; 1 John 2:24; 2 John 9).

15:3,4 according to the Scriptures. The OT spoke of the suffering and resurrection of Christ (*see Luke 24:25-27; Acts 2:25-31; 26:22,23*). Jesus, Peter, and Paul quoted or referred to such OT passages regarding the work of Christ as Pss. 16:8-11; 22; Is. 53.

15:5-7 The testimony of eyewitnesses, recorded in the NT, was added to support the reality of the resurrection. These included: 1) John and Peter together (John 20:19,20), but probably also separately before (Luke 24:34); 2) the 12 (John 20:19,20; Luke 24:36; Acts 1:22); 3) the 500, only referred to here (*see note on 2 Pet. 3:15,16*), had

Appearances of the Risen Christ

Central to Christian faith is the bodily resurrection of Jesus. By recording the resurrection appearances, the New Testament leaves no doubt about this event.

- In or around Jerusalem
  - To Mary Magdalene (John 20:11-18)
  - To the other women (Matt. 28:8-10)
  - To Peter (Luke 24:34)
  - To ten disciples (Luke 24:36-43; John 20:19-25)
  - To the Eleven, including Thomas (John 20:26-29)
  - At His ascension (Luke 24:50-53; Acts 1:4-12)
- To the disciples on the Emmaus road (Luke 24:13-35)
- In Galilee (Matt. 28:16-20; John 21:1-24)
- To five hundred people (1 Cor. 15:6)
- To James and the apostles (1 Cor. 15:6)
- To Paul on the road to Damascus (Acts 9:1-6; 18:9,10; 22:1-8; 23:11; 26:12-18; 1 Cor. 15:8)

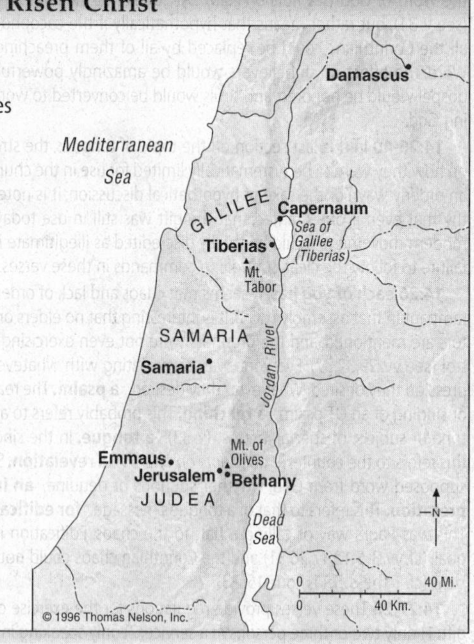

He was seen by over five hundred
brethren at once, of whom the greater part
remain to the present, but some have [2]fall-
en asleep. 7 After that He was seen by
James, then [k]by all the apostles. 8 [l]Then
last of all He was seen by me also, as by
one born out of due time.

9 For I am [m]the least of the apostles,
who am not worthy to be called an apostle, because [n]I persecuted the church of
God. 10 But [o]by the grace of God I am
what I am, and His grace toward me was
not in vain; but I labored more abundantly than they all, [p]yet not I, but the grace of
God *which was* with me. 11 Therefore,
whether *it was* I or they, so we preach and
so you believed.

The Risen Christ, Our Hope

12 Now if Christ is preached that He has
been raised from the dead, how do some
among you say that there is no resurrection of the dead? 13 But if there is no resurrection of the dead, [q]then Christ is not
risen. 14 And if Christ is not risen, then
our preaching *is* empty and your faith *is*
also empty. 15 Yes, and we are found false
witnesses of God, because [r]we have testified of God that He raised up Christ,
whom He did not raise up—if in fact the
dead do not rise. 16 For if *the* dead do not
rise, then Christ is not risen. 17 And if
Christ is not risen, your faith *is* futile;
[s]you are still in your sins! 18 Then also
those who have [3]fallen [t]asleep in Christ
have perished. 19 [u]If in this life only we
have hope in Christ, we are of all men the
most pitiable.

The Last Enemy Destroyed

20 But now [v]Christ is risen from the
dead, *and* has become [w]the firstfruits of
those who have [4]fallen asleep. 21 For
[x]since by man *came* death, [y]by Man also
came the resurrection of the dead. 22 For as
in Adam all die, even so in Christ all shall
[z]be made alive. 23 But [a]each one in his
own order: Christ the firstfruits, after-

6 [2] Died
7 [k] Luke 24:50; Acts 1:3,4
8 [l] [Acts 9:3-8; 22:6-11; 26:12-18]; 1 Cor. 9:1
9 [m] 2 Cor. 12:11; Eph. 3:8; 1 Tim. 1:15 [n] Acts 8:3
10 [o] Eph. 3:7,8 [p] Matt. 10:20; Rom. 15:18; Gal. 2:8; Phil. 2:13
13 [q] [1 Thess. 4:14]
15 [r] Acts 2:24
17 [s] [Rom. 4:25]
18 [t] Job 14:12; Ps. 13:3 [3] Died
19 [u] 1 Cor. 4:9; 2 Tim. 3:12
20 [v] Acts 2:24; 1 Pet. 1:3 [w] Acts 26:23; 1 Cor. 15:23; Rev. 1:5 [4] Died
21 [x] Gen. 3:19; Ezek. 18:4; Rom. 5:12; 6:23; Heb. 9:27 [y] John 11:25
22 [z] [John 5:28,29]
23 [a] [1 Thess. 4:15-17]

all seen the risen Christ (cf. Matt. 28:9; Mark 16:9,12,14; Luke 24:31-39; John 21:1-23); 4) James, either one of the two so-named apostles (son of Zebedee or son of Alphaeus; cf. Mark 3:17,18) or even James the half-brother of the Lord, the author of the epistle by that name and the key leader in the Jerusalem church (Acts 15:13-21); and 5) the apostles (John 20:19-29). Such unspecified appearances occurred over a 40 day period (Acts 1:3) to all the apostles.

15:8 born out of due time. Paul was saved too late to be one of the 12 apostles. Christ had ascended before he was converted. But through a miraculous appearance (Acts 9:1-8; cf. 18:9,10; 23:11; 2 Cor. 12:1-7), Christ revealed Himself to Paul and, according to divine purpose, Paul was made an apostle. *See note on 1:1.* He was "last of all" the apostles, and felt himself to be the "least" (vv. 9,10; 1 Tim. 1:12-17).

15:10 labored more...they all. In terms of years and extent of ministry, he exceeded all those named (vv. 5-7). John outlived him but did not have the extensive ministry of Paul.

15:12 some among you say. The Corinthian Christians believed in Christ's resurrection, or else they could not have been Christians (cf. John 6:44; 11:25; Acts 4:12; 2 Cor. 4:14; 1 Thess. 4:16). But some had particular difficulty accepting and understanding the resurrection of believers. Some of this confusion was a result of their experiences with pagan philosophies and religions. A basic tenet of much of ancient Gr. philosophy was dualism, which taught that everything physical was intrinsically evil; so the idea of a resurrected body was repulsive and disgusting (Acts 17:32). In addition, perhaps some Jews in the Corinthian church formerly may have been influenced by the Sadducees, who did not believe in the resurrection even though it is taught in the OT (Job 19:26; Pss. 16:8-11; 17:15; Dan. 12:2). On the other hand, NT teaching in the words of our Lord Himself was extensive on the resurrection (John 5:28,29; 6:44; 11:25; 14:19) and it was the theme of the apostolic preaching (Acts 4:1,2). In spite of that clarity, the church at Corinth was in doubt about the resurrection.

15:13-19 In these verses, Paul gives 6 disastrous consequences if there were no resurrection: 1) preaching Christ would be senseless (v. 14); 2) faith in Christ would be useless (v. 14); 3) all the witnesses and preachers of the resurrection would be liars (v. 15); 4) no one would be redeemed from sin (v. 17); 5) all former believers would have perished (v. 18); and 6) Christians would be the most pitiable people on earth (v. 19).

15:13,16 The two resurrections, Christ's and believers', stand or fall together; if there is no resurrection, then Christ is dead. Cf. Rev. 1:17,18.

15:17 still in your sins. *See notes on Acts 5:30,31; Rom. 4:24,25.*

15:18 fallen asleep. A common euphemism for death (cf. vv. 6,20; 11:30; Matt. 27:52; Acts 7:60; 2 Pet. 3:4). This is not soul sleep, in which the body dies and the soul, or spirit, supposedly rests in unconsciousness.

15:19 most pitiable. This is because of the sacrifices made in this life in light of the hope of life to come. If there is no life to come, we would be better "to eat, drink and be merry" before we die.

15:20 firstfruits. This speaks of the first installment of harvest to eternal life, in which Christ's resurrection will precipitate and guarantee that all of the saints who have died will be resurrected also. See John 14:19. **fallen asleep.** *See note on v. 18.*

15:21,22 man...Man. Adam, who through his sin brought death on the whole human race, was human. So was Christ, who by His resurrection brought life to the race. *See notes on Rom. 5:12-19.*

15:22 all...all. The two "alls" are alike only in the sense that they both apply to descendants. The second "all" applies only to believers (see Gal. 3:26,29; 4:7; Eph. 3:6; cf. Acts 20:32; Titus 3:7) and does not imply universalism (the salvation of everyone without faith). Countless other passages clearly teach the eternal punishment of the unbelieving (e.g., Matt. 5:29; 10:28; 25:41,46; Luke 16:23; 2 Thess. 1:9; Rev. 20:15).

15:23 in his own order. Christ was first, as the firstfruits of the resurrection harvest (vv. 20-23a). Because of His resurrection, "those who are Christ's" will be raised and enter the eternal heavenly state in 3 stages at Christ's coming (cf. Matt. 24:36,42,44,50; 25:13): 1) those who have come to saving faith from Pentecost to the Rapture will be joined by living saints at the Rapture to meet the Lord in the air and ascend to heaven (1 Thess. 4:16,17); 2) those who come to faith during the Tribulation, with the OT saints as well, will be raised up to reign with Him during the Millennium (Rev. 20:4; cf. Dan. 12:2; cf. Is. 26:19,20); and 3) those who die during the millennial kingdom may well be instantly transformed at death into their eternal bodies and

ward those *who are* Christ's at His coming.
24 Then *comes* the end, when He delivers
[b]the kingdom to God the Father, when He
puts an end to all rule and all authority
and power. 25 For He must reign [c]till He
has put all enemies under His feet.
26 [d]The last enemy *that* will be destroyed
is death. 27 For [e]*"He has put all things*
under His feet." But when He says "all
things are put under *Him,*" *it is* evident
that He who put all things under Him is
excepted. 28 [f]Now when all things are
made subject to Him, then [g]the Son Himself will also be subject to Him who put
all things under Him, that God may be all
in all.

Effects of Denying the Resurrection

29 Otherwise, what will they do who are
baptized for the dead, if the dead do not
rise at all? Why then are they baptized for
the dead? 30 And [h]why do we stand in
[5]jeopardy every hour? 31 I affirm, by [i]the
boasting in you which I have in Christ Jesus our Lord, [j]I die daily. 32 If, in the manner of men, [k]I have fought with beasts at
Ephesus, what advantage *is it* to me? If *the*
dead do not rise, [l]*"Let us eat and drink, for*
tomorrow we die!"
33 Do not be deceived: [m]"Evil company
corrupts good habits." 34 [n]Awake to righteousness, and do not sin; [o]for some do not
have the knowledge of God. [p]I speak *this*
to your shame.

A Glorious Body

35 But someone will say, [q]"How are the
dead raised up? And with what body do

24 [b] [Dan. 2:44; 7:14, 27; 2 Pet. 1:11]
25 [c] Ps. 110:1; Matt. 22:44
26 [d] [2 Tim. 1:10; Rev. 20:14; 21:4]
27 [e] Ps. 8:6
28 [f] [Phil. 3:21] [g] 1 Cor. 3:23; 11:3; 12:6
30 [h] 2 Cor. 11:26 [5] *danger*
31 [i] 1 Thess. 2:19 [j] Rom. 8:36
32 [k] 2 Cor. 1:8 [l] Eccl. 2:24; Is. 22:13; 56:12; Luke 12:19
33 [m] [1 Cor. 5:6]
34 [n] Rom. 13:11; Eph. 5:14 [o] [1 Thess. 4:5] [p] 1 Cor. 6:5
35 [q] Ezek. 37:3

spirits. The only people left to be raised will be the ungodly and that will occur at the end of the Millennium at the Great White Throne Judgment of God (*see notes on Rev. 20:11-15*; cf. John 5:28,29), which will be followed by eternal hell (Rev. 21:8).

15:24 Then *comes* the end. This third aspect of the resurrection involves the restoration of the earth to the rule of Christ, the rightful King. "End" can refer not only to what is over, but to what is complete and fulfilled. **He delivers the kingdom to God.** In the culmination of the world's history, after Christ has taken over the restored world for His Father and reigned for 1,000 years, all things will be returned to the way they were designed by God to be in the sinless glory of the new heavens and new earth (see Rev. 21,22). **end to all rule.** Christ will permanently conquer every enemy of God and take back the earth that He created and that is rightfully His. During the Millennium, under Christ's rule, rebelliousness will still exist and Christ will have to "rule them with a rod of iron" (Rev. 19:15). At the end of that 1,000 years, Satan will be unleashed briefly to lead a final insurrection against God (Rev. 20:7-9). But with all who follow his hatred of God and Christ, he will be banished to hell with his fallen angels to suffer forever in the lake of fire (Rev. 20:10-15).

15:25 all enemies under His feet. This figure comes from the common practice of kings always sitting enthroned above their subjects, so that when the subjects bowed or kneeled, they were lower than the sovereign's feet. With enemies, the monarch might put his foot on the neck of a conquered ruler, symbolizing that enemy's total subjugation. In the millennial kingdom, Christ's foes will be in subjection to Him.

15:26,27 last enemy...death. Christ has broken the power of Satan, who held the power of death (Heb. 2:14), at the cross. But Satan will not be permanently divested of his weapon of death until the end of the Millennium (*see notes on Rev. 20:1-10*). At that point, having fulfilled completely the prophecy of Ps. 8:6 (v. 27a), Christ then will deliver the kingdom to His Father, and the eternal glory of Rev. 21,22 will begin.

15:27 *it is* evident. Lest anyone misunderstand what should be "evident," Paul does not mean by "all things being put under Christ," that God the Father is so included. It is actually the Father who gave Christ His authority (Matt. 28:18; John 5:26,27) and whom the Son perfectly serves.

15:28 all in all. Christ will continue to rule because His reign is eternal (Rev. 11:15), but He will reign in His former, full, and glorious place within the Trinity, subject to God (v. 28) in the way eternally designed for Him in full Trinitarian glory.

15:29-34 Paul points out that the resurrection gives men compelling incentives for salvation (v. 19), for service (vv. 30-32), and for sanctification (vv. 33,34).

15:29 This difficult verse has numerous possible interpretations. Other Scripture passages, however, clarify certain things which it does *not* mean. It does not teach, for example, that a dead person can be saved by another person's being baptized on his behalf, because baptism never has a part in a person's salvation (Eph. 2:8; cf. Rom. 3:28; 4:3; 6:3,4). A reasonable view seems to be that "they...who are baptized" refers to living believers who give outward testimony to their faith in baptism by water because they were first drawn to Christ by the exemplary lives, faithful influence, and witness of believers who had subsequently died. Paul's point is that if there is no resurrection and no life after death, then why are people coming to Christ to follow the hope of those who have died?

15:30,31 I die daily. Paul continually risked his life in self-sacrificing ministry. Why would he risk death daily, even hourly, if there were no life after death, no reward, and no eternal joy for all his pain? Cf. 1 Pet. 1:3,4.

15:32 beasts at Ephesus. Perhaps literal wild animals, or, metaphorically, the fierce crowd of Ephesians incited against him by Demetrius (Acts 19:23-34). In either case, these were life-threatening dangers (cf. 2 Cor. 11:23-28). ***eat...drink...die.*** A direct quote from Is. 22:13 reflecting the hopelessness of the backslidden Israelites. Cf. Heb. 11:33,34,38 for a litany of suffers who were willing to die because they looked forward to resurrection (v. 35).

15:33,34 Evil company. The Gr. term behind this word can also refer to a spoken message. By word or example, evil friends are a corrupting influence. Hope in the resurrection is sanctifying; it leads to godly living, not corruption. Some in the church did not know God and were a corrupting influence, but not for those who hoped for life in God's presence (see 1 John 3:2,3).

15:35 They had the truth but shamefully did not believe and follow it (cf. 2 Cor. 13:5); thus, these questions did not reflect a genuine interest in the resurrection but were mocking taunts, by those who denied the resurrection, perhaps under the influence of gnostic-oriented philosophy. But supposing it were true, they queried as to how it could ever happen. Cf. Acts 26:8.

15:36-49 To the questions posed in v. 35, Paul here gives 4 responses: 1) an illustration from nature (vv. 36-38); 2) a description of resurrection bodies (vv. 39-42a); 3) contrasts of earthly and resurrection bodies (vv. 42b-44); and 4) a reminder of the prototype resurrection of Jesus Christ (vv. 45-49).

they come?" 36 Foolish one, [r]what you sow
is not made alive unless it dies. 37 And
what you sow, you do not sow that body
that shall be, but mere grain—perhaps
wheat or some other *grain.* 38 But God
gives it a body as He pleases, and to each
seed its own body.
39 All flesh *is* not the same flesh, but *there*
is one *kind* [6]*of* flesh of men, another flesh of
animals, another of fish, *and* another of
birds.
40 *There are* also [7]celestial bodies and
[8]terrestrial bodies; but the glory of the celestial *is* one, and the *glory* of the terrestrial
is another. 41 *There is* one glory of the sun,
another glory of the moon, and another
glory of the stars; for *one* star differs from
another star in glory.
42 [s]So also *is* the resurrection of the
dead. *The body* is sown in corruption, it is
raised in incorruption. 43 [t]It is sown in dishonor, it is raised in glory. It is sown in
weakness, it is raised in power. 44 It is
sown a natural body, it is raised a spiritual body. There is a natural body, and there
is a spiritual body. 45 And so it is written,
[u]*"The first man Adam became a living*
being." [v]The last Adam *became* [w]a life-giving spirit.
46 However, the spiritual is not first, but
the natural, and afterward the spiritual.
47 [x]The first man *was* of the earth, [y]*made*[9]
of dust; the second Man *is* [1]the Lord [z]from
heaven. 48 As *was* the [2]*man* of dust, so also
are those *who are* [2]*made* of dust; [a]and as *is*
the heavenly *Man,* so also *are* those *who are*
heavenly. 49 And [b]as we have borne the
image of the *man* of dust, [c]we[3] shall also
bear the image of the heavenly *Man.*

Our Final Victory

50 Now this I say, brethren, that [d]flesh
and blood cannot inherit the kingdom of
God; nor does corruption inherit incorruption. 51 Behold, I tell you a [4]mystery: [e]We
shall not all sleep, [f]but we shall all be
changed— 52 in a moment, in the twinkling of an eye, at the last trumpet. [g]For the
trumpet will sound, and the dead will be
raised incorruptible, and we shall be
changed. 53 For this corruptible must put
on incorruption, and [h]this mortal *must* put
on immortality. 54 So when this corruptible
has put on incorruption, and this mortal
has put on immortality, then shall be
brought to pass the saying that is written:
[i]*"Death is swallowed up in victory."*

55 *"O[j][5] Death, where is your sting?*
O Hades, where is your victory?"

56 The sting of death *is* sin, and [k]the
strength of sin *is* the law. 57 [l]But thanks *be*
to God, who gives us [m]the victory through
our Lord Jesus Christ.
58 [n]Therefore, my beloved brethren, be
steadfast, immovable, always abounding
in the work of the Lord, knowing [o]that
your labor is not in vain in the Lord.

Collection for the Saints

16 Now concerning [a]the collection for
the saints, as I have given orders to
the churches of Galatia, so you must do

36 [r] John 12:24
39 [6] NU, M omit *of flesh*
40 [7] *heavenly* [8] *earthly*
42 [s] [Dan. 12:3; Matt. 13:43]
43 [t] [Phil. 3:21; Col. 3:4]
45 [u] Gen. 2:7 [v] [Rom. 5:14] [w] John 5:21; 6:57; [Rom. 8:2; Phil. 3:21; Col. 3:4]
47 [x] John 3:31 [y] Gen. 2:7; 3:19 [z] John 3:13 [9] *earthy* [1] NU omits *the Lord*
48 [a] Phil. 3:20 [2] *earthy*
49 [b] Gen. 5:3 [c] Rom. 8:29; [2 Cor. 3:18; Phil. 3:21; 1 John 3:2] [3] M *let us also bear*
50 [d] Matt. 16:17; [John 3:3, 5]
51 [e] [1 Thess. 4:15] [f] [Phil. 3:21] [4] *hidden truth*
52 [g] Zech. 9:14; Matt. 24:31; John 5:25
53 [h] 2 Cor. 5:4
54 [i] Is. 25:8; [Rev. 20:14]
55 [j] Hos. 13:14 [5] NU *O Death, where is your victory? O Death, where is your sting?*
56 [k] [Rom. 3:20; 4:15; 7:8]
57 [l] [Rom. 7:25]; 2 Cor. 2:14 [m] Rom. 8:37; [Heb. 2:14; 1 John 5:4]; Rev. 21:4
58 [n] 2 Pet. 3:14 [o] [1 Cor. 3:8]

CHAPTER 16

1 [a] Acts 11:29; Gal. 2:10

15:36-38 When a seed is planted in the ground it dies; decomposing, it ceases to exist in its seed form, but life comes from inside that dead seed (see John 12:24). Just as God gives a new body to that plant that rises from the dead seed, so He can give a resurrection body to a man who dies.

15:39-42a As there are vastly different bodies and forms in God's created universe which are suited for all kinds of existence, so God can design a body perfect for resurrection life.

15:42b-44 Focusing directly on the resurrection body, Paul gives 4 sets of contrasts to show how the new body will differ from the present ones (cf. v. 54; Phil. 3:20,21): 1) no more sickness and death ("corruption"); 2) no more shame because of sin ("dishonor"); 3) no more frailty in temptation ("weakness"); and 4) no more limits to the time/space sphere ("natural").

15:45-49 Here Paul answers the question (v. 35) more specifically by showing that the resurrection body of Jesus Christ is the prototype. He begins with a quotation from Gen. 2:7 with the addition of two words, "first" and "Adam." Adam was created with a natural body, not perfect, but good in every way (Gen. 3:1). The "last Adam" is Jesus Christ (Rom. 5:19,21). He is saying that through the first Adam we received our natural bodies, but through the last Adam we will receive our spiritual bodies in resurrection. Adam's body was the prototype of the natural, Christ's body of the resurrection. We will bear the image of His body fit for heaven (Acts 1:11; Phil. 3:20,21; 1 John 3:1-3) as we have borne the image of Adam's on earth.

15:50 People cannot live in God's eternal heavenly glory the way they are. *See notes on Rom. 8:23.* We have to be changed (v. 51).

15:51 mystery. This term refers to truth hidden in the past and revealed in the NT. *See notes on 2:7 and Eph. 3:4,5.* In this case, the rapture of the church was never revealed in the OT. It was first mentioned in John 14:1-3, when it is specifically explained and is detailed in 1 Thess. 4:13-18 (*see notes there*). **sleep.** *See note on v. 18.*

15:52 twinkling of an eye. This was Paul's way of showing how brief the "moment" will be. The Gr. word for "twinkling" refers to any rapid movement. Since the eye can move more rapidly than any other part of our visible bodies, it seems to well illustrate the sudden transformation of raptured believers. **trumpet will sound.** To herald the end of the church era, when all believers will be removed from the earth at the rapture (1 Thess. 4:16). **dead...raised.** According to 1 Thess. 4:16, they are first and the living saints follow (1 Thess. 4:17).

15:54-57 Paul enhanced his joy at the reality of resurrection by quoting from Is. 25:8 and Hos. 13:14. The latter quote taunts death as if it were a bee whose sting was removed. That sting was the sin that was exposed by the law of God (*see notes on Rom. 3:23; 4:15; 6:23; Gal. 3:10-13*), but conquered by Christ in His death (*see notes on Rom. 5:17; 2 Cor. 5:21*).

15:58 The hope of resurrection makes all the efforts and sacrifices in the Lord's work worth it. No work done in His name is wasted in light of eternal glory and reward.

16:1 collection. An offering for destitute believers in the over-

also: 2 [b]On the first *day* of the week let each
one of you lay something aside, storing up
as he may prosper, that there be no collections when I come. 3 And when I come,
[c]whomever you approve by *your* letters I
will send to bear your gift to Jerusalem.
4 [d]But if it is fitting that I go also, they will
go with me.

Personal Plans

5 Now I will come to you [e]when I pass
through Macedonia (for I am passing
through Macedonia). 6 And it may be that
I will remain, or even spend the winter
with you, that you may [f]send me on my
journey, wherever I go. 7 For I do not wish
to see you now on the way; but I hope to
stay a while with you, [g]if the Lord permits.

8 But I will tarry in Ephesus until [h]Pen-
tecost. 9 For [i]a great and effective door has
opened to me, and [j]*there are* many adversaries.

10 And [k]if Timothy comes, see that he
may be with you without fear; for [l]he does
the work of the Lord, as I also *do*. 11 [m]There-
fore let no one despise him. But send him
on his journey [n]in peace, that he may come
to me; for I am waiting for him with the
brethren.

12 Now concerning *our* brother [o]Apollos,
I strongly urged him to come to you with
the brethren, but he was quite unwilling to
come at this time; however, he will come
when he has a convenient time.

Final Exhortations

13 [p]Watch, [q]stand fast in the faith, be
brave, [r]be strong. 14 [s]Let all *that* you *do* be
done with love.

15 I urge you, brethren—you know [t]the
household of Stephanas, that it is [u]the firstfruits of Achaia, and *that* they have devoted themselves to [v]the ministry of the
saints— 16 [w]that you also submit to such,
and to everyone who works and [x]labors
with *us*.

17 I am glad about the coming of
Stephanas, Fortunatus, and Achaicus,
[y]for what was lacking on your part they
supplied. 18 [z]For they refreshed my spirit
and yours. Therefore [a]acknowledge such
men.

Greetings and a Solemn Farewell

19 The churches of Asia greet you.
Aquila and Priscilla greet you heartily in
the Lord, [b]with the church that is in their
house. 20 All the brethren greet you.

2 [b] Acts 20:7
3 [c] 2 Cor. 3:1; 8:18
4 [d] 2 Cor. 8:4, 19
5 [e] Acts 19:21; 2 Cor. 1:15, 16
6 [f] Acts 15:3; Rom. 15:24; 1 Cor. 16:11
7 [g] Acts 18:21; James 4:15
8 [h] Lev. 23:15-22
9 [i] Acts 14:27; 2 Cor. 2:12; Col. 4:3 [j] Acts 19:9
10 [k] Acts 19:22; 2 Tim. 1:2 [l] Phil. 2:20; 1 Thess. 3:2
11 [m] 1 Tim. 4:12; Titus 2:15 [n] Acts 15:33
12 [o] Acts 18:24; 1 Cor. 1:12; 3:5
13 [p] Matt. 24:42 [q] 1 Cor. 15:1; Gal. 5:1; Phil. 1:27; 4:1; 1 Thess. 3:8; 2 Thess. 2:15 [r] [Ps. 31:24; Eph. 3:16; 6:10; Col. 1:11]
14 [s] [1 Pet. 4:8]
15 [t] 1 Cor. 1:16 [u] Rom. 16:5 [v] 2 Cor. 8:4
16 [w] Eph. 5:21; 1 Thess. 5:12; Heb. 13:17 [x] [Heb. 6:10]
17 [y] 2 Cor. 11:9; Phil. 2:30
18 [z] Col. 4:8 [a] Phil. 2:29
19 [b] Rom. 16:5

populated, famine stricken city of Jerusalem (v. 3; see Acts 11:28). Paul had previously solicited funds from the churches of Galatia, Macedonia, and Achaia (Rom. 15:26; cf. Luke 10:25-37; 2 Cor. 8:1-5; 9:12-15; Gal. 6:10; 1 John 3:17).

16:2 first *day* of the week. This evidences that the early church met on Sunday (Acts 20:7). The point is that giving must occur regularly, not just when one feels generous, particularly led to do so, or instructed to do so for some special purpose (cf. Luke 6:38; cf. 2 Cor. 9:6,7). **as he may prosper.** No required amount or percentage for giving to the Lord's work is specified in the NT. All giving to the Lord is to be free will giving and completely discretionary (see Luke 6:38; 2 Cor. 9:6-8). This is not to be confused with the OT required giving of 3 tithes (see Lev. 27:30; Num. 18:21-26; Deut. 14:28,29; Mal. 3:8-10) which totaled about 23 percent annually to fund the national government of Israel, take care of public festivals, and provide welfare. Modern parallels to the OT tithe are found in the taxation system of countries (Rom. 13:6). OT giving to God was not regulated as to amount (see Ex. 25:1,2; 35:21; 36:6; Prov. 3:9,10; 11:24).

16:3,4 This matter of getting the money to Jerusalem was important enough for Paul to go, if necessary.

16:5 At the end of a 3 year stay in Ephesus, Paul wrote his letter and probably gave it to Timothy to deliver (v. 10). Paul originally planned to follow Timothy a short while after (4:19), visiting Corinth on the way to and from Macedonia (2 Cor. 1:15,16). He had to change his plan and visit only after a longer stay in Ephesus (v. 8), then on to Corinth after Macedonia, to stay for a while (vv. 6,7).

16:9 many adversaries. Perhaps no NT church had such fierce opposition as the one in Ephesus (see 2 Cor. 1:8-10 where he described his experience in Ephesus; cf. Acts 19:1-21). In spite of that opposition, the door for the gospel was open wide (cf. 2 Cor. 2:12,13 where Paul also had an open door, but no heart to remain and preach) and Paul stayed. At the end of the experience of opposition described in 2 Cor. 1:8-10, he wrote 1 Corinthians.

16:10 Timothy. Paul had sent him with Erastus to Macedonia (Acts 19:22) and then he was to travel to Corinth, perhaps to carry this epistle (4:17). **without fear.** I.e., of intimidation or frustration by believers in Corinth.

16:12 Apollos. *See note on Acts 18:24.* Paul felt Apollos should accompany the other brothers, Timothy and Erastus, to Corinth. Apollos refused, staying in Ephesus longer. Paul respected his convictions.

16:13,14 Paul gives 5 final commands. The Corinthians are to be alert, firm, mature, strong, and loving.

16:13 the faith. The Christian faith, i.e., sound doctrine, as in Phil. 1:27; 1 Tim. 6:12; Jude 3.

16:15 firstfruits. The members of the household of Stephanas were among the first converts in Corinth, which is located in Achaia, the southern province of Greece. Stephanas was one of the Corinthian believers Paul baptized personally (1:16), and was visiting with Paul in Ephesus at the time this epistle was written. With Fortunatus and Achaicus (v. 17), he probably delivered the earlier letter from Corinth mentioned in 7:1 (*see note there*).

16:17,18 Paul was glad about the arrival of his 3 friends in Ephesus who went there to be with him (cf. Prov. 25:25). The Corinthians were to give those men respect for their service to the Lord (cf. 1 Thess. 5:12,13).

16:19 Aquila and Priscilla. *See note on Acts 18:2.* They had become good friends with Paul, since he stayed in their house during his first ministry in Corinth (Acts 18:1-3). He may have stayed with them the entire year and a half (cf. Acts 18:18,19,24-26). **in their house.** The early church used homes of believers for worship and many other activities (see, e.g., Acts 2:46; 5:42; 10:23,27-48; 20:7,8; 28:23).

[c]Greet one another with a holy kiss.
21 [d]The salutation with my own hand—
Paul's.
22 If anyone [e]does not love the Lord Jesus Christ, [f]let him be [1]accursed. [g]O[2] Lord,
come!

23 [h]The grace of our Lord Jesus Christ *be*
with you. 24 My love *be* with you all in
Christ Jesus. Amen.

20 [c] Rom. 16:16
21 [d] Rom. 16:22; Gal. 6:11; Col. 4:18; 2 Thess. 3:17; Philem. 19
22 [e] Eph. 6:24 [f] Gal. 1:8, 9 [g] Jude 14, 15
[1] Gr. *anathema*
[2] Aram. *Marana tha;* possibly *Maran atha, Our Lord has come*
23 [h] Rom. 16:20

16:20 kiss. A pure expression of Christian love between men with men and women with women, with no sexual overtones (cf. Rom. 16:16; 2 Cor. 13:12; 1 Thess. 5:26; 1 Pet. 5:14).

16:21 my own hand. Paul dictated the main part of the letter to a scribe (Rom. 16:22), but finished and signed it himself.

16:22 accursed. I.e., devoted to destruction. **O Lord, come!** In this context, Paul perhaps appeals for the Lord to take away the nominal, false Christians who threatened the spiritual well-being of the church. This was also an expression of eagerness for the Lord's return (cf. Rev. 22:20). The Aram. words are transliterated "Maranatha" (see marginal note).

The Second Epistle of Paul to the

CORINTHIANS

Title

This is the second NT epistle the Apostle Paul wrote to the Christians in the city of Corinth (see Introduction to 1 Corinthians).

Author and Date

That the Apostle Paul wrote 2 Corinthians is uncontested; the lack of any motive for a forger to write this highly personal, biographical epistle has led even the most critical scholars to affirm Paul as its author.

Several considerations establish a feasible date for the writing of this letter. Extrabiblical sources indicate that July, A.D. 51 is the most likely date for the beginning of Gallio's proconsulship (cf. Acts 18:12). Paul's trial before him at Corinth (Acts 18:12-17) probably took place shortly after Gallio assumed office. Leaving Corinth (probably in A.D. 52), Paul sailed for Palestine (Acts 18:18), thus concluding his second missionary journey. Returning to Ephesus on his third missionary journey (probably in A.D. 52), Paul ministered there for about 2 ½ years (Acts 19:8,10). The apostle wrote 1 Corinthians from Ephesus toward the close of that period (1 Cor. 16:8), most likely in A.D. 55. Since Paul planned to stay in Ephesus until the following spring (cf. the reference to Pentecost in 1 Cor. 16:8), and 2 Corinthians was written after he left Ephesus (see Background and Setting), the most likely date for 2 Corinthians is late A.D. 55 or very early A.D. 56.

Background and Setting

Paul's association with the important commercial city of Corinth (see Introduction to 1 Corinthians: Title) began on his second missionary journey (Acts 18:1-18), when he spent 18 months (Acts 18:11) ministering there. After leaving Corinth, Paul heard of immorality in the Corinthian church and wrote a letter (since lost) to confront that sin, referred to in 1 Cor. 5:9. During his ministry in Ephesus, he received further reports of trouble in the Corinthian church in the form of divisions among them (1 Cor. 1:11). In addition, the Corinthians wrote Paul a letter (1 Cor. 7:1) asking for clarification of some issues. Paul responded by writing the letter known as 1 Corinthians. Planning to remain at Ephesus a little longer

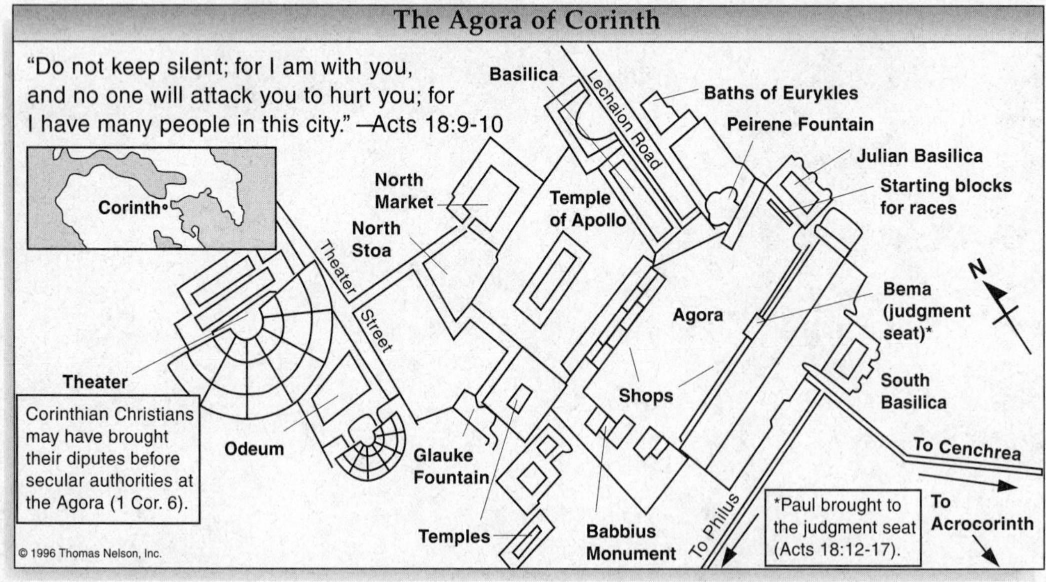

(1 Cor. 16:8,9), Paul sent Timothy to Corinth (1 Cor. 4:17; 16:10,11). Disturbing news reached the apostle (possibly from Timothy) of further difficulties at Corinth, including the arrival of self-styled false apostles (11:13; *see note on 11:4*).

To create the platform to teach their false gospel, they began by assaulting the character of Paul. They had to convince the people to turn from Paul to them if they were to succeed in preaching demon doctrine. Temporarily abandoning the work at Ephesus, Paul went immediately to Corinth. The visit (known as the "painful visit," 2:1) was not a successful one from Paul's perspective; someone in the Corinthian church (possibly one of the false apostles) even openly insulted him (2:5-8,10; 7:12). Saddened by the Corinthians' lack of loyalty to defend him, seeking to spare them further reproof (cf. 1:23), and perhaps hoping time would bring them to their senses, Paul returned to Ephesus. From Ephesus, Paul wrote what is known as the "severe letter" (2:4) and sent it with Titus to Corinth (7:5-16). Leaving Ephesus after the riot sparked by Demetrius (Acts 19:23–20:1), Paul went to Troas to meet Titus (2:12,13). But Paul was so anxious for news of how the Corinthians had responded to the "severe letter" that he could not minister there though the Lord had opened the door (2:12; cf. 7:5). So he left for Macedonia to look for Titus (2:13). To Paul's immense relief and joy, Titus met him with the news that the majority of the Corinthians had repented of their rebellion against Paul (7:7). Wise enough to know that some rebellious attitudes still smoldered under the surface, and could erupt again, Paul wrote (possibly from Philippi, cf. 11:9 with Phil. 4:15; also, some early manuscripts list Philippi as the place of writing) the Corinthians the letter called 2 Corinthians. In this letter, though the apostle expressed his relief and joy at their repentance (7:8-16), his main concern was to defend his apostleship (chaps. 1–7), exhort the Corinthians to resume preparations for the collection for the poor at Jerusalem (chaps. 8,9), and confront the false apostles head on (chaps. 10–13). He then went to Corinth, as he had written (12:14; 13:1,2). The Corinthians' participation in the Jerusalem offering (Rom. 15:26) implies that Paul's third visit to that church was successful.

Historical and Theological Themes

Second Corinthians complements the historical record of Paul's dealings with the Corinthian church recorded in Acts and 1 Corinthians. It also contains important biographical data on Paul throughout.

Although an intensely personal letter, written by the apostle in the heat of battle against those attacking his credibility, 2 Corinthians contains several important theological themes. It portrays God the Father as a merciful comforter (1:3; 7:6), the Creator (4:6), the One who raised Jesus from the dead (4:14; cf. 13:4), and who will raise believers as well (1:9). Jesus Christ is the One who suffered (1:5), who fulfilled God's promises (1:20), who was the proclaimed Lord (4:5), who manifested God's glory (4:6), and the One who in His incarnation became poor for believers (8:9; cf. Phil. 2:5-8). The letter portrays the Holy Spirit as God (3:17,18) and the guarantee of believers' salvation (1:22; 5:5). Satan is identified as the "god of this age" (4:4; cf. 1 John 5:19), a deceiver (11:14), and the leader of human and angelic deceivers (11:15). The end times include both the believer's glorification (4:16–5:8) and his judgment (5:10). The glorious truth of God's sovereignty in salvation is the theme of 5:14-21, while 7:9,10 sets forth man's response to God's offer of salvation—genuine repentance. Second Corinthians also presents the clearest, most concise summary of the substitutionary atonement of Christ to be found anywhere in Scripture (5:21; cf. Is. 53) and defines the mission of the church to proclaim reconciliation (5:18-20). Finally, the nature of the New Covenant receives its fullest exposition outside the book of Hebrews (3:6-16).

Interpretive Challenges

The main challenge confronting the interpreter is the relationship of chaps. 10–13 to chaps. 1–9 (*see note on 10:1–13:14*). The identity of Paul's opponents at Corinth has produced various interpretations, as has the identity of the brother who accompanied Titus to Corinth (8:18,22). Whether the offender mentioned in 2:5-8 is the incestuous man of 1 Cor. 5 is also uncertain. It is difficult to explain Paul's vision (12:1-5) and to identify specifically his "thorn in the flesh," the "messenger of Satan [sent] to buffet [him]" (12:7). These and other interpretive problems will be dealt with in the notes on the appropriate passages.

Outline

- I. Paul's Greeting (1:1-11)
- II. Paul's Ministry (1:12–7:16)
  - A. Paul's Plans (1:12–2:4)
  - B. The Offender's Punishment (2:5-11)
  - C. Titus' Absence (2:12,13)
  - D. The Ministry's Nature (2:14–6:10)
    1. The triumph of the ministry (2:14-17)
    2. The commendation of the ministry (3:1-5)
    3. The basis of the ministry (3:6-18)
    4. The theme of the ministry (4:1-7)
    5. The trials of the ministry (4:8-18)
    6. The motivation of the ministry (5:1-10)
    7. The message of the ministry (5:11-21)
    8. The conduct of the ministry (6:1-10)
  - E. The Corinthians Exhorted (6:11–7:16)
    1. To open their hearts to Paul (6:11-13)
    2. To separate themselves from unbelievers (6:14–7:1)
    3. To be assured of Paul's love (7:2-16)
- III. Paul's Collection (8:1–9:15)
  - A. The Patterns of Giving (8:1-9)
    1. The Macedonians (8:1-7)
    2. Jesus Christ (8:8,9)
  - B. The Purpose of Giving (8:10-15)
  - C. The Procedures of Giving (8:16–9:5)
  - D. The Promise of Giving (9:6-15)
- IV. Paul's Apostleship (10:1–12:13)
  - A. Apostolic Authority (10:1-18)
  - B. Apostolic Conduct (11:1-15)
  - C. Apostolic Suffering (11:16-33)
  - D. Apostolic Credentials (12:1-13)
- V. Paul's Visit (12:14–13:14)
  - A. Paul's Unselfishness (12:14-18)
  - B. Paul's Warnings (12:19–13:10)
  - C. Paul's Benediction (13:11-14)

Greeting

1 Paul, [a]an apostle of Jesus Christ by the
will of God, and [b]Timothy *our* brother,

To the church of God which is at
Corinth, [c]with all the saints who are in all
Achaia:

2 [d]Grace to you and peace from God our
Father and the Lord Jesus Christ.

Comfort in Suffering

3 [e]Blessed *be* the God and Father of our
Lord Jesus Christ, the Father of mercies
and God of all comfort, 4 who [f]comforts us
in all our tribulation, that we may be able
to comfort those who are in any [1]trouble,
with the comfort with which we ourselves
are comforted by God. 5 For as [g]the sufferings of Christ abound in us, so our [2]conso-
lation also abounds through Christ. 6 Now
if we are afflicted, [h]*it is* for your consolation and salvation, which is effective for
enduring the same sufferings which we
also suffer. Or if we are comforted, *it is* for
your consolation and salvation. 7 And our
hope for you *is* steadfast, because we know
that [i]as you are partakers of the sufferings,
so also *you will partake* of the consolation.

Delivered from Suffering

8 For we do not want you to be ignorant,
brethren, of [j]our [3]trouble which came to us
in Asia: that we were burdened beyond
measure, above strength, so that we despaired even of life. 9 Yes, we had the sentence of death in ourselves, that we should
[k]not trust in ourselves but in God who

CHAPTER 1
1 [a]1 Cor. 1:1; Eph. 1:1; Col. 1:1; 1 Tim. 1:1; 2 Tim. 1:1 [b]Acts 16:1; 1 Cor. 16:10 [c]Phil. 1:1; Col. 1:2
2 [d]Rom. 1:7
3 [e]Eph. 1:3; 1 Pet. 1:3
4 [f]Is. 51:12; 66:13; 2 Cor. 7:6, 7, 13
[1]tribulation
5 [g][Acts 9:4]; 2 Cor. 4:10; Phil. 3:10; Col. 1:24
[2]comfort
6 [h]2 Cor. 4:15; 12:15; Eph. 3:1, 13; 2 Tim. 2:10
7 [i][Rom. 8:17; 2 Tim. 2:12]
8 [j]Acts 19:23; 1 Cor. 15:32; 16:9
[3]tribulation
9 [k]Jer. 17:5, 7

1:1 apostle. This refers to Paul's official position as a messenger sent by Christ (*see note on Rom. 1:1*; Introduction to 1 Corinthians: Author and Date). **by the will of God.** Paul's mission was not a self-appointed one, or based on his own achievements. Rather, his credentials were by divine appointment and his letter reflected not his own message but the words of Christ (see Introduction to Romans: Author and Date; cf. Acts 26:15-18). **Timothy *our* brother.** Paul's cherished son in the faith and a dominant person in Paul's life and ministry (see Introduction to 1 Timothy: Background and Setting; *see note on 1 Tim. 1:2*). Paul first met Timothy in Derbe and Lystra on his second missionary journey (Acts 16:1-4). Timothy was with him during the founding of the church in Corinth (Acts 18:1-5), which, along with Paul's mention of Timothy in 1 Corinthians (4:17; 16:10,11), indicated the Corinthians knew Timothy. Perhaps Paul mentioned him here to remind them Timothy was indeed a brother and to smooth over any hard feelings left from his recent visit (*see notes on 1 Cor. 16:10*).

1:2 Grace...peace. Part of Paul's normal salutation in his letters (*see note on Rom. 1:7*). "Grace" is God's unmerited favor, and "peace" one of its benefits.

1:3 God and Father of our Lord Jesus Christ. Paul praised the true God who revealed Himself in His Son, who is of the same essence with the Father (*see notes on John 1:14,18; 17:3-5*; cf. John 5:17; 14:9-11; Eph. 1:3; Heb. 1:2,3; 2 John 3). He is the anointed one (Christ) and sovereign (Lord) Redeemer (Jesus). Although the Son enjoyed this lofty position, He was willing to become a servant and submit Himself in His incarnation (*see notes on Phil. 2:5-8*). This great benediction comprehends the entire gospel. **Father of mercies.** Paul borrowed from Jewish liturgical language and a synagogue prayer that called for God to treat the sinful individual with kindness, love, and tenderness (*see note on Rom. 12:1*; cf. 2 Sam. 24:14; Ps. 103:13,14; Mic. 7:18-20). **God of all comfort.** An OT description of God (cf. Is. 40:1; 51:3,12; 66:13), who is the ultimate source of every true act of comfort. The Gr. word for "comfort" is related to the familiar word *paraclete,* "one who comes alongside to help," another name for the Holy Spirit (*see notes on John 14:26; Phil. 2:1*). "Comfort" often connotes softness and ease, but that is not its meaning here. Paul was saying that God came to him in the middle of his sufferings and troubles to strengthen him and give him courage and boldness (cf. vv. 4-10).

1:4 tribulation. This term refers to crushing pressure, because in Paul's life and ministry there was always something attempting to weaken him, restrict or confine his ministry, or even crush out his life. But no matter what confronted him, Paul knew God would sustain and strengthen him (*see notes on 12:9,10; Rom. 8:31-38*; cf. Phil. 1:6). **that we may be able to comfort.** Comfort from God is not an end in itself. Its purpose is that believers also might be comforters. Having humiliated and convicted the Corinthians, God used Paul to return to them with a strengthening message after he himself had received divine strengthening (6:1-13; 12:6-11; cf. Luke 22:31,32).

1:5 sufferings of Christ abound. God's comfort to believers extends to the boundaries of their suffering for Christ. The more they endure righteous suffering, the greater will be their comfort and reward (cf. 1 Pet. 4:12-14). Paul knew first hand that these many sufferings would seem never-ending (4:7-11; 6:5-10; 11:23-27; cf. Gal. 6:17; Phil. 3:10; Col. 1:24), and all genuine believers should expect the same (cf. Matt. 10:18-24).

1:6 Paul was referring to the body of Christ's partnership of suffering, which mutually builds godly patience and endurance (1 Cor. 12:26). All believers need to realize this process, avoid any sense of self-pity when suffering for Him, and share in each others' lives the encouragement of divine comfort they receive from their experiences. **consolation.** Comfort (*see note on v. 3*). **salvation.** This refers to the Corinthians' ongoing perseverance to final, completed salvation when they will be glorified (*see note on Rom. 13:11*). Paul's willingness, by God's grace and the Spirit's power, to suffer and be comforted and then comfort and strengthen the Corinthians enabled them to persevere.

1:7 partakers of the sufferings. Some in the church at Corinth, perhaps the majority, were suffering for righteousness, as Paul was. Although that church had caused him much pain and concern, Paul saw its members as partners to be helped, because of their faithfulness in mutual suffering.

1:8 our. An editorial plural, which Paul used throughout the letter. It usually was a humble reference to Paul himself, but in this instance it could include others as well. **trouble which came to us in Asia.** This was a recent occurrence (following the writing of 1 Corinthians) that happened in or around the city of Ephesus. The details of this situation are not known. **despaired even of life.** Paul faced something that was beyond human survival and was extremely discouraging because he believed it threatened to end his ministry prematurely. The Gr. word for "despaired" lit. means "no passage," the total absence of an exit (cf. 2 Tim. 4:6). The Corinthians were aware of what had happened to Paul, but did not realize the utter severity of it, or what God was doing through those circumstances.

1:9 the sentence of death. The word for "sentence" is a technical term that indicated the passing of an official resolution, in this case the death sentence. Paul was so absolutely sure he was going to die for the gospel that he had pronounced the sentence upon himself. **not trust in ourselves but in God.** God's ultimate purpose for Paul's

raises the dead, 10 [l]who delivered us from
so great a death, and [4]does deliver us; in
whom we trust that He will still deliver *us,*
11 you also [m]helping together in prayer for
us, that thanks may be given by many persons on [5]our behalf [n]for the gift *granted* to
us through many.

Paul's Sincerity

12 For our boasting is this: the testimony
of our conscience that we conducted ourselves in the world in [6]simplicity and
[o]godly sincerity, [p]not with fleshly wisdom
but by the grace of God, and more abundantly toward you. 13 For we are not writing any other things to you than what you
read or understand. Now I trust you will
understand, even to the end 14 (as also you
have understood us in part), [q]that we are
your boast as [r]you also *are* ours, in the day
of the Lord Jesus.

Sparing the Church

15 And in this confidence [s]I intended to
come to you before, that you might have [t]a
second benefit— 16 to pass by way of you
to Macedonia, [u]to come again from Macedonia to you, and be helped by you on my
way to Judea. 17 Therefore, when I was
planning this, did I do it lightly? Or the
things I plan, do I plan [v]according to the
flesh, that with me there should be Yes,
Yes, and No, No? 18 But *as* God *is* [w]faithful,
our [7]word to you was not Yes and No.
19 For [x]the Son of God, Jesus Christ, who
was preached among you by us—by me,
[y]Silvanus, and [z]Timothy—was not Yes and
No, [a]but in Him was Yes. 20 [b]For all the

10 [l][2 Pet. 2:9] [4]NU *shall*
11 [m]Rom. 15:30; Phil. 1:19; Philem. 22 [n]2 Cor. 4:15; 9:11 [5]M *your behalf*
12 [o]2 Cor. 2:17 [p][1 Cor. 2:4] [6]The opposite of duplicity
14 [q]2 Cor. 5:12 [r]Phil. 2:16; 1 Thess. 2:19
15 [s]1 Cor. 4:19 [t]Rom. 1:11; 15:29
16 [u]Acts 19:21; 1 Cor. 16:3-6
17 [v]2 Cor. 10:2; 11:18
18 [w]1 John 5:20 [7]*message*
19 [x]Mark 1:1; Luke 1:35; John 1:34; 20:31; 1 John 5:5, 20 [y]1 Thess. 1:1; 2 Thess. 1:1; 1 Pet. 5:12 [z]Acts 18:5; 2 Cor. 1:1 [a][Heb. 13:8]
20 [b][Rom. 15:8, 9]

horrible extremity. The Lord took him to the point at which he could not fall back on any intellectual, physical, or emotional human resource (cf. 12:9,10). **who raises the dead.** A Jewish descriptive term for God used in synagogue worship language (*see note on v. 3*). Paul understood that trust in God's power to raise the dead was the only hope of rescue from his extreme circumstances.

1:10 He will still deliver *us.* *See notes on 2 Tim. 4:16,17; 2 Pet. 2:9.*

1:11 helping together in prayer. Intercessory prayer is crucial to the expression of God's power and sovereign purpose. In this regard, Paul wanted the faithful Corinthians to know he needed their prayers then and in the future (cf. Eph. 6:18; James 5:16). **thanks may be given.** Prayer's duty is not to change God's plans, but to glorify Him and give thanks for them. Paul was confident that God's sovereign purpose would be accomplished, balanced by the prayerful participation of believers. **the gift.** Probably better translated "favor," or "blessing," as in God's undeserved favor or the divine answer to prayer Paul would receive in being delivered from death.

1:12 Paul faced his critics' many accusations against his character and integrity (they had accused him of being proud, self-serving, untrustworthy and inconsistent, mentally unbalanced, incompetent, unsophisticated, and an incompetent preacher) by appealing to the highest human court, his conscience. **boasting.** Paul often used this word, and it can also be rendered "proud confidence." Used negatively, it refers to unwarranted bragging about one's own merits and achievements; but Paul used it positively to denote legitimate confidence in what God had done in his life (cf. Jer. 9:23,24; Rom. 15:18; 1 Cor. 1:31; 15:9,10; 1 Tim. 1:12-17). **conscience.** The soul's warning system, which allows human beings to contemplate their motives and actions and make moral evaluations of what is right and wrong (*see note on Rom. 2:14,15*). In order to work as God designed it, the conscience must be informed to the highest moral and spiritual level and best standard, which means submitting it to the Holy Spirit through God's Word (cf. Rom. 12:1,2; 1 Tim. 1:19; 2 Tim. 2:15; Heb. 9:14; 10:22). Paul's fully enlightened conscience exonerated him completely (cf. Acts 23:1; 24:16; 1 Tim. 1:5; 3:9; 2 Tim. 1:3). But ultimately, only God can accurately judge a man's motives (1 Cor. 4:1-5). **fleshly wisdom.** Wisdom that is based on worldly, human insight (*see note on James 3:15*).

1:13 This broadly answers the accusation that Paul had engaged in deceptive personal relationships (cf. 7:2; 11:9). His continuing flow of information to the Corinthians was always clear, straightforward and understandable, consistent, and genuine. Paul wanted them to know that he was not holding anything back, nor did he have any secret agenda (10:11). He simply wanted them to understand all that he had written and spoken to them.

1:14 in part. As the Corinthians read and heard Paul's unfolding instruction to them, they continued to understand more. **we are your boast.** More clearly translated, "we are your reason to be proud" (*see note on v. 12*). **the day of the Lord Jesus.** When He returns (*see notes on Phil. 1:6; 2 Tim. 1:12; 4:8*). Paul eagerly longed for the Lord's coming when they would rejoice over each other in glory (cf. 1 Thess. 2:19,20).

1:15 a second benefit. Or, "twice receive a blessing." Paul's original plan was to visit the Corinthians twice so that they might receive a double blessing. His travel plans were not the result of selfishness, but of the genuine relationship he enjoyed with the Corinthians and their mutual loyalty and godly pride in each other.

1:16 come again. Paul had planned to leave Ephesus, stop at Corinth on the way to Macedonia, and return to Corinth again after his ministry in Macedonia (cf. 1 Cor. 16:5-7). For some reason, Paul's plans changed and he was unable to stop in Corinth the first time. The false apostles who had invaded the church seized upon that honest change of schedule as evidence of his untrustworthiness and tried to use it to discredit him.

1:17 Paul is probably quoting some actual accusations of dishonesty brought by his opponents. **Therefore...did I do it lightly?** The Gr. words that introduce this question call for an indignant, negative answer. Paul declared that he was in no way operating as a vacillating, fickle, unstable person who could not be trusted. **according to the flesh.** Purely from a human viewpoint, apart from the leading of the Holy Spirit, this is someone who is unregenerate (*see notes on Gal. 5:19-21*). He affirmed that his "yes" and "no" words to them really meant what they said.

1:18 *as* God *is* faithful. Paul may have been making an oath and calling God to give testimony (cf. 11:10,31; Rom. 1:9; Gal. 1:20; Phil. 1:8; 1 Thess. 2:5,10). Whatever the case, he refers to God's trustworthiness and the fact that he represented such a God as an honest spokesman. **not Yes and No.** He was not saying "yes" and meaning "no." There was no duplicity with Paul (nor with Timothy and Silas). He said what he meant and did what he said, unless there was compelling reason to change his plans.

1:19 The firmness of Paul's statement, and his use of Jesus' full title, indicates that the person and work of Christ were under attack from the false teachers at Corinth. The proof of his truthfulness with them was the truthful gospel which he faithfully preached. **Silvanus.** The Lat. name for Silas, Paul's companion on his second missionary journey (Acts 16–18) and fellow preacher at Corinth (*see note on Acts 15:22*). **Timothy.** *See note on v. 1.*

promises of God in Him *are* Yes, and in
Him Amen, to the glory of God through
us. 21 Now He who establishes us with you
in Christ and [c]has anointed us *is* God,
22 who [d]also has sealed us and [e]given us
the Spirit in our hearts as a guarantee.
23 Moreover [f]I call God as witness against
my soul, [g]that to spare you I came no more
to Corinth. 24 Not [h]that we [8]have dominion
over your faith, but are fellow workers for
your joy; for [i]by faith you stand.

2 But I determined this within myself,
[a]that I would not come again to you in
sorrow. 2 For if I make you [b]sorrowful,
then who is he who makes me glad but the
one who is made sorrowful by me?

Forgive the Offender

3 And I wrote this very thing to you, lest,
when I came, [c]I should have sorrow over
those from whom I ought to have joy,
[d]having confidence in you all that my joy
is *the joy* of you all. 4 For out of much [1]af-
fliction and anguish of heart I wrote to
you, with many tears, [e]not that you should
be grieved, but that you might know the
love which I have so abundantly for you.
5 But [f]if anyone has caused grief, he has
not [g]grieved me, but all of you to some extent—not to be too severe. 6 This punishment which *was inflicted* [h]by the majority *is*
sufficient for such a man, 7 [i]so that, on the
contrary, you *ought* rather to forgive and
comfort *him,* lest perhaps such a one be
swallowed up with too much sorrow.
8 Therefore I urge you to reaffirm *your* love
to him. 9 For to this end I also wrote, that I
might put you to the test, whether you are
[j]obedient in all things. 10 Now whom you
forgive anything, I also *forgive.* For [2]if in-

21 [c] [1 John 2:20,27]
22 [d] [Eph. 4:30] [e] Rom. 8:16; 2 Cor. 5:5; [Eph. 1:14]
23 [f] Rom. 1:9; Gal. 1:20; Phil. 1:8 [g] 1 Cor. 4:21; 2 Cor. 2:3; 12:20
24 [h] 1 Cor. 3:5; 2 Cor. 4:5; 11:20; [1 Pet. 5:3] [i] Rom. 11:20; 1 Cor. 15:1 [8] *rule*

CHAPTER 2

1 [a] 2 Cor. 1:23
2 [b] 2 Cor. 7:8
3 [c] 1 Cor. 4:21; 2 Cor. 12:21 [d] 2 Cor. 8:22; Gal. 5:10; 2 Thess. 3:4; Philem. 21
4 [e] [2 Cor. 2:9; 7:8, 12] [1] *tribulation*
5 [f] [1 Cor. 5:1] [g] Gal. 4:12
6 [h] 1 Cor. 5:4, 5; 2 Cor. 7:11; 1 Tim. 5:20
7 [i] Gal. 6:1; Eph. 4:32
9 [j] 2 Cor. 7:15; 10:6
10 [2] NU *indeed, what I have forgiven, if I have forgiven anything, I did it for your sakes*

1:20 in Him *are* Yes. All God's OT and NT promises of peace, joy, love, goodness, forgiveness, salvation, sanctification, fellowship, hope, glorification, and heaven are made possible and fulfilled in Jesus Christ (cf. Luke 24:44). **Amen.** The Heb. word of affirmation (cf. Matt. 5:18; John 3:3; Rom. 1:25). Paul reminded them that they had said a collective "yes" to the truth of his preaching and teaching.

1:21 He who establishes us. Christ's saving work of grace stabilizes believers and places them on a firm foundation in Him (cf. Rom. 16:25; 1 Cor. 15:58; 1 Pet. 5:10).

1:21,22 Christ...God...Spirit. A clear reference to the 3 members of the Trinity. The authenticity of Paul's spiritual life and that of every genuine believer is verified by these 4 divine works ("establishes us," "anointed us," "sealed us," "given us the Spirit") accomplished in their lives. For the critics to attack Paul's authenticity was equal to tearing down God's work as well as the church's unity.

1:21 anointed. This word is borrowed from a commissioning service that would symbolically set apart kings, prophets, priests, and special servants. The Holy Spirit sets apart believers and empowers them for the service of gospel proclamation and ministry (cf. Acts 1:8; 1 John 2:20,27).

1:22 sealed us. Refers to the ancient practice of placing soft wax on a document and imprinting the wax with a stamp that indicated authorship or ownership, authenticity, and protection. The Holy Spirit attaches all these meanings to His act of spiritually sealing believers (*see notes on Eph. 1:13*; cf. Hag. 2:23; Eph. 4:30). **guarantee.** A pledge or down payment. The Spirit is the down payment on the believer's eternal inheritance (*see note on Eph. 1:14*; cf. 2 Pet. 1:4,11).

1:23 God as witness. *See note on v. 18.* **to spare you.** Paul finally explained why he said he was coming, but did not. He did not come earlier because he wanted them to have time to repent of and correct their sinful behavior (see Introduction to 1 Corinthians: Background and Setting; *see note on 1 Cor. 4:21*). He waited instead for a report from Titus before taking further action (see chap. 7), hoping he would not have to come again, as he had earlier, to face their rebellion.

1:24 Not that we have dominion over your faith. Paul did not want to lord it over the Corinthians when he ministered and worked among them (*see notes on 1 Pet. 5:2,3*).

2:1 come again...in sorrow. Paul, who had already had a painful confrontation at Corinth (see Introduction: Background and Setting), was not eager to have another one (*see note on 1:23*).

2:2 Although Paul was sensitive to the Corinthians' pain and sadness from the past confrontation, because of his commitment to purity he would confront them again if necessary. "The one who is made sorrowful" refers to one convicted by his sin. In particular, there was apparently on Paul's last visit, a man in the church who confronted him with the accusations taken from the false teachers. The church had not dealt with that man in Paul's defense, and Paul was deeply grieved over that lack of loyalty. The only thing that would bring Paul joy would be repentance from such a one and any who agreed with him, and Paul had been waiting for it.

2:3 I wrote this very thing. Paul's reason for writing was that those in sin would repent—then there could be mutual joy when the apostle came.

2:4 Paul again wanted them to know that his motive in dealing with them in the severe letter (see Introduction: Background and Setting) and 1 Corinthians (see Introduction to 1 Corinthians: Background and Setting) was not harsh but loving.

2:5-11 This passage is one of the best texts in all of Scripture on the godly motivation and rationale for forgiveness.

2:5 if anyone has caused grief. The Gr. construction of this clause assumes the condition to be true—Paul is acknowledging the reality of the offense and its ongoing effect, not on him, but on the church. With this deflection of any personal vengeance, he sought to soften the charge against the penitent offender and allow the church to deal with the man and those who were with him objectively, apart from Paul's personal anguish or offense.

2:6 punishment...*inflicted* by the majority. This indicates that the church in Corinth had followed the biblical process in disciplining the sinning man (cf. Matt. 18:15-20; 1 Cor. 5:4-13; 2 Thess. 3:6,14). The Gr. word for "punishment," used frequently in secular writings but only here in the NT, denoted an official legal penalty or commercial sanction that was enacted against an individual or group (city, nation). ***is* sufficient.** The process of discipline and punishment was enough; now it was time to show mercy because the man had repented (cf. Matt. 18:18,23-35; Gal. 6:1,2; Eph. 4:32; Col. 3:13; Heb. 12:11).

2:7 to forgive. It was time to grant forgiveness so the man's joy would be restored (cf. Ps. 51:12,14; Is. 42:2,3). Paul knew there was—and is—no place in the church for man-made limits on God's grace, mercy, and forgiveness toward repentant sinners. Such restrictions could only rob the fellowship of the joy of unity (cf. Matt. 18:34,35; Mark 11:25,26).

deed I have forgiven anything, I have forgiven that one for your sakes in the presence of Christ, **11** lest Satan should take advantage of us; for we are not ignorant of
his devices.

Triumph in Christ

12 Furthermore, [k]when I came to Troas
to *preach* Christ's gospel, and [l]a [3]door was
opened to me by the Lord, **13** [m]I had no rest
in my spirit, because I did not find Titus
my brother; but taking my leave of them, I
departed for Macedonia.
14 Now thanks *be* to God who always
leads us in triumph in Christ, and through
us [4]diffuses the fragrance of His knowledge in every place. **15** For we are to God
the fragrance of Christ [n]among those who
are being saved and [o]among those who are
perishing. **16** [p]To the one *we are* the aroma
of death *leading* to death, and to the other
the aroma of life *leading* to life. And [q]who
is sufficient for these things? **17** For we are
not, as [5]so many, [r]peddling[6] the word of
God; but as [s]of sincerity, but as from God,
we speak in the sight of God in Christ.

Christ's Epistle

3 Do [a]we begin again to commend ourselves? Or do we need, as some *others*,
[b]epistles of commendation to you or *letters*
of commendation from you? **2** [c]You are our

12 [k]Acts 16:8 [l]1 Cor. 16:9 [3]Opportunity
13 [m]2 Cor. 7:6, 13; 8:6; Gal. 2:1, 3; 2 Tim. 4:10; Titus 1:4
14 [4]*manifests*
15 [n][1 Cor. 1:18] [o][2 Cor. 4:3]
16 [p]Luke 2:34; [John 9:39; 1 Pet. 2:7] [q][1 Cor. 15:10]
17 [r]2 Pet. 2:3 [s]1 Cor. 5:8; 2 Cor. 1:12; 1 Thess. 2:4; 1 Pet. 4:11 [5]*M the rest* [6]*adulterating for gain*

CHAPTER 3

1 [a]2 Cor. 5:12; 10:12, 18; 12:11 [b]Acts 18:27
2 [c]1 Cor. 9:2

2:10 in the presence of Christ. Paul was constantly aware that his entire life was lived in the sight of God, who knew everything he thought, did, and said (cf. v. 17; 4:2; 2 Tim. 4:1).

2:11 devices. The devil wants to produce sin and animosity that will destroy church unity. He uses every possible approach to accomplish this—from legalism to libertinism, intolerance to excessive tolerance (cf. 11:13,14; Eph. 4:14; 6:11,12; 1 Pet. 5:8). Paul used a different word (but with similar meaning) for "devices" (wiles) in Eph. 6:11. It, along with the words for "take advantage" and "ignorant," strongly implies that Satan targets the believer's mind, but God has provided protection by unmasking Satan's schemes in Scripture, along with providing the counteracting truth.

2:12 when I came to Troas. "Troas" was a seaport city N of Ephesus in the western Asia Minor province of Mysia (cf. Acts 16:7). The riots in Ephesus probably caused Paul to leave for Troas, but his main reason for going was to meet Titus, returning from Corinth after delivering "the severe letter" (v. 4), and to hear how the Corinthians had responded to that letter (see Introduction: Background and Setting). **a door was opened to me.** God sovereignly provided a great evangelistic opportunity for Paul, which may have led to the planting of the church in Troas (cf. Acts 20:5-12). Because of the success of his preaching, Paul was assured that this opportunity was from God (cf. 1 Cor. 16:8,9).

2:13 I had no rest in my spirit. Paul's concern for the problems in the Corinthian church and how its members were responding to both those problems and his instructions caused Paul debilitating restlessness and anxiety (cf. 7:5,6). These concerns became so heavy and distracting that he was unable to give full attention to his ministry. **Titus.** One of Paul's most important Gentile converts and closest associates in ministry (*see notes on v. 12; Gal. 2:1;* see Introduction to Titus: Background and Setting). **taking my leave of them.** Because of his troubled heart and mind and his anxiety to see Titus, Paul turned his back on the open door in Troas. **Macedonia.** A province that bordered the NW shore of the Aegean Sea, N of Achaia (see Introduction to 1 Thessalonians: Background and Setting; *see note on Acts 16:9*). Paul headed there in hopes of intersecting with Titus, whom he knew would have to pass through there on his journey back from Corinth.

2:14 Now thanks *be* to God. Paul made an abrupt transition from his narrative and looked above and beyond his troubles to praise and thank God. By turning from the difficulties of ministry and focusing on the privileges of his position in Christ, Paul regained his joyful perspective. He picked the narrative back up in 7:5. **leads us in triumph in Christ.** Paul drew from the imagery of the official and exalted Roman ceremony called the Triumph, in which a victorious general was honored with a festive, ceremonial parade through the streets of Rome. First, Paul gave thanks for being led by a sovereign God at all times (cf. 1 Tim. 1:17); and second, for the promised victory in Jesus Christ (cf. Matt. 16:18; Rom. 8:37; Rev. 6:2). **diffuses the fragrance of His knowledge.** Paul was also grateful for the privilege of being used as an influence for Christ (cf. Rom. 10:14,15) wherever he went. The imagery comes from the strong, sweet smell of incense from censers in the Triumph parade, which, along with the fragrance of crushed flowers strewn under horses' hooves, produced a powerful aroma that filled the city. By analogy, every believer is transformed and called by the Lord to be an influence for His gospel throughout the world.

2:15 to God the fragrance of Christ. Paul was further thankful for the privilege of pleasing God. Continuing his analogy, Paul pictured God as the emperor at the end of the Triumph who also smells the pervasive fragrance and is pleased with the victorious efforts it represents. Wherever God's servant is faithful and is an influence for the gospel, God is pleased (cf. 5:9; Matt. 25:21).

2:16 the aroma of death...life. Paul used the style of Heb. superlatives to emphasize the twofold effect of gospel preaching. To some, the message brings eternal life and ultimate glorification. To others, it is a stumbling stone of offense that brings eternal death (cf. 1 Pet. 2:6-8). **sufficient for these things.** No one in his own strength is adequate or competent to serve God in the ways and with the power that Paul has been describing (cf. 3:5; 1 Cor. 15:10; Gal. 2:20; Eph. 1:19; 3:20; Phil. 2:13; Col. 1:29).

2:17 not, as so many. Or, "not as the majority." This specifically refers to the false teachers in Corinth and to the many other teachers and philosophers of that day who operated by human wisdom (cf. 1 Cor. 1:19,20). **peddling.** From a Gr. verb that means "to corrupt," this word came to refer to corrupt hucksters, or con men who by their cleverness and deception were able to sell as genuine an inferior product that was only a cheap imitation. The false teachers in the church were coming with clever, deceptive rhetoric to offer a degraded, adulterated message that mixed paganism and Jewish tradition. They were dishonest men seeking personal profit and prestige at the expense of gospel truth and people's souls. **in the sight of God.** *See note on v. 10.*

3:1-6 The false teachers in Corinth constantly attacked Paul's competency as a minister of the gospel; these verses form his defense.

3:1 Because Paul did not want to allow the false teachers to accuse him of being proud, he began his defense by posing two questions rather than making any overt claims. **Do we begin again to commend ourselves?** The Gr. word for "commend" means "to introduce." Thus Paul was asking the Corinthians if he needed to reintroduce himself, as if they had never met, and prove himself once more. The form of the question demanded a negative answer. ***letters* of commendation.** The false teachers also accused Paul of not possessing the appropriate documents to prove his legitimacy. Such letters were often used to introduce and authenticate someone to the first-

epistle written in our hearts, known and
read by all men; 3 clearly *you are* an epistle
of Christ, [d]ministered by us, written not
with ink but by the Spirit of the living God,
not [e]on tablets of stone but [f]on tablets of
flesh, *that is,* of the heart.

The Spirit, Not the Letter

4 And we have such trust through Christ
toward God. 5 [g]Not that we are sufficient
of ourselves to think of anything as *being*
from ourselves, but [h]our sufficiency *is*
from God, 6 who also made us sufficient as
[i]ministers of [j]the new covenant, not [k]of the
letter but of the [1]Spirit; for [l]the letter kills,
[m]but the Spirit gives life.

3 [d] 1 Cor. 3:5 [e] Ex. 24:12; 31:18; 32:15; 2 Cor. 3:7 [f] Ps. 40:8
5 [g] [John 15:5] [h] 1 Cor. 15:10
6 [i] 1 Cor. 3:5; Eph. 3:7 [j] Jer. 31:31; Matt. 26:28; Luke 22:20 [k] Rom. 2:27 [l] [Rom. 3:20]; Gal. 3:10 [m] John 6:63; Rom. 8:2 [1] Or *spirit*
7 [n] Rom. 7:10 [o] Ex. 34:1; Deut. 10:1 [p] Ex. 34:29
8 [q] [Gal. 3:5]
9 [r] [Rom. 1:17; 3:21]

Glory of the New Covenant

7 But if [n]the ministry of death, [o]written
and engraved on stones, was glorious, [p]so
that the children of Israel could not look
steadily at the face of Moses because of the
glory of his countenance, which *glory* was
passing away, 8 how will [q]the ministry of
the Spirit not be more glorious? 9 For if the
ministry of condemnation *had* glory, the
ministry [r]of righteousness exceeds much
more in glory. 10 For even what was made
glorious had no glory in this respect, because of the glory that excels. 11 For if what
is passing away *was* glorious, what remains *is* much more glorious.
12 Therefore, since we have such hope,

century churches (cf. 1 Cor. 16:3,10,11). The false teachers undoubtedly arrived in Corinth with such letters, which they may have forged (cf. Acts 15:1,5) or obtained under false pretenses from prominent members of the Jerusalem church. Paul's point was that he did not need secondhand testimony when the Corinthians had firsthand proof of his sincere and godly character, as well as the truth of his message that regenerated them.

3:2 written in our hearts. An affirmation of Paul's affection for the believers in Corinth—he held them close to his heart (cf. 12:15). **known and read by all men.** The transformed lives of the Corinthians were Paul's most eloquent testimonial, better than any secondhand letter. Their changed lives were like an open letter that could be seen and read by all men as a testimony to Paul's faithfulness and the truth of his message.

3:3 epistle of Christ. The false teachers did not have a letter of commendation signed by Christ, but Paul had the Corinthian believers' changed lives as proof that Christ had transformed them. **written not with ink.** Paul's letter was no human document written with ink that can fade. It was a living one. **Spirit of the living God.** Paul's letter was alive, written by Christ's divine, supernatural power through the transforming work of the Holy Spirit (cf. 1 Cor. 2:4,5; 1 Thess. 1:5). **tablets of stone.** A reference to the Ten Commandments (*see notes on Ex. 24:12; 25:16*). **tablets of flesh...of the heart.** More than just writing His law on stone, God was writing His law on the hearts of those people He transformed (cf. Jer. 31:33; 32:38,39; Ezek. 11:19; 36:26,27). The false teachers claimed external adherence to the Mosaic law as the basis of salvation, but the transformed lives of the Corinthians proved that salvation was an internal change wrought by God in the heart.

3:4 such trust. The Gr. word for "trust" can mean "to win." Paul was confident in his ministry, and that confidence resulted in his ability to stay the course and continue moving toward the goal (cf. Acts 4:13,29).

3:5 sufficient. *See note on 2:16.* **to think of anything.** The Gr. word for "think" can also mean "to consider" or "to reason." Paul disdained his own ability to reason, judge, or assess truth. Left to his own abilities, he was useless. He was dependent on divine revelation and the Holy Spirit's power. **our sufficiency *is* from God.** Only God can make a person adequate to do his work, and Paul realized that truth (*see note on 2:16*; cf. 9:8,10; 2 Thess. 2:13).

3:6 new covenant. The covenant that provides forgiveness of sins through the death of Christ (*see notes on Jer. 31:31-34; Matt. 26:28; Heb. 8:7-12*). **the letter.** A shallow, external conformity to the law that missed its most basic requirement of absolutely holy and perfect love for God and man (Matt. 22:34-40) and distorted its true intention, which was to make a person recognize his sinfulness (cf. Rom. 2:27-29). **the Spirit.** The Holy Spirit. **the letter kills, but the Spirit gives life.** The letter kills in two ways: 1) it results in a living death. Before Paul was converted, he thought he was saved by keeping the law, but all it did was kill his peace, joy, and hope; and 2) it results in spiritual death. His inability to truly keep the law sentenced him to an eternal death (*see notes on Rom. 7:9-11*; cf. Rom. 5:12; Gal. 3:10). Only Jesus Christ through the agency of the Holy Spirit can produce eternal life in one who believes.

3:7-18 A true minister of God preaches the New Covenant, thus Paul featured the glory of the New Covenant in these verses.

3:7 the ministry of death. The law is a killer (v. 6) in the sense that it brings knowledge of sin. It acts as a ministry of death because no one can satisfy the demands of the law on his own and is therefore condemned (cf. Gal. 3:22; *see notes on Rom. 7:1-13; 8:4; Gal. 3:10-13; 3:19–4:5*). **was glorious.** When God gave Moses the law, His glory appeared on the mountain (Ex. 19:10-25; 20:18-26). Paul was not depreciating the law; he was acknowledging that it was glorious because it reflected God's nature, will, and character (*see notes on Ex. 33:18–34:9*). **could not look steadily at the face of Moses.** The Israelites could not look intently or stare at Moses' face for too long because the reflective glory of God was too bright for them. It was similar to staring into the sun (*see notes on Ex. 34:29-35*). **the glory of his countenance.** When God manifested Himself, He did so by reducing His attributes to visible light. That's how God manifested Himself to Moses (Ex. 34:29), whose face in turn reflected the glory of God to the people (cf. the Transfiguration of Jesus in Matt. 17:1-8; 2 Pet. 1:16-18; and His second coming in Matt. 24:29,30; 25:31).

3:8,9 ministry of the Spirit...exceeds much more in glory. The "ministry of the Spirit" is Paul's descriptive term for the New Covenant (*see notes on Jer. 31:31-34; Matt. 26:28; 1 Cor. 11:25; Heb. 8:8,13; 9:15; 12:24*). Paul is arguing that if such glory attended the giving of the law under the ministry that brought death, how much more glorious will be the ministry of the Spirit in the New Covenant which brings righteousness. The law pointed to the superior New Covenant and thus a glory that must also be superior.

3:9 ministry of condemnation. Another name for the ministry of death (*see note on v. 7*). **ministry of righteousness.** The New Covenant. The emphasis here is on the righteousness it provides (cf. Rom. 3:21,22; Phil. 3:9).

3:11 what is passing away. The law had a fading glory (cf. v. 7). It was not the final solution or the last word on the plight of sinners. **what remains.** The New Covenant is "what" remains because it is the consummation of God's plan of salvation. It has permanent glory.

3:12 such hope. The belief that all the promises of the New Covenant will occur. It is hope in total and complete forgiveness of sins for those who believe the gospel (cf. Rom. 8:24,25; Gal. 5:5; Eph.

[s]we use great boldness of speech— 13 unlike Moses, [t]*who* put a veil over his face so
that the children of Israel could not look
steadily at [u]the end of what was passing
away. 14 But [v]their minds were blinded.
For until this day the same veil remains
unlifted in the reading of the Old Testament, because the *veil* is taken away in
Christ. 15 But even to this day, when Moses
is read, a veil lies on their heart. 16 Nevertheless [w]when one turns to the Lord, [x]the
veil is taken away. 17 Now [y]the Lord is the
Spirit; and where the Spirit of the Lord *is,*
there *is* [z]liberty. 18 But we all, with unveiled face, beholding [a]as in a mirror [b]the
glory of the Lord, [c]are being transformed
into the same image from glory to glory,
just as [2]by the Spirit of the Lord.

12 [s]Acts 4:13,29; 2 Cor. 7:4; Eph. 6:19 **13** [t]Ex. 34:33-35; 2 Cor. 3:7 [u]Rom. 10:4; [Gal. 3:23] **14** [v]Is. 6:10; 29:10; Acts 28:26; Rom. 11:7,8; 2 Cor. 4:4 **16** [w]Ex. 34:34; Rom. 11:23 [x]Is. 25:7 **17** [y][1 Cor. 15:45] [z]John 8:32; Gal. 5:1, 13 **18** [a]1 Cor. 13:12 [b][2 Cor. 4:4, 6] [c][Rom. 8:29, 30] [2]Or *from the Lord, the Spirit*

CHAPTER 4

1 [a]1 Cor. 7:25 [b]Luke 18:1; 2 Cor. 4:16; Gal. 6:9; Eph. 3:13; 2 Thess. 3:13

The Light of Christ's Gospel

4 Therefore, since we have this ministry, [a]as we have received mercy, we
[b]do not lose heart. 2 But we have renounced the hidden things of shame, not
walking in craftiness nor [1]handling the
word of God deceitfully, but by manifestation of the truth [c]commending ourselves to every man's conscience in the
sight of God. 3 But even if our gospel is
veiled, [d]it is veiled to those who are perishing, 4 whose minds [e]the god of this age
[f]has blinded, who do not believe, lest [g]the
light of the gospel of the glory of Christ,
[h]who is the image of God, should shine

2 [c]2 Cor. 5:11 [1]*adulterating the word of God* **3** [d][1 Cor. 1:18]; 2 Cor. 2:15 **4** [e]John 12:31; [Eph. 6:12] [f]John 12:40 [g][2 Cor. 3:8, 9] [h][John 1:18]; Phil. 2:6; Col. 1:15; Heb. 1:3

1:18; 1 Pet. 1:3,13,21). **boldness of speech.** The Gr. word for "boldness" means "courageously." Because of his confidence, Paul preached the New Covenant fearlessly, without any hesitation or timidity.

3:13 Moses, *who* put a veil over his face. This physical action pictured the fact that Moses did not have the confidence or boldness of Paul because the Old Covenant was veiled. It was shadowy. It was made up of types, pictures, symbols, and mystery. Moses communicated the glory of the Old Covenant with a certain obscurity (cf. 1 Pet. 1:10,11).

3:14,15 the same veil remains...a veil lies on their heart. The "veil" here represents unbelief. Those Israelites did not grasp the glory of the Old Covenant because of their unbelief. As a result, the meaning of the Old Covenant was obscure to them (cf. Heb. 3:8,15; 4:7). Paul's point was that just as the Old Covenant was obscure to the people of Moses' day, it was still obscure to those who trusted in it as a means of salvation in Paul's day. The veil of ignorance obscures the meaning of the Old Covenant to the hardened heart (cf. John 5:38).

3:14 the *veil* is taken away in Christ. Without Christ the OT is unintelligible. But when a person comes to Christ, the veil is lifted and his spiritual perception is no longer impaired (Is. 25:6-8). With the veil removed, believers are able to see the glory of God revealed in Christ (John 1:14). They understand that the law was never given to save them, but to lead them to the One who would.

3:17 the Lord is the Spirit. Yahweh of the OT is the same Lord who is saving people in the New Covenant through the agency of the Holy Spirit. The same God is the minister of both the Old and New Covenants. **there *is* liberty.** Freedom from sin and the futile attempt to keep the demands of the law as a means of earning righteousness (cf. John 8:32-36; Rom. 3:19,20). The believer is no longer in bondage to the law's condemnation and Satan's dominion.

3:18 we all. Not just Moses, or prophets, apostles, and preachers, but all believers. **with unveiled face.** Believers in the New Covenant have nothing obstructing their vision of Christ and His glory as revealed in the Scripture. **beholding as in a mirror.** Paul's emphasis here is not so much on the reflective capabilities of the mirror as it is on the intimacy of it. A person can bring a mirror right up to his face and get an unobstructed view. Mirrors in Paul's day were polished metal (*see note on James 1:23*), and thus offered a far from perfect reflection. Though the vision is unobstructed and intimate, believers do not see a perfect representation of God's glory now, but will one day (cf. 1 Cor. 13:12). **being transformed.** A continual, progressive transformation (*see note on Rom. 12:2*). **into the same image.** As they gaze at the glory of the Lord, believers are continually being transformed into Christlikeness. The ultimate goal of the believer is to be like Christ (cf. Rom. 8:29; Phil. 3:12-14; 1 John 3:2), and by continually focusing on Him the Spirit transforms the believer more and more into His image. **from glory to glory.** From one level of glory to another level of glory—from one level of manifesting Christ to another. This verse describes progressive sanctification. The more believers grow in their knowledge of Christ, the more He is revealed in their lives (cf. Phil. 3:12-14).

4:1 this ministry. The New Covenant gospel of Jesus Christ. **lose heart.** A strong Gr. term which refers to abandoning oneself to cowardly surrender. That was not how Paul responded to the continual attacks he faced. The task of ministering the New Covenant was too noble to lose heart over (cf. Gal. 6:9; Eph. 3:13). Since God had called him to proclaim it, Paul could not abandon his calling. Instead, he trusted God to strengthen him (cf. Acts 20:24; 1 Cor. 9:16,17; Col. 1:23,25).

4:2 we have renounced the hidden things of shame. "Renounced" means "to turn away from" or "to repent," and "shame" means "ugly" or "disgraceful." The phrase "hidden things of shame" refers to secret immoralities, hypocrisies, and the sins hidden deep in the darkness of one's life. At salvation every believer repents and turns away from such sin and devotes his life to the pursuit of godliness. This appears to be a reply by Paul to a direct and slanderous accusation against him, that he was a hypocrite, whose mask of piety hid a corrupt and shameful life. **handling...deceitfully.** This Gr. word means "to tamper with," and was used in nonbiblical sources to speak of the dishonest business practice of diluting wine with water. The false teachers accused Paul of being a deceiver ("craftiness") who was twisting and perverting the teaching of Jesus and the OT Scripture.

4:3 if our gospel is veiled...to those who are perishing. The false teachers accused Paul of preaching an antiquated message. So Paul showed that the problem was not with the message or the messenger, but with the hearers headed for hell (cf. 1 Cor. 2:14). The preacher cannot persuade people to believe; only God can do that.

4:4 the god of this age. Satan (cf. Matt. 4:8; John 12:31; 14:30; 16:11; Eph. 2:2; 2 Tim. 2:26; 1 John 5:19). **this age.** The current world mind-set expressed by the ideals, opinions, goals, hopes, and views of the majority of people. It encompasses the world's philosophies, education, and commerce. *See notes on 10:5.* **has blinded.** Satan blinds men to God's truth through the world system he has created. Without a godly influence, man left to himself will follow that system, which panders to the depravity of unbelievers and deepens their moral darkness (cf. Matt. 13:19). Ultimately, it is God who allows such blindness (John 12:40). **image of God.** Jesus Christ is the exact representation of God Himself (*see notes on Col. 1:15; 2:9; Heb. 1:3*).

on them. 5 [i]For we do not preach ourselves,
but Christ Jesus the Lord, and [j]ourselves
your bondservants for Jesus' sake. 6 For it is
the God [k]who commanded light to shine
out of darkness, who has [l]shone in our
hearts to *give* the light of the knowledge of
the glory of God in the face of Jesus Christ.

Cast Down but Unconquered

7 But we have this treasure in earthen
vessels, [m]that the excellence of the power
may be of God and not of us. 8 *We are*
[n]hard-pressed on every side, yet not
crushed; *we are* perplexed, but not in despair; 9 persecuted, but not [o]forsaken;
[p]struck down, but not destroyed— 10 [q]al-
ways carrying about in the body the dying
of the Lord Jesus, [r]that the life of Jesus also
may be manifested in our body. 11 For we
who live [s]are always delivered to death for
Jesus' sake, that the life of Jesus also may
be manifested in our mortal flesh. 12 So
then death is working in us, but life in you.
13 And since we have [t]the same spirit of
faith, according to what is written, [u]*"I believed and therefore I spoke,"* we also believe and therefore speak, 14 knowing that
[v]He who raised up the Lord Jesus will also
raise us up with Jesus, and will present *us*
with you. 15 For [w]all things *are* for your
sakes, that [x]grace, having spread through
the many, may cause thanksgiving to
abound to the glory of God.

Seeing the Invisible

16 Therefore we [y]do not lose heart. Even
though our outward man is perishing, yet
the inward *man* is [z]being renewed day by
day. 17 For [a]our light affliction, which is
but for a moment, is working for us a far
more exceeding *and* eternal weight of
glory, 18 [b]while we do not look at the

5 [i] 1 Cor. 1:13 [j] 1 Cor. 9:19
6 [k] Gen. 1:3 [l] Is. 9:2; Mal. 4:2; Luke 1:78; 2 Pet. 1:19
7 [m] Judg. 7:2; 1 Cor. 2:5
8 [n] 2 Cor. 1:8; 7:5
9 [o] Ps. 129:2; [Heb. 13:5] [p] Ps. 37:24
10 [q] Phil. 3:10 [r] Rom. 8:17
11 [s] Rom. 8:36
13 [t] 2 Pet. 1:1 [u] Ps. 116:10
14 [v] [Rom. 8:11]
15 [w] Col. 1:24 [x] 1 Cor. 9:19; 2 Cor. 1:11
16 [y] 2 Cor. 4:1; Gal. 6:9 [z] [Is. 40:29, 31; Col. 3:10]
17 [a] Matt. 5:12; Rom. 8:18; 1 Pet. 1:6
18 [b] Rom. 8:24; [2 Cor. 5:7; Heb. 11:1, 13]

4:5 we do not preach ourselves. The false teachers accused Paul of preaching for his own benefit, yet they were the ones guilty of doing so. In contrast, Paul was always humble (12:5,9; cf. 1 Cor. 2:3); he never promoted himself, but always preached Christ Jesus as Lord (1 Cor. 2:2).

4:6 commanded light to shine out of darkness. A direct reference to God as Creator, who commanded physical light into existence (Gen. 1:3). **the light of the knowledge of the glory of God.** The same God who created physical light in the universe is the same God who must create supernatural light in the soul and usher believers from the kingdom of darkness to His kingdom of light (Col. 1:13). The light is expressed as "the knowledge of the glory of God." That means to know that Christ is God incarnate. To be saved, one must understand that the glory of God shone in Jesus Christ. That is the theme of John's gospel (*see note on John 1:4*).

4:7 this treasure. *See note on v. 1.* **earthen vessels.** The Gr. word means "baked clay," and refers to clay pots. They were cheap, breakable, and replaceable, but they served necessary household functions. Sometimes they were used as a vault to store valuables, such as money, jewelry, or important documents. But they were most often used for holding garbage and human waste. The latter is the use Paul had in mind, and it was how Paul viewed himself—as lowly, common, expendable, and replaceable (cf. 1 Cor. 1:20-27; 2 Tim. 2:20,21). **excellence of the power may be of God and not of us.** By using frail and expendable people, God makes it clear that salvation is the result of His power and not any power His messengers could generate (cf. 2:16). The great power of God overcomes and transcends the clay pot. The messenger's weakness is not fatal to what he does; it is essential (cf. 12:9,10).

4:8,9 Here Paul gave 4 contrasting metaphors to show that his weakness did not cripple him, but actually strengthened him (cf. 6:4-10; 12:7-10).

4:10 always carrying about in the body the dying of the Lord Jesus. "Always" indicates that the suffering Paul experienced was endless. And the suffering was a result of attacks against the "Lord Jesus," not Paul and other believers. Those who hated Jesus took out their vengeance on those who represented Him (cf. John 15:18-21; Gal. 6:17; Col. 1:24). **that the life of Jesus also may be manifested in our body.** Through Paul's weakness, Christ was put on display (cf. Gal. 2:20). His suffering, the false apostles said, was evidence that God was not with him and he was a fraud. On the contrary, Paul affirmed that his suffering was the badge of his loyalty to Christ and the source of his power (12:9,10).

4:11 delivered to death. Refers to the transferring of a prisoner to the executioner. It was used to refer to Christ's being delivered to those who crucified Him (Matt. 27:2). In this case, it refers to the potential physical death constantly faced by those who represented Christ. **our mortal flesh.** Another term for Paul's humanness—his physical body (cf. v. 10; 5:3).

4:12 Paul faced death every day, yet he was willing to pay that price if it meant salvation for those to whom he preached (cf. Phil. 2:17; Col. 1:24; 2 Tim. 2:10).

4:13 Paul remained true to his convictions, no matter the cost. He was not a pragmatist who would alter his message to suit his listeners. He was convinced of the power of God to act through the message he preached. **spirit of faith.** The attitude of faith, not the Holy Spirit. Paul had the same conviction about the power of the message as did the psalmist (*see following note*). ***I believed and therefore I spoke.*** A quotation from the LXX (the Gr. translation of the OT) version of Ps. 116:10. In the midst of his troubles, the psalmist confidently asked God to deliver him out of his troubles. He could confidently do so because he believed God would answer his prayer.

4:15 to the glory of God. The ultimate goal of all that the believer does (*see note on 1 Cor. 10:31*).

4:16 we do not lose heart. *See note on v. 1.* **our outward man is perishing.** The physical body is in the process of decay and will eventually die. On the surface Paul was referring to the normal aging process, but with the added emphasis that his lifestyle sped up that process. While not an old man, Paul wore himself out in ministry, both in the effort and pace he maintained, plus the number of beatings and attacks he absorbed from his enemies (cf. 6:4-10; 11:23-27). **inward *man*.** The soul of every believer i.e., the new creation—the eternal part of the believer (cf. Eph. 4:24; Col. 3:10). **being renewed.** The growth and maturing process of the believer is constantly occurring. While the physical body is decaying, the inner self of the believer continues to grow and mature into Christlikeness (cf. Eph. 3:16-20).

4:17 our light affliction...for a moment. The Gr. word for "light" means "a weightless trifle" and "affliction" refers to intense pressure. From a human perspective, Paul's own testimony lists a seemingly unbearable litany of sufferings and persecutions he endured throughout his life (11:23-33), yet he viewed them as weightless and lasting for only a brief moment. **eternal weight of glory.** The Gr. word for "weight" refers to a heavy mass. For Paul, the future glory he

things which are seen, but at the things
which are not seen. For the things which
are seen *are* temporary, but the things
which are not seen *are* eternal.

Assurance of the Resurrection

5 For we know that if [a]our earthly
[1]house, *this* tent, is destroyed, we have
a building from God, a house [b]not made
with hands, eternal in the heavens. 2 For
in this [c]we groan, earnestly desiring to be
clothed with our [2]habitation which is
from heaven, 3 if indeed, [d]having been
clothed, we shall not be found naked.
4 For we who are in *this* tent groan, being
burdened, not because we want to be unclothed, [e]but further clothed, that mortality may be swallowed up by life. 5 Now He
who has prepared us for this very thing *is*
God, who also [f]has given us the Spirit as
[3]a guarantee.
6 So *we are* always confident, knowing
that while we are at home in the body we
are absent from the Lord. 7 For [g]we walk
by faith, not by sight. 8 We are confident,
yes, [h]well pleased rather to be absent from
the body and to be present with the Lord.

The Judgment Seat of Christ

9 Therefore we make it our aim, whether
present or absent, to be well pleasing to
Him. 10 [i]For we must all appear before the
judgment seat of Christ, [j]that each one
may receive the things *done* in the body, ac-

CHAPTER 5

1 [a] Job 4:19; 1 Cor. 15:47; 2 Cor. 4:7 [b] Mark 14:58; Acts 7:48; Heb. 9:11, 24 [1] Physical body
2 [c] Rom. 8:23; 2 Cor. 5:4 [2] *dwelling*
3 [d] Rev. 3:18
4 [e] 1 Cor. 15:53
5 [f] Rom. 8:23; [2 Cor. 1:22]; Eph. 1:14 [3] *down payment, earnest*
7 [g] Rom. 8:24; Heb. 11:1
8 [h] Phil. 1:23
10 [i] Matt. 16:27; Acts 10:42; Rom. 2:16; 14:10, 12 [j] Gal. 6:7; Eph. 6:8

would experience with the Lord far outweighed any suffering he experienced in this world (cf. Rom. 8:17,18; 1 Pet. 1:6,7). Paul understood that the greater the suffering, the greater would be his eternal glory (cf. 1 Pet. 4:13).

4:18 things which are seen...not seen. Endurance is based on one's ability to look beyond the physical to the spiritual; beyond the present to the future, and beyond the visible to the invisible. Believers must look past what is temporary—what is perishing (i.e., the things of the world). **things...not seen *are* eternal.** Pursuing God, Christ, the Holy Spirit, and the souls of men should consume the believer.

5:1 earthly house...tent. Paul's metaphor for the physical body (cf. 2 Pet. 1:13,14). The imagery was quite natural for that time because many people were nomadic tent dwellers, and Paul as a tentmaker (Acts 18:3) knew much about tents' characteristics. Also, the Jewish tabernacle had symbolized God's presence among the people as they left Egypt and became a nation. Paul's point is that like a temporary tent, man's earthly existence is fragile, insecure, and lowly (cf. 1 Pet. 2:11). **a building from God.** Paul's metaphor for the believer's resurrected, glorified body (cf. 1 Cor. 15:35-50). "Building" implies solidity, security, certainty, and permanence, as opposed to the frail, temporary, uncertain nature of a tent. Just as the Israelites replaced the tabernacle with the temple, so believers ought to long to exchange their earthly bodies for glorified ones (*see notes on 4:16; Rom. 8:19-23; 1 Cor. 15:35-50; Phil. 3:20,21*). **a house...in the heavens.** A heavenly, eternal body. Paul wanted a new body that would forever perfectly express his transformed nature. **not made with hands.** A glorified body, by definition, is not of this earthly creation (*see notes on Mark 14:58; Heb. 9:11*; cf. John 2:19; Col. 2:11).

5:2 we groan. Paul had a passionate longing to be free from his earthly body and all the accompanying sins, frustrations, and weaknesses that were so relentless (*see notes on Rom. 7:24; 8:23*). **clothed with our habitation...from heaven.** The perfections of immortality (*see notes on v. 1*).

5:3 we shall not be found naked. Paul clarified the fact that the believer's hope for the next life is not a disembodied spiritual life, but a real, eternal, resurrection body. Unlike the pagans who viewed matter as evil and spirit as good, Paul knew that Christian death would not mean being released into a nebulous, spiritual infinity. Rather, it would mean the receiving of a glorified, spiritual, immortal, perfect, qualitatively different but nonetheless real body, just as Jesus received (*see notes on 1 Cor. 15:35-44; Phil. 3:20,21*; cf. 1 John 3:2).

5:4 unclothed...further clothed. *See notes on vv. 2,3.* Paul reiterated that he could hardly wait to get his glorified body (cf. Phil. 1:21-23). **mortality...swallowed up by life.** Paul wanted the fullness of all that God had planned for him in eternal life, when all that is earthly and human will cease to be.

5:5 for this very thing. More precisely translated "purpose." Paul emphatically states that the believer's heavenly existence will come to pass according to God's sovereign purpose (*see notes on Rom. 8:28-30*; cf. John 6:37-40,44). **God...has given us the Spirit.** *See notes on 1:22; Rom. 5:5; Eph. 1:13*; cf. Phil. 1:6. **guarantee.** *See notes on 1:22; Eph. 1:13.*

5:6 at home in the body...absent from the Lord. While a believer is alive on earth he is away from the fullness of God's presence. However, Paul was not saying he had absolutely no contact, because there is prayer, the indwelling Spirit, and fellowship through the Word. Paul was simply expressing a heavenly homesickness, a strong yearning to be at home with his Lord (cf. Ps. 73:25; 1 Thess. 4:17; Rev. 21:3,23; 22:3).

5:7 The Christian can hope for a heaven he has not seen. He does so by believing what Scripture says about it and living by that belief (*see note on Heb. 11:1*; cf. John 20:29).

5:8 absent from the body...present with the Lord. Because heaven is a better place than earth, Paul would rather have been there, with God. This sentiment simply states Paul's feelings and longings of v. 6 from a reverse perspective (*see notes on Phil. 1:21,23*).

5:9 we make it our aim. Paul was speaking of his ambition in life, but not the kind of proud, selfish desire that "ambition" expresses in English. "Aim" is from the Gr. word that means "to love what is honorable." Paul demonstrated that it is right and noble for the believer to strive for excellence, spiritual goals, and all that is honorable before God (cf. Rom. 15:20; 1 Tim. 3:1). **whether present or absent.** *See notes on vv. 6,8.* Paul's ambition was not altered by his state of being—whether he should be in heaven or on earth—he cared how he lived for the Lord (*see notes on Rom. 14:6; Phil. 1:20*; cf. 1 Cor. 9:27). **well pleasing to Him.** This was Paul's highest goal (cf. 1 Cor. 4:1-5), and should be so for every believer (cf. Rom. 12:2; Eph. 5:10; Col. 1:9; 1 Thess. 4:1). The term translated "well pleasing" is the same one used in Titus 2:9 to describe slaves who were passionate to please their masters.

5:10 This describes the believer's deepest motivation and highest aim in pleasing God—the realization that every Christian is inevitably and ultimately accountable to Him. **the judgment seat of Christ.** "Judgment seat" metaphorically refers to the place where the Lord will sit to evaluate believers' lives for the purpose of giving them eternal rewards. It is translated from the Gr. word *bēma,* which was an elevated platform where victorious athletes (e.g., during the Olympics) went to receive their crowns. The term is also used in the NT to refer to the place of judging, as when Jesus stood before Pontius Pilate (Matt. 27:19; John 19:13), but here the reference is definitely from the athletic analogy. Corinth had such a platform where both athletic rewards and legal justice were dispensed (Acts 18:12-16), so the Corinthians understood Paul's reference. **the things *done* in the body.** Actions

cording to what he has done, whether
good or bad. 11 Knowing, therefore, [k]the
terror of the Lord, we persuade men; but
we are well known to God, and I also trust
are well known in your consciences.

Be Reconciled to God

12 For [l]we do not commend ourselves
again to you, but give you opportunity
[m]to boast on our behalf, that you may
have *an answer* for those who boast in appearance and not in heart. 13 For [n]if we
are beside ourselves, *it is* for God; or if we
are of sound mind, *it is* for you. 14 For the
love of Christ compels us, because we
judge thus: that [o]if One died for all, then
all died; 15 and He died for all, [p]that those
who live should live no longer for themselves, but for Him who died for them
and rose again.
16 [q]Therefore, from now on, we regard
no one according to the flesh. Even though
we have known Christ according to the
flesh, [r]yet now we know *Him thus* no
longer. 17 Therefore, if anyone [s]*is* in Christ,
he is [t]a new creation; [u]old things have
passed away; behold, all things have become [v]new. 18 Now all things *are* of God,

11 [k][Heb. 10:31; 12:29; Jude 23]
12 [l]2 Cor. 3:1 [m]2 Cor. 1:14; Phil. 1:26
13 [n]Mark 3:21; 2 Cor. 11:1, 16; 12:11
14 [o][Rom. 5:15; 6:6; Gal. 2:20; Col. 3:3]
15 [p][Rom. 6:11]
16 [q]2 Cor. 10:3 [r][Matt. 12:50]
17 [s][John 6:63] [t][Rom. 8:9] [u]Is. 43:18; 65:17; [Eph. 4:24]; Rev. 21:4 [v][Rom. 6:3-10; Col. 3:3]

which happened during the believer's time of earthly ministry. This does not include sins, since their judgment took place at the cross (Eph 1:7). Paul was referring to all those activities believers do during their lifetimes, which relate to their eternal reward and praise from God. What Christians do in their temporal bodies will, in His eyes, have an impact for eternity (*see notes on 1 Cor. 4:3-5*; cf. Rom. 12:1,2: Rev. 22:12). **whether good or bad.** These Gr. terms do not refer to moral good and moral evil. Matters of sin have been completely dealt with by the death of the Savior. Rather, Paul was comparing worthwhile, eternally valuable activities with useless ones. His point was not that believers should not enjoy certain wholesome, earthly things, but that they should glorify God in them and spend most of their energy and time with what has eternal value (*see notes on 1 Cor. 3:8-14*).

5:11 the terror of the Lord. This is more clearly rendered, "the fear of the Lord." It is not referring to being afraid, but to Paul's worshipful reverence for God as his essential motivation to live in such a way as to honor his Lord and maximize his reward for his Lord's glory (cf. 7:1; Prov. 9:10; Acts 9:31). **we persuade men.** The Gr. word for "persuade" means to seek someone's favor, as in getting the other person to see you in a certain favorable or desired way (cf. Gal. 1:10). This term can mean gospel preaching (Acts 18:4; 28:23), but here Paul was persuading others not about salvation, but about his own integrity. The Corinthians' eternal reward would be affected if they defected to the false teachers and left the divine teaching of Paul. **well known.** Paul's true spiritual condition of sincerity and integrity was manifest to God (*see notes on 1:12*; cf. Acts 23:1; 24:16), and he also wanted the Corinthians to believe the truth about him.

5:12 boast in appearance. Those who have no integrity, such as Paul's opponents at Corinth, have to take pride in externals, which can be any false doctrine accompanied by showy hypocrisy (cf. Matt. 5:20; 6:1; Mark 7:6,7).

5:13 beside ourselves. This Gr. phrase usually means to be insane, or out of one's mind, but here Paul used the expression to describe himself as one dogmatically devoted to truth. In this way, he answered those critics who claimed he was nothing more than an insane fanatic (cf. John 8:48; Acts 26:22-24). **of sound mind.** The original word meant to be moderate, sober minded, and in complete control. Paul also behaved this way among the Corinthians as he defended his integrity and communicated truth to them.

5:14 the love of Christ. Christ's love for Paul and all believers at the cross (cf. Rom. 5:6-8). Christ's loving, substitutionary death motivated Paul's service for Him (cf. Gal. 2:20; Eph. 3:19). **compels.** This refers to pressure that causes action. Paul emphasized the strength of his desire to offer his life to the Lord. **One died for all.** This expresses the truth of Christ's substitutionary death. The preposition "for" indicates He died "in behalf of," or "in the place of" all (cf. Is. 53:4-12; Gal. 3:13; Heb. 9:11-14). This truth is at the heart of the doctrine of salvation. God's wrath against sin required death; Jesus took that wrath and died in the sinner's place. Thus He took away God's wrath and satisfied God's justice as a perfect sacrifice (*see notes on v. 21; Rom. 5:6-11,18,19; 1 Tim. 2:5,6*; cf. Eph. 5:2; 1 Thess. 5:10; Titus 2:14; 1 Pet. 2:24). **then all died.** Everyone who died in Christ receives the benefits of His substitutionary death (*see notes on Rom. 3:24-26; 6:8*). With this short phrase, Paul defined the extent of the atonement and limited its application. This statement logically completes the meaning of the preceding phrase, in effect saying, "Christ died for all who died in Him," or "One died for all, therefore all died" (*see notes on vv. 19-21*; cf. John 10:11-16; Acts 20:28). Paul was overwhelmed with gratitude that Christ loved him and was so gracious as to make him a part of the "all" who died in Him.

5:15 As he defended his integrity to the Corinthians, Paul wanted them to know that his old, self-centered life was finished and that he had an all-out desire to live righteously. For all genuine believers, their death in Christ is not only a death to sin, but a resurrection to a new life of righteousness (*see notes on Rom. 6:3,4,8,10*; cf. Gal. 2:19,20; Col. 3:3).

5:16 Since Paul's conversion, his priority was to meet people's spiritual needs (cf. Acts 17:16; Rom. 1:13-16; 9:1-3; 10:1). **according to the flesh.** Paul no longer evaluated people according to external, human, worldly standards (cf. 10:3). **we know *Him thus* no longer.** Paul, as a Christian, also no longer had merely a fallible, human assessment of Jesus Christ (cf. Acts 9:1-6; 26:9-23).

5:17 in Christ. These two words comprise a brief but most profound statement of the inexhaustible significance of the believer's redemption, which includes the following: 1) the believer's security in Christ, who bore in His body God's judgment against sin; 2) the believer's acceptance in Him with whom God alone is well pleased; 3) the believer's future assurance in Him who is the resurrection to eternal life and the sole guarantor of the believer's inheritance in heaven; and 4) the believer's participation in the divine nature of Christ, the everlasting Word (cf. 2 Pet. 1:4). **new creation.** This describes something that is created at a qualitatively new level of excellence. It refers to regeneration or the new birth (cf. John 3:3; Eph. 2:1-3; Titus 3:5; 1 Pet. 1:23; 1 John 2:29; 3:9; 5:4). This expression encompasses the Christian's forgiveness of sins paid for in Christ's substitutionary death (cf. Gal. 6:15; Eph. 4:24). **old things have passed away.** After a person is regenerate, old value systems, priorities, beliefs, loves, and plans are gone. Evil and sin are still present, but the believer sees them in a new perspective (*see note on v. 16*), and they no longer control him. **all things...new.** The Gr. grammar indicates that this newness is a continuing condition of fact. The believer's new spiritual perception of everything is a constant reality for him, and he now lives for eternity, not temporal things. James identifies this transformation as the faith that produces works (*see notes on Eph. 2:10; James 2:14-26*).

5:18 all things *are* of God. Many modern translations add the article "these" before "things," which connects the word "things" to all that Paul has just asserted in vv. 14-17. All the aspects related to someone's conversion and newly transformed life in Christ are accomplished by sovereign God. Sinners on their own cannot decide to participate in these new realities (*see note on Rom. 5:10*; cf. 1 Cor. 8:6;

[w]who has reconciled us to Himself
through Jesus Christ, and has given us the
ministry of reconciliation, 19 that is, that
[x]God was in Christ reconciling the world
to Himself, not [4]imputing their trespasses
to them, and has committed to us the word
of reconciliation.
20 Now then, we are [y]ambassadors for
Christ, as though God were pleading
through us: we implore *you* on Christ's behalf, be reconciled to God. 21 For [z]He made
Him who knew no sin *to be* sin for us, that
we might become [a]the righteousness of
God in Him.

18 [w]Rom. 5:10; [Eph. 2:16; Col. 1:20]
19 [x][Rom. 3:24] [4]*reckoning*
20 [y]Mal. 2:7; Eph. 6:20
21 [z]Is. 53:6, 9 [a][Rom. 1:17; 3:21]; 1 Cor. 1:30

CHAPTER 6

1 [a]1 Cor. 3:9 [b]2 Cor. 5:20
2 [c]Is. 49:8
3 [d]Rom. 14:13

Marks of the Ministry

6 We then, *as* [a]workers together *with Him*
also [b]plead with *you* not to receive the
grace of God in vain. 2 For He says:

> [c]*"In an acceptable time I have heard*
> *you,*
> *And in the day of salvation I have*
> *helped you."*

Behold, now *is* the accepted time; behold,
now *is* the day of salvation.
3 [d]We give no offense in anything, that
our ministry may not be blamed. 4 But in

11:12; Eph. 2:1). **ministry of reconciliation.** This speaks to the reality that God wills to be reconciled with sinners (cf. Rom. 5:10; Eph. 4:17-24). God has called believers to proclaim the gospel of reconciliation to others (cf. 1 Cor. 1:17). The concept of service, such as waiting on tables, derives from the Gr. word for "ministry." Lit. God wants Christians to accept the privilege of serving unbelievers by proclaiming a desire to be reconciled.

5:19 God was in Christ. God by His own will and design used His Son, the only acceptable and perfect sacrifice, as the means to reconcile sinners to Himself (*see notes on v. 18; Acts 2:23; Col. 1:19,20*; cf. John 14:6; Acts 4:12; 1 Tim. 2:5,6). **reconciling the world.** God initiates the change in the sinner's status in that He brings him from a position of alienation to a state of forgiveness and right relationship with Himself. This again is the essence of the gospel. The word "world" should not be interpreted in any universalistic sense, which would say that everyone will be saved, or even potentially reconciled. "World" refers rather to the entire sphere of mankind or humanity (cf. Titus 2:11; 3:4), the category of beings to whom God offers reconciliation—people from every ethnic group, without distinction. The intrinsic merit of Christ's reconciling death is infinite and the offer is unlimited. However, actual atonement was made only for those who believe; cf. John 10:11,15; 17:9; Acts 13:48; 20:28; Rom. 8:32,33; Eph. 5:25). The rest of humanity will pay the price personally for their own sin in eternal hell. **imputing.** This may also be translated "reckoning," or "counting." This is the heart of the doctrine of justification whereby God declares the repentant sinner righteous and does not count his sins against him because He covers him with the righteousness of Christ the moment he places wholehearted faith in Christ and His sacrificial death (*see notes on Rom. 3:24–4:5*; cf. Ps. 32:2; Rom. 4:8). **word of reconciliation.** *See note on v. 18.* Here Paul presents another aspect to the meaning of the gospel. He used the Gr. word for "word" (cf. Acts 13:26), which indicated a true and trustworthy message, as opposed to a false or unsure one. In a world filled with false messages, believers have the solid, truthful message of the gospel.

5:20 ambassadors. A term that is related to the more familiar Gr. word often translated "elder." It described an older, more experienced man who served as a representative of a king from one country to another. Paul thus described his role—and the role of all believers—as a messenger representing the King of heaven with the gospel, who pleads with the people of the world to be reconciled to God, who is their rightful King (cf. Rom. 10:13-18). **as though God were pleading.** As believers present the gospel, God speaks (lit. "calls," or "begs") through them and urges unbelieving sinners to come in an attitude of faith and accept the gospel, which means to repent of their sins and believe on Jesus (cf. Acts 16:31; James 4:8).

5:21 Here Paul summarized the heart of the gospel, resolving the mystery and paradox of vv. 18-20, and explaining how sinners can be reconciled to God through Jesus Christ. These 15 Gr. words express the doctrines of imputation and substitution like no other single verse. **who knew no sin.** Jesus Christ, the sinless Son of God (*see notes on Gal. 4:4,5*; cf. Luke 23:4,14,22,47; John 8:46; Heb. 4:15; 7:26; 1 Pet. 1:19; 2:22-24; 3:18; Rev. 5:2-10). **sin for us.** God the Father, using the principle of imputation (*see note on v. 19*), treated Christ as if He were a sinner though He was not, and had Him die as a substitute to pay the penalty for the sins of those who believe in Him (cf. Is. 53:4-6; Gal. 3:10-13; 1 Pet. 2:24). On the cross, He did not become a sinner (as some suggest), but remained as holy as ever. He was treated as if He were guilty of all the sins ever committed by all who would ever believe, though He committed none. The wrath of God was exhausted on Him and the just requirement of God's law met for those for whom He died. **the righteousness of God.** Another reference to justification and imputation. The righteousness that is credited to the believer's account is the righteousness of Jesus Christ, God's Son (*see notes on Rom. 1:17; 3:21-24; Phil. 3:9*). As Christ was not a sinner, but was treated as if He were, so believers who have not yet been made righteous (until glorification) are treated as if they were righteous. He bore their sins so that they could bear His righteousness. God treated Him as if He committed believers' sins, and treats believers as if they did only the righteous deeds of the sinless Son of God.

6:1 to receive the grace of God in vain. Most of the Corinthians were saved but hindered by legalistic teaching regarding sanctification (*see notes on 11:3; Gal. 6:1*). Some were not truly saved but deceived by a gospel of works (cf. 13:5; Gal. 5:4), which was being taught by the false teachers. In either case, Paul's proclamation of the gospel of grace would not have been having its desired effect, and he would have had cause for serious concern that his many months of ministry at Corinth were for nothing. Both cases also prevented the people from effectively assuming any "ministry of reconciliation."

6:2 Paul emphasized his point by quoting Is. 49:8. He was passionately concerned that the Corinthians adhere to the truth because it was God's time to save and they were messengers for helping to spread that message. **now *is* the day of salvation.** Paul applied Isaiah's words to the present situation. There is a time in God's economy when He listens to sinners and responds to those who are repentant—and it was and is that time (cf. Prov. 1:20-23; Is. 55:6; Heb. 3:7,8; 4:7). However, there will also be an end to that time (cf. Gen. 6:3; Prov. 1:24-33; John 9:4), which is why Paul's exhortation was so passionate.

6:3-10 Like Paul, any believer who engages in a faithful ministry of reconciliation should expect to be rejected and accepted, to be hated and loved, to encounter joy and hardship. This is what Jesus had already taught His disciples (cf. Matt. 5:10-16; Luke 12:2-12).

6:3 We give no offense in anything. The faithful ambassador of Christ does nothing to discredit his ministry, but everything he can to protect its integrity, the gospel's integrity, and God's integrity (cf. Rom. 2:24; 1 Cor. 9:27; Titus 2:1-10).

all *things* we commend ourselves [e]as ministers of God: in much [1]patience, in tribulations, in needs, in distresses, **5** [f]in stripes,
in imprisonments, in tumults, in labors, in
sleeplessness, in fastings; **6** by purity, by
knowledge, by longsuffering, by kindness,
by the Holy Spirit, by [2]sincere love, **7** [g]by
the word of truth, by [h]the power of God,
by [i]the armor of righteousness on the right
hand and on the left, **8** by honor and dishonor, by evil report and good report; as
deceivers, and *yet* true; **9** as unknown, and
[j]*yet* well known; [k]as dying, and behold we
live; [l]as chastened, and *yet* not killed; **10** as
sorrowful, yet always rejoicing; as poor,
yet making many [m]rich; as having nothing,
and *yet* possessing all things.

Be Holy

11 O Corinthians! [3]We have spoken
openly to you, [n]our heart is wide open.
12 You are not restricted by us, but [o]you are
restricted by your *own* affections. **13** Now
in return for the same [p](I speak as to children), you also be open.
14 [q]Do not be unequally yoked together
with unbelievers. For [r]what [4]fellowship
has righteousness with lawlessness? And
what [5]communion has light with darkness? **15** And what accord has Christ with
Belial? Or what part has a believer with an
unbeliever? **16** And what agreement has the
temple of God with idols? For [s]you[6] are the
temple of the living God. As God has said:

[t]*"I will dwell in them*
And walk among them.
I will be their God,
And they shall be My people."

17 Therefore

[u]*"Come out from among them*
And be separate, says the Lord.
Do not touch what is unclean,
And I will receive you."

4 [e] 1 Cor. 4:1 [1] *endurance*
5 [f] 2 Cor. 11:23
6 [2] Lit. *unhypocritical*
7 [g] 2 Cor. 7:14 [h] 1 Cor. 2:4 [i] Rom. 13:12; 2 Cor. 10:4
9 [j] 2 Cor. 4:2; 5:11 [k] 1 Cor. 4:9, 11 [l] Ps. 118:18
10 [m] 1 Cor. 1:5; [2 Cor. 8:9]
11 [n] Is. 60:5; 2 Cor. 7:3 [3] Lit. *Our mouth is open*
12 [o] 2 Cor. 12:15
13 [p] 1 Cor. 4:14
14 [q] Deut. 7:2, 3; 22:10; 1 Cor. 5:9 [r] 1 Sam. 5:2, 3; 1 Kin. 18:21; Eph. 5:6, 7, 11; 1 John 1:6 [4] *in common* [5] *fellowship*
16 [s] [1 Cor. 3:16, 17; 6:19]; Eph. 2:21; [Heb. 3:6] [t] Ex. 29:45; Lev. 26:12; Jer. 31:33; 32:38; Ezek. 37:26, 27; Zech. 8:8 [6] NU *we*
17 [u] Num. 33:51-56; Is. 52:11; Rev. 18:4

6:4 we commend ourselves as ministers of God. "Commend" means "introduce," with the connotation of proving oneself (*see note on 3:1*). The most convincing proof is the patient endurance of character reflected in Paul's hardships (v. 5) and the nature of his ministry (vv. 6,7).

6:5 Here Paul commended himself to them by mentioning his faithfulness in enduring persecution and citing his diligence in ministry labors, to the point of anguished deprivations when necessary (*see note on 4:17*).

6:6 Paul commended himself positively by listing the important elements of the righteousness God had granted to him. **by the Holy Spirit.** Paul lived and walked by the power of the Spirit (*see note on Gal. 5:16*). It was the central reason that all the other positive elements of his endurance were a reality.

6:7 by the word of truth. The Scriptures, the revealed Word of God (cf. Col. 1:5; James 1:18). During his entire ministry, Paul never operated beyond the boundaries of the direction and guidance of divine revelation. **by the power of God.** Paul did not rely on his own strength when he ministered (*see notes on 1 Cor. 1:18; 2:1-5*; cf. Rom. 1:16). **by the armor of righteousness.** Paul did not fight Satan's kingdom with human resources, but with spiritual virtue (*see notes on 10:3-5; Eph. 6:10-18*). **the right hand...the left.** Paul had both offensive tools, such as the sword of the Spirit, and defensive tools, such as the shield of faith and the helmet of salvation, at his disposal (*see notes on Eph. 6:16,17*).

6:8-10 The mark of a ministry that has genuine character is paradoxical, and here Paul gave a series of paradoxes regarding his service for Christ.

6:8 as deceivers. Paul's opponents at Corinth had accused him of being an impostor and a false apostle (cf. John 7:12).

6:9 as unknown. This is a twofold reference to: 1) the fact that Christians did not know him before he began persecuting them (cf. Acts 8:1; 1 Tim. 1:12,13); and 2) his rejection by the community of leading Jews and Pharisees following his conversion. He had become unknown to his former world, and well-known and well-loved by the Christian community.

6:10 making many rich. The spiritual wealth Paul possessed and imparted did much to make his hearers spiritually wealthy (cf. Acts 3:6).

6:11-13 Paul proved his genuine love for the Corinthians by defining love's character. This passage confirms the reality of his profession of love for them (cf. 2:4; 3:2; 12:15,19).

6:11 our heart is wide open. Lit. "our heart is enlarged" (cf. 1 Kin. 4:29). The evidence of Paul's genuine love for the Corinthians was that no matter how some of them had mistreated him, he still loved them and had room for them in his heart (cf. Phil. 1:7).

6:14 unequally yoked together. An illustration taken from OT prohibitions to Israel regarding the work-related joining together of two different kinds of livestock (*see note on Deut. 22:10*). By this analogy, Paul taught that it is not right to join together in common spiritual enterprise with those who are not of the same nature (unbelievers). It is impossible under such an arrangement for things to be done to God's glory. **with unbelievers.** Christians are not to be bound together with non-Christians in any spiritual enterprise or relationship that would be detrimental to the Christian's testimony within the body of Christ (*see notes on 1 Cor. 5:9-13*; cf. 1 Cor. 6:15-18; 10:7-21; James 4:4; 1 John 2:15). This was especially important for the Corinthians because of the threats from the false teachers and the surrounding pagan idolatry. But this command does not mean believers should end all associations with unbelievers; that would defy the purpose for which God saved believers and left them on earth (cf. Matt. 28:19,20; 1 Cor. 9:19-23). The implausibility of such religious alliances is made clear in vv. 14b-17.

6:15 Belial. An ancient name for Satan, the utterly worthless one (*see note on Deut. 13:13*). This contrasts sharply with Jesus Christ, the worthy One with whom believers are to be in fellowship.

6:16 agreement...temple of God with idols. The temple of God (true Christianity) and idols (idolatrous, demonic false religions) are utterly incompatible (cf. 1 Sam. 4-6; 2 Kin. 21:1-15; Ezek. 8). **you are the temple of the living God.** Believers individually are spiritual houses (cf. 5:1) in which the Spirit of Christ dwells (*see notes on 1 Cor. 3:16,17; 6:19,20; Eph. 2:22*). **As God has said.** Paul supported his statement by referring to a blend of OT texts (Lev. 26:11,12; Jer. 24:7; 31:33; Ezek. 37:26,27; Hos. 2:2,3).

6:17 Paul drew from Is. 52:11 and elaborated on the command to be spiritually separated. It is not only irrational and sacrilegious but disobedient to be bound together with unbelievers. When believers are saved, they are to disengage themselves from all forms of false religion and make a clean break from all sinful habits and old idolatrous patterns (*see notes on Eph. 5:6-12; 2 Tim. 2:20-23*; cf. Rev. 18:4). ***be separate.*** This is a command for believers to be as Christ was (Heb. 7:26).

18 *"I [v]will be a Father to you,*
And you shall be My [w]sons and
daughters,
Says the LORD Almighty."

7 Therefore, [a] having these promises,
beloved, let us cleanse ourselves from
all filthiness of the flesh and spirit, perfecting holiness in the fear of God.

The Corinthians' Repentance

2 Open *your hearts* to us. We have
wronged no one, we have corrupted no
one, [b]we have cheated no one. 3 I do not
say *this* to condemn; for [c]I have said before
that you are in our hearts, to die together
and to live together. 4 [d]Great *is* my boldness of speech toward you, [e]great *is* my
boasting on your behalf. [f]I am filled with
comfort. I am exceedingly joyful in all our
tribulation.

18 [v] 2 Sam. 7:14; Jer. 31:1, 9; [Rev. 21:7] [w] [John 1:12; Rom. 8:14; Gal. 4:5-7]; Phil. 2:15; 1 John 3:1

CHAPTER 7

1 [a] [1 John 3:3]
2 [b] Acts 20:33
3 [c] 2 Cor. 6:11, 12
4 [d] 2 Cor. 3:12 [e] 1 Cor. 1:4 [f] Phil. 2:17; Col. 1:24

5 [g] Rom. 15:26; 2 Cor. 2:13 [h] 2 Cor. 4:8 [i] Deut. 32:25
6 [j] Is. 49:13; 2 Cor. 1:3, 4 [k] 2 Cor. 2:13; 7:13
7 [1] *comfort*
8 [l] 2 Cor. 2:2 [m] 2 Cor. 2:4
10 [n] 2 Sam. 12:13; Ps. 32:10; Matt. 26:75

5 For indeed, [g]when we came to Macedonia, our bodies had no rest, but [h]we
were troubled on every side. [i]Outside *were*
conflicts, inside *were* fears. 6 Nevertheless
[j]God, who comforts the downcast, comforted us by [k]the coming of Titus, 7 and not
only by his coming, but also by the [1]conso-
lation with which he was comforted in
you, when he told us of your earnest desire, your mourning, your zeal for me, so
that I rejoiced even more.
8 For even if I made you [l]sorry with my
letter, I do not regret it; [m]though I did regret it. For I perceive that the same epistle
made you sorry, though only for a while.
9 Now I rejoice, not that you were made
sorry, but that your sorrow led to repentance. For you were made sorry in a godly
manner, that you might suffer loss from us
in nothing. 10 For [n]godly sorrow produces
repentance *leading* to salvation, not to be

6:18 As a result of separating themselves from false doctrine and practice, believers will know the full richness of what it means to be children of God (*see notes on Rom. 8:14-17*; cf. 2 Sam. 7:14; Ezek. 20:34).

7:1 these promises. The OT promises Paul quoted in 6:16-18. Scripture often encourages believers to action based on God's promises (cf. Rom. 12:1; 2 Pet. 1:3). **let us cleanse ourselves.** The form of this Gr. verb indicates that this is something each Christian must do in his own life. **filthiness.** This Gr. word, which appears only here in the NT, was used 3 times in the Greek OT to refer to religious defilement, or unholy alliances with idols, idol feasts, temple prostitutes, sacrifices, and festivals of worship. **flesh and spirit.** False religion panders to the human appetites, represented by both "flesh and spirit." While some believers for a time might avoid succumbing to fleshly sins associated with false religion, the Christian who exposes his mind to false teaching cannot avoid contamination by the devilish ideologies and blasphemies that assault the purity of divine truth and blaspheme God's name. *See note on 6:17.* **perfecting holiness.** The Gr. word for "perfecting" means "to finish" or "to complete" (cf. 8:6). "Holiness" refers to separation from all that would defile both the body and the mind. Complete or perfect holiness was embodied only in Christ, thus believers are to pursue Him (cf. 3:18; Lev. 20:26; Matt. 5:48; Rom. 8:29; Phil. 3:12-14; 1 John 3:2,3).

7:2 We have wronged no one. The Gr. word for "wronged" means "to treat someone unjustly," "to injure someone," or "to cause someone to fall into sin." Paul could never be accused of injuring or leading any Corinthian into sin (*see notes on Matt. 18:5-14*). **we have corrupted no one.** "Corrupted" could refer to corruption by doctrine or money, but probably refers to corrupting one's morals (cf. 1 Cor. 15:33). Paul could never be accused of encouraging any immoral conduct.

7:3 Paul had a forgiving heart. Rather than only condemning the Corinthians for believing the false teachers and rejecting him, Paul reminded them of his love for them and his readiness to forgive them.

7:4 Great *is* my boldness. "Boldness" can be translated "confidence." Paul was confident of God's ongoing work in their lives (cf. Phil. 1:6)—another proof of Paul's love for the Corinthian believers.

7:5-16 These verses catalog the restoration of Paul's joy over the repentance of the Corinthian believers.

7:5 Here, Paul continued the narrative he left off in 2:13. When he arrived in Macedonia after leaving Troas, he had no rest from external "conflicts." The Gr. word is used of quarrels and disputes, and probably refers to the ongoing persecution Paul faced. He was also burdened by internal "fears"—the concern he had for the church and the anti-Paul faction prevalent there. **Macedonia.** *See note on 2:13.*

7:6 the downcast. This refers not to the spiritually humble, but to those who are humiliated. Such people are lowly in the economic, social, or emotional sense (cf. Rom. 12:16).

7:6,7 comforted us by the coming of Titus...when he told us. The Gr. word for "coming" refers to the actual presence of Titus with Paul. But comforting Paul beyond just the arrival of Titus, which was a blessing, was the encouraging report he gave regarding the repentance of the Corinthians and their positive response to Paul's letter carried by Titus.

7:7 Paul was encouraged by the manner in which the Corinthians comforted Titus, since he brought them such a confrontational letter (see Introduction: Background and Setting). Paul was also encouraged by their response to himself, which was manifested in 3 ways: 1) "earnest desire"—they longed to see Paul again and resume their relationship with him; 2) "mourning"—they were sorrowful over their sin and the breach it created between themselves and Paul; and 3) "zeal"—they loved Paul to such a degree that they were willing to defend him against those who sought to harm him, specifically the false teachers.

7:8 I made you sorry. This can also be translated "I caused you sorrow" (*see note on 2:1*). **my letter.** The severe letter that confronted the mutiny in the church at Corinth (*see note on 2:3*; see Introduction: Background and Setting).

7:8,9 I do not regret it...I did regret it.... Now I rejoice. Paul did not regret sending the letter, even though it caused them sorrow, because he knew that sorrow over their sin would affect in them repentance leading to obedience. Yet Paul did regret having sent it for a brief time while awaiting Titus' return, fearing that his letter was too harsh, and that he might have driven them further away from him. In the end, however, he rejoiced because the letter accomplished what he had hoped.

7:9 your sorrow led to repentance. The letter produced a sorrow in the Corinthian believers that led them to repent of their sins. "Repentance" refers to the desire to turn from sin and restore one's relationship to God (*see notes on Matt. 3:2,8*).

7:10 godly sorrow produces repentance *leading* to salvation. "Godly sorrow" refers to sorrow that is according to the will of God and produced by the Holy Spirit (*see note on 2 Tim. 2:25*). True re-

regretted; [o]but the sorrow of the world
produces death. 11 For observe this very
thing, that you sorrowed in a godly manner: What diligence it produced in you,
what [p]clearing *of yourselves, what* indignation, *what* fear, *what* vehement desire, *what*
zeal, *what* vindication! In all *things* you
proved yourselves to be [q]clear in this matter. 12 Therefore, although I wrote to you, *I*
did not *do it* for the sake of him who had
done the wrong, nor for the sake of him
who suffered wrong, [r]but that our care for
you in the sight of God might appear to
you.

The Joy of Titus

13 Therefore we have been comforted in
your comfort. And we rejoiced exceedingly more for the joy of Titus, because his
spirit [s]has been refreshed by you all. 14 For
if in anything I have boasted to him about
you, I am not ashamed. But as we spoke all
things to you in truth, even so our boasting
to Titus was found true. 15 And his affections are greater for you as he remembers
[t]the obedience of you all, how with fear
and trembling you received him. 16 Therefore I rejoice that [u]I have confidence in you
in everything.

Excel in Giving

8 Moreover, brethren, we make known to
you the grace of God bestowed on the
churches of Macedonia: 2 that in a great trial
of affliction the abundance of their joy and
[a]their deep poverty abounded in the riches
of their liberality. 3 For I bear witness that according to *their* ability, yes, and beyond *their*
ability, *they were* freely willing, 4 imploring
us with much urgency [1]that we would receive the gift and [b]the fellowship of the ministering to the saints. 5 And not *only* as we

10 [o] Prov. 17:22
11 [p] Eph. 5:11 [q] 2 Cor. 2:5-11
12 [r] 2 Cor. 2:4
13 [s] Rom. 15:32
15 [t] 2 Cor. 2:9; Phil. 2:12
16 [u] 2 Cor. 2:3; 8:22; 2 Thess. 3:4; Philem. 8, 21

CHAPTER 8

2 [a] Mark 12:44
4 [b] Acts 11:29; 24:17; Rom. 15:25, 26; 1 Cor. 16:1, 3, 4; 2 Cor. 9:1
[1] NU, M omit *that we would receive,* thus changing text to *urgency for the favor and fellowship*

pentance cannot occur apart from such a genuine sorrow over one's sin. The word "leading" is supplied by the translators; Paul was saying that repentance belongs to the realm or sphere of salvation. Repentance is at the very heart of and proves one's salvation: unbelievers repent of their sin initially when they are saved, and then as believers, repent of their sins continually to keep the joy and blessing of their relationship to God (*see notes on 1 John 1:7-9*). **sorrow of the world produces death.** Human sorrow is unsanctified remorse and has no redemptive capability. It is nothing more than the wounded pride of getting caught in a sin and having one's lusts go unfulfilled. That kind of sorrow leads only to guilt, shame, despair, depression, self-pity, and hopelessness. People can die from such sorrow (cf. Ps. 32:3,4).

7:11 This verse provides a look at how genuine repentance will manifest itself in one's attitudes. **diligence.** Better translated, "earnestness" or "eagerness." It is the initial reaction of true repentance to eagerly and aggressively pursue righteousness. This is an attitude that ends indifference to sin and complacency about evil and deception. ***what* clearing *of yourselves.*** A desire to clear one's name of the stigma that accompanies sin. The repentant sinner restores the trust and confidence of others by making his genuine repentance known. **indignation.** Often associated with righteous indignation and holy anger. Repentance leads to anger over one's sin and displeasure at the shame it has brought on the Lord's name and His people. **fear.** This is reverence toward God, who is the One most offended by sin. Repentance leads to a healthy fear of the One who chastens and judges sin. **vehement desire.** This could be translated "yearning," or "a longing for," and refers to the desire of the repentant sinner to restore the relationship with the one who was sinned against. **zeal.** This refers to loving someone or something so much that one hates anyone or anything that harms the object of this love (*see note on v. 7*). **vindication.** This could be translated "avenging of wrong," and refers to the desire to see justice done. The repentant sinner no longer tries to protect himself; he wants to see the sin avenged no matter what it might cost him. **to be clear in this matter.** The essence of repentance is an aggressive pursuit of holiness, which was characteristic of the Corinthians. The Gr. word for "clear" means "pure" or "holy." They demonstrated the integrity of their repentance by their purity.

7:12 him who had done the wrong. The leader of the mutiny in the Corinthian church (*see note on 12:7*).

7:15 fear and trembling. Reverence toward God and a healthy fear of judgment (*see note on 1 Cor. 2:3*).

8:1–9:15 While this section specifically deals with Paul's instruction to the Corinthians about a particular collection for the saints in Jerusalem, it also provides the richest, most detailed model of Christian giving in the NT.

8:1 grace of God. The generosity of the churches of Macedonia was motivated by God's grace. Paul did not merely commend those churches for a noble human work, but instead gave the credit to God for what He did through them. **churches of Macedonia.** Macedonia was the northern Roman province of Greece. Paul's reference was to the churches at Philippi, Thessalonica, and Berea (cf. Acts 17:11). This was basically an impoverished province that had been ravaged by many wars and even then was being plundered by Roman authority and commerce.

8:2 abundance of their joy. "Abundance" means "surplus." In spite of their difficult circumstances, the churches' joy rose above their pain because of their devotion to the Lord and the causes of His kingdom. **deep poverty.** "Deep" means "according to the depth," or "extremely deep." "Poverty" refers to the most severe type of economic deprivation, the kind that caused a person to become a beggar. **riches of their liberality.** The Gr. word for "liberality" can be translated "generosity" or "sincerity." It is the opposite of duplicity or being double-minded. The Macedonian believers were rich in their single-minded, selfless generosity to God and to others.

8:3 Paul highlighted 3 elements of the Macedonians' giving which summed up the concept of freewill giving: 1) "according to their ability." Giving is proportionate—God sets no fixed amount or percentage and expects His people to give based on what they have (Luke 6:38; 1 Cor. 16:2); 2) "beyond their ability." Giving is sacrificial. God's people are to give according to what they have, yet it must be in proportions that are sacrificial (cf. Matt. 6:25-34; Mark 12:41-44; Phil. 4:19); and 3) "freely willing"—lit. "one who chooses his own course of action." Giving is voluntary—God's people are not to give out of compulsion, manipulation, or intimidation. Freewill giving has always been God's plan (cf. 9:6; Gen. 4:2-4; 8:20; Ex. 25:1,2; 35:4,5,21,22; 36:5-7; Num. 18:12; Deut. 16:10,17; 1 Chr. 29:9; Prov. 3:9,10; 11:24; Luke 19:1-8). Freewill giving is not to be confused with tithing, which related to the national taxation system of Israel (*see note on Lev. 27:30*) and is paralleled in the NT and the present by paying taxes (*see notes on Matt. 22:21; Rom. 13:6,7*).

8:4 the gift and the fellowship. "Gift" means "grace." The Macedonian Christians implored Paul for the special grace of being able to have fellowship and be partners in supporting the poor saints in Jerusalem. They viewed giving as a privilege, not an obligation (cf. 9:7).

had hoped, but they first [c]gave themselves
to the Lord, and *then* to us by the [d]will of
God. 6 So [e]we urged Titus, that as he had
begun, so he would also complete this grace
in you as well. 7 But as [f]you abound in
everything—in faith, in speech, in knowledge, in all diligence, and in your love for
us—*see* [g]that you abound in this grace also.

Christ Our Pattern

8 [h]I speak not by commandment, but I
am testing the sincerity of your love by the
diligence of others. 9 For you know the
grace of our Lord Jesus Christ, [i]that
though He was rich, yet for your sakes He
became poor, that you through His poverty might become [j]rich.
10 And in this [k]I give advice: [l]It is to
your advantage not only to be doing what
you began and [m]were desiring to do a year
ago; 11 but now you also must complete
the doing *of it;* that as *there was* a readiness
to desire *it,* so *there* also *may be* a completion out of what *you* have. 12 For [n]if there is

5 [c][Rom. 12:1, 2] [d][Eph. 6:6]
6 [e]2 Cor. 8:17; 12:18
7 [f][1 Cor. 1:5; 12:13] [g]2 Cor. 9:8
8 [h]1 Cor. 7:6
9 [i]Matt. 8:20; Luke 9:58; Phil. 2:6, 7 [j]Rom. 9:23; [Eph. 1:7; Rev. 3:18]
10 [k]1 Cor. 7:25, 40 [l][Prov. 19:17; Matt. 10:42; 1 Tim. 6:18, 19; Heb. 13:16] [m]1 Cor. 16:2; 2 Cor. 9:2
12 [n]Mark 12:43, 44; Luke 21:3, 4; 2 Cor. 9:7
15 [o]Ex. 16:18
16 [2]NU *has put*
18 [p]1 Cor. 16:3; 2 Cor. 12:18
19 [q]Acts 14:23; 1 Cor. 16:3, 4 [r]2 Cor. 4:15

first a willing mind, *it is* accepted according to what one has, *and* not according to
what he does not have.
13 For *I do* not *mean* that others should be
eased and you burdened; 14 but by an equality, *that* now at this time your abundance
may supply their lack, that their abundance
also may supply your lack—that there may
be equality. 15 As it is written, [o]*"He who
gathered much had nothing left over, and he
who gathered little had no lack."*

Collection for the Judean Saints

16 But thanks *be* to God who [2]puts the
same earnest care for you into the heart of
Titus. 17 For he not only accepted the exhortation, but being more diligent, he went
to you of his own accord. 18 And we have
sent with him [p]the brother whose praise *is*
in the gospel throughout all the churches,
19 and not only *that,* but who was also [q]cho-
sen by the churches to travel with us with
this gift, which is administered by us [r]to
the glory of the Lord Himself and *to show*

8:5 not *only* as we had hoped. The response of the Macedonian churches was far more than Paul had expected. **first.** Refers not to time but priority. Of first priority to the Macedonians was to present themselves as sacrifices to God (cf. Rom. 12:1,2; 1 Pet. 2:5). Generous giving follows personal dedication.

8:6 we urged Titus. Titus initially encouraged the Corinthians to begin the collection at least one year earlier. When he returned to Corinth with the severe letter (see Introduction: Background and Setting), Paul encouraged him to help the believers finish the collection of the money for the support of the poor saints in Jerusalem.

8:7 you abound in everything. The giving of the Corinthians was to be in harmony with other Christian virtues that Paul already recognized in them: "faith"—sanctifying trust in the Lord; "speech"—sound doctrine; "knowledge"—the application of doctrine; "diligence"—eagerness and spiritual passion; and "love"—the love of choice, inspired by their leaders.

8:8 not by commandment. Freewill giving is never according to obligation or command (*see note on v. 3*).

8:9 though He was rich. A reference to the eternality and pre-existence of Christ. As the second person of the Trinity, Christ is as rich as God is rich. He owns everything, and possesses all power, authority, sovereignty, glory, honor, and majesty (cf. Is. 9:6; Mic. 5:2; John 1:1; 8:58; 10:30; 17:5; Col. 1:15-18; 2:9; Heb. 1:3). **He became poor.** A reference to Christ's incarnation (cf. John 1:14; Rom. 1:3; 8:3; Gal. 4:4; Col. 1:20; 1 Tim. 3:16; Heb. 2:7). He laid aside the independent exercise of all His divine prerogatives, left His place with God, took on human form, and died on a cross like a common criminal (Phil. 2:5-8). **that you...might become rich.** Believers become spiritually rich through the sacrifice and impoverishment of Christ (Phil. 2:5-8). They become rich in salvation, forgiveness, joy, peace, glory, honor, and majesty (cf. 1 Cor. 1:4,5; 3:22; Eph. 1:3; 1 Pet. 1:3,4). They become joint heirs with Christ (Rom. 8:17).

8:10 advice. Paul was not commanding the Corinthians to give any specific amount. It was his opinion, however, that it was to their advantage to give generously so they might receive abundantly more from God in either material blessings, spiritual blessings, or eternal reward (cf. 9:6; Luke 6:38).

8:11 complete the doing *of it.* The Corinthians needed to finish what they had started by completing the collection (cf. Luke 9:62; 1 Cor. 16:2). They needed this reminder since they likely stopped the process due to the influence of the false teachers, who probably accused Paul of being a huckster who would keep the money for himself (cf. 2:17).

8:12 willing mind. Paul spoke of a readiness and eagerness to give. God is most concerned with the heart attitude of the giver, not the amount he gives (cf. 9:7; Mark 12:41-44). **according to what one has.** Whatever one has is the resource out of which he should give (*see note on v. 3*). That is why there are no set amounts or percentages for giving anywhere stated in the NT. The implication is that if one has much, he can give much; if he has little, he can give only little (cf. 9:6). **not according to what he does not have.** Believers do not need to go into debt to give, nor lower themselves to a poverty level. God never asks believers to impoverish themselves. The Macedonians received a special blessing of grace from God to give the way they did.

8:14 equality. This Gr. word gives us the Eng. word "isostasy," which refers to a condition of equilibrium. Thus the term could also be translated "balance" or "equilibrium." The idea is that in the body of Christ some believers who have more than they need should help those who have far less than they need (cf. 1 Tim. 6:17,18). This is not, however, a scheme of Paul's to redistribute wealth within the church, but rather to meet basic needs.

8:15 as it is written. Quoted from Ex. 16:18. The collecting of the manna by the Israelites in the wilderness was an appropriate illustration of sharing of resources. Some were able to gather more than others, and apparently shared it so that no one lacked what they needed.

8:16 Titus. *See note on v. 6.*

8:18 the brother. This man is unnamed because he was so well known, prominent and unimpeachable. He was a distinguished preacher, and he was able to add credibility to the enterprise of taking the collection to Jerusalem.

8:19 chosen by the churches. To protect Paul and Titus from false accusations regarding the mishandling of the money, the churches picked the unbiased brother (v. 18) as their representative to lend accountability to the enterprise. **to the glory of the Lord Himself.** Paul wanted careful scrutiny as protection against bringing dishonor to Christ for any misappropriation of the money. He wanted to avoid any offenses worthy of justifiable criticisms or accusations.

your ready mind, 20 avoiding this: that
anyone should blame us in this lavish gift
which is administered by us— 21 [s]provid-
ing honorable things, not only in the sight
of the Lord, but also in the sight of men.
22 And we have sent with them our
brother whom we have often proved diligent in many things, but now much more
diligent, because of the great confidence
which *we have* in you. 23 If *anyone inquires*
about [t]Titus, *he is* my partner and fellow
worker concerning you. Or if our brethren
are inquired about, they are [u]messengers[3] of
the churches, the glory of Christ. 24 Therefore show to them, [4]and before the churches the proof of your love and of our [v]boast-
ing on your behalf.

Administering the Gift

9 Now concerning [a]the ministering to
the saints, it is superfluous for me to
write to you; 2 for I know your willingness,
about which I boast of you to the Macedonians, that Achaia was ready a [b]year
ago; and your zeal has stirred up the majority. 3 [c]Yet I have sent the brethren, lest
our boasting of you should be in vain in
this respect, that, as I said, you may be
ready; 4 lest if *some* Macedonians come
with me and find you unprepared, we (not
to mention you!) should be ashamed of
this [1]confident boasting. 5 Therefore I
thought it necessary to [2]exhort the
brethren to go to you ahead of time, and
prepare your generous gift beforehand,
which *you had* previously promised, that it
may be ready as *a matter of* generosity and
not as a [3]grudging obligation.

The Cheerful Giver

6 [d]But this *I say:* He who sows sparingly
will also reap sparingly, and he who sows
[4]bountifully will also reap [4]bountifully.
7 *So let* each one *give* as he purposes in his
heart, [e]not grudgingly or of [5]necessity; for
[f]God loves a cheerful giver. 8 [g]And God *is*
able to make all grace abound toward you,
that you, always having all sufficiency in
all *things,* may have an abundance for
every good work. 9 As it is written:

21 [s] Rom. 12:17; Phil. 4:8; 1 Pet. 2:12
23 [t] 2 Cor. 7:13, 14 [u] [John 13:16]; Phil. 2:25 [3] Lit. *apostles,* "sent ones"
24 [v] 2 Cor. 7:4, 14; 9:2 [4] NU, M omit *and*

CHAPTER 9

1 [a] Acts 11:29; Rom. 15:26; 1 Cor. 16:1; 2 Cor. 8:4; Gal. 2:10
2 [b] 2 Cor. 8:10
3 [c] 2 Cor. 8:6, 17
4 [1] NU *confidence.*
5 [2] *encourage* [3] Lit. *covetousness*
6 [d] Prov. 11:24; 22:9; Gal. 6:7, 9 [4] *with blessings*
7 [e] Deut. 15:7 [f] Deut. 15:10; 1 Chr. 29:17; [Prov. 11:25]; Rom. 12:8; [2 Cor. 8:12] [5] *compulsion*
8 [g] [Prov. 11:24]

8:21 providing honorable things. A better rendering is "have regard for what is honorable," or "take into consideration what is honorable." Paul cared greatly about what people thought of his actions, especially considering how large the gift was.

8:22 our brother. A third member of the delegation sent to deliver the gift, also unnamed.

8:23 partner and fellow worker. Titus was Paul's "partner"—his close companion—and fellow laborer among the Corinthians. They already knew of his outstanding character. **messengers of the churches.** The two men who went with Titus were apostles in the sense of being commissioned and sent by the churches. They were not apostles of Christ (11:13; 1 Thess. 2:6), because they were not eyewitnesses of the resurrected Lord or commissioned directly by Him (*see note on Rom. 1:1*). **glory of Christ.** The greatest of all commendations is to be characterized as bringing glory to Christ. Such was the case of the two messengers.

9:1 ministering to the saints. The offering they were collecting for the believers in Jerusalem (*see note on 8:4*).

9:2 Paul was simply calling the Corinthians back to their original eagerness and readiness to participate in the offering project. The confusion and lies spread by the false teachers (i.e., Paul was a deceiver ministering only for the money) had sidetracked the believers on this issue. **the Macedonians.** Believers in the churches in the province of Macedonia, which was the northern part of Greece (*see notes on 8:1-5; Acts 16:9;* see Introduction to 1 Thessalonians: Background and Setting). **Achaia.** A province in southern Greece, where Corinth was located (*see note on Acts 18:12;* see Introduction to 1 Corinthians: Background and Setting).

9:5 your generous gift. On first hearing of the need, the Corinthians had undoubtedly promised Paul that they would raise a large amount. **grudging obligation.** More clearly translated "covetousness," or "greed," it denotes a grasping to get more and keep it at the expense of others. This attitude emphasizes selfishness and pride, which can have a very detrimental effect on giving, and is natural for unbelievers but should not be for professed believers (cf. Ps. 10:3; Eccl. 5:10; Mic. 2:2; Mark 7:22; Rom. 1:29; 1 Cor. 5:11; 6:9,10; Eph. 5:3-5; 1 Tim. 6:10; 2 Pet. 2:14).

9:6 The simple, self-evident agrarian principle—which Paul applied to Christian giving—that the harvest is directly proportionate to the amount of seed sown (cf. Prov. 11:24,25; 19:17; Luke 6:38; Gal. 6:7). **bountifully.** This is derived from the Gr. word which gives us the word "eulogy" ("blessing"). When a generous believer gives by faith and trust in God, with a desire to produce the greatest possible blessing, that person will receive that kind of a harvest of blessing (cf. Prov. 3:9,10; 28:27; Mal. 3:10). God gives a return on the amount one invests with Him. Invest a little, receive a little, and vice versa (cf. Luke 6:38).

9:7 as he purposes. The term translated "purposes" occurs only here in the NT and indicates a premeditated, predetermined plan of action that is done from the heart voluntarily, but not impulsively. This is an age-old biblical principle of giving (*see note on 8:3;* cf. Ex. 25:2). **grudgingly.** Lit. "with grief," "sorrow," or "sadness," which indicates an attitude of depression, regret, and reluctance that accompanies something done strictly out of a sense of duty and obligation, but not joy. **of necessity.** Or "compulsion." This refers to external pressure and coercion, quite possibly accompanied by legalism. Believers are not to give based on the demands of others, or according to any arbitrary standards or set amounts. **God loves a cheerful giver.** God has a unique, special love for those who are happily committed to generous giving. The Gr. word for "cheerful" is the word from which we get "hilarious," which suggests that God loves a heart that is enthusiastically thrilled with the pleasure of giving.

9:8 all grace abound toward you. God possesses an infinite amount of grace, and He gives it lavishly, without holding back (cf. 1 Chr. 29:14). Here "grace" does not refer to spiritual graces, but to money and material needs. When the believer generously—and wisely—gives of his material resources, God graciously replenishes them so he always has plenty and will not be in need (cf. 2 Chr. 31:10). **all sufficiency.** In secular Greek philosophy, this was the proud contentment of self-sufficiency that supposedly led to true happiness. Paul sanctifies the secular term and says that God, not man, will supply everything needed for real happiness and contentment (cf. Phil. 4:19). **abundance for every good work.** God gives back lavishly to generous, cheerful givers, not so they may satisfy selfish, nonessential desires, but so they may meet the variety of needs others have (cf. Deut. 15:10,11).

[h]"He has dispersed abroad,
He has given to the poor;
His righteousness endures
forever."

10 Now [6]may He who [i]supplies seed to
the sower, and bread for food, [7]supply and
multiply the seed you have *sown* and increase the fruits of your [j]righteousness,
11 while *you are* enriched in everything for
all liberality, [k]which causes thanksgiving
through us to God. 12 For the administration of this service not only [l]supplies the
needs of the saints, but also is abounding
through many thanksgivings to God,
13 while, through the proof of this ministry,
they [m]glorify God for the obedience of
your confession to the gospel of Christ,
and for *your* liberal [n]sharing with them
and all *men,* 14 and by their prayer for you,
who long for you because of the exceeding
[o]grace of God in you. 15 Thanks *be* to God
[p]for His indescribable gift!

The Spiritual War

10 Now [a]I, Paul, myself am pleading
with you by the meekness and gentleness of Christ—[b]who in presence *am*
lowly among you, but being absent am
bold toward you. 2 But I beg *you* [c]that
when I am present I may not be bold with
that confidence by which I intend to be

9 [h]Ps. 112:9
10 [i]Is. 55:10 [j]Hos. 10:12 [6]NU omits *may* [7]NU *will supply*
11 [k]2 Cor. 1:11
12 [l]2 Cor. 8:14
13 [m][Matt. 5:16] [n][Heb. 13:16]
14 [o]2 Cor. 8:1
15 [p][John 3:16; 4:10; Rom. 6:23; 8:32; Eph. 2:8; James 1:17]

CHAPTER 10

1 [a]Rom. 12:1 [b]1 Thess. 2:7
2 [c]1 Cor. 4:21; 2 Cor. 13:2, 10

9:9 Paul marshals OT support (Ps. 112:9) for what he has been saying about the divine principles of giving. God replenishes and rewards the righteous giver both in time and eternity.

9:10 Paul drew on Is. 55:10 for additional OT support. The same God who is faithful to supply all His creatures' physical needs and is kind to all men, is uniquely gracious to His children. He always fulfills His promise to replenish their generosity. **fruits of your righteousness.** God's temporal and eternal blessings to the cheerful giver (cf. Hos. 10:12).

9:12 administration of this service. "Administration," which may also be translated "service," is a priestly word from which we get "liturgy." Paul viewed the entire collection project as a spiritual, worshipful enterprise that was primarily being offered to God to glorify Him. **supplies the needs of the saints.** The Gr. word for "supplies" is a doubly intense term that could be rendered "really, fully supplying." This indicates the Jerusalem church had an extremely great need. Many of its members had gone to Jerusalem as pilgrims to celebrate the feast of Pentecost (*see notes on Acts 2:1,5-11*), had been converted through Peter's message, and had then remained in the city without adequate financial support. Many residents of Jerusalem had undoubtedly lost their jobs in the waves of persecution that came after the martyrdom of Stephen (Acts 8:1). However, the Corinthians were wealthy enough (they had not yet suffered persecution and deprivation like the Macedonians; 8:1-4) to help meet the huge need with a generous monetary gift (*see note on 9:5*).

9:13 proof of this ministry. The collection also provided an important opportunity for the Corinthians to test the genuineness of their faith (cf. James 1:22; 1 John 2:3,4). The Jewish believers, who already doubted the validity of Gentile salvation, were especially skeptical of the Corinthians since their church had so many problems. The Corinthians' involvement in the collection would help to put those doubts to rest. **obedience of your confession.** Obedient submission to God's Word is always evidence of a true confession of Christ as Lord and Savior (Eph. 2:10; James 2:14-20; cf. Rom. 10:9,10). If the Corinthians had a proper response to and participation in Paul's collection ministry, the Jewish believers would know the Gentile conversions had been real.

9:14 This verse illustrates the truth that mutual prayer is at the heart of authentic Christian unity. When the Jerusalem believers recognized God was at work in the Corinthian church as a result of its outreach through the collection (*see notes on v. 13*), they would have become friends in Christ and prayed for the Corinthians, thanking God for their loving generosity. **the exceeding grace of God.** The Spirit of God was at work in the Corinthians in a special way (*see note on v. 13*).

9:15 Paul summarized his discourse by comparing the believer's act of giving with what God did in giving Jesus Christ (cf. Rom. 8:32), "His indescribable gift." God buried His Son and reaped a vast harvest of those who put their faith in the resurrected Christ (cf. John 12:24). That makes it possible for believers to joyfully, sacrificially, and abundantly sow and reap. As they give in this manner, they show forth Christ's likeness (cf. John 12:25,26; Eph. 5:1,2).

10:1–13:14 The abrupt change in tone from chaps. 1–9 has prompted various explanations of the relationship between chaps. 10–13 and 1–9. Some argue that chaps. 10–13 were originally part of the "severe letter" (2:4), and hence belong chronologically before chaps. 1–9. Chapters 10–13 cannot, however, have been written before chaps. 1–9, since they refer to Titus' visit as a past event (12:18; cf. 8:6). Further, the offender whose defiance of Paul prompted the "severe letter" (2:5-8) is nowhere mentioned in chaps. 10–13. Others agree that chaps. 10–13 belong after chaps. 1–9, but believe they form a separate letter. They assume that Paul, after sending chaps. 1–9 to the Corinthians, received reports of new trouble at Corinth and wrote chaps. 10–13 in response. A variation of this view is that Paul paused in his writing of 2 Corinthians after chaps. 1–9, then heard bad news from Corinth before he resumed writing chaps. 10–13. This view preserves the unity of 2 Corinthians; however Paul does not mention anywhere in chaps. 10–13 that he received any fresh news from Corinth. The best interpretation views 2 Corinthians as a unified letter, with chaps. 1–9 addressed to the repentant majority (cf. 2:6) and chaps. 10–13 to the minority still influenced by the false teachers. The support for this view is that: 1) there is no historical evidence (from Gr. manuscripts, the writings of the church Fathers, or early translations) that chaps. 10–13 ever circulated as a separate letter; all Gr. manuscripts have them following chaps. 1–9; 2) the differences in tone between chaps. 10–13 and 1–9 have been exaggerated (cf. 11:11; 12:14 with 6:11; 7:2); and 3) chaps. 10–13 form the logical conclusion to chaps. 1–9, as Paul prepared the Corinthians for his promised visit (1:15,16; 2:1-3).

10:1 meekness. The humble and gentle attitude that expresses itself in patient endurance of unfair treatment. A meek person is not bitter or angry, and he does not seek revenge when wronged. *See note on Matt. 5:5.* **gentleness.** This is similar in meaning to meekness. When applied to someone in a position of authority it refers to leniency. Gentle people refuse to retaliate, even when it is in their power to do so (Phil. 4:5). **lowly...bold toward you.** Paul sarcastically repeated another feature of the Corinthians' accusation against him; sadly, they had mistaken his gentleness and meekness toward them for weakness. Further, they accused him of cowardice, of being bold only when writing to them from a safe distance (cf. v. 10).

10:2 Paul was quite capable of bold, fearless confrontation (cf. Gal. 2:11). But seeking to spare the Corinthians (cf. 1:23), the apostle begged the rebellious minority not to force him to display his boldness by confronting them—something he would do, he warned, if necessary.

bold against some, who think of us as if we
walked according to the flesh. **3** For though
we walk in the flesh, we do not war according to the flesh. **4** [d]For the weapons [e]of
our warfare *are* not [1]carnal but [f]mighty in
God [g]for pulling down strongholds,
5 [h]casting down arguments and every high
thing that exalts itself against the knowledge of God, bringing every thought into
captivity to the obedience of Christ, **6** [i]and
being ready to punish all disobedience
when [j]your obedience is fulfilled.

Reality of Paul's Authority

7 [k]Do you look at things according to the
outward appearance? [l]If anyone is convinced in himself that he is Christ's, let him
again consider this in himself, that just as
he *is* Christ's, even [2]so [m]we *are* Christ's.
8 For even if I should boast somewhat more
[n]about our authority, which the Lord gave
[3]us for [4]edification and not for your destruction, [o]I shall not be ashamed— **9** lest I
seem to terrify you by letters. **10** "For *his* letters," they say, "*are* weighty and powerful,
but [p]*his* bodily presence *is* weak, and *his*
[q]speech contemptible." **11** Let such a person consider this, that what we are in word
by letters when we are absent, such *we will*
also *be* in deed when we are present.

Limits of Paul's Authority

12 [r]For we dare not class ourselves or
compare ourselves with those who commend themselves. But they, measuring
themselves by themselves, and comparing

4 [d]Eph. 6:13 [e]1 Cor. 9:7; [2 Cor. 6:7]; 1 Tim. 1:18 [f]Acts 7:22 [g]Jer. 1:10; [2 Cor. 10:8; 13:10] [1]*of the flesh*
5 [h]1 Cor. 1:19
6 [i]2 Cor. 13:2, 10 [j]2 Cor. 7:15
7 [k][John 7:24]; 2 Cor. 5:12 [l]1 Cor. 1:12; 14:37
[m][Rom. 14:8]; 1 Cor. 3:23 [2]NU *as we are.*
8 [n]2 Cor. 13:10 [o]2 Cor. 7:14 [3]NU omits *us* [4]*building up*
10 [p]1 Cor. 2:3, 4; 2 Cor. 12:7; Gal. 4:13 [q][1 Cor. 1:17]; 2 Cor. 11:6
12 [r]2 Cor. 5:12

10:3 walk in the flesh. Paul's opponents at Corinth had wrongly accused him of walking in the flesh in a moral sense (cf. Rom. 8:4). Playing off that, Paul affirmed that he did walk in the flesh in a physical sense; though possessing the power and authority of an apostle of Jesus Christ, he was a real human being (cf. 4:7,16; 5:1). **war according to the flesh.** Although a man, Paul did not fight the spiritual battle for men's souls using human ingenuity, worldly wisdom, or clever methodologies (cf. 1 Cor. 1:17-25; 2:1-4). Such impotent weapons are powerless to free souls from the forces of darkness and bring them to maturity in Christ. They cannot successfully oppose satanic assaults on the gospel, such as those made by the false apostles at Corinth.

10:4 our warfare. The motif of the Christian life as warfare is a common one in the NT (cf. 6:7; Eph. 6:10-18; 1 Tim. 1:18; 2 Tim. 2:3,4; 4:7). **carnal.** Human. *See note on v. 3.* **strongholds.** The metaphor would have been readily understandable to the Corinthians since Corinth, like most ancient cities, had a fortress (on top of a hill S of the city) in which its residents could take refuge. The formidable spiritual strongholds manned by the forces of hell can be demolished only by spiritual weapons wielded by godly believers—singularly the "sword of the Spirit" (Eph. 6:17), since only the truth of God's Word can defeat satanic falsehoods. This is the true spiritual warfare. Believers are not instructed in the NT to assault demons or Satan (*see note on Jude 9*), but to assault error with the truth. That is our battle (cf. John 17:17; Heb. 4:12).

10:5 arguments. Thoughts, ideas, speculations, reasonings, philosophies, and false religions are the ideological forts in which men barricade themselves against God and the gospel (cf. 1 Cor. 3:20). **every thought into captivity.** Emphasizes the total destruction of the fortresses of human and satanic wisdom and the rescuing of those inside from the damning lies that had enslaved them.

10:6 Paul would not stand idly by while enemies of the faith assaulted a church under his care. He was ready to purge them out (as he did at Ephesus; 1 Tim. 1:19,20) as soon as the Corinthian church was complete in its obedience. When that happened, the lines would be clearly drawn between the repentant, obedient majority and the recalcitrant, disobedient minority.

10:7 look...outward appearance. The Gr. verb "look" is better translated as an imperative, or command: "Look at what is obvious, face the facts, consider the evidence." In light of what they knew about him (cf. 1 Cor. 9:1,2), how could some of the Corinthians possibly believe that Paul was a false apostle and the false teachers were true apostles? Unlike Paul, the false apostles had founded no churches, and had suffered no persecution for the cause of Christ. Paul could call on his companions and even Ananias as witnesses to the reality of his Damascus Road experience; there were no witnesses to verify the false apostles' alleged encounters with the risen, glorified Christ. **If anyone is convinced...that he is Christ's.** The false apostles' claim to belong to Christ can be understood in 4 ways: 1) that they were Christians; 2) that they had known Jesus during His earthly life; 3) that they had an apostolic commission from Him; or 4) that they had an elevated, secret knowledge of Him. Their claim that some or all of those things were true about themselves implies that they denied all of them to be true of Paul. **we *are* Christ's.** For the sake of argument, Paul did not at this point deny the false apostles' claims (as he did later in 11:13-15). He merely pointed out that he, too, can and does claim to belong to Christ. To decide between the conflicting personal claims, the Corinthians needed only to consider the objective evidence, as he commanded them to do earlier in this verse.

10:8 The debate with the false apostles had forced Paul to emphasize his authority more than he cared to; Paul's claims for his authority normally were restrained by his humility. But no matter how much he said about his authority, Paul would never be ashamed. Since he had the authority of which he spoke, he would never be proved guilty of making an empty boast. The Lord gave Paul his authority to edify and strengthen the church; that he had done so at Corinth proves the genuineness of his claim to apostolic calling. Far from edifying the Corinthian church, the false apostles had brought confusion, divisiveness, and turmoil to it. That showed that their authority did not come from the Lord, who seeks only to build His church (cf. Matt. 16:18), not tear it down.

10:9 terrify you by letters. The false apostles had accused Paul of being an abusive leader, of trying to intimidate the Corinthians in his letters (such as the "severe letter," see Introduction: Background and Setting). Paul's goal, however, was not to terrify the Corinthians, but to bring them to repentance (cf. 7:9,10), because he loved them (cf. 7:2,3; 11:11; 12:15).

10:10 In their continuing attempt to discredit Paul, the false apostles claimed that in contrast to his bold, forceful letters, in person he lacked the presence, charisma, and personality of a truly great leader. They no doubt supported their point by portraying Paul's departure after his "painful" visit (2:1; cf. Introduction: Background and Setting) as a retreat of abject failure. And in a culture that highly valued skillful rhetoric and eloquent oration, Paul's "contemptible" speech was also taken as evidence that he was a weak, ineffective person.

10:11 Paul denied the false charges against him and affirmed his integrity. What he was in his letters he was to be when present with them.

10:12 class ourselves or compare ourselves. It is a mark of Paul's humility that he refused to compare himself with others, or engage in self-promotion. His only personal concern was what the Lord

themselves among themselves, are not
wise. 13 [s]We, however, will not boast beyond measure, but within the limits of the
sphere which God appointed us—a sphere
which especially includes you. 14 For we
are not overextending ourselves (as
though *our authority* did not extend to
you), [t]for it was to you that we came with
the gospel of Christ; 15 not boasting of
things beyond measure, *that is,* [u]in other
men's labors, but having hope, *that* as your
faith is increased, we shall be greatly enlarged by you in our sphere, 16 to preach
the gospel in the *regions* beyond you, *and*
not to boast in another man's sphere of accomplishment.
17 But [v]*"he who glories, let him glory in the* LORD." 18 For [w]not he who commends
himself is approved, but [x]whom the Lord
commends.

13 [s]2 Cor. 10:15
14 [t]1 Cor. 3:5, 6
15 [u]Rom. 15:20
17 [v]Is. 65:16; Jer. 9:24; 1 Cor. 1:31
18 [w]Prov. 27:2 [x]Rom. 2:29; [1 Cor. 4:5]

CHAPTER 11

1 [a]Matt. 17:17; 2 Cor. 11:4, 16, 19
2 [b]Gal. 4:17 [c]Hos. 2:19; [Eph. 5:26] [d]Col. 1:28 [e]Lev. 21:13
3 [f]Gen. 3:4, 13; John 8:44; 1 Thess. 3:5; 1 Tim. 2:14; [Rev. 12:9, 15] [g]Eph. 6:24 [1]NU adds *and purity*
4 [h]Gal. 1:6-8
5 [i][1 Cor. 15:10]; 2 Cor. 12:11; Gal. 2:6

Concern for Their Faithfulness

11 Oh, that you would bear with me in
a little [a]folly—and indeed you do
bear with me. 2 For I am [b]jealous for you
with godly jealousy. For [c]I have betrothed
you to one husband, [d]that I may present
you [e]*as* a chaste virgin to Christ. 3 But I fear,
lest somehow, as [f]the serpent deceived Eve
by his craftiness, so your minds [g]may be
corrupted from the [1]simplicity that is in
Christ. 4 For if he who comes preaches another Jesus whom we have not preached,
or *if* you receive a different spirit which
you have not received, or a [h]different
gospel which you have not accepted—you
may well put up with it!

Paul and False Apostles

5 For I consider that [i]I am not at all inferior to the most eminent apostles. 6 Even

thought of him (cf. 1 Cor. 4:4), though he needed to defend his apostleship so the Corinthians would not, in turning from him, turn from the truth to lies. **comparing themselves among themselves.** Paul pointed out the folly of the false apostles' boasting. They invented false standards that they could meet, then proclaimed themselves superior for meeting them.

10:13 not boast beyond measure. In contrast to the proud, arrogant, boastful false apostles, Paul refused to say anything about himself or his ministry that was not true and God-given. **the limits of the sphere which God appointed us.** Paul was content to stay within the bounds of the ministry God had given him—that of being the apostle to the Gentiles (Rom. 1:5; 11:13; 1 Tim. 2:7; 2 Tim. 1:11). Thus, contrary to the claims of the false apostles, Paul's sphere of ministry included Corinth. The apostle again demonstrated his humility by refusing to boast of his own accomplishments, preferring to speak only of what Christ had done through him (Rom. 15:18; Col. 1:29).

10:15 enlarged…in our sphere. When the crisis in Corinth had been resolved and the Corinthians' faith strengthened, Paul would, with their help, expand his ministry into new areas.

10:16 *regions* beyond you. Areas such as Rome (Acts 19:21) and Spain (Rom. 15:24,28).

10:17 The thought of self-glory was repugnant to Paul; he boasted only in the Lord (cf. Jer. 9:23,24; 1 Cor. 1:31; *see note on v. 13*).

10:18 whom the Lord commends. *See note on v. 12.* Self-commendation is both meaningless and foolish; the only true, meaningful commendation comes from God.

11:1 a little folly. Having just pointed out the folly of self-commendation (10:18), Paul certainly did not want to engage in it. But the Corinthians' acceptance of the false apostles' claims forced Paul to set forth his own apostolic credentials (cf. 12:11); that was the only way he could get them to see the truth (*see note on 10:7*). Unlike the false apostles, however, Paul's boasting was in the Lord (10:17) and motivated by concern for the Corinthians' well-being under the threat of false teaching (cf. v. 2; 12:19).

11:2 I am jealous for you. The reason for Paul's "folly" (*see note on v. 1*) was his deep concern for the Corinthians—concern to the point of jealousy, not for his own reputation, but zeal for their spiritual purity (*see note on v. 3*). **godly jealousy.** Jealousy inspired by zeal for God's causes, and thus similar to God's own jealousy for His holy name and His people's loyalty (cf. Ex. 20:5; 34:14; Deut. 4:24; 5:9; 6:15; 32:16,21; Josh. 24:19; Ps. 78:58; Ezek. 39:25; Nah. 1:2). **I have betrothed you to one husband.** As their spiritual father (12:14; 1 Cor. 4:15; cf. 9:1,2), Paul portrayed the Corinthians like a daughter, whom he betrothed to Jesus Christ (at their conversion). The OT pictures Israel as the wife of the Lord (cf. Is. 54:5; Jer. 3:14; Hos. 2:19,20), while the NT pictures the church as the bride of Christ (Eph. 5:22-32; Rev. 19:7). **chaste virgin.** Having betrothed or pledged the Corinthians to Christ, Paul wanted them to be pure until the marriage day finally arrived (cf. Rev. 19:7). It was that passionate concern which provoked Paul's jealousy (*see note on v. 1*) and prompted him to set forth his apostolic credentials.

11:3 Paul compared the danger facing the Corinthian church to Eve's deception by Satan. He feared the Corinthians, like Eve, would fall prey to satanic lies and have their minds corrupted. The tragic result would be the abandonment of their simple devotion to Christ in favor of the sophisticated error of the false apostles. Paul's allusion to Gen. 3 implies that the false apostles were Satan's emissaries—a truth that he later made explicit (vv. 13-15).

11:4 he who comes. The false apostles came into the Corinthian church from the outside—just as Satan did into the Garden. Likely they were Palestinian Jews (cf. v. 22; Acts 6:1) who allegedly sought to bring the Corinthians under the sway of the Jerusalem church. They were in a sense Judaizers, seeking to impose Jewish customs on the Corinthians. Unlike the Judaizers who plagued the Galatian churches (cf. Gal. 5:2), however, the false apostles at Corinth apparently did not insist that the Corinthians be circumcised. Nor did they practice a rigid legalism; in fact, they apparently encouraged licentiousness (cf. 12:21). Their fascination with rhetoric and oratory (cf. 10:10) suggests they had been influenced by Greek culture and philosophy. They claimed (falsely, cf. Acts 15:24) to represent the Jerusalem church, even possessing letters of commendation (*see note on 3:1*). Claiming to be the most eminent of apostles (v. 5), they scorned Paul's apostolic claims. Though their teaching may have differed from the Galatian Judaizers, it was just as deadly. **another Jesus…a different spirit…a different gospel.** Despite their vicious attacks on him, Paul's quarrel with the false apostles was not personal, but doctrinal. He could tolerate those hostile to him, as long as they preached the gospel of Jesus Christ (cf. Phil. 1:15-18). Those who adulterated the true gospel, however, received Paul's strongest condemnation (cf. Gal. 1:6-9). Though the precise details of what the false apostles taught are unknown and don't matter, they preached "another Jesus" and "a different spirit," which added up to "a different gospel." **you may well put up with it!** Paul's fear that the Corinthians would embrace the damning lies of the false apostles prompted his jealous concern for them (*see notes on vv. 2,3*).

11:5 the most eminent apostles. Possibly a reference to the 12 apostles, in which case Paul was asserting that, contrary to the claims

though [j]*I am* untrained in speech, yet *I am*
not [k]in knowledge. But [l]we have [2]been
thoroughly manifested among you in all
things.
7 Did I commit sin in [3]humbling myself
that you might be exalted, because I
preached the gospel of God to you [m]free of
charge? 8 I robbed other churches, taking
wages *from them* to minister to you. 9 And
when I was present with you, and in need,
[n]I was a burden to no one, for what I lacked
[o]the brethren who came from Macedonia
supplied. And in everything I kept myself
from being burdensome to you, and so I
will keep *myself.* 10 [p]As the truth of Christ is
in me, [q]no one shall stop me from this
boasting in the regions of Achaia. 11 Why?
[r]Because I do not love you? God knows!
12 But what I do, I will also continue to
do, [s]that I may cut off the opportunity
from those who desire an opportunity to
be regarded just as we are in the things of
which they boast. 13 For such [t]*are* false
apostles, [u]deceitful workers, transforming
themselves into apostles of Christ. 14 And
no wonder! For Satan himself transforms
himself into [v]an angel of light. 15 Therefore
it is no great thing if his ministers also
transform themselves into ministers of
righteousness, [w]whose end will be according to their works.

Reluctant Boasting

16 I say again, let no one think me a fool.
If otherwise, at least receive me as a fool,
that I also may boast a little. 17 What I
speak, [x]I speak not according to the Lord,
but as it were, foolishly, in this confidence
of boasting. 18 Seeing that many boast according to the flesh, I also will boast. 19 For

6 [j][1 Cor. 1:17] [k][1 Cor. 12:8; Eph. 3:4] [l][2 Cor. 12:12] [2]NU omits *been*
7 [m]Acts 18:3; 1 Cor. 9:18; 2 Cor. 12:13 [3]*putting myself down*
9 [n]Acts 20:33 [o]Phil. 4:10
10 [p]Rom. 1:9; 9:1; 2 Cor. 1:23; [Gal. 2:20] [q]1 Cor. 9:15
11 [r]2 Cor. 6:11; 12:15
12 [s]1 Cor. 9:12
13 [t]Acts 15:24; Rom. 16:18; Gal. 1:7; Phil. 1:15; 2 Pet. 2:1; Rev. 2:2 [u]Phil. 3:2; Titus 1:10
14 [v]Gal. 1:8
15 [w][Phil. 3:19]
17 [x]1 Cor. 7:6

of the false apostles (who said they were sent from the Jerusalem church; *see note on v. 4*), he was in no way inferior to the 12 (cf. 1 Cor. 15:7-9). More likely, Paul was making a sarcastic reference to the false apostles, based on their exalted view of themselves. It is unlikely that he would refer to the 12 in the context of false teaching (cf. vv. 1-4), nor does the comparison that follows seem to be between Paul and the 12 (Paul certainly would not have had to defend his speaking skills against those of the 12; cf. Acts 4:13).

11:6 untrained in speech. Paul acknowledged his lack of training in the rhetorical skills so prized in Greek culture (*see note on 10:10*; cf. Acts 18:24); he was a preacher of the gospel, not a professional orator. ***I am* not in knowledge.** Whatever deficiencies Paul may have had as an orator, he had none in terms of knowledge. Paul did not refer here to his rabbinic training under Gamaliel (Acts 22:3), but to his knowledge of the gospel (cf. 1 Cor. 2:6-11; Eph. 3:1-5), which he had received directly from God (Gal. 1:12).

11:7 free of charge. Greek culture measured the importance of a teacher by the fee he could command. The false apostles therefore accused Paul of being a counterfeit, since he refused to charge for his services (cf. 1 Cor. 9:1-15). They convinced the Corinthians to be offended by Paul's refusal to accept support from them, offering that as evidence that he did not love them (cf. v. 11). Paul's resort to manual labor to support himself (Acts 18:1-3) also embarrassed the Corinthians, who felt such work to be beneath the dignity of an apostle. With biting irony Paul asked his accusers how foregoing his right to support could possibly be a sin. In fact, by refusing support he had humbled himself so they could be exalted; that is, lifted out of their sin and idolatry.

11:8 I robbed other churches. "Robbed" is a very strong word, used in extrabiblical Gr. to refer to pillaging. Paul, of course, did not take money from churches without their consent; his point is that the churches who supported him while he ministered in Corinth received no direct benefit from the support they gave him. Why Paul refused to accept the support he was entitled to from the Corinthians (1 Cor. 9:15) is not clear; perhaps some of them were suspicious of his motives in promoting the offering for the Jerusalem church (cf. 12:16-18).

11:9 brethren who came from Macedonia. Silas and Timothy (Acts 18:5), bringing money from Philippi (Phil. 4:15) and, possibly, Thessalonica (cf. 1 Thess. 3:6). The Macedonians' generous financial support allowed Paul to devote himself full time to preaching the gospel.

11:10 this boasting. About his ministering free of charge (*see note on v. 7*; cf. 1 Cor. 9:15,18). **the regions of Achaia.** The Roman province of which Corinth was the capital and leading city (*see note on 9:2*). The false apostles apparently were affecting more than just the city of Corinth.

11:12 continue to do. That Paul refused to accept financial support from the Corinthians was a source of embarrassment to the false apostles, who eagerly sought money for their services. Paul intended to keep his ministry free of charge and thereby undermine the false apostles' claims that they operated on the same basis as he did.

11:13-15 No longer speaking with veiled irony or defending himself, Paul bluntly and directly exposed the false apostles for what they were—emissaries of Satan. Not only was their claim to apostleship false, so also was their doctrine (*see note on v. 4*). As satanic purveyors of false teaching, they were under the curse of Gal. 1:8,9. Paul's forceful language may seem harsh, but it expressed the godly jealousy he felt for the Corinthians (*see note on v. 2*). Paul was unwilling to sacrifice truth for the sake of unity. Cf. 1 Tim. 4:12; 2 Pet. 2:1-17; Jude 8-13.

11:13 false apostles. *See note on v. 4.*

11:14,15 Since the Prince of Darkness (cf. Luke 22:53; Acts 26:18; Eph. 6:12; Col. 1:13) masquerades as an angel of light—that is, deceptively, disguised as a messenger of truth—it is not surprising that his emissaries do as well. Satan deceived Eve (*see notes on v. 3; Gen 3:1-7*) and holds unbelievers captive (4:4; cf. Eph. 2:1-3); his emissaries were attempting to deceive and enslave the Corinthians. The terrifying "end" these self-styled "ministers of righteousness" will face is God's judgment—the fate of all false teachers (Rom. 3:8; 1 Cor. 3:17; Phil. 3:19; 2 Thess. 2:8; 2 Pet. 2:1,3,17; Jude 4,13).

11:16-33 After digressing to discuss the issue of financial support (vv. 7-12) and to expose the false teachers as emissaries of Satan (vv. 13-15), Paul returned to the "foolish" boasting the Corinthians had forced him into (vv. 1-6; *see note on v. 1*).

11:16 let no one think me a fool. *See note on v. 1.* Since some of the Corinthians (following the false apostles' lead) were comparing Paul unfavorably to the false apostles, he decided to answer fools according to their folly (Prov. 26:5). Paul's concern was not personal preservation; rather, the apostle knew that by rejecting him in favor of the false apostles, the Corinthians would be rejecting the true gospel for a false one. So by establishing himself and his ministry as genuine, Paul was defending the true gospel of Jesus Christ.

11:17,18 Paul acknowledged that boasting is "not according to the Lord" (cf. 10:1), but the desperate situation in Corinth (where the false apostles made their "boast according to the flesh") forced him to boast, not for self-glorification (Gal. 6:14), but to counter the false doctrine threatening the Corinthian church (*see note on v. 16*).

you put up with fools gladly, [y]since you
yourselves are wise! 20 For you put up with
it [z]if one brings you into bondage, if one
devours *you,* if one takes *from you,* if one
exalts himself, if one strikes you on the
face. 21 To *our* shame [a]I say that we were
too weak for that! But [b]in whatever anyone
is bold—I speak foolishly—I am bold also.

Suffering for Christ

22 Are they [c]Hebrews? So *am* I. Are they
Israelites? So *am* I. Are they the seed of
Abraham? So *am* I. 23 Are they ministers of
Christ?—I speak as a fool—I *am* more: [d]in
labors more abundant, [e]in stripes above
measure, in prisons more frequently, [f]in
deaths often. 24 From the Jews five times I
received [g]forty [h]*stripes* minus one. 25 Three
times I was [i]beaten with rods; [j]once I was
stoned; three times I [k]was shipwrecked; a
night and a day I have been in the deep;
26 *in* journeys often, *in* perils of waters, *in*
perils of robbers, [l]*in* perils of *my own* countrymen, [m]*in* perils of the Gentiles, *in* perils
in the city, *in* perils in the wilderness, *in*
perils in the sea, *in* perils among false
brethren; 27 in weariness and toil, [n]in
sleeplessness often, [o]in hunger and thirst,
in [p]fastings often, in cold and nakedness—
28 besides the other things, what comes
upon me daily: [q]my deep concern for all
the churches. 29 [r]Who is weak, and I am
not weak? Who is made to stumble, and I
do not burn *with indignation?*

30 If I must boast, [s]I will boast in the
things which concern my [4]infirmity.
31 [t]The God and Father of our Lord Jesus
Christ, [u]who is blessed forever, knows that
I am not lying. 32 [v]In Damascus the governor, under Aretas the king, was guarding

19 [y]1 Cor. 4:10
20 [z]2 Cor. 1:24; [Gal. 2:4; 4:3, 9; 5:1]
21 [a]2 Cor. 10:10 [b]Phil. 3:4
22 [c]Acts 22:3; Rom. 11:1; Phil. 3:4-6
23 [d]1 Cor. 15:10 [e]Acts 9:16 [f]1 Cor. 15:30
24 [g]Deut. 25:3 [h]2 Cor. 6:5
25 [i]Acts 16:22, 23; 21:32 [j]Acts 14:5, 19 [k]Acts 27:1-44
26 [l]Acts 9:23, 24; 13:45, 50; 17:5, 13; 1 Thess. 2:15 [m]Acts 14:5, 19; 19:23; 27:42
27 [n]Acts 20:31 [o]1 Cor. 4:11; Phil. 4:12 [p]Acts 9:9; 13:2, 3; 14:23
28 [q]Acts 20:18; [Rom. 1:14]; 2 Cor. 7:12; 12:20; Gal. 4:11; 1 Thess. 3:10
29 [r][1 Cor. 8:9, 13; 9:22] 30 [s][2 Cor. 12:5, 9, 10] [4]*weakness*
31 [t]Rom. 1:9; Gal. 1:20; 1 Thess. 2:5 [u]Rom. 9:5 32 [v]Acts 9:19-25

11:19-21 These verses contain some of the most scathing sarcasm Paul ever penned, demonstrating the seriousness of the situation at Corinth and revealing the jealous concern of a godly pastor (*see note on v. 2*). Paul did not view his disagreement with the false apostles as a mere academic debate; the souls of the Corinthians and the purity of the gospel were at stake.

11:19 The Corinthians, wrote Paul sarcastically, should have no trouble bearing with a "fool" like him, since they themselves were so wise (cf. 1 Cor. 4:10)!

11:20 brings you into bondage. The Gr. verb translated by this phrase appears elsewhere in the NT only in Gal. 2:4, where it speaks of the Galatians' enslavement by the Judaizers. The false apostles had robbed the Corinthians of their freedom in Christ (cf. Gal. 5:1). **devours *you.*** Or "preys upon you." This probably refers to the false teachers' demands for financial support (the same verb appears in Luke 20:47 where Jesus denounces the Pharisees for devouring widows' houses). **takes *from you.*** Better translated "takes advantage of you" (it is translated "I caught you by cunning" in 12:16). The false apostles were attempting to catch the Corinthians like fish in a net (cf. Luke 5:5,6). **exalts himself.** This refers to one who is presumptuous, puts on airs, acts arrogantly, or lords it over people (cf. 1 Pet. 5:3). **strikes you on the face.** The false apostles may have physically abused the Corinthians, but the phrase is more likely used in a metaphorical sense (cf. 1 Cor. 9:27) to speak of the false teachers' humiliation of the Corinthians. To strike someone on the face was a sign of disrespect and contempt (cf. 1 Kin. 22:24; Luke 22:64; Acts 23:2).

11:21 too weak for that. Paul's sarcasm reached its peak as he noted that he was "too weak" to abuse the Corinthians as the false apostles had done (v. 20).

11:22-33 The third and most comprehensive list recorded in this letter of Paul's sufferings for the cause of Christ (cf. 4:8-12; 6:4-10).

11:22 Are they Hebrews...Israelites...the seed of Abraham? To each of these questions Paul replied simply and powerfully, "so am I" (cf. Phil. 3:5).

11:23 Are they ministers of Christ? Paul had already emphatically denied that they were (v. 13); however, some of the Corinthians still believed they were. Paul accepted that belief for the sake of argument, then went on to show that his ministry was in every way superior to the false apostles' so-called "ministry." **I speak as a fool.** *See note on v. 1.* Once again Paul expressed his extreme distaste for the boasting the Corinthians had forced him into. **in labors...in deaths often.** A general summation of Paul's sufferings for the gospel; the next few verses give specific examples, many of which are not found in Acts. Paul was often in danger of death (Acts 9:23,29; 14:5,19,20; 17:5; 21:30-32).

11:24 forty *stripes* minus one. Deuteronomy 25:1-3 set 40 as the maximum number that could legally be administered; in Paul's day the Jews reduced that number by one to avoid accidentally going over the maximum. Jesus warned that His followers would receive such beatings (Matt. 10:17).

11:25 beaten with rods. Refers to Roman beatings with flexible sticks tied together (cf. Acts 16:22,23). **once I was stoned.** At Lystra (Acts 14:19,20). **three times I was shipwrecked.** Not including the shipwreck on his journey as a prisoner to Rome (Acts 27), which had not yet taken place. Paul had been on several sea voyages up to this time (cf. Acts 9:30; 11:25,26; 13:4,13; 14:25,26; 16:11; 17:14,15; 18:18,21), giving ample opportunity for the 3 shipwrecks to have occurred. **a night and a day I have been in the deep.** At least one of the shipwrecks was so severe that Paul spent an entire day floating on the wreckage, waiting to be rescued.

11:26,27 *in* perils. Those connected with his frequent travels. "Waters" (rivers) and "robbers" posed a serious danger to travelers in the ancient world. Paul's journey from Perga to Pisidian Antioch (Acts 13:14), for example, required him to travel through the robber-infested Taurus Mountains, and to cross two dangerous, flood-prone rivers. Paul was frequently in danger from his "own countrymen" (Acts 9:23,29; 13:45; 14:2,19; 17:5; 18:6,12-16; 20:3,19; 21:27-32) and, less often, from "Gentiles" (Acts 16:16-40; 19:23–20:1).

11:26 false brethren. Those who appeared to be Christians, but were not, such as the false apostles (v. 13) and the Judaizers (Gal. 2:4).

11:28,29 Far worse than the occasional physical suffering Paul endured was the constant, daily burden of concern for the churches that he felt. Those who were "weak" (cf. Rom. 14; 1 Cor. 8) in faith, or were "made to stumble" into sin caused him intense emotional pain. Cf. 1 Thess. 5:14.

11:30 I will boast...my infirmity. To do so magnified God's power at work in him (cf. 4:7; Col. 1:29; 2 Tim. 2:20,21).

11:31 Realizing how incredible the list of his sufferings must have seemed, Paul called on God to witness that he was telling the truth (cf. v. 10; 1:23; Rom. 1:9; 9:1; Gal. 1:20; 1 Thess. 2:5,10; 1 Tim. 2:7)—that these things really happened.

11:32,33 Paul related his humiliating escape from Damascus (cf.

the city of the Damascenes with a garrison,
desiring to arrest me; **33** but I was let down
in a basket through a window in the wall,
and escaped from his hands.

The Vision of Paradise

12 It is [1]doubtless not profitable for me
to boast. I will come to [a]visions and
[b]revelations of the Lord: **2** I know a man
[c]in Christ who fourteen years ago—
whether in the body I do not know, or
whether out of the body I do not know,
God knows—such a one [d]was caught up to
the third heaven. **3** And I know such a
man—whether in the body or out of the
body I do not know, God knows— **4** how
he was caught up into [e]Paradise and heard
inexpressible words, which it is not lawful
for a man to utter. **5** Of such a one I will
boast; yet of myself I will not [f]boast, except
in my infirmities. **6** For though I might desire to boast, I will not be a fool; for I will
speak the truth. But I refrain, lest anyone
should think of me above what he sees me
to be or hears from me.

The Thorn in the Flesh

7 And lest I should be exalted above
measure by the abundance of the revelations, a [g]thorn in the flesh was given to me,
[h]a messenger of Satan to [2]buffet me, lest I
be exalted above measure. **8** [i]Concerning
this thing I pleaded with the Lord three
times that it might depart from me. **9** And
He said to me, "My grace is sufficient for
you, for My strength is made perfect in
weakness." Therefore most gladly [j]I will
rather boast in my infirmities, [k]that the
power of Christ may rest upon me.
10 Therefore [l]I take pleasure in infirmities,

CHAPTER 12

1 [a] Acts 16:9; 18:9; 22:17, 18; 23:11; 26:13-15; 27:23 [b] Acts 9:3-6; 1 Cor. 14:6; 2 Cor. 12:7; [Gal. 1:12; 2:2; Eph. 3:3-6] [1] NU *necessary, though not profitable, to boast*
2 [c] Rom. 16:7; Gal. 1:22 [d] Acts 22:17
4 [e] Luke 23:43; [Rev. 2:7]
5 [f] 2 Cor. 11:30
7 [g] Num. 33:55; Ezek. 28:24; Hos. 2:6; Gal. 4:13, 14 [h] Job 2:7; Matt. 4:10; Luke 13:16; [1 Cor. 5:5] [2] *beat*
8 [i] Deut. 3:23; Matt. 26:44
9 [j] 2 Cor. 11:30 [k] [1 Pet. 4:14]
10 [l] [Rom. 5:3; 8:35]

Acts 9:23-25) as the crowning example of the weakness and infirmity in which he boasted (v. 30). The Acts narrative names the hostile Jews as those who sought Paul's life, whereas Paul here mentioned the governor under the Nabatean Arab king Aretas (9 B.C.–A.D. 40) as the one who sought him. Evidently the Jews stirred up the secular authorities against him, as they were later to do repeatedly in Acts (cf. Acts 13:50; 14:2; 17:13).

12:1-7 Paul continued, reluctantly, with his boasting (*see note on 11:1*). Though it was "not profitable," since it could tempt his own flesh to be proud, the Corinthians' fascination with the alleged visions and revelations of the false apostles left him little choice (v. 11).

12:1 visions and revelations. Six of Paul's visions are recorded in Acts (9:12; 16:9,10; 18:9; 22:17,18; 23:11; 27:23,24), and his letters speak of revelations he had received (cf. Gal. 1:12; 2:2; Eph. 3:3).

12:2-4 Since it took place 14 years before the writing of 2 Corinthians, the specific vision Paul relates cannot be identified with any incident recorded in Acts. It probably took place between his return to Tarsus from Jerusalem (Acts 9:30) and the start of his missionary journeys (Acts 13:1-3). **caught up to the third heaven...caught up into Paradise.** Paul was not describing two separate visions; "the third heaven" and "Paradise" are the same place (cf. Rev. 2:7, which says the tree of life is in Paradise, with Rev. 22:14, which says it is in heaven). The first heaven is the earth's atmosphere (Gen. 8:2; Deut. 11:11; 1 Kin. 8:35); the second is interplanetary and interstellar space (Gen. 15:5; Ps. 8:3; Is. 13:10); and the third the abode of God (1 Kin. 8:30; 2 Chr. 30:27; Ps. 123:1).

12:2 a man in Christ. Though Paul's reluctance to boast caused him to refer to himself in the third person, the context makes it obvious that he was speaking about himself; relating the experience of another man would hardly have enhanced Paul's apostolic credentials. Also, Paul's thorn in the flesh afflicted him, not someone else (v. 7).

12:2,3 whether in...or...out of the body. Paul was so overwhelmed by his heavenly vision that he did not know the precise details. However, whether he was caught up bodily into heaven (like Enoch, Gen. 5:24 and Elijah, 2 Kin. 2:11), or his spirit was temporarily separated from his body, was not important.

12:4 inexpressible words...not lawful...to utter. Because the words were for him alone, Paul was forbidden to repeat them, even if he could have expressed them coherently.

12:5 Of such a one I will boast. *See note on v. 2.*

12:6 If Paul wished to boast about his unique experience (vv. 1-4) he would not be a fool, because it really happened. He refrained from boasting about it, however, because he wanted the Corinthians to judge him based on their observations of his ministry, not on his visions.

12:7 the revelations. *See note on v. 1.* **a thorn in the flesh...a messenger of Satan.** This was sent to him by God, to keep him humble. As with Job, Satan was the immediate cause, but God was the ultimate cause. Paul's use of the word "messenger" (Gr., *angellos,* or angel) from Satan suggests the "thorn in the flesh" (lit. "a stake for the flesh") was a demon person, not a physical illness. Of the 188 uses of the Gr. word, *angellos,* in the NT, at least 180 are in reference to angels. This angel was from Satan, a demon afflicting Paul. Possibly, the best explanation for this demon was that he was indwelling the ring leader of the Corinthian conspiracy, the leader of the false apostles. Through them he was tearing up Paul's beloved church and thus driving a painful stake through Paul. Further support for this view comes from the context of chaps. 10–13, which is one of fighting adversaries (the false prophets). The verb translated "buffet" always refers to ill treatment from other people (Matt. 26:67; Mark 14:65; 1 Cor. 4:11; 1 Pet. 2:20). Finally, the OT describes Israel's personal opponents as thorns (Num. 33:55; Josh. 23:13; Judg. 2:3; Ezek. 28:24). **lest I be exalted above measure.** The assault was painful, but purposeful. God was allowing Satan to bring this severe trouble in the church for the purpose of humbling Paul who, having had so many revelations, including a trip to heaven and back, would have been proud. The demonized false apostle attacking his work in Corinth was the stake being driven through his otherwise proud flesh.

12:8 I pleaded...three times. Paul, longing for relief from this painful hindrance to his ministry, went to his Lord, begging Him (the use of the definite article with "Lord" shows Paul's prayer was directed to Jesus) to remove it. The demons are only subject to His authority. The 3-fold repetition of Paul's request parallels that of Jesus in Gethsemane (Mark 14:32-41). Both Paul and Jesus had their requests denied, but were granted grace to endure their ordeals.

12:9 My grace is sufficient for you. The present tense of the verb translated "is sufficient" reveals the constant availability of divine grace. God would not remove the thorn, as Paul had requested, but would continually supply him with grace to endure it (cf. 1 Cor. 15:10; Phil. 4:13; Col. 1:29). **My strength is made perfect in weakness.** Cf. 4:7-11. The weaker the human instrument, the more clearly God's grace shines forth.

12:9,10 Paul took no pleasure in the pain itself, but rejoiced in the power of Christ that it revealed through him.

in reproaches, in needs, in persecutions, in
distresses, for Christ's sake. [m]For when I
am weak, then I am strong.

Signs of an Apostle

11 I have become [n]a fool [3]in boasting; you
have compelled me. For I ought to have
been commended by you; for [o]in nothing
was I behind the most eminent apostles,
though [p]I am nothing. 12 [q]Truly the signs of
an apostle were accomplished among you
with all perseverance, in signs and [r]won-
ders and mighty [s]deeds. 13 For what is it in
which you were inferior to other churches,
except that I myself was not burdensome to
you? Forgive me this wrong!

Love for the Church

14 [t]Now *for* the third time I am ready to
come to you. And I will not be burdensome to you; for [u]I do not seek yours, but
you. [v]For the children ought not to lay up
for the parents, but the parents for the children. 15 And I will very gladly spend and
be spent [w]for your souls; though [x]the more
abundantly I love you, the less I am loved.
16 But be that *as it may,* [y]I did not burden
you. Nevertheless, being crafty, I caught
you by cunning! 17 Did I take advantage of
you by any of those whom I sent to you?
18 I urged Titus, and sent our [z]brother with

10 [m] 2 Cor. 13:4
11 [n] 2 Cor. 5:13; 11:1, 16; 12:6 [o] 1 Cor. 15:10; 2 Cor. 11:5 [p] 1 Cor. 3:7; 13:2; 15:9 [3] NU omits *in boasting*
12 [q] Acts 14:3; Rom. 15:18 [r] Acts 15:12 [s] Acts 14:8-10; 16:16-18; 19:11, 12; 20:6-12; 28:1-10
14 [t] 2 Cor. 1:15; 13:1, 2 [u] Acts 20:33; [1 Cor. 10:24-33] [v] 1 Cor. 4:14; Gal. 4:19
15 [w] John 10:11; Rom. 9:3; 2 Cor. 1:6; Phil. 2:17; Col. 1:24; 1 Thess. 2:8; [2 Tim. 2:10] [x] 2 Cor. 6:12, 13
16 [y] 2 Cor. 11:9
18 [z] 2 Cor. 8:18
19 [a] 2 Cor. 5:12 [b] [Rom. 9:1, 2]; 2 Cor. 11:31 [c] 1 Cor. 10:33 [4] NU *You have been thinking for a long time that we*
20 [d] 1 Cor. 4:21; 2 Cor. 13:2, 10
21 [e] 2 Cor. 2:1, 4 [f] 2 Cor. 13:2 [g] 1 Cor. 5:1

CHAPTER 13

1 [a] 2 Cor. 12:14 [b] Num. 35:30; Deut. 17:6; 19:15; Matt. 18:16; John 8:17; Heb. 10:28

him. Did Titus take advantage of you? Did
we not walk in the same spirit? Did *we* not
walk in the same steps?
19 [a]Again,[4] do you think that we excuse
ourselves to you? [b]We speak before God in
Christ. [c]But *we do* all things, beloved, for
your edification. 20 For I fear lest, when I
come, I shall not find you such as I wish,
and *that* [d]I shall be found by you such as
you do not wish; lest *there be* contentions,
jealousies, outbursts of wrath, selfish ambitions, backbitings, whisperings, conceits,
tumults; 21 lest, when I come again, my
God [e]will humble me among you, and I
shall mourn for many [f]who have sinned
before and have not repented of the
uncleanness, [g]fornication, and lewdness
which they have practiced.

Coming with Authority

13 This *will be* [a]the third *time* I am coming to you. [b]*"By the mouth of two or
three witnesses every word shall be established."* 2 [c]I have told you before, and foretell as if I were present the second time, and
now being absent [1]I write to those [d]who
have sinned before, and to all the rest, that
if I come again [e]I will not spare— 3 since
you seek a proof of Christ [f]speaking in me,

2 [c] 2 Cor. 10:2 [d] 2 Cor. 12:21 [e] 2 Cor. 1:23; 10:11 [1] NU omits *I write*
3 [f] Matt. 10:20; [1 Cor. 5:4; 7:40]

12:11 become a fool. *See note on 11:1,16*; cf. 11:17,21,23. **you have compelled me.** *See note on 11:1.* **the most eminent apostles.** *See note on 11:5.*

12:12 the signs of an apostle. Including, but not limited to, "signs and wonders and mighty deeds" (the miracle of the Corinthians' salvation was also a mark of Paul's apostleship, 1 Cor. 9:2). The purpose of miraculous signs was to authenticate the apostles as God's messengers (cf. Acts 2:22,43; 4:30; 5:12; 14:3; Rom. 15:18,19; Heb. 2:3,4).

12:13 Paul had not slighted the Corinthians except by refusing to be a burden (*see note on 11:7*). With a touch of irony, he begged their forgiveness for that "wrong."

12:14 *for* the third time. The first was the visit recorded in Acts 18; the second was the "painful visit" (2:1; see Introduction: Background and Setting). **not be burdensome.** On his upcoming visit, Paul wished to continue his practice of refusing to accept support from the Corinthians. **I do not seek yours, but you.** Paul sought the Corinthians (cf. 6:11-13; 7:2,3), not their money. **children...parents...parents...children.** To reinforce his point, Paul cited the axiomatic truth that parents are financially responsible for their children, not children (when they are young, cf. 1 Tim. 5:4) for their parents.

12:15 Far from seeking to take from the Corinthians, Paul sought to give. The verb translated "spend" refers to spending money, and probably describes Paul's willingness to work to support himself while in Corinth (Acts 18:3). "Be spent" describes Paul's willingness to give of himself—even to the point of sacrificing his life.

12:16-18 Although it was obvious to all that Paul had not personally taken advantage of the Corinthians, his opponents circulated an even more vicious rumor—that he was using craftiness and cunning to deceive the Corinthians (cf. 4:2). Specifically, the false apostles accused Paul of sending his assistants to collect the Jerusalem offering from the Corinthians while intending to keep some of it for himself. Thus, according to his opponents, Paul was both a deceitful hypocrite (because he really did take money from the Corinthians after all, despite his words in vv. 14,15) and a thief. This charge was all the more painful to Paul because it impugned the character of his friends. Outraged that the Corinthians could believe such ridiculous lies, Paul pointed out that his associates did not take advantage of the Corinthians during their earlier visits regarding the collection (8:6,16-22). The simple truth was that neither Paul nor his representatives had in any way defrauded the Corinthians.

12:19 Lest the Corinthians view themselves as judges before whom Paul was on trial, the apostle quickly set them straight: only God was his judge (cf. 5:10; 1 Cor. 4:3-5). Paul sought to edify the Corinthians, not exonerate himself.

12:21 When he visited them, Paul did not want to find the Corinthians in the same sorry spiritual condition as on his last visit (the "painful visit," 2:1; see Introduction: Background and Setting). If he found that they were not what he wished (i.e., still practicing the sins he listed), they would find him not as they wished—he would have had to discipline them (cf. 13:2). To find the Corinthians still living in unrepentant sin would both humiliate and sadden Paul. This warning (and the one in 13:2) was designed to prevent that from happening.

13:1 the third *time.* *See note on 12:14.* ***two or three witnesses.*** Not a reference to Paul's 3 visits to Corinth, since he could be only one witness no matter how many visits he made. Paul informed the Corinthians that he would deal biblically (cf. Deut. 19:15; Matt. 18:16; John 8:17; Heb. 10:28) with any sin he found in Corinth.

13:2 I will not spare. *See note on 12:21.*

13:3 a proof of Christ speaking in me. Those Corinthians still seeking proof that Paul was a genuine apostle would have it when he arrived. They may have gotten more than they bargained for, however, for Paul was going to use his apostolic authority and power to deal

who is not weak toward you, but mighty
[g]in you. 4 [h]For though He was crucified in
weakness, yet [i]He lives by the power of
God. For [j]we also are weak in Him, but we
shall live with Him by the power of God
toward you.
5 Examine yourselves *as to* whether you
are in the faith. Test yourselves. Do you not
know yourselves, [k]that Jesus Christ is in
you?—unless indeed you [2]are [l]disquali-
fied. 6 But I trust that you will know that
we are not disqualified.

Paul Prefers Gentleness

7 Now [3]I pray to God that you do no
evil, not that we should appear approved,
but that you should do what is honorable,
though [m]we may seem disqualified. 8 For
we can do nothing against the truth, but
for the truth. 9 For we are glad [n]when we
are weak and you are strong. And this also
we pray, [o]that you may be made complete.
10 [p]Therefore I write these things being absent, lest being present I should use sharp-
ness, according to the [q]authority which the
Lord has given me for edification and not
for destruction.

Greetings and Benediction

11 Finally, brethren, farewell. Become
complete. [r]Be of good comfort, be of one
mind, live in peace; and the God of love
[s]and peace will be with you.
12 [t]Greet one another with a holy kiss.
13 All the saints greet you.
14 [u]The grace of the Lord Jesus Christ,
and the love of God, and [v]the [4]communion
of the Holy Spirit *be* with you all. Amen.

3 [g][1 Cor. 9:2]
4 [h]Phil. 2:7, 8; [1 Pet. 3:18] [i][Rom. 1:4; 6:4; 1 Cor. 6:14] [j][2 Cor. 10:3, 4]
5 [k]Rom. 8:10; [Gal. 4:19] [l]1 Cor. 9:27 [2]*do not stand the test*
7 [m]2 Cor. 6:9 [3]NU *we*
9 [n]1 Cor. 4:10 [o]1 Cor. 1:10; 2 Cor. 13:11; Eph. 4:12; [1 Thess. 3:10]
10 [p]1 Cor. 4:21 [q]1 Cor. 5:4; 2 Cor. 10:8
11 [r]Rom. 12:16, 18 [s]Rom. 15:33; Eph. 6:23
12 [t]Rom. 16:16
14 [u]Rom. 16:24 [v]Phil. 2:1 [4]*fellowship*

with any sin and rebellion he found there (v. 2; *see note on 12:21*). **who is not weak.** Christ's power was to be revealed through Paul against the sinning Corinthians (cf. 1 Cor. 11:30-32). By rebelling against Christ's chosen apostle (1:1), they were rebelling against Him.

13:4 Paul was to come to Corinth armed with the irresistible power of the risen, glorified Christ (cf. Phil. 3:10).

13:5,6 The Gr. grammar places great emphasis on the pronouns "yourselves" and "you." Paul turned the tables on his accusers; instead of presuming to evaluate his apostleship, they needed to test the genuineness of their faith (cf. James 2:14-26). He pointed out the incongruity of the Corinthians' believing (as they did) that their faith was genuine and his apostleship false. Paul was their spiritual father (1 Cor. 4:15); if his apostleship was counterfeit, so was their faith. The genuineness of their salvation was proof of the genuineness of his apostleship.

13:5 disqualified. Lit. "not approved." Here it referred to the absence of genuine saving faith.

13:7 do what is honorable. Paul's deepest longing was for his spiritual children to lead godly lives (cf. 7:1)—even if they persisted in doubting him. Paul was even willing to appear "disqualified," as long as the Corinthians turned from their sin (cf. Rom. 9:3).

13:8,9 Lest anyone think his reference to being disqualified (v. 7) was an admission of wrongdoing on his part, Paul hastened to add that he had not violated "the truth" of the gospel. The apostle may also have meant that he needed to take no action against the Corinthians if he found them living according to "the truth." In that case, he would rejoice in his "weakness" (that is, his lack of opportunity to exercise his apostolic power), because that would mean that the Corinthians were spiritually "strong."

13:10 A one-sentence summary of Paul's purpose in writing this letter.

13:11 Paul's concluding exhortations expressed the attitudes he prayed (v. 9) would characterize the Corinthians. **the God of love and peace will be with you.** An encouragement to the Corinthians to carry out the exhortations in the first part of the verse. Only here in the NT is God called "the God of love" (cf. 1 John 4:8).

13:12 a holy kiss. A sign of greeting in biblical times (Matt. 26:49; Luke 7:45), much like the modern handshake. For Christians, it further expressed brotherly love and unity (Rom. 16:16; 1 Cor. 16:20; 1 Thess. 5:26; 1 Pet. 5:14).

13:13 All the saints. Those in Macedonia (possibly Philippi; see Introduction: Background and Setting), from where Paul wrote 2 Corinthians. While encouraging unity within the Corinthian church, Paul did not want the Corinthians to lose sight of their unity with other churches.

13:14 The Trinitarian benediction reminded the Corinthians of the blessings they had received: "grace" from the Lord Jesus Christ (cf. 8:9), "love" from God the Father (cf. v. 11), and "communion" with God and each other through the Holy Spirit (cf. 1:22; 5:5). Jesus was mentioned before the Father because His sacrificial death is the ultimate expression of God's love.

The Epistle of Paul to the

GALATIANS

Title

Galatians derives its title (*pros Galatas*) from the region in Asia Minor (modern Turkey) where the churches addressed were located. It is the only one of Paul's epistles specifically addressed to churches in more than one city (1:2; cf. 3:1; 1 Cor. 16:1).

Author and Date

There is no reason to question the internal claims that the apostle Paul wrote Galatians (1:1; 5:2). Paul was born in Tarsus, a city in the province of Cilicia, not far from Galatia. Under the famous rabbi, Gamaliel, Paul received a thorough training in the OT Scriptures and in the rabbinic traditions at Jerusalem (Acts 22:3). A member of the ultra-orthodox sect of the Pharisees (Acts 23:6), he was one of first-century Judaism's rising stars (1:14; cf. Phil. 3:5,6).

The course of Paul's life took a sudden and startling turn when, on his way to Damascus from Jerusalem to persecute Christians, he was confronted by the risen, glorified Christ (*see notes on Acts 9*). That dramatic encounter turned Paul from Christianity's chief persecutor to its greatest missionary. His 3 missionary journeys and trip to Rome turned Christianity from a faith that included only a small group of Palestinian Jewish believers into an Empire-wide phenomenon. Galatians is one of 13 inspired letters he addressed to Gentile congregations or his fellow workers. For further biographical information on Paul, see Introduction to Romans: Author and Date.

In chap. 2, Paul described his visit to the Jerusalem Council of Acts 15 (*see note on 2:1*), so he must have written Galatians after that event. Since most scholars date the Jerusalem Council about A.D. 49, the most likely date for Galatians is shortly thereafter.

Background and Setting

In Paul's day, the word *Galatia* had two distinct meanings. In a strict ethnic sense, Galatia was the region of central Asia Minor inhabited by the Galatians. They were a Celtic people who had migrated to that region from Gaul (modern France) in the third century B.C. The Romans conquered the Galatians in 189 B.C. but allowed them to have some measure of independence until 25 B.C. when Galatia became a Roman province, incorporating some regions not inhabited by ethnic Galatians (e.g., parts of Lycaonia, Phrygia, and Pisidia). In a political sense, *Galatia* came to describe the entire Roman province, not merely the region inhabited by the ethnic Galatians.

Paul founded churches in the southern Galatian cities of Antioch, Iconium, Lystra, and Derbe (Acts 13:14–14:23). These cities, although within the Roman province of Galatia, were not in the ethnic Galatian region. There is no record of Paul's founding churches in that northern, less populated region.

Those two uses of the word *Galatia* make it more difficult to determine who the original recipients of the epistle were. Some interpret *Galatia* in its strict racial sense and argue that Paul addressed this epistle to churches in the northern Galatian region, inhabited by the ethnic descendants of the Gauls. Although the apostle apparently crossed the border into the fringes of ethnic Galatia on at least two occasions (Acts 16:6; 18:23), Acts does not record that he founded any churches or engaged in any evangelistic ministry there.

Because neither Acts nor Galatians mentions any cities or people from northern (ethnic) Galatia, it is reasonable to believe that Paul addressed this epistle to churches located in the southern part of the Roman province, but outside of the ethnic Galatian region. Acts records the apostle's founding of such churches at Pisidian Antioch (13:14-50), Iconium (13:51–14:7; cf. 16:2), Lystra (14:8-19; cf. 16:2), and Derbe (14:20,21; cf. 16:1). In addition, the churches Paul addressed had apparently been established before the Jerusalem Council (2:5), and the churches of southern Galatia fit that criterion, having been founded during Paul's first missionary journey before the Council met. Paul did not visit northern (ethnic) Galatia until after the Jerusalem Council (Acts 16:6).

Paul wrote Galatians to counter judaizing false teachers who were undermining the central NT doctrine of justification by faith (*see note on Rom. 3:34*). Ignoring the express decree of the Jerusalem Council (Acts 15:23-29), they spread their dangerous teaching that Gentiles must first become Jewish proselytes and submit to all the Mosaic law before they could become Christians (see 1:7; 4:17,21; 5:2-12; 6:12,13). Shocked by the Galatians' openness to that damning heresy (cf. 1:6), Paul wrote this letter to defend justification by faith, and warn these churches of the dire consequences of abandoning that essential doctrine. Galatians is the only epistle Paul wrote that does not contain a commendation for its readers—that obvious omission reflects how urgently he felt about confronting the defection and defending the essential doctrine of justification.

Historical and Theological Themes

Galatians provides valuable historical information about Paul's background (chaps. 1,2), including his 3-year stay in Nabatean Arabia (1:17,18), which Acts does not mention; his 15-day visit with Peter after his stay in Arabia (1:18,19); his trip to the Jerusalem Council (2:1-10); and his confrontation of Peter (2:11-21).

As already noted, the central theme of Galatians (like that of Romans) is justification by faith. Paul defends that doctrine (which is the heart of the gospel) both in its theological (chaps. 3,4) and practical (chaps. 5,6) ramifications. He also defends his position as an apostle (chaps. 1,2) since, as in Corinth, false teachers had attempted to gain a hearing for their heretical teaching by undermining Paul's credibility. The main theological themes of Galatians are strikingly similar to those of Romans, e.g., the inability of the law to justify (2:16; cf. Rom. 3:20); the believer's deadness to the law (2:19; cf. Rom. 7:4); the believer's crucifixion with Christ (2:20; cf. Rom. 6:6); Abraham's justification by faith (3:6; cf. Rom. 4:3); that believers are Abraham's spiritual children (3:7; cf. Rom. 4:10,11) and therefore blessed (3:9; cf. Rom. 4:23,24); that the law brings not salvation but God's wrath (3:10; cf. Rom. 4:15); that the just shall live by faith (3:11; cf. Rom. 1:17); the universality of sin (3:22; cf. Rom. 11:32); that believers are spiritually baptized into Christ (3:27; cf. Rom. 6:3); believers' adoption as God's spiritual children (4:5-7; cf. Rom. 8:14-17); that love fulfills the law (5:14; cf. Rom. 13:8-10); the importance of walking in the Spirit (5:16; cf. Rom. 8:4); the warfare of the flesh against the Spirit (5:17; cf. Rom. 7:23,25); and the importance of believers bearing one anothers' burdens (6:2; cf. Rom. 15:1).

Interpretive Challenges

First, Paul described a visit to Jerusalem and a subsequent meeting with Peter, James, and John (2:1-10). There is a question to be resolved in that text, as to whether that was his visit to the Jerusalem Council (Acts 15), or his earlier visit bringing famine relief to the Jerusalem church (Acts 11:27-30). Second, those who teach baptismal regeneration (the false doctrine that baptism is necessary for salvation) support their view from 3:27. Third, others have used this epistle to support their attacks on the biblical roles of men and women, claiming that the spiritual equality taught in 3:28 is incompatible with the traditional concept of authority and submission. Fourth, those who reject the doctrine of eternal security argue that the phrase "you have fallen from grace" (5:4) describes believers who lost their salvation. Fifth, there is disagreement whether Paul's statement "see with what large letters I have written to you with my own hand!" refers to the entire letter, or merely the concluding verses. Finally, many claim that Paul erased the line between Israel and the church when he identified the church as the "Israel of God" (6:16). Those challenges will be addressed in the notes to the appropriate passages.

Outline

I. Personal: The Preacher of Justification (1:1–2:21)
   A. Apostolic Chastening (1:1-9)
   B. Apostolic Credentials (1:10–2:10)
   C. Apostolic Confidence (2:11-21)

II. Doctrinal: The Principles of Justification (3:1–4:31)
   A. The Experience of the Galatians (3:1-5)
   B. The Blessing of Abraham (3:6-9)
   C. The Curse of the Law (3:10-14)
   D. The Promise of the Covenant (3:15-18)
   E. The Purpose of the Law (3:19-29)
   F. The Sonship of Believers (4:1-7)
   G. The Futility of Ritualism (4:8-20)
   H. The Illustration from Scripture (4:21-31)

III. Practical: The Privileges of Justification (5:1–6:18)
   A. Freedom from Ritual (5:1-6)
   B. Freedom from Legalists (5:7-12)
   C. Freedom in the Spirit (5:13-26)
   D. Freedom from Spiritual Bondage (6:1-10)
   E. Conclusion (6:11-18)

Greeting

CHAPTER 1

1 Paul, an apostle (not from men nor
through man, but [a]through Jesus
Christ and God the Father [b]who raised
Him from the dead), 2 and all the brethren
who are with me,

To the churches of Galatia:

3 Grace to you and peace from God the
Father and our Lord Jesus Christ, 4 [c]who
gave Himself for our sins, that He might
deliver us [d]from this present evil age, according to the will of our God and Father,
5 to whom *be* glory forever and ever.
Amen.

Only One Gospel

6 I marvel that you are turning away so
soon [e]from Him who called you in the
grace of Christ, to a different gospel,
7 [f]which is not another; but there are some
[g]who trouble you and want to [h]pervert[1]
the gospel of Christ. 8 But even if [i]we, or an
angel from heaven, preach any other
gospel to you than what we have preached
to you, let him be [2]accursed. 9 As we have
said before, so now I say again, if anyone
preaches any other gospel to you [j]than
what you have received, let him be accursed.
10 For [k]do I now [l]persuade men, or God?
Or [m]do I seek to please men? For if I still
pleased men, I would not be a bondservant
of Christ.

1 [a] Acts 9:6 [b] Acts 2:24
4 [c] [Matt. 20:28] [d] Heb. 2:5
6 [e] [Rom. 8:28]; Gal. 1:15; 5:8
7 [f] 2 Cor. 11:4 [g] Acts 15:1; Gal. 5:10, 12 [h] 2 Cor. 2:17 [1] *distort*
8 [i] 1 Cor. 16:22 [2] Gr. *anathema*
9 [j] Deut. 4:2
10 [k] [1 Cor. 10:33]; 1 Thess. 2:4 [l] 1 Sam. 24:7 [m] 1 Thess. 2:4

1:1 Paul. See Introduction to Romans: Author and Date; *see note on Acts 9:1*. **apostle.** In general terms, it means "one who is sent with a commission." The apostles of Jesus Christ—the 12 and Paul—were special ambassadors or messengers chosen and trained by Christ to lay the foundation of the early church and be the channels of God's completed revelation (*see note on Rom. 1:1*; cf. Acts 1:2; 2:42; Eph. 2:20). **not from men...but through Jesus Christ.** To defend his apostleship against the false teachers' attack, Paul emphasized that Christ Himself appointed him as an apostle before he met the other apostles (cf. vv. 17,18; Acts 9:3-9). **raised Him from the dead.** *See notes on Rom. 1:4*. Paul included this important fact to show that the risen and ascended Christ Himself appointed him (*see notes on Acts 9:1-9,15*), thus Paul was a qualified witness of His resurrection (cf. Acts 1:22).

1:2 churches of Galatia. The churches Paul founded at Antioch of Pisidia, Iconium, Lystra, and Derbe during his first missionary journey (Acts 13:14–14:23; see Introduction: Background and Setting).

1:3-5 Paul's deep concern over the churches' defection from the gospel is evident from his greeting, which lacks his customary commendations and courtesies, and is instead brief and impersonal.

1:3 Grace to you and peace. *See note on Rom. 1:1*. Even Paul's typical greeting attacked the Judaizers' legalistic system. If salvation is by works as they claimed, it is not of "grace" and cannot result in "peace," since no one can be sure he has enough good works to be eternally secure.

1:4 for our sins. No one can avoid sin by human effort or law-keeping (Rom. 3:20); therefore it must be forgiven, which Christ accomplished through His atoning death on the cross (3:13; *see notes on 2 Cor. 5:19-21; 1 Pet. 2:24*). **present evil age.** The Gr. word for "age" does not refer to a period of time but an order or system, and in particular to the current world system ruled by Satan (*see notes on Rom. 12:2; 1 John 2:15,16; 5:19*). **the will of our God.** The sacrifice of Christ for salvation was the will of God designed and fulfilled for His glory. Cf. Matt. 26:42; John 6:38-40; Acts 2:22,23; Rom. 8:3,31,32; Eph. 1:7,11; Heb. 10:4-10.

1:6 turning away. This is better translated "deserting." The Gr. word was used of military desertion, which was punishable by death. The form of this Gr. verb indicates that the Galatian believers were voluntarily deserting grace to pursue the legalism taught by the false teachers (*see notes on 5:4*). **so soon.** This Gr. word can mean either "easily" or "quickly" and sometimes both. No doubt both senses characterized the Galatians' response to the false teachers' heretical doctrines. **called you.** This could be translated, "who called you once and for all" (cf. 2 Thess. 2:13,14; 2 Tim. 1:8,9; 1 Pet. 1:15), and refers to God's effectual call to salvation (*see note on Rom. 1:7*). **grace of Christ.** God's free and sovereign act of mercy in granting salvation through the death and resurrection of Christ, totally apart from any human work or merit (*see note on Rom. 3:24*). **different gospel.** Cf. 2 Cor. 11:4. The Judaizers' perversion of the true gospel. They added the requirements, ceremonies, and standards of the Old Covenant as necessary prerequisites to salvation. *See notes on 3:3; 4:9; 5:7; Phil. 3:2*.

1:7 trouble. The Gr. word could be translated "disturb" and means "to shake back and forth," meaning to agitate or stir up. Here, it refers to the deep emotional disturbance the Galatian believers experienced. **pervert.** To turn something into its opposite. By adding law to the gospel of Christ, the false teachers were effectively destroying grace, turning the message of God's undeserved favor toward sinners into a message of earned and merited favor. **the gospel of Christ.** The good news of salvation by grace alone through faith alone in Christ alone (*see notes on Rom. 1:1; 1 Cor. 15:1-4*).

1:8,9 Throughout history God has devoted certain objects, individuals, and groups of people to destruction (Josh. 6:17,18; 7:1,25,26). The NT offers many examples of one such group: false teachers (Matt. 24:24; John 8:44; 1 Tim. 1:20; Titus 1:16). Here the Judaizers are identified as members of this infamous company.

1:8 we, or an angel from heaven. Paul's point is hypothetical, calling on the most unlikely examples for false teaching—himself and holy angels. The Galatians should receive no messenger, regardless of how impeccable his credentials, if his doctrine of salvation differs in the slightest degree from God's truth revealed through Christ and the apostles. **accursed.** The translation of the familiar Gr. word *anathema*, which refers to devoting someone to destruction in eternal hell (cf. Rom. 9:3; 1 Cor. 12:3; 16:22).

1:9 As we have said before. This refers to what Paul taught during an earlier visit to these churches, not to a previous comment in this epistle. **anyone.** Paul turns from the hypothetical case of v. 8 (the apostle or heavenly angels preaching a false gospel) to the real situation faced by the Galatians. The Judaizers were doing just that, and were to be devoted to destruction because of their damning heresy.

1:10-12 Because the false teachers sought to undermine Paul's spiritual credentials, he set out to defend his apostleship, explaining once again (cf. v. 1) that he was appointed by God and not by men.

1:10 still pleased men. Paul's previous motivation when he used to persecute Christians on behalf of his fellow Jews. **a bond servant of Christ.** *See note on Rom. 1:1*. Paul had become a willing slave of Christ, which cost him a great deal of suffering from others (6:17). Such personal sacrifice is exactly opposite the goal of pleasing men (6:12).

Call to Apostleship

11 [n]But I make known to you, brethren,
that the gospel which was preached by me
is not according to man. 12 For [o]I neither
received it from man, nor was I taught *it,*
but *it came* [p]through the revelation of Jesus
Christ.
13 For you have heard of my former conduct in Judaism, how [q]I persecuted the
church of God beyond measure and [r]*tried
to* destroy it. 14 And I advanced in Judaism
beyond many of my contemporaries in my
own nation, [s]being more exceedingly zealous [t]for the traditions of my fathers.
15 But when it pleased God, [u]who separated me from my mother's womb and
called *me* through His grace, 16 [v]to reveal
His Son in me, that [w]I might preach Him
among the Gentiles, I did not immediately
confer with [x]flesh and blood, 17 nor did I
go up to Jerusalem to those *who were* apostles before me; but I went to Arabia, and returned again to Damascus.

Contacts at Jerusalem

18 Then after three years [y]I went up to
Jerusalem to see [3]Peter, and remained with
him fifteen days. 19 But [z]I saw none of the
other apostles except [a]James, the Lord's
brother. 20 (Now *concerning* the things
which I write to you, indeed, before God, I
do not lie.)
21 [b]Afterward I went into the regions of
Syria and Cilicia. 22 And I was unknown by
face to the churches of Judea which [c]*were* in
Christ. 23 But they were [d]hearing only, "He
who formerly [e]persecuted us now preaches
the faith which he once *tried to* destroy."
24 And they [f]glorified God in me.

11 [n][Rom. 2:16]; 1 Cor. 15:1
12 [o]1 Cor. 15:1 [p][Eph. 3:3-5]
13 [q]Acts 9:1 [r]Acts 8:3; 22:4, 5
14 [s]Acts 26:9; Phil. 3:6 [t]Jer. 9:14; Matt. 15:2; Mark 7:3; [Col. 2:8]
15 [u]Is. 49:1, 5; Jer. 1:5; Acts 9:15; Rom. 1:1; Gal. 1:6
16 [v][2 Cor. 4:5-7] [w]Acts 9:15; Gal. 2:9 [x]Matt. 16:17
18 [y]Acts 9:26 [3]NU *Cephas*
19 [z]1 Cor. 9:5 [a]Matt. 13:55
21 [b]Acts 9:30
22 [c]Rom. 16:7
23 [d]Acts 9:20, 21 [e]Acts 8:3
24 [f]Acts 11:18

1:11 make known to you. The strong Gr. verb Paul used here often introduced an important and emphatic statement (1 Cor. 12:3; 2 Cor. 8:1). **the gospel...not according to man.** The gospel Paul preached was not human in origin or it would have been like all other human religion, permeated with works righteousness born of man's pride and Satan's deception (Rom. 1:16).

1:12 neither received it from man, nor was I taught *it*. In contrast to the Judaizers, who received their religious instruction from rabbinic tradition. Most Jews did not study the actual Scriptures; instead they used human interpretations of Scripture as their religious authority and guide. Many of their traditions not only were not taught in Scripture but also contradicted it (Mark 7:13). **through the revelation.** This refers to the unveiling of something previously kept secret—in this case, Jesus Christ. While he knew about Christ, Paul subsequently met Him personally on the road to Damascus and received the truth of the gospel from Him (Acts 9:1-16).

1:13–2:21 Paul offers a brief biographical sketch of important events in his life to further defend his apostleship and prove the authenticity of the gospel of grace he proclaimed.

1:13 Judaism. The Jewish religious system of works righteousness, based not primarily on the OT text, but on rabbinic interpretations and traditions. In fact, Paul will argue that a proper understanding of the OT can lead only to Christ and His gospel of grace through faith (3:6-29). **persecuted.** The tense of this Gr. verb emphasizes Paul's persistent and continual effort to hurt and ultimately exterminate Christians. *See notes on Acts 8:1-3; 9:1; 1 Cor. 15:9; 1 Tim. 1:12-14.*

1:14 advanced...beyond. The Gr. word for "advanced" means "to chop ahead," much like one would blaze a trail through a forest. Paul blazed his path in Judaism (cf. Phil. 3:5,6), and because he saw Jewish Christians as obstacles to its advancement, he worked to cut them down. **exceedingly zealous.** Paul demonstrated this by the extent to which he pursued and persecuted Christians (cf. Acts 8:1-3; 26:11). **traditions of my fathers.** The oral teachings about OT law commonly known as the "Halakah." This collection of interpretations of the law eventually carried the same authority as, or even greater than, the law (Torah) itself. Its regulations were so hopelessly complex and burdensome that even the most astute rabbinical scholars could not master it by either interpretation or conduct.

1:15 separated me from my mother's womb. Paul is not talking about being born, separated physically from his mother, but being separated or set apart to God for service from the time of his birth. The phrase refers to God's election of Paul without regard for his personal merit or effort (cf. Is. 49:1; Jer. 1:5; Luke 1:13-17; Rom. 9:10-23). **called *me* through His grace.** This refers to God's effectual call (*see notes on Rom. 1:7; 8:30*). On the Damascus Road God actually brought Saul, whom He had already chosen, to salvation.

1:16 reveal His Son in me. Not only was Christ revealed *to* Paul on the Damascus Road, but *in* him as God gave him the life, light, and faith to believe in Him. **preach Him among the Gentiles.** Paul's specific call to proclaim the gospel to non-Jews (*see notes on Acts 9:15; 26:15-18*; cf. Rom. 1:13-16; 11:13; 15:18). **confer with flesh and blood.** Paul did not look to Ananias or other Christians at Damascus for clarification of or addition to the revelation he received from Christ (Acts 9:19,20).

1:17 Jerusalem...Arabia...Damascus. Rather than immediately travel to Jerusalem to be instructed by the apostles, Paul instead went to Nabatean Arabia, a wilderness desert that stretched E of Damascus down to the Sinai peninsula. After being prepared for ministry by the Lord, he returned to minister in nearby Damascus.

1:18 three years. The approximate time from Paul's conversion to his first journey to Jerusalem. During those years he made a visit to Damascus and resided in Arabia, under the instruction of the Lord. This visit is discussed in Acts 9:26-30 (*see note on Acts 9:23*). **up to Jerusalem.** Travelers in Israel always speak of going up to Jerusalem because of its higher elevation (*see note on Acts 18:22*). **see.** Better translated, "to become acquainted with." **Peter.** *See notes on Matt. 10:2;* see Introduction to 1 Peter: Author and Date. The apostle who was the personal companion of the Lord and the most powerful spokesman in the early years of the Jerusalem church (Acts 1–12).

1:19 James, the Lord's brother. Cf. 2:9,12; *see note on Acts 15:13;* see Introduction to James: Author and Date.

1:20 The directness of this statement indicates that Paul had been accused by the Jewish legalists of being a liar, who was shameless or deluded.

1:21 Syria and Cilicia. *See note on Acts 15:23*; cf. Acts 9:30. This area included his home town of Tarsus. He was preaching in that region for several years. When word of revival in that area reached Jerusalem, they sent Barnabas (see Acts 11:20-26). Paul stayed on in that region as a pastor in the church at Antioch. With Barnabas, they went from there on the first missionary journey (Acts 13:1-3), and afterward returned to Antioch (Acts 13:1-3) from where they were sent to the Jerusalem Council (Acts 14:26–15:4).

1:22 Judea. *See note on Acts 1:8.*

1:23 Over the 14 years before the Jerusalem Council (*see note on 2:1*), Paul had come only twice to Jerusalem (Acts 9:26-30; 11:30) so the Christians there only knew him by reputation.

1:24 they glorified God in me. Proof that the gospel Paul

Defending the Gospel

2 Then after fourteen years [a]I went up
again to Jerusalem with Barnabas, and
also took Titus with *me.* 2 And I went up
[1]by revelation, and communicated to them
that gospel which I preach among the Gentiles, but [b]privately to those who were of
reputation, lest by any means [c]I might run,
or had run, in vain. 3 Yet not even Titus
who *was* with me, being a Greek, was compelled to be circumcised. 4 And *this occurred* because of [d]false brethren secretly
brought in (who came in by stealth to spy
out our [e]liberty which we have in Christ
Jesus, [f]that they might bring us into
bondage), 5 to whom we did not yield submission even for an hour, that [g]the truth of
the gospel might continue with you.

6 But from those [h]who seemed to be
something—whatever they were, it makes
no difference to me; [i]God [2]shows personal favoritism to no man—for those who
seemed *to be something* [j]added nothing to
me. 7 But on the contrary, [k]when they saw
that the gospel for the uncircumcised [l]had
been committed to me, as *the gospel* for the
circumcised *was* to Peter 8 (for He who
worked effectively in Peter for the apostleship to the [m]circumcised [n]also [o]worked
effectively in me toward the Gentiles),
9 and when James, [3]Cephas, and John,
who seemed to be [p]pillars, perceived [q]the
grace that had been given to me, they
gave me and Barnabas the right hand of

CHAPTER 2

1 [a] Acts 15:2
2 [b] Acts 15:1-4 [c] [Rom. 9:16; 1 Cor. 9:24]; Gal. 5:7; Phil. 2:16; 1 Thess. 3:5; 2 Tim. 4:7; Heb. 12:1 [1] *because of*
4 [d] Acts 15:1, 24; 2 Cor. 11:13, 26; Gal. 1:7 [e] Gal. 3:25; 5:1, 13; [James 1:25] [f] Gal. 4:3, 9
5 [g] [Gal. 1:6; 2:14; 3:1]; Col. 1:5
6 [h] Gal. 2:9; 6:3 [i] Acts 10:34; Rom. 2:11 [j] 2 Cor. 11:5; 12:11 [2] Lit. *does not receive the face of a man*
7 [k] Acts 9:15; 13:46; 22:21; Rom. 11:13 [l] 1 Cor. 9:17; 1 Thess. 2:4; 1 Tim. 1:11
8 [m] 1 Pet. 1:1 [n] Acts 9:15 [o] [Gal. 3:5] **9** [p] Matt. 16:18 [q] Rom. 1:5 [3] Peter

---

preached was the same one the other apostles had taught the Judean believers.

2:1-10 By recounting the details of his most significant trip to Jerusalem after his conversion, Paul offered convincing proof that the message he proclaimed was identical to that of the other 12 apostles.

2:1 fourteen years...again to Jerusalem. This was the period from the time of his first visit to Jerusalem (1:18) to the one Paul refers to here, which probably was for the Jerusalem Council (Acts 15:1-22) called to resolve the issue of Gentile salvation. Linguistically, the word "again" need not refer to the next visit; it can just as easily mean "once again" without respect to how many visits took place in between. And in fact, Paul did visit Jerusalem during that 14-year period to deliver famine relief to the church there (Acts 11:27-30; 12:24,25), but he does not refer to that visit here since it had no bearing on his apostolic authority. **Barnabas.** *See note on Acts 4:36.* Paul's first ally who vouched for him before the apostles at Jerusalem (Acts 9:27), and became his traveling companion on his first missionary journey (Acts 13:2,3). **Titus.** A spiritual child of Paul and a co-worker (Titus 1:4,5). As an uncircumcised Gentile, Titus was fitting proof of the effectiveness of Paul's ministry. See Introduction to Titus: Author and Date.

2:2 by revelation. This revelation from God was the voice of the Holy Spirit (*see notes on Acts 13:2-4*). He refers to the divine commissioning of his visit in order to refute any suggestion by the Judaizers that they had sent Paul to Jerusalem to have the apostles correct his doctrine. **gospel.** *See note on 1:7.* **those who were of reputation.** The 3 main leaders of the Jerusalem church: Peter, James (the Lord's brother, 1:19), and John (cf. v. 9). This phrase was typically used of authorities and implied a position of honor. Paul refers to them in a similar way two other times (vv. 6,9), suggesting a hint of sarcasm directed toward the Judaizers, who claimed they had apostolic approval for their doctrine and Paul did not. They had likely made a habit of exalting these 3 leaders at the expense of Paul. **might run...in vain.** Paul hoped the Jerusalem leaders would support his ministry to the Gentiles and not soften their opposition to legalism. He did not want to see his ministry efforts wasted because of conflict with the other apostles.

2:3 Greek. *See note on Rom. 1:14.* **compelled to be circumcised.** At the core of the Judaizers' works system was the Mosaic prescription of circumcision (*see notes on Gen. 17:9-14; Rom. 4:9-12*). They were teaching that there could be no salvation without circumcision (Acts 15:1,5,24). Paul and the apostles denied that and it was settled at the Jerusalem Council (Acts 15:1-22). *See notes on 5:2-12; 6:15; Rom. 4:10-12; 1 Cor. 7:19.* As a true believer, Titus was living proof that circumcision and the Mosaic regulations were not prerequisites or necessary components of salvation. The apostles' refusal to require Titus' circumcision verified the church's rejection of the Judaizers' doctrine (cf. Timothy, Acts 16:1-3).

2:4 false brethren. The Judaizers, who pretended to be true Christians. Yet, their doctrine, because it claimed allegiance to Christ, was opposed to traditional Judaism, and because it demanded circumcision and obedience to the Mosaic law as prerequisites for salvation, was opposed to Christianity. **to spy out.** This Gr. word pictures spies or traitors entering by stealth into an enemy's camp. The Judaizers were Satan's undercover agents sent into the midst of the church to sabotage the true gospel. **liberty.** Christians are free from the law as a means of salvation, from its external ceremonial regulations as a way of living, and from its curse for disobedience to the law—a curse that Christ bore for all believers (3:13). This freedom is not, however, a license to sin (5:13; Rom. 6:18; 1 Pet. 2:16). **bondage.** Conveys the idea of absolute slavery to an impossible system of works righteousness.

2:5 we did not yield. Paul and Titus (v. 3) never budged from their position of salvation by grace alone through faith alone. **truth of the gospel.** The true gospel as opposed to the different (1:6-8) and false one propagated by the Judaizers (*see note on Rom. 1:1*).

2:6 those who seemed to be something. Another reference to Peter, James, and John (*see note on v. 2*). **personal favoritism.** The unique privileges of the 12 did not make their apostleship more legitimate or authoritative than Paul's—Christ commissioned them all (cf. Rom. 2:11). Paul never saw himself as apostolically inferior (see 2 Cor. 12:11,12).

2:7 The Judaizers claimed Paul was preaching a deviant gospel, but the apostles confirmed that he proclaimed the true gospel. It was the same gospel Peter proclaimed, but to a different audience. **for the uncircumcised.** Better translated "*to* the uncircumcised." Paul preached the gospel primarily to the Gentiles (also to Jews in Gentile lands, as his pattern was to go to the synagogue first; cf. Acts 13:5). **circumcised...Peter.** Peter's ministry was primarily to the Jews.

2:8 He who worked effectively in Peter...in me. The Holy Spirit, who has but one gospel, empowered both Peter and Paul in their ministries.

2:9 James, Cephas, and John. This James was Jesus' half-brother (1:19), who had risen to a prominent role in the Jerusalem church (see Introduction to James). Cephas (Peter) and John (the brother of James the apostle, martyred in Acts 12:2), were two of Christ's closest companions and became the main apostles in the Jerusalem church (see Acts 2–12). **pillars.** Emphasizing the role of James, Peter, and John in establishing and supporting the church. **grace...given to me.** The only conclusion these leaders could make was that God's grace was responsible for the powerful preaching of the gospel and

fellowship, [r]that we *should go* to the Gentiles and they to the circumcised. **10** *They*
desired only that we should remember the
poor, [s]the very thing which I also was
eager to do.

No Return to the Law

11 [t]Now when [4]Peter had come to Antioch, I [5]withstood him to his face, because
he was to be blamed; **12** for before certain
men came from James, [u]he would eat with
the Gentiles; but when they came, he withdrew and separated himself, fearing [6]those
who were of the circumcision. **13** And the
rest of the Jews also played the hypocrite
with him, so that even Barnabas was carried away with their hypocrisy.

14 But when I saw that they were not
straightforward about [v]the truth of the
gospel, I said to Peter [w]before *them* all, [x]"If
you, being a Jew, live in the manner of
Gentiles and not as the Jews, [7]why do you
compel Gentiles to live as [8]Jews? **15** [y]We
who are Jews by nature, and not [z]sinners of
the Gentiles, **16** [a]knowing that a man is not
[9]justified by the works of the law but [b]by
faith in Jesus Christ, even we have believed in Christ Jesus, that we might be justified by faith in Christ and not [c]by the
works of the law; for by the works of the
law no flesh shall be justified.

17 "But if, while we seek to be justified by
Christ, we ourselves also are found [d]sinners,
is Christ therefore a minister of sin? Certain-

9 [r]Acts 13:3
10 [s]Acts 11:30
11 [t]Acts 15:35 [4]NU *Cephas* [5]*opposed*
12 [u][Acts 10:28; 11:2, 3] [6]Jewish Christians
14 [v]Gal. 1:6; 2:5; Col. 1:5 [w]1 Tim. 5:20 [x][Acts 10:28]; Gal. 2:12 [7]NU *how can you* [8]Some interpreters stop the quotation here.
15 [y][Acts 15:10] [z]Matt. 9:11
16 [a]Acts 13:38, 39; Gal. 3:11 [b]Rom. 1:17 [c]Ps. 143:2; Rom. 3:20 [9]*declared righteous*
17 [d][1 John 3:8]

the building of the church through Paul's efforts. **Barnabas.** *See notes on v. 1; Acts 4:36.* **the right hand of fellowship.** In the Near East, this represented a solemn vow of friendship and a mark of partnership. This act signified the apostles' recognition of Paul as a teacher of the true gospel and a partner in ministry. **we *should go* to the Gentiles.** Further confirmation of Paul's divine call to ministry and a blow to the Judaizers, since the apostles directed him to continue in his already flourishing ministry to the Gentiles. **circumcised.** *See note on v. 7.*

2:10 remember the poor. A practical reminder for Paul and the growing ranks of Gentile Christians. The number of Christians in Jerusalem grew rapidly at first (cf. Acts 2:41-45; 6:1) and many who were visiting the city for the feast of Pentecost (Acts 2:1,5) remained and never returned to their homes. While the believers initially shared their resources (Acts 2:45; 4:32-37), many had little money. For years the Jerusalem church was economically pressed. *See notes on Acts 11:29,30.*

2:11-13 A brief account of the darkest of days in the history of the gospel. By withdrawing from the Gentile believers to fellowship with the Judaizers who held a position he knew was wrong, Peter had in appearance supported their doctrine and nullified Paul's divine teaching, especially the doctrine of salvation by grace alone through faith alone. *See notes on 2 Cor. 6:14-18; 2 John 10,11.*

2:11 Antioch. *See note on Acts 11:19.* The location of the first Gentile church. **to be blamed.** Better translated, "stood condemned." Peter was guilty of sin by aligning himself with men he knew to be in error and because of the harm and confusion he caused his Gentile brethren.

2:12 certain men...from James. Peter, knowing the decision the Jerusalem Council had made (Acts 15:7-29), had been in Antioch for some time, eating with Gentiles. When Judaizers came, pretending to be sent by James, they lied, giving false claims of support from the apostles. Peter had already given up all Mosaic ceremony (Acts 10:9-22) and James had at times held only to some of it (Acts 21:18-26). **withdrew.** The Gr. term refers to strategic military withdrawal. The verb's form may imply that Peter's withdrawal was gradual and deceptive. To eat with the Judaizers and decline invitations to eat with the Gentiles, which he had previously done, meant that Peter was affirming the very dietary restrictions he knew God had abolished (Acts 10:15) and thus striking a blow at the gospel of grace. **fearing those...of the circumcision.** The true motivation behind Peter's defection. He was afraid of losing popularity with the legalistic, Judaizing segment of people in the church, even though they were self-righteous hypocrites promoting a heretical doctrine.

2:13 the rest of the Jews. The Jewish believers in Antioch. **hypocrite.** This Gr. word refers to an actor who wore a mask to depict a mood or certain character. In the spiritual sense, it refers to someone who masks his true character by pretending to be something he is not (cf. Matt. 6:1-6). They were committed to the gospel of grace, but pretended to accept Jewish legalism.

2:14 straightforward. Lit. to walk "straight" or "uprightly." By withdrawing from the Gentile Christians, Peter and the other Jewish believers were not walking in line with God's Word. **truth of the gospel.** *See note on v. 5.* **live in the manner of Gentiles.** Before his gradual withdrawal, Peter regularly had fellowship and ate with the Gentiles, thus modeling the ideal of Christian love and liberty between Jew and Gentile. **compel Gentiles to live as Jews.** By his Judaizing mandate, he was declaring theirs was the right way.

2:15,16 Paul's rebuke of Peter serves as one of the most dynamic statements in the NT on the absolute and unwavering necessity of the doctrine of justification by grace through faith (*see note on Rom. 3:24*). Peter's apparent repentance acknowledged Paul's apostolic authority and his own submission to the truth (cf. 2 Pet. 3:15,16).

2:15 sinners of the Gentiles. This is used in the legal sense since Gentiles were sinners by nature because they had no revealed divine written law to guide them toward salvation or living righteously.

2:16 works...faith. Three times in this verse Paul declares that salvation is only through faith in Christ and not by law. The first is general, "a *man* is not justified"; the second is personal, "*we* might be justified"; and the third is universal, "no *flesh* shall be justified." **justified.** This basic forensic Gr. word describes a judge declaring an accused person not guilty and therefore innocent before the law. Throughout Scripture it refers to God's declaring a sinner not guilty and fully righteous before Him by imputing to him the divine righteousness of Christ and imputing the man's sin to his sinless Savior for punishment, (*see notes on Rom. 3:24; Phil. 3:8,9*). **works of the law.** Keeping the law is a totally unacceptable means of salvation because the root of sinfulness is in the fallenness of man's heart, not his actions. The law served as a mirror to reveal sin, not a cure for it (*see notes on 3:22-24; Rom. 7:7-13; 1 Tim. 1:8-11*).

2:17 we...are found sinners. If the Judaizers' doctrine was correct, then Paul, Peter, Barnabas, and the other Jewish believers fell back into the category of sinners because they had been eating and fellowshiping with Gentiles, who according to the Judaizers were unclean. **minister of sin.** If the Judaizers were right, then Christ was wrong and had been teaching people to sin because He taught that food could not contaminate a person (Mark 7:19; cf. Acts 10:13-15). He also declared that all who belong to Him are one with Him and therefore each other (John 17:21-23). Paul's airtight logic condemned Peter, because by his actions he had in effect made it appear as if Christ was lying. This thought is utterly objectionable and causes Paul to use the strongest Gr. negative ("certainly not"; cf. 3:21; Rom. 6:1,2; 7:13).

ly not! 18 For if I build again those things
which I destroyed, I make myself a transgressor. 19 For I [e]through the law [f]died to the
law that I might [g]live to God. 20 I have been
[h]crucified with Christ; it is no longer I who
live, but Christ lives in me; and the *life* which
I now live in the flesh [i]I live by faith in the
Son of God, [j]who loved me and gave Himself for me. 21 I do not set aside the grace of
God; for [k]if righteousness *comes* through the
law, then Christ died [1]in vain."

Justification by Faith

3 O foolish Galatians! Who has bewitched you [1]that you should not obey
the truth, before whose eyes Jesus Christ
was clearly portrayed [2]among you as crucified? 2 This only I want to learn from you:
Did you receive the Spirit by the works of
the law, [a]or by the hearing of faith? 3 Are
you so foolish? [b]Having begun in the Spirit, are you now being made perfect by [c]the
flesh? 4 [d]Have you suffered so [3]many
things in vain—if indeed *it was* in vain?
5 Therefore He who supplies the Spirit to
you and works miracles among you, *does
He do it* by the works of the law, or by the
hearing of faith?— 6 just as Abraham [e]*"believed God, and it was accounted to him
for righteousness."* 7 Therefore know that
only [f]those who are of faith are sons of
Abraham. 8 And [g]the Scripture, foreseeing
that God would justify the Gentiles by
faith, preached the gospel to Abraham beforehand, *saying,* [h]*"In you all the nations
shall be blessed."* 9 So then those who *are* of
faith are blessed with believing Abraham.

The Law Brings a Curse

10 For as many as are of the works of the
law are under the curse; for it is written,
[i]*"Cursed is everyone who does not continue in all things which are written in the
book of the law, to do them."* 11 But that

19 [e] Rom. 8:2 [f] [Rom. 6:2, 14; 7:4]; 1 Cor. 9:20 [g] [Rom. 6:11]
20 [h] [Rom. 6:6; Gal. 5:24; 6:14] [i] Rom. 6:8-11; 2 Cor. 5:15; [Eph. 2:4-6; Col. 3:1-4] [j] Is. 53:12; Eph. 5:2
21 [k] Heb. 7:11 [1] *for nothing*

CHAPTER 3

1 [1] NU omits *that you should not obey the truth* [2] NU omits *among you*
2 [a] Rom. 10:16, 17
3 [b] [Gal. 4:9] [c] Heb. 7:16
4 [d] Heb. 10:35 [3] *Or great*
6 [e] Gen. 15:6
7 [f] John 8:39
8 [g] Rom. 9:17 [h] Gen. 12:3; 18:18; 22:18; 26:4; 28:14
10 [i] Deut. 27:26

2:18 things which I destroyed. The false system of salvation through legalism (*see note on 1:13*), done away with by the preaching of salvation by grace alone through faith alone.

2:19 died to the law. When a person is convicted of a capital crime and executed, the law has no further claim on him. So it is with the Christian who has died in Christ (who paid the penalty for his sins in full) and rises to new life in Him—justice has been satisfied and he is forever free from any further penalty. *See notes on Rom. 7:1-6.*

2:20 I have been crucified with Christ. *See notes on Rom. 6:2-6.* When a person trusts in Christ for salvation, he spiritually participates with the Lord in His crucifixion and His victory over sin and death. **no longer I who live, but Christ lives in me.** The believer's old self is dead (*see note on Eph. 4:22*), having been crucified with Christ (Rom. 6:3,5). The believer's new man has the privilege of the indwelling Christ empowering him and living through him (*see notes on Rom. 8:9,10*). **gave Himself for me.** The manifestation of Christ's love for the believer through His sacrificial death on the cross (John 10:17,18; Rom. 5:6-8; Eph. 5:25-30).

2:21 Paul concluded that Peter, by taking his stand with the Judaizers and thus against Christ, was in effect denying the need for God's grace and thereby nullifying the benefit of Christ's death. **righteousness.** *See note on Rom. 1:17.* **Christ died in vain.** This can be better translated, "Christ died needlessly." Those who insist they can earn salvation by their own efforts undermine the foundation of Christianity and render unnecessary the death of Christ.

3:1 foolish. This refers not to lack of intelligence, but to lack of obedience (cf. Luke 24:25; 1 Tim. 6:9; Titus 3:3). Paul expressed his shock, surprise, and outrage at the Galatians' defection. **Who...?** The Judaizers, the Jewish false teachers were plaguing the Galatian churches (see Introduction: Background and Setting). **bewitched.** Charmed or misled by flattery and false promises. The term suggests an appeal to the emotions by the Judaizers. **clearly portrayed.** The Gr. word describes the posting of official notices in public places. Paul's preaching had publicly displayed the true gospel of Jesus Christ before the Galatians. **crucified.** The crucifixion of Christ was a one time historical fact with continuing results into eternity. Christ's sacrificial death provides eternal payment for believers' sins (cf. Heb. 7:25), and does not need to be supplemented by any human works.

3:2 Did you receive the Spirit...? The answer to Paul's rhetorical question is obvious. The Galatians had received the Spirit when they were saved (Rom. 8:9; 1 Cor. 12:13; 1 John 3:24; 4:13), not through keeping the law, but through saving faith granted when hearing the gospel (cf. Rom. 10:17). The hearing *of* faith is actually hearing *with* faith. Paul appealed to the Galatians' own salvation to refute the Judaizers' false teaching that keeping the law is necessary for salvation.

3:3 Are you so foolish? Incredulous at how easily the Galatians had been duped, Paul asked a second rhetorical question, again rebuking them for their foolishness. **begun in the Spirit...by the flesh.** The notion that sinful, weak (Matt. 26:41; Rom. 6:19), fallen human nature could improve on the saving work of the Holy Spirit was ludicrous to Paul.

3:4 suffered. The Gr. word has the basic meaning of "experienced," and does not necessarily imply pain or hardship. Paul used it to describe the Galatians' personal experience of salvation in Jesus Christ. **many things.** This refers to all the blessings of salvation from God, Christ, and the Holy Spirit (cf. Eph. 1:3). **if indeed *it was* in vain.** See Luke 8:13; Acts 8:13,21; 1 Cor. 15:2; 2 Cor. 6:1; 13:5,6.

3:5 hearing of faith. *See note on v. 2.*

3:6 As he does in Romans (*see note on Rom. 4:3*), Paul uses Abraham as proof that there has never been any other way of salvation than by grace through faith. Even the OT teaches justification by faith.

3:7 sons of Abraham. Quoted from Gen. 15:6. Believing Jews and Gentiles are the true spiritual children of Abraham because they follow his examples of faith (cf. v. 29; Rom. 4:11,16).

3:8 Scripture, foreseeing. Personifying the Scriptures was a common Jewish figure of speech (cf. 4:30; John 7:38,42; 19:37; Rom. 9:17; 10:11; 11:2; 1 Tim. 5:18). Because Scripture is God's Word, when it speaks, God speaks. **preached the gospel to Abraham.** The "good news" to Abraham was the news of salvation for all the nations (quoted from Gen. 12:3; 18:18). See Gen. 22:18; John 8:56; Acts 26:22,23. Salvation has always, in every age, been by faith.

3:9 those who *are* of faith...Abraham. Whether Jew or Gentile. The OT predicted that Gentiles would receive the blessings of justification by faith, as did Abraham. Those blessings are poured out on all because of Christ (cf. John 1:16; Rom. 8:32; Eph. 1:3; 2:6,7; Col. 2:10; 1 Pet. 3:9; 2 Pet. 1:3,4).

3:10 as many as are of the works of the law. Those attempting to earn salvation by keeping the law. **under the curse.** Quoted from Deut. 27:26 to show that failure to perfectly keep the law brings divine judgment and condemnation. One violation of the law deserves the curse of God. Cf. Deut. 27,28. ***all things.*** See James 2:10. No one

no one is [4]justified by the law in the sight
of God *is* evident, for [j]*"the just shall live by*
faith." **12** Yet [k]the law is not of faith, but
[l]*"the man who does them shall live by*
them."

13 [m]Christ has redeemed us from the
curse of the law, having become a curse for
us (for it is written, [n]*"Cursed is everyone*
who hangs on a tree"), **14** [o]that the blessing
of Abraham might come upon the [p]Gen-
tiles in Christ Jesus, that we might receive
[q]the promise of the Spirit through faith.

The Changeless Promise

15 Brethren, I speak in the manner of
men: [r]Though *it is* only a man's covenant,
yet *if it is* confirmed, no one annuls or adds
to it. **16** Now to Abraham and his Seed
were the promises made. He does not say,
"And to seeds," as of many, but as of [s]one,
[t]*"And to your Seed,"* who is [u]Christ.
17 And this I say, *that* the law, [v]which was
four hundred and thirty years later, cannot
annul the covenant that was confirmed before by God [5]in Christ, [w]that it should
make the promise of no effect. **18** For if [x]the
inheritance *is* of the law, [y]*it is* no longer of
promise; but God gave *it* to Abraham by
promise.

Purpose of the Law

19 What purpose then *does* the law *serve?*
[z]It was added because of transgressions,
till the [a]Seed should come to whom the
promise was made; *and it was* [b]appointed
through angels by the hand [c]of a mediator.
20 Now a mediator does not *mediate* for one
only, [d]but God is one.

11 [j] Hab. 2:4; Rom. 1:17; Heb. 10:38 [4] *declared righteous* **12** [k] Rom. 4:4, 5 [l] Lev. 18:5; Rom. 10:5 **13** [m] [Rom. 8:3] [n] Deut. 21:23 **14** [o] [Rom. 4:1-5, 9, 16; Gal. 3:28] [p] Is. 42:1, 6; 49:6; Luke 2:32; Rom. 3:29, 30 [q] Is. 32:15 **15** [r] Heb. 9:17 **16** [s] Gen. 22:18 [t] Gen. 12:3, 7; 13:15; 24:7 [u] [1 Cor. 12:12] **17** [v] Gen. 15:13; Ex. 12:40; Acts 7:6 [w] [Rom. 4:13] [5] NU omits *in Christ* **18** [x] [Rom. 8:17] [y] Rom. 4:14 **19** [z] John 15:22 [a] Gal. 4:4 [b] Acts 7:53 [c] Ex. 20:19; Deut. 5:5 **20** [d] [Rom. 3:29]

---

can keep all the commands of the law—not even strict Pharisees like Saul of Tarsus (Rom. 7:7-12).

3:11 no one is justified by the law. Cf. Rom. 3:20. **justified.** Made righteous before God. *See note on Rom. 3:24.* ***the just shall live by faith.*** *See note on Rom. 1:17.* Paul's earlier OT quote (v. 10; cf. Deut. 27:26) showed that justification does not come from keeping the law; this quote from Hab. 2:4 shows that justification is by faith alone (cf. Heb. 10:38).

3:12 the law is not of faith. Justification by faith and justification by keeping the law are mutually exclusive, as Paul's OT quote from Lev. 18:5 proves.

3:13 Christ has redeemed us from the curse of the law. The Gr. word translated "redeemed" was often used to speak of buying a slave's or debtor's freedom. Christ's death, because it was a death of substitution for sin, satisfied God's justice and exhausted His wrath toward His elect, so that Christ actually purchased believers from slavery to sin and from the sentence of eternal death (4:5; Titus 2:14; 1 Pet. 1:18; cf. Rom. 3:24; 1 Cor. 1:30; Eph. 1:7; Col. 1:14; Heb. 9:12). **having become a curse for us.** By bearing God's wrath for believers' sins on the cross (*see note on 2 Cor. 5:21*; cf. Heb. 9:28; 1 Pet. 2:24; 3:18), Christ took upon Himself the curse pronounced on those who violated the law (*see note on v. 10*). **it is written.** The common NT way (61 times) of introducing OT quotes, (*see note on Rom. 3:10*). Deut. 21:23 is quoted.

3:14 the blessing of Abraham. Faith in God's promise of salvation. *See note on v. 9.* **promise of the Spirit.** From God the Father. Cf. Is. 32:15; 44:3; 59:19-21; Ezek. 36:26,27; 37:14; 39:29; Joel 2:28,29; Luke 11:13; 24:49; John 7:37-39; 14:16,26.

3:15-22 Paul anticipated and refuted a possible objection to his use of Abraham to prove the doctrine of justification by faith: that the giving of the law at Sinai after Abraham brought about a change and a better method of salvation. The apostle dismissed that argument by showing the superiority of the Abrahamic Covenant (vv. 15-18), and the inferiority of the law (vv. 19-22).

3:15 Brethren. This term of endearment reveals Paul's compassionate love for the Galatians—which they may have begun to question in light of his stern rebuke (vv. 1,3). **manner of man...man's covenant.** Even human covenants, once confirmed, are considered irrevocable and unchangeable, how much more a covenant made by an unchanging God (Mal. 3:6; James 1:17).

3:16 Seed. Cf. v. 19. The quote is from Gen. 12:7. The singular form of the Heb. word, like its Eng. and Gr. counterparts, can be used in a collective sense. Paul's point is that in some OT passages (e.g., Gen. 3:15; 22:18), "seed" refers to the greatest of Abraham's descendants, Jesus Christ. **promises.** Those associated with the Abrahamic Covenant (Gen. 12:3,7; 13:15,16; 15:5,18; 17:8; 22:16-18; 26:3,4; 28:13,14). Because they were made both to Abraham and his descendants, they did not become void when Abraham died, or when the law came.

3:17 four hundred and thirty years. From Israel's sojourn in Egypt (cf. Ex. 12:40) to the giving of the law at Sinai (ca. 1445 B.C.) The law actually came 645 years after the initial promise to Abraham (ca. 2090 B.C.; cf. Gen. 12:4; 21:5; 25:26; 47:9), but the promise was repeated to Isaac (Gen. 26:24) and later to Jacob (ca. 1928 B.C.; Gen. 28:15). The last known reaffirmation of the Abrahamic Covenant to Jacob occurred in Gen. 46:2-4 (ca. 1875 B.C.) just before he went to Egypt—430 years before the Mosaic law was given. **the covenant.** The Abrahamic Covenant (*see note on v. 16*). For a discussion of the biblical covenants, *see notes on Gen. 9:16; 12:1-3; Rom. 9:4.* **confirmed before by God.** *See note on v. 15.* The term means "ratified." Once God ratified the covenant officially (*see notes on Gen. 15:9-21*), it had lasting authority so that nothing and no one could annul it. The Abrahamic Covenant was unilateral (God made the promise to Himself), eternal (it provided for everlasting blessing), irrevocable (it will never cease), unconditional (in that it depended on God, not man), but its complete fulfillment awaits the salvation of Israel and the millennial kingdom of Jesus Christ.

3:18 Paul again emphasized that there is no middle ground between law (works) and promise (grace); the two principles are mutually exclusive ways of salvation (cf. Rom 4:14). An "inheritance" by definition is something granted, not worked for, as proven in the case of Abraham.

3:19-22 Having shown the superiority of the promise to Abraham (vv. 15-18), Paul described the inferiority of the law, and its purpose.

3:19 was added because of transgressions. Paul's persuasive argument that the promise is superior to the law raises an obvious question: What was the purpose of the law? Paul's answer is that the law reveals man's utter sinfulness, inability to save himself, and desperate need of a Savior—it was never intended to be the way of salvation (cf. Rom. 7:1-13). **Seed.** *See note on v. 16.* **through angels.** The Bible teaches that angels were involved in the giving of the law (cf. Acts 7:53; Heb. 2:2), but does not explain the precise role they played.

3:20 mediator. Paul's point is apparently that a "mediator" is required when more than one party is involved, but God alone ratified the covenant with Abraham (*see notes on Gen. 15:7-21*).

21 *Is* the law then against the promises of
God? Certainly not! For if there had been a
law given which could have given life,
truly righteousness would have been by
the law. 22 But the Scripture has confined
[e]all under sin, [f]that the promise by faith in
Jesus Christ might be given to those who
believe. 23 But before faith came, we were
kept under guard by the law, [6]kept for the
faith which would afterward be revealed.
24 Therefore [g]the law was our [7]tutor *to
bring us* to Christ, [h]that we might be justified by faith. 25 But after faith has come,
we are no longer under a tutor.

Sons and Heirs

26 For you [i]are all sons of God through
faith in Christ Jesus. 27 For [j]as many of you
as were baptized into Christ [k]have put on
Christ. 28 [l]There is neither Jew nor Greek,
[m]there is neither slave nor free, there is neither male nor female; for you are all [n]one
in Christ Jesus. 29 And [o]if you *are* Christ's,
then you are Abraham's [p]seed, and [q]heirs
according to the promise.

4 Now I say *that* the heir, as long as he is
a child, does not differ at all from a
slave, though he is master of all, 2 but is
under guardians and stewards until the
time appointed by the father. 3 Even so we,
when we were children, [a]were in bondage
under the elements of the world. 4 But

22 [e]Rom. 11:32 [f]Rom. 4:11 **23** [6]Lit. *confined* **24** [g]Rom. 10:4 [h]Acts 13:39 [7]In a household, the guardian responsible for the care and discipline of the children **26** [i]John 1:12 **27** [j]Matt. 28:19; [Rom. 6:3]; 1 Cor. 10:2 [k]Rom. 10:12; 13:14 **28** [l][John 10:16]; Rom. 3:22; 10:12; [Eph. 2:14]; Col. 3:11 [m][1 Cor. 12:13] [n]John 17:11; [1 Cor. 12:13; Eph. 2:15, 16] **29** [o]Gen. 21:10; Heb. 11:18 [p]Rom. 4:11; Gal. 3:7 [q]Gen. 12:3; 18:18; Rom. 8:17 **CHAPTER 4** **3** [a]Gal. 4:9; Col. 2:8, 20; Heb. 5:12; 9:10

3:21 Paul uses the strongest Gr. negative (*see note on 2:17*) to disdain the idea that the law and the promise are at opposite purposes. Since God gave them both and does not work against Himself, law and promise work in harmony; the law reveals man's sinfulness and need for the salvation freely offered in the promise. If the law could have provided righteousness and eternal life, there would be no gracious promise.

3:22 confined all under sin. The Gr. verb translated "confined" means "to enclose on all sides." Paul portrays all mankind as hopelessly trapped in sin, like a school of fish caught in a net. That all people are sinners is the express teaching of Scripture (*see note on Rom. 3:19;* cf. 1 Kin. 8:46; Ps. 143:2; Prov. 20:9; Eccl. 7:20; Is. 53:6; Rom. 3:9-19,23; 11:32).

3:23 before faith came. From the viewpoints of both the history of redemption and through all times in the area of individual salvation (cf. vv. 19,24,25; 4:1-4), only saving faith unlocks the door of the prison where the law keeps men bound. **kept under guard by the law.** Paul personifies the law as a jailer of guilty, condemned sinners, on death row awaiting God's judgment (Rom. 6:23). **the faith which would afterward be revealed.** Again Paul was looking at the coming of Christ, historically and at each believer's salvation, individually. Faith in Christ alone releases people from bondage to law, whether the Mosaic law, or the law written on the hearts of Gentiles (Rom. 2:14-16).

3:24 tutor. The Gr. word denotes a slave whose duty it was to take care of a child until adulthood. The "tutor" escorted the children to and from school and watched over their behavior at home. Tutors were often strict disciplinarians, causing those under their care to yearn for the day when they would be free from their tutor's custody. The law was our tutor which, by showing us our sins, was escorting us to Christ.

3:25,26 Believers, through faith in Jesus Christ, have come of age as God's children. Thus, they are not under the tutelage of the law (Rom. 6:14), although they are still obligated to obey God's holy and unchanging righteous standards which are now given authority in the New Covenant (6:2; Rom. 8:4; 1 Cor. 9:21).

3:26 sons of God. While God is the Father of all people in a general sense because He created them (Acts 17:24-28), only those who have put their faith in Jesus Christ are God's true spiritual children. Unbelievers are the children of Satan (Matt. 13:38; John 8:38,41,44; Acts 13:10; 1 John 3:10; cf. Eph. 2:3; 1 John 5:19).

3:27 baptized into Christ. This is not water baptism, which cannot save (*see notes on Acts 2:38; 22:16*). Paul used the word "baptized" in a metaphorical manner to speak of being "immersed," or "placed into" Christ (cf. 2:20) by the spiritual miracle of union with Him in His death and resurrection. *See notes on Rom. 6:3-5*; cf. 1 Cor. 6:17. **put on Christ.** The result of the believer's spiritual union with Christ. Paul was emphasizing the fact that we have been united with Christ through salvation. Positionally before God, we have put on Christ, His death, resurrection, and righteousness (*see notes on Phil. 3:8-10*). Practically, we need to "put on Christ" before men, in our conduct (Rom. 13:14).

3:28 you are all one in Christ Jesus. All those who are one with Jesus Christ are one with each other. This verse does not deny that God has designed for racial, social, and sexual distinctions among Christians, but it affirms that those do not imply spiritual inequality before God. Nor is this spiritual equality incompatible with the God-ordained roles of headship and submission in the church, society, and at home. Jesus Christ, though fully equal with the Father, assumed a submissive role during His incarnation (Phil. 2:5-8).

3:29 Abraham's seed. *See note on v. 7.* Not all physical children of Abraham are the "Israel of God" (cf. 6:16), that is, true spiritual children of Abraham (Rom. 9:6-8). Gentile believers who are not physical children of Abraham are, however, his spiritual children in the sense that they followed the pattern of his faith (*see note on Rom. 4:11*). **heirs according to the promise.** All believers are heirs of the spiritual blessing that accompanied the Abrahamic Covenant—justification by faith (Gen. 15:6; cf. Rom. 4:3-11).

4:1-7 Paul expands on the analogy of a child's coming of age (3:24-26), contrasting believers' lives before salvation (as children and servants), with their lives after salvation (as adults and sons). Both Paul's Jewish and Gentile readers readily understood this imagery, since the Jews, Greeks, and Romans all had a ceremony to mark a child's coming of age.

4:1 child. The Gr. word refers to a child too young to talk; a minor, spiritually and intellectually immature and not ready for the privileges and responsibilities of adulthood.

4:2 guardians and stewards. "Guardians" were slaves entrusted with the care of underage boys, while "stewards" managed their property for them until they came of age. Along with the tutor (3:24), they had almost complete charge of the child—so that, for all practical purposes, a child under their care did not differ from a slave.

4:3 when we were children...in bondage. Before our "coming of age" when we came to saving faith in Jesus Christ. **the elements of the world.** "Elements" is from a Gr. word meaning "row," or "rank," and was used to speak of basic, foundational things like the letters of the alphabet. In light of its use in v. 9, it is best to see it here as a reference to the basic elements and rituals of human religion (*see note on Col. 2:8*). Paul describes both Jewish and Gentile religions as elemental because they are merely human, never rising to the level of the divine. Both Jewish religion and Gentile religion centered on man-made systems of works. They were filled with laws and ceremonies to be performed so as to achieve divine acceptance. All such rudimentary elements are immature, like behaviors of children under bondage to a guardian.

[b]when the fullness of the time had come,
God sent forth His Son, [c]born [1] [d]of a
woman, [e]born under the law, 5 [f]to redeem
those who were under the law, [g]that we
might receive the adoption as sons.
6 And because you are sons, God has sent
forth [h]the Spirit of His Son into your hearts,
crying out, [2]"Abba, Father!" 7 Therefore
you are no longer a slave but a son, [i]and if
a son, then an heir [3]of God [4]through Christ.

Fears for the Church

8 But then, indeed, [j]when you did not
know God, [k]you served those which by nature are not gods. 9 But now [l]after you
have known God, or rather are known by
God, [m]how *is it that* you turn again to [n]the
weak and beggarly elements, to which you
desire again to be in bondage? 10 [o]You observe days and months and seasons and
years. 11 I am afraid for you, [p]lest I have labored for you in vain.
12 Brethren, I urge you to become like
me, for I *became* like you. [q]You have not injured me at all. 13 You know that [r]because
of physical infirmity I preached the gospel
to you at the first. 14 And my trial which
was in my flesh you did not despise or reject, but you received me [s]as an [5]angel of
God, [t]*even* as Christ Jesus. 15 [6]What then
was the blessing you *enjoyed?* For I bear
you witness that, if possible, you would
have plucked out your own eyes and given

4 [b] [Gen. 49:10] [c] [John 1:14]; Rom. 1:3; 8:3; [Phil. 2:7] [d] Gen. 3:15; [Is. 7:14; Matt. 1:25] [e] [Matt. 5:17]; Luke 2:21, 27 [1] Or *made*
5 [f] [Matt. 20:28; Gal. 3:13] [g] [John 1:12]
6 [h] [Acts 16:7; Rom. 5:5; 8:9, 15, 16; 2 Cor. 3:17] [2] Lit., in Aram., *Father*
7 [i] [Rom. 8:16, 17] [3] NU *through God* [4] NU omits *through Christ*
8 [j] 1 Cor. 1:21; Eph. 2:12; 1 Thess. 4:5; 2 Thess. 1:8 [k] Rom. 1:25
9 [l] [1 Cor. 8:3] [m] Gal. 3:1-3; Col. 2:20 [n] Heb. 7:18
10 [o] Rom. 14:5; Col. 2:16 11 [p] 1 Thess. 3:5 12 [q] 2 Cor. 2:5
13 [r] 1 Cor. 2:3 14 [s] Mal. 2:7 [t] [Luke 10:16] [5] Or *messenger*
15 [6] NU *Where*

4:4 the fullness of the time. In God's timetable, when the exact religious, cultural, and political conditions demanded by His perfect plan were in place, Jesus came into the world. **God sent forth His Son.** As a father set the time for the ceremony of his son becoming of age and being released from the guardians, stewards, and tutors, so God sent His Son at the precise moment to bring all who believe out from under bondage to the law—a truth Jesus repeatedly affirmed (John 5:30,36,37; 6:39,44,57; 8:16,18,42; 12:49; 17:21,25; 20:21). That the Father sent Jesus into the world teaches His pre-existence as the eternal second member of the Trinity. *See notes on Phil. 2:6,7; Heb. 1:3-5*; cf. Rom. 8:3,4. **born of a woman.** This emphasizes Jesus' full humanity, not merely His virgin birth (Is. 7:14; Matt. 1:20-25). Jesus had to be fully God for His sacrifice to be of the infinite worth needed to atone for sin. But, He also had to be fully man so He could take upon Himself the penalty of sin as the substitute for man. See Luke 1:32,35; John 1:1,14,18. **under the law.** Like all men, Jesus was obligated to obey God's law. Unlike anyone else, however, He perfectly obeyed that law (John 8:46; 2 Cor. 5:21; Heb. 4:15; 7:26; 1 Pet. 2:22; 1 John 3:5). His sinlessness made Him the unblemished sacrifice for sins, who "fulfilled all righteousness," i.e., perfectly obeyed God in everything. That perfect righteousness is what is imputed to those who believe in Him.

4:5 to redeem. *See note on 3:13.* **those...under the law.** Guilty sinners who are under the law's demands and its curses (*see notes on 3:10,13*) and in need of a savior (*see note on 3:23*). **the adoption as sons.** "Adoption" is the act of bringing someone who is the offspring of another into one's own family. Since unregenerate people are by nature children of the devil (*see note on 3:26*), the only way they can become God's children is by spiritual adoption (Rom. 8:15,23; Eph. 1:5).

4:6 Spirit of His Son. It is the Holy Spirit's work to confirm to believers their adoption as God's children (*see note on Rom. 8:15*). Assurance of salvation is a gracious work of the Holy Spirit and does not come from any human source. **Abba.** An Aram. term of endearment, used by young children to speak to their fathers; the equivalent of the word "Daddy" (*see note on Rom. 8:15*).

4:8-11 While salvation is the free gift of God (Rom. 5:15,16,18; 6:23; Eph. 2:8), it brings with it serious responsibility (cf. Luke 12:48). God requires believers to live a holy life because they are children of a holy God and desire to love and worship Him (Matt. 5:48; 1 Pet. 1:15-18). That obligation was to the unchanging moral and spiritual principles that forever reflect the nature of God; however, it did not include the rituals and ceremonies unique to Israel under Mosaic law as the Judaizers falsely claimed.

4:8 when you did not know God. Before coming to saving faith in Christ, no unsaved person knows God. *See notes on Eph. 4:17-19; 2 Cor. 4:3-6.* **by nature are not gods.** The Greco-Roman pantheon of non-existent deities the Galatians had imagined they worshiped before their conversion (cf. Rom. 1:23; 1 Cor. 8:4; 10:19,20; 12:2; 1 Thess. 1:9).

4:9 known by God. We can know God only because He first knew us, just as we choose Him only because He first chose us (John 6:44; 15:16), and we love Him only because He first loved us (1 John 4:19). **turn again.** *See notes on 3:1-3.* **weak...elements...again... bondage.** *See note on v. 3.*

4:10 days...years. The rituals, ceremonies, and festivals of the Jewish religious calendar which God had given, but were never required for the church. Paul warns the Galatians, as he did the Colossians (*see notes on Rom. 14:1-6; Col. 2:16,17*), against legalistically observing them as if they were required by God or could earn favor with Him.

4:11 labored...in vain. Paul feared that his effort in establishing and building the Galatian churches might prove to be futile if they fell back into legalism (cf. 3:4; 1 Thess. 3:5).

4:12-20 Having sternly rebuked the Galatians, Paul changes his approach and makes an appeal based on his strong affection for them.

4:12 become like me, for I *became* like you. Paul had been a proud, self-righteous Pharisee, trusting in his own righteousness to save him (cf. Phil. 3:4-6). But when he came to Christ, he abandoned all efforts to save himself, trusting wholly in God's grace (Phil. 3:7-9). He urged the Galatians to follow his example and avoid the legalism of the Judaizers. **You have not injured me.** Though the Jews persecuted him when he first went to Galatia, the Galatian believers had not harmed Paul, but had enthusiastically received him when he preached the gospel to them (cf. Acts 13:42-50; 14:19). How, he asked, could they reject him now?

4:13 physical infirmity. Some think the illness Paul refers to was malaria, possibly contracted in the coastal lowlands of Pamphylia. That could explain why Paul and Barnabas apparently did not preach at Perga, a city in Pamphylia (cf. Acts 13:13,14). The cooler and healthier weather in Galatia and especially at Pisidian Antioch (3,600 ft. above sea level), where Paul went when he left Perga, would have brought some relief to the fever caused by malaria. Although malaria is a serious, debilitating disease, its attacks are not continuous; Paul could have ministered between bouts with fever.

4:14 you received me. The Galatians welcomed Paul in spite of his illness, which in no way was a barrier to his credibility or acceptance. **as Christ Jesus.** *See notes on Matt. 18:5-10.*

4:15 blessing you *enjoyed*. "Blessing" can also be translated "happiness," or "satisfaction." Paul points out that the Galatians had been happy and content with his gospel preaching (cf. Acts 13:48) and wonders why they had turned against him. **plucked out your own eyes.** This may be a figure of speech (cf. Matt. 5:29; 18:9), or an indication that Paul's bodily illness (*see note on v. 13*) had somehow

them to me. 16 Have I therefore become
your enemy because I tell you the truth?
17 They [u]zealously court you, *but* for no
good; yes, they want to exclude you, that
you may be zealous for them. 18 But it is
good to be zealous in a good thing always,
and not only when I am present with you.
19 [v]My little children, for whom I labor in
birth again until Christ is formed in you,
20 I would like to be present with you now
and to change my tone; for I have doubts
about you.

Two Covenants

21 Tell me, you who desire to be under
the law, do you not hear the law? 22 For it
is written that Abraham had two sons:
[w]the one by a bondwoman, [x]the other by a
freewoman. 23 But he *who was* of the bondwoman [y]was born according to the flesh,
[z]and he of the freewoman through
promise, 24 which things are symbolic. For
these are [7]the two covenants: the one from
Mount [a]Sinai which gives birth to
bondage, which is Hagar— 25 for this
Hagar is Mount Sinai in Arabia, and corresponds to Jerusalem which now is, and is
in bondage with her children— 26 but the
[b]Jerusalem above is free, which is the
mother of us all. 27 For it is written:

> [c]*"Rejoice, O barren,*
> *You who do not bear!*
> *Break forth and shout,*
> *You who are not in labor!*
> *For the desolate has many more*
> *children*
> *Than she who has a husband."*

28 Now [d]we, brethren, as Isaac *was,* are
[e]children of promise. 29 But, as [f]he who
was born according to the flesh then persecuted him *who was born* according to the
Spirit, [g]even so *it is* now. 30 Nevertheless

17 [u] Rom. 10:2
19 [v] 1 Cor. 4:15
22 [w] Gen. 16:15 [x] Gen. 21:2
23 [y] Rom. 9:7, 8; Gal. 4:29 [z] Gen. 16:15; 17:15-19; 18:10; 21:1; Gal. 4:28; Heb. 11:11
24 [a] Ex. 24:6-8; Deut. 33:2 [7] NU, M omit *the*
26 [b] [Is. 2:2]
27 [c] Is. 54:1
28 [d] Rom. 9:7, 8; Gal. 3:29 [e] Acts 3:25
29 [f] Gen. 21:9 [g] Gal. 5:11

affected his eyes (cf. 6:11). In either case, it reflects the great love the Galatians had initially expressed for the apostle.

4:16 your enemy. The Galatians had become so confused that, in spite of their previous affection for Paul, some had come to regard him as their enemy. The apostle reminds them that he had not harmed them, but merely told them the truth—a truth that had once brought them great joy (*see note on v. 15*).

4:17 They. The Judaizers (see Introduction: Background and Setting). **zealously.** With a serious concern, or warm interest (the same word is used in 1:14 to describe Paul's former zeal for Judaism). The Judaizers appeared to have a genuine interest in the Galatians, but their true motive was to exclude the Galatians from God's gracious salvation and win recognition for themselves.

4:18 not only when I am present. Paul encouraged the Galatians to have the same zeal for the true gospel of grace that they had had when he was with them.

4:19 My little children. Paul's only use of this affectionate phrase, which John uses frequently (1 John 2:1,18,28; 3:7,18; 4:4; 5:21). **until Christ is formed in you.** In contrast to the evil motives of the Judaizers (*see note on 3:1*), Paul sought to bring the Galatians to Christlikeness. This is the goal of salvation (*see notes on Rom. 8:29*).

4:20 doubts. The verb means "to be at wits end." Cf. v. 6.

4:21–5:1 Paul, continuing to contrast grace and law, faith and works, employs an OT story as an analogy or illustration of what he has been teaching.

4:21 under the law. *See note on 3:10.*

4:22 two sons. Ishmael, son of Sarah's Egyptian maid Hagar (Gen. 16:1-16), and Isaac, Sarah's son (Gen 21:1-7).

4:23 according to the flesh. Ishmael's birth was motivated by Abraham and Sarah's lack of faith in God's promise and fulfilled by sinful human means. **through promise.** God miraculously enabled Abraham and Sarah to have Isaac when Sarah was well past childbearing age and had been barren her entire life.

4:24 symbolic. The Gr. word was used of a story that conveyed a meaning beyond the literal sense of the words. In this passage, Paul uses historical people and places from the OT to illustrate spiritual truth. This is not an allegory, nor are there any allegories in Scripture. An allegory is a fictional story where real truth is the secret, mysterious, hidden meaning. The story of Abraham, Sarah, Hagar, Ishmael, and Isaac is actual history and has no secret or hidden meaning. Paul uses it only as an illustration to support his contrast between law and grace. **two covenants.** Paul uses the two mothers, their two sons, and two locations as a further illustration of two covenants. Hagar, Ishmael, and Mt. Sinai (earthly Jerusalem) represent the covenant of law; Sarah, Isaac and the heavenly Jerusalem the covenant of promise. However, Paul cannot be contrasting these two covenants as different ways of salvation, one way for OT saints, another for NT saints—a premise he has already denied (2:16; 3:10-14,21,22). The purpose of the Mosaic Covenant was only to show all who were under its demands and condemnation their desperate need for salvation by grace alone (3:24)—it was never intended to portray the way of salvation. Paul's point is that those, like the Judaizers, who attempt to earn righteousness by keeping the law receive only bondage and condemnation (3:10,23). While those who partake of salvation by grace—the only way of salvation since Adam's sin—are freed from the law's bondage and condemnation. **Mount Sinai.** An appropriate symbol for the old covenant, since it was at Mt. Sinai that Moses received the law (Ex. 19). **Hagar.** Since she was Sarah's slave (Gen. 16:1), Hagar is a fitting illustration of those under bondage to the law (cf. vv. 5,21; 3:23). She was actually associated with Mt. Sinai through her son Ishmael, whose descendants settled in that region.

4:25 corresponds to Jerusalem. The law was given at Sinai and received its highest expression in the temple worship at Jerusalem. The Jewish people were still in bondage to the law.

4:26 Jerusalem above is free. Heaven (Heb. 12:18,22). Those who are citizens of heaven (Phil. 3:20) are free from the Mosaic law, works, bondage, and trying endlessly and futilely to please God by the flesh. **the mother.** Believers are children of the heavenly Jerusalem, the "mother-city" of heaven. In contrast to the slavery of Hagar's children, believers in Christ are free (5:1; Is. 61:1; Luke 4:18; John 8:36; Rom. 6:18,22; 8:2; 2 Cor. 3:17).

4:27 Paul applies the passage from Is. 54:1 to the Jerusalem above.

4:28 children of promise. Just as Isaac inherited the promises made to Abraham (Gen. 26:1-3), so also are believers the recipients of God's redemptive promises (1 Cor. 3:21-23; Eph. 1:3), because they are spiritual heirs of Abraham (*see note on 3:29*).

4:29 he who was born according to the flesh. Ishmael. *See note on v. 23.* **persecuted him *who was born* according to the Spirit.** Isaac, whom Ishmael mocked at the feast celebrating Isaac's weaning (see Gen. 21:8,9). **even so *it is* now.** Ishmael's descendants

what does [h]the Scripture say? [i]*"Cast out*
the bondwoman and her son, for [j]*the son*
of the bondwoman shall not be heir with
the son of the freewoman." 31 So then,
brethren, we are not children of the bondwoman but of the free.

Christian Liberty

5 Stand[a] [1] fast therefore in the liberty by
which Christ has made us free, and do
not be entangled again with a [b]yoke of
bondage. 2 Indeed I, Paul, say to you that
[c]if you become circumcised, Christ will
profit you nothing. 3 And I testify again to
every man who becomes circumcised [d]that
he is [2]a debtor to keep the whole law.
4 [e]You have become estranged from Christ,
you who *attempt to* be justified by law; [f]you
have fallen from grace. 5 For we through
the Spirit eagerly [g]wait for the hope of
righteousness by faith. 6 For [h]in Christ Jesus neither circumcision nor uncircumcision avails anything, but [i]faith working
through love.

Love Fulfills the Law

7 You [j]ran well. Who hindered you from
obeying the truth? 8 This persuasion does
not *come* from Him who calls you. 9 [k]A little
leaven leavens the whole lump. 10 I have
confidence in you, in the Lord, that you will
have no other mind; but he who troubles
you shall bear his judgment, whoever he is.
11 And I, brethren, if I still preach circumcision, [l]why do I still suffer persecution? Then [m]the offense of the cross has

30 [h] [Gal. 3:8, 22] [i] Gen. 21:10, 12 [j] [John 8:35]

CHAPTER 5

1 [a] Phil. 4:1 [b] Acts 15:10; Gal. 2:4 [1] NU *For freedom Christ has made us free; stand fast therefore, and*
2 [c] Acts 15:1; Gal. 5:3, 6, 11
3 [d] [Deut. 27:26; Rom. 2:25; Gal. 3:10] [2] *obligated*
4 [e] [Rom. 9:31] [f] Heb. 12:15; 2 Pet. 3:17
5 [g] Rom. 8:24
6 [h] [1 Cor. 7:19; Gal. 6:15; Col. 3:11] [i] Col. 1:4; 1 Thess. 1:3; [James 2:18, 20, 22]
7 [j] 1 Cor. 9:24
9 [k] 1 Cor. 5:6
11 [l] 1 Cor. 15:30 [m] Rom. 9:33; [1 Cor. 1:23]

(Arabs) have always persecuted Isaac's (Jews). So unbelievers have always persecuted believers (cf. Matt. 5:11; 10:22-25; Mark 10:30; John 15:19,20; 16:2,33; 17:14; Acts 14:22; 2 Tim. 3:12; Heb. 11:32-37; 1 Pet. 2:20,21; 3:14; 4:12-14).

4:30 *Cast out the bondwoman.* Quoted from Gen. 21:10 to illustrate that those who are attempting to be justified on the basis of keeping the law will be cast out of God's presence forever (Matt. 8:12; 22:12,13; 25:30; Luke 13:28; 2 Thess. 1:9).

4:31 we are not children of the bondwoman. *See notes on 4:24,26.*

5:1 Stand fast. Stay where you are, Paul asserts, because of the benefit of being free from law and the flesh as a way of salvation and the fullness of blessing by grace. **free.** Deliverance from the curse that the law pronounces on the sinner who has been striving unsuccessfully to achieve his own righteousness (3:13,22-26; 4:1-7), but who has now embraced Christ and the salvation granted to him by grace (*see notes on 2:4; 4:26*; cf. Rom. 7:3; 8:2). **entangled again.** Better translated "to be burdened by," "to be oppressed by," or "to be subject to," because of its connection with a yoke. **yoke of bondage.** "Yoke" refers to the apparatus used to control a domesticated animal. The Jews referred to the "yoke of the law" as a good thing, the essence of true religion. Paul argued that for those who pursued it as a way of salvation, the law was a yoke of slavery. *See notes on Matt. 11:29,30.*

5:2 circumcised. *See notes on 2:3.* Paul had no objection to circumcision itself (cf. Acts 16:1-3; Phil. 3:5). But he objected to the notion that it had some spiritual benefit or merit with God and was a prerequisite or necessary component of salvation. Circumcision had meaning in Israel when it was a physical symbol of a cleansed heart (cf. Deut. 30:6; Jer. 4:4; 9:24-26) and served as a reminder of God's covenant of salvation promise (Gen. 17:9,10). **Christ...profit you nothing.** The atoning sacrifice of Christ cannot benefit anyone who trusts in law and ceremony for salvation.

5:3 a debtor to keep the whole law. God's standard is perfect righteousness, thus a failure to keep only one part of the law falls short of the standard (*see note on 3:10*).

5:4 justified. *See notes on 2:16; Rom. 3:24.* **estranged from Christ...fallen from grace.** The Gr. word for "estranged" means "to be separated," or "to be severed." The word for "fallen" means "to lose one's grasp on something." Paul's clear meaning is that any attempt to be justified by the law is to reject salvation by grace alone through faith alone. Those once exposed to the gracious truth of the gospel, who then turn their backs on Christ (Heb. 6:4-6) and seek to be justified by the law are separated from Christ and lose all prospects of God's gracious salvation. Their desertion of Christ and the gospel only proves that their faith was never genuine (cf. Luke 8:13,14; 1 John 2:19).

5:5 the hope of righteousness by faith. Christians already possess the imputed righteousness of Christ, but they still await the completed and perfected righteousness that is yet to come at glorification (Rom. 8:18,21).

5:6 neither circumcision nor uncircumcision avails anything. Cf. 6:15. Nothing done or not done in the flesh, even religious ceremony, makes any difference in one's relationship to God. What is external is immaterial and worthless, unless it reflects genuine internal righteousness (cf. Rom. 2:25-29). **faith working through love.** Saving faith proves its genuine character by works of love. The one who lives by faith is internally motivated by love for God and Christ (cf. Matt. 22:37-40), which supernaturally issues forth in reverent worship, genuine obedience, and self-sacrificing love for others.

5:7 You ran well. Cf. 3:3. Paul compares the Galatians' life of faith with a race, a figure he used frequently (2:2; Rom. 9:16; 1 Cor. 9:24). They had a good beginning—they had received the gospel message by faith and had begun to live their Christian lives by faith as well. **obeying the truth.** *See note on 1 Peter 1:22.* A reference to believers' true way of living, including both their response to the true gospel in salvation (cf. Acts 6:7; Rom. 2:8; 6:17; 2 Thess. 1:8), and their consequent response to obey the Word of God in sanctification. Paul wrote more about salvation and sanctification being a matter of obedience in Rom. 1:5; 6:16,17; 16:26. The legalistic influence of the Judaizers prevented the unsaved from responding in faith to the gospel of grace and true believers from living by faith.

5:8 This persuasion. Salvation by works. God does not promote legalism. Any doctrine that claims His gracious work is insufficient to save is false (*see notes on 1:6,7*).

5:9 leaven. A common axiomatic saying (cf. 1 Cor. 5:6) regarding the influence of yeast in dough. Leaven is often used in Scripture to denote sin (Matt. 16:6,12) because of its permeating power.

5:10 confidence in you. Paul expresses encouraging assurance that the Lord will be faithful to keep His own from falling into the gross heresy. See John 6:39,40; 10:28,29; Rom. 8:31-39; Phil. 1:6,7. They will persevere and be preserved (Jude 24). **judgment.** All false teachers will incur strict and devastating eternal condemnation. *See notes on 2 Pet. 2:2,3,9.*

5:11 still preach circumcision. Apparently the Judaizers had falsely claimed that Paul agreed with their teaching. But he makes the point that if he was preaching circumcision as necessary for salvation, why were the Judaizers persecuting him instead of supporting him? **offense of the cross.** The Gr. word for "offense" can mean "trap,"

ceased. 12 [n]I could wish that those [o]who
trouble you would even [3]cut themselves
off!

13 For you, brethren, have been called to
liberty; only [p]do not *use* liberty as an [q]op-
portunity for the flesh, but [r]through love
serve one another. 14 For [s]all the law is fulfilled in one word, *even* in this: [t]*"You shall
love your neighbor as yourself."* 15 But if
you bite and devour one another, beware
lest you be consumed by one another!

Walking in the Spirit

16 I say then: [u]Walk in the Spirit, and
you shall not fulfill the lust of the flesh.
17 For [v]the flesh lusts against the Spirit,
and the Spirit against the flesh; and these
are contrary to one another, [w]so that you
do not do the things that you wish. 18 But
[x]if you are led by the Spirit, you are not
under the law.

19 Now [y]the works of the flesh are evident, which are: [4]adultery, [5]fornication,
uncleanness, lewdness, 20 idolatry, sorcery,
hatred, contentions, jealousies, outbursts
of wrath, selfish ambitions, dissensions,
heresies, 21 envy, [6]murders, drunkenness,
revelries, and the like; of which I tell you
beforehand, just as I also told *you* in time
past, that [z]those who practice such things
will not inherit the kingdom of God.

22 But [a]the fruit of the Spirit is [b]love, joy,

12 [n] Josh. 7:25 [o] Acts 15:1, 2 [3] *mutilate themselves* **13** [p] [Rom. 8:2]; 1 Cor. 8:9; Gal. 5:1 [q] Rom. 6:1; 1 Pet. 2:16 [r] 1 Cor. 9:19; Eph. 5:21 **14** [s] Matt. 7:12; 22:40; Rom. 13:8, 10; Gal. 6:2 [t] Lev. 19:18; Matt. 22:39; Rom. 13:9 **16** [u] Rom. 6:12 **17** [v] Rom. 7:18, 22, 23; 8:5 [w] Rom. 7:15 **18** [x] [Rom. 6:14; 7:4; 8:14; 1 Tim. 1:9] **19** [y] Rom. 1:26-31; Eph. 5:3, 11; 2 Tim. 3:2-4 [4] NU omits *adultery* [5] *sexual immorality*

21 [z] 1 Cor. 6:9, 10 [6] NU omits *murders* **22** [a] [John 15:2] [b] [Rom. 5:1-5; 1 Cor. 13:4; Col. 3:12-15]

"snare," or "stumbling block." Any offer of salvation that strips man of the opportunity to earn it by his own merit breeds opposition (cf. Rom. 9:33).

5:12 cut themselves off. Better translated "mutilate themselves." The Gr. word was often used of castration, such as in the cult of Cybele, whose priests were self-made eunuchs. Paul's ironic point is that since the Judaizers were so insistent on circumcision as a means of pleasing God, they should go to the extreme of religious devotion and mutilate themselves.

5:13 liberty. *See note on 2:4.* **opportunity for the flesh.** The Gr. word for "opportunity" was often used to refer to a central base of military operations (cf. Rom. 7:8). In the context, "flesh" refers to the sinful inclinations of fallen man (*see note on Rom. 7:5*). The freedom Christians have is not a base from which they can sin freely and without consequence. **serve one another.** Christian freedom is not for selfish fulfillment, but for serving others. Cf. Rom. 14:1-15.

5:14 all the law. The ethics of the former OT law are the same as those of the NT gospel as indicated in the quote from Lev. 19:18 (*see notes on Rom. 7:12; 8:4*; cf. James 2:8-10). When a Christian genuinely loves others, he fulfills all the moral requirements of the former Mosaic law concerning them (Matt. 22:36-40; cf. Deut. 6:5; Rom. 13:8-10). This is the ruling principle of Christian freedom (vv. 6,13).

5:15 bite and devour one another. The imagery is of wild animals savagely attacking and killing each other—a graphic picture of what happens in the spiritual realm when believers do not love and serve each other.

5:16 Walk in the Spirit. All believers have the presence of the indwelling Holy Spirit (cf. Rom. 8:9; 1 Cor. 6:19,20) as the personal power for living to please God. The form of the Gr. verb translated "walk" indicates continuous action, or a habitual lifestyle. Walking also implies progress; as a believer submits to the Spirit's control—that is, responds in obedience to the simple commands of Scripture—he grows in his spiritual life (*see notes on Rom. 8:13; Eph. 5:18; Col. 3:16*). **the flesh.** This is not simply the physical body, but includes the mind, will, and emotions which are all subject to sin. It refers in general to our unredeemed humanness. *See notes on Rom. 7:5; 8:23*; cf. v. 13.

5:17 contrary to one another. The flesh opposes the work of the Spirit and leads the believer toward sinful behavior he would not otherwise be compelled to do (*see notes on Rom. 7:14-25*).

5:18 led by the Spirit...not under the law. Take your choice; these are mutually exclusive. Either you live by the power of the Holy Spirit which results in righteous behavior and spiritual attitudes (vv. 22-29) or by the law which can only produce unrighteous behavior and attitudes (vv. 19-21). Cf. 1 Cor. 15:56.

5:19-21 These sins characterize all unredeemed mankind living under the impotent commands of the law which produces only iniquity, though not every person manifests all these sins nor exhibits them to the same degree. Paul's list, which is not exhaustive, encompasses 3 areas of human life: sex, religion, and human relationships. For other such lists, see Rom. 1:24-32; 1 Cor. 6:9,10.

5:19 evident. The flesh manifests itself in obvious and certain ways. **fornication.** The Gr. word is *porneia,* from which the Eng. word "pornography" comes. It refers to all illicit sexual activity, including (but not limited to) adultery, premarital sex, homosexuality, bestiality, incest, and prostitution. **lewdness.** The word originally referred to any excessive behavior or lack of restraint, but eventually became associated with sexual excess and indulgence.

5:20 sorcery. The Gr. word *pharmakeia,* from which the Eng. word "pharmacy" comes, originally referred to medicines in general, but eventually only to mood- and mind-altering drugs, as well as the occult, witchcraft, and magic. Many pagan religious practices required the use of these drugs to aid in the communication with deities. **contentions...heresies.** Many of these sins manifested in the area of human relationships have to do with some form of anger: "Hatred" results in "contentions" (strife). "Jealousies" (hateful resentment) result in "outbursts of wrath" (sudden, unrestrained expressions of hostility). The next 4 represent animosity between individuals and groups.

5:21 drunkenness, revelries. Probably a specific reference to the orgies that characterized pagan, idolatrous worship. Generally, it refers to all rowdy, boisterous, and crude behavior. **practice.** Here is the key word in Paul's warning. The sense of this Gr. verb describes continual, habitual action. Although believers undoubtedly can commit these sins, those people whose basic character is summed up in the uninterrupted and unrepentant practice of them cannot belong to God (*see notes on 1 Cor. 6:11; 1 John 3:4-10*). **will not inherit the kingdom of God.** *See note on Matt. 5:3.* The unregenerate are barred from entering the spiritual kingdom of redeemed people over whom Christ now rules, and they will be excluded from His millennial kingdom and the eternal state of blessing that follows it. *See note on Eph. 5:5.*

5:22 fruit of the Spirit. Godly attitudes that characterize the lives of only those who belong to God by faith in Christ and possess the Spirit of God. The Spirit produces fruit which consists of 9 characteristics or attitudes that are inextricably linked with each and are commanded of believers throughout the NT. **love.** One of several Gr. words for love, *agape,* is the love of choice, referring not to an emotional affection, physical attraction, or a familial bond, but to respect, devotion, and affection that leads to willing, self-sacrificial service (John 15:13; Rom. 5:8; 1 John 3:16,17). **joy.** A happiness based on unchanging divine promises and eternal spiritual realities. It is the sense of well being experienced by one who knows all is well between himself and the Lord (1 Pet. 1:8). Joy is not the result of favorable circumstances, and even occurs when those circumstances are the most painful and severe

peace, longsuffering, kindness, [c]goodness,
[d]faithfulness, **23** [7]gentleness, self-control.
[e]Against such there is no law. **24** And those
who are Christ's [f]have crucified the flesh
with its passions and desires. **25** [g]If we live
in the Spirit, let us also walk in the Spirit.
26 [h]Let us not become conceited, provoking one another, envying one another.

Bear and Share the Burdens

6 Brethren, if a man is [1]overtaken in any
trespass, you who *are* spiritual restore
such a one in a spirit of [a]gentleness, considering yourself lest you also be tempted.
2 [b]Bear one another's burdens, and so fulfill [c]the law of Christ. **3** For [d]if anyone
thinks himself to be something, when [e]he
is nothing, he deceives himself. **4** But [f]let
each one examine his own work, and then
he will have rejoicing in himself alone, and
[g]not in another. **5** For [h]each one shall bear
his own load.

Be Generous and Do Good

6 [i]Let him who is taught the word share
in all good things with him who teaches.
7 Do not be deceived, God is not
mocked; for [j]whatever a man sows, that
he will also reap. **8** For he who sows to
his flesh will of the flesh reap corruption,
but he who sows to the Spirit will of the
Spirit reap [k]everlasting life. **9** And [l]let us
not grow weary while doing good, for in
due season we shall reap [m]if we do not
lose heart. **10** [n]Therefore, as we have opportunity, [o]let us do good to all, [p]espe-
cially to those who are of the household
of faith.

22 [c] Rom. 15:14 [d] 1 Cor. 13:7
23 [e] 1 Tim. 1:9 [7] *meekness*
24 [f] Rom. 6:6; [Gal. 2:20; 6:14]
25 [g] [Rom. 8:4, 5]
26 [h] Phil. 2:3

CHAPTER 6

1 [a] Eph. 4:2 [1] *caught*
2 [b] Acts 20:35; Rom. 15:1; 1 Thess. 5:14 [c] [James 2:8]
3 [d] Rom. 12:3 [e] [2 Cor. 3:5; James 1:22]
4 [f] 1 Cor. 11:28 [g] Luke 18:11
5 [h] [Rom. 2:6]
6 [i] 1 Cor. 9:11, 14
7 [j] [Rom. 2:6]
8 [k] [Rom. 6:8]
9 [l] 1 Cor. 15:58; 2 Cor. 4:1; 2 Thess. 3:13 [m] [Matt. 24:13]; Heb. 12:3, 5; [James 5:7, 8]
10 [n] Prov. 3:27; [John 9:4; 12:35] [o] Titus 3:8 [p] Rom. 12:13

(John 16:20-22). Joy is a gift from God, and as such, believers are not to manufacture it but to delight in the blessing they already possess (Rom. 14:17; Phil. 4:4). **peace.** The inner calm that results from confidence in one's saving relationship with Christ. The verb form denotes binding together and is reflected in the expression "having it all together." Like joy, peace is not related to one's circumstances (John 14:27; Rom. 8:28; Phil. 4:6,7,9). **longsuffering.** Patience which refers to the ability to endure injuries inflicted by others and the willingness to accept irritating or painful situations (Eph. 4:2; Col. 3:12; 1 Tim. 1:15,16). **kindness.** Tender concern for others, reflected in a desire to treat others gently, just as the Lord treats all believers (Matt. 11:28,29; 19:13,14; 2 Tim. 2:24). **goodness.** Moral and spiritual excellence manifested in active kindness (Rom. 5:7). Believers are commanded to exemplify goodness (6:10; 2 Thess. 1:11). **faithfulness.** Loyalty and trustworthiness (Lam. 3:22; Phil. 2:7-9; 1 Thess. 5:24; Rev. 2:10).

5:23 gentleness. Better translated "meekness." It is a humble and gentle attitude that is patiently submissive in every offense, while having no desire for revenge or retribution. In the NT, it is used to describe 3 attitudes: submission to the will of God (Col. 3:12), teachability (James 1:21), and consideration of others (Eph. 4:2). **self-control.** This refers to restraining passions and appetites (1 Cor. 9:25; 2 Pet. 1:5,6). **no law.** When a Christian walks by the Spirit and manifests His fruit, he needs no external law to produce the attitudes and behavior that please God (cf. Rom. 8:4).

5:24 have crucified the flesh. One of 4 uses of "crucified" that does not refer to Christ's crucifixion (Rom. 2:20; 6:6,14). Here Paul states that the flesh has been executed, yet the spiritual battle still rages in the believer (*see notes on Rom. 7:14-25*). Paul's use looks back to the cross of Christ, where the death of the flesh and its power to reign over believers was actually accomplished (Rom. 6:1-11). Christians must wait until their glorification before they are finally rid of their unredeemed humanness (Rom. 8:23), yet by walking in the Spirit they can please God in this world.

5:25 walk in the Spirit. *See note on v. 16.*

6:1 overtaken. Lit. "caught," which may imply the person was actually seen committing the sin or that he was caught or snared by the sin itself. **you...spiritual.** Those believers who are walking in the Spirit (*see note on 5:16*), filled with the Spirit (*see notes on Eph. 5:18-20; Col. 3:16*), and evidencing the fruit of the Spirit (*see notes on 5:22,23*). **restore.** Sometimes used metaphorically of settling disputes or arguments, it lit. means "to mend" or "repair," and was used of setting a broken bone or repairing a dislocated limb (Heb. 12:12,13; *see notes on Rom. 15:1; 1 Thess. 5:14*). The basic process of restoration is outlined in Matt. 18:15-20 (*see notes there*). **spirit of gentleness.** *See note on 5:23* (cf. 2 Cor. 2:7; 2 Thess. 3:15). **considering.** Also "looking to, observing." The Gr. form strongly emphasizes a continual, diligent attentiveness.

6:2 Bear one another's burdens. "Burdens" are extra heavy loads, which here represent difficulties or problems people have trouble dealing with. "Bear" connotes carrying something with endurance. **the law of Christ.** The law of love which fulfills the entire law (*see notes on 5:14; John 13:34; Rom. 13:8,10*).

6:4 examine. Lit. "to approve something after testing it." Believers first must be sure their lives are right with God before giving spiritual help to others (cf. Matt. 7:3-5). **have rejoicing in himself.** If a believer rejoices or boasts, it should be only boasting in the Lord for what God has done in him (cf. 2 Cor. 10:12-18), not for what he supposedly has accomplished compared to other believers (*see note on 1 Cor. 1:31*).

6:5 bear his own load. This is not a contradiction to v. 2. "Load" has no connotation of difficulty; it refers to life's routine obligations and each believer's ministry calling (cf. Matt. 11:30; 1 Cor. 3:12-15; 2 Cor. 5:10). God requires faithfulness in meeting those responsibilities.

6:6 all good things. Although this expression could refer to material compensation, the context suggests that Paul is referring to the spiritually and morally excellent things learned from the Word, in which they fellowship together. Paul uses this same term to describe the gospel (Rom. 10:15; cf. Heb. 9:11).

6:7 whatever a man sows...reap. This agricultural principle, applied metaphorically to the moral and spiritual realm, is universally true (cf. Job 4:8; Prov. 1:31-33; Hos. 8:7; 10:12). This law is a form of God's wrath. *See note on Rom. 1:18.*

6:8 sows to his flesh. *See notes on 5:16-19; Rom. 7:18; 8:23.* Here it means pandering to the flesh's evil desires. **corruption.** From the Gr. word for degeneration, as in decaying food. Sin always corrupts and, when left unchecked, always makes a person progressively worse in character (cf. Rom. 6:23). **sows to the Spirit.** To walk by the Holy Spirit (*see notes on 5:16-18; Eph. 5:18*; cf. John 8:31; 15:7; Rom. 12:1,2; Col. 2:6; 3:2). **everlasting life.** This expression describes not only a life that endures forever but, primarily, the highest quality of living that one can experience (cf. Ps. 51:12; John 10:10; Eph. 1:3,18).

6:10 opportunity. This Gr. word refers to a distinct, fixed time period, rather than occasional moments. Paul's point is that the believer's entire life provides the unique privilege by which he can serve others in Christ's name. **especially...the household of faith.** Our love for fellow Christians is the primary test of our love for God (*see notes on John 13:35; Rom. 12:10-13; 1 John 4:20,21*).

Glory Only in the Cross

11 See with what large letters I have
written to you with my own hand! 12 As
many as desire to make a good showing in
the flesh, these *would* compel you to be circumcised, [q]only that they may not suffer
persecution for the cross of Christ. 13 For
not even those who are circumcised keep
the law, but they desire to have you circumcised that they may boast in your
flesh. 14 But God forbid that I should boast
except in the [r]cross of our Lord Jesus
Christ, by [2]whom the world has been crucified to me, and [s]I to the world. 15 For [t]in
Christ Jesus neither circumcision nor
uncircumcision avails anything, but a new
creation.

Blessing and a Plea

16 And as many as walk according to
this rule, peace and mercy *be* upon them,
and upon the Israel of God.

17 From now on let no one trouble me,
for I bear in my body the marks of the Lord
Jesus.

18 Brethren, the grace of our Lord Jesus
Christ *be* with your spirit. Amen.

12 [q] Gal. 5:11; Phil. 3:8
14 [r] [1 Cor. 1:18] [2] Or *which,* the cross
[s] [Gal. 2:20]; Col. 2:20
15 [t] [Rom. 2:26, 28]; 1 Cor. 7:19; [Gal. 5:6]

6:11-17 This closing section of the letter is Paul's final rhetorical attack against the Judaizers' doctrine (*see notes on 1:7-9*) and motives. It is also a positive statement of his own godly motives in preaching the true gospel.

6:11 with what large letters. This can be interpreted in two ways: 1) Paul's poor eyesight forced him to use large letters (cf. 4:13,15); or 2) instead of the normal cursive style of writing used by professional scribes, he used the large, block letters (frequently employed in public notices) to emphasize the letter's content rather than its form. It was a visible picture that contrasted his concern with the content of the gospel for the Judaizers' only concern: appearances. The expression served as a transition to his concluding remarks. **I have written…my own hand.** As a good translation of the Gr. verb, this indicates that Paul wrote the entire letter by his own hand, not merely penning a brief statement at the end of dictation to a secretary as he did other times (cf. 1 Cor. 16:21; Col. 4:18; 2 Thess. 3:17). Paul wrote this letter himself to make sure the Galatians knew he—not some forger—was writing it, and to personalize the document, given the importance and severity of its contents.

6:12 good showing. The Judaizers were motivated by religious pride and wanted to impress others with their external piety (cf. Matt. 6:1-7). **compel you to be circumcised.** *See notes on 2:3; 5:2-6.* **may not suffer persecution.** The Judaizers were more concerned about their personal safety than correct doctrine. By adhering more to the Mosaic law than to the gospel of Jesus, they hoped to avoid social and financial ostracism from other Jews and maintain their protected status as Jews within the Roman Empire.

6:13 circumcised. Specifically, in this case, the Judaizers (*see notes on 2:7,8*; cf. Acts 10:45; 11:2). **boast in your flesh.** They zealously worked to win Gentile converts to the law so they could brag about their effective proselytizing (cf. Matt. 23:15).

6:14 boast except in the cross. The Gr. word for "boast" is a basic expression of praise, unlike the Eng. word, which necessarily includes the aspect of pride. Paul glories and rejoices in the sacrifice of Jesus Christ (cf. Rom. 8:1-3; 1 Cor. 2:2; 1 Pet. 2:24). **the world.** The evil, Satanic system (*see notes on 1 John 2:15,16; 5:19*). **crucified to me, and I to the world.** The world is spiritually dead to believers, and they are dead to the world (*see notes on 2:20; Rom. 6:2-10; 1 John 5:4,5*; cf. Phil. 3:20,21).

6:15 circumcision nor uncircumcision. *See notes on 5:6.* **a new creation.** The new birth (*see notes on John 3:3; 2 Cor. 5:17*).

6:16 peace and mercy. The results of salvation: "Peace" is the believer's new relationship to God (Rom. 5:1; 8:6; Col. 3:15), and "mercy" is the forgiveness of all his sins and the setting aside of God's judgment (Ps. 25:6; Dan. 9:18; Matt. 5:7; Luke 1:50; Rom. 12:1; Eph. 2:4; Titus 3:5). **Israel of God.** All Jewish believers in Christ, i.e., those who are both physical and spiritual descendants of Abraham (*see notes on 3:7,18; Rom. 2:28,29; 9:6,7*).

6:17 marks. The physical results of persecution (scars, wounds, etc.) that identified Paul as one who had suffered for the Lord (cf. Acts 14:19; 16:22; 2 Cor. 11:25; *see notes on 2 Cor. 1:5; 4:10; Col. 1:24*).

6:18 Even Paul's final benediction implicitly extols the superiority of the gospel of grace over any man-made system of works righteousness.

The Epistle of Paul to the

EPHESIANS

Title

The letter is addressed to the church in the city of Ephesus, capital of the Roman province of Asia (Asia Minor, modern Turkey). Because the name Ephesus is not mentioned in every early manuscript, some scholars believe the letter was an encyclical, intended to be circulated and read among all the churches in Asia Minor and was simply sent first to believers in Ephesus.

Author and Date

There is no indication that the authorship of Paul should be in question. He is indicated as author in the opening salutation (1:1; 3:1). The letter was written from prison in Rome (Acts 28:16-31) sometime between A.D. 60–62 and is, therefore, often referred to as a prison epistle (along with Philippians, Colossians, and Philemon). It may have been composed almost contemporaneously with Colossians and initially sent with that epistle and Philemon by Tychicus (Eph. 6:21,22; Col. 4:7,8). See Introduction to Philippians: Author and Date for a discussion of the city from which Paul wrote.

Background and Setting

It is likely that the gospel was first brought to Ephesus by Priscilla and Aquila, an exceptionally gifted couple (see Acts 18:26) who were left there by Paul on his second missionary journey (Acts 18:18,19). Located at the mouth of the Cayster River, on the east side of the Aegean Sea, the city of Ephesus was perhaps best known for its magnificent temple of Artemis, or Diana, one of the 7 wonders of the ancient world. It was also an important political, educational, and commercial center, ranking with Alexandria in Egypt, and Antioch of Pisidia, in southern Asia Minor.

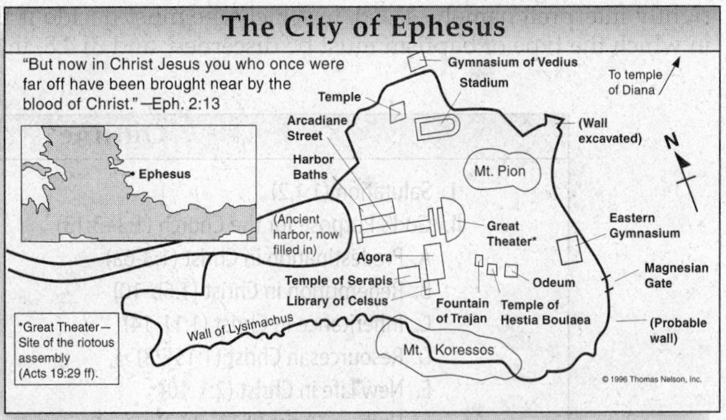

The City of Ephesus

The fledgling church begun by Priscilla and Aquila was later firmly established by Paul on his third missionary journey (Acts 19) and was pastored by him for some 3 years. After Paul left, Timothy pastored the congregation for perhaps a year and a half, primarily to counter the false teaching of a few influential men (such as Hymenaeus and Alexander), who were probably elders in the congregation there (1 Tim. 1:3,20). Because of those men, the church at Ephesus was plagued by "fables and endless genealogies" (1:4) and by such ascetic and unscriptural ideas as the forbidding of marriage and abstaining from certain foods (4:3). Although those false teachers did not rightly understand Scripture, they propounded their ungodly interpretations with confidence (1:7), which produced in the church harmful "disputes rather than godly edification which is in faith" (1:4). Thirty years or so later, Christ gave to the Apostle John a letter for this church indicating its people had left their first love for Him (Rev. 2:1-7).

Historical and Theological Themes

The first 3 chapters are theological, emphasizing NT doctrine, whereas the last 3 chapters are practical and focus on Christian behavior. Perhaps, above all, this is a letter of encouragement and admonition, written to remind believers of their immeasurable blessings in Jesus Christ; and not only to be thankful for those blessings, but also to live in a manner worthy of them. Despite, and partly even because of, a Christian's great blessings in Jesus Christ, he is sure to be tempted by Satan to self-satisfaction and complacency. It was for that reason that, in the last chapter, Paul reminds believers of the full and sufficient spiritual armor supplied to them through God's Word and by His Spirit (6:10-17) and of their need for vigilant and persistent prayer (6:18).

A key theme of the letter is the mystery (meaning a heretofore unrevealed truth) of the church, which is "that the Gentiles should be fellow heirs, of the same body, and partakers of His promise in Christ through the gospel" (3:6), a truth completely hidden from the OT saints (cf. 3:5,9). All believers in Jesus Christ, the Messiah, are equal before the Lord as His children and as citizens of His eternal kingdom, a marvelous truth that only believers of this present age possess. Paul also speaks of the mystery of the church as the bride of Christ (5:32; cf. Rev. 21:9).

A major truth emphasized is that of the church as Christ's present spiritual, earthly body, also a distinct and formerly unrevealed truth about God's people. This metaphor depicts the church, not as an organization, but as a living organism composed of mutually related and interdependent parts. Christ is Head of the body and the Holy Spirit is its lifeblood, as it were. The body functions through the faithful use of its members' various spiritual gifts, sovereignly and uniquely bestowed by the Holy Spirit on each believer.

Other major themes include the riches and fullness of blessing to believers. Paul writes of "the riches of His [God's] grace (1:7), "the unsearchable riches of Christ" (3:8), and "the riches of His glory" (3:16). Paul admonishes believers to "be filled with all the fullness of God" (3:19), to "come to the unity of the faith and of the knowledge of the Son of God, to a perfect man, to the measure of the stature of the fullness of Christ" (4:13), and to "be filled with the Spirit" (5:18). Their riches in Christ are based on His grace (1:2,6,7; 2:7), His peace (1:2), His will (1:5), His pleasure and purpose (1:9), His glory (1:12,14), His calling and inheritance (1:18), His power and strength (1:19; 6:10), His love (2:4), His workmanship (2:10), His Holy Spirit (3:16), His offering and sacrifice (5:2), and His armor (6:11,13). The word "riches" is used 5 times in this letter; "grace" is used 12 times; "glory" 8 times; "fullness" or "filled" 6 times; and the key phrase "in Christ" (or "in Him") some 12 times.

Interpretive Challenges

The general theology of Ephesians is direct, unambiguous, and presents no ideas or interpretations whose meanings are seriously contended. There are, however, some texts that require careful thought to rightly interpret, namely: 1) 2:8, in which one must decide if the salvation or the faith is the gift; 2) 4:5, in which the type of baptism must be discerned; and 3) 4:8, in its relationship to Ps. 68:18.

Outline

- I. Salutation (1:1,2)
- II. God's Purpose for the Church (1:3–3:13)
  - A. Predestination in Christ (1:3-6a)
  - B. Redemption in Christ (1:6b-10)
  - C. Inheritance in Christ (1:11-14)
  - D. Resources in Christ (1:15-23)
  - E. New Life in Christ (2:1-10)
  - F. Unity in Christ (2:11–3:13)
- III. God's Fullness for the Church (3:14-21)
- IV. God's Plan for Faithful Living in the Church (4:1-6)
- V. God's Son Endows and Builds the Church (4:7-16)
- VI. God's Pattern and Principles for Members of the Church (4:17-32)
- VII. God's Standards for Faithfulness in the Church (5:1-21)
  - A. Walking in Love (5:1-7)
  - B. Living in Light (5:8-14)
  - C. Walking in Wisdom and Sobriety (5:15-18a)
  - D. Filled with God's Spirit (5:18b-21)
- VIII. God's Standards for Authority and Submission in the Church (5:22–6:9)
  - A. Husbands and Wives (5:22-33)
  - B. Parents and Children (6:1-4)
  - C. Employers and Employees (6:5-9)
- IX. God's Provision for His Children's Spiritual Battles (6:10-17)
  - A. The Believer's Warfare (6:10-13)
  - B. The Believer's Armor (6:14-17)
- X. God's Appeal for Prayer in the Church (6:18-20)
- XI. Benediction (6:21-24)

Greeting

1 Paul, an apostle of Jesus Christ by the
will of God,

To the saints who are in Ephesus, and
faithful in Christ Jesus:

2 Grace to you and peace from God our
Father and the Lord Jesus Christ.

Redemption in Christ

3 [a]Blessed *be* the God and Father of our
Lord Jesus Christ, who has blessed us with
every spiritual blessing in the heavenly
places in Christ, 4 just as [b]He chose us in
Him [c]before the foundation of the world,
that we should [d]be holy and without
blame before Him in love, 5 [e]having predestined us to [f]adoption as sons by Jesus
Christ to Himself, [g]according to the good
pleasure of His will, 6 to the praise of the
glory of His grace, [h]by which He [1]made us
accepted in [i]the Beloved.
7 [j]In Him we have redemption through
His blood, the forgiveness of sins, according to [k]the riches of His grace 8 which He
made to abound toward us in all wisdom
and [2]prudence, 9 [l]having made known to
us the mystery of His will, according to
His good pleasure [m]which He purposed in
Himself, 10 that in the dispensation of [n]the
fullness of the times [o]He might gather together in one [p]all things in Christ, [3]both
which are in heaven and which are on

CHAPTER 1

3 [a] 2 Cor. 1:3
4 [b] Rom. 8:28 [c] 1 Pet. 1:2 [d] Luke 1:75
5 [e] Acts 13:48; [Rom. 8:29] [f] John 1:12 [g] [1 Cor. 1:21]
6 [h] [Rom. 3:24] [i] Matt. 3:17 [1] Lit. *bestowed grace (favor) upon us*
7 [j] [Heb. 9:12] [k] [Rom. 3:24, 25]
8 [2] *understanding*
9 [l] [Rom. 16:25] [m] [2 Tim. 1:9]
10 [n] Gal. 4:4 [o] 1 Cor. 3:22 [p] Eph. 3:15; [Phil. 2:9; Col. 1:16, 20] [3] NU, M omit *both*

1:1 apostle. The word means "messenger" and served as an official title for Paul and the 12 disciples (including Matthias, Acts 1:26), who were eyewitnesses of the resurrected Jesus and were chosen by God to lay the foundation for the church by preaching, teaching, and writing Scripture, accompanied by miracles (cf. 2 Cor. 12:12). *See note on 4:11.* **saints...faithful.** Designates those whom God has set apart from sin to Himself, made holy through their faith in Jesus Christ.

1:2 Grace to you and peace. A common greeting in the early church which Paul used in all his letters. **God our Father and the Lord Jesus Christ.** From them came the authority with which Paul spoke (v. 1) as well as the blessings of grace and peace to all believers. The conjunction "and" indicates equivalence; that is, the Lord Jesus Christ is equally divine with the Father.

1:3-14 This passage describes God's master plan for salvation in terms of the past (election, vv. 3-6a), the present (redemption, vv. 6b-11), and the future (inheritance, vv. 12-14). It can also be viewed as emphasizing the Father (vv. 3-6), the Son (vv. 7-12), and the Spirit (vv. 13-16).

1:3 Blessed. Derived from the same Gr. word as "eulogy," which means to praise or commend. This is the supreme duty of all creatures (*see notes on Rom. 1:18-21*; cf. Rev. 5:13). **God...who has blessed us with every spiritual blessing.** In His providential grace, God has already given believers total blessing (Rom 8:28; Col. 2:10; James 1:17; 2 Pet. 1:3). "Spiritual" does not refer to immaterial blessings as opposed to material ones, but rather to the work of God, who is the divine and spiritual source of all blessings. **in the heavenly *places*.** Lit. "in the heavenlies." This refers to the realm of God's complete, heavenly domain, from which all his blessings come (cf. v. 20; 2:6; 3:10; 6:12). **in Christ.** God's superabundant blessings belong only to believers who are His children, by faith in Christ, so that what He has is theirs—including His righteousness, resources, privilege, position, and power (cf. Rom 8:16,17).

1:4 He chose us. The doctrine of election is emphasized throughout Scripture (cf. Deut. 7:6; Is. 45:4; John 6:44; Acts 13:48; Rom 8:29; 9:11; 1 Thess. 1:3,4; 2 Thess. 2:13; 2 Tim 2:10; *see note on 1 Pet. 1:2*). The form of the Gr. verb behind "chose" indicates that God not only chose *by* Himself but *for* Himself to the praise of His own glory (vv. 6,12,14). God's election or predestination does not operate apart from or nullify man's responsibility to believe in Jesus as Lord and Savior (cf. Matt. 3:1,2; 4:17; John 5:40). **before the foundation of the world.** Through God's sovereign will before the creation of the world and, therefore, obviously independent of human influence and apart from any human merit, those who are saved have become eternally united with Christ Jesus. Cf. 1 Pet. 1:20; Rev. 13:8; 17:8. **holy and without blame before Him.** This describes both a purpose and a result of God's choosing those who are to be saved. Unrighteous persons are declared righteous, unworthy sinners are declared worthy of salvation, all because they are chosen "in Him" (Christ). This refers to Christ's imputed righteousness granted to us (*see notes on 2 Cor. 5:21; Phil 3:9*), a perfect righteousness which places believers in a holy and blameless position before God (5:27; Col. 2:10), though daily living inevitably falls far short of His holy standard. **in love.** This phrase belongs at the start of v. 5, since it introduces the divine motive for God's elective purpose. Cf. 2:45; Deut. 7:8.

1:5 having predestined us to adoption as sons. Human parents can bestow their love, resources, and inheritance on an adopted child, but not their own distinct characteristics. But God miraculously gives His own nature to those whom He has elected and who have trusted in Christ. He makes them his children in the image of His divine Son, giving them not just Christ's riches and blessings but also His very nature (cf. John 15:15; Rom. 8:15).

1:6 to the praise of the glory of His grace. The ultimate purpose of election to salvation is the glory of God (cf. vv. 12,14; Phil. 2:13; 2 Thess. 1:11,12). **by which...accepted in the Beloved.** "Which" refers to the divine grace (undeserved love and favor) that has made it possible for sinners to be accepted by God through the substitutionary death and imputed righteousness provided by Jesus Christ ("the Beloved," cf. Matt. 3:17; Col. 1:13). Because believers are accepted in Him, then they, like Him, are beloved of God.

1:7 redemption through His blood. The term used here relates to paying the required ransom to God for the release of a person from bondage. Christ's sacrifice on the cross paid that price for every elect person enslaved by sin, buying them out of the slave market of iniquity (*see notes on 2 Cor. 5:18,19*). The price of redemption was death (cf. Lev. 17:11; Rom. 3:24,25; Heb. 9:22; 1 Pet. 1:18,19; Rev. 5:8-10).

1:7b,8 the forgiveness of sins...in all wisdom and prudence. Redemption brings in the limitless grace of God (Rom. 5:20) and forgiveness of sin (cf. Matt. 26:28; Acts 13:38,39; Eph 4:32; Col. 2:13; 1 John 1:9). It brings divinely-bestowed spiritual understanding. Cf. 1 Cor. 2:6,7,12,16.

1:10 He might gather. At the end of this world's history, God will gather believers together in the millennial kingdom, called here the "dispensation of the fullness of the times," meaning the completion of history (Rev. 20:1-6). After that, God will gather everything to Himself in eternity future, and the new heaven and new earth will be created (Rev. 21:1ff.). The new universe will be totally unified under Christ (cf. 1 Cor. 15:27,28; Phil. 2:10,11).

earth—in Him. 11 [q]In Him also we have
obtained an inheritance, being predestined
according to [r]the purpose of Him who
works all things according to the counsel
of His will, 12 [s]that we [t]who first trusted in
Christ should be to the praise of His glory.
13 In Him you also *trusted,* after you
heard [u]the word of truth, the gospel of
your salvation; in whom also, having believed, [v]you were sealed with the Holy
Spirit of promise, 14 [w]who[4] is the [5]guaran-
tee of our inheritance [x]until the redemption of [y]the purchased possession, [z]to the
praise of His glory.

Prayer for Spiritual Wisdom

15 Therefore I also, [a]after I heard of your
faith in the Lord Jesus and your love for all
the saints, 16 [b]do not cease to give thanks
for you, making mention of you in my
prayers: 17 that [c]the God of our Lord Jesus
Christ, the Father of glory, [d]may give to
you the spirit of wisdom and revelation in
the knowledge of Him, 18 [e]the eyes of your
[6]understanding being enlightened; that
you may know what is [f]the hope of His
calling, what are the riches of the glory of
His inheritance in the saints, 19 and what *is*
the exceeding greatness of His power toward us who believe, [g]according to the
working of His mighty power 20 which He
worked in Christ when [h]He raised Him
from the dead and [i]seated *Him* at His right
hand in the heavenly *places,* 21 [j]far above
all [k]principality[7] and [8]power and [9]might
and dominion, and every name that is
named, not only in this age but also in that
which is to come.
22 And [l]He put all *things* under His feet,
and gave Him [m]*to be* head over all *things* to
the church, 23 [n]which is His body, [o]the fullness of Him [p]who fills all in all.

By Grace Through Faith

2 And [a]you *He made alive,* [b]who were
dead in trespasses and sins, 2 [c]in which
you once walked according to the [1]course
of this world, according to [d]the prince of
the power of the air, the spirit who now
works in [e]the sons of disobedience,
3 [f]among whom also we all once conducted ourselves in [g]the lusts of our flesh, ful-

11 [q]Rom. 8:17 [r]Is. 46:10
12 [s]2 Thess. 2:13 [t]James 1:18
13 [u]John 1:17 [v][2 Cor. 1:22]
14 [w]2 Cor. 5:5 [x]Rom. 8:23 [y][Acts 20:28] [z]1 Pet. 2:9 [4]NU *which* [5]*down payment, earnest*
15 [a]Col. 1:4; Philem. 5
16 [b]Rom. 1:9
17 [c]John 20:17; Rom. 15:6 [d]Is. 11:2; Col. 1:9
18 [e]Acts 26:18; 2 Cor. 4:6; Heb. 6:4 [f]Eph. 2:12 [6]NU, M *hearts*
19 [g]Col. 2:12
20 [h]Acts 2:24 [i]Ps. 110:1
21 [j]Is. 9:6, 7; Luke 1:32, 33; Phil. 2:9, 10; Rev. 19:12 [k][Rom. 8:38, 39] [7]*rule* [8]*authority* [9]*power*
22 [l]Ps. 8:6; 110:1; Matt. 28:18; 1 Cor. 15:27 [m]Heb. 2:7
23 [n]Rom. 12:5 [o]Col. 2:9 [p][1 Cor. 12:6]

CHAPTER 2

1 [a]Eph. 2:5; Col. 2:13 [b]Eph. 4:18
2 [c]Col. 1:21 [d][John 12:31]; Eph. 6:12 [e]Col. 3:6 [1]Gr. *aion,* aeon
3 [f]1 Pet. 4:3 [g]Gal. 5:16

1:11 In Him also we have obtained an inheritance. Christ is the source of the believer's divine inheritance, which is so certain that it is spoken of as if it has already been received. Cf. 1 Cor. 3:22,23; 2 Pet. 1:3,4. **being predestined.** Before the earth was formed, God sovereignly determined that every elect sinner—however vile, useless, and deserving of death—by trusting in Christ would be made righteous. *See note on v. 4.* **who works all things.** The word translated "works" is the same one from which "energy," "energetic," and "energize" are derived. When God created the world, He gave it sufficient energy to begin immediately to operate as He had planned. It was not simply ready to function, but was created functioning. As God works out His plan according "to the counsel of His will," He energizes every believer with the power necessary for his spiritual completion (cf. Phil 1:6; 2:13).

1:12 to the praise of His glory. God's glory is the supreme purpose of redemption (cf. vv. 6,14).

1:13 *trusted,* after you heard the word. The God-revealed gospel of Jesus Christ must be heard (Rom. 10:17) and believed (John 1:12) to bring salvation.

1:13,14 sealed with the Holy Spirit. God's own Spirit comes to indwell the believer and secures and preserves his eternal salvation. The sealing of which Paul speaks refers to an official mark of identification placed on a letter, contract, or other document. That document was thereby officially under the authority of the person whose stamp was on the seal. Four primary truths are signified by the seal: 1) security (cf. Dan. 6:17; Matt. 27:62-66); 2) authenticity (cf. 1 Kin. 21:6-16); 3) ownership (cf. Jer. 32:10); and 4) authority (cf. Esth. 8:8-12). The Holy Spirit is given by God as His pledge of the believer's future inheritance in glory (cf. 2 Cor. 1:21).

1:15 your love for all the saints. Love for other believers evidences saving faith (cf. John 13:34,35; 1 John 4:16-18; 4:20; 5:1) and is a cause of thanksgiving (v. 16).

1:17 the God of our Lord Jesus Christ. This is a designation of God that links Father and Son in essential nature as deity (cf. v. 3a; Rom. 1:5,6; 1 Cor. 1:3; Phil 2:9-11; 1 Pet. 1:3; 2 John 3).

1:17,18 the spirit of wisdom...understanding. Paul was praying that believers will have the disposition of godly knowledge and insight of which the sanctified mind is capable (v. 8), so as to grasp the greatness of the hope (Rom. 8:29; 1 John 3:2) and the inheritance that is theirs in Christ (vv. 3-14).

1:18 the eyes of your understanding being enlightened. A spiritually enlightened mind is the only means of truly understanding and appreciating the hope and inheritance in Christ and of living obediently for Him.

1:19,20 exceeding greatness of His power. God's great power, that very power which raised Jesus from the dead and lifted Him by ascension back to glory to take His seat at God's right hand, is given to every believer at the time of salvation and is always available (cf. Acts 1:8; Col. 1:29). Paul therefore did not pray that God's power be given to believers but that they be aware of the power they already possessed in Christ and use it (cf. 3:20).

1:21 Paul wanted believers to comprehend the greatness of God compared to other heavenly beings. "Principality, power, might, and dominion" were traditional Jewish terms to designate angelic beings having a high rank among God's hosts. God is above them all (cf. Rev. 20:10-15).

1:22 feet...head. This is a quote from Ps. 8:6 indicating that God has exalted Christ over everything (cf. Heb. 2:8), including His church (cf. Col. 1:18). Christ is clearly the authoritative Head (not "source") because all things have been placed under His feet. *See notes on 4:15; 5:23.*

1:23 His body. A metaphor for God's redeemed people, used exclusively in the NT of the church (cf. 4:12-16; 1 Cor. 12:12-27).

2:1 dead in trespasses and sins. A sobering reminder of the total sinfulness and lostness from which believers have been redeemed. "In" indicates the realm or sphere in which unregenerate sinners exist. They are not dead because of sinful acts that have been committed but because of their sinful nature (cf. Matt. 12:35; 15:18,19).

2:2 course of this world. *See note on John 1:9.* This refers to the world order, i.e., humanity's values and standards apart from God and

filling the desires of the flesh and of the
mind, and [h]were by nature children of
wrath, just as the others.
4 But God, [i]who is rich in mercy, because
of His [j]great love with which He loved us,
5 [k]even when we were dead in trespasses,
[l]made us alive together with Christ (by
grace you have been saved), 6 and raised
us up together, and made *us* sit together
[m]in the heavenly *places* in Christ Jesus,
7 that in the ages to come He might show
the exceeding riches of His grace in [n]His
kindness toward us in Christ Jesus. 8 [o]For
by grace you have been saved [p]through
faith, and that not of yourselves; [q]*it is* the
gift of God, 9 not of [r]works, lest anyone
should [s]boast. 10 For we are [t]His workmanship, created in Christ Jesus for good
works, which God prepared beforehand
that we should walk in them.

Brought Near by His Blood

11 Therefore remember that you, once
Gentiles in the flesh—who are called Uncircumcision by what is called [u]the Circumcision made in the flesh by hands— 12 that at
that time you were without Christ, being
aliens from the commonwealth of Israel
and strangers from the covenants of
promise, having no hope and without God
in the world. 13 But now in Christ Jesus you
who once were far off have been brought
near by the blood of Christ.

Christ Our Peace

14 For He Himself is our peace, who has
made both one, and has broken down the
middle wall of separation, 15 having abolished in His flesh the enmity, *that is,* the law
of commandments *contained* in ordinances,
so as to create in Himself one [v]new man

3 [h] [Ps. 51:5]
4 [i] Ps. 103:8-11; Rom. 10:12 [j] John 3:16; 1 John 4:9, 10
5 [k] Rom. 5:6, 8 [l] [Rom. 6:4, 5]
6 [m] Eph. 1:20
7 [n] Titus 3:4
8 [o] [2 Tim. 1:9] [p] Rom. 4:16 [q] [John 1:12, 13]
9 [r] Rom. 4:4, 5; 11:6 [s] Rom. 3:27
10 [t] Is. 19:25
11 [u] [Rom. 2:28; Col. 2:11]
15 [v] Gal. 6:15

Christ. In 2 Cor. 10:4,5, Paul refers to these ideologies that are like fortresses in which people are imprisoned, need to be set free, and brought captive to Christ and obedience to the truth (*see notes there*). **the prince of the power of the air.** Satan. Cf. John 12:31; 14:30; 16:11; 2 Cor. 4:4.

2:4 mercy…love. Salvation is for God's glory by putting on display His boundless mercy and love for those who are spiritually dead because of their sinfulness.

2:5 when we were dead…made us alive. Far more than anything else, a spiritually dead person needs to be made alive by God. Salvation brings spiritual life to the dead. The power that raises believers out of death and makes them alive (cf. Rom. 6:1-7) is the same power that energizes every aspect of Christian living (cf. Rom. 6:11-13).

2:6 raised *us* up together, and made *us* sit together. The tense of "raised" and "made" indicates that these are immediate and direct results of salvation. Not only is the believer dead to sin and alive to righteousness through Christ's resurrection, but he also enjoys his Lord's exaltation and shares in His pre-eminent glory. **in the heavenly *places*.** The supernatural realm where God reigns. In 3:10 and 6:12, however, it also refers to the supernatural sphere where Satan temporarily rules. This spiritual realm is where believers' blessings are (cf. 1:3), their inheritance is (1 Pet. 1:4), their affections should be (Col. 3:3), and where they enjoy fellowship with the Lord. It is the realm from which all divine revelation has come and where all praise and petitions go.

2:7 riches of His grace. Salvation, of course, is very much for the believer's blessing, but it is even more for the purpose of eternally glorifying God for bestowing on believers His endless and limitless grace and kindness. The whole of heaven glorifies Him for what He has done in saving sinners (cf. 3:10; Rev. 7:10-12).

2:8 faith, and that not of yourselves. "That" refers to the entire previous statement of salvation, not only the grace but the faith. Although men are required to believe for salvation, even that faith is part of the gift of God which saves and cannot be exercised by one's own power. God's grace is preeminent in every aspect of salvation (cf. Rom. 3:20; Gal. 2:16).

2:10 created in…for good works. Good works cannot produce salvation but are subsequent and resultant God-empowered fruits and evidences of it (cf. John 15:8; Phil. 2:12,13; 2 Tim. 3:17; Titus 2:14; James 2:16-26). **which God prepared beforehand.** Like his salvation, a believer's sanctification and good works were ordained before time began (*see notes on Rom. 8:29,30*).

2:11,12 Gentiles (the "uncircumcision") experienced two types of alienation. The first was social, resulting from the animosity that had existed between Jews and Gentiles for thousands of years. Jews considered Gentiles to be outcasts, objects of derision, and reproach. The second and more significant type of alienation was spiritual, because Gentiles as a people were cut off from God in 5 different ways: 1) they were "without Christ," the Messiah, having no Savior and Deliverer and without divine purpose or destiny. 2) They were "aliens from the commonwealth of Israel." God's chosen people, the Jews, were a nation whose supreme King and Lord was God Himself, and from whose unique blessing and protection they benefitted. 3) Gentiles were "strangers from the covenants of promise," not able to partake of God's divine covenants in which He promised to give His people a land, a priesthood, a people, a nation, a kingdom, and a King—and to those who believe in Him, eternal life and heaven. 4) They had "no hope" because they had been given no divine promise. 5) They were "without God in the world." While Gentiles had many gods, they did not recognize the true God because they did not want Him (*see Rom. 1:18-26*).

2:13 far off. A common term in rabbinical writings used to describe Gentiles, those who were apart from the true God (cf. Is. 57:19; Acts 2:39). **brought near.** Every person who trusts in Christ alone for salvation, Jew or Gentile, is brought into spiritual union and intimacy with God. This is the reconciliation of 2 Cor. 5:18-21. The atoning work accomplished by Christ's death on the cross washes away the penalty of sin and ultimately even its presence.

2:14 He Himself. This emphatically indicates that Jesus alone is the believer's source of peace (cf. Is. 9:6). **the middle wall of separation.** This alludes to a wall in the temple that partitioned off the Court of the Gentiles from the areas accessible only to Jews. Paul referred to that wall as symbolic of the social, religious, and spiritual separation that kept Jews and Gentiles apart.

2:15 abolished in His flesh the enmity. Through His death, Christ abolished OT ceremonial laws, feasts, and sacrifices which uniquely separated Jews from Gentiles. God's moral law (as summarized in the Ten Commandments and written on the hearts of all men, Rom. 2:15) was not abolished but subsumed in the New Covenant, however, because it reflects His own holy nature (Matt. 5:17-19.) *See notes on Matt. 22:37-40; Rom. 13:8-10.* **one new man.** Christ does not exclude anyone who comes to Him, and those who are His are not spiritually distinct from one another. "New" translates a Gr. word that refers to something completely unlike what it was before. It refers to being different in kind and quality. Spiritually, a new person in Christ is no longer Jew or Gentile, only Christian (cf. Rom. 10:12,13; Gal. 3:28).

from the two, *thus* making peace, 16 and that
He might [w]reconcile them both to God in
one body through the cross, thereby [x]put-
ting to death the enmity. 17 And He came
and preached peace to you who were afar
off and to those who were near. 18 For
[y]through Him we both have access [z]by one
Spirit to the Father.

Christ Our Cornerstone

19 Now, therefore, you are no longer
strangers and foreigners, but fellow citizens with the saints and members of the
household of God, 20 having been [a]built
[b]on the foundation of the [c]apostles and
prophets, Jesus Christ Himself being [d]the
chief corner*stone,* 21 in whom the whole
building, being fitted together, grows into
[e]a holy temple in the Lord, 22 [f]in whom
you also are being built together for a
[g]dwelling place of God in the Spirit.

The Mystery Revealed

3 For this reason I, Paul, the prisoner of
Christ Jesus for you Gentiles— 2 if indeed you have heard of the [1]dispensation
of the grace of God [a]which was given to
me for you, 3 [b]how that by revelation [c]He
made known to me the mystery (as I have
briefly written already, 4 by which, when
you read, you may understand my knowledge in the mystery of Christ), 5 which in
other ages was not made known to the
sons of men, as it has now been revealed
by the Spirit to His holy apostles and
prophets: 6 that the Gentiles [d]should be fellow heirs, of the same body, and partakers
of His promise in Christ through the
gospel, 7 [e]of which I became a minister [f]ac-

16 [w]2 Cor. 5:18; [Col. 1:20-22] [x][Rom. 6:6]
18 [y]John 10:9 [z]1 Cor. 12:13; Eph. 4:4
20 [a]1 Pet. 2:4 [b]Matt. 16:18; 1 Cor. 3:10, 11; Rev. 21:14 [c]1 Cor. 12:28; Eph. 3:5 [d]Ps. 118:22; Luke 20:17
21 [e]1 Cor. 3:16, 17
22 [f]1 Pet. 2:5 [g]John 17:23

CHAPTER 3

2 [a]Acts 9:15 [1]*stewardship*
3 [b]Acts 22:17, 21; 26:16 [c][Rom. 11:25; 16:25; Eph. 3:4, 9; 6:19]; Col. 1:26; 4:3
6 [d]Gal. 3:28, 29
7 [e]Rom. 15:16 [f]Rom. 1:5

2:16 reconcile them both to God. As Jews and Gentiles are brought to God through Christ Jesus, they are brought together with each other. This was accomplished by the cross where Jesus became a curse (Gal. 3:10-13), taking God's wrath so that divine justice was satisfied and reconciliation with God became a reality (*see notes on 2 Cor. 5:19-21*). For more on reconciliation, see Rom. 5:8-10; Col. 1:19-23.

2:17 preached peace. The Gr. word for "preached" lit. means "to bring or announce good news," and in the NT is almost always used of proclaiming the good news that sinners can be reconciled to God by the salvation which is through Jesus Christ. In this context, Christ, the One who "Himself is our peace" (v. 14), also announced the good news of peace. **afar off and…near.** That is to Gentiles and Jews alike.

2:18 access by one Spirit to the Father. No sinner has any right or worthiness in himself for access to God, but believers have been granted that right through faith in Christ's sacrificial death (cf. 3:12; Rom. 5:2). The resources of the Trinity belong to believers the moment they receive Christ, and the Holy Spirit presents them before the heavenly throne of God the Father, where they are welcome to come with boldness at any time. *See notes on Rom. 8:15-17; Gal. 4:6,7; Heb. 4:16.*

2:19 fellow citizens with the saints. God's kingdom is made up of the people from all time who have trusted in Him. There are no strangers, foreigners, or second-class citizens there (cf. Phil. 3:20). **members of the household of God.** Redeemed sinners not only become heavenly citizens but also members of God's own family. The Father bestows on believers the same infinite love He gives His Son. *See note on 1:5*; cf. Heb. 3:6.

2:20 the foundation of the apostles and prophets. For discussion of these gifted men, *see note on 4:11.* As important as they were, it was not them personally, but the divine revelation they taught, as they authoritatively spoke the word of God to the church before the completion of the NT, that provided the foundation (cf. Rom. 15:20). **corner*stone*.** Cf. Ps. 118:22; Is. 28:16; Matt. 21:42; Acts 4:11; 1 Pet. 2:6,7. This stone set the foundation and squared the building.

2:21 a holy temple in the Lord. Every new believer is a new stone in Christ's temple, the church, Christ's body of believers (*see note on 1 Pet. 2:5*). Christ's building of His church will not be complete until every person who will believe in Him has done so (2 Pet. 3:9).

2:22 a dwelling place of God in the Spirit. The term for "dwelling" connotes a permanent home. God the Holy Spirit takes up permanent residence in His earthly sanctuary, the church, the vast spiritual body of all the redeemed (cf. 1 Cor. 6:19,20; 2 Cor. 6:16).

3:1 For this reason. This refers back to the truths about the unity of believers that Paul has just discussed and introduces the motive for his prayer which begins in v. 14. **the prisoner of Christ Jesus.** Although Paul had been a prisoner for about two years in Caesarea and two years in Rome, he did not consider himself to be a prisoner of any government or person. Rather, he knew he was under Christ's control, and every aspect of his life was in the Lord's hands. He suffered imprisonment for preaching to Gentiles. See 2 Cor. 4:8-15.

3:2-13 In this parenthetical passage, Paul interrupted the thought begun in v. 1 to re-emphasize and to expand upon the truths he had just written. He was compelled to affirm his authority for teaching the oneness of Jew and Gentile in Christ (vv. 2-7), a new and far-reaching truth that most of the Ephesians doubtless found difficult to comprehend or accept.

3:2 dispensation…given to me. "Dispensation" means a stewardship, an administration, or management. Paul did not choose the stewardship of his apostleship or ministry. God had sovereignly commissioned him with the calling, spiritual gifts, opportunities, knowledge, and authority to minister as the apostle to the Gentiles (see Acts 9:1-19; 1 Tim 1:12,13; cf. Rom 15:15,16; 1 Cor. 4:1; 9:16,17; Gal. 2:9).

3:4 the mystery of Christ. *See notes on 1:9-12; 2:11,12; Matt. 13:11; 1 Cor. 2:7; Col. 4:3.* There were many truths hidden and later revealed in the NT that are called mysteries. Here is one: Jew and Gentile brought together in one body in the Messiah. For others, *see notes on 1 Cor. 15:51; Col. 1:27; 1 Tim. 3:16.* Paul not only wrote of the mystery that, in Christ, Jew and Gentile become one in God's sight and in His kingdom and family, but also explained and clarified that truth. He realized that spiritual knowledge must precede practical application. What is not properly understood cannot properly be applied.

3:5 in other ages was not made known. Though God had promised universal blessing through Abraham (Gen. 12:3), the full meaning of that promise became clear when Paul wrote Gal. 3:28. Isaiah 49:6 predicted salvation to all races, but it was Paul who wrote of the fulfillment of that pledge (Acts 13:46,47). Paul disclosed a truth that not even the greatest prophets understood—that within the church, composed of all the saved since Pentecost in one united body, there would be no racial, social, or spiritual distinctions.

3:6 Gentiles should be fellow heirs. A summary of 2:11-22. *See notes on 1 Cor. 12:12,13; Gal. 3:29.*

3:7 became a minister. No man can make himself a minister (lit. servant) of God, because the calling, message, work, and empowering of genuine ministry to and for God are His prerogative alone to give. See Acts 26:16; 1 Cor. 15:10; Col. 1:23,25,29.

cording to the gift of the grace of God
given to me by [g]the effective working of
His power.

Purpose of the Mystery

8 To me, [h]who am less than the least of
all the saints, this grace was given, that I
should preach among the Gentiles [i]the unsearchable riches of Christ, 9 and to make
all see what *is* the [2]fellowship of the mystery, which from the beginning of the ages
has been hidden in God who [j]created all
things [3]through Jesus Christ; 10 [k]to the intent that now [l]the [4]manifold wisdom of
God might be made known by the church
[m]to the [5]principalities and powers in the
heavenly *places,* 11 [n]according to the eternal purpose which He accomplished in
Christ Jesus our Lord, 12 in whom we have
boldness and access [o]with confidence
through faith in Him. 13 [p]Therefore I ask

7 [g] Rom. 15:18
8 [h] [1 Cor. 15:9] [i] [Col. 1:27; 2:2, 3]
9 [j] John 1:3; Col. 1:16; Heb. 1:2 [2] NU, M *stewardship* (dispensation) [3] NU omits *through Jesus Christ*
10 [k] 1 Pet. 1:12 [l] [1 Tim. 3:16] [m] Eph. 1:21; 6:12; Col. 1:16; 2:10, 15 [4] *variegated* or *many-sided* [5] *rulers*
11 [n] [Eph. 1:4, 11]
12 [o] 2 Cor. 3:4; Heb. 4:16; 10:19, 35; [1 John 2:28; 3:21]
13 [p] Phil. 1:14 [q] 2 Cor. 1:6
14 [r] Eph. 1:3 [6] NU omits *of our Lord Jesus Christ*
16 [s] [Eph. 1:7; 2:4; Phil. 4:19] [t] 1 Cor. 16:13; Phil. 4:13; Col. 1:11 [u] Rom. 7:22

that you do not lose heart at my tribulations for you, [q]which is your glory.

Appreciation of the Mystery

14 For this reason I bow my knees to the
[r]Father [6]of our Lord Jesus Christ, 15 from
whom the whole family in heaven and
earth is named, 16 that He would grant
you, [s]according to the riches of His glory,
[t]to be strengthened with might through
His Spirit in [u]the inner man, 17 [v]that Christ
may dwell in your hearts through faith;
that you, [w]being rooted and grounded in
love, 18 [x]may be able to comprehend with
all the saints [y]what *is* the width and length
and depth and height— 19 to know the
love of Christ which passes knowledge;
that you may be filled [z]with all the fullness
of God.

17 [v] John 14:23; Rom. 8:9; 2 Cor. 13:5; [Eph. 2:22] [w] Col. 1:23
18 [x] Eph. 1:18 [y] Rom. 8:39 19 [z] Eph. 1:23

3:8 the least of all the saints. In light of God's perfect righteousness, Paul's assessment of himself was not false humility but simple honesty. He knew his unworthiness. See 1 Tim. 1:12,13 (cf. Judg. 6:15,16; Is. 6:1-9). **the unsearchable riches of Christ.** All God's truths, all His blessings, all that He is and has (cf. 1:3; Col. 2:3; 2 Pet. 1:3).

3:9 fellowship...mystery. *See notes on vv. 4,5.*

3:10 principalities and powers. Angels, both holy and unholy (1:21; 6:12; *see note on Col. 1:16*). God, through the church manifests His glory to all the angels. The holy angels rejoice (see Luke 15:10; cf. 1 Pet. 1:12) because they are involved with the church (see 1 Cor. 11:10; Heb. 1:14). Although they have no desire or capacity to praise God, even fallen angels see the glory of God in the salvation and preservation of the church. **in the heavenly *places*.** As in 1:3; 6:12, this refers to the entire realm of spiritual beings.

3:11 the eternal purpose. The supreme purpose of the church is to glorify God, which includes the displaying of His wisdom (v. 10) before the angels, who then honor Him with even greater praise.

3:12 access with confidence. Every person who comes to Christ in faith can come before God at any time, not in self-confidence but in Christ-confidence. *See notes on Heb. 4:15,16.*

3:13 tribulations...your glory. Through trouble and suffering, God produces glory. *See note on Rom. 8:18.*

3:14 For this reason. Paul repeated what he wrote in v. 1 (*see note there*) as he began his prayer. Because of their new identity in Christ, stated in chap. 2, believers are spiritually alive (v. 5), they are unified into God's household (v. 19), and, as the church, they are the dwelling place of God, built on the words and work of the apostles and prophets (vv. 20-22). **I bow my knees.** Not an instruction for physical posture during prayer, but suggesting an attitude of submission, reverence, and intense passion (cf. Ezra 9:5,6; Ps. 95:1-6; Dan. 6:10; Acts 20:36).

3:15 whole family in heaven and earth is named. Paul was not teaching the universal fatherhood of God and the universal brotherhood of man (cf. John 8:39-42; 1 John 3:10), but was simply referring to believers from every era of history, those who are dead (in heaven) and those who are alive (on earth).

3:16 that He would grant you. Paul's prayers are almost always for the spiritual welfare of others (cf. Phil. 1:4; Col. 1:9-11; 1 Thess. 1:2). **according to the riches of His glory.** They are limitless and available to every believer. **strengthened...His Spirit in the inner man.** Spiritual power is a mark of every Christian who submits to God's Word and Spirit. It is not reserved for some special class of Christian, but for all those who discipline their minds and spirits to study the Word, understand it, and live by it. Although the outer, physical person becomes weaker with age (cf. 2 Cor. 4:16), the inner, spiritual person should grow stronger through the Holy Spirit, who will energize, revitalize, and empower the obedient, committed Christian (cf. Acts 1:8; Rom. 8:5-9,13; Gal. 5:16).

3:17 that Christ may dwell in your hearts. Every believer is indwelt by Christ at the moment of salvation (Rom. 8:9; 1 Cor. 12:13), but He is "at home," finding comfort and satisfaction, only where hearts are cleansed of sin and filled with His Spirit (cf. John 14:23). **through faith.** This speaks of Christians' continuing trust in Christ to exercise His lordship over them. **rooted and grounded in love.** I.e., established on the strong foundation of self-giving, serving love for God and for His people (cf. Matt. 22:37-39; 1 John 4:9-12,19-21).

3:18 able to comprehend. A believer cannot understand the fullness of God's love apart from genuine, Spirit-empowered love in his own life. **with all the saints.** Love is both granted to (Rom. 5:5; 1 Thess. 4:9) and commanded of (John 13:34,35) every Christian, not just those who have a naturally pleasant temperament or have great spiritual maturity. **width...length...depth...height.** Not 4 different features of love, but an effort to suggest its vastness and completeness.

3:19 to know the love of Christ. Not the love believers have for Christ, but the love of and from Christ that He places in their hearts before they can truly and fully love Him or anyone else (Rom. 5:5). **which passes knowledge.** Knowledge of Christ's love is far beyond the capability of human reason and experience. It is only known by those who are God's children (cf. Phil. 4:7). **filled with all the fullness of God.** To be so strong spiritually, so compelled by divine love, that one is totally dominated by the Lord with nothing left of self. Human comprehension of the fullness of God is impossible, because even the most spiritual and wise believer cannot completely grasp the full extent of God's attributes and characteristics—His power, majesty, wisdom, love, mercy, patience, kindness, and everything He is and does. But believers can experience the greatness of God in their lives as a result of total devotion to Him. Note the fullness of God, here; the fullness of Christ in 4:13; and the fullness of the Spirit in 5:18. Paul prayed for believers to become as Godlike as possible (Matt. 5:48; 1 Pet. 1:15,16).

20 Now [a]to Him who is able to do exceedingly abundantly [b]above all that we
ask or think, [c]according to the power that
works in us, 21 [d]to Him *be* glory in the
church by Christ Jesus to all generations,
forever and ever. Amen.

Walk in Unity

4 I, therefore, the prisoner [1]of the Lord,
[2]beseech you to [a]walk worthy of the
calling with which you were called, 2 with
all lowliness and gentleness, with longsuffering, bearing with one another in love,
3 endeavoring to keep the unity of the Spirit [b]in the bond of peace. 4 [c]*There is* one
body and one Spirit, just as you were
called in one hope of your calling; 5 [d]one
Lord, [e]one faith, [f]one baptism; 6 [g]one God
and Father of all, who *is* above all, and
[h]through all, and in [3]you all.

Spiritual Gifts

7 But [i]to each one of us grace was given
according to the measure of Christ's gift.
8 Therefore He says:

> [j]*"When He ascended on high,*
> *He led captivity captive,*
> *And gave gifts to men."*

9 [k](Now this, *"He ascended"*—what does
it mean but that He also [4]first descended
into the lower parts of the earth? 10 He

20 [a] Rom. 16:25 [b] 1 Cor. 2:9 [c] Col. 1:29 **21** [d] Rom. 11:36

CHAPTER 4

1 [a] Eph. 2:10; [Col. 1:10; 2:6]; 1 Thess. 2:12 [1] Lit. *in* [2] *exhort, encourage* **3** [b] Col. 3:14 **4** [c] Rom. 12:5 **5** [d] 1 Cor. 1:13 [e] [1 Cor. 15:1-8]; Jude 3 [f] 1 Cor. 12:12, 13; [Heb. 6:6] **6** [g] Mal. 2:10; 1 Cor. 8:6; 12:6

[h] Rom. 11:36 [3] NU omits *you;* M *us* **7** [i] [1 Cor. 12:7, 11] **8** [j] Ps. 68:18; [Col. 2:15] **9** [k] Luke 23:43; John 3:13; 20:17; [1 Pet. 3:19, 20] [4] NU omits *first*

3:20 When the conditions of vv. 16-19 are met, God's power working in and through believers is unlimited and far beyond their comprehension.

3:21 to Him *be* glory. Only when His children meet this level of faithfulness will Christ be fully glorified with the honor He deserves from His church.

4:1 therefore. This word marks the transition from doctrine to duty, principle to practice, position to behavior. This is typical of Paul (see Rom. 12:1; Gal. 5:1; Phil. 2:1; Col. 3:5; 1 Thess. 4:1). **the prisoner of the Lord.** By mentioning his imprisonment again (see 3:1), Paul gently reminded Ephesian believers that the faithful Christian walk can be costly and that he had paid a considerable personal price because of his obedience to the Lord. **walk worthy.** "Walk" is frequently used in the N.T. to refer to daily conduct. It sets the theme for the final 3 chapters. "Worthy" has the idea of living to match one's position in Christ. The apostle urged his readers to be everything the Lord desires and empowers them to be. **calling.** This refers to God's sovereign call to salvation, as always in the epistles. *See note on Rom. 8:30.* The effectual call that saves is mentioned in 1:18; Rom. 11:29; 1 Cor. 1:26; Phil. 3:14; 2 Thess. 1:11; 2 Tim. 1:9; Heb. 3:1.

4:2 lowliness. "Humility" is a term not found in the Rom. or Gr. vocabularies of Paul's day. The Gr. word apparently was coined by Christians, perhaps even by Paul himself, to describe a quality for which no other word was available. Humility, the most foundational Christian virtue (James 4:6), is the quality of character commanded in the first beatitude (Matt. 5:3), and describes the noble grace of Christ (Phil. 2:7,8). **gentleness.** "Meekness," an inevitable product of humility, refers to that which is mild-spirited and self-controlled (cf. Matt. 5:5; 11:29; Gal. 5:23; Col. 3:12). **longsuffering.** The Gr. word lit. means long-tempered, and refers to a resolved patience that is an outgrowth of humility and gentleness (cf. 1 Thess. 5:14; James 5:10). **bearing with one another in love.** Humility, gentleness, and patience are reflected in a forbearing love for others that is continuous and unconditional (cf. 1 Pet. 4:8).

4:3 unity of the Spirit. The Spirit-bestowed oneness of all true believers (see 1 Cor. 6:17; 12:11-13; Phil. 1:27; 2:2) has created the bond of peace, the spiritual cord that surrounds and binds God's holy people together. This bond is love (Col. 3:14).

4:4-6 In this passage, Paul lists the particular areas of oneness, or unity: body, Spirit, hope, Lord, faith, baptism, and God and Father. He focuses on the Trinity—the Spirit in v. 4, the Son in v. 5, and the Father in v. 6. His point is not to distinguish between the Persons of the Godhead but to emphasize that, although they have unique roles, they are completely unified in every aspect of the divine nature and plan.

4:4 one body. The church, the body of Christ, is composed of every believer since Pentecost without distinction, by the work of the "one Spirit" (see 1 Cor. 12:11-13). **one hope.** This is the pledge and promise of eternal inheritance given each believer (1:11-14) and sealed to each believer by the one Spirit (v. 13).

4:5 one Lord. See Acts 4:12; Rom. 10:12; Gal. 1:8. **one faith.** The body of doctrine revealed in the NT (cf. Jude 3). **one baptism.** This probably refers to the water baptism following salvation, a believer's public confession of faith in Jesus Christ. Spiritual baptism, by which all believers are placed into the body of Christ (1 Cor. 12:11-13) is implied in v. 4.

4:6 one God. This is the basic doctrine of God taught in Scripture (see Deut. 4:35; 6:4; 32:39; Is. 45:14; 46:9; 1 Cor. 8:4-6).

4:7 But to each one. This could be translated "in spite of that," or "on the other hand," contrasting what has just been said with what is about to be said, moving from the subject of the unity of believers ("all," v. 6) to that of the uniqueness of believers ("each one"). **grace.** Grace is a single-word definition of the gospel, the good news of God's offering salvation to sinful and unworthy mankind. God is the God of grace because He is a God who freely gives; His giving has nothing to do with anything we have done, but is unmerited, unearned, and undeserved. *See notes on 2:7-9.* **the measure of Christ's gift.** Each believer has a unique spiritual gift that God individually portions out according to His sovereign will and design. The Gr. term for "gift" focuses not on the Spirit as the source like the term used in 1 Cor. 12:1, nor on the grace that prompted it in Rom. 12:6, but on the freeness of the gift. For discussions of the gifts, *see notes on Rom. 12:6-8; 1 Cor. 12:4-10; 1 Pet. 4:10.*

4:8 *When He ascended on high.* Paul used an interpretive rendering of Ps. 68:18 as a parenthetical analogy to show how Christ received the right to bestow the spiritual gifts (v. 7). Psalm 68 is a victory hymn composed by David to celebrate God's conquest of the Jebusite city of Jerusalem and the triumphant assent of God up to Mt. Zion (cf. 2 Sam. 6,7; 1 Chr. 13). After such a triumph, the king would bring home the spoils and the prisoners. Here Paul depicts Christ returning from His battle on earth back into the glory of the heavenly city with the trophies of His great victory at Calvary (*see notes on 2 Cor. 2:14-16*). ***led captivity captive.*** Through His crucifixion and resurrection, Christ conquered Satan and death, and in triumph returned to God those who were once sinners and prisoners of Satan (cf. Col. 2:15). ***gave gifts to men.*** He distributes the spoils throughout His kingdom. After His ascension came all the spiritual gifts empowered by the Spirit, who was then sent (see John 7:39; 14:12; Acts 2:33).

4:9 *ascended.* Jesus' ascension from earth to heaven (Acts 1:9-11), where He forever reigns with His Father. **first descended.** This refers to Christ's incarnation, when He came down from heaven as a man into the earth of suffering and death. **the lower parts of the earth.**

who descended is also the One [l]who ascended far above all the heavens, [m]that He
might fill all things.)
11 And He Himself gave some *to be* apostles, some prophets, some evangelists, and
some pastors and teachers, 12 for the
equipping of the saints for the work of
ministry, [n]for the [5]edifying of [o]the body of
Christ, 13 till we all come to the unity of the
faith [p]and of the knowledge of the Son of
God, to [q]a perfect man, to the measure of
the stature of the fullness of Christ; 14 that
we should no longer be [r]children, tossed to
and fro and carried about with every wind
of doctrine, by the trickery of men, in the
cunning craftiness of [s]deceitful plotting,
15 but, speaking the truth in love, may
grow up in all things into Him who is the
[t]head—Christ— 16 [u]from whom the whole
body, joined and knit together by what
every joint supplies, according to the effective working by which every part does its
share, causes growth of the body for the
edifying of itself in love.

10 [l] Acts 1:9 [m] [Acts 2:33; Eph. 1:23]
12 [n] 1 Cor. 14:26 [o] Col. 1:24 [5] *building up*
13 [p] Col. 2:2 [q] 1 Cor. 14:20; Col. 1:28; Heb. 5:14
14 [r] 1 Cor. 14:20 [s] Rom. 16:18
15 [t] Eph. 1:22
16 [u] [Rom. 12:4]; Col. 2:19

These are in contrast to the highest heavens to which He afterward ascended (cf. Ps. 139:8,15; Is. 44:23). The phrase here does not point to a specific place, but to the great depth, as it were, of the incarnation, including Christ's descent, between His crucifixion and resurrection beyond the earth, the grave, and death, into the very pit of the demons, "the spirits in prison" (*see notes on Col. 2:14,15; 1 Pet. 3:18,19*).

4:10 that He might fill all things. After the Lord ascended, having fulfilled all prophecies and all His divinely-ordained redemptive tasks, He gained the right to rule the church and to give gifts, as He was then filling the entire universe with His divine presence, power, sovereignty, and blessing (cf. Phil. 2:9-11).

4:11 He Himself gave some *to be*. As evidenced by His perfect fulfillment of His Father's will, Christ possessed the authority and sovereignty to assign the spiritual gifts (v. 7,8) to those He has called into service in His church. He gave not only gifts, but gifted men. **apostles.** *See note on 2:20.* A term used particularly of the 12 disciples who had seen the risen Christ (Acts 1:22), including Matthias, who replaced Judas. Later, Paul was uniquely set apart as the apostle to the Gentiles (Gal. 1:15-17) and was numbered with the other apostles. He, too, miraculously encountered Jesus at his conversion on the Damascus Road (Acts 9:1-9; Gal. 1:15-17). Those apostles were chosen directly by Christ, so as to be called "apostles of Christ" (Gal. 1:1; 1 Pet. 1:1). They were given 3 basic responsibilities: 1) to lay the foundation of the church (2:20); 2) to receive, declare and write God's Word (3:5; Acts 11:28; 21:10,11); and 3) to give confirmation of that Word through signs, wonders, and miracles (2 Cor. 12:12; cf. Acts 8:6,7; Heb. 2:3,4). The term "apostle" is used in more general ways of other men in the early church, such as Barnabas (Acts 14:4), Silas, Timothy, (1 Thess. 2:6) and others (Rom. 16:7; Phil. 2:25). They are called "apostles of the churches" (2 Cor. 8:23), rather than "apostles of Jesus Christ" like the 13. They were not self-perpetuating, nor was any apostle who died replaced. **prophets.** *See note on 2:20.* Not ordinary believers who had the gift of prophecy but specially commissioned men in the early church. The office of prophet seems to have been exclusively for work within a local congregation. They were not "sent ones" as were the apostles (see Acts 13:1), but, as with the apostles, their office ceased with the completion of the NT. They sometimes spoke practical direct revelation for the church from God (Acts 11:21-28) or expounded revelation already given (implied in Acts 13:1). They were not used for the reception of Scripture. Their messages were to be judged by other prophets for validity (1 Cor. 14:32) and had to conform to the teaching of the apostles (v. 37). Those two offices were replaced by the evangelists and teaching pastors. **evangelists.** Men who proclaim the good news of salvation in Jesus Christ to unbelievers. Cf. the use of this term in Acts 21:8; 2 Tim. 4:5. The related verb translated "to preach the gospel" is used 54 times and the related noun translated "gospel" is used 76 times in the NT. **pastors and teachers.** This phrase is best understood in context as a single office of leadership in the church. The Gr. word translated "and" can mean "in particular" (see 1 Tim. 5:17). The normal meaning of pastor is "shepherd," so the two functions together define the teaching shepherd. He is identified as one who is under the "great Pastor" Jesus (Heb. 13:20,21; 1 Pet. 2:25). One who holds this office is also called an "elder" (*see notes on Titus 1:5-9*) and "bishop" (*see notes on 1 Tim. 3:1-7*). Acts 20:28 and 1 Pet. 5:1,2 bring all 3 terms together.

4:12 equipping. This refers to restoring something to its original condition, or its being made fit or complete. In this context, it refers to leading Christians from sin to obedience. Scripture is the key to this process (*see notes on 2 Tim. 3:16,17*; cf. John 15:3). **saints.** All who believe in Jesus Christ. *See note on 1:1.* **the work of ministry.** The spiritual service required of every Christian, not just of church leaders (cf. 1 Cor. 15:58). **the edifying of the body of Christ.** The spiritual edification, nurturing, and development of the church (cf. Acts 20:32).

4:13 unity of the faith. Faith here refers to the body of revealed truth that constitutes Christian teaching, particularly featuring the complete content of the gospel. Oneness and harmony among believers is possible only when it is built on the foundation of sound doctrine. **the knowledge of the Son of God.** This does not refer to salvation knowledge but to the deep knowledge of Christ that a believer comes to have through prayer, faithful study of His Word, and obedience to His commands (cf. Phil. 3:8-10,12; Col. 1:9,10; 2:2; *see note on 1 John 2:12-14*). **the fullness of Christ.** God wants every believer to manifest the qualities of His Son, who is Himself the standard for their spiritual maturity and perfection. *See notes on Rom. 8:29; 2 Cor. 3:18; Col. 1:28,29.*

4:14 carried about with every wind of doctrine. Spiritually immature believers who are not grounded in the knowledge of Christ through God's Word are inclined to uncritically accept every sort of beguiling doctrinal error and fallacious interpretation of Scripture promulgated by deceitful, false teachers in the church. They must learn discernment (1 Thess. 5:21,22). See 3:1; 14:20. The NT is replete with warnings of such danger (Acts 20:30,31; Rom. 16:17,18; Gal. 1:6,7; 1 Tim. 4:1-7; 2 Tim. 2:15-18; 2 Pet. 2:1-3).

4:15 speaking the truth in love. Evangelism is most effective when the truth is proclaimed in love. This can be accomplished only by the spiritually mature believer who is thoroughly equipped in sound doctrine. Without maturity, the truth can be cold and love little more than sentimentality. **grow up...into Him.** Christians are to be completely yielded and obedient to the Lord's will, subject to His controlling power and Christlike in all areas of their lives (cf. Gal. 2:20; Phil. 1:21). **the head.** Given the picture of the church as a body whose head is Christ, "head" is used in the sense of authoritative leader, not "source," which would have required a different anatomical picture. See 1:22; 5:23.

4:16 from whom. This refers to the Lord. Power for producing mature, equipped believers comes not from the effort of those believers alone but from their Head, the Lord Jesus Christ (cf. Col. 2:19). **every part does its share.** Godly, biblical church growth results from every member of the body fully using his spiritual gift, in submission to the Holy Spirit and in cooperation with other believers (cf. Col. 2:19).

The New Man

17 This I say, therefore, and testify in the
Lord, that you should [v]no longer walk as
[6]the rest of the Gentiles walk, in the futility of their mind, 18 having their understanding darkened, being alienated from
the life of God, because of the ignorance
that is in them, because of the [w]blindness
of their heart; 19 [x]who, being past feeling,
[y]have given themselves over to lewdness,
to work all uncleanness with greediness.
20 But you have not so learned Christ,
21 if indeed you have heard Him and have
been taught by Him, as the truth is in Jesus: 22 that you [z]put off, concerning your
former conduct, the old man which grows
corrupt according to the deceitful lusts,
23 and [a]be renewed in the spirit of your
mind, 24 and that you [b]put on the new man
which was created according to God, in
true righteousness and holiness.

Do Not Grieve the Spirit

25 Therefore, putting away lying, [c]*"Let
each one of you speak truth with his neighbor,"* for [d]we are members of one another.
26 [e]*"Be angry, and do not sin"*: do not let
the sun go down on your wrath, 27 [f]nor
give [7]place to the devil. 28 Let him who
stole steal no longer, but rather [g]let him
labor, working with *his* hands what is good,
that he may have something [h]to give him
who has need. 29 [i]Let no corrupt word proceed out of your mouth, but [j]what is good
for necessary [8]edification, [k]that it may impart grace to the hearers. 30 And [l]do not

17 [v] Eph. 2:2; 4:22 [6] NU omits *the rest of*
18 [w] Rom. 1:21
19 [x] 1 Tim. 4:2 [y] 1 Pet. 4:3
22 [z] Col. 3:8
23 [a] [Rom. 12:2; Col. 3:10]
24 [b] [Rom. 6:4; 7:6; 12:2; 2 Cor. 5:17; Col. 3:10]
25 [c] Zech. 8:16; Eph. 4:15; Col. 3:9 [d] Rom. 12:5
26 [e] Ps. 4:4; 37:8
27 [f] [Rom. 12:19; James 4:7]; 1 Pet. 5:9 [7] *an opportunity*
28 [g] Acts 20:35; 1 Cor. 4:12; Gal. 6:10 [h] Luke 3:11; 1 Thess. 4:12
29 [i] Matt. 12:34; Eph. 5:4; Col. 3:8 [j] 1 Thess. 5:11 [k] Col. 3:16 [8] *building up*
30 [l] Is. 7:13

4:17 no longer walk. "Walk" expresses daily conduct and refers back to what Paul has said about the believer's high calling in Christ Jesus (v. 1). Because Christians are part of the body of Christ, have been spiritually gifted by the Holy Spirit, and are edified through other believers, they should not continue to live like the rest of the ungodly (1 John 2:6). **Gentiles.** All ungodly, unregenerate pagans (cf. 1 Thess. 4:5 which defines them).

4:17-19 In these verses, Paul gives 4 characteristics of the ungodly lifestyles which believers are to forsake.

4:17 the futility of their mind. First, unbelievers are intellectually unproductive. As far as spiritual and moral issues are concerned, their rational processes are distorted and inadequate, inevitably failing to produce godly understanding or moral living. Their life is empty, vain, and without meaning (cf. Rom. 1:21-28; 1 Cor. 2:14; Col. 2:18).

4:18 alienated from the life of God. Second, unbelievers are spiritually separated form God, thus ignorant of God's truth (1 Cor. 2:14), and their willing spiritual darkness and moral blindness is the result (cf. Rom. 1:21-24; 2 Tim. 3:7). They are blind, or "hard" like a rock.

4:19 being past feeling. Third, unbelievers are morally insensitive. As they continue to sin and turn away from God, they become still more apathetic about moral and spiritual things (cf. Rom. 1:32). **lewdness...uncleanness.** Fourth, unbelievers are behaviorally depraved (cf. Rom. 1:28). As they willingly keep succumbing to sensuality and licentiousness, they increasingly lose moral restraint, especially in the area of sexual sins. Impurity is inseparable from greediness, which is a form of idolatry (5:5; Col. 3:5). That some souls may not reach the extremes of vv. 17-19 is due only to God's common grace and the restraining influence of the Holy Spirit.

4:20,21 learned...heard...taught. Three figurative descriptions of salvation, the new birth.

4:21 as the truth is in Jesus. The truth about salvation leads to the fullness of truth about God, man, creation, history, life, purpose, relationships, heaven, hell, judgment, and everything else that is truly important. John summed this up in 1 John 5:20.

4:22 put off. To strip away, as in taking off old, filthy clothes. This describes repentance from sin and submission to God at the point of salvation. *See notes on Col. 3:3-9* (cf. Is. 55:6,7; Matt. 19:16-22; Acts 2:38-40; 20:21; 1 Thess. 1:9). **the old man.** The worn out, useless, and unconverted sinful nature corrupted by deceit. Salvation is a spiritual union with Jesus Christ that is described as the death plus burial of the old self and the resurrection of the new self walking in newness of life. This transformation is Paul's theme in Rom. 6:2-8 (*see notes there*).

4:23 be renewed in the spirit of your mind. Salvation involves the mind (*see notes on Rom. 12:2; 2 Cor. 10:5*), which is the center of thought, understanding, and belief, as well as of motive and action (cf. Col. 3:1,2,10). When a person becomes a Christian, God gives him a completely new spiritual and moral capability that a mind apart from Christ could never achieve (cf. 1 Cor. 2:9-16).

4:24 put on the new man. The renewal of the mind in salvation brings not simply a renovation of character, but transformation of the old to the new self (cf. 2 Cor. 5:17). **which was created according to God.** In Christ, the old self no longer exists as it had in the past; the new self is created in the very likeness of God (cf. Gal. 2:20). **in true righteousness and holiness.** Righteousness relates to the Christian's moral responsibility to his fellow men reflecting the second table of the law (Ex. 20:12-17), while holiness refers to his responsibilities to God, reflecting the first table (Ex. 20:3-11). There is still sin in the believer's unredeemed human flesh (*see notes on Rom. 7:17,18,20,23,25; 8:23*).

4:25 putting away lying. More than simply telling direct falsehoods, lying also includes exaggeration and adding fabrications to something that is true. Cheating, making foolish promises, betraying a confidence, and making false excuses are all forms of lying, with which Christians should have no part (cf. John 8:44; 1 Cor. 6:9; Rev. 21:8). ***speak truth with his neighbor.*** Quoted from Zech. 8:16. God's work in the world is based on truth, and neither the church nor individual believers can be fit instruments for the Lord to use if they are not truthful.

4:26 *Be angry, and do not sin.* Quoted from Ps. 4:4. By NT standards, anger can be either good or bad, depending on motive and purpose. Paul may have been sanctioning righteous indignation, anger at evil. This type of anger hates injustice, immorality, ungodliness, and every other sin. When such anger is unselfish and based on love for God and others, it not only is permissible but commanded. Jesus expressed this righteous anger (see Matt. 21:12; Mark 3:5; John 2:15). **sun go down.** Even righteous anger can turn to bitterness, so should be set aside by the end of each day. If anger is prolonged, it may become hostile and violate the instruction of Rom. 12:17-21.

4:28 steal no longer. Stealing in any form is a sin and has no part in the life of a Christian. Rather, let him work, producing what is beneficial (cf. Ex. 20:15). The alternative to stealing is to provide for oneself, one's family, and others what is God-honoring through honest, honorable means (cf. 2 Thess. 3:10,11; 1 Tim. 5:8). **give him who has need.** A Christian not only should harm no one but should continually endeavor to help those who are in need. See Luke 14:13,14; Acts 20:33-35.

4:29 corrupt word. The word for "corrupt" refers to that which is foul or rotten, such as spoiled fruit or putrid meat. Foul language of any sort should never pass a Christian's lips, because it is totally out of character with his new life in Christ (see Col. 3:8; James 3:6-8; cf. Ps. 141:3). **good for necessary edification.** The Christian's speech should be instructive, encouraging, uplifting, (even when it must be

grieve the Holy Spirit of God, by whom
you were sealed for the day of redemption.
31 [m]Let all bitterness, wrath, anger, [9]clamor,
and [n]evil speaking be put away from you,
[o]with all malice. 32 And [p]be kind to one another, tenderhearted, [q]forgiving one another, even as God in Christ forgave you.

Walk in Love

5 Therefore[a] be imitators of God as dear
[b]children. 2 And [c]walk in love, [d]as
Christ also has loved us and given Himself
for us, an offering and a sacrifice to God
[e]for a sweet-smelling aroma.
3 But fornication and all [f]uncleanness or
[g]covetousness, let it not even be named
among you, as is fitting for saints; 4 [h]nei-
ther filthiness, nor [i]foolish talking, nor
coarse jesting, [j]which are not fitting, but
rather [k]giving of thanks. 5 For [1]this you
know, that no fornicator, unclean person,
nor covetous man, who is an idolater, has
any [l]inheritance in the kingdom of Christ
and God. 6 Let no one deceive you with
empty words, for because of these things
the wrath of God comes upon the sons of
disobedience. 7 Therefore do not be [m]par-
takers with them.

Walk in Light

8 For you were once darkness, but now
you are [n]light in the Lord. Walk as children

31 [m]Rom. 3:14; Col. 3:8, 19 [n]James 4:11 [o]Titus 3:3 [9]*loud quarreling*
32 [p][Matt. 6:14]; 2 Cor. 6:10 [q][Mark 11:25; Luke 6:37]

CHAPTER 5

1 [a][Matt. 5:48]; Luke 6:36; Eph. 4:32 [b]1 Pet. 1:14-16
2 [c]1 Thess. 4:9 [d]John 15:9; Gal. 1:4; 1 John 3:16 [e]Ex. 29:18, 25; 2 Cor. 2:14, 15
3 [f]Col. 3:5-7 [g][Luke 12:15]
4 [h]Matt. 12:34, 35; Eph. 4:29; Col. 3:8; James 1:21 [i]Titus 3:9 [j]Rom. 1:28 [k]Phil. 4:6; Col. 3:17; [1 Thess. 5:18]
5 [l]1 Cor. 6:9, 10; Col. 3:5 [1]NU *know this*
7 [m]1 Tim. 5:22
8 [n]1 Thess. 5:5

corrective), and suited for the moment (cf. Prov. 15:23; 25:11; 24:26). **grace to the hearers.** Cf. Col. 4:6. Because believers have been saved by grace and kept by grace, they should live and speak with grace. Our Lord set the standard (Luke 4:22).

4:30 do not grieve the Holy Spirit of God. God is grieved when His children refuse to change the old ways of sin for those righteous ways of the new life. It should be noted that such responses by the Holy Spirit indicate He is a person. His personhood is also indicated by personal pronouns (John 14:17; 16:13), His personal care of believers (John 14:16,26; 15:26), His intellect (1 Cor. 2:11), feelings (Rom. 8:27; 15:30), will (1 Cor. 12:11), speaking (Acts 13:2), convicting (John 16:8-11), interceding (Rom. 8:26), guiding (John 16:13), glorifying Christ (John 16:14), and serving God (Acts 16:6,7). **sealed for the day of redemption.** The Holy Spirit is the guarantor of eternal redemption in Christ for those who believe in Him (*see notes on 1:13,14*).

4:31,32 These verses summarize the changes in the life of a believer mentioned in vv. 17-30. "Bitterness" reflects a smoldering resentment. "Wrath" has to do with rage, the passion of a moment. "Anger" is a more internal, deep hostility. "Clamor" is the outcry of strife out of control. "Evil speaking" is slander. "Malice" is the general Gr. term for evil, the root of all vices.

4:32 even as God in Christ forgave you. Those who have been forgiven so much by God should, of all people, forgive the relatively small offenses against them by others. The most graphic illustration of this truth is the parable of Matt. 18:21-35.

5:1 be imitators of God. The Christian has no greater calling or purpose than that of imitating his Lord (*see notes on 3:16,19*). That is the very purpose of sanctification, growing in likeness to the Lord while serving Him on earth (cf. Matt. 5:48). The Christian life is designed to reproduce godliness as modeled by the Savior and Lord, Jesus Christ, in whose image believers have been recreated through the new birth (cf. Rom. 8:29; 2 Cor. 3:18; 1 Pet. 1:14-16). As God's dear children, believers are to become more and more like their heavenly Father (Matt. 5:48; 1 Pet. 1:15,16).

5:2 Christ also has loved us and given Himself for us. The Lord is the supreme example in His self-sacrificing love for lost sinners (4:32; Rom. 5:8-10). He took human sin upon Himself and gave up His very life that men might be redeemed from their sin, receive a new and holy nature, and inherit eternal life (*see note on 2 Cor. 5:21*). They are henceforth to be imitators of His great love in the newness and power of the Holy Spirit, who enables them to demonstrate divine love. **a sweet-smelling aroma.** Christ's offering of Himself for fallen man pleased and glorified His heavenly Father, because it demonstrated in the most complete and perfect way God's sovereign, perfect, unconditional, and divine kind of love. Leviticus describes 5 offerings commanded by God for Israel. The first 3 were: 1) the burnt offering (Lev. 1:1-17), depicting Christ's perfection; 2) the grain offering (Lev. 2:1-16), depicting Christ's total devotion to God in giving His life to please the Father; and 3) the peace offering (Lev. 3:1-17; 4:27-31), depicting His peacemaking between God and man. All 3 of these were a "soothing aroma to the Lord" (Lev. 1:9,13,17; 2:2,9,12; 3:5,16). The other two offerings, the sin offering (Lev. 4:1-26,32-35) and the trespass offering (Lev. 5:1-19), were repulsive to God because, though they depicted Christ, they depicted Him as bearing sin (cf. Matt. 27:46). In the end, when redemption was accomplished, the whole work pleased God completely.

5:3 fornication...covetousness. In absolute contrast to God's holiness and love, such sins as these exist (also in v. 5), by which Satan seeks to destroy God's divine work in His children and turn them as far away as possible from His image and will. As do many other Scriptures, this verse shows the close connection between sexual sin and other forms of impurity and greed. An immoral person is inevitably greedy. Such sins are so godless that the world should never have reason even to suspect their presence in Christians.

5:4 not fitting. These 3 inappropriate sins of the tongue include any speech that is obscene and degrading or foolish and dirty, as well as suggestive and immoral wit. All such are destructive of holy living and godly testimony and should be confessed, forsaken, and replaced by open expressions of thankfulness to God (cf. Col. 3:8).

5:5 For this you know. Paul had taught this truth many times when he pastored the church at Ephesus and it should have been clear in their minds. God never tolerates sin, which has no place at all in His kingdom, nor will any person whose life pattern is one of habitual immorality, impurity, and greed (see v. 3) be in His kingdom, because no such person is saved (*see notes on 1 Cor. 6:9,10; Gal. 5:17-21; 1 John 3:9,10*). **the kingdom of Christ and God.** A reference to the sphere of salvation where Christ rules the redeemed. *See note on Acts 1:3.*

5:6 deceive you. No Christian will be sinless in this present life, but it is dangerously deceptive for Christians to offer assurance of salvation to a professing believer whose life is characterized by persistent sin and who shows no shame for that sin or hunger for the holy and pure things of God. They are headed for wrath (2:2) and believers must not partner in any of their wickedness (v. 7).

5:8 darkness...light. "Darkness" describes the character of the life of the unconverted as void of truth and virtue in intellectual and moral matters (cf. 1 John 1:5-7). The realm of darkness is presided over by the "power of darkness," (Luke 22:53; Col. 1:13) who rules those headed for "eternal darkness" (Matt. 8:12; 2 Pet. 2:17). Tragically, sinners love the darkness (John 3:19-21). It is that very darkness from which salvation in Christ delivers sinners (*see notes on John 8:12; Col. 1:13; 1 Pet. 2:9*; cf. Ps. 27:1).

of light **9** (for [o]the fruit of the [2]Spirit *is* in
all goodness, righteousness, and truth),
10 [p]finding out what is acceptable to the
Lord. **11** And have [q]no fellowship with the
unfruitful works of darkness, but rather
[3]expose *them.* **12** [r]For it is shameful even to
speak of those things which are done by
them in secret. **13** But [s]all things that are
[4]exposed are made manifest by the light,
for whatever makes manifest is light.
14 Therefore He says:

> [t]"Awake, you who sleep,
> Arise from the dead,
> And Christ will give you light."

9 [o]Gal. 5:22 [2]NU *light*
10 [p][Rom. 12:1, 2]
11 [q]1 Cor. 5:9; 2 Cor. 6:14 [3]*reprove*
12 [r]Rom. 1:24
13 [s][John 3:20, 21] [4]*reproved*
14 [t][Is. 26:19; 60:1; Rom. 13:11]
15 [u]Col. 4:5 [5]*carefully*
16 [v]Col. 4:5 [w]Eccl. 11:2
17 [x]Col. 4:5 [y][Rom. 12:2]; Col. 1:9 [z]1 Thess. 4:3
18 [a]Prov. 20:1; 23:31; Rom. 13:13; 1 Cor. 5:11; 1 Thess. 5:7

Walk in Wisdom

15 [u]See then that you walk [5]circum-
spectly, not as fools but as wise, **16** [v]redeem-
ing the time, [w]because the days are evil.
17 [x]Therefore do not be unwise, but [y]un-
derstand [z]what the will of the Lord *is.*
18 And [a]do not be drunk with wine, in
which is dissipation; but be filled with the
Spirit, **19** speaking to one another [b]in
psalms and hymns and spiritual songs,
singing and making [c]melody in your heart
to the Lord, **20** [d]giving thanks always for
all things to God the Father [e]in the name of

19 [b]Acts 16:25 [c]James 5:13 **20** [d]Ps. 34:1 [e][1 Pet. 2:5]

5:9 fruit of the spirit. Better, as in marginal reading, "fruit of the light." This speaks of that which is produced by walking in the light (cf. 1 John 1:5-7), namely moral excellence of heart, righteous behavior, and truthfulness (honesty or integrity). *See notes on Gal. 5:22,23.*

5:10 finding out what is acceptable to the Lord. "Finding out" carries the idea of testing or proving to learn by clear and convincing evidence what is truly honoring to God. The point is that, as believers walk in the light of the truth, the knowledge of the Lord's will becomes clear. See Rom. 12:1,2 where Paul says the same thing, stating that it is only after presenting ourselves as living sacrifices to God that we can know His acceptable will. This relates to assurance of salvation also (see 1 Pet. 1:5-11).

5:11 no fellowship with…darkness. Paul's instruction is plain and direct: Christians are to faithfully live in righteousness and purity and have nothing at all to do with the evil ways and works of Satan and the world. The two ways of living are unalterably opposed to each other and mutually exclusive. Cf. 1 Cor. 5:9-11; 2 Cor. 6:14-18; 2 Thess. 3:6,14. **but rather expose *them*.** The Christian's responsibility does not stop with his own rejection of evil. He is also responsible for exposing and opposing darkness wherever it is found, especially when it is found in the church. *See notes on Matt. 18:15-17; Gal. 6:1-3.*

5:12 shameful even to speak. Some sins are so despicable that they should be sealed off from direct contact and not even mentioned, much less discussed, except in order to contradict and oppose them. Merely talking about them can be morally and spiritually corruptive. Positive proclamation of the pure truth in the light of the Word exposes all evil (cf. Prov. 6:23; 2 Tim. 3:16).

5:13 for whatever makes manifest is light. This phrase should probably be part of v. 14, and is better translated, "for it is light that makes everything visible." The pure and illuminating light of God's Word exposes all the secrets of sin.

5:14 Using this quotation from Is. 60:1, Paul extended an invitation for salvation to the unsaved, in order that they may be transformed from children of darkness into children of God's holy light (cf. Prov. 4:18). These words may have been part of an early church Easter hymn used as an invitation to unbelievers. They express a capsule view of the gospel. Cf. the invitations in Is. 55:1-3,6,7 and in James 4:6-10.

5:15 circumspectly, not as fools but as wise. This term means "accurately or precisely with great care" (cf. Ps. 1:1; Matt. 7:14). To live morally is to live wisely. Biblically, a "fool" is not so named because of intellectual limits, but because of unbelief and the consequent abominable deeds (Ps. 14:1; Rom. 1:22). He lives apart from God and against God's law (Prov. 1:7,22; 14:9), and can't comprehend the truth (1 Cor. 2:14) or his true condition (Rom. 1:21,22). Certainly believers are to avoid behaving like fools (see Luke 24:25; Gal. 3:1-3).

5:16 redeeming the time. The Gr. word for "time" denotes a fixed, measured, allocated season; with the definite article "the," it likely refers to one's lifetime as a believer. We are to make the most of our time on this evil earth in fulfilling God's purposes, lining up every opportunity for useful worship and service. *See note on 1 Pet. 1:17.* Be aware of the brevity of life (Pss. 39:4,5; 89:46,47; James 4:14,17).

5:17 Therefore do not be unwise, but understand what the will of the Lord *is*. Knowing and understanding God's will through His Word is spiritual wisdom. For example, God's will revealed to us is that people should be saved (1 Tim. 2:3,4), Spirit-filled (v. 18), sanctified (1 Thess. 4:3), submissive (1 Pet. 2:13-15), suffering (1 Pet. 2:20) and thankful (1 Thess. 5:18). Jesus is the supreme example for all (see John 4:4; 5:19,30; 1 Pet. 4:1,2).

5:18 And do not be drunk with wine. Although Scripture consistently condemns all drunkenness (*see notes on Prov. 23:20,21,29-35; 31:4,5; Is. 5:11,12; 28:7,8*; cf. 1 Cor. 5:11; 1 Pet. 4:3), the context suggests that Paul is here speaking especially about the drunken orgies commonly associated with many pagan worship ceremonies of that day. They were supposed to induce some ecstatic communion with the deities. Paul refers to such as the "cup of demons" (*see notes on 1 Cor. 10:20,21*). **but be filled with the Spirit.** *See notes on Acts 2:4; 4:8,31; 6:3.* True communion with God is not induced by drunkenness, but by the Holy Spirit. Paul is not speaking of the Holy Spirit's indwelling (Rom. 8:9) or the baptism by Christ with the Holy Spirit (1 Cor. 12:13), because every Christian is indwelt and baptized by the Spirit at the time of salvation. He is rather giving a command for believers to live continually under the influence of the Spirit by letting the Word control them (*see note on Col. 3:16*), pursuing pure lives, confessing all known sin, dying to self, surrendering to God's will, and depending on His power in all things. Being filled with the Spirit is living in the conscious presence of the Lord Jesus Christ, letting His mind, through the Word, dominate everything that is thought and done. Being filled with the Spirit is the same as walking in the Spirit (*see notes on Gal. 5:16-23*). Christ exemplified this way of life (Luke 4:1).

5:19-21 These verses summarize the immediate personal consequences of obeying the command to be filled with the Spirit, namely singing, giving thanks, and humbly submitting to others. The rest of the epistle features instruction based on obedience to this command

5:19 speaking to one another. This is to be public (Heb. 2:12). Cf. Pss. 33:1; 40:3; 96:1,2; 149:1; Acts 16:25; Rev. 14:3. **psalms.** Old Testament psalms put to music, primarily, but the term was used also of vocal music in general. The early church sang the Psalms. **hymns.** Perhaps songs of praise distinguished from the Psalms which exalted God, in that they focused on the Lord Jesus Christ. **spiritual songs.** Probably songs of personal testimony expressing truths of the grace of salvation in Christ. **making melody.** Lit. means to pluck a stringed instrument, so it could refer primarily to instrumental music, while including vocal also. **in your heart to the Lord.** Not just public, but private. The Lord Himself is both the source and the object of the believer's song-filled heart. That such music pleases God can be seen in the account of the temple dedication, when the singing so honored the Lord that His glory came down (2 Chr. 5:12,14).

our Lord Jesus Christ, 21 [f]submitting to
one another in the fear of [6]God.

Marriage—Christ and the Church

22 Wives, [g]submit to your own husbands, as to the Lord. 23 For [h]the husband
is head of the wife, as also [i]Christ is head
of the church; and He is the Savior of the
body. 24 Therefore, just as the church is
subject to Christ, so *let* the wives *be* to their
own husbands [j]in everything.

25 [k]Husbands, love your wives, just as
Christ also loved the church and [l]gave
Himself for her, 26 that He might [7]sanctify
and cleanse her [m]with the washing of
water [n]by the word, 27 [o]that He might present her to Himself a glorious church, [p]not
having spot or wrinkle or any such thing,
but that she should be holy and without
blemish. 28 So husbands ought to love their
own wives as their own bodies; he who
loves his wife loves himself. 29 For no one
ever hated his own flesh, but nourishes
and cherishes it, just as the Lord *does* the
church. 30 For [q]we are members of His
body, [8]of His flesh and of His bones.
31 [r]*"For this reason a man shall leave his
father and mother and be joined to his
wife, and the* [s]*two shall become one flesh."*
32 This is a great mystery, but I speak concerning Christ and the church. 33 Nevertheless [t]let each one of you in particular so
love his own wife as himself, and let the
wife *see* that she [u]respects *her* husband.

Children and Parents

6 Children, [a]obey your parents in the
Lord, for this is right. 2 [b]*"Honor your*

21 [f][Phil. 2:3]; 1 Pet. 5:5 [6]NU *Christ*
22 [g]Eph. 5:22–6:9; Col. 3:18–4:1; 1 Pet. 3:1-6
23 [h][1 Cor. 11:3] [i]Col. 1:18
24 [j]Titus 2:4, 5
25 [k]Eph. 5:28, 33; Col. 3:19; [1 Pet. 3:7] [l]Acts 20:28
26 [m]John 3:5 [n][John 15:3; 17:17; Rom. 10:8; Eph. 6:17] [7]*set it apart*
27 [o][2 Cor. 4:14; 11:2]; Col. 1:22 [p]Song 4:7
30 [q]Gen. 2:23 [8]NU omits the rest of v. 30.
31 [r]Gen. 2:24; Matt. 19:5; Mark 10:7 [s][1 Cor. 6:16]
33 [t]Col. 3:19 [u]1 Pet. 3:1, 6

CHAPTER 6 1 [a]Prov. 6:20; 23:22; Col. 3:20 2 [b]Ex. 20:12; Deut. 5:16

5:20 giving thanks always for all things. *See note on 1 Thess. 5:18*; cf. 2 Cor. 4:15; 9:12,15; Phil. 4:6; Col. 2:7; Heb. 13:15. Believers' thankfulness is for who God is and for what He has done through His Son, their Savior and Lord.

5:21 submitting to one another. Paul here made a transition and introduced his teaching about specific relationships of authority and submission among Christians (5:22–6:9) by declaring unequivocally that every spirit-filled Christian is to be a humble, submissive Christian. This is foundational to all the relationships in this section. No believer is inherently superior to any other believer. In their standing before God, they are equal in every way (Gal 3:28). **in the fear of God.** The believer's continual reverence for God is the basis for his submission to other believers. Cf. Prov. 9:10.

5:22 Wives, submit to your own husbands. Having established the foundational principle of submission (v. 21), Paul applied it first to the wife. The command is unqualified, applying to every Christian wife, no matter what her own abilities, education, knowledge of Scripture, spiritual maturity, or any other qualifications might be in relation to those of her husband. The submission is not the husband's to command but for the wife to willingly and lovingly offer. "Your own husbands" limits her submission to the one man God has placed over her, and also gives a balancing emphasis that he is hers as a personal intimate possession (Song 2:16; 6:3; 7:10). She submits to the man she possesses as her own. **as to the Lord.** Because the obedient, spiritual wife's supreme submission is to the Lord, her attitude is that she lovingly submits as an act of obedience to the Lord who has given this command as His will for her, regardless of her husband's personal worthiness or spiritual condition. Cf. vv. 5-9.

5:23 husband is head...Christ is head. The Spirit-filled wife recognizes that her husband's role in giving leadership is not only God-ordained, but is a reflection of Christ's own loving, authoritative headship of the church. *See notes on 1 Cor. 11:3*; cf. 1:22,23; 4:15; Col. 1:18; Titus 2:4,5. **Savior.** As the Lord delivered His church from the dangers of sin, death, and hell, so the husband provides for, protects, preserves, and loves his wife, leading her to blessing as she submits. Cf. Titus 1:4; 2:13; 3:6.

5:25 love your wives. Though the husband's authority has been established (vv. 22-24), the emphasis moves to the supreme responsibility of husbands in regard to their wives, which is to love them with the same unreserved, selfless, and sacrificial love that Christ has for His church. Christ gave everything He had, including His own life, for the sake of His church, and that is the standard of sacrifice for a husband's love of his wife. Cf. Col. 3:19.

5:26,27 sanctify...cleanse...holy...without blemish. This speaks of the love of Christ for His church. Saving grace makes believers holy by the agency of the Word of God (Titus 2:1-9; 3:5) so that they may be a pure bride. For husbands to love their wives as Christ does His church, demands a purifying love. Since divine love seeks to completely cleanse those who are loved from every form of sin and evil, a Christian husband should not be able to bear the thought of anything sinful in the life of his wife that displeases God. His greatest desire for her should be that she become perfectly conformed to Christ, so he leads her to purity. *See note on 2 Cor. 11:23.*

5:28 as their own bodies. Here is one of the most poignant and compelling descriptions of the oneness that should characterize Christian marriage. A Christian husband is to care for his wife with the same devotion that he naturally manifests as he cares for himself (v. 29)—even more so, since his self-sacrificing love causes him to put her first (cf. Phil. 2:1-4). **loves his wife loves himself.** In the end, a husband who loves his wife in these ways brings great blessing to himself from her and from the Lord.

5:29 nourishes and cherishes. These express the twin responsibilities of providing for her needs so as to help her grow mature in Christ and to provide warm and tender affection to give her comfort and security.

5:30 members of His body. The Lord provides for His church because it is so intimately and inseparably connected to Him. If He did not care for His church, He would be diminishing His own glory which the church brings to Him by praise and obedience. So, in marriage, the husband's life is so intimately joined to the wife's that they are one. When he cares for her, he cares for himself (v. 29).

5:31 Quoted from Gen. 2:24 (*see note there*). Paul reinforces the divine plan for marriage which God instituted at creation, emphasizing its permanence and unity. The union of marriage is intimate and unbreakable. "Joined" is a word used to express having been glued or cemented together, emphasizing the permanence of the union (*see notes on Mal. 2:16; Matt. 19:6-9*).

5:32 a great mystery. In the NT, "mystery" identifies some reality hidden in the past and revealed in the NT age to be written in Scripture. Marriage is a sacred reflection of the magnificent and beautiful mystery of union between the Messiah and His church, completely unknown until the NT. *See notes on 3:4,5; Matt. 13:11; 1 Cor. 2:7.*

5:33 let each one of you. The intimacy and sacredness of the love relationship between believing marriage partners is to be a visual expression of the love between Christ and His church.

6:1 obey...in the Lord. See Col. 3:20. The child in the home is to

father and mother," which is the first commandment with promise: 3 *"that it may be
well with you and you may live long on
the earth."*
4 And [c]you, fathers, do not provoke
your children to wrath, but [d]bring them up
in the training and admonition of the Lord.

Bondservants and Masters

5 [e]Bondservants, be obedient to those
who are your masters according to the
flesh, [f]with fear and trembling, [g]in sincerity of heart, as to Christ; 6 [h]not with eyeservice, as men-pleasers, but as bondservants
of Christ, doing the will of God from the
heart, 7 with goodwill doing service, as to
the Lord, and not to men, 8 [i]knowing that
whatever good anyone does, he will receive the same from the Lord, whether *he is*
a slave or free.
9 And you, masters, do the same things
to them, giving up threatening, knowing
that [1]your own [j]Master also is in heaven,
and [k]there is no partiality with Him.

The Whole Armor of God

10 Finally, my brethren, be strong in the
Lord and in the power of His might. 11 [l]Put
on the whole armor of God, that you may
be able to stand against the [2]wiles of the

4 [c]Col. 3:21 [d]Gen. 18:19; Deut. 6:7; 11:19; Ps. 78:4; Prov. 22:6; 2 Tim. 3:15
5 [e]Col. 3:22; [1 Tim. 6:1]; Titus 2:9; 1 Pet. 2:18 [f]2 Cor. 7:15 [g]1 Chr. 29:17
6 [h]Col. 3:22
8 [i]Rom. 2:6
9 [j]Job 31:13; John 13:13; Col. 4:1 [k]Deut. 10:17; Acts 10:34; Rom. 2:11; Col. 3:25 [1]NU *He who is both their Master and yours is*
11 [l][2 Cor. 6:7] [2]*schemings*

be willingly under the authority of parents with obedient submission to them as the agents of the Lord placed over him, obeying parents as if obeying the Lord Himself. The reasoning here is simply that such is the way God has designed and required it ("right"). Cf. Hos. 14:9.

6:2,3 ***Honor.*** While v. 1 speaks of action, this term speaks of attitude, as Paul deals with the motive behind the action. When God gave His law in the Ten Commandments, the first law governing human relationships was this one (Ex. 20:12; Deut. 5:16). It is the only command of the 10 that relates to the family because that principle alone secures the family's fulfillment. Cf. Ex. 21:15,17; Lev. 20:9; Matt. 15:3-6. Proverbs affirms this principle (see 1:8; 3:1; 4:1-4; 7:1-3; 10:1; 17:21; 19:13,26; 28:24).

6:2 the first commandment with promise. Although submission to parents should first of all be for the Lord's sake, He has graciously added the promise of special blessing for those who obey this command. *See note on Ex. 20:12*, the verse from which Paul quotes (cf. Deut. 5:16).

6:4 fathers. The word technically refers to male parents, but was also used of parents in general. Since Paul had been speaking of both parents (vv. 1-3) he probably had both in mind here. The same word is used in Heb. 11:23 for Moses' parents. **do not provoke.** In the pagan world of Paul's day, and even in many Jewish households, most fathers ruled their families with rigid and domineering authority. The desires and welfare of wives and children were seldom considered. The apostle makes clear that a Christian father's authority over his children does not allow for unreasonable demands and strictures that might drive his children to anger, despair, and resentment. **training and admonition of the Lord.** This calls for systematic discipline and instruction, which brings children to respect the commands of the Lord as the foundation of all of life, godliness, and blessing. Cf. Prov. 13:24; Heb. 12:5-11.

6:5 Bondservants, be obedient. *See notes on Col. 3:22-24.* Slaves in both Greek and Roman culture had no rights legally and were treated as commodities. There was much abuse and seldom good treatment of slaves. The Bible does not speak against slavery itself, but against its abuses (cf. Ex. 21:16,26,27; Lev. 25:10; Deut. 23:15,16). Paul's admonition applies equally well to all employees. The term "obedient" refers to continuous, uninterrupted submission to one's earthly master or employer, the only exception being in regard to a command that involves clear disobedience of God's Word as illustrated in Acts 4:19,20. *See notes on 1 Tim. 6:1,2; Titus 2:9,10; 1 Pet. 2:18-20.* **according to the flesh.** Human masters, that is. **with fear and trembling.** This is not fright, but respect for their authority. Even if an employer does not deserve respect in his own right (see 1 Pet. 2:18), it should nevertheless be given to him with genuine sincerity as if one was serving Christ Himself. To serve one's employer well is to serve Christ well. Cf. Col. 3:23,24.

6:6 eyeservice. Working well only when being watched by the boss. **men-pleasers.** Working only to promote one's welfare, rather than to honor the employer and the Lord, whose servants we really are.

6:7,8 Cf. Col. 3:23. God's credits and rewards will be appropriate to the attitude and action of our work. No good thing done for His glory will go unrewarded.

6:9 And you, masters, do the same things to them. There should be mutual honor and respect from Christian employers to their employees, based on their common allegiance to the Lord. **giving up threatening.** The Spirit-filled boss uses his authority and power with justice and grace—never putting people under threats, never abusive or inconsiderate. He realizes that he has a heavenly Master who is impartial (cf. Acts 10:34; Rom. 2:11; James 2:9).

6:10-17 The true believer described in chaps. 1–3, who lives the Spirit-controlled life of 4:1–6:9, can be sure to be in a spiritual war, as described here. Paul closes this letter with both warning about that war and instructions on how to win it. The Lord provides His saints with sufficient armor to combat and thwart the adversary. In vv. 10-13, the apostle briefly sets forth the basic truths regarding the believer's necessary spiritual preparation as well as truths regarding his enemy, his battle, and his victory. In vv. 14-17, he specifies the 6 most necessary pieces of spiritual armor with which God equips His children to resist and overcome Satan's assaults.

6:10 be strong in the Lord and in the power of His might. Cf. Phil. 4:13; 2 Tim. 2:1. Ultimately, Satan's power over Christians is already broken and the great war is won through Christ's crucifixion and resurrection, which forever conquered the power of sin and death (Rom. 5:18-21; 1 Cor. 15:56,57; Heb. 2:14). However, in life on earth, battles of temptation go on regularly. The Lord's power, the strength of His Spirit, and the force of biblical truth are required for victory (*see notes on 2 Cor. 10:3-5*).

6:11 Put on the whole armor of God. "Put on" conveys the idea of permanence, indicating that armor should be the Christian's sustained, life-long attire. Paul uses the common armor worn by Roman soldiers as the analogy for the believer's spiritual defense and affirms its necessity if one is to hold his position while under attack. **wiles.** This is the Gr. word for "schemes," carrying the idea of cleverness, crafty methods, cunning, and deception. Satan's schemes are propagated through the evil world system over which he rules, and are carried out by his demon hosts. "Wiles" is all-inclusive, encompassing every sin, immoral practice, false theology, false religion, and worldly enticement. *See note on 2 Cor. 2:11.* **the devil.** Scripture refers to him as "the anointed cherub" (Ezek. 28:14), "the ruler of the demons" (Luke 11:15), "the god of this world" (2 Cor. 4:4), and "the prince of the power of the air" (2:2). Scripture depicts him opposing God's work (Zech. 3:1), perverting God's Word (Matt. 4:6), hindering God's servant (1 Thess. 2:18), hindering the gospel (2 Cor. 4:4), snaring the righteous (1 Tim. 3:7), and holding the world in his power (1 John 5:19).

devil. 12 For we do not wrestle against
flesh and blood, but against [m]principali-
ties, against powers, against [n]the rulers of
[3]the darkness of this age, against spiritual
hosts of wickedness in the heavenly *places.*
13 [o]Therefore take up the whole armor of
God, that you may be able to withstand
[p]in the evil day, and having done all, to
stand.
14 Stand therefore, [q]having girded your
waist with truth, [r]having put on the breastplate of righteousness, 15 [s]and having shod
your feet with the preparation of the
gospel of peace; 16 above all, taking [t]the
shield of faith with which you will be able
to quench all the fiery darts of the wicked
one. 17 And [u]take the helmet of salvation,
and [v]the sword of the Spirit, which is the
word of God; 18 [w]praying always with all
prayer and supplication in the Spirit, [x]be-
ing watchful to this end with all perseverance and [y]supplication for all the saints—
19 and for me, that utterance may be given
to me, [z]that I may open my mouth boldly
to make known the mystery of the gospel,
20 for which [a]I am an ambassador in

12 [m] Rom. 8:38 [n] Luke 22:53 [3] NU *this darkness,*
13 [o] [2 Cor. 10:4] [p] Eph. 5:16
14 [q] Is. 11:5; Luke 12:35; 1 Pet. 1:13 [r] Is. 59:17; Rom. 13:12; Eph. 6:13; 1 Thess. 5:8
15 [s] Is. 52:7; Rom. 10:15
16 [t] 1 John 5:4
17 [u] 1 Thess. 5:8 [v] Is. 49:2; Hos. 6:5; [Heb. 4:12]
18 [w] Luke 18:1; Col. 1:3; 4:2; 1 Thess. 5:17 [x] [Matt. 26:41] [y] Phil. 1:4
19 [z] Acts 4:29; Col. 4:3
20 [a] 2 Cor. 5:20; Philem. 9

6:12 wrestle. A term used of hand-to-hand combat. Wrestling features trickery and deception, like Satan and his hosts when they attack. Coping with deceptive temptation requires truth and righteousness. The 4 designations describe the different strata and rankings of those demons and the evil supernatural empire in which they operate. Satan's forces of darkness are highly structured for the most destructive purposes. Cf. Col. 2:15; 1 Pet. 3:22. **not...against flesh and blood.** See 2 Cor. 10:3-5. **spiritual *hosts* of wickedness.** This possibly refers to the most depraved abominations, including such things as extreme sexual perversions, occultism, and Satan worship. *See note on Col. 1:16.* **in the heavenly *places*.** As in 1:3; 3:10, this refers to the entire realm of spiritual beings.

6:13 Therefore take up the whole armor of God. Paul again emphasized the necessity of the Christian's appropriating God's full spiritual armor by obedience in taking it up, or putting it on (v. 11). The first 3 pieces of armor (girdle, breastplate, and shoes/boots, vv. 14,15) were worn continually on the battlefield; the last 3 (shield, helmet, and sword, vv. 16,17) were kept ready for use when actual fighting began. **the evil day.** Since the fall of man, every day has been evil, a condition that will persist until the Lord returns and establishes His own righteous kingdom on earth. **having done all, to stand.** Standing firm against the enemy without wavering or falling is the goal. *See notes on James 4:17; 1 Pet. 5:8,9.*

6:14 Stand therefore. For the third time (see vv. 11,13), the apostle calls Christians to take a firm position in the spiritual battle against Satan and his minions. Whether confronting Satan's efforts to distrust God, forsaking obedience, producing doctrinal confusion and falsehood, hindering service to God, bring division, serving God in the flesh, living hypocritically, being worldly, or in any other way reject biblical obedience, this armor is our defense. **girded...with truth.** The soldier wore a tunic of loose-fitting cloth. Since ancient combat was largely hand-to-hand, a loose tunic was a potential hindrance and danger. A belt was necessary to cinch up the loosely hanging material. Cf. Ex. 12:11; Luke 12:35; 1 Pet. 1:13. Girding up was a matter of pulling in the loose ends as preparation for battle. The belt that pulls all the spiritual loose ends in is "truth" or better, "truthfulness." The idea is of sincere commitment to fight and win without hypocrisy—self-discipline in devotion to victory. Everything that hinders is tucked away. Cf. 2 Tim. 2:4; Heb. 12:1. **the breastplate of righteousness.** The breastplate was usually a tough, sleeveless piece of leather or heavy material with animal horn or hoof pieces sewn on, covering the soldier's full torso, protecting his heart and other vital organs. Because righteousness, or holiness, is such a distinctive characteristic of God Himself, it is not hard to understand why that is the Christian's chief protection against Satan and his schemes. As believers faithfully live in obedience to and communion with Jesus Christ, His own righteousness produces in them the practical, daily righteousness that becomes their spiritual breastplate. Lack of holiness, on the other hand, leaves them vulnerable to the great enemy of their souls (cf. Is. 59:17; 2 Cor. 7:1; 1 Thess. 5:8).

6:15 shod...with...the gospel of peace. Roman soldiers wore boots with nails in them to grip the ground in combat. The gospel of peace pertains to the good news that, through Christ, believers are at peace with God and He is on their side (Rom. 5:6-10). It is that confidence of divine support which allows the believer to stand firm, knowing that since he is at peace with God, and God is his strength (see Rom. 8:31,37-39).

6:16 the shield of faith. This Gr. word usually refers to the large shield (2.5 x 4.5 ft.) that protected the entire body. The faith to which Paul refers is not the body of Christian doctrine (as the term is used in 4:13) but basic trust in God. The believer's continual trust in God's word and promise is "above all" absolutely necessary to protect him from temptations to every sort of sin. All sin comes when the victim falls to Satan's lies and promises of pleasure, rejecting the better choice of obedience and blessing. **fiery darts.** Temptations are likened to the flaming arrows shot by the enemy and quenched by the oil-treated leather shield (cf. Ps. 18:30; Prov. 30:5,6; 1 John 5:4).

6:17 the helmet of salvation. The helmet protected the head, always a major target in battle. Paul is speaking to those who are already saved, and is therefore not speaking here about attaining salvation. Rather, Satan seeks to destroy a believer's assurance of salvation with his weapons of doubt and discouragement. This is clear from Paul's reference to "the helmet of the hope of salvation" (Is. 59:17; *see note on 1 Thess. 5:8*). But although a Christian's feelings about his salvation may be seriously damaged by Satan-inspired doubt, his salvation itself is eternally protected and he need not fear its loss. Satan wants to curse the believer with doubts, but the Christian can be strong in God's promises of eternal salvation in Scripture (see John 6:37-39; 10:28,29; Rom. 5:10; 8:31-39; Phil. 1:6; 1 Pet. 1:3-5). Security is a fact; assurance is a feeling that comes to the obedient Christian (1 Pet. 1:3-10). **the sword of the Spirit.** As the sword was the soldier's only weapon, so God's Word is the only needed weapon, infinitely more powerful than any of Satan's. The Gr. term refers to a small weapon (6-18 in. long). It was used both defensively to fend off Satan's attacks, and offensively to help destroy the enemy's strategies. It is the truth of Scripture. *See notes on 2 Cor. 10:3-5; Heb. 4:12.*

6:18 This verse introduces the general character of a believer's prayer life: 1) "all prayer and supplication" focuses on the variety; 2) "always" focuses on the frequency (cf. Rom. 12:12; Phil. 4:6; 1 Thess. 5:17); 3) "in the Spirit" focuses on submission, as we line up with the will of God (cf. Rom. 8:26,27); 4) "being watchful" focuses on the manner (cf. Matt. 26:41; Mark 13:33); 5) "all perseverance" focuses on the persistence (cf. Luke 11:9; 18:7,8); and 6) "all saints" focuses on the objects (cf. 1 Sam. 12:23).

6:19,20 Paul does not ask for prayer for his personal well-being or physical comfort in the imprisonment from which he wrote, but for boldness and faithfulness to continue proclaiming the gospel to the unsaved no matter what the cost. **mystery.** *See notes on 3:4.* **ambassador.** *See notes on 2 Cor. 5:18-20.*

chains; that in it I may speak boldly, as I ought to speak.

A Gracious Greeting

21 But that you also may know my affairs *and* how I am doing, [b]Tychicus, a beloved brother and [c]faithful minister in the Lord, will make all things known to you; 22 [d]whom I have sent to you for this very purpose, that you may know our affairs, and *that* he may [e]comfort your hearts.

23 Peace to the brethren, and love with faith, from God the Father and the Lord Jesus Christ. 24 Grace *be* with all those who love our Lord Jesus Christ in sincerity. Amen.

21 [b] Acts 20:4; 2 Tim. 4:12; Titus 3:12 [c] 1 Cor. 4:1, 2
22 [d] Col. 4:8 [e] 2 Cor. 1:6

6:21,22 Tychicus. A convert from Asia Minor (modern Turkey) who was with the apostle during his first imprisonment in Rome, from where this epistle was written (see 3:1). He accompanied Paul in taking an offering to the church in Jerusalem (Acts 20:4-6) and was sent by him on several missions (2 Tim. 4:12; Titus 3:12).

6:23,24 This beautiful benediction sums up the major themes of this very personal letter, reminding readers of the peace (v. 15; 1:2; 2:14,15,17; 4:3), love (1:15; 4:2,15,16; 5:25,28,33), and faith (v. 16; 1:15; 2:8; 3:12,17; 4:5,13) from God and Jesus Christ.

The Epistle of Paul to the

PHILIPPIANS

Title

Philippians derives its name from the Greek city where the church to which it was addressed was located. Philippi was the first town in Macedonia where Paul established a church.

Author and Date

The unanimous testimony of the early church was that the Apostle Paul wrote Philippians. Nothing in the letter would have motivated a forger to write it.

The question of when Philippians was written cannot be separated from that of where it was written. The traditional view is that Philippians, along with the other Prison Epistles (Ephesians, Colossians, Philemon), was written during Paul's first imprisonment at Rome (ca. A.D. 60–62). The most natural understanding of the references to the "palace guard" (1:13) and the "saints…of Caesar's household" (4:22) is that Paul wrote from Rome, where the emperor lived. The similarities between the details of Paul's imprisonment given in Acts and in the Prison Epistles also argue that those epistles were written from Rome (e.g., Paul was guarded by soldiers, Acts 28:16; cf. 1:13,14; was permitted to receive visitors, Acts 28:30; cf. 4:18; and had the opportunity to preach the gospel, Acts 28:31; cf. 1:12-14; Eph. 6:18-20; Col. 4:2-4).

Some have held that Paul wrote the Prison Epistles during his two-year imprisonment at Caesarea (Acts 24:27). But Paul's opportunities to receive visitors and proclaim the gospel were severely limited during that imprisonment (cf. Acts 23:35). The Prison Epistles express Paul's hope for a favorable verdict (1:25; 2:24; cf. Philem. 22). In Caesarea, however, Paul's only hope for release was either to bribe Felix (Acts 24:26), or agree to stand trial at Jerusalem under Festus (Acts 25:9). In the Prison Epistles, Paul expected the decision in his case to be final (1:20-23; 2:17,23). That could not have been true at Caesarea, since Paul could and did appeal his case to the emperor.

Another alternative has been that Paul wrote the Prison Epistles from Ephesus. But at Ephesus, like Caesarea, no final decision could be made in his case because of his right to appeal to the emperor. Also, Luke was with Paul when he wrote Colossians (Col. 4:14), but he apparently was not with the apostle at Ephesus. Acts 19, which records Paul's stay in Ephesus, is not in one of the "we sections" of Acts (see Introduction to Acts: Author and Date). The most telling argument against Ephesus as the point of origin for the Prison Epistles, however, is that there is no evidence that Paul was ever imprisoned at Ephesus.

In light of the serious difficulties faced by both the Caesarean and Ephesian views, there is no reason to reject the traditional view that Paul wrote the Prison Epistles—including Philippians—from Rome.

Paul's belief that his case would soon be decided (2:23,24) points to Philippians being written toward the close of the apostle's two-year Roman imprisonment (ca. A.D. 61).

Background and Setting

Originally known as Krenides ("The Little Fountains") because of the numerous nearby springs, Philippi ("city of Philip") received its name from Philip II of Macedon (the father of Alexander the Great). Attracted by the nearby gold mines, Philip conquered the region in the fourth century B.C. In the second century B.C., Philippi became part of the Roman province of Macedonia.

The city existed in relative obscurity for the next two centuries until one of the most famous events in Roman history brought it recognition and expansion. In 42 B.C., the forces of Antony and Octavian defeated those of Brutus and Cassius at the Battle of Philippi, thus ending the Roman Republic and ushering in the Empire. After the battle, Philippi became a Roman colony (cf. Acts 16:12), and many veterans of the Roman army settled there. As a colony, Philippi had autonomy from the provincial government and the same rights granted to cities in Italy, including the use of Roman law, exemption from some taxes, and Roman citizenship for its residents (Acts 16:21). Being a colony was also the source of much civic pride for the Philippians, who used Latin as their official language, adopted Roman customs, and modeled their city government after that of Italian cities. Acts and Philippians both reflect Philippi's status as a Roman colony.

Paul's description of Christians as citizens of heaven (3:20) was appropriate, since the Philippians prided themselves on being citizens of Rome (cf. Acts 16:21). The Philippians may well have known some of the members of the palace guard (1:13) and Caesar's household (4:22).

The church at Philippi, the first one founded by Paul in Europe, dates from the apostle's second missionary journey (Acts 16:12-40). Philippi evidently had a very small Jewish population. Because there were not enough men to form a synagogue (the requirement was for 10 Jewish men who were heads of a household), some devout women met outside the city at a place of prayer (Acts 16:13) alongside the Gangites River. Paul preached the gospel to them and Lydia, a wealthy merchant dealing in expensive purple dyed goods (Acts 16:14), became a believer (16:14,15). It is likely that the Philippian church initially met in her spacious home.

Satanic opposition to the new church immediately arose in the person of a demon-possessed, fortune-telling slave girl (Acts 16:16,17). Not wanting even agreeable testimony from such an evil source, Paul cast the demon out of her (Acts 16:18). The apostle's act enraged the girl's masters, who could no longer sell her services as a fortune-teller (Acts 16:19). They hauled Paul and Silas before the city's magistrates (Acts 16:20) and inflamed the civic pride of the Philippians by claiming the two preachers were a threat to Roman customs (Acts 16:20,21). As a result, Paul and Silas were beaten and imprisoned (Acts 16:22-24).

The two preachers were miraculously released from prison that night by an earthquake, which unnerved the jailer and opened his heart and that of his household to the gospel (Acts 16:25-34). The next day the magistrates, panicking when they learned they had illegally beaten and imprisoned two Roman citizens, begged Paul and Silas to leave Philippi.

Paul apparently visited Philippi twice during his third missionary journey, once at the beginning (cf. 2 Cor. 8:1-5), and again near the end (Acts 20:6). About 4 or 5 years after his last visit to Philippi, while a prisoner at Rome, Paul received a delegation from the Philippian church. The Philippians had generously supported Paul in the past (4:15,16), and had also contributed abundantly for the needy at Jerusalem (2 Cor. 8:1-4). Now, hearing of Paul's imprisonment, they sent another contribution to him (4:10), and along with it Epaphroditus to minister to Paul's needs. Unfortunately Epaphroditus suffered a near-fatal illness (2:26,27), either while en route to Rome, or after he arrived. Accordingly, Paul decided to send Epaphroditus back to Philippi (2:25,26) and wrote the letter to the Philippians to send back with him.

Paul had several purposes in composing this epistle. First, he wanted to express in writing his thanks for the Philippians' gift (4:10-18). Second, he wanted the Philippians to know why he decided to return Epaphroditus to them, so they would not think his service to Paul had been unsatisfactory (2:25,26). Third, he wanted to inform them about his circumstances at Rome (1:12-26). Fourth, he wrote to exhort them to unity (2:1,2; 4:2). Finally, he wrote to warn them against false teachers (3:1–4:1).

Historical and Theological Themes

Since it is primarily a practical letter, Philippians contains little historical material (there are no OT quotes), apart from the momentous treatment of Paul's spiritual autobiography (3:4-7). There is, likewise, little direct theological instruction, also with one momentous exception. The magnificent passage describing Christ's humiliation and exaltation (2:5-11) contains some of the most profound and crucial teaching on the Lord Jesus Christ in all the Bible. The major theme of pursuing Christlikeness, as the most defining element of spiritual growth and the one passion of Paul in his own life, is presented in 3:12-14. In spite of Paul's imprisonment, the dominant tone of the letter is joyful (1:4,18,25,26; 2:2,16-18,28; 3:1,3; 4:1,4,10).

Interpretive Challenges

The major difficulty connected with Philippians is determining where it was written (see Author and Date). The text itself presents only one significant interpretive challenge: the identity of the "enemies of the cross" (*see notes on 3:18,19*).

Outline

I. Paul's Greeting (1:1-11)

II. Paul's Circumstances (1:12-26)

III. Paul's Exhortations (1:27–2:18)

- A. To Stand Firm Amid Persecution (1:27-30)
- B. To Be United by Humility (2:1-4)
- C. To Remember the Example of Christ (2:5-11)
- D. To Be Light in a Dark World (2:12-18)

IV. Paul's Companions (2:19-30)

- A. Timothy (2:19-24)
- B. Epaphroditus (2:25-30)

V. Paul's Warnings (3:1–4:1)

- A. Against Legalism (3:1-16)
- B. Against Lawlessness (3:17–4:1)

VI. Paul's Admonition (4:2-9)

VII. Paul's Thankfulness (4:10-20)

VIII. Paul's Farewell (4:21-23)

Greeting

1 Paul and Timothy, bondservants of Jesus Christ,

To all the saints in Christ Jesus who are
in Philippi, with the [1]bishops and [a]dea-
cons:

2 Grace to you and peace from God our
Father and the Lord Jesus Christ.

Thankfulness and Prayer

3 [b]I thank my God upon every remembrance of you, 4 always in [c]every prayer of
mine making request for you all with joy,
5 [d]for your fellowship in the gospel from
the first day until now, 6 being confident of
this very thing, that He who has begun [e]a
good work in you will complete *it* until the
day of Jesus Christ; 7 just as it is right for
me to think this of you all, because I have
you in my heart, inasmuch as both in my
chains and in the defense and confirmation
of the gospel, you all are partakers with me
of grace. 8 For God is my witness, how
greatly I long for you all with the affection
of Jesus Christ.

9 And this I pray, that your love may
abound still more and more in knowledge
and all discernment, 10 that you may approve the things that are excellent, that you
may be sincere and without offense till the
day of Christ, 11 being filled with the fruits
of righteousness [f]which *are* by Jesus Christ,
[g]to the glory and praise of God.

CHAPTER 1

1 [a] [1 Tim. 3:8–13] [1] Lit. *overseers*
3 [b] 1 Cor. 1:4
4 [c] Eph. 1:16; 1 Thess. 1:2
5 [d] [Rom. 12:13]
6 [e] [John 6:29]
11 [f] [Eph. 2:10]; Col. 1:6 [g] John 15:8

1:1,2 First century letters normally began by identifying the sender and the recipient with a basic greeting. One notable variation here is that Paul includes Timothy's name because Timothy was an important gospel co-worker in and around Philippi and a trusted, corroborating witness to the truths Paul expounded.

1:1 Paul. See Introduction to Romans: Author and Date; *see note on Acts 9:1.* Paul wrote this letter from a Roman prison (see Introduction: Author and Date). **Timothy.** Timothy, Paul's beloved son in the faith (see Introduction to 1 Timothy: Author and Date; Acts 16:1-3), was not the co-author of the letter, but possibly the one to whom Paul dictated it. Regardless, Paul had good reason for including Timothy's name (*see note on vv. 1,2*). **bondservants.** This denotes a willing slave who was happily and loyally linked to his master (*see note on Rom. 1:1*; cf. James 1:1; 2 Pet. 1:1; Jude 1). **saints.** *See note on 1 Cor. 1:2.* These were believers in the church at Philippi, including those who led the assembly. **in Christ Jesus.** This describes the Philippian believers' union with Christ in His death and resurrection (*see notes on Rom. 6:2-9; Gal. 2:20*), which was the reason they could be called "saints." **Philippi.** See Introduction: Background and Setting. **bishops.** Lit. "overseers"; *see note on 1 Tim. 3:1.* This is a term used to emphasize the leadership responsibilities of those who are elders, who are also called pastors. All 3 terms are used to describe the same men in Acts 20:28 (*see note there*). **deacons.** Lit. "those who serve"; *see note on 1 Tim. 3:8.*

1:2 Grace...peace. Paul's standard greeting (*see note on Rom. 1:7*) reminded the believers of their relationship to God.

1:3 I thank my God. Paul's letters usually included such commendation (*see note on Gal. 1:3-5*).

1:4 in every prayer...with joy. The Gr. word for "prayer" denotes a petition for, or a request made on behalf of, someone else. It was a delight for him to intercede for fellow believers.

1:5 fellowship. This can also be translated "participation" or "partnership." Cf. 2 Cor. 8:4. **from the first day.** These believers eagerly assisted Paul in evangelizing Philippi from the beginning of the church there (Acts 16:12-40).

1:6 He...will complete *it*. The Gr. verb translated "has begun" is used only here and in Gal. 3:3—both times in reference to salvation itself. When God begins a work of salvation in a person, He finishes and perfects that work. Thus the verb "will complete" points to the eternal security of the Christian (*see notes on John 6:39,40,44; Rom. 5:10; 8:29-39; Eph. 1:13,14; Heb. 7:25; 12:2*). **day of Jesus Christ.** This phrase is not to be confused with the "Day of the Lord" (see Introduction to Joel: Historical and Theological Themes), which describes final divine judgment and wrath (cf. Is. 13:9; Joel 1:15; 2:11; 1 Thess. 5:2; 2 Pet. 3:10). "Day of Jesus Christ" is also called the "Day of Christ" (v. 10; 2:16) and the "Day of our Lord Jesus Christ" (1 Cor. 1:8), which looks to the final salvation, reward, and glorification of believers. Cf. 1 Cor. 3:10-15; 4:5; 2 Cor. 5:9,10.

1:7 heart. A common biblical word used to describe the center of thought and feeling (cf. Prov. 4:23). **defense and confirmation.** Two judicial terms referring either to the first phase of Paul's trial in Rome in which he defended his gospel ministry or in a general sense to his continual defense of the faith, which was the heart of his ministry. **partakers with me of grace.** *See notes on v. 5.* During his imprisonment, the Philippians sent Paul money and Epaphroditus' services to support the apostle, thus sharing in God's gracious blessing on his ministry (cf. 2:30).

1:8 affection. The word lit. refers to the internal organs, which are the part of the body that reacts to intense emotion. It became the strongest Gr. word to express compassionate love—a love that involves one's entire being.

1:9 in knowledge. This is from the Gr. word that describes genuine, full, or advanced knowledge. Biblical love is not an empty sentimentalism but is anchored deeply in the truth of Scripture and regulated by it (cf. Eph. 5:2,3; 1 Pet. 1:22). **discernment.** The Eng. word "aesthetic" comes from this Gr. word, which speaks of moral perception, insight, and the practical application of knowledge. Love is not blind, but perceptive, and it carefully scrutinizes to distinguish between right and wrong. *See notes on 1 Thess. 5:21,22.*

1:10 approve the...excellent. "Approve" in classical Gr. described the assaying of metals or the testing of money for authenticity (cf. Luke 12:56; 14:19). "Excellent" means "to differ." Believers need the ability to distinguish those things that are truly important so they can establish the right priorities. **sincere and without offense.** "Sincere" means "genuine," and may have originally meant "tested by sunlight." In the ancient world, dishonest pottery dealers filled cracks in their inferior products with wax before glazing and painting them, making worthless pots difficult to distinguish from expensive ones. The only way to avoid being defrauded was to hold the pot to the sun, making the wax-filled cracks obvious. Dealers marked their fine pottery that could withstand "sun testing" as *sine cera*—"without wax." "Without offense" can be translated "blameless," referring to relational integrity. Christians are to live lives of true integrity that do not cause others to sin (*see notes on Rom. 12:9; 1 Cor. 10:31,32; 2 Cor. 1:12*; cf. Rom. 14; 1 Cor. 8). **the day of Christ.** *See note on v. 6.*

1:11 fruits of righteousness. This is better translated, "the fruit righteousness produces" (*see note on Rom. 1:13*; cf. Prov. 11:30; Amos 6:12; James 3:17,18). **which *are* by Jesus Christ.** See John 15:1-5; Eph. 2:10. This speaks of the salvation transformation provided by our Lord and His ongoing work of power through His Spirit in us. **to the glory and praise of God.** See John 15:8; Eph. 1:12-14; 3:20,21. The ultimate end of all Paul's prayers was that God be glorified.

Christ Is Preached

12 But I want you to know, brethren, that
the things *which happened* to me have actually turned out for the furtherance of the
gospel, 13 so that it has become evident [h]to
the whole [2]palace guard, and to all the
rest, that my chains are in Christ; 14 and
most of the brethren in the Lord, having
become confident by my chains, are much
more bold to speak the word without fear.
15 Some indeed preach Christ even from
envy and strife, and some also from goodwill: 16 [3]The former preach Christ from
selfish ambition, not sincerely, supposing
to add affliction to my chains; 17 but the latter out of love, knowing that I am appointed for the defense of the gospel. 18 What
then? Only *that* in every way, whether in
pretense or in truth, Christ is preached; and
in this I rejoice, yes, and will rejoice.

To Live Is Christ

19 For I know that [i]this will turn out for
my deliverance through your prayer and
the supply of the Spirit of Jesus Christ, 20 according to my earnest expectation and hope
that in nothing I shall be ashamed, but [j]with
all boldness, as always, so now also Christ
will be magnified in my body, whether by
life [k]or by death. 21 For to me, to live *is*
Christ, and to die *is* gain. 22 But if *I* live on in
the flesh, this *will mean* fruit from *my* labor;
yet what I shall choose I [4]cannot tell. 23 [5]For
I am hard-pressed between the two, having
a [l]desire to depart and be with Christ, *which*
is [m]far better. 24 Nevertheless to remain in
the flesh *is* more needful for you. 25 And
being confident of this, I know that I shall re-

13 [h] Phil. 4:22 [2] Or *Praetorium*
16 [3] NU reverses vv. 16 and 17.
19 [i] Job 13:16, LXX
20 [j] Eph. 6:19, 20 [k] [Rom. 14:8]
22 [4] *do not know*
23 [l] [2 Cor. 5:2, 8]; 2 Tim. 4:6 [m] [Ps. 16:11] [5] NU, M *But*

1:12 things *which happened* to me. Paul's difficult circumstances, namely, his journey to Rome and imprisonment there (see Introduction: Background and Setting; Acts 21–28). **for the furtherance.** Better translated, "for the progress," which refers to the forward movement of something—often of armies—in spite of obstacles, dangers, and distractions. Paul's imprisonment proved to be no hindrance to spreading the message of salvation (cf. Acts 28:30,31). Actually, it created new opportunities (*see note on 4:22*).

1:13 evident...chains are in Christ. People around him recognized that Paul was no criminal, but had become a prisoner because of preaching Jesus Christ and the gospel (cf. Eph. 6:20). **whole palace guard.** The Gr. word for "palace," often simply used in its transliterated form "praetorion," can denote either a special building (e.g., a commander's headquarters, the emperor's palace) or the group of men in the Imperial guard. Because Paul was in a private house in Rome, "palace guard" probably refers to the members of the Imperial guard who guarded Paul day and night. Cf. Acts 28:16. **all the rest.** Everyone else in the city of Rome who met and heard him (cf. Acts 28:23,24,30,31).

1:14 most of the brethren. With the exception of those detractors identified in vv. 15,16, who were attacking Paul. **much more bold to speak.** Paul's example of powerful witness to the gospel as a prisoner demonstrated God's faithfulness to His persecuted children and that their imprisonment would not halt the progress of the gospel. This encouraged others to be bold and not fear imprisonment.

1:15 from envy and strife. The attitude of Paul's detractors, who really did preach the gospel but were jealous of his apostolic power and authority, his success and immense giftedness. "Strife" connotes contention, rivalry, and conflict, which resulted when Paul's critics began discrediting him. **from goodwill.** "Goodwill" speaks of satisfaction and contentment, the attitude that Paul's supporters had for him personally and for his ministry.

1:16 selfish ambition. This describes those who were interested only in self-advancement, or who ruthlessly sought to get ahead at any cost. Paul's detractors used his incarceration as an opportunity to promote their own prestige by accusing Paul of being so sinful the Lord had chastened him by imprisonment. **not sincerely.** *See note on v. 10.* Paul's preacher critics did not have pure motives.

1:17 the latter out of love. Paul's supporters were motivated by genuine affection for him and confidence in his virtue (cf. 1 Cor. 13:1,2). **appointed.** The Gr. word describes a soldier's being placed on duty. Paul was in prison because he was destined to be there by God's will, so as to be in a strategic position to proclaim the gospel. **defense of the gospel.** *See note on v. 7.*

1:18 I rejoice...will rejoice. Paul's joy was not tied to his circumstances or his critics (cf. Ps. 4:7,8; Rom. 12:12; 2 Cor. 6:10). He was glad when the gospel was proclaimed with authority, no matter who received credit. He endured the unjust accusations without bitterness at his accusers. Rather, he rejoiced that they preached Christ, even in a pretense of godliness.

1:19 my deliverance. "Deliverance" is from the basic Gr. term for salvation. But it can also be rendered "well-being" or "escape," which presents 4 possible interpretations: 1) it refers to Paul's ultimate salvation; 2) it alludes to his deliverance from threatened execution; 3) he would finally be vindicated by the emperor's ruling; or 4) Paul is talking about his eventual release from prison. Whatever Paul's precise meaning, he was certain he would be freed from his temporary distress (Job 13:16; cf. Job 19:26; Pss. 22:4,5,8; 31:1; 33:18,19; 34:7; 41:1). **Spirit of Jesus Christ.** The Holy Spirit (Rom. 8:9; Gal. 4:6). Paul had supreme confidence in the Spirit (cf. Zech. 4:6; John 14:16; Rom. 8:26; Eph. 3:20).

1:20 earnest expectation. This Gr. word indicates keen anticipation of the future, as when someone stretches his neck to see what lies ahead. Paul was very confident and excited about Christ's promise (see Matt. 10:32). **nothing...ashamed.** See Is. 49:23; Rom. 9:33; cf. Pss. 25:2,3; 40:15,16; 119:80; Is. 1:27-29; 45:14-17; Jer. 12:13; Zeph. 3:11.

1:21 to me, to live *is* Christ. For Paul, life is summed up in Jesus Christ; Christ was his reason for being. *See notes on 3:12-14.* **to die *is* gain.** Death would relieve him of earthly burdens and let him focus totally on glorifying God (*see notes on vv. 23,24;* cf. Acts 21:13).

1:22 the flesh. Cf. v. 24. Here this word refers not to one's fallen humanness (as in Rom. 7:5,18; 8:1), but simply to physical life (as in 2 Cor. 10:3; Gal. 2:20). **fruit.** *See notes on Rom. 1:13.* Paul knew that the only reason to remain in this world was to bring souls to Christ and build up believers to do the same. *See note on 2 Cor. 4:15.*

1:23 hard-pressed. The Gr. word pictures a traveler on a narrow path, a rock wall on either side allowing him to go only straight ahead. **depart and be with Christ.** Paul knew if he died he would have complete, conscious, intimate, unhindered fellowship with his Lord (*see notes on 2 Cor. 5:1,8; 2 Tim. 4:6-8*). **far better.** Lit. "very much better," the highest superlative.

1:24 more needful for you. Paul yielded his personal desire to be with his Lord for the necessity of the building of the church (see 2:3,4).

1:25 confident...I shall remain. Paul's conviction—not a supernatural revelation—that their need would determine that he stay on

main and continue with you all for your
progress and joy of faith, 26 that [n]your rejoicing for me may be more abundant in Jesus Christ by my coming to you again.

Striving and Suffering for Christ

27 Only [o]let your conduct be worthy of
the gospel of Christ, so that whether I come
and see you or am absent, I may hear of
your affairs, that you stand fast in one spirit,
[p]with one mind [q]striving together for the
faith of the gospel, 28 and not in any way terrified by your adversaries, which is to them
a proof of perdition, but [6]to you of salvation,
and that from God. 29 For to you [r]it has been
granted on behalf of Christ, [s]not only to believe in Him, but also to [t]suffer for His sake,
30 [u]having the same conflict [v]which you saw
in me and now hear *is* in me.

26 [n] 2 Cor. 1:14
27 [o] Eph. 4:1; 1 Thess. 2:12 [p] 1 Cor. 1:10; Eph. 4:3 [q] Jude 3
28 [6] NU *of your salvation*
29 [r] [Matt. 5:11, 12; Acts 5:41; Rom. 5:3] [s] Eph. 2:8 [t] [2 Tim. 3:12]
30 [u] Col. 1:29; 2:1; 1 Thess. 2:2; 1 Tim. 6:12; 2 Tim. 4:7; Heb. 10:32; 12:1 [v] Acts 16:19–40; Phil. 1:13; 1 Thess. 2:2

CHAPTER 2

1 [a] Col. 3:12 [1] Or *encouragement*
2 [b] John 3:29 [c] Rom. 12:16 [d] Phil. 4:2
3 [e] Gal. 5:26; James 3:14 [f] Rom. 12:10; Eph. 5:21

Unity Through Humility

2 Therefore if *there is* any [1]consolation in
Christ, if any comfort of love, if any fellowship of the Spirit, if any [a]affection and
mercy, 2 [b]fulfill my joy [c]by being like-
minded, having the same love, *being* of
[d]one accord, of one mind. 3 [e]*Let* nothing *be*
done through selfish ambition or conceit,
but [f]in lowliness of mind let each esteem
others better than himself. 4 [g]Let each of
you look out not only for his own interests,
but also for the interests of [h]others.

The Humbled and Exalted Christ

5 [i]Let this mind be in you which was
also in Christ Jesus, 6 who, [j]being in the
form of God, did not consider it [2]robbery

4 [g] 1 Cor. 13:5 [h] Rom. 15:1, 2 **5** [i] [Matt. 11:29]; Rom. 15:3
6 [j] 2 Cor. 4:4 [2] Or *something to be held onto to be equal*

earth longer. **progress…of faith.** "Progress" pictures trail blazing so that an army can advance (*see note on v. 12*). Paul wanted to cut a new path for the Philippians to follow to victory; the increasing of their faith would result in the increasing of their joy.

1:26 rejoicing for me…in Jesus Christ. The Gr. word order is "that your rejoicing may be more abundant in Jesus Christ for me." The point is, as Paul lived on fruitfully, their joy and confidence would overflow because of Christ's working in him, not because of anything he himself did by his own ability.

1:27 worthy of the gospel. Believers are to have integrity, i.e., to live consistent with what they believe, teach, and preach. Cf. Eph. 4:1; Col. 1:10; 1 Thess. 2:11,12; 4:1; Titus 2:10; 2 Pet. 3:11,14. **one spirit…one mind.** This introduces Paul's theme of unity that continues through 2:4. His call for genuine unity of heart and mind is based on 1) the necessity of oneness to win the spiritual battle for the faith (vv. 28-30); 2) the love of others in the fellowship (2:1,2); 3) genuine humility and self-sacrifice (2:3,4); and 4) the example of Jesus Christ who proved that sacrifice produces eternal glory (2:5-11). **striving together.** Lit. "to struggle along with someone." Paul changed the metaphor from that of a soldier standing at his post ("stand fast") to one of a team struggling for victory against a common foe. **the faith of the gospel.** The Christian faith as revealed by God and recorded in the Scripture (Jude 3; cf. Rom. 1:1; Gal. 1:7).

1:28 proof of perdition. When believers willingly suffer without being "terrified," it is a sign that God's enemies will be destroyed and eternally lost (*see notes on 2 Thess. 1:4-8*).

1:29 granted…to suffer. *See notes on 3:10; 1 Pet. 2:20,21*; cf. Matt. 5:10-12; Acts 5:41. The Gr. verb translated "granted" is from the noun for grace. Believers' suffering is a gift of grace which brings power (2 Cor. 7:9,10; 1 Pet. 5:10) and eternal reward (1 Pet. 4:13).

1:30 same conflict. The same kind of suffering Paul had experienced (vv. 12-14; Acts 16:22-24). **you saw.** This refers to what the Philippians witnessed when Paul and Silas were imprisoned at Philippi (Acts 16:19-40).

2:1 consolation in Christ. "Consolation" can also be translated "encouragement," and is from the Gr. word that means "to come alongside and help, counsel, exhort" (*see notes on John 14:26; Rom. 12:1*), which our beloved Lord does for His own. **comfort of love.** The Gr. word translated "comfort" portrays the Lord coming close and whispering words of gentle cheer or tender counsel in a believer's ear. **fellowship of the Spirit.** "Fellowship" refers to the partnership, of common eternal life, provided by the indwelling Holy Spirit (1 Cor. 3:16; 12:13; 2 Cor. 13:14; 1 John 1:4-6). **affection and mercy.** God has extended His deep affection (*see note on 1:8*) and compassion to every believer (cf. Rom. 12:1; 2 Cor. 1:3; Col. 3:12) and that reality should result in unity.

2:2 fulfill my joy. This can also be translated "make my joy complete." Paul's joy was tied to concern for the unity of believers (cf. Heb. 13:17). **like-minded.** Cf. 3:15,16; 4:2; 1 Pet. 3:8. The Gr. word means "think the same way." This exhortation is not optional or obscure, but is repeated throughout the NT (cf. Rom. 15:5; 1 Cor. 1:10; 2 Cor. 13:11-13). **same love.** Believers are to love others in the body of Christ equally—not because they are all equally attractive, but by showing the same kind of sacrificial, loving service to all that was shown to them by Christ (John 15:13; Rom. 12:10; 1 John 3:17; cf. John 3:16). **one accord.** This may also be translated "united in spirit" and perhaps is a term specially coined by Paul. It lit. means "one-souled" and describes people who are knit together in harmony, having the same desires, passions, and ambitions. **one mind.** "Intent on one purpose" is an alternative translation.

2:3 selfish ambition. This Gr. word, which is sometimes rendered "strife" because it refers to factionalism, rivalry, and partisanship (*see note on Gal. 5:20*), speaks of the pride that prompts people to push for their own way. **conceit.** Lit. "empty glory," and often translated "empty conceit." This word refers to the pursuit of personal glory, which is the motivation for selfish ambition. **lowliness of mind.** This translates a Gr. word that Paul and other NT writers apparently coined. It was a term of derision, with the idea of being low, shabby, and humble (cf. 1 Cor. 15:9; 1 Tim. 1:15). **esteem others better than himself.** The basic definition of true humility (cf. Rom. 12:10; Gal. 5:13; Eph. 5:21; 1 Pet. 5:5).

2:5 Christ is the ultimate example of selfless humility (cf. Matt. 11:29; John 13:12-17).

2:6-11 This is the classic Christological passage in the NT, dealing with the Incarnation. It was probably sung as a hymn in the early church (*see note on Col. 3:16*).

2:6 being in the form of God. Paul affirms that Jesus eternally has been God. The usual Gr. word for "being" is not used here. Instead, Paul chose another term that stresses the essence of a person's nature—his continuous state or condition. Paul also could have chosen one of two Gr. words for "form," but he chose the one that specifically denotes the essential, unchanging character of something—what it is in and of itself. The fundamental doctrine of Christ's deity has always encompassed these crucial characteristics (cf. John 1:1,3,4,14; 8:58; Col. 1:15-17; Heb. 1:3). **not…robbery.** The Gr. word is translated "robbery" here because it originally meant "a thing seized by robbery." It eventually came to mean anything clutched, embraced, or

to be equal with God, 7 [k]but [3]made Himself of no reputation, taking the form [l]of a
bondservant, *and* [m]coming in the likeness
of men. 8 And being found in appearance
as a man, He humbled Himself and [n]be-
came [o]obedient to *the point of* death, even
the death of the cross. 9 [p]Therefore God
also [q]has highly exalted Him and [r]given
Him the name which is above every name,
10 [s]that at the name of Jesus every knee
should bow, of those in heaven, and of
those on earth, and of those under the
earth, 11 and [t]*that* every tongue should
confess that Jesus Christ *is* Lord, to the
glory of God the Father.

Light Bearers

12 Therefore, my beloved, [u]as you have
always obeyed, not as in my presence only,
but now much more in my absence, [v]work
out your own salvation with [w]fear and
trembling; 13 for [x]it is God who works in
you both to will and to do [y]for *His* good
pleasure.

7 [k] Ps. 22:6 [l] Is. 42:1 [m] [John 1:14]; Rom. 8:3; Gal. 4:4; [Heb. 2:17] [3] *emptied Himself* of His privileges **8** [n] Ps. 40:6–8; Matt. 26:39; John 10:18; [Rom. 5:19] [o] Heb. 5:8 **9** [p] [Matt. 28:18]; Heb. 2:9 [q] Ps. 68:18; 110:1; Is. 52:13; Acts 2:33 [r] Is. 9:6; Luke 1:32; Eph. 1:21 **10** [s] Is. 45:23; Rom. 14:11; Rev. 5:13 **11** [t] John 13:13; [Rom. 10:9; 14:9] **12** [u] Phil. 1:5, 6; 4:15 [v] John 6:27, 29; 2 Pet. 1:10 [w] Eph. 6:5 **13** [x] Rom. 12:3; 1 Cor. 12:6; 15:10; 2 Cor. 3:5; Heb. 13:20, 21 [y] Eph. 1:5

prized, and thus is sometimes translated "grasped" or "held onto." Though Christ had all the rights, privileges, and honors of deity—which He was worthy of and could never be disqualified from—His attitude was not to cling to those things or His position but to be willing to give them up for a season. *See notes on John 17:1-5.* **equal with God.** The Gr. word for "equal" defines things that are exactly the same in size, quantity, quality, character, and number. In every sense, Jesus is equal to God and constantly claimed to be so during His earthly ministry (cf. John 5:18; 10:33,38; 14:9; 20:28; Heb. 1:1-3).

2:7 made Himself of no reputation. This is more clearly translated "emptied Himself." From this Gr. word comes the theological word "kenosis"; i.e., the doctrine of Christ's self-emptying in His incarnation. This was a self-renunciation, not an emptying Himself of deity nor an exchange of deity for humanity (*see notes on v. 6*). Jesus did, however, renounce or set aside His privileges in several areas: 1) heavenly glory—while on earth He gave up the glory of a face-to-face relationship with God and the continuous outward display and personal enjoyment of that glory (cf. John 17:5); 2) independent authority—during His incarnation Christ completely submitted Himself to the will of His Father (*see note on v. 8*; cf. Matt. 26:39; John 5:30; Heb. 5:8); 3) divine prerogatives—He set aside the voluntary display of His divine attributes and submitted Himself to the Spirit's direction (cf. Matt. 24:36; John 1:45-49); 4) eternal riches—while on earth Christ was poor and owned very little (cf. 2 Cor. 8:9); and 5) a favorable relationship with God—He felt the Father's wrath for human sin while on the cross (cf. Matt. 27:46; *see note on 2 Cor. 5:21*). **form of a bondservant.** Again, Paul uses the Gr. word "form," which indicates exact essence (*see note on v. 6*). As a true servant (*see note on 1:1*), Jesus submissively did the will of His Father (cf. Is. 52:13,14). **the likeness of men.** Christ became more than God in a human body, but He took on all the essential attributes of humanity (Luke 2:52; Gal. 4:4; Col. 1:22), even to the extent that He identified with basic human needs and weaknesses (cf. Heb. 2:14,17; 4:15). He became the God-Man: fully God and fully man.

2:8 in appearance as a man. This is not simply a repetition of the last phrase in v. 7, but a shift from the heavenly focus to an earthly one. Christ's humanity is described from the viewpoint of those who saw Him. Paul is implying that although He outwardly looked like a man, there was much more to Him (His deity) than many people recognized naturally (cf. John 6:42; 8:48). **He humbled Himself.** After the humbling of incarnation, Jesus further humbled Himself in that He did not demand normal human rights, but subjected Himself to persecution and suffering at the hands of unbelievers (cf. Is. 53:7; Matt. 26:62-64; Mark 14:60,61; 1 Pet. 2:23). **obedient...death.** Beyond even persecution, Jesus went to the lowest point or furthest extent in His humiliation in dying as a criminal, following God's plan for Him (cf. Matt. 26:39; Acts 2:23). **the cross.** *See notes on Matt. 27:29-50.* Even further humiliation was His because Jesus' death was not by ordinary means, but was accomplished by crucifixion—the cruelest, most excruciating, most degrading form of death ever devised. The Jews hated this manner of execution (Deut. 21:23; *see note on Gal. 3:13*).

2:9 Therefore God. Christ's humiliation (vv. 5-8) and exaltation by God (vv. 9-11) are causally and inseparably linked. **highly exalted Him.** Christ's exaltation was fourfold. The early sermons of the apostles affirm His resurrection and coronation (His position at the right hand of God), and allude to His intercession for believers (Acts 2:32,33; 5:30,31; cf. Eph. 1:20,21; Heb. 4:15; 7:25,26). Hebrews 4:14 refers to the final element, His ascension. The exaltation did not concern Christ's nature or eternal place within the Trinity, but His new identity as the God-Man (cf. John 5:22; Rom. 1:4; 14:9; 1 Cor. 15:24,25). In addition to receiving back His glory (John 17:5), Christ's new status as the God-Man meant God gave Him privileges He did not have prior to the Incarnation. If He had not lived among men, He could not have identified with them as the interceding High-Priest. Had He not died on the cross, He could not have been elevated from that lowest degree back to heaven as the substitute for sin. **name...above every name.** Christ's new name which further describes His essential nature and places Him above and beyond all comparison is "Lord." This name is the NT synonym for OT descriptions of God as sovereign ruler. Both before (Is. 45:21-23; Mark 15:2; Luke 2:11; John 13:13; 18:37; 20:28) and after (Acts 2:36; 10:36; Rom. 14:9-11; 1 Cor. 8:6; 15:57; Rev. 17:14; 19:16) the exaltation, Scripture affirms that this was Jesus' rightful title as the God-Man.

2:10,11 bow...confess. The entire intelligent universe is called to worship Jesus Christ as Lord (cf. Ps. 2). This mandate includes the angels in heaven (Rev. 4:2-9), the spirits of the redeemed (Rev. 4:10,11), obedient believers on earth (Rom. 10:9), the disobedient rebels on earth (2 Thess. 1:7-9), demons and lost humanity in hell (1 Pet. 3:18-22). The Gr. word for "confess" means "to acknowledge," "affirm," or "agree" which is what everyone will eventually do in response to Christ's lordship, willingly and blessedly or unwillingly and painfully.

2:10 at the name of Jesus. "Jesus" was the name bestowed at His birth (Matt. 1:21), not His new name. The name for Jesus given in the fullest sense after His exaltation, was "Lord" (*see note on v. 11*).

2:11 Lord. *See note on v. 9.* "Lord" primarily refers to the right to rule, and in the NT it denotes mastery over or ownership of people and property. When applied to Jesus, it certainly implies His deity, but it mainly refers to sovereign authority. **glory of God the Father.** The purpose of Christ's exaltation (cf. Matt. 17:5; John 5:23; 13:31,32; 1 Cor. 15:28).

2:12 obeyed. Their faithful response to the divine commands Paul had taught them (cf. Rom. 1:5; 15:18; 2 Cor. 10:5,6). **work out your own salvation.** The Gr. verb rendered "work out" means "to continually work to bring something to fulfillment or completion." It cannot refer to salvation by works (cf. Rom. 3:21-24; Eph. 2:8,9), but it does refer to the believer's responsibility for active pursuit of obedience in the process of sanctification (*see notes on 3:13,14; Rom. 6:19*; cf. 1 Cor. 9:24-27; 15:58; 2 Cor. 7:1; Gal. 6:7-9; Eph. 4:1; Col. 3:1-17; Heb. 6:10,11; 12:1,2; 2 Pet. 1:5-11). **fear and trembling.** The attitude with which Christians are to pursue their sanctification. It involves a healthy fear of offending God and a righteous awe and respect for Him (cf. Prov. 1:7; 9:10; Is. 66:1,2).

2:13 God who works in you. Although the believer is responsi-

14 Do all things [z]without [4]complaining
and [a]disputing,[5] 15 that you may become
blameless and [6]harmless, children of God
without fault in the midst of a crooked and
perverse generation, among whom you
shine as [b]lights in the world, 16 holding
fast the word of life, so that [c]I may rejoice
in the day of Christ that [d]I have not run in
vain or labored in [e]vain.
17 Yes, and if [f]I am being poured out *as a*
drink offering on the sacrifice [g]and service
of your faith, [h]I am glad and rejoice with
you all. 18 For the same reason you also be
glad and rejoice with me.

Timothy Commended

19 But I trust in the Lord Jesus to send
[i]Timothy to you shortly, that I also may be
encouraged when I know your [7]state.
20 For I have no one [j]like-minded, who
will sincerely care for your state. 21 For all
seek their own, not the things which are
of Christ Jesus. 22 But you know his
proven character, [k]that as a son with *his*
father he served with me in the gospel.
23 Therefore I hope to send him at once, as
soon as I see how it goes with me. 24 But I
trust in the Lord that I myself shall also
come shortly.

Epaphroditus Praised

25 Yet I considered it necessary to send to
you [l]Epaphroditus, my brother, fellow

14 [z] 1 Cor. 10:10; 1 Pet. 4:9 [a] Rom. 14:1 [4] *grumbling* [5] *arguing*
15 [b] Matt. 5:15, 16 [6] *innocent*
16 [c] 2 Cor. 1:14 [d] Gal. 2:2 [e] Is. 49:4; Gal. 4:11; 1 Thess. 3:5
17 [f] 2 Cor. 12:15; 2 Tim. 4:6 [g] Num. 28:6, 7; Rom. 15:16 [h] 2 Cor. 7:4
19 [i] Rom. 16:21 [7] *condition*
20 [j] 1 Cor. 16:10; 2 Tim. 3:10
22 [k] 1 Cor. 4:17
25 [l] Phil. 4:18

ble to work (v. 12), the Lord actually produces the good works and spiritual fruit in the lives of believers (John 15:5; 1 Cor. 12:6). This is accomplished because He works through us by His indwelling Spirit (Acts 1:8: 1 Cor. 3:16,17; 6:19,20; cf. Gal. 3:3). **to will and to do.** God energizes both the believer's desires and his actions. The Gr. word for "will" indicates that He is not focusing on mere desires or whimsical emotions but on the studied intent to fulfill a planned purpose. God's power makes His church willing to live godly lives (cf. Ps. 110:3). **good pleasure.** God wants Christians to do what satisfies Him. Cf. Eph. 1:5,9; 2 Thess. 1:11.

2:14 without complaining and disputing. The Gr. word for "complaining" is a term that actually sounds like what it means. Its pronunciation is much like muttering or grumbling in a low tone of voice. It is an emotional rejection of God's providence, will, and circumstances for one's life. The word for "disputing" is more intellectual and here means "questionings," or "criticisms" directed negatively toward God.

2:15 that you may become. This introduces the reasons believers should have the right attitude in pursuing godliness. "Become" indicates a process—they are to be growing toward something they do not yet fully possess as children of God (cf. Eph. 5:1; Titus 2:1). **blameless and harmless.** "Blameless" describes a life that cannot be criticized because of sin or evil. "Harmless," which can also be translated "innocent," describes a life that is pure, unmixed, and unadulterated with sin, much like high quality metal without any alloy (cf. Matt. 10:16; Rom. 16:19; 2 Cor. 11:3; Eph. 5:27). **without fault.** Can also be translated "above reproach." In the Gr. OT, it is used several times of the kind of sacrifice to be brought to God, i.e., spotless and without blemish (cf. Num. 6:14; 19:2; 2 Pet. 3:14). **crooked and perverse generation.** See Deut. 32:5. "Crooked" is the word from which the Eng. "scoliosis" (curvature of the spinal column) comes. It describes something that is deviated from the standard, which is true of all who stray from God's path (cf. Prov. 2:15; Is. 53:6). "Perverse" intensifies this meaning by referring to one who has strayed so far off the path that his deviation is severely twisted and distorted (cf. Luke 9:41). Paul applies this condition to the sinful world system. **shine as lights.** A metaphorical reference to spiritual character. "Shine" can be more precisely rendered "you have to shine," which means believers must show their character in the midst of a dark culture, as the sun, moon, and stars shine in an otherwise dark sky (*see notes on Matt. 5:14; 2 Cor. 4:6; Eph. 5:8*).

2:16 holding fast. A slightly different translation—"holding forth"—more accurately reflects the verb in the original text. Here it refers to believers' holding out or offering something for others to take. **the word of life.** The gospel which, when believed, produces spiritual and eternal life (cf. Eph. 2:1). **I may rejoice.** *See notes on v. 2; 4:1; 1 Thess. 2:19,20.* **day of Christ.** *See note on 1:6.* **run...or labored in vain.** *See note on Gal. 2:2.* Paul wanted to look back on his ministry and see that all his efforts were worthwhile (cf. 1 Cor. 9:27; 1 Thess. 5:12; 2 Tim. 4:7; Heb. 13:17; 3 John 4).

2:17,18 I...rejoice...you also...rejoice. An attitude of mutual joy ought to accompany any sacrificial Christian service (*see notes on 1:4,18,26*; cf. 2 Cor. 7:4; Col. 1:24; 1 Thess. 3:9).

2:17 being poured out. From the Gr. that means "to be offered as a libation or drink offering." Some connect this with Paul's future martyrdom, but the verb is in the present tense, which means he is referring to his sacrificial ministry among the Philippians. ***drink offering.*** This refers to the topping off of an ancient animal sacrifice. The offerer poured wine either in front of or on top of the burning animal and the wine would be vaporized. That steam symbolized the rising of the offering to the deity for whom the sacrifice was made (cf. Ex. 29:38-41; 2 Kin. 16:13; Jer. 7:18; Hos. 9:4). Paul viewed his entire life as a drink offering, and here it was poured on the Philippians' sacrificial service. **service of your faith.** "Service" comes from a word that refers to sacred, priestly service (cf. Rom. 12:1; 1 Cor. 9:12) and was so used in the Gr. OT. Paul sees the Philippians as priests who were offering their lives sacrificially and faithfully in service to God (cf. 1 Pet. 2:9).

2:19-23 Paul tells the Philippians of his plans to send Timothy to Philippi to set him forth as a model spiritual servant.

2:19 Timothy. *See note on 1:1.*

2:20 I have no one like-minded. *See notes on v. 2.* Lit. "one souled," and often translated "kindred spirit." Timothy was one in thought, feeling, and spirit with Paul in love for the church. He was unique in being Paul's protege (*see note on 1 Cor. 4:17*; cf. 1 Tim. 1:2; 2 Tim. 1:2). Paul had no other like Timothy because, sadly, "all" the others were devoted to their own purposes rather than Christ's. *See notes on 2 Tim. 1:15.*

2:23,24 Paul was eventually released from prison (cf. Acts 28:30), after which he may have visited the church at Philippi.

2:24 in the Lord. Paul knew his plans were subject to God's sovereignty (cf. James 4:13-17).

2:25-30 This passage is a compelling look at love and unity among believers. All the parties show selfless affection for each other.

2:25 Epaphroditus. Paul wanted to send Timothy (v. 23) and come himself (v. 24), but found it necessary to send this man, a native Philippian of whom, outside this passage, little is known. His name was a common Gr. one, taken from a familiar word that originally meant "favorite of Aphrodite" (Gr. goddess of love). Later, the name came to mean "lovely" or "loving." He was sent to Paul with gifts (4:18) and was to remain and serve Paul as he could (v. 30). **messenger.** This comes from the same word that yields the Eng. "apostle." He was not an apostle of Christ (*see note on Rom. 1:1*), but an apostle ("sent one") in the broader sense (*see note on Rom. 1:5*) that he was an apostle of the church in Philippi, sent to Paul with their monetary love gift

worker, and [m]fellow soldier, [n]but your
messenger and [o]the one who ministered to
my need; 26 [p]since he was longing for you
all, and was distressed because you had
heard that he was sick. 27 For indeed he
was sick almost unto death; but God had
mercy on him, and not only on him but on
me also, lest I should have sorrow upon
sorrow. 28 Therefore I sent him the more
eagerly, that when you see him again you
may rejoice, and I may be less sorrowful.
29 Receive him therefore in the Lord with
all gladness, and hold such men in esteem;
30 because for the work of Christ he came
close to death, [8]not regarding his life, [q]to
supply what was lacking in your service
toward me.

25 [m] Philem. 2 [n] John 13:16; 2 Cor. 8:23 [o] 2 Cor. 11:9
26 [p] Phil. 1:8
30 [q] 1 Cor. 16:17; Phil. 4:10 [8] *risking*

CHAPTER 3

1 [a] 1 Thess. 5:16
2 [b] Ps. 22:16, 20; Gal. 5:15; Rev. 22:15 [c] Ps. 119:115 [d] Rom. 2:28
3 [e] Deut. 30:6; Rom. 2:28, 29; 9:6; [Gal. 6:15] [f] John 4:24; Rom. 7:6 [1] NU, M *in the Spirit of God*
4 [g] 2 Cor. 5:16; 11:18 [h] 2 Cor. 11:22, 23
5 [i] Rom. 11:1 [j] 2 Cor. 11:22 [k] Acts 23:6
6 [l] Acts 8:3; 22:4, 5; 26:9–11

All for Christ

3 Finally, my brethren, [a]rejoice in the
Lord. For me to write the same things
to you *is* not tedious, but for you *it is* safe.
2 [b]Beware of dogs, beware of [c]evil workers, [d]beware of the mutilation! 3 For we are
[e]the circumcision, [f]who worship [1]God in
the Spirit, rejoice in Christ Jesus, and have
no confidence in the flesh, 4 though [g]I also
might have confidence in the flesh. If anyone else thinks he may have confidence in
the flesh, I [h]more so: 5 circumcised the
eighth day, of the stock of Israel, [i]*of* the
tribe of Benjamin, [j]a Hebrew of the Hebrews; concerning the law, [k]a Pharisee;
6 concerning zeal, [l]persecuting the church;
concerning the righteousness which is in
the law, blameless.

(*see note on 1:7*; cf. 2 Cor. 8:23). Paul's sending him back to the church with this letter needed an explanation, lest they think Epaphroditus had not served Paul well.

2:26 distressed. The Gr. term describes the confused, chaotic, heavy state of restlessness that results from a time of turmoil or great trauma. Epaphroditus was more concerned about the Philippians' worry for him than he was about his own difficult situation.

2:27 sick almost unto death. Perhaps by the time he arrived in Rome, he had become seriously ill, but now was recovered enough to go back home to labor with the church, who needed him more than Paul did.

2:28 sorrowful. More accurately translated "concern" or "anxiety." Paul had a great burden for all the people in the churches (cf. 2 Cor. 11:2), and he was concerned here because the Philippians were so distressed about Epaphroditus (*see note on 1:8*).

2:29 esteem. Men like him are worthy of honor. *See notes on 1 Thess. 5:12,13.*

2:30 close to death. This refers to the same thing mentioned as sickness in vv. 26,27.

3:1 Finally. Paul has reached a transition point—not a conclusion, since 44 verses remain. Cf. 4:8. **rejoice in the Lord.** Cf. 4:1. Paul's familiar theme throughout the epistle (see Introduction: Historical and Theological Themes), which has already been heard in chaps. 1,2. This, however, is the first time he adds "in the Lord," which signifies the sphere in which the believers' joy exists—a sphere unrelated to the circumstances of life, but related to an unassailable, unchanging relationship to the sovereign Lord. **the same things.** What he is about to teach them in the verses that follow, he had previously given them instruction in, regarding their opponents (cf. 1:27-30). ***is* safe.** A safeguard to protect the Philippians from succumbing to the false teachers.

3:2 dogs. During the first century, dogs roamed the streets and were essentially wild scavengers. Because dogs were such filthy animals, the Jews loved to refer to Gentiles as dogs. Yet here Paul refers to Jews, specifically the Judaizers, as dogs to describe their sinful, vicious, and uncontrolled character. For more on those who taught that circumcision was necessary for salvation, see Introduction to Galatians: Background and Setting; *see notes on Acts 15:1-5; Gal. 2:3.* **evil workers.** The Judaizers prided themselves on being workers of righteousness. Yet Paul described their works as evil, since any attempt to please God by one's own efforts and draw attention away from Christ's accomplished redemption is the worst kind of wickedness. **mutilation.** In contrast to the Gr. word for "circumcision," which means "to cut around," this term means "to cut down (off)." Like the prophets of Baal (1 Kin. 18:28) and pagans who mutilated their bodies in their frenzied rituals, which were forbidden in the OT (Lev. 19:28; 21:5; Deut. 14:1; Is. 15:2; Hos. 7:14), the Judaizers' circumcision was, ironically, no spiritual symbol; it was merely physical mutilation (*see note on Gal. 5:12*).

3:3 we are the circumcision. The true people of God do not possess merely a symbol of the need for a clean heart (*see note on Gen. 17:10*), they actually have been cleansed of sin by God (*see notes on Rom. 2:25-29*). **worship God in the Spirit.** The first characteristic Paul uses to define a true believer. The Gr. word for "worship" means to render respectful spiritual service, while "Spirit" should have a small "s," to indicate the inner person. *See notes on John 4:23,24.* **rejoice in Christ Jesus.** The Gr. word for "rejoice" means "to boast with exultant joy." The true Christian gives all the credit for all that he is to Christ (cf. Rom. 15:17; 1 Cor. 1:31; 2 Cor. 10:17; *see note on v. 1*). **no confidence in the flesh.** By "flesh" Paul is referring to man's unredeemed humanness, his own ability and achievements apart from God (*see note on Rom. 7:5*). The Jews placed their confidence in being circumcised, being descendants of Abraham, and performing the external ceremonies and duties of the Mosaic law—things that could not save them (*see notes on Rom. 3:20; Gal. 5:1-12*). The true believer views his flesh as sinful, without any capacity to merit salvation or please God.

3:4-7 To counteract the Judaizers' claim that certain ceremonies and rituals of Judaism were necessary for salvation, Paul described his own lofty attainments as a Jew, which were greater than those his opponents could claim, but were of no benefit for salvation.

3:5 the eighth day. Paul was circumcised on the prescribed day (Gen. 17:12; 21:4; Lev. 12:3). **of Israel.** All true Jews were direct descendants of Abraham, Isaac, and Jacob (Israel). Paul's Jewish heritage was pure. ***of* the tribe of Benjamin.** Benjamin was the second son of Rachel (Gen. 35:18), and one of the elite tribes of Israel, who along with Judah, remained loyal to the Davidic dynasty and formed the southern kingdom (1 Kin. 12:21). **Hebrew of the Hebrews.** Paul was born to Hebrew parents and maintained the Hebrew tradition and language, even while living in a pagan city (cf. Acts 21:40; 26:4,5). **a Pharisee.** The legalistic fundamentalists of Judaism, whose zeal to apply the OT Scriptures directly to life led to a complex system of tradition and works righteousness (*see note on Matt. 3:7*). Paul may have come from a line of Pharisees (cf. Acts 22:3; 23:6; 26:5).

3:6 zeal, persecuting the church. To the Jew, "zeal" was the highest single virtue of religion. It combines love and hate; because Paul loved Judaism, he hated whatever might threaten it (*see notes on Acts 8:3 and 9:1*). **the righteousness which is in the law.** The standard of righteous living advocated by God's law. Paul outwardly kept this, so that no one could accuse him of violation. Obviously his heart was sinful and self-righteous. He was not an OT believer, but a proud and lost legalist.

7 But [m]what things were gain to me,
these I have counted loss for Christ. 8 Yet
indeed I also count all things loss [n]for the
excellence of the knowledge of Christ Jesus
my Lord, for whom I have suffered the loss
of all things, and count them as rubbish,
that I may gain Christ 9 and be found in
Him, not having [o]my own righteousness,
which *is* from the law, but [p]that which *is*
through faith in Christ, the righteousness
which is from God by faith; 10 that I may
know Him and the [q]power of His resurrection, and [r]the fellowship of His sufferings,
being conformed to His death, 11 if, by any
means, I may [s]attain[2] to the resurrection
from the dead.

7 [m]Matt. 13:44
8 [n]Is. 53:11; Jer. 9:23; John 17:3; 1 Cor. 2:2; [Eph. 4:13]
9 [o]Rom. 10:3 [p]Rom. 1:17
10 [q]Eph. 1:19, 20 [r][Rom. 6:3–5]; 2 Cor. 1:5; 1 Pet. 4:13
11 [s]Acts 26:6–8; [1 Cor. 15:23; Rev. 20:5] [2]Lit. *arrive at*
12 [t]1 Cor. 9:24; [1 Tim. 6:12, 19] [u]Heb. 12:23 [3]*obtained it*
13 [v]Luke 9:62 [w]Heb. 6:1 [4]*laid hold of it*
14 [x]2 Tim. 4:7 [y]Heb. 3:1
15 [z]Matt. 5:48; 1 Cor. 2:6 [a]Gal. 5:10 [b]Hos. 6:3; James 1:5
16 [c]Gal. 6:16 [5]*arrived*

Pressing Toward the Goal

12 Not that I have already [t]attained,[3] or
am already [u]perfected; but I press on, that
I may lay hold of that for which Christ Jesus has also laid hold of me. 13 Brethren, I
do not count myself to have [4]appre-
hended; but one thing *I do*, [v]forgetting
those things which are behind and [w]reach-
ing forward to those things which are
ahead, 14 [x]I press toward the goal for the
prize of [y]the upward call of God in Christ
Jesus.
15 Therefore let us, as many as are [z]ma-
ture, [a]have this mind; and if in anything
you think otherwise, [b]God will reveal even
this to you. 16 Nevertheless, to *the degree*
that we have already [5]attained, [c]let us

3:7 what things were gain…I have counted loss. The Gr. word for "gain" is an accounting term that means "profit." The Gr. word for "loss" also is an accounting term, used to describe a business loss. Paul used the language of business to describe the spiritual transaction that occurred when Christ redeemed him. All his Jewish religious credentials that he thought were in his profit column, were actually worthless and damning (cf. Luke 18:9-14). Thus, he put them in his loss column when he saw the glories of Christ (cf. Matt. 13:44,45; 16:25,26).

3:8-11 Paul described the benefits that accrued to his profit column when he came to Christ.

3:8 knowledge of Christ Jesus. To "know" Christ is not simply to have intellectual knowledge about Him; Paul used the Gr. verb that means to know "experientially" or "personally" (cf. John 10:27; 17:3; 2 Cor. 4:6; 1 John 5:20). It is equivalent to shared life with Christ (*see note on Gal. 2:20*). It also corresponds to a Heb. word used of God's knowledge of His people (Amos 3:2) and their knowledge of Him in love and obedience (Jer. 31:34; Hos. 6:3; 8:2). **rubbish.** The Gr. word refers to garbage or waste, and can even be translated "dung" or "manure."

3:9 be found in Him. Paul was "in Christ" (*see note on 1:1*). His union with Christ was possible only because God imputed Christ's righteousness to him so that it was reckoned by God as his own (*see notes on Rom. 1:17; 3:24*). **not having my own righteousness…from the law.** This is the proud self-righteousness of external morality, religious ritual and ceremony, and good works. It is the righteousness produced by the flesh, which cannot save from sin (Rom. 3:19,20; Gal. 3:6-25). **faith in Christ.** Faith is the confident, continuous confession of total dependence on and trust in Jesus Christ for the necessary requirement to enter God's kingdom (*see note on Rom. 1:16*). And that requirement is the righteousness of Christ, which God imputes to every believer (*see note on Rom. 3:24*).

3:10 I may know Him. *See note on v. 8.* Paul's emphasis here is on gaining a deeper knowledge and intimacy with Christ. **the power of His resurrection.** Christ's resurrection most graphically demonstrated the extent of His power. By raising Himself from the dead, Christ displayed His power over both the physical and spiritual worlds. **fellowship of His sufferings.** This refers to a partnership—a deep communion of suffering that every believer shares with Christ, who is able to comfort suffering Christians because He has already experienced the same suffering, and infinitely more (Heb. 2:18; 4:15; 12:2-4; cf. 2 Cor. 5:21; 1 Pet. 2:21-24). **conformed to His death.** As Christ died for the purpose of redeeming sinners, so Paul had that same purpose in a lesser sense; he lived and would willingly die to reach sinners with the gospel. His life and death, though not redemptive, were for the same purpose as his Lord's.

3:11 by any means. Reflecting his humility, he didn't care how God brought it to pass, but longed for death and for the fulfillment of his salvation in his resurrection body (cf. Rom. 8:23). **the resurrection from the dead.** Lit. "the resurrection out from the corpses." This is a reference to the resurrection which accompanies the rapture of the church (1 Thess. 4:13-17 ; cf. 1 Cor. 15:42-44).

3:12-14 Paul uses the analogy of a runner to describe the Christian's spiritual growth. The believer has not reached his goal of Christlikeness (cf. vv. 20,21), but like the runner in a race, he must continue to pursue it. That this is the goal for every believer is also clear from Rom. 8:29; 2 Thess. 2:14; 1 John 3:2 (*see notes there*).

3:12 Not that I have already attained. The race toward Christlikeness begins with a sense of honesty and dissatisfaction. **press on.** The Gr. word was used of a sprinter, and refers to aggressive, energetic action. Paul pursued sanctification with all his might, straining every spiritual muscle to win the prize (1 Cor. 9:24-27; 1 Tim. 6:12; Heb. 12:1). **lay hold…laid hold of me.** "Lay hold" means "to make one's own possession." Christ chose Paul for the ultimate purpose of conforming Paul to His glorious image (Rom. 8:29), and that is the very goal Paul pursued to attain.

3:13 apprehended. The same Gr. word translated "laid hold" in v. 12. **one thing *I do*.** Paul had reduced the whole of sanctification to the simple and clear goal of doing "one thing"—pursuing Christlikeness (*see notes on 2 Cor. 11:1-3*). **forgetting…which are behind.** The believer must refuse to rely on past virtuous deeds and achievements in ministry or to dwell on sins and failures. To be distracted by the past debilitates one's efforts in the present.

3:14 the goal. Christlikeness here and now (*see note on v. 12*). **the prize.** Christlikeness in heaven (cf. vv. 20,21; 1 John 3:1,2). **the upward call of God.** The time when God calls each believer up to heaven and into His presence will be the moment of receiving the prize which has been an unattainable goal in earthly life.

3:15 as many as are mature. Since the spiritual perfection of Christlikeness is possible only when the believer receives the upward call, Paul is referring here to mature spirituality. He could be referring to the mature believers who were like-minded with him in this pursuit or he may also have used "mature" here to refer sarcastically to the Judaizers, who thought they had reached perfection. **have this mind.** A better translation is "attitude." Believers are to have the attitude of pursuing the prize of Christlikeness. **if…you think otherwise.** Those who continue to dwell on the past and make no progress toward the goal. **God will reveal.** The Gr. word for "reveal" means "to uncover" or "unveil." Paul left in God's hands those who were not pursuing spiritual perfection. He knew God would reveal the truth to them eventually, even if it meant chastening (Heb. 12:5-11).

3:16 to *the degree*…already attained, let us walk. The Gr.

walk [d]by the same [6]rule, let us be of the
same mind.

Our Citizenship in Heaven

17 Brethren, [e]join in following my example, and note those who so walk, as [f]you
have us for a pattern. 18 For many walk, of
whom I have told you often, and now tell
you even weeping, *that they are* [g]the enemies of the cross of Christ: 19 [h]whose end *is*
destruction, [i]whose god *is their* belly, and
[j]*whose* glory *is* in their shame—[k]who set
their mind on earthly things. 20 For [l]our
citizenship is in heaven, [m]from which we
also [n]eagerly wait for the Savior, the Lord
Jesus Christ, 21 [o]who will transform our
lowly body that it may be [p]conformed to
His glorious body, [q]according to the working by which He is able even to [r]subdue all
things to Himself.

4 Therefore, my beloved and [a]longed-for
brethren, [b]my joy and crown, so [c]stand
fast in the Lord, beloved.

Be United, Joyful, and in Prayer

2 I implore Euodia and I implore Synty-
che [d]to be of the same mind in the Lord.
3 [1]And I urge you also, true companion,
help these women who [e]labored with me
in the gospel, with Clement also, and the
rest of my fellow workers, whose names
are in [f]the Book of Life.

16 [d] Rom. 12:16; 15:5 [6] NU omits *rule* and the rest of v. 16.
17 [e] [1 Cor. 4:16; 11:1]; Phil. 4:9 [f] Titus 2:7, 8; 1 Pet. 5:3
18 [g] Gal. 1:7
19 [h] 2 Cor. 11:15 [i] 1 Tim. 6:5 [j] Hos. 4:7 [k] Rom. 8:5; Col. 3:2
20 [l] Eph. 2:6, 19; Phil. 1:27; [Col. 3:1; Heb. 12:22] [m] Acts 1:11 [n] 1 Cor. 1:7
21 [o] [1 Cor. 15:43–53] [p] 1 John 3:2 [q] Eph. 1:19 [r] [1 Cor. 15:28]

CHAPTER 4

1 [a] Phil. 1:8 [b] 2 Cor. 1:14 [c] 1 Cor. 16:13; Phil. 1:27 2 [d] Phil. 2:2; 3:16 3 [e] Rom. 16:3 [f] Ex. 32:32; Luke 10:20 [1] NU, M *Yes*

word for "walk" refers to walking in line. Paul's directive for the Philippian believers was to stay in line spiritually and keep progressing in sanctification by the same principles that had brought them to this point in their spiritual growth (cf. 1 Thess. 3:10; 1 Pet. 2:2).

3:17 my example. Lit. "be imitators of me." Since all believers are imperfect, they need examples of less imperfect people who know how to deal with imperfection and who can model the process of pursuing the goal of Christlikeness. Paul was that model (1 Cor. 11:1; 1 Thess. 1:6). **note those who so walk.** The Philippian believers were to focus on other godly examples, such as Timothy and Epaphroditus (2:19,20), and see how they conducted themselves in service to Christ.

3:18 told you often. Apparently Paul had warned the Philippians on numerous occasions about the dangers of false teachers, just as he did the Ephesians (Acts 20:28-30). **weeping.** Paul had a similar response as he warned the Ephesian elders about the dangers of false teachers (Acts 20:31). **enemies of the cross.** Implied in Paul's language is that these men did not claim to oppose Christ, His work on the cross, or salvation by grace alone through faith alone, but they did not pursue Christlikeness in manifest godliness. Apparently, they were posing as friends of Christ, and possibly had even reached positions of leadership in the church.

3:19 These enemies of the cross could have been either Jews (the Judaizers; v. 2) or Gentile libertines—precursors of Gnosticism, who maintained a dualistic philosophy that tended toward antinomianism, which is a discarding of any moral law. **end *is* destruction.** The Gr. word for "end" refers to one's ultimate destiny. The Judaizers were headed for eternal damnation because they depended on their works to save them. The Gentile libertines were headed for the same destiny because they trusted in their human wisdom and denied the transforming power of the gospel. **god...belly.** This may refer to the Judaizers' fleshly accomplishments, which were mainly religious works. It could also refer to their observance of the dietary laws they believed were necessary for salvation. If the Gentile libertines are in view, it could easily refer to their sensual desires and fleshly appetites. As always, false teachers are evident by their wickedness. *See notes on 2 Pet. 2:10-19; Jude 8-13.* **glory...shame.** The Judaizers boasted of their self-effort; but even the best of their accomplishments were no better than filthy rags or dung (vv. 7,8; Is. 64:6). The Gentile libertines boasted about their sin and abused Christian liberty to defend their behavior (1 Cor. 6:12). **earthly things.** The Judaizers were preoccupied with ceremonies, feasts, sacrifices, and other kinds of physical observances. The Gentile libertines simply loved the world itself and all the things in it (cf. James 4:4; 1 John 2:15).

3:20 our citizenship. The Gr. term refers to a colony of foreigners. In one secular source, it was used to describe a capital city that kept the names of its citizens on a register. **in heaven.** The place where God dwells and where Christ is present. It is the believers' home (John 14:2,3), where their names are registered (Luke 10:20) and their inheritance awaits (1 Pet. 1:4). Other believers are there (Heb. 12:23). We belong to the kingdom under the rule of our heavenly King, and obey heaven's laws. Cf. 1 Pet. 2:11. **eagerly wait.** The Gr. verb is found in most passages dealing with the second coming and expresses the idea of waiting patiently, but with great expectation (Rom. 8:23; 2 Pet. 3:11,12).

3:21 transform our lowly body. The Gr. word for "transform" gives us the word "schematic," which is an internal design of something. Those who are already dead in Christ, but alive with Him in spirit in heaven (1:23; 2 Cor. 5:8; Heb. 12:23), will receive new bodies at the resurrection and rapture of the church, when those alive on earth will have their bodies transformed (*see notes on Rom. 8:18-23; 1 Cor. 15:51-54; 1 Thess. 4:16*). **conformed to His glorious body.** The believer's new body will be like Christ's after His resurrection, and will be redesigned and adapted for heaven (1 Cor. 15:42,43; 1 John 3:2). **subdue.** The Gr. word means "to subject" and refers to arranging things in order of rank or managing something. Christ has the power both to providentially create natural laws and miraculously overrule them (1 Cor. 15:23-27).

4:1 beloved and longed-for. Paul reveals his deep affection for the Philippian believers. The Gr. term for "longed-for" refers to the deep pain of separation from loved ones. **my joy and crown.** Paul did not derive his joy from circumstances, but from his fellow believers in Philippi (cf. 1 Thess. 2:19,20; 3:9). The Gr. term for "crown" refers to the laurel wreath received by an athlete for winning a contest (1 Cor. 9:25) or by a person honored by his peers at a banquet as a symbol of success or a fruitful life. The Philippian believers were proof that Paul's efforts were successful (cf. 1 Cor. 9:2). **stand fast.** This Gr. word was often used to describe a soldier standing at his post; here it is a military command (cf. 1:27) which is the dominant expression of vv. 1-9.

4:2 I implore. The Gr. term means "to urge," or "to appeal." **Euodia...Syntyche.** These two women were prominent church members (v. 3), who may have been among the women meeting for prayer when Paul first preached the gospel in Philippi (Acts 16:13). Apparently, they were leading two opposing factions in the church, most likely over a personal conflict. **the same mind.** Another possible translation is "harmony" (*see note on 2:2*). Spiritual stability depends on the mutual love, harmony, and peace between believers. Apparently the disunity in the Philippian church was about to destroy the integrity of its testimony.

4:3 companion. The Gr. word pictures two oxen in a yoke, pulling the same load. A companion is a partner or an equal in a specific endeavor—in this case a spiritual one. It is possible that this individual

4 [g]Rejoice in the Lord always. Again I
will say, rejoice!
5 Let your [2]gentleness be known to all
men. [h]The Lord *is* at hand.
6 [i]Be anxious for nothing, but in everything by prayer and supplication, with
[j]thanksgiving, let your requests be made
known to God; 7 and [k]the peace of God,
which surpasses all understanding, will
guard your hearts and minds through
Christ Jesus.

Meditate on These Things

8 Finally, brethren, whatever things are
[l]true, whatever things *are* [m]noble, whatever things *are* [n]just, [o]whatever things *are*
pure, whatever things *are* [p]lovely, whatever things *are* of good report, if *there is*
any virtue and if *there is* anything
praiseworthy—meditate on these things.
9 The things which you learned and received and heard and saw in me, these
do, and [q]the God of peace will be with
you.

Philippian Generosity

10 But I rejoiced in the Lord greatly that
now at last [r]your[3] care for me has flourished again; though you surely did care,
but you lacked opportunity. 11 Not that I
speak in regard to need, for I have learned
in whatever state I am, [s]to be content: 12 [t]I
know how to [4]be abased, and I know how
to [5]abound. Everywhere and in all things I
have learned both to be full and to be hungry, both to abound and to suffer need. 13 I
can do all things [u]through [6]Christ who
strengthens me.
14 Nevertheless you have done well that
[v]you shared in my distress. 15 Now you
Philippians know also that in the beginning of the gospel, when I departed from

4 [g] Rom. 12:12
5 [h] 1 Cor. 16:22; Heb. 10:25, 37; [James 5:7–9]; Rev. 22:7, 20 [2] *graciousness* or *forbearance*
6 [i] Ps. 55:22; Matt. 6:25; 1 Pet. 5:7 [j] [1 Thess. 5:17, 18]
7 [k] [Is. 26:3; John 14:27]; Phil. 4:9; Col. 3:15
8 [l] Eph. 4:25 [m] 2 Cor. 8:21 [n] Deut. 16:20 [o] 1 Thess. 5:22; James 3:17 [p] 1 Cor. 13:4–7
9 [q] Rom. 15:33; Heb. 13:20
10 [r] 2 Cor. 11:9; Phil. 2:30 [3] *you have revived your care*
11 [s] 2 Cor. 9:8; 1 Tim. 6:6, 8; Heb. 13:5
12 [t] 1 Cor. 4:11 [4] *live humbly* [5] *live in prosperity*
13 [u] John 15:5 [6] NU *Him who*
14 [v] Phil. 1:7

is unnamed, but it is best to take the Gr. word translated "companion" as a proper name ("Syzygos"). He was likely one of the church elders (1:1). **with Clement.** Nothing is known of him. **Book of Life.** In eternity past, God registered all the names of His elect in that book which identifies those inheritors of eternal life (*see note on Rev. 3:5*; cf. Dan. 12:1; Mal. 3:16,17; Luke 10:20; Rev. 17:8; 20:12).

4:4 Rejoice in the Lord. *See note on 3:1.*

4:5 gentleness. This refers to contentment with and generosity toward others. It can also refer to mercy or leniency toward the faults and failures of others. It can even refer to patience in someone who submits to injustice or mistreatment without retaliating. Graciousness with humility encompasses all the above. **at hand.** Can refer to nearness in space or time. The context suggests nearness in space: the Lord encompasses all believers with His presence (Ps. 119:151).

4:6 Be anxious for nothing. *See notes on Matt. 6:25-34.* Fret and worry indicate a lack of trust in God's wisdom, sovereignty, or power. Delighting in the Lord and meditating on His Word are a great antidote to anxiety (Ps. 1:2). **in everything.** All difficulties are within God's purposes. **prayer and supplication, with thanksgiving...requests.** Gratitude to God accompanies all true prayer.

4:7 peace of God. *See note on v. 9.* Inner calm or tranquillity is promised to the believer who has a thankful attitude based on unwavering confidence that God is able and willing to do what is best for His children (cf. Rom. 8:28). **surpasses all understanding.** This refers to the divine origin of peace. It transcends human intellect, analysis, and insight (Is. 26:3; John 16:33). **guard.** A military term meaning "to keep watch over." God's peace guards believers from anxiety, doubt, fear, and distress. **hearts...minds.** Paul was not making a distinction between the two—he was giving a comprehensive statement referring to the whole inner person. Because of the believer's union with Christ, He guards his inner being with His peace.

4:8 true. What is true is found in God (2 Tim. 2:25), in Christ (Eph. 4:20,21), in the Holy Spirit (John 16:13), and in God's Word (John 17:17). **noble.** The Gr. term means "worthy of respect." Believers are to meditate on whatever is worthy of awe and adoration, i.e., the sacred as opposed to the profane. **just.** This refers to what is right. The believer is to think in harmony with God's divine standard of holiness. **pure.** That which is morally clean and undefiled. **lovely.** The Gr. term means "pleasing" or "amiable." By implication, believers are to focus on whatever is kind or gracious. **of good report.** That which is highly regarded or thought well of. It refers to what is generally considered reputable in the world, such as kindness, courtesy, and respect for others.

4:9 in me. The Philippians were to follow the truth of God proclaimed, along with the example of that truth lived by Paul before them (*see note on Heb. 13:7*). **the God of peace.** *See note on Rom. 15:33*; cf. 1 Cor. 14:33. God is peace (Rom. 16:20; Eph. 2:14), makes peace with sinners through Christ (2 Cor. 5:18-20), and gives perfect peace in trouble (v. 7).

4:10-19 Paul expressed his gratitude to the Philippians for their kind expressions of love and the generous gift they sent him and thus provides a powerful example of how a Christian can be content regardless of his circumstances.

4:10 at last...you lacked opportunity. About ten years had passed since the Philippians first gave a gift to Paul to help meet his needs when he was first in Thessalonica (vv. 15,16). Paul was aware of their desire to continue to help, but he realized, within God's providence, that they had not had the "opportunity" (season) to help.

4:11 whatever state I am. Paul defined the circumstances in the following verse. **content.** The Gr. term means "to be self-sufficient" or "to be satisfied." It is the same word translated "sufficiency" in 2 Cor. 9:8. It indicates independence from any need for help (cf. Luke 3:14; 1 Thess. 4:12; 1 Tim. 6:6,8; Heb. 13:5).

4:12 abased...abound. Paul knew how to get along with humble means (food, clothing, daily necessities) and how to live in prosperity ("to overflow"). **to be full and to be hungry.** The Gr. word translated "to be full" was used of feeding and fattening animals. Paul knew how to be content when he had plenty to eat and when he was deprived of enough to eat.

4:13 I can do all things. Paul uses a Gr. verb that means "to be strong" or "to have strength" (cf. Acts 19:16,20; James 5:16). He had strength to withstand "all things" (vv. 11,12), including both difficulty and prosperity in the material world. **through Christ who strengthens me.** The Gr. word for strengthen means "to put power in." Because believers are in Christ (Gal. 2:20), He infuses them with His strength to sustain them until they receive some provision (Eph. 3:16-20; 2 Cor. 12:10).

4:14 Paul adds a word of clarification here so the Philippians would not think he was being ungrateful for their most recent gift, because of what he just wrote (vv. 11-13). **shared.** To join in a partnership with someone.

4:15 in the beginning of the gospel. When Paul first preached the gospel in Philippi (Acts 16:13). **when I departed.** When Paul

Macedonia, [w]no church shared with me
concerning giving and receiving but you
only. 16 For even in Thessalonica you sent
aid once and again for my necessities.
17 Not that I seek the gift, but I seek [x]the
fruit that abounds to your account. 18 Indeed I [7]have all and abound. I am full,
having received from [y]Epaphroditus the
things *sent* from you, [z]a sweet-smelling
aroma, [a]an acceptable sacrifice, well pleasing to God. 19 And my God [b]shall supply
all your need according to His riches in
glory by Christ Jesus. 20 [c]Now to our God
and Father *be* glory forever and ever.
Amen.

15 [w] 2 Cor. 11:8,9
17 [x] Titus 3:14
18 [y] Phil. 2:25 [z] Heb. 13:16 [a] Rom. 12:1; 2 Cor. 9:12 [7] Or *have received all*
19 [b] Ps. 23:1; 2 Cor. 9:8
20 [c] Rom. 16:27
21 [d] Gal. 1:2
23 [8] NU *your spirit*

Greeting and Blessing

21 Greet every saint in Christ Jesus. The
brethren [d]who are with me greet you.
22 All the saints greet you, but especially
those who are of Caesar's household.
23 The grace of our Lord Jesus Christ be
with [8]you all. Amen.

first left Philippi approximately 10 years before (Acts 16:40). **Macedonia.** In addition to Philippi, Paul also ministered in two other towns in Macedonia: Thessalonica and Berea (Acts 17:1-14). **concerning giving and receiving.** Paul used 3 business terms. "Concerning" could be translated "account." "Giving and receiving" refer to expenditures and receipts. Paul was a faithful steward of God's resources and kept careful records of what he received and spent. **but you only.** Only the Philippians sent Paul provisions to meet his needs.

4:16 even in Thessalonica. *See note on Acts 17:1*; see also Introduction to 1 Thessalonians. Paul preached there for a few months, during his second missionary journey.

4:17 the fruit. The Gr. word can be translated "profit." **abounds to your account.** The Philippians were in effect storing up for themselves treasure in heaven (Matt. 6:20). The gifts they gave to Paul were accruing eternal dividends to their spiritual account (Prov. 11:24,25; 19:17; Luke 6:38; 2 Cor. 9:6).

4:18 Epaphroditus. *See note on 2:25.* **a sweet-smelling aroma, an acceptable sacrifice, well-pleasing to God.** In the OT sacrificial system, every sacrifice was to provide a fragrant aroma and be acceptable to God. Only if it was offered with the correct attitude would it be pleasing to Him (Gen. 8:20,21; Ex. 29:18; Lev. 1:9,13,17). The Philippians' gift was a spiritual sacrifice (cf. Rom. 12:1; 1 Pet. 2:5) that pleased God.

4:19 all your need. Paul addressed all the Philippians' material needs, which had probably been depleted to some extent because of their gracious gift (Prov. 3:9). **according to His riches.** God would give increase to the Philippians in proportion to His infinite resources, not just a small amount out of His riches.

4:20 This doxology is Paul's praise in direct response to the great truth that God supplies all the needs of the saints. In a more general sense, this is praise in response to the character of God and His faithfulness.

4:21 every saint. *See note on 1:1.* Instead of using the collective "all," Paul used the individualistic "every" to declare that each saint was worthy of his concern. **brethren who are with me.** They certainly included Timothy and Epaphroditus (2:19,25). Others who were preaching the gospel in Rome were present (1:14). It is possible that Tychicus, Aristarchus, Onesimus, and Jesus Justus were also there (Col. 4:7,9-11).

4:22 Caesar's household. A significant number of people, not limited to Caesar's family, which would include courtiers, princes, judges, cooks, food-tasters, musicians, custodians, builders, stablemen, soldiers, accountants. Within that large group, Paul had in mind those who, through the proclamation of the gospel by members of the church at Rome, had been saved prior to his coming. Newly added to their number were those led to Christ by Paul himself, including those soldiers who were chained to him while he was a prisoner (1:13).

4:23 The common conclusion to Paul's epistles (*see note on Rom. 16:24*). **Amen.** A confessional affirmation that underscores the preceding truth.

The Epistle of Paul to the COLOSSIANS

Title

Colossians is named for the city of Colosse, where the church it was addressed to was located. It was also to be read in the neighboring church at Laodicea (4:16).

Author and Date

Paul is identified as author at the beginning (1:1; cf. v. 23; 4:18), as customarily in his epistles. The testimony of the early church, including such key figures as Irenaeus, Clement of Alexandria, Tertullian, Origen, and Eusebius, confirms that the opening claim is genuine. Additional evidence for Paul's authorship comes from the book's close parallels with Philemon, which is universally accepted as having been written by Paul. Both were written (ca. A.D. 60–62) while Paul was a prisoner in Rome (4:3,10,18; Philem. 9,10,13,23); plus the names of the same people (e.g., Timothy, Aristarchus, Archippus, Mark, Epaphras, Luke, Onesimus, and Demas) appear in both epistles, showing that both were written by the same author at about the same time. For biographical information on Paul see Introduction to Romans: Author and Date.

Background and Setting

Colosse was a city in Phrygia, in the Roman province of Asia (part of modern Turkey), about 100 mi. E of Ephesus in the region of the 7 churches of Rev. 1–3. The city lay alongside the Lycus River, not far from where it flowed into the Maender River. The Lycus Valley narrowed at Colosse to a width of about two mi., and Mt. Cadmus rose 8,000 feet above the city.

Colosse was a thriving city in the fifth century B.C. when the Persian king Xerxes (Ahasuerus, cf. Esth. 1:1) marched through the region. Black wool and dyes (made from the nearby chalk deposits) were important products. In addition, the city was situated at the junction of the main north-south and east-west trade routes. By Paul's day, however, the main road had been rerouted through nearby Laodicea, thus bypassing Colosse and leading to its decline and the rise of the neighboring cities of Laodicea and Hierapolis.

Although Colosse's population was mainly Gentile, there was a large Jewish settlement dating from the days of Antiochus the Great (223–187 B.C.). Colosse's mixed population of Jews and Gentiles manifested itself both in the composition of the church and in the heresy that plagued it, which contained elements of both Jewish legalism and pagan mysticism.

The church at Colosse began during Paul's 3-year ministry at Ephesus (Acts 19). Its founder was not Paul, who had never been there (2:1); but Epaphras (1:5-7), who apparently was saved during a visit to Ephesus, then likely started the church in Colosse when he returned home. Several years after the Colossian church was founded, a dangerous heresy arose to threaten it—one not identified with any particular historical system. It contained elements of what later became known as Gnosticism: that God is good, but matter is evil, that Jesus Christ was merely one of a series of emanations descending from God and being less than God (a belief that led them to deny His true humanity), and that a secret, higher knowledge above Scripture was necessary for enlightenment and salvation. The Colossian heresy also embraced aspects of Jewish legalism, e.g., the necessity of circumcision for salvation, observance of the ceremonial rituals of the OT law (dietary laws, festivals, Sabbaths), and rigid asceticism. It also called for the worship of angels and mystical experience. Epaphras was so concerned about this heresy that he made the long journey from Colosse to Rome (4:12,13), where Paul was a prisoner.

This letter was written from prison in Rome (Acts 28:16-31) sometime between A.D. 60–62 and is, therefore, referred to as a Prison Epistle (along with Ephesians, Philippians, and Philemon). It may have been composed almost contemporaneously with Ephesians and initially sent with that epistle and Philemon by Tychicus (Eph. 6:21,22; Col. 4:7,8). See Introduction to Philippians: Author and Date for a discussion of the city from which Paul wrote. He wrote this letter to warn the Colossians against the heresy they faced, and sent the letter to them with Tychicus, who was accompanying the runaway slave Onesimus back to his master, Philemon, a member of the Colossian church (4:7-9; see Introduction to Philemon: Background and Setting). Epaphras remained behind in Rome (cf. Philem. 23), perhaps to receive further instruction from Paul.

Historical and Theological Themes

Colossians contains teaching on several key areas of theology, including the deity of Christ (1:15-20; 2:2-10), reconciliation (1:20-23), redemption (1:13,14; 2:13,14; 3:9-11), election (3:12), forgiveness (3:13), and the nature of the church (1:18,24,25; 2:19; 3:11,15). Also, as noted above, it refutes the heretical teaching that threatened the Colossian church (chap. 2).

Interpretive Challenges

Those cults that deny Christ's deity have seized upon the description of Him as "the firstborn over all creation" (1:15) as proof that He was a created being. Paul's statement that believers will be "holy, and blameless, and above reproach" if they "continue in the faith" (1:22,23) has led some to teach that believers can lose their salvation. Some have argued for the existence of purgatory based on Paul's statement, "I…fill up in my flesh what is lacking in the afflictions of Christ" (1:24), while others see support for baptismal regeneration (2:12). The identity of the "epistle from Laodicea" (4:16) has also prompted much discussion. These issues will be treated in the notes.

Outline

I. Personal Matters (1:1-14)
  A. Paul's Greeting (1:1,2)
  B. Paul's Thankfulness (1:3-8)
  C. Paul's Prayer (1:9-14)

II. Doctrinal Instruction (1:15–2:23)
  A. About Christ's Deity (1:15-23)
  B. About Paul's Ministry (1:24–2:7)
  C. About False Philosophy (2:8-23)

III. Practical Exhortations (3:1–4:18)
  A. Christian Conduct (3:1-17)
  B. Christian Households (3:18–4:1)
  C. Christian Speech (4:2-6)
  D. Christian Friends (4:7-18)

The Glories of Christ

"Not that we are sufficient of ourselves to think of anything as *being* from ourselves, but our sufficiency is from God…" (2 Cor. 3:5)

One of the great tenets of Scripture is the claim that Jesus Christ is completely sufficient for all matters of life and godliness (2 Pet. 1:3, 4)! He is sufficient for creation (Col. 1:16, 17), salvation (Heb. 10:10-12), sanctification (Eph. 5:26, 27), and glorification (Rom. 8:30). So pure is He that there is no blemish, stain, spot of sin, defilement, lying, deception, corruption, error, or imperfection (1 Pet. 1:18-20).

So complete is He that there is no other God besides Him (Is. 45:5); He is the only begotten Son (John 1:14, 18); all the treasures of wisdom and knowledge are in Him (Col. 2:3); the fullness of the Godhead dwells bodily in Him (Col. 2:9); He is heir of all things (Heb. 1:2); He created all things and all things were made by Him, through Him, and for Him (Col. 1:16); He upholds all things by the word of His power (Col. 1:17; Heb. 1:3); He is the firstborn of all creation (Col. 1:15); He is the exact representation of God (Heb. 1:3).

He is the only Mediator between God and man; He is the Sun that enlightens; the Physician that heals; the Wall of Fire that defends; the Friend that comforts; the Pearl that enriches; the Ark that supports; and the Rock to sustain under the heaviest of pressures; He is seated at the right hand of the throne of the Majesty on high (Heb. 1:3; 8:1); He is better than the angels (Heb. 1:4-14); better than Moses; better than Aaron; better than Joshua; better than Melchizedek; better than all the prophets; greater than Satan (Luke 4:1-12); and stronger than death (1 Cor. 15:55).

He has no beginning and no end (Rev. 1:17, 18); He is the spotless Lamb of God; He is our Peace (Eph. 2:14); He is our Hope (1 Tim. 1:1); He is our Life (Col. 3:4); He is the living and true Way (John 14:6); He is the Strength of Israel (1 Sam. 15:29); He is the Root and Offspring of David, the Bright and Morning Star (Rev. 22:16); He is Faithful and True (Rev. 19:11); He is the Author and Finisher of our faith (Heb. 12:1, 2); He is the Captain of our Salvation (Heb. 2:10); He is the Champion; He is the Elect One (Is. 42:1); He is the Apostle and High-Priest of our confession (Heb. 3:1); He is the Righteous Servant (Is. 53:11).

He is the Lord of Hosts, the Redeemer—the Holy One of Israel, the God of the whole earth (Is. 54:5); He is the Man of Sorrows (Is. 53:3); He is the Light; He is the Son of Man (Matt. 20:28); He is the Vine; He is the Bread of Life; He is the Door; He is Lord (Phil. 2:10-13); He is Prophet, Priest and King (Heb. 1:1-3); He is our Sabbath rest (Heb. 4:9); He is our Righteousness (Jer. 23:6); He is the Wonderful Counselor, the Mighty God, the Everlasting Father, the Prince of Peace (Is. 9:6); He is the Chief Shepherd (1 Pet. 5:4); He is Lord God of hosts; He is Lord of the nations; He is the Lion of Judah; the Living Word; the Rock of Salvation; the Eternal Spirit; He is the Ancient of Days; Creator and Comforter; Messiah; and He is the great I AM (John 8:58)!

Greeting

1 Paul, [a]an apostle of Jesus Christ by the
will of God, and Timothy our brother,

2 To the saints [b]and faithful brethren in
Christ *who are* in Colosse:

[c]Grace to you and peace from God our
Father [1]and the Lord Jesus Christ.

Their Faith in Christ

3 [d]We give thanks to the God and Father
of our Lord Jesus Christ, praying always for
you, 4 [e]since we heard of your faith in
Christ Jesus and of [f]your love for all the
saints; 5 because of the hope [g]which is laid
up for you in heaven, of which you heard
before in the word of the truth of the gospel,
6 which has come to you, [h]as *it has* also in all
the world, and [i]is bringing forth [2]fruit, as *it
is* also among you since the day you heard
and knew [j]the grace of God in truth; 7 as
you also learned from [k]Epaphras, our dear
fellow servant, who is [l]a faithful minister of
Christ on your behalf, 8 who also declared
to us your [m]love in the Spirit.

Preeminence of Christ

9 [n]For this reason we also, since the day
we heard it, do not cease to pray for you,
and to ask [o]that you may be filled with [p]the
knowledge of His will [q]in all wisdom and
spiritual understanding; 10 [r]that you may
walk worthy of the Lord, [s]fully pleasing
Him, [t]being fruitful in every good work
and increasing in the [u]knowledge of God;
11 [v]strengthened with all might, according
to His glorious power, [w]for all patience and
longsuffering [x]with joy; 12 [y]giving thanks
to the Father who has qualified us to be
partakers of [z]the inheritance of the saints in
the light. 13 He has delivered us from [a]the
power of darkness [b]and [3]conveyed *us* into

CHAPTER 1

1 [a]Eph. 1:1
2 [b]1 Cor. 4:17 [c]Gal. 1:3 [1]NU omits *and the Lord Jesus Christ*
3 [d]1 Cor. 1:4; Eph. 1:16; Phil. 1:3
4 [e]Eph. 1:15 [f][Heb. 6:10]
5 [g][1 Pet. 1:4]
6 [h]Matt. 24:14 [i]John 15:16 [j]Eph. 3:2 [2]NU, M add *and growing*
7 [k]Col. 4:12; Philem. 23 [l]1 Cor. 4:1, 2; 2 Cor. 11:23
8 [m]Rom. 15:30
9 [n]Eph. 1:15-17 [o]1 Cor. 1:5 [p][Rom. 12:2]; Eph. 5:17 [q]Eph. 1:8
10 [r]Eph. 4:1; Phil. 1:27; 1 Thess. 2:12 [s]1 Thess. 4:1 [t]Heb. 13:21 [u]2 Pet. 3:18
11 [v][Eph. 3:16; 6:10] [w]Eph. 4:2 [x][Acts 5:41]; 2 Cor. 8:2; [Heb. 10:34]
12 [y][Eph. 5:20] [z]Eph. 1:11
13 [a]Eph. 6:12 [b]2 Pet. 1:11 [3]*transferred*

1:1 Paul. For details on the Apostle Paul, see Introduction to Romans: Author and Date; *see note on Acts 9:1.* **Timothy.** Paul's co-laborer and true child in the faith (see Introduction to 1 Timothy: Background and Setting; *see note on Acts 16:1*) was able to be with him because, although Paul was a prisoner, he had personal living quarters (Acts 28:16-31).

1:2 saints. Those who have been separated from sin and set apart to God—the believers in Colosse (*see note on 1 Cor. 1:2*). **faithful.** A word used in the NT exclusively for believers. Cf. v. 4. **Colosse.** One of 3 cities in the Lycus River valley in the region of Phrygia, in the Roman province of Asia (part of modern Turkey), about 100 mi. E of Ephesus (see Introduction: Background and Setting). **Grace...and peace.** Paul's greeting in all 13 of his epistles (*see note on Rom. 1:7*).

1:3 God and Father of our Lord Jesus Christ. This designation was often used to show that Jesus was one in nature with God, as any true son is with his father. It was an affirmation of Christ's deity (cf. Rom. 15:6; 2 Cor. 1:3; 11:13; Eph. 1:3; 3:14; 1 Pet. 1:3).

1:4 faith in Christ Jesus. For discussion of saving faith *see notes on Rom. 1:16; 10:4-17; James 2:14-26.* **love for all the saints.** Cf. v. 8. One of the visible fruits of true saving faith is love for fellow believers (John 13:34,35; Gal. 5:22; 1 John 2:10; 3:14-16).

1:5 the hope which is laid up. The believer's hope is inseparable from his faith. *See notes on Rom. 5:2; 1 Pet. 1:3-5.* **the gospel.** *See note on Rom. 1:1.* The Gr. word lit. means "good news," and was used in classical Greek to express the good news of victory in a battle. The gospel is the good news of Christ's victory over Satan, sin, and death.

1:6 in all the world. Cf. v. 23, "every creature under heaven." The gospel was never intended for an exclusive group of people; it is good news for the whole world (Matt. 24:14; 28:19,20; Mark 16:15; Rom. 1:8,14,16; 1 Thess. 1:8). It transcends all ethnic, geographic, cultural, and political boundaries. **fruit.** Refers to the saving effect of gospel preaching and to the growth of the church. *See notes on Rom. 1:13; Phil. 1:22;* cf. Matt. 13:3-8,31,32.

1:7 Epaphras. The likely founder of the church at Colosse (see Introduction: Background and Setting).

1:9 the knowledge of His will. The Gr. word for "knowledge" is the usual one, with an added preposition that intensifies its meaning. This is not an inner impression or feeling, but a deep and thorough knowledge of the will of God that is finally and completely revealed in the Word of God (3:16; Eph. 5:17; 1 Thess. 4:3; 5:18; 1 Tim. 2:4; 1 Pet. 2:13,15; 4:19). **wisdom and spiritual understanding.** "Spiritual" modifies both "wisdom" (the ability to accumulate and organize principles from Scripture) and "understanding" (the application of those principles to daily living).

1:10 walk worthy. This is a key NT concept which calls the believer to live in a way that is consistent with his identification with the Lord who saved Him. *See notes on Eph. 4:1; Phil. 1:27.* **being fruitful in every good work.** *See notes on Rom. 1:13; Phil. 4:17.* Spiritual fruit is the by-product of a righteous life. The Bible identifies spiritual fruit as leading people to Christ (1 Cor. 16:15), praising God (Heb. 13:15), giving money (Rom. 15:26-28), living a godly life (Heb. 12:11), and displaying holy attitudes (Gal. 5:22,23). **increasing in the knowledge of God.** Spiritual growth cannot occur apart from this knowledge (1 Pet. 2:2; 2 Pet. 3:18). The evidences of spiritual growth include a deeper love for God's Word (Ps. 119:97), a more perfect obedience (1 John 2:3-5), a strong doctrinal foundation (1 John 2:12-14), an expanding faith (2 Thess. 1:3; cf. 2 Cor. 10:5), and a greater love for others (Phil. 1:9).

1:11 strengthened with all might. *See notes on Eph. 3:16-20.* **patience and longsuffering.** These terms are closely related and refer to the attitude one has during trials. "Patience" looks more at enduring difficult circumstances while "longsuffering" looks at enduring difficult people.

1:12 qualified us. The Gr. word means "to make sufficient," "to empower," or "to authorize." God qualifies us only through the finished work of the Savior. Apart from God's grace through Jesus Christ, all people would be qualified only to receive His wrath. **inheritance.** Lit. "for the portion of the lot." Each believer will receive his own individual portion of the total divine inheritance (*see note on Rom. 8:17*), an allusion to the partitioning of Israel's inheritance in Canaan (cf. Num. 26:52-56; 33:51-54; Josh. 14:1,2). *See notes on 1 Pet. 1:3-5.* **in the light.** Scripture represents "light" intellectually as divine truth (Ps. 119:130) and morally as divine purity (Eph. 5:8-14; 1 John 1:5). The saints' inheritance exists in the spiritual realm of truth and purity where God Himself dwells (1 Tim. 6:16). Light, then, is a synonym for God's kingdom. Cf. John 8:12; 2 Cor. 4:6; Rev. 21:23; 22:5.

1:13 delivered us. The Gr. term means "to draw to oneself" or "to rescue," and refers to the believer's spiritual liberation by God from Satan's kingdom, which, in contrast to the realm of light with truth and purity, is the realm of darkness (cf. Luke 22:53) with only deception and wickedness (1 John 2:9,11). *See note on Acts 26:18.*

the kingdom of the Son of His love, **14** [c]in
whom we have redemption [4]through His
blood, the forgiveness of sins.
15 He is [d]the image of the invisible God,
[e]the firstborn over all creation. **16** For [f]by
Him all things were created that are in
heaven and that are on earth, visible and
invisible, whether thrones or [g]dominions
or [5]principalities or [6]powers. All things
were created [h]through Him and for Him.
17 [i]And He is before all things, and in Him
[j]all things consist. **18** And [k]He is the head
of the body, the church, who is the beginning, [l]the firstborn from the dead, that in
all things He may have the preeminence.

Reconciled in Christ

19 For it pleased *the Father that* [m]in Him
all the fullness should dwell, **20** and [n]by
Him to reconcile [o]all things to Himself, by
Him, whether things on earth or things in
heaven, [p]having made peace through the
blood of His cross.
21 And you, [q]who once were alienated

14 [c]Eph. 1:7 [4]NU, M omit *through His blood*
15 [d]2 Cor. 4:4; Heb. 1:3 [e]Ps. 89:27; Rev. 3:14
16 [f]John 1:3; Heb. 1:2, 3 [g][Eph. 1:20, 21; Col. 2:15] [h]John 1:3; Rom. 11:36; 1 Cor. 8:6; Heb. 2:10 [5]*rulers* [6]*authorities*
17 [i][John 17:5] [j]Heb. 1:3
18 [k]1 Cor. 11:3; Eph. 1:22 [l]Rev. 1:5
19 [m]John 1:16 **20** [n]Rom. 5:1; Eph. 2:14 [o]2 Cor. 5:18 [p]Eph. 1:10
21 [q][Eph. 2:1]

kingdom. In its basic sense, a group of people ruled by a king. More than just the future, earthly millennial kingdom, this everlasting kingdom (2 Pet. 1:11) speaks of the realm of salvation in which all believers live in current and eternal spiritual relationship with God under the care and authority of Jesus Christ (*see note on Matt. 3:2*). **the Son of His love.** Cf. Matt. 3:17; 12:18; 17:5; Mark 1:11; 9:7; Luke 3:22; 9:35; Eph. 1:6; 2 Pet. 1:17; *see notes on John 17:23-26.* The Father gave this kingdom to the Son He loves, as an expression of eternal love. That means that every person the Father calls and justifies is a love gift from Him to the Son. *See notes on John 6:37,44.*

1:14 redemption. The Gr. word means "to deliver by payment of a ransom," and was used of freeing slaves from bondage. Here it refers to Christ freeing believing sinners from slavery to sin (cf. Eph. 1:7; 1 Cor. 1:30; *see note on Rom. 3:24*). **through His blood.** Cf. v. 20. A reference, not limited to the fluid as if the blood had saving properties in its chemistry, but an expression pointing to the totality of Christ's atoning work as a sacrifice for sin. This is a frequently used metonym in the NT (see Eph. 1:7; 2:13; Heb. 9:14; 1 Pet. 1:19). The word "cross" (as in v. 20) is used similarly to refer to the whole atoning work (see 1 Cor. 1:18; Gal. 6:12,14; Eph. 2:16). *See note on Rom. 5:9.* **the forgiveness of sins.** The Gr. word is a composite of two words that mean "to pardon" or "grant remission of a penalty." Cf. Ps. 103:12; Mic. 7:19; Eph. 1:7; *see notes on 2 Cor. 5:19-21.*

1:15-20 One component in the heresy threatening the Colossian church was the denial of the deity of Christ. Paul combats that damning element of heresy with an emphatic defense of Christ's deity.

1:15 image of the invisible God. *See note on Heb. 1:3.* The Gr. word for "image" is *eikōn,* from which the Eng. word "icon" derives. It means, "copy" or "likeness." Jesus Christ is the perfect image—the exact likeness—of God and is in the very form of God (Phil. 2:6; cf. John 1:14; 14:9), and has been so from all eternity. By describing Jesus in this manner, Paul emphasizes that He is both the representation and manifestation of God. Thus, He is fully God in every way (cf. 2:9; John 8:58; 10:30-33; Heb. 1:8). **the firstborn over all creation.** Cf. v. 18. The Gr. word for "firstborn" can refer to one who was born first chronologically, but most often refers to pre-eminence in position, or rank (*see note on Heb. 1:6*; cf. Rom. 8:29). In both Greek and Jewish culture, the firstborn was the ranking son who had received the right of inheritance from his father, whether he was born first or not. It is used of Israel who, not being the first nation, was however the preeminent nation (cf. Ex. 4:22; Jer. 31:9). Firstborn in this context clearly means highest in rank, not first created (cf. Ps. 89:27; Rev. 1:5) for several reasons: 1) Christ cannot be both "first begotten" and "only begotten" (cf. John 1:14,18; 3:16,18; 1 John 4:9); 2) when the "firstborn" is one of a class, the class is in the plural form (cf. v. 18; Rom. 8:29), but "creation," the class here, is in a singular form; 3) if Paul was teaching that Christ was a created being, he was agreeing with the heresy he was writing to refute; and 4) it is impossible for Christ to be both created, and the Creator of everything (v. 16). Thus Jesus is the firstborn in the sense that He has the preeminence (v. 18) and possesses the right of inheritance "over all creation" (cf. Heb. 1:2; Rev. 5:1-7,13). He existed before the creation and is exalted in rank above it. *See notes on Ps. 2:7; Rom. 8:29.*

1:16 thrones or dominions or principalities or powers. Cf. 2:15; Rom. 8:38; Eph. 1:21; 3:10; 6:12; 1 Pet. 3:22; Jude 6. These are various categories of angels whom Christ created and rules over. There is no comment regarding whether they are holy or fallen, since He is Lord of both groups. The false teachers had incorporated into their heresy the worship of angels (*see note on 2:18*), including the lie that Jesus was one of them, merely a spirit created by God and inferior to Him. Paul rejected that and made it clear that angels, whatever their rank, whether holy or fallen, are mere creatures, and their Creator is none other than the preeminent One, the Lord Savior, Jesus Christ. The purpose of His catalog of angelic ranks is to show the immeasurable superiority of Christ over any being the false teachers might suggest. **All things were created through Him and for Him.** Cf. Rom. 11:33-36. *See notes on John 1:3; Heb. 1:2.* As God, Jesus created the material and spiritual universe for His pleasure and glory.

1:17 He is before all things. When the universe had its beginning, Christ already existed, thus by definition He must be eternal (Mic. 5:2; John 1:1,2; 8:58; 1 John 1:1; Rev. 22:13). **consist.** Lit. "to hold together." Christ sustains the universe, maintaining the power and balance necessary to life's existence and continuity (cf. Heb. 1:3).

1:18 head of the body. Cf. 2:19. Paul uses the human body as a metaphor for the church, of which Christ serves as the "head." Just as a body is controlled from the brain, so Christ controls every part of the church and gives it life and direction. Cf. Eph. 4:15; 5:23. For a detailed discussion of the church as a body, *see notes on 1 Cor. 12:4-27.* **the beginning.** This refers to both source and preeminence. The church had its origins in the Lord Jesus (Eph. 1:4), and He gave life to the church through His sacrificial death and resurrection to become its Sovereign. **the firstborn from the dead.** *See note on v. 15.* Jesus was the first chronologically to be resurrected, never to die again. Of all who have been or ever will be raised from the dead, and that includes all men (John 5:28,29), Christ is supreme (*see notes on v. 15; Phil. 2:8-11*).

1:19 all the fullness. A term likely used by those in the Colossian heresy to refer to divine powers and attributes they believed were divided among various emanations (see Introduction: Background and Setting). Paul countered that by asserting that the fullness of deity—all the divine powers and attributes—was not spread out among created beings, but completely dwelt in Christ alone (cf. 2:9).

1:20 reconcile all things to Himself. The Gr. word for "reconcile" means "to change" or "exchange." Its NT usage refers to a change in the sinner's relationship to God. *See notes on Rom. 5:10; 2 Cor. 5:18-21.* Man is reconciled to God when God restores man to a right relationship with Him through Jesus Christ. An intensified form for "reconcile" is used in this verse to refer to the total and complete reconciliation of believers and ultimately "all things" in the created universe (cf. Rom. 8:21; 2 Pet. 3:10-13; Rev. 21:1). This text does not teach that, as a result, all will believe; rather it teaches that all will ultimately submit (cf. Phil. 2:9-11). **having made peace.** *See note on Rom. 5:1.* God and those He saved are no longer at enmity with each other. **the blood of His cross.** *See note on v. 14.*

and enemies in your mind [r]by wicked
works, yet now He has [s]reconciled 22 [t]in the
body of His flesh through death, [u]to present
you holy, and blameless, and above reproach in His sight— 23 if indeed you continue [v]in the faith, grounded and steadfast,
and are [w]not moved away from the hope of
the gospel which you heard, [x]which was
preached to every creature under heaven,
[y]of which I, Paul, became a minister.

Sacrificial Service for Christ

24 [z]I now rejoice in my sufferings [a]for
you, and fill up in my flesh [b]what is lacking in the afflictions of Christ, for [c]the sake
of His body, which is the church, 25 of
which I became a minister according to
[d]the [7]stewardship from God which was
given to me for you, to fulfill the word of
God, 26 [e]the [8]mystery which has been hidden from ages and from generations, [f]but
now has been revealed to His saints. 27 [g]To
them God willed to make known what are
[h]the riches of the glory of this mystery
among the Gentiles: [9]which is [i]Christ in
you, [j]the hope of glory. 28 Him we preach,
[k]warning every man and teaching every
man in all wisdom, [l]that we may present
every man perfect in Christ Jesus. 29 To this
end I also labor, striving according to His
working which works in me [m]mightily.

Not Philosophy but Christ

2 For I want you to know what a great
[a]conflict[1] I have for you and those in
Laodicea, and *for* as many as have not seen

21 [r]Titus 1:15 [s]2 Cor. 5:18, 19 **22** [t]2 Cor. 5:18; [Eph. 2:14-16] [u][Eph. 5:27]; Col. 1:28 **23** [v]Eph. 3:17; Col. 2:7 [w][John 15:6]; 1 Cor. 15:58 [x]Mark 16:15; Acts 2:5; Rom. 10:18; Col. 1:6 [y]Acts 1:17; Eph. 3:7; Col. 1:25 **24** [z]2 Cor. 7:4 [a]Eph. 3:1, 13 [b][Rom. 8:17; 2 Cor. 1:5; 12:15]; Phil. 2:17 [c]Eph. 1:23 **25** [d]Gal. 2:7 [7]*dispensation or administration* **26** [e][1 Cor. 2:7] [f][2 Tim. 1:10] [8]*secret or hidden truth* **27** [g]2 Cor. 2:14 [h]Rom. 9:23 [i][Rom. 8:10, 11] [j]1 Tim. 1:1 [9]*M who* **28** [k]Acts 20:20 [l]Eph. 5:27 **29** [m]Eph. 3:7
CHAPTER 2 **1** [a]Phil. 1:30; Col. 1:29; 4:12; 1 Thess. 2:2 [1]*struggle*

1:21 alienated...enemies. The Gr. term for "alienated" means "estranged," "cut off," or "separated." Before they were reconciled, all people were completely estranged from God (cf. Eph. 2:12,13). The Gr. word for "enemies" can also be translated "hateful." Unbelievers hate God and resent His holy standard because they love "wicked works" (cf. John 3:19,20; 15:18,24,25). Actually, there is alienation from both sides, since God "hates all workers of iniquity" (Ps. 5:5). **reconciled.** *See note on v. 20.*

1:21,22 reconciled...through death. Christ's substitutionary death on the cross that paid the full penalty for the sin of all who believe made reconciliation possible and actual. *See notes on 2 Cor. 5:18-21*; cf. Rom. 3:25; 5:9,10; 8:3.

1:22 holy...in His sight. "Holy" refers to the believer's positional relationship to God—he is separated from sin and set apart to God by imputed righteousness. This is justification (*see notes on Rom. 3:24-26; Phil. 3:8,9*). As a result of the believer's union with Christ in His death and resurrection, God considers Christians as holy as His Son (Eph. 1:4; 2 Cor. 5:21). Christians are also "blameless" (without blemish) and "above reproach" (no one can bring a charge against them; Rom. 8:33; cf. Phil. 2:15). We are to be presented to Christ, when we meet Him, as a chaste bride (Eph. 5:25-27; 2 Cor. 11:2).

1:23 continue in the faith. Cf. Acts 11:23; 14:22. Those who have been reconciled will persevere in faith and obedience because, in addition to being declared righteous, they are actually made new creatures (2 Cor. 5:17) with a new disposition that loves God, hates sin, desires obedience, and is energized by the indwelling Holy Spirit (cf. John 8:30-32; 1 John 2:19). Rather than defect from the gospel they heard, true believers will remain solid on Christ who is the only foundation (1 Cor. 3:11), and faithful by the enabling grace of God (Phil. 1:6; 2:11-13). For discussion on perseverance of the saints, *see note on Matt. 24:13.* **preached to every creature.** Cf. Mark 16:15. The gospel has no racial boundaries. Having reached Rome, where Paul was when he wrote Colossians, it had reached the center of the known world.

1:24 my sufferings. Paul's present imprisonment (Acts 28:16,30; see Introduction to Ephesians: Background and Setting). **fill up... what is lacking.** Paul was experiencing the persecution intended for Christ. In spite of His death on the cross, Christ's enemies had not gotten their fill of inflicting injury on Him. So they turned their hatred on those who preached the gospel (cf. John 15:18,24; 16:1-3). It was in that sense that Paul filled up what was lacking in Christ's afflictions (*see notes on 2 Cor. 1:5; Gal. 6:17*). **the sake of His body.** Paul's motivation for enduring suffering was to benefit and build Christ's church. Cf. Phil. 1:13,29,30; *see notes on 2 Cor. 4:8-15; 6:4-10; 11:23-28; 12:9,10.*

1:25 stewardship. Cf. 1 Cor. 4:1,2; 9:17. A steward was a slave who managed his master's household, supervising the other servants, dispensing resources, and handling business and financial affairs. Paul viewed his ministry as a stewardship from the Lord. The church is God's household (1 Tim. 3:16), and Paul was given the task of caring for, feeding, and leading the churches, for which he was accountable to God (cf. Heb. 13:17). All believers are responsible for managing the abilities and resources God gives them (*see note on 1 Pet. 4:10*). **to fulfill the word of God.** This refers to Paul's single-minded devotion to completely fulfill the ministry God gave him to preach the whole counsel of God to those to whom God sent him (Acts 20:27; 2 Tim. 4:7).

1:26 mystery. Cf. 2:2; 4:3. *See notes on Matt. 13:11; 1 Cor. 2:7; Eph. 3:4,5.* This refers to truth, hidden until now, but revealed for the first time to the saints in the NT. Such truth includes the mystery of the incarnate God (2:2,3,9), Israel's unbelief (Rom. 11:25), lawlessness (2 Thess. 2:7), the unity of Jew and Gentile made one in the church (Eph. 3:3-6), and the rapture of the church (1 Cor. 15:51). In this passage, the mystery is specifically identified in v. 27.

1:27 Gentiles...Christ in you. The OT predicted the coming of the Messiah and that the Gentiles would partake of salvation (cf. Is. 42:6; 45:21,22; 49:6; 52:10; 60:1-3; Pss. 22:27; 65:5; 98:2,3), but it did not reveal that the Messiah would actually live in each member of His redeemed church, made up mostly of Gentiles. That believers, both Jew and Gentile, now possess the surpassing riches of the indwelling Christ is the glorious revealed mystery (John 14:23; Rom. 8:9,10; Gal. 2:20; Eph. 1:7,17,18; 3:8-10,16-19). **the hope of glory.** The indwelling Spirit of Christ is the guarantee to each believer of future glory (Rom. 8:11; Eph. 1:13,14; 1 Pet. 1:3,4).

1:28 perfect. To be complete or mature—to be like Christ. *See notes on Rom. 8:29; 1 Cor. 11:1; Phil. 3:12-14,19,20; 1 John 2:6; 3:2.* This spiritual maturity is defined in 2:2.

1:29 I...labor, striving according to His working. Here is the balance of Christian living. Paul gave the effort to serve and honor God with all his might. "Labor" refers to working to the point of exhaustion. The Gr. word for "striving" gives us the Eng. word "agonize" and refers to the effort required to compete in an athletic event. At the same time, he knew the effective "striving" or work, with spiritual and eternal results was being done by God through him (*see notes on Phil. 2:11-13*; cf. 1 Cor. 15:10,58).

2:1 great conflict. The word means "striving" and comes from the same root as in 1:29. Both the Colossians and Laodiceans were among those for whom Paul struggled so hard in order to bring them to maturity. **Laodicea.** The chief city of Phrygia in the Roman province of Asia, located just S of Hierapolis in the Lycus River valley (see Introduction: Background and Setting; *see note on Rev. 3:14*; cf. 4:13).

my face in the flesh, **2** that their hearts may
be encouraged, being knit together in love,
and *attaining* to all riches of the full assurance of understanding, to the knowledge
of the mystery of God, [2]both of the Father
and of Christ, **3** [b]in whom are hidden all
the treasures of wisdom and knowledge.
4 Now this I say [c]lest anyone should deceive you with persuasive words. **5** For
[d]though I am absent in the flesh, yet I am
with you in spirit, rejoicing [3]to see [e]your
good order and the [f]steadfastness of your
faith in Christ.
6 [g]As you therefore have received Christ
Jesus the Lord, so walk in Him, **7** [h]rooted
and built up in Him and established in the
faith, as you have been taught, abounding
[4]in it with thanksgiving.
8 Beware lest anyone [5]cheat you through
philosophy and empty deceit, according to
[i]the tradition of men, according to the [j]ba-
sic principles of the world, and not according to Christ. **9** For [k]in Him dwells all the
fullness of the Godhead [6]bodily; **10** and
you are complete in Him, who is the [l]head
of all [7]principality and power.

Not Legalism but Christ

11 In Him you were also [m]circumcised
with the circumcision made without
hands, by [n]putting off the body [8]of the sins
of the flesh, by the circumcision of Christ,
12 [o]buried with Him in baptism, in which
you also were raised with *Him* through
[p]faith in the working of God, [q]who raised
Him from the dead. **13** And you, being
dead in your trespasses and the uncircumcision of your flesh, He has made alive together with Him, having forgiven you all
trespasses, **14** [r]having wiped out the

2 [2] NU omits *both of the Father and*
3 [b] 1 Cor. 1:24, 30
4 [c] Rom. 16:18; 2 Cor. 11:13; Eph. 4:14; 5:6
5 [d] 1 Thess. 2:17 [e] 1 Cor. 14:40 [f] 1 Pet. 5:9 [3] Lit. *and seeing*
6 [g] 1 Thess. 4:1
7 [h] Eph. 2:21 [4] NU omits *in it*
8 [i] Gal. 1:14 [j] Gal. 4:3, 9, 10; Col. 2:20 [5] Lit. *plunder you* or *take you captive*
9 [k] [John 1:14]; Col. 1:19 [6] *in bodily form*
10 [l] [Eph. 1:20, 21; 1 Pet. 3:22] [7] *rule and authority*
11 [m] Deut. 10:16 [n] Rom. 6:6; 7:24; Gal. 5:24; Col. 3:5 [8] NU omits *of the sins*
12 [o] Rom. 6:4 [p] Eph. 1:19, 20 [q] Acts 2:24
14 [r] [Eph. 2:15, 16]; Col. 2:20

2:2 full assurance of understanding. "Understanding" of the fullness of the gospel, along with inner encouragement and shared love, mark mature believers who, thereby, enjoy the "assurance" of salvation (*see notes on 2 Pet. 1:5-8*). **mystery.** *See note on 1:26.* **of God...Christ.** Cf. 4:3. Leaving out the phrase between "God" and "Christ" (see marginal note), which was probably not in the original text, changes nothing. The point is that the mystery Paul referred to here is that the Messiah Christ is God incarnate Himself (cf. 1 Tim. 3:16).

2:3 all the treasures. Cf. vv. 9,10; 1:19. The false teachers threatening the Colossians claimed to possess a secret wisdom and transcendent knowledge available only to the spiritual elite. In sharp contrast, Paul declared that all the richness of truth necessary for either salvation, sanctification, or glorification is found in Jesus Christ, who Himself is God revealed. Cf. John 1:14; Rom. 11:33-36; 1 Cor. 1:24,30; 2:6-8; Eph. 1:8,9; 3:8,9.

2:4 lest anyone should deceive you. Paul did not want the Colossians to be deceived by the persuasive rhetoric of the false teachers which assaulted the person of Christ. That is why throughout chaps. 1,2 he stressed Christ's deity, and His sufficiency both to save believers and bring them to spiritual maturity.

2:5 absent in the flesh...with you in spirit. Because he was a prisoner, Paul was unable to be present with the Colossians. That did not mean, however, that his love and concern for them was any less (cf. 1 Cor. 5:3,4; 1 Thess. 2:17). Their "good order" and "steadfast faith" (both military terms depicting a solid rank of soldiers drawn up for battle) brought great joy to the apostle's heart.

2:6 walk in Him. "Walk" is the familiar NT term denoting the believer's daily conduct (1:10; 4:5; Rom. 6:4; 8:1,4; 13:13; 1 Cor. 7:17; 2 Cor. 5:7; 10:3; 12:18; Gal. 5:16,25; 6:16; Eph. 2:10; 4:1,17; 5:2,8,15; Phil. 3:16-18; 1 Thess. 2:12; 4:1,12; 2 Thess. 3:11; 1 John 1:6,7; 2:6; 2 John 6; 3 John 3,4). To walk in Christ is to live a life patterned after His.

2:7 the faith. The sense here is objective, referring to the truth of Christian doctrine. Spiritual maturity develops upward from the foundation of biblical truth as taught and recorded by the apostles. Cf. 3:16. This rooting, building, and establishing is in sound doctrine (cf. 1 Tim. 4:6; 2 Tim. 3:16,17; Titus 2:1).

2:8 cheat you. Here is the term for robbery. False teachers who are successful in getting people to believe lies, rob them of truth, salvation, and blessing. **philosophy and empty deceit.** "Philosophy" (lit. "love of wisdom") appears only here in the NT. The word referred to more than merely the academic discipline, but described any theory about God, the world, or the meaning of life. Those embracing the Colossian heresy used it to describe the supposed higher knowledge they claimed to have attained. Paul, however, equates the false teachers' philosophy with "empty deceit"; that is, with worthless deception. Cf. 1 Tim. 6:20; *see note on 2 Cor. 10:5.* **the basic principles of the world.** *See note on v. 20; Gal. 4:3.* Far from being advanced, profound knowledge, the false teachers' beliefs were simplistic and immature like all the rest of the speculations, ideologies, philosophies, and psychologies the fallen satanic and human system invents.

2:9 fullness of the Godhead. Christ possesses the fullness of the divine nature and attributes (*see notes on 1:19; John 1:14-16*). **bodily.** In Greek philosophical thought, matter was evil; spirit was good. Thus, it was unthinkable that God would ever take on a human body. Paul refutes that false teaching by stressing the reality of Christ's incarnation. Jesus was not only fully God, but fully human as well. *See notes on Phil. 2:5-11.*

2:10 complete in Him. *See notes on vv. 3,4*; cf. John 1:16; Eph. 1:3. Believers are complete in Christ, both positionally by the imputed perfect righteousness of Christ (*see note on 1:22*), and the complete sufficiency of all heavenly resources for spiritual maturity (*see notes on 2 Pet. 1:3,4*). **the head of all principality and power.** Jesus Christ is the creator and ruler of the universe and all its spiritual beings (*see note on 1:16*), not a lesser being emanating from God as the Colossian errorists maintained (see Introduction: Background and Setting).

2:11,12 circumcision made without hands. *See note on circumcision in Gen. 17:11.* Circumcision symbolized man's need for cleansing of the heart (cf. Deut. 10:16; 30:6; Jer. 4:4; 9:26; Acts 7:51; Rom. 2:29) and was the outward sign of that cleansing of sin that comes by faith in God (Rom. 4:11; Phil. 3:3). At salvation, believers undergo a spiritual "circumcision" "by putting off the body of the sins of the flesh" (cf. Rom. 6:6; 2 Cor. 5:17; Phil 3:3; Titus 3:5). This is the new birth, the new creation in conversion. The outward affirmation of the already accomplished inner transformation is now the believer's baptism by water (Acts 2:38).

2:13 dead in your trespasses. *See notes on Eph. 2:1,5.* So bound in the sphere of sin, the world (Eph. 2:12), the flesh (Rom. 8:8), and the devil (1 John 5:19) as to be unable to respond to spiritual stimuli; totally devoid of spiritual life. Paul further defines this condition of the unsaved in 1 Cor. 2:14; Eph. 4:17-19; Titus 3:3. **He has made alive together with Him.** *See notes on Eph. 2:1,5.* Only through union with Jesus Christ (vv. 10-12) can those hopelessly dead in their sins receive eternal life (cf. Eph. 2:5). Note that God takes the initiative and exerts the life-giving power to awaken and unite sinners with His Son; the spiritually dead have no ability to make themselves alive (cf. Rom. 4:17; 2 Cor. 1:9). **forgiven you all trespasses.** Cf. 1:14. God's free (Rom. 3:24) and complete (Rom. 5:20; Eph. 1:7) forgiveness of guilty

[9]handwriting of requirements that was
against us, which was contrary to us. And
He has taken it out of the way, having
nailed it to the cross. **15** [s]Having disarmed
[t]principalities and powers, He made a
public spectacle of them, triumphing over
them in it.

16 So let no one [u]judge you in food or in
drink, or regarding a [1]festival or a new
moon or sabbaths, **17** [v]which are a shadow
of things to come, but the [2]substance is of
Christ. **18** Let no one cheat you of your reward, taking delight in *false* humility and
worship of angels, intruding into those
things which he has [3]not seen, vainly
puffed up by his fleshly mind, **19** and not
holding fast to [w]the Head, from whom all
the body, nourished and knit together by
joints and ligaments, [x]grows with the increase *that is* from God.

20 [4]Therefore, if you [y]died with Christ
from the basic principles of the world, [z]why,
as *though* living in the world, do you subject
yourselves to regulations— **21** [a]"Do not
touch, do not taste, do not handle," **22** which
all concern things which perish with the
using—[b]according to the commandments
and doctrines of men? **23** [c]These things indeed have an appearance of wisdom in self-
imposed religion, *false* humility, and [5]ne-
glect of the body, *but are* of no value against
the indulgence of the flesh.

14 [9] *certificate of debt with its*
15 [s] [Is. 53:12; Heb. 2:14] [t] Eph. 6:12
16 [u] Rom. 14:3 [1] *feast day*
17 [v] Heb. 8:5; 10:1 [2] Lit. *body*
18 [3] NU omits *not*
19 [w] Eph. 4:15 [x] Eph. 1:23; 4:16
20 [y] Rom. 6:2-5 [z] Gal. 4:3, 9 [4] NU, M omit *Therefore*
21 [a] 1 Tim. 4:3
22 [b] Is. 29:13; Matt. 15:9; Titus 1:14
23 [c] Rom. 13:14; 1 Tim. 4:8 [5] *severe treatment, asceticism*

CHAPTER 3

1 [a] Rom. 6:5; Eph. 2:6; Col. 2:12

Not Carnality but Christ

3 If then you were [a]raised with Christ,
seek those things which are above,

sinners who put their faith in Jesus Christ is the most important reality in Scripture (cf. Pss. 32:1; 130:3,4; Is. 1:18; 55:7; Mic. 7:18; Matt. 26:28; Acts 10:43; 13:38,39; Titus 3:4-7; Heb. 8:12).

2:14 wiped out the handwriting. The Gr. work translated "handwriting" referred to the handwritten certificate of debt by which a debtor acknowledged his indebtedness. All people (Rom. 3:23) owe God an unpayable debt for violating His law (Gal. 3:10; James 2:10; cf. Matt. 18:23-27), and are thus under sentence of death (Rom. 6:23). Paul graphically compares God's forgiveness of believers' sins to wiping ink off a parchment. Through Christ's sacrificial death on the cross, God has totally erased our certificate of indebtedness and made our forgiveness complete. **nailed it to the cross.** This is another metaphor for forgiveness. The list of the crimes of a crucified criminal were nailed to the cross with that criminal to declare the violations he was being punished for (as in the case of Jesus, as noted in Matt. 27:37). Believers' sins were all put to Christ's account, nailed to His cross as He paid the penalty in their place for them all, thus satisfying the just wrath of God against crimes requiring punishment in full.

2:15 Having disarmed. In yet another element of the cross work, Paul tells that the cross spelled the ultimate doom of Satan and his evil host of fallen angels (cf. Gen. 3:15; John 12:31; 16:11; Heb. 2:14). **principalities and powers.** *See note on 1:16.* While His body was dead, His living, divine spirit actually went to the abode of demons and announced His triumph over sin, Satan, death, and hell. *See notes on 1 Pet. 3:18,19.* **made a public spectacle...triumphing over them.** The picture is that of a victorious Roman general parading his defeated enemies through the streets of Rome (*see notes on 2 Cor. 2:14-16*). Christ won the victory over the demon forces on the cross, where their efforts to halt God's redemptive plan were ultimately defeated. For more on that triumphant imagery, *see notes on 2 Cor. 2:14-16.*

2:16,17 Paul warns the Colossians against trading their freedom in Christ for a set of useless, man-made, legalistic rules (cf. Gal. 5:1). Legalism is powerless to save or to restrain sin.

2:16 food...drink. The false teachers sought to impose some sort of dietary regulations, probably based on those of the Mosaic law (cf. Lev. 11). Since they were under the New Covenant, the Colossians (like all Christians) were not obligated to observe the OT dietary restrictions (cf. Mark 7:14-19; Acts 10:9-15; Rom. 14:17; 1 Cor. 8:8; 1 Tim. 4:1-5; Heb. 9:9,10). **festival.** The annual religious celebrations of the Jewish calendar (e.g., Passover, Pentecost, or Tabernacles; cf. Lev. 23). **new moon.** The monthly sacrifice offered on the first day of each month (Num. 10:10; 28:11-14; Ps. 81:3). **sabbaths.** The weekly celebration of the seventh day, which pictured God's rest from creation. The NT clearly teaches that Christians are not required to keep it (*see notes on Acts 20:7; Rom. 14:5,6*).

2:17 shadow...substance. The ceremonial aspects of the OT law (dietary regulations, festivals, sacrifices) were mere shadows pointing to Christ. Since Christ, the reality has come, the shadows have no value. Cf. Heb. 8:5; 10:1.

2:18 cheat you. Paul warns the Colossians not to allow the false teachers to cheat them of their temporal blessings or eternal reward (cf. 2 John 8) by luring them into irrational mysticism. ***false* humility.** Since the false teachers took great delight in it, their "humility" was actually pride, which God hates (Prov. 6:16,17). **worship of angels.** The beginning of a heresy that was to plague the region around Colosse for several centuries and far beyond—a practice the Bible clearly prohibits (Matt. 4:10; Rev. 19:10; 22:8,9). **which he has not seen.** Like virtually all cults and false religions, the Colossian false teachers based their teaching on visions and revelations they had supposedly received. Their claims were false, since Jesus Christ is God's final and complete (*see notes on vv. 3,4*) revelation to mankind (Heb. 1:1,2). **fleshly mind.** *See note on Rom. 8:6.* This describes the unregenerate and is further defined in Eph. 4:17-19.

2:19 Cf. 1:18; *see note on Eph. 4:15,16.* There is no spiritual growth for the body (the church) apart from union with the Head, Christ (cf. John 15:4,5; 2 Pet. 1:3).

2:20 died with Christ. Refers to the believer's union with Christ in His death and resurrection (*see notes on Rom. 6:1-11*) by which he has been transformed to new life from all worldly folly. **basic principles.** *See note on v. 8.* These are the same as "the commandments and doctrines of men" (v. 22).

2:21-23 These verses point out the futility of asceticism, which is the attempt to achieve holiness by rigorous self-neglect (v. 23), self-denial (v. 21), and even self-infliction. Since it focuses on temporal "things which perish with the using," asceticism is powerless to restrain sin or bring one to God. While reasonable care and discipline of one's body is of temporal value (1 Tim. 4:8), it has no eternal value, and the extremes of asceticism serve only to gratify the flesh. All too often, ascetics seek only to put on a public show of their supposed holiness (Matt. 6:16-18).

3:1 If. Better translated, "since." **you were raised.** This verb actually means "to be co-resurrected." Because of their union with Christ, believers spiritually entered His death and resurrection at the moment of their conversion (*see notes on Rom. 6:3,4; Gal. 2:20*) and have been and are now alive in Him so as to understand spiritual truths, realities, blessings, and the will of God. Those glorious benedictions (cf. Eph. 1:3) are the privileges and riches of the heavenly kingdom, all of which are at our disposal. Paul called them "things above." To understand what these are, *see note on 2:3.* **sitting at the right hand of God.** The position of honor and majesty (cf. Ps. 110:1; Luke 22:69; Acts 2:33; 5:31;

[b]where Christ is, sitting at the right hand of
God. 2 Set your mind on things above, not
on things on the [c]earth. 3 [d]For you died,
[e]and your life is hidden with Christ in God.
4 [f]When Christ *who is* [g]our life appears, then
you also will appear with Him in [h]glory.
5 [i]Therefore put to death [j]your members which are on the earth: [k]fornication,
uncleanness, passion, evil desire, and covetousness, [l]which is idolatry. 6 [m]Because
of these things the wrath of God is coming
upon [n]the sons of disobedience, 7 [o]in
which you yourselves once walked when
you lived in them.

1 [b] Ps. 68:18; 110:1; [Rom. 8:34]; Eph. 1:20 2 [c] [Matt. 6:19-21] 3 [d] [Rom. 6:2; 2 Cor. 5:14; Gal. 2:20]; Col. 2:20 [e] [2 Cor. 5:7] 4 [f] [1 John 3:2] [g] John 14:6 [h] 1 Cor. 15:43 5 [i] [Rom. 8:13] [j] [Rom. 6:13] [k] Eph. 5:3 [l] Mark 7:21; 1 Cor. 6:9, 18; 2 Cor. 12:21; Gal. 5:19; Eph. 4:19; 5:3, 5 6 [m] Rom. 1:18; Eph. 5:6; Rev. 22:15 [n] [Eph. 2:2] 7 [o] 1 Cor. 6:11; [Eph. 2:2]; Titus 3:3

7:56; Eph. 1:20; Heb. 1:3; 8:1; 1 Pet. 3:22) that Christ enjoys as the exalted Son of God (*see note on Phil. 2:9*). That exaltation makes Him the fountain of blessing for His people (John 14:13,14; cf. 2 Cor. 1:20).

3:2 Set your mind. This can also be translated "think," or "have this inner disposition." As a compass points N, the believer's entire disposition should point itself toward the things of heaven. Heavenly thoughts can only come by understanding heavenly realities from Scripture (cf. Rom. 8:5; 12:2; Phil. 1:23; 4:8; 1 John 2:15-17; *see note on Matt. 6:33*).

3:3 you died. *See notes on Rom. 6:1-11; 2 Cor. 5:17; Gal. 6:14.* The verb's tense indicates that a death occurred in the past, in this case at the death of Jesus Christ, where believers were united with Him, their penalty of sin was paid, and they arose with Him in new life. **hidden with Christ in God.** This rich expression has a threefold meaning: 1) believers have a common spiritual life with the Father and Son (1 Cor. 6:17; 2 Pet. 1:4); 2) the world cannot understand the full import of the believer's new life (Rom. 8:19; 1 Cor. 2:14; 1 John 3:2); and 3) believers are eternally secure, protected from all spiritual enemies, and with access to all God's blessings (John 10:28; Rom. 8:31-39; Heb. 7:25; 1 Pet. 1:4).

3:4 When Christ…appears. At His second coming (cf. Rev. 19:11-13,15,16).

3:5 put to death. *See note on Rom. 8:13*; cf. Zech. 4:6; Eph. 5:18; 6:17; 1 John 2:14. This refers to a conscious effort to slay the remaining sin in our flesh. **fornication.** Also translated "immorality," it refers to any form of sexual sin (*see note on Gal. 5:19*; cf. 1 Thess. 4:3). **uncleanness.** Also translated "impurity," this term goes beyond sexual acts of sin to encompass evil thoughts and intentions as well (*see note on Gal. 5:19*; cf. Matt. 5:28; Mark 7:21,22; 1 Thess. 4:7). **passion, evil desire.** Similar terms that refer to sexual lust. "Passion" is the physical side of that vice, and "evil desire" is the mental side (*see notes on Rom. 1:26; 1 Thess. 4:5*; cf. James 1:15). **covetousness.** Also rendered "greed," lit. it means "to have more." It is the insatiable desire to gain more, especially of things that are forbidden (cf. Ex. 20:17; Deut. 5:21; James 4:2). **which is idolatry.** When people engage in either greed or the sexual sins Paul has cataloged, they follow their desires rather than God's, in essence worshiping themselves—which is idolatry (Num. 25:1-3; Eph. 5:3-5).

3:6 wrath of God. His constant, invariable reaction against sin (*see notes on John 3:36; Rom. 1:18; Rev. 11:18*). **sons of disobedience.** *See note on Eph. 2:2.* This expression designates unbelievers as bearing the very nature and character of the disobedient, rebellious sinfulness they love.

3:7 in which you…once walked. Before their conversion (cf. Eph. 2:1-5; Titus 3:3,4).

Titles of Christ

Name or Title	Significance	Biblical Reference
Adam, Last Adam	First of the new race of the redeemed	1 Cor. 15:45
Alpha and Omega	The beginning and ending of all things	Rev. 21:6
Bread of Life	The one essential food	John 6:35
Chief Cornerstone	A sure foundation for life	Eph. 2:20
Chief Shepherd	Protector, sustainer, and guide	1 Pet. 5:4
Firstborn from the Dead	Leads us into resurrection and eternal life	Col. 1:18
Good Shepherd	Provider and caretaker	John 10:11
Great Shepherd of the Sheep	Trustworthy guide and protector	Heb. 13:20
High Priest	A perfect sacrifice for our sins	Heb. 3:1
Holy One of God	Sinless in His nature	Mark 1:24
Immanuel (God With Us)	Stands with us in all life's circumstances	Matt. 1:23
King of Kings, Lord of Lords	The Almighty, before whom every knee will bow	Rev. 19:16
Lamb of God	Gave His life as a sacrifice on our behalf	John 1:29
Light of the World	Brings hope in the midst of darkness	John 9:5
Lord of Glory	The power and presence of the living God	1 Cor. 2:8
Mediator between God and Men	Brings us into God's presence redeemed and forgiven	1 Tim. 2:5
Only Begotten of the Father	The unique, one-of-a-kind Son of God	John 1:14
Prophet	Faithful proclaimer of the truths of God	Acts 3:22
Savior	Delivers from sin and death	Luke 1:47
Seed of Abraham	Mediator of God's covenant	Gal. 3:16
Son of Man	Identifies with us in our humanity	Matt. 18:11
The Word	Present with God at the creation	John 1:1

8 [p]But now you yourselves are to put off
all these: anger, wrath, malice, blasphemy,
filthy language out of your mouth. 9 Do
not lie to one another, since you have put
off the old man with his deeds, 10 and have
put on the new *man* who [q]is renewed in
knowledge [r]according to the image of Him
who [s]created him, 11 where there is neither
[t]Greek nor Jew, circumcised nor uncircumcised, barbarian, Scythian, slave *nor* free,
[u]but Christ *is* all and in all.

Character of the New Man

12 Therefore, [v]as *the* elect of God, holy
and beloved, [w]put on tender mercies,
kindness, humility, meekness, longsuffering; 13 [x]bearing with one another, and forgiving one another, if anyone has a complaint against another; even as Christ
forgave you, so you also *must do.* 14 [y]But
above all these things [z]put on love, which
is the [a]bond of perfection. 15 And let [b]the
peace of God rule in your hearts, [c]to which
also you were called [d]in one body; and [e]be
thankful. 16 Let the word of Christ dwell in
you richly in all wisdom, teaching and admonishing one another [f]in psalms and
hymns and spiritual songs, singing with
grace in your hearts to the Lord. 17 And
[g]*whatever* you do in word or deed, *do* all in

8 [p]Eph. 4:22; 1 Pet. 2:1
10 [q]Rom. 12:2; 2 Cor. 4:16 [r][Rom. 8:29] [s][Eph. 2:10]
11 [t]Rom. 10:12; [1 Cor. 12:13]; Gal. 3:27, 28 [u]Eph. 1:23
12 [v][1 Pet. 1:2] [w]Luke 1:78; Phil. 2:1; 1 John 3:17
13 [x][Mark 11:25]
14 [y]1 Pet. 4:8 [z][1 Cor. 13] [a]Eph. 4:3
15 [b][John 14:27; Phil. 4:7] [c]1 Cor. 7:15 [d]Eph. 4:4 [e][1 Thess. 5:18]
16 [f]Eph. 5:19
17 [g]1 Cor. 10:31

3:8 put off. A Gr. word used for taking off clothes (cf. Acts 7:58; Rom. 13:12-14; 1 Pet. 2:1). Like one who removes his dirty clothes at day's end, believers must discard the filthy garments of their old, sinful lives. **anger.** A deep, smoldering bitterness; the settled heart attitude of an angry person (cf. Eph. 4:31; James 1:19,20). **wrath.** Unlike God's settled and righteous wrath (*see note on Rom. 1:18*), this is a sudden outburst of sinful anger, usually the eruption that flows out of "anger" (*see note on Gal. 5:20*; cf. Luke 4:28; Acts 19:28; Eph. 4:31). **malice.** From the Gr. term that denotes general moral evil. Here it probably refers to the damage caused by evil speech (cf. 1 Pet. 2:1). **blasphemy.** The normal translation when this word refers to God. But here, since it refers to people, it is better translated "slander." To slander people, however, is to blaspheme God (James 3:9; cf. Matt. 5:22; James 3:10).

3:9,10 put off...put on. *See notes on v. 8; Eph. 4:24,25.* These words are the basis for the command of v. 8. Because the old man died in Christ, and the new man lives in Christ—because that is the fact of new creation or regeneration (2 Cor. 5:17)—believers must put off remaining sinful deeds and be being continually renewed into the Christlikeness to which they are called.

3:9 old man. The old, unregenerate self, originating in Adam (*see notes on Rom. 5:12-14; 6:6*; cf. Eph. 4:22).

3:10 new *man*. The new, regenerate self, which replaces the old man; this is the essence of what believers are in Christ (cf. Eph. 4:17; 5:1,8,15). The reason believers still sin is their unredeemed flesh (*see notes on Rom. 6:6,12; 7:5*). **renewed.** *See note on 2 Cor. 4:16*; cf. Rom. 12:2; 2 Cor. 3:18. This Gr. verb contains a sense of contrast with the former reality. It describes a new quality of life that never before existed (cf. Rom. 12:2; Eph. 4:22). Just like a baby is born complete but immature, the new man is complete, but has the capacity to grow. **knowledge.** *See note on 1:9.* A deep, thorough knowledge, without which there can be no spiritual growth or renewal (2 Tim. 3:16,17; 1 Pet. 2:2). **image of Him who created him.** It is God's plan that believers become progressively more like Jesus Christ, the one who made them (cf. Rom. 8:29; 1 Cor. 15:49; 1 John 3:2). *See notes on Phil. 3:12-14,19,20.*

3:11 Even as individual believers must discard old, sinful habits, the body of Christ must realize its unity and destroy the old barriers that separated people (cf. Gal. 3:28; Eph. 2:15). **Greek.** A Gentile, or non-Jew (*see note on Rom. 1:14*). **Jew.** A descendant of Abraham through Isaac (*see note on Rom. 2:17*). **barbarian.** *See note on Rom. 1:14.* **Scythian.** An ancient nomadic and warlike people that invaded the Fertile Crescent in the seventh century B.C. Noted for their savagery, they were the most hated and feared of all the so-called barbarians. **slave *nor* free.** A social barrier had always existed between slaves and freemen; Aristotle had referred to slaves as "a living tool." But faith in Christ removed the separation (1 Cor. 12:13; Gal. 3:28; cf. Philem. 6). **Christ *is* all and in all.** Because Jesus Christ is the Savior of all believers, He is equally the all-sufficient Lord of them all.

3:12 Therefore. In view of what God has done through Jesus Christ for the believer, Paul described the behavior and attitude God expects in response (vv. 12-17). **elect of God.** This designates true Christians as those who have been chosen by God. No one is converted solely by his own choice, but only in response to God's effectual, free, uninfluenced, and sovereign grace (*see notes on John 15:16; Rom. 8:29; 9:10-24; Eph. 1:4; 2 Thess. 2:13; 2 Tim. 1:8,9; 1 Pet. 1:1,2*; cf. Acts 13:46-48; Rom. 11:4,5). **beloved.** Election means believers are the objects of God's incomprehensible special love (cf. John 13:1; Eph. 1:4,5). **put on.** *See note on vv. 9,10.* **tender mercies.** This may also be rendered "heart of compassion." It is a Hebraism that connotes the internal organs of the human body as used figuratively to describe the seat of the emotions (cf. Matt. 9:36; Luke 6:36; James 5:11). **kindness.** Refers to a goodness toward others that pervades the entire person, mellowing all harsh aspects (cf. Matt. 11:29,30; Luke 10:25-37). **humility.** *See notes on Rom. 12:3,10; Phil. 2:3*; cf. Matt. 18:4; John 13:14-16; James 4:6,10. This is the perfect antidote to the self-love that poisons human relationships. **meekness.** *See notes on Matt. 5:5, Gal. 5:23.* Sometimes translated "gentleness," it is the willingness to suffer injury or insult rather than to inflict such hurts. **longsuffering.** *See note on 1:11*; cf. Rom. 2:4. It is also translated "patience," the opposite of quick anger, resentment, or revenge and thus epitomizes Jesus Christ (1 Tim. 1:16; cf. 2 Pet. 3:15). It endures injustice and troublesome circumstances with hope for coming relief.

3:13 as Christ forgave you. *See notes on Matt. 18:23-35; Eph. 4:32.* Because Christ as the model of forgiveness has forgiven all our sins totally (1:14; 2:13,14), believers must be willing to forgive others.

3:14 bond of perfection. A better rendering is "perfect bond of unity" (*see notes on Eph. 4:3; Phil. 1:27; 2:2*). Supernatural love poured into the hearts of believers is the adhesive of the church. Cf. Rom. 5:5; 1 Thess. 4:9.

3:15 the peace of God. The Gr. word "peace" here refers to both the call of God to salvation and consequent peace with Him (*see note on Rom. 5:1*), and the attitude of rest or security (Phil. 4:7) believers have because of that eternal peace.

3:16 word of Christ. This is Scripture, the Holy Spirit inspired Scripture, the word of revelation He brought into the world. **dwell in you richly.** *See notes on Eph. 5:18.* "Dwell" means "to live in" or "to be at home," and "richly" may be more fully rendered "abundantly or extravagantly rich." Scripture should permeate every aspect of the believer's life and control every thought, word, and deed (cf. Ps. 119:11; Matt. 13:9; Phil. 2:16; 2 Tim. 2:15). This concept is parallel to being filled with the Spirit in Eph. 5:18 since the results of each are the same. In Eph. 5:18, the power and motivation for all the effects is the filling of the Holy Spirit; here it is the word richly dwelling. Those two realities are really one. The Holy Spirit fills the life controlled by His Word. This emphasizes that the filling of the Spirit is not some ecstatic or emotional experience, but a steady controlling of the life by obedience to the truth of God's Word. **psalms and hymns and spiritual songs.** *See note on Eph. 5:19.*

the name of the Lord Jesus, giving thanks
to God the Father through Him.

The Christian Home

18 [h]Wives, submit to your own husbands, [i]as is fitting in the Lord.
19 [j]Husbands, love your wives and do
not be [k]bitter toward them.
20 [l]Children, obey your parents [m]in all
things, for this is well pleasing to the Lord.
21 [n]Fathers, do not provoke your children, lest they become discouraged.
22 [o]Bondservants, obey in all things your
masters according to the flesh, not with
eyeservice, as men-pleasers, but in sincerity
of heart, fearing God. 23 [p]And whatever
you do, do it heartily, as to the Lord and not
to men, 24 [q]knowing that from the Lord you
will receive the reward of the inheritance;
[r]for[1] you serve the Lord Christ. 25 But he
who does wrong will be repaid for what he
has done, and [s]there is no partiality.

4 Masters,[a] give your bondservants
what is just and fair, knowing that you
also have a Master in heaven.

18 [h]1 Pet. 3:1 [i][Col. 3:18–4:1; Eph. 5:22–6:9]
19 [j][Eph. 5:25; 1 Pet. 3:7] [k]Eph. 4:31
20 [l]Eph. 6:1 [m]Eph. 5:24
21 [n]Eph. 6:4
22 [o]Eph. 6:5; [1 Tim. 6:1]; Titus 2:9; 1 Pet. 2:18
23 [p][Eccl. 9:10]
24 [q]Eph. 6:8 [r]1 Cor. 7:22 [1]NU omits *for*
25 [s]Rom. 2:11

CHAPTER 4

1 [a]Eph. 6:9
2 [b]Luke 18:1 [c]Col. 2:7
3 [d]Eph. 6:19 [e]1 Cor. 16:9 [f]Eph. 3:3, 4; 6:19 [g]Eph. 6:20 [1]*hidden truth*
5 [h]Eph. 5:15 [i][Matt. 10:16] [j]Eph. 5:16
6 [k]Eccl. 10:12 [l]Mark 9:50 [m]1 Pet. 3:15
7 [n]Acts 20:4; Eph. 6:21; 2 Tim. 4:12; Titus 3:12
8 [o]Eph. 6:22

Christian Graces

2 [b]Continue earnestly in prayer, being
vigilant in it [c]with thanksgiving; 3 [d]mean-
while praying also for us, that God would
[e]open to us a door for the word, to speak
[f]the [1]mystery of Christ, [g]for which I am
also in chains, 4 that I may make it manifest, as I ought to speak.
5 [h]Walk in [i]wisdom toward those *who are*
outside, [j]redeeming the time. 6 *Let* your
speech always *be* [k]with grace, [l]seasoned
with salt, [m]that you may know how you
ought to answer each one.

Final Greetings

7 [n]Tychicus, a beloved brother, faithful
minister, and fellow servant in the Lord,
will tell you all the news about me. 8 [o]I am
sending him to you for this very purpose,
that [2]he may know your circumstances
and comfort your hearts, 9 with [p]Onesi-
mus, a faithful and beloved brother, who is

[2]NU *you may know our circumstances and he may comfort*
9 [p]Philem. 10

3:17 *do* all in the name of the Lord Jesus. This simply means to act consistently with who He is and what He wants (*see note on 1 Cor. 10:31*).

3:18–4:1 Paul discusses the new man's relationships to others. This passage is also a brief parallel to Eph. 5:19–6:9 (*see notes there*).

3:18 submit. *See notes on Eph. 5:22-24.* The Gr. verb means "to subject oneself," which denotes willingly putting oneself under someone or something (cf. Luke 2:51; 10:17,20; Rom. 8:7; 13:1,5; 1 Cor. 15:27,28; Eph. 1:22).

3:19 love. *See notes on Eph. 5:25-29.* This is a call for the highest form of love which is rendered selflessly (cf. Gen. 24:67; Eph. 5:22-28; 1 Pet. 3:7). **be bitter.** The form of this Gr. verb is better translated "stop being bitter," or "do not have the habit of being bitter." Husbands must not be harsh or angrily resentful toward their wives.

3:20 in all things. *See notes on Eph. 6:1-3.* The only limit on a child's obedience is when parents demand something contrary to God's Word. For example, some children will act contrary to their parents' wishes even in coming to Christ (cf. Luke 12:51-53; 14:26).

3:21 provoke. *See notes on Eph. 6:4.* Also translated "do not exasperate," this word has the connotation of not stirring up or irritating.

3:22–4:1 *See notes on Eph. 6:5-9;* see Introduction to Philemon: Historical and Theological Themes. Paul upholds the duties of slave and master, of which the modern parallel is the duties of employee and employer. Scripture never advocates slavery, but recognizes it as an element of ancient society that could have been more beneficial if slaves and masters had treated each other properly. Here, Paul followed Christ's example and used slavery as a motif for spiritual instruction, likening the believer to one who is a slave and servant to Jesus Christ and seeing service to an earthly master as a way to serve the Lord.

3:22 Bondservants. I.e., slaves (*see note on Rom. 1:1*). **according to the flesh.** I.e., human inclination (cf. 2 Cor. 10:2,3). **eyeservice.** *See notes on Eph. 6:6.* Better translated, "external service." It refers to working only when the master is watching, rather than recognizing the Lord is always watching, and how our work concerns Him (vv. 23,24). Cf. 1 Tim. 6:1,2; Titus 2:9,10; 1 Pet. 2:18-21.

3:24 reward of the inheritance. *See note on Eph. 6:8.* The Lord ensures the believer that he will receive a just, eternal compensation for his efforts (cf. Rev. 20:12,13), even if his earthly boss or master does not compensate fairly (v. 25). God deals with obedience and disobedience impartially (cf. Acts 10:34; Gal. 6:7). Christians are not to presume on their faith in order to justify disobedience to an authority or employer (cf. Philem. 18).

4:1 Masters. *See note on Eph. 6:9.*

4:2 Continue earnestly. The Gr. word means "to be courageously persistent" or "to hold fast and not let go" and refers here to persistent prayer (Acts 1:14; Rom. 12:12; Eph. 6:18; 1 Thess. 5:17; cf. Luke 11:5-10; 18:1-8). **being vigilant.** In its most general sense this means to stay awake while praying. But Paul has in mind the broader implication of staying alert for specific needs about which to pray, rather than being vague and unfocused. Cf. Matt. 26:41; Mark 14:38; Luke 21:36.

4:3 a door. An opportunity (1 Cor. 16:8,9; 2 Cor. 2:12). **the mystery of Christ.** *See notes on 1:26,27; 2:2,3.*

4:5 those…outside. This refers to unbelievers. *See notes on Eph. 5:15,16.* Believers are called to so live that they establish the credibility of the Christian faith and that they make the most of every evangelistic opportunity.

4:6 with grace. To speak what is spiritual, wholesome, fitting, kind, sensitive, purposeful, complimentary, gentle, truthful, loving, and thoughtful (*see notes on Eph. 4:29-31*). **seasoned with salt.** Just as salt not only flavors, but prevents corruption, the Christian's speech should act not only as a blessing to others, but as a purifying influence within the decaying society of the world.

4:7 Tychicus. The name means, "fortuitous" or "fortunate." He was one of the Gentile converts Paul took to Jerusalem as a representative of the Gentile churches (Acts 20:4). He was a reliable companion of Paul and a capable leader, since he was considered as a replacement for Titus and Timothy on separate occasions (2 Tim. 4:12; Titus 3:12). He had the responsibility to deliver Paul's letters to the Colossians, the Ephesians (Eph. 6:21), and Philemon (v. 9).

4:9 Onesimus. The runaway slave whose return to his master was the basis for Paul's letter to Philemon (see Introduction to Philemon: Background and Setting).

one of you. They will make known to you
all things which *are happening* here.
10 [q]Aristarchus my fellow prisoner greets
you, with [r]Mark the cousin of Barnabas
(about whom you received instructions: if
he comes to you, welcome him), 11 and Jesus who is called Justus. These *are my* only
fellow workers for the kingdom of God
who are of the circumcision; they have
proved to be a comfort to me.
12 [s]Epaphras, who is *one* of you, a
bondservant of Christ, greets you, always
[t]laboring fervently for you in prayers, that
you may stand [u]perfect and [3]complete in
all the will of God. 13 For I bear him witness that he has a great [4]zeal for you, and
those who are in Laodicea, and those in
Hierapolis. 14 [v]Luke the beloved physician
and [w]Demas greet you. 15 Greet the
brethren who are in Laodicea, and
[5]Nymphas and [x]the church that *is* in [6]his
house.

Closing Exhortations and Blessing

16 Now when [y]this epistle is read among
you, see that it is read also in the church of
the Laodiceans, and that you likewise read
the epistle from Laodicea. 17 And say to
[z]Archippus, "Take heed to [a]the ministry
which you have received in the Lord, that
you may fulfill it."
18 [b]This salutation by my own hand—
Paul. [c]Remember my chains. Grace *be* with
you. Amen.

10 [q] Acts 19:29; 20:4; 27:2; Philem. 24 [r] Acts 15:37; 2 Tim. 4:11
12 [s] Col. 1:7; Philem. 23 [t] Rom. 15:30 [u] Matt. 5:48; 1 Cor. 2:6 [3] NU *fully assured*
13 [4] NU *concern*
14 [v] 2 Tim. 4:11; Philem. 24 [w] 2 Tim. 4:10
15 [x] Rom. 16:5; 1 Cor. 16:19 [5] NU *Nympha* [6] NU *her*
16 [y] 1 Thess. 5:27; 2 Thess. 3:14
17 [z] Philem. 2 [a] 1 Tim. 4:6; 2 Tim. 4:5
18 [b] 1 Cor. 16:21; 2 Thess. 3:17 [c] Heb. 13:3

4:10 Aristarchus. The Gr. name of a Jewish (cf. v. 11) native of Thessalonica (Acts 20:4; 27:2). He was one of Paul's companions who was seized by a rioting mob in Ephesus (Acts 19:29) and also accompanied Paul on his trip to Jerusalem and his voyage to Rome (Acts 27:4). **Mark.** *See notes on Acts 13:5,13;* see Introduction to Mark: Author and Date. After having fallen out of favor with Paul for some time, Mark is seen here as one of Paul's key helpers (cf. 2 Tim. 4:11).

4:11 Jesus who is called Justus. Possibly one of the Roman Jews who believed Paul's message (Acts 28:24). **kingdom of God.** *See note on 1:13.*

4:12 Epaphras. See Introduction: Background and Setting. **perfect and complete.** His goal for the Colossian believers was the same as Paul's (cf. 1:28–2:2).

4:13 Laodicea. *See note on 2:1.* **Hierapolis.** A city in Phrygia 20 mi. W of Colosse and 6 mi. N of Laodicea (see Introduction: Background and Setting).

4:14 Luke. Paul's personal physician and close friend who traveled frequently with him on his missionary journeys and wrote the Gospel of Luke and Acts (see Introductions to the Gospel of Luke and Acts: Author and Date). **Demas.** A man who demonstrated substantial commitment to the Lord's work before the attraction of the world led him to abandon Paul and the ministry (2 Tim. 4:9,10; Philem. 24).

4:15 Nymphas and the church...in his house. Other manuscripts make the name feminine (*Nympha*) and indicate the church met in her house, probably in Laodicea.

4:16 when this epistle is read among you. This letter was to be publicly read in the churches in Colosse and in Laodicea. **epistle from Laodicea.** A separate letter from Paul, usually identified as the epistle to the Ephesians. The oldest manuscripts of Ephesians do not contain the words "in Ephesus," indicating that in all likelihood it was a circular letter intended for several churches in the region. Tychicus may have delivered Ephesians to the church at Laodicea first.

4:17 Archippus. Most likely the son of Philemon (Philem. 2). Paul's message to him to fulfill his ministry is similar to the exhortation to Timothy (2 Tim. 4:5).

4:18 by my own hand. Paul usually dictated his letters to an amanuensis (recording secretary), but would often add his own greeting in his own writing at the end of his letters (cf. 1 Cor. 16:21; Gal. 6:11; 2 Thess. 3:17; Philem. 19). **Remember my chains.** *See note on Phil. 1:16;* see Introduction to Ephesians: Background and Setting. Cf. Heb. 13:3.

The First Epistle of Paul to the THESSALONIANS

Title

In the Greek NT, 1 Thessalonians is listed literally as "To *the* Thessalonians." This represents the Apostle Paul's first canonical correspondence to the church in the city of Thessalonica (cf. 1:1).

Author and Date

The Apostle Paul identified himself twice as the author of this letter (1:1; 2:18). Silvanus (Silas) and Timothy (3:2,6), Paul's traveling companions on the second missionary journey when the church was founded (Acts 17:1-9), were also mentioned in Paul's greeting (1:1). Though Paul was the single inspired author, most of the first person plural pronouns (we, us, our) refer to all 3. However, during Timothy's visit back to Thessalonica, they refer only to Paul and Silvanus (3:1,2,6). Paul commonly used such editorial plurals because the letters came with the full support of his companions.

Paul's authorship has not been questioned until recently by radical critics. Their attempts to undermine Pauline authorship has failed in light of the combined weight of evidence favoring Paul such as: 1) the direct assertions of Paul's authorship (1:1; 2:18); 2) the letter's perfect correlation with Paul's travels in Acts 16–18; 3) the multitude of intimate details regarding Paul; and 4) the confirmation by multiple, early historical verifications starting with Marcion's canon in A.D. 140.

The first of Paul's two letters written from Corinth to the church at Thessalonica is dated ca. A.D. 51. This date has been archeologically verified by an inscription in the temple of Apollos at Delphi (near Corinth) which dates Gallio's service as proconsul in Achaia to A.D. 51–52 (Acts 18:12-17). Since Paul's letter to the churches of Galatia was probably written ca. A.D. 49–50, this was his second piece of canonical correspondence.

Background and Setting

Thessalonica (modern Salonica) lies near the ancient site of Therma on the Thermaic Gulf at the northern reaches of the Aegean Sea. This city became the capital of Macedonia (ca. 168 B.C.) and enjoyed the status of a "free city" which was ruled by its own citizenry (Acts 17:6) under the Roman Empire. Because it was located on the main east-west highway, Via Egnatia, Thessalonica served as the hub of political and commercial activity in Macedonia, and became known as "the mother of all Macedonia." The population in Paul's day reached 200,000 people.

Paul had originally traveled 100 mi. from Philippi via Amphipolis and Apollonia to Thessalonica on his second missionary journey (A.D. 50; Acts 16:1–18:22). As his custom was upon arrival, he sought out the synagogue in which to teach the local Jews the gospel (Acts 17:1,2). On that occasion, he dialogued with them from the OT concerning Christ's death and resurrection in order to prove that Jesus of Nazareth was truly the promised Messiah (Acts 17:2,3). Some Jews believed and soon after, Hellenistic proselytes and some wealthy women of the community also were converted (Acts 17:4). Mentioned among these new believers were Jason (Acts 17:5), Gaius (Acts 19:29), Aristarchus (Acts 20:4), and Segundus (Acts 20:4).

Because of their effective ministry, the Jews had Paul's team evicted from the city (Acts 17:5-9), so they went south to evangelize Berea (Acts 17:10). There Paul had a similar experience to Thessalonica with conversions followed by hostility, so the believers sent Paul away. He headed for Athens, while Silvanus and Timothy remained in Berea (Acts 17:11-14). They rejoined Paul in Athens (cf. Acts 17:15,16 with 3:1), from which Timothy was later dispatched back to Thessalonica (3:2). Apparently, Silas afterwards traveled from Athens to Philippi while Paul journeyed on alone to Corinth (Acts 18:1). It was after Timothy and Silvanus rejoined Paul in Corinth (Acts 18:5), that he wrote 1 Thessalonians in response to Timothy's good report of the church.

Paul undoubtedly had multiple reasons for writing, all coming out of his supreme concern for the flock from which he had been separated. Some of Paul's purposes clearly included: 1) encouraging the church (1:2-10); 2) answering false allegations (2:1-12); 3) comforting the persecuted flock (2:13-16); 4) expressing his joy in their faith (2:17–3:13); 5) reminding them of the importance of moral purity (4:1-8); 6) condemning the sluggard lifestyle (4:9-12); 7) correcting a wrong understanding of prophetic events

(4:13–5:11); 8) defusing tensions within the flock (5:12-15); and 9) exhorting the flock in the basics of Christian living (5:16-22).

Historical and Theological Themes

Both letters to Thessalonica have been referred to as "the eschatological epistles." However, in light of their more extensive focus upon the church, they would better be categorized as the church epistles. Five major themes are woven together in 1 Thessalonians: 1) an apologetic theme with the historical correlation between Acts and 1 Thessalonians; 2) an ecclesiastical theme with the portrayal of a healthy, growing church; 3) a pastoral theme with the example of shepherding activities and attitudes; 4) an eschatological theme with the focus on future events as the church's hope; and 5) a missionary theme with the emphasis on gospel proclamation and church planting.

Interpretive Challenges

Primarily the challenges for understanding this epistle involve the sections that are eschatological in nature: 1) the coming wrath (1:10; 5:9); 2) Christ's return (2:19; 3:13; 4:15; 5:23); 3) the rapture of the church (4:13-18); and 4) the meaning and time of the Day of the Lord (5:1-11).

Outline

I. Paul's Greeting (1:1)

II. Paul's Personal Thoughts (1:2–3:13)
   - A. Thanksgiving for the Church (1:2-10)
   - B. Reminders for the Church (2:1-16)
   - C. Concerns for the Church (2:17–3:13)

III. Paul's Practical Instructions (4:1–5:22)
   - A. On Moral Purity (4:1-8)
   - B. On Disciplined Living (4:9-12)
   - C. On Death and the Rapture (4:13-18)
   - D. On Holy Living and the Day of the Lord (5:1-11)
   - E. On Church Relationships (5:12-15)
   - F. On the Basics of Christian Living (5:16-22)

IV. Paul's Benediction (5:23,24)

V. Paul's Final Remarks (5:25-28)

Greeting

1 Paul, [a]Silvanus, and Timothy,

To the church of the [b]Thessalonians in
God the Father and the Lord Jesus Christ:

Grace to you and peace [1]from God our
Father and the Lord Jesus Christ.

Their Good Example

2 [c]We give thanks to God always for you
all, making mention of you in our prayers,
3 remembering without ceasing [d]your
work of faith, [e]labor of love, and patience
of hope in our Lord Jesus Christ in the
sight of our God and Father, 4 knowing,
beloved brethren, [f]your election by God.
5 For [g]our gospel did not come to you in
word only, but also in power, [h]and in the
Holy Spirit [i]and in much assurance, as you
know what kind of men we were among
you for your sake.
6 And [j]you became followers of us and of
the Lord, having received the word in much
affliction, [k]with joy of the Holy Spirit, 7 so
that you became examples to all in Macedonia and Achaia who believe. 8 For from
you the word of the Lord [l]has sounded
forth, not only in Macedonia and Achaia,
but also [m]in every place. Your faith toward
God has gone out, so that we do not need to
say anything. 9 For they themselves declare
concerning us [n]what manner of entry we
had to you, [o]and how you turned to God
from idols to serve the living and true God,
10 and [p]to wait for His Son from heaven,
whom He raised from the dead, *even* Jesus
who delivers us [q]from the wrath to come.

CHAPTER 1

1 [a] 1 Pet. 5:12 [b] Acts 17:1-9 [1] NU omits *from God our Father and the Lord Jesus Christ*
2 [c] Rom. 1:8; 2 Thess. 1:3
3 [d] John 6:29 [e] Rom. 16:6
4 [f] Col. 3:12
5 [g] Mark 16:20 [h] 2 Cor. 6:6 [i] Heb. 2:3
6 [j] 1 Cor. 4:16; 11:1 [k] Acts 5:41; 13:52; 2 Cor. 6:10; Gal. 5:22
8 [l] Rom. 10:18 [m] Rom. 1:8; 16:19; 2 Cor. 2:14; 2 Thess. 1:4
9 [n] 1 Thess. 2:1 [o] 1 Cor. 12:2
10 [p] [Rom. 2:7] [q] Matt. 3:7; Rom. 5:9

1:1 Paul. Biographical details for the former Saul of Tarsus (Acts 9:11) can be found in Acts 9:1-30; 11:19–28:31; *see note on Rom. 1:1.* For autobiographical material, see 2 Cor. 11:16–12:10; Gal. 1:11–2:21; Phil. 3:4-6; and 1 Tim. 1:12-17. **Silvanus.** A companion of Paul on the second missionary journey (Acts 15–18), later a writer for Peter (1 Pet. 5:12), also called Silas. **Timothy.** Paul's most notable disciple (Phil. 2:17-23) who traveled on the second and third missionary journeys and stayed near Paul during his first Roman imprisonment (Phil. 1:1; Col. 1:1; Philem. 1). Later he served in Ephesus (1 Tim. 1:3) and spent some time in prison (Heb. 13:23). Paul's first letter to Timothy, while he was ministering in the church at Ephesus, instructed him regarding life in the church (cf. 1 Tim. 3:15). In his second letter, Paul called Timothy to be strong (2 Tim. 2:1) and faithfully preach as he faced death and was about to turn his ministry over to Timothy (2 Tim. 4:1-8). **God the Father and the Lord Jesus Christ.** Since Paul's initial converts were Jewish, he made it unmistakably clear that this "church" was not a Jewish assembly, but rather one which gathered in the name of Jesus, the Son of God (Acts 17:2,3), who is both Lord God and Messiah. This emphasis on the equality between God and the Lord Jesus is a part of the introduction in all Paul's epistles (cf. 1 John 2:23).

1:2 our prayers. Paul and his companions prayed frequently for the entire flock and 3 of those prayers are offered in this letter (1:2,3; 3:11-13; 5:23,24).

1:3 work of faith. The 3-fold combination of faith, hope, and love is a Pauline favorite (5:8; 1 Cor. 13:13; Col. 1:4,5). Paul refers here to the fulfillment of ministry duties which resulted from these three spiritual attitudes (cf. vv. 9,10).

1:4 your election by God. The church is commonly called "the elect" (cf. Rom. 8:33; Col. 3:12; 2 Tim. 2:10; Titus 1:1). In salvation, the initiating will is God's not man's (cf. John 1:13; Acts 13:46-48; Rom. 9:15,16; 1 Cor. 1:30; Col. 1:13; 2 Thess. 2:13; 1 Pet. 1:1,2; *see notes on Eph. 1:4,5*). Man's will participates in response to God's promptings as Paul makes clear when he says the Thessalonians received the Word (v. 6) and they turned to God from idols (v. 9). These two responses describe faith and repentance, which God repeatedly calls sinners to do throughout Scripture (e.g., Acts 20:21).

1:5 our gospel. Paul called his message "our gospel," because it was for him and all sinners to believe and especially for him to preach. He knew it did not originate with him, but was divinely authored; thus he also called it "the gospel of God" (2:2,9; Rom. 1:1). Because the person who made forgiveness possible is the Lord Jesus, he also referred to it as "the gospel of Christ" (3:2). **word only.** It had to come in word (cf. Rom. 10:13-17), and not word only, but in Holy Spirit power (cf. 2 Cor. 2:4,5) and in confidence (cf. Is. 55:11). **what kind of men.** The quality of the message was confirmed by the character of the lives of the preachers. Paul's exemplary life served as an open book for all men to read, establishing the credibility of the power and grace of God essential to making the message of redemption believable to sinners (*see note on 2 Cor. 1:12*).

1:6 followers. The Thessalonians had become third generation mimics of Christ. Christ is the first; Paul is the second; and the Thessalonians are the third (1 Cor. 4:16; 11:1). **joy of the Holy Spirit.** Cf. Rom. 14:17. Joy in the midst of suffering evidenced the reality of their salvation, which included the indwelling Holy Spirit (1 Cor. 3:16; 6:19).

1:7 examples. The Gr. word was used to describe a seal that marked wax or a stamp that minted coins. Paul commended the Thessalonians for being model believers leaving their mark on others. **Macedonia and Achaia.** The two Roman provinces which compromised Greece, Macedonia being to the N and Achaia to the S.

1:8 sounded forth. The idea is to reverberate. Wherever the Thessalonians went, the gospel given by the word of the Lord was heard. It resulted in a local outreach to Thessalonica, a national outreach to Macedonia and Achaia, and an international outreach to regions beyond. **we do not need to say anything.** Though it may appear that this church developed such a testimony in only 3 Sabbaths of preaching (cf. Acts 17:2) spanning as little as 15 days, it is better to understand that Paul preached 3 Sabbaths in the synagogue before he had to relocate elsewhere in the city. In all likelihood, Paul spent months not weeks, which accounts for: 1) the two collections he received from Philippi (Phil. 4:16); 2) the time he worked night and day (2:9; 2 Thess. 3:8); and 3) the depth of pastoral care evidenced in the letter (2:7,8,11).

1:9 turned. This word describes what the Bible elsewhere calls repentance (Matt. 3:1,2; 4:17; Acts 2:38; 3:19; 5:31; 20:21). Salvation involves a person's turning from sin and trusting in false gods to Christ. Cf. notes on 2 Cor. 7:8-11. **to serve the living and true God.** Those converted to Christ abandoned the worship of dead idols to become willing slaves to the living God.

1:10 to wait. This is a recurring theme in the Thessalonian letters (3:13; 4:15-17; 5:8,23; 2 Thess. 3:6-13; cf. Acts 1:11; 2 Tim. 4:8; Titus 2:11-13). These passages indicate the imminency of the deliverance; it was something Paul felt could happen in their lifetime. **delivers us from the wrath to come.** This can mean to evacuate out of a current distress (Rom. 7:24; Col. 1:13) or to exempt from entering into a distress (John. 12:27; 2 Cor. 1:10). The wrath can refer either to God's temporal wrath to come on the earth (Rev. 6:16,17; 19:15) or to God's eternal wrath (John. 3:36; Rom. 5:9,10). First Thessalonians 5:9 develops the same idea (*see note there*). The emphasis in both passages on Christ's

Paul's Conduct

2 For you yourselves know, brethren,
that our coming to you was not in vain.
2 But [1]even after we had suffered before
and were spitefully treated at [a]Philippi, as
you know, we were [b]bold in our God to
speak to you the gospel of God in much
conflict. 3 [c]For our exhortation *did* not *come*
from error or uncleanness, nor *was it* in deceit.
4 But as [d]we have been approved by
God [e]to be entrusted with the gospel, even
so we speak, [f]not as pleasing men, but God
[g]who tests our hearts. 5 For [h]neither at any
time did we use flattering words, as you
know, nor a [2]cloak for covetousness—
[i]God *is* witness. 6 [j]Nor did we seek glory
from men, either from you or from others,
when [k]we might have [l]made demands [m]as
apostles of Christ. 7 But [n]we were gentle
among you, just as a nursing *mother* cherishes her own children. 8 So, affectionately
longing for you, we were well pleased [o]to

CHAPTER 2

2 [a] Acts 14:5; 16:19-24; Phil. 1:30 [b] Acts 17:1-9 [1] NU, M omit *even*
3 [c] 2 Cor. 7:2
4 [d] 1 Cor. 7:25 [e] Titus 1:3 [f] Gal. 1:10 [g] Prov. 17:3
5 [h] 2 Cor. 2:17 [i] Rom. 1:9; 1 Thess. 2:10 [2] *pretext for greed*
6 [j] 1 Tim. 5:17 [k] 1 Cor. 9:4 [l] 2 Cor. 11:9 [m] 1 Cor. 9:1
7 [n] 1 Cor. 2:3
8 [o] Rom. 1:11

work of salvation from sin favors this being understood as the deliverance from the eternal wrath of God in hell because of salvation.

2:1 not in vain. Paul's ministry among the Thessalonians was so fruitful that not only were people saved and a vibrant, reproducing church planted, but the church also grew and flourished even after Paul left (cf. 1:5-8).

2:2 spitefully treated at Philippi. Paul and Silas had been brutalized in Philippi before coming to Thessalonica (cf. Acts 16:19-24,37). They suffered physically when beaten (Acts 16:22,23) and incarcerated (Acts 16:24). They were arrogantly mistreated with false accusations (Acts 16:20,21) and illegally punished in spite of their Roman citizenship (Acts 16:37). **much conflict.** Like their treatment in Philippi, Paul's team was falsely accused of civil treason in Thessalonica (Acts 17:7) and suffered physical intimidation (Acts 17:5,6).

2:3 error or uncleanness…deceit. Paul used 3 distinctly different words to affirm the truthfulness of his ministry, each expressing a contrast with what was characteristic of false teachers. He first asserted that "his message" was true and not erroneously false. His "manner of life" was pure, not sexually wicked. His "method of ministry" was authentic, not deceptive (*see notes on 2 Cor. 4:2*).

2:4 approved by God. It could be that some false teachers came into the church to discredit Paul's ministry. This would account for his emphasis in vv. 1-12 on his divine appointment, approval, integrity, and devotion to them. Cf. Acts 9:15; 16:9,10.

2:5,6 flattering words. Paul used 3 disclaimers to affirm the purity of his motives for ministry: 1) he denied being a smooth talking preacher who tried to make favorable impressions in order to gain influence for selfish advantage; 2) he did not pretend to be poor and work night and day (cf. v. 9) as a pretense to get rich in the ministry at their expense; and 3) he didn't use his honored position as an apostle to seek personal glory, only God's glory (cf. 1 Cor. 10:31).

2:6 apostles of Christ. This plural is designed to include Paul with the 12 for the sake of emphasizing his unique authority. Silvanus and Timothy were "apostles (messengers) of the church" (cf. Rom. 16:7; Phil. 2:15).

2:7,8 gentle…as a nursing *mother*. Paul may have had in mind Moses' portrayal of himself as a nursing mother to Israel (cf. Num. 11:12). He used the same tender picture with the Corinthians (cf. 2 Cor. 12:14,15) and the Galatians (cf. Gal. 4:19). Paul's affection for the Thessalonians was like that felt by a mother willing to sacrifice her life for her child as was Christ who was willing to give up His own life for those who would be born again into the family of God (cf. Matt. 20:28)

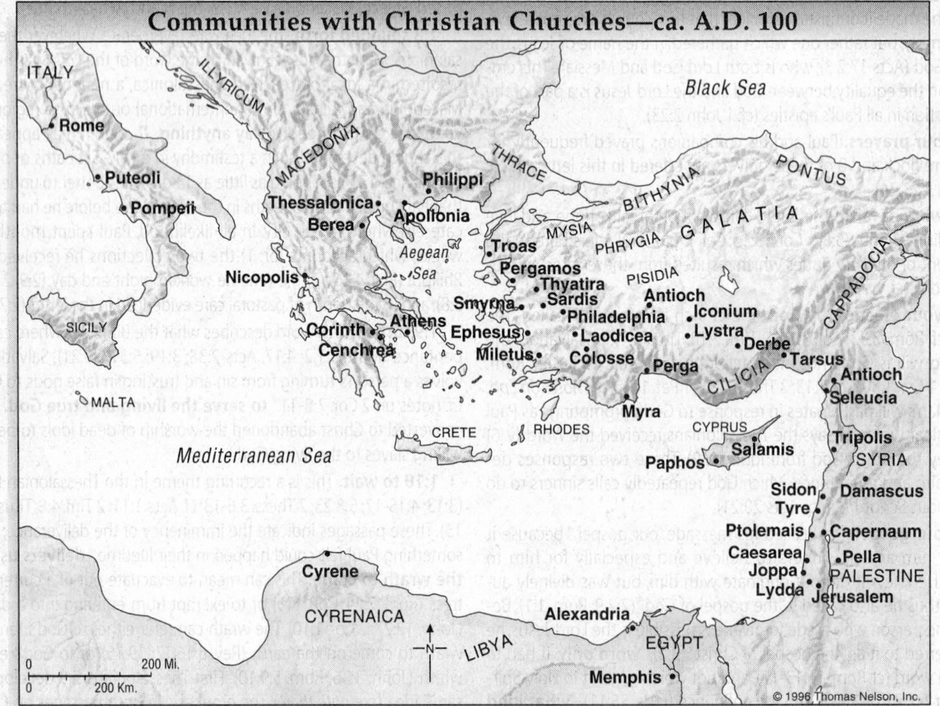

impart to you not only the gospel of God,
but also [p]our own lives, because you had
become dear to us. 9 For you remember,
brethren, our [q]labor and toil; for laboring
night and day, [r]that we might not be a burden to any of you, we preached to you the
gospel of God.
10 [s]You *are* witnesses, and God *also*,
[t]how devoutly and justly and blamelessly
we behaved ourselves among you who believe; 11 as you know how we exhorted,
and comforted, and [3]charged every one of
you, as a father *does* his own children,
12 [u]that you would walk worthy of God
[v]who calls you into His own kingdom and
glory.

Their Conversion

13 For this reason we also thank God
[w]without ceasing, because when you [x]re-
ceived the word of God which you heard
from us, you welcomed *it* [y]not *as* the
word of men, but as it is in truth, the
word of God, which also effectively
[z]works in you who believe. 14 For you,
brethren, became imitators [a]of the
churches of God which are in Judea in
Christ Jesus. For [b]you also suffered the
same things from your own countrymen,
just as they *did* from the Judeans, 15 [c]who
killed both the Lord Jesus and [d]their own
prophets, and have persecuted us; and
they do not please God [e]and are [4]con-
trary to all men, 16 [f]forbidding us to
speak to the Gentiles that they may be
saved, so as always [g]to fill up *the measure
of* their sins; [h]but wrath has come upon
them to the uttermost.

Longing to See Them

17 But we, brethren, having been taken
away from you for a short time [i]in presence, not in heart, endeavored more eagerly to see your face with great desire.
18 Therefore we wanted to come to you—
even I, Paul, time and again—but [j]Satan
hindered us. 19 For [k]what *is* our hope, or
joy, or [l]crown of rejoicing? *Is it* not even

8 [p]2 Cor. 12:15; 1 John 3:16
9 [q]Acts 18:3; 20:34, 35; 1 Cor. 4:12; 2 Thess. 3:7, 8 [r]2 Cor. 12:13
10 [s]2 Cor. 1:12; 1 Thess. 1:5 [t]2 Cor. 7:2
11 [3]NU, M *implored*
12 [u]Eph. 4:1; Col. 1:10 [v]Rom. 8:28; 1 Cor. 1:9; 1 Thess. 5:24; 2 Thess. 2:14; [2 Tim. 1:9]
13 [w]Rom. 1:8; 1 Thess. 1:2, 3 [x]Mark 4:20 [y][Matt. 10:20; Gal. 4:14] [z][1 Pet. 1:23]
14 [a]Gal. 1:22 [b]Acts 17:5; 1 Thess. 3:4; 2 Thess. 1:4
15 [c]Luke 24:20; Acts 2:23 [d]Jer. 2:30; Matt. 5:12; 23:34, 35; Acts 7:52 [e]Esth. 3:8 [4]*hostile*
16 [f]Luke 11:52 [g]Gen. 15:16; Dan. 8:23; Matt. 23:32 [h]Matt. 24:6
17 [i]1 Cor. 5:3
18 [j]Rom. 1:13; 15:22
19 [k]2 Cor. 1:14 [l]Prov. 16:31

2:9 laboring night and day. Paul explained this in 2 Thess. 3:7-9. He did not ask for any money from the Thessalonians but rather lived on what he earned and what the Philippians sent (Phil. 4:16), so that his motives could not be questioned, unlike the false teachers who always sought money (cf. 1 Pet. 5:2). **the gospel of God.** Cf. Rom. 1:1. The good news from God which Paul preached included these truths: 1) the authority and truthfulness of Scripture (v. 13); 2) the deity of Christ (Rom. 10:9); 3) the sinfulness of mankind (Rom. 3:23); 4) Christ's death and resurrection (1 Cor. 15:4,5); and 5) salvation by God's grace through man's faith (Eph. 2:8,9). Paul's summary of the gospel is in 1 Cor. 15:1-5.

2:10 you *are* witnesses. Under OT law it took two or more witnesses to verify truth (Num. 35:30; Deut. 17:6; 19:15; 2 Cor. 13:1). Here Paul called on both the Thessalonians and God as witnesses to affirm his holy conduct in the ministry. Cf. 2 Cor. 1:12.

2:11 exhorted...comforted...charged. Paul used these 3 words to describe his fatherly relationship with the Thessalonians since they were his children in the faith. They emphasized the personal touch of a loving father (cf. 1 Cor. 4:14,15).

2:12 His own kingdom and glory. This speaks of the sphere of eternal salvation (cf. Col. 1:13,14) culminating in the splendor of heaven.

2:13 the word of God. Paul's message from God is equated with the OT (Mark 7:13). It was the message taught by the apostles (Acts 4:31; 6:2). Peter preached it to the Gentiles (Acts 11:1). It was the word Paul preached on his first missionary journey (Acts 13:5,7,44,48,49), his second (Acts 16:32; 17:13; 18:11), and his third (Acts 19:10). Cf. Col. 1:25. **effectively works.** The work of God's Word includes: saving (Rom. 10:17; 1 Pet. 1:23); teaching and training (2 Tim. 3:16,17); guiding (Ps. 119:105); counseling (Ps. 119:24); reviving (Ps. 119:154); restoring (Ps. 19:7); warning and rewarding (Ps. 19:11); nourishing (1 Pet. 2:2); judging (Heb. 4:12); sanctifying (John 17:17); freeing (John 8:31,32); enriching (Col. 3:16); protecting (Ps. 119:11); strengthening (Ps. 119:28); making wise (Ps. 119:17-100); rejoicing the heart (Ps. 19:8); and prospering (Josh. 1:8,9). All this is summarized in Ps. 19:7-9 (*see notes there*).

2:14 imitators. Not only were the Thessalonians imitators of Paul and the Lord (cf. 1:6), but also of the churches in Judea in the sense that they both were persecuted for Christ's sake (cf. Acts 4:1-4; 5:26; 8:1). They drank Christ's cup of suffering (Matt. 26:39) and walked in the way of the OT prophets (Matt. 21:33-46; Luke 13:34).

2:15 who killed...the Lord Jesus. There is no question that the Jews were responsible for the death of their Messiah, though the Romans carried out the execution. It was the Jews who brought the case against Him and demanded His death (cf. Luke 23:1-24,34-38), just as they had killed the prophets (cf. Matt. 22:37; Mark 5:1-8; Acts 7:51,52).

2:15,16 contrary to all men. Just as it is God's will that all men be saved (1 Tim. 2:4; 2 Pet. 3:9), so it was the will of the Jews that no one find salvation in Christ (v. 16). Paul at one time had embraced this blasphemy of trying to prevent gospel preaching (cf. 1 Tim. 1:12-17).

2:16 wrath has come upon them. God's wrath (cf. 1:10; 5:9) on the Jews who "pile up their sins to the maximum limit" (cf. Matt. 23:32; Rom. 2:5), thus filling up the cup of wrath, can be understood: 1) historically of the Babylonian exile (Ezek. 8–11); 2) prophetically of Jerusalem's destruction in A.D. 70; 3) eschatologically of Christ's second coming in judgment (Rev. 19); or 4) soteriologically in the sense that God's promised eternal wrath for unbelievers is so certain that it is spoken of as having come already as does the Apostle John (cf. John 3:18,36). This context relates to the fourth option.

2:17 having been taken away. Paul had been forcedly separated from his spiritual children (cf. Acts 17:5-9). His motherly (v. 7) and fatherly instincts (v. 11) had been dealt a severe blow. Lit. the Thessalonians had been orphaned by Paul's forced departure.

2:18 Satan hindered us. Satan, which means "adversary," continually attempted to tear down the church that Christ promised to build (cf. Matt. 16:18). He was said to be present at the churches of Jerusalem (Acts 5:1-10), Smyrna (Rev. 2:9,10), Pergamum (Rev. 2:13), Thyatira (Rev. 2:24), Philadelphia (Rev. 3:9), Ephesus (1 Tim. 3:6,7), and Corinth (2 Cor. 2:1-11). He thwarted Paul in the sense that a military foe would hinder the advance of his enemy. This could very possibly refer to the pledge that Jason made (Acts 17:9), if that pledge was a promise that Paul would not return to Thessalonica.

2:19 crown of rejoicing. The Bible speaks of eternal life like a wreath awarded for an athletic victory. It is spoken of in terms of: 1) the imperishable wreath that celebrates salvation's victory over corruption (1 Cor. 9:25); 2) the righteous wreath that celebrates salvation's victory over unrighteousness (2 Tim. 4:8); 3) the unfading wreath of glory that celebrates salvation's victory over defilement

you in the [m]presence of our Lord Jesus
Christ [n]at His coming? 20 For you are our
glory and joy.

Concern for Their Faith

3 Therefore, when we could no longer
endure it, we thought it good to be left
in Athens alone, 2 and sent [a]Timothy, our
brother and minister of God, and our fellow laborer in the gospel of Christ, to establish you and encourage you concerning
your faith, 3 [b]that no one should be shaken
by these afflictions; for you yourselves
know that [c]we are appointed to this. 4 [d]For,
in fact, we told you before when we were
with you that we would suffer tribulation,
just as it happened, and you know. 5 For
this reason, when I could no longer endure
it, I sent to know your faith, [e]lest by some
means the tempter had tempted you, and
[f]our labor might be in vain.

19 [m]Jude 24 [n]1 Cor. 15:23

CHAPTER 3

2 [a]Rom. 16:21
3 [b]Eph. 3:13 [c]John 16:2; Acts 9:16; 14:22; 1 Cor. 4:9; 2 Tim. 3:12; 1 Pet. 2:21
4 [d]Acts 20:24
5 [e]1 Cor. 7:5 [f]Gal. 2:2
6 [g]Acts 18:5 [h]Phil. 1:8
7 [i]2 Cor. 1:4
8 [j][Eph. 6:13, 14]; Phil. 4:1
10 [k]2 Cor. 13:9; Col. 4:12
11 [l]Mark 1:3
12 [m]Phil. 1:9; 1 Thess. 4:1, 10; 2 Thess. 1:3

Encouraged by Timothy

6 [g]But now that Timothy has come to us
from you, and brought us good news of
your faith and love, and that you always
have good remembrance of us, greatly desiring to see us, [h]as we also *to see* you—
7 therefore, brethren, in all our affliction
and distress [i]we were comforted concerning you by your faith. 8 For now we live, if
you [j]stand fast in the Lord.
9 For what thanks can we render to God
for you, for all the joy with which we rejoice for your sake before our God, 10 night
and day praying exceedingly that we may
see your face [k]and perfect what is lacking
in your faith?

Prayer for the Church

11 Now may our God and Father Himself, and our Lord Jesus Christ, [l]direct our
way to you. 12 And may the Lord make
you increase and [m]abound in love to one

(1 Pet. 5:4); 4) the wreath of life that celebrates salvation's victory over death (James 1:12, Rev. 2:10); and here 5) the wreath of exultation which celebrates salvation's victory over Satan and mankind's persecution of believers. **at His coming.** "Coming" or *parousia,* lit. means "to be present." It can be understood as: 1) actual presence (Phil. 2:2); 2) moment of arrival (1 Cor. 16:17); or 3) expected coming (2 Cor. 7:6). In regard to Christ and the future, it can refer to: 1) Christ's coming at the Rapture (4:15), or 2) Christ's second coming prior to His 1,000 year millennial reign (Matt. 24:37; Rev. 19:11–20:6). Paul referred directly to Christ's coming 4 times in 1 Thess. (see also 3:13; 4:15; 5:23) and once indirectly (1:10). Context indicates Paul most likely refers here to Christ's coming for the rapture of the church.

3:1 no longer endure it. The agony of separation between spiritual parent Paul and his children in Thessalonica became unbearably painful (cf. v. 5). **in Athens alone.** Paul and Silas stayed behind while Timothy returned (v. 2). This would not be the last time that Timothy went to a church in Paul's place (cf. 1 Cor. 4:17; 16:10; Phil. 2:19-24; 1 Tim. 1:3).

3:2 establish...encourage...your faith. This was a common ministry concern and practice of Paul (cf. Acts 14:22; 15:32; 18:23). Paul's concern did not focus on health, wealth, self-esteem, or ease of life, but rather the spiritual quality of life. Their faith was of supreme importance in Paul's mind as evidenced by 5 mentions in vv. 1-10 (see also vv. 5,6,7,10). Faith includes the foundation of the body of doctrine (cf. Jude 3) and their believing response to God in living out that truth (cf. Heb. 11:6).

3:3 appointed. God had promised Paul future sufferings when He commended him to ministry through Ananias (Acts 9:16). Paul reminded the Thessalonians of this divine appointment so that they would not think that: 1) God's plan was not working out as evidenced by Paul's troubles, or 2) Paul's afflictions demonstrated God's displeasure with him. To think that way would upset the church's confidence in Paul and fulfill Satan's deceptive purposes (v. 5). Cf. 2 Cor. 4:8-15; 6:1-10; 11:23-27; 12:7-10.

3:4 suffer tribulation. Paul had told them to expect him to suffer as he had already suffered before his Thessalonian experience (2:14-16; Acts 13,14). During (Acts 17:1-9) and following (Acts 17:10–18:11) his time at Thessalonica, Paul also knew tribulation.

3:5 the tempter. Satan had already been characterized as a hinderer (2:18) and now as a tempter in the sense of trying/testing for the purpose of causing failure (cf. Matt. 4:3; 1 Cor. 7:5; James 1:12-18). Paul was not ignorant of Satan's schemes (2 Cor. 2:11; 11:23) nor vulnerable to his methods (Eph. 6:11), so Paul took action to counterattack Satan's expected maneuver and to assure that all his efforts were not useless (cf. 2:1).

3:6 your faith and love. Timothy returned to report the Thessalonians' trust in God, their response to one another, and to Paul's ministry. This news convinced Paul that Satan's plans to disrupt God's work had not been successful and settled Paul's anxiety (v. 7).

3:8 stand fast. Pictured here is an army that refuses to retreat even though it is being assaulted by the enemy. This is a frequent Pauline injunction (1 Cor. 16:13; Gal. 5:1; Eph. 6:11,13,14; Phil. 1:27; 4:1; 2 Thess. 2:15).

3:9 joy. Paul, like John (3 John 4), found the highest sense of ministry joy in knowing that his children in the faith were growing and walking in the truth. It led him to the worship of God in thanksgiving and rejoicing.

3:10 praying. As to frequency, Paul prayed night and day just as he worked night and day (2:9). As to fervency, Paul prayed superabundantly (cf. Eph. 3:20). **lacking.** Paul was not criticizing the church but rather acknowledging that they had not yet reached their full potential, for which he prayed and labored (v. 10). The themes of chaps. 4,5 deal with areas of this lack.

3:11 direct our way. Paul knew that Satan had hindered his return (2:18). Even though Timothy had visited and returned with a good report, Paul still felt the urgency to see his spiritual children again. Paul followed the biblical admonition of the Psalms (Ps. 37:1-5) and Proverbs (Prov. 3:5,6) to entrust difficult situations to God.

3:12 love to one another. With over 30 positive and negative "one anothers" in the NT, love appears by far most frequently (cf. 4:9; Rom. 12:10; 13:8; 2 Thess. 1:3; 1 Pet. 1:22; 1 John 3:11,23; 4:7,11; 2 John 5). It is the overarching term that includes all of the other "one anothers." Its focus is on believers in the church. **to all.** In light of the fact that God loved the world and sent His son to die for human sin (John 3:16), believers who were loved when they were unlovely (Rom. 5:8) are to love unbelievers (*see notes on Matt. 5:43,44*). Other NT commands concerning all men include pursuing peace (Rom. 12:18), doing good (Gal. 6:10), being patient (Phil. 4:5), praying (1 Tim. 2:1), showing consideration (Titus 3:2), and honoring (1 Pet. 2:17).

another and to all, just as we *do* to you,
13 so that He may establish [n]your hearts
blameless in holiness before our God and
Father at the coming of our Lord Jesus
Christ with all His saints.

Plea for Purity

4 Finally then, brethren, we urge and exhort in the Lord Jesus [a]that you should
abound more and more, [b]just as you received from us how you ought to walk and
to please God; 2 for you know what commandments we gave you through the Lord
Jesus.
3 For this is [c]the will of God, [d]your sanctification: [e]that you should abstain from
sexual immorality; 4 [f]that each of you
should know how to possess his own vessel in sanctification and honor, 5 [g]not in
passion of lust, [h]like the Gentiles [i]who do
not know God; 6 that no one should take
advantage of and defraud his brother in
this matter, because the Lord [j]*is* the
avenger of all such, as we also forewarned
you and testified. 7 For God did not call us
to uncleanness, [k]but in holiness. 8 [l]There-
fore he who rejects *this* does not reject man,
but God, [m]who[1] has also given us His
Holy Spirit.

A Brotherly and Orderly Life

9 But concerning brotherly love you
have no need that I should write to you, for
[n]you yourselves are taught by God [o]to
love one another; 10 and indeed you do so
toward all the brethren who are in all Macedonia. But we urge you, brethren, [p]that
you increase more and more; 11 that you
also aspire to lead a quiet life, [q]to mind
your own business, and [r]to work with
your own hands, as we commanded you,
12 [s]that you may walk properly toward
those who are outside, and *that* you may
lack nothing.

The Comfort of Christ's Coming

13 But I do not want you to be ignorant,
brethren, concerning those who have fallen
[2]asleep, lest you sorrow [t]as others [u]who
have no hope. 14 For [v]if we believe that

13 [n] 2 Thess. 2:17

CHAPTER 4

1 [a] 1 Cor. 15:58 [b] Phil. 1:27; Col. 1:10
3 [c] [Rom. 12:2] [d] Eph. 5:27 [e] [1 Cor. 6:15-20; Col. 3:5]
4 [f] Rom. 6:19
5 [g] Col. 3:5 [h] Eph. 4:17, 18 [i] 1 Cor. 15:34
6 [j] 2 Thess. 1:8
7 [k] Lev. 11:44; [Heb. 12:14]; 1 Pet. 1:14-16
8 [l] Luke 10:16 [m] 1 Cor. 2:10 [1] NU *who also gives*
9 [n] [Jer. 31:33, 34]; John 6:45; 15:12, 17; [1 John 2:27] [o] Matt. 22:39
10 [p] 1 Thess. 3:12
11 [q] 2 Thess. 3:11; 1 Pet. 4:15 [r] Acts 20:35
12 [s] Rom. 13:13; Col. 4:5; [1 Pet. 2:12]
13 [t] Lev. 19:28 [u] [Eph. 2:12] [2] Died
14 [v] 1 Cor. 15:13

3:13 blameless in holiness. Paul prayed that there would be no grounds of accusation because of unholiness. Cf. 1 Cor. 1:8; 2 Cor. 11:2; Eph. 5:25-27; 1 Pet. 5:16,17; Jude 24. **His saints.** Since this exact term is not used elsewhere in the NT of angels (*see note on Jude 14*), but is commonly used for believers, it is best to understand the coming of the Lord to rapture all His church (*see notes on 4:13-18*) and take them to heaven to enjoy His presence (*see notes on John 14:1-3*).

4:1 in the Lord Jesus. To give added weight to his words, Paul appealed here to the fact that he wrote with the authority of Christ Himself (see vv. 2,15; 5:27; 2 Thess. 3:6,12; cf. 2:4,15; 2 Cor. 5:9; Eph. 5:10,17; Col. 1:10; Heb. 11:6; 13:15,16; 1 John 3:22). This is done by obedience to the Word of God (cf. v. 3).

4:3 the will of God. All of God's Word contains God's will—both affirmations and prohibitions. Specifically, God's will includes salvation (1 Tim. 2:4), self-sacrifice (Rom. 12:1,2), Spirit filling (Eph. 5:18), submission (1 Pet. 2:13-15), suffering (1 Pet. 3:17), satisfaction (5:18), settledness (Heb. 10:36), and particularly here—sanctification, which literally refers to a state of being set apart from sin to holiness. In this context, it means being set apart from sexual impurity in particular, holding oneself away from immorality by following the instruction in vv. 4-8.

4:4 possess his own vessel. Two interpretations of "vessel" are usually offered. The term can mean: 1) the wife (cf. Ruth 4:10 LXX; 1 Pet. 3:7) which one acquires, or 2) the body (2 Cor. 4:7; 2 Tim. 2:21) which one possesses. The latter is most likely since: 1) vessel in 1 Pet. 3:7 is used only in a comparative sense ("weaker vessel") referring to vessel in terms of general humanity not femaleness; 2) being married does not guarantee sexual purity; 3) Paul would be contradicting what he taught in 1 Cor. 7 about the superlative state of singleness (cf. 7:8,9); and 4) if taken in the sense of "acquiring a wife," Paul would be talking to men only and ignoring how women were to stay pure. Therefore, "possess his own body" is the preferred translation/interpretation. Cf. note on 1 Cor. 9:27.

4:5 the Gentiles. Used here in a spiritual sense referring to non-Christians, and indicated by the defining statement, "who do not know God." *See notes on Eph. 4:17,18.*

4:6 defraud his brother. The context, which remains unchanged throughout vv. 1-8, demands that this refer to all the destructive social and spiritual implications of illegitimate sexual activity. *See notes on Matt. 18:6-10.* **avenger.** This means it is God who ultimately works out just recompense for such sins (cf. Col. 3:4-7; Heb. 13:4).

4:7 call us. Whenever the epistles refer to the "call" of God, it is always a reference to His effectual, saving call, never to a general plea. It is linked to justification (cf. Rom. 8:30).

4:8 given us His Holy Spirit. God's Spirit is a free gift to all who believe in the Lord Jesus Christ for salvation. Cf. Acts 2:38; Rom. 8:9; 1 Cor. 3:16; 12:13; 2 Cor. 6:16.

4:9,10 taught by God to love. Through God's Word (Ps. 119:97-102) and by God Himself, they were loving believers (cf. Rom. 5:5; 1 John 2:7-11; 3:14; 4:7,8,12).

4:11 a quiet life. This refers to one who does not present social problems (*see note on 1 Tim. 2:2*) or generate conflict among those people in his life, but whose soul rests easy even in the midst of difficulty (cf. 1 Pet. 3:4). Paul later deals with those who did not "mind their own business" at Thessalonica (cf. 2 Thess. 3:6-15). **work with your own hands.** Greek culture looked down on manual labor but Paul exalts it (*see note on Eph. 4:28*).

4:12 those...outside. Non-Christians are in view here (cf. 1 Cor. 5:2; Col. 4:5; 1 Tim. 3:7).

4:13-18 Even though Paul's ministry in Thessalonica was brief, it is clear the people had come to believe in and hope for the reality of their Savior's return (cf. 1:3,9,10; 2:19; 5:1,2; 2 Thess. 2:1,5). They were living in expectation of that coming, eagerly awaiting Christ. Verse 13 (cf. 2 Thess. 2:1-3) indicates they were even agitated about some things that were happening to them that might affect their participation in it. They knew Christ's return was the climactic event in redemptive history and didn't want to miss it. The major question they had was "What happens to the Christians who die before He comes? Do they miss His return?" Clearly, they had an imminent view of Christ's return and Paul had left the impression it could happen in their lifetime. Their confusion came as they were being persecuted, an experience they thought they were to be delivered from by the Lord's return (cf. 3:3,4).

4:13 those who have fallen asleep. Sleep is the familiar NT euphemism for death which describes the appearance of the deceased (*see note on 1 Cor. 11:30*). It describes the dead body, not the soul (cf. 2 Cor. 5:1-9; Phil. 1:23). Sleep is used of Jarius' daughter (Matt. 9:24)

Jesus died and rose again, even so God will
bring with Him [w]those who [3]sleep in Jesus.
15 For this we say to you [x]by the word of
the Lord, that [y]we who are alive *and* remain until the coming of the Lord will by
no means precede those who are [4]asleep.
16 For [z]the Lord Himself will descend from
heaven with a shout, with the voice of an
archangel, and with [a]the trumpet of God.
[b]And the dead in Christ will rise first.
17 [c]Then we who are alive *and* remain shall
be caught up together with them [d]in the
clouds to meet the Lord in the air. And
thus [e]we shall always be with the Lord.
18 [f]Therefore comfort one another with
these words.

The Day of the Lord

5 But concerning [a]the times and the seasons, brethren, you have no need that I
should write to you. 2 For you yourselves
know perfectly that [b]the day of the Lord so

14 [w] 1 Cor. 15:20, 23 [3] *Or through Jesus sleep* **15** [x] 1 Kin. 13:17; 20:35; 2 Cor. 12:1; Gal. 1:12 [y] 1 Cor. 15:51, 52; 1 Thess. 5:10 [4] *Dead* **16** [z] [Matt. 24:30, 31] [a] [1 Cor. 15:52] [b] [1 Cor. 15:23]; 2 Thess. 2:1; Rev. 14:13; 20:6 **17** [c] [1 Cor. 15:51-53]; 1 Thess. 5:10 [d] Dan. 7:13; Acts 1:9; Rev. 11:12 [e] John 14:3; 17:24 **18** [f] 1 Thess. 5:11 CHAPTER 5 **1** [a] Matt. 24:3 **2** [b] Luke 21:34; 1 Thess. 5:4; [2 Pet. 3:10]; Rev. 3:3; 16:15

whom Jesus raised from the dead and Stephen who was stoned to death (Acts 7:60; cf. John 11:11; 1 Cor. 7:39; 15:6,18,51; 2 Pet. 3:4). Those who sleep are identified in v. 16 as "the dead in Christ." The people, in ignorance, had come to the conclusion that those who die miss the Lord's return and they were grieved over their absence at such a glorious event. Thus the departure of a loved one brought great anguish to the soul. But there is no reason for Christians to sorrow when a brother dies as if some great loss to that person has come.

4:14 God will bring with Him. As Jesus died and rose, so also will those who die believing in Him rise again so they can be taken to heaven with the Lord *(see notes on John 14:1-3; 1 Cor. 15:51-58).* These texts describe the rapture of the church, which takes place when Jesus comes to collect His redeemed and take them back to heaven. Those who have died before that time (called "those who sleep") will be gathered and taken back to heaven with the Lord.

4:15 the word of the Lord. Was Paul referring to some saying of Jesus found in the gospels? No. There are none exact or even close. The only explicit reference to the Rapture in the gospel is John 14:1-3. Some suggest that Jesus had said the words while on earth, their substance being recorded later in such places as Matt. 24:30,31 and John 6:39,40; 11:25,26. Similarities between this passage in 1 Thess. and the gospel accounts include a trumpet (Matt. 24:31), a resurrection (John 1:26), and a gathering of the elect (Matt. 24:31). Yet dissimilarities between it and the canonical sayings of Christ far outweigh the resemblances. Some of the differences between Matt. 24:30,31 and vv. 15-17 are as follows: 1) in Matt. the Son of Man is coming on the clouds (but see Mark 13:26; Luke 21:27), in 1 Thess. ascending believers are in them; 2) in the former the angels gather, in the latter Christ does personally; 3) in the former nothing is said about resurrection, while in the latter this is the main theme; and 4) Matthew records nothing about the order of ascent, which is the principal lesson in Thessalonians. On the other hand, did he mean a statement of Jesus that was spoken but not recorded in the gospels (Acts 20:35)? No. There is reason to conclude this since Paul affirmed that he taught the Rapture as a heretofore hidden truth (1 Cor. 15:51), i.e., "mystery." Apparently, the Thessalonians were informed fully about the Day of the Lord judgment (cf. 5:1,2), but not the preceding event—the rapture of the church. Until Paul revealed it as the revelation from God to him, it had been a secret, with the only prior mention being Jesus' teaching in John 14:1-3. This was new revelation of what had previously been an unrevealed mystery. **we who are alive *and* remain.** This refers to Christians alive at the time of the Rapture, those who live on this earth to see the coming of the Lord for His own. Since Paul didn't know God's timing, he lived and spoke as if it could happen in his lifetime. As with all early Christians, he believed the event was near (cf. Rom. 13:11; 1 Cor. 6:14; 10:11; 16:22; Phil. 3:20,21; 1 Tim. 6:14; Titus 2:13). Those alive at the Rapture will follow those dead who rise first (v. 16).

4:16 the Lord Himself will descend. This fulfills the pledge of John 14:1-3 (cf. Acts 1:11). Until then, He remains in heaven (cf. 1:10; Heb. 1:1-3). **archangel.** Very little is known about the organization or rank of angels (cf. Col. 1:17). While only Michael is named as an archangel (Jude 9), there seems to be more than one in the angelic ranks (Dan. 10:13). Perhaps it is Michael, the archangel, whose voice is heard as he is identified with Israel's resurrection in Dan. 12:1-3. At that moment (cf. 1 Cor. 15:52, "twinkling of an eye"), the dead rise first. They will not miss the Rapture, but be the first participants. **trumpet of God.** Cf. 1 Cor. 15:52. This trumpet is not the judgment trumpets of Rev. 8–11, but is illustrated by the trumpet of Ex. 19:16-19, which called the people out of the camp to meet God. It will be a trumpet of deliverance (cf. Zeph. 1:16; Zech. 9:14).

4:17 caught up. After the dead come forth, their spirits, already with the Lord (2 Cor. 5:8; Phil. 1:23), now being joined to resurrected new bodies *(see notes on 1 Cor. 15:35-50)*, the living Christians will be raptured, lit. snatched away (cf. John 10:28; Acts 8:39). This passage, along with John 14:1-3 and 1 Cor. 15:51,52, form the biblical basis for "the Rapture" of the church. The time of the Rapture cannot be conclusively determined from this passage alone. However, when other texts such as Rev. 3:10 and John 14:3 are consulted and compared to the texts about Christ's coming in judgment (Matt. 13:34-50; 24:29-44; Rev. 19:11-21) at the end of a 7 year tribulation, it has to be noted that there is a clear difference between the character of the "Rapture" in that there is no mention of any judgment, while the other texts feature judgment. So then, it is best to understand that the Rapture occurs at a time different from the coming of Christ in judgment. Thus, the Rapture has been described as pretribulational (before the wrath of God unfolded in the judgments of Rev. 6–19). This event includes complete transformation (cf. 1 Cor. 15:51,52; Phil 3:20,21) and union with the Lord Jesus Christ that never ends.

4:18 comfort one another. The primary purpose of this passage is not to teach a scheme of prophecy, but rather to provide encouragement to those Christians whose loved ones have died. The comfort here is based on the following: 1) the dead will be resurrected and will participate in the Lord's coming for His own; 2) when Christ comes the living will be reunited forever with their loved ones; and 3) they all will be with the Lord eternally (v. 17).

5:1 But. Paul used familiar Gr. words here to indicate a change of topics within the same general subject of prophecy (cf. 4:9,13; 1 Cor. 7:1,25; 8:1; 12:1; 16:1). The expression here points to the idea that within the broader context of the end time coming of the Lord Jesus, the subject is changing from a discussion of the blessings of the rapture of believers to the judgment of unbelievers. **times and the seasons.** These two terms mean the measurement of time and the character of the times respectively (cf. Dan. 2:21; Acts 1:7). Many of them expected the Lord to come in their lifetime and were confused and grieved when their fellow believers died before His coming (*see notes on 4:13-18*). They were concerned about the delay. Apparently, the Thessalonians knew all that God intended believers to know about coming judgment, and Paul had taught them what they hadn't known about the Rapture (4:13-18), so Paul exhorted them to live godly lives in light of coming judgment on the world, rather than to be distracted by probing into issues of prophetic timing. They could not know the timing of God's final judgment, but they knew well that it was coming unexpectedly (v. 2).

5:2 day of the Lord. There are 19 indisputable uses of "the Day of

comes as a thief in the night. 3 For when
they say, "Peace and safety!" then [c]sud-
den destruction comes upon them, [d]as
labor pains upon a pregnant woman. And
they shall not escape. 4 [e]But you,
brethren, are not in darkness, so that this
Day should overtake you as a thief. 5 You
are all [f]sons of light and sons of the day.
We are not of the night nor of darkness.
6 [g]Therefore let us not sleep, as others *do,*
but [h]let us watch and be [1]sober. 7 For
[i]those who sleep, sleep at night, and those
who get drunk [j]are drunk at night. 8 But
let us who are of the day be sober, [k]put-
ting on the breastplate of faith and love,
and *as* a helmet the hope of salvation.

3 [c] Is. 13:6-9 [d] Hos. 13:13
4 [e] [Acts 26:18]; Rom. 13:12; Eph. 5:8; 1 John 2:8
5 [f] Eph. 5:8
6 [g] Matt. 25:5 [h] Matt. 25:13; Mark 13:35; [1 Pet. 5:8] [1] *self-controlled*
7 [i] [Luke 21:34] [j] Acts 2:15; 2 Pet. 2:13
8 [k] Is. 59:17; Eph. 6:14
9 [l] Rom. 9:22 [m] [2 Thess. 2:13]
10 [n] 2 Cor. 5:15
11 [2] Or *encourage* [3] *build one another up*
12 [o] 1 Cor. 16:18; 1 Tim. 5:17; Heb. 13:7, 17 [4] *instruct* or *warn*
13 [p] Mark 9:50

9 For [l]God did not appoint us to wrath,
[m]but to obtain salvation through our Lord
Jesus Christ, 10 [n]who died for us, that
whether we wake or sleep, we should live
together with Him.
11 Therefore [2]comfort each other and
[3]edify one another, just as you also are
doing.

Various Exhortations

12 And we urge you, brethren, [o]to recognize those who labor among you, and are
over you in the Lord and [4]admonish you,
13 and to esteem them very highly in love
for their work's sake. [p]Be at peace among
yourselves.

---

the Lord" in the OT and 4 in the NT (cf. Acts 2:20; 2 Thess. 2:2; 2 Pet. 3:10). The OT prophets used "Day of the Lord" to describe near historical judgments (see Is. 13:6-22; Ezek. 30:2-19; Joel 1:15; 3:14; Amos 5:18-20; Zeph. 1:14-18) or far eschatological divine judgments (see Joel 2:30-32; Zech. 14:1; Mal. 4:1,5). Six times it is referred to as the "day of doom" and 4 times "day of vengeance." The NT calls it a day of "wrath," day of "visitation," and the "Great Day of God Almighty" (Rev. 16:4). These are terrifying judgments from God (cf. Joel 2:30,31; 2 Thess. 1:7-10) for the overwhelming sinfulness of the world. The future "Day of the Lord" which unleashes God's wrath, falls into two parts: 1) the end of the 7 year tribulation period (cf. Rev. 19:11-21), and 2) the end of the Millennium. These two are actually 1,000 years apart and Peter refers to the end of the 1,000 year period in connection with the final "Day of the Lord" (cf. 2 Pet. 3:10; Rev. 20:7-15). Here, Paul refers to that aspect of the "Day of the Lord," which concludes the tribulation period. **a thief in the night.** This phrase is never used to refer to the rapture of the church. It is used of Christ's coming in judgment on the Day of the Lord at the end of the 7 year tribulation which is distinct from the rapture of the church (*see note on 4:15*) and it is used of the judgment which concludes the Millennium (2 Pet. 3:10). As a thief comes unexpectedly and without warning, so will the Day of the Lord come in both its final phases.

5:3 "Peace and safety!" Just as false prophets of old fraudulently forecast a bright future, in spite of the imminence of God's judgment (Jer. 6:14; 8:11; 14:13,14; Lam. 2:14; Ezek. 13:10,16; Mic. 3:5), so they will again in future days just before the final Day of the Lord destruction. **labor pains.** The Lord used this same illustration in the Olivet Discourse (*see note on Matt. 24:8*). It portrays the inevitability, suddenness, inescapable nature, and painfulness of the Day of the Lord.

5:4 But you, brethren. Paul dramatically shifts from the third person plural pronoun (3 times in v. 3) to the second person plural. Because the church is raptured before the judgment of the Day of the Lord, believers will not be present on earth to experience its terrors and destruction (v. 3). **not in darkness.** Believers have no part in the Day of the Lord, because they have been delivered from the domain of darkness and transferred to the kingdom of light (Col. 1:13). Jesus taught that to believe in Him would remove a person from spiritual darkness (John 8:12; 12:46). The contrast between believers and the lost is emphatic and Paul draws it out all the way through v. 7. Believers will not experience the wrath of God because they are different in nature. Unbelievers are in darkness (cf. v. 2, "in the night"), engulfed in mental, moral, and spiritual darkness because of sin and unbelief (cf. John 1:5; 3:19; 8:12; 2 Cor. 4:6; Eph. 4:17,18; 5:8,11). All these people are children of Satan (cf. John 8:44) who is called "the power of darkness" (Luke 22:53). The Day of the Lord will "overtake" them suddenly and with deadly results.

5:5 sons of light. This is a Heb. expression that characterizes believers as children of God, their heavenly Father, who is light and in whom is no darkness at all (1 John 1:5-7). Cf. Luke 16:8; John 8:12; 12:36. Believers live in a completely different sphere of life than those who will be in the Day of the Lord.

5:6 let us not sleep. Because believers have been delivered from the domain of darkness, they are taken out of the night of sin and ignorance and put into the light of God. Because Christians are in the light, they should not sleep in spiritual indifference and comfort, but be alert to the spiritual issues around them. They are not to live like the sleeping, darkened people who will be jolted out of their coma by the Day of the Lord (v. 7), but to live alert, balanced, godly lives under control of the truth.

5:8 breastplate. Paul pictured the Christian life in military terms as being a life of soberness (alertness) and proper equipping. The "breastplate" covers the vital organs of the body. "Faith" is an essential protection against temptations, because it is trust in God's promise, plan, and truth. It is unwavering belief in God's Word that protects us from temptation's arrows. Looking at it negatively, it is unbelief that characterizes all sin. When believers sin, they have believed Satan's lie. Love for God is essential, as perfect love for Him yields perfect obedience to Him. Elsewhere the warrior's breastplate has been used to represent righteousness (Is. 59:17; Eph. 6:14). Faith elsewhere is represented by a soldier's shield (Eph. 6:16). The "helmet" is always associated with salvation in its future aspects (cf. Is. 59:17; Eph. 6:17). Our future salvation is guaranteed, nothing can take it away (Rom. 13:11). Paul again combined faith, love, and hope (cf. 1:3). *See notes on Eph. 6:10-17.*

5:9 wrath. This is the same wrath referred to in 1:9 (*see notes there*). In this context (note especially the contrast), it appears obvious that this wrath refers to God's eternal wrath, not His temporal wrath during the tribulation period (cf. Rom. 5:9).

5:10 wake or asleep. This analogy goes back to 4:13-15 and refers to being physically alive or dead with the promise that, in either case, we will one day live together (cf. 4:17; John 14:1-3) forever with the Savior who died as the substitute for our sins. Cf. Rom. 4:9; Gal. 1:4; 2 Cor. 5:15,21.

5:12 recognize. This does not mean simple face recognition, but that the people are to lit. know their pastors well enough to have an intimate appreciation for them and to respect them because of their value. The work of pastors is summarized in a 3-fold description which includes: 1) laboring, working to the point of exhaustion; 2) overseeing, lit. standing before the flock to lead them in the way of righteousness; and 3) admonishing, instructing in the truths of God's Word. Cf. Heb. 13:7,17.

5:13 esteem. In addition to knowing pastors *(see notes on v. 12)*, congregations are to think rightly and lovingly of their pastors, not because of their charm or personality, but because of the fact that they work for the Chief Shepherd as His special servants (cf. 1 Pet. 5:2-4). They are also to submit to their leadership so that "peace" prevails in the church.

14 Now we [5]exhort you, brethren, [q]warn
those who are [6]unruly, [r]comfort the fainthearted, [s]uphold the weak, [t]be patient
with all. 15 [u]See that no one renders evil
for evil to anyone, but always [v]pursue
what is good both for yourselves and for
all.
16 [w]Rejoice always, 17 [x]pray without
ceasing, 18 in everything give thanks; for
this is the will of God in Christ Jesus for
you.
19 [y]Do not quench the Spirit. 20 [z]Do not
despise prophecies. 21 [a]Test all things;
[b]hold fast what is good. 22 Abstain from
every form of evil.

14 [q] 2 Thess. 3:6, 7, 11 [r] Heb. 12:12 [s] Rom. 14:1; 15:1; 1 Cor. 8:7 [t] Gal. 5:22 [5] *encourage* [6] *insubordinate* or *idle*
15 [u] Lev. 19:18 [v] Rom. 12:9; Gal. 6:10; 1 Thess. 5:21
16 [w] [2 Cor. 6:10]
17 [x] Eph. 6:18
19 [y] Eph. 4:30
20 [z] Acts 13:1; 1 Cor. 14:1, 31
21 [a] 1 Cor. 14:29; 1 John 4:1 [b] Phil. 4:8
23 [c] Phil. 4:9 [d] 1 Thess. 3:13

Blessing and Admonition

23 Now may [c]the God of peace Himself
[d]sanctify [7] you completely; and may your
whole spirit, soul, and body [e]be preserved
blameless at the coming of our Lord Jesus
Christ. 24 He who calls you *is* [f]faithful,
who also will [g]do *it*.
25 Brethren, pray for us.
26 Greet all the brethren with a holy kiss.
27 I charge you by the Lord that this
[8]epistle be read to all the [9]holy brethren.
28 The grace of our Lord Jesus Christ *be*
with you. Amen.

[e] 1 Cor. 1:8, 9 [7] *set you apart* 24 [f] [1 Cor. 10:13]; 2 Thess. 3:3 [g] Phil. 1:6 27 [8] *letter* [9] NU omits *holy*

5:14,15 we exhort you. Paul has discussed how the pastors are to serve the people and how the people are to respond to the pastors (vv. 12,13). In these verses, he presents how the people are to treat each other in the fellowship of the church. The "unruly," those out of line, must be warned and taught to get back in line. The "fainthearted," those in fear and doubt, must be encouraged and made bold. The "weak," those without spiritual and moral strength, must be held up firmly. Patience, forgiveness and acts of goodness must prevail between all the people.

5:16-22 Paul gave a summary of the Christian's virtues. These verses provide the foundational principles for a sound spiritual life in brief, staccato statements that, in spite of their brevity, give believers the priorities for successful Christian living.

5:16 Rejoice. Joy is appropriate at all times. Cf. Phil. 2:17,18; 3:1; 4:4.

5:17 pray. This does not mean pray repetitiously or continuously without a break (cf. Matt. 6:7,8), but rather pray persistently (cf. Luke 11:1-13; 18:1-8) and regularly (cf. Eph. 6:18; Phil. 4:6; Col. 4:2,12).

5:18 give thanks. Thanklessness is a trait of unbelievers (cf. Rom. 1:21; 2 Tim. 3:1-5). "This is the will of God" includes vv. 16,17.

5:19 quench. The fire of God's Spirit is not to be doused with sin. Believers are also instructed to not grieve the Holy Spirit (Eph. 4:30), but to be controlled by the Holy Spirit (Eph. 5:18) and to walk by the Holy Spirit (Gal. 5:16).

5:20 prophecies. This word can refer to a spoken revelation from God (cf. Acts 11:27,28; 1 Tim. 1:18; 4:14), but most often refers to the written word of Scripture (cf. Matt. 13:14; 2 Pet. 1:19-21; Rev. 1:3; 22:7,10,18,19). These "prophecies" are authoritative messages from God through a well recognized spokesman for God that, because of their divine origin, are not to be treated lightly. When God's Word is preached or read, it is to be received with great seriousness.

5:21,22 Test all things. This call for careful examination and discernment is in response to the command of v. 20. One is never to downgrade the proclamation of God's Word, but to examine the preached word carefully (cf. Acts 17:10,11). What is found to be "good" is to be wholeheartedly embraced. What is "evil" or unbiblical is to be shunned.

5:23 God...sanctify you. Having concluded all the exhortations beginning in 4:1, and especially from vv. 16-22, Paul's ending benediction acknowledged the source for obeying and fulfilling them all. It is not within human power to be sanctified in all these ways (cf. Zech. 4:6; 1 Cor. 2:4,5; Eph. 3:20,21; Col. 1:29). Only God (cf. Rom. 15:33; 16:20; Phil. 4:9; Heb. 13:20 for references to God as "peace") "Himself" can separate us from sin to holiness "completely." **whole spirit, soul, and body.** This comprehensive reference makes the term "completely" more emphatic. By using spirit and soul, Paul was not indicating that the immaterial part of man could be divided into two substances (cf. Heb. 4:12). The two words are used interchangeably throughout Scripture (cf. Heb. 6:19; 10:39; 1 Pet. 2:11; 2 Pet. 2:8). There can be no division of these realities, but rather they are used as other texts use multiple terms for emphasis (cf. Deut. 6:5; Matt. 22:37; Mark 12:30; Luke 10:27). Nor was Paul a believer in a 3-part human composition (cf. Rom. 8:10; 1 Cor. 3:11; 5:3-5; 7:34; 2 Cor. 7:1; Gal. 6:18; Col. 2:5; 2 Tim. 4:22), but rather two parts: material and immaterial. **at the coming.** This fourth mention of Christ's *parousia* refers to the rapture of the church as it has previously at 2:19; 3:13; 4:15.

5:24 calls you. This, as every time the divine call is mentioned in the NT, refers to God's effectual call of His chosen ones to salvation (cf. 2:12; 4:7; Rom. 1:6,7; 8:28; 1 Cor. 1:9; Eph. 4:1,4; 2 Tim. 1:9; 1 Pet. 2:9; 5:10; 2 Pet. 1:10). The God who calls will also bring those whom He calls to glory and none will be lost (cf. John 6:37-44; 10:28,29; Rom. 8:28-39; Phil. 1:6; Jude 24).

5:26 holy kiss. This gesture of affection is commanded 5 times in the NT (Rom. 16:16; 1 Cor. 16:20; 2 Cor. 13:12; 1 Pet. 5:14) and refers to the cultural hug and kiss greeting of the first century which for Christians was to be done righteously in recognition that believers are brothers and sisters in the family of God.

5:27 Public reading was the foundation of spiritual accountability (cf. Gal. 4:16; 2 Thess. 3:14).

5:28 Cf. Rom. 16:20,24; 2 Thess. 3:18.

The Second Epistle of Paul to the THESSALONIANS

Title

In the Greek NT, 2 Thessalonians is listed as "To *the* Thessalonians." This represents the Apostle Paul's second canonical correspondence to the fellowship of believers in the city of Thessalonica (cf. 1:1).

Author and Date

Paul, as in 1 Thessalonians, identified himself twice as the author of this letter (1:1; 3:17). Silvanus (Silas) and Timothy, Paul's co-laborers in founding the church, were present with him when he wrote. Evidence, both within this letter and with regard to vocabulary, style, and doctrinal content, strongly supports Paul as the only possible author. The time of this writing was surely a few months after the first epistle, while Paul was still in Corinth with Silas and Timothy (1:1; Acts 18:5) in late A.D. 51 or early A.D. 52 (see Introduction to 1 Thessalonians: Author and Date).

Background and Setting

For the history of Thessalonica, see Introduction to 1 Thessalonians: Background and Setting. Some have suggested that Paul penned this letter from Ephesus (Acts 18:18-21), but his 18 month stay in Corinth provided ample time both for the Thessalonian epistles to be authored (Acts 18:11).

Apparently, Paul had stayed appraised of the happenings in Thessalonica through correspondence and/or couriers. Perhaps the bearer of the first letter brought Paul back an update on the condition of the church, which had matured and expanded (1:3); but pressure and persecution had also increased. The seeds of false doctrine concerning the Lord had been sown, and the people were behaving disorderly. So Paul wrote to his beloved flock who were: 1) discouraged by persecution and needed incentive to persevere; 2) deceived by false teachers who confused them about the Lord's return; and 3) disobedient to divine commands, particularly by refusing to work. Paul wrote to address those 3 issues by offering: 1) comfort for the persecuted believers (1:3-12); 2) correction for the falsely taught and frightened believers (2:1-15); and 3) confrontation for the disobedient and undisciplined believers (3:6-15).

Historical and Theological Themes

Although chaps. 1,2 contain much prophetic material because the main issue was a serious misunderstanding generated by false teachers about the coming Day of the Lord (Paul reveals that the Day had not come and would not until certain other events occur), it is still best to call this "a pastoral letter." The emphasis is on how to maintain a healthy church with an effective testimony in proper response to sound eschatology and obedience to the truth.

Eschatology dominates the theological issues. One of the clearest statements on personal eschatology for unbelievers is found in 1:9. Church discipline is the major focus of 3:6-15, which needs to be considered along with Matt. 18:15-20; 1 Cor. 5:1-13; Gal. 6:1-5, and 1 Tim. 5:19,20 for understanding the complete Biblical teaching on this theme.

Interpretive Challenges

Eternal reward and retribution are discussed in 1:5-12 in such general terms that it is difficult to precisely identify some of the details with regard to exact timing. Matters concerning the Day of the Lord (2:2), the restrainer (2:6,7), and the lawless one (2:3,4,8-10) provide challenging prophetic material to interpret.

Outline

I. Paul's Greeting (1:1,2)

II. Paul's Comfort for Affliction (1:3-12)

- A. By Way of Encouragement (1:3,4)
- B. By Way of Exhortation (1:5-12)

III. Paul's Correction for Prophetic Error (2:1-17)

- A. Prophetic Crisis (2:1,2)
- B. Apostolic Correction (2:3-12)
- C. Pastoral Comfort (2:13-17)

IV. Paul's Concern for the Church

- A. Regarding Prayer (3:1-5)
- B. Regarding Undisciplined Living (3:6-15)

V. Paul's Benediction (3:16-18)

Greeting

1 Paul, Silvanus, and Timothy,
To the church of the Thessalonians in
God our Father and the Lord Jesus Christ:

2 [a]Grace to you and peace from God our
Father and the Lord Jesus Christ.

God's Final Judgment and Glory

3 We are bound to thank God always for
you, brethren, as it is fitting, because your
faith grows exceedingly, and the love of
every one of you all abounds toward each
other, 4 so that [b]we ourselves boast of you
among the churches of God [c]for your patience and faith [d]in all your persecutions
and [1]tribulations that you endure, 5 *which*
is [e]manifest[2] evidence of the righteous
judgment of God, that you may be counted
worthy of the kingdom of God, [f]for which
you also suffer; 6 [g]since *it is* a righteous
thing with God to repay with [3]tribulation
those who trouble you, 7 and to *give* you
who are troubled [h]rest with us when [i]the
Lord Jesus is revealed from heaven with
His mighty angels, 8 in flaming fire taking
vengeance on those who do not know
God, and on those who do not obey the
gospel of our Lord Jesus Christ. 9 [j]These
shall be punished with everlasting destruction from the presence of the Lord
and [k]from the glory of His power, 10 when
He comes, in that Day, [l]to be [m]glorified in
His saints and to be admired among all
those who [4]believe, because our testimony
among you was believed.
11 Therefore we also pray always for you
that our God would [n]count you worthy of
this calling, and fulfill all the good pleasure

CHAPTER 1
2 [a] 1 Cor. 1:3
4 [b] 2 Cor. 7:4; [1 Thess. 2:19] [c] 1 Thess. 1:3 [d] 1 Thess. 2:14 [1] *afflictions*
5 [e] Phil. 1:28 [2] *plain* [f] 1 Thess. 2:14
6 [g] Rev. 6:10 [3] *affliction*
7 [h] Rev. 14:13 [i] [1 Thess. 4:16]; Jude 14
9 [j] Phil. 3:19; 1 Thess. 5:3 [k] Deut. 33:2
10 [l] Matt. 25:31 [m] Is. 49:3; John 17:10; 1 Thess. 2:12 [4] NU, M *have believed*
11 [n] Col. 1:12

1:1,2 *See note on 1 Thess. 1:1.*

1:3 bound to thank. There is a spiritual obligation to thank God in prayer when He accomplishes great things in the lives of His saints. That was the case with the obedient Thessalonians, who had demonstrated growth in faith and love since the first letter. This was in direct answer to Paul's prayers (cf. 1 Thess. 1:3; 3:12).

1:4 patience and faith. Nowhere was their growth in faith and love (v. 3) more evident than in the way they patiently and faithfully endured hostilities and suffering from the enemies of Christ. Although there was no need to speak, since the Thessalonians' lives spoke clearly enough (1 Thess. 1:8), Paul's joy before the Lord over their perseverance bubbled up.

1:5 suffer. Having a right attitude toward suffering is essential, and that required attitude is concern for the kingdom of God. They were not self-centered, but concentrated on God's kingdom. Their focus was not on personal comfort, fulfillment, and happiness, but on the glory of God and the fulfillment of His purposes. They were not moaning about the injustice of their persecutions. Rather, they were patiently enduring the sufferings they did not deserve (v. 4). This very attitude was "manifest evidence" or positive proof that God's wise process of purging, purifying, and perfecting through suffering was working to make His beloved people worthy of the kingdom (cf. 2:12) by being perfected (cf. James 1:2-4; 1 Pet. 5:10). For believers, afflictions are to be expected (cf. 1 Thess. 3:3) as they live and develop Christian character in a satanic world. Suffering is not to be thought of as evidence that God has forsaken them, but evidence that He is with them, perfecting them (cf. Matt. 5:10; Rom 8:18; 2 Cor. 12:10). So the Thessalonians demonstrated that their salvation, determined by faith alone in the Lord Jesus Christ, was genuine because they, like Christ, were willing to suffer on account of God and His kingdom. They suffered unjustly as objects of man's wrath against Christ and His kingdom (Acts 5:41; Phil. 3:10; Col. 1:24). "Kingdom of God" is used here in its spiritual sense of salvation (*see note on Matt. 3:2*).

1:6 God to repay. Just as the righteous judgment of God works to perfect believers (v. 5), so it works to "repay" the wicked (cf. v. 8). Vindication and retribution are to be exercised by God, not man, in matters of spiritual persecution (cf. Deut. 32:35; Prov. 25:21,22; Rom. 12:19-21; 1 Thess. 5:15; Rev. 19:2). When God repays and how God repays are to be determined by Him.

1:7 rest with us. Paul was a fellow-sufferer for the just cause of Christ. He, like the Thessalonians, hoped for that ultimate rest and reward for their suffering for the kingdom that was to come when Christ returned to judge the ungodly. The Lord Jesus promised this two-fold coming for rest and retribution (cf. Matt. 13:40-43; 24:39-41; 25:31-33; Luke 21:27,28,34-36; John 5:24-29). **when the Lord Jesus is revealed.** This undoubtedly refers to Christ being unveiled in His coming as Judge. The first aspect of this revealing occurs at the end of the 7 year tribulation period (cf. Matt. 13:24-30,36-43; 24:29-51; 25:31-46; Rev. 19:11-15). The final and universal revelation of Christ as Judge occurs at the Great White Throne judgment following Christ's millennial reign on the earth (Rev. 20:11-15). Angels always accompany Christ in His coming for judgment (cf. Matt 13:41,49; 24:30,31; 25:31; Rev. 14:14,15).

1:8 in flaming fire. Fire is a symbol of judgment (cf. Ex. 3:2; 19:16-20; Deut. 5:4; Ps. 104:4; Is. 66:15,16; Matt. 3:11,12; Rev. 19:12). **taking vengeance.** Lit. these words mean "to give full punishment" (cf. Deut. 32:35; Is. 59:17; 66:15; Ezek. 25:14; Rom. 12:19). **do not know God.** Cf. 1 Thess. 4:5. This speaks to the lack of a personal relationship with God through Jesus Christ (cf. John 17:3; Gal. 4:8; Eph. 2:12; 4:17,18; Titus 1:16). Retribution is not dealt out because of persecuting Christians, but rather because they did not obey God's command to believe (cf. Acts 17:30,31; Rom. 1:5; 10:16; 15:18; 16:19) and call upon the name of the Lord to be saved from their sin (Rom. 10:9-13; 1 Cor. 16:22; Heb. 10:26-31). Salvation is never obtained by works but always by placing one's faith alone in the Lord Jesus Christ (Eph. 2:8-10).

1:9 everlasting destruction. *See note on Matt. 25:46.* Paul explained the duration and extent of what is elsewhere in Scripture called "hell." First, it is forever, thus it is not a reversible experience. Second, destruction means ruin and does not involve annihilation, but rather a new state of conscious being which is significantly worse than the first (cf. Rev. 20:14,15). This is described as the absence of God's presence and glory (cf. Matt. 8:12; 22:13; 25:30; Luke 16:24-26).

1:10 when He comes. When the Day of the Lord arrives bringing retribution and ruin for unbelievers. As Christ's great glory is displayed the result will be rest and relief for believers and the privilege of sharing His glory (cf. Phil. 3:21; 1 John 3:2). This is the "glorious manifestation" of believers of which Paul spoke (Rom. 8:18,19). At the time, all believers will adore and worship Him, including those in the Thessalonian church who believed Paul's testimony of the gospel.

1:11 we also pray. Paul's prayer life is exemplified 4 times in this letter (cf. v. 12; 2:16,17; 3:1-5,16). Here he prayed as he did in v. 5, that they might behave in ways consistent with their identity as Christians (cf. 1 Thess. 2:19; Eph. 4:1; Col. 1:10), living up to their "calling to salvation" (cf. Rom 8:30; 11:29; Gal. 4:13-15; 1 Cor. 1:26; Col. 1:3-5; 1 Thess. 2:12) with lives marked by goodness and powerful works of faith.

of *His* goodness and [o]the work of faith
with power, 12 [p]that the name of our Lord
Jesus Christ may be glorified in you, and
you in Him, according to the grace of our
God and the Lord Jesus Christ.

The Great Apostasy

2 Now, brethren, [a]concerning the coming of our Lord Jesus Christ [b]and our
gathering together to Him, we ask you,
2 [c]not to be soon shaken in mind or troubled, either by spirit or by word or by letter, as if from us, as though the day of
[1]Christ had come. 3 Let no one deceive
you by any means; for *that Day will not*
come [d]unless the falling away comes first,
and [e]the man of [2]sin is revealed, [f]the son
of perdition, 4 who opposes and [g]exalts
himself [h]above all that is called God or
that is worshiped, so that he sits [3]as God
in the temple of God, showing himself
that he is God.
5 Do you not remember that when I was
still with you I told you these things?
6 And now you know what is restraining,
that he may be revealed in his own time.

11 [o] 1 Thess. 1:3
12 [p] [Col. 3:17]

CHAPTER 2

1 [a] Mark 13:26; [1 Thess. 4:15-17] [b] Matt. 24:31
2 [c] Matt. 24:4 [1] NU *the Lord*
3 [d] 1 Tim. 4:1 [e] Dan. 7:25; 8:25; 11:36; 2 Thess. 2:8; Rev. 13:5 [f] John 17:12 [2] NU *lawlessness*
4 [g] Is. 14:13, 14; Ezek. 28:2 [h] 1 Cor. 8:5 [3] NU omits *as God*

1:12 that. The worthy walk of v. 11 allows God to be glorified in us, the light of all purposes (cf. 2:14; 1 Cor. 10:31; 1 Pet. 4:11).

2:1 coming of our Lord Jesus Christ. This is the fifth mention of Christ's coming in the Thessalonian letters (cf. 1 Thess. 2:19; 3:13; 4:15; 5:23; *see note at 1 Thess. 2:19*). The aspect of His particular coming in view here is identified by the next phrase "our gathering together," which conveys the idea of all believers meeting together with the Lord Jesus, obviously referring to the rapture of the church described in 1 Thess. 4:13-18 and John 14:1-3. Cf. Heb. 10:25 for the only other use of this phrase in the NT. This was the event the Thessalonians were anticipating (cf. 1 Thess. 1:10; 3:13; 5:9).

2:2 soon shaken. This term has been used of an earthquake (Acts 16:26) and a ship at anchor slipping its mooring in the midst of a heavy wind. Along with the word "troubled," it describes the state of agitation and alarm that had gripped the church. They were greatly distressed because they had expected the Rapture, the gathering together to the Lord, to take place before the Day of the Lord. They had expected to be taken to glory and heavenly rest, not left to persecution and divine wrath. Paul must have taught them that they would miss the Day of the Lord (1 Thess. 5:2-5; cf. Rev. 3:10), but they had become confused by the persecution they were experiencing, thinking they may have been in the Day of the Lord. This error had been reinforced by some messages to them claiming that they were indeed in the Day of the Lord. Paul noted the source of these as "spirit," "word," and "letter." A "spirit" would most likely refer to a false prophet claiming divine revelation as in 1 John 4:1-3. A "word" would refer to a sermon or speech given, while a "letter" indicated a written report. The powerful but harmful effect of this false information was gained by claiming it was from the Apostle Paul ("as if from us"). Whoever was telling them they were in the Day of the Lord claimed that it came from Paul who heard it, preached it, and wrote it. Thus their lie was given supposed apostolic sanction. The result was shock, fear, and alarm. Obviously, they had expected the Rapture before the Day of the Lord. For if they had expected it after, they would have rejoiced because Christ's coming was to be soon. Apostolic authenticity in this letter which corrects the error was important and accounts for Paul's care to close the letter in his distinctive handwriting (3:17; cf. Gal. 6:11). **the day of Christ.** The better text sources indicate "the Lord" rather than "Christ," (*see note on 1 Thess. 5:2* for discussion of this "day"). The idea that the Day of the Lord had already come conflicted with what Paul had previously taught them about the Rapture. This error, which so upset the Thessalonians, is what Paul corrected in vv. 3-12, where he showed that the day hadn't come and couldn't until certain realities were in place, most especially "the man of sin" (v. 3).

2:3,4 the falling away. The Day of the Lord cannot occur until a deliberate abandonment of a formerly professed position, allegiance, or commitment occurs, (the term was used to refer to military, political, or religious rebellion). Some have suggested, on questionable linguistic evidence, that this refers to "departure" in the sense of the Rapture. Context, however, points to a religious defection, which is further described in v. 4. The language indicates a specific event, not general apostasy which exists now and always will. Rather, Paul has in mind *the* apostasy. This is an event which is clearly and specifically identifiable and unique, the consummate act of rebellion, an event of final magnitude. The key to identifying the event is to identify the main person, which Paul does, calling him the "man of sin." Some texts have "man of lawlessness," but there is no real difference in meaning since sin equals lawlessness (1 John 3:4). This is the one who is called "the prince who is to come" (Dan. 9:26) and "the little horn" (Dan. 7:8), whom John calls "the beast" (Rev. 13:2-10,18) and most know as the Antichrist. The context and language clearly identify a real person in future times who actually does the things prophesied of him in Scripture. He is also called "the son of perdition" or destruction, a term used of Judas Iscariot (John 17:12). "The falling away" is the abomination of desolation that takes place at the midpoint of the Tribulation, spoken of in Dan. 9:27; 11:31 and Matt. 24:15 (*see notes there*). This man is not Satan, although Satan is the force behind him (v. 9) and he has motives like the desires of the devil (cf. Is. 14:13,14). Paul is referring to the very act of ultimate apostasy which reveals the final Antichrist and sets the course for the events that usher in the Day of the Lord. Apparently, he will be seen as supportive of religion so that God and Christ will not appear as his enemies until the apostasy. He exalts himself and opposes God by moving into the temple, the place for worship of God, declaring himself to be God and demanding the worship of the world. In this act of Satanic self-deification, he commits the great apostasy in defiance of God. For the first 3½ years of the Tribulation, he maintains relations with Israel, but halts those (cf. Dan. 9:27); and for the last 3½ years, there is great tribulation under his reign (cf. Dan. 7:25; 11:36-39; Matt. 24:15-21; Rev. 13:1-8) culminating with the Day of the Lord.

2:5 I told you. The imperfect tense is used indicating repeated action in past time. Apparently, Paul on numerous occasions had taught them the details of God's future plans. Here, he reminded them of the issues which proved the false teachers wrong about the Day of the Lord. Paul had before told them that the revealing of the Antichrist preceded the Day of the Lord; since he has not yet been revealed they could not possibly be in that Day.

2:6 restraining. While the Thessalonians already had been taught and thus knew what was restraining the coming of the Antichrist, Paul does not say specifically in this letter; thus many suggestions have been made to identify the restraining force of vv. 6,7. These include: 1) human government; 2) preaching of the gospel; 3) the binding of Satan; 4) the providence of God; 5) the Jewish state; 6) the church; 7) the Holy Spirit; and 8) Michael. Whatever now restrains the Antichrist of vv. 3,4,8-10 from being revealed in the fullness of his apostasy and evil, must be more than human or even angelic power. The power that holds back Satan from bringing the final apostasy and unveiling of his Satan-possessed false Christ must be divinely supernatural. It must be God's power in operation that holds back Satan, so that the man of sin, the son of destruction, won't be able to come until God permits it by removing the restraining power. The reason for the restraint was so that Antichrist would be revealed at God's appointed time and no sooner, just as was Christ (cf. Gal. 4:4), because God controls Satan.

7 For [i]the [4]mystery of lawlessness is already at work; only [5]He who now restrains *will do so* until [5]He is taken out of
the way. 8 And then the lawless one will
be revealed, [j]whom the Lord will consume [k]with the breath of His mouth and
destroy [l]with the brightness of His coming. 9 The coming of the *lawless one* is [m]ac-
cording to the working of Satan, with all
power, [n]signs, and lying wonders, 10 and
with all unrighteous deception among
[o]those who perish, because they did not
receive [p]the love of the truth, that they
might be saved. 11 And [q]for this reason
God will send them strong delusion, [r]that
they should believe the lie, 12 that they all
may be condemned who did not believe
the truth but [s]had pleasure in unrighteousness.

Stand Fast

13 But we are [6]bound to give thanks to
God always for you, brethren beloved by
the Lord, because God [t]from the beginning
[u]chose you for salvation [v]through [7]sancti-
fication by the Spirit and belief in the truth,
14 to which He called you by our gospel,
for [w]the obtaining of the glory of our Lord
Jesus Christ. 15 Therefore, brethren, [x]stand
fast and hold [y]the traditions which you
were taught, whether by word or our
[8]epistle.

16 Now may our Lord Jesus Christ Himself, and our God and Father, [z]who has
loved us and given *us* everlasting consolation and [a]good hope by grace, 17 comfort
your hearts [b]and [9]establish you in every
good word and work.

Pray for Us

3 Finally, brethren, [a]pray for us, that the
word of the Lord may run *swiftly* and
be glorified, just as *it is* with you, 2 and
[b]that we may be delivered from unreasonable and wicked men; [c]for not all have
faith.

7 [i]1 John 2:18 [4]*hidden truth* [5]Or he
8 [j]Dan. 7:10 [k]Is. 11:4; Rev. 2:16; 19:15 [l]Heb. 10:27
9 [m]John 8:41 [n]Deut. 13:1
10 [o]2 Cor. 2:15 [p]1 Cor. 16:22
11 [q]Rom. 1:28 [r]1 Tim. 4:1
12 [s]Rom. 1:32; 1 Cor. 13:6
13 [t]Eph. 1:4 [u]1 Thess. 1:4 [v]1 Thess. 4:7; [1 Pet. 1:2] [6]*under obligation* [7]*being set apart by*
14 [w]1 Pet. 5:10
15 [x]1 Cor. 16:13 [y]Rom. 6:17; 1 Cor. 11:2; 2 Thess. 3:6; Jude 3 [8]*letter*
16 [z][Rev. 1:5] [a]Titus 3:7; 1 Pet. 1:3
17 [b]1 Cor. 1:8 [9]*strengthen*

CHAPTER 3
1 [a]Eph. 6:19
2 [b]Rom. 15:31 [c]Acts 28:24

2:7 the mystery of lawlessness. This is the spirit of lawlessness already prevalent in society (cf. 1 John 3:4; 5:17), but still a mystery in that it is not fully revealed as it will be in the one who so blatantly opposes God that he blasphemously assumes the place of God on earth which God has reserved for Jesus Christ. The spirit of such a man is already in operation (cf. 1 John 2:18; 4:3), but the man who fully embodies that spirit has not come. For more on mystery, *see notes on Matt. 13:11; 1 Cor. 2:7; Eph. 3:4,5.* **taken out of the way.** This refers not to spatial removal (therefore it could not be the rapture of the church) but rather "a stepping aside." The idea is "out of the way," not gone (cf. Col. 2:14 where our sins are taken out of the way as a barrier to God); *see note on vv. 3,4.* This restraint will be in place until the Antichrist is revealed, at the midpoint of the Tribulation, leaving him 42 months to reign (Dan. 7:25; Rev. 13:5).

2:8 And then the…revealed. At the divinely decreed moment in the middle of the Tribulation when God removes the divine restraint, Satan, who has been promoting the spirit of lawlessness (v. 7), is finally allowed to fulfill his desire to imitate God by indwelling a man who will perform his will as Jesus did God's. This also fits God's plan for the consummation of evil and the judgment of the Day of the Lord. **the Lord will consume.** Death occurs at God's hand (cf. Dan 7:26; Rev. 17:11) and this man and his partner, the false prophet, will be cast alive into the lake of fire which burns with brimstone, where he will be eternally separated from God. (Rev. 19:20; 20:10). **His coming.** The aspect of His coming in view here is not the rapture of the church, but the Lord's coming in judgment on that day when He conquers the forces of Satan and sets up his millennial kingdom (Rev. 19:11-21).

2:9,10 the *lawless one*. He will do mighty acts pointing to himself as supernaturally empowered. His whole operation will be deceptive, luring the world to worship him and be damned. The career of the coming lawless one is more fully described in Rev. 13:1-18 (*see notes there*).

2:10 those who perish. His influence is limited to deceiving the unsaved, who will believe his lies (cf. Matt. 24:24; John 8:41-44). They perish in the deception because of Satan-imposed blindness to the truth of the saving gospel. Cf. John 3:19,20; 2 Cor. 4:4.

2:11 strong delusion. People who prefer to love sin and lies rather than gospel truth will receive severe, divine recompense, as do all sinners. God Himself will send judgment that insures their fate in the form of a deluding influence so that they continue to believe what is false. They accept evil as good and a lie as the truth. Thus does God use Satan and Antichrist as His instruments of judgment (cf. 1 Kin. 22:19-23).

2:12 condemned. As God has always judged willful rejection by giving men over to impurity and degrading passions (Rom. 1:24-28), so in the last days God will sovereignly seal the fate of those who persist in following Satan and his counterfeit Christ. As in all ages, those who habitually reject the truth are judged by being left to the consequences of their sin.

2:13,14 salvation…sanctification. Just as there were specific elements in the character of the Antichrist (vv. 10-12), so there are characteristics of the saved. In these two verses, Paul swept through the features of salvation, noting that believers are "beloved by the Lord," chosen for salvation from eternity past (cf. Rev. 13:8; 17:18), set apart from sin by the Spirit, and called to eternal glory, i.e., the sharing of the very "glory of our Lord Jesus Christ." Paul's main point in this section was to remind the Thessalonians that there was no need to be agitated or troubled (v. 2) thinking they had missed the rapture and thus were in the Day of Lord judgment. They were destined for glory, not judgment and would not be included with those deceived and judged in that Day.

2:15 stand fast…hold. This direct exhortation called for appropriate response to the great truths Paul had just written. In place of agitation should come strength and a firm stand. In place of false teaching should come faithful adherence to the truth.

2:16,17 Now may. This is one of many benedictions Paul has given in his letters. In it, he invoked God's power based on His love and grace, as the true source of encouragement and strength (cf. 3:5,16).

3:1 pray for us. Paul frequently enlisted prayer support from the churches for his ministry (cf. Rom. 15:30-32; Eph. 6:18,19; Col. 4:2,3; 1 Thess. 5:25; Philem. 22). In particular, he asked them to pray that the word of God would continue to spread rapidly as it had been already (cf. Acts 6:7; 12:24; 13:44-49), and be received with the honor it deserved.

3:2 unreasonable and wicked men. These were Paul's enemies at Corinth, where he ministered when he wrote (cf. Acts 18:9-17), who were perverse and aggressively unrighteous in their opposition of him and the gospel.

3 But [d]the Lord is faithful, who will establish you and [e]guard *you* from the evil
one. 4 And [f]we have confidence in the
Lord concerning you, both that you do and
will do the things we command you.
5 Now may [g]the Lord direct your hearts
into the love of God and into the patience
of Christ.

Warning Against Idleness

6 But we command you, brethren, in the
name of our Lord Jesus Christ, [h]that you
withdraw [i]from every brother who walks
[j]disorderly and not according to the tradition which [1]he received from us. 7 For you
yourselves know how you ought to follow
us, for we were not disorderly among you;
8 nor did we eat anyone's bread [2]free of
charge, but worked with [k]labor and toil
night and day, that we might not be a burden to any of you, 9 not because we do not
have [l]authority, but to make ourselves an
example of how you should follow us.
10 For even when we were with you, we
commanded you this: If anyone will not
work, neither shall he eat. 11 For we hear
that there are some who walk among you
in a disorderly manner, not working at all,
but are [m]busybodies. 12 Now those who
are such we command and [3]exhort
through our Lord Jesus Christ [n]that they
work in quietness and eat their own bread.
13 But *as for* you, brethren, [o]do not grow
weary *in* doing good. 14 And if anyone
does not obey our word in this [4]epistle,
note that person and [p]do not keep company with him, that he may be ashamed.
15 [q]Yet do not count *him* as an enemy, [r]but
[5]admonish *him* as a brother.

Benediction

16 Now may [s]the Lord of peace Himself
give you peace always in every way. The
Lord *be* with you all.
17 [t]The salutation of Paul with my own
hand, which is a sign in every [6]epistle; so I
write.
18 [u]The grace of our Lord Jesus Christ *be*
with you all. Amen.

3 [d] 1 Cor. 1:9; 1 Thess. 5:24 [e] John 17:15
4 [f] 2 Cor. 7:16
5 [g] 1 Chr. 29:18
6 [h] Rom. 16:17 [i] 1 Cor. 5:1 [j] 1 Thess. 4:11 [1] NU, M *they*
8 [k] 1 Thess. 2:9 [2] Lit. *for nothing*
9 [l] 1 Cor. 9:4, 6-14
11 [m] 1 Tim. 5:13; 1 Pet. 4:15
12 [n] Eph. 4:28; 1 Thess. 4:11, 12 [3] *encourage*
13 [o] 2 Cor. 4:1; Gal. 6:9
14 [p] Matt. 18:17 [4] *letter*
15 [q] Lev. 19:17 [r] Titus 3:10 [5] *warn*
16 [s] John 14:27; Rom. 15:33; Phil. 4:9
17 [t] 1 Cor. 16:21 [6] *letter*
18 [u] Rom. 16:20, 24; 1 Thess. 5:28

3:3 the Lord is faithful. Cf. Lam. 3:23. God is faithful in regard to creation (Ps. 119:90), His promises (Deut. 7:9; 2 Cor. 1:18; Heb. 10:23), salvation (1 Thess. 5:24), temptation (1 Cor. 10:13), suffering (1 Pet. 4:19), and here faithful to strengthen and protect from Satan (cf. John 17:15; Eph. 6:16; 1 Thess. 3:5).

3:5 Another of Paul's benedictions (cf. v. 16; 2:16,17), so common in his letters.

3:6 we command you. Paul's directions were not mere suggestions but rather they carried the weight and authority of a judge's court order which the apostle delivered and enforced (cf. vv. 4,6,10,12). Here, he required separation so that obedient Christians were not to fellowship with habitually disobedient believers. This is further explained at v. 14. **the tradition.** There were false traditions (Mark 7:2-13; Col. 2:8) and true (cf. 2:15). Paul's traditions were the inspired teachings he had given.

3:7 follow us. Paul called for them to imitate him (cf. v. 9; 1 Thess. 1:6) because he imitated Christ's example (cf. 1 Cor. 4:16; 11:1; Eph. 5:1).

3:8-10 worked. The specific issue related to working diligently to earn one's living. Though Paul had the "authority" as an apostle to receive support, he chose rather to earn his own living to set an example (cf. 1 Cor. 9:3-14; Gal. 5:4,6; 1 Tim. 5:17,18).

3:11,12 we hear. Word had come that, in spite of Paul teaching them to work and writing to them about it (1 Thess. 4:11), some were still not willing to work (cf. 1 Tim. 5:13). These were commanded to settle down and begin an ordered life of work.

3:13 do not grow weary. The hard working believers were tired of having to support the lazy, and were ready to stop all help to those in need, giving up all charity. Paul reminded them that the truly needy still required help and that the Thessalonians must not be negligent toward them.

3:14 do not keep company. This means to "mix it up" in the sense of social interaction. Blatantly disobedient Christians were to be disfellowshipped (v. 6) to produce shame and, hopefully, repentance if they refused to obey the Word of God. See Matt. 18:15-17; 1 Cor. 5:9-13; Gal. 6:1 for additional details on how to deal with those engaged in unrepentant and repeated sin.

3:15 enemy...brother. The purpose of this disfellowship discipline is not final rejection. While an unrepentant pattern of sin is to be dealt with decisively, it is to be continually kept in mind that the one with whom one deals is a brother in the Lord, so all further warnings to him about his sin are done with a brotherly attitude. For instruction on the manner of church discipline, *see notes on Matt. 18:15-20.*

3:16 the Lord of peace. Paul knew this characteristic of God would be most meaningful to reflect upon in light of the intense spiritual battle that raged all around the Thessalonians (cf. 1:2; 1 Thess. 1:1; 5:23). Cf. Paul's other benedictions to this church in v. 5; 2:16,17; 1 Thess. 3:11-13; 5:23.

3:17 a sign. Paul often wrote through a secretary (cf. Rom. 16:22). When that was the case, as most likely with this letter, Paul added an identifying signature (cf. 1 Cor. 16:21; Col. 4:18) so that readers could be sure he was truly the author *(see note on 2:2).*

3:18 Cf. 1 Thess. 5:28.

The First Epistle of Paul to TIMOTHY

Title

This is the first of two inspired letters Paul wrote to his beloved son in the faith. Timothy received his name, which means "one who honors God," from his mother (Eunice) and grandmother (Lois), devout Jews who became believers in the Lord Jesus Christ (2 Tim. 1:5) and taught Timothy the OT Scriptures from his childhood (2 Tim. 3:15). His father was a Greek (Acts 16:1) who may have died before Timothy met Paul.

Timothy was from Lystra (Acts 16:1-3), a city in the Roman province of Galatia (part of modern Turkey). Paul led Timothy to Christ (1:2,18; 1 Cor. 4:17; 2 Tim. 1:2), undoubtedly during his ministry in Lystra on his first missionary journey (Acts 14:6-23). When he revisited Lystra on his second missionary journey, Paul chose Timothy to accompany him (Acts 16:1-3). Although Timothy was very young (probably in his late teens or early twenties, since about 15 years later Paul referred to him as a young man, 4:12), he had a reputation for godliness (Acts 16:2). Timothy was to be Paul's disciple, friend, and colaborer for the rest of the apostle's life, ministering with him in Berea (Acts 17:14), Athens (Acts 17:15), Corinth (Acts 18:5; 2 Cor. 1:19), and accompanying him on his trip to Jerusalem (Acts 20:4). He was with Paul in his first Roman imprisonment and went to Philippi (2:19-23) after Paul's release. In addition, Paul frequently mentions Timothy in his epistles (Rom. 16:21; 2 Cor. 1:1; Phil. 1:1; Col. 1:1; 1 Thess. 1:1; 2 Thess. 1:1; Philem. 1). Paul often sent Timothy to churches as his representative (1 Cor. 4:17; 16:10; Phil. 2:19; 1 Thess. 3:2), and 1 Timothy finds him on another assignment, serving as pastor of the church at Ephesus (1:3). According to Heb. 13:23, Timothy was imprisoned somewhere and released.

Author and Date

Many modernist critics delight in attacking the plain statements of Scripture and, for no good reason, deny that Paul wrote the Pastoral Epistles (1, 2 Tim., Titus). Ignoring the testimony of the letters themselves (1:1; 2 Tim. 1:1; Titus 1:1) and that of the early church (which is as strong for the Pastoral Epistles as for any of Paul's epistles, except Rom. and 1 Cor.), these critics maintain that a devout follower of Paul wrote the Pastoral Epistles in the second century. As proof, they offer 5 lines of supposed evidence: 1) The historical references in the Pastoral Epistles cannot be harmonized with the chronology of Paul's life given in Acts; 2) The false teaching described in the Pastoral Epistles is the fully-developed Gnosticism of the second century; 3) The church organizational structure in the Pastoral Epistles is that of the second century, and is too well developed for Paul's day; 4) The Pastoral Epistles do not contain the great themes of Paul's theology; 5) The Greek vocabulary of the Pastoral Epistles contains many words not found in Paul's other letters, nor in the rest of the NT.

While it is unnecessary to dignify such unwarranted attacks by unbelievers with an answer, occasionally such an answer does enlighten. Thus, in reply to the critics' arguments, it can be pointed out that: 1) This contention of historical incompatibility is valid only if Paul was never released from his Roman imprisonment mentioned in Acts. But he was released, since Acts does not record Paul's execution, and Paul himself expected to be released (Phil. 1:19,25,26; 2:24; Philem. 22). The historical events in the Pastoral Epistles do not fit into the chronology of Acts because they happened after the close of the Acts narrative which ends with Paul's first imprisonment in Rome. 2) While there are similarities between the heresy of the Pastoral Epistles and second-century Gnosticism (see Introduction to Colossians: Background and Setting), there are also important differences. Unlike second-century Gnosticism, the false teachers of the Pastoral Epistles were still within the church (cf. 1:3-7) and their teaching was based on Judaistic legalism (1:7; Titus 1:10,14; 3:9). 3) The church organizational structure mentioned in the Pastoral Epistles is, in fact, consistent with that established by Paul (Acts 14:23; Phil. 1:1). 4) The Pastoral Epistles do mention the central themes of Paul's theology, including the inspiration of Scripture (2 Tim. 3:15-17); election (2 Tim. 1:9; Titus 1:1,2); salvation (Titus 3:5-7); the deity of Christ (Titus 2:13); His mediatorial work (2:5), and substitutionary atonement (2:6). 5) The different subject matter in the Pastoral Epistles required a different vocabulary from that in Paul's other epistles. Certainly a pastor today would use a different vocabulary in a personal letter to a fellow pastor than he would in a work of systematic theology.

The idea that a "pious forger" wrote the Pastoral Epistles faces several further difficulties: 1) The early church did not approve of such practices and surely would have exposed this as a ruse, if there had actually been one (cf. 2 Thess. 2:1,2; 3:17). 2) Why forge 3 letters that include similar material and no deviant doctrine? 3) If a counterfeit, why not invent an itinerary for Paul that would have harmonized with Acts? 4) Would a later, devoted follower of Paul have put the words of 1:13,15 into his master's mouth? 5) Why would he include warnings against deceivers (2 Tim. 3:13; Titus 1:10), if he himself were one?

The evidence seems clear that Paul wrote 1 Timothy and Titus shortly after his release from his first Roman imprisonment (ca. A.D. 62–64), and 2 Timothy from prison during his second Roman imprisonment (ca. A.D. 66–67), shortly before his death.

Background and Setting

After being released from his first Roman imprisonment (cf. Acts 28:30), Paul revisited several of the cities in which he had ministered, including Ephesus. Leaving Timothy behind there to deal with problems that had arisen in the Ephesian church, such as false doctrine (1:3-7; 4:1-3; 6:3-5), disorder in worship (2:1-15), the need for qualified leaders (3:1-14), and materialism (6:6-19), Paul went on to Macedonia, from where he wrote Timothy this letter to help him carry out his task in the church (cf. 3:14,15).

Historical and Theological Themes

First Timothy is a practical letter containing pastoral instruction from Paul to Timothy (cf. 3:14,15). Since Timothy was well versed in Paul's theology, the apostle had no need to give him extensive doctrinal instruction. This epistle does, however, express many important theological truths, such as the proper function of the law (1:5-11), salvation (1:14-16; 2:4-6); the attributes of God (1:17); the Fall (2:13,14); the person of Christ (3:16; 6:15,16); election (6:12); and the second coming of Christ (6:14,15).

Interpretive Challenges

There is disagreement over the identity of the false teachers (1:3) and the genealogies (1:4) involved in their teaching. What it means to be "delivered to Satan" (1:20) has also been a source of debate. The letter contains key passages in the debate over the extent of the atonement (2:4-6; 4:10). Paul's teaching on the role of women (2:9-15) has generated much discussion, particularly his declaration that they are not to assume leadership roles in the church (2:11,12). How women can be saved by bearing children (2:15) has also confused many. Whether the fact that an elder must be "the husband of one wife" excludes divorced or unmarried men has been disputed, as well as whether Paul refers to deacons' wives or deaconesses (3:11). Those who believe Christians can lose their salvation cite 4:1 as support for their view. There is a question about the identity of the widows in 5:3-16—are they needy women ministered to by the church, or an order of older women ministering to the church? Does "double honor" accorded to elders who rule well (5:17,18) refer to respect or money? These will all be dealt with in their respective notes.

Outline

I. Greeting (1:1,2)

II. Instructions Concerning False Doctrine (1:3-20)
   - A. The False Doctrine at Ephesus (1:3-11)
   - B. The True Doctrine of Paul (1:12-17)
   - C. The Exhortation to Timothy (1:18-20)

III. Instructions Concerning the Church (2:1–3:16)
   - A. The Importance of Prayer (2:1-8)
   - B. The Role of Women (2:9-15)
   - C. The Qualifications for Leaders (3:1-13)
   - D. The Reason for Paul's Letter (3:14-16)

IV. Instructions Concerning False Teachers (4:1-16)
   - A. The Description of False Teachers (4:1-5)
   - B. The Description of True Teachers (4:6-16)

V. Instructions Concerning Pastoral Responsibilities (5:1–6:2)
   - A. The Responsibility to Sinning Members (5:1,2)
   - B. The Responsibility to Widows (5:3-16)
   - C. The Responsibility to Elders (5:17-25)
   - D. The Responsibility to Slaves (6:1,2)

VI. Instructions Concerning the Man of God (6:3-21)
   - A. The Peril of False Teaching (6:3-5)
   - B. The Peril of Loving Money (6:6-10)
   - C. The Proper Character and Motivation of a Man of God (6:11-16)
   - D. The Proper Handling of Treasure (6:17-19)
   - E. The Proper Handling of Truth (6:20,21)

Greeting

1
Paul, an apostle of Jesus Christ, by the
commandment of God our Savior and
the Lord Jesus Christ, our hope,

2 To Timothy, a [a]true son in the faith:

[b]Grace, mercy, *and* peace from God our
Father and Jesus Christ our Lord.

No Other Doctrine

3 As I urged you [c]when I went into Macedonia—remain in Ephesus that you may
[1]charge some [d]that they teach no other
doctrine, 4 [e]nor give heed to fables and
endless genealogies, which cause disputes
rather than godly edification which is in
faith. 5 Now [f]the purpose of the commandment is love [g]from a pure heart, *from*
a good conscience, and *from* [2]sincere faith,
6 from which some, having strayed, have
turned aside to [h]idle talk, 7 desiring to be
teachers of the law, understanding neither
what they say nor the things which they
affirm.
8 But we know that the law *is* [i]good if
one uses it lawfully, 9 knowing this: that
the law is not made for a righteous person,

CHAPTER 1

2 [a] Acts 16:1, 2; Rom. 1:7; 2 Tim. 1:2; Titus 1:4 [b] Gal. 1:3
3 [c] Acts 20:1, 3 [d] Rom. 16:17; 2 Cor. 11:4; Gal. 1:6, 7; 1 Tim. 6:3 [1] *command*
4 [e] 1 Tim. 6:3, 4, 20; Titus 1:14
5 [f] Rom. 13:8-10; Gal. 5:14 [g] Eph. 6:24 [2] Lit. *unhypocritical*
6 [h] 1 Tim. 6:4, 20
8 [i] Rom. 7:12, 16

1:1 apostle of Jesus Christ. *See notes on 2 Cor. 12:11,12;* cf. Acts 1:2; 2:42; Rom. 1:1; Eph. 2:20. **God our Savior.** A title unique to the Pastoral Epistles (1, 2 Tim., Titus) that has its roots in the OT (Pss. 18:46; 25:5; 27:9; Mic. 7:7; Hab. 3:18). God is by nature a saving God and the source of our salvation, which He planned from eternity past (*see note on 4:10;* cf. 2 Thess. 2:13). **Jesus Christ, our hope.** Christians have hope for the future because Christ purchased salvation for them on the cross in the past (Rom. 5:1,2), sanctifies them through His Spirit in the present (Gal. 5:16-25), and will lead them to glory in the future (Col. 1:27; 1 John 3:2,3).

1:2 Timothy. See Introduction: Title. **true son in the faith.** Only Timothy (2 Tim. 1:2; 2:1) and Titus (1:4) received this special expression of Paul's favor. The Gr. word for "son" is better translated "child," which emphasizes Paul's role as spiritual father to Timothy. "True" speaks of the genuineness of Timothy's faith (cf. 2 Tim. 1:5). Timothy was Paul's most cherished pupil, and protégé (1 Cor. 4:17; Phil. 2:19-22). **Grace, mercy, *and* peace.** Paul's familiar greeting that appears in all his epistles (*see note on Rom. 1:7*), but with the addition here of "mercy" (cf. 2 Tim. 1:2). Mercy frees believers from the misery that accompanies the consequences of sin.

1:3-11 In his opening charge to halt the spread of false teaching in the church at Ephesus, Paul characterizes the false teachers and their doctrine.

1:3 when I went into Macedonia—remain in Ephesus. Before Paul left Ephesus, he likely began the confrontation with the expulsion of Hymenaeus and Alexander (v. 20), then assigned Timothy to stay on and complete what he had begun. **charge.** This refers to a military command—it demands that a subordinate obey an order from a superior (cf. 2 Tim. 4:1). **some.** The false teachers were few in number, yet had a wide influence. Several reasons point toward these men being elders in the church at Ephesus and in the churches in the surrounding region: 1) they presumed to be teachers (v. 7), a role reserved for elders (3:2; 5:17). 2) Paul himself had to excommunicate Hymenaeus and Alexander, which implies they occupied the highest pastoral positions. 3) Paul detailed the qualifications of an elder (3:1-7), implying that unqualified men, who needed to be replaced by qualified ones, were occupying those roles. 4) Paul stressed that sinning elders were to be publicly disciplined (5:19-22). **teach no other doctrine.** A compound word made up of two Gr. words that mean "of a different kind" and "to teach." The false teachers were teaching doctrine different than apostolic doctrine (cf. 6:3,4; Acts 2:42; Gal. 1:6,7). This had to do with the gospel of salvation. Apparently they were teaching another gospel (*see notes on Gal. 1:6-9*) and not the "glorious gospel of the blessed God" (v. 11).

1:4 fables and endless genealogies. Legends and fanciful stories manufactured from elements of Judaism (v. 7; cf. Titus 1:14), which probably dealt with allegorical or fictitious interpretations of OT genealogical lists. In reality, they were "doctrines of demons" (4:1), posing as God's truth (cf. 4:7).

1:5 the commandment. *See note on v. 3,* where the verb form "charge" is used (also in v. 8). The purpose of the charge in vv. 3,4 is the spiritual virtue defined in v. 5. Timothy was to deliver this charge to the church. The goal of preaching the truth and warning of error is to call men to true salvation in Christ, which produces a love for God from a purified heart (2 Tim. 2:22; 1 Pet. 1:22), a cleansed conscience (Heb. 9:22; 10:14), and genuine faith (Heb. 10:22). **love.** This is the love of choice and the will, characterized by self-denial and self-sacrifice for the benefit of others, and it is the mark of a true Christian (John 13:35; Rom. 13:10; 1 John 4:7,8; *see notes on 1 Cor. 13:1-7*). In contrast, false doctrine produces only conflict and resultant "disputes" (v. 4; 6:3-5). **good conscience.** Cf. v. 19; 3:9; 4:2; *see note on 2 Cor. 1:12.* The Gr. word for "good" refers to that which is perfect and produces pleasure and satisfaction. God created man with a "conscience" as his self-judging faculty. Because God has written His law on man's heart (*see note on Rom. 2:15*), man knows the basic standard of right and wrong. When he violates that standard, his conscience produces guilt, which acts as the mind's security system that produces fear, guilt, shame, and doubt as warnings of threats to the soul's well-being (cf. John 8:9; 1 Cor. 8:7,10,12; Titus 1:15; Heb. 10:22). On the other hand, when a believer does God's will, he enjoys the affirmation, assurance, peace, and joy of a good conscience (cf. Acts 23:1; 24:16; 2 Tim. 1:3; Heb. 13:18; 1 Pet. 3:16,21).

1:6 idle talk. Cf. Titus 1:10. Refers to speech that is aimless and has no logical end. It is essentially irrelevant and will not accomplish anything spiritual or edifying to believers. It can also be translated "fruitless discussion." False doctrine leads nowhere, but to the deadening end of human speculation and demonic deception (cf. 6:3-5).

1:7 desiring to be teachers. The false teachers wanted the kind of prestige enjoyed by Jewish rabbis; but they were not concerned at all about truly learning the law and teaching it to others (cf. 6:4; Matt. 23:5-7). Instead, they imposed on believers in Ephesus a legalistic heresy that offered salvation by works.

1:7,8 the law. The Mosaic law is in view here, not just law in general. These were Jewish would-be teachers who wanted to impose circumcision and the keeping of Mosaic ceremonies on the church as necessary for salvation. They plagued the early church (*see notes on Gal. 3–5; Phil. 3:1-8*).

1:8 the law *is* good. The Gr. word for "good" can be translated "useful." The law is good or useful because it reflects God's holy will and righteous standard (Ps. 19:7; Rom. 7:12) which accomplishes its purpose in showing sinners their sin (Rom. 3:19) and their need for a savior (Gal. 3:24). The law forces people to recognize that they are guilty of disobeying God's commands, and it thereby condemns every person and sentences them to hell (*see notes on Rom. 3:19,20*).

1:9 not made for a righteous person. Those who think they are righteous will never be saved (Luke 5:32) because they do not understand the true purpose of the law. The false teachers, with their works system of personally achieved self-righteousness (in their own minds),

but for *the* lawless and insubordinate, for
the ungodly and for sinners, for *the* unholy
and profane, for murderers of fathers and
murderers of mothers, for manslayers,
10 for fornicators, for sodomites, for kidnappers, for liars, for perjurers, and if there
is any other thing that is [3]contrary to
sound doctrine, 11 according to the glorious gospel of the [j]blessed God which was
[k]committed to my trust.

Glory to God for His Grace

12 And I thank Christ Jesus our Lord
who has [l]enabled me, [m]because He counted me faithful, [n]putting *me* into the ministry, 13 although [o]I was formerly a blasphemer, a persecutor, and an [4]insolent
man; but I obtained mercy because [p]I did *it*
ignorantly in unbelief. 14 [q]And the grace of
our Lord was exceedingly abundant, [r]with
faith and love which are in Christ Jesus.
15 [s]This *is* a faithful saying and worthy of
all acceptance, that [t]Christ Jesus came into
the world to save sinners, of whom I am
chief. 16 However, for this reason I obtained mercy, that in me first Jesus Christ
might show all longsuffering, as a pattern
to those who are going to believe on Him
for everlasting life. 17 Now to [u]the King
eternal, [v]immortal, [w]invisible, to [5]God
[x]who alone is wise, [y]*be* honor and glory
forever and ever. Amen.

10 [3] *opposed*
11 [j] 1 Tim. 6:15 [k] 1 Cor. 9:17
12 [l] 1 Cor. 15:10 [m] 1 Cor. 7:25 [n] Col. 1:25
13 [o] Acts 8:3; 1 Cor. 15:9 [p] John 4:21 [4] *violently arrogant*
14 [q] Rom. 5:20; 1 Cor. 3:10; 2 Cor. 4:15; Gal. 1:13-16 [r] 1 Thess. 1:3; 1 Tim. 2:15; 4:12; 6:11; 2 Tim. 1:13; 2:22; Titus 2:2
15 [s] 1 Tim. 3:1; 4:9; 2 Tim. 2:11; Titus 3:8 [t] Is. 53:5; 61:1; Hos. 6:1-3; Matt. 1:21; 9:13
17 [u] Ps. 10:16 [v] Rom. 1:23 [w] Heb. 11:27 [x] Rom. 16:27 [y] 1 Chr. 29:11 [5] NU *the only God,*

had shown clearly that they misunderstood the law completely. It was not a means to self-righteousness, but a means to self-condemnation, sin, conviction, repentance, and pleading to God for mercy (v. 15). *See notes on Luke 18:9-14; Rom. 5:20; Gal. 3:10-13,19.* **lawless...profane.** These first 6 characteristics, expressed in 3 couplets, delineate sins from the first half of the Ten Commandments, which deal with a person's relationship to God. "Lawless" describes those who have no commitment to any law or standard, which makes such people "insubordinate," or rebellious. Those who are "ungodly" have no regard for anything sacred, which means they are "sinners" because they disregard God's law. "Unholy" people are indifferent to what is right, which leads them to be the "profane," who step on or trample what is sacred (cf. Heb. 10:29).

1:9,10 murderers of fathers...perjurers. These sins are violations of the second half of the Ten Commandments—those dealing with relationships among people. These specific sins undoubtedly characterized the false teachers, since they are characteristic behaviors related to false doctrine (v. 10). "Murderers of fathers" and "mothers" is a violation of the fifth commandment (Ex. 20:12; cf. 21:15-17), which forbids everything from dishonor to murder. "Manslayers" (or "murderers") is in violation of the sixth commandment (Ex. 20:13). "Fornicators" and "sodomites" (or "homosexuals") violate the seventh commandment (Ex. 20:14), which prohibits sexual activity outside the marriage bed. Because the theft of children was commonplace in Paul's day, he mentions "kidnappers" in connection with the eighth commandment (Ex. 20:15), which prohibits stealing. Finally, "liars" and "perjurers" are violators of the ninth commandment (Ex. 20:16).

1:10 sound doctrine. A familiar emphasis in the Pastoral Epistles (cf. 2 Tim. 4:3; Titus 1:9; 2:1). "Sound" refers to that which is healthy and wholesome. It is the kind of teaching that produces spiritual life and growth, which implies that false doctrine produces spiritual disease and debilitation.

1:11 the glorious gospel. The gospel reveals God's glory; that is, the perfections of His person or His attributes, including His holiness (hatred of sin) and justice (demand of punishment for violations of His law) and grace (forgiveness of sin). Those particular attributes are key to any effective gospel presentation. **committed.** This Gr. word refers to committing something of value to another, and can be translated "entrusted." God entrusted Paul with the communication and guardianship of His revealed truth. Cf. 2:7; 6:20,21; Rom. 15:15,16; 1 Cor. 4:1,2; 9:17; 2 Cor. 5:18-20; Gal. 2:7; Col. 1:25; 1 Thess. 2:4.

1:12-17 Paul's testimony of his own salvation in these verses provides a contrast between his proper understanding of the law and the misconceptions of the false teachers, and between the glory of the true gospel and the emptiness of false doctrine.

1:12 counted me faithful. God's sovereign purpose for Paul and for all believers works through personal faith. Until Paul was turned by the Holy Spirit from self-righteous works (see Phil. 3:4-7) to faith alone in Christ, he could not be used by God. He was in the same condition as the useless false teachers (vv. 6,7).

1:13 a blasphemer, a persecutor, and an insolent man. This verse indicates that experience of Paul when he saw himself, in the light of God's law, for who he really was (*see notes on Rom. 7:7-12*). A "blasphemer" speaks evil of and slanders God. Paul violated the first half of the Ten Commandments through his overt attacks against Christ (cf. Acts 9:4,5; 22:7,8; 26:9,14,15). As a "persecutor" and an "insolent man," Paul violated the second half through his attacks on believers. The Gr. word for "insolent man" can be translated "violent aggressor," indicating the violence Paul heaped on Christians. Cf. note on v. 20. **because I did *it* ignorantly in unbelief.** Paul was neither a Jewish apostate nor a Pharisee who clearly understood Jesus' teaching and still rejected Him. He was a zealous, fastidious Jew trying to earn his salvation, thus lost and damned (*see notes on Phil. 3:4-7*). His plea of ignorance was not a claim to innocence nor an excuse denying his guilt. It was simply a statement indicating that he did not understand the truth of Christ's gospel and was honestly trying to protect his religion. His willing repentance when confronted by Christ (cf. Rom. 7:9; Phil. 3:8,9) is evidence that he had not understood the ramifications of his actions—he truly thought he was doing God a service (Acts 26:9).

1:14 grace. God's loving forgiveness, by which He grants salvation apart from any merit on the part of those He saves (*see notes on Rom. 3:24; Gal. 1:6*). **faith and love.** Attitudes frequently linked with salvation in the NT (cf. Eph. 1:15; 3:17; Col. 1:4,23). They are gifts of God's grace in Christ.

1:15 This *is* a faithful saying. A phrase unique to the Pastoral Epistles (cf. 3:1; 4:9; 2 Tim. 2:11; Titus 3:8), which announces a statement summarizing key doctrines. The phrase "worthy of all acceptance" gives the statement added emphasis. Apparently, these sayings were well known in the churches, as concise expressions of cardinal gospel truth. **to save sinners.** This faithful saying was based on the statements of Jesus recorded in Matt. 9:13; Luke 19:10. **I am chief.** Lit. "first," in rank. Few could be considered a worse sinner than someone who blasphemed God and persecuted His church (*see notes on 1 Cor. 15:9; Eph. 3:8*). Paul's attitude toward himself dramatically changed (cf. Phil. 3:7-9; *see notes on Rom 7:7-12*).

1:16 for this reason. Paul was saved so that God could display to all His gracious and merciful patience with the most wretched sinners. **longsuffering.** Refers to patience with people (cf. Rom. 2:4). **a pattern.** A model or example. Paul was living proof that God could save any sinner, no matter how great a one he might be. The account of Paul's conversion has been instrumental in the salvation of many. Paul's testimony is repeated 6 other times in the NT (Acts 9,22,26; Gal. 1,2; Phil. 3:1-14).

1:17 God receives all the praise for sovereignly saving Paul. This is one of the many doxologies Paul wrote (cf. Rom. 11:33-36).

Fight the Good Fight

18 This [6]charge I commit to you, son
Timothy, according to the prophecies previously made concerning you, that by
them you may wage the good warfare,
19 having faith and a good conscience,
which some having rejected, concerning
the faith have suffered shipwreck, 20 of
whom are [z]Hymenaeus and [a]Alexander,
whom I delivered to Satan that they may
learn not to [b]blaspheme.

18 [6] *command*
20 [z] 2 Tim. 2:17, 18 [a] 2 Tim. 4:14 [b] Acts 13:45

CHAPTER 2

1 [1] *encourage*
2 [a] Ezra 6:10 [b] [Rom. 13:1] [2] *a prominent place* [3] *dignity*
3 [c] Rom. 12:2 [d] 2 Tim. 1:9
4 [e] Ezek. 18:23, 32; John 3:17; 1 Tim. 4:10; Titus 2:11; 2 Pet. 3:9 [f] [John 17:3]
5 [g] 1 Cor. 8:6; Gal. 3:20 [h] [Heb. 9:15]

Pray for All Men

2 Therefore I [1]exhort first of all that supplications, prayers, intercessions, *and*
giving of thanks be made for all men, 2 [a]for
kings and [b]all who are in [2]authority, that
we may lead a quiet and peaceable life in
all godliness and [3]reverence. 3 For this *is*
[c]good and acceptable in the sight [d]of God
our Savior, 4 [e]who desires all men to be
saved [f]and to come to the knowledge of
the truth. 5 [g]For *there is* one God and [h]one
Mediator between God and men, *the* Man

1:18 Timothy. See Introduction: Title. **prophecies previously made concerning you.** The Gr. word for "previously made" lit. means "leading the way to," implying that a series of prophecies had been given about Timothy in connection with his receiving his spiritual gift (*see note on 4:14*). These prophecies specifically and supernaturally called Timothy into God's service. **wage the good warfare.** Paul urged Timothy to fight the battle against the enemies of Christ and the gospel. Cf. 2 Cor. 10:3-5; 2 Tim. 2:3,4; 4:7.

1:19 faith...faith. The first is subjective and means continuing to believe the truth. The second is objective, referring to the content of the Christian gospel. **a good conscience.** *See note on v. 5.* **shipwreck.** A good conscience serves as the rudder that steers the believer through the rocks and reefs of sin and error. The false teachers ignored their consciences and the truth, and as a result, suffered shipwreck of the Christian faith (the true doctrine of the gospel), which implies severe spiritual catastrophe. This does not imply loss of salvation of a true believer (*see notes on Rom. 8:31-39*), but likely indicates the tragic loss that comes to the apostate. They had been in the church, heard the gospel and rejected it in favor of the false doctrine defined in vv. 3-7. Apostasy is a turning away from the gospel, having once known it. *See notes on Heb. 2:3,4; 3:12-15; 6:1-8; 10:26-31.*

1:20 Hymenaeus and Alexander. Hymenaeus is mentioned in 2 Tim. 2:17 in connection with Philetus, another false teacher. Alexander may be the opponent of the faith referred to in 2 Tim. 4:14,15. Nothing else is known about these two men (*see note on v. 3*). **I delivered to Satan.** Paul put both men out of the church, thus ending their influence and removing them from the protection and insulation of God's people. They were no longer in the environment of God's blessing but under Satan's control. In some instances God has turned believers over to Satan for positive purposes, such as revealing the genuineness of saving faith, keeping them humble and dependent on Him, enabling them to strengthen others, or offering God praise (cf. Job. 1:1-22; Matt. 4:1-11; Luke 22:31-33; 2 Cor. 12:1-10; Rev. 7:9-15). God hands some people over to Satan for judgment, such as King Saul (1 Sam. 16:12-16; 28:4-20), Judas (John 13:27), and the sinning member in the Corinthian church (*see notes on 1 Cor. 5:1-5*). **may learn not to blaspheme.** *See note on v. 13.* Paul learned not to blaspheme when confronted by the true understanding of the law and the gospel. That was what those men needed. God, the inspired text seems to indicate, would teach them and show them grace as he had Paul. But that evangelistic work could not go on at the expense of the purity of the church.

2:1-8 The Ephesian church had evidently stopped praying for the lost, since Paul urged Timothy to make it a priority again. The Judaistic false teachers in Ephesus, by a perverted gospel and the teaching that salvation was only for Jews and Gentile proselytes to Judaism, would have certainly restricted evangelistic praying. Religious exclusivism (salvation only for the elite) would preclude the need for prayer for the lost.

2:1 supplications. The Gr. word is from a root that means "to lack," "to be deprived," or "to be without." Thus this kind of prayer occurs because of a need. The lost have a great need for salvation, and believers should always be asking God to meet that need. **intercessions.** This word comes from a root meaning "to fall in with someone," or "to draw near so as to speak intimately." The verb from which this word derives is used of Christ's and the Spirit's intercession for believers (Rom. 8:26; Heb. 7:25). Paul's desire is for the Ephesian Christians to have compassion for the lost, to understand the depths of their pain and misery, and to come intimately to God pleading for their salvation. *See notes on Titus 3:3,4.* **all men.** The lost in general, not the elect only. God's decree of election is secret—believers have no way of knowing who is elect until they respond. The scope of God's evangelistic efforts is broader than election (Matt. 22:14; John 17:21,23; *see note on v. 4*).

2:2 kings and all who are in authority. Because so many powerful and influential political rulers are hostile to God, they are often the targets of bitterness and animosity. But Paul urges believers to pray that these leaders might repent of their sins and embrace the gospel, which meant that the Ephesians were even to pray for the salvation of the Roman emperor, Nero, a cruel and vicious blasphemer and persecutor of the faith. **a quiet and peaceable life.** "Quiet" refers to the absence of external disturbances; "peaceable" refers to the absence of internal ones. While it remains uncompromising in its commitment to the truth, the church is not to agitate or disrupt the national life. When it manifests love and goodness to all and prays passionately for the lost, including rulers, the church may experience a certain amount of religious freedom. Persecution should only be the result of righteous living, not civil disobedience (*see notes on Titus 3:1-4; 1 Pet. 2:13-23*). **godliness and reverence.** "Godliness" is a key word in this letter (3:16; 4:7,8; 6:3,5,6,11; cf. 2 Tim. 3:5; Titus 1:1), indicating that there needed to be a call back to holy living, which had been negatively affected by the false doctrine. Godliness refers to having the proper attitude and conduct before God in everything; "reverence" can be translated "moral earnestness," and refers to moral dignity and holy behavior before men.

2:3 God our Savior. *See note on 1:1.*

2:4 desires all men to be saved. The Gr. word for "desires" is not that which normally expresses God's will of decree (His eternal purpose), but God's will of desire. There is a distinction between God's desire and His eternal saving purpose, which must transcend His desires. God does not want men to sin. He hates sin with all His being (Pss. 5:4; 45:7); thus, He hates its consequences—eternal wickedness in hell. God does not want people to remain wicked forever in eternal remorse and hatred of Himself. Yet, God, for His own glory, and to manifest that glory in wrath, chose to endure "vessels...prepared for destruction" for the supreme fulfillment of His will (Rom. 9:22). In His eternal purpose, He chose only the elect out of the world (John 17:6) and passed over the rest, leaving them to the consequences of their sin, unbelief, and rejection of Christ (cf. Rom. 1:18-32). Ultimately, God's choices are determined by His sovereign, eternal purpose, not His desires. *See note on 2 Pet. 3:9.* **the knowledge of the truth.** Meaning "to be saved." *See note on 2 Tim. 3:7.*

2:5 *there is* one God. There is no other way of salvation (Acts 4:12); hence there is the need to pray for the lost to come to know the one true God (cf. Deut. 4:35,39; 6:4; Is. 43:10; 44:6; 45:5,6,21,22; 46:9; 1 Cor. 8:4,6). **Mediator.** This refers to someone who intervenes between two parties to resolve a conflict or ratify a covenant. Jesus Christ is the only "Mediator" who can restore peace between God and

Christ Jesus, **6** [i]who gave Himself a ransom for all, to be testified in due time, **7** [j]for
which I was appointed a preacher and an
apostle—I am speaking the truth [4]in Christ
and not lying—[k]a teacher of the Gentiles in
faith and truth.

Men and Women in the Church

8 I desire therefore that the men pray
[l]everywhere, [m]lifting up holy hands, without wrath and doubting; **9** in like manner
also, that the [n]women adorn themselves in
modest apparel, with propriety and [5]mod-
eration, not with braided hair or gold or
pearls or costly clothing, **10** [o]but, which is
proper for women professing godliness,
with good works. **11** Let a woman learn in
silence with all submission. **12** And [p]I do
not permit a woman to teach or to have authority over a man, but to be in silence.

6 [i] Mark 10:45
7 [j] Eph. 3:7, 8; 1 Tim. 1:11; 2 Tim. 1:11 [k] [Gal. 1:15, 16] [4] NU omits *in Christ*
8 [l] Luke 23:34 [m] Ps. 134:2
9 [n] 1 Pet. 3:3 [5] *discretion*
10 [o] 1 Pet. 3:4
12 [p] 1 Cor. 14:34; Titus 2:5

sinners (Heb. 8:6; 9:15; 12:24). ***the* Man Christ Jesus.** The absence of the article before "Man" in the Gr. suggests the translation, "Christ Jesus, Himself a man." Only the perfect God-Man could bring God and man together. Cf. Job 9:32,33.

2:6 a ransom. This describes the result of Christ's substitutionary death for believers, which He did voluntarily (John 10:17,18) and reminds one of Christ's own statement in Matt. 20:28, "a ransom for many." The "all" is qualified by the "many." Not all will be ransomed (though His death would be sufficient), but only the many who believe by the work of the Holy Spirit and for whom the actual atonement was made. *See note on 2 Pet. 3:9.* Christ did not pay a ransom only; He became the object of God's just wrath in the believer's place—He died his death and bore his sin (cf. 2 Cor. 5:21; 1 Pet. 2:24). **for all.** This should be taken in two senses: 1) there are temporal benefits of the atonement that accrue to all men universally (*see note on 4:10*), and 2) Christ's death was sufficient to cover the sins of all people. Yet the substitutionary aspect of His death is applied to the elect alone (*see above and notes on 2 Cor. 5:14-21*). Christ's death is therefore unlimited in its sufficiency, but limited in its application. Because Christ's expiation of sin is indivisible, inexhaustible, and sufficient to cover the guilt of all the sins that will ever be committed, God can clearly offer it to all. Yet only the elect will respond and be saved, according to His eternal purpose (cf. John 17:12). **in due time.** At the proper time in God's redemptive plan (*see note on Gal. 4:4*).

2:7 for which. Paul's divine commission was based on the truths delineated in vv. 3-6. **preacher.** The Gr. word derives from the verb that means, "to herald," "to proclaim," or "to speak publicly." Paul was a public herald proclaiming the gospel of Christ. **apostle.** *See note on 1:1.* **I am speaking the truth…not lying.** Paul's emphatic outburst of his apostolic authority and integrity is to emphasize that he was a teacher of the Gentiles. **teacher of the Gentiles.** The distinctive feature of Paul's apostolic appointment, which demonstrates the universal scope of the gospel. Paul's need to make this distinction suggests he was dealing with some form of Jewish exclusivism that had crippled the Ephesians' interest in praying for Gentiles to be saved.

2:8 men. The Gr. word for "men" as opposed to women. God intends for men to be the leaders when the church meets for corporate worship. When prayer for the lost is offered during those times, the men are to lead it. **everywhere.** Paul's reference to the official assembly of the church (cf. 1 Cor. 1:2; 2 Cor. 2:14; 1 Thess. 1:8). **lifting up holy hands.** Paul is not emphasizing a specific posture necessary for prayer, but a prerequisite for effective prayer (cf. Ps. 66:18). Though this posture is described in the OT (1 Kin. 8:22; Pss. 28:2; 63:4; 134:2), so are many others. The Gr. word for "holy" means "unpolluted" or "unstained by evil." "Hands" symbolize the activities of life; thus "holy hands" represent a holy life. This basis of effective prayer is a righteous life (James 5:16). **without wrath and doubting.** "Wrath" and righteousness are mutually exclusive (James 1:20; cf. Luke 9:52-56). A better translation for "doubting" is "dissension," and refers to a hesitant reluctance to be committed to prayer. "Effectual, fervent" prayer is effective (James 5:16). The two refer to one's inner attitude.

2:9-15 Women in the church were living impure and self-centered lives (cf. 5:6,11-15; 2 Tim. 3:6), and that practice carried over into the worship service, where they became distractions. Because of the centrality of worship in the life of the church, Paul calls on Timothy to confront the problem.

2:9 adorn…modest apparel. The Gr. word for "adorn" means "to arrange," "to put in order," or "to make ready." A woman is to arrange herself appropriately for the worship service, which includes wearing decent clothing which reflects a properly adorned chaste heart. **propriety and moderation.** The Gr. word for "propriety" refers to modesty mixed with humility, which carries the underlying idea of shame. It can also refer to a rejection of anything dishonorable to God, or refer to grief over sin. "Moderation" basically refers to self-control over sexual passions. Godly women hate sin and control their passions so as not to lead another into sin. *See notes on 1 Pet. 3:3,4.* **braided hair or gold or pearls or costly clothing.** Specific practices that were causing distraction and discord in the church. Women in the first century often wove "gold, pearls," or other jewelry into their hair styles ("braided hair") to call attention to themselves and their wealth or beauty. The same was true of those women who wore "costly clothing." By doing so they would draw attention to themselves and away from the Lord, likely causing the poorer women to be envious. Paul's point was to forbid the preoccupation of certain women with flaunting their wealth and distracting people from worshiping the Lord.

2:10 Those women who have publicly committed themselves to pursuing godliness should support that claim not only in their demeanor, wardrobe, and appearance, but by being clothed with righteous behavior.

2:11 Let a woman learn. Women are not to be the public teachers when the church assembles, but neither are they to be shut out of the learning process. The form of the Gr. verb translated "let…learn" is an imperative: Paul is commanding that women be taught in the church. That was a novel concept, since neither first century Judaism nor Greek culture held women in high esteem. Some of the women in Ephesus probably overreacted to the cultural denigration they had typically suffered and took advantage of their opportunity in the church by seeking a dominant role in leadership. **in silence with all submission.** "Silence" ("quiet") and "submission" ("to line up under") were to characterize the role of a woman as a learner in the context of the church assembly. Paul explains his meaning in v. 12: Women are to be silent by not teaching, and they are to demonstrate submission by not usurping the authority of the pastors or elders.

2:12 I do not permit. The Gr. word for "permit" is used in the NT to refer to allowing someone to do what he desires. Paul may have been addressing a real situation in which several women in Ephesus desired to be public preachers. **to teach.** Paul used a verbal form of this Gr. word that indicates a condition or process and is better translated: "to be a teacher." This was an important, official function in the church (*see Acts 13:1; 1 Cor. 12:28; Eph. 4:11*). Thus Paul is forbidding women from filling the office and role of the pastor or teacher. He is not prohibiting them from teaching in other appropriate conditions and circumstances (cf. Acts 18:26; Titus 2:3,4). **to have authority over.** Paul forbids women from exercising any type of authority over men in the church assembly, since the elders are those who rule (5:17). They are all to be men (as is clear from the requirements in 3:2,5). **in silence.** *See note on v. 11.*

13 For Adam was formed first, then Eve.
14 And Adam was not deceived, but the
woman being deceived, fell into transgression. 15 Nevertheless she will be saved in
childbearing if they continue in faith, love,
and holiness, with self-control.

CHAPTER 3

1 [1] Lit. *overseer*

Qualifications of Overseers

3 This *is* a faithful saying: If a man desires the position of a [1]bishop, he desires a good work. 2 A bishop then must be
blameless, the husband of one wife, temperate, sober-minded, of good behavior,

2:13,14 A woman's subordinate role did not result after the Fall as a cultural, chauvinistic corruption of God's perfect design; rather, God established her role as part of His original creation (v. 13). God made woman after man to be his suitable helper (*see note on Gen. 2:18*; cf. 1 Cor. 11:8,9). The Fall actually corroborates God's divine plan of creation (*see notes on Gen. 3:1-7*). By nature Eve was not suited to assume the position of ultimate responsibility. By leaving Adam's protection and usurping his headship, she was vulnerable and fell, thus confirming how important it was for her to stay under the protection and leadership of her husband (*see notes on 5:11,12; 2 Tim. 3:6,7*). Adam then violated his leadership role, followed Eve in her sin, and plunged the human race into sinfulness—all connected with violating God's planned roles for the sexes. Ultimately, the responsibility for the Fall still rests with Adam, since he chose to disobey God apart from being deceived (Rom. 5:12-21; 1 Cor. 15:21,22).

2:15 she. That Paul does not have Eve in mind here is clear because the verb translated "will be saved" is future, and he also uses the plural pronoun "they." He is talking about women after Eve. **will be saved.** Better translated in this context, "will be preserved." The Gr. word can also mean "to rescue," "to preserve safe and unharmed," "to heal," or "to deliver from." It appears several times in the NT without reference to spiritual salvation (cf. Matt. 8:25; 9:21,22; 24:22; 27:40,42,49; 2 Tim. 4:18). Paul is not advocating that women are eternally saved from sin through childbearing or that they maintain their salvation by having babies, both of which would be clear contradictions of the NT teaching of salvation by grace alone through faith alone (Rom. 3:19,20) sustained forever (Rom. 8:31-39). Paul is teaching that even though a woman bears the stigma of being the initial instrument who led the race into sin, it is women through childbearing who may be preserved or freed from that stigma by raising a generation of godly children (cf. 5:10). **in childbearing.** Because mothers have a unique bond and intimacy with their children, and spend far more time with them than do fathers, they have far greater influence in their lives and thus a unique responsibility and opportunity for rearing godly children. While a woman may have led the human race into sin, women have the privilege of leading many out of sin to godliness. Paul is speaking in general terms; God does not want all women to be married (1 Cor. 7:25-40), let alone bear children. **if they continue in faith, love, and holiness, with self-control.** The godly appearance, demeanor, and behavior commanded of believing women in the church (vv. 9-12) is motivated by the promise of deliverance from any inferior status and the joy of raising godly children.

3:1-13 Paul's purpose in writing this letter was to instruct Timothy regarding the church (vv. 14,15). Of primary importance to any church is that its leaders be qualified to teach and set the example for the rest. These verses delineate those qualifications for pastors and deacons (*see also notes on Titus 1:5-9*).

3:1 This *is* a faithful saying: *See note on 1:15.* **desires…desires.** Two different Gr. words are used. The first means "to reach out after." It describes external action, not internal motive. The second means "a strong passion," and refers to an inward desire. Taken together, these two words aptly describe the type of man who belongs in the ministry—one who outwardly pursues it because he is driven by a strong internal desire. **bishop.** The word means "overseer" and identifies the men who are responsible to lead the church (cf. 5:17; 1 Thess. 5:12; Heb. 13:7). In the NT the words "bishop," "elder," "overseer," and "pastor" are used interchangeably to describe the same men (Acts 20:17,28; Titus 1:5-9; 1 Pet. 5:1,2). Bishops (pastors, overseers, elders) are responsible to lead (5:17), preach and teach (5:17), help the spiritually weak (1 Thess. 5:12-14), care for the church (1 Pet. 5:1,2), and ordain other leaders (4:14).

3:2 must. The use of this Gr. particle stresses emphatically that living a blameless life is absolutely necessary for church leaders. **blameless.** Lit. "not able to be held" in a criminal sense; there is no valid accusation of wrongdoing that can be made against him. No overt, flagrant sin can mar the life of one who must be an example for his people to follow (cf. v. 10; 4:17; 5:7; Ps. 101:6; Phil. 3:17; 2 Thess. 3:9; Heb. 13:7; 1 Pet. 5:3). This is the overarching requirement for elders; the rest of the qualifications elaborate on what it means to be blameless. Titus 1:6,7 uses another Gr. word to mean the same thing. **the husband of one wife.** Lit. in Gr. a "one-woman man." This says nothing about marriage or divorce (for comments on that, *see note on v. 4*). The issue is not the elder's marital status, but his moral and sexual purity. This qualification heads the list, because it is in this area that leaders are most prone to fail. Various interpretations of this qualification have been offered. Some see it as a prohibition against polygamy—an unnecessary injunction since polygamy was not common in Roman society and clearly forbidden by Scripture (Gen 2:24), the teaching of Jesus (Matt. 19:5,6; Mark 10:6-9), and Paul (Eph. 5:31). A polygamist could not even have been a church member, let alone a church leader. Others see this requirement as barring those who remarried after the death of their wives. But, as already noted, the issue is sexual purity, not marital status. Further, the Bible encourages remarriage after widowhood (5:14; 1 Cor. 7:39). Some believe that Paul here excludes divorced men from church leadership. That again ignores the fact that this qualification does not deal with marital status. Nor does the Bible prohibit all remarriage after divorce (*see notes on Matt. 5:31,32; 19:9; 1 Cor. 7:15*). Finally, some think that this requirement excludes single men from church leadership. But if that were Paul's intent, he would have disqualified himself (1 Cor. 7:8). A "one-woman man" is one totally devoted to his wife, maintaining singular devotion, affection and sexual purity in both thought and deed. To violate this is to forfeit blamelessness and no longer be "above reproach" (Titus 1:6,7). Cf. Prov. 6:32,33. **temperate.** The Gr. word lit. means "wineless," but is here used metaphorically to mean "alert," "watchful," "vigilant," or "clear-headed." Elders must be able to think clearly. **sober-minded.** A "sober-minded" man is disciplined, knows how to properly order his priorities, and is serious about spiritual matters. **good behavior.** The Gr. word means "orderly." Elders must not lead chaotic lives; if they cannot order their own lives, how can they bring order to the church? **hospitable.** From a compound Gr. word meaning "love of strangers" (*see notes on Rom. 12:13; Heb. 13:2*; cf. 1 Pet. 4:9). As with all spiritual virtues, elders must set the example; their lives and homes are to be open so all can see their spiritual character. **able to teach.** Used only here and in 2 Tim. 2:24. The only qualification relating to an elder's giftedness and spiritual ability, and the only one that distinguishes elders from deacons. The preaching and teaching of God's Word is the overseer/pastor/elder's primary duty (4:6,11,13; 5:17; 2 Tim. 2:15,24; Titus 2:1).

3:3 not given to wine. More than a mere prohibition against drunkenness (*see note on Eph. 5:18*). An elder must not have a reputation as a drinker; his judgment must never be clouded by alcohol (cf. Prov. 31:4,5; 1 Cor. 6:12), his lifestyle must be radically different from the world and lead others to holiness, not sin (Rom. 14:21). *See note on 5:23.* **not violent.** Lit. "not a giver of blows." Elders must react to difficult situations calmly and gently (2 Tim. 2:24,25), and under no circumstances

hospitable, able to teach; 3 not [2]given to
wine, not violent, [3]not greedy for money,
but gentle, not quarrelsome, not [4]covetous;
4 one who rules his own house well, having *his* children in submission with all reverence 5 (for if a man does not know how
to rule his own house, how will he take
care of the church of God?); 6 not a [5]novice,
lest being puffed up with pride he fall into
the *same* condemnation as the devil.
7 Moreover he must have a good testimony
among those who are outside, lest he fall
into reproach and the [a]snare of the devil.

Qualifications of Deacons

8 Likewise deacons *must be* reverent, not
double-tongued, [b]not given to much wine,
not greedy for money, 9 holding the [6]mys-
tery of the faith with a pure conscience.
10 But let these also first be tested; then let
them serve as deacons, being *found* blameless. 11 Likewise, *their* wives *must be* reverent, not [7]slanderers, temperate, faithful in
all things. 12 Let deacons be the husbands
of one wife, ruling *their* children and their
own houses well. 13 For those who have
served well as deacons [c]obtain for themselves a good standing and great boldness
in the faith which is in Christ Jesus.

The Great Mystery

14 These things I write to you, though I
hope to come to you shortly; 15 but if I am
delayed, *I write* so that you may know

3 [2] *addicted* [3] NU omits *not greedy for money* [4] *loving money*
6 [5] *new convert*
7 [a] 1 Tim. 6:9; 2 Tim. 2:26
8 [b] Ezek. 44:21
9 [6] *hidden truth*
11 [7] *malicious gossips*
13 [c] Matt. 25:21

with physical violence. **not greedy for money.** The better Gr. manuscripts omit this phrase. *See note below on "not covetous."* The principle is included, however, in Titus 1:7; 1 Pet. 5:2. **gentle.** Considerate, genial, gracious, quick to pardon failure, and one who does not hold a grudge. **not quarrelsome.** "Peaceful," "reluctant to fight"; one who does not promote disunity or disharmony. **not covetous.** Elders must be motivated by love for God and His people, not money (cf. 1 Pet. 5:2). A leader who is in the ministry for money reveals a heart set on the world, not the things of God (Matt. 6:24; 1 John 2:15). Covetousness characterizes false teachers (Titus 1:11; 2 Pet. 2:1-3,14; Jude 11), but not Paul's ministry (Acts 20:33; 1 Cor. 9:1-16; 2 Cor. 11:9; 1 Thess. 2:5).

3:4 who rules his own house well. The elder's home life, like his personal life, must be exemplary. He must be one who "rules" (presides over, has authority over) "his own house" (everything connected with his home, not merely his wife and children) "well" (intrinsically good; excellently). Issues of divorce should be related to this matter. A divorced man gives no evidence of a well-managed home, but rather that divorce shows weakness in his spiritual leadership. If there has been a biblically permitted divorce, it must have been so far in the past as to have been overcome by a long pattern of solid family leadership and the rearing of godly children (v. 4; Titus 1:6). **submission.** A military term referring to soldiers ranked under one in authority. An elder's children must be believers (*see note on "faithful" in Titus 1:6*), well-behaved, and respectful.

3:5 take care of the church of God. An elder must first prove in the intimacy and exposure of his own home his ability to lead others to salvation and sanctification. There he proves God has gifted him uniquely to spiritually set the example of virtue, to serve others, resolve conflicts, build unity, and maintain love. If he cannot do those essential things there, why would anyone assume he would be able to do them in the church?

3:6 not a novice, lest…puffed up with pride. Putting a new convert into a leadership role would tempt him to pride. Elders, therefore, are to be drawn from the spiritually mature men of the congregation (*see notes on 5:22*). **fall into the *same* condemnation as the devil.** Satan's condemnation was due to pride over his position. It resulted in his fall from honor and authority (Is. 14:12-14; Ezek. 28:11-19; cf. Prov. 16:18). The same kind of fall and judgment could easily happen to a new and weak believer put in a position of spiritual leadership.

3:7 good testimony…outside. A leader in the church must have an unimpeachable reputation in the unbelieving community, even though people there may disagree with his moral and theological stands. How can he make a spiritual impact on those who do not respect him? Cf. Matt. 5:48; Phil. 2:15.

3:8 deacons. From a word group meaning "to serve." Originally referring to menial tasks such as waiting on tables (*see notes on Acts 6:1-4*), "deacon" came to denote any service in the church. Deacons serve under the leadership of elders, helping them exercise oversight in the practical matters of church life. Scripture defines no official or specific responsibilities for deacons; they are to do whatever the elders assign them or whatever spiritual ministry is necessary. **reverent.** Serious in mind and character; not silly or flippant about important matters. **not double-tongued.** Deacons must not say one thing to some people and something else to others; their speech must not be hypocritical, but honest and consistent. **not given to much wine.** Not preoccupied with drink (*see note on v. 3*). **not greedy.** Like elders (*see note on v. 3*), deacons must not abuse their office to make money. Such a qualification was especially important in the early church, where deacons routinely handled money, distributing it to those in need.

3:9 the mystery. *See notes on Matt. 13:11; 1 Cor. 2:7; Eph. 3:4,5.* Appearing frequently in Paul's writings (cf. Rom. 11:25; 16:25; Eph. 1:9; 3:9; 6:19; Col. 2:2), the word "mystery" describes truth previously hidden, but now revealed, including Christ's incarnation (v. 16), Christ's indwelling of believers (Col. 1:26,27), the unity of Jews and Gentiles in the church (Eph. 3:4-6), the gospel (Col. 4:3), lawlessness (2 Thess. 2:7), and the rapture of the church (1 Cor. 15:51,52). **a pure conscience.** *See note on 1:5.*

3:10 first be tested. The present tense of this verb indicates an ongoing evaluation of deacons' character and service by the church. **being *found* blameless.** *See note on v. 2.*

3:11 *their* wives. The Gr. word rendered "wives" can also be translated "women." Paul likely here refers not to deacons' wives, but to the women who serve as deacons. The use of the word "likewise" as an introduction (cf. v. 8) suggests a third group in addition to elders and deacons. Also, since Paul gave no requirements for elders' wives, there is no reason to assume these would be qualifications for deacons' wives. **reverent.** *See note on v. 8.* **not slanderers.** "Slanderers" is the plural form of *diabolos*—a title frequently given to Satan (Matt. 4:5,8,11; 13:39; Luke 4:3,5,6,13; 8:12; 1 Pet. 5:8; 1 John 3:8; Rev. 2:10; 12:9,12; 20:2,10). The women who serve must not be gossips. **temperate.** *See note on v. 2.* **faithful in all things.** Women servants in the church, like their male counterparts (*see note on v. 2*), must be absolutely trustworthy in all aspects of their lives and ministries.

3:12 the husbands of one wife. *See note on v. 2.* **ruling…their own houses well.** *See note on v. 4.*

3:14-16 These verses mark a transition point between the positive instruction of the first 3 chapters and the warnings of the last 3. They reveal the heart of the church's mission (v. 15) and message (v. 16).

3:14,15 I hope to come to you shortly. The Gr. grammar suggests Paul's meaning is "These things I write, although I had hoped to come to you sooner." Delayed in Macedonia (see Introduction: Background and Setting), Paul sent Timothy this letter.

how you ought to conduct yourself in the
house of God, which is the church of the
living God, the pillar and [8]ground of the
truth. 16 And without controversy great is
the [9]mystery of godliness:

[d]God[1] was manifested in the flesh,
[e]Justified in the Spirit,
[f]Seen by angels,
[g]Preached among the Gentiles,
[h]Believed on in the world,
[i]Received up in glory.

The Great Apostasy

4 Now the Spirit [1]expressly says that in
latter times some will depart from the
faith, giving heed [a]to deceiving spirits and
doctrines of demons, 2 [b]speaking lies in
hypocrisy, having their own conscience
[c]seared with a hot iron, 3 forbidding to
marry, *and commanding* to abstain from
foods which God created to be received
with thanksgiving by those who believe
and know the truth. 4 For every creature of
God *is* good, and nothing is to be refused if
it is received with thanksgiving; 5 for it is
[2]sanctified by the word of God and prayer.

A Good Servant of Jesus Christ

6 If you instruct the brethren in these
things, you will be a good minister of Jesus

15 [8] *foundation, mainstay*
16 [d] [John 1:14; 1 Pet. 1:20; 1 John 1:2; 3:5, 8] [e] [Matt. 3:16; Rom. 1:4] [f] Matt. 28:2 [g] Acts 10:34; Rom. 10:18 [h] Rom. 16:26; 2 Cor. 1:19; Col. 1:6, 23 [i] Luke 24:51 [9] *hidden truth* [1] NU *Who*

CHAPTER 4

1 [a] 2 Tim. 3:13; Rev. 16:14 [1] *explicitly*
2 [b] Matt. 7:15 [c] Eph. 4:19
5 [2] *set apart*

3:15 how you ought to conduct yourself. The second half of this verse expresses the theme of this epistle—setting things right in the church. **house of God.** This is better translated "household." Believers are members of God's household (Gal. 6:10; Eph. 2:19; Heb. 3:6; 1 Pet. 4:17) and must act accordingly. This is not a reference to any building, but to the people who make up the true church. **church of the living God.** The church is God's possession (Acts 20:28; Eph. 1:14; Titus 2:14; 1 Pet. 2:9). The title "the living God" has a rich OT heritage (Deut. 5:26; Josh. 3:10; 1 Sam. 17:26,36; 2 Kin. 19:4,16; Pss. 42:2; 84:2; Is. 37:4,17; Jer. 10:10; 23:26; Dan. 6:20,26; Hos. 1:10). **pillar and ground.** Paul's imagery may have referred to the magnificent temple of Diana (Artemis) in Ephesus, which was supported by 127 gold-plated marble pillars. The word translated "ground" appears only here in the NT and denotes the foundation on which a building rests. The church upholds the truth of God's revealed Word. **the truth.** The content of the Christian faith recorded in Scripture and summed up in v. 16.

3:16 This verse contains part of an early church hymn, as its uniformity, rhythm, and parallelism indicate. Its 6 lines form a concise summary of the truth of the gospel. **mystery of godliness.** "Mystery" is that term used by Paul to indicate truth hidden in the OT age and revealed in the NT (*see note on v. 9*). Godliness refers to the truths of salvation and righteousness in Christ, which produce holiness in believers; namely, the manifestation of true and perfect righteousness in Jesus Christ. **God was manifested.** The better manuscripts read "He who" instead of "God." In either case, the reference is clearly to Christ, who manifested the invisible God to mankind (John 1:1-4; 14:9; Col. 1:15; Heb. 1:3; 2 Pet. 1:16-18). **in the flesh.** Not sinful, fallen human nature here (cf. Rom. 7:18,25; 8:8; Gal. 5:16,17), but merely humanness (cf. John 1:14; Rom. 1:3; 8:3; 9:5; 1 Pet. 3:18; 1 John 4:2,3; 2 John 7). **Justified in the Spirit.** "Justified" means "righteous," so that "spirit" may be written with lower case "s" indicating a declaration of Christ's sinless spiritual righteousness (John 8:46; 2 Cor. 5:21; Heb. 4:15; 5:9; 7:26; 1 Pet. 2:21,22; 1 John 2:1), or it could refer to His vindication by the Holy Spirit (Rom. 1:4). **Seen by angels.** Both by fallen (*see notes on Col. 2:15; 1 Pet. 3:18-20*) and elect (Matt. 28:2; Luke 24:4-7; Acts 1:10,11; Heb. 1:6-9) angels. **Preached among the Gentiles.** Or, nations. See Matt. 24:14; 26:13; 28:19,20; Mark 13:10; Acts 1:8. **Received up in glory.** See Acts 1:9,10; Phil. 2:8-11; Heb. 1:3. Christ's ascension and exaltation showed that the Father was pleased with Him and accepted His work fully.

4:1-5 After already noting the presence of false teachers at Ephesus (1:3-7,18-20), and countering some of their erroneous teaching with the positive instruction of chaps. 2,3, Paul deals directly with the false teachers themselves in this passage, focusing on their origin and content.

4:1 the Spirit expressly says. Paul repeats to Timothy the warning he had given many years earlier to the Ephesian elders (Acts 20:29,30). The Holy Spirit through the Scriptures has repeatedly warned of the danger of apostasy (cf. Matt. 24:4-12; Acts 20:29,30; 2 Thess. 2:3-12; Heb. 3:12; 5:11–6:8; 10:26-31; 2 Pet. 3:3; 1 John 2:18; Jude 18). **in latter times.** The period from the first coming of Christ until His return (Acts 2:16,17; Heb. 1:1,2; 9:26; 1 Pet. 1:20; 1 John 2:18). Apostasy will exist throughout that period, reaching a climax shortly before Christ returns (cf. Matt. 24:12). **depart from the faith.** Those who fall prey to the false teachers will abandon the Christian faith. The Gr. word for "depart" is the source of the Eng. word "apostatize," and refers to someone moving away from an original position. These are professing or nominal Christians who associate with those who truly believe the gospel, but defect after believing lies and deception, thus revealing their true nature as unconverted. *See notes on 1 John 2:19; Jude 24.* **deceiving spirits.** Those demonic spirits, either directly or through false teachers, who have wandered away from the truth and lead others to do the same. The most defining word to describe the entire operation of Satan and his demons is "deception" (cf. John 8:44; 1 John 4:1-6). **doctrines of demons.** Not teaching about demons, but false teaching that originates from them. To sit under such teaching is to hear lies from the demonic realm (Eph. 6:12; James 3:15; 2 John 7-11). The influence of demons will reach its peak during the Tribulation (2 Thess. 2:9; Rev. 9:2-11; 16:14; 20:2,3,8,10). Satan and demons constantly work the deceptions that corrupt and pervert God's Word.

4:2 speaking lies in hypocrisy. Lit. "hypocritical lie-speakers." These are the human false teachers who propagate demon doctrine (cf. 1 John 4:1). **conscience.** *See note on 1:5.* **seared.** A medical term referring to cauterization. False teachers can teach their hypocritical lies because their consciences have been desensitized (cf. Eph. 4:19), as if all the nerves that make them feel had been destroyed and turned into scar tissue by the burning of demonic deception.

4:3 forbidding to marry, *and commanding* to abstain from foods. A sample of the false teaching at Ephesus. Typically, it contained elements of truth, since Scripture commends both singleness (1 Cor. 7:25-35) and fasting (Matt. 6:16,17; 9:14,15). The deception came in making such human works a prerequisite for salvation—a distinguishing mark of all false religion. This ascetic teaching was probably influenced both by the Jewish sect known as the Essenes, and contemporary Greek thought (which viewed matter as evil and spirit as good). Paul addressed this asceticism in Col. 2:21-23 (*see notes there*). Neither celibacy nor any form of diet saves or sanctifies.

4:4 every creature of God *is* good. The false teachers' asceticism contradicted Scripture, which teaches that since God created both marriage and food (Gen. 1:28-31; 2:18-24; 9:3), they are intrinsically good (Gen. 1:31) and to be enjoyed with gratitude by believers. Obviously food and marriage are essential for life and procreation.

4:5 sanctified. Set apart or dedicated to God for holy use. The means for so doing are thankful prayer and an understanding that the Word of God has set aside the temporary Mosaic dietary restrictions (Mark 7:19; Acts 10:9-15; Rom. 14:1-12; Col. 2:16,17). Contrast the unbeliever whose inner corruption and evil motives corrupt every good thing (Titus 1:15).

Christ, [d]nourished in the words of faith
and of the good doctrine which you have
carefully followed. 7 But [e]reject profane
and old wives' fables, and [f]exercise yourself toward godliness. 8 For [g]bodily exercise profits a little, but godliness is profitable for all things, [h]having promise of the
life that now is and of that which is to
come. 9 This *is* a faithful saying and worthy of all acceptance. 10 For to this *end* [3]we
both labor and suffer reproach, because we
trust in the living God, [i]who is *the* Savior
of all men, especially of those who believe.
11 These things command and teach.

6 [d]2 Tim. 3:14
7 [e]2 Tim. 2:16; Titus 1:14 [f]Heb. 5:14
8 [g]1 Cor. 8:8 [h]Ps. 37:9
10 [i]Ps. 36:6 [3]NU *we labor and strive,*
12 [j]Phil. 3:17; Titus 2:7; 1 Pet. 5:3 [4]*look down on your youthfulness* [5]NU omits *in spirit*
13 [6]*teaching*
14 [k]2 Tim. 1:6 [l]Acts 6:6; 1 Tim. 5:22

Take Heed to Your Ministry

12 Let no one [4]despise your youth, but
be an [j]example to the believers in word, in
conduct, in love, [5]in spirit, in faith, in purity. 13 Till I come, give attention to reading,
to exhortation, to [6]doctrine. 14 [k]Do not neglect the gift that is in you, which was
given to you by prophecy [l]with the laying
on of the hands of the eldership. 15 Meditate on these things; give yourself entirely
to them, that your progress may be evident
to all. 16 Take heed to yourself and to the
doctrine. Continue in them, for in doing

4:6 nourished...words of faith...good doctrine. Continual feeding on the truths of Scripture is essential to the spiritual health of all Christians (2 Tim. 3:16,17), but especially of spiritual leaders like Timothy. Only by reading the Word, studying it, meditating on it, and mastering its contents can a pastor fulfill his mandate (2 Tim. 2:15). Timothy had been doing so since childhood (2 Tim. 3:15), and Paul urged him to continue (cf. v. 16; 2 Tim. 3:14). "Words of faith" is a general reference to Scripture, God's revealed truth. "Good doctrine" indicates the theology Scripture teaches.

4:7 reject profane and old wives' fables. In addition to being committed to God's Word (*see note on v. 6*), believers must avoid all false teaching. Paul denounced such error as "profane" (worldly; the opposite of what is holy) "fables" (*muthos,* from which the Eng. word "myths" derives), fit only for "old wives" (a common epithet denoting something fit only for the uneducated and philosophically unsophisticated). *See notes on 2 Tim. 2:14-18.* **exercise...toward godliness.** "Godliness" (a proper attitude and response toward God; *see note on 2:2*) is the prerequisite from which all effective ministry flows. "Exercise" is an athletic term denoting the rigorous, self-sacrificing training an athlete undergoes. Spiritual self-discipline is the path to godly living (cf. 1 Cor. 9:24-27).

4:8 profits a little. Bodily exercise is limited both in extent and duration; it affects only the physical body during this earthly life. **profitable for all things.** In time and eternity.

4:9 faithful saying. *See note on 1:15.*

4:10 trust. Or "hope." Believers are saved in hope (*see note on Rom. 8:24*), and live and serve in light of that hope of eternal life (Titus 1:2; 3:7; *see note on Rom. 5:2*). Working to the point of exhaustion and suffering rejection and persecution are acceptable because believers understand they are doing God's work—which is the work of salvation. That makes it worth all of the sacrifices (Phil. 1:12-18,27-30; 2:17; Col. 1:24,25; 2 Tim. 1:6-12; 2:3,4,9,10; 4:5-8). ***the* Savior of all men, especially of those who believe.** Paul is obviously not teaching universalism, that all men will be saved in the spiritual and eternal sense, since the rest of Scripture clearly teaches that God will not save everyone. Most will reject Him and spend eternity in hell (Matt. 25:41,46; Rev. 20:11-15). Yet, the Gr. word translated "especially" must mean that all men enjoy God's salvation in some way like those who believe enjoy His salvation. The simple explanation is that God is the Savior of all men, only in a temporal sense, while of believers in an eternal sense. Paul's point is that while God graciously delivers believers from sin's condemnation and penalty because He was their substitute (2 Cor. 5:21), all men experience some earthly benefits from the goodness of God. Those benefits are: 1) common grace—a term that describes God's goodness shown to all mankind universally (Ps. 145:9) in restraining sin (Rom. 2:15) and judgment (Rom. 2:3-6), maintaining order in society through government (Rom. 13:1-5), enabling man to appreciate beauty and goodness (Ps. 50:2), and showering him with temporal blessings (Matt. 5:45; Acts 14:15-17; 17:25); 2) compassion—the broken-hearted love of pity God shows to undeserving, unregenerate sinners (Ex. 34:6,7; Ps. 86:5; Dan. 9:9; Matt. 23:37; Luke 19:41-44; cf. Is. 16:11-13; Jer. 48:35-37); 3) admonition to repent—God constantly warns sinners of their fate, demonstrating the heart of a compassionate Creator who has no pleasure in the death of the wicked (Ezek. 18:30-32; 33:11); 4) the gospel invitation—salvation in Christ is indiscriminately offered to all (Matt. 11:28,29; 22:2-14; John 6:35-40; Rev. 22:17; cf. John 5:39,40). God is, by nature, a saving God. That is, He finds no pleasure in the death of sinners. His saving character is revealed even in how He deals with those who will never believe, but only in those 4 temporal ways. *See notes on 2:6.*

4:12 Let no one despise your youth. Greek culture placed great value on age and experience. Since Timothy was in his thirties, still young by the standards of that culture, he would have to earn respect by being a godly example. Because he had been with Paul since a young teenager, Timothy had much experience to mature him, so that looking down on him because he was under 40 was inexcusable. **be an example...in purity.** Paul lists 5 areas (the better Gr. manuscripts omit "in spirit") in which Timothy was to be an example to the church: "word" (speech; cf. Matt. 12:34-37; Eph. 4:25,29,31); "conduct" (righteous living; cf. Titus 2:10; 1 Pet. 1:15; 2:12; 3:16); "love" (self-sacrificial service for others; cf. John 15:13); "faith" (not belief, but faithfulness or commitment; cf. 1 Cor. 4:2); "purity" (especially sexual purity; cf. 3:2). Timothy's exemplary life in those areas would offset the disadvantage of his youth.

4:13 Till I come. *See note on 3:14.* **give attention...to doctrine.** These things were to be Timothy's constant practice; his way of life. "Reading" refers to the custom of public reading of Scripture in the church's worship service, followed by the exposition of the passage that had been read (cf. Neh. 8:1-8; Luke 4:16-27). "Exhortation" challenges those who hear the Word to apply it in their daily lives. It may involve rebuke, warning, encouragement, or comfort. "Doctrine" (teaching) refers to systematic instruction from the Word of God (cf. 3:2; Titus 1:9).

4:14 the gift. That grace given to Timothy and to all believers at salvation which consisted of a God-designed, Spirit-empowered spiritual ability for the use of ministry (*see notes on Rom. 12:4-8; 1 Cor. 12:4-12; 1 Pet. 4:10,11*). Timothy's gift (cf. 2 Tim. 1:6) was leadership with special emphasis on preaching (2 Tim. 4:2), and teaching (vv. 6,11,13; 6:2). **by prophecy.** Timothy's gift was identified by a revelation from God (*see note on 1:18*) and apostolic confirmation (2 Tim. 1:6), probably when he joined Paul on the apostle's second missionary journey (Acts 16:1-3). **laying on of the hands of the eldership.** *See note on 5:22.* This public affirmation of Timothy's call to the ministry likely took place at the same time as the prophecy (cf. 2 Tim. 1:6). His call to the ministry was thus confirmed subjectively (by means of his spiritual gift), objectively (through the prophecy made about him), and collectively (by the affirmation of apostles and the church, represented by the elders).

4:15 progress. The word was used in military terms of an advancing force and in general terms of advancement in learning, under-

this you will save both yourself and those
who hear you.

Treatment of Church Members

5 Do not rebuke an older man, but exhort *him* as a father, younger men as
brothers, 2 older women as mothers,
younger women as sisters, with all purity.

Honor True Widows

3 Honor widows who are really widows.
4 But if any widow has children or
grandchildren, let them first learn to show
piety at home and [a]to repay their parents;
for this is [1]good and acceptable before
God. 5 Now she who is really a widow, and
left alone, trusts in God and continues in
supplications and prayers [b]night and day.
6 But she who lives in [2]pleasure is dead
while she lives. 7 And these things command, that they may be blameless. 8 But if
anyone does not provide for his own, [c]and
especially for those of his household, [d]he
has denied the faith [e]and is worse than an
unbeliever.
9 Do not let a widow under sixty years
old be taken into the number, *and not unless*
she has been the wife of one man, 10 well
reported for good works: if she has
brought up children, if she has lodged
strangers, if she has washed the saints'
feet, if she has relieved the afflicted, if she
has diligently followed every good work.
11 But [3]refuse *the* younger widows; for

CHAPTER 5

4 [a] Gen. 45:10 [1] NU, M omit *good and*

5 [b] Acts 26:7

6 [2] *indulgence*

8 [c] Is. 58:7; 2 Cor. 12:14 [d] 2 Tim. 3:5 [e] Matt. 18:17

11 [3] Refuse to enroll

standing, or knowledge. Paul exhorted Timothy to let his progress toward Christlikeness be evident to all.

4:16 to yourself and to the doctrine. The priorities of a godly leader are summed up in his personal holiness and public teaching. All of Paul's exhortations in vv. 6-16 fit into one or the other of those two categories. **you will save…yourself.** Perseverance in believing the truth always accompanies genuine conversion (*see note on Matt. 24:13*; cf. John 8:31; Rom. 2:7; Phil. 2:12,13; Col. 1:23). **those who hear you.** By careful attention to his own godly life and faithful preaching of the Word, Timothy would continue to be the human instrument God used to bring the gospel and to save some who heard him. Though salvation is God's work, it is His pleasure to do it through human instruments.

5:1 rebuke. Some translations add "sharply" to the word "rebuke," which fills out the intensity of the Gr. term. An older sinning believer is to be shown respect by not being addressed with harsh words (cf. 2 Tim. 2:24,25). **an older man.** In this context, the Gr. is indicating older men generally, not the office of elder. The younger Timothy was to confront sinning older men with deference and honor, which is clearly inferred from OT principles (cf. Lev. 19:32; Job 32:4,6; Prov. 4:1-4; 16:31; 20:29). **exhort.** This Gr. word, which is related to a title for the Holy Spirit (*paraclētos;* cf. John 14:16,26; 15:26; 16:7), refers to coming alongside someone to help. It may best be translated "strengthen." We are to strengthen our fellow believers (cf. Gal. 6:1,2) in the same way the Scripture (Rom. 15:4) and the Holy Spirit do.

5:3-16 This section supports the mandate of Scripture that women who have lost the support of their husbands are to be cared for (cf. Ex. 22:22-24; Deut. 27:19; Is. 1:17). God's continual compassion for widows only reinforces this command (cf. Ps. 68:5; 146:9; Mark 12:41-44; Luke 7:11-17).

5:3 Honor. "To show respect or care," "to support," or "to treat graciously." Although it includes meeting all kinds of needs, Paul had in mind here not only this broad definition, but primarily financial support (cf. Ex. 20:12; Matt. 15:1-6; 27:9). **really widows.** Not all widows are truly alone and without resources. Financial support from the church is mandatory only for widows who have no means to provide for their daily needs.

5:4 widow has children or grandchildren. Families, not the church, have the first responsibility for their own widows. **repay their parents.** Children and grandchildren are indebted to those who brought them into the world, reared them, and loved them. Fulfilling this responsibility is a mark of godly obedience (cf. Ex. 20:12).

5:5 left alone. *See note on v. 3.* The form of this Gr. word denotes a permanent condition of being forsaken and left without resources. She is "really" a widow, since there is no family to support her. **trusts in God.** A continual state or settled attitude of hope in God (cf. 1 Kin. 17:8-16; Jer. 49:11). Since she has no one else, she pleads with God as her only hope.

5:6 dead while she lives. A widow who lives a worldly, immoral, ungodly life may be alive physically, but her lifestyle proves she is unregenerate and spiritually dead (cf. Eph. 2:1).

5:7 blameless. *See notes on 3:2; Phil. 2:15.* "Blameless" means "above reproach," so that no one can fault their conduct.

5:8 if. Better translated, "since." Paul negatively restated the positive principle of v. 4, using the Gr. construction that implies the condition is true, suggesting that there were numerous violations of that principle at Ephesus. Any believer who fails to obey this command is guilty of: 1) denying the principle of compassionate Christian love (cf. John 13:35; Rom. 5:5; 1 Thess. 4:9); and 2) being "worse than an unbeliever." Most pagans naturally fulfill this duty, so believers who have God's command and power to carry it out and do not, behave worse than pagans. Cf. 1 Cor. 5:1,2.

5:9 under sixty. In NT culture, 60 was considered retirement age. By that age, older women would have completed their child rearing and would have the time, maturity, and character to devote their lives in service to God and the church. They also would not be likely to remarry and become preoccupied with that commitment. **be taken into the number.** More clearly rendered, "be put on the list." This was not a list of those widows eligible for specially recognized church support (all widows in the church who had no other means of support were; v. 3), but rather those eligible for specially recognized church ministry (cf. Titus 2:3-5). **the wife of one man.** Lit. "one-man woman" (cf. 3:2,12). It does not exclude women who have been married more than once (cf. v. 14; 1 Cor. 7:39), but it refers to a woman totally devoted and faithful to her husband, a wife who had displayed purity of thought and action in her marriage.

5:10 has brought up children. This views the godly widow as a Christian mother who has nourished or reared children that have followed the Lord (*see note on 2:15*). **washed the saints' feet.** The menial duty of slaves. It is used literally and metaphorically of widows who have humble servants' hearts (*see notes on John 13:5-17*). **every good work.** Cf. Dorcas in Acts 9:36-39.

5:11 to grow wanton. Better translated "to feel the impulses of sensual desires"—an expression that includes all that is involved in the marriage relationship, including sexual passion. Paul saw the danger that younger widows might want to escape from their vows to remain single (*see note on v. 12*) and be devoted only to God's service (cf. Num. 30:9); he knew the negative impact such feelings could have on young widows' personal lives and ministry within the church. Such women were also marked out by false teachers as easy prey (2 Tim. 3:6,7), causing them to leave the truth (v. 15).

when they have begun to grow wanton
against Christ, they desire to marry, 12 having condemnation because they have cast
off their first [4]faith. 13 And besides they
learn *to be* idle, wandering about from
house to house, and not only idle but also
gossips and busybodies, saying things
which they ought not. 14 Therefore I desire
that *the* younger *widows* marry, bear children, manage the house, give no opportunity to the adversary to speak reproachfully. 15 For some have already turned aside
after Satan. 16 If any believing [5]man or
woman has widows, let them [6]relieve
them, and do not let the church be burdened, that it may relieve those who are
really widows.

Honor the Elders

17 Let the elders who rule well be counted worthy of double honor, especially
those who labor in the word and doctrine.
18 For the Scripture says, [f]*"You shall not
muzzle an ox while it treads out the grain,"*
and, [g]"The laborer *is* worthy of his wages."
19 Do not receive an accusation against an
elder except [h]from two or three witnesses.
20 Those who are sinning rebuke in the
presence of all, that the rest also may fear.
21 I charge *you* before God and the Lord
Jesus Christ and the [7]elect angels that you
observe these things without [i]prejudice,
doing nothing with partiality. 22 Do not lay
hands on anyone hastily, nor [j]share in
other people's sins; keep yourself pure.

12 [4] Or *solemn promise*
16 [5] NU omits *man or* [6] *give aid to*
18 [f] Deut. 25:4; 1 Cor. 9:7-9 [g] Lev. 19:13; Deut. 24:15; Matt. 10:10; Luke 10:7; 1 Cor. 9:14
19 [h] Deut. 17:6; 19:15; Matt. 18:16
21 [i] Deut. 1:17 [7] *chosen*
22 [j] Eph. 5:6,7; 2 John 11

5:12 cast off their first faith. In classical Gr., "faith" could also mean "pledge." Taken that way here, it refers to a specific covenant young widows made when asking to be included on the widows' list. Likely, they promised to devote the rest of their lives in service to the church and the Lord. Though well-meaning at the time of their need and bereavement, they were surely to desire marriage again (see v. 11), and thus renege on their original pledge.

5:13 gossips. Such people speak nonsense, talk idly, make empty charges, or even accuse others with malicious words. This idleness and talk also made them suitable targets for the false teachers (1:6). **busybodies.** Lit. "one who moves around." The implication is that such people pry into things that do not concern them; they do not mind their own business.

5:14 bear children. The younger widows were still of childbearing age. Although they had lost their first husbands, there was still the potential privilege and blessing of remarrying and having children (*see notes on 2:15*; cf. Ps. 127:3,5). **manage the house.** The Gr. term denotes all the aspects of household administration, not merely the rearing of children. The home is the domain where a married woman fulfills herself in God's design. *See notes on Titus 2:4,5.*

5:15 Some of the young widows had given up their commitment to serve Christ (*see notes on vv. 11,12*), perhaps either by following false teachers and spreading their false doctrine or by marrying unbelievers and bringing disgrace upon the church. **Satan.** The devil, the believer's adversary (*see notes on Job 1:6-12; 2:1-7; Is. 14:12-15; Ezek. 28:12-15; Rev. 12:9*).

5:16 woman. Paul restates the message of vv. 4-8 with the addition that as the situation warrants, Christian women are included in this responsibility for support of widows.

5:17-25 The source of much of the Ephesian church's difficulties was the inadequacy of the pastors. So Paul explains to Timothy how to restore proper pastoral oversight. He sets forth the church's obligations in regard to honoring, protecting, rebuking, and selecting elders.

5:17 elders. This identifies the "bishop" (3:1) or overseer, who is also called pastor (Eph. 4:11). *See notes on 3:1-7; Titus 1:6-9.* **rule well.** Elders are spiritual rulers in the church. Cf. 1 Thess. 5:12,13; Heb. 13:7,17. **double honor.** Elders who serve with greater commitment, excellence, and effort should have greater acknowledgment from their congregations. This expression does not mean such men should receive exactly twice as much remuneration as others, but because they have earned such respect they should be paid more generously. **especially.** Means "chiefly" or "particularly." Implicit is the idea that some elders will work harder than others and be more prominent in ministry. **labor.** Lit. "work to the point of fatigue or exhaustion." The Gr. word stresses the effort behind the work more than the amount of work. **word and doctrine.** Or better, "preaching and teaching" (*see note on 4:13*). The first emphasizes proclamation, along with exhortation and admonition, and calls for a heart response to the Lord. The second is an essential fortification against heresy and puts more stress on instruction.

5:18 For the Scripture says. A typical formula for introducing biblical references, in this instance both an OT (Deut. 25:4) and NT (Luke 10:7) one. It is also very significant that this is a case of one NT writer (Paul) affirming the inspiration of another by referring to Luke's writing as "Scripture" (cf. 2 Pet. 3:15,16), which shows the high view that the early church took of NT Scripture.

5:19 two or three witnesses. Serious accusations against elders must be investigated and confirmed by the same process as established in Matt. 18:15-20 (*see notes there*). This process for the whole church also applies to elders. This demand does not place elders beyond successful accusation, but protects them from frivolous, evil accusers, by demanding the same process of confirmation of sin as for all in the church.

5:20 Those who are sinning. Elders who continue in any kind of sin after the confrontation of 2 or 3 witnesses, especially any that violates the qualifications to serve (3:2-7). **in the presence of all.** The other elders and the congregation. The third step of confrontation, established in Matt. 18:17, is to tell the church, so that they can all confront the person and call him to repentance.

5:21 charge...God...Lord. Cf. 6:13; *see note on 2 Tim. 4:1.* **the elect angels.** "Chosen angels," or the unfallen angels, as opposed to Satan and his demons. This indicates that God's sovereign purpose to choose those beings who would be part of His eternal kingdom included angels whom He chose to eternal glory. Christians are also called "elect" (Rom. 8:33; 11:7; Col. 3:12; 2 Tim. 2:10; Titus 1:1; 1 Pet. 1:2; 2 John 1,13). **without prejudice...partiality.** All discipline of elders is to be done fairly, without prejudgment or personal preference, according to the standards of Scripture.

5:22 Do not lay hands on...hastily. The ceremony that affirmed a man's suitability for and acceptance into public ministry as an elder/pastor/overseer. This came from the OT practice of laying hands on a sacrificial animal to identify with it (Ex. 29:10,15,19; Lev. 4:15; cf. Num. 8:10; 27:18-23; Deut. 34:9; Matt. 19:15; Acts 8:17,18; 9:17; Heb. 6:2). "Hastily" refers to proceeding with this ceremony without a thorough investigation and preparation period to be certain of the man's qualifications (as in 3:1-7). **nor share in other people's sins.** This refers to the sin of hasty ordination, which makes those responsible culpable for the man's sin of serving as an unqualified elder and, thus, misleading people. **keep yourself pure.** Some versions translate "pure" as "free from sin." Paul wanted Timothy, by not participating in the recognition of unqualified elders, to remain untainted by others' sins. The church desperately needed qualified spiritual leaders, but the selection had to be carefully executed.

23 No longer drink only water, but use a
little wine for your stomach's sake and
your frequent [8]infirmities.
24 Some men's sins are [k]clearly evident,
preceding *them* to judgment, but those of
some *men* follow later. 25 Likewise, the
good works *of some* are clearly evident, and
those that are otherwise cannot be hidden.

Honor Masters

6 Let as many [a]bondservants as are under
the yoke count their own masters worthy of all honor, so that the name of God
and *His* doctrine may not be blasphemed.
2 And those who have believing masters, let
them not despise *them* because they are
brethren, but rather serve *them* because
those who are benefited are believers and
beloved. Teach and exhort these things.

Error and Greed

3 If anyone teaches otherwise and does
not consent to [b]wholesome words, *even* the
words of our Lord Jesus Christ, [c]and to the
[1]doctrine which accords with godliness,
4 he is proud, knowing nothing, but is obsessed with disputes and arguments over
words, from which come envy, strife, reviling, evil suspicions, 5 [2]useless wranglings
of men of corrupt minds and destitute of
the truth, who suppose that godliness is a
means of gain. [3]From [d]such withdraw yourself.
6 Now godliness with [e]contentment is

23 [8] *illnesses*
24 [k] Gal. 5:19-21

CHAPTER 6

1 [a] Eph. 6:5; Titus 2:9; 1 Pet. 2:18
3 [b] 2 Tim. 1:13 [c] Titus 1:1 [1] *teaching*
5 [d] 2 Tim. 3:5 [2] NU, M *constant friction* [3] NU omits the rest of v. 5.
6 [e] Phil. 4:11; Heb. 13:5

5:23 No longer drink only water. "Water" in the ancient world was often polluted and carried many diseases. Therefore Paul urged Timothy not to risk illness, not even for the sake of a commitment to abstinence from wine. Apparently Timothy avoided wine, so as not to place himself in harm's way (*see note on 3:3*). **use a little wine...infirmities.** Paul wanted Timothy to use wine which, because of fermentation, acted as a disinfectant to protect his health problems due to the harmful effects of impure water. With this advice, however, Paul was not advocating that Timothy lower the high standard of behavior for leaders (cf. Num. 6:1-4; Prov. 31:4,5).

5:24 sins are clearly evident. The sins of some men are manifest for all to see, thus disqualifying them out of hand for service as elders. **preceding *them* to judgment.** The known sins of the unqualified announce those men's guilt and unfitness before all. "Judgment" refers to the church's process for determining men's suitability to serve as elders. **follow later.** The sins of other candidates for elder will come to light in time, perhaps even during the scrutiny of the evaluation process.

5:25 The same is true of good works. Some are evident; others come to light later. Time and truth go hand in hand. The whole emphasis in this instruction regarding choosing elders, according to the qualifications of 3:1-7, is to be patient, fair, impartial, and pure (vv. 21-25). Such an approach will yield the right choices.

6:1,2 The Ephesian believers may have been struggling to maintain a biblical work ethic in the world of slavery, so these verses form Paul's instruction on that subject. Essentially, first century slaves resembled the indentured servants of the American colonial period. In many cases, slaves were better off than day-laborers, since much of their food, clothing, and shelter was provided. The system of slavery served as the economic structure in the Roman world, and the master-slave relationship closely parallels the twentieth-century employer-employee relationship. For more on slaves, see Introduction to Philemon: Background and Setting.

6:1 bondservants. This can be translated "slaves." They are people who are in submission to another. It carries no negative connotation and is often positive when used in connection with the Lord serving the Father (Phil. 2:7), and believers serving God (1 Pet. 2:16), the Lord (Rom. 1:1; Gal. 1:10; 2 Tim. 2:24; James 1:1), non-Christians (1 Cor. 9:19), and other believers (Gal. 5:13). **under the yoke.** A colloquial expression describing submissive service under another's authority, not necessarily describing an abusive relationship (cf. Matt. 11:28-30). **masters.** The Gr. word for "master," while giving us the Eng. word "despot," does not carry a negative connotation. Instead, it refers to one with absolute and unrestricted authority. **all honor.** This translates into diligent and faithful labor for one's employer. *See notes on Eph. 6:5-9; Col. 3:22-25.* ***His* doctrine.** The revelation of God summed up in the gospel. How believers act while under the authority of another affects how people view the message of salvation Christians proclaim (*see notes on Titus 2:5-14*). Displaying a proper attitude of submission and respect, and performing quality work, help make the gospel message believable (Matt. 5:48).

6:2 believing masters. The tendency might be to assume one's equality in Christ with a Christian master, and disdain the authority related to work roles. On the contrary, working for a Christian should produce more loyal and diligent service out of love for the brethren. **exhort.** Lit. "to call to one's side." The particular emphasis here is on a strong urging, directing, and insisting on following the principles for correct behavior in the workplace.

6:3 Paul identifies 3 characteristics of false teachers: 1) they "teach otherwise"—a different doctrine, or any teaching that contradicts God's revelation in Scripture (*see notes on Gal. 1:6-9*); 2) they do "not consent to wholesome words"—they do not agree with sound, healthy teaching, specifically the teaching contained in Scripture (2 Pet. 3:16); and 3) they reject "doctrine which accords with godliness"—teaching not based on Scripture will always result in an unholy life. Instead of godliness, false teachers will be marked by sin (*see notes on 2 Pet. 2:10-22*; cf. Jude 4,8-16).

6:4 disputes and arguments over words. "Disputes" refers to idle speculation; "arguments over words" lit. means "word battles." Because proud, ignorant false teachers do not understand divine truth (2 Cor. 2:14), they obsess over terminology and attack the reliability and authority of Scripture. Every kind of strife is mentioned to indicate that false teachers produce nothing of benefit out of their fleshly, corrupt, and empty minds (v. 5).

6:5 destitute of the truth. False teachers are in a state of apostasy; that is, although they once knew and seemed to embrace the truth, they turned to openly reject it. The Gr. word for "destitute" means "to steal," "to rob," or "to deprive" and its form here indicates that someone or something was pulled away from contact with the truth (it does not mean they were ever saved; *see note on 1:19*; cf. 2 Tim. 2:18; 3:7,8; Heb. 6:4-6; 2 Pet. 2:1,4-9). ***a means of* gain.** Almost always behind all the efforts of the hypocritical, lying (4:2) false teachers is the driving motivation of monetary gain (cf. Acts 8:18-23; 2 Pet. 2:15). **From such withdraw yourself.** This phrase does not appear in the better manuscripts, although the idea expressed is self-evident.

6:6 contentment. This Gr. word means "self-sufficiency," and was used by Stoic philosophers to describe a person who was unflappable and unmoved by external circumstances. Christians are to be satisfied and sufficient, and not to seek for more than what God has already given them. He is the source of true contentment (2 Cor. 3:5; 9:8; Phil. 4:11-13,19).

great gain. 7 For we brought nothing into
this world, [4]*and it is* [f]certain we can carry
nothing out. 8 And having food and clothing, with these we shall be [g]content. 9 But
those who desire to be rich fall into temptation and a snare, and *into* many foolish
and harmful lusts which drown men in destruction and perdition. 10 For the love of
money is a root of all *kinds of* evil, for
which some have strayed from the faith in
their greediness, and pierced themselves
through with many sorrows.

The Good Confession

11 But you, O man of God, flee these
things and pursue righteousness, godliness, faith, love, patience, gentleness.
12 Fight the good fight of faith, lay hold on
eternal life, to which you were also called
and have confessed the good confession in
the presence of many witnesses. 13 I urge
you in the sight of God who gives life to all
things, and *before* Christ Jesus [h]who witnessed the good confession before Pontius
Pilate, 14 that you keep *this* commandment
without spot, blameless until our Lord Jesus Christ's appearing, 15 which He will
manifest in His own time, *He who is* the
blessed and only [5]Potentate, the King of
kings and Lord of lords, 16 who alone has
immortality, dwelling in [i]unapproachable
light, [j]whom no man has seen or can see,
to whom *be* honor and everlasting power.
Amen.

Instructions to the Rich

17 Command those who are rich in this
present age not to be haughty, nor to

7 [f] Job 1:21; Ps. 49:17; Eccl. 5:15 [4] NU omits *and it is certain*
8 [g] Prov. 30:8, 9
13 [h] Matt. 27:2; John 18:36, 37
15 [5] *Sovereign*
16 [i] Dan. 2:22 [j] John 6:46

6:8 having food and clothing…be content. The basic necessities of life are what ought to make Christians content. Paul does not condemn having possessions, as long as God graciously provides them (v. 17). He does, however, condemn a self-indulgent desire for money, which results from discontentment. *See note on Matt. 6:33.*

6:9 desire to be rich fall into temptation. "Desire" refers to a settled wish born of reason, and clearly describes those guilty of greed. The form of the Gr. verb for "fall" indicates that those who have such a desire are continually falling into temptation. Greedy people are compulsive—they are continually trapped in sins by their consuming desire to acquire more. **destruction and perdition.** Such greed may lead these people to suffer the tragic end of destruction and hell. These terms refer to the eternal punishment of the wicked.

6:10 love of money. Lit. "affection for silver." In the context, this sin applies to false teachers specifically, but the principle is true universally. Money itself is not evil since it is a gift from God (Deut. 8:18); Paul condemns only the love of it (cf. Matt. 6:24) which is so characteristic of false teachers (*see notes on 1 Pet. 5:2; 2 Pet. 2:1-3,15*). **strayed from the faith.** From the body of Christian truth. Gold has replaced God for these apostates, who have turned away from pursuing the things of God in favor of money.

6:11 O man of God. Cf. 2 Tim. 3:17. This is a term used in the NT only for Timothy; as a technical term it is used about 70 times in the OT, always to refer to a man who officially spoke for God (*see note on Deut. 33:1*). This, along with 1:2; 2:1, indicates that the letter is primarily directed to Timothy, exhorting him to be faithful and strong in light of persecution and difficulty—and particularly with Paul's death near (see Introduction to 2 Timothy: Background and Setting). The man of God is known by what he: 1) flees from (v. 11); 2) follows after (v. 11); 3) fights for (v. 12); and 4) is faithful to (vv. 13,14). The key to his success in all these endeavors is the perfection produced in him by the Scripture (2 Tim. 3:16,17). **these things.** Love of money and all that goes with it (vv. 6-10), along with the other proud obsessions of false teachers (vv. 3-5). **righteousness, godliness.** "Righteousness" means to do what is right, in relation to both God and man, and it emphasizes outward behavior. "Godliness" (*see note on 2:2*) refers to one's reverence for God, and could be translated "God-likeness."

6:12 Fight the good fight of faith. The Gr. word for "fight" gives us the Eng. word "agonize," and was used in both military and athletic endeavors to describe the concentration, discipline, and extreme effort needed to win. The "good fight of faith" is the spiritual conflict with Satan's kingdom of darkness in which all men of God are necessarily involved. *See notes on 2 Cor. 10:3-5; 2 Tim. 4:2.* **lay hold on eternal life.** Paul is here admonishing Timothy to "get a grip" on the reality of the matters associated with eternal life, so that he would live and minister with a heavenly and eternal perspective (cf. Phil. 3:20; Col. 3:2). **to which you were also called.** Refers to God's effectual, sovereign call of Timothy to salvation (*see note on Rom. 1:7*). **good confession.** Timothy's public confession of faith in the Lord Jesus Christ, which likely occurred at his baptism and again when he was ordained to the ministry (4:14; 2 Tim. 1:6).

6:13 urge…God…Christ. Cf. 5:21; *see note on 2 Tim. 4:1.* **the good confession before Pontius Pilate.** Knowing that such a confession would cost Him His life, Jesus nevertheless confessed that He was truly the King and Messiah (John 18:33-37). He never evaded danger; He boldly and trustfully committed Himself to God who raises the dead (cf. Col. 2:12).

6:14 *this* commandment. The entire revealed Word of God, which Paul charged Timothy to preach (2 Tim. 4:2). Paul also repeatedly encouraged Timothy to guard it (v. 20; 1:18,19; 4:6,16; 2 Tim. 1:13,14; 2:15-18). **appearing.** When the Lord returns to earth in glory (cf. 2 Tim. 4:1,8; Titus 2:13) to judge and to establish His kingdom (Matt. 24:27,29,30; 25:31). Because Christ's return is imminent, that ought to be motivation enough for the man of God to remain faithful to his calling until he dies or the Lord returns (cf. Acts 1:8-11; 1 Cor. 4:5; Rev. 22:12).

6:15 in His own time. The time, known only to Him, that God established in eternity past for Christ to return (Mark 13:32; Acts 1:7). **Potentate.** This word comes from a Gr. word group that basically means "power," but here it is best translated "Sovereign." God is absolutely sovereign and omnipotently rules everything everywhere. **King of kings and Lord of lords.** A title used of Christ (Rev. 17:14; 19:16) is here used of God the Father. Paul probably used this title for God to confront the cult of emperor worship, intending to communicate that only God is sovereign and worthy of worship.

6:16 whom no man has seen or can see. God in spirit is invisible (cf. 1:17; Job 23:8,9; John 1:18; 5:37; Col. 1:15) and, therefore, unapproachable in the sense that sinful man has never seen nor can he ever see His full glory (cf. Ex. 33:20; Is. 6:1-5).

6:17-19 Paul counsels Timothy what to teach those who are rich in material possessions, those who have more than the mere essentials of food, clothing, and shelter. Paul does not condemn such people, nor command them to get rid of their wealth. He does call them to be good stewards of their God-given resources (cf. Deut. 8:18; 1 Sam. 2:7; 1 Chr. 29:12).

6:17 haughty. "To have an exalted opinion of oneself." Those who have an abundance are constantly tempted to look down on others

trust in uncertain [k]riches but in the living God, who gives us richly all things
[l]to enjoy. **18** *Let them* do good, that they
be rich in good works, ready to give,
willing to share, **19** [m]storing up for themselves a good foundation for the time to
come, that they may lay hold on eternal
life.

17 [k] Jer. 9:23; 48:7 [l] Eccl. 5:18, 19
19 [m] [Matt. 6:20, 21; 19:21]
20 [n] [2 Tim. 1:12, 14] [o] Titus 1:14 [6] *empty chatter*

Guard the Faith

20 O Timothy! [n]Guard what was committed to your trust, [o]avoiding the profane
and [6]idle babblings and contradictions of
what is falsely called knowledge— **21** by
professing it some have strayed concerning the faith.
Grace *be* with you. Amen.

and act superior. Riches and pride often go together, and the wealthier a person is, the more he is tempted to be proud (Prov. 18:23; 28:11; James 2:1-4). **uncertain riches...gives us richly.** Those who have much tend to trust in their wealth (cf. Prov. 23:4,5). But God provides far more security than any earthly investment can ever give (Eccl. 5:18-20; Matt. 6:19-21).

6:18 ready to give. The Gr. word means "liberal," or "bountiful." Those believers who have money must use it in meeting the needs of others, unselfishly and generously (*see notes on Acts 4:32-37; 2 Cor. 8:1-4*).

6:19 storing up…a good foundation. "Storing up" can be translated "amassing a treasure," while "foundation" can refer to a fund. The idea is that the rich in this world should not be concerned with receiving a return on their earthly investment. Those who make eternal investments will be content to receive their dividends in heaven. *See notes on Luke 16:1-13.* **lay hold on eternal life.** *See note on v. 12.*

6:20,21 The church's main responsibility is to guard and proclaim the truths of Scripture, so Paul here instructs Timothy on how to guard and protect the Word of God.

6:20 what was committed to your trust. This translates one Gr. word, which means "deposit." The deposit Timothy was to guard is the truth—the divine revelation that God committed to his care. Every Christian, especially if he is in ministry, has that sacred trust to guard the revelation of God (cf. 1 Cor. 4:1; 1 Thess. 2:3,4). **what is falsely called knowledge.** False doctrine—anything claiming to be the truth that is in fact a lie. False teachers typically claim to have the superior knowledge (as in gnosticism). They claim to know the transcendent secrets, but actually are ignorant and infantile in their understanding (*see notes on Col. 2:8*).

6:21 Grace *be* with you. Paul's closing salutation is plural, i.e., "you all"—it goes beyond Timothy to the entire congregation at Ephesus. All believers require the grace of God to preserve the truth and pass it on to the next generation.

Names of Satan

	Name	Meaning	Reference
1.	Abaddon	Destruction	Rev. 9:11
2.	Accuser	Opposes believers before God	Rev. 12:10
3.	Adversary	Against God	1 Pet. 5:8
4.	Apollyon	Destroyer	Rev. 9:11
5.	Beelzebub	Lord of the fly	Matt. 12:24
6.	Belial	Worthless	2 Cor. 6:15
7.	Devil	Slanderer	Matt. 4:1
8.	Dragon	Destructive	Rev. 12:3, 7, 9
9.	Enemy	Opponent	Matt. 13:28
10.	Evil one	Intrinsically evil	John 17:15
11.	God of this age	Influences thinking of world	2 Cor. 4:4
12.	Liar	Perverts the truth	John 8:44
13.	Murderer	Leads people to eternal death	John 8:44
14.	Prince of the power of the air	Control of unbelievers	Eph. 2:2
15.	Roaring lion	One who destroys	1 Pet. 5:8
16.	Ruler of demons	Leader of fallen angels	Mark 3:22
17.	Ruler of this world	Rules in world system	John 12:31
18.	Satan	Adversary	1 Tim. 5:15
19.	Serpent of old	Deceiver in garden	Rev. 12:9; 20:2
20.	Tempter	Solicits people to sin	1 Thess. 3:5

The Second Epistle of Paul to

TIMOTHY

Title

This epistle is the second of two inspired letters Paul the apostle wrote to his son in the faith, Timothy (1:2; 2:1). For biographical information on Timothy, see Introduction to 1 Timothy: Title. It is titled, as are the other personal letters of Paul to individuals (1 Timothy, Titus, and Philemon), with the name of the addressee (1:2).

Author and Date

The issue of Paul's authorship of the Pastoral Epistles is discussed in the Introduction to 1 Timothy: Author and Date. Paul wrote 2 Timothy, the last of his inspired letters, shortly before his martyrdom (ca. A.D. 67).

Background and Setting

Paul was released from his first Roman imprisonment for a short period of ministry during which he wrote 1 Timothy and Titus. Second Timothy, however, finds Paul once again in a Roman prison (1:16; 2:9), apparently rearrested as part of Nero's persecution of Christians. Unlike Paul's confident hope of release during his first imprisonment (Phil. 1:19,25,26; 2:24; Philem. 22), this time he had no such hopes (4:6-8). In his first imprisonment in Rome (ca. A.D. 60–62), before Nero had begun the persecution of Christians (A.D. 64), he was only under house arrest and had opportunity for much interaction with people and ministry (Acts 28:16-31). At this time, 5 or 6 years later (ca. A.D. 66–67), however, he was in a cold cell (4:13), in chains (2:9), and with no hope of deliverance (4:6). Abandoned by virtually all of those close to him for fear of persecution (cf. 1:15; 4:9-12,16) and facing imminent execution, Paul wrote to Timothy, urging him to hasten to Rome for one last visit with the apostle (4:9,21). Whether Timothy made it to Rome before Paul's execution is not known. According to tradition, Paul was not released from this second Roman imprisonment, but suffered the martyrdom he had foreseen (4:6).

In this letter, Paul, aware the end was near, passed the non-apostolic mantle of ministry to Timothy (cf. 2:2) and exhorted him to continue faithful in his duties (1:6), hold on to sound doctrine (1:13,14), avoid error (2:15-18), accept persecution for the gospel (2:3,4; 3:10-12), put his confidence in the Scripture, and preach it relentlessly (3:15–4:5).

Historical and Theological Themes

It seems that Paul may have had reason to fear that Timothy was in danger of weakening spiritually. This would have been a grave concern for Paul since Timothy needed to carry on Paul's work (cf. 2:2). While there are no historical indications elsewhere in the NT as to why Paul was so concerned, there is evidence in the epistle itself from what he wrote. This concern is evident, for example, in Paul's exhortation to "stir up" his gift (1:6), to replace fear with power, love, and a sound mind (1:7), to not be

A Comparison of Paul's Two Roman Imprisonments

First Imprisonment	Second Imprisonment
Acts 28—Wrote the Prison Epistles	2 Timothy
Accused by Jews of heresy and sedition	Persecuted by Rome and arrested as a criminal against the Empire
Local sporadic persecutions (A.D. 60–63)	Neronian persecution (A.D. 64–68)
Decent living conditions in a rented house (Acts 28:30,31)	Poor conditions, in a cold, dark dungeon
Many friends visited him	Virtually alone (only Luke with him)
Many opportunities for Christian witness were available	Opportunities for witness were restricted
Was optimistic for release and freedom (Phil. 1:24-26)	Anticipated his execution (2 Tim. 4:6)

ashamed of Paul and the Lord, but willingly suffer for the gospel (1:8), and to hold on to the truth (1:13,14). Summing up the potential problem of Timothy, who might be weakening under the pressure of the church and the persecution of the world, Paul calls him to 1) generally "be strong" (2:11), the key exhortation of the first part of the letter, and to 2) continue to "preach the word" (4:2), the main admonition of the last part. These final words to Timothy include few commendations but many admonitions, including about 25 imperatives.

Since Timothy was well versed in Paul's theology, the apostle did not instruct him further doctrinally. He did, however, allude to several important doctrines, including salvation by God's sovereign grace (1:9,10; 2:10), the person of Christ (2:8; 4:1,8), and perseverance (2:11-13); plus Paul wrote the crucial text of the NT on the inspiration of Scripture (3:16,17).

Interpretive Challenges

There are no major challenges in this letter involving theological issues. There is limited data regarding several individuals named in the epistle; e.g., Phygellus and Hermogenes (1:15), Onesiphorus (1:17; cf. 4:19), Hymenaeus and Philetus (2:17,18), Jannes and Jambres (3:8), and Alexander (4:14).

Outline

I. Greeting and Thanksgiving (1:1-5)

II. The Perseverance of a Man of God (1:6-18)
- A. The Exhortation (1:6-11)
- B. The Examples (1:12-18)
  - 1. Paul (1:12-14)
  - 2. Onesiphorus (1:15-18)

III. The Patterns of a Man of God (2:1-26)
- A. Paul (2:1,2)
- B. A Soldier (2:3,4)
- C. An Athlete (2:5)
- D. A Farmer (2:6,7)
- E. Jesus (2:8-13)
- F. A Worker (2:14-19)
- G. A Vessel (2:20-23)
- H. A Servant (2:24-26)

IV. The Perils of a Man of God (3:1-17)
- A. Facing Apostasy (3:1-9)
- B. Defeating Apostasy (3:10-17)

V. The Preaching of the Man of God (4:1-5)
- A. The Charge to Preach (4:1,2)
- B. The Need for Preaching (4:3-5)

VI. Concluding Remarks (4:6-18)
- A. Paul's Triumph (4:6-8)
- B. Paul's Needs (4:9-18)

VII. Paul's Farewells (4:19-22)

Greeting

1 Paul, an apostle of [1]Jesus Christ by the
will of God, according to the [a]promise
of life which is in Christ Jesus,

2 To Timothy, a [b]beloved son:

Grace, mercy, *and* peace from God the
Father and Christ Jesus our Lord.

Timothy's Faith and Heritage

3 I thank God, whom I serve with a pure
conscience, as *my* [c]forefathers *did,* as without ceasing I remember you in my prayers
night and day, 4 greatly desiring to see
you, being mindful of your tears, that I
may be filled with joy, 5 when I call to remembrance [d]the [2]genuine faith that is in
you, which dwelt first in your grandmother Lois and [e]your mother Eunice, and I am
persuaded is in you also. 6 Therefore I remind you [f]to stir up the gift of God which
is in you through the laying on of my
hands. 7 For [g]God has not given us a spirit
of fear, [h]but of power and of love and of a
sound mind.

Not Ashamed of the Gospel

8 [i]Therefore do not be ashamed of [j]the
testimony of our Lord, nor of me [k]His prisoner, but share with me in the sufferings
for the gospel according to the power of
God, 9 who has saved us and called *us*
with a holy calling, [l]not according to our
works, but [m]according to His own purpose
and grace which was given to us in Christ
Jesus [n]before time began, 10 but [o]has now

CHAPTER 1

1 [a] Titus 1:2 [1] NU, M *Christ Jesus*
2 [b] 1 Tim. 1:2; 2 Tim. 2:1; Titus 1:4
3 [c] Acts 24:14
5 [d] 1 Tim. 1:5; 4:6 [2] Lit. *unhypocritical* [e] Acts 16:1
6 [f] 1 Tim. 4:14
7 [g] John 14:27; Rom. 8:15; 1 John 4:18 [h] [Acts 1:8]
8 [i] [Mark 8:38; Luke 9:26; Rom. 1:16]; 2 Tim. 1:12, 16 [j] 1 Tim. 2:6 [k] Eph. 3:1; 2 Tim. 1:16
9 [l] [Rom. 3:20]; Eph. 2:8, 9 [m] Rom. 8:28 [n] Rom. 16:25; Eph. 1:4; Titus 1:2
10 [o] Eph. 1:9

1:1,2 Paul reminded Timothy that, despite their intimate spiritual relationship, the apostle wrote to him with spiritual authority given him by God. This established the necessity that not only Timothy, but also all others comply with the inspired mandates of the epistle.

1:1 apostle of Jesus Christ by the will of God. *See note on 1 Tim. 1:1.* His call was according to God's sovereign plan and purpose (cf. 1 Cor. 1:1; 2 Cor. 1:1; Eph. 1:1; Col. 1:1). **promise of life...in Christ Jesus.** The gospel, which promises that those who are spiritually dead, but by faith embrace the gospel's message, will be united to Christ and find eternal life in Him (John 3:16; 10:10; 14:6; Col. 3:4).

1:2 Timothy, a beloved son. *See note on 1 Tim. 1:2.* **Grace...our Lord.** *See note on 1 Tim. 1:2.* More than a standard greeting by Paul, this expressed his genuine desire for God's best in Timothy's life.

1:3 I thank God...in my prayers. *See notes on Phil. 1:3,4.* **pure conscience.** *See note on 1 Tim. 1:5.*

1:4 greatly desiring to see you. Because of Paul's affection for Timothy and the urgency of the hour in Paul's life, as he faced death, Paul had an intense yearning to see Timothy again (cf. 4:9,13,21). **mindful of your tears.** Paul perhaps remembered this occurring at their latest parting, which occurred after a short visit to Ephesus, following the writing of 1 Timothy, and prior to Paul's arrest at Troas (*see note on 4:13*) and his second imprisonment in Rome. Years before, Paul had a similar parting with the elders at Ephesus (Acts 20:36-38).

1:5 Lois...Eunice. Mention of their names suggests that Paul knew them personally, perhaps because he (with Barnabas) led them to faith in Christ during his first missionary journey (cf. Acts 13:13–14:21). The women were true OT Jewish believers, who understood the Scripture well enough to prepare themselves and Timothy (3:15) to immediately accept Jesus as Messiah when they first heard the gospel from Paul.

1:6 stir up the gift of God. This seems to indicate Paul was unsatisfied with Timothy's level of current faithfulness. "Stir up" means lit. "to keep the fire alive," and "gift" refers to the believer's spiritual gift (*see notes on Rom. 12:4-8; 1 Cor. 12:7-11*; regarding Timothy's spiritual gift, *see notes on 4:2-6; 1 Tim. 4:14*). Paul reminds Timothy that as a steward of his God-given gift for preaching, teaching, and evangelizing, he could not let it fall into disuse (cf. 4:2-5). **laying on of my hands.** *See notes on 1 Tim. 4:14; 5:22*; cf. 6:12. Paul might have done this at the time of Timothy's conversion, in which case it would have corresponded to when Timothy received his spiritual gift. The expression may also refer to an extraordinary spiritual endowment, which was received or enhanced at some point after his conversion.

1:7 a spirit of fear. The Gr. word, which can also be translated "timidity," denotes a cowardly, shameful fear caused by a weak, selfish character. The threat of Roman persecution, which was escalating under Nero, the hostility of those in the Ephesian church who resented Timothy's leadership, and the assaults of false teachers with their sophisticated systems of deceptions may have been overwhelming Timothy. But if he was fearful, it didn't come from God. **power.** Positively, God has already given believers all the spiritual resources they need for every trial and threat (cf. Matt. 10:19,20). Divine power—effective, productive spiritual energy belongs to believers (Eph. 1:18-20; 3:20; cf. Zech. 4:6). **love.** *See note on 1 Tim. 1:5.* This kind of love centers on pleasing God and seeking others' welfare before one's own (cf. Rom. 14:8; Gal. 5:22,25; Eph. 3:19; 1 Pet. 1:22; 1 John 4:18). **sound mind.** Refers to a disciplined, self-controlled, and properly prioritized mind. This is the opposite of fear and cowardice that causes disorder and confusion. Focusing on the sovereign nature and perfect purposes of our eternal God allows believers to control their lives with godly wisdom and confidence in every situation (cf. Rom. 12:3; 1 Tim. 3:2; Titus 1:8; 2:2).

1:8 the testimony of our Lord. The gospel message concerning Jesus Christ. Paul did not want Timothy to be "ashamed" to name the name of Christ because he was afraid of the potential persecution (cf. vv. 12,16). **me His prisoner.** See Introduction: Author and Date; *see notes on Eph. 3:1; Phil. 1:12-14.* Being linked to Paul, who was a prisoner because of his preaching of the gospel, could have put Timothy's life and freedom in jeopardy (cf. Heb. 13:23).

1:9 with a holy calling. As always in the NT epistles, this calling is not a general invitation to sinners to believe the gospel and be saved (as in Matt. 20:16), but refers to God's effectual call of the elect to salvation (*see note on Rom. 1:7*). This calling results in holiness, imputed (justification) and imparted (sanctification), and finally completed (glorification). **not...works, but...grace.** This truth is the foundation of the gospel. Salvation is by grace through faith, apart from works (*see notes on Rom. 3:20-25; Gal. 3:10,11; Eph. 2:8,9; Phil. 3:8,9*). Grace is also the basis for God's sustaining work in believers (cf. Phil. 1:6; Jude 24,25). **in Christ Jesus.** His sacrifice made God's salvation plan possible, because He became the substitute sacrifice for the sins of God's people (*see notes on 2 Cor. 5:21*). **according to His own purpose.** God's sovereign plan of election (*see notes on 2:10; John 6:37-40,44; Acts 13:48; Rom. 8:29; 9:10-24; Eph. 1:4; 3:11; 2 Thess. 2:13; Titus 1:1,2; 1 Pet. 1:2*). **before time began.** The same Gr. phrase appears in Titus 1:2. The destiny of God's chosen was determined and sealed from eternity past (John 17:24; cf. Eph. 1:4,5; Phil. 1:29; 1 Pet. 1:2).

been revealed by the appearing of our Savior Jesus Christ, *who* has abolished death
and brought life and immortality to light
through the gospel, 11 [p]to which I was
appointed a preacher, an apostle, and a
teacher [3]of the Gentiles. 12 For this reason I
also suffer these things; nevertheless I am
not ashamed, [q]for I know whom I have believed and am persuaded that He is able to
keep what I have committed to Him until
that Day.

Be Loyal to the Faith

13 [r]Hold fast [s]the pattern of [t]sound
words which you have heard from me, in
faith and love which are in Christ Jesus.
14 That good thing which was committed
to you, keep by the Holy Spirit who dwells
in us.
15 This you know, that all those in Asia
have turned away from me, among whom
are Phygellus and Hermogenes. 16 The
Lord grant mercy to the [u]household of Onesiphorus, for he often refreshed me, and
was not ashamed of my chain; 17 but when
he arrived in Rome, he sought me out very
zealously and found *me.* 18 The Lord
[v]grant to him that he may find mercy from
the Lord [w]in that Day—and you know
very well how many ways he [x]ministered
[4]*to me* at Ephesus.

Be Strong in Grace

2 You therefore, [a]my son, [b]be strong in
the grace that is in Christ Jesus. 2 And
the things that you have heard from me
among many witnesses, commit these to
faithful men who will be able to teach others also. 3 You therefore must [c]endure[1]
hardship [d]as a good soldier of Jesus Christ.

11 [p] Acts 9:15 [3] NU omits *of the Gentiles*
12 [q] 1 Pet. 4:19
13 [r] 2 Tim. 3:14; Titus 1:9 [s] Rom. 2:20; 6:17 [t] 1 Tim. 6:3
16 [u] 2 Tim. 4:19
18 [v] Matt. 6:4; Mark 9:41 [w] 2 Thess. 1:10 [x] Heb. 6:10 [4] *to me* from Vg., a few Gr. mss.

CHAPTER 2

1 [a] 1 Tim. 1:2 [b] Eph. 6:10
3 [c] 2 Tim. 4:5 [d] 1 Cor. 9:7; 1 Tim. 1:18 [1] NU *You must share*

1:10 appearing. "Epiphany" is the Eng. equivalent of this Gr. word, most often used of Christ's second coming (4:18; 1 Tim. 6:14; Titus 2:13), but here of His first coming. **abolished death…immortality to light.** "Abolished" means "rendered inoperative." Physical death still exists, but it is no longer a threat or an enemy for Christians (1 Cor. 15:54,55; Heb. 2:14). It was not until the incarnation and the gospel that God chose to fully make known the truth of immortality and eternal life, a reality only partially understood by OT believers (cf. Job 19:26).

1:11 preacher…teacher. *See notes on 1 Tim. 2:7.*

1:12 I also suffer. Cf. v. 8; *see notes on 2 Cor. 4:8-18; 6:4-10; 11:23-28; Gal. 6:17; Phil. 3:10.* **I am not ashamed.** *See notes on v. 8; Rom. 1:16; 1 Pet. 4:16.* Paul had no fear of persecution and death from preaching the gospel in a hostile setting, because he was so confident God had sealed his future glory and blessing. **know whom I have believed.** "Know" describes the certainty of Paul's intimate, saving knowledge—the object of which was God Himself. The form of the Gr. verb translated "I have believed" refers to something that began in the past and has continuing results (*see note on Rom. 1:16*). This knowing is equal to "the knowledge of the truth" (3:7; 1 Tim. 2:4). **He is able to keep.** *See notes on Jude 24,25.* **what I have committed.** Paul's life in time and eternity had been given to his Lord. He lived with unwavering confidence and boldness because of the revealed truth about God's power and faithfulness, and his own experience of an unbreakable relationship to the Lord (Rom. 8:31-39). **that Day.** Cf. vv. 18; 4:8; *see notes on Phil. 1:6.* Also called "Day of Christ" (*see notes on Phil. 1:10*), when believers will stand before the judgment seat and be rewarded (*see notes on 1 Cor. 3:13; 2 Cor. 5:10; 1 Pet. 1:5*).

1:13 sound words. Cf. 1 Tim. 4:6; 6:3. The Scripture and the doctrine it teaches (*see notes on 3:15-17*). **from me.** Paul had been the source of this divine revelation (cf. 2:2; 3:10,14; Phil. 4:9; *see notes on Eph. 3:1-5*). **faith and love…in Christ Jesus.** "Faith" is confidence that God's Word is true, and "love" is kindness and compassion in teaching that truth (cf. Eph. 4:15).

1:14 That good thing…committed to you. The treasure of the good news of salvation revealed in the Scripture (*see note on 1 Tim. 6:20*).

1:15 Asia. A Roman province that is part of modern Turkey; this is not a reference to the entire region of Asia Minor. **Phygellus and Hermogenes.** Nothing else is known about these two men, who apparently had shown promise as leaders, had been close to Paul, and were well known among the Asian churches, but deserted Paul under the pressure of persecution.

1:16 Onesiphorus. One of Paul's loyal co-workers who had not deserted Paul, but befriended him in prison and was not ashamed or afraid to visit the apostle there regularly and minister to his needs. Since Paul asks Timothy to greet those in his house (4:19), the family obviously lived in or near Ephesus.

1:17 when he arrived in Rome. For notes on Rome, see Introduction to Romans: Background and Setting. Onesiphorus was perhaps on a business trip and the text implies that his search involved time, effort, and possibly even danger.

1:18 that Day. *See note on v. 12.* **Ephesus.** See Introduction to Ephesians: Background and Setting. Onesiphorus' faithfulness began here many years earlier, when Paul ministered on his third or fourth missionary journey.

2:1 my son. Paul had led Timothy to Christ during his first missionary journey (cf. 1 Cor. 4:17; 1 Tim. 1:2,18). **be strong.** Here is the main admonition in the first part of the letter. Paul is calling for Timothy to overcome his apparent drift toward weakness and renew his commitment to his ministry (see Introduction: Historical and Theological Themes).

2:2 heard from me. *See notes on 1:13*; cf. 3:14. During Timothy's many years of close association with Paul (see Introduction to 1 Timothy: Author and Date), he had heard divine truth which God had revealed through the apostle. **among many witnesses.** Such as Silas, Barnabas, and Luke, and many others in the churches who could attest to the divine authenticity of Paul's teaching—a needed reminder to Timothy in light of the many defections at Ephesus (cf. 1:15). **faithful men who will be able to teach others.** Timothy was to take the divine revelation he had learned from Paul and teach it to other faithful men—men with proven spiritual character and giftedness, who would in turn pass on those truths to another generation. From Paul to Timothy to faithful men to others encompasses 4 generations of godly leaders. That process of spiritual reproduction, which began in the early church, is to continue until the Lord returns.

2:3 a good soldier. The metaphor of the Christian life as warfare (against the evil world system, the believer's sinful human nature, and Satan) is a familiar one in the NT (cf. 2 Cor. 10:3-5; Eph. 6:10-20; 1 Thess. 4:8; 1 Tim. 1:18; 4:7; 6:12). Here Paul is dealing with the conflict against the hostile world and the persecution (cf. v. 9; 1:8; 3:11,12; 4:7).

4 [e]No one engaged in warfare entangles
himself with the affairs of *this* life, that he
may please him who enlisted him as a soldier. 5 And also [f]if anyone competes in athletics, he is not crowned unless he competes according to the rules. 6 The
hardworking farmer must be first to partake of the crops. 7 Consider what I say,
and [2]may the Lord [g]give you understanding in all things.
8 Remember that Jesus Christ, [h]of the
seed of David, [i]was raised from the dead
[j]according to my gospel, 9 [k]for which I suffer trouble as an evildoer, [l]*even* to the point
of chains; [m]but the word of God is not
chained. 10 Therefore [n]I endure all things
for the sake of the [3]elect, [o]that they also
may obtain the salvation which is in Christ
Jesus with eternal glory.
11 *This is* a faithful saying:

For [p]if we died with *Him*,
We shall also live with *Him*.
12 [q]If we endure,
We shall also reign with *Him*.
[r]If we deny *Him*,
He also will deny us.
13 If we are faithless,
He remains faithful;
He [s]cannot deny Himself.

Approved and Disapproved Workers

14 Remind *them* of these things, [t]charg-
ing *them* before the Lord not to [4]strive
about words to no profit, to the ruin of the
hearers. 15 [u]Be diligent to present yourself
approved to God, a worker who does not
need to be ashamed, rightly dividing the
word of truth. 16 But shun profane *and*
[5]idle babblings, for they will [6]increase to
more ungodliness. 17 And their message

4 [e][2 Pet. 2:20]
5 [f][1 Cor. 9:25]
7 [g]Prov. 2:6 [2]NU *the Lord will give you*
8 [h]Rom. 1:3,4 [i]1 Cor. 15:4 [j]Rom. 2:16
9 [k]Acts 9:16 [l]Eph. 3:1 [m]Acts 28:31; [2 Tim. 4:17]
10 [n]Eph. 3:13 [o]2 Cor. 1:6; 1 Thess. 5:9 [3]*chosen ones*
11 [p]Rom. 6:5, 8; 1 Thess. 5:10
12 [q][Matt. 19:28]; Luke 22:29; [Rom. 5:17; 8:17] [r]Matt. 10:33; Luke 12:9; 1 Tim. 5:8
13 [s]Num. 23:19; Titus 1:2
14 [t]1 Tim. 5:21; 6:4; 2 Tim. 2:23; Titus 3:9 [4]*battle*
15 [u]1 Tim. 4:13; 2 Pet. 1:10
16 [5]*empty chatter* [6]*lead*

2:4 entangles himself. Just as a soldier called to duty is completely severed from the normal affairs of civilian life, so also must the good soldier of Jesus Christ refuse to allow the things of the world to distract him (cf. James 4:4; 1 John 2:15-17).

2:5 competes in athletics. The Gr. verb (*athleō*) expresses the effort and determination needed to compete successfully in an athletic event (cf. 1 Cor. 9:24). This is a useful picture of spiritual effort and untiring pursuit of the victory to those familiar with events such as the Olympic Games and the Isthmian Games (held in Corinth). **crowned...rules.** All an athlete's hard work and discipline will be wasted if he or she fails to compete according to the rules. This is a call to obey the Word of God in the pursuit of spiritual victory.

2:6 The hardworking farmer. "Hardworking" is from a Gr. verb meaning "to labor to the point of exhaustion." Ancient farmers worked long hours of backbreaking labor under all kinds of conditions, with the hope that their physical effort would be rewarded by a good harvest. Paul is urging Timothy not to be lazy or indolent, but to labor intensely (cf. Col. 1:28,29) with a view to the harvest. *See notes on 1 Cor. 3:6,7.*

2:7 Consider. The Gr. word denotes clear perception, full understanding, and careful consideration. The form of the verb suggests a strong admonition by Paul, not mere advice, to give deep thought to what he was writing.

2:8 Remember...Jesus Christ. The supreme model of a faithful teacher (v. 2), soldier (vv. 3,4), athlete (v. 5), and farmer (v. 6). Timothy was to follow His example in teaching, suffering, pursuing the prize, and planting the seeds of truth for a spiritual harvest. **of the seed of David.** *See notes on Rom. 1:3; Rev. 22:16.* As David's descendant, Jesus is the rightful heir to his throne (Luke 1:32,33). The Lord's humanity is stressed. **raised from the dead.** The resurrection of Christ is the central truth of the Christian faith (1 Cor. 15:3,4,17,19). By it, God affirmed the perfect redemptive work of Jesus Christ (*see note on Rom. 1:4*).

2:9 I suffer...but the word...is not chained. Paul contrasts his imprisonment for the sake of the gospel to the unfettered power of the Word of God.

2:10 for the sake of the elect. Those of the elect, having been chosen for salvation from before the world began (*see note on 1:9*), who had not yet come to faith in Jesus Christ (*see notes on Acts 18:10; Titus 1:1*). **the salvation which is in Christ Jesus.** There is salvation in no one else (Acts 4:12; cf. Rom. 8:29; Eph. 1:4,5). The gospel must be proclaimed (Matt. 28:19; Acts 1:8) because the elect are not saved apart from faith in Christ (Rom. 10:14). **eternal glory.** The ultimate outcome of salvation (*see notes on Rom. 5:2; 8:17*).

2:11 faithful saying. The saying is in vv. 11-13. *See note on 1 Tim. 1:15.* **died with *Him*...live with *Him*.** This refers to believers' spiritual participation in Christ's death and resurrection (Rom. 6:4-8), including also the possibility of suffering martyrdom for the sake of Christ, as the context would indicate.

2:12 endure. Believers who persevere give evidence of the genuineness of their faith (*see note on Matt. 10:22*; cf. 24:13; John 8:31; Rom. 2:7; Col. 1:23). **reign with *Him*.** In His future eternal kingdom (Rev. 1:6; 5:10; 20:4,6). **If we deny *Him*, He also will deny us.** Speaks of a final, permanent denial, such as that of an apostate (*see note on 1 Tim. 1:19*), not the temporary failure of a true believer like Peter (Matt. 26:69-75). Those who so deny Christ give evidence that they never truly belonged to Him (1 John 2:19) and face the fearful reality of one day being denied by Him (Matt. 10:33).

2:13 faithless. This refers to a lack of saving faith, not to weak or struggling faith. Unbelievers will ultimately deny Christ because their faith was not genuine (cf. James 2:14-26). **He remains faithful; He cannot deny Himself.** As faithful as Jesus is to save those who believe in Him (John 3:16), He is equally faithful to judge those who do not (John 3:18). To act any other way would be inconsistent with His holy, unchangeable nature. Cf. Heb. 10:23.

2:14 strive about words. Arguing with false teachers, i.e., deceivers who use human reason to subvert God's Word, is not only foolish (Prov. 14:7) and futile (Matt. 7:6), but dangerous (vv. 16,17; cf. v. 23). This is the first of 3 warnings to avoid useless arguments (*see notes on vv. 16,23*). *See notes on 1 Tim. 4:6,7; 6:3-5; 2 Pet. 1–3.* **ruin.** The Gr. word means "overturned," or "overthrown." It appears only one other time in the NT (2 Pet. 2:6), where it describes the destruction of Sodom and Gomorrah. Because it replaces the truth with lies, false teaching brings spiritual catastrophe to those who heed it. The ruin can be eternal.

2:15 Be diligent. This word denotes zealous persistence in accomplishing a goal. Timothy, like all who preach or teach the Word, was to give his maximum effort to impart God's Word completely, accurately, and clearly to his hearers. This is crucial to counter the disastrous effects of false teaching (vv. 14,16,17). **rightly dividing.** Lit. "cutting it straight"—a reference to the exactness demanded by such trades as carpentry, masonry, and Paul's trade of leather working and tentmaking. Precision and accuracy are required in biblical interpretation, beyond all other enterprises because the interpreter is handling God's Word. Anything less is shameful. **the word of truth.** All of Scripture in general (John 17:17), and the gospel message in particular (Eph. 1:13; Col. 1:5).

2:16 shun profane *and* idle babblings. *See notes on v. 14; 1 Tim.*

will spread like cancer. [v]Hymenaeus and
Philetus are of this sort, 18 who have
strayed concerning the truth, [w]saying that
the resurrection is already past; and they
overthrow the faith of some. 19 Nevertheless [x]the solid foundation of God stands,
having this seal: "The Lord [y]knows those
who are His," and, "Let everyone who
names the name of [7]Christ depart from iniquity."

20 But in a great house there are not only
[z]vessels of gold and silver, but also of
wood and clay, some for honor and some
for dishonor. 21 Therefore if anyone cleanses himself from the latter, he will be a vessel for honor, [8]sanctified and useful for the
Master, [a]prepared for every good work.
22 [b]Flee also youthful lusts; but pursue
righteousness, faith, love, peace with those
who call on the Lord out of a pure heart.
23 But avoid foolish and ignorant disputes,
knowing that they generate strife. 24 And
[c]a servant of the Lord must not quarrel but
be gentle to all, [d]able to teach, [e]patient,
25 [f]in humility correcting those who are in
opposition, [g]if God perhaps will grant
them repentance, [h]so that they may know
the truth, 26 and *that* they may come to
their senses *and* [i]*escape* the snare of the
devil, having been taken captive by him to
do his will.

17 [v] 1 Tim. 1:20
18 [w] 1 Cor. 15:12
19 [x] Matt. 24:24; [1 Cor. 3:11] [y] Num. 16:5; [Nah. 1:7]; John 10:14, 27 [7] NU, M *the Lord*
20 [z] Rom. 9:21
21 [a] 2 Cor. 9:8; [Eph. 2:10]; 2 Tim. 3:17 [8] *set apart*
22 [b] 1 Tim. 6:11
24 [c] Titus 3:2 [d] Titus 1:9 [e] 1 Tim. 3:3; Titus 1:7
25 [f] Gal. 6:1; Titus 3:2; 1 Pet. 3:15 [g] Acts 8:22 [h] 1 Tim. 2:4
26 [i] 1 Tim. 3:7

CHAPTER 3

1 [a] 1 Tim. 4:1; 2 Pet. 3:3; 1 John 2:18; Jude 17, 18 [1] *times of stress*
3 [2] *irreconcilable*

Perilous Times and Perilous Men

3 But know this, that [a]in the last days
[1]perilous times will come: 2 For men
will be lovers of themselves, lovers of
money, boasters, proud, blasphemers,
disobedient to parents, unthankful, unholy, 3 unloving, [2]unforgiving, slanderers,
without self-control, brutal, despisers of

6:20; cf. Titus 3:9. Such destructive heresy leads only to "more ungodliness." Heresy can't save or sanctify. This is Paul's second such warning. Cf. vv. 14,23.

2:17 cancer. The word refers to a disease which spreads rapidly in a deadly manner. The metaphor emphasizes the insidious danger of false teaching. It attacks and consumes one's life. **Hymenaeus.** *See note on 1 Tim. 1:20.* **Philetus.** Alexander's replacement (1 Tim. 1:20) as Hymenaeus' accomplice.

2:18 the resurrection is already past. Like the false teachers who troubled the Corinthians (1 Cor. 15:12), Hymenaeus and Philetus denied the reality of believers' bodily resurrection. They probably taught that believers' spiritual identification with Christ's death and resurrection (Rom. 6:4,5,8) was the only resurrection they would experience and that had already happened. Such heretical teaching reflects the contemporary Greek philosophical view that matter was evil and spirit was good. **overthrow the faith.** This speaks of those whose faith was not genuine (cf. Matt. 24:24). Genuine saving faith cannot be finally and completely overthrown (*see note on v. 12*). False, non-saving faith is common (cf. 4:10). *See notes on Matt. 7:21-27; 13:18-22; John 2:23-25; 6:64-66; 8:31; 1 John 2:19.*

2:19 the solid foundation of God. This is likely a reference to the church (cf. 1 Tim. 3:15), which cannot be overcome by the forces of hell (Matt. 16:18) and is made up of those who belong to Him. **seal.** A symbol of ownership and authenticity. Paul gives two characteristics of those with the divine seal of authenticity. **"The Lord knows those who are His."** This is likely a reference to Num. 16:5. He "knows," not the sense of awareness, but as a husband knows his wife in the sense of intimate relationship (*see notes on John 10:27,28; Gal. 4:9*). God has known His own ever since He chose them before time began. *See note on 1:9.* **"Let everyone...depart from iniquity."** This statement is likely adapted from Num. 16:26, and reflects a second mark of God's ownership of believers, which is their pursuit of holiness (cf. 1 Cor. 6:19,20; 1 Pet. 1:15,16).

2:20 vessels. The Gr. word is very general and was used to describe various tools, utensils, and furniture found in the home. In this "great house" analogy, Paul contrasts two kinds of utensils or serving dishes. **some for honor.** In a wealthy home, the ones made of precious "gold and silver" were used for honorable purposes such as serving food to the family and guests. **some for dishonor.** Those made of "wood and clay" were not for any honorable use, but rather those uses which were repulsive—disposing of garbage and the filthy waste of the household. *See notes on 2 Cor. 4:7.*

2:21 anyone. Whoever wants to be useful to the Lord for noble purposes. Even a common wood bucket or clay pot becomes useful when purged and made holy. **cleanses himself.** *See note on v. 19.* The Gr. word means "to thoroughly clean out," or "to completely purge." For any wastebucket in the house to be used for a noble purpose, it would have had to be vigorously scoured, cleansed, and purged of all vestiges of its former filth. **the latter.** The vessels of dishonor (v. 20). Associating with anyone who teaches error and lives in sin is corrupting (Prov. 1:10-19; 13:20; 1 Cor. 5:6,11; 15:33; Titus 1:16)—all the more so when they are leaders in the church. This is clearly a call to separate from all who claim to serve God, but do so as filthy implements useful only for the most dishonorable duties.

2:22 youthful lusts. Not merely illicit sexual desires, but also such lusts as pride, desire for wealth and power, jealousy, self-assertiveness, and an argumentative spirit.

2:23 disputes...strife. Paul's third warning to avoid useless arguments with false teachers (*see notes on vv. 14,16*).

2:24 able to teach. This is one word in Gr. meaning "skilled in teaching." *See note on 1 Tim. 3:2.*

2:25 those who are in opposition. Primarily unbelievers (captive to Satan, v. 26), but also could include believers deceived by the "foolish and ignorant" (v. 23) speculations of the false teachers; and, possibly, the false teachers themselves. **God...will grant them repentance.** Cf. Acts 11:18; see 2 Cor. 7:9,10. All true repentance is produced by God's sovereign grace (Eph. 2:7), and without such grace human effort to change is futile (cf. Jer. 13:23). **know the truth.** *See note on 3:7.* When God, by grace, grants saving faith it includes the granting of repentance from sin. Neither is a human work.

2:26 the snare of the devil. Deception is Satan's trap. He is an inveterate, scheming, clever, and subtle purveyor of lies. *See notes on Gen. 3:4-6; John 8:44; 2 Cor. 11:13-15; Rev. 12:9.*

3:1 the last days. This phrase refers to this age, the time since the first coming of the Lord Jesus. *See note on 1 Tim. 4:1.* **perilous times.** "Perilous" is used to describe the savage nature of two demon-possessed men (Matt. 8:28). The word for "times" had to do with epochs, rather than clock or calendar time. Such savage, dangerous eras or epochs will increase in frequency and severity as the return of Christ approaches (v. 13). The church age is fraught with these dangerous movements accumulating strength as the end nears. Cf. Matt. 7:15; 24:11,12,24; 2 Pet. 2:1,2.

3:2-4 This list of attributes characterizing the leaders of the dangerous seasons is a description of unbelievers similar to the Lord's in Mark 7:21,22.

good, 4 [b]traitors, headstrong, haughty,
lovers of pleasure rather than lovers of
God, 5 [c]having a form of godliness but
[d]denying its power. And [e]from such people turn away! 6 For [f]of this sort are those
who creep into households and make captives of gullible women loaded down with
sins, led away by various lusts, 7 always
learning and never able [g]to come to the
knowledge of the truth. 8 [h]Now as Jannes
and Jambres resisted Moses, so do these
also resist the truth: [i]men of corrupt
minds, [j]disapproved concerning the faith;
9 but they will progress no further, for their
folly will be manifest to all, [k]as theirs also
was.

The Man of God and the Word of God

10 [l]But you have carefully followed my
doctrine, manner of life, purpose, faith,
longsuffering, love, perseverance, 11 persecutions, afflictions, which happened to me
[m]at Antioch, [n]at Iconium, [o]at Lystra—what
persecutions I endured. And [p]out of *them*
all the Lord delivered me. 12 Yes, and [q]all
who desire to live godly in Christ Jesus
will suffer persecution. 13 [r]But evil men
and impostors will grow worse and worse,
deceiving and being deceived. 14 But you
must [s]continue in the things which you
have learned and been assured of, knowing from whom you have learned *them*,
15 and that from childhood you have
known [t]the Holy Scriptures, which are
able to make you wise for salvation
through faith which is in Christ Jesus.
16 [u]All Scripture *is* given by inspiration
of God, [v]and *is* profitable for doctrine, for

4 [b]2 Pet. 2:10
5 [c]Titus 1:16 [d]1 Tim. 5:8 [e]Matt. 23:3; 2 Thess. 3:6; 1 Tim. 6:5
6 [f]Matt. 23:14; Titus 1:11
7 [g]1 Tim. 2:4
8 [h]Ex. 7:11, 12, 22; 8:7; 9:11 [i]1 Tim. 6:5 [j]Rom. 1:28
9 [k]Ex. 7:11, 12; 8:18; 9:11
10 [l]Phil. 2:20, 22; 1 Tim. 4:6
11 [m]Acts 13:44-52 [n]Acts 14:1-6, 19 [o]Acts 14:8-20 [p]Ps. 34:19
12 [q][Ps. 34:19]
13 [r]2 Thess. 2:11
14 [s]2 Tim. 1:13; Titus 1:9
15 [t]Ps. 119:97-104; John 5:39
16 [u][2 Pet. 1:20] [v]Rom. 4:23; 15:4

3:5 having a form of godliness but denying its power. "Form" refers to outward shape or appearance. Like the unbelieving scribes and Pharisees, false teachers and their followers are concerned with mere external appearances (cf. Matt. 23:25; Titus 1:16). Their outward form of Christianity and virtue makes them all the more dangerous.

3:6 gullible women. Weak in virtue and the knowledge of the truth, and weighed down with emotional and spiritual guilt over their sins, these women were easy prey for the deceitful false teachers. *See notes on 1 Tim. 2:13,14; 5:11,12.*

3:7 the knowledge of the truth. First Timothy 2:4 uses this same phrase, equating it with being saved. Here Paul identified those women (v. 6) and men who were often jumping from one false teacher or cult to another without ever coming to an understanding of God's saving truth in Jesus Christ. The present age, since the coming of Jesus Christ, has been loaded with perilous false teaching that can't save, but does damn (cf. vv. 14,16,17; 1 Tim. 4:1).

3:8 Jannes and Jambres. Although their names are not mentioned in the OT, they were likely two of the Egyptian magicians that opposed Moses (Ex. 7:11,22; 8:7,18,19; 9:11). According to Jewish tradition, they pretended to become Jewish proselytes, instigated the worship of the golden calf, and were killed with the rest of the idolaters (Ex. 32). Paul's choice of them as examples may indicate the false teachers at Ephesus were practicing deceiving signs and wonders. **the truth.** *See note on v. 7.* **disapproved.** The same word is translated "debased" in Rom. 1:28 (*see note there*) and comes from a Gr. word meaning "useless" in the sense of being tested (like metal) and shown to be worthless.

3:9 folly...manifest. Sooner or later, it will be clear that these false teachers are lost fools, as it became clear in the case of Jannes and Jambres.

3:11 persecutions. From a Gr. verb that lit. means "to put to flight." Paul had been forced to flee from Damascus (Acts 9:23-25), Pisidian Antioch (Acts 13:50), Iconium (Acts 14:6), Thessalonica (Acts 17:10), and Berea (Acts 17:14). **Antioch...Iconium...Lystra.** As a native of Lystra (Acts 16:1), Timothy vividly recalled the persecution Paul faced in those 3 cities. **the Lord delivered me.** Cf. 4:17,18; Pss. 34:4,6,19; 37:40; 91:2-6,14; Is. 41:10; 43:2; Dan. 3:17; Acts 26:16,17; 2 Cor. 1:10. The Lord's repeated deliverance of Paul should have encouraged Timothy in the face of persecution by those at Ephesus who opposed the gospel.

3:12 who desire to live godly in Christ Jesus will suffer persecution. Faithful believers must expect persecution and suffering at the hands of the Christ-rejecting world (cf. John 15:18-21; Acts 14:22).

3:13 All the dangerous movements of the false teachers (cf. vv. 1-9) will become increasingly more successful until Christ comes. Cf. 2 Thess. 2:11.

3:14 from whom you have learned. *See note on 1:13.* To further encourage Timothy to stand firm, Paul reminds him of his godly heritage. The plural form of the pronoun "whom" suggests Timothy was indebted not just to Paul, but to others as well (1:5).

3:15 from childhood. Lit. "from infancy." Two people whom Timothy was especially indebted to were his mother and grandmother (*see note on 1:5*), who faithfully taught him the truths of OT Scripture from his earliest childhood, so that he was ready to receive the gospel when Paul preached it. **you have known the Holy Scriptures.** Lit. "the sacred writings," a common designation of the OT by Greek-speaking Jews. **wise for salvation.** The OT Scriptures pointed to Christ (John 5:37-39) and revealed the need for faith in God's promises (Gen. 15:6; cf. Rom. 4:1-3). Thus, they were able to lead people to acknowledge their sin and need for justification in Christ (Gal. 3:24). Salvation is brought by the Holy Spirit using the Word. *See notes on Rom. 10:14-17; Eph. 5:26; 1 Pet. 1:23-25.* **faith which is in Christ Jesus.** Though not understanding all the details involved (cf. 1 Pet. 1:10-12), OT believers including Abraham (John 8:56) and Moses (Heb. 11:26) looked forward to the coming of the Messiah (Is. 7:14; 9:6) and His atonement for sin (Is. 53:5,6). So did Timothy, who responded when he heard the gospel.

3:16 All Scripture. Grammatically similar Gr. constructions (Rom. 7:12; 2 Cor. 10:10; 1 Tim. 1:15; 2:3; 4:4) argue persuasively that the translation "all Scripture *is* given by inspiration..." is accurate. Both OT and NT Scripture are included (*see notes on 2 Pet. 3:15,16,* which identify NT writings as Scripture). **given by inspiration of God.** Lit. "breathed out by God," or "God-breathed." Sometimes God told the Bible writers the exact words to say (e.g., Jer. 1:9), but more often He used their minds, vocabularies, and experiences to produce His own perfect infallible, inerrant Word (*see notes on 1 Thess. 2:13; Heb. 1:1; 2 Pet. 1:20,21*). It is important to note that inspiration applies only to the original autographs of Scripture, not the Bible writers; there are no inspired Scripture writers, only inspired Scripture. So identified is God with His Word that when Scripture speaks, God speaks (cf. Rom. 9:17; Gal. 3:8). Scripture is called "the oracles of God" (Rom. 3:2; 1 Pet. 4:11), and cannot be altered (John 10:35; Matt. 5:17,18; Luke 16:17; Rev. 22:18,19). **doctrine.** The divine instruction or doctrinal content of both the OT and the NT (cf. 2:15; Acts 20:18,20,21,27; 1 Cor. 2:14-16; Col. 3:16; 1 John 2:20,24,27). The Scripture provides the comprehensive and complete body of divine truth necessary for life and godliness. Cf. Ps. 119:97-105. **reproof.** Rebuke for wrong behavior or wrong belief. The Scripture exposes sin (Heb. 4:12,13) that can then be dealt with

reproof, for correction, for [3]instruction in
righteousness, 17 [w]that the man of God
may be complete, [x]thoroughly equipped
for every good work.

Preach the Word

4 I [a]charge *you* [1]therefore before God and
the Lord Jesus Christ, [b]who will judge
the living and the dead [2]at His appearing
and His kingdom: 2 Preach the word! Be
ready in season *and* out of season. [c]Con-
vince, [d]rebuke, [e]exhort, with all longsuffering and teaching. 3 [f]For the time will come
when they will not endure [g]sound doctrine,
[h]but according to their own desires, *because*
they have itching ears, they will heap up for
themselves teachers; 4 and they will turn
their ears away from the truth, and [i]be
turned aside to fables. 5 But you be watchful in all things, [j]endure afflictions, do the
work of [k]an evangelist, fulfill your ministry.

Paul's Valedictory

6 For [l]I am already being poured out as a
drink offering, and the time of [m]my depar-

16 [3] *training, discipline*
17 [w] 1 Tim. 6:11 [x] 2 Tim. 2:21; Heb. 13:21

CHAPTER 4

1 [a] 1 Tim. 5:21; 2 Tim. 4:1 [b] Acts 10:42 [1] NU omits *therefore* [2] NU *and by*
2 [c] Titus 2:15 [d] 1 Tim. 5:20; Titus 1:13; 2:15 [e] 1 Tim. 4:13
3 [f] 2 Tim. 3:1 [g] 1 Tim. 1:10; 2 Tim. 1:13 [h] Is. 30:9-11; Jer. 5:30, 31; 2 Tim. 3:6
4 [i] 1 Tim. 1:4
5 [j] 2 Tim. 1:8 [k] Acts 21:8 **6** [l] Phil. 2:17 [m] [Phil. 1:23]; 2 Pet. 1:14

through confession and repentance. **correction.** The restoration of something to its proper condition. The word appears only here in the NT, but was used in extrabiblical Gr. of righting a fallen object, or helping back to their feet those who had stumbled. Scripture not only rebukes wrong behavior, but also points the way back to godly living. Cf. Ps. 119:9-11; John 15:1,2. **instruction in righteousness.** Scripture provides positive training ("instruction" originally referred to training a child) in godly behavior, not merely rebuke and correction of wrong behavior (Acts 20:32; 1 Tim. 4:6; 1 Pet. 2:1,2).

3:17 man of God. A technical term for an official preacher of divine truth. *See note on 1 Tim. 6:11.* **complete.** Capable of doing everything one is called to do (cf. Col. 2:10). **thoroughly equipped.** Enabled to meet all the demands of godly ministry and righteous living. The Word not only accomplishes this in the life of the man of God but in all who follow him (Eph. 4:11-13).

4:1 I charge *you*. Or better "command." The Gr. has the idea of issuing a forceful order or directive (cf. 2:14; 1 Tim. 1:18; 5:21). **before God and the Lord Jesus Christ.** The Gr. construction also allows the translation "in the presence of God, even Christ Jesus," which is probably the best rendering since He is about to be introduced as the judge (cf. John 5:22). Everyone who ministers the Word of God is under the omniscient scrutiny of Christ (*see notes on 2 Cor. 2:17; Heb. 13:17*). **Christ, who will judge.** The grammatical construction suggests imminency—that Christ is about to judge. Paul is emphasizing the unique accountability that all believers, and especially ministers of the Word of God, have to Christ as Judge. Service to Christ is rendered both under His watchful eye and with the knowledge that as Judge He will one day appraise the works of every believer (*see notes on 1 Cor. 3:12-15; 4:1-5; 2 Cor. 5:10*). That is not a judgment of condemnation, but one of evaluation. With regard to salvation, believers have been judged already and declared righteous—they are no longer subject to the condemnation of sin (Rom. 8:1-4). **the living and the dead.** Christ will ultimately judge all men in 3 distinct settings: 1) the judgment of believers after the Rapture (1 Cor. 3:12-15; 2 Cor. 5:10); 2) the sheep and goats judgment of the nations, in which believers will be separated from unbelievers (Matt. 25:31-33, for entrance into the millennial kingdom); and 3) the Great White Throne judgment of unbelievers only (Rev. 20:11-15). Here, the apostle is referring to judgment in a general sense, encompassing all those elements. **His appearing.** The Gr. word translated "appearing" lit. means "a shining forth" and was used by the ancient Greeks of the supposed appearance to men of a pagan god. Here, Paul is referring generally to Christ's second coming, when He will judge "the living and the dead" (*see previous note*) and establish His millennial and eternal kingdom (*see note on 1 Tim. 6:14*).

4:2 the word. The entire written Word of God, His complete revealed truth as contained in the Bible (cf. 3:15,16; Acts 20:27). **Be ready.** The Gr. word has a broad range of meanings, including suddenness (Luke 2:9; Acts 12:7) or forcefulness (Luke 20:1; Acts 4:1; 6:12; 23:27). Here the form of the verb suggests the complementary ideas of urgency, preparedness, and readiness. It was used of a soldier prepared to go into battle or a guard who was continually alert for any surprise attack—attitudes which are imperative for a faithful preacher (Jer. 20:9; Acts 21:11-13; Eph. 5:15,16; 1 Pet. 3:15). **in season *and* out of season.** The faithful preacher must proclaim the Word when it is popular and/or convenient, and when it is not; when it seems suitable to do so, and when it seems not. The dictates of popular culture, tradition, reputation, acceptance, or esteem in the community (or in the church) must never alter the true preacher's commitment to proclaim God's Word. **Convince, rebuke.** The negative side of preaching the Word (the "reproof" and "correction"; cf. 3:16). The Gr. word for "convince" refers to correcting behavior or false doctrine by using careful biblical argument to help a person understand the error of his actions. The Gr. word for "rebuke" deals more with correcting the person's motives by convicting him of his sin and leading him to repentance. **exhort...teaching.** The positive side of preaching (the "doctrine" and "instruction"; cf. 3:16).

4:3 not endure. This refers to holding up under adversity, and can be translated "tolerate." Paul here warns Timothy that, in the dangerous seasons of this age, many people would become intolerant of the confrontive, demanding preaching of God's Word (1:13,14; 1 Tim. 1:9,10; 6:3-5). **sound doctrine.** *See notes on 1:13; 1 Tim. 4:6; Titus 2:1.* **their own desires...itching ears.** Professing Christians, nominal believers in the church follow their own desires and flock to preachers who offer them God's blessings apart from His forgiveness, and His salvation apart from their repentance. They have an itch to be entertained by teachings that will produce pleasant sensations and leave them with good feelings about themselves. Their goal is that men preach "according to their own desires." Under those conditions, people will dictate what men preach, rather than God dictating it by His Word.

4:4 fables. This refers to false idealogies, viewpoints, and philosophies in various forms that oppose sound doctrine (*see notes on 2 Cor. 10:3-5; 1 Tim. 1:4; 4:7*; cf. Titus 1:14; 2 Pet. 1:16).

4:5 an evangelist. Used only two other times in the NT (*see notes on Acts 21:8; Eph. 4:11*), this word always refers to a specific office of ministry for the purpose of preaching the gospel to non-Christians. Based on Eph. 4:11, it is very basic to assume that all churches would have both pastor-teachers and evangelists. But the related verb "to preach the gospel" and the related noun "gospel" are used throughout the NT not only in relation to evangelists, but also to the call for every Christian, especially preachers and teachers, to proclaim the gospel. Paul did not call Timothy to the office of an evangelist, but to "do the work" of one.

4:6-8 As Paul neared the end of his life, he was able to look back without regret or remorse. In these verses, he examines his life from 3 perspectives: the present reality of the end of his life, for which he was ready (v. 6); the past, when he had been faithful (v. 7); and the future, as he anticipated his heavenly reward (v. 8).

4:6 already. Meaning his death was imminent. **a drink offering.** In the OT sacrificial system, this was the final offering that followed the burnt and grain offerings prescribed for the people of Israel (Num. 15:1-16). Paul saw his coming death as his final offering to

ture is at hand. 7 [n]I have fought the good
fight, I have finished the race, I have kept
the faith. 8 Finally, there is laid up for me
[o]the crown of righteousness, which the
Lord, the righteous [p]Judge, will give to me
[q]on that Day, and not to me only but also
to all who have loved His appearing.

The Abandoned Apostle

9 Be diligent to come to me quickly;
10 for [r]Demas has forsaken me, [s]having
loved this present world, and has departed
for Thessalonica—Crescens for Galatia, Titus for Dalmatia. 11 Only Luke is with me.
Get [t]Mark and bring him with you, for he
is useful to me for ministry. 12 And [u]Tychi-
cus I have sent to Ephesus. 13 Bring the
cloak that I left with Carpus at Troas when
you come—and the books, especially the
parchments.

14 [v]Alexander the coppersmith did me
much harm. May the Lord repay him according to his works. 15 You also must beware of him, for he has greatly resisted our
words.

16 At my first defense no one stood with
me, but all forsook me. [w]May it not be
charged against them.

7 [n] 1 Cor. 9:24-27; Phil. 3:13, 14
8 [o] [1 Cor. 9:25; 2 Tim. 2:5]; James 1:12 [p] John 5:22 [q] 2 Tim. 1:12
10 [r] Col. 4:14; Philem. 24 [s] 1 John 2:15
11 [t] Acts 12:12, 25; 15:37-39; Col. 4:10
12 [u] Acts 20:4; Eph. 6:21, 22; Col. 4:7; Titus 3:12
14 [v] Acts 19:33; 1 Tim. 1:20
16 [w] Acts 7:60; [1 Cor. 13:5]

God in a life that had already been full of sacrifices to Him (*see note on Phil. 2:17*). **my departure.** Paul's death. The Gr. word essentially refers to the loosening of something, such as the mooring ropes of a ship or the ropes of a tent; thus it eventually acquired the secondary meaning of "departure."

4:7 The form of the 3 Gr. verbs "have fought, have finished, have kept," indicate completed action with continuing results. Paul saw his life as complete—he had been able to accomplish through the Lord's power all that God called him to do. He was a soldier (2:3,4; 2 Cor. 10:3; 1 Tim. 6:12; Philem. 2), an athlete (1 Cor. 9:24-27; Eph. 6:12), and a guardian (1:13,14; 1 Tim. 6:20,21). **the faith.** The truths and standards of the revealed Word of God.

4:8 the crown of righteousness. The Gr. word for "crown" lit. means "surrounding," and it was used of the plaited wreaths or garlands placed on the heads of dignitaries and victorious military officers or athletes. Linguistically, "of righteousness" can mean either that righteousness is the source of the crown, or that righteousness is the nature of the crown. Like the "crown of life" (James 1:12), the "crown of rejoicing" (1 Thess. 2:19), the "imperishable crown" (1 Cor. 9:25), and the "crown of glory" (1 Pet. 5:4), in which life, rejoicing, imperishability, and glory describe the nature of the crown, the context here seems to indicate that the crown represents eternal righteousness. Believers receive the imputed righteousness of Christ (justification) at salvation (Rom. 4:6,11). The Holy Spirit works practical righteousness (sanctification) in the believer throughout his lifetime of struggle with sin (Rom. 6:13,19; 8:4; Eph. 5:9; 1 Pet. 2:24). But only when the struggle is complete will the Christian receive Christ's righteousness perfected in him (glorification) when he enters heaven (*see note on Gal. 5:5*). **the righteous Judge.** *See note on v. 1.* **that Day.** *See note on 1:12.* **His appearing.** *See notes on v. 1; 1 Tim. 6:14.*

4:9-22 In these closing verses, Paul brings Timothy up to date on the spiritual condition, activities, and whereabouts of certain men and women who either helped or harmed his ministry.

4:9 Be diligent to come to me quickly. Paul longed to see his beloved co-worker, but it was imperative that Timothy make haste because Paul knew his days were numbered (v. 6).

4:10 Demas. He had been one of Paul's closest associates along with Luke and Epaphras (*see notes on Col. 4:14; Philem. 24*). **forsaken.** This Gr. word means "to utterly abandon," with the idea of leaving someone in a dire situation. Demas was a fair-weather disciple who had never counted the cost of genuine commitment to Christ. His kind are described by our Lord in Matt. 13:20,21; cf. John 8:31; 1 John 2:1. **loved this present world.** *See notes on James 4:4; 1 John 2:15-17.* **Thessalonica.** Demas may have considered this city a safe haven (see Introduction to 1 Thessalonians: Background and Setting). **Crescens.** In contrast to Demas, Crescens must have been faithful and dependable, since Paul sent him to Galatia, a Roman province in central Asia Minor, where Paul ministered on each of his 3 missionary journeys. **Titus.** Paul's closest friend and co-worker next to Timothy (Titus 1:5; see Introduction to Titus: Title). **Dalmatia.** Also known as Illyricum (Rom. 15:19), a Roman province on the E coast of the Adriatic Sea, just N of Macedonia.

4:11 Luke. The author of the Gospel of Luke and Acts, and Paul's devoted friend and personal physician, who could not carry the burden of ministry in Rome by himself (see Introductions to Luke and Acts: Author and Date). **Get Mark and bring him with you.** Evidently Mark lived somewhere along the route Timothy would take from Ephesus to Rome. The one who was the author of the Gospel of Mark (sometimes called John), cousin of Barnabas (Col. 4:10), and devoted fellow worker (Philem. 24), had once left Paul and Barnabas in shame (*see notes on Acts 13:13; 15:36-39*), but had become by this time a valued servant (see Introduction to Mark: Author and Date).

4:12 Tychicus. Paul had either sent him to Ephesus earlier, or he was sending him there to deliver this second letter to Timothy, just as Tychicus had previously delivered Paul's letters to the churches at Ephesus (Eph. 6:12), Colosse (Col. 4:7), and possibly to Titus (Titus 3:12; *see note on Col. 4:7*). **Ephesus.** See Introduction to Ephesians: Background and Setting; *see notes on Rev. 2:1.*

4:13 cloak. A large, heavy wool garment that doubled as a coat and blanket in cold weather, which Paul would soon face (v. 21). **Carpus.** An otherwise unknown acquaintance of Paul whose name means "fruit." **Troas.** A seaport of Phrygia, in Asia Minor. **the books, especially the parchments.** "Books" refers to papyrus scrolls, possibly OT books. "Parchments" were vellum sheets made of treated animal hides, thus they were extremely expensive. They may have been copies of letters he had written or blank sheets for writing other letters. That Paul did not have these already in his possession leads to the possible conclusion that he was arrested in Troas and had no opportunity to retrieve them.

4:14 Alexander the coppersmith. Probably not the same man whom Paul delivered to Satan along with Hymenaeus (1 Tim. 1:20), since Paul singles him out as the one who was a "coppersmith." This Alexander, however, may have been an idol maker (cf. Acts 19:24). **did me much harm.** Alexander opposed Paul's teaching and likely spread his own false doctrine. He may have been instrumental in Paul's arrest and may even have borne false witness against him. Cf. Acts 19:23ff. **May the Lord repay him.** Paul left vengeance in God's hands (Deut. 32:35; Rom. 12:19).

4:16 first defense. The Gr. word for "defense" gives us the Eng. words "apology" and "apologetics." It referred to a verbal defense used in a court of law. In the Roman legal system, an accused person received two hearings: the *prima actio,* much like a contemporary arraignment, established the charge and determined if there was a need for a trial. The *secunda actio* then established the accused's guilt or innocence. The defense Paul referred to was the *prima actio.* **May it not be charged against them.** Like Stephen (Acts 7:60) and the Lord Himself (Luke 23:24).

The Lord Is Faithful

17 [x]But the Lord stood with me and
strengthened me, [y]so that the message
might be preached fully through me, and
that all the Gentiles might hear. Also I was
delivered [z]out of the mouth of the lion.
18 [a]And the Lord will deliver me from
every evil work and preserve *me* for His
heavenly kingdom. [b]To Him *be* glory forever and ever. Amen!

Come Before Winter

19 Greet [c]Prisca and Aquila, and the
household of [d]Onesiphorus. 20 [e]Erastus
stayed in Corinth, but [f]Trophimus I have
left in Miletus sick.
21 Do your utmost to come before winter.
Eubulus greets you, as well as Pudens,
Linus, Claudia, and all the brethren.

Farewell

22 The Lord [3]Jesus Christ be with your
spirit. Grace be with you. Amen.

17 [x]Deut. 31:6; Acts 23:11 [y]Acts 9:15; Phil. 1:12 [z]1 Sam. 17:37; Ps. 22:21
18 [a]Ps. 121:7; [2 Pet. 2:9] [b]Rom. 11:36; Gal. 1:5; Heb. 13:21; 2 Pet. 3:18
19 [c]Acts 18:2; Rom. 16:3 [d]2 Tim. 1:16
20 [e]Acts 19:22; Rom. 16:23 [f]Acts 20:4; 21:29
22 [3]NU omits *Jesus Christ*

4:17 But the Lord stood with me. The Lord fulfills His promise never to "leave or forsake" His children (Deut. 31:6,8; Josh. 1:5; Heb. 13:5). **the message might be preached fully through me.** As he had done in the past (Acts 26:2-29), Paul was able to proclaim the gospel before a Roman tribunal. **all the Gentiles might hear.** By proclaiming the gospel to such a cosmopolitan, pagan audience, Paul could say that he had reached all the Gentiles with the gospel. This was a fulfillment of his commission (Acts 9:15,16; 26:15-18). **the mouth of the lion.** Cf. Dan. 6:26,27. A common figure for mortal danger (Pss. 22:21; 35:17) and a common occurrence for Paul (cf. Acts 14:19; 2 Cor. 4:8-12; 6:4-10; 11:23-27). Peter pictured Satan as a lion in 1 Pet. 5:8.

4:18 will deliver me from every evil work. On the basis of the Lord's present work—strengthening Paul and standing with him (v. 17)—Paul had hope for the Lord's future work. He knew God would deliver him from all temptations and plots against him (2 Cor. 1:8-10). **preserve *me* for His heavenly kingdom.** Paul knew the completion of his own salvation was nearer than when he first believed (cf. Rom. 13:11; 2 Cor. 5:8; Phil. 1:21).

4:19 Prisca and Aquila. Paul first met these two faithful friends in Corinth after they fled Italy (*see note on Acts 18:2*). They ministered for some time in Ephesus (Acts 18:18,19), later returned to Rome for a period of time (Rom. 16:3), and had returned to Ephesus. **the household of Onesiphorus.** *See note on 1:16.*

4:20 Erastus. Probably the city treasurer of Corinth, who sent greetings through Paul to the church at Rome (*see note on Rom. 16:23*). **Corinth.** The leading city in Greece (*see note on Acts 18:1*; see Introduction to 1 Corinthians: Title). **Trophimus.** A native of Asia, specifically Ephesus, who had accompanied Paul from Greece to Troas (*see note on Acts 20:4*). **Miletus.** A city and seaport in the province of Lycia, located 40 mi. S of Ephesus (*see note on Acts 20:15*).

4:21 before winter. In view of the coming season and the cold Roman jail cell, Paul needed the cloak for warmth. He would also have less opportunity to use the books and parchments as the duration of light grew shorter in winter. **Eubulus...Pudens, Linus, Claudia.** The first 3 names are Latin, which could indicate they were from Italy and had been members in the church at Rome. "Claudia" was a believer and close friend of whom nothing else is known.

4:22 Grace be with you. This is the same benediction as in Paul's previous letter to Timothy (*see note on 1 Tim. 6:21*). The "you" is plural, which means it extended to the entire Ephesian congregation.

The Epistle of Paul to
TITUS

Title

This epistle is named for its recipient, Titus, who is mentioned by name 13 times in the NT (1:4; Gal. 2:1,3; 2 Tim 4:10; for the 9 times in 2 Cor., see Background and Setting). The title in the Greek NT literally reads "To Titus." Along with 1, 2 Timothy, these letters to Paul's sons in the faith are traditionally called "The Pastoral Epistles."

Author and Date

Authorship by the Apostle Paul (1:1) is essentially uncontested (see Introduction to 1 Timothy). Titus was written between A.D. 62–64, while Paul ministered to Macedonian churches between his first and second Roman imprisonments, from either Corinth or Nicopolis (cf. 3:12). Most likely, Titus served with Paul on both the second and third missionary journeys. Titus, like Timothy (2 Tim. 1:2), had become a beloved disciple (1:4) and fellow worker in the gospel (2 Cor. 8:23). Paul's last mention of Titus (2 Tim. 4:10) reports that he had gone for ministry in Dalmatia—modern Yugoslavia. The letter probably was delivered by Zenas and Apollos (3:13).

Background and Setting

Although Luke did not mention Titus by name in the book of Acts, it seems probable that Titus, a Gentile (Gal. 2:3), met and may have been led to faith in Christ by Paul (1:4) before or during the apostle's first missionary journey. Later, Titus ministered for a period of time with Paul on the Island of Crete and was left behind to continue and strengthen the work (1:5). After Artemas or Tychicus (3:12) arrived to direct the ministry there, Paul wanted Titus to join him in the city of Nicopolis, in the province of Achaia in Greece, and stay through the winter (3:12).

Because of his involvement with the church at Corinth during Paul's third missionary journey, Titus is mentioned 9 times in 2 Corinthians (2:13; 7:6,13,14; 8:6,16,23; 12:18), where Paul refers to him as "my brother" (2:13) and "my partner and fellow worker" (8:23). The young elder was already familiar with Judaizers, false teachers in the church, who among other things insisted that all Christians, Gentile as well as Jew, were bound by the Mosaic law. Titus had accompanied Paul and Barnabas years earlier to the Council of Jerusalem where that heresy was the subject (Acts 15; Gal. 2:1-5).

Crete, one of the largest islands in the Mediterranean Sea, measuring 160 mi. long by 35 mi. at its widest, lying S of the Aegean Sea, had been briefly visited by Paul on his voyage to Rome (Acts 27:7-9,12,13,21). He returned there for ministry and later left Titus to continue the work, much as he left Timothy at Ephesus (1 Tim. 1:3), while he went on to Macedonia. He most likely wrote to Titus in response to a letter from Titus or a report from Crete.

Historical and Theological Themes

Like Paul's two letters to Timothy, the apostle gives personal encouragement and counsel to a young pastor who, though well-trained and faithful, faced continuing opposition from ungodly men within the churches where he ministered. Titus was to pass on that encouragement and counsel to the leaders he was to appoint in the Cretan churches (1:5).

In contrast to several of Paul's other letters, such as those to the churches in Rome and Galatia, the book of Titus does not focus on explaining or defending doctrine. Paul had full confidence in Titus' theological understanding and convictions, evidenced by the fact that he entrusted him with such a demanding ministry. Except for the warning about false teachers and Judaizers, the letter gives no theological correction, strongly suggesting that Paul also had confidence in the doctrinal grounding of most church members there, despite the fact that the majority of them were new believers. Doctrines that this epistle affirms include: 1) God's sovereign election of believers (1:1,2); 2) His saving grace (2:11; 3:5); 3) Christ's deity and second coming (2:13); 4) Christ's substitutionary atonement (2:14); and 5) the regeneration and renewing of believers by the Holy Spirit (3:5).

God and Christ are regularly referred to as Savior (1:3,4; 2:10,13; 3:4,6) and the saving plan is so emphasized in 2:11-14 that it indicates the major thrust of the epistle is that of equipping the churches of

Crete for effective evangelism. This preparation required godly leaders who not only would shepherd believers under their care (1:5-9), but also would equip those Christians for evangelizing their pagan neighbors, who had been characterized by one of their own famous natives as liars, evil beasts, and lazy gluttons (1:12). In order to gain a hearing for the gospel among such people, the believers' primary preparation for evangelization was to live among themselves with the unarguable testimony of righteous, loving, selfless, and godly lives (2:2-14) in marked contrast to the debauched lives of the false teachers (1:10-16). How they behaved with reference to governmental authorities and unbelievers was also crucial to their testimony (3:1-8).

Several major themes repeat themselves throughout Titus. They include: work(s) (1:16; 2:7,14; 3:1,5,8,14); soundness in faith and doctrine (1:4,9,13; 2:1,2,7,8,10; 3:15); and salvation (1:3,4; 2:10,13; 3:4,6).

Interpretive Challenges

The letter to Titus presents itself in a straightforward manner which should be taken at face value. The few interpretive challenges include: 1) Are the children of 1:6 merely "faithful" or are they "believing"? and 2) What is the "blessed hope" of 2:13?

Outline

- I. Salutation (1:1-4)
- II. Essentials for Effective Evangelism (1:5–3:11)
  - A. Among Leaders (1:5-16)
    - 1. Recognition of elders (1:5-9)
    - 2. Rebuke of false teachers (1:10-16)
  - B. In the Church (2:1-15)
    - 1. Holy living (2:1-10)
    - 2. Sound doctrine (2:11-15)
  - C. In the World (3:1-11)
    - 1. Holy living (3:1-4)
    - 2. Sound doctrine (3:5-11)
- III. Conclusion (3:12-14)
- IV. Benediction (3:15)

Greeting

1 Paul, a bondservant of God and an
apostle of Jesus Christ, according to
the faith of God's elect and [a]the acknowledgment of the truth [b]which accords with
godliness, **2** in hope of eternal life which
God, who [c]cannot lie, promised before
time began, **3** but has in due time manifested His word through preaching, which
was committed to me according to the
commandment of God our Savior;

4 To [d]Titus, a true son in *our* common
faith:

Grace, mercy, *and* peace from God the
Father and [1]the Lord Jesus Christ our
Savior.

Qualified Elders

5 For this reason I left you in Crete, that
you should [e]set in order the things that are
lacking, and appoint elders in every city as
I commanded you— **6** if a man is blameless, the husband of one wife, [f]having
faithful children not accused of [2]dissipa-
tion or insubordination. **7** For a [3]bishop
must be blameless, as a steward of God,
not self-willed, not quick-tempered, [g]not
given to wine, not violent, not greedy for

CHAPTER 1

1 [a] 2 Tim. 2:25 [b] [1 Tim. 3:16]
2 [c] Num. 23:19
4 [d] 2 Cor. 2:13; 8:23; Gal. 2:3; 2 Tim. 4:10

[1] NU *Christ Jesus*
5 [e] 1 Cor. 11:34
6 [f] 1 Tim. 3:2-4; Titus 1:6-8 [2] *debauchery,* lit. *incorrigibility*
7 [g] Lev. 10:9 [3] Lit. *overseer*

1:1-3 This salutation emphasizes the nature of Paul's service as an apostle of Jesus Christ. He proclaimed: 1) salvation: God's purpose to save the elect by the gospel; 2) sanctification: God's purpose to build up the saved by the Word of God; and 3) glorification: God's purpose to bring believers to eternal glory.

1:1 Paul. See Introduction: Title; Author and Date; Background and Setting. **bondservant.** Paul pictures himself as the most menial slave of NT times (*see notes on 2:9; 1 Cor. 4:1,2*), indicating his complete and willing servitude to the Lord, by whom all believers have been "bought at a price" (1 Cor. 6:20; cf. 1 Pet. 1:18,19). This the only time Paul referred to himself as a "bondservant of God" (cf. Rom. 1:1; Gal. 1:10; Phil. 1:1). He was placing himself alongside OT men of God (cf. Rev. 15:3). **apostle.** Cf. Rom. 1:1; 1 Cor. 1:1; 2 Cor. 1:1; Eph. 1:1. The word has the basic meaning of messenger or lit. "sent one" and, though often used of royal emissaries who ministered with the extended authority of their sovereign, Paul's exalted position as "an apostle" also was an extension of his bondservice to "God," which came with great authority, responsibility, and sacrifice. *See note on Acts 20:24.* **God's elect.** *See note on Eph. 1:4,5.* Those who have been graciously chosen for salvation "before the foundation of the world" (Eph. 1:4), but who must exercise personal faith prompted and empowered by the Holy Spirit. God's choice of believers always precedes and enables their choice of Him (cf. John 15:16; Acts 13:46-48; Rom. 9:15-21; 2 Thess. 2:13; 2 Tim. 1:8,9; 2:10; 1 Pet. 1:1,2). **the truth.** Paul had in mind gospel truth, the saving message of the death and resurrection of Jesus Christ (1 Tim. 2:3,4; 2 Tim. 2:25). It is that saving truth that leads to "godliness" or sanctification (see 2:11,12).

1:2 hope. This is divinely promised and divinely guaranteed to all believers, providing endurance and patience (cf. John 6:37-40; Rom. 8:18-23; 1 Cor. 15:51-58; Eph. 1:13,14; Phil. 3:8-11,20,21; 1 Thess. 4:13-18; 1 John 3:2,3). *See notes on 1 Pet. 1:3-9.* **cannot lie.** Cf. 1 Sam. 15:29; Heb. 6:18. Because God Himself is truth and the source of truth, it is impossible for Him to say anything untruthful (John 14:6,17; 15:26; cf. Num. 23:19; Ps. 146:6). **before time began.** God's plan of salvation for sinful mankind was determined and decreed before man was even created. The promise was made to God the Son (*see notes on John 6:37-44; Eph. 1:4,5; 2 Tim. 1:9*).

1:3 His word...preaching. God's Word is the sole source of content for all faithful preaching and teaching. Cf. 1 Cor. 1:18-21; 9:16,17; 2:1-4; Gal. 1:15,16; Col 1:25. **God our Savior.** Cf. 2:10; 3:4. The plan of salvation originated in eternity past with God.

1:4 true son. A spiritual son, a genuine believer in Christ, like Timothy (1 Tim. 1:2). **common faith.** This may refer to saving faith or to the content of the Christian faith, e.g., "The faith which was once for all delivered to the saints" (Jude 3). **our Savior.** Christ is called Savior each time He is mentioned after v. 1 (cf. 2:13; 3:6).

1:5-9 God's standards for all believers are high; His requirement for church leaders is to set that standard and model it. Such leaders are not qualified on the basis of natural ability, intelligence, or education but on the basis of moral and spiritual character and the ability to teach with skill as the Spirit sovereignly has equipped them.

1:5 Crete. See Introduction: Background and Setting. **set in order.** Titus was to correct wrong doctrine and practices in the Cretan churches, a task that Paul had been unable to complete. This ministry is mentioned nowhere else. **elders.** Cf. similar qualifications in 1 Tim. 3:1-7. Mature spiritual leaders of the church, also called bishops (v. 7; cf. 1 Tim. 3:2) or overseers (see 1 Pet. 2:25 where the same Gr. word is used of Christ), and pastors (lit. shepherds; see Eph. 4:11) were to care for each city's congregation. See also Acts 20:17,28; 1 Pet. 5:1,2. This ministry of appointing leaders is consistently Pauline (cf. Acts 14:23). **commanded you.** A reminder of past apostolic instructions.

1:6 blameless. This word does not refer to sinless perfection but to a personal life that is beyond legitimate accusation and public scandal. It is a general and primary requirement of spiritual leaders that is repeated (v. 7) and explained in the next verses (cf. 1 Tim. 3:2,10). **husband of one wife.** Lit. "a one-woman man," i.e., a husband who is consistently, both inwardly and outwardly, devoted and faithful to his wife (cf. 1 Tim. 3:2). An otherwise qualified single man is not necessarily disqualified. This is not speaking of divorce, but of internal and external purity in the sexual area. *See note on Prov. 6:32,33.* This necessity was motivation for Paul's commitment to control his body (1 Cor. 9:27). **faithful children.** "Faithful" is always used in the NT of believers and never for unbelievers, so this refers to children who have saving faith in Christ and reflect it in their conduct. Since 1 Tim. 3:4 requires children to be in submission, it may be directed at young children in the home, while this text looks at those who are older. **dissipation or insubordination.** "Dissipation" connotes debauchery, suggesting, again, that the reference is to grown children. "Insubordination" carries the idea of rebelliousness to the gospel. Here the elder shows his ability to lead his family to salvation and sanctification (see 1 Tim. 3:4,5), an essential prerequisite for leading the church.

1:7 bishop. This is not a hierarchial title, but a word meaning "overseer." Cf. Acts 20:28; Heb. 13:17; 1 Pet. 5:2. **steward.** The term refers to one who manages someone else's properties for the well-being of those his master cares for. In this context, one who manages spiritual truths, lives on God's behalf, and is wholly accountable to Him. The church is God's (Acts 20:28; 1 Tim. 3:15; 1 Pet. 5:2-4) and elders or bishops are accountable to him for the way they lead it (Heb. 13:17). **wine.** Applies to drinking any alcoholic beverage in any way that dulls the mind or subdues inhibitions (cf. Prov. 23:29-35; 31:4-7). By application, it also indicts any other substance, e.g., drugs, which would cloud the mind. **greedy.** Even in the early church, some men became pastors in order to gain wealth (see v. 11; 1 Pet. 5:3; cf. 2 Pet. 2:1-3).

money, 8 but hospitable, a lover of what is
good, sober-minded, just, holy, self-controlled, 9 holding fast the faithful word as
he has been taught, that he may be able, by
sound doctrine, both to exhort and convict
those who contradict.

The Elders' Task

10 For there are many insubordinate,
both idle [h]talkers and deceivers, especially
those of the circumcision, 11 whose mouths
must be stopped, who subvert whole
households, teaching things which they
ought not, [i]for the sake of dishonest gain.
12 [j]One of them, a prophet of their own,
said, "Cretans *are* always liars, evil beasts,
lazy gluttons." 13 This testimony is true.
[k]Therefore rebuke them sharply, that they
may be sound in the faith, 14 not giving
heed to Jewish fables and [l]commandments
of men who turn from the truth. 15 [m]To the
pure all things are pure, but to those who
are defiled and unbelieving nothing is
pure; but even their mind and conscience
are defiled. 16 They profess to [n]know God,
but [o]in works they deny Him, being
[4]abominable, disobedient, [p]and disqualified for every good work.

Qualities of a Sound Church

2 But as for you, speak the things which
are proper for sound doctrine: 2 that
the older men be sober, reverent, temperate, sound in faith, in love, in patience;
3 the older women likewise, that they be
reverent in behavior, not slanderers, not
given to much wine, teachers of good
things— 4 that they admonish the young
women to love their husbands, to love
their children, 5 to be discreet, chaste,
[a]homemakers, good, [b]obedient to their

10 [h] James 1:26
11 [i] 1 Tim. 6:5
12 [j] Acts 17:28
13 [k] 2 Cor. 13:10; 2 Tim. 4:2
14 [l] Is. 29:13
15 [m] Luke 11:41; Rom. 14:14, 20; 1 Cor. 6:12
16 [n] Matt. 7:20-23; 25:12; 1 John 2:4 [o] [2 Tim. 3:5, 7] [p] Rom. 1:28 [4] *detestable*

CHAPTER 2

5 [a] 1 Tim. 5:14 [b] 1 Cor. 14:34; 1 Tim. 2:11

1:8 hospitable. The word actually means "a lover of strangers." **sober-minded.** Serious, with the right priorities, sensible.

1:9 faithful word. Sound biblical doctrine not only should be taught but also adhered to with deep conviction. Cf. 1 Tim. 4:6; 5:17; 2 Tim. 2:15; 3:16,17; 4:2-4. **exhort and convict.** The faithful teaching and defending of Scripture which encourages godliness and confronts sin and error (those who contradict). *See notes on vv. 10-16; 3:10,11; Acts 20:29,30.*

1:10-16 The false teachers in the Cretan churches were much like those with whom Timothy had to deal in Ephesus (see 1 Tim. 1:3-7; cf. Rom. 16:17,18; 2 Pet. 2:1-3).

1:10 insubordinate. Because those men were so numerous, Titus' job was especially difficult, which made the appointment of additional godly elders (v. 5) all the more crucial. Some of the false teachers may have opposed even Paul's apostolic authority during his brief ministry on Crete. **deceivers.** Cf. Jer. 14:14; 23:2,21,32. **the circumcision.** Cf. Acts 10:45; 11:2. These were Jews who taught that salvation required the physical cutting of circumcision (*see note on Gen. 17:9-14*) and adherence to Mosaic ceremonies. *See notes on Acts 15:1-12; Gal. 3:1-12; Eph. 2:11; Col. 2:12.*

1:11 whole households. Cf. 2 Tim. 3:6. **dishonest gain.** False teachers are always in it for the money (1 Tim. 6:4; 1 Pet. 5:2).

1:12 a prophet. Epimenides, the highly esteemed sixth century B.C. Greek poet and native of Crete, had characterized his own people as the dregs of Greek culture. Elsewhere, Paul also quoted pagan sayings (cf. Acts 17:28; 1 Cor. 15:33). This quote is directed at the false teachers' character.

1:13 sound in the faith. True and pure doctrine was to be required of all who spoke to the church. Any who fell short of that were to be rebuked.

1:14 fables and commandments of men. Paul reemphasized (see v. 10, "those of the circumcision") that most of the false teachers were Jewish. They taught the same kind of externalism and unscriptural laws and traditions that both Isaiah and Jesus railed against (Is. 29:13; Matt. 15:1-9; Mark 7:5-13).

1:15,16 False teachers are corrupt on the inside ("mind and conscience") and the outside ("works" and "disobedient"). Cf. Matt. 7:15,16.

1:15 defiled. The outwardly despicable things that those men practiced (vv. 10-12) were simply reflections of their inner corruption. *See notes on Matt. 15:15-20.* **mind and conscience.** If the mind is defiled, it cannot accurately inform the conscience, so conscience cannot warn the person. When conscience is accurately and fully infused with God's truth, it functions as the warning system God designed. *See notes on 2 Cor. 1:12; 4:2; 1 Tim. 1:19,20.*

1:16 profess...deny. Some of the false teachers in the church were not believers at all. Eventually, even the seemingly noble "works" of unbelievers will betray them. **disqualified.** They can do nothing that pleases God. *See note on 1 Cor. 9:27;* cf. 2 Tim. 3:8.

2:1-10 Sound doctrine for older men (v. 2), older women (v. 3), younger women (vv. 4,5), young men (vv. 6-8), and bond servants (vv. 9,10) reflects the duty of everyone in the church.

2:1 sound. Meaning healthy—Paul uses this word 9 times in the pastoral epistles (5 times in Titus), always in the sense that the truth produces spiritual well-being. The "things" Paul mentions in vv. 2-10 pertain to truths, attitudes, and actions that correspond to and are based on biblical truth. In order not only to please God, but also to have an effective witness to unbelievers, God's people must know the truth that leads to spiritual health.

2:2 older men. Paul used this term for himself (Philem. 9) when he was over 60. It refers to those of advanced age, using a different term from the one translated "elder" in 1:5. **reverent.** This requirement is not limited to reverence for God, which is assumed, but also refers to being honorable and dignified. They are to be sensible and spiritually healthy.

2:3 older women. Those who no longer had child-rearing responsibilities, typically around age 60 (cf. 1 Tim. 5:3-10). **reverent.** *See note on v. 2.* Cf. 1 Tim. 2:9-11,15. **not slanderers.** A term used 34 times in the NT to describe Satan, the arch-slanderer. **good things.** Those that please God (cf. 1:16), particularly the lessons in vv. 4,5.

2:4 admonish the young women. Their own examples of godliness (v. 3) give older women the right and the credibility to instruct younger women in the church. The obvious implication is that older women must exemplify the virtues (vv. 4,5) that they "admonish." **love their husbands.** Like the other virtues mentioned here, this one is unconditional. It is based on God's will, not on a husband's worthiness. The Gr. word *phileō* emphasizes affection. *See notes on Eph. 5:22-24.*

2:5 discreet. I.e., pure. Cf. 1 Tim. 2:9-11,15; 1 Pet. 3:3-6. **homemakers.** Cf. 1 Tim. 5:14. Keeping a godly home with excellence for one's husband and children is the Christian woman's non-negotiable responsibility. **obedient.** The ideas of radical feminism were an inte-

own husbands, [c]that the word of God may
not be blasphemed.
6 Likewise, exhort the young men to be
sober-minded, 7 in all things showing
yourself *to be* [d]a pattern of good works; in
doctrine *showing* integrity, reverence, [e]in-
corruptibility,[1] 8 sound speech that cannot
be condemned, that one who is an opponent may be ashamed, having nothing evil
to say of [2]you.
9 *Exhort* [f]bondservants to be obedient to
their own masters, to be well pleasing in
all *things,* not answering back, 10 not [3]pil-
fering, but showing all good [4]fidelity, that
they may adorn the doctrine of God our
Savior in all things.

5 [c]Rom. 2:24
7 [d]Phil. 3:17; 1 Tim. 4:12 [e]Eph. 6:24
[1]NU omits *incorruptibility*
8 [2]NU, M *us*
9 [f]Eph. 6:5; 1 Tim. 6:1
10 [3]*thieving* [4]*honesty*
11 [g][Rom. 5:15]
13 [h]1 Cor. 1:7 [i][Col. 3:4]
14 [j]Is. 53:12; Gal. 1:4 [k]Ezek. 37:23; [Heb. 1:3; 9:14; 1 John 1:7] [l]Ex. 15:16
15 [m]1 Tim. 4:13; 5:20; 2 Tim. 4:2

Trained by Saving Grace

11 For [g]the grace of God that brings salvation has appeared to all men, 12 teaching us that, denying ungodliness and
worldly lusts, we should live soberly,
righteously, and godly in the present age,
13 [h]looking for the blessed [i]hope and glorious appearing of our great God and Savior Jesus Christ, 14 [j]who gave Himself for
us, that He might redeem us from every
lawless deed [k]and purify for Himself [l]*His*
own special people, zealous for good
works.
15 Speak these things, [m]exhort, and rebuke with all authority. Let no one despise
you.

gral part of ancient Babylonian and Assyrian mythology as well as of Greek gnosticism, which flourished throughout the Roman Empire during NT times and posed a constant danger to the early church. Modern feminism is neither new nor progressive; it is age-old and regressive. *See notes on Eph. 5:22.* **not be blasphemed.** This is the purpose of godly conduct—to eliminate any reproach on Scripture. For a person to be convinced God can save from sin, one needs to see someone who lives a holy life. When Christians claim to believe God's Word but do not obey it, the Word is dishonored. Many have mocked God and His truth because of the sinful behavior of those who claim to be Christians. Cf. Matt. 5:16; 1 Pet. 2:9.

2:6 young men. Males, 12 and older.

2:6,7 sober-minded. Sensible (see v. 2).

2:7 in all things. This rightly goes at the end of v. 6, qualifying young men and emphasizing the comprehensiveness of this admonition. **pattern.** Titus had a special obligation to exemplify the moral and spiritual qualities about which he was to admonish others. Cf. 1 Cor. 4:16; 11:1; Phil. 3:17; 2 Thess. 3:8,9; 1 Tim. 4:12; Heb. 13:7. **in doctrine.** All 3 terms—"integrity," "reverence," and "incorruptibility"—qualify the appropriate commitment to doctrine.

2:8 sound speech. Daily conversation. Cf. Eph. 4:31; Col. 3:16,17; 4:6. **cannot be condemned.** Beyond reproach. **nothing evil to say.** Again, as in v. 5, the purpose of godly living is to silence the opponents of Christianity and the gospel (*see notes on 1 Pet. 2:11,12*), and make the power of Christ believable.

2:9 bondservants. The term applies generally to all employees, but direct reference is to slaves—men, women, and children who, in the Roman Empire and in much of the ancient world, were owned by their masters. They had few, if any, civil rights and often were accorded little more dignity or care than domestic animals. The NT nowhere condones or condemns the practice of slavery, but it everywhere teaches that freedom from the bondage of sin is infinitely more important than freedom from any human bondage a person may have to endure (see Rom. 6:22). **obedient...well pleasing.** Paul clearly teaches that, even in the most servile of circumstances, believers are "to be obedient" and seek to please those for whom they work, whether their "masters" are believers or unbelievers, fair or unfair, kind or cruel. How much more obligated are believers to respect and obey employers for whom they work voluntarily! As with wives' obedience to their husbands (v. 5), the only exception would involve a believer's being required to disobey God's Word. Cf. Eph. 6:5-9; Col. 3:22–4:1; 1 Tim. 6:1,2.

2:10 not pilfering. A term used to refer to embezzlement. **all good fidelity.** Loyalty. **adorn the doctrine.** Again (cf. v. 5), Paul stresses that the supreme purpose of a virtuous life is to make attractive the teaching that God saves sinners.

2:11-13 This is the heart of the letter, emphasizing that God's sovereign purpose in calling out elders (1:5) and in commanding His people to live righteously (vv. 1-10) is to provide the witness that brings God's plan and purpose of salvation to fulfillment. Paul condensed the saving plan of God into 3 realities: 1) salvation from the penalty (v. 11); 2) the power (v. 12); and 3) the presence (v. 13) of sin.

2:11 grace of God. Not simply the divine attribute of grace, but Jesus Christ Himself, grace incarnate, God's supremely gracious gift to fallen mankind. Cf. John 1:14. **all men.** This does not teach universal salvation. "All men" is used as "man" in 3:4, to refer to humanity in general, as a category, not to every individual. *See notes on 2 Cor. 5:19; 2 Pet. 3:9.* Jesus Christ made a sufficient sacrifice to cover every sin of every one who believes (John 3:16-18; 1 Tim. 2:5,6; 4:10; 1 John 2:2). Paul makes clear in the opening words of this letter to Titus that salvation becomes effective only through "the faith of God's elect" (1:1). *See note on 3:2.* Out of all humanity, only those who believe will be saved (John 1:12; 3:16; 5:24,38,40; 6:40; 10:9; Rom. 10:9-17).

2:12 denying...live. Salvation is transforming (2 Cor. 5:17; Eph. 2:8-10), and transformation (new birth) produces a new life in which the power of sin has been broken (*see notes on Rom 6:4-14; Phil. 3:8,9; Col. 3:9,10*).

2:13 blessed hope. A general reference to the second coming of Jesus Christ, including the resurrection (cf. Rom. 8:22,23; 1 Cor. 15:51-58; Phil. 3:20,21; 1 Thess. 4:13-18; 1 John 3:2,3) and the reign of the saints with Christ in glory (2 Tim. 2:10). **glorious appearing.** Cf. 2 Tim. 1:10. Lit. "the appearing of the glory." This will be our salvation from the presence of sin. **God and Savior.** A clear reference to the deity of Jesus. Cf. 2 Pet. 1:1.

2:14 redeem...purify. Another expression (cf. v. 12) summarizes the dual effect of salvation (regeneration and sanctification). To "redeem" is to release someone held captive, on the payment of a ransom. The price was Christ's blood paid to satisfy God's justice. *See notes on Acts 20:28; Gal. 1:4; 2:20; 1 Pet. 1:18,19;* cf. Mark 10:45. **special people.** People who are special by virtue of God's decree and confirmed by the grace of salvation which they have embraced (*see notes on 1:1-4*). Cf. 1 Cor. 6:19,20; 1 Pet. 2:9. **zealous.** Cf. 3:8. Good works are the product, not the means, of salvation. Cf. Eph. 2:10.

2:15 Speak...exhort...rebuke. These 3 verbs identify the need for proclamation, application, and correction by the Word. **authority.** "Authority" to command people in the spiritual realm comes only from God's Word. Cf. Matt. 7:28,29.

2:15 Let no one despise you. See 3:9-11. Rebellion against the truth has to be dealt with. Cf. Matt. 18:15-20; 1 Cor. 5:9-13; 2 Thess. 3:14,15.

Graces of the Heirs of Grace

3 Remind them [a]to be subject to rulers
and authorities, to obey, [b]to be ready
for every good work, 2 to speak evil of no
one, to be peaceable, gentle, showing all
humility to all men. 3 For [c]we ourselves
were also once foolish, disobedient, deceived, serving various lusts and pleasures, living in malice and envy, hateful
and hating one another. 4 But when [d]the
kindness and the love of [e]God our Savior
toward man appeared, 5 [f]not by works of
righteousness which we have done, but according to His mercy He saved us, through
[g]the washing of regeneration and renewing of the Holy Spirit, 6 [h]whom He poured
out on us abundantly through Jesus Christ
our Savior, 7 that having been justified by
His grace [i]we should become heirs according to the hope of eternal life.

CHAPTER 3

1 [a] [Rom. 13:1]; 1 Pet. 2:13 [b] Col. 1:10
3 [c] 1 Cor. 6:11; 1 Pet. 4:3
4 [d] Titus 2:11 [e] 1 Tim. 2:3
5 [f] [Rom. 3:20]; Eph. 2:4-9 [g] John 3:3
6 [h] Ezek. 36:26
7 [i] [Matt. 25:34]; Mark 10:17; [Rom. 8:17, 23, 24; Titus 1:2]
8 [j] 1 Tim. 1:15
9 [k] 1 Tim. 1:4; 2 Tim. 2:23
10 [l] Matt. 18:17
[1] warning
12 [m] Acts 20:4; Eph. 6:21; Col. 4:7; 2 Tim. 4:12
13 [n] Acts 18:24; 1 Cor. 16:12

8 [j]This is a faithful saying, and these
things I want you to affirm constantly, that
those who have believed in God should be
careful to maintain good works. These
things are good and profitable to men.

Avoid Dissension

9 But [k]avoid foolish disputes, genealogies, contentions, and strivings about the
law; for they are unprofitable and useless.
10 [l]Reject a divisive man after the first and
second [1]admonition, 11 knowing that such
a person is warped and sinning, being self-
condemned.

Final Messages

12 When I send Artemas to you, or
[m]Tychicus, be diligent to come to me at Nicopolis, for I have decided to spend the
winter there. 13 Send Zenas the lawyer and
[n]Apollos on their journey with haste, that

3:1-11 In his closing remarks, Paul admonished Titus to remind believers under his care of their attitudes toward: 1) the unsaved rulers (v. 1) and people in general (v. 2); 2) their previous state as unbelievers lost in sin (v. 3); 3) of their gracious salvation through Jesus Christ (vv. 4-7); 4) of their righteous testimony to the unsaved world (v. 8); 5) and of their responsibility to oppose false teachers and factious members within the church (vv. 9-11). All of these matters are essential to effective evangelism.

3:1 subject. Submission to the authority of Scripture demands submission to human authorities as part of a Christian's testimony (*see notes on Rom. 13:1-7; 1 Pet. 2:12-17*).

3:2 all men. Christians are to exemplify these godly virtues in their dealings with everyone. The admonition applies especially to dealings with unbelievers. The use of this phrase here to refer to mankind in general (particularly those who cross our paths), rather than every person who lives, supports the fact that it has the same meaning in 2:11.

3:3 ourselves. It is not that every believer has committed every sin listed here, but rather that before salvation every life is characterized by such sins. That sobering truth should make believers humble in dealing with the unsaved, even those who are grossly immoral and ungodly. If it weren't for God's grace to His own, they would all be wicked. *See note on 1 Pet. 3:15*; cf. 2 Tim. 2:25. For other lists of sins, see Rom. 1:18-32; 1 Cor. 6:9,10; Gal. 5:19-21; Eph. 4:17-19.

3:4 kindness...appeared. As in 2:11, Paul is speaking of Jesus Christ, who was kindness and love incarnate, appearing in human form. Cf. Eph. 2:4-6.

3:5 not by works. Salvation has never been by works (*see notes on Eph. 2:8,9*; cf. Rom. 3:19-28.) **according to His mercy.** Cf. Eph. 2:4; 1 Tim. 1:13; 1 Pet. 1:3; 2:10. **washing of regeneration.** *See notes on Ezek. 36:25-29; Eph. 5:26; James 1:18; 1 Pet. 1:23.* Salvation brings divine cleansing from sin and the gift of a new, Spirit-generated, Spirit-empowered, and Spirit-protected life as God's own children and heirs (v. 7). This is the new birth (cf. John 3:5; 1 John 2:29; 3:9; 4:7; 5:1). **renewing of the Holy Spirit.** Cf. Rom. 8:2. He is the agent of the "working of regeneration."

3:6 abundantly. When believers are saved, Christ's Spirit blesses them beyond measure (cf. Acts 2:38,39; 1 Cor. 12:7,11,13; Eph. 3:20; 5:18).

3:7 justified. The central truth of salvation is justification by faith alone. When a sinner repents and places his faith in Jesus Christ, God declares him just, imputes the righteousness of Christ to him, and gives him eternal life by virtue of the substitutionary death of Christ as the penalty for that sinner's iniquity. *See notes on Rom. 3:21–5:21; Gal. 3:6-22; Phil. 3:8,9.* **heirs.** As adopted children of God through faith in Jesus Christ, believers become "heirs of God and joint heirs with Christ" (Rom. 8:17; cf. 1 Pet. 1:3,4).

3:8 faithful saying. A common expression in the early church, used 5 times in the pastoral epistles (cf. 1 Tim. 1:15; 3:1; 4:9; 2 Tim. 2:11). **profitable to men.** That is, for the sake of evangelism. Again "men" (cf. v. 2; 2:11) is general, referring to those who respond by the holy witness to the gospel.

3:9 foolish disputes. Paul again warns against becoming embroiled in senseless discussions with the many false teachers on Crete (see 1:10,14-16), especially the Judaizers who contended that a Christian must be obedient to "the (Mosaic) law," a view that assaulted the doctrine of justification by grace through faith alone and, contrary to holy living, which was good and profitable, was "unprofitable and useless." Proclaiming the truth, not arguing error, is the biblical way to evangelize.

3:10 Reject. Anyone in the church who is unsubmissive, self-willed, and divisive should be expelled. Two warnings are to be given, following the basic pattern for church discipline set forth by Christ (*see notes on Matt. 18:15-17*; cf. Rom. 16:17,18; 2 Thess. 3:14,15).

3:11 self-condemned. By his own ungodly behavior, a factious believer brings judgment on himself.

3:12-14 Paul gives Titus special instructions and a warning about a particularly dangerous opponent of Paul's.

3:12 Artemis. Nothing is known of this man beyond Paul's obvious confidence in him. **Tychicus.** This "beloved brother [and] faithful minister" (Col. 4:7) accompanied Paul from Corinth to Asia Minor (Acts 20:4), carried the apostle's letter to the Colossian church (Col. 4:7), and possibly his letter to Ephesus (see Eph. 6:21). **Nicopolis.** The name means "city of victory," and this was but one of perhaps 9 different cities so named because of decisive military battles that were won in or near them. This particular Nicopolis was probably in southern Greece, on the W coast of Achaia, which was a good place "to spend the winter."

3:13 Zenas. Nothing is known of this believer whose expertise was either in biblical law or Roman law. **Apollos.** Originally from Alexandria, he was an outstanding teacher of Scripture who was converted to Christ after being acquainted only with the teaching of John the Baptist (Acts 18:24-28). Some of his followers apparently formed a faction in the church at Corinth (1 Cor. 1:11,12; 3:4).

they may lack nothing. 14 And let our *peo-*
ple also learn to maintain good works, to
meet urgent needs, that they may not be
unfruitful.

Farewell

15 All who *are* with me greet you. Greet
those who love us in the faith.
Grace *be* with you all. Amen.

3:14 good works. Again the emphasis is on good works as the platform for witnessing effectively (cf. v. 8; 1:13-16; 2:5,8,10,12,14).

3:15 All who *are* with me. Cf. 1 Cor. 16:20; 2 Cor. 13:12; Phil. 4:22; cf. also Rom. 16:21-23; Col. 4:10-14, where those with Paul are mentioned by name.

The Epistle of Paul to

PHILEMON

Title

Philemon, the recipient of this letter, was a prominent member of the church at Colosse (vv. 1,2; cf. Col. 4:9), which met in his house (v. 2). The letter was for him, his family, and the church.

Author and Date

The book claims that the Apostle Paul was its writer (vv. 1,9,19), a claim that few in the history of the church have disputed, especially since there is nothing in Philemon that a forger would have been motivated to write. It is one of the Prison Epistles, along with Ephesians, Philippians, and Colossians. Its close connection with Colossians, which Paul wrote at the same time (ca. A.D. 60–62; cf. vv. 1,16), brought early and unquestioned vindication of Paul's authorship by the early church fathers (e.g., Jerome, Chrysostom, and Theodore of Mopsuestia). The earliest of NT canons, the Muratorian (ca. A.D. 170), includes Philemon. For biographical information on Paul, see Introduction to Romans: Author and Date; for the date and place of Philemon's writing, see Introductions to Ephesians and Philippians: Author and Date.

Background and Setting

Philemon had been saved under Paul's ministry, probably at Ephesus (v. 19), several years earlier. Wealthy enough to have a large house (cf. v. 2), Philemon also owned at least one slave, a man named Onesimus (lit."useful"; a common name for slaves). Onesimus was not a believer at the time he stole some money (v. 18) from Philemon and ran away. Like countless thousands of other runaway slaves, Onesimus fled to Rome, seeking to lose himself in the Imperial capital's teeming and nondescript slave population. Through circumstances not recorded in Scripture, Onesimus met Paul in Rome and became a Christian.

The apostle quickly grew to love the runaway slave (vv. 12,16) and longed to keep Onesimus in Rome (v. 13), where he was providing valuable service to Paul in his imprisonment (v. 11). But by stealing and running away from Philemon, Onesimus had both broken Roman law and defrauded his master. Paul knew those issues had to be dealt with, and decided to send Onesimus back to Colosse. It was too hazardous for him to make the trip alone (because of the danger of slave-catchers), so Paul sent him back with Tychicus, who was returning to Colosse with the epistle to the Colossians (Col. 4:7-9). Along with Onesimus, Paul sent Philemon this beautiful personal letter, urging him to forgive Onesimus and welcome him back to service as a brother in Christ (vv. 15-17).

Historical and Theological Themes

Philemon provides valuable historical insights into the early church's relationship to the institution of slavery. Slavery was widespread in the Roman Empire (according to some estimates, slaves constituted one third, perhaps more, of the population) and an accepted part of life. In Paul's day, slavery had virtually eclipsed free labor. Slaves could be doctors, musicians, teachers, artists, librarians, or accountants; in short, almost all jobs could be and were filled by slaves.

Slaves were not legally considered persons, but were the tools of their masters. As such, they could be bought, sold, inherited, exchanged, or seized to pay their master's debt. Their masters had virtually unlimited power to punish them, and sometimes did so severely for the slightest infractions. By the time of the NT, however, slavery was beginning to change. Realizing that contented slaves were more productive, masters tended to treat them more leniently. It was not uncommon for a master to teach a slave his own trade, and some masters and slaves became close friends. While still not recognizing them as persons under the law, the Roman Senate in A.D. 20 granted slaves accused of crimes the right to a trial. It also became more common for slaves to be granted (or to purchase) their freedom. Some slaves enjoyed very favorable and profitable service under their masters and were better off than many freemen because they were assured of care and provision. Many freemen struggled in poverty.

The NT nowhere directly attacks slavery; had it done so, the resulting slave insurrections would have been brutally suppressed and the message of the gospel hopelessly confused with that of social reform. Instead, Christianity undermined the evils of slavery by changing the hearts of slaves and masters. By stressing the spiritual equality of master and slave (v. 16; Gal. 3:28; Eph. 6:9; Col. 4:1; 1 Tim. 6:1,2), the Bible did away with slavery's abuses. The rich theological theme that alone dominates the letter is forgiveness, a featured theme throughout NT Scripture (cf. Matt. 6:12-15; 18:21-35; Eph. 4:32; Col. 3:13). Paul's instruction here provides the biblical definition of forgiveness, without ever using the word.

Interpretive Challenges

There are no significant interpretive challenges in this personal letter from Paul to his friend Philemon.

Outline

I. Greeting (1-3)

II. The Character of One Who Forgives (4-7)

III. The Actions of One Who Forgives (8-18)

IV. The Motives of One Who Forgives (19-25)

Greeting

Paul, a [a]prisoner of Christ Jesus, and
Timothy *our* brother,

To Philemon our beloved *friend* and fellow laborer, 2 to [1]the beloved Apphia, [b]Ar-
chippus our fellow soldier, and to the
church in your house:

3 Grace to you and peace from God our
Father and the Lord Jesus Christ.

Philemon's Love and Faith

4 [c]I thank my God, making mention of
you always in my prayers, 5 [d]hearing of
your love and faith which you have toward the Lord Jesus and toward all the
saints, 6 that the sharing of your faith may
become effective [e]by the acknowledgment
of [f]every good thing which is in [2]you in
Christ Jesus. 7 For we [3]have great [4]joy and
[5]consolation in your love, because the
[6]hearts of the saints have been refreshed
by you, brother.

1 [a] Eph. 3:1
2 [b] Col. 4:17 [1] NU *our sister Apphia*
4 [c] Eph. 1:16; 1 Thess. 1:2; 2 Thess. 1:3
5 [d] Eph. 1:15; Col. 1:4; 1 Thess. 3:6
6 [e] Phil. 1:9; [Col. 1:9; 3:10; James 2:14-17] [f] [1 Thess. 5:18] [2] NU, M *us*
7 [3] NU *had* [4] M *thanksgiving* [5] *comfort* [6] Lit. *inward parts,* heart, liver, and lungs
10 [g] Col. 4:9
12 [7] NU *back to you in person, that is, my own heart,* [8] See v. 7.
14 [h] 2 Cor. 9:7; 1 Pet. 5:2
16 [i] Eph. 6:5; Col. 3:22

The Plea for Onesimus

8 Therefore, though I might be very bold
in Christ to command you what is fitting,
9 *yet* for love's sake I rather appeal *to you*—
being such a one as Paul, the aged, and
now also a prisoner of Jesus Christ— 10 I
appeal to you for my son [g]Onesimus,
whom I have begotten *while* in my chains,
11 who once was unprofitable to you, but
now is profitable to you and to me.
12 I am sending him [7]back. You therefore
receive him, that is, my own [8]heart,
13 whom I wished to keep with me, that on
your behalf he might minister to me in my
chains for the gospel. 14 But without your
consent I wanted to do nothing, [h]that your
good deed might not be by compulsion, as
it were, but voluntary.
15 For perhaps he departed for a while
for this *purpose,* that you might receive him
forever, 16 no longer as a slave but more
than a slave—a beloved brother, especially
to me but how much more to you, both in
the [i]flesh and in the Lord.

1,2 Following first century custom, the salutation contains the names of the letter's author and its recipient. This is a very personal letter and Philemon was one of only 3 individuals (Timothy and Titus are the others) to receive a divinely inspired letter from Paul.

1 prisoner of Christ Jesus. At the time of writing, Paul was a prisoner in Rome (see Introductions to Ephesians and Philippians: Author and Date). Paul was imprisoned for the sake of and by the sovereign will of Christ (cf. Eph. 3:1; 4:1; 6:19,20; Phil. 1:13; Col. 4:3). By beginning with his imprisonment and not his apostolic authority, Paul made this letter a gentle and singular appeal to a friend. A reminder of Paul's severe hardships was bound to influence Philemon's willingness to do the comparatively easy task Paul was about to request. **Timothy.** See Introduction to 1 Timothy: Background and Setting; *see notes on Acts 16:1-3; 1 Tim. 1:2; Phil. 1:1.* He was not the co-author of this letter, but probably had met Philemon at Ephesus and was with Paul when the apostle wrote the letter. Paul mentions Timothy here and in the other epistles (e.g., 2 Cor. 1:1; Phil. 1:1; Col. 1:1; 1 Thess. 1:1; 2 Thess. 1:1) because he wanted him recognized as a leader and the non-apostolic heir apparent to Paul. **Philemon.** A wealthy member of the Colossian church which met in his house (see Introduction: Background and Setting). Church buildings were unknown until the third century.

2 Apphia, Archippus. Philemon's wife and son, respectively. **in your house.** First century churches met in homes, and Paul wanted this personal letter read in the church that met at Philemon's. This reading would hold Philemon accountable, as well as instruct the church on the matter of forgiveness.

3 Grace to you. The standard greeting that appears in all 13 of Paul's NT letters. It highlighted salvation's means (grace) and its results (peace) and linked the Father and Son, thus affirming the deity of Christ.

5 In the Gr. text, this verse is arranged in what is called a chiastic construction. "Love" relates to the final phrase "toward all the saints." This love of will, choice, self-sacrifice, and humility (Gal. 5:22) was a manifestation of Philemon's genuine faith "toward the Lord Jesus" (cf. Rom. 5:5; Gal. 5:6; 1 John 3:14).

6 sharing. Usually rendered "fellowship," the Gr. word means much more than simply enjoying one another's company. It refers to a mutual sharing of all life, which believers do because of their common life in Christ and mutual partnership or "belonging to each other" in the "faith." **effective.** Lit. "powerful." Paul wanted Philemon's actions to send a powerful message to the church about the importance of forgiveness. **acknowledgment.** The deep, rich, full, experiential knowledge of the truth (*see notes on Col. 1:9; 3:10*).

7 hearts. This Gr. word denotes the seat of human feelings (*see note on Col. 3:12* where the same Gr. word is translated "tender mercies"). **refreshed.** This comes from the Gr. military term that describes an army at rest from a march.

8 bold...to command. Because of his apostolic authority (*see notes on Rom. 1:1; 1 Thess. 2:6*), Paul could have ordered Philemon to accept Onesimus.

9 I rather appeal. In this situation, however, Paul did not rely on his authority but called for a response based on the bond of love between himself and Philemon (v. 7; cf. 1 Cor. 10:1). **the aged.** More than a reference to his chronological age (which at the time of this letter was about 60), this description includes the toll that all the years of persecution, illnesses, imprisonments, difficult journeys, and constant concern for the churches had taken on Paul (*see notes on 2 Cor. 11:23-30*), making him feel and appear even older than he actually was. **prisoner.** *See note on v. 1.*

10 my son Onesimus. See Introduction: Background and Setting. To Paul, he was a son in the faith (*see note on 1 Tim. 1:2*). **begotten...in my chains.** While in prison at Rome, Paul had led him to faith in Christ.

11 unprofitable...profitable. Better translated "useless...useful," this is the same Gr. root word from which "Onesimus" comes. Paul was making a play on words that basically said, "Useful formerly was useless, but now is useful"—Paul's point is that Onesimus had been radically transformed by God's grace.

14 voluntary. Or "of your own personal will." Paul wanted Onesimus to minister alongside him, but only if Philemon openly and gladly agreed to release him.

15 perhaps. Paul was suggesting that God providentially ordered the overturning of the evil of Onesimus' running away to produce eventual good (cf. Gen. 50:20; Rom. 8:28).

16 more than a slave...beloved brother. Paul did not call for Onesimus' freedom (cf. 1 Cor. 7:20-22), but that Philemon would

Philemon's Obedience Encouraged

17 If then you count me as a partner, receive him as *you would* me. 18 But if he has
wronged you or owes anything, put that
on my account. 19 I, Paul, am writing with
my own [j]hand. I will repay—not to mention to you that you owe me even your
own self besides. 20 Yes, brother, let me
have joy from you in the Lord; refresh my
heart in the Lord.
21 [k]Having confidence in your obedience, I write to you, knowing that you will
do even more than I say. 22 But, meanwhile, also prepare a guest room for me,
for [l]I trust that [m]through your prayers I
shall be granted to you.

Farewell

23 [n]Epaphras, my fellow prisoner in
Christ Jesus, greets you, 24 *as do* [o]Mark,
[p]Aristarchus, [q]Demas, [r]Luke, my fellow
laborers.
25 [s]The grace of our Lord Jesus Christ *be*
with your spirit. Amen.

19 [j] 1 Cor. 16:21; Gal. 6:11; 2 Thess. 3:17
21 [k] 2 Cor. 7:16
22 [l] Phil. 1:25; 2:24 [m] 2 Cor. 1:11
23 [n] Col. 1:7; 4:12
24 [o] Acts 12:12, 25; 15:37-39; Col. 4:10 [p] Acts 19:29; 27:2; Col. 4:10 [q] Col. 4:14; 2 Tim. 4:10 [r] 2 Tim. 4:11
25 [s] 2 Tim. 4:22

receive his slave now as a fellow-believer in Christ (cf. Eph. 6:9; Col. 4:1; 1 Tim. 6:2). Christianity never sought to abolish slavery, but rather to make the relationships within it just and kind. **in the flesh.** In this physical life (*see note on Phil. 1:22*), as they worked together. **in the Lord.** The master and slave were to enjoy spiritual oneness and fellowship as they worshiped and ministered together.

17-19 Paul offered to pay whatever restitution was necessary for Onesimus to be reconciled to Philemon, following the example of Jesus in reconciling sinners to God.

19 with my own hand. *See notes on Gal. 6:11; Col. 4:18*; cf. 2 Thess. 3:17. **even your own self.** Philemon owed Paul something far greater than the material debt Paul was offering to repay, since Paul had led him to saving faith, a debt Philemon could never repay.

20 let me have joy. *See note on Phil. 2:2.* By forgiving Onesimus, Philemon would keep the unity in the church at Colosse and bring joy to the chained apostle (cf. v. 7).

21 even more than I say. The more than forgiveness that Paul was urging upon Philemon was either: 1) to welcome Onesimus back enthusiastically, not grudgingly (cf. Luke 15:22-24); 2) to permit Onesimus, in addition to his menial tasks, to minister spiritually with Philemon; or 3) to forgive any others who might have wronged Philemon. Whichever Paul intended, he was not subtly urging Philemon to grant Onesimus freedom (*see note on v. 16*).

22 a guest room. Lit. "a lodging," a place where Paul could stay when he visited Colosse. **I shall be granted to you.** Paul expected to be released from prison in the near future (cf. Phil. 2:23,24), after which he could be with Philemon and the other Colossians again.

23 Epaphras. *See note on Col. 4:12.*

24 Mark, Aristarchus. *See note on Col. 4:10.* The story of the once severed but now mended relationship between Paul and Mark (Acts 15:38-40; 2 Tim. 4:11) would have been well known to the believers in Colosse (Col. 4:10). Listing Mark's name here would serve to remind Philemon that Paul himself had worked through the issues of forgiveness, and that the instructions he was passing on to his friend were ones the apostle himself had already implemented in his relationship with John Mark. **Demas, Luke.** *See note on Col. 4:14.*

The Epistle to the HEBREWS

Title

When the various NT books were formally brought together into one collection shortly after A.D. 100, the titles were added for convenience. This epistle's title bears the traditional Greek title, "To the Hebrews," which was attested by at least the second century A.D. Within the epistle itself, however, there is no identification of the recipients as either Hebrews (Jews) or Gentiles. Since the epistle is filled with references to Hebrew history and religion and does not address any particular Gentile or pagan practice, the traditional title has been maintained.

Author and Date

The author of Hebrews is unknown. Paul, Barnabas, Silas, Apollos, Luke, Philip, Priscilla, Aquila, and Clement of Rome have been suggested by different scholars, but the epistle's vocabulary, style, and various literary characteristics do not clearly support any particular claim. It is significant that the writer includes himself among those people who had received confirmation of Christ's message from others (2:3). That would seem to rule out someone like Paul who claimed that he had received such confirmation directly from God and not from men (Gal. 1:12). Whoever the author was, he preferred citing OT references from the Greek OT (LXX) rather than from the Hebrew text. Even the early church expressed various opinions on authorship, and current scholarship admits the puzzle still has no solution. Therefore, it seems best to accept the epistle's anonymity. Ultimately, of course, the author was the Holy Spirit (2 Pet. 1:21).

The use of the present tense in 5:1-4; 7:21,23,27,28; 8:3-5,13; 9:6-9,13,25; 10:1,3,4,8,11; and 13:10,11 would suggest that the Levitical priesthood and sacrificial system were still in operation when the epistle was composed. Since the temple was destroyed by General (later Emperor) Titus Vespasian in A.D. 70, the epistle must have been written prior to that date. In addition, it may be noted that Timothy had just been released from prison (13:23) and that persecution was becoming severe (10:32-39; 12:4; 13:3). These details suggest a date for the epistle around A.D. 67–69.

Background and Setting

Emphases on the Levitical priesthood and on sacrifices, as well as the absence of any reference to the Gentiles, support the conclusion that a community of Hebrews was the recipient of the epistle. Although these Hebrews were primarily converts to Christ, there were probably a number of unbelievers in their midst, who were attracted by the message of salvation, but who had not yet made a full commitment of faith in Christ (see Interpretive Challenges). One thing is clear from the contents of the epistle: the community of Hebrews was facing the possibility of intensified persecution (10:32-39; 12:4). As they confronted this possibility, the Hebrews were tempted to cast aside any identification with Christ. They may have considered demoting Christ from God's Son to a mere angel. Such a precedent had already been set in the Qumran community of messianic Jews living near the Dead Sea. They had dropped out of society, established a religious commune, and included the worship of angels in their brand of reformed Judaism. The Qumran community had even gone so far as to claim that the angel Michael was higher in status than the coming Messiah. These kinds of doctrinal aberrations could explain the emphasis in Hebrews chapter one on the superiority of Christ over the angels.

Possible locations for the recipients of the epistle include Palestine, Egypt, Italy, Asia Minor, and Greece. The community that was the primary recipient may have circulated the epistle among those of Hebrew background in neighboring areas and churches. Those believers probably had not seen Christ personally. Apparently, they had been evangelized by "those who heard" Christ and whose ministries had been authenticated "with signs and wonders, with various miracles" (2:3,4). Thus the recipients could have been in a church outside Judea and Galilee or in a church in those areas, but established among people in the generation following those who had been eyewitnesses of Christ. The congregation was not new or untaught ("by this time you ought to be teachers") yet some of them still needed "milk and not solid food" (5:12).

"Those from Italy" (13:24) is an ambiguous reference since it could mean either those who had left

Italy and were living elsewhere, or those who were still in Italy and being singled out as native residents of that country. Greece or Asia Minor must also be considered because of the apparently early establishment of the church there, and because of the consistent use of the LXX.

The generation of Hebrews receiving this epistle had practiced the Levitical sacrifices at the temple in Jerusalem. Jews living in exile had substituted the synagogue for the temple but still felt a deep attraction to the temple worship. Some had the means to make regular pilgrimages to the temple in Jerusalem. The writer of this epistle emphasized the superiority of Christianity over Judaism and the superiority of Christ's once-for-all sacrifice over the repeated and imperfect Levitical sacrifices observed in the temple.

Historical and Theological Themes

Since the book of Hebrews is grounded in the work of the Levitical priesthood, an understanding of the book of Leviticus is essential for properly interpreting Hebrews. Israel's sin had continually interrupted God's fellowship with His chosen and covenant people, Israel. Therefore, He graciously and sovereignly established a system of sacrifices that symbolically represented the inner repentance of sinners and His divine forgiveness. However, the need for sacrifices never ended because the people and priests continued to sin. The need of all mankind was for a perfect priest and a perfect sacrifice that would once and for all actually remove sin. God's provision for that perfect priest and sacrifice in Christ is the central message of Hebrews.

The epistle to the Hebrews is a study in contrast, between the imperfect and incomplete provisions of the Old Covenant, given under Moses, and the infinitely better provisions of the New Covenant offered by the perfect High-Priest, God's only Son and the Messiah, Jesus Christ. Included in the "better" provisions are: a better hope, testament, promise, sacrifice, substance, country, and resurrection. Those who belong to the New Covenant dwell in a completely new and heavenly atmosphere, they worship a heavenly Savior, have a heavenly calling, receive a heavenly gift, are citizens of a heavenly country, look forward to a heavenly Jerusalem, and have their very names written in heaven.

One of the key theological themes in Hebrews is that all believers now have direct access to God under the New Covenant and, therefore, may approach the throne of God boldly (4:16; 10:22). One's hope is in the very presence of God, into which he follows the Savior (6:19,20; 10:19,20). The primary teaching symbolized by the tabernacle service was that believers under the covenant of law did not have direct access to the presence of God (9:8), but were shut out of the Holy of Holies. The book of Hebrews may briefly be summarized in this way: Believers in Jesus Christ, as God's perfect sacrifice for sin, have the perfect High-Priest through whose ministry everything is new and better than under the covenant of law.

This epistle is more than a doctrinal treatise, however. It is intensely practical in its application to everyday living (see chap. 13). The writer himself even refers to his letter as a "word of exhortation" (13:22; cf. Acts 13:15). Exhortations designed to stir the readers into action are found throughout the text. Those exhortations are given in the form of 6 warnings:

Warning against drifting from "the things we have heard" (2:1-4)
Warning against disbelieving the "voice" of God (3:7-14)
Warning against degenerating from "the elementary principles of Christ" (5:11–6:20)
Warning against despising "the knowledge of the truth" (10:26-39)
Warning against devaluing "the grace of God" (12:15-17)
Warning against departing from Him "who speaks" (12:25-29)

Another significant aspect of this epistle is its clear exposition of selected OT passages. The writer was clearly a skilled expositor of the Word of God. His example is instructive for preachers and teachers:

1:1–2:4	Exposition of verses from Pss.; 2 Sam. 7; Deut. 32
2:5-18	Exposition of Ps. 8:4-6
3:1–4:13	Exposition of Ps. 95:7-11
4:14–7:28	Exposition of Ps. 110:4
8:1–10:18	Exposition of Jer. 31:31-34
10:32–12:3	Exposition of Hab. 2:3,4
12:4-13	Exposition of Prov. 3:11,12
12:18-29	Exposition of Ex. 19,20

Interpretive Challenges

A proper interpretation of this epistle requires the recognition that it addresses 3 distinct groups of Jews: 1) believers; 2) unbelievers who were intellectually convinced of the gospel; and 3) unbelievers who were attracted by the gospel and the person of Christ but who had reached no final conviction about Him. Failure to acknowledge these groups leads to interpretations inconsistent with the rest of Scripture.

The primary group addressed were Hebrew Christians who suffered rejection and persecution by fellow Jews (10:32-34), although none as yet had been martyred (12:4). The letter was written to give them encouragement and confidence in Christ, their Messiah and High-Priest. They were an immature group of believers who were tempted to hold on to the symbolic and spiritually powerless rituals and traditions of Judaism.

The second group addressed were Jewish unbelievers who were convinced of the basic truths of the gospel but who had not placed their faith in Jesus Christ as their own Savior and Lord. They were intellectually persuaded but spiritually uncommitted. These unbelievers are addressed in such passages as 2:1-3; 6:4-6; 10:26-29; and 12:15-17.

The third group addressed were Jewish unbelievers who were not convinced of the gospel's truth but had had some exposure to it. Chapter 9 is largely devoted to them (see especially vv. 11,14,15,27,28).

By far, the most serious interpretive challenge is found in 6:4-6. The phrase "once enlightened" is often taken to refer to Christians, and the accompanying warning taken to indicate the danger of losing their salvation if "they fall away" and "crucify again for themselves the Son of God." But there is no mention of their being saved and they are not described with any terms that apply only to believers (such as holy, born again, righteous, or saints). This problem arises from inaccurately identifying the spiritual condition of the ones being addressed. In this case, they were unbelievers who had been exposed to God's redemptive truth, and perhaps made a profession of faith, but had not exercised genuine saving faith. In 10:26, the reference once again is to apostate Christians, not to genuine believers who are often incorrectly thought to lose their salvation because of their sins.

Outline

- I. The Superiority of Jesus Christ's Position (1:1–4:13)
  - A. A Better Name (1:1-3)
  - B. Better Than the Angels (1:4–2:18)
    - 1. A greater messenger (1:4-14)
    - 2. A greater message (2:1-18)
      - a. A greater salvation (2:1-4)
      - b. A greater savior (2:5-18)
  - C. Better Than Moses (3:1-19)
  - D. A Better Rest (4:1-13)
- II. The Superiority of Jesus Christ's Priesthood (4:14–7:28)
  - A. Christ as High-Priest (4:14–5:10)
  - B. Exhortation to Full Commitment to Christ (5:11–6:20)
  - C. Christ's Priesthood like Melchizedek's (7:1-28)
- III. The Superiority of Jesus Christ's Priestly Ministry (8:1–10:18)
  - A. Through a Better Covenant (8:1-13)
  - B. In a Better Sanctuary (9:1-12)
  - C. By a Better Sacrifice (9:13–10:18)
- IV. The Superiority of the Believer's Privileges (10:19–12:29)
  - A. Saving Faith (10:19-25)
  - B. False Faith (10:26-39)
  - C. Genuine Faith (11:1-3)
  - D. Heroes of the Faith (11:4-40)
  - E. Persevering Faith (12:1-29)
- V. The Superiority of Christian Behavior (13:1-21)
  - A. In Relation to Others (13:1-3)
  - B. In Relation to Ourselves (13:4-9)
  - C. In Relation to God (13:10-21)
- Postscript (13:22-25)

God's Supreme Revelation

1 God, who [1]at various times and [a]in
various ways spoke in time past to the
fathers by the prophets, **2** has in these last
days spoken to us by *His* Son, whom He
has appointed heir of all things, through
whom also He made the [2]worlds; **3** [b]who
being the brightness of *His* glory and the
express [c]image of His person, and [d]up-
holding all things by the word of His
power, [e]when He had [3]by Himself
[4]purged [5]our sins, [f]sat down at the right
hand of the Majesty on high, **4** having become so much better than the angels, as
[g]He has by inheritance obtained a more excellent name than they.

CHAPTER 1

1 [a] Num. 12:6, 8; Joel 2:28 [1] Or *in many portions*
2 [2] Or *ages*, Gr. *aiones*, aeons
3 [b] John 1:14 [c] 2 Cor. 4:4; Col. 1:15 [d] Col. 1:17 [e] [Heb. 7:27] [f] Ps. 110:1 [3] NU omits *by Himself* [4] *cleansed* [5] NU omits *our*
4 [g] Is. 9:6, 7; Luke 1:32, 33; [Phil. 2:9, 10]
5 [h] Ps. 2:7; Acts 13:33; Heb. 5:5 [i] 2 Sam. 7:14
6 [j] Ps. 89:27; [Rom. 8:29] [k] Deut. 32:43, LXX, DSS; Ps. 97:7; 1 Pet. 3:22; Rev. 5:11-13

The Son Exalted Above Angels

5 For to which of the angels did He ever
say:

[h]"You are My Son,
Today I have begotten You"?

And again:

[i]"I will be to Him a Father,
And He shall be to Me a Son"?

6 But when He again brings [j]the firstborn into the world, He says:

[k]"Let all the angels of God worship
Him."

1:1 various times. The meaning is "many portions" (as of books). Over the course of possibly 1,800 years (from Job, ca. 2200 B.C. [?] to Nehemiah, ca. 400 B.C.) the OT was written in 39 different books reflecting different historical times, locations, cultures, and situations. **various ways.** These included visions, symbols, and parables, written in both poetry and prose. Though the literary form and style varied, it was always God's revelation of what He wanted His people to know. The progressive revelation of the OT described God's program of redemption (1 Pet. 1:10-12) and His will for His people (Rom. 15:4; 2 Tim. 3:16,17).

1:2 last days. Jews understood the "last days" to mean the time when Messiah (Christ) would come (cf. Num. 24:14; Jer. 33:14-16; Mic. 5:1,2; Zech. 9:9,16). The fulfillment of the messianic prophecies commenced with the advent of the Messiah. Since He came, it has been the "last days" (cf. 1 Cor. 10:11; James 5:8; 1 Pet. 1:20; 4:7; 1 John 2:18). In the past God gave revelation through His prophets, but in these times, beginning with the Messiah's advent, God spoke the message of redemption through the Son. **heir.** Everything that exists will ultimately come under the control of the Son of God, the Messiah (cf. Pss. 2:8,9; 89:27; Rom. 11:36; Col. 1:16). This "inheritance" is the full extension of the authority which the Father has given to the Son (cf. Dan. 7:13,14; Matt. 28:18), as the "firstborn" (*see note on v. 6*). **worlds.** The word can also be translated "ages." It refers to time, space, energy, and matter—the entire universe and everything that makes it function (cf. John 1:3).

1:3 brightness. The term is used only here in the NT. It expresses the concept of sending forth light or shining (cf. John 8:12; 2 Cor. 4:4,6). The meaning of "reflection" is not appropriate here. The Son is not just reflecting God's glory, He is God and radiates His own essential glory. **express image of His person.** The term translated "express image" is used only here in the NT. In extrabiblical literature, it was employed for an engraving on wood, an etching in metal, a brand on an animal hide, an impression in clay, and a stamped image on coins. "Person" is a word expressing nature, being, or essence. The Son is the perfect imprint, the exact representation of the nature and essence of God in time and space (cf. John 14:9; Col. 1:15; 2:9). **upholding.** The universe and everything in it is constantly sustained by the Son's powerfully effective word (Col. 1:17). The term also conveys the concept of movement or progress—the Son of God directs all things toward the consummation of all things according to God's sovereign purpose. He who spoke all things into existence also sustains His creation and consummates His purpose by His word. **purged our sins.** By the substitutionary sacrifice of Himself on the cross (cf. Titus 2:14; Rev. 1:5). **sat down at the right hand.** The right hand is the place of power, authority, and honor (cf. v. 13; Rom. 8:34; 1 Pet. 3:22). It is also the position of subordination, implying that the Son is under the authority of the Father (cf. 1 Cor. 15:27,28). The seat that Christ has taken is the throne of God (8:1; 10:12; 12:2) where He rules as sovereign Lord. This depicts a victorious Savior, not a defeated martyr. While the primary thrust of this phrase is the enthronement of Christ, His sitting might also imply the completion of His atoning work.

1:4 having become. The Gr. verb used here refers to a change of state, not a change of existence. The Son in His divine essence has eternally existed, but for a while He was made lower than the angels (2:9) and afterward was exalted to an infinitely higher position by virtue of what He had accomplished in His redemptive work (*see notes on Phil. 2:9-11*). **angels.** Spirit beings created by God to minister to Him and do His bidding. The Jews held angels in very high regard as the highest beings next to God. The sect of Judaism which had established a community at Qumran taught that the archangel Michael's authority rivaled or surpassed that of the Messiah. The writer of Hebrews clearly disclaims any such concept. The Son of God is superior to the angels. **more excellent name.** That name is Lord (*see notes on Phil 2:9-11*). No angel is Sovereign Lord (vv. 6,13,14).

1:5 Quoting from Ps. 2:7 and 2 Sam. 7:14, the writer presents the unique relationship which the Son has with the Father. No angel ever experienced such a relationship. ***Son.*** A title of Christ expressing the voluntary submission of the Second Person of the Godhead to the First Person for the purpose of fulfilling the program of redemption established in eternity past (*see note on 2 Tim. 1:9*). Cf. vv. 2,8; 3:6; 4:14; 5:5,8; 6:6; 7:3,28; 10:29; 11:17 and many other references in the NT. His sonship was also expressed in the OT (cf. Ps. 2:12; Prov. 30:4). The word "today" indicates that God's Son was born in a point of time. He was always God, but He fulfilled His role as Son in space and time at His incarnation and was affirmed as such by His resurrection (Rom. 1:4).

1:6 again. This adverb can be taken with "brings" as a reference to the second coming of Christ or with "says" to indicate yet another quotation from the OT ("and again, when He brings the firstborn into the world, He says"; cf. v. 5; 2:13). The NKJV has chosen the former sense. **firstborn.** *See notes on Rom. 8:29; Col. 1:15*, where it refers to prominence of position or title, not to the order of time. Christ was not the first to be born on the earth, but He holds the highest position of sovereignty. As "firstborn" He is also set apart to the service of God and, being preeminent, is entitled to the inheritance (cf. v. 2; Gen. 43:33; Ex. 13:2; 22:29; Deut. 21:17; Ps. 89:27). ***Let all the angels.*** Quoted from the LXX translation of Deut. 32:43 (cf. Ps. 97:7). Since the angels are commanded to worship the Messiah, the Messiah must be superior to them. Five of the 7 OT passages quoted in this first chapter of Hebrews are in contexts related to the Davidic Covenant, which emphasizes the concepts of sonship, kingship, and kingdom. Although Deut. 32:43 is not in a Davidic Covenant context, it has an affinity to the teaching of Ps. 89:6 (a psalm of the Davidic Covenant), which declares that the heavenly beings themselves must recognize the lordship of God. Ref-

7 And of the angels He says:

[l] "Who makes His angels spirits
And His ministers a flame of fire."

8 But to the Son *He says:*

[m] "Your throne, O God, *is* forever and ever;
A [6] scepter of righteousness *is* the scepter of Your kingdom.
9 You have loved righteousness and hated lawlessness;
Therefore God, Your God, [n] has anointed You
With the oil of gladness more than Your companions."

10 And:

[o] "You, LORD, in the beginning laid the foundation of the earth,
And the heavens are the work of Your hands.
11 [p] They will perish, but You remain;
And [q] they will all grow old like a garment;
12 Like a cloak You will fold them up,
And they will be changed.
But You are the [r] same,
And Your years will not fail."

13 But to which of the angels has He ever said:

[s] "Sit at My right hand,
Till I make Your enemies Your footstool"?

14 [t] Are they not all ministering spirits sent
forth to minister for those who will [u] inherit salvation?

Do Not Neglect Salvation

2 Therefore we must give [1] the more
earnest heed to the things we have
heard, lest we drift away. 2 For if the word
[a] spoken through angels proved steadfast,
and [b] every transgression and disobedience
received a just [2] reward, 3 [c] how shall we escape if we neglect so great a salvation,

7 [l] Ps. 104:4
8 [m] Ps. 45:6, 7 [6] A ruler's staff
9 [n] Is. 61:1, 3
10 [o] Ps. 102:25-27
11 [p] [Is. 34:4] [q] Is. 50:9; 51:6; Heb. 8:13
12 [r] Heb. 13:8
13 [s] Ps. 110:1; Matt. 22:44; Heb. 1:3
14 [t] Ps. 103:20; Dan. 7:10 [u] Rom. 8:17

CHAPTER 2

1 [1] *all the more careful attention*
2 [a] Deut. 33:2; Acts 7:53; Gal. 3:19 [b] Num. 15:30 [2] *retribution* or *penalty*
3 [c] Heb. 10:28

erence is made to "the firstborn" in the introduction to the Deuteronomy quote. In addition, "firstborn" is mentioned in Ps. 89:27.

1:7 of the angels. The writer continues biblical proofs that the angels are subservient to the Son of God by citing Ps. 104:4. This is the only one of the 7 OT quotations in chap. 1 which has no connection at all to the Davidic Covenant. The quote merely defines the primary nature and purpose of angels.

1:8,9 ***He says.*** Quoting from Ps. 45:6,7, the writer argues for the deity and the lordship of the Son over creation (cf. v. 3). The text is all the more significant since the declaration of the Son's deity is presented as the words of the Father Himself (cf. Is. 9:6; Jer. 23:5,6; John 5:18; Titus 2:13; 1 John 5:20). It is clear that the writer of Hebrews had the 3 messianic offices in mind: Prophet (v. 1), Priest (v. 3), and King (vv. 3,8). Induction into those 3 offices required anointing (v. 9). The title Messiah (Christ) means "anointed one" (cf. Is. 61:1-3; Luke 4:16-21).

1:9 ***companions.*** The term is used only in Hebrews (3:1,14; 6:4; 12:8) and in Luke 5:7. In this occurrence, it might refer to angels or to other men who were similarly anointed for their offices: the OT prophets, priests, and kings. If the "oil of gladness" is the same as "oil of joy" referred to in Is. 61:3, the reference would clearly be to those who had mourned in Zion but who would one day be clothed with praise and called "trees of righteousness"—references to men, not angels. No matter how noble such men were, Christ is superior.

1:10-12 Quoted from Ps. 102:25-27. The Son who created the universe (John 1:1-3), one day will destroy the heavens and earth that He created (*see notes on 2 Pet. 3:10-12; Rev. 6:14*), but He remains unchanged. Immutability is yet another characteristic of the divine essence. Once again the OT testifies of the Son's deity.

1:13,14 The writer re-emphasizes the lordship of the Son by quoting Ps. 110:1. While Christ's destiny is to reign (cf. v. 3; Matt. 22:44; Acts 2:35), the angels' destiny is to serve the recipients of salvation (*see note on 1 Cor. 6:3*). This is the seventh and final quotation from the OT to bolster the argument that as Son and Lord the Messiah is superior to the angels.

1:13 ***enemies Your footstool.*** This quote from Ps. 110:1 is repeated in the NT at 10:13; Matt. 22:44; Mark 12:36; Luke 20:43; Acts 2:35, and expresses the sovereignty of Christ over all (cf. Phil. 2:10).

1:14 *See note on Matt. 18:10.*

2:1-4 In order to drive home the importance of the superiority of the Son of God over angels, the writer urges the readers to respond. "We" includes all those who are Hebrews. Some had given intellectual assent to the doctrine of Messiah's superiority to the angels, but had not yet committed themselves to Him as God and Lord. He deserves their worship as much as He deserves the worship of the angels.

2:1 earnest heed...drift away. Both phrases have nautical connotations. The first refers to mooring a ship, tying it up at the dock. The second was often used of a ship that had been allowed to drift past the harbor. The warning is to secure oneself to the truth of the gospel, being careful not to pass by the only harbor of salvation. The closest attention must be paid to these very serious matters of the Christian faith. The readers in their tendency to apathy are in danger of making shipwreck of their lives (cf. 6:19; *see note on 1 Tim. 1:18*).

2:2 if. The Gr. term assumes a fulfilled condition and here carries the idea: "In view of the fact that...." **angels.** Angels were instrumental in bringing God's law to His people at Mt. Sinai (cf. Deut. 33:1,2; Ps. 68:17; Acts 7:38,53; Gal. 3:19). **transgression and disobedience.** The former means to step across the line, in an overt sin of commission. The latter carries the idea of shutting one's ears to God's commands, thereby committing a sin of omission. Both are willful, serious, and require just judgment.

2:3 how shall we escape. If disobedience to the older covenant of law brought swift judgment, how much more severe will be the judgment of disobedience to the New Covenant gospel of salvation, which was mediated by the Son who is superior to the angels (cf. Matt. 10:14,15; 11:20-24)? The messenger and message of the New Covenant are greater than the messengers and message of the older covenant. The greater the privilege, the greater the punishment for disobedience or neglect (10:29; cf. Luke 12:47). **by those who heard** ***Him.*** This phrase reveals the succession of evangelism. That generation of Hebrews would not have heard if the previous generation of witnesses had not passed the message along (cf. 1 Tim. 2:5-7).

[d]which at the first began to be spoken by
the Lord, and was [e]confirmed to us by
those who heard *Him,* **4** [f]God also bearing
witness [g]both with signs and wonders,
with various miracles, and [h]gifts[3] of the
Holy Spirit, [i]according to His own will?

The Son Made Lower than Angels

5 For He has not put [j]the world to come,
of which we speak, in subjection to angels.
6 But one testified in a certain place, saying:

[k]"What is man that You are mindful
of him,
Or the son of man that You take
care of him?
7 *You have made him [4]a little lower*
than the angels;
You have crowned him with glory
and honor,
[5]And set him over the works of
Your hands.
8 *[l]You have put all things in*
subjection under his feet."

For in that He put all in subjection under
him, He left nothing *that is* not put under
him. But now [m]we do not yet see all things
put under him. **9** But we see Jesus, [n]who
was made [6]a little lower than the angels,
for the suffering of death [o]crowned with
glory and honor, that He, by the grace of
God, might taste death [p]for everyone.

Bringing Many Sons to Glory

10 For it was fitting for Him, [q]for whom
are all things and by whom *are* all things, in
bringing many sons to glory, to make the
captain of their salvation [r]perfect through
sufferings. **11** For [s]both He who [7]sanctifies
and those who are being sanctified [t]*are* all
of one, for which reason [u]He is not
ashamed to call them brethren, **12** saying:

[v]"I will declare Your name to My
brethren;
In the midst of the assembly I will
sing praise to You."

13 And again:

[w]"I will put My trust in Him."

3 [d]Matt. 4:17 [e]Mark 16:20; Luke 1:2; 1 John 1:1
4 [f]Mark 16:20 [g]Acts 2:22, 43; 2 Cor. 12:2 [h]1 Cor. 12:4, 7, 11; Eph. 4:7 [i]Eph. 1:5, 9 [3]*distributions*
5 [j][2 Pet. 3:13]
6 [k]Job 7:17; Ps. 8:4-6
7 [4]Or *for a little while* [5]NU, M omit the rest of v. 7.
8 [l]Matt. 28:18 [m]Ps. 8:6; 1 Cor. 15:25, 27
9 [n]Phil. 2:7-9; Heb. 1:9 [o]Acts 2:33; 3:13; 1 Pet. 1:21 [p]Is. 53:12; [John 3:16] [6]Or *for a little while*
10 [q]Col. 1:16 [r]Heb. 5:8, 9; 7:28
11 [s]Heb. 10:10 [t]Acts 17:26 [u]Matt. 28:10 [7]*sets apart*
12 [v]Ps. 22:22
13 [w]2 Sam. 22:3; Is. 8:17

2:4 signs…wonders…miracles…gifts. The supernatural powers demonstrated by Jesus and by His apostles were the Father's divine confirmation of the gospel of Jesus Christ, His Son (cf. John 10:38; Acts 2:22; Rom. 15:19; 1 Cor. 14:22; *see note on 2 Cor. 12:12*). This authentication of the message was the purpose of such miraculous deeds. **the Holy Spirit.** The epistle's first reference to the Holy Spirit refers in passing to His ministry of confirming the message of salvation by means of miraculous gifts. Mentioned elsewhere in the epistle are the Holy Spirit's involvement in the revelation of Scripture (3:7; 10:15), in teaching (9:8), in pre-salvation operations (6:4, perhaps His convicting work; 10:29, common grace), and in ministry to Christ (9:14).

2:5 world. The term refers to the inhabited earth. The reference is to the great millennial kingdom (cf. Zech. 14:9; Rev. 20:1-5). Angels will not reign over the messianic kingdom.

2:6-8 Quoted from Ps. 8:4-6 (cf. 1 Cor. 15:27,28; Eph. 1:22).

2:6 in a certain place. This is not an indication that the writer was ignorant of the source of the quotation that follows. The location of the quotation is not as significant as its divine authorship. Perhaps it is significant that the author of Hebrews is not identified either. The writer may have desired that his readers understand that the Holy Spirit is the real author of all Scripture (cf. 2 Tim. 3:16; 2 Pet. 1:21). ***man…son of man.*** Both refer to mankind, not to Christ. The passage asks why God would ever bother with man. As the following verses demonstrate (vv. 9,10), the incarnation of Christ is the greatest proof of God's love and regard for mankind. Christ was not sent in the form of an angel. He was sent in the form of a man.

2:7 *angels.* Angels were given supernatural powers by the Creator. They have continual access to the throne of God (cf. Job 1:6; 2:1; Rev. 5:11) and are not subject to death.

2:8 *subjection.* In spite of the superiority of angels to mankind, God had originally placed the administration of the earth into the hands of mankind (Gen. 1:26-28). Due to the Fall (Gen. 3), however, mankind has been incapable of fulfilling that divinely ordained position.

2:9 glory and honor. Because Jesus "became obedient to the point of death…God also has highly exalted Him" (Phil. 2:8,9). By His redemptive work, Christ has fulfilled all that is required as the supreme representative of mankind. By His incarnation, substitutionary sacrifice, and victory over sin and death (cf. Rom. 6:23; 1 John 4:10), He has fulfilled man's original purpose. As the Second Adam (1 Cor. 15:47), He was for a short time lower than the angels. Now He has glory and honor, and all things (including angels) are subject to Him. **taste death for everyone.** Everyone who believes, that is. The death of Christ can only be applied in its efficacy to those who come to God repentantly in faith, asking for saving grace and forgiveness of sins. *See notes on 2 Cor. 5:21; 1 Tim. 2:6; 4:10; Titus 2:11.*

2:10 fitting. What God did through the humiliation of Jesus Christ was perfectly consistent with His sovereign righteousness and holiness. Without Christ's humiliation and suffering, there could be no redemption. Without redemption, there could be no glorification (cf. Rom. 8:18,29,30). **captain.** The term is also used in 12:2 and Acts 5:31. It could be translated "pioneer," "leader," or "originator." Christ is the source (cf. "author" in 5:9, which has the meaning of cause), the initiator, and the leader in regard to salvation. He has led the way into heaven as our forerunner (6:20). **perfect.** In His divine nature, Christ was already perfect. However, His human nature was perfected through obedience, including suffering in order that He might be an understanding High-Priest, an example for believers (cf. 5:8,9; 7:25-28; Phil. 2:8; 1 Pet. 2:21), and establish the perfect righteousness (Matt. 3:15) to be imputed to believers (2 Cor. 5:21; Phil. 3:8,19).

2:11 sanctifies. Sanctification sets a person apart for service through purification from sin and conformity to the holiness of God (cf. 10:10).

2:12 *My brethren.* Quoted from Ps. 22:22. Jesus had taught that those who do the will of the Father in obedience to His word are His brothers and mother (Matt. 12:50; Luke 8:21). He never directly referred to His disciples by the title of "brethren" until after His resurrection (Matt. 28:10; John 20:17). Not until He had paid the price for their salvation, did they truly become His spiritual brothers and sisters. The use of the term demonstrates His full identification with mankind in order to provide complete redemption (Phil. 2:7-9).

2:13 The citation of Is. 8:17,18 (cf. 2 Sam. 22:3) emphasizes the point made in vv. 9-11: that Christ had fully identified Himself with mankind

And again:

[x]*"Here am I and the children whom*
God has given Me."

14 Inasmuch then as the children have
partaken of flesh and blood, He [y]Himself
likewise shared in the same, [z]that through
death He might destroy him who had the
power of [a]death, that is, the devil, **15** and release those who [b]through fear of death were
all their lifetime subject to bondage. **16** For
indeed He does not [8]give aid to angels, but
He does [9]give aid to the seed of Abraham.
17 Therefore, in all things He had [c]to be
made like *His* brethren, that He might be [d]a
merciful and faithful High Priest in things
pertaining to God, to make propitiation for
the sins of the people. **18** [e]For in that He
Himself has suffered, being [1]tempted, He is
able to aid those who are tempted.

The Son Was Faithful

3 Therefore, holy brethren, partakers of
the heavenly calling, consider the
Apostle and High Priest of our confession,
Christ Jesus, **2** who was faithful to Him
who appointed Him, as [a]Moses also *was*
faithful in all His house. **3** For this One has
been counted worthy of more glory than
Moses, inasmuch as [b]He who built the
house has more honor than the house.

13 [x] Is. 8:18
14 [y] John 1:14 [z] Col. 2:15 [a] [1 Cor. 15:54-57]; 2 Tim. 1:10
15 [b] Ps. 68:18; Is. 42:7; 45:13; 49:9; 61:1; [Luke 1:74]
16 [8] Or *take on* the nature of [9] Or *take on*
17 [c] Phil. 2:7; Heb. 2:14 [d] [Heb. 4:15; 5:1-10]
18 [e] [Heb. 4:15, 16] [1] *tested*

CHAPTER 3

2 [a] Ex. 40:16; Num. 12:7; Heb. 3:5
3 [b] Zech. 6:12, 13

by taking a human nature. He demonstrated the reality of His human nature by His reliance upon God during His earthly sojourn.

2:14 partaken...shared. The Gr. word for "partaken" means fellowship, communion, or partnership. "Shared" means to take hold of something that is not related to one's own kind. The Son of God was not by nature "flesh and blood," but took upon Himself that nature for the sake of providing redemption for mankind. **death...power of death.** This is the ultimate purpose of the incarnation: Jesus came to earth to die. By dying, He was able to conquer death in His resurrection (John 14:19). By conquering death, He rendered Satan powerless against all who are saved. Satan's using the power of death is subject to God's will (cf. Job 2:6).

2:15 fear of death. For the believer, "death is swallowed up in victory" (1 Cor. 15:54). Therefore, the fear of death and its spiritual bondage has been brought to an end through the work of Christ.

2:16 give aid. The literal meaning is to "take hold of." The sense of "giving aid" is from the picture of a taking hold of someone in order to push or pull them to safety, to rescue them. However, there was no thought in Judaism that the Messiah's entrance into the world would be to give aid to the angels. The contrast, using this translation, is weak in comparison with all that has been previously said about Christ's superiority to the angels. The context presents the identification of Christ with mankind in His incarnation—He took upon Himself a human nature (vv. 9-14,17). When the writer wished to express the concept of giving aid, he chose a different Gr. word in v. 18 (also, 4:16). Therefore, the translation, "take on *the nature of,*" is to be preferred. **seed of Abraham.** Christ is that promised seed (*see notes on Gal. 3:16*). Since the readers are Hebrews, they would certainly identify themselves with this description. The Messiah had been born in the line of Abraham in fulfillment of the OT prophecies (Matt. 1:1). One of the chief purposes for the incarnation was the salvation of Israel (Matt. 1:21). Yet another purpose was the fulfillment of the Abrahamic Covenant in regard to the promised seed. Of all peoples, the Hebrews should be first to recognize the significance and importance of the incarnation.

2:17 propitiation. The word means "to conciliate" or "satisfy." *See note on Rom. 3:25.* Christ's work of propitiation is related to His high-priestly ministry. By His partaking of a human nature, Christ demonstrated His mercy to mankind and His faithfulness to God by satisfying God's requirement for sin and thus obtaining for His people full forgiveness. Cf. 1 John 2:2; 4:10.

2:18 tempted. The genuineness of Christ's humanity is demonstrated by the fact that He was subject to temptation. By experiencing temptation, Jesus became fully capable of understanding and sympathizing with His human brethren (cf. 4:15). He felt the full force of temptation. Though we often yield to temptation before we feel its full force, Jesus resisted temptation even when the greatest enticement for yielding had become evident (cf. Luke 4:1-13). **able to aid...tempted.** *See notes on 4:15,16; 1 Cor. 10:13.*

3:1-6 This section presents the superiority of Jesus over the highly revered Moses. The Lord had spoken with Moses "face to face, as a man speaks to his friend" (Ex. 33:11) and had given the law to him (Neh. 9:13,14). The commandments and rituals of the law were the Jews' supreme priorities, and to them Moses and the law were synonymous. Both the OT and the NT refer to the commands of God as the "law of Moses" (Josh. 8:31; 1 Kin. 2:3; Luke 2:22; Acts 13:39). Yet, as great as Moses was, Jesus was infinitely greater.

3:1 holy brethren. The phrase occurs only here and in 1 Thess. 5:27, where some manuscripts omit "holy." The writer addresses believers who have a "heavenly calling" (cf. Phil. 3:14). They are elsewhere described as desiring a "heavenly country" (11:16) and as coming to "the heavenly Jerusalem" (12:22). They are "holy" in the sense that they are set apart unto God and identified with the heavenly realm—citizens of heaven more than citizens of earth. **calling.** The reference, as always in the NT epistles, is to the effective summons to salvation in Christ (cf. Rom. 8:30; 1 Cor. 7:21). **consider.** The writer asks for the readers' complete attention and diligent observation of the superiority of Jesus Christ. **Apostle and High Priest.** An apostle is a "sent one" who has the rights, power, and authority of the one who sends him. Jesus was sent to earth by the Father (cf. John 3:17,34; 5:36-38; 8:42). The topic of the High-Priesthood of Christ, which was begun in 2:17,18 and is mentioned again here, will be taken up again in greater detail in 4:14–10:18. Meanwhile, the writer presents the supremacy of Christ to Moses (vv. 1-6), to Joshua (4:8), and to all other national heroes and OT preachers whom Jews held in high esteem. Jesus Himself spoke of His superiority to Moses in the same context in which He spoke of His being sent by the Father (John 5:36-38,45-47; cf. Luke 16:29-31). Moses had been sent by God to deliver His people from historical Egypt and its bondage (Ex. 3:10). Jesus was sent by God to deliver His people from spiritual Egypt and its bondage (2:15). **of our confession.** Christ is the center of our confession of faith in the gospel, both in creed and public testimony. The term is used again in 4:14 and 10:23 (cf. 2 Cor. 9:13; 1 Tim. 6:12). In all 3 uses in Hebrews there is a sense of urgency. Surely, the readers would not give up Christ, whom they had professed, and reject what He had done for them, if they could understand the superiority of His person and work.

3:2 house. The term refers to a family of people rather than a building or dwelling (cf. v. 6; 1 Tim. 3:15). Those who were stewards of a household must above all be faithful (1 Cor. 4:2). Both Moses (Num. 12:7) and Christ (2:17) faithfully fulfilled their individual, divine appointments to care for the people of God.

3:3,4 He who built. Moses was only a part of God's household of faith, whereas Jesus was the creator of that household (cf. 2 Sam. 7:13; Zech. 6:12,13; Eph. 2:19-22; 1 Pet. 2:4,5) and, therefore, is greater than Moses and equal to God.

4 For every house is built by someone, but
[c]He who built all things *is* God. 5 [d]And
Moses indeed *was* faithful in all His house
as [e]a servant, [f]for a testimony of those
things which would be spoken *afterward,*
6 but Christ as [g]a Son over His own house,
[h]whose house we are [i]if we hold fast the
confidence and the rejoicing of the hope
[1]firm to the end.

Be Faithful

7 Therefore, as [j]the Holy Spirit says:

[k]"Today, if you will hear His voice,
8 *Do not harden your hearts as in*
the rebellion,
In the day of trial in the wilderness,
9 *Where your fathers tested Me,*
tried Me,
And saw My works forty years.
10 *Therefore I was angry with that*
generation,
And said, 'They always go astray
in their heart,
And they have not known My
ways.'
11 *So I swore in My wrath,*
'They shall not enter My rest.'"

12 Beware, brethren, lest there be in any
of you an evil heart of unbelief in departing from the living God; 13 but [2]exhort one
another daily, while it is called *"Today,"*
lest any of you be hardened through the
deceitfulness of sin. 14 For we have become
partakers of Christ if we hold the beginning of our confidence steadfast to the end,
15 while it is said:

[l]"Today, if you will hear His
voice,
Do not harden your hearts as in
the rebellion."

4 [c] [Eph. 2:10]
5 [d] Ex. 40:16; Num. 12:7; Heb. 3:2 [e] Ex. 14:31; Num. 12:7 [f] Deut. 18:15, 18, 19
6 [g] Ps. 2:7; 110:4; Heb. 1:2 [h] [1 Cor. 3:16]; 1 Tim. 3:15 [i] [Matt. 10:22] [1] NU omits *firm to the end*
7 [j] Acts 1:16 [k] Ps. 95:7-11; Heb. 3:15; 4:7
13 [2] *encourage*
15 [l] Ps. 95:7, 8

3:5,6 servant...Son. The term for "servant" implies a position of dignity and freedom, not slavery (cf. Ex. 14:31; Josh. 1:2). However, even as the highest-ranking servant, Moses could never hold the position of Son, which is Christ's alone (cf. John 8:35).

3:5 spoken *afterward.* Moses was faithful primarily as a testimony to that which was to come in Christ (cf. 11:24-27; *see note on John 5:46*).

3:6 whose house we are. *See notes on v. 2; Eph. 2:22; 1 Tim. 3:15; 1 Pet. 2:5; 4:17.* **if we hold fast.** Cf. v. 14. This is not speaking of how to be saved or remain saved (cf. 1 Cor. 15:2). It means rather that perseverance in faithfulness is proof of real faith. The one who returns to the rituals of the Levitical system to contribute to his own salvation proves he was never truly part of God's household (*see note on 1 John 2:19*), whereas the one who abides in Christ gives evidence of his genuine membership in that household (cf. Matt. 10:22; Luke 8:15; John 8:31; 15:4-6). The promise of God will fulfill this holding fast (1 Thess. 5:24; Jude 24,25). *See note on Matt. 24:13.* **hope.** See the writer's further description of this hope in 6:18,19. This hope rests in Christ Himself, whose redemptive work has accomplished our salvation (Rom. 5:1,2; *see note on 1 Pet. 1:3*).

3:7-11 The writer cites Ps. 95:7-11 as the words of its ultimate author, the Holy Spirit (cf. 4:7; 9:8; 10:15). This passage describes the Israelites' wilderness wanderings after their delivery from Egypt. Despite God's miraculous works and His gracious, providential faithfulness to them, the people still failed to commit themselves to Him in faith (cf. Ex. 17; Num. 14:22,23; Ps. 78:40-53). The writer of Hebrews presents a 3-point exposition of the OT passage: 1) beware of unbelief (vv. 12-19); 2) be afraid of falling short (4:1-10); and 3) be diligent to enter (4:11-13). The themes of the exposition include urgency, obedience (including faith), perseverance, and rest.

3:7 *Today.* The reference is to the present moment while the words of God are fresh in the mind. There is a sense of urgency to immediately give heed to the voice of God. This urgency is emphasized by repeating the reference to "today" from Ps. 95:7 three more times (vv. 13,15; 4:7) and is the theme of the writer's exposition (cf. 2 Cor. 6:2).

3:11 *My rest.* The earthly rest which God promised to give was life in the land of Canaan which Israel would receive as their inheritance (Deut. 12:9,10; Josh. 21:44; 1 Kin. 8:56). Because of rebellion against God, an entire generation of the children of Israel was prohibited from entering into that rest in the Promised Land (cf. Deut. 28:65; Lam. 1:3). The application of this picture is to an individual's spiritual rest in the Lord, which has precedent in the OT (cf. Ps. 116:7; Is. 28:12). At salvation, every believer enters the true rest, the realm of spiritual promise, never again laboring to achieve through personal effort a righteousness that pleases God. God wanted both kinds of rest for that generation who was delivered from Egypt.

3:12 brethren. This admonition is addressed to those having the same potential characteristics as the generation which perished in the wilderness without ever seeing the Land of Promise. They were unbelieving Jewish brethren who were in the company of the "holy brethren" (v. 1). They were admonished to believe and be saved before it was too late. See Introduction: Interpretive Challenges. **an evil heart.** All men are born with such a heart (Jer. 17:9). In the case of these Hebrews, that evil manifested itself in disbelief of the gospel which moved them in the opposite way from God.

3:13 exhort one another daily. Both individual accountability and corporate responsibility are intended in this admonition. As long as the distressing days were upon them and they were tempted to return to the ineffective Levitical system, they were to encourage one another to identify completely with Jesus Christ. **hardened.** Repeated rejection of the gospel concerning Jesus results in a progressive hardening of the heart and will ultimately result in outright antagonism to the gospel. Cf. 6:4-6; 10:26-29; Acts 19:9. **deceitfulness.** Sin lies and deceives, using every trickery and stratagem possible (cf. Rom. 7:11; 2 Thess. 2:10; James 1:14-16). The Hebrews deceived themselves with the reasoning that their rejection of Jesus Christ was being faithful to the older system. Their willingness to hang on to the Levitical system was really a rejection of the living Word (4:12) of the "living God" (v. 12), who through Christ had opened up a "new and living way" (10:20). Choosing the path of unbelief always leads only to death (v. 17; 10:26-29; cf. 2:14,15; Jude 5).

3:14 The exhortation is similar to that in v. 6. It repeats the theme of perseverance.

3:15-19 The quotation from Ps. 95:7,8 is repeated (cf. v. 7). The first quotation was followed with exposition emphasizing "today" and the urgency that word conveys. This second quotation is followed with exposition emphasizing the word "rebellion" (vv. 15,16) and presenting the theme of obedience by means of its antithesis, disobedience. Four different terms are employed to drive the point of rebellion home: "rebelled" (v. 16), "sinned" (v. 17), "did not obey" (v. 18), and "unbelief" (v. 19). This initial third (*see notes on vv. 7-11*) of the writer's exposition of Ps. 95:7-11 is summed up by the obvious conclusion that the Israelites who died in the wilderness were victims of their own unbelief (v. 19).

Failure of the Wilderness Wanderers

16 [m]For who, having heard, rebelled? Indeed, *was it* not all who came out of Egypt,
led by Moses? 17 Now with whom was He
angry forty years? *Was it* not with those
who sinned, [n]whose corpses fell in the
wilderness? 18 And [o]to whom did He
swear that they would not enter His rest,
but to those who did not obey? 19 So we
see that they could not enter in because of
[p]unbelief.

The Promise of Rest

4 Therefore, since a promise remains of
entering His rest, [a]let us fear lest any of
you seem to have come short of it. 2 For indeed the gospel was preached to us as well
as to them; but the word which they heard
did not profit them, [1]not being mixed with
faith in those who heard *it.* 3 For we who
have believed do enter that rest, as He has
said:

[b]"So I swore in My wrath,
'They shall not enter My rest,' "

although the works were finished from the
foundation of the world. 4 For He has spoken in a certain place of the seventh *day* in
this way: [c]*"And God rested on the seventh*
day from all His works"; 5 and again in
this *place:* [d]*"They shall not enter My rest."*
6 Since therefore it remains that some
must enter it, and those to whom it was
first preached did not enter because of
disobedience, 7 again He designates a certain day, saying in David, *"Today,"* after
such a long time, as it has been said:

[e]"Today, if you will hear His voice,
Do not harden your hearts."

8 For if [2]Joshua had [f]given them rest,
then He would not afterward have spoken
of another day. 9 There remains therefore a
rest for the people of God. 10 For he who
has entered His rest has himself also
ceased from his works as God *did* from
His.

The Word Discovers Our Condition

11 [g]Let us therefore be diligent to enter
that rest, lest anyone fall according to the
same example of disobedience. 12 For the
word of God *is* [h]living and powerful, and
[i]sharper than any [j]two-edged sword,

16 [m] Num. 14:2, 11, 30; Deut. 1:35, 36, 38
17 [n] Num. 14:22, 23
18 [o] Num. 14:30
19 [p] Num. 14:1-39; 1 Cor. 10:11, 12

CHAPTER 4

1 [a] 2 Cor. 6:1; [Gal. 5:4]; Heb. 12:15
2 [1] NU, M *since they were not united by faith with those who heeded it*
3 [b] Ps. 95:11; Heb. 3:11
4 [c] Gen. 2:2; Ex. 20:11; 31:17
5 [d] Ps. 95:11
7 [e] Ps. 95:7, 8
8 [f] Josh. 22:4 [2] Gr. *Jesus,* same as Heb. *Joshua*
11 [g] 2 Pet. 1:10
12 [h] Ps. 147:15 [i] Is. 49:2 [j] Eph. 6:17; Rev. 2:12

4:1-10 The second section of the writer's exposition of Ps. 95:7-11 goes beyond the description of unbelief and its dire consequences (3:12-19) to define the nature of the "rest" which the disobedient had forfeited. The first section had dealt primarily with Ps. 95:7,8; the second section deals primarily with Ps. 95:11.

4:1 promise. This is the first use of this important word in Hebrews. The content of this promise is defined as "entering His rest." **His rest.** *See note on 3:11.* This is the rest which God gives, therefore it is called "My rest" (Ps. 95:11) and "His rest." For believers, God's rest includes His peace, confidence of salvation, reliance on His strength, and assurance of a future heavenly home (cf. Matt. 11:29). **come short.** The entire phrase could be translated "lest you think you have come too late to enter into the rest of God" (cf. 12:15). With reverential fear all are to examine their own spiritual condition (cf. 1 Cor. 10:12; 2 Cor. 13:5) and to actively press for commitment on the part of others (cf. Jude 23).

4:2 faith. Mere knowledge of God's message is not sufficient. It must be appropriated by saving faith. Later in the epistle a much longer exposition will take up this topic of faith (10:19–12:29). The writer's point of comparison is that, like the Jews who left Egypt (3:16-19), his generation had also received God's message through the preaching of the gospel—they had been evangelized.

4:3 we...do enter. Those who exercise faith in the message of God will enter into their spiritual rest. This is the corollary of Ps. 95:11 which states the opposite side: that the unbeliever will not enter into the rest which God provides. **finished from the foundation of the world.** The spiritual rest which God gives is not something incomplete or unfinished. It is a rest which is based upon a finished work which God purposed in eternity past, just like the rest which God took after He finished creation (v. 4).

4:4,5 By way of explanation for the statement in v. 3, the writer cites the illustration of the seventh day of creation and quotes Gen. 2:2. Then he repeats the last part of Ps. 95:11.

4:6,7 The opportunity to enter God's rest remains open (cf. "a promise remains" in v. 1). It is not yet too late. God had offered the rest to His people in Moses' time and continued to offer it in David's time. He is still patiently inviting His people to enter His rest (cf. Rom. 10:21). Quoting Ps. 95:7,8 once again (see 3:7,15), the author urges an immediate, positive response. The themes of urgency and obedience are thus combined in a clear invitation to the readers.

4:8-10 God's true rest did not come through Joshua or Moses, but through Jesus Christ, who is greater than either one. Joshua led the nation of Israel into the land of their promised rest (*see note on 3:11;* Josh. 21:43-45). However, that was merely the earthly rest which was but the shadow of what was involved in the heavenly rest. The very fact that, according to Ps. 95, God was still offering His rest in the time of David (long after Israel had been in the Land) meant that the rest being offered was spiritual—superior to that which Joshua obtained. Israel's earthly rest was filled with the attacks of enemies and the daily cycle of work. The heavenly rest is characterized by the fullness of heavenly promise (Eph. 1:3) and the absence of any labor to obtain it.

4:9 rest. A different Gr. word for "rest" meaning "Sabbath rest" is introduced here, and this is its only appearance in the NT. The writer chose the word to draw the readers' attention back to the "seventh day" mentioned in v. 4 and to set up the explanation in v. 10 ("ceased from his works as God *did* from His").

4:11-13 The concluding third part of the exposition of Ps. 95:7-11 emphasizes the accountability which comes to those who have heard the Word of God. Scripture records the examples of those in the wilderness with Moses, those who entered Canaan with Joshua, and those who received the same opportunity in David's day. It is the Word which must be believed and obeyed and the Word which will judge the disobedient (cf. 1 Cor. 10:5-13).

4:12 two-edged sword. While the Word of God is comforting and nourishing to those who believe, it is a tool of judgment and execution for those who have not committed themselves to Jesus Christ. Some of the Hebrews were merely going through the motions

piercing even to the division of soul and
spirit, and of joints and marrow, and is [k]a
discerner of the thoughts and intents of the
heart. 13 [l]And there is no creature hidden
from His sight, but all things *are* [m]naked
and open to the eyes of Him to whom we
must give account.

Our Compassionate High Priest

14 Seeing then that we have a great
[n]High Priest who has passed through the
heavens, Jesus the Son of God, [o]let us
hold fast *our* confession. 15 For [p]we do
not have a High Priest who cannot sym-
pathize with our weaknesses, but [q]was in
all *points* tempted as *we are,* [r]*yet* without
sin. 16 [s]Let us therefore come boldly to
the throne of grace, that we may obtain
mercy and find grace to help in time of
need.

12 [k] [John 12:48]; 1 Cor. 14:24, 25
13 [l] 2 Chr. 16:9; Ps. 33:13-15; 90:8 [m] Job 26:6; Prov. 15:11
14 [n] Heb. 2:17; 7:26 [o] Heb. 10:23
15 [p] Is. 53:3-5 [q] Luke 22:28 [r] 2 Cor. 5:21; Heb. 7:26
16 [s] [Eph. 2:18; Heb. 10:19, 22]

CHAPTER 5

1 [a] Heb. 2:17; 8:3
2 [b] Heb. 7:28 [1] *deal gently with*
3 [c] Lev. 9:7; 16:6; [Heb. 7:27; 9:7]
4 [d] Ex. 28:1; Num. 16:40; 1 Chr. 23:13
5 [e] John 8:54 [f] Ps. 2:7

Qualifications for High Priesthood

5 For every high priest taken from
among men [a]is appointed for men in
things *pertaining* to God, that he may offer
both gifts and sacrifices for sins. 2 He can
[1]have compassion on those who are ignorant and going astray, since he himself is
also subject to [b]weakness. 3 Because of this
he is required as for the people, so also for
[c]himself, to offer *sacrifices* for sins. 4 And
no man takes this honor to himself, but he
who is called by God, just as [d]Aaron *was.*

A Priest Forever

5 [e]So also Christ did not glorify Himself
to become High Priest, *but it* was He who
said to Him:

> [f]*"You are My Son,*
> *Today I have begotten You."*

of belonging to Christ. Intellectually, they were at least partly persuaded, but inside they were not committed to Him. God's Word would expose their shallow beliefs and even their false intentions (cf. 1 Sam. 16:7; 1 Pet. 4:5). **division of soul and spirit.** These terms do not describe two separate entities (any more than "thoughts and intents" do) but are used as one might say "heart and soul" to express fullness (cf. Luke 10:27; Acts 4:32; *see note on 1 Thess. 5:23*). Elsewhere these two terms are used interchangeably to describe man's immaterial self, his eternal inner person.

4:13 open to the eyes of Him. "Open" is a specialized term used just this one time in the NT. It originally meant to expose the neck either in preparation for sacrifice or for beheading. Perhaps the use of "sword" in the previous verse triggered the term. Each individual is judged not only by the Word of God (cf. John 12:48), but by God Himself. We are accountable to the living, written Word (cf. John 6:63,68; Acts 7:38) and to the living God who is its author.

4:14–7:28 Next, the writer expounds on Ps. 110:4, quoted in 5:6. Not only is Christ as Apostle superior to Moses and to Joshua, but as High-Priest, He is superior to Aaron (4:14–5:10; cf. 3:1). In the midst of his exposition, the writer gives an exhortation related to the spiritual condition of his readers (5:11–6:20). At the conclusion of the exhortation, he then returns to the subject of Christ's priesthood (7:1-28).

4:14 passed through the heavens. Just as the High-Priest under the Old Covenant passed through 3 areas (the outer court, the Holy Place, and the Holy of Holies) to make the atoning sacrifice, Jesus passed through 3 heavens (the atmospheric heaven, the stellar heaven, and God's abode; cf. 2 Cor. 12:2-4) after making the perfect, final sacrifice. Once a year on the Day of Atonement the High-Priest of Israel would enter the Holy of Holies to make atonement for the sins of the people (Lev. 16). That tabernacle was but a limited copy of the heavenly reality (cf. 8:1-5). When Jesus entered into the heavenly Holy of Holies, having accomplished redemption, the earthly facsimile was replaced by the reality of heaven itself. Freed from that which is earthly, the Christian faith is characterized by the heavenly (3:1; Eph. 1:3; 2:6; Phil. 3:20; Col. 1:5; 1 Pet. 1:4). **Jesus the Son of God.** The use of both the title of humanity (Jesus) and of deity (Son of God) is significant. One of the few cases of such a juxtaposition is in 1 John 1:7, where His sacrifice for sins is emphasized (cf. 1 Thess. 1:10; 1 John 4:15; 5:5). **hold fast *our* confession.** *See notes on 3:1,6; 10:23.*

4:15 all *points* tempted. *See notes on 2:17,18.* The writer here adds to his statements in 2:18 that Jesus was sinless. He was able to be tempted (Matt. 4:1-11), but not able to sin (*see notes on 7:26*).

4:16 come boldly to the throne of grace. Most ancient rulers were unapproachable by anyone but their highest advisers (cf. Esth. 4:11). In contrast, the Holy Spirit calls for all to come confidently before God's throne to receive mercy and grace through Jesus Christ (cf. 7:25; 10:22; Matt. 27:51; see Introduction: Historical and Theological Themes). The ark of the covenant was viewed as the place on earth where God sat enthroned between the cherubim (cf. 2 Kin. 19:15; Jer. 3:16,17). Oriental thrones included a footstool—yet another metaphor for the ark (cf. Ps. 132:7). It was at the throne of God that Christ made atonement for sins, and it is there that grace is dispensed to believers for all the issues of life (cf. 2 Cor. 4:15; 9:8; 12:9; Eph. 1:7; 2:7). "Grace to you" became a standard greeting among believers who celebrated this provision (Rom. 1:7; 16:20,24; 1 Cor. 1:3; 16:23; 2 Cor. 1:2; 13:14; Gal 1:3; 6:18; Eph. 1:2; 6:24; Phil. 1:2; 4:18; Col. 1:2; 4:18; 1 Thess. 1:1; 5:28; 2 Thess. 1:2; 3:18; 1 Tim. 1:2; 6:21; 2 Tim. 1:2; 4:22; Titus 1:4; 3:15; Philem. 3,25). **to help in time of need.** *See notes on 2:16,18.*

5:1-4 No angel with supernatural power could serve as High-Priest. Only men with the weaknesses of humanity could serve as High-Priest (v. 2; 7:28). The position of High-Priest in the Levitical system was by appointment only. No man could legitimately appoint himself High-Priest. The use of the present tense in these verses would seem to indicate that the Levitical system still was being practiced at the time of this epistle (see Introduction: Author and Date).

5:1 gifts and sacrifices. The first term might refer especially to the grain offerings under the Old Covenant, which were for thanksgiving or dedication. That would leave the second term to refer to blood offerings for the expiation of sins (see Lev. 1–5). However, "gifts" is used in 8:4 to refer to all of the various sacrifices (cf. 8:3). The 3 occurrences of the phrase in the NT (cf. 8:3; 9:9) employ a Gr. construction which expresses a closer relationship between the two terms than is normally indicated by the word "and." This could indicate that no distinction should be made between the terms, and that "for sins" should be taken with both.

5:2 have compassion. This verb occurs only here in the NT. It carries the idea of maintaining a controlled but gentle attitude in the treatment of those who are spiritually ignorant and wayward. Impatience, loathing, and indignation have no part in priestly ministry. Such moderation and gentleness comes from realizing one's own human frailty. The priest would be reminded of his own sinful humanity every time he offered sacrifices for his own sins (v. 3).

5:4 called by God. A High-Priest was selected and called by God into service (cf. Ex. 28; Num. 16:1-40; 1 Sam. 16:1-3).

5:5,6 With the quotations of Pss. 2:7 and 110:4, the writer demonstrates that Christ's Sonship (*see notes on 1:5*) and His priesthood

6 As *He* also *says* in another *place:*

[g]"*You are a priest forever*
According to the order of
Melchizedek";

7 who, in the days of His flesh, when He
had [h]offered up prayers and supplications,
[i]with vehement cries and tears to Him
[j]who was able to save Him from death,
and was heard [k]because of His godly fear,
8 though He was a Son, *yet* He learned
[l]obedience by the things which He suffered. 9 And [m]having been perfected, He
became the author of eternal salvation to
all who obey Him, 10 called by God as
High Priest [n]"*according to the order of*
Melchizedek," 11 of whom [o]we have much
to say, and hard to explain, since you have
become [p]dull of hearing.

Spiritual Immaturity

12 For though by this time you ought to
be teachers, you need *someone* to teach you
again the first principles of the [2]oracles of
God; and you have come to need [q]milk and
not solid food. 13 For everyone who par-
takes *only* of milk *is* unskilled in the word of
righteousness, for he is [r]a babe. 14 But solid
food belongs to those who are [3]of full age,

6 [g] Ps. 110:4; Heb. 7:17
7 [h] Matt. 26:39, 42, 44; Mark 14:36, 39; Luke 22:41, 44 [i] Ps. 22:1 [j] Matt. 26:53 [k] Matt. 26:39
8 [l] Phil. 2:8
9 [m] Heb. 2:10
10 [n] Ps. 110:4
11 [o] [John 16:12]; Heb. 7:1-22 [p] [Matt. 13:15]
12 [q] 1 Cor. 3:1-3; 1 Pet. 2:2 [2] *sayings, Scriptures*
13 [r] Eph. 4:14
14 [3] *mature*

were both by divine appointment (cf. John 8:54). That means that the two titles are titles of subordination—the subordination not being in regard to essence or nature (cf. John 10:30; 14:9,11), but in regard to the fulfillment of the program of redemption. Neither office diminishes the eternal deity of Christ or the equality of the Trinity. Both offices had a beginning. It is noteworthy that Ps. 2 recognizes the Son as both King and Messiah. Christ is the King-Priest.

5:6 Quoted from Ps. 110:4, from which this whole section is expounded (*see note on 4:14–7:28*). ***Melchizedek.*** As king of Salem and priest of the Most High God in the time of Abraham, he was also a king-priest (Gen. 14:18-20). The Melchizedekan priesthood is discussed in detail in chap. 7.

5:7,8 Having established the first requirement that a High-Priest be appointed (vv. 1,4,5,6), the writer focused on the requirement of being humanly sympathetic (vv. 2,3).

5:7 who. The subsequent context makes it clear that this refers back to Christ, the main subject in v. 5. In Gethsemane, Jesus agonized and wept, but committed Himself to do the Father's will in accepting the cup of suffering which would bring His death (Matt. 26:38-46; Luke 22:44,45). Anticipating bearing the burden of judgment for sin, Jesus felt its fullest pain and grief (cf. Is. 52:14; 53:3-5,10). Though He bore the penalty in silence and did not seek to deliver Himself from it (Is. 53:7), He did cry out from the agony of the fury of God's wrath poured on His perfectly holy and obedient person (Matt. 27:46; cf. 2 Cor. 5:21). Jesus asked to be saved from remaining in death, i.e., to be resurrected (cf. Ps. 16:9,10).

5:8 learned obedience. Christ did not need to suffer in order to conquer or correct any disobedience. In His deity (as the Son of God), He understood obedience completely. As the incarnate Lord, He humbled Himself to learn (cf. Luke 2:52). He learned obedience for the same reasons He bore temptation: to confirm His humanity and experience its sufferings to the fullest (*see notes on 2:10*; cf. Luke 2:52; Phil. 2:8). Christ's obedience was also necessary so that He could fulfill all righteousness (Matt. 5:13) and thus prove to be the perfect sacrifice to take the place of sinners (1 Pet. 3:18). He was the perfectly righteous One, whose righteousness would be imputed to sinners (cf. Rom. 3:24-26).

5:9 perfected...author of eternal salvation. *See notes on 2:10.* Because of the perfect righteousness of Jesus Christ and His perfect sacrifice for sin, He became the cause of salvation. **obey Him.** True salvation evidences itself in obedience to Christ, from the initial obedience to the gospel command to repent and believe (cf. Acts 5:32; Rom. 1:5; 2 Thess. 1:8; 1 Pet. 1:2,22; 4:17) to a life pattern of obedience to the Word (cf. Rom. 6:16).

5:10 Quoting from Ps. 110:4 a second time (cf. v. 6), the writer mentions again the call of God to the priesthood (v. 4).

5:11 of whom. An alternate translation would be "of which" (meaning the relationship of Christ's High-Priesthood to that of Melchizedek). Logically and stylistically, v. 11 appears to introduce the entire section from 5:11–6:12. The same Gr. verb "become" forms brackets around the section: "become dull" (v. 11) and "become sluggish" (6:12). **dull.** The Hebrews' spiritual lethargy and slow response to gospel teaching prevented additional teaching at this time. This is a reminder that failure to appropriate the truth of the gospel produces stagnation in spiritual advancement and the inability to understand or assimilate additional teaching (cf. John 16:12). Such a situation exists also among the Gentiles who have received revelatory truth (natural or general revelation) from God in the creation (Rom. 1:18-20). Rejection of that revelation results in a process of hardening (Rom. 1:21-32). The Hebrews had not only received the same general revelation, they had also received special revelation consisting of the OT Scriptures (Rom. 9:4), the Messiah Himself (Rom. 9:5), and the teaching of the apostles (2:3,4). Until the Hebrews obeyed the revelation they had received and obtained eternal salvation (v. 8), additional teaching about the Messiah's Melchizedekan priesthood would be of no profit to them.

5:12 teachers. Every believer is to be a teacher (Col. 3:16; 1 Pet. 3:15; cf. Deut. 6:7; 2 Tim. 3:15). If these Hebrews had really obeyed the gospel of Christ, they would have been passing that message on to others. The Jews were instructed in the law and prided themselves because they taught the law, but had not really understood or appropriated its truths to themselves (*see notes on Rom. 2:17-23*). **oracles.** These are contained in the OT Scripture, which had laid the foundation for the gospel and had been committed into the care of the Hebrews (Rom. 3:1,2). The ABC's of the law tutored the Hebrews in order to lead them to faith in the Messiah (Gal. 3:23,24). They had also heard the NT gospel (2:2-4; 1 Pet. 4:11).

5:12,13 milk. Knowledge without obedience does not advance a person. In fact, by rejecting saving faith, the Hebrews were regressing in their understanding concerning the Messiah. They had long enough been exposed to the gospel to be teaching it to others, but were babies, too infantile and unskilled to comprehend, let alone teach, the truth of God.

5:13 word of righteousness. This is the message about the righteousness of Christ which we have by faith (Rom. 3:21,22; 1 Cor. 1:30; 2 Cor. 5:21; Phil. 3:9; Titus 3:5). The phrase is equivalent to the gospel of salvation by faith rather than works.

5:14 of full age. The same Gr. root is translated "perfection" in 6:1 and is elsewhere translated "perfect" (7:11,19,28; 9:9; 10:1,14; 11:40; 12:23). It is used in Hebrews, including this text, as a synonym for salvation. In that sense, it refers to the completion which comes when one becomes a believer in Christ, rather than referring to a Christian who has become mature, as is typical Pauline usage (see marginal note, cf. Col. 4:12). Jesus invited unbelieving Jews to the salvation perfection which came only through following Him in faith (Matt. 19:21). Paul wrote that those who had come to Christ by faith were thereby

that is, those who by reason of [4]use have
their senses exercised [s]to discern both good
and evil.

The Peril of Not Progressing

6 Therefore, [a]leaving the discussion of
the elementary *principles* of Christ, let
us go on to [1]perfection, not laying again
the foundation of repentance from [b]dead
works and of faith toward God, 2 [c]of the
doctrine of baptisms, [d]of laying on of
hands, [e]of resurrection of the dead, [f]and of
eternal judgment. 3 And this [2]we will do if
God permits.
4 For *it is* impossible for those who
were once enlightened, and have tasted
[g]the heavenly gift, and [h]have become
partakers of the Holy Spirit, 5 and have
tasted the good word of God and the
powers of the age to come, 6 [3]if they fall
away, to renew them again to repentance,
[i]since they crucify again for themselves
the Son of God, and put *Him* to an open
shame.

14 [s] Is. 7:15; Phil. 1:9 [4] *practice*

CHAPTER 6

1 [a] Heb. 5:12 [b] [Heb. 9:14] [1] *maturity*
2 [c] John 3:25; Acts 19:3-5 [d] [Acts 8:17] [e] Acts 17:31 [f] Acts 24:25
3 [2] M *let us do*
4 [g] [John 4:10]; Eph. 2:8 [h] [Gal. 3:2, 5]; Heb. 2:4
6 [i] Heb. 10:29 [3] Or *and have fallen away*

mature and able to receive the wisdom of God (1 Cor. 2:6). He described believers as "mature" when he referred to those whose righteousness was in Christ (Phil. 3:2-20), as opposed to those who had confidence in the flesh. Paul also declared that the apostles warned and taught everyone "that we may present every man perfect in Christ Jesus" (Col. 1:28). **exercised.** The deeper, more "solid" truths about the priesthood of the Lord Jesus could only be given to those who knew Him as Savior. Athletic training and competition form the metaphor implied by this particular word (cf. 1 Tim. 4:7,8). The one who has come to Christ for spiritual completion is then trained by the Word to discern truth from error and holy behavior from unholy (cf. 2 Tim. 3:16,17).

6:1 leaving. This "leaving" does not mean to despise or abandon the basic doctrines. They are the place to start, not stop. They are the gate of entrance on the road to salvation in Christ. **elementary *principles* of Christ.** As "the oracles of God" in 5:12 refers to the OT, so does this phrase. The writer is referring to basic OT teaching that prepared the way for Messiah—the beginning teaching about Christ. These OT "principles" include the 6 features listed in vv. 1,2. **go on to perfection.** Salvation by faith in Messiah Jesus. *See note on 5:14.* The verb is passive, so as to indicate "let us be carried to salvation." That is not a matter of learners being carried by teachers, but both being carried forward by God. The writer warns his Jewish readers that there is no value in stopping with the OT basics and repeating ("laying again") what was only intended to be foundational. **repentance from dead works.** This OT form of repentance is the turning away from evil deeds that bring death (cf. Ezek. 18:4; Rom. 6:23) and turning to God. Too often the Jew only turned to God in a superficial fashion—fulfilling the letter of the law as evidence of his repentance. The inner man was still dead (Matt. 23:25-28; Rom. 2:28,29). Such repentance was not the kind which brought salvation (v. 6; 12:17; cf. Acts 11:18; 2 Cor. 7:10). Under the New Covenant, however, "repentance toward God" is coupled with "faith in our Lord Jesus Christ" (Acts 20:21). Christ's atoning sacrifice saves from "dead works" (9:14; cf. John 14:6). **faith toward God.** Faith directed only toward the Father is unacceptable without faith in His Son, Jesus Christ (Acts 4:12; cf. James 2:14-20).

6:2 baptisms. A better translation would be "washings" as in 9:10. The Gr. term is never used of Christian baptism. The plural also is inconsistent with the singular concept of Christian baptism. In the OT Levitical system, there were many ceremonial cleansings, which were outward signs of heart cleansing (cf. Ex. 30:18-21; Lev. 16:4,24,26,28; Mark 7:4,8). The New Covenant called for an inner washing (Titus 3:5) that regenerated the soul. **laying on of hands.** Under the Old Covenant, the person who brought a sacrifice placed his hands on it to symbolize his identification with it as a substitute sacrifice for sin (Lev. 1:4; 3:8,13; 16:21). There could also be a reference here to solemn priestly blessings (cf. Matt. 19:13). **resurrection...and of eternal judgment.** The Pharisees believed in the resurrection from the dead (Acts 23:8) but were still spiritually dead (Matt. 23:27). They also believed in the judgment of God and were headed for it. It is significant that all of the doctrines listed in vv. 1,2 can be associated with the Pharisees, who were attracted to and sometimes associated with Jesus (Luke 7:36-50; 13:31; 14:1; John 3:1). Paul was a Pharisee before his conversion (Phil. 3:5). The Pharisees were products of the pursuit of righteousness by works of the law rather than by faith (Rom. 9:30-32; 10:1-3). A portion of the Hebrews to whom this epistle was written may have been Pharisees.

6:3 we will do. The writer is likely both giving his own testimony about going on from OT teaching to embrace the New Covenant in Jesus Christ and also identifying himself with the readers. Salvation always requires God's enablement (cf. John 6:44).

6:4-6 See Introduction: Interpretive Challenges. Five advantages possessed by the Jews are yet insufficient for their salvation.

6:4 enlightened. They had received instruction in biblical truth which was accompanied by intellectual perception. Understanding the gospel is not the equivalent of regeneration (cf. 10:26,32). In John 1:9 it is clear that enlightening is not the equivalent of salvation. Cf. 10:29. **tasted the heavenly gift.** Tasting in the figurative sense in the NT refers to consciously experiencing something (cf. 2:9). The experience might be momentary or continuing. Christ's "tasting" of death (2:9) was obviously momentary and not continuing or permanent. All men experience the goodness of God, but that does not mean they are all saved (cf. Matt. 5:45; Acts 17:25). Many Jews, during the Lord's earthly ministry experienced the blessings from heaven He brought—in healings and deliverance from demons, as well as eating the food He created miraculously (John 6). Whether the gift refers to Christ (cf. John 6:51; 2 Cor. 9:15) or to the Holy Spirit (cf. Acts 2:38; 1 Pet. 1:12), experiencing either one was not the equivalent of salvation (cf. John 16:8; Acts 7:51). **partakers of the Holy Spirit.** *See notes on 2:4.* Even though the concept of partaking is used in 3:1; 3:14; and 12:8 of a relationship which believers have, the context must be the final determining factor. This context in vv. 4-6 seems to preclude a reference to true believers. It could be a reference to their participation, as noted above, in the miraculous ministry of Jesus who was empowered by the Spirit (*see notes on Matt. 12:18-32*; cf. Luke 4:14,18) or in the convicting ministry of the Holy Spirit (John 16:8) which obviously can be resisted without experiencing salvation (cf. Acts 7:51).

6:5 tasted. *See note on v. 4.* This has an amazing correspondence to what was described in 2:1-4 (*see notes there*). Like Simon Magus (Acts 8:9-24), these Hebrews had not yet been regenerated in spite of all they had heard and seen (cf. Matt. 13:3-9; John 6:60-66). They were repeating the sins of those who died in the wilderness after seeing the miracles performed through Moses and Aaron and hearing the voice of God at Sinai.

6:6 fall away. This Gr. term occurs only here in the NT. In the LXX, it was used to translate terms for severe unfaithfulness and apostasy (cf. Ezek. 14:13; 18:24; 20:27). It is equivalent to the apostasy in 3:12. The seriousness of this unfaithfulness is seen in the severe description of rejection within this verse: they re-crucify Christ and treat Him contemptuously (see also the strong descriptions in 10:29). The "impossible" of v. 4 goes with "to renew them again to repentance." Those who sinned against Christ in such a way had no hope of restoration or forgiveness (cf. 2:2,3; 10:26,27; 12:25). The reason is that they had rejected Him with full knowledge and conscious experience

7 For the earth which drinks in the rain
that often comes upon it, and bears herbs
useful for those by whom it is cultivated,
[j]receives blessing from God; 8 [k]but if it
bears thorns and briers, *it is* rejected and
near to being cursed, whose end *is* to be
burned.

A Better Estimate

9 But, beloved, we are confident of better
things concerning you, yes, things that
accompany salvation, though we speak in
this manner. 10 For [l]God *is* not unjust to
forget [m]your work and [4]labor of love
which you have shown toward His name,
in that you have [n]ministered to the saints,
and do minister. 11 And we desire that
each one of you show the same diligence
[o]to the full assurance of hope until the end,
12 that you do not become [5]sluggish, but
imitate those who through faith and patience [p]inherit the promises.

God's Infallible Purpose in Christ

13 For when God made a promise to
Abraham, because He could swear by no
one greater, [q]He swore by Himself, 14 saying, [r]*"Surely blessing I will bless you, and*
multiplying I will multiply you." 15 And so,
after he had patiently endured, he obtained
the [s]promise. 16 For men indeed swear by
the greater, and [t]an oath for confirmation *is*
for them an end of all dispute. 17 Thus God,
determining to show more abundantly to
[u]the heirs of promise [v]the [6]immutability of
His counsel, [7]confirmed *it* by an oath,
18 that by two [8]immutable things, in which
it *is* impossible for God to [w]lie, we [9]might
have strong consolation, who have fled for
refuge to lay hold of the hope [x]set before *us.*

7 [j]Ps. 65:10
8 [k]Is. 5:6
10 [l]Rom. 3:4 [m]1 Thess. 1:3 [n]Rom. 15:25; Heb. 10:32-34 [4]NU omits *labor of*
11 [o]Col. 2:2
12 [5]*lazy* [p]Heb. 10:36
13 [q]Gen. 22:16, 17; Luke 1:73
14 [r]Gen. 22:16, 17
15 [s]Gen. 12:4; 21:5
16 [t]Ex. 22:11
17 [u]Rom. 8:17; Heb. 11:9 [v]Rom. 11:29 [6]*unchangeableness of His purpose* [7]*guaranteed*
18 [w]Num. 23:19; 1 Sam. 15:29; Titus 1:2 [x][Col. 1:5]; Heb. 3:6; 7:19; 12:1 [8]*unchangeable* [9]M omits *might*

(as described in the features of vv. 5,6). With full revelation they rejected the truth, concluding the opposite of the truth about Christ, and thus had no hope of being saved. They can never have more knowledge than they had when they rejected it. They have concluded that Jesus should have been crucified, and they stand with his enemies. There is no possibility of these verses referring to losing salvation. Many Scripture passages make unmistakably clear that salvation is eternal (cf. John 10:27-29; Rom. 8:35,38,39; Phil. 1:6; 1 Pet. 1:4,5). Those who want to make this verse mean that believers can lose salvation will have to admit that it would then also say that one could never get it back again. See Introduction: Interpretive Challenges.

6:7,8 Here are illustrations showing that those who hear the gospel message and respond in faith are blessed; those who hear and reject it are cursed (cf. Matt. 13:18-23).

6:8 rejected. See the use of the term in Rom. 1:28 ("debased"); 2 Cor. 13:5 ("disqualified"); and 2 Tim. 3:8 ("disapproved").

6:9 beloved. This term shows a change of audience and a change from a message of warning to a message of encouragement. That the address is to believers is further confirmed by the expression of confidence that "better things" could be said of them (as compared to those who were being warned in the preceding verses). The "things that accompany salvation" are their works which verify their salvation (v. 10; cf. Eph. 2:10; James 2:18,26). The very statement implies that the things described in 5:11–6:5 do not accompany salvation but are indicative of unbelief and apostasy. **though we speak in this manner.** Though it had been necessary to speak about judgment in the preceding verses, the writer assures the "beloved," those who are believers, that he is confident of their salvation.

6:10 work and labor of love. See 1 Thess. 1:3,4. **toward His name.** Throughout this epistle "name" has the Hebraic sense of the authority, character, and attributes of the Son of God (1:4) or of God the Father (2:12; 13:15; cf. John 14:13,14). **saints.** All true Christians are saints, or "holy ones" (cf. 13:24; Acts 9:13; Rom. 1:7; *see note on 1 Cor. 1:2*).

6:11 you. The author is speaking again to unbelievers but appears to intentionally distance this particular group from the would-be apostates of vv. 4-6, who are in danger of being impossible to restore. **diligence.** This term can carry the idea of eagerness or haste. It is a plea for unbelieving Jews to come to Christ immediately. If these uncommitted Jews followed the example of the active faith of the saints (vv. 9,10,12), they would obtain the salvation which gives "full assurance of hope until the end" (cf. 10:22; Col. 2:2). Salvation should not be postponed.

6:12 sluggish. *See note on 5:11,* where the same Gr. word is translated "dull." **imitate.** This concept is repeated in 13:7 and is inherent in the many illustrations of faith given in chap. 11. **inherit the promises.** The inheritance and the promises of salvation are a theme of this epistle (cf. vv. 13,15,17; 1:14; 4:1,3; 9:15; 10:36; 11:7,8,9,11,13, 17,33,39).

6:13-20 The persecution and trials which the believing Hebrews faced required patient perseverance. That persevering faith would enable them to inherit the promises of God, which at the time of suffering seemed so distant. Regardless of their circumstances, they were to remember that God is faithful (cf. v. 10) and that in Him their hope was secure (cf. v. 11).

6:13 Abraham. To encourage the Hebrews to rely upon faith as opposed to holding on to the Levitical system of worship, the writer cited the example of Abraham, who, as the great model of faith (cf. Rom. 4), should be imitated (v. 12). **swore by Himself.** As recorded in Gen. 22:15-19, God promised unilaterally to fulfill the Abrahamic Covenant.

6:14 Quoted from Gen. 22:17, this summarizes the essence of God's promise. The fact that God had said it assured its fulfillment. It is significant that the quote in Genesis is in the context of Abraham's sacrifice of Isaac, who was the immediate fulfillment of God's promise to Abraham. Ultimate fulfillment would also take place through Isaac and his descendants.

6:15 patiently endured. Abraham was an example of the patience mentioned in v. 12. He received the promise in the beginning of its fulfillment by the birth of Isaac (*see note on v. 14*), but he did not live to see all the promises fulfilled (11:13).

6:16-18 God's Word does not need any confirmation from someone else. It is reliable because God Himself is faithful. People confirm their promises by appealing to someone greater (especially to God) as witness. Since no one is greater than God, He can only provide an oath from Himself. By doing so He is willingly (v. 17) accommodating Himself to human beings who desire the confirmation because of the characteristic unreliability of human promises.

6:18 two immutable things. These are God's promise and His oath. The Gr. term behind "immutable" was used of a legal will, which was unchangeable by anyone but the maker of the will. **fled for refuge.** In the LXX, the Gr. word is used for the cities of refuge God provided for those who sought protection from avengers for an accidental killing (Num. 35:9-34; Deut. 19:1-13; Josh. 20:1-9; cf. Acts 14:5,6). **hope.** *See note on 3:6.* Hope is one of the themes of Hebrews. It is also the product of OT studies (Rom. 15:4). Hope for the fulfillment of God's

19 This *hope* we have as an anchor of the
soul, both sure and steadfast, [y]and which
enters the Presence *behind* the veil,
20 [z]where the forerunner has entered for
us, *even* Jesus, [a]having become High Priest
forever according to the order of Melchizedek.

The King of Righteousness

7 For this [a]Melchizedek, king of Salem,
priest of the Most High God, who met
Abraham returning from the slaughter of
the kings and blessed him, **2** to whom also
Abraham gave a tenth part of all, first
being translated "king of righteousness,"
and then also king of Salem, meaning
"king of peace," **3** without father, without
mother, without genealogy, having neither
beginning of days nor end of life, but made
like the Son of God, remains a priest continually.

4 Now consider how great this man *was*,
to whom even the patriarch Abraham gave
a tenth of the [1]spoils. **5** And indeed [b]those
who are of the sons of Levi, who receive
the priesthood, have a commandment to
receive tithes from the people according to
the law, that is, from their brethren, though
they have come from the loins of Abraham;
6 but he whose genealogy is not derived
from them received tithes from Abraham
[c]and blessed [d]him who had the promises.
7 Now beyond all contradiction the lesser
is blessed by the better. **8** Here mortal men
receive tithes, but there he *receives them*, [e]of
whom it is witnessed that he lives. **9** Even
Levi, who receives tithes, paid tithes
through Abraham, so to speak, **10** for he
was still in the loins of his father when
Melchizedek met him.

Need for a New Priesthood

11 [f]Therefore, if perfection were through
the Levitical priesthood (for under it the
people received the law), what further
need *was there* that another priest should
rise according to the order of Melchizedek,
and not be called according to the order
of Aaron? **12** For the priesthood being
changed, of necessity there is also a change
of the law. **13** For He of whom these things

19 [y]Lev. 16:2, 15; Heb. 9:3, 7
20 [z][John 14:2; Heb. 4:14] [a]Gen. 14:17-19; Ps. 110:4; Heb. 3:1; 5:10, 11

CHAPTER 7

1 [a]Gen. 14:18-20; Heb. 7:6
4 [1]*plunder*
5 [b]Num. 18:21-26; 2 Chr. 31:4
6 [c]Gen. 14:19, 20 [d][Rom. 4:13]
8 [e]Heb. 5:6; 6:20; [Rev. 1:18]
11 [f][Rom. 7:7-14]; Gal. 2:21; Heb. 7:18; 8:7

salvation promises is the "anchor of the soul" (v. 19) keeping the believer secure during the times of trouble and turmoil.

6:19,20 Our hope is embodied in Christ Himself who has entered into God's presence in the heavenly Holy of Holies on our behalf (*see note on 4:14*). By this line of reasoning the writer returned to the topic which he left in 5:10, the Melchizedekan priesthood.

7:1-28 Using the two OT references to Melchizedek (Gen. 14:18-20; Ps. 110:4), chap. 7 explains the superiority of Christ's priesthood to that of this unique High-Priest, who was a type of Christ in certain respects (*see note on 5:6*). Chapter 7 is the focal point of the epistle to the Hebrews because of its detailed comparison of the priesthood of Christ and the Levitical High-Priesthood.

7:1,2 A summary of the account of Melchizedek in Gen. 14:18-20 (*see notes there*).

7:3 The Levitical priesthood was hereditary, but Melchizedek's was not. His parentage and origin are unknown because they were irrelevant to his priesthood. Contrary to some interpretations, Melchizedek did have a father and a mother. The ancient Syriac Peshitta gives a more accurate translation of what was intended by the Gr. phrase: "whose father and mother are not written in genealogies." No record existed of Melchizedek's birth or death. This is quite a contrast to the details of Aaron's death (Num. 20:22-29). **like.** Lit. "made to be like"; this word is used nowhere else in the NT. The implication is that the resemblance to Christ rests upon the way Melchizedek's history is reported in the OT, not upon Melchizedek himself. Melchizedek was not the pre-incarnate Christ, as some maintain, but was similar to Christ in that his priesthood was universal (v. 1), royal (v. 1,2; cf. Zech. 6:13), righteous (v. 2; cf. Ps. 72:2; Jer. 23:5; 1 Cor. 1:30), peaceful (v. 2; cf. Ps. 72:7; Is. 9:6; Rom. 5:1), and unending (v. 3; cf. vv. 24,25).

7:4-28 This section presents the superiority of the Melchizedekan priesthood to the Levitical. The major arguments for superiority are related to the receiving of tithes (vv. 2-10), the giving of blessing (vv. 1,6,7), the replacement of the Levitical priesthood (vv. 11-19), and the perpetuity of the Melchizedekan priesthood (vv. 3,8,16,17,20-28).

7:4 In antiquity, it was common for people to give a tithe to a god or his representative. Abraham, the father of the Hebrew faith, gave a tithe to Melchizedek. That proves that Melchizedek was superior to Abraham. The lesser person tithes to the greater (v. 7).

7:5 By the authority invested in them after the establishment of the Mosaic law, the Levitical priests collected tithes from their fellow Israelites (*see notes on Num. 18:21,26*). The submission of the Israelites was not to honor the priests but to honor the law of God.

7:6,7 Melchizedek not only received a tithe from Abraham, he also blessed him. This proves again Melchizedek's superiority.

7:8 Here...there. The adverbs have reference to the Levitical law whose system was still active at the time ("here") and to the earlier historical incident recorded in Gen. 14 ("there"). The Levitical priesthood changed as each priest died until it passed away altogether, whereas Melchizedek's priesthood is perpetual since the record about his priesthood does not record his death (cf. v. 3).

7:9,10 In an argument based upon seminal headship, the writer observes that it is possible to speak of Levi paying tithes to Melchizedek. It is the same kind of argument Paul employed to demonstrate that when Adam sinned we all sinned (*see note on Rom. 5:12-14*).

7:11-28 In this section the argument is extended a step further. Since the Melchizedekan priesthood is superior to the Levitical priesthood (vv. 1-10), Christ's priesthood is also superior to the Levitical priesthood, since Christ's priesthood is Melchizedekan rather than Levitical.

7:11 perfection. *See note on 5:14.* Throughout Hebrews, the term refers to complete reconciliation with and access to God—salvation. The Levitical system and its priesthood could not save anyone from their sins. *See notes on 10:1-4.*

7:12-14 Since Christ is the Christian's High-Priest and He was of the tribe of Judah, not Levi (cf. Matt. 2:1,6; Rev. 5:5), His priesthood is clearly beyond the law which was the authority for the Levitical priesthood (cf. v. 11). This is proof that the Mosaic law had been abrogated. The Levitical system was replaced by a new Priest, offering a new sacrifice, under a New Covenant. He abrogated the law by fulfilling it (cf. Matt. 5:17) and providing the perfection which the law could never accomplish (cf. Matt. 5:20).

are spoken belongs to another tribe, from
which no man has [2]officiated at the altar.
14 For *it is* evident that [g]our Lord arose
from [h]Judah, of which tribe Moses spoke
nothing concerning [3]priesthood. 15 And it
is yet far more evident if, in the likeness of
Melchizedek, there arises another priest
16 who has come, not according to the law
of a fleshly commandment, but according
to the power of an endless life. 17 For [4]He
testifies:

[i]"You are a priest forever
According to the order of
Melchizedek."

18 For on the one hand there is an annulling of the former commandment because of [j]its weakness and unprofitableness, 19 for [k]the law made nothing
[5]perfect; on the other hand, *there is the*
bringing in of [l]a better hope, through
which [m]we draw near to God.

Greatness of the New Priest

20 And inasmuch as *He was* not *made*
priest without an oath 21 (for they have become priests without an oath, but He with
an oath by Him who said to Him:

[n]"The LORD has sworn
And will not relent,
'You are a priest [6]forever
According to the order of
Melchizedek' "),

22 by so much more Jesus has become a
[7]surety of a [o]better covenant.
23 Also there were many priests, because
they were prevented by death from continuing. 24 But He, because He continues forever, has an unchangeable priesthood.
25 Therefore He is also [p]able to save [8]to the
uttermost those who come to God through
Him, since He always lives [q]to make intercession for them.
26 For such a High Priest was fitting for
us, [r]*who is* holy, [9]harmless, undefiled, separate from sinners, [s]and has become higher than the heavens; 27 who does not need
daily, as those high priests, to offer up sacrifices, first for His [t]own sins and then for
the people's, for this He did once for all
when He offered up Himself. 28 For the

13 [2] *served*
14 [g] Gen. 49:8-10; Num. 24:17; Is. 1:1; Mic. 5:2; Matt. 1:3; 2:6; Rev. 5:5 [h] Matt. 1:2 [3] NU *priests*
17 [i] Ps. 110:4; Heb. 5:6; 6:20; 7:21 [4] NU *it is testified*
18 [j] [Rom. 8:3]; Gal. 3:21; Heb. 7:11
19 [k] [Acts 13:39]; Rom. 3:20; 7:7; Gal. 2:16; 3:21; Heb. 9:9; 10:1 [l] Heb. 6:18, 19 [m] Lam. 3:57; Rom. 5:2; [Eph. 2:18]; Heb. 4:16; James 4:8 [5] *complete*
21 [n] Ps. 110:4; Heb. 5:6; 7:17 [6] NU ends the quotation after *forever.*
22 [o] Heb. 8:6 [7] *guarantee*
25 [p] Jude 24 [q] Rom. 8:34; 1 Tim. 2:5; Heb. 9:24; 1 John 2:1 [8] *completely* or *forever*
26 [r] [2 Cor. 5:21]; Heb. 4:15 [s] Eph. 1:20 [9] *innocent*
27 [t] Lev. 9:7; 16:6; Heb. 5:3

7:13,15 another. In both cases, the term is "another of a different kind" (*heteros*) emphasizing the contrast with the Levitical priesthood.

7:16 fleshly commandment. The law dealt only with the temporal existence of Israel. The forgiveness which could be obtained even on the Day of Atonement was temporary. Those who ministered as priests under the law were mortals receiving their office by heredity. The Levitical system was dominated by matters of physical existence and transitory ceremonialism. **power of an endless life.** Because He is the eternal Second Person of the Godhead, Christ's priesthood cannot end. He obtained His priesthood, not by virtue of the law, but by virtue of His deity.

7:17 Quoted from Ps. 110:4 again (*see notes on 5:6,10*).

7:18 annulling. *See note on vv. 12-14.* The law was weak in that it could not save or bring about inward change in a person (cf. Rom. 8:3; Gal. 4:9).

7:19 the law made nothing perfect. *See note on v. 11.* The law saved no one (cf. Rom. 3:19,20); rather it cursed everyone (cf. Gal. 3:10-13). **a better hope.** *See notes on 3:6; 6:18.* **draw near to God.** See Introduction: Historical and Theological Themes; *see note on 4:16.* This is the key phrase in this passage. Drawing near to God is the essence of Christianity as compared with the Levitical system, which kept people outside His presence. As believer priests, we are all to draw near to God—that is a characteristic of priesthood (cf. Ex. 19:22; *see notes on Matt. 27:51*).

7:20,21 oath. God's promises are unchangeable, sealed with an oath (cf. 6:17). The Melchizedekan priesthood of Christ is confirmed with God's oath in Ps. 110:4. God's mind on this matter will not change ("relent," v. 21).

7:22 surety. This is the only use of the Gr. term in the NT and could also be translated "guarantor." Jesus Himself guarantees the success of His New Covenant of salvation. **a better covenant.** The New Covenant (8:8,13; 9:15). *See notes on Jer. 31:31-34; Matt. 26:28.* The first mention of "covenant" in this epistle is coupled with one of the key themes of the book ("better," cf. v. 19; see Introduction: Historical and Theological Themes). This covenant will be more fully discussed in chap. 8.

7:23,24 *See notes on vv. 3,8,16.*

7:23 many. It is claimed that there were 84 High-Priests who served from Aaron until the destruction of the temple by the Romans in A.D. 70. The lesser priests' numbers were much larger.

7:25 uttermost. Virtually the same concept as was expressed in "perfection" (v. 11) and "make perfect" (v. 19). The Gr. term is used only here and in Luke 13:11 (the woman's body could not be straightened completely). **who come to God.** *See note on 4:16* (cf. John 6:37). **intercession.** The word means "to intercede on behalf of another." It was used to refer to bringing a petition to a king on behalf of someone. *See note on Rom. 8:34.* Cf. the High-Priestly intercessory prayer of Christ in John 17. Since rabbis assigned intercessory powers to angels, perhaps the people were treating angels as intercessors. The writer makes it clear that only Christ is the intercessor (cf. 1 Tim. 2:5).

7:26-28 Christ's divine and holy character is yet another proof of the superiority of His priesthood.

7:26 In His relationship to God, Christ is "holy" (piety without any pollution; Matt. 3:17; 17:5; Mark 1:24; Luke 4:24; Acts 2:27; 13:35). In His relationship to man, He is "harmless" (without evil or malice; John 8:46). In relationship to Himself, He is "undefiled" (free from contamination; 1 Pet. 1:19) and "separate from sinners" (He had no sin nature which would be the source of any act of sin; cf. "without sin" in 4:15). *See notes on 2 Cor. 5:21.* **higher than the heavens.** *See notes on 1:3; 4:14.*

7:27 daily. Whenever the Levitical High-Priest sinned, he was required to offer sacrifices for himself (Lev. 4:3). Whenever the people sinned, he also had to offer a sacrifice for them (Lev. 4:13). These occasions could be daily. Then, annually, on the Day of Atonement, he had to again offer sacrifices for himself and for the people (Lev. 16:6,11, 15). Christ had no sin and needed no sacrifice for Himself. And only one sacrifice (by Him) was needed—one time only, for all men, for all time. **once for all.** A key emphasis in Hebrews. The sacrificial work of Christ never needed to be repeated, unlike the OT priestly sacrifices. Cf. 9:12,26,28; 10:2,10; 1 Pet. 3:18.

law appoints as high priests men who
have weakness, but the word of the oath,
which came after the law, *appoints* the Son
who has been perfected forever.

The New Priestly Service

8 Now *this is* the main point of the things
we are saying: We have such a High
Priest, [a]who is seated at the right hand of
the throne of the Majesty in the heavens,
2 a Minister of [b]the [1]sanctuary and of [c]the
true tabernacle which the Lord erected,
and not man.
3 For [d]every high priest is appointed to
offer both gifts and sacrifices. Therefore [e]*it*
is necessary that this One also have something to offer. 4 For if He were on earth, He
would not be a priest, since there are
priests who offer the gifts according to the
law; 5 who serve [f]the copy and [g]shadow of
the heavenly things, as Moses was divinely instructed when he was about to make
the tabernacle. For He said, [h]*"See that you*
make all things according to the pattern
shown you on the mountain." 6 But now
[i]He has obtained a more excellent ministry,
inasmuch as He is also Mediator of a [j]bet-
ter covenant, which was established on
better promises.

A New Covenant

7 For if that [k]first *covenant* had been
faultless, then no place would have been
sought for a second. 8 Because finding
fault with them, He says: [l]*"Behold, the*
days are coming, says the LORD, *when I*
will make a new covenant with the house
of Israel and with the house of Judah—
9 *not according to the covenant that I made*
with their fathers in the day when I took
them by the hand to lead them out of the
land of Egypt; because they did not contin-
ue in My covenant, and I disregarded
them, says the LORD. 10 *For this is the*
covenant that I will make with the house of
Israel after those days, says the [m]LORD: *I*
will put My laws in their mind and write
them on their hearts; and [n]*I will be their*
God, and they shall be My people.
11 [o]*None of them shall teach his neighbor,*
and none his brother, saying, 'Know the
[p]LORD,' *for all shall know Me, from the*
least of them to the greatest of them. 12 *For*
I will be merciful to their unrighteousness,
[q]*and their sins* [2]*and their lawless deeds I*
will remember no more."
13 [r]In that He says, *"A new covenant,"*
He has made the first obsolete. Now what
is becoming obsolete and growing old is
ready to vanish away.

The Earthly Sanctuary

9 Then indeed, even the first *covenant*
had ordinances of divine service and
[a]the earthly sanctuary. 2 For a tabernacle
was prepared: the first *part,* in which *was*
the lampstand, the table, and the showbread, which is called the [1]sanctuary;

CHAPTER 8
1 [a] Ps. 68:18; 110:1; Eph. 1:20; Col. 3:1; Heb. 2:17; 3:1; 10:12
2 [b] Heb. 9:8, 12 [c] Heb. 9:11, 24 [1] Lit. *holies*
3 [d] [Rom. 4:25; 5:6, 8; Gal. 2:20; Eph. 5:2]; Heb. 5:1; 8:4 [e] [Eph. 5:2; Heb. 9:14]
5 [f] Heb. 9:23, 24 [g] Col. 2:17; Heb. 10:1 [h] Ex. 25:40
6 [i] [2 Cor. 3:6-8] [j] [Luke 22:20]; Heb. 7:22
7 [k] Ex. 3:8; 19:5
8 [l] Jer. 31:31-34
10 [m] Jer. 31:33; Rom. 11:27; Heb. 10:16 [n] Zech. 8:8
11 [o] Is. 54:13; John 6:45; [1 John 2:27] [p] Jer. 31:34
12 [q] Rom. 11:27 [2] NU omits *and their lawless deeds*
13 [r] [2 Cor. 5:17]; Heb. 1:11

CHAPTER 9
1 [a] Ex. 25:8; [Heb. 8:2; 9:11, 24]
2 [1] *holy place,* lit. *holies*

7:28 word of the oath. God confirmed Christ as High-Priest. *See notes on vv. 20,21; 6:16-18.* **perfected forever.** *See note on 2:10.*

8:1–10:18 This entire section is an exposition of the New Covenant promised in Jer. 31:31-34 and its contrast to the Old Covenant of Law.

8:1-5 A brief description of Jesus' priesthood in the heavenly sanctuary, which is better than Aaron's because He serves in a better sanctuary (vv. 1-5; cf. 9:1-12).

8:1 main point. Here the writer arrived at his central message. The fact is that "we have" (current possession) a superior High-Priest, Jesus Christ, who is the fulfillment of all that was foreshadowed in the OT. **seated.** *See notes on 1:3,13.*

8:2 Minister. This is the same word used of the angels in 1:7. In Jer. 33:21 it was used of the priests. **sanctuary.** Cf. 9:3. The holiest place where God dwelt (cf. Ex. 15:17; 25:8; 26:23,24; 1 Chr. 22:17). **true tabernacle.** The definition is given in the phrase "which the Lord erected, and not man," as well as in 9:11,24 (cf. v. 5). It refers to the heavenly dwelling place of God.

8:3 gifts and sacrifices. *See note on 5:1.*

8:4 not be a priest. Jesus was not qualified to be a Levitical priest because He was not of the tribe of Levi. *See note on 7:12-14.* Because of its use of the present tense, this verse indicates that the Levitical system was still in operation at the time of writing, indicating it was before the destruction of the temple in A.D. 70 (*see note on 5:1-4*).

8:5 The quote is from Ex. 25:40. **copy and shadow.** This does not mean that there are actual buildings in heaven which were copied in the tabernacle, but rather that the heavenly realities were adequately symbolized and represented in the earthly tabernacle model.

8:6 Mediator. Cf. 9:15. The word describes a go-between or an arbitrator, in this case between man and God. *See note on 1 Tim. 2:5* (cf. Gal. 3:19,20). **better covenant...better promises.** *See notes on 7:19,22; John 1:17.* This covenant is identified as the "new covenant" in vv. 8,13; 9:15.

8:7 Cf. the same argument in 7:11. The older covenant, incomplete and imperfect, was only intended to be temporary.

8:8-12 Quoted from Jer. 31:31-34 (*see notes there*).

8:9 ***I disregarded them.*** Jeremiah 31:32 says, "though I was a husband to them." The NT writer is quoting from the LXX, which uses a variant reading that does not essentially change the meaning.

8:10 ***mind...hearts.*** By its nature, the Covenant of Law was primarily external, but the New Covenant is internal (cf. Ezek. 36:26,27).

8:12 The LXX represents a slight expansion of the last sentence of Jer. 31:34.

8:13 ready to vanish. Soon after the book of Hebrews was written, the temple in Jerusalem was destroyed and its Levitical worship ended (*see note on 5:1-4;* see Introduction: Author and Date).

9:1-10 In these verses, the author gives a brief description of the tabernacle, to which some 50 chaps. in the OT are devoted, including the tabernacle service (cf. Ex. 25–40). The section is marked off by its beginning with a reference to "ordinances" (v. 1) and closing with a reference to "ordinances" (v. 10).

9:2 first *part*...sanctuary. This is the Holy Place, the first room of the tabernacle (Ex. 26:33). For the items in the Holy Place, see Ex. 25:23-40; 40:22-25; Lev. 24:5-9.

3 [b]and behind the second veil, the part of
the tabernacle which is called the Holiest
of All, 4 which had the [c]golden censer and
[d]the ark of the covenant overlaid on all
sides with gold, in which *were* [e]the golden
pot that had the manna, [f]Aaron's rod that
budded, and [g]the tablets of the covenant;
5 and [h]above it were the cherubim of glory
overshadowing the mercy seat. Of these
things we cannot now speak in detail.

Limitations of the Earthly Service

6 Now when these things had been thus
prepared, [i]the priests always went into the
first part of the tabernacle, performing *the
services.* 7 But into the second part the high
priest *went* alone [j]once a year, not without
blood, which he offered for [k]himself and
for the people's sins *committed* in ignorance; 8 the Holy Spirit indicating this,
that [l]the way into the Holiest of All was
not yet made manifest while the first
tabernacle was still standing. 9 It *was* symbolic for the present time in which both
gifts and sacrifices are offered [m]which
cannot make him who performed the service perfect in regard to the conscience—
10 *concerned* only with [n]foods and drinks,
[o]various [2]washings, [p]and fleshly ordinances imposed until the time of reformation.

The Heavenly Sanctuary

11 But Christ came *as* High Priest of [q]the
good things [3]to come, with the greater and
more perfect tabernacle not made with
hands, that is, not of this creation. 12 Not
[r]with the blood of goats and calves, but
[s]with His own blood He entered the Most
Holy Place [t]once for all, [u]having obtained

3 [b]Ex. 26:31-35; 40:3
4 [c]Lev. 16:12 [d]Ex. 25:10 [e]Ex. 16:33 [f]Num. 17:1-10 [g]Ex. 25:16; 34:29; Deut. 10:2-5
5 [h]Ex. 25:17, 20; Lev. 16:2; 1 Kin. 8:7
6 [i]Num. 18:2-6; 28:3
7 [j]Ex. 30:10; Lev. 16:34; Heb. 10:3 [k]Heb. 5:3
8 [l][John 14:6; Heb. 10:20]
9 [m][Gal. 3:21]; Heb. 7:19
10 [n]Lev. 11:2; Col. 2:16 [o]Num. 19:7 [p]Eph. 2:15 [2]Lit. *baptisms*
11 [q][Eph. 1:3-11]; Heb. 10:1 [3]NU *that have come*
12 [r]Heb. 10:4 [s]Is. 53:12; Eph. 1:7 [t]Zech. 3:9 [u][Dan. 9:24]
13 [v]Lev. 16:14, 15; Heb. 9:19; 10:4

9:3 Holiest of All. This is the Most Holy Place where the ark of the covenant and the mercy seat dwelt—the place of atonement (Ex. 26:33,34).

9:4 golden censer. This is best understood as being the golden altar of incense. *See note on Ex. 30:1-10* (cf. Ex. 40:5,26,27). Though it was outside the Holy Place (Ex. 30:6), the writer of Hebrews pictures the golden altar inside the Most Holy Place because uppermost in his mind is its role in the liturgy of the Day of Atonement. On that day, the High-Priest brought incense from that altar into the Most Holy Place (Lev. 16:12,13). The altar of golden incense marked the boundary of the Holy of Holies as well as the curtain. The High-Priest went beyond the altar of incense only once a year. **the ark.** *See notes on Ex. 25:10-18; 26:31-34.* **golden pot that had the manna.** *See notes on Ex. 16:32-36.* **Aaron's rod.** *See notes on Num. 17:2-10.* **tablets of the covenant.** *See note on Ex. 25:16* (cf. 1 Kin. 8:9).

9:5 cherubim...mercy seat. *See note on Ex. 25:17,18.* **cannot now speak in detail.** The writer has no desire to obscure his main point with details (cf. 8:1).

9:7 This was the Day of Atonement. *See notes on 4:14; 7:27; Lev. 16:16,20-22,30.* **not without blood.** *See note on v. 22.* This is the first of many references to the blood of sacrifice. The term is especially central to 9:1–10:18 where it identifies the deaths of OT sacrifices and of Christ (cf. vv. 12-14). Note, however, that the shedding of blood in and of itself is an insufficient sacrifice. Christ had not only to shed His blood, but to die. Hebrews 10:10 indicates that He gave His body as the sacrificial offering. Without His death, His blood had no saving value. *See notes on v. 14,18,22; 10:10.*

9:8 The Levitical system did not provide any direct access into God's presence for His people. Rather, it kept them away. Nearness had to be provided by another way (v. 12). This is the primary lesson which the Holy Spirit taught concerning the tabernacle. It teaches how inaccessible God is apart from the death of Jesus Christ. See Introduction: Historical and Theological Themes. See the counterpart to this lesson in 10:20. **Holy Spirit.** *See note on 2:4.* By the Spirit-inspired instruction given for the Holiest of All, He was indicating that there was no way to God in the ceremonial system. Only Christ could open the way (cf. John 14:6).

9:9 symbolic. The Gr. word is *parabolē*, from which the Eng. word "parable" is derived. The Levitical system was a parable, an object lesson, about what was to come in Christ. **for the present time.** "For" is ambiguous enough to allow for two different meanings and interpretations: 1) "during" the time of the OT, or 2) "until" and "pointing to" the current Christian era. The NKJV's translation "in which" indicates the first interpretation. The second interpretation is "according to which" (from an alternate Gr. reading) referring to the "parable" rather than to the time, "It was an object lesson from the past pointing to the present time." This latter interpretation is preferable because of the explanation in v. 10. "The present time" is "the time of reformation." **gifts and sacrifices.** *See note on 5:1.* **perfect...conscience.** Again, this term refers to salvation. *See notes on 5:14; 7:11; 10:1* (cf. 7:25). The sacrifices of the OT did not remove the offerers' guilty conscience or provide them with full forgiveness for their sins (cf. 10:1-4). It was only "symbolic" of something else that would—namely Christ. The conscience is a divinely given warning device that reacts to sin and produces accusation and guilt (*see notes on Rom. 2:14,15*) that cannot be relieved apart from the work of Christ (cf. v. 14; 10:22). At the time of salvation it is quieted from its convicting ravings, but it is not deactivated. Rather, it continues its work, warning the believer about sin. Believers should seek a clear conscience (*see notes on 2 Cor. 1:12*).

9:10 foods and drinks. *See notes on Lev. 11:1-47; Deut. 14:3-21* (cf. Col. 2:16). **washings.** *See note on 6:2.* **fleshly ordinances.** The Levitical ordinances regulated the visible actions without changing the inner man (cf. 10:4). **reformation.** The Gr. term means "restoring what is out of line." All things are set straight in Christ. The reformation is the New Covenant and its application. *See note on v. 9.*

9:11 the good things to come. The reference appears to be to the "eternal redemption" (v. 12). In 10:1, the "good things" refer back to the "salvation" of v. 28 (cf. Rom. 10:15). Most Gr. editions of the NT accept the reading "that have come." In the context, both readings refer to the things of the New Covenant. It is just a matter of perspective: whether from the view point of the Levitical system where the realities of redemption were "to come," or the viewpoint of those in the Christian era where the realities of redemption "have come" because Christ has completed His work. **not of this creation.** The phrase is the explanation of "not made with hands"—it is the creation of God alone. The sanctuary where Christ serves is heaven itself (cf. v. 24; 8:2).

9:12 goats and calves. Only one of each was sacrificed on the Day of Atonement (cf. Lev. 16:5-10). The plural here represents the numbers sacrificed as the Day of Atonement was observed year after year. **with His own blood.** A better translation would be "through His own blood." The same phrase is used in 13:12. Nothing is said which would indicate that Christ carried His actual physical blood with Him into the heavenly sanctuary. The Sacrificer was also the Sacrifice. **once for all.** *See note on 7:27.* **eternal redemption.** This word for redemption is found only here and in Luke 1:68; 2:38. Its original use was for the release of slaves by payment of a ransom.

eternal redemption. **13** For if [v]the blood of
bulls and goats and [w]the ashes of a heifer,
sprinkling the unclean, [4]sanctifies for the
[5]purifying of the flesh, **14** how much more
shall the blood of Christ, who through the
eternal Spirit offered Himself without
[6]spot to God, [x]cleanse your conscience
from [y]dead works [z]to serve the living
God? **15** And for this reason [a]He is the Mediator of the new covenant, by means of
death, for the redemption of the transgressions under the first covenant, that [b]those
who are called may receive the promise of
the eternal inheritance.

13 [w]Num. 19:2 [4]*sets apart* [5]*cleansing*
14 [x]1 John 1:7 [y]Heb. 6:1 [z]Luke 1:74 [6]*blemish*
15 [a]Rom. 3:25 [b]Heb. 3:1

The Mediator's Death Necessary

16 For where there *is* a testament, there
must also of necessity be the death of the
testator. **17** For [c]a testament *is* in force after
men are dead, since it has no power at all
while the testator lives. **18** [d]Therefore not
even the first *covenant* was dedicated without blood. **19** For when Moses had spoken
every [7]precept to all the people according
to the law, [e]he took the blood of calves and
goats, [f]with water, scarlet wool, and hyssop, and sprinkled both the book itself and
all the people, **20** saying, [g]*"This is the*
[h]*blood of the covenant* which *God has*

17 [c]Gal. 3:15
18 [d]Ex. 24:6
19 [e]Ex. 24:5,6 [f]Lev. 14:4,7; Num. 19:6, 18 [7]*command*
20 [g][Matt. 26:28] [h]Ex. 24:3-8

9:13-22 Christ's death was necessary for the fulfillment of the older covenant and the establishment of the new.

9:13 ashes of a heifer. *See notes on Num. 19.* It is said that, in the history of Israel, only 6 red heifers were killed and their ashes used. One heifer's ashes would suffice for centuries since only a minute amount of the ash was required. **unclean.** The Gr. term is literally "common" or "profane." Not that it was ceremonially unclean, but that it was not sanctified or set apart unto God. The word was used in Jesus' discourse on what defiles a man (cf. Matt. 15:11,18,20; Mark 7:15,18,20,23), in the Jews' complaint that Paul had defiled the temple by bringing Gentiles into it (Acts 21:28), and in reference to the meats which Peter had been invited to eat (Acts 10:15; 11:9). According to the Mosaic regulation, the red heifer's ashes were to be placed "outside the camp" and used in a ceremony for symbolic purifying from sin (Num. 19:9; cf. 13:11-13).

9:14 how much more. Superior to the cleansing capability of the ashes of an animal is the cleansing power of the sacrifice of Christ. **the blood of Christ.** This is an expression that refers not simply to the fluid, but the whole atoning sacrificial work of Christ in His death. Blood is used as a substitute word for death (cf. Matt. 23:30,35; 27:6,8,24,25; John 6:54-56; Acts 18:6; 20:26). *See notes on Matt. 26:28; Rom. 3:25; 5:9; Col. 1:14.* **the eternal Spirit.** *See note on 2:4* (cf. Is. 42:1; 61:1; Luke 4:1,14). Some interpreters argue that the lack of the definite article in the Gr. makes this a reference to Christ's own "eternal spirit" (in the sense of an endless life, cf. 7:16). However, the references to the Holy Spirit in 2:4 and 6:4 are also without the definite article. The use of "eternal" as a qualifier serves to relate the Spirit to the "eternal redemption" (v. 12) and the "eternal inheritance" (v. 15) which Christ accomplished by His sacrificial death. **offered Himself.** *See notes on v. 7; John 10:17,18.* The animals in the Levitical system were brought involuntarily and without understanding to their deaths. Christ came of His own volition with a full understanding of the necessity and consequences of His sacrifice. His sacrifice was not just His blood, it was His entire human nature (cf. 10:10). **without spot.** In the LXX, the term is used for describing acceptable sacrifices including the red heifer (Num. 19:3; cf. Ex. 29:1; Lev. 1:3). A similar reference is found in 1 Pet. 1:19 (*see note there*). **conscience.** *See note on v. 9.* **dead works.** *See note on 6:1.* The works are dead because the unregenerate are "dead in trespasses and sins" (Eph. 2:1), their works are worthless and unproductive (Gal. 2:16; 5:19-21), and they end in death (Rom. 6:23). **to serve the living God.** Salvation is not an end in itself. The believer has been freed from sin to serve God, saved to serve (cf. Rom. 6:16-18; 1 Thess. 1:9). The contrast between dead works and the living God (cf. 3:12; 10:31; 12:22) is basic. Cf. James 2:14-26.

9:15 Mediator. *See note on 8:6.* **death.** In the making of some biblical covenants, sacrifices were involved. When God made the covenant with Abraham, 5 different animals were sacrificed in the ceremony (Gen. 15:9,10). The Mosaic Covenant was affirmed by animal sacrifices (Ex. 24:5-8). **redemption.** The compound term used here is found more frequently than the term used in v. 12 (cf. 11:35; Luke 21:28; Rom. 3:24). Jesus' death retroactively redeemed all those who had believed in God under the Old Covenant (cf. Rom. 3:24-26). This is in keeping with symbolism of the Day of Atonement. Annually the High-Priest would atone for or cover the sins that the people had committed in the preceding year (Lev. 16:16,21,30). **first covenant.** *See note on Gen. 9:16.* The actual first covenant historically was made with Noah (Gen. 6:18; 9:9). Next came the covenant made with Abraham (Gen. 15:18). By context, however, the older covenant under discussion in this epistle is that which is called the Mosaic Covenant or the Covenant of Law (Ex. 19:1–20:21). "First" in this verse, therefore, means the former, older covenant with which the Levitical system is connected. **those who are called.** Lit. "the ones having been called," looking back to those under the Old Covenant who were called to salvation by God on the basis of the sacrifice of Jesus Christ to come long after most of them had died. The reference, as always in the NT epistles, is to the effectual calling related to salvation (cf. 3:1), which in this context refers to OT believers. **promise of the eternal inheritance.** That is, salvation in its fullness (*see notes on "rest" in 3:11; 4:1,9; 6:12; 1 Pet. 1:3-5*).

9:16,17 A last will and testament illustrates the necessity of Christ's death. "Testament" is the same Gr. word translated "covenant," but the term takes on the more specialized meaning in this context. The benefits and provisions of a will are only promises until the one who wrote the will dies. Death activates the promises into realities.

9:18-20 The shedding of blood in the covenant ratification ceremony at Sinai (Ex. 24:1-8) also illustrates the necessity of Christ's death (*see note on v. 15*).

9:18 blood. "Death" in vv. 15,16 is replaced by "blood" (*see notes on vv. 7,14*). The term is used to emphasize the violent aspect of His sacrificial death.

9:19 water, scarlet wool, and hyssop. These items were used at the Passover in Egypt (Ex. 12:22) for sprinkling of blood, and in the ritual cleansing for lepers (Lev. 14:4), and in the red heifer ceremony (Num. 19:6). More of those are in view here. These elements were a part of the sprinkling of blood in the covenant ceremony described in Ex. 24:1-8, though not mentioned there. The added details came either by direct revelation to the writer or had been preserved in other records or traditions known to the writer and his readers. **the book...the people.** *See notes on Ex. 24:1-8.* The consecration of Aaron and his sons to the priesthood is the only other occasion in the OT when any persons were sprinkled with blood (Ex. 29:21; Lev. 8:30; cf. 1 Pet. 1:2). The detail about the book also being sprinkled with the blood is not recorded in the Exodus account.

9:20 ***This is the blood.*** Cf. Ex. 24:8 with Matt. 26:28. The same formula was utilized in the inaugural ceremonies for the Mosaic Covenant and for the New Covenant.

commanded you.” 21 Then likewise [i]he
sprinkled with blood both the tabernacle
and all the vessels of the ministry. 22 And
according to the law almost all things are
[8]purified with blood, and [j]without shedding of blood there is no [9]remission.

Greatness of Christ's Sacrifice

23 Therefore *it was* necessary that [k]the
copies of the things in the heavens should
be [1]purified with these, but the heavenly
things themselves with better sacrifices than
these. 24 For [l]Christ has not entered the holy
places made with hands, *which are* [2]copies of
[m]the true, but into heaven itself, now [n]to appear in the presence of God for us; 25 not
that He should offer Himself often, as [o]the
high priest enters the Most Holy Place every
year with blood of another— 26 He then
would have had to suffer often since the
foundation of the world; but now, once at
the end of the ages, He has appeared to put
away sin by the sacrifice of Himself. 27 [p]And
as it is appointed for men to die once, [q]but
after this the judgment, 28 so [r]Christ was [s]of-
fered once to bear the sins [t]of many. To those
who [u]eagerly wait for Him He will appear a
second time, apart from sin, for salvation.

Animal Sacrifices Insufficient

10 For the law, having a [a]shadow of
the good things to come, *and* not the
very image of the things, [b]can never with
these same sacrifices, which they offer continually year by year, make those who approach perfect. 2 For then would they not

21 [i] Ex. 29:12, 36
22 [j] Lev. 17:11 [8] *cleansed* [9] *forgiveness*
23 [k] Heb. 8:5 [1] *cleansed*
24 [l] Heb. 6:20 [m] Heb. 8:2 [n] Rom. 8:34 [2] *representations*
25 [o] Heb. 9:7
27 [p] Gen. 3:19; Eccl. 3:20 [q] [2 Cor. 5:10]; 1 John 4:17
28 [r] Rom. 6:10 [s] Is. 53:12; 1 Pet. 2:24 [t] Matt. 26:28 [u] 1 Cor. 1:7; Titus 2:13

CHAPTER 10

1 [a] Heb. 8:5 [b] Heb. 7:19; 9:9

9:21 likewise. The dedication of the tabernacle and its vessels was accompanied by a blood sprinkling ritual similar to that observed at the inauguration of the Mosaic Covenant (cf. Ex. 29:10-15,21,36,37).

9:22 almost all. There were a few exceptions. Water, incense, and fire were also used to purify (cf. Ex. 19:10; Lev. 15:5; Num. 16:46,47; 31:21-24). Those who were too poor to bring even a small animal for sacrifice were allowed to bring fine flour instead (Lev. 5:11). **blood…remission.** "It *is* the blood *that* makes atonement for the soul" (Lev. 17:11). The phraseology is reminiscent of Christ's own words (Matt. 26:28). "Shedding of blood" refers to death (*see notes on vv. 7,14,18*). "Remission" (meaning forgiveness) is the emphatic last word in this section (vv. 18-22) of the Gr. NT, and it forms the transition to the next section (vv. 23-28).

9:23-28 Christ's High-Priestly ministry is to be exercised in the perfect tabernacle of heaven. The real High-Priest who offered the real sacrifice for sin serves in the real tabernacle. He is the complete fulfillment of the shadowy copies in the Levitical system.

9:23 copies. *See note on 8:5.* The earthly tabernacle and its vessels were only symbolic replicas of the true heavenly tabernacle (8:2), and were also made unclean by the transgressions of the people (Lev. 16:16). **the heavenly things.** As the preceding context indicated, the inauguration of the Mosaic Covenant by sacrifices was necessary (vv. 18-21). That concept is here applied to the heavenly sanctuary—it is dedicated or inaugurated as the central sanctuary of the New Covenant by Christ's sacrifice. The better covenant required a better sacrifice. **better sacrifices.** Christ's superior sacrifice is a major theme in 9:13–10:18. The many sacrifices of the Levitical system were to be superseded by better sacrifices that would be represented in the one, all-inclusive, perfect sacrifice of Christ (cf. 10:12). *See note on 7:22.*

9:24 copies. The term is not the same as that used in v. 23 and 8:5. This is lit. "antitype." It is used only twice in the NT. The antitype either prefigures the type (as here), or is a later illustration of the type (as in 1 Pet. 3:21). In both cases, the antitype is not the real thing, but only a copy of it. The earthly "holy places" in the tabernacle were only types of the heavenly abode of God. **now to appear.** On the Day of Atonement, the High-Priest entered the Most Holy Place where God made an appearance (Lev. 16:2). The High-Priest, however, was hidden from the presence of God by the cloud of incense (Lev. 16:12,13). See also "has appeared" (v. 26) and "will appear" (v. 28). Each verb is a different term in the Gr. The term for Christ's present appearance in heaven (v. 24) alludes to His official presentation to report to the Father on the fulfillment of His mission. The concept of making an appearance or being revealed is involved in the incarnational appearance in order to die once for sin (v. 26). At Christ's appearing at the Second Advent (v. 28), the term used stresses the visible nature of the appearance (cf. 2:8; 12:14). All 3 tenses of Christ's soteriological ministry are also covered: 1) His First Advent to save us from the penalty of sin; 2) His present intercessory ministry in heaven to save us from the power of sin; and 3) His Second Advent to deliver us from the presence of sin. **for us.** Christ is our representative and the provider of our spiritual benefits (cf. 2:9; 6:20; 7:25; John 14:12-14; Eph. 1:3).

9:26 since the foundation of the world. This is a reference to creation (*see notes on 4:3*). **end of the ages.** All the eras and ages came together and were consummated in the coming of the Messiah. The eschatological era was inaugurated (*see note on 1:2*; cf. Gal. 4:4).

9:27 to die once. This is a general rule for all mankind. There have been very rare exceptions (e.g., Lazarus and the multitude who were resuscitated at Christ's resurrection died twice; cf. John 11:43,44; Matt. 27:51-53). Those, like Lazarus, who were raised from the dead by a miraculous act of our Lord were not resurrected to a glorified body and unending life. They only experienced resuscitation. Another exception will be those who don't die even once, but who will be "caught up…to meet the Lord in the air" (1 Thess. 4:17; cf. Enoch, Gen. 5:24; Elijah, 2 Kin. 2:11). **the judgment.** A general term encompassing the judgment of all people, believers (*see note on 2 Cor. 5:10*) and unbelievers (*see notes on Rev. 20:11-15*).

9:28 to bear the sins of many. *See note on Is. 53:12* (cf. 2 Cor. 5:21; 1 Pet. 2:24). **eagerly wait.** *See note on Phil. 3:20.* **second time.** On the Day of Atonement, the people eagerly waited for the High-Priest to come back out of the Holy of Holies. When he appeared, they knew that the sacrifice on their behalf had been accepted by God. In the same way, when Christ appears at His second coming, it will be confirmation that the Father has been fully satisfied with the Son's sacrifice on behalf of believers. At that point salvation will be consummated (cf. 1 Pet. 1:3-5). **apart from sin.** *See notes on 2:17,18; 4:15.* This phrase testifies to the completed work of Christ in removing sins by His sacrifice at His first coming. No such burden will be upon Him in His second coming.

10:1-18 Christ's offering was a once-for-all sacrifice which is superior to all the sacrifices of the Levitical system.

10:1 shadow. *See note on 8:5.* The Gr. term translated "shadow" refers to a pale reflection, as contrasted with a sharp, distinct one. The term behind "very image," on the other hand, indicates an exact and distinct replica (cf. Col. 2:17). **good things.** *See note on 9:11.* **perfect.** This term is used repeatedly in Hebrews to refer to salvation. *See notes on 5:14; 7:11; 9:9.* As much as those living under the law desired to approach God, the Levitical system provided no way to enter His holy presence (cf. Pss. 15:1; 16:11; 24:3,4).

have ceased to be offered? For the worshipers, once [1]purified, would have had
no more consciousness of sins. **3** But in
those *sacrifices there is* a reminder of sins
every year. **4** For [c]*it is* not possible that the
blood of bulls and goats could take away
sins.

Christ's Death Fulfills God's Will

5 Therefore, when He came into the
world, He said:

[d]*"Sacrifice and offering You did not*
desire,
But a body You have prepared for
Me.
6 *In burnt offerings and sacrifices for*
sin
You had no pleasure.
7 *Then I said, 'Behold, I have come—*
In the volume of the book it is
written of Me—
To do Your will, O God.' "

8 Previously saying, *"Sacrifice and offer-*
ing, burnt offerings, and offerings for sin
You did not desire, nor had pleasure in
them" (which are offered according to the
law), **9** then He said, *"Behold, I have come*
to do Your will, [2]*O God."* He takes away
the first that He may establish the second.
10 [e]By that will we have been [3]sanctified
[f]through the offering of the body of Jesus
Christ once *for all.*

Christ's Death Perfects the Sanctified

11 And every priest stands [g]ministering
daily and offering repeatedly the same sacrifices, which can never take away sins.
12 [h]But this Man, after He had offered one
sacrifice for sins forever, sat down [i]at the
right hand of God, **13** from that time waiting [j]till His enemies are made His footstool. **14** For by one offering He has perfected forever those who are being
[4]sanctified.

15 But the Holy Spirit also witnesses to
us; for after He had said before,

16 [k]*"This is the covenant that I will make*
with them after those days, says the LORD:
I will put My laws into their hearts, and in
their minds I will write them," **17** *then He*
adds, [l]*"Their sins and their lawless deeds I*
will remember no more." **18** Now where
there is [5]remission of these, *there is* no
longer an offering for sin.

2 [1] *cleansed*
4 [c] Mic. 6:6, 7
5 [d] Ps. 40:6-8
9 [2] NU, M omit *O God*
10 [e] John 17:19; [Eph. 5:26; Heb. 2:11; 10:14, 29; 13:12] [f] [Heb. 9:12] [3] *set apart*
11 [g] Num. 28:3
12 [h] Col. 3:1; Heb. 1:3 [i] Ps. 110:1
13 [j] Ps. 110:1; Heb. 1:13
14 [4] *set apart*
16 [k] Jer. 31:33, 34; Heb. 8:10
17 [l] Jer. 31:34
18 [5] *forgiveness*

10:2 consciousness of sins. This is the same word translated "conscience" in v. 22; 9:9; 13:18. *See note on 9:9.* If sin had really been overpowered by that system of sacrifices, the OT believers' consciences would have been cleansed from condemning guilt (cf. v. 22). There was not freedom of conscience under the Old Covenant.

10:3 reminder. The OT sacrifices not only could not remove sin, but their constant repetition was a constant reminder of that deficiency. The promise of the New Covenant was that the sin would be removed and even God would "remember" their sins "no more" (8:12, quoting Jer. 31:34).

10:4 not possible. The Levitical system was not designed by God to remove or forgive sins. It was preparatory for the coming of the Messiah (Gal. 3:24) in that it made the people expectant (cf. 1 Pet. 1:10). It revealed the seriousness of their sinful condition, in that even temporary covering required the death of an animal. It revealed the reality of God's holiness and righteousness by indicating that sin had to be covered. Finally, it revealed the necessity of full and complete forgiveness so that God could have desired fellowship with His people.

10:5-7 Quoted from Ps. 40:6-8.

10:5,6 ***You did not desire.*** God was not pleased with sacrifices given by a person who did not give them out of a sincere heart (cf. Ps. 51:17; Is. 1:11; Jer. 6:20; Hos. 6:6; Amos 5:21-25). To sacrifice only as a ritual, without obedience, was a mockery and worse than no sacrifice at all (cf. Is. 1:11-18).

10:5 ***a body You have prepared for Me.*** Psalm 40:6 reads, "My ears you have opened." This does not represent a significant alteration in the meaning of the psalm, as indicated by the fact that the writer quoted the LXX version of the Heb. idiom, which was an accurate representation for Greek readers. The Greek translators regarded the Heb. words as a figure of speech, in which a part of something signified the whole, i.e., the hollowing out of ears was part of the total work of fashioning a human body. And ears were selected as the part to emphasize because they were symbols of obedience as the organ of the reception of God's Word and will (cf. 1 Sam. 15:22). Christ needed a body in order to offer Himself as the final sacrifice (2:14).

10:7 ***To do Your will.*** Cf. Matt. 26:39,42.

10:8,9 The writer quotes from Ps. 40:6-8 again, but in a condensed form.

10:9 first...second. The old, repetitious sacrificial system was removed to make way for the new, once-for-all sacrifice of Christ, who had obediently done God's will (cf. 5:8; Phil. 2:8).

10:10 sanctified. "Sanctify" means to "make holy," to be set apart from sin for God (cf. 1 Thess. 4:3). When Christ fulfilled the will of God, He provided for the believer a continuing, permanent condition of holiness (Eph. 4:24; 1 Thess. 3:13). This is the believer's positional sanctification as opposed to the progressive sanctification that results from daily walking by the will of God (*see notes on Rom. 6:19; 12:1,2; 2 Cor. 7:1*). **body.** Refers to His atoning death, as the term "blood" has been used to do (9:7,12,14,18,22). Mention of the body of Christ in such a statement is unusual in the NT, but it is logically derived from the quotation from Ps. 40:6.

10:11,12 The old and new are contrasted: thousands of priests versus one Priest; the old priests continually standing versus the sitting down of the new; repeated offerings versus a once-for-all offering; and the ineffective sacrifices that only covered sin versus the effective sacrifice that completely removes sin.

10:11 stands. *See note on 1:3.* In 2 Chr. 6:10,12, Solomon sat on his throne as king, but stood at the altar when acting in a priestly role (cf. Deut. 17:12; 18:7).

10:13 footstool. *See note on 1:13.* This is yet another reference to Ps. 110:1. This prediction will be fulfilled when Christ returns and all creation acknowledges His lordship by bowing at His feet (Phil. 2:10).

10:14 perfected. *See note on v. 1.* This involves a perfect standing before God in the righteousness of Christ (*see notes on Rom. 3:22; Phil. 3:8,9*). **sanctified.** *See notes on v. 10.*

10:15-17 The writer confirms his interpretation of Ps. 40:7-9 by repeating from Jer. 31:31-34 what he had already quoted in 8:8-12.

Hold Fast Your Confession

19 Therefore, brethren, having [m]bold-
ness[6] to enter [n]the Holiest by the blood of
Jesus, 20 by a new and [o]living way which
He consecrated for us, through the veil,
that is, His flesh, 21 and *having* a High
Priest over the house of God, 22 let us
[p]draw near with a true heart [q]in full assurance of faith, having our hearts sprinkled
from an evil conscience and our bodies
washed with pure water. 23 Let us hold fast
the confession of *our* hope without wavering, for [r]He who promised *is* faithful.
24 And let us consider one another in order
to stir up love and good works, 25 [s]not forsaking the assembling of ourselves together, as *is* the manner of some, but exhorting
one another, and [t]so much the more as you
see [u]the Day approaching.

The Just Live by Faith

26 For [v]if we sin willfully [w]after we have

19 [m] [Eph. 2:18]; Heb. 4:16 [n] Heb. 9:8, 12 [6] *confidence*
20 [o] John 14:6; [Heb. 7:24, 25]
22 [p] Heb. 7:19; 10:1 [q] Eph. 3:12
23 [r] 1 Cor. 1:9; 10:13; 1 Thess. 5:24; Heb. 11:11
25 [s] Acts 2:42 [t] Rom. 13:11 [u] Phil. 4:5
26 [v] Num. 15:30 [w] 2 Pet. 2:20

10:19-25 For the second time (cf. 8:1-6 for the first), the writer gives a summary of the arguments for the superiority of Christ's priestly ministry.

10:19 brethren. *See note on 3:12.* As on the earlier occasion, the writer addresses his Jewish brethren with an invitation to leave behind the Levitical system and to appropriate the benefits of the New Covenant in Christ. **boldness.** Or "confidence," an important emphasis in the epistle (*see note on 4:16*). Because of the high-priestly ministry of Christ and His finished sacrifice, the Hebrews can enter boldly into the presence of God.

10:20 new. In Gr., this word originally meant "newly slain," but was understood as "recent" when the epistle was written. The way is new because the covenant is new. It is not a way provided by the Levitical system. **living way.** Though it is the path of eternal life, it was not opened by Christ's sinless life—it required His death. *See notes on 2:17,18; 4:16.* The Hebrews were invited to embark on this way which is characterized by the eternal life of the Son of God who loved them and gave Himself for them (cf. John 14:6; Gal. 2:20). The Christian faith was known as "the Way" among the Jews of Jerusalem (Acts 9:2) as well as among the Gentiles (Acts 19:23). Those receiving this epistle understood quite clearly that the writer was inviting them to become Christians—to join those who had been persecuted for their faith. True believers in their midst were even then suffering persecution, and those who had not committed themselves to the Way were asked to become targets of the same persecution. **veil...flesh.** When Jesus' flesh was torn at His crucifixion, so was the temple veil that symbolically separated men from God's presence (Matt. 27:51). When the High-Priest on the Day of Atonement entered the Holy of Holies, the people waited outside for him to return. When Christ entered the heavenly temple He did not return. Instead, He opened the curtain and exposed the Holy of Holies so that we could follow Him. Here "flesh" is used as was "body" (v. 10) and "blood" (9:7,12,14,18,22) to refer to the sacrificial death of the Lord Jesus.

10:21 the house of God. *See note on 3:6.*

10:22 let us draw near. *See note on 7:19.* Based on what had been written, this was the heart of the invitation to those in the assembly who had not come to Christ. The same invitation is found in the first NT book to be written (James 4:8), where James reveals the corollary of drawing near to God: God will draw near to you. Asaph taught that it is a good thing to draw near to God (Ps. 73:28). The full restoration of Israel to God's blessing is dependent upon them drawing near to Him (Jer. 30:18-22). In other words, it is an eschatological invitation coming to them in "these last days" (1:2). This verse describes the prerequisites for entering the presence of God (cf. Ps. 15): sincerity, security, salvation, and sanctification. **true heart.** The Gr. term behind "true" carries the ideas of being sincere, genuine, and without ulterior motive (cf. Jer. 24:7; Matt. 15:8). This one thing these particular Hebrews lacked: genuine commitment to Christ. **full assurance of faith.** *See note on 6:11.* Utter confidence in the promises of God is intended by the phrase. Such confidence will result in heartfelt assurance or security which will allow them to persevere through the coming trials. This is the first of a familiar triad: faith, hope (v. 23), and love (v. 24). **hearts sprinkled.** *See notes on 9:9,14; 10:1-4; 1 Pet. 1:2.* **pure water.** The imagery in this verse is taken from the sacrificial ceremonies of the Old Covenant, where blood was sprinkled as a sign of cleansing, and the priests were continually washing themselves and the sacred vessels in basins of clear water. The "washing with pure water" does not refer to Christian baptism, but to the Holy Spirit's purifying one's life by means of the Word of God (cf. Eph. 5:25,26; Titus 3:5). This is purely a New Covenant picture (Jer. 31:33; Ezek. 36:25,26).

10:23 hold fast. Holding on, or the perseverance of the saints, is the human side of eternal security. It is not something done to maintain salvation, but is rather an evidence of salvation. *See note on 3:6.* **confession of *our* hope.** Affirmation of salvation. *See note on 3:1.* **without wavering.** The idea is not to follow any inclination that leads back to the old covenant. In other ancient literature, the same Gr. term is used of enduring torture. Persecution will come (2 Tim. 3:12), but God is faithful. Temptations will abound, but God is faithful to provide an escape (cf. 1 Cor. 10:13). God's promises are reliable (1 Cor. 10:13; 1 Thess. 5:24; Jude 24,25). With that confidence, the believer can persevere.

10:24 consider. The same verb is used about Jesus in 3:1. The invitation must be responded to individually, but the response also has a corporate side. They are members of a community of Hebrews whose initial attraction to Christ is in danger of eroding. They have been considering a return to the Levitical system of Judaism to avoid the persecution (cf. John 12:42,43). Mutual encouragement to make full commitment is crucial. **stir up.** The Eng. word "paroxysm" is derived from the Gr. term used here. The meaning in this context is that of stimulating or inciting someone to do something. **love and good works.** An example of such mutual effort in the midst of persecution was to be found at Corinth (cf. 2 Cor. 8:1-7).

10:25 not forsaking the assembling. Collective and corporate worship is a vital part of spiritual life. The warning here is against apostasy in an eschatological context (cf. 2 Thess. 2:1). The reference is to the approaching "Day" (the second coming of Christ; cf. Rom. 13:12; 1 Cor. 3:13; 1 Thess. 5:4). **exhorting.** Exhortation takes the form of encouragement, comfort, warning, or strengthening. There is an eschatological urgency to the exhortation which requires an increased activity as the coming of Christ approaches (cf. 3:13; cf. 1 Thess. 4:18).

10:26-39 *See notes on 6:1-8.* This warning passage deals with the sin of apostasy, an intentional falling away, or defection. Apostates are those who move toward Christ, hear and understand His gospel, and are on the verge of saving belief, but then rebel and turn away. This warning against apostasy is one of the most serious warnings in all of Scripture. Not all of the Hebrews would respond to the gentle invitation of vv. 19-25. Some were already beyond response.

10:26 we. The author is speaking rhetorically. In v. 39, he excludes himself and genuine believers from this category. **sin willfully.** The Gr. term carries the idea of deliberate intention that is habitual. The sin is rejecting Christ deliberately. These are not isolated acts. According to the Mosaic legislation, such acts of deliberate, premeditated sin required exclusion from the congregation of Israel (cf. Num. 15:30,31) and from its worship (cf. Ex. 21:14). Such sins also excluded the individual from sanctuary in the cities of refuge (cf. Deut. 19:11-13). **knowledge.**

received the knowledge of the truth, there
[x]no longer remains a sacrifice for sins,
27 but a certain fearful expectation of judgment, and [y]fiery indignation which will
devour the adversaries. **28** Anyone who
has rejected Moses' law dies without
mercy on the testimony of two or three
[z]witnesses. **29** [a]Of how much worse punishment, do you suppose, will he be
thought worthy who has trampled the Son
of God underfoot, [b]counted the blood of
the covenant by which he was sanctified a
common thing, [c]and insulted the Spirit of
grace? **30** For we know Him who said,
[d]*"Vengeance is Mine, I will repay,"* [7]says
the Lord. And again, [e]*"The LORD will*
judge His people." **31** [f]It is a fearful thing to
fall into the hands of the living God.
32 But [g]recall the former days in which,
after you were [8]illuminated, you endured
a great struggle with sufferings: **33** partly
while you were made [h]a spectacle both by
reproaches and tribulations, and partly
while [i]you became companions of those
who were so treated; **34** for you had compassion on [9]me [j]in my chains, and [k]joy-
fully accepted the plundering of your
[1]goods, knowing that [l]you have a better
and an enduring possession for yourselves
[2]in heaven. **35** Therefore do not cast away
your confidence, [m]which has great reward.
36 [n]For you have need of endurance, so
that after you have done the will of God,
[o]you may receive the promise:

37 *"For [p]yet a little while,*
And [q]He[3] who is coming will come
and will not [4]tarry.

26 [x]Heb. 6:6
27 [y]Zeph. 1:18
28 [z]Deut. 17:2-6; 19:15; Matt. 18:16; Heb. 2:2
29 [a][Heb. 2:3] [b]1 Cor. 11:29 [c][Matt. 12:31]
30 [d]Deut. 32:35; Rom. 12:19 [e]Deut. 32:36 [7]NU omits *says the Lord*
31 [f][Luke 12:5]
32 [g]Gal. 3:4; Heb. 6:9, 10 [8]*enlightened*
33 [h]1 Cor. 4:9; Heb. 12:4 [i]Phil. 1:7
34 [j]2 Tim. 1:16 [k]Matt. 5:12 [l]Matt. 6:20 [9]NU *the prisoners* instead of *me in my chains* [1]*possessions* [2]NU omits *in heaven*
35 [m]Matt. 5:12
36 [n]Luke 21:19; Heb. 12:1 [o][Col. 3:24] **37** [p]Luke 18:8 [q]Hab. 2:3, 4; Heb. 10:25; Rev. 22:20 [3]Or *that which* [4]*delay*

The Gr. term denotes specific knowledge, not general spiritual knowledge (cf. 6:4; cf. 1 Tim. 2:4). Though the knowledge was not defective or incomplete, the application of the knowledge was certainly flawed. Judas Iscariot is a good example of a disciple who had no lack of knowledge, but lacked faith and became the arch-apostate. **no longer.** *See note on 6:6.* The apostate is beyond salvation because he has rejected the only sacrifice that can cleanse him from sin and bring him into God's presence. To turn away from that sacrifice leaves him with no saving alternative. This is parallel to Matt. 12:31 (*see note there*).

10:27 fearful expectation. The judgment is certain to happen, so it engenders fear. **judgment and fiery indignation.** The description is similar to that in Is. 26:11 and Zeph. 1:18 (cf. 2 Thess. 1:7-9). Ultimately, such judgment is that of eternity in the lake of fire (cf. Matt. 13:38-42,49,50). **adversaries.** Actual opposition against God and toward the program of God in salvation (*see notes on Phil. 3:18,19*).

10:28 Cf. Deut. 17:2-7.

10:29 how much worse punishment. There will be degrees of punishment in hell. This is also clearly indicated in Matt. 11:22-24 (*see notes there*). **trampled.** In the ancient Near East one of the gestures used to show contempt for someone was to "lift up the foot" against or toward them (cf. Ps. 41:9). To walk on top of someone or something was a more extreme gesture showing utter contempt and scorn (cf. 2 Kin. 9:33; Is. 14:19; Mic. 7:10; Zech. 10:5). Such contempt demonstrates a complete rejection of Christ as Savior and Lord. **counted...common.** To reckon Christ's blood as something "common" is the same thing as saying that it is unclean or defiled (*see note on 9:13*) and implies that Christ was a sinner and a blemished sacrifice. Such thinking is truly blasphemous. **blood of the covenant.** *See notes on 9:14,15.* Christ's death inaugurated or ratified the New Covenant. **sanctified.** This refers to Christ, in that He was set apart unto God (cf. John 17:19). It cannot refer to the apostate, because only true believers are sanctified. See Introduction: Interpretive Challenges. **insulted the Spirit of grace.** *See notes on 6:4 and 9:14.* The same title is utilized in Zech. 12:10. Rejecting Christ insults the Spirit who worked through Him (Matt. 12:31,32) and who testifies of Him (John 15:26; 16:8-11).

10:30 Quoted from Deut. 32:35,36 (cf. Ps. 135:4; Rom. 12:19).

10:31 living God. *See note on 3:12.*

10:32-39 In this section, a word of encouragement is presented to counterbalance the preceding grave warning (vv. 19-31). The writer points out that the Hebrews' former experiences should stimulate them, the nearness of reward should strengthen them, and the fear of God's displeasure should prevent them from going back to Judaism.

10:32 recall. Carries the idea of carefully thinking back and reconstructing something in one's mind, not merely remembering (cf. Acts 5:41; 2 Cor. 7:15). **illuminated.** *See note on 6:4* (cf. "full knowledge of the truth" in v. 26). **a great struggle.** The word is only here in the NT. It is a picture of the struggling athlete engaged in a rigorous contest (cf. 2 Tim. 2:5). After being enlightened, they suffered (v. 33), became offended, and began to fall away (*see notes on Matt. 13:20,21*).

10:33 a spectacle. The theater is alluded to with regard to the actors being placed on a stage where they can be observed by everyone. In the context of this verse, the idea is exposure to disgrace and ridicule (cf. 1 Cor. 4:9). **companions.** These unconverted Hebrews had been close to persecution when it happened to the believers they associated with. They perhaps had actually suffered for that identification, including the seizure of their property, but had not yet turned away because they were still interested in the prospects of heaven (v. 34). In the NT, there are examples of those who willingly exposed themselves to possible arrest and harassment because they sought to help those who were persecuted for their faith. Surprisingly, on one occasion, the Pharisees were among them. The Pharisees warned Jesus about Herod's pending attempt on Jesus' life (Luke 13:31). Among genuine believers who might be given as examples of helping the persecuted, there was Onesiphorus (2 Tim. 1:16-18).

10:34 in my chains. This is one of the supposed indicators used for identifying the author of this epistle as the Apostle Paul (cf. Eph. 3:1; 2 Tim. 1:8). However, many other Christians were also imprisoned. **joyfully accepted.** Cf. Acts 5:41; 16:24,25; Rom. 5:3; James 1:2. **a better and an enduring possession.** *See note on 9:15* (cf. Matt. 6:19,20; 1 Pet. 1:4).

10:35 cast away. Due to their current persecutions, they were tempted to run away from their outward identification with Christ and Christians and to apostatize (cf. v. 23; Deut. 32:15,18). **reward.** They are closer than ever to the eternal reward. It is no time to turn back.

10:36 done the will of God. To trust in Christ fully by living daily in the will of the Father. *See notes on Matt. 7:21-27; James 1:22-25*; cf. John 6:29. **receive the promise.** *See notes on 4:1; 6:12; 9:15.* If they would but remain with the New Covenant and put their trust exclusively in Christ, they would obtain the promise of salvation for themselves.

10:37,38 The loose reference to Hab. 2:3,4 (cf. Rom. 1:17; Gal. 3:11) is introduced by a phrase taken from Is. 26:20. This is the second reference to the Isaiah passage (cf. v. 27) which is part of a song of salvation. The passage in Is. 26 (or, its greater context, Is. 24–27) is perhaps uppermost in the writer's mind. The Habakkuk reference is altered considerably so that it is more of an interpretive paraphrase drawing

38 *Now* [r] *the*[5] *just shall live by faith;*
But if anyone draws back,
My soul has no pleasure in him."

39 But we are not of those [s] who draw back
to [6] perdition, but of those who [t] believe to
the saving of the soul.

By Faith We Understand

11 Now faith is the [1] substance of
things hoped for, the [2] evidence [a] of
things not seen. 2 For by it the elders obtained a *good* testimony.
3 By faith we understand that [b] the
[3] worlds were framed by the word of God,
so that the things which are seen were not
made of things which are visible.

38 [r] Hab. 2:3, 4; Rom. 1:17; Gal. 3:11 [5] NU *My just one*
39 [s] 2 Pet. 2:20 [t] Acts 16:31 [6] *destruction*

CHAPTER 11

1 [a] Rom. 8:24; [2 Cor. 4:18; 5:7]; Heb. 11:7, 27 [1] *realization* [2] Or *confidence*
3 [b] Gen. 1:1; Ps. 33:6; [John 1:3]; 2 Pet. 3:5 [3] Or *ages*, Gr. *aiones*, aeons
4 [c] Gen. 4:3-5; Matt. 23:35; 1 John 3:12 [d] Gen. 4:8-10; Heb. 12:24
5 [e] Gen. 5:21-24
7 [f] Gen. 6:13-22

Faith at the Dawn of History

4 By faith [c] Abel offered to God a more
excellent sacrifice than Cain, through
which he obtained witness that he was
righteous, God testifying of his gifts; and
through it he being dead still [d] speaks.
5 By faith Enoch was taken away so that
he did not see death, [e] *"and was not found,*
because God had taken him"; for before he
was taken he had this testimony, that he
pleased God. 6 But without faith *it is* impossible to please *Him,* for he who comes
to God must believe that He is, and *that* He
is a rewarder of those who diligently seek
Him.
7 By faith [f] Noah, being divinely warned
of things not yet seen, moved with godly

on other OT concepts and contexts. Habakkuk 2:4,5 is descriptive of the proud who do not live by faith. It is the proud who are self-sufficient and who fail to realize the necessity of patient endurance and trust in God. The proud Jew will be rejected if he does not exercise faith. He will be judged along with the nations.

10:38 ***the just shall live by faith.*** *See note on Rom. 1:17.* The opposite of apostasy is faith. This is a preview of the subsequent chapter. It is faith which pleases God. The individual who draws back from the knowledge of the gospel and faith will prove his apostasy

10:39 draw back to perdition. The writer expresses confidence that believing readers ("we") will not be counted among "those" who fall away to destruction. Apostates will draw back from Christ but there are some who are near to believing who can be pulled "out of the fire" (cf. Jude 23). "Perdition" is commonly used in the NT of the everlasting punishment or judgment of unbelievers (cf. Matt. 7:13; Rom. 9:22; Phil. 1:28; 3:19; 1 Tim. 6:9). Judas and the Man of Sin are called "son of perdition" (a Semitism meaning "perdition bound"; John 17:12; 2 Thess. 2:3). **saving of the soul.** Preservation from eschatological destruction is the concept of "saving" in this context. In the context of Is. 26:20,21 (v. 19) the eschatological preservation includes resurrection from the dead. The writer connects faith and resurrection in the example of Abraham (11:19).

11:1-40 The 11th chapter is a moving account of faithful OT saints and given such titles as, "The Saints' Hall of Fame," "The Honor Roll of OT Saints," and "Heroes of Faith." They all attest to the value of living by faith. They compose "the cloud of witnesses" (12:1) who give powerful testimony to the Hebrews that they should come to faith in God's truth in Christ.

11:1 This verse is written in a style of Heb. poetry (used often in the Psalms), in which two parallel and nearly identical phrases are used to state the same thing. Cf. 1 Pet. 1:7—God tests our faith in the crucible. **substance.** This is from the same Gr. word translated "express image" in 1:3 and "confidence" in 3:14. The faith described here involves the most solid possible conviction, the God-given present assurance of a future reality. **evidence of things not seen.** True faith is not based on empirical evidence but on divine assurance, and is a gift of God (Eph. 2:8).

11:2 elders. Meaning "men of old." In this context, the term refers to all saints, both men and women, under the older covenant, a select few of whom are described in vv. 4-40. **obtained a *good* testimony.** Lit. "were testified to" or "had witness given about them" (cf. vv. 4,39). God bears witness on the behalf of these saints that they lived by faith and divine approval is granted to them.

11:3 By faith. Each example of faith in vv. 3-31 is formally introduced with this specific phrase. True saving faith works in obedience to God (*see notes on James 2:14-26*). **we.** This refers to the writer and all other true believers, present and past. **worlds.** The physical universe itself, as well as its operation and administration. **were framed.** The concept involved in this verb (used also in 13:21) is that of equipping so that something might be made ready to fulfill its purpose. **word of God.** God's divine utterance (see, e.g., Gen. 1:3,6,9,11,14). **not made.** God created the universe out of something which cannot be seen. There is the possibility that the invisible something was God's own energy or power. For more on creation, *see notes on Gen. 1:1-31.*

11:4-40 Adam and Eve are passed over in this portion regarding creation because they had seen God, fellowshipped with Him, and talked with Him. Their children were the first to exercise faith in the unseen God.

11:4 Abel. See Gen. 4:1-15. **more excellent.** The precise reason for the excellence of Abel's sacrifice is not specifically revealed by the writer of Hebrews, but implied in 12:24 (*see notes there*). Here his concern is with Abel's faith. Both brothers knew what God required. Abel obeyed and Cain did not. Abel acted in faith, Cain in unbelief (*see notes on Gen. 4:4,5*). **through which...it.** The antecedent of both "which" and "it" is Abel's faith, not his offering. Through that faith, he left testimony to all succeeding generations that a person comes to God by faith to receive righteousness. **righteous.** Because of his faith, evidenced in obedience to God's requirement for sacrifice, Abel was accounted as righteous by God (cf. Rom. 4:4-8). Christ Himself referred to the righteousness of Abel (Matt. 23:35). Cain's sacrifice was evidence that he was just going through the motions of ritual in a disobedient manner, not evidencing authentic faith. Without faith no one can receive imputed righteousness (cf. Gen. 15:6). **testifying of his gifts.** Abel's offering proved something about his faith that was not demonstrated by Cain's offering.

11:5 The quoted is from Gen. 5:24. **Enoch.** *See note on Gen. 5:24.* The LXX translated the Heb. idiom "Enoch walked with God" with "he pleased God." The writer combines both in the reference. Enoch was miraculously taken to heaven without dying (cf. 1 Thess. 4:17).

11:6 impossible to please. Enoch pleased God because he had faith. Without such faith it is not possible for anyone to "walk with God" or "please Him" (cf. 10:38). **He is.** The emphasis here is on "He," the true God. Genuine faith does not simply believe that *a* divine being exists, but that the God of Scripture is the *only* real and true God who exists. Not believing that God exists is equivalent to calling Him a liar (cf. 1 John 5:10). **rewarder.** A person must believe not only that the true God exists, but also that He will reward men's faith in Him with forgiveness and righteousness, because He has promised to do so (cf. 10:35; Gen. 15:1; Deut. 4:29; 1 Chr. 28:9; Ps. 58:11; Is. 40:10).

11:7 Noah. *See Gen. 5:28–9:29; Ezek. 14:14.* **things not yet seen.** *See notes on vv. 1,6.* The world had not seen anything resembling the great Flood (not even rain; *see notes on Gen. 7:11*), yet Noah spent 120

fear, [g]prepared an ark for the saving of his
household, by which he condemned the
world and became heir of [h]the righteousness which is according to faith.

Faithful Abraham

8 By faith [i]Abraham obeyed when he
was called to go out to the place which he
would receive as an inheritance. And he
went out, not knowing where he was
going. 9 By faith he dwelt in the land of
promise as *in* a foreign country, [j]dwelling
in tents with Isaac and Jacob, [k]the heirs
with him of the same promise; 10 for he
waited for [l]the city which has foundations,
[m]whose builder and maker *is* God.
11 By faith [n]Sarah herself also received
strength to conceive seed, and [o]she[4] bore a
child when she was past the age, because
she judged Him [p]faithful who had
promised. 12 Therefore from one man, and
him as good as [q]dead, were born *as many*
as the [r]stars of the sky in multitude—innumerable as the sand which is by the
seashore.

The Heavenly Hope

13 These all died in faith, [s]not having received the [t]promises, but [u]having seen
them afar off [5]were assured of them, embraced *them* and [v]confessed that they were
strangers and pilgrims on the earth. 14 For
those who say such things [w]declare plainly that they seek a homeland. 15 And truly
if they had called to mind [x]that *country*
from which they had come out, they
would have had opportunity to return.
16 But now they desire a better, that is, a
heavenly *country*. Therefore God is not
ashamed [y]to be called their God, for He
has [z]prepared a city for them.

The Faith of the Patriarchs

17 By faith Abraham, [a]when he was tested, offered up Isaac, and he who had received the promises offered up his only begotten *son*, 18 [6]of whom it was said, [b]*"In
Isaac your seed shall be called,"* 19 concluding that God [c]*was* able to raise *him* up,
even from the dead, from which he also received him in a figurative sense.
20 By faith [d]Isaac blessed Jacob and Esau
concerning things to come.
21 By faith Jacob, when he was dying,
[e]blessed each of the sons of Joseph, and
worshiped, *leaning* on the top of his staff.

7 [g] 1 Pet. 3:20 [h] Rom. 3:22
8 [i] Gen. 12:1-4; Acts 7:2-4
9 [j] Gen. 12:8; 13:3, 18; 18:1, 9 [k] Heb. 6:17
10 [l] [Heb. 12:22; 13:14] [m] [Rev. 21:10]
11 [n] Gen. 17:19; 18:11-14; 21:1, 2 [o] Luke 1:36 [p] Heb. 10:23 [4] NU omits *she bore a child*
12 [q] Rom. 4:19 [r] Gen. 15:5; 22:17; 32:12
13 [s] Heb. 11:39 [t] Gen. 12:7 [u] John 8:56; Heb. 11:27 [v] Gen. 23:4; 47:9; 1 Chr. 29:15; Ps. 39:12; Eph. 2:19; 1 Pet. 1:17; 2:11 [5] NU, M omit *were assured of them*
14 [w] Heb. 13:14
15 [x] Gen. 11:31
16 [y] Gen. 26:24; 28:13; Ex. 3:6, 15; 4:5 [z] [John 14:2]; Heb. 11:10; [Rev. 21:2]
17 [a] Gen. 22:1-14; James 2:21
18 [b] Gen. 21:12; Rom. 9:7 [6] *to*
19 [c] Rom. 4:17
20 [d] Gen. 27:26-40
21 [e] Gen. 48:1, 5, 16, 20

years (Gen. 6:3) fulfilling God's command to build the massive ark, (Gen. 6:13-22). **godly fear.** Noah treated God's message with great respect and awe (cf. 5:7). His faith was expressed in obedience (cf. Gen. 6:22; 7:5). **condemned.** Noah warned the people of his time about God's impending judgment (cf. 1 Pet. 3:20), and is called "a preacher of righteousness" (2 Pet. 2:5). **heir of the righteousness.** *See notes on 6:12; 9:15.* He who was a preacher of righteousness (2 Pet. 2:5) also became an heir of righteousness. He believed the message he preached. Like Enoch before him (*see notes on v. 5*), Noah walked with God in faith and obedience (Gen. 6:9).

11:8-19 Abraham. *See Gen. 11:27–25:11.*

11:8 the place…inheritance. The land of Canaan, far from his original home in Ur of the Chaldees (Gen. 11:31). He went by faith.

11:9 promise. Neither Abraham, Isaac, nor Jacob were able to settle permanently in or possess the land God promised to them (v. 10). Abraham first went there in faith, and they all lived there in faith, believing in a promise of possession that would not be fulfilled for many generations beyond their lifetimes (Gen. 12:7).

11:10 city. Abraham's ultimate and permanent Promised Land was heaven which, through faith, he knew he would ultimately inherit. This city is mentioned again in v. 16; 12:22; 13:14.

11:11,12 Sarah. See Gen. 11:27–23:2; 1 Pet. 3:5,6.

11:11 past the age. At 90 (Gen. 17:17), she was long past child-bearing age and had never been able to conceive. God enabled her, however, because of her faith in His promise (Gen. 21:1-3).

11:12 as good as dead. At 99, Abraham was well beyond the age to father children apart from divine intervention (Gen. 17:1,15-17; 21:1-5). **stars…sand.** This is hyperbole to stress the vastness of the population that would come from Abraham's loins. See Gen. 15:4,5; 22:17.

11:13 These all. The reference is to the patriarchs only (Abraham, Isaac, and Jacob). This interpretation is supported by the fact that the promises began with Abraham (cf. Acts 7:17; Rom. 4:13; Gal. 3:14-18) and were passed on to Isaac (Gen. 26:2-5,24) and Jacob (Gen. 28:10-15). In addition, only those individuals fit the description in v. 15 and Enoch did not die. *See note on 6:15.* These people of faith didn't know when they would inherit the promise. They had a life in the land, but did not possess it.

11:13-16 strangers and pilgrims. See Gen. 23:4. Their faith was patient and endured great hardships because they believed God had something better. They had no desire to go back to Ur, but did long for heaven (Job 19:25,26; Ps. 27:4).

11:16 their God. God referred to Himself as "the God of Abraham, the God of Isaac, and the God of Jacob" (Ex. 3:6; cf. Gen. 28:13; Matt. 22:32). This is a significant covenant formula whereby an individual or a people identified with God and He with them (cf. Lev. 26:12). **a city.** *See note on 12:22.*

11:17-19 See Gen. 22:1-18. Abraham again proved his faith by his willingness to give back to God his son of promise, Isaac, whom he had miraculously received because of his faith. It would take an even greater miracle for them to replace Isaac by natural means. He trusted God for a resurrection. Cf. Rom. 4:16-21.

11:17,18 only begotten. Isaac was not the only son of Abraham—there was also Ishmael through Hagar (Gen. 16:1-16). The term refers to someone who is unique, one of a kind (cf. John 1:14). Isaac was the only son born according to God's promise and was the only heir of that promise. The quotation from Gen. 21:12 proves this latter point.

11:19 even from the dead. Believing that God's promise regarding Isaac was unconditional, Abraham came to the conclusion that God would fulfill that promise even if it required raising Isaac from the dead (cf. Gen. 22:5). **figurative sense.** The word is the same as in 9:9, which is the basis for the Eng. word "parable." Abraham received Isaac back from the dead, as it were, even though Isaac had not been slain.

11:20 Isaac. See Gen. 27:1–28:5.

11:21 Jacob. See Gen. 47:28–49:33. **each of the sons.** Both of Joseph's sons, Ephraim and Manasseh, received a blessing from Jacob. Consequently, two tribes descended from Joseph, whereas only one tribe descended from each of his brothers (see Gen. 47:31; 48:1,5,16). **top of his staff.** According to Gen. 47:31, Jacob leaned upon his

22 By faith [f]Joseph, when he was dying,
made mention of the departure of the children of Israel, and gave instructions concerning his bones.

The Faith of Moses

23 By faith [g]Moses, when he was born,
was hidden three months by his parents,
because they saw *he was* a beautiful child;
and they were not afraid of the king's
[h]command.
24 By faith [i]Moses, when he became of
age, refused to be called the son of Pharaoh's daughter, 25 choosing rather to suffer
affliction with the people of God than to
enjoy the [7]passing pleasures of sin, 26 esteeming [j]the [8]reproach of Christ greater
riches than the treasures [9]in Egypt; for he
looked to the [k]reward.
27 By faith [l]he forsook Egypt, not fearing
the wrath of the king; for he endured as
seeing Him who is invisible. 28 By faith
[m]he kept the Passover and the sprinkling
of blood, lest he who destroyed the firstborn should touch them.
29 By faith [n]they passed through the Red
Sea as by dry *land, whereas* the Egyptians,
attempting *to do* so, were drowned.

By Faith They Overcame

30 By faith [o]the walls of Jericho fell down
after they were encircled for seven days.
31 By faith [p]the harlot Rahab did not perish
with those who [1]did not believe, when
[q]she had received the spies with peace.
32 And what more shall I say? For the
time would fail me to tell of [r]Gideon and
[s]Barak and [t]Samson and [u]Jephthah, also
of [v]David and [w]Samuel and the prophets:
33 who through faith subdued kingdoms,
worked righteousness, obtained promises, [x]stopped the mouths of lions,
34 [y]quenched the violence of fire, escaped
the edge of the sword, out of weakness

22 [f]Gen. 50:24, 25; Ex. 13:19
23 [g]Ex. 2:1-3 [h]Ex. 1:16, 22
24 [i]Ex. 2:11-15
25 [7]*temporary*
26 [j]Heb. 13:13 [k]Rom. 8:18; 2 Cor. 4:17 [8]*reviling because of* [9]NU, M *of*
27 [l]Ex. 10:28
28 [m]Ex. 12:21
29 [n]Ex. 14:22-29; Jude 5
30 [o]Josh. 6:20
31 [p]Josh. 2:9; 6:23; James 2:25 [q]Josh. 2:1 [1]*were disobedient*
32 [r]Judg. 6:11; 7:1-25 [s]Judg. 4:6-24 [t]Judg. 13:24–16:31 [u]Judg. 11:1-29; 12:1-7 [v]1 Sam. 16; 17 [w]1 Sam. 7:9-14
33 [x]Judg. 14:6; 1 Sam. 17:34; Dan. 6:22
34 [y]Dan. 3:23-28

"bed." The two words (staff, bed) in Heb. have exactly the same consonants. Old Testament Heb. mss. were copied without vowels. Later Heb. mss., between the sixth and ninth centuries A.D., took the word as "bed." The LXX, in the third century B.C., rendered it "staff," which seems more likely although both could be factual.

11:22 Joseph. See Gen. 37:1–50:26. Joseph spent all of his adult life in Egypt and, even though he was a fourth-generation heir of the promise given to Abraham, he never returned to Canaan while he was alive. Yet, facing death, he still had faith that God would fulfill His promise and demonstrated that confidence by making his brothers promise to take his bones back to Canaan for burial (Gen. 50:24,25; cf. Ex. 13:19; Josh. 24:32).

11:23-29 Moses. See Ex. 1–15; Acts 7:17-36.

11:23 beautiful child. Meaning "favored," in this case divinely favored (Acts 7:20; cf. Ex. 2:2). The faith described here is actually that exercised by Moses' parents, although it is unclear how much Moses' parents understood about God's plan for their child.

11:24 Moses refused the fame he could have in Egypt if he would have capitalized on his position as the adopted son of Pharaoh's daughter (cf. Ex. 2:10).

11:25 with the people of God. Moses would have sinned had he refused to take on the responsibility God gave him regarding Israel, and he had a clear and certain conviction that "God would deliver them by his hand" (Acts 7:25). Moses repudiated the pleasures of Egypt.

11:26 reproach of Christ. Moses suffered reproach for the sake of Christ in the sense that he identified with Messiah's people in their suffering (v. 25). In addition, Moses identified himself with the Messiah because of his own role as leader and prophet (cf. 12:2; Deut. 18:15; Pss. 69:9; 89:51). Moses knew of the sufferings and glory of the Messiah (cf. John 5:46; Acts 26:22,23; 1 Pet. 1:10-12). Anyone who suffers because of genuine faith in God and for the redemptive gospel suffers for the sake of Christ (cf. 13:12,13; 1 Pet. 4:14).

11:27 forsook Egypt. Moses left Egypt for the first time when he fled for his life after killing the Egyptian slave master (Ex. 2:14,15). That time he did fear Pharaoh's wrath. On the second occasion, he turned his back on Egypt and all that it represented. This leaving was not for fear of Pharoah, so it is the one in view here. **seeing Him.** Moses' faith was such that he responded to God's commands as though God were standing visibly before him. This was the basis for his loyalty to God, and it should be a believer's example for loyalty (cf. 2 Cor. 4:16-18).

11:28 Passover. See Ex. 12.

11:29 Red Sea. See Ex. 14,15. When they first reached the shores of the Red Sea, the people feared for their lives (Ex. 14:11,21). But upon hearing Moses' pronouncement of God's protection (Ex. 14:13,14), they went forward in faith.

11:30 Jericho. See Josh. 6. The people did nothing militarily to cause the fall of Jericho; they simply followed God's instructions in faith. Cf. 2 Cor. 10:4.

11:31 Rahab. See Josh. 2:1-24; 6:22-25; Matt. 1:5; James 2:25.

11:32 All of the men listed in this verse held a position of power or authority, but none of them is praised for his personal status or abilities. Instead, they are recognized for what each one had accomplished by faith in God. They are not listed chronologically, but are listed in pairs with the more important member mentioned first (cf. 1 Sam. 12:11). See Judg. 6–9 (Gideon); 4,5 (Barak); 13–16 (Samson); 11,12 (Jephthah). **David.** David is the only king mentioned in this verse. All the others are judges or prophets. David could also be considered a prophet (see 4:7; 2 Sam. 23:1-3; Mark 12:36). Cf. 1 Sam. 13:14; 16:1,12; Acts 13:22. **Samuel and the prophets.** Samuel was the last of the judges and the first of the prophets (cf. 1 Sam. 7:15; Acts 3:24; 13:20). He anointed David as king (1 Sam. 16:13) and was known as a man of intercessory prayer (1 Sam. 12:19,23; Jer. 15:1).

11:33-38 The many accomplishments and sufferings described in these verses apply generally to those faithful saints. Some experienced great success, whereas others suffered great affliction. The point is that they all courageously and uncompromisingly followed God, regardless of the earthly outcome. They placed their trust in Him and in His promises (cf. 6:12; 2 Tim. 3:12).

11:33 subdued kingdoms. Joshua, the judges, David, and others. **worked righteousness.** Righteous kings like David, Solomon, Asa, Jehoshaphat, Joash, Hezekiah, and Josiah. **obtained promises.** Abraham, Moses, David, and Solomon. **stopped the mouths of lions.** Samson (Judg. 14:5,6), David (1 Sam. 17:34,35), Daniel (Dan. 6:22).

11:34 quenched the violence of fire. Shadrach, Meshach, and Abednego (Dan. 3:19-30). **escaped the edge of the sword.** David (1 Sam. 18:4,11; 19:9,10), Elijah (1 Kin. 19:1-3,10), and Elisha (2 Kin. 6:15-19). **weakness.** Ehud (Judg. 3:12-30), Jael (Judg. 4:17-24), Gideon (Judg. 6:15,16; 7:1-25), Samson (Judg. 16:21-30), and Hezekiah (Is. 38:1-6). Cf. 1 Cor. 1:27; 2 Cor. 12:10.

were made strong, became valiant in battle, turned to flight the armies of the
aliens. **35** [z]Women received their dead
raised to life again.
Others were [a]tortured, not accepting deliverance, that they might obtain a better
resurrection. **36** Still others had trial of
mockings and scourgings, yes, and [b]of
chains and imprisonment. **37** [c]They were
stoned, they were sawn in two, [2]were
tempted, were slain with the sword. [d]They
wandered about [e]in sheepskins and
goatskins, being destitute, afflicted, tormented— **38** of whom the world was not
worthy. They wandered in deserts and
mountains, [f]*in* dens and caves of the earth.
39 And all these, [g]having obtained a
good testimony through faith, did not receive the promise, **40** God having provided
something better for us, that they should
not be [h]made perfect apart from us.

35 [z] 1 Kin. 17:22; 2 Kin. 4:35-37 [a] Acts 22:25
36 [b] Gen. 39:20; 1 Kin. 22:27; 2 Chr. 18:26; Jer. 20:2; 37:15
37 [c] 1 Kin. 21:13; 2 Chr. 24:21; Acts 7:58 [d] 2 Kin. 1:8; Matt. 3:4 [e] 1 Kin. 19:13, 19; 2 Kin. 2:8, 13; Zech. 13:4 [2] NU omits *were tempted*
38 [f] 1 Kin. 18:4, 13; 19:9
39 [g] Heb. 11:2, 13
40 [h] Heb. 5:9

CHAPTER 12

1 [a] Col. 3:8 [b] 1 Cor. 9:24; Gal. 2:2; Heb. 10:39 [c] Rom. 12:12; Heb. 10:36
2 [d] Luke 24:26 [e] Ps. 69:7, 19; Phil. 2:8; [Heb. 2:9] [f] Ps. 110:1 [1] *originator* [2] *perfecter*
3 [g] Matt. 10:24 [h] Gal. 6:9; Heb. 12:5
4 [i] [1 Cor. 10:13]

The Race of Faith

12 Therefore we also, since we are surrounded by so great a cloud of witnesses, [a]let us lay aside every weight, and
the sin which so easily ensnares *us*, and
[b]let us run [c]with endurance the race that is
set before us, **2** looking unto Jesus, the [1]au-
thor and [2]finisher of *our* faith, [d]who for the
joy that was set before Him [e]endured the
cross, despising the shame, and [f]has sat
down at the right hand of the throne of
God.

The Discipline of God

3 [g]For consider Him who endured such
hostility from sinners against Himself,
[h]lest you become weary and discouraged
in your souls. **4** [i]You have not yet resisted
to bloodshed, striving against sin. **5** And
you have forgotten the exhortation which
speaks to you as to sons:

11:35 Women received their dead. The widow of Zarephath (1 Kin. 17:22) and the woman of Shunem (2 Kin. 4:34). **tortured.** The word indicates that they were beaten to death while strapped to some sort of rack (cf. 2 Macc. 6,7 about Eleazar and the mother with 7 sons who were martyrs). **better resurrection.** *See note on 9:27.* The deliverance from certain death or near death would be like returning from the dead, but would not be the promised resurrection. This was especially true of those who had died and were raised. The first time they were raised from the dead was merely resuscitation, not the true and glorious final resurrection (Dan. 12:2; cf. Matt. 5:10; James 1:12).

11:36 others. Joseph (Gen. 39:20), Micaiah (1 Kin. 22:27), Elisha (2 Kin. 2:23), Hanani (2 Chr. 16:10), Jeremiah (Jer. 20:1-6; 37:15), and others (2 Chr. 36:16).

11:37 stoned. The prophet Zechariah (son of Jehoiada) was killed in this fashion (*see notes on 2 Chr. 24:20-22;* see Introduction to Zechariah: Author and Date). **sawn in two.** According to tradition, this was the method Manasseh employed to execute Isaiah. **slain with the sword.** Uriah the prophet died in this fashion (Jer. 26:23; cf. 1 Kin. 19:10). However, the expression here may refer to the mass execution of God's people; several such incidents occurred during the time of the Maccabees in the 400 years between the OT and NT (see Introduction to the Intertestamental Period). **wandered about.** Many of God's people suffered from poverty and persecution (cf. Ps. 107:4-9).

11:38 See 1 Kin. 18:4,13; 19:9.

11:39,40 something better. They had faith in the ultimate fulfillment of the eternal promises in the covenant (v. 13). See Introduction: Historical and Theological Themes.

11:40 apart from us. The faith of OT saints looked forward to the promised salvation, whereas the faith of those after Christ looks back to the fulfillment of the promise. Both groups are characterized by genuine faith and are saved by Christ's atoning work on the cross (cf. Eph. 2:8,9).

12:1 Therefore. This is a very crucial transition word offering an emphatic conclusion (cf. 1 Thess. 4:8) to the section which began in 10:19. **witnesses.** The deceased people of chap. 11 give witness to the value and blessing of living by faith. Motivation for running "the race" is not in the possibility of receiving praise from "observing" heavenly saints. Rather, the runner is inspired by the godly examples those saints set during their lives. The great crowd are not comprised of spectators but rather are ones whose past life of faith encourages others to live that way (cf. 11:2,4,5,33,39). **let us.** The reference is to those Hebrews who had made a profession of Christ, but had not gone all the way to full faith. They had not yet begun the race, which starts with salvation. The writer has invited them to accept salvation in Christ and join the race. **every weight.** Different from the "sin" mentioned next, this refers to the main encumbrance weighing down the Hebrews which was the Levitical system with its stifling legalism. The athlete would strip away every piece of unnecessary clothing before competing in the race. The outward things emphasized by the Levitical system not only impede, they "ensnare." **sin.** In this context, this focuses first on the particular sin of unbelief—refusing to turn away from the Levitical sacrifices to the perfect sacrifice, Jesus Christ (cf. John 16:8-11), as well as other sins cherished by the unbeliever. **endurance.** Endurance is the steady determination to keep going, regardless of the temptation to slow down or give up (cf. 1 Cor. 9:24,25). **race.** The athletic metaphor presents the faith-filled life as a demanding, grueling effort. The Eng. word "agony" is derived from the Gr. word used here. *See note on Matt. 7:14.*

12:2 looking. They were to fix their eyes on Jesus as the object of faith and salvation (cf. 11:26,27; Acts 7:55,56; Phil. 3:8). **author.** *See note on 2:10.* The term means originator or preeminent example. **finisher.** *See note on 5:14.* The term is lit. "perfecter," having the idea of carrying through to perfect completion (cf. John 19:30). **the joy.** Jesus persevered so that He might receive the joy of accomplishment of the Father's will and exaltation (cf. 1:9; Ps. 16:9-11; Luke 10:21-24). **right hand.** *See note on 1:3.*

12:3 consider Him. Jesus is the supreme example of willingness to suffer in obedience to God. He faced "hostility" (the same word as "spoken against" in Luke 2:34) and endured even the cruel cross. The same opposition is faced by all who follow Him (Acts 28:22; Gal. 6:17; Col. 1:24; 2 Tim. 3:12). **weary and discouraged.** Believers' pressures, exhaustion, and persecutions (cf. Gal. 6:9) are as nothing compared to Christ's.

12:4 bloodshed. None of the Hebrews had experienced such intense exhaustion or persecution that it brought them to death or martyrdom. Since Stephen (Acts 7:60), James (Acts 12:1), and others (cf. Acts 9:1; 22:4; 26:10) had faced martyrdom in Jerusalem, it would appear to rule out that city as the residence of this epistle's recipients (see Introduction: Author and Date).

12:5,6 Here the writer recalls and expounds Prov. 3:11,12. Trials and sufferings in the Christian's life come from God who uses them to educate and discipline believers by such experiences. Such dealings are evidence of God's love for His own children (cf. 2 Cor. 12:7-10).

[j]"My son, do not despise the
[3]chastening of the LORD,
Nor be discouraged when you are
rebuked by Him;
6 *For [k]whom the* LORD *loves He*
chastens,
And scourges every son whom He
receives."

7 [l]If[4] you endure chastening, God deals
with you as with sons; for what [m]son is
there whom a father does not chasten?
8 But if you are without chastening, [n]of
which all have become partakers, then you
are illegitimate and not sons. 9 Furthermore, we have had human fathers who
corrected *us*, and we paid *them* respect.
Shall we not much more readily be in subjection to [o]the Father of spirits and live?
10 For they indeed for a few days chastened *us* as seemed *best* to them, but He for
our profit, [p]that *we* may be partakers of His
holiness. 11 Now no [5]chastening seems to
be joyful for the present, but painful; nevertheless, afterward it yields [q]the peaceable fruit of righteousness to those who
have been trained by it.

Renew Your Spiritual Vitality

12 Therefore [r]strengthen the hands
which hang down, and the feeble knees,
13 and make straight paths for your feet, so
that what is lame may not be *dislocated*, but
rather be healed.
14 [s]Pursue peace with all *people*, and holiness, [t]without which no one will see the
Lord: 15 looking carefully lest anyone [u]fall
short of the grace of God; lest any [v]root of
bitterness springing up cause trouble, and
by this many become defiled; 16 lest there
be any [w]fornicator or [6]profane person like
Esau, [x]who for one morsel of food sold his
birthright. 17 For you know that afterward,
when he wanted to inherit the blessing, he
was [y]rejected, for he found no place for repentance, though he sought it diligently
with tears.

The Glorious Company

18 For you have not come [7]to [z]the mountain that may be touched and that burned
with fire, and to blackness and [8]darkness
and tempest, 19 and the sound of a trumpet
and the voice of words, so that those who
heard *it* [a]begged that the word should not
be spoken to them anymore. 20 (For they
could not endure what was commanded:
[b]*"And if so much as a beast touches the*
mountain, it shall be stoned [9]*or shot with*
an arrow." 21 And so terrifying was the
sight *that* Moses said, [c]*"I am exceedingly*
afraid and trembling.")

5 [j]Job 5:17; Prov. 3:11, 12 [3]*discipline*
6 [k]Ps. 94:12; Rev. 3:19
7 [l]Deut. 8:5; 2 Sam. 7:14 [m]Prov. 13:24; 19:18; 23:13 [4]NU, M *It is for discipline that you endure; God*
8 [n]1 Pet. 5:9
9 [o][Job 12:10]
10 [p]Lev. 11:44
11 [q]Is. 32:17; 2 Tim. 4:8; James 3:17, 18 [5]*discipline*
12 [r]Is. 35:3
14 [s]Ps. 34:14 [t]Matt. 5:8; [Heb. 9:28]
15 [u]2 Cor. 6:1; Gal. 5:4; Heb. 4:1 [v]Deut. 29:18
16 [w][1 Cor. 6:13-18] [x]Gen. 25:33 [6]*godless*
17 [y]Gen. 27:30-40
18 [z]Ex. 19:12, 16; 20:18; Deut. 4:11; 5:22 [7]NU *to that which* [8]NU *gloom*
19 [a]Ex. 20:18-26; Deut. 5:25; 18:16
20 [b]Ex. 19:12, 13 [9]NU, M omit the rest of v. 20.
21 [c]Deut. 9:19

12:6 *scourges.* This refers to flogging with a whip, a severe and painful form of beating that was a common Jewish practice (cf. Matt. 10:17; 23:34).

12:7,8 sons. Because all are imperfect and need discipline and training, all true children of God are chastened at one time or another, in one way or another.

12:8 illegitimate. The word is found only here in the NT, but is used elsewhere in Gr. literature of those born to slaves or concubines. There could be in this an implied reference to Hagar and Ishmael (Gen. 16), Abraham's concubine and illegitimate son.

12:9 subjection. Respect for God equals submission to His will and law, and those who willingly receive the Lord's chastening will have a richer, more abundant life (cf. Ps. 119:165). **Father of spirits.** Probably best translated as "Father of our spirits," it is in contrast to "human fathers" (lit. "fathers of our flesh").

12:10 *our* profit. Imperfect human fathers discipline imperfectly; but God is perfect and therefore His discipline is perfect and always for the spiritual good of His children.

12:11 fruit of righteousness. This is the same phrase as in James 3:18. **trained.** The same word was used in 5:14 and translated "exercised" (*see note there*; cf. 1 Tim. 4:17).

12:12-17 This passage exhorts believers to act on the divine truths laid out in the previous passages. Truth that is known but not obeyed becomes a judgment rather than a benefit (cf. 13:22).

12:12,13 The author returns to the race metaphor begun in vv. 1-3 (cf. Prov. 4:25-27) and incorporates language taken from Is. 35:3 to describe the disciplined individual's condition like a weary runner whose arms drop and knees wobble. When experiencing trials in his life, the believer must not allow the circumstances to get the best of him. Instead, he must endure and get his second wind so as to be renewed to continue the race.

12:14 Pursue...holiness. In this epistle, it is explained as 1) a drawing near to God with full faith and a cleansed conscience (10:14,22), and 2) a genuine acceptance of Christ as the Savior and sacrifice for sin, bringing the sinner into fellowship with God. Unbelievers will not be drawn to accept Christ if believers' lives do not demonstrate the qualities God desires, including peace and holiness (cf. John 13:35; 1 Tim. 4:3; 5:23; 1 Pet. 1:16).

12:15 looking carefully. Believers are to watch their own lives, so as to give a testimony of peace and holiness, as well as to look out for and help those in their midst who are in need of salvation. **fall short of the grace of God.** *See notes on 4:1; 6:6; 10:26.* This means to come too late and be left out. Here is another mention of the intellectually convinced Jews in that assembly, who knew the gospel and were enamored with Christ, but still stood on the edge of apostasy. **root of bitterness.** This is the attitude of apostates within the church who are corruptive influences. Cf. Deut. 29:18.

12:16,17 See Gen. 25:29-34 and 27:1-39. Esau desired God's blessings, but he did not want God. He regretted what he had done, but he did not repent. Esau is an example of those who willfully sin against God and who are given no second chance because of their exposure to the truth and their advanced state of hardness (cf. 6:6; 10:26). Esau was an example of the "profane" person.

12:16 fornicator. In this context, it refers to the sexually immoral in general. Apostasy is often closely linked with immorality (cf. 2 Pet. 2:10,14,18; Jude 8,16,18).

12:18-29 The writer proceeds to give an exposition based upon Israel's encounter with God at Mt. Sinai (see Ex. 19,20; Deut. 4:10-24).

12:18 See Ex. 19:12,13; Deut. 4:11; 5:22.

12:19 sound of a trumpet. See Ex. 19:16,19; Deut. 4:12.

12:20 Quoted from Ex. 19:12,13 (cf. 20:19; Deut. 5:23,24).

12:21 Quoted from Deut. 9:19.

[22] But you have come to Mount Zion
and to the city of the living God, the heavenly Jerusalem, to an innumerable company of angels, [23] to the [1]general assembly
and church of [d]the firstborn [e]*who are* registered in heaven, to God [f]the Judge of all, to
the spirits of just men [g]made perfect, [24] to
Jesus [h]the Mediator of the new covenant,
and to [i]the blood of sprinkling that speaks
better things [j]than *that of* Abel.

Hear the Heavenly Voice

[25] See that you do not refuse Him who
speaks. For [k]if they did not escape who refused Him who spoke on earth, much
more *shall we not escape* if we turn away
from Him who *speaks* from heaven,
[26] whose voice then shook the earth; but
now He has promised, saying, [l]*"Yet once
more I [2]shake not only the earth, but also
heaven."* [27] Now this, *"Yet once more,"* indicates the [m]removal of those things that
are being shaken, as of things that are
made, that the things which cannot be
shaken may remain.

[28] Therefore, since we are receiving a
kingdom which cannot be shaken, let us
have grace, by which we [3]may [n]serve God
acceptably with reverence and godly fear.
[29] For [o]our God *is* a consuming fire.

Concluding Moral Directions

13 Let [a]brotherly love continue. [2] [b]Do
not forget to entertain strangers, for
by so *doing* [c]some have unwittingly entertained angels. [3] [d]Remember the prisoners
as if chained with them—those who are
mistreated—since you yourselves are in
the body also.

[4] [e]Marriage *is* honorable among all, and
the bed undefiled; [f]but fornicators and
adulterers God will judge.

[5] *Let your* conduct *be* without covetousness; *be* content with such things as you
have. For He Himself has said, [g]*"I will never*

23 [d][James 1:18] [e]Luke 10:20 [f]Gen. 18:25; Ps. 50:6; 94:2 [g][Phil. 3:12] [1]*festal gathering*
24 [h]1 Tim. 2:5; Heb. 8:6; 9:15 [i]Ex. 24:8 [j]Gen. 4:10; Heb. 11:4
25 [k]Heb. 2:2, 3
26 [l]Hag. 2:6 [2]NU *will shake*
27 [m][Is. 34:4; 54:10; 65:17; Rom. 8:19, 21]; 1 Cor. 7:31; Heb. 1:10
28 [n]Heb. 13:15, 21 [3]M omits *may*
29 [o]Ex. 24:17

CHAPTER 13

1 [a]Rom. 12:10
2 [b]Matt. 25:35; Rom. 12:13 [c]Gen. 18:1–22; 19:1
3 [d]Matt. 25:36; Heb. 10:34
4 [e]Prov. 5:18, 19 [f]1 Cor. 6:9; Gal. 5:19, 21; 1 Thess. 4:6
5 [g]Gen. 28:15; Deut. 31:6, 8; Josh. 1:5

12:22 Mount Zion. As opposed to Mt. Sinai, where God gave the Mosaic law which was forbidding and terrifying, Mt. Zion here is not the earthly one in Jerusalem, but God's heavenly abode, which is inviting and gracious. No one could please God on Sinai's terms, which was perfect fulfillment of the law (Gal. 3:10-12). Zion, however, is accessible to all who come to God through Jesus Christ (cf. Ps. 132:13,14; Is. 46:13; Zech. 2:10; Gal. 4:21-31). **Mount Zion...city of the living God... heavenly Jerusalem.** These are synonyms for heaven itself. For a description of the abode of God, the city of Jerusalem in heaven, *see notes on Rev. 21:1–22:5.* **innumerable.** The Gr. word is often translated 10,000. See Rev. 5:11,12.

12:23 general assembly. The term here means "a gathering for public festival." It does not likely describe a distinct group as if different from the church, but describes the attitude of the innumerable angels in heaven in a festal gathering around the throne of God. **church of the firstborn.** The firstborn is Jesus Christ (*see note on 1:6*). The "church" is comprised of believers who are fellow heirs with Christ, the preeminent One among many brethren (Rom. 8:17,29). **just men made perfect.** *See notes on 5:14* (cf. 11:40). These are the OT saints in distinction from the "church of the firstborn," who are the NT believers.

12:24 Mediator. *See note on 7:22* (cf. 8:6-10; 9:15). **better things.** *See notes on 6:9; 9:23.* Abel's sacrifice was pleasing to God because it was offered in faith and obedience (cf. 11:4), but it had no atoning power. Jesus' blood alone was sufficient to cleanse sin (cf. 1 John 1:7). The sacrifice of Christ brought redemption (9:12), forgiveness (9:26), and complete salvation (10:10,14). **than *that of* Abel.** The blood of Abel's sacrifice only provided a temporary covering, but Christ's blood sacrifice declares eternal forgiveness (cf. Col. 1:20).

12:25 refused. *See note on v. 19,* where the same word describes the conduct of the Israelites at Mt. Sinai. **much more.** The consequences for apostates is dire indeed. The judgment to be experienced and the expected terror is far in excess of that on Mt. Sinai.

12:26 Quoted from Hag. 2:6.

12:26,27 shook the earth. At Mt. Sinai, God shook the earth. From Zion, He will shake the heavens, the entire universe (cf. Is. 13:13; 34:4; 65:17,22; 2 Pet. 3:10-13; Rev. 6:12-14; 20:11; 21:1).

12:27 Everything physical ("things...being shaken") will be destroyed; only eternal things ("which cannot be shaken") will remain.

12:28 kingdom. God will create "a new heaven and a new earth...the holy city, New Jerusalem" (Rev. 21:1,2), which will be eternal and immovable. **let us have grace.** *See note on 4:16.* **with reverence and godly fear.** *See note on 5:7* (cf. 11:7). The second word has to do with the apprehension felt due to being in God's presence.

12:29 consuming fire. See Deut. 4:24. God's law given at Sinai prescribed many severe punishments, but the punishment is far worse for those who reject His offer of salvation through His own Son, Jesus Christ (cf. Luke 3:16,17). This verse is to be related to 10:29-31.

13:1 The last chapter of the epistle focuses on some of the essential practical ethics of Christian living. These ethics help portray the true gospel to the world, encourage others to believe in Christ, and bring glory to God. The first of these is love for fellow believers (cf. John 13:35). Although the primary reference would be to Christians, the writer must have had emotions similar to those of the Apostle Paul when it came to considering his fellow Hebrews (see Rom. 9:3,4).

13:2 entertain. The second grace needing development was the extension of love to those who were strangers (cf. Rom. 12:3; 1 Tim. 3:2). Hospitality in the ancient world often included putting up a guest overnight or longer. This is hardest to do when experiencing a time of persecution. The Hebrews would not know whether a guest would prove to be a spy or a fellow believer being pursued. **angels.** This is not given as the ultimate motivation for hospitality but to reveal that one never knows how far-reaching an act of kindness might be (cf. Matt. 25:40,45). This is exactly what happened to Abraham and Sarah (Gen. 18:1-3), Lot (Gen. 19:1,2), Gideon (Judg. 6:11-24), and Manoah (Judg. 13:6-20).

13:3 yourselves. Believers should be able to identify with the suffering of others because they also suffer physical ("in the body") pain and hardship.

13:4 honorable. God highly honors marriage, which He instituted at creation (Gen. 2:24); but some people in the early church considered celibacy to be holier than marriage, an idea Paul strongly denounces in 1 Tim. 4:3 (*see notes on 1 Cor. 7*). Sexual activity in a marriage is pure, but any sexual activity outside marriage brings one under divine judgment. **God will judge.** God prescribes serious consequences for sexual immorality (*see notes on Eph. 5:3-6*).

13:5 covetousness. Lusting after material riches is "a root of all *kinds of* evil, for which some have strayed from the faith in their greediness" (1 Tim. 6:10; cf. 1 Tim. 3:3). ***I will never.*** Quoted from Gen.

leave you nor forsake you." 6 So we may
boldly say:

> [h]*"The LORD is my helper;*
> *I will not fear.*
> *What can man do to me?"*

Concluding Religious Directions

7 Remember those who [1]rule over you,
who have spoken the word of God to you,
whose faith follow, considering the outcome of *their* conduct. 8 Jesus Christ *is* [i]the
same yesterday, today, and forever. 9 Do
not be carried [2]about with various and
strange doctrines. For *it is* good that the
heart be established by grace, not with
foods which have not profited those who
have been occupied with them.
10 We have an altar from which those
who serve the tabernacle have no right to
eat. 11 For the bodies of those animals,
whose blood is brought into the sanctuary
by the high priest for sin, are burned outside the camp. 12 Therefore Jesus also, that
He might [3]sanctify the people with His
own blood, suffered outside the gate.
13 Therefore let us go forth to Him, outside
the camp, bearing [j]His reproach. 14 For
here we have no continuing city, but we
seek the one to come. 15 [k]Therefore by Him
let us continually offer [l]the sacrifice of
praise to God, that is, [m]the fruit of *our* lips,
[4]giving thanks to His name. 16 [n]But do not
forget to do good and to share, for [o]with
such sacrifices God is well pleased.
17 [p]Obey those who [5]rule over you, and
be submissive, for [q]they watch out for
your souls, as those who must give account. Let them do so with joy and not
with grief, for that would be unprofitable
for you.

Prayer Requested

18 [r]Pray for us; for we are confident that
we have [s]a good conscience, in all things
desiring to live honorably. 19 But I especially urge *you* to do this, that I may be restored to you the sooner.

Benediction, Final Exhortation, Farewell

20 Now may [t]the God of peace [u]who
brought up our Lord Jesus from the dead,
[v]that great Shepherd of the sheep,
[w]through the blood of the everlasting cov-

6 [h] Ps. 27:1; 118:6
7 [1] *lead*
8 [i] [John 8:58]; 2 Cor. 1:19; Heb. 1:12
9 [2] NU, M *away*
12 [3] *set apart*
13 [j] 1 Pet. 4:14
15 [k] Eph. 5:20 [l] Lev. 7:12 [m] Is. 57:19; Hos. 14:2 [4] Lit. *confessing*
16 [n] Rom. 12:13 [o] 2 Cor. 9:12; Phil. 4:18
17 [p] Phil. 2:29 [q] Is. 62:6; Ezek. 3:17; Acts 20:28 [5] *lead*
18 [r] Eph. 6:19 [s] Acts 23:1
20 [t] Rom. 5:1, 2, 10; 15:33 [u] Ps. 16:10, 11; Hos. 6:2; Rom. 4:24 [v] Ps. 23:1; Is. 40:11; 63:11; John 10:11; 1 Pet. 2:25; 5:4 [w] Zech. 9:11; Heb. 10:29

28:15; Deut. 31:6,8; Josh. 1:5; 1 Chr. 28:20. Believers can be content in every situation because of this promise. Five negatives are utilized in this statement to emphasize the impossibility of Christ deserting believers. It is like saying "there is absolutely no way whatsoever that I will ever, ever leave you."

13:6 boldly. Not the usual word for boldness, this word has the idea of being confident and courageous. Cf. its use in Matt. 9:2; 2 Cor. 5:6,8. Quoted from Ps. 118:6.

13:7 In addition to the roll of the faithful in chap. 11, the writer reminds the Hebrews of their own faithful leaders within the church. In so doing, he outlines the duties of pastors: 1) rule; 2) speak the Word of God; and 3) establish the pattern of faith for the people to follow. Cf. Acts 20:28; 1 Tim. 3:1-7; Titus 1:5-9.

13:9 various and strange doctrines. These would include any teaching contrary to God's Word. The NT contains countless warnings against false teaching and false teachers (cf. Acts 20:29,30; Rom. 16:17; 2 Cor. 10:4,5; Gal. 1:6-9; Eph. 4:14; 2 Tim. 3:16). **established by grace.** Those who are experiencing God's grace in Christ have hearts and minds that remain stable. **foods.** The Mosaic law had regulations for everything, including food (Lev. 11). But for Christians, those laws have been abrogated (Acts 10:9-16; cf. 1 Cor. 8:8; Rom. 14:17; 1 Tim. 4:1-5).

13:10-13 *See notes on 11:26; 12:2.* The writer presents an analogy for the believers' identification with Christ in His rejection by Jews. The bodies of animals offered on the Day of Atonement were not eaten but burned "outside the camp" (Lev. 4:21; 16:27). Jesus, who was the ultimate atoning sacrifice, was similarly crucified outside the gates of Jerusalem (John 19:17). Figuratively, believers must join Him outside the camp of the world, no longer being a part of its unholy systems and practices (cf. 2 Tim. 2:4). By extension, this would also depict the departure from the Levitical system. The uncommitted Hebrews needed to take the bold step of leaving that system and being outside the camp of Old Covenant Israel.

13:10 an altar. The altar, the offerer, and the sacrifice are all closely related. Association with an altar identifies the offerer with the sacrifice. With certain offerings, the individual further identified himself with the altar and sacrifice by eating some of the sacrifice. The Apostle Paul referred to this relationship to an altar when giving instruction to the Corinthians regarding eating meat offered to idols (1 Cor. 9:13) and regarding the observation of the Lord's Supper (1 Cor. 10:18). Here, the altar is equivalent to the sacrifice of Christ, especially as seen in the comparison to the Day of Atonement.

13:15 praise...thanks. As seen throughout the book of Hebrews, sacrifices were extremely important under the Old Covenant. Under the New Covenant, God desires the praise and thanksgiving of His people rather than offerings of animals or grain. Since NT believers are all priests (1 Pet. 2:5,9), they have offerings of praise and thanks to God (cf. Rom. 12:1). The "sacrifice of praise" is also mentioned in Lev. 7:12; Ps. 54:8. For "fruit of the lips" see Is. 57:19; Hos. 14:3.

13:16 do good...share. The sacrifices of praise coming from the lips of God's people please Him only when accompanied by loving action (cf. Is. 58:6,7; James 1:27; 1 John 3:18).

13:17 rule over you. *See note on v. 7.* The pastors/elders of the church exercise the very authority of Christ when they preach, teach, and apply Scripture (*see notes on Acts 20:28; 1 Thess. 5:12,13*). They serve the church on behalf of Christ and must give Him an account of their faithfulness. *See notes on 1 Cor. 4:1-5; 1 Pet. 5:1-4.* These may include both secular and spiritual rulers. Even those who do not acknowledge God are nevertheless ordained and used by Him (cf. Rom. 13:1,4). **joy.** The church is responsible to help its leaders do their work with satisfaction and delight. *See notes on 1 Thess. 5:12,13.*

13:19 restored. The author had been with these Hebrews and was anxious to once again be in their fellowship.

13:20,21 This benediction is among the most beautiful in Scripture (cf. Num. 6:24-26; 2 Cor. 13:14; Jude 24,25). It is an example of how grace can be manifested in mutual blessing and prayer.

13:20 God of peace. Paul uses this title 6 times in his epistles (cf. 1 Thess. 5:23). **great Shepherd of the sheep.** *See Is. 63:11.* The fig-

enant, 21 make you [6]complete in every
good work to do His will, [x]working in
[7]you what is well pleasing in His sight,
through Jesus Christ, to whom *be* glory forever and ever. Amen.

22 And I appeal to you, brethren, bear
with the word of exhortation, for I have
written to you in few words. 23 Know that
our brother Timothy has been set free, with
whom I shall see you if he comes shortly.

24 Greet all those who [8]rule over you,
and all the saints. Those from Italy greet
you.

25 Grace *be* with you all. Amen.

21 [x] Phil. 2:13 [6] *perfect* [7] NU, M *us*
24 [8] *lead*

ure of the Messiah as a Shepherd is found frequently in Scripture (cf. Ps. 23; Is. 40:11; Ezek. 34:23; John 10:11; 1 Pet. 2:25; 5:4). **through the blood of the everlasting covenant.** This must refer, in the context of Hebrews, to the New Covenant that is eternal (in a future sense) compared to the Mosaic Covenant that was temporary and had been abrogated (*see notes on 8:6-13; 9:15*).

13:21 make you complete. This is not the Gr. word for "perfect" or "perfection" used throughout Hebrews to indicate salvation (*see note on 5:14*) but is a word which is translated "prepared" in 10:5 and "framed" in 11:3. It refers to believers being edified. The verb has the idea of equipping by means of adjusting, shaping, mending, restoring, or preparing (*see note on 11:3*; cf. 1 Cor. 1:10; 2 Cor. 13:11; 2 Tim. 3:17).

13:22 bear with. Readers are encouraged to receive this message with open minds and warm hearts, in contrast to those who "will not endure sound doctrine" (2 Tim. 4:3). **word of exhortation.** Cf. 3:13. This is the writer's own description of his epistle (see Introduction: Historical and Theological Themes).

13:23 set free. The details of Timothy's imprisonment are unknown (cf. 2 Tim. 4:11,21).

13:24 Those from Italy. The group to which the author wrote may have been in Italy, or the meaning might be that Italian Christians who were with him sent their greetings (see Introduction: Author and Date). The use of similar phrases elsewhere is ambiguous since some are clearly referring to people still in their location (Acts 10:23; 17:13) and those who were away from their homes (Acts 21:27).

The Epistle of JAMES

Title

James, like all of the general epistles except Hebrews, is named after its author (v. 1).

Author and Date

Of the 4 men named James in the NT, only two are candidates for authorship of this epistle. No one has seriously considered James the Less, the son of Alphaeus (Matt. 10:3; Acts 1:13), or James the father of Judas, not Iscariot (Luke 6:16; Acts 1:13). Some have suggested James the son of Zebedee and brother of John (Matt. 4:21), but he was martyred too early to have written it (Acts 12:2). That leaves only James, the oldest half-brother of Christ (Mark 6:3) and brother of Jude (Matt. 13:55), who also wrote the epistle that bears his name (Jude 1). James had at first rejected Jesus as Messiah (John 7:5), but later believed (1 Cor. 15:7). He became the key leader in the Jerusalem church (cf. Acts 12:17; 15:13; 21:18; Gal. 2:12), being called one of the "pillars" of that church, along with Peter and John (Gal. 2:9). Also known as James the Just because of his devotion to righteousness, he was martyred ca. A.D. 62, according to the first century Jewish historian Josephus. Comparing James' vocabulary in the letter he wrote which is recorded in Acts 15 with that in the epistle of James further corroborates his authorship.

James		Acts 15
1:1	"greetings"	15:23
1:16,19; 2:5	"beloved"	15:25
1:21; 5:20	"your souls"	15:24,26
1:27	"visit"	15:14
2:10	"keep"	15:24
5:19,20	"turn"	15:19

James wrote with the authority of one who had personally seen the resurrected Christ (1 Cor. 15:7), who was recognized as an associate of the apostles (Gal. 1:19), and who was the leader of the Jerusalem church.

James most likely wrote this epistle to believers scattered (1:1) as a result of the unrest recorded in Acts 12 (ca. A.D. 44). There is no mention of the Council of Jerusalem described in Acts 15 (ca. A.D. 49), which would be expected if that Council had already taken place. Therefore, James can be reliably dated ca. A.D. 44–49, making it the earliest written book of the NT canon.

Background and Setting

The recipients of this book were Jewish believers who had been dispersed (1:1), possibly as a result of Stephen's martyrdom (Acts 7, A.D. 31–34), but more likely due to the persecution under Herod Agrippa I (Acts 12, ca. A.D. 44). The author refers to his audience as "brethren" 15 times (1:2,16,19; 2:1,5,14; 3:1,10,12; 4:11; 5:7,9,10,12,19), which was a common epithet among the first century Jews. Not surprisingly, then, James is Jewish in its content. For example, the Gr. word translated "assembly" (2:2) is the word for "synagogue." Further, James contains more than 40 allusions to the OT (and more than 20 to the Sermon on the Mount, Matt. 5–7).

Historical and Theological Themes

James, with its devotion to direct, pungent statements on wise living, is reminiscent of the book of Proverbs. It has a practical emphasis, stressing not theoretical knowledge, but godly behavior. James wrote with a passionate desire for his readers to be uncompromisingly obedient to the Word of God. He used at least 30 references to nature (e.g., "wave of the sea" [1:6]; "reptile" [3:7]; and "heaven gave rain" [5:18]), as befits one who spent a great deal of time outdoors. He complements Paul's emphasis on justification by faith with his own emphasis on spiritual fruitfulness demonstrating true faith.

Interpretive Challenges

At least two significant texts challenge the interpreter: 1) In 2:14-26, what is the relationship between faith and works? Does James' emphasis on works contradict Paul's focus on faith? 2) In 5:13-18, do the promises of healing refer to the spiritual or physical realm? These difficult texts are treated in the notes.

Outline

There are a number of ways to outline the book to grasp the arrangement of its content. One way is to arrange it around a series of tests by which the genuineness of a person's faith may be measured.

Outline

Introduction (1:1)

I. The Test of Perseverance in Suffering (1:2-12)

II. The Test of Blame in Temptation (1:13-18)

III. The Test of Response to the Word (1:19-27)

IV. The Test of Impartial Love (2:1-13)

V. The Test of Righteous Works (2:14-26)

VI. The Test of the Tongue (3:1-12)

VII. The Test of Humble Wisdom (3:13-18)

VIII. The Test of Worldly Indulgence (4:1-12)

IX. The Test of Dependence (4:13-17)

X. The Test of Patient Endurance (5:1-11)

XI. The Test of Truthfulness (5:12)

XII. The Test of Prayerfulness (5:13-18)

XIII. The Test of True Faith (5:19,20)

Greeting to the Twelve Tribes

1 James, [a]a bondservant of God and of
the Lord Jesus Christ,

To the twelve tribes which are scattered
abroad:

Greetings.

Profiting from Trials

2 My brethren, [b]count it all joy [c]when
you fall into various trials, 3 [d]knowing that
the testing of your faith produces [1]pa-
tience. 4 But let patience have *its* perfect
work, that you may be [2]perfect and complete, lacking nothing. 5 [e]If any of you
lacks wisdom, [f]let him ask of God, who
gives to all liberally and without reproach,
and [g]it will be given to him. 6 [h]But let him
ask in faith, with no doubting, for he who
doubts is like a wave of the sea driven and
tossed by the wind. 7 For let not that man
suppose that he will receive anything from
the Lord; 8 *he is* [i]a double-minded man,
unstable in all his ways.

The Perspective of Rich and Poor

9 Let the lowly brother glory in his exaltation, 10 but the rich in his humiliation,
because [j]as a flower of the field he will
pass away. 11 For no sooner has the sun
risen with a burning heat than it withers

CHAPTER 1

1 [a] Acts 12:17
2 [b] Acts 5:41 [c] 1 Pet. 1:6
3 [d] Rom. 5:3-5
[1] *endurance* or *perseverance*
4 [2] *mature*
5 [e] 1 Kin. 3:9; James 3:17
[f] Prov. 2:3-6; Matt. 7:7
[g] Jer. 29:12
6 [h] [Mark 11:23, 24]; Acts 10:20
8 [i] James 4:8
10 [j] Job 14:2

1:1 James. The half-brother of the Lord Jesus (see Introduction: Author and Date; cf. Gal. 1:19; 2:9). **bondservant.** *See note on Rom. 1:1.* **twelve tribes.** A common NT title for Jews (cf. Matt. 19:28; Acts 26:7; Rev. 7:4). When the kingdom split after Solomon's reign, 10 tribes constituted the northern kingdom, called Israel, and Benjamin and Judah combined to form the southern kingdom, called Judah. After the fall and deportation of the northern kingdom to Assyria (722 B.C.), some of the remnant of those in the 10 northern tribes filtered down into Judah and came to Jerusalem to worship (2 Chr. 29,30,34), thus preserving all 12 tribes in Judah's land. Although tribal identity could not be established with certainty after the southern kingdom was led captive by Babylon (586 B.C.), the prophets foresaw a time when God would reconstitute the whole nation and delineate each person's tribal membership once again (cf. Is. 11:12,13; Jer. 3:18; 50:4; Ezek. 37; Rev. 7:5-8). **scattered abroad.** The Gr. word *diaspora,* which lit. means "through a sowing" (cf. John 7:35), became a technical term referring to Jews living outside the land of Palestine (cf. 1 Pet. 1:1). Besides the expulsions from the land by the Assyrians (2 Kin. 17; 1 Chr. 5) and Babylonians (2 Kin. 24,25; 2 Chr. 36), many Jews were taken to Rome as slaves when the Romans conquered them ca. 63 B.C. In addition, during the centuries leading up to Christ's first coming, thousands of Jews drifted out of Palestine and settled throughout the Mediterranean world (*see notes on Acts 2:5-11*). But James' primary audience was those who were scattered because of persecution (see Introduction: Background and Setting).

1:2 brethren. Believing Jews among those scattered (cf. 1 Pet. 1:1,2; *see note on Acts 8:1*). **count it all joy.** The Gr. word for "count" may also be translated "consider" or "evaluate." The natural human response to trials is not to rejoice; therefore the believer must make a conscious commitment to face them with joy (*see note on Phil. 3:1*). **trials.** This Gr. word connotes trouble, or something that breaks the pattern of peace, comfort, joy, and happiness in someone's life. The verb form of this word means "to put someone or something to the test," with the purpose of discovering that person's nature or that thing's quality. God brings such tests to prove—and increase—the strength and quality of one's faith and to demonstrate its validity (vv. 2-12). Every trial becomes a test of faith designed to strengthen: if the believer fails the test by wrongly responding, that test then becomes a temptation, or a solicitation to evil (*see notes on vv. 13-15*).

1:3 testing. This means "proof," or "proving" (see Introduction: Outline). **patience.** Better translated "endurance," or "perseverance." Through tests, a Christian will learn to withstand tenaciously the pressure of a trial until God removes it at His appointed time and even cherish the benefit. *See notes on 2 Cor. 12:7-10.*

1:4 perfect. Not a reference to sinless perfection (cf. 3:2), but to spiritual maturity (cf. 1 John 2:14). The testing of faith drives believers to deeper communion and greater trust in Christ—qualities that in turn produce a stable, godly, and righteous character (*see note on 1 Pet. 5:10*; cf. Gal. 4:19). **complete.** From a compound Gr. word that lit. means "all the portions whole."

1:5 wisdom. James' Jewish audience recognized this as the understanding and practical skill that was necessary to live life to God's glory. It was not a wisdom of philosophical speculation, but the wisdom contained in the pure and peaceable absolutes of God's will revealed in His Word (cf. 3:13,17) and lived out. Only such divine wisdom enables believers to be joyous and submissive in the trials of life. **ask of God.** This command is a necessary part of the believer's prayer life (cf. Job 28:12-23; Prov. 3:5-7; 1 Thess. 5:17). God intends that trials will drive believers to greater dependency on Him, by showing them their own inadequacy. As with all His riches (Eph. 1:7; 2:7; 3:8; Phil. 4:19), God has wisdom in abundance (Rom. 11:33) available for those who seek it. *See notes on Prov. 2:1-7.*

1:6 ask in faith. Prayer must be offered with confident trust in a sovereign God (*see note on Heb. 11:1*). **with no doubting.** This refers to having one's thinking divided within himself, not merely because of mental indecision but an inner moral conflict or distrust in God (*see note on v. 8*). **wave of the sea.** The person who doubts God's ability or willingness to provide this wisdom is like the billowing, restless sea, moving back and forth with its endless tides, never able to settle (cf. Josh. 24:15; 1 Kin. 18:21; Rev. 3:16).

1:8 double-minded man. A lit. translation of the Gr. expression that denotes having one's mind or soul divided between God and the world (*see note on 4:4*). This man is a hypocrite, who occasionally believes in God but fails to trust Him when trials come, and thus receives nothing. The use of this expression in 4:8 makes it clear that it refers to an unbeliever. **unstable.** *See notes on v. 6.*

1:9,10 lowly brother…the rich. Trials make all believers equally dependent on God and bring them to the same level with each other by keeping them from becoming preoccupied with earthly things. Poor Christians and wealthy ones can rejoice that God is no respecter of persons and that they both have the privilege of being identified with Christ.

1:9 glory. This word refers to the boasting of a privilege or possession; it is the joy of legitimate pride. Although having nothing in this world, the poor believer can rejoice in his high spiritual standing before God by grace and the hope which that brings (cf. Rom. 8:17,18; 1 Pet. 1:4).

1:10 his humiliation. Refers to the rich believer's being brought low by trials. Such experiences help him rejoice and realize that genuine happiness and contentment depend on the true riches of God's grace, not earthly wealth.

the grass; its flower falls, and its beautiful
appearance perishes. So the rich man also
will fade away in his pursuits.

Loving God Under Trials

12 [k]Blessed *is* the man who endures
temptation; for when he has been approved, he will receive [l]the crown of life
[m]which the Lord has promised to those
who love Him. 13 Let no one say when he
is tempted, "I am tempted by God"; for
God cannot be tempted by evil, nor does
He Himself tempt anyone. 14 But each one
is tempted when he is drawn away by his
own desires and enticed. 15 Then, [n]when
desire has conceived, it gives birth to sin;
and sin, when it is full-grown, [o]brings
forth death.
16 Do not be deceived, my beloved
brethren. 17 [p]Every good gift and every
perfect gift is from above, and comes down
from the Father of lights, [q]with whom
there is no variation or shadow of turning.
18 [r]Of His own will He brought us forth by
the [s]word of truth, [t]that we might be a
kind of firstfruits of His creatures.

Qualities Needed in Trials

19 [3]So then, my beloved brethren, let
every man be swift to hear, [u]slow to speak,
[v]slow to wrath; 20 for the wrath of man
does not produce the righteousness of God.

12 [k]Job 5:17; Luke 6:22; Heb. 10:36; James 5:11; [1 Pet. 3:14; 4:14] [l][1 Cor. 9:25] [m]Matt. 10:22
15 [n]Job 15:35; Ps. 7:14; Is. 59:4
[o][Rom. 5:12; 6:23]
17 [p]John 3:27
[q]Num. 23:19
18 [r]John 1:13
[s]2 Cor. 6:7; 1 Thess. 2:13; 2 Tim. 2:15; [1 Pet. 1:3, 23]
[t][Eph. 1:12, 13]; Heb. 12:23; Rev. 14:4
19 [u]Prov. 10:19; 17:27
[v]Prov. 14:17; 16:32; Eccl. 7:9 [3]NU *Know this* or *This you know*

1:11 grass...flower. A picture of Palestine's flowers and flowering grasses, which colorfully flourish in Feb. and dry up by May. This is a clear allusion to Is. 40:6-8, which speaks of the scorching sirocco wind that burns and destroys plants in its path. This picture from nature illustrates how divinely wrought death and judgment can quickly end the wealthy person's dependence on material possessions (*see note on v. 10*; cf. Prov. 27:24).

1:12 Blessed. *See notes on Matt. 5:4,10,11.* Believers who successfully endure trials are truly happy (cf. 5:11). **endures.** *See note on v. 3.* In this context, it also describes the passive, painful survival of a trial and focuses on the victorious outcome. Such a person never relinquishes his saving faith in God; thus this concept is closely related to the doctrine of eternal security and perseverance of the believer (*see note on Matt. 24:13*; cf. John 14:15,23; 1 John 2:5,6,15,19; 4:19; 1 Pet. 1:6-8). **temptation.** This is better translated "trials" (*see note on v. 2*). **approved.** Lit. "passed the test" (*see note on v. 2*, "trials"). The believer has successfully and victoriously gone through his trials, indicating he is genuine because his faith has endured like Job's. **crown of life.** Best translated "the crown which is life." "Crown" was the wreath put on the victor's head after ancient Greek athletic events. Here, it denotes the believer's ultimate reward, eternal life, which God has promised to him and will grant in full at death or at Christ's coming (*see notes on 2 Tim. 4:8; Rev. 2:10*; cf. 1 Pet. 5:4).

1:13 The same Gr. word translated "trials" (vv. 2-12) is also translated "temptation" here. James' point is that every difficult circumstance that enters a believer's life can either strengthen him if he obeys God and remains confident in His care, or become a solicitation to evil if the believer chooses instead to doubt God and disobey His Word. **God cannot be tempted.** God by His holy nature has no capacity for evil, or vulnerability to it (Hab. 1:13; cf. Lev. 19:2; Is. 6:3; 1 Pet. 1:16). **nor does He Himself tempt anyone.** God purposes trials to occur and in them He allows temptation to happen, but He has promised not to allow more than believers can endure and never without a way to escape (1 Cor. 10:13). They choose whether to take the escape God provides or to give in (*see note on v. 14*; cf. 2 Sam. 24:1; 1 Chr. 21:1).

1:14 drawn away. This Gr. word was used to describe wild game being lured into traps. Just as animals can be drawn to their deaths by attractive baits, temptation promises people something good, which is actually harmful. **his own desires.** This refers to lust, the strong desire of the human soul to enjoy or acquire something to fulfill the flesh. Man's fallen nature has the propensity to strongly desire whatever sin will satisfy it (*see notes on Rom. 7:8-25*). "His own" describes the individual nature of lust—it is different for each person as a result of inherited tendencies, environment, upbringing, and personal choices. The Gr. grammar also indicates that these "desires" are the direct agent or cause of one's sinning. Cf. Matt. 15:18-20. **enticed.** A fishing term that means "to capture" or "to catch with bait" (cf. 2 Pet. 2:14,18). It is a parallel to "drawn away."

1:15 Sin is not merely a spontaneous act, but the result of a process. The Gr. words for "has conceived" and "brings forth" liken the process to physical conception and birth. Thus James personifies temptation and shows that it can follow a similar sequence and produce sin with all its deadly results. While sin does not result in spiritual death for the believer, it can lead to physical death (1 Cor. 11:30; 1 John 5:16).

1:16 Do not be deceived. The Gr. expression refers to erring, going astray, or wandering. Christians are not to make the mistake of blaming God rather than themselves for their sin.

1:17 Every good...perfect gift is from above. Two different Gr. words for "gift" emphasize the perfection and inclusiveness of God's graciousness. The first denotes the act of giving, and the second is the object given. Everything related to divine giving is adequate, complete, and beneficial. **Father of lights.** An ancient Jewish expression for God as the Creator, with "lights" referring to the sun, moon, and stars (cf. Gen. 1:14-19). **no variation or shadow of turning.** From man's perspective, the celestial bodies have different phases of movement and rotation, change from day to night, and vary in intensity and shadow. But God does not follow that pattern—He is changeless (cf. Mal. 3:6; 1 John 1:5).

1:18 Of His own will. This phrase translates a Gr. word that makes the point that regeneration is not just a wish, but an active expression of God's will, which He always has the power to accomplish. This phrase occurs at the beginning of the Gr. sentence, which means James intends to emphasize that the sovereign will of God is the source of this new life. **He brought us forth.** The divine act of regeneration, or the new birth (*see notes on John 3:3-8; 1 Pet. 1:23*; cf. Ezek. 36:25-27; John 1:12,13; Eph. 2:5,6; 5:26). **word of truth.** Cf. John 17:17. Scripture, or the Word of God. He regenerates sinners through the power of that Word (cf. 2 Cor. 6:7; Col. 1:5; 1 Thess. 2:13; Titus 3:5; 1 Pet. 1:23-25). **firstfruits.** Originally an OT expression referring to the first and best harvest crops, which God expected as an offering (cf. Ex. 23:19; Lev. 23:9-14; Deut. 26:1-19). Giving God that initial crop was an act of faith that He would fulfill His promise of a full harvest to come (Prov. 3:9,10). In the same way, Christians are the first evidence of God's new creation that is to come (cf. 2 Pet. 3:10-13) and enjoy presently in their new life a foretaste of future glory (*see notes on Rom. 8:19-23*).

1:19 swift to hear, slow to speak. Believers are to respond positively to Scripture, and eagerly pursue every opportunity to know God's Word and will better (cf. Ps. 119:11; 2 Tim. 2:15). But at the same time, they should be cautious about becoming a preacher or teacher too quickly (*see notes on 3:1,2*; cf. Ezek. 3:17; 33:6,7; 1 Tim. 3:6; 5:22).

1:20 wrath. From the Gr. word that describes a deep, internal resentment and rejection, in this context, of God's Word (*see notes on 4:1-3*; cf. Gal. 4:16).

Doers—Not Hearers Only

21 Therefore [w]lay aside all filthiness and
[4]overflow of wickedness, and receive with
meekness the implanted word, [x]which is
able to save your souls.
22 But [y]be doers of the word, and not
hearers only, deceiving yourselves. 23 For
[z]if anyone is a hearer of the word and not
a doer, he is like a man observing his natural face in a mirror; 24 for he observes
himself, goes away, and immediately forgets what kind of man he was. 25 But [a]he
who looks into the perfect law of liberty
and continues *in it,* and is not a forgetful
hearer but a doer of the work, [b]this one
will be blessed in what he does.
26 If anyone [5]among you thinks he is religious, and [c]does not bridle his tongue but
deceives his own heart, this one's religion
is useless. 27 [d]Pure and undefiled religion
before God and the Father is this: [e]to visit
orphans and widows in their trouble, [f]and
to keep oneself unspotted from the world.

Beware of Personal Favoritism

2 My brethren, do not hold the faith of
our Lord Jesus Christ, [a]*the Lord* of
glory, with [b]partiality. 2 For if there should
come into your assembly a man with gold
rings, in [1]fine apparel, and there should
also come in a poor man in [2]filthy clothes,
3 and you [3]pay attention to the one wearing the fine clothes and say to him, "You sit
here in a good place," and say to the poor

21 [w]Col. 3:8 [x]Acts 13:26 [4]*abundance*
22 [y]Matt. 7:21-28; Luke 6:46-49; [Rom. 2:13; James 1:22-25; 2:14-20]
23 [z]Luke 6:47
25 [a][John 8:32; Rom. 8:2; 2 Cor. 3:17]; Gal. 2:4; 6:2; James 2:12; 1 Pet. 2:16 [b]John 13:17
26 [c]Ps. 34:13 [5]NU omits *among you*
27 [d]Matt. 25:34-36 [e]Is. 1:17 [f][Rom. 12:2]

CHAPTER 2

1 [a]Acts 7:2; 1 Cor. 2:8 [b]Lev. 19:15
2 [1]*bright* [2]*vile*
3 [3]Lit. *look upon*

1:21 lay aside. Lit. "having put off," as one would do with dirty clothes (*see notes on Rom. 13:12-14; Eph. 4:22; Col. 3:8; Heb. 12:1; 1 Pet. 2:1,2*). The tense of this Gr. verb stresses the importance of putting off sin prior to receiving God's Word. **filthiness...wickedness.** The first term was used of moral vice as well as dirty garments. Sometimes it was even used of ear wax—here, of sin that would impede the believer's spiritual hearing. "Wickedness" refers to evil desire or intent. **implanted word.** *See note on v. 18.*

1:22 be doers. The fact that James calls professing believers to be "doers," rather than simply *to do,* emphasizes that their entire personality should be characterized in that way. *See notes on Matt. 7:21-27.* **deceiving.** Lit. "reasoning beside or alongside" (as in "beside oneself"). This word was used in mathematics to refer to a miscalculation. Professing Christians who are content with only hearing the Word have made a serious spiritual miscalculation.

1:23 observing. A forceful Gr. word meaning to look carefully and cautiously, as opposed to taking a casual glance. **mirror.** First century mirrors were not glass but metallic, made of bronze, silver—or for the wealthy—gold. The metals were beaten flat and polished to a high gloss, and the image they reflected was adequate but not perfect (cf. 1 Cor. 13:12).

1:24 forgets what kind of man he was. Unless professing Christians act promptly after they hear the Word, they will forget the changes and improvements that their reflection showed them they need to make.

1:25 perfect law. In both the OT and NT, God's revealed, inerrant, sufficient, and comprehensive Word is called "law" (cf. Ps. 19:7). The presence of His grace does not mean there is no moral law or code of conduct for believers to obey. Believers are enabled by the Spirit to keep it (*see note on Rom. 8:4*). **liberty.** Genuine freedom from sin. As the Holy Spirit applies the principles of Scripture to believers' hearts, they are freed from sin's bondage and enabled to obey God (John 8:34-36).

1:26 religious. This refers to ceremonial public worship (cf. Acts 26:5). James chose this term, instead of one referring to internal godliness, to emphasize the external trappings, rituals, routines, and forms that were not followed sincerely. **bridle his tongue.** "Bridle" means "control," or as another translation renders it, "keep a tight rein." Purity of heart is often revealed by controlled and proper speech (*see note on Matt. 12:36,37*).

1:27 Pure and undefiled religion. James picks two synonymous adjectives to define the most spotless kind of religious faith—that which is measured by compassionate love (cf. John 13:35). **orphans and widows.** Those without parents or husbands were and are an especially needy segment of the church (*see notes on 1 Tim. 5:3;* cf. Ex. 22:22; Deut. 14:28,29; Ps. 68:5; Jer. 7:6,7; 22:16; Acts 6:1-6). Since they are usually unable to reciprocate in any way, caring for them clearly demonstrates true, sacrificial, Christian love. **world.** The evil world system (*see notes on 4:4; 1 John 2:15*).

2:1 the faith. This refers not to the act of believing, but to the entire Christian faith (cf. Jude 3), which has as its central focus Jesus Christ. ***the Lord* of glory.** Christ is the One who reveals the glory of God (*see note on Rev. 1:6*; cf. John 1:14; 2 Cor. 4:4-6; Heb. 1:1-3). In His incarnation, He showed only impartiality (cf. Matt. 22:16)—for example, consider the non-elite people included in His genealogy (*see notes on Matt. 1:1-16*), His choice of the humble village of Nazareth as His residence for 30 years, and His willingness to minister in Galilee and Samaria, both regions held in contempt by Israel's leaders. **partiality.** Originally, this word referred to raising someone's face or elevating the person, but it came to refer to exalting someone strictly on a superficial, external basis, such as appearance, race, wealth, rank, or social status (Lev. 19:15; Job 34:19; cf. Deut. 10:17; 15:7-10; 2 Chr. 19:7; Prov. 24:23; 28:21; Matt. 22:8-10; Acts 10:34,35; Rom. 2:11; Eph. 6:9; Col. 3:25; 4:1; 1 Pet. 1:17).

2:2 assembly. Lit. "a gathering together" or "synagogue." Since James was writing early in the church's history (see Introduction: Author and Date) to Jewish believers (1:1), he used both this general word and the normal Gr. word for "church" (5:14) to describe the church's corporate meetings during that period of transition. **gold rings.** While Jews commonly wore rings (cf. Luke 15:22), few could afford gold ones. However, there are some reports that in the ancient world the most ostentatious people wore rings on every finger but the middle one to show off their economic status (some ancient sources indicate that there were even ring rental businesses). **fine apparel.** This word refers to bright, shining garments and is used of the gorgeous garment Herod's soldiers put on Jesus to mock him (Luke 23:11) and of the apparel of an angel (Acts 10:30). It can also refer to bright, flashy color and to brilliant, glittering, sparkling ornamentation. James is not condemning this unbeliever for his distracting dress, but the church's flattering reaction to it. **a poor man.** Although there were people of means in the early church (Matt. 27:57-60; John 19:38,39; Acts 4:36,37; 8:27; 10:1,2; 16:14; 17:4; 1 Tim. 6:17-19), it consisted mostly of common, poor people (cf. v. 5; Acts 2:45; 4:35-37; 6:1-6; 1 Cor. 1:26; 2 Cor. 8:2,14). Throughout Scripture the poor are objects of God's special concern (1:27; Lev. 25:25,35-37,39; Pss. 41:1; 68:10; 72:4,12; 113:7; Prov. 17:5; 21:13; 28:27; 29:7; 31:9,20; Is. 3:14,15; 10:1,2; 25:4; Gal. 2:10).

2:3 sit...in a good place. A more comfortable, prominent place of honor. The synagogues and assembly halls of the first century sometimes had benches around the outside wall and a couple of benches in front. Most of the congregation either sat cross-legged on the floor or stood. There were a limited number of good seats; they were the ones the Pharisees always wanted (Mark 12:38,39).

man, "You stand there," or, "Sit here at my
footstool," 4 have you not [4]shown partiality among yourselves, and become judges
with evil thoughts?
5 Listen, my beloved brethren: [c]Has God
not chosen the poor of this world *to be*
[d]rich in faith and heirs of the kingdom
[e]which He promised to those who love
Him? 6 But [f]you have dishonored the poor
man. Do not the rich oppress you [g]and
drag you into the courts? 7 Do they not
blaspheme that noble name by which you
are [h]called?
8 If you really fulfill *the* royal law according to the Scripture, [i]*"You shall love
your neighbor as yourself,"* you do well;
9 but if you [5]show partiality, you commit
sin, and are convicted by the law as [j]trans-
gressors. 10 For whoever shall keep the
whole law, and yet [k]stumble in one *point,*
[l]he is guilty of all. 11 For He who said,
[m]*"Do not commit adultery,"* also said,
[n]*"Do not murder."* Now if you do not
commit adultery, but you do murder, you
have become a transgressor of the law.
12 So speak and so do as those who will be
judged by [o]the law of liberty. 13 For [p]judg-
ment is without mercy to the one who has
shown [q]no [r]mercy. [s]Mercy triumphs over
judgment.

Faith Without Works Is Dead

14 [t]What *does it* profit, my brethren, if
someone says he has faith but does not
have works? Can faith save him? 15 [u]If a
brother or sister is naked and destitute of
daily food, 16 and [v]one of you says to
them, "Depart in peace, be warmed and

4 [4] *differentiated*
5 [c] Job 34:19; John 7:48; 1 Cor. 1:27 [d] Luke 12:21; 1 Tim. 6:18; Rev. 2:9 [e] Ex. 20:6
6 [f] 1 Cor. 11:22 [g] Acts 13:50
7 [h] Acts 11:26; 1 Pet. 4:16
8 [i] Lev. 19:18
9 [j] Lev. 19:15; Deut. 1:17 [5] Lit. *receive the face*
10 [k] Gal. 3:10
[l] Deut. 27:26
11 [m] Ex. 20:14; Deut. 5:18 [n] Ex. 20:13; Deut. 5:17
12 [o] James 1:25
13 [p] Job 22:6 [q] Prov. 21:13; Matt. 18:32-35; [Luke 6:37] [r] Mic. 7:18; [Matt. 5:7] [s] Rom. 12:8
14 [t] Matt. 7:21-23, 26; 21:28-32 15 [u] Matt. 25:35; Luke 3:11
16 [v] [1 John 3:17, 18]

2:4 shown partiality. *See note on v. 1.* The true nature of the sin in this passage, not the lavish apparel or rings of the rich man or that he was given a good seat. **judges with evil thoughts.** This is better translated "judges with vicious intentions." James feared that his readers would behave just like the sinful world by catering to the rich and prominent while shunning the poor and common.

2:5 Has God not chosen. *See note on Rom. 8:29;* cf. 1 Cor. 1:26-29. **the kingdom.** *See note on Matt. 3:2.* Here James intends the kingdom in its present sense of the sphere of salvation—those over whom Christ rules—as well as its future millennial and eternal glory.

2:6 oppress. Lit. "to tyrannize." **drag you into the courts.** A reference to civil court.

2:7 blaspheme that noble name. Probably a reference to religious courts. Wealthy Jewish opponents of Christ were harassing these poor Christians. Cf. John 16:2-4.

2:8 royal law. This is better translated "sovereign law." The idea is that this law is supreme or binding. ***love your neighbor as yourself.*** This sovereign law (quoted from Lev. 19:18), when combined with the command to love God (Deut. 6:4,5), summarizes all the Law and the Prophets (Matt. 22:36-40; Rom. 13:8-10). James is not advocating some kind of emotional affection for oneself—self-love is clearly a sin (2 Tim. 3:2). Rather, the command is to pursue meeting the physical health and spiritual well-being of one's neighbors (all within the sphere of our influence; Luke 10:30-37) with the same intensity and concern as one does naturally for one's self (cf. Phil. 2:3,4).

2:9 if. Better translated as "since," the Gr. construction of this conditional statement indicates that this practice was in fact happening among James' readers. **show partiality.** *See note on v. 1.* The form of this Gr. verb indicates that their behavior was not an occasional slip but a continual practice. **convicted by the law.** Specifically by the commands in Deut. 1:17 and 16:19. **transgressors.** This refers to one who goes beyond the law of God. Respect of persons makes one a violator of God's law.

2:10 whole law...one *point.* *See notes on Gal. 3:10-13.* The law of God is not a series of detached injunctions but a basic unity that requires perfect love of Him and our neighbors (Matt. 22:36-40). Although all sins are not equally damaging or heinous, they all shatter that unity and render men transgressors, much like hitting a window with a hammer at only one point will shatter and destroy the whole window. **guilty of all.** Not in the sense of having violated every command, but in the sense of having violated the law's unity. One transgression makes fulfilling the law's most basic commands—to love God perfectly and to love one's neighbor as oneself—impossible.

2:11 These quotations are taken from Ex. 20:13,14 and Deut. 5:17,18.

2:12 judged. Cf. Rom. 2:6-16. **law of liberty.** *See note on 1:25.*

2:13 A person who shows no mercy and compassion for people in need demonstrates that he has never responded to the great mercy of God, and as an unredeemed person will receive only strict, unrelieved judgment in eternal hell (cf. Matt. 5:7). **Mercy triumphs over judgment.** The person whose life is characterized by mercy is ready for the day of judgment, and will escape all the charges that strict justice might bring against him because by showing mercy to others he gives genuine evidence of having received God's mercy.

2:14-26 James continues his series of tests by which his readers can evaluate whether their faith is living or dead (see Introduction: Background and Setting). This passage contains the composite test—the one test that pulls the others together: the test of works, or righteous behavior that obeys God's Word and manifests a godly nature (cf. 1:22-25). James' point is not that a person is saved by works (he has already strongly and clearly asserted that salvation is a gracious gift from God; 1:17,18; cf. Eph. 2:8,9), but that there is a kind of apparent faith that is dead and does not save (vv. 14,17,20,24,26; cf. Matt. 3:7,8; 5:16; 7:21; 13:18-23; John 8:30,31; 15:6). It is possible James was writing to Jews (cf. 1:1) who had jettisoned the works righteousness of Judaism but, instead, had embraced the mistaken notion that since righteous works and obedience to God's will were not efficacious for salvation, they were not necessary at all. Thus, they reduced faith to a mere mental assent to the facts about Christ.

2:14 if someone says. This important phrase governs the interpretation of the entire passage. James does not say that this person actually has faith, but that he claims to have it. **faith.** This is best understood in a broad sense, speaking of any degree of acceptance of the truths of the gospel. **does not have.** Again, the verb's form describes someone who continually lacks any external evidence of the faith he routinely claims. **works.** This refers to all righteous behavior that conforms to God's revealed Word, but specifically, in the context, to acts of compassion (v. 15). **Can faith save him?** Better translated, "Can that kind of faith save?" James is not disputing the importance of faith. Rather, he is opposing the notion that saving faith can be a mere intellectual exercise void of a commitment to active obedience (cf. Matt. 7:16-18). The grammatical form of the question demands a negative answer. *See notes on Rom. 2:5-10.*

2:15,16 James illustrates his point by comparing faith without works to words of compassion without acts of compassion (cf. Matt. 25:31-46).

filled," but you do not give them the things
which are needed for the body, what *does it*
profit? 17 Thus also faith by itself, if it does
not have works, is dead.
18 But someone will say, "You have faith,
and I have works." [w]Show me your faith
without [6]your works, [x]and I will show you
my faith by [7]my works. 19 You believe that
there is one God. You do well. Even the
demons believe—and tremble! 20 But do
you want to know, O foolish man, that
faith without works is [8]dead? 21 Was not
Abraham our father justified by works
[y]when he offered Isaac his son on the altar?
22 Do you see [z]that faith was working together with his works, and by [a]works faith
was made [9]perfect? 23 And the Scripture
was fulfilled which says, [b]*"Abraham be-*
lieved God, and it was [1]*accounted to him*
for righteousness." And he was called [c]the
friend of God. 24 You see then that a man is
justified by works, and not by faith only.
25 Likewise, [d]was not Rahab the harlot
also justified by works when she received
the messengers and sent *them* out another
way?
26 For as the body without the spirit is
dead, so faith without works is dead also.

The Untamable Tongue

3 My brethren, [a]let not many of you become teachers, [b]knowing that we
shall receive a stricter judgment. 2 For [c]we
all stumble in many things. [d]If anyone
does not stumble in word, [e]he *is* a [1]perfect
man, able also to bridle the whole body.

18 [w] Col. 1:6; 1 Thess. 1:3; Heb. 6:10 [x] [Gal. 5:6]; James 3:13 [6] NU omits *your* [7] NU omits *my*
20 [8] NU *useless*
21 [y] Gen. 22:9, 10, 12, 16-18
22 [z] [John 6:29]; Heb. 11:17 [a] John 8:39 [9] *complete*
23 [b] Gen. 15:6; Rom. 4:3 [c] 2 Chr. 20:7; Is. 41:8 [1] *credited*
25 [d] Heb. 11:31

CHAPTER 3

1 [a] [Matt. 23:8]; Rom. 2:21; 1 Tim. 1:7 [b] Luke 6:37
2 [c] 1 Kin. 8:46 [d] Ps. 34:13 [e] [Matt. 12:34-37; James 3:2-12] [1] *mature*

2:17 faith by itself...is dead. Just as professed compassion without action is phony, the kind of faith that is without works is mere empty profession, not genuine saving faith.

2:18 someone. Interpreters disagree on whether 1) "someone" is James' humble way of referring to himself or whether it refers to one of James' antagonists who objected to his teaching; and 2) how much of the following passage should be attributed to this antagonist as opposed to James himself. Regardless, James' main point is the same: the only possible evidence of true faith is works (cf. 2 Pet. 1:3-11).

2:19 You believe that there is one God. A clear reference to the passage most familiar to his Jewish readers: the *Shema* (Deut. 6:4,5), the most basic doctrine of the OT. **demons believe.** Even fallen angels affirm the oneness of God and tremble at its implications. Demons are essentially orthodox in their doctrine (cf. Matt. 8:29,30; Mark 5:7; Luke 4:41; Acts 19:15). But orthodox doctrine by itself is no proof of saving faith. They know the truth about God, Christ, and the Spirit, but hate it and them.

2:20 foolish. Lit. "empty, defective." The objector's claim of belief is fraudulent, and his faith is a sham. **faith without works is dead?** Lit. "the faith without the works." James is not contrasting two methods of salvation (faith versus works). Instead, he contrasts two kinds of faith: living faith that saves and dead faith that does not (cf. 1 John 3:7-10).

2:21-26 James cites 3 illustrations of living faith: 1) Abraham (vv. 21-24); 2) Rahab (v. 25); and 3) the human body and spirit (v. 26).

2:21 justified by works. This does not contradict Paul's clear teaching that Abraham was justified before God by grace alone through faith alone (Rom. 3:20; 4:1-25; Gal. 3:6,11). For several reasons, James cannot mean that Abraham was constituted righteous before God because of his own good works: 1) James already stressed that salvation is a gracious gift (1:17,18); 2) in the middle of this disputed passage (v. 23), James quoted Gen. 15:6, which forcefully claims that God credited righteousness to Abraham solely on the basis of his faith (*see notes on Rom. 1:17; 3:24; 4:1-25*); and 3) the work that James said justified Abraham was his offering up of Isaac (Gen. 22:9,12), an event that occurred many years after he first exercised faith and was declared righteous before God (Gen. 12:1-7; 15:6). Instead, Abraham's offering of Isaac demonstrated the genuineness of his faith and the reality of his justification before God. James is emphasizing the vindication before others of a man's claim to salvation. James' teaching perfectly complements Paul's writings; salvation is determined by faith alone (Eph. 2:8,9) and demonstrated by faithfulness to obey God's will alone (Eph. 2:10).

2:22 was made perfect. This refers to bringing something to its end, or to its fullness. Just as a fruit tree has not arrived at its goal until it bears fruit, faith has not reached its end until it demonstrates itself in a righteous life.

2:23 the Scripture...says. Quoted from Gen. 15:6; *see notes on Rom. 4:1-5.* **friend of God.** Abraham is so called in 2 Chr. 20:7 and Is. 41:8 because of his obedience (John 15:14,15).

2:24 justified by works, and not by faith only. *See note on v. 21.*

2:25 Rahab the harlot. The OT records the content of her faith, which was the basis of her justification before God (*see note on Josh. 2:11*). She demonstrated the reality of her saving faith when, at great personal risk she protected the messengers of God (Josh. 2:4,15; 6:17; cf. Heb. 11:31). James did not intend, however, for those words to be a commendation of her occupation or her lying. **justified by works.** *See note on v. 21.*

3:1-12 In this passage, James used the common Jewish literary device of attributing blame to a specific bodily member (cf. Rom. 3:15; 2 Pet. 2:14). He personified the tongue as being representative of human depravity and wretchedness. In this way, he echoed the scriptural truth that the mouth is a focal point and vivid indicator of man's fallenness and sinful heart condition (cf. Is. 6:5; Matt. 15:11,16-19; Mark 7:20-23; Rom. 3:13,14).

3:1 teachers. This word is translated "master" in the gospels and refers to a person who functions in an official teaching or preaching capacity (cf. Luke 4:16-27; John 3:10; Acts 13:14,15; 1 Cor. 12:28; Eph. 4:11). **stricter judgment.** The word translated "judgment" usually expresses a negative verdict in the NT, and here refers to a future judgment: 1) for the unbelieving false teacher, at the second coming (Jude 14,15); and 2) for the believer, when he is rewarded before Christ (1 Cor. 4:3-5). This is not meant to discourage true teachers, but to warn the prospective teacher of the role's seriousness (cf. Ezek. 3:17,18; 33:7-9; Acts 20:26,27; Heb. 13:17).

3:2 Scripture contains much about all the evil which the tongue can cause (cf. Pss. 5:9; 34:13; 39:1; 52:4; Prov. 6:17; 17:20; 26:28; 28:23; Is. 59:3; Rom. 3:13). The tongue has immense power to speak sinfully, erroneously, and inappropriately—human speech is a graphic representation of human depravity (*see notes on vv. 1-12*). **stumble.** This refers to sinning, or offending God's Person. The form of the Gr. verb emphasizes that everyone continually fails to do what is right. **perfect man.** "Perfect" may refer to true perfection, in which case James is saying that, hypothetically, if a human being were able to perfectly control his tongue, he would be a perfect man. But, of course, no one is actually immune from sinning with his tongue. More likely, "perfect" is describing those who are spiritually mature and thus able to control their tongues.

3 [2]Indeed, [f]we put bits in horses' mouths
that they may obey us, and we turn their
whole body. 4 Look also at ships: although they are so large and are driven by
fierce winds, they are turned by a very
small rudder wherever the pilot desires.
5 Even so [g]the tongue is a little member
and [h]boasts great things.

See how great a forest a little fire kindles! 6 And [i]the tongue *is* a fire, a world of
[3]iniquity. The tongue is so set among our
members that it [j]defiles the whole body,
and sets on fire the course of [4]nature; and
it is set on fire by [5]hell. 7 For every kind of
beast and bird, of reptile and creature of
the sea, is tamed and has been tamed by
mankind. 8 But no man can tame the
tongue. *It is* an unruly evil, [k]full of deadly
poison. 9 With it we bless our God and Father, and with it we curse men, who have
been made [l]in the [6]similitude of God.
10 Out of the same mouth proceed blessing
and cursing. My brethren, these things
ought not to be so. 11 Does a spring send
forth fresh *water* and bitter from the same
opening? 12 Can a [m]fig tree, my brethren,
bear olives, or a grapevine bear figs?
[7]Thus no spring yields both salt water and
fresh.

Heavenly Versus Demonic Wisdom

13 [n]Who *is* wise and understanding
among you? Let him show by good conduct *that* his works *are done* in the meekness of wisdom. 14 But if you have [o]bitter
envy and [8]self-seeking in your hearts, [p]do
not boast and lie against the truth. 15 [q]This
wisdom does not descend from above, but
is earthly, sensual, demonic. 16 For [r]where
envy and self-seeking *exist*, confusion and
every evil thing *are* there. 17 But [s]the wisdom that is from above is first pure, then
peaceable, gentle, willing to yield, full of
mercy and good fruits, [t]without partiality

3 [f]Ps. 32:9 [2]NU *Now if*
5 [g]Prov. 12:18; 15:2; James 1:26 [h]Ps. 12:3; 73:8
6 [i]Ps. 120:2, 3; Prov. 16:27 [j][Matt. 12:36; 15:11, 18] [3]*unrighteousness* [4]*existence* [5]Gr. *Gehenna*
8 [k]Ps. 140:3; Eccl. 10:11; Rom. 3:13
9 [l]Gen. 1:26; 5:1; 9:6; 1 Cor. 11:7 [6]*likeness*
12 [m]Matt. 7:16-20 [7]NU *Neither can a salty spring produce fresh water.*
13 [n]Gal. 6:4
14 [o]Rom. 13:13 [p]Rom. 2:17 [8]*selfish ambition*
15 [q]Phil. 3:19
16 [r]1 Cor. 3:3
17 [s]1 Cor. 2:6, 7 [t]James 2:1

3:3-5 James provided several analogies that show how the tongue, even though small, has the power to control one's whole person and influence everything in his life.

3:6 tongue *is* a fire. Like fire, the tongue's sinful words can spread destruction rapidly, or as its accompanying smoke, those words can permeate and ruin everything around it. **defiles.** This means "to pollute or contaminate" (cf. Mark 7:20; Jude 23). **the course of nature.** Better translated "the circle of life," this underscores that the tongue's evil can extend beyond the individual to affect everything in his sphere of influence. **hell.** *See note on Matt. 25:46.* A translation of the Gr. word *gehenna* (or valley of Hinnom). In Christ's time this valley that lay SW of Jerusalem's walls served as the city dump and was known for its constantly burning fire. Jesus used that place to symbolize the eternal place of punishment and torment (cf. Mark 9:43,45). To James "hell" conjures up not just the place but the satanic host that will some day inherit it—they use the tongue as a tool for evil.

3:8 no man can tame the tongue. Only God, by His power, can do this (cf. Acts 2:1-11).

3:9 bless...curse. It was traditional for Jews to add "blessed be He" to a mention of God's name (cf. Ps. 68:19,35). However, the tongue also wishes evil on people made in God's image. This points out the hypocritical inconsistency of the tongue's activities. **made in the similitude of God.** Man was made in God's image (*see notes on Gen. 1:26*).

3:11,12 Three illustrations from nature demonstrate the sinfulness of cursing. The genuine believer will not contradict his profession of faith by the regular use of unwholesome words.

3:13-18 In v. 13, James makes a transition from discussing teachers and the tongue to dealing with wisdom's impact on everyone's life. He supports the truth of OT wisdom literature (Job to Song of Solomon), that wisdom is divided into two realms—man's and God's.

3:13 wise and understanding. "Wise" is the common Gr. word for speculative knowledge and philosophy, but the Hebrews infused it with the much richer meaning of skillfully applying knowledge to the matter of practical living. The word for "understanding" is used only here in the NT and means a specialist or professional who could skillfully apply his expertise to practical situations. James is asking who is truly skilled in the art of living. **meekness.** Also rendered "gentleness," it is the opposite of arrogance and self-promotion (*see note on Matt. 5:5*; cf. 1:21; Num. 12:3; Gal. 5:23). The Greeks described it as power under control. **wisdom.** The kind that comes only from God (*see note on 1:5*; cf. Job 9:4; 28; Pss. 104:24; 111:10; Prov. 1:7; 2:1-7; 3:19,20; 9:10; Jer. 10:7,12; Dan. 1:17; 2:20-23; Rom. 11:33; 1 Cor. 1:30; Eph. 3:10; Col. 2:3).

3:14 bitter envy. The Gr. term for "bitter" was used of undrinkable water. When combined with "envy" it defines a harsh, resentful attitude toward others. **self-seeking.** Sometimes translated "strife," it refers to selfish ambition that engenders antagonism and factionalism. The Gr. word came to describe anyone who entered politics for selfish reasons and sought to achieve his agenda at any cost (i.e., even if that meant trampling on others).

3:15 from above. *See notes on v. 13.* Self-centered wisdom that is consumed with personal ambition is not from God. **earthly, sensual, demonic.** A description of man's wisdom as: 1) limited to earth; 2) characterized by humanness, frailty, an unsanctified heart, and an unredeemed spirit; and 3) generated by Satan's forces (cf. 1 Cor. 2:14; 2 Cor. 11:14,15).

3:16 confusion. This is the disorder that results from the instability and chaos of human wisdom (*see notes on 1:6,8*; cf. v. 8). **every evil thing.** Lit. "every worthless (or vile) work." This denotes things that are not so much intrinsically evil as they are simply good for nothing.

3:17 wisdom...from above. *See note on v. 13.* **pure.** This refers to spiritual integrity and moral sincerity. Every genuine Christian has this kind of heart motivation (cf. Pss. 24:3,4; 51:7; Matt. 5:8; Rom. 7:22,23; Heb. 12:14). **peaceable.** Means "peace loving" or "peace promoting" (cf. Matt. 5:9). **gentle.** This word is difficult to translate, but most nearly means a character trait of sweet reasonableness. Such a person will submit to all kinds of mistreatment and difficulty with an attitude of kind, courteous, patient humility, without any thought of hatred or revenge (cf. Matt. 5:10,11). **willing to yield.** The original term described someone who was teachable, compliant, easily persuaded, and who willingly submitted to military discipline or moral and legal standards. For believers, it defines obedience to God's standards (cf. Matt. 5:3-5). **full of mercy.** The gift of showing concern for those who suffer pain and hardship, and the ability to forgive quickly (cf. Matt. 5:7; Rom. 12:8). **without partiality.** The Gr. word occurs only here in the NT and denotes a consistent, unwavering person who is undivided in his commitment and conviction and does not make unfair distinctions (*see notes on 2:1-13*).

[u]and without hypocrisy. 18 [v]Now the fruit
of righteousness is sown in peace by those
who make peace.

Pride Promotes Strife

4 Where do [1]wars and fights *come* from
among you? Do *they* not *come* from
your *desires for* pleasure [a]that war in your
members? 2 You lust and do not have. You
murder and covet and cannot obtain. You
fight and [2]war. [3]Yet you do not have because you do not ask. 3 [b]You ask and do
not receive, [c]because you ask amiss, that
you may spend *it* on your pleasures.
4 [4]Adulterers and adulteresses! Do you not
know that [d]friendship with the world is
enmity with God? [e]Whoever therefore
wants to be a friend of the world makes
himself an enemy of God. 5 Or do you
think that the Scripture says in vain, [f]"The
Spirit who dwells in us yearns jealously"?
6 But He gives more grace. Therefore He
says:

> [g]"*God resists the proud,*
> *But gives grace to the humble."*

Humility Cures Worldliness

7 Therefore submit to God. [h]Resist the
devil and he will flee from you. 8 [i]Draw
near to God and He will draw near to
you. [j]Cleanse *your* hands, *you* sinners; and

17 [u] Rom. 12:9; 2 Cor. 6:6; 1 Pet. 1:22
18 [v] Prov. 11:18; Is. 32:17; Hos. 10:12; Amos 6:12; [Gal. 6:8; Phil. 1:11]

CHAPTER 4

1 [a] Rom. 7:23; [Gal. 5:17]; 1 Pet. 2:11 [1] *battles*
2 [2] *battle* [3] NU, M omit *Yet*
3 [b] Job 27:8, 9 [c] [Ps. 66:18]
4 [d] Rom. 8:7; 1 John 2:15 [e] Gal. 1:4 [4] NU omits *Adulterers and*
5 [f] Gen. 6:5
6 [g] Job 22:29; Ps. 138:6; Prov. 3:34; Matt. 23:12; 1 Pet. 5:5
7 [h] [Eph. 4:27; 6:11]; 1 Pet. 5:8 **8** [i] 2 Chr. 15:2; Zech. 1:3; Mal. 3:7; Heb. 7:19 [j] Job 17:9; Is. 1:16; 1 Tim. 2:8

3:18 fruit of righteousness. Good works that result from salvation (cf. v. 17; Matt. 5:6; *see notes on 2:14-20; Gal. 5:22,23; Phil. 1:11*). **those who make peace.** *See note on v. 17.* Righteousness flourishes in a climate of spiritual peace.

4:1 wars and fights...among you. These are between people in the church, not internal conflict in individual people. "Wars" speaks of the conflict in general; "fights" of its specific manifestations. Discord in the church is not by God's design (John 13:34,35; 17:21; 2 Cor. 12:20; Phil. 1:27), but results from the mix of tares (false believers) and wheat (truly redeemed people) that make up the church. ***desires.*** The Gr. word (from which the Eng. word "hedonism" derives) always has a negative connotation in the NT. The passionate desires for worldly pleasures that mark unbelievers (1:14; Eph. 2:3; 2 Tim. 3:4; Jude 18) are the internal source of the external conflict in the church. Cf. 1:14,15. **your members.** Not church members, but bodily members (*see note on Rom. 6:13*). James, like Paul, uses "members" to speak of sinful, fallen human nature (cf. Rom. 6:19; 7:5,23). Unbelievers (who are in view here) fight (unsuccessfully) against the evil desires they cannot control.

4:2 murder. The ultimate result of thwarted desires. James had in mind actual murder, and the gamut of sins (hate, anger, bitterness) leading up to it. The picture is of unbelievers so driven by their uncontrollable evil desires that they will fight to the death to fulfill them. **you do not ask.** True joy, peace, happiness, meaning, hope, and fulfillment in life come only from God. Unbelievers, however, are unwilling to ask for them on His terms—they refuse to submit to God or acknowledge their dependence on Him.

4:3 amiss. This refers to acting in an evil manner, motivated by personal gratification and selfish desire. Unbelievers seek things for their own pleasures, not the honor and glory of God.

4:4 Adulterers and adulteresses! A metaphorical description of spiritual unfaithfulness (cf. Matt. 12:39; 16:4; Mark 8:38). It would have been especially familiar to James' Jewish readers, since the OT often describes unfaithful Israel as a spiritual harlot (cf. 2 Chr. 21:11,13; Jer. 2:20; 3:1,6,8,9; Ezek. 16:26-29; Hos. 1:2; 4:15; 9:1). James has in view professing Christians, outwardly associated with the church, but holding a deep affection for the evil world system. **friendship.** Appearing only here in the NT, the Gr. word describes love in the sense of a strong emotional attachment. Those with a deep and intimate longing for the things of the world give evidence that they are not redeemed (1 John 2:15-17). **world.** *See note on 1:27.* **enmity with God.** The necessary corollary to friendship with the world. The sobering truth that unbelievers are God's enemies is taught throughout Scripture (cf. Deut. 32:41-43; Pss. 21:8; 68:21; 72:9; 110:1,2; Is. 42:13; Nah. 1:2,8; Luke 19:27; Rom. 5:10; 8:5-7; 1 Cor. 15:25).

4:5 Scripture says. A common NT way of introducing an OT quote (John 19:37; Rom. 4:3; 9:17; 10:11; 11:2; Gal. 4:30; 1 Tim. 5:18). The quote that follows, however, is not found as such in the OT; it is a composite of general OT teaching. **The Spirit...yearns jealously.** This difficult phrase is best understood by seeing the "spirit" as a reference not to the Holy Spirit, but to the human spirit, and translating the phrase "yearns jealously" in the negative sense of "lusts to envy." James' point is that an unbelieving person's spirit (inner person) is bent on evil (cf. Gen. 6:5; 8:21; Prov. 21:10; Eccl. 9:3; Jer. 17:9; Mark 7:21-23). Those who think otherwise defy the biblical diagnosis of fallen human nature; and those who live in worldly lusts give evidence that their faith is not genuine (cf. Rom. 8:5-11; 1 Cor. 2:14).

4:6 more grace. The only ray of hope in man's spiritual darkness is the sovereign grace of God, which alone can rescue man from his propensity to lust for evil things. That God gives "more grace" shows that His grace is greater than the power of sin, the flesh, the world, and Satan (cf. Rom. 5:20). The OT quote (from Prov. 3:34; cf. 1 Pet. 5:5) reveals who obtains God's grace—the humble, not the proud enemies of God. The word "humble" does not define a special class of Christians, but encompasses all believers (cf. Is. 57:15; 66:2; Matt. 18:3,4).

4:7-10 In a series of 10 commands (10 imperative verbs in the Gr. text), James reveals how to receive saving grace. These verses delineate man's response to God's gracious offer of salvation, and disclose what it means to be humble.

4:7 submit. Lit. "to line up under." The word was used of soldiers under the authority of their commander. In the NT, it describes Jesus' submission to His parents' authority (Luke 2:51), submission to human government (Rom. 13:1), the church's submission to Christ (Eph. 5:24), and servants' submission to their masters (Titus 2:9; 1 Pet. 2:18). James used the word to describe a willing, conscious submission to God's authority as sovereign ruler of the universe. A truly humble person will give his allegiance to God, obey His commands, and follow His leadership (cf. Matt. 10:38). **Resist the devil and he will flee from you.** The flip side of the first command. "Resist" literally means "take your stand against." All people are either under the lordship of Christ or the lordship of Satan (John 8:44; Eph. 2:2; 1 John 3:8; 5:19); there is no middle ground. Those who transfer their allegiance from Satan to God will find that Satan "will flee from" them; he is a defeated foe.

4:8 Draw near. Pursue an intimate love relationship with God (cf. Phil. 3:10). The concept of drawing near to God was associated originally with the Levitical priests (Ex. 19:22; Lev. 10:3; Ezek. 44:13), but eventually came to describe anyone's approach to God (Ps. 73:28; Is. 29:13; Heb. 4:16; 7:19; 10:22). Salvation involves more than submitting to God and resisting the devil; the redeemed heart longs for communion with God (Pss. 27:8; 42:1,2; 63:1,2; 84:2; 143:6; Matt. 22:37). **Cleanse *your* hands.** The OT priests had to ceremonially wash their hands before approaching God (Ex. 30:19-21), and sinners (a term used only for unbelievers; *see note on 5:20*) who would approach Him

[k]purify *your* hearts, *you* double-minded.
9 [l]Lament and mourn and weep! Let your
laughter be turned to mourning and *your*
joy to gloom. 10 [m]Humble yourselves in
the sight of the Lord, and He will lift you
up.

Do Not Judge a Brother

11 [n]Do not speak evil of one another,
brethren. He who speaks evil of a brother
[o]and judges his brother, speaks evil of the
law and judges the law. But if you judge
the law, you are not a doer of the law but a
judge. 12 There is one [5]Lawgiver, [p]who is
able to save and to destroy. [q]Who[6] are you
to judge [7]another?

Do Not Boast About Tomorrow

13 Come now, you who say, "Today or
tomorrow [8]we will go to such and such a
city, spend a year there, buy and sell, and
make a profit"; 14 whereas you do not
know what *will happen* tomorrow. For what
is your life? [r]It is even a vapor that appears
for a little time and then vanishes away.
15 Instead you *ought* to say, [s]"If the Lord
wills, we shall live and do this or that."
16 But now you boast in your arrogance.
[t]All such boasting is evil.
17 Therefore, [u]to him who knows to do
good and does not do *it,* to him it is sin.

Rich Oppressors Will Be Judged

5 Come now, *you* [a]rich, weep and howl
for your miseries that are coming upon
you! 2 Your [b]riches [1]are corrupted, and
[c]your garments are moth-eaten. 3 Your
gold and silver are corroded, and their cor-
rosion will be a witness against you and
will eat your flesh like fire. [d]You have
heaped up treasure in the last days. 4 Indeed [e]the wages of the laborers who
mowed your fields, which you kept back
by fraud, cry out; and [f]the cries of the
reapers have reached the ears of the Lord
of [2]Sabaoth. 5 You have lived on the earth

8 [k] Jer. 4:14; James 3:17; 1 Pet. 1:22; 1 John 3:3
9 [l] Matt. 5:4
10 [m] Job 22:29; Luke 14:11; 18:14; 1 Pet. 5:6
11 [n] 2 Cor. 12:20; Eph. 4:31; James 5:9; 1 Pet. 2:1-3 [o] [Matt. 7:1-5]; Rom. 14:4
12 [p] [Matt. 10:28] [q] Rom. 14:4 [5] NU adds *and Judge* [6] NU, M *But who* [7] NU *a neighbor*
13 [8] M *let us*
14 [r] Job 7:7; Ps. 102:3; 1 Pet. 1:24
15 [s] Acts 18:21; 1 Cor. 4:19
16 [t] 1 Cor. 5:6
17 [u] [Luke 12:47]; John 9:41; 2 Pet. 2:21

CHAPTER 5

1 [a] Prov. 11:28; [Luke 6:24; 1 Tim. 6:9]
2 [b] Jer. 17:11; Matt. 6:19 [c] Job 13:28

[1] *have rotted* 3 [d] Rom. 2:5 4 [e] Lev. 19:13; Job 24:10; Jer. 22:13; Mal. 3:5 [f] Ex. 2:23; Deut. 24:15; Job 31:38 [2] Lit., in Heb., *Hosts*

must recognize and confess their sin. **purify *your* hearts.** Cleansing the hands symbolizes external behavior; this phrase refers to the inner thoughts, motives, and desires of the heart (Ps. 24:3,4; Jer. 4:4; Ezek. 18:31; 36:25,26; 1 Tim. 1:5; 2 Tim. 2:22; 1 Pet. 1:22). **double-minded.** *See note on 1:8.*

4:9 Lament. Be afflicted, wretched, and miserable. This is the state of those truly broken over their sin. **mourn.** *See note on Matt. 5:4.* God will not turn away a heart broken and contrite over sin (Ps. 51:17; 2 Cor. 7:10). Mourning is the inner response to such brokenness. **weep.** The outward manifestation of inner sorrow over sin (cf. Mark 14:72). **laughter.** Used only here in the NT, the word signifies the flippant laughter of those foolishly indulging in worldly pleasures. The picture is of people who give no thought to God, life, death, sin, judgment, or holiness. James calls on such people to mourn over their sin (cf. Luke 18:13,14).

4:10 See Ps. 75:6; Matt. 23:12. This final command sums up the preceding 9 (*see notes on vv. 7-10*) commands, which mark the truly humble person. "Humble" comes from a word meaning "to make oneself low." Those conscious of being in the presence of the majestic, infinitely holy God are humble (cf. Is. 6:5).

4:11 speak evil. This means to slander or defame. James does not forbid confronting those in sin, which is elsewhere commanded in Scripture (Matt. 18:15-17; Acts 20:31; 1 Cor. 4:14; Col. 1:28; Titus 1:13; 2:15; 3:10). Rather, he condemns careless, derogatory, critical, slanderous accusations against others (cf. Ex. 23:1; Pss. 50:20; 101:5; 140:11; Prov. 10:18; 11:9; 16:28; 17:9; 26:20; Rom. 1:29; 2 Cor. 12:20; Eph. 4:31; 1 Tim. 3:11; 2 Tim. 3:3; Titus 2:3; 3:2). **speaks evil of a brother...speaks evil of the law.** Those who speak evil of other believers set themselves up as judges and condemn them (cf. 2:4). They thereby defame and disregard God's law, which expressly forbids such slanderous condemnation. **judges the law.** By refusing to submit to the law, slanderers place themselves above it as its judges.

4:12 one Lawgiver. God, who gave the law (cf. Is. 33:22). He alone has the authority to save those who repent from its penalty, and destroy those who refuse to repent.

4:13 James does not condemn wise business planning, but rather planning that leaves out God. The people so depicted are practical atheists, living their lives and making their plans as if God did not exist. Such conduct is inconsistent with genuine saving faith, which submits to God (*see note on v. 7*).

4:14 know what *will happen*. See Prov. 27:1. James exposes the presumptuous folly of the practical atheists he condemned in v. 13—those who do not know what the future holds for them (cf. Luke 12:16-21). God alone knows the future (cf. Is. 46:9,10). **vapor.** This refers either to a puff of smoke or one's breath that appears for a moment in cold air. It stresses the transitory nature of life (cf. 1:10; Job 7:6,7; 9:25,26; 14:1,2; Pss. 39:5,11; 62:9; 89:47; 90:5,6,10).

4:15 If the Lord wills. The true Christian submits his plans to the lordship of Christ (*see note on v. 7*; cf. Prov. 19:21; Acts 18:21; 21:14; Rom. 1:10; 15:32; 1 Cor. 4:19; 16:7).

4:16 boasting. Arrogant bragging about their anticipated business accomplishments (*see note on v. 13*).

4:17 sin. The implication is that they also did what they shouldn't do. Sins of omission lead directly to sins of commission.

5:1 rich. Those with more than they need to live. James condemns them not for being wealthy, but for misusing their resources. Unlike the believing rich in Timothy's congregation (1 Tim. 6:17-19), these are the wicked wealthy who profess Christian faith and have associated themselves with the church, but whose real god is money. For prostituting the goodness and generosity of God, they can anticipate only divine punishment (v. 5).

5:2,3 corrupted...moth-eaten...corroded. James points out the folly of hoarding food, expensive clothing, or money—all of which is subject to decay, theft, fire, or other forms of loss.

5:3 last days. The period between Christ's first and second comings (*see note on 1 Tim. 4:1*). James rebukes the rich for living as if Jesus were never coming back.

5:4 wages...you kept back. The rich had gained some of their wealth by oppressing and defrauding their day laborers—a practice strictly forbidden in the OT (cf. Lev. 19:13; Deut. 24:14,15). **the Lord of Sabaoth.** An untranslated Gr. word meaning "hosts." The One who hears the cries of the defrauded laborers, James warns, is the Lord of hosts (a name for God used frequently in the OT), the commander of the armies of heaven (angels). The Bible teaches that angels will be involved in the judgment of unbelievers (Matt. 13:39-41,49; 16:27; 25:31; 2 Thess. 1:7,8).

in pleasure and [3]luxury; you have [4]fat-
tened your hearts [5]as in a day of slaughter.
6 You have condemned, you have murdered the just; he does not resist you.

Be Patient and Persevering

7 Therefore be patient, brethren, until the
coming of the Lord. See *how* the farmer
waits for the precious fruit of the earth,
waiting patiently for it until it receives the
early and latter rain. **8** You also be patient.
Establish your hearts, for the coming of the
Lord [6]is at hand.

9 Do not [7]grumble against one another,
brethren, lest you be [8]condemned. Behold,
the Judge is standing at the door! **10** [g]My
brethren, take the prophets, who spoke in
the name of the Lord, as an example of
suffering and [h]patience. **11** Indeed [i]we
count them blessed who [j]endure. You
have heard of [k]the perseverance of Job
and seen [l]the end *intended by* the Lord—
that [m]the Lord is very compassionate and
merciful.

12 But above all, my brethren, [n]do not
swear, either by heaven or by earth or with
any other oath. But let your "Yes" be "Yes,"
and *your* "No," "No," lest you fall into
[9]judgment.

Meeting Specific Needs

13 Is anyone among you suffering? Let
him [o]pray. Is anyone cheerful? [p]Let him
sing psalms. **14** Is anyone among you sick?
Let him call for the elders of the church,
and let them pray over him, [q]anointing
him with oil in the name of the Lord.
15 And the prayer of faith will save the
sick, and the Lord will raise him up. [r]And
if he has committed sins, he will be forgiv-
en. **16** [1]Confess *your* trespasses to one another, and pray for one another, that you

5 [3] *indulgence* [4] Lit. *nourished* [5] NU omits *as*
8 [6] *has drawn near*
9 [7] Lit. *groan* [8] NU, M *judged*
10 [g] Matt. 5:12 [h] Heb. 10:36
11 [i] [Ps. 94:12; Matt. 5:10]; James 1:2 [j] [James 1:12] [k] Job 1:21, 22; 2:10 [l] Job 42:10 [m] Num. 14:18
12 [n] Matt. 5:34-37 [9] M *hypocrisy*
13 [o] Ps. 50:14, 15 [p] Eph. 5:19
14 [q] Mark 6:13; 16:18
15 [r] Is. 33:24
16 [1] NU *Therefore confess your sins*

5:5 pleasure and luxury. After robbing their workers to accumulate their wealth, the rich indulged themselves in an extravagant lifestyle. "Pleasure" has the connotation of wanton pleasure. "Luxury" leads to vice when a person becomes consumed with the pursuit of pleasure, since a life without self-denial soon becomes out of control in every area. **a day of slaughter.** Like fattened cattle ready to be slaughtered, the rich that James condemns had indulged themselves to the limit. This is a vivid depiction of divine judgment, in keeping with the metaphor likening the overindulgent rich to fattened cattle.

5:6 condemned...murdered. This describes the next step in the sinful progression of the rich. Hoarding led to fraud, which led to self-indulgence. Finally, that overindulgence has consumed the rich to the point that they will do anything to sustain their lifestyle. "Condemned" comes from a word meaning "to sentence." The implication is that the rich were using the courts to commit judicial murder (cf. 2:6).

5:7 patient. The word emphasizes patience with people (cf. 1 Thess. 5:14), not trials or circumstances (as in 1:3). Specifically, James has in mind patience with the oppressive rich. **the coming.** The second coming of Christ (*see note on Matt. 24:27*). Realizing the glory that awaits them at Christ's return should motivate believers to patiently endure mistreatment (Rom. 8:18). **the early and latter rain.** The "early" rain falls in Israel during October and November and softens the ground for planting. The "latter" rain falls in March and April, immediately before the spring harvest. Just as the farmer waits patiently from the early rain to the latter for his crop to ripen, so must Christians patiently wait for the Lord's return (cf. Gal. 6:9; 2 Tim. 4:8; Titus 2:13).

5:8 Establish your hearts. A call for resolute, firm courage and commitment. James exhorts those about to collapse under the weight of persecution to shore up their hearts with the hope of the second coming. **at hand.** The imminency of Christ's return is a frequent theme in the NT (cf. Rom. 13:12; Heb. 10:25; 1 Pet. 4:7; 1 John 2:18).

5:9 Do not grumble...the Judge is standing at the door! James pictured Christ as a judge about to open the doors to the courtroom and convene His court. Knowing that the strain of persecution could lead to grumbling, James cautioned his readers against that sin (Phil. 2:14), lest they forfeit their full reward (2 John 8).

5:11 the perseverance of Job. Job is the classic example of a man who patiently endured suffering and was blessed by God for his persevering faith. James reassured his readers that God had a purpose for their suffering, just as He did for Job's. Cf. Job 42. **compassionate and merciful.** Remembering the Lord's character is a great comfort in suffering. The Scriptures repeatedly affirm His compassion and mercy (Ex. 34:6; Num. 14:18; 1 Chr. 21:13; 2 Chr. 30:9; Pss. 25:6; 78:38; 86:5,15; 103:8,13; 116:5; 136:1; 145:8; Lam. 3:22; Joel 2:13; Jon. 4:2; Mic. 7:18; Luke 6:36).

5:12 above all. Or "especially." As he has done repeatedly in his epistle, James stressed that a person's speech provides the most revealing glimpse of his spiritual condition (cf. 1:26; 2:12; 3:2-11; 4:11). **do not swear...any other oath.** As Jesus did before him (Matt. 5:33-36; 23:16-22), James condemned the contemporary Jewish practice of swearing false, evasive, deceptive oaths by everything other than the name of the Lord (which alone was considered binding). **"Yes" be "Yes."** Again echoing Jesus (*see note on Matt. 5:37*), James called for straightforward, honest, plain speech. To speak otherwise is to invite God's judgment.

5:13 suffering. The antidote to the suffering caused by evil treatment or persecution is seeking God's comfort through prayer (cf. Pss. 27:13,14; 55:22; Jon. 2:7; Phil. 4:6; 1 Pet. 5:7). **Let him sing psalms.** The natural response of a joyful heart is to sing praise to God.

5:14,15 sick. James directs those who are "sick," meaning weakened by their suffering to call for the elders of the church for strength, support, and prayer.

5:14 anointing him with oil. Lit. "rubbing him with oil": 1) possibly this is a reference to ceremonial anointing (*see notes on Lev. 14:18; Mark 6:13*); 2) on the other hand, James may have had in mind medical treatment of believers physically bruised and battered by persecution. Perhaps it is better to understand the anointing in a metaphorical sense of the elders' encouraging, comforting, and strengthening the believer.

5:15 prayer of faith. The prayer offered on their behalf by the elders. **save the sick.** Deliver them from their suffering because they have been weakened by their infirmity, not from their sin, which was confessed. **committed sins...be forgiven.** Not by the elders, since God alone can forgive sins (Is. 43:25; Dan. 9:9; Mark 2:7). That those who are suffering called for the elders implies they had a contrite, repentant heart, and that part of their time with the overseers would involve confessing their sins to God.

5:16 Confess *your* trespasses. Mutual honesty, openness, and sharing of needs will enable believers to uphold each other in the

may be healed. [s]The effective, [2]fervent
prayer of a righteous man avails much.
17 Elijah was a man [t]with a nature like
ours, and [u]he prayed earnestly that it
would not rain; and it did not rain on the
land for three years and six months.
18 And he prayed [v]again, and the heaven
gave rain, and the earth produced its fruit.

16 [s]Num. 11:2
[2]*supplication*
17 [t]Acts 14:15
[u]1 Kin. 17:1; 18:1
18 [v]1 Kin. 18:1, 42
19 [w]Matt. 18:15; Gal. 6:1
20 [x]Rom. 11:14; 1 Cor. 1:21; James 1:21
[y]Prov. 10:12; [1 Pet. 4:8] [3]NU *his soul*

Bring Back the Erring One

19 Brethren, if anyone among you wanders from the truth, and someone [w]turns
him back, 20 let him know that he who
turns a sinner from the error of his way
[x]will save [3]a soul from death and [y]cover a
multitude of sins.

---

spiritual struggle. **The effective…avails much.** The energetic, passionate prayers of godly men have the power to accomplish much. Cf. Num. 11:2.

5:17,18 Elijah…prayed…he prayed again. Elijah provides one of the most notable illustrations of the power of prayer in the OT. His prayers (not mentioned in the OT account) both initiated and ended a 3 year, 6 month drought (cf. Luke 4:25).

5:19 if anyone among you. This introduces a third category of people in the church (cf. vv. 13,14)—those professing believers who have strayed from the truth. **wanders from the truth.** Apostatizes from the faith they once professed (cf. Heb. 5:12–6:9; 10:29; 1 John 2:19). Such people are in grave danger (v. 20), and the church must call them back to the true faith.

5:20 sinner. Cf. 4:8. A word used to describe the unregenerate (cf. Prov. 11:31; 13:6,22; Matt. 9:13; Luke 7:37,39; 15:7,10; 18:13; Rom. 5:8; 1 Tim. 1:9,15; 1 Pet. 4:18). James has in mind here those with dead faith (cf. 2:14-26), not sinning, true believers. **the error of his way.** Those who go astray doctrinally (v. 19) will also manifest an errant lifestyle, one not lived according to biblical principles. **save a soul from death.** A person who wanders from the truth puts his soul in jeopardy. The "death" in view is not physical death, but eternal death—eternal separation from God and eternal punishment in hell (cf. Is. 66:24; Dan. 12:2; Matt. 13:40,42,50; 25:41,46; Mark 9:43-49; 2 Thess. 1:8,9; Rom. 6:23; Rev. 20:11-15; 21:8). Knowing how high the stakes are should motivate Christians to aggressively pursue such people. **cover a multitude of sins.** See Ps. 5:10. Since even one sin is enough to condemn a person to hell, James' use of the word "multitude" emphasizes the hopeless condition of lost, unregenerate sinners. The good news of the gospel is that God's forgiving grace (which is greater than any sin; Rom. 5:20) is available to those who turn from their sins and exercise faith in the Lord Jesus Christ (Eph. 2:8,9).

The First Epistle of PETER

Title

The letter has always been identified (as are most general epistles, like James, John, and Jude) with the name of the author, Peter, and with the notation that it was his first inspired letter.

Author and Date

The opening verse of the epistle claims it was written by Peter, who was clearly the leader among Christ's apostles. The gospel writers emphasize this fact by placing his name at the head of each list of apostles (Matt. 10; Mark 3; Luke 6; Acts 1), and including more information about him in the 4 gospels than any person other than Christ. Originally known as Simon (Gr.) or Simeon (Heb.), cf. Mark 1:16; John 1:40,41, Peter was the son of Jonas (Matt. 16:17) who was also known as John (John 1:42), and a member of a family of fishermen who lived in Bethsaida and later in Capernaum. Andrew, Peter's brother, brought him to Christ (John 1:40-42). He was married, and his wife apparently accompanied him in his ministry (Mark 1:29-31; 1 Cor. 9:5).

Peter was called to follow Christ in His early ministry (Mark 1:16,17), and was later appointed to apostleship (Matt. 10:2; Mark 3:14-16). Christ renamed him Peter (Gr.), or Cephas (Aram.), both words meaning "stone" or "rock" (John 1:42). The Lord clearly singled out Peter for special lessons throughout the gospels (e.g., Matt. 10; 16:13-21; 17:1-9; 24:1-7; 26:31-33; John 6:6; 21:3-7,15-17). He was the spokesman for the 12, articulating their thoughts and questions as well as his own. His triumphs and weaknesses are chronicled in the gospels and Acts 1–12.

After the resurrection and ascension, Peter initiated the plan for choosing a replacement for Judas (Acts 1:15). After the coming of the Holy Spirit (Acts 2:1-4), he was empowered to become the leading gospel preacher from the Day of Pentecost on (Acts 2–12). He also performed notable miracles in the early days of the church (Acts 3–9), and opened the door of the gospel to the Samaritans (Acts 8) and to the Gentiles (Acts 10). According to tradition, Peter had to watch as his wife was crucified, but encouraged her with the words, "Remember the Lord." When it came time for him to be crucified, he reportedly pled that he was not worthy to be crucified like his Lord, but rather should be crucified upside down (ca. A.D. 67–68), which tradition says he was.

Because of his unique prominence, there was no shortage in the early church of documents falsely claiming to be written by Peter. That the Apostle Peter is the author of 1 Peter, however, is certain. The material in this letter bears definite resemblance to his messages in the book of Acts. The letter teaches, for example, that Christ is the Stone rejected by the builder (2:7,8; Acts 4:10,11), and that Christ is no respecter of persons (1:17; Acts 10:34). Peter teaches his readers to "gird yourself with humility" (5:5), an echo of the Lord's girding Himself with a towel and washing the disciples' feet (John 13:3-5). There are other statements in the letter similar to Christ's sayings (4:14; 5:7,8). Moreover, the author claims to have been a witness of the sufferings of Christ (5:1; cf. 3:18; 4:1). In addition to these internal evidences, it is noteworthy that the early Christians universally recognized this letter as the work of Peter.

The only significant doubt to be raised about Peter's authorship arises from the rather classical style of Greek employed in the letter. Some have argued that Peter, being an "unlearned" fisherman (Acts 4:13), could not have written in sophisticated Greek, especially in light of the less classical style of Greek employed in the writing of 2 Peter. However, this argument is not without a good answer. In the first place, that Peter was "unlearned" does not mean that he was illiterate, but only that he was without formal, rabbinical training in the Scriptures. Moreover, though Aramaic may have been Peter's primary language, Greek would have been a widely spoken second language in Palestine. It is also apparent that at least some of the authors of the NT, though not highly educated, could read the Greek of the OT Septuagint (see James' use of the LXX in Acts 15:14-18).

Beyond these evidences of Peter's ability in Greek, Peter also explained (5:12) that he wrote this letter "by Silvanus," also known as Silas. Silvanus was likely the messenger designated to take this letter to its intended readers. But more is implied by this statement in that Peter is acknowledging that Silvanus served as his secretary, or amanuensis. Dictation was common in the ancient Roman world (cf. Paul and Tertius; Rom. 16:22), and secretaries often could aid with syntax and grammar. So, Peter, under the superintendence of the Spirit of God, dictated the letter to Silvanus, while Silvanus, who also was a prophet (Acts 15:32), may have aided in some of the composition of the more classical Greek.

First Peter was most likely written just before or shortly after July, A.D. 64 when the city of Rome burned, thus a writing date of ca. A.D. 64–65.

Background and Setting

When the city of Rome burned, the Romans believed that their emperor, Nero, had set the city on fire, probably because of his incredible lust to build. In order to build more, he had to destroy what already existed.

The Romans were totally devastated. Their culture, in a sense, went down with the city. All the religious elements of their life were destroyed—their great temples, shrines, and even their household idols were burned up. This had great religious implications because it made them believe that their deities had been unable to deal with this conflagration and were also victims of it. The people were homeless and hopeless. Many had been killed. Their bitter resentment was severe, so Nero realized that he had to redirect the hostility.

The emperor's chosen scapegoat was the Christians, who were already hated because they were associated with Jews, and because they were seen as being hostile to the Roman culture. Nero spread the word quickly that the Christians had set the fires. As a result, a vicious persecution against Christians began, and soon spread throughout the Roman Empire, touching places N of the Taurus mountains, like Pontus, Galatia, Cappadocia, Asia, and Bithynia (1:1), and impacting the Christians, whom Peter calls "pilgrims." These "pilgrims," who were probably Gentiles, for the most part (1:14,18; 2:9,10; 4:3), possibly led to Christ by Paul and his associates, and established on Paul's teachings. But they needed spiritual strengthening because of their sufferings. Thus the Apostle Peter, under the inspiration of the Holy Spirit, wrote this epistle to strengthen them.

Peter wrote that he was in "Babylon" when he penned the letter (5:13). Three locations have been suggested for this "Babylon." First, a Roman outpost in northern Egypt was named Babylon; but that place was too obscure, and there are no reasons to think that Peter was ever there. Second, ancient Babylon in Mesopotamia is a possibility; but it would be quite unlikely that Peter, Mark, and Silvanus were all at this rather small, distant place at the same time. Third, "Babylon" is an alias for Rome; perhaps even a code word for Rome. In times of persecution, writers exercised unusual care not to endanger Christians by identifying them. Peter, according to some traditions, followed James and Paul and died as a martyr near Rome about two years after he wrote this letter, thus he had written this epistle near the end of his life, probably while staying in the imperial city. He did not want the letter to be found and the church to be persecuted, so he may have hidden its location under the code word, "Babylon," which aptly fit because of the city's idolatry (cf. Rev. 17,18).

Historical and Theological Themes

Since the believers addressed were suffering escalating persecution (1:6; 2:12,19-21; 3:9,13-18; 4:1,12-16,19), the purpose of this letter was to teach them how to live victoriously in the midst of that hostility: 1) without losing hope; 2) without becoming bitter; 3) while trusting in their Lord; and 4) while looking for His second coming. Peter wished to impress on his readers that by living an obedient, victorious life under duress, a Christian can actually evangelize his hostile world (cf. 1:14; 2:1,12,15; 3:1-6,13-17; 4:2; 5:8,9).

Believers are constantly exposed to a world system energized by Satan and his demons. Their effort is to discredit the church and to destroy its credulity and integrity. One way these spirits work is by finding Christians whose lives are not consistent with the Word of God, and then parading them before the unbelievers to show what a sham the church is. Christians, however, must stand against the enemy and silence the critics by the power of holy lives.

In this epistle, Peter is rather effusive in reciting two categories of truth. The first category is positive and includes a long list of blessings bestowed on Christians. As he speaks about the identity of Christians and what it means to know Christ, Peter mentions one privilege and blessing after another. Interwoven into this list of privileges is the catalog of suffering. Christians, though most greatly privileged, should also know that the world will treat them unjustly. Their citizenship is in heaven and they are strangers in a hostile, Satan-energized world. Thus the Christian life can be summed up as a call to victory and glory through the path of suffering. So, the basic question that Peter answers in this epistle is: How are Christians to deal with animosity? The answer features practical truths and focuses on Jesus Christ as the model of one who maintained a triumphant attitude in the midst of hostility.

First Peter also answers other important practical questions about Christian living such as: Do Christians need a priesthood to intercede with God for them (2:5-9)? What should be the Christian's attitude to secular government and civil disobedience (2:13-17)? What should a Christian employee's attitude be toward a hostile employer (2:18)? How should a Christian lady conduct herself (3:3,4)? How can a believing wife win her unsaved husband to Christ (3:1,2)?

Interpretive Challenges

First Peter 3:18-22 stands as one of the most difficult NT texts to translate and then interpret. For example, does "Spirit" in 3:18 refer to the Holy Spirit, or to Christ's Spirit? Did Christ preach through Noah before the Flood, or did He preach Himself after the crucifixion (3:19)? Was the audience to this preaching composed of the humans in Noah's day, or demons in the abyss (3:19)? Does 3:20,21 teach baptismal regeneration (salvation), or salvation by faith alone in Christ? Answers to these questions will be found in the notes.

Outline

Salutation (1:1,2)

I. Remember Our Great Salvation (1:3–2:10)
- A. The Certainty of Our Future Inheritance (1:3-12)
  1. Preserved by the power of God (1:3-5)
  2. Proven by the trials of persecution (1:6-9)
  3. Predicted by the prophets of God (1:10-12)
- B. The Consequences of Our Future Inheritance (1:13–2:10)
  1. Perseverance of hope (1:13-16)
  2. Persistence of wonder (1:17-21)
  3. Power of love (1:22–2:3)
  4. Praises of Christ (2:4-10)

II. Remember Our Example Before Men (2:11–4:6)
- A. Honorable Living Before Unbelievers (2:11–3:7)
  1. Submission to the government (2:11-17)
  2. Submission to masters (2:18-25)
  3. Submission in the family (3:1-7)
- B. Honorable Living Before Believers (3:8-12)
- C. Honorable Living in the Midst of Suffering (3:13–4:6)
  1. The principle of suffering for righteousness (3:13-17)
  2. The paragon of suffering for righteousness (3:18-22)
  3. The purpose of suffering for righteousness (4:1-6)

III. Remember Our Lord Will Return (4:7–5:11)
- A. The Responsibilities of Christian Living (4:7-11)
- B. The Rewards of Christian Suffering (4:12-19)
- C. The Requirements for Christian Leadership (5:1-4)
- D. The Realization of Christian Victory (5:5-11)

Conclusion (5:12-14)

Greeting to the Elect Pilgrims

1 Peter, an apostle of Jesus Christ,

To the [1]pilgrims [a]of the Dispersion in
Pontus, Galatia, Cappadocia, Asia, and Bithynia, 2 [b]elect [c]according to the foreknowledge of God the Father, [d]in sanctification of the Spirit, for [e]obedience and
[f]sprinkling of the blood of Jesus Christ:

[g]Grace to you and peace be multiplied.

CHAPTER 1

1 [a]John 7:35; James 1:1 [1]*sojourners, temporary residents*
2 [b]Eph. 1:4 [c][Rom. 8:29]; 1 Pet. 1:20 [d]2 Thess. 2:13 [e]Rom. 1:5 [f]Is. 52:15; Heb. 10:22; 12:24 [g]Rom. 1:7
3 [h]Eph. 1:3 [i]Gal. 6:16; Titus 3:5 [j][John 3:3, 5] [k]1 Cor. 15:20; 1 Pet. 3:21

A Heavenly Inheritance

3 [h]Blessed *be* the God and Father of our
Lord Jesus Christ, who [i]according to His
abundant mercy [j]has begotten us again to
a living hope [k]through the resurrection of
Jesus Christ from the dead, 4 to an inheritance [2]incorruptible and undefiled and
that does not fade away, [l]reserved in heav-
en for you, 5 [m]who are kept by the power

4 [l]Col. 1:5 [2]*imperishable* 5 [m]John 10:28; [Phil. 4:7]

1:1 Peter. See Introduction: Author and Date. **apostle of Jesus Christ.** Peter was one of a unique group of men who were personally called (Matt. 10:1-4) and commissioned (John 20:19-23) by Christ, and who ministered with Christ after His resurrection. *See note on 5:1.* The church was built upon the foundation of their teaching (*see notes on Acts 2:42; Eph. 2:20*). **pilgrims.** These were strangers dispossessed in a land not their own—temporary residents or foreigners. Like all believers, they were residents of an eternal city (Phil. 3:20; Heb. 13:13,14). **the Dispersion.** With the Gr. definite article, "dispersion" is sometimes a technical term for the scattering of the Jews from Israel throughout the world (John 7:35; James 1:1). But here, without the article, it is used in a non-technical sense referring to spiritual pilgrims, aliens to the earth, whether Jews or Gentiles (cf. v. 17; 2:11), i.e., the church. **Pontus...Bithynia.** Peter's letter is addressed to churches in provinces located in modern-day Turkey, which were part of the Roman empire.

1:2 elect. From the Gr. word which connotes the "called out ones." The word means "to pick out" or "to select." In the OT, it was used of Israel (Deut. 7:6), indicating that God sovereignly chose Israel from among all the nations of the world to believe in and belong to Him (cf. Deut. 14:12; Pss. 105:43; 135:4). Here the word is used as a term for Christians, those chosen by God for salvation (cf. Rom. 8:33; Col. 3:12; 2 Tim. 2:10). The word is also used for those who receive Christ during the tribulation time (Matt. 24:22,24), and holy, unfallen angels (1 Tim. 5:21). To be reminded that they were elected by God was a great comfort to those persecuted Christians (*see notes on Eph. 1:3-14*). **foreknowledge.** The same Gr. word is translated "foreordained" in v. 20. In both verses, the word does not refer to awareness of what is going to happen, but it clearly means a predetermined relationship in the knowledge of God. God brought the salvation relationship into existence by decreeing it into existence ahead of time. Christians are foreknown for salvation in the same way Christ was foreordained before the foundation of the world to be a sacrifice for sins (cf. Acts 2:23). "Foreknowledge" means that God planned before, not that He observed before (cf. Ex. 33:17; Jer. 1:5; Amos 3:2; Matt. 7:23). Thus, God prethought and pre-determined or predestined each Christian's salvation (*see notes on Rom. 8:29; Eph. 1:4*). **sanctification of the Spirit.** To sanctify means "to consecrate," "to set apart." The objective of election is salvation, which comes to the elect through the sanctifying work of the Spirit. The Holy Spirit thus makes God's chosen holy, by savingly setting them apart from sin and unbelief unto faith and righteousness (cf. 1 Thess. 1:4; 2 Thess. 2:13). Sanctification thus begins with justification (declaring the sinner just before God by graciously imputing Christ's righteousness to him, cf. Phil. 3:9), and continues as a process of purification that goes on until glorification, when the Christian sees Jesus face to face. **for obedience.** Believers are set apart from sin to God in order that they might obey Jesus Christ. True salvation produces obedience to Christ (cf. Eph. 2:10; 1 Thess. 1:4-10). **sprinkling of the blood of Jesus Christ.** This phrase is based on Moses' sprinkling sacrificial blood on the people of Israel as a symbol sealing their covenant as they promised to obey God's Word (*see notes on Ex. 24:3-8*). Likewise, in the New Covenant, faith in the shedding of Christ's blood on the cross not only activates God's promise to give the believer perfect atonement for sin, but also brings the believer into the covenant by one's promise of obedience to the Lord and His Word.

1:3 Father of our Lord Jesus Christ. Though God was known as Creator and Redeemer in the OT, He was rarely called Father. Christ, however, always addressed God as His Father in the gospels (as John 5:17), except in the separation on the cross (Matt. 27:46). In so doing, Christ was claiming to be of the same nature, being, or essence as the Father (cf. Matt. 11:27; John 10:29-39; 14:6-11; 2 Cor. 1:3; Eph. 1:3,17; 2 John 3). Also, by speaking of "our" Lord, Peter personalized the Christian's intimate relationship with the God of the universe through His Son (cf. 1 Cor. 6:17), an important truth for suffering Christians to remember. **abundant mercy.** The reason God provided a glorious salvation for mankind is that He is merciful. Sinners need God's mercy because they are in a pitiful, desperate, wretched condition as sinners (cf. Eph. 2:4; Titus 3:5; see also Ex. 34:6; Ps. 108:4; Is. 27:4; Lam. 3:22; Mic. 7:18). **has begotten us again.** God gave the new birth as part of His provision in salvation. When a sinner comes to Christ and puts His faith in Him, he is born anew into God's family and receives a new nature (*see notes on v. 23; John 1:13; 3:1-21*). **a living hope.** The living hope is eternal life. "Hope" means confident optimism, and: 1) comes from God (Ps. 43:5); 2) is a gift of grace (2 Thess. 2:16); 3) is defined by Scripture (Rom. 15:4); 4) is a reasonable reality (3:15); 5) is secured by the resurrection of Jesus Christ (John 11:25,26; 14:19; 1 Cor. 15:17); 6) is confirmed in the Christian by the Holy Spirit (Rom. 15:13); 7) defends the Christian against Satan's attacks (1 Thess. 5:8); 8) is confirmed through trials (Rom. 5:3,4); 9) produces joy (Ps. 146:5); and 10) is fulfilled in Christ's return (Titus 2:13).

1:4 inheritance. Peter showed those persecuted Christians how to look past their troubles to their eternal inheritance. Life, righteousness, joy, peace, perfection, God's presence, Christ's glorious companionship, rewards, and all else God has planned is the Christian's heavenly inheritance (v. 5; cf. Matt. 25:34; Acts 26:18; Eph. 1:11; Col. 1:12; Heb. 9:15; also Pss. 16:5; 23; 26; 72; Lam. 3:24). According to Eph. 1:14, the indwelling Holy Spirit is the resident guarantee of that inheritance. **incorruptible.** The inheritance is not subject to passing away, nor liable to decay. The word was used in secular Greek of something that was unravaged by an invading army (cf. Matt. 6:19-21). **undefiled.** This word means unpolluted, unstained with evil. The undefiled inheritance of the Christian is in marked contrast to an earthly inheritance, all of which is corrupted and defiled. **does not fade away.** "Fading" was often used of flowers that wither and decay. Though earthly inheritances eventually fade away, the eternal inheritance of a Christian has no decaying elements.

1:5 kept by the power of God. Supreme power, omniscience, omnipotence, and sovereignty, not only keep the inheritance (v. 4), but also keep the believer secure. No one can steal the Christian's treasure, and no one can disqualify him from receiving it. *See notes on Rom. 8:31-39.* **through faith.** The Christian's response to God's election and the Spirit's conviction is faith, but even faith is empowered by God (*see note on Eph. 2:8,9*). Moreover, the Christian's continued faith in God is the evidence of God's keeping power. At the time of salvation, God energizes faith, and continues to preserve it. Saving faith is permanent; it never dies. *See notes on Matt. 24:13; Heb. 3:14.*

of God through faith for salvation ready to
be revealed in the last time.
6 [n]In this you greatly rejoice, though
now [o]for a little while, if need be, [p]you
have been [3]grieved by various trials, 7 that
[q]the genuineness of your faith, *being* much
more precious than gold that perishes,
though [r]it is tested by fire, [s]may be found
to praise, honor, and glory at the revelation
of Jesus Christ, 8 [t]whom having not [4]seen
you love. [u]Though now you do not see
Him, yet believing, you rejoice with joy inexpressible and full of glory, 9 receiving the
end of your faith—the salvation of *your*
souls.
10 Of this salvation the prophets have
inquired and searched carefully, who
prophesied of the grace *that would come* to
you, 11 searching what, or what manner of
time, [v]the Spirit of Christ who was in
them was indicating when He testified beforehand the sufferings of Christ and the
glories that would follow. 12 To them it
was revealed that, not to themselves, but
to [5]us they were ministering the things
which now have been reported to you
through those who have preached the
gospel to you by the Holy Spirit sent from
heaven—things which [w]angels desire to
look into.

Living Before God Our Father

13 Therefore gird up the loins of your
mind, be sober, and rest *your* hope fully
upon the grace that is to be brought to you
at the revelation of Jesus Christ; 14 as obedient children, not [x]conforming yourselves to the former lusts, *as* in your ignorance; 15 [y]but as He who called you *is* holy,
you also be holy in all *your* conduct, 16 because it is written, [z]*"Be holy, for I am
holy."*
17 And if you call on the Father, who
[a]without partiality judges according to

6 [n]Matt. 5:12 [o]2 Cor. 4:17 [p]James 1:2; 1 Pet. 4:12 [3]distressed
7 [q]James 1:3 [r]Job 23:10 [s][Rom. 2:7]
8 [t]1 John 4:20 [u]John 20:29 [4]M *known*
11 [v]2 Pet. 1:21
12 [w]Eph. 3:10 [5]NU, M *you*
14 [x][Rom. 12:2]; 1 Pet. 4:2
15 [y][2 Cor. 7:1]
16 [z]Lev. 11:44, 45; 19:2; 20:7
17 [a]Acts 10:34

1:6 greatly rejoice. That is, to be exceedingly glad, exuberantly jubilant. This kind of joy is not based on changing, temporal circumstances, but is used of joy that comes from the unchanging, eternal relationship with God. Peter relates this joy to 1) the assurance of one's protected eternal inheritance (vv. 4,5; cf. John 16:16-33) and 2) the assurance from one's proven faith (v. 7). **various trials.** Peter teaches several important principles about trouble in this verse: 1) trouble does not last ("little while"); 2) trouble serves a purpose ("if need be"); 3) trouble brings distress ("grieved"); 4) trouble comes in various forms ("various trials"); and 5) trouble should not diminish the Christian's joy ("greatly rejoice").

1:7 genuineness of your faith. God's purpose in allowing trouble is to test the reality of one's faith. But the benefit of such a testing, or "fire," is immediately for the Christian, not God. When a believer comes through a trial still trusting the Lord, he is assured that his faith is genuine (cf. Gen. 22:1-12; Job 1:20-22). **revelation of Jesus Christ.** The revelation or unveiling of Christ refers to His second coming, particularly focusing on the time when He comes to call and reward His redeemed people (cf. v. 13; 4:13; 1 Cor. 1:7), i.e., the Rapture (1 Thess. 4:13-18).

1:8 having not seen. This is in the sense of His appearing (v. 7). Cf. 2 Cor. 5:7. At that time, the fiery trials that believers have endured will benefit God by bringing Him "praise, honor, and glory" eternally.

1:9 receiving...salvation. "Receiving" could lit. be translated "presently receiving for yourselves." In one sense, Christians now possess the result of their faith, a constant deliverance from the power of sin. In another sense, we are waiting to receive the full salvation of eternal glory in the redemption of our bodies (Rom. 8:23).

1:10 this salvation. In this section, Peter looks at the greatness of salvation from the viewpoint of the divine agents who made it possible: 1) OT prophets (vv. 10,11); 2) the Holy Spirit (vv. 11,12); 3) the NT apostles (v. 12); and 4) the angels (v. 12). **inquired and searched carefully.** The OT prophets studied their own writings in order to know more about the promised salvation. Though they believed and were personally saved from their sin by that faith (through the sacrifice God would provide in Christ), they could not fully understand what was involved in the life and death of Jesus Christ (cf. Num. 24:17; Heb. 11:13,39,40). **grace *that would come.*** God is by nature gracious and was so, even under the conditional Old Covenant (cf. Ex. 33:19; Jon. 4:2). But the prophets foretold an even greater exhibit of grace than what they had ever known (Is. 45:20-25; 52:14,15; 55:1-7; 61:1-3; cf. Rom. 9:24-33; 10:11,13,20; 15:9-21).

1:11 what, or what manner of time. "Who would be the person?" and "When would He come?" were the questions the OT prophets searched to know. **Spirit of Christ who was in them.** Jesus Christ, in the person of the Holy Spirit, took up residence within the writers of the OT, enabling them to write about the glorious salvation to be consummated in the future (2 Pet. 1:19-21).

1:12 to us they were ministering. The OT prophets who wrote of the coming of salvation (vv. 10,11) knew it was a future Savior who would come, and thus they were really writing for those who are on this side of the cross. **those who have preached the gospel.** The NT apostles and preachers of the gospel had the privilege of proclaiming that the prophecies written by the OT prophets had come to pass (cf. 2 Cor. 6:1,2).

1:13 gird up the loins of your mind. The ancient practice of gathering up one's robes when needing to move in a hurry; here, it is metaphorically applied to one's thought process. The meaning is to pull in all the loose ends of one's thinking, by rejecting the hindrances of the world and focusing on the future grace of God (cf. Eph. 6:14; Col. 3:2). **be sober.** Spiritual sober-mindedness includes the ideas of steadfastness, self-control, clarity of mind, and moral decisiveness. The sober Christian is correctly in charge of his priorities and not intoxicated with the various allurements of the world. **rest *your* hope fully.** In light of their great salvation, Christians, especially those undergoing suffering, should unreservedly live for the future, anticipating the consummation of their salvation at the second coming of Christ (see v. 7). Cf. Col. 3:2-4. **grace that is to be brought to you.** Christ's future ministry of glorifying Christians and giving them eternal life in His presence will be the final culmination of the grace initiated at salvation (cf. Eph. 2:7).

1:15 you also be holy. Holiness essentially defines the Christian's new nature and conduct in contrast with his pre-salvation lifestyle. The reason for practicing a holy manner of living is that Christians are associated with the holy God and must treat Him and His Word with respect and reverence. We therefore glorify Him best by being like Him (see vv. 16,17; Matt. 5:48; Eph. 5:1; cf. Lev. 11:44,45; 18:30; 19:2; 20:7; 21:6-8).

1:17 if you call on the Father. This is another way of saying, "if you are a Christian." The believer who knows God and that He judges the works of all His children fairly, will respect God and His evaluation of his life, and long to honor his heavenly Father.

each one's work, conduct yourselves
throughout the time of your [6]stay *here* in
fear; **18** knowing that you were not redeemed with [7]corruptible things, *like* silver or gold, from your aimless conduct *received* by tradition from your fathers,
19 but [b]with the precious blood of Christ,
[c]as of a lamb without blemish and without
spot. **20** [d]He indeed was foreordained before the foundation of the world, but was
[8]manifest [e]in these last times for you
21 who through Him believe in God, [f]who
raised Him from the dead and [g]gave Him
glory, so that your faith and hope are in
God.

The Enduring Word

22 Since you [h]have purified your souls in
obeying the truth [9]through the Spirit in
[1]sincere [i]love of the brethren, love one another fervently with a pure heart, **23** [j]hav-
ing been born again, not of [2]corruptible
seed but [3]incorruptible, [k]through the word
of God which lives and abides [4]forever,
24 because

[l]*"All flesh is as grass,*
And all [5]the glory of man as the
flower of the grass.
The grass withers,
And its flower falls away,
25 [m]*But the [6]word of the LORD endures*
forever."

[n]Now this is the word which by the gospel
was preached to you.

2 Therefore, [a]laying aside all malice, all
deceit, hypocrisy, envy, and all evil
speaking, **2** [b]as newborn babes, desire the
pure [c]milk of the word, that you may grow
[1]thereby, **3** if indeed you have [d]tasted that
the Lord *is* gracious.

The Chosen Stone and His Chosen People

4 Coming to Him *as to* a living stone, [e]re-
jected indeed by men, but chosen by God
and precious, **5** you also, as living stones,
are being built up a spiritual house, a holy
priesthood, to offer up spiritual sacrifices
acceptable to God through Jesus Christ.
6 Therefore it is also contained in the Scripture,

17 [6] *sojourning, dwelling* as resident aliens
18 [7] *perishable*
19 [b] Acts 20:28; 1 Pet. 1:2 [c] Ex. 12:5; Is. 53:7
20 [d] Rom. 3:25 [e] Gal. 4:4 [8] *revealed*
21 [f] Acts 2:24 [g] Acts 2:33
22 [h] Acts 15:9 [i] John 13:34; Rom. 12:10; Heb. 13:1; 1 Pet. 2:17; 3:8 [9] NU omits *through the Spirit* [1] Lit. *unhypocritical*
23 [j] John 1:13 [k] 1 Thess. 2:13; James 1:18 [2] *perishable* [3] *imperishable* [4] NU omits *forever*
24 [l] Is. 40:6-8; James 1:10 [5] NU *its glory as*
25 [m] Is. 40:8 [n] [John 1:1] [6] *spoken word*

CHAPTER 2

1 [a] Heb. 12:1
2 [b] [Matt. 18:3; 19:14; Mark 10:15; Luke 18:17]; 1 Cor. 14:20 [c] 1 Cor. 3:2 [1] NU adds *up to salvation*
3 [d] Ps. 34:8; Titus 3:4; Heb. 6:5
4 [e] Ps. 118:22

1:18 redeemed. *See note on 1 Tim. 2:6.* That is, to buy back someone from bondage by the payment of a price; to set free by paying a ransom. "Redemption" was a technical term for money paid to buy back a prisoner of war. Here it is used of the price paid to buy the freedom of one in the bondage of sin and under the curse of the law (i.e., eternal death, cf. Gal. 3:13). The price paid to a holy God was the shed blood of His own Son (cf. Ex. 12:1-13; 15:13; Ps. 78:35; Acts 20:28; Rom. 3:24; Gal. 4:4,5; Eph. 1:7; Col. 1:14; Titus 2:14; Heb. 9:11-17).

1:20 foreordained. In eternity past, before Adam and Eve sinned, God planned the redemption of sinners through Jesus Christ (cf. Acts 2:23; 4:27,28; 2 Tim. 1:9). *See note on v. 2.* **last times.** The "last times" are the times of the Messiah, from His first coming to His second coming (cf. Acts 2:17; 1 Tim. 4:1; 1 John 2:18).

1:21 gave Him glory. God, through the ascension, returned Christ to the glory that He had with Him before the world began (cf. Luke 24:51-53; John 17:4,5; Acts 1:9-11; Phil. 2:9-11; Heb. 1:1-3; 2:9).

1:22 love one another fervently. The love indicated here by Peter is the love of choice, the kind of love that can respond to a command. "Fervently" means to stretch to the limits (cf. Luke 22:44; Acts 12:5; also Luke 10:27ff.). Only those whose "souls" have been "purified," i.e., saved, have the capacity to love like this. Such love exhibits itself by meeting others at the point of their need (cf. 2:17; 3:8; 4:8; also John 13:34; Rom. 12:10; Phil. 2:1-8; Heb. 13:1; 1 John 3:11).

1:23 not of corruptible seed. The spiritual life implanted by the Holy Spirit to produce the new birth is unfailing and permanent. **through the word of God.** The Spirit uses the Word to produce life. It is the truth of the gospel that saves. *See note on Rom. 10:17.*

1:24,25 Peter enforces his point about the power of the Word to regenerate by quoting from Is. 40:6-8 (*see notes there*).

2:1 laying aside. The Christian's new life can't grow unless sins are renounced. When that purging takes place, then the Word does its work (v. 2). **malice.** The Gr. word for evil is used 11 times in the NT to indicate that wickedness which comes from within a person (cf. v. 16; Rom. 1:29; Eph. 4:31; Titus 3:3).

2:2 desire the pure milk of the word. Spiritual growth is always marked by a craving for and a delight in God's Word with the intensity with which a baby craves milk (cf. Job 23:12; Pss. 1:1,2; 19:7-11; 119:16,24,35,47,48,72,92,97,103,111,113,127,159,167,174; Jer. 15:16). A Christian develops a desire for the truth of God's Word by: 1) remembering his life's source (1:25; cf. Is. 55:10,11; John 15:3; Heb. 4:12); 2) eliminating sin from his life (v. 1); 3) admitting his need for God's truth (v. 2, "as newborn babes"; cf. Matt. 4:4); 4) pursuing spiritual growth (v. 2, "that you may grow thereby"); and 5) surveying his blessings (v. 3, "Lord is gracious").

2:3 tasted. At salvation, all believers experience how gracious the Lord is to those who trust Him. That should compel believers to seek more of that grace in pursuing His Word.

2:4 Coming to Him. "Coming," in the Gr. here means to come with the idea of remaining. Here it means to remain in Christ's presence with intimate fellowship (cf. John 15:5-15). **a living stone.** Both a metaphor and a paradox, this phrase from the OT (see vv. 6-8) emphasizes that Christ, the "cornerstone" and "stone of stumbling," is alive from the dead and has a living relationship with saved humanity (v. 5; cf. 1 Cor. 15:45; 1 John 5:11,12). **rejected...but chosen.** See v. 7. The messianic credentials of Jesus were examined by the false religious leaders of Israel and contemptuously rejected (vv. 6-8; cf. Matt. 12:22-24; John 1:10,11). But Jesus Christ was God's precious and elect Son, ultimately authenticated through His resurrection from the dead (cf. Ps. 2:10,11; Matt. 3:17; Acts 2:23,24,32; 4:11,12; 5:30,31; 10:39).

2:5 you also, as living stones. Christians are so closely identified and united with Christ that the very life that exists in Christ exists in them also (cf. Gal. 2:20; Col. 3:3,4; 2 Pet. 2:4). **built up a spiritual house.** Metaphorically, God is building a spiritual house, putting all believers in place, integrating each one with others, and each one with the life of Christ (cf. Eph. 2:19; Heb. 3:6). **a holy priesthood.** OT priests and NT believer-priests share a number of characteristics: 1) priesthood is an elect privilege (Ex. 28:1; John 15:16); 2) priests are cleansed of sins (Lev. 8:6-36; Titus 2:14); 3) priests are clothed for service (5:5; Ex. 28:42; Lev. 8:7ff.; Ps. 132:9,16); 4) priests are anointed for service (Lev. 8:12,30; 1 John 2:20,27); 5) priests are prepared for service (Lev. 8:33; 9:4,23; Gal. 1:16; 1 Tim. 3:6); 6) priests are ordained to obedience (v. 4; Lev. 10:1ff.); 7) priests are to honor the Word of God (v. 2; Mal. 2:7); 8) priests are to walk with God (Mal. 2:6; Gal. 5:16,25);

[f]"Behold, I lay in Zion
A chief cornerstone, elect, precious,
And he who believes on Him will by no means be put to shame."

7 Therefore, to you who believe, *He is* precious; but to those who [2]are disobedient,

[g]"The stone which the builders rejected
Has become the chief cornerstone,"

8 and

[h]"A stone of stumbling
And a rock of offense."

[i]They stumble, being disobedient to the
word, [j]to which they also were appointed.
9 But you *are* a chosen generation, a
royal priesthood, a holy nation, His own
special people, that you may proclaim the
praises of Him who called you out of
[k]darkness into His marvelous light;
10 [l]who once *were* not a people but *are* now
the people of God, who had not obtained
mercy but now have obtained mercy.

Living Before the World

11 Beloved, I beg *you* as sojourners and
pilgrims, abstain from fleshly lusts [m]which
war against the soul, 12 [n]having your conduct honorable among the Gentiles, that
when they speak against you as evildoers,
[o]they may, by *your* good works which they

6 [f] Is. 28:16; Rom. 9:32, 33; 10:11; 1 Pet. 2:8
7 [g] Ps. 118:22; Matt. 21:42; Luke 2:34 [2] NU *disbelieve*
8 [h] Is. 8:14
[i] 1 Cor. 1:23; Gal. 5:11 [j] Rom. 9:22
9 [k] Is. 9:2; 42:16; [Acts 26:18; 2 Cor. 4:6]
10 [l] Hos. 1:9, 10; 2:23; Rom. 9:25; 10:19
11 [m] [Rom. 8:13]; Gal. 5:17; James 4:1
12 [n] 2 Cor. 8:21; Phil. 2:15; Titus 2:8; 1 Pet. 2:15; 3:16 [o] Matt. 5:16; 9:8; John 13:31; 1 Pet. 4:11, 16

9) priests are to impact sinners (Mal. 2:6; Gal. 6:1); and 10) priests are messengers of God (Mal. 2:7; Matt. 28:19,20). The main privilege of a priest, however, is access to God. **to offer up spiritual sacrifices.** Spiritual sacrifices mean God-honoring works done because of Christ under the direction of the Holy Spirit and the guidance of the Word of God. These would include: 1) offering the strength of one's body to God (Rom. 12:1,2); 2) praising God (Heb. 13:15); 3) doing good (Heb. 13:16); 4) sharing one's resources (Heb. 13:16); 5) bringing people to Christ (Rom. 15:16); 6) sacrificing one's desires for the good of others (Eph. 5:2); and 7) praying (Rev. 8:3).

2:6-8 Three OT passages employing the "stone" metaphor are used by Peter to show that Christ's position as chief cornerstone of the new spiritual house was foreordained by God. That same stone is also going to be the stumbling stone that brings down the unbelieving in judgment (cf. Matt. 21:42,44).

2:6 Zion. Quoted from Is. 28:16. Figuratively, Zion, i.e., Jerusalem, is in the realm of the New Covenant, as Sinai is in the realm of the Old Covenant.

2:6,7 *cornerstone.* *See note on Eph. 2:20*; cf. Ps. 118:22.

2:7 disobedient. Unbelieving (v. 8).

2:8 *A stone of stumbling...a rock of offense.* Quoted from Is. 8:14. To every human being, Christ is either the means of salvation if they believe, or the means of judgment if they reject the gospel. He is like a stone in the road that causes a traveler to fall. **disobedient to the word.** Unbelief is their disobedience, since the call of the gospel to repent and believe is a command from God. **they also were appointed.** These were not appointed by God to disobedience and unbelief. Rather, these were appointed to doom because of their disobedience and unbelief. Judgment on unbelief is as divinely appointed as salvation by faith. *See notes on Rom. 9:22; 2 Cor. 2:15,16.*

2:9 a chosen generation. Peter uses OT concepts to emphasize the privileges of NT Christians (cf. Deut. 7:6-8). In strong contrast to the disobedient who are appointed by God to wrath (v. 8), Christians are chosen by God to salvation (cf. 1:2). **a royal priesthood.** The concept of a kingly priesthood is drawn from Ex. 19:6. Israel temporarily forfeited this privilege because of its apostasy and because its wicked leaders executed the Messiah. At the present time, the church is a royal priesthood united with the royal priest, Jesus Christ. A royal priesthood is not only a priesthood that belongs to and serves the king, but is also a priesthood which exercises rule. This will ultimately be fulfilled in Christ's future kingdom (1 Cor. 6:1-4; Rev. 5:10; 20:6). **a holy nation.** Another allusion to Ex. 19:6 (cf. Lev. 19:2; 20:26; Deut. 7:6; Is. 62:12). Tragically, Israel temporarily forfeited the great privilege of being the unique people of God through unbelief. Until Israel's future acceptance of its Messiah, God has replaced the nation with the church. *See notes on Rom. 11:1,2,25-29* for Israel's salvation. **His own special people.** This combines phraseology found in Ex. 19:5; Is. 43:21; Mal. 3:17. Cf. Titus 2:14. **proclaim the praises.** "Proclaim," an unusual word found in no other place in the NT, means to tell forth, to tell something not otherwise known. "Praises" are excellencies, virtues, eminent qualities. **darkness...light.** Cf. Acts 26:18; Eph. 5:8; Col. 1:13.

2:10 the people of God. The ideas of this verse come from Hos. 1:6-10; 2:23. Cf. Rom. 9:23-26 where the reference is explicitly to the calling of a people made up of Jews and Gentiles. **now have obtained mercy.** God generally has temporal mercy and the compassion of common grace on His creation as a whole (Ps. 145:9; Lam. 3:22). Paul made reference to this when he said that God is the "Savior of all men" (*see note on 1 Tim. 4:10*). But God has eternal mercy on His elect church by forgiving their sins and eliminating their judgment (cf. Rom. 9:15; Titus 3:5). In the OT, the prophet Hosea promised that Israel, though remaining outside of God's blessings for a long period of time, would eventually come under God's mercy. God's dealing with Israel was somewhat of a pattern for His dealings with the believers under the New Covenant, who previously were outside God's covenant, but have been brought under the mercy of God by faith in Christ (cf. Eph. 2:4-13).

2:11 sojourners and pilgrims. In this section, Peter called his readers to a righteous life in a hostile world. Christians are foreigners in a secular society because their citizenship is in heaven. There are 3 perspectives from which Christians can look at their obligations: 1) pilgrims (vv. 11,12); 2) citizens (vv. 13-17); and 3) servants (vv. 18-20). In vv. 21-25, Peter shows how Christ set the example by living a perfect life in the midst of His hostile environment. **abstain from fleshly lusts.** Perhaps more lit. "hold yourself away from fleshly lusts." In order to have an impact on the world for God, Christians must be disciplined in an inward and private way by avoiding the desires of the fallen nature (cf. Gal. 5:19-21, where "fleshly lusts" include much more than sexual temptations). **which war against the soul.** "War," i.e., to carry on a military campaign. Fleshly lusts are personified as if they were an army of rebels or guerrillas who incessantly search out and try to destroy the Christian's joy, peace and usefulness (cf. 4:2,3).

2:12 conduct honorable. The Gr. word for "honorable" is rich in meaning and implies the purest, highest, noblest kind of goodness. It means "lovely," "winsome," "gracious," "noble," and "excellent." Having been disciplined in the inward and private side, the Christian must outwardly live among non-Christians in a way which reflects that inward discipline. **evildoers.** The early Christians were falsely accused

observe, glorify God in the day of visitation.

Submission to Government

[13] [p]Therefore submit yourselves to
every [3]ordinance of man for the Lord's
sake, whether to the king as supreme,
[14] or to governors, as to those who are
sent by him for the punishment of evildoers and *for the* praise of those who do
good. [15] For this is the will of God, that by
doing good you may put to silence the ignorance of foolish men— [16] [q]as free, yet
not [r]using liberty as a cloak for [4]vice, but
as bondservants of God. [17] Honor all *people.* Love the brotherhood. Fear [s]God.
Honor the king.

Submission to Masters

[18] [t]Servants, *be* submissive to *your* masters with all fear, not only to the good and
gentle, but also to the harsh. [19] For this *is*
[u]commendable, if because of conscience
toward God one endures grief, suffering
wrongfully. [20] For [v]what credit *is it* if,
when you are beaten for your faults, you
take it patiently? But when you do good
and suffer, if you take it patiently, this *is*
commendable before God. [21] For [w]to this
you were called, because Christ also suffered for [5]us, [x]leaving [6]us an example, that
you should follow His steps:

[22] *"Who[y] committed no sin,*
Nor was deceit found in His
mouth";

[23] [z]who, when He was reviled, did not revile in return; when He suffered, He did
not threaten, but [a]committed *Himself* to
Him who judges righteously; [24] [b]who
Himself bore our sins in His own body on

13 [p] Matt. 22:21 [3] *institution*
16 [q] Rom. 6:14, 20, 22; 1 Cor. 7:22; [Gal. 5:1] [r] Gal. 5:13 [4] *wickedness*
17 [s] Prov. 24:21
18 [t] Eph. 6:5-8
19 [u] Matt. 5:10
20 [v] Luke 6:32-34
21 [w] Matt. 16:24; 1 Thess. 3:3, 4 [x] [1 John 2:6] [5] NU *you* [6] NU, M *you*
22 [y] Is. 53:9; 2 Cor. 5:21
23 [z] Is. 53:7; Heb. 12:3; 1 Pet. 3:9 [a] Luke 23:46
24 [b] Is. 53:4, 11; 1 Cor. 15:3; [Heb. 9:28]

of rebellion against the government with such false accusations as: terrorism (burning Rome; see Introduction: Background and Setting), atheism (no idols or emperor worship), cannibalism (rumors about the Lord's Supper), immorality (because of their love for one another), damaging trade and social progress, and leading slaves into insurrection. Cf. Acts 16:18-21; 19:19,24-27. **day of visitation.** A common phrase in the OT (Is. 10:3; Jer. 27:22) warning of God's "visitation," His drawing near to people or nations in either judgment or blessing. In the NT, "visitation" speaks of redemption (Luke 1:68; 7:16; 19:44). Peter was teaching that when the grace of God visits the heart of an unbeliever, he will respond with saving faith and glorify God because he remembers the testimony of believers he had observed. Those who don't believe will experience the visitation of His wrath in the final judgment.

2:13 submit yourselves. "Submit" is a military term meaning "to arrange in military fashion under the commander," "to put oneself in an attitude of submission." As citizens in the world and under civil law and authority, God's people are to live in a humble, submissive way in the midst of any hostile, godless, slandering society (cf. vv. 21-23; Prov. 24:21; Jer. 29:4-14; Matt. 22:21; Rom. 13:1ff., 1 Tim. 2:1; Heb. 10:32-34). **for the Lord's sake.** Though the Christian's true citizenship is in heaven, (Phil. 3:20) he still must live as an obedient citizen in this world so that God will be honored and glorified. Rebellious conduct by a Christian brings dishonor on Christ. *See notes on Rom. 13:1-5; Titus 3:1,2.*

2:14 governors. Christians are to live in obedience to every institution of civil and social order on earth. This includes obedience to the national government (v. 13, "king"), the state government, the police, and judges. Only when the government tries to force a Christian to do what is against the law of God explicitly stated in Scripture, should he refuse to submit (cf. Acts 4:18-20; 5:28,29; Titus 1:6; 3:1,2).

2:15 silence...foolish men. Here is the purpose for our submission to authority, in order that we should avoid condemnation and win commendation that shuts the mouth of those obstinately set against the faith who are looking for reasons to criticize believers.

2:16 liberty as a cloak for vice. Believers should enjoy their freedom in Christ, but ought not to put on a veil or mask of freedom to cover what really is wickedness. Christian freedom is never to be an excuse for self-indulgence or license. Cf. 1 Cor. 7:22; 8:9-13; 2 Thess. 3:7-9; *see notes on Rom. 14:1–15:3.*

2:17 Honor. Highly esteem is the idea, and it refers not just to obedient duty but inner respect. **brotherhood.** The church. Cf. 1:22; 3:8; 4:8; 5:14.

2:18 Servants, *be* submissive. One's Christianity does not give the right to rebel against one's superior in the social structure (*see notes on 1 Cor. 7:20-24; Eph. 6:5-7; Col. 3:22-25; Philem.*; see also Ex. 21:26,27; Lev. 25:39-43; Deut. 23:15,16), no matter how unfair or harsh he may be.

2:19,20 commendable before God. Favor with God is found when an employee, treated unjustly, accepts his poor treatment with faith in God's sovereign care, rather than responding in anger, hostility, discontent, pride, or rebellion (cf. Matt. 5:11).

2:21 to this. Patient endurance (v. 20). **you were called.** The "call," as always in the NT epistles, is the efficacious call to salvation (v. 9; 5:10; Rom. 8:30). Peter's point is that a person called to salvation will, sometimes at least, have to endure unfair treatment. Commendable behavior on the part of the believer in the midst of such trials results in the strengthening and perfecting of the Christian on earth (5:10; cf. James 1:2-4), and his increased eternal capacity to glorify God (cf. Matt. 20:21-23; 2 Cor. 4:17,18; 2 Tim. 2:12). **leaving us an example.** The word "example" lit. means "writing under." It was writing put under a piece of paper on which to trace letters, thus a pattern. Christ is the pattern for Christians to follow in suffering with perfect patience. His death was efficacious primarily, as an atonement for sin (2 Cor. 5:21); but it was also exemplary, as a model of endurance in unjust suffering.

2:22 This is a quote from Is. 53:9. He was the perfect example of patient endurance in unjust suffering because He was sinless, as the prophet said He would be. Cf. 1:19.

2:23 reviled. To "revile" is to pile up abusive and vile language against someone. Though verbally abused, Christ never retaliated with vicious words and threats (3:9; cf. Matt. 26:57-65; 27:12-14; Luke 23:7-11). **committed *Himself.*** "To commit" was "to hand over to someone to keep." Christ was "handed over" to Pilate (John 19:11); Pilate "handed Him over" to the Jews (John 19:16); Christ "handed over" Himself to God, suffering in surprising silence, because of His perfect confidence in the sovereignty and righteousness of His Father (cf. Is. 53:7).

2:24 bore our sins. Christ suffered not simply as the Christian's pattern (vv. 21-23), but far more importantly as the Christian's substitute. To bear sins was to be punished for them (cf. Num. 14:33; Ezek. 18:20). Christ bore the punishment and the penalty for believers, thus satisfying a holy God (3:18; *see notes on 2 Cor. 5:21; Gal. 3:13*). This great doctrine of the substitutionary atonement is the

the tree, [c]that we, having died to sins,
might live for righteousness—[d]by whose
[7]stripes you were healed. 25 For [e]you were
like sheep going astray, but have now returned [f]to the Shepherd and [8]Overseer of
your souls.

Submission to Husbands

3 Wives, likewise, *be* [a]submissive to your
own husbands, that even if some do
not obey the word, [b]they, without a word,
may [c]be won by the conduct of their wives,
2 [d]when they observe your chaste conduct
accompanied by fear. 3 [e]Do not let your
adornment be *merely* outward—arranging
the hair, wearing gold, or putting on *fine*
apparel— 4 rather *let it be* [f]the hidden person of the heart, with the [1]incorruptible
beauty of a gentle and quiet spirit, which is
very precious in the sight of God. 5 For in
this manner, in former times, the holy
women who trusted in God also adorned
themselves, being submissive to their own
husbands, 6 as Sarah obeyed Abraham,
[g]calling him lord, whose daughters you
are if you do good and are not afraid with
any terror.

A Word to Husbands

7 [h]Husbands, likewise, dwell with *them*
with understanding, giving honor to the
wife, [i]as to the weaker vessel, and as *being*
heirs together of the grace of life, [j]that your
prayers may not be hindered.

24 [c]Rom. 7:6 [d]Is. 53:5 [7]*wounds* **25** [e]Is. 53:5, 6 [f]Is. 40:11; [Ezek. 34:23]; Zech. 13:7 [8]Gr. *Episkopos*

CHAPTER 3

1 [a]Gen. 3:16; 1 Cor. 14:34; Eph. 5:22; Col. 3:18 [b]1 Cor. 7:16 [c]Matt. 18:15 **2** [d]1 Pet. 2:12; 3:6 **3** [e]Is. 3:18; 1 Tim. 2:9 **4** [f]Rom. 2:29 [1]*imperishable* **6** [g]Gen. 18:12 **7** [h]1 Cor. 7:3; [Eph. 5:25]; Col. 3:19 [i]1 Cor. 12:23 [j]Job 42:8

heart of the gospel. Actual atonement, sufficient for the sins of the whole world, was made for all who would ever believe, namely, the elect (cf. Lev. 16:17; 23:27-30; John 3:16; 2 Cor. 5:19; 1 Tim. 2:6; 2 Tim. 4:10; Titus 2:11; Heb. 2:9; 1 John 2:2; 4:9,10). **we, having died to sins.** This is true by the miracle of being in Christ. We died to sin in the sense that we paid its penalty, death, by being in Christ when He died as our substitute. *See notes on Rom. 6:1-11.* **live for righteousness.** Not only have we been declared just, the penalty for our sins paid by His death, but we have risen to walk in new life, empowered by the Holy Spirit (*see notes on Rom. 6:12-22*). **by whose stripes you were healed.** From Is. 53:5 (*see note*). Through the wounds of Christ at the cross, believers are healed spiritually from the deadly disease of sin. Physical healing comes at glorification only, when there is no more physical pain, illness, or death (Rev. 21:4). *See notes on Is. 53:4-6; Matt. 8:17* for comments on healing in the atonement.

2:25 returned. Means "to turn toward," and refers to the repentant faith a person has at salvation. **Shepherd and Overseer.** Christ is not only the Christian's standard (vv. 21-23) and substitute (v. 24), but He is also the Christian's shepherd (5:4; cf. Is. 53:6; John 10:11). In the OT, the title of "shepherd" for the Lord was often messianic (Ezek. 34:23,24; 37:24; cf. John 10:1-18). Beyond that, "Shepherd and Overseer" were the most appropriate descriptions of Christ for Peter to use in order to comfort Christians who were being persecuted and slandered (v. 12). These two terms are also used for human spiritual leaders. "Shepherd" is the word for pastor, and "overseer" is the word for bishop (cf. Eph. 4:11; Titus 1:7), both referring to the same persons who lead the church (cf. Acts 20:28).

3:1 likewise. In chap. 2, Peter taught that living successfully as a Christian in a hostile world would require relating properly in two places: the civil society (2:13-17), and the work-place (2:18-25). At the start of this chapter, he added two more places: the family (vv. 1-7) and the local church (vv. 8,9). ***be* submissive.** Peter insisted that if Christians are to be a witness for their Lord, they must submit not only to the civil, but also to the social order which God has designed. **own husbands.** Women are not inferior to men in any way, any more than submissive Christians are inferior to pagan rulers or non-Christian bosses (cf. Gal. 3:28). But wives have been given a role which puts them in submission to the headship which resides in their own husbands (*see notes on 1 Cor. 11:1-9; Eph. 5:22; Col. 3:18; Titus 2:4,5*). **some do not obey the word.** Since obedience has been used in this letter to refer to believers and disobedience to non-believers (*see notes on 1:2; 2:8*), this is a non-Christian husband. In a culture in which women were viewed as lower than men, the potential for conflict and embarrassment in the marriage of a believer and unbeliever was significant, even as it is in contemporary society. Peter did not urge the Christian wife to leave her husband (cf. 1 Cor. 7:13-16), to preach to her husband ("without a word"), or to demand her rights ("be submissive"). **won by the conduct of their wives.** The loving, gracious submission of a Christian woman to her unsaved husband is the strongest evangelistic tool she has. Added to submission is modesty, meekness, and respect for the husband (vv. 2-6).

3:2 chaste...fear. Purity of life with reverence for God is what the unsaved husband should observe consistently.

3:3 outward. Peter was not here condemning all outward adornment. His condemnation is for incessant preoccupation with the outward to the disregard of one's character (v. 4; cf. 1 Tim. 2:9,10). But every Christian woman is especially to concentrate on developing that chaste and reverent Christlike character.

3:4 gentle and quiet spirit. Here is beauty that never decays, as the outward body does. "Gentle" is actually "meek or humble" and "quiet" describes the character of her action and reaction to her husband and life in general. Such is precious not only to her husband, but also to God.

3:5 holy women. Certain OT saints (particularly Sarah, v. 6) are models of inner beauty, character, modesty, and submissiveness to their husbands (*see notes on Prov. 31:10-31*).

3:6 not afraid with any terror. There are potential fears for a Christian woman who sets out to be submissive to her unsaved husband, as to where such submission might lead. But Peter's instruction to the wife is not to be intimidating or fearful, but as a principle, she is to submit to her husband. This precludes any coercion to sin, disobedience to God's Word, or imposition of physical harm (cf. Acts 4:18-20; 5:28,29; Titus 1:6).

3:7 Husbands, likewise. Submission is the responsibility of a Christian husband as well (cf. Eph. 5:21). Though not submitting to his wife as a leader, a believing husband must submit to the loving duty of being sensitive to the needs, fears, and feelings of his wife. In other words, a Christian husband needs to subordinate his needs to hers, whether she is a Christian or not. Peter specifically notes consideration, chivalry, and companionship. **weaker vessel.** While she is fully equal in Christ and not inferior spiritually because she is a woman (see Gal. 3:28), she is physically weaker, and in need of protection, provision, and strength from her husband. **heirs together of the grace of life.** Here the "grace of life" is not salvation, but marriage—the best relationship earthly life has to offer. The husband must cultivate companionship and fellowship with his wife, Christian or not (cf. Eccl. 9:9). **prayers may not be hindered.** This refers specifically to the husband's prayer for the salvation of his wife (*see note on v. 1*). Such a prayer would be hindered if he were not respectful of her needs and fellowship.

Called to Blessing

8 Finally, all *of you be* of one mind, having compassion for one another; love as
brothers, *be* tenderhearted, *be* [2]courteous;
9 [k]not returning evil for evil or reviling for
reviling, but on the contrary [l]blessing,
knowing that you were called to this, [m]that
you may inherit a blessing. 10 For

[n]"He who would love life
And see good days,
[o]Let him [3]refrain his tongue from evil,
And his lips from speaking deceit.
11 *Let him [p]turn away from evil and do good;*
[q]Let him seek peace and pursue it.
12 *For the eyes of the LORD are on the righteous,*
[r]And His ears are open to their prayers;
But the face of the LORD is against those who do evil."

8 [2]NU *humble*
9 [k][Prov. 17:13] [l]Matt. 5:44 [m]Matt. 25:34
10 [n]Ps. 34:12-16 [o]James 1:26 [3]*restrain*
11 [p]Ps. 37:27 [q]Rom. 12:18
12 [r]John 9:31
13 [s]Prov. 16:7
14 [t]James 1:12 [u]Is. 8:12
15 [v]Ps. 119:46 [w][Titus 3:7] [4]*set apart* [5]NU *Christ as Lord*
16 [x]1 Tim. 1:5; Heb. 13:18; 1 Pet. 3:21
18 [6]NU, M *you*

Suffering for Right and Wrong

13 [s]And who *is* he who will harm you if
you become followers of what is good?
14 [t]But even if you should suffer for righteousness' sake, *you are* blessed. [u]*"And do*
not be afraid of their threats, nor be trou-
bled." 15 But [4]sanctify [5]the Lord God in
your hearts, and always [v]*be* ready to *give* a
defense to everyone who asks you a reason
for the [w]hope that is in you, with meekness
and fear; 16 [x]having a good conscience,
that when they defame you as evildoers,
those who revile your good conduct in
Christ may be ashamed. 17 For *it is* better, if
it is the will of God, to suffer for doing
good than for doing evil.

Christ's Suffering and Ours

18 For Christ also suffered once for sins,
the just for the unjust, that He might bring
[6]us to God, being put to death in the flesh
but made alive by the Spirit, 19 by whom
also He went and preached to the spirits in

3:8 *be* of one mind. From two Gr. words, meaning "to think the same," "to be like-minded." The idea is to maintain inward unity of heart. All Christians are to be examples and purveyors of peace and unity, not disruption and disharmony (John 13:35; 17; Rom. 12:16; 15:5; 1 Cor. 1:10; Phil. 2:1,2). **love as brothers.** A recurring theme in 1 Peter (see 1:22; 2:17; 4:8; 5:14).

3:9 on the contrary blessing. "Blessing" means "to speak well of," "to eulogize." The blessing that a Christian is to give to the reviler includes finding ways to serve him, praying for his salvation or spiritual progress, expressing thankfulness for him, speaking well of him, and desiring his well-being (2:23; cf. Lev. 19:18; Prov. 20:22; Luke 6:38). **you were called to this.** A person to whom God has given undeserved blessings instead of judgment, should seek the blessing he will receive when giving a free gift of forgiveness to someone who has wronged him (cf. v. 21; Matt. 18:21-35).

3:10 *love life and see good days.* Peter employed apt scriptural confirmation of his exhortation in v. 9, by quoting from Ps. 34:12-16. The believer has been granted the legacy to enjoy his life (John 10:10). In this section, Peter gave straightforward advice on how to experience that rich joy and fullness of life, even in the midst of a hostile environment. The requirements of the fulfilled life include a humble, loving attitude towards everyone (v. 8), a non-vindictive response toward revilers (v. 9), pure and honest speech (v. 10), a disdain for sin and pursuit of peace (v. 11), and a right motive, i.e., to work the righteousness that pleases the omniscient Lord (v. 12; cf. Matt. 5:38-48; Rom. 12:14,17; 1 Cor. 4:12; 5:11; 1 Thess. 5:15).

3:13 who will harm you. It is unusual for people to mistreat those who are zealous for good. Even a hostile world is slow to hurt people who are benefactors of society, who are kind and caring (cf. 4:12), but it does happen (v. 14).

3:14 blessed. Here the idea is "privileged" or "honored" (cf. Matt. 5:10). ***do not be afraid.*** The idea here is borrowed from Is. 8:12,13.

3:15 sanctify the Lord God in your hearts. "Christ" is to be preferred here, so the reading is "set apart in your hearts Christ as Lord." The heart is the sanctuary in which He prefers to be worshiped. Live in submissive communion with the Lord Jesus, loving and obeying Him—and you have nothing to fear. **always *be* ready to *give* a defense.** The Eng. word "apologetics" comes from the Gr. word here translated "defense." Peter is using the word in an informal sense (cf. Phil. 1:16,17) and is insisting that the believer must understand what he believes and why one is a Christian, and then be able to articulate one's beliefs humbly, thoughtfully, reasonably, and biblically. **the hope that is in you.** Salvation with its anticipation of eternal glory.

3:16 a good conscience. The conscience accuses (cf. Rom. 2:14,15) by notifying the person of sin by producing guilt, shame, doubt, fear, anxiety, or despair. A life free of ongoing and unconfessed sin, lived under the command of the Lord, will produce a conscience "without offense" (Acts 24:16; *see notes on 2 Cor. 1:12; 4:2*). This will cause your false accusers to feel the "shame" of their own consciences (cf. 2:12,15).

3:18 For Christ also suffered. Peter wished to encourage his readers in their suffering by again reminding them that even Christ suffered unjustly because it was God's will (v. 11). Ultimately, however, Christ was marvelously triumphant to the point of being exalted to the right hand of God while all of those demon beings who were behind His suffering were made forever subject to Him (v. 22). God also caused Peter's suffering readers to triumph. **once for sins.** Under the Old Covenant, the Jewish people offered sacrifice after sacrifice, and then repeated it all the next year, especially at the Passover. But Christ's one sacrifice for sins was of such perpetual validity that it was sufficient for all and would never need to be repeated (*see notes on Heb. 7:27; 9:26-28*). **the just for the unjust.** This is another statement of the sinlessness of Jesus (cf. Heb. 7:26) and of His substitutionary and vicarious atonement. He, who personally never sinned and had no sin nature, took the place of sinners (cf. 2:24; 2 Cor. 5:21). In so doing, Christ satisfied God's just penalty for sin required by the law and opened the way to God for all who repentantly believe (cf. John 14:6; Acts 4:12). **bring us to God.** In this life spiritually, and in the next life, wholly (cf. Mark 15:38). **put to death in the flesh.** A violent physical execution that terminated His earthly life (cf. Heb. 5:7). **alive by the Spirit.** This is not a reference to the Holy Spirit, but to Jesus' true inner life, His own spirit. Contrasted with His flesh (humanness) which was dead for 3 days, His spirit (deity) was alive, lit. "in spirit" (cf. Luke 23:46).

3:19 preached. Between Christ's death and resurrection, His living spirit went to the demon spirits bound in the abyss and proclaimed that, in spite of His death, He had triumphed over them (*see notes on Col. 2:14,15*). **spirits in prison.** This refers to fallen angels (demons), who were permanently bound because of heinous

prison, **20** who formerly were disobedient, [7]when once the Divine longsuffering
waited in the days of Noah, while *the* ark
was being prepared, in which a few, that
is, eight souls, were saved through water.
21 [y]There is also an antitype which now
saves us—baptism [z](not the removal of
the filth of the flesh, [a]but the answer of a
good conscience toward God), through
the resurrection of Jesus Christ, **22** who
has gone into heaven and [b]is at the right
hand of God, [c]angels and authorities and
powers having been made subject to
Him.

20 [7] NU, M *when the longsuffering of God waited patiently*
21 [y] Acts 16:33; Eph. 5:26 [z] [Titus 3:5] [a] [Rom. 10:10]
22 [b] Ps. 110:1 [c] Rom. 8:38; Heb. 1:6

CHAPTER 4

1 [1] NU omits *for us*
2 [a] John 1:13
3 [2] NU *time*
5 [b] Acts 10:42; Rom. 14:9; 2 Tim. 4:1

4

Therefore, since Christ suffered [1]for us
in the flesh, arm yourselves also with
the same mind, for he who has suffered in
the flesh has ceased from sin, **2** that he no
longer should live the rest of *his* time in the
flesh for the lusts of men, [a]but for the will
of God. **3** For we *have spent* enough of our
past [2]lifetime in doing the will of the Gentiles—when we walked in lewdness, lusts,
drunkenness, revelries, drinking parties,
and abominable idolatries. **4** In regard to
these, they think it strange that you do not
run with *them* in the same flood of dissipation, speaking evil of *you*. **5** They will give
an account to Him who is ready [b]to judge

wickedness. The demons who are not so bound resist such a sentence (cf. Luke 8:31). In the end, they will all be sent to the eternal lake of fire (Matt. 25:41; Rev. 20:10).

3:20 disobedient...in the days of Noah. Peter further explains that the abyss is inhabited by bound demons who have been there since the time of Noah, and who were sent there because they severely overstepped the bounds of God's tolerance with their wickedness. The demons of Noah's day were running riot through the earth, filling the world with their wicked, vile, anti-God activity, including sexual sin, so that even 120 years of Noah's preaching, while the ark was being built, could not convince any of the human race beyond the 8 people in Noah's family to believe in God (*see notes on 2 Pet. 2:4,5; Jude 6,7*; cf. Gen. 6:1-8). Thus God bound these demons permanently in the abyss until their final sentencing. **saved through water.** They had been rescued in spite of the water not because of the water. Here, water was the agent of God's judgment not the means of salvation (*see note on Acts 2:38*).

3:21 an antitype which now saves us. In the NT, an antitype is an earthly expression of a spiritual reality. It indicates a symbol, picture, or pattern of some spiritual truth. Peter is teaching that the fact that 8 people were in an ark and went through the whole judgment, and yet were unharmed, is analogous to the Christian's experience in salvation by being in Christ, the ark of one's salvation. **baptism... through the resurrection of Jesus Christ.** Peter is not at all referring to water baptism here, but rather a figurative immersion into union with Christ as an ark of safety from the judgment of God. The resurrection of Christ demonstrates God's acceptance of Christ's substitutionary death for the sins of those who believe (Acts 2:30,31; Rom. 1:4). Judgment fell on Christ just as the judgment of the flood waters fell on the ark. The believer who is in Christ is thus in the ark of safety that will sail over the waters of judgment into eternal glory (cf. Rom. 6:1-4). **not the removal of the filth of the flesh.** To be sure he is not misunderstood, Peter clearly says he is not speaking of water baptism. In Noah's flood, they were kept out of the water while those who went into the water were destroyed. Being in the ark and thus saved from God's judgment on the world prefigures being in Christ and thus saved from eternal damnation. **the answer of a good conscience toward God.** The word for "answer" has the idea of a pledge, agreeing to certain conditions of a covenant (the New Covenant) with God. What saves a person plagued by sin and a guilty conscience is not some external rite, but the agreement with God to get in the ark of safety, the Lord Jesus, by faith in His death and resurrection (cf. Rom. 10:9,10; Heb. 9:14; 10:22).

3:22 right hand of God. After Jesus accomplished His cross work and was raised from the dead, He was exalted to the place of prominence, honor, majesty, authority, and power (cf. Rom. 8:34; Eph. 1:20,21; Phil. 2:9-11; Heb. 1:3-9; 6:20; 8:1; 12:2). The point of application to Peter's readers is that suffering can be the context for one's greatest triumph, as seen in the example of the Lord Jesus.

4:1 Therefore. In light of the triumphant suffering and death of Christ, Peter's readers should also be willing to suffer in the flesh, knowing that it potentially produces the greatest triumph. **suffered for us in the flesh.** A reference to Christ's death on the cross (*see note on 3:18*). **the same mind.** The Christian should be armed (terminology that realizes a battle) with the same thought that was manifest in the suffering of Christ, namely that one can be triumphant in suffering, even the suffering of death. In other words, the Christian should voluntarily accept the potential of death as a part of the Christian life (cf. Matt. 10:38,39; 2 Cor. 4:8-11). Peter would have his opportunity to live this principle himself, when he faced martyrdom (see John 21:18,19). **has ceased from sin.** The perfect tense of the verb emphasizes a permanent eternal condition free from sin. The worst that can happen to a believer suffering unjustly is death, and that is the best that can happen because death means the complete and final end of all sins. If the Christian is armed with the goal of being delivered from sin, and that goal is achieved through his death, the threat and experience of death is precious (cf. Rom. 7:5,18; 1 Cor. 1:21; 15:42,49). Moreover, the greatest weapon that the enemy has against the Christian, the threat of death, is not effective.

4:2 no longer should live...for the lusts of men. If the goal of the Christian's life is the freedom from sin which comes at death, then he should live the remainder of his life on earth pursuing the holy will of God rather than the ungodly lusts of the flesh.

4:3 lewdness...abominable idolatries. "Lewdness" describes unbridled, unrestrained sin, an excessive indulgence in sensual pleasure. "Revelries" has the idea of an orgy. The Gr. word was used in extrabiblical literature to refer to a band of drunken, wildly acting people, swaggering and staggering through public streets, wreaking havoc. Thus the pleasures of the ungodly are described here from the perspective of God as despicable acts of wickedness. Though Peter's readers had indulged in such sins before salvation, they must never do so again. Sin in the believer is a burden which afflicts him rather than a pleasure which delights him.

4:4 they think it strange. The former friends are surprised, offended, and resentful because of the Christian's lack of interest in ungodly pleasures. **the same flood of dissipation.** "Dissipation" refers to the state of evil in which a person thinks about nothing else. The picture here is of a large crowd running together in a mad, wild race—a melee pursuing sin.

4:5 give an account. This verb means "to pay back." People who have "walked in lewdness" (v. 3) and who malign believers (v. 4) are amassing a debt to God which they will spend all eternity paying back (*see note on Matt. 18:23*; cf. Matt. 12:36; Rom. 14:11,12; Heb. 4:13). **to judge the living and the dead.** All the unsaved, currently alive or dead, will be brought before the Judge, the Lord Jesus Christ at the Great White Throne Judgment (Rev. 20:11-15; cf. Rom. 3:19; 2 Thess. 1:6-10).

the living and the dead. 6 For this reason
[c]the gospel was preached also to those
who are dead, that they might be judged
according to men in the flesh, but [d]live according to God in the spirit.

Serving for God's Glory

7 But [e]the end of all things is at hand;
therefore be serious and watchful in your
prayers. 8 And above all things have fervent love for one another, for [f]*"love will
cover a multitude of sins."* 9 [g]*Be* hospitable
to one another [h]without grumbling. 10 [i]As
each one has received a gift, minister it to
one another, [j]as good stewards of [k]the
manifold grace of God. 11 [l]If anyone
speaks, *let him speak* as the [3]oracles of God.
If anyone ministers, *let him do it* as with the
ability which God supplies, that [m]in all
things God may be glorified through Jesus
Christ, to whom belong the glory and the
[4]dominion forever and ever. Amen.

Suffering for God's Glory

12 Beloved, do not think it strange concerning the fiery trial which is to try you,
as though some strange thing happened to
you; 13 but rejoice [n]to the extent that you
partake of Christ's sufferings, that [o]when
His glory is revealed, you may also be glad

6 [c] 1 Pet. 1:12; 3:19 [d] [Rom. 8:9, 13]; Gal. 5:25
7 [e] Rom. 13:11; Heb. 9:26; James 5:8, 9; 1 John 2:18
8 [f] [Prov. 10:12]; 1 Cor. 13:4; James 5:20
9 [g] 1 Tim. 3:2; Heb. 13:2 [h] 2 Cor. 9:7
10 [i] Rom. 12:6-8 [j] Matt. 24:45; 1 Cor. 4:1, 2 [k] [1 Cor. 12:4]
11 [l] Eph. 4:29 [m] [1 Cor. 10:31]; Eph. 5:20 [3] *utterances* [4] *sovereignty*
13 [n] James 1:2 [o] 2 Tim. 2:12

4:6 to those who are dead. The preaching of the gospel not only offers a rich life (3:10), a ceasing from sin (v. 1), and a good conscience (3:21), but also an escape from final judgment. Peter had in mind believers who had heard and accepted the gospel of Christ when they were still alive, but who had died by the time Peter wrote this letter. Some of them, perhaps, had been martyred for their faith. Though these were dead physically, they were triumphantly alive in their spirits (cf. Heb. 12:23). All their judgment had been fully accomplished while they were alive in this world ("in the flesh"), so they will live forever in God's presence.

4:7 the end of all things. The Gr. word for "end" is never used in the NT as a chronological end, as if something simply stops. Instead, the word means a consummation, a goal achieved, a result attained, or a realization. Having emphasized triumphant suffering through death, Peter here begins to emphasize triumphant suffering through the second coming of Christ (cf. 1:3; 2:12), which is the goal of all things. He is calling believers to live obediently and expectantly in the light of Christ's return. **is at hand.** The idea is that of a process consummated with a resulting nearness; that is, "imminent." Peter is reminding the readers of this letter that the return of Jesus Christ could be at any moment (cf. Rom. 13:12; 1 Thess. 1:10; James 5:7,8; Rev. 22:20). **be serious and watchful.** To be "serious" implies here not to be swept away by emotions or passions, thus maintaining a proper eternal perspective on life. The doctrine of the imminent return of Christ should not turn the Christian into a zealous fanatic who does nothing but wait for it to occur. Instead, it should lead the believer into a watchful pursuit of holiness. Moreover, a watchful attitude creates a pilgrim mentality (2:11). It reminds the Christian that he is a citizen of heaven only sojourning on earth. It should also remind him that he will face the record of his service to God and be rewarded for what stands the test at the judgment seat of Christ, which follows the return of Christ to rapture His church (see 1 Cor. 3:10-15; 4:1-5; 2 Cor. 5:9,10). **watchful...prayers.** A mind victimized by emotion and passion, out of control, or knocked out of balance by worldly lusts and pursuits, is a mind that cannot know the fullness of holy communion in prayer with God (cf. 3:7). A mind fixed on His return is purified (1 John 3:3) and enjoys the fullness of fellowship with the Lord.

4:8 fervent love. "Fervent" means "to be stretched," "to be strained." It is used of a runner who is moving at maximum output with taut muscles straining and stretching to the limit (cf. 1:22). This kind of love requires the Christian to put another's spiritual good ahead of his own desires in spite of being treated unkindly, ungraciously, or even with hostility (cf. 1 Cor. 13:4-7; Phil. 2:1-4). ***"love will cover a multitude of sins."*** Quoted from Prov. 10:12. It is the nature of true spiritual love, whether from God to man or Christian to Christian, to cover sins (cf. Rom. 5:8). This teaching does not preclude the discipline of a sinning, unrepentant church member (cf. Matt. 18:15-18; 1 Cor. 5). It means specifically that a Christian should overlook sins against him if possible, and always be ready to forgive insults and unkindnesses.

4:9 *Be* hospitable to one another. The Gr. word means "love of strangers." Love is intensely practical, not just emotional. In Peter's day, love included opening one's home and caring for other needy Christians, such as traveling preachers. It also included opening one's home for church services. Scripture also teaches that Christians should be hospitable to strangers (Ex. 22:21; Deut. 14:28,29; Heb. 13:1,2).

4:10 received a gift. A spiritual gift is a graciously given supernaturally designed ability granted to every believer by which the Holy Spirit ministers to the body of Christ. The Gr. word (*charisma*) emphasizes the freeness of the gift. A spiritual gift cannot be earned, pursued, or worked up. It is merely "received" through the grace of God (cf. 1 Cor. 12:4,7,11,18). The pursuit of the exercise of the best gifts (especially prophecy) in the ministry of a local church was encouraged by Paul (1 Cor. 12:31). The categories of spiritual gifts are given in Rom. 12:3-8 and 1 Cor. 12:4-10 (*see notes there*). Each believer has one specific gift, often a combination of the various categories of gifts blended together uniquely for each Christian. **minister it to one another.** Spiritual gifts were used, not for the exaltation of the one with the gift, but in loving concern for the benefit of others in the church (cf. 1 Cor. 12:7; 13). **good stewards.** A steward is responsible for another's resources. A Christian does not own his gifts, but God has given him gifts to manage for the church and His glory. **manifold grace of God.** This emphasizes the vast designs of God for these gifts.

4:11 speaks...ministers. Peter is implying that there are two categories of gifts: speaking gifts and serving gifts. Such distinctions are clear in the lists in Rom. 12 and 1 Cor. 12. For a discussion of the gifts, *see notes on 1 Cor. 12–14.* **oracles of God.** Elsewhere used of Scripture, the very words out of God's mouth (cf. Rom. 3:2; Acts 7:38). **God may be glorified.** That is the goal of everything. Cf. Rom. 11:33-36; Eph. 3:21; 2 Tim. 4:18; 2 Pet. 3:18; Rev. 1:6.

4:12 the fiery trial. Peter probably wrote this letter shortly before or after the burning of Rome (see Introduction: Background and Setting), and at the beginning of the horrors of a 200 year period of Christian persecution. Peter explains that 4 attitudes are necessary in order to be triumphant in persecution: 1) expect it (v. 12); 2) rejoice in it (vv. 13,14); 3) evaluate its cause (vv. 15-18); and 4) entrust it to God (v. 19). **some strange thing happened.** "Happened" means "to fall by chance." A Christian must not think that his persecution is something that happened accidentally. God allowed it and designed it for the believer's testing, purging, and cleansing.

4:13 to the extent...sufferings. The Christian who is persecuted for his faith is a partner in the same kind of suffering Jesus endured—suffering for doing what is right (cf. Matt. 5:10-12; Gal. 6:17; Phil. 1:29; 3:10; Col. 1:24). **when His glory is revealed.** That is, at Christ's second coming (cf. Matt. 24:30; 25:31; Luke 17:30). While Jesus is presently glorified in heaven, His glory is not yet fully revealed on earth. **be glad with exceeding joy.** That is, exult and rejoice with a rapturous joy (cf. James 1:2). A Christian who is persecuted for righ-

with exceeding joy. **14** If you are [5]re-
proached for the name of Christ, [p]blessed
are you, for the Spirit of glory and of God
rests upon you. [6]On their part He is blasphemed, [q]but on your part He is glorified.
15 But let none of you suffer as a murderer,
a thief, an evildoer, or as a [7]busybody in
other people's matters. **16** Yet if *anyone suffers* as a Christian, let him not be ashamed,
but let him glorify God in this [8]matter.
17 For the time *has come* [r]for judgment to
begin at the house of God; and if *it begins*
with us first, [s]what will *be* the end of those
who do not obey the gospel of God? **18** Now

[t]"If the righteous one is scarcely
saved,
Where will the ungodly and the
sinner appear?"

19 Therefore let those who suffer according
to the will of God [u]commit their souls *to*
Him in doing good, as to a faithful Creator.

Shepherd the Flock

5 The elders who are among you I exhort,
I who am a fellow elder and a [a]witness
of the sufferings of Christ, and also a partaker of the [b]glory that will be revealed:
2 [c]Shepherd the flock of God which is
among you, serving as overseers, [d]not by
compulsion but [1]willingly, [e]not for dishonest gain but eagerly; **3** nor as [f]being [2]lords
over [g]those entrusted to you, but [h]being examples to the flock; **4** and when [i]the Chief

14 [p] Matt. 5:11; Luke 6:22; Acts 5:41 [q] Matt. 5:16 [5] *insulted or reviled* [6] NU omits the rest of v. 14. **15** [7] *meddler* **16** [8] NU *name* **17** [r] Is. 10:12 [s] Luke 10:12 **18** [t] Prov. 11:31 **19** [u] Ps. 37:5-7; 2 Tim. 1:12

CHAPTER 5

1 [a] Matt. 26:37 [b] Rom. 8:17, 18 **2** [c] John 21:16; Acts 20:28 [d] 1 Cor. 9:17 [e] 1 Tim. 3:3 [1] NU adds *according to God* **3** [f] Ezek. 34:4; Matt. 20:25 [g] Ps. 33:12 [h] John 13:15; Phil. 3:17; 1 Thess. 1:7; 2 Thess. 3:9; 1 Tim. 4:12; Titus 2:7 [2] *masters* **4** [i] Is. 40:11; Zech. 13:7; Heb. 13:20; 1 Pet. 2:25

teousness in this life will have overflowing joy in the future because of his reward (*see notes on Matt. 20:20-23*). Such an awareness of future joy enables him also to "rejoice" (v. 13) at the present time (cf. Luke 6:22; *see note on Rom. 8:17*).

4:14 reproached for the name of Christ. Insulted and treated unfairly for being a representative of all that Christ is, and for the public proclamation of the name of Christ (cf. Acts 4:12; 5:41; 9:15,16; 15:26). **blessed.** Not a general, nondescript happiness so much as a specific benefit, in that suffering triumphantly for Christ shows God's approval. **Spirit of glory.** That is, the Spirit who has glory, or who is glorious. In the OT, the glory of God was represented by the Shekinah light, that luminous glow which signified the presence of God (see Ex. 33:15–34:9). **rests upon you.** When a believer suffers, God's presence specially rests and lifts him to strength and endurance beyond the physical dimension (cf. Acts 6:8–7:60; 2 Cor. 12:7-10).

4:15 busybody in other people's matters. Someone who intrudes into matters that belong to someone else. Peter is dealing with matters that would lead to persecution, such as getting involved in revolutionary, disruptive activity, or interfering in the function and flow of government. It might also refer to being a troublesome meddler in the workplace. As a general rule, a Christian living in a non-Christian culture is to do his work faithfully, exalt Jesus Christ, and live a virtuous life, rather than try to overturn or disrupt his culture (2:13-16; cf. 1 Thess. 4:11; 2 Thess. 3:11; *see notes on 1 Tim. 2:1-3*).

4:16 Christian. In the earliest days of the church, "Christian" was a derisive term given to those followers of Christ (cf. Acts 11:26; 26:28). Eventually, followers of Christ came to love and adopt this name.

4:17 judgment...house of God. Not condemnation, but the purging, chastening, and purifying of the church by the loving hand of God. It is far better and more important to kingdom work to endure suffering as the Lord purges and strengthens the church, than to endure the eternal sufferings of the unbeliever in the lake of fire. And, if God so strongly and painfully judges His church which He loves, what will be His fury on the ungodly?

4:18 Quoted from the LXX of Prov. 11:31, and reinforces the point that if the justified sinner is saved only with great difficulty, suffering, pain, and loss—what will be the end of the ungodly? Cf. 2 Thess. 1:4-10.

4:19 commit their souls *to Him*. "Commit" is a banking term meaning "to deposit for safe keeping." **faithful Creator.** Peter uses the word "Creator," to remind the readers of this letter that when they committed their lives to God, they were simply giving back to God what He had created. As Creator, God knows best the needs of His beloved creatures (2:23; cf. 2 Tim. 1:12).

5:1 elders...I exhort. Times of suffering and persecution in the church call for the noblest leadership. The "elder" is the same leader as the "shepherd" (i.e., pastor, v. 2), and "overseer" (i.e., bishop, v. 2; *see note on Acts 20:28*). The word "elder" emphasizes their spiritual maturity. As in almost all other uses of the word (with the exception of Peter's reference to himself here and John's in 2 John 1 and 3 John 1), Peter wrote in the plural, indicating it was usual to have a plurality of godly leaders who oversaw and fed the flock. **fellow elder and a witness...and...partaker of the glory.** Peter loaded this exhortation to the elders with some rich motivation. First, there was motivation by identification with Peter, who refers to himself as a fellow-elder. As such, he could give relevant exhortation to the spiritual leaders. Second, there was motivation by authority. By noting that he had been an eyewitness of Christ's suffering, Peter was affirming his apostleship (cf. Luke 24:45; Acts 1:21,22). Third, there was the motivation by anticipation. The fact that Christian leaders will one day receive from the hand of Christ a reward for their service should be a stimulant to faithful duty. The basis of this anticipation was Peter's experience in observing the transfiguration of Christ (cf. Matt. 17:1-8; 2 Pet. 1:16). At that momentous event, he did partake of the Lord's glory.

5:2 Shepherd the flock of God. After the motivation (v. 1) comes the exhortation (vv. 2-4). Since the primary objective of shepherding is feeding; that is, teaching, every elder must be able to teach (cf. John 21:15-17; *see notes on 1 Tim. 3:2; Titus 1:9*). Involved with the feeding of the flock is also protecting the flock (cf. Acts 20:28-30). In both duties, it must be remembered that the flock belongs to God, not to the pastor. God entrusts some of His flock to the pastor of a church to lead, care for, and feed (v. 3). **not by compulsion but willingly.** Specifically, Peter may be warning the elders against a first danger—laziness. The divine calling (cf. 1 Cor. 9:16), along with the urgency of the task (Rom. 1:15), should prevent laziness and indifference. Cf. 2 Cor. 9:7. **not for dishonest gain.** False teachers are always motivated by a second danger, money, and use their power and position to rob people of their own wealth (*see notes on 2 Pet. 2:1-3*). Scripture is clear that churches should pay their shepherds well (1 Cor. 9:7-14; 1 Tim. 5:17,18); but a desire for undeserved money must never be a motive for ministers to serve (cf. 1 Tim. 3:3; 6:9-11; 2 Tim. 2:4; Titus 1:7; 2 Pet. 2:3; see also Jer. 6:13; 8:10; Mic. 3:11; Mal. 1:10).

5:3 nor as being lords. This is the third major temptation for a pastor: 1) laziness (v. 2); 2) dishonest finances (v. 2); and 3) demagoguery. In this context, "lords" means to dominate someone or some situation. It implies leadership by manipulation and intimidation. *See notes on Matt. 20:25-28.* Rather, true spiritual leadership is by example (see 1 Tim. 4:12).

5:4 Chief Shepherd appears. The Chief Shepherd is Jesus Christ (cf. Is. 40:11; Zech. 13:7; John 10:2,11,12,16; Heb. 13:20,21). When He ap-

Shepherd appears, you will receive [j]the
crown of glory that does not fade away.

Submit to God, Resist the Devil

5 Likewise you younger people, submit
yourselves to *your* elders. Yes, [k]all of *you* be
submissive to one another, and be clothed
with humility, for

> [l]"*God resists the proud,*
> *But* [m]*gives grace to the humble.*"

6 Therefore humble yourselves under the
mighty hand of God, that He may exalt
you in due time, 7 casting all your care
upon Him, for He cares for you.
8 Be [3]sober, be [4]vigilant; [5]because your adversary the devil walks about like a roaring
lion, seeking whom he may devour. 9 Resist
him, steadfast in the faith, knowing that the
same sufferings are experienced by your
brotherhood in the world. 10 But [6]may the
God of all grace, [n]who called [7]us to His eternal glory by Christ Jesus, after you have suffered a while, [8]perfect, establish, strengthen,
and settle *you.* 11 [o]To Him *be* the glory and
the dominion forever and ever. Amen.

Farewell and Peace

12 By [p]Silvanus, our faithful brother as I
consider him, I have written to you briefly,
exhorting and testifying [q]that this is the
true grace of God in which you stand.
13 She who is in Babylon, elect together
with *you,* greets you; and *so does* [r]Mark my
son. 14 Greet one another with a kiss of love.
Peace to you all who are in Christ Jesus.
Amen.

4 [j] 2 Tim. 4:8 **5** [k] Rom. 12:10; Eph. 5:21 [l] Prov. 3:34; James 4:6 [m] Is. 57:15 **8** [3] *self-controlled* [4] *watchful* [5] NU, M omit *because* **10** [n] 1 Cor. 1:9; 1 Thess. 2:12 [6] NU *the God of all grace,* [7] NU, M *you* [8] NU *will perfect* **11** [o] Rev. 1:6 **12** [p] 2 Cor. 1:19; 1 Thess. 1:1; 2 Thess. 1:1 [q] Acts 20:24 **13** [r] Acts 12:12, 25; 15:37, 39; Col. 4:10; Philem. 24

pears at the second coming, He will evaluate the ministry of pastors at the judgment seat of Christ (cf. 1 Cor. 3:9-15; 4:5; 2 Cor. 5:9,10). **crown of glory.** Lit. the crown which is eternal glory. In the NT world, crowns were given as marks of victorious achievements (cf. 1 Cor. 9:24,25). Believers are promised crowns of glory, life (James 1:12), righteousness (2 Tim. 4:8), and rejoicing (1 Thess. 2:19), and all are imperishable (1 Cor. 9:25). All the crowns describe certain characteristics of eternal life. *See note on 1 Thess. 2:19.* **that does not fade away.** The Gr. word for "not fade away" is the name of a flower, the amaranth.

5:5 submit yourselves. See 2:18–3:9. **elders.** The elders are the pastors, the spiritual leaders of the church (cf. v. 1; notes on 1 Tim. 3:1-7; Titus 1:5-9). The church members, especially the young people, are to give honor, deference, and respect to spiritual leadership. Submission is a fundamental attitude of spiritual maturity (cf. 1 Cor. 16:15; 1 Thess. 5:12-14; Titus 3:1,2; Heb. 13:7,17). Lack of submission to the elders not only makes the ministry difficult, but also forfeits God's grace, as noted in the quote from Prov. 3:34 (*see note on James 4:6*). **be clothed with humility.** To "be clothed" lit. means to tie something on oneself with a knot or a bow. This term was often used of a slave putting on an apron over his clothes in order to keep his clothes clean. "Humility" is lit. "lowly mindedness," an attitude that one is not too good to serve. Humility was not considered a virtue by the ancient world, any more than it is today (but cf. John 13:3-17; Phil. 2:3,4; see also Prov. 6:16; 8:13; Is. 57:15).

5:6 under the mighty hand of God. This is an OT symbol of the power of God working in the experience of men, always accomplishing His sovereign purpose (cf. Ex. 3:19,20; Job 30:20,21; Ezek. 20:33,37; Mic. 6:8). The readers of Peter's letter were not to fight the sovereign hand of God, even when it brought them through testings. One of the evidences of lack of submission and humility is impatience with God in His work of humbling believers (*see notes on 2 Cor. 12:7-10*). **exalt you in due time.** Cf. Luke 14:11. God will lift up the suffering, submissive believers in His wisely appointed time. *See notes on Job 42.*

5:7 casting all your care upon Him. This verse partly quotes and partly interprets Ps. 55:22. "Casting" means "to throw something on something," as to throw a blanket on a donkey (Luke 19:35). Christians are to cast all of their discontent, discouragement, despair, and suffering on the Lord, and trust Him for knowing what He's doing with their lives (cf. 1 Sam. 1:10-18). Along with submission (v. 5) and humility (vv. 5,6), trust in God is the third attitude necessary for victorious Christian living.

5:8 Be sober. *See notes on 1:13 and 4:7.* **be vigilant.** Strong confidence in God's sovereign care does not mean that the believer may live carelessly. The outside evil forces which come against the Christian demand that the Christian stay alert. **your adversary.** Gr. for a legal opponent in a lawsuit. **the devil...a roaring lion.** The Gr. word for "devil" means "slanderer"; thus a malicious enemy who maligns believers. He and his forces are always active, looking for opportunities to overwhelm the believer with temptation, persecution, and discouragement (cf. Pss. 22:13; 104:21; Ezek. 22:25). Satan sows discord, accuses God to men, men to God, and men to men. He will do what he can to drag the Christian out of fellowship with Christ and out of Christian service (cf. Job 1; Luke 22:3; John 13:27; 2 Cor. 4:3,4; Rev. 12). And he constantly accuses believers before God's throne, attempting to convince God to abandon them (Job 1:6-12; Rev. 12:10).

5:9 Resist him, steadfast in the faith. Cf. James 4:7. "Resist" means "to stand up against." The way to resist the devil is not with special formulas, or words directed at him and his demons, but by remaining firm in the Christian faith. This means to continue to live in accord with the truth of God's Word (*see notes on 2 Cor. 10:3-5*). As the believer knows sound doctrine and obeys God's truth, Satan is withstood (cf. Eph. 6:17). **the same sufferings.** The whole brotherhood, the entire Christian community, is always going through similar trials brought on by the roaring lion who never stops trying to devour believers (cf. 1 Cor. 10:13).

5:10 who called us. As always in the NT epistles, an effectual, saving call. *See notes on 1:5; 2:9,21; 3:9.* **after you have suffered a while.** Christians are to live with the understanding that God's purposes realized in the future require some pain in the present. While the believer is being personally attacked by the enemy, he is being personally perfected by the Lord, as the next phrase attests (cf. 1:6; also 2 Cor. 1:3-7). **perfect, establish, strengthen, and settle.** These 4 words all speak of strength and resoluteness. God is working through the Christian's struggles to produce strength of character. In vv. 5-14, Peter elucidated briefly, but in wonderful richness, those attitudes which are necessary for the believer to grow in Christ to effective maturity. These include submission (v. 5), humility (vv. 5,6), trust (v. 7), sobermindedness (v. 8), vigilant defense (vv. 8,9), hope (v. 10), worship (v. 11), faithfulness (v. 12), and affection (vv. 13,14).

5:12 Silvanus. This is the Silas who traveled with Paul and is often mentioned in his epistles. He was a prophet (Acts 15:32) and a Roman citizen (Acts 16:37); he was apparently the one who wrote down Peter's words and later took this letter to its intended recipients (cf. Introduction: Author and Date).

5:13 She who is in Babylon. This refers to a church (cf. 2 John 1,13) in Rome (cf. Rev. 17,18; Introduction: Background and Setting). **Mark my son.** Mark, called John Mark, was the spiritual son of Peter. Tradition indicates that Peter helped him write the Gospel of Mark (cf. Acts 12:12). This is the same Mark who once failed Paul (Acts 13:13; 15:38,39; Col. 4:10), but later became useful again for ministry (2 Tim. 4:11).

The Second Epistle of PETER

Title

The clear claim to authorship in 1:1 by the Apostle Peter gives the epistle its title. To distinguish it from Peter's first epistle, it was given the Greek title "*Petrou B*," or 2 Peter.

Author and Date

The author of 2 Peter is the Apostle Peter (see Introduction to 1 Peter). In 1:1, he makes that claim; in 3:1, he refers to his first letter; in 1:14, he refers to the Lord's prediction of his death (John 21:18,19); and in 1:16-18, he claims to have been at the Transfiguration (Matt. 17:1-4). However, critics have generated more controversy over 2 Peter's authorship and rightful place in the canon of Scripture than over any other NT book. The church fathers were slow in giving it their acceptance. No church father refers to 2 Peter by name until Origen near the beginning of the third century. The ancient church historian, Eusebius, only included 2 Peter in his list of disputed books, along with James, Jude, 2 John, and 3 John. Even the leading Reformers only hesitatingly accepted it.

The question about differences in Greek style between the two letters has been satisfactorily answered. Peter wrote that he used an amanuensis, Silvanus, in 1 Peter (cf. 1 Pet. 5:12). In 2 Peter, Peter either used a different amanuensis or wrote the letter by himself. The differences in vocabulary between the two letters can be explained by the differences in themes. First Peter was written to help suffering Christians. Second Peter was written to expose false teachers. On the other hand, there are remarkable similarities in the vocabulary of the two books. The salutation, "grace to you and peace be multiplied," is essentially the same in each book. The author uses such words as "precious," "virtue," "putting off," and "eyewitness," to name just a few examples, in both letters. Certain rather unusual words found in 2 Peter are also found in Peter's speeches in the Acts of the Apostles. These include "obtained" (1:2; Acts 1:17); "godliness" (1:3,6,7; 3:11; Acts 3:12); and "wages of iniquity" (2:13,15; Acts 1:18). Both letters also refer to the same OT event (2:5; 1 Pet. 3:18-20). Some scholars have pointed out that there are as many similarities in vocabulary between 1 and 2 Peter as there are between 1 Timothy and Titus, two letters almost universally believed to have been written by Paul.

The differences in themes also explains certain emphases, such as why one letter teaches that the second coming is near, and one deals with its delay. First Peter, ministering especially to suffering Christians, focuses on the imminency of Christ as a means of encouraging the Christians. Second Peter, dealing with scoffers, emphasizes the reasons why that imminent return of Christ has not yet occurred. Other proposed differences invented by the critics, such as the contradiction between including the resurrection of Christ in one letter and the Transfiguration of Christ in the other, seem to be contrived.

Moreover, it is seemingly irrational that a false teacher would spuriously write a letter against false teachers. No unusual, new, or false doctrines appear in 2 Peter. So, if 2 Peter were a forgery, it would be a forgery written by a fool for no reason at all. This is too much to believe. The conclusion to the question of authorship is that, when the writer introduced the letter and referred to himself as Peter, he was writing the truth.

Nero died in A.D. 68, and tradition says Peter died in Nero's persecution. The epistle may have been written just before his death (1:14; ca. A.D. 67–68).

Background and Setting

Since the time of the writing and sending his first letter, Peter had become increasingly concerned about false teachers who were infiltrating the churches in Asia Minor. Though these false teachers had already caused trouble, Peter expected that their heretical doctrines and immoral life-styles would result in more damage in the future. Thus Peter, in an almost last will and testament (1:13-15), wrote to warn the beloved believers in Christ about the doctrinal dangers they were facing.

Peter does not explicitly say where he was when he wrote this letter, as he does in 1 Peter (1 Pet. 5:13). But the consensus seems to be that Peter wrote this letter from prison in Rome, where he was facing imminent death. Shortly after this letter was written, Peter was martyred, according to reliable tradition, by being crucified upside down (*see note on John 21:18*).

Peter says nothing in the salutation about the recipients of this letter. But according to 3:2, Peter was writing another epistle to the same people to whom he wrote 1 Peter. In his first letter, he spelled out that he was writing "to the pilgrims of the Dispersion in Pontus, Galatia, Cappadocia, Asia, and Bithynia" (1 Pet. 1:1). These provinces were located in an area of Asia Minor, which is modern Turkey. The Christians to whom Peter wrote were mostly Gentiles (*see note on 1:1*).

Historical and Theological Themes

Second Peter was written for the purpose of exposing, thwarting, and defeating the invasion of false teachers into the church. Peter intended to instruct Christians in how to defend themselves against these false teachers and their deceptive lies. This book is the most graphic and penetrating exposé of false teachers in Scripture, comparable only to Jude.

The description of the false teachers is somewhat generic. Peter does not identify some specific false religion, cult, or system of teaching. In a general characterization of false teachers, he informs that they teach destructive heresies. They deny Christ and twist the Scriptures. They bring true faith into disrepute. And they mock the second coming of Christ. But Peter was just as concerned to show the immoral character of these teachers as he was to expose their teaching. Thus, he describes them in more detail than he describes their doctrines. Wickedness is not the product of sound doctrine, but of "destructive heresies" (2:1).

Other themes for this letter can be discerned in the midst of Peter's polemic against the false teachers. He wanted to motivate his readers to continue to develop their Christian character (1:5-11). In so doing, he explains wonderfully how a believer can have assurance of his salvation. Peter also wanted to persuade his readers of the divine character of the apostolic writings (1:12-21). Near the end of the letter, he presents reasons for the delay in Christ's second coming (3:1-13).

Another recurring theme is the importance of knowledge. The word, "knowledge," appears in some form 16 times in these 3 short chapters. It is not too much to say that Peter's primary solution to false teaching is knowledge of true doctrine. Other distinctive features of 2 Peter include a precise statement on the divine origin of Scripture (1:20,21); the future destruction of the world by fire (3:8-13); and the recognition of Paul's letters as inspired Scripture (3:15,16).

Interpretive Challenges

Perhaps the most important challenge in the epistle is to rightly interpret 1:19-21, because of its far-reaching implications with regard to the nature and authenticity of Scripture. That passage, along with 2 Tim. 3:15-17, is vital to a sound view of the Bible's inspiration. Peter's remark that the Lord "bought" false teachers (2:1) poses a challenge interpretively and theologically with regard to the nature of the atonement. The identity of the angels who sinned (2:4) also challenges the interpreter. Many who believe that the saved can be lost again, use 2:18-22 for their argument. That passage, directed at false teachers, must be clarified so as not to contradict a similar statement to believers in 1:4. Further, whom does God not want to perish (3:9)? All of these matters will be treated in the notes.

Outline

Salutation (1:1,2)

I. Know Your Salvation (1:3-11)
   - A. Sustained by God's Power (1:3,4)
   - B. Confirmed by Christian Graces (1:5-7)
   - C. Honored by Abundant Reward (1:8-11)

II. Know Your Scriptures (1:12-21)
   - A. Certified by Apostolic Witness (1:12-18)
   - B. Inspired by the Holy Spirit (1:19-21)

III. Know Your Adversaries (2:1-22)
   - A. Deceptive in Their Infiltration (2:1-3)
   - B. Doomed by Their Iniquity (2:4-10a)
   - C. Disdainful in Their Impurity (2:10b-17)
   - D. Devastating in Their Impact (2:18-22)

IV. Know Your Prophecy (3:1-18)
   - A. The Sureness of the Day of the Lord (3:1-10)
   - B. The Sanctification of God's People (3:11-18)

Greeting the Faithful

1 Simon Peter, a bondservant and [a]apos-
tle of Jesus Christ,

To those who have [1]obtained [b]like[2] precious faith with us by the righteousness of
our God and Savior Jesus Christ:

2 [c]Grace and peace be multiplied to you
in the knowledge of God and of Jesus our
Lord, 3 as His [d]divine power has given to
us all things that *pertain* to life and godliness, through the knowledge of Him [e]who
called us by glory and virtue, 4 [f]by which
have been given to us exceedingly great
and precious promises, that through these
you may be [g]partakers of the divine nature, having escaped the [3]corruption *that is*
in the world through lust.

Fruitful Growth in the Faith

5 But also for this very reason, [h]giving
all diligence, add to your faith virtue, to
virtue [i]knowledge, 6 to knowledge self-

CHAPTER 1

1 [a] Gal. 2:8 [b] Eph. 4:5 [1] *received* [2] *faith of the same value*
2 [c] Dan. 4:1
3 [d] 1 Pet. 1:5 [e] 1 Thess. 2:12; 2 Thess. 2:14; 1 Pet. 5:10
4 [f] 2 Cor. 1:20; 7:1 [g] [2 Cor. 3:18] [3] *depravity*
5 [h] 2 Pet. 3:18 [i] 2 Pet. 1:2

1:1 Simon Peter. See Introduction. **a bondservant and apostle.** Peter identifies himself with a balance of humility and dignity. As a servant, he was on equal basis with other Christians—an obedient slave of Christ. As an apostle, he was unique, divinely called, and commissioned as an eyewitness to the resurrection of Christ (*see notes on Rom. 1:1*). **To those.** The recipients of this letter are the same as those who received Peter's first letter (cf. 3:1; 1 Pet. 1:1; see Introductions to 1, 2 Peter). **obtained.** An uncommon word often referring to obtaining something by lot (cf. Acts 1:17). It is often translated "received," and can mean "attaining by divine will." Here, Peter was emphasizing that salvation was not attained by personal effort, skill, or worthiness, but came purely from God's grace. **like precious.** Generally the Gr. word which is translated "like precious" was used to designate equal in rank, position, honor, standing, price, or value. It was used in the ancient world with strangers and foreigners who were given equal citizenship in a city. Here, Peter was emphasizing that Christians have all received the same precious, priceless saving faith. There are no first and second class Christians in spiritual, racial, or gender distinctions (cf. Gal. 3:28). Since Peter was writing to mostly Gentiles, he may have been emphasizing that they have received the same faith as the Jews (cf. Acts 10:44-48; 11:17,18). **faith.** Peter is speaking of a subjective faith, i.e., the Christian's power to believe for his salvation. Faith is the capacity to believe (Eph. 2:8,9). Even though faith and belief express the human side of salvation, God still must grant that faith. God initiates faith when the Holy Spirit awakens the dead soul in response to hearing the Word of God (cf. Acts 11:21; Eph. 2:8; Phil. 1:2). **by the righteousness.** Peter's point is that believers share the equal gift of salvation because God's righteousness is imputed to them. That righteousness recognizes no distinction between people except that the sins of some are more heinous than others. So, not only do they have faith because God gives it to them, they are saved only because God imputes righteousness to them (*see notes on Rom. 3:26; 4:5; 2 Cor. 5:21; Phil. 3:8,9*). **our God and Savior Jesus Christ.** The Gr. construction has only one article before this phrase, making the entire phrase refer to the same person. Thus, Peter is identifying Jesus Christ as both Savior and God (cf. Is. 43:3,11; 45:15,21; 60:16; Rom. 9:5; Col. 2:9; Titus 2:13; Heb. 1:8).

1:2 knowledge. This is a strengthened form of "knowledge" implying a larger, more thorough, and intimate knowledge. The Christian's precious faith is built on knowing the truth about God (cf. v. 3). Christianity is not a mystical religion, but is based in objective, historical, revealed, rational truth from God and intended to be understood and believed. The deeper and wider that knowledge of the Lord, the more "grace and peace" are multiplied.

1:3 His divine power. "His" refers to Jesus Christ. Christ's power is the source of the believer's sufficiency and perseverance (cf. Matt. 24:30; Mark 5:30; Luke 4:14; 5:17; Rom. 1:4; 2 Cor. 12:9). **all things that *pertain* to life.** The genuine Christian is eternally secure in his salvation and will persevere and grow because he has received everything necessary to sustain eternal life through Christ's power. **godliness.** To be godly is to live reverently, loyally, and obediently toward God. Peter means that the genuine believer ought not to ask God for something more (as if something necessary to sustain his growth, strength, and perseverance was missing) to become godly, because he already has every spiritual resource to manifest, sustain, and perfect godly living. **knowledge of Him.** "Knowledge" is a key word in 2 Peter (vv. 2,5,6,8; 2:20; 3:18). Throughout Scripture, it implies an intimate knowledge (Amos 3:2), and is even used for sexual intercourse (Gen. 4:1) The knowledge of Christ emphasized here is not a superficial knowledge, or a mere surface awareness of the facts about Christ, but a genuine, personal sharing of life with Christ, based on repentance from sin and personal faith in Him (cf. Matt. 7:21). **called us by glory and virtue.** This call, as always when mentioned in the NT epistles, is the effectual call to salvation (cf. 1 Pet. 1:15; 2:21; 5:10; *see note on Rom. 8:30*). This saving call is based on the sinner's understanding of Christ's revealed majesty and moral excellence evidencing that He is Lord and Savior. This implies that there must be a clear presentation of Christ's person and work as the God-Man in evangelism, which attracts men to salvation (cf. 1 Cor. 2:1,2). The cross and resurrection most clearly reveal His "glory and virtue."

1:4 exceedingly great and precious promises. That is, the promises of abundant and eternal life. **partakers of the divine nature.** This expression is not different from the concepts of being born again, born from above (cf. John 3:3; James 1:18; 1 Pet. 1:23), being in Christ (cf. Rom. 8:1), or being the home of the Trinity (John 14:17-23). The precious promises of salvation result in becoming God's children in the present age (John 1:12; Rom. 8:9; Gal. 2:20; Col. 1:27), and thereby sharing in God's nature by the possession of His eternal life. Christians do not become little gods, but they are "new creations" (2 Cor. 5:17) and have the Holy Spirit living in them (1 Cor. 6:19,20). Moreover, believers will partake of the divine nature in a greater way when they bear a glorified body like Jesus Christ (Phil. 3:20,21; 1 John 3:1-3). **escaped the corruption.** The word "corruption" has the idea of something decomposing or decaying. "Escaped" depicts a successful flight from danger. At the time of salvation, the believer escapes from the power which the rottenness in the world has over him through his fallen, sinful nature.

1:5 for this very reason. Because of all the God-given blessings in vv. 3,4, the believer cannot be indifferent or self-satisfied. Such an abundance of divine grace calls for total dedication. **giving all diligence.** That is, making maximum effort. The Christian life is not lived to the honor of God without effort. Even though God has poured His divine power into the believer, the Christian himself is required to make every disciplined effort alongside of what God has done (cf. Phil. 2:12,13; Col. 1:28,29). **add to your faith.** "Add" is to give lavishly and generously. In Greek culture, the word was used for a choirmaster who was responsible for supplying everything that was needed for his choir. The word never meant to equip sparingly, but to supply lavishly for a noble performance. God has given us faith and all the graces necessary for godliness (vv. 3,4). We add to those by our diligent devotion to personal righteousness. **virtue.** First in Peter's list of moral excellencies is a word that, in classical Gr., meant the God-given ability to perform heroic deeds. It also came to mean that quality of life which made someone stand out as excellent. It never meant

control, to self-control [4]perseverance, to
perseverance godliness, **7** to godliness
brotherly kindness, and [j]to brotherly kindness love. **8** For if these things are yours
and abound, *you will be* neither [5]barren
[k]nor unfruitful in the knowledge of our
Lord Jesus Christ. **9** For he who lacks these
things is [l]shortsighted, even to blindness,
and has forgotten that he was cleansed
from his old sins.

10 Therefore, brethren, be even more
diligent [m]to make your call and election
sure, for if you do these things you will
never stumble; **11** for so an entrance will be
supplied to you abundantly into the everlasting kingdom of our Lord and Savior Jesus Christ.

Peter's Approaching Death

12 For this reason [n]I will not be negligent
to remind you always of these things,
[o]though you know and are established in
the present truth. **13** Yes, I think it is right,
[p]as long as I am in this [6]tent, [q]to stir you up
by reminding *you,* **14** [r]knowing that shortly
I *must* [7]put off my tent, just as [s]our Lord Jesus Christ showed me. **15** Moreover I will
be careful to ensure that you always have a
reminder of these things after my [8]decease.

The Trustworthy Prophetic Word

16 For we did not follow [t]cunningly devised fables when we made known to you
the [u]power and [v]coming of our Lord Jesus
Christ, but were [w]eyewitnesses of His

6 [4] *patience*
7 [j] Gal. 6:10
8 [k] [John 15:2] [5] *useless*
9 [l] 1 John 2:9-11
10 [m] 2 Cor. 13:5; 1 John 3:19
12 [n] Phil. 3:1; 1 John 2:21; Jude 5 [o] 1 Pet. 5:12
13 [p] [2 Cor. 5:1, 4]; 2 Pet. 1:14 [q] 2 Pet. 3:1 [6] Body
14 [r] [2 Cor. 5:1; 2 Tim. 4:6] [s] John 13:36; 21:18, 19 [7] Die and leave this body
15 [8] Lit. *exodus,* *departure*
16 [t] 1 Cor. 1:17 [u] [Matt. 28:18; Eph. 1:19-22] [v] [1 Pet. 5:4] [w] Matt. 17:1-5; Luke 1:2

cloistered virtue, or virtue of attitude, but virtue which is demonstrated in life. Peter is here writing of moral energy, the power that performs deeds of excellence. **knowledge.** This means understanding, correct insight, truth properly comprehended and applied. This virtue involves a diligent study and pursuit of truth in the Word of God.

1:6 self-control. Lit. "holding oneself in." In Peter's day, self-control was used of athletes who were to be self-restrained and self-disciplined. Thus, a Christian is to control the flesh, the passions, and the bodily desires, rather than allowing himself to be controlled by them (cf. 1 Cor. 9:27; Gal. 5:23). Virtue, guided by knowledge, disciplines desire and makes it the servant, not the master, of one's life. **perseverance.** That is, patience or endurance in doing what is right, never giving in to temptation or trial. Perseverance is that spiritual staying power that will die before it gives in. It is the virtue which can endure, not simply with resignation, but with a vibrant hope. **godliness.** *See note on v. 3.*

1:7 brotherly kindness. I.e., brotherly affection, mutual sacrifice for one another (cf. 1 John 4:20). **love.** See 1 Cor. 13; 1 Pet. 4:8.

1:8 neither barren. To be barren is to be inactive, indolent, and useless (cf. Titus 1:12; James 2:20-22). With these virtues increasing in one's life (vv. 5-7), a Christian will not be useless or ineffective. **nor unfruitful.** I.e., unproductive (cf. Matt. 13:22; Eph. 5:11; 2 Thess. 3:14; Jude 12). When these Christian qualities are not present in a believer's life (vv. 5-7), he will be indistinguishable from an evildoer or a superficial believer. But when these qualities are increasing in a Christian's life, there is the manifestation of "the divine nature" within the believer (*see note on v. 4*).

1:9 these things. The qualities mentioned in vv. 5-7 (see v. 10). **shortsighted, even to blindness.** A professing Christian who is missing the virtues mentioned above is, therefore, unable to discern his true spiritual condition, and thus can have no assurance of his salvation. **forgotten.** The failure to diligently pursue spiritual virtues produces spiritual amnesia. Such a person, unable to discern his spiritual condition, will have no confidence about his profession of faith. He may be saved and possess all the blessings of vv. 3,4, but without the excellencies of vv. 5-7, he will live in doubt and fear.

1:10 make your call and election sure. This expresses the bull's-eye Peter has been shooting at in vv. 5-9. Though God is "sure" who His elect are and has given them an eternally secure salvation (*see notes on 1 Pet. 1:1-5*; cf. Rom. 8:31-39), the Christian might not always have assurance of his salvation. Security is the Holy Spirit revealed fact that salvation is forever. Assurance is one's confidence that he possesses that eternal salvation. In other words, the believer who pursues the spiritual qualities mentioned above guarantees to himself by spiritual fruit that he was called (cf. v. 3; Rom. 8:30; 1 Pet. 2:21) and chosen (cf. 1 Pet. 1:2) by God to salvation. **never stumble.** As the Christian pursues the qualities enumerated by Peter (vv. 5-7) and sees that his life is useful and fruitful (v. 8), he will not stumble into doubt, despair, fear, or questioning, but enjoy assurance that he is saved.

1:11 abundantly into the everlasting kingdom. Peter piles up the words to bring joy to the weary Christian's heart. An abundant entrance into eternal heaven is the hope and reality for a Christian who lives a faithful, fruitful life here on earth. Peter's point is that a Christian who pursues the listed virtues (vv. 5-7) will not only enjoy assurance in the present, but a full, rich reward in the future life (cf. 1 Cor. 4:5; Rev. 22:12)

1:12,13 this reason. Truth always needs repetition because believers forget so easily. Cf. 2 Thess. 2:5; Jude 5.

1:13,14 tent. Death is described aptly as laying aside one's tent (cf. 2 Cor. 5:1). Peter was likely in his seventies as he wrote this letter (likely from a Roman prison) and anticipated dying soon. Nero's persecution had begun and he was martyred in it, soon after writing this epistle. Tradition says he was crucified upside down, refusing to be crucified like his Lord.

1:14 Christ showed me. Christ had prophesied the death Peter would die almost 40 years earlier (*see notes on John 21:18,19*).

1:15 after my decease. Peter wanted to make certain that after he died, God's people would have a permanent reminder of the truth, thus he penned this inspired letter.

1:16 cunningly devised fables. The word for "fables" was used to refer to mythical stories about gods and miracles (cf. 1 Tim. 1:4; 4:7; 2 Tim. 4:5; Titus 1:14). Realizing that false leaders and their followers would try to discredit this letter, and that he was probably already being accused of concocting fables and myths in order to get people to follow him so he could amass wealth, power, and prestige as false teachers were motivated to do, Peter gave evidences in the following verses to prove that he wrote the truth of God as a genuinely inspired writer. **made known.** This word is a somewhat technical term for imparting a new revelation—something previously hidden, but now revealed. **the power and coming of our Lord Jesus Christ.** Since there is only one definite article with this phrase, the meaning is, "the powerful coming," or "the coming in power." The false teachers who were opposing Peter had tried to debunk the doctrine of the second coming of Christ (see 3:3,4) about which Peter had spoken and written (1 Pet. 1:3-7,13; 4:13). **eyewitnesses of His majesty.** The "we" that begins this verse refers to the apostles. In one sense, all of the apostles had been eyewitnesses to Christ's majesty, especially His miracles, resurrection body, and ascension into heaven. Peter, however, is referring to a more specific event which he will describe in the next verse. The kingdom splendor of Christ revealed at this event was intended as a preview of His majesty to be manifested at the His second coming (cf. Matt. 16:28; *see notes on 17:1-8*). The Transfiguration was a

majesty. 17 For He received from God the
Father honor and glory when such a voice
came to Him from the Excellent Glory:
[x]"This is My beloved Son, in whom I am
well pleased." 18 And we heard this voice
which came from heaven when we were
with Him on [y]the holy mountain.
19 [9]And so we have the prophetic word
confirmed, which you do well to heed as a
[z]light that shines in a dark place, [a]until
[b]the day dawns and the morning star rises
in your [c]hearts; 20 knowing this first, that
[d]no prophecy of Scripture is of any private
[1]interpretation, 21 for [e]prophecy never
came by the will of man, [f]but [2]holy men of
God spoke *as they were* moved by the Holy
Spirit.

Destructive Doctrines

2 But there were also false prophets
among the people, even as there will
be [a]false teachers among you, who will secretly bring in destructive heresies, even
denying the Lord who bought them, *and*
bring on themselves swift destruction.

17 [x]Ps. 2:7; Is. 42:1; Matt. 17:5; Mark 9:7; Luke 1:35; 9:35 **18** [y]Matt. 17:1 **19** [z][John 1:4, 5, 9] [a]Prov. 4:18 [b]Rev. 2:28; 22:16 [c][2 Cor. 4:5-7] [9]Or *We also have the more sure prophetic word* **20** [d][Rom. 12:6] [1]Or *origin* **21** [e]Jer. 23:26; [2 Tim. 3:16] [f]2 Sam. 23:2; Luke 1:70; Acts 1:16; 3:18; 1 Pet. 1:11 [2]NU *men spoke from God*

CHAPTER 2 **1** [a]Matt. 24:5, 24; 1 Tim. 4:1, 2

glimpse of the glory to be unveiled at the final revelation, the apocalypse of Christ (Rev. 1:1). It must be noted that Jesus' earthly ministry of healing, teaching, and gathering souls into His kingdom was a preview of the character of the earthly kingdom He will establish at His return.

1:17 Excellent Glory. A reference to the glory cloud on the Mt. of Transfiguration from which God spoke to the disciples (Matt. 17:5). **This is My beloved Son.** This means, "This One is in essence with Me." The Father is thus affirming the deity of Christ (cf. Matt. 17:5; Luke 9:27-36).

1:18 when we were with Him. Peter implied that there was no reason to believe the false teachers who denied the majesty and second coming of Christ, since they were not on the Mt. of Transfiguration to see the preview of the kingdom and glory of Christ, as were he, James, and John.

1:19 the prophetic word. The "prophetic word" refers not just to the OT major and minor prophets, but to the entire OT. Of course, all of the OT was written by "prophets" in the truest sense, since they spoke and wrote God's Word, which was the task of a prophet, and they looked forward, in some sense, to the coming Messiah (cf. Luke 24:27). **confirmed.** This translation could indicate that the eyewitness account of Christ's majesty at the Transfiguration confirmed the Scriptures. However, the Gr. word order is crucial in that it does not say that. It says, "And we have more sure the prophetic word." That original arrangement of the sentence supports the interpretation that Peter is ranking Scripture over experience. The prophetic word (Scripture) is more complete, more permanent, and more authoritative than the experience of anyone. More specifically, the Word of God is a more reliable verification of the teachings about the person, atonement, and second coming of Christ than even the genuine first hand experiences of the apostles themselves. **you do well to heed.** Peter was warning believers that since they would be exposed to false teachers, they must pay careful attention to Scripture. **a light that shines in a dark place.** The murky darkness of this fallen world keeps people from seeing the truth until the light shines. The light is the lamp of revelation, the Word of God (cf. Ps. 119:105; John 17:17). **the day dawns and the morning star rises.** These simultaneous images mark the *parousia,* i.e., the appearing of Jesus Christ (cf. Luke 1:78; Rev. 2:28; 22:16). **the morning star rises in your hearts.** The second coming will have not only an externally transforming impact on the universe (3:7-13), but also an internally transforming impact on those believers who are alive when Jesus returns, forever removing any of their remaining doubts. The perfect, but limited, revelation of the Scriptures will be replaced with the perfect and complete revelation of Jesus Christ at the second coming (cf. John 14:7-11; 21:25;). Then the Scriptures will have been fulfilled; and believers, made like Christ (1 John 3:1,2), will have perfect knowledge and all prophecy will be abolished (*see notes on 1 Cor. 13:8-12*).

1:20 knowing this first. A call to recognize His truth as priority, namely that Scripture is not of human origin. **prophecy of Scripture.** I.e., all of Scripture. This refers primarily to all of the OT, and then by implication to all of the NT (*see notes on 3:15,16*). **private interpretation.** The Gr. word for "interpretation" has the idea of a "loosing," as if to say no Scripture is the result of any human being privately, "untying" and "loosing" the truth. Peter's point is not so much about how to interpret Scripture, but rather how Scripture originated, and what its source was. The false prophets untied and loosed their own ideas. But no part of God's revelation was unveiled or revealed from a human source or out of the prophet's unaided understanding (see v. 21).

1:21 by the will of man. As Scripture is not of human origin, neither is it the result of human will. The emphasis in the phrase is that no part of Scripture was ever at any time produced because men wanted it so. The Bible is not the product of human effort. The prophets, in fact, sometimes wrote what they could not fully understand (1 Pet. 1:10,11), but were nonetheless faithful to write what God revealed to them. **moved by the Holy Spirit.** Grammatically, this means that they were continually carried or borne along by the Spirit of God (cf. Luke 1:70; Acts 27:15,17). The Holy Spirit thus is the divine author and originator, the producer of the Scriptures. In the OT alone, the human writers refer to their writings as the words of God over 3800 times (e.g., Jer. 1:4; cf. 3:2; Rom. 3:2; 1 Cor. 2:10). Though the human writers of Scripture were active rather than passive in the process of writing Scripture, God the Holy Spirit superintended them so that, using their own individual personalities, thought processes, and vocabulary, they composed and recorded without error the exact words God wanted written. The original copies of Scripture are therefore inspired, i.e., God-breathed (cf. 2 Tim. 3:16) and inerrant, i.e., without error (John 10:34,35; 17:17; Titus 1:2). Peter defined the process of inspiration which created an inerrant original text (cf. Prov. 30:5; 1 Cor. 14:36; 1 Thess. 2:13).

2:1 false prophets. Peter described false teachers in detail in this chapter so that Christians would always recognize their characteristics and methods. The greatest sin of Christ-rejecters and the most damning work of Satan is misrepresentation of the truth and its consequent deception. Nothing is more wicked than for someone to claim to speak for God to the salvation of souls when in reality he speaks for Satan to the damnation of souls (cf. Deut. 13:1-18; 18:20; Jer. 23; Ezek. 13; Matt. 7:15; 23:1-36; 24:4,5; Rom. 16:17; 2 Cor. 11:13,14; Gal. 3:1,2; 2 Tim. 4:3,4). **among the people.** "The people" is used in the NT of Israel (cf. Acts 26:17,23). Peter's point, though, is that Satan has always endeavored to infiltrate groups of believers with the deceptions of false teachers (cf. John 8:44). Since Eve, he has been in the deceit business (*see notes on 2 Cor. 11:3,4*). **secretly bring in destructive heresies.** The false teachers parade themselves as Christian pastors, teachers, and evangelists (cf. Jude 4). "Heresies" means self-designed religious lies which lead to division and faction (cf. 1 Cor. 11:19; Gal. 5:20). The Gr. word for "destructive" basically means damnation. This word is used 6 times in this letter and always speaks of final damnation (vv. 1-3; 3:7,16). This is why it is so tragic when a church makes a virtue out of the toleration of unscriptural teachings and ideas in the name of love and unity (see 2 Thess. 3:14; 1 Tim. 4:1-5; Titus 3:9-11). **denying the Lord.** This phrase exposes the depth of the crime and guilt of the false teachers. This unusual Gr. word for "Lord" appears 10

2 And many will follow their destructive
ways, because of whom the way of truth
will be blasphemed. 3 By covetousness
they will exploit you with deceptive
words; for a long time their judgment has
not been idle, and their destruction [1]does
not slumber.

Doom of False Teachers

4 For if God did not spare the angels
who sinned, but cast *them* down to [2]hell
and delivered *them* into chains of darkness,
to be reserved for judgment; 5 and did not
spare the ancient world, but saved Noah,
one of eight *people,* a preacher of righteousness, bringing in the flood on the world of
the ungodly; 6 and turning the cities of
[b]Sodom and Gomorrah into ashes, condemned *them* to destruction, making *them*
an example to those who afterward would
live ungodly; 7 and [c]delivered righteous
Lot, *who was* oppressed by the filthy conduct of the wicked 8 (for that righteous
man, dwelling among them, [d]tormented
his righteous soul from day to day by seeing and hearing *their* lawless deeds)—

3 [1] M *will not*
4 [2] Lit. *Tartarus*
6 [b] Gen. 19:1-26; Jude 7
7 [c] Gen. 19:16,29
8 [d] Ps. 119:139

times in the NT and means one who has supreme authority, whether human authority or divine authority. Peter here warns that false prophets deny the sovereign lordship of Jesus Christ. Though their heresies may include the denial of the virgin birth, deity, bodily resurrection, and second coming of Christ, the false teachers' basic error is that they will not submit their lives to the rule of Christ. All false religions have an erroneous Christology. **who bought them.** The terms which Peter used here are more analogical than theological, speaking of a human master over a household. The master bought slaves, and the slaves owed the master allegiance as their sovereign. (For an OT parallel, see Deut. 32:5,6, where God is said to have bought Israel, though they rejected Him.). Doctrinally, this analogy can be viewed as responsibility for submission to God which the false teachers had refused. Beyond this, they are probably claiming that they were Christians, so that the Lord had bought them actually and personally. With some sarcasm, Peter mocks such a claim by writing of their coming damnation. Thus, the passage is describing the sinister character of the false teachers who claim Christ, but deny His lordship over their lives. **swift destruction.** This refers to either physical death or judgment at the return of Christ (Prov. 29:1; 2 Thess. 1:7-10).

2:2 many will follow their destructive ways. Many people will profess to be Christians but deny Christ's lordship over their lives, refusing to live as obedient servants to Christ and His Word, following instead the lusts of the flesh, the world, and the devil. Such nominal Christians tragically will be included in the Lord's condemnation of hypocrites at the judgment (Matt. 7:21-23; cf. Jude 4,7). Denying the lordship of Christ while claiming to be a believer destructively infects other people and discredits the gospel. **the way of truth will be blasphemed.** The world mocks and scoffs at the gospel of Jesus Christ because of nominal Christians who do not follow the Lord they claim, and have been unmasked as hypocritical people.

2:3 By covetousness. That is, uncontrolled greed. Peter observed that the underlying motive of the false teachers was not love of the truth, but love of money (see v. 14). They exploited people through their lies. **their judgment has not been idle.** The principle that God is going to damn false teachers was set in place in eternity past, repeated throughout the OT, and "has not been idle" in the sense that it has not worn out or become ineffective. It is still potent and will come to pass (see Jude 4). **their destruction does not slumber.** Peter is personifying destruction as if destruction were an executioner who is fully awake and alert, ready to act. Because God is by nature a God of truth, He will judge all liars and deceivers (cf. Prov. 6:19; 19:5,9; Is. 9:15; 28:15,22; Jer. 9:3,5; 14:14; 23:25,26; Rev. 21:8,27).

2:4 if. This is better translated "since" because there is no doubt about the history of judgment which Peter is about to recount. Verses 4-10 are one long sentence with the conclusion to the "since" clause beginning in v. 9. Lest anyone think that God is too loving and merciful to judge the wicked false teachers and their deceived people, Peter gives 3 powerful illustrations of past divine judgment on the wicked. These illustrations set the precedents for the future and final judgment on liars and deceivers. Though God has no pleasure in the death of the wicked (Ezek. 33:11), He must judge wickedness because His holiness requires it (2 Thess. 1:7-9). **the angels who sinned.** These angels, according to Jude 6, "did not keep their proper domain," i.e., they entered men who promiscuously cohabited with women. Apparently this is a reference to the fallen angels of Gen. 6 (sons of God): 1) before the flood (v. 5; Gen. 6:1-3) who left their normal state and lusted after women, and 2) before the destruction of Sodom and Gomorrah (v. 6; Gen. 19). *See notes on Gen. 6:1,2; Jude 6.* **cast *them* down to hell.** Peter borrows a word from Greek mythology for hell, "*tartarus.*" The Greeks taught that *tartarus* was a place lower than Hades reserved for the most wicked of human beings, gods, and demons. The Jews eventually came to use this term to describe the place where fallen angels were sent. It defined for them the lowest hell, the deepest pit, the most terrible place of torture and eternal suffering. Jesus, in spirit, entered that place when His body was in the grave, and proclaimed triumph over the demons during the time between His death and resurrection (*see notes on Col. 2:14; 1 Pet. 3:18,19*). **chains of darkness.** The demons feared going there and begged Jesus during His life on earth not to send them there (cf. Matt. 8:29; Luke 8:31). Not all demons are bound. Many roam the heavens and earth (cf. Rev. 12:7-9). Some are temporarily bound (*see notes on Rev. 9:1-12*). These were, because of their sin in Gen. 6, permanently bound in darkness. **reserved for judgment.** These permanently incarcerated demons are like prisoners who are incarcerated awaiting final sentencing. *Tartarus* is only temporary in the sense that in the day of judgment, the wicked angels confined there will be ultimately cast into the lake of fire (Rev. 20:10).

2:5 did not spare the ancient world. The second illustration serving as precedent for God's future judgment on false teachers is the judgment on the ancient world through the world-wide flood (cf. Gen. 6–8). The human race was reduced to 8 people by that judgment (cf. 1 Pet. 3:20). **a preacher of righteousness.** See Gen. 6:9; 7:1. His life spoke of righteousness as he called people to repent and avoid the flood judgment.

2:6 Sodom and Gomorrah. The third precedent for a future divine judgment on the wicked is the total destruction of Sodom and Gomorrah and the other lesser surrounding cities (cf. Gen. 13; 18:16-33; 19:1-38; Deut. 29:23). This judgment destroyed every person in the area by incineration. *See notes on Jude 7.* **making *them* an example.** That is, a model, or a pattern. God sent an unmistakable message to all future generations that wickedness results in judgment.

2:7,8 delivered righteous Lot. He was righteous, as all the saved are, by faith in the true God. Righteousness was imputed to him, by grace through faith, as it was to Abraham (Gen. 15:6; Rom. 4:3,11,22, 23). There was spiritual weakness in Lot (Gen. 19:6), e.g., immorality (Gen. 19:8) and drunkenness (Gen. 19:33-35). His heart was in Sodom (Gen. 19:16), yet he did hate the sins of his culture and strongly sought ways to protect God's angels from harm. He obeyed the Lord in not looking back at Sodom (Gen. 19). In both of the illustrations where God rendered a wholesale judgment on all living people (once on the whole earth, and once in the whole region of the plain S of the

9 *then* [e]the Lord knows how to deliver the
godly out of temptations and to reserve the
unjust under punishment for the day of
judgment, 10 and especially [f]those who
walk according to the flesh in the lust of
uncleanness and despise authority. [g]*They*
are presumptuous, self-willed. They are
not afraid to speak evil of [3]dignitaries,
11 whereas [h]angels, who are greater in
power and might, do not bring a reviling
accusation against them before the Lord.

Depravity of False Teachers

12 But these, [i]like natural brute beasts
made to be caught and destroyed, speak
evil of the things they do not understand,
and will utterly perish in their own corruption, 13 [j]*and* will receive the wages of
unrighteousness, *as* those who count it
pleasure [k]to [4]carouse in the daytime. [l]*They*
are spots and blemishes, [5]carousing in
their own deceptions while [m]they feast
with you, 14 having eyes full of [6]adultery
and that cannot cease from sin, enticing
unstable souls. [n]*They have* a heart trained
in covetous practices, *and are* accursed children. 15 They have forsaken the right way
and gone astray, following the way of [o]Ba-
laam the *son* of Beor, who loved the wages
of unrighteousness; 16 but he was rebuked
for his iniquity: a dumb donkey speaking
with a man's voice restrained the madness
of the prophet.

9 [e] Ps. 34:15-19; 1 Cor. 10:13; Rev. 3:10
10 [f] Jude 4, 7, 8 [g] Ex. 22:28; Jude 8
[3] *glorious ones*, lit. *glories*
11 [h] Jude 9
12 [i] Jude 10
13 [j] Phil. 3:19 [k] Rom. 13:13 [l] Jude 12 [m] 1 Cor. 11:20, 21
[4] *revel* [5] *reveling*
14 [n] Jude 11 [6] Lit. *an adulteress*
15 [o] Num. 22:5, 7; Deut. 23:4; Neh. 13:2; Jude 11; Rev. 2:14

Dead Sea), Peter pointed out that God's people were rescued (v. 5; cf. v. 9). The Gr. word for "oppressed" implies that Lot was troubled deeply and tortured (the meaning of "tormented") with the immoral, outrageous behavior of the people living in and around Sodom and Gomorrah. Tragically, it is ordinary for believers today no longer to be shocked by the rampant sin in their society.

2:9 to deliver the godly out of temptations. The Gr. word for "temptations" can mean "an attack with intent to destroy" (cf. Mark 8:11; Luke 4:12; 22:28; Acts 20:29; Rev. 3:10) and refers to severe divine judgment. The pattern of the plan of God is to rescue the godly before His judgment falls on the wicked. **to reserve the unjust.** The wicked are kept like prisoners awaiting the sentencing that will send them to their eternal prison (cf. v. 4). The final judgment on the wicked is called the Great White Throne Judgment (Rev. 20:11-15) where all the ungodly of all the ages will be raised, judged finally, and cast into the lake of fire.

2:10 walk according to the flesh. Cf. Jude 6. Like the wicked of Noah's and Lot's time, the false teachers of Peter's era were slaves to the corrupt desires of the flesh. **despise authority.** "Authority" comes from the same Gr. word as "lord" (v. 1). The false teachers identified with Christ outwardly, but they would not live under His lordship. The two major characteristics of false teachers are emphasized in this verse: 1) lust and 2) arrogance. **presumptuous, self-willed.** "Presumptuous" is to be brazen, audacious, and defiant. "Self-willed" is to be obstinate, determined in one's own way. **speak evil of dignitaries.** Cf. Jude 8. To speak evil is to ridicule and blaspheme. "Dignitaries" refers to angels, probably wicked angels. Wicked angels have a level of existence in the supernatural world that has a dignity and a transcendent quality about it that is beyond humanity (Eph. 6:12). A certain honor belongs to those who transcend time. Consequently, there must be no flippancy regarding Satan and his angels. It may even be that these teachers tried to excuse their wicked lusts by pointing to the angels in Genesis 6 "who did not keep their proper domain" (Jude 6). The blasphemy of even bad angels by the false teachers demonstrated their arrogance and antipathy towards any authority, be it good or bad.

2:11 angels, who are greater in power. A reference to the holy angels, who are greater in power than human beings. **do not bring a reviling accusation.** Unlike false teachers who are defiant towards higher powers, the holy angels so revere their Lord that they will not speak insults against any authority. Even the archangel, Michael, recognizing the great presence and power of Satan, refused to speak evil of him (*see notes on Jude 8,9*), but called on the Lord to do so (*see note on Zech. 3:2*). No believer should be so boldly foolish as to mock or command the power of supernatural demons, especially Satan.

2:12 like natural brute beasts. Cf. Jude 10. The false teachers have no sensitivity to the power and presence of demons or holy angels, but like wild animals, insubordinate, insolent, and arrogant, they charge into the supernatural realm, cursing away at persons and matters they don't understand. **utterly perish.** Since they live like beasts who are "made to be caught and destroyed," the false teachers will be killed like beasts. False teachers cannot get beyond their own instincts and thus will be destroyed by the folly of those passions.

2:13 the wages of unrighteousness. Immorality and arrogant boldness will not pay in the end. It will rob and destroy. **carouse in the daytime.** Sinning during the day without the cover of darkness was a sign of low-level wickedness in Roman society (cf. 1 Thess. 5:7). But these false teachers are so consumed with lust and rebellion that they are pleased not to wait for the night. Their unbridled passions consume them. **spots and blemishes.** Cf. Jude 10. That is, dirt spots and scabs. They are opposite to the character of Christ (1 Pet. 1:19). The church should be like her Lord (Eph. 5:27). **carousing...while they feast with you.** The false teachers, feigning to be teachers of truth while sitting with Christians at church love-feasts, were behaving arrogantly and immorally even on such occasions intended for Christian fellowship. Though attempting to cover their corruption with religious talk, they were filthy defects on these church gatherings (cf. 2 John 9-11; Jude 12).

2:14 eyes full of adultery. The false teachers had so totally lost moral control that they could not look at any woman without seeing her as a potential adulteress (cf. Matt. 5:28). They were uncontrollably driven by lust, never resting from their sins. **enticing unstable souls.** The metaphor is from fishing and appears also in v. 8. To beguile is to catch with bait. False teachers do not capture those strong in the Word, but prey on the weak, the unstable, and the young in the faith (see 3:16; cf. Eph. 4:14; 1 John 2:13). **heart trained in covetous practices.** The word "trained," was often used for training in athletics. The false teachers have trained, prepared, and equipped their minds to concentrate on nothing but the forbidden things for which their passions lust. They are well schooled in the craft of self-fulfillment. **accursed children.** This is a Hebraism for the curse of sin being the dominant thing in their lives, thus saying that they are damned to hell for their blatant wickedness. Cf. Gal. 3:10,13; Eph. 2:1-3; 1 Pet. 1:14.

2:15 forsaken the right way. The "right way" is an OT metaphor for obedience to God (cf. Acts 13:10). **Balaam.** Cf. Jude 11. Balaam served as an illustration and example of such false prophets. He was an OT compromising prophet for sale to whomever paid him, who preferred wealth and popularity over faithfulness and obedience to God (Num. 22–24). Through a talking donkey, God kept him from cursing Israel (v. 16; cf. Num 22:21-35).

17 [p]These are wells without water,
[7]clouds carried by a tempest, for whom is
reserved the blackness of darkness [8]forever.

Deceptions of False Teachers

18 For when they speak great swelling
words of emptiness, they allure through the
lusts of the flesh, through lewdness, the
ones who [9]have actually escaped from
those who live in error. 19 While they
promise them liberty, they themselves are
slaves of [1]corruption; [q]for by whom a person is overcome, by him also he is brought
into [2]bondage. 20 For if, after they [r]have
escaped the pollutions of the world
through the knowledge of the Lord and
Savior Jesus Christ, they are [s]again entangled in them and overcome, the latter end
is worse for them than the beginning.
21 For [t]it would have been better for them
not to have known the way of righteousness, than having known *it,* to turn from
the holy commandment delivered to them.
22 But it has happened to them according
to the true proverb: [u]*"A dog returns to his
own vomit,"* and, "a sow, having washed,
to her wallowing in the mire."

God's Promise Is Not Slack

3 Beloved, I now write to you this second epistle (in *both of* which [a]I stir up
your pure minds by way of reminder),
2 that you may be mindful of the words
[b]which were spoken before by the holy
prophets, [c]and of the commandment of
[1]us, the apostles of the Lord and Savior,

17 [p]Jude 12,13 [7]NU *and mists* [8]NU omits *forever*
18 [9]NU *are barely escaping*
19 [q]John 8:34; Rom. 6:16 [1]*depravity* [2]*slavery*
20 [r]Matt. 12:45 [s]Luke 11:26; [Heb. 6:4-6]
21 [t]Luke 12:47
22 [u]Prov. 26:11

CHAPTER 3

1 [a]2 Pet. 1:13
2 [b]2 Pet. 1:21 [c]Jude 17 [1]NU, M *the apostles of your Lord and Savior* or *your apostles of the Lord and Savior*

2:17 wells without water. In this verse, Peter uses two poetic figures ("wells" and "clouds") which represent a precious commodity in the Middle East. A well without water would be a major disappointment in a hot and dry land. Likewise, false teachers have a pretense of spiritual water to quench the thirsty soul, but they actually have nothing to give. **clouds carried by a tempest.** The coming of clouds would seem to promise rain, but sometimes the storm would blow the clouds on by, leaving the land dry and hot. The false teachers might seem to promise spiritual refreshment, but were all show with no substance (cf. Jude 12). **the blackness of darkness.** That is, hell (cf. Matt. 8:12; Jude 13.)

2:18 great swelling *words* of emptiness. Cf. Jude 16. That is, ostentatious verbosity. The false teachers deceive the weak with high sounding words that masquerade as scholarship or profound spiritual insight, and even as direct revelation from God. They may contradict the plain historic teachings of Scripture which in some cases they are not able to explain properly because of their lack of adequate training and divine wisdom (cf. 1 Cor. 2:14). In reality, they say nothing genuinely scholarly, or spiritual, or divine. **allure through...lewdness.** Nevertheless, in spite of all the empty talk, false teachers entice others to their philosophies by appealing to people on the baser level. Seduction, rather than the winsomeness of truth, is their ploy. They offer people a kind of religion that they can embrace and still hold on to their fleshly desires and sensuality. Peter may also be implying that false teachers particularly aim to seduce women through sensual methods. **actually escaped...error.** The preferred translation is "barely escaping" or "trying to escape." This is a description not of saved people, but of people who are vulnerable because they have high levels of guilt and anxieties—people with broken marriages, people who are lonely and tired of the consequences of sin and are looking for a new start, even for religion or help from God. The false teachers exploit these kinds of people.

2:19 promise them liberty. False teachers promise those "trying to escape" the struggles of life, the very freedom they seek. **slaves of corruption.** The false teachers can't deliver the freedom they promise, because they themselves are enslaved to the very corruption which people are trying to escape. **overcome...bondage.** Whoever puts himself, in the name of freedom, into the hands of a false teacher, who is a prisoner himself, also becomes a prisoner. Bondage to corruption awaits all followers of false teachers.

2:20 escaped the pollutions of the world. "Pollutions" has the idea of putrid or poisonous vapors. Morally, the world gives off a deadly influence. Peter notes that at some point in time, these false teachers and their followers wanted to escape the moral contamination of the world system and sought religion, even Jesus Christ (on their terms, not His; *see notes on v. 1*). But these false teachers had never genuinely been converted to Christ. They heard the true gospel and moved toward it, but then rejected the Christ of that gospel. That is apostasy, like the people of Heb. 10:26,27. Their last end is far worse than the first (for examples of apostasy, see Luke 11:24-26; 12:47,48; 1 Cor. 10:1-12; Heb. 3:12-18; 6:6; 10:26; 38ff; 1 John 2:19; Jude 4-6).

2:21 to turn from the holy commandment. Lit., "to turn back." This verse describes the perversion and defection of the false teachers. They professed the Christian experience (the way of righteousness; cf. Matt. 21:32), and even had access to the true teachings of Scripture. But by their lives they demonstrated that they ultimately had chosen to reject Christ (cf. Heb. 10:26-31). Such false teachers as Peter was describing were not made outside Christianity. They are always bred in the church, half in and half out; but eventually they reject the truth and try to seduce others in their attempt to fulfill their self-gratification.

2:22 *dog*...sow. Two graphic analogies of an apostate. The first from Proverbs 26:11; the second is Peter's own.

3:1 Beloved. This attitude toward the readers of his letter reflects Peter's pastoral concern (cf. 1 Pet. 5:1-4). **this second epistle.** That is, second to 1 Peter (see Introduction). **your pure minds.** A good commendation which demonstrates that Peter believed that his readers were genuine Christians. "Pure" means uncontaminated, unmixed by the seductive influences of the world, the flesh, and the devil. How different the true believers were from the corrupt apostate false teachers (2:10-22). Peter sought to impress on his readers the truth they already knew so that their sanctified reason and spiritual discernment would be able to detect and refute the purveyors of false doctrine.

3:2 holy prophets. The OT prophets are in view, who were holy in contrast to the unholy false teachers. God's Word was written by those prophets in the Scriptures (*see notes on 1:19-21*). In particular those prophets warned about coming judgment (e.g., Ps. 50:1-4; Is. 13:10-13; 24:19-23; Mic. 1:4; Mal. 4:1,2), and even about the coming of the Lord (Zech. 14:1-9). **the commandment of us.** Peter is referring to the warnings which he and the other apostles had written regarding judgment (Jude 17). **apostles of the Lord.** The apostles (*see notes on Rom. 1:1; Eph. 4:11*) of Christ filled the 260 chapters of the NT with about 300 references to the second coming. NT revelation about the Christ coming to gather His own, warnings about eschatological judgments, information about the establishment of His kingdom, and teaching concerning God's bringing in eternal righteousness, are the irrefutable proof for the second coming of Christ and the judgment of the wicked.

3 knowing this first: that scoffers will come
in the last days, [d]walking according to
their own lusts, 4 and saying, "Where is the
promise of His coming? For since the fathers fell asleep, all things continue as *they*
were from the beginning of [e]creation." 5 For
this they willfully forget: that [f]by the word
of God the heavens were of old, and the
earth [g]standing out of water and in the
water, 6 [h]by which the world *that* then existed perished, being flooded with water.
7 But [i]the heavens and the earth *which* are
now preserved by the same word, are reserved for [j]fire until the day of judgment
and [2]perdition of ungodly men.
8 But, beloved, do not forget this one
thing, that with the Lord one day *is* as a
thousand years, and [k]a thousand years as

3 [d] 2 Pet. 2:10
4 [e] Gen. 6:1-7
5 [f] Gen. 1:6, 9; Heb. 11:3 [g] Ps. 24:2; 136:6
6 [h] Gen. 7:11, 12, 21-23; Matt. 24:37-39; Luke 17:26, 27; 2 Pet. 2:5
7 [i] 2 Pet. 3:10, 12 [j] Matt. 25:41; [2 Thess. 1:8] [2] *destruction*
8 [k] Ps. 90:4

3:3 knowing this first. "First," here means the preeminent matter, not the first in a list. Peter's priority in this section of his letter is to warn Christians about how the false teachers would try to deny this judgment and steal the hope of believers. **scoffers will come.** False teachers argue against the second coming of Christ or any teaching of Scripture through ridicule (cf. Is. 5:19; Jude 18). **in the last days.** This phrase refers to that entire period of time from the arrival of the Messiah to His return (cf. Acts 2:17; Gal. 4:4; 2 Tim. 3:1; Heb. 1:2; 1 Pet. 1:20; 1 John 2:18,19; James 5:3; Jude 18). The entire age will be marked by saboteurs of the Christian truth and especially the hope of Christ's return. **walking according to their own lusts.** "Walking" speaks of the way of conduct, the course of lifestyle. Peter again speaks of the lifestyle of the false teachers, which was characterized by sexual lusts (cf. 2:2,10,13,14,18), pounding home his warning. False teachers who know not the truth and know not God have nothing to restrain their lusts. They particularly mock the second coming of Jesus Christ because they want to pursue impure sexual pleasure without consequence, or without having to face divine retribution. They want an eschatology that fits their conduct (cf. 1 John 2:28,29; 3:2,3).

3:4 Where is the promise of His coming? The early church believed that Jesus was coming back imminently (cf. 1 Cor. 15:51; 1 Thess. 1:10; 2:19; 4:15-18; 5:1,2). These scoffers employed an emotional argument against imminency rather than a biblical argument. Their argument played on ridicule and disappointment. **the fathers.** The OT patriarchs, Abraham, Isaac, and Jacob (cf. Rom. 9:5; Heb. 1:1). **all things continue as *they were*.** This argument against the second coming of Christ is based on the theory of uniformitarianism, which says that all natural phenomena have operated uniformly since the beginning of the earth. The false teachers were also implying that God is absent from earth affairs. In effect, they were teaching that, "There will not be a great cataclysmic judgmental event at the end of history, because that is not how the universe works. There never has been such a judgment, so why should we expect one in the future. Instead, everything in the universe is stable, closed, fixed, and governed by never varying patterns and principles of evolution. Nothing catastrophic has ever happened in the past, so nothing catastrophic ever will happen in the future. There will be no divine invasion, no supernatural judgment on mankind."

3:5 they willfully forget. The false teachers, in their quest to avoid the doctrine of judgment, deliberately ignore the two major previous divine cataclysmic events—creation and the flood. **by the word of God the heavens were of old.** Creation was God's stepping into the emptiness and bringing the universe into existence, not by uniformitarianism, but by an instantaneous, explosive 6-day creation. Everything has not gone along in some consistent, unvarying evolutionary process. In six, 24 hour days the whole universe was created mature and complete (*see notes on Gen. 1; 2*). **earth standing out of water and in the water.** The earth was formed between two realms of watery mass. During the early part of the creation week, God collected the upper waters into a canopy around the whole earth, and the lower waters into underground reservoirs, rivers, lakes, and seas. *See notes on Gen. 1:2-9.*

3:6 by which. That is, by water. God, by creating water above and below, built into His creation the tool of its destruction. **the world *that* then existed.** A reference to the pre-flood world order. This world included the physical arrangement with the canopy above, the waters in the underground reservoirs, rivers, lakes, and seas below, and the heavens in the middle. The pre-flood world, sheltered from the sun's destructive ultraviolet rays, and with a gentle climate without rain, storms, and winds, was characterized by long life of humans (Gen. 5) and the ability of the earth (like a green house) to produce extensively. **perished, being flooded with water.** The second great divine cataclysm that defeats the idea of uniformitarianism, was the universal flood which drowned the whole earth and altered that originally created world order. According to Genesis 7:11ff., the flood occurred from two directions: first, the bursting open of the sources of water below as the earth cracked open and gas, dust, water, and air burst up; then came the breakup of the canopy when hit by all that upward flow, which sent the water from above crashing down on the earth. The deluge was so cataclysmic that the inhabitants of the earth were all destroyed, except 8 people and a representation of every kind of animal (*see notes on Gen. 7:11-24*). Clearly, by those two great events, it is clear that the world is not in a uniformitarian process.

3:7 *which* are now. Humanity, since the flood, lives in the second world order. One of the obvious differences between the two world-orders is that people live 70 years in the present world not 900 years, which was a common age of pre-Flood human beings. And Peter was making the point that there is a third form of the heavens and earth yet to come following another cataclysm. **are now preserved by the same word.** The present world system is reserved for future judgment, which will come by the Word of God just as creation and the flood came. God will speak it into existence as well, after the present order is again destroyed. **reserved for fire.** God put the rainbow in the sky to signify that He would never destroy the world again by water (Gen. 9:13). In the future, God will destroy the heavens and the earth by fire (cf. Is. 66:15; Dan. 7:9,10; Mic. 1:4; Mal. 4:1; Matt. 3:11,12; 2 Thess. 1:7,8). In the present universe, the heavens are full of stars, comets, and asteroids. The core of the earth is also filled with a flaming, boiling, liquid lake of fire, the temperature of which is some 12,400 degrees Fahrenheit. The human race is separated from the fiery core of the earth by only a thin 10 mile crust. Far more than that, the whole of creation is a potential fire bomb due to its atomic structure. As man from atoms creates destructive bombs that burn a path of death, so God can disintegrate the whole universe in an explosion of atomic energy (*see notes on vv. 10-12*). **until the day of judgment...of ungodly men.** The earth waits for the day of judgment and destruction of ungodly men. The godly will not be present on earth when God speaks into existence the judgment by fire (cf. 1 Thess. 1:10; 5:9).

3:8 one day *is* as a thousand years. God understands time much differently from man. From man's viewpoint, Christ's coming seems like a long time away (cf. Ps. 90:4). From God's viewpoint, it will not be long. Beyond that general reference, this may be a specific indication of the fact that there are actually 1,000 years between the first phase of the Day of the Lord at the end of the Tribulation (Rev. 6:17), and the last phase 1,000 years later at the end of the millennial kingdom when the Lord creates the new heaven and new earth (*see notes on vv. 10,13; Rev. 20:1–21:1*).

one day. 9 [l]The Lord is not slack concerning *His* promise, as some count slackness,
but [m]is longsuffering toward [3]us, [n]not
willing that any should perish but [o]that all
should come to repentance.

The Day of the Lord

10 But [p]the day of the Lord will come as
a thief in the night, in which [q]the heavens
will pass away with a great noise, and the
elements will melt with fervent heat; both
the earth and the works that are in it will
be [4]burned up. 11 Therefore, since all these
things will be dissolved, what manner *of*
persons ought you to be [r]in holy conduct
and godliness, 12 [s]looking for and hastening the coming of the day of God, because
of which the heavens will [t]be dissolved,
being on fire, and the elements will [u]melt
with fervent heat? 13 Nevertheless we, according to His promise, look for [v]new
heavens and a [w]new earth in which righteousness dwells.

Be Steadfast

14 Therefore, beloved, looking forward
to these things, be diligent [x]to be found by
Him in peace, without spot and blameless;
15 and consider *that* [y]the longsuffering of
our Lord *is* salvation—as also our beloved

9 [l] Hab. 2:3; Rom. 13:11; Heb. 10:37 [m] Ps. 86:15; Is. 30:18 [n] Ezek. 33:11 [o] Matt. 20:28; [Rom. 2:4] [3] NU *you*
10 [p] Matt. 24:42, 43; Luke 12:39; 1 Thess. 5:2; Rev. 3:3; 16:15 [q] Gen. 1:6-8; Ps. 102:25, 26; Is. 51:6; Rev. 20:11 [4] NU *laid bare*, lit. *found*
11 [r] 1 Pet. 1:15
12 [s] 1 Cor. 1:7, 8; Titus 2:13-15 [t] Ps. 50:3 [u] Is. 24:19; 34:4; Mic. 1:4
13 [v] Is. 65:17; 66:22 [w] [Rom. 8:21]; Rev. 21:1
14 [x] 1 Cor. 1:8; 15:58; [1 Thess. 3:12, 13; 5:23] **15** [y] Ps. 86:15; Rom. 2:4; 1 Pet. 3:20

3:9 not slack. That is, not loitering or late (cf. Gal. 4;4; Titus 1:6; Heb. 6:18; 10:23,37; Rev. 19:11). **longsuffering toward us.** "Us" is the saved, the people of God. He waits for them to be saved. God has an immense capacity for patience before He breaks forth in judgment (cf. v. 15; Joel 2:13; Luke 15:20; Rom. 9:22; 1 Pet. 3:15). God endures endless blasphemies against His name, along with rebellion, murders, and the ongoing breaking of His law, waiting patiently while He is calling and redeeming His own. It is not impotence or slackness that delays final judgment; it is patience. **not willing that any should perish.** The "any" must refer to those whom the Lord has chosen and will call to complete the redeemed, i.e., the "us." Since the whole passage is about God's destroying the wicked, his patience is not so He can save all of them, but so that He can receive all His own. He can't be waiting for everyone to be saved, since the emphasis is that He will destroy the world and the ungodly. Those who do perish and go to hell, go because they are depraved and worthy only of hell and have rejected the only remedy, Jesus Christ, not because they were created for hell and predetermined to go there. The path to damnation is the path of a non-repentant heart; it is the path of one who rejects the person and provision of Jesus Christ and holds on to sin (cf. Is. 55:1; Jer. 13:17; Ezek. 18:32; Matt. 11:28; 13:37; Luke 13:3; John 3:16; 8:21,24; 1 Tim. 2:3,4; Rev. 22:17). **all should come to repentance.** "All" (cf. "us," "any") must refer to all who are God's people who will come to Christ to make up the full number of the people of God. The reason for the delay in Christ's coming and the attendant judgments is not because He is slow to keep His promise, or because He wants to judge more of the wicked, or because He is impotent in the face of wickedness. He delays His coming because He is patient and desires the time for His people to repent.

3:10 The day of the Lord. See Introduction to Joel: Historical and Theological Themes; *see note on 1 Thess. 5:2.* "The Day of the Lord" is a technical term pointing to the special interventions of God in human history for judgment. It ultimately refers to the future time of judgment whereby God judges the wicked on earth and ends this world system in its present form. The OT prophets saw the final Day of the Lord as unequaled darkness and damnation, a day when the Lord would act in a climactic way to vindicate His name, destroy His enemies, reveal His glory, establish His kingdom, and destroy the world (cf. Is. 2:10-21; 13:6-22; Ezek. 13:30; Joel 1,2; Amos 5; Obad. 15; Zech. 14; Mal. 4; 2 Thess. 1:7; 2:2). It occurs at the time of the tribulation on earth (Rev. 6:17), and again 1,000 years later at the end of the millennial kingdom before the creation of the new heavens and new earth (v. 13; Rev. 20:1–21:1). **as a thief in the night.** The Day of the Lord will have a surprise arrival, sudden, unexpected, and disastrous to the unprepared (*see notes on 1 Thess. 5:2*). **the heavens will pass away with a great noise.** The "heavens" refer to the physical universe. The "great noise" connotes a whistling or a crackling sound as of objects being consumed by flames. God will incinerate the universe, probably in an atomic reaction that disintegrates all matter as we know it (vv. 7,11,12,13). **the elements will melt with fervent heat.** The "elements" are the atomic components into which matter is ultimately divisible, which make up the composition of all the created matter. Peter means that the atoms, neutrons, protons, and electrons are all going to disintegrate (v. 11). **the earth and the works.** The whole of the physical, natural earth in its present form, with its entire universe will be consumed. Cf. Is. 24:19,20; 34:4.

3:11 what manner *of persons* ought you to be. This is an exclamation rather than a question. It means, "How astoundingly excellent you ought to be!" This is a straightforward challenge for Christians to conform their lives to God's standards in light of the reality of coming judgment and eternity (cf. 1 Cor. 4:15; 2 Cor. 5:9). **holy conduct and godliness.** "Holy conduct" refers to the way a Christian should live life—separate from sin. "Godliness" refers to the spirit of reverence which should permeate a Christian's attitude—that which rules the heart.

3:12 looking for and hastening. One of the motives for holy conduct and godliness is expectation. "Hastening" means "eagerly desiring" that something will happen. Christians are not to fear the future day of God, but eagerly hope for it (cf. 1 Cor. 1:7; 16:22; 1 John 2:28; 3:3). **the day of God.** The "day of God" is not the same as the "Day of the Lord." The "day of God" refers to the eternal state, in preparation of which the heavens and the earth are burned up and the new creation is made. It is likely so named because of what Paul had in mind in 1 Cor. 15:28, the eternal glory of the new creation, with God being all in all. When the day of God comes, man's "day" will be over. The corrupting of the universe by man and Satan will have been terminated and judged, finally and forever. **the heavens will be dissolved.** *See notes on vv. 7,10,11.* The new world in which righteousness dwells (v. 13), requires the Lord to first destroy the old, sin-cursed universe (cf. Rom. 8:19-22).

3:13 new heavens and a new earth. The "promise" of a new universe is rooted in the OT (e.g., Ps. 102:25; Is. 65:17; 66:22). The word "new" means new in quality, i.e., different from before, not just new in chronology. **righteousness dwells.** The universe is new in quality because righteousness has settled in and taken up permanent and exclusive residence (cf. Is. 60:19-22; Rev. 21:1-7).

3:14 in peace. When Christ returns, each Christian should be found enjoying the peace of Christ which knows no worry or fear about the Day of the Lord or the judgment of Christ (cf. Phil. 4:6,7). To have this peace means that the Christian has a strong sense of assurance of his salvation and a life of obedience to Christ (cf. 1 John 4:17). **without spot and blameless.** Christians should have a spotless character and a blameless reputation. These characteristics are in graphic contrast to the false teachers (cf. 2:13), but like Christ (1 Pet. 1:18).

3:15 the longsuffering of our Lord *is* salvation. In addition to

brother Paul, according to the wisdom
given to him, has written to you, 16 as also
in all his [z]epistles, speaking in them of
these things, in which are some things
hard to understand, which untaught and
unstable *people* twist to their own destruction, as *they do* also the [a]rest of the Scriptures.

17 You therefore, beloved, [b]since you
know *this* beforehand, [c]beware lest you also
fall from your own steadfastness, being led
away with the error of the wicked; 18 [d]but
grow in the grace and knowledge of our
Lord and Savior Jesus Christ.

[e]To Him *be* the glory both now and forever. Amen.

16 [z] Rom. 8:19; 1 Cor. 15:24; 1 Thess. 4:15; 2 Thess. 1:10 [a] 2 Tim. 3:16
17 [b] Mark 13:23 [c] Eph. 4:14
18 [d] Eph. 4:15 [e] Rom. 11:36; 2 Tim. 4:18; Rev. 1:6

what he has already explained in v. 9 about the Lord's patience being the reason He delays judgment, here he adds that during the time of God's patience, Christians should engage in seeking the salvation of souls.

3:15b,16 hard to understand. Since Paul had (by the time Peter wrote) written all his letters and died, the readers of 2 Peter would have already received letters about future events from Paul. Some of Paul's explanations were difficult (not impossible) to interpret. Nevertheless, Peter uses Paul as a support for his teaching.

3:16 untaught and unstable…twist. In Peter's day (as today), there was a proliferation of foolish and hurtful perverting of apostolic teaching about the future (cf. vv. 3,4; 2 Thess. 2:1-5; 3:6-12). **to their own destruction.** The fact that distorting Paul's writings leads to eternal damnation proves that Paul's writings were inspired of God. **the rest of the Scriptures.** This is one of the most clear-cut statements in the Bible to affirm that the writings of Paul are Scripture. Peter's testimony is that Paul wrote Scripture, but the false teachers distorted it. The NT apostles were aware that they spoke and wrote the Word of God (1 Thess. 2:13) as surely as did the OT prophets. Peter realized that the NT writers brought the divine truth that completed the Bible (1 Pet. 1:10-12).

3:17 know *this* beforehand. Since Christians now know that there will be false teachers who will appear, twisting and distorting the Scriptures, they should be all the more on their guard. **beware lest you also fall.** Any time a believer seriously listens to a false teacher, he runs the risk of being led astray (cf. 2 Tim. 2:14-18; Titus 1:10-16).

3:18 grow in the grace and knowledge. Peter ends this letter with a summary statement of the same instruction with which he began it (1:2-11). Pursuing Christian maturity and a deepening knowledge of the Lord Jesus Christ will lead to doctrinal stability and prevent a Christian from being led astray. **To Him *be* the glory.** Such a call for glory to Christ demonstrates again that Peter considered Jesus Christ to be deity, equal in honor with God the Father (cf. 1:1; John 5:23).

The First Epistle of JOHN

Title

The epistle's title has always been "1 John." It is the first and largest in a series of 3 epistles that bear the Apostle John's name. Since the letter identifies no specific church, location, or individual to whom it was sent, its classification is as a "general epistle." Although 1 John does not exhibit some of the general characteristics of an epistle common to that time (e.g., no introduction, greeting, or concluding salutation), its intimate tone and content indicate that the term "epistle" still applies to it.

Author and Date

The epistle does not identify the author, but the strong, consistent and earliest testimony of the church ascribes it to John the disciple and apostle (cf. Luke 6:13,14). This anonymity strongly affirms the early church's identification of the epistle with John the apostle, for only someone of John's well known and preeminent status as an apostle would be able to write with such unmistakable authority, expecting complete obedience from his readers, without clearly identifying himself (e.g., 4:6). He was well known to the readers so he didn't need to mention his name.

John and James, his older brother (Acts 12:2), were known as "the sons of Zebedee" (Matt. 10:2-4), whom Jesus gave the name "Sons of Thunder" (Mark 3:17). John was one of the 3 most intimate associates of Jesus (along with Peter and James—cf. Matt. 17:1; 26:37), being an eyewitness to and participant in Jesus' earthly ministry (1:1-4). In addition to the 3 epistles, John also authored the fourth gospel, in which he identified himself as the disciple "whom Jesus loved" and as the one who reclined on Jesus' breast at the Last Supper (John 13:23; 19:26; 20:2; 21:7,20). He also wrote the book of Revelation (Rev. 1:1).

Precise dating is difficult because no clear historical indications of date exist in 1 John. Most likely John composed this work in the latter part of the first century. Church tradition consistently identifies John in his advanced age as living and actively writing during this time at Ephesus in Asia Minor. The tone of the epistle supports this evidence since the writer gives the strong impression that he is much older than his readers (e.g., "my little children"—2:1,18,28). The epistle and John's gospel reflect similar vocabulary and manner of expression (see Historical and Theological Themes). Such similarity causes many to date the writing of John's epistles as occurring soon after he composed his gospel. Since many date the gospel during the later part of the first century, they also prefer a similar date for the epistles. Furthermore, the heresy John combats most likely reflects the beginnings of Gnosticism (see Background and Setting) which was in its early stages during the latter third of the first century when John was actively writing. Since no mention is made of the persecution under Domitian, which began about A.D. 95, it may have been written before that began. In light of such factors, a reasonable date for 1 John is ca. A.D. 90–95. It was likely written from Ephesus to the churches of Asia Minor over which John exercised apostolic leadership.

Background and Setting

Although he was greatly advanced in age when he penned this epistle, John was still actively ministering to churches. He was the sole remaining apostolic survivor who had intimate, eyewitness association with Jesus throughout His earthly ministry, death, resurrection, and ascension. The church Fathers (e.g., Justin Martyr, Irenaeus, Clement of Alexandria, Eusebius) indicate that after that time, John lived at Ephesus in Asia Minor, carrying out an extensive evangelistic program, overseeing many of the churches that had arisen, and conducting an extensive writing ministry (e.g., epistles, The Gospel of John, and Revelation). One church Father (Papias) who had direct contact with John described him as a "living and abiding voice." As the last remaining apostle, John's testimony was highly authoritative among the churches. Many eagerly sought to hear the one who had first-hand experience with the Lord Jesus.

Ephesus (cf. Acts 19:10) lay within the intellectual center of Asia Minor. As predicted years before by the Apostle Paul (Acts 20:28-31), false teachers arising from within the church's own ranks, saturated with the prevailing climate of philosophical trends, began infecting the church with false doctrine, perverting fundamental apostolic teaching. These false teachers advocated new ideas which eventually became known as "Gnosticism" (from the Gr. word "knowledge"). After the Pauline battle for freedom from the law, Gnosticism was the most dangerous heresy that threatened the early church during the first

3 centuries. Most likely, John was combating the beginnings of this virulent heresy that threatened to destroy the fundamentals of the faith and the churches (see Interpretive Challenges).

Gnosticism, influenced by such philosophers as Plato, advocated a dualism asserting that matter was inherently evil and spirit was good. As a result of this presupposition, these false teachers, although attributing some form of deity to Christ, denied his true humanity to preserve Him from evil. It also claimed elevated knowledge, a higher truth known only to those in on the deep things. Only the initiated had the mystical knowledge of truth that was higher even than the Scripture

Instead of divine revelation standing as judge over man's ideas, man's ideas judged God's revelation (2:15-17). The heresy featured two basic forms. First, some asserted that Jesus' physical body was not real but only "seemed" to be physical (known as "Docetism" from a Gr. word that means "to appear"). John forcefully affirmed the physical reality of Jesus by reminding his readers that he was an eyewitness to Him ("heard," "seen," " handled," "Jesus Christ has come in the flesh"—1:1-4; 4:2,3). According to early tradition (Irenaeus), another form of this heresy which John may have attacked was led by a man named Cerinthus, who contended that the Christ's "spirit" descended on the human Jesus at his baptism but left him just before his crucifixion. John wrote that the Jesus who was baptized at the beginning of His ministry was the same person who was crucified on the cross (5:6).

Such heretical views destroy not only the true humanity of Jesus, but also the atonement, for Jesus must not only have been truly God, but also the truly human (and physically real) man who actually suffered and died upon the cross in order to be the acceptable substitutionary sacrifice for sin (cf. Heb. 2:14-17). The biblical view of Jesus affirms His complete humanity as well as His full deity.

The gnostic idea that matter was evil and only spirit was good led to the idea that either the body should be treated harshly, a form of asceticism (e.g., Colossians 2:21-23), or sin committed in the body had no connection or effect on one's spirit. This led some, especially John's opponents, to conclude that sin committed in the physical body did not matter; absolute indulgence in immorality was permissible; one could deny sin even existed (1:8-10) and disregard God's law (3:4). John emphasized the need for obedience to God's laws, for he defined the true love of God as obedience to His commandments (5:3).

A lack of love for fellow believers characterizes false teachers, especially as they react against anyone rejecting their new way of thinking (3:10-18). They separated their deceived followers from the fellowship of those who remained faithful to apostolic teaching, leading John to reply that such separation outwardly manifested that those who followed false teachers lacked genuine salvation (2:19). Their departure left the other believers, who remained faithful to apostolic doctrine, shaken. Responding to this crisis, the aged apostle wrote to reassure those remaining faithful and to combat this grave threat to the church. Since the heresy was so acutely dangerous and the time period was so critical for the church in danger of being overwhelmed by false teaching, John gently, lovingly, but with unquestionable apostolic authority, sent this letter to churches in his sphere of influence to stem this spreading plague of false doctrine.

Historical and Theological Themes

In light of the circumstances of the epistle, the overall theme of 1 John is "a recall to the fundamentals of the faith" or "back to the basics of Christianity." The apostle deals with certainties, not opinions or conjecture. He expresses the absolute character of Christianity in very simple terms; terms that are clear and unmistakable, leaving no doubt as to the fundamental nature of those truths. A warm, conversational, and above all, loving tone occurs, like a father having a tender, intimate conversation with his children.

First John also is pastoral, written from the heart of a pastor who has concern for his people. As a shepherd, John communicated to his flock some very basic, but vitally essential, principles reassuring them regarding the basics of the faith. He desired them to have joy regarding the certainty of their faith rather than being upset by the false teaching and current defections of some (1:4).

The book's viewpoint, however, is not only pastoral but also polemical; not only positive but also negative. John's refutes the defectors from sound doctrine, exhibiting no tolerance for those who pervert divine truth. He labels those departing from the truth as "false prophets" (4:1), "those who try to deceive" (2:26; 3:7), and "antichrists" (2:18). He pointedly identifies the ultimate source of all such defection from sound doctrine as demonic (4:1-7).

The constant repetition of 3 sub-themes reinforces the overall theme regarding faithfulness to the basics of Christianity: happiness (1:4), holiness (2:1), and security (5:13). By faithfulness to the basics, his readers will experience these 3 results continually in their lives. These 3 factors also reveal the key cycle of true spirituality in 1 John: a proper belief in Jesus produces obedience to His commands; obedience issues in love for God and fellow believers (e.g., 3:23,24). When these 3 (sound faith, obedience, love) operate in concert together, they result in happiness, holiness and assurance. They constitute the evidence, the litmus test, of a true Christian.

Interpretive Challenges

Theologians debate the precise nature of the false teachers' beliefs in 1 John, because John does not directly specify their beliefs, but rather combats the heretics mainly through a positive restatement of the fundamentals of the faith. The main feature of the heresy, as noted above, seems to be a denial of the incarnation, i.e., Christ had not come in the flesh. This was most likely an incipient or beginning form of Gnosticism, as was pointed out.

The interpreter is also challenged by the rigidity of John's theology. John presents the basics or fundamentals of the Christian life in absolute, not relative, terms. Unlike Paul, who presented exceptions, and dealt so often with believers' failures to meet the divine standard, John does not deal with the "what if I fail" issues. Only in 2:1,2 does he give some relief from the absolutes. The rest of the book presents truths in black and white rather than shades of gray, often through a stark contrast, e.g., "light" vs. "darkness" (1:5,7; 2:8-11); truth vs. lies (2:21,22; 4:1); children of God vs. children of the devil (3:10). Those who claim to be Christians must absolutely display the characteristics of genuine Christians: sound doctrine, obedience, and love. Those who are truly born again have been given a new nature, which gives evidence of itself. Those who do not display characteristics of the new nature don't have it, so were never truly born again. The issues do not center (as much of Paul's writing does) in maintaining temporal or daily fellowship with God but the application of basic tests in one's life to confirm that salvation has truly occurred. Such absolute distinctions were also characteristic of John's gospel.

In a unique fashion, John challenges the interpreter by his repetition of similar themes over and over to emphasize the basic truths about genuine Christianity. Some have likened John's repetition to a spiral that moves outward, becoming larger and larger, each time spreading the same truth over a wider area and encompassing more territory. Others have seen the spiral as moving inward, penetrating deeper and deeper into the same themes while expanding on his thoughts. However one views the spiraling pattern, John uses repetition of basic truths as a means to accentuate their importance and to help his readers understand and remember them.

Outline

I. The Fundamental Tests of Genuine Fellowship—SPIRAL I (1:1–2:17)
- A. The Fundamental Tests of Doctrine (1:1–2:2)
  - 1. A biblical view of Christ (1:1-4)
  - 2. A biblical view of sin (1:5–2:2)
- B. The Fundamental Tests of Morals (2:3-17)
  - 1. A biblical view of obedience (2:3-6)
  - 2. A biblical view of love (2:7-17)
    - a. The love that God requires (2:7-11)
    - b. The love that God hates (2:12-17)

II. The Fundamental Tests of Genuine Fellowship—SPIRAL II (2:18–3:24)
- A. Part 2 of the Doctrinal Test (2:18-27)
  - 1. Antichrists depart from Christian fellowship (2:18-21)
  - 2. Antichrists deny the Christian faith (2:22-25)
  - 3. Antichrists deceive the Christian faithful (2:26,27)
- B. Part 2 of the Moral Test (2:28–3:24)
  - 1. The purifying hope of the Lord's return (2:28–3:3)
  - 2. The Christian's incompatibility with sin (3:4-24)
    - a. The requirement of righteousness (3:4-10)
    - b. The requirement of love (3:11-24)

III. The Fundamental Tests of Genuine Fellowship—SPIRAL III (4:1-21)
- A. Part 3 of the Doctrinal Test (4:1-6)
  - 1. The demonic source of false doctrine (4:1-3)
  - 2. The need for sound doctrine (4:4-6)
- B. Part 3 of the Moral Test (4:7-21)
  - 1. God's character of love (4:7-10)
  - 2. God's requirement of love (4:11-21)

IV. The Fundamental Tests of Genuine Fellowship—SPIRAL IV (5:1-21)
- A. The Victorious Life in Christ (5:1-5)
- B. The Witness of God for Christ (5:6-12)
- C. Christian Certainties Because of Christ (5:13-21)
  - 1. The certainty of eternal life (5:13)
  - 2. The certainty of answered prayer (5:14-17)
  - 3. The certainty of victory over sin and Satan (5:18-21)

What Was Heard, Seen, and Touched

1 That [a]which was from the beginning,
which we have heard, which we have
[b]seen with our eyes, [c]which we have
looked upon, and [d]our hands have handled, concerning the [e]Word of life— 2 [f]the
life [g]was manifested, and we have seen,
[h]and bear witness, and declare to you that
eternal life which was [i]with the Father and
was manifested to us— 3 that which we
have seen and heard we declare to you,
that you also may have fellowship with us;
and truly our fellowship *is* [j]with the Father
and with His Son Jesus Christ. 4 And these
things we write to you [k]that [1]your joy may
be full.

CHAPTER 1

1 [a][John 1:1]; 1 John 2:13, 14 [b]Luke 1:2; John 1:14 [c]2 Pet. 1:16 [d]Luke 24:39; John 20:27 [e][John 1:1, 4, 14]
2 [f]John 1:4; [1 John 3:5, 8; 5:20] [g]Rom. 16:26; 1 Tim. 3:16 [h]John 21:24 [i][John 1:1, 18; 16:28]
3 [j]John 17:21; 1 Cor. 1:9; 1 John 2:24
4 [k]John 15:11; 16:24; 1 Pet. 1:8 [1]NU, M *our*
5 [l]John 1:19; 1 John 3:11 [m][1 Tim. 6:16]; James 1:17

Fellowship with Him and One Another

5 [l]This is the message which we have
heard from Him and declare to you, that
[m]God is light and in Him is no darkness at
all. 6 [n]If we say that we have fellowship
with Him, and walk in darkness, we lie and
do not practice the truth. 7 But if we [o]walk
in the light as He is in the light, we have fellowship with one another, and [p]the blood of
Jesus Christ His Son cleanses us from all sin.
8 If we say that we have no sin, we deceive ourselves, and the truth is not in us.
9 If we [q]confess our sins, He is [r]faithful
and just to forgive us *our* sins and to

6 [n][John 8:12]; 2 Cor. 6:14; [1 John 2:9-11] 7 [o]Is. 2:5 [p][1 Cor. 6:11]
9 [q]Ps. 32:5; Prov. 28:13 [r][Rom. 3:24-26]

1:1-4 As an apostolic eyewitness to Jesus' ministry, including his death and resurrection, and as one of the 3 most intimate associates of the Lord (John, Peter, James), John affirms the physical reality of Jesus Christ's having come "in the flesh" (cf. 4:2,3). In this way, John accentuated the gravity of the false teaching by immediately focusing on a strongly positive affirmation of the historic reality of Jesus' humanity and the certainty of the gospel. Although the false teachers claimed to believe in Christ, their denial of the true nature of Christ (i.e., his humanity) demonstrated their lack of genuine salvation (2:22,23). The affirmation of a proper view of Christ constitutes the first test of genuine fellowship (v. 3; see 1:5–2:2 for test two).

1:1 That which. This phrase refers to the proclamation of the gospel that centers in Christ's person, words, and works as contained in apostolic testimony. **from the beginning.** Although John's gospel uses a similar phrase meaning eternity past (John 1:1, "in the beginning"), the phrase here, in the context of vv. 1-4, refers to the beginnings of gospel preaching when the readers first heard about Jesus (cf. 2:7,24). The phrase also emphasizes the stability of the gospel message; its contents do not change but remain stable from the very beginning; it is not subject to change due to current worldly fads or philosophical thinking. **we have heard...we have seen...we have looked upon...our hands have handled.** The words used here point to the vivid recollection of the person of Jesus that John still had even in his old age. For John, even 60 years later, those memories were permanently etched on his mind as if the events had just happened. He uses terms that strongly affirm the physical reality of Jesus, for a spirit cannot be heard, gazed at for long periods ("looked upon") or touched ("handled") as Jesus was by John during His earthly ministry and even after His resurrection. **the Word of life.** This refers not only to Jesus Christ but the proclamation of His gospel.

1:2,3 manifested...seen...bear witness...heard...declare. John dramatically reemphasizes through repetition of these terms in vv. 2,3 (cf. v. 1) the authority of his own personal experience as an eyewitness of Jesus' life. Such repetition pointedly reminds his readers that John's personal testimony refutes the false teachers who boasted arrogantly and wrongly about the Christ they had never seen or known.

1:2 that eternal life...with the Father and...manifested to us. With this phrase, John accentuates the eternality of Christ in his pre-incarnate glory (cf. 5:12; John 1:4; 5:26,40; 11:25; 14:6).

1:3 fellowship with us. Fellowship does not mean social relations, but that his readers were to be partakers (or, partners) with John in possessing eternal life (cf. Phil. 1:5; 1 Pet. 5:1; 2 Pet. 1:4). John writes not only to affirm the physical reality of Jesus (vv. 1,2) but also to produce salvation in the readers. That genuine Christians are never "out of fellowship" is clear, since this verse equates fellowship with salvation.

1:4 your joy may be full. A main goal for this epistle is to create joy in the readers. The proclamation of the reality of the gospel (vv. 1,2) produces a fellowship in eternal life (v. 3), and in turn, fellowship in eternal life produces joy (v. 4).

1:5–2:2 To counter the false teachers who denied the existence or importance of sin, John affirms its reality. This affirmation of sin's reality constitutes the second test of true fellowship (cf. vv. 1-4 for test one and 2:3-6 for test three). Those who deny the reality of sin demonstrate their lack of genuine salvation. The "we" in vv. 6,8,10 is not a reference to genuine Christians but a general reference to anyone claiming fellowship, but denying sin. The "we" in vv. 7,9 and 2:1,2 is a specific reference to genuine Christians.

1:5 we have heard from Him. The message that John and the other apostles preached came from God not from men (cf. Gal. 1:12). **God is light.** In Scripture, light and darkness are very familiar symbols. Intellectually, "light" refers to biblical truth while "darkness" refers to error or falsehood (cf. Ps. 119:105; Prov. 6:23; John 1:4; 8:12). Morally, "light" refers to holiness or purity while "darkness" refers to sin or wrongdoing (Rom. 13:11-14; 1 Thess. 5:4-7). The heretics claimed to be the truly enlightened, walking in the real light, but John denied that because they do not recognize their sin. About that basic reality, they were unenlightened. **no darkness at all.** With this phrase, John forcefully affirms that God is absolutely perfect and nothing exists in God's character that impinges upon His truth and holiness (cf. James 1:17).

1:6 In spite of their claims to enlightenment and although the false teachers may have claimed fellowship with Christ, their walking in darkness refuted such claims, and consequently, demonstrated their lack of genuine salvation. The reference to "lie" in v. 6b refers to the claim of fellowship in v. 6a. **do not practice.** This points to their habitual failure regarding the practice of the truth.

1:7 A genuine Christian walks habitually in the light (truth and holiness), not in darkness (falsehood and sin). *See note on 3:9.* Their walk also results in cleansing from sin as the Lord continually forgives His own. Since those walking in the light share in the character of God, they will be habitually characterized by His holiness (3 John 11), indicating their true fellowship with Him (James 1:27). A genuine Christian does not walk in darkness but only in the light (2 Cor. 6:14; Eph. 5:8; Col. 1:12,13), and cleansing from sin continually occurs (cf. v. 9).

1:8 Not only did the false teachers walk in darkness (i.e., sin; v. 6) but went so far as to deny totally the existence of a sin nature in their lives. If someone never admits to being a sinner, salvation cannot result (see Matt. 19:16-22 for the account of the young man who refused to recognize his sin). Not only did the false teachers make false claims to fellowship and disregard sin (v. 6), they are also characterized by deceit regarding sinlessness (Eccl. 7:20; Rom. 3:23).

1:9 Continual confession of sin is an indication of genuine salvation. While the false teachers would not admit their sin, the genuine

[s]cleanse us from all unrighteousness. **10** If
we say that we have not sinned, we [t]make
Him a liar, and His word is not in us.

2 My little children, these things I write
to you, so that you may not sin. And if
anyone sins, [a]we have an Advocate with
the Father, Jesus Christ the righteous.
2 And [b]He Himself is the propitiation for
our sins, and not for ours only but [c]also for
the whole world.

The Test of Knowing Him

3 Now by this we know that we know
Him, if we keep His commandments. **4** He
who says, "I know Him," and does not keep
His commandments, is a [d]liar, and the truth
is not in him. **5** But [e]whoever keeps His
word, truly the love of God [1]is perfected [f]in
him. By this we know that we are in Him.
6 [g]He who says he abides in Him [h]ought
himself also to walk just as He walked.

7 [2]Brethren, I write no new commandment to you, but an old commandment
which you have had [i]from the beginning.
The old commandment is the word which
you heard [3]from the beginning. **8** Again, [j]a
new commandment I write to you, which
thing is true in Him and in you, [k]because

9 [s]Ps. 51:2
10 [t]John 3:33; 1 John 5:10

CHAPTER 2

1 [a]Rom. 8:34; 1 Tim. 2:5; Heb. 7:25; 9:24
2 [b][Rom. 3:25]; Heb. 2:17; 1 John 4:10 [c]John 1:29
4 [d]Rom. 3:4
5 [e]John 14:21, 23 [f][1 John 4:12] [1]*has been completed*
6 [g]John 15:4 [h]Matt. 11:29; John 13:15; 15:10; 1 Pet. 2:21
7 [i]John 13:34; 1 John 3:11, 23; 4:21; 2 John 5 [2]NU *Beloved* [3]NU omits *from the beginning*
8 [j]John 13:34; 15:12 [k]Rom. 13:12; Eph. 5:8; 1 Thess. 5:4

Christian admitted and forsook it (Ps. 32:3-5; Prov. 28:13). The term "confess" means to say the same thing about sin as God does; to acknowledge His perspective about sin. While v. 7 is from God's perspective, v. 9 is from the Christian's perspective. Confession of sin characterizes genuine Christians, and God continually cleanses those who are confessing (cf. v. 7). Rather than focusing on confession for every single sin as necessary, John has especially in mind here a settled recognition and acknowledgment that one is a sinner in need of cleansing and forgiveness (Eph. 4:32; Col. 2:13).

1:10 make Him a liar. Since God has said that all people are sinners (cf. Ps. 14:3; 51:5; Is. 53:6; Jer. 17:5,6; Rom. 3:10-19,23; 6:23), to deny that fact is to blaspheme God with slander that defames His name.

2:1 so that you may not sin. Although a Christian must continually acknowledge and confess sin (1:9), he is not powerless against it. Fulfilling the duty of confession does not give license to sin. Sin can and should be conquered through the power of the Holy Spirit (see Rom. 6:12-14; 8:12,13; 1 Cor. 15:34; Titus 2:11,12; 1 Pet. 1:13-16). **Advocate.** John 16:7 translates this word as "Helper" (lit. "one called alongside"). Perhaps a modern concept of the term would be a defense attorney. Although Satan prosecutes believers night and day before the Father due to sin (Rev. 12:10), Christ's High-Priestly ministry guarantees not only sympathy but also acquittal (Heb. 4:14-16).

2:2 propitiation. Cf. 4:10. The word means "appeasement" or "satisfaction." The sacrifice of Jesus on the cross satisfied the demands of God's holiness for the punishment of sin (cf. Rom. 1:18; 2 Cor. 5:21; Eph. 2:3). So Jesus propitiated or satisfied God. *See note on Heb. 9:5* for a clear illustration of propitiation. **for the whole world.** This is a generic term, referring not to every single individual, but to mankind in general. Christ actually paid the penalty only for those who would repent and believe. A number of Scriptures indicate that Christ died for the world (John 1:29; 3:16; 6:51; 1 Tim. 2:6; Heb. 2:9). Most of the world will be eternally condemned to hell to pay for their own sins, so they could not have been paid for by Christ. The passages which speak of Christ's dying for the whole world must be understood to refer to mankind in general (as in Titus 2:3,4). "World" indicates the sphere, the beings toward whom God seeks reconciliation and has provided propitiation. God has mitigated His wrath on sinners temporarily, by letting them live and enjoy earthly life (*see note on 1 Tim. 4:10*). In that sense, Christ has provided a brief, temporal propitiation for the whole world. But He actually satisfied fully the wrath of God eternally only for the elect who believe. Christ's death in itself had unlimited and infinite value because He is Holy God. Thus His sacrifice was sufficient to pay the penalty for all the sins of all whom God brings to faith. But the actual satisfaction and atonement was made only for those who believe (cf. John 10:11,15; 17:9,20; Acts 20:28; Rom. 8:32,37; Eph. 5:25). The pardon for sin is offered to the whole world, but received only by those who believe (cf. 4:9,14; John 5:24). There is no other way to be reconciled to God.

2:3-6 Obedience to God's commands constitutes a third test of genuine fellowship. First John presents two external tests that demonstrate salvation: doctrinal and moral. The doctrinal test consists of confessing a proper view of Christ and of sin (see 1:1-4 and 1:5–2:2), while the moral test consists of obedience and love (see also vv. 7-11). While subjective assurance of salvation comes through the internal witness of the Holy Spirit (5:10; Rom. 8:14-16; 2 Cor. 1:12), the test of obedience constitutes objective assurance that one is genuinely saved. Obedience is the external, visible proof of salvation (*see notes on James 2:14-26; 2 Pet. 2:5-11*). The false teachers' failure to obey God's commands objectively demonstrated that they were not saved (Luke 6:46). Those who are truly enlightened and know God are obedient to His Word.

2:3,4 know...keep. The repetition of these words emphasizes that those genuinely born again display the habit of obedience. Obedience results in assurance of salvation (cf. Eph. 2:2; 1 Pet. 1:14). That these two words are among John's favorites is clear since he uses "know" approximately 40 times and "keep" approximately 10 times in this epistle.

2:6 abides. This word is one of John's favorite terms for salvation (*see notes on John 15:4-10*). **just as He walked.** Jesus' life of obedience is the Christian's pattern. Those who claim to be Christians ought to live as He did (cf. John 6:38) since they possess His Spirit's presence and power.

2:7-11 Love of the brethren constitutes the fourth test of genuine fellowship. The primary focus of the moral test is obedience to the command of love because love is the fulfillment of the law (Matt. 22:34-40; Rom. 13:8-10; James 2:8) and is also Christ's new command (John 13:34; 15:12,17). True enlightenment is to love. God's light is the light of live, so to walk in light is to walk in love.

2:7 new. Not referring to "new" in the sense of time but something that is fresh in quality, kind or form; something that replaces something else that has been worn out. **new commandment... old commandment.** John makes a significant word play here. Though he doesn't state here what the command is, he does in 2 John 5,6. It is to love. Both of these phrases refer to the same commandment of love. The commandment of love was "new" because Jesus personified love in a fresh, new way and it was shed abroad in believers' hearts (Rom. 5:5) and energized by the Holy Spirit (Gal. 5:22; 1 Thess. 4:9). He raised love to a higher standard for the church and commanded His disciples to imitate His love ("as I have loved you"; cf. 3:16; John 13:34). The command was also "old" because the OT commanded love (Lev. 19:18; Deut. 6:5) and the readers of John's epistle had heard about Jesus' command to love when they first heard the gospel. **from the beginning.** This phrase refers not to the beginning of time but the beginning of their Christian lives, as indicated by v. 24; 3:11; 2 John 6. This was part of the ethical instruction they received from the day of their salvation and not some innovation invented by John, as the heretics may have said.

the darkness is passing away, and [l]the true
light is already shining.
9 [m]He who says he is in the light, and
hates his brother, is in darkness until now.
10 [n]He who loves his brother abides in the
light, and [o]there is no cause for stumbling
in him. 11 But he who [p]hates his brother is
in darkness and [q]walks in darkness, and
does not know where he is going, because
the darkness has blinded his eyes.

Their Spiritual State

12 I write to you, little children,
Because [r]your sins are forgiven
you for His name's sake.
13 I write to you, fathers,
Because you have known Him
who is [s]from the beginning.
I write to you, young men,
Because you have overcome the
wicked one.
I write to you, little children,
Because you have [t]known the
Father.
14 I have written to you, fathers,
Because you have known Him
who is from the beginning.
I have written to you, young men,
Because [u]you are strong, and the
word of God abides in you,
And you have overcome the
wicked one.

Do Not Love the World

15 [v]Do not love the world or the things in
the world. [w]If anyone loves the world, the
love of the Father is not in him. 16 For all that
is in the world—the lust of the flesh, [x]the
lust of the eyes, and the pride of life—is not
of the Father but is of the world. 17 And [y]the
world is passing away, and the lust of it; but
he who does the will of God abides forever.

8 [l][John 1:9; 8:12; 12:35]
9 [m][1 Cor. 13:2]; 1 John 3:14
10 [n][1 John 3:14] [o]2 Pet. 1:10
11 [p][1 John 2:9; 3:15; 4:20] [q]John 12:35; 1 John 1:6
12 [r][1 Cor. 6:11]
13 [s]John 1:1; Rev. 22:13
[t][Rom. 8:15-17; Gal. 4:6]
14 [u]Eph. 6:10
15 [v][Rom. 12:2]; Gal. 1:4; James 1:27 [w]Matt. 6:24; James 4:4
16 [x][Eccl. 5:10, 11]
17 [y]1 Cor. 7:31; 1 Pet. 1:24

2:9 hates. The original language conveys the idea of someone who habitually hates or is marked by a lifestyle of hate. **in darkness until now.** Those who profess to be Christians, yet are characterized by hate, demonstrate by such action that they have never been born again. The false teachers made claims to enlightenment, transcendent knowledge of God, and salvation, but their actions, especially the lack of love, proved all such claims false (see also v. 11).

2:12-14 Only two families exist from God's perspective: children of God and children of Satan (see John 8:39-44). John reminds his readers in these verses that as Christians they have been forgiven and come to know God as their heavenly Father. As a result, they are a part of God's family. They must not love Satan's family or give their allegiance to the world controlled by him (see v. 15). The word "little children" in v. 12 is general for offspring of any age, in contrast to a different Gr. word for "little children" in v. 13, which refers to young children (*see note on vv. 13,14*). **I write...I have written.** John repeats the message in these verses to emphasize the certainty of their belonging to God's family. "I write" is from John's perspective, while "I have written" anticipates his readers' perspective when they received the letter.

2:13,14 fathers...young men...little children. These very clear distinctions identify 3 stages of spiritual growth in God's family. "Fathers," the most mature, have a deep knowledge of the Eternal God. The pinnacle of spiritual maturity is to know God in His fullness (cf. Phil. 3:10). "Young men" are those who, while not yet having the mature experience of knowing God in the Word and through life, do know sound doctrine. They are strong against sin and error because they have His Word in them. Thus they overcome the wiles of the devil, who makes havoc of children (cf. Eph. 4:14). Since Satan's efforts are in falsehood and deception, they have overcome him. "Little children" are those who have only the basic awareness of God and need to grow. All are in God's family and manifest Christ's character at different levels.

2:15 Do not love the world. Although John often repeats the importance of love and that God is love (4:7,8), he also reveals that God hates a certain type of love: love of the world (John 15:18-20). In this text, John expresses a particular form of the fourth test (i.e., the test of love). Positively, the Christian loves God and fellow Christians. Negatively, an absence of love for the world must habitually characterize the love life of those to be considered genuinely born again. "Love" here signifies affection and devotion. God, not the world, must have the first place in the Christian's life (Matt. 10:37-39; Phil. 3:20) **the world.** This is not a reference to the physical, material world but the invisible spiritual system of evil dominated by Satan (*see notes on 2 Cor. 10:3-5*) and all that it offers in opposition to God, His Word, and His people (cf. 5:19; John 12:31; 1 Cor. 1:21; 2 Cor. 4:4; James 4:4; 2 Pet. 1:4). **the love of the Father is not in him.** Either one is a genuine Christian marked by love and obedience to God, or one is a non-Christian in rebellion against God, i.e., in love with and enslaved by the satanically controlled world system (Eph. 2:1-3; Col. 1:13; James 4:4). No middle ground between these two alternatives exists for someone claiming to be born again. The false teachers had no such singular love, but were devoted to the world's philosophy and wisdom, thereby revealing their love for the world and their unsaved state (cf. Matt. 6:24; Luke 16:13; 1 Tim. 6:20; 2 Pet. 2:12-22).

2:16 all that *is* in the world. Cf. James 4:4. While the world's philosophies and ideologies and much that it offers may appear attractive and appealing, that is deception. Its true and pervasive nature is evil, harmful, ruinous, and satanic. Its deadly theories are raised up against the knowledge of God and hold the souls of men captive (2 Cor. 10:3-5). **lust.** John uses the term negatively here for a strong desire for evil things. **flesh.** The term refers to the sin nature of man; the rebellious self dominated by sin and in opposition to God (Rom. 7:15-25; 8:2-8; Gal. 5:19-21). Satan uses the evil world system to incite the flesh. **eyes.** Satan uses the eyes as a strategic avenue to incite wrong desires (Josh. 7:20,21; 2 Sam. 11:2; Matt. 5:27-29). Satan's temptation of Eve involved being attracted to something beautiful in appearance, but the result was spiritual death (Gen. 3:6 "pleasant to the eyes"). **the pride of life.** The phrase has the idea of arrogance over one's circumstances, which produced haughtiness or exaggeration, parading what one possessed to impress other people (James 4:16). **not of the Father.** The world is the enemy of the Christian because it is in rebellion and opposition against God and controlled by Satan (5:19; Eph. 2:2; 2 Cor. 4:4; 10:3-5). The 3 openings presented, if allowing access to sin, result in tragedy. Not only must the Christian reject the world for what it is but also for what it does.

2:17 the world is passing away. The Christian also must not love the satanic world system because of its temporary nature. It is in the continual process of disintegration, headed for destruction (Rom. 8:18-22). **he who does the will of God abides forever.** In contrast to the temporary world, God's will is permanent and unchangeable. Those who follow God's will abide as His people forever. While God offers eternal life to His children, the present age is doomed (cf. 1 Cor. 7:3; 2 Cor. 4:18).

Deceptions of the Last Hour

18 [z]Little children, [a]it is the last hour;
and as you have heard that [b]the[4] Antichrist is coming, [c]even now many antichrists have come, by which we know
[d]that it is the last hour. 19 [e]They went out
from us, but they were not of us; for [f]if
they had been of us, they would have continued with us; but *they went out* [g]that they
might be made manifest, that none of them
were of us.

20 But [h]you have an anointing [i]from the
Holy One, and [j]you[5] know all things. 21 I
have not written to you because you do
not know the truth, but because you know
it, and that no lie is of the truth.

22 [k]Who is a liar but he who denies that
[l]Jesus is the Christ? He is antichrist who
denies the Father and the Son. 23 [m]Who-
ever denies the Son does not have the [n]Fa-
ther either; [o]he who acknowledges the Son
has the Father also.

Let Truth Abide in You

24 Therefore let that abide in you [p]which
you heard from the beginning. If what you
heard from the beginning abides in you,
[q]you also will abide in the Son and in the
Father. 25 [r]And this is the promise that He
has promised us—eternal life.

26 These things I have written to you
concerning those who *try to* [6]deceive you.
27 But the [s]anointing which you have received from Him abides in you, and [t]you
do not need that anyone teach you; but as
the same anointing [u]teaches you concerning all things, and is true, and is not a lie,
and just as it has taught you, you [7]will
abide in Him.

The Children of God

28 And now, little children, abide in
Him, that [8]when He appears, we may have
[v]confidence and not be ashamed before

18 [z] John 21:5 [a] Rom. 13:11; 1 Tim. 4:1; Heb. 1:2; 1 Pet. 4:7 [b] 2 Thess. 2:3 [c] Matt. 24:5, 24; 1 John 2:22; 4:3; 2 John 7 [d] 1 Tim. 4:1 [4] NU omits *the* **19** [e] Deut. 13:13 [f] Matt. 24:24 [g] 1 Cor. 11:19 **20** [h] 2 Cor. 1:21; Heb. 1:9; 1 John 2:27 [i] Acts 3:14 [j] Prov. 28:5; [John 16:13]; 1 Cor. 2:15, 16 [5] NU *you all know.* **22** [k] 2 John 7 [l] 1 John 4:3 **23** [m] John 15:23 [n] John 5:23 [o] 1 John 4:15; 5:1; 2 John 9 **24** [p] 2 John 5, 6 [q] John 14:23; 1 John 1:3; 2 John 9 **25** [r] John 3:14-16; 6:40; 17:2, 3; 1 John 1:2 **26** [6] *lead you astray* **27** [s] [John 14:16; 16:13]; 1 John 2:20 [t] [Jer. 31:33] [u] [John 14:16; 1 Cor. 2:12]; 1 Thess. 4:9 [7] NU omits *will* **28** [v] Eph. 3:12; 1 John 3:21; 4:17; 5:14 [8] NU *if*

2:18 the Antichrist. This is the first occurrence of the term "antichrist." Its usage is found only in John's epistles (4:3; 2 John 7). Here it is a proper name and refers to the coming final world ruler energized by Satan who will seek to replace and oppose the true Christ (Dan. 8:9-11; 11:31-38; 12:11; Matt. 24:15; 2 Thess. 2:1-12; *see notes on Rev. 13:1-5; 19:20; 20:10*). **many antichrists have come.** While the term's first occurrence refers to a particular person prophesied in Scripture, this one is plural and refers to many individuals. John uses the plural to identify and characterize the false teachers who were troubling John's congregations because their false doctrine distorted the truth and opposed Christ (Matt. 24:24; Mark 13:22; Acts 20:28-30). The term, therefore, refers to a principle of evil, incarnated in men, who are hostile and opposed to God (cf. 2 Cor. 10:4,5). John writes to expose the false teachers, the wolves in sheep's clothing, who purvey damning lies (cf. Eph. 5:11). **the last hour.** The phrase refers to the "latter times" or "last days," i.e., the time period between the first and second comings of Christ (1 Tim. 4:1; James 5:3; 1 Pet. 4:7; 2 Pet. 3:3; Jude 18).

2:19 They went out from us…none of them were of us. The first characteristic mentioned of antichrists, i.e., false teachers and deceivers (vv. 22-26), is that they depart from the faithful (see vv. 22,23 for the second characteristic and v. 26 for the third). They arise from within the church and depart from true fellowship and lead people out with them. The verse also places emphasis on the doctrine of the perseverance of the saints. Those genuinely born again endure in faith and fellowship and the truth (1 Cor. 11:19; 2 Tim. 2:12). The ultimate test of true Christianity is endurance (Mark 13:13; Heb. 3:14). The departure of people from the truth and the church is their unmasking.

2:20,21 Two characteristics mark genuine Christians in contrast to the antichrists. First, the Holy Spirit ("an anointing," v. 27) guards them from error (cf. Acts 10:38; 2 Cor. 1:21). Christ as the Holy One (Luke 4:34; Acts 3:14) imparts the Holy Spirit as their illuminating guardian from deception. Second, the Holy Spirit guides the believer into knowing "all things" (John 14:26; 16:13). True Christians have a built in lie detector and persevere in the truth. Those who remain in heresy and apostasy manifest the fact that they were never genuinely born again (cf. v. 19).

2:22,23 denies the Father and the Son. A second characteristic of antichrists is that they deny the faith (i.e., sound doctrine). Anyone denying the true nature of Christ as presented in the Scripture is an antichrist (cf. 4:2; 2 Thess. 2:11). The denial of Christ also constitutes a denial of God Himself, who testified to His Son (5:9; John 5:32-38; 8:18).

2:24,25 heard from the beginning. The gospel that cannot change. Let it remain, do not follow false teachers (cf. 2 Tim. 3:1,7,13; 4:3). Christian truth is fixed and unalterable (Jude 3). If we stay faithful to the truth, we continue to experience intimate communion with God and Christ and persevere to the full eternal life (cf. 5:11,12).

2:26 A third characteristic of antichrists is that they try to deceive the faithful (cf. also 1 Tim. 4:1).

2:27 anointing. *See note on vv. 20,21.* John is not denying the importance of gifted teachers in the church (1 Cor. 12:28; Eph. 4:11) but indicates that neither those teachers nor those believers are dependent on human wisdom or the opinions of men for the truth. God's Holy Spirit guards and guides the true believer into the truth (see vv. 20,21). If God is true (cf. 2 Chr. 15:3; Jer. 10:10; John 17:3; 1 Thess. 1:9) and Christ is the truth (cf. John 14:6), so is the Holy Spirit (cf. 5:6; John 15:26; 16:17). **abide in Him.** In response to such deceivers, the task of the genuine believer is to "walk in the truth," i.e., persevere in faithfulness and sound doctrine (see vv. 20-21; 2 John 4; 3 John 4).

2:28–3:3 This section deals with the "purifying hope" of every Christian, i.e., the return of Christ. John uses this purifying hope to reiterate and elaborate on the moral test (love and obedience) of a true Christian. The hope of Christ's return has a sanctifying effect on moral behavior. In anticipation of Christ's return and reward (cf. 1 Cor. 3:10-17; 4:1-5; 2 Cor. 5:9,10; Rev. 22:12), a genuine Christian walks in holiness of life. Those who do not evidence such behavior manifest an unsaved life. In these 5 verses, John has given 5 features of the believer's hope.

2:28 abide in Him. John repeats his emphasis on abiding (v. 27) to introduce it as the first feature of the believer's hope in 2:27–3:3. Whenever John refers to abiding he is referring to persevering in the faith of salvation; which is evidence of being a true believer (John 15:1-6). The hope of Christ's return produces the effect of continual abiding in every true believer as they long for the glorious future prepared for them. Paul called it "loving His appearing" (2 Tim. 4:8) and said those who do that are the ones who will be crowned with eternal righteousness in heaven. Abiding signifies a permanent remaining in Christ and guarantees the believer's hope. Those who truly abide continue in the faith and in fellowship with the saints (v. 19). In contrast to v. 27 ("you will abide"), however, he commands (impera-

Him at His coming. **29** [w]If you know that
He is righteous, you know that [x]everyone
who practices righteousness is born of
Him.

3 Behold [a]what manner of love the Father has bestowed on us, that [b]we
should be called children of [1]God! Therefore the world does not know [2]us, [c]be-
cause it did not know Him. **2** Beloved,
[d]now we are children of God; and [e]it has
not yet been revealed what we shall be,
but we know that when He is revealed,

29 [w]Acts 22:14 [x]John 7:18; 1 John 3:7, 10

CHAPTER 3

1 [a][John 3:16; Eph. 2:4-7; 1 John 4:10] [b][John 1:12] [c]John 15:18, 21; 16:3 [1]NU adds *And we are.* [2]M *you*
2 [d][Is. 56:5; Rom. 8:15, 16] [e][Rom. 8:18, 19, 23] [f]Rom. 8:29; 2 Pet. 1:4 [g][Ps. 16:11]

[f]we shall be like Him, for [g]we shall see
Him as He is. **3** [h]And everyone who has
this hope in Him purifies himself, just as
He is pure.

Sin and the Child of God

4 Whoever commits sin also commits
lawlessness, and [i]sin is lawlessness. **5** And
you know [j]that He was manifested [k]to
take away our sins, and [l]in Him there is no

3 [h]1 John 4:17 **4** [i]Rom. 4:15; 1 John 5:17 **5** [j]1 John 1:2; 3:8 [k][Is. 53:5, 6]; John 1:29; [2 Cor. 5:21; Heb. 9:26] [l][2 Cor. 5:21]; 1 John 2:29

tive) believers to abide. The command signals that abiding is not passive; continual, active abiding must be pursued by every genuine believer (Phil. 2:12). Salvation is eternal because of the Lord's side—He holds us (cf. John 6:37-44) and because of our side—we persevere in faith and obedience (cf. John 8:31,32). It is not unlike salvation in which God sovereignly saves, but not apart from personal faith from the one He saves. Or in the case of sanctification, God conforms us to His Son but not apart from obedience. The NT is rich with statements about God's work and the work of the believer. Paul said it well in Col. 1:29. **when He appears.** This refers especially to the Rapture and gathering of the church (cf. John 14:1-6; 1 Cor. 15:51-54; 1 Thess. 4:13-18) and the Judgment Seat of Christ to follow (cf. 1 Cor. 4:5; 2 Cor. 5:9,10). **confidence...not be ashamed before Him.** The word "confidence" means "outspokenness" or "freedom of speech." Those who are saved will have confidence at Christ's coming because they will be blameless in holiness based on abiding in Christ (Eph. 5:27; Col. 1:22; 1 Thess. 3:13; 5:23). In contrast, there will be many, like the soils in Matthew 13, who are temporary look-alike believers (see 13:20-22; cf. John 8:31), who did not believe, who did not persevere in abiding, and consequently, face only shame at His appearance.

2:29 everyone who practices righteousness is born of Him. This is the second feature of the believer's hope in 2:28–3:3. The hope of Christ's return not only sustains faith (v. 28), but makes righteousness a habit. The term for "born" is the same verb used in John 3:7 where Jesus told Nicodemus that he must be "born" again. Those truly born again as God's children have their heavenly Father's righteous nature (1 Pet. 1:3,13-16). As a result, they will display characteristics of God's righteousness. John looks from effect (righteous behavior) to cause (being truly born again) to affirm that righteous living is the proof of being born again (James 2:20,26; 2 Pet. 3:11).

3:1 what manner of love the Father has bestowed on us. This outburst of wonder introduces the third feature of the believer's hope in 2:28–3:3. The believer's hope is strengthened by the fact that God's love initiated his salvation (Eph. 1:3-6). Christ's return will unite the believer with the heavenly Father who loves His child with an immeasurable love. John expresses utter astonishment at God's love for believers in making them His children (Rom. 8:17). **Therefore the world does not know us.** The real aliens in the world are not extraterrestrials but Christians. Having been born again, given a new nature of heavenly origin, Christians display a nature and lifestyle like their Savior and heavenly Father; a nature totally foreign (other worldly) to the unsaved (1 Cor. 2:15,16; 1 Pet. 4:3,4). No wonder Scripture describes Christians as "pilgrims," "sojourners," and "strangers" (Heb. 11:13; 1 Pet. 1:1; 2:11). The Lord Jesus was unearthly in origin, and so are those born again. Our true transformed lives have not yet been manifested (*see notes on Rom. 8:18-25*).

3:2 now we are children of God. Everyone who exercises genuine saving faith becomes a child of God at the moment of belief (John 1:12; Rom. 8:16; 2 Pet. 1:4), though the truly heavenly, divine life in that person (cf. Eph. 4:24; Col. 3:10) will not be revealed until Jesus appears (*see note on Rom. 8:19*). In the meantime, the Holy Spirit is working into us the image of Christ (*see note on 2 Cor. 3:18*). **we shall be like Him.** This phrase introduces the fourth feature of the believer's hope in 2:28–3:3. When Christ returns He shall conform every believer to His image, i.e., His nature. A tension exists between the first part of the verse ("now we are children") and the latter part ("we shall be like Him"). Such tension finds resolution in the solid hope that at Christ's return the believer shall experience ultimate conformity to His likeness (*see notes on Rom. 8:29; 1 Cor. 15:42-49; Phil. 3:21*). The glorious nature of that conformity defies description, but as much as glorified humanity can be like incarnate deity, believers will be, without becoming deity.

3:3 purifies himself, just as He is pure. This is the key verse to 2:28–3:3 and introduces the fifth feature of the believer's hope in this section. Living in the reality of Christ's return makes a difference in a Christian's behavior. Since Christians someday will be like Him, a desire should grow within the Christian to become like Him now. That was Paul's passion, expressed in Phil. 3:12-14 (*see notes there*). That calls for a purifying of sin, in which we play a part (*see notes on 2 Cor. 7:1; 1 Tim. 5:22; 1 Pet. 1:22*).

3:4-24 The primary aim of this section is to combat false teachers who are corrupting the fundamentals of the faith. These verses further amplify, reiterate and emphasize the moral test already presented by John (see 2:3-6,7-11). Verses 4-10 convey that genuine believers practice righteousness, while vv. 11-24 relate that genuine believers practice love toward fellow believers. John was very concerned that Christians know how to tell the true from the false; the genuine from the artificial; true believers from false ones. He presents tests here and throughout this letter to help determine the validity of anybody's claims to be a Christian.

3:4-10 These verses deal with the Christian's incompatibility with sin. The false teachers that John combated, because of their gnostic-like concepts (see Introduction: Background and Setting), discounted the significance of sin and the need for obedience. Because of their philosophical dualism, they viewed matter as inherently bad, and as a result, any sins committed in the physical realm as inconsequential. In this section, John gives 4 reasons why true Christians cannot habitually practice sin (John 8:31,34-36; Rom. 6:11; 2 John 9).

3:4 commits sin. The verb, "commits," in the Gr. conveys the idea of making sin a habitual practice. Although genuine Christians have a sin nature (1:8), and do commit and need to confess sin (1:9; 2:1), that is not the unbroken pattern of their lives. A genuinely born again believer has a built-in check or guard against habitual sinning due to a new nature ("born of God"—v. 9; Rom. 6:12). **sin is lawlessness.** The first reason why Christians cannot practice sin is because sin is incompatible with the law of God which they love (Ps. 119:34,77,97; Rom. 7:12,22). The term "lawlessness" conveys more than transgressing God's law. It conveys the ultimate sense of rebellion, i.e., living as if there was no law or ignoring what laws exist (James 4:17).

3:5 He was manifested to take away our sins. A second reason why Christians cannot practice sin is because it is incompatible with the work of Christ. Christ died to sanctify (i.e., make holy) the believer (2 Cor. 5:21; Eph. 5:25-27). To sin is contrary to Christ's work of breaking the dominion of sin in the believer's life (Rom. 6:1-15).

sin. [6] Whoever abides in Him does not sin.
Whoever sins has neither seen Him nor
known Him.
[7] Little children, let no one deceive you.
He who practices righteousness is righteous, just as He is righteous. [8] [m]He who
sins is of the devil, for the devil has sinned
from the beginning. For this purpose the
Son of God was manifested, [n]that He might
destroy the works of the devil. [9] Whoever
has been [o]born of God does not sin, for
[p]His seed remains in him; and he cannot
sin, because he has been born of God.

8 [m] Matt. 13:38; John 8:44; 1 John 3:10 [n] Luke 10:18; [Heb. 2:14]
9 [o] John 1:3; 3:3; [1 John 2:29; 4:7; 5:1, 4, 18]; 3 John 11 [p] 1 Pet. 1:23
11 [q] [John 13:34; 15:12]; 1 John 4:7, 11, 21; 2 John 5
12 [r] Gen. 4:4, 8
13 [s] [John 15:18; 17:14]

The Imperative of Love

[10] In this the children of God and the
children of the devil are manifest: Whoever does not practice righteousness is not of
God, nor *is* he who does not love his brother. [11] For this is the message that you heard
from the beginning, [q]that we should love
one another, [12] not as [r]Cain *who* was of the
wicked one and murdered his brother. And
why did he murder him? Because his
works were evil and his brother's righteous.
[13] Do not marvel, my brethren, if [s]the

3:6 does not sin. Like the phrase "commits sin" of verse 4, the sense conveyed here is the idea of habitual, constant sinning. **Whoever sins has neither seen Him nor known Him.** If no check against habitual sin exists in someone who professes to be a Christian, John's pronouncement is absolutely clear—salvation never took place.

3:7 let no one deceive you. The word "deceive" means "to be lead astray." Since false teachers were attempting to pervert the fundamentals of the faith, the possibility existed that some Christians might be fooled into accepting what they were advocating. To prevent this deception from occurring, John repeatedly emphasized the basics of Christianity, e.g., the need for obedience, the need for love, and the need for a proper view of Christ (see Introduction: Historical and Theological Themes). **practices righteousness.** The genuine believer's habitual lifestyle of righteousness stands in sharp contrast to those false teachers who practiced sin (cf. vv. 4,6). Since Christ died on the cross to transform sinners, those truly born again have replaced the habit of sin with the habit of righteous living (Rom. 6:13,14). **just as He is righteous.** Those who are truly born again reflect the divine nature of the Son. They behave like Him, manifesting the power of His life in them (Gal. 2:20).

3:8 He who sins. This phrase means "who habitually practice sin" (*see notes on vv. 4,6*). **of the devil.** The phrase gives the source of the false teachers' actions. The term "devil" means "accuser" or "slanderer." Not only does Satan ("adversary") oppose God and his plan, but is the originator and instigator of sin and rebellion against God and His law (v. 4; *see notes on Eph. 6:10-17*). Therefore, all the unsaved are under the diabolic influence of Satan. Their sinful lifestyle reflects their satanic origin (*see note on Eph. 2:1*). John contrasts the children of God with the children of Satan in terms of their actions. While those who are truly born again reflect the habit of righteousness, Satan's children practice sin. **from the beginning.** Since Satan was originally created as perfect and only later rebelled against God (Is. 14:12-14; Ezek. 24:12-17), John probably means the moment of his rebellion against God, the beginning of his rebellious career. Since sin characterizes him completely, so everyone characterized by sin must derive from him (cf. John 8:44). **For this purpose...that He might destroy.** A third reason why Christians cannot practice sin is because Christ came to destroy the works of the arch-sinner, Satan. The devil is still operating, but he has been defeated and in Christ we escape his tyranny. The day will come when all of Satan's activity will cease in the universe and he will be sent to hell forever (Rev. 20:10). **works of the devil.** This summarizes a variety of the devil's activities: sin, rebellion, temptation, ruling the world, persecution and accusation of saints, instigation of false teachers, power of death (e.g., Luke 8:12; John 8:44; Acts 5:3; 1 Cor. 7:5; 2 Cor. 4:4; Eph. 6:11,12; 1 Thess. 2:18; Heb. 2:14; Rev. 12:10).

3:9 The fourth reason why Christians cannot practice sin is because it is incompatible with the ministry of the Holy Spirit, who has imparted a new nature to the believer (John 3:5-8). **born of God.** John wrote here of the new birth (John 3:7). When people become Christians, God makes them new creatures with new natures (2 Cor. 5:17). Believers have God's characteristics because they have been born into God's family. This new nature exhibits the habitual character of righteousness produced by the Holy Spirit (Gal. 5:22-24). John repeats this phrase twice for emphasis. **His seed.** The new birth involves the acquisition of a seed, which refers to the principle of life of God imparted to the believer at salvation's new birth. John uses this image of a planted seed to picture the divine element involved in being born again. *See notes on 1 Peter 1:23-25.* **remains.** The word conveys the idea of the permanence of the new birth which cannot be reversed, for those who are truly born again are permanently transformed into a new creation (2 Cor. 5:17; Gal. 6:15; Eph. 2:10). **he cannot sin.** This phrase once again conveys the idea of habitual sinning (see vv. 4,6).

3:10 This summary verse is the key to vv. 4-10. Only two kinds of children exist in the world: children of God and children of Satan. No one can belong to both families simultaneously. Either one belongs to God's family and exhibits His righteous character or one belongs to Satan's family and exhibits his sinful nature.

3:10b he who does not love his brother. This phrase introduces the readers to the second aspect of the moral test, i.e., the test of love (as in 2:7-11). John develops this thought through vv. 11-24. The false teachers not only had an erroneous view of Christ's nature and displayed disobedience to God's commands, but they also displayed a distinct lack of love for true believers, who rejected their heretical teaching.

3:11-24 John elaborates on the love life of genuine believers. For those who are truly born again, love is an indispensable characteristic. The new nature or "seed" (v. 9) that God imparts not only exhibits holiness but also love as a habitual characteristic (John 13:35; Rom. 5:5; 1 Thess. 4:9). Those who practice love give proof of the new birth. Those who do not have never been born again.

3:11 from the beginning. Since the beginning of gospel proclamation, love has been a central theme of Christianity (*see notes on 1:1; 2:7*). John emphasizes what they heard "from the beginning" (1:1; 2:7,24) to emphasize that the false teachers were preventing that which God, through the apostles, proclaimed. **we should love one another.** This phrase highlights the habit of love displayed by those possessing the new nature. Love is not merely an optional duty for someone claiming to be a Christian, but proof positive that one truly has been born again (John 15:12; 1 Pet. 1:22,23).

3:12-24 As noted throughout this epistle, John often repeated the same truths, expanding on them to allow his readers to hear them in new and fresh ways. Each time he presents the same truths in "new" packages, which expand on a particular aspect of their significance or approach the subject from a slightly different angle. Verses 12-17 address the characteristic lack of love displayed by the children of the devil, while in vv. 18-24 he talks about the characteristics of love displayed by the children of God (see also comments on v. 10).

3:12 Cain. Scripture presents Cain outwardly as a God-worshiper who even offered sacrifice (Gen. 4:3-5). Cain's murderous actions, however, revealed that inwardly he was a child of the Devil (cf. John 8:44). ***who* was of the wicked one and murdered his brother.** In

world hates you. 14 We know that we have
passed from death to life, because we love
the brethren. He who does not love [3]*his*
brother abides in death. 15 [t]Whoever hates
his brother is a murderer, and you know that
[u]no murderer has eternal life abiding in him.

The Outworking of Love

16 [v]By this we know love, [w]because He
laid down His life for us. And we also
ought to lay down *our* lives for the
brethren. 17 But [x]whoever has this world's
goods, and sees his brother in need, and
shuts up his heart from him, how does the
love of God abide in him?
18 My little children, [y]let us not love in
word or in tongue, but in deed and in truth.
19 And by this we [4]know [z]that we are of the
truth, and shall [5]assure our hearts before
Him. 20 [a]For if our heart condemns us, God
is greater than our heart, and knows all
things. 21 Beloved, if our heart does not
condemn us, [b]we have confidence toward
God. 22 And [c]whatever we ask we receive
from Him, because we keep His commandments [d]and do those things that are pleasing in His sight. 23 And this is His commandment: that we should believe on the
name of His Son Jesus Christ [e]and love one
another, as He gave [6]us commandment.

The Spirit of Truth and the Spirit of Error

24 Now [f]he who keeps His commandments [g]abides in Him, and He in him. And
[h]by this we know that He abides in us, by
the Spirit whom He has given us.
4 Beloved, do not believe every spirit,
but [a]test the spirits, whether they are
of God; because [b]many false prophets have
gone out into the world. 2 By this you

14 [3] NU omits *his brother*
15 [t] Matt. 5:21; John 8:44 [u] [Gal. 5:20, 21; Rev. 21:8]
16 [v] [John 3:16] [w] John 10:11; 15:13; Gal. 2:20
17 [x] Deut. 15:7
18 [y] Ezek. 33:31
19 [z] John 18:37 [4] NU *shall know* [5] *persuade, set at rest*
20 [a] [1 Cor. 4:4, 5]
21 [b] [Heb. 10:22; 1 John 2:28; 5:14]
22 [c] Ps. 34:15; [John 15:7]; 1 John 5:14, 15 [d] John 8:29; Heb. 13:21
23 [e] Matt. 22:39 [6] M omits *us*
24 [f] John 14:23 [g] John 14:21; 17:21 [h] John 14:17; Rom. 8:9, 14, 16; 1 Thess. 4:8; 1 John 4:13

CHAPTER 4 1 [a] 1 Cor. 14:29 [b] Matt. 24:5

vv. 12-17, John presents the first of three behaviors of the devil's children manifesting their lack of love—murder, the ultimate expression of hate. **his works were evil.** Cain's offering was not acceptable because he was sinful (cf. Gen. 4:5). Jealousy was behind his hate and murder, as in the case of the religious leaders who had Christ executed.

3:13 the world hates you. History is filled with stories of the persecution of the saints by the world (Heb. 11:36-40). This does not surprise believers because hateful Satan is their father (v. 10).

3:14 passed from death to life, because we love. Becoming a Christian is a resurrection from death to life, and a turning of hate to love (cf. Gal. 5:6,22). A lack of love indicates that one is spiritually dead. Love is the sure test of whether someone has experienced the new birth or is still in the darkness of spiritual death (2:9,11). **abides in death.** Someone who is characterized by hate has never experienced the new birth.

3:15 Whoever hates his brother is a murderer. John presents the second of 3 characteristics of the devil's children with respect to their lack of love. Hatred is spiritually the same as murder in the eyes of God, i.e., the attitude is equal to the act. Hate is the seed that leads to murder, as seen in the example of the hatred of Cain for Abel that resulted in murder (*see notes on Matt. 5:20-22*; cf. Gal. 5:19-21; Rev. 22:15).

3:16 By this we know love. With this phrase, John introduces the standard of love that is reflected in genuine Christianity. It becomes the measuring stick for every expression of love (see v. 18). John presents the third characteristics of Satan's children in terms of their lack of love. Satan's children are marked by indifference toward other's needs (see also vv. 12,15). **He laid down His life for us.** This expression is unique to John (John 10:11,15,17,18; 13:37,38; 15:13) and speaks of divesting oneself of something. Christian love is self-sacrificing and giving. Christ's giving up his life for believers epitomized the true nature of Christian love (John 15:12,13; Phil. 2:5-8; 1 Pet. 2:19-23). **we also ought to lay down *our* lives for the brethren.** God calls Christians to that same standard of love for one another as He had for us (see v. 16a).

3:17 whoever has this world's goods...and shuts up his heart. True love is not limited to supreme sacrifices (v. 16), but shows up in lesser ones. Genuine Christian love expresses itself in sacrificial giving to other Christian's needs (i.e., "his brother"). It is a practical love that finds motivation in helping others (1 Tim. 6:17-19; Heb. 13:16; James 2:14-17). Where it does not exist, it is questionable that God's love is present. If that is so, it is also questionable whether the person is the Lord's child (v. 14).

3:18 in word or in tongue...in deed and in truth. Claiming to love is not enough. Love is not sentiment, but deeds.

3:19 by this we know. A lifestyle of love in action is the demonstrable proof of salvation (see v. 16). **shall assure our hearts before Him.** John gives 3 benefits of love for the true Christian. The first benefit is assurance of salvation since love in action is the test of Christian profession (cf. 4:7; John 13:34,35).

3:20 if our heart condemns us, God is greater. God knows those who are truly His (2 Tim. 2:19) and wants to assure His own of their salvation. Although Christians may have insecurities and doubts about salvation, God does not condemn them (Rom. 8:10). Displaying love as a pattern of life, is the proof that believers stand uncondemned before God.

3:21 confidence toward God. Love banishes self-condemnation. When a Christian recognizes in his life the manifestation of love in deeds and actions, it results in confidence about his relationship with God.

3:22 The second benefit of love is answered prayer (see v. 19). Since love is the heart of obedience to the law (cf. Matt. 22:37-40; Rom. 13:8-10), its presence in a life evidences submission to God which He blesses by answered prayers.

3:23,24 Cf. 4:13. These verses again repeat the 3 features of this epistle—believing, loving, and obeying—which are the major evidences of true salvation. The third benefit of love is the abiding presence and empowering of the Holy Spirit.

4:1-6 John turns from the importance of love to the importance of belief in God's truth. He focuses once again on the doctrinal test and emphasizes the need to obey sound teaching (Matt. 24:11; 2 Pet. 2,3; Jude 3). Scripture presents stern warnings against false doctrine. From his temptation of Eve on, Satan has sought to distort and deny God's Word (Gen. 3:1-5). He is the ultimate demonic source behind all false teachers and false doctrine (2 Cor. 11:13,14). In this section, John gives two doctrinal tests to determine truth from error and false teachers from true teachers.

4:1 do not believe every spirit. The mention of the Holy Spirit in 3:24 prompts John to inform his readers that those other spirits exist, i.e., demonic spirits, who produce false prophets and false teachers to propagate their false doctrine (*see notes on 1 Tim. 4:1,2*). Christians are to have a healthy skepticism regarding any teaching, unlike some among John's congregations who were too open minded to anyone

know the Spirit of God: [c]Every spirit that
confesses that Jesus Christ has come in the
flesh is of God, **3** and every spirit that does
not confess [1]that Jesus [2]Christ has come in
the flesh is not of God. And this is the *spirit* of the Antichrist, which you have heard
was coming, and is now already in the
world.
4 You are of God, little children, and
have overcome them, because He who is
in you is greater than [d]he who is in the
world. **5** [e]They are of the world. Therefore they speak *as* of the world, and [f]the
world hears them. **6** We are of God. He
who knows God hears us; he who is not
of God does not hear us. [g]By this we
know the spirit of truth and the spirit of
error.

Knowing God Through Love

7 [h]Beloved, let us love one another, for
love is of God; and everyone who [i]loves is
born of God and knows God. **8** He who
does not love does not know God, for
God is love. **9** [j]In this the love of God was
manifested toward us, that God has sent
His only begotten [k]Son into the world,
that we might live through Him. **10** In this
is love, [l]not that we loved God, but that
He loved us and sent His Son [m]*to be* the

2 [c] [Rom. 10:8-10]; 1 Cor. 12:3; 1 John 5:1
3 [1] NU omits *that* [2] NU omits *Christ has come in the flesh*
4 [d] John 14:30; 16:11
5 [e] John 3:31 [f] John 15:19; 17:14
6 [g] [1 Cor. 2:12-16]
7 [h] 1 John 3:10, 11, 23 [i] 1 Thess. 4:9; [1 John 3:14]
9 [j] Rom. 5:8 [k] Is. 9:6, 7; John 3:16
10 [l] Titus 3:5 [m] 1 John 2:2

claiming a new teaching regarding the faith. Christians are to be like the Bereans who, as students of the Word, examined the Scriptures to determine truth and error (Acts 17:11,12). **test.** The word "test" is a metallurgist's term used for assaying metals to determine their purity and value. Christians must test any teaching with a view to approving or disapproving it (*see notes on 1 Thess. 5:20-22*), rigorously comparing any teaching to the Scripture. **the spirits...many false prophets.** By juxtaposing "spirits" with "false prophets" John reminds his readers that behind human teachers who propagate false doctrine and error are demons inspired by Satan (*see notes on 1 Thess. 5:20-22*; cf. Acts 20:28-30). Human false prophets and teachers are the physical expressions of demonic, spiritual sources (Matt. 7:15; Mark 13:22).

4:2 By this you know the Spirit of God. John gives a measuring stick to determine whether the propagator of the message is a demon spirit or the Holy Spirit. **Jesus Christ has come in the flesh.** This is the first test of a true teacher: they acknowledge and proclaim that Jesus is God incarnate in human flesh. The Gr. construction does not mean that they confess Christ as having come to earth, but that they confess that He came in the flesh to the earth, i.e., his human body was physically real. Both the full humanity and full deity of Jesus must be equally maintained by the teacher who is to be considered genuinely of the Spirit. The Holy Spirit testifies to the true nature of the Son, while Satan and his forces distort and deny that true nature. John accentuates the crucial importance of sound doctrine expressed in God's Word as the only absolute and trustworthy standard (cf. Is. 8:20).

4:3 the *spirit* of the Antichrist. These false teachers who denied the true nature of the Son (see Introduction: Background and Setting) are to be identified among the antichrists in 2:28,29 (2 John 7). The same demonic deception that will work to produce the final world ruler (*see notes on Rev. 13:1-8*) who rules as the false Christ is always actively seeking to distort Jesus Christ's true nature, perverting the gospel. The final Antichrist will not be something new, but will be the ultimate embodiment of all the antichrist spirits that have perverted truth and propagated satanic lies since the beginning. This is similar to 2 Thess. 2:3-8, where the man of lawlessness (Antichrist) is still to be revealed, but the mystery of lawlessness is already at work.

4:4 He who is in you is greater. Believers need to be aware and alert to false teaching, but not afraid, since those who have experienced the new birth with its indwelling of the Holy Spirit gave an built-in check against false teaching (cf. 2:20,27). The Holy Spirit leads into sound doctrine for genuine Christians evidencing that salvation has actually occurred (cf. Rom. 8:17). True believers have nothing to fear, for even Satan's hosts with their perversions can't take them out of the Lord's hand. Here, as in 2:18-27, protection against error or victory over it are guaranteed by sound doctrine and the indwelling Holy Spirit who illumines the mind.

4:5,6 they speak *as* of the world...He who knows God hears us. John gives the second test of a true teacher: they speak God's word, following apostolic doctrine.

4:6 By this we know the spirit of truth and the spirit of error. The OT and NT are the sole standards by which all teaching is to be tested. In contrast, demonically inspired teachers either reject the teaching of God's Word or add elements to it (2 Cor. 4:2; Rev. 22:18,19).

4:7-21 True to his pattern to develop the same subjects, each time broadening, expanding, and enhancing their significance, John returns once again to the moral test of love. These verses constitute one long unit describing what perfect love is and that it is available to men. In John's third and last discussion of love in this letter (see also 2:7-11; 3:10-14), he gives 5 reasons why Christians love.

4:7,8 love is of God...God is love. John introduces the reader to the first of 5 reasons why Christians love: because God is the essence of love. The gnostics believed that God was immaterial spirit and light, but never defined the source of love as coming from His inmost being. As He is spirit (John 4:24), light (1:5), and a consuming fire (Heb. 12:9), so He is love. Love is inherent in all He is and does. Even His judgment and wrath is perfectly harmonized with His love.

4:7 let us love one another. This phrase in v. 7 is the key to the entire section (see v. 21). The original conveys the idea of making sure that love is a habitual practice. He has already written that those who are truly born again do exhibit the characteristic habit of love (cf. 2:10,11; 3:14). **everyone who loves is born of God.** Those who are born again receive God's nature (cf. 2 Pet. 1:4). Since God's nature exhibits love as a chief characteristic (see also v. 8), God's children will also reflect that love.

4:8 He who does not love does not know God. Someone may profess to be a Christian but only those who display love like their heavenly Father actually possess His divine nature and are truly born again.

4:9 John introduces the reader to the second of 5 reasons why Christians love: to follow the supreme example of God's sacrificial love in sending His Son for us. The judgment of sin on the cross was the supreme example of God's love, for He poured out His wrath on His beloved Son in place of sinners (John 3:14-16; Rom. 5:8; 2 Cor. 5:21; Eph. 5:1,2; *see note on Titus 3:4*). **only begotten.** Over half of the NT's uses of this term are by John (e.g., John 1:14,18; 3:16,18). John always uses it of Christ to picture His unique relationship to the Father, His pre-existence, and His distinctness from creation. The term emphasizes the uniqueness of Christ, as the only one of His kind. It was He whom the Father sent into the world as the greatest gift ever given (John 17:3; 2 Cor. 8:9) so that we might have life eternal (cf. John 3:14,15,49-52; 12:24).

propitiation for our sins. 11 Beloved, [n]if
God so loved us, we also ought to love
one another.

Seeing God Through Love

12 [o]No one has seen God at any time. If
we love one another, God abides in us, and
His love has been perfected in us. 13 [p]By
this we know that we abide in Him, and
He in us, because He has given us of His
Spirit. 14 And [q]we have seen and testify
that [r]the Father has sent the Son *as* Savior
of the world. 15 [s]Whoever confesses that
Jesus is the Son of God, God abides in him,
and he in God. 16 And we have known and
believed the love that God has for us. God
is love, and [t]he who abides in love abides
in God, and God [u]in him.

The Consummation of Love

17 Love has been perfected among us in
this: that [v]we may have boldness in the
day of judgment; because as He is, so are
we in this world. 18 There is no fear in love;
but perfect love casts out fear, because fear
involves torment. But he who fears has not
been made perfect in love. 19 [w]We love
[3]Him because He first loved us.

Obedience by Faith

20 [x]If someone says, "I love God," and
hates his brother, he is a liar; for he who
does not love his brother whom he has
seen, [4]how can he love God [y]whom he has
not seen? 21 And [z]this commandment we
have from Him: that he who loves God
must love his brother also.

5 Whoever believes that [a]Jesus is the
Christ is [b]born of God, and everyone
who loves Him who begot also loves him
who is begotten of Him. 2 By this we know
that we love the children of God, when we
love God and [c]keep His commandments.
3 [d]For this is the love of God, that we keep
His commandments. And [e]His commandments are not burdensome. 4 For [f]what-

11 [n] Matt. 18:33
12 [o] John 1:18; 1 Tim. 6:16; 1 John 4:20
13 [p] John 14:20
14 [q] John 1:14 [r] John 3:17; 4:42; 1 John 2:2
15 [s] [Rom. 10:9]; 1 John 3:23; 4:2; 5:1,5
16 [t] [1 John 3:24] [u] [John 14:23]
17 [v] [James 2:13]; 1 John 2:28
19 [w] 1 John 4:10 [3] NU omits *Him*
20 [x] [1 John 2:4] [y] 1 Pet. 1:8; 1 John 4:12 [4] NU *he cannot*
21 [z] Lev. 19:18; [Matt. 5:43, 44; 22:39]; John 13:34

CHAPTER 5

1 [a] 1 John 2:22; 4:2, 15 [b] John 1:13
2 [c] John 15:10; 2 John 6
3 [d] John 14:15; 2 John 6 [e] Mic. 6:8; Matt. 11:30; 23:4
4 [f] John 16:33

4:10 propitiation for our sins. For the word's meaning, *see note on 2:2.* Hebrews 9:5 translates a form of this word as "the mercy seat." Christ lit. became our mercy seat like the one in the Holy of Holies, where the High-Priest splattered the blood of the sacrifice on the Day of Atonement (Lev. 16:15). Christ did this when His blood, spilled on behalf of others, satisfied the demands of God's holy justice and wrath against sin.

4:11 God's sending His Son gives Christians not only salvation privilege, but obligation to follow this pattern of sacrificial love. Christian love must be self-sacrificing like God's love.

4:12 John introduces the reader to the third of 5 reasons why Christians love: because love is the heart of Christian witness. Nobody can see God loving since His is invisible. Jesus no longer is in the world to manifest the love of God. The only demonstration of God's love in this age is the church. That testimony is critical (John 13:35; 2 Cor. 5:18-20). John's argument in vv. 7-12 can be summed up as: love originated in God, was manifested in His Son, and demonstrated in His people.

4:13-16 John introduces the reader to the fourth of 5 reasons why Christians love: because love is the Christian's assurance (*see notes on 3:16-23*).

4:15 whoever confesses. *See note on v. 2.* This refers to the doctrinal test (cf. vv. 1-6; 1:1-4; 2:23).

4:17-20 John introduces the reader to the fifth reason why Christians love: because love is the Christian's confidence in judgment (*see notes on 3:16-23*).

4:17 Love…perfected among us. He is not suggesting sinless perfection, but rather mature love marked by confidence in the face of judgment. Confidence is a sign that love is mature. **as He is, so are we.** Jesus was God's Son in whom He was well pleased on earth; we also are God's children (3:11) and the objects of His gracious goodness. If Jesus called God Father, so may we, since we are accepted in the Beloved (Eph. 1:6). In v. 18, the same truth is stated negatively. The love that builds confidence also banishes fears. We love God and reverence Him, but we do not love God and come to Him in love, and at the same time, hide from Him in terror (cf. Rom. 8:14,15; 2 Tim. 1:7). Fear involves torment or punishment, a reality the sons of God will never experience, because they are forgiven.

4:21 This verse summarizes chap. 4. One cannot love God without first loving his fellow believer. A claim to love God is a delusion if not accompanied by unselfish love for other Christians.

5:1-5 John introduces the subject of the victorious life. While the Bible uses many terms to describe what Christians are (e.g., believers, friends, brothers, sheep, saints, soldiers, witnesses, etc.), John highlights one particular term in this chapter: the overcomer (*see especially the note on 5:4* for the meaning of the term). Of the 24 times the word occurs in the NT, John uses it 21 times (cf. also Rev. 2:7,11,17; 2:26; 3:5,12,21). Several different forms of this term appear in these verses to emphasize the victorious nature of the believer.

5:1 Whoever believes. Saving faith is the first characteristic of an overcomer. The term "believes" conveys the idea of continuing faith, making the point that the mark of genuine believers is that they continue in faith throughout their life. Saving belief is not simply intellectual acceptance, but whole-hearted dedication to Jesus Christ that is permanent. **Jesus is the Christ.** The object of the believer's faith is Jesus, particularly that He is the promised Messiah or "Anointed One" whom God sent to be the Savior from sin. Whoever places faith in Jesus Christ as the only Savior has been born again and, as a result, is an overcomer (v. 5). **born of God.** This is a reference to the new birth and is the same word that Jesus used in John 3:7. The tense of the Gr. verb indicates that ongoing faith is the result of the new birth and, therefore, the evidence of the new birth. The sons of God will manifest the reality that they have been born again by continuing to believe in God's Son, the Savior. The new birth brings us into a permanent faith relationship with God and Christ. **everyone who loves Him who begot also loves him who is begotten of Him.** Love is the second characteristic of the overcomer. The overcomer not only believes in God, but loves both God and fellow believers. The moral test is again in view.

5:2,3 keep His commandments. John repeats this phrase twice in these two verses. Obedience is the third characteristic of an overcomer. In these 5 verses, John weaves faith, love, and obedience all together inextricably. They exist mutually in a dynamic relationship i.e., as the genuine proof of love is obedience, so the genuine proof of faith is love. The word "keep" conveys the idea of constant obedience (cf. John 8:31,32; 14:15,21; 15:10).

5:3 His commandments are not burdensome. For example, in contrast to the burdensome man-made religious traditions of the Jewish leaders (Matt. 23:4), the yoke of Jesus is easy and the burden light (11:30).

ever is born of God overcomes the world.
And this is the victory that [g]has overcome
the world—[1]our faith. 5 Who is he who
overcomes the world, but [h]he who believes
that Jesus is the Son of God?

The Certainty of God's Witness

6 This is He who came [i]by water and
blood—Jesus Christ; not only by water, but
by water and blood. [j]And it is the Spirit
who bears witness, because the Spirit is
truth. 7 For there are three that bear witness [2]in heaven: the Father, [k]the Word, and
the Holy Spirit; [l]and these three are one.
8 And there are three that bear witness on
earth: [m]the Spirit, the water, and the blood;
and these three agree as one.
9 If we receive [n]the witness of men, the
witness of God is greater; [o]for this is the
witness of [3]God which He has testified of
His Son. 10 He who believes in the Son of
God [p]has the witness in himself; he who
does not believe God [q]has made Him a liar,
because he has not believed the testimony
that God has given of His Son. 11 And this
is the testimony: that God has given us
eternal life, and this life is in His Son.
12 [r]He who has the Son has [4]life; he who
does not have the Son of God does not
have [4]life. 13 These things I have written to
you who believe in the name of the Son of
God, that you may know that you have
eternal life, [5]and that you may *continue to*
believe in the name of the Son of God.

4 [g] 1 John 2:13; 4:4 [1] M *your*
5 [h] 1 Cor. 15:57
6 [i] John 1:31-34; [Eph. 5:26, 27] [j] [John 14:17]
7 [k] [John 1:1] [l] John 10:30 [2] NU, M omit the words from *in heaven* (v. 7) through *on earth* (v. 8). Only 4 or 5 very late mss. contain these words in Greek.
8 [m] John 15:26
9 [n] John 5:34, 37; 8:17, 18
[o] [Matt. 3:16, 17]; John 5:32, 37 [3] NU *God, that*
10 [p] [Rom. 8:16]; Gal. 4:6; Rev. 12:17 [q] John 3:18, 33; 1 John 1:10
12 [r] [John 3:15, 36; 6:47; 17:2, 3] [4] Or *the life* **13** [5] NU omits the rest of v. 13.

5:4 overcomes. John clearly defines who these overcomers are: They are all who believe that Jesus is God's Son, and all that means. The overcomers are believers—all of them (cf. 2:13). The word for "overcomer" comes from a Gr. word meaning "to conquer," "to have victory," "to have superiority" or "conquering power." The word reflects a genuine superiority that leads to overwhelming success. The victory is demonstrable; it involves overthrowing an enemy so that the victory is seen by all. Jesus also used this word to describe himself (John 16:33). Because of believers' union with Christ, they too partake in His victory (Rom. 8:37; 2 Cor. 2:14). The word "overcomes" in the original language conveys the idea that the believer has continual victory over the world.

5:4,5 the world. Satan's worldwide system of deception and wickedness. *See notes on 2:15.* Through Christ and His provision of salvation, the believer is a victor (v. 5) over the invisible system of demonic and human evil that Satan operates to capture men's souls for hell. John repeats the reference to overcoming the world 3 times—to press it home. **our faith...he who believes.** Faith in Jesus Christ and dedication of one's life to Him make one an overcomer. John repeats the truth for emphasis.

5:6-12 The term "witness" is the theme of this section. The passage concerns the witness or testimony of God and the Spirit to the world regarding the great truth of the deity of Jesus Christ. The previous passage (5:1-5) described overcomers as those who believed in Jesus as Lord and Savior, and here John presents God's own testimony to confirm that Jesus is the Christ (John 5:31-37; 8:13-18). He gives two kinds of testimony: external (vv. 6-9) and internal (vv. 10-12).

5:6 water and blood. Water and the blood constitute external, objective witnesses to who Jesus Christ is. They refer to Jesus' baptism (water) and death (blood). John combats the dualism of false teachers who asserted that "Christ-spirit" departed from the man Jesus just prior to His death on the cross (see Introduction: Background and Setting). John writes to show that God has given testimony to the deity of Jesus through both His baptism and death. **bears witness.** Both the verb "bear witness" and the noun "testimony" come from the same Gr. word and are used a total of 9 times in this section. The basic meaning is "someone who has personal and immediate knowledge of something." **the Spirit is truth.** John no longer stresses apostolic testimony (1:1-4; 4:14) but writes of the testimony of God that comes through the Holy Spirit. Since the Spirit of God cannot lie, His testimony is sure.

5:7 three that bear witness. The OT law required "the testimony of two or three witnesses" to establish the truth of a particular matter (Deut. 17:6; 19:15; cf. John 8:17,18; 1 Tim. 5:19).

5:7,8 in heaven: the Father, the Word, and the Holy Spirit... three that bear witness on earth. These words are a direct reference to the Trinity and what they say is accurate. External manuscript evidence, however, is against them being in the original epistle. They do not appear in any Gr. mss. dated before ca. tenth century A.D. Only 8 very late Gr. mss. contain the reading, and these contain the passage in what appears to be a translation from a late recension of the Latin Vulgate. Furthermore, 4 of those 8 mss. contain the passage as a variant reading written in the margin as a later addition to the manuscript. No Greek or Latin Father, even those involved in Trinitarian controversies, quote them; no ancient version except the Latin records them (not the Old Latin in its early form or the Vulgate). Internal evidence also militates against their presence, since they disrupt the sense of the writer's thoughts. Most likely, the words were added much later to the text. There is no verse in Scripture which so explicitly states the obvious reality of the Trinity, although many passages imply it strongly. See 2 Cor. 13:14.

5:8 the Spirit, the water, and the blood. At the baptism of Jesus, the Father and the Spirit testified to the Son (see Matt. 3:16,17). The death of Jesus Christ also witnessed to who He was (Matt. 27:54; Heb. 9:14). The Holy Spirit testified throughout Jesus' life as to His identity (Mark 1:12; Luke 1:35; Acts 10:38).

5:10 has the witness in himself. John writes of the internal subjective witness to the Son within the believer's heart (Rom. 8:15,16; Gal. 4:6). **made Him a liar.** If someone refuses the testimony of God regarding His Son, such rejection is the ultimate form of blasphemy for it is tantamount to calling God a liar (Titus 1:2; Heb. 6:18).

5:11,12 This summarizes the blessing of the believer's subjective witness—the very life that we possess in Christ expressed in the grace and power He provides all the time. It is the very experience of knowing Christ in one's life. Life is only in Him, so it is impossible to have it without Him.

5:13-21 John concludes his letter with a discussion regarding 5 Christian certainties that constitute a powerful climax to the entire epistle. He accentuates their certainty by using the word "know" 7 times in this section.

5:13 These things. This has reference to all that John has written in his letter. **that you may know that you have eternal life.** Assurance of eternal life constitutes the first Christian certainty. While John wrote his gospel to bring unbelievers to faith (John 20:31), he wrote the epistle to give believers confidence that they possessed eternal life. The false brethren's departure left John's congregations shaken (2:19). He assured those who remained that since they adhered to the fundamentals of the faith (a proper view of Christ, obedience, love), their salvation was sure. **eternal life.** This does not refer primarily to a period of time but a person (v. 20; John 17:3). Eternal life is a relationship with the person of Jesus Christ and possessing His nature (as in vv. 11,12).

Confidence and Compassion in Prayer

14 Now this is the confidence that we
have in Him, that [s]if we ask anything according to His will, He hears us. 15 And if
we know that He hears us, whatever we
ask, we know that we have the petitions
that we have asked of Him.

16 If anyone sees his brother sinning a
sin *which does* not *lead* to death, he will ask,
and [t]He will give him life for those who
commit sin not *leading* to death. [u]There is
sin *leading* to death. [v]I do not say that he
should pray about that. 17 [w]All unrighteousness is sin, and there is sin not *leading*
to death.

Knowing the True—Rejecting the False

18 We know that [x]whoever is born of
God does not sin; but he who has been
born of God [y]keeps[6] [7]himself, and the
wicked one does not touch him.

19 We know that we are of God, and [z]the
whole world lies *under the sway of* the
wicked one.

20 And we know that the [a]Son of God
has come and [b]has given us an understanding, [c]that we may know Him who is
true; and we are in Him who is true, in His
Son Jesus Christ. [d]This is the true God [e]and
eternal life.

21 Little children, keep yourselves from
idols. Amen.

14 [s] [1 John 2:28; 3:21,22]
16 [t] Job 42:8 [u] [Matt. 12:31] [v] Jer. 7:16; 14:11
17 [w] 1 John 3:4
18 [x] [1 Pet. 1:23]; 1 John 3:9 [y] James 1:27 [6] *guards* [7] NU *him*
19 [z] John 12:31; 17:15; Gal. 1:4
20 [a] 1 John 4:2 [b] Luke 24:45 [c] John 17:3; Rev. 3:7 [d] Is. 9:6 [e] 1 John 5:11,12

5:14-17 Answered prayer is the second Christian certainty.

5:14 confidence. For the meaning of the term, *see note on 3:21.* Christians can know with absolute confidence that God answers prayer when they approach the throne of grace (Heb. 4:14). **according to His will.** This phrase constitutes a strategic key to answered prayer. To pray according to God's will is to pray in accord with what He would want, not what we would desire or insist that He do for us (John 14:13,14). John already specified that answered prayer also depends on obedience to God's commandments and avoidance of sin (3:21; Ps. 66:18; John 15:7; 1 Pet. 3:7). Since genuine believers know God's Word (i.e., His will) and practice those things that are pleasing to Him, they never insist on their own will, but supremely seek God's desires (Matt. 27:39-44). **He hears us.** The word "hear" signifies that God always hears the prayers of His children (Ps. 34:15-17), but not always in the manner they were presented.

5:16,17 John illustrates praying according to God's will with the specific example of the "sin leading to death." Such a sin could be any premeditated and unconfessed sin that causes the Lord to determine to end a believer's life. It is not one particular sin like homosexuality or lying, but whatever sin is the final one in the tolerance of God. Failure to repent of and forsake sin may eventually lead to physical death as a judgment of God (Acts 5:1-11; 1 Cor. 5:5; 11:30). No intercessory prayer will be effective for those who have committed such deliberate high-handed sin, i.e., God's discipline with physical death is inevitable in such cases as He seeks to preserve the purity of His church (*see notes on 1 Cor. 5:5-7*). The contrast to the phrase "there is sin leading to death" with "there is sin not leading to death" signifies that the writer distinguishes between sins that may lead to physical death and those that do not. That is not to identify a certain kind of mortal or non-mortal sin, but to say not all sins are so judged by God.

5:18 Victory over sin and Satan is the third Christian certainty (3:9; Rom. 6:15-22). **himself.** This word is not in the best manuscripts. The better reading in the original language is "keeps him," referring to the fact that God protects the believer. **wicked one.** This is a reference to Satan. **does not touch him.** John uses this word only here and in John 20:17. The word suggests "to lay hold of" or "to grasp" in order to harm. Because the believer belongs to God, Satan must operate within God's sovereignty and cannot function beyond what God allows, as in the example of Job (Job 2:5; Rom. 16:20). While Satan may persecute, tempt, test, and accuse the believer, God protects His children and places definite limits on Satan's influence or power (2:13; John 10:28; 17:12-15).

5:19 we are of God. That Christians belong to God is the fourth Christian certainty. Only two types of people exist in the world according to John: children of God and children of Satan (*see note on 3:10*). One belongs either to God or to the evil world system that is Satan's domain. Because the whole world belongs to Satan, Christians should avoid its contamination.

5:20 true. The word means "genuine" as opposed to what is false (cf. v. 21). **God and eternal life.** That Jesus Christ is the true God is the fifth Christian certainty. This verse constitutes the summation of John's whole letter. The greatest certainty of all, the Incarnation, guarantees the certainty of the rest. This is the doctrinal foundation, out of which comes love and obedience.

5:21 keep yourselves from idols. John contrasts the term "idols" with "the true God" of v. 20. He has reference here to the false teachers that withdrew from the brotherhood with which they had been formerly associated (2:19). Their false beliefs and practices are the idols from which the readers are commanded to protect themselves. The false teachers upheld the world's philosophy as superior to God's revelation as demonstrated in their perversion of basic Christian teaching (faith, love, and obedience). In closing, John once again highlights the importance of adherence to the fundamentals of the faith.

The Second Epistle of JOHN

Title

The epistle's title is "2 John." It is the second in a series of 3 epistles that bear the Apostle John's name. Second and Third John present the closest approximation in the NT to the conventional letter form of the contemporary Greco-Roman world, since they were addressed from an individual to individuals. Second and Third John are the shortest epistles in the NT, each containing less than 300 Greek words. Each letter could fit on a single papyrus sheet (cf. 3 John 13).

Author and Date

The author is the Apostle John. He describes himself in 2 John 1 as "The Elder" which conveys the advanced age of the apostle, his authority, and status during the foundational period of Christianity when he was involved with Jesus' ministry. The precise date of the epistle cannot be determined. Since the wording, subject matter, and circumstances of 2 John closely approximate 1 John (v. 5 [cf. 1 John 2:7; 3:11]; v. 6 [cf. 1 John 5:3]; v. 7 [cf. 1 John 2:18-26]; v. 9 [cf. 1 John 2:23]; v. 12; [cf. 1 John 1:4]), most likely John composed the letter at the same time or soon after 1 John, ca. A. D. 90–95, during his ministry at Ephesus in the latter part of his life.

Background and Setting

Second John deals with the same problem as 1 John (see Introduction to 1 John: Background and Setting). False teachers influenced by the beginnings of Gnostic thought were threatening the church (v. 7; cf. 1 John 2:18,19,22,23; 4:1-3). The strategic difference is that while 1 John has no specific individual or church specified to whom it was addressed, 2 John has a particular local group or house-church in mind (v. 1).

The focus of 2 John is that the false teachers were conducting an itinerant ministry among John's congregations, seeking to make converts, and taking advantage of Christian hospitality to advance their cause (vv. 10,11; cf. Rom. 12:13; Heb. 13:2; 1 Pet. 4:9). The individual addressed in the greeting (v. 1) inadvertently or unwisely may have shown these false prophets hospitality, or John may have feared that the false teachers would attempt to take advantage of her kindness (vv. 10,11). The apostle seriously warns his readers against showing hospitality to such deceivers (vv. 10,11). Although his exhortation may appear on the surface to be harsh or unloving, the acutely dangerous nature of their teaching justified such actions, especially since it threatened to destroy the very foundations of the faith (v. 9).

Historical and Theological Themes

The overall theme of 2 John closely parallels 1 John's theme of a "recall to the fundamentals of the faith" or "back to the basics of Christianity" (vv. 4-6). For John, the basics of Christianity are summarized by adherence to the truth (v. 4), love (v. 5), and obedience (v. 6).

The apostle, however, conveys an additional but related theme in 2 John: "the biblical guidelines for hospitality." Not only are Christians to adhere to the fundamentals of the faith, but the gracious hospitality that is commanded of them (Rom. 12:13) must be discriminating. The basis of hospitality must be common love of or interest in the truth, and Christians must share their love within the confines of that truth. They are not called to universal acceptance of anyone who claims to be a believer. Love must be discerning. Hospitality and kindness must be focused on those who are adhering to the fundamentals of the faith. Otherwise, Christians may actually aid those who are attempting to destroy those basic truths of the faith. Sound doctrine must serve as the test of fellowship and the basis of separation between those who profess to be Christians and those who actually are (vv. 10,11; cf. Rom. 16:17; Gal. 1:8,9; 2 Thess. 3:6,14; Titus 3:10).

Interpretive Challenges

Second John stands in direct antithesis to the frequent cry for ecumenism and Christian unity among believers. Love and truth are inseparable in Christianity. Truth must always guide the exercise of love (cf. Eph. 4:15). Love must stand the test of truth. The main lesson of this book is that truth determines the bounds of love, and as a consequence, of unity. Therefore, truth must exist before love can unite, for truth generates love (1 Pet. 1:22). When someone compromises the truth, true Christian love and unity are destroyed. Only a shallow sentimentalism exists where the truth is not the foundation of unity.

The reference to the "elect lady and her children" (v. 1) should be understood in a normal, plain sense referring to a particular woman and her children rather than interpreted in a non-literal sense as a church and its membership. Similarly, the reference to "the children of your elect sister" (v. 13) should be understood as a reference to the nieces and/or nephews of the individual addressed in verse 1, rather than metaphorically to a sister church and its membership. In these verses, John conveys greetings to personal acquaintances that he has come to know through his ministry.

Outline

I. The Basis of Christian Hospitality (1-3)

II. The Behavior of Christian Hospitality (4-6)

III. The Bounds of Christian Hospitality (7-11)

IV. The Blessings of Christian Hospitality (12,13)

Greeting the Elect Lady

The Elder,
To the [1]elect lady and her children,
whom I love in truth, and not only I, but
also all those who have known [a]the truth,
2 because of the truth which abides in us
and will be with us forever:

3 [b]Grace, mercy, *and* peace will be with
[2]you from God the Father and from the
Lord Jesus Christ, the Son of the Father, in
truth and love.

Walk in Christ's Commandments

4 I [c]rejoiced greatly that I have found
some of your children walking in truth, as
we received commandment from the Father. 5 And now I plead with you, lady,
not as though I wrote a new commandment to you, but that which we have had
from the beginning: [d]that we love one another. 6 [e]This is love, that we walk according to His commandments. This is
the commandment, that [f]as you have
heard from the beginning, you should
walk in it.

Beware of Antichrist Deceivers

7 For [g]many deceivers have gone out
into the world [h]who do not confess Jesus
Christ *as* coming in the flesh. [i]This is a deceiver and an antichrist. 8 [j]Look to yourselves, [k]that [3]we do not lose those things
we worked for, but *that* [3]we may receive a
full reward.
9 [l]Whoever [4]transgresses and does not
abide in the doctrine of Christ does not
have God. He who abides in the doctrine
of Christ has both the Father and the Son.
10 If anyone comes to you and [m]does not
bring this doctrine, do not receive him into

1 [a]Col. 1:5 [1]*chosen*
3 [b]Rom. 1:7; 1 Tim. 1:2 [2]NU, M *us*
4 [c]1 Thess. 2:19, 20; 3 John 3, 4
5 [d][John 13:34, 35; 15:12, 17]; 1 John 3:11; 4:7, 11
6 [e]John 14:15; 1 John 2:5; 5:3 [f]1 John 2:24
7 [g]1 John 2:19; 4:1 [h]1 John 4:2 [i]1 John 2:22
8 [j]Mark 13:9 [k]Gal. 3:4 [3]NU *you*
9 [l]John 7:16; 8:31; 1 John 2:19, 23, 24 [4]NU *goes ahead*
10 [m]1 Kin. 13:16; Rom. 16:17; 2 Thess. 3:6, 14; Titus 3:10

1 The Elder. John uses this title to emphasize his advanced age, his spiritual authority over the congregations in Asia Minor, and the strength of his own personal eyewitness testimony to the life of Jesus and all that He taught (vv. 4-6). **the elect lady and her children.** Some think that this phrase refers metaphorically to a particular local church, while "her children" would refer to members of the congregation. The more natural understanding in context, however, is that it refers to a particular woman and her children (i.e., offspring) who were well known to John. **whom I love in truth.** The basis of Christian hospitality is the truth (vv. 1-3). John accentuates the need for truth by repeating the term "truth" 5 times in the opening 4 verses. Truth refers to the basics or fundamentals of the faith that John has discussed in 1 John (sound belief in Christ, obedience, love) as well the truths expressed in 2 John (e.g., vv. 4-6). Truth is the necessary condition of unity and, as a result, the basis of hospitality.

2 truth...abides in us...will be with us forever. This is the cognitive truth of God's Word (cf. Col. 3:16).

3 Grace, mercy, *and* peace...in truth and love. John's succession from grace to mercy and then peace marks the order from the first motion of God to the final satisfaction of man. The confines of these threefold blessings are within the sphere of truth and love.

4 children walking in truth, as we received commandment. The behavior of hospitality involves obedience to the truth (see vv. 5,6). The word "walking" has reference to continual walking in the truth, i.e., making obedience to the truth a habit in one's life.

5 new commandment...that we love one another. John ties the commandment of truth to the commandment of love (cf. 1 John 2:7-11; 4:7-12). The word "love" has reference to practicing love as a habit in one's life. Both walking in the truth and in love is the behavior of hospitality.

6 This is love, that we walk according to His commandments. John defines love, not as a sentiment or an emotion, but as obedience to God's commands (*see notes on 1 John 5:2,3*). Those who are obedient to the truth as contained in God's commandments, the fundamentals of the faith (1 John 2:3-11), are identified as walking in love. Cf. John 14:15,21; 15:10.

7 many deceivers. Cf. Mark 13:22,23; 1 Tim. 4:1-4; 2 Pet. 2:1ff.; 1 John 4:1. In vv. 7-11, John gives limits for Christian hospitality. This is the centerpiece of John's thought in this epistle and expands the first two points. Since Satan comes as an angel of light (2 Cor. 11:13-15), believers must be on guard against error by having an intimate acquaintance with the truth. **who do not confess Jesus Christ *as* coming in the flesh.** The original language conveys the idea of a habitual denial of the undiminished deity and humanity of Christ. A biblical Christology maintains that Jesus Christ's nature was both fully God and fully man with all the implications for the fulfillment of redemptive purposes. The essence of the severest error in false religions, heresies, and cults centers in a denial of the true nature of Jesus Christ.

8 do not lose those things we worked for. Although a reward is generally promised Christians for hospitality (e.g., Matt. 10:41; 25:40; Mark 9:41), the idea here is of the fullness of a believer's reward for all the good he has done (see 1 Cor. 3:10-17; 2 Cor. 5:9,10). A loss of that reward may occur to any believer who does not discriminate fellowship on the basis of adherence to the truth (Col. 2:18,19; 3:24,25). This is a potent warning. All the eternal reward one earns by seeing Christ purely, eagerly, effectively in the Spirit can be diminished by any aiding or abetting of false teaching.

9 does not abide in the doctrine of Christ does not have God. A failure to be faithful to the fundamental, sound doctrines of the faith (a proper view of the person and work of Christ, love, obedience) marks a person as having never been born again (1 John 2:23; 3:6-10; 4:20,21; 5:1-3). The word "abide" has the idea of constant adherence and warns that these fundamentals are not open to change or subject to the latest trends or philosophical fads.

10 do not receive him into your house nor greet him. John's prohibition is not a case of entertaining people who disagree on minor matters. These false teachers were carrying on a regular campaign to destroy the basic, fundamental truths of Christianity. Complete disassociation from such heretics is the only appropriate course of action for genuine believers. No benefit or aid of any type (not even a greeting) is permissible. Believers should aid only those who proclaim the truth (vv. 5-8).

11 shares in his evil deeds. Hospitality to such leaders aids the spread of their heresy and inevitably leaves the impression of sanctioning the teachings of these antichrists (cf. 1 John 2:22). Supreme loyalty to God and His Word alone must characterize the actions of every true believer.

your house nor greet him; 11 for he who
greets him shares in his evil deeds.

John's Farewell Greeting

12 [n]Having many things to write to you,
I did not wish *to do so* with paper and ink;
but I hope to come to you and speak face to
face, [o]that our joy may be full.
13 [p]The children of your elect sister greet
you. Amen.

12 [n]3 John 13,14 [o]John 17:13
13 [p]1 Pet. 5:13

12 paper and ink. The word "paper" refers to a papyrus sheet. One papyrus sheet could contain the whole letter of 2 John. The term "ink" means "black" and refers to a mixture of water, charcoal, and gum resin that was used to write. **face to face.** John lit. wrote "mouth to mouth." Cf. Num. 12:8 where God spoke to Moses "mouth to mouth." **that our joy may be full.** The blessing of hospitality is full joy (vv. 12,13). John uses this same wording in 1 John 1:4. When believers uphold the biblical standards for fellowship, the result is genuine joy among believers because the truths of the Word are maintained.

13 The children of your elect sister. John refers to the nieces and/or nephews of the woman ("elect lady") addressed in v. 1 who sent their greetings via John.

The Third Epistle of JOHN

Title

The epistle's title is "3 John." It is the third in a series of 3 epistles that bear the Apostle John's name. Third John and 2 John present the closest approximation in the New Testament to the conventional letter form of the contemporary Greco-Roman world, since they were addressed from an individual to individuals. Both 2 and 3 John are the shortest epistles in the NT, each containing less than 300 Greek words, so as to fit on a single papyrus sheet (cf. v. 13).

Author and Date

The author is the Apostle John. He describes himself in v. 1 as "The Elder" which conveys the advanced age of the apostle, his authority and his eyewitness status especially during the foundational period of Christianity when John was involved with Jesus' ministry (cf. 2 John 1). The precise date of the epistle cannot be determined. Since the structure, style, and vocabulary closely approximate 2 John (v. 1 [cf. 2 John 1]; v. 4 [cf. 2 John 4]; v. 13 [cf. 2 John 12]; v. 14 [cf. 2 John 12]), most likely John composed the letter at the same time or soon after 2 John, ca. A.D. 90–95. As with 1 and 2 John, the apostle probably composed the letter during his ministry at Ephesus in the latter part of his life.

Background and Setting

Third John is perhaps the most personal of John's 3 epistles. While 1 John appears to be a general letter addressed to congregations scattered throughout Asia Minor, and 2 John was sent to a lady and her family (2 John 1), in 3 John the apostle clearly names the sole recipient as "the beloved Gaius" (v. 1). This makes the epistle one of a few letters in the NT addressed strictly to an individual (cf. Philemon). The name "Gaius" was very common in the first century (e.g., Acts 19:29; 20:4; Rom. 16:23; 1 Cor. 1:14), but nothing is known of this individual beyond John's salutation, from which it is inferred that he was a member of one of the churches under John's spiritual oversight.

As with 2 John, 3 John focuses on the basic issue of hospitality but from a different perspective. While 2 John warns against showing hospitality to false teachers (2 John 7-11), 3 John condemns the lack of hospitality shown to faithful ministers of the Word (vv. 9,10). Reports came back to the apostle that itinerant teachers known and approved by him (vv. 5-8) had traveled to a certain congregation where they were refused hospitality (e.g., lodging and provision) by an individual named Diotrephes who domineered the assembly (v. 10). Diotrephes went even further, for he also verbally slandered the Apostle John with malicious accusations and excluded anyone from the assembly who dared challenge him (v. 10).

In contrast, Gaius, a beloved friend of the apostle and faithful adherent to the truth (vv. 1-4), extended the correct standard of Christian hospitality to itinerant ministers. John wrote to commend the type of hospitality exhibited by Gaius to worthy representatives of the gospel (vv. 6-8) and to condemn the high-handed actions of Diotrephes (v. 10). The apostle promised to correct the situation personally and sent this letter through an individual named Demetrius, whom he commended for his good testimony among the brethren (vv. 10-12).

Historical and Theological Themes

The theme of 3 John is the commendation of the proper standards of Christian hospitality and the condemnation for failure to follow those standards.

Interpretive Challenges

Some think that Diotrephes may either have been a heretical teacher or at least favored the false teachers who were condemned by 2 John. However, the epistle gives no clear evidence to warrant such a conclusion, especially since one might expect that John would have mentioned Diotrephes' heretical views. The epistle indicates that his problems centered around arrogance and disobedience, which is a problem for the orthodox as well as the heretic.

Outline

I. The Commendation Regarding Christian Hospitality (1-8)

II. The Condemnation Regarding Violating Christian Hospitality (9-11)

III. The Conclusion Regarding Christian Hospitality (12-14)

Greeting to Gaius

The Elder,

To the beloved Gaius, [a]whom I love in
truth:

2 Beloved, I pray that you may prosper
in all things and be in health, just as your
soul prospers. 3 For I [b]rejoiced greatly
when brethren came and testified of the
truth *that is* in you, just as you walk in the
truth. 4 I have no greater [c]joy than to hear
that [d]my children walk in [1]truth.

Gaius Commended for Generosity

5 Beloved, you do faithfully whatever
you do for the brethren [2]and for strangers, 6 who have borne witness of your
love before the church. *If* you send them
forward on their journey in a manner
worthy of God, you will do well, 7 because they went forth for His name's
sake, [e]taking nothing from the Gentiles.
8 We therefore ought to [f]receive[3] such,
that we may become fellow workers for
the truth.

Diotrephes and Demetrius

9 I wrote to the church, but Diotrephes,
who loves to have the preeminence among
them, does not receive us. 10 Therefore, if I
come, I will call to mind his deeds which

1 [a] 2 John 1
3 [b] 2 John 4
4 [c] 1 Thess. 2:19, 20; 2 John 4 [d] [1 Cor. 4:15] [1] NU *the truth*
5 [2] NU *and especially for*
7 [e] 1 Cor. 9:12, 15
8 [f] Matt. 10:40; Rom. 12:13; Heb. 13:2; 1 Pet. 4:9 [3] NU *support*

1 The Elder. John uses the same term for himself as he did in 2 John 1. The term probably has reference to his age, his apostolic eyewitness status of Jesus' life and also that he had an official position of authority in the church. **the beloved.** The term "beloved" is only used of Christians in the NT (Col. 3:12; Philem. 1,2; 2 Pet. 3:14; 1 John 4:1). **Gaius.** Nothing is known of Gaius beyond the mention of his name in the salutation. The name was one of 18 common names from which Roman parents usually chose a name for one of their sons, making any specific identification doubtful. John, his fellow believers, and even strangers to whom Gaius extended hospitality held him in great esteem for his Christian walk and conduct (vv. 1-6). John conveyed his own appreciation for Gaius by calling him "beloved" 4 times in the letter (vv. 1,2,5,11). He probably was a member of a church somewhere in Asia Minor that was under John's sphere of influence. The apostle planned to visit him sometime in the near future (v. 13). **whom I love in truth.** Because Christians have common knowledge of the truth, they have the common source of love (2 John 1). While some have taken the phrase to mean simply "truly" or "really" (Mark 12:32; John 1:47), John's usage of this phrase elsewhere in these letters where truth takes on such a significant meaning suggests that the elder intended the kind of love that is consistent with the fundamental truths of the faith (cf. v. 4; 1 John 2:21; 3:19).

2 I pray. John's prayer for Gaius is significant. Gaius' spiritual state was so excellent that John prayed that his physical health would match his spiritual vigor. To ask about one's health was standard custom in ancient letters, but John adapted this convention in a unique manner to highlight Gaius' vibrant spiritual state.

3 when brethren came and testified. The phrase indicates that Christians continually praised Gaius' exemplary obedience to the fundamentals of the faith. His spiritual reputation was well known. **you walk in the truth.** Gaius' walk matched his talk. His reputation for practicing what he preached was exemplary (2 John 4). John's commendation of him is one of the greatest given in the NT, since the commendation centers not only in the fact that he knew the truth but that he faithfully practiced it. Gaius' actions were in stark contrast to Diotrephes' negative reputation (v. 10).

4 I have no greater joy. John's personal affection for Gaius radiated especially from his personal conduct (Luke 6:46). **my children.** The word "my" is emphatic in the original. John's heart delighted in the proper conduct of his spiritual children in the faith. Those who walk (conduct) in the truth (belief) have integrity; there is no dichotomy between professing and living. He had strong fatherly affection for them (cf. 1 Cor. 4:14-16; 1 Thess. 2:11; 3:1-10).

5 you do faithfully. Genuine faith always produces genuine good works (James 2:14-17). **brethren and for strangers.** Gaius practiced hospitality not only toward those whom he knew but also to those whom he did not know. The reference concerns especially itinerant gospel preachers that Gaius aided on their journeys.

6 who have borne witness of your love before the church. Gaius' reputation for hospitality and kindness (as well as obedience—v. 3) was also well known throughout the churches in the region. **in a manner worthy of God.** Cf. Col. 1:10; 1 Thess. 2:12. The phrase has the connotation of treating people as God would treat them (see Matt. 10:40), and becomes the key manner in which hospitality should be practiced (Matt. 25:40-45). **you will do well.** John encouraged Gaius to keep practicing hospitality, especially because of the actions of Diotrephes who conducted a heavy-handed campaign against it (v. 10).

7,8 John gives several grounds for practicing hospitality in a "manner worthy of God." First, one must show hospitality to those who have pure motives. These itinerant missionaries went out "for the sake of the name" (v. 7; cf. Rom. 1:5). They must be doing their ministry for God's glory not their own. Second, one must show hospitality to those who are not in ministry for money. Since the missionaries were "taking nothing from the Gentiles" (v. 7), the church was their only means of support. They were free from avarice (2 Cor. 2:17; 1 Tim. 5:17,18). Third, those who show hospitality participate in the ministries of those to whom hospitality is shown (v. 8). Verse 8 gives the same reason to demonstrate hospitality to genuine teachers as does 2 John 10 in forbidding hospitality toward false teachers, i.e., that those who extend hospitality share in the deeds (i.e., good or bad) of those receiving it.

9 I wrote to the church. John apparently had written a previous letter to the church, perhaps on the subject of hospitality, but it was lost. Perhaps Diotrephes never read it to the church because he rejected John's authority (cf. vv. 9,10). **Diotrephes, who loves to have the preeminence.** In the second part of his epistle, John condemned the violation of hospitality toward faithful ministers of the Word. The word "preeminence" has the idea of "desiring to be first." It conveys the idea of someone who is selfish, self-centered, and self-seeking. The language suggests a self-promoting demagogue, who served no one, but wanted all to serve only him. Diotrephes' actions directly contradict Jesus' and the NT's teaching on servant-leadership in the church (cf. Matt. 20:20-28; Phil 2:5-11; 1 Tim. 3:3; 1 Pet. 5:3). **does not receive us.** Diotrephes modeled the opposite of kindness and hospitality to God's servants, even denying John's apostolic authority over the local congregation, and as a result, denying the revelation of God that came through that authority. His pride endeavored to supplant the rule of Christ through John in the church. Diotrephes' character was the very opposite of the gentle and loving Gaius who readily showed hospitality.

10 if I come, I will call to mind his deeds. John's apostolic authority meant that Diotrephes had to answer for his behavior. The

he does, [g]prating[4] against us with malicious words. And not content with that, he
himself does not receive the brethren, and
forbids those who wish to, putting *them*
out of the church.
11 Beloved, [h]do not imitate what is evil,
but what is good. [i]He who does good is of
God, [5]but he who does evil has not seen
[j]God.
12 Demetrius [k]has a *good* testimony from
all, and from the truth itself. And we also
[6]bear witness, [l]and you know that our testimony is true.

Farewell Greeting

13 [m]I had many things to write, but I do
not wish to write to you with pen and ink;
14 but I hope to see you shortly, and we
shall speak face to face.
Peace to you. Our friends greet you.
Greet the friends by name.

10 [g] Prov. 10:8, 10 [4] *talking nonsense*
11 [h] Ps. 34:14; 37:27; Rom. 14:19; 1 Thess. 5:15; 1 Tim. 6:11; 2 Tim. 2:22 [i] [1 John 2:29; 3:10] [j] [1 John 3:10] [5] NU, M omit *but*
12 [k] Acts 6:3; 1 Tim. 3:7 [l] John 19:35; 21:24 [6] *testify*
13 [m] 2 John 12

apostle did not overlook this usurping of Christ's place in the church. Verse 10 indicates that Diotrephes was guilty of 4 things: 1) "prating against us." The word "prating" comes from a word meaning "to bubble up" and has the idea of useless, empty jabber, i.e., talking nonsense. The charges against John were completely unjustified; 2) "with malicious words." Not only were Diotrephes' charges false, they were evil; 3) "does not receive the brethren." He not only slandered John but also deliberately defied other believers; and 4) "putting *them* out of the church." The original language indicates that Diotrephes' habit was to excommunicate those who resisted his authority. **does not receive the brethren.** To accept John's authority (v. 9), as well as being hospitable to the traveling ministers, directly threatened the authority that Diotrephes coveted.

11 do not imitate what is evil, but what is good. The verse begins the introduction to the commendation of Demetrius in v. 12. Gaius was to imitate Demetrius as the correct role model for his actions. **He who does good is of God, but he who does evil has not seen God.** John's statement indicates that Diotrephes' actions proved that he was never a Christian. This is a practical application of the moral test (*see notes on 1 John 5:2,3*).

12 Demetrius. As with Gaius, Demetrius was a very common name in the Roman world (Acts 19:24,38). Nothing is known of him apart from this epistle. He may have delivered this letter, which also would serve to commend him to Gaius. **has a *good* testimony from all.** Like Gaius, Demetrius' reputation was well known in the region. **from the truth itself.** Demetrius was an excellent role model preeminently because he practiced the truth of God's Word in his life.

13 pen and ink…face to face. *See note on 2 John 12.*

The Epistle of JUDE

Title

Jude, which is rendered "Judah" in Hebrew and "Judas" in Greek, was named after its author (v. 1), one of the 4 half-brothers of Christ (Matt. 13:55; Mark 6:3). As the fourth shortest NT book (Philem., 2 John, and 3 John are shorter), Jude is the last of 8 general epistles. Jude does not quote the OT directly, but there are at least 9 obvious allusions to it. Contextually, this "epistolary sermon" could be called "The Acts of the Apostates."

Author and Date

Although Jude (Judas) was a common name in Palestine (at least 8 are named in the NT), the author of Jude generally has been accepted as Jude, Christ's half-brother. He is to be differentiated from the Apostle Judas, the son of James (Luke 6:16; Acts 1:13). Several lines of thought lead to this conclusion: 1) Jude's appeal to being the "brother of James," the leader of the Jerusalem Council (Acts 15) and another half-brother of Jesus (v. 1; cf. Gal. 1:19); 2) Jude's salutation being similar to James (cf. James 1:1); and 3) Jude's not identifying himself as an apostle (v. 1), but rather distinguishing between himself and the apostles (v. 17).

The doctrinal and moral apostasy discussed by Jude (vv. 4-18) closely parallels that of 2 Peter (2:1–3:4), and it is believed that Peter's writing predated Jude for several reasons: 1) 2 Peter anticipates the coming of false teachers (2 Pet. 2:1,2; 3:3), while Jude deals with their arrival (vv. 4,11,12,17,18); and 2) Jude quotes directly from 2 Pet. 3:3 and acknowledges that it is from an apostle (vv. 17,18). Since no mention of Jerusalem's destruction in A.D. 70 was made by Jude, though Jude most likely came after 2 Peter (ca. A.D. 68–70), it was almost certainly written before the destruction of Jerusalem. Although Jude did travel on missionary trips with other brothers and their wives (1 Cor. 9:5), it is most likely that he wrote from Jerusalem. The exact audience of believers with whom Jude corresponded is unknown, but seems to be Jewish in light of Jude's illustrations. He undoubtedly wrote to a region recently plagued by false teachers.

Although Jude had earlier rejected Jesus as Messiah (John 7:1-9), he, along with other half-brothers of our Lord, was converted after Christ's resurrection (Acts 1:14). Because of his relation to Jesus, his eyewitness knowledge of the resurrected Christ, and the content of this epistle, it was acknowledged as inspired and was included in the Muratorian Canon (A.D. 170). The early questions about its canonicity also tend to support that it was written after 2 Peter. If Peter had quoted Jude, there would have been no question about canonicity, since Peter would thereby have given Jude apostolic affirmation. Clement of Rome (ca. A.D. 96) plus Clement of Alexandria (ca. A.D. 200) also alluded to the authenticity of Jude. Its diminutive size and Jude's quotations from uninspired writings, account for any misplaced questions about its canonicity.

Background and Setting

Jude lived at a time when Christianity was under severe political attack from Rome and aggressive spiritual infiltration from gnostic-like apostates and libertines who sowed abundant seed for a gigantic harvest of doctrinal error. It could be that this was the forerunner to full blown Gnosticism which the Apostle John would confront over 25 years later in his epistles. Except for John, who lived at the close of the century, all of the other apostles had been martyred, and Christianity was thought to be extremely vulnerable. Thus, Jude called the church to fight, in the midst of intense spiritual warfare, for the truth.

Historical and Theological Themes

Jude is the only NT book devoted exclusively to confronting "apostasy," meaning defection from the true, biblical faith (vv. 3,17). Apostates are described elsewhere in 2 Thess. 2:10; Heb. 10:29; 2 Pet. 2:1-22; 1 John 2:18-23. He wrote to condemn the apostates and to urge believers to contend for the faith. He called for discernment on the part of the church and a rigorous defense of biblical truth. He followed the earlier examples of: 1) Christ (Matt. 7:15ff.; 16:6-12; 24:11ff; Rev. 2,3); 2) Paul (Acts 20:29,30; 1 Tim. 4:1; 2 Tim. 3:1-5; 4:3,4); 3) Peter (2 Pet. 2:1,2; 3:3,4); and 4) John (1 John 4:1-6; 2 John 6-11).

Jude is replete with historical illustrations from the OT which include: 1) the Exodus (v. 5); 2) Satan's rebellion (v. 6); 3) Sodom and Gomorrah (v. 7); 4) Moses' death (v. 9); 5) Cain (v. 11); 6) Balaam (v. 11); 7) Korah (v. 11); 8) Enoch (vv. 14,15); and 9) Adam (v. 14).

Jude also vividly described the apostates in terms of their character and unconscionable activities (vv. 4,8,10,16,18,19). Additionally, he borrowed from nature to illustrate the futility of their teaching (vv. 12,13). While Jude never commented on the specific content of their false teaching, it was enough to demonstrate that their degenerate personal lives and fruitless ministries betrayed their attempts to teach error as though it were truth. This emphasis on character repeats the constant theme regarding false teachers—their personal corruption. While their teaching is clever, subtle, deceptive, enticing, and delivered in myriads of forms, the common way to recognize them is to look behind their false spiritual fronts and see their wicked lives (2 Pet. 2:10,12,18,19).

Interpretive Challenges

Because there are no doctrinal issues discussed, the challenges of this letter have to do with interpretation in the normal process of discerning the meaning of the text. Jude does quote from non-canonical, pseudepigraphal (i.e., the actual author was not the one named in its title) sources such as *1 Enoch* (v. 14) and the *Assumption of Moses* (v. 9) to support his points. Was this acceptable? Since Jude was writing under the inspiration of the Holy Spirit (2 Tim. 3:16; 2 Pet. 1:20,21) and included material that was accurate and true in its affirmations, he did no differently than Paul (cf. Acts 17:28; 1 Cor. 15:33; Titus 1:12).

Outline

I. Desires of Jude (1,2)
II. Declaration of War Against Apostates (3,4)
III. Damnable Outcome of Apostates (5-7)
IV. Denunciation of Apostates (8-16)
V. Defenses Against Apostates (17-23)
VI. Doxology of Jude (24,25)

Greeting to the Called

Jude, a bondservant of Jesus Christ, and
[a]brother of James,

To those who are [b]called, [1]sanctified by
God the Father, and [c]preserved in Jesus
Christ:

2 Mercy, [d]peace, and love be multiplied
to you.

Contend for the Faith

3 Beloved, while I was very diligent to
write to you [e]concerning our common salvation, I found it necessary to write to you
exhorting [f]you to contend earnestly for the
faith which was once for all delivered to
the saints. 4 For certain men have crept in
unnoticed, who long ago were marked out
for this condemnation, ungodly men, who
turn the grace of our God into lewdness
and deny the only Lord [2]God and our
Lord Jesus Christ.

Old and New Apostates

5 But I want to remind you, though you
once knew this, that [g]the Lord, having
saved the people out of the land of Egypt,
afterward destroyed those who did not be-

1 [a] Acts 1:13 [b] Rom. 1:7 [c] John 17:11, 12 [1] NU *beloved*
2 [d] 1 Pet. 1:2; 2 Pet. 1:2
3 [e] Titus 1:4 [f] Phil. 1:27
4 [2] NU omits *God*
5 [g] Ex. 12:51; 1 Cor. 10:5-10; Heb. 3:16

1 Jude. See Introduction: Author and Date. **bondservant.** Before the crucifixion and resurrection, Jude had denied Jesus as Messiah (Matt. 13:55; Mark 6:3; John 7:5), but afterward came to humbly acknowledge himself as His slave, having submitted to Christ's lordship. **brother of James.** James was the well known leader of the Jerusalem church (Acts 12:17; 15:13; 21:18; Gal. 2:9) and author of the epistle that carried his name. **called.** As always in the epistles, this refers not to a general invitation to salvation, but to God's irresistible, elective call to salvation (cf. Rom. 1:7; 1 Cor. 1:23,24; 1 Thess. 5:24; 2 Thess. 2:13,14). This call yields: 1) fellowship with Christ (1 Cor. 1:9); 2) peace (1 Cor. 7:15); 3) freedom (Gal. 5:13); 4) a worthy walk (Eph. 4:1); 5) hope (Eph. 4:4); 6) holiness (1 Pet. 1:15); 7) blessing (1 Pet. 3:9); and 8) eternal glory (1 Pet. 5:10). Cf. "grace of our God" (v. 4). **sanctified.** The better Gr. texts have "beloved" (see marginal note). Cf. John 13:1; 14:23; 16:27; 17:20,23; Rom. 5:8; 1 John 3:1, which expand on the idea of unconditional, thus unending, love from God to the believer in Christ. It is certainly because of that love that believers are "sanctified," set apart from sin to God by the transformation of conversion. **God the Father.** The plan of salvation and its fulfillment come from God, who is not only Father in the sense of creation and origin of all that exists, but is also "God our Savior" (v. 25; cf. 1 Tim. 2:4; Titus 1:3; 2:10; 3:4). *See note on 1 Tim. 4:10.* **preserved.** *See note on v. 24.* God not only initiates salvation but He also completes it through Christ, thus preserving or keeping the believer secure for eternal life (cf. John 6:37-44; 10:28-30; 17:11,15; Rom. 8:31-39; 2 Tim. 4:18; Heb. 7:25; 9:24; 1 Pet. 1:3-5).

2 Mercy, peace, and love. "Mercy and peace" was a common Jewish greeting; "love" was added to make this distinctively Christian. Only here in the NT do these 3 qualities appear so closely together. Where law and works prevail, there is failure and death. Where grace prevails, there is mercy (Eph. 2:4; Heb. 4:16), peace (Rom. 5:1), and love (Rom. 5:5) in abundance.

3 Beloved. Cf. vv. 17,20. **I found it necessary.** Cf. 1 Cor. 9:16. This verse implies that Jude had intended to write a letter on salvation as the common blessing enjoyed by all believers, perhaps to emphasize unity and fellowship among believers, and remind them that God is no respecter of persons. But he was compelled, instead, to write a call to battle for the truth in light of the arrival of apostate teachers. **contend earnestly.** While the salvation of those to whom he wrote was not in jeopardy, false teachers preaching and living out a counterfeit gospel were misleading those who needed to hear the true gospel. Jude wrote this urgent imperative for Christians to wage war against error in all forms and fight strenuously for the truth, like a soldier who has been entrusted with a sacred task of guarding a holy treasure (cf. 1 Tim. 6:12; 2 Tim. 4:7). **the faith.** This is the whole body of revealed salvation truth contained in the Scriptures (cf. Gal. 1:23; Eph. 4:5,13; Phil. 1:27; 1 Tim. 4:1). Cf. v. 20. Here is a call to know sound doctrine (Eph. 4:14; Col. 3:16: 1 Pet. 2:2; 1 John 2:12-14), to be discerning in sorting out truth from error (1 Thess. 5:20-22), and to be willing to confront and attack error (*see notes on 2 Cor. 10:3-5; Phil. 1:17,27; 1 Tim. 1:18; 6:12; 2 Tim. 1:13; 4:7,8; Titus 1:13*). **once for all delivered...saints.** God's revelation was delivered once as a unit, at the completion of the Scripture, and is not to be edited by either deletion or addition (cf. Deut. 4:2; 12:32; Prov. 30:6; Rev. 22:18,19). Scripture is complete, sufficient, and finished; therefore it is fixed for all time. Nothing is to be added to the body of the inspired Word (*see notes on 2 Tim. 3:16,17; 2 Pet. 1:19-21*) because nothing else is needed. It is the responsibility of believers now to study the Word (2 Tim. 2:15), preach the Word (2 Tim. 4:2), and fight for its preservation. **saints.** Believers are identified as holy, since they are set apart from sin to God. *See note on 1 Cor. 1:2.*

4 certain men...crept in unnoticed. These were infiltrating, false teachers pretending to be true, who on the surface looked like the real thing, but whose intentions were to lead God's people astray (cf. Matt. 7:15; Acts 20:29; Gal. 2:4,5; 1 Tim. 4:1-3; 2 Pet. 2:1,20; 1 John 2:18-23). These apostates were Satan's counterfeits, most likely posing as itinerant teachers (cf. 2 Cor. 11:13-15; 2 Pet. 2:1-3; 2 John 7-11). Their stealth made them dangerous. They were characterized by 3 features: 1) they were ungodly; 2) they perverted grace; and 3) they denied Christ. **long ago...marked out.** Apostasy and apostates in general were written about and condemned many centuries before, such as illustrated in vv. 5-7 and spoken of as Enoch did in vv. 14-16. Cf. Is. 8:19-21; 47:9-15; Hos. 9:9; Zeph. 3:1-8. Their doom was "pre-written" in Scripture as a warning to all who would come later. Jesus had warned about them in Matt. 7:15-20 (cf. Acts 20:29). The most recent warning had been 2 Pet. 2:3,17; 3:7. **this condemnation.** This refers to the judgment spoken of by others "long ago." Jude's present exposé of apostates placed them in the path of the very judgment of God, written of previously. **ungodly men.** Lit. "impious" or "without worship." Their lack of reverence for God was demonstrated by the fact that they infiltrated the church of God to corrupt it and gain riches from its people. Cf. vv. 15,16,18,19. **lewdness.** Lit. "unrestrained vice" or "gross immorality," which describes the shameless lifestyle of one who irreverently flaunts God's grace by indulging in unchecked and open immorality (cf. Rom. 6:15). **deny...Lord...Lord Jesus Christ.** *See note on 2 Pet. 2:1.* Two Gr. words for Lord are used here. The apostates disowned Christ as sovereign Lord (*despotēs*) and disdained any recognition of Christ as honorable Lord (*kurios*) by their wicked behavior. The better NT mss. omit "God" in the text (see marginal note), placing the emphasis clearly on one person, the Lord Jesus Christ, and emphasizing that apostates deny Him. *See note on 2 Pet. 2:1.* Cf. Matt. 10:33; 2 Tim. 2:12; Titus 1:16; 1 John 2:22,23. It is always true of apostates, false teachers, and false religions that they pervert what Scripture declares is true about the Lord Jesus Christ.

5-7 Jude provided 3 well known acts of apostasy from the OT as brief reminders (v. 5) to illustrate their damnable outcome as declared in v. 4.

5 saved...destroyed. Cf. Heb. 3:16-19. God miraculously delivered the nation of Israel out of Egyptian bondage (Ex. 12:51; Deut. 4:34) only to have them respond in unbelief, doubting, and defecting from faith in God that He could bring them into the Promised Land

lieve. 6 And the angels who did not keep
their [3]proper domain, but left their own
abode, He has reserved in everlasting
chains under darkness for the judgment of
the great day; 7 as [h]Sodom and Gomorrah,
and the cities around them in a similar
manner to these, having given themselves
over to sexual immorality and gone after
strange flesh, are set forth as an example,
suffering the [4]vengeance of eternal fire.
8 [i]Likewise also these dreamers defile the
flesh, reject authority, and [j]speak evil of
[5]dignitaries. 9 Yet Michael the archangel, in
[6]contending with the devil, when he disputed about the body of Moses, dared not
bring against him a reviling accusation, but
said, [k]"The Lord rebuke you!" 10 [l]But these
speak evil of whatever they do not know;
and whatever they know naturally, like
brute beasts, in these things they corrupt
themselves. 11 Woe to them! For they have
gone in the way [m]of Cain, [n]have run greedily in the error of Balaam for profit, and
perished [o]in the rebellion of Korah.

Apostates Depraved and Doomed

12 These are [7]spots in your love feasts,
while they feast with you without fear,
serving *only* themselves. *They are* clouds
without water, carried [8]about by the

6 [3] *own*
7 [h] Gen. 19:24; 2 Pet. 2:6 [4] *punishment*
8 [i] 2 Pet. 2:10 [j] Ex. 22:28 [5] *glorious ones*, lit. *glories*
9 [k] Zech. 3:2 [6] *arguing*
10 [l] 2 Pet. 2:12
11 [m] Gen. 4:3-8; Heb. 11:4; 1 John 3:12 [n] Num. 31:16; 2 Pet. 2:15; Rev. 2:14 [o] Num. 16:1-3, 31-35
12 [7] *stains*, or *hidden reefs* [8] NU, M *along*

(Num. 13:25–14:4), even to the extent of worshiping an idol of their own making, as well as murmuring against God instead of adoring Him (Ex. 16:7-12; 1 Cor. 10:10,11). That apostate generation died during 38 years of wilderness wanderings (Num. 14:22-30,35).

6 angels...did not keep. This apostasy of fallen angels is described in Gen. 6:1-3 as possessing men who then cohabited with women. *See note on 2 Pet. 2:4.* The transition to Sodom and Gomorrah in v. 7 points to the similitude of the sin of homosexuality and what these angels did in Gen. 6. **judgment...great day.** This refers to the final judgment when all demons and Satan are forever consigned to the "lake of fire" prepared for them (Matt. 25:41; Rev. 20:10) and all the ungodly (Rev. 20:15).

7 Sodom...Gomorrah. *See notes on 2 Pet. 2:6-10.* The destruction of these cities at the SE corner of the Dead Sea is used over 20 times in Scripture as an illustration of God's judgment during the days of Abraham and Lot (cf. Gen. 18:22–19:29). This destruction was in view of their apostasy, since it occurred about 450 years after the Flood, when at least one of Noah's sons, Shem (Gen. 11:10,11) was still living. Since this was only 100 years after Noah's death (Gen. 9:28), people would have known about the message of righteousness and judgment from God which Noah preached, and which they rejected. **similar...to these.** This points back to v. 6. **sexual immorality...strange flesh.** This refers to both the heterosexual (Gen. 19:8) and homosexual lusts (Gen. 19:4,5) of the residents. Cf. Lev. 18:22; 20:13; Rom. 1:27; 1 Cor. 6:9; 1 Tim. 1:10 for the absolute condemnation of homosexual activity. **eternal fire.** Sodom and Gomorrah illustrate God's fire of earthly judgment (cf. Rev. 16:8,9; 20:9) which was only a preview of the fire that can never be quenched in eternal hell (cf. Matt. 3:12; 18:8; 25:41; Mark 9:43,44,46,48; Luke 3:17; Rev. 19:20; 20:14,15; 21:8).

8 these dreamers. *See notes on 2 Pet. 2:10-12.* This refers to a confused state of the soul or abnormal imagination, producing delusions and sensual confusion. These men's minds were numb to the truth of God's Word so that, being beguiled and deluded, they fantasized wicked perversions, being blind and deaf to reality and truth. Perhaps they falsely claimed these were dreams/visions from God. "These" occurs 5 more times (vv. 10,12,14,16,19) in reference to the apostates, who are characterized in 3 ways (v. 8). **defile the flesh.** Similar to the inhabitants of Sodom and Gomorrah (v. 7), apostates have few, if any, moral restraints and thus are frequently characterized by immoral lifestyles (v. 4). Cf. Titus 1:15; Heb. 12:15; 2 Pet. 2:10-19; 3:3. **reject authority.** Like the sinning angels (v. 6), these pretenders rejected all authority, civil and spiritual, thus rejecting the Scriptures and denying Christ (v. 4). **speak evil...dignitaries.** Cf. v. 10. That the dignitaries (lit. "glories") are likely angels is supported by the illustration in v. 9.

9 Michael...archangel. The chief angel of God who especially watches over Israel (Dan. 10:13,21; 12:1) and leads the holy angels (Rev. 12:7). Nowhere else in Scripture is this struggle over the body of Moses mentioned. Michael had to fight with Satan to do God's bidding, as he did on another occasion in Dan. 10:13 (*see note there*). **the devil.** Another name for Satan which means "accuser" or "slanderer" (cf. Rev. 12:9,10). **body of Moses.** Moses died on Mt. Nebo in Moab without having entered the Promised Land and was secretly buried in a place not known to man (Deut. 34:5,6). It would likely be that this confrontation took place as Michael buried Moses to prevent Satan from using Moses' body for some diabolical purpose not stated. Perhaps Satan wanted to use it as an idol, an object of worship for Israel. God sent Michael, however, to be certain it was buried. This account was recorded in the pseudepigraphal *Assumption of Moses* (see Introduction: Interpretive Challenges). **reviling accusation.** *See note on 2 Pet. 2:11.* Rather than personally cursing such a powerful angel as Satan, Michael deferred to the ultimate, sovereign power of God following the example of the Angel of the Lord in Zech. 3:2. This is the supreme illustration of how Christians are to deal with Satan and demons. Believers are not to address them, but rather to seek the Lord's intervening power against them.

10 speak evil. Lit. "blaspheme." Cf. v. 8. Apostate teachers, in their brash, bold, egotistical infatuation with imagined power and authority, rail on that which they don't even understand. **whatever...whatever.** *See note on 2 Pet. 2:12.* Apostates are intellectually arrogant and spiritually ignorant in that they don't know because they are blinded by Satan (2 Cor. 4:4) and spiritual matters are beyond their unregenerate capacity to understand (1 Cor. 2:14). In divine matters, they are no brighter than the dumbest beasts. **corrupt themselves.** This speaks of spiritual and moral self-destruction.

11 Woe. In declaring ultimate spiritual judgment on the apostates, Jude followed the example of the prophets (cf. Is. 5:8-23) and of Christ (cf. Matt. 23:13,15,16,23,25,27,29). The severest judgment of all (Heb. 10:26), will come on apostates because they too followed the same path as Cain, Balaam, and Korah. **way of Cain.** Cain openly rebelled against God's revealed will regarding sacrifice (*see notes on Gen. 4:1-15*; cf. Heb. 11:4; 1 John 3:12). **error of Balaam.** Cf. Num. 22–25; *see note on 2 Pet. 2:15.* For a large financial reward, Balaam devised a plan for Balak, king of Moab, to entice Israel into a compromising situation with idolatry and immorality which would bring God's own judgment on His people (cf. Num. 31:16; Rev. 2:14). **rebellion of Korah.** *See notes on Num. 16:1-35.* Korah, plus 250 Jewish leaders, rejected the God-appointed leadership of Moses and Aaron in an attempt to impose his will upon God and the people. Apostates will unquestionably meet the same end as Korah—divine judgment.

12,13 *See notes on 2 Pet. 2:13-17.*

12 spots...love feasts. *See note on 2 Pet. 2:13.* "Spots" can be taken as "hidden rocks" or "reefs" or as "stains" (see marginal note). These apostates were dirt spots, filth on the garment of the church; or more likely, what God intended for the church as smooth sailing, they turned into a potential shipwreck through their presence. "Love feasts" were the regular gathering of the early church to partake of the bread and cup, plus share a common meal (cf. 1 Cor. 11:20-30). **clouds without water.** *See*

winds; late autumn trees without fruit,
twice dead, pulled up by the roots; 13 [p]rag-
ing waves of the sea, [q]foaming up their
own shame; wandering stars [r]for whom is
reserved the blackness of darkness forever.
14 Now Enoch, the seventh from Adam,
prophesied about these men also, saying,
"Behold, the Lord comes with ten thousands of His saints, 15 to execute judgment
on all, to convict all who are ungodly
among them of all their ungodly deeds
which they have committed in an ungodly
way, and of all the [s]harsh things which ungodly sinners have spoken against Him."

13 [p] Is. 57:20 [q] [Phil. 3:19] [r] 2 Pet. 2:17; Jude 6
15 [s] 1 Sam. 2:3
16 [t] 2 Pet. 2:18 [u] Prov. 28:21
17 [v] 2 Pet. 3:2
18 [w] Acts 20:29; [1 Tim. 4:1]; 2 Tim. 3:1; 4:3; 2 Pet. 3:3
19 [9] *soulish* or *worldly*

Apostates Predicted

16 These are grumblers, complainers,
walking according to their own lusts; and
they [t]mouth great swelling *words,* [u]flatter-
ing people to gain advantage. 17 [v]But you,
beloved, remember the words which were
spoken before by the apostles of our Lord
Jesus Christ: 18 how they told you that
[w]there would be mockers in the last time
who would walk according to their own
ungodly lusts. 19 These are [9]sensual persons, who cause divisions, not having the
Spirit.

note on 2 Pet. 2:17. Apostates promise spiritual life but are empty clouds which bring the hope of rain, but actually deliver nothing but dryness and death (cf. Prov. 25:14). They preach a false gospel that leads only to hell. **trees without fruit.** Apostates hold out the claim of providing a spiritual feast, but instead deliver famine (cf. Luke 16:6-9). Doubly dead trees will never yield fruit and, regardless of what they say, will always be barren because they are uprooted. Cf. Matt. 7:17-20.

13 raging waves. Apostates promise powerful ministry, but are quickly exposed as wreakers of havoc and workers of worthless shame (cf. Is. 57:20). **wandering stars.** This most likely refers to a meteor or shooting star which has an uncontrolled moment of brilliance and then fades away forever into nothing. Apostates promise enduring spiritual direction, but deliver a brief, aimless, and worthless flash.

14 Enoch. Following the genealogy of Gen. 5:1-24; 1 Chr. 1:1-3, Enoch was the seventh in the line of Adam. Because Enoch "walked with God," he was taken directly to heaven without having to die (cf. Gen. 5:24; Heb. 11:5). **prophesied about these men.** *See note on v. 4.* The source of this information was the Holy Spirit who inspired Jude. The fact that it was recorded in the nonbiblical and pseudepigraphal *Book of Enoch* had no effect on its accuracy. See Introduction: Interpretive Challenges. **Behold...Lord...saints.** Enoch, before the Flood, prophesied about Christ's second coming in judgment (cf. 1 Thess. 3:13). "Saints" can refer to either angels or believers. Since both angels (Matt. 24:31; 25:31; Mark 8:38; 2 Thess 1:7) and believers (Col. 3:4; 1 Thess. 3:13; Rev. 19:14) will accompany Him, it may refer to both (cf. Zech. 14:5), but the focus on judgment in v. 15 seems to favor angels, who are often seen in judgment action. While believers will have a role of judging during the Lord's earthly kingdom (*see note on 1 Cor. 6:2*) and will return when Christ comes to judge (Rev. 19:14), angels are the executioners of God at the second coming of Christ (see Matt. 13:39-41,49,50; 24:29-31; 25:31; 2 Thess. 1:7-10).

15 execute judgment. The sentence will be eternal hell (see Rev. 20:11-15). Cf. Matt. 5:22; 7:19; 8:12; 10:28; 13:40-42; 25:41,46). **ungodly.** *See note on v. 4.* The 4-fold use of this word as a description of the apostates (cf. vv 4,18) identifies the core iniquity, which is failure to reverence God. See Peter's use of the term in 2 Pet. 2:5,6; 3:7. It was for such that Christ died (Rom. 5:6).

16 grumblers. *See note on v. 5.* The word, found only here in the NT, is used in the LXX to describe the murmurings of Israel against God (Ex. 16:7-9; Num. 14:27,29; 1 Cor. 10:10). **complainers.** Lit. "finding fault." They gave vent to dissatisfaction with God's will and way as was the case with Israel, Sodom, the fallen angels, Cain, Korah, and Balaam (cf. vv. 5-7,11). **walking...own lusts.** *See notes on 2 Pet. 2:10,18; 3:3.* This is a common phrase used to describe the unconverted (v. 18; 2 Tim. 4:3). Apostates are especially driven by a desire for sinful self-satisfaction. **mouth great...*words.*** *See note on 2 Pet. 2:18.* They speak arrogantly, pompously, and even magnificently, but with empty, lifeless words of no spiritual value. Their message has external attractiveness, but is void of the powerful substance of divine truth. **flattering people.** They tell people what they want to hear for their own profit (cf. 2 Tim. 4:3,4), rather than proclaiming the truth of God's Word for the auditors' benefit. Cf. Pss. 5:9; 12:2,3; Prov. 26:28; 29:5; Rom. 3:13; 16:18.

17,18 *See notes on 2 Pet. 3:1-3.*

17 words...by the apostles. The apostles had warned the coming generation about apostates, so that they would be prepared and not be taken by surprise (cf. Acts 20:28-31; 1 Tim. 4:1,2; 2 Tim. 3:1-5; 4:1-3; 2 Pet. 2:1–3:4; 1 John 2:18; 2 John 7-11). God's Word is designed to warn and protect (Acts 20:31; 1 Cor. 4:14); as v. 18 indicates, there had been continually repeated warnings.

18 mockers. *See note on 2 Pet. 3:3.* These are the scoffers at God's future plans who pretend to know the truth but deny that judgment will ever come. **last time.** Lit. at the chronological end of the current epoch or season (cf. 2 Tim. 3:1). This term refers to the time of Messiah from His first coming until His second (*see notes on 2 Tim. 3:1; 2 Pet. 3:3; 1 John 2:18*). These characteristics will prevail until Christ returns. **walk...ungodly lust.** *See note on v. 16.*

19 sensual persons. Apostate teachers advertise themselves as having the highest spiritual knowledge, but are actually attracted to the most debased levels of life. They are "soulish" not "spiritual." Cf. James 3:15. **cause divisions.** They fractured the church rather than united it (cf. Eph. 4:4-6; Phil. 2:2). **not having the Spirit.** To not have

Profile of an Apostate

1. Ungodly (v. 4)
2. Morally perverted (v. 4)
3. Deny Christ (v. 4)
4. Defile the flesh (v. 8)
5. Rebellious (v. 8)
6. Revile holy angels (v. 8)
7. Dreamers (v. 10)
8. Ignorant (v. 10)
9. Corrupted (v. 10)
10. Grumblers (v. 16)
11. Fault finders (v. 16)
12. Self seeking (v. 16)
13. Arrogant speakers (v. 16)
14. Flatterers (v. 16)
15. Mockers (v. 18)
16. Cause division (v. 19)
17. Worldly minded (v. 19)
18. Without the Spirit (v. 19)

Maintain Your Life with God

20 But you, beloved, [x]building yourselves up on your most holy faith, [y]pray-
ing in the Holy Spirit, 21 keep yourselves
in the love of God, [z]looking for the mercy
of our Lord Jesus Christ unto eternal life.
22 And on some have compassion, [1]mak-
ing a distinction; 23 but [a]others save [2]with
fear, [b]pulling *them* out of the [3]fire, hating
even [c]the garment defiled by the flesh.

Glory to God

24 [d]Now to Him who is able to keep
[4]you from stumbling,
And [e]to present *you* faultless
Before the presence of His glory
With exceeding joy,
25 To [5]God our Savior,
[6]Who alone is wise,
Be glory and majesty,
Dominion and [7]power,
Both now and forever.
Amen.

20 [x] Col. 2:7; 1 Thess. 5:11 [y] [Rom. 8:26] **21** [z] Titus 2:13; Heb. 9:28; 2 Pet. 3:12 **22** [1] NU *who are doubting* (or *making distinctions*) **23** [a] Rom. 11:14 [b] Amos 4:11; Zech. 3:2; 1 Cor. 3:15 [c] [Zech. 3:4, 5]; Rev. 3:4 [2] NU omits *with fear* [3] NU adds *and on some have mercy with fear* **24** [d] [Eph. 3:20] [4] M *them* [e] Col. 1:22

25 [5] NU *the only God our* [6] NU *Through Jesus Christ our Lord, Be glory* [7] NU adds *Before all time,*

the Spiri, is to not have spiritual life at all (*see notes on Rom. 8:9; 1 Cor. 6:19,20*) or, in other words, to be an unbeliever.

20 building. True believers have a sure foundation (1 Cor. 3:11) and cornerstone (Eph. 2:20) in Jesus Christ. The truths of the Christian faith (cf. v. 3) have been provided in the teaching of the apostles and prophets (Eph. 2:20), so that Christians can build themselves up by the Word of God (Acts 20:32). **praying in the Holy Spirit.** *See note on Eph 6:18.* This is not a call to some ecstatic form of prayer, but simply a call to pray consistently in the will and power of the Spirit, as one would pray in the name of Jesus Christ (cf. Rom. 8:26,27).

21 keep. Cf. Acts 13:43. This imperative establishes the believer's responsibility to be obedient and faithful by living out his salvation (cf. Phil. 2:12), while God works out His will (cf. Phil. 2:13). It means to remain in the place of obedience where God's love is poured out on His children, as opposed to being disobedient and incurring His chastening (cf. 1 Cor. 11:27-31; Heb. 12:5-11). This refers to the perseverance of the saints, the counterbalance to God's sovereign preservation of believers in Christ (cf. v. 1). This is accomplished by: 1) building one's self up in the Word of God (v. 20); 2) praying in the Holy Spirit (v. 20); and 3) looking for the finalization of eternal life (v. 21). For a related discussion of the perseverance of the saints, *see note on Matt. 24:13.* **looking.** An eager anticipation of Christ's second coming to provide eternal life in its ultimate, resurrection form (cf. Titus 2:13; 1 John 3:1-3), which is the supreme expression of God's mercy on one to whom Christ's righteousness has undeservedly been imputed (cf. v. 2). Paul called this "loving His appearing" (2 Tim. 3:8) and John wrote that such a steady anticipation was purifying (1 John 3:3).

22,23 some. There are several textual variants here which could result in either two or three groups being indicated. They are: 1) sincere doubters who deserve compassion (v. 22; see marginal note); 2) those who are deeper in unbelief and urgently need to be pulled from the fire (v. 23); and 3) those declared disciples of apostasy who still deserve mercy, but are to be handled with much fear (v. 23; see marginal note), lest the would-be-rescuer also be spiritually sullied. Given the mss. evidence and Jude's pattern of writing in triads, 3 groups is the more likely scenario.

22 compassion. These victims of the apostate teachers need mercy and patience because they have not yet reached a firm conclusion about Christ and eternal life, and so remain doubters (see marginal note) who could possibly be swayed to the truth.

23 others save. Others, who are committed to the errors taught by the apostates, need immediate and forthright attention before they are further entrenched on the road to the fire of hell (cf. v. 7) as a result of embracing deceptive lies. **with fear.** See marginal note for this phrase. This third group also needs mercy, even though they are thoroughly polluted by apostate teaching. These people are to be given the true gospel, but with great fear, lest the deliverer be contaminated also. The defiled garment pictures the apostate's debauched life, which can spread its contagion to the well-meaning evangel.

24,25 Jude's lovely benediction/doxology stands as one of the most splendid in the NT (cf. Rom. 11:33-36; 16:25-27; 2 Cor. 13:14; Heb. 13:20,21). It returned to the theme of salvation which Jude had hoped to develop at the beginning (cf. v. 3) and bolstered the courage of believers to know that Christ would protect them from the present apostasy.

24 Him who is able. This speaks of omnipotent God. Cf. Gen. 18:15; Deut. 7:21; 1 Sam. 14:6; Matt. 19:26. **keep you from stumbling.** *See notes on v. 1; 1 Pet. 1:3-5.* The power of Christ would sustain the sincere believer from falling to the temptation of apostasy (cf. Job 42:2; Pss. 37:23,24; 121:3; Jer. 32:17; Matt. 19:26; Luke 1:37; John 6:39,40,44; 10:27-30; Eph. 3:20). **present *you* faultless.** Cf. 2 Cor. 11:1; Eph. 5:27. Christians possess Christ's imputed righteousness through justification by faith and have been made worthy of eternal life in heaven (*see notes on Rom. 8:31-39*). **with exceeding joy.** This refers primarily to the joy of the Savior (cf. Heb. 12:2) but also includes the joy of believers (cf. 1 Pet. 1:8). Joy is the dominant expression of heaven (see Matt. 25:23). **God our Savior.** God is by nature a saving God, unlike the reluctant and indifferent false deities of human and demon invention (*see notes on 1 Tim. 2:2; 4:10; 2 Tim. 1:10; Titus 1:3; 2:10; 3:4; 2 Pet. 1:1; 1 John 4:14*).

25 alone is wise. Divine wisdom is embodied by Christ alone (cf. 1 Cor. 1:24,30; Col. 2:3) and not by any human person or group, like the apostates. **glory...power.** Both Jude on earth and the angels and saints in heaven (Rev. 4:10,11; 5:12-14) ascribed these qualities to our God and the Lord Jesus Christ.

THE REVELATION

of Jesus Christ

Title

Unlike most books of the Bible, Revelation contains its own title: "The Revelation of Jesus Christ" (1:1). "Revelation" (Gr., *apokalupsis*) means "an uncovering," "an unveiling," or "a disclosure." In the NT, this word describes the unveiling of spiritual truth (Rom. 16:25; Gal. 1:12; Eph. 1:17; 3:3), the revealing of the sons of God (Rom. 8:19), Christ's incarnation (Luke 2:32), and His glorious appearing at His second coming (2 Thess. 1:7; 1 Pet. 1:7). In all its uses, "revelation" refers to something or someone, once hidden, becoming visible. What this book reveals or unveils is Jesus Christ in glory. Truths about Him and His final victory, that the rest of Scripture merely allude to, become clearly visible through revelation about Jesus Christ (see Historical and Theological Themes). This revelation was given to Him by God the Father, and it was communicated to the Apostle John by an angel (1:1).

Author and Date

Four times the author identifies himself as John (1:1,4,9; 22:8). Early tradition unanimously identified him as John the apostle, author of the fourth gospel and three epistles. For example, important second century witnesses to the Apostle John's authorship include Justin Martyr, Irenaeus, Clement of Alexandria, and Tertullian. Many of the book's original readers were still alive during the lifetimes of Justin Martyr and Irenaeus—both of whom held to apostolic authorship.

There are differences in style between Revelation and John's other writings, but they are insignificant and do not preclude one man from writing both. In fact, there are some striking parallels between Revelation and John's other works. Only John's gospel and Revelation refer to Jesus Christ as the Word (19:13; John 1:1). Revelation (1:7) and John's gospel (19:37) translate Zech. 12:10 differently from the Septuagint, but in agreement with each other. Only Revelation and the Gospel of John describe Jesus as the Lamb (5:6,8; John 1:29); both describe Jesus as a witness (cf. 1:5; John 5:31,32).

Revelation was written in the last decade of the first century (ca. A.D. 94–96), near the end of Emperor Domitian's reign (A.D. 81–96). Although some date it during Nero's reign (A.D. 54–68), their arguments are unconvincing and conflict with the view of the early church. Writing in the second century, Irenaeus declared that Revelation had been written toward the end of Domitian's reign. Later writers, such as Clement of Alexandria, Origen, Victorinus (who wrote one of the earliest commentaries on Revelation), Eusebius, and Jerome affirm the Domitian date.

The spiritual decline of the 7 churches (chaps. 2,3) also argues for the later date. Those churches were strong and spiritually healthy in the mid-60s, when Paul last ministered in Asia Minor. The brief time between Paul's ministry there and the end of Nero's reign was too short for such a decline to have occurred. The longer time gap also explains the rise of the heretical sect known as the Nicolaitans (2:6,15), who are not mentioned in Paul's letters, not even to one or more of these same churches (Ephesians). Finally, dating Revelation during Nero's reign does not allow time for John's ministry in Asia Minor to reach the point at which the authorities would have felt the need to exile him.

Background and Setting

Revelation begins with John, the last surviving apostle and an old man, in exile on the small, barren island of Patmos, located in the Aegean Sea southwest of Ephesus. The Roman authorities had banished him there because of his faithful preaching of the gospel (1:9). While on Patmos, John received a series of visions that laid out the future history of the world.

When he was arrested, John was in Ephesus, ministering to the church there and in the surrounding cities. Seeking to strengthen those congregations, he could no longer minister to them in person and, following the divine command (1:11), John addressed Revelation to them (1:4). The churches had begun to feel the effects of persecution; at least one man—probably a pastor—had already been martyred (2:13), and John himself had been exiled. But the storm of persecution was about to break in full fury upon the 7 churches so dear to the apostle's heart (2:10). To those churches, Revelation provided a message of hope: God is in sovereign control of all the events of human history, and though evil often seems pervasive and wicked men all powerful, their ultimate doom is certain. Christ will come in glory to judge and rule.

Historical and Theological Themes

Since it is primarily prophetic, Revelation contains little historical material, other than that in chaps. 1–3. The 7 churches to whom the letter was addressed were existing churches in Asia Minor (modern Turkey). Apparently, they were singled out because John had ministered in them.

Revelation is first and foremost a revelation about Jesus Christ (1:1). The book depicts Him as the risen, glorified Son of God ministering among the churches (1:10ff.), as "the faithful witness, the firstborn from the dead, and the ruler over the kings of the earth" (1:5), as "the Alpha and the Omega, the Beginning and the End" (1:8), as the one "who is and who was and who is to come, the Almighty" (1:8), as the First and the Last (1:11), as the Son of Man (1:13), as the one who was dead, but now is alive forevermore (1:18), as the Son of God (2:18), as the one who is holy and true (3:7), as "the Amen, the Faithful and True Witness, the Beginning of the creation of God" (3:14), as the Lion of the tribe of Judah (5:5), as the Lamb in heaven, with authority to open the title deed to the earth (6:1ff.), as the Lamb on the throne (7:17), as the Messiah who will reign forever (11:15), as the Word of God (19:13), as the majestic King of kings and Lord of lords, returning in glorious splendor to conquer His foes (19:11ff.), and as "the Root and the Offspring of David, the Bright and Morning Star" (22:16).

Many other rich theological themes find expression in Revelation. The church is warned about sin and exhorted to holiness. John's vivid pictures of worship in heaven both exhort and instruct believers. In few other books of the Bible is the ministry of angels so prominent. Revelation's primary theological contribution is to eschatology, i.e., the doctrine of last things. In it we learn about: the final political setup of the world; the last battle of human history; the career and ultimate defeat of Antichrist; Christ's 1,000 year earthly kingdom; the glories of heaven and the eternal state; and the final state of the wicked and the righteous. Finally, only Daniel rivals this book in declaring that God providentially rules over the kingdoms of men and will accomplish His sovereign purposes regardless of human or demonic opposition.

Interpretive Challenges

No other NT book poses more serious and difficult interpretive challenges than Revelation. The book's vivid imagery and striking symbolism have produced 4 main interpretive approaches:

The *preterist* approach interprets Revelation as a description of first century events in the Roman Empire (see Author and Date). This view conflicts with the book's own often repeated claim to be prophecy (1:3; 22:7,10,18,19). It is impossible to see all the events in Revelation as already fulfilled. The second coming of Christ, for example, obviously did not take place in the first century.

The *historicist* approach views Revelation as a panoramic view of church history from apostolic times to the present—seeing in the symbolism such events as the barbarian invasions of Rome, the rise of the Roman Catholic Church (as well as various individual popes), the emergence of Islam, and the French Revolution. This interpretive method robs Revelation of any meaning for those to whom it was written. It also ignores the time limitations the book itself places on the unfolding events (cf. 11:2; 12:6,14; 13:5). Historicism has produced many different—and often conflicting—interpretations of the actual historical events contained in Revelation.

The *idealist* approach interprets Revelation as a timeless depiction of the cosmic struggle between the forces of good and evil. In this view, the book contains neither historical allusions nor predictive prophecy. This view also ignores Revelation's prophetic character and, if carried to its logical conclusion, severs the book from any connection with actual historical events. Revelation then becomes merely a collection of stories designed to teach spiritual truth.

The *futurist* approach insists that the events of chaps. 6–22 are yet future, and that those chapters literally and symbolically depict actual people and events yet to appear on the world scene. It describes the events surrounding the second coming of Jesus Christ (chaps. 6–19), the Millennium and final judgment (chap. 20), and the eternal state (chaps. 21,22). Only this view does justice to Revelation's claim to be prophecy and interprets the book by the same grammatical-historical method as chaps. 1–3 and the rest of Scripture.

Outline

- I. The Things which You Have Seen (1:1-20)
  - A. The Prologue (1:1-8)
  - B. The Vision of the Glorified Christ (1:9-18)
  - C. The Apostle's Commission to Write (1:19,20)
- II. The Things which Are (2:1–3:22)
  - A. The Letter to the Church at Ephesus (2:1-7)
  - B. The Letter to the Church at Smyrna (2:8-11)
  - C. The Letter to the Church at Pergamos (2:12-17)
  - D. The Letter to the Church at Thyatira (2:18-29)
  - E. The Letter to the Church at Sardis (3:1-6)
  - F. The Letter to the Church at Philadelphia (3:7-13)
  - G. The Letter to the Church at Laodicea (3:14-22)
- III. The Things which Will Take Place after This (4:1–22:21)
  - A. Worship in Heaven (4:1–5:14)
  - B. The Great Tribulation (6:1–18:24)
  - C. The Return of the King (19:1-21)
  - D. The Millennium (20:1-10)
  - E. The Great White Throne Judgment (20:11-15)
  - F. The Eternal State (21:1–22:21)

Introduction and Benediction

1 The Revelation of Jesus Christ, [a]which
God gave Him to show His servants—
things which must [1]shortly take place.
And [b]He sent and signified *it* by His angel
to His servant John, **2** [c]who bore witness to
the word of God, and to the testimony of
Jesus Christ, to all things [d]that he saw.
3 [e]Blessed *is* he who reads and those who
hear the words of this prophecy, and keep
those things which are written in it; for [f]the
time *is* near.

Greeting the Seven Churches

4 John, to the seven churches which are
in Asia:

Grace to you and peace from Him [g]who
is and [h]who was and who is to come, [i]and
from the seven Spirits who are before His
throne, **5** and from Jesus Christ, [j]the faithful [k]witness, the [l]firstborn from the dead,
and [m]the ruler over the kings of the earth.

To Him [n]who [2]loved us [o]and washed us
from our sins in His own blood, **6** and has
[p]made us [3]kings and priests to His God
and Father, [q]to Him *be* glory and dominion
forever and ever. Amen.

7 Behold, He is coming with [r]clouds,
and every eye will see Him, even [s]they
who pierced Him. And all the tribes of the
earth will mourn because of Him. Even so,
Amen.

8 [t]"I am the Alpha and the Omega, [4]*the*
Beginning and *the* End," says the [5]Lord,
[u]"who is and who was and who is to come,
the [v]Almighty."

Vision of the Son of Man

9 I, John, [6]both your brother and [w]com-
panion in the tribulation and [x]kingdom and
patience of Jesus Christ, was on the island
that is called Patmos for the word of God
and for the testimony of Jesus Christ. **10** [y]I

CHAPTER 1

1 [a] John 3:32 [b] Rev. 22:6 [1] *quickly* or *swiftly*
2 [c] 1 Cor. 1:6 [d] 1 John 1:1
3 [e] Luke 11:28; Rev. 22:7 [f] James 5:8; Rev. 22:10
4 [g] Ex. 3:14 [h] John 1:1 [i] [Is. 11:2]; Zech. 3:9; Rev. 3:1; 4:5; 5:6
5 [j] John 8:14; Prov. 14:5 [k] Is. 55:4 [l] Ps. 89:27; 1 Cor. 15:20; [Col. 1:18] [m] Rev. 17:14 [n] John 13:34 [o] Heb. 9:14 [2] NU *loves us and freed;* M *loves us and washed*
6 [p] 1 Pet. 2:5,9 [q] 1 Tim. 6:16 [3] NU, M *a kingdom*
7 [r] Matt. 24:30 [s] Zech. 12:10-14; John 19:37
8 [t] Is. 41:4; Rev. 21:6; 22:13 [u] Rev. 4:8; 11:17 [v] Is. 9:6

[4] NU, M omit *the Beginning and the End* [5] NU, M *Lord God* **9** [w] Phil. 1:7 [x] [Rom. 8:17; 2 Tim. 2:12] [6] NU, M omit *both* **10** [y] Acts 10:10

1:1 The Revelation. The Gr. word from which the Eng. word "apocalypse" comes lit. means "to uncover, or to reveal." When it refers to a person, it means that person becomes clearly visible (see Introduction: Title; cf. Luke 2:30-32; Rom. 8:19; 1 Cor. 1:7; 1 Pet. 1:7). **Jesus Christ.** The gospels unveil Christ at His first coming in humiliation; Revelation reveals Him in His exaltation: 1) in blazing glory (vv. 7-20); 2) over His church, as its Lord (chaps. 2,3); 3) in His second coming, as He takes back the earth from the usurper, Satan, and establishes His kingdom (chaps. 4–20); and 4) as He lights up the eternal state (chaps. 21,22). The NT writers eagerly anticipate this unveiling (1 Cor. 1:7; 2 Thess. 1:7; 1 Pet. 1:7). **God gave Him.** As a reward for Christ's perfect submission and atonement, the Father now presented to Him the great record of His future glory (cf. Phil. 2:5-11). Readers eavesdrop on the gift of this book, from the Father to His Son. **shortly.** The primary meaning of this word (lit. "soon"; cf. 2:5,16; 3:11; 11:14; 22:12; 2 Tim. 4:9) underscores the imminence of Christ's return.

1:3 Blessed. This is the only biblical book that comes with a blessing for the one who listens to it being read and explained and then responds in obedience. This is the first of 7 beatitudes in the book (v. 3; 14:13; 16:15; 19:9; 20:6; 22:7,14). **time *is* near.** "Time" refers to epochs, eras, or seasons. The next great epoch of God's redemptive history is imminent. But although Christ's coming is the next event, it may be delayed so long that people begin to question whether He will ever come (cf. Matt. 24:36-39; 2 Pet. 3:3,4).

1:4 seven churches which are in Asia. Asia Minor, equivalent to modern Turkey, was composed of 7 postal districts. At the center of those districts were 7 key cities which served as central points for the dissemination of information. It is to the churches in those cities that John writes. **who is and who was and who is to come.** God's eternal presence is not limited by time. He has always been present and will come in the future. **the seven Spirits.** There are two possible meanings: 1) a reference to Isaiah's prophecy concerning the 7-fold ministry of the Holy Spirit (Is. 11:2); or 2) more likely, it is a reference to the lampstand with 7 lamps (a menorah) in Zechariah—also a description of the Holy Spirit (*see notes on 4:5; 5:6; Zech. 4:1-10*). In either case, 7 is the number of completeness, so John is identifying the fullness of the Holy Spirit.

1:5 firstborn. Of all who have been or will be raised from the dead, He is the preeminent one, the only one who is the rightful heir (cf. 3:14; Ps. 89:27; Col. 1:15).

1:6 kings and priests. More accurately, "a kingdom and priests." All who believe live in the sphere of God's rule, a kingdom entered by faith in Jesus Christ. And as priests, believers have the right to enter God's presence.

1:7 coming with clouds. This echoes the promise of Daniel: The Son of Man will come with the clouds of heaven (Dan. 7:13)—not ordinary clouds but clouds of glory. In the OT, God often manifested Himself in an energized, blazing light, called the Shekinah or glory cloud. No one could see it fully and live (Ex. 33:20), so it had to be veiled. But when Christ returns, the glory will be completely visible. cf. Matt. 24:29,30; 25:31; *see notes on 6:12-17*. **they who pierced.** Not a reference to the 4 Roman soldiers usually involved in crucifixion, but to the Jews who were actually responsible for Christ's death (Acts 2:22,23; 3:14,15). Zechariah identified the ones who pierced Him as "the house of David" and "the inhabitants of Jerusalem" and prophesied that they will weep tears of genuine repentance because of what they did to their Messiah (Zech. 12:10). **all the tribes...will mourn.** The mourning of the rest of the earth's inhabitants is not that which accompanies genuine repentance (cf. 9:21). It is the result of guilt for sin and fear of punishment (6:16; cf. Gen. 3:8-10).

1:8 Alpha and the Omega. These are the first and last letters of the Greek alphabet. An alphabet is an ingenious way to store and communicate knowledge. The 26 letters in the English alphabet, arranged in almost endless combinations, can hold and convey all knowledge. Christ is the supreme, sovereign alphabet; there is nothing outside His knowledge, so as there are no unknown factors that can sabotage His second coming. (cf. Col. 2:3). **the Almighty.** "Almighty God" occurs 8 times in Revelation, underscoring that God's power is supreme over all the cataclysmic events it records (see also 4:8; 11:17; 15:3; 16:7,14; 19:15; 21:22). He exercises sovereign control over every person, object, and event, and not one molecule in the universe is outside that dominion.

1:9-17 This vision of Christ is equaled in grandeur only by the vision of His final return as King of kings and Lord of lords (19:11-16).

1:9 tribulation and kingdom and patience. Four characteristics that John and his believing readers share: 1) persecution for their faith; 2) membership in the redeemed community over which Christ serves as Lord and King; 3) eager anticipation of the glory of His coming millennial reign on earth; and 4) endurance and perseverance in spite of difficult times. **island...called Patmos.** Located in the Aegean Sea

was in the Spirit on [z]the Lord's Day, and I
heard behind me [a]a loud voice, as of a trumpet, 11 saying, [7]"I am the Alpha and the
Omega, the First and the Last," and, "What
you see, write in a book and send *it* to the
seven churches [8]which are in Asia: to Ephesus, to Smyrna, to Pergamos, to Thyatira, to
Sardis, to Philadelphia, and to Laodicea."
12 Then I turned to see the voice that
spoke with me. And having turned [b]I saw
seven golden lampstands, 13 [c]and in the
midst of the seven lampstands [d]*One* like
the Son of Man, [e]clothed with a garment
down to the feet and [f]girded about the
chest with a golden band. 14 His head and
[g]hair *were* white like wool, as white as
snow, and [h]His eyes like a flame of fire;
15 [i]His feet *were* like fine brass, as if refined
in a furnace, and [j]His voice as the sound of
many waters; 16 [k]He had in His right hand
seven stars, [l]out of His mouth went a
sharp two-edged sword, [m]and His countenance *was* like the sun shining in its
strength. 17 And [n]when I saw Him, I fell at
His feet as dead. But [o]He laid His right
hand on me, saying [9]to me, "Do not be
afraid; [p]I am the First and the Last. 18 [q]I *am*
He who lives, and was dead, and behold,
[r]I am alive forevermore. Amen. And [s]I
have the keys of [1]Hades and of Death.
19 [2]Write the things which you have [t]seen,
[u]and the things which are, [v]and the things
which will take place after this. 20 The
[3]mystery of the seven stars which you saw
in My right hand, and the seven golden
lampstands: The seven stars are [w]the [4]an-
gels of the seven churches, and [x]the seven
lampstands [5]which you saw are the seven
churches.

The Loveless Church

2 "To the [1]angel of the church of Ephesus write,
'These things says [a]He who holds the
seven stars in His right hand, [b]who walks
in the midst of the seven golden lampstands: 2 [c]"I know your works, your labor,

10 [z]Acts 20:7 [a]Rev. 4:1 **11** [7]NU, M omit *"I am the Alpha and the Omega, the First and the Last," and,* [8]NU, M omit *which are in Asia* **12** [b]Ex. 25:37; Zech. 4:2; Rev. 1:20; 2:1 **13** [c]Rev. 2:1 [d]Ezek. 1:26; Dan. 7:13; 10:16; Rev. 14:14 [e]Dan. 10:5 [f]Rev. 15:6 **14** [g]Dan. 7:9 [h]Dan. 10:6; Rev. 2:18; 19:12 **15** [i]Ezek. 1:7; Dan. 10:6; Rev. 2:18 [j]Ezek. 1:24; 43:2; Rev. 14:2; 19:6 **16** [k]Rev. 1:20; 2:1; 3:1 [l]Is. 49:2; [Heb. 4:12]; Rev. 2:12, 16; 19:15 [m]Matt. 17:2; Acts 26:13; Rev. 10:1 **17** [n]Ezek. 1:28 [o]Dan. 8:18; 10:10, 12 [p]Is. 41:4; 44:6; 48:12; Rev. 2:8; 22:13 [9]NU, M omit *to me* **18** [q]Rom. 6:9; Rev. 2:8; 10:6; 15:7 [r]Rev. 4:9 [s]Ps. 68:20 [1]Lit. *Unseen;* the unseen realm

19 [t]Rev. 1:9-18 [u]Rev. 2:1 [v]John 16:13; Rev. 4:1 [2]NU, M *Therefore, write* **20** [w]Mal. 2:7; Rev. 2:1 [x]Ex. 25:37; 37:23; Zech. 4:2; Matt. 5:15; Phil. 2:15 [3]*hidden truth* [4]Or *messengers* [5]NU, M omit *which you saw*
CHAPTER 2 **1** [a]Rev. 1:16 [b]Rev. 1:13 [1]Or *messenger* **2** [c]Ps. 1:6

off the coast of Asia Minor (modern Turkey) and part of a group of about 50 islands, Patmos is a barren, rocky, crescent-shaped island that is about 10 mi. long and less than 6 mi. at its widest point. It served as a Roman penal colony. According to early Christian historian, Eusebius, the emperor Nerva (A.D. 96–98) released John from Patmos.

1:10 in the Spirit. This was not a dream. John was supernaturally transported out of the material world awake—not sleeping—to an experience beyond the normal senses. The Holy Spirit empowered his senses to perceive revelation from God (cf. Acts 10:11). **Lord's Day.** This phrase appears in many early Christian writings and refers to Sunday, the day of the Lord's resurrection. Some have suggested this phrase refers to "the Day of the Lord," but the context doesn't support that interpretation, and the grammatical form of the word "Lord" is adjectival, thus "the Lord's day." **loud voice.** Throughout Revelation, a loud sound or voice indicates the solemnity of what God is about to reveal.

1:11 book. The Gr. word refers to a scroll made of parchment formed from papyrus, a reed that grows plentifully along the Nile.

1:12 lampstands. These were portable gold lampstands that held small oil lamps. Each lampstand represented a church (v. 20), from which the light of life shone. Throughout Scripture, 7 is the number of completeness, so these 7 lampstands are representative of all the churches.

1:13 Son of Man. According to the gospels, this is the title Christ used most often for Himself during His earthly ministry (81 times in the gospels). Taken from the heavenly vision in Dan. 7:13, it is an implied claim to deity. **garment.** Most occurrences of this word in the Septuagint, the Gr. OT, refer to the garment of the High-Priest. The golden sash across His chest completes the picture of Christ serving in His priestly role (cf. Lev. 16:1-4; Heb. 2:17).

1:14 white like wool. "White" does not refer to a flat white color but a blazing, glowing, white light (cf. Dan. 7:9). Like the glory cloud (or Shekinah), it is a picture of His holiness. **eyes...flame of fire.** Like two lasers, the eyes of the exalted Lord look with penetrating gaze into the depths of His church (2:18; 19:12; Heb. 4:13).

1:15 feet...fine brass. The altar of burnt offering was covered with brass and its utensils were made of the same material (cf. Ex. 38:1-7). Glowing hot, brass feet are a clear reference to divine judgment. Jesus Christ with feet of judgment is moving through His church to exercise His chastening authority upon sin. **voice... sound of many waters.** No longer was His voice like the crystal clear note of a trumpet (v. 10), but John likened it to the crashing of the surf against the rocks of the island (cf. Ezek. 43:2). It was the voice of authority.

1:16 seven stars. These are the messengers who represent the 7 churches (*see note on v. 20*). Christ holds them in His hand, which means that He controls the church and its leaders. **a sharp two-edged sword.** A large, two-edged broad sword. It signifies judgment (cf. 2:16; 19:15) on those who attack His people and destroy His church.

1:17 fell at His feet. A common response to seeing the awesome glory of the Lord (Gen. 17:3; Num. 16:22; Ezek. 1:28; Is. 6:1-8; Acts 9:4). **First and the Last.** Jesus Christ applies this OT name for Yahweh (22:13; Is. 41:4; 44:6; 48:12) to Himself, clearly claiming to be God. Idols will come and go. He was before them, and He will remain after them.

1:18 keys of Hades and of Death. *See note on Luke 16:23.* Death and Hades are essentially synonyms, but death is the condition and Hades, equivalent to the OT Sheol, the place of the dead (*see note on 20:13*). Christ decides who lives, who dies, and when.

1:19 This verse provides a simple outline for the entire book: "the things which you have seen" refers to the vision John has just seen (chap. 1); "the things which are" denotes the letters to the churches (chaps. 2,3); and "the things which will take place after this" refers to the revelation of future history (chaps. 4–22).

1:20 the angels. The word lit. means "messenger." Although it can mean angel—and does throughout the book—it cannot refer to angels here because angels are never leaders in the church. Most likely, these messengers are the 7 key elders representing each of those churches (*see note on v. 16*).

2:1–3:22 Although these 7 churches were actual, historical churches in Asia Minor, they represent the types of churches that perennially exist throughout the church age. What Christ says to these churches is relevant in all times.

2:1 angel. The elder or pastor from the church (*see note on 1:20*). **Ephesus.** It was an inland city 3 mi. from the sea, but the broad

your [2]patience, and that you cannot [3]bear
those who are evil. And [d]you have tested
those [e]who say they are apostles and are
not, and have found them liars; **3** and you
have persevered and have patience, and
have labored for My name's sake and have
[f]not become weary. **4** Nevertheless I have
this against you, that you have left your
first love. **5** Remember therefore from
where you have fallen; repent and do the
first works, [g]or else I will come to you
quickly and remove your lampstand from
its place—unless you repent. **6** But this you
have, that you hate the deeds of the Nicolaitans, which I also hate.

7 [h]"He who has an ear, let him hear what
the Spirit says to the churches. To him who
overcomes I will give [i]to eat from [j]the tree
of life, which is in the midst of the Paradise
of God."'

The Persecuted Church

8 "And to the [4]angel of the church in
Smyrna write,

'These things says [k]the First and the Last,
who was dead, and came to life: **9** "I know
your works, tribulation, and poverty (but
you are [l]rich); and *I know* the blasphemy of
[m]those who say they are Jews and are not,
[n]but *are* a [5]synagogue of Satan. **10** [o]Do not
fear any of those things which you are
about to suffer. Indeed, the devil is about to
throw *some* of you into prison, that you
may be tested, and you will have tribulation ten days. [p]Be faithful until death, and I
will give you [q]the crown of life.

2 [d]John 6:6; 1 John 4:1 [e]2 Cor. 11:13 [2]*perseverance* [3]*endure*
3 [f]Gal. 6:9; Heb. 12:3, 5
5 [g]Matt. 21:41
7 [h]Matt. 11:15; Rev. 2:11, 17; 3:6, 13, 22; 13:9 [i][Rev. 22:2, 14] [j][Gen. 2:9; 3:22]
8 [k]Rev. 1:8, 17, 18 [4]*Or messenger*
9 [l]Luke 12:21 [m]Rom. 2:17 [n]Rev. 3:9 [5]*congregation*
10 [o]Matt. 10:22 [p]Matt. 24:13 [q]James 1:12

mouth of the Cayster River allowed access and provided the greatest harbor in Asia Minor. Four great trade roads went through Ephesus; therefore, it became known as the gateway to Asia. It was the center of the worship of Artemis (Greek), or Diana (Roman), whose temple was one of the 7 Wonders of the Ancient World. Paul ministered there for 3 years (Acts 20:31), and later met with the Ephesian elders on his way to Jerusalem (Acts 20). Timothy, Tychicus, and the Apostle John all served this church. John was in Ephesus when he was arrested by Domitian and exiled 50 mi. SW to Patmos. **seven stars.** *See note on 1:16.* **seven golden lampstands.** *See note on 1:12.*

2:2 who say they are apostles. The Ephesian church exercised spiritual discernment. It knew how to evaluate men who claimed spiritual leadership by their doctrine and behavior (cf. 1 Thess. 5:20,21).

2:3 not become weary. For over 40 years, since its founding, this church had remained faithful to the Word and the Lord. Through difficulty and persecution, the members had endured, always driven by the right motive, i.e., for Christ's name and reputation.

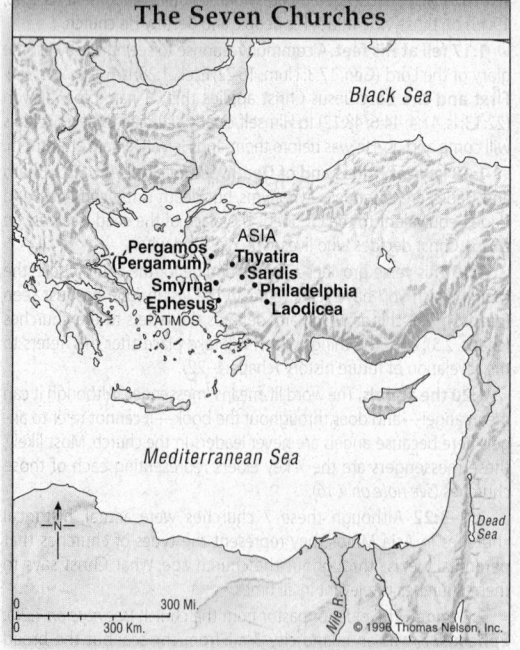

The Seven Churches

Black Sea
ASIA
Pergamos (Pergamum)
Thyatira
Sardis
Smyrna
Philadelphia
Ephesus
Laodicea
PATMOS
Mediterranean Sea
Dead Sea
Nile R.
N
0 300 Mi.
0 300 Km.

2:4 left your first love. To be a Christian is to love the Lord Jesus Christ (John 14:21,23; 1 Cor. 16:22). But the Ephesians' passion and fervor for Christ had become cold, mechanical orthodoxy. Their doctrinal and moral purity, their undiminished zeal for the truth, and their disciplined service were no substitute for the love for Christ they had forsaken.

2:5 remove your lampstand. God's judgment would bring an end to the Ephesian church.

2:6 the deeds of the Nicolaitans. A problem in Pergamos also (vv. 12-15), this heresy was similar to the teaching of Balaam (vv. 14,15). Nicolas means "one who conquers the people." Irenaeus writes that Nicolas, who was made a deacon in Acts 6, was a false believer who later became apostate; but because of his credentials he was able to lead the church astray. And, like Balaam, he led the people into immorality and wickedness. The Nicolaitans, followers of Nicolas, were involved in immorality and assaulted the church with sensual temptations. Clement of Alexander says, "They abandoned themselves to pleasure like goats, leading a life of self-indulgence." Their teaching perverted grace and replaced liberty with license.

2:7 him who overcomes. According to John's own definition, to be an overcomer is to be a Christian (*see note on 1 John 5:5*; cf. vv. 11,17,26; 3:5,12,21). **tree of life.** True believers enjoy the promise of heaven (*see notes on 22:2; Gen. 2:9*).

2:8 angel. *See note on v. 1.* **Smyrna.** Smyrna means "myrrh," the substance used for perfume and often for anointing a dead body for aromatic purposes. Called the crown of Asia, this ancient city (modern Izmir, Turkey) was the most beautiful in Asia Minor and a center of science and medicine. Always on the winner's side in the Roman wars, Smyrna's intense loyalty to Rome resulted in a strong emperor-worship cult. Fifty years after John's death, Polycarp, the pastor of the church in Smyrna, was burned alive at the age of 86 for refusing to worship Caesar. A large Jewish community in the city also proved hostile to the early church. **the First and the Last.** *See note on 1:17.*

2:9 who say they are Jews. Although they were Jews physically, they were not true Jews but spiritual pagans (cf. Rom. 2:28). Who allied with other pagans in putting Christians to death as they attempted to stamp out the Christian faith. **synagogue of Satan.** With the rejection of its Messiah, Judaism becomes as much a tool of Satan as emperor worship.

2:10 devil. The Gr. name for God's archenemy means "accuser." For discussion of Satan, *see notes on Eph. 6:10-17.* **tribulation ten days.** Their imprisonment will be brief. **crown of life.** It is the crown which is life, or the reward which is life, not an actual crown to adorn the head. "Crown" here does not refer to the kind royalty wear, but to the wreath awarded winning athletes.

11 [r]"He who has an ear, let him hear
what the Spirit says to the churches. He
who overcomes shall not be hurt by [s]the
second death."'

The Compromising Church

12 "And to the [6]angel of the church in
Pergamos write,
'These things says [t]He who has the
sharp two-edged sword: 13 "I know your
works, and where you dwell, where Satan's throne *is*. And you hold fast to My
name, and did not deny My faith even in
the days in which Antipas *was* My faithful
martyr, who was killed among you, where
Satan dwells. 14 But I have a few things
against you, because you have there those
who hold the doctrine of [u]Balaam, who
taught Balak to put a stumbling block before the children of Israel, [v]to eat things
sacrificed to idols, [w]and to commit sexual
immorality. 15 Thus you also have those
who hold the doctrine of the Nicolaitans,
[7]which thing I hate. 16 Repent, or else I will
come to you quickly and [x]will fight against
them with the sword of My mouth.
17 "He who has an ear, let him hear what
the Spirit says to the churches. To him who
overcomes I will give some of the hidden
[y]manna to eat. And I will give him a white
stone, and on the stone [z]a new name written which no one knows except him who
receives *it*."'

The Corrupt Church

18 "And to the [8]angel of the church in
Thyatira write,
'These things says the Son of God, [a]who
has eyes like a flame of fire, and His feet
like fine brass: 19 [b]"I know your works,
love, [9]service, faith, and your [1]patience;
and *as* for your works, the last *are* more
than the first. 20 Nevertheless I have [2]a few
things against you, because you allow
[3]that woman [c]Jezebel, who calls herself a
prophetess, [4]to teach and seduce My servants [d]to commit sexual immorality and
eat things sacrificed to idols. 21 And I gave
her time [e]to [5]repent of her sexual immorality, and she did not repent. 22 Indeed I will
cast her into a sickbed, and those who
commit adultery with her into great tribulation, unless they repent of [6]their deeds.
23 I will kill her children with death, and
all the churches shall know that I am He
who [f]searches [7]the minds and hearts. And

11 [r]Rev. 13:9 [s][Rev. 20:6, 14; 21:8]
12 [t]Is. 49:2; Rev. 1:16; 2:16 [6]Or *messenger*
14 [u]Num. 31:16 [v]Num. 25; Acts 15:29; [1 Cor. 10:20]; Rev. 2:20 [w]1 Cor. 6:13
15 [7]NU, M *likewise.*
16 [x]Is. 11:4; 2 Thess. 2:8; Rev. 19:15
17 [y]Ex. 16:33, 34; [John 6:49, 51] [z]Is. 56:5; 62:2; 65:15; Rev. 3:12
18 [a]Rev. 1:14, 15 [8]Or *messenger*
19 [b]Rev. 2:2 [9]NU, M *faith, service* [1]*perseverance*
20 [c]1 Kin. 16:31; 21:25; 2 Kin. 9:7, 22, 30 [d]Ex. 34:15 [2]NU, M *against you that you tolerate* [3]M *your wife Jezebel* [4]NU, M *and teaches and seduces*
21 [e]Rom. 2:5; Rev. 9:20; 16:9, 11 [5]NU, M *repent, and she does not want to repent of her sexual immorality.*
22 [6]NU, M *her*
23 [f]Ps. 7:9; 26:2; 139:1; Jer. 11:20; 17:10; Matt. 16:27; Luke 16:15; Acts 1:24; Rom. 8:27 [7]*examines*

2:11 who overcomes. This identifies every Christian (*see note on v. 7*). **the second death.** The first death is only physical; the second is spiritual and eternal (cf. 20:14).

2:12 angel. *See note on 1:20.* **Pergamos.** Pergamos lit. means "citadel" and is the word from which we get parchment—a writing material developed from animal skin, which apparently was first developed in that area. Pergamos (modern Bergama) was built on a 1,000-foot hill in a broad, fertile plain about 20 mi. inland from the Aegean Sea. It had served as the capital of the Roman province of Asia Minor for over 250 years. It was an important religious center for the pagan cults of Athena, Asklepios, Dionysius (or Bacchus, the god of drunkenness), and Zeus. It was the first city in Asia to build a temple to Caesar (29 B.C.) and became the capital of the cult of Caesar worship. **two-edged sword.** *See note on 1:16.*

2:13 where Satan's throne *is*. The headquarters of satanic opposition and a Gentile base for false religions. On the acropolis in Pergamos was a huge, throne-shaped altar to Zeus. In addition, Asklepios, the god of healing, was the god most associated with Pergamos. His snake-like form is still the medical symbol today. The famous medical school connected to his temple mingled medicine with superstition. One prescription called for the worshiper to sleep on the temple floor, allowing snakes to crawl over his body and infuse him with their healing power. **Antipas.** Probably the pastor of the church. **faithful martyr.** Tradition says Antipas was burned to death inside a brass bull. "Martyr," a transliteration of the Gr. word, means witness. Because so many of the witnesses faithful to Christ were put to death, the word "martyr" developed its current definition.

2:14 doctrine of Balaam. Balaam tried unsuccessfully to prostitute his prophetic gift and curse Israel for money offered him by Balak, king of Moab. So he devised a plot to have Moabite women seduce Israelite men into intermarriage. The result was the blasphemous union of Israel with fornication and idolatrous feasts (for the story of Balaam, see Num. 22–25). **things sacrificed to idols.** See Acts 15:19-29.

2:15 Thus you also. The teaching of the Nicolaitans led to the same behavior as Balaam's schemes. **doctrine of the Nicolaitans.** *See note on v. 6.*

2:16 sword of My mouth. *See note on 1:16.*

2:17 overcomes. *See note on v. 7.* **hidden manna.** Just as Israel received manna, God promises to give the true believer the spiritual bread the unbelieving world cannot see: Jesus Christ (cf. John 6:51). **white stone.** When an athlete won in the games, he was often given, as part of his prize, a white stone which was an admission pass to the winner's celebration afterwards. This may picture the moment when the overcomer will receive his ticket to the eternal victory celebration in heaven. **new name.** A personal message from Christ to the ones He loves, which serves as their admission pass into eternal glory. It is so personal that only the person who receives it will know what it is.

2:18 angel. *See note on 1:20.* **Thyatira.** Located halfway between Pergamos and Sardis, this city had been under Roman rule for nearly 3 centuries (ca. 190 B.C.). Since the city was situated in a long valley that swept 40 mi. to Pergamos, it had no natural defenses and had a long history of being destroyed and rebuilt. Originally populated by soldiers of Alexander the Great, it was little more than a military outpost to guard Pergamos. Lydia came from this city on business and was converted under Paul's ministry (Acts 16:14,15). **eyes like a flame of fire.** *See note on 1:14.* **feet like fine brass.** Cf. 19:15; *see note on 1:15.*

2:20 Jezebel. Probably a pseudonym for a woman who influenced the church in the way Jezebel influenced the OT Jews into idolatry and immorality (cf. 1 Kin. 21:25,26). **sexual immorality and eat things sacrificed to idols.** Cf. Acts 15:19-29; *see note on v. 14.*

2:22 sickbed. Lit. "bed." Having given this woman time to repent, God was to judge her upon a bed. Since she used a luxurious bed to commit her immorality, and the reclining couch at the idol feast to eat things offered to false gods, He was to give her a bed in hell where she would lie forever.

2:23 her children. The church was about 40 years old as John wrote, and her teaching had produced a second generation, advocating the same debauchery. **who searches the minds and hearts.**

I will give to each one of you according to
your works.
24 "Now to you I say, [8]and to the rest in
Thyatira, as many as do not have this doctrine, who have not known the [g]depths of
Satan, as they say, [h]I [9]will put on you no
other burden. 25 But hold fast [i]what you
have till I come. 26 And he who overcomes,
and keeps [j]My works until the end, [k]to
him I will give power over the nations—

27 *'He[l] shall rule them with a rod of*
iron;
They shall be dashed to pieces like
the potter's vessels'—

as I also have received from My Father;
28 and I will give him [m]the morning star.
29 "He who has an ear, let him hear what
the Spirit says to the churches."'

The Dead Church

3 "And to the [1]angel of the church in
Sardis write,
'These things says He who [a]has the
seven Spirits of God and the seven stars: "I
know your works, that you have a name
that you are alive, but you are dead. 2 Be
watchful, and strengthen the things which
remain, that are ready to die, for I have not
found your works perfect before [2]God.
3 [b]Remember therefore how you have received and heard; hold fast and [c]repent.
[d]Therefore if you will not watch, I will
come upon you [e]as a thief, and you will
not know what hour I will come upon you.
4 [3]You have [f]a few names [4]even in Sardis
who have not [g]defiled their garments; and
they shall walk with Me [h]in white, for they
are worthy. 5 He who overcomes [i]shall be
clothed in white garments, and I will not
[j]blot out his name from the [k]Book of Life;
but [l]I will confess his name before My Father and before His angels.
6 [m]"He who has an ear, let him hear
what the Spirit says to the churches."'

The Faithful Church

7 "And to the [5]angel of the church in
Philadelphia write,
'These things says [n]He who is holy, [o]He
who is true, [p]*"He who has the key of Da-*
vid, [q]*He who opens and no one shuts, and*
[r]*shuts and no one opens"*: 8 [s]"I know your
works. See, I have set before you [t]an open
door, [6]and no one can shut it; for you have

24 [g] 2 Tim. 3:1-9 [h] Acts 15:28 [8] NU, M omit *and* [9] NU, M omit *will*
25 [i] Rev. 3:11
26 [j] [John 6:29] [k] [Matt. 19:28]
27 [l] Ps. 2:8, 9; Rev. 12:5; 19:15
28 [m] 2 Pet. 1:19; Rev. 22:16

CHAPTER 3

1 [a] Rev. 1:4, 16 [1] Or *messenger*
2 [2] NU, M *My God*
3 [b] 1 Tim. 6:20 [c] Rev. 3:19 [d] Matt. 24:42, 43; Luke 12:39 [e] 1 Thess. 5:2; [2 Pet. 3:10; Rev. 16:15]
4 [f] Acts 1:15 [g] [Jude 23] [h] Rev. 4:4; 6:11 [3] NU, M *Nevertheless you* [4] NU, M omit *even*
5 [i] [Rev. 19:8] [j] Ex. 32:32; Ps. 69:28; Luke 10:20; [Rev. 13:8; 17:8; 20:12, 15; 21:27] [k] Phil. 4:3 [l] Matt. 10:32; Luke 12:8
6 [m] Rev. 2:7
7 [n] Acts 3:14 [o] John 14:6; 1 John 5:20; Rev. 3:14; 19:11 [p] Is. 9:7; 22:22; Jer. 23:5 [q] [Matt. 16:19; Rev. 1:18] [r] Job 12:14 [5] Or *messenger*
8 [s] Rev. 3:1 [t] 1 Cor. 16:9 [6] NU, M *which no one can shut*

God has perfect, intimate knowledge of every human heart; no evil can be hidden from Him (Ps. 7:9; Prov. 24:12; Jer. 11:20; 17:10; 20:12). **according to your works.** Always the basis for future judgment (20:12,13; Matt. 16:27; Rom. 2:6). Works do not save (Eph. 2:8,9), but they do evidence salvation (James 2:14-26).

2:24 the depths of Satan. This unbelievable libertinism and license was the fruit of pre-gnostic teaching that one was free to engage and explore the sphere of Satan and participate in evil with the body without harming the spirit (see Introduction to 1 John: Background and Setting).

2:26 overcomes. *See note on v. 7.*

2:27 *rule them with a rod of iron.* Lit. "shepherd them with an iron rod." During the millennial kingdom, Christ will enforce His will and protect his sheep with His iron scepter from any who would seek to harm them (cf. Ps. 2:8).

2:28 the morning star. John later reveals Christ to be "the morning star." Although the morning star has already dawned in our hearts (2 Pet. 1:19), someday we will have Him in His fullness.

3:1 angel. Messenger or pastor (*see note on 1:20*). **Sardis.** Situated on a natural acropolis rising 1,500 feet above the valley floor, the city (modern Sart) was nearly impregnable. Around 1200 B.C. it gained prominence as the capital of the Lydian kingdom. Its primary industry was harvesting wool, dying it, and making garments from it. The famous author, Aesop, came from Sardis, and tradition says that Mileto, a member of the church in Sardis, wrote the first-ever commentary on certain passages in the book of Revelation. The church in Sardis was dead; that is, basically populated by unredeemed, unregenerate people. **seven Spirits.** *See note on 1:4.* **seven stars.** The pastors of these 7 churches (*see notes on 1:16,20*).

3:3 come upon you as a thief. Here the reference is not to Christ's second coming (cf. 16:15; 1 Thess. 5:2; 2 Pet. 3:10), but to His sudden and unexpected coming to His unrepentant, dead church to inflict harm and destruction.

3:4 who have not defiled their garments. Defiled means "to smear, to pollute," or "to stain," and garments refer to character. There were a few whose character was still godly (cf. Jude 23). **in white.** The white garments of all the redeemed (cf. 6:11; 7:9,13;19:8,14), speak of holiness and purity. Such white robes are reserved for Christ (Matt. 17:2; Mark 9:3), holy angels (Matt. 28:3; Mark 16:5), and the glorified church (19:8,14). In the ancient world, white robes were commonly worn at festivals and celebrations.

3:5 overcomes. All true Christians (*see note on 2:7*). **Book of Life.** A divine journal records the names of all those whom God has chosen to save and who, therefore, are to possess eternal life (13:8; 17:8; 20:12,15; 21:27; 22:19; cf. Dan. 12:1; Luke 10:20). Under no circumstances will He erase those names (*see notes on Ex. 32:33; Pss. 69:28; 139:16; Heb. 12:23; Phil 4:3*), as city officials often did of undesirable people on their roles.

3:7 angel. *See note on 1:20.* **Philadelphia.** Located on a hillside about 30 mi. SE of Sardis, the city (modern Alashehir) was founded around 190 B.C. by Attalus II, king of Pergamos. His unusual devotion to his brother earned the city its name, "brotherly love." The city was an important commercial stop on a major trade route called the Imperial Post Road, a first century mail route. Although Scripture does not mention this church elsewhere, it was probably the fruit of Paul's extended ministry in Ephesus (cf. Acts 19:10). **holy...true.** A common description in this book (4:8; 6:10; 15:3; 16:7; 19:2,11). Christ shares the holy, sinless, pure nature of His Father (Ps. 16:10; Is. 6:3; 40:25; 43:15; Hab. 3:3; Mark 1:11,24; John 6:69; Acts 3:14); that is, He is absolutely pure and separate from sin. "True" can refer both to one who speaks truth, and who is genuine or authentic as opposed to fake. ***the key of David.*** Christ has the sovereign authority to control entrance into the kingdom (Is. 22:22; cf. Matt. 16:19; John 14:6). In 1:18 He is pictured holding the keys to death and hell—here, the keys to salvation and blessing.

3:8 open door. This is either admission into the kingdom (see v. 7), or an opportunity for service (cf. 1 Cor. 16:9; 2 Cor. 2:12; Col. 4:3).

a little strength, have kept My word, and
have not denied My name. 9 Indeed I will
make [u]*those* of the synagogue of Satan,
who say they are Jews and are not, but
lie—indeed [v]I will make them come and
worship before your feet, and to know
that I have loved you. 10 Because you have
kept [7]My command to persevere, [w]I also
will keep you from the hour of trial which
shall come upon [x]the whole world, to test
those who dwell [y]on the earth. 11 [8]Behold,
[z]I am coming quickly! [a]Hold fast what
you have, that no one may take [b]your
crown. 12 He who overcomes, I will make
him [c]a pillar in the temple of My God, and
he shall [d]go out no more. [e]I will write on
him the name of My God and the name of
the city of My God, the [f]New Jerusalem,
which [g]comes down out of heaven from
My God. [h]And *I will write on him* My new
name.
13 [i]"He who has an ear, let him hear
what the Spirit says to the churches."'

9 [u] Rev. 2:9 [v] Is. 45:14; 49:23; 60:14
10 [w] 2 Tim. 2:12; 2 Pet. 2:9 [x] Luke 2:1 [y] Is. 24:17 [7] Lit. *the word of My patience*
11 [z] Phil. 4:5 [a] Rev. 2:25 [b] [Rev. 2:10] [8] NU, M omit *Behold*
12 [c] 1 Kin. 7:21; Jer. 1:18; Gal. 2:9 [d] Ps. 23:6 [e] [Rev. 14:1; 22:4] [f] [Heb. 12:22] [g] Rev. 21:2 [h] [Rev. 2:17; 22:4]
13 [i] Rev. 2:7
14 [j] Is. 65:16; 2 Cor. 1:20 [k] Rev. 1:5; 3:7; 19:11 [l] [Col. 1:15] [9] Or *messenger* [1] NU, M *in Laodicea*
15 [m] Rev. 3:1
16 [2] NU, M *hot nor cold*
17 [n] Hos. 12:8; Zech. 11:5; [Matt. 5:3]; 1 Cor. 4:8
18 [o] Is. 55:1; Matt. 13:44 [p] 2 Cor. 5:3
19 [q] Job 5:17 [r] Prov. 3:12; [2 Cor. 11:32]; Heb. 12:6 [3] *discipline* [4] *eager*
20 [s] Song 5:2 [t] Luke 12:36, 37; John 10:3

The Lukewarm Church

14 "And to the [9]angel of the church [1]of
the Laodiceans write,
[j]'These things says the Amen, [k]the Faithful and True Witness, [l]the Beginning of the
creation of God: 15 [m]"I know your works,
that you are neither cold nor hot. I could
wish you were cold or hot. 16 So then, because you are lukewarm, and neither [2]cold
nor hot, I will vomit you out of My mouth.
17 Because you say, [n]'I am rich, have become wealthy, and have need of nothing'—and do not know that you are
wretched, miserable, poor, blind, and
naked— 18 I counsel you [o]to buy from Me
gold refined in the fire, that you may be
rich; and [p]white garments, that you may
be clothed, *that* the shame of your nakedness may not be revealed; and anoint your
eyes with eye salve, that you may see.
19 [q]As many as I love, I rebuke and [r]chas-
ten. [3] Therefore be [4]zealous and repent.
20 Behold, [s]I stand at the door and knock.
[t]If anyone hears My voice and opens the

3:9 synagogue of Satan. *See note on 2:9.* **who say they are Jews.** *See note on 2:9.*

3:10 keep you from the hour of trial. Christ's description—an event still future that for a short time severely tests the whole world—must refer to the time of tribulation, the 7 year period before Christ's earthly kingdom is consummated, featuring the unleashing of divine wrath in judgments expressed as seals, trumpets, and bowls. This period is described in detail throughout chaps. 6–19. The latter half is called "the Great Tribulation" (7:14; Matt. 24:21) and is identified as to time in 11:2,3; 12:6,14; 13:5. The verb "to keep" is followed by a preposition whose normal meaning is "from" or "out of"—this phrase, "keep...from" supports the pretribulational rapture of the church (*see notes on John 14:1-3; 1 Cor. 15:51,52 1; Thess. 4:13-17*). This period is the same as Daniel's 70th week (*see notes on Dan. 9:24-27*) and "the time of Jacob's trouble" (*see notes on Jer. 30:7*).

3:11 I am coming quickly! This isn't the threatening temporal judgment described in v. 3; 2:5,16, nor the final judgment of chap. 19; it is a hopeful event. Christ will return to take His church out of the hour of trial (*see note on 2 Thess. 2:1*).

3:12 He who overcomes. All Christians (*see note on 2:7*). **a pillar.** Believers will enjoy an unshakable, eternal, secure place in the presence of God. **temple.** *See note on 7:15.* **write...name of My God.** In biblical times, one's name spoke of his character. Writing His name on us speaks of imprinting His character on us and identifying us as belonging to Him. **New Jerusalem.** The capital city of heaven (*see notes on 21:1-27*). The overcomer will enjoy eternal citizenship. **My new name.** At the moment we see Christ, whatever we may have called Him and understood by that name will pale in the reality of what we see. And He will give us a new, eternal name by which we will know Him.

3:14 angel. The pastor-messenger designated to deliver this letter (*see note on 1:20*). **Laodiceans.** Located in the Lycus River Valley, the SW area of Phrygia, Laodicea became the wealthiest, most important commercial center in the region. It was primarily known for 3 industries: banking, wool, and medicine (notably its eye salve). An inadequate local water supply forced the city to build an underground aqueduct. All 3 industries, as well as the inadequate water supply, played a major part in this letter. The church began through the ministry of Epaphras, while Paul was ministering in Ephesus (cf. Col. 1:7; Paul never personally visited Laodicea). **the Amen.** A common biblical expression signifying certainty and veracity (cf. Is. 65:16, "the God of truth"). According to 2 Cor. 1:20, all the promises of God are fulfilled in Christ; that is, all God's promises and unconditional covenants are guaranteed and affirmed by the person and work of Jesus Christ. **Faithful and True Witness.** He is a completely trustworthy and perfectly accurate witness to the truth of God (John 14:6). **Beginning of the creation.** This corrects a heresy, apparently present in Laodicea as in Colosse, that Christ was a created being (cf. Col. 1:15-20). Instead, He is the "Beginning" (lit. "beginner, originator, initiator") of creation (cf. John 1:3; 3:14) and the "firstborn of creation"; that is, the most preeminent, supreme person ever born (Col. 1:15). As a man, he had a beginning, but as God, He was the beginning. Sadly, this heresy concerning the person of Christ had produced an unregenerate church in Laodicea.

3:16 lukewarm. I.e., tepid. Nearby Hierapolis was famous for its hot springs, and Colosse for its cold, refreshing mountain stream. But Laodicea had dirty, tepid water that flowed for miles through an underground aqueduct. Visitors, unaccustomed to it, immediately spat it out. The church at Laodicea was neither cold, openly rejecting Christ, nor hot, filled with spiritual zeal. Instead, its members were lukewarm, hypocrites professing to know Christ, but not truly belonging to Him (cf. Matt. 7:21ff.). **I will vomit you out of My mouth.** Just like the dirty, tepid water of Laodicea, these self-deceived hypocrites sickened Christ.

3:18 gold...white garments...eye salve. *See note on v. 4.* He was offering them the spiritual counterparts to their 3 major industries. Each item was a way to refer to genuine salvation.

3:19 As many as I love...chasten. Both vv. 18,20 indicate that Christ was speaking here to unbelievers. God certainly loves the unconverted (cf. John 3:16). And "chasten" (lit. "reprove") often refers to God's convicting and punishing the unregenerate (Matt. 18:17; 1 Cor. 14:24; 2 Tim. 2:25).

3:20 I stand at the door and knock. Rather than allowing for the common interpretation of Christ's knocking on a person's heart, the context demands that Christ was seeking to enter this church that bore His name but lacked a single true believer. This poignant letter was His knocking. If one member would recognize his spiritual bankruptcy and respond in saving faith, He would enter the church.

door, [u]I will come in to him and dine with
him, and he with Me. **21** To him who overcomes [v]I will grant to sit with Me on My
throne, as I also overcame and sat down
with My Father on His throne.

22 [w]"He who has an ear, let him hear
what the Spirit says to the churches." ' "

The Throne Room of Heaven

4 After these things I looked, and behold, a door *standing* [a]open in heaven.
And the first voice which I heard *was* like a
[b]trumpet speaking with me, saying,
"Come up here, and I will show you things
which must take place after this."

2 Immediately [c]I was in the Spirit; and
behold, [d]a throne set in heaven, and *One*
sat on the throne. **3** [1]And He who sat there
was [e]like a jasper and a sardius stone in
appearance; [f]and *there was* a rainbow
around the throne, in appearance like an
emerald. **4** [g]Around the throne *were* twenty-four thrones, and on the thrones I saw
twenty-four elders sitting, [h]clothed in
white [2]robes; and they had crowns of gold
on their heads. **5** And from the throne proceeded [i]lightnings, [3]thunderings, and
voices. [j]Seven lamps of fire *were* burning
before the throne, which are [k]the[4] seven
Spirits of God.

20 [u][John 14:23]
21 [v]Matt. 19:28; 2 Tim. 2:12; [Rev. 2:26; 20:4]
22 [w]Rev. 2:7

CHAPTER 4

1 [a]Ezek. 1:1; Rev. 19:11 [b]Rev. 1:10
2 [c]Rev. 1:10 [d]1 Kin. 22:19; Is. 6:1; Ezek. 1:26; Dan. 7:9; Rev. 3:21; 4:9
3 [e]Matt. 5:8; Rev. 21:11 [f]Gen. 9:13-17; Ezek. 1:28; Rev. 10:1 [1]M omits *And He who sat there was*, making the following a description of the throne.
4 [g]Rev. 11:16 [h]Rev. 3:4, 5 [2]NU, M *robes, with crowns*
5 [i]Gen. 49:9, 10; Ex. 19:16; Rev. 8:5; 11:19; 16:18 [j]Ex. 37:23 [k]2 Sam. 7:12; [Rev. 1:4] [3]NU, M *voices, and thunderings.* [4]M omits *the*
6 [l]Ex. 38:8; Ezek. 1:22; Rev. 15:2 [m]Ezek. 1:5; Rev. 4:8; 5:6; 6:1, 6; 7:11; 14:3; 15:7; 19:4 [5]NU, M add *something like*
7 [n]Ezek. 1:10; 10:14
8 [o]Is. 6:2 [p]Is. 6:3 [q]Rev. 1:8 [r]Rev. 1:4

6 Before the throne *there* [5]*was* [l]a sea of
glass, like crystal. [m]And in the midst of the
throne, and around the throne, *were* four
living creatures full of eyes in front and in
back. **7** [n]The first living creature *was* like a
lion, the second living creature like a calf,
the third living creature had a face like a
man, and the fourth living creature *was*
like a flying eagle. **8** *The* four living creatures, each having [o]six wings, were full of
eyes around and within. And they do not
rest day or night, saying:

[p]"Holy,[6] holy, holy,
[q]Lord God Almighty,
[r]Who was and is and is to come!"

9 Whenever the living creatures give
glory and honor and thanks to Him who
sits on the throne, [s]who lives forever and
ever, **10** [t]the twenty-four elders fall down
before Him who sits on the throne and worship Him who lives forever and ever, and
cast their crowns before the throne, saying:

11 "You[u] are worthy, [7]O Lord,
To receive glory and honor and
power;

[6]M has *holy* nine times. **9** [s]Rev. 1:18 **10** [t]Rev. 5:8, 14; 7:11; 11:16; 19:4 **11** [u]Rev. 1:6; 5:12 [7]NU, M *our Lord and God*

3:21 overcomes. All true Christians (*see note on 2:7*). **sit with Me on My throne.** A figurative expression meaning that we will share the privilege and authority that Christ enjoys as we reign with Him (1:6; Matt. 19:28; Luke 22:29,30).

4:1 Come up here. This is not a veiled reference to the rapture of the church, but a command for John to be temporarily transported to heaven "in the Spirit" (*see note on 1:10*) to receive revelation about future events. **things which must take place after this.** According to the outline given in 1:19, this begins the third and final section of the book, describing the events that will follow the church age.

4:2 I was in the Spirit. *See note on 1:10.* **throne.** Not so much a piece of furniture, but a symbol of sovereign rule and authority (7:15; 11:19; 16:17,18; cf. Is. 6:1). It is the focus of chap. 4, occurring 13 times, 11 times referring to God's throne.

4:3 jasper. John later describes this stone as "crystal clear" (21:11), probably referring to a diamond, which refracts all the colors of the spectrum in wondrous brilliance. **sardius.** A fiery bright ruby stone named for the city near which it was found. **emerald.** A cool, emerald-green hue dominates the multi-colored rainbow surrounding God's throne (cf. Ezek. 1:28). From the time of Noah, the rainbow became a sign of God's faithfulness to His Word, His promises, and His Noahic covenant (Gen. 9:12-17).

4:4 twenty-four elders. Their joint rule with Christ, their white garments (19:7,8), and their golden crowns (2:10) all seem to indicate that these 24 represent the redeemed (vv. 9-11; 5:5-14; 7:11-17; 11:16-18; 14:3; 19:4). The question is which redeemed? Not Israel, since the nation is not yet saved, glorified, and coronated. That is still to come at this point in the events of the end. Their resurrection and glory will come at the end of the 7 year tribulation time (cf. Dan. 12:1-3). Tribulation saints aren't yet saved (7:9,10). Only one group will be complete and glorified at that point—the church. Here elders represent the church, which sings the song of redemption (5:8-10). They are the overcomers who have their crowns and live in the place prepared for them, where they have gone with Jesus (cf. John 14:1-4).

4:5 lightnings, thunderings. Not the fury of nature, but the firestorm of righteous fury about to come from an awesome, powerful God upon a sinful world (8:5; 11:19; 16:18). **seven Spirits of God.** The Holy Spirit (*see note on 1:4*).

4:6 sea of glass. There is no sea in heaven (21:1), but the crystal pavement that serves as the floor of God's throne stretches out like a great, glistening sea (cf. Ex. 24:10; Ezek. 1:22). **four living creatures.** Lit. "four living ones or beings." These are the cherubim (sing., cherub), those angels frequently referred to in the OT in connection with God's presence, power, and holiness. Although John's description is not identical to Ezekiel's, they are obviously both referring to the same supernatural and indescribable beings (Pss. 80:1; 99:1; *see notes on Ezek. 1:4-25; 10:15*). **full of eyes.** Although not omniscient—an attribute reserved for God alone—these angels have a comprehensive knowledge and perception. Nothing escapes their scrutiny (cf. v. 8).

4:7 first...like a lion. In what is obviously intended as symbolic language, John compares these 4 beings with 4 of God's earthly creations. Ezekiel indicates that every cherub has these 4 attributes. The likeness to a lion symbolizes strength and power. **second...like a calf.** The image of a calf demonstrates that these beings render humble service to God. **third...face like a man.** Their likeness to man shows they are rational beings. **fourth...like a flying eagle.** The cherubim fulfill their service to God with the swiftness of eagles' wings.

4:8 full of eyes. *See note on v. 6.* **Holy, holy, holy.** Often God is extolled for His holiness in this 3-fold form, because it is the summation of all that He is—His most salient attribute (*see note on Is. 6:3*). **Who was and is and is to come!** *See note on 1:4.*

4:10 cast their crowns. Aware that God alone is responsible for the rewards they have received, they divest themselves of all honor and cast it at the feet of their King (*see note on 2:10*).

[v]For You created all things,
And by [w]Your will they [8]exist and
were created."

The Lamb Takes the Scroll

5 And I saw in the right *hand* of Him
who sat on the throne [a]a scroll written
inside and on the back, [b]sealed with seven
seals. 2 Then I saw a strong angel proclaiming with a loud voice, [c]"Who is worthy to open the scroll and to loose its
seals?" 3 And no one in heaven or on the
earth or under the earth was able to open
the scroll, or to look at it.
4 So I wept much, because no one was
found worthy to open [1]and read the scroll,
or to look at it. 5 But one of the elders said
to me, "Do not weep. Behold, [d]the Lion of
the tribe of [e]Judah, [f]the Root of David, has
[g]prevailed to open the scroll [h]and [2]to loose
its seven seals."
6 And I looked, [3]and behold, in the
midst of the throne and of the four living
creatures, and in the midst of the elders,
stood [i]a Lamb as though it had been slain,
having seven horns and [j]seven eyes, which
are [k]the seven Spirits of God sent out into
all the earth. 7 Then He came and took the
scroll out of the right hand [l]of Him who sat
on the throne.

Worthy Is the Lamb

8 Now when He had taken the scroll,
[m]the four living creatures and the twenty-
four elders fell down before the Lamb,
each having a harp, and golden bowls full
of incense, which are the [n]prayers of the
saints. 9 And [o]they sang a new song, saying:

[p]"You are worthy to take the scroll,
And to open its seals;
For You were slain,
And [q]have redeemed us to God
[r]by Your blood
Out of every tribe and tongue and
people and nation,
10 And have made [4]us [s]kings [5] and
[t]priests to our God;
And [6]we shall reign on the earth."

11 Then I looked, and I heard the voice of
many angels around the throne, the living
creatures, and the elders; and the number
of them was ten thousand times ten thousand, and thousands of thousands, 12 saying with a loud voice:

11 [v]Gen. 1:1; John 1:3 [w]Col. 1:16 [8]NU, M *existed*

CHAPTER 5

1 [a]Ezek. 2:9, 10 [b]Is. 29:11; Dan. 12:4
2 [c]Rev. 4:11; 5:9
4 [1]NU, M omit *and read*
5 [d]Gen. 49:9 [e]Heb. 7:14 [f]Is. 11:1, 10; Rom. 15:12; Rev. 22:16 [g]Rev. 3:21 [h]Rev. 6:1 [2]NU, M omit *to loose*
6 [i]Is. 53:7; [John 1:29; 1 Pet. 1:19] [j]Zech. 3:9; 4:10 [k]Rev. 1:4; 3:1; 4:5 [3]NU, M *I saw in the midst . . . a Lamb standing*
7 [l]Rev. 4:2
8 [m]Rev. 4:8-10; 19:4 [n]Ps. 141:2; Rev. 8:3
9 [o]Rev. 14:3 [p]Rev. 4:11 [q]John 1:29 [r][Heb. 9:12; 1 Pet. 1:18, 19]
10 [s]Ex. 19:6 [t]Is. 61:6 [4]NU, M *them* [5]NU *a kingdom* [6]NU, M *they*

4:11 You created all things. It is the Creator God who set out to redeem His creation.

5:1 a scroll. *See note on 1:11.* **written inside and on the back.** This is typical of various kinds of contracts in the ancient world, including deeds, marriage contracts, rental and lease agreements, and wills. The inside of the scroll contained all the details of the contract, and the outside—or back—contained a summary of the document. In this case it almost certainly is a deed—the title deed to the earth (cf. Jer. 32:7ff.) **sealed with seven seals.** Romans sealed their wills 7 times—on the edge at each roll—to prevent unauthorized entry. Hebrew title deeds required a minimum of 3 witnesses and 3 separate seals, with more important transactions requiring more witnesses and seals.

5:2 strong angel. The identity of this angel is uncertain, but it may refer to the angel Gabriel, whose name means "strength of God" (Dan. 8:16).

5:3 heaven or on the earth or under the earth. A common biblical expression denoting the entire universe and not intended to teach 3 precise divisions.

5:5 the Lion of the tribe of Judah. One of the earliest titles for the Messiah (*see notes on Gen. 49:8-10*), it speaks of His fierceness and strength, which although glimpsed in His first coming, do not appear in their fullness until the moment anticipated here. **the Root of David.** Another clearly messianic title (*see notes on Is. 11:1ff.*), it anticipates His being a descendant of David, who with devastating force will compel the wicked of the earth to succumb to His authority.

5:6 Lamb. Hearing of a lion, John turns to see a lamb (lit. "a little, pet lamb"). God required the Jews to bring the Passover lamb into their houses for 4 days, essentially making it a pet, before it was to be violently slain (Ex. 12:3,6). This is the true Passover Lamb, God's Son (cf. Is. 53:7; Jer. 11:19; John 1:29). **as though it had been slain.** The scars from its slaughter are still clearly visible, but it is standing—it is alive. **seven horns.** In Scripture, horns always symbolize power, because in the animal kingdom they are used to exert power and inflict wounds in combat. Seven horns signify complete or perfect power. Unlike other defenseless lambs, this One has complete, sovereign power. **seven eyes...seven Spirits.** Cf. 4:5; *see note on 1:4.*

5:8 harp. These ancient stringed instruments not only accompanied the songs of God's people (1 Chr. 25:6; Ps. 33:2), but also accompanied prophecy (cf. 1 Sam. 10:5). The 24 elders, representative of the redeemed church, played their harps in praise and in a symbolic indication that all the prophets had said was about to be fulfilled. **bowls full of incense.** These golden, wide-mouth saucers were common in the tabernacle and temple. Incense was a normal part of the OT ritual. Priests stood twice daily before the inner veil of the temple and burned incense so that the smoke would carry into the Holy of Holies and be swept into the nostrils of God. That symbolized the people's prayers rising to Him. **prayers of the saints.** Specifically, these prayers represent all that the redeemed have ever prayed concerning ultimate and final redemption. This becomes a major theme throughout the book (cf. 11:17,18; 13:7,9,10; 14:12; 16:6; 17:6; 18:20,24; 19:8; 20:9).

5:9 new song. Cf. 15:3. The OT is filled with references to a new song that flows from a heart that has experienced God's redemption or deliverance (cf. 14:3; Pss. 33:3; 96:1; 144:9). This new song anticipates the final, glorious redemption that God is about to begin. **redeemed us to God by Your blood.** The sacrificial death of Christ on behalf of sinners made Him worthy to take the scroll (cf. 1 Cor. 6:20; 7:23; 2 Cor. 5:21; Gal. 3:3; 1 Pet. 1:18,19; 2 Pet. 2:1).

5:10 kings and priests. *See note on 1:6.* **reign on the earth.** *See note on 1:6.*

5:11 ten thousand times ten thousand. Lit. "myriads of myriads." The number is to express an amount beyond calculation. The Gr. expression can also be translated "innumerable" (Luke 12:1; Heb. 12:22).

"Worthy is the Lamb who was slain
To receive power and riches and wisdom,
And strength and honor and glory and blessing!"

13 And [u]every creature which is in heav-
en and on the earth and under the earth
and such as are in the sea, and all that are
in them, I heard saying:

[v]"Blessing and honor and glory and power
Be to Him [w]who sits on the throne,
And to the Lamb, forever and [7]ever!"

14 Then the four living creatures said,
"Amen!" And the [8]twenty-four elders fell
down and worshiped [9]Him who lives forever and ever.

First Seal: The Conqueror

6 Now [a]I saw when the Lamb opened
one of the [1]seals; and I heard [b]one of
the four living creatures saying with a
voice like thunder, "Come and see." 2 And
I looked, and behold, [c]a white horse. [d]He
who sat on it had a bow; [e]and a crown was
given to him, and he went out [f]conquering
and to conquer.

Second Seal: Conflict on Earth

3 When He opened the second seal, [g]I
heard the second living creature saying,
"Come [2]and see." 4 [h]Another horse, fiery
red, went out. And it was granted to the one
who sat on it to [i]take peace from the earth,
and that *people* should kill one another; and
there was given to him a great sword.

Third Seal: Scarcity on Earth

5 When He opened the third seal, [j]I
heard the third living creature say, "Come
and see." So I looked, and behold, [k]a black
horse, and he who sat on it had a pair of
[l]scales[3] in his hand. 6 And I heard a voice
in the midst of the four living creatures
saying, "A [4]quart of wheat for a [5]denarius,
and three quarts of barley for a denarius;
and [m]do not harm the oil and the wine."

Fourth Seal: Widespread Death on Earth

7 When He opened the fourth seal, [n]I
heard the voice of the fourth living creature saying, "Come and see." 8 [o]So I
looked, and behold, a pale horse. And the
name of him who sat on it was Death, and
Hades followed with him. And [6]power

13 [u]Phil. 2:10; Rev. 5:3 [v]1 Chr. 29:11; Rom. 9:5; 1 Tim. 6:16; 1 Pet. 4:11 [w]Rev. 4:2, 3; 6:16; 20:11 [7]M adds *Amen*
14 [8]NU, M omit *twenty-four* [9]NU, M omit *Him who lives forever and ever*

CHAPTER 6

1 [a]Is. 53:7; [John 1:29; Rev. 5:5-7, 12; 13:8] [b]Rev. 4:7 [1]NU, M *seven seals*
2 [c]Zech. 1:8; 6:3 [d]Ps. 45:4, 5, LXX [e]Zech. 6:11; Rev. 9:7; 14:14; 19:12 [f]Matt. 24:5; Rev. 3:21
3 [g]Rev. 4:7 [2]NU, M omit *and see*
4 [h]Zech. 1:8; 6:2 [i]Matt. 24:6, 7
5 [j]Rev. 4:7 [k]Zech. 6:2, 6 [l]Matt. 24:7 [3]*balances*
6 [m]Rev. 7:3; 9:4 [4]Gr. *choinix*, about 1 quart [5]About 1 day's wage for a worker
7 [n]Rev. 4:7
8 [o]Zech. 6:3 [6]*authority*

5:12 power...and blessing. This doxology records 7 qualities intrinsic to God and to the Lamb that demand our praise.

5:13 heaven and on the earth and under the earth. *See note on v. 3.*

5:14 four living creatures. *See note on 4:6.* **twenty-four elders.** *See note on 4:4.*

6:1–19:21 This lengthy section details the judgments and events of the time of tribulation (*see notes on 3:10*) from its beginning with the opening of the first seal (vv. 1,2) through the 7 seal, trumpet, and bowl judgments to the return of Christ to destroy the ungodly (19:11-21).

6:1 the seals. In chap. 5, Christ was the only One found worthy to open the little scroll—the title deed to the universe. As he breaks the 7 seals that secure the scroll, each seal unleashes a new demonstration of God's judgment on the earth in the future tribulation period (*see notes on 5:1; Matt. 24:3-9*). These seal judgments include all the judgments to the end. The seventh seal contains the 7 trumpets; the seventh trumpet contains the 7 bowls.

6:2 white horse. The animal represents an unparalleled time of world peace—a false peace that is to be short-lived (*see note on v. 4*). This peace will be ushered in by a series of false messiahs, culminating with the Antichrist (Matt. 24:3-5). **He who sat on it.** The 4 horses and their riders do not represent specific individuals, but forces. Some, however, identify this rider with Antichrist. Although he will be the leading figure, John's point is that the entire world will follow him, being obsessed with pursuing this false peace. **bow.** The bow is a symbol of war, but the absence of arrows implies that this victory is a bloodless one—a peace won by covenant and agreement, not by war (cf. Dan. 9:24-27). **crown.** This word refers to the kind of laurel wreath awarded winning athletes. It "was given to him." Antichrist becomes king, elected by the world's inhabitants regardless of the cost, and will conquer the entire earth in a bloodless coup.

6:4 Another horse, fiery red. Its blood-red appearance speaks of the holocaust of war (cf. Matt. 24:7). God will grant this horse and its rider the power to create worldwide war. But as horrible as this judgment is, it will be only the "birth pangs," the beginning pains of God's wrath (Matt. 24:8; Mark 13:7,8; Luke 21:9). ***people* should kill one another.** Violent slaughter will become commonplace. **sword.** Not the long, broad sword, but the shorter, more easily maneuvered one that assassins often used and that soldiers carried into battle. It depicts assassination, revolt, massacre, and wholesale slaughter (cf. Dan. 8:24).

6:5 black horse. Black signifies famine (cf. Lam. 5:8-10). Worldwide war will destroy the food supply which spawns global hunger. **pair of scales.** The common measuring device—two small trays hung from each end of a balance beam—indicates that the scarcity of food will lead to rationing and food lines.

6:6 quart of wheat. The approximate amount necessary to sustain one person for one day. **denarius.** One day's normal wages. One day's work will provide enough food for only one person. **three quarts of barley.** Usually fed to animals, this grain was low in nutrients and cheaper than wheat. A day's wages provides enough for only a small family's daily supply. **oil and the wine.** Although the point could be that these foods will not be affected by the famine, a more straightforward meaning is that bare staples—oil was used in the preparation of bread, and wine was considered necessary for cooking and purifying water—suddenly will become luxuries that have to be carefully protected.

6:8 pale horse. "Pale," the Gr. word from which the Eng. word "chlorophyll" comes, describes the pale, ashen-green, pallor characteristic of the decomposition of a corpse. God grants this horseman the authority to bring death to 25 percent of the world's population. **Hades.** *See note on Luke 16:23.* The place of the dead, which is identified as a common and fitting partner for death (20:13; *see note on 1:18*).

was given to them over a fourth of the
earth, [p]to kill with sword, with hunger,
with death, [q]and by the beasts of the earth.

Fifth Seal: The Cry of the Martyrs

9 When He opened the fifth seal, I saw
under [r]the altar [s]the souls of those who had
been slain [t]for the word of God and for [u]the
testimony which they held. 10 And they
cried with a loud voice, saying, [v]"How
long, O Lord, [w]holy and true, [x]until You
judge and avenge our blood on those who
dwell on the earth?" 11 Then a [y]white robe
was given to each of them; and it was said
to them [z]that they should rest a little while
longer, until both *the number of* their fellow
servants and their brethren, who would be
killed as they *were,* was completed.

Sixth Seal: Cosmic Disturbances

12 I looked when He opened the sixth
seal, [a]and [7]behold, there was a great earthquake; and [b]the sun became black as sackcloth of hair, and the [8]moon became like
blood. 13 [c]And the stars of heaven fell to the
earth, as a fig tree drops its late figs when it
is shaken by a mighty wind. 14 [d]Then the
sky [9]receded as a scroll when it is rolled up,
and [e]every mountain and island was
moved out of its place. 15 And the [f]kings of
the earth, the great men, [1]the rich men, the
commanders, the mighty men, every slave
and every free man, [g]hid themselves in the
caves and in the rocks of the mountains,
16 [h]and said to the mountains and rocks,
"Fall on us and hide us from the face of Him
who [i]sits on the throne and from the wrath
of the Lamb! 17 For the great day of His
wrath has come, [j]and who is able to stand?"

The Sealed of Israel

7 After these things I saw four angels
standing at the four corners of the earth,
[a]holding the four winds of the earth, [b]that
the wind should not blow on the earth, on
the sea, or on any tree. 2 Then I saw another
angel ascending from the east, having the
seal of the living God. And he cried with a
loud voice to the four angels to whom it was
granted to harm the earth and the sea, 3 saying, [c]"Do not harm the earth, the sea, or the
trees till we have sealed the servants of our
God [d]on their foreheads." 4 [e]And I heard the
number of those who were sealed. [f]One

8 [p] Jer. 14:12; 15:2; 24:10; 29:17; Ezek. 5:12, 17; 14:21; 29:5; Matt. 24:9 [q] Lev. 26:22
9 [r] Rev. 8:3 [s] [Rev. 20:4] [t] Rev. 1:2, 9 [u] 2 Tim. 1:8
10 [v] Ps. 13:1-6; Zech. 1:12 [w] Rev. 3:7 [x] Rev. 11:18
11 [y] Rev. 3:4, 5; 7:9 [z] Heb. 11:40
12 [a] Matt. 24:7; Rev. 8:5; 11:13; 16:18 [b] Is. 13:10; Joel 2:10, 31; 3:15; Matt. 24:29; Mark 13:24 [7] NU, M omit *behold* [8] NU, M *whole moon*
13 [c] Matt. 24:29; Mark 13:25; Rev. 8:10; 9:1
14 [d] Ps. 102:26; Is. 34:4; [2 Pet. 3:10]; Rev. 20:11; 21:1 [e] Jer. 3:23; Rev. 16:20 [9] Or *split apart*
15 [f] Ps. 2:2-4 [g] Is. 2:10, 19, 21; 24:21; Rev. 19:18 [1] NU, M *the commanders, the rich men,*
16 [h] Hos. 10:8; Luke 23:29, 30; Rev. 9:6 [i] Rev. 20:11
17 [j] Is. 63:4; Jer. 30:7; Joel 1:15; 2:1, 11, 31; Zeph. 1:14; Rev. 16:14

CHAPTER 7 **1** [a] Jer. 49:36; Dan. 7:2; Zech. 6:5; Matt. 24:31 [b] Rev. 7:3; 8:7; 9:4 **3** [c] Rev. 6:6 [d] Ezek. 9:4, 6; Rev. 22:4 **4** [e] Rev. 9:16 [f] Rev. 14:1, 3

6:9 fifth seal. This seal describes the force of the saints' prayers for God's vengeance. Its events will begin in the first half and mark the mid-point and events following, in the 7 year period, which is called the Great Tribulation (2:22; 7:14; *see note on Matt. 24:9,15; Dan. 9:24-27; 2 Thess. 2:4*). The second 3½ year period (11:2; 12:6; 13:5) features the Day of the Lord, in which God unleashes His judgment and wrath on the earth in intensifying waves (*see note on 2 Thess. 5:2*). **under the altar.** Probably a reference to the altar of incense, which pictured the saints' prayers ascending to God (5:8; cf. Ex. 40:5). **the souls of those who had been slain.** Christians martyred for their faith (cf. 7:9,13-15; 17:6; Matt. 24:9-14; see also Mark 13:9-13; Luke 21:12-19).

6:11 white robe. *See note on 3:5.* **rest a little while longer.** God will answer their prayer for vengeance, but in His time. **until both *the number* . . . was completed.** God has predetermined the number of the righteous whose death He will allow before moving to destroy the rebels.

6:12 sixth seal. The force described in this seal is overpowering fear (cf. Luke 21:26). While the first 5 seals will result from human activity God used to accomplish His purposes, at this point He begins direct intervention (cf. Matt. 24:29; Luke 21:25). The previous 5 seals will be precursors to the full fury of the Day of the Lord which will begin with the sixth seal (v. 17). The events described in this seal unleash the seventh, which contains the trumpet judgments (chaps. 8,9; 11:15ff.) and the bowl judgments (chap. 16). **great earthquake.** There have been many earthquakes prior to this (Matt. 24:7), but this will be more than an earthquake. All the earth's faults will begin to fracture simultaneously, resulting in a cataclysmic, global earthquake. **moon became like blood.** Accompanying the earthquake will be numerous volcanic eruptions; and large amounts of ash and debris will be blown into the earth's atmosphere, blackening the sun and giving the moon a blood-red hue (cf. Zech. 14:6,7).

6:13 stars of heaven fell. The word "stars" can refer to any celestial body, large or small, and is not limited to normal English usage. The best explanation is a massive asteroid or meteor shower. **late figs.** Winter figs that grow without the protection of leaves and are easily blown from the tree.

6:14 sky receded as a scroll. The earth's atmosphere will be somehow dramatically affected and the sky as we know it disappears (cf. Is. 34:4). **every mountain and island was moved.** Under the stress created by the global earthquake, great segments of the earth's plates will begin to slip and shift, realigning whole continents.

6:16 wrath of the Lamb. Earth's inhabitants will recognize for the first time the source of all their trouble (*see note on 4:6*). Incredibly, prior to this they will be living life as usual (Matt. 24:37-39).

6:17 great day. The sixth seal will commence what the prophets call "the Day of the Lord." See Introduction to Joel: Historical and Theological Themes.

7:1-17 Chapter 7 forms a parenthesis between the sixth seal (6:12-17) and the seventh seal (8:1) and answers the question posed at the end of chap. 6. Two distinct groups will survive the divine fury: 1) 144,000 Jewish evangelists on earth (vv. 1-8) and 2) their converts in heaven (vv. 9-17).

7:1 four corners. The 4 quadrants of the compass; that is, the angels will take up key positions on earth. **four winds.** A figurative expression, indicating all the earth's winds—those from S, E, N, and W. The 4 angels will turn off, for a brief interlude, the essential engine of our earth's atmosphere.

7:2 seal of the living God. "Seal" often refers to a signet ring used to press its image into wax melted on a document. The resulting imprint implied authenticity and ownership and protected the contents (cf. 9:4; Ezek. 9:3,4). In this case, the mark is the name of God (14:1).

7:4 One hundred *and* forty-four thousand. A missionary corps of redeemed Jews who are instrumental in the salvation of many Jews and Gentiles during the Tribulation (vv. 9-17). They will be the firstfruits of a new redeemed Israel (v. 4; Zech. 12:10). Finally, Israel will be the witness nation she refused to be in the OT (*see notes on Rom.*

hundred *and* forty-four thousand [g]of all the
tribes of the children of Israel *were* sealed:

5 of the tribe of Judah twelve
thousand *were* sealed;
of the tribe of Reuben twelve
thousand *were* [1]sealed;
of the tribe of Gad twelve
thousand *were* sealed;
6 of the tribe of Asher twelve
thousand *were* sealed;
of the tribe of Naphtali twelve
thousand *were* sealed;
of the tribe of Manasseh twelve
thousand *were* sealed;
7 of the tribe of Simeon twelve
thousand *were* sealed;
of the tribe of Levi twelve
thousand *were* sealed;
of the tribe of Issachar twelve
thousand *were* sealed;
8 of the tribe of Zebulun twelve
thousand *were* sealed;
of the tribe of Joseph twelve
thousand *were* sealed;
of the tribe of Benjamin twelve
thousand *were* sealed.

A Multitude from the Great Tribulation

9 After these things I looked, and behold, [h]a great multitude which no one
could number, [i]of all nations, tribes, peoples, and tongues, standing before the
throne and before the Lamb, [j]clothed with
white robes, with palm branches in their
hands, 10 and crying out with a loud voice,
saying, [k]"Salvation *belongs* to our God
[l]who sits on the throne, and to the Lamb!"
11 [m]All the angels stood around the throne
and the elders and the four living creatures, and fell on their faces before the
throne and [n]worshiped God, 12 [o]saying:

"Amen! Blessing and glory and
wisdom,
Thanksgiving and honor and
power and might,
Be to our God forever and ever.
Amen."

13 Then one of the elders answered, saying to me, "Who are these arrayed in [p]white
robes, and where did they come from?"
14 And I said to him, [2]"Sir, you know."
So he said to me, [q]"These are the ones
who come out of the great tribulation, and
[r]washed their robes and made them white
in the blood of the Lamb. 15 Therefore they
are before the throne of God, and serve
Him day and night in His temple. And He
who sits on the throne will [s]dwell among
them. 16 [t]They shall neither hunger anymore nor thirst anymore; [u]the sun shall not
strike them, nor any heat; 17 for the Lamb
who is in the midst of the throne [v]will
shepherd them and lead them to [3]living
fountains of waters. [w]And God will wipe
away every tear from their eyes."

Seventh Seal: Prelude to the Seven Trumpets

8 When[a] He opened the seventh seal,
there was silence in heaven for about
half an hour. 2 [b]And I saw the seven angels
who stand before God, [c]and to them were
given seven trumpets. 3 Then another angel,

4 [g]Gen. 49:1-27
5 [1]NU, M omit *sealed* in vv. 5b-8b.
9 [h]Is. 60:1-5; Rom. 11:25 [i]Rev. 5:9 [j]Rev. 3:5, 18; 4:4; 6:11
10 [k]Ps. 3:8; Is. 43:11; Jer. 3:23; Hos. 13:4; Rev. 19:1 [l]Rev. 5:13
11 [m]Rev. 4:6 [n]Rev. 4:11; 5:9, 12, 14; 11:16
12 [o]Rev. 5:13, 14
13 [p]Rev. 7:9
14 [q]Rev. 6:9 [r]Is. 1:18; Zech. 3:3-5; [Heb. 9:14] [2]NU, M *My lord*
15 [s]Is. 4:5, 6; Rev. 21:3
16 [t]Ps. 121:5; Is. 49:10 [u]Ps. 121:6; Rev. 21:4
17 [v]Ps. 23:1; Matt. 2:6; [John 10:11, 14] [w]Is. 25:8; Matt. 5:4; Rev. 21:4 [3]NU, M *fountains of the waters of life*

CHAPTER 8

1 [a]Rev. 6:1
2 [b][Matt. 18:10]; Luke 1:19 [c]2 Chr. 29:25-28

11:25-27). **all the tribes of the children of Israel.** By sovereign election, God will seal 12,000 from each of the 12 tribes, promising His protection while they accomplish their mission.

7:9 a great multitude. While the tribulation period will be a time of judgment, it will also be a time of unprecedented redemption (cf. v. 14; 6:9-11; 20:4; Is. 11:10; Matt. 24:14). **all nations, tribes, peoples, and tongues.** All the earth's people groups. **white robes.** *See note on 3:4.* **palm branches.** In ancient times, they were associated with celebrations, including the Feast of Tabernacles (Lev. 23:40; Neh. 8:17; John 12:13).

7:10 Salvation *belongs* to our God. Salvation is the theme of their worship, and they recognize that it comes solely from Him.

7:11 elders. *See note on 4:4.* **four living creatures.** *See note on 4:6.*

7:12 Blessing...and might. *See note on 5:12.*

7:13 white robes. *See note on 6:11.*

7:14 the great tribulation. *See notes on 3:10; 6:1,9,12.* These people didn't go with the raptured church, since they were not yet saved. During the 7 year period they will be saved, martyred, and enter heaven. Though it is a time of unparalleled judgment, it is also a time of unparalleled grace in salvation (cf. Matt. 24:12-14). **washed their robes.** Cf. 19:8. Salvation's cleansing is in view (see Titus 2:11-14). **blood of the Lamb.** This refers to the atoning sacrifice of Christ (cf. 1:5; 5:9; Rom. 3:24,25; 5:9).

7:15 His temple. This refers to the heavenly throne of God (*see note on 11:19*). During the Millennium there will also be a temple on earth—a special holy place where God dwells in a partially restored, but still fallen universe (see Ezek. 40–48). In the final, eternal state with its new heavens and earth, there is no temple; God Himself, who will fill all, will be its temple (21:22). **dwell among them.** The preferred reading is that He "will spread His tent over them." God's presence will become their canopy of shelter to protect them from all the terrors of a fallen world and the indescribable horrors they have experienced on the earth during the time of tribulation.

7:17 shepherd. In a beautiful mix of images, the Lamb has always been the Shepherd (Ps. 23; John 10:14ff.; Heb. 13:20).

8:1 the seventh seal. This seal includes not only an earthquake, but the 7 trumpet judgments (8:1–9:21; 11:15ff.) and the 7 bowl judgments (16:1-21), with the bowl judgments flowing out of the seventh trumpet and coming in rapid succession just before Christ's return (*see note on 6:1*). **silence in heaven.** The silence of awe and anticipation at the grim reality of the judgments God is about to unleash.

8:2 seven trumpets. In Revelation, trumpets primarily announce impending judgment. The trumpets are of greater intensity than the seals, but not as destructive as the final bowl judgments will be (cf. 16:1-21). They occur during the final 3½ years, but the time of each is indefinite, except the effects of the fifth trumpet judgment, which will last 5 months (9:10). The first 4 announce the divine destruction of

having a golden censer, came and stood at
the altar. He was given much incense, that
he should offer *it* with [d]the prayers of all the
saints upon [e]the golden altar which was before the throne. 4 And [f]the smoke of the incense, with the prayers of the saints, ascended before God from the angel's hand. 5 Then
the angel took the censer, filled it with fire
from the altar, and threw *it* to the earth. And
[g]there were noises, thunderings, [h]light-
nings, [i]and an earthquake.
6 So the seven angels who had the seven
trumpets prepared themselves to sound.

First Trumpet: Vegetation Struck

7 The first angel sounded: [j]And hail and
fire followed, mingled with blood, and
they were thrown [k]to the [1]earth. And a
third [l]of the trees were burned up, and all
green grass was burned up.

Second Trumpet: The Seas Struck

8 Then the second angel sounded: [m]And
something like a great mountain burning
with fire was thrown into the sea, [n]and a
third of the sea [o]became blood. 9 [p]And a
third of the living creatures in the sea died,
and a third of the ships were destroyed.

Third Trumpet: The Waters Struck

10 Then the third angel sounded: [q]And a
great star fell from heaven, burning like a

3 [d]Rev. 5:8 [e]Ex. 30:1; Rev. 8:3
4 [f]Ps. 141:2; Luke 1:10
5 [g]Ex. 19:16; Rev. 11:19; 16:18 [h]Rev. 4:5 [i]2 Sam. 22:8; 1 Kin. 19:11; Acts 4:31
7 [j]Ex. 9:23; Is. 28:2; Ezek. 38:22; Joel 2:30 [k]Rev. 16:2 [l]Is. 2:13; Rev. 9:4,15-18 [1]NU, M add *and a third of the earth was burned up*
8 [m]Jer. 51:25; Amos 7:4 [n]Ex. 7:17; Rev. 11:6; 16:3 [o]Ezek. 14:19
9 [p]Rev. 16:3
10 [q]Is. 14:12; Rev. 6:13; 9:1 [r]Rev. 14:7; 16:4
11 [s]Ruth 1:20 [t]Ex. 15:23
12 [u]Is. 13:10; Joel 2:31; Amos 8:9; Matt. 24:29; Rev. 6:12 [2]*had no light*
13 [v]Rev. 14:6; 19:17 [w]Rev. 9:12; 11:14; 12:12 [3]NU, M *eagle*

CHAPTER 9

1 [a]Luke 10:18; Rev. 8:10 [b]Luke 8:31; Rev. 9:2, 11; 17:8 [1]Lit. *shaft of the abyss*
2 [c]Joel 2:2, 10
3 [d]Ex. 10:4; Judg. 7:12

torch, [r]and it fell on a third of the rivers and
on the springs of water. 11 [s]The name of the
star is Wormwood. [t]A third of the waters
became wormwood, and many men died
from the water, because it was made bitter.

Fourth Trumpet: The Heavens Struck

12 [u]Then the fourth angel sounded: And
a third of the sun was struck, a third of the
moon, and a third of the stars, so that a
third of them were darkened. A third of the
day [2]did not shine, and likewise the night.
13 And I looked, [v]and I heard an [3]angel
flying through the midst of heaven, saying
with a loud voice, [w]"Woe, woe, woe to the
inhabitants of the earth, because of the remaining blasts of the trumpet of the three
angels who are about to sound!"

Fifth Trumpet: The Locusts from the Bottomless Pit

9 Then the fifth angel sounded: [a]And I
saw a star fallen from heaven to the
earth. To him was given the key to [b]the
[1]bottomless pit. 2 And he opened the bottomless pit, and smoke arose out of the pit
like the smoke of a great furnace. So the
[c]sun and the air were darkened because of
the smoke of the pit. 3 Then out of the
smoke locusts came upon the earth. And to
them was given power, [d]as the scorpions of
the earth have power. 4 They were com-

earth's ecology (vv. 6-12), while the final 3 involve demonic devastation of earth's inhabitants (9:1-21; 11:15ff.).

8:3 censer. A golden pan, suspended on a rope or chain, that was used to transport fiery coals from the brazen altar to the altar of incense, in order to ignite the incense, symbolizing the prayers of the people (5:8; Ex. 27:3; cf. Luke 1:8,9). This occurred twice daily at the time of the morning and evening sacrifices.

8:5 thunderings, lightnings. *See note on 4:5.* **an earthquake.** Surely of equal or greater intensity than one described in the sixth seal (*see note on 6:12*).

8:7 hail and fire followed, mingled with blood. This may describe volcanic eruptions that could certainly result from the earthquake in v. 5. The steam and water thrown into the sky by such eruptions could easily condense into hail and fall to earth along with the fiery lava (cf. Ex. 9:13-25). Dust and gases may so contaminate falling liquid water that it appears blood red. **a third of the trees were burned up.** The lava storm will create a blazing fire that devastates one-third of the earth's forests.

8:8 like a great mountain. Probably a huge meteor or asteroid surrounded by gases that will ignite as it enters earth's atmosphere. Its impact will create a tidal wave, destroying a one-third of the world's ships. **sea became blood.** This may refer to an event known as red tides, caused by billions of dead micro-organisms poisoning the water—in this case the result of the meteor's collision. Or it may be actual blood, a clear act of eschatological judgment.

8:10 great star fell. Another celestial body, perhaps a comet in this case since it leaves a fiery trail (*see notes on v. 8; 6:13*). It will disintegrate as it nears the earth, scattering over the globe.

8:11 Wormwood. A bitter, poisonous substance, derived from a root, that causes drunkenness and eventually death (Deut. 29:18; Prov. 5:4; Jer. 9:15; Lam. 3:15).

8:12 a third of the sun was struck. God will supernaturally reduce the intensity of the celestial bodies by one-third. The loss of solar heat will cause a radical drop in temperature, producing severe changes in meteorological, botanical, and biological cycles (Luke 21:25; cf. Ex. 10:21-23). But this is temporary (cf. 16:8,9).

8:13 Woe, woe, woe. One for each remaining trumpet blast. Although the first 4 trumpets are unimaginable, they will be nothing like the 3 to come (9:1-21; 11:15ff.).

9:1 a star fallen from heaven. Unlike the other stars that will have fallen (6:13; 8:8), this one will be an angelic being (cf. v. 2)—probably Satan himself (v. 4; 12:7; *see notes on Is. 14:12-15; Luke 10:18*). **bottomless pit.** Lit. "pit of the abyss." Mentioned 7 times in Revelation, it always refers to the prison where some of the demonic hordes are incarcerated, the place of severest torment and isolation (vv. 1,2,11; 11:7; 17:8; 20:1,3; *see notes on Luke 8:31; 2 Pet. 2:4; Jude 6,7*).

9:3 locusts. A grasshopper-like insect that descends in swarms so thick they can obscure the sun and strip bare all vegetation. In the 1950s a locust swarm devoured every growing thing for several hundred thousand square miles in the Middle East. These are not normal locusts, however, but specially prepared ones that are merely the outward form of demons, who, like locusts, will bring swarming desolation (*see notes on Joel 2:1-5*). "Like" appears 9 times in John's description; he finds it difficult to describe what he sees in a way the reader can understand. **scorpions.** An arachnid that inhabits warm, dry regions and has an erect tail tipped with a venomous stinger. A scorpion's victim often rolls on the ground in agony, foams at the mouth, and grinds his teeth in pain. The demons in locust form are able to inflict the physical—and perhaps, spiritual—pain like the scorpion (v. 5).

manded [e]not to harm [f]the grass of the earth,
or any green thing, or any tree, but only
those men who do not have [g]the seal of God
on their foreheads. 5 And [2]they were not
given *authority* to kill them, [h]but to torment
them *for* five months. Their torment *was* like
the torment of a scorpion when it strikes a
man. 6 In those days [i]men will seek death
and will not find it; they will desire to die,
and death will flee from them.
7 [j]The shape of the locusts was like horses prepared for battle. [k]On their heads
were crowns of something like gold, [l]and
their faces *were* like the faces of men.
8 They had hair like women's hair, and
[m]their teeth were like lions' *teeth*. 9 And
they had breastplates like breastplates of
iron, and the sound of their wings *was*
[n]like the sound of chariots with many
horses running into battle. 10 They had
tails like scorpions, and there were stings
in their tails. Their power *was* to hurt men
five months. 11 And they had as king over
them [o]the angel of the bottomless pit,
whose name in Hebrew *is* [3]Abaddon, but
in Greek he has the name [4]Apollyon.
12 [p]One woe is past. Behold, still two
more woes are coming after these things.

Sixth Trumpet: The Angels from the Euphrates

13 Then the sixth angel sounded: And I
heard a voice from the four horns of the
[q]golden altar which is before God, 14 saying to the sixth angel who had the trumpet,
"Release the four angels who are bound [r]at
the great river Euphrates." 15 So the four
angels, who had been prepared for the
hour and day and month and year, were
released to kill a [s]third of mankind.
16 Now [t]the number of the army [u]of the
horsemen *was* two hundred million; [v]I
heard the number of them. 17 And thus I
saw the horses in the vision: those who sat
on them had breastplates of fiery red, hy-
acinth blue, and sulfur yellow; [w]and the
heads of the horses *were* like the heads of
lions; and out of their mouths came fire,
smoke, and brimstone. 18 By these three
plagues a third of mankind was killed—by
the fire and the smoke and the brimstone
which came out of their mouths. 19 For
[5]their power is in their mouth and in their
tails; [x]for their tails *are* like serpents, having heads; and with them they do harm.
20 But the rest of mankind, who were not
killed by these plagues, [y]did not repent of
the works of their hands, that they should
not worship [z]demons, [a]and idols of gold,
silver, brass, stone, and wood, which can
neither see nor hear nor walk. 21 And they
did not repent of their murders [b]or their
[6]sorceries or their sexual immorality or
their thefts.

4 [e]Rev. 6:6 [f]Rev. 8:7 [g]Ex. 12:23; Ezek. 9:4; Rev. 7:2, 3
5 [h][Rev. 9:10; 11:7] [2]The locusts
6 [i]Job 3:21; 7:15; Is. 2:19; Jer. 8:3; Rev. 6:16
7 [j]Joel 2:4 [k]Nah. 3:17 [l]Dan. 7:8
8 [m]Joel 1:6
9 [n]Jer. 47:3; Joel 2:5-7
11 [o]Eph. 2:2 [3]Lit. *Destruction* [4]Lit. *Destroyer*
12 [p]Rev. 8:13; 11:14
13 [q]Rev. 8:3
14 [r]Gen. 15:18; Deut. 1:7; Josh. 1:4; Rev. 16:12
15 [s]Rev. 8:7-9; 9:18
16 [t]Ps. 68:17; Dan. 7:10 [u]Ezek. 38:4 [v]Rev. 7:4
17 [w]1 Chr. 12:8; Is. 5:28, 29
19 [x]Is. 9:15 [5]NU, M *the power of the horses*
20 [y]Deut. 31:29 [z]Lev. 17:7; Deut. 32:17; Ps. 106:37; 1 Cor. 10:20 [a]Ps. 115:4-7; 135:15-17; Dan. 5:23
21 [b]Rev. 21:8; 22:15 [6]NU, M *drugs*

9:4 men who do not have the seal of God. Everyone on earth except the two groups mentioned in chap. 7—the 144,000 Jewish evangelists and their converts (*see note on 7:3*).

9:5 five months. The normal life cycle of locusts is 5 months, usually from May to Sep.

9:6 seek death and will not find it. The tormented will find no relief. Even their unimaginable attempts to end their misery in suicide will be unsuccessful.

9:7 faces of men. Probably a reference to these demonic creatures as rational, intelligent beings.

9:8 women's hair. Jeremiah 51:27 refers to locusts having bristles like hair. **lions' *teeth*.** They are fierce, powerful, and deadly (cf. Jer. 51:27).

9:9 breastplates of iron. Breastplates were designed to protect the vital organs and sustain the life of the warrior. These creatures are invulnerable.

9:10 five months. *See note on v. 5.*

9:11 Abaddon…Apollyon. Although locusts normally have no king (Prov. 30:27), these demonic creatures do. His name in both Heb. and Gr. means "destroyer." There is a hierarchy of power among the demons, just as among the holy angels. Apparently, "the angel of the bottomless pit" is one of Satan's most trusted leaders.

9:12 One woe. The first of the final 3 trumpets (*see note on 8:13*).

9:13 horns of the golden altar. God's design for the golden altar of incense included small protrusions (horns) on each corner (Ex. 30:2; *see note on 6:9*). Normally a place of mercy, as God responded to His people's prayers, the altar will resound with a cry for vengeance.

9:14 four angels. Scripture never refers to holy angels as being bound. These are fallen angels—another segment of Satan's force whom God had bound but will free to accomplish His judgment through their horsemen (vv. 15-19). God's control extends even to the demonic forces—they are bound or freed at His command. **Euphrates.** One of the 4 rivers that flowed through the Garden of Eden (*see note on 16:12*; cf. Gen. 2:14). Starting with Babel, this region has spawned many of the world's pagan religions.

9:15 the hour and day and month and year. God works according to His predetermined plan (cf. Matt. 24:36; Acts 1:7).

9:16 the army. Some see this as a reference to forces accompanying the kings of the east (16:12) and identify them with a human army coming from Asia. But that event occurs in connection with the seventh trumpet, not the sixth. The language is better understood as referring to a demon force that makes war with the earth's inhabitants and kills one-third of humanity (v. 15).

9:17 breastplates. *See note on v. 9.* **brimstone.** Brimstone is a yellowish, sulfuric rock that often attends fire and smoke in Revelation (14:10; 19:20; 20:10). Common in the Dead Sea region, when ignited such deposits melt and produce burning streams and suffocating gas.

9:19 tails *are* like serpents, having heads. John's language represents the demons' ability to vent their destructive power in both directions.

9:20,21 God lists 5 sins that are representative of their defiance.

9:20 demons. Reminiscent of Paul's comments about idolatry (*see note on 1 Cor. 10:20*); demons impersonate the stone and wood idols men make.

9:21 they did not repent. Cf. 16:9,11,21. **sorceries.** This Gr. word is the root of the Eng. word "pharmacy." Drugs in the ancient world were used to dull the senses and induce a state suitable for religious experiences such as seances, witchcraft, incantations, and cavorting with mediums (21:8; 22:15). *See note on Eph. 5:18.*

The Mighty Angel with the Little Book

10 I saw still another mighty angel
coming down from heaven, clothed
with a cloud. [a]And a rainbow *was* on [b]his
head, his face *was* like the sun, and [c]his feet
like pillars of fire. 2 He had a little book
open in his hand. [d]And he set his right foot
on the sea and *his* left *foot* on the land,
3 and cried with a loud voice, as *when* a
lion roars. When he cried out, [e]seven thunders uttered their voices. 4 Now when the
seven thunders [1]uttered their voices, I was
about to write; but I heard a voice from
heaven saying [2]to me, [f]"Seal up the things
which the seven thunders uttered, and do
not write them."
5 The angel whom I saw standing on the
sea and on the land [g]raised up his [3]hand to
heaven 6 and swore by Him who lives forever and ever, [h]who created heaven and
the things that are in it, the earth and the
things that are in it, and the sea and the
things that are in it, [i]that there should be
delay no longer, 7 but [j]in the days of the
sounding of the seventh angel, when he is
about to sound, the mystery of God would
be finished, as He declared to His servants
the prophets.

John Eats the Little Book

8 Then the voice which I heard from
heaven spoke to me again and said, "Go,
take the little book which is open in the
hand of the angel who stands on the sea
and on the earth."
9 So I went to the angel and said to him,
"Give me the little book."
And he said to me, [k]"Take and eat it; and
it will make your stomach bitter, but it will
be as sweet as honey in your mouth."
10 Then I took the little book out of the
angel's hand and ate it, [l]and it was as
sweet as honey in my mouth. But when I
had eaten it, [m]my stomach became bitter.
11 And [4]he said to me, "You must prophesy again about many peoples, nations,
tongues, and kings."

The Two Witnesses

11 Then I was given [a]a reed like a measuring rod. [1]And the angel stood,
saying, [b]"Rise and measure the temple of
God, the altar, and those who worship
there. 2 But leave out [c]the court which is
outside the temple, and do not measure it,
[d]for it has been given to the Gentiles. And
they will [e]tread the holy city underfoot *for*

CHAPTER 10

1 [a] Ezek. 1:26-28; Rev. 4:3 [b] Matt. 17:2; Rev. 1:16 [c] Rev. 1:15
2 [d] Ps. 95:5; Matt. 28:18
3 [e] Ps. 29:3-9; Rev. 4:5; 8:5
4 [f] Dan. 8:26; 12:4,9; Rev. 22:10 [1] NU, M *sounded,* [2] NU, M omit *to me*
5 [g] Ex. 6:8; Deut. 32:40; Dan. 12:7 [3] NU, M *right hand*
6 [h] Gen. 1:1; Ex. 20:11; Neh. 9:6; Rev. 4:11 [i] Dan. 12:7; Rev. 16:17
7 [j] Rev. 11:15
9 [k] Jer. 15:16; Ezek. 2:8; 3:1-3
10 [l] Ezek. 3:3 [m] Ezek. 2:10
11 [4] NU, M *they*

CHAPTER 11

1 [a] Ezek. 40:3–42:20; Zech. 2:1; Rev. 21:15 [b] Num. 23:18 [1] NU, M omit *And the angel stood*
2 [c] Ezek. 40:17,20 [d] Ps. 79:1; Luke 21:24 [e] Dan. 8:10

10:1–11:14 These verses serve as an interlude between the sixth trumpet and the seventh trumpet (11:15). The seals and the bowls also have a brief interlude between their sixth and seventh judgments (7:1-17; 16:15). God's intention is to encourage and comfort His people in the midst of the fury and to remind them that He is still sovereign, that He remembers His people, and that they will ultimately be victorious.

10:1 another mighty angel. Many commentators understand this to be Jesus Christ. But the Gr. word translated "another" means one of the same kind, that is, a created being. This is not one of the 7 angels responsible for sounding the trumpets (8:2), but one of the highest ranking in heaven, filled with splendor, greatness, and strength (cf. 5:2; 8:3; 18:1). **rainbow.** *See note on 4:3.* Perhaps God included this to remind John, that even in judgment, He will always remember His Noahic Covenant and protect His own. **feet like pillars of fire.** This angel's feet and legs indicate the firm resolve with which He will execute the Day of the Lord.

10:2 little book. The 7 sealed scroll that is the title deed to the earth (*see note on 5:1*) will be fully opened and all the final judgments made visible. **right foot on the sea and *his* left *foot* on the land.** Although Satan has temporarily usurped the sea and the earth, this symbolic act demonstrates that all creation belongs to the Lord and He rules it with sovereign authority.

10:3 seven thunders. *See note on 4:5*; cf. 6:1; 8:5.

10:4 Seal up. John was told he must conceal the message of the 7 thunders until God's time (cf. 22:10; Dan. 8:26,27; 12:9).

10:5 raised up his hand. This Gr. verb appears often in the technical sense of raising the hand to take an oath or a solemn vow (cf. Dan. 12:7; *see notes on Matt. 5:33-37*). The hand is raised toward heaven because that is where God dwells. The angel is taking an oath.

10:6 there should be delay no longer. This initiates the last plagues of the Day of the Lord (11:15), indicating that the time the disciples anticipated has come (Matt. 24:3; Acts 1:6). The prayers of the saints will be answered (6:9-11; Matt. 6:10).

10:7 the mystery. A Gr. term meaning "to shut" or "to close." In the NT, a "mystery" is a truth that God concealed but has revealed through Christ and His apostles (*see notes on Eph. 3:3-5*; cf. Rom. 16:25). Here the mystery is the final consummation of all things as God destroys sinners and establishes His righteous kingdom on earth. **as He declared.** This mystery, though not fully revealed, was declared to God's prophets (cf. Amos 3:7).

10:9 Take and eat it. This act graphically illustrates taking in God's Word. John's physical reactions demonstrate what every believer's proper response to God's judgment should be (cf. Ezek. 3:1)—sweet anticipation of God's glory and our victory, and at the same time, the bitterness of seeing God's wrath poured out on those who reject His Son. **your stomach bitter.** As he truly digests what the seal, trumpet, and bowl judgments hold in store for the sinner, John becomes nauseated. **sweet as honey in your mouth.** But still God's final victory and vindication are sweet realities to the believer.

10:11 prophesy again. A call for John to warn men about the bitter judgment in the seventh trumpet and the 7 bowls. **peoples, nations, tongues, and kings.** *See note on 7:9.*

11:1 a reed. A hollow, bamboo-like cane plant that grew in the Jordan Valley. Because of its light weight and rigidity, it was commonly used as a measuring rod (cf. Ezek. 40:3,5). Measuring the temple signified God's ownership of it (cf. 21:15; Zech. 2:1-5). **the temple of God.** Refers to the Holy of Holies and the Holy Place, not the entire temple complex (cf. v. 2). A rebuilt temple will exist during the time of the Tribulation (Dan. 9:27; 12:11; Matt. 24:15; 2 Thess. 2:4). **altar.** The reference to worshipers suggests this is the bronze altar in the courtyard, not the incense altar in the Holy Place, since only the priests were permitted inside the Holy Place (cf. Luke 1:8-10).

11:2 court which is outside. The court of the Gentiles, separated from the inner court in the Herodian temple by a low wall. Gentiles were forbidden to enter the inner court on penalty of death. That John is instructed not to measure the outer court symbolizes God's rejection of the unbelieving Gentiles who have oppressed His covenant people. **tread the holy city underfoot.** Assyria, Babylon,

[f]forty-two months. 3 And I will give *power*
to my two [g]witnesses, [h]and they will
prophesy [i]one thousand two hundred and
sixty days, clothed in sackcloth."
4 These are the [j]two olive trees and the
two lampstands standing before the [2]God
of the earth. 5 And if anyone wants to
harm them, [k]fire proceeds from their
mouth and devours their enemies. [l]And if
anyone wants to harm them, he must be
killed in this manner. 6 These [m]have power
to shut heaven, so that no rain falls in the
days of their prophecy; and they have
power over waters to turn them to blood,
and to strike the earth with all plagues, as
often as they desire.

The Witnesses Killed

7 When they [n]finish their testimony, [o]the
beast that ascends [p]out of the bottomless
pit [q]will make war against them, overcome
them, and kill them. 8 And their dead bodies *will lie* in the street of [r]the great city
which spiritually is called Sodom and
Egypt, [s]where also [3]our Lord was crucified. 9 [t]Then *those* from the peoples, tribes,
tongues, and nations [4]will see their dead
bodies three-and-a-half days, [u]and not
allow their dead bodies to be put into
graves. 10 [v]And those who dwell on the
earth will rejoice over them, make merry,
[w]and send gifts to one another, [x]because
these two prophets tormented those who
dwell on the earth.

The Witnesses Resurrected

11 [y]Now after the three-and-a-half days
[z]the breath of life from God entered them,
and they stood on their feet, and great
fear fell on those who saw them. 12 And
[5]they heard a loud voice from heaven saying to them, "Come up here." [a]And they
ascended to heaven [b]in a cloud, [c]and their
enemies saw them. 13 In the same hour

2 [f]Dan. 7:25; 12:7; Rev. 12:6; 13:5
3 [g]Deut. 17:6; Rev. 20:4 [h]Rev. 19:10 [i]Rev. 12:6
4 [j]Ps. 52:8; Jer. 11:16; Zech. 4:2, 3, 11, 14 [2]NU, M *Lord*
5 [k]2 Kin. 1:10-12; Jer. 1:10; 5:14; Ezek. 43:3; Hos. 6:5; Rev. 9:17 [l]Num. 16:29
6 [m]1 Kin. 17:1; Luke 4:25; [James 5:16, 17]
7 [n]Luke 13:32 [o]Rev. 13:1, 11; 17:8 [p]Rev. 9:1, 2 [q]Dan. 7:21; Rev. 13:7
8 [r]Rev. 14:8 [s]Heb. 13:12 [3]NU, M *their*
9 [t]Rev. 17:15 [u]1 Kin. 13:22; Ps. 79:2, 3 [4]NU, M *see . . . and will not allow*
10 [v]Rev. 12:12 [w]Neh. 8:10, 12; Esth. 9:19, 22 [x]Rev. 16:10
11 [y]Rev. 11:9 [z]Ezek. 37:5, 9, 10
12 [a]Is. 14:13 [b]Is. 60:8; Acts 1:9 [c]2 Kin. 2:11, 12 [5]M *I*

Medo-Persia, Greece, and Rome all oppressed Jerusalem in ancient times (cf. 2 Kin. 25:8-10; Ps. 79:1; Is. 63:18; Lam. 1:10). This verse refers to the future devastating destruction and oppression of Jerusalem by the forces of the Antichrist. **forty-two months.** This 3½ year period covers the second half of the Tribulation and coincides with the visibly evil career of the Antichrist (v. 3; 12:6; 13:5). During this same time, the Jews will be sheltered by God in the wilderness (12:6,14).

11:3 two witnesses. Individuals granted special power and authority by God to preach a message of judgment and salvation during the second half of the Tribulation. The OT required two or more witnesses to confirm testimony (cf. Deut. 17:6; 19:15; Matt. 18:16; John 8:17; Heb. 10:28), and these two prophets will be the culmination of God's testimony to Israel: a message of judgment from God and of His gracious offer of the gospel to all who will repent and believe. **one thousand two hundred and sixty days.** Forty-two months or 3½ years (cf. 12:6; 13:5; *see note on v. 2*). **sackcloth.** Coarse, rough cloth made from goat or camel hair. Wearing garments made from it expressed penitence, humility, and mourning (cf. Gen. 37:34; 2 Sam. 3:31; 2 Kin. 6:30; 19:1; Esth. 4:1; Is. 22:12; Jer. 6:26; Matt. 11:21). The witnesses are mourning because of the wretched wickedness of the world, God's judgment on it, and the desecration of the temple and the holy city by the Antichrist.

11:4 This imagery is drawn from Zech. 3,4 (*see notes there*). Zechariah's vision had both a near fulfillment (the rebuilding of the temple by Joshua and Zerubbabel) and a far future fulfillment (the two witnesses, whose ministry points toward Israel's final restoration in the Millennium). **two olive trees and the two lampstands.** Olive oil was commonly used in lamps; together the olive trees and lampstands symbolize the light of spiritual revival. The two witnesses' preaching will spark a revival, just as Joshua's and Zerubbabel's did in Israel after the Babylonian captivity.

11:5,6 While it is impossible to be dogmatic about the identity of these two witnesses, several observations suggest they might be Moses and Elijah: 1) like Moses, they strike the earth with plagues, and like Elijah, they have the power to keep it from raining; 2) Jewish tradition expected both Moses (cf. Deut. 18:15-18) and Elijah (cf. Mal. 4:5,6) to return in the future (cf. John 1:21); 3) both Moses and Elijah were present at the Transfiguration, the preview of Christ's second coming; 4) both Moses and Elijah used supernatural means to provoke repentance; 5) Elijah was taken up alive into heaven, and God buried Moses' body where it would never be found; and 6) the length of the drought the two witnesses bring (3½ years; cf. v. 3) is the same as that brought by Elijah (James 5:17).

11:5 fire proceeds . . . and devours. Probably this refers to literal fire. These two will be invincible during their ministry, protected by supernatural power. The false prophet will counterfeit this sign (13:3).

11:6 power to shut heaven. Miracles have often authenticated God's messengers. Here, bringing a 3½ year drought (as did Elijah before them) will add immeasurable torment to those experiencing the worldwide disasters of the Tribulation—and exacerbate their hatred of the two witnesses. **waters to turn them to blood.** The earth's water, already devastated by the effects of the second and third trumpets, will become undrinkable, adding immensely to the suffering caused by the drought.

11:7 the beast. The first of 36 references to this person in Revelation, who is none other than the Antichrist (see chap. 13). That he will ascend out of the bottomless pit indicates that his power is satanic. **kill them.** Their ministry completed, God will withdraw the two witnesses' supernatural protection. The beast will then be able to accomplish what many had died trying to do.

11:8 bodies *will lie* in the street. Refusing to bury one's enemies was a way to dishonor and show contempt for them (cf. Acts 14:19). The OT expressly forbids this practice (Deut. 21:22,23). **the great city.** Identifying Jerusalem as a city like Sodom and Egypt stresses the city's wickedness. Its Jewish population will apparently be the focus of the witnesses' ministry, leading to the conversions of v. 13.

11:9 three-and-a-half days. The entire world will watch (undoubtedly on the latest form of visual media) and glorify the Antichrist as the bodies of the dead prophets who have been killed begin to decay.

11:10 rejoice . . . make merry . . . send gifts. Wild with joy over the death of their tormentors, those who dwell on the earth (a phrase used 11 times in Revelation to speak of unbelievers) will celebrate the two witnesses' deaths as a holiday.

11:11 breath of life from God entered them. The festivities, however, are short-lived as God vindicates His faithful witnesses by resurrecting them.

11:12 ascended to heaven in a cloud. Some may wonder why God will not allow them to preach, assuming their message would have more force following their resurrection. But that ignores Christ's clear statement to the contrary (Luke 16:31). **enemies saw them.**

[d]there was a great earthquake, [e]and a tenth
of the city fell. In the earthquake seven
thousand people were killed, and the rest
were afraid [f]and gave glory to the God of
heaven.
14 [g]The second woe is past. Behold, the
third woe is coming quickly.

Seventh Trumpet: The Kingdom Proclaimed

15 Then [h]the seventh angel sounded:
[i]And there were loud voices in heaven,
saying, [j]"The [6]kingdoms of this world
have become *the kingdoms* of our Lord and
of His Christ, [k]and He shall reign forever
and ever!" 16 And [l]the twenty-four elders
who sat before God on their thrones fell on
their faces and [m]worshiped God, 17 saying:

"We give You thanks, O Lord God
Almighty,
The One [n]who is and who was
[7]and who is to come,
Because You have taken Your great
power [o]and reigned.
18 The nations were [p]angry, and Your
[8]wrath has come,
And the time of the [q]dead, that
they should be judged,
And that You should reward Your
servants the prophets and the
saints,
And those who fear Your name,
small and great,
And should destroy those who
destroy the earth."

19 Then [r]the temple of God was opened
in heaven, and the ark of [9]His covenant
was seen in His temple. And [s]there were
lightnings, noises, thunderings, an earthquake, [t]and great hail.

The Woman, the Child, and the Dragon

12 Now a great sign appeared in heav-
en: a woman clothed with the sun,
with the moon under her feet, and on her

13 [d]Rev. 6:12; 8:5; 11:19; 16:18 [e]Rev. 16:19 [f]Josh. 7:19; John 9:24; Rev. 14:7; 16:9; 19:7
14 [g]Rev. 8:13; 9:12
15 [h]Rev. 8:2; 10:7 [i]Is. 27:13 [j]Rev. 12:10 [k]Ex. 15:18; Dan. 2:44; 7:14, 27; Luke 1:33 [6]NU, M *kingdom . . . has become the kingdom*
16 [l]Matt. 19:28; Rev. 4:4 [m]Rev. 4:11; 5:9, 12, 14; 7:11
17 [n]Rev. 16:5 [7]NU, M omit *and who is to come*
[o]Rev. 19:6
18 [p]Ps. 2:1 [q]Dan. 7:10; [Rev. 20:12, 13] [8]*anger*
19 [r]Rev. 4:1; 15:5, 8 [s]Rev. 8:5 [t]Rev. 16:21 [9]M *the covenant of the Lord*

Those who hated and dishonored the two witnesses will watch their vindication.

11:13 earthquake. God punctuates the ascension of His prophets with a shattering earthquake. The destruction and loss of life may be primarily among the leaders of the Antichrist's forces. **the rest.** This refers to the Jews still living, who will not yet have come to faith in Christ. **gave glory to the God of heaven.** A genuine experience of the salvation of Jews (cf. Luke 17:18,19), in contrast to those who blaspheme and refuse to glorify God (16:9). This makes a key fulfilment of Zechariah's prophecy (12:10; 13:1) and Paul's (Rom. 11:25-27).

11:14 second woe. The sixth trumpet (*see note on 9:12*). The interlude between the sixth and seventh trumpets ends (*see note on 10:1*). Israel's repentance will shortly usher in the millennial kingdom (Acts 3:19-21; Rom. 11:25,26). But first will come the final, climactic judgments.

11:15 seventh angel sounded. The seventh trumpet includes the 7 bowl, final judgments depicted in chap. 16 and all the events leading up to the establishing of the millennial kingdom (chap. 20) and the coronation of Jesus as King (chap. 19). ***kingdoms* of our Lord and of His Christ.** The singular (kingdom) is the preferred reading. Despite its many political and cultural divisions, the Bible views the world spiritually as one kingdom, with one ruler—Satan (John 12:31; 14:30; 16:11; 2 Cor. 4:4). Following Satan's lead, the human rulers of this world are generally hostile to Christ (Ps. 2:2; Acts 4:26). The long rebellion of the world kingdom will end with the victorious return of the Lord Jesus Christ to defeat His enemies and establish His messianic kingdom (Is. 2:2,3; Dan. 2:44; 7:13,14,18,22,27; Luke 1:31-33). This kingdom also belongs to God the Father (*see notes on Dan. 4:3; 6:26; 1 Cor. 15:24*).

11:16 twenty-four elders. *See note on 4:4.*

11:17 One who is and who was. The final phrase, "who is to come," (used in 1:4,8; 4:8) is omitted in the most reliable Gr. manuscripts. The coming of the kingdom is no longer future, it will be immediate.

11:18 nations were angry. No longer terrified (cf. 6:15-17), they will be filled with defiant rage. Their hostility will shortly manifest itself in a foolish attempt to fight against Christ—a doomed, futile effort that is the apex of human rebellion against God (16:14; 19:17-21). **Your wrath.** Almighty God answers the feeble, impotent fury of the nations (cf. Ps. 2:1-9). The 24 elders speak of God's future wrath (20:11-15) as if it were already present, signifying its certainty. That God will one day pour out His wrath on rebellious men is a major theme in Scripture (cf. Is. 24:17-23; 26:20,21; 30:27-33; Ezek. 38:16ff.; 2 Thess. 1:5-10). **dead...judged.** The final outpouring of God's wrath includes judging the dead (cf. Matt. 25:31-46; John 5:25-29). The judgment has two parts: 1) God rewards OT saints (Dan. 12:1-3; cf. 22:12; 1 Cor. 3:8; 4:5), the raptured church (1 Cor. 15:51,52; 1 Thess. 4:13-18), and Tribulation saints (20:4); and 2) God condemns unbelievers to the lake of fire forever (20:15).

11:19 temple of God...heaven. See 3:12; 7:15; 14:15,17; 15:5-8; 16:1,17. The heavenly Holy of Holies (*see notes on Ex. 26:31-37*) where God dwells in transcendent glory, already is identified as His throne (chaps. 4,5). Cf. Heb 9:24. John had seen the throne (4:5), the altar (6:9; 8:3-5), and here the Holy of Holies. **ark of His covenant.** This piece of furniture in the OT tabernacle and temple (*see notes on Ex. 25:10-22*) symbolized God's presence, atonement, and covenant with His people. That earthly ark was only a picture of this heavenly one (see Heb. 9:23; 10:20). It was there God provided mercy and atonement for sin. As the earthly Holy of Holies was open when the price of sin was paid (Matt. 27:51; Heb. 10:19,20), so the Holy of Holies in heaven is opened to speak of God's saving New Covenant and redeeming purpose in the midst of judgment. **lightnings, noises, thunderings, an earthquake, and great hail.** What was anticipated in 4:5 and 8:5 will become a terrifying reality. These events occur as part of the seventh bowl (16:17-21) and are the climax of the seventh trumpet. Since heaven is the source of vengeance, judgment also comes out of God's Holy of Holies (14:15; 17; 15:5-8; 16:1,7,17). *See note on 6:1.*

12:1 sign. A symbol pointing to something else. This is the first of 7 signs in the last half of Revelation. Cf. v. 3; 13:13,14; 15:1; 16:14; 19:20. **a woman.** Not an actual woman, but a symbolic representation of Israel, pictured in the OT as the wife of God (Is. 54:5,6; Jer. 3:6-8; 31:32; Ezek. 16:32; Hos. 2:16). Three other symbolic women appear in Revelation: 1) Jezebel, who represents paganism (2:20); 2) the scarlet woman (17:3-6), symbolizing the apostate church; and 3) the wife of the Lamb (19:7), symbolizing the true church. That this woman

head a garland of twelve stars. 2 Then
being with child, she cried out [a]in labor
and in pain to give birth.
3 And another sign appeared in heaven:
behold, [b]a great, fiery red dragon having
seven heads and ten horns, and seven diadems on his heads. 4 [c]His tail drew a third
[d]of the stars of heaven [e]and threw them to
the earth. And the dragon stood [f]before the
woman who was ready to give birth, [g]to
devour her Child as soon as it was born.
5 She bore a male Child [h]who was to rule
all nations with a rod of iron. And her
Child was [i]caught up to God and His
throne. 6 Then [j]the woman fled into the
wilderness, where she has a place prepared by God, that they should feed her
there [k]one thousand two hundred and
sixty days.

Satan Thrown Out of Heaven

7 And war broke out in heaven: [l]Michael
and his angels fought [m]with the dragon;
and the dragon and his angels fought,
8 but they [1]did not prevail, nor was a place
found for [2]them in heaven any longer. 9 So
[n]the great dragon was cast out, [o]that serpent of old, called the Devil and Satan,
[p]who deceives the whole world; [q]he was
cast to the earth, and his angels were cast
out with him.
10 Then I heard a loud voice saying in
heaven, [r]"Now salvation, and strength,
and the kingdom of our God, and the
power of His Christ have come, for the accuser of our brethren, [s]who accused them
before our God day and night, has been
cast down. 11 And [t]they overcame him by
the blood of the Lamb and by the word of
their testimony, [u]and they did not love
their lives to the death. 12 Therefore [v]re-
joice, O heavens, and you who dwell in
them! [w]Woe to the inhabitants of the earth
and the sea! For the devil has come down
to you, having great wrath, [x]because he
knows that he has a short time."

The Woman Persecuted

13 Now when the dragon saw that he had
been cast to the earth, he persecuted [y]the

CHAPTER 12

2 [a] Is. 26:17; 66:6-9; Mic. 4:9; Gal. 4:19
3 [b] Rev. 13:1; 17:3, 7, 9
4 [c] Rev. 9:10, 19 [d] Rev. 8:7, 12 [e] Dan. 8:10 [f] Rev. 12:2 [g] Ex. 1:16; Matt. 2:16
5 [h] Ps. 2:9; Is. 7:14; 9:6; Rev. 2:27; 19:15 [i] Luke 24:51; Acts 1:9-11
6 [j] Rev. 12:4, 14 [k] Rev. 11:3; 13:5
7 [l] Dan. 10:13, 21; 12:1; Jude 9 [m] Rev. 20:2
8 [1] *were not strong enough* [2] M *him*
9 [n] Luke 10:18; John 12:31 [o] Gen. 3:1, 4; 2 Cor. 11:3; Rev. 12:15; 20:2 [p] Rev. 20:3 [q] Rev. 9:1
10 [r] Rev. 11:15 [s] Job 1:9, 11; 2:5; Zech. 3:1
11 [t] Rom. 16:20 [u] Luke 14:26; [Rev. 2:10]
12 [v] Ps. 96:11; Is. 44:23; Rev. 18:20 [w] Rev. 8:13 [x] Rev. 10:6
13 [y] Rev. 12:5

does not represent the church is clear from the context. **clothed with the sun…moon under her feet…twelve stars.** Cf. Gen. 37:9-11. Being clothed with the sun speaks of the glory, dignity, and exalted status of Israel, the people of promise who will be saved and given a kingdom. The picture of the moon under her feet possibly describes God's covenant relationship with Israel, since new moons were associated with worship (1 Chr. 23:31; 2 Chr. 2:4; 8:13; Ezra 3:5; Ps. 81:3). The 12 stars represent the 12 tribes of Israel.

12:2 cried out…in pain. Israel, often pictured as a mother giving birth (cf. Is. 26:17,18; 54:1; 66:7-12; Hos. 13:13; Mic. 4:10; 5:2,3; Matt. 24:8), had agonized and suffered for centuries, longing for the Messiah to come and destroy Satan, sin, and death, and usher in the kingdom.

12:3 great, fiery red dragon. The woman's mortal enemy is Satan, who appears as a dragon 13 times in this book (cf. v. 9; 20:2). Red speaks of bloodshed (cf. John 8:44). **seven heads…ten horns…seven diadems.** Figurative language depicting Satan's domination of 7 past worldly kingdoms and 10 future kingdoms (cf. Dan. 7:7,20,24). *See notes on 13:1; 17:9,10.* Satan has and will rule the world until the seventh trumpet blows (11:15). He has inflicted relentless pain on Israel (Dan. 8:24), desiring to kill the woman before she could bring forth the child that would destroy him (*see notes on Esth. 3:6-15*).

12:4 a third of the stars of heaven. Satan's original rebellion (cf. Is. 14:12ff.; Ezek. 28:11ff.) resulted in one-third of the angelic host joining his insurrection and becoming demons. **to devour her Child.** Unable to prevent the virgin birth of Christ, Satan tried to kill the child in a general massacre of male children commanded by Herod (Matt. 2:13-18; cf. Luke 4:28,29).

12:5 a male Child. Jesus Christ in His incarnation was of Jewish descent (Matt. 1:1; 2 Tim. 2:8). Despite Satan's efforts to destroy Israel and the messianic line, Jesus' birth took place as predicted by the prophets (cf. Is. 7:14; 9:6; Mic. 5:2). **rod of iron.** Describes Jesus' coronation as King over the nations of the world (cf. 11:15; 19:15; Ps. 2:6-9). **her Child was caught up to God.** Christ's ascension is in view (Acts 1:9; 2:33; Heb. 1:1-3; 12:2).

12:6 wilderness. God will protect Israel from Satan by hiding her in the wilderness, perhaps in the region of Moab, Ammon, and Edom, east of Palestine. Interestingly, those countries will be specifically spared from the Antichrist's attack against the Holy Land (cf. Dan. 11:41). **one thousand two hundred and sixty days.** At the midpoint of the Tribulation, the Antichrist breaks his covenant with Israel, puts a stop to temple worship, sets up the abomination of desolation (Dan. 9:27; Matt. 24:15), and devastates Jerusalem (11:2). At that time, many Jews flee for their lives (Matt. 24:16ff.). God will preserve them during the last 1,260 days (42 months; 3½ years) constituting the Great Tribulation. *See notes on 3:10; 6:1,9.*

12:7 war broke out in heaven. The tumultuous events on earth during the Tribulation find their counterpart in heaven. A state of war has existed since the fall of Satan (cf. v. 4; cf. Dan. 10:13; Jude 9). Something will intensify that warfare—possibly the raptured saints passing through the realm of the prince of the power of the air (cf. Eph. 2:2).

12:9 dragon was cast…to the earth. Satan and his demons were cast out of heaven at the time of their original rebellion, but still have access to it (cf. Job 1:6; 2:1). That access will then be denied, and they will be forever barred from heaven. **Devil and Satan.** Cf. 20:2. "Devil" comes from a Gr. verb meaning "to slander" or "to falsely accuse." He is a malignant liar (John 8:44; 1 John 3:8). His accusations against believers (v. 10) are unsuccessful because of Christ our Advocate (1 John 2:1). Satan, meaning "adversary," or "enemy," appears especially in Job and the gospels. **deceives the whole world.** As he has throughout human history, Satan will deceive people during the Tribulation (cf. 13:14; 20:3; John 8:44). After his temporary release from the bottomless pit at the end of the Millennium, he will briefly resume his deceitful ways (20:8,10).

12:10 accuser. *See note on v. 9.* Satan will no longer accuse believers before the throne of God because he will no longer have access to heaven.

12:11 blood of the Lamb. No accusation can stand against those whose sins have been forgiven because of Christ's sacrificial death (see Rom. 8:33-39).

12:12 he has a short time. Knowing that his time is limited, Satan will intensify his efforts against God and mankind, and specifically target Israel (v. 13,17).

woman who gave birth to the male *Child.*
14 [z]But the woman was given two wings of
a great eagle, [a]that she might fly [b]into the
wilderness to her place, where she is nourished [c]for a time and times and half a time,
from the presence of the serpent. 15 So the
serpent [d]spewed water out of his mouth
like a flood after the woman, that he might
cause her to be carried away by the flood.
16 But the earth helped the woman, and the
earth opened its mouth and swallowed up
the flood which the dragon had spewed out
of his mouth. 17 And the dragon was enraged with the woman, and he went to
make war with the rest of her offspring,
who keep the commandments of God and
have the testimony of Jesus [3]Christ.

The Beast from the Sea

13 Then [1]I stood on the sand of the sea.
And I saw [a]a beast rising up out of
the sea, [b]having [2]seven heads and ten
horns, and on his horns ten crowns, and on
his heads a [c]blasphemous name. 2 Now
the beast which I saw was like a leopard,
his feet were like *the feet of* a bear, and his
mouth like the mouth of a lion. The [d]drag-
on gave him his power, his throne, and
great authority. 3 And *I saw* one of his
heads [e]as if it had been mortally wounded,
and his deadly wound was healed. And
[f]all the world marveled and followed the
beast. 4 So they worshiped the dragon who
gave authority to the beast; and they worshiped the beast, saying, [g]"Who *is* like the
beast? Who is able to make war with him?"
5 And he was given [h]a mouth speaking
great things and blasphemies, and he was
given authority to [3]continue for [i]forty-two
months. 6 Then he opened his mouth in
blasphemy against God, to blaspheme His
name, [j]His tabernacle, and those who
dwell in heaven. 7 It was granted to him
[k]to make war with the saints and to over-

14 [z]Ex. 19:4; Deut. 32:11; Is. 40:31 [a]Rev. 12:6 [b]Rev. 17:3 [c]Dan. 7:25; 12:7
15 [d]Is. 59:19
17 [3]NU, M omit *Christ*

CHAPTER 13
1 [a]Dan. 7:2,7 [b]Rev. 12:3 [1]NU *he* [2]NU, M *ten horns and seven heads* [c]Dan. 7:8; 11:36; Rev. 17:3
2 [d]Rev. 12:3, 9; 13:4, 12
3 [e]Rev. 13:12, 14 [f]Rev. 17:8
4 [g]Ex. 15:11; Is. 46:5; Rev. 18:18
5 [h]Dan. 7:8, 11, 20, 25; 11:36; 2 Thess. 2:3 [i]Rev. 11:2 [3]M *make war*
6 [j][John 1:14; Col. 2:9]
7 [k]Dan. 7:21; Rev. 11:7

12:14 wings of a great eagle. Not actual birds' wings, but a graphic depiction of God's providential protection of Israel (cf. Ex. 19:4). Wings often speak of protection (cf. Deut. 32:9-12; Ps. 91:4; Is. 40:31). Eagles—probably vulture-like griffins—were the largest birds known in Palestine. **a time and times and half a time.** Three and one-half years; the second half of the Tribulation (cf. v. 6; 11:2,3; 13:5).

12:16 earth opened its mouth. A great army will come against Israel like a flood (v. 15; cf. Jer. 46:8; 47:2), only to be swallowed up, perhaps in conjunction with one of the numerous earthquakes that occur during that period (6:12; 8:5; 11:13,19; 16:18; Matt. 24:7).

12:17 rest of her offspring. Satan will turn his frustrated rage against every follower of the Lamb he can find—Jew or Gentile. **commandments of God...testimony of Jesus.** The revealed truth from God and Christ contained in Scripture. Obedience to God's Word always marks a genuine believer. Cf. John 8:32.

13:1 Then I stood. Most manuscripts read "He stood," referring again to the dragon, or Satan (cf. 12:9,17). He takes a position in the midst of the nations of his world, represented by the sand of the sea. **a beast.** Lit. "a monster" (cf. 11:7), which describes a vicious, killing animal. In this context, the term represents both a person (Antichrist) and his system (the world). The final satanic world empire will be inseparable from the demon-possessed man who leads it. For a discussion of Antichrist, *see notes on 2 Thess. 2:3-11.* He is also described in Dan. 7:8,21-26; 8:23-25; 9:24-27; 11:36-45. **rising up out of the sea.** The sea represents the abyss or pit, the haunt of demons (cf. 11:7; 17:8; 20:1; Luke 8:31). The picture is of Satan summoning a powerful demon from the abyss, who then activates and controls the beast (Antichrist) and his empire. **seven heads and ten horns.** This description is like that of Satan in 12:3. The heads may represent successive world empires—Egypt, Assyria, Babylon, Medo-Persia, Greece, Rome, and the final kingdom of Antichrist (*see notes on 17:9,10*). The final one is made up on all the kingdoms represented by the horns (*see notes for 17:12*). Ten is a number that symbolizes the totality of human military and political power assisting the beast (Antichrist) as he controls the world. Horns always represent power, as in the animal kingdom—both offensive power (attack) and defensive power (protection). Daniel shows that the human Antichrist will rise up from these 10 kings (Dan. 7:16-24). John picks up the numerical imagery of Dan. 2:41,42, which refers to the 10 toes on the statue's clay and iron feet. The apostle sees the beast as the final world government—the anti-Christ, anti-God coalition—headed by a revived Roman Empire, having the strengths of various world powers, yet mixed with weakness and ultimately crushed (cf. Dan. 2:32-45; 7:7,8,19-25; *see note on 12:3*). The crowns show the regal dominion of this confederate kingdom. **blasphemous name.** Throughout history, every time a monarch has identified himself as a god, he has blasphemed the true God. Each ruler who contributes to the beast's final coalition has an identity, wears a crown, exerts dominion and power, and therefore blasphemes God.

13:2 leopard. A metaphor for ancient Greece, alluding to the Greeks' swiftness and agility as their military moved forward in conquest, particularly under Alexander the Great (cf. Dan. 7:6). The leopard and subsequent animal symbols were all native wildlife in Palestine, familiar to John's readers. **bear.** A metaphor for the ancient Medo-Persian Empire, depicting that kingdom's ferocious strength, combined with its great stability (cf. Dan. 7:5). **lion.** A metaphor for the ancient Babylonian Empire, referring to the Babylonians' fierce, all-consuming power as they extended their domain (cf. Dan. 7:4). **The dragon gave him his power.** *See note on v. 1.* **dragon.** *See notes on v. 1; 12:9.*

13:3 his deadly wound was healed. This statement could refer to one of the kingdoms that was destroyed and revived (i.e., the Roman Empire). But more likely it refers to a fake death and resurrection enacted by the Antichrist, as part of his lying deception. Cf. vv. 12,14; 17:8,11; 2 Thess. 2:9. **world marveled.** People in the world will be astounded and fascinated when Antichrist appears to rise from the dead. His charisma, brilliance, and attractive but deluding powers will cause the world to follow him unquestioningly (v. 14; 2 Thess. 2:8-12).

13:5 was given. The sovereign God will establish the limits within which Antichrist will be allowed to speak and operate. God will allow him to utter his blasphemies, to bring the rage of Satan to its culmination on earth for 3½ years (v. 5; 11:2,3; 12:6,13,14). **forty-two months.** The final 3½ years—1,260 days—of the "time of Jacob's trouble" (Jer. 30:7) and Daniel's 70th week (Dan. 9:24-27), known as the Great Tribulation (*see notes on 11:2; 12:6*; cf. Dan. 7:25). This last half is launched by the abomination of desolations (*see note on Matt. 24:15*).

13:6 His name. This identifies God and summarizes all His attributes (cf. Ex. 3:13,14). **His tabernacle.** This is symbolic of heaven (cf. Heb. 9:23,24). **those who dwell in heaven.** The angels and glorified saints who are before the throne of God and serve Him day and night.

13:7 make war with the saints. The Antichrist will be allowed to massacre those who are God's children (cf. 6:9-11; 10:17; 11:7; 17:14; Dan. 7:23-25; 8:25; 9:27; 11:38; 12:10; Matt. 24:16-22). *See note on 17:6.*

come them. And [l]authority was given him
over every [4]tribe, tongue, and nation. 8 All
who dwell on the earth will worship him,
[m]whose names have not been written in
the Book of Life of the Lamb slain [n]from
the foundation of the world.
9 [o]If anyone has an ear, let him hear.
10 [p]He who leads into captivity shall go
into captivity; [q]he who kills with the
sword must be killed with the sword.
[r]Here is the [5]patience and the faith of the
saints.

The Beast from the Earth

11 Then I saw another beast [s]coming up
out of the earth, and he had two horns like
a lamb and spoke like a dragon. 12 And he
exercises all the authority of the first beast
in his presence, and causes the earth and
those who dwell in it to worship the first
beast, [t]whose deadly wound was healed.
13 [u]He performs great signs, [v]so that he
even makes fire come down from heaven
on the earth in the sight of men. 14 [w]And
he deceives [6]those who dwell on the earth
[x]by those signs which he was granted to
do in the sight of the beast, telling those
who dwell on the earth to make an image
to the beast who was wounded by the
sword [y]and lived. 15 He was granted
power to give breath to the image of the
beast, that the image of the beast should
both speak [z]and cause as many as would
not worship the image of the beast to be
killed. 16 He causes all, both small and
great, rich and poor, free and slave, [a]to receive a mark on their right hand or on
their foreheads, 17 and that no one may
buy or sell except one who has [7]the mark
or [b]the name of the beast, [c]or the number
of his name.
18 [d]Here is wisdom. Let him who has

7 [l]Rev. 11:18 [4]NU, M add *and people*
8 [m]Ex. 32:32; [Rev. 20:12-15] [n]Matt. 25:34; Rev. 17:8
9 [o]Rev. 2:7
10 [p]Is. 33:1; Jer. 15:2; 43:11 [q]Gen. 9:6; Matt. 26:52; Rev. 11:18 [r]Heb. 6:12; Rev. 14:12 [5]*perseverance*
11 [s]Rev. 11:7
12 [t]Rev. 13:3, 4
13 [u]Deut. 13:1; Matt. 24:24; 2 Thess. 2:9; Rev. 16:14 [v]1 Kin. 18:38; 2 Kin. 1:10; Luke 9:54; Rev. 11:5; 20:9
14 [w]Rev. 12:9 [x]2 Thess. 2:9 [y]2 Kin. 20:7 [6]M *my own people*
15 [z]Rev. 16:2
16 [a]Gal. 6:17; Rev. 7:3; 14:9; 20:4
17 [b]Rev. 14:9-11 [c]Rev. 15:2 [7]NU, M *the mark, the name*
18 [d]Rev. 17:9

13:8 Book of Life. *See note on 3:5.* **Lamb slain.** The Lord Jesus who died to purchase the salvation of those whom God had chosen was fulfilling an eternal plan. **from the foundation of the world.** According to God's eternal, electing purpose before creation, the death of Christ seals the redemption of the elect forever (cf. Acts 2:23; 4:27,28). Antichrist can never take away the salvation of the elect. The eternal registry of the elect will never be altered, nor will the saved in the Antichrist's day worship him.

13:9 Cf. 2:7,11 17,29; 3:6,13,22. This phrase omits "what the Spirit says to the churches" as in the 7 letters to the churches, perhaps because they have been raptured.

13:10 A call for believers to accept persecution from Antichrist with perseverance and endurance. God has chosen some believers to be imprisoned and executed which they must not resist (cf. Matt. 26:51-54; 2 Cor. 10:4), but accept with patience such suffering as God ordains for them (cf. 1 Pet. 2:19-24).

13:11 another beast. This is the final false prophet (called such in 16:13; 19:20; 20:10) who promotes Antichrist's power and convinces the world to worship him as God. This companion beast will be the chief, most persuasive proponent of satanic religion (cf. 16:13; 19:20; 20:10). Antichrist will be primarily a political and military leader, but the false prophet will be a religious leader. Politics and religion will unite in a worldwide religion of worshiping the Antichrist (see 17:1-9,15-17). **out of the earth.** Likely another reference to the abyss that lies below the earth. The false prophet will be sent forth and controlled by a powerful demon from below. The earth imagery, in contrast to that of the foreboding, mysterious sea in v. 1, may imply that the false prophet is subtler and more winsome than Antichrist. **two horns like a lamb.** This describes the relative weakness of the false prophet compared to Antichrist, who has 10 horns. A lamb has only two small bumps on its head, very inferior to the 10 horned beast. **like a lamb.** The lamb imagery may also imply that the false prophet will be also a false Christ masquerading as the true Lamb. Unlike Antichrist, the false prophet will come not as a killing, destroying animal, but as one who appears gentle and deceptively attractive. **spoke like a dragon.** The false prophet will be Satan's mouthpiece and thus his message will be like the dragon, Satan—the source of all false religion (cf. 2 Cor. 11:14).

13:12 exercises all the authority of the first beast. The false prophet exercises the same kind of satanic power as Antichrist because he is empowered by the same source. He, too, will have worldwide influence and reputation as a miracle worker and speaker. **causes...to worship.** "He causes" is used 8 times of him. He wields influence to establish a false world religion headed by Antichrist and to entice people to accept that system. **whose deadly wound was healed.** *See notes on v. 3; 17:8.* This likely refers to the carefully crafted deception of a false resurrection, a false murder to inspire allegiance for the world.

13:13 great signs. The same phrase is used of Jesus' miracles (John 2:11,23; 6:2), which indicates the false prophet performs signs that counterfeit Christ's. Satan, who has done supernatural works in the past (e.g., Ex. 7:11; 2 Tim. 3:8), must use his strategy of false miracles to convince the world that Antichrist is more powerful than God's true witnesses (chap. 11), including Jesus Christ. **fire come down from heaven.** The context indicates that the false prophet does counterfeit pyrotechnic signs continually to convince men of his power, and also in imitation of the two witnesses (11:5).

13:14 make an image. This refers to replication of Antichrist that is related to the throne he will erect during the abomination of desolation, halfway into the Tribulation period. This will happen in the Jerusalem temple when Antichrist abolishes the former false world religion and seeks to have people worship him alone as God (cf. Dan. 9:27; 11:31; 12:11; Matt. 24:15; 2 Thess. 2:4). The false prophet and Antichrist again will deceive the world with a clever imitation of Christ, who will later return and reign from the true throne in Jerusalem.

13:15 speak. The false prophet will give the image of Antichrist the appearance of life, and the image will seem to utter words—contrary to what is normally true of idols (cf. Ps. 135:15,16; Hab. 2:19). **cause...to be killed.** His gentleness is a lie, since he is a killer (7:9-17). Some Gentiles will be spared to populate the kingdom (Matt. 25:31-40) and Jews will be protected (12:17).

13:16 a mark. In the Roman Empire, this was a normal identifying symbol, or brand, that slaves and soldiers bore on their bodies. Some of the ancient mystical cults delighted in such tattoos, which identified members with a form of worship. Antichrist will have a similar requirement, one that will need to be visible on the hand or forehead.

13:17 buy or sell. Antichrist's mark will allow people to engage in daily commerce, including the purchase of food and other necessities. Without the identifying mark, individuals will be cut off from the necessities of life. **number of his name.** The beast (Antichrist) will have a name inherent in a numbering system. It is not clear from the text exactly what this name and number system will be or what its significance will be.

[e]understanding calculate [f]the number of
the beast, [g]for it is the number of a man:
His number *is* 666.

The Lamb and the 144,000

14 Then I looked, and behold, [1]a
[a]Lamb standing on Mount Zion,
and with Him [b]one hundred *and* forty-four
thousand, [2]having His Father's name
[c]written on their foreheads. **2** And I heard
a voice from heaven, [d]like the voice of
many waters, and like the voice of loud
thunder. And I heard the sound of [e]harp-
ists playing their harps. **3** They sang as it
were a new song before the throne, before
the four living creatures, and the elders;
and no one could learn that song [f]except
the hundred *and* forty-four thousand who
were redeemed from the earth. **4** These are
the ones who were not defiled with
women, [g]for they are virgins. These are the
ones [h]who follow the Lamb wherever He
goes. These [i]were [3]redeemed from *among*
men, [j]*being* firstfruits to God and to the
Lamb. **5** And [k]in their mouth was found no
[4]deceit, for [l]they are without fault [5]before
the throne of God.

The Proclamations of Three Angels

6 Then I saw another angel [m]flying in the
midst of heaven, [n]having the everlasting
gospel to preach to those who dwell on the
earth—[o]to every nation, tribe, tongue, and
people— **7** saying with a loud voice,
[p]"Fear God and give glory to Him, for the
hour of His judgment has come; [q]and worship Him who made heaven and earth, the
sea and springs of water."
8 And another angel followed, saying,
[r]"Babylon[6] is fallen, is fallen, that great city,
because [s]she has made all nations drink of
the wine of the wrath of her fornication."
9 Then a third angel followed them, saying with a loud voice, [t]"If anyone worships the beast and his image, and receives
his [u]mark on his forehead or on his hand,
10 he himself [v]shall also drink of the wine

18 [e][1 Cor. 2:14] [f]Rev. 15:2 [g]Rev. 21:17

CHAPTER 14

1 [a]Rev. 5:6 [b]Rev. 7:4; 14:3 [c]Ezek. 9:4; Rev. 7:3; 22:4 [1]NU, M *the* [2]NU, M add *His name and*
2 [d]Rev. 1:15; 19:6 [e]Rev. 5:8
3 [f]Rev. 5:9
4 [g][Matt. 19:12; 2 Cor. 11:2; Eph. 5:27] [h]Rev. 3:4; 7:17 [i]Rev. 5:9 [j]Heb. 12:23; James 1:18 [3]M adds *by Jesus*
5 [k]Ps. 32:2; Zeph. 3:13; Mal. 2:6; John 1:47; 1 Pet. 2:22 [l]Eph. 5:27 [4]NU, M *falsehood* [5]NU, M omit the rest of v. 5.
6 [m]Rev. 8:13 [n]Eph. 3:9 [o]Rev. 13:7
7 [p]Rev. 11:18 [q]Neh. 9:6
8 [r]Is. 21:9; Jer. 51:8; Rev. 18:2 [s]Jer. 51:7; Rev. 17:2

[6]NU *Babylon the great is fallen, is fallen, which has made;* M *Babylon the great is fallen. She has made* **9** [t]Rev. 13:14, 15; 14:11 [u]Rev. 13:16
10 [v]Ps. 75:8

13:18 His number *is* 666. This is the essential number of a man. The number 6 falls one short of God's perfect number, 7, and thus represents human imperfection. Antichrist, the most powerful human the world will ever know, will still be a man, i.e., a 6. The ultimate in human and demonic power is a 6, not perfect, as God is. The 3-fold repetition of the number is intended to reiterate and underscore man's identity. When Antichrist is finally revealed, there will be some way to identify him with this basic number of a man, or his name may have the numerical equivalent of 666. (In many languages, including Heb., Gr., and Lat., letters have numerical equivalents.) Because this text reveals very little about the meaning of 666, it is unwise to speculate beyond what is said.

14:1 a Lamb. *See note on 5:6.* **Mount Zion.** The city of Jerusalem, where Messiah will return and plant His feet (cf. Pss. 2; 48:1,2; Is. 24:23). **one hundred *and* forty-four thousand.** *See note on 7:4.* **name.** The counterpart to the mark of the beast. It is the stamp that will identify the 144,000 as belonging to God (*see note on 13:6*).

14:2 harps. *See note on 5:8.*

14:3 new song. The song of redemption, which is being sung by all the redeemed saints in one gigantic choir. They are rejoicing over the accomplishment of God's entire redemptive work before Christ's return (cf. Pss. 33:1-3; 40:3; 96:1; 144:9,10; 149; Luke 15:10; *see note on 5:9*). **the four living creatures, and the elders.** *See notes on 4:4,6.*

14:4 not defiled with women. An illustration of God's ability to keep believers remarkably pure in the midst of great difficulty. This phrase indicates that the 144,000 Jewish evangelists will have not only resisted the perverse system of Antichrist, but they will have also resisted all temptations to illicit sex. Cf. 2 Cor. 11:2. **follow the Lamb.** This indicates partisanship for Jesus Christ. The victorious 144,000 are unwaveringly loyal to Him, whatever the cost (cf. Matt. 16:24; Mark 10:21; Luke 9:23; John 10:27; 12:26; 14:15). **firstfruits.** Like the OT firstfruits offerings, these men will be set apart for special service to God (cf. Deut. 26:1-11). Some see firstfruits as the first large group of redeemed Israel (*see note on 11:13*), saved much earlier, and representative of more converts to follow (cf. Rom. 16:5; 1 Cor. 16:15), the first fruits of a redeemed Israel (Rom. 11:1-5,11-15,25-27).

14:5 no deceit. The 144,000 speak God's truth accurately and precisely, with no exaggeration or understatement (cf. Zeph. 3:13). **without fault.** Not sinless, but sanctified (see Eph. 1:4; 5:27; Col. 1:22).

14:6 midst of heaven. From a Gr. term ("mid-heaven") denoting the point in the noonday sky where the sun reaches its zenith. This is the highest and brightest point, where all can see and hear. **the everlasting gospel.** The angel is preaching the good news concerning everlasting life and entrance into the kingdom of God (cf. Matt. 24:14; 1 Cor. 15:1-10). He is urging the people of the world to change their allegiance from the beast to the Lamb. It is also called in the NT the gospel of God, the gospel of grace, the gospel of Christ, the gospel of peace, the glorious gospel, and the gospel of the kingdom. It is good news that God saves by the forgiveness of sin and opens His kingdom to all who will repent and believe. The whole world will hear this preaching by the angel as God graciously calls all to salvation.

14:7 Fear God. Not Satan, nor Antichrist. This is the theme of Scripture, calling people to give honor, glory, worship, and reverence to God (cf. Prov. 23:17; 1 Pet. 2:17). *See notes on Rom. 1:18-21.* **hour of His judgment has come.** The last moment arrives to repent and believe before God's wrath is poured out. This is the book's first use of the word judgment, a term that has the same meaning as wrath (see 6:17; 12:12). **Him who made heaven and earth.** Creation is the great proof of God, which preachers will appeal to as the ground for all people to believe in Him and worship Him (cf. 4:11; 10:6; John 1:9; Acts 14:15-17; 17:23-28).

14:8 Babylon is fallen. Lack of response to the first angel's message causes a second angel to pronounce this judgment. Babylon refers to the entire worldwide political, economic, and religious kingdom of Antichrist. (cf. 16:17-19 for details of this fall.) The original city of Babylon was the birthplace of idolatry where the residents built the Tower of Babel, a monument to rebelliousness and false religion. Such idolatry was subsequently spread when God confounded man's language and scattered them around the world (cf. Gen. 11:1-9). **wine of the wrath of her fornication.** This pictures Babylon causing the world to become intoxicated with her pleasures and enter an orgy of rebellion, hatred, and idolatry toward God. Fornication is spiritual prostitution to Antichrist's false system, which will fall for such iniquity.

14:9 worships the beast. *See notes on 13:14,15;* cf. 13:8.

of the wrath of God, which is [w]poured out
full strength into [x]the cup of His indignation. [y]He shall be tormented with [z]fire and
brimstone in the presence of the holy angels and in the presence of the Lamb.
11 And [a]the smoke of their torment ascends forever and ever; and they have no
rest day or night, who worship the beast
and his image, and whoever receives the
mark of his name."
12 [b]Here is the [7]patience of the saints;
[c]here[8] *are* those who keep the commandments of God and the faith of Jesus.
13 Then I heard a voice from heaven
saying [9]to me, "Write: [d]'Blessed *are* the
dead [e]who die in the Lord from now
on.' "
"Yes," says the Spirit, [f]"that they may
rest from their labors, and their works follow [g]them."

Reaping the Earth's Harvest

14 Then I looked, and behold, a white
cloud, and on the cloud sat *One* like the
Son of Man, having on His head a golden
crown, and in His hand a sharp sickle.
15 And another angel [h]came out of the
temple, crying with a loud voice to Him
who sat on the cloud, [i]"Thrust in Your
sickle and reap, for the time has come [1]for
You to reap, for the harvest [j]of the earth is
ripe." 16 So He who sat on the cloud thrust
in His sickle on the earth, and the earth
was reaped.

Reaping the Grapes of Wrath

17 Then another angel came out of the
temple which is in heaven, he also having
a sharp sickle.
18 And another angel came out from the
altar, [k]who had power over fire, and he
cried with a loud cry to him who had the
sharp sickle, saying, [l]"Thrust in your
sharp sickle and gather the clusters of the
vine of the earth, for her grapes are fully
ripe." 19 So the angel thrust his sickle into
the earth and gathered the vine of the
earth, and threw *it* into [m]the great winepress of the wrath of God. 20 And [n]the
winepress was trampled [o]outside the city,
and blood came out of the winepress, [p]up
to the horses' bridles, for one thousand six
hundred [2]furlongs.

10 [w]Rev. 18:6 [x]Rev. 16:19 [y]Rev. 20:10 [z]Gen. 19:24; Ezek. 38:22; 2 Thess. 1:7; Rev. 19:20
11 [a]Is. 34:8-10; Rev. 18:9, 18; 19:3
12 [b]Rev. 13:10 [c]Rev. 12:17 [7]*steadfastness, perseverance* [8]NU, M omit *here are those*
13 [d]Eccl. 4:1, 2 [e]1 Cor. 15:18; [1 Thess. 4:16] [f]2 Thess. 1:7; Heb. 4:9, 10; Rev. 6:11 [g][1 Cor. 3:11-15; 15:58] [9]NU, M omit *to me*
15 [h]Rev. 16:17 [i]Joel 3:13; Mark 4:29; Rev. 14:18 [j]Jer. 51:33; [Matt. 13:39-41] [1]NU, M omit *for You*
18 [k]Rev. 16:8 [l]Joel 3:13; Mark 4:29; Rev. 14:15
19 [m]Is. 63:2; Rev. 19:15
20 [n]Is. 63:3; Lam. 1:15; Rev. 19:15 [o]Heb. 13:12; Rev. 11:8 [p]Is. 34:3 [2]Lit. *stadia*, about 184 miles in all

14:10 cup of His indignation. Anyone loyal to the Antichrist and his kingdom will suffer the outpouring of God's collected wrath, done with the full force of His divine anger and unmitigated vengeance (cf. Ps. 75:8; Is. 51:17; Jer. 25:15,16). Divine wrath is not an impulsive outburst of anger aimed capriciously at people God does not like. It is the settled, steady, merciless, graceless, and compassionless response of a righteous God against sin. **fire and brimstone.** These are two elements that are often associated in Scripture with the torment of divine punishment (Gen. 19:24,25; Is. 34:8-10). Here the reference is to hell, the lake of fire (cf. 19:20; 20:10; 21:8). Brimstone is a fiery sulfur (*see note on 9:17*).

14:11 torment ascends forever and ever. A reference to the eternality of hell (cf. Matt. 3:12; 13:41,42; 25:41; Mark 9:48). Torment is the ceaseless infliction of unbearable pain (cf. Luke 16:23,24), here prescribed for all who are loyal to Satan's leader.

14:12 This is excellent scriptural support for the doctrine of perseverance, which assures all true believers in Christ that they will never lose their faith. The regenerate will continually endure, right to the end, in obedience to the truth, no matter what may come against them (*see notes on Rom. 8:31-39; Phil. 1:6*; cf. Jer. 32:40; Matt. 24:13; John 6:35-40; 10:27-30; 1 John 5:4,11-13,20).

14:13 Blessed. *See note on 1:3.*

14:14 Son of Man. *See note on 1:13.* The imagery of the Lord on a cloud is from Dan. 7:13,14 and emphasizes magnificent majesty (cf. 1:7; Matt. 24:30; 26:64; Acts 1:9-11). **golden crown.** The victor's crown, a laurel wreath, worn by those who celebrated victory in war or athletic competition. Christ now wears this particular crown, in this case made of gold, as a triumphant conqueror coming out of heaven to prevail over His enemies. **sickle.** A harvesting tool with a razor-sharp, curved steel or iron blade and a wooden handle, commonly used by ancient farmers to cut grain. It represents swift and devastating judgment.

14:15 harvest of the earth. The grain—in this case the ungodly people of the world—is ready to be gathered up and judged.

14:17 temple. *See note on 11:19.* This refers to the heavenly dwelling place of God, not the Tribulation temple in Jerusalem (cf. 11:1).

14:18 another angel...who had power over fire. This angel is associated with fire on the altar, which represents the prayers of the saints (6:9-11; 8:3-5). Fire refers to the constantly burning fire on the brass altar of the Jerusalem temple. Twice daily the priest would burn incense with that fire and offer the burning incense in the Holy Place as a symbol of the people's prayers (*see notes on 5:8; 6:9; 8:3*). This angel is coming from the heavenly altar to ensure that all the prayers of all the saints for judgment and the coming of the kingdom are answered. He calls for judgment to start. **sickle.** *See note on v. 14.*

14:19 winepress. This vivid imagery signifies a horrendous slaughter or bloodbath (cf. Is. 63:2,3; Lam. 1:15; Joel 3:13). Here it refers to the slaughter of all the enemies of God who are still alive, facing the destruction at Armageddon, the final battle against God's enemies, staged on the Plain of Esdraelon. The bloody imagery comes from the fresh juice of stomped grapes splattering and running down a trough from the upper vat to the lower vat of a stone winepress.

14:20 outside the city. God will determine that this bloodbath will occur outside Jerusalem, as if God wants to protect the city from the carnage all around. Zechariah 14:1-5 makes clear that Jerusalem will be attacked, but will not be destroyed in the end, but spared for the glory of the kingdom, and the believing remnant will be saved as the Lord defends them and the city against the nations. They will escape through a newly created valley as the Lord finishes judgment and sets up His kingdom. **up to the horses' bridles.** The severity of the slaughter is indicated in the imagery of the blood of those killed in the Battle of Armageddon splattering as high (about 4 ft.) as the bridles of the horses involved. Equally likely, if the battle occurs near the central valley of Israel, the tremendous volume and flow of blood could easily form troughs 4 ft. deep in some places. This event clearly is described in 19:11-21. Ezekiel 39:8-16 may be describing the clean up. **one thousand six hundred furlongs.** See marginal note. The approximate distance from Armageddon in the N of Palestine to Edom in the S. The great battle will rage across that entire area and even slightly beyond.

Prelude to the Bowl Judgments

15 Then [a]I saw another sign in heaven,
great and marvelous: [b]seven angels
having the seven last plagues, [c]for in them
the wrath of God is complete.
2 And I saw *something* like [d]a sea of glass
[e]mingled with fire, and those who have the
victory over the beast, [f]over his image and
[1]over his mark *and* over the [g]number of his
name, standing on the sea of glass, [h]having
harps of God. 3 They sing [i]the song of Moses, the servant of God, and the song of the
[j]Lamb, saying:

[k]"Great and marvelous *are* Your
works,
Lord God Almighty!
[l]Just and true *are* Your ways,
O King of the [2]saints!
4 [m]Who shall not fear You, O Lord,
and glorify Your name?
For *You* alone *are* [n]holy.
For [o]all nations shall come and
worship before You,
For Your judgments have been
manifested."

5 After these things I looked, and [3]be-
hold, [p]the [4]temple of the tabernacle of the
testimony in heaven was opened. 6 And
out of the [5]temple came the seven angels
having the seven plagues, [q]clothed in pure
bright linen, and having their chests girded with golden bands. 7 [r]Then one of the
four living creatures gave to the seven angels seven golden bowls full of the wrath
of God [s]who lives forever and ever. 8 [t]The
temple was filled with smoke [u]from the
glory of God and from His power, and no
one was able to enter the temple till the
seven plagues of the seven angels were
completed.

16 Then I heard a loud voice from the
temple saying [a]to the seven angels,
"Go and pour out the [1]bowls [b]of the wrath
of God on the earth."

First Bowl: Loathsome Sores

2 So the first went and poured out his
bowl [c]upon the earth, and a [2]foul and
[d]loathsome sore came upon the men [e]who
had the mark of the beast and those [f]who
worshiped his image.

Second Bowl: The Sea Turns to Blood

3 Then the second angel poured out his
bowl [g]on the sea, and [h]it became blood as
of a dead *man;* [i]and every living creature in
the sea died.

CHAPTER 15

1 [a]Rev. 12:1, 3 [b]Rev. 21:9 [c]Rev. 14:10
2 [d]Rev. 4:6 [e][Matt. 3:11] [f]Rev. 13:14, 15 [g]Rev. 13:17 [h]Rev. 5:8 [1]NU, M omit *over his mark*
3 [i]Ex. 15:1-21 [j]Rev. 15:3 [k]Deut. 32:3, 4; Ps. 92:5; Rom. 11:33 [l]Ps. 145:17; Rev. 16:7 [2]NU, M *nations*
4 [m]Ex. 15:14 [n]Lev. 11:44; 1 Pet. 1:16; Rev. 4:8 [o]Ps. 86:9; Is. 66:23
5 [p]Ex. 38:21; Num. 1:50; Heb. 8:5; Rev. 13:6 [3]NU, M omit *behold* [4]*sanctuary,* the inner shrine
6 [q]Ex. 28:6 [5]*sanctuary,* the inner shrine
7 [r]Rev. 4:6 [s]1 Thess. 1:9
8 [t]Ex. 19:18; 40:34; Lev. 16:2; 1 Kin. 8:10; 2 Chr. 5:13; Is. 6:4 [u]2 Thess. 1:9

CHAPTER 16

1 [a]Rev. 15:1 [b]Rev. 14:10 [1]NU, M *seven bowls*
2 [c]Rev. 8:7 [d]Ex. 9:9-11; Deut. 28:35; Rev. 16:11 [e]Rev. 13:15-17; 14:9 [f]Rev. 13:14 [2]*severe and malignant,* lit. *bad and evil*
3 [g]Rev. 8:8; 11:6 [h]Ex. 7:17-21 [i]Rev. 8:9

15:1-8 Chapter 15 introduces the 7 bowls of wrath, God's final judgments at the end of the 7 year Tribulation period. The bowl judgments come in a rapid-fire, staccato fashion, each one stronger in fury and intensity. The bowls are the last plagues that issue from the blast of the seventh trumpet, and will conclude the seventh seal (*see note on 6:1*).

15:1 wrath of God. *See notes on 11:18; 14:10; 16:19; 19:15*; cf. Rom. 1:18-21.

15:2 sea of glass. God's heavenly throne sits on a transparent crystal platform or pavement (*see note on 4:6*). **victory over the beast.** All the saints from every nation, including Israel, ultimately triumph over Satan's Antichrist and his system because of their faith in Jesus Christ. **number of his name.** *See note on 13:17.* **harps.** *See note on 5:8.*

15:3 song of Moses. Sung by the people of Israel immediately after their passage through the Red Sea and their deliverance from the Egyptian armies (Ex. 15:1-21; cf. Deut. 32:1-43), this was a song of victory and deliverance that the redeemed who overcome Antichrist and his system will readily identify with. **song of the Lamb.** See 5:8-14. These two songs celebrate two great redemptive events: 1) deliverance of Israel by God from Egypt through Moses; and 2) deliverance of sinners by God from sin through Christ. **Great and marvelous *are* Your works.** This statement from the song of the Lamb extols God's powerful works in creation as He providentially upholds the universe (cf. Ps. 139:14). **Almighty.** God is omnipotent (cf. Amos 4:13). **King of the saints.** God is sovereign over the redeemed of every nation (cf. Jer. 10:7).

15:4 God's holy and perfect character inevitably demands that He judge (cf. Ps. 19:9; Nah. 1:3,6). After God's righteous judgment is complete, He will set up Christ's millennial kingdom on earth and the elect from every nation will come and worship Him (cf. Ps. 66:4; Is. 66:23; Phil. 2:9-11).

15:5 the temple of the tabernacle of the testimony. This refers to the ark of the covenant in the Holy of Holies (temple) where God dwells (*see note on 11:19*; cf. Num. 10:11).

15:6 seven plagues. The final, most severe judgments from God, described in chap. 16 (*see note on v. 1*). **linen...golden bands.** The fabric represents holiness and purity (19:14). These are belts or girdles, running from the shoulder to the waist, that each of the 7 angels wear over his garments. The bands demonstrate riches, royalty, and untarnished glory.

15:7 four living creatures. *See notes on 4:6-9.* **seven golden bowls.** These are shallow saucers, familiar items often associated with various functions of the temple worship (1 Kin. 7:50; 2 Kin. 12:13; 25:15), such as wine (Amos 6:6) and blood sacrifice (Ex. 27:3). Their flat shallowness pictures how the divine judgments will be emptied instantly rather than slowly poured, drowning those who refused to drink the cup of salvation. **wrath of God.** *See notes on 11:18; 14:10.*

15:8 filled with smoke. Cf. Ex. 19:16-18; 40:34-35; 1 Kin. 8:10,11; Is. 6:4.

16:2 first...bowl...a foul and loathsome sore. The Septuagint (LXX) uses the same Gr. word to describe the boils that plagued the Egyptians (Ex. 9:9-11) and afflicted Job (Job 2:7). In the NT, it describes the open sores that covered the beggar Lazarus (Luke 16:21). All over the world, people will be afflicted with incurable, open, oozing sores. **mark of the beast.** Only the worshipers of Antichrist will be afflicted (*see note on 13:16*; cf. 14:9-11).

16:3 second...bowl...every living creature in the sea died. This is reminiscent of the second trumpet (8:8,9), and of the first plague against Egypt (Ex. 7:20-25). This plague, however, will be far more widespread. The water in the world's oceans will become thick, dark, and coagulated, like the blood of a corpse. The death and decay of billions of sea creatures will only add to the misery of this judgment.

Third Bowl: The Waters Turn to Blood

4 Then the third angel poured out his
bowl [j]on the rivers and springs of water,
[k]and they became blood. 5 And I heard the
angel of the waters saying:

> [l]"You are righteous, [3]O Lord,
> The One [m]who is and who [4]was
> and who is to be,
> Because You have judged these
> things.
> 6 For [n]they have shed the blood [o]of
> saints and prophets,
> [p]And You have given them blood to
> drink.
> [5]For it is their just due."

7 And I heard [6]another from the altar
saying, "Even so, [q]Lord God Almighty,
[r]true and righteous *are* Your judgments."

Fourth Bowl: Men Are Scorched

8 Then the fourth angel poured out his
bowl [s]on the sun, [t]and power was given to
him to scorch men with fire. 9 And men
were scorched with great heat, and they
[u]blasphemed the name of God who has
power over these plagues; [v]and they did
not repent [w]and give Him glory.

Fifth Bowl: Darkness and Pain

10 Then the fifth angel poured out his
bowl [x]on the throne of the beast, [y]and his
kingdom became full of darkness; [z]and
they gnawed their tongues because of the
pain. 11 They blasphemed the God of heav-
en because of their pains and their sores,
and did not repent of their deeds.

Sixth Bowl: Euphrates Dried Up

12 Then the sixth angel poured out his
bowl [a]on the great river Euphrates, [b]and
its water was dried up, [c]so that the way of
the kings from the east might be prepared.
13 And I saw three unclean [d]spirits like
frogs *coming* out of the mouth of [e]the dragon, out of the mouth of the beast, and out
of the mouth of [f]the false prophet. 14 For

4 [j] Rev. 8:10 [k] Ex. 7:17-20; Ps. 78:44; Rev. 11:6
5 [l] Rev. 15:3,4 [m] Rev. 1:4,8 [3] NU, M omit *O Lord* [4] NU, M *was, the Holy One*
6 [n] Matt. 23:34 [o] Rev. 11:18 [p] Is. 49:26; Luke 11:49-51 [5] NU, M omit *For*
7 [q] Rev. 15:3 [r] Rev. 13:10; 19:2 [6] NU, M omit *another from*
8 [s] Rev. 8:12 [t] Rev. 9:17, 18
9 [u] Rev. 16:11 [v] Dan. 5:22 [w] Rev. 11:13
10 [x] Rev. 13:2 [y] Ex. 10:21; Is. 8:22; Rev. 8:12; 9:2 [z] Rev. 11:10
12 [a] Rev. 9:14 [b] Jer. 50:38 [c] Is. 41:2, 25; 46:11
13 [d] 1 John 4:1 [e] Rev. 12:3, 9 [f] Rev. 13:11, 14; 19:20; 20:10

16:4 third...bowl...rivers and springs of water. Fresh water, already in short supply because of the prolonged drought (11:6), will now suffer the fate of the oceans (cf. Ex. 7:19ff.). In addition to suffering from thirst, the worshipers of Antichrist will have no clean water with which to wash their sores.

16:5 who is and who was and who is to be. This phrase expresses God's eternality (cf. 1:4,8; 4:8; 11:17). Verse 6 says that the eternal God will judge justly because they have killed the believers and preachers of the gospel (6:9-11; 7:9-17; 11:18; 17:6; 18:20). This slaughter will have no parallel in history (Matt. 24:21) and neither will the vengeance of God (cf. Rom. 12:19-21).

16:6 given them blood to drink. The thick, blood-like substance which the fresh waters have become is all that is available to drink (cf. v. 4). **For it is their just due.** The angel exonerates God from any charge that His judgments are too harsh. The unspeakably wicked generation then alive will shed more blood than any before it, including that of saints (6:9; 17:6) and prophets (11:7-10). God's judgment is fair and proper (cf. Ex. 21:25-27; Lev. 24:19,20; Heb. 10:26-31).

16:7 altar. The personified altar echoes the words of the angel, reinforcing the truth that God is just in all judgment (19:1,2; cf. Gen. 18:25; Ps. 51:4; Rom. 3:4).

16:8 fourth...bowl...scorch...with fire. The sun that normally provides light, warmth, and energy will become a deadly killer. With no fresh water to drink, earth's inhabitants will face extreme heat. The scorching heat will melt the polar ice caps, which some estimate would raise the level of the world's oceans by 200 ft., inundating many of the world's major cities and producing further catastrophic loss of life (cf. Amos 9:5,6). The resulting disruption of ocean transportation will make it difficult to distribute the dwindling resources of food and water.

16:9 they did not repent. Incredibly, sinners will still refuse to repent (cf. vv. 11,21), and instead blaspheme God—the One they know has caused their afflictions.

16:10 throne of the beast. This refers to either Antichrist's actual throne, or his capital city, but extends to all his dominion. Regardless of where the darkness begins, it eventually covers Antichrist's entire kingdom. **full of darkness.** Worldwide darkness is elsewhere associated with the judgment of God (cf. Is. 60:2; Joel 2:2; Mark 13:24,25). **gnawed their tongues.** A futile attempt to alleviate the pain from their sores, the drought, and the fierce heat.

16:11 blasphemed the God of heaven. A sign of their continued loyalty to Antichrist and their anger at God for the cumulative miseries brought about by the first 5 bowls. "God of heaven," a frequent OT title for God, appears in the NT only here and in 11:13. **their sores.** The lingering effects of the first bowl are the chief cause of their blasphemy.

16:12 Euphrates. Called "the great river" 5 times in Scripture (cf. 9:14; Gen. 15:18; Deut. 1:7; Josh. 1:4), it flows some 1,800 mi. from its source on the slopes of Mt. Ararat to the Persian Gulf (*see note on 9:14*). It forms the eastern boundary of the land God promised to Israel (Gen. 15:18; Deut. 1:7; 11:24; Josh. 1:4). With its flow already reduced by the prolonged drought and intensified heat, God supernaturally will dry it up to make way for the eastern confederacy to reach Palestine (Is. 11:15). **the kings from the east.** God providentially draws these kings and their armies in order to destroy them in the battle of Armageddon (v. 14). Their reason for coming may be to rebel against Antichrist, whose failure to alleviate the world's suffering will no doubt erode his popularity. Or, this may be a final act of rabid anti-Semitism intent on destroying Israel, perhaps in retaliation for the plagues sent by her God. Since the sun may have melted the ice caps on Ararat, flooding the valley of the Euphrates as the river overflows its banks and bridges, the land will be swamped. God will have to dry it up miraculously for the eastern army to get to Armageddon.

16:13 three unclean spirits. A common NT designation for demons (cf. Matt. 12:43; Mark 1:23; Luke 8:29). These are especially vile, powerful, and deceitful (v. 14). **like frogs.** This figure further emphasizes their vileness (cf. Lev. 10:11,41). Frogs were unclean animals according to OT dietary laws (Lev. 11:10,11,41). Persian mythology viewed them as plague-inducing creatures. The demons are thus described as slimy, cold-blooded, loathsome beings. **the dragon...the beast...the false prophet.** The "unholy trinity," composed of Satan (the dragon; *see note on 12:3*), the Antichrist (the beast; *see note on 11:7*), and Antichrist's associate (the false prophet; *see note on 13:11*), spew out this plague.

they are spirits of demons, [g]performing
signs, *which* go out to the kings [7]of the
earth and of [h]the whole world, to gather
them to [i]the battle of that great day of God
Almighty.
15 [j]"Behold, I am coming as a thief.
Blessed *is* he who watches, and keeps his
garments, [k]lest he walk naked and they see
his shame."
16 [l]And they gathered them together to
the place called in Hebrew, [8]Arma-
geddon.

Seventh Bowl: The Earth Utterly Shaken

17 Then the seventh angel poured out his
bowl into the air, and a loud voice came
out of the temple of heaven, from the
throne, saying, [m]"It is done!" 18 And
[n]there were noises and thunderings and
lightnings; [o]and there was a great earthquake, such a mighty and great earthquake [p]as had not occurred since men
were on the earth. 19 Now [q]the great city
was divided into three parts, and the cities
of the nations fell. And [r]great Babylon
[s]was remembered before God, [t]to give her
the cup of the wine of the fierceness of His
wrath. 20 Then [u]every island fled away,
and the mountains were not found. 21 And
great hail from heaven fell upon men, *each
hailstone* about the weight of a talent. Men
blasphemed God because of the plague of
the hail, since that plague was exceedingly
great.

The Scarlet Woman and the Scarlet Beast

17 Then [a]one of the seven angels who
had the seven bowls came and
talked with me, saying [1]to me, "Come, [b]I
will show you the judgment of [c]the great
harlot [d]who sits on many waters, 2 [e]with
whom the kings of the earth committed
fornication, and [f]the inhabitants of the
earth were made drunk with the wine of
her fornication."
3 So he carried me away in the Spirit
[g]into the wilderness. And I saw a woman
sitting [h]on a scarlet beast *which was* full of
[i]names of blasphemy, having seven heads
and ten horns. 4 The woman [j]was arrayed

14 [g] 2 Thess. 2:9 [h] Luke 2:1 [i] 1 Kin. 22:21-23; Rev. 17:14; 19:19; 20:8 [7] NU, M omit *of the earth and*
15 [j] Matt. 24:43; Luke 12:39; Rev. 3:3, 11 [k] 2 Cor. 5:3
16 [l] Rev. 19:19 [8] Lit. *Mount Megiddo;* M *Megiddo*
17 [m] Rev. 10:6; 21:6
18 [n] Rev. 4:5 [o] Rev. 11:13 [p] Dan. 12:1; Matt. 24:21
19 [q] Rev. 14:8 [r] Rev. 17:5, 18 [s] Rev. 14:8; 18:5 [t] Is. 51:17; Rev. 14:10
20 [u] Rev. 6:14; 20:11

CHAPTER 17

1 [a] Rev. 1:1; 21:9 [b] Rev. 16:19 [c] Is. 1:21; Jer. 2:20; Nah. 3:4; Rev. 17:5, 15; 19:2 [d] Jer. 51:13; Rev. 17:15 [1] NU, M omit *to me*
2 [e] Rev. 2:22; 18:3, 9 [f] Jer. 51:7; Rev. 14:8
3 [g] Rev. 12:6, 14; 21:10 [h] Rev. 12:3 [i] Rev. 13:1
4 [j] Ezek. 28:13; Rev. 18:12, 16

16:14 signs. These are supernatural wonders (cf. 13:12-15) designed to deceive (cf. 19:20; 1 Kin. 22:20-23; Mark 13:22) the kings into invading Palestine. Their impact will be so great that the unclean spirits are able to induce the kings to make the journey to Palestine in spite of their sores, the intense heat, drought, and darkness. **kings of the earth.** No longer just the eastern confederacy, but now all the world begins to gather in Palestine for the final, climactic battle (Ps. 2:2,3; Joel 3:2-4; Zech. 14:1-3). **the battle of that great day of God Almighty.** The Battle of Armageddon (v. 16). It is the great war with God and Christ (*see notes on 2 Thess. 1:7-10*; cf. Joel 2:11; 3:2,4). The war will end when Christ arrives (19:17-20).

16:15 Blessed. *See note on 1:3.* **watches, and keeps his garments.** Our Lord stresses the need for constant readiness for His return (cf. 1 John 2:28). The imagery pictures a soldier ready for battle, or a homeowner watchful for the arrival of a thief (see also 3:3; 1 Thess. 5:2,4; 2 Pet. 3:10).

16:16 Armageddon. The Heb. name for Mt. Megiddo, 60 mi. N of Jerusalem. The battle will rage on the nearby plains, site of Barak's victory over the Canaanites (Judg. 4), and Gideon's victory over the Midianites (Judg. 7). Napoleon called this valley the greatest battlefield he had ever seen. But the Battle of Armageddon will not be limited to the Megiddo plains—it will encompass the length of Palestine (*see note on 14:20*).

16:17 seventh...bowl..."It is done!" This bowl will complete God's wrath (except for final judgment on the rebellion at the end of the Millennium; 20:7-10) and immediately precedes the second coming of Christ. It will usher in the worst calamity in the history of the world. The voice from the temple in heaven is undoubtedly that of God Himself. "It is done!" is best translated, "It has been and will remain done" (cf. John 19:30). God will punctuate the completion of His wrath with a devastating earthquake—the most powerful in earth's history (cf. vv. 19-21).

16:19 the great city. Cf. 11:13; 21:10; *see notes on Zech 14:1-8*. Jerusalem will be split into 3 parts (Zech. 14:4), not as a judgment (cf. 11:13), but as an improvement. The additional water supply (Zech. 14:8) and topographical changes (Zech. 14:4,5) will prepare the city for its central place in the millennial kingdom. Jerusalem is the only city to be spared the judgment (cf. 1 Chr. 23:25; Ps. 125:1,2; Mic. 4:7) and will be made more beautiful (Ps. 48:2), because of her repentance (see 11:13). **cities of the nations.** God's purpose is very different for the rest of the world's cities—they are to be destroyed. **Babylon.** The capital of the Antichrist's empire will receive a special outpouring of God's wrath as prophesied in Is. 13:6-13. Chapters 17,18 give details of its destruction.

16:20 every island fled...mountains...not found. This powerful earthquake will radically alter all the earth's topography, preparing it for the coming millennial kingdom. Cf. 6:12-14; Is. 40:4,5; Jer. 4:23-27.

16:21 a talent. The heaviest weight a normal man could carry (about 75 lbs.). The huge size of the hailstones indicates unparalleled atmospheric convulsions. Such massive chunks of ice will cause unimaginable devastation and death.

17:1 seven angels. The reference to these angels links chaps. 17,18 with the bowl judgments (chap. 16), which extend to the second coming of Christ (*see note on 16:17*). Chapters 17,18 focus on one aspect of those bowl judgments, the judgment of Babylon. The judgments already described are identified as targeting the final world system. **great harlot.** *See note on 14:8.* Prostitution frequently symbolizes idolatry or religious apostasy (cf. Jer. 3:6-9; Ezek. 16:30ff.; 20:30; Hos. 4:15; 5:3; 6:10; 9:1). Nineveh (Nah. 3:1,4), Tyre (Is. 23:17), and even Jerusalem (Is. 1:21) are also depicted as harlot cities. **sits on many waters.** This picture emphasizes the sovereign power of the harlot. The picture is of a ruler seated on a throne, ruling the waters, which symbolize the nations of the world (see v. 15).

17:2 kings...committed fornication. The harlot will ally herself with the world's political leaders. Fornication here does not refer to sexual sin, but to idolatry (*see note on 14:8*). All the world rulers will be absorbed into the empire of Satan's false christ. **wine of her fornication.** The harlot's influence will extend beyond the world's rulers to the rest of mankind (cf. v. 15; 13:8,14). The imagery does not describe actual wine and sexual sin, but pictures the world's people being swept up into the intoxication and sin of a false system of religion.

17:3 in the Spirit. Cf. 1:10; 4:2; 21:10. The Holy Spirit transports John into the wilderness (a deserted, lonely, desolate wasteland), perhaps to give him a better understanding of the vision. **a woman.** The harlot of v. 1, Babylon. **scarlet beast.** The Antichrist (cf. 13:1,4;

in purple and scarlet, [k]and adorned with
gold and precious stones and pearls, [l]hav-
ing in her hand a golden cup [m]full of
abominations and the filthiness of [2]her fornication. **5** And on her forehead a name
was written:

[n]MYSTERY,
BABYLON THE GREAT,
THE MOTHER OF HARLOTS
AND OF THE ABOMINATIONS
OF THE EARTH.

6 I saw [o]the woman, drunk [p]with the blood
of the saints and with the blood of [q]the
martyrs of Jesus. And when I saw her, I
marveled with great amazement.

The Meaning of the Woman and the Beast

7 But the angel said to me, "Why did you
marvel? I will tell you the [3]mystery of the
woman and of the beast that carries her,
which has the seven heads and the ten
horns. **8** The beast that you saw was, and is
not, and [r]will ascend out of the bottomless
pit and [s]go to [4]perdition. And those who
[t]dwell on the earth [u]will marvel, [v]whose
names are not written in the Book of Life
from the foundation of the world, when
they see the beast that was, and is not, and
[5]yet is.

9 [w]"Here *is* the mind which has wisdom:
[x]The seven heads are seven mountains on
which the woman sits. **10** There are also
seven kings. Five have fallen, one is, *and*
the other has not yet come. And when he
comes, he must [y]continue a short time.
11 The [z]beast that was, and is not, is himself also the eighth, and is of the seven, and
is going to [6]perdition.

12 [a]"The ten horns which you saw are ten
kings who have received no kingdom as
yet, but they receive authority for one hour
as kings with the beast. **13** These are of one
mind, and they will give their power and
authority to the beast. **14** [b]These will make

4 [k]Dan. 11:38 [l]Jer. 51:7; Rev. 18:6 [m]Rev. 14:8 [2]M *the fornication of the earth*
5 [n]2 Thess. 2:7; Rev. 1:20; 17:7
6 [o]Rev. 18:24 [p]Rev. 13:15 [q]Rev. 6:9, 10
7 [3]*hidden truth*
8 [r]Rev. 11:7 [s]Rev. 13:10; 17:11 [t]Rev. 3:10 [u]Rev. 13:3 [v]Matt. 25:34; Rev. 13:8 [4]*destruction* [5]NU, M *shall be present*
9 [w]Rev. 13:18 [x]Rev. 13:1
10 [y]Rev. 13:5
11 [z]Rev. 13:3, 12, 14; 17:8 [6]*destruction*
12 [a]Dan. 7:20
14 [b]Rev. 16:14; 19:19

14:9; 16:10), who for a time will support and use the false religious system to affect world unity. Then he will assume political control (cf. v. 16). Scarlet is the color of luxury, splendor, and royalty. **full of names of blasphemy.** Because of his self-deification (cf. 13:1; Dan. 7:25; 11:36; 2 Thess. 2:4). **having seven heads and ten horns.** This pictures the extent of Antichrist's political alliances (*see notes on vv. 9-12; 13:1*).

17:4 purple and scarlet. The colors of royalty, nobility, and wealth. The woman is portrayed as a prostitute who has plied her trade successfully and become extremely wealthy. **adorned.** Prostitutes often dress in fine clothes and precious jewels to allure their victims (cf. Prov. 7:10). The religious harlot Babylon is no different, adorning herself to lure the nations into her grasp. **a golden cup.** Still another evidence of the harlot's great wealth (cf. Jer. 51:7); but the pure gold is defiled by the filthiness of her immorality. Just as a prostitute might first get her victim drunk, so the harlot system deceives the nations into committing spiritual fornication with her.

17:5 forehead. It was customary for Roman prostitutes to wear a headband with their name on it (cf. Jer. 3:3) parading their wretchedness for all to see. The harlot's forehead is emblazoned with a 3-fold title descriptive of the world's final false religious system. **MYSTERY.** A NT mystery is truth once hidden, but in the NT revealed. *See notes on Matt. 13:11; Eph. 3:4,5.* Spiritual Babylon's true identity is yet to be revealed. Thus, the precise details of how it will be manifested in the world are not yet known. **BABYLON THE GREAT.** This Babylon is distinct from the historical, geographical city of Babylon (which still existed in John's day). The details of John's vision cannot be applied to any historical city (*see note on 14:8*). **MOTHER OF HARLOTS.** All false religion stems ultimately from Babel, or Babylon (cf. Gen. 11; *see note on 14:8*).

17:6 the blood of the saints...martyrs of Jesus. Some see the first group as OT saints, and the second as NT saints—an unimportant distinction since this pictures the martyrs of the Tribulation. John's point is that the harlot is a murderer. False religion has killed millions of believers over the centuries, and the final false system will be far more deadly than any that preceded it.

17:7 mystery. Not that Babylon is a false system of religion, because that is already known, but that the beast will fully support the harlot and together exert vast influence over the whole earth.

17:8 The beast. Both a king and kingdom are referred to in this term. **was, and is not, and will ascend.** A reference to the Antichrist's false resurrection (13:3,4,12-14; *see note on 13:3*). **out of the bottomless pit.** After his "resurrection," the Antichrist will become possessed by a great demon from the abyss (*see notes on 13:1,3*). **perdition.** Eternal destruction (cf. v. 11; Matt. 7:13; John 17:12; Phil. 1:28; 3:19; 2 Thess. 2:3; Heb. 10:39; 2 Pet. 2:3; 3:7,16). This is the lake of fire, the place of Antichrist's destruction (19:20). **Book of Life.** The roll of the elect, written in eternity past by God (*see note on 3:5*). Only the elect will escape the Antichrist's deception (Matt. 24:24). **from the foundation of the world.** *See note on 13:8*; cf. 1 Tim. 1:9; Titus 1:2 ("before time began"). A frequent phrase (Matt. 13:35; 25:34; Luke 11:50; John 17:24; Eph. 1:4; Heb. 4:3; 9:26; 1 Pet. 1:20) referring to God's pre-creation plan.

17:9 seven mountains. The Gr. word is often used of hills (Matt. 5:1; 15:29; John 6:15; 8:1). Many commentators interpret this expression to mean Rome, which sits on 7 hills. It is true that the final worldwide system of false religion includes, but is not necessarily limited to, Rome; but specifically, the 7 mountains in context likely symbolize the 7 kingdoms and their kings of v. 10.

17:10 seven kings. Representatives of the 7 great world empires (Egypt, Assyria, Babylon, Medo-Persia, Greece, Rome, and that of the Antichrist). Cf. Daniel's image in Dan. 2:37-45. **Five have fallen, one is, *and* the other.** When John wrote, the Egyptian, Assyrian, Babylonian, Medo-Persian and Greek empires had gone out of existence; Rome still existed; and the Antichrist's empire had not yet come. When it does, it will be brief (12:12; 13:5) and he will end in perdition (v. 11; *see note on v. 8*).

17:11 and is not...the eighth. The Antichrist's kingdom is said to be both the seventh and eighth kingdoms because of his supposed demise and resurrection. He is the seventh king before and the eighth king after his "resurrection" when he destroys the harlot's religious empire and demands exclusive worship of himself (v. 16).

17:12 ten kings. *See notes on 12:3; 13:1* (cf. Dan. 2:41,42). These kings are sub-rulers under the Antichrist, whose empire will apparently be divided into 10 administrative districts. **no kingdom as yet.** Thus, the kings cannot be identified with any historical figures. **one hour.** Symbolic of the brief 3½ year period of time (cf. 11:2,3; 12:6,12,14; 13:5; 18:10,17,19).

war with the Lamb, and the Lamb will
[c]overcome them, [d]for He is Lord of lords
and King of kings; [e]and those *who are* with
Him *are* called, chosen, and faithful."
15 Then he said to me, [f]"The waters
which you saw, where the harlot sits, [g]are
peoples, multitudes, nations, and tongues.
16 And the ten horns which you [7]saw on
the beast, [h]these will hate the harlot, make
her [i]desolate [j]and naked, eat her flesh and
[k]burn her with fire. **17** [l]For God has put it
into their hearts to fulfill His purpose, to be
of one mind, and to give their kingdom to
the beast, [m]until the words of God are fulfilled. **18** And the woman whom you saw
[n]is that great city [o]which reigns over the
kings of the earth."

The Fall of Babylon the Great

18 After[a] these things I saw another
angel coming down from heaven,
having great authority, [b]and the earth was
illuminated with his glory. **2** And he cried
[1]mightily with a loud voice, saying, [c]"Babylon the great is fallen, is fallen, and [d]has
become a dwelling place of demons, a
prison for every foul spirit, and [e]a cage for
every unclean and hated bird! **3** For all the
nations [f]have drunk of the wine of the
wrath of her fornication, the kings of the
earth have committed fornication with her,
[g]and the merchants of the earth have become rich through the [2]abundance of her
luxury."
4 And I heard another voice from heav-
en saying, [h]"Come out of her, my people,
lest you share in her sins, and lest you receive of her plagues. **5** [i]For her sins [3]have
reached to heaven, and [j]God has remembered her iniquities. **6** [k]Render to her just
as she rendered [4]to you, and repay her
double according to her works; [l]in the cup
which she has mixed, [m]mix double for her.
7 [n]In the measure that she glorified herself
and lived [5]luxuriously, in the same measure give her torment and sorrow; for she
says in her heart, 'I sit *as* [o]queen, and am
no widow, and will not see sorrow.'
8 Therefore her plagues will come [p]in one
day—death and mourning and famine.
And [q]she will be utterly burned with fire,
[r]for strong *is* the Lord God who [6]judges
her.

The World Mourns Babylon's Fall

9 [s]"The kings of the earth who committed fornication and lived luxuriously with
her [t]will weep and lament for her, [u]when

14 [c]Rev. 19:20 [d]Deut. 10:17; 1 Tim. 6:15; Rev. 19:16 [e]Jer. 50:44
15 [f]Is. 8:7; Jer. 47:2; Rev. 17:1 [g]Rev. 13:7
16 [h]Jer. 50:41 [i]Rev. 18:17, 19 [j]Ezek. 16:37, 39 [k]Rev. 18:8 [7]NU, M *saw, and the beast*
17 [l]2 Thess. 2:11 [m]Rev. 10:7
18 [n]Rev. 11:8; 16:19 [o]Rev. 12:4

CHAPTER 18

1 [a]Rev. 17:1, 7 [b]Ezek. 43:2
2 [c]Is. 13:19; 21:9; Jer. 51:8; Rev. 14:8 [d]Is. 13:21; 34:11, 13-15; Jer. 50:39; 51:37; Zeph. 2:14 [e]Is. 14:23 [1]NU, M omit *mightily*
3 [f]Jer. 51:7; Rev. 14:8 [g]Is. 47:15 [2]Lit. *strengths*
4 [h]Is. 48:20
5 [i]Gen. 18:20 [j]Rev. 16:19 [3]NU, M *have been heaped up*
6 [k]Ps. 137:8; Jer. 50:15, 29 [l]Rev. 14:10 [m]Rev. 16:19 [4]NU, M omit *to you*
7 [n]Ezek. 28:2-8 [o]Is. 47:7, 8; Zeph. 2:15 [5]*sensually*
8 [p]Is. 47:9; Jer. 50:31; Rev. 18:10 [q]Rev. 17:16 [r]Jer. 50:34; Heb. 10:31; Rev. 11:17 [6]NU, M *has judged*
9 [s]Ezek. 26:16; 27:35 [t]Jer. 50:46; Rev. 17:2; 18:3 [u]Rev. 19:3

17:14 make war. A reference to the battle of Armageddon (16:14-16), where the Lamb will utterly destroy the kings (19:17-21). **Lord of lords and King of kings.** A title for God (19:16; 1 Tim. 6:15; cf. Deut. 10:17; Ps. 136:3) that emphasizes His sovereignty over all other rulers to whom He has delegated authority.

17:15 *See note on v. 1.*

17:16 these will hate the harlot. After using the false religious system to unify the world kingdoms and gain control of all, the Antichrist—with the help of his 10 sub-rulers—will turn against the system, plunder and destroy it, and seize all power and worship for himself. They will be carrying out God's will (v. 17). Cf. Gen. 50:20.

17:18 great city. Here is another identification of the capital city of Babylon, centerpiece of Antichrist's empire. Cf. 18:10,18,21.

18:1 earth was illuminated with his glory. The fifth bowl (16:10) will have plunged the world into darkness. Against that backdrop, the sudden, blazing appearance of another angel (not the same as in 17:1,7,15) will certainly rivet the world's attention on him and his message of judgment on Babylon (cf. 14:8).

18:2 Babylon the great is fallen. Cf. 14:8; *see note on Is. 21:9,* the verse from which these words come. The Gr. text views the results of this as if it had already taken place (*see note on 14:8*). But the seventh bowl is being referred to here and it is yet to come at this point (16:17-21). When it comes, devastation and annihilation will take place, leaving the place to demons and scavenger birds.

18:3 wine...of her fornication. Religious Babylon (chap. 17) lures the nations into spiritual drunkenness and fornication with false gods (17:2,4); commercial Babylon (chap. 18) seduces the unbelieving world into a materialistic stupor, so that the people of the world will become drunk with passion because of their relationship with Babylon. **kings...merchants.** Political rulers and corporate leaders alike are swept up in this worldwide system of commerce (14:8; 17:2).

18:4 Come out of her, my people. God will call His own to disentangle themselves from this evil system. This may also be God's calling the elect to abandon the world system and come to faith in the Savior. In either case, the message is to abandon the system before it is destroyed (cf. 2 Cor. 6:17; 1 John 2:15). The judgment of God on that society living in sinful, arrogant self-indulgence can be avoided. Cf. Isaiah's and Jeremiah's message to their people to leave Babylon (Is. 48:20; Jer. 50:8; 51:6-9,45).

18:5 remembered. See 16:19. God does not remember the iniquities of His people (Jer. 31:34), but does remember to protect them (Mal. 3:16–4:2). For unrepentant Babylon, there will be no such forgiveness, only judgment.

18:6,7a repay. The angel calls for God to recompense wrath to Babylon in her own cup to repay her according to her deeds (*see note on 17:4*). This is an echo of the OT law of retaliation (Ex. 21:24) which will be implemented by God (Rom 12:17-21).

18:6 double. Has the sense of "full," or "overflowing." The punishment will fit the crime (cf. Jer. 16:18). **cup.** The cup of wickedness from which so many have drunk (14:8; 17:2,4,6) will call for the cup of wrath (14:10; 16:19).

18:7b am no widow. A proud, but empty, boast of self-sufficiency, also made by historical Babylon (Is. 47:8). Cf. 1 Cor. 10:12.

18:8 her plagues. These could include those of 16:1ff., but must be the special destruction of the city as well, described as "death, mourning and famine." **in one day.** See vv. 10,16,17. The special judgments on Babylon take place in a brief period of time. Daniel 5:30 records that Babylon of old fell in one day.

18:9-20 This section records the lament over Babylon's destruction, not her sin, by those who were part of her system.

18:9 kings. The political leaders of the world will weep because the loss of his capital city will signal the doom of Antichrist's empire, and with it, the source of their power. Cf. v. 3; 17:2. **weep and lament for her.** "Weep" means "to sob openly." "Lament" translates the same

they see the smoke of her burning,
10 standing at a distance for fear of her torment, saying, [v]'Alas, alas, that great city
Babylon, that mighty city! [w]For in one
hour your judgment has come.'
11 "And [x]the merchants of the earth will
weep and mourn over her, for no one buys
their merchandise anymore: 12 [y]merchan-
dise of gold and silver, precious stones and
pearls, fine linen and purple, silk and scarlet, every kind of citron wood, every kind
of object of ivory, every kind of object of
most precious wood, bronze, iron, and
marble; 13 and cinnamon and incense, fragrant oil and frankincense, wine and oil,
fine flour and wheat, cattle and sheep,
horses and chariots, and bodies and [z]souls
of men. 14 The fruit that your soul longed
for has gone from you, and all the things
which are rich and splendid have [7]gone
from you, and you shall find them no more
at all. 15 The merchants of these things,
who became rich by her, will stand at a distance for fear of her torment, weeping and
wailing, 16 and saying, 'Alas, alas, [a]that
great city [b]that was clothed in fine linen,
purple, and scarlet, and adorned with gold
and precious stones and pearls! 17 [c]For in
one hour such great riches [8]came to nothing.' [d]Every shipmaster, all who travel by
ship, sailors, and as many as trade on the
sea, stood at a distance 18 [e]and cried out
when they saw the smoke of her burning,
saying, [f]'What *is* like this great city?'
19 [g]"They threw dust on their heads and
cried out, weeping and wailing, and saying, 'Alas, alas, that great city, in which all
who had ships on the sea became rich by
her wealth! [h]For in one hour she [9]is made
desolate.'
20 [i]"Rejoice over her, O heaven, and *you*
[1]holy apostles and prophets, for [j]God has
avenged you on her!"

Finality of Babylon's Fall

21 Then a mighty angel took up a stone
like a great millstone and threw *it* into the
sea, saying, [k]"Thus with violence the great
city Babylon shall be thrown down, and
[l]shall not be found anymore. 22 [m]The sound
of harpists, musicians, flutists, and trumpeters shall not be heard in you anymore.
No craftsman of any craft shall be found in
you anymore, and the sound of a millstone
shall not be heard in you anymore. 23 [n]The
light of a lamp shall not shine in you anymore, [o]and the voice of bridegroom and
bride shall not be heard in you anymore.
For [p]your merchants were the great men of
the earth, [q]for by your sorcery all the nations were deceived. 24 And [r]in her was
found the blood of prophets and saints, and
of all who [s]were slain on the earth."

Heaven Exults over Babylon

19 After these things [a]I [1]heard a loud
voice of a great multitude in heaven,
saying, "Alleluia! [b]Salvation and glory and
honor and power *belong* to [2]the Lord our

10 [v]Is. 21:9 [w]Rev. 18:17, 19
11 [x]Ezek. 27:27-34
12 [y]Ezek. 27:12-22; Rev. 17:4
13 [z]1 Chr. 5:21; Ezek. 27:13
14 [7]NU, M *been lost to you*
16 [a]Rev. 17:18 [b]Rev. 17:4
17 [c]Rev. 18:10 [d]Is. 23:14 [8]*have been laid waste*
18 [e]Ezek. 27:30 [f]Rev. 13:4
19 [g]Josh. 7:6; Job 2:12; Lam. 2:10; Ezek. 27:30

[h]Rev. 18:8 [9]*have been laid waste*
20 [i]Is. 44:23; 49:13; Jer. 51:48; Rev. 12:12 [j]Luke 11:49; Rev. 19:2 [1]NU, M *saints and apostles*
21 [k]Jer. 51:63, 64 [l]Rev. 12:8; 16:20
22 [m]Eccl. 12:4; Jer. 7:34; 16:9; 25:10; Rev. 14:1-3
23 [n]Jer. 25:10 [o]Jer. 7:34; 16:9 [p]Is. 23:8; Rev. 6:15; 18:3 [q]2 Kin. 9:22
24 [r]Rev. 16:6; 17:6 [s]Jer. 51:49

CHAPTER 19

1 [a]Jer. 51:48; Rev. 11:15; 19:6 [b]Rev. 4:11 [1]NU, M add *something like* [2]NU, M omit *the Lord*

Gr. word used to express the despair of the unbelieving world at the return of Christ (1:7).

18:10 one hour. Cf. vv. 8,16,17.

18:12,13 Over half of their commodities appear in the list of Ezek. 27:12-22.

18:12 purple. This refers to garments laboriously dyed with purple dye extracted from shellfish. Lydia (Acts 16:14) was a seller of such expensive garments. A distinctive mark of the Caesars was their purple robes. **citron wood.** Wood from North African citrus trees, highly valued because of its color, which was used to make extremely expensive pieces of furniture. **marble.** Marble, imported from Africa, Egypt, and Greece, was widely used in Roman buildings.

18:13 fragrant oil. A very costly perfume (cf. Matt. 26:7,12; John 12:3). **frankincense.** A fragrant gum or resin imported from Arabia and used in incense and perfume (Song 3:6; Matt. 2:11). **bodies and souls of men.** The slave trade, long banned by the civilized nations of the world, will reappear in Antichrist's debauched commercial system.

18:17 shipmaster. Ship captains will mourn the loss of Babylon and the lucrative transport business that went with it.

18:19 threw dust on their heads. An ancient expression of grief (cf. Josh. 7:6; 1 Sam. 4:12; 2 Sam. 1:2; 15:32; Job 2:12; Lam. 2:10; Ezek. 27:30). **in one hour.** Not just 60 minutes, but one brief period of swift judgment (*see note on v. 8*).

18:20 God has avenged you on her. The angel will exhort the tribulation martyrs (6:9-11) to rejoice, not over the deaths of those doomed to eternal hell, but, because God's righteousness and justice will have prevailed.

18:21 great millstone. Millstones were large, heavy stones used to grind grain. This metaphor portrays the violence of Babylon's overthrow. Cf. Jer. 51:61-64; *see note on Matt. 18:6*.

18:22,23 The fall of Babylon ends whatever semblance of normalcy will still exist in the world after all the seals, trumpets, and bowls. Life will be totally disrupted and the end near. No more music, no industry, no preparing of food ("millstone"), no more power for light, and no more weddings because God will destroy the deceivers and deceived.

18:24 blood of prophets and saints. The religious and commercial/political systems embodied in Babylon will commit unspeakable atrocities against God's people (cf. 6:10; 11:7; 13:7,15; 17:6; 19:2). God will avenge that slaughter of His people (19:2).

19:1-6 Alleluia. The transliteration of this Heb. word appears 4 times in the NT, all in this chapter (vv. 1,3,4,6). This exclamation, meaning "Praise the Lord," occurs frequently in the OT (cf. Pss. 104:35; 105:45; 106:1; 111:1; 112:1; 113:1; 117:1; 135:1; 146:1). Five reasons for their praise emerge: 1) God's deliverance of His people from their enemies (v. 1); 2) God's meting out of justice (v. 2); 3) God's permanent crushing of man's rebellion (v. 3); 4) God's sovereignty (v. 6); and 5) God's communion with His people (v. 7).

19:1 After these things. This is a time key. After the destruction of Babylon at the end of the Great Tribulation, just before the kingdom is established (chap. 20). This section bridges the Tribulation and the millennial kingdom. **great multitude.** Probably angels, since the saints join in later (vv. 5ff.; cf. 5:11,12; 7:11,12). The imminent return of the Lord Jesus Christ prompts this outburst of praise.

God! 2 For [c]true and righteous *are* His judgments, because He has judged the great harlot who corrupted the earth with her fornication; and He [d]has avenged on her the
blood of His servants *shed* by her." 3 Again
they said, "Alleluia! [e]Her smoke rises up
forever and ever!" 4 And [f]the twenty-four
elders and the four living creatures fell
down and worshiped God who sat on the
throne, saying, [g]"Amen! Alleluia!" 5 Then a
voice came from the throne, saying, [h]"Praise
our God, all you His servants and those who
fear Him, [i]both[3] small and great!"
6 [j]And I heard, as it were, the voice of a
great multitude, as the sound of many waters and as the sound of mighty thunderings, saying, "Alleluia! For [k]the[4] Lord God
Omnipotent reigns! 7 Let us be glad and rejoice and give Him glory, for [l]the marriage
of the Lamb has come, and His wife has
made herself ready." 8 And [m]to her it was
granted to be arrayed in fine linen, clean
and bright, [n]for the fine linen is the righteous acts of the saints.
9 Then he said to me, "Write: [o]'Blessed
are those who are called to the marriage
supper of the Lamb!' " And he said to me,
[p]"These are the true sayings of God."
10 And [q]I fell at his feet to worship him.
But he said to me, [r]"See *that you do* not *do
that!* I am your [s]fellow servant, and of your
brethren [t]who have the testimony of Jesus.
Worship God! For the [u]testimony of Jesus
is the spirit of prophecy."

Christ on a White Horse

11 [v]Now I saw heaven opened, and behold, [w]a white horse. And He who sat on
him *was* called [x]Faithful and True, and [y]in
righteousness He judges and makes war.
12 [z]His eyes *were* like a flame of fire, and on
His head *were* many crowns. [a]He [5]had a
name written that no one knew except

2 [c]Rev. 15:3; 16:7 [d]Deut. 32:43; 2 Kin. 9:7; Luke 18:7, 8; Rev. 6:10
3 [e]Is. 34:10; Rev. 14:11
4 [f]Rev. 4:4, 6, 10 [g]1 Chr. 16:36
5 [h]Ps. 134:1 [i]Rev. 11:18 [3]NU, M omit *both*
6 [j]Ezek. 1:24; Rev. 1:15; 14:2 [k]Rev. 11:15 [4]NU, M *our*
7 [l][Matt. 22:2; 25:10]; Luke 12:36; John 3:29; [2 Cor. 11:2]; Eph. 5:23, 32; Rev. 19:9
8 [m]Ps. 45:13; Ezek. 16:10 [n]Ps. 132:9
9 [o]Matt. 22:2; Luke 14:15 [p]Rev. 22:6
10 [q]Rev. 22:8 [r]Acts 10:26; Rev. 22:9 [s][Heb. 1:14] [t]1 John 5:10 [u]Luke 24:27; John 5:39
11 [v]Rev. 15:5 [w]Ps. 45:3, 4; Rev. 6:2; 19:19, 21 [x]Rev. 3:7, 14 [y]Ps. 96:13; Is. 11:4

12 [z]Dan. 10:6; Rev. 1:14 [a]Rev. 2:17; 19:16 [5]M adds *names written, and*

19:2 judgments. Saints long for the day of judgment (cf. 6:10; 16:7; Is. 9:7; Jer. 23:5). Godly people love righteousness and hate sin, for righteousness honors God and sin mocks Him. Believers long for a world of justice and it will come (v. 15; 2:27; 12:5).

19:3 smoke rises. This is because of the fire (cf. 17:16,18; 18:8,9,18; 14:8-11).

19:4 twenty-four elders. Best understood as representatives of the church (*see note on 4:4*). **four living creatures.** A special order of angelic beings (*see note on 4:6*). These compose the same group as in 7:11 and are associated with worship frequently (4:8,11; 5:9-12,14; 11:16-18).

19:5 small and great. All distinctions and ranks are to be transcended.

19:6 Omnipotent. Or "Almighty." Used 9 times in Revelation as a title for God (cf. v. 15; 1:8; 4:8; 11:17; 15:3; 16:7,14; 21:22). The great praise of the multitude sounds like a massive crashing of waves.

19:7 marriage of the Lamb. Hebrew weddings consisted of 3 phases: 1) betrothal (often when the couple were children); 2) presentation (the festivities, often lasting several days, that preceded the ceremony); and 3) the ceremony (the exchanging of vows). The church was betrothed to Christ by His sovereign choice in eternity past (Eph. 1:4; Heb. 13:20) and will be presented to Him at the Rapture (John 14:1-3; 1 Thess. 4:13-18). The final supper will signify the end of the ceremony. This symbolic meal will take place at the establishment of the millennial kingdom and last throughout that 1,000 year period (cf. 21:2). While the term "bride" often refers to the church, and does so here (2 Cor. 11:2; Eph. 5:22-24), it ultimately expands to include all the redeemed of all ages, which becomes clear in the remainder of the book.

19:8 righteous acts of the saints. Not Christ's imputed righteousness granted to believers at salvation, but the practical results of that righteousness in believers' lives, i.e., the outward manifestation of inward virtue.

19:9 Blessed. *See note on 1:3.* **those who are called.** This is not the bride (the church) but the guests. The bride doesn't get invited, she invites. These are those saved before Pentecost, all the faithful believers saved by grace through faith up to the birth of the church (Acts 2:1ff.). Though they are not the bride, they still are glorified and reign with Christ in the millennial kingdom. It is really differing imagery rather than differing reality. The guests also will include tribulation saints and believers alive in earthly bodies in the kingdom. The church is the bride, pure and faithful—never a harlot, like Israel was (see Hos. 2). So the church is the bride during the presentation feast in heaven, then comes to earth for the celebration of the final meal (the Millennium). After that event, the new order comes and the marriage is consummated (*see notes on 21:1,2*). **true sayings of God.** This refers to everything since 17:1. It is all true—the marriage will take place after judgment.

19:10 fell at his feet. Overwhelmed by the grandeur of the vision, John collapsed in worship before the angel (cf. 1:17; 22:8). ***do not do that.*** Cf. 22:8,9. The Bible forbids the worship of angels (Col. 2:18,19). **the testimony of Jesus is the spirit of prophecy.** The central theme of both OT prophecy and NT preaching is the gospel of the Lord Jesus Christ.

19:11 heaven opened. The One who ascended to heaven (Acts 1:9-11) and had been seated at the Father's right hand (Heb. 8:1; 10:12; 1 Pet. 3:22) will return to take back the earth from the usurper and establish His kingdom (5:1-10). The nature of this event shows how it differs from the Rapture. At the Rapture, Christ meets His own in the air—in this event He comes with them to earth. At the Rapture, there is no judgment, in this event it is all judgment. This event is preceded by blackness—the darkened sun, moon gone out, stars fallen, smoke—then lightning and blinding glory as Jesus comes. Such details are not included in Rapture passages (John 14:1-3; 1 Thess. 4:13-18). **white horse.** In the Roman triumphal processions, the victorious general rode his white war horse up the Via Sacra to the temple of Jupiter on the Capitoline Hill. Jesus' first coming was in humiliation on a colt (Zech. 9:9). John's vision portrays Him as the conqueror on His war horse, coming to destroy the wicked, to overthrow the Antichrist, to defeat Satan, and to take control of the earth (cf. 2 Cor. 2:14). **Faithful and True.** True to His word, Jesus will return to earth (Matt. 24:27-31; *see note on 3:14*). **in righteousness He judges.** See 20:11-15; cf. Matt. 25:31ff.; John 5:25-30; Acts 17:31. **makes war.** This startling statement, appearing only here and 2:16, vividly portrays the holy wrath of God against sinners (cf. Ps. 7:11). God's patience will be exhausted with sinful, rebellious mankind.

19:12 His eyes *were* like a flame of fire. Nothing escapes His penetrating vision, so His judgments are always just and accurate (*see notes on 1:14; 2:18*). **a name...no one knew.** John could see the name, but was unable to comprehend it (cf. 2 Cor. 12:4). There are unfathomable mysteries in the Godhead that even glorified saints will be unable to grasp.

Himself. 13 [b]He *was* clothed with a robe
dipped in blood, and His name is called
[c]The Word of God. 14 [d]And the armies in
heaven, [e]clothed in [6]fine linen, white and
clean, followed Him on white horses.
15 Now [f]out of His mouth goes a [7]sharp
sword, that with it He should strike the nations. And [g]He Himself will rule them
with a rod of iron. [h]He Himself treads the
winepress of the fierceness and wrath of
Almighty God. 16 And [i]He has on *His* robe
and on His thigh a name written:

[j]KING OF KINGS
AND LORD OF LORDS.

The Beast and His Armies Defeated

17 Then I saw an angel standing in the
sun; and he cried with a loud voice, saying
to all the birds that fly in the midst of heav-
en, [k]"Come and gather together for the
[8]supper of the great God, 18 [l]that you may
eat the flesh of kings, the flesh of captains,
the flesh of mighty men, the flesh of horses and of those who sit on them, and the
flesh of all *people,* [9]free and slave, both
small and great."
19 [m]And I saw the beast, the kings of the
earth, and their armies, gathered together
to make war against Him who sat on the
horse and against His army. 20 [n]Then the
beast was captured, and with him the false
prophet who worked signs in his presence, by which he deceived those who received the mark of the beast and [o]those
who worshiped his image. [p]These two
were cast alive into the lake of fire [q]burn-
ing with brimstone. 21 And the rest [r]were
killed with the sword which proceeded
from the mouth of Him who sat on the
horse. [s]And all the birds [t]were filled with
their flesh.

Satan Bound 1000 Years

20 Then I saw an angel coming down
from heaven, [a]having the key to the
bottomless pit and a great chain in his
hand. 2 He laid hold of [b]the dragon, that

13 [b] Is. 63:2, 3 [c] [John 1:1, 14]
14 [d] Rev. 14:20 [e] Matt. 28:3 [6] NU, M *pure white linen*
15 [f] Is. 11:4; 2 Thess. 2:8; Rev. 1:16 [g] Ps. 2:8, 9 [h] Is. 63:3-6; Rev. 14:20 [7] M *sharp two-edged*
16 [i] Rev. 2:17; 19:12 [j] Dan. 2:47
17 [k] 1 Sam. 17:44; Jer. 12:9; Ezek. 39:17 [8] NU, M *great supper of God*
18 [l] Ezek. 39:18-20
[9] NU, M *both free*
19 [m] Rev. 16:13-16
20 [n] Rev. 16:13 [o] Rev. 13:8, 12, 13 [p] Is. 30:33; Dan. 7:11 [q] Rev. 14:10
21 [r] Rev. 19:15 [s] Rev. 19:17, 18 [t] Rev. 17:16

CHAPTER 20

1 [a] Rev. 1:18; 9:1
2 [b] Is. 24:22; 2 Pet. 2:4; Jude 6

19:13 a robe dipped in blood. This is not from the battle of Armageddon, which will not have begun until v. 15. Christ's blood-spattered garments symbolize the great battles He has already fought against sin, Satan, and death and been stained with the blood of His enemies. **The Word.** Only John uses this title for the Lord (see Introduction: Author and Date). As the Word of God, Jesus is the image of the invisible God (Col. 1:15); the express image of His person (Heb. 1:3); and the final, full revelation from God (Heb. 1:1,2).

19:14 armies in heaven. Composed of the church (v. 8), tribulation saints (7:13), OT believers (Jude 14; cf. Dan. 12:1,2), and even angels (Matt. 25:31). They return not to help Jesus in the battle (they are unarmed), but to reign with Him after He defeats His enemies (20:4; 1 Cor. 6:2; 2 Tim. 2:12). Cf. Ps. 149:5-9.

19:15 sharp sword. This symbolizes Christ's power to kill His enemies (1:16; cf. Is. 11:4; Heb. 4:12,13). That the sword comes out of His mouth indicates that He wins the battle with the power of His word. Though the saints return with Christ to reign and rule, they are not the executioners. That is His task, and that of His angels (Matt. 13:37-50). **rod of iron.** Swift, righteous judgment will mark Christ's rule in the kingdom. Believers will share His authority (2:26; 1 Cor. 6:2; *see notes on 2:27; 12:5; Ps. 2:8,9*). **winepress.** A vivid symbol of judgment (*see note on 14:19*). Cf. Is. 63:3; Joel 3:13.

19:16 on His thigh. Jesus will wear a banner across His robe and down His thigh with a title emblazoned on it that emphasizes His absolute sovereignty over all human rulers (*see note on 17:14*).

19:17-21 These verses depict the frightening holocaust unparalleled in human history—the Battle of Armageddon, the pinnacle of the Day of the Lord (*see note on 1 Thess. 5:2*). It is not so much a battle as an execution, as the remaining rebels are killed by the Lord Jesus (v. 21; *see notes on 14:19,20*; cf. Ps. 2:1-9; Is. 66:15,16; Ezek. 39:1ff.; Joel 3:12ff.; Matt. 24,25; 2 Thess. 1:7-9). This Day of the Lord was seen by Isaiah (66:15,16), Joel (3:12-21), Ezekiel (39:1-4,17-20), Paul (2 Thess. 1:6ff.; 2:8) and our Lord (Matt. 25:31-46).

19:17,18 supper of the great God. Cf. Ezek. 39:17. Also called "the battle of that great day of God Almighty" (16:14), it will begin with an angel summoning birds to feed on the corpses of those who will be slain (cf. Matt. 24:27,28). God will declare His victory before the battle even begins. The OT frequently pictures the indignity of carrion birds feasting on human dead (Deut. 28:26; Ps. 79:2; Is. 18:6; Jer. 7:33; 16:4; 19:7; 34:20; Ezek. 29:5).

19:19 kings of the earth. See 17:12-17. **their armies.** See 16:13,14. **His army.** Zechariah describes this army of the Lord as "all the saints" (14:5).

19:20 beast was captured, and...the false prophet. In an instant, the world's armies are without their leaders. The beast is Antichrist (*see note on 13:1-4*); the false prophet is his religious cohort (*see notes on 13:11-17*). **cast alive.** The bodies of the beast and the false prophet will be transformed, and they will be banished directly to the lake of fire (Dan. 7:11)—the first of countless millions of unregenerate men (20:15) and fallen angels (cf. Matt. 25:41) to arrive in that dreadful place. That these two still appear there 1,000 years later (20:10) refutes the false doctrine of annihilationism (cf. 14:11; Is. 66:24; Matt. 25:41; Mark 9:48; Luke 3:17; 2 Thess. 1:9). **lake of fire.** The final hell, the place of eternal punishment for all unrepentant rebels, angelic or human (cf. 20:10,15). The NT says much of eternal punishment (cf. 14:10,11; Matt. 13:40-42; 25:41; Mark 9:43-48; Luke 3:17; 12:47,48). **fire...brimstone.** *See note on 9:17.* These two are frequently associated with divine judgment (14:10; 20:10; 21:8; Gen. 19:24; Ps. 11:6; Is. 30:33; Ezek. 38:22; Luke 17:29).

19:21 sword. See v. 15; cf. Zech. 14:1-13. **birds were filled with their flesh.** All remaining sinners in the world will have been executed, and the birds will gorge themselves on their corpses.

20:1–22:21 Chapter 19 ends with the Battle of Armageddon and Christ's second coming—events that mark the close of the Tribulation. The events of chap. 20—the binding of Satan, Christ's 1,000 year earthly kingdom, Satan's final rebellion, and the Great White Throne Judgment—fit chronologically between the close of the Tribulation and the creation of the new heaven and the new earth described in chaps. 21,22.

20:1 bottomless pit. The place where demons are incarcerated pending their final sentencing to the lake of fire (*see notes on 9:1; 2 Pet. 2:4*).

20:2 laid hold. This includes not only Satan, but the demons as well. Their imprisonment will dramatically alter the world during the kingdom, since their destructive influence in all areas of human thought and life will be removed. **dragon.** Likening Satan to a dragon

serpent of old, who is *the* Devil and Satan,
and bound him for a thousand years; **3** and
he cast him into the bottomless pit, and
shut him up, and [c]set a seal on him, [d]so
that he should deceive the nations no more
till the thousand years were finished. But
after these things he must be released for a
little while.

The Saints Reign with Christ 1000 Years

4 And I saw [e]thrones, and they sat on
them, and [f]judgment was committed to
them. Then *I saw* [g]the souls of those who
had been beheaded for their witness to Jesus and for the word of God, [h]who had not
worshiped the beast [i]or his image, and had
not received *his* mark on their foreheads or
on their hands. And they [j]lived and
[k]reigned with Christ for [1]a thousand years.
5 But the rest of the dead did not live again

3 [c] Dan. 6:17; Matt. 27:66 [d] Rev. 12:9; 20:8, 10
4 [e] Dan. 7:9; Matt. 19:28; Luke 22:30 [f] Dan. 7:22; [1 Cor. 6:2, 3] [g] Rev. 6:9 [h] Rev. 13:12 [i] Rev. 13:15 [j] John 14:19 [k] Rom. 8:17; 2 Tim. 2:12 [1] M *the*
6 [l] [Rev. 2:11; 20:14] [m] Is. 61:6; 1 Pet. 2:9; Rev. 1:6 [n] Rev. 20:4
8 [o] Rev. 12:9; 20:3, 10 [p] Ezek. 38:2; 39:1, 6 [q] Rev. 16:14
9 [r] Is. 8:8; Ezek. 38:9, 16

until the thousand years were finished.
This *is* the first resurrection. **6** Blessed and
holy *is* he who has part in the first resurrection. Over such [l]the second death has
no power, but they shall be [m]priests of God
and of Christ, [n]and shall reign with Him a
thousand years.

Satanic Rebellion Crushed

7 Now when the thousand years have
expired, Satan will be released from his
prison **8** and will go out [o]to deceive the nations which are in the four corners of the
earth, [p]Gog and Magog, [q]to gather them
together to battle, whose number *is* as the
sand of the sea. **9** [r]They went up on the
breadth of the earth and surrounded the
camp of the saints and the beloved city.
And fire came down from God out of
heaven and devoured them. **10** The devil,

emphasizes his ferocity, and cruelty (*see note on 12:3*). **serpent of old.** A reference to Satan's first appearance in the Garden of Eden (Gen. 3:1ff.), where he deceived Eve (cf. 2 Cor. 11:3; 1 Tim. 2:14). **Devil...Satan.** *See note on 12:9.* **a thousand years.** This is the first of 6 references to the length of the millennial kingdom (cf. vv. 3,4,5,6,7). There are 3 main views of the duration and nature of this period: 1) Premillennialism sees this as a literal 1,000 year period during which Jesus Christ, in fulfillment of numerous OT prophecies (e.g., 2 Sam. 7:12-16; Ps. 2; Is. 11:6-12; 24:23; Hos. 3:4,5; Joel 3:9-21; Amos 9:8-15; Mic. 4:1-8; Zeph. 3:14-20; Zech. 14:1-11; Matt. 24:29-31,36-44), reigns on the earth. Using the same general principles of interpretation for both prophetic and non-prophetic passages leads most naturally to Premillennialism. Another strong argument supporting this view is that so many biblical prophecies have already been literally fulfilled, suggesting that future prophecies will likewise be fulfilled literally. 2) Postmillennialism understands the reference to a 1,000 year period as only symbolic of a golden age of righteousness and spiritual prosperity. It will be ushered in by the spread of the gospel during the present church age and brought to completion when Christ returns. According to this view, references to Christ's reign on earth primarily describe His spiritual reign in the hearts of believers in the church. 3) Amillennialism understands the 1,000 years to be merely symbolic of a long period of time. This view interprets OT prophecies of a Millennium as being fulfilled spiritually now in the church (either on earth or in heaven) or as references to the eternal state. Using the same literal, historical, grammatical principles of interpretation so as to determine the normal sense of language, one is left with the inescapable conclusion that Christ will return and reign in a real kingdom on earth for 1,000 years. There is nothing in the text to render the conclusion that "a thousand years" is symbolic. Never in Scripture when "year" is used with a number is its meaning not literal (*see note on 2 Pet. 3:10*).

20:3 released for a little while. Satan will be released so God can make a permanent end of sin before establishing the new heaven and earth. All who survive the Tribulation and enter the kingdom will be believers. However, despite that and the personal presence and rule of the Lord Jesus Christ, many of their descendants will refuse to believe in Him. Satan will then gather those unbelievers for one final, futile rebellion against God. It will be quickly and decisively crushed, followed by the Great White Throne Judgment and the establishment of the eternal state. **bottomless pit.** All 7 times that this appears in Revelation, it refers to the place where fallen angels and evil spirits are kept captive, waiting to be sent to the lake of fire—the final hell prepared for them (Matt. 25:41).

20:4 the souls of those who had been beheaded. These are tribulation martyrs (cf. 6:9; 18:24; 19:2). The Gr. word translated "beheaded" became a general term for execution, not necessarily a particular method. ***his* mark.** *See note on 13:16.* Tribulation martyrs will be executed for refusing the mark of the beast. **reigned.** Tribulation believers, along with the redeemed from both the OT and NT eras, will reign with Christ (1 Cor. 6:2; 2 Tim. 2:12) during the 1,000 year kingdom.

20:5 the rest of the dead. The bodies of unbelievers of all ages will not be resurrected until the Great White Throne judgment (vv. 12,13). **first resurrection.** Scripture teaches two kinds of resurrections: the "resurrection of life" and "the resurrection of condemnation" (John 5:29; cf. Dan. 12:2; Acts 24:15). The first kind of resurrection is described as "the resurrection of the just" (Luke 14:14), the resurrection of "those who are Christ's at His coming" (1 Cor. 15:23), and the "better resurrection" (Heb. 11:35). It includes only the redeemed of the church age (1 Thess. 4:13-18), the OT (Dan. 12:2), and the Tribulation (v. 4). They will enter the kingdom in resurrection bodies, along with believers who survived the Tribulation. The second kind of resurrection, then, will be the resurrection of the unconverted who will receive their final bodies suited for torment in hell.

20:6 Blessed. Those who die in the Lord (14:13) are blessed with the privilege of entering His kingdom (*see note on 1:3*). **second death.** The first death is spiritual and physical, the second is eternal in the lake of fire, the final, eternal hell (v. 14). It could exist outside the created universe as we know it, outside of space and time, and be presently unoccupied (*see note on 19:20*). **thousand years.** *See note on v. 2.*

20:7 Satan...released. He is loosed to bring cohesive leadership to the world of rebels born to the believers who entered the kingdom at the beginning. He is loosed to reveal the character of Christ-rejecting sinners who are brought into judgment for the last time ever.

20:8 Gog and Magog. The name given to the army of rebels and its leader at the end of the Millennium. They were names of ancient enemies of the Lord. Magog was the grandson of Noah (Gen. 10:2) and founder of a kingdom located N of the Black and Caspian Seas. Gog is apparently the leader of a rebel army known collectively as Magog. The battle depicted in vv. 8,9 is like the one in Ezek. 38,39; it is best to see this one as taking place at the end of the Millennium. For the difference, *see notes on Ezek. 38,39.*

20:9 beloved city. Jerusalem (cf. Pss. 78:68; 87:2), the capital city during Christ's millennial reign (Jer. 3:17). The saints will be living around the city where Christ reigns (cf. Is. 24:23; Jer. 3:17; Zech. 14:9-11). **fire.** Frequently associated in Scripture with divine judgment of wicked men (Gen. 19:24; 2 Kin. 1:10,12,14; Luke 9:54; 17:29).

who deceived them, was cast into the lake of fire and brimstone [s]where[2] the beast and the false prophet *are.* And they [t]will be tormented day and night forever and ever.

The Great White Throne Judgment

11 Then I saw a great white throne and
Him who sat on it, from whose face [u]the
earth and the heaven fled away. [v]And
there was found no place for them. **12** And
I saw the dead, [w]small and great, standing
before [3]God, [x]and books were opened.
And another [y]book was opened, which is
the Book of Life. And the dead were judged
[z]according to their works, by the things
which were written in the books. **13** The
sea gave up the dead who were in it, [a]and
Death and Hades delivered up the dead
who were in them. [b]And they were judged,
each one according to his works. **14** Then
[c]Death and Hades were cast into the lake
of fire. [d]This is the second [4]death. **15** And
anyone not found written in the Book of
Life [e]was cast into the lake of fire.

All Things Made New

21 Now [a]I saw a new heaven and a
new earth, [b]for the first heaven and
the first earth had passed away. Also there
was no more sea. **2** Then I, [1]John, saw [c]the
holy city, New Jerusalem, coming down
out of heaven from God, prepared [d]as a
bride adorned for her husband. **3** And I
heard a loud voice from heaven saying,
"Behold, [e]the tabernacle of God *is* with
men, and He will dwell with them, and
they shall be His people. God Himself will
be with them *and be* their God. **4** [f]And God
will wipe away every tear from their eyes;
[g]there shall be no more death, [h]nor sorrow,
nor crying. There shall be no more pain, for
the former things have passed away."

10 [s]Rev. 19:20; 20:14, 15 [t]Rev. 14:10 [2]NU, M *where also* **11** [u]2 Pet. 3:7; Rev. 21:1 [v]Dan. 2:35; Rev. 12:8 **12** [w]Rev. 19:5 [x]Dan. 7:10 [y]Ps. 69:28; Dan. 12:1; Phil. 4:3; Rev. 3:5 [z]Jer. 17:10; Matt. 16:27; Rom. 2:6; Rev. 2:23; 20:12 [3]NU, M *the throne* **13** [a]1 Cor. 15:26; Rev. 1:18; 6:8; 21:4 [b]Matt. 16:27; Rev. 2:23; 20:12 **14** [c]1 Cor. 15:26; Rev. 1:18; 6:8; 21:4 [d]Rev. 21:8 [4]NU, M *death, the lake of fire.* **15** [e]Rev. 19:20

CHAPTER 21

1 [a]Is. 65:17; 66:22; [2 Pet. 3:13] [b][2 Pet. 3:10]; Rev. 20:11 **2** [c]Is. 52:1; [Gal. 4:26]; Heb. 11:10 [d]Is. 54:5; 2 Cor. 11:2 [1]NU, M omit *John* **3** [e]Lev. 26:11; Ezek. 43:7; 2 Cor. 6:16 **4** [f]Is. 25:8; Rev. 7:17 [g]1 Cor. 15:26; Rev. 20:14 [h]Is. 35:10; 51:11; 65:19

20:10 deceived. Just as his demons will entice the world's armies into the Battle of Armageddon, Satan will draw them into a suicidal assault against Christ and His people (16:13,14). **lake of fire and brimstone.** *See note on 19:20.* **tormented day and night.** *See note on 14:11.* Continuous, unrelieved torment will be the final state of Satan, fallen angels, and unredeemed men.

20:11-15 These verses describe the final judgment of all the unbelievers of all ages (Matt. 10:15; 11:22,24; 12:36,41,42; Luke 10:14; John 12:48; Acts 17:31; 24:25; Rom. 2:5,16; Heb. 9:27; 2 Pet. 2:9; 3:7; Jude 6). Our Lord referred to this event as the "resurrection of condemnation" (John 5:29). This judgment takes place in the indescribable void between the end of the present universe (v. 11) and the creation of the new heaven and earth (21:1).

20:11 great white throne. Nearly 50 times in Revelation there is the mention of a throne. This is a judgment throne, elevated, pure, and holy. God sits on it as judge (cf. 4:2,3,9; 5:1,7,13; 6:16; 7:10,15) in the person of the Lord Jesus Christ. See 21:5,6; John 5:22-29; Acts 17:31. **earth and the heaven fled away.** John saw the contaminated universe go out of existence. Peter described this moment in 2 Pet. 3:10-13 (*see notes there*). The universe is "uncreated," going into nonexistence (cf. Matt. 24:35).

20:12 standing before God. In a judicial sense, as guilty, condemned prisoners before the bar of divine justice. There are no living sinners left in the destroyed universe since all sinners were killed and all believers glorified. **books.** These books record every thought, word, and deed of sinful men—all recorded by divine omniscience (*see note on Dan. 7:10*, the verse that is the source of this text). They will provide the evidence for eternal condemnation. Cf. 18:6,7. ***Book* of Life.** It contains the names of all the redeemed (Dan. 12:1; *see notes on 3:5*). **judged according to their works.** Their thoughts (Luke 8:17; Rom. 2:16), words (Matt. 12:37), and actions (Matt. 16:27) will be compared to God's perfect, holy standard (Matt. 5:48; 1 Pet. 1:15,16) and will be found wanting (Rom. 3:23). This also implies that there are degrees of punishment in hell (cf. Matt. 10:14,15; 11:22; Mark 12:38-40; Luke 12:47,48; Heb. 10:29).

20:13 Death and Hades. *See note on 1:18.* Both terms describe the state of death. All unrighteous dead will appear at the Great White Throne Judgment; none will escape. All the places that have held the bodies of the unrighteous dead will yield up new bodies suited for hell.

20:14 second death. *See note on v. 6.*

20:15 lake of fire. *See note on 19:20.*

21:1 As the chapter opens, all the sinners of all the ages, both demons and men, including Satan, the beast, and false prophet, are in the lake of fire forever. The whole universe has been destroyed, and God creates a new universe to be the eternal dwelling place of the redeemed. **a new heaven and a new earth.** The entire universe as we now know it will be destroyed (2 Pet. 3:10-13) and be replaced by a new creation that will last forever. This is an OT reality (Ps. 102:25,26; Is. 65:17; 66:22), as well as a NT one (Luke 21:33; Heb. 1:10-12). *See note on 20:11-15.* **no more sea.** Currently three-fourths of the earth's surface is water, but the new environment will no longer be water-based and will have completely different climatic conditions. *See notes on 22:1,2.*

21:2–22:5 By this point in the chronology of Revelation, OT saints, tribulation saints, and all those converted during the millennial kingdom will be incorporated into the ultimate redeemed bride and will dwell in the New Jerusalem. John described the consummation of all things in Christ and the New Jerusalem descending into the eternal state (cf. 19:7; 20:6; 1 Cor. 15:28; Heb. 12:22-24).

21:2 New Jerusalem. Cf. 3:12; Heb. 11:10; 12:22-24; 13:14. This is the capital city of heaven, a place of perfect holiness. It is seen "coming down out of heaven" indicating it already existed; but it descends into the new heavens and new earth from its place on high. This is the city where the saints will live (cf. John 14:1-3). **bride.** An important NT metaphor for the church (cf. Matt. 25:1-13; Eph. 5:25-27). John's imagery here extends from the third part of the Jewish wedding, the ceremony. Believers (the bride) in the New Jerusalem come to meet Christ (the bridegroom) in the final ceremony of redemptive history (*see note on 19:7*). The whole city, occupied by all the saints, is called the bride, so that all saints must be finally included in the bride imagery and bridal blessing. God has brought home a bride for His beloved Son. All the saints live with Christ in the Father's house (a promise made before the church began).

21:3 the tabernacle of God. The word translated "tabernacle" means place of abode. This is God's house, the place where He lives (cf. Lev. 26:11,12; Deut. 12:5).

21:4 wipe away every tear. Since there will never be a tear in heaven, nothing will be sad, disappointing, deficient, or wrong (cf. Is. 53:4,5; 1 Cor. 15:54-57).

5 Then [i]He who sat on the throne said,
[j]"Behold, I make all things new." And He
said [2]to me, "Write, for [k]these words are
true and faithful."
6 And He said to me, [l]"It[3] is done! [m]I am
the Alpha and the Omega, the Beginning
and the End. [n]I will give of the fountain of
the water of life freely to him who thirsts.
7 He who overcomes [4]shall inherit all
things, and [o]I will be his God and he shall
be My son. 8 [p]But the cowardly, [5]unbeliev-
ing, abominable, murderers, sexually immoral, sorcerers, idolaters, and all liars
shall have their part in [q]the lake which
burns with fire and brimstone, which is the
second death."

The New Jerusalem

9 Then one of [r]the seven angels who had
the seven bowls filled with the seven last
plagues came [6]to me and talked with me,
saying, "Come, I will show you [s]the
[7]bride, the Lamb's wife." 10 And he carried
me away [t]in the Spirit to a great and high
mountain, and showed me [u]the [8]great city,
the [9]holy Jerusalem, descending out of
heaven from God, 11 [v]having the glory of
God. Her light *was* like a most precious
stone, like a jasper stone, clear as crystal.
12 Also she had a great and high wall with
[w]twelve gates, and twelve angels at the
gates, and names written on them, which
are *the names* of the twelve tribes of the
children of Israel: 13 [x]three gates on the
east, three gates on the north, three gates
on the south, and three gates on the west.
14 Now the wall of the city had twelve
foundations, and [y]on them were the
[1]names of the twelve apostles of the Lamb.
15 And he who talked with me [z]had a gold
reed to measure the city, its gates, and its
wall. 16 The city is laid out as a square; its
length is as great as its breadth. And he
measured the city with the reed: twelve
thousand [2]furlongs. Its length, breadth,
and height are equal. 17 Then he measured
its wall: one hundred *and* forty-four cubits,
according to the measure of a man, that is,
of an angel. 18 The construction of its wall
was *of* jasper; and the city *was* pure gold,
like clear glass. 19 [a]The foundations of the
wall of the city *were* adorned with all kinds
of precious stones: the first foundation *was*
jasper, the second sapphire, the third chalcedony, the fourth emerald, 20 the fifth sardonyx, the sixth sardius, the seventh
chrysolite, the eighth beryl, the ninth
topaz, the tenth chrysoprase, the eleventh

5 [i] Rev. 4:2, 9; 20:11 [j] Is. 43:19; 2 Cor. 5:17 [k] Rev. 19:9; 22:6 [2] NU, M omit *to me*
6 [l] Rev. 10:6; 16:17 [m] Rev. 1:8; 22:13 [n] Is. 12:3; 55:1; John 4:10; Rev. 7:17; 22:17 [3] M omits *It is done*
7 [o] Zech. 8:8; Heb. 8:10 [4] M *I shall give him these things*
8 [p] 1 Cor. 6:9; Gal. 5:19; Eph. 5:5; 1 Tim. 1:9; [Heb. 12:14] [q] Rev. 20:14 [5] M adds *and sinners,*
9 [r] Rev. 15:1 [s] Rev. 19:7; 21:2 [6] NU, M omit *to me* [7] M *woman, the Lamb's bride*
10 [t] Rev. 1:10 [u] Ezek. 48 [8] NU, M omit *great* [9] NU, M *holy city, Jerusalem*
11 [v] Is. 60:1; Ezek. 43:2; Rev. 15:8; 21:23; 22:5
12 [w] Ezek. 48:31-34
13 [x] Ezek. 48:31-34
14 [y] Matt. 16:18; Luke 22:29, 30; Gal. 2:9; Eph. 2:20 [1] NU, M *twelve names*
15 [z] Ezek. 40:3; Zech. 2:1; Rev. 11:1
16 [2] Lit. *stadia,* about 1,380 miles in all
19 [a] Ex. 28:17-20; Is. 54:11; Ezek. 28:13

21:5 true and faithful. Cf. 3:14; 19:11. God always speaks truth (John 17:17).

21:6 the Alpha and the Omega. *See note on 1:8.* **water of life.** Cf. 7:17; 22:1,17. The lasting spiritual water of which Jesus spoke (John 4:13,14; 7:37,38; cf. Is. 55:1,2). **him who thirsts.** Heaven belongs to those who, knowing their souls are parched by sin, have earnestly sought the satisfaction of salvation and eternal life (cf. Ps. 42:1,2; Is. 55:1,2; John 7:37,38).

21:7 He who overcomes. Cf. 1 John 5:4,5. Anyone who exercises saving faith in Jesus Christ (*see note on 2:7*). **inherit.** The spiritual inheritance all believers will receive (1 Pet. 1:4; cf. Matt. 25:23) is the fullness of the new creation. Cf. Rom. 8:16,17.

21:8 A solemn, serious warning about the kinds of people who will be outcasts from the new heaven and the new earth in the lake of fire. The NT often goes beyond just citing unbelief in listing character and lifestyle traits of the outcast, so that believers can identify such people (1 Cor. 6:9,10; Gal. 5:19; cf. John 8:31). **sorcerers.** *See note on 9:21.* **lake which burns with fire.** *See note on 19:20.* **brimstone.** *See note on 9:17.* **second death.** *See note on 20:6.*

21:9 seven bowls. *See note on 15:7.* **seven last plagues.** *See note on 15:1-8.*

21:9,10 the Lamb's wife. The New Jerusalem takes on the character of its inhabitants, the redeemed (*see notes on v. 2; 19:7-9*).

21:10 in the Spirit. *See note on 1:10.*

21:11 jasper. A transliteration, not a translation, of the Gr. word. Rather than the modern opaque jasper, the term actually refers to a completely clear diamond, a perfect gem with the brilliant light of God's glory shining out of it and streaming over the new heaven and the new earth (cf. 4:3).

21:12-14 wall. No measurements are given for the length of the wall.

21:15 gold reed. *See note on Ezek. 40:3.* The reed was about 10 ft. long, which was a standard for measure. **measure the city.** This action indicates that the capital of heaven belongs to God and He is measuring what is His (cf. 11:1; Ezek. 40:3).

21:16 length, breadth, and height. The city has the symmetrical dimensions of a perfect cube, which parallels its closest earthly counterpart, the inner sanctuary in the tabernacle and temple (cf. 1 Kin. 6:20). **twelve thousand furlongs.** This would be nearly 1,400 mi. cubed or over two million square miles, offering plenty of room for all the glorified saints to live.

21:17 one hundred *and* forty-four cubits. 72 yards or 216 feet. This is likely the width of the wall.

21:18 jasper. *See note on v. 11.* This is the material of the thick wall—diamond! **pure gold, like clear glass.** Unlike earth's gold, this gold will be transparent so the overpowering radiance of God's glory can refract and glisten through the entire city.

21:19,20 Because some of the names of these gems have changed through the centuries, it is difficult to identify each one with certainty. Eight of the 12 stones are found in the breastplate of the High-Priest (Ex. 28,39), and the other 4 may also be related to the breastplate. The gems picture a brilliant, indescribable panoply of beautiful colors that send forth the light of God's glory. The following are possible identifications for these gems.

21:19 chalcedony. This name derives from Chalcedon, an ancient name for a city in modern Turkey. The gem is a sky-blue agate stone with translucent, colored stripes.

21:20 sardonyx. A variety of chalcedony with parallel layers of red and white (*see note on v. 19*). **sardius.** A common stone from the quartz family, which ranged in color from orange-red to brownish-red to blood-red (4:3). **chrysolite.** A gem with a transparent gold or yellowish tone. **beryl.** A mineral with several varieties of gems, ranging from the green emerald to the golden yellow beryl to the light blue aquamarine. **topaz.** Ancient topaz was a softer stone with a yellow or yellow-green color. **chrysoprase.** The modern form of this

jacinth, and the twelfth amethyst. 21 The
twelve gates *were* twelve [b]pearls: each individual gate was of one pearl. [c]And the
street of the city *was* pure gold, like transparent glass.

The Glory of the New Jerusalem

22 [d]But I saw no temple in it, for the Lord
God Almighty and the Lamb are its temple. 23 [e]The city had no need of the sun or
of the moon to shine [3]in it, for the [4]glory of
God illuminated it. The Lamb *is* its light.
24 [f]And the nations [5]of those who are
saved shall walk in its light, and the kings
of the earth bring their glory and honor
[6]into it. 25 [g]Its gates shall not be shut at all
by day [h](there shall be no night there).
26 [i]And they shall bring the glory and the
honor of the nations into [7]it. 27 But [j]there
shall by no means enter it anything [8]that
defiles, or causes an abomination or a lie,
but only those who are written in the
Lamb's [k]Book of Life.

The River of Life

22 And he showed me [a]a [1]pure river of
water of life, clear as crystal, proceeding from the throne of God and of the
Lamb. 2 [b]In the middle of its street, and on
either side of the river, *was* [c]the tree of life,
which bore twelve fruits, each *tree* yielding
its fruit every month. The leaves of the tree
were [d]for the healing of the nations. 3 And
[e]there shall be no more curse, [f]but the
throne of God and of the Lamb shall be in
it, and His [g]servants shall serve Him.
4 [h]They shall see His face, and [i]His name
shall be on their foreheads. 5 [j]There shall be
no night there: They need no lamp nor
[k]light of the sun, for [l]the Lord God gives
them light. [m]And they shall reign forever
and ever.

The Time Is Near

6 Then he said to me, [n]"These words *are*
faithful and true." And the Lord God of the
[2]holy prophets [o]sent His angel to show His
servants the things which must [p]shortly
take place.
7 [q]"Behold, I am coming quickly!
[r]Blessed *is* he who keeps the words of the
prophecy of this book."
8 Now I, John, [3]saw and heard these
things. And when I heard and saw, [s]I fell
down to worship before the feet of the
angel who showed me these things.
9 Then he said to me, [t]"See *that you do*
not *do that.* [4]For I am your fellow servant,
and of your brethren the prophets, and of
those who keep the words of this book.
Worship God." 10 [u]And he said to me,

21 [b] Matt. 13:45, 46 [c] Rev. 22:2
22 [d] Matt. 24:2; John 4:21, 23
23 [e] Is. 24:23; 60:19, 20; Rev. 21:25; 22:5 [3] NU, M omit *in it* [4] M *very glory*
24 [f] Is. 60:3, 5; 66:12 [5] NU, M omit *of those who are saved* [6] M *of the nations to Him*
25 [g] Is. 60:11 [h] Is. 60:20; Zech. 14:7
26 [i] Rev. 21:24 [7] M adds *that they may enter in.*
27 [j] Is. 35:8; Joel 3:17 [k] Phil. 4:3 [8] NU, M *profane, nor one who causes*

CHAPTER 22

1 [a] Ps. 46:4; Ezek. 47:1; [Zech. 14:8] [1] NU, M omit *pure*
2 [b] Ezek. 47:12 [c] Gen. 2:9; [Rev. 2:7; 22:14, 19] [d] Rev. 21:24
3 [e] Zech. 14:11 [f] Ezek. 48:35 [g] Rev. 7:15
4 [h] [Ps. 17:15; 42:2; Matt. 5:8; 1 Cor. 13:12; 1 John 3:2] [i] Rev. 14:1
5 [j] Is. 60:19; Rev. 21:23 [k] Rev. 7:15 [l] Ps. 36:9 [m] Dan. 7:18, 27; Matt. 19:28; [Rom. 5:17]; 2 Tim. 2:12; Rev. 20:4
6 [n] Rev. 19:9 [o] Rev. 1:1 [p] Heb. 10:37 [2] NU, M *spirits of the prophets*
7 [q] [Rev. 3:11] [r] Rev. 1:3 **8** [s] Rev. 19:10 [3] NU, M *am the one who heard and saw* **9** [t] Rev. 19:10 [4] NU, M omit *For* **10** [u] Dan. 8:26; Rev. 10:4

jewel is an apple-green variety of quartz. The Gr. name suggests a gold-tinted, green gemstone. **jacinth.** Today this stone is a transparent zircon, usually red or reddish-brown. The one John saw was blue or shining violet in color. **amethyst.** A clear quartz crystal that ranges in color from a faint purple tint to an intense purple.

21:21 one pearl. Each of the gates of the city is a single, 1,500-mile-high pearl. Even as earthly pearls are formed in response to the wounding of oyster flesh, so these gigantic, supernatural pearls will remind saints throughout eternity of the magnitude of Christ's suffering and its eternal benefit.

21:22 no temple. Several passages affirm that there is a temple in heaven (3:12; 7:15; 11:19; 15:5). Here, it is clear there is none in eternity. How can this be? The temple is not a building; it is the Lord God Himself. Revelation 7:15 implies this when it says, "He who sits on the throne will dwell among them." Verse 23 continues the thought of no temple, except God and the Lamb. The glory of God which illuminates all heaven defines it as His temple. There is no need for a temple in the eternal state since God Himself will be the temple in which everything exists. The presence of God lit. fills the entire new heaven and new earth (cf. v. 3). Going to heaven will be entering the limitless presence of the Lord (cf. John 14:3; 1 Thess. 4:17).

21:24 the nations. Lit. "the peoples." Redeemed people from every nation and ethnic group will dwell in heaven's light. In the eternal city, there will be no more divisions, barriers, or exclusions because of race or politics. All kinds of peoples in eternity dissolve into the people of God, and they will move freely in and about the city.

21:27 Lamb's Book of Life. *See note on 3:5.*

22:1 river…of life. This river is unlike any on earth because no hydrological cycle exists. Water of life symbolizes the continual flow of eternal life from God's throne to heaven's inhabitants (*see note on 21:6*).

22:2 tree of life. A symbol of both eternal life and continual blessing (*see note on Gen. 2:9*). The tree bears 12 fruits, one for each month, and is symbolic of the abundant variety in heaven. The Eng. word "therapeutic" comes from the Gr. word translated "healing." The leaves somehow enrich heavenly life, making it full and satisfying.

22:3 no more curse. The curse on humanity and the earth as a result of Adam's and Eve's disobedience (Gen. 3:16-19) will be totally finished. God will never have to judge sin again, since it will never exist in the new heaven and new earth. **His servants shall serve Him.** *See note on 7:15.*

22:4 see His face. No unglorified human could see God's face and live (Ex. 33:20-23). But the residents of heaven can look on God's face without harm because they are now holy (cf. John 1:18; 1 Tim. 6:16; 1 John 3:20). **His name.** They are God's personal possession (*see note on 3:12*).

22:5 they shall reign. Heaven's citizens are more than servants (*see note on 3:21*).

22:6 His servants. The members of the 7 churches of Asia Minor who received this letter (1:11), and then all believers who have read, or will read it since. **things which must shortly take place.** This involves the entire revelation which John has just related (*see note on 1:1*).

22:7 I am coming quickly! Jesus' return is imminent (*see note on 3:11*). **Blessed.** *See note on 1:3.*

22:8 heard and saw. John resumes speaking for the first time since chap. 1 and confirms the veracity of the revelation with his own eyewitness testimony—the basis of any reliable witness. **fell down to worship.** *See note on 19:10.*

"Do not seal the words of the prophecy of
this book, [v]for the time is at hand. 11 He
who is unjust, let him be unjust still; he
who is filthy, let him be filthy still; he who
is righteous, let him [5]be righteous still; he
who is holy, let him be holy still."

Jesus Testifies to the Churches

12 "And behold, I am coming quickly,
and [w]My reward *is* with Me, [x]to give to
every one according to his work. 13 [y]I am
the Alpha and the Omega, *the* [6]Beginning
and *the* End, the First and the Last."
14 [z]Blessed *are* those who [7]do His commandments, that they may have the right
[a]to the tree of life, [b]and may enter through
the gates into the city. 15 [8]But [c]outside *are*
[d]dogs and sorcerers and sexually immoral
and murderers and idolaters, and whoever
loves and practices a lie.
16 [e]"I, Jesus, have sent My angel to testify to you these things in the churches. [f]I
am the Root and the Offspring of David,
[g]the Bright and Morning Star."

10 [v] Rev. 1:3
11 [5] NU, M *do right*
12 [w] Is. 40:10; 62:11 [x] Rev. 20:12
13 [y] Is. 41:4 [6] NU, M *First and the Last, the Beginning and the End.*
14 [z] Dan. 12:12; [1 John 3:24] [a] [Prov. 11:30]; Rev. 2:7 [b] Rev. 21:27 [7] NU *wash their robes,*
15 [c] Matt. 8:12; 1 Cor. 6:9; Gal. 5:19; Col. 3:6; Rev. 21:8 [d] Deut. 23:18; Matt. 7:6; Phil. 3:2 [8] NU, M omit *But*
16 [e] Rev. 1:1 [f] 2 Sam. 7:12; Is. 9:7; Jer. 23:5; Rev. 5:5 [g] Num. 24:17; Luke 1:78; 2 Pet. 1:19
17 [h] [Rev. 21:2, 9] [i] Is. 55:1; Rev. 21:6
18 [j] Deut. 4:2; 12:32; Prov. 30:6 [9] NU, M omit *For* [1] M *may God add*
19 [k] Ex. 32:33 [2] M *may God take away* [3] NU, M *tree of life*
21 [4] NU *with all;* M *with all the saints*

17 And the Spirit and [h]the bride say,
"Come!" And let him who hears say,
"Come!" [i]And let him who thirsts come.
Whoever desires, let him take the water of
life freely.

A Warning

18 [9]For I testify to everyone who hears
the words of the prophecy of this book: [j]If
anyone adds to these things, [1]God will
add to him the plagues that are written in
this book; 19 and if anyone takes away
from the words of the book of this
prophecy, [k]God [2] shall take away his part
from the [3]Book of Life, from the holy city,
and *from* the things which are written in
this book.

I Am Coming Quickly

20 He who testifies to these things says,
"Surely I am coming quickly."
Amen. Even so, come, Lord Jesus!
21 The grace of our Lord Jesus Christ *be*
[4]with you all. Amen.

22:10 Do not seal the words. Cf. 10:11. Previous prophecies were sealed up (Dan. 8:26; 12:4-10). These prophecies are to be proclaimed so they can produce obedience and worship. **the time is at hand.** This refers to imminency, which means that the end is next.

22:11 Those who reject God's warnings will fix their eternal destiny in hell, where they will retain their evil and filthy natures for all eternity. Those who respond to the warnings will fix their eternal destiny in glory and realize perfect righteousness and holiness in heaven.

22:12 I am coming quickly. *See note on 3:11.* Again, imminence is the issue (cf. Mark 13:33-37). **according to his work.** Only those works which survive God's testing fire have eternal value and are worthy of reward (1 Cor. 3:10-15; 4:1-5; 2 Cor. 5:10).

22:13 the Alpha and the Omega. *See note on 1:8.*

22:14 Blessed *are* those who do His commandments. *See note on 1:3.* The preferred reading is "Blessed are those who wash their robes," symbolizing those who have been forgiven of their sins—who have been cleansed by the blood of the Lamb of God (Heb. 9:14; 1 Pet. 1:18,19; *see note on 7:14*). **tree of life.** *See notes on v. 2; Gen. 2:9.*

22:15 dogs. Considered despicable creatures in NT times, the term when applied to people referred to anyone of low moral character. Unfaithful leaders (Is. 56:10) and homosexual prostitutes (Deut. 23:18) are among those who received such a designation. **sorcerers.** *See note on 9:21.*

22:16 My angel. See 1:1. **the churches.** The 7 churches of Asia Minor who were the book's original recipients (1:11). **the Root and the Offspring of David.** Christ is the source (root) of David's life and line of descendants, which establishes His deity. He is also a descendant of David (offspring), which establishes His humanity. This phrase gives powerful testimony to Christ as the God-Man (cf. 2 Tim. 2:8). **Bright and Morning Star.** This is the brightest star announcing the arrival of the day. When Jesus comes, He will be the brightest star who will shatter the darkness of man's night and herald the dawn of God's glorious day (*see note on 2:28*).

22:17 "Come!" This is the Spirit's and church's answer to the promise of His coming. **let him.** This is an unlimited offer of grace and salvation to all who desire to have their thirsty souls quenched. Cf. Is. 55:1,2. **water of life.** *See note on v. 1.*

22:18 Jesus offers extended testimony on the authority and finality of the prophecy. He commissioned John to write it, but He was its author.

22:18,19 These are not the first such warnings (cf. Deut. 4:2; 12:32; Prov. 30:6; Jer. 26:2). These warnings against altering the biblical text represent the close of the NT canon. Anyone who tampers with the truth by attempting to falsify, mitigate, alter, or misinterpret it will incur the judgments described in these verses.

22:20 "Surely I am coming quickly." *See note on 3:11.* In light of this future expectation, what is now required of believers is outlined by Peter (see 2 Pet. 3:11-18).

Appendices

- Topical Index
- Read Through the Bible in a Year
- The Character of Genuine Saving Faith
- Overview of Theology
- Monies, Weights, Measures
- Color Maps

The Topical Index

Access to God.

Is of God. Ps 65:4.
Is by Christ. John 10:7,9; 14:6; Rom 5:2; Eph 2:13; 3:12; Heb 7:9,25; 10:19; 1 Pet 3:18.
Is by the Holy Spirit. Eph 2:18.
Obtained through faith. Acts 14:27; Rom 5:2; Eph 3:12; Heb 11:6.
Follows upon reconciliation to God. Col 1:21,22.
In prayer. See Prayer. Deut 4:7; Matt 6:6; 1 Pet 1:17.
In his temple. Ps 15:1; 27:4; 43:3; 65:4.
To obtain mercy and grace. Heb 4:16.
A privilege of saints. Deut 4:7; Ps 15:1; 23:6; 24:3,4.
Saints have, with confidence. Eph 3:12; Heb 4:16; 10:19,20.
Vouchsafed to repenting sinners. See Repentance. Hos 14:2; Joel 2:12.
Saints earnestly seek. Ps 27:4; 42:1,2; 43:3; 84:1,2.
The wicked commanded to seek. Is 55:6; James 4:8.
Urge others to seek. Is 2:3; Jer 31:6.
Promises connected with. Ps 145:18; Is 55:3; Matt 6:6; James 4:8.
Blessedness connected with. Ps 16:11; 65:4; 73:28.
Typified. Lev 16:12-15; Heb 10:19-22.
Exemplified
Moses. Ex 24:2; 34:4-7.

Adoption.

Explained. 2 Cor 6:18.
Is according to promise. Rom 9:8; Gal 3:29.
Is by faith. Gal 3:7,26.
Is of God's grace. Ezek 16:3-6; Rom 4:16,17; Eph 1:5,6,11.
Is through Christ. John 1:12; Gal 4:4,5; Eph 1:5; Heb 2:10,13.
Saints predestinated to. Rom 8:29; Eph 1:5,11.
Of Gentiles, predicted. Hos 2:23; Rom 9:24-26; Eph 3:6.
The adopted are gathered together in one by Christ. John 11:52.
New birth connected with. John 1:12,13.
The Holy Spirit is a witness of. Rom 8:16.
Being led by the Spirit is an evidence of. Rom 8:14.
Saints receive the Spirit of. Rom 8:15; Gal 4:6.
A privilege of saints. John 1:12; 1 John 3:1.
Saints become brethren of Christ by. John 20:17; Heb 2:11,12.
Saints wait for final consummation of. Rom 8:19,23; 1 John 3:2.
Subjects saints to the fatherly discipline of God. Deut 8:5; 2 Sam 7:14; Prov 3:11,12; Heb 12:5-11.
God is long-suffering and merciful towards the partakers of. Jer 31:1,9,20.
Should lead to holiness. 2 Cor 6:17,18; 7:1; Phil 2:15; 1 John 3:2,3.
Should produce
Likeness to God. Matt 5:44,45,48; Eph 5:1.
Child-like confidence in God. Matt 6:25-34.
A desire for God's glory. Matt 5:16.
A spirit of prayer. Matt 7:7-11.
A love of peace. Matt 5:9.
A forgiving spirit. Matt 6:14.
A merciful spirit. Luke 6:35,36.
An avoidance of ostentation. Matt 6:1-4,6,18.
Safety of those who receive. Prov 14:26.
Confers a new name. See Titles of Saints. Num 6:27; Is 62:2; Acts 15:17.
Entitles to an inheritance. Matt 13:43; Rom 8:17; Gal 3:29; 4:7; Eph 3:6.
Is to be pleaded in prayer. Is 63:16; Matt 6:9.
Illustrated
Joseph's sons. Gen 48:5,14,16,22.
Moses. Ex 2:10.
Esther. Esth 2:7.
Typified
Israel. Ex 4:22; Hos 11:1; Rom 9:4.
Exemplified
Solomon. 1 Chr 28:6.

Affections, The.

Should be supremely set upon God. Deut 6:3; Mark 12:30.
Should be set
Upon the commandments of God. Ps 19:8-10; 119:20,97,103,167.
Upon the house and worship of God. 1 Chr 29:3; Ps 26:8; 27:4; 84:1,2.
Upon the people of God. Ps 16:3; Rom 12:10; 2 Cor 7:13-15; 1 Thess 2:8.
Upon heavenly things. Col 3:1,2.
Should be zealously engaged for God. Ps 69:9; 119:139; Gal 4:18.
Christ claims the first place in. Matt 10:37; Luke 14:26.
Enkindled by communion with Christ. Luke 24:32.
Blessedness of making God the object of. Ps 91:14.
Should not grow cold. Ps 106:12,13; Matt 24:12; Gal 4:15; Rev 2:4.
Of saints, supremely set on God. Ps 42:1; 73:25; 119:10.
Of the wicked, not sincerely set on God. Is 58:1,2; Ezek 33:31,32; Luke 8:13.
Carnal affections should be mortified. Rom 8:13; 13:14; 1 Cor 9:27; Col 3:5; 1 Thess 4:5.
Carnal affections crucified in saints. Rom 6:6; Gal 5:24.
False teachers seek to captivate. Gal 1:10; 4:17; 2 Tim 3:6; 2 Pet 2:3,18; Rev 2:14,20.
Of the wicked, are unnatural and perverted. Rom 1:31; 2 Tim 3:3; 2 Pet 2:10.

Afflicted, Duty Toward The.

To pray for them. Acts 12:5; Phil 1:16,19; James 5:14-16.
To sympathise with them. Rom 12:15; Gal 6:2.
To pity them. Job 6:14.
To bear them in mind. Heb 13:3.
To visit them. James 1:27.
To comfort them. Job 16:5; 29:25; 2 Cor 1:4; 1 Thess 4:18.
To relieve them. Job 31:19,20; Is 58:10; Phil 4:14; 1 Tim 5:10.
To protect them. Ps 82:3; Prov 22:22; 31:5.

Afflicted Saints.

God is with. Ps 46:5,7; Is 43:2.
God is a refuge and strength to. Ps 27:5,6; Is 25:4; Jer 16:19; Nah 1:7.
God comforts. Is 49:13; Jer 31:13; Matt 5:4; 2 Cor 1:4,5; 7:6.
God preserves. Ps 34:20.
God delivers. Ps 34:4,19; Prov 12:13; Jer 39:17,18.
Christ is with. John 14:18.
Christ supports. 2 Tim 4:17; Heb 2:18.
Christ comforts. Is 61:2; Matt 11:28-30; Luke 7:13; John 14:1; 16:33.
Christ preserves. Is 63:9; Luke 21:18.
Christ delivers. Rev 3:10.
Should praise God. Ps 13:5,6; 56:8-10; 57:6,7; 71:20-23.
Should imitate Christ. Heb 12:1-3; 1 Pet 2:21-23.
Should imitate the prophets. James 5:10.
Should be patient. Luke 21:19; Rom 12:12; 2 Thess 1:4; James 1:4; 1 Pet 2:20.
Should be resigned. 1 Sam 3:18; 2 Kin 20:19; Job 1:21; Ps 39:9.
Should not despise chastening. Job 5:17; Prov 3:11; Heb 12:5.
Should acknowledge the justice of their chastisements. Neh 9:33; Job 2:10; Is 64:5-7; Lam 3:39; Mic 7:9.
Should avoid sin. Job 34:31,32; John 5:14; 1 Pet 2:12.
Should trust in the goodness of God. Job 13:15; Ps 71:20; 2 Cor 1:9.
Should turn and devote themselves to God. Ps 116:7-9; Jer 50:3,4; Hos 6:1.
Should keep the pious resolutions made during afflictions. Ps 66:13-15.

Should be frequent in prayer. See "Affliction, Prayer Under." Ps 50:15-17.
Should take encouragement from former mercies. Ps 27:9; 2 Cor 1:10.
Examples of afflicted saints:
Joseph. Gen 39:20-23; Ps 105:17-19.
Moses. Heb 11:25.
Eli. 1 Sam 3:18.
Nehemiah. Neh 1:4.
Job. Job 1:20-22.
David. 2 Sam 12:15-23.
Paul. Acts 20:22-24; 21:13.
Apostles. 1 Cor 4:13; 2 Cor 6:4-10.

Affliction, Consolation Under.

God is the Author and Giver of. Ps 23:4; Rom 15:5; 2 Cor 1:3; 7:6; Col 1:11; 2 Thess 2:16,17.
Christ is the Author and Giver of. Is 61:2; John 14:18; 2 Cor 1:5.
The Holy Spirit is the Author and Giver of. John 14:16,17; 15:26; 16:7; Acts 9:31.
Promised. Is 51:3,12; 66:13; Ezek 14:22,23; Hos 2:14; Zech 1:17.
Through the Holy Scriptures. Ps 119:50,76; Rom 15:4.
By ministers of the gospel. Is 40:1,2; 1 Cor 14:3; 2 Cor 1:4,6.
Is abundant. Ps 71:21; Is 66:11.
Is strong. Heb 6:18.
Is everlasting. 2 Thess 2:16.
Is a cause of praise. Is 12:1; 49:13.
Pray for. Ps 119:82.
Saints should administer to each other. 1 Thess 4:18; 5:11,14.
Is sought in vain from the world. Ps 69:20; Eccl 4:1; Lam 1:2.
To those who mourn for sin. Ps 51:17; Is 1:18; 40:1,2; 61:1; Mic 7:18,19; Luke 4:18.
To the troubled in mind. Ps 42:5; 94:19; John 14:1,27; 16:20,22.
To those deserted by friends. Ps 27:10; 41:9-12; John 14:18; 15:18,19.
To the persecuted. Deut 33:27.
To the poor. Ps 10:14; 34:6,9,10.
To the sick. Ps 41:3.
To the tempted. Rom 16:20; 1 Cor 10:13; 2 Cor 12:9; James 1:12; 4:7; 2 Pet 2:9; Rev 2:10.
In prospect of death. Job 19:25,26; Ps 23:4; John 14:2; 2 Cor 5:1; 1 Thess 4:14; Heb 4:9; Rev 7:14-17; 14:13.
Under the infirmities of age. Ps 71:9,18.

Affliction, Prayer Under.

Exhortation to. James 5:13.
That God would consider our trouble. 2 Kin 19:16; Neh 9:32; Ps 9:13; Lam 5:1.
For the presence and support of God. Ps 10:1; 102:2.
That the Holy Spirit may not be withdrawn. Ps 51:11.
For divine comfort. Ps 4:6; 119:76.
For mitigation of troubles. Ps 39:12,13.
For deliverance. Ps 25:17,22; 39:10; Is 64:9-12; Jer 17:14.
For pardon and deliverance from sin. Ps 39:8; 51:1; 79:8.
That we may be turned to God. Ps 80:7; 85:4-6; Jer 31:18.
For divine teaching and direction. Job 34:32; Ps 27:11; 143:10.
For increase of faith. Mark 9:24.
For mercy. Ps 6:2; Hab 3:2.
For restoration to joy. Ps 51:8,12; 69:29; 90:14,15.
For protection and preservation from enemies. 2 Kin 19:19; 2 Chr 20:12; Ps 17:8,9.
That we may know the causes of our trouble. Job 6:24; 10:2; 13:23,24.
That we may be taught the uncertainty of life. Ps 39:4.
That we may be quickened. Ps 143:11.

Afflictions.

God appoints. 2 Kin 6:33; Job 5:6,17; Ps 66:11; Amos 3:6; Mic 6:9.
God dispenses, as He will. Job 11:10; Is 10:15; 45:7.
God regulates the measure of. Ps 80:5; Is 9:1; Jer 46:28.
God determines the continuance of. Gen 15:13,14; Num 14:33; Is 10:25; Jer 29:10.
God does not willingly send. Lam 3:33.
Man is born to. Job 5:6,7; 14:1.
Saints appointed to. 1 Thess 3:3.
Consequent upon the fall. Gen 3:16-19.
Sin produces. Job 4:8; 20:11; Prov 1:31.
Sin visited with. 2 Sam 12:14; Ps 89:30-32; Is 57:17; Acts 13:10,11.
Often severe. Job 16:7-16; Ps 42:7; 66:12; Jon 2:3; Rev 7:14.
Always less than we deserve. Ezra 9:13; Ps 103:10.
Frequently terminate in good. Gen 50:20; Ex 1:11,12; Deut 8:15,16; Jer 24:5,6; Ezek 20:37.
Tempered with mercy. Ps 78:38,39; 106:43-46; Is 30:18-21; Lam 3:32; Mic 7:7-9; Nah 1:12.
Saints are to expect. John 16:33; Acts 14:22.
Of saints, are comparatively light. Acts 20:23,24; Rom 8:18; 2 Cor 4:17.
Of saints, are but temporary. Ps 30:5; 103:9; Is 54:7,8; John 16:20; 1 Pet 1:6; 5:10.
Saints have joy under. Job 5:17; James 5:11.
Of saints, end in joy and blessedness. Ps 126:5,6; Is 61:2,3; Matt 5:4; 1 Pet 4:13,14.
Often arise from the profession of the gospel. Matt 24:9; John 15:21; 2 Tim 3:11,12.
Exhibit the love and faithfulness of God. Deut 8:5; Ps 119:75; Prov 3:12; 1 Cor 11:32; Heb 12:6,7; Rev 3:19.

Afflictions Made Beneficial.

In promoting the glory of God. John 9:1-3; 11:3,4; 21:18,19.
In exhibiting the power and faithfulness of God. Ps 34:19,20; 2 Cor 4:8-11.
In teaching us the will of God. Ps 119:71; Is 26:9; Mic 6:9.
In turning us to God. Deut 4:30,31; Neh 1:8,9; Ps 78:34; Is 10:20,21; Hos 2:6,7.
In keeping us from again departing from God. Job 34:31,32; Is 10:20; Ezek 14:10,11.
In leading us to seek God in prayer. Judg 4:3; Jer 31:18; Lam 2:17-19; Hos 5:14,15; Jon 2:1.
In convincing us of sin. Job 36:8,9; Ps 119:67; Luke 15:16-18.
In leading us to confession of sin. Num 21:7; Ps 32:5; 51:3,5.
In testing and exhibiting our sincerity. Job 23:10; Ps 66:10; Prov 17:3.
In trying our faith and obedience. Gen 22:1,2; Heb 11:17; Ex 15:23-25; Deut 8:2,16; 1 Pet 1:7; Rev 2:10.
In humbling us. Deut 8:3,16; 2 Chr 7:13,14; Lam 3:19,20; 2 Cor 12:7.
In purifying us. Eccl 7:2,3; Is 1:25,26; 48:10; Jer 9:6,7; Zech 13:9; Mal 3:2,3.
In exercising our patience. Ps 40:1; Rom 5:3; James 1:3; 1 Pet 2:20.
In rendering us fruitful in good works. John 15:2; Heb 12:10,11.
In furthering the gospel. Acts 8:3,4; 11:19-21; Phil 1:12; 2 Tim 2:9,10; 4:16,17.
Exemplified
Joseph's brethren. Gen 42:21.
Joseph. Gen 45:5,7,8.
Israel. Deut 8:3,5.
Josiah. 2 Kin 22:19.
Hezekiah. 2 Chr 32:25,26.
Manasseh. 2 Chr 33:12.
Jonah. Jon 2:7.
Prodigal's son. Luke 15:21.

Afflictions of the Wicked, The.

God is glorified in. Ex 14:4; Ezek 38:22,23.
God holds in derision. Ps 37:13; Prov 1:26,27.
Are multiplied. Deut 31:17; Job 20:12-18; Ps 32:10.
Are continual. Job 15:20; Eccl 2:23; Is 32:10.
Are often sudden. Ps 73:10; Prov 6:15; Is 30:13; Rev 18:10.
Are often judicially sent. Job 21:17; Ps 107:17; Jer 30:15.
Are for examples to others. Ps 64:7-9; Zeph 3:6,7; 1 Cor 10:5-11; 2 Pet 2:6.
Are ineffectual of themselves, for their conversion. Ex 9:30; Is 9:13; Jer 2:30; Hag 2:17.
Their persecution of saints, a cause of. Deut 30:7; Ps 55:19; Zech 2:9; 2 Thess 1:6.
Impenitence is a cause of. Prov 1:30,31; Ezek 24:13; Amos 4:6-12; Zech 7:11,12; Rev 2:21,22.
Sometimes humble them. 1 Kin 21:27.
Frequently harden. Neh 9:28,29; Jer 5:3.
Produce slavish fear. Job 15:24; Ps 73:19; Jer 49:3,5.
Saints should not be alarmed at. Prov 3:25,26.
Exemplified
Pharaoh and the Egyptians. Ex 9:14,15; 14:24,25.
Ahaziah. 2 Kin 1:1-4.
Gehazi. 2 Kin 5:27.
Jehoram. 2 Chr 21:12-19.
Uzziah. 2 Chr 26:19-21.
Ahaz, etc. 2 Chr 28:5-8,22.

Agriculture or Husbandry.

The cultivation of the earth. Gen 3:23.

The occupation of man before the fall. Gen 2:15.
Rendered laborious by the curse on the earth. Gen 3:17-19.
Man doomed to labour in, after the fall. Gen 3:23.
Contributes to the support of all. Eccl 5:9.
The providence of God to be acknowledged in the produce of. Jer 5:24; Hos 2:8.
Requires
 Wisdom. Is 28:26.
 Diligence. Prov 27:23-27; Eccl 11:6.
 Toil. 2 Tim 2:6.
 Patience in waiting. James 5:7.
Diligence in, abundantly recompensed. Prov 12:11; 13:23; 28:19; Heb 6:7.
Persons engaged in, called
 Tillers of the ground. Gen 4:2.
 Husbandmen. 2 Chr 26:10.
 Labourers. Matt 9:37; 20:1.
Peace favourable to. Is 2:4; Jer 31:24.
War destructive to. Jer 50:16; 51:23.
Patriarchs engaged in. Gen 4:2; 9:20.
The labour of, supposed to be lessened by Noah. Gen 5:29; 9:20.
The Jews loved and followed. Judg 6:11; 1 Kin 19:19; 2 Chr 26:10.
Soil of Canaan suited to. Gen 13:10; Deut 8:7-9.
Climate of Canaan favourable to. Deut 11:10,11.
Was promoted amongst the Jews by
 Allotments to each family. Num 36:7-9.
 The rights of redemption. Lev 25:23-28.
 Separation from other nations. Ex 33:16.
 The prohibition against usury. Ex 22:25.
 The promises of God's blessings on. Lev 26:4; Deut 7:13; 11:14,15.
Enactments to protect
 Not to covet the fields of another. Deut 5:21.
 Not to move landmarks. Deut 19:14; Prov 22:28.
 Not to cut down crops of another. Deut 23:25.
 Against the trespass of cattle. Ex 22:5.
 Against injuring the produce of. Ex 22:5.
Often performed by hirelings. 1 Chr 27:26; 2 Chr 26:10; Matt 20:8; Luke 17:7.
Not to be engaged in during the Sabbatical year. Ex 23:10,11.
Produce of, given as rent for land. Matt 21:33,34.
Produce of, often blasted because of sin. Is 5:10; 7:23; Jer 12:13; Joel 1:10,11.
Grief occasioned by the failure of the fruits of. Joel 1:11; Amos 5:16,17.
Produce of, exported. 1 Kin 5:11; Ezek 27:17.
Operations in
 Hedging. Is 5:2,5; Hos 2:6.
 Ploughing. Job 1:14.
 Digging. Is 5:6; Luke 13:8; 16:3.
 Manuring. Is 25:10; Luke 14:34,35.
 Harrowing. Job 39:10; Is 28:24.
 Gathering out the stones. Is 5:2.
 Sowing. Eccl 11:4; Is 32:20; Matt 13:3.
 Planting. Prov 31:16; Is 44:14; Jer 31:5.
 Watering. Deut 11:10; 1 Cor 3:6-8.
 Weeding. Matt 13:28.
 Grafting. Rom 11:17-19,24.
 Pruning. Lev 25:3; Is 5:6; John 15:2.
 Mowing. Ps 129:7; Amos 7:1.
 Reaping. Is 17:5.
 Binding. Gen 37:7; Matt 13:30.
 Gleaning. Lev 19:9; Ruth 2:3.
 Stacking. Ex 22:6.
 Threshing. Deut 25:4; Judg 6:11.
 Winnowing. Ruth 3:2; Matt 3:12.
 Storing in barns. Matt 6:26; 13:30.
Beasts used in
 The ox. Deut 25:4.
 The ass. Deut 22:10.
 The horse. Is 28:28.
Implements of
 The plough. 1 Sam 13:20.
 The harrow. 2 Sam 12:31.
 The mattock. 1 Sam 13:20; Is 7:25.
 The sickle. Deut 16:9; 23:25.
 The pruning-hook. Is 18:5; Joel 3:10.
 The fork. 1 Sam 13:21.
 The axe. 1 Sam 13:20.
 The teethed threshing instrument. Is 41:15.
 The flail, etc. Is 28:27.
 The cart. 1 Sam 6:7; Is 28:27,28.
 The shovel. Is 30:24.
 The sieve. Amos 9:9.
 The fan. Is 30:24; Matt 3:12.
Illustrative of
 Culture of the Church. 1 Cor 3:9.
 Culture of the heart. Jer 4:3; Hos 10:12.

Alliance and Society With the Enemies of God.

Forbidden. Ex 23:32; 34:12; Deut 7:2,3; 13:6,8; Josh 23:6,7; Judg 2:2; Ezra 9:12; Prov 1:10,15; 2 Cor 6:14-17; Eph 5:11.
Lead to idolatry. Ex 34:15,16; Num 25:1-8; Deut 7:4; Judg 3:5-7; Rev 2:20.
Have led to murder and human sacrifice. Ps 106:37,38.
Provoke the anger of God. Deut 7:4; 31:16,17; 2 Chr 19:2; Ezra 9:13,14; Ps 106:29,40; Is 2:6.
Provoke God to leave mean to reap the fruits of them. Josh 23:12,13; Judg 2:1-3.
Are ensnaring. Ex 23:33; Num 25:18; Deut 12:30; 13:6; Ps 106:36.
Are enslaved. 2 Pet 2:18,19.
Are defiling. Ezra 9:1,2.
Are degrading. Is 1:23.
Are ruinous to spiritual interest. Prov 29:24; Heb 12:14,15; 2 Pet 3:17.
Are ruinous to moral character. 1 Cor 15:33.
Are a proof of folly. Prov 12:11.
Children who enter into, bring shame upon their parents. Prov 28:7.
Evil consequences of. Prov 28:19; Jer 51:7.
The wicked are prone to. Ps 50:18; Jer 2:25.
The wicked tempt saints to. Neh 6:2-4.
Sin of, to be confessed, deeply repented of, and forsaken. Ezra 10:1-44.
Involve saints in their guiltiness. 2 John 9-11; Rev 18:4.
Involve saints in their punishment. Num 16:26; Jer 51:6; Rev 18:4.
Unbecoming in those called saints. 2 Chr 19:2; 2 Cor 6:14-16; Phil 2:15.
Exhortations to shun all inducements to. Prov 1:10-15; 4:14,15; 2 Pet 3:17.
Exhortations to hate and avoid. Prov 14:7; Rom 16:17; 1 Cor 5:9-11; Eph 5:6,7; 1 Tim 6:5; 2 Tim 3:5.
A call to come out from. Num 16:26; Ezra 10:11; Jer 51:6,45; 2 Cor 6:17; 2 Thess 3:6; Rev 18:4.
Means of preservation from. Prov 2:10-20; 19:27.
Blessedness of avoiding. Ps 1:1.
Blessedness of forsaking. Ezra 9:12; Prov 9:6; 2 Cor 6:17,18.
Saints grieve to meet with, in their intercourse with the world. Ps 57:4; 120:5,6; 2 Pet 2:7,8.
Saints grieve to witness in their brethren. Gen 26:35; Ezra 9:3; 10:6.
Saints hate and avoid. Ps 26:4,5; 31:6; 101:7; Rev 2:2.
Saints deprecate. Gen 49:6; Ps 6:8; 15:4; 101:4,7; 119:115; 139:19.
Saints are separate from. Ex 33:16; Ezra 6:21.
Saints should be circumspect when unintentionally thrown into. Matt 10:16; Col 4:5; 1 Pet 2:12.
Pious parents prohibit, to their children. Gen 28:1.
Persons in authority should denounce. Ezra 10:9-11; Neh 13:23-27.
Punishment of. Num 33:56; Deut 7:4; Josh 23:13; Judg 2:3; 3:5-8; Ezra 9:7,14; Ps 106:41,42; Rev 2:16,22,23.
Exemplified
 Solomon. 1 Kin 11:1-8.
 Rehoboam. 1 Kin 12:8,9.
 Jehoshaphat. 2 Chr 18:3; 19:2; 20:35-37.
 Jehoram. 2 Chr 21:6.
 Ahaziah. 2 Chr 22:3-5.
 Israelites. Ezra 9:1,2.
 Israel. Ezek 44:7.
 Judas Iscariot. Matt 26:14-16.
Examples of avoiding
 Man of God. 1 Kin 13:7-10.
 Nehemiah, etc. Neh 6:2-4; 10:29-31.
 David. Ps 101:4-7; 119:115.
 Jeremiah. Jer 15:17.
 Joseph of Arimathaea. Luke 23:51.
 Church of Ephesus. Rev 2:6.
Examples of forsaking
 Israelites. Num 16:27; Ezra 6:21,22; 10:3,4,16,17.
 Sons of the priests. Ezra 10:18,19.
Examples of the judgments of God against
 Korah, etc. Num 16:32.
 Ahaziah. 2 Chr 22:7,8.
 Judas Iscariot. Acts 1:18.

Altars.

Designed for sacrifice. Ex 20:24.
To be made of earth, or unhewn stone. Ex 20:24,25; Deut 27:5,6.
Of brick, hateful to God. Is 65:3.
Natural rocks sometimes used as. Judg 6:19-21; 13:19,20.
Were not to have steps up to them. Ex 20:26.

For idolatrous worship, often erected on roofs of houses. 2 Kin 23:12; Jer 19:13; 32:29.
Idolaters planted groves near. Judg 6:30; 1 Kin 16:32,33; 2 Kin 21:3.
The Jews not to plant groves near. Deut 16:21.
For idolatrous worship, to be destroyed. Ex 34:13; Deut 7:5.
Probable origin of inscriptions on. Deut 27:8.
Mentioned in Scripture
- Of Noah. Gen 8:20.
- Of Abraham. Gen 12:7,8; 13:18; 22:9.
- Of Isaac. Gen 26:25.
- Of Jacob. Gen 33:20; 35:1,3,7.
- Of Moses. Ex 17:15; 24:4.
- Of Balaam. Num 23:1,14,29.
- Of Joshua. Josh 8:30,31.
- Of the temple of Solomon. 2 Chr 4:1,19.
- Of the second temple. Ezra 3:2,3.
- Of Reubenites, etc. east of Jordan. Josh 22:10.
- Of Gideon. Judg 6:26,27.
- Of the people of Israel. Judg 21:4.
- Of Samuel. 1 Sam 7:17.
- Of David. 2 Sam 24:21,25.
- Of Jeroboam at Bethel. 1 Kin 12:33.
- Of Ahaz. 2 Kin 16:10-12.
- Of the Athenians. Acts 17:23.
- For burnt offering. Ex 27:1-8.
- For incense. Ex 30:1-6.

Protection afforded by. 1 Kin 1:50,51.
Afforded no protection to murderers. Ex 21:14; 1 Kin 2:18-34.

ALTAR OF BURNT OFFERING, THE.

Dimensions, etc. of. Ex 27:1; 38:1.
Horns on the corners of. Ex 27:2; 38:2.
Covered with brass. Ex 27:2.
All its vessels of brass. Ex 27:3; 38:3.
A net-working grate of brass placed in. Ex 27:4,5; 38:4.
Furnished with rings and staves. Ex 27:6,7; 38:5-7.
Made after a divine pattern. Ex 27:8.
Called
- The brazen altar. Ex 39:39; 1 Kin 8:64.
- The altar of God. Ps 43:4.
- The altar of the Lord. Mal 2:13.

Placed in the court before the door of the tabernacle. Ex 40:6,29.
Sanctified by God. Ex 29:44.
Anointed and sanctified with holy oil. Ex 40:10; Lev 8:10,11.
Cleansed and purified with blood. Ex 29:36,37.
Was most holy. Ex 40:10.
Sanctified whatever touched it. Ex 29:37.
All sacrifices to be offered on. Ex 29:38-42; Is 56:7.
All gifts to be presented at. Matt 5:23,24.
Nothing polluted or defective to be offered on. Lev 22:22; Mal 1:7,8.
Offering at the dedication of. Num 7:1-89.
The fire upon
- Came from before the Lord. Lev 9:24.
- Was continually burning. Lev 6:13.
- Consumed the sacrifices. Lev 1:8,9.

Sacrifices bound to the horns of. Ps 118:27.
The blood of sacrifices put on the horns and poured at the foot of. Ex 29:12; Lev 4:7,18,25; 8:15.
The priests
- Alone to serve. Num 18:3,7.
- Derived support from. 1 Cor 9:13.

Ahaz removed and profaned. 2 Kin 16:10-16.
The Jews condemned for swearing lightly by. Matt 23:18,19.
A type of Christ. Heb 13:10.

ALTAR OF INCENSE.

Dimensions, etc. of. Ex 30:1,2; 37:25.
Covered with gold. Ex 30:3; 37:26.
Top of, surrounded with a crown of gold. Ex 30:3; 37:26.
Had four rings of gold under the crown for the staves. Ex 30:4; 37:27.
Staves of, covered with gold. Ex 30:5.
Called the golden altar. Ex 39:38.
Placed before the vail in the outer sanctuary. Ex 30:6; 40:5,26.
Said to be before the Lord. Lev 4:7; 1 Kin 9:25.
Anointed with holy oil. Ex 30:26,27.
The priest burned incense on every morning and evening. Ex 30:7,8.
No strange incense nor any sacrifice to be offered on. Ex 30:9.
Atonement made for, by the high priest once every year. Ex 30:10; Lev 16:18,19.
The blood of all sin offerings put on the horns of. Lev 4:7,18.
Punishment for
- Offering strange fire on. Lev 10:1,2.
- Unauthorised offering on. 2 Chr 26:16-19.

Covered by the priest before removal from the sanctuary. Num 4:11.
A type of Christ. Rev 8:3; 9:3.

AMALEKITES, THE.

Descent of. Gen 36:12,16.
Character of
- Wicked. 1 Sam 15:18.
- Oppressive. Judg 10:12.
- Warlike and cruel. 1 Sam 15:33.

Governed by Kings. 1 Sam 15:20,32.
A powerful and influential nation. Num 24:7.
Possessed cities. 1 Sam 15:5.
Country of
- In the south of Canaan. Num 13:29; 1 Sam 27:8.
- Extended from Havilah to Shur. 1 Sam 15:7.
- Was the scene of ancient warfare. Gen 14:7.

Part of the Kenites dwelt amongst. 1 Sam 15:6.
Were the first to oppose Israel. Ex 17:8.
Discomfited at Rephidim through the intercession of Moses. Ex 17:9-13.
Doomed to utter destruction for opposing Israel. Ex 17:14,16; Deut 25:19.
Their utter destruction foretold. Num 24:20.
Presumption of Israel punished by. Num 14:45.
United with Eglon against Israel. Judg 3:13.
Part of their possessions taken by Ephraim. Judg 5:14; 12:15.
With Midian, oppressed Israel. Judg 6:3-5.
Overcome by Gideon. Judg 6:33,34; 7:21,22.
Saul
- Overcame, and delivered Israel. 1 Sam 14:48.
- Commissioned to destroy. 1 Sam 15:1-3.
- Massacred. 1 Sam 15:4-8.
- Condemned for not utterly destroying. 1 Sam 15:9-26; 28:18.

Agag, king of, slain by Samuel. 1 Sam 15:32,33.
Invaded by David. 1 Sam 27:8,9.
Pillaged and burned Ziklag. 1 Sam 30:1,2.
Pursued and slain by David. 1 Sam 30:10-20.
Spoil taken from, consecrated. 2 Sam 8:11,12.
Confederated against Israel. Ps 83:7.
Remnant of, completely destroyed during the reign of Hezekiah. 1 Chr 4:41-43.

AMBITION.

God condemns. Gen 11:7; Is 5:8.
Christ condemns. Matt 18:1,3,4; 20:25,26; 23:11,12.
Saints avoid. Ps 131:1,2.
Vanity of. Job 20:5-9; 24:24; Ps 49:11-20.
Leads to strife and contention. James 4:1,2.
Punishment of. Prov 17:19; Is 14:12-15; Ezek 31:10,11; Obad 3,4.
Connected with
- Pride. Hab 2:5.
- Covetousness. Hab 2:8,9.
- Cruelty. Hab 2:12.

Exemplified
- Adam and Eve. Gen 3:5,6.
- Builders of Babel. Gen 11:4.
- Miriam and Aaron. Num 12:2.
- Korah, etc. Num 16:3.
- Absalom. 2 Sam 15:4; 18:18.
- Adonijah. 1 Kin 1:5.
- Sennacherib. 2 Kin 19:23.
- Shebna. Is 22:16.
- Sons of Zebedee. Matt 20:21.
- Antichrist. 2 Thess 2:4.
- Diotrephes. 3 John 9.

AMMONITES, THE.

Descent of. Gen 19:38.
Called the
- Children of Lot. Deut 2:19.
- Children of Ammon. Jer 25:21.

Governed by hereditary kings. 2 Sam 10:1.
Country of
- Belonged to the Zamzummims. Deut 2:20,21.
- Bordered on the Amorites. Num 21:24.
- Was fertile. Jer 49:4.
- Well fortified. Num 21:24.
- Half of, given to the Gadites. Josh 13:25.

Character of
- Cruel and covetous. Amos 1:13.
- Proud and reproachful. Zeph 2:10.

Vindictive. Ezek 25:3,6.
Fond of ornaments. 2 Chr 20:25.
Idolatrous. Judg 10:6; 1 Kin 11:7,33; 2 Kin 23:13.
Superstitious. Jer 27:3,9.
Chief cities of
Rabbah. 2 Sam 12:26,27; Jer 49:3.
Ai. Jer 49:3.
Jewish laws respecting
Perpetual exclusion from the congregation. Deut 23:3; Neh 13:1.
No covenant to be made with. Deut 23:6.
Not to be distressed. Deut 2:19; 2 Chr 20:10.
Assisted Eglon against Israel. Judg 3:12,13.
With the Philistines oppressed Israel for eighteen years. Judg 10:6-9.
Jephthah raised up to deliver Israel from. Judg 10:15-18; 11:4-33.
Proposed a disgraceful treaty to Jabesh-gilead. 1 Sam 11:1-3.
Saul's victories over. 1 Sam 11:11; 14:47.
Ill-treated David's ambassadors. 2 Sam 10:1-4.
Hired the Syrians against David. 2 Sam 10:6.
Victories of Joab over. 2 Sam 10:7-14; 12:26-29.
The royal treasure of, taken. 2 Sam 12:30.
Of Rabbah reduced to hard bondage. 2 Sam 12:31.
Spoil of, consecrated to God. 2 Sam 8:11,12.
One of David's mighty men was of. 2 Sam 23:37.
Solomon intermarried with, and introduced idols of into Israel. 1 Kin 11:1-5.
Confederated against Jehoshaphat. 2 Chr 20:1; Ps 83:7.
Miraculous defeat of. 2 Chr 20:5-24.
Submitted to Uzziah. 2 Chr 26:8.
Defeated by Jotham. 2 Chr 27:5.
Seized upon the possessions of Gad. Jer 49:1.
Aided the Chaldeans against Judah. 2 Kin 24:2.
Vexed the Jews after captivity. Neh 4:3,7,8.
The Jews reprobated for intermarrying with. Ezra 9:1-3; Neh 13:23-28.
Predictions respecting
Subjection to Babylon. Jer 25:9-21; 27:3,6.
Destructions for hatred to Israel. Ezek 25:2-10; Zeph 2:8,9.
Punishment for oppressive cruelty. Jer 49:1-5; Amos 1:13-15.
Restoration. Jer 49:6.
Subjection to the Jews. Is 11:14.

Amorites, The.

Descent of. Gen 10:15,16; 1 Chr 1:13,14.
One of the seven nations of Canaan. Gen 15:21; Ex 3:8,17.
Governed by many independent kings. Josh 5:1; 9:10.
Kings of, great and powerful. Ps 136:18,20.
Originally inhabited a mountain district in the south. Num 13:29; Deut 1:7,20; Judg 1:36.
Acquired an extensive territory from Moab east of Jordan. Num 21:26,30.
Had many and strong cities. Num 32:17,33.
Of gigantic strength and stature. Amos 2:9.
Character of
Profane and wicked. Gen 15:16.
Idolatrous. Josh 24:15.
Defeated by Chedorlaomer, etc. Gen 14:7.
Joined Abraham against the kings. Gen 14:13,24.
Jacob took a portion from. Gen 48:22.
Forbearance of God towards. Gen 15:16.
Doomed to utter destruction. Deut 20:17,18.
Refused a passage to Israel. Num 21:21-23; Deut 2:30.
Deprived of their eastern territory by Israel. Num 21:24-35.
Land of, given to Reubenites, etc. Josh 13:15-31.
Western kings of, confederated against Israel. Josh 10:1-5.
Miraculous overthrow of. Josh 10:11-14.
Kings of, degraded and slain. Josh 10:24-27.
The Gibeonites a tribe of, deceived Israel into a league. 2 Sam 21:2, Josh 9:3-16.
The Israelites unable to expel, but extracted tribute from. Judg 1:34,35.
Had peace with Israel in the days of Samuel. 1 Sam 7:14.
Brought into bondage by Solomon. 1 Kin 9:20,21.
Ahab followed the abominations of. 1 Kin 21:26.
Manasseh exceeded abominations of. 2 Kin 21:11.
The Jews after the captivity condemned for intermarrying with. Ezra 9:1,2.
Descent from, illustrative of man's natural state. Ezek 16:3.

Amusements and Pleasures, Worldly.

Belong to the works of the flesh. Gal 5:19,21.
Are transitory. Job 21:12,13; Heb 11:25.
Are all vanity. Eccl 2:11.
Choke the word of God in the heart. Luke 8:14.
Formed a part of idolatrous worship. Ex 32:4,6,19; 1 Cor 10:7; Judg 16:23-25.
Lead to
Rejection of God. Job 21:14,15.
Poverty. Prov 21:17.
Disregard of the judgments and works of God. Is 5:12; Amos 6:1-6.
Terminate in sorrow. Prov 14:13.
Are likely to lead to greater evil. Job 1:5; Matt 14:6-8.
The wicked seek for happiness in. Eccl 2:1,8.
Indulgence in
A proof of folly. Eccl 7:4.
A characteristic of the wicked. Is 47:8; Eph 4:17,19; 2 Tim 3:4; Titus 3:3; 1 Pet 4:3.
A proof of spiritual death. 1 Tim 5:6.
An abuse of riches. James 5:1,5.
Wisdom of abstaining from. Eccl 7:2,3.
Shunned by the saints. 1 Pet 4:3.
Abstinence from, seems strange to the wicked. 1 Pet 4:4.
Denounced by God. Is 5:11,12.
Punishment of. Eccl 11:9; 2 Pet 2:13.
Renunciation of, Exemplified
Moses. Heb 11:25.

Anakim, The.

Descent of. Num 13:22; Josh 15:13.
Were called
The sons of Anak. Num 13:33.
The sons of the Anakim. Deut 1:28.
The children of the Anakims. Deut 9:2.
Divided into three tribes. Josh 15:14.
Inhabited the mountains of Judah. Josh 11:21.
Hebron, chief city of. Josh 14:15; 21:11.
Of gigantic strength and stature. Deut 2:10,11,21.
Israel terrified by. Num 14:1; 13:33.
Hebron a possession of, given to Caleb for his faithfulness. Josh 14:6-14.
Driven from Hebron by Caleb. Josh 15:13,14.
Driven from Kirjathsepher or Debir by Othniel. Josh 15:15-17; Judg 1:12,13.
Almost annihilated. Josh 11:21,22.

Angels.

Created by God and Christ. Neh 9:6; Col 1:16.
Worship God and Christ. Neh 9:6; Phil 2:9-11; Heb 1:6.
Are ministering spirits. 1 Kin 19:5; Ps 68:17; 104:4; Luke 16:22; Acts 12:7-11; 27:23; Heb 1:7,14.
Communicate the will of God and Christ. Dan 8:16,17; 9:21-23; 10:11; 12:6,7; Matt 2:13,20; Luke 1:19,28; Acts 5:20; 8:26; 10:5; 27:23; Rev 1:1.
Obey the will of God. Ps 103:20; Matt 6:10.
Execute the purposes of God. Num 22:22; Ps 103:21; Matt 13:39-42; 28:2; John 5:4; Rev 5:2.
Execute the judgments of God. 2 Sam 24:16; 2 Kin 19:35; Ps 35:5,6; Acts 12:23; Rev 16:1.
Celebrate the praises of God. Job 38:7; Ps 148:2; Is 6:3; Luke 2:13,14; Rev 5:11,12; 7:11,12.
The law given by the ministration of. Ps 68:17; Acts 7:53; Heb 2:2.
Announced
The conception of Christ. Matt 1:20,21; Luke 1:31.
The birth of Christ. Luke 2:10-12.
The resurrection of Christ. Matt 28:5-7; Luke 24:23.
The ascension and second coming of Christ. Acts 1:11.
The conception of John the Baptist. Luke 1:13,36.
Minister to Christ. Matt 4:11; Luke 22:43; John 1:51.
Are subject to Christ. Eph 1:21; Col 1:16; 2:10; 1 Pet 3:22.
Shall execute the purposes of Christ. Matt 13:41; 24:31.
Shall attend Christ at his second coming. Matt 16:27; 25:31; Mark 8:38; 2 Thess 1:7.

Know and delight in the gospel of Christ. Eph 3:9,10; 1 Tim 3:16; 1 Pet 1:12.
Ministration of, obtained by prayer. Matt 26:53; Acts 12:5,7.
Rejoice over every repentant sinner. Luke 15:7,10.
Have charge over the children of God. Ps 34:7; 91:11,12; Dan 6:22; Matt 18:10.
Are of different orders. Is 6:2; 1 Thess 4:16; 1 Pet 3:22; Jude 1:9; Rev 12:7.
Not to be worshipped. Col 2:18; Rev 19:10; 22:9.
Are examples of meekness. 2 Pet 2:11; Jude 1:9.
Are wise. 2 Sam 14:20.
Are mighty. Ps 103:20.
Are holy. Matt 25:31.
Are elect. 1 Tim 5:21.
Are innumerable. Job 25:3; Heb 12:22.

ANGER.

Forbidden. Eccl 7:9; Matt 5:22; Rom 12:19.
A work of the flesh. Gal 5:20.
A characteristic of fools. Prov 12:16; 14:29; 27:3; Eccl 7:9.
Connected with
 Pride. Prov 21:24.
 Cruelty. Gen 49:7; Prov 27:3,4.
 Clamour and evil-speaking. Eph 4:31.
 Malice and blasphemy. Col 3:8.
 Strife and contention. Prov 21:19; 29:22; 30:33.
Brings its own punishment. Job 5:2; Prov 19:19; 25:28.
Grievous words stir up. Judg 12:4; 2 Sam 19:43; Prov 15:1.
Should not betray us into sin. Ps 37:8; Eph 4:26.
In prayer be free from. 1 Tim 2:8.
May be averted by wisdom. Prov 29:8.
Meekness pacifies. Prov 15:1; Eccl 10:4.
Children should not be provoked to. Eph 6:4; Col 3:21.
Be slow to. Prov 15:18; 16:32; 19:11; Titus 1:7; James 1:19.
Avoid those given to. Gen 49:6; Prov 22:24.
Justifiable—Exemplified
 Our Lord. Mark 3:5.
 Jacob. Gen 31:36.
 Moses. Ex 11:8; 32:19; Lev 10:16; Num 16:15.
 Nehemiah. Neh 5:6; 13:17,25.
Sinful—Exemplified
 Cain. Gen 4:5,6.
 Esau. Gen 27:45.
 Simeon and Levi. Gen 49:5-7.
 Moses. Num 20:10,11.
 Balaam. Num 22:27.
 Saul. 1 Sam 20:30.
 Ahab. 1 Kin 21:4.
 Naaman. 2 Kin 5:11.
 Asa. 2 Chr 16:10.
 Uzziah. 2 Chr 26:19.
 Haman. Esth 3:5.
 Nebuchadnezzar. Dan 3:13.
 Jonah. Jon 4:4.
 Herod. Matt 2:16.
 Jews. Luke 4:28.
 High Priest, etc. Acts 5:17; 7:54.

ANGER OF GOD, THE.

Averted by Christ. Luke 2:11,14; Rom 5:9; 2 Cor 5:18,19; Eph 2:14,17; Col 1:20; 1 Thess 1:10.
Is averted from them that believe. John 3:14-18; Rom 3:25; 5:1.
Is averted upon confession of sin and repentance. Job 33:27,28; Ps 106:43-45; Jer 3:12,13; 18:7,8; 31:18-20; Joel 2:12-14; Luke 15:18-20.
Is slow. Ps 103:8; Is 48:9; Jon 4:2; Nah 1:3.
Is righteous. Ps 58:10,11; Lam 1:18; Rom 2:6,8; 3:5,6; Rev 16:6,7.
The justice of, not to be questioned. Rom 9:18,20,22.
Manifested in terrors. Ex 14:24; Ps 76:6-8; Jer 10:10; Lam 2:20-22.
Manifested in judgments and afflictions. Job 21:17; Ps 78:49-51; 90:7; Is 9:19; Jer 7:20; Ezek 7:19; Heb 3:17.
Cannot be resisted. Job 9:13; 14:13; Ps 76:7; Nah 1:6.
Aggravated by continual provocation. Num 32:14.
Specially reserved for the day of wrath. Zeph 1:14-18; Matt 25:41; Rom 2:5,8; 2 Thess 1:8; Rev 6:17; 11:18; 19:15.
Against
 The wicked. Ps 7:11; 21:8,9; Is 3:8; 13:9; Nah 1:2,3; Rom 1:18; 2:8; Eph 5:6; Col 3:6.
 Those who forsake him. Ezra 8:22; Is 1:4.
 Unbelief. Ps 78:21,22; Heb 3:18,19; John 3:36.
 Impenitence. Ps 7:12; Prov 1:30,31; Is 9:13,14; Rom 2:5.
 Apostasy. Heb 10:26,27.
 Idolatry. Deut 29:20,27,28; 32:19,20,22; Josh 23:16; 2 Kin 22:17; Ps 78:58,59; Jer 44:3.
 Sin, in saints. Ps 89:30-32; 90:7-9; 99:8; 102:9,10; Is 47:6.
Extreme, against those who oppose the gospel. Ps 2:2,3,5; 1 Thess 2:16.
Folly of provoking. Jer 7:19; 1 Cor 10:22.
To be dreaded. Ps 2:12; 76:7; 90:11; Matt 10:28.
To be deprecated. Ex 32:11; Ps 6:1; 38:1; 74:1,2; Is 64:9.
Removal of, should be prayed for. Ps 39:10; 79:5; 80:4; Dan 9:16; Hab 3:2.
Tempered with mercy to saints. Ps 30:5; Is 26:20; 54:8; 57:15,16; Jer 30:11; Mic 7:11.
To be born with submission. 2 Sam 24:17; Lam 3:39,43; Mic 7:9.
Should lead to repentance. Is 42:24,25; Jer 4:8.
Exemplified against
 The old world. Gen 7:21-23.
 Builders of Babel. Gen 11:8.
 Cities of the plain. Gen 19:24,25.
 Egyptians. Ex 7:20; 8:6,16,24; 9:3,9,23; 10:13,22; 12:29; 14:27.
 Israelites. Ex 32:35; Num 11:1,33; 14:40-45; 21:6; 25:9; 2 Sam 24:1,15.
 Enemies of Israel. 1 Sam 5:6; 7:10.
 Nadab, etc. Lev 10:2.
 The spies. Num 14:37.
 Korah, etc. Num 16:31,35.
 Aaron and Miriam. Num 12:9,10.
 Five kings. Josh 10:25.
 Abimelech. Judg 9:56.
 Men of Bethshemesh. 1 Sam 6:19.
 Saul. 1 Sam 31:6.
 Uzzah. 2 Sam 6:7.
 Saul's family. 2 Sam 21:1.
 Sennacherib. 2 Kin 19:28,35,37.

ANOINTING.

With oil. Ps 92:10.
With ointment. John 11:2.
Was used for
 Decorating the person. Ruth 3:3.
 Refreshing the body. 2 Chr 28:15.
 Purifying the body. Esth 2:12; Is 57:9.
 Curing the sick. Mark 6:13; James 5:14.
 Healing wounds. Is 1:6; Luke 10:34.
 Preparing weapons for war. Is 21:5.
 Preparing the dead for burial. Matt 26:12; Mark 16:1; Luke 23:56.
 The Jews were very fond of. Prov 27:9; Amos 6:6.
Was applied to
 The head. Ps 23:5; Eccl 9:8.
 The face. Ps 104:15.
 The feet. Luke 7:38,39; John 12:3.
 The eyes. Rev 3:18.
Ointment for
 Richly perfumed. Song 4:10; John 12:3.
 Most expensive. 2 Kin 20:13; Amos 6:6; John 12:3,5.
 Prepared by the apothecary. Eccl 10:1.
 An article of commerce. Ezek 27:17; Rev 18:13.
 Neglected in times of affliction. 2 Sam 12:20; 14:2; Dan 10:3.
Neglect of, to guests, a mark of disrespect. Luke 7:46.
A token of joy. Eccl 9:7,8.
Deprivation of, threatened as a punishment. Deut 28:40; Mic 6:15.
Why recommended by Christ in times of fasting. Matt 6:17,18.

ANOINTING OF THE HOLY SPIRIT.

Is from God. 2 Cor 1:21.
That christ should receive
 Foretold. Ps 45:7; Is 61:1; Dan 9:24.
 Fulfilled. Luke 4:18,21; Acts 4:27; 10:38; Heb 1:9.
God preserves those who receive. Ps 18:50; 20:6; 89:20-23.
Saints receive. Is 61:3; 1 John 2:20.
Is abiding in saints. 1 John 2:27.
Guides into all truth. 1 John 2:27.
Typified. Ex 40:13-15; Lev 8:12; 1 Sam 16:13; 1 Kin 19:16.

ANOINTING, SACRED.

Antiquity of. Gen 28:18; 35:14.
Consecrates to God's service. Ex 30:29.
Persons who received
 Prophets. 1 Kin 19:16; Is 61:1.
 Priests. Ex 40:13-15.
 Kings. Judg 9:8; 1 Sam 9:16; 1 Kin 1:34.
Things which received
 Tabernacle, etc. Ex 30:26,27; 40:9.
 Brazen altar. Ex 29:36; 40:10.
 Brazen laver. Ex 40:11.
Those who partook of
 Protected by God. 1 Chr 16:22; Ps 105:15.

Not to be injured or insulted. 1 Sam 24:6; 26:9; 2 Sam 1:14,15; 19:21.

Oil or ointment for

Divinely prescribed. Ex 30:23-25.

Compounded by the priests. 1 Chr 9:30.

An holy anointing oil for ever. Ex 30:25,31.

Not to be imitated. Ex 30:32.

To be put on no stranger. Ex 30:33.

Jews condemned for imitating. Ezek 23:41.

Illustrative of the anointing

Of Christ with the Holy Spirit. Ps 45:7; Is 61:1; Luke 4:18.

Of saints with the Holy Spirit. 1 John 2:27.

Antichrist.

Denies the Father and the Son. 1 John 2:22.

Denies the incarnation of Christ. 1 John 4:3; 2 John 7.

Spirit of, prevalent in apostolic times. 1 John 2:18.

Deceit, a characteristic of. 2 John 7.

Apostates.

Described. Deut 13:13; Heb 3:12.

Persecution tends to make. Matt 24:9,10; Luke 8:13.

A worldly spirit tends to make. 2 Tim 4:10.

Never belonged to Christ. 1 John 2:19.

Saints do not become. Ps 44:18,19; Heb 6:9; 10:39.

It is impossible to restore. Heb 6:4-6.

Guilt and punishment of. Zeph 1:4-6; Heb 10:25-31,39; 2 Pet 2:17,20-22.

Cautions against becoming. Heb 3:12; 2 Pet 3:17.

Shall abound in the latter days. Matt 24:12; 2 Thess 2:3; 1 Tim 4:1-3.

Exemplified

Amaziah. 2 Chr 25:14,27.

Professed disciples. John 6:66.

Hymenaeus and Alexander. 1 Tim 1:19,20.

Apostles, The.

Christ pre-eminently called "The Apostle." Heb 3:1.

Ordained by Christ. Mark 3:14; John 15:16.

Received their title from Christ. Luke 6:13.

Called by

God. 1 Cor 1:1; 12:28; Gal 1:1,15,16.

Christ. Matt 10:1; Mark 3:13; Acts 20:24; Rom 1:5.

The Holy Spirit. Acts 20:24; Rom 1:5.

Were unlearned men. Acts 4:13.

Selected from obscure stations. Matt 4:18.

Sent first to the house of Israel. Matt 10:5,6; Luke 24:47; Acts 13:46.

Sent to preach the gospel to all nations. Matt 28:19,20; Mark 16:15; 2 Tim 1:11.

Christ always present with. Matt 28:20.

Warned against a timid profession of Christ. Matt 10:27-33.

The Holy Spirit given to. John 20:22; Acts 2:1-4; 9:17.

Guided by the Spirit into all truth. John 14:26; 15:26; 16:13.

Instructed by the Spirit to answer adversaries. Matt 10:19,20; Luke 12:11,12.

Specially devoted to the office of the ministry. Acts 6:4; 20:27.

Humility urged upon. Matt 20:26,27; Mark 9:33-37; Luke 22:24-30.

Self-denial urged upon. Matt 10:37-39.

Mutual love urged upon. John 15:17.

Equal authority given to each of. Matt 16:19; 18:18; 2 Cor 11:5.

Were not of the world. John 15:19; 17:16.

Were hated by the world. Matt 10:22; 24:9; John 15:18.

Persecutions and sufferings of. Matt 10:16,18; Luke 21:16; John 15:20; 16:2.

Saw Christ in the flesh. Luke 1:2; Acts 1:22; 1 Cor 9:1; 1 John 1:1.

Witnesses of the resurrection and ascension of Christ. Luke 24:33-41,51; Acts 1:2-9; 10:40,41; 1 Cor 15:8.

Empowered to work miracles. Matt 10:1,8; Mark 16:20; Luke 9:1; Acts 2:43.

Ark of the Covenant.

Dimensions, etc. of. Ex 25:10; 37:1.

Entirely covered with gold. Ex 25:11; 37:2.

Surrounded with a crown of gold. Ex 25:11.

Furnished with rings and staves. Ex 25:12-15; 37:3-5.

Tables of testimony alone placed in. Ex 25:16,21; 1 Kin 8:9,21; 2 Chr 5:10; Heb 9:4.

Mercy-seat laid upon. Ex 25:21; 26:34.

Placed in the Holy of Holies. Ex 26:33; 40:21; Heb 9:3,4.

The pot of manna and Aaron's rod laid up before. Heb 9:4; Ex 16:33,34; Num 17:10.

A copy of the law laid in the side of. Deut 31:26.

Anointed with sacred oil. Ex 30:26.

Covered with the vail by the priests before removal. Num 4:5,6.

Was called the

Ark of God. 1 Sam 3:3.

Ark of God's strength. 2 Chr 6:41; Ps 132:8.

Ark of the covenant of the Lord. Num 10:33.

Ark of the testimony. Ex 30:6; Num 7:89.

A symbol of the presence and glory of God. Num 14:43,44; Josh 1:6; 1 Sam 14:18,19; Ps 132:8.

Esteemed the glory of Israel. 1 Sam 4:21,22.

Was holy. 2 Chr 35:3.

Sanctified its resting place. 2 Chr 8:11.

The Israelites enquired of the Lord before. Josh 7:6-9; Judg 20:27; 1 Chr 13:3.

Was carried

By priests of Levites alone. Deut 10:8; Josh 3:14; 2 Sam 15:24; 1 Chr 15:2.

Before the Israelites in their journeys. Num 10:33; Josh 3:6.

Sometimes to the camp in war. 1 Sam 4:4,5.

Profanation of, punished. Num 4:5,15; 1 Sam 6:19; 1 Chr 15:13.

Protecting of, rewarded. 1 Chr 13:14.

Captured by the Philistines. 1 Sam 4:11.

Miracles connected with

Jordan divided. Josh 4:7.

Fall of the walls of Jericho. Josh 6:6-20.

Fall of Dagon. 1 Sam 5:1-4.

Philistines plagued. 1 Sam 5:6-12.

Manner of its restoration. 1 Sam 6:1-18.

At Kirjath-jearim twenty years. 1 Sam 7:1,2.

Removed from Kirjath-jearim to the house of Obed-edom. 2 Sam 6:1-11.

David made a tent for. 2 Sam 6:17; 1 Chr 15:1.

Brought into the city of David. 2 Sam 6:12-15; 1 Chr 15:25-28.

Brought by Solomon into the temple with great solemnity. 1 Kin 8:1-6; 2 Chr 5:2-9.

A type of Christ. Ps 40:8; Rev 11:19.

Armies.

Antiquity of. Gen 14:1-8.

Ancient, often numerous. Josh 11:4; 1 Sam 13:5.

Of different nations often confederated. Josh 9:2; 10:5; Judg 3:13; 1 Kin 20:1.

Troops often hired for. 1 Chr 19:7; 2 Chr 25:6.

Were composed of

Bowmen and slingers. 1 Chr 12:2; Jer 4:29.

Spearmen or heavy troops. Ps 68:30; Acts 23:23.

Cavalry. Ex 14:9; 1 Kin 20:20.

War chariots. Josh 17:16; Judg 4:3.

Often consisted of the whole effective strength of nations. Num 21:23; 1 Sam 29:1.

Furnished with standards. Song 6:4; Is 10:18; Jer 4:21.

Accompanied by beasts of burden and wagons for baggage. Judg 7:12; 2 Kin 7:7; Ezek 23:2.

Generally in three divisions. Gen 14:15; Job 1:17.

Were led by

Kings in person. 2 Kin 18:13; 25:1.

Experienced captains. 2 Kin 18:17,24.

Called the

Wings of a nation. Is 8:8; Jer 48:40.

Power of kings. 2 Chr 32:9.

Hosts. Josh 10:5; Judg 8:10.

Bands. 2 Kin 24:2; 1 Chr 7:4.

Began their campaigns in the spring. 2 Sam 11:1.

Often went on foreign service. Jer 5:15; 50:3.

Marched

Often in open line. Hab 1:6,8.

With order and precision. Is 5:27; Joel 2:7,8.

With rapidity. Jer 48:40; Hab 1:8.

With noise and tumult. Is 17:12,13; Joel 2:5.

Employed in

Fighting battles. 1 Sam 17:2,3; 1 Chr 19:17.

Besieging cities. Deut 20:12; Is 29:3.
Assaulting cities. Josh 7:3,4; Judg 9:45.
Often surprised their enemies. Josh 8:2; 2 Chr 13:15; Jer 51:12.
Commenced battles with a shout. 1 Sam 17:20; 2 Chr 13:15; Jer 51:14.
Toil and fatigue often endured by. Ezek 29:18.
Divided the spoil. Ex 15:9; Zech 14:1.
Sent out foraging parties. 2 Kin 5:2.
Exercised savage cruelties on the vanquished. Jer 50:42; Lam 5:11-13; Amos 1:13.
Frequently the instrument of God's vengeance. Is 13:5.
In latter ages received pay. Luke 3:14; 1 Cor 9:7.
Encamped
In the open fields. 2 Sam 11:11; 1 Chr 11:15.
Before cities. Josh 10:5; 1 Sam 11:1.
Fear occasioned by. Num 22:3; Jer 6:25.
Devastation occasioned by. Is 37:18; Jer 5:17.
Often destroyed by
Their enemies. Ex 17:13; Josh 10:10,20; Judg 11:33; 2 Sam 18:7; 1 Kin 20:21.
Themselves through divine intervention. Judg 7:22; 1 Sam 14:15,16; 2 Chr 20:23.
Supernatural means. Josh 10:11; 2 Kin 19:35.
Brought their idols with them. 1 Chr 14:12.
Compared to
Whirlwinds. Jer 25:32.
Waters of a river. Is 8:7.
Caterpillars. Jer 51:14,27.
Grasshoppers. Judg 6:3-5; 7:12.
Locusts. Is 33:4; Rev 9:3,7.
Flies. Is 7:18,19.
Clouds. Ezek 38:9-16.
Overflowing torrents. Is 28:2; Dan 11:10,26.
Illustrative of
Multitudes of angels. 1 Kin 22:19; Ps 148:2; Dan 4:35; Matt 26:53.
The Church. Dan 8:10-13; Song 6:4,10.
Numerous and heavy afflictions. Job 19:12.

ARMIES OF ISRAEL, THE.

First mention of. Ex 7:4.
Collected by
Sound of trumpets. Judg 3:27; 6:34.
Special messengers. Judg 6:35; 2 Sam 20:14.
Extraordinary means. Judg 19:29; 20:1; 1 Sam 11:7.
Enroled by the chief scribe. 2 Kin 25:19.
Called
The host. Deut 23:9; 1 Sam 28:19.
The armies of the living God. 1 Sam 17:26.
Composed of infantry. Num 11:21; Judg 5:15.
Horsemen and chariots introduced into, after David's reign. 1 Kin 1:5; 4:26.
Divided into
Three divisions. Judg 7:16; 1 Sam 11:11.
Van and rear. Josh 6:9.
Companies of thousands, etc. Num 31:14; 2 Kin 1:9,11; 1 Chr 13:1; 27:1.
Commanded by the captain of the host. 2 Sam 2:8; 17:25; 20:23.
Often led by the king in person. 1 Sam 8:20; 15:4,5; 2 Sam 12:29; 1 Kin 22:1-53.
Inferior officers of, appointed by
The chief officers. Deut 20:9.
The king. 2 Sam 18:1; 2 Chr 25:5.
The captain of the host. 2 Sam 18:11; 2 Kin 4:13.
Persons liable to serve in. Num 1:2,3.
Persons exempted from serving in
Who had built a house. Deut 20:5.
Who had planted a vineyard. Deut 20:6.
Who were lately betrothed. Deut 20:7.
Who were newly married. Deut 24:5.
Refusing to join, stigmatised. Judg 5:15-17.
Refusing to join, often punished. Judg 21:5,8-11; 1 Sam 11:7.
The fearful allowed to leave. Deut 20:8; Judg 7:3.
Sometimes consisted of the whole nation. Judg 20:11; 1 Sam 11:7.
Strict discipline observed in. Josh 7:16-21; 1 Sam 14:24-44.
Educated in the art of war. Is 2:4; Mic 4:3.
Often supplied with arms from public armouries. 2 Chr 11:12; 26:14.
Before going to war
Were numbered and reviewed. 2 Sam 18:1,2,4; 1 Kin 10:15,27.
Required to keep from iniquity. Deut 23:9.
Consulted the Lord. Judg 1:1; 20:27,28.
Encouraged by their commanders. 2 Chr 20:20.
Ark of God frequently brought with. Josh 6:6,7; 1 Sam 4:4,5; 2 Sam 11:11; 15:24.
Attended by priest with trumpets. Num 10:9; 31:6; 2 Chr 13:13,14.
Praises of God often sung before. 2 Chr 20:21,22.
Often disposed to battle with judgment, etc. 2 Sam 10:9.
Bravery and fidelity in, rewarded. Josh 15:16; 1 Sam 17:25; 18:17; 2 Sam 18:11; 1 Chr 11:6.
Men selected from, for difficult enterprises. Ex 17:9; Num 31:5,6; Josh 7:4; 8:3; Judg 7:5,6; 2 Sam 17:1.
Directed in their movements by God. Josh 8:1,2; Judg 1:2; 2 Sam 5:25; 1 Chr 14:16.
With the aid of God all-powerful. Lev 26:3,7,8; Deut 7:24; 32:30; Josh 1:5.
Without God easily overcome. Lev 26:17; Num 14:42,45.
Mode of supplying
Food brought by themselves. Josh 1:11.
Food sent by their families. 1 Sam 17:17.
Contribution levied. Judg 8:5; 1 Sam 25:4-8.
By presents. 2 Sam 17:27-29.
Congratulated on returning victorious. 1 Sam 18:6,7; Ex 15:1-21.
Purified on returning from war. Num 31:19-24.
Disbanded after war. 1 Sam 13:2; 1 Kin 22:36.
Part of, retained in times of peace by the kings. 1 Sam 13:1,2; 1 Chr 27:1-15.

ARMS, MILITARY.

Made of iron, steel, or brass. Job 20:24; 1 Sam 17:5,6.
Offensive
Sword. Judg 20:15; Ezek 32:27.
Two-edged sword. Ps 149:6; Prov 5:4.
Dagger. Judg 3:16,21,22.
Dart or javelin. 1 Sam 18:10,11; 2 Sam 18:14.
Spear or lance. 1 Sam 26:7; Jer 50:42.
Battle-axe. Ezek 26:9; Jer 51:20.
Bow and arrows. Gen 48:22; 1 Kin 22:34.
Sling. 1 Sam 17:50; 2 Kin 3:25.
Hand staff. Matt 26:47.
Called weapons of war. 2 Sam 1:27.
Called instruments of war. 1 Chr 12:33,37.
Called instruments of death. Ps 7:13.
Defensive
Helmet. 1 Sam 17:5,38; 2 Chr 26:14.
Coat of mail, breastplate, habergeon, or brigandine. 1 Sam 17:5,38; Ex 28:32; Jer 46:4; Rev 9:9.
Girdle. 1 Sam 18:4; 2 Sam 18:11.
Target. 1 Sam 17:6.
Greaves. 1 Sam 17:6.
Shield. 1 Kin 10:16,17; 14:26,27.
Buckler. 1 Chr 5:18; Ezek 26:8.
Called harness. 1 Kin 22:34.
Called armour. Luke 11:22.
For sieges
Battering rams. 2 Sam 20:15; Ezek 4:2.
Engines for casting stones, etc. 2 Chr 26:15.
Not worn in ordinary times. 1 Sam 21:8.
Put on at the first alarm. Is 8:9; Jer 46:3,4.
Armouries built for. 2 Kin 20:13; Song 4:4.
Great stores of, prepared. 2 Chr 32:5.
Were provided
By individuals themselves. 1 Chr 12:33,37.
From the public arsenals. 2 Chr 11:12; 26:14.
Often given as presents. 1 Kin 10:25.
Before using
Tried and proved. 1 Sam 17:39.
Burnished. Jer 46:4; Ezek 21:9-11,28.
Anointed. Is 21:5.
Part of, borne by armour-bearers. Judg 9:54; 1 Sam 14:1; 16:21.
Hung of the walls of cities. Ezek 27:10,11.
Of the vanquished
Taken off them. 2 Sam 2:21; Luke 11:22.
Sometimes kept as trophies. 1 Sam 17:54.
Sometime burned. Ezek 39:9,10.

Of conquered nations taken away to prevent rebellion. Judg 5:8; 1 Sam 13:19-22.
Inferior to wisdom. Eccl 9:18.
Illustrative of
Spiritual armour. Rom 13:12; 2 Cor 6:7; Eph 6:11-14; 1 Thess 5:8.
Spiritual weapons. 2 Cor 10:4; Eph 6:17.
Judgments of God. Is 13:5; Jer 50:25.

Arrows.

Deadly and destructive weapons. Prov 26:18.
Called shafts. Is 49:2.
Sharp. Ps 120:4; Is 5:28.
Bright and polished. Is 49:2; Jer 51:11.
Sometimes poisoned. Job 6:4.
Carried in a quiver. Gen 27:3; Is 49:2; Jer 5:16; Lam 3:13.
Discharged
From a bow. Ps 11:2; Is 7:24.
From engines. 2 Chr 26:15.
At a mark for amusement. 1 Sam 20:20-22.
At the beasts of the earth. Gen 27:3.
Against enemies. 2 Kin 19:32; Jer 50:14.
With great force. Num 24:8; 2 Kin 9:24.
Fleetness of, alluded to. Zech 9:14.
The ancients divined by. Ezek 21:21.
Illustrative
Of Christ. Is 49:2.
Of the word of Christ. Ps 45:5.
Of God's judgment. Deut 32:23-42; Ps 7:13; 21:12; 64:7; Ezek 5:16.
Of severe afflictions. Job 6:4; Ps 38:2.
Of bitter words. Ps 64:3.
Of slanderous tongues. Jer 9:8.
Of false witnesses. Prov 25:18.
Of devices of the wicked. Ps 11:2.
Of young children. Ps 127:5.
Of lightnings. Ps 77:17,18; Hab 3:11.
(Broken), of destruction of power. Ps 76:3.
(Falling from the hand), of the paralysing power. Ezek 39:3.

Arts of The.

Apothecary or perfumer. Ex 30:25,35.
Armourer. 1 Sam 8:12.
Baker. Gen 40:1; 1 Sam 8:13.
Brick-maker. Gen 11:3; Ex 5:7,8,18.
Brazier. Gen 4:22; 2 Tim 4:14.
Blacksmith. Gen 4:22; 1 Sam 13:19.
Carver. Ex 31:5; 1 Kin 6:18.
Carpenter. 2 Sam 5:11; Mark 6:3.
Calker. Ezek 27:9,27.
Confectioner. 1 Sam 8:13.
Dyer. Ex 25:5.
Embroiderer. Ex 35:35; 38:23.
Embalmer. Gen 50:2,3,26.
Engraver. Ex 28:11; Is 49:16; 2 Cor 3:7.
Founder. Judg 17:4; Jer 10:9.
Fuller. 2 Kin 18:17; Mark 9:3.
Gardener. Jer 29:5; John 20:15.
Goldsmith. Is 40:19.
Husbandman. Gen 4:2; 9:20.
Mariner, etc. Ezek 27:8,9.
Mason. 2 Sam 5:11; 2 Chr 24:12.
Musician. 1 Sam 18:6; 1 Chr 15:16.
Potter. Is 64:8; Jer 18:3; Lam 4:2; Zech 11:13.
Refiner of metals. 1 Chr 28:18; Mal 3:2,3.
Rope maker. Judg 16:11.
Silversmith. Acts 19:24.
Stone cutter. Ex 20:25; 1 Chr 22:15.
Ship builder. 1 Kin 9:26.
Smelter of metals. Job 28:2.
Spinner. Ex 35:25; Prov 31:19.
Tailor. Ex 28:3.
Tanner. Acts 9:43; 10:6.
Tent-maker. Gen 4:20; Acts 18:3.
Weaver. Ex 35:35; John 19:23.
Wine-maker. Neh 13:15; Is 63:3.
Writer. Judg 5:14.

Ascension of Christ, The.

Prophecies respecting. Ps 24:7; 68:18; Eph 4:7,8.
Foretold by himself. John 6:62; 7:33; 14:28; 16:5; 20:17.
Forty days after his resurrection. Acts 1:3.
Described. Acts 1:9.
From Mount Olivet. Luke 24:50; Mark 11:1; Acts 1:12.
While blessing his disciples. Luke 24:50.
When he had atoned for sin. Heb 9:12; 10:12.
Was triumphant. Ps 68:18.
Was to supreme power and dignity. Luke 24:26; Eph 1:20,21; 1 Pet 3:22.
As the forerunner of his people. Heb 6:20.
To intercede. Rom 8:34; Heb 9:24.
To send the Holy Spirit. John 16:7; Acts 2:33.
To receive gifts for men. Ps 68:18; Eph 4:8,11.
To prepare a place for his people. John 14:2.
His second coming shall be in like manner as. Acts 1:10,11.
Typified. Lev 16:15; Heb 6:20; 9:7,9,12.

Asher, the Tribe Of.

Descended from Jacob's eighth son. Gen 30:12,13.
Predictions concerning. Gen 49:20; Deut 33:24,25.
Strength of, on leaving Egypt. Num 1:40,41.
Persons selected from
To number the people. Num 1:13.
To spy out the land. Num 13:13.
To divide the land. Num 34:27.
The centre of the fourth division of Israel in its journeys. Num 10:25,26.
Encamped next to, and under the standard of Dan, north of the tabernacles. Num 2:25,27.
Offering of, at the dedication. Num 7:72-77.
Families of. Num 26:44-47.
Strength of on entering Canaan. Num 26:47.
On Ebal, said amen to the curses of the law. Deut 27:13.
Bounds of their inheritance. Josh 19:24-31.
Bordered on the sea. Josh 19:29; Judg 5:17.
Did not fully drive out Canaanites. Judg 1:31,32.
Reproved for not aiding against Sisera. Judg 5:17.
Assisted Gideon against the Midianites. Judg 6:35; 7:23.
Some of, at coronation of David. 1 Chr 12:36.
Officers place over, by Solomon. 1 Kin 4:16.
Aided in Hezekiah's reformation. 2 Chr 30:11.
Remarkable persons of. 1 Chr 7:30-40; Luke 2:36.

Asp, or Adder.

Dangerous to travellers. Gen 49:17.
Described as
Venomous. Job 20:14,16.
Not to be charmed. Ps 58:5.
Illustrative
Of obstinate rejecters of God's Word. Ps 58:4,5.
Of the enemies of God's people. Ps 91:13.
(Venom of), of the speech of the wicked. Ps 140:3; Rom 3:13.
(Venom of), of injurious effects of wine. Deut 32:33; Prov 23:32.
(Deprived of its venom), of the effects of conversion. Is 11:8,9.

Ass, the Domestic.

Unclean. Lev 11:2,3,26; Ex 13:13.
Described as
Not devoid of instinct. Is 1:3.
Strong. Gen 49:14.
Fond of ease. Gen 49:14,15.
Often fed on vine-leaves. Gen 49:11.
Formed a part of patriarchal wealth. Gen 12:16; 30:43; Job 1:3; 42:12.
Was used
In agriculture. Is 30:6,24.
For bearing burdens. Gen 42:26; 1 Sam 25:18.
For riding. Gen 22:3; Num 22:21.
In harness. Is 21:7.
In war. 2 Kin 7:7,10.
Governed by a bridle. Prov 26:3.
Urged on with a staff. Num 22:23,27.
Women often rode on. Josh 15:18; 1 Sam 25:20.
Persons of rank rode on. Judg 10:3,4; 2 Sam 16:2.
Judges of Israel rode on white. Judg 5:10.
Young, most valued for labour. Is 30:6,24.
Trusty persons appointed to take care of. Gen 36:24; 1 Sam 9:3; 1 Chr 27:30.
Often taken unlawfully by corrupt rulers. Num 16:15; 1 Sam 8:16; 12:3.
Later counted as an ignoble creature. Jer 22:19.
Laws respecting
Not to be coveted. Ex 20:17.
Fallen under a burden, to be assisted. Ex 23:5.
Astray, to be brought back to its owners. Ex 23:4; Deut 22:1.
Astray, to be taken care of till its owner appeared. Deut 22:2,3.
Not to be yoked with an ox. Deut 22:10.
To enjoy the rest of the Sabbath. Deut 5:14.
Firstborn of, if not redeemed, to have its neck broken. Ex 13:13; 34:20.

Christ entered Jerusalem on. Zech 9:9; John 12:14.
Miracles connected with
Mouth of Balaam's opened to speak. Num 22:28; 2 Pet 2:16.
A thousand men slain by Samson with a jaw-bone of. Judg 15:19.
Water brought from the jaw-bone of. Judg 15:19.
Not torn by a lion. 1 Kin 13:28.
Eaten during famine in Samaria. 2 Kin 6:25.

Ass, the Wild.

Inhabits wild and solitary places. Job 39:6; Is 32:14; Dan 5:21.
Ranges the mountains for food. Job 39:8.
Brays when hungry. Job 6:5.
Suffers in time of scarcity. Jer 14:6.
Described as
Fond of liberty. Job 39:5.
Intractable. Job 11:12.
Unsocial. Hos 8:9.
Despises his pursuers. Job 39:7.
Supported by God. Ps 104:10,11.
Illustrative of
Intractableness of natural man. Job 11:12.
The wicked in their pursuit of sin. Job 24:5.
Israel in their love of idols. Jer 2:23,24.
The Assyrian power. Hos 8:9.
The Ishmaelites (Hebrew). Gen 16:12.

Assurance.

Produced by faith. Eph 3:12; 2 Tim 1:12; Heb 10:22.
Made full by hope. Heb 6:11,19.
Confirmed by love. 1 John 3:14,19; 4:18.
Is the effect of righteousness. Is 32:17.
Is abundant in the understanding of the gospel. Col 2:2; 1 Thess 1:5.
Saints privileged to have, of
Their election. Ps 4:3; 1 Thess 1:4.
Their redemption. Job 19:25.
Their adoption. Rom 8:16; 1 John 3:2.
Their salvation. Is 12:2.
Eternal life. 1 John 5:13.
The unalienable love of God. Rom 8:38,39.
Union with God and Christ. 1 Cor 6:15; 2 Cor 13:5; Eph 5:30; 1 John 2:5; 4:13.
Peace with God by Christ. Rom 5:1.
Preservation. Ps 3:6,8; 27:3-5; 46:1-3.
Answers to prayer. 1 John 3:22; 5:14,15.
Continuance in grace. Phil 1:6.
Comfort in affliction. Ps 73:26; Luke 4:18,19; 2 Cor 4:8-10,16-18.
Support in death. Ps 23:4.
A glorious resurrection. Job 19:26; Ps 17:15; Phil 3:21; 1 John 3:2.
A kingdom. Heb 12:28; Rev 5:10.
A crown. 2 Tim 4:7,8; James 1:12.
Give diligence to attain to. 2 Pet 1:10,11.
Strive to maintain. Heb 3:14,18.
Confident hope in God restores. Ps 42:11.
Exemplified
David. Ps 23:4; 73:24-26.
Paul. 2 Tim 1:12; 4:18.

Assyria.

Antiquity and origin of. Gen 10:8-11.
Situated beyond the Euphrates. Is 7:20.
Watered by the river Tigris. Gen 2:14.
Called
The land of Nimrod. Mic 5:6.
Shinar. Gen 11:2; 14:1.
Asshur. Hos 14:3.
Nineveh, chief city of. Gen 10:11; 2 Kin 19:36.
Governed by kings. 2 Kin 15:19,29.
Celebrated for
Fertility. 2 Kin 18:32; Is 36:17.
Extent of conquests. 2 Kin 18:33-35; 19:11-13; Is 10:9-14.
Extensive commerce. Ezek 27:23,24.
Idolatry, the religion of. 2 Kin 19:37.
As a power, was
Most formidable. Is 28:2.
Intolerant and oppressive. Nah 3:19.
Cruel and destructive. Is 10:7.
Selfish and reserved. Hos 8:9.
Unfaithful, etc. 2 Chr 28:20,21.
Proud and haughty. 2 Kin 19:22-24; Is 10:8.
An instrument of God's vengeance. Is 7:18,19; 10:5,6.
Chief men of, described. Ezek 23:6,12,23.
Armies of, described. Is 5:26-29.
Pul king of
Invaded Israel. 2 Kin 15:19.
Brought off by Menahem. 2 Kin 15:19,20.
Tiglathpileser king of
Ravaged Israel. 2 Kin 15:29.
Asked to aid Ahaz against Syria. 2 Kin 16:7,8.
Took money from Ahaz, but strengthened him not. 2 Chr 28:20,21.
Conquered Syria. 2 Kin 16:9.
Shalmaneser king of
Reduced Israel to tribute. 2 Kin 17:3.
Was conspired against by Hoshea. 2 Kin 17:4.
Imprisoned Hoshea. 2 Kin 17:4.
Carried Israel captive. 2 Kin 17:5,6.
Re-peopled Samaria from Assyria. 2 Kin 17:24.
Sennacherib king of
Invaded Judah. 2 Kin 18:13.
Bought off by Hezekiah. 2 Kin 18:14-16.
Insulted and threatened Judah. 2 Kin 18:17-32; 19:10-13.
Blasphemed the Lord. 2 Kin 18:33-35.
Prayed against by Hezekiah. 2 Kin 19:14-19.
Reproved for pride and blasphemy. 2 Kin 19:12-34; Is 37:21-29.
His army destroyed by God. 2 Kin 19:35.
Assassinated by his sons. 2 Kin 19:36.
Condemned for oppressing God's people. Is 52:4.
Manasseh taken captive to. 2 Chr 33:11.
The re-peopling of Samaria from, completed by Asnappar. Ezra 4:10.
Idolatry of, brought into Samaria. 2 Kin 17:29.
Judah condemned for trusting to. Jer 2:18,36.
Israel condemned for trusting to. Hos 5:13; 7:11; 8:9.
The Jews condemned for following the idolatries of. Ezek 16:28; 23:5,7-49.
The greatness, extent, duration, and fall, illustrated. Ezek 31:3-17.
Predictions respecting
Conquest of the Kenites by. Num 24:22.
Conquest of Syria by. Is 8:4.
Conquest and captivity of Israel by. Is 8:4; Hos 9:3; 10:6; 11:5.
Invasion of Judah by. Is 5:26; 7:17-20; 8:8; 10:5,6,12.
Restoration of Israel from. Is 27:12,13; Hos 11:11; Zech 10:10.
Destruction of. Is 10:12-19; 14:24,25; 30:31-33; 31:8,9; Zech 10:11.
Participation in the blessings of the gospel. Is 19:23-25; Mic 7:12.

Atonement, The.

Explained. Rom 5:8-11; 2 Cor 5:18,19; Gal 1:4; 1 John 2:2; 4:10.
Foreordained. Rom 3:25; 1 Pet 1:11,20; Rev 13:8.
Foretold. Is 53:4-6,8-12; Dan 9:24-27; Zech 13:1,7; John 11:50,51.
Effected by Christ alone. John 1:29,36; Acts 4:10,12; 1 Thess 1:10; 1 Tim 2:5,6; Heb 2:9; 1 Pet 2:24.
Was voluntary. Ps 40:6-8; Heb 10:5-9; John 10:11,15,17,18.
Exhibits the
Grace and mercy of God. Rom 8:32; Eph 2:4,5,7; 1 Tim 2:4; Heb 2:9.
Love of God. Rom 5:8; 1 John 4:9,10.
Love of Christ. John 15:13; Gal 2:20; Eph 5:2,25; Rev 1:5.
Reconciles the justice and mercy of God. Is 45:21; Rom 3:25,26.
Necessity for. Is 59:16; Luke 19:10; Heb 9:22.
Made but once. Heb 7:27; 9:24-28; 10:10,12,14; 1 Pet 3:18.
Acceptable to God. Eph 5:2.
Reconciliation to God effected by. Rom 5:10; 2 Cor 5:18-20; Eph 2:13-16; Col 1:20-22; Heb 2:17; 1 Pet 3:18.
Access to God by. Heb 10:19,20.
Remission of sins by. John 1:29; Rom 3:25; Eph 1:7; 1 John 1:7; Rev 1:5.
Justification by. Rom 5:9; 2 Cor 5:21.
Sanctification by. 2 Cor 5:15; Eph 5:26,27; Titus 2:14; Heb 10:10; 13:12.
Redemption by. Matt 20:28; Acts 20:28; 1 Tim 2:6; Heb 9:12; Rev 5:9.
Has delivered saints from the
Power of sin. Rom 8:3; 1 Pet 1:18,19.
Power of the World. Gal 1:4; 6:14.
Power of the devil. Col 2:15; Heb 2:14,15.
Saints glorify God for. 1 Cor 6:20; Gal 2:20; Phil 1:20,21.
Saints rejoice in God for. Rom 5:11.
Saints praise God for. Rev 5:9-13.
Faith in, indispensable. Rom 3:25; Gal 3:13,14.
Commemorated in the Lord's Supper. Matt 26:26-28; 1 Cor 11:23-26.
Ministers should fully set forth. Acts 5:29-31,42; 1 Cor 15:3; 2 Cor 5:18-21.
Typified. Gen 4:4; Heb 11:4; Gen 22:2; Heb 11:17,19; Ex 12:5,11,14; 1 Cor 5:7;

Ex 24:8; Heb 9:20; Lev 16:30,34; Heb 9:7,12,28; Lev 17:11; Heb 9:22.

ATONEMENT, THE DAY OF.

Tenth day of seventh month. Lev 23:26,27.
A day of humiliation. Lev 16:29,31; 23:27.
Observed as a sabbath. Lev 23:28,32.
Offerings to be made on. Lev 16:3,5-15.
The high priest entered into the holy place on. Lev 16:2,3; Heb 9:7.
Atonement made on
 For the holy place. Ex 30:10; Lev 16:15,16.
 For the high priest. Lev 16:11; Heb 9:7.
 For the whole congregation. Lev 16:17,24; 23:28; Heb 9:7.
The sins of the people borne off by the scapegoat on. Lev 16:21.
Punishment for not observing. Lev 23:29,30.
Year of Jubilee commenced on. Lev 25:9.
Typical. Heb 9:8,24.

ATONEMENT, UNDER THE LAW.

Made by sacrifice. Lev 1:4,5.
By priests alone. 1 Chr 6:49; 2 Chr 29:24.
Necessary for
 Propitiating God. Ex 32:30; Lev 23:27,28; 2 Sam 21:3.
 Ransoming. Ex 30:15,16; Job 33:24.
 Purifying. Ex 29:36.
Offered for
 The congregation. Num 15:25; 2 Chr 29:24.
 The priests. Ex 29:31-33; Lev 8:34.
 Persons sinning ignorantly. Lev 4:20-35.
 Persons sinning wilfully. Lev 6:7.
 Persons swearing rashly. Lev 5:4,6.
 Persons withholding evidence. Lev 5:1,6.
 Persons unclean. Lev 5:2,3,6.
 Women after childbirth. Lev 12:8.
 The altar. Ex 29:36,37; Lev 16:18,19.
 The holy place. Lev 16:16,17.
 The healed leper. Lev 14:18.
 The leprous house healed. Lev 14:53.
Extraordinary cases of. Ex 32:30-34; Num 16:47; 25:10-13.
Typical of Christ's atonement. Rom 5:6-11.

BABYLON.

Origin of. Gen 10:8,10.
Origin of the name. Gen 11:8,9.
Was called
 Land of the Chaldeans. Ezek 12:13.
 Land of Shinar. Dan 1:2; Zech 5:11.
 Land of Merathaim. Jer 50:1,21.
 Desert of the sea. Is 21:1,9.
 Sheshach. Jer 25:12,26.
 Lady of kingdoms. Is 47:5.
Situated beyond the Euphrates. Gen 11:31; Josh 24:2,3.
Formerly a part of Mesopotamia. Acts 7:2.
Founded by the Assyrians, and a part of their empire. 2 Kin 17:24; Is 23:13.
Watered by the rivers Euphrates and Tigris. Ps 137:1; Jer 51:13.
Composed of many nations. Dan 3:4; 3:29.
Governed by kings. 2 Kin 20:12; Dan 5:1.
With Media and Persia divided by Darius into 120 provinces. Dan 6:1.
Presidents placed over. Dan 2:48; 6:1.
Babylon the chief province of. Dan 3:1.
Babylon the capital of
 Its antiquity. Gen 11:4,9.
 Enlarged by Nebuchadnezzar. Dan 4:30.
 Surrounded with a great wall and fortified. Jer 51:53,58.
 Called the golden city. Is 14:4.
 Called the glory of kingdoms. Is 13:19.
 Called beauty of Chaldees, etc. Is 13:19.
 Called the city of merchants. Ezek 17:4.
 Called Babylon the great. Dan 4:30.
Remarkable for
 Antiquity. Jer 5:15.
 Naval power. Is 43:14.
 Military power. Jer 5:16; 50:23.
 National greatness. Is 13:19; Jer 51:41.
 Wealth. Jer 50:37; 51:13.
 Commerce. Ezek 17:4.
 Manufacture of garments. Josh 7:21.
 Wisdom of senators. Is 47:10; Jer 50:35.
Inhabitants of
 Idolatrous. Jer 50:38; Dan 3:18.
 Addicted to magic. Is 47:9,12,13; Dan 2:1,2.
 Profane and sacrilegious. Dan 5:1-3.
 Wicked. Is 47:10.
As a power was
 Arrogant. Is 14:13,14; Jer 50:29,31,32.
 Secure and self-confident. Is 47:7,8.
 Grand and stately. Is 47:1,5.
 Covetous. Jer 51:13.
 Oppressive. Is 14:4.
 Cruel and destructive. Is 14:17; 47:6; Jer 51:25; Hab 1:6,7.
 An instrument of God's vengeance on other nations. Jer 51:7; Is 47:6.
Languages spoken in. Dan 1:4; 2:4.
Armies of, described. Hab 1:7-9.
Represented by
 A great eagle. Ezek 17:3.
 A head of gold. Dan 2:32,37,38.
 A lion with eagle's wings. Dan 7:4.
Ambassadors of, sent to Hezekiah. 2 Kin 20:12.
Nebuchadnezzar king of
 Made Jehoiakim tributary. 2 Kin 24:1.
 Besieged Jerusalem. 2 Kin 24:10,11.
 Took Jehoiachin, etc. captive to Babylon. 2 Kin 24:12,14-16; 2 Chr 36:10.
 Spoiled the temple. 2 Kin 24:13.
 Made Zedekiah king. 2 Kin 24:17.
 Rebelled against by Zedekiah. 2 Kin 24:20.
 Besieged and took Jerusalem. 2 Kin 25:1-4.
 Burned Jerusalem, etc. 2 Kin 25:9,10.
 Took Zedekiah, etc. captive to Babylon. 2 Kin 25:7,11,18-21; 2 Chr 36:20.
 Spoiled and burned the temple. 2 Kin 25:9,13-17; 2 Chr 36:18,19.
Revolt of the Jews from, and their punishment illustrated. Ezek 17:1-24.
The Jews exhorted to be subject to, and settle in. Jer 27:17; 29:1-7.
Treatment of the Jews in. 2 Kin 25:27-30; Dan 1:3-7.
Grief of the Jews in. Ps 137:1-6.
Destroyed by the Medes. Dan 5:30,31.
Restoration of the Jews from. 2 Chr 36:23; Ezra 1:1-2:67.
The gospel preached in. 1 Pet 5:13.
A type of Antichrist. Rev 16:19; 17:5.
Predictions respecting
 Conquests by. Jer 21:3-10; 27:2-6; 49:28-33; Ezek 21:19-32; 29:18-20.
 Captivity of the Jews by. Jer 20:4-6; 22:20-26; 25:9-11; Mic 4:10.
 Restoration of the Jews from. Is 14:1-4; 44:28; 48:20; Jer 29:10; 50:4,8,19.
 Destruction of. Is 13:1-22; 14:4-22; 21:1-10; 47:1-15; Jer 25:12; 50:1-51:64.
 Perpetual desolation of. Is 13:19-22; 14:22,23; Jer 50:13,39; 51:37.
 Preaching of the gospel in. Ps 87:4.

BACKSLIDING.

Is turning from God. 1 Kin 11:9.
Is leaving the first love. Rev 2:4.
Is departing form the simplicity of the gospel. 2 Cor 11:3; Gal 3:1-3; 5:4,7.
God is displeased at. Ps 78:57,59.
Warnings against. Ps 85:8; 1 Cor 10:12.
Guilt and consequences of. Num 14:43; Ps 125:5; Is 59:2,9-11; Jer 5:6; 8:5,13; 15:6; Luke 9:62.
Brings its own punishment. Prov 14:14; Jer 2:19.
A haughty spirit leads to. Prov 16:18.
Proneness to. Prov 24:16; Hos 11:7.
Liable to continue and increase. Jer 8:5; 14:7.
Exhortations to return from. 2 Chr 30:6; Is 31:6; Jer 3:12,14,22; Hos 6:1.
Pray to be restored from. Ps 80:3; 85:4; Lam 5:21.
Punishment of tempting others to the sin of. Prov 28:10; Matt 18:6.
Not hopeless. Ps 37:24; Prov 24:16.
Endeavour to bring back those guilty of. Gal 6:1; James 5:19,20.
Sin of, to be confessed. Is 59:12-14; Jer 3:13,14; 14:7-9.
Pardon of, promised. 2 Chr 7:14; Jer 3:12; 31:20; 36:3.
Healing of, promised. Jer 3:22; Hos 14:4.
Afflictions sent to heal. Hos 5:15.
Blessedness of those who keep from. Prov 28:14; Is 26:3,4; Col 1:21-23.
Hateful to saints. Ps 101:3.
Exemplified
 Israel. Ex 32:8; Neh 9:26; Jer 3:11; Hos 4:16.
 Saul. 1 Sam 15:11.
 Solomon. 1 Kin 11:3,4.
 Peter. Matt 26:70-74.

BAPTISM.

As administered by John. Matt 3:5-12; John 3:23; Acts 13:24; 19:4.
Sanctioned by Christ's submission to it. Matt 3:13-15; Luke 3:21.
Adopted by Christ. John 3:22; 4:1,2.
Appointed an ordinance of the Christian church. Matt 28:19,20; Mark 16:15,16.

To be administered in the name of the Father, Son, and Holy Spirit. Matt 28:19.
Water, the outward and visible sign in. Acts 8:36; 10:47.
Regeneration, the inward and spiritual grace of. John 3:3,5,6; Rom 6:3,4,11.
Remission of sins, signified by. Acts 2:38; 22:16.
Unity of the Church effected by. 1 Cor 12:13; Gal 3:27,28.
Confession of sin necessary to. Matt 3:6.
Repentance necessary to. Acts 2:38.
Faith necessary to. Acts 8:37; 18:8.
There is but one. Eph 4:5.
Administered to
  Individuals. Acts 8:38; 9:18.
  Households. Acts 16:15; 1 Cor 1:16.
  Only to professing believers. Acts 2:38; Matt 3:6; Mark 16:16; Acts 8:12,37; 10:47,48.
  Scriptures supporting infant baptism. Prov 30:6.
Administered by immersing the whole body of the person in water. Matt 3:16; Acts 8:38,39.
Emblematic of the influences of the Holy Spirit. Matt 3:11; Titus 3:5.
Typified. 1 Cor 10:2; 1 Pet 3:20,21.

Baptism with the Holy Spirit.

Foretold. Ezek 36:25.
Is through Christ. Titus 3:6.
Christ administered. Matt 3:11; John 1:33.
Promised to saints. Acts 1:5; 2:38,39; 11:16.
All saints partake of. 1 Cor 12:13.
Necessity for. John 3:5; Acts 19:2-6.
Renews and cleanses the soul. Titus 3:5; 1 Pet 3:20,21.
The Word of God instrumental to. Acts 10:44; Eph 5:26.
Typified. Acts 2:1-4.

Bear, The.

Inhabits woods. 2 Kin 2:24.
Described as
  Voracious. Dan 7:5.
  Cunning. Lam 3:10.
  Cruel. Amos 5:19.
Often attacks men. 2 Kin 2:24; Amos 5:19.
Attacks the flock in the presence of the shepherd. 1 Sam 17:34.
Particularly fierce when deprived of its young. 2 Sam 17:8; Prov 17:12.
Growls when annoyed. Is 59:11.
Miraculously killed by David. 1 Sam 17:36,37.
Illustrative of
  God in his judgments. Lam 3:10; Hos 13:8.
  The natural man. Is 11:7.
  Wicked rulers. Prov 28:15.
  The kingdom of the Medes. Dan 7:5.
  The kingdom of Antichrist. Rev 13:2.

Beard, The.

The Jews never appeared without. 2 Sam 10:5.
Worn even by the priests. Ps 133:2.
Laying hold of, a token of respect. 1 Sam 20:9.
Shaving of, a great offence. 2 Sam 10:4,6,7.
Plucking of, a sign of scorn. Is 50:6.
Dribbling on, a sign of derangement. 1 Sam 21:13.
In affliction
  Was neglected and untrimmed. 2 Sam 19:24.
  Was clipped. Jer 48:37.
  Was shorn. Jer 41:5.
  Sometimes plucked out. Ezra 9:3.
Corners of, not to be marred for the dead. Lev 19:27; 21:5.
Subject to leprosy. Lev 13:29,30.
Of the healed leper to be shaved. Lev 14:9.
Shaving, illustrative of severe judgments. Is 7:20; 15:2; Ezek 5:1.

Beasts.

Created by God. Gen 1:24,25; 2:19.
Creation of, exhibits God's power. Jer 27:5.
Made for the praise and glory of God. Ps 148:10.
Differ in flesh from birds and fishes. 1 Cor 15:39.
Herb of the field given to, for food. Gen 1:30.
Power over, given to man. Gen 1:26,28; Ps 8:7.
Instinctively fear man. Gen 9:2.
Received their names from Adam. Gen 2:19,20.
Given to man for food after the flood. Gen 9:3.
Not to be eaten alive or with blood. Gen 9:4; Deut 12:16,23.
That died naturally or were torn, not to be eaten. Ex 22:31; Lev 17:15; 22:8.
Supply clothing to man. Gen 3:21; Job 31:20.
The property of God. Ps 50:10.
Subjects of God's care. Ps 36:6; 104:10,11.
Described as
  Devoid of speech. 2 Pet 2:16.
  Devoid of understanding. Ps 32:9; 73:22.
  Devoid of immortality. Ps 49:12-15.
  Possessed of instinct. Is 1:3.
  Being four-footed. Acts 10:12.
  By nature wild, etc. Ps 50:11; Mark 1:13.
  Capable of being tamed. James 3:7.
Many kinds of, noisome and destructive. Lev 26:6; Ezek 5:17.
Many kinds of, domestic. Gen 36:6; 45:17.
Lessons of wisdom to be learned from. Job 12:7.
Found in
  Deserts. Is 13:21.
  Fields. Deut 7:22; Joel 2:22.
  Mountains. Song 4:8.
  Forests. Is 56:9; Mic 5:8.
Habitations of
  Dens and caves. Job 37:8; 38:40.
  Under spreading trees. Dan 4:12.
  Deserted cities. Is 13:21,22; Zeph 2:15.
Liable to diseases. Ex 9:3.
Frequently suffered on account of the sins of men. Joel 1:18,20; Hag 1:11.
Often cut off for the sins of men. Gen 6:7; 7:23; Ex 11:5; Hos 4:3.
Early distinguished into clean and unclean. Gen 7:2.
Clean
  Ox. Ex 21:28; Deut 14:4.
  Wild ox. Deut 14:5.
  Sheep. Deut 7:13; 14:4.
  Goat. Deut 14:4.
  Hart. Deut 14:5; Job 39:1.
  Roebuck. Deut 14:5; 2 Sam 2:18.
  Wild goat. Deut 14:5.
  Fallow deer. Deut 14:5.
  Chamois. Deut 14:5.
  Pygarg. Deut 14:5.
  How distinguished. Lev 11:3; Deut 14:6.
  Used for food. Lev 11:2; Deut 12:15.
  Used for sacrifice. Gen 8:20.
  Firstborn of, not redeemed. Num 18:17.
Unclean
  Camel. Gen 24:64; Lev 11:4.
  Dromedary. 1 Kin 4:28; Esth 8:10.
  Horse. Job 39:19-25.
  Ass. Gen 22:3; Matt 21:2.
  Wild Ass. Job 6:5; 39:5-8.
  Mule. 2 Sam 13:29; 1 Kin 10:25.
  Lion. Judg 14:5,6.
  Leopard. Song 4:8.
  Bear. 2 Sam 17:8.
  Wolf. Gen 49:27; John 10:12.
  Unicorn. Num 23:22.
  Behemoth. Job 40:15.
  Ape. 1 Kin 10:22.
  Fox. Ps 63:10; Song 2:5.
  Dog. Ex 22:31; Luke 16:2.
  Swine. Lev 11:7; Is 66:17.
  Hare. Lev 11:6; Deut 14:7.
  Coney. Lev 11:5; Ps 104:18.
  Mouse. Lev 11:29; Is 66:17.
  Mole. Lev 11:30; Is 2:20.
  Weasel. Lev 11:29.
  Ferret. Lev 11:30.
  Badger. Ex 25:5; Ezek 16:10.
  How distinguished. Lev 11:26.
  Not eaten. Lev 11:4-8; Deut 1:7,8.
  Not offered in sacrifice. Lev 27:11.
  Firstborn of, redeemed. Num 18:15.
  Caused uncleanness when dead. Lev 5:2.
Domestic
  To enjoy the Sabbath. Ex 20:10; Deut 5:14.
  To be taken care of. Lev 25:7; Deut 25:4.
  Not to be cruelly used. Num 22:27-32; Prov 12:10.
No likeness of, to be worshipped. Deut 4:17.
Representations of, worshipped by the heathen. Rom 1:23.
History of, written by Solomon. 1 Kin 4:33.
Often used as instruments of punishment. Lev 26:22; Deut 32:24; Jer 15:3; Ezek 5:17.
Man by nature no better than. Eccl 3:18,19.
Illustrative of
  The wicked. Ps 49:20; Titus 1:12.

Ungodly professors. 2 Pet 2:12; Jude 1:10.
Persecutors. 1 Cor 15:32; 2 Tim 4:17.
Kingdoms. Dan 7:11,17; 8:4.
People of different nations. Dan 4:12,21,22.
Antichrist. Rev 13:2; 20:4.

BEDS.

Antiquity of. Gen 47:31; Ex 8:3.
Couches or divans used as. Job 7:13; Ps 6:6.
A small pallet or mattress used as. 1 Sam 19:15.
Considered necessary. 2 Kin 4:10.
Made of
Iron. Deut 3:11.
Ivory. Amos 6:4.
Gold and Silver. Esth 1:6.
Wood. Song 3:7-9.
Supplied with pillows. 1 Sam 19:13; 26:7.
Covered with tapestry and linen. Prov 7:16.
Often perfumed. Prov 7:17; Ezek 23:41.
Of the poor covered with upper garment. Ex 22:26,27; Deut 24:12,13.
Used for
Sleeping on. Job 33:15; Luke 11:7.
Reclining on by day. 2 Sam 4:5; 11:2.
Reclining on at meals. 1 Sam 28:23-25; Amos 6:4-6; Luke 7:36-38; John 13:23.
Not used in affliction. 2 Sam 12:16; 13:31.
Persons sometimes took to, in grief. 1 Kin 21:4; Hos 7:14.
Saints meditate and praise God while on. Ps 4:4; 149:5; Song 3:1.
The wicked devise mischief while on. Ps 36:4; Mic 2:1.
The slothful too fond of. Prov 26:14.
Of the poor often sold for debt. Prov 22:27.
Subject to ceremonial defilement. Lev 15:4.
Purification of. Mark 7:4.
Illustrative
Of the grave. Is 57:2.
(Made in darkness,) of extreme misery. Job 17:13.
(Made in sickness,) of divine support and comfort. Ps 41:3.
(Made on high,) of carnal security. Is 57:7.
(Too short,) of plans which afford no rest or peace. Is 28:20.

BENJAMIN, TRIBE OF.

Descended from Jacob's twelfth son. Gen 35:18.
Predictions respecting. Gen 49:27; Deut 33:12.
Persons selected from
To number the people. Num 1:11.
To spy out the land. Num 13:9.
To divide the land. Num 34:21.
Strength of, on leaving Egypt. Num 1:36,37.
Formed the rear of the third division of Israel in their journeys. Num 10:22,24.
Encamped on west side of the tabernacle under the standard of Ephrain. Num 2:18,22.
Offering of, at dedication. Num 7:60-65.
Families of. Num 26:38-40.
Strength of, entering Canaan. Num 26:41.
On Gerizim said amen to the blessings. Deut 27:12.
Cities and bounds of inheritance. Josh 18:11-28.
Celebrated as bowmen and slingers. 1 Chr 12:2.
Assisted against Sisera. Judg 5:14.
Oppressed by the Ammonites. Judg 10:9.
Almost annihilated for protecting the men of Gibeah. Judg 20:12-48.
Remnant of, provided with wives to preserve the tribe. Judg 21:1-23.
Furnished the first king to Israel. 1 Sam 9:1,2,15-17; 10:20,21; 2 Sam 2:8-10.
Adhered for a time to the house of Saul against David. 2 Sam 2:9,15,25,31.
Some of, assisted David. 1 Chr 12:1-7,16.
Revolted from the house of Saul. 2 Sam 3:19.
Some of, at David's coronation. 1 Chr 12:29.
A 1000 of, with Shimei came to meet David on his return to Jerusalem. 2 Sam 19:16,17.
Very numerous in David's time. 1 Chr 7:6-12.
Captains appointed over. 1 Kin 4:18; 1 Chr 27:12.
Remained faithful to Judah. 1 Kin 12:21.
Furnished an army to Jehoshaphat. 2 Chr 17:17.
Numbers of, returned from the captivity and dwelt at Jerusalem. Ezra 1:5; Neh 11:4.
Celebrated persons of
Ehud. Judg 3:15.
Kish. 1 Sam 9:1.
Saul. 1 Sam 9:1; 10:1.
Abner. 1 Sam 14:51; 17:55.
Elhanan. 2 Sam 21:19.
Paul. Phil 3:5.

BIRDS.

Created by God. Gen 1:20,21; 2:19.
Created for the glory of God. Ps 148:10.
Herb of the field given as food to. Gen 1:30.
Differ in flesh from beasts and fishes. 1 Cor 15:39.
Power over given to man. Gen 1:26; Ps 8:8.
Names given to, by Adam. Gen 2:19,20.
Instinctively fear man. Gen 9:2.
Instinct of, inferior to man's reason. Job 35:11.
Lessons of wisdom to be learned from. Job 12:7.
Can all be tamed. James 3:7.
Given as food to man. Gen 9:2,3.
The blood of, not to be eaten. Lev 7:26.
The property of God. Ps 50:11.
God provides for. Ps 104:1-12; Matt 6:26; Luke 12:23,24.
Called
Fowls of the air. Gen 7:3.
Fowls of heaven. Job 35:11.
Feathered fowl. Ezek 39:17.
Winged fowl. Deut 4:17.
Birds of the air. Matt 8:20.
Many kinds of, graniverous. Matt 13:4.
Many kinds of, carnivorous. Gen 15:11; 40:19; Deut 28:26.
Furnished with claws. Dan 4:33.
Propagated by eggs. Deut 22:6; Jer 17:11.
Make, and dwell in nests. Matt 8:20.
Are hostile to strange kinds. Jer 12:9.
Have each their peculiar note or song. Ps 104:12; Eccl 12:4; Song 2:12.
Fly above the earth. Gen 1:20.
Rapid flight of, alluded to. Is 31:5; Hos 9:11; 11:11.
Many kinds of, migratory. Jer 8:7.
Often remove from places suffering calamities. Jer 4:25; 9:10.
Rest on trees. Dan 4:12; Matt 13:32.
Inhabit
Mountains. Ps 50:11.
Deserts. Ps 102:6.
Marshes. Is 14:23.
Deserted cities. Is 34:11,14,15.
Make their nests
In trees. Ps 104:17; Ezek 31:6.
On the ground. Deut 22:6.
In clefts of rocks. Num 24:21; Jer 48:28.
In deserted cities. Is 34:15.
Under the roofs of houses. Ps 84:3.
Early distinguished into clean and unclean. Gen 8:20.
Clean
Dove. Gen 8:8.
Turtle. Lev 14:22; Song 2:12.
Pigeon. Lev 1:14; 12:6.
Quail. Ex 16:12,13; Num 11:31,32.
Sparrow. Lev 14:4; Matt 10:29-31.
Swallow. Ps 84:3; Is 38:14.
Cock and hen. Matt 23:37; 26:34,74.
Partridge. 1 Sam 26:20; Jer 17:11.
Crane. Is 38:14; Jer 8:7.
To be eaten. Deut 14:11,20.
Offered in sacrifice. Gen 8:20; Lev 1:14.
Unclean
Eagle. Lev 11:13; Job 39:27.
Ossifrage. Lev 11:13.
Osprey. Lev 11:13.
Vulture. Lev 11:14; Job 28:7; Is 34:15.
Glede. Deut 14:13.
Kite. Lev 11:14.
Raven. Lev 11:15; Job 38:41.
Owl. Lev 11:16; Job 30:29.
Nighthawk. Lev 11:16.
Cuckoo. Lev 11:16.
Hawk. Lev 11:17; Job 39:26.
Little owl. Lev 11:17.
Cormorant. Lev 11:17; Is 34:11.
Great owl. Lev 11:17.
Swan. Lev 11:18.
Pelican. Lev 11:18; Ps 102:6.
Gier Eagle. Lev 11:18.
Stork. Lev 11:19; Ps 104:17.
Heron. Lev 11:19.
Lapwing. Lev 11:19.
Bat. Lev 11:19; Is 2:20.
Ostrich. Job 39:13,18.
Bittern. Is 14:23; 34:11.
Peacock. 1 Kin 10:22; Job 39:13.
Not to be eaten. Lev 11:13,17; Deut 14:12.
Not to be eaten with their young. Deut 22:6,7.

Taken in snares or nets. Prov 1:17.
Often suffered for man's sin. Gen 6:7; Jer 12:4; Ezek 38:20; Hos 4:3.
Solomon wrote the history of. 1 Kin 4:33.
Confinement of, in cages alluded to. Jer 5:27.
No likeness of, to be made for worship. Deut 4:17.
Often worshipped by idolaters. Rom 1:23.
Illustrative
Of cruel and rapacious kings. Is 46:11.
Of hostile nations. Jer 12:9.
Of people of different countries. Ezek 31:6; Matt 13:32.
Of unsettled person, etc. Prov 27:8; Is 16:2.
Of the devil and his spirits. Matt 13:4,19.
(Snaring,) of death. Eccl 9:12.
(Snaring,) of designs of the wicked. Ps 124:7; Prov 1:10-17; 7:23.

BLASPHEMY.

Christ assailed with. Matt 10:25; Luke 22:64,65; 1 Pet 4:14.
Charged upon Christ. Matt 9:2,3; 26:64,65; John 10:33,36.
Charged upon saints. Acts 6:11,13.
Proceeds from the heart. Matt 15:19.
Forbidden. Ex 20:7; Col 3:8.
The wicked addicted to. Ps 74:18; Is 52:5; 2 Tim 3:2; Rev 18:11,21.
Idolatry counted as. Is 65:7; Ezek 20:27,28.
Hypocrisy counted as. Rev 2:9.
Saints grieved to hear. Ps 44:15,16; 74:10,18,22.
Gives no occasion for. 2 Sam 12:14; 1 Tim 6:1.
Against the Holy Spirit, unpardonable. Matt 12:31,32.
Connected with folly and pride. 2 Kin 19:22; Ps 74:18.
Punishment of. Lev 24:16; Is 65:7; Ezek 20:27-33; 35:11,12.
Exemplified
The Danite. Lev 24:11.
Sennacherib. 2 Kin 19:4,10,22.
The Jews. Luke 22:65.
Hymenaeus. 1 Tim 1:20.

BLESSED, THE.

Whom God chooses. Ps 65:4; Eph 1:3,4.
Whom God calls. Is 51:2; Rev 19:9.
Who know Christ. Matt 16:16,17.
Who know the gospel. Ps 89:15.
Who are not offended at Christ. Matt 11:6.
Who believe. Luke 1:45; Gal 3:9.
Whose sins are forgiven. Ps 32:1,2; Rom 4:7.
To whom God imputes righteousness without works. Rom 4:6-9.
Whom God chastens. Job 5:17; Ps 94:12.
Who suffer for Christ. Luke 6:22.
Who have the Lord for their God. Ps 144:15.
Who trust in God. Ps 2:12; 34:8; 40:4; 84:12; Jer 17:7.
Who fear God. Ps 112:1; 128:1,4.
Who hear and keep the word of God. Ps 119:2; James 1:24; Matt 13:16; Luke 11:28; Rev 1:3; 22:7.
Who delight in the commandments of God. Ps 112:1.
Who keep the commandments of God. Rev 22:14.
Who wait for the Lord. Is 30:18.
Whose strength is in the Lord. Ps 84:5.
Who hunger and thirst after righteousness. Matt 5:6.
Who frequent the house of God. Ps 65:4; 84:5.
Who avoid the wicked. Ps 1:1.
Who endure temptation. James 1:12.
Who watch against sin. Rev 16:15.
Who rebuke sinners. Prov 24:25.
Who watch for the Lord. Luke 12:37.
Who die in the Lord. Rev 14:13.
Who have part in the first resurrection. Rev 20:6.
Who favour saints. Gen 12:3; Ruth 2:10.
The undefiled. Ps 119:1.
The pure in heart. Matt 5:8.
The just. Ps 106:3; 10:6.
The children of the just. Prov 20:7.
The righteous. Ps 5:12.
The generation of the upright. Ps 112:2.
The faithful. Prov 28:20.
The poor in spirit. Matt 5:3.
The meek. Matt 5:5.
The merciful. Matt 5:7.
The bountiful. Deut 15:10; Ps 41:1; Prov 22:9; Luke 14:13,14.
The peace-makers. Matt 5:9.
Holy mourners. Matt 5:4; Luke 6:21.
Saints at the judgment day. Matt 25:34.
Who shall eat bread in the kingdom of God. Luke 14:15; Rev 19:9.

BLINDNESS, SPIRITUAL.

Explained. John 1:5; 1 Cor 2:14.
The effect of sin. Is 29:10; Matt 6:23; John 3:19,20.
Unbelief, the effect of. Rom 11:8; 2 Cor 4:3,4.
Uncharitableness, a proof of. 1 John 2:9,11.
A work of the devil. 2 Cor 4:4.
Leads to all evil. Eph 4:17-19.
Is inconsistent with communion with God. 1 John 1:6,7.
Of ministers, fatal to themselves and to the people. Matt 15:14.
The wicked are in. Ps 82:5; Jer 5:21.
The self-righteous are in. Matt 23:19,26; Rev 3:17.
The wicked wilfully guilty of. Is 26:11; Rom 1:19-21.
Judicially inflicted. Ps 69:23; Is 29:10; 44:18; Matt 13:13,14; John 12:40.
Pray for the removal of. Ps 13:3; 119:18.
Christ appointed to remove. Is 42:7; Luke 4:18; John 8:12; 9:39; 2 Cor 4:6.
Christ's ministers are lights to remove. Matt 5:14; Acts 26:18.
Saints are delivered from. John 8:12; Eph 5:8; Col 1:13; 1 Thess 5:4,5; 1 Pet 2:9.
Removal of, illustrated. John 9:7,11,25; Acts 9:18; Rev 3:18.
Exemplified
Israel. Rom 11:25; 2 Cor 3:15.
Scribes and Pharisees. Matt 23:16,24.
Churches of Laodicea. Rev 3:17.

BLOOD.

The life of animals. Gen 9:4; Lev 17:11,14.
Fluid. Deut 12:16.
Red. 2 Kin 3:22; Joel 2:31.
Of all men the same. Acts 17:26.
Eating of, forbidden to
Man after the flood. Gen 9:4.
The Israelites under the law. Lev 3:17; 17:10,12.
The early Christians. Acts 15:20,29.
The Jews often guilty of eating. 1 Sam 14:32,33; Ezek 33:25.
Of animals slain for good to be poured on the earth and covered. Lev 17:13; Deut 12:16,24.
Birds of prey delight in. Job 39:30.
Beasts of prey delight in. Num 23:24; Ps 68:23.
Shedding of human
Forbidden. Gen 9:5.
Hateful to God. Prov 6:16,17.
Defiling to the land. Ps 106:38.
Defiling to the person. Is 59:3.
Jews often guilty of. Jer 22:17; Ezek 22:4.
Always punished. Gen 9:6.
Mode of clearing those accused of. Deut 21:1-9.
The price of, not to be consecrated. Matt 27:6.
Of legal sacrifices
For atonement. Ex 30:10; Lev 17:11.
For purification. Heb 9:13,19-22.
How disposed of. Ex 29:12; Lev 4:7.
Not offered with leaven. Ex 23:18; 34:25.
Ineffectual to remove sin. Heb 10:4.
Idolaters made drink offerings of. Ps 16:4.
Water turned into, as a sign. Ex 4:30.
Waters of Egypt turned into, as a judgment. Ex 7:17-21.
Illustrative
(Washing the feet in,) of victories. Ps 58:10; 68:23.
(Building with,) of oppression and cruelty. Hab 2:12.
(Preparing to,) of ripening for destruction. Ezek 35:6.
(On one's own head,) of guilt. Lev 20:9; 2 Sam 1:16; Ezek 18:13.
(Given to drink,) of severe judgments. Ezek 16:38; Rev 16:6.

BOLDNESS, HOLY.

Christ set an example of. John 7:26.
Is through faith in Christ. Eph 3:12; Heb 10:19.
A characteristic of saints. Prov 28:1.
Produced by
Trust in God. Is 50:7.
The fear of God. Acts 4:19; 5:29.
Faithfulness to God. 1 Tim 3:13.
Express your trust in God with. Heb 13:6.
Have, in prayer. Eph 3:12; Heb 4:16.
Saints shall have, in judgment. 1 John 4:17.
Exhortations to. Josh 1:7; 2 Chr 19:11; Jer 1:8; Ezek 3:9.
Pray for. Acts 4:29; Eph 6:19,20.
Ministers should exhibit, in

Faithfulness to their people. 2 Cor 7:4; 10:1.
Preaching. Acts 4:31; Phil 1:14.
Reproving sin. Is 58:1; Mic 3:8.
The face of opposition. Acts 13:46; 1 Thess 2:2.
Exemplified
Abraham. Gen 18:22-32.
Jacob. Gen 32:24-29.
Moses. Ex 32:31,32; 33:18.
Aaron. Num 16:47,48.
David. 1 Sam 17:45.
Elijah. 1 Kin 18:15,18.
Nehemiah. Neh 6:11.
Shadrach. Dan 3:17,18.
Daniel. Dan 6:10.
Joseph of Arimathaea. Mark 15:43.
Peter and John. Acts 4:8-13.
Stephen. Acts 7:51.
Paul. Acts 9:27,29; 19:8.
Barnabas. Acts 14:3.
Apollos. Acts 18:26.

BONDAGE, SPIRITUAL.

Is to the devil. 1 Tim 3:7; 2 Tim 2:26.
Is to the fear of death. Heb 2:14,15.
Is to sin. John 8:34; Acts 8:23; Rom 6:16; 7:23; Gal 4:3; 2 Pet 2:19.
Deliverance from, promised. Is 42:6,7.
Christ delivers from. Luke 4:18,21; John 8:36; Rom 7:24,24; Eph 4:8.
The gospel, the instrument of deliverance from. John 8:32; Rom 8:2.
Saints are delivered from. Rom 6:18,22.
Deliverance from, illustrated. Deut 4:20.
Typified
Israel in Egypt. Ex 1:13,14.

BOOKS.

Probable origin of. Job 19:23,24.
Made of
Papyrus or paper reed. Is 19:7.
Parchment. 2 Tim 4:13.
Made in a roll. Is 34:4; Jer 36:2; Ezek 2:9.
Written with pen and ink. Jer 36:18; 3 John 13.
Often written on both sides. Ezek 2:10.
Often sealed. Is 29:11; Dan 12:4; Rev 5:1.
Often dedicated to persons of distinction. Luke 1:3; Acts 1:1.
Were numerous and most expensive. Acts 19:19.
The ancients fond of making. Eccl 12:12.
Divine communications recorded in. Ex 17:14; Is 30:8; Jer 36:2; Rev 1:19.
Important events recorded in. Ezra 4:15; 6:1,2; Esth 2:23.
Erasures in, alluded to. Ex 32:33; Num 5:23.
Not extant, but mentioned in scripture
Wars of the Lord. Num 21:14.
Jasher. Josh 10:13; 2 Sam 1:18.
Samuel concerning the kingdom. 1 Sam 10:25.
Chronicles of David. 1 Chr 27:24.
Acts of Solomon. 1 Kin 11:41.
Natural history by Solomon. 1 Kin 4:32,33.
History of the kings. 1 Chr 9:1.
Samuel the seer. 1 Chr 29:29.
Nathan. 1 Chr 29:29; 2 Chr 9:29.
Shemaiah. 2 Chr 12:15.
Gad the seer. 1 Chr 29:29.
Ahijah the Shilonite. 2 Chr 9:29.
Visions of Iddo. 2 Chr 9:29; 12:15.
Jehu the son of Hanani. 2 Chr 20:34.
Sayings of the seers. 2 Chr 33:19.
Illustrative of
Memorials of God's providence. Ps 56:8; 139:16.
Memorials of conversation and conduct of men. Dan 7:10; Mal 3:16; Rev 20:12.
The record of the church of Christ. Dan 12:1; Heb 12:23; Rev 20:12,15; 22:19.

BOTTLES.

First mention of, in Scripture. Gen 21:14.
Ancients often drank from. Hab 2:15.
Used for holding
Water. Gen 21:14,15,19.
Milk. Judg 4:19.
Wine. 1 Sam 1:24; 16:20.
Some, made of earthenware. Jer 19:1.
Made of skins
Shrivelled and dried by smoke. Ps 119:83.
Marred by age and use. Josh 9:14,13.
When old, unfit for holding new wine. Matt 9:17; Mark 2:22.
Sometimes probably of large dimensions. 1 Sam 25:18; 2 Sam 16:1.
Illustrative
Of the clouds. Job 38:37.
Of God's remembrance. Ps 56:8.
Of sinners ripe for judgment. Jer 13:12-14.
(Dried up,) of the afflicted. Ps 119:83.
(Ready to burst,) of the impatient. Job 32:19.
(Broken,) of severe judgments. Is 30:14; Jer 19:10; 48:12.

BOW, THE.

An instrument of war. Gen 48:22; Is 7:24.
Sometimes used in hunting. Gen 27:3.
For shooting arrows. 1 Chr 12:2.
Called the battle bow. Zech 9:10; 10:4.
Those who used, called
Bowmen. Jer 4:29.
Archers. 1 Sam 31:3; Jer 51:3.
Usually of steel. 2 Sam 22:35; Job 20:24.
Held in the left hand. Ezek 39:3.
Drawn with full force. 2 Kin 9:24.
The Jews taught to use. 2 Sam 1:18.
Used expertly by
Lydians. Jer 46:9.
Elamites. Jer 49:35.
Philistines. 1 Sam 31:2,3.
Sons of Reuben, Gad, and Manasseh. 1 Chr 5:18.
Benjamites. 1 Chr 12:2; 2 Chr 14:8.
Given as a token of friendship. 1 Sam 18:4.
Often furnished by the state. 2 Chr 26:14.
Of the vanquished, broken and burned. Ps 37:15; Ezek 39:9.
Illustrative
Of strength and power. Job 29:20.
Of the tongue of the wicked. Ps 11:2; Jer 9:3.
(When deceitful,) of the hypocrite. Ps 78:57; Hos 7:16.
(When broken,) of the overthrow of power. 1 Sam 2:4; Jer 49:35; Hos 1:5; 2:18.

BRASS, OR COPPER.

Dug out of the mountains. Deut 8:9.
Purified by smelting. Job 28:2.
Characterised by
Strength. Job 40:18.
Hardness. Lev 26:19.
Yellow colour. Ezra 8:27.
Fusibility. Ezek 22:18,20.
Sonorousness. 1 Cor 13:1.
Takes a high polish. 2 Chr 4:16; Ezek 1:7.
Inferior in value to gold and silver. Is 60:17; Dan 2:32,39.
Antiquity of working in. Gen 4:22.
Extensive commerce in. Ezek 27:13; Rev 18:12.
Working in, a trade. Gen 4:22; 1 Kin 7:14; 2 Chr 24:12; 2 Tim 4:14.
Canaan abounded in. Deut 8:9; 33:25.
Taken in war
Often in great quantities. Josh 22:8; 2 Sam 8:8; 2 Kin 25:13-16.
Cleansed by fire. Num 31:21-23.
Generally consecrated to God. Josh 6:19,24; 2 Sam 8:10,11.
Offerings of, for the tabernacle. Ex 38:29.
Collected by David for the temple. 1 Chr 22:3,14,16; 29:2.
Offerings of, for the temple. 1 Chr 29:6,7.
Coined for money. Matt 10:9; Mark 12:41.
Made into
Mirrors. Ex 38:8.
Gates. Ps 107:16; Is 45:2.
Bars for gates. 1 Kin 4:13.
Fetters. Judg 16:21; 2 Kin 25:7.
Shields. 1 Kin 14:27; 2 Chr 12:10.
Helmets. 1 Sam 17:5.
Greaves for the legs. 1 Sam 17:6.
Household vessels. Mark 7:4.
Sacred vessels. Ex 27:3; 1 Kin 7:45.
Altars. Ex 27:2; 39:39.
Sockets for pillars. Ex 38:10,11,17.
Lavers. Ex 30:18; 1 Kin 7:38.
Pillars. 1 Kin 7:15,16.
Idols. Dan 5:4; Rev 9:20.
Instruments of music. 1 Chr 15:19.
Moses made the serpent of. Num 21:9; 2 Kin 18:4.
Illustrative of
Obstinate sinners. Is 48:4; Jer 6:28.
The decrees of God. Zech 6:1.
The strength and firmness of Christ. Dan 10:6; Rev 1:15.
Strength given to saints. Jer 15:20; Mic 4:13.
Macedonian empire. Dan 2:39.
Extreme drought. Deut 28:23.
The earth made barren. Lev 26:19.

BREAD.

Given by God. Ruth 1:6; Matt 6:11.
Yielded by the earth. Job 28:5; Is 55:10.
Made of
Wheat. Ex 29:2; Ps 81:16.
Barley. Judg 7:13; John 6:9.
Beans, millet, etc. Ezek 4:9.
Manna (in the wilderness). Num 11:8.
Corn ground for making. Is 28:28.
Was kneaded. Gen 18:6; Jer 7:18; Hos 7:4.
Troughs used for kneading. Ex 12:34.

Usually leavened. Lev 23:17; Matt 13:33.
Sometimes unleavened. Ex 12:18; 1 Cor 5:8.
Was formed into
  Loaves. 1 Sam 10:3,4; Matt 14:17.
  Cakes. 2 Sam 6:19; 1 Kin 17:13.
  Wafers. Ex 16:31; 29:23.
Was baked
  On hearths. Gen 18:6.
  On coals of fire. Is 44:19; John 21:9.
  In ovens. Lev 26:26; Hos 7:4-7.
Making of, a trade. Gen 40:2; Jer 37:21.
Ordinary, called common bread. 1 Sam 21:4.
Sacred, called hallowed bread. 1 Sam 21:4,6.
Nutritious and strengthening. Ps 104:15.
When old, dry and mouldy. Josh 9:5,12.
Often put for the whole substance of man. Gen 3:19; 39:6; Matt 6:11.
The principal food used by the ancients. Gen 18:5; 21:14; 27:17; Judg 19:5.
Broken for use. Lam 4:4; Matt 14:19.
Kept in baskets. Gen 40:16; Ex 29:32.
Publicly sold. Matt 14:15; 15:33.
In times of scarcity, sold by weight. Lev 26:26; Ezek 4:16.
Scarceness of, sent as a punishment. Ps 105:16; Is 3:1; Ezek 5:16.
Plenty of, promised to the obedient. Lev 26:5.
Often given as a present. 1 Sam 25:18; 2 Sam 16:12; 1 Chr 12:40.
Served round after funerals. Ezek 24:17-22.
With water, the food of prisons. 1 Kin 22:27.
Crumb of, used to wipe the fingers, thrown under the table. Matt 15:27; Luke 16:21.
First fruit of, offered to God. Num 15:19,20.
Offered with sacrifices. Ex 29:2,23; Num 28:2.
Placed on table of showbread. Ex 25:30.
Multitudes miraculously fed by Christ with. Matt 14:19-21; 15:34-37.
Illustrative
  Of Christ. John 6:33-35.
  (When broken,) of the death of Christ. Matt 26:26; 1 Cor 11:23,24.
  (Partaking of,) of communion of saints. Acts 2:46; 1 Cor 10:17.
  (Want of,) of extreme poverty. Prov 12:9; Is 3:7.
  (Seeking of begging,) of extreme poverty. 1 Sam 2:36; Ps 37:25; Lam 1:11.
  (Fulness of,) of abundance. Ezek 16:49.
  (Eating without scarceness,) of plenty. Deut 8:9.
  (Of adversity,) of heavy affliction. Is 30:20.
  (Of tears,) of sorrow. Ps 80:5.
  (Of deceit,) of unlawful gain. Prov 20:17.
  (Of wickedness,) of oppression. Prov 4:17.
  (Of idleness,) of sloth. Prov 31:27.

Breastplate.

A part of defensive armour. 1 Kin 22:34.
A part of the high priest's dress. Ex 28:4.
For soldiers
  Made of iron. Rev 9:9.
  Bright and shining. Rev 9:17.
For the high priest
  Materials of. Ex 28:15; 39:8.
  Form and dimensions of. Ex 28:16; 39:9.
  Made from the offering of the people. Ex 35:9.
Had names of the tribes engraved on precious stones. Ex 28:17-21; 39:10,14.
Inseparably united to the ephod. Ex 28:22-28; 39:15-21.
The Urim and Thummim placed in. Ex 28:30; Lev 8:8.
Worn as a memorial. Ex 28:29; Is 49:16.
Illustrative of the
  Righteous judgment of Christ. Is 59:17.
  Defence of righteousness. Eph 6:14.
  Defence of faith and love. 1 Thess 5:8.

Brooks.

Canaan abounded with. Deut 8:7.
Often ran over pebbles. 1 Sam 17:40; Job 22:24.
Borders of, favourable to
  Grass. 1 Kin 18:5.
  Willows. Lev 23:40; Job 40:22.
  Reeds. Is 19:7.
Abounded with fish. Is 19:8.
Afforded protection to a country. Is 19:6.
Mentioned in Scripture
  Arnon. Num 21:14,15.
  Besor. 1 Sam 30:9.
  Gaash. 2 Sam 23:30; 1 Chr 11:32.
  Cherith. 1 Kin 17:3,5.
  Eshcol. Num 13:23,24.
  Kidron. 2 Sam 15:23; 1 Kin 15:13; John 18:1.
  Kishon. 1 Kin 18:40; Ps 83:9.
  Zered. Deut 2:13.
  Of the willows. Is 15:7.
Illustrative
  Of wisdom. Prov 18:4.
  Of temporal abundance. Job 20:17.
  (Deceptive,) of false friends. Job 6:15.
  (Drinking of, by the way,) of help in distress. Ps 110:7.

Burial.

Probable origin of. Gen 4:9,10.
Design of. Gen 23:3,4.
Attended by
  Family of the dead. Gen 50:5,6,8; Matt 8:21.
  Numbers of friends, etc. Gen 50:7,9; 2 Sam 3:31; Luke 7:12.
  Female friends. Mark 15:47; Luke 7:13.
  Hired mourners. Jer 9:17,18.
  Great lamentation at. Gen 50:10,11; 2 Sam 3:31,32.
Orations sometimes made at. 2 Sam 3:33,34.
The body was
  Washed before. Acts 9:37.
  Anointed for. Matt 26:12.
  Wound in linen for. John 11:44; 19:40.
  Preserved with spices. John 19:39,40.
  Sometimes burned before. 1 Sam 31:12.
  Carried on a bier to. 2 Sam 3:31; Luke 7:14.
Perfumes burned at. 2 Chr 16:14; Jer 34:5.
Antiquity of coffins for. Gen 50:26.
Often took place immediately after death. John 11:17,39; Acts 5:6,10.
Of persons embalmed, deferred for seventy days. Gen 50:3,4.
Of persons hanged, always on the days of execution. Deut 21:23; John 19:31.
The right of all nations. Judg 16:31; John 19:38.
Of enemies, sometimes performed by the conquerors. 1 Kin 11:15; Ezek 39:11-14.
Of the friendless, a kind act. 2 Sam 2:5.
Places used for
  Natural caves. Gen 23:19; John 11:38.
  Caves hewn out of rocks. Is 22:16; Matt 27:60.
  Gardens. 2 Kin 21:18,26; John 19:41.
  Under trees. Gen 35:8; 1 Sam 31:13.
  Tops of the hills. Josh 24:33; 2 Kin 23:16.
  Houses of the deceased. 1 Sam 25:1; 1 Kin 2:34.
  The city of David for the kings of Judah. 1 Kin 2:10; 2 Chr 21:20; 24:16.
Antiquity of purchasing places for. Gen 23:7-16.
Places of
  Frequently prepared and pointed out during life. Gen 50:5; 2 Chr 16:14; Matt 27:60.
  Members of a family interred in the same. Gen 25:10; 49:31; 2 Sam 2:32.
  Held in high veneration. Neh 2:3,5.
  Provided for the common people. Jer 26:23.
  Provided for aliens and strangers. Matt 27:7.
  Visited by sorrowing friends. John 11:31.
  Pillars erected on. Gen 35:20.
  Tombs erected over. Matt 23:27-29.
  Sometimes had inscriptions. 2 Kin 23:17.
  Sometimes not apparent. Luke 11:44.
  For criminals, marked by heaps. Josh 7:26.
  Were ceremonially unclean. Num 19:16,18.
  Often desecrated by idolatry. Is 65:3,4.
The Jews anxious to be interred in their family places of. Gen 47:29-31; 49:29,30; 50:25; 2 Sam 19:37.
Followed by a feast. 2 Sam 3:35; Jer 16:7,8; Hos 9:4.
Privation of, considered a calamity. Eccl 6:3.
Privation of, threatened as a punishment. 2 Kin 9:10; Jer 8:2; 16:4.
An ignominious, compared to the burial of an ass. Jer 22:19.
Illustrative of regeneration. Rom 6:4; Col 2:12.

Burnt Offering, The.

To be offered only to the Lord. Judg 13:16.
Specially acceptable. Gen 8:21; Lev 1:9,13,17.

The most ancient of all sacrifices. Gen 4:4; 8:20; 22:2,13; Job 1:5.
Offered by the Jews before the law. Ex 10:25; 24:5.
To be taken from
 The flock or herd. Lev 1:2.
 The fowls. Lev 1:14.
Was an atonement for sin. Lev 9:7.
Guilt transferred to, by imposition of hands. Lev 1:4; Num 8:12.
Required to be
 Killed, if a beast, by the person who brought it. Lev 1:5,11.
 Killed, if a bird, by the priest. Lev 1:15.
 For the people at large, killed and prepared by the Levites. Ezek 44:11.
 A male without blemish. Lev 1:3; 22:19.
 Voluntary. Lev 1:3; 22:18,19.
 Presented at the door of the tabernacle. Lev 1:3; Deut 12:6,11,14.
 Offered by priests only. Lev 1:9; Ezek 44:15.
 Offered in righteousness. Ps 51:19.
 Entirely burned. Lev 1:8,9,12,13; 6:9.
 Blood of, sprinkled round about upon the altar. Lev 1:5,11.
Blood of, sprinkled round about upon the altar. Lev 1:5,11.
If a bird, the blood was wrung out at the side of the altar. Lev 1:15.
Ashes of, collected at foot of the altar, and conveyed without the camp. Lev 6:11.
Skin of, given to the priests for clothing. Lev 7:8; Gen 3:21.
Was offered
 Every morning and evening. Ex 29:38-42.
 Every Sabbath day. Num 28:9,10.
 The first day of every month. Num 28:11.
 The seven days of unleavened bread. Num 28:19,24.
 The Day of Atonement. Lev 16:3,5; Num 29:8.
 At consecration of Levites. Num 8:12.
 At consecration priests. Lev 9:2,12-14.
 At consecration of kings. 1 Chr 29:21-23.
 At purification of women. Lev 12:6.
 For Nazirites after defilement, or at the end of their vow. Num 6:11,14.
 For the healed leper. Lev 14:13,19,20.
 At dedication of sacred places. Num 7:15; 1 Kin 8:64.
 After great mercies. 1 Sam 6:14; 2 Sam 24:22,25.
 Before going to war. 1 Sam 7:9.
 With sounds of trumpets at feasts. Num 10:10.
The fat, etc. of all peace offerings laid on, and consumed with the daily. Lev 3:5; 6:12.
Of the wicked, not accepted by God. Is 1:10,11; Jer 6:19,20; Amos 5:22.
Obedience better than. 1 Sam 15:22; Jer 7:21-23.
Knowledge of God better than. Hos 6:6.
Love of God better than. Mark 12:33.
Abraham tried by the command to offer Isaac as. Gen 22:1-24.
Incapable of removing sin, and reconciling to God. Ps 40:6; 50:8; Heb 10:6.
The most costly, no adequate tribute to God. Is 40:16; Ps 50:9-13.
Guilt of unauthorised persons offering. 1 Sam 13:12,13.
Guilt of offering, except in the place appointed. Lev 17:8,9.
Of human victims execrated. Deut 12:31; 2 Kin 3:27; Jer 7:31; 19:5.
Illustrative of
 The offering of Christ. Eph 5:2; Heb 10:8-10.
 Devotedness to God. Rom 12:1.

Busy-Bodies.

Fools are. Prov 20:3.
The idle are. 2 Thess 3:11; 1 Tim 5:13.
Are mischievous tale-bearers. 1 Tim 5:13.
Bring mischief upon themselves. 2 Kin 14:10; Prov 26:17.
Christians must not be. 1 Pet 4:15.

Calf, The.

The young of the herd. Job 21:10; Jer 31:12.
Playfulness of, alluded to. Ps 29:6.
Fed on
 Milk. 1 Sam 6:10.
 Branches of trees, etc. Is 27:10.
Fattened in stalls, etc. 1 Sam 28:24; Amos 6:4.
Offered in sacrifice. Lev 9:2,3; Heb 9:12,19.
Of a year old best for sacrifice. Mic 6:6.
If firstborn not redeemed. Num 18:17.
Eaten in the patriarchal age. Gen 18:7,8.
When fattened considered a delicacy. 1 Sam 28:24,25; Amos 6:4; Luke 15:23,27.
Illustrative of
 Saints nourished by grace. Mal 4:2.
 Sacrifices of praise. Hos 14:2; Heb 13:5.
 Patient endurance. Ezek 1:7; Rev 4:7.

Calf of Gold.

Made on account of the delay of Moses in the mount. Ex 32:1.
Was made
 Of the ornaments of the women, etc. Ex 32:2,3.
 To represent God. Ex 32:4,5; Ps 106:20.
 After an Egyptian model. Acts 7:39,41.
 To go before the congregation. Ex 32:1.
Molten in the fire. Ex 32:4; Ps 106:19.
Fashioned with a graven tool. Ex 32:4.
An altar built before. Ex 32:5.
Sacrifices offered to. Ex 32:6; Acts 7:41.
Worshipped with profane revelry. Ex 32:6,18,19,25; 1 Cor 10:7.
Making of
 A very great sin. Ex 32:21,30,31.
 A forgetting of God. Ps 106:21.
 A turning aside from the divine command. Ex 32:8; Deut 9:12,16.
 Excited wrath against Aaron. Deut 9:20.
 Excited wrath against Israel. Ex 32:10; Deut 9:14,19.
 Caused Moses to break the tables of the testimony. Ex 32:19; Deut 9:17.
 Israel punished for. Ex 32:26-29,35.
Moses interceded for those who worshipped. Ex 32:11-14,30-34; Deut 9:18-20.
Destroyed by Moses. Ex 32:20; Deut 9:21.
Punishment of those who worshipped a warning to others. 1 Cor 10:5-7.

Call of God, The.

By Christ. Is 55:5; Rom 1:6.
By his Spirit. Rev 22:17.
By his works. Ps 19:2,3; Rom 1:20.
By his ministers. Jer 35:15; 2 Cor 5:20.
By his gospel. 2 Thess 2:14.
Is from darkness. 1 Pet 2:9.
Addressed to all. Is 45:22; Matt 20:16.
Most reject. Prov 1:24; Matt 20:16.
Effectual to saints. Ps 110:3; Acts 2:47; 13:48; 1 Cor 1:24.
To man is
 Of grace. Gal 1:15; 2 Tim 1:9.
 According to the purpose of God. Rom 8:28; 9:11,23,24.
 High. Phil 3:14.
 Holy. 1 Tim 1:9.
 Heavenly. Heb 3:1.
 To fellowship with Christ. 1 Cor 1:9.
 To holiness. 1 Thess 4:7.
 To liberty. Gal 5:13.
 To peace. 1 Cor 7:15; Col 3:15.
 To glory and virtue. 2 Pet 1:3.
 To the eternal glory of Christ. 2 Thess 2:14; 1 Pet 5:10.
 To eternal life. 1 Tim 6:12.
Partakers of, justified. Rom 8:30.
Walk worthy of. Eph 4:1.
Blessedness of receiving. Rev 19:9.
Praise God for. 1 Pet 2:9.
Illustrated. Prov 9:3,4; Matt 23:3-9.
Rejection of, leads to
 Judicial blindness. Is 6:9; Acts 28:24-27; Rom 11:8-10.
 Delusion. Is 66:4; 2 Thess 2:10,11.
Withdrawal of the means of grace. Jer 26:4-6; Acts 13:46; 18:6; Rev 2:5.
Temporal judgments. Is 28:12; Jer 6:16,19; 35:17; Zech 7:12-14.
Rejection by God. Prov 1:14-32; Jer 6:19,30.
Condemnation. John 12:48; Heb 2:1-3; 12:25.
Destruction. Prov 29:1; Matt 22:3-7.

Calves of Jeroboam.

Made of gold. 1 Kin 12:28.
Made to prevent the Israelites going to Jerusalem. 1 Kin 12:26,27.
Called the
 Golden calves. 2 Kin 10:29; 2 Chr 13:8.
 Calves of Bethaven. Hos 10:5.
 Calves of Samaria. Hos 8:5.
Placed in Dan and Bethel. 1 Kin 12:29.
Probably from an Egyptian model. 1 Kin 11:40.
Designed to represent God. 1 Kin 12:28.
Priests appointed for. 1 Kin 12:31; 2 Chr 11:15.
Sacrifices offered to. 1 Kin 12:32; 13:1.
Feasts appointed for. 1 Kin 12:32,33.
Were kissed in adoration. Hos 13:2.
Worship of
 Denounced by a prophet. 1 Kin 13:1-3.

Adopted by succeeding kings. 1 Kin 15:34; 16:26; 2 Kin 10:29,31; 14:24.
Became the sin of Israel. 1 Kin 12:30; 2 Kin 10:31; 2 Chr 13:8.
God's people refused to worship. 1 Kin 19:18; 2 Chr 11:16.
Guilt of making. 1 Kin 14:9,10.
Guilt of worshipping. 1 Kin 14:15,16; 2 Kin 17:22,23.
Predictions respecting
Captivity. Hos 10:6.
Destruction. Hos 8:6; 10:8.
Punishment of the worshippers. Hos 8:13,14.

Camel, The.

Unclean. Lev 11:4; Deut 14:7.
Found in deserted places. Ezek 25:5.
Characterised by
The bunches on its back. Is 30:6.
Its docility. Gen 24:11.
The dromedary a species of, remarkable for swiftness. Jer 2:23.
Abounded in the east. 1 Chr 5:21; Is 60:6.
A part of patriarchal wealth. Gen 12:16; 30:43; Job 1:3.
Kept in numbers by kings. 1 Chr 27:30.
Used for
Riding. Gen 24:61.
Drawing chariots. Is 21:7.
Carrying burdens. Gen 37:25; 1 Kin 10:2; 2 Kin 8:9.
Conveying posts and messengers. Esth 8:10.
War. Judg 7:12; 1 Sam 30:17.
Of the rich adorned with chains. Judg 8:21,26.
Furniture of, alluded to. Gen 31:34.
Subject to plagues. Ex 9:3; Zech 14:15.
Treated with great care. Gen 24:31,32.
Esteemed a valuable booty. 1 Chr 5:20,21; 2 Chr 14:15; Job 1:17; Jer 49:29,32.
Coarse cloth made from its hair. Matt 3:4.
Referred to in illustrations by Christ. Matt 19:24; 23:24.

Canaanites, The.

Descended from Ham. Gen 10:6.
An accursed race. Gen 9:25,26.
Different families of. Gen 10:15-18.
Comprised seven distinct nations. Deut 7:1.
Possessions of, how bounded. Gen 10:19.
Country of, fertile. Ex 3:17; Num 13:27.
Described as
Great and mighty. Num 13:28; Deut 7:1.
Idolatrous. Deut 29:17.
Superstitious. Deut 18:9-11.
Profane and wicked. Lev 18:27.
Extremely numerous. Deut 7:17.
Had many strong cities. Num 13:28; Deut 1:28.
Expelled for wickedness. Deut 9:4; 18:12.
Abraham
Called to dwell amongst. Gen 12:1-5.
Was promised the country of, of inheritance. Gen 13:14-17; 15:18; 17:8.
Had his faith tried by dwelling amongst. Gen 12:6; 13:7.
Kind to the patriarchs. Gen 14:13; 23:6.
Israel commanded
To make no league with. Deut 7:2; Judg 2:2.
Not to intermarry with. Deut 7:3; Josh 23:12.
Not to follow idols of. Ex 23:24; Deut 7:25.
Not to follow customs of. Lev 18:26,27.
To destroy, without mercy. Deut 7:2,24.
To destroy all vestiges of their idolatry. Ex 23:24; Deut 7:5,25.
Not to fear. Deut 7:17,18; 31:7.
Terrified at the approach of Israel. Ex 15:15,16; Josh 2:9-11; 5:1.
Partially subdued by Israel. Josh 10:1-11:23; Judg 1:1-36.
Part of left
To try Israel. Judg 2:21,22; 3:1-4.
To chastise Israel. Num 33:55; Judg 2:3; 4:2.
Israel ensnared by. Judg 2:3,19; Ps 106:36-38.
Some descendants of, in our Lord's time. Matt 15:22; Mark 7:26.

Candlestick.

A part of household furniture. 2 Kin 4:10.
Used for holding
Candles or torches. Matt 5:15.
Lamps. Ex 25:31,37; Zech 4:2.
For the tabernacle
Form, etc. of. Ex 25:31-36; 37:17-22.
Held seven golden lamps. Ex 25:37; 37:23.
Had snuffers, etc. of gold. Ex 25:38; 37:23.
Weighed a talent of gold. Ex 25:39.
After a divine pattern. Ex 25:40; Num 8:4.
Called the lamp of God. 1 Sam 3:3.
Called the pure candlestick. Lev 24:4.
Placed in the outer sanctuary over against the table. Ex 40:24; Heb 9:2.
Lighted with olive oil. Ex 27:20; Lev 24:2.
Lighted etc. by priests. Ex 27:21; Lev 24:3,4.
Directions for removing. Num 4:9,10.
Illustrative Of
Christ. Zech 4:2; John 8:12; Heb 9:2.
The church. Rev 1:13,20.
Ministers. Matt 5:14-16.

Care, Overmuch.

About earthly things, forbidden. Matt 6:25; Luke 12:22,29; John 6:27.
God's providential goodness should keep us from. Matt 6:26,28,30; Luke 22:35.
God's promises should keep us from. Heb 13:5.
Trust in God should free us from. Jer 17:7,8; Dan 3:16.
Should be cast on God. Ps 37:5; 55:22; Prov 16:3; 1 Pet 5:7.
An obstruction to the gospel. Matt 13:22; Luke 8:14; 14:18-20.
Be without. 1 Cor 7:32; Phil 4:6.
Unbecoming in saints. 2 Tim 2:4.
Uselessness of. Matt 6:27; Luke 12:25,26.
Vanity of. Ps 39:6; Eccl 4:8.
Warning against. Luke 21:34.
Sent as a punishment to the wicked. Ezek 4:16; 12:19.
Exemplified
Martha. Luke 10:41.
Persons who offered to follow Christ. Luke 9:57.

Caves.

Natural. Heb 11:38.
Artificial. Judg 6:2.
Found in the
Open fields. Gen 23:20.
Rocks. Is 2:19.
Were used as
Dwelling-places. Gen 19:30.
Places of concealment. 1 Sam 13:6; 14:11; 1 Kin 18:4; Heb 11:38.
Resting places. 1 Sam 24:3; 1 Kin 19:9.
Burial places. Gen 23:19; John 11:38.
Haunts of robbers. Jer 7:11; Matt 21:13.
Hiding placed of wild beasts. Nah 2:12.
Often capacious. 1 Sam 22:1,2; 24:3.
Afford no protection from the judgments of God. Is 2:19; Ezek 33:27; Rev 6:15.
Mentioned in Scripture
Adullam. 1 Sam 22:1.
Engedi. 1 Sam 23:29; 24:1,3.
Machpelah. Gen 23:9.
Makkedah. John 10:16,17.

Cedar, The.

Planted by God. Ps 104:16; Is 41:19.
Made to glorify God. Ps 148:9.
Lebanon celebrated for. Judg 9:15; Ps 92:12.
Banks of rivers favourable to the growth of. Num 24:6.
Imported largely by Solomon. 1 Kin 10:27.
Described as
High. Is 37:24; Ezek 17:22; Amos 2:9.
Spreading. Ps 80:10,11.
Fragrant. Song 4:11.
Graceful and beautiful. Ps 80:10; Ezek 17:23.
Strong and durable. Is 9:10.
Considered the first of trees. 1 Kin 4:33.
Extensive commerce in. 1 Kin 5:10,11; Ezra 3:7.
Used in
Building temples. 1 Kin 5:5,6; 6:9,10.
Building palaces. 2 Sam 5:11; 1 Kin 7:2,3.
Making masts of ships. Ezek 27:5.
Making wardrobes. Ezek 27:24.
Making chariots. Song 3:9.
Purifying the leper. Lev 14:4-7,49-52.
Preparing the water of separation. Num 19:6.
Making idols. Is 44:14.
The eagle alluded to as
Making its nest in. Jer 22:23.
Perching on the high branches of. Ezek 17:3.
Instrumental in propagating. Ezek 17:4,5.
Destruction of, a punishment. Jer 22:7.

Destruction of, exhibits God's power. Ps 29:5.
Illustrative of
- Majesty, strength, and glory of Christ. Song 5:15; Ezek 17:22,23.
- Beauty and glory of Israel. Num 24:6.
- Saints in their rapid growth. Ps 92:12.
- Powerful nations. Ezek 31:3; Amos 2:9.
- Arrogant rulers. Is 2:13; 10:33,34.

Censers.

For burning incense. Lev 10:1; 2 Chr 26:19.
Made of
- Brass. Num 16:39.
- Gold. 1 Kin 7:50.

One of gold in the most holy place. Heb 9:4.
Directions for removing. Num 4:14.
Often used in idolatrous worship. Ezek 8:11.
Of Korah, etc. made into plates to cover the altar. Num 16:18,39.
Typical of Christ's intercession. Rev 8:3,5.

Character of Saints.

Attentive to Christ's voice. John 10:3,4.
Blameless and harmless. Phil 2:15.
Bold. Prov 28:1; Rom 13:3.
Contrite. Is 57:15; 66:2.
Devout. Acts 8:2; 22:12.
Faithful. Rev 17:14.
Fearing God. Matt 3:16; Acts 10:2.
Following Christ. John 10:4,27.
Godly. Ps 4:3; 2 Pet 2:9.
Guileless. John 1:47.
Holy. Deut 7:6; 14:2; Col 3:12.
Humble. Ps 34:2; 1 Pet 5:5.
Hungering after righteousness. Matt 5:6.
Just. Gen 6:9; Hab 2:4; Luke 2:25.
Led by the Spirit. Rom 8:14.
Liberal. Is 32:8; 2 Cor 9:13.
Loving. Col 1:4; 1 Thess 4:9.
Lowly. Prov 16:19.
Meek. Is 29:19; Matt 5:5.
Merciful. Ps 37:26; Matt 5:7.
New creatures. 2 Cor 5:17; Eph 2:10.
Obedient. Rom 16:19; 1 Pet 1:14.
Poor in spirit. Ps 51:17; Matt 5:3.
Prudent. Prov 16:21.
Pure in heart. Matt 5:8; 1 John 3:3.
Righteous. Is 60:21; Luke 1:6.
Sincere. 2 Cor 1:12; 2:17.
Steadfast. Acts 2:42; Col 2:5.
Taught of God. Is 54:13; 1 John 2:27.
True. 2 Cor 6:8.
Undefiled. Ps 119:1.
Upright. 1 Kin 3:6; Ps 15:2.
Watchful. Luke 12:37.
Zealous of good works. Titus 2:14; 3:8.

Character of the Wicked.

Abominable. Rev 21:8.
Alienated from God. Eph 4:18; Col 1:21.
Blasphemous. Luke 22:65; Rev 16:9.
Blinded. 2 Cor 4:4; Eph 4:18.
Boastful. Ps 10:3; 49:6.
Conspiring against God's people. Neh 4:8; 6:2; Ps 38:12.
Covetous. Mic 2:2; Rom 1:29.
Deceitful. Ps 5:6; Rom 3:13.
Delighting in the iniquity of others. Prov 2:14; Rom 1:32.
Despising the works of the faithful. Neh 2:19; 4:2; 2 Tim 3:3,4.
Destructive. Is 59:7.
Disobedient. Neh 9:26; Titus 3:3; 1 Pet 2:7.
Enticing to evil. Prov 1:10-14; 2 Tim 3:6.
Envious. Neh 2:10; Titus 3:3.
Fearful. Prov 28:1; Rev 21:8.
Fierce. Prov 16:29; 2 Tim 3:3.
Foolish. Deut 32:6; Ps 5:5.
Forgetting God. Job 8:13.
Fraudulent. Ps 37:21; Mic 6:11.
Froward. Prov 21:8; Is 57:17.
Glorying in their shame. Phil 3:19.
Hard-hearted. Ezek 3:7.
Hating the light. Job 24:13; John 3:20.
Heady and high-minded. 2 Tim 3:4.
Hostile to God. Rom 8:7; Col 1:21.
Hypocritical. Is 29:13; 2 Tim 3:5.
Ignorant of God. Hos 4:1; 2 Thess 1:8.
Impudent. Ezek 2:4.
Incontinent. 2 Tim 3:3.
Infidel. Ps 10:4; 14:1.
Loathsome. Prov 13:5.
Lovers of pleasure more than of God. 2 Tim 3:4.
Lying. Ps 58:3; 62:4; Is 59:4.
Mischievous. Prov 24:8; Mic 7:3.
Murderous. Ps 10:8; 94:6; Rom 1:29.
Prayerless. Job 21:15; Ps 53:4.
Persecuting. Ps 69:26; 109:16.
Perverse. Deut 32:5.
Proud. Ps 59:12; Obad 3:2; 2 Tim 3:2.
Rejoicing in the affliction of saints. Ps 35:15.
Reprobate. 2 Cor 13:5; 2 Tim 3:8; Titus 1:16.
Selfish. 2 Tim 3:2.
Sensual. Phil 3:19; Jude 1:19.
Sold under sin. 1 Kin 21:20; 2 Kin 17:17.
Stiff-hearted. Ezek 2:4.
Stiff-necked. Ex 33:5; Acts 7:51.
Uncircumcised in heart. Jer 9:26; Acts 7:51.
Unjust. Prov 11:7; Is 26:10.
Unmerciful. Rom 1:31.
Ungodly. Prov 16:27.
Unholy. 2 Tim 3:2.
Unprofitable. Matt 25:30; Rom 3:12.
Unruly. Titus 1:10.
Unthankful. Luke 6:35; 2 Tim 3:2.
Untoward. Acts 2:40.
Unwise. Deut 32:6.

Chariots.

Carriages for travelling, etc. Gen 46:29.
Carriages used in war. 1 Kin 20:25.
Wheels of, described. 1 Kin 7:33.
Bound with traces. Mic 1:13.
Drawn by
- Horses. 2 Kin 10:2; Song 1:9.
- Asses and camels. Is 21:7.

Value of in Solomon's time. 1 Kin 10:29.
Drivers generally employed for. 1 Kin 22:34; 2 Chr 18:33.
Sometimes driven by the owners. 2 Kin 9:16,20.
Sometimes driven furiously. 2 Kin 9:20; Is 5:28; Jer 4:13.
Bounding motion of, referred to. Nah 3:2.
Noise occasioned by, referred to. 2 Kin 7:6; Joel 2:5; Nah 3:2; Rev 9:9.
Introduced into Israel by David. 2 Sam 8:4.
Multiplied by Solomon. 1 Kin 10:26.
Imported from Egypt. 1 Kin 10:28,29.
For war
- Armed with iron. Josh 17:16; Judg 1:19.
- Lighted by night with torches. Nah 2:3.
- Commanded by captains. Ex 14:7; 1 Kin 16:9.
- Advantageously manoeuvred in a flat country. Judg 1:19; 1 Kin 20:23-25.
- Formed part of the line of battle. 1 Kin 20:25.
- Used in pursuing enemies. Ex 14:9; 2 Sam 1:6.
- Kept in chariot cities. 1 Kin 9:19; 10:26.

Used in war by the
- Egyptians. Ex 14:7; 2 Kin 18:24.
- Canaanites. Josh 17:16; Judg 4:3.
- Philistines. 1 Sam 13:5.
- Syrians. 2 Sam 10:18; 1 Kin 20:1.
- Assyrians. 2 Kin 19:23.
- Ethiopians. 2 Chr 14:9; 16:8.
- Babylonians. Ezek 23:23; 26:7.
- Jews. 2 Kin 8:21; 10:2.

Kings rode in, to battle. 1 Kin 22:35.
Kings used, in common. 1 Kin 12:18; 18:44.
Persons of distinction used. Gen 41:43; 2 Kin 5:9,21; Jer 17:25; Acts 8:28.
Often attended by running footmen. 1 Sam 8:11; 2 Sam 15:1; 1 Kin 1:5.
Consecrated to the sun. 2 Kin 23:11.
The Jews condemned for
- Multiplying. Is 2:7.
- Trusting to. Is 22:18; 31:1.
- Taken in war, often destroyed. Josh 11:6,9; Jer 51:21; Mic 5:10; Nah 2:13.

Illustrative of
- The clouds. Ps 104:3.
- The judgments of God. Is 66:15.
- Angels. 2 Kin 6:16,17; Ps 68:17.
- Prophets. 2 Kin 2:12; 13:14.
- Christ's love to his church. Song 6:12.

Elijah taken to heaven in one of fire. 2 Kin 2:11.

Charity.

Explained. 1 Cor 13:4-7.
Enjoined. See "Love to man." Col 3:14.

Chastity.

Commanded. Ex 20:14; Prov 31:3; Acts 15:20; Rom 13:13; Col 3:5; 1 Thess 4:3.
Required in look. Job 31:1; Matt 5:28.
Required in heart. Prov 6:25.
Required in speech. Eph 5:3.
Keep the body in. 1 Cor 6:13,15-18.
Preserved by wisdom. Prov 2:10,11,16; 7:1-5.
Saints are kept in. Eccl 7:26.
Advantages of. 1 Pet 3:1,2.
Shun those devoid of. 1 Cor 5:11; 1 Pet 4:3.
The wicked are devoid of. Rom 1:29; Eph 4:19; 2 Pet 2:14; Jude 1:8.

Temptation to deviate from, dangerous. 2 Sam 11:2-4.
Consequences of associating with those devoid of. Prov 7:25-27; 22:14.
Want of, excludes from heaven. Gal 5:19-21.
Drunkenness destructive to. Prov 23:31-33.
Breach of, punished. 1 Cor 3:16,17; Eph 5:5,6; Heb 13:4; Rev 22:15.
Motives for. 1 Cor 6:19; 1 Thess 4:7.
Exemplified
  Abimelech. Gen 20:4,5; 26:10,11.
  Joseph. Gen 39:7-10.
  Ruth. Ruth 3:10,11.
  Boaz. Ruth 3:13.

CHERUBIM.

Form and appearance of. Ezek 1:5-11,13,14.
Animated by the Spirit of God. Ezek 1:12,20.
Engaged in accomplishing the purposes of God. Ezek 1:15,21; 10:9-11,16,17.
The glory of God exhibited upon. Ezek 1:22,26-28; 10:4,18,20.
Sound of their wings was as the voice of God. Ezek 1:24; 10:5.
Placed at the entrance of Eden. Gen 3:24.
Of gold
  Formed out of, and at each end of the mercy seat. Ex 25:18-20.
  Placed over the ark of the covenant. 1 Sam 4:4; 1 Kin 8:6,7; 2 Chr 5:7,8.
  God's presence manifested between. 2 Sam 6:2; 2 Kin 19:15; Ps 80:1; 99:1.
  The oracles or answers of God delivered from between. Ex 25:22; Num 7:89.
Called the cherubim of glory. Heb 9:5.
Representations of, made on the
  Curtains of the tabernacle. Ex 26:1,31.
  Vail of the tabernacle. Ex 26:31.
  Vail of the temple. 2 Chr 3:14.
  Doors of the temple. 1 Kin 6:32,35.
  Walls of the temple. 2 Chr 3:7.
  Bases of brazen lavers. 1 Kin 7:29,36.
Riding on, illustrative of majesty and power of God. 2 Sam 22:11; Ps 18:10.

CHILDREN.

Christ was an example to. Luke 2:51; John 19:26,27.
Are a gift from God. Gen 33:5; Ps 127:3.
Are capable of glorifying God. Ps 8:2; 148:12,13; Matt 21:15,16.
Should be
  Brought to Christ. Mark 10:13-16.
  Brought early to the house of God. 1 Sam 1:24.
  Instructed in the ways of God. Deut 31:12,13; Prov 22:6.
  Judiciously trained. Prov 22:15; 29:17; Eph 6:4.
Should
  Obey God. Deut 30:2.
  Fear God. Prov 24:21.
  Remember God. Eccl 12:1.
  Attend to parental teaching. Prov 1:8,9.
  Honour parents. Ex 20:12; Heb 12:9.
  Fear parents. Lev 19:3.
  Obey parents. Prov 6:20; Eph 6:1.
  Take care of parents. 1 Tim 5:4.
  Honour the aged. Lev 19:32; 1 Pet 5:5.
  Not imitate bad parents. Ezek 20:18.
An heritage from the Lord. Ps 113:9; 127:3.
Not to have
  Considered an affliction. Gen 15:2,3; Jer 22:30.
  A reproach in Israel. 1 Sam 1:6,7; Luke 1:25.
Anxiety of the Jews for. Gen 30:1; 1 Sam 1:5,8.
Often prayed for. 1 Sam 1:10,11; Luke 1:13.
Often given in answer to prayer. Gen 25:21; 1 Sam 1:27; Luke 1:13.
Treatment of, after birth, noticed. Ezek 16:4.
Mostly nursed by the mothers. 1 Sam 1:22; 1 Kin 3:21; Ps 22:9; Song 8:1.
Weaning of, a time of joy and feasting. Gen 21:8; 1 Sam 1:24.
Circumcised on the eighth day. Phil 3:5.
Named at circumcision. Luke 1:59; 2:21.
Were named
  After relatives. Luke 1:59,61.
  From remarkable events. Gen 21:3,6; 18:13; Ex 2:10; 18:3,4.
  From circumstances connected with their birth. Gen 25:25,26; 35:18; 1 Chr 4:9.
  Often by God. Is 8:3; Hos 1:4,6,9.
  Often numerous. 2 Kin 10:1; 1 Chr 4:27.
  Numerous, considered an especial blessing. Ps 115:14; 127:4,5.
  Sometimes born when parents were old. Gen 15:3,6; 17:17; Luke 1:18.
Male
  If firstborn, belonged to God and were redeemed. Ex 13:12,13,15.
  Birth of, announced to the father by a messenger. Jer 20:15.
  Under the care of tutors, till they came of age. 2 Kin 10:1; Gal 4:1,2.
  Usefully employed. 1 Sam 9:3; 17:15.
  Inherited the possessions of their father. Deut 21:16,17; Luke 12:13,14.
  Received the blessing of their father before his death. Gen 27:1-4; 48:15; 49:1-33.
Female
  Taken care of by nurses. Gen 35:8.
  Usefully employed. Gen 24:13; Ex 2:16.
  Inherited property in default of sons. Num 27:1-8; Josh 17:1-6.
Fondness and care of mothers for. Ex 2:2-10; 1 Sam 2:19; 1 Kin 3:27; Is 49:15; 1 Thess 2:7,8.
Of God's people, holy. Ezra 9:2; 1 Cor 7:14.
Of God's people, interested in the promises. Deut 29:29; Acts 2:39.
Prosperity of, greatly depended on obedience of parents. Deut 4:40; 12:25,28; Ps 128:1-3.
Frequently bore the curse of parents. Ex 20:5; Ps 109:9,10.
Were required
  To honour their parents. Ex 20:12.
  To attend to instruction. Deut 4:9; 11:19.
  To submit to discipline. Prov 29:17; Heb 12:9.
  To respect the aged. Lev 19:32.
Mode of giving public instruction to. Luke 2:46; Acts 22:3.
Power of parents over, during the patriarchal age. Gen 9:24,25; 21:14; 38:24.
Often wicked and rebellious. 2 Kin 2:23.
Rebellious, punished by the civil power. Ex 21:15-17; Deut 21:18-21.
Sometimes devoted their property to avoid supporting parents. Matt 15:5; Mark 7:11,12.
Could demand their portion during father's life. Luke 15:12.
Amusements of. Zech 8:5; Matt 11:16,17.
Casting out of weak, etc. alluded to. Ezek 16:5.
Inhuman practice of offering to idols. 2 Kin 17:31; 2 Chr 28:3; 33:6.
Illegitimate
  Had no inheritance. Gen 21:10,14; Gal 4:30.
  Not cared for by the father. Heb 12:8.
  Excluded from the congregation. Deut 23:2.
  Sometimes sent away with gifts. Gen 25:6.
  Despised by their brethren. Judg 11:2.
Destruction of, a punishment. Lev 26:22; Ezek 9:6; Luke 19:44.
Grief occasioned by loss of. Gen 37:35; 44:27-29; 2 Sam 13:37; Jer 6:26; 31:15.
Resignation manifested at loss of. Lev 10:19,20; 2 Sam 12:18-23; Job 1:19-21.

CHILDREN, GOOD.

The Lord is with. 1 Sam 3:19.
Know the Scriptures. 2 Tim 3:15.
Observe the law of God. Prov 28:7.
Their obedience to parents is well pleasing to God. Col 3:20.
Partake of the promises of God. Acts 2:39.
Shall be blessed. Prov 3:1-4; Eph 6:2,3.
Show love to parents. Gen 46:29.
Obey parents. Gen 28:7; 47:30.
Attend to parental teaching. Prov 13:1.
Take care of parents. Gen 45:9,11; 47:12.
Make their parents' hearts glad. Prov 10:1; 29:17.
Honour the aged. Job 32:6,7.
Adduced as a motive for submission to God. Heb 12:9.
Spirit of, a requisite for the kingdom of heaven. Matt 18:3.
Illustrative of a teachable spirit. Matt 18:4.
Exemplified
  Isaac. Gen 22:6-10.
  Joseph. Gen 45:9; 46:29.
  Jephthah's daughter. Judg 11:34,36.
  Samson. Judg 13:24.
  Samuel. 1 Sam 3:19.
  Obadiah. 1 Kin 18:12.
  Josiah. 2 Chr 34:3.
  Esther. Esth 2:20.
  Job. Job 29:4.
  David. 1 Sam 17:20; Ps 71:5.
  Daniel. Dan 1:6.
  John the Baptist. Luke 1:80.
  Children in the temple. Matt 21:15,16.
  Timothy. 2 Tim 3:15.

Children, Wicked.

Know not God. 1 Sam 2:12.
Are void of understanding. Prov 7:7.
Are proud. Is 3:5.
With regard to parents
  Hearken not to them. 1 Sam 2:25.
  Despise them. Prov 15:5,20; Ezek 22:7.
  Curse them. Prov 30:11.
  Bring reproach on them. Prov 19:26.
  Are a calamity to them. Prov 19:13.
  Are a grief to them. Prov 17:25.
  Despised their elders. Job 19:18.
Punishment of, for
  Setting light by parents. Deut 27:16.
  Disobeying parents. Deut 21:21.
  Mocking parents. Prov 30:17.
  Cursing parents. Ex 21:15; Mark 7:10.
  Smiting parents. Ex 21:15.
  Mocking of a prophet. 2 Kin 2:23,24.
  Gluttony and drunkenness. Deut 21:20,21.
Their guilt in robbing parents. Prov 28:24.
Exemplified
  Esau. Gen 26:34,35.
  Sons of Eli. 1 Sam 2:,12,17.
  Sons of Samuel. 1 Sam 8:3.
  Absalom. 2 Sam 15:10.
  Adonijah. 1 Kin 1:5,6.
  Children at Bethel. 2 Kin 2:23.
  Adrammelech and Sharezer. 2 Kin 19:37.

Christ, Character Of.

Altogether lovely. Song 5:16.
Holy. Luke 1:35; Acts 4:27; Rev 3:7.
Righteous. Is 53:11; Heb 1:9.
Good. Matt 19:16.
Faithful. Is 11:5; 1 Thess 5:24.
True. John 1:14; 7:18; 1 John 5:20.
Just. Zech 9:9; John 5:30; Acts 22:14.
Guileless. Is 53:9; 1 Pet 2:22.
Sinless. John 8:46; 2 Cor 5:21.
Spotless. 1 Pet 1:19.
Innocent. Matt 27:4.
Harmless. Heb 7:26.
Resisting temptation. Matt 4:1-10.
Obedient to God the Father. Ps 40:8; John 4:34; 15:10.
Zealous. Luke 2:49; John 2:17; 8:29.
Meek. Is 53:7; Zech 9:9; Matt 11:29.
Lowly in heart. Matt 11:29.
Merciful. Heb 2:17.
Patient. Is 53:7; Matt 27:14.
Long-suffering. 1 Tim 1:16.
Compassionate. Is 40:11; Luke 19:41.
Benevolent. Matt 4:23,24; Acts 10:38.
Loving. John 13:1; 15:13.
Self-denying. Matt 8:20; 2 Cor 8:9.
Humble. Luke 22:27; Phil 2:8.
Resigned. Luke 22:42.
Forgiving. Luke 23:34.
Subject to His parents. Luke 2:51.
Saints are conformed to. Rom 8:29.

Christ is God.

As Jehovah. Is 40:3; Matt 3:3.
As Jehovah of glory. Ps 24:7,10; 1 Cor 2:8; James 2:1.
As Jehovah, our Righteousness. Jer 23:5,6; 1 Cor 1:30.
As Jehovah, above all. Ps 97:9; John 3:31.
As Jehovah, the First and the Last. Is 44:6; Rev 1:17; Is 48:12-16; Rev 22:13.
As Jehovah's Fellow and Equal. Zech 13:7; Phil 2:6.
As Jehovah of Hosts. Is 6:1-3; John 12:41; Is 8:13,14; 1 Pet 2:8.
As Jehovah, the Shepherd. Is 40:11; Heb 13:20.
As Jehovah, for whose glory all things were created. Prov 16:4; Col 1:16.
As Jehovah, the Messenger of the covenant. Mal 3:1; Mark 1:2; Luke 2:27.
Invoked as Jehovah. Joel 2:32; Acts 2:21; 1 Cor 1:2.
As the Eternal God and Creator. Ps 102:24-27; Heb 1:8,10-12.
As the mighty God. Is 9:6.
As the Great God and Saviour. Hos 1:7; Titus 2:13.
As God over all. Ps 45:6,7; Rom 9:5.
As the true God. Jer 10:10; 1 John 5:20.
As God the Word. John 1:1.
As God, the Judge. Eccl 12:14; 1 Cor 4:5; 2 Cor 5:10; 2 Tim 4:1.
As Emmanuel. Is 7:14; Matt 1:23.
As King of kings and Lord of lords. Dan 10:17; Rev 1:5; 17:14.
As the Holy One. 1 Sam 2:2; Acts 3:14.
As the Lord from heaven. 1 Cor 15:47.
As Lord of the Sabbath. Gen 2:3; Matt 12:8.
As Lord of all. Acts 10:36; Rom 10:11-13.
As Son of God. Matt 26:63-67.
As the Only-begotten Son of the Father. John 1:14,18; 3:16,18; 1 John 4:9.
His blood is called the blood of God. Acts 20:28.
As one with the Father. John 10:30,38; 12:45; 14:7-10; 17:10.
As sending the Spirit, equally with the Father. John 14:16; 15:26.
As entitled to equal honour with the Father. John 5:23.
As Owner of all things, equally with the Father. John 16:15.
As unrestricted by the law of the Sabbath, equally with the Father. John 5:17.
As the Source of grace, equally with the Father. 1 Thess 3:11; 2 Thess 2:16,17.
As unsearchable, equally with the Father. Prov 30:4; Matt 11:27.
As Creator of all things. Is 40:28; John 1:3; Col 1:16; Heb 1:2.
As Supporter and Preserver of all things. Neh 9:6; Col 1:17; Heb 1:3.
As possessed of the fulness of the God head. Col 2:9; Heb 1:3.
As raising the dead. John 5:21; 6:40,54.
As raising himself from the dead. John 2:19,21; 10:18.
As Eternal. Is 9:6; Mic 5:2; John 1:1; Col 1:17; Heb 1:8-10; Rev 1:8.
As Omnipresent. Matt 18:20; 28:20; John 3:13.
As Omnipotent. Ps 45:3; Phil 3:21; Rev 1:8.
As Omniscient. John 16:30; 21:17.
As discerning the thoughts of the heart. 1 Kin 8:39; Luke 5:22; Ezek 11:5; John 2:24,25; Rev 2:23.
As unchangeable. Mal 3:6; Heb 1:12; 13:8.
As having power to forgive sins. Col 3:13; Mark 2:7,10.
As Giver of pastors to the Church. Jer 3:15; Eph 4:11-13.
As Husband of the Church. Is 54:5; Eph 5:25-32; Is 62:5; Rev 21:2,9.
As the object of divine worship. Acts 7:59; 2 Cor 12:8,9; Heb 1:6; Rev 5:12.
As the object of faith. Ps 2:12; 1 Pet 2:6; Jer 17:5,7; John 14:1.
As God, he redeems and purifies the Church to himself. Rev 5:9; Titus 2:14.
As God, he presents the Church to himself. Eph 5:27; Jude 1:24,25.
Saints live to him as God. Rom 6:11; Gal 2:19; 2 Cor 5:15.
Acknowledged by his apostles. John 20:28.
Acknowledged by the Old Testament saints. Gen 17:1; 48:15,16; 32:24-30; Hos 12:3-5; Judg 6:22-24; 13:21,22; Job 19:25-27.

Christ, the Head of the Church.

Predicted. Ps 118:22; Matt 21:42.
Appointed by God. Eph 1:22.
Declared by himself. Matt 21:42.
As his mystical body. Eph 4:12,15; 5:23.
Has the pre-eminence in all things. 1 Cor 11:3; Eph 1:22; Col 1:18.
Commissioned his apostles. Matt 10:1,7; 28:19; John 20:21.
Instituted the ordinances. Matt 28:19; Luke 22:19,20.
Imparts gifts. Ps 68:18; Eph 4:8.
Saints are complete in. Col 2:10.
Perverters of the truth do not hold. Col 2:18,19.

Christ, the High Priest.

Appointed and called by God. Heb 3:1,2; 5:4,5.
After the order of Melchizedek. Ps 110:4; Heb 5:6; 6:20; 7:15,17.
Superior to Aaron and the Levitical priests. Heb 7:11,16,22; 8:1,2,6.
Consecrated with an oath. Heb 7:20,21.
Has an unchangeable priesthood. Heb 7:23,28.
Is of unblemished purity. Heb 7:26,28.
Faithful. Heb 3:2.
Needed no sacrifice for himself. Heb 7:27.
Offered himself a sacrifice. Heb 9:14,26.
His sacrifice superior to all others. Heb 9:13,14,23.
Offered sacrifice but once. Heb 7:27; 9:25,26.
Made reconciliation. Heb 2:17.
Obtained redemption for us. Heb 9:12.
Entered into heaven. Heb 4:14; 10:12.
Sympathises with those who are tempted. Heb 2:18; 4:15.
Intercedes. Heb 7:25; 9:24.
Blesses. Num 6:23-26; Acts 3:26.
On his throne. Zech 6:13.
Appointment of, and encouragement to steadfastness. Heb 4:14.
Typified
  Melchizedek. Gen 14:18-20.
  Aaron, etc. Ex 40:12-15.

Christ, the King.

Foretold. Num 24:17; Ps 2:6; 45:1-17; Is 9:7; Jer 23:5; Mic 5:2.
Glorious. Ps 24:7-10; 1 Cor 2:8; James 2:1.
Supreme. Ps 89:27; Rev 1:5; 19:16.
Sits in the throne of God. Rev 3:21.
Sits on the throne of David. Is 9:7; Ezek 37:24,25; Luke 1:32; Acts 2:30.
Is King of Zion. Ps 2:6; Is 52:7; Zech 9:9; Matt 21:5; John 12:12-15.
Has a righteous kingdom. Ps 45:6; Heb 1:8,9; Is 32:1; Jer 23:5.
Has an everlasting kingdom. Dan 2:44; 7:14; Luke 1:33.
Has an universal kingdom. Ps 2:8; 72:8; Zech 14:9; Rev 11:15.
His kingdom not of this world. John 18:36.
Saints, the subjects of. Col 1:13; Rev 15:3.
Saints receive a kingdom from. Luke 22:29,30; Heb 12:28.
Acknowledged by
- The wise men from the East. Matt 2:2.
- Nathanael. John 1:49.
- His followers. Luke 19:38; John 12:13.

Declared by himself. Matt 25:34; John 18:37.
Written on His cross. John 19:19.
The Jews shall seek to. Hos 3:5.
Saints shall behold. Is 33:17; Rev 22:3,4.
Kings shall do homage to. Ps 72:10; Is 49:7.
Shall overcome all his enemies. Ps 110:1; Mark 12:36; 1 Cor 15:25; Rev 17:14.
Typified
- Melchizedek. Gen 14:18.
- David. 1 Sam 16:1,12,13; Luke 1:32.
- Solomon. 1 Chr 28:6,7.

Christ, the Mediator.

In virtue of his atonement. Eph 2:13-18; Heb 9:15; 12:24.
The only one between God and man. 1 Tim 2:5.
Of the gospel covenant. Heb 8:6; 12:24.
Typified
- Moses. Deut 5:5; Gal 3:19.
- Aaron. Num 16:48.

Christ, the Prophet.

Foretold. Deut 18:15,18; Is 52:7; Nah 1:15.
Anointed with the Holy Spirit. Is 42:1; 61:1; Luke 4:18; John 3:34.
Alone knows and reveals God. Matt 11:27; John 3:2,13,34; 17:6,14,26; Heb 1:1,2.
Declared his doctrine to be that of the Father. John 8:26,28; 12:49,50; 14:10,24; 15:15; 17:8,16.
Preached the gospel, and worked miracles. Matt 4:23; 11:5; Luke 4:43.
Foretold things to come. Matt 24:3-35; Luke 19:41,44.
Faithful to his trust. Luke 4:43; John 17:8; Heb 3:2; Rev 1:5; 3:14.
Abounded in wisdom. Luke 2:40,47,52; Col 2:3.
Mighty in deed and word. Matt 13:54; Mark 1:27; Luke 4:32; John 7:46.
Meek and unostentatious in his teaching. Is 42:2; Matt 12:17-20.
God commands us to hear. Deut 18:15; Matt 17:25; Acts 3:22; 7:37.
God will severely visit our neglect of. Deut 18:19; Acts 3:23; Heb 2:3.
Typified
- Moses. Deut 18:15.

Christ, the Shepherd.

Foretold. Gen 49:24; Is 40:11; Ezek 34:23; 37:24.
The chief. 1 Pet 5:4.
The good. John 10:11,14.
The great. Mic 5:4; Heb 13:20.
His sheep
- He knows. John 10:14,27.
- He calls. John 10:3.
- He gathers. Is 40:11; John 10:16.
- He guides. Ps 23:3; John 10:3,4.
- He feeds. Ps 23:1,2; John 10:9.
- He cherishes tenderly. Is 40:11.
- He protects and preserves. Jer 31:10; Ezek 34:10; Zech 9:16; John 10:28.
- He laid down his life for. Zech 13:7; Matt 26:31; John 10:11,15; Acts 20:28.
- He gives eternal life to. John 10:28.

Typified
- David. 1 Sam 16:11.

Church, The.

Belongs to God. 1 Tim 3:15.
The body of Christ. Eph 1:23; Col 1:24.
Christ, the foundation-stone of. 1 Cor 3:11; Eph 2:20; 1 Pet 2:4,5.
Christ, the head of. Eph 1:22; 5:23.
Loved by Christ. Song 7:10; Eph 5:25.
Purchased by the blood of Christ. Acts 20:28; Eph 5:25; Heb 9:12.
Sanctified and cleansed by Christ. 1 Cor 6:11; Eph 5:26,27.
Subject to Christ. Rom 7:4; Eph 5:24.
The object of the grace of God. Is 27:3; 2 Cor 8:1.
Displays the wisdom of God. Eph 3:10.
Shows forth the praises of God. Is 60:6.
God defends. Ps 89:18; Is 4:5; 49:25; Matt 16:18.
God provides ministers for. Jer 3:15; Eph 4:11,12.
Glory to be ascribed to God by. Eph 3:21.
Elect. 1 Pet 5:13.
Glorious. Ps 45:13; Eph 5:27.
Clothed in righteousness. Rev 19:8.
Believers continually added to, by the Lord. Acts 2:27; 5:14; 11:24.
Unity of. Rom 12:5; 1 Cor 10:17; 12:12; Gal 3:28.
Saints baptised into, by one Spirit. 1 Cor 12:13.
Ministers commanded to feed. Acts 20:28.
Is edified by the Word. 1 Cor 14:4,13; Eph 4:15,16.
The wicked persecute. Acts 8:1-3; 1 Thess 2:14,15.
Not to be despised. 1 Cor 11:22.
Defiling of, will be punished. 1 Cor 3:17.
Extent of, predicted. Is 2:2; Ezek 17:22-24; Dan 2:34,35; Hab 2:14.

Church of Israel.

Established by God. Deut 4:5-14; 26:18; Acts 7:35,38.
Admission into, by circumcision. Gen 17:10-14.
All Israelites members of. Rom 9:4.
Was relatively holy. Ex 31:13; Num 16:3.
Had
- An appointed place of worship. Deut 12:5.
- Appointed ordinances. Ex 18:20; Heb 9:1,10.
- Appointed feasts. Lev 23:2; Is 1:14.
- An ordained ministry. Ex 29:9; Deut 10:8.
- The divine presence manifested in it. Ex 29:45,46; Lev 26:11,12; 1 Kin 8:10,11.
- A spiritual church within it. Rom 9:6-8; 11:2-7.

In covenant with God. Deut 4:13,23; Acts 3:25.
The depository of holy writ. Rom 3:2.
Called the
- Congregation of Israel. Ex 12:47; Lev 4:13.
- Congregation of the Lord. Num 27:17; 31:16.

Privileges of. Rom 9:4.
Proselytes admitted into. Num 9:14; 15:15,29.
Supported by the people. Ex 34:20; Deut 16:17.
Worship of, consisted in
- Sacrifice. Ex 10:25; Lev 1:2; Heb 10:1.
- Prayer. Ex 24:11; Ps 5:7; 95:6.
- Praise. 2 Chr 5:13; 30:21.
- Reading God's word. Ex 24:7; Deut 31:11.
- Preaching. Neh 8:4,5.

Attachment of the Jews to. John 9:28,29; Acts 6:11.
Members of
- Required to know its statutes. Lev 10:11.
- Required to keeps its statutes. Deut 16:12.
- Required to attend its worship. Ex 23:17.
- Separated from, while unclean. Lev 13:46; 15:31; Num 5:2-4.
- Excommunicated for heavy offences. Num 15:30,31; 19:20.

Persons excluded from. Ex 12:48; Deut 23:1-4; Ezek 44:7,9.
A type of the church of Christ. Gal 4:24-26; Heb 12:23.

Circumcision.

Instituted by God. Gen 17:9,10.
Described. Gen 17:11; Ex 4:25.
Enforced by the law. Lev 12:3; John 7:22.
Called the
- Covenant of circumcision. Acts 7:8.
- Circumcision in the flesh. Eph 2:11.
- Concision. Phil 3:2.

A painful and bloody rite. Ex 4:26; Josh 5:8.
Promises to Abraham previous to. Rom 4:9,13.
A seal of the covenant. Gen 17:11; Rom 4:11.
Introductory Jewish ordinances. Gal 5:3.

Outward sign of. Rom 2:28.
Inward grace. Rom 2:29.
Necessary to enjoying the privileges of the Jewish State. Ex 12:48; Ezek 44:7.
Was performed
On males home-born and bought. Gen 17:12,13.
On the eighth day. Gen 17:12; Lev 12:3.
Even on the sabbath day. John 7:22,23.
With knives of flint. Ex 4:25; Josh 5:3.
By the heads of families. Gen 17:23; Ex 4:25.
By persons in authority. Josh 5:3.
In the presence of the family, etc. Luke 1:58-61.
Accompanied with naming the child. Gen 21:3,4; Luke 1:59; 2:21.
First performed on Abraham and his family. Gen 17:24-27.
Not performed in the wilderness. Josh 5:5.
Performed by Joshua at Gilgal. Josh 5:2,7.
Punishment for neglecting. Gen 17:14; Ex 4:24,26.
Without faith, vain. Rom 3:30; Gal 5:6.
Without obedience, vain. Rom 2:25; 1 Cor 7:19.
The Jews
Denominated by. Acts 10:45; Gal 2:9.
Held it unlawful to intermarry with those not of the. Gen 34:14; Judg 14:3.
Held no intercourse with those not of the. Acts 10:28; 11:3; Gal 2:12.
Despised as unclean those not of the. 1 Sam 14:6; 17:26; Matt 15:26,27; Eph 2:11,15.
Sometimes performed on slain enemies. 1 Sam 18:25-27; 2 Sam 3:14.
Abolished by the gospel. Eph 2:11,15; Col 3:11.
Performed on Timothy as a matter or expediency because of the Jews. Acts 16:3.
Necessity of, denied by Paul. Gal 2:3-5.
Necessity of, asserted by false teachers. Acts 15:24; Gal 6:12; Titus 1:10.
Trusting to, a denial of Christ. Gal 3:3,4; 5:3,4.
Paul denounced for opposing. Acts 21:21.
Saints the true spiritual. Phil 3:3; Col 2:11.
Illustrative of
Readiness to hear and obey. Jer 6:10.
Purity of heart. Deut 10:16; 30:6.
Purity of speech. Ex 6:12.

Cities.

First mention of. Gen 4:17.
Designed for habitations. Ps 107:7,36.
Often built to perpetuate a name. Gen 11:4.
Often founded and enlarged by blood and rapine. Mic 3:10; Hab 2:12.
Built
Of brick and slime. Gen 11:3.
Of stone and wood. Ps 102:14; Ezek 26:12.
Of brick and mortar. Ex 1:11,14.
On solid foundations. Ezra 6:3; Rev 21:14.
With compactness. Ps 122:3.
Often of a square form. Rev 21:16.
Beside rivers. Ps 46:4; 137:1.
On hills. Matt 5:14; Luke 4:29; Rev 17:9.
In plains. Gen 11:2,4; 13:12.
In desert places. 2 Chr 8:4; Ps 107:35,36.
In pleasant situations. 2 Kin 2:19; Ps 48:2.
Arranged in streets and lanes. Num 22:39; Zech 8:5; Luke 14:21.
Entered through gates. Gen 34:24; Neh 13:19,22.
Surrounded with walls. Deut 1:28; 3:5.
Often fortified by nature. Ps 125:2; Is 33:16.
Often fortified by art. 2 Chr 11:5-10,23; Ps 48:12,13; Jer 4:5; Dan 11:15.
Sometimes had suburbs. Num 35:2; Josh 21:3.
Were called for
The family of the founder. Gen 4:17; Judg 18:29.
The proprietor of the land. 1 Kin 16:24.
The country in which built. Dan 4:29,30.
Numerous. Josh 15:21; 1 Chr 2:22; Jer 2:28.
Densely inhabited. Jon 4:11; Nah 3:8.
Often great and goodly. Gen 10:12; Deut 6:10; Dan 4:30; Jon 3:3.
Often of great antiquity. Gen 10:11,12.
Often insignificant. Gen 19:20; Eccl 9:14.
Different kinds of
Royal. Num 21:26; Josh 10:2; 2 Sam 12:26.
Fenced. Josh 10:20; Is 36:1.
Treasure. Ex 1:11.
Commercial. Is 23:11; Ezek 27:3.
Chariot. 2 Chr 1:14; 9:25.
Store. 2 Chr 8:4,6.
Levitical. Lev 25:32,33; Num 35:7,8.
Refuge. Num 35:6.
Inhabitants of, called citizens. Acts 21:39.
Prosperity of, increased by commerce. Gen 49:13; Deut 33:18,19; Ezek 28:5.
Artificial mode of supplying water to. 2 Kin 18:17; 20:20.
Infested by dogs. 1 Kin 14:11; Ps 59:6,14.
Under governors. 2 Chr 33:14; 2 Cor 11:32.
Provided with judges. Deut 16:18; 2 Chr 19:5.
Protected at night by watchmen. Ps 127:1; Song 5:7; Is 21:11.
Furnished with stores. 2 Chr 11:11,12.
Garrisoned in war. 2 Chr 17:2,19.
Often had citadels. Judg 9:51.
A great defence to a country. 2 Chr 11:5.
Afforded refuge in times of danger. Jer 8:14-16.
Often deserted on the approach of an enemy. 1 Sam 31:7; Jer 4:20.
Were frequently
Stormed. Josh 8:3-7; Judg 9:44.
Besieged. Deut 28:52; 2 Kin 19:24,25.
Pillaged. Is 13:16; Jer 20:5.
Wasted by pestilence. 1 Sam 5:11.
Wasted by famine. Jer 52:6; Amos 4:6.
Depopulated. Is 17:9; Ezek 26:19.
Burned. Judg 20:38,40; Is 1:7.
Made heaps of ruins. Is 25:2.
Razed and sown with salt. Judg 9:45.
Difficulty of taking, alluded to. Prov 18:19; Jer 1:18,19.
Perishable nature of. Heb 13:14.
Illustrative of
Saints. Matt 5:14.
Visible church. Song 3:2,3; Rev 11:2.
Church triumphant. Rev 21:2; 22:19.
Heavenly inheritance. Heb 11:16.
The apostasy. Rev 16:10; 17:18.
Riches. Prov 10:15.

Cities of Refuge.

Design of. Ex 21:13; Num 35:11; Josh 20:3.
Names etc. of. Deut 4:41-43; Josh 20:7,8.
Required to be
Easy of access. Deut 19:3; Is 62:10.
Open to all manslayers. Josh 20:4.
Strangers might take advantage of. Num 35:15.
Those admitted to
Were put on their trial. Num 35:12,24.
Not protected outside of. Num 35:26,27.
Obliged to remain in, until the high priest's death. Num 35:25,28.
Afforded no asylum to murderers. Ex 21:14; Num 35:16-21.
Illustrative
Of Christ. Ps 91:2; Is 25:4.
Of the hope of the gospel. Heb 6:18.
(The way to,) of Christ. Is 35:8; John 14:6.

Clouds.

Formed from the sea. 1 Kin 18:44; Amos 9:6.
Are garment of the sea. Job 38:9.
God
Established. Prov 8:28.
Balanced in the air. Job 37:16.
Disposed in order. Job 37:15.
Brings over the earth. Gen 9:14.
Binds up. Job 26:8.
Spreads out. Job 26:9.
Scatters. Job 37:11.
Power and wisdom of God exhibited in forming. Ps 135:6,7; 147:5,8; Jer 10:13; 51:16.
Power and wisdom of God exhibited in condensing. Job 36:27,28; 37:10,11; Prov 3:20.
Made for the glory of God. Ps 148:4.
Called the
Clouds of heaven. Dan 7:13; Matt 24:30.
Windows of heaven. Gen 7:11; Is 24:18.
Bottles of heaven. Job 38:37.
Chambers of God. Ps 104:3,13.
Waters above the firmament. Gen 1:7.
Dust of God's feet. Nah 1:3.
Different kinds of, mentioned
White. Rev 14:14.
Bright. Job 37:11; Zech 10:1.
Thick. Job 22:14; 37:11.
Black. 1 Kin 18:45.
Swift. Is 19:1.
Great. Ezek 1:4.
Small. 1 Kin 18:44.

Often cover the heavens. Ps 147:8.
Often obscure the sun, etc. Job 36:32; Ezek 32:7.
Often dispersed by the wind. Hos 13:3.
Uses of
To give rain. Judg 5:4; Ps 104:13,14.
To supply dew. Prov 3:20; Is 18:4.
To moderate heat. Is 25:5.
From the west, bring rain. Luke 12:54.
Though small, often bring much rain. 1 Kin 18:44,45.
Thunder and lightning come from. Ps 77:17,18.
The rainbow appears in. Gen 9:13,14.
Frequently the instrument of God's judgments. Gen 7:11,12; Job 37:13; Ps 77:17.
Man
Ignorant of the spreading of. Job 36:29.
Ignorant of the disposing of. Job 37:15.
Ignorant of the balancing of. Job 37:16.
Cannot number. Job 38:37.
Cannot cause to rain. Job 38:34.
Cannot stay. Job 38:37.
Illustrative
Of multitudes of persons. Is 60:8; Heb 12:1.
Of hostile armies. Jer 4:13; Ezek 38:9,16.
Of sins of men. Is 44:22.
Of judgments of God. Lam 2:1; Ezek 30:3; 34:12; Joel 2:2.
Of unsearchableness of God. 2 Sam 22:12; Ps 97:2; Ezek 1:4.
(Riding upon,) of the power and greatness of God. Ps 104:3; Is 19:1.
(Passing away,) of the goodness and prosperity of hypocrites. Hos 6:4; 13:3.
(Without water,) of false teachers. Jude 1:12.
(Carried away by a tempest,) of false teachers. 2 Pet 2:17.
(Without rain,) of the fraudulent. Prov 25:14.
(A morning without,) of wise rulers. 2 Sam 23:3,4.
(When seasonable,) of the favour of good rulers. Prov 16:15.

Cloud of Glory.

First manifestation of. Ex 13:20,21.
Called
The cloud. Ex 34:5.
Pillar of cloud and pillar of fire. Ex 13:22.
Cloudy pillar. Ex 33:9,10.
Cloud of the Lord. Num 10:34.
The presence of God. Ex 33:14,15.
God's glory manifested in. Ex 16:10; 40:35.
God came down in. Ex 34:5; Num 11:25.
God spoke from. Ex 24:16; Ps 99:7.
Was designed to
Regulate the movements of Israel. Ex 40:36,37; Num 9:17-23.
Guide Israel. Ex 13:21; Neh 9:19.
Show light to Israel. Ps 105:39.
Defend Israel. Ex 14:19; Ps 105:39.
Cover the tabernacle. Ex 40:34; Num 9:15.
Was dark to the enemies of Israel. Ex 14:20.
Was the Shekinah over the mercy-seat. Lev 16:2.
Continued during the journeyings of Israel. Ex 13:22; 40:38.
Manifested in the temple of Solomon. 1 Kin 8:10,11; 2 Chr 5:13; Ezek 10:4.
Special appearances of;
At the murmuring for bread. Ex 16:10.
At giving of the law. Ex 19:9,16; 24:16-18.
At sedition of Aaron and Miriam. Num 12:5.
At the murmuring of Israel on the report of the spies. Num 14:10.
At the rebellion of Korah etc. Num 16:19.
At the murmuring of Israel on account of Korah's death. Num 16:42.
At Christ's transfiguration. Matt 17:5.
At Christ's ascension. Acts 1:9.
Our Lord shall make his second appearance in. Luke 21:27; Acts 1:11.
Illustrative of
The glory of Christ. Rev 10:1.
The protection of the church. Is 4:5.

Commandments, the Ten.

Spoken by God. Ex 20:1; Deut 5:4,22.
Written by God. Ex 32:16; 34:1,28; Deut 4:13; 10:4.
Enumerated. Ex 20:3-17.
Summed up Christ. Matt 22:35-40.
Law of, is spiritual. See "Law of God." Matt 5:28; Rom 7:14.

Commerce.

The barter of one commodity for another. 1 Kin 5:8,11.
The exchange of commodities for money. 1 Kin 10:28,29.
Called
Trade. Gen 34:10; Matt 25:16.
Traffic. Gen 42:34; Ezek 17:4.
Buying and selling. James 4:13.
Articles of, called
Merchandise. Ezek 26:12; Matt 22:5.
Wares. Jer 10:17; Ezek 27:16; Jon 1:5.
Persons engaged in, called
Merchants. Gen 37:28; Prov 31:24.
Chapmen. 2 Chr 9:14.
Traffickers. Is 23:8.
Sellers and buyers. Is 24:2.
Carried on in fairs, etc. Ezek 27:12,19; Matt 11:16.
Inland, by caravans. Job 6:19; Is 21:13.
Maritime, by ships. 2 Chr 8:18; 9:21.
Persons of distinction engaged in. Is 23:8.
Increased the wealth of nations and individuals. 2 Chr 9:20-22; Prov 31:14-18; Ezek 28:4,5.
Carried on by
Ishmaelites. Gen 37:25.
Egyptians. Gen 42:2-34.
Ethiopians. Is 45:14.
Ninevites. Nah 3:16.
Syrians. Ezek 27:16,18.
People of Tarshish. Ezek 27:25.
People of Tyre. Ezek 28:5,13,16.
Jews. Ezek 27:17.
Of the Jews
Under strict laws. Lev 19:36,37; 25:14,17.
Commenced after their settlement in Canaan. Gen 49:13; Judg 5:17.
Greatly extended by Solomon. 1 Kin 9:26,27; 2 Chr 9:21.
Checked in Jehoshaphat's time. 1 Kin 22:48,49.
Success in, led to pride, etc. Ezek 28:2,16-18.
Evil practices connected with. Prov 20:14; Ezek 22:13; Hos 12:7.
Denunciations connected with abuses of. Is 23:11; Ezek 7:12,13; 27:32-36; 28:16-18.
Articles of
Blue cloth. Ezek 27:24.
Brass. Ezek 27:13.
Corn. 1 Kin 5:11; Ezek 27:17.
Cattle. Ezek 27:21.
Chests of rich apparel. Ezek 27:24.
Chariots. 1 Kin 10:29.
Clothes for chariots. Ezek 27:20.
Embroidery. Ezek 27:16,24.
Gold. 2 Chr 8:18.
Honey. Ezek 27:17.
Horses. 1 Kin 10:29; Ezek 27:14.
Ivory. 2 Chr 9:21; Ezek 27:15.
Iron and steel. Ezek 27:12,19.
Land. Gen 23:13-16; Ruth 4:3.
Lead. Ezek 27:12.
Linen. 1 Kin 10:28.
Oil. 1 Kin 5:11; Ezek 27:17.
Perfumes. Song 3:6.
Precious stones. Ezek 27:16,22; 28:13,16.
Purple. Ezek 27:16.
Slaves. Gen 37:28,36; Deut 24:7.
Silver. 2 Chr 9:21.
Timber. 1 Kin 5:6,8.
Tin. Ezek 27:12.
White wool. Ezek 27:18.
Wine. 2 Chr 2:15; Ezek 27:18.
Illustrative of intercourse with the apostasy. Rev 18:3-19.

Communication—A Biblical Approach.

Key texts. Prov 10:11-14,18-21; 25:11-14; 26:17-28; James 3:1-8.
Communication
The power of words. Prov 11:9; 12:18; 15:4; 18:21; Matt 12:37; James 3:1-8.
The value of words. Prov 20:15; 25:11-14.
The source of words. Prov 6:12; 15:28; 16:23,24; Matt 12:34.
Handling Communication Properly
Be listening. Prov 18:13; 19:20; James 1:19.
Do not talk too much. Prov 10:19; 13:2,3; 17:27-28; Eccl 10:12-14; Col 4:6.
Do not nag. Prov 21:19; 26:21.
Do not meddle. Prov 26:27.
Do not gossip. Prov 11:13; 20:19; 26:20.
Do not brag. Prov 14:23; 27:2.
Be slow to speak. Prov 15:28; 29:20; James 1:19.
Be wise in timing. Prov 15:23; Eph 4:29.

Admit wrongs. Prov 29:23; James 5:16.
Do not lie. Ps 34:13; Prov 12:19,22; 26:18,19; Eph 4:15,25.
Do not respond in anger. Prov 15:1; Eph 4:26.
Avoid quarrels. Prov 17:14; 20:3.
Communication Guidelines
Set a guard over my lips. Ps 141:3.
Deliver me from lying lips. Ps 120:3.
May my lips offer up a sacrifice of praise. Heb 13:15.
Let me speak encouragingly. Eph 4:29.
Bridle my tongue. James 1:26.

COMMUNION OF SAINTS.

According to the prayer of Christ. John 17:20,21.
Is with
God. 1 John 1:3.
Saints in heaven. Heb 12:22-24.
Each other. Gal 2:9; 1 John 1:3,7.
God marks, with his approval. Mal 3:16.
Christ is present in. Matt 18:20.
In public and social worship. Ps 34:3; 55:14; Acts 1:14; Heb 10:25.
In the Lord's Supper. 1 Cor 10:17.
In holy conversation. Mal 3:16.
In prayer for each other. 2 Cor 1:11; Eph 6:18.
In exhortation. Col 3:16; Heb 10:25.
In mutual comfort and edification. 1 Thess 4:18; 5:11.
In mutual sympathy and kindness. Rom 12:15; Eph 4:32.
Delight of. Ps 16:3; 42:4; 133:1-3; Rom 15:32.
Exhortation to. Eph 4:1-3.
Opposed to communion with the wicked. 2 Cor 6:14-17; Eph 5:11.
Exemplified
Jonathan. 1 Sam 23:16.
David. Ps 119:63.
Daniel. Dan 2:17,18.
Apostles. Acts 1:14.
The Church. Acts 2:42; 5:12.
Paul. Acts 20:36-38.

COMMUNION OF THE LORD'S SUPPER.

Prefigured. Ex 12:21-28; 1 Cor 5:7,8.
Instituted. Matt 26:26; 1 Cor 11:23.
Object of. Luke 22:19; 1 Cor 11:24,26.
Is the communion of the body and blood of Christ. 1 Cor 10:16.
Both bread and wine are necessary to be received in. Matt 26:27; 1 Cor 11:26.
Self-examination commanded before partaking of. 1 Cor 11:28,31.
Newness of heart and life necessary to the worthy partaking of. 1 Cor 5:7,8.
Partakers of, be wholly separate to God. 1 Cor 10:21.
Was continually partaken of, by the Church. Acts 2:42; 20:7.
Unworthy partakers of
Are guilty of the body and blood of Christ. 1 Cor 11:27.
Discern not the Lord's body. 1 Cor 11:29.
Are visited with judgments. 1 Cor 11:30.

COMMUNION WITH GOD.

Is communion with the Father. 1 John 1:3.
Is communion with the Son. 1 Cor 1:9; 1 John 1:3; Rev 3:20.
Is communion with the Holy Spirit. 1 Cor 12:13; 2 Cor 13:14; Phil 2:1.
Reconciliation must precede. Amos 3:3.
Holiness essential to. 2 Cor 6:14-16.
Promised to the obedient. John 14:23.
Saints
Desire. Ps 42:1; Phil 1:23.
Have, in meditation. Ps 63:5,6.
Have, in prayer. Phil 4:6; Heb 4:16.
Have, in the Lord's Supper. 1 Cor 10:16.
Should always enjoy. Ps 16:8; John 14:16-18.
Exemplified
Enoch. Gen 5:24.
Noah. Gen 6:9.
Abraham. Gen 18:33.
Jacob. Gen 32:24-29.
Moses. Ex 33:11-23.

COMPASSION AND SYMPATHY.

Christ set an example of. Luke 19:41,42.
Exhortation to. Rom 12:15; 1 Pet 3:8.
Exercise towards
The afflicted. Job 6:14; Heb 13:3.
The chastened. Is 22:4; Jer 9:1.
Enemies. Ps 35:13.
The poor. Prov 19:17.
The weak. 2 Cor 11:29; Gal 6:2.
Saints. 1 Cor 12:25,26.
Inseparable from love to God. 1 John 3:17; John 4:20.
Motives to
The compassion of God. Matt 13:27,33.
The sense of our infirmities. Heb 5:2.
The wicked made to feel, for saints. Ps 106:46.
Promise to those who show. Prov 19:17; Matt 10:42.
Illustrated. Luke 10:33; 15:20.
Exemplified
Pharaoh's daughter. Ex 2:6.
Shobi, etc. 2 Sam 17:27-29.
Elijah. 1 Kin 17:18,19.
Nehemiah. Neh 1:4.
Job's friends. Job 2:11.
Job. Job 30:25.
David. Ps 35:13,14.
Jews. John 11:19.
Paul. 1 Cor 9:22.

COMPASSION AND SYMPATHY OF CHRIST, THE.

Necessary to his priestly office. Heb 5:2,7.
Manifested for the
Weary and heavy-laden. Matt 11:28-30.
Weak in faith. Is 40:11; 42:3; Matt 12:20.
Tempted. Heb 2:18.
Afflicted. Luke 7:13; John 11:33,35.
Diseased. Matt 14:14; Mark 1:41.
Poor. Mark 8:2.
Perishing sinners. Matt 9:36; Luke 19:41; John 3:16.
An encouragement to prayer. Heb 4:15.

CONDEMNATION.

The sentence of God against sin. Matt 25:41.
Universal, caused by the offence of Adam. Rom 5:12,16,18.
Inseparable consequence of sin. Prov 12:2; Rom 6:23.
Increased by
Impenitence. Matt 11:20-24.
Unbelief. John 3:18,19.
Pride. 1 Tim 3:6.
Oppression. James 5:1-5.
Hypocrisy. Matt 23:14.
Conscience testifies to the justice of. Job 9:20; Rom 2:1; Titus 3:11.
The law testifies to the justice of. Rom 3:19.
According to men's deserts. Matt 12:37; 2 Cor 11:15.
Saints are delivered from, by Christ. John 3:18; 5:24; Rom 8:1,33,34.
Of the wicked, an example. 2 Pet 2:7; Jude 1:7.
Chastisements are designed to rescue us from. Ps 94:12,13; 1 Cor 11:32.
Apostates ordained to. Jude 1:4.
Unbelievers remain under. John 3:18,36.
The law is the ministration of. 2 Cor 3:9.

CONDUCT, CHRISTIAN.

Believing God. Mark 11:22; John 14:11,12.
Fearing God. Eccl 12:13; 1 Pet 2:17.
Loving God. Deut 6:5; Matt 22:37.
Following God. Eph 5:1; 1 Pet 1:15,16.
Obeying God. Luke 1:6; 1 John 5:3.
Rejoicing in God. Ps 33:1; Hab 3:18.
Believing in Christ. John 6:29; 1 John 3:23.
Loving Christ. John 21:15; 1 Pet 1:7,8.
Following the example of Christ. John 13:15; 1 Pet 2:21-24.
Obeying Christ. John 14:21; 15:14.
Living
To Christ. Rom 14:8; 2 Cor 5:15.
To righteousness. Mic 6:8; Rom 6:18; 1 Pet 2:24.
Soberly, righteously, and godly. Titus 2:12.
Walking
Honestly. 1 Thess 4:12.
Worthy of God. 1 Thess 2:12.
Worthy of the Lord. Col 1:10.
In the Spirit. Gal 5:25.
After the Spirit. Rom 8:1.
In newness of life. Rom 6:4.
Worthy of vocation. Eph 4:1.
As children of light. Eph 5:8.
Rejoicing in Christ. Phil 3:1; 4:4.
Loving one another. John 15:12; Rom 12:10; 1 Cor 13:1-13; Eph 5:2; Heb 13:1.
Striving for the faith. Phil 1:27; Jude 1:3.
Putting away all sin. 1 Cor 5:7; Heb 12:1.
Abstaining from all appearance of evil. 1 Thess 5:22.
Perfecting holiness. Matt 5:48; 2 Cor 7:1; 2 Tim 3:17.
Hating defilement. Jude 1:23.
Following after that which is good. Phil 4:8; 1 Thess 5:15; 1 Tim 6:11.
Overcoming the world. 1 John 5:4,5.
Adorning the gospel. Matt 5:16; Titus 2:10.

Showing a good example. 1 Tim 4:12; 1 Pet 2:12; Titus 2:7.
Abounding in the work of the Lord. 1 Cor 15:58; 2 Cor 8:7; 1 Thess 4:1.
Shunning the wicked. Ps 1:1; 2 Thess 3:6.
Controlling the body. 1 Cor 9:27; Col 3:5.
Subduing the temper. Eph 4:26; James 1:19.
Submitting to injuries. Matt 5:39-41; 1 Cor 6:7.
Forgiving injuries. Matt 6:14; Rom 12:20.
Living peaceably with all. Rom 12:18; Heb 12:14.
Visiting the afflicted. Matt 25:36; James 1:27.
Doing as we would be done by. Matt 7:12; Luke 6:31.
Sympathising with others. Gal 6:2; 1 Thess 5:14.
Honouring others. Ps 15:4; Rom 12:10.
Fulfilling domestic duties. Eph 6:1-8; 1 Pet 3:1-7.
Submitting to authorities. Rom 13:1-7.
Being liberal to others. Acts 20:35; Rom 12:13.
Being contented. Phil 4:11; Heb 13:5.
Blessedness of maintaining. Ps 1:1-3; 19:9-11; 50:23; Matt 5:3-12; John 15:10; 7:17.

Confessing Christ.

Influences of the Holy Spirit necessary to. 1 Cor 12:3; 1 John 4:2.
A test of being saints. 1 John 2:23; 4:2,3.
An evidence of union with God. 1 John 4:15.
Necessary to salvation. Rom 10:9,10.
Ensures his confessing us. Matt 10:32.
The fear of man prevents. John 7:13; 12:42,43.
Persecution should not prevent us from. Mark 8:35; 2 Tim 2:12.
Must be connected with faith. Rom 10:9.
Consequences of not. Matt 10:33.
Exemplified
- Nathanael. John 1:49.
- Peter. John 6:68,69; Acts 2:22-36.
- Man born blind. John 9:25,33.
- Martha. John 11:27.
- Peter and John. Acts 4:7-12.
- Apostles. Acts 5:29-32,42.
- Stephen. Acts 7:52,59.
- Paul. Acts 9:29.
- Timothy. 1 Tim 6:12.
- John. Rev 1:9.
- Church in Pergamos. Rev 2:13.
- Martyrs. Rev 20:4.

Confession of Sin.

God requires. Lev 5:5; Hos 5:15.
God regards. Job 33:27,28; Dan 9:20-23.
Exhortation to. Josh 7:19; Jer 3:13; James 5:16.
Promises to. Lev 26:40-42; Prov 28:13.
Should be accompanied with
- Submission to punishment. Lev 26:41; Neh 9:33; Ezra 9:13.
- Prayer for forgiveness. 2 Sam 24:10; Ps 25:11; 51:1; Jer 14:7-9,20.
- Self-abasement. Is 64:5,6; Jer 3:25.
- Godly sorrow. Ps 38:18; Lam 1:20.
- Forsaking sin. Prov 28:13.
- Restitution. Num 5:6,7.

Should be full and unreserved. Ps 32:5; 51:3; 106:6.
Followed by pardon. Ps 32:5; 1 John 1:9.
Illustrated. Luke 15:21; 18:13.
Exemplified
- Aaron. Num 12:11.
- Israelites. Num 21:6,7; 1 Sam 7:6; 12:19.
- Saul. 1 Sam 15:24.
- David. 2 Sam 24:10.
- Ezra. Ezek 9:6.
- Nehemiah. Neh 1:6,7.
- Levites. Neh 9:4,33,34.
- Job. Job 7:20.
- Daniel. Dan 9:4.
- Peter. Luke 5:8.
- Thief. Luke 23:41.

Conscience.

Witnesses in man. Prov 20:27; Rom 2:15.
Accuses of sin. Gen 42:21; 2 Sam 24:10; Matt 27:3; Acts 2:37.
We should have the approval of. Job 27:6; Acts 24:16; Rom 9:1; 14:22.
The blood of Christ alone can purify. Heb 9:14; 10:2-10,22.
Keep the faith in purity of. 1 Tim 1:19; 3:9.
Of saints, pure and good. Heb 13:18; 1 Pet 3:16,21.
Submit to authority for. Rom 13:5.
Suffer patiently for. 1 Pet 2:19.
Testimony of, a source of joy. 2 Cor 1:12; 1 John 3:21.
Of others, not to be offended. Rom 14:21; 1 Cor 10:28-32.
Ministers should commend themselves to that of their people. 2 Cor 4:2; 5:11.
Of the wicked, seared. 1 Tim 4:2.
Of the wicked, defiled. Titus 1:15.
Without spiritual illumination, a false guide. Acts 23:1; 26:9.

Contempt.

Sin of. Job 31:13,14; Prov 14:21.
Folly of. Prov 11:12.
A characteristic of the wicked. Prov 18:3; Is 5:24; 2 Tim 3:3.
Forbidden towards
- Parents. Prov 23:22.
- Christ's little ones. Matt 18:10.
- Weak brethren. Rom 14:3.
- Young ministers. 1 Cor 16:11.
- Believing masters. 1 Tim 6:2.
- The poor. James 2:1-3.

Self-righteous prompts to. Is 65:5; Luke 18:9,11.
Pride and prosperity prompt to. Ps 123:4.
Ministers should give no occasion for. 1 Tim 4:12.
Of ministers, is a despising of God. Luke 10:16; 1 Thess 4:8.
Towards the church
- Often turned into respect. Is 60:14.
- Often punished. Ezek 28:26.

Causes saints to cry to God. Neh 4:4; Ps 123:3.
The wicked exhibit towards
- Christ. Ps 22:6; Is 53:3; Matt 27:29.
- Saints. Ps 119:141.
- Authorities. 2 Pet 2:10; Jude 1:8.
- Parents. Prov 15:5,20.
- The afflicted. Job 19:18.
- The poor. Ps 14:6; Eccl 9:16.

Saints sometimes guilty of. James 2:6.
Exemplified
- Hagar. Gen 16:4.
- Children of Belial. 1 Sam 10:27.
- Nabal. 1 Sam 25:10,11.
- Michal. 2 Sam 6:16.
- Sanballat, etc. Neh 2:19; 4:2,3.
- False teachers. 2 Cor 10:10.

Contentment.

With godliness is great gain. Ps 37:16; 1 Tim 6:6.
Saints should exhibit
- In their respective callings. 1 Cor 7:20.
- With appointed wages. Luke 3:14.
- With what things they have. Heb 13:5.
- With food and raiment. 1 Tim 6:8.

God's promises should lead to. Heb 13:5.
The wicked want. Is 5:8; Eccl 5:10.
Exemplified
- Barzillai. 2 Sam 19:33-37.
- Shunammite. 2 Kin 4:13.
- David. Ps 16:6.
- Agur. Prov 30:8,9.
- Paul. Phil 4:11,12.

Conversion.

By God. 1 Kin 18:37; John 6:44; Acts 21:19.
By Christ. Acts 3:26; Rom 15:18.
By the power of the Holy Spirit. Prov 1:23.
Is of grace. Acts 11:21,23.
Follows repentance. Acts 3:19; 26:20.
Is the result of faith. Acts 11:21.
Through the instrumentality of
- The Scriptures. Ps 19:7.
- Ministers. Acts 26:18; 1 Thess 1:9.
- Self-examination. Ps 119:59; Lam 3:40.
- Affliction. Ps 78:34.

Of sinners, a cause of joy
- To God. Ezek 18:23; Luke 15:32.
- To saints. Acts 15:3; Gal 1:23,24.

Is necessary. Matt 18:3.
Commanded. Job 36:10.
Exhortations to. Prov 1:23; Is 31:6; 55:7; Jer 3:7; Ezek 33:11.
Promises connected with. Neh 1:9; Is 1:27; Jer 3:14; Ezek 18:27.
Pray for. Ps 80:7; 85:4; Jer 31:18; Lam 5:21.
Is accompanied by confession of sin, and prayer. 1 Kin 8:35.
Danger of neglecting. Ps 7:12; Jer 44:5,11; Ezek 3:19.
Duty of leading sinners to. Ps 51:13.
Encouragement for leading sinners to. Dan 12:3; James 5:19,20.
Of Gentiles, predicted. Is 2:2; 11:10; 60:5; 66:12.
Of Israel, predicted. Ezek 36:25-27.

Counsels and Purposes of God, The.

Are great. Jer 32:19.
Are wonderful. Is 28:29.

Are immutable. Ps 33:11; Prov 19:21; Jer 4:28; Rom 9:11; Heb 6:17.
Are sovereign. Is 40:13,14; Dan 4:35.
Are eternal. Eph 3:11.
Are faithfulness and truth. Is 25:1.
None can disannul. Is 14:27.
Shall be performed. Is 14:24; 46:11.
The sufferings and death of Christ were according to. Acts 2:23; 4:28.
Saints called and save according to. Rom 8:28; 2 Tim 1:9.
The union of all saints in Christ, is according to. Eph 1:9,10.
The works of God according to. Eph 1:11.
Should be declared by ministers. Acts 20:27.
Attend to. Jer 49:20; 50:45.
Secret not to be searched into. Deut 29:29; Matt 24:36; Acts 1:7.
The wicked
- Understand not. Mic 4:12.
- Despise. Is 5:19.
- Reject. Luke 7:30.

Courts of Justice.

Have authority from God. Rom 13:1-5.
Superior court
- Held first by Moses alone in the wilderness. Ex 18:13-20.
- Consisted subsequently of priests and Levites. Deut 17:9; Mal 2:7.
- Presided over by the governor or the high priest. Deut 17:12; Judg 4:4,5.
- Held at the seat of government. Deut 17:8.
- Decided on all appeals and difficult cases. Ex 18:26; Deut 1:17; 17:8,9.
- Decisions of, conclusive. Deut 17:10,11.

Inferior court
- In all cities. Deut 16:18; 2 Chr 19:5-7.
- Held at the gates. Gen 34:20; Deut 16:18; 21:19; Job 5:4.
- Judges of, appointed by the governor. Ex 18:21,25; Deut 1:9-15; 2 Sam 15:3.
- All minor cases decided by. Ex 18:26; 2 Sam 15:4.
- All transfers of property made before. Gen 23:17-20; Ruth 4:1,2.

Re-established by Jehoshaphat. 2 Chr 19:5-10.
Re-established by Ezra. Ezra 7:25.
Sanhedrim or court of the seventy
- Probably derived from the seventy elders appointed by Moses. Ex 24:9; Num 11:16,17,24-30.
- Mentioned in the latter part of sacred history. Luke 22:66; John 11:47; Acts 5:27.
- Consisted of chief priest, etc. Matt 26:57,59.
- Presided over by high priest. Matt 26:62-66.
- Sat in high priest's palace. Matt 26:57,58.

Of the Romans in Judea
- Presided over by the governor or deputy. Matt 27:2,11; Acts 18:12.
- Place of, called the hall of judgment. John 18:28,33; 19:9.
- Never interfered in any dispute about minor matters or about religion. Acts 18:14,15.
- Could alone award death. John 18:31.
- Never examined their own citizens by torture. Acts 22:25-29.
- Appeals from, made to the emperor. Acts 25:11; 26:32; 28:19.

Generally held in the morning. Jer 21:12; Matt 27:1; Luke 22:66; Acts 5:21.
Sometimes held in synagogues. Matt 10:17; Acts 22:19; 26:11; James 2:2.
Provided with
- Judges. Deut 16:18.
- Officers. Deut 16:18; Matt 5:25.
- Tormentors or executioners. Matt 18:34.

Judges of
- Called elders. Deut 25:7; 1 Sam 16:4.
- Called magistrates. Luke 12:58.
- Rode often on white asses. Judg 5:10.
- To judge righteously. Lev 19:15; Deut 1:6.
- To judge without respect of persons. Ex 23:3,6; Lev 19:15; Deut 1:17; Prov 22:22.
- To investigate every case. Deut 19:18.
- Not to take bribes. Ex 23:8; Deut 16:19.
- To judge as for God. 2 Chr 19:6,7,9.
- To decide according to the law. Ezek 44:24.
- To promote peace. Zech 8:16.
- Sat on the judgment-seat while hearing causes. Ex 18:13; Judg 5:10; Is 28:6; Matt 27:19.
- Examined the parties. Acts 24:8.
- Conferred together before giving judgment. Acts 5:34-40; 25:12; 26:30,31.
- Pronounced the judgment of the court. Matt 26:65,66; Luke 23:24; Acts 5:40.

Both the accusers and accused required to appear before. Deut 25:1; Acts 25:16.
Causes in, were opened by
- The complainant. 1 Kin 3:17-21; Acts 16:19-21.
- An advocate. Acts 24:1.

The accused
- Stood before the judge. Num 35:12; Matt 27:11.
- Permitted to plead their own cause. 1 Kin 3:22; Acts 24:10; 26:1.
- Might have advocates. Prov 31:8,9; Is 1:17.
- Exhorted to confess. Josh 7:19.
- Examined on oath. Lev 5:1; Matt 26:63.
- Sometimes examined by torture. Acts 22:24,29.
- Sometimes treated with insult. Matt 26:67; John 18:22,23; Acts 23:2,3.
- The evidence of two or more witnesses required in. Deut 17:6; 19:15; John 8:17; 2 Cor 13:1.
- Witnesses sometimes laid their hands on the criminal's head before punishment. Lev 24:14.

False witnesses in to receive the punishment of the accused. Deut 19:19.
Corruption and bribery often practised in. Is 10:1; Amos 5:12; 8:6.
The judgment of
- Not given till accused was heard. John 7:51.
- Recorded in writing. Is 10:1.
- Immediately executed. Deut 25:2; Josh 7:25; Mark 15:15-20.
- Witnesses first to execute. Deut 17:7; Acts 7:58.
- Allusions to. Job 5:4; Ps 127:5; Matt 5:22.
- Illustrative of the last judgment. Matt 19:28; Rom 14:10; 1 Cor 6:2.

Covenants.

Agreements between two parties. Gen 26:28; Dan 11:6.
Designed for
- Establishing friendship. 1 Sam 18:3.
- Procuring assistance in war. 1 Kin 15:18,19.
- Mutual protection. Gen 26:28,29; 31:50-52.
- Establishing peace. Josh 9:15,16.
- Promoting commerce. 1 Kin 5:6-11.
- Selling land. Gen 23:14-16.

Conditions of
- Clearly specified. 1 Sam 11:1,2.
- Conformed by oath. Gen 21:23,31; 26:31.
- Witnessed. Gen 23:17,18; Ruth 4:9-11.
- Written and sealed. Neh 9:38; 10:1.

God often called to witness. Gen 31:50,53.
When confirmed, unalterable. Gal 3:15.
Made by passing between the pieces of the divided sacrifices. Gen 15:9-17; Jer 34:18,19.
Salt a sign of perpetuity in. Num 18:19; 2 Chr 13:5.
Ratified by joining hands. Prov 11:21; Ezek 17:18.
Followed by a feast. Gen 26:30; 31:54.
Presents given as tokens. Gen 21:27-30; 1 Sam 18:3,4.
Pillars raised in token of. Gen 31:45,46.
Names given to places where made. Gen 21:31; 31:47-49.
The Jews
- Forbidden to make, with the nations of Canaan. Ex 23:32; Deut 7:2.
- Frequently made with other nations. 1 Kin 5:12; 2 Kin 17:4.
- Condemned for making, with idolatrous nations. Is 30:2-5; Hos 12:1.
- Regarded, as sacred. Josh 9:16-19; Ps 15:4.

Violated by the wicked. Rom 1:31; 2 Tim 3:3.
Illustrative
- Of the contract of marriage. Mal 2:14.
- Of God's promises to man. Gen 9:9-11; Eph 2:12.
- Of the united determination of a people to serve God. 2 Kin 11:17; 2 Chr 15:12; Neh 10:29.
- Of good resolutions. Job 31:1.
- (With death and hell,) of carnal security. Is 28:15,18.
- (With stones and beasts, of the earth,) of peace and prosperity. Job 5:23; Hos 2:18.

Covenant, The.

Christ, the substance of. Is 42:6; 49:8.
Christ, the Mediator of. Heb 8:6; 9:15; 12:24.
Christ, the Messenger of. Mal 3:1.

Made with
Abraham. Gen 15:7-18; 17:2-14; Luke 1:72-75; Acts 3:25; Gal 3:16.
Isaac. Gen 17:19,21; 26:3,4.
Jacob. Gen 28:13,14; 1 Chr 16:16,17.
Israel. Ex 6:4; Acts 3:25.
David. 2 Sam 23:5; Ps 89:3,4.
Renewed under the gospel. Jer 31:31-33; Rom 11:27; Heb 8:8-10,13.
Fulfilled in Christ. Luke 1:68-79.
Confirmed in Christ. Gal 3:17.
Ratified by the blood of Christ. Heb 9:11-14,16-23.
Is a covenant of peace. Is 54:9,10; Ezek 34:25; 37:26.
Is unalterable. Ps 89:34; Is 54:10; 59:21; Gal 3:17.
Is everlasting. Ps 111:9; Is 55:3; 61:8; Ezek 16:60-63; Heb 13:20.
All saints interested in. Ps 25:14; 89:29-37; Heb 8:10.
The wicked have no interest in. Eph 2:12.
Blessings connected with. Is 56:4-7; Heb 8:10-12.
God is faithful to. Deut 7:9; 1 Kin 8:23; Neh 1:5; Dan 9:4.
God is ever mindful of. Ps 105:8; 111:5; Luke 1:72.
Be mindful of. 1 Chr 16:15.
Caution against forgetting. Deut 4:23.
Plead, in prayer. Ps 74:20; Jer 14:21.
Punishment for despising. Heb 10:29,30.

Covetousness.

Comes from the heart. Mark 7:22,23.
Engrosses the heart. Ezek 33:31; 2 Pet 2:14.
Is idolatry. Eph 5:5; Col 3:5.
Is the root of all evil. 1 Tim 6:10.
Is never satisfied. Eccl 5:10; Hab 2:5.
Is vanity. Ps 39:6; Eccl 4:8.
Is inconsistent
In saints. Eph 5:3; Heb 13:5.
Specially in ministers. 1 Tim 3:3.
Leads to
Injustice and oppression. Prov 28:20; Mic 2:2.
Foolish and hurtful lusts. 1 Tim 6:9.
Departure from the faith. 1 Tim 6:10.
Lying. 2 Kin 5:22-25.
Murder. Prov 1:18,19; Ezek 22:12.
Theft. Josh 7:21.
Poverty. Prov 28:22.
Misery. 1 Tim 6:10.
Domestic affliction. Prov 15:27.
Abhorred by God. Ps 10:3.
Forbidden. Ex 20:17.
A characteristic of the wicked. Rom 1:29.
A characteristic of the slothful. Prov 21:26.
Commended by the wicked alone. Ps 10:3.
Hated by saints. Ex 18:21; Acts 20:33.
To be mortified by saints. Col 3:5.
Woe denounced against. Is 5:8; Hab 2:9.
Punishment of. Job 20:15; Is 57:17; Jer 22:17-19; Mic 2:2,3.
Excludes from heaven. 1 Cor 6:10; Eph 5:5.
Beware of. Luke 12:15.
Avoid those guilty of. 1 Cor 5:11.
Pray against. Ps 119:36.
Reward of those who hate. Prov 28:16.
Shall abound in the last days. 2 Tim 3:2; 2 Pet 2:1-3.
Exemplified
Laban. Gen 31:41.
Achan. Josh 7:21.
Eli's sons. 1 Sam 2:12-14.
Samuel's sons. 1 Sam 8:3.
Saul. 1 Sam 15:9,19.
Ahab. 1 Kin 21:2-4.
Gehazi. 2 Kin 5:20-24.
Nobles of the Jews. Neh 5:7; Is 1:23.
Jewish people. Is 56:11; Jer 6:13.
Babylon. Jer 51:13.
Young man. Matt 19:22.
Judas. Matt 26:14,15; John 12:6.
Pharisees. Luke 16:14.
Ananias etc. Acts 5:1-10.
Felix. Acts 24:26.
Balaam. 2 Pet 2:15; Jude 1:11.

Creation.

The formation of things which had no previous existence. Rom 4:17; Heb 11:3.
Effected
By God. Gen 1:1; 2:4,5; Prov 26:10.
By Christ. John 1:3,10; Col 1:16.
By the Holy Spirit. Job 26:13; Ps 104:30.
By the command of God. Ps 33:9; Heb 11:3.
In the beginning. Gen 1:1; Matt 24:21.
In six normal days. Ex 20:11; 31:17.
According to God's purpose. Ps 135:6.
For God's pleasure. Prov 16:4; Rev 4:11.
For Christ. Col 1:16.
By faith we believe, to be God's work. Heb 11:3.
Order of
First day, making light and dividing it from darkness. Gen 1:3-5; 2 Cor 4:6.
Second day, making the firmament or atmosphere, and separating the waters. Gen 1:6-8.
Third day, separating the land from the water, and making it fruitful. Gen 1:9-13.
Fourth day, placing the sun, moon, and stars to give light, etc. Gen 1:14-19.
Fifth day, making birds, insects, and fishes. Gen 1:20-23.
Sixth day, making beasts of the earth, and man. Gen 1:24,28.
God rested from, on the seventh day. Gen 2:2,3.
Approved of by God. Gen 1:31.
A subject of joy to angels. Job 38:7.
Exhibits
The deity of God. Rom 1:20.
The power of God. Is 40:26,28; Rom 1:20.
The glory and handiwork of God. Ps 19:1.
The wisdom of God. Ps 104:24; 136:5.
The goodness of God. Ps 33:5.
God as the sole object of worship. Is 45:16,18; Acts 17:24,27.
Glorifies God. Ps 145:10; 148:5.
God to be praised for. Neh 9:6; Ps 146:5,6.
Leads to confidence. Ps 124:8; 146:5,6.
Insignificance of man seen from. Ps 8:3,4; Is 40:12,17.
Groans because of sin. Rom 8:22.
Illustrative of
The new birth. 2 Cor 5:17; Eph 2:10.
Daily renewal of saints. Ps 51:10; Eph 4:24.
Renewal of the earth. Is 65:17; 2 Pet 3:11,13.

Creditors.

Defined. Philem 18.
Might demand
Pledges. Deut 24:10,11; Prov 22:27.
Security of others. Prov 6:1; 22:26.
Mortgages on property. Neh 5:3.
Bills or promissory notes. Luke 16:6,7.
To return before sunset, garments taken in pledge. Ex 22:26,27; Deut 24:12,13; Ezek 18:7,12.
Prohibited from
Taking millstones in pledge. Deut 24:6.
Violently selecting pledges. Deut 24:10.
Exacting usury from brethren. Ex 22:25; Lev 25:36,37.
Exacting debts from brethren during sabbatical year. Deut 15:2,3.
Might take interest from strangers. Deut 23:20.
Sometimes entirely remitted debts. Neh 5:10-12; Matt 18:27; Luke 7:42.
Often cruel in exacting debts. Neh 5:7-9; Job 24:3-9; Matt 18:28-30.
Often exacted debts
By selling the debtor or taking him for a servant. Matt 18:25; Ex 21:2.
By selling the debtor's property. Matt 18:25.
By selling the debtor's family. 2 Kin 4:1; Job 24:9; Matt 18:25.
By imprisonment. Matt 5:25,26; 18:34.
From the sureties. Prov 11:15; 22:26,27.
Were often defrauded. 1 Sam 22:2; Luke 16:5-7.
Illustrative of
God's claim upon men. Matt 5:25,26; 18:23,25; Luke 7:41,47.
The demands of the law. Gal 5:3.

Daily Sacrifice, The.

Ordained in Mount Sinai. Num 28:6.
A lamb as a burnt offering morning and evening. Ex 29:38,39; Num 28:3,4.
Doubled on the Sabbath. Num 28:9,10.
Required to be
With a meat and drink offering. Ex 29:40,41; Num 28:5-8.
Slowly and entirely consumed. Lev 6:9-12.
Perpetually observed. Ex 29:42; Num 28:3,6.
Peculiarly acceptable. Num 28:8; Ps 141:2.
Secured God's presence and favour. Ex 29:43,44.
Times of offering, were seasons of prayer. Ezra 9:5; Dan 9:20,21; Acts 3:1.

Restored after the captivity. Ezra 3:3.
The abolition of, foretold. Dan 9:26,27; 11:31.
Illustrative of
  Christ. John 1:29,36; 1 Pet 1:19.
  Acceptable prayer. Ps 141:2.

Dan, the Tribe Of.

Descended from Jacob's fifth son. Gen 30:6.
Predictions respecting. Gen 49:16,17; Deut 33:22.
Persons selected from
  To number the people. Num 1:12.
  To spy out the land. Num 13:12.
  To divide the land. Num 34:22.
Strength of, on leaving Egypt. Num 1:38,39.
Led the fourth and last division of Israel. Num 2:31; 10:25.
Encamped north of the tabernacle. Num 2:25.
Offering of, at dedication. Num 7:66-71.
Families of. Num 26:42.
Strength of, entering Canaan. Num 26:43.
On Ebal, said amen to the curses. Deut 27:13.
Bounds of its inheritance. Josh 19:40-46.
A commercial people. Judg 5:17; Ezek 27:19.
Restricted to the hills by Amorites. Judg 1:34.
A part of
  Sent to seek new settlements. Judg 18:1,2.
  Tool Laish and called it Dan. Josh 19:47; Judg 18:8-13,27-29.
  Plundered Micah of his idols and his ephod. Judg 18:17-21,27.
  Set up Micah's idols in Dan. Judg 18:30,31.
Reproved for not aiding against Sisera. Judg 5:17.
Samson was of. Judg 13:2,24,25.
Some of, at coronation of David. 1 Chr 12:35.
Ruler appointed over, by David. 1 Chr 27:22.

Darkness.

Created by God. Ps 104:20; Is 45:7.
Originally covered the earth. Gen 1:2.
Separated from the light. Gen 1:4.
Called night. Gen 1:5.
Caused by the setting of the sun. Gen 15:17; John 6:17.
Inexplicable nature of. Job 38:19,20.
Exhibits God's power and greatness. Job 38:8,9.
Degrees of, mentioned
  Great. Gen 15:12.
  That may be felt. Ex 10:21.
  Thick. Deut 5:22; Joel 2:2.
  Gross. Jer 13:16.
  Outer or extreme. Matt 8:12.
Effects of
  Keeps us from seeing objects. Ex 10:23.
  Causes us to go astray. John 12:35; 1 John 2:11.
  Causes us to stumble. Is 59:10.
Often put for night. Ps 91:6.
Called the swaddling band of the sea. Job 38:9.
Cannot hide us from God. Ps 139:11,12.
The wicked
  The children of. 1 Thess 5:5.
  Live in. Ps 107:10.
  Walk in. Ps 82:5.
  Perpetuate their designs in. Job 24:16.
  Are full of. Matt 6:23.
Miraculous
  On Mount Sinai. Ex 19:16; Heb 12:18.
  Over the land of Egypt. Ex 10:21,22.
  At the death of Christ. Matt 27:45.
  Before the destruction of Jerusalem. Matt 24:29.
Illustrative of
  Greatness and unsearchableness of God. Ex 20:21; 2 Sam 22:10,12; 1 Kin 8:12; Ps 97:2.
  Abstruse and deep subjects. Job 28:3.
  Secrecy. Is 45:19; Matt 10:27.
  Ignorance and error. Job 37:19; Is 60:2; John 1:5; 3:19; 12:35; Acts 26:18.
  Anything hateful. Job 3:4-9.
  A course of sin. Prov 2:13; Eph 5:11.
  Heavy afflictions. Job 23:17; Ps 112:4; Eccl 5:17; Is 5:30; 8:22; 59:9.
  The power of Satan. Eph 6:12; Col 1:13.
  The grave. 1 Sam 2:9; Job 10:21,22.
  The punishment of devils and wicked men. Matt 22:13; 2 Pet 2:4,17; Jude 1:6,13.

Day.

The light first called. Gen 1:5.
Natural, from evening to evening. Gen 1:5; Lev 23:32.
Artificial, the time of the sun's continuance above the horizon. Gen 31:39,40; Neh 4:21,22.
Prophetical, a year. Ezek 4:6; Dan 12:12.
Artificial, divided into
  Break of. Gen 32:24,26; Song 2:17.
  Morning. Ex 29:39; 2 Sam 23:4.
  Noon. Gen 43:16; Ps 55:17.
  Decline of. Judg 19:8,9; Luke 9:12; 24:29.
  Evening. Gen 8:11; Ps 104:23; Jer 6:4.
Sometimes divided into four parts. Neh 9:3.
Later subdivided into twelve hours. Matt 20:3,5,6; John 11:9.
Time of, ascertained by the dial. 2 Kin 20:11.
Succession of, secured by covenant. Gen 8:22.
Made for the glory of God. Ps 74:16.
Proclaims the glory of God. Ps 19:2.
Under the control of God. Amos 5:8; 8:9.
A time of judgment called a day of
  Anger. Lam 2:21.
  Wrath. Job 20:28; Zeph 1:15,18; Rom 2:5.
  Visitation. Mic 7:4.
  Destruction. Job 21:30.
  Darkness. Joel 2:2; Zeph 1:15.
  Trouble. Ps 102:2.
  Calamity. Deut 32:35; Jer 18:17.
  Adversity. Prov 24:10.
  Vengeance. Prov 6:34; Is 61:2.
  Slaughter. Is 30:25; Jer 12:3.
  Evil. Jer 17:17; Amos 6:3; Eph 6:13.
  The Lord. Is 2:12; 13:6; Zeph 1:14.
A time of mercy called a day of
  Salvation. 2 Cor 6:2.
  Redemption. Eph 4:30.
  Visitation. Jer 27:22; 1 Pet 2:12.
  God's power. Ps 110:3.
A time of festivity called a
  Good day. Esth 8:17; 9:19.
  Day of good tidings. 2 Kin 7:9.
  Day which the Lord has made. Ps 118:24.
  Solemn day. Num 10:10; Hos 9:5.
  Day of gladness. Num 10:10.
The time for labour. Ps 104:22.
Wild beasts hide during. Ps 104:22.
Illustrative of
  Time of judgment. 1 Cor 3:13; 4:3.
  Spiritual light. 1 Thess 5:5,8; 2 Pet 1:19.
  The path of the just. Prov 4:18.

Dead, The.

They who have departed this life. Gen 23:2; 25:8; Job 1:19.
Terms used to express
  Corpses. 2 Kin 19:35; Nah 3:3.
  Carcases. Num 14:29,32,33; 1 Kin 13:24.
  Those who are not. Matt 2:18.
  Deceased. Is 26:14; Matt 22:25.
Characterised by
  Being without the Spirit. James 2:26.
  Being incapable of motion. Matt 28:4; Rev 1:17.
  Ignorance of all human affairs. Eccl 9:5.
  Absence of all human passions. Eccl 9:6.
  Inability to glorify God. Ps 115:17.
Return not to this life. Job 7:9,10; 14:10,14.
Eyes of, closed by nearest of kin. Gen 46:4.
Were washed and laid out. Acts 9:37.
Were wrapped in lined with spices. John 19:40.
Mourning for, often
  Very great. Gen 27:35; Jer 31:15; Matt 2:18; John 11:33.
  Loud and clamorous. Jer 16:6; Mark 5:38.
  By hired mourners. Jer 9:17,18; Amos 5:16.
  With plaintive music. Jer 48:36; Matt 9:23.
  Testified by change of apparel. 2 Sam 14:2.
  Testified by taring the hair. Jer 16:7.
  Testified by covering the head. 2 Sam 19:4.
  Testified by rending the garments. Gen 37:34; 2 Sam 3:31.
  Lasted many days. Gen 37:34; 50:3,10.
Regard often shown to the memory of. Ruth 1:8.
Too soon forgotten. Ps 31:12; Eccl 9:5.
Heathenish expressions of grief for, forbidden. Lev 19:28; Deut 14:1,2.
All offerings to, forbidden. Deut 26:14.
Touching of, caused uncleanness. Num 19:11,13,16; 9:6,7.

In a house rendered it unclean. Num 19:14,15.
Even bones of, caused uncleanness. Num 19:16; 2 Chr 34:5.
A priest not to mourn for, except when near of kin. Lev 21:1-3; Ezek 44:25.
High priest in no case to mourn for. Lev 21:10,11.
Nazirites not to touch or mourn for. Num 6:6,7.
Those defiled by, removed from the camp. Num 5:2.
Uncleanness contracted from, removed by the water separation. Num 19:12,18.
Idolaters
  Tore themselves for. Jer 16:7.
  Offered sacrifices for. Ps 106:28.
  Invoked and consulted. 1 Sam 28:7,8.
  Consecrated part of their crops to. Deut 26:14.
The Jews looked for a resurrection from. Is 26:19; Acts 24:15.
Instances of, restored to life before Christ. 1 Kin 17:22; 2 Kin 4:34-36; 13:21.
Instances of, restored by Christ. Matt 9:25; Luke 7:15; John 11:44; Acts 9:40; 20:12.
Illustrative of
  Man's state by nature. 2 Cor 5:4; Eph 2:1,5.
  A state of deep affliction, etc. Ps 88:5,6; 143:3; Is 59:10.
  Freedom from the power of sin. Rom 6:2,8,11; Col 3:3.
  Freedom from the law. Rom 7:4.
  Faith without works. 1 Tim 5:6; James 2:17,26.
  Diviners etc. Is 8:19.
  Impotence. Gen 20:3; Rom 4:19.

DEATH, ETERNAL.

The necessary consequence of sin. Rom 6:16,21; 8:13; James 1:15.
The wages of sin. Rom 6:23.
The portion of the wicked. Matt 25:41,46; Rom 1:32.
The way to, described. Ps 9:17; Matt 7:13.
Self-righteousness leads to. Prov 14:12.
God alone can inflict. Matt 10:28; James 4:12.
Is described as
  Banishment from God. 2 Thess 1:9.
  Society with the devil etc. Matt 25:41.
  A lake of fire. Rev 19:20; 21:8.
  The worm that dies not. Mark 9:44.
  Outer darkness. Matt 25:30.
  A mist of darkness for ever. 2 Pet 2:17.
  Indignation, wrath, etc. Rom 2:8,9.
Is called
  Destruction. Rom 9:22; 2 Thess 1:9.
  Perishing. 2 Pet 2:12.
  The wrath to come. 1 Thess 1:10.
  The second death. Rev 2:11.
  A resurrection to damnation. John 5:29.
  A resurrection to shame etc. Dan 12:2.
  Damnation of hell. Matt 23:33.
  Everlasting punishment. Matt 25:46.
Shall be inflicted by Christ. Matt 25:31,41; 2 Thess 1:7,8.
Christ, the only way of escape from. John 3:16; 8:51; Acts 4:12.
Saints shall escape. Rev 2:11; 20:6.
Strive to preserve others from. James 5:20.
Illustrated. Luke 16:23-26.

DEATH, NATURAL.

By Adam. Gen 3:19; 1 Cor 15:21,22.
Consequence of sin. Gen 2:17; Rom 5:12.
Lot of all. Eccl 8:8; Heb 9:27.
Ordered by God. Deut 32:39; Job 14:5.
Puts an end to earthly projects. Eccl 9:10.
Strips of earthly possessions. Job 1:21; 1 Tim 6:7.
Levels all ranks. Job 3:17-19.
Conquered by Christ. Rom 6:9; Rev 1:18.
Abolished by Christ. 2 Tim 1:10.
Shall finally be destroyed by Christ. Hos 13:14; 1 Cor 15:26.
Christ delivers from the fear of. Heb 2:15.
Regard, as at hand. Job 14:1,2; Ps 39:4,5; 90:9; 1 Pet 1:24.
Prepare for. 2 Kin 20:1.
Pray to be prepared for. Ps 39:4,13; 90:12.
Consideration of, a motive to diligence. Eccl 9:10; John 9:4.
When averted for a season, is a motive to increased devotedness. Ps 56:12,13; 118:17; Is 38:18,20.
Enoch and Elijah were exempted from. Gen 5:24; Heb 11:5; 2 Kin 2:11.
All shall be raised from. Acts 24:15.
None subject to in heaven. Luke 20:36; Rev 21:4.
Illustrates the change produced in conversion. Rom 6:2; Col 2:20.
Is described as
  A sleep. Deut 31:16; John 11:11.
  The earthly house of this tabernacle being dissolved. 2 Cor 5:1.
  Putting off this tabernacle. 2 Pet 1:14.
  God requiring the soul. Luke 12:20.
  Going the way whence there is no return. Job 16:22.
  Gathering to our people. Gen 49:33.
  Going down into silence. Ps 115:17.
  Yielding up the spirit. Acts 5:10.
  Returning to dust. Gen 3:19; Ps 104:29.
  Being cut down. Job 14:2.
  Fleeing as a shadow. Job 14:2.
  Departing. Phil 1:23.

DEATH OF CHRIST, THE.

Foretold. Is 53:8; Dan 9:26; Zech 13:7.
Appointed by God. Is 53:6,10; Acts 2:23.
Necessary for the redemption of man. Luke 24:46; Acts 17:3.
Acceptable, as a sacrifice to God. Matt 20:28; Eph 5:2; 1 Thess 5:10.
Was voluntary. Is 53:12; Matt 26:53; John 10:17,18.
Was undeserved. Is 53:9.
Mode of
  Foretold by Christ. Matt 20:18,19; John 12:32,33.
  Prefigured. Num 21:8; John 3:14.
  Ignominious. Heb 12:2.
  Accursed. Gal 3:13.
  Exhibited His humility. Phil 2:8.
  A stumbling block to Jews. 1 Cor 1:23.
  Foolishness to Gentiles. 1 Cor 1:18,23.
Demanded by the Jews. Matt 27:22,23.
Inflicted by the Gentiles. Matt 27:26-35.
In the company of malefactors. Is 53:12; Matt 27:38.
Accompanied by supernatural signs. Matt 27:45,51-53.
Emblematical of the death to sin. Rom 6:3-8; Gal 2:20.
Commemorated in the ordinance of the Lord's Supper. Luke 22:19,20; 1 Cor 11:26-29.

DEATH OF SAINTS, THE.

Asleep in Christ. 1 Cor 15:18; 1 Thess 4:14.
Is blessed. Rev 14:13.
Is gain. Phil 1:21.
Is full of
  Faith. Heb 11:13.
  Peace. Is 57:2.
  Hope. Prov 14:32.
Sometimes desired. Luke 2:29.
Waited for. Job 14:14.
Met with resignation. Gen 50:24; Josh 23:14; 1 Kin 2:2.
Met without fear. 1 Cor 15:55.
Precious in God's sight. Ps 116:15.
God preserves them to. Ps 48:14.
God is with them in. Ps 23:4.
Removes from coming evil. 2 Kin 22:20; Is 57:1.
Leads to
  Rest. Job 3:17; 2 Thess 1:7.
  Comfort. Luke 16:25.
  Christ's presence. 2 Cor 5:8; Phil 1:23.
  A crown of life. 2 Tim 4:8; Rev 2:10.
  A joyful resurrection. Is 26:19; Dan 12:2.
Disregarded by the wicked. Is 57:1.
Survivors consoled for. 1 Thess 4:13-18.
The wicked wish theirs to resemble. Num 23:10.
Illustrated. Luke 16:22.
Exemplified
  Abraham. Gen 25:8.
  Isaac. Gen 35:29.
  Jacob. Gen 49:33.
  Aaron. Num 20:28.
  Moses. Deut 34:5.
  Joshua. Josh 24:29.
  Elisha. 2 Kin 13:14,20.
  One thief. Luke 23:43.
  Dorcas. Acts 9:37.

DEATH OF THE WICKED, THE.

Is in their sins. Ezek 3:19; John 8:21.
Is without hope. Prov 11:7.
Sometimes without fear. Jer 34:5; 2 Chr 36:11-13.
Frequently sudden and unexpected. Job 21:13,23; 27:21; Prov 29:1.
Frequently marked by terror. Job 18:11-15; 27:19-21; Ps 73:19.
Punishment follows. Is 14:9; Acts 1:25.
The remembrance of them perishes in. Job 18:17; Ps 34:16; Prov 10:7.
God has no pleasure in. Ezek 18:23,32.

Like the death of beasts. Ps 49:14.
Illustrated. Luke 12:20; 16:22,23.
Exemplified
- Korah, etc. Num 16:32.
- Absalom. 2 Sam 18:9,10.
- Ahab. 1 Kin 22:34.
- Jezebel. 2 Kin 9:33.
- Athaliah. 2 Chr 23:15.
- Haman. Esth 7:10.
- Belshazzar. Dan 5:30.
- Judas. Matt 27:5; Acts 1:18.
- Ananias, etc. Acts 5:5,9,10.
- Herod. Acts 12:23.

Death, Spiritual.

Alienation from God is. Eph 4:18.
Carnal-mindedness is. Rom 8:6.
Walking in trespasses and sins is. Eph 2:1; Col 2:13.
Spiritual ignorance is. Is 9:2; Matt 4:16; Luke 1:79; Eph 4:18.
Unbelief is. John 3:36; 1 John 5:12.
Living in pleasure is. 1 Tim 5:6.
Hypocrisy is. Rev 3:1,2.
Is a consequence of the Fall. Rom 5:15.
Is the state of all men by nature. Rom 6:13; 8:6.
The fruits of, are dead works. Heb 6:1; 9:14.
A call to arise from. Eph 5:14.
Deliverance from, is through Christ. John 5:24,25; Eph 2:5; 1 John 5:12.
Saints are raised from. Rom 6:13.
Love of the brethren, a proof of being raised from. 1 John 3:14.
Illustrated. Ezek 37:2,3; Luke 15:24.

Deceit.

Is falsehood. Ps 119:118.
The tongue, the instrument of. Rom 3:13.
Comes from the heart. Mark 7:22.
Characteristic of the heart. Jer 17:9.
God abhors. Ps 5:6.
Forbidden. Prov 24:28; 1 Pet 3:10.
Christ was perfectly free from. Is 53:9; 1 Pet 2:22.
Saints
- Free from. Ps 24:4; Zeph 3:13; Rev 14:5.
- Purposed against. Job 27:4.
- Avoid. Job 31:5.
- Shun those addicted to. Ps 101:7.
- Pray for deliverance from those who use. Ps 43:1; 120:2.
- Delivered from those who use. Ps 72:14.
- Should beware of those who teach. Eph 5:6; Col 2:8.
- Should lay aside, in seeking truth. 1 Pet 2:1.

Ministers should lay aside. 2 Cor 4:2; 1 Thess 2:3.
The wicked
- Are full of. Rom 1:29.
- Devise. Ps 35:20; 38:12; Prov 12:5.
- Utter. Ps 10:7; 36:3.
- Work. Prov 11:18.
- Increase in. 2 Tim 3:13.
- Use, to each other. Jer 9:5.
- Use, to themselves. Jer 37:9; Obad 3:7.
- Delight in. Prov 20:17.

False teachers
- Are workers of. 2 Cor 11:13.
- Preach. Jer 14:14; 23:26.
- Impose on others by. Rom 16:18; Eph 4:14.
- Sport themselves with. 2 Pet 2:13.

Hypocrites devise. Job 15:35.
Hypocrites practise. Hos 11:12.
False witnesses use. Prov 12:17; 14:5.
A characteristic of Antichrist. 2 John 7.
A characteristic of the apostasy. 2 Thess 2:10.
Evil of
- Keeps from knowledge of God. Jer 9:6.
- Keeps from turning to God. Jer 8:5.
- Leads to pride and oppression. Jer 5:27,28.
- Leads to lying. Prov 14:25.

Often accompanied by fraud and injustice. Ps 10:7; 43:1.
Hatred often concealed by. Prov 26:24-28.
The folly of fools is. Prov 14:8.
The kisses of an enemy are. Prov 27:6.
Blessedness of being free from. Ps 24:4,5; 32:2.
Punishment of. Ps 55:23; Jer 9:7-9.
Exemplified
- The devil. Gen 3:1,4,5; John 8:44.
- Rebecca and Jacob. Gen 27:9,19.
- Laban. Gen 31:7.
- Joseph's brothers. Gen 37:31,32.
- Pharaoh. Ex 8:29.
- David. 1 Sam 21:13.
- Job's friends. Job 6:15.
- Doeg. Ps 52:1,2.
- Herod. Matt 2:8.
- Pharisees. Matt 22:16.
- Chief priests. Mark 14:1.

Decision.

Necessary to the service of God. Luke 9:62.
Exhortations to. Josh 24:14,15.
Exhibited in
- Seeking God with the heart. 2 Chr 15:12.
- Keeping the commandments of God. Neh 10:29.
- Being on the Lord's side. Ex 32:26.
- Following God fully. Num 14:24; 32:12; Josh 14:8.
- Serving God. Is 56:6.
- Loving God perfectly. Deut 6:5.
- Blessedness of. Josh 1:7.

Opposed to
- A divided service. Matt 6:24.
- Doublemindedness. James 1:8.
- Halting between two opinions. 1 Kin 18:21.
- Turning to the right or left. Deut 5:32.
- Not setting the heart aright. Ps 78:8,37.

Exemplified
- Moses. Ex 32:26.
- Caleb. Num 13:30.
- Joshua. Josh 24:15.
- Ruth. Ruth 1:16.
- Asa. 2 Chr 15:8.
- David. Ps 17:3.
- Peter. John 6:68.
- Paul. Acts 21:13.
- Abraham. Heb 11:8.

Dedication.

Consecration of a place of worship. 2 Chr 2:4.
Solemn confirmation of a covenant. Heb 9:18.
Devoting anything to sacred uses. 1 Chr 28:12.
Subjects of
- Tabernacle. Num 7:1-89.
- Temple of Solomon. 1 Kin 8:1-63; 2 Chr 7:5.
- Second temple. Ezra 6:16,17.
- Persons. Ex 22:29; 1 Sam 1:11.
- Property. Lev 27:28; Matt 15:5.
- Spoils of war. 2 Sam 8:11; 1 Chr 18:11.
- Tribute from foreigners. 2 Sam 8:10,11.
- Walls of cities. Neh 12:27.
- Houses when built. Deut 20:5; Ps 30:1.

By idolaters in setting up idols. Dan 3:2,3.
Things dedicated to God
- Esteemed holy. Lev 27:28; 2 Kin 12:18.
- Placed with the treasures of the Lord's house. 1 Kin 7:51; 2 Chr 5:1.
- Special chambers prepared for. 2 Chr 31:11,12.
- Levites place over. 1 Chr 26:20,26; 2 Chr 31:12.
- Applied to the repair and maintenance of the temple. 2 Kin 12:4,5; 1 Chr 26:27.
- For support of priests. Num 18:14; Ezek 44:29.
- Given to propitiate enemies. 2 Kin 12:17,18.
- Law respecting the release of. Lev 27:1-34.

Of property often perverted. Mark 7:9-13.
Illustrated of devotedness to God. Ps 119:38.

Defilement.

Forbidden to the Jews. Lev 11:44,45.
Things liable to ceremonial
- The person. Lev 5:3.
- Garments. Lev 13:59.
- Furniture, etc. Lev 15:9,10; Num 19:14,15.
- Houses. Lev 14:44.
- The land. Lev 18:25; Deut 21:23.
- The sanctuary. Lev 20:3; Zeph 3:4.

Ceremonial caused by
- Eating unclean things. Lev 11:8; Acts 10:11,14.
- Eating things that died. Lev 17:15.
- Touching a dead body or a bone. Num 9:6,7; 19:11,16.
- Touching a grave. Num 19:16.
- Touching a dead beast. Lev 5:2; 11:24-28.
- Being alone with a dead body. Num 19:14.
- Mourning for the dead. Lev 21:1-3.
- Having a leprosy. Lev 13:3,11; Num 5:2,3.
- Having an issue, etc. Lev 15:2; Num 5:2.
- Touching anything defiled by an issue, etc. Lev 15:5-11.

Going into a leprous house. Lev 14:46.
Sacrificing the red heifer. Num 19:7.
Burning the red heifer. Num 19:8.
Gathering the ashes of the red heifer. Num 19:10.
Touching an unclean person. Num 19:22.
Child bearing. Lev 12:2.
Causes of, improperly enlarged by tradition. Mark 7:2; Matt 15:20.
Moral, caused by
Following the sins of the heathen. Lev 18:24.
Seeking after wizards. Lev 19:31.
Giving children to Molech. Lev 20:3.
Making and serving idols. Ezek 20:17,18; 22:3,4; 23:7.
Blood shedding. Is 59:3.
Moral, punished. Lev 18:24,25,28,29.
Those under, removed from the camp. Num 5:3,4; Deut 23:14.
Priests
To decide in all cases of. Lev 10:10; 13:3.
Specially required to avoid. Lev 21:1-6,11,12.
Not to eat holy things while under. Lev 22:2,4-6.
Punished for eating of the holy things while under. Lev 22:3.
Cleansed by legal offerings. Num 19:18,19; Heb 9:13.
Neglecting purification from, punished by cutting off. Num 19:13,20.
Ceremonial, abolished under the gospel. Acts 10:15; Rom 14:14; Col 2:20-22.
Illustrative of
Sin. Matt 15:11,18; Jude 1:8.
Unholy doctrines. 1 Cor 3:16,17.

Delighting in God.

Commanded. Ps 37:4.
Reconciliation leads to. Job 22:21,26.
Observing the Sabbath leads to. Is 58:13,14.
Saints' experience in
Communion with God. Song 2:3.
The law of God. Ps 1:1; 119:24,35.
The goodness of God. Neh 9:25.
The comforts of God. Ps 94:19.
Hypocrites
Pretend to. Is 58:2.
In heart despise. Job 27:10; Jer 6:10.
Promise to. Ps 37:4.
Blessedness. Ps 112:1.

Deluge, The.

Sent as a punishment for the extreme wickedness of man. Gen 6:5-7,11-13,17.
Called the
Flood. Gen 9:28.
Waters of Noah. Is 54:9.
Noah forewarned of. Gen 6:13; Heb 11:7.
Long-suffering of God exhibited in deferring. Gen 6:3; 1 Pet 3:20.
The wicked warned of. 1 Pet 3:19,20; 2 Pet 2:5.
Noah, etc., saved from. Gen 6:18-22; 7:13,14.
Date of its commencement. Gen 7:11.
Came suddenly and unexpectedly. Matt 24:38,39.
Produced by
Forty days' incessant rain. Gen 7:4,12,17.
Opening up of the fountains of the great deep. Gen 7:11.
Increased gradually. Gen 7:17,18.
Extreme height of. Gen 7:19,20.
Time of its increase and prevailing. Gen 7:24.
Causes of its abatement. Gen 8:1,2.
Decrease of gradual. Gen 8:3,5.
Date of its complete removal. Gen 8:13.
Complete destruction of whole earth effected by. Gen 7:23.
Entire face of the earth changed by. 2 Pet 3:5,6.
Traditional notice of. Job 22:15-17.
That it shall never again occur
Promised. Gen 8:21,22.
Confirmed by covenant. Gen 9:9-11.
The rainbow a token. Gen 9:12-17.
A pledge of God's faithfulness. Is 54:9,10.
Illustrative
Of the destruction of sinners. Ps 32:6; Is 28:2,18.
Of baptism. 1 Pet 3:20,21.
(Unexpectedness of,) of suddenness of Christ's coming. Matt 24:36-39; Luke 17:26,27-30.

Denial of Christ.

In doctrine. Mark 8:38; 2 Tim 1:8.
In practice. Phil 3:18,10; Titus 1:16.
A characteristic of false teachers. 2 Pet 2:1; Jude 1:4.
Is the spirit of Antichrist. 1 John 2:22,23; 4:3.
Christ will deny those guilty of. Matt 10:33; 2 Tim 2:12.
Leads to destruction. 2 Pet 2:1; Jude 1:4,15.
Exemplified
Peter. Matt 26:69-75.
The Jews. John 18:40; Acts 3:13,14.

Desert, Journey of Israel Through The.

Date of its commencement. Ex 12:41,42.
Their number commencing. Ex 12:37.
Their healthy state commencing. Ps 105:37.
A mixed multitude accompanied them in. Ex 12:38; Num 11:4.
Commenced in haste. Ex 12:39.
Conducted with regularity. Ex 13:18.
Under Moses as leader. Ex 3:10-12; Acts 7:36,38.
By a circuitous route. Ex 13:17,18.
Order of marching during. Num 10:14-29.
Order of encamping during. Num 2:1-34.
Difficulty and danger of. Deut 8:15.
Continued forty years
As a punishment. Num 14:33,34.
To prove and humble them, etc. Deut 8:2.
To teach them to live on God's word. Deut 8:3.
Under God's guidance. Ex 13:21,22; 15:13; Neh 9:12; Ps 78:52; Is 63:11-14.
Under God's protection. Ex 14:19,20; Ps 105:39; Ex 23:20; Ps 78:53.
With miraculous provision. Ex 16:35; Deut 8:3.
Their clothing preserved during. Deut 8:4; 29:5; Neh 9:21.
Worship of God celebrated during. Ex 24:5-8; 29:38-42; 40:24-29.
Justice administered during. Ex 18:13,26.
Circumcision omitted during. Josh 5:5.
Caused universal terror and dismay. Ex 15:14-16; Num 22:3,4.
Obstructed, etc. by the surrounding nations. Ex 17:8; Num 20:21.
Territory acquired during. Deut 29:7,8.
Marked by constant murmurings and rebellions. Ps 78:40; 95:10; 106:7-39.
Constant goodness and mercy of God to them during. Ps 106:10,43-46; 107:6,13.
Commenced from Rameses in Egypt. Ex 12:37.
To Succoth. Ex 12:37; Num 33:5.
To Etham. Ex 13:20; Num 33:6.
Between Baalzephon and Pihahiroth. Ex 14:2; Num 33:7.
Overtaken by Pharaoh. Ex 14:9.
Exhorted to look to God. Ex 14:13,14.
The cloud removed to the rear. Ex 14:19,20.
Red Sea divided. Ex 14:16,21.
Through the Red Sea. Ex 14:22,29.
Faith exhibited in passing. Heb 11:29.
Pharaoh and his host destroyed. Ex 14:23-28; Ps 106:11.
Israel's song of praise. Ex 15:1-21; Ps 106:12.
Through the wilderness of Shur or Etham. Ex 15:22; Num 33:8.
To Marah. Ex 15:23; Num 33:8.
Murmuring of the people on account of bitter water. Ex 15:24.
Water sweetened. Ex 15:25.
To Elim. Ex 15:27; Num 33:9.
By the Red Sea. Num 33:10.
Through the wilderness of Sin. Ex 16:1; Num 33:11.
Murmuring for bread. Ex 16:2,3.
Quails given for one night. Ex 16:8,12,13.
Manna sent. Ex 16:4,8,16-31.
To Dophkah. Num 33:12.
To Alush. Num 33:13.
To Rephidim. Ex 17:1; Num 33:14.
Murmuring for water. Ex 17:2,3.
Water brought from the rock. Ex 17:5,6.
Called Massah and Meribah. Ex 17:7.
Amalek opposes Israel. Ex 17:8.
Amalek overcome. Ex 17:9-13.
To Mount Sinai. Ex 19:1,2; Num 33:15.
Jethro's visit. Ex 18:1-6.
Judges appointed. Ex 18:14-26; Deut 1:9-15.
Moral law given. Ex 19:3; 20:1-26.
Covenant made. Ex 24:3-8.
Moral law written on tables. Ex 31:18.
Order for making the tabernacle, etc. Ex 24:1-27:21.
Tribe of Levi taken instead of the firstborn. Num 3:11-13.

Aaron and his sons selected for priesthood. Ex 28:1-29:46; Num 3:1-3,10.
Levites set apart. Num 3:5-9.
Golden calf made. Ex 32:1,4.
Tables of testimony broken. Ex 32:19.
People punished for idolatry. Ex 32:25-29,35.
God's glory shown to Moses. Ex 33:18-23; 34:5-8.
The tables of testimony renewed. Ex 34:1-4,27-29; Deut 10:1-5.
Tabernacle first set up. Ex 40:1-38.
Nadab and Abihu destroyed for offering strange fire. Lev 10:1,2; Num 3:4.
Passover first commemorated. Num 9:1-5.
Second numbering of the people. Num 1:1-46; Ex 38:25,26.
To Kibrothhattaavah. Num 33:16.
Complaining punished by fire. Num 11:1-3.
Called Taberah. Num 11:3.
Murmuring of the mixed multitude and of Israel, for flesh. Num 11:4-9.
Flesh promised. Num 11:10-15,18-23.
Seventy elders appointed to assist Moses. Num 11:16,17,24-30.
Quails sent for a month. Num 11:19,20,31,32.
Their murmuring punished. Num 11:33; Ps 78:30,31.
Why called Kibrothhattaavah. Num 11:34.
To Hazeroth. Num 11:35; 33:17.
Aaron and Miriam envy Moses. Num 12:1,2.
Miriam punished by leprosy. Num 12:10.
Delayed seven days for Miriam. Num 12:14,15.
To Kadeshbarnea in wilderness of Rithmah or Paran. Deut 1:19; Num 32:8; 12:16; 33:18.
The people anxious to have the land of Canaan searched. Deut 1:22.
Moses commanded to send spies. Num 13:1,2.
Persons selected as spies. Num 13:3-16.
Spies sent. Josh 14:7; Num 13:17-20.
Spies bring back evil report. Num 13:26-33.
The people terrified and rebel. Num 14:1-4.
Punishment for rebellion. Num 14:26,35; 32:11-13; Deut 1:35,36,40.
Guilty spies slain by plague. Num 14:36,37.
People smitten by Amalek for going up without the Lord. Num 14:40-45; Deut 1:41-44.
Returned by the way to the Red Sea. Num 14:25; Deut 1:40; 2:1.
Sabbath breaker stoned. Num 15:32-36.
Rebellion of Korah. Num 16:1-19.
Korah, etc. punished. Num 16:30-35.
Plague sent. Num 16:41-46.
Plague stayed. Num 16:47-50.
God's choice of Aaron confirmed. Num 17:1-13.

To Rimmonparez. Num 33:19.
To Libnah or Laban. Num 33:20; Deut 1:1.
To Rissah. Num 33:21.
To Kehelathah. Num 33:22.
To Mount Shapher. Num 33:23.
To Haradah. Num 33:24.
To Makheloth. Num 33:25.
To Tahath. Num 33:26.
To Tarah. Num 33:37.
To Mithcah. Num 33:28.
To Hashmonah. Num 33:29.
To Moseroth or Mosera. Num 33:30.
To Bene-Jaakan. Num 33:31.
To Horhagidgad or Gud-Godah. Num 33:32; Deut 10:7.
To Jotbathah or land of rivers. Num 33:33; Deut 10:7.
Several of these stations probably revisited. Deut 10:6,7; Num 33:30-32.
To Ebronah. Num 33:34.
To Eziongaber. Num 33:35.
To Kadesh in the wilderness of Zin. Num 20:1; 33:36; Judg 11:16.
Miriam dies and is buried. Num 20:1.
Second murmuring for water. Num 20:2-6.
Moses striking the rock instead of speaking to it, disobeys God. Num 20:7-11.
Moses and Aaron punished. Num 20:12.
Called Meribah to commemorate the murmuring. Num 20:13; 27:14.
Orders given respecting Edom. Deut 2:3-6.
The king of Edom refuses a passage. Num 20:14-21; Judg 11:17.
To Mount Hor. Num 20:22; 33:37.
Aaron dies. Num 20:28,29; 33:38,39.
Arad conquered. Num 21:1-3; 33:40.
Called Hormah. Num 21:2,3.
To Zalmonah. Num 33:41.
Murmuring of the people. Num 21:4,5.
Fiery serpents sent. Num 21:6.
Brazen serpent raised up. Num 21:7-9.
To Punon. Num 33:42.
To Oboth. Num 21:10; 33:43.
To Ijeabarim before Moab. Num 21:11; 33:44.
Orders given respecting Moab. Deut 2:8,9.
To Zared or Dibon-Gad. Num 21:12; 33:45.
To Almondiblathaim. Num 33:46.
Across the brook Zered. Deut 2:13.
Time occupied in going from Kadeshbarnea to this station. Deut 2:14.
Order to pass through Ar. Deut 2:18.
Orders given respecting Ammon. Deut 2:19.
Across the Arnon. Num 21:13-15; Deut 2:24.
To Beer or The Well. Num 21:16.
To Mattanah. Num 21:18.
To Nahaliel. Num 21:19.
To Bamoth. Num 21:19.
To the mountains of Abarim. Num 21:20; 33:47.
The Amorites refuse a passage to Israel. Num 21:21-23; Deut 2:26-30.

Sihon conquered. Num 21:23-32; Deut 2:32-36.
Og conquered. Num 21:33-35; Deut 3:1-11.
Reubenites, etc. obtained the land taken from the Amorites. Num 32:1-42; Deut 3:12-17.
Return to the plains of Moab. Num 22:1; 33:48,49.
Balak sends for Balaam. Num 22:5,6,15-17.
Balaam not permitted to curse Israel. Num 22:9-41; 23:1-24:25.
Israel seduced to idolatry, etc. by advice of Balaam. Num 25:1-3; Rev 2:14.
Israel punished. Num 25:5,9.
Third numbering. Num 26:1-62.
All formerly numbered over twenty years old, except Caleb and Joshua, dead. Num 26:63-65; 14:29.
The law of female inheritance settled. Num 27:1-11; 36:1-9.
Appointment of Joshua. Num 27:15-23.
Midianites destroyed and Balaam slain. Num 31:1-54; 25:17,18.
The law rehearsed. Deut 1:3.
The law written by Moses. Deut 31:9.
Moses beholds Canaan. Deut 34:1-4.
Moses dies and is buried. Deut 34:5,6.
Joshua ordered to cross Jordan. Josh 1:2.
Two spies sent to Jericho. Josh 2:1.
Across the river Jordan. Josh 4:10.
Illustrative of the pilgrimage of the church. Song 8:5; 1 Pet 1:17.

Deserts.

Vast barren plains. Ex 5:3; John 6:13.
Uninhabited places. Matt 14:15; Mark 6:31.
Described as
Uninhabited and lonesome. Jer 2:6.
Uncultivated. Num 20:5; Jer 2:2.
Desolate. Ezek 6:14.
Dry and without water. Ex 17:1; Deut 8:15.
Trackless. Is 43:19.
Great and terrible. Deut 1:19.
Waste and howling. Deut 32:10.
Infested with wild beasts. Is 13:21; Mark 1:13.
Infested with serpents. Deut 8:15.
Infested with robbers. Jer 3:2; Lam 4:19.
Danger of travelling in. Ex 14:3; 2 Cor 11:26.
Guides required in. Num 10:31; Deut 32:10.
Phenomena of, alluded to
Mirage or deceptive appearance of water. Jer 15:18.
Simoom or deadly wind. 2 Kin 19:7; Jer 4:11.
Tornadoes or whirlwinds. Is 21:1.
Clouds of sand and dust. Deut 28:24; Jer 4:12,13.
Mentioned in Scripture
Arabian or great desert. Ex 23:31.
Bethaven. Josh 18:12.
Beersheba. Gen 21:14; 1 Kin 19:3,4.
Damascus. 1 Kin 19:15.
Edom. 2 Kin 3:8.

Engedi. 1 Sam 24:1.
Gibeon. 2 Sam 2:24.
Judea. Matt 3:1.
Jeruel. 2 Chr 20:16.
Kedemoth. Deut 2:26.
Kadesh. Ps 29:8.
Maon. 1 Sam 23:24,25.
Paran. Gen 21:21; Num 10:12.
Shur. Gen 16:7.
Sin. Ex 16:1.
Sinai. Ex 19:1,2; Num 33:16.
Ziph. 1 Sam 23:14,15.
Zin. Num 20:1; 27:14.
Of the Red Sea. Ex 13:18.
Near Gaza. Acts 8:26.
Heath often found in. Jer 17:6.
Parts of, afforded pasture. Gen 36:24; Ex 3:1.
Inhabited by wandering tribes. Gen 21:20,21; Ps 72:9; Jer 25:24.
The persecuted fled to. 1 Sam 23:14; Heb 11:38.
The disaffected fled to. 1 Sam 22:2; Acts 21:38.
Illustrative of
Barrenness. Ps 106:9; 107:33,35.
Those deprived of blessings. Hos 2:3.
The world. Song 3:6; 8:5.
The Gentiles. Is 35:1,6; 41:19.
What affords no support. Jer 2:31.
Desolation by armies. Jer 12:10-13; 50:12.

Despair.

Produced in the wicked by divine judgments. Deut 28:34,67; Rev 9:6; 16:10.
Leads to
Continuing in sin. Jer 2:25; 18:12.
Blasphemy. Is 8:21; Rev 16:10,11.
Shall seize upon the wicked at the appearing of Christ. Rev 6:16.
Saints sometimes tempted to. Job 7:6; Lam 3:18.
Saints enabled to overcome. 2 Cor 4:8,9.
Trust in God, a preservative against. Ps 42:5,11.
Exemplified
Cain. Gen 4:13,14.
Ahithophel. 2 Sam 17:23.
Judas. Matt 27:5.

Devil, The.

Sinned against God. 2 Pet 2:4; 1 John 3:8.
Cast out of heaven. Luke 10:18.
Cast down to hell. 2 Pet 2:4; Jude 1:6.
The author of the fall. Gen 3:1,6,14,24.
Tempted Christ. Matt 4:3-10.
Perverts the Scripture. Matt 4:6; Ps 91:11,12.
Opposes God's work. Zech 3:1; 1 Thess 2:18.
Hinders the gospel. Matt 13:19; 2 Cor 4:4.
Works lying wonders. 2 Thess 2:9; Rev 16:14.
Assumes the form of an angel of light. 2 Cor 11:14.
The wicked
Are the children of. Matt 13:38; Acts 13:10; 1 John 3:10.
Turn aside after. 1 Tim 5:15.
Do the lusts of. John 8:44.
Possessed by. Luke 22:3; Acts 5:3; Eph 2:2.
Blinded by. 2 Cor 4:4.
Deceived by. 1 Kin 22:21,22; Rev 20:7,8.
Ensnared by. 1 Tim 3:7; 2 Tim 2:26.
Troubled by. 1 Sam 16:14.
Punished, together with. Matt 25:41.
Saints
Afflicted by, only as God permits. Job 1:12; 2:4-7.
Tempted by. 1 Chr 21:1; 1 Thess 3:5.
Sifted by. Luke 22:31.
Should resist. James 4:7; 1 Pet 5:9.
Should be armed against. Eph 6:11-16.
Should be watchful against. 2 Cor 2:11.
Overcome. 1 John 2:13; Rev 12:10,11.
Shall finally triumph over. Rom 16:20.
Triumph over, by Christ
Predicted. Gen 3:15.
In resisting his temptations. Matt 4:11.
In casting out the spirits of. Luke 11:20; 13:32.
In empowering his disciples to cast out. Matt 10:1; Mark 16:17.
In destroying the works of. 1 John 3:8.
Completed by his death. Col 2:15; Heb 2:14.
Illustrated. Luke 11:21,22.
Character of
Presumptuous. Job 1:6; Matt 4:5,6.
Proud. 1 Tim 3:6.
Powerful. Eph 2:2; 6:12.
Wicked. 1 John 2:13.
Malignant. Job 1:9; 2:4.
Subtle. Gen 3:1; 2 Cor 11:3.
Deceitful. 2 Cor 11:14; Eph 6:11.
Fierce and cruel. Luke 8:29; 9:39,42; 1 Pet 5:8.
Cowardly. James 4:7.
The apostasy is of. 2 Thess 2:9; 2 Tim 4:1.
Shall be condemned at the judgment. Jude 1:6; Rev 20:10.
Everlasting fire is prepared for. Matt 25:41.
Compared to
A fowler. Ps 91:3.
Fowls. Matt 13:4.
A sower of tares. Matt 13:25,28.
A wolf. John 10:12.
A roaring lion. 1 Pet 5:8.
A serpent. Rev 12:9; 20:2.

Devotedness to God.

A characteristic of saints. Job 23:12.
Christ, an example of. John 4:34; 17:4.
Grounded upon
The mercies of God. Rom 12:1.
The goodness of God. 1 Sam 12:24.
The call of God. 1 Thess 2:12.
The death of Christ. 2 Cor 5:15.
Our creation. Ps 86:9.
Our preservation. Is 46:4.
Our redemption. 1 Cor 6:19,20.
Should be
With our spirit. 1 Cor 6:20; 1 Pet 4:6.
With our bodies. Rom 12:1; 1 Cor 6:20.
With our members. Rom 6:12,13; 1 Pet 4:2.
With our substance. Ex 22:29; Prov 3:9.
Unreserved. Matt 6:24; Luke 14:33.
Abounding. 1 Thess 4:1.
Persevering. Luke 1:74,75; 9:62.
In life and death. Rom 14:8; Phil 1:20.
Should be exhibited in
Loving God. Deut 6:5; Luke 10:27.
Serving God. 1 Sam 12:24; Rom 12:11.
Walking worthy of God. 1 Thess 2:12.
Doing all to God's glory. 1 Cor 10:31.
Bearing the cross. Mark 8:34.
Self-denial. Mark 8:34.
Living to Christ. 2 Cor 5:15.
Giving up all for Christ. Matt 19:21,28,29.
Want of, condemned. Rev 3:16.
Exemplified
Joshua. Josh 24:15.
Peter, Andrew, James, John. Matt 4:20-22.
Joanna, etc. Luke 8:3.
Paul. Phil 1:21.
Timothy. Phil 2:19-22.
Epaphroditus. Phil 2:30.

Diet of the Jews, The.

In patriarchal age. Gen 18:7,8; 27:4.
In Egypt. Ex 16:3; Num 11:5.
In the wilderness. Ex 16:4-12.
Of the poor, frugal. Ruth 2:14; Prov 15:17.
Of the rich, luxurious. Prov 23:1-3; Lam 4:5; Amos 6:4,5; Luke 16:19.
Articles used for
Milk. Gen 49:12; Prov 27:27.
Butter. Deut 32:14; 2 Sam 17:29.
Cheese. 1 Sam 17:18; Job 10:10.
Bread. Gen 18:5; 1 Sam 17:17.
Parched corn. Ruth 2:14; 1 Sam 17:17.
Flesh. 2 Sam 6:19; Prov 9:2.
Fish. Matt 7:10; Luke 24:42.
Herbs. Prov 15:17; Rom 14:2; Heb 6:7.
Fruit. 2 Sam 16:2.
Dried fruit. 1 Sam 25:18; 30:12.
Honey. Song 5:1; Is 7:15.
Oil. Deut 12:17; Prov 21:17; Ezek 16:13.
Vinegar. Num 6:3; Ruth 2:14.
Wine. 2 Sam 6:19; John 2:3,10.
Water. Gen 21:14; Matt 10:42.
Expressed by bread and water. 1 Kin 13:9,16.
Generally prepared by females. Gen 27:9; Prov 31:15; Is 8:13.
Was taken
In the morning, sparingly. Judg 19:5; Eccl 10:16,17.
At noon. Gen 43:16; John 4:6,8.
In the evening. Gen 24:11,33; Luke 24:29,30.
Often sitting. Gen 27:19; 43:33.
Often reclining. Amos 6:4; John 13:23.
With the hand. Matt 26:23; Luke 22:21.
Thanks given before. Mark 8:6; Acts 27:35.
Purification before. 2 Kin 3:11; Matt 15:2.
A hymn sung after. Matt 26:30.
Men and women did not partake of together. Gen 18:8,9; Esth 1:3,9.

Articles of, often sent as presents. 1 Sam 17:18; 25:18,27; 2 Sam 16:1,2.

Diligence.

Christ, an example. Mark 1:35; Luke 2:49.
Required by God in
- Seeking him. 1 Chr 22:19; Heb 11:6.
- Obeying him. Deut 6:17; 11:13.
- Hearkening to him. Is 55:2.
- Striving after perfection. Phil 3:13,14.
- Cultivating Christian graces. 2 Pet 1:5.
- Keeping the souls. Deut 4:9.
- Keeping the heart. Prov 4:23.
- Labours of love. Heb 6:10-12.
- Following every good work. 1 Tim 5:10.
- Guarding against defilement. Heb 12:15.
- Seeking to be found spotless. 2 Pet 3:14.
- Making our call, etc., sure. 2 Pet 1:10.
- Self-examination. Ps 77:6.
- Lawful business. Prov 27:23; Eccl 9:10.
- Teaching religion. 2 Tim 4:2; Jude 1:3.
- Instructing children. Deut 11:19.
- Discharging official duties. Deut 19:18.

Saints should abound in. 2 Cor 8:7.
In the service of God
- Should be preserved in. Gal 6:9.
- Is not in vain. 1 Cor 15:58.
- Preserves from evil. Ex 15:26.
- Leads to assured hope. Heb 6:11.

God rewards. Deut 11:14; Heb 11:6.
In temporal matters, leads to
- Favour. Prov 11:27.
- Prosperity. Prov 10:4; 13:4.
- Honour. Prov 12:24; 22:29.

Illustrated. Prov 6:6-8.
Exemplified
- Jacob. Gen 31:40.
- Ruth. Ruth 2:17.
- Hezekiah. 2 Chr 31:21.
- Nehemiah, etc. Neh 4:6.
- Psalmist. Ps 119:60.
- Apostles. Acts 5:42.
- Apollos. Acts 18:25.
- Titus. 2 Cor 8:22.
- Paul. 1 Thess 2:9.
- Onesiphorus. 2 Tim 1:17.

Discipline of the Church.

Ministers authorised to establish. Matt 16:19; 18:18.
Consists in
- Maintaining sound doctrine. 1 Tim 1:3; Titus 1:13.
- Ordering its affairs. 1 Cor 11:34; Titus 1:5.
- Rebuking offenders. 1 Tim 5:20; 2 Tim 4:2.
- Removing obstinate offenders. 1 Cor 5:3-5,13; 1 Tim 1:20.

Should be submitted to. Heb 13:17.
Is for edification. 2 Cor 10:8; 13:10.
Decency and order, the objects of. 1 Cor 14:40.
Exercise, in a spirit of charity. 1 Cor 2:6-8.
Prohibits women preaching. 1 Cor 14:34; 1 Tim 2:12.

Diseases.

Often sent as punishment. Deut 28:21; John 5:14.
Often brought from other countries. Deut 7:15.
Often through Satan. 1 Sam 16:14-16; Job 2:7.
Regarded as visitations. Job 2:7-10; Ps 38:2,7.
Intemperance a cause of. Hos 7:5.
Sins of youth a cause of. Job 20:11.
Over-excitement a cause of. Dan 8:27.
Were many and divers. Matt 4:24.
Mentioned in Scripture
- Ague. Lev 26:16.
- Abscess. 2 Kin 20:7.
- Atrophy. Job 16:8; 19:20.
- Blindness. Job 29:15; Matt 9:27.
- Boils and blains. Ex 9:10.
- Consumption. Lev 26:16; Deut 28:22.
- Demoniacal possession. Matt 15:22; Mark 5:15.
- Deafness. Ps 38:13; Mark 7:32.
- Debility. Ps 102:23; Ezek 7:17.
- Dropsy. Luke 14:2.
- Dumbness. Prov 31:8; Matt 9:32.
- Dysentery. 2 Chr 21:12-19; Acts 28:8.
- Emerods. Deut 28:27; 1 Sam 5:6,12.
- Fever. Deut 28:22; Matt 8:14.
- Impediment speech. Mark 7:32.
- Itch. Deut 28:27.
- Inflammation. Deut 28:22.
- Issue of blood. Matt 9:20.
- Lameness. 2 Sam 4:4; 2 Chr 16:12.
- Leprosy. Lev 13:2; 2 Kin 5:1.
- Loss of appetite. Job 33:20; Ps 107:18.
- Lunacy. Matt 4:24; 17:15.
- Melancholy. 1 Sam 16:14.
- Palsy. Matt 8:6; 9:2.
- Plague. Num 11:33; 2 Sam 24:15,21,25.
- Scab. Deut 28:27.
- Sunstroke. 2 Kin 4:18-20; Is 49:10.
- Ulcers. Is 1:6; Luke 16:20.
- Worms. Acts 12:23.

Children subject to. 2 Sam 12:15; 1 Kin 17:17.
Frequently
- Loathsome. Ps 38:7; 41:8.
- Painful. 2 Chr 21:15; Job 33:19.
- Tedious. Deut 28:59; John 5:5; Luke 13:16.
- Complicated. Deut 28:60,61; Acts 28:8.
- Incurable. 2 Chr 21:18; Jer 14:19.

Physicians undertook the cure of. Jer 8:22; Matt 9:12; Luke 4:23.
Medicine used for curing. Prov 17:22; Is 1:6.
Art of curing, defective. Job 13:4; Mark 5:26.
God often entreated to cure. 2 Sam 12:16; 2 Kin 20:1-3; Ps 6:2; James 5:14.
Not looking to God in, condemned. 2 Chr 16:12.
Those afflicted with
- Anointed. Mark 6:13; James 5:14.
- Often laid in the streets to receive advice from passers by. Mark 6:56; Acts 5:15.
- Often divinely supported. Ps 41:3.
- Often divinely cured. 2 Kin 20:5; James 5:15.

Illustrative of sin. Is 1:5.

Disobedience to God.

Provokes his anger. Ps 78:10,40; Is 3:8.
Forfeits his favour. 1 Sam 13:14.
Forfeits his promised blessings. Josh 5:6; 1 Sam 2:30; Jer 18:10.
Brings a curse. Deut 11:28; 28:15.
A characteristic of the wicked. Eph 2:2; Titus 1:16; 3:3.
The wicked persevere in. Jer 2:21.
Heinousness of, illustrated. Jer 35:14.
Men prone to excuse. Gen 3:12,13.
Shall be punished. Is 42:24,25; Heb 2:2.
Acknowledge the punishment of, to be just. Neh 9:32,33; Dan 9:10,11,14.
Warnings against. 1 Sam 12:15; Jer 12:17.
Bitter results of, illustrated. Jer 9:13,15.
Exemplified
- Adam and Eve. Gen 3:6,11.
- Pharaoh. Ex 5:2.
- Nadab, etc. Lev 10:1.
- Moses, etc. Num 20:8,11,24.
- Saul. 1 Sam 28:18.
- The prophet. 1 Kin 13:20-23.
- Israel. 2 Kin 18:9-12.
- Jonah. Jon 1:2,3.

Divination.

An abominable practice. 1 Sam 15:23.
All who practised it, abominable. Deut 18:12.
Practised by
- Diviners. Deut 18:14.
- Enchanters. Deut 18:10; Jer 27:9.
- Witches. Ex 22:18; Deut 18:10.
- Charmers. Deut 18:11.
- Wizards. Deut 18:11; 1 Sam 28:3.
- Consulters of familiar spirits. Deut 18:11.
- Magicians. Gen 41:8; Dan 4:7.
- Astrologers. Is 47:13; Dan 4:7.
- Sorcerers. Jer 27:9; Acts 13:6,8.
- Necromancers. Deut 18:11.
- Soothsayers. Is 2:6; Dan 2:27.
- False prophets. Jer 14:14; Ezek 13:3,6.

Effected through
- Enchantments. Ex 7:11; Num 24:1.
- Sorcery. Is 47:12; Acts 8:11.
- Observing times. 2 Kin 21:6.
- Observing heavenly bodies. Is 37:13.
- Raising the dead. 1 Sam 28:11,12.
- Inspecting the inside of beasts. Ezek 21:21.
- The flight of arrows. Ezek 21:21,22.
- Cups. Gen 44:2,5.
- Rods. Hos 4:12.
- Dreams. Jer 29:8; Zech 10:2.
- Connected with idolatry. 2 Chr 33:5,6.
- Books of, numerous and expensive. Acts 19:19.
- A lucrative employment. Num 22:7; Acts 16:16.

Those who practised
- Regarded as wise men. Dan 2:12,27.
- Regarded with awe. Acts 8:9,11.
- Consulted in difficulties. Dan 2:2; 4:6,7.
- Used mysterious words and gestures. Is 8:19.

A system of fraud. Ezek 13:6,7; Jer 29:8.
Frustrated by God. Is 44:25.
Could not injure the Lord's people. Num 23:23.

The law
Forbade to the Israelites the practice of. Lev 19:26; Deut 18:10,11.
Forbade seeking to. Lev 19:31; Deut 18:14.
Punished with death those who used. Ex 22:18; Lev 20:27.
Punished those who sought to. Lev 20:6.
The Jews prone to. 2 Kin 17:17; Is 2:6.

Divisions.

Forbidden in the church. 1 Cor 1:10.
Condemned in the church. 1 Cor 1:11-13; 11:18.
Unbecoming in the church. 1 Cor 12:24,25.
Are contrary to the
Unity of Christ. 1 Cor 1:13; 12:13.
Desire of Christ. John 17:21-23.
Purpose of Christ. John 10:16.
Spirit of the church. 1 Cor 11:16.
Are proof of a carnal spirit. 1 Cor 3:3.
Avoid those who cause. Rom 16:17.
Evil of, illustrated. Matt 12:25.

Divorce.

Law of marriage against. Gen 2:24; Matt 19:6.
Permitted
By the Mosaic law. Deut 24:1.
On account of hardness of heart. Matt 19:8.
Often sought by the Jews. Mic 2:9; Mal 2:14.
Sought on slight grounds. Matt 5:31; 19:3.
Not allowed to those who falsely accused their wives. Deut 22:18,19.
Women
Could obtain. Prov 2:17; Mark 10:12.
Could marry after. Deut 24:2.
Responsible for vows after. Num 30:9.
Married after, could not return to first husband. Deut 24:3,4; Jer 3:1.
Afflicted by. Is 54:4,6.
Priests not to marry women after. Lev 21:14.
Of servants, regulated by law. Ex 21:7,11.
Of captives, regulated by law. Deut 21:13,14.
Forced on those who had idolatrous wives. Ezra 10:2-17; Neh 13:23,30.
Jews condemned for love of. Mal 2:14-16.
Forbidden by Christ except for adultery. Matt 5:32; 19:9.
Prohibition of, offended the Jews. Matt 19:10.
Illustrative of God's casting off of the Jewish church. Is 50:1; Jer 3:8.

Doctrines, False.

Destructive to faith. 2 Tim 2:18.
Hateful to God. Rev 2:14,15.
Unprofitable and vain. Titus 3:9; Heb 13:9.
Should be avoided by
Ministers. 1 Tim 1:4; 6:20.
Saints. Eph 4:14; Col 2:8.
All men. Jer 23:16; 29:8.
The wicked love. 2 Tim 4:3,4.
The wicked given up to believe. 2 Thess 2:11.
Teachers of
Not to be countenanced. 2 John 10.
Should be avoided. Rom 16:17,18.
Bring reproach on religion. 2 Pet 2:2.
Speak perverse things. Acts 20:30.
Attract many. 2 Pet 2:2.
Deceive many. Matt 24:5.
Shall abound in the latter days. 1 Tim 4:1.
Pervert the gospel of Christ. Gal 1:6,7.
Shall be exposed. 2 Tim 3:9.
Teachers of, are described as
Cruel. Acts 20:29.
Deceitful. 2 Cor 11:13.
Covetous. Titus 1:11; 2 Pet 2:3.
Ungodly. Judg 1:4,8.
Proud and ignorant. 1 Tim 6:3,4.
Corrupt and reprobate. 2 Tim 3:8.
Try, by Scripture. Is 8:20; 1 John 4:1.
Curse on those who teach. Gal 1:8,9.
Punishment on those who teach. Mic 3:6,7; 2 Pet 2:1,3.

Doctrines of the Gospel, The.

Are from God. John 7:16; Acts 13:12.
Are taught by Scripture. 2 Tim 3:16.
Are godly. 1 Tim 6:3; Titus 1:1.
Immorality condemned by. 1 Tim 1:9-11.
Lead to fellowship with the Father and with the Son. 1 John 1:3; 2 John 9.
Lead to holiness. Rom 6:17-22; Titus 2:12.
Bring no reproach on. 1 Tim 6:1; Titus 2:5.
Ministers should
Be nourished up in. 1 Tim 4:6.
Attend to. 1 Tim 4:13,16.
Hold, in sincerity. 2 Cor 2:17; Titus 2:7.
Hold steadfastly. 2 Tim 1:13; Titus 1:9.
Continue in. 1 Tim 4:16.
Speak things which become. Titus 2:1.
Saints obey, from the heart. Rom 6:17.
Saints abide in. Acts 2:42.
A faithful walk adorns. Titus 2:10.
The obedience of saints leads to surer knowledge of. John 7:17.
Those who oppose are
Proud. 1 Tim 6:3,4.
Ignorant. 1 Tim 6:4.
Doting about questions, etc. 1 Tim 6:4.
Not to be received. 2 John 10.
To be avoided. Rom 16:17.
Not endured by the wicked. 2 Tim 4:3.

Dog, The.

Despised by the Jews. 2 Sam 3:8.
Described as
Impatient of injury. Prov 26:17.
Unclean. Luke 16:21; 2 Pet 2:22.
Carnivorous. 1 Kin 14:11; 2 Kin 9:35,36.
Fond of blood. 1 Kin 21:19; 22:38.
Dangerous and destructive. Ps 22:16.
Infested cities by night. Ps 59:14,15.
Nothing holy to be given to. Matt 7:6; 15:26.
Things torn by beasts given to. Ex 22:31.
Sacrificing of, an abomination. Is 66:3.
Price of, not to be consecrated. Deut 23:18.
When domesticated
Employed in watching flocks. Job 30:1.
Fed with the crumbs, etc. Matt 15:27.
Manner of, in drinking alluded to. Judg 7:5.
Illustrative
Of Gentiles. Matt 15:22,26.
Of covetous ministers. Is 56:11.
Of fools. Prov 26:11.
Of apostates. 2 Pet 2:22.
Of persecutors. Ps 22:16,20.
Of obstinate sinners. Matt 7:6; Rev 22:15.
Of false teachers. Phil 3:2.
(Dumb,) of unfaithful ministers. Is 56:10.
(Dead,) of the mean. 1 Sam 24:14; 2 Sam 9:8.

Dove, The.

Clean and used as food. Deut 14:11.
Offered in sacrifice. Gen 15:9; Lev 1:14.
Impiously sold in the court of the temple. Matt 21:12; John 2:16.
Characterised by
Simplicity. Matt 10:16.
Comeliness of countenance. Song 2:14.
Softness of eyes. Song 1:15.
Sweetness of voice. Song 2:14.
Richness of plumage. Ps 68:13.
Mournful tabering of, alluded to. Nah 2:7.
Dwells in rocks. Song 2:14; Jer 48:28.
Frequents streams and rivers. Song 5:12.
Sent from the ark by Noah. Gen 8:8,10,12.
Why considered the emblem of peace. Gen 8:11.
The harbinger of spring. Song 2:12.
Illustrative
Of the Holy Spirit. Matt 3:16; John 1:32.
Of the meekness of Christ. Song 5:12.
Of the church. Song 2:14; 5:2.
Of mourners. Is 38:14; 59:11.
Of converts to the church. Is 60:8.
(In its flight,) of the return of Israel from captivity. Hos 11:11.

Dragon, The.

Often of a red colour. Rev 12:3.
Described as
Powerful. Rev 12:4.
Poisonous. Deut 32:33.
Of solitary habits. Job 30:29.
Its mournful voice alluded to. Mic 1:8.
Its wailing alluded to. Mic 1:8.
Its snuffing up the air alluded to. Jer 14:6.
Its swallowing of its prey alluded to. Jer 51:34.
Found in
The wilderness. Mal 1:3.
Deserted cities. Is 13:22; Jer 9:11.
Dry places. Is 34:13; 43:20.
A species of, in rivers. Ps 74:13; Is 27:1.

Illustrative
- Of cruel and persecuting kings. Is 27:1; 51:9; Ezek 29:3.
- Of enemies of the church. Ps 9:13.
- Of wicked men. Ps 44:19.
- Of the devil. Rev 13:2; 20:2,7.
- (Poison of,) of wine. Deut 32:33.

Dreams.

Visions in sleep. Job 33:15; Dan 2:28.
Often imaginary. Job 20:8; Is 29:8.
Excess of business frequently leads to. Eccl 5:3.
God's will often revealed in. Num 12:6; Job 33:15.
False prophets
- Pretend to. Jer 23:25-28; 29:8.
- Not to be regarded in. Deut 13:1-3; Jer 27:9.
- Condemned for pretending to. Jer 23:32.

Vanity of trusting to natural. Eccl 5:7.
The ancients
- Put great faith in. Judg 7:15.
- Often perplexed by. Gen 40:6; 41:8; Job 7:14; Dan 2:1; 4:5.
- Anxious to have, explained. Gen 40:8; Dan 2:3.
- Consulting magicians on. Gen 41:8; Dan 2:2-4.

God the only interpreter of. Gen 40:8; 41:16; Dan 2:27-30; 7:16.
Mentioned in Scripture
- Abimelech. Gen 20:3-7.
- Jacob. Gen 28:12; 31:10.
- Laban. Gen 31:24.
- Joseph. Gen 37:5-9.
- Pharaoh's butler and baker. Gen 40:5-19.
- Pharaoh. Gen 41:1-7.
- Midianite. Judg 7:13-15.
- Solomon. 1 Kin 3:5-15.
- Nebuchadnezzar. Dan 2:1,31; 4:5,8.
- Daniel. Dan 7:1-28.
- Joseph. Matt 1:20,21; 2:13,19,20.
- Wise men. Matt 2:11,12.
- Pilate's wife. Matt 27:19.

Illustrative of
- Prosperity of sinners. Job 20:5-8, Ps 73:19,20.
- Impure imaginations. Jude 1:8.
- Enemies of the church. Is 29:7,8.

Drink Offering.

Antiquity of. Gen 35:14.
Sacrifices accompanied by. Ex 29:40; Lev 23:13.
Quantity appointed to be used for each kind of sacrifice. Num 15:3-10.
For public sacrifices provided by the state. Ezra 7:17; Ezek 45:17.
Not poured on the altar of incense. Ex 30:9.
Omission of, caused by bad vintage. Joel 1:9,13.
Idolatrous Jews
- Offered to the queen of heaven. Jer 7:18; 44:17-19.
- Reproved for offering, to idols. Is 57:5,6; 65:11; Jer 19:13; Ezek 20:28.

Idolaters often used blood for. Ps 16:4.
Vanity of offering, to idols. Deut 32:37,38.
Illustrative of the
- Offering of Christ. Is 53:12.
- Pouring out of the Spirit. Joel 2:28.
- Devotedness of ministers. Phil 2:17.

Drunkenness.

Forbidden. Eph 5:18.
Caution against. Luke 21:34.
Is a work of the flesh. Gal 5:21.
Is debasing. Is 28:8.
Is inflaming. Is 5:11.
Overcharges the heart. Luke 21:34.
Takes away the heart. Hos 4:11.
Leads to
- Poverty. Prov 21:17; 23:21.
- Strife. Prov 23:29,30.
- Woe and sorrow. Prov 23:29,30.
- Error. Is 28:7.
- Contempt of God's works. Is 5:12.
- Scorning. Hos 7:5.
- Rioting and wantonness. Rom 13:13.

The wicked addicted to. Dan 5:1-4.
False teachers often addicted to. Is 56:12.
Folly of yielding to. Prov 20:1.
Avoid those given to. Prov 23:20; 1 Cor 5:11.
Denunciations against
- Those given to. Is 5:11,12; 28:1-3.
- Those who encourage. Hab 2:15.

Excludes from heaven. 1 Cor 6:10; Gal 5:21.
Punishment of. Deut 21:20; Joel 1:5,6; Amos 6:6,7; Matt 24:49-51.
Exemplified
- Noah. Gen 9:21.
- Nabal. 1 Sam 25:36.
- Uriah. 2 Sam 11:13.
- Elah. 1 Kin 16:9,10.
- Benhadad. 1 Kin 20:16.
- Belshazzar. Dan 5:4.
- Corinthians. 1 Cor 11:21.

Eagle, The.

A bird of prey. Job 9:26; Matt 24:28.
Unclean. Lev 11:13; Deut 14:12.
Different kinds of. Lev 11:13,18; Ezek 17:3.
Called the eagle of the heavens. Lam 4:19.
Described as
- Long-sighted. Job 39:29.
- Swift. 2 Sam 1:23.
- Soaring to heaven. Prov 23:5.

Strength of its feathers alluded to. Dan 4:33.
Greatness of its wings alluded to. Ezek 17:3,7.
Peculiarity of its flight alluded to. Prov 30:19.
Delights in the lofty cedars. Ezek 17:3,4.
Dwells in the high rocks. Job 39:27,28.
Feeds her young with blood. Job 39:29,30.
Illustrative
- Of wisdom and zeal of God's ministers. Ezek 1:10; Rev 4:7.
- Of great and powerful kings. Ezek 17:3; Hos 8:1.
- (Renewed strength and beauty of,) of the renewal of saints. Ps 103:5.
- (Mode of teaching her young to fly,) of God's care of his church. Ex 19:4; Deut 32:11.
- (Wings of,) of protection afforded to the church. Rev 12:14.
- (Upward flight of,) of the saint's rapid progress toward heaven. Is 40:31.
- (Swiftness of,) of the melting away of riches. Prov 23:5.
- (Swiftness of,) of the swiftness of hostile armies. Deut 28:49; Jer 4:13; 48:40; Lam 4:19.
- (Height and security of its dwelling,) of the fancied but fatal security of the wicked. Jer 49:16; Obad 4.
- (Increase baldness of, in the moulting season,) of calamities. Mic 1:16.
- (Hasting to the prey,) of the swiftness of man's days. Job 9:26.

Was the standard of the Roman armies. Matt 24:15,28.

Ear, The.

The organ of hearing. Job 13:1; 29:11.
Capable of trying and distinguishing words. Job 12:11.
God
- Made. Prov 20:12.
- Planted. Ps 94:9.
- Opens. Job 33:16; 36:10.
- Judicially closed. Is 6:10; Matt 13:15.

Christ opens. Is 35:5; 43:8,10.
Instruction received through. Is 30:21.
That hears and receives the word of God, blessed. Ex 15:26; Matt 13:16.
Should
- Seek knowledge. Prov 18:15.
- Be bowed down to instructions. Prov 5:1.
- Be inclined to wisdom. Prov 2:2.
- Be given to the law of God. Is 1:10.
- Receive the word of God. Jer 9:20.
- Hear and obey reproof. Prov 15:31; 25:12.

Not satisfied with earthly things. Eccl 1:8.
Of the wicked
- Uncircumcised. Jer 6:10; Acts 7:51.
- Itching. 2 Tim 4:3.
- Not inclined to hear God. Jer 7:24; 35:15.
- Turned away from God's law. Prov 28:9.
- Stopped against God's word. Ps 58:4; Zech 7:11.

Not to be stopped at cry of the poor. Prov 21:13.
Blood put on the right ear of
- Priests at consecration. Ex 29:20; Lev 8:23.
- The healed leper in cleansing him. Lev 14:14.

Often adorned with rings. Ezek 16:12; Hos 2:13.
Of servants who refused to leave their masters, bored to the door. Ex 21:6; Deut 15:17.

Early Rising.

Christ set an example of. Mark 1:35; Luke 21:38; John 8:2.
Requisite for
- Devotion. Ps 5:3; 59:16; 63:1; 88:13; Is 26:9.
- Executing God's commands. Gen 22:3.

Discharge of daily duties. Prov 31:15.
Neglect of, leads to poverty. Prov 6:9-11.
Practised by the wicked, for
Deceit. Prov 27:14.
Executing plans of evil. Mic 2:1.
Illustrates spiritual diligence. Rom 13:11,12.
Exemplified
Abraham. Gen 19:27.
Isaac, etc. Gen 26:31.
Jacob. Gen 28:18.
Joshua, etc. Josh 3:1.
Gideon. Judg 6:38.
Samuel. 1 Sam 15:12.
David. 1 Sam 17:20.
Mary, etc. Mark 16:2.
Apostles. Acts 5:21.

EARTH, THE.

The world in general. Gen 1:2.
The dry land as divided from waters. Gen 1:10.
God
Created. Gen 1:1; Neh 9:6.
Laid the foundation of. Job 38:4; Ps 102:25.
Formed. Ps 90:2.
Spread abroad. Is 42:5; 44:24.
Suspended in space. Job 26:7.
Supports. Ps 75:3.
Establishes. Ps 78:69; 119:90.
Enlightens. Gen 1:14-16; Jer 33:25.
Waters. Ps 65:9; 147:8.
Makes fruitful. Gen 1:11; 27:28.
Inspects. Zech 4:10.
Governs supremely. Job 34:13; Ps 135:6.
Reigns in. Ex 8:22; Ps 97:1.
Shall be exalted in. Ps 46:10.
Is the Lord's. Ex 9:29; 1 Cor 10:26.
Created to be inhabited. Is 45:18.
First division of. Gen 10:25.
Ideas of the ancients respecting the form of. Job 11:9; 38:18; Prov 25:3.
Diversified by hills and mountains. Hab 3:6.
Full of minerals. Deut 8:9; Job 28:1-5,15-19.
Described as
God's footstool. Is 66:1; Matt 5:35.
Full of God's goodness. Ps 33:5.
Full of God's riches. Ps 104:24.
Full of God's mercy. Ps 119:64.
Full of God's glory. Num 14:21; Is 6:3.
Shining with God's glory. Ezek 43:2.
Trembling before God. Ps 68:8; Jer 10:10.
Melting at God's voice. Ps 46:6.
Burning at God presence. Nah 1:5.
Man
Formed out of. Gen 2:7; Ps 103:14.
Given dominion over. Gen 1:26; Ps 115:16.
By nature is of. 1 Cor 15:47-48.
By nature minds the thing of. Phil 3:19.
Brought a curse on. Gen 3:17.
Shall return to. Gen 3:19; Ps 146:4.
Subject to God's judgments. Ps 46:8; Is 11:4.
Corrupted by sin. Gen 6:11,12; Is 24:5.
Made barren by sin. Deut 28:23; Ps 107:34.
Made to mourn and languish by sin. Is 24:4; Jer 4:28; 12:4; Hos 4:3.
Satan goes to and fro in. Job 1:7; 1 Pet 5:8.
Shall be filled with the knowledge of God. Is 11:9; Hab 2:14.
Once inundated. Gen 7:17-24.
Not to be again inundated. Gen 9:11; 2 Pet 3:6,7.
To be dissolved by fire. 2 Pet 3:7,10,12.
To be renewed. Is 65:17; 2 Pet 3:13.
Saints shall inherit. Ps 25:13; Matt 5:5.

EARTHQUAKES.

Islands and mountainous districts liable to. Ps 114:4,6; Rev 6:14; 16:18,20.
Frequently accompanied by
Volcanic eruptions. Ps 104:32; Nah 1:5.
Convulsion and receding of the sea. 2 Sam 22:8,16; Ps 18:7,15; 46:3.
Opening of the earth. Num 16:31,32.
Overturning of mountains. Ps 46:2; Zech 14:4.
Rending of rocks. Matt 27:51.
Are visible tokens of
God's power. Job 9:6; Heb 12:26.
God's presence. Ps 68:7,8; 114:7.
God's anger. Ps 18:7; 60:2; Is 13:13.
Men always terrified by. Num 16:34; Zech 14:5; Matt 27:54; Rev 11:13.
Mentioned in Scripture
At Mount Sinai. Ex 19:18.
In the wilderness. Num 16:31,32.
In strongholds of Philistines. 1 Sam 14:15.
When Elijah fled from Jezebel. 1 Kin 19:11.
In Uzziah's reign. Amos 1:1; Zech 14:5.
At our Lord's death. Matt 27:51.
At out Lord's resurrection. Matt 28:2.
At Philippi. Acts 16:26.
Before destruction of Jerusalem, predicted. Matt 24:7; Luke 21:11.
At Christ's second coming, predicted. Zech 14:4.
Illustrative of
The judgments of God. Is 24:19,20; 29:6; Jer 4:24; Rev 8:5.
The overthrow of kingdoms. Hag 2:6,22; Rev 6:12,13; 16:18,19.

EDIFICATION.

Described. Eph 4:12-16.
Is the object of
The ministerial office. Eph 4:11,12.
Ministerial gifts. 1 Cor 14:3-5,12.
Ministerial authority. 2 Cor 10:8; 13:10.
The Church's union in Christ. Eph 4:16.
The gospel, the instrument of. Acts 20:32.
Love leads to. 1 Cor 8:1.
Exhortation to. Jude 1:20,21.
Mutual, commanded. Rom 14:19; 1 Thess 5:11.
All to be done to. 2 Cor 12:19; Eph 4:29.
Use self-denial to promote, in others. 1 Cor 10:23,33.
The peace of the Church favours. Acts 9:31.
Foolish questions opposed to. 1 Tim 1:4.

EDOMITES, THE.

Descended from Esau. Gen 36:9.
Dwelt in Mount Seir. Gen 32:3; Deut 2:4,5.
Were called
Children of Esau. Deut 2:4.
Brethren of Israel. Num 20:14.
Governed by dukes. Gen 36:15-30,40-43; Ex 15:15.
Afterwards had kings. Gen 36:31-29; Num 20:14.
Under a deputy or viceroy while subject to Judah. 1 Kin 22:47.
Character of
Wise. Jer 49:7.
Proud and self-confident. Jer 49:16; Obad 3.
Strong and cruel. Jer 49:19.
Vindictive. Ezek 25:12.
Idolatrous. 2 Chr 25:14,20.
Superstitious. Jer 27:3,9.
Carried on extensive commerce. Ezek 27:20.
Country of
Specially given to them. Deut 2:5.
Fertile and rich. Gen 27:39.
Mountainous and rocky. Jer 49:16; Mal 1:3.
Traversed by roads. Num 20:17.
Well fortified. Ps 60:9.
Called Mount Seir. Ezek 35:2.
Called Mount of Esau. Obad 21.
Called Dumah. Is 21:11.
Called Idumea. Is 34:6; Mark 3:8.
Called Edom. Is 63:1.
Cities of
Dinhabah or Dedan. Gen 36:32; Jer 49:8.
Avith. Gen 36:35.
Pau. Gen 36:39.
Bozrah. Jer 49:22; Amos 1:12.
Teman. Jer 49:7; Ezek 25:13.
Eziongeber, a sea port. 1 Kin 9:26.
Implacable enemies of Israel. Ezek 35:5.
Israel forbidden to hate. Deut 23:7.
Israel forbidden to spoil. Deut 2:4,6; 2 Chr 20:10.
Might be received into the congregation in third generation. Deut 23:8.
Refused Israel a passage. Num 20:21; Judg 11:17.
Saul made war against. 1 Sam 14:47.
David subdued, etc. 2 Sam 8:14; 1 Chr 18:11,13.
Slaughter of, by Joab and Abishai. 1 Kin 11:16; 1 Chr 18:12.
Took refuge in Egypt. 1 Kin 11:17-19.
Returned after David's death. 1 Kin 11:21-22.
Were stirred up against Solomon. 1 Kin 11:14.
Confederated with enemies of Israel against Jehoshaphat. 2 Chr 20:10; Ps 83:4-6.
Miraculous overthrow of. 2 Chr 20:22.
Revolted from Joram, king of Judah. 2 Kin 8:20-22; 2 Chr 21:8-10.
Reconquered by Amaziah. 2 Kin 14:7,10; 2 Chr 25:11,12.
The Jews ensnared by the idols of, and punished. 2 Chr 25:14,15,20.
Rebelled against Ahaz. 2 Chr 28:17.
Aided Babylon against Judah. Ps 137:7; Obad 11.

Predictions respecting
Subjection to Israel. Gen 25:23; 27:29,37.
Revolt from Israel. Gen 27:40.
Israel's occupation of their country. Num 24:18; Obad 17-19.
To share in the punishment of the nations. Jer 9:26; 25:15-27; Ezek 32:29.
Punishment for persecuting Israel. Is 34:5-8; 63:1-4; Lam 4:21; Ezek 25:13,14; Amos 1:11,12; Obad 10,15.
Exterminating slaughter of. Obad 18.
Utter desolation of their country. Is 34:9-17; Ezek 35:7-15.
The king of Babylon an instrument of their punishment. Jer 27:3-6.
Israel an instrument of their punishment. Ezek 25:14; Obad 18.
Their ruin to be an astonishment. Jer 49:17,21.
Their future subjection to the Jews. Is 11:14; Amos 9:12.
Remarkable persons of
Doeg. 1 Sam 22:18.
Hadad. 1 Kin 11:14,19.
Eliphaz. Job 2:11.

EGYPT.

Peopled by Mizraim's posterity. Gen 10:6,13,14.
Boundaries of. Ezek 29:10.
Dry climate of. Deut 11:10,11.
Watered by the Nile. Gen 41:1-3; Ex 1:22.
Inundations of, alluded to. Amos 8:8.
Subject to plague, etc. Deut 7:15; 28:27,60.
Sometimes visited by famine. Gen 41:30.
Called
The land of Ham. Ps 105:23; 106:22.
The South. Jer 13:19; Dan 11:14,25.
Sihor. Is 23:3.
Rahab. Ps 87:4; 89:10.
House of Bondmen. Ex 13:3,14; Deut 7:8.
Celebrated for
Fertility. Gen 13:10; 45:18.
Wealth. Heb 11:26.
Literature. 1 Kin 4:30; Acts 7:22.
Fine horses. 1 Kin 10:28,29.
Fine linen, etc. Prov 7:16; Is 19:9.
Commerce. Gen 41:57; Ezek 27:7.
Religion of, idolatrous. Ex 12:12; Num 33:4; Is 19:1; Ezek 29:7.
Idolatry of, followed by Israel. Ex 32:4; Ezek 20:8,19.
Magic practised in. Ex 7:11,12,22; 8:7.
Ruled by kings who assumed the name of Pharaoh. Gen 12:14,15; 40:1,2; Ex 1:8,22.
Under a governor. Gen 41:41-44.
Had princes and counsellors. Gen 12:15; Is 19:11.
As a power was
Proud and arrogant. Ezek 29:3; 30:6.
Pompous. Ezek 32:12.
Mighty. Is 30:2,3.
Ambitious of conquests. Jer 46:8.
Treacherous. Is 36:6; 29:6,7.
Inhabitants of
Superstitious. Is 19:3.
Hospitable. Gen 47:5,6; 1 Kin 11:18.
Often intermarried with strangers. Gen 21:21; 1 Kin 3:1; 11:19; 1 Chr 2:34,35.
Abhorred shepherds. Gen 46:34.
Abhorred the sacrifice of oxen, etc. Ex 8:26.
Not to be abhorred by Israel. Deut 23:7.
Might be received into the congregation in the third generation. Deut 23:8.
Mode of entertaining in. Gen 43:32-34.
Diet used in. Num 11:5.
Mode of embalming in. Gen 50:3.
Often a refuge to strangers. Gen 12:10; 47:4; 1 Kin 11:17,40; 2 Kin 25:26; Matt 2:12,13.
The armies of
Described. Ex 14:7-9.
Destroyed in the Red Sea. Ex 14:23-28.
Captured and burned Gezer. 1 Kin 9:16.
Besieged and plundered Jerusalem in Rehoboam's time. 1 Kin 14:25,26.
Invaded Assyria and killed Josiah who assisted it. 2 Kin 23:29.
Deposed Jehoahaz and made Judea tributary. 2 Kin 23:31-35.
Assistance of, sought by Judah against the Chaldees. Ezek 17:15; Jer 37:5,7.
History of Israel in
Their sojourn in it, foretold. Gen 15:13.
Joseph sold into. Gen 37:28; 39:1.
Potiphar blessed for Joseph's sake. Gen 39:2-6.
Joseph unjustly cast into prison. Gen 39:7-20.
Joseph interprets the chief baker's and the chief butler's dreams. Gen 40:5-19.
Joseph interprets Pharaoh's dreams. Gen 41:14-32.
Joseph counsels Pharaoh. Gen 41:33-36.
Joseph made governor. Gen 41:41-44.
Joseph's successful provision against the years of famine. Gen 41:46-56.
Joseph's ten brethren arrive. Gen 42:1-6.
Joseph recognises his brethren. Gen 42:7,8.
Benjamin brought. Gen 43:15.
Joseph makes himself known to his brethren. Gen 45:1-8.
Joseph sends for his father. Gen 45:9-11.
Pharaoh invites Jacob into. Gen 45:16-20.
Jacob's journey. Gen 46:5-7.
Jacob, etc. presented to Pharaoh. Gen 47:1-10.
Israel placed in the land of Goshen. Gen 46:34; 47:11,27.
Joseph enriches the king. Gen 47:13-26.
Jacob's death and burial. Gen 49:33; 50:1-13.
Israel increases and are oppressed. Ex 1:1-14.
Male children destroyed. Ex 1:15-22.
Moses born and hid for three months. Ex 2:2.
Moses exposed on the Nile. Ex 2:3,4.
Moses adopted and brought up by Pharaoh's daughter. Ex 2:5-10.
Moses slays an Egyptian. Ex 2:11,12.
Moses flies to Midian. Ex 2:15.
Moses sent to Pharaoh. Ex 3:2-10.
Pharaoh increases their affliction. Ex 5:1-23.
Moses proves his divine mission by miracles. Ex 4:29-31; 7:10.
Egypt is plagued for Pharaoh's obstinacy. Ex 7:14-10:29.
The Passover instituted. Ex 12:1-28.
Destruction of the firstborn. Ex 12:29,30.
Israel spoils the Egyptians. Ex 12:35,36.
Israel driven out of. Ex 12:31-33.
Date of the Exodus. Ex 12:41; Heb 11:27.
Pharaoh pursues Israel and is miraculously destroyed. Ex 14:5-25.
Prophecies respecting
Dismay of its inhabitants. Is 19:1,16,17.
Infatuation of its princes. Is 19:3,11-14.
Failure of internal resources. Is 19:5-10.
Civil war and domestic strife. Is 19:2.
Armies destroyed by Babylon. Jer 46:2-12.
Invasion by Babylon. Jer 46:13,24; Ezek 32:11.
Destruction of its power. Ezek 30:24,25.
Destruction of its cities. Ezek 30:14-18.
Destruction of its idols. Jer 43:12,13; 46:25; Ezek 30:13.
Spoil of, a reward to Babylon for services against Tyre. Ezek 29:18-20.
Captivity of its people. Is 20:4; Jer 46:19,24,26; Ezek 30:4.
Utter desolation of, for forty years. Ezek 29:8-12; 30:12; 32:15.
Allies to share its misfortunes. Ezek 30:4,6.
The Jews who practised its idolatry to share its punishments. Jer 44:7-28.
Terror occasioned by its fall. Ezek 32:9,10.
Ever to be a base kingdom. Ezek 29:15.
Christ to be called out of. Hos 11:1; Matt 2:15.
Conversion of. Is 19:18-20.
To be numbered and blessed along with Israel. Is 19:23-25.
Prophetic illustration of its destruction. Jer 43:9,10; Ezek 30:21,22; 32:4-6.

ELECTION.

Of Christ, as Messiah. Is 42:1; 1 Pet 2:6.
Of good angels. 1 Tim 5:21.
Of Israel. Deut 7:6; Is 45:5.
Of ministers. Luke 6:13; Acts 9:15.
Of churches. 1 Pet 5:13.
Of saints, is
Of God. 1 Thess 1:4; Titus 1:1.
By Christ. John 13:18; 15:16.
In Christ. Eph 1:4.

Personal. Matt 20:16; John 6:44; Acts 22:14; 2 John 13.
According to the purpose of God. Rom 9:11; Eph 1:11.
According to the foreknowledge of God. Rom 8:29; 1 Pet 1:2.
Eternal. Eph 1:4.
Sovereign. Rom 9:15,16; 1 Cor 1:27; Eph 1:11.
Irrespective of merit. Rom 9:11.
Of grace. Rom 11:5.
Recorded in heaven. Luke 10:20.
For the glory of God. Eph 1:6.
Through faith. 2 Thess 2:13.
Through sanctification of the Spirit. 1 Pet 1:2.
To adoption. Eph 1:5.
To salvation. 2 Thess 2:13.
To conformity with Christ. Rom 8:29.
To good works. Eph 2:10.
To spiritual warfare. 2 Tim 2:4.
To eternal glory. Rom 9:23.
Ensures to saints
Effectual calling. Rom 8:30.
Divine teaching. John 17:6.
Belief in Christ. Acts 13:48.
Acceptance with God. Rom 11:7.
Protection. Mark 13:20.
Vindication of their wrongs. Luke 18:7.
Working of all things for good. Rom 8:28.
Blessedness. Ps 33:12; 65:4.
The inheritance. Is 65:9; 1 Pet 1:4,5.
Should lead to cultivation of graces. Col 3:12.
Should be evidenced by diligence. 2 Pet 1:10.
Saints may have assurance of. 1 Thess 1:4.
Exemplified
Isaac. Gen 21:12.
Abram. Neh 9:7.
Zerubbabel. Hag 2:23.
Apostles. John 13:18; 15:19.
Jacob. Rom 9:12,13.
Rufus. Rom 16:13.
Paul. Gal 1:15.

EMBALMING.

Unknown to early patriarchs. Gen 23:4.
Learned by the Jews in Egypt. Gen 50:2,26.
Time required for. Gen 50:3.
How performed by the Jews. 2 Chr 16:14; Luke 23:56; John 19:40.
Not always practised by the Jews. John 11:39.
An attempt to defeat God's purpose. Gen 3:19.

EMBLEMS OF THE HOLY SPIRIT, THE.

Water. John 3:5; 7:38,39.
Cleansing. Ezek 16:9; 36:25; Eph 5:26; Heb 10:22.
Fertilising. Ps 1:3; Is 27:3,6; 44:3,4; 58:11.
Refreshing. Ps 46:4; Is 41:17,18.
Abundant. John 7:37,38.
Freely given. Is 55:1; John 4:14; Rev 22:17.
Fire
Purifying. Is 4:4; Mal 3:2,3.
Illuminating. Ex 13:21; Ps 78:14.
Searching. Zeph 1:12; 1 Cor 2:10.
Wind
Independent. John 3:8; 1 Cor 12:11.
Powerful. 1 Kin 19:11; Acts 2:2.
Sensible in its effects. John 3:8.
Reviving. Ezek 37:9,10,14.
Oil. Ps 45:7.
Healing. Luke 10:34; Rev 3:18.
Comforting. Is 61:3; Heb 1:9.
Illuminating. Matt 25:3,4; 1 John 2:20,27.
Consecrating. Ex 29:7; 30:30; Is 61:1.
Rain and dew. Ps 72:6.
Fertilising. Ezek 34:26,27; Hos 6:3; 10:12; 14:5.
Refreshing. Ps 68:9; Is 18:5.
Abundant. Ps 133:3.
Imperceptible. 2 Sam 17:12; Mark 4:26-28.
A dove. Matt 3:16.
Gentle. Matt 10:16; Gal 5:22.
A voice. Is 6:8.
Speaking. Matt 10:20.
Guiding. Is 30:21; John 16:13.
Warning. Heb 3:7-11.
A seal. Rev 7:2.
Securing. Eph 1:13,14; 4:30.
Authenticating. John 6:27; 2 Cor 1:22.
Cloven tongues. Acts 2:3,6-11.

ENEMIES.

Christ prayed for his. Luke 23:34.
The lives of, to be spared. 1 Sam 24:10; 2 Sam 16:10,11.
The goods of, to be taken care of. Ex 23:4,5.
Should be
Loved. Matt 5:44.
Prayed for. Acts 7:60.
Assisted. Prov 25:21; Rom 12:20.
Overcome by kindness. 1 Sam 26:21.
Rejoice not at the misfortunes of. Job 31:29.
Rejoice not at the failings of. Prov 24:17.
Desire not the death of. 1 Kin 3:11.
Curse them not. Job 31:30.
Be affectionately concerned for. Ps 35:13.
The friendship of, deceitful. 2 Sam 20:9,10; Prov 26:26; 27:6; Matt 26:48,49.
God defends against. Ps 59:9; 61:3.
God delivers from. 1 Sam 12:11; Ezra 8:31; Ps 18:48.
Made to be at peace with saints. Prov 16:7.
Pray for deliverance from. 1 Sam 12:10; Ps 17:9; 59:1; 64:1.
Of saints, God will destroy. Ps 60:12.
Praise God for deliverance from. Ps 136:24.

ENTERTAINMENTS.

Often great. Gen 21:8; Dan 5:1; Luke 5:29.
Given on occasions of
Marriage. Matt 22:2.
Birthdays. Mark 6:21.
Weaning children. Gen 21:8.
Taking leave of friends. 1 Kin 19:21.
Return of friends. 2 Sam 12:4; Luke 15:23.
Ratifying covenants. Gen 26:30; 31:54.
Sheep-shearing. 1 Sam 25:2,36; 2 Sam 13:23.
Harvest home. Ruth 3:2-7; Is 9:3.
Vintage. Judg 9:27.
Coronation of kings. 1 Kin 1:9,18,19; 1 Chr 12:39,40; Hos 7:5.
Offering voluntary sacrifice. Gen 31:54; Deut 12:6,7; 1 Sam 1:4,5,9.
Festivals. 1 Sam 20:5,24-26.
National deliverance. Esth 8:17; 9:17-19.
Preparations made for. Gen 18:6,7; Prov 9:2; Matt 22:4; Luke 15:23.
Kinds of, mentioned in Scripture
Dinner. Gen 43:16; Matt 22:4; Luke 14:12.
Supper. Luke 14:12; John 12:2.
Banquet of wine. Esth 5:6.
Under the direction of a master of the feast. John 2:8,9.
Served often by hired servants. Matt 22:13; John 2:5.
Served often by members of the family. Gen 18:8; Luke 10:40; John 12:2.
Invitations to
Often addressed to many. Luke 14:16.
Often only to relatives and friends. 1 Kin 1:9; Luke 14:12.
Often by the master in person. 2 Sam 13:24; Esth 5:4; Zeph 1:7; Luke 7:36.
Repeated through servants when all things were ready. Prov 9:1-5; Luke 14:17.
Should be sent to the poor, etc. Deut 14:29; Luke 14:13.
Often given in
The house. Luke 5:29.
The air, beside fountains. 1 Kin 1:9.
The court of the house. Esth 1:5,6; Luke 7:36,37.
The upper room or guest chamber. Mark 14:14,15.
Guests at
Saluted by the master. Luke 7:45.
Usually anointed. Ps 23:5; Luke 7:46.
Had their feet washed when they came a distance. Gen 18:4; 43:24; Luke 7:38,44.
Arranged according to rank. Gen 43:33; 1 Sam 9:22; Luke 14:10.
Often had separate dishes. Gen 43:34; 1 Sam 1:4.
Often ate from the same dish. Matt 26:23.
Forwardness to take chief seats at, condemned. Matt 23:6; Luke 14:7,8.
A choice portion reserved in, for principal guests. Gen 43:34; 1 Sam 1:5; 9:23,24.
Custom of presenting the sop at, to one of the guests, alluded to. John 13:26.
Portions of, often sent to the absent. 2 Sam 11:8; Neh 8:10; Esth 9:19.
Offence given by refusing to go to. Luke 14:18,24.
Anxiety to have many guests at, alluded to. Luke 14:22,23.
Men and women did not usually meet at. Esth 1:8,9; Mark 6:21; Matt 14:11.
None admitted to, after the master had risen and shut the door. Luke 13:24,25.

Began with thanksgiving. 1 Sam 9:13; Mark 8:6.
Concluded with a hymn. Mark 14:26.
None asked to eat or drink more than he liked at. Esth 1:8.
Music and dancing often introduced at. Amos 6:5; Mark 6:22; Luke 15:25.
Often scenes of great intemperance. 1 Sam 25:36; Dan 5:3,4; Hos 7:5.
Given by the guests in return. Job 1:4; Luke 14:12.

ENVY.

Forbidden. Prov 3:31; Rom 13:13.
Produced by foolish disputation. 1 Tim 6:4.
Excited by good deeds of others. Eccl 4:4.
A work of the flesh. Gal 5:21; James 4:5.
Hurtful to the envious. Job 5:2; Prov 14:30.
None can stand before. Prov 27:4.
A proof of carnal-mindedness. 1 Cor 3:1,3.
Inconsistent with the gospel. James 3:14.
Hinders growth in grace. 1 Pet 2:1,2.
The wicked
- Are full of. Rom 1:29.
- Live in. Titus 3:3.

Leads to every evil work. James 3:16.
Prosperity of the wicked should not excite. Ps 37:1,35; 73:3,17-20.
Punishment of. Is 26:11.
Exemplified
- Cain. Gen 4:5.
- Philistines. Gen 26:14.
- Laban's sons. Gen 31:1.
- Joseph's brethren. Gen 37:11.
- Joshua. Num 11:28,29.
- Aaron, etc. Num 12:2.
- Korah, etc. Num 16:3; Ps 106:16.
- Saul. 1 Sam 18:8.
- Sanballat, etc. Neh 2:10.
- Haman. Esth 5:13.
- Edomites. Ezek 35:11.
- Princes of Babylon. Dan 6:3,4.
- Chief Priests. Mark 15:10.
- Jews. Acts 13:45; 17:5.

EPHOD, THE.

The emblem of the priestly office. Hos 3:4.
Worn by
- The high priest. 1 Sam 2:28; 14:3.
- Ordinary priests. 1 Sam 22:18.
- Persons engaged in the service of God. 1 Sam 2:18; 2 Sam 6:14.
- Generally of linen. 1 Sam 2:18; 2 Sam 6:14.

For the high priest
- Commanded to be made. Ex 28:4.
- Made of offerings of the people. Ex 25:4,7.
- Made of gold, blue, purple, scarlet, etc. Ex 28:6; 29:2,3.
- Shoulders of, joined by onyx stones engraved with names of the twelve tribes of Israel. Ex 28:7,9-12; 39:4,6,7.
- Had a girdle of curious work. Ex 28:8.
- Breastplate of judgment inseparably united to. Ex 28:25-28; 39:20,21.
- Worn over the robe. Ex 28:31; Lev 8:7.
- Fastened on with its own girdle. Lev 8:7.
- Worn or held by him when consulted. 1 Sam 23:6,9-12; 30:7,8.

Used by idolatrous priests. Judg 8:27; 17:5; 18:14.
Israel deprived of, for sin. Hos 3:4.

EPHRAIM, TRIBE OF.

Descended from Joseph's second son adopted by Jacob. Gen 41:52; 48:5.
Predictions respecting. Gen 48:20; Deut 33:13-17.
Persons selected from
- To number the people. Num 1:10.
- To spy out the land. Num 13:8.
- To divide the land. Num 34:24.

Strength of, on leaving Egypt. Num 1:32,33.
Led the third division of Israel. Num 10:22.
Encamped west of the tabernacle. Num 2:18.
Offering of, at the dedication. Num 7:48-53.
Families of. Num 26:35,36.
Strength of, on entering Canaan. Num 26:37.
On Gerizim, said amen to blessings. Deut 27:12.
Bounds of its inheritance. Josh 16:5-9.
Could not drive out the Canaanites but made them tributary. Josh 16:10; Judg 1:29.
Assisted
- Manasseh in taking Bethel. Judg 1:22-25.
- Deborah and Barak against Sisera. Judg 5:14.
- Gideon against Midian. Judg 7:24,25.

Remonstrated with Gideon for not calling them sooner against Midian. Judg 8:1-3.
Quarrelled with Jephthah for not seeking their aid against Ammon. Judg 12:1-4.
Defeated and many slain. Judg 12:5,6.
Some of, at coronation of David. 1 Chr 12:30.
Officers appointed over, by David. 1 Chr 27:10,20.
The leading tribe of the kingdom of Israel. Is 7:2-17; Jer 31:9,20.
Many of, joined Judah under Asa. 2 Chr 15:9.
Many of, joined in Hezekiah's Passover and reformation. 2 Chr 30:18; 31:1.
The tabernacle continued a long time in Shiloh, a city of. Josh 18:1; 19:51.
One of Jeroboam's calves set up in Bethel, a city of. 1 Kin 12:29.
Remarkable persons of
- Joshua. Num 13:8; Josh 1:1.
- Abdon. Judg 12:13-15.
- Zichri. 2 Chr 28:7.

EUPHRATES, THE.

A branch of the river of Eden. Gen 2:14.
Called
- The river. Ex 23:31; Neh 2:7; Ps 72:8.
- The great river. Gen 15:18; Deut 1:7.
- The flood. Josh 24:2.

Waters of, considered wholesome. Jer 2:18.
Often overflowed its banks. Is 8:7,8.
Assyria bounded by. 2 Kin 23:29; Is 7:20.
Babylon situated on. Jer 51:13,36.
Extreme eastern boundary of the promised land. Gen 15:18; Deut 1:7; 11:24.
Egyptian army destroyed at. Jer 46:2,6,10.
Frequented by the captive Jews. Ps 137:1.
Captivity of Judah represented by the marring of Jeremiah's girdle in. Jer 13:3-9.
Prophecies respecting Babylon thrown into, as a sign. Jer 51:63.
Shall be the scene of future judgments. Rev 16:12.

EVENING, THE.

The day originally began with. Gen 1:5.
Divided into two, commencing at 3 o'clock, and sunset. Ex 12:6; Num 9:3.
Called
- Even. Gen 19:1; Deut 28:67.
- Eventide. Josh 8:29; Acts 4:3.
- Cool of the day. Gen 3:8.

Stretches out its shadows. Jer 6:4.
The outgoings of, praise God. Ps 65:8.
Man ceases from labour in. Ruth 2:17; Ps 104:23.
Wild beasts come forth in. Ps 59:6,14; Jer 5:6.
A season for
- Meditation. Gen 24:63.
- Prayer. Ps 55:17; Matt 14:15,23.
- Exercise. 2 Sam 11:2.
- Taking food. Mark 14:17,18; Luke 24:29,30.

Humiliation often continued until. Josh 7:6; Judg 20:23,26; 21:2; Ezra 9:4,5.
Custom of sitting at the gates in. Gen 19:1.
All defiled persons uncleaned until. Lev 11:24-28; 15:5-7; 17:15; Num 19:19.
Part of the daily sacrifice offered in. Ex 29:41; Ps 141:2; Dan 9:21.
Paschal lamb killed in. Ex 12:6,18.
The golden candlestick lighted in. Ex 27:21; 30:8.
The sky red in, a token of fair weather. Matt 16:2.

EXAMPLE OF CHRIST, THE.

Is perfect. Heb 7:26.
Conformity to, required in
- Holiness. 1 Pet 1:15,16; Rom 1:6.
- Righteousness. 1 John 2:6.
- Purity. 1 John 3:3.
- Love. John 13:34; Eph 5:2; 1 John 3:16.
- Humility. Luke 22:27; Phil 2:5,7.
- Meekness. Matt 11:29.
- Obedience. John 15:10.
- Self-denial. Matt 16:24; Rom 15:3.
- Ministering to others. Matt 20:28; John 13:14,15.
- Benevolence. Acts 20:35; 2 Cor 8:7,9.
- Forgiving injuries. Col 3:13.
- Overcoming the world. John 16:33; 1 John 5:4.
- Being not of the world. John 17:16.
- Being guileless. 1 Pet 2:21-22.
- Suffering wrongfully. 1 Pet 2:21-23.

Suffering for righteousness. Heb 12:3,4.
Saints predestinated to follow. Rom 8:29.
Conformity to, progressive. 2 Cor 3:18.

Excellency and Glory of Christ, The.

As God. John 1:1-5; Phil 2:6,9,10.
As the Son of God. Matt 3:17; Heb 1:6,8.
As one with the Father. John 10:30,38.
As the Firstborn. Col 1:15,18.
As the First-begotten. Heb 1:6.
As Lord of lords, etc. Rev 17:14.
As the image of God. Col 1:15; Heb 1:3.
As Creator. John 1:3; Col 1:16; Heb 1:2.
As the Blessed of God. Ps 45:2.
As Mediator. 1 Tim 2:5; Heb 8:6.
As Prophet. Deut 18:15,16; Acts 3:22.
As Priest. Ps 110:4; Heb 4:15.
As King. Is 6:1-5; John 12:41.
As Judge. Matt 16:27; 25:31,33.
As Shepherd. Is 40:10,11; John 10:11,14.
As Head of the Church. Eph 1:22.
As the true Light. Luke 1:78,79; John 1:4,9.
As the foundation of the Church. Is 28:16.
As the way. John 14:6; Heb 10:19,20.
As the truth. 1 John 5:20; Rev 3:7.
As the life. John 11:25; Col 3:4; 1 John 5:11.
As incarnate. John 1:14.
In his words. Luke 4:22; John 7:46.
In his works. Matt 13:54; John 2:11.
In his sinless perfection. Heb 7:26-28.
In the fulness of his grace and truth. Ps 45:2; John 1:14.
In his transfiguration. Matt 17:2; 2 Pet 1:16-18.
In his exaltation. Acts 7:55,56; Eph 1:21.
In the calling of the Gentiles. Ps 72:17; John 12:21,23.
In the restoration of the Jews. Ps 102:16.
In his triumph. Is 63:1-3; Rev 19:11,16.
Followed his sufferings. 1 Pet 1:10,11.
Followed his resurrection. 1 Pet 1:21.
Is unchangeable. Heb 1:10-12.
Is incomparable. Song 5:10; Phil 2:9.
Imparted to saints. John 17:22; 2 Cor 3:18.
Celebrated by the redeemed. Rev 5:8-14; 7:9-12.
Revealed in the gospel. Is 40:5.
Saints shall rejoice at the revelation of. 1 Pet 4:13.
Saints shall behold, in heaven. John 17:24.

Excellency and Glory of the Church, The.

Derived from God. Is 28:5.
Derived from Christ. Is 60:1; Luke 2:34.
Result from the favour of God. Is 43:4.
God delights in. Ps 45:11; Is 62:3-5.
Saints delight in. Is 66:11.
Consist in its
- Being the seat of God's worship. Ps 96:6.
- Being the temple of God. 1 Cor 3:16,17; Eph 2:21,22.
- Being the body of Christ. Eph 1:22,23.
- Being the bride of Christ. Ps 45:13,14; Rev 19:7,8; 21:2.
- Being established. Ps 48:8; Is 33:20.
- Eminent position. Ps 48:2; Is 2:2.
- Graces of character. Song 2:14.
- Perfection of beauty. Ps 50:2.
- Members being righteous. Is 60:21; Rev 19:8.
- Strength and defence. Ps 48:12,13.
- Sanctification. Eph 5:26,27.

Augmented by increase of its members. Is 49:18; 60:4-14.
Are abundant. Is 66:11.
Sin obscures. Lam 2:14,15.

Eye, The.

The light of the body. Matt 6:22; Luke 11:34.
God
- Made. Prov 20:12.
- Formed. Ps 94:9.
- Opens. 2 Kin 6:17; Ps 146:8.
- Enlightens. Ezra 9:8; Ps 13:3.

Frequently fair. 1 Sam 16:12.
Sometimes tender. Gen 29:17.
Sometimes blemished. Lev 21:20.
Parts of mentioned in Scripture
- The apple or ball. Deut 32:10.
- The lid. Job 16:16.
- The brow. Lev 14:9.

Actions of, mentioned in Scripture
- Seeing. Job 7:8; 28:10.
- Winking. Prov 10:1.
- Weeping. Job 16:20; Ps 88:9; Lam 1:16.
- Directing. Num 10:31; Ps 32:8.

The light of, rejoices the heart. Prov 15:30.
Not satisfied with seeing. Prov 27:20; Eccl 1:8.
Not satisfied with riches. Eccl 4:8.
Not evil thing to be set before. Ps 101:3.
A guard to be set on. Job 31:1; Prov 23:31.
Made red by wine. Gen 49:12; Prov 23:29.
Grows dim by sorrow. Job 17:7.
Grows dim by age. Gen 27:1; 1 Sam 3:2.
Consumed by grief. Ps 6:7; 31:9.
Consumed by sickness. Lev 26:16.
The Jews
- Wore their phylacteries between. Ex 13:16; Matt 23:5.
- Not to make baldness between. Deut 14:1.
- Raised up, in prayer. Ps 121:1; 123:1.
- Cast, on the ground in humiliation. Luke 18:13.

The Jewish women often painted. 2 Kin 9:30; Jer 4:30; Ezek 23:40.
Often put out as a punishment. Judg 16:21; 1 Sam 11:2; 2 Kin 25:7.
Punishment for injuring. Ex 21:24,26; Lev 24:20; Matt 5:38.
Illustrative
- Of the mind. Matt 6:22,23.
- (Open,) of spiritual illumination. Ps 119:18,37.
- (Anointing with eyesalve,) of healing by the Spirit. Rev 3:18.

Faith.

Is the substance of things hoped for. Heb 11:1.
Is the evidence of things not seen. Heb 11:1.
Commanded. Matt 11:22; 1 John 3:23.
The objects of, are
- God. John 14:1.
- Christ. John 6:29; Acts 20:21.
- Writings of Moses. John 5:46; Acts 24:14.
- Writings of the prophets. 2 Chr 20:20; Acts 26:27.
- The gospel. Mark 1:15.
- Promises of God. Rom 4:21; Heb 11:13.

In Christ is
- The gift of God. Rom 12:3; Eph 2:8; 6:23; Phil 1:29.
- The work of God. Acts 11:21; 1 Cor 2:5.
- Precious. 2 Pet 1:1.
- Most holy. Jude 1:20.
- Fruitful. 1 Thess 1:3.
- Accompanied by repentance. Mark 1:15; Luke 24:47.
- Followed by conversion. Acts 11:21.

Christ is the Author and Finisher of. Heb 12:2.
Is a gift of the Holy Spirit. 1 Cor 12:9.
The Scriptures designed to produce. John 20:31; 2 Tim 3:15.
Preaching designed to produce. John 17:20; Acts 8:12; Rom 10:14,15,17; 1 Cor 3:5.
Through it is
- Remission of sins. Acts 10:43; Rom 3:25.
- Justification. Acts 13:39; Rom 3:21,22,28,30; 5:1; Gal 2:16.
- Salvation. Mark 16:16; Acts 16:31.
- Sanctification. Acts 15:9; 26:18.
- Spiritual light. John 12:36,46.
- Spiritual life. John 20:31; Gal 2:20.
- Eternal life. John 3:15,16; 6:40,47.
- Rest in heaven. Heb 4:3.
- Edification. 1 Tim 1:4; Jude 1:20.
- Preservation. 1 Pet 1:5.
- Adoption. John 1:12; Gal 3:26.
- Access to God. Rom 5:2; Eph 3:12.
- Inheritance of the promises. Gal 3:22; Heb 6:12.
- The gift of the Holy Spirit. Acts 11:15-17; Gal 3:14; Eph 1:13.

Impossible to please God without. Heb 11:6.
Justification is by, to be of grace. Rom 4:16.
Essential to the profitable reception of the gospel. Heb 4:2.
Necessary in the Christian warfare. 1 Tim 1:18,19; 6:12.
The gospel effectual in those who have. 1 Thess 2:13.
Excludes self-justification. Rom 10:3,4.
Excludes boasting. Rom 3:27.
Works by love. Gal 5:6; 1 Tim 1:5; Philem 5.
Produces
- Hope. Rom 5:2.
- Joy. Acts 16:34; 1 Pet 1:8.
- Peace. Rom 15:13.
- Confidence. Is 28:16; 1 Pet 2:6.
- Boldness in preaching. Ps 116:10; 2 Cor 4:13.

Christ is precious to those having. 1 Pet 2:7.
Christ dwells in the heart by. Eph 3:17.

Necessary in prayer. Matt 21:22; James 1:6.
Those who are not Christ's have not. John 10:26,27.
An evidence of the new birth. 1 John 5:1.
By it saints
Live. Gal 2:20.
Stand. Rom 11:20; 2 Cor 1:24.
Walk. Rom 4:12; 2 Cor 5:7.
Obtain a good report. Heb 11:2.
Overcome the world. 1 John 5:4,5.
Resist the devil. 1 Pet 5:9.
Overcome the devil. Eph 6:16.
Are supported. Ps 27:13; 1 Tim 4:10.
Saints die in. Heb 11:13.
Saints should
Be sincere in. 1 Tim 1:5; 2 Tim 1:5.
Abound in. 2 Cor 8:7.
Continue in. Acts 14:22; Col 1:23.
Be strong in. Rom 4:20-24.
Stand fast in. 1 Cor 16:13.
Be grounded and settled in. Col 1:23.
Hold, with a good conscience. 1 Tim 1:19.
Pray for the increase of. Luke 17:5.
Have full assurance of. 2 Tim 1:12; Heb 10:22.
True, evidenced by its fruits. James 2:21-25.
Without fruits, is dead. James 2:17,20,26.
Examine whether you be in. 2 Cor 13:5.
All difficulties overcome by. Matt 17:20; 21:21; Mark 9:23.
All things should be done in. Rom 14:22.
Whatever is not of, is sin. Rom 14:23.
Often tried by affliction. 1 Pet 1:6,7.
Trial of, works patience. James 1:3.
The wicked often profess. Acts 8:13,21.
The wicked destitute of. John 10:25; 12:37; Acts 19:9; 2 Thess 3:2.
Protection of, illustrated
A shield. Eph 6:16.
A breastplate. 1 Thess 5:8.
Exemplified
Caleb. Num 13:30.
Job. Job 19:25.
Shadrach, etc. Dan 3:17.
Daniel. Dan 6:10,23.
Peter. Matt 16:16.
Woman who was a sinner. Luke 7:50.
Nathanael. John 1:49.
Samaritans. John 4:39.
Martha. John 11:27.
The disciples. John 16:30.
Thomas. John 20:28.
Stephen. Acts 6:5.
Priests. Acts 6:7.
Ethiopian. Acts 8:37.
Barnabas. Acts 11:24.
Sergius Paulus. Acts 13:12.
Philippian jailor. Acts 16:31,34.
Romans. Rom 1:8.
Colossians. Col 1:4.
Thessalonians. 1 Thess 1:3.
Lois. 2 Tim 1:5.
Paul. 2 Tim 4:7.
Abel. Heb 11:4.
Enoch. Heb 11:5.
Noah. Heb 11:7.
Abraham. Heb 11:8,17.
Isaac. Heb 11:20.
Jacob. Heb 11:21.
Joseph. Heb 11:22.
Moses. Heb 11:24,27.
Rahab. Heb 11:31.
Gideon etc. Heb 11:32,33,39.

FAITHFULNESS.

A characteristic of saints. Eph 1:1; Col 1:2; 1 Tim 6:2; Rev 17:14.
Exhibited in
The service of God. Matt 24:45.
Declaring the word of God. Jer 23:28; 2 Cor 2:17; 4:2.
The care of dedicated things. 2 Chr 31:12.
Helping the brethren. 3 John 5.
Bearing witness. Prov 14:5.
Reproving others. Prov 27:6; Ps 141:5.
Situations of trust. 2 Kin 12:15; Neh 13:13; Acts 6:1-3.
Doing work. 2 Chr 34:12.
Keeping secrets. Prov 11:13.
Conveying messages. Prov 13:17; 25:13.
All things. 1 Tim 3:11.
The smallest matters. Luke 16:10-12.
Should be to death. Rev 2:10.
Especially required in
Ministers. 1 Cor 4:2; 2 Tim 2:2.
The wives of ministers. 1 Tim 3:11.
The children of ministers. Titus 1:6.
Difficulty of finding. Prov 20:6.
The wicked devoid of. Ps 5:9.
Associate with those who exhibit. Ps 101:6.
Blessedness of. 1 Sam 26:23; Prov 28:20.
Blessedness of, illustrated. Matt 24:45,46; 25:21,23.
Exemplified
Joseph. Gen 39:22,23.
Moses. Num 12:7; Heb 3:2,5.
David. 1 Sam 22:14.
Hananiah. Neh 7:2.
Abraham. Neh 9:8; Gal 3:9.
Daniel. Dan 6:4.
Paul. Acts 20:20,27.
Timothy. 1 Cor 4:17.
Tychicus. Eph 6:21.
Epaphras. Col 1:7.
Onesimus. Col 4:9.
Silvanus. 1 Pet 5:12.
Antipas. Rev 2:13.

FAITHFULNESS OF GOD, THE.

Is part of his character. Is 49:7; 1 Cor 1:9; 1 Thess 5:24.
Declared to be
Great. Lam 3:23.
Established. Ps 89:2.
Incomparable. Ps 89:8.
Unfailing. Ps 89:33; 2 Tim 2:13.
Infinite. Ps 36:5.
Everlasting. Ps 119:90; 146:6.
Should be pleaded in prayer. Ps 143:1.
Should be proclaimed. Ps 40:10; 89:1.
Manifested
In his counsels. Is 25:1.
In afflicting his saints. Ps 119:75.
In fulfilling his promises. 1 Kin 8:20; Ps 132:11; Mic 7:20; Heb 10:23.
In keeping his covenant. Deut 7:9; Ps 111:5.
In executing his judgments. Jer 23:20; 51:29.
In forgiving sins. 1 John 1:9.
To his saints. Ps 89:24; 2 Thess 3:3.
Saints encouraged to depend on. 1 Pet 4:19.
Should be magnified. Ps 89:5; 92:2.

FALL OF MAN, THE.

By the disobedience of Adam. Gen 3:6,11,12; Rom 5:12,15,19.
Through temptation of the devil. Gen 3:1-5; 2 Cor 11:3; 1 Tim 2:14.
Man in consequence of
Made in the image of Adam. Gen 5:3; 1 Cor 15:48,49.
Born in sin. Job 15:14; 25:4; Ps 51:5; Is 48:8; John 3:6.
A child of wrath. Eph 2:3.
Evil in heart. Gen 6:5; 8:21; Jer 16:12; Matt 15:19.
Blinded in heart. Eph 4:18.
Corrupt and perverse in his ways. Gen 6:12; Ps 10:5; Rom 3:12-16.
Depraved in mind. Rom 8:5-7; Eph 4:17; Col 1:21; Titus 1:15.
Without understanding. Ps 14:2,3; Rom 3:11; 1:31.
Receives not the things of God. 1 Cor 2:14.
Comes short of God's glory. Rom 3:23.
Defiled in conscience. Titus 1:15; Heb 10:22.
Intractable. Job 11:12.
Estranged from God. Gen 3:8; Ps 58:3; Eph 4:18; Col 1:21.
In bondage to sin. Rom 6:19; 7:5,23; Gal 5:17; Titus 3:3.
In bondage to the devil. 2 Tim 2:26; Heb 2:14,15.
Constant in evil. Ps 10:5; 2 Pet 2:14.
Conscious of guilt. Gen 3:7,8,10.
Unrighteous. Eccl 7:20; Rom 3:10.
Abominable. Job 15:16; Ps 14:3.
Turned to his own way. Is 53:6.
Loves darkness. John 3:19.
Corrupt, etc. in speech. Rom 3:13,14.
Devoid of the fear of God. Rom 3:18.
Totally depraved. Gen 6:5; Rom 7:18.
Dead in sin. Eph 2:1; Col 2:13.
All men partake of the effects of. 1 Kin 8:46; Gal 3:22; 1 John 1:8; 5:19.
Punishment consequent upon
Banishment from Paradise. Gen 3:24.
Condemnation to labour and sorrow. Gen 3:16,19; Job 5:6,7.
Temporal death. Gen 3:19; Rom 5:12; 1 Cor 15:22.
Eternal death. Job 21:30; Rom 5:18,21; 6:23.
Cannot be remedied by man. Prov 20:9; Jer 2:22; 13:23.
Remedy for, provided by God. Gen 3:15; John 3:16.

FAMILIES.

Of saints blessed. Ps 128:3-6.
Should
Be taught the Scriptures. Deut 4:9,10.
Worship God together. 1 Cor 16:19.
Be duly regulated. Prov 31:27; 1 Tim 3:4,5,12.
Live in unity. Gen 45:24; Ps 133:1.
Live in mutual forbearance. Gen 50:17-21; Matt 18:21,22.

Rejoice together before God. Deut 14:26.
Deceivers and liars should be removed from. Ps 101:7.
Warning against departing from God. Deut 29:18.
Punishment of irreligious. Jer 10:25.
Good—Exemplified
Abraham. Gen 18:19.
Jacob. Gen 35:2.
Joshua. Josh 24:15.
David. 2 Sam 6:20.
Job. Job 1:5.
Lazarus of Bethany. John 11:1-5.
Cornelius. Acts 10:2,33.
Lydia. Acts 16:15.
Jailor of Philippi. Acts 16:31-34.
Crispus. Acts 18:8.
Lois. 2 Tim 1:5.

Famine.

Sent by God. Ps 10:16.
Often on account of sin. Lev 26:21,26; Lam 4:4-6.
One of God's four sore judgments. Ezek 14:21.
Caused by
God's blessing withheld. Hos 2:8,9; Hag 1:6.
Want of seasonable rain. 1 Kin 17:1; Jer 14:1-4; Amos 4:7.
Rotting of the seed in the ground. Joel 1:17.
Swarms of insects. Deut 28:38,42; Joel 1:4.
Blasting and mildew. Amos 4:9; Hag 2:17.
Devastation by enemies. Deut 28:33,51.
Often long continued. Gen 41:27; 2 Kin 8:1,2.
Often severe. Gen 12:10; 1 Kin 18:2; Jer 52:6.
Expressed by
Taking away the stay of bread, etc. Is 3:1.
Cleanness of teeth. Amos 4:6.
The arrows of famine. Ezek 5:16.
Often accompanied by war. Jer 14:15; 29:18.
Often followed by pestilence. Jer 42:17; Ezek 7:15; Matt 24:7.
Things eaten during
Wild herbs. 2 Kin 4:39,40.
Ass's flesh. 2 Kin 6:25.
Dung. 2 Kin 6:25; Lam 4:5.
Human flesh. Lev 26:29; 2 Kin 6:28,29.
Provisions sold by weight during. Ezek 4:16.
Suffering of brute creation from. Jer 14:5,6.
Caused
Burning and fever. Deut 32:24.
Blackness of the skin. Lam 4:8; 5:10.
Grief and mourning. Joel 1:11-13.
Faintness. Gen 47:13.
Wasting of the body. Lam 4:8; Ezek 4:17.
Death. 2 Kin 7:4; Jer 11:22.
God provided for his people during. 1 Kin 17:4,9; Job 5:20; Ps 33:19; 37:19.
Instances of, in Scripture
In the days of Abraham. Gen 12:10.
In the days of Isaac. Gen 26:1.
In the days of Joseph. Gen 41:53-56.
In the days of the Judges. Ruth 1:1.
In the reign of David. 2 Sam 21:1.
In the reign of Ahab. 1 Kin 17:1; 18:5.
In the time of Elisha. 2 Kin 4:38.
During the siege of Samaria. 2 Kin 6:25.
Of seven years foretold by Elisha. 2 Kin 8:1.
In the time of Jeremiah. Jer 14:1.
During the siege of Jerusalem. 2 Kin 25:3.
After the captivity. Neh 5:3.
In the reign of Claudius Caesar. Acts 11:28.
Before destruction of Jerusalem. Matt 24:7.
The Jews in their restored state not to be afflicted by. Ezek 36:29,30.
Illustrative of
A dearth of the means of grace. Amos 8:11,12.
Destruction of idols. Zeph 2:11.

Fasting.

Spirit of, explained. Is 58:6,7.
Not to be made a subject of display. Matt 6:16-18.
Should be to God. Zech 7:5; Matt 6:18.
For the chastening of the soul. Ps 69:10.
For the humbling of the soul. Ps 35:13.
Observed on occasions of
Judgments of God. Joel 1:14; 2:12.
Public calamities. 2 Sam 1:12.
Afflictions of the Church. Luke 5:33-35.
Afflictions of others. Ps 35:13; Dan 6:18.
Private afflictions. 2 Sam 12:16.
Approaching danger. Esth 4:16.
Ordination of ministers. Acts 13:3; 14:23.
Accompanied by
Prayer. Ezra 8:23; Dan 9:3.
Confession of sin. 1 Sam 7:6; Neh 9:1,2.
Mourning. Joel 2:12.
Humiliation. Deut 9:18; Neh 9:1.
Promises connected with. Is 58:8-12; Matt 6:18.
Of hypocrites
Described. Is 58:4,5.
Ostentatious. Matt 6:16.
Boasted of, before God. Luke 18:12.
Rejected. Is 58:3; Jer 14:12.
Extraordinary—Exemplified
Our Lord. Matt 4:2.
Moses. Ex 34:28; Deut 9:9,18.
Elijah. 1 Kin 19:8.
National—Exemplified
Israel. Judg 20:26; Ezra 8:21; Esth 4:3,16; Jer 36:9.
Men of Jabesh-gilead. 1 Sam 31:13.
Ninevites. Jon 3:5-8.
Of Saints—Exemplified
David. 2 Sam 12:16; Ps 109:24.
Nehemiah. Neh 1:4.
Esther. Esth 4:16.
Daniel. Dan 9:3.
Disciples of John. Matt 9:14.
Anna. Luke 2:37.
Cornelius. Acts 10:30.
Christians. Acts 13:2.
Apostles. 2 Cor 6:5.
Paul. 2 Cor 11:27.
Of the wicked—Exemplified
Elders of Jezreel. 1 Kin 21:12.
Ahab. 1 Kin 21:27.
Pharisees. Mark 2:18; Luke 18:12.

Fatherless.

Find mercy in God. Hos 14:3.
God will
Be a father of. Ps 68:5.
Be a helper of. Ps 10:14.
Hear the cry of. Ex 22:23.
Execute the judgment of. Deut 10:18; Ps 10:18.
Punish those who oppress. Ex 22:24; Is 10:1-3; Mal 3:5.
Punish those who judge not. Jer 5:28,29.
Visit in affliction. James 1:27.
Let them share in our blessings. Deut 14:29.
Defend. Ps 82:3; Is 1:17.
Wrong not, in judgment. Deut 24:17.
Defraud not. Prov 23:10.
Afflict not. Ex 22:22.
Oppress not. Zech 7:10.
Do no violence to. Jer 22:3.
Blessedness of taking care of. Deut 14:29; Job 29:12,13; Jer 7:6,7.
The wicked
Rob. Is 10:2.
Overwhelm. Job 6:27.
Vex. Ezek 22:7.
Oppress. Job 24:3.
Murder. Ps 94:6.
Judge not for. Is 1:23; Jer 5:28.
A curse on those who oppress. Deut 27:19.
Promises with respect to. Jer 49:11.
A type of Zion in affliction. Lam 5:3.
Exemplified
Lot. Gen 11:27,28.
Daughters of Zelophehad. Num 27:1-5.
Jotham. Judg 9:16-21.
Mephibosheth. 2 Sam 9:3.
Joash. 2 Kin 11:1-12.
Esther. Esth 2:7.

Favour of God, The.

Christ the special object of. Luke 2:52.
Is the source of
Mercy. Is 60:10.
Spiritual life. Ps 30:5.
Spiritual wisdom leads to. Prov 8:35.
Mercy and truth lead to. Prov 3:3,4.
Saints
Obtain. Prov 12:2.
Encompassed by. Ps 5:12.
Strengthened by. Ps 30:7.
Victorious through. Ps 44:3.
Preserved through. Job 10:12.
Exalted in. Ps 89:17.
Sometimes tempted to doubt. Ps 77:7.
Domestic blessings traced to. Prov 18:22.
Disappointment of enemies an assured evidence of. Ps 41:11.
Given in answer to prayer. Job 33:26.
Pray for. Ps 106:4; 119:58.
Plead, in prayer. Ex 33:12; Num 11:15.
To be acknowledged. Ps 85:1.

The wicked
  Uninfluenced by. Is 26:10.
  Do not obtain. Is 27:11; Jer 16:13.
Exemplified
  Naphtali. Deut 33:23.
  Samuel. 1 Sam 2:26.
  Job. Job 10:12.
  The Virgin Mary. Luke 1:28,30.
  David. Acts 7:46.

FEAR, GODLY.

God is the object of. Is 8:13.
God is the author of. Jer 32:39,40.
Searching the Scriptures gives the understanding of. Prov 2:3-5.
Described as
  Hatred of evil. Prov 8:13.
  Wisdom. Job 28:28; Ps 111:10.
  A treasure to saints. Prov 15:16; Is 33:6.
  A fountain of life. Prov 14:27.
  Sanctifying. Ps 19:9.
  Filial and reverential. Heb 12:9,28.
Commanded. Deut 13:4; Ps 22:23; Eccl 12:13; 1 Pet 2:17.
Motives to
  The holiness of God. Rev 15:4.
  The greatness of God. Deut 10:12,17.
  The goodness of God. 1 Sam 12:24.
  The forgiveness of God. Ps 130:4.
  Wondrous works of God. Josh 4:23,24.
  Judgments of God. Rev 14:7.
A characteristic of saints. Mal 3:16.
Should accompany the joy of saints. Ps 2:11.
Necessary to
  The worship of God. Ps 5:7; 89:7.
  The service of God. Ps 2:11; Heb 12:28.
  Avoiding of sin. Ex 20:20.
  Righteous government. 2 Sam 23:3.
  Impartial administration of justice. 2 Chr 19:6-9.
  Perfecting holiness. 2 Cor 7:1.
Those who have
  Afford pleasure to God. Ps 147:11.
  Are pitied by God. Ps 103:13.
  Are accepted of God. Acts 10:35.
  Receive mercy from God. Ps 103:11,17; Luke 1:50.
  Are blessed. Ps 112:1; 115:13.
  Confide in God. Ps 115:11; Prov 14:26.
  Depart from evil. Prov 16:6.
  Converse together of holy things. Mal 3:16.
  Should not fear man. Is 8:12,13; Matt 10:28.
  Desires of, fulfilled by God. Ps 145:19.
  Days of, prolonged. Prov 10:27.
Should be
  Prayed for. Ps 86:11.
  Exhibited in our callings. Col 3:22.
  Exhibited in giving a reason for our hope. 1 Pet 3:15.
  Constantly maintained. Deut 14:23; Josh 4:24; Prov 23:17.
  Taught to others. Ps 34:11.
Advantages of. Prov 15:16; 19:23; Eccl 8:12,13.
The wicked destitute of. Ps 36:1; Prov 1:29; Jer 2:19; Rom 3:18.
Exemplified
  Abraham. Gen 22:12.
  Joseph. Gen 39:9; 42:18.
  Obadiah. 1 Kin 18:12.
  Nehemiah. Neh 5:15.
  Job. Job 1:1,8.
  Christians. Acts 9:31.
  Cornelius. Acts 10:2.
  Noah. Heb 11:7.

FEAR, UNHOLY.

A characteristic of the wicked. Rev 21:8.
Is described as
  A fear of idols. 2 Kin 17:38.
  A fear of man. 1 Sam 15:24; John 9:22.
  A fear of judgments. Is 2:19; Luke 21:26; Rev 6:16,17.
  A fear of future punishment. Heb 10:27.
  Overwhelming. Ex 15:16; Job 15:21,24.
  Consuming. Ps 73:19.
A guilty conscience leads to. Gen 3:8,10; Ps 53:5; Prov 28:1.
Seizes the wicked. Job 15:24; 18:11.
Surprises the hypocrite. Is 33:14,18.
The wicked judicially filled with. Lev 26:16,17; Deut 28:65-67; Jer 49:5.
Shall be realised. Prov 1:27; 10:24.
God mocks. Prov 1:26.
Saints sometimes tempted to. Ps 55:5.
Saints delivered from. Prov 1:33; Is 14:3.
Trust in God, a preservative from. Ps 27:1.
Exhortations against. Is 8:12; John 14:27.
Exemplified
  Adam. Gen 3:10.
  Cain. Gen 4:14.
  Midianites. Judg 7:21,22.
  Philistines. 1 Sam 14:15.
  Saul. 1 Sam 28:5,20.
  Adonijah's guests. 1 Kin 1:49.
  Haman. Esth 7:6.
  Ahaz. Is 7:2.
  Belshazzar. Dan 5:6.
  Pilate. John 19:8.
  Felix. Acts 24:25.

FEAST OF DEDICATION, THE.

To commemorate the cleansing of the temple after its defilement by Antiochus. Dan 11:31.
Held in the winter month, Chisleu. John 10:22.

FEAST OF JUBILEE, THE.

Held every fiftieth year. Lev 25:8,10.
Began upon the Day of Atonement. Lev 25:9.
Called the
  Year of liberty. Ezek 46:17.
  Year of the redeemed. Is 63:4.
  Acceptable year. Is 61:2.
Was specially holy. Lev 25:12.
Proclaimed by trumpets. Lev 25:9; Ps 89:15.
Enactments respecting
  Cessation of all field labour. Lev 25:11.
  The fruits of the earth to be common property. Lev 25:12.
  Redemption of sold property. Lev 25:23-27.
  Restoration of all inheritances. Lev 25:10,13,28; 27:24.
  Release of Hebrew servants. Lev 25:40,41,54.
Houses in walled cities not redeemed within a year, exempted from the benefit of. Lev 25:30.
Sale of property calculated from. Lev 25:15,16.
Value of devoted property calculated from. Lev 27:14-23.
Illustrative of the gospel. Is 61:1,2; Luke 4:18,19.

FEAST OF THE NEW MOON, THE.

Held first day of the month. Num 10:10.
Celebrated with blowing of trumpets. Num 10:10; Ps 81:3,4.
Sacrifices at. Num 28:11-15.
A season for
  Inquiring of God's messengers. 2 Kin 4:23.
  Worship in God's house. Is 66:23; Ezek 46:1.
  Entertainments. 1 Sam 20:5,18.
Observed with great solemnity. 1 Chr 23:31; 2 Chr 2:4; 8:13; 31:3.
Restored after captivity. Ezra 3:5; Neh 10:33.
Mere outward observance of, hateful to God. Is 1:13,14.
Disliked by the ungodly. Amos 8:5.
The Jews deprived of, for sin. Hos 2:11.
Observance of, by Christians, condemned. Col 2:16; Gal 4:10.

FEAST OF PENTECOST, THE.

Held fiftieth day after offering first sheaf of barley harvest. Lev 23:15,16; Deut 16:9.
Called the
  Feast of harvest. Ex 23:16.
  Feast of weeks. Ex 34:22; Deut 16:10.
  Day of the firstfruits. Num 28:26.
  Day of Pentecost. Acts 2:1.
To be perpetually observed. Lev 23:21.
All males to attend. Ex 23:16,17; Deut 16:16.
A holy convocation. Lev 23:21; Num 28:26.
A time of holy rejoicing. Deut 16:11,12.
The firstfruits of bread presented at. Lev 23:17; Deut 16:10.
Sacrifices at. Lev 23:18,19; Num 28:27-31.
The law given from Mount Sinai upon. Ex 12:6,12; 19:1,11.
The Holy Spirit given to apostles at. Acts 2:1-3.
Observed by the church. Acts 20:16; 1 Cor 16:8.

FEAST OF PURIM, OR LOTS, THE.

Instituted by Mordecai. Esth 9:20.
To commemorate the defeat of Haman's wicked design. Esth 3:7-15; 9:24-26.
Began fourteenth of twelfth month. Esth 9:17.
Lasted two days. Esth 9:21.
Mode of celebrating. Esth 9:17-19,22.
The Jews bound themselves to keep. Esth 9:27,28.
Confirmed by royal authority. Esth 9:29-32.

FEAST OF SABBATICAL YEAR, THE.

A sabbath for the land. Lev 25:2.
Kept every seventh year. Ex 23:11; Lev 25:4.
Surplus of sixth year to provide for. Lev 25:20-22.
Enactments respecting
  Cessation of all field labour. Lev 25:4,5.
  The fruits of the earth to be common property. Ex 23:11; Lev 25:6,7.
  Remission of debts. Deut 15:1-3; Neh 10:31.
  Release of all Hebrew servants. Ex 21:2; Deut 15:12.
  Public reading of the law at feast of tabernacles. Deut 31:10-13.
  No release to strangers during. Deut 15:3.
Release of, not to hinder the exercise of benevolence. Deut 15:9-11.
Jews threatened for neglecting. Lev 26:34,35,43; Jer 34:13-18.
The seventy years captivity a punishment for neglecting. 2 Chr 36:20,21.
Restored after the captivity. Neh 10:31.

FEAST OF TABERNACLES, THE.

Held after harvest and vintage. Deut 16:13.
Began fifteenth of seventh month. Lev 23:34,39.
Lasted seven days. Lev 23:34,41; Deut 16:13,15.
Called the feast of ingathering. Ex 23:16,17.
All males obliged to appear at. Ex 23:16,17.
First and last days of, holy convocations. Lev 23:35,39; Num 29:12,35.
Sacrifices during. Lev 23:36,37; Num 29:13-39.
To be observed
  With rejoicing. Deut 16:14,15.
  Perpetually. Lev 23:41.
The people dwelt in booths during. Lev 23:42; Neh 8:15,16.
The law publicly read every seventh year at. Deut 31:10-12; Neh 8:18.
Customs observed at
  Bearing branches of palms. Lev 23:40; Rev 7:9.
  Drawing water from the pool of Siloam. Is 12:3; John 7:2,37-39.
  Singing hosannas. Ps 118:24-29; Matt 21:8,9.
To commemorate the sojourn of Israel in the desert. Lev 23:43.
Remarkable celebrations of
  At the dedication of Solomon's temple. 1 Kin 8:2,65.
  After the captivity. Ex 3:4; Neh 8:17.

FEAST OF THE PASSOVER, THE.

Ordained by God. Ex 12:1,2.
Commenced the fourteenth of the first month at even. Ex 12:2,6,18; Lev 23:5; Num 9:3.
Lasted seven days. Ex 12:15; Lev 23:6.
Called the
  Passover. Num 9:5; John 2:23.
  Jew's Passover. John 2:13; 11:55.
  Lord's Passover. Ex 12:11,27.
  Feast of unleavened bread. Mark 14:1; Luke 22:1.
  Days of unleavened bread. Acts 12:3; 20:6.
All males to appear at. Ex 23:17; Deut 16:16.
Paschal lamb eaten first day of. Ex 12:6,8.
Unleavened bread eaten at. Ex 12:15; Deut 16:3.
Leaven
  Not to be in their houses during. Ex 12:19.
  Not to be in any of their quarters. Ex 13:7; Deut 16:4.
  Nothing with, to be eaten. Ex 12:20.
  Punishment for eating. Ex 12:15,19.
First and last days of, holy convocations. Ex 12:16; Num 28:18,25.
Sacrifices during. Lev 23:8; Num 28:19-24.
The first sheaf of barley harvest offered the day after the Sabbath in. Lev 23:10-14.
To commemorate the
  Passing over the firstborn. Ex 12:12,13.
  Deliverance of Israel from bondage of Egypt. Ex 12:17,42; 13:9; Deut 16:3.
To be perpetually observed during the Mosaic age. Ex 12:14; 13:10.
Children to be taught the nature and design of. Ex 12:26,27; 13:8.
Purification necessary to the due observance of. 2 Chr 30:15-19; John 11:55.
Might be kept in the second month by those who were unclean at the appointed time. Num 9:6-11; 2 Chr 30:2,3,15.
No uncircumcised person to keep. Ex 12:43,45.
Strangers and servants when circumcised might keep. Ex 12:44,48.
Neglect of, punished with death. Num 9:13.
Improper keeping of, punished. 2 Chr 30:18,20.
Remarkable celebrations of
  On leaving Egypt. Ex 12:28,50.
  In the wilderness of Sinai. Num 9:3-5.
  On entering the land of promise. Josh 5:10,11.
  In Hezekiah's reign. 2 Chr 30:1.
  In Josiah's reign. 2 Kin 23:22,23; 2 Chr 35:1,18.
  After the captivity. Ezra 6:19,20.
  Before the death of Christ. Luke 22:15.
Moses kept through faith. Heb 11:28.
Christ always observed. Matt 26:17-20; Luke 22:15; John 2:13,23.
The people of Jerusalem lent their rooms to strangers for. Luke 22:11,12.
The Lord's Supper instituted at. Matt 26:26-28.
Custom of releasing a prisoner at. Matt 27:15; Luke 23:16,17.
The Sabbath in, a high day. John 19:31.
The day before the Sabbath in, called the preparation. John 19:14,31.
Illustrative of redemption through Christ. 1 Cor 5:7,8.

FEASTS OF TRUMPETS, THE.

Held the first day of seventh month. Lev 23:24; Num 29:1.
A memorial of blowing of trumpets. Lev 23:24.
A holy convocation and rest. Lev 23:24,25.
Sacrifices at. Num 29:2-6.

FEASTS, THE ANNIVERSARY.

Instituted by God. Ex 23:14.
Enumerated. Ex 23:15,16.
Called
  Appointed feasts. Is 1:14.
  Feasts of the Lord. Lev 23:4.
  Solemn feasts. 2 Chr 8:13; Lam 1:4.
  Solemn meetings. Is 1:13.
Were a time of thankfulness. Ps 122:4.
All males to attend. Ex 23:17; 34:23.
Children commenced attending, when twelve years old. Luke 2:42.
Females often attended. 1 Sam 1:3,9; Luke 2:41.
The Jews attended gladly. Ps 122:1,2.
The Jews went up to, in large companies. Ps 42:4; Luke 2:44.
The dangers and difficulties encountered in going up to, alluded to. Ps 84:6,7.
The land divinely protected during. Ex 34:24.
Offerings to made at. Ex 34:20; Deut 16:16,17.
Were seasons of
  Joy and gladness. Ps 42:4; Is 30:20.
  Sacrificing. 1 Sam 1:3; 1 Kin 9:25; 2 Chr 8:13.
  Entertainments. 1 Sam 1:4,9.
  The ten tribes seduced by Jeroboam from attending. 1 Kin 12:27.
  The Jews dispersed in distant parts often attended. Acts 2:5-11; 8:27.
  Christ attended. John 5:1; 7:10.
  Rendered unavailing by the impiety of the Jews. Is 1:13,14; Amos 5:21.
  Illustrative of general assembly of the Church. Heb 12:23.

FEET, THE.

Necessary members of the body. 1 Cor 12:15,21.
Parts of, mentioned in Scripture
  Heel. Ps 41:9; 49:5; Hos 12:3.
  Sole. Deut 11:24; 1 Kin 5:3.
  Toes. Ex 29:20; 2 Sam 21:20; Dan 2:41.
Often swift. 2 Sam 2:18; 22:34.
Were liable to
  Disease. 1 Kin 15:23.
  Swelling from walking. Deut 8:4.
  Injury from stones, etc. Ps 91:12.
Early use of shoes. Ex 12:11.
Of women often adorned with tingling ornaments. Is 3:16,18.
Of the Jews
  Neglected in affliction. 2 Sam 19:24; Ezek 24:17.
  Bare in affliction. 2 Sam 15:30.
  Washed frequently. 2 Sam 11:8; Song 5:3.
Stamped on the ground in extreme joy or grief. Ezek 6:11; 25:6.
Washing for others, a menial office. 1 Sam 25:41; John 13:5-14.

Of strangers and travellers washed. Gen 18:4; 19:2; 24:32; 1 Tim 5:10.
Neglect of washing, disrespectful to guest. Luke 7:44.
Respect exhibited by falling at. 1 Sam 25:24; 2 Kin 4:37; Esth 8:3; Mark 5:22; Acts 10:25.
Reverence expressed by kissing. Luke 7:38,45.
Sleep expressed by covering. 1 Sam 24:3.
Subjection expressed by licking the dust of. Is 49:23.
Condemnation expressed by shaking the dust from. Matt 10:14; Mark 6:11.
Subjugation of enemies expressed by placing on their necks. Josh 10:24; Ps 110:1.
Origin of uncovering in consecrated places. Ex 3:5; Josh 5:15.
Of enemies often maimed and cut off. Judg 1:6,7; 2 Sam 4:12.
Of criminals
  Bound with fetters. Ps 105:18.
  Placed in stocks. Job 13:27; Acts 16:24.
Path of, to be pondered. Prov 4:26.
To be refrained from evil. Prov 1:15; Heb 12:13.
To be turned to God's testimonies. Ps 119:59.
To be directed by God's word. Ps 119:105.
To be guided by wisdom and discretion. Prov 3:21,23,26.
Of the wicked
  Swift to mischief. Prov 6:18.
  Swift to shed blood. Prov 1:16; Rom 3:15.
  Ensnared. Job 18:8; Ps 9:15.
Of saints
  At liberty. Ps 18:36; 31:8.
  Kept by God. 1 Sam 2:9; Ps 116:8.
  Established by God. Ps 66:9; 121:3.
  Guided by Christ. Is 48:17; Luke 1:79.
Illustrative
  (Set on a rock,) of stability. Ps 40:2.
  (Set in a large place,) of liberty. Ps 31:8.
  (Sliding,) of yielding to temptation. Job 12:5; Ps 17:5; 38:16; 94:18.
  (Treading under,) of complete destruction. Is 18:7; Lam 1:15.
  (Washed or dipped in oil,) of abundance. Deut 33:24; Job 29:6.
  (Dipped in blood,) of victory. Ps 68:23.

FIG TREE, THE.

Produces a rich sweet fruit. Judg 9:11.
Not found in desert places. Num 20:5.
Abounded in
  Egypt. Ps 105:33.
  Canaan. Num 13:23; Deut 8:8.
Often grew wild. Amos 7:14.
Sometimes planted in vineyards. Luke 13:6.
Propagated by the Jews. Amos 4:9.
Required cultivation. Luke 13:8.
Fruit of, formed after winter. Song 2:11,13.
Leaves of, put forth, a sign of the approach of summer. Matt 24:32.
Reasonableness of expecting fruit upon, when full of leaves. Mark 11:13.
Fruit of
  Eaten fresh from the tree. Matt 21:18,19.
  Eaten dried in cakes. 1 Sam 30:12.
  Gathered and kept in baskets. Jer 24:1.
  First ripe esteemed. Jer 24:2; Hos 9:10.
  Used in the miraculous healing of Hezekiah. 2 Kin 20:7; Is 38:21.
  Sold in the markets. Neh 13:15.
  Sent as presents. 1 Sam 25:18; 1 Chr 12:40.
A species of, produced vile and worthless fruit. Jer 29:17.
Leaves of, used by Adam for covering. Gen 3:7.
Afforded a thick shade. John 1:48,50.
Often unfruitful. Luke 13:7.
Failure of, a great calamity. Hab 3:17.
The Jews punished by
  God's breaking down. Hos 2:12.
  Failure of fruit on. Jer 8:13; Hag 2:19.
  Enemies devouring fruit of. Jer 5:17.
  Barking and eating of, by locusts. Joel 1:4,7,12; Amos 4:9.
Illustrative
  (Barren,) of mere professors of religion. Matt 21:19; Luke 13:6,7.
  (Sitting under one's own,) of prosperity and peace. 1 Kin 4:25; Mic 4:4.
Fruit of, illustrative
  Of good works. Matt 7:16.
  (Good,) of saints. Jer 24:2,3.
  (Bad,) of wicked men. Jer 24:2-8.
  (First ripe,) of the fathers of the Jewish church. Hos 9:10.
  (Untimely and dropping,) of the wicked ripe for judgment. Is 34:4; Nah 3:12; Rev 6:13.

FIRE.

Can be increased in intensity. Dan 3:19,22.
Though small, kindles a great matter. James 3:5.
Things connected with
  Burning coals. Prov 26:21.
  Flame. Song 8:6; Is 66:15.
  Sparks. Job 18:5; Is 1:31.
  Ashes. 1 Kin 13:3; 2 Pet 2:6.
  Smoke. Is 34:10; Joel 2:30.
Kept alive by fuel. Prov 26:20; Is 9:5.
Characterised as
  Bright. Ezek 1:13.
  Spreading. James 3:5.
  Enlightening. Ps 78:14; 105:39.
  Heating. Mark 14:54.
  Melting. Ps 68:2; Is 64:2.
  Purifying. Num 31:23; 1 Pet 1:7; Rev 3:18.
  Drying. Job 15:30; Joel 1:20.
  Consuming. Judg 15:4,5; Ps 46:9; Is 10:16,17.
  Insatiable. Prov 30:16.
Sacred
  Came from before the Lord. Lev 9:24.
  Always burning on the altar. Lev 6:13.
  All burnt offerings consumed by. Lev 6:9,12.
  Incense burned with. Lev 16:12; Num 16:46.
  Guilt of burning incense without. Lev 10:1.
  Restored to the temple. 2 Chr 7:1-3.
Frequently employed as an instrument of divine vengeance. Ps 97:3; Is 47:14; 66:16.
Miraculous
  In the burning bush. Ex 3:2.
  Plagued the Egyptians. Ex 9:23,24.
  Led the people of Israel in the desert. Ex 13:22; 40:38.
  On Mount Sinai at giving of law. Deut 4:11,37.
  Destroyed Nadab and Abihu. Lev 10:2.
  Destroyed the people at Taberah. Num 11:1.
  Consumed the company of Korah. Num 16:35.
  Consumed the sacrifice of Gideon. Judg 6:21.
  Angel ascended in. Judg 13:20.
  Consumed the sacrifice of Elijah. 1 Kin 18:38.
  Destroyed the enemies of Elijah. 2 Kin 1:10,12.
  Elijah taken up in a chariot of. 2 Kin 2:11.
God appeared in. Ex 3:2; 19:18.
Christ shall appear in. Dan 7:10; 2 Thess 1:8.
Punishment of the wicked shall be in. Matt 13:42; 25:41.
In houses
  Lighted in the winter. Jer 36:22.
  Lighted in spring mornings. John 18:18.
  Not to be lighted on the Sabbath. Ex 35:3.
  Made of charcoal. John 18:18.
  Made of wood. Acts 28:3.
Injury from, to be made good by the person who kindled it. Ex 22:6.
Illustrative of
  God's protection. Num 9:16; Zech 2:5.
  God's vengeance. Deut 4:24; Heb 12:29.
  Christ as judge. Is 10:17; Mal 3:2.
  The Holy Spirit. Is 4:4; Acts 2:3.
  The church destroying her enemies. Obad 18.
  The word of God. Jer 5:14; 23:29.
  Zeal of saints. Ps 39:3; 119:139.
  Zeal of angels. Ps 104:4; Heb 1:7.
  God's enemies. Is 10:17; Obad 18.
  Lust. Prov 6:27,28.
  Wickedness. Is 9:18.
  The tongue. Prov 16:27; James 3:6.
  The self-righteous. Is 65:5.
  The hope of hypocrites. Is 50:11.
  Persecution. Luke 12:49-53.
  Affliction. Is 43:2.
  Judgments. Jer 48:45; Lam 1:13; Ezek 39:6.

FIRSTBORN, THE.

Of man and beast dedicated to God. Ex 13:2,12; 22:29.
Dedicated to commemorate the sparing of the firstborn of Israel. Ex 13:15; Num 3:13; 8:17.

Of clean beasts
- Not to labour. Deut 15:19.
- Not shorn. Deut 15:19.
- Not taken from the dam for seven days. Ex 22:30; Lev 22:27.
- Offered in sacrifice. Num 18:17.
- Could not be a free-will offering. Lev 27:26.
- Antiquity of offering. Gen 4:4.
- Flesh of, the priest's portion. Num 18:18.

Of clean beasts
- To be redeemed. Num 18:15.
- Law of redemption for. Num 18:16.

Of the ass to be redeemed with lamb or its neck broken. Ex 13:13; 34:20.

Of Israel
- Tribe of Levi taken for. Num 3:12,40-43; 8:18.
- To be redeemed. Ex 34:20; Num 18:15.
- Price of redemption for. Num 3:46,47.
- Price of, given to the priests. Num 3:48-51.

Laws respecting, restored after the captivity. Neh 10:36.

Laws respecting, observed at Christ's birth. Luke 2:22,23.

The beginning of strength and excellency of power. Gen 49:3; Deut 21:17.

Precious and valuable. Mic 6:7; Zech 12:10.

Objects of special love. Gen 25:28; Jer 31:9,20.

Privileges of
- Precedence in the family. Gen 48:13,14.
- Authority over the younger children. Gen 27:29; 1 Sam 20:29.
- Special blessing by the father. Gen 27:4,35.
- The father's title and power. 2 Chr 21:3.
- A double portion of inheritance. Deut 21:17.
- In case of death the next brother to raise up seed to. Deut 25:5,6; Matt 22:24-28.
- Not to be alienated by parents through caprice. Deut 21:15,16.
- Could be forfeited by misconduct. Gen 49:3,4,8; 1 Chr 5:1.
- Could be sold. Gen 25:31,33; Heb 12:16,17.

Instances of, superseded
- Cain. Gen 4:4,5.
- Japheth. Gen 10:21.
- Ishmael. Gen 17:19-21.
- Esau. Gen 25:23; Rom 9:12,13.
- Manasseh. Gen 48:15-20.
- Reuben, etc. 1 Chr 5:1,2.
- Aaron. Ex 7:1,2; Num 12:2,8.
- David's brothers. 1 Sam 16:6-12.
- Adonijah. 1 Kin 2:15,22.

Illustrative of
- The dignity, etc. of Christ. Ps 89:27; Rom 8:29; Col 1:18.
- The dignity, etc. of the church. Heb 12:23.

FIRSTFRUITS, THE.

To be brought to God's house. Ex 34:26.

Different kinds of
- Barley harvest. Lev 23:10-14.
- Wheat harvest. Ex 23:16; Lev 23:16,17.
- Wine and oil. Deut 18:4.
- Wool. Deut 18:4.
- Honey. 2 Chr 31:5.
- Fruit of new trees in fourth year. Lev 19:23,24.
- All agricultural produce. Deut 26:2.

To be the very best of their kind. Num 18:12.

Holy to the Lord. Ezek 48:14.

God honoured by the offering of. Prov 3:9.

Offering of, consecrated the whole. Rom 11:16.

To be offered
- Without delay. Ex 22:29.
- In a basket. Deut 26:2.
- With thanksgiving. Deut 26:3-10.

Allotted to the priests. Num 18:12,13; Lev 23:20; Deut 18:3-5.

Law of, restored after the captivity. Neh 10:35,37; 13:31.

Illustrative of
- The Jewish church. Jer 2:3.
- First converts in any place. Rom 16:5.
- Church of Christ. James 1:18; Rev 14:4.
- Resurrection of Christ. 1 Cor 15:20,23.

FISHES.

Created by God. Gen 1:20,21; Ex 20:11.

Made for God's glory. Job 12:8,9; Ps 69:34.

Inhabit
- Seas. Num 11:22; Ezek 47:10.
- Rivers. Ex 7:18; Ezek 29:5.
- Ponds. Song 7:4; Is 19:10.

Number and variety of. Ps 104:25.

Different in flesh from beasts, etc. 1 Cor 15:39.

Cannot live without water. Is 50:2.

Man given dominion over. Gen 1:26,28; Ps 8:8.

Man permitted to eat. Gen 9:2,3.

Used as food
- By the Egyptians. Num 11:5.
- By the Jews. Matt 7:10.

Mode of cooking alluded to. Luke 24:42; John 21:9.

The people of Tyre traded in. Neh 13:16.

Sold near the fish gate at Jerusalem. 2 Chr 33:14; Zeph 1:10.

Distinction between clean and unclean. Lev 11:9-12; Deut 14:9,10.

Mentioned in Scripture
- Leviathan. Job 41:1; Ps 74:14.
- Whale. Gen 1:21; Matt 12:40.

Solomon wrote the history of. 1 Kin 4:33.

No likeness of, to be made for worship. Ex 20:4; Deut 4:18.

Catching of, a trade. Matt 4:18; Luke 5:2.

Taken with
- Nets. Luke 5:4-6; John 21:6-8.
- Hooks. Amos 4:2; Matt 17:27.
- Spears. Job 41:7.
- Often suffered for man's sin. Ex 7:21; Ezek 38:20.

Miracles connected with
- Multiplying a few. Matt 14:17-21; 15:34.
- Immense draughts of. Luke 5:6,9; John 21:6,11.
- Procuring tribute money from. Matt 17:27.
- Dressed on the shore. John 21:9.

Illustrative
- Of the whole population of Egypt. Ezek 29:4,5.
- Of the visible church. Matt 13:48.
- Of men ignorant of future events. Eccl 9:12.
- Of those ensnared by the wicked. Hab 1:14.
- (Good,) of saints. Matt 13:48,49.
- (Bad,) of mere professors. Matt 13:48,49.

FLATTERY.

Saints should not use. Job 32:21,22.

Ministers should not use. 1 Thess 2:5.

The wicked use, to
- Others. Ps 5:9; 12:2.
- Themselves. Ps 36:2.

Hypocrites use, to
- God. Ps 78:36.
- Those in authority. Dan 11:34.

False prophets and teachers use. Ezek 12:24; Rom 16:18.

Wisdom, a preservative against. Prov 4:5.

Worldly advantage obtained by. Dan 11:21,22.

Seldom gains respect. Prov 28:23.

Avoid those given to. Prov 20:19.

Danger of. Prov 7:21-23; 20:5.

Punishment of. Job 17:5; Ps 12:3.

Exemplified
- Woman of Tekoah. 2 Sam 14:17,20.
- Absalom. 2 Sam 15:2-6.
- False prophets. 1 Kin 22:13.
- Darius's courtiers. Dan 6:7.
- Pharisees, etc. Matt 12:14.
- People of Tyre, etc. Acts 12:22.

FLOWERS.

Wild in fields. Ps 103:15.

Cultivated in gardens. Song 6:2,3.

Described as
- Beautiful. Matt 6:29.
- Sweet. Song 5:13.
- Evanescent. Ps 103:16; Is 40:8.
- Appear in spring. Song 2:12.

Mentioned in Scripture
- The lily. Hos 14:5; Matt 6:28.
- The lily of the valley. Song 2:1.
- The rose. Is 35:1.
- The rose of Sharon. Song 2:1.
- Of the grass. 1 Pet 1:24.

Garlands of, used in worship of idols. Acts 14:13.

Representations of, on the
- Golden candlestick. Ex 25:31,33; 2 Chr 4:21.
- Sea of brass. 1 Kin 7:26; 2 Chr 4:5.
- Woodwork of the temple. 1 Kin 6:18,29,33,35.

Illustrative of
- The graces of Christ. Song 5:13.
- Shortness of man's life. Job 14:2; Ps 103:15.
- Kingdom of Israel. Is 28:1.
- Glory of man. 1 Pet 1:24.
- Rich men. James 1:10,11.

Fools.

All men are, without the knowledge of God. Titus 3:3.
Deny God. Ps 14:1; 53:1.
Blaspheme God. Ps 74:18.
Reproach God. Ps 74:22.
Make a mock at sin. Prov 14:9.
Despise instruction. Prov 1:7; 15:5.
Hate knowledge. Prov 1:22.
Delight not in understanding. Prov 18:2.
Sport themselves in mischief. Prov 10:23.
Walk in darkness. Eccl 2:14.
Hate to depart from evil. Prov 13:19.
Worship of, hateful to God. Eccl 5:1.
Are
- Corrupt and abominable. Ps 14:1.
- Self-sufficient. Prov 12:15; Rom 1:22.
- Self-confident. Prov 14:16.
- Self-deceivers. Prov 14:8.
- Mere professors of religion. Matt 25:2-12.
- Full of words. Eccl 10:14.
- Given to meddling. Prov 20:3.
- Slanderers. Prov 10:18.
- Liars. Prov 10:18.
- Slothful. Eccl 4:5.
- Angry. Eccl 7:9.
- Contentious. Prov 18:6.
- A grief to parents. Prov 17:25; 19:13.

Come to shame. Prov 3:35.
Destroy themselves by their speech. Prov 10:8,14; Eccl 10:12.
The company of, ruinous. Prov 13:20.
Lips of, a snare to the soul. Prov 18:7.
Cling to their folly. Prov 26:11; 27:22.
Worship idols. Jer 10:8; Rom 1:22,23.
Trust to their own hearts. Prov 28:26.
Depend upon their wealth. Luke 12:20.
Hear the gospel and obey it not. Matt 7:26.
The mouth of, pours out folly. Prov 15:2.
Honour is unbecoming for. Prov 26:1,8.
God has no pleasure in. Eccl 5:4.
Shall not stand in the presence of God. Ps 5:5.
Avoid them. Prov 9:6; 14:7.
Exhorted to seek wisdom. Prov 8:5.
Punishment of. Ps 107:17; Prov 19:29; 26:10.
Exemplified
- Rehoboam. 1 Kin 12:8.
- Israel. Jer 4:22.
- Pharisees. Matt 23:17,19.

Forests.

Tracts of land covered with trees. Is 44:14.
Underbrush often in. Is 9:18.
Infested by wild beasts. Ps 50:10; 104:20; Is 56:9; Jer 5:6; Mic 5:8.
Abounded with wild honey. 1 Sam 14:25,26.
Often afforded pasture. Mic 7:14.
Mentioned in Scripture
- Bashan. Is 2:13; Ezek 27:6; Zech 11:2.
- Hareth. 1 Sam 22:5.
- Ephraim. 2 Sam 18:6,8.
- Lebanon. 1 Kin 7:2; 10:17.
- Carmel. 2 Kin 19:23; Is 37:24.
- Arabian. Is 21:13.
- The south. Ezek 20:46,47.
- The king's. Neh 2:8.

Supplied timber for building. 1 Kin 5:6-8.
Were places of refuge. 1 Sam 22:5; 23:16.
Jotham built towers, etc., in. 2 Chr 27:4.
The power of God extends over. Ps 29:9.
Called on to rejoice at God's mercy. Is 44:23.
Often destroyed by enemies. 2 Kin 19:23; Is 37:24; Jer 46:23.
Illustrative
- Of the unfruitful world. Is 32:19.
- (A fruitful field turned into,) of the Jews rejected by God. Is 29:17; 32:15.
- (Destroyed by fire,) of destruction of the wicked. Is 9:18; 10:17,18; Jer 21:14.

Forgetting God.

A characteristic of the wicked. Prov 2:17; Is 65:11.
Backsliders are guilty of. Jer 3:21,22.
Is forgetting his
- Covenant. Deut 4:23; 2 Kin 17:38.
- Works. Ps 78:7,11; 106:13.
- Benefits. Ps 103:2; 106:7.
- Word. Heb 12:5; James 1:25.
- Law. Ps 119:153,176; Hos 4:6.
- Past deliverance. Judg 8:34; Ps 78:42.
- Power to deliver. Is 51:13-15.

Encouraged by false teachers. Jer 23:27.
Prosperity often leads to. Deut 8:12-14; Hos 13:6.
Trials should not lead to. Ps 44:17-20.
Resolve against. Ps 119:16,93.
Cautions against. Deut 6:12; 8:11.
Exhortation to those guilty of. Ps 50:22.
Punishment of. Job 8:12,13; Ps 9:17; Is 17:10,11; Ezek 23:35; Hos 8:14.

Forgiveness of Injuries.

Christ set an example of. Luke 23:34.
Commanded. Mark 11:25; Rom 12:19.
To be unlimited. Matt 18:22; Luke 17:4.
A characteristic of saints. Ps 7:4.
Motives to
- The mercy of God. Luke 6:36.
- Our need of forgiveness. Mark 11:25.
- God's forgiveness of us. Eph 4:32.
- Christ's forgiveness of us. Col 3:13.

A glory to saints. Prov 19:11.
Should be accompanied by
- Forbearance. Col 3:13.
- Kindness. Gen 45:5-11; Rom 12:20.
- Blessing and prayer. Matt 5:44.

Promises to. Matt 6:14; Luke 6:37.
No forgiveness without. Matt 6:15; James 2:13.
Illustrated. Matt 18:23-35.
Exemplified
- Joseph. Gen 50:20,21.
- David. 1 Sam 24:7; 2 Sam 18:5; 19:23.
- Solomon. 1 Kin 1:53.
- Stephen. Acts 7:60.
- Paul. 2 Tim 4:16.

Forsaking God.

Idolaters guilty of. 1 Sam 8:8; 1 Kin 11:33.
The wicked guilty of. Deut 28:20.
Backsliders guilty of. Jer 15:6.
Is forsaking
- His house. 2 Chr 29:6.
- His covenant. Deut 29:25; 1 Kin 19:10; Jer 22:9; Dan 11:30.
- His commandments. Ezra 9:10.
- The right way. 2 Pet 2:15.

Trusting in man is. Jer 17:5.
Leads men to follow their own devices. Jer 2:13.
Prosperity tempts to. Deut 31:20; 32:15.
Wickedness of. Jer 2:13; 5:7.
Unreasonableness and ingratitude of. Jer 2:5,6.
Brings confusion. Jer 17:13.
Followed by remorse. Ezek 6:9.
Brings down his wrath. Ezra 8:22.
Provokes God to forsake men. Judg 10:13; 2 Chr 15:2; 24:20,24.
Resolve against. Josh 24:16; Neh 10:29-39.
Curse pronounced upon. Jer 17:5.
Sin of, to be confessed. Ezra 9:10.
Warnings against. Josh 24:20; 1 Chr 28:9.
Punishment of. Deut 28:20; 2 Kin 22:16,17; Is 1:28; Jer 1:16; 5:19.
Exemplified
- Children of Israel. 1 Sam 12:10.
- Saul. 1 Sam 15:11.
- Ahab. 1 Kin 18:18.
- Amon. 2 Kin 21:22.
- Kingdom of Judah. 2 Chr 12:1,5; 21:10; Is 1:4; Jer 15:6.
- Kingdom of Israel. 2 Chr 13:11; 2 Kin 17:7-18.
- Many disciples. John 6:66.
- Phygellus, etc. 2 Tim 1:15.
- Balaam. 2 Pet 2:15.

Fortresses.

Places strong by nature. Num 24:21.
Places fortified by art. Jer 51:53.
The security of a nation. Is 33:16; Dan 11:10.
Places used as
- Cities. Judg 9:31; Neh 4:2.
- Strong-holds. Judg 6:2; 2 Chr 11:11.
- Forts. 2 Sam 5:9; Is 25:12.
- Strong towers. 2 Chr 26:9.

Afforded protection in danger. Judg 6:2.
Defended against enemies. Nah 2:1.
Often
- Entered by the enemy. Dan 11:7.
- Spoiled. Hos 10:14.
- Levelled. Is 25:12.
- Deserted, etc. Is 34:13.
- Destruction of, threatened. Is 17:3.

Illustrative of
- God's protection. Ps 18:2; Jer 16:19.
- Christ, the defence of saints. Is 33:16.
- Protection afforded to ministers. Jer 6:27.

Foundation.

The lowest part of a building, and on which it rests. Luke 14:29; Acts 16:26.
Figuratively applied to
- The heavens. 2 Sam 22:8.
- The earth. Job 38:4; Ps 104:5.
- The world. Ps 18:15; Matt 13:35.
- The mountains. Deut 32:22.
- The ocean. Ps 104:8.
- Kingdoms. Ex 9:18.

Laid for
- Cities. Josh 6:26; 1 Kin 16:34.

Walls. Ezra 4:12; Rev 21:14.
Houses. Luke 6:48.
Temples. 1 Kin 6:37; Ezra 3:10.
Towers. Luke 14:28,29.
Described as
Of stone. 1 Kin 5:17.
Deep laid. Luke 6:48.
Strongly laid. Ezra 6:3.
Joined together by corner stones. Ezra 4:12; 1 Pet 2:6; Eph 2:20.
Security afforded by. Matt 7:25; Luke 6:48.
Illustrative of
Christ. Is 28:16; 1 Cor 3:11.
Doctrines of the apostles, etc. Eph 2:20.
First principles of the gospel. Heb 6:1,2.
Decrees and purposes of God. 2 Tim 2:19.
Magistrates. Ps 82:5.
The righteous. Prov 10:25.
Hope of saints. Ps 87:1.
Security of saints' inheritance. Heb 11:10.

Fountains and Springs.

Created by God. Ps 74:15; 104:10.
God to be praised for. Rev 14:7.
Come from the great deep. Gen 7:11; Job 38:16.
Found in hills and valleys. Deut 8:7; Ps 104:10.
Send forth each but one kind of water. James 3:11.
Afford
Drink to the beasts. Ps 104:11.
Refreshment to the birds. Ps 104:12.
Fruitfulness to the earth. 1 Kin 18:5; Joel 3:18.
Frequented by travellers. Gen 16:7.
Abound in Canaan. Deut 8:7; 1 Kin 18:5.
Sometimes dried up. Is 58:11.
Drying up of, a severe punishment. Ps 107:33,34; Hos 13:15.
Constantly flowing
Especially esteemed. Is 58:11.
Could not be ceremonially defiled. Lev 11:36.
Sometimes stopped or turned off to distress enemies. 2 Chr 32:3,4.
Mentioned in Scripture
In the way to Shur. Gen 16:7.
Of the waters of Nephtoah. Josh 15:9.
Of Jezreel. 1 Sam 29:1.
Of Pisgah. Deut 4:49.
Upper and nether springs. Josh 15:19; Judg 1:15.
Illustrative
Of God. Ps 36:9; Jer 2:13; 17:13.
Of Christ. Zech 13:1.
Of the Holy Spirit. John 7:38,39.
Of constant supplies of grace. Ps 87:7.
Of eternal life. John 4:14; Rev 21:6.
Of the means of grace. Is 41:18; Joel 3:18.
Of a good wife. Prov 5:18.
Of a numerous posterity. Deut 33:28.
Of spiritual wisdom. Prov 16:22; 18:4.
Of the law of the wise. Prov 13:14.
Of godly fear. Prov 14:27.
(Sealed up,) of the church. Song 4:12.
(Not failing,) of the church. Is 58:11.
(Always flowing,) of unceasing wickedness of the Jews. Jer 6:7.
(Corrupt,) of the natural heart. James 3:11; Matt 15:18,19.
(Troubled,) of saints led astray. Prov 25:26.

Fox, The.

Found in deserts. Ezek 13:4.
Abounded in Palestine. Judg 15:4; Lam 5:18.
Described as
Active. Neh 4:3.
Crafty. Luke 13:32.
Carnivorous. Ps 63:10.
Destructive to vines. Song 2:15.
Dwells in holes. Matt 8:20; Luke 9:58.
Illustrative of
False prophets. Ezek 13:4.
Cunning and deceitful persons. Luke 13:32.
Enemies of the church. Song 2:15.
Used by Samson for annoying the Philistines. Judg 15:4-6.

Fruits.

The produce of corn, etc. Deut 22:9; Ps 107:37.
The produce of trees. Gen 1:29; Eccl 2:5.
Called the
Fruit of the ground. Gen 4:3; Jer 7:20.
Fruit of the earth. Is 4:2.
Increase of the land. Ps 85:12.
Given by God. Acts 14:17.
Preserved to us by God. Mal 3:11.
Require
A fruitful land. Ps 107:31.
Rain from heaven. Ps 104:13; James 5:18.
Influence of the sun and moon. Deut 33:14.
Produced in their due seasons. Matt 21:41.
First of, devoted to God. Deut 26:2.
Divided into
Hasty or precocious. Is 28:4.
Summer fruits. 2 Sam 16:1.
New and old. Song 7:13.
Goodly. Jer 11:16.
Pleasant. Song 4:16.
Precious. Deut 33:14.
Evil or bad. Matt 7:17.
To be waited for with patience. James 5:7.
Often sent as presents. Gen 43:11.
Often destroyed
In God's anger. Jer 7:20.
By blight. Joel 1:12.
By locusts, etc. Deut 28:38,39; Joel 1:4.
By enemies. Ezek 25:4.
By drought. Hag 1:10.
Illustrative
Of effects of repentance. Matt 3:8.
Of works of the Spirit. Gal 5:22,23; Eph 5:9.
Of doctrines of Christ. Song 2:3.
Of good works. Matt 7:17,18; Phil 4:17.
Of a holy conversation. Prov 12:14; 18:20.
Of praise. Heb 13:15.
Of the example, etc. of the godly. Prov 11:30.
Of effects of industry. Prov 31:16,31.
Of the reward of saints. Is 3:10.
Of the reward of the wicked. Jer 17:9,10.
Of converts to the church. Ps 72:16; John 4:36.
(Bad,) of the conduct and conversation of evil men. Matt 12:33.

Gad, the Tribe Of.

Descended from Jacob's seventh son. Gen 30:11.
Predictions respecting. Gen 49:19; Deut 33:20,21.
Persons selected from
To number the people. Num 1:14.
To spy out the land. Num 13:15.
Strength of, on leaving Egypt. Num 1:24,25.
The rear of second division of Israel in their journeys. Num 10:18-20.
Encamped south of the tabernacle under the standard of Reuben. Num 2:10,14.
Offering of, at the dedication. Num 7:42-47.
Families of. Num 26:15-17.
Strength of, on entering Canaan. Num 26:18.
On Ebal, said amen to the curse. Deut 27:13.
Sought and obtained its inheritance east of Jordan. Num 32:1-33.
Bounds of its inheritance. Josh 13:24-28.
Cities built by. Num 32:34-36.
Assisted in conquest of Canaan. Josh 4:12,13.
After the conquest, returned home. Josh 22:9.
Assisted in building the altar of witness which excited the jealousy of Israel. Josh 22:10-29.
Many from other tribes sought refuge with, from the Philistines. 1 Sam 13:7.
Eleven of, swam the Jordan, and joined David in the hold. 1 Chr 12:8-15.
Some of, at coronation of David. 1 Chr 12:37,38.
David appointed rulers over. 1 Chr 26:32.
Spoiled the Hagarites. 1 Chr 5:18-22.
Subdued by Hazael king of Syria. 2 Kin 10:33.
Taken captive to Assyria. 2 Kin 15:29; 1 Chr 5:22,26.
Land of, seized by the Moabites and Ammonites. Jer 48:18-24; 49:1.

Galilee.

Separated from Judea by Samaria. John 4:3,4.
Upper part of, called Galilee of the Gentiles. Is 9:1; Matt 4:15.
Lake of Gennesaret, called the Sea of. Matt 15:29; Luke 5:1.
Kadesh the city of refuge for. Josh 21:32.
Inhabitants of
Called Galilaeans. Acts 2:7.
Used a peculiar dialect. Matt 26:73; Mark 14:70.
Despised by the Jews. John 7:41,52.
Opposed the Roman taxation. Acts 5:37.
Cruelly treated by Pilate. Luke 13:1.

Twenty cities of, given to Hiram. 1 Kin 9:11.
Conquered by the Syrians. 1 Kin 15:20.
Conquered by the Assyrians. 2 Kin 15:29.
Jurisdiction of, granted to Herod by the Romans. Luke 3:1; 23:6,7.
Supplied Tyre, etc. with provisions. Acts 12:20.
Christ
  Brought up in. Matt 2:22; Luke 2:39,51.
  Despised as of. Matt 26:69; John 7:52.
  Chose his apostles from. Matt 4:18,21; John 1:43,44; Acts 1:11.
  Preaching in, predicted. Is 9:1,2; Matt 4:14,15.
  Preached throughout. Mark 1:39; Luke 4:44.
  Commenced, and wrought many miracles in. Matt 4:23,24; 15:29-31.
  Kindly received in. John 4:45.
  Followed by the people of. Matt 4:25.
  Ministered to by women of. Matt 27:55; Mark 15:41; Luke 8:3.
  Sought refuge in. John 4:1,3.
  Appeared in, to his disciples after his resurrection. Matt 26:32; 28:7.
Modern towns of
  Accho or Ptolemais. Judg 1:31.
  Tiberias. John 6:23.
  Nazareth. Matt 2:22,23; Luke 1:26.
  Cana. John 2:1; 21:2.
  Capernaum. Matt 4:13.
  Chorazin. Matt 11:21.
  Bethsaida. Mark 6:45; John 1:44.
  Nain. Luke 7:11.
  Caesarea. Acts 9:30; 10:24.
  Caesarea Philippi. Matt 16:13; Mark 8:27.
Christian churches established in. Acts 9:31.

Gardens.

Often made by the banks of rivers. Num 24:6.
Kinds of, mentioned in Scripture
  Herbs. Deut 11:10; 1 Kin 21:2.
  Cucumbers. Is 1:8.
  Fruit trees. Eccl 2:5,6.
  Spices, etc. Song 4:16; 6:2.
Often enclosed. Song 4:12.
Often refreshed by fountains. Song 4:15.
Taken care of by gardeners. John 20:15.
Lodges erected in. Is 1:8.
Often used for
  Entertainments. Song 5:1.
  Retirement. John 18:1.
  Burial places. 2 Kin 21:18,26; John 19:41.
  Idolatrous worship. Is 1:29; 65:3.
Blasting of, a punishment. Amos 4:9.
Jews ordered to plant, in Babylon. Jer 29:5,28.
Of Eden
  Planted by the Lord. Gen 2:8.
  Called the garden of the Lord. Gen 13:10.
  Called the garden of God. Ezek 28:13.
  Had every tree good for food. Gen 2:9.
  Watered by a river. Gen 2:10-14.
  Man placed in, to dress and keep. Gen 2:8,15.
  Man driven from, after the fall. Gen 3:23,24.
  Fertility of Canaan like. Gen 13:10; Joel 2:3.
  The future state of the Jews shall be like. Is 51:3; Ezek 36:35.
Illustrative
  Of the church. Song 5:1; 6:2,11.
  (Enclosed,) of the pleasantness, fruitfulness, and security of the church. Song 4:12.
  (Well watered,) of spiritual prosperity of the church. Is 58:11; Jer 31:12.
  (When dried up,) of the wicked. Is 1:30.

Garments.

Origin of. Gen 3:7,21.
Called
  Raiment. Gen 28:20; Deut 8:4.
  Clothes. Prov 6:27; Ezek 16:39.
  Clothing. Job 22:6; 31:19.
  Vesture. Gen 41:42; Rev 19:16.
Materials used for
  Wool. Prov 27:26; Ezek 34:3.
  Silk. Prov 31:22.
  Linen. Lev 6:10; Esth 8:15.
  Camel's hair. Matt 3:4.
  Skins. Heb 11:37.
  Sackcloth. 2 Sam 3:31; 2 Kin 19:1.
Not to be made of mixed materials. Deut 22:11.
Of the sexes, not to be interchanged. Deut 22:5.
Colours of, mentioned
  White. Eccl 9:8.
  Blue. Ezek 23:6.
  Purple. Ezek 7:27; Luke 16:19.
  Scarlet. 2 Sam 1:24; Dan 5:7.
  Different colours. Gen 37:3; 2 Sam 13:18.
Were often fringed and bordered. Num 15:38; Deut 22:12.
Scribes and Pharisees condemned for making broad the borders of. Matt 23:5.
Worn long and flowing. Luke 20:46; Rev 1:13.
Girt up during employment. Luke 17:8; John 13:4.
Mentioned in Scripture
  Hyke or upper garment. Deut 24:13; Matt 21:8.
  Burnouse or cloak. Luke 6:29; 2 Tim 4:13.
  Tunic or coat. John 19:23; 21:7.
  Girdle. 1 Sam 18:4; Acts 21:11.
  Bonnet or hat. Lev 8:13; Dan 3:21.
  Shoe or sandal. Ex 3:5; Mark 6:9.
  Vail. Gen 24:65.
Liable to plague and leprosy. Lev 13:47-59.
Cleansed by water from ceremonial uncleanness. Lev 11:32; Num 31:20.
Of the rich
  Of the finest materials. Matt 11:8.
  Gay. James 2:23.
  Gorgeous. Luke 7:25; Acts 12:21.
  Embroidered. Ps 45:14; Ezek 16:18.
  Perfumed. Ps 45:8; Song 4:11.
  Multiplied and heaped up. Job 27:17; Is 3:22.
  Often moth-eaten. Job 13:28; James 5:2.
Of the poor
  Provided specially by God. Deut 10:18.
  Vile. James 2:2.
  Used as a covering by night. Deut 24:13.
  Not to be retained in pledge. Deut 24:12,13.
Grew old and wore out. Josh 9:5; Ps 102:26.
Of Israel preserved for forty years. Deut 8:4.
Were often changed. Gen 35:2; 41:14.
Of those slain with a sword not used. Is 14:19.
Given as a token of covenants. 1 Sam 18:4.
Given as presents. Gen 45:22; 2 Kin 5:22.
Often rent in affliction. 2 Sam 15:32; Ezra 9:3,5.
Illustrative
  (White,) of righteousness. Matt 28:3; Rev 3:18.
  (Rolled in blood,) of victory. Is 9:5.
  (Washed in wine,) of abundance. Gen 49:11.

Gates.

Design of. Is 62:10.
Made of
  Brass. Ps 107:16; Is 45:2.
  Iron. Acts 12:10.
Often two-leaved. Is 45:1.
Fastened with bars of iron. Ps 107:16; Is 45:2.
Made to
  Cities. 1 Kin 17:10.
  Houses. Luke 16:20; Acts 12:14.
  Temples. Acts 3:2.
  Palaces. Esth 5:13.
  Prisons. Acts 12:10.
  Camps. Ex 32:26.
  Rivers. Nah 2:6.
Of cities
  Chief places of concourse. Prov 1:21.
  Courts of justice held at. Deut 16:18; 2 Sam 15:2; Prov 22:22,23.
  Land sold at. Gen 23:10,16.
  Land redeemed at. 2 Kin 7:1,18.
  Markets held at. 2 Kin 7:1,18.
  Proclamations made at. Prov 1:21; Jer 17:19.
  Councils of state held at. 2 Chr 18:9; Jer 39:3.
  Conferences held at. Gen 34:20; 2 Sam 3:27.
  Public commendation given at. Prov 31:23,31.
  Public censure passed at. Job 5:4; Is 29:21.
  Shut at night-fall. Josh 2:5; Neh 13:19.
  Chief points of attack in war. Judg 5:8; Is 22:7; Ezek 21:15.
  Battering rams used against. Ezek 21:22.
  Experienced officers placed over. 2 Kin 7:17.
  Troops reviewed at, going to war. 2 Sam 18:4.
  Often razed and burned. Neh 1:3; Lam 2:9.
  Idolatrous rites performed at. Acts 14:13.

Criminals punished at. Deut 17:5; Jer 20:2.
Custom of sitting at, in the evening, alluded to. Gen 19:1.
Of the temple
Called gates of Zion. Lam 1:4.
Called gates of righteousness. Ps 118:19.
Called gates of the Lord. Ps 118:20.
Overlaid with gold. 2 Kin 18:16.
One specially beautiful. Acts 3:2.
Levites the porters of. 2 Chr 8:14; 23:4.
Charge of, given by lot. 1 Chr 26:13-19.
The treasury placed at. 2 Chr 24:8; Mark 12:41.
The pious Israelites delighted to enter. Ps 118:19,20; 100:4.
Frequented by beggars. Acts 3:2.
Of Jerusalem
High gate of Benjamin. Jer 20:2; 37:13.
Fish gate. 2 Chr 33:14; Neh 3:3.
Sheep gate. Neh 3:1; John 5:2.
Gate of Miphkad. Neh 3:31.
Gate of Ephraim. Neh 12:39.
Valley gate. 2 Chr 26:9; Neh 2:13.
Water gate. Neh 3:26; 8:3.
Horse gate. 2 Chr 23:15; Neh 3:28.
Old gate. Neh 3:6; 12:39.
Corner gate. 2 Chr 26:9.
Dung gate. Neh 3:14; 12:31.
Gate of the fountain. Neh 3:15.
Carcase of sin offering burned without. Lev 4:12; Heb 13:11-13.
Criminals generally punished without. Lev 24:23; John 19:17; Heb 13:12.
Illustrative
Of Christ. John 10:9.
(Of heaven,) of access to God. Gen 28:12-17.
(Of hell,) of Satan's power. Matt 16:18.
(Of the grave,) of death. Is 38:10.
(Strait,) of the entrance to life. Matt 7:14.
(Wide,) of the entrance to ruin. Matt 7:13.

GENEALOGIES.

The Jews reckoned by. 1 Chr 9:1; 2 Chr 31:19.
Public registers kept of. 2 Chr 12:15; Neh 7:5.
Of Christ
Given. Matt 1:1-17; Luke 3:23-38.
Prove his descent from Judah. Heb 7:14.
Priests who could not prove their own, excluded from the priesthood. Ezra 2:62; Neh 7:64.
Subject of, to be avoided. 1 Tim 1:4; Titus 3:9.
Illustrative of the record of saints in the book of life. Luke 10:20; Heb 12:23; Rev 3:5.

GENTILES.

Comprehend all nations except the Jews. Rom 2:9; 3:9; 9:24.
Called
Heathen. Ps 2:1; Gal 3:8.
Nations. Ps 9:20; 22:28; Is 9:1.
Uncircumcised. Is 14:6; 52:1.
Uncircumcision. Rom 2:26.
Greeks. Rom 1:16; 10:12.
Strangers. Is 14:1; 60:10.
Ruled by God. 2 Chr 20:6; Ps 47:8.
Chastised by God. Ps 9:5; 94:10.
Counsel of, brought to nought. Ps 33:10.
Characterised as
Ignorant of God. Rom 1:21; 1 Thess 4:5.
Refusing to know God. Rom 1:28.
Without the law. Rom 2:14.
Idolatrous. Rom 1:23,25; 1 Cor 12:2.
Superstitious. Deut 18:14.
Depraved and wicked. Rom 1:28-32; Eph 4:19.
Blasphemous and reproachful. Neh 5:9.
Constant to their false gods. Jer 2:11.
Hated and despised the Jews. Esth 9:1,5; Ps 44:13,14; 123:3.
Often ravaged and defiled the holy land and sanctuary. Ps 79:1; Lam 1:10.
The Jews
Not to follow the ways of. Lev 18:3; Jer 10:2.
Not to intermarry with. Deut 7:3.
Permitted to have, as servants. Lev 25:44.
Despised, as if dogs. Matt 15:26.
Never associated with. Acts 10:28; 11:2,3.
Often corrupted by. 2 Kin 17:7,8.
Dispersed amongst. John 7:35.
Excluded from Israel's privileges. Eph 2:11,12.
Not allowed to enter the temple. Acts 21:28,29.
Outer court of temple for. Eph 2:14; Rev 11:2.
Given to Christ as His inheritance. Ps 2:8.
Christ given as a light to. Is 42:6; Luke 2:32.
Conversion of, predicted. Is 2:2; 11:10.
United with the Jews against Christ. Acts 4:27.
The gospel not to be preached to, till preached to the Jews. Matt 10:5; Luke 24:47; Acts 13:46.
First special introduction of the gospel to. Acts 10:34-45; 15:14.
First general introduction of the gospel to. Acts 13:48,49,52; 15:12.
Paul the apostle of. Acts 9:15; Gal 2:7,8.
Jerusalem trodden down by, etc. Luke 21:24.
Israel rejected till the fulness of. Rom 11:25.

GIBEONITES.

Descended from the Hivites and Amorites. Josh 9:3,7; 2 Sam 21:2.
A mighty and warlike people. Josh 10:2.
Cities of. Josh 9:17.
Israel
Deceived by. Josh 9:4-13.
Made a league with. Josh 9:15.
Spared on account of their oath. Josh 9:18,19.
Appointed, hewers of wood, etc. Josh 9:20-27.
Attacked by the kings of Canaan. Josh 10:1-5.
Delivered by Israel. Josh 10:6-10.
Saul sought to destroy. 2 Sam 21:2.
Israel plagued for Saul's cruelty to. 2 Sam 21:1.
Effected the destruction of the remnant of Saul's house. 2 Sam 21:4-9.
The office of the Nethinim probably originated in. 1 Chr 9:2.
Part of, returned from the captivity. Neh 7:25.

GIFT OF THE HOLY SPIRIT, THE.

By the Father. Neh 9:20; Luke 11:13.
By the Son. John 20:22.
To Christ without measure. John 3:34.
Given
According to promise. Acts 2:38,39.
Upon the exaltation. Ps 68:18; John 7:39.
Through the intercession of Christ. John 14:16.
In answer to prayer. Luke 11:13; Eph 1:16,17.
For instruction. Neh 9:20.
For comfort of saints. John 14:16.
To those who repent and believe. Acts 2:38.
To those who obey God. Acts 5:32.
To the Gentiles. Acts 10:44,45; 11:17; 15:8.
Is abundant. Ps 68:9; John 7:38,39.
Is permanent. Is 59:21; Hag 2:5; 1 Pet 4:14.
Is fruit bearing. Is 32:15.
Received through faith. Gal 3:14.
An evidence of union with Christ. 1 John 3:24; 4:13.
An earnest of the inheritance of the saints. 2 Cor 1:22; 5:5; Eph 1:14.
A pledge of the continued favour of God. Ezek 39:29.

GIFTS OF GOD, THE.

All blessings are. James 1:17; 2 Pet 1:3.
Are dispensed according to his will. Eccl 2:26; Dan 2:21; Rom 12:6; 1 Cor 7:7.
Are free and abundant. Num 14:8; Rom 8:32.
Spiritual
Christ the chief of. Is 42:6; 55:4; John 3:16; 4:10; 6:32,33.
Are through Christ. Ps 68:18; Eph 4:7,8; John 6:27.
The Holy Spirit. Luke 11:13; Acts 8:20.
Grace. Ps 84:11; James 4:6.
Wisdom. Prov 2:6; James 1:5.
Repentance. Acts 11:18.
Faith. Eph 2:8; Phil 1:29.
Righteousness. Rom 5:16,17.
Strength and power. Ps 68:35.
A new heart. Ezek 11:19.
Peace. Ps 29:11.
Rest. Matt 11:28; 2 Thess 1:7.
Glory. Ps 84:11; John 17:22.
Eternal life. Rom 6:23.
Not repented of by him. Rom 11:29.
To be used for mutual profit. 1 Pet 4:10.
Pray for. Matt 7:7,11; John 16:23,24.
Acknowledge. Ps 4:7; 21:2.
Temporal
Life. Is 42:5.

Food and raiment. Matt 6:25-33.
Rain and fruitful seasons. Gen 27:28; Lev 26:4,5; Is 30:23.
Wisdom. 2 Chr 1:12.
Peace. Lev 26:6; 1 Chr 22:9.
All good things. Ps 34:10; 1 Tim 6:17.
To be used and enjoyed. Eccl 3:13; 5:19,20; 1 Tim 4:4,5.
Should cause us to remember God. Deut 8:18.
All creatures partake of. Ps 136:25; 145:15,16.
Pray for. Zech 10:1; Matt 6:11.
Illustrated. Matt 25:15-30.

GIRDLES.

Worn upon the loins. 1 Kin 2:5; Jer 13:1,11.
Worn by priests about the breasts. Rev 1:13.
Made of
Fine linen. Ezek 16:10.
Twined linen with blue purple, etc. Ex 39:29.
Gold. Rev 1:13; 15:6.
Leather. 2 Kin 1:8; Matt 3:4.
Sackcloth. Is 3:24; Lam 2:10.
Made for sale by industrious women. Prov 31:24.
Used for
Strengthening the loins. Prov 31:17; Is 22:21; 23:10.
Girding up the garments when walking. 1 Kin 18:46; 2 Kin 4:29.
Girding up the garments when working. Luke 12:37; 17:8; John 13:4.
Suspending the sword. 2 Sam 20:8; Neh 4:18.
Suspending the inkhorn. Ezek 9:2.
Holding money. Matt 10:9; Mark 6:8.
Taken off when at rest. Is 5:27; John 13:4.
Given as
A token of friendship. 1 Sam 18:4.
A reward of military service. 2 Sam 18:11.
Illustrative of
Strength. Ps 18:39; Is 22:21.
Gladness. Ps 30:11.
Righteousness of Christ. Is 11:5.
Faithfulness of Christ. Is 11:5.
Truth. Eph 6:14.

GLORIFYING GOD.

Commanded. 1 Chr 16:28; Ps 22:23; Is 42:12.
Due to him. 1 Chr 16:29.
For his
Holiness. Ps 99:9; Rev 15:4.
Mercy and truth. Ps 115:1; Rom 15:9.
Faithfulness and truth. Is 25:1.
Wondrous works. Matt 15:31; Acts 4:21.
Judgments. Is 25:3; Ezek 28:22; Rev 14:7.
Deliverance. Ps 50:15.
Grace to others. Acts 11:18; 2 Cor 9:13; Gal 1:24.
Obligation of saints to. 1 Cor 6:20.
Is acceptable through Christ. Phil 1:11; 1 Pet 4:11.
Christ, an example of. John 17:4.
Accomplished by
Relying on his promises. Rom 4:20.
Praising him. Ps 50:23.
Doing all to him. 1 Cor 10:31.
Dying for him. John 21:19.
Confessing Christ. Phil 2:11.
Suffering for Christ. 1 Pet 4:14,16.
Glorifying Christ. Acts 19:17; 2 Thess 1:12.
Bringing forth fruits of righteousness. John 15:8; Phil 1:11.
Patience in affliction. Is 24:15.
Faithfulness. 1 Pet 4:11.
Required in body and spirit. 1 Cor 6:20.
Shall be universal. Ps 86:9; Rev 5:13.
Saints should
Resolve on. Ps 69:30; 118:28.
Unite in. Ps 34:3; Rom 15:6.
Persevere in. Ps 86:12.
All the blessings of God are designed to lead to. Is 60:21; 61:3.
The holy example of saints may lead others to. Matt 5:16; 1 Pet 2:12.
All, by nature, fail in. Rom 3:23.
The wicked averse to. Dan 5:23; Rom 1:21.
Punishment for not. Dan 5:23,30; Mal 2:2; Acts 12:23; Rom 1:21.
Heavenly host engaged in. Rev 4:11.
Exemplified
David. Ps 57:5.
The Multitude. Matt 9:8; 15:31.
The Virgin Mary. Luke 1:46.
Angels. Luke 2:14.
Shepherds. Luke 2:20.
Man sick of the palsy. Luke 5:25.
Woman with infirmity. Luke 13:13.
Leper. Luke 17:15.
Blind man. Luke 18:43.
Centurion. Luke 23:47.
The Church at Jerusalem. Acts 11:18.
Gentiles at Antioch. Acts 13:48.
Abraham. Rom 4:20.
Paul. Rom 11:36.

GLORY.

God is, to his people. Ps 3:3; Zech 2:5.
Christ is, to his people. Is 60:1; Luke 2:32.
The gospel ordained to be, to saints. 1 Cor 2:7.
Of the gospel, exceeds that of the law. 2 Cor 3:9,10.
The joy of saints is full of. 1 Pet 1:8.
Spiritual
Is given by God. Ps 84:11.
Is given by Christ. John 17:22.
Christ. John 17:22.
Is the work of the Holy Spirit. 2 Cor 3:18.
Eternal
Procured by the death of Christ. Heb 2:10.
Accompanies salvation by Christ. 2 Tim 2:10.
Inherited by saints. 1 Sam 2:8; Ps 73:24; Prov 3:35; Col 3:4; 1 Pet 5:10.
Saints called to. 2 Thess 2:14; 1 Pet 5:10.
Saints afore prepared to. Rom 9:23.
Enhanced by present afflictions. 2 Cor 4:17.
Present afflictions not worthy to be compared with. Rom 8:18.
Of the Church shall be rich and abundant. Is 60:11-13.
The bodies of saints shall be raised in. 1 Cor 15:43; Phil 3:21.
Saints shall be, of their ministers. 1 Thess 2:19,20.
Temporal
Is given by God. Dan 2:37.
Passes away. 1 Pet 1:24.
The devil tries to seduce by. Matt 4:8.
Of hypocrites turned to shame. Hos 4:7.
Seek not, from man. Matt 6:2; 1 Thess 2:6.
Of the wicked
Is in their shame. Phil 3:19.
Ends in destruction. Is 5:14.

GLORY OF GOD, THE.

Exhibited in Christ. John 1:14; 2 Cor 4:6; Heb 1:3.
Exhibited in
His name. Deut 28:58; Neh 9:5.
His majesty. Job 37:22; Ps 93:1; 104:1; 145:5,12; Is 2:10.
His power. Ex 15:1,6; Rom 6:4.
His works. Ps 19:1; 111:3.
His holiness. Ex 15:11.
Described as
Great. Ps 138:5.
Eternal. Ps 104:31.
Rich. Eph 3:16.
Highly exalted. Ps 8:1; 113:4.
Exhibited to
Moses. Ex 34:5-7; 33:18-23.
Stephen. Acts 7:55.
His Church. Deut 5:24; Ps 102:16.
Enlightens the Church. Is 60:1,2; Rev 21:11,23.
Saints desire to behold. Ps 63:2; 90:16.
God is jealous. Is 42:8.
Reverence. Is 59:19.
Plead in prayer. Ps 79:9.
Declare. 1 Chr 16:24; Ps 145:5,11.
Magnify. Ps 57:5.
The earth is full of. Is 6:3.
The knowledge of, shall fill the earth. Hab 2:14.

GLUTTONY.

Christ was falsely accused of. Matt 11:19.
The wicked addicted to. Phil 3:19; Jude 1:12.
Leads to
Carnal security. Is 22:13; 1 Cor 15:32; Luke 12:19.
Poverty. Prov 23:21.
Of princes, ruinous to their people. Eccl 10:16,17.
Is inconsistent in saints. 1 Pet 4:3.
Caution against. Prov 23:2,3; Luke 21:34; Rom 13:13,14.
Pray against temptations to. Ps 141:4.
Punishment of. Num 11:33,34; Ps 78:31; Deut 21:21; Amos 6:4,7.
Danger of, illustrated. Luke 12:45,46.
Exemplified
Esau. Gen 25:30-34; Heb 12:16,17.
Israel. Num 11:4; Ps 78:18.
Sons of Eli. 1 Sam 2:12-17.
Belshazzar. Dan 5:1.

GOAT, THE.

Clean and fit for food. Deut 14:4,5.

Offered in sacrifice. Gen 15:9; Lev 16:5,7.
The male, best for sacrifice. Lev 22:19; Ps 50:9.
Firstborn of, not redeemed. Num 18:17.
Jews had large flocks of. Gen 32:14; 1 Sam 25:2.
Most profitable to the owner. Prov 27:26.
Milk of, used as food. Prov 27:27.
The young of
Called kids. Gen 37:31.
Kept in small flocks. 1 Kin 20:27.
Fed near the shepherds' tents. Song 1:8.
Not to be seethed in milk of mother. Ex 23:19.
Offered in sacrifice. Lev 4:23; 5:6.
Offered at the Passover. Ex 12:5; 2 Chr 35:7.
Considered a delicacy. Gen 27:9; Judg 6:19.
Given as a present. Gen 38:17; Judg 15:1.
The hair of
Offered for tabernacle. Ex 25:4; 35:23.
Made into curtains, for covering the tabernacle. Ex 35:26; 36:14-18.
Made into pillows. 1 Sam 19:13.
Skin of, often used as clothing. Heb 11:37.
Bashan celebrated for. Deut 32:14.
The Arabians traded in. Ezek 27:21.
Flocks of, always led by a male. Jer 50:8.
When wild dwelt in the hills and rocks. 1 Sam 24:2; Job 39:1; Ps 104:18.
Illustrative
Of Macedonian empire. Dan 8:5,21.
Of the wicked. Zech 10:3; Matt 25:32,33.
(Flock of,) of the Church. Song 4:1.

God.

Is a spirit. John 4:24; 2 Cor 3:17.
Is declared to be
Light. Is 60:19; James 1:17; 1 John 1:5.
Love. 1 John 4:8,16.
Invisible. Job 23:8,9; John 1:18; 5:37; Col 1:15; 1 Tim 1:17.
Unsearchable. Job 11:7; 37:23; Ps 145:3; Is 40:28; Rom 11:33.
Incorruptible. Rom 1:23.
Eternal. Deut 33:27; Ps 90:2; Rev 4:8-10.
Immortal. 1 Tim 1:17; 6:16.
Omnipotent. Gen 17:1; Ex 6:3.
Omniscient. Ps 139:1-6; Prov 5:21.
Omnipresent. Ps 139:7; Jer 23:23.
Immutable. Ps 102:26,27; James 1:17.
Only-wise. Rom 16:27; 1 Tim 1:17.
Glorious. Ex 15:11; Ps 145:5.
Most High. Ps 83:18; Acts 7:48.
Perfect. Matt 5:48.
Holy. Ps 99:9; Is 5:16.
Just. Deut 32:4; Is 45:21.
True. Jer 10:10; John 17:3.
Upright. Ps 25:8; 92:15.
Righteous. Ezra 9:15; Ps 145:17.
Good. Ps 25:8; 119:68.
Great. 2 Chr 2:5; Ps 86:10.
Gracious. Ex 34:6; Ps 116:5.
Faithful. 1 Cor 10:13; 1 Pet 4:19.
Merciful. Ex 34:6,7; Ps 86:5.
Long-suffering. Num 14:18; Mic 7:1.
Jealous. Josh 24:19; Nah 1:2.
Compassionate. 2 Kin 13:23.
A consuming fire. Heb 12:29.
None beside him. Deut 4:35; Is 44:6.
None before him. Is 43:10.
None like to him. Ex 9:14; Deut 33:26; 2 Sam 7:22; Is 46:5,9; Jer 10:6.
None good but he. Matt 19:17.
Fills heaven and earth. 1 Kin 8:27; Jer 23:24.
Should be worshipped in spirit and in truth. John 4:24.

Gold.

Found in the earth. Job 28:1,6.
Abounded in
Havilah. Gen 2:11.
Ophir. 1 Kin 9:28; Ps 45:9.
Sheba. Ps 72:15; Is 60:6.
Parvaim. 2 Chr 3:6.
Belongs to God. Joel 3:5; Hag 2:8.
Described as
Yellow. Ps 68:13.
Malleable. Ex 39:3; 1 Kin 10:16,17.
Fusible. Ex 32:3,4; Prov 17:3.
Precious. Ezra 8:27; Is 13:12.
Valuable. Job 28:15,16.
Most valuable when pure and fine. Job 28:19; Ps 19:10; 21:3; Prov 3:14.
Refined and tried by fire. Zech 13:9; 1 Pet 1:7.
Working in, a trade. Neh 3:8; Is 40:19.
An article of commerce. Ezek 27:22.
The patriarchs were rich in. Gen 13:2.
Imported by Solomon. 1 Kin 9:11,28; 10:11.
Abundance of, in Solomon's reign. 2 Chr 1:15.
Offerings of, for tabernacle. Ex 35:22.
Offerings of, for temple. 1 Chr 22:14; 29:4,7.
Used as money. Matt 10:9; Acts 3:6.
Priestly and royal garments adorned with. Ex 28:4-6; Ps 45:9,13.
Was used for
Overlaying the tabernacle. Ex 36:34,38.
Overlaying the temple. 1 Kin 6:21,22.
Overlaying cherubims in temple. 2 Chr 3:10.
Overlaying the ark, etc. Ex 25:11-13.
Overlaying floor of temple. 1 Kin 6:30.
Overlaying throne of Solomon. 1 Kin 10:18.
Mercy seat and cherubims. Ex 25:17,18.
Sacred candlesticks. Ex 25:31; 2 Chr 4:7,20.
Sacred utensils. Ex 25:29,38; 2 Chr 4:19-22.
Crowns. 2 Sam 12:30; Ps 21:3.
Sceptres. Esth 4:11.
Chains. Gen 41:42; Dan 5:29.
Rings. Song 5:14; James 2:2.
Earrings. Judg 8:24,26.
Ornaments. Jer 4:30.
Shields. 2 Sam 8:7; 1 Kin 10:16,17.
Vessels. 1 Kin 10:21; Esth 1:7.
Idols. Ex 20:23; Ps 115:4; Dan 5:4.
Couches. Esth 1:6.
Footstools. 2 Chr 9:18.
Estimated by weight. 1 Chr 28:14.
Given as presents. 1 Kin 15:19; Matt 2:11.
Exacted as tribute. 1 Kin 20:3,5; 2 Kin 23:33,35.
Taken in war, dedicated to God. Josh 6:19; 2 Sam 8:11; 1 Kin 15:15.
Kings of Israel not to multiply. Deut 17:17.
Jews condemned for multiplying. Is 2:7.
Vanity of heaping up. Eccl 2:8,11.
Liable to
Grow dim. Lam 4:1.
Canker and rust. James 5:3.
Illustrative of
Saints after affliction. Job 23:10.
Tried faith. 1 Pet 1:7.
The doctrines of grace. Rev 3:18.
True converts. 1 Cor 3:12.
Babylonish empire. Dan 2:38.

Goodness of God, The.

Is part of his character. Ps 25:8; Nah 1:7; Matt 19:17.
Declared to be
Great. Neh 9:35; Zech 9:17.
Rich. Ps 104:24; Rom 2:4.
Abundant. Ex 34:6; Ps 33:5.
Satisfying. Ps 65:4; Jer 31:12,14.
Enduring. Ps 23:6; 52:1.
Universal. Ps 145:9; Matt 5:45.
Manifested
To his Church. Ps 31:19; Lam 3:25.
In doing good. Ps 119:68; 145:9.
In supplying temporal wants. Acts 14:17.
In providing for the poor. Ps 68:10.
In forgiving sins. 2 Chr 30:18; Ps 86:5.
Leads to repentance. Rom 2:4.
Recognise, in his dealings. Ezra 8:18; Neh 2:18.
Pray for the manifestation of. 2 Thess 1:11.
Despise not. Rom 2:4.
Reverence. Jer 33:9; Hos 3:5.
Magnify. Ps 107:8; Jer 33:11.
Urge others to confide in. Ps 34:8.
The wicked disregard. Neh 9:35.

Gospel, The.

Is good tidings of great joy for all people. Luke 2:10,11,31,32.
Foretold. Is 41:27; 52:7; 61:1-3; Mark 1:15.
Preached under the Old Testament. Heb 4:2.
Exhibits the grace of God. Acts 14:3; 20:32.
The knowledge of the glory of God is by. 2 Cor 4:4,6.
Life and immortality are brought to light by Jesus through. 2 Tim 1:10.
Is the power of God to salvation. Rom 1:16; 1 Cor 1:18; 1 Thess 1:5.
Is glorious. 2 Cor 4:4.
Is everlasting. 1 Pet 1:25; Rev 14:6.
Preached by Christ. Matt 4:23; Mark 1:14.
Ministers have a stewardship to preach. 1 Cor 9:17.
Preached beforehand to Abraham. Gen 22:18; Gal 3:8.
Preached to
The Jews first. Luke 24:47; Acts 13:46.
The Gentiles. Mark 13:10; Gal 2:2,9.

The poor. Matt 11:5; Luke 4:18.
Every creature. Mark 16:15; Col 1:23.
Must be believed. Mark 1:15; Heb 4:2.
Brings peace. Luke 2:10,14; Eph 6:15.
Produces hope. Col 1:23.
Saints have fellowship in. Phil 1:5.
There is fulness of blessing in. Rom 15:29.
Those who receive, should
Adhere to the truth of. Gal 1:6,7; 2:14; 2 Tim 1:13.
Not be ashamed of. Rom 1:16; 2 Tim 1:8.
Live in subjection to. 2 Cor 9:13.
Have their conversation becoming. Phil 1:27.
Earnestly contend for the faith of. Phil 1:17,27; Jude 1:3.
Sacrifice friends and property for. Matt 10:37.
Sacrifice life itself for. Mark 8:35.
Profession of, attended by afflictions. 2 Tim 3:12.
Promises to sufferers. Mark 8:35; 10:30.
Be careful not to hinder. 1 Cor 9:12.
Is hid to them that are lost. 2 Cor 4:3.
Testifies to the final judgment. Rom 2:16.
Let him who preached another, be accursed. Gal 1:8.
Awful consequences of not obeying. 2 Thess 1:8,9.
Is called the
Dispensation of the grace of God. Eph 3:2.
Gospel of peace. Eph 6:15.
Gospel of God. Rom 1:1; 1 Thess 2:8; 1 Pet 4:17.
Gospel of Christ. Rom 1:9,16; 2 Cor 2:12; 1 Thess 3:2.
Gospel of the grace of God. Acts 20:24.
Gospel of the kingdom. Matt 24:14.
Gospel of salvation. Eph 1:13.
Glorious gospel of Jesus Christ. 2 Cor 4:4.
Preaching of Jesus Christ. Rom 16:25.
Mystery of the gospel. Eph 6:19.
Word of God. 1 Thess 2:13.
Word of Christ. Col 3:16.
Word of grace. Acts 14:3; 20:32.
Word of salvation. Acts 13:26.
Word of reconciliation. 2 Cor 5:19.
Word of truth. Eph 1:13; James 1:18.
Word of faith. Rom 10:8.
Word of life. Phil 2:16.
Ministration of the Spirit. 2 Cor 3:8.
Doctrine according to godliness. 1 Tim 6:3.
Form of sound words. 2 Tim 1:13.
Rejection of, by many, foretold. Is 53:1; Rom 10:15,16.
Rejection of, by the Jews, a means of blessing to the Gentiles. Rom 11:28.

GRACE.

God is the God of all. 1 Pet 5:10.
God is the Giver of. Ps 84:11; James 1:17.
God's throne, the throne of. Heb 4:16.
The Holy Spirit is the Spirit of. Zech 12:10; Heb 10:29.
Was upon Christ. Luke 2:40; John 3:24.
Christ spoke with. Ps 45:2; Luke 4:22.
Christ was full of. John 1:14.
Came by Christ. John 1:17; Rom 5:15.
Given by Christ. 1 Cor 1:4.
Foretold by the prophets. 1 Pet 1:10.
Riches of, exhibited in God's kindness through Christ. Eph 2:7.
Glory of, exhibited in our acceptance in Christ. Eph 1:6.
Is described as
Great. Acts 4:33.
Sovereign. Rom 5:21.
Rich. Eph 1:7; 2:7.
Exceeding. 2 Cor 9:14.
Manifold. 1 Pet 4:10.
All-sufficient. 2 Cor 12:9.
All-abundant. Rom 5:15,17,20.
Glorious. Eph 1:6.
The gospel, a declaration of. Acts 20:24,32.
Is the source of
Election. Rom 11:5.
The call of God. Gal 1:15.
Justification. Rom 3:24; Titus 3:7.
Faith. Acts 18:27.
Forgiveness of sins. Eph 1:7.
Salvation. Acts 15:11; Eph 2:5,8.
Consolation. 2 Thess 2:16.
Hope. 2 Thess 2:16.
Necessary to the service of God. Heb 12:28.
God's work completed in saints by. 2 Thess 1:11,12.
The success and completion of the work of God to be attributed to. Zech 4:7.
Inheritance of the promises by. Rom 4:16.
Justification by, opposed to that by works. Rom 4:4,5; 11:6; Gal 5:4.
Saints
Are heirs of. 1 Pet 3:7.
Are under. Rom 6:14.
Receive, from Christ. John 1:16.
Are what they are by. 1 Cor 15:10; 2 Cor 1:12.
Abound in gifts of. Acts 4:33; 2 Cor 8:1; 9:8,14.
Should be established in. Heb 13:9.
Should be strong in. 2 Tim 2:1.
Should grow in. 2 Pet 3:18.
Should speak with. Eph 4:29; Col 4:6.
Specially given
To ministers. Rom 12:3,6; 15:15; 1 Cor 3:10; Gal 2:9; Eph 3:7.
To the humble. Prov 3:34; James 4:6.
To those who walk uprightly. Ps 84:11.
Not to be received in vain. 2 Cor 6:1.
Pray for
For yourselves. Heb 4:16.
For others. 2 Cor 13:14; Eph 6:24.
Beware lest you fail of. Heb 12:15.
Manifestation of, in others, a cause of gladness. Acts 11:23; 1 John 1:3,4.
Special manifestation of, at the second coming of Christ. 1 Pet 1:13.
Not to be abused. Rom 3:8; 6:1,15.
Antinomians abused. Jude 1:4.

GRASS.

A green herb. Mark 6:39.
Called
Grass of the earth. Rev 9:4.
Grass of the field. Num 22:4.
Springs out of the earth. 2 Sam 23:4.
God
Originally created. Gen 1:11,12.
The giver of. Deut 11:15.
Causes to grow. Ps 104:14; 147:8.
Adorns and clothes. Matt 6:30.
Often grew on the tops of houses. Ps 129:6.
When young, soft and tender. Prov 27:25.
Refreshed by rain and dew. Deut 32:2; Prov 19:12.
Cattle fed upon. Job 6:5; Jer 50:11.
Ovens often heated with. Matt 6:30.
Destroyed by
Locusts. Rev 9:4.
Hail and lightning. Rev 8:7.
Drought. 1 Kin 17:1; 18:5.
Failure of, a great calamity. Is 15:5,6.
Sufferings of cattle from failure of, described. Jer 14:5,6.
Illustrative
Of shortness and uncertainty of life. Ps 90:5,6; 103:15; Is 40:6,7; 1 Pet 1:24.
Of prosperity of the wicked. Ps 92:7.
(Refreshed by dew and showers,) of the saints refreshed by grace. Ps 72:6; Mic 5:7.
(On tops of houses,) of the wicked. 2 Kin 19:26; Is 37:27.

GROVES.

Antiquity of. Gen 21:33.
Often on tops of hills. 1 Kin 14:23; Hos 4:13.
Often used as resting places. 1 Sam 22:6.
Idols were worshipped in. Deut 12:2.
Not to be planted near God's altar. Deut 16:21.
Of Canaanites, to be destroyed. Ex 34:13; Deut 7:5; 12:3.
For idol worship planted
By Ahab. 1 Kin 16:33.
By Manasseh. 2 Kin 21:3.
By Israelites. 2 Kin 17:16.
Fondness of Israel for. Jer 17:2.
Punishment for making and serving. 1 Kin 14:15; Is 1:28,29; Mic 5:14.
Destroyed by
Gideon. Judg 6:25-28.
Hezekiah. 2 Kin 18:4.
Asa. 2 Chr 14:3.
Jehoshaphat. 2 Chr 17:6.
Josiah. 2 Kin 23:14; 2 Chr 34:3,7.
God promised to wean Israel from. Is 17:7,8.

HAIR, THE.

The natural covering of the head. Ps 68:21.
Innumerable. Ps 40:12; 69:4.
Growth of. Judg 16:22.
God
Numbers. Matt 10:30.
Takes care of. Dan 3:27; Luke 21:18.
Black, particularly esteemed. Song 5:11.
White or gray
A token of age. 1 Sam 12:2; Ps 71:18.
A token of weakness and decay. Hos 7:9.
An emblem of wisdom. Dan 7:9; Job 12:12.

With righteousness, a crown of glory. Prov 16:31.
To be reverenced. Lev 19:32.
Man cannot even change the colour or. Matt 5:36.
Of women
Worn long for a covering. 1 Cor 11:15.
Plaited and broidered. 1 Tim 2:9; 1 Pet 3:3.
Well set and ornamented. Is 3:24.
Neglected in grief. Luke 7:38; John 12:3.
Sometimes worn long by men. 2 Sam 14:26.
Men condemned for wearing long. 1 Cor 11:14.
Often expensively anointed. Eccl 9:8.
Of Nazirites
Not to be cut or shorn during their vow. Num 6:5; Judg 16:17,19,20.
Shorn after completion of vow. Num 6:18.
Of the healed leper to be shorn. Lev 14:9.
Colour of, changed by leprosy. Lev 13:3,10.
Cut off in affliction. Jer 7:29.
Plucked out in extreme grief. Ezra 9:3.
Plucking out of, a reproach. Neh 13:25; Is 50:6.
Judgments expressed by
Sending baldness for. Is 3:24; Jer 47:5.
Shaving. Is 7:20.

HANDS, THE.

Necessary members of the body. 1 Cor 12:21.
Parts of, mentioned
The palm. Is 49:16; Matt 26:67.
The thumb. Ex 29:20; Lev 14:14,17.
The fingers. 2 Sam 21:20; Dan 5:5.
God strengthens. Gen 49:24.
God makes impotent. Job 5:12.
Operations of, mentioned
Feeling. Ps 115:7; 1 John 1:1.
Taking. Gen 3:22; Ex 4:4.
Holding. Judg 7:20; Rev 10:2.
Working. Prov 31:19; 1 Thess 4:11.
Writing. Is 44:5; Gal 6:11.
Making signs. Is 13:2; Acts 12:17.
Striking. Mark 14:65; John 19:3.
Distinguished as
The right. Acts 3:7.
The left. Gen 14:15; Acts 21:3.
Many alike expert with both. 1 Chr 12:2.
Many had more command of the left. Judg 3:15,21; 20:16.
The right hand
Place of honour. 1 Kin 2:19; Ps 45:9.
Place of power. Ps 110:1; Mark 14:62.
Signet worn on. Jer 22:24.
Given in token of friendship. Gal 2:9.
Used in embracing. 2 Sam 20:9; Song 2:6; 8:3.
Sworn by. Is 62:8.
The accuser stood at, of the accused. Ps 109:6; Zech 3:1.
Of priests touched with blood of consecration-ram. Ex 29:20; Lev 8:23,24.
Of healed leper touched with blood of his sacrifice. Lev 14:14,17,25.
Of healed leper touched with oil. Lev 14:28.
The Jews carried a staff in, when walking. Ex 12:11; 2 Kin 4:29.
The Jews eat with. Matt 26:23.
Were washed
Before eating. Matt 15:2; Mark 7:3.
After touching an unclean person. Lev 15:11.
In token of innocency. Deut 21:6,7; Matt 27:24.
Custom of domestics pouring water upon, alluded to. 2 Kin 3:11.
Servants directed by movements of. Ps 123:2.
Kissed in idolatrous worship. Job 31:27.
Treaties made by joining. 2 Kin 10:15; Prov 11:21.
Suretiship entered into by striking. Job 17:3; Prov 6:1; 17:18; 22:26.
Were lifted up
In prayer. Ps 141:2; Lam 3:41.
In praise. Ps 134:2.
In taking an oath. Gen 14:22; Rev 10:5.
In blessing. Lev 9:22.
Often spread out in prayer. Ps 68:31; Is 1:15.
Placed under the thigh of a person to whom an oath was made. Gen 24:2,3; 47:29,31.
Clapped together in joy. 2 Kin 11:12; Ps 47:1.
Smitten together in extreme anger. Num 24:10; Ezek 21:14,17.
Stretched out in derision. Hos 7:5; Zeph 2:15.
Imposition of, used in
Transferring guilt of sacrifices. Lev 1:4; 3:2; 16:21,22.
Setting apart the Levites. Num 8:10.
Conferring civil power. Num 27:18; Deut 34:9.
Blessing. Gen 48:14; Mark 10:16.
Ordaining ministers. Acts 6:6; 1 Tim 4:14.
Imparting the gifts of the Holy Spirit. Acts 8:17; 19:6.
Imposition of, a first principle of the doctrine of Christ. Heb 6:1,2.
Should be employed
Industriously. Eph 4:28; 1 Thess 4:11.
In God's service. Neh 2:18; Zech 8:9,13.
In acts of benevolence. Prov 3:27; 31:20.
Of the wicked, described as
Bloody. Is 1:15; 59:3.
Violent. Ps 58:2; Is 59:6.
Mischievous. Ps 26:10; Mic 7:3.
Slothful. Prov 6:10; 21:25.
Ensnaring to themselves. Ps 9:16.
The wicked recompensed for the work of. Ps 28:4; Prov 12:14; Is 3:11.
Saints blessed in the work of. Deut 2:7; 30:9; Job 1:10; Ps 90:17.
Criminals often
Bound by. Matt 22:13.
Deprived of. Deut 25:12; 2 Sam 4:12.
Mutilated in. Judg 1:6,7.
Hung by. Lam 5:12.
Illustrative
Of power. 1 Kin 18:46; 2 Kin 13:5.
(Lifted up against another,) of rebellion. 2 Sam 20:21.
(Opened,) of liberality. Deut 15:8; Ps 104:28.
(Shut,) of illiberality. Deut 15:7.
Right hand, illustrative
Of strength and power. Ex 15:6; Ps 17:7.
(Holding by,) of support. Ps 73:23; Is 41:13.
(Standing at,) of protection. Ps 16:8; 109:31; 110:5.
(Full of bribes,) of corruption. Ps 26:10.
(Full of falsehood,) of deceitfulness. Ps 144:8,11; Is 44:20.
(Withdrawn,) of support withheld. Ps 74:11.
(Cutting off,) of extreme self-denial. Matt 5:30.

HAPPINESS OF SAINTS IN THIS LIFE.

Is in God. Ps 73:25,26.
Only found in the ways of wisdom. Prov 3:17,18.
Described by Christ in the beatitudes. Matt 5:3-12.
Is derived from
Fear of God. Ps 128:1,2; Prov 28:14.
Trust in God. Prov 16:20; Phil 4:6,7.
The words of Christ. John 17:13.
Obedience to God. Ps 40:8; John 13:17.
Salvation. Deut 33:29; Is 12:2,3.
Hope in the Lord. Ps 146:5.
Hope of glory. Rom 5:2.
God being their Lord. Ps 144:15.
God being their help. Ps 146:5.
Praising God. Ps 135:3.
Their mutual love. Ps 133:1.
Divine chastening. Job 5:17; James 5:11.
Suffering for Christ. 2 Cor 12:10; 1 Pet 3:14; 4:13,14.
Having mercy on the poor. Prov 14:21.
Finding wisdom. Prov 3:13.
Is abundant and satisfying. Ps 36:8; 63:5.

HAPPINESS OF THE WICKED, THE.

Is limited to this life. Ps 17:14; Luke 16:25.
Is short. Job 20:5.
Is uncertain. Luke 12:20; James 4:13,14.
Is vain. Eccl 2:1; 7:6.
Is derived from
Their wealth. Job 21:13; Ps 52:7.
Their power. Job 21:7; Ps 37:35.
Their worldly prosperity. Ps 17:14; 73:3,4,7.
Popular applause. Acts 12:22.
Gluttony. Is 22:13; Hab 1:16.
Drunkenness. Is 5:11; 56:12.
Vain pleasure. Job 21:12; Is 5:12.
Successful oppression. Hab 1:15; James 5:6.
Marred by jealousy. Esth 5:13.
Often interrupted by judgments. Num 11:33; Job 15:21; Ps 73:18-20; Jer 25:10-11.
Leads to sorrow. Prov 14:13.

Leads to recklessness. Is 22:13.
Sometimes a stumbling-block to saints. Ps 73:3,16; Jer 12:1; Hab 1:13.
Saints often permitted to see the end of. Ps 73:17-20.
Envy not. Ps 37:1.
Woe against. Amos 6:1; Luke 6:25.
Illustrated. Ps 37:35,36; Luke 12:16-20; 16:19-25.
Exemplified
- Israel. Num 11:33.
- Haman. Esth 5:9-11.
- Belshazzar. Dan 5:1.
- Herod. Acts 12:21-23.

HART, THE.

Clean and used as food. Deut 12:15; 14:5.
Often hunted. Lam 1:6.
Female of
- Called the hind. Song 2:7.
- Delights in freedom. Gen 49:21.
- Kind and affectionate. Prov 5:19.
- Brings forth at appointed time. Job 39:1,2.
- Brings forth with difficulty. Job 39:3.
- Brings forth at the voice of God. Ps 29:9.
- Forsakes her young in famine. Jer 14:5.

Young of, abundantly provided for. Job 39:4.
Illustrative
- Of Christ. Song 2:9,17; 8:14.
- Of converted sinners. Is 35:6.
- (Sure-footedness of,) of experienced saints. Ps 18:33; Hab 3:19.
- (Panting for water,) of afflicted saints longing for God. Ps 42:1,2.
- (Without pasture,) of the persecuted. Lam 1:6.

HARVEST, THE.

Ingathering of fruits of the fields. Mark 4:29.
To continue without intermission. Gen 8:22.
Called the
- Appointed weeks of harvest. Jer 5:24.
- Harvest time. 2 Sam 23:13; Jer 50:16.

Fields appeared white before. John 4:35.
Of barley at the Passover. Lev 23:6,10; Ruth 1:22.
Of wheat at Pentecost. Ex 34:22; 1 Sam 12:17.
Men and women engaged in. Ruth 2:8,9.
Persons engaged in
- Reapers. Ruth 2:4.
- Binders. Gen 37:7; Ps 129:7.
- Called harvest-men. Is 17:5.
- Called labourers. Matt 9:37.
- Fed by the husbandman during. Ruth 2:14.
- Received wages. John 4:35.
- Often defrauded of their wages. James 5:4.

Former and latter rain necessary to abundance of. Jer 5:24; Amos 4:7.
Patience required in waiting for. James 5:7.
Not to be commenced until the first-fruits had been offered to God. Lev 23:10,14.
A time of great joy. Ps 126:6; Is 9:3.
Omitted in the sabbatical year. Lev 25:5.
Omitted in year of jubilee. Lev 25:11,12.
The Sabbath to observed during. Ex 34:21.
Legal provision for the poor during. Lev 19:9,10; 23:22; Deut 24:19.
Failure of
- Occasioned by drought. Amos 4:7.
- Occasioned by locusts. Joel 1:4.
- Sometimes continued for years. Gen 45:6.
- A cause of great grief. Is 16:9; Joel 1:11.
- A punishment for sin. Is 17:10,11.

Slothfulness during, ruinous. Prov 10:5.
Miraculous thunder, etc. in. 1 Sam 12:17,18.
Illustrative
- Of seasons of grace. Jer 8:20.
- Of the end of the world. Matt 13:30,39.
- Of a time when many are ready to receive the gospel. Matt 9:37,38; John 4:35.
- Of a time of judgment. Jer 51:33; Hos 6:11.
- Of ripeness for wrath. Joel 3:13; Rev 14:15.
- (Dew in,) of God's protection. Is 18:4.
- (Cold in,) of a refreshing message. Prov 25:13.
- (Rain in,) of honour given to fools. Prov 26:1.

HATRED.

Forbidden. Lev 19:17; Col 3:8.
Is murder. 1 John 3:15.
A work of the flesh. Gal 5:20.
Often cloaked by deceit. Prov 10:18; 26:26.
Leads to deceit. Prov 26:24,25.
Stirs up strife. Prov 10:12.
Embitters life. Prov 15:17.
Inconsistent with
- The knowledge of God. 1 John 2:9,11.
- The love of God. 1 John 4:20.
- Liars prone to. Prov 26:28.

The wicked exhibit
- Towards God. Rom 1:30.
- Towards saints. Ps 25:19; Prov 29:10.
- Towards each other. Titus 3:3.

Christ experienced. Ps 35:19; John 7:7; 15:18,24,25.
Saints should
- Expect. Matt 10:22; John 15:18,19.
- Not marvel at. 1 John 3:13.
- Return good for. Ex 23:5; Matt 5:44.
- Not rejoice in the calamities of those who exhibit. Job 31:29,30; Ps 35:13,14.
- Give no cause for. Prov 25:17.

Punishment of. Ps 34:21; 44:7; 89:23; Amos 1:11.
We should exhibit against
- False ways. Ps 119:104,128.
- Lying. Ps 119:163.
- Evil. Ps 97:10; Prov 8:13.
- Backsliding. Ps 101:3.
- Hatred and opposition to God. Ps 139:21,22.

Exemplified
- Cain. Gen 4:5,8.
- Esau. Gen 27:41.
- Joseph's brethren. Gen 37:4.
- Men of Gilead. Judg 11:7.
- Saul. 1 Sam 18:8,9.
- Ahab. 1 Kin 22:8.
- Haman. Esth 3:5,6.
- Enemies of the Jews. Esth 9:1,5; Ezek 35:5,6.
- Chaldeans. Dan 3:12.
- Enemies of Daniel. Dan 6:4-15.
- Herodias. Matt 14:3,8.
- The Jews. Acts 23:12,14.

HATRED TO CHRIST.

Is without cause. Ps 69:4; John 15:25.
Is on account of his testimony against the world. John 7:7.
Involves
- Hatred to his Father. John 15:23,24.
- Hatred to his people. John 15:18.

Punishment of. Ps 2:2,9; 21:8.
No escape for those who persevere in. 1 Cor 15:25; Heb 10:29-31.
Illustrated. Luke 19:12-14,17.
Exemplified
- Chief priests etc. Matt 27:1,2; Luke 22:5.
- Jews. Matt 27:22,23.
- Scribes etc. Mark 11:18; Luke 11:53,54.

HEAD.

The uppermost and chief member of the body. Is 1:6; 2 Kin 6:31.
All the other members necessary to. 1 Cor 12:21.
The body supported and supplied by. Eph 4:16.
Put for the whole person. Gen 49:26; Prov 10:6.
Put for the life. Dan 1:10; 1 Sam 28:2.
Parts of, mentioned
- The skull. 2 Kin 9:35; Matt 27:33.
- The crown. Gen 49:26; Is 3:17.
- The forehead. 1 Sam 17:49; Ezek 9:4.
- The temples. Judg 4:21,22; Song 4:3.
- The face. Gen 48:12; 2 Kin 9:30.
- The hair. Judg 16:22; Ps 40:12.
- The scalp. Ps 68:21.

Often anointed. Eccl 9:8; Matt 6:17.
Bowed down
- In worshipping God. Gen 24:26; Ex 4:31.
- As a token of respect. Gen 43:23.

In grief
- Covered up. 2 Sam 15:30; Esth 6:12.
- Shorn. Job 1:20.
- Sprinkled with dust. Josh 7:6; 2:12.
- The hands placed on. 2 Sam 13:19; Jer 2:37.

Priests forbidden to shave. Lev 21:5,10.
Nazirites forbidden to shave. Num 6:5.
Derision expressed by shaking. 2 Kin 19:21; Ps 22:7; 109:25; Matt 27:39.
The Jews censured for swearing by. Matt 5:36.
When hoary with age to be respected. Lev 19:32.
Liable to
- Leprosy. Lev 13:42-44.
- Scab. Is 3:17.
- Internal disease. 2 Kin 4:19; Is 1:5.
- Baldness. Lev 13:40,41; Is 15:2.

Of the leper always uncovered. Lev 13:45.

Of women generally covered in public. Gen 24:65; 1 Cor 11:5.
Of criminals often cut off. Matt 14:10.
Of enemies slain in war, often cut off. Judg 5:26; 1 Sam 17:51,57; 31:9.
Illustrative
 Of God. 1 Cor 11:3.
 Of Christ. 1 Cor 11:3; Eph 1:22; Col 2:19.
 Of rulers. 1 Sam 15:17; Dan 2:38.
 Of chief men. Is 9:14,15.
 Of the chief city of a kingdom. Is 7:8.
 (Covered,) of defence and protection. Ps 140:7.
 (Covered,) of subjection. 1 Cor 11:5,10.
 (Made bald,) of heavy judgments. Is 3:24; 15:2; 22:12; Mic 1:16.
 (Lifted up,) of joy and confidence. Ps 3:3; Luke 21:28.
 (Lifted up,) of pride, etc. Ps 83:2.
 (Lifted up,) of exaltation. Gen 40:13; Ps 27:6.
 (Anointed,) of joy and prosperity. Ps 23:5; 92:10.

Heart, The.

Issues of life are out of. Prov 4:23.
God
 Tries. 1 Chr 29:17; Jer 12:3.
 Knows. Ps 44:21; Jer 20:12.
 Searches. 1 Chr 28:9; Jer 17:10.
 Understands the thoughts of. 1 Chr 28:9; Ps 139:2.
 Ponders. Prov 21:2; 24:12.
 Influences. 1 Sam 10:26; Ezra 6:22; 7:27; Prov 21:1; Jer 20:9.
 Creates a new. Ps 51:10; Ezek 36:26.
 Prepares. 1 Chr 29:18; Prov 16:1.
 Opens. Acts 16:14.
 Enlightens. 2 Cor 4:6; Eph 1:18.
 Strengthens. Ps 27:14.
 Establishes. Ps 112:8; 1 Thess 3:13.
Should be
 Prepared to God. 1 Sam 7:3.
 Given to God. Prov 23:26.
 Perfect with God. 1 Kin 8:61.
 Applied to wisdom. Ps 90:12; Prov 2:2.
 Guided in the right. Prov 23:19.
 Purified. James 4:8.
 Single. Eph 6:5; Col 3:22.
 Tender. Eph 4:32.
 Kept with diligence. Prov 4:23.
We should
 Believe with. Acts 8:37; Rom 10:10.
 Serve God with all. Deut 11:13.
 Keep God's statutes with all. Deut 26:16.
 Walk before God with all. 1 Kin 2:4.
 Trust in God with all. Prov 3:5.
 Love God with all. Matt 22:37.
 Return to God with all. Deut 30:2.
 Do the will of God from. Eph 6:6.
 Sanctify God in. 1 Pet 3:15.
 Love one another with a pure. 1 Pet 1:22.
No man can cleanse. Prov 20:9.
Faith, the means of purifying. Acts 15:9.
Renewal of, promised under the gospel. Ezek 11:19; 36:26; Heb 3:10.
When broken and contrite, not despised by God. Ps 51:17.
The pure in, shall see God. Matt 5:8.
Pray that it may be
 Cleansed. Ps 51:10.
 Inclined to God's testimonies. Ps 119:36.
 United to fear God. Ps 86:11.
 Directed into the love of God. 2 Thess 3:5.
Harden not, against God. Ps 95:8; Heb 4:7.
Harden not, against the poor. Deut 15:7.
Regard not iniquity in. Ps 66:18.
Take heed lest it be deceived. Deut 11:16.
Know the plague of. 1 Kin 8:38.
He that trusts in, is a fool. Prov 28:26.

Heart, Character of the Renewed.

Prepared to seek God. 2 Chr 19:3; Ezra 7:10; Ps 10:17.
Fixed on God. Ps 57:7; 112:7.
Joyful in God. 1 Sam 2:1; Zech 10:7.
Perfect with God. 1 Kin 8:61; Ps 101:2.
Upright. Ps 97:11; 125:4.
Clean. Ps 73:1.
Pure. Ps 24:4; Matt 5:8.
Tender. 1 Sam 24:5; 2 Kin 22:19.
Single and sincere. Acts 2:46; Heb 10:22.
Honest and good. Luke 8:15.
Broken, contrite. Ps 34:18; 51:17.
Obedient. Ps 119:112; Rom 6:17.
Filled with the law of God. Ps 40:8; 119:11.
Awed by the Word of God. Ps 119:161.
Filled with the fear of God. Jer 32:40.
Meditative. Ps 4:4; 77:6.
Circumcised. Deut 30:6; Rom 2:29.
Void of fear. Ps 27:3.
Desirous of God. Ps 84:2.
Enlarged. Ps 119:32; 2 Cor 6:11.
Faithful to God. Neh 9:8.
Confident in God. Ps 112:7.
Sympathising. Jer 4:19; Lam 3:51.
Prayerful. 1 Sam 1:13; Ps 27:8.
Inclined to obedience. Ps 119:112.
Wholly devoted to God. Ps 9:1; 119:10,69,145.
Zealous. 2 Chr 17:6; Jer 20:9.
Wise. Prov 10:8; 14:33; 23:15.
A treasury of good. Matt 12:35.

Heart, Character of the Unrenewed.

Hateful to God. Prov 6:16,18; 11:20.
Full of evil. Eccl 9:3.
Full of evil imaginations. Gen 6:5; 8:21; Prov 6:18.
Full of vain thoughts. Jer 4:14.
Fully set to do evil. Eccl 8:11.
Desperately wicked. Jer 17:9.
Far from God. Is 29:13; Matt 15:8.
Not perfect with God. 1 Kin 15:3; Acts 8:21; Prov 6:18.
Not prepared to seek God. 2 Chr 12:14.
A treasury of evil. Matt 12:35; Mark 7:21.
Darkened. Rom 1:21.
Prone to error. Ps 95:10.
Prone to depart from God. Deut 29:18; Jer 17:5.
Impenitent. Rom 2:5.
Unbelieving. Heb 3:12.
Blind. Eph 4:18.
Uncircumcised. Lev 26:41; Acts 7:51.
Of little worth. Prov 10:20.
Deceitful. Jer 17:9.
Deceived. Is 44:20; James 1:26.
Divided. Hos 10:2.
Double. 1 Chr 12:33; Ps 12:2.
Hard. Ezek 3:7; Mark 10:5; Rom 2:5.
Haughty. Prov 18:12; Jer 48:29.
Influenced by the devil. John 13:2.
Carnal. Rom 8:7.
Covetous. Jer 22:17; 2 Pet 2:14.
Despiteful. Ezek 25:15.
Ensnaring. Eccl 7:26.
Foolish. Prov 12:23; 22:15.
Froward. Ps 101:4; Prov 6:14; 17:20.
Fretful against the Lord. Prov 19:3.
Idolatrous. Ezek 14:3,4.
Mad. Eccl 9:3.
Mischievous. Ps 28:3; 140:2.
Proud. Ps 101:5; Jer 49:16.
Rebellious. Jer 5:23.
Perverse. Prov 12:8.
Stiff. Ezek 2:4.
Stony. Ezek 11:19; 36:26.
Stout. Is 10:12; 46:12.
Elated by sensual indulgence. Hos 13:3.
Elated by prosperity. 2 Chr 26:16; Dan 5:20.
Studies destruction. Prov 24:2.
Often judicially stupefied. Is 6:10; Acts 28:26,27.
Often judicially hardened. Ex 4:21; Josh 11:20.

Heathen, The.

Are without God and Christ. Eph 2:12.
Described as
 Ignorant. 1 Cor 1:21; Eph 4:18.
 Idolatrous. Ps 135:15; Rom 1:23,25.
 Worshippers of the devil. 1 Cor 10:20.
 Cruel. Ps 74:20; Rom 1:31.
 Filthy. Ezra 6:21; Eph 4:19; 5:12.
 Persecuting. Ps 2:1,2; 2 Cor 11:26.
 Scoffing at saints. Ps 79:10.
 Strangers to the covenant of promise. Eph 2:12.
 Having no hope. Eph 2:12.
 Degradation of. Lev 25:44.
Have
 Evidence of the power of God. Rom 1:19,20; Acts 17:27.
 Evidence of the goodness of God. Acts 14:17.
 The testimony of conscience. Rom 2:14,15.
Evil of imitating. 2 Kin 16:3; Ezek 11:12.
Cautions against imitating. Jer 10:2; Matt 6:7.
Danger of intercourse with. Ps 106:35.
Employed to chastise the Church. Lev 26:33; Jer 49:14; Lam 1:3; Ezek 7:24; 25:7; Dan 4:27; Hab 1:5-9.
The Church shall be avenged of. Ps 149:7; Jer 10:25; Obad 15.
God
 Rules over. 2 Chr 20:6; Ps 47:8.
 Brings to nought the counsels of. Ps 33:10.
 Will be exalted among. Ps 46:10; 102:15.
 Punishes. Ps 44:2; Joel 3:11-13; Mic 5:15; Hab 3:12; Zech 14:18.
 Will finally judge. Rom 2:12-16.
Given to Christ. Ps 2:8; Dan 7:14.

Salvation of, foretold. Gen 12:3; Gal 3:8; Is 2:2-4; 52:10; 60:1-8.
Salvation provided for. Acts 28:28; Rom 15:9-12.
The glory of God to be declared among. 1 Chr 16:24; Ps 96:3.
The gospel to be preached to. Matt 24:14; 28:19; Rom 16:26; Gal 1:16.
Necessity for preaching to. Rom 10:14.
The gospel received by. Acts 11:1; 13:48; 15:3,23.
Baptism to be administered to. Matt 28:19.
The Holy Spirit poured out upon. Acts 10:44,45; 15:8.
Praise God for success of the gospel among. Ps 98:1-3; Acts 11:18.
Pray for. Ps 67:2-5.
Aid missions to. 2 Cor 11:9; 3 John 6,7.
Conversion of, acceptable to God. Acts 10:35; Rom 15:16.

Heaven.

Created by God. Gen 1:1; Rev 10:6.
Everlasting. Ps 89:29; 2 Cor 5:1.
Immeasurable. Jer 31:37.
High. Ps 103:11; Is 57:15.
Holy. Deut 26:15; Ps 20:6; Is 57:15.
God's dwelling-place. 1 Kin 8:30; Matt 6:9.
God's throne. Is 66:1; Acts 7:49.
God
  Is the Lord of. Dan 5:23; Matt 11:25.
  Reigns in. Ps 11:4; 135:6; Dan 4:35.
  Fills. 1 Kin 8:27; Jer 23:24.
  Answers his people from. 1 Chr 21:26; 2 Chr 7:14; Neh 9:27; Ps 20:6.
  Sends his judgments from. Gen 19:24; 1 Sam 2:10; Dan 4:13,14; Rom 1:18.
Christ
  As Mediator, entered into. Acts 3:21; Heb 6:20; 9:12,24.
  Is all-powerful in. Matt 28:18; 1 Pet 3:22.
Angels are in. Matt 18:10; 24:36.
Names of saints are written. Luke 10:20; Heb 12:23.
Saints rewarded in. Matt 5:12; 1 Pet 1:4.
Repentance occasions joy in. Luke 15:7.
Lay up treasure in. Matt 6:20; Luke 12:33.
Flesh and blood cannot inherit. 1 Cor 15:50.
Happiness of, described. Rev 7:16,17.
Is called
  A garner. Matt 3:12.
  The kingdom of Christ and of God. Eph 5:5.
  The Father's house. John 14:2.
  A heavenly country. Heb 11:16.
  A rest. Heb 4:9.
  Paradise. 2 Cor 12:2,4.
The wicked excluded from. Gal 5:21; Eph 5:5; Rev 22:15.
Enoch and Elijah were translated into. Gen 5:24; Heb 11:5; 2 Kin 2:11.

Heave Offering.

To brought to God's house. Deut 12:6.
Consisted of
  Firstfruits of bread. Num 15:19-21.
  Right shoulder of peace offerings. Lev 7:32.
  Part of the meat offering of all peace offerings. Lev 7:14.
  Shoulder of the priest's consecration-ram. Ex 29:27.
  Tenth of all tithes. Num 18:26.
  Part of all gifts. Num 18:29.
  Part of spoil taken in war. Num 31:26-47.
To be the best of their kind. Num 18:29.
To be heaved up by the priest. Ex 29:27.
Sanctified the whole offering. Num 18:27,30.
Given to the priests. Ex 29:28; Lev 7:34.
To be eaten in a clean place. Lev 10:12-15.

Hedges.

Antiquity of. 1 Chr 4:23.
Designed for protection. Is 5:2.
Often made of thorns. Mic 7:4.
Placed around
  Gardens. Song 4:12; Lam 2:6.
  Vineyards. Matt 21:33; Mark 12:1.
Difficulty of breaking through. Prov 15:19.
Danger of breaking through. Eccl 10:8.
Desolation caused by removing. Ps 80:12,13.
Filled with grasshoppers. Nah 3:17.
Poor travellers sought rest under. Luke 14:23.
Afforded protection in danger. Jer 49:3.
Making up gaps in, alluded to. Ezek 13:5; 22:30.
Illustrative
  Of God's protection. Job 1:10.
  Of numerous afflictions. Job 3:23; 19:8.
  Of heavy judgments. Lam 3:7; Hos 2:6.
  Of holy ordinances. Is 5:2; Matt 21:33.
  Of the way of the slothful. Prov 15:19.
  (Broken down,) of the taking away of protection. Ps 80:12; Is 5:5.

Heedfulness.

Commanded. Ex 23:13; Prov 4:25-27.
Necessary
  In the care of the soul. Deut 4:9.
  In the house and worship of God. Eccl 5:1.
  In what we hear. Mark 4:24.
  In how we hear. Luke 8:18.
  In keeping God's commandments. Josh 22:5.
  In conduct. Eph 5:15.
  In speech. Prov 13:3; James 1:19.
  In worldly company. Ps 39:1; Col 4:5.
  In giving judgment. 1 Chr 19:6,7.
  Against sin. Heb 12:15,16.
  Against unbelief. Heb 3:12.
  Against idolatry. Deut 4:15,16.
  Against false Christs, and false prophets. Matt 24:4,5,23,24.
  Against false teachers. Phil 3:2; Col 2:8; 2 Pet 3:16,17.
  Against presumption. 1 Cor 10:12.
  Promises to. 1 Kin 2:4; 1 Chr 22:13.

Hell.

The place of disembodied spirits. Acts 2:31.
  Which Christ visited. Luke 23:43; Acts 2:31; 1 Pet 3:19.
  Contains, a place of rest, Abraham's bosom. Luke 16:23.
  Paradise. Luke 23:43.
  And a place of torment. Luke 16:23.
The place of future punishment
  Destruction from the presence of God. 2 Thess 1:9.
Described as
  Everlasting punishment. Matt 25:46.
  Everlasting fire. Matt 25:41.
  Everlasting burnings. Is 33:14.
  A furnace of fire. Matt 13:42,50.
  A lake of fire. Rev 20:15.
  Fire and brimstone. Rev 14:10.
  Unquenchable fire. Matt 3:12.
  Devouring fire. Is 33:14.
Prepared for the devil, etc. Matt 25:41.
Devils are confined in, until the judgment day. 2 Pet 2:4; Jude 1:6.
Punishment of, is eternal. Is 33:14; Rev 20:10.
The wicked shall be turned into. Ps 9:17.
Human power cannot preserve from. Ezek 32:27.
The body suffers in. Matt 5:29; 10:28.
The soul suffers in. Matt 10:28.
The wise avoid. Prov 15:24.
Endeavour to keep others from. Prov 23:14; Jude 1:23.
The society of the wicked leads to. Prov 5:5; 9:18.
The beast, false prophets, and the devil shall be cast into. Rev 19:20; 20:10.
The powers of, cannot prevail against the Church. Matt 16:18.
Illustrated. Is 30:33.

Herbs, Etc.

Called the green herbs. 2 Kin 19:26.
God
  Created. Gen 1:11,12; 2:5.
  Causes to grow. Job 38:27; Ps 104:14.
Each kind of, contains its own seed. Gen 1:11,12.
Given as food to man. Gen 1:28,29; 9:3.
Found in
  The fields. Jer 12:4.
  The mountains. Prov 27:25.
  The marshes. Job 8:11.
  The deserts. Job 24:5; Jer 17:6.
Cultivated in gardens. Deut 11:10; 1 Kin 21:2.
Cultivated for food. Prov 15:17; Heb 6:7.
Require rain dew. Deut 32:2; Job 38:26,27.
Mode of watering, alluded to. Deut 11:10.
Mentioned in Scripture
  Aloe. Song 4:14.
  Anise. Matt 23:23.
  Barley. Ex 9:31; 2 Sam 14:30.
  Beans. 2 Sam 17:28.
  Bulrushes. Ex 2:3; Is 58:5.
  Calamus. Song 4:14.
  Cummin. Is 28:27; Matt 23:23.
  Cucumber. Num 11:5; Is 1:8.
  Fitches. Is 28:25,27.
  Flag. Ex 2:3; Job 8:11.
  Flax. Ex 9:31.
  Garlic. Num 11:5.

Gourds. 2 Kin 4:39.
Grass. Num 22:4.
Heath. Jer 17:6; 48:6.
Hyssop. Ex 12:22; 1 Kin 4:33.
Leeks. Num 11:5.
Lentiles. Gen 25:34.
Mandrakes. Gen 30:14; Song 7:13.
Mallows. Job 30:4.
Millet. Ezek 4:9.
Melon. Num 11:5.
Mint. Matt 23:23.
Myrrh. Song 4:14.
Onions. Num 11:5.
Reeds. Job 40:21; Is 19:6.
Rushes. Job 8:11.
Rye. Ex 9:32.
Saffron. Song 4:14.
Spikenard. Song 4:14.
Tares or Darnel. Matt 13:30.
Wheat. Ex 9:32; Jer 12:13.
Bitter, used at Passover. Ex 12:8; Num 9:11.
Poisonous, not fit for man's use. 2 Kin 4:39,40.
Destroyed by
Hail and lightning. Ex 9:22-25.
Locusts, etc. Ex 10:12,15; Ps 105:34,35.
Drought. Is 42:15.
Tithable among the Jews. Luke 11:42.
Were sometimes used instead of animal food by weak saints. Rom 14:2.
Illustrative
Of the wicked. 2 Kin 19:26; Ps 37:2.
(Dew on,) of grace given to saints. Is 18:4.

HIGH PLACES.

Used for idolatrous worship. 1 Kin 11:7,8.
God sometimes worshipped on. 1 Sam 9:12; 1 Kin 3:2,4; 2 Chr 33:17.
Mentioned in Scripture
Gibeon. 1 Kin 3:4.
Arnon. Num 21:28.
Baal. Num 22:41.
Tophet. Jer 7:31.
Bamah. Ezek 20:29.
Aven. Hos 10:8.
Adorned with tapestry. Ezek 16:16.
Surrounded with groves. 1 Kin 14:23.
Built by
Solomon. 1 Kin 11:7.
Jeroboam. 1 Kin 12:31.
Jehoram. 2 Chr 21:11.
Ahaz. 2 Chr 28:25.
Manasseh. 2 Kin 21:3; 2 Chr 33:3.
People of Judah. 1 Kin 14:23.
People of Israel. 2 Kin 17:9.
Priests ordained for. 1 Kin 12:32; 13:33.
Sacrifices and incense offered to idols upon. 2 Kin 12:3; 16:4.
Enchantments used upon. Num 23:3; 24:1.
Of the Canaanites to be destroyed. Num 33:52.
The Jews
Built, in their cities. 2 Kin 17:9.
Built, in all their streets. Ezek 16:24,31.
Condemned for building. Ezek 16:23-35.
Provoked God with. 1 Kin 14:22,23; Ps 78:58.
Threatened with destruction of. Lev 26:30.
Punished for. 2 Kin 17:11,18.
Destroyed
Asa, partially. 2 Chr 14:3,5; 15:17.
Jehoshaphat. 2 Chr 17:6.
Hezekiah. 2 Kin 18:4; 2 Chr 31:1.
Josiah. 2 Kin 23:8; 2 Chr 34:3.
Not removed
Jehoash. 2 Kin 12:3.
Amaziah. 2 Kin 14:4.
Azariah. 2 Kin 15:4.
Jotham. 2 Kin 15:35.

HIGH PRIEST, THE.

Specially called of God. Ex 28:1,2; Heb 5:4.
Consecrated to his office. Ex 40:13; Lev 8:12.
Was called
The priest. Ex 29:30; Neh 7:65.
God's high priest. Acts 23:4.
Ruler of the people. Ex 22:28; Acts 23:5.
The office of, hereditary. Ex 29:29.
Next in rank to the king. Lam 2:6.
Often exercised chief civil power. 1 Sam 4:18.
Duties of
Offering gifts and sacrifices. Heb 5:1.
Lighting the sacred lamps. Ex 30:8; Num 8:3.
Making atonement in the most holy place once a year. Lev 16:1-34; Heb 9:7.
Bearing before the Lord the names of Israel for a memorial. Ex 28:12,29.
Enquiring of God by Urim and Thummim. 1 Sam 23:9-12; 30:7,8.
Consecrating the Levites. Num 9:11-21.
Appointing priests to offices. 1 Sam 2:36.
Taking charge of money collected in the sacred treasury. 2 Kin 12:10; 22:4.
Presiding in the superior court. Matt 26:3,57-62; Acts 5:21-28; 23:1-5.
Taking the census of the people. Num 1:3.
Blessing the people. Lev 9:22,23.
Sometimes enabled to prophesy. John 11:49-52.
Assisted by a deputy. 2 Sam 15:24; Luke 3:2.
The deputy of
Called the second priest. 2 Kin 25:18.
Had oversight of the tabernacle. Num 4:16.
Had oversight of the Levites. Num 3:32.
To marry a virgin of Aaron's family. Lev 21:13,14.
Forbidden to mourn for any. Lev 21:1-12.
To be tender and compassionate. Heb 5:2.
Needed to sacrifice for himself. Heb 5:1-3.
Special garments of
Ephod with its curious girdle. Ex 28:6,7.
Girdle. Ex 28:4,39.
Broidered coat. Ex 28:4,39.
Robe of the ephod. Ex 28:31-35.
Breastplate. Ex 28:15-29.
Linen mitre. Ex 28:4,39.
Plate or crown of gold, etc. Ex 28:36-38.
Made by divine wisdom given to Bezaleel, etc. Ex 28:3; 36:1; 39:1.
Were for beauty and ornament. Ex 28:2.
Worn at his consecration. Lev 8:7,9.
Worn seven days after consecration. Ex 29:30.
Descended to his successors. Ex 29:29.
Wore the ordinary priest's garments when making atonement in the holy place. Lev 16:4.
Office of, promised to the posterity of Phinehas for his zeal. Num 25:12,13.
Family of Eli degraded from office of, for bad conduct. 1 Sam 2:27-36.
Sometimes deposed by the kings. 1 Kin 2:27.
Office of, made annual by the Romans. John 11:49-51; Acts 4:6.
Typified Christ in
Being called of God. Heb 5:4,5.
His title. Heb 3:1.
His appointment. Is 61:1; John 1:32-34.
Making atonement. Lev 16:33; Heb 2:17.
Splendid dress. Ex 28:2; John 1:14.
Being liable to temptation. Heb 2:18.
Compassion and sympathy for the weak and ignorant. Heb 4:15; 5:1,2.
Marrying a virgin. Lev 21:13,14; 2 Cor 11:2.
Holiness of office. Lev 21:15; Heb 7:26.
Performing by himself all the services on Day of Atonement. Lev 16:1-34; Heb 1:3.
Bearing the names of Israel upon his heart. Ex 28:29; Song 8:6.
Alone entering into most holy place. Heb 9:7,12,24; 4:14.
Interceding. Num 16:43-48; Heb 7:25.
Blessing. Lev 9:22,23; Acts 3:26.
Inferior to Christ in
Needing to make atonement for his own sins. Heb 5:2,3; 7:26-28; 9:7.
Being of the order of Aaron. Heb 6:20; 7:11-17; 8:4,5,1,2,6.
Being made without an oath. Heb 7:20-22.
Not being able to continue. Heb 7:23,24.
Offering oftentimes the same sacrifices. Heb 9:25,26,28; 10:11,12,14.
Entering into holiest every year. Heb 9:7,12,25.

HIGHWAYS.

Roads for public use. Num 20:19; Deut 2:27.
Called the king's highway. Num 20:17.
Marked out by heaps of stones. Jer 31:21.
Generally broad. Judg 20:32,45; Matt 7:13.
Generally straight. 1 Sam 6:12; Is 40:3.
Made to all cities of refuge. Deut 19:2,3.
Often made in deserts. Is 40:3.

Infested with
Serpents. Gen 49:17.
Wild beasts. 1 Kin 13:24; Is 35:9.
Robbers. Jer 3:2; Luke 10:30-33.
Beggars sat by sides of. Matt 20:30; Mark 10:46.
Often obstructed. Jer 18:15.
All obstructions removed from, before persons of distinction. Is 40:3,4; Matt 3:3.
By-paths more secure in times of danger. Judg 5:6.
Desolation of, threatened as a punishment. Lev 26:22; Is 33:8.
Illustrative
Of Christ. John 14:6.
Of the way of holiness. Is 35:8.
Of facilities for the restoration of the Jews. Is 11:16; 62:10.
(Made in the deserts,) of facilities for the spread of the gospel. Is 40:3; 43:19.
(Narrow,) of the way of life. Matt 7:14.
(Broad,) of the way to destruction. Matt 7:13.

Hittites.

Descended from Canaan's son, Heth. Gen 10:15.
Called the
Sons of Heth. Gen 23:3,20.
Children of Heth. Gen 23:5.
One of the seven nations of Canaan. Deut 7:1.
Dwelt in Hebron. Gen 23:2,3,19.
Governed by kings. 1 Kin 10:29; 2 Kin 7:6.
Land of, promised to Israel. Gen 15:20; Ex 3:8.
Israel commanded to destroy. Deut 7:1,2,24.
Part of their land given to Caleb. Josh 14:13.
Not entirely destroyed by Israel. Judg 3:5.
The remnant of, made tributary in the reign of Solomon. 1 Kin 9:20,21.
Luz built in the country of. Judg 1:26.
Intermarriages with, by
Esau. Gen 36:2.
Solomon. 1 Kin 11:1,2.
Israel after conquest of Canaan. Judg 3:5,6.
Israelites after the captivity. Ezra 9:1.
Descent from, illustrative of the degradation of the Jews. Ezek 16:3.
Remarkable persons of
Ephron. Gen 49:30.
Abimelech. 1 Sam 26:6.
Uriah. 2 Sam 11:6,21.

Hivites.

Descended from Canaan. Gen 10:15,17.
Supposed to be the ancient Avim, or Avites. Deut 2:33; Josh 13:3.
One of the seven nations of Canaan. Deut 7:1.
Dwelt near Lebanon. Judg 3:3.
The Shechemites a people of. Gen 34:2.
The Gibeonites a people of. Josh 9:3,7.
Esau intermarried with. Gen 36:2.
Land of, promised to Israel. Ex 3:8; 23:23.
Israel commanded to destroy. Deut 7:1,2,24.
A part of, left to prove Israel. Judg 3:3.
Remnant of, made tributary in the reign of Solomon. 1 Kin 9:20,21.

Holiness.

Commanded. Lev 11:45; 20:7; Eph 5:8; Col 3:12; Rom 12:1.
Christ
Desires, for his people. John 17:17.
Effects, in his people. Eph 5:25-27.
An example of. Heb 7:26; 1 Pet 2:21,22.
The character of God, the standard of. Lev 19:2; 1 Pet 1:15,16; Eph 5:1.
The character of Christ, the standard of. Rom 8:29; 1 John 2:6; Phil 2:5.
The gospel the way of. Is 35:8.
Necessary to God's worship. Ps 24:3,4.
None shall see God without. Eph 5:5; Heb 12:14.
Saints
Elected to. Rom 8:29; Eph 1:4.
Called to. 1 Thess 4:7; 2 Tim 1:9.
New created in. Eph 4:24.
Possess. 1 Cor 3:17; Heb 3:1.
Have their fruit to. Rom 6:22.
Should follow after. Heb 12:14.
Should serve God in. Luke 1:74,75.
Should yield their members as instruments of. Rom 6:13,19.
Should present their bodies to God in. Rom 12:1.
Should have their conversation in. 1 Pet 1:15; 2 Pet 3:11.
Should continue in. Luke 1:75.
Should seek perfection in. 2 Cor 7:1.
Shall be presented to God in. Col 1:22; 1 Thess 3:13.
Shall continue in, for ever. Rev 22:11.
Behaviour of aged women should be as becomes. Titus 2:3.
Promise to women who continue in. 1 Tim 2:15.
Promised to the Church. Is 35:8; Obad 17; Zech 14:20,21.
Becoming to the Church. Ps 93:5.
The Church is the beauty of. 1 Chr 16:29; Ps 29:2.
The Word of God the means of producing. John 17:17; 2 Tim 3:16,17.
Is the result of
The manifestation of God's grace. Titus 2:3,11,12.
Subjection to God. Rom 6:22.
God's keeping. John 17:15.
Union with Christ. John 15:4,5; 17:9.
Required in prayer. 1 Tim 2:8.
Ministers should
Possess. Titus 1:8.
Avoid everything inconsistent with. Lev 21:6; Is 52:11.
Be examples of. 1 Tim 4:12.
Exhort to. Heb 12:14; 1 Pet 1:14-16.
Motives to
The glory of God. John 15:8; Phil 1:11.
The love of Christ. 2 Cor 5:14,15.
The mercies of God. Rom 12:1,2.
The dissolution of all things. 2 Pet 3:11.
Chastisements are intended to produce, in saints. Heb 12:10; James 1:2,3.
Should lead to separation from the wicked. Num 16:21,26; 2 Cor 6:17,18.
The wicked are without. 1 Tim 1:9; 2 Tim 3:2.
Exemplified
David. Ps 86:2.
Israel. Jer 2:3.
John the Baptist. Mark 6:20.
Prophets. Luke 1:70.
Paul. 1 Thess 2:10.
Wives of patriarchs. 1 Pet 3:5.

Holiness of God, The.

Is incomparable. Ex 15:11; 1 Sam 2:2.
Exhibited in his
Character. Ps 22:3; John 17:11.
Name. Is 57:15; Luke 1:49.
Words. Ps 60:6; Jer 23:9.
Works. Ps 145:17.
Kingdom. Ps 47:8; Matt 13:41; Rev 21:27; 1 Cor 6:9,10.
Is pledged for the fulfilment of
His promises. Ps 89:35.
His judgments. Amos 4:2.
Saints are commanded to imitate. Lev 11:44; 1 Pet 1:15,16.
Saints should praise. Ps 30:4.
Should produce reverential fear. Rev 15:4.
Requires holy service. Josh 24:19; Ps 93:5.
Heavenly hosts adore. Is 6:3; Rev 4:8.
Should be magnified. 1 Chr 16:10; Ps 48:1; 99:3,5; Rev 15:4.

Holy Spirit, the Comforter, The.

Proceeds from the Father. John 15:26.
Given
By the Father. John 14:16.
By Christ. Is 61:3.
Through Christ's intercession. John 14:16.
Sent in the name of Christ. John 14:26.
Sent by Christ from the Father. John 15:26; 16:7.
As such he
Communicates joy to saints. Rom 14:17; Gal 5:22; 1 Thess 1:6.
Edifies the Church. Acts 9:31.
Testifies of Christ. John 15:26.
Imparts the love of God. Rom 5:3-5.
Imparts hope. Rom 15:13; Gal 5:5.
Teaches saints. John 14:26.
Dwells with, and in saints. John 14:17.
Abides for ever with saints. John 14:16.
Is known by saints. John 14:17.
The world cannot receive. John 14:17.

Holy Spirit, The, is God.

As Jehovah. Ex 17:7; Heb 3:7-9; Num 12:6; 2 Pet 1:21.
As Jehovah of hosts. Is 6:3,8-10; Acts 28:25.
As Jehovah, Most High. Ps 78:17,21; Acts 7:51.
Being invoked as Jehovah. Luke 2:26-29; Acts 4:23-25; 1:16,20; 2 Thess 3:5.
As called God. Acts 5:3,4.
As joined with the Father and the Son in the baptismal formula. Matt 28:19.
As eternal. Heb 9:14.

As omnipresent. Ps 139:7-13.
As omniscient. 1 Cor 2:10.
As omnipotent. Luke 1:35; Rom 15:19.
As the Spirit of glory and of God. 1 Pet 4:14.
As Creator. Gen 1:26,27; Job 33:4.
As equal to, and one with the Father. Matt 28:19; 2 Cor 13:14.
As Sovereign Disposer of all things. Dan 4:35; 1 Cor 12:6,11.
As Author of the new birth. John 3:5,6; 1 John 5:4.
As raising Christ from the dead. Acts 2:24; 1 Pet 3:18; Heb 13:20; Rom 1:4.
As inspiring Scripture. 2 Tim 3:16; 2 Pet 1:21.
As the source of wisdom. 1 Cor 12:8; Is 11:2; John 16:13; 14:26.
As the source of miraculous power. Matt 12:28; Luke 11:20; Acts 19:11; Rom 15:19.
As appointing and sending ministers. Acts 13:2,4; 9:38; 20:28.
As directing where the gospel should be preached. Acts 16:6,7,10.
As dwelling in saints. John 14:17; 1 Cor 14:25; 3:16; 6:19.
As Comforter of the Church. Acts 9:31; 2 Cor 1:3.
As sanctifying the Church. Ezek 37:28; Rom 15:16.
As the Witness. Heb 10:15; 1 John 5:9.
As convincing of sin, of righteousness, and of judgment. John 16:8-11.

HOLY SPIRIT, THE PERSONALITY OF.

He creates and gives life. Job 33:4.
He appoints and commissions ministers. Is 48:16; Acts 13:2; 20:28.
He directs ministers where to preach. Acts 8:29; 10:19,20.
He directs ministers where not to preach. Acts 16:6,7.
He instructs ministers what to preach. 1 Cor 2:13.
He spoke in, and by, the prophets. Acts 1:16; 1 Pet 1:11,12; 2 Pet 1:21.
He strives with sinners. Gen 6:3.
He reproves. John 16:8.
He comforts. Acts 9:31.
He helps our infirmities. Rom 8:26.
He teaches. John 14:26; 1 Cor 12:3.
He guides. John 16:13.
He sanctifies. Rom 15:16; 1 Cor 6:11.
He testifies of Christ. John 15:26.
He glorifies Christ. John 16:14.
He has a power of his own. Rom 15:13.
He searches all things. Rom 11:33,34; 1 Cor 2:10,11.
He works according to his own will. 1 Cor 12:11.
He dwells with saints. John 14:17.
He can be grieved. Eph 4:30.
He can be vexed. Is 63:10.
He can be resisted. Acts 7:51.
He can be tempted. Acts 5:9.

HOLY SPIRIT, THE TEACHER, THE.

Promised. Prov 1:23.
As the Spirit of wisdom. Is 11:2; 40:13,14.
Given
In answer to prayer. Eph 1:16,17.
To saints. Neh 9:20; 1 Cor 2:12,13.
Necessity for. 1 Cor 2:9,10.
As such he
Reveals the things of God. 1 Cor 2:10,13.
Reveals the things of Christ. John 16:14.
Reveals the future. Luke 2:26; Acts 21:11.
Brings the words of Christ to remembrance. John 14:26.
Directs in the way of godliness. Is 30:21; Ezek 36:27.
Teaches saints to answer persecutors. Mark 13:11; Luke 12:12.
Enables ministers to teach. 1 Cor 12:8.
Guides into all truth. John 14:26; 16:13.
Directs the decisions of the Church. Acts 15:28.
Attend to the instruction of. Rev 2:7,11,29.
The natural man will not receive the things of. 1 Cor 2:14.

HOLY LAND.

Extremely fruitful. Ex 3:8; Num 13:27; Deut 8:7-9; 11:10-12.
Abounded in minerals. Deut 8:9; 33:25.
Called
The land. Lev 26:42; Luke 4:25.
The Lord's land. Hos 9:3.
Land of Canaan. Gen 11:31; Lev 14:34.
Land of Israel. 1 Sam 13:19; Matt 2:20,21.
Land of Judah. Is 26:1.
Land of the Hebrews. Gen 40:15.
Land of promise. Heb 11:9.
Land of Immanuel. Is 8:8.
Pleasant land. Ps 106:24; Dan 8:9.
Good land. Num 14:7; Deut 3:25.
Glorious land. Dan 11:16.
Palestine. Ex 15:14; Is 14:29,31.
Original inhabitants of, expelled for wickedness. Gen 15:16; Ex 23:23; Lev 18:25; Deut 18:12.
Promised to
Abraham. Gen 12:7; 13:15; 17:8.
Isaac. Gen 26:3.
Jacob. Gen 28:13,15; 35:12.
Given by covenant to Israel. Ex 6:4.
Extent of
As promised. Gen 15:18; Deut 1:7; Josh 1:4.
As at first divided. Num 34:1-12.
Under Solomon. 1 Kin 4:21,24; 2 Chr 9:26.
Twelve men sent to spy. Num 13:1-33.
Conquered by Joshua. Josh 6:1-12:24.
Divided by lot. Num 34:16-29; Josh 13:7-14.
Allotment of, specified. Josh 14:1-19:51.
All inheritances in, inalienable. Lev 25:10,23.
A sabbath of rest appointed for. Lev 25:2-5.
Obedience the condition of continuing in. Lev 26:3; Deut 5:33; 11:16,17,22-25.
Divided into
Twelve provinces by Solomon. 1 Kin 4:7-19.
Two kingdoms in the time of Rehoboam. 1 Kin 11:35,36; 12:19,20.
Four provinces by the Romans. Luke 3:1.
Numerous population of, in Solomon's reign. 1 Kin 3:8; 2 Chr 1:9.
Extensive commerce of, in Solomon's reign. 1 Kin 9:26-28; 10:22-29.
Prosperity of, in Solomon's reign. 1 Kin 4:20.
Was the burial place of the patriarchs. Gen 49:29-31; 50:13,25; Josh 24:32.
A type of the rest that remains for saints. Heb 4:1,2,9; 1 Pet 1:4.

HOLY OF HOLIES.

Divided from the outward tabernacle by a vail. Ex 26:31-33.
Was called the
Sanctuary. Lev 4:6; Ps 20:2.
Holy sanctuary. Lev 16:33.
Holy place. Ex 28:29; Lev 16:2,3.
Most holy place. Ex 26:31-33.
Holiest of all. Heb 9:3.
Oracle. 1 Kin 6:5,16,20.
Contained
Ark of testimony. Ex 26:33; 40:3,21.
Mercy-seat. Ex 26:34.
Cherubim. Ex 25:18-22; 1 Kin 6:23-28.
Golden censer. Heb 9:4.
Pot of manna. Ex 16:33; Heb 9:4.
Aaron's rod. Num 17:10; Heb 9:4.
A written copy of the divine law. Deut 31:26; 2 Kin 22:8.
God appeared in. Ex 25:22; Lev 16:2.
The high priest
Not to enter, at all times. Lev 16:2.
Alone to enter, once a year. Heb 9:7.
Entered, in ordinary priest's dress. Lev 16:4.
Entered, not without blood of atonement. Lev 16:14,15; Heb 9:7.
Offered incense in. Lev 16:12.
Made atonement for. Lev 16:15,16,20,33.
The priests allowed to enter, and prepare the holy things for removal. Num 4:5.
Laid open to view at Christ's death. Matt 27:51.
A type of heaven. Ps 102:19; Heb 9:12,13,24.
Saints have boldness to enter the true. Heb 10:19.

HOMICIDE.

Distinguished from murder. Ex 21:13,14; Num 35:16-21,25.
Justifiable, described as
Killing persons condemned by law. Gen 9:6; Ex 35:2; Lev 24:16.
Killing a thief in the night. Ex 22:2.
Killing enemies in battle. Num 31:7,8.
Killing a manslayer by next of kin. Num 35:27.
Unjustifiable, described as
Killing without enmity. Num 35:22.
Killing without lying in wait. Ex 21:13; Num 35:22.
Killing by accident. Num 35:23; Deut 19:5.
The avenger of blood might slay those guilty of unjustifiable. Num 35:19,27.

Protection afforded in the cities of refuge to those guilty of unjustified. Num 35:11,15.
Confinement in the city of refuge the punishment for unjustifiable. Num 35:25,28.

Honey.

God the giver of. Ps 81:16; Ezek 16:19.
Gathered and prepared by bees. Judg 14:18.
Found in
- Rocks. Deut 32:13; Ps 81:16.
- Woods. 1 Sam 14:25,26; Jer 41:8.
- Carcases of dead animals. Judg 14:8.

Sweetness of. Judg 14:18.
In the honeycomb sweetest and most valuable. Prov 16:24; 24:13.
Abounded in
- Egypt. Num 16:13.
- Assyria. 2 Kin 18:32.
- Canaan. Ex 3:8; Lev 20:24; Deut 8:8.

Esteemed a wholesome food. Prov 24:13.
Moderation needful in the use of. Prov 25:16,27.
Loathed by those who are full. Prov 27:7.
Was eaten
- Plain. 1 Sam 14:25,26,29.
- With the honeycomb. Song 5:1; Luke 24:42.
- With milk. Song 4:11.
- With butter. Is 7:15,22.
- With locusts. Matt 3:4; Mark 1:6.
- Mixed with flour. Ex 16:31; Ezek 16:13.

Not to be offered with any sacrifice. Lev 2:11.
Firstfruits of, offered to God. 2 Chr 31:5.
Often sent as a present. Gen 43:11; 1 Kin 14:3.
Exported from Canaan. Ezek 27:17.
Illustrative of
- The word of God. Ps 19:10; 119:103.
- Wisdom. Prov 24:13,14.
- Holy speech of saints. Song 4:11.
- Pleasant words. Prov 16:24.
- Lips of a strange woman. Prov 5:3.

Hope.

In God. Ps 39:7; 1 Pet 1:21.
In Christ. 1 Cor 15:19; 1 Tim 1:1.
In God's promises. Acts 26:6,7; Titus 1:2.
In the mercy of God. Ps 33:18.
Is the work of the Holy Spirit. Rom 15:13; Gal 5:5.
Obtained through
- Grace. 2 Thess 2:16.
- The word. Ps 119:81.
- Patience and comfort of the Scriptures. Rom 15:4.
- The gospel. Col 1:5,23.
- Faith. Rom 5:1,2; Gal 5:5.

The result of experience. Rom 5:4.
A better hope brought in by Christ. Heb 7:19.
Described as
- Good. 2 Thess 2:16.
- Lively. 1 Pet 1:3.
- Sure and steadfast. Heb 6:19.
- Gladdening. Prov 10:28.
- Blessed. Titus 2:13.

Makes not ashamed. Rom 5:5.
Triumphs over difficulties. Rom 4:18.
Is an encouragement to boldness in preaching. 2 Cor 3:12.
Saints
- Are called to. Eph 4:4.
- Rejoice in. Rom 5:2; 12:12.
- Have all, the same. Eph 4:4.
- Have, in death. Prov 14:32.
- Should abound in. Rom 15:13.
- Should look for the object of. Titus 2:13.
- Should not be ashamed of. Ps 119:16.
- Should hold fast. Heb 3:6.
- Should not be moved from. Col 1:23.
- Should continue in. Ps 71:14; 1 Pet 1:13.

Connected with faith and love. 1 Cor 13:13.
Objects of
- Salvation. 1 Thess 5:8.
- Righteousness. Gal 5:5.
- Christ's glorious appearing. Titus 2:13.
- A resurrection. Acts 23:6; 24:15.
- Eternal life. Titus 1:2; 3:7.
- Glory. Rom 5:2; Col 1:27.

Leads to purity. 1 John 3:3.
Leads to patience. Rom 8:25; 1 Thess 1:3.
Seek for full assurance of. Heb 6:11.
Be ready to give an answer concerning. 1 Pet 3:15.
Encouragement to. Hos 2:15; Zech 9:12.
Encourage others to. Ps 130:7.
Happiness of. Ps 146:5.
Life is the season of. Eccl 9:4; Is 38:18.
The wicked have no ground for. Eph 2:12.
Of the wicked
- Is in their worldly possessions. Job 31:24.
- Shall make them ashamed. Is 20:5,6; Zech 9:5.
- Shall perish. Job 8:13; 11:20; Prov 10:28.
- Shall be extinguished in death. Job 27:8.

Illustrated by
- An Anchor. Heb 6:19.
- A helmet. 1 Thess 5:8.

Exemplified
- David. Ps 39:7.
- Paul. Acts 24:15.
- Abraham. Rom 4:18.
- Thessalonians. 1 Thess 1:3.

Horns.

Natural weapons on heads of animals. Dan 7:20.
Animals with, mentioned
- The ox. Ps 69:31.
- The ram. Gen 22:13.
- The goat. Dan 8:5.
- The unicorn. Ps 22:21; 92:10.

Tusks of the elephant so called. Ezek 27:15.
Used offensively. Ex 21:29; Ezek 34:21.
Were used
- For holding oil. 1 Sam 16:1; 1 Kin 1:39.
- As musical instruments. Josh 6:4,5; 1 Chr 25:5.

Representations of, placed at the four corners of the altars. Ex 27:2; 30:2.
Wearing of, alluded to. Ps 75:5,10.
Illustrative
- Of power of God. Ps 18:2; Hab 3:4.
- Of power of Christ. Luke 1:69; Rev 5:6.
- Of power of Ephraim, etc. Deut 33:17.
- Of power of the wicked. Ps 22:21; 75:10.
- Of kings. Dan 7:7,8,24; 8:3,5,20.
- Of antichristian powers. Rev 13:1; 17:3,7.
- (Budding of,) of the commencement or revival of a nation. Ps 132:17; Ezek 29:21.
- (Raising up,) of arrogance. Ps 75:4,5.
- (Exalting,) of increase of power and glory. 1 Sam 2:1,10; Ps 89:17,24; 92:10; 112:9.
- (Pushing with,) of conquests. Deut 33:17; 1 Kin 22:11; Mic 4:13.
- (Bringing down,) of degradation. Job 16:15.
- (Cutting off,) of destruction of power. Ps 75:10; Jer 48:25; Lam 2:3.

Horse, The.

Endued with strength by God. Job 39:19.
Described as
- Strong. Ps 33:17; 147:10.
- Swift. Is 30:16; Jer 4:13; Hab 1:8.
- Fearless. Job 39:20,22.
- Fierce and impetuous. Job 39:21,24.
- Warlike in disposition. Job 39:21; Jer 8:6.
- Sure footed. Is 63:13.

Want of understanding in, alluded to. Ps 32:9.
Hard hoofs of, alluded to. Is 5:28.
Loud snorting of, alluded to. Jer 8:16; Job 39:20.
Colours of, mentioned
- White. Zech 1:8; 6:3; Rev 6:2.
- Black. Zech 6:2,6; Rev 6:5.
- Red. Zech 1:8; 6:2; Rev 6:4.
- Speckled. Zech 1:8.
- Bay. Zech 6:3,7.
- Grisled. Zech 6:3,6.
- Pale or ash colour. Rev 6:8.

Fed on grain and herbs. 1 Kin 4:23; 18:5.
Used for
- Mounting cavalry. Ex 14:9; 1 Sam 13:5.
- Drawing chariots. Mic 1:13; Zech 6:2.
- Bearing burdens. Ezra 2:66; Neh 7:68.
- Hunting. Job 39:18.
- Conveying posts, etc. 2 Kin 9:17-19; Esth 8:10.

Kings and princes rode on. Esth 6:8-11; Ezek 23:23.
Governed by bit and bridle. Ps 32:9; James 3:3.
Urged on by whips. Prov 26:3.
Adorned with bells on the neck. Zech 14:20.
Numbers of, kept for war. Jer 51:27; Ezek 26:10.
Prepared and trained for war. Prov 21:31.
In battle protected by armour. Jer 46:4.
Vanity of trusting to. Ps 33:17; Amos 2:15.
The Jews
- Forbidden to multiply. Deut 17:16.
- Imported from Egypt. 1 Kin 10:28,29.

Multiplied in Solomon's reign. 1 Kin 4:26.
Condemned for multiplying. Is 2:7.
Not to trust in. Hos 14:3.
Condemned for trusting to. Is 30:16; 31:3.
Brought back many, from Babylon. Ezra 2:66.
Notice of early traffic in. Gen 47:17.
Sold in fairs and markets. Ezek 27:14; Rev 18:13.
Often suffered
From blindness. Zech 12:4.
From plague. Zech 14:15.
From murrain. Ex 9:3.
From bites of serpents. Gen 49:17.
In the hoof from prancing. Judg 5:22.
In battle. Jer 51:21; Hag 2:22.
Dedicated to the sun by idolaters. 2 Kin 23:11.
Illustrative of
Beauty of the church. Song 1:9; Zech 10:3.
Glorious and triumphant deliverance of the church. Is 63:13.
A dull headstrong disposition. Ps 32:9.
Impetuosity of the wicked in sin. Jer 8:6.

HOSPITALITY.

Commanded. Rom 12:13; 1 Pet 4:9.
Required in ministers. 1 Tim 3:2; Titus 1:8.
A test of Christian character. 1 Tim 5:10.
Specially to be shown to
Strangers. Heb 13:2.
The poor. Is 58:7; Luke 14:13.
Enemies. 2 Kin 6:22,23; Rom 12:20.
Encouragement to. Luke 14:14; Heb 13:2.
Exemplified
Melchizedek. Gen 14:18.
Abraham. Gen 18:3-8.
Lot. Gen 19:2,3.
Laban. Gen 24:31.
Jethro. Ex 2:20.
Manoah. Judg 13:15.
Samuel. 1 Sam 9:22.
David. 2 Sam 6:19.
Barzillai. 2 Sam 19:32.
Shunammite. 2 Kin 4:8.
Nehemiah. Neh 5:17.
Job. Job 31:17,32.
Zacchaeus. Luke 19:6.
Samaritans. John 4:40.
Lydia. Acts 16:15.
Jason. Acts 17:7.
Mnason. Acts 21:16.
People of Melita. Acts 28:2.
Publius. Acts 28:7.
Gaius. 3 John 5,6.

HOUSES.

Antiquity of. Gen 12:1; 19:3.
Deep and solid foundations required for. Matt 7:24; Luke 6:48.
Sometimes built without foundation. Matt 7:26; Luke 6:49.
Built of
Clay. Job 4:19.
Bricks. Ex 1:11-14; Is 9:10.
Stone and wood. Lev 14:40,42; Hab 2:11.
Hewn or cut stone. Is 3:10; Amos 5:11.
In cities, built in streets. Gen 19:2; Josh 2:19.
Often built on city walls. Josh 2:15; 2 Cor 11:33.
The flat roofs of
Surrounded with battlements. Deut 22:8.
Had often booths on them. 2 Sam 16:22; Neh 8:16; Prov 2:19.
Had often idolatrous altars on them. 2 Kin 23:12; Jer 19:13; Zeph 1:5.
Used for drying flax. Josh 2:6.
Used for exercise. 2 Sam 11:2; Dan 4:29.
Used for devotion. Acts 10:9.
Used for making proclamations. Luke 12:3.
Used for secret conference. 1 Sam 9:25,26.
Resorted to in grief. Is 15:3; Jer 48:38.
Often covered with weak grass. Ps 129:6,7.
Accessible from the outside. Matt 24:17.
The courts of, large and used as apartments. Esth 1:5; Luke 5:19.
Entered by a gate or door. Gen 43:19; Ex 12:22; Luke 16:20; Acts 10:17.
Doors of, low and small for safety. Prov 17:19.
Doors of, how fastened. 2 Sam 13:18; Song 5:5; Luke 11:7.
Admission to, gained by knocking at the door. Acts 12:13; Rev 3:20.
Walls of, plastered. Lev 14:42,43.
Serpents often lodged in walls of. Amos 5:19.
Custom of fastening nails, etc., in walls of, alluded to. Eccl 12:11; Is 22:23.
Had often several stories. Ezek 41:16; Acts 20:9.
Divided into apartments. Gen 43:30; Is 26:20.
Apartments of, were often
Large and airy. Jer 22:14.
Ceiled and painted. Jer 22:14; Hag 1:4.
Inlaid with ivory. 1 Kin 22:39; Amos 3:15.
Hung with rich tapestries. Esth 1:6.
Warmed with fires. Jer 36:22; John 18:18.
Upper apartments of, the best, and used for entertainments. Mark 14:15.
Had often detached apartments for secrecy and for strangers. Judg 3:20-23; 2 Kin 4:10,11; 9:2,3.
Lighted by windows. 1 Kin 7:4.
Street windows of, high and dangerous. 2 Kin 1:2; 9:30,33; Acts 20:9.
Of the rich
Great. Is 5:9; Amos 6:11; 2 Tim 2:20.
Goodly. Deut 8:12.
Pleasant. Ezek 26:12; Mic 2:9.
Of brick or clay
Plastered. Ezek 13:10,11.
Easily broken through. Job 24:16; Ezek 12:5.
Often swept away by torrents. Ezek 13:13,14.
When finished were usually dedicated. Deut 20:5; Ps 30:1.
For summer residence. Amos 3:15.
Liable to leprosy. Lev 14:34-53.
Not to be coveted. Ex 20:17; Mic 2:2.
Were hired. Acts 28:30.
Were mortgaged. Neh 5:3.
Were sold. Acts 4:34.
Law respecting the sale of. Lev 25:29-33.
Of criminals, desolated. Dan 2:5; 3:29.
Desolation of, threatened as a punishment. Is 5:9; 13:16,21,22; Ezek 16:41; 26:12.
Often broken down to repair city walls before sieges. Is 22:10.
Illustrative
Of the body. Job 4:19; 2 Cor 5:1.
Of the grave. Job 30:23.
Of the church. Heb 3:6; 1 Pet 2:5.
Of saints' inheritance. John 14:2; 2 Cor 5:1.
(On sand,) of the delusive hope of hypocrites. Matt 7:24,25.
(On a rock,) of the hope of saints. Matt 7:24,25.
(Insecurity of,) of earthly trust. Matt 6:19,20.
(Building of,) of great prosperity. Is 65:21; Ezek 28:26.
(Built and not inhabited,) of calamity. Deut 28:30; Amos 5:11; Zeph 1:13.
(To inhabit those, built by others,) of abundant feelings. Deut 6:10,11.

HUMAN NATURE OF CHRIST, THE.

Was necessary to his mediatorial office. 1 Tim 2:5; Heb 2:17; Gal 4:4,5; 1 Cor 15:21; Rom 6:15,19.
Is proved by his
Conception in the Virgin's womb. Matt 1:18; Luke 1:31.
Birth. Matt 1:16,25; 2:2; Luke 2:7,11.
Partaking of flesh and blood. John 1:14; Heb 2:14.
Having a human soul. Matt 26:38; Luke 23:46; Acts 2:31.
Circumcision. Luke 2:21.
Increase in wisdom and stature. Luke 2:52.
Weeping. Luke 19:41; John 11:35.
Hungering. Matt 4:2; 21:18.
Thirsting. John 4:7; 19:28.
Sleeping. Matt 8:24; Mark 4:38.
Being subject to weariness. John 4:6.
Being a man of sorrows. Is 53:3,4; Luke 22:44; John 11:33; 12:27.
Being buffeted. Matt 26:67; Luke 22:64.
Enduring indignities. Luke 23:11.
Being scourged. Matt 27:26; Luke 22:64.
Being nailed to the cross. Ps 22:16; Luke 23:33.
Death. John 19:30.
Side being pierced. John 19:34.
Burial. Matt 27:59,60; Mark 15:46.
Resurrection. Acts 3:15; 2 Tim 2:8.
Was like our own in all things except sin. Acts 3:22; Phil 2:7,8; Heb 2:17.
Was without sin. Heb 7:26,28; 1 John 3:5; 1 Pet 2:22; Heb 4:15; John 18:38; 8:46.
Was submitted to the evidence of the senses. Luke 24:39; John 20:27; 1 John 1:1,2.

Was of the seed of
The woman. Gen 3:15; Is 7:4; Jer 31:22; Luke 1:31; Gal 4:4.
Abraham. Gen 22:18; Gal 3:16; Heb 2:16.
David. 2 Sam 7:12,16; Ps 89:35,36; Jer 23:5; Matt 22:42; Mark 10:47; Acts 2:30; 13:23; Rom 1:3.
Genealogy of. Matt 1:1-17; Luke 3:23-38.
Attested by himself. Matt 8:20; 16:13.
Confession of, a test of belonging to God. John 4:2.
Acknowledged by men. Mark 6:3; John 7:27; 19:5; Acts 2:22.
Denied by Antichrist. 1 John 4:3; 2 John 7.

Humility.

Necessary to the service of God. Mic 6:8.
Christ an example of. Matt 11:29; John 13:14,15; Phil 2:5-8.
A characteristic of saints. Ps 34:2.
Those who have
Regarded by God. Ps 138:6; Is 66:2.
Heard by God. Ps 9:12; Is 10:17.
Enjoy the presence of God. Is 57:15.
Delivered by God. Job 22:29.
Lifted up by God. James 4:10.
Exalted by God. Luke 14:11; 18:14.
Are greatest in Christ's kingdom. Matt 18:4; 20:26-28.
Receive more grace. Prov 3:34; James 4:6.
Upheld by honour. Prov 18:12; 29:23.
Is before honour. Prov 15:33.
Leads to riches, honour, and life. Prov 22:4.
Saints should
Put on. Col 3:12.
Be clothed with. 1 Pet 5:5.
Walk with. Eph 4:1,2.
Beware of false. Col 2:18,23.
Afflictions intended to produce. Lev 26:41; Deut 8:3; Lam 3:20.
Want of, condemned. 2 Chr 33:23; 36:12; Jer 44:10; Dan 5:22.
Temporal judgments averted by. 2 Chr 7:14; 12:6,7.
Excellency of. Prov 16:19.
Blessedness of. Matt 5:3.
Exemplified
Abraham. Gen 18:27.
Jacob. Gen 32:10.
Moses. Ex 3:11; 4:10.
Joshua. Josh 7:6.
Gideon. Judg 6:15.
David. 1 Chr 29:14.
Hezekiah. 2 Chr 32:26.
Manasseh. 2 Chr 33:12.
Josiah. 2 Chr 34:27.
Job. Job 40:4; 42:6.
Isaiah. Is 6:5.
Jeremiah. Jer 1:6.
John the Baptist. Matt 3:14.
Centurion. Matt 8:8.
Woman of Canaan. Matt 15:27.
Elizabeth. Luke 1:43.
Peter. Luke 5:8.
Paul. Acts 20:19.

Humility of Christ, The.

Declared by himself. Matt 11:29.
Exhibited in his
Taking our nature. Phil 2:7; Heb 2:16.
Birth. Luke 2:4-7.
Subjection to his parents. Luke 2:51.
Station in life. Matt 13:55; John 9:29.
Poverty. Luke 9:58; 2 Cor 8:9.
Partaking of our infirmities. Heb 4:15; 5:7.
Submitting to ordinances. Matt 3:13-15.
Becoming a servant. Matt 20:28; Luke 22:27; Phil 2:7.
Associating with the despised. Matt 9:10,11; Luke 15:1,2.
Refusing honours. John 5:41; 6:15.
Entry into Jerusalem. Zech 9:9; Matt 21:5,7.
Washing his disciples' feet. John 13:5.
Obedience. John 6:38; Heb 10:9.
Submitting to sufferings. Is 50:6; 53:7; Acts 8:32; Matt 26:37-39.
Exposing himself to reproach and contempt. Ps 22:6; 69:9; Rom 15:3; Is 53:3.
Death. John 10:15,17,18; Phil 2:8; Heb 12:2.
Saints should imitate. Phil 2:5-8.
On account of, he was despised. Mark 6:3; John 9:29.
His exaltation, the result of. Phil 2:9.

Husbands.

Should have but one wife. Gen 2:24; Mark 10:6-8; 1 Cor 7:2-4.
Have authority over their wives. Gen 3:16; 1 Cor 11:3; Eph 5:23.
Duty of, to wives
To respect them. 1 Pet 3:7.
To love them. Eph 5:25-33; Col 3:19.
To regard them as themselves. Gen 2:23; Matt 19:5.
To be faithful to them. Prov 5:19; Mal 2:14,15.
To dwell with them for life. Gen 2:24; Matt 19:3-9.
To comfort them. 1 Sam 1:8.
To consult with them. Gen 31:4-7.
Not to leave them, though unbelieving. 1 Cor 7:11,12,14,16.
Duties of, not to interfere with their duties to Christ. Luke 14:26; Matt 19:29.
Good—Exemplified
Isaac. Gen 24:67.
Elkanah. 1 Sam 1:4,5.
Bad—Exemplified
Solomon. 1 Kin 11:1.
Ahasuerus. Esth 1:10,11.

Hyke or Upper Garment.

Law respecting fringes of. Num 15:38; Deut 22:12.
Used by the poor as a covering by night. Ex 22:26,27; Deut 24:13.
Burdens often bound up in. Ex 12:34.
The skirts of, used to hold things in. 2 Kin 4:39; Neh 5:13; Hag 2:12; Luke 6:38.
Probably used by women as a vail. Ruth 3:15.
Required to be girt up
For running. 1 Kin 18:46.
For labour. Luke 17:8.
Often laid aside. Matt 24:18; Mark 10:50.
The Jews said to be naked without. 2 Sam 6:20; Mark 14:51,52; John 21:7.
Was the garment
Rent in token of anger. Matt 26:65.
Rent in token of grief. Joel 2:13.
Of Samuel rent by Saul. 1 Sam 15:27.
Of Saul which David cut. 1 Sam 24:4,5.
Of Jeroboam rent by Ahijah. 1 Kin 11:30.
Laid aside by Christ. John 13:4.
Spread before Christ by the Jews. Matt 21:8.
The Jews condemned for making broad the borders of. Matt 23:5.

Hypocrites.

God knows and detects. Is 29:15,16.
Christ knew and detected. Matt 22:18.
God has no pleasure in. Is 9:17.
Shall not come before God. Job 13:16.
Described as
Wilfully blind. Matt 23:17,19,26.
Vile. Is 32:6.
Self-righteous. Is 65:5; Luke 18:11.
Covetous. Ezek 33:31; 2 Pet 2:3.
Ostentatious. Matt 5:2,5,16; 23:5.
Censorious. Matt 7:3-5; Luke 13:14,15.
Regarding tradition more than the word of God. Matt 15:1-3.
Exact in minor, but neglecting important duties. Matt 23:23,24.
Having but a form of godliness. 2 Tim 3:5.
Seeking only outward purity. Luke 11:39.
Professing but not practising. Ezek 33:31,32; Matt 23:3; Rom 2:17-23.
Using but lip-worship. Is 29:13; Matt 15:8.
Glorying in appearance only. 2 Cor 5:12.
Trusting in privileges. Jer 7:4; Matt 3:9.
Apparently zealous in the things of God. Is 58:2.
Zealous in making proselytes. Matt 23:15.
Devouring widows' houses. Matt 23:14.
Loving pre-eminence. Matt 23:6,7.
Worship of, not acceptable to God. Is 1:11-15; 58:3-5; Matt 15:9.
Joy of, but for a moment. Job 20:5.
Hope of perishes. Job 8:13; 27:8,9.
Heap up wrath. Job 36:13.
Fearfulness shall surprise. Is 33:14.
Destroy others by slander. Prov 11:9.
In power, are a snare. Job 34:30.
The Apostasy to abound with. 1 Tim 4:2.
Beware the principles of. Luke 12:1.
Spirit of, hinders growth in grace. 1 Pet 2:1.
Woe to. Is 29:15; Matt 23:13.
Punishment of. Job 15:34; Is 10:6; Jer 42:20,22; Matt 24:51.
Illustrated. Matt 23:27,28; Luke 11:44.
Exemplified
Cain. Gen 4:3.
Absalom. 2 Sam 15:7,8.
The Jews. Jer 3:10.
Pharisees, etc. Matt 16:3.
Judas. Matt 26:49.
Herodians. Mark 12:13,15.

- Ananias. Acts 5:1-8.
- Simon. Acts 8:13-23.

Idleness and Sloth.

Forbidden. Rom 12:11; Heb 6:12.
Produce apathy. Prov 12:27; 26:15.
Akin to extravagance. Prov 18:9.
Accompanied by conceit. Prov 26:16.
Lead to
- Poverty. Prov 10:4; 20:13.
- Want. Prov 20:4; 24:34.
- Hunger. Prov 19:15; 20:13.
- Bondage. Prov 12:24.
- Disappointment. Prov 13:4; 21:25.
- Ruin. Prov 24:30,31; Eccl 10:18.
- Tattling and meddling. 1 Tim 5:13.

Effects of, afford instruction to others. Prov 24:30-32.
Remonstrance against. Prov 6:6,9.
False excuses for. Prov 20:4; 22:13.
Illustrated. Prov 26:14; Matt 25:18,26.
Exemplified
- Watchmen. Is 56:10.
- Athenians. Acts 17:21.
- Thessalonians. 2 Thess 3:11.

Idolatry.

Forbidden. Ex 20:2,3; Deut 5:7.
Consists in
- Bowing down to images. Ex 20:5; Deut 5:9.
- Worshipping images. Is 44:17; Dan 3:5,10,15.
- Sacrificing to images. Ps 106:38; Acts 7:41.
- Worshipping other gods. Deut 30:17; Ps 81:9.
- Swearing by other gods. Ex 23:13; Josh 23:7.
- Walking after other gods. Deut 8:19.
- Speaking in the name of other gods. Deut 18:20.
- Looking to other gods. Hos 3:1.
- Serving other gods. Deut 7:4; Jer 5:19.
- Fearing other gods. 2 Kin 17:35.
- Sacrificing to other gods. Ex 22:20.
- Worshipping the true God by an image, etc. Ex 32:4-6; Ps 106:19,20.
- Worshipping angels. Col 2:18.
- Worshipping the host of heaven. Deut 4:19; 17:3.
- Worshipping demons. Matt 4:9-10; Rev 9:20.
- Worshipping dead men. Ps 106:28.
- Setting up idols in the heart. Ezek 14:3,4.
- Covetousness. Eph 5:5; Col 3:5.
- Sensuality. Phil 3:19.

Is changing the glory of God into an image. Rom 1:23; Acts 17:29.
Is changing the truth of God into a lie. Rom 1:25; Is 44:20.
Is a work of the flesh. Gal 5:19,20.
Incompatible with the service of God. Gen 35:2,3; Josh 24:23; 1 Sam 7:3; 1 Kin 18:21; 2 Cor 6:15,16.
Described as
- An abomination to God. Deut 7:25.
- Hateful to God. Deut 16:22; Jer 44:4.
- Vain and foolish. Ps 115:4-8; Is 44:19; Jer 10:3.
- Bloody. Ezek 23:39.
- Abominable. 1 Pet 4:3.
- Unprofitable. Judg 10:14; Is 46:7.
- Irrational. Acts 17:29; Rom 1:21-23.
- Defiling. Ezek 20:7; 36:18.

They who practise
- Forget God. Deut 8:19; Jer 18:15.
- Go astray from God. Ezek 44:10.
- Pollute the name of God. Ezek 20:39.
- Defile the sanctuary of God. Ezek 5:11.
- Are estranged from God. Ezek 14:5.
- Forsake God. 2 Kin 22:17; Jer 16:11.
- Hate God. 2 Chr 19:2,3.
- Provoke God. Deut 31:20; Is 65:3; Jer 25:6.
- Are vain in their imaginations. Rom 1:21.
- Are ignorant and foolish. Rom 1:21,22.
- Inflame themselves. Is 57:5.
- Hold fast their deceit. Jer 8:5.
- Carried away by it. 1 Cor 12:2.
- Go after it in heart. Ezek 20:16.
- Are mad upon it. Jer 50:38.
- Boast of it. Ps 97:7.
- Have fellowship with devils. Hos 4:12.
- Ask counsel of their idols. Hos 4:12.
- Look to idols for deliverance. Is 44:17; 45:20.
- Swear by their idols. Amos 8:14.

Objects of, numerous. 1 Cor 8:5.
Objects of described as
- Strange gods. Gen 35:2,4; Josh 24:20.
- Other gods. Judg 2:12,17; 1 Kin 14:9.
- New gods. Deut 32:17; Judg 5:8.
- Gods that cannot save. Is 45:20.
- Gods that have not made the heavens. Jer 10:11.
- No gods. Jer 5:7; Gal 4:8.
- Molten gods. Ex 34:17; Lev 19:4.
- Molten images. Deut 27:15; Hab 2:18.
- Graven images. Is 45:20; Hos 11:2.
- Senseless idols. Deut 4:28; Ps 115:5,7.
- Dumb idols. Hab 2:18.
- Dumb Stones. Hab 2:19.
- Stocks. Jer 3:9; Hos 4:12.
- Abominations. Is 44:19; Jer 32:34.
- Images of abomination. Ezek 7:20.
- Idols of abomination. Ezek 16:36.
- Stumbling blocks. Ezek 14:3.
- Teachers of lies. Hab 2:18.
- Wind and confusion. Is 41:29.
- Nothing. Is 41:24; 1 Cor 8:4.
- Helpless. Jer 10:5.
- Vanity. Jer 18:15.
- Vanities of the Gentiles. Jer 14:22.

Making idols for the purpose of, described and ridiculed. Is 44:10-20.
Obstinate sinners judicially given up to. Deut 4:28; 28:64; Hos 4:17.
Warnings against. Deut 4:15-19.
Exhortations to turn from. Ezek 14:6; 20:7; Acts 14:15.
Renounced on conversion. 1 Thess 1:9.
Led to abominable sins. Rom 1:26-32; Acts 15:20.
Saints should
- Keep from. Josh 23:7; 1 John 5:21.
- Flee from. 1 Cor 10:14.
- Not have anything connected with in their houses. Deut 7:26.
- Not partake of any thing connected with. 1 Cor 10:19,20.
- Not have religious intercourse with those who practise. Josh 23:7; 1 Cor 5:11.
- Not covenant with those who practise. Ex 34:12,15; Deut 7:2.
- Not intermarry with those who practise. Ex 34:16; Deut 7:3.
- Testify against. Acts 14:15; 19:26.
- Refuse to engage in, though threatened with death. Dan 3:18.

Saints preserved by God from. 1 Kin 19:18; Rom 11:4.
Saints refuse to receive the worship of. Acts 10:25,26; 14:11-15.
Angels refuse to receive the worship of. Rev 22:8,9.
Destruction of, promised. Ezek 36:25; Zech 13:2.
Everything connected with, should be destroyed. Ex 34:13; Deut 7:5; 2 Sam 5:21; 2 Kin 23:14.
Woe denounced against. Hab 2:19.
Curse denounced against. Deut 27:15.
Punishment of
- Judicial death. Deut 17:2-5.
- Dreadful judgments which end in death. Jer 8:2; 16:1-11.
- Banishment. Jer 8:3; Hos 8:5-8; Amos 5:26,27.
- Exclusion from heaven. 1 Cor 6:9,10; Eph 5:5; Rev 22:15.
- Eternal torments. Rev 14:9-11; 21:8.

Exemplified
- Israel. Ex 32:1; 2 Kin 17:12.
- Philistines. Judg 16:23.
- Micah. Judg 17:4,5.
- Jeroboam. 1 Kin 12:28.
- Maachah. 1 Kin 15:13.
- Ahab. 1 Kin 16:31.
- Jezebel. 1 Kin 18:19.
- Sennacherib. 2 Kin 19:37.
- Manasseh. 2 Kin 21:4-7.
- Amon. 2 Kin 21:21.
- Ahaz. 2 Chr 28:3.
- Judah. Jer 11:13.
- Nebuchadnezzar. Dan 3:1.
- Belshazzar. Dan 5:23.
- People of Lystra. Acts 14:11,12.
- Athenians. Acts 17:16.
- Ephesians. Acts 19:28.

Zeal against—Exemplified
- Asa. 1 Kin 15:12.
- Josiah. 2 Kin 23:5.
- Jehoshaphat. 2 Chr 17:6.
- Israel. 2 Chr 31:1.
- Manasseh. 2 Chr 33:15.

All forms of, forbidden by the law of Moses. Ex 20:4,5.
All heathen nations given up to. Ps 96:5; Rom 1:23,25; 1 Cor 12:2.
Led the heathen to think that their gods visited the earth in bodily shapes. Acts 14:11.
Led the heathen to consider their gods to have but a local influence. 1 Kin 20:23; 2 Kin 17:26.
Objects of
- The heavenly bodies. 2 Kin 23:5; Acts 7:42.
- Angels. Col 2:18.
- Departed spirits. 1 Sam 28:14,15.
- Earthly creatures. Rom 1:23.
- Images. Deut 29:17; Ps 115:4; Is 44:17.

Temples built for. Hos 8:14.
Altars raised for. 1 Kin 18:26; Hos 8:11.
Accompanied by feasts. 2 Kin 10:20; 1 Cor 10:27,28.

Objects of, worshipped
With sacrifices. Num 22:40; 2 Kin 10:24.
With libations. Is 57:6; Jer 19:13.
With incense. Jer 48:35.
With prayer. 1 Kin 18:26; Is 44:17.
With singing and dancing. Ex 32:18,19; 1 Kin 18:26; 1 Cor 10:7.
By bowing to them. 1 Kin 19:18; 2 Kin 5:18.
By kissing them. 1 Kin 19:18; Hos 13:2.
By kissing the hand to them. Job 31:26,27.
By cutting the flesh. 1 Kin 18:28.
By burning children. Deut 12:31; 2 Chr 33:6; Jer 19:4,5; Ezek 16:21.
In temples. 2 Kin 5:18.
On high places. Num 22:41; Jer 2:20.
In groves. Ex 34:13.
Under trees. Is 57:5; Jer 2:20.
In private houses. Judg 17:4,5.
On the tops of houses. 2 Kin 23:12; Zeph 1:5.
In secret places. Is 57:8.
Rites of, obscene and impure. Ex 32:25; Num 25:1-3; 2 Kin 17:9; Is 57:6,8,9; 1 Pet 4:3.
Divination connected with. 2 Chr 33:6.
Victims sacrificed in, often adorned with garlands. Acts 14:13.
Idols, mentioned in Scripture
Adrammelech. 2 Kin 17:31.
Anammelech. 2 Kin 17:31.
Ashima. 2 Kin 17:30.
Ashtoreth. Judg 2:13; 1 Kin 11:33.
Baal. Judg 2:11-13; 6:25.
Baal-berith. Judg 8:33; 9:4,46.
Baal-peor. Num 25:1-3.
Baalzebub. 2 Kin 1:2,16.
Baal-zephon. Ex 14:2.
Bel. Jer 50:2; 51:44.
Chemosh. Num 21:29; 1 Kin 11:33.
Chiun. Amos 5:26.
Dagon. Judg 16:23; 1 Sam 5:1-3.
Diana. Acts 19:24,27.
Huzzab. Nah 2:7.
Jupiter. Acts 14:12.
Mercury. Acts 14:12.
Molech or Milcom. Lev 18:21; 1 Kin 11:5,33.
Merodach. Jer 50:2.
Nergal. 2 Kin 17:30.
Nebo. Is 46:1.
Nibhaz and Tartak. 2 Kin 17:31.
Nisroch. 2 Kin 19:37.
Queen of heaven. Jer 44:17,25.
Remphan. Acts 7:43.
Rimmon. 2 Kin 5:18.
Succothbenoth. 2 Kin 17:30.
Tammuz. Ezek 8:14.
Objects of, carried in procession. Is 46:7; Amos 5:26; Acts 7:43.
Early notice of, amongst God's professing people. Gen 31:19,30; 35:1-4; Josh 24:2.
The Jews
Practised, in Egypt. Josh 24:14; Ezek 23:3,19.
Brought, out of Egypt with them. Ezek 23:8; Acts 7:39-41.
Forbidden to practise. Ex 20:1-5; 23:24.
Often mixed up, with God's worship. Ex 32:1-5; 1 Kin 12:27,28.
Followed the Canaanites in. Judg 2:11-13; 1 Chr 5:25.
Followed the Moabites in. Num 25:1-3.
Followed the Assyrians in. Ezek 16:28-30; 23:5-7.
Followed the Syrians in. Judg 10:6.
Adopted by Solomon. 1 Kin 11:5-8.
Adopted by the wicked kings. 1 Kin 21:26; 2 Kin 21:21; 2 Chr 28:2-4; 33:3,7.
Example of the kings encouraged Israel in. 1 Kin 12:30; 2 Kin 21:11; 2 Chr 33:9.
Great prevalence of, in Israel. Is 2:8; Jer 2:28; Ezek 8:10.
A virtual forsaking of God. Jer 2:9-13.
The good kings of Judah endeavoured to destroy. 2 Chr 15:16; 34:7.
Captivity of Israel on account of. 2 Kin 17:6-18.
Captivity of Judah on account of. 2 Kin 17:19-23.

Ignorance of God.

Ignorance of Christ is. John 8:19.
Evidenced by
Want of love. 1 John 4:8.
Not keeping his commands. 1 John 2:4.
Living in sin. Titus 1:16; 1 John 3:6.
Leads to
Error. Matt 22:29.
Idolatry. Is 44:19; Acts 17:29,30.
Alienation from God. Eph 4:18.
Sinful lusts. 1 Thess 4:5; 1 Pet 1:14.
Persecuting saints. John 15:21; 16:3.
Is no excuse for sin. Lev 4:2; Luke 12:48.
The wicked, in a state of. Jer 9:3; John 15:21; 17:25; Acts 17:30.
The wicked choose. Job 21:14; Rom 1:28.
Punishment of. Ps 79:6; 2 Thess 1:8.
Ministers should
Compassionate those in. Heb 5:2; 2 Tim 2:24,25.
Labour to remove. Acts 17:23.
Exemplified
Pharaoh. Ex 5:2.
Israelites. Ps 95:10; Is 1:3.
False prophets. Is 56:10,11.
Jews. Luke 23:34.
Nicodemus. John 3:10.
Gentiles. Gal 4:8.
Paul. 1 Tim 1:13.

Incense.

Brought from Sheba. Jer 6:20.
Called frankincense. Song 4:6,14.
An article of extensive commerce. Rev 18:13.
Common, not to be offered to God. Ex 30:9.
For God's service mixed with sweet spices. Ex 25:6; 37:29.
Receipt for mixing. Ex 30:34-36.
None but priest to offer. Num 16:40; Deut 33:10.
Offered
In censers. Lev 10:1; Num 16:17,46.
On the altar of gold. Ex 30:1,6; 40:5.
Morning and evening. Ex 30:7,8.
Perpetually. Ex 30:8.
By the high priest in the most holy place on the day of atonement. Lev 16:12,13.
With fire from off the altar of burnt offering. Lev 16:12; Num 16:46.
Offering of, allotted to the priests. Luke 1:9.
The Jews prayed at time of offering. Luke 1:10.
Designed for atonement. Num 16:46,47.
Put on meat offerings. Lev 2:1,2,15,16; 6:15.
Levites had charge of. 1 Chr 9:29.
Used in idolatrous worship. Jer 48:35.
The Jews
Not accepted in offering, on account of sin. Is 1:13; 66:3.
Offered, to idols on altars of brick. Is 65:3.
Punished for offering, to idols. 2 Chr 34:25.
Nadab and Abihu destroyed for offering, with strange fire. Lev 10:1,2.
Korah and his company punished for offering. Num 16:16-35.
Uzziah punished for offering. 2 Chr 26:16-21.
Presented to Christ by the wise men. Matt 2:11.
Illustrative of
The merits of Christ. Rev 8:3,4.
Prayer. Ps 141:2; Mal 1:11; Rev 5:8.

Industry.

Commanded. Eph 4:28; 1 Thess 4:11.
Required of man in a state of innocence. Gen 2:15.
Required of man after the fall. Gen 3:23.
To be suspended on the Sabbath. Ex 20:10.
Characteristic of godly women. Prov 31:13-31.
Early rising necessary to. Prov 31:15.
Requisite to supply
Our own wants. Acts 20:34; 1 Thess 2:9.
Wants of others. Acts 20:35; Eph 4:28.
The slothful devoid of. Prov 24:30,31.
Leads to
Increase of substance. Prov 13:11.
Affection of relatives. Prov 31:28.
General commendation. Prov 31:31.
Illustrated. Prov 6:6-8.
Exemplified
Rachel. Gen 29:9.
Jacob. Gen 31:6.
Jethro's daughters. Ex 2:10.
Ruth. Ruth 2:2,3.
Jeroboam. 1 Kin 11:28.
David. 1 Sam 16:11.
Jewish elders. Ezra 6:14,15.
Dorcas. Acts 9:39.
Paul. Acts 18:3; 1 Cor 4:12.

Indwelling of the Holy Spirit, The.

In his Church, as his temple. 1 Cor 3:16.
In the body of saints, as his temple. 1 Cor 6:19; 2 Cor 6:16.
Promised to saints. Ezek 36:27.
Saints enjoy. Is 63:11; 2 Tim 1:14.
Saints full of. Acts 6:5; Eph 5:18.
Is the means of
Quickening. Rom 8:11.

Guiding. John 16:13; Gal 5:18.
Fruit bearing. Gal 5:22.
A proof of being Christ's. Rom 8:9; 1 John 4:13.
A proof of adoption. Rom 8:15; Gal 4:5.
Is abiding. 1 John 2:27.
Those who have not
Are sensual. Jude 1:19.
Are without Christ. Rom 8:9.
Opposed by the carnal nature. Gal 5:17.

INGRATITUDE.

A characteristic of the wicked. Ps 38:20; 2 Tim 3:2.
Often exhibited
By relations. Job 19:14.
By servants. Job 19:15,16.
To benefactors. Ps 109:5; Eccl 9:15.
To friends in distress. Ps 38:11.
Saints should avoid the guilt of. Ps 7:4,5.
Should be met with
Prayers. Ps 35:12,13; 109:4.
Faithfulness. Gen 31:38-42.
Persevering love. 2 Cor 12:15.
Punishment of. Prov 17:13; Jer 18:20,21.
Exemplified
Laban. Gen 31:6,7.
Chief butler. Gen 40:23.
Israel. Ex 17:4.
Men of Keilah. 1 Sam 23:5,12.
Saul. 1 Sam 24:17.
Nabal. 1 Sam 25:5-11,21.
Absalom. 2 Sam 15:6.
Joash. 2 Chr 24:22.

INGRATITUDE TO GOD.

A characteristic of the wicked. Rom 1:21.
Inexcusable. Is 1:2,3; Rom 1:21.
Unreasonable. Jer 2:5,6,31; Mic 6:2,3.
Exceeding folly of. Deut 32:6.
Guilt of. Ps 106:7,21; Jer 2:11-13.
Prosperity likely to produce. Deut 31:20; 32:15; Jer 5:7-11.
Warnings against. Deut 8:11-14; 1 Sam 12:24,25.
Punishment of. Neh 9:20-27; Hos 2:8,9.
Illustrated. Is 5:1-7; Ezek 16:1-15.
Exemplified
Israel. Deut 32:18.
Saul. 1 Sam 15:17-19.
David. 2 Sam 12:7-9.
Nebuchadnezzar. Dan 5:18-21.
Lepers. Luke 17:17,18.

INJUSTICE.

Forbidden. Lev 19:15,35; Deut 16:19.
Specially to be avoided toward
The poor. Ex 23:6; Prov 22:16,22,23.
The stranger and fatherless. Ex 22:21,22; Deut 24:17; Jer 22:3.
Servants. Job 31:13,14; Deut 24:14; Jer 22:13.
Of the least kind, condemned. Luke 16:10.
God
Regards. Eccl 5:8.
Approves not of. Lam 3:35,36.
Abominates. Prov 17:15; 20:10.
Hears the cry of those who suffer. James 5:4.
Provoked to avenge. Ps 12:5.
Brings a curse. Deut 27:17,19.
A bad example leads to. Ex 23:2.
Intemperance leads to. Prov 31:5.
Covetousness leads to. Jer 6:13; Ezek 22:12; Mic 2:2.
Saints should
Hate. Prov 29:27.
Testify against. Ps 58:1,2; Mic 3:8,9.
Bear, patiently. 1 Cor 6:7.
Take no vengeance for. Matt 5:39.
The wicked
Deal with. Is 26:10.
Judge with. Ps 82:2; Eccl 3:16; Hab 1:4.
Practise, without shame. Jer 6:13,15; Zeph 3:5.
Punishment of. Prov 11:7; 28:8; Amos 5:11,12; 8:5,8; 1 Thess 4:6.
Exemplified
Potiphar. Gen 39:20.
Sons of Samuel. 1 Sam 8:3.
Ahab. 1 Kin 21:10,15,16.
Jews. Is 59:14.
Princes etc. Dan 6:4.
Judas. Matt 27:4.
Pilate. Matt 27:24-26.
Priests etc. Acts 4:3.
Festus. Acts 24:27.

INSECTS.

Created by God. Gen 1:24,25.
Divided into
Clean and fit for food. Lev 11:21,22.
Unclean and abominable. Lev 11:23,24.
Mentioned in Scripture
Ant. Prov 6:6; 30:25.
Bee. Judg 14:8; Ps 118:12; Is 7:18.
Beetle. Lev 11:22.
Caterpillar. Ps 78:46; Is 33:4.
Cankerworm. Joel 1:4; Nah 3:15,16.
Earthworm. Job 25:6; Mic 7:17.
Flea. 1 Sam 24:14.
Fly. Ex 8:22; Eccl 10:1; Is 7:18.
Gnat. Matt 23:24.
Grasshopper. Lev 11:22; Judg 6:5; Job 39:20.
Hornet. Deut 7:20.
Locust. Ex 10:12,13.
Bald locust. Lev 11:22.
Lice. Ex 8:16; Ps 105:31.
Maggot. Ex 16:20.
Moth. Job 4:19; 27:18; Is 50:9.
Palmer-worm. Joel 1:4; Amos 4:9.
Spider. Job 8:14; Prov 30:28.
Fed by God. Ps 104:25,27; 145:9,15.

INSPIRATION OF THE HOLY SPIRIT, THE.

Foretold. Joel 2:28; Acts 2:16-18.
All Scripture given by. 2 Sam 23:2; 2 Tim 3:16; 2 Pet 1:21.
Design of
To reveal future events. Acts 1:16; 28:25; 1 Pet 1:11.
To reveal the mysteries of God. Amos 3:7; 1 Cor 2:10.
To give power to ministers. Mic 3:8; Acts 1:8.
To direct ministers. Ezek 3:24-27; Acts 11:12; 13:2.
To control ministers. Acts 16:6.
To testify against sin. 2 Kin 17:13; Neh 9:30; Mic 3:8; John 16:8,9.
Modes of
Various. Heb 1:1.
By secret impulse. Judg 13:25; 2 Pet 1:21.
By a voice. Is 6:8; Acts 8:29; Rev 1:10.
By visions. Num 12:6; Ezek 11:24.
By dreams. Num 12:6; Dan 7:1.
Necessary to prophesying. Num 11:25-27; 2 Chr 20:14-17.
Is irresistible. Amos 3:8.
Despisers of, punished. 2 Chr 36:15,16; Zech 7:12.

IRON.

Dug out of the earth. Job 28:2.
Described as
Strong and durable. Job 40:18; Dan 2:40.
Fusible. Ezek 22:20.
Malleable. Is 2:4.
Of greater gravity than water. 2 Kin 6:5.
Admits of a high polish. Ezek 27:19.
Hardened into steel. 2 Sam 22:35; Job 20:24.
Of small comparative value. Is 60:17.
The land of Canaan abounded with. Deut 8:9; 33:25.
From the north hardest and best. Jer 15:12.
Used from the earliest age. Gen 4:22.
Made into
Armour. 2 Sam 23:7; Rev 9:9.
Weapons of war. 1 Sam 13:19; 17:7.
Chariots. Judg 4:3.
Implements for husbandry. 1 Sam 13:20,21; 2 Sam 12:31.
Tools for artificers. Josh 8:31; 1 Kin 6:7.
Graving tools. Job 19:24; Jer 17:1.
Gates. Acts 12:10.
Nails and hinges. 1 Chr 22:3.
Bars. Ps 107:16; Is 45:2.
Fetters. Ps 105:18; 149:8.
Yokes. Deut 28:48; Jer 28:13,14.
Idols. Dan 5:4,23.
Bedsteads. Deut 3:11.
Pillars. Jer 1:18.
Rods. Ps 2:9; Rev 2:27.
Sharpens things made of. Prov 27:17.
Working in, a trade. 1 Sam 13:19; 2 Chr 2:7,14.
An article of commerce. Ezek 27:12,19; Rev 18:12.
Great quantity of, provided for the temple. 1 Chr 22:3,14,16; 29:2.
Taken in war, often dedicated to God. Josh 6:19,24.
Mode of purifying, taken in war. Num 31:21-23.
Miraculously made to swim. 2 Kin 6:6.
Illustrative
Of strength. Dan 2:33,40.
Of stubbornness. Is 48:4.
Of severe affliction. Deut 4:20; Ps 107:10.
Of a hard barren soil. Deut 28:23.
Of severe exercise of power. Ps 2:9; Rev 2:27.
(Seared with,) of insensibility of conscience. 1 Tim 4:2.

ISHMAELITES, THE.

Descended from Abraham's son, Ishmael. Gen 16:15,16; 1 Chr 1:28.
Divided into twelve tribes. Gen 25:16.

Heads of tribes. Gen 25:13-15; 1 Chr 1:29-31.
Called
Hagarites. 1 Chr 5:10.
Hagarenes. Ps 83:6.
Arabians. Is 13:20.
Original possessions of. Gen 25:18.
Governed by kings. Jer 25:24.
Dwelt in tents. Is 13:20.
Rich in cattle. 1 Chr 5:21.
Wore ornaments of gold. Judg 8:24.
Were the merchants of the east. Gen 37:25; Ezek 27:20,21.
Travelled in large companies or caravans. Gen 37:25; Job 6:19.
Waylaid and plundered travellers. Jer 3:2.
Often confederate against Israel. Ps 83:6.
Overcome by
Gideon. Judg 8:10-24.
Reubenites and Gadites. 1 Chr 5:10,18-20.
Uzziah. 2 Chr 26:7.
Sent presents to Solomon. 1 Kin 10:15; 2 Chr 9:14.
Sent flocks to Jehoshaphat. 2 Chr 17:11.
Predictions respecting
To be numerous. Gen 16:10; 17:20.
To be wild and savage. Gen 16:12.
To be warlike and predatory. Gen 16:12.
To be divided into twelve tribes. Gen 17:20.
To continue independent. Gen 16:12.
To be a great nation. Gen 21:13,18.
To be judged with the nations. Jer 25:23-25.
Their glory, etc. to be diminished. Is 21:13-17.
Their submission to Christ. Ps 72:10,15.
Probably preached to by Paul. Gal 1:17.

ISSACHAR, THE TRIBE OF.

Descended from Jacob's fifth son. Gen 30:17,18.
Predictions respecting. Gen 49:14,15; Deut 33:18,19.
Persons selected from
To number the people. Num 1:8.
To spy out the land. Num 13:7.
To divide the land. Num 34:26.
Strength of, on leaving Egypt. Num 1:28,29; 2:6.
Encamped under the standard of Judah east of the tabernacle. Num 2:5.
Next to and under standard of Judah in the journeys of Israel. Num 10:14,15.
Offering of, at the dedication. Num 7:18-23.
Families of. Num 26:23,24.
Strength of, on entering Canaan. Num 26:25.
On Gerizim said amen to the blessings. Deut 27:12.
Bounds of their inheritance. Josh 19:17-23.
Assisted Deborah against Sisera. Judg 5:15.
Officers of, appointed by David. 1 Chr 27:18.
Officers of, appointed by Solomon. 1 Kin 4:17.
Some of, at David's coronation. 1 Chr 12:32.
Number of warriors belonging to, in David's time. 1 Chr 7:2,5.
Many of, at Hezekiah's Passover. 2 Chr 30:18.
Remarkable persons of. Judg 10:1; 1 Kin 15:27.

JEHOVAH, THE ONLY TRUE GOD.

Jehovah is "Alpha and Omega" and "the First and the Last." Rev 1:7,8; 22:12,13,20; Is 48:12,13.
Death and life of "the First and the Last." Rev 2:8; 1:17,18; Matt 28:5,6.
There is only one true God, Jehovah. Is 43:10,11; John 1:1; * compare NW, Watchtower's rendering; Is 44:6,8; John 1:1; * compare KJV, RSV, NKJV, NIV, JB, etc.; Heb 1:3; Col 2:9 * Read in NIV.

JERUSALEM.

The ancient Salem. Gen 14:18; Ps 76:2.
The ancient Jebusi or Jebus. Josh 15:8; 18:28; Judg 19:10.
The king of, defeated and slain by Joshua. Josh 10:5-23.
Allotted to the tribe of Benjamin. Josh 18:28.
Partly taken and burned by Judah. Judg 1:8.
The Jebusites
Formerly dwelt in. Judg 19:10,11.
Held possession of, with Judah and Benjamin. Josh 15:63; Judg 1:21.
Finally dispossessed of, by David. 2 Sam 5:6-8.
Enlarged by David. 2 Sam 5:9.
Made the royal city. 2 Sam 5:9; 20:3.
Specially chosen by God. 2 Chr 6:6; Ps 135:21.
The seat of government under the Romans for a time. Matt 27:2,19.
Roman government transferred from, to Caesarea. Acts 23:23,24; 25:1-13.
Called
City of God. Ps 46:4; 48:1.
City of the Lord. Is 60:14.
City of Judah. 2 Chr 25:28.
City of the great king. Ps 48:2; Matt 5:5.
City of solemnities. Is 33:20.
City of righteousness. Is 1:26.
City of truth. Zech 8:3.
A city not forsaken. Is 62:12.
Faithful city. Is 1:21,26.
Holy city. Neh 11:1; Is 48:2; Matt 4:5.
Throne of the Lord. Jer 3:17.
Zion. Ps 48:12; Is 33:20.
Zion of the holy one of Israel. Is 60:14.
Surrounded by mountains. Ps 125:2.
Surrounded by a wall. 1 Kin 3:1.
Protected by forts and bulwarks. Ps 48:12,13.
Entered by gates. Ps 122:2; Jer 17:19-21.
Hezekiah made an aqueduct for. 2 Kin 20:20.
Spoils of war placed in. 1 Sam 17:54; 2 Sam 8:7.
Described as
Beautiful for situation. Ps 48:2.
Compact. Ps 122:3.
Comely. Song 6:4.
The perfection of beauty. Lam 2:15.
Joy of the whole earth. Ps 48:2; Lam 2:15.
Princess among the provinces. Lam 1:1.
Great. Jer 22:8.
Populous. Lam 1:1.
Full of business and tumult. Is 22:3.
Wealth, etc. in the time of Solomon. 1 Kin 10:26,27.
Protected by God. Is 31:5.
Instances of God's care and protection of. 2 Sam 24:16; 2 Kin 19:32-34; 2 Chr 12:7.
The temple built in. 2 Chr 3:1; Ps 68:29.
The Jews
Went up to, at the feasts. Luke 2:42; Ps 122:4.
Loved. Ps 137:5,6.
Lamented the affliction of. Neh 1:2-4.
Prayed for the prosperity of. Ps 51:18; 122:6.
Prayed toward. Dan 6:10; 1 Kin 8:41.
Wickedness of. Is 1:1-4; Jer 5:1-5; Mic 3:10.
Idolatry of. 2 Chr 28:4; Ezek 8:7-10.
Wickedness of, the cause of its calamities. 2 Kin 21:12-15; 2 Chr 24:18; Lam 1:8; Ezek 5:5-8.
Was the tomb of the prophets. Luke 13:33,34.
Christ
Preached in. Luke 21:37,38; John 18:20.
Did many miracles in. John 4:45.
Publicly entered, as king. Matt 21:9,10.
Lamented over. Matt 23:37; Luke 19:41.
Put to death at. Luke 9:31; Acts 13:27,29.
Gospel first preached at. Luke 24:47; Acts 2:14.
Miraculous gift of the Holy Spirit first given at. Acts 1:4; 2:1-5.
Persecution of the Christian church commenced at. Acts 4:1; 8:1.
First Christian council held at. Acts 15:4,6.
Calamities of, mentioned
Taken and plundered by Shishak. 1 Kin 14:25,26; 2 Chr 12:1-4.
Taken and plundered by Jehoash king of Israel. 2 Kin 14:13,14.
Besieged but not taken by Rezin and Pekah. Is 7:1; 2 Kin 16:5.
Besieged but not taken by Sennacherib. 2 Kin 18:17; 19:1-37.
Taken and made tributary by Pharaoh-Necho. 2 Kin 23:33-35.
Besieged by Nebuchadnezzar. 2 Kin 24:10,11.
Taken and burned by Nebuchadnezzar. 2 Kin 25:1-30; Jer 39:1-8.
Threatened by Sanballat. Neh 4:7,8.
Rebuilt after the captivity by order of Cyrus. Ezra 1:1-4.
Prophecies respecting
To be taken by king of Babylon. Jer 20:5.
To be made a heap of ruins. Jer 9:11; 26:18.
To be a wilderness. Is 64:10.

To be rebuilt by Cyrus. Is 44:26-28.
To be a quiet habitation. Is 33:20.
To be a terror to her enemies. Zech 12:2,3.
Christ to enter, as king. Zech 9:9.
The gospel to go forth from. Is 2:3; 40:9.
To be destroyed by the Romans. Luke 19:42-44.
Its capture accompanied by severe calamities. Matt 24:21,29; Luke 21:23,24.
Signs preceding its destruction. Matt 24:6-15; Luke 21:7-11,25,28.

Illustrative
Of the church. Gal 4:25,26; Heb 12:22.
Of the church glorified. Rev 3:12; 21:2,10.
(Its strong position,) of saints under God's protection. Ps 125:2.

Jews, The.

Descended from Abraham. Is 51:2; John 8:39.
Divided into twelve tribes. Gen 35:22; 49:28.
Called
Hebrews. Gen 14:13; 40:15; 2 Cor 11:22.
Israelites. Ex 9:7; Josh 3:17.
Seed of Abraham. Ps 105:6; Is 41:8.
Seed of Jacob. Jer 33:26.
Seed of Israel. 1 Chr 16:13.
Children of Jacob. 1 Chr 16:13.
Children of Israel. Gen 50:25; Is 27:12.
Jeshurun. Deut 32:15.
Chosen and loved by God. Deut 7:6,7.
Circumcised in token of their covenant relation. Gen 17:10,11; Acts 7:8.
Separated from all other nations. Ex 33:16; Lev 20:24; 1 Kin 8:53.
Described as
A peculiar people. Deut 14:2.
A peculiar treasure. Ex 19:5; Ps 135:4.
A holy nation. Ex 19:6.
A holy people. Deut 7:6; 14:21.
A kingdom of priests. Ex 19:6.
A special people. Deut 7:6.
The Lord's portion. Deut 32:9.
Sojourned in Egypt. Ex 12:40,41.
Brought out of Egypt by God. Ex 12:42; Deut 5:15; 6:12.
In the desert forty years. Num 14:33; Josh 5:6.
Settled in Canaan. Num 32:18; Josh 14:1-5.
Under the theocracy until the time of Samuel. Ex 19:4-6; 1 Sam 8:7.
Desired and obtained kings. 1 Sam 8:5,22.
Divided into two kingdoms after Solomon. 1 Kin 11:31,32; 12:19,20.
Often subdued and made tributary. Judg 2:13,14; 4:2; 6:2,6; 2 Kin 23:33.
Taken captive to Assyria and Babylon. 2 Kin 17:32; 18:11; 24:16; 25:11.
Restored to their own land by Cyrus. Ezra 1:1-4.
Had courts of justice. Deut 16:18.
Had an ecclesiastical establishment. Ex 28:1; Num 18:6; Mal 2:4-7.
Had a series of prophets to promote national reformation. Jer 7:25; 26:4,5; 35:15; 44:4; Ezek 38:17.
The only people who had knowledge of God. Ps 76:1; 1 Thess 4:5; Ps 48:3; Rom 1:28.
The only people who worshipped God. Ex 5:17; Ps 96:5; 115:3,4; John 4:22.
Religion of, according to rites prescribed by God. Lev 18:4; Deut 12:8-11; Heb 9:1.
Religion of, typical. Heb 9:8-11; 10:1.
Their national greatness. Gen 12:2; Deut 33:29.
Their national privileges. Rom 3:2; 9:4,5.
Their vast numbers. Gen 22:17; Num 10:36.
National character of
Pride of descent, etc. Jer 13:9; John 8:33,41.
Love of country. Ps 137:6.
Fondness for their brethren. Ex 2:11,12; Rom 9:1-3.
Attachment to Moses. John 9:28,29; Acts 6:11.
Attachment to customs of the law. Acts 6:14; 21:21; 22:3.
Fondness for traditionary customs. Jer 44:17; Ezek 20:18,30,21; Mark 7:3,4.
Stubborn and stiffnecked. Ex 32:9; Acts 7:51.
Prone to rebellion. Deut 9:7,24; Is 1:2.
Prone to backsliding. Jer 2:11-13; 8:5.
Prone to idolatry. Is 2:8; 57:5.
Prone to formality in religion. Is 29:13; Ezek 33:31; Matt 15:7-9.
Self-righteous. Is 65:5; Rom 10:3.
Unfaithful to covenant engagements. Jer 3:6-8; 31:32; Ezek 16:59.
Ungrateful to God. Deut 32:15; Is 1:2.
Ignorant of the true sense of Scripture. Acts 13:27; 2 Cor 3:13-15.
Distrustful of God. Num 14:11; Ps 78:22.
Covetous. Jer 6:13; Ezek 33:31; Mic 2:2.
Cowardly. Ex 14:10; Num 14:3; Is 51:12.
Trusted to their privileges for salvation. Jer 7:4; Matt 3:9.
Distinction of castes among, noticed. Is 65:5; Luke 7:39; 15:2; Acts 26:5.
Degenerated as they increased in national greatness. Amos 6:4.
Often displeased God by their sins. Num 25:3; Deut 32:16; 1 Kin 16:2; Is 1:4; 5:24,25.
A spiritual seed of true believers always among. 1 Kin 19:18; Is 6:13; Rom 9:6,7; 11:1,5.
Modern, divided into
Hebrews or pure Jews. Acts 6:1; Phil 3:5.
Hellenists or Grecians. Acts 6:1; 9:29.
Many sects and parties. Matt 16:6; Mark 8:15.
An agricultural people. Gen 46:32.
A commercial people. Ezek 27:17.
Obliged to unite against enemies. Num 32:20-22; Judg 19:29; 20:1-48; 1 Sam 11:7,8.
Often distinguished in war. Judg 7:19-23; 1 Sam 14:6-13; 17:32,33; Neh 4:16-22.
Strengthened by God in war. Lev 26:7,8; Josh 5:13,14; 8:1,2.
Under God's special protection. Deut 32:10,11; 33:27-29; Ps 105:13-15; 121:3-5.
Enemies of, obliged to acknowledge them as divinely protected. Josh 2:9-11; Esth 6:13.
Prohibited from
Associating with others. Acts 10:28.
Covenanting with others. Ex 23:32; Deut 7:2.
Marry with others. Deut 7:3; Josh 23:12.
Following practices of others. Deut 12:29-31; 18:9-14.
Despised all strangers. 1 Sam 17:36; Matt 16:26,27; Eph 2:11.
Held no intercourse with strangers. John 4:9; Acts 11:2,3.
Condemned for associating with other nations. Judg 2:1-3; Jer 2:18.
Received proselytes from other nations. Acts 2:10; Ex 12:44,48.
Gentiles made one with, under the gospel. Acts 10:15,28; 15:8,9; Gal 3:28; Eph 2:14-16.
All other nations
Envied. Neh 4:1; Is 26:11; Ezek 35:11.
Hated. Ps 44:10; Ezek 35:5.
Oppressed. Ex 3:9; Judg 2:18; 4:3.
Persecuted. Lam 1:3; 5:5.
Rejoiced at calamities of. Ps 44:13,14; 80:5,6; Ezek 36:4.
None hated or oppressed, with impunity. Ps 137:8,9; Ezek 25:15,16; 35:6; Obad 10-16.
Christ
Promised to. Gen 49:10; Dan 9:25.
Expected by. Ps 14:7; Matt 11:3; Luke 2:25,38; John 8:56.
Regarded as the restorer of national greatness. Matt 20:21; Luke 24:21; Acts 1:6.
Sprang from. Rom 9:5; Heb 7:14.
Rejected by. Is 53:3; Mark 6:3; John 1:11.
Murdered by. Acts 7:52; 1 Thess 2:15.
Imprecated the blood of Christ upon themselves and their children. Matt 27:25.
Many of, believed the gospel. Acts 21:20.
Unbelieving, persecuted the Christians. Acts 17:5,13; 1 Thess 2:14-16.
Cast off for unbelief. Rom 11:17,20.
Scattered and peeled. Is 18:2,7; James 1:1.
Shall finally be saved. Rom 11:26,27.
Punishment of, for rejecting and killing Christ, illustrated. Matt 21:37-43.
Descendants of Abraham. Ps 105:6; Is 51:2; John 8:33; Rom 9:7.
The people of God. Deut 32:9; 2 Sam 7:24; Is 51:16.
Separated to God. Ex 33:16; Num 23:9; Deut 4:34.
Beloved for their father's sake. Deut 4:37; 10:15; Rom 11:28.
Christ descended from. John 4:22; Rom 9:5.
The objects of
God's love. Deut 7:8; 23:5; Jer 31:3.
God's choice. Deut 7:6.
God's protection. Ps 105:15; Zech 2:8.

The covenant established with. Ex 6:4; 24:6-8; 34:27.
Promises respecting made to
  Abraham. Gen 12:1-3; 13:14-17; 15:18; 17:7,8.
  Isaac. Gen 26:2-5,24.
  Jacob. Gen 28:12-15; 35:9-12.
  Themselves. Ex 6:7,8; 19:5,6; Deut 26:18,19.
Privileges of. Ps 76:1,2; Rom 3:1,2; 9:4,5.
Punished for
  Idolatry. Ps 78:58-64; Is 65:3-7.
  Unbelief. Rom 11:20.
  Breaking covenant. Is 24:5; Jer 11:10.
  Transgressing the law. Is 1:4,7; 24:5,6.
  Changing the ordinances. Is 24:5.
  Killing the prophets. Matt 23:37,38.
  Imprecating upon themselves the blood of Christ. Matt 27:25.
Scattered among the nations. Deut 28:64; Ezek 6:8; 36:19.
Despised by the nations. Ezek 36:3.
Their country trodden under foot by the Gentiles. Deut 28:49-52; Luke 21:24.
Their house left desolate. Matt 24:38.
Deprived of civil and religious privileges. Hos 3:4.
Denunciations against those who
  Cursed. Gen 27:29; Num 24:9.
  Contended with. Is 41:11; 49:25.
  Oppressed. Is 49:26; 51:21-23.
  Hated. Ps 129:5; Ezek 35:5,6.
  Aggravated the afflictions of. Zech 1:14,15.
  Slaughtered. Ps 79:1-7; Ezek 35:5,6.
God, mindful of. Ps 98:3; Is 49:15,16.
Christ was sent to. Matt 15:24; 21:37; Acts 3:20,22,26.
Compassion of Christ for. Matt 23:37; Luke 19:41.
The gospel preached to, first. Matt 10:6; Luke 24:47; Acts 1:8.
Blessedness of blessing. Gen 27:29.
Blessedness of favouring. Gen 12:3; Ps 122:6.
Pray importunately for. Ps 122:6; Is 62:1,6,7; Jer 31:7; Rom 10:1.
Saints remember. Ps 102:14; 137:5; Jer 51:50.
Promises respecting
  The pouring out of the Spirit upon them. Ezek 39:29; Zech 12:10.
  The removal of their blindness. Rom 11:25; 2 Cor 3:14-16.
  Their return and seeking to God. Hos 3:5.
  Their humiliation for the rejection of Christ. Zech 12:10.
  Pardon of sin. Is 44:22; Rom 11:27.
  Salvation. Is 59:20; Rom 11:26.
  Sanctification. Jer 33:8; Ezek 36:25; Zech 12:1,9.
  Joy occasioned by conversion of. Is 44:23; 49:13; 52:8,9; 66:10.
  Blessing to the Gentiles by conversion of. Is 2:1-5; 60:5; 66:19; Rom 11:12,15.
  Reunion of. Jer 3:18; Ezek 37:16,17,20-22; Hos 1:11; Mic 2:12.
  Restoration to their own land. Is 11:15,16; 14:1-3; 27:12,13; Jer 16:14,15; Ezek 36:24; 37:21,25; 39:25,28; Luke 21:24.
  Gentiles assisting in their restoration. Is 49:22,23; 60:10,14; 61:4-6.
  Subjection of Gentiles to. Is 60:11,12,14.
  Future glory of. Is 60:19; 62:3,4; Zeph 3:19,20; Zech 2:5.
  Future prosperity of. Is 60:6,7,9,17; 61:4-6; Hos 14:5,6.
  That Christ shall appear amongst. Is 59:20; Zech 14:4.
  That Christ shall dwell amongst. Ezek 43:7,9; Zech 2:11.
  That Christ shall reign over. Ezek 34:23,24; 37:24,25.
Conversion of, illustrated. Ezek 37:1-14; Rom 11:24.

Jordan, the River.

Eastern boundary of Canaan. Num 34:12.
Often overflowed. Josh 3:15; 1 Chr 12:15.
Overflowing of, called the swelling of Jordan. Jer 12:5; 49:19.
Empties itself into the Dead Sea. Num 34:12.
The plains of
  Thickly wooded. 2 Kin 6:2.
  Exceeding fertile. Gen 13:10.
  Infested with lions. Jer 49:19; 50:44.
  Afforded clay for moulding brass, etc. 1 Kin 7:46; 2 Chr 4:17.
  Chosen by Lot for a residence. Gen 13:11.
Fordable in some places. Josh 2:7; Judg 12:5,6.
Ferry boats often used on. 2 Sam 19:18.
Remarkable events connected with
  Division of its waters to let Israel pass over. Josh 3:12-16; 5:1.
  Return of its waters to their place. Josh 4:18.
  Slaughter of Moabites. Judg 3:28,29.
  Slaughter of the Ephraimites. Judg 12:4-6.
  Its division by Elijah. 2 Kin 2:8.
  Its division by Elisha. 2 Kin 2:14.
  Healing of Naaman the leper. 2 Kin 5:10,14.
  Baptism of multitudes by John the Baptist. Matt 3:6; Mark 1:5; John 1:28.
  Baptism of our Lord. Matt 3:13,15; Mark 1:9.
Passage of Israel over
  Promised. Deut 4:22; 9:1; 11:31.
  In an appointed order. Josh 3:1-8.
  Preceded by priests with the ark. Josh 3:6,11,14.
  Successfully effected. Josh 3:17; 4:1,10,11.
  Commemorated by a pillar of stones raised in it. Josh 4:9.
  Commemorated by a pillar of stones in Gilgal. Josh 4:2-8,20-24.
  Alluded to. Ps 74:15; 114:3,5.
  A pledge that God would drive the Canaanites, etc. out of their land. Josh 3:10.
The Jews had great pride in. Zech 11:3.
Despised by foreigners. 2 Kin 5:12.
Moses not allowed to cross. Deut 3:27; 31:2.

Joy.

God gives. Eccl 2:26; Ps 4:7.
Christ appointed to give. Is 61:3.
Is a fruit of the Spirit. Gal 5:22.
The gospel, good tidings of. Luke 2:10,11.
God's word affords. Neh 8:12; Jer 15:16.
The gospel to be received with. 1 Thess 1:6.
Promised to saints. Ps 132:16; Is 35:10; 55:12; 56:7.
Prepared for saints. Ps 97:11.
Enjoined to saints. Ps 32:11; Phil 3:1.
Fulness of, in God's presence. Ps 16:11.
Vanity of seeking, from earthly things. Eccl 2:10,11; 11:8.
Experienced by
  Believers. Luke 24:52; Acts 16:34.
  Peace-makers. Prov 12:20.
  The just. Prov 21:15.
  The wise, and discreet. Prov 15:23.
  Parents of good children. Prov 23:24.
Increased to the meek. Is 29:19.
Of saints is
  In God. Ps 89:16; 149:2; Hab 3:18; Rom 5:11.
  In Christ. Luke 1:47; Phil 3:3.
  In the Holy Spirit. Rom 14:17.
  For election. Luke 10:20.
  For salvation. Ps 21:1; Is 61:10.
  For deliverance from bondage. Ps 105:43; Jer 31:10-13.
  For manifestation of goodness. 2 Chr 7:10.
  For temporal blessings. Joel 2:23,24.
  For supplies of grace. Is 12:3.
  For divine protection. Ps 5:11; 16:8,9.
  For divine support. Ps 28:7; 63:7.
  For the victory of Christ. John 16:33.
  For the hope of glory. Rom 5:2.
  For the success of the gospel. Acts 15:3.
Of saints should be
  Great. Zech 9:9; Acts 8:8.
  Abundant. 2 Cor 8:2.
  Exceeding. Ps 21:6; 68:3.
  Animated. Ps 32:11; Luke 6:23.
  Unspeakable. 1 Pet 1:8.
  Full of glory. 1 Pet 1:8.
  Constant. 2 Cor 6:10; Phil 4:4.
  For evermore. 1 Thess 5:16.
  With awe. Ps 2:11.
  In hope. Rom 12:12.
  In sorrow. 2 Cor 6:10.
  Under trials. James 1:2; 1 Pet 1:6.
  Under persecutions. Matt 5:11,12; Luke 6:22,23; Heb 10:34.
  Under calamities. Hab 3:17,18.
  Expressed in hymns. Eph 5:19; James 5:13.
Afflictions of saints succeeded by. Ps 30:5; 126:5; Is 35:10; John 16:20.
Pray for restoration of. Ps 51:8,12; 85:6.
Promote, in the afflicted. Job 29:13.
Of saints, made full by
  The favour of God. Acts 2:28.
  Faith in Christ. Rom 15:13.
  Abiding in Christ. John 15:10,11.
  The word of Christ. John 17:13.
  Answers to prayer. John 16:24.
  Communion of saints. 2 Tim 1:4; 1 John 1:3,4; 2 John 12.
Saints should afford, to their minsters. Phil 2:2; Philem 20.

Ministers should
Esteem their people as their. Phil 4:1; 1 Thess 2:20.
Promote, in their people. 2 Cor 1:24; Phil 1:25.
Pray for, for their people. Rom 15:13.
Have, in the faith and holiness of their people. 2 Cor 7:4; 1 Thess 3:9; 3 John 4.
Come to their people with. Rom 15:32.
Finish their course with. Acts 20:24.
Desire to render an account with. Phil 2:16; Heb 13:17.
Serve God with. Ps 100:2.
Liberality in God's service should cause. 1 Chr 29:9,17.
Is strengthening to saints. Neh 8:10.
Saints should engage in all religious services with. Ezra 6:22; Ps 42:4.
Saints should have, in all their undertakings. Deut 12:18.
Saints shall be presented to God with exceeding. 1 Pet 4:13; Jude 1:24.
The coming of Christ will afford to saints, exceeding. 1 Pet 4:13.
Shall be the final reward of saints at the judgment day. Matt 25:21.
Of the wicked
Is derived from earthly pleasures. Eccl 2:10; 11:9.
Is derived from folly. Prov 15:21.
Is delusive. Prov 14:13.
Is short-lived. Job 20:5; Eccl 7:6.
Should be turned into mourning. James 4:9.
Shall be taken away. Is 16:10.
Holy—Illustrated. Is 9:3; Matt 13:44.
Holy—Exemplified
Hannah. 1 Sam 2:1.
David. 1 Chr 29:9.
Wise men. Matt 2:10.
The Virgin Mary. Luke 1:47.
Zacchaeus. Luke 19:6.
Converts. Acts 2:46; 13:52.
Peter, etc. Acts 5:41.
Samaritans. Acts 8:8.
Jailor. Acts 16:34.

Joy of God Over His People, The.

Greatness of, described. Zeph 3:17.
On account of their
Repentance. Luke 15:7,10.
Faith. Heb 11:5,6.
Fear of him. Ps 147:11.
Praying to him. Prov 15:8.
Hope in his mercy. Ps 147:11.
Meekness. Ps 149:4.
Uprightness. 1 Chr 29:17; Prov 11:20.
Leads to him
Prosper them. Deut 30:9.
Do them good. Deut 28:63; Jer 32:41.
Deliver them. 2 Sam 22:20.
Comfort them. Is 65:19.
Give them the inheritance. Num 14:8.
Illustrated. Is 62:5; Luke 15:23,24.
Exemplified
Solomon. 1 Kin 10:9.

Judah, the Tribe Of.

Descended from Jacob's fourth son. Gen 29:35.
Predictions respecting. Gen 49:8-12; Deut 33:7.
Persons selected from
To number the people. Num 1:7.
To spy out the land. Num 13:6.
To divide the land. Num 34:19.
Strength of, on leaving Egypt. Num 1:26,27; 2:4.
Encamped with its standard east of the tabernacle. Num 2:3.
Led the first division of Israel in their journeys. Num 10:14.
Offering of, at dedication. Num 7:12-17.
Families of. Num 26:19-21.
Strength of on entering Canaan. Num 26:22.
On Gerizim said amen to the blessings. Deut 27:12.
Bounds of inheritance. Josh 15:1-12.
First and most vigorous in driving out the Canaanites. Judg 1:3-20.
Went first against Gibeah. Judg 20:18.
Furnished to Israel the first judge. Judg 3:9.
Aided Saul in his wars. 1 Sam 11:8; 15:4.
After Saul's rebellion appointed to furnish kings to Israel. 1 Sam 13:14; 15:28; 16:6,13; 2 Sam 2:4; 7:16,17.
The first to submit to David. 2 Sam 2:10.
Reigned over alone by David seven years and a half. 2 Sam 2:11; 5:5.
Officer placed over by David. 1 Chr 27:18.
Reproved for tardiness in bringing back David after Absalom's rebellion. 2 Sam 19:11-15.
Other tribes jealous of, on account of David. 2 Sam 19:41-42; 20:1,2.
With Benjamin alone, adhered to the house of David. 1 Kin 12:21.
The last tribe carried into captivity. 2 Kin 17:18,20; 25:21.
Out Lord sprang from. Matt 1:3-16; Luke 3:23-33; Heb 7:14.
Remarkable persons of
Achan. Josh 7:18.
Elimelech. Ruth 1:1,2.
Boaz. Ruth 2:1.
Obed. Ruth 4:21.
Jesse. Ruth 4:22; 1 Sam 16:1.
David. 1 Sam 16:1,13.
Solomon. 1 Kin 1:32-39.
Elihu. 1 Chr 27:18.
Pethahiah. Neh 11:24.
Bezaleel. Ex 31:2; 35:30.
Nahshon. Num 7:12.
Caleb. Num 14:24.
Absalom. 2 Sam 15:1.
Elhanan. 2 Sam 21:19; 23:24.
Adonijah. 1 Kin 1:5,6.
Jonathan. 2 Sam 21:21.
Kings of Judah (See 1st and 2nd Books of Kings)

Judea, Modern.

One of the divisions of the Holy Land under the Romans. Luke 3:1.
Comprised the whole of the ancient kingdom of Judah. 1 Kin 12:21-24.
Called
The land of Judah. Matt 2:6.
Jewry. Dan 5:13; John 7:1.
A mountainous district. Luke 1:39,65.
Parts of, desert. Matt 3:1; Acts 8:26.
Jerusalem the capital of. Matt 4:25.
Towns of
Arimathea. Matt 27:57; John 19:38.
Azotus or Ashdod. Acts 8:40.
Bethany. John 11:1,18.
Bethlehem. Matt 2:1,6,16.
Bethphage. Matt 21:1.
Emmaus. Luke 24:13.
Ephraim. John 11:54.
Gaza. Acts 8:26.
Jericho. Luke 10:30; 19:1.
Joppa. Acts 9:36; 10:5,8.
Lydda. Acts 9:32,35,38.
John the Baptist preached in. Matt 3:1.
Our Lord
Born in. Matt 2:1,5,6.
Tempted in the wilderness of. Matt 4:1.
Frequently visited. John 11:7.
Often left, to escape persecution. John 4:1-3.
Several Christian churches in. Acts 9:31; 1 Thess 2:14.

Judges, Extraordinary.

Raised up to deliver Israel. Judg 2:16.
Upheld and strengthened by God. Judg 2:18.
Remarkable for their faith. Heb 11:32.
Names of
Othniel. Judg 3:9,10.
Ehud. Judg 3:15.
Shamgar. Judg 3:31.
Deborah. Judg 4:4.
Gideon. Judg 6:11.
Abimelech. Judg 9:6.
Tola. Judg 10:1.
Jair. Judg 10:3.
Jephthah. Judg 11:1.
Ibzan. Judg 12:8.
Elon. Judg 12:11.
Abdon. Judg 12:13.
Samson. Judg 13:24,25; 16:31.
Eli. 1 Sam 4:18.
Samuel. 1 Sam 7:6,15-17.
During four hundred and fifty years. Acts 13:20.
Not without intermission. Judg 17:6; 18:1; 19:1; 21:25.
The office of, not always for life, or hereditary. Judg 8:23,29.
Israel not permanently or spiritually benefitted by. Judg 2:17-19.

Judgments.

Are from God. Deut 32:39; Job 12:23; Amos 3:6; Mic 6:9.
Different kinds of
Blotting out the name. Deut 29:20.
Abandonment by God. Hos 4:17.
Cursing men's blessings. Mal 2:2.
Pestilence. Deut 28:21,22; Amos 4:10.
Enemies. 2 Sam 24:13.
Famine. Deut 28:38-40; Amos 4:7-9.
Famine of hearing the word. Amos 8:11.
The sword. Ex 22:24; Jer 19:7.
Captivity. Deut 28:41; Ezek 39:23.
Continued sorrows. Ps 32:10; 78:32,33; Ezek 24:23.
Desolation. Ezek 33:29; Joel 3:19.
Destruction. Job 31:3; Ps 34:16; Prov 2:22; Is 11:4.

Inflicted upon
Nations. Gen 15:14; Jer 51:20,21.
Individuals. Deut 29:20; Jer 23:34.
False gods. Ex 12:12; Num 33:4.
Posterity of sinners. Ex 20:5; Ps 37:28; Lam 5:7.
All enemies of saints. Jer 30:16.
Sent for correction. Job 37:13; Jer 30:11.
Sent for the deliverance of saints. Ex 6:6.
Are sent, as punishment for
Disobedience to God. Lev 26:14-16; 2 Chr 7:19,20.
Despising the warnings of God. 2 Chr 36:16; Prov 1:24-31; Jer 44:4-6.
Murmuring against God. Num 14:29.
Idolatry. 2 Kin 22:17; Jer 16:18.
Iniquity. Is 26:21; Ezek 24:13,14.
Persecuting saints. Deut 32:43.
Sins of rulers. 1 Chr 21:2,12.
Manifest the righteous character of God. Ex 9:14-16; Ezek 39:21; Dan 9:14.
Are in all the earth. 1 Chr 16:14.
Are frequently tempered with mercy. Jer 4:27; 5:10,15-18; Amos 9:8.
Should lead to
Humiliation. Josh 7:6; 2 Chr 12:6; Lam 3:1-20; Joel 1:13; Jon 3:5,6.
Prayer. 2 Chr 20:9.
Contrition. Neh 1:4; Esth 4:3; Is 22:12.
Learning righteousness. Is 26:9.
Should be a warning to others. Luke 13:3,5.
May be averted by
Humiliation. Ex 33:3,4,14; 2 Chr 7:14.
Prayer. Judg 3:9-11; 2 Chr 7:13,14.
Forsaking iniquity. Jer 18:7,8.
Turning to God. Deut 30:1-3.
Saints
Preserved during. Job 5:19,20; Ps 91:7; Is 26:20; Ezek 9:6; Rev 7:3.
Provided for, during. Gen 47:12; Ps 33:19; 37:19.
Pray for those under. Ex 32:11-13; Num 11:2; Dan 9:3.
Sympathise with those under. Jer 9:1; 13:17; Lam 3:48.
Acknowledge the justice of. 2 Sam 24:17; Ezra 9:13; Neh 9:33; Jer 14:17.
Upon nations - Exemplified
The old world. Gen 6:7,17.
Sodom, etc. Gen 19:24.
Egypt. Ex 9:14.
Israel. Num 14:29,35; 21:6.
People of Ashdod. 1 Sam 5:6.
People of Bethshemesh. 1 Sam 6:19.
Amalekites. 1 Sam 15:3.
Upon individuals - Exemplified
Cain. Gen 4:11,12.
Canaan. Gen 9:25.
Korah, etc. Num 16:33-35.
Achan. Josh 7:25.
Hophni, etc. 1 Sam 2:34.
Saul. 1 Sam 15:23.
Uzzah. 2 Sam 6:7.
Jeroboam. 1 Kin 13:4.
Ahab. 1 Kin 22:38.
Gehazi. 2 Kin 5:27.
Jezebel. 2 Kin 9:35.
Nebuchadnezzar. Dan 4:31.
Belshazzar. Dan 5:30.
Zacharias. Luke 1:20.
Ananias, etc. Acts 5:1-10.
Herod. Acts 12:23.
Elymas. Acts 13:11.
Preservation during - Exemplified
Noah. Gen 7:1,16.
Lot. Gen 19:15-17.
Joseph, etc. Gen 45:7.
Elijah. 1 Kin 17:9.
Elisha, etc. 2 Kin 4:38-41.
Shunammite. 2 Kin 8:1,2.

Judgment, The.

Predicted in the Old Testament. 1 Chr 16:33; Ps 9:7; 96:13; Eccl 3:17.
A first principle of the gospel. Heb 6:2.
A day appointed for. Acts 17:31; Rom 2:16.
Time of, unknown to us. Mark 13:32.
Called the
Day of wrath. Rom 2:5; Rev 6:17.
Revelation of the righteous judgment of God. Rom 2:5.
Day of judgment and perdition of ungodly men. 2 Pet 3:7.
Day of destruction. Job 21:30.
Judgment of the great day. Jude 1:6.
Shall be administered by Christ. John 5:22,27; Acts 10:42; Rom 14:10; 2 Cor 5:10.
Saints shall sit with Christ in. 1 Cor 6:2; Rev 20:4.
Shall take place at the coming of Christ. Matt 25:31; 2 Tim 4:1.
Of Heathen, by the law of conscience. Rom 2:12,14,15.
Of Jews, by the law of Moses. Rom 2:12.
Of Christians, by the gospel. James 2:12.
Shall be held upon
All nations. Matt 25:32.
All men. Heb 9:27; 12:23.
Small and great. Rev 20:12.
The righteous and wicked. Eccl 3:17.
Quick and dead. 2 Tim 4:1; 1 Pet 4:5.
Shall be in righteousness. Ps 98:9; Acts 17:31.
The books shall be opened at. Dan 7:10.
Shall be of all
Actions. Eccl 11:9; 12:14; Rev 20:13.
Words. Matt 12:36,37; Jude 1:15.
Thoughts. Eccl 12:14; 1 Cor 4:5.
None, by nature can stand in. Ps 130:3; 143:2; Rom 3:19.
Saints shall, through Christ, be enabled to stand in. Rom 8:33,34.
Christ will acknowledge saints at. Matt 25:34-40; Rev 3:5.
Perfect love will give boldness in. 1 John 4:17.
Saints shall be rewarded at. 2 Tim 4:8; Rev 11:18.
The wicked shall be condemned in. Matt 7:22,23; 25:41.
Final punishment of the wicked will succeed. Matt 13:40-42; 25:46.
The word of Christ shall be a witness against the wicked in. John 12:48.
The certainty of, a motive to
Repentance. Acts 17:30,31.
Faith. Is 28:16,17.
Holiness. 2 Cor 5:9,10; 2 Pet 3:11,14.
Prayer and watchfulness. Mark 13:33.
Warn the wicked of. Acts 24:25; 2 Cor 5:11.
The wicked dread. Acts 24:25; Heb 10:27.
Neglected advantages increase condemnation at. Matt 11:20-24; Luke 11:31,32.
Devils shall be condemned at. 2 Pet 2:4; Jude 1:6.

Justice.

Commanded. Deut 16:20; Is 56:1.
Christ, an example of. Ps 98:9; Is 11:4; Jer 23:5.
Specially required in rulers. 2 Sam 23:3; Ezek 45:9.
To be done
In executing judgment. Deut 16:18; Jer 21:12.
In buying and selling. Lev 19:36; Deut 25:15.
To the poor. Prov 29:14; 31:9.
To the fatherless and widows. Is 1:17.
To servants. Col 4:1.
Gifts impede. Ex 23:8.
God
Requires. Mic 6:8.
Sets the highest value on. Prov 2:13.
Delights in. Prov 11:1.
Gives wisdom to execute. 1 Kin 3:11,12; Prov 2:6,9.
Displeased with the want of. Eccl 5:8.
Brings its own reward. Jer 22:15.
Saints should
Study the principles of. Phil 4:8.
Receive instruction in. Prov 1:3.
Pray for wisdom to execute. 1 Kin 3:9.
Always do. Ps 119:121; Ezek 18:8,9.
Take pleasure in doing. Prov 21:15.
Teach others to do. Gen 18:19.
Promises to. Is 33:15,16; Jer 7:5,7.
The wicked
Scorn. Prov 19:28.
Abhor. Mic 3:9.
Call not for. Is 59:4.
Banish. Is 59:14.
Pass over. Luke 11:42.
Afflict those who act with. Job 12:4; Amos 5:12.
Exemplified
Moses. Num 16:15.
Samuel. 1 Sam 12:4.
David. 2 Sam 8:15.
Solomon. 1 Kin 3:16-27.
Josiah. Jer 22:15.
Joseph. Luke 23:50,51.
Apostles. 1 Thess 2:10.

Justice of God, The.

Is a part of his character. Deut 32:4; Is 45:21.
Declared to be
Plenteous. Job 37:23.
Incomparable. Job 4:1.
Incorruptible. Deut 10:17; 2 Chr 19:7.
Impartial. 2 Chr 19:7; Jer 32:19.
Unfailing. Zeph 3:5.
Undeviating. Job 8:3; 34:12.
Without respect of persons. Rom 2:11; Col 3:25; 1 Pet 1:17.
The habitation of his throne. Ps 89:14.
Not to be sinned against. Jer 50:7.
Denied by the ungodly. Ezek 33:17,20.
Exhibited in
Forgiving sins. 1 John 1:9.
Redemption. Rom 3:26.
His government. Ps 9:4; Jer 9:24.

His judgments. Gen 18:25; Rev 19:2.
All his ways. Ezek 18:25,29.
The final judgment. Acts 17:31.
Acknowledge. Ps 51:4; Rom 3:4.
Magnify. Ps 98:9; 99:3,4.

JUSTIFICATION BEFORE GOD.

Promised in Christ. Is 45:25; 53:11.
Is the act of God. Is 50:8; Rom 8:33.
Under law
Requires perfect obedience. Lev 18:5; Rom 10:5; 2:13; James 2:10.
Man cannot attain to. Job 9:2,3,20; 25:4; Ps 130:3; 143:2; Rom 3:20; 9:31,32.
Under the gospel
Is not of works. Acts 13:39; Rom 8:3; Gal 2:16; 3:11.
Is not of faith and works united. Acts 15:1-29; Rom 3:28; 11:6; Gal 2:14-21; 5:4.
Is by faith alone. John 5:24; Acts 13:39; Rom 3:30; 5:1; Gal 2:16.
Is of grace. Rom 3:24; 4:16; 5:17-21.
In the name of Christ. 1 Cor 6:11.
By imputation of Christ's righteousness. Is 61:10; Jer 23:6; Rom 3:22; 5:18; 1 Cor 1:30; 2 Cor 5:21.
By the blood of Christ. Rom 5:9.
By the resurrection of Christ. Rom 4:25; 1 Cor 15:17.
Blessedness of. Ps 32:1,2; Rom 4:6-8.
Frees from condemnation. Is 50:8,9; 54:17; Rom 8:33,34.
Entitles to an inheritance. Titus 3:7.
Ensures glorification. Rom 8:30.
The wicked shall not attain to. Ex 23:7.
By faith
Revealed under the Old Testament age. Hab 2:4; Rom 1:17.
Excludes boasting. Rom 3:27; 4:2; 1 Cor 1:29,31.
Does not make void the law. Rom 3:30,31; 1 Cor 9:21.
Typified. Zech 3:4,5.
Illustrated. Luke 18:14.
Exemplified
Abraham. Gen 15:6.
Paul. Phil 3:8,9.

KENITES, THE.

Originally a people of Canaan. Gen 15:19.
Connected with the Midianites. Num 10:29; Judg 4:11.
Dwelt in strongholds. Num 24:21.
Had many cities. 1 Sam 30:29.
Moses
Intermarried with. Ex 2:21; Judg 1:16.
Invited, to accompany Israel. Num 10:29-32.
Part of, dwelt with Israel. Judg 1:16; 4:11.
Part of, dwelt with the Amalekites. 1 Sam 15:6.
Showed kindness to Israel in the desert. Ex 18:1-27.
Not destroyed with the Amalekites. 1 Sam 15:6.
The Rechabites descended from. 1 Chr 2:55.
Sisera slain by Jael one of. Judg 4:22; 5:24.
David
Pretended that he invaded. 1 Sam 27:10.
Sent part of the spoil of war to. 1 Sam 30:29.
Ruin of, predicted. Num 24:21,22.

KINGS.

Israel warned against seeking. 1 Sam 8:9-18.
Sin of Israel in seeking. 1 Sam 12:17-20.
Israel in seeking, rejected God as their king. 1 Sam 8:7; 10:19.
Israel asked for, that they might be like the nations. 1 Sam 8:5,19,20.
First given to Israel in anger. Hos 13:11.
God reserved to himself the choice of. Deut 17:14,15; 1 Sam 9:16,17; 16:12.
When first established in Israel, not hereditary. Deut 17:20; 1 Sam 13:13,14; 15:28,29.
Rendered hereditary in the family of David. 2 Sam 7:12-16; Ps 89:35-37.
Of Israel not to be foreigners. Deut 17:15.
Laws for the government of the kingdom by, written by Samuel. 1 Sam 10:25.
Forbidden to multiply
Horses. Deut 17:16.
Wives. Deut 17:17.
Treasure. Deut 17:17.
Required to write and keep by them, a copy of the divine law. Deut 17:18-20.
Had power to make war and peace. 1 Sam 11:5-7.
Often exercised power arbitrarily. 1 Sam 22:17,18; 2 Sam 1:15; 4:9-12; 1 Kin 2:23,25,31.
Ceremonies at inauguration of
Anointing. 1 Sam 10:1; 16:13; Ps 89:20.
Crowning. 2 Kin 11:12; 2 Chr 23:11; Ps 21:3.
Proclaiming with trumpets. 2 Sam 15:10; 1 Kin 1:34; 2 Kin 9:13; 11:14.
Enthroning. 1 Kin 1:35,46; 2 Kin 11:19.
Girding on the sword. Ps 45:3.
Putting into their hands the books of the law. 2 Kin 11:12; 2 Chr 23:11.
Covenanting to govern lawfully. 2 Sam 5:3.
Receiving homage. 1 Sam 10:1; 1 Chr 29:24.
Shouting "God save the king." 1 Sam 10:24; 2 Sam 16:16; 2 Kin 11:12.
Offering sacrifice. 1 Sam 11:15.
Feasting. 1 Chr 12:38,39; 29:22.
Attended by a body-guard. 1 Sam 13:2; 2 Sam 8:18; 1 Chr 11:25; 2 Chr 12:10.
Dwelt in royal palaces. 2 Chr 9:11; Ps 45:15.
Arrayed in royal apparel. 1 Kin 22:30; Matt 6:29.
Names of, often changed at their accession. 2 Kin 23:34; 24:17.
Officers of
Prime minister. 2 Chr 19:11; 28:7.
First Counsellor. 1 Chr 27:33.
Confidant or king's special friend. 1 Kin 4:5; 1 Chr 27:33.
Comptroller of the household. 1 Kin 4:6; 2 Chr 28:7.
Scribe or secretary. 2 Sam 8:17; 1 Kin 4:3.
Captain of the host. 2 Sam 8:16; 1 Kin 4:4.
Captain of the guard. 2 Sam 8:18; 20:23.
Recorder. 2 Sam 8:16; 1 Kin 4:3.
Providers for the king's table. 1 Kin 4:7-19.
Master of the wardrobe. 2 Kin 22:14; 2 Chr 34:22.
Treasurer. 1 Chr 27:25.
Storekeeper. 1 Chr 27:25.
Overseer of the tribute. 1 Kin 4:6; 12:18.
Overseer of royal farms. 1 Chr 27:26.
Overseer of royal vineyards. 1 Chr 27:27.
Overseer of royal plantations. 1 Chr 27:28.
Overseer of royal herds. 1 Sam 21:7; 1 Chr 27:29.
Overseer of royal camels. 1 Chr 27:30.
Overseer of royal flocks. 1 Chr 27:31.
Armour-bearer. 1 Sam 16:21.
Cup-bearer. 1 Kin 10:5; 2 Chr 9:5.
Approached with greatest reverence. 1 Sam 24:8; 2 Sam 9:8; 14:22; 1 Kin 1:23.
Presented with gifts by strangers. 1 Kin 10:2,10,25; 2 Kin 5:5; Matt 2:11.
Right hand of, the place of honour. 1 Kin 2:19; Ps 45:9; 110:1.
Attendants of, stood in their presence. 1 Kin 10:8; 2 Kin 25:19.
Exercised great hospitality. 1 Sam 20:25-27; 2 Sam 9:7-13; 19:33; 1 Kin 4:22,23,28.
Their revenues derived from
Voluntary contributions. 1 Sam 10:27; 16:20; 1 Chr 12:39,40.
Tribute from foreign nations. 1 Kin 4:21,24,25; 2 Chr 8:8; 17:11.
Tax on produce of the land. 1 Kin 4:7-19.
Tax on foreign merchandise. 1 Kin 10:15.
Their own flocks and herds. 2 Chr 32:29.
Produce of their own lands. 2 Chr 26:10.
Sometimes nominated their successors. 1 Kin 1:33,34; 2 Chr 11:22,23.
Punished for transgressing the divine law. 2 Sam 12:7-12; 1 Kin 21:18-24.
Who reigned over all Israel
Saul. 1 Sam 11:15-31:13; 1 Chr 10:1-10:14.
David. 2 Sam 2:4-1Ki 2:11; 1 Chr 11:1-29:30.
Solomon. 1 Kin 1:39-11:43; 2 Chr 1:1-9:31.
Rehoboam (first part of his reign). 1 Kin 12:1-20; 2 Chr 10:1-16.
Who reigned over Judah
Rehoboam (latter part of his reign). 1 Kin 12:21-24; 14:21-31; 2 Chr 10:17-12:16.
Abijam or Abijah. 1 Kin 15:1-8; 2 Chr 13:1-22.
Asa. 1 Kin 15:9-24; 2 Chr 14:1-16:14.
Jehoshaphat. 1 Kin 22:41-50; 2 Chr 17:1-21:1.

Jehoram or Joram. 2 Kin 8:16-24; 2 Chr 21:1-20.
Ahaziah. 2 Kin 8:25-29; 9:16-29; 2 Chr 22:1-9.
Athaliah, mother of Ahaziah (usurper). 2 Kin 11:1-3; 2 Chr 22:10-12.
Joash or Jehoash. 2 Kin 11:4-12:21; 2 Chr 23:1-24:27.
Amaziah. 2 Kin 14:1-20; 2 Chr 25:1-28.
Azariah or Uzziah. 2 Kin 14:21,22; 15:1-7; 2 Chr 26:1-23.
Jotham. 2 Kin 15:32-38; 2 Chr 27:1-9.
Ahaz. 2 Kin 16:1-20; 2 Chr 28:1-27.
Hezekiah. 2 Kin 18:1-20:21; 2 Chr 29:1-32:33.
Manasseh. 2 Kin 21:1-18; 2 Chr 33:1-20.
Amon. 2 Kin 21:19-26; 2 Chr 33:21-25.
Josiah. 2 Kin 22:1-23:30; 2 Chr 34:1-35:27.
Jehoahaz. 2 Kin 23:31-33; 2 Chr 36:1-4.
Jehoiakim. 2 Kin 23:34-24:6; 2 Chr 36:5-8.
Jehoiachin. 2 Kin 24:8-16; 2 Chr 36:9,10.
Zedekiah. 2 Kin 24:17-25:7; 2 Chr 36:11-21.
Who reigned over Israel
Jeroboam. 1 Kin 12:20; 12:25-14:20.
Nadab. 1 Kin 15:25-27,32.
Baasha. 1 Kin 15:28-16:7.
Elah. 1 Kin 16:8-14.
Zimri. 1 Kin 16:11,12,15,20.
Omri. 1 Kin 16:23-28.
Ahab. 1 Kin 16:29-22:40.
Ahaziah. 1 Kin 22:51-53; 2 Kin 1:18.
Jehoram or Joram. 2 Kin 3:1-9:26.
Jehu. 2 Kin 9:3-10:36.
Jehoahaz. 2 Kin 13:1-9.
Jehoash or Joash. 2 Kin 13:10-25; 14:8-16.
Jeroboam the Second. 2 Kin 14:23-29.
Zachariah. 2 Kin 15:8-12.
Shallum. 2 Kin 15:13-15.
Menahem. 2 Kin 15:16-22.
Pekahiah. 2 Kin 15:23-26.
Pekah. 2 Kin 15:27-31; 16:5.
Hoshea. 2 Kin 17:1-6.
Called the Lord's anointed. 1 Sam 16:6; 24:6; 2 Sam 19:21.
Conspiracies against
Absalom against David. 2 Sam 15:10.
Adonijah against Solomon. 1 Kin 1:5-7.
Jeroboam against Rehoboam. 1 Kin 12:12,16.
Baasha against Nadab. 1 Kin 15:27.
Zimri against Elah. 1 Kin 16:9,10.
Omri against Zimri. 1 Kin 16:17.
Jehu against Joram. 2 Kin 9:14.
Shallum against Zachariah. 2 Kin 15:10.
Menahem against Shallum. 2 Kin 15:14.
Pekah against Menahem. 1 Kin 15:25.
God chooses. Deut 17:15; 1 Chr 28:4-6.
God ordains. Rom 13:1.
God anoints. 1 Sam 16:12; 2 Sam 12:7.
Set up by God. 1 Sam 12:13; Dan 2:21.
Removed by God. 1 Kin 11:11; Dan 2:21.
Christ is the Prince of. Rev 1:5.
Christ is the King of. Rev 17:14.
Reign by direction of Christ. Prov 8:15.
Supreme judges of nations. 1 Sam 8:5.
Resistance to, is resistance to the ordinance of God. Rom 13:2.
Able to enforce their commands. Eccl 8:4.
Numerous subjects the honour of. Prov 14:28.
Not save by their armies. Ps 33:16.
Dependent on the earth. Eccl 5:9.
Should
Fear God. Deut 17:19.
Serve Christ. Ps 2:10-12.
Keep the law of God. 1 Kin 2:3.
Study the Scriptures. Deut 17:19.
Promote the interests of the Church. Ezra 1:2-4; 6:1-12.
Nourish the Church. Is 49:23.
Rule in the fear of God. 2 Sam 23:3.
Maintain the cause of the poor and oppressed. Prov 31:8,9.
Investigate all matters. Prov 25:2.
Not pervert judgment. Prov 31:5.
Prolong their reign by hating covetousness. Prov 28:16.
Throne of, established by righteousness and justice. Prov 16:12; 29:14.
Specially warned against
Impurity. Prov 31:3.
Lying. Prov 17:7.
Hearkening to lies. Prov 29:12.
Intemperance. Prov 31:4,5.
The gospel to be preached to. Acts 9:15; 26:27,28.
Without understanding, are oppressors. Prov 28:16.
Often reproved by God. 1 Chr 16:21.
Judgments upon, when opposed to Christ. Ps 2:2,5,9.
When good
Regard God as their strength. Ps 99:4.
Speak righteously. Prov 16:10.
Love righteous lips. Prov 16:13.
Abhor wickedness. Prov 16:12.
Discountenance evil. Prov 20:8.
Punish the wicked. Prov 20:8.
Favour the wise. Prov 14:35.
Honour the diligent. Prov 22:29.
Befriend the good. Prov 22:14.
Are pacified by submission. Prov 16:14; 25:15.
Evil counsellors should be removed from. 2 Chr 22:3,4; Prov 25:5.
Curse not, even in thought. Ex 22:28; Eccl 10:20.
Speak no evil of. Job 34:18; 2 Pet 2:10.
Pay tribute to. Matt 22:21; Rom 13:6,7.
Be not presumptuous before. Prov 25:6.
Should be
Honoured. Rom 13:7; 1 Pet 2:17.
Feared. Prov 24:21.
Reverenced. 1 Sam 24:8; 1 Kin 1:23,21.
Obeyed. Rom 13:1,5; 1 Pet 2:13.
Prayed for. 1 Tim 2:1,2.
Folly of resisting. Prov 19:12; 20:2.
Punishment for resisting the lawful authority of. Rom 13:2.
Guilt and danger of stretching out the hand against. 1 Sam 26:9; 2 Sam 1:14.
They that walk after the flesh despise. 2 Pet 2:10; Jude 1:8.
Good—Exemplified
David. 2 Sam 8:15.
Asa. 1 Kin 15:11.
Jehoshaphat. 1 Kin 22:43.
Amaziah. 2 Kin 15:3.
Uzziah. 2 Kin 15:34.
Hezekiah. 2 Kin 18:3.
Josiah. 2 Kin 22:2.

LAMB, THE.

The young of the flock. Ex 12:5; Ezek 45:15.
Described as
Patient. Is 53:7.
Playful. Ps 114:4,6.
Exposed to danger from wild beasts. 1 Sam 17:34.
The shepherd's care for. Is 40:11.
Used for
Food. Deut 32:14; 2 Sam 12:4.
Clothing. Prov 27:26.
Sacrifice. 1 Chr 29:21; 2 Chr 29:32.
Considered a great delicacy. Amos 6:4.
Offered in sacrifice
Males. Ex 12:5.
Females. Num 6:14.
While sucking. 1 Sam 7:9.
At a year old. Ex 12:5; Num 6:14.
From the earliest times. Gen 4:4; 22:7,8.
Every morning and evening. Ex 29:38,39; Num 28:3,4.
At the Passover. Ex 12:3,6,7.
By the wicked not accepted. Is 1:11; 66:3.
Numbers of, given by Josiah to the people for sacrifice. 2 Chr 35:7.
The firstborn of an ass to be redeemed with. Ex 13:13; 34:20.
An extensive commerce in. Ezra 7:17; Ezek 27:21.
Tribute often paid in. 2 Kin 3:4; Is 16:1.
Covenants confirmed by gift of. Gen 21:28-30.
The image of, was the first impression of on money. Gen 33:19; Josh 24:32.
Illustrative
Of purity of Christ. 1 Pet 1:19.
Of Christ as a sacrifice. John 1:29; Rev 5:6.
Of any thing dear or cherished. 2 Sam 12:3,9.
Of the Lord's people. Is 5:17; 11:6.
Of weak believers. Is 40:11; John 21:15.
(Patience of,) of the patience of Christ. Is 53:7; Acts 8:32.
(Among wolves,) of ministers among the ungodly. Luke 10:3.
(Deserted and exposed,) of Israel deprived of God's protection. Hos 4:16.
(Brought to slaughter,) of the wicked under judgments. Jer 51:40.
(Consumed in sacrifice,) of complete destruction of the wicked. Ps 37:20.

LAMPS.

Design of. 2 Pet 1:19.
Described as
Burning. Gen 15:17.
Shining. John 5:35.
Lighted with oil. Matt 25:3,8.
Oil for, carried in vessels. Matt 25:4.
Sometimes supplied with oil form a bowl through pipes. Zech 4:2.
Required to be constantly trimmed. Matt 25:7.

Used for lighting
The tabernacle. Ex 25:37.
Private apartments. Acts 20:8.
Chariots of war by night. Nah 2:3,4.
Marriage processions. Matt 25:1.
Persons going out at night. John 18:3.
Often kept lighting all night. Prov 31:18.
Placed on a stand to give light to all in the house. Matt 5:15.
Illumination of the tents of Arab chiefs by, alluded to. Job 29:3,4.
Probable origin of dark lantern. Judg 7:16.
Illustrative
Of the word of God. Ps 119:105; Prov 6:23.
Of omniscience of Christ. Dan 10:6; Rev 1:14.
Of graces of the Holy Spirit. Rev 4:5.
Of salvation of God. Gen 15:17; Is 62:1.
Of God's guidance. 2 Sam 22:29; Ps 18:28.
Of glory of the cherubim. Ezek 1:13.
Of spirit of man. Prov 20:27.
Of ministers. John 5:35.
Of wise rulers. 2 Sam 21:17.
Of severe judgments. Rev 8:10.
Of a succession of heirs. 1 Kin 11:36; 15:4.
(Put out,) of destruction of the wicked. Job 18:5,6; 21:17; 13:9.
(Totally quenched,) of complete destruction of those who curse parents. Prov 20:20.

LANGUAGE.

Of all mankind one at first. Gen 11:1,6.
Called
Speech. Mark 14:70; Acts 14:11.
Tongue. Acts 1:19; Rev 5:9.
Confusion of
A punishment for presumption, etc. Gen 11:2-6.
Originated the varieties in. Gen 11:7.
Scattered men over the earth. Gen 11:8,9.
Divided men into separated nations. Gen 10:5,20,31.
Great variety of, spoken by men. 1 Cor 14:10.
Ancient kingdoms often comprehended nations of different. Esth 1:22; Dan 3:4; 6:25.
Kinds of, mentioned
Hebrew. 2 Kin 18:28; Acts 26:14.
Chaldea. Dan 1:4.
Syriack. 2 Kin 18:26; Ezra 4:7.
Greek. Acts 21:37.
Latin. Luke 23:38.
Lycaonian. Acts 14:11.
Arabic, etc. Acts 2:11.
Egyptian. Ps 84:5; 114:1; Acts 2:10.
Of some nations difficult. Ezek 3:5,6.
The term barbarian applied to those who spoke a strange. 1 Cor 14:11.
Power of speaking different
A gift of the Holy Spirit. 1 Cor 12:10.
Promised. Mark 16:17.
Given on the day of Pentecost. Acts 2:3,4.
Followed receiving the gospel. Acts 10:44-46.
Conferred by laying on of the apostles' hands. Acts 8:17,18; 19:6.
Necessary to spread of the gospel. Acts 2:7-11.
A sign to unbelievers. 1 Cor 14:22.
Sometimes abused. 1 Cor 14:2-12,23.
Ceased when the written Bible completed. 1 Cor 13:8-10.
Interpretation of
Antiquity of engaging persons for. Gen 42:23.
A gift of the Holy Spirit. 1 Cor 12:10.
Most important in the early church. 1 Cor 14:5,13,27,28.
The Jews punished by being given up to people of a strange. Deut 28:49; Is 28:11; Jer 5:15.

LAVER OF BRASS.

Moses was commanded to make. Ex 30:18.
Wisdom given to Bezaleel to make. Ex 31:2,9.
Made of brazen mirrors of the women. Ex 38:8.
Was placed in the court between the altar and the tabernacle. Ex 30:18; 40:7,30.
Was anointed with holy oil. Ex 40:11; Lev 8:11.
The priests washed in
Before consecration. Ex 40:12.
Before entering the tabernacle. Ex 30:19,20.
Before approaching the altar. Ex 30:20.
One made by Solomon for the temple. 1 Kin 7:23-26; 2 Kin 25:13.
Called the Brazen sea. 2 Kin 25:13; Jer 52:17.
Illustrative of
Christ the fountain for sin. Zech 13:1; Rev 1:5.
Regeneration. Titus 3:5; Eph 5:26.

LAW OF GOD, THE.

Is absolute and perpetual. Matt 5:18.
Given
To Adam. Gen 2:16,17; Rom 5:12-14.
To Noah. Gen 9:6.
To the Israelites. Ex 20:2-17; Ps 78:5.
Through Moses. Ex 31:18; John 7:19.
Through the ministration of angels. Acts 7:53; Gal 3:19; Heb 2:2.
Described as
Pure. Ps 19:8.
Spiritual. Rom 7:14.
Holy, just, and good. Rom 7:12.
Exceeding broad. Ps 119:96.
Perfect. Ps 19:7; Rom 12:2.
Truth. Ps 119:142.
Not grievous. 1 John 5:3.
Requires obedience of the heart. Ps 51:6; Matt 5:28; 22:37.
Requires perfect obedience. Deut 27:26; Gal 3:10; James 2:10.
Love is the fulfilling of. Rom 13:8,10; Gal 3:10; James 2:10.
It is man's duty to keep. Eccl 12:13.
Man, by nature, not in subjection to. Rom 7:5; 8:7.
Man cannot render perfect obedience to. 1 Kin 8:46; Eccl 7:20; Rom 3:10.
Sin is a transgression of. 1 John 3:4.
All men have transgressed. Rom 3:9,19.
Man cannot be justified by. Acts 13:39; Rom 3:20,28; Gal 2:16; 3:11.
Gives the knowledge of sin. Rom 3:20; 7:7.
Works wrath. Rom 4:15.
Conscience testifies to. Rom 2:15.
Designed to lead to Christ. Gal 3:24.
Obedience to
A characteristic of saints. Rev 12:17.
A test of love. 1 John 5:3.
Of prime importance. 1 Cor 7:19.
Blessedness of keeping. Ps 119:1; Matt 5:19; 1 John 3:22,24; Rev 22:14.
Christ
Came to fulfil. Matt 5:17.
Magnified. Is 42:21.
Explained. Matt 7:12; 22:37-40.
The love of, produces peace. Ps 119:165.
Saints
Freed from the bondage of. Rom 6:14; 7:4,6; Gal 3:13.
Freed from the curse of. Gal 3:13.
Have, written on their hearts. Jer 31:33; Heb 8:10.
Love. Ps 119:97,113.
Delight in. Ps 119:77; Rom 7:22.
Prepare their hearts to seek. Ezra 7:10.
Pledge themselves to walk in. Neh 10:29.
Keep. Ps 119:55.
Pray to understand. Ps 119:18.
Pray for power to keep. Ps 119:34.
Should remember. Mal 4:4.
Should make the subject of their conversation. Ex 13:9.
Lament over the violation of, by others. Ps 119:136.
The wicked
Despise. Amos 2:4.
Forget. Hos 4:6.
Forsake. 2 Chr 12:1; Jer 9:13.
Refuse to hear. Is 30:9; Jer 6:19.
Refuse to walk in. Ps 78:10.
Cast away. Is 5:24.
Is the rule of life to saints. 1 Cor 9:21; Gal 5:13,14.
Is the rule of the judgment. Rom 2:12.
To be used lawfully. 1 Tim 1:8.
Established by faith. Rom 3:31.
Punishment for disobeying. Neh 9:26,27; Is 65:11-13; Jer 9:13-16.

LAW OF MOSES, THE.

Is the law of God. Lev 26:46.
Given
In the desert. Ezek 20:10,11.
At Horeb. Deut 4:10,15; 5:2.
From the Mount Sinai. Ex 19:11,20.
By disposition of angels. Acts 7:53.
Through Moses as mediator. Deut 5:5,27,28; John 1:17; Gal 3:19.
To the Jews. Lev 26:46; Ps 78:5.
After the exodus. Deut 4:45; Ps 81:4,5.
To no other nation. Deut 4:8; Ps 147:20.
None to approach the Mount while God gave. Ex 19:13,21-24; Heb 12:20.
Remarkable phenomena connected with, at giving of. Ex 19:16-19.
Terror of Israel at receiving. Ex 19:16; 20:18-20; Deut 5:5,23-25.
Additions made to, in the plains of Moab by Jordan. Num 36:13.

Called
A fiery law. Deut 33:2.
Word spoken by angels. Heb 2:2.
Ministration of death. 2 Cor 3:7.
Ministration of condemnation. 2 Cor 3:9.
Lively oracles. Acts 7:38.
Royal law. James 2:8.
Book of the law. Deut 30:10; Josh 1:8.
Book of Moses. 2 Chr 25:4; 35:12.
Rehearsed by Moses. Deut 1:1-3.
Entire of, written in a book. Deut 31:9.
Book of, laid up in the sanctuary. Deut 31:26.
Tables of, laid up in the ark. Deut 10:5.
Divided into
Moral, embodied in the ten commandments. Deut 5:22; 10:4.
Ceremonial, relating to manner of worshipping God. Lev 7:37,38; Heb 9:1-7.
Civil, relating to administration of justice. Deut 17:9-11; Acts 23:3; 24:6.
A covenant of works to the Jews as a nation. Deut 28:1,15; Jer 31:32.
Taught the Jews
To love and fear God. Deut 6:5; 10:12,13; Matt 22:36,38.
To love their neighbour. Lev 19:18; Matt 22:39.
Strict justice and impartiality. Lev 19:35,36.
All punishments awarded according to. John 8:5; 19:7; Heb 10:28.
All Israelites required
To know. Ex 18:16.
To observe. Deut 4:6; 6:2.
To lay up, in their hearts. Deut 6:6; 11:18.
To remember. Mal 4:4.
To teach their children. Deut 6:7; 11:19.
Kings to write and study. Deut 17:18,19.
Good kings enforced. 2 Kin 23:24,25; 2 Chr 31:21.
Priests and Levites to teach. Deut 33:8-10; Neh 8:7; Mal 2:7.
The scribes were learned in, and expounded. Ezra 7:6; Matt 23:2.
Public instruction given to youth in. Luke 2:46; Acts 22:3.
Publicly read
At the feast of tabernacles in the sabbatical year. Deut 31:10-13.
By Joshua. Josh 8:34,35.
By Ezra. Neh 8:2,3.
In the synagogues every Sabbath day. Acts 13:15; 15:21.
A means of national reformation. 2 Chr 34:19-21; Neh 8:13-18.
A shadow of good things to come. Heb 10:1.
Could not give righteous and life. Gal 3:21; Rom 8:3,4; Heb 10:1.
A schoolmaster to lead to Christ. Gal 3:24.
Christ
Made under. Gal 4:4.
Circumcised according to. Luke 2:21; Rom 15:8.
Came not to destroy but to fulfil. Matt 5:17,18.
Attended all feasts of. John 2:23; 7:2,10,37.
Fulfilled all precepts of. Ps 40:7,8.
Fulfilled all types and shadows of. Heb 9:8,11-14; 10:1,11-14.
Magnified and made honourable. Is 42:21.
Bore the curse of. Deut 21:23; Gal 3:13.
Abrogated, as a covenant of works. Rom 7:4.
Was not the manifestation of the grace of God. John 1:17; Rom 8:3,4.
Could not disannul the covenant of grace made in Christ. Gal 3:17.
Jewish converts would have all Christians observe. Acts 15:1.
The Jews
Jealous for. John 9:28,29; Acts 21:20.
Held those ignorant of, accursed. John 7:49.
From regard to, rejected Christ. Rom 9:31-33.
Accused Christ of breaking. John 19:7.
Accused Christians of speaking. Acts 6:11-14; 21:28.
Broke it themselves. John 7:19.
Dishonoured God by breaking. Rom 2:23.
Shall be judged by. John 5:45; Rom 2:12.
Was a burdensome yoke. Acts 15:10.
Darkness, etc. at giving of, illustrative of obscurity of Mosaic age. Heb 12:18-24.

LEAVEN.

Used in making bread. Hos 7:4.
Diffusive properties of. 1 Cor 5:6.
Forbidden
During the feast of the Passover. Ex 12:15-20.
To be offered with blood. Ex 34:25.
To be offered, etc. with meat offerings which were burned. Lev 2:11; 10:12.
Used with thank offerings. Lev 7:13; Amos 4:5.
Firstfruits of wheat offered with. Lev 23:17.
Illustrative of
The rapid spread of the gospel. Matt 13:33; Luke 13:21.
Doctrines of Pharisees, etc. Matt 16:6,12.
Ungodly professors. 1 Cor 5:6,7.
False teachers. Gal 5:8,9.
Malice and wickedness. 1 Cor 5:8.

LEBANON.

Bounded the land of Canaan on the north. Deut 1:7; 11:24.
Given to Israel. Josh 13:5,6.
Celebrated for
Cedars. Ps 29:5; 92:12; Is 14:8.
Flowers. Nah 1:4.
Fragrance. Song 4:11.
Fragrance of its wines. Hos 14:7.
Glorious appearance. Is 35:2.
Great part of, not conquered by the Israelites. Josh 13:2,5; Judg 3:1-4.
Called
The mountains. 2 Chr 2:2.
Mount Lebanon. Judg 3:3.
That goodly mountain. Deut 3:25.
Lofty tops of, covered with snow. Jer 18:14.
Part of, barren. Is 29:17.
Forests of, infested with wild beasts. Song 4:8; Is 40:16; Hab 2:17.
Many streams came from. Song 4:15.
Formerly inhabited by the Hivites. Judg 3:3.
Moses anxious to behold. Deut 3:25.
Furnished
Wood for Solomon's temple. 1 Kin 5:5,6.
Stones for Solomon's temple. 1 Kin 5:14,18.
Wood for second temple. Ezra 3:7.
Solomon built
The house of the forest of. 1 Kin 7:2.
Storehouses in. 1 Kin 9:19.
Difficulties of passing, surmounted by Assyrian army. 2 Kin 19:23.
Illustrative
Of great and powerful monarchs. Is 10:24,34.
Of the Gentile world. Is 29:17.
Of the Jewish nation. Jer 22:6,23; Heb 2:17.
Of the temple. Zech 11:1.
(Glory of,) of the glory of the church. Is 35:2; 60:13.
(Fragrance of,) of the graces of the church. Song 4:11; Hos 14:6,7.
(Shaking of its forests,) of prodigious growth of the church. Ps 72:16.
(Mourning of,) of deep affliction. Ezek 31:15.

LEOPARD.

Inhabited mountains of Canaan. Song 4:8.
Described as
Spotted. Jer 13:23.
Fierce and cruel. Jer 5:6.
Swift. Hab 1:8.
Lies in wait for its prey. Jer 5:6; Hos 13:7.
Illustrative
Of God in his judgments. Hos 13:7.
Of the Macedonian empire. Dan 7:6.
Of antichrist. Rev 13:2.
(Tamed,) of the wicked subdued by the gospel. Is 11:6.

LEPROSY.

A common disease among the Jews. Luke 4:27.
Infected
Men. Luke 17:12.
Women. Num 12:10.
Houses. Lev 14:34.
Garments. Lev 13:47.
An incurable disease. 2 Kin 5:7.
Often sent as a punishment for sin. Num 12:9,10; 2 Chr 26:19.
Often hereditary. 2 Sam 3:29; 2 Kin 5:27.
Parts affected by
The hand. Ex 4:6.
The head. Lev 13:44.
The forehead. 2 Chr 26:19.
The beard. Lev 13:30.
The whole body. Luke 5:12.
Often began with a bright red spot. Lev 13:2,24.

Turned the skin white. Ex 4:6; 2 Kin 5:27.
Turned the hair white or yellow. Lev 13:3,10,30.
The priests
Judges and directors in cases of. Deut 24:8.
Examined persons suspected of. Lev 13:2,9.
Shut up persons suspected of, seven days. Lev 13:4.
Had rules for distinguishing. Lev 13:5-44.
Examined all persons healed of. Lev 14:2; Matt 8:4; Luke 17:14.
Ceremonies at cleansing of. Lev 17:14.
Those afflicted with
Ceremonially unclean. Lev 13:8,11,22,44.
Separated from intercourse with others. Num 5:2; 12:14,15.
Associated together. 2 Kin 7:3; Luke 17:12.
Dwelt in a separate house. 2 Kin 15:5.
Cut off from God's house. 2 Chr 26:21.
Excluded from priest's office. Lev 22:2-4.
To have their heads bare, clothes rent, and lip covered. Lev 13:45.
To cry unclean when approached. Lev 13:45.
Less inveterate when it covered the whole body. Lev 13:13.
Power of God manifested in curing. Num 12:13,14; 2 Kin 5:8-14.
Power of Christ manifested in curing. Matt 8:3; Luke 5:13; 17:13,14.
Christ gave power to heal. Matt 10:8.
Garments
Suspected of, shown to priest. Lev 13:49.
Suspected of, shut up seven days. Lev 13:50.
Infected with, to have the piece first torn out. Lev 13:56.
Incurable infected with, burned. Lev 13:51,52.
Suspected of, but not having, washed and pronounced clean. Lev 13:53,54,58,59.
Houses
Suspected of, reported to priest. Lev 14:35.
Suspected of, emptied. Lev 14:36.
Suspected of, inspected by priest. Lev 14:37.
Suspected of, shut up seven days. Lev 14:38.
To have the part infected with, first removed, and the rest scraped, etc. Lev 14:39,42.
Incurably infected with, pulled down and removed. Lev 14:43-45.
Infected with, communicated uncleanness to everyone who entered them. Lev 14:46,47.
Suspected of, but not infected, pronounced clean. Lev 14:48.
Ceremonies at cleansing of. Lev 14:49-53.

LEVIATHAN.

Created by God. Ps 104:26.
Nature and habits of. Job 41:1-34.
God's power, exhibited in destroying. Ps 74:14.
Illustrative of
Powerful and cruel kings. Is 27:1.
Power and severity of God. Job 41:10.

LEVITES, THE.

Descended from Jacob's third son. Gen 29:34; Heb 7:9,10.
Prophecies respecting. Gen 49:5,7; Deut 33:8-11.
Originally consisted for three families or divisions. Num 3:17; 1 Chr 6:16-48.
Not numbered with Israel. Num 1:47-49.
Numbered separately after the people from a month old. Num 3:14-16,39.
Families, as numbered
Of Gershom. Num 3:18,21,22.
Of Kohath. Num 3:19,27,28.
Of Merari. Num 3:20,33,34.
Chosen by God for service of the sanctuary. 1 Chr 15:2; Num 3:6.
Were consecrated. Num 8:6,14.
Taken instead of the firstborn of Israel. Num 3:12,13,40-45; 8:16-18.
Zeal against idolatry a cause of their appointment. Ex 32:26-28; Deut 33:9,10.
Entered on their service at twenty-five years of age. Num 8:24.
Numbered as ministers at thirty. Num 4:3,23-49.
Superannuated at fifty. Num 8:25.
When superannuated required to perform the less arduous duties. Num 8:26.
Ceremonies at consecration of
Cleansing and purifying. Num 8:7.
Making a sin offering for. Num 8:8,12.
Elders of Israel laying their hands on them. Num 8:9,10.
Presenting them to God as an offering for the people. Num 8:11,15.
Setting before the priest and presenting them as their offering to God. Num 8:13.
Given to Aaron and sons. Num 3:9; 8:19.
Encamped round the tabernacle. Num 1:50,52,53; 3:23,29,35.
Marched in the centre of Israel. Num 2:17.
Services of
Ministering to the Lord. Deut 10:8.
Ministering to priests. Num 3:6,7; 18:2.
Ministering to the people. 2 Chr 35:3.
Keeping the charge of the sanctuary. Num 18:3; 1 Chr 23:32.
Keeping sacred instruments and vessels. Num 3:8; 1 Chr 9:28,29.
Keeping sacred oil, flour, etc. 1 Chr 9:29,30.
Keeping sacred treasures. 1 Chr 26:20.
Taking charge of the tithes, offerings, etc. 2 Chr 31:11-19; Neh 12:44.
Doing the service of tabernacle. Num 8:19,22.
Taking down, putting up, and carrying the tabernacle, etc. Num 1:50,51; 4:5-33.
Preparing the sacrifices for the priests. 1 Chr 23:31; 2 Chr 35:11.
Preparing the show bread. 1 Chr 9:31,32; 23:29.
Purifying the holy things. 1 Chr 23:28.
Regulating weights and measures. 1 Chr 23:29.
Teaching the people. 2 Chr 17:8,9; 30:22; 35:3; Neh 8:7.
Blessing the people. Deut 10:8.
Keeping the gates of the temple. 1 Chr 9:17-26; 23:5; 2 Chr 35:15; Neh 12:25.
Conducting the sacred music. 1 Chr 23:5-30; 2 Chr 5:12,13; Neh 12:24,27-43.
Singing praises before the army. 2 Chr 20:21,22.
Judging and deciding in controversies. Deut 17:9; 1 Chr 23:4; 2 Chr 19:8.
Guarded king's person and house in times of danger. 2 Kin 11:5-9; 2 Chr 23:5-7.
Had no inheritance in Israel. Deut 10:9; Josh 13:33; 14:3.
The Jews to be kind and benevolent to. Deut 12:12,18,19; 14:29; 16:11,14.
Eight and forty cities with extensive suburbs, appointed for. Num 35:2-8.
The tithes given to, for their support. Num 18:21,24; 2 Chr 31:4,5; Neh 12:44,45; Heb 7:5.
Bound to give a tenth of their tithes to the priests. Num 18:26-32.
Had a part of their offerings. Deut 18:1,2.
David
Numbered them first from thirty years old. 1 Chr 23:2-3.
Divided them into four classed. 1 Chr 23:4-6.
By his last words had them numbered from twenty years old. 1 Chr 23:24,27.
Made them serve from twenty on account of the lightness of their duties. 1 Chr 23:26,28-32.
Subdivided into 24 courses. 1 Chr 23:6; 25:8-31.
Made them attend in courses. 2 Chr 8:14; 31:17.
Served in courses after captivity. Ezra 6:18.
Had chiefs or officers over them. Num 3:24,30,35; 1 Chr 15:4-10; 2 Chr 35:9; Ezra 8:29.
Were all under control of the high priest's deputy. Num 3:32; 1 Chr 9:20.
While in attendance lodged around the temple. 1 Chr 9:27.
Punished with death for encroaching on the priestly office. Num 18:3.
Punishment of Korah and others of, for offering incense. Num 16:1-35.

LIBERALITY.

Pleasing to God. 2 Cor 9:7; Heb 13:16.
God never forgets. Heb 6:10.
Christ set an example of. 2 Cor 8:9.
Characteristic of saints. Ps 112:9; Is 32:8.
Unprofitable, without love. 1 Cor 13:3.

Should be exercised
In the service of God. Ex 35:21-29.
Toward saints. Rom 12:13; Gal 6:10.
Toward servants. Deut 15:12-14.
Toward the poor. Deut 15:11; Is 58:7.
Toward strangers. Lev 25:35.
Toward enemies. Prov 25:21.
Toward all men. Gal 6:10.
In leading to those in want. Matt 5:42.
In giving alms. Luke 12:33.
In relieving the destitute. Is 58:7.
In forwarding missions. Phil 4:14-16.
In rendering personal services. Phil 2:30.
Without ostentation. Matt 6:1-3.
With simplicity. Rom 12:8.
According to ability. Deut 16:10,17; 1 Cor 16:2.
Willingly. Ex 25:2; 2 Cor 8:12.
Abundantly. 2 Cor 8:7; 9:11-13.
Exercise of, provokes others to. 2 Cor 9:2.
Labour to be enabled to exercise. Acts 20:35; Eph 4:28.
Want of
Brings many a curse. Prov 28:27.
A proof of not loving God. 1 John 3:17.
A proof of not having faith. James 2:14-16.
Blessings connected with. Ps 41:1; Prov 22:9; Acts 20:35.
Promises to. Ps 112:9; Prov 11:25; 28:27; Eccl 11:1,2; Is 58:10.
Exhortations to. Luke 3:11; 11:41; Acts 20:35; 1 Cor 16:1; 1 Tim 6:17,18.
Exemplified
Princes of Israel. Num 7:2.
Boaz. Ruth 2:16.
David. 2 Sam 9:7,10.
Barzillai, etc. 2 Sam 17:28.
Araunah. 2 Sam 24:22.
Shunammite. 2 Kin 4:8,10.
Judah. 2 Chr 24:10,11.
Nehemiah. Neh 7:70.
Jews. Neh 7:71,72.
Job. Job 29:15,16.
Nebuzaradan. Jer 40:4,5.
Joanna, etc. Luke 8:3.
Zacchaeus. Luke 19:8.
Christians. Acts 2:45.
Barnabas. Acts 4:36,37.
Dorcas. Acts 9:36.
Cornelius. Acts 16:2.
Church of Antioch. Acts 11:29,30.
Lydia. Acts 16:15.
Paul. Acts 20:34.
Stephanas, etc. 1 Cor 16:17.
Extraordinary - Exemplified
Israelites. Ex 36:5.
Poor widow. Mark 12:42-44.
Churches of Macedonia. 2 Cor 8:1-5.

LIBERTY, CHRISTIAN.

Foretold. Is 42:7; 61:1.
Conferred
By God. Col 1:13.
By Christ. Gal 4:3-5; 5:1.
By the Holy Spirit. Rom 8:15; 2 Cor 3:17.
Through the gospel. John 8:32.
Confirmed by Christ. John 8:36.
Proclaimed by Christ. Is 61:1; Luke 4:18.
The service of Christ is. 1 Cor 7:22.
Is freedom from
The law. Rom 7:6; 8:2.
The curse of the law. Gal 3:13.
The fear of death. Heb 2:15.
Sin. Rom 6:7,18.
Corruption. Rom 8:21.
Bondage of man. 1 Cor 9:19.
Jewish ordinances. Gal 4:3; Col 2:20.
Called the glorious liberty of the children of God. Rom 8:21.
Saints are called to. Gal 5:13.
Saints should
Praise God for. Ps 116:16,17.
Assert. 1 Cor 10:29.
Walk in. Ps 119:45.
Stand fast in. Gal 2:5; 5:1.
Not abuse. Gal 5:13; 1 Pet 2:16.
Not offend others by. 1 Cor 8:9; 10:29,32.
The gospel is the law of. James 1:25; 2:12.
False teachers
Promise, to others. 2 Pet 2:19.
Abuse. Jude 1:4.
Try to destroy. Gal 2:4.
The wicked, devoid of. John 8:34; Rom 6:20.
Typified. Lev 25:10-17; Gal 4:22-26,31.

LIFE, ETERNAL.

Christ is. 1 John 1:2; 5:20.
Revealed by Christ. John 6:68; 2 Tim 1:10.
To know God and Christ is. John 17:3.
Given
By God. Ps 133:3; Rom 6:23.
By Christ. John 6:27; 10:28.
In Christ. 1 John 5:11.
Through Christ. Rom 5:21; 6:23.
To all given to Christ. John 17:2.
To those who believe in God. John 5:24.
To those who believe in Christ. John 3:15,16; 6:40,47.
To those who hate life for Christ. John 12:25.
In answer to prayer. Ps 21:4.
Revealed in the Scriptures. John 5:39.
Results from
Drinking the water of life. John 4:14.
Eating the bread of life. John 6:50-58.
Eating of the tree of life. Rev 2:7.
They who are ordained to, believe the gospel. Acts 13:48.
Saints
Have promises of. 1 Tim 4:8; 2 Tim 1:1; Titus 1:2; 1 John 2:25.
Have hope of. Titus 1:2; 3:7.
May have assurance of. 2 Cor 5:1; 1 John 5:13.
Shall reap, through the Spirit. Gal 6:8.
Shall inherit. Matt 19:29.
Look for the mercy of God to. Jude 1:21.
Should lay hold of. 1 Tim 6:12,19.
Are preserved to. John 10:28,29.
Shall rise to. Dan 12:2; John 5:29.
Shall go into. Matt 25:46.
Shall reign in. Dan 7:18; Rom 5:17.
The self-righteous think to inherit, by works. Mark 10:17.
Cannot be inherited by works. Rom 2:7; 3:10-19.
The wicked
Have not. 1 John 3:15.
Judge themselves unworthy of. Acts 13:46.
Exhortation to seek. John 6:27.

LIFE, NATURAL.

God is the author of. Gen 2:7; Acts 17:28.
God preserves. Ps 36:6; 66:9.
Is in the hand of God. Job 12:10; Dan 5:23.
Forfeited by sin. Gen 2:17; 3:17-19.
Of others, not to be taken away. Ex 20:13.
Described as
Vain. Eccl 6:12.
Limited. Job 7:1; 14:5.
Short. Job 14:1; Ps 89:47.
Uncertain. James 4:13-15.
Full of trouble. Job 14:1.
God's lovingkindness better than. Ps 63:3.
The value of. Job 2:4; Matt 6:25.
Preserved by discretion. Prov 13:3.
Sometimes prolonged, in answer to prayer. Is 38:2-5; James 5:15.
Obedience to God, tends to prolong. Deut 30:20.
Obedience to parents, tends to prolong. Ex 20:12; Prov 4:10.
Cares and pleasures of, dangerous. Luke 8:14; 21:34; 2 Tim 2:4.
Saints have true enjoyment of. Ps 128:2; 1 Tim 4:8.
Of saints, specially protected by God. Job 2:6; Acts 18:10; 1 Pet 3:13.
Of the wicked, not specially protected by God. Job 36:6; Ps 78:50.
The wicked have their portion of good, during. Ps 17:14; Luke 6:24; 16:25.
Should be spent in
The fear of God. 1 Pet 1:17.
The service of God. Luke 1:75.
Living to God. Rom 14:8; Phil 1:21.
Peace. Rom 12:18; 1 Tim 2:2.
Doing good. Eccl 3:12.
Should be taken all due care of. Matt 10:23; Acts 27:34.
Should be laid down, if necessary, for Christ. Matt 10:39; Luke 14:26; Acts 20:24.
Should be laid down, if necessary, for the brethren. Rom 16:4; 1 John 3:16.
Be thankful for
The preservation of. Ps 103:4; John 2:6.
The supply of its wants. Gen 48:15.
The dissatisfied despise. Eccl 2:17.
We know not what is good for us in. Eccl 6:12.
Be not over-anxious to provide for its wants. Matt 6:25.
The enjoyment of, consists not in abundance of possessions. Luke 12:15.
Is compared to
An eagle hasting to the prey. Job 9:26.
A pilgrimage. Gen 47:9.
A tale told. Ps 90:9.
A swift post. Job 9:25.
A swift ship. Job 9:26.
A hand-breadth. Ps 39:5.
A shepherd's tent removed. Is 38:18.
A dream. Ps 73:20.
A sleep. Ps 90:5.

A vapour. James 4:14.
A shadow. Eccl 6:12.
A thread cut by the weaver. Is 38:12.
A weaver's shuttle. Job 7:6.
A flower. Job 14:2.
Grass. 1 Pet 1:24.
Water spilt on the ground. 2 Sam 14:14.
Wind. Job 7:7.
Shortness of, should lead to spiritual improvement. Deut 32:29; Ps 90:12.
Sometimes judicially shortened. 1 Sam 2:32,33; Job 36:14.
Miraculously restored by Christ. Matt 9:18,25; Luke 7:15,22; John 11:43.

Life, Spiritual.

God is the Author of. Ps 36:9; Col 2:13.
Christ is the Author of. John 5:21,25; 6:33,51-53; 14:6; 1 John 4:9.
The Holy Spirit is the Author of. Ezek 37:14; Rom 8:9-13.
The word of God is the instrument of. Is 55:3; 2 Cor 3:6; 1 Pet 4:6.
Is hidden with Christ. Col 3:3.
The fear of God is. Prov 14:27; 19:23.
Spiritual-mindedness is. Rom 8:6.
Is maintained by
Christ. John 6:57; 1 Cor 10:3,4.
Faith. Gal 2:20.
The word of God. Deut 8:3; Matt 4:4.
Prayer. Ps 69:32.
Has its origin in the new-birth. John 3:3-8.
Has its infancy. Luke 10:21; 1 Cor 3:1,2; 1 John 2:12.
Has its youth. 1 John 2:13,14.
Has its maturity. Eph 4:13; 1 John 2:13,14.
Is described as
A life to God. Rom 6:11; Gal 2:19.
Newness of life. Rom 6:4.
Living in the Spirit. Gal 5:25.
Revived by God. Ps 85:6; Hos 6:2.
Evidenced by love to the brethren. 1 John 3:14.
All saints have. Eph 2:1,5; Col 2:13.
Should animate the services of saints. Rom 12:1; 1 Cor 14:15.
Saints praise God for. Ps 119:175.
Seek to grow in. Eph 4:15; 1 Pet 2:2.
Pray for the increase of. Ps 119:25; 143:11.
The wicked alienated from. Eph 4:18.
Lovers of pleasure destitute of. 1 Tim 5:6.
Hypocrites destitute of. Jude 1:12; Rev 3:1.
Illustrated. Ezek 37:9,10; Luke 15:24.

Light.

God the only source of. James 1:17.
Created by God. Gen 1:3; Is 45:7.
Separated from darkness. Gen 1:4.
Sun, moon, and stars appointed to communicate to the earth. Gen 1:14-17; Jer 31:35.
Divided into
Natural. Job 24:14; Is 5:30.
Extraordinary or miraculous. Ex 14:20; Ps 78:14; Acts 9:3; 12:7.
Artificial. Jer 25:10; Acts 16:29.
Communicated to the body through the eye. Prov 15:30; Matt 6:22.
Described as
White and pure. Matt 17:2.
Bright. Job 37:21.
Shining. 2 Sam 23:4; Job 41:18.
Diffusive. Job 25:3; 36:30.
Useful and precious. Eccl 2:13.
Agreeable. Eccl 11:7.
Manifesting objects. John 3:20,21; Eph 5:13.
The theory of, beyond man's comprehension. Job 38:19,20,24.
Illustrative of
Glory of God. Ps 104:2; 1 Tim 6:16.
Purity of God. 1 John 1:5.
Wisdom of God. Dan 2:22.
Guidance of God. Ps 27:1; 36:9.
Favour of God. Ps 4:6; Is 2:5.
Christ the source of all wisdom. Luke 2:32; John 1:4,9; 8:12; 12:46.
Glory of Christ. Acts 9:3,5; 26:13.
Purity of Christ. Matt 17:2.
Word of God. Ps 119:105,130; 2 Pet 1:19.
Gospel. 2 Cor 4:4; 1 Pet 2:9.
Ministers. Matt 5:14; John 5:35.
Wise rulers. 2 Sam 21:17; 23:4.
The soul of man. Job 18:5,6.
Saints. Luke 16:8; Eph 5:8; Phil 2:15.
Future glory of saints. Ps 97:11; Col 1:12.
The path of the just. Prov 4:18.
The glory of the church. Is 60:1-3.
Whatever makes manifest. John 3:21; Eph 5:13.

Lion, The.

Canaan infested by. 2 Kin 17:25,26.
Described as
Superior in strength. Judg 14:18; Prov 30:30.
Active. Deut 33:22.
Courageous. 2 Sam 17:10.
Fearless even of man. Is 31:4; Nah 2:11.
Fierce. Job 10:16; 28:8.
Voracious. Ps 17:12.
Majestic in movement. Prov 30:29,30.
Greatness of its teeth alluded to. Ps 58:6; Joel 1:6.
God's power exhibited in restraining. 1 Kin 13:28; Dan 6:22,27.
God provides for. Job 38:39; Ps 104:21,28.
Lurks for its prey. Ps 10:9.
Roars when seeking prey. Ps 104:21; Is 31:4.
Rends its prey. Deut 33:20; Ps 7:2.
Often carries its prey to its den. Nah 2:12.
Conceals itself by day. Ps 104:22.
Often perishes for lack of food. Job 4:11.
Inhabits
Forests. Jer 5:6.
Thickets. Jer 4:7.
Mountains. Song 4:8.
Deserts. Is 30:6.
Attacks the sheepfolds. 1 Sam 17:34; Amos 3:12; Mic 5:8.
Attacks and destroys men. 1 Kin 13:24; 20:36.
Universal terror caused by roaring of. Jer 2:15; Amos 3:8.
Criminals often thrown to. Dan 6:7,16,24.
Hunting of, alluded to. Job 10:16.
Slain by
Samson. Judg 14:5,6.
David. 1 Sam 17:35,36.
Benaiah. 2 Sam 23:20.
A swarm of bees found in the carcass of, by Samson. Judg 14:8.
Disobedient prophet slain by. 1 Kin 13:24,26.
Illustrative
Of Israel. Num 24:9.
Of the tribe of Judah. Gen 49:9.
Of the tribe of Gad. Deut 33:20.
Of Christ. Rev 5:5.
Of God in protecting his church. Is 31:4.
Of God in executing judgments. Is 38:13; Lam 3:10; Hos 5:14; 13:8.
Of boldness of saints. Prov 28:1.
Of brave men. 2 Sam 1:23; 23:20.
Of cruel and powerful enemies. Is 5:29; Jer 49:19; 51:38.
Of persecutors. Ps 22:13; 2 Tim 4:17.
Of the devil. 1 Pet 5:8.
Of imaginary fears of the slothful. Prov 22:13; 26:13.
(Tamed,) of the natural man subdued by grace. Is 11:7; 65:25.
(Roaring of,) of a king's wrath. Prov 19:12; 20:2.

Locust, The.

A small insect. Prov 30:24,27.
Clean and fit for food. Lev 11:21,22.
Described as
Wise. Prov 30:24,27.
Voracious. Ex 10:15.
Rapid in movement. Is 33:4.
Like to horses prepared for battle. Joel 2:4; Rev 9:7.
Carried every way by the wind. Ex 10:13,19.
Immensely numerous. Ps 105:34; Nah 3:15.
Flies in bands and with order. Prov 30:27.
One of the plagues of Egypt. Ex 10:4-15.
The Jews
Used as food. Matt 3:4.
Threatened with, as a punishment for sin. Deut 28:38,42.
Deprecated the plague of. 1 Kin 8:37,38.
Often plagued by. Joel 1:4; 2:25.
Promised deliverance from the plague of, on humiliation, etc. 2 Chr 7:13,14.
Illustrative
Of destructive enemies. Joel 1:6,7; 2:2-9.
Of false teachers of the apostasy. Rev 9:3.
Of ungodly rulers. Nah 3:17.
(Destruction of,) of destruction of God's enemies. Nah 3:15.

Long-Suffering of God, The.

Is part of his character. Ex 34:6; Num 14:18; Ps 86:15.
Salvation, the object of. 2 Pet 3:15.
Through Christ's intercession. Luke 13:8.
Should lead to repentance. Rom 2:4; 2 Pet 3:9.

An encouragement to repent. Joel 2:13.
Exhibited in forgiving sins. Rom 3:25.
Exercised toward
His people. Is 30:18; Ezek 20:17.
The wicked. Rom 9:22; 1 Pet 3:20.
Plead in prayer. Jer 15:15.
Limits set to. Gen 6:3; Jer 44:22.
The wicked
Abuse. Eccl 8:11; Matt 24:48,49.
Despise. Rom 2:4.
Punished for despising. Neh 9:30; Matt 24:48-51; Rom 2:5.
Illustrated. Luke 13:6,9.
Exemplified
Manasseh. 2 Chr 33:10-13.
Israel. Ps 78:38; Is 48:9.
Jerusalem. Matt 23:37.
Paul. 1 Tim 1:16.

LOVE OF CHRIST, THE.

To the Father. Ps 91:14; John 14:31.
To his church. Song 4:8,9; 5:1; John 15:9; Eph 5:24.
To those who love him. Prov 8:17; John 14:21.
Manifested in his
Coming to seek the lost. Luke 19:10.
Praying for his enemies. Luke 23:34.
Giving himself for us. Gal 2:20.
Dying for us. John 15:13; 1 John 3:16.
Washing away our sins. Rev 1:5.
Interceding for us. Heb 7:25; 9:24.
Sending the Spirit. Ps 68:18; John 16:7.
Rebukes and chastisements. Rev 3:19.
Passes knowledge. Eph 3:19.
To be imitated. John 13:34; 15:12; Eph 5:2; 1 John 3:16.
To saints, is
Unquenchable. Song 8:7.
Constraining. 2 Cor 5:14.
Unchangeable. John 13:1.
Indissoluble. Rom 8:35.
Obedient saints abide in. John 15:10.
Saints obtain victory through. Rom 8:37.
Is the banner over his saints. Song 2:4.
Is the ground of his saints love to him. Luke 7:47.
To saints, shall be acknowledge even by enemies. Rev 3:9.
Illustrated. Matt 18:11-13.
Exemplified towards
Peter. Luke 22:32,61.
Lazarus, etc. John 11:5,36.
His apostles. John 13:1,34.
John. John 13:23.

LOVE OF GOD, THE.

Is a part of his character. 2 Cor 13:11; 1 John 4:8.
Christ, the special object of. John 15:9; 17:26.
Christ abides in. John 15:10.
Described as
Sovereign. Deut 7:8; 10:15.
Great. Eph 2:4.
Abiding. Zeph 3:17.
Unfailing. Is 49:15,16.
Unalienable. Rom 8:39.
Constraining. Hos 11:4.
Everlasting. Jer 31:3.
Irrespective of merit. Deut 7:7; Job 7:17.
Manifested towards
Perishing sinners. John 3:16; Titus 3:4.
His saints. John 16:27; 17:23; 2 Thess 2:16; 1 John 4:16.
The destitute. Deut 10:18.
The cheerful giver. 2 Cor 9:7.
Exhibited in
The giving of Christ. John 3:16.
The sending of Christ. 1 John 4:9.
Christ's dying for us while sinners. Rom 5:8; 1 John 4:10.
Election. Mal 1:2,3; Rom 9:11-13.
Adoption. 1 John 3:1.
Redemption. Is 43:3,4; 63:9.
Freeness of salvation. Titus 3:4-7.
Forgiving sin. Is 38:17.
Quickening of souls. Eph 2:4,5.
Drawing us to himself. Hos 11:4.
Temporal blessings. Deut 7:13.
Chastisements. Heb 12:6.
Defeating evil counsels. Deut 23:5.
Shed abroad in the heart by the Holy Spirit. Rom 5:5.
Saints know and believe. 1 John 4:16.
Saints should abide in. Jude 1:21.
Perfected in saints
By obedience. 1 John 2:5.
By brotherly love. 1 John 4:12.
The source of our love to him. 1 John 4:19.
To be sought in prayer. 2 Cor 13:14.

LOVE TO CHRIST.

Exhibited by God. Matt 17:5; John 5:20.
Exhibited by saints. 1 Pet 1:8.
His personal excellence is deserving of. Song 5:9-16.
His love to us a motive to. 2 Cor 5:14.
Manifested in
Seeking him. Song 3:2.
Obeying him. John 14:15,21,23.
Ministering to him. Matt 27:55; 25:40.
Preferring him to all others. Matt 10:37.
Taking up the cross for Him. Matt 10:38.
A characteristic of saints. Song 1:4.
An evidence of adoption. John 8:42.
Should be
Sincere. Eph 6:24.
With the soul. Song 1:7.
In proportion to our mercies. Luke 7:47.
Supreme. Matt 10:37.
Ardent. Song 2:5; 8:6.
Unquenchable. Song 8:7.
Even to death. Acts 21:13; Rev 12:11.
Promises to. 2 Tim 4:8; James 1:12.
Increase of, to be prayed for. Phil 1:9.
Pray for grace to those who have. Eph 6:24.
They who have
Are loved by the Father. John 14:21,23; 16:27.
Are loved by Christ. Prov 8:17; John 14:21.
Enjoy communion with God and Christ. John 14:23.
Decrease of, rebuked. Rev 2:4.
Want of, denounced. 1 Cor 16:22.
The wicked, destitute of. Ps 35:19; John 15:18,25.
Exemplified
Joseph of Arimathaea. Matt 27:57-60.
Penitent woman. Luke 7:47.
Certain women. Luke 23:28.
Thomas. John 11:16.
Mary Magdalene. John 20:11.
Peter. John 21:15-17.
Paul. Acts 21:13.

LOVE TO GOD.

Commanded. Deut 11:1; Josh 22:5.
The first great commandment. Matt 22:38.
With all the heart. Deut 6:5; Matt 22:37.
Better than all sacrifices. Mark 12:33.
Produced by
The Holy Spirit. Gal 5:22; 2 Thess 3:5.
The love of God to us. 1 John 4:19.
Answers to prayer. Ps 116:1.
Exhibited by Christ. John 14:31.
A characteristic of saints. Ps 5:11.
Should produce
Joy. Ps 5:11.
Love to saints. 1 John 5:1.
Hatred of sin. Ps 97:10.
Obedience to God. Deut 30:20; 1 John 5:3.
Perfected in obedience. 1 John 2:5.
Perfected, gives boldness. 1 John 4:17,18.
God, faithful to those who have. Deut 7:9.
They who have
Are known of him. 1 Cor 8:3.
Are preserved by him. Ps 145:20.
Are delivered by him. Ps 91:14.
Partake of his mercy. Ex 20:6; Deut 7:9.
Have all things working for their good. Rom 8:28.
Persevere in. Jude 1:21.
Exhort one another to. Ps 31:23.
Pray for. 2 Thess 3:5.
The love of the world is a proof of not having. 1 John 2:15.
They who love not others, are without. 1 John 4:20.
Hypocrites, without. Luke 11:42; John 5:42.
The uncharitable, without. 1 John 3:17.
God tries the sincerity of. Deut 13:3.
Promises connected with. Deut 11:13-15; Ps 69:36; Is 56:6,7; James 1:12.

LOVE TO MAN.

Is of God. 1 John 4:7.
Commanded by God. 1 John 4:21.
Commanded by Christ. John 13:34; 15:12; 1 John 3:23.
After the example of Christ. John 13:34; 15:12; Eph 5:2.
Taught by God. 1 Thess 4:9.
Faith works by. Gal 5:6.
A fruit of the Spirit. Gal 5:22; Col 1:8.
Purity of heart leads to. 1 Pet 1:22.
Explained. 1 Cor 13:4-7.
Is an active principle. 1 Thess 1:3; Heb 6:10.
Is an abiding principle. 1 Cor 13:8,13.
Is the second great commandment. Matt 22:37-39.
Is the end of the commandment. 1 Tim 1:5.
Supernatural gifts are nothing without. 1 Cor 13:1,2.

The greatest sacrifices are nothing without. 1 Cor 13:3.
Especially enjoined upon ministers. 1 Tim 4:12; 2 Tim 2:22.
Saints should
- Put on. Col 3:14.
- Follow after. 1 Cor 14:1.
- Abound in. Phil 1:9; 1 Thess 3:12.
- Continue in. 1 Tim 2:15; Heb 13:1.
- Provoke each other to. 2 Cor 8:7; 9:2; Heb 10:24.
- Be sincere in. Rom 12:9; 2 Cor 6:6; 8:8; 1 John 3:18.
- Be disinterested in. 1 Cor 10:24; 13:5; Phil 2:4.
- Be fervent in. 1 Pet 1:22; 4:8.

Should be connected with brotherly kindness. Rom 12:10; 2 Pet 1:7.
Should be with a pure heart. 1 Pet 1:22.
All things should be done with. 1 Cor 16:14.
Should be exhibited, toward
- Saints. 1 Pet 2:17; 1 John 5:1.
- Ministers. 1 Thess 5:13.
- Our families. Eph 5:25; Titus 2:4.
- Fellow-countrymen. Ex 32:32; Rom 9:2,3; 10:1.
- Strangers. Lev 19:34; Deut 10:19.
- Enemies. Ex 23:4,5; 2 Kin 6:22; Matt 5:44; Rom 12:14,20; 1 Pet 3:9.
- All men. Gal 6:10.

Should be exhibited, in
- Ministering to the wants of others. Matt 25:35; Heb 6:10.
- Loving each other. Gal 5:13.
- Relieving strangers. Lev 25:35; Matt 25:36.
- Clothing the naked. Is 58:7; Matt 25:36.
- Visiting the sick, etc. Job 31:16-22; James 1:27.
- Sympathising. Rom 12:15; 1 Cor 12:26.
- Supporting the weak. Gal 6:2; 1 Thess 5:14.
- Covering the faults of others. Prov 10:12; 1 Pet 4:8.
- Forgiving injuries. Eph 4:32; Col 3:13.
- Forbearing. Eph 4:2.
- Rebuking. Lev 19:17; Matt 18:15.

Necessary to true happiness. Prov 15:17.
The love of God is a motive to. John 13:34; 1 John 4:11.
An evidence of
- Being in the light. 1 John 2:10.
- Discipleship with Christ. John 13:35.
- Spiritual life. 1 John 3:14.

Is the fulfilling of the law. Rom 13:8-10; Gal 5:14; James 2:8.
Love to self is the measure of. Mark 12:33.
Is good and pleasant. Ps 133:1,2.
Is a bond of union. Col 2:2.
Is the bond of perfectness. Col 3:14.
Hypocrites, devoid of. 1 John 2:9,11; 4:20.
The wicked devoid of. 1 John 3:10.
Exemplified
- Joseph. Gen 45:15.
- Ruth. Ruth 1:16,17.
- Jonathan, etc. 1 Sam 20:17,41,42.
- Obadiah. 1 Kin 18:4.
- Centurion. Luke 7:5.
- The Church. Acts 2:46; Heb 10:33,34.
- Lydia. Acts 16:15.
- Aquila. Rom 16:3,4.
- Paul. 2 Cor 6:11,12.
- Epaphroditus. Phil 2:25,26,30.
- Philippians. Phil 4:15-19.
- Colossians. Col 1:4.
- Thessalonians. 1 Thess 3:6.
- Onesiphorus. 2 Tim 1:16-18.
- Philemon. Philem 7-9.
- Moses. Heb 11:25.

Lovingkindness of God, The.

Is through Christ. Eph 2:7; Titus 3:4-6.
Described as
- Great. Neh 9:17.
- Excellent. Ps 36:7.
- Good. Ps 69:16.
- Marvellous. Ps 17:7; 31:21.
- Multitudinous. Is 63:7.
- Everlasting. Is 54:8.
- Merciful. Ps 117:2.
- Better than life. Ps 63:3.

Consideration of the dealings of God gives a knowledge of. Ps 107:43.
Saints
- Betrothed in. Hos 2:19.
- Drawn by. Jer 31:3.
- Preserved by. Ps 40:11.
- Quickened after. Ps 119:88.
- Comforted by. Ps 119:76.
- Look for mercy through. Ps 51:1.
- Receive mercy through. Is 54:8.
- Are heard according to. Ps 119:149.
- Are ever mindful of. Ps 26:3; 48:9.
- Should expect, in affliction. Ps 42:7,8.
- Crowned with. Ps 103:4.

Never utterly taken from saints. Ps 89:33; Is 54:10.
Former manifestations of, to be pleaded in prayer. Ps 25:6; 89:49.
Pray for the
- Exhibition of. Ps 17:7; 143:8.
- Continuance of. Ps 36:10.
- Extension of. Gen 24:12; 2 Sam 2:6.

Praise God for. Ps 92:2; 138:2.
Proclaim. Ps 40:10.

Lying.

Forbidden. Lev 19:11; Col 3:9.
Hateful to God. Prov 6:16-19.
An abomination to God. Prov 12:22.
A hindrance to prayer. Is 59:2,3.
The devil, the father of. John 8:44.
The devil excites men to. 1 Kin 22:22; Acts 5:3.
Saints
- Hate. Ps 119:163; Prov 13:5.
- Avoid. Is 63:8; Zeph 3:13.
- Respect not those who practise. Ps 40:4.
- Reject those who practise. Ps 101:7.
- Pray to be preserved from. Ps 119:29; Prov 30:8.

Unbecoming in rulers. Prov 17:7.
The evil of rulers hearkening to. Prov 29:12.
False prophets addicted to. Jer 23:14; Ezek 22:28.
False witnesses addicted to. Prov 14:5,25.
Antinomians guilty of. 1 John 1:6; 2:4.
Hypocrites addicted to. Hos 11:12.
Hypocrites, a seed of. Is 57:4.
The wicked
- Addicted to, from their infancy. Ps 58:3.
- Love. Ps 52:3.
- Delight in. Ps 62:4.
- Seek after. Ps 4:2.
- Prepare their tongues for. Jer 9:3,5.
- Bring forth. Ps 7:14.
- Give heed to. Prov 17:4.

A characteristic of the Apostasy. 2 Thess 2:9; 1 Tim 4:2.
Leads to
- Hatred. Prov 26:28.
- Love of impure conversation. Prov 17:4.

Often accompanied by gross crimes. Hos 4:1,2.
Folly of concealing hatred by. Prov 10:18.
Vanity of getting riches by. Prov 21:6.
Shall be detected. Prov 12:19.
Poverty preferable to. Prov 19:22.
Excludes from heaven. Rev 21:27; 22:15.
They who are guilty of, shall be cast into hell. Rev 21:8.
Punishment for. Ps 5:6; 120:3,4; Prov 19:5; Jer 50:36.
Exemplified
- The devil. Gen 3:4.
- Cain. Gen 4:9.
- Sarah. Gen 18:15.
- Jacob. Gen 27:19.
- Joseph's brethren. Gen 37:31,32.
- Gibeonites. Josh 9:9-13.
- Samson. Judg 16:10.
- Saul. 1 Sam 15:13.
- Michal. 1 Sam 19:14.
- David. 1 Sam 21:2.
- Prophet of Bethel. 1 Kin 13:18.
- Gehazi. 2 Kin 5:22.
- Job's friends. Job 13:4.
- Ninevites. Nah 3:1.
- Peter. Matt 26:72.
- Ananias, etc. Acts 5:5.
- Cretans. Titus 1:12.

Macedonian Empire, The.

Called the kingdom of Grecia. Dan 11:2.
Illustrated by the
- Brazen part of the image in Nebuchadnezzar's dream. Dan 2:32,39.
- Leopard with four wings and four heads. Dan 7:16,17.
- Rough goat with notable horn. Dan 8:5,21.

Philippi the chief city of. Acts 16:12.
Predictions respecting
- Conquest of the Medo-Persian kingdom. Dan 8:6,7; 11:2,3.
- Power and greatness of Alexander its last king. Dan 8:8; 11:3.
- Division of it into four kingdoms. Dan 8:8,22.
- Divisions of it ruled by strangers. Dan 11:4.
- History of its four divisions. Dan 11:4-29.
- The little horn to arise out of one of its divisions. Dan 8:8-12,23-25.

Gospel preached in, by God's desire. Acts 16:9,10.
Liberality of the churches of. 2 Cor 8:1-5.

MAGISTRATES.

Are appointed by God. Rom 13:1.
Are ministers of God. Rom 13:4,6.
Purpose of their appointment. Rom 13:4; 1 Pet 2:14.
Their office to be respected. Acts 23:5.
Are not a terror to the good, but to the evil. Rom 13:3.
To be wisely selected and appointed. Ex 18:21; Ezra 7:25.
To be prayed for. 1 Tim 2:1,2.
Should
  Seek wisdom from God. 1 Kin 3:9.
  Rule in the fear of God. 2 Sam 23:3; 2 Chr 19:7.
  Know the law of God. Ezra 7:25.
  Be faithful to the Sovereign. Dan 6:4.
  Enforce the laws. Ezra 7:26.
  Judge wisely. 1 Kin 3:16-28.
  Hate covetousness. Ex 18:21.
  Not take bribes. Ex 23:8; Deut 16:19.
  Defend the poor. Job 29:12,16.
  Judge for God, not for man. 2 Chr 19:6.
  Judge righteously. Deut 1:16; 16:18; 25:1.
  Be impartial. Ex 23:6; Deut 1:17.
  Be diligent in ruling. Rom 12:8.
  Subjection to their authority enjoined. Matt 23:2,3; Rom 13:1; 1 Pet 2:13,14.
Wicked—Illustrated. Prov 28:15.
Good—Exemplified
  Joseph. Gen 41:46.
  Gideon. Judg 8:35.
  Samuel. 1 Sam 12:3,4; Ezra 10:1-9.
  Nehemiah. Neh 3:15.
  Job. Job 29:16.
  Daniel. Dan 6:3.
Wicked—Exemplified
  Sons of Samuel. 1 Sam 8:3.
  Pilate. Matt 27:24,26.
  Magistrates in Philippi. Acts 16:22,23.
  Gallio. Acts 18:16,17.
  Felix. Acts 24:26.

MALICE.

Springs from an evil heart. Matt 15:19,20; Gal 5:19.
Forbidden. 1 Cor 14:20; Col 3:8; Eph 4:26,27.
A hindrance to growth in grace. 1 Pet 2:1,2.
Incompatible with the worship of God. 1 Cor 5:7,8.
Christian liberty not to be a cloak for. 1 Pet 2:16.
Saints avoid. Job 31:29,30; Ps 35:12-14.
The wicked
  Speak with. 3 John 10.
  Live in. Titus 3:3.
  Conceive. Ps 7:14.
  Filled with. Rom 1:29.
  Visit saints with. Ps 83:3; Matt 22:6.
Pray for those who injure you through. Matt 5:44.
Brings its own punishment. Ps 7:15,16.
God requites. Ps 10:14; Ezek 36:5.
Punishment of. Amos 1:11,12; Obad 10-15.
Exemplified
  Cain. Gen 4:5.
  Esau. Gen 27:41.
  Joseph's brethren. Gen 37:19,20.
  Saul. 1 Sam 18:9-11.
  Shimei. 2 Sam 16:5; 1 Kin 2:8,9.
  Joab. 2 Sam 3:27; 1 Kin 2:5,28-33.
  Sanballat. Neh 2:10.
  Haman. Esth 3:5,6.
  Edomites. Ezek 35:5.
  Presidents, etc. Dan 6:4-9.
  Herodias. Mark 6:19.
  Scribes, etc. Mark 11:18; Luke 11:54.
  Diotrephes. 3 John 10.

MAN.

Made for God. Prov 16:4; Rev 4:11.
God's purpose in creation completed by making. Gen 2:5,7.
Cannot profit God. Job 22:2; Ps 16:2.
Unworthy of God's favour. Job 7:17; Ps 8:4.
Created
  By God. Gen 1:27; Is 45:12.
  By Christ. John 1:3; Col 1:16.
  By the Holy Spirit. Job 33:4.
  After consultation, by the Trinity. Gen 1:26.
  On the sixth day. Gen 1:31.
  Upon the earth. Deut 4:32; Job 20:4.
  From the dust. Gen 2:7; Job 33:6.
  In the image of God. Gen 1:26,27; 1 Cor 11:7.
  After the likeness of God. Gen 1:26; James 3:9.
  Male and female. Gen 1:27; 5:2.
  A living soul. Gen 2:7; 1 Cor 15:45.
  In uprightness. Eccl 7:29.
  In knowledge (inferred). Col 3:10.
  Under obligations to obedience. Gen 2:16,17.
  A type of Christ. Rom 5:14.
Approved of by God. Gen 1:31.
Blessed by God. Gen 1:28; 5:2.
Placed in the garden of Eden. Gen 2:15.
Every herb and tree given to, for food. Gen 1:29.
Allowed to eat flesh after the flood. Gen 9:3.
Not good for, to be alone. Gen 2:18.
Woman formed to be a help for. Gen 21:2-25.
Possessed of
  A Body. Matt 6:25.
  A soul. Luke 12:20; Acts 14:22; 1 Pet 4:19.
  A spirit. Prov 18:14; 20:17; 1 Cor 2:11.
  Understanding. Eph 1:18; 4:18.
  Will. 1 Cor 9:17; 2 Pet 1:21.
  Affections. 1 Chr 29:3; Col 3:2.
  Conscience. Rom 2:15; 1 Tim 4:2.
  Memory. Gen 41:9; 1 Cor 15:2.
Made by God in his successive generations. Job 10:8-11; 31:15.
Fearfully and wonderfully made. Ps 139:14.
Of every nation, made of one blood. Acts 17:26.
Quickened by the breath of God. Gen 2:7; 7:22; Job 33:4.
Made wise by the inspiration of the Almighty. Job 32:8,9.
Inferior to angels. Ps 8:5; Heb 2:7.
Is of the earth earthy. 1 Cor 15:47.
Nature and constitution of, different from other creatures. 1 Cor 15:39.
More valuable than other creatures. Matt 6:26; 10:31; 12:12.
Wiser than other creatures. Job 35:11.
Received dominion over other creatures. Gen 1:28; Ps 8:6-8.
Gave names to other creatures. Gen 2:19,20.
Intellect of, matured by age. 1 Cor 13:11.
Called
  The potsherd of the earth. Is 45:9.
  A worm. Job 25:6.
  Vain man. Job 11:12; James 2:20.
  Flesh. Gen 6:12; Joel 2:28.
Compared to
  Grass. Is 40:6-8; 1 Pet 1:24.
  Clay in the potter's hand. Is 64:8; Jer 18:2,6.
  Vanity. Ps 144:4.
  A sleep. Ps 90:5.
  A wild ass's colt. Job 11:12.
Originally naked and not ashamed. Gen 2:25.
Disobeyed God by eating part of the forbidden fruit. Gen 3:1-12.
Filled with shame after the fall. Gen 3:10.
Covered himself with fig leaves. Gen 3:7.
Clothed by God with skins. Gen 3:21.
Punished for disobedience. Gen 3:16-19.
Banished from paradise. Gen 3:23,24.
Involved posterity in his ruin. Rom 5:12-19.
Has sought out many inventions. Eccl 7:29.
Born in sin. Ps 51:5.
Born to trouble. Job 5:7.
Has an appointed time on the earth. Job 7:1.
Days of, compared to a shadow. 1 Chr 29:15.
Days of, as the days of a hireling. Job 7:1.
Has but few days. Job 14:1.
Ordinary limit of his life. Ps 90:10.
Ignorant of what is good for him. Eccl 10:2.
Ignorant of what is to come after him. Eccl 10:14.
Not profited by all his labour and travail. Eccl 2:22; 6:12.
Cannot direct his ways. Jer 10:23; Prov 20:24.
Walks in a vain show. Ps 39:6.
God
  Instructs. Ps 94:10.
  Orders the goings of. Prov 5:21; 20:24.
  Prepares the heart of. Prov 16:1.
  Enables to speak. Prov 16:1.
  Preserves. Job 7:20; Ps 36:6.
  Provides for. Ps 145:15,16.
  Destroys the hopes of. Job 14:19.
  Makes the wrath of, to praise him. Ps 76:10.
  Makes his beauty consume away. Ps 39:11.
  Turns to destruction. Ps 90:3.
Cannot be just with God. Job 9:2; 25:4; Ps 143:2; Rom 3:20.
Cannot cleanse himself. Job 15:14; Jer 2:22.
All the ways of, clean in his own eyes. Prov 16:2.
Christ
  Knew what was in. John 2:25.

Took on him nature of. John 1:14; Heb 2:14,16.
Made in the image of. Phil 2:7.
Was found in fashion as. Phil 2:8.
Approved of God as. Acts 2:22.
Called the second, as covenant head of the church. 1 Cor 15:47.
Is the head of every. 1 Cor 11:3.
A refuge as, to sinners. Is 32:2.
As such, is the cause of the resurrection. 1 Cor 15:21,22.
Shall be recompensed according to his works. Ps 62:12; Rom 2:6.
Cannot retain his spirit from death. Eccl 8:8.
Would give all his possessions for the preservation of life. Job 2:4.
Able to sustain bodily affliction. Prov 18:14.
Sinks under trouble of mind. Prov 18:14.
No trust to be placed in. Ps 118:8; Is 2:22.
The help of, vain. Ps 60:11.
The whole duty of. Eccl 12:13.

Manasseh, the Tribe Of.

Descended from Joseph's eldest son adopted by Jacob. Gen 41:51; 48:5.
Predictions respecting. Gen 48:20; 49:22-26; Deut 33:13-17.
Persons selected from
To number the people. Num 1:10.
To spy out the land. Num 13:11.
To divide the land. Num 34:23.
Strength of, on leaving Egypt. Num 1:34,35.
Part of third division of Israel in their journeys. Num 10:22,23.
Encamped next to, and under the standard of Ephraim west of tabernacle. Num 2:18,20.
Offering of, at dedication. Num 7:54-59.
Families of. Num 26:29-33.
Strength of, on entering Canaan. Num 26:34.
On Gerizim said amen to the blessing. Deut 27:12.
Half of, obtained inheritance east of Jordan. Num 32:33,39-42; Josh 13:29-31.
Inheritance of the other half. Josh 17:1-11.
Could not drive out the Canaanites but made them tributary. Josh 17:12,13; Judg 1:27,28.
Some of
Aided David against Saul. 1 Chr 12:19-21.
At coronation of David. 1 Chr 12:31-37.
Returned to their allegiance to the house of David in Asa's reign. 2 Chr 15:9.
At Hezekiah's Passover. 2 Chr 30:1,11,18.
David appointed rulers and captains over. 1 Chr 26:32; 27:20,21.
Often at war with Ephraim. Judg 12:1,6; Is 9:21.
Country of, purified from idols by Hezekiah and Josiah. 2 Chr 31:1; 34:6.
Remarkable persons of
Daughters of Zelophehad. Num 27:1-7.
Gideon. Judg 6:15.
Abimelech. Judg 9:1.
Jotham. Judg 9:5,7,21.
Jair. Judg 10:3.
Jephthah. Judg 11:1.
Barzillai. 2 Sam 17:27.
Elijah. 1 Kin 17:1.

Manna.

Miraculously given to Israel for food in the wilderness. Ex 16:4,15; Neh 9:15.
Called
God's manna. Neh 9:20.
Bread of heaven. Ps 105:40.
Bread from heaven. Ex 16:4; John 6:31.
Corn of heaven. Ps 78:24.
Angel's food. Ps 78:25.
Spiritual meat. 1 Cor 10:3.
Previously unknown. Deut 8:3,16.
Described as
Like coriander seed. Ex 16:31; Num 11:7.
White. Ex 16:31.
Like in colour to bdellium. Num 11:7.
Like in taste to wafers made with honey. Ex 16:31.
Like in taste to oil. Num 11:18.
Like hoar frost. Ex 16:14.
Fell after the evening dew. Num 11:9.
None fell on the Sabbath day. Ex 16:26,27.
Gathered every morning. Ex 16:21.
An omer of, gathered for each person. Ex 16:16.
Two portions of, gathered the sixth day on account of the Sabbath. Ex 16:5,22-26.
He that gathered much or little had sufficient and nothing over. Ex 16:18.
Melted away by the sun. Ex 16:21.
Given
When Israel murmured for bread. Ex 16:2,3.
In answer to prayer. Ps 105:40.
Through Moses. John 6:31,32.
To exhibit God's glory. Ex 16:7.
As a sign of Moses's divine mission. John 6:30,31.
For forty years. Neh 9:21.
As a test of obedience. Ex 16:4.
To teach that man does not live by bread only. Deut 8:3; Matt 4:4.
To humble and prove Israel. Deut 8:16.
Kept longer than a day (except on the Sabbath) became corrupt. Ex 16:19,20.
The Israelites
At first covetous of. Ex 16:17.
Ground, made into cakes and baked in pans. Num 11:8.
Counted inferior to food of Egypt. Num 11:4-6.
Loathed. Num 21:5.
Punished for despising. Num 11:10-20.
Punished for loathing. Num 21:6.
Ceased when Israel entered Canaan. Ex 16:35; Josh 5:12.
Illustrative of
Christ. John 6:32-35.
Blessedness given to saints. Rev 2:17.
A golden pot of, laid up in the holiest for a memorial. Ex 16:32-34; Heb 9:4.

Marriage.

Divinely instituted. Gen 2:24.
A covenant relationship. Mal 2:4.
Designed for
The happiness of man. Gen 2:18.
Increasing the human population. Gen 1:28; 9:1.
Raising up godly seed. Mal 2:15.
Preventing fornication. 1 Cor 7:2.
The expectation of the promised seed of the woman an incentive to, in the early age. Gen 3:15; 4:1.
Lawful in all. 1 Cor 7:2,28; 1 Tim 5:14.
Honourable for all. Heb 13:4.
Should be only in the Lord. 1 Cor 7:39.
Expressed by
Joining together. Matt 19:6.
Making affinity. 1 Kin 3:1.
Taking to wife. Ex 2:1.
Giving daughters to sons, and sons to daughters. Deut 7:3; Ezra 9:12.
Indissoluble during the joint lives of the parties. Matt 19:6; Rom 7:2,3; 1 Cor 7:39.
Early introduction of polygamy. Gen 4:19.
Contracted in patriarchal age with near relations. Gen 20:12; 24:24; 28:2.
Often contracted by parents for children. Gen 24:49-51; 34:6,8.
Should be with consent of parents. Gen 28:8; Judg 14:2,3.
Consent of the parties necessary to. Gen 24:57,58; 1 Sam 18:20; 25:41.
Parents might refuse to give their children in. Ex 22:17; Deut 7:3.
The Jews
Forbidden to contract, with their near relations. Lev 18:6.
Forbidden to contract with idolaters. Deut 7:3,4; Josh 23:12; Ezra 9:11,12.
Often contracted with foreigners. 1 Kin 11:1; Neh 13:23.
Sometimes guilty of polygamy. 1 Kin 11:1,3.
Careful in contracting for their children. Gen 24:2,3; 28:1,2.
Betrothed themselves some time before. Deut 20:7; Judg 14:5,7,8; Matt 1:18.
Contracted when young. Prov 2:17; Joel 1:8.
Often contracted, in their own tribe. Ex 2:1; Num 36:6-13; Luke 1:5,27.
Obliged to contract with a brother's wife who died without seed. Deut 25:5; Matt 22:24.
Considered being debarred from, a reproach. Is 4:1.
Considered being debarred from, a cause of grief. Judg 11:38.
Often punished by being debarred from. Jer 7:34; 16:9; 25:10.
Were allowed divorce from, because of hardness of their hearts. Deut 24:1; Matt 19:7,8.
Exempted from going to war immediately after. Deut 20:7.
Priest not to contract, with divorced or improper persons. Lev 21:7.
The high priest not to contract, with a widow or a divorced or profane person. Lev 21:14.

Contracted at the gate and before witnesses. Ruth 4:1,10,11.
Modes of demanding women in. Gen 24:3,4; 34:6,8; 1 Sam 25:39,40.
Elder daughters usually given in, before the younger. Gen 29:26.
A dowry given to the woman's parents before. Gen 29:18; 34:12; 1 Sam 18:27,28; Hos 3:2.
Celebrated
  With great rejoicing. Jer 33:11; John 3:29.
  With feasting. Gen 29:22; Judg 14:10; Matt 22:2,3; John 2:1-10.
  For seven days. Judg 14:12.
A benediction pronounced after. Gen 24:60; Ruth 4:11,12.
The bride
  Received presents before. Gen 24:53.
  Given a handmaid at. Gen 24:59; 29:24,29.
  Adorned with jewels for. Is 49:18; 61:10.
  Gorgeously apparelled. Ps 45:13,14.
  Attended by bridesmaids. Ps 45:9.
  Stood on the right of bridegroom. Ps 45:9.
  Called to forget her father's house. Ps 45:10.
The bridegroom
  Adorned with ornaments. Is 61:10.
  Attended by many friends. Judg 14:11; John 3:29.
  Presented with gifts. Ps 45:12.
  Crowned with garlands. Song 3:11.
  Rejoiced over the bride. Is 62:5.
  Returned with the bride to his house at night. Matt 25:1-6.
Garments provided for guests at. Matt 22:12.
Infidelity of those contracted in, punished as if married. Deut 22:23,24; Matt 1:19.
Illustrative of
  God's union with the Jewish nation. Is 54:5; Jer 3:14; Hos 2:19,20.
  Christ's union with his church. Eph 5:23,24,32.

MARTYRDOM.

Is death endured for the word of God, and testimony of Christ. Rev 6:9; 20:4.
Saints
  Forewarned of. Matt 10:21; 24:9; John 16:2.
  Should not fear. Matt 10:28; Rev 2:10.
  Should be prepared for. Matt 16:24,25; Acts 21:13.
  Should resist sin to. Heb 12:4.
Reward of. Rev 2:10; 6:11.
Inflicted at the instigation of the devil. Rev 2:10,13.
The Apostasy guilty of inflicting. Rev 17:6; 18:24.
Of saints, shall be avenged. Luke 11:50,51; Rev 18:20-24.
Exemplified
  Abel. Gen 4:8; 1 John 3:12.
  Ahimelech and his fellow priests. 1 Sam 22:18,19.
  Prophets and Saints of old. 1 Kin 18:4; 19:10; Luke 11:50,51; Heb 11:37.
  Urijah. Jer 26:23.
  John the Baptist. Mark 6:27.
  Peter. John 21:18,19.
  Stephen. Acts 7:58.
  Christians. Acts 9:1; 22:4; 26:10.
  James. Acts 12:2.
  Antipas. Rev 2:13.

MASTERS.

Authority of, established. Col 3:22; 1 Pet 2:18.
Should, with their households,
  Worship God. Gen 35:3.
  Fear God. Acts 10:2.
  Serve God. Josh 24:15.
  Observe the Sabbath. Ex 20:10; Deut 5:12-14.
  Put away idols. Gen 35:2.
Should select faithful servants. Gen 24:2; Ps 101:6,7.
Should receive faithful advice from servants. 2 Kin 5:13,14.
Duty of, toward servants;
  To act justly. Job 31:13,15; Col 4:1.
  To deal with them in the fear of God. Eph 6:9; Col 4:1.
  To esteem them highly, if saints. Philem 16.
  To take care of them in sickness. Luke 7:3.
  To forbear threatening them. Eph 6:9.
  Not to defraud them. Gen 31:7.
  Not to keep back their wages. Lev 19:13; Deut 24:15.
  Not to rule over them with rigour. Lev 25:43; Deut 24:14.
Benevolent, blessed. Deut 15:18.
Unjust, denounced. Jer 22:13; James 5:4.
Good—Exemplified
  Abraham. Gen 18:19.
  Jacob. Gen 35:2.
  Joshua. Josh 24:15.
  Centurion. Luke 7:2,3.
  Cornelius. Acts 10:2.
Bad—Exemplified
  Egyptians. Ex 1:13,14.
  Nabal. 1 Sam 25:17.
  Amalekite. 1 Sam 30:13.

MEASURES.

Unjust, an abomination to God. Prov 20:10.
The Jews not to be unjust in. Lev 19:35; Deut 25:14,15.
The Jews often used unjust. Mic 6:10.
Of liquids and solids
  Log. Lev 14:10,15.
  Cab. 2 Kin 6:25.
  Omer or tenth-deal (the tenth of an ephah). Ex 16:36; Lev 5:11; 14:10.
  Hin. Ex 29:40.
  Bath or ephah. Is 5:10; Ezek 45:11.
  Homer or Cor. Is 5:10; Ezek 45:14.
  Firkin. John 2:6.
Of length
  Handbreadth. Ex 25:25; Ps 39:5.
  Span. Ex 28:16; 1 Sam 17:4.
  Cubit. Gen 6:15,16; Deut 3:11.
  Fathom. Acts 27:28.
  Furlong. Luke 24:13; John 11:13.
  Mile. Matt 5:41.
Distances measured by rods and lines. 2 Sam 8:2; Jer 31:39; Ezek 40:3; Rev 21:16.
Were regulated by the standard of the sanctuary. 1 Chr 23:29.
Illustrative
  (Correcting in measure,) of mitigated afflictions. Jer 30:11.
  (Drinking tears in great measure,) of severe afflictions. Ps 80:5.
  (Weighing the waters in a measure,) of God's infinite wisdom. Job 28:23,25.
  (Measuring the dust of the earth,) of God's greatness. Is 40:12.
  (The measure of our days,) of the shortness of life. Ps 39:4.
  (Drinking water, by measure) of severe famine. Ezek 4:11,16.
  (The measure of the stature of Christ,) of perfection. Eph 4:13.
  (Opening the mouth without measure,) of the insatiableness of hell. Is 5:14.

MEAT OFFERINGS.

Were most holy. Lev 6:17.
Consisted of
  Fine flour. Lev 2:1.
  Unleavened cakes baked in the oven. Lev 2:4.
  Fine flour baked in a pan. Lev 2:5.
  Fine flour baked in a frying pan. Lev 2:7.
  Green ears of corn parched. Lev 2:5.
  Barley meal. Num 5:15.
Oil and incense used with. Lev 2:1,4,15.
Of jealousy, without oil or incense. Num 5:15.
Always seasoned with salt. Lev 2:13.
No leaven used with. Lev 2:11; 6:17.
Not to be offered on altar of incense. Ex 30:9.
Offered
  On the altar of burnt offering. Ex 40:29.
  With the daily sacrifices. Ex 29:40-42.
  With all burnt offerings. Num 15:3-12.
  By the poor for a trespass offering. Lev 5:11.
  By the high priest every day, half in the morning and half in the evening. Lev 6:20-22.
A small part of, was consumed on the altar for a memorial. Lev 2:2,9,16; 6:15.
When offered for a priest entirely consumed by fire. Lev 6:23.
High priest's deputy had care of. Num 4:16.
Laid up in a chamber of the temple. Neh 10:39; 13:5; Ezek 42:13.
The priest's portion. Lev 2:3; 6:17.
To be eaten by the males of the house of Aaron alone. Lev 6:18.
To be eaten in the holy place. Lev 6:16.
The Jews
  Often not accepted in. Amos 5:22.
  Condemned for offering, to idols. Is 57:6.
  Often prevented from offering, by judgments. Joel 1:9,13.
Materials for public, often provided by the princes. Num 7:13,19,25; Ezek 45:16.

MEDO-PERSIAN KINGDOM.

Extended from India to Ethiopia. Esth 1:1.
Peopled by descendants of Eliam. Gen 10:22.
Illustrated by
  Silver part of image in Nebuchadnezzar's dream. Dan 2:32,39.
  A bear. Dan 7:5.
  A ram with two horns. Dan 8:3,20.
Shushan a chief city of. Esth 1:2; 8:15.
Achmetha or Ecbatana a chief city of. Ezra 6:2.
Divided into many provinces. Esth 1:1; Dan 6:1.
Laws of, unalterable. Dan 6:12,15.
Ruled by, absolute kings. Esth 3:8,11; 7:9.
Kings of, mentioned in Scripture
  Cyrus. Ezra 1:1.
  Ahasuerus or Cambyses. Ezra 4:6.
  Artaxerxes Smerdis (an usurper). Ezra 4:7.
  Darius Hystaspes. Ezra 6:1; Dan 5:31.
  Xerxes. Dan 11:2.
  Artaxerxes Longimanus or Ahasuerus. Ezra 6:14; 7:1; Esth 1:1.
Kings of
  Called kings of Assyria. Ezra 6:22.
  Called kings of Babylon. Neh 13:6.
  Styled themselves king of kings. Ezra 7:12.
  Dwelt in royal palaces. Esth 1:2; 8:14.
  Were exceeding rich. Esth 1:4; Dan 12:2.
  Entertained magnificently. Esth 1:3,5,7.
  Held in their hand a golden sceptre. Esth 5:2.
  Put to death all who approached them without permission. Esth 4:11,16.
Celebrated for wise men. Esth 1:13; Matt 2:1.
People of, warlike. Ezek 27:10; 38:5.
Peculiar customs in. Esth 1:8; 2:12,13.
Babylon taken by the king of. Dan 5:20,31.
The Jews delivered from captivity by means of. 2 Chr 36:20,22,23; Ezra 1:1-4.
Predictions respecting
  Extensive conquest. Dan 8:4.
  Conquest of Babylon. Is 21:1,2; Dan 5:28.
  Deliverance of the Jews. Is 44:28; 45:1-4.
  Invasion of Greece under Xerxes. Dan 11:2.
  Downfall by Alexander. Dan 8:6,7; 11:3.

MEEKNESS.

Christ set an example of. Ps 45:4; Is 53:7; Matt 11:29; 21:5; 2 Cor 10:1; 1 Pet 2:21-23.
His teaching. Matt 5:38-45.
A fruit of the Spirit. Gal 5:22,23.
Saints should
  Seek. Zeph 2:3.
  Put on. Col 3:12-13.
  Receive the word of God with. James 1:21.
  Exhibit, in conduct, etc. James 3:13.
  Answer for their hope with. 1 Pet 3:15.
  Show to all men. Titus 3:2.
  Restore the erring with. Gal 6:1.
Precious in the sight of God. 1 Pet 3:4.
Ministers should
  Follow after. 1 Tim 6:11.
  Instruct opposers with. 2 Tim 2:24,25.
  Urge, on their people. Titus 3:1,2.
A characteristic of wisdom. James 3:17.
Necessary to a Christian walk. Eph 4:1,2; 1 Cor 6:7.
Those who are gifted with
  Are preserved. Ps 76:9.
  Are exalted. Ps 147:6; Matt 23:12.
  Are guided and taught. Ps 25:9.
  Are richly provided for. Ps 22:26.
  Are beautified with salvation. Ps 149:4.
  Increase their joy. Is 29:19.
  Shall inherit the earth. Ps 37:11.
The gospel to be preached to those who possess. Is 61:1.
Blessedness of. Matt 5:5.
Exemplified
  Moses. Num 12:3.
  David. 1 Sam 30:6; 2 Sam 16:9-12.
  Paul. 1 Cor 4:12; 1 Thess 2:7.

MERCY.

After the example of God. Luke 6:36.
Enjoined. 2 Kin 6:21-23; Hos 12:6; Rom 12:20,21; Col 3:12.
To be engraved on the heart. Prov 3:3.
Characteristic of saints. Ps 37:26; Is 57:1.
Should be shown
  With cheerfulness. Rom 12:8.
  To our brethren. Zech 7:9.
  to those that are in distress. Luke 10:37.
  To the poor. Prov 14:31; Dan 4:27.
  To backsliders. Luke 15:18-20; 2 Cor 2:6-8.
  To animals. Prov 12:10.
Upholds the throne of kings. Prov 20:28.
Beneficial to those who exercise. Prov 11:17.
Blessedness of showing. Prov 14:21; Matt 5:7.
Hypocrites devoid of. Matt 23:23.
Denunciations against those devoid of. Hos 4:1,3; Matt 18:23-25; James 2:13.

MERCY OF GOD, THE.

Is part of his character. Ex 34:6,7; Ps 62:12; Neh 9:17; Jon 4:2,10,11; 2 Cor 1:3.
Described as
  Great. Num 14:18; Is 54:7.
  Rich. Eph 2:4.
  Manifold. Neh 9:27; Lam 3:32.
  Plenteous. Ps 86:5,15; 103:8.
  Abundant. 1 Pet 1:3.
  Sure. Is 55:3; Mic 7:20.
  Everlasting. 1 Chr 16:34; Ps 89:28; 106:1; 107:1; 136:1-26.
  Tender. Ps 25:6; 103:4; Luke 1:78.
  New every morning. Lam 3:23.
  High as heaven. Ps 36:5; 103:11.
  Filling the earth. Ps 119:64.
  Over all his works. Ps 145:9.
Is his delight. Mic 7:18.
Manifested
  In the sending of Christ. Luke 1:78.
  In salvation. Titus 3:5.
  In long-suffering. Lam 3:22; Dan 9:9.
  To his people. Deut 32:43; 1 Kin 8:23.
  To them that fear him. Ps 103:17; Luke 1:50.
  To returning backsliders. Jer 3:12; Hos 14:4; Joel 2:13.
  To repentant sinners. Ps 32:5; Prov 28:13; Is 55:7; Luke 15:18-20.
  To the afflicted. Is 49:13; 54:7.
  To the fatherless. Hos 14:3.
  To whom he will. Hos 2:23; Rom 9:15,18.
  With everlasting kindness. Is 54:8.
A ground of hope. Ps 130:7; 147:11.
A ground of trust. Ps 52:8.
Should be
  Sought for ourselves. Ps 6:2.
  Sought for others. Gal 6:16; 1 Tim 1:2; 2 Tim 1:18.
  Pleaded in prayer. Ps 6:4; 25:6; 51:1.
  Rejoiced in. Ps 31:7.
  Magnified. 1 Chr 16:34; Ps 115:1; 118:1-4,29; Jer 33:11.
Typified
  Mercy seat. Ex 25:17.
Exemplified
  Lot. Gen 19:16,19.
  Epaphroditus. Phil 2:27.
  Paul. 1 Tim 1:13.

MERCY SEAT.

Moses commanded to make. Ex 25:17.
Bezaleel given wisdom to make. Ex 31:2,3,7.
Made of pure gold. Ex 25:17; 37:6.
The cherubim formed out of, and at each end of it. Ex 25:18-20; Heb 9:5.
Placed upon the ark of testimony. Ex 25:21; 26:34; 40:20.
God
  Appeared over in the cloud. Lev 16:2.
  Dwelt over. Ps 80:1.
  Spoke from above. Ex 25:22; Num 7:89.
Covered with a cloud of incense on the day of atonement. Lev 16:13.
The blood of sacrifices on the day of atonement sprinkled upon and before. Lev 16:14,15.
Illustrative of
  Christ. Rom 3:25; Heb 9:3.
  The throne of grace. Heb 4:16.

METALS.

Dug out of the earth. Job 28:1,2,6.
Mentioned in Scripture
  Gold. Gen 2:11,12.
  Silver. Gen 44:2.
  Brass. Ex 27:2,4; 2 Chr 12:10.
  Copper. Ezra 8:27; 2 Tim 4:14.
  Iron. Num 35:16; Prov 27:17.
  Lead. Ex 15:10; Jer 6:29.
  Tin. Num 31:22.
Comparative value of. Is 60:17; Dan 2:32-45.
Often mixed with dross. Is 1:25.
The holy land abounded in. Deut 8:9.
Antiquity of the art of working in. Gen 4:21.
Freed from dross by fire. Ezek 22:18,20.

Ceremonially cleansed by fire. Num 31:21-23.
Cast in mould. Judg 17:4; Jer 6:29.
Clay of Jordan used for moulding. 1 Kin 7:46.
An extensive commerce in. Ezek 27:12.

Midianites.

Descended form Midian, son of Abraham by Keturah. Gen 25:1,2; 1 Chr 1:32.
Dwelt east of Jordan, beside Moab. Num 22:1,4.
A small part of
- Dwelt near Horeb. Ex 2:15; 3:1.
- Retained the knowledge and worship of Jehovah. Ex 2:16; 18:9-12.

Governed by kings. Num 31:8; Judg 8:5.
Dwelt in tents. Hab 3:7.
Engaged in commerce. Gen 37:28,36.
Conquered by Hadad. Gen 36:25; 1 Chr 1:46.
Excited by Moab against Israel. Num 22:4.
Terrified at approach of Israel. Hab 3:3-7.
With the moabites
- Sent for Balaam to curse Israel. Num 22:5-7.
- Seduced Israel to idolatry. Num 25:1-6.
- Punished for seducing Israel. Num 25:16-18; 31:1-12.

Allowed to oppress Israel. Judg 6:1-6.
Gideon raised up against. Judg 6:11-14.
With Amalek, etc. opposed Gideon. Judg 6:33.
Miraculously defeated and destroyed by Gideon. Judg 7:16-22; 8:10,11.
Princes of, slain. Judg 7:24,25; 8:12,21.
Completeness of their destruction, alluded to. Ps 83:9-11; Is 9:4; 10:26.
Shall minister to future glory of the church. Is 60:6.

Milk.

An animal secretion, of a white colour. Lam 4:7.
Used as food by the Jews. Gen 18:8; Judg 5:25.
Different kinds mentioned
- Of cows. Deut 32:14; 1 Sam 6:7.
- Of camels. Gen 32:15.
- Of goats. Prov 27:27.
- Of sheep. Deut 32:14.
- Of sea-monsters. Lam 4:3.

Flocks and herds fed for supply of. Prov 27:23,27; Is 7:21,22; 1 Cor 9:7.
Canaan abounded with. Ex 3:8,17; Josh 5:6.
Made into
- Butter. Prov 30:33.
- Cheese. Job 10:10.

Kept by the Jews in bottles. Judg 4:19.
Young animals not to be seethed in that of the mother. Ex 23:19.
Illustrative of
- Temporal blessings. Gen 49:12.
- Blessings of the gospel. Is 55:1; Joel 3:18.
- First principles of God's word. 1 Cor 3:2; Heb 5:12; 1 Pet 2:2.
- Godly and edifying discourses. Song 4:11.
- Wealth of the Gentiles. Is 60:16.
- Doctrines of the gospel. Song 5:1.

Mills.

Antiquity of. Ex 11:5.
Used for grinding
- Manna in the wilderness. Num 11:8.
- Corn. Is 47:2.

Female servants usually employed at. Ex 11:5; Matt 24:41.
Male captives often employed at. Judg 16:24; Lam 5:13.
Stones used in
- Hard. Job 41:24.
- Heavy. Matt 18:6.
- Large. Rev 18:21.
- Not to be taken in pledge. Deut 24:6.
- Often thrown down on enemies during sieges. Judg 9:53; 2 Sam 11:21.

Illustrative
- (Grinding at,) of degradation. Is 47:1,2.
- (Ceasing,) of desolation. Jer 25:10; Rev 18:22.

Ministers.

Called by God. Ex 28:1; Heb 5:4.
Qualified by God. Is 6:5-7; 2 Cor 3:5,6.
Commissioned by Christ. Matt 28:19.
Sent by the Holy Spirit. Acts 13:2,4.
Have authority from God. 2 Cor 10:8; 13:10.
Authority of, is for edification. 2 Cor 10:8; 13:10.
Separated to the gospel. Rom 1:1.
Entrusted with the gospel. 1 Thess 2:4.
Described as
- Ambassadors for Christ. 2 Cor 5:20.
- Ministers of Christ. 1 Cor 4:1.
- Stewards of the mysteries of God. 1 Cor 4:1.
- Defenders of the faith. Phil 1:7.
- The servants of Christ's people. 2 Cor 4:5.

Specially protected by God. 2 Cor 1:10.
Necessity for. Matt 9:37,38; Rom 10:14.
Excellency of. Rom 10:15.
Labours of, vain, without God's blessing. 1 Cor 3:7; 15:10.
Compared to earthen vessels. 2 Cor 4:7.
Should be
- Pure. Is 52:11; 1 Tim 3:9.
- Holy. Ex 28:36; Lev 21:6; Titus 1:8.
- Humble. Acts 20:19.
- Patient. 2 Cor 6:4; 2 Tim 2:24.
- Blameless. 1 Tim 3:2; Titus 1:7.
- Willing. Is 6:8; 1 Pet 5:2.
- Disinterested. 2 Cor 12:14; 1 Thess 2:6.
- Impartial. 1 Tim 5:21.
- Gentle. 1 Thess 2:7; 2 Tim 2:24.
- Devoted. Acts 20:24; Phil 1:20,21.
- Strong in grace. 2 Tim 2:1.
- Self-denying. 1 Cor 9:27.
- Sober, just, and temperate. Lev 10:9; Titus 1:8.
- Hospitable. 1 Tim 3:2; Titus 1:8.
- Apt to teach. 1 Tim 3:2; 2 Tim 2:24.
- Studious and meditative. 1 Tim 4:13,15.
- Watchful. 2 Tim 4:5.
- Prayerful. Eph 3:14; Phil 1:4.
- Strict in ruling their own families. 1 Tim 3:4,12.
- Affectionate to their people. Phil 1:7; 1 Thess 2:8,11.
- Ensample to the flock. Phil 3:17; 2 Thess 3:9; 1 Tim 4:12; 1 Pet 5:3.

Should not be
- Lords over God's heritage. 1 Pet 5:3.
- Greedy of filthy lucre. Acts 20:33; 1 Tim 3:3,8; 1 Pet 5:2.
- Contentious. 1 Tim 3:3; Titus 1:7.
- Crafty. 2 Cor 4:2.
- Men-pleasers. Gal 1:10; 1 Thess 2:4.
- Easily dispirited. 2 Cor 4:8,9; 6:10.
- Entangled by cares. Luke 9:60; 2 Tim 2:4.
- Given to wine. 1 Tim 3:3; Titus 1:7.

Should seek the salvation of their flock. 1 Cor 10:33.
Should avoid giving unnecessary offence. 1 Cor 10:32,33; 2 Cor 6:3.
Should make full proof of their ministry. 2 Tim 4:5.
Are bound to
- Preach the gospel to all. Mark 16:16; 1 Cor 1:17.
- Feed the Church. Jer 3:15; John 21:15-17; Acts 20:28; 1 Pet 5:2.
- Build up the Church. 2 Cor 12:19; Eph 4:12.
- Watch for souls. Heb 13:17.
- Pray for their people. Joel 2:17; Col 1:9.
- Strengthen the faith of their people. Luke 22:32; Acts 14:22.
- Teach. 2 Tim 2:2.
- Exhort. Titus 1:9; 2:15.
- Warn affectionately. Acts 20:31.
- Rebuke. Titus 1:13; 2:15.
- Comfort. 2 Cor 1:4-6.
- Convince gainsayers. Titus 1:9.
- War a good warfare. 1 Tim 1:18; 2 Tim 4:7.
- Endure hardness. 2 Tim 2:3.

Should preach
- Christ crucified. Acts 8:5,35; 1 Cor 2:2.
- Repentance and faith. Acts 20:21.
- According to the oracles of God. 1 Pet 4:11.
- Everywhere. Mark 16:20; Acts 8:4.
- Not with enticing words of man's wisdom. 1 Cor 1:17; 2:1,4.
- Not setting forth themselves. 2 Cor 4:5.
- Without deceitfulness. 2 Cor 2:17; 4:2; 1 Thess 2:3,5.
- Fully, and without reserve. Acts 5:20; 20:20,27; Rom 15:19.
- With boldness. Is 58:1; Ezek 2:6; Matt 10:27,28.
- With plainness of speech. 2 Cor 3:12.
- With zeal. 1 Thess 2:8.
- With constancy. Acts 6:4; 2 Tim 4:2.
- With consistency. 2 Cor 1:18,19.
- With heedfulness. 1 Tim 4:16.
- With good will and love. Phil 1:15-17.
- With faithfulness. Ezek 3:17,18.
- Without charge, if possible. 1 Cor 9:18; 1 Thess 2:9.

Woe to those who do not preach the gospel. 1 Cor 9:16.
When faithful
- Approve themselves as the ministers of God. 2 Cor 6:4.

Thank God for his gifts to their people. 1 Cor 1:4; Phil 1:3; 1 Thess 3:9.
Glory in their people. 2 Cor 7:4.
Rejoice in the faith and holiness of their people. 1 Thess 3:6-9.
Commend themselves to the consciences of men. 2 Cor 4:2.
Are rewarded. Matt 24:47; 1 Cor 3:14; 9:17,18; 1 Pet 5:4.
When unfaithful
Described. Is 56:10-12; Titus 1:10,11.
Deal treacherously with their people. John 10:12.
Delude men. Jer 6:14; Matt 15:14.
Seek gain. Mic 3:11; 2 Pet 2:3.
Shall be punished. Ezek 33:6-8; Matt 24:48-51.
Their people are bound, to
Regard them as God's messengers. 1 Cor 4:1; Gal 4:14.
Not to despise them. Luke 10:16; 1 Tim 4:12.
Attend to their instructions. Mal 2:7; Matt 23:3.
Follow their holy example. 1 Cor 11:1; Phil 3:17.
Imitate their faith. Heb 13:7.
Hold them in reputation. Phil 2:29; 1 Thess 5:13; 1 Tim 5:17.
Love them. 2 Cor 8:7; 1 Thess 3:6.
Pray for them. Rom 15:30; 2 Cor 1:11; Eph 6:19; Heb 13:18.
Obey them. 1 Cor 16:16; Heb 13:17.
Give them joy. 2 Cor 1:14; 2:3.
Help them. Rom 16:9; Phil 4:3.
Support them. 2 Chr 31:4; 1 Cor 9:7-11; Gal 6:6.
Pray for the increase of. Matt 9:38.
Faithful—Exemplified
The Eleven Apostles. Matt 28:16-19.
The seventy. Luke 10:1,17.
Matthias. Acts 1:26.
Philip. Acts 8:5.
Barnabas. Acts 11:23.
Simeon, etc. Acts 13:1.
Paul. Acts 28:31.
Tychicus. Eph 6:21.
Timothy. Phil 2:22.
Epaphroditus. Phil 2:24.
Archippus. Col 4:17.
Titus. Titus 1:5.

Miracles.

Power of God necessary to. John 3:2.
Described as
Marvellous things. Ps 78:12.
Marvellous works. Is 29:14; Ps 105:5.
Signs and wonders. Jer 32:21; John 4:48; 2 Cor 12:12.
Manifest
The glory of God. John 11:4.
The glory of Christ. John 2:11; 11:4.
The works of God. John 9:3.
Were evidences of a divine commission. Ex 4:1-5; Mark 16:20.
The Messiah was expected to perform. Matt 11:2,3; John 7:31.
Jesus was proved to be the Messiah by. Matt 11:4-6; Luke 7:20-22; John 5:36; Acts 2:22.
Jesus was followed on account of. Matt 4:23-25; 14:35,36; John 6:2,26; 12:18.
A gift of the Holy Spirit. 1 Cor 12:10.
Were performed
By the power of God. Ex 8:19; Acts 14:3; 15:12; 19:11.
By the power of Christ. Matt 10:1.
By the power of the Holy Spirit. Matt 12:28; Rom 15:19.
In the name of Christ. Matt 16:17; Acts 3:16; 4:30.
First preaching of the gospel confirmed by. Mark 16:20; Heb 2:4.
The who wrought, disclaimed all power of their own. Acts 3:12.
Should produce faith. John 2:23; 20:30,31.
Should produce obedience. Deut 11:1-3; 29:2,3,9.
Instrumental to the early propagation of the gospel. Acts 8:6; Rom 15:18,19.
Faith required in
Those who performed. Matt 17:20; 21:21; John 14:12; Acts 3:16; 6:8.
Those for whom they were performed. Matt 9:28; 13:58; Mark 9:22-24; Acts 14:9.
Should be remembered. 1 Chr 16:12; Ps 105:5.
Should be told to future generations. Ex 10:2; Judg 6:13.
Insufficient of themselves, to produce conversion. Luke 16:31.
The wicked
Desire to see. Matt 27:42; Luke 11:29; 23:8.
Often acknowledge. John 11:47; Acts 4:16.
Do not understand. Ps 106:7.
Do not consider. Mark 6:52.
Forget. Neh 9:17; Ps 78:1,11.
Proof against. Num 14:22; John 12:37.
Guilt of rejecting the evidence afforded by. Matt 11:20-24; John 15:24.

Miracles of Christ, The.

Water turned to wine. John 2:6-10.
Nobleman's son healed. John 4:46-53.
Centurion's servant healed. Matt 9:5-13.
Draughts of fish. Luke 5:4-6; John 21:6.
Devils cast out. Matt 8:28-32; 9:32,33; 15:22-28; 17:14-18; Mark 1:23-27.
Peter's wife's mother healed. Matt 8:14,15.
Lepers cleansed. Matt 8:3; Luke 17:14.
Paralytic healed. Mark 2:3-12.
Withered hand restored. Matt 12:10-13.
Impotent man healed. John 5:5-9.
The dead raised to life. Matt 9:18; 19:23-25; Luke 7:12-15; John 11:11-44.
Issue of blood stopped. Matt 9:20-22.
The blind restored to sight. Matt 9:27-30; Mark 8:22-25; John 9:1-7.
The deaf and mute cured. Mark 7:32-35.
The multitude fed. Matt 14:15-21; 15:32-38.
His walking on the sea. Matt 14:25-27.
Peter walking on the sea. Matt 14:29.
Tempest stilled. Matt 8:23-26; 14:32.
Sudden arrival of the ship. John 6:21.
Tribute money. Matt 17:27.
Woman healed of infirmity. Luke 13:11-13.
Dropsy cured. Luke 14:2-4.
Fig tree blighted. Matt 21:19.
Malchus healed. Luke 22:50,51.
Performed before the messengers of John. Luke 7:21,22.
Many and divers diseases healed. Matt 4:23,24; 14:14; 15:30; Mark 1:34; Luke 6:17-19.
His transfiguration. Matt 17:1-8.
His resurrection. Luke 24:6; John 10:18.
His appearance to his disciples, the doors being shut. John 20:19.
His ascension. Acts 1:9.

Miracles Through Evil Agents.

Performed through the power of the devil. 2 Thess 2:9; Rev 16:14.
Wrought
In support of false religions. Deut 13:1-2.
By false christs. Matt 24:24.
By false prophets. Matt 24:24; Rev 19:20.
A mark of the Apostasy. 2 Thess 2:3,9; Rev 13:13.
Not to be regarded. Deut 13:3.
Deceive the ungodly. 2 Thess 2:10-12; Rev 13:14; 19:20.
Exemplified
Magicians of Egypt. Ex 7:11,22; 8:7.
Witch of Endor. 1 Sam 28:7-14.
Simon Magus. Acts 8:9-11.

Miracles Wrought Through Servants of God.

Moses and Aaron
Rod turned into a serpent. Ex 4:3; 7:10.
Rod restored. Ex 4:4.
Hand made leprous. Ex 4:6.
Hand healed. Ex 4:7.
Water turned into blood. Ex 4:9,30.
River turned into blood. Ex 7:20.
Frogs brought. Ex 8:6.
Frogs removed. Ex 8:13.
Lice brought. Ex 8:17.
Flies brought. Ex 8:21-24.
Flies removed. Ex 8:31.
Murrain of beasts. Ex 9:3-6.
Boils and blains brought. Ex 9:10,11.
Hail brought. Ex 9:23.
Hail removed. Ex 9:33.
Locusts brought. Ex 10:13.
Locust removed. Ex 10:19.
Darkness brought. Ex 10:22.
The firstborn destroyed. Ex 12:29.
The Red Sea divided. Ex 14:21,22.
Egyptians overwhelmed. Ex 14:26-28.
Water sweetened. Ex 15:25.
Water from rock in Horeb. Ex 17:6.
Amalek vanquished. Ex 17:11-13.
Destruction of Korah. Num 16:28-32.
Water from rock in Kadesh. Num 20:11.
Healing by brazen serpent. Num 21:8,9.
Joshua
Waters of Jordan divided. Josh 3:10-17.
Jordan restored to its course. Josh 4:18.
Jericho taken. Josh 6:6-20.
The sun and moon stayed. Josh 10:12-14.
Gideon
Midianites destroyed. Judg 7:16-22.

Samson
- A lion killed. Judg 14:6.
- Philistines killed. Judg 14:19; 15:15.
- The gates of Gaza carried away. Judg 16:3.
- Dagon's house pulled down. Judg 16:30.

Samuel
- Thunder and rain in harvest. 1 Sam 12:18.

The prophet of Judah
- Jeroboam's hand withered. 1 Kin 13:4.
- The altar rent. 1 Kin 13:5.
- The withered hand restored. 1 Kin 13:6.

Elijah
- Drought caused. 1 Kin 17:1; James 5:17.
- Meal and oil multiplied. 1 Kin 17:14-16.
- A child restored to life. 1 Kin 17:22,23.
- Sacrifice consumed by fire. 1 Kin 18:36,38.
- Men destroyed by fire. 2 Kin 1:10-12.
- Rain brought. 1 Kin 18:41-45; James 5:18.
- Waters of Jordan divided. 2 Kin 2:8.
- Taken to heaven. 2 Kin 2:11.

Elisha
- Waters of Jordan divided. 2 Kin 2:14.
- Waters healed. 2 Kin 2:21,22.
- Children torn by bears. 2 Kin 2:24.
- Oil multiplied. 2 Kin 4:1-7.
- Child restored to life. 2 Kin 4:32-35.
- Naaman healed. 2 Kin 5:10,14.
- Gehazi struck with leprosy. 2 Kin 5:27.
- Iron caused to swim. 2 Kin 6:6.
- Syrians smitten with blindness. 2 Kin 6:20.
- Syrians restored to sight. 2 Kin 6:20.
- A man restored to life. 2 Kin 13:21.

Isaiah
- Hezekiah healed. 2 Kin 20:7.
- Shadow put back on the dial. 2 Kin 20:11.

The seventy disciples
- Various miracles. Luke 10:9,17.

The apostles
- Many miracles. Acts 2:43; 5:12.

Peter
- Lame man cured. Acts 3:7.
- Death of Ananias. Acts 5:5.
- Death of Sapphira. Acts 5:10.
- The sick healed. Acts 5:15,16.
- Aeneas made whole. Acts 9:34.
- Dorcas restored to life. Acts 9:40.

Stephen
- Great miracles. Acts 6:8.

Philip
- Various miracles. Acts 8:6,7,13.

Paul
- Elymas smitten with blindness. Acts 13:11.
- Lame man cured. Acts 14:10.
- An unclean spirit cast out. Acts 16:18.
- Special miracles. Acts 19:11,12.
- Eutychus restored to life. Acts 20:10-12.
- Viper's bite made harmless. Acts 28:5.
- Father of Publius healed. Acts 28:8.

Paul and Barnabas
- Various miracles. Acts 14:3.

Miraculous Gifts of the Holy Spirit.

Foretold. Is 35:4-6; Joel 2:28,29.
Of different kinds. 1 Cor 12:4-6.
Enumerated. 1 Cor 12:8-10,28; 14:1.
Christ was endued with. Matt 12:28.
Poured out on the day of Pentecost. Acts 2:1-4.
Communicated
- Upon the preaching of the gospel. Acts 10:44-46.
- By the laying on of the Apostles' hands. Acts 8:17,18; 19:6.
- For the confirmation of the gospel. Mark 16:20; Acts 14:3; Rom 15:19; Heb 2:4.
- For the edification of the Church. 1 Cor 12:7; 14:12,13.

Dispensed according to his sovereign will. 1 Cor 12:11.
Were to be sought after. 1 Cor 12:31; 14:1.
Temporary nature of. 1 Cor 13:8.
Were not to be
- Neglected. 1 Tim 4:14; 2 Tim 1:6.
- Despised. 1 Thess 5:20.
- Purchased. Acts 8:20.

Might be possessed without saving grace. Matt 7:22,23; 1 Cor 13:1,2.
Counterfeited by Antichrist. Matt 24:24; 2 Thess 2:9; Rev 13:13,14.

Missionaries, All Christians Should Be As.

After the example of Christ. Acts 10:38.
Women and children as well as men. Ps 8:2; Prov 31:26; Matt 21:15,16; Phil 4:3; 1 Tim 5:10; Titus 2:3-5; 1 Pet 3:1.
The zeal of idolaters should provoke to. Jer 7:18.
The zeal of hypocrites should provoke to. Matt 23:15.
An imperative duty. Judg 5:23; Luke 19:40.
The principle on which. 2 Cor 5:14,15.
However weak they may be. 1 Cor 1:27.
From their calling as saints. Ex 19:6; 1 Pet 2:9.
As faithful stewards. 1 Pet 4:10,11.
In youth. Ps 71:17; 148:12,13.
In old age. Deut 32:7; Ps 71:18.
In the family. Deut 6:7; Ps 78:5-8; Is 38:19; 1 Cor 7:16.
In their intercourse with the world. Matt 5:16; Phil 2:15,16; 1 Pet 2:12.
In first giving their own selves to the Lord. 2 Cor 8:5.
In declaring what God has done for them. Ps 66:16; 116:16-19.
In hating life for Christ. Luke 14:26.
In openly confessing Christ. Matt 10:32.
In following Christ. Luke 14:27; 18:22.
In preferring Christ above all relations. Luke 14:26; 1 Cor 2:2.
In joyfully suffering for Christ. Heb 10:34.
In forsaking all for Christ. Luke 5:11.
In a holy example. Matt 5:16; Phil 2:15; 1 Thess 1:7.
In holy conduct. 1 Pet 2:12.
In holy boldness. Ps 119:46.
In dedicating themselves to the service of God. Josh 24:15; Ps 27:4.
In devoting all property to God. 1 Chr 29:2,3,14,16; Eccl 11:1; Matt 6:19,20; Mark 12:44; Luke 12:33; 18:22,28; Acts 2:45; 4:32-34.
In holy conservation. Ps 37:30; Prov 10:31; 15:7; Eph 4:29; Col 4:6.
In talking of God and his works. Ps 71:24; 77:12; 119:27; 145:11,12.
In showing forth God's praises. Is 43:21.
In inviting forth God's praises. Is 43:21.
In inviting others to embrace the gospel. Ps 34:8; Is 2:3; John 1:46; 4:29.
In seeking the edification of others. Rom 14:19; 15:2; 1 Thess 5:11.
In admonishing others. 1 Thess 5:14; 2 Thess 3:15.
In reproving others. Lev 19:17; Eph 5:11.
In teaching and exhorting. Ps 34:11; 51:13; Col 3:16; Heb 3:13; 10:25.
In interceding for others. Col 4:3; Heb 13:18; James 5:16.
In aiding ministers in their labours. Rom 16:3,9; 2 Cor 11:9; Phil 4:14-16; 3 John 6.
In giving a reason for their faith. Ex 12:26,27; Deut 6:20,21; 1 Pet 3:15.
In encouraging the weak. Is 35:3,4; Rom 14:1; 15:1; 1 Thess 5:14.
In visiting and relieving the poor, the sick, etc. Lev 25:35; Ps 112:9; 2 Cor 9:9; Matt 25:36; Acts 20:35; James 1:27.
With a willing heart. Ex 35:29; 1 Chr 29:9,14.
With a superabundant liberality. Ex 36:5-7; 2 Cor 8:3.
Encouragement to. Prov 11:25,30; 1 Cor 1:27; James 5:19,20.
Blessedness of. Dan 12:3.
Illustrated. Matt 25:14; Luke 19:13.
Exemplified
- Hannah. 1 Sam 2:1-10.
- Captive maid. 2 Kin 5:3.
- Chief of the Fathers, etc. Ezra 1:5.
- Shadrach, etc. Dan 3:16-18.
- Restored demoniac. Mark 5:20.
- Shepherds. Luke 2:17.
- Anna. Luke 2:38.
- Joanna, etc. Luke 8:3.
- Leper. Luke 17:15.
- Disciples. Luke 19:37,38.
- Centurion. Luke 23:47.
- Andrew. John 1:41,42.
- Philip. John 1:46.
- Woman of Samaria. John 4:29.
- Barnabas. Acts 4:36,37.
- Persecuted Saints. Acts 8:4; 11:19,20.
- Apollos. Acts 18:25.
- Aquila, etc. Acts 18:26.
- Various individuals. Rom 16:1-27.
- Onesiphorus. 2 Tim 1:16.
- Philemon. Philem 1-6.

Missionary Work By Ministers.

Commanded. Matt 28:19; Mark 16:15.
Warranted by predictions concerning the heathen, etc. Is 42:10-12; 66:19.
Is according to the purpose of God. Luke 24:46,47; Gal 1:15,16; Col 1:25-27.
Directed by the Holy Spirit. Acts 13:2.

Required. Luke 10:2; Rom 10:14,15.
The Holy Spirit calls to. Acts 13:2.
Christ engaged in. Matt 4:17,23; 11:1; Mark 1:38,39; Luke 8:1.
Christ sent his disciples to labour in. Mark 3:14; 6:7; Luke 10:1-11.
Obligations to engage in. Acts 4:19,20; Rom 1:13-15; 1 Cor 9:16.
Excellency of. Is 52:7; Rom 10:15.
Worldly concerns should not delay. Luke 9:59-62.
God qualifies for. Ex 3:11,18; 4:11,12,15; Is 6:5-9.
God strengthens for. Jer 1:7-9.
Guilt and danger of shrinking from. Jon 1:3,4.
Requires wisdom and meekness. Matt 10:16.
Be ready to engage in. Is 6:8.
Aid those engaged in. Rom 16:1,2; 2 Cor 11:9; 3 John 5-8.
Harmony should subsist amongst those engaged in. Gal 2:9.
Success of
- To be prayed for. Eph 6:18,19; Col 4:3.
- A cause of joy. Acts 15:3.
- A cause of praise. Acts 11:18; 21:19,20.

No limits to the sphere of. Is 11:9; Mark 16:15; Rev 14:6.
Opportunities for, not to be neglected. 1 Cor 16:9.
Exemplified
- Levites. 2 Chr 17:8,9.
- Jonah. Jon 3:2.
- The Seventy. Luke 10:1,17.
- Apostles. Mark 6:12; Acts 13:2-5.
- Philip. Acts 8:5.
- Paul, etc. Acts 13:2-4.
- Silas. Acts 15:40,41.
- Timotheus. Acts 16:3.
- Noah. 2 Pet 2:5.

Moabites.

Descended from Lot. Gen 19:37.
Called
- Children of Lot. Deut 2:9.
- People of Chemosh. Num 21:29; Jer 48:46.

Are given to, as a possession. Deut 2:9.
Separated from the Amorites by the river Arnon. Num 21:13.
Expelled the ancient Emims. Deut 2:9-11.
Possessed many and great cities. Num 21:28,30; Is 15:1-4; Jer 48:21-24.
Governed by kings. Num 23:7; Josh 24:9.
Described as
- Proud and arrogant. Is 16:6; Jer 48:29.
- Idolatrous. 1 Kin 11:7.
- Superstitious. Jer 27:3,9.
- Rich and confident. Jer 48:7.
- Prosperous and at ease. Jer 48:11.
- Mighty men of war. Jer 48:14.

Deprived of a large part of their territories by the Amorites. Num 21:26.
Refused to let Israel pass. Judg 11:17,18.
Alarmed at the number, etc. of Israel. Num 22:3.
With Midian send for Balaam to curse Israel. Num 22:1-24:25.
Israelites
- Enticed to idolatry by. Num 25:1-3.
- Forbidden to spoil. Deut 2:9; Judg 11:15.
- Forbidden to make leagues with. Deut 23:6.
- Sometimes intermarried with. Ruth 1:4; 1 Kin 11:1; 1 Chr 8:8; Neh 13:23.

Excluded from the congregation of Israel forever. Deut 23:3,4; Neh 13:1,2.
Always hostile to Israel. Ps 83:6; Ezek 25:8.
Harassed and subdued by Saul. 1 Sam 14:47.
Gave an asylum to David's family. 1 Sam 22:4.
Made tributary to David. 2 Sam 8:2,12.
Benaiah slew two champions of. 2 Sam 23:20.
Paid tribute of sheep and wool to the king of Israel. 2 Kin 3:4; Is 16:1.
Revolted from Israel after the death of Ahab. 2 Kin 1:1; 3:5.
Israel and Judah joined against. 2 Kin 3:6,7.
Miraculously deceived by the colour of the water. 2 Kin 3:21-24.
Conquered by Israel and Judah. 2 Kin 3:24-26.
King of, sacrificed his son to excite animosity against Israel. 2 Kin 3:27.
Joined Babylon against Judah. 2 Kin 24:2.
Prophesies respecting
- Terror on account of Israel. Ex 15:15.
- Desolation and grief. Is 15:1-9; 16:2-11.
- Inability to avert destruction. Is 16:12.
- To destroyed in three years. Is 16:13,14.
- To be captives in Babylon. Jer 27:3,8; 48:7.
- Their desolation as a punishment for their hatred of Israel. Jer 48:26,27; Ezek 25:8,9.
- Restoration from captivity. Jer 48:47.
- Subjugation to Messiah. Num 24:17; Is 25:10.
- Subjugation to Israel. Is 11:14.

Money.

Gold and silver used as. Gen 13:2; Num 22:18.
Brass introduced as, by the Romans. Matt 10:9.
Originally stamped with the image of a lamb. Gen 23:15; 33:19.
Of the Romans, stamped with the image of Caesar. Matt 22:20,21.
Usually taken by weight. Gen 23:16; Jer 32:10.
Pieces of mentioned
- Talent of gold. 1 Kin 9:14; 2 Kin 23:23.
- Talent of silver. 1 Kin 16:24; 2 Kin 5:22,23.
- Shekel of silver. Judg 17:10; 2 Kin 15:20.
- Half shekel or bekah. Ex 30:15.
- Third of a shekel. Neh 10:32.
- Fourth of a shekel. 1 Sam 9:8.
- Gerah the twentieth of a shekel. Num 3:47.
- Pound. Luke 19:13.
- Penny. Matt 20:2; Mark 6:37.
- Farthing. Matt 5:26; Luke 12:6.
- Mite. Mark 12:42; Luke 21:2.

Of the Jews regulated by the standard of sanctuary. Lev 5:15; Num 3:47.
Was current with the merchants. Gen 23:16.
Jews forbidden to take usury for. Lev 25:37.
Changing of, a trade. Matt 21:12; John 2:15.
Was given
- For lands. Gen 23:9; Acts 4:37.
- For slaves. Gen 37:28; Ex 21:21.
- For merchandise. Gen 43:12; Deut 2:6.
- For tribute. 2 Kin 23:33; Matt 22:19.
- As wages. Ezra 3:7; Matt 20:2; James 5:4.
- As offerings. 2 Kin 12:7-9; Neh 10:32.
- As alms. 1 Sam 2:36; Acts 3:3,6.
- Custom of presenting a piece of. Job 42:11.
- Power and usefulness of. Eccl 7:12; 10:19.
- Love of, the root of all evil. 1 Tim 6:10.

Months.

Sun and moon designed to mark out. Gen 1:14.
The patriarchs computed time by. Gen 29:14.
The Jews computed time by. Judg 11:37; 1 Sam 6:1; 1 Kin 4:7.
Commenced with first appearance of new moon. Num 10:10; Ps 81:3.
Originally had no names. Gen 7:11; 8:4.
The year composed of twelve. 1 Chr 27:2-15; Esth 2:12; Rev 22:2.
Names of the twelve
- First, Nisan or Abib. Ex 13:4; Neh 2:1.
- Second, Zif. 1 Kin 6:1,37.
- Third, Sivan. Esth 8:9.
- Fourth, Tammuz. Zech 8:19.
- Fifth, Av. Zech 7:3.
- Sixth, Elul. Neh 6:15.
- Seventh, Ethanim. 1 Kin 8:2.
- Eighth, Bul. 1 Kin 6:38.
- Ninth, Chisleu. Zech 7:1.
- Tenth, Tebeth. Esth 2:16.
- Eleventh, Sebat. Zech 1:7.
- Twelfth, Adar. Ezra 6:15; Esth 3:7.

Idolaters prognosticated by. Is 47:13.
Observance of, condemned. Gal 4:10.

Moon, The.

Created by God. Gen 1:14; Ps 8:3.
Made to glorify God. Ps 148:3.
Called the lesser light. Gen 1:16.
Described as
- Fair. Song 6:10.
- Bright. Job 31:26.

Has a glory of its own. 1 Cor 15:41.
Appointed
- To divide day from night. Gen 1:14.
- For signs and seasons. Gen 1:14; Ps 104:19.
- For a light in the firmament. Gen 1:15.
- To light the earth by night. Jer 31:35.
- To rule the night. Gen 1:16; Ps 136:9.
- By an ordinance for ever. Ps 72:5,7; 89:37; Jer 31:36.
- For the benefit of all. Deut 4:19.

Influences vegetation. Deut 33:14.
First appearance of, a time of festivity. 1 Sam 20:5,6; Ps 81:3.
Miracles connected with
Standing still in Ajalon. Josh 10:12,13.
Signs in, before the destruction of Jerusalem. Luke 21:25.
Lunacy attributed to the influence of. Ps 121:6; Matt 4:24.
Worshipped as the queen of heaven. Jer 7:18; 44:17-19,25.
Worshipping of
Forbidden to the Jews. Deut 4:19.
Condemned as atheism. Job 31:26,28.
To be punished with death. Deut 17:3-6.
Jews often guilty of. 2 Kin 23:5; Jer 8:2.
Jews punished for. Jer 8:1-3.
Illustrative
Of glory of Christ in the Church. Is 60:20.
Of fairness of the Church. Song 6:10.
Of changeableness of the world. Rev 12:1.
(Becoming blood,) of judgments. Rev 6:12.
(Withdrawing her light,) of deep calamities. Is 13:10; Joel 2:10; 3:15; Matt 24:29.

MORNING.

The second part of the day at the creation. Gen 1:5,8,13,19,23,31.
The first part of the natural day. Mark 16:2.
Ordained by God. Job 38:12.
Began with first dawn. Josh 6:15; Ps 119:147.
Continued until noon. 1 Kin 18:26; Neh 8:3.
First dawning of, called the eyelids of the morning. Job 3:9; 41:18.
The outgoings of, made to rejoice. Ps 65:8.
The Jews
Generally rose early in. Gen 28:18; Judg 6:28.
Eat but little in. Eccl 10:16.
Went to the temple in. Luke 21:38; John 8:2.
Offered a part of the daily sacrifice in. Ex 29:38,39; Num 28:4-7.
Devoted a part of, to prayer and praise. Ps 5:3; 59:16; 88:13.
Gathered the manna in. Ex 16:21.
Began their journeys in. Gen 22:3.
Held courts of justice in. Jer 21:12; Matt 27:1.
Contracted covenants in. Gen 26:31.
Transacted business in. Eccl 11:6; Matt 20:1.
Was frequently cloudless. 2 Sam 23:4.
A red sky in, a sign of bad weather. Matt 16:3.
Ushered in by the morning star. Job 38:7.
Illustrative
Of the resurrection day. Ps 49:14.
(Breaking forth,) of the glory of the church. Song 6:10; Is 58:8.
(Star of,) of the glory of Christ. Rev 22:16.
(Star of,) of reward of saints. Rev 2:28.
(Clouds in,) of the short lived profession of hypocrites. Hos 6:4.
(Wings of,) of rapid movements. Ps 139:9.
(Spread upon the mountains,) of heavy calamities. Joel 2:2.

MOTH, THE.

Destructive to garments. Matt 6:19; James 5:2.
Destroyed by the slightest touch. Job 4:19.
Illustrative
Of God in the execution of his judgments. Hos 5:12.
(Eating a garment,) of God's judgments. Is 50:9; 51:8.
(Garments eaten by,) of those who have suffered severe judgments. Job 13:28.
(Making its house in garments,) of man's folly in providing earthly things. Job 27:18.

MOUNTAINS.

The elevated parts of the earth. Gen 7:19,20.
God
Formed. Amos 4:13.
Set fast. Ps 65:6.
Gives strength to. Ps 95:4.
Weighs, in a balance. Is 40:12.
Waters, from his chambers. Ps 104:13.
Parches, with draught. Hag 1:11.
Causes, to smoke. Ps 104:32; 144:5.
Sets the foundations of, on fire. Deut 32:22.
Makes waste. Is 42:15.
Causes, to tremble. Nah 1:5; Hab 3:10.
Causes, to skip. Ps 114:4,6.
Causes, to melt. Judg 5:5; Ps 97:5; Is 64:1,3.
Removes. Job 9:5.
Overturns. Job 9:5; 28:9.
Scatters. Hab 3:6.
Made to glorify God. Ps 148:9.
Called
God's mountains. Is 49:11.
The ancient mountains. Deut 33:15.
The everlasting mountains. Hab 3:6.
Perpetual hills. Heb 3:6.
Everlasting hills. Gen 49:26.
Pillars of heaven. Job 26:11.
Many exceedingly high. Ps 104:18; Is 2:14.
Collect the vapours which ascend from the earth. Ps 104:6,8.
Are the sources of springs and rivers. Deut 8:7; Ps 104:8-10.
Canaan abounded in. Deut 11:11.
Volcanic fires of, alluded to. Is 64:1,2; Jer 51:25; Nah 1:5,6.
Mentioned in Scripture
Ararat. Gen 8:4.
Abarim. Num 33:47,48.
Amalek. Judg 12:15.
Bashan. Ps 68:15.
Bethel. 1 Sam 13:2.
Carmel. Josh 15:55; 19:26; 2 Kin 19:23.
Ebal. Deut 11:29; 27:13.
Ephraim. Josh 17:15; Judg 2:9.
Gerizim. Deut 11:29; Judg 9:7.
Gilboa. 1 Sam 31:1; 2 Sam 1:6,21.
Gilead. Gen 31:21,25; Song 4:1.
Hachilah. 1 Sam 23:19.
Hermon. Josh 13:11.
Hor. Num 20:22; 34:7,8.
Horeb. Ex 3:1.
Lebanon. Deut 3:25.
Mizar. Ps 42:6.
Moreh. Judg 7:1.
Moriah. Gen 22:2; 2 Chr 3:1.
Nebo (part of Abarim). Num 32:3; Deut 34:1.
Olives or mount of corruption. 1 Kin 11:7; 2 Kin 23:13; Luke 21:37.
Pisgah (part of Abarim). Num 21:20; Deut 34:1.
Seir. Gen 14:6; 36:8.
Sinai. Ex 19:2; 18:20,23; 31:18.
Sion. 2 Sam 5:7.
Tabor. Judg 4:6,12,14.
A defence to a country. Ps 125:2.
Afford refuge in time of danger. Gen 14:10; Judg 6:2; Matt 24:16; Heb 11:38.
Afforded pasturage. Ex 3:1; 1 Sam 25:7; 1 Kin 22:17; Ps 147:8; Amos 4:1.
Abounded with
Herbs. Prov 27:25.
Minerals. Deut 8:9.
Precious things. Deut 33:15.
Stone for building. 1 Kin 5:14,17; Dan 2:45.
Forests. 2 Kin 19:23; 2 Chr 2:2,8-10.
Vineyards. 2 Chr 26:10; Jer 31:5.
Spices. Song 4:6; 8:14.
Deer. 1 Chr 12:8; Song 2:8.
Game. 1 Sam 26:20.
Wild beasts. Song 4:8; Hab 2:17.
Often inhabited. Gen 36:8; Josh 11:21.
Sometimes selected as places for divine worship. Gen 22:2,5; Ex 3:12; Is 2:2.
Often selected as places for idolatrous worship. Deut 12:2; 2 Chr 21:11.
Proclamations often made from. Is 40:9.
Beacons or ensigns often raised upon. Is 13:2; 30:17.
Illustrative
Of difficulties. Is 40:4; Zech 4:7; Matt 17:20.
Of persons in authority. Ps 72:3; Is 44:23.
Of the church of God. Is 2:2; Dan 2:35,44,45.
Of God's righteousness. Ps 36:6.
Of proud and haughty persons. Is 2:14.
(Burning,) of destructive enemies. Jer 51:25; Rev 8:8.
(Breaking forth into singing,) of exceeding joy. Is 44:23; 55:12.
(Threshing of,) of heavy judgments. Is 41:15.
(Made waste,) of desolation. Is 42:15; Mal 1:3.
(Dropping new wine,) of abundance. Amos 9:13.

MULE, THE.

First mention of. Gen 36:24.
Stupid and intractable. Ps 32:9.
Used for
Riding, by persons of distinction. 2 Sam 13:29; 18:9; 1 Kin 1:33.

Carrying burdens. 2 Kin 5:17; 1 Chr 12:40.
Conveying posts and messengers. Esth 8:10,14.
Liable to the plague. Zech 14:15.
Food of. 1 Kin 4:28; 18:5.
The Jews
Forbidden to breed. Lev 19:19.
Set a great value upon. 1 Kin 18:5.
Brought many, from Babylon. Ezra 2:66.
Shall be used, at the restoration. Is 66:20.
Of Togarmah, sold in fairs of Tyre. Ezek 27:14.
Often given as tribute. 1 Kin 10:25.

MURDER.

Forbidden by Mosaic law. Ex 20:13; Deut 5:17.
Why forbidden by God. Gen 9:6.
The law made to restrain. 1 Tim 1:9.
Described as killing
With premeditation. Ex 21:14.
From hatred. Num 35:20,21; Deut 19:11.
By lying in wait. Num 35:20; Deut 19:11.
By an instrument of iron. Num 35:16.
By the blow of a stone. Num 35:17.
By a hand weapon of wood. Num 35:18.
Killing a thief in the day, counted as. Ex 22:3.
Early introduction of. Gen 4:8.
Represented as a sin crying to heaven. Gen 4:10; Heb 12:24; Rev 6:10.
The Jews often guilty of. Is 1:21.
Persons guilty of
Fearful and cowardly. Gen 4:14.
Wanderers and vagabonds. Gen 4:14.
Flee from God's presence. Gen 4:16.
Not protected in refuge cities. Deut 19:11,12.
Had no protection from altars. Ex 21:14.
Not to be pitied or spared. Deut 19:13.
Often committed by night. Neh 6:10; Job 24:14.
Imputed to the nearest city when the murderer was unknown. Deut 21:1-3.
Mode of clearing those suspected of. Deut 21:3-9; Matt 27:24.
To be proved by two witnesses at least. Num 35:30; Deut 19:11,15.
Punishment for
The curse of God. Gen 4:11.
Death. Gen 9:5,6; Ex 21:12; Num 35:16.
Not to be commuted. Num 35:32.
Inflicted by the nearest of kin. Num 35:19,21.
Forbidden. Gen 9:6; Ex 20:13; Deut 5:17; Rom 13:9.
Explained by Christ. Matt 5:21,22.
Hatred is. 1 John 3:15.
Is a work for the flesh. Gal 5:21.
Comes from the heart. Matt 15:19.
Defiles the
Hands. Is 59:3.
Person and garments. Lam 4:13,14.
Land. Num 35:33; Ps 106:38.
Not concealed from God. Is 26:21; Jer 2:34.
Cries for vengeance. Gen 4:10.
God
Abominates. Prov 6:16,17.
Makes inquisition for. Ps 9:12.
Will avenge. Deut 32:43; 1 Kin 21:19; Hos 1:4.
Requires blood for. Gen 9:5; Num 35:33; 1 Kin 2:32.
Rejects the prayers of those guilty of. Is 1:15; 59:2,3.
Curses those guilty of. Gen 4:11.
The law made to restrain. 1 Tim 1:9.
Saints
Specially warned against. 1 Pet 4:15.
Deprecate the guilt of. Ps 51:14.
Should warn others against. Gen 37:22; Jer 26:15.
Connected with idolatry. Ezek 22:3,4; 2 Kin 3:27.
The wicked
Filled with. Rom 1:29.
Devise. Gen 27:41; 37:18.
Intent on. Jer 22:17.
Lie in wait to commit. Ps 10:8-10.
Swift to commit. Prov 1:16; Rom 3:15.
Perpetrate. Job 24:14; Ezek 22:3.
Have hands full of. Is 1:15.
Encourage others to commit. 1 Kin 21:8-10; Prov 1:11.
Characteristic of the devil. John 8:44.
Punishment of. Gen 4:12-15; 9:6; Num 35:30; 2 Kin 9:36,37; Jer 19:4-9.
Punishment of, not commuted under the Law. Num 35:31.
Of saints, specially avenged. Deut 32:43; Matt 23:35; Rev 18:20,24.
Excludes from heaven. Gal 5:21; Rev 22:15.
Exemplified
Cain. Gen 4:8.
Esau. Gen 27:41.
Joseph's brethren. Gen 37:20.
Pharaoh. Ex 1:22.
Abimelech. Judg 9:5.
Men of Shechem. Judg 9:24.
Amalekite. 2 Sam 1:16.
Rechab. 2 Sam 4:5-7.
David. 2 Sam 12:9.
Absalom. 2 Sam 13:29.
Joab. 1 Kin 2:31,32.
Baasha. 1 Kin 15:27.
Zimri. 1 Kin 16:10.
Jezebel. 1 Kin 21:10.
Elders of Jezreel. 1 Kin 21:13.
Ahab. 1 Kin 21:19.
Hazael. 2 Kin 8:12,15.
Adrammelech, etc. 2 Kin 19:37.
Manasseh. 2 Kin 21:16.
Ishmael. Jer 41:7.
Princes of Israel. Ezek 11:6.
People of Gilead. Hos 6:8.
The Herods. Matt 2:16; 14:10; Acts 12:2.
Herodias and her daughter. Matt 14:8-11.
Chief priests. Matt 27:1.
Judas. Matt 27:4.
Barabbas. Mark 15:7.
Jews. Acts 7:52; 1 Thess 2:15.

MURMURING.

Forbidden. 1 Cor 10:10; Phil 2:14.
Against
God. Prov 19:3.
The sovereignty of God. Rom 9:19,20.
The service of God. Mal 3:14.
Christ. Luke 5:30; 15:2; 19:7; John 6:41-43,52.
Ministers of God. Ex 17:3; Num 16:41.
Disciples of Christ. Matt 7:2; Luke 5:30; 6:2.
Unreasonableness of. Lam 3:39.
Tempts God. Ex 17:2.
Provokes God. Num 14:2,11; Deut 9:8,22.
Saints cease from. Is 29:23,24.
Characteristic of the wicked. Jude 1:16.
Guilt of encouraging others in. Num 13:31-33; 14:36,37.
Punishment of. Num 11:1; 14:27-29; 16:45,46; Ps 106:25,26.
Illustrated. Matt 20:11; Luke 15:29,30.
Exemplified
Cain. Gen 4:13,14.
Moses. Ex 5:22,23.
Israelites. Ex 14:11; 15:24; 16:2; 17:2,3; Num 11:1-4; 21:5.
Aaron, etc. Num 12:1,2,8.
Korah, etc. Num 16:3.
Elijah. 1 Kin 19:4.
Job. Job 3:1-26.
Jeremiah. Jer 20:14-18.
Jonah. Jon 4:8,9.
Disciples. Mark 14:4,5; John 6:61.
Pharisees. Luke 15:2; 19:7.
Jews. John 6:41-43.
Grecians. Acts 6:1.

MUSIC.

Early invention of. Gen 4:21.
Divided into
Vocal. 2 Sam 19:35; Acts 16:25.
Instrumental. Dan 6:18.
Designed to promote joy. Eccl 2:8,10.
Vanity of all unsanctified. Eccl 2:8,11.
Considered efficacious in mental disorders. 1 Sam 16:14-17,23.
Effects produced on the prophets of old by. 1 Sam 10:5,6; 2 Kin 3:15.
Instruments of
Cymbals. 1 Chr 16:5; Ps 150:5.
Cornet. Ps 98:6; Hos 5:8.
Dulcimer. Dan 3:5.
Flute. Dan 3:5.
Harp. Ps 137:2; Ezek 26:13.
Organ. Gen 4:21; Job 21:12; Ps 150:4.
Pipe. 1 Kin 1:40; Is 5:12; Jer 48:36.
Psaltery. Ps 33:2; 71:22.
Sackbut. Dan 3:5.
Tabret. 1 Sam 10:5; Is 24:8.
Timbrel. Ex 15:20; Ps 68:25.
Trumpet. 2 Kin 11:14; 2 Chr 29:27.
Viol. Is 14:11; Amos 5:23.
Made of fir wood. 2 Sam 6:5.
Made of almug wood. 1 Kin 10:12.
Made of brass. 1 Cor 13:1.
Made of silver. Num 10:2.
Made of horns of animals. Josh 6:8.
Many, with strings. Ps 33:2; 150:4.
Early invention of. Gen 4:21.
Invented by David. 1 Chr 23:5; 2 Chr 7:6.
The Jews celebrated for inventing. Amos 6:5.
Often expensively ornamented. Ezek 28:13.
Great diversity of. Eccl 2:8.

Appointed to be used in the temple. 1 Chr 16:4-6; 23:5,6; 25:1; 2 Chr 29:25.
Custom of sending away friends with. Gen 31:27.
The Jews used
In sacred processions. 2 Sam 6:4,5,15; 1 Chr 13:6-8; 15:27,28.
At laying foundation of temple. Ezra 3:9,10.
At consecration of temple. 2 Chr 5:11-13.
At coronation of kings. 2 Chr 23:11,13.
At dedication of city walls. Neh 12:27,28.
To celebrate victories. Ex 15:20; 1 Sam 18:6,7.
In religious feasts. 2 Chr 30:21.
In private entertainments. Is 5:12; Amos 6:5.
In dances. Matt 11:17; Luke 15:25.
In funeral ceremonies. Matt 9:23.
In commemorating great men. 2 Chr 35:25.
Used in idol worship. Dan 3:5.
The movements of armies regulated by. Josh 6:8; 1 Cor 14:8.
Generally put aside in times of affliction. Ps 137:2-4; Dan 6:18.
Illustrative
Of joy and gladness. Zeph 3:17; Eph 5:19.
Of heavenly felicity. Rev 5:8,9.
(Ceasing of,) of calamities. Is 24:8,9; Rev 18:22.

Naphtali, the Tribe of.

Descended from Jacob's sixth son. Gen 30:7,8.
Predictions respecting. Gen 49:21; Deut 33:23.
Persons selected from
To number the people. Num 1:15.
To spy out the land. Num 13:14.
To divide the land. Num 34:28.
Strength of, on leaving Egypt. Num 1:42,43.
The rear of the fourth division of Israel in their journeys. Num 10:25,27.
Encamped under the standard of Dan north of the tabernacle. Num 2:25,29.
Offering of, at the dedication. Num 7:78-83.
Families of. Num 26:48,49.
Strength of, on entering Canaan. Num 26:50.
On Ebal, said amen to the curses. Deut 27:13.
Bounds of their inheritance. Josh 19:32-39.
Did not drive out the Canaanites, but made them tributary. Judg 1:33.
Chosen from Zebulun to go with Barak against Sisera. Judg 4:6,10.
Praised for aiding against Sisera. Judg 5:18.
Joined Gideon in the pursuit and overthrow of the Midianites. Judg 7:23.
Some of, at David's coronation. 1 Chr 12:34.
Officer placed over, by David. 1 Chr 27:19.
Officer placed over, by Solomon. 1 Kin 4:15.
Land of, ravaged by Benhadad. 1 Kin 15:20.
Land of, purged of idols by Josiah. 2 Chr 34:6.
Taken captive by Tiglathpileser. 2 Kin 15:29.
Specially favoured by our Lord's ministry. Is 9:1,2; Matt 4:13-15.
Remarkable persons of
Barak. Judg 4:6.
Hiram. 1 Kin 7:14.

Nazirites.

Persons separated to the service of God. Num 6:2.
Different kinds of
From the womb. Judg 13:5; Luke 1:15.
By a particular vow. Num 6:2.
Required to be holy. Num 6:8.
Esteemed pure. Lam 4:7.
Prohibited from
Wine or strong drink. Num 6:3; Luke 1:15.
Grapes or anything made from the vine. Num 6:3,4; Judg 13:14.
Cutting or shaving the head. Num 6:5; Judg 13:5; 16:17.
Defiling themselves by the dead. Num 6:6,7.
Raised up for good of the nation. Amos 2:11.
Ungodly Jews tried to corrupt. Amos 2:12.
Defiled during vow
To shave the head the seventh day. Num 6:9.
To bring two turtle doves for a burnt offering. Num 6:10,11.
To recompense their vow with a trespass offering. Num 6:12.
On completion of vow
To be brought to tabernacle door. Num 6:13.
To offer sacrifices. Num 6:14-17.
To shave their heads. Num 6:18; Acts 18:18; 21:24.
To have the left shoulder of the ram of the peace offering waved upon their hands by the priest. Num 6:19,20; Lev 7:32.
Illustrative of
Christ. Heb 7:26.
Saints. 2 Cor 6:17; James 1:27.

Nethinim.

Were the servants of the Levites. Ezra 8:20.
Probably originated in the appointment of the Gibeonites. Josh 9:27.
The remnant of the Canaanites appointed as, by Solomon. 1 Kin 9:20,21; Ezra 2:58.
With the priests and Levites
Had cities to reside in. 1 Chr 9:2; Ezra 2:70.
Exempted from tribute. Ezra 7:24.
Had chiefs or captains over them. Neh 11:21.
A large number of, returned from the captivity. Ezra 2:43-54; Neh 7:46-56,60.
Were zealous for the covenant. Neh 10:28,29.

New Birth, The.

The corruption of human nature requires. John 3:6; Rom 8:7,8.
None can enter heaven without. John 3:3.
Effected by
God. John 1:13; 1 Pet 1:3.
Christ. 1 John 2:29.
The Holy Spirit. John 3:6; Titus 3:5.
Through the instrumentality of
The Word of God. James 1:18; 1 Pet 1:23.
The resurrection of Christ. 1 Pet 1:3.
The ministry of the gospel. 1 Cor 4:15.
Is of the will of God. James 1:18.
Is of the mercy of God. Titus 3:5.
Is for the glory of God. Is 43:7.
Described as
A new creation. 2 Cor 5:17; Gal 6:15; Eph 2:10.
Newness of life. Rom 6:4.
A spiritual resurrection. Rom 6:4-6; Eph 2:1,5; Col 2:12; 3:1.
A new heart. Ezek 36:26.
A new spirit. Ezek 11:19; Rom 7:6.
Putting on the new man. Eph 4:24.
The inward man. Rom 7:22; 2 Cor 4:16.
Circumcision of the heart. Deut 30:6; Rom 2:29; Col 2:11.
Partaking of the divine nature. 2 Pet 1:4.
The washing of regeneration. Titus 3:5.
All saints partake of. Rom 8:16,17; 1 Pet 2:2; 1 John 5:1.
Produces
Likeness to God. Eph 4:24; Col 3:10.
Likeness to Christ. Rom 8:29; 2 Cor 3:18; 1 John 3:2.
Knowledge of God. Jer 24:7; Col 3:10.
Hatred of sin. 1 John 3:9; 5:18.
Victory over the world. 1 John 5:4.
Delight in God's law. Rom 7:22.
Evidenced by
Faith in Christ. 1 John 5:1.
Righteousness. 1 John 2:29.
Brotherly love. 1 John 4:7.
Connected with adoption. Is 43:6,7; John 1:12,13.
The ignorant cavil at. John 3:4.
Manner of effecting—Illustrated. John 3:8.
Preserves from Satan's devices. 1 John 5:18.

Night.

The darkness first called. Gen 1:5.
Caused by God. Ps 104:20.
Belongs to God. Ps 74:16.
The heavenly bodies designed to separate day from. Gen 1:14.
The moon and stars designed to rule and give light by. Gen 1:16-18; Jer 31:35.
Commenced at sunset. Gen 28:11.
Continued until sunrise. Ps 104:22; Matt 28:1; Mark 16:2.
Regular succession of
Established by covenant. Gen 8:22; Jer 33:20.
Ordained for the glory of God. Ps 19:2.

Originally divided into three watches. Lam 2:19; Judg 7:19; Ex 14:24.
Divided into four watches by the Romans. Luke 12:38; Matt 14:25; Mark 13:35.
Frequently
Exceeding dark. Prov 7:9.
Cold and frosty. Gen 31:40; Jer 36:30.
Accompanied by heavy dew. Num 11:9; Judg 6:38,40; Job 29:19; Song 5:2.
Unsuitable for labour. John 9:4.
Unsuitable for travelling. John 11:10.
Designed for rest. Ps 104:23.
Wearisome to the afflicted. Job 7:3,4.
Favourable to the purposes of the wicked. Gen 31:39; Job 24:14,15; Obad 5; 1 Thess 5:2.
Wild beasts go forth in search of prey during. 2 Sam 21:10; Ps 104:21,22.
The Jews
Forbidden to keep the wages of servants during. Lev 19:13.
Forbidden to allow malefactors to hang during. Deut 21:23.
In affliction spent, in sorrow and humiliation. Ps 6:6; 30:5; Joel 1:13.
In affliction spent, in prayer. Ps 22:2.
Often kept lamps burning during. Prov 31:18.
Eastern shepherds watched over their flocks during. Gen 31:40; Luke 2:8.
Eastern fishermen continued their employment during. Luke 5:5; John 21:3.
God frequently
Revealed his will in. Gen 31:24; 46:2; Num 22:30; Dan 7:2.
Visited his people in. 1 Kin 3:5; Ps 17:3.
Executed his judgments in. Ex 12:12; 2 Kin 19:35; Job 27:20; Dan 5:30.
Illustrative of
Spiritual darkness. Rom 13:12.
Seasons of severe calamities. Is 21:12; Amos 5:8.
Seasons of spiritual desertion. Song 3:1.
Death. John 9:4.

NILE, THE RIVER.

Empties itself into the Mediterranean Sea by seven streams. Is 11:15.
Called
The river. Gen 41:1,3.
The Egyptian sea. Is 11:15.
The stream of Egypt. Is 27:12.
Sihor. Josh 13:3; Jer 2:18.
Abounded in
Crocodiles. Ezek 29:3.
Fish. Ex 7:21; Ezek 29:4.
Reeds and flags. Is 19:6,7.
Annual overflow of its banks alluded to. Jer 46:8; Amos 8:8; 9:5.
The Egyptians
Took great pride in. Ezek 29:9.
Carried on extensive commerce by. Is 23:3.
Bathed in. Ex 2:5.
Drank of. Ex 7:21,24.
Punished by failure of its waters. Is 19:5,6.
Punished by destruction of its fish. Is 19:8.
Remarkable events connected with
Male children drowned in. Ex 1:22.
Moses exposed on its banks. Ex 2:3.
Its waters turned into blood. Ex 7:15,20.
Miraculous generation of frogs. Ex 8:3.

NINEVEH.

Origin and antiquity of. Gen 10:11.
Situated on the river Tigris. Nah 2:6,8.
The ancient capital of Assyria. 2 Kin 19:36; Is 37:37.
Called the bloody city. Nah 3:1.
Described as
Great. Jon 1:2; 3:2.
Extensive. Jon 3:3.
Rich. Nah 2:9.
Strong. Nah 3:12.
Commercial. Nah 3:16.
Populous. Jon 4:11.
Vile. Nah 1:14.
Wicked. Jon 1:2.
Idolatrous. Nah 1:14.
Full of joy and carelessness. Zeph 2:15.
Full of lies and robbery. Nah 3:1.
Full of witchcraft. Nah 3:4.
Jonah sent to proclaim the destruction of. Jon 1:2; 3:1,2,4.
Inhabitants of, repented at Jonah's preaching. Jon 3:5-9; Matt 12:41; Luke 11:32.
Destruction of, averted. John 3:10; 4:11.
Predictions respecting
Coming up of the Babylonish armies against. Nah 2:1-4; 3:2.
Destruction of its people. Nah 1:12; 3:3.
Spoiling of its treasures. Nah 2:9.
Destruction of its idols. Nah 1:14; 2:7.
Degradation and contempt put on. Nah 3:5-7; Zeph 2:15.
Utter destruction. Nah 1:8,9.
Complete desolation. Zeph 2:13-15.
Feebleness of its people. Nah 3:13.
Being taken while people were drunk. Nah 1:10; 3:11.
Captivity of its people. Nah 3:10.

OAK TREE, THE.

The hill of Bashan celebrated for. Is 2:13.
Described as
Strong. Amos 2:9.
Thick spreading. 2 Sam 18:9; Ezek 6:13.
Casting its leaves in winter. Is 6:13.
The people of Tyre made oars of. Ezek 27:6.
Idolaters often made idols of. Is 44:14.
The ancients often
Rested under. Judg 6:11,19; 1 Kin 13:14.
Buried their dead under. Gen 35:8; 1 Chr 10:12.
Erected monuments under. Josh 24:26.
Performed idolatrous rites under. Is 1:29; 57:5; Ezek 6:13; Hos 4:13.
Absalom in his flight intercepted by, and suspended from. 2 Sam 18:9,10,14.
Jacob buried his family idols under. Gen 35:4.
Illustrative
Of the church. Is 6:13.
Of strong and powerful men. Amos 2:9.
Of wicked rulers. Is 2:13; Zech 11:2.
(Fading,) of the wicked under judgments. Is 1:30.

OATHS.

The lawful purpose of, explained. Heb 6:16.
Antiquity of. Gen 14:22; 24:3,8.
Used for
Confirming covenants. Gen 26:28; 31:44,53; 1 Sam 20:16,17.
Deciding controversies in courts of law. Ex 22:11; Num 5:19; 1 Kin 8:31.
Pledging allegiance to sovereigns. 2 Kin 11:4; Eccl 8:2.
Binding to performance of sacred duties. Num 30:2; 2 Chr 15:14,15; Neh 10:29; Ps 132:2.
Binding to performance of any particular act. Gen 24:3,4; 50:25; Josh 2:12.
Judicial form of administering. 1 Kin 22:16; Matt 26:63.
Often accompanied by raising up the hand. Gen 14:22; Dan 12:7; Rev 10:5,6.
Often accompanied by placing the hand under the thigh of the person sworn to. Gen 24:2,9; 47:29.
To be taken in fear and reverence. Eccl 9:2.
The Jews
Forbidden to take, in name of idols. Josh 23:7.
Forbidden to take, in the name of any created thing. Matt 5:34-36; James 5:12.
Forbidden to take false. Lev 6:3; Zech 8:17.
Forbidden to take rash, or unholy. Lev 5:4.
To use God's name alone in. Deut 6:13; 10:20; Is 65:16.
To take, in truth, judgment, etc. Jer 4:2.
Generally respected the obligation of. Josh 9:19,20; 2 Sam 21:7; Ps 15:4; Matt 14:9.
Fell into many errors respecting. Matt 23:16-22.
Often guilty of rashly taking. Judg 21:7; Matt 14:7; 26:72.
Often guilty of falsely taking. Lev 6:3; Jer 5:2; 7:9.
Condemned for false. Zech 5:4; Mal 3:5.
Condemned for profane. Jer 23:10; Hos 4:2.
Instances of rash
Joshua, etc. Josh 9:15,16.
Jephthah. Judg 11:30-36.
Saul. 1 Sam 14:27,44.
Herod. Matt 14:7-9.
The Jews who sought to kill Paul. Acts 23:21.
Custom of swearing by the life of the king. Gen 42:15,16.

Expressions used as
- By the fear of Isaac. Gen 31:53.
- As the Lord liveth. Judg 8:19; Ruth 3:13.
- The Lord do so to me, and more also. Ruth 1:17.
- God do so to thee, and more also. 1 Sam 3:17.
- By the Lord. 2 Sam 19:7; 1 Kin 2:42.
- Before God I lie not. Gal 1:20.
- I call God for a record. 2 Cor 1:23.
- God is witness. 1 Thess 2:5.
- I charge you by the Lord. 1 Thess 5:27.
- As thy soul liveth. 1 Sam 1:26; 25:26.

God used, to show the immutability of his counsel. Gen 22:16; Num 14:28; 6:17.

Obedience to God.

Commanded. Deut 13:4.
Without faith, is impossible. Heb 11:6.
Includes
- Obeying his voice. Ex 19:5; Jer 7:23.
- Obeying his law. Deut 11:27; Is 42:24.
- Obeying Christ. Ex 23:21; 2 Cor 10:5.
- Obeying the gospel. Rom 1:5; 6:17; 10:16,17.
- Keeping his commandments. Eccl 12:13.
- Submission to higher powers. Rom 13:1.

Better than sacrifice. 1 Sam 15:22.
Justification obtained by that of Christ. Rom 5:19.
Christ, an example of. Matt 3:15; John 15:20; Phil 2:5-8; Heb 5:8.
Angels engaged in. Ps 103:20.
A characteristic of saints. 1 Pet 1:14.
Saints elected to. 1 Pet 1:2.
Obligations to. Acts 4:19,20; 5:29.
Exhortations to. Jer 26:13; 38:20.
Should be
- From the heart. Deut 11:13; Rom 6:17.
- With willingness. Ps 18:44; Is 1:19.
- Unreserved. Josh 22:2,3.
- Undeviating. Deut 28:14.
- Constant. Phil 2:12.

Resolve upon. Ex 24:7; Josh 24:24.
Confess your failure in. Dan 9:10.
Prepare the heart for. 1 Sam 7:3; Ezra 7:10.
Pray to be taught. Ps 119:35; 143:10.
Promises to. Ex 23:22; 1 Sam 12:14; Is 1:19; Jer 7:23.
To be universal in the latter days. Dan 7:27.
Blessedness of. Deut 11:27; 28:1-13; Luke 11:28; James 1:25.
The wicked refuse. Ex 5:2; Neh 9:17.
Punishment of refusing. Deut 11:28; 28:15-68; Josh 5:6; Is 1:20.
Exemplified
- Noah. Gen 6:22.
- Abram. Gen 12:1-4; Heb 11:8; Gen 22:3,12.
- Israelites. Ex 12:28; 24:7.
- Caleb, etc. Num 32:12.
- Asa. 1 Kin 15:11.
- Elijah. 1 Kin 17:5.
- Hezekiah. 2 Kin 18:6.
- Josiah. 2 Kin 22:2.
- David. Ps 119:106.
- Zerubbabel. Hag 1:12.
- Joseph. Matt 1:24.
- Wise men. Matt 2:12.
- Zacharias, etc. Luke 1:6.
- Paul. Acts 26:19.
- Saints of Rome. Rom 16:19.

Offence.

Occasions of, must arrive. Matt 18:7.
Occasions of, forbidden. 1 Cor 10:32; 2 Cor 6:3.
Persecution, a cause of, to mere professors. Matt 13:21; 24:10; 26:31.
The wicked take, at
- The low station of Christ. Is 53:1-3; Matt 13:54-57.
- Christ, as the corner-stone. Is 8:14; Rom 9:33; 1 Pet 2:8.
- Christ, as the bread of life. John 6:58-61.
- Christ crucified. 1 Cor 1:23; Gal 5:11.
- The righteousness of faith. Rom 9:32.
- The necessity of inward purity. Matt 15:11,12.

Blessedness of not taking, at Christ. Matt 11:6.
Saints warned against taking. John 16:1.
Saints should
- Be without. Phil 1:10.
- Be cautious of giving. Ps 73:15; Rom 14:13; 1 Cor 8:9.
- Have a conscience void of. Acts 24:16.
- Cut off what causes, to themselves. Matt 5:29,30; Mark 9:43-47.
- Not let their liberty occasion, to others. 1 Cor 8:9.
- Use self-denial rather than occasion. Rom 14:21; 1 Cor 8:13.
- Avoid those who cause. Rom 16:17.
- Reprove those who cause. Ex 32:21; 1 Sam 2:24.

Ministers should
- Be cautious of giving. 2 Cor 6:3.
- Remove that which causes. Is 57:14.

All things that cause, shall be gathered out of Christ's kingdom. Matt 13:41.
Denunciation against those who cause. Matt 18:7; Mark 9:42.
Punishment for occasioning. Ezek 44:12; Mal 2:8,9; Matt 18:6,7.
Exemplified
- Aaron. Ex 32:2-6.
- Balaam, etc. Num 31:16; Rev 2:14.
- Gideon. Judg 8:27.
- Sons of Eli. 1 Sam 2:12-17.
- Jeroboam. 1 Kin 12:26-30.
- Old prophet. 1 Kin 13:18-26.
- Priests. Mal 2:8.
- Peter. Matt 16:23.

Offences Against the Holy Spirit.

Exhortations against. Eph 4:30; 1 Thess 5:19.
Exhibited in
- Tempting him. Acts 5:9.
- Vexing him. Is 63:10.
- Grieving him. Eph 4:30.
- Quenching him. 1 Thess 5:19.
- Lying to him. Acts 5:3,4.
- Resisting him. Acts 7:51.
- Undervaluing his gifts. Acts 8:19,20.
- Danger of trifling with the Holy Spirit. Heb 6:4-6.
- Doing despite to him. Heb 10:29.
- Disregarding his testimony. Neh 9:30.

Blasphemy against him, unpardonable. Matt 12:31,32; 1 John 5:16.

Offerings.

To be made to God alone. Ex 22:20; Judg 13:16.
Antiquity of. Gen 4:3,4.
Different kinds of
- Burnt. Lev 1:3-17; Ps 66:15.
- Sin. Lev 4:3-35; 6:25; 10:17.
- Trespass. Lev 5:16-19; 6:6; 7:1.
- Peace. Lev 3:1-17; 7:11.
- Heave. Ex 29:27,28; 7:14; Num 15:19.
- Wave. Ex 29:26; Lev 7:30.
- Meat. Lev 2:1-16; Num 15:4.
- Drink. Gen 35:14; Ex 29:40; Num 15:5.
- Thank. Lev 7:12; 22:29; Ps 50:14.
- Free-will. Lev 23:38; Deut 16:10; 23:23.
- Incense. Ex 30:8; Mal 1:11; Luke 1:9.
- First-fruits. Ex 22:29; Deut 18:4.
- Tithe. Lev 27:30; Num 18:21; Deut 14:22.
- Gifts. Ex 35:22; Num 7:2-88.
- Jealousy. Num 5:15.
- Personal, for redemption. Ex 30:13,15.

Declared to be most holy. Num 18:9.
Required to be
- Perfect. Lev 22:21.
- The best of their kind. Mal 1:14.
- Offered willingly. Lev 22:19.
- Offered in righteousness. Mal 3:3.
- Offered in love and charity. Matt 5:23,24.
- Brought in a clean vessel. Is 66:20.
- Brought to the place appointed of God. Deut 12:6; Ps 27:6; Heb 9:9.
- Laid before the altar. Matt 5:23,24.
- Presented by the priest. Heb 5:1.
- Brought without delay. Ex 22:29,30.

Unacceptable, without gratitude. Ps 50:8,14.
Could not make the offerer perfect. Heb 9:9.
Things forbidden as
- The price of fornication. Deut 23:18.
- The price of a dog. Deut 23:18.
- Whatever was blemished. Lev 22:20.
- Whatever was imperfect. Lev 22:24.
- Whatever was unclean. Lev 27:11,27.

Laid up in the temple. 2 Chr 31:12; Neh 10:37.
Hezekiah prepared chambers for. 2 Chr 31:11.
The Jews often
- Slow in presenting. Neh 13:10-12.
- Defrauded God of. Mal 3:8.
- Gave the worst they had as. Mal 1:8,13.
- Rejected in, because of sin. Is 1:13; Mal 1:10.
- Abhorred, on account of the sins of the priests. 1 Sam 2:17.
- Presented to idols. Ezek 20:28.

Made by strangers, to be the same as by the Jews. Num 15:14-16.

Many offences under the law, beyond the efficacy of. 1 Sam 3:14; Ps 51:16.
Illustrative of
Christ's offering of himself. Eph 5:2.
The conversion of the Gentiles. Rom 15:16.
The conversion of the Jews. Is 66:20.

OIL.

Given by God. Ps 104:14,15; Jer 31:12; Joel 2:19,24.
Comes form the earth. Ps 104:14,15; Hos 2:22.
Kinds of, mentioned
Olive. Ex 30:24; Lev 24:2.
Myrrh. Esth 2:12.
Extracted by presses. Hag 2:16; Mic 6:15.
The poor employed in extracting. Job 24:11.
Canaan abounded in. Deut 8:8.
Described as
Soft. Ps 55:21.
Smooth. Prov 5:3.
Penetrating. Ps 109:18.
Healing. Is 1:6; Luke 10:34.
The ointments of the Jews made of perfumes mixed with. Ex 30:23-25; John 12:3.
Jews often extravagant in the use of. Prov 21:17.
Was tithable by the law. Deut 12:17.
First-fruits of, given to God. Deut 18:4; 2 Chr 31:5; Neh 10:37.
Used
For food. 1 Kin 17:12; Ezek 16:13.
For anointing the person. Ps 23:5; 104:15; Luke 7:46.
For anointing to offices of trust. Ex 29:7; 1 Sam 10:1; 1 Kin 19:16.
For anointing the sick. Mark 6:13; James 5:14.
In God's worship. Lev 7:10; Num 15:4-10.
In idolatrous worship. Hos 2:5,8.
For lamps. Ex 25:6; 27:20; Matt 25:3.
When fresh, especially esteemed. Ps 92:10.
Dealing in, a trade. 2 Kin 4:7.
Exported. 1 Kin 5:11; Ezek 27:17; Hos 12:1.
Sold by measure. 1 Kin 5:11; Luke 16:6.
Kept in
Boxes. 2 Kin 9:1.
Horns. 1 Kin 1:39.
Pots. 2 Kin 4:2.
Cruises. 1 Kin 17:12.
Cellars. 1 Chr 27:28.
Storehouses. 2 Chr 32:28.
Stores of, laid up in fortified cities. 2 Chr 11:11.
Failure of, a severe calamity. Hag 1:11.
Miraculous increase of. 2 Kin 4:2-6.
Illustrative of
The unction of the Holy Spirit. Ps 45:7; 89:20; Zech 4:12.
The consolation of the gospel. Is 61:3.
Kind reproof. Ps 141:5.

OLIVE TREE, THE.

Often grew wild. Rom 11:17.
Cultivated
In olive yards. 1 Sam 8:14; Neh 5:11.
Among rocks. Deut 32:13.
On the sides of mountains. Matt 21:1.
Canaan abounded in. Deut 6:11; 8:8.
Assyria abounded in. 2 Kin 18:32.
Kings of Israel largely cultivated. 1 Chr 27:28.
Described as
Green. Jer 11:16.
Fair and beautiful. Jer 11:16; Hos 14:6.
Fat and unctuous. Judg 9:9; Rom 11:17.
Bearing goodly fruit. Jer 11:16; James 3:12.
Grafting of, alluded to. Rom 11:24.
Pruning of, alluded to. Rom 11:18,19.
Often cast its flowers. Job 15:33.
Often cast its fruit. Deut 28:40.
Often suffered from caterpillars. Amos 4:9.
Good for the service of God and man. Judg 9:9.
Oil procured from. Ex 27:20; Deut 8:8.
Used for making
The cherubim in the temple. 1 Kin 6:23.
The doors and posts of the temple. 1 Kin 6:31-33.
Booths at feast of tabernacles. Neh 8:15.
Beaten to remove the fruit. Deut 24:20.
Shaken when fully ripe. Is 17:6.
Gleaning of, left for the poor. Deut 24:20.
Fruit of, during sabbatical year left for the poor, etc. Ex 23:11.
The fruit of, trodden in presses to extract the oil. Mic 6:15; Hag 2:16.
Failure of, a great calamity. Hab 3:17,18.
Illustrative
Of Christ. Rom 11:17,24; Zech 4:3,12.
Of the Jewish church. Jer 11:16.
Of the righteous. Ps 52:8; Hos 14:6.
Of children of pious parents. Ps 128:3.
Of the two witnesses. Rev 11:3,4.
(When wild,) of the Gentiles. Rom 11:17,24.
(Gleaning of,) of the remnant of grace. Is 17:6; 24:13.
Probably origin of its being the emblem of peace. Gen 8:11.

OSTRICH, THE.

Unclean and unfit for food. Lev 11:13.
Furnished with wings and feathers. Job 39:13.
Lays her eggs in the sand. Job 39:14.
Described as
Void of wisdom. Job 39:17.
Imprudent. Job 39:15.
Cruel to her young. Job 39:16.
Rapid in movement. Job 39:18.
Illustrative
Of the unnatural cruelty of the Jews in their calamities. Lam 4:3.
(Companionship with,) of extreme desolation. Job 30:29.

OWL, THE.

Varieties of. Lev 11:16,17; Deut 14:15,16.
Unclean and not to be eaten. Lev 11:13,16.
Described as
Mournful in voice. Mic 1:8.
Solitary in disposition. Ps 102:6.
Careful of its young. Is 34:15.
Inhabits deserted cities and houses. Is 13:21; 34:11-14; Jer 50:39.
Illustrative of mourners. Ps 102:6.

OX, THE.

Often found wild. Deut 14:5.
Includes the
Bull. Gen 32:15; Job 21:10.
Bullock. Ps 50:9; Jer 46:21.
Cow. Num 18:17; Job 21:10.
Heifer. Gen 15:9; Num 19:2.
Was clean and fit for food. Deut 14:4.
Described as
Strong. Ps 144:14; Prov 14:4.
Beautiful. Jer 46:20; Hos 10:11.
Not without sagacity. Is 1:3.
Horns and hoofs of, alluded to. Ps 69:31.
Lowing of, alluded to. 1 Sam 15:14; Job 6:5.
Was fed
With grass. Job 40:15; Ps 106:20; Dan 4:25.
With corn. Is 30:24.
With straw. Is 11:7.
On the hills. Is 7:25.
In the valleys. 1 Chr 27:29; Is 65:10.
In stalls. Hab 3:17.
Rapid manner of collecting its food alluded to. Num 22:4.
Formed a part of the patriarchal wealth. Gen 13:2,5; 26:14; Job 1:3.
Formed a part of the wealth of Israel in Egypt. Gen 50:8; Ex 10:9; 12:32.
Formed a part of the wealth of the Jews. Num 32:4; Ps 144:14.
Required great care and attention. Prov 27:23.
Herdmen appointed over. Gen 13:7; 1 Sam 21:7.
Urged on by the goad. Judg 3:31.
Used for
Drawing wagons, etc. Num 7:3; 1 Sam 6:7.
Carrying burdens. 1 Chr 12:40.
Ploughing. 1 Kin 19:19; Job 1:14; Amos 6:12.
Earing the ground. Is 30:24; 32:20.
Treading out the corn. Hos 10:11.
Sacrifice. Ex 20:24; 2 Sam 24:22.
Food. 1 Kin 1:9; 19:21; 2 Chr 18:2.
Often stall-fed for slaughter. Prov 15:17.
Goes to the slaughter unconscious. Prov 7:22.
Young of, considered a great delicacy. Gen 18:7; Amos 6:4.
Male firstlings of, belonged to God. Ex 34:19.
Tithe of, given to the priests. 2 Chr 31:6.
Laws respecting
To rest on the Sabbath. Ex 23:12; Deut 5:14.
Not to be yoked with an ass in the same plough. Deut 22:10.
Not to be muzzled when treading out the corn. Deut 25:4; 1 Cor 9:9.
If stolen to be restored double. Ex 22:4.
Of others not to be coveted. Ex 20:17; Deut 5:21.
Of others if lost or hurt through neglect, to be made good. Ex 22:9-13.

Killing a man, to be stoned. Ex 21:28-32.
Mode of reparation for one, killing another. Ex 21:35,36.
Straying to be brought back to its owner. Ex 23:4; Deut 22:1,2.
Fallen under its burden to be raised up again. Deut 22:4.
Fat of, not to be eaten. Lev 7:23.
Increase of, promised. Deut 7:13; 28:4.
Publicly sold. 2 Sam 24:24; Luke 14:19.
Often given as a present. Gen 12:16; 20:14.
The wicked often took, in pledge from the poor. Job 24:3.
Custom of sending the pieces of, to collect the people to war. 1 Sam 11:7.
Sea of brass rested on figures of. 1 Kin 7:25.
Illustrative
(Engaged in husbandry,) of ministers. Is 30:24; 32:20.
(Not muzzled in treading corn,) of minister's right to support. 1 Cor 9:9,10.
(Prepared for a feast,) of the provision of the gospel. Prov 9:2; Matt 22:4.
(Led to slaughter,) of a rash youth. Prov 7:22.
(Led to slaughter,) of saints under persecution. Jer 11:19.
(Stall fed,) of sumptuous living. Prov 15:17.
Bull or bullock—illustrative
Of fierce enemies. Ps 22:12; 68:30.
(Firstling of,) of the glory of Joseph. Deut 33:17.
(In a net,) of the impatient under judgment. Is 51:20.
(Fatted,) of greedy mercenaries. Jer 46:21.
(Unaccustomed to the yoke,) of intractable sinners. Jer 31:18.
Kine—illustrative
Of proud and wealthy rules. Amos 4:1.
(Well favoured,) of years of plenty. Gen 41:2,26,29.
(Lean,) of years of scarcity. Gen 41:3; 27:30.
Heifer—illustrative
Of a beloved wife. Judg 14:18.
(Sliding back,) of backsliding Israel. Hos 4:16.
(Taught, etc.) of Israel's fondness for ease in preference to obedience. Hos 10:11.
(Of three years old,) of Moab in affliction. Is 15:5; Jer 48:34.
(Fair,) of the beauty and wealth of Egypt. Jer 46:20.
(At grass,) of the luxurious Chaldees. Jer 50:11.

PALACES.

Jerusalem celebrated for. Ps 48:3,13.
The term applied to
Residences of kings. Dan 4:4; 6:18.
Houses of great men. Amos 3:9; Mic 5:5.
The temple of God. 1 Chr 29:1,19.
The house of the high priest. Matt 26:58.
Described as
High. Ps 78:69.
Polished. Ps 144:12.
Pleasant. Is 13:22.
Of kings
Called the king's house. 2 Kin 25:9; 2 Chr 7:11.
Called the house of the kingdom. 2 Chr 2:1,12.
Called the king's palace. Esth 1:5.
Called the royal house. Esth 1:9.
Splendidly furnished. Esth 1:6.
Surrounded with gardens. Esth 1:5.
Surrounded with terraces. 2 Chr 9:11.
Under governors. 1 Kin 4:6; Neh 7:2.
Often attended by eunuchs as servants. 2 Kin 20:18; Dan 1:3,4.
Were strictly guarded. 2 Kin 11:5.
Afforded support to all the king's retainers. Ezra 4:14; Dan 1:5.
Royal decrees issued from. Esth 3:15; 8:14.
Royal decrees laid up in. Ezra 6:2.
Contained treasures of the king. 1 Kin 15:18; 2 Chr 12:9; 25:24.
Gorgeous apparel suited to, alone. Luke 7:25.
Were entered by gates. Neh 2:8.
Often the storehouses of rapine. Amos 3:10.
Often as punishment
Spoiled. Amos 3:11.
Forsaken. Is 32:14.
Desolate. Ps 69:25; Ezek 19:7.
Scenes of bloodshed. Jer 9:21.
Burned with fire. 2 Chr 36:19; Jer 17:27.
Overgrown with thorns, etc. Is 34:13.
The habitation of dragons, etc. Is 13:22.
The spider makes its way even into. Prov 30:28.
Illustrative of
The splendour of the church. Song 8:9.
The godly children of saints. Ps 144:12.
The place of Satan's dominion. Luke 11:21.

PALM TREE, THE.

First mention of, in Scripture. Ex 15:27.
Jericho celebrated for. Deut 34:3; Judg 1:16.
Described as
Tall. Song 7:7.
Upright. Jer 10:5.
Flourishing. Ps 92:12.
Fruitful to a great age. Ps 92:14.
The fruit of, called dates. 2 Chr 31:5.
Requires a moist and fertile soil. Ex 15:27.
Tents often pitched under the shade of. Judg 4:5.
The branches of, were
The emblem of victory. Rev 7:9.
Carried at feast of tabernacles. Lev 23:40.
Used for constructing booths. Neh 8:15.
Spread before Christ. John 12:13.
Blasted as a punishment. Joel 1:12.
Represented in carved work on the walls and doors of the temple of Solomon. 1 Kin 6:29,32,35; 2 Chr 3:5.
Illustrative of
The church. Song 7:7,8.
The righteous. Ps 92:12.
The upright appearance of idols. Jer 10:5.

PARABLES.

Remarkable parables of the Old Testament. Judg 9:8-15; 2 Sam 12:1-4; 14:5-7.
Parables of Christ
Wise and foolish builders. Matt 7:24-27.
Children of the bride chamber. Matt 9:15.
New cloth and old garment. Matt 9:16.
New wine and old bottles. Matt 9:17.
Unclean spirit. Matt 12:43.
Sower. Matt 13:3-23; Luke 8:5-15.
Tares. Matt 13:24-30,36-43.
Mustard-seed. Matt 13:31,32; Luke 13:19.
Leaven. Matt 13:33.
Treasure hid in a field. Matt 13:44.
Pearl of great price. Matt 13:45,46.
Net cast into the sea. Matt 13:47-50.
Meats defiling not. Matt 15:10-15.
Unmerciful servant. Matt 18:23-35.
Labourers hired. Matt 20:1-16.
Two sons. Matt 21:28-32.
Wicked husbandmen. Matt 21:33-45.
Marriage-feast. Matt 22:2-14.
Fig-tree leafing. Matt 24:32-34.
Man of the house watching. Matt 24:43.
Faithful, and evil servants. Matt 24:45-51.
Ten virgins. Matt 25:1-13.
Talents. Matt 25:14-30.
Kingdom, divided against itself. Mark 3:24.
House, divided against itself. Mark 3:25.
Strong man armed. Mark 3:27; Luke 11:21.
Seed growing secretly. Mark 4:26-29.
Lighted candle. Mark 4:21; Luke 11:33-36.
Man taking a far journey. Mark 13:34-37.
Blind leading the blind. Luke 6:39.
Beam and mote. Luke 6:41,42.
Tree and its fruit. Luke 6:43-45.
Creditor and debtors. Luke 7:41-47.
Good Samaritan. Luke 10:30-37.
Importunate friend. Luke 11:5-9.
Rich fool. Luke 12:16-21.
Cloud and wind. Luke 12:54-57.
Barren fig-tree. Luke 13:6-9.
Men bidden to a feast. Luke 14:7-11.
Builder of a tower. Luke 14:28-30,33.
King going to war. Luke 14:31-33.
Savour of salt. Luke 14:34,35.
Lost sheep. Luke 15:3-7.
Lost piece of silver. Luke 15:8-10.
Prodigal son. Luke 15:11-32.
Unjust steward. Luke 16:1-8.
Rich man and Lazarus. Luke 16:19-31.
Importunate widow. Luke 18:1-8.
Pharisee and Publican. Luke 18:9-14.
Pounds. Luke 19:12-27.
Good Shepherd. John 10:1-6.
Vine and branches. John 15:1-5.

Pardon.

Promised. Is 1:18; Jer 31:34; Heb 8:12; Jer 50:20.
None without shedding of blood. Lev 17:11; Heb 9:22.
Legal sacrifices, ineffectual for. Heb 10:4.
Outward purifications, ineffectual for. Job 9:30,31; Jer 2:22.
The blood of Christ, alone, is efficacious for. Zech 13:1; 1 John 1:7.
Is granted
By God alone. Dan 9:9; Mark 2:7.
By Christ. Mark 2:5; Luke 7:48.
Through Christ. Luke 1:69,77; Acts 5:31; 13:38.
Through the blood of Christ. Matt 26:28; Rom 3:25; Col 1:14.
For the name's sake of Christ. 1 John 2:12.
According to the riches of grace. Eph 1:7.
On the exaltation of Christ. Acts 5:31.
Freely. Is 43:25.
Readily. Neh 9:17; Ps 86:5.
Abundantly. Is 55:7; Rom 5:20.
To those who confess their sins. 2 Sam 12:13; Ps 32:5; 1 John 1:9.
To those who repent. Acts 2:38.
To those who believe. Acts 10:43.
Should be preached in the name of Christ. Luke 24:47.
Exhibits the
Compassion of God. Mic 7:18,19.
Grace of God. Rom 5:15,16.
Mercy of God. Ex 34:7; Ps 51:1.
Goodness of God. 2 Chr 30:18; Ps 86:5.
Forbearance of God. Rom 3:25.
Lovingkindness of God. Ps 51:1.
Justice of God. 1 John 1:9.
Faithfulness of God. 1 John 1:9.
Expressed by
Forgiving transgression. Ps 32:1.
Removing transgression. Ps 103:12.
Blotting out transgression. Is 44:22.
Covering sin. Ps 32:1.
Blotting out sin. Acts 3:19.
Casting sins into the sea. Mic 7:19.
Not imputing sin. Rom 4:8.
Not mentioning transgression. Ezek 18:22.
Remembering sins no more. Heb 10:17.
All saints enjoy. Col 2:13; 1 John 2:12.
Blessedness of. Ps 32:1; Rom 4:7.
Should lead to
Returning to God. Is 44:22.
Loving God. Luke 7:47.
Fearing God. Ps 130:4.
Praising God. Ps 103:2,3.
Ministers are appointed to proclaim. Is 40:1,2; 2 Cor 5:19.
Pray for
Yourselves. Ps 25:11,18; 51:1; Matt 6:12; Luke 11:4.
Others. James 5:15; 1 John 5:16.
Encouragement to pray for. 2 Chr 7:14.
Withheld from
The unforgiving. Mark 11:26; Luke 6:37.
The unbelieving. John 8:21,24.
The impenitent. Luke 13:2-5.
Blasphemers against the Holy Spirit. Matt 12:32; Mark 3:28,29.
Apostates. Heb 10:26,27; 1 John 5:16.
Illustrated. Luke 7:42; 15:20-24.
Exemplified
Israelites. Num 14:20.
David. 2 Sam 12:13.
Manasseh. 2 Chr 33:13.
Hezekiah. Is 38:17.
The paralytic. Matt 9:2.
The penitent. Luke 7:47.

Parents.

Receive their children from God. Gen 33:5; 1 Sam 1:27; Ps 127:3.
Their duty to their children is
To love them. Titus 2:4.
To bring them to Christ. Matt 19:13,14.
To train them up for God. Prov 22:6; Eph 6:4.
To instruct them in God's Word. Deut 4:9; 11:19; Is 38:19.
To tell them of God's judgments. Joel 1:3.
To tell them of the miraculous works of God. Ex 10:2; Ps 78:4.
To command them to obey God. Deut 32:46; 1 Chr 28:9.
To bless them. Gen 48:15; Heb 11:20.
To pity them. Ps 103:13.
To provide for them. Job 42:15; 2 Cor 12:14; 1 Tim 5:8.
To rule them. 1 Tim 3:4,12.
To correct them. Prov 13:24; 19:18; 23:13; 29:17; Heb 12:7.
Not to provoke them. Eph 6:4; Col 3:21.
Not to make unholy connections for them. Gen 24:1-4; 28:1,2.
Wicked children, a cause of grief to. Prov 10:1; 17:25.
Should pray for their children
For their spiritual welfare. Gen 17:18; 1 Chr 29:19.
When in temptation. Job 1:5.
When in sickness. 2 Sam 12:16; Mark 5:23; John 4:46,49.
When faithful
Are blessed by their children. Prov 31:28.
Leave a blessing to their children. Ps 112:2; Prov 11:21; Is 65:23.
Sins of, visited on their children. Ex 20:5; Is 14:20; Lam 5:7.
Negligence of, sorely punished. 1 Sam 3:13.
When wicked
Instruct their children in evil. Jer 9:14; 1 Pet 1:18.
Set a bad example to their children. Ezek 20:18; Amos 2:4.
Good—Exemplified
Abraham. Gen 18:19.
Jacob. Gen 44:20,30.
Joseph. Gen 48:13-20.
Mother of Moses. Ex 2:2,3.
Manoah. Judg 13:8.
Hannah. 1 Sam 1:28.
David. 2 Sam 18:5,33.
Shunammite. 2 Kin 4:19,20.
Job. Job 1:5.
Mother of Lemuel. Prov 31:1.
Nobleman. John 4:49.
Lois and Eunice. 2 Tim 1:5.
Bad—Exemplified
Mother of Micah. Judg 17:3.
Eli. 1 Sam 3:13.
Saul. 1 Sam 20:33.
Athaliah. 2 Chr 22:3.
Manasseh. 2 Chr 33:6.
Herodias. Mark 6:24.

Paschal Lamb, Typical Nature Of.

A type of Christ. Ex 12:3; 1 Cor 5:7.
A male of the first year. Ex 12:5; Is 9:6.
Without blemish. Ex 12:5; 1 Pet 1:19.
Taken out of the flock. Ex 12:5; Heb 2:14,17.
Chosen before-hand. Ex 12:3; 1 Pet 2:4.
Shut up four days that it might be closely examined. Ex 12:6; John 8:46; 18:38.
Killed by the people. Ex 12:6; Acts 2:23.
Killed at the place where the Lord put his name. Deut 16:2,5-7; 2 Chr 35:1; Luke 13:33.
Killed in the evening. Ex 12:6; Mark 15:34,37.
Its blood to be shed. Ex 12:7; Luke 22:20.
Blood of, sprinkled on lintel and door-posts. Ex 12:22; Heb 9:13,14; 10:22; 1 Pet 1:2.
Blood of, not sprinkled on threshold. Ex 12:7; Heb 10:29.
Not a bone of, broken. Ex 12:46; John 19:36.
Not eaten raw. Ex 12:9; 1 Cor 11:28,29.
Roasted with fire. Ex 12:8; Ps 22:14,15.
Eaten with bitter herbs. Ex 12:8; Zech 12:10.
Eaten with unleavened bread. Ex 12:39; 1 Cor 5:7,8; 2 Cor 1:12.
Eaten in haste. Ex 12:11; Heb 6:18.
Eaten with the loins girt. Ex 12:11; Luke 12:35; Eph 6:14; 1 Pet 1:13.
Eaten with staff in hand. Ex 12:11; Ps 23:4.
Eaten with shoes on. Ex 12:11; Eph 6:15.
Not taken out of the house. Ex 12:46; Eph 3:17.
What remained of it till morning to be burned. Ex 12:10; Matt 7:6; Luke 11:3.

Patience.

God, is the God of. Rom 15:5.
Christ, an example of. Is 53:7; Acts 8:32; Matt 27:14.
Enjoined. Titus 2:2; 2 Pet 1:6.
Should have its perfect work. James 1:4.
Trials of saints lead to. Rom 5:3; James 1:3.
Produces
Experience. Rom 5:4.
Hope. Rom 15:4.
Suffering with, for well-doing, is acceptable with God. 1 Pet 2:20.
To be exercised
Running the race set before us. Heb 12:1.
Bringing forth fruits. Luke 8:15.
Well-doing. Rom 2:7; Gal 6:9.
Waiting for God. Ps 37:7; 40:1.
Waiting for Christ. 1 Cor 1:7; 2 Thess 3:5.
Waiting for the hope of the gospel. Rom 8:25; Gal 5:5.

Waiting for God's salvation. Lam 3:26.
Bearing the yoke. Lam 3:27.
Tribulation. Luke 21:19; Rom 12:12.
Necessary to the inheritance of the promises. Heb 6:12; 10:36.
Exercise, towards all. 1 Thess 5:14.
They who are in authority, should exercise. Matt 18:26; Acts 26:3.
Ministers should follow after. 1 Tim 6:11.
Ministers approved by. 2 Cor 6:4.
Should be accompanied by
Godliness. 2 Pet 1:6.
Faith. 2 Thess 1:4; Heb 6:12; Rev 13:10.
Temperance. 2 Pet 1:6.
Long-suffering. Col 1:11.
Joyfulness. Col 1:11.
Saints strengthened to all. Col 1:11.
Commended. Eccl 7:8; Rev 2:2,3.
Illustrated. James 5:7.
Exemplified
Job. Job 1:21; James 5:11.
Simeon. Luke 2:25.
Paul. 2 Tim 3:10.
Abraham. Heb 6:15.
Prophets. James 5:10.
John. Rev 1:9.

Patriarchal Government.

Vested in the heads of families. Gen 18:19.
Exercised in
Training, etc. their servants for war. Gen 14:14.
Vindicating their wrongs. Gen 14:12,15,16.
Forming treaties and alliances. Gen 14:13; 21:22-32; 26:28-33.
Acting as priests. Gen 8:20; 12:7,8; 35:1-7; Job 1:5.
Acting as judges. Gen 38:24.
Arbitrarily disinheriting and putting away servants and children. Gen 21:14; 1 Chr 5:1.
Blessing and cursing their children. Gen 9:25,26; 27:28,29; 49:1-33.
The authority of heads of families for, acknowledged. Gen 23:6.

Peace.

God is the Author of. Ps 147:14; Is 45:7; 1 Cor 14:33.
Results from
Heavenly wisdom. James 3:17.
The government of Christ. Is 2:4.
Praying for rulers. 1 Tim 2:2.
Seeking the peace of those with whom we dwell. Jer 29:7.
Necessary to the enjoyment of life. Ps 34:12,14; 1 Pet 3:10,11.
God bestows upon those who
Obey him. Lev 26:6.
Please him. Ps 16:7.
Endure his chastisements. Job 5:17,23,24.
Is a bond of union. Eph 4:3.
The fruit of righteousness should be sown in. James 3:18.
The church shall enjoy. Ps 125:5; 128:6; Is 2:4; Hos 2:18.
Saints should
Love. Zech 8:19.
Seek. Ps 34:14; 1 Pet 3:11.
Follow. 2 Tim 2:22.
Follow the things which make for. Rom 14:19.
Cultivate. Ps 120:7.
Speak. Esth 10:3.
Live in. 2 Cor 13:11.
Have, with each other. Mark 9:50; 1 Thess 5:13.
Endeavour to have will all men. Rom 12:18; Heb 12:14.
Pray for that of the church. Ps 122:6-8.
Exhort others to. Gen 45:24.
Ministers should exhort to. 2 Thess 3:12.
Advantages of. Prov 17:1; Eccl 4:6.
Blessedness of. Ps 133:1.
Blessedness of promoting. Matt 5:9.
The wicked
Hypocritically speak. Ps 28:3.
Speak not. Ps 35:20.
Enjoy not. Is 48:22; Ezek 7:25.
Opposed to. Ps 120:7.
Hate. Ps 120:6.
Shall abound in the latter days. Is 2:4; 11:13; 32:18.
Exemplified
Abraham. Gen 13:8,9.
Abimelech. Gen 26:29.
Mordecai. Esth 10:3.
David. Ps 120:7.

Peace Offerings.

A male or female of herd or flock. Lev 3:1,6,12.
The offerer required
To give it freely. Lev 19:5.
To bring it himself. Lev 7:29,30.
To lay his hand upon its head. Lev 3:2,8,13.
To kill it at tabernacle door. Lev 3:2; 8:13.
Required to be perfect and free from blemish. Lev 3:1,6; 22:21.
The priest
Prepared. Ezek 46:2.
Sprinkled the blood on the altar. Lev 3:2,8,13.
Offered the inside fat, etc. by fire. Lev 3:3,4,9,10.
Laid it upon the daily burnt offering to be consumed with it. Lev 3:5; 6:12,13.
Waved the breast as a wave offering. Ex 29:26,28; Lev 7:29,30.
Heaved the right shoulder as an heave offering. Ex 29:22-27.
Had the shoulder and breast as his portion. Ex 29:28; Lev 7:31-34.
An offering most acceptable. Lev 3:5,16.
Generally accompanied by a burnt offering. Judg 21:4; 1 Sam 10:8; 1 Kin 3:15.
Often accompanied by a sin offering. Lev 23:19.
Was offered
As a thanksgiving offering. Lev 7:12,13.
As a votive offering. Lev 7:16.
For reconciliation. Ezek 45:15; Eph 2:13,14.
For confirming the legal covenant. Ex 24:5.
At consecration of priests. Ex 29:22,29.
For the people at large. Lev 9:4.
At expiration of Nazarite's vow. Num 6:14.
At all the festivals. Num 10:10.
At dedication of tabernacle. Num 7:17,23.
At dedication of temple. 1 Kin 8:62-64.
At coronation of kings. 1 Sam 11:15.
By Joshua after his victories. Josh 8:31.
By Israel after their defeat. Judg 20:26.
By David on bringing up the ark. 2 Sam 6:17.
By David after the plague. 2 Sam 24:25.
By Solomon three times a year. 1 Kin 9:25.
By Manasseh on repairing and restoring the altar. 2 Chr 33:15,16.
If a thanksgiving offering to be eaten the day offered. Lev 7:15.
If a votive offering to be eaten the same day or the next. Lev 7:16,17; 19:6-8.
To be eaten before the Lord. Deut 12:17,18.
No unclean person to eat of. Lev 7:20,21.

Peace, Spiritual.

God is the God of. Rom 15:33; 2 Cor 13:11; 1 Thess 5:23; Heb 13:20.
God ordains. Is 26:12.
God speaks, to his saints. Ps 85:8.
Christ is the Lord of. 2 Thess 3:16.
Christ is the Prince of. Is 9:6.
Christ gives. 2 Thess 3:16.
Christ guides into the way of. Luke 1:79.
Christ is our. Eph 2:14.
Is through the atonement of Christ. Is 53:5; Eph 2:14,15; Col 1:20.
Bequeathed by Christ. John 14:27.
Preached
By Christ. Eph 2:17.
Through Christ. Acts 10:36.
By ministers. Is 52:7; Rom 10:15.
Announced by angels. Luke 2:14.
Follows upon justification. Rom 5:1.
A fruit of the Spirit. Rom 14:17; Gal 5:22.
Divine wisdom is the way of. Prov 3:17.
Accompanies
Faith. Rom 15:13.
Righteousness. Is 32:17.
Acquaintance with God. Job 22:21.
The love of God's law. Ps 119:165.
Spiritual-mindedness. Rom 8:6.
Established by covenant. Is 54:10; Ezek 34:25; Mal 2:5.
Promised to
The Church. Is 66:12.
The Gentiles. Zech 9:10.
Saints. Ps 72:3,7; Is 55:12.
The meek. Ps 37:11.
Those who confide in God. Is 26:3.
Returning backsliders. Is 57:18,19.
We should love. Zech 8:19.
The benediction of ministers should be. Num 6:26; Luke 10:5.

Saints
- Have in Christ. John 16:33.
- Have, with God. Is 27:5; Rom 5:1.
- Enjoy. Ps 119:165.
- Repose in. Ps 4:8.
- Blessed with. Ps 29:11.
- Kept in perfect. Is 26:3.
- Ruled by. Col 3:15.
- Kept by. Phil 4:7.
- Die in. Ps 37:37; Luke 2:29.
- Wish, to each other. Gal 6:16; Phil 1:2; Col 1:2; 1 Thess 1:1.

Of saints
- Great. Ps 119:165; Is 54:13.
- Abundant. Ps 72:7; Jer 33:6.
- Secure. Job 34:29.
- Passes all understanding. Phil 4:7.
- Consummated after death. Is 57:2.

The gospel is good tidings of. Rom 10:15.

The wicked
- Know not the way of. Is 57:2; Rom 3:17.
- Know not the things of. Luke 19:42.
- Promise, to themselves. Deut 29:19.
- Are promised, by false teachers. Jer 6:14.
- There is none for. Is 48:22; 57:21.

Supports under trials. John 14:27; 16:33.

PERFECTION.

Is of God. Ps 18:32; 138:8.
All saints have, in Christ. 1 Cor 2:6; Phil 3:15; Col 2:10.
God's perfection the standard of. Matt 5:48.
Implies
- Entire devotedness. Matt 19:21.
- Purity and holiness in speech. James 3:2.

Saints commanded to aim at. Gen 17:1; Deut 18:13.
Saints claim not. Job 9:20; Phil 3:12.
Saints follow after. Prov 4:18; Phil 3:12.
Ministers appointed to lead saints to. Eph 4:12; Col 1:28.
Exhortation to. 2 Cor 7:1; 13:11.
Impossibility of attaining to. 2 Chr 6:36; Ps 119:96.
The Word of God is
- The rule of. James 1:25.
- Designed to lead us to. 2 Tim 3:16,17.

Charity is the bond of. Col 3:14.
Patience leads to. James 1:4.
Pray for. Heb 13:20,21; 1 Pet 5:10.
The Church shall attain to. John 17:23; Eph 4:13.
Blessedness of. Ps 37:37; Prov 2:21.

PERSECUTION.

Christ suffered. Ps 69:26; John 5:16.
Christ voluntarily submitted to. Is 50:6.
Christ was patient under. Is 53:7.
Saints may expect. Mark 10:30; Luke 21:12; John 15:20.
Saints suffer, for the sake of God. Jer 15:15.
Of saints, is a persecution of Christ. Zech 2:8; Acts 9:4,5.
All that live godly in Christ, shall suffer. 2 Tim 3:12.
Originates
- Ignorance of God and Christ. John 16:3.
- Hated to God and Christ. John 15:20,24.
- Hatred to the gospel. Matt 13:21.
- Pride. Ps 10:2.
- Mistaken zeal. Acts 13:50; 26:9-11.

Is inconsistent with the spirit of the gospel. Matt 26:52.
Men by nature addicted to. Gal 4:29.
Preacher of the gospel subject to. Gal 5:11.
Is sometimes to death. Acts 22:4.
God forsakes not his saints under. 2 Cor 4:9.
God delivers out of. Dan 3:25,28; 2 Cor 1:10; 2 Tim 3:11.
Cannot be separated from Christ. Rom 8:35.
Lawful means may be used to escape. Matt 2:13; 10:23; 12:14,15.
Saints suffering, should
- Commit themselves to God. 1 Pet 4:19.
- Exhibit patience. 1 Cor 4:12.
- Rejoice. Matt 5:12; 1 Pet 4:13.
- Glorify God. 1 Pet 4:16.
- Pray for deliverance. Ps 7:1; 119:86.
- Pray for those who inflict. Matt 5:44.
- Return blessing for. Rom 12:14.

The hope of future blessedness supports under. 1 Cor 15:19,32; Heb 10:34,35.
Blessedness of enduring, for Christ's sake. Matt 5:10; Luke 6:22.
Pray for those suffering. 2 Thess 3:2.
Hypocrites cannot endure. Matt 4:17.
False teachers shrink from. Gal 6:12.
The wicked
- Addicted to. Ps 10:2; 69:26.
- Active in. Ps 143:3; Lam 4:19.
- Encourage each other in. Ps 71:11.
- Rejoice in its success. Ps 13:4; Rev 11:10.
- Punishment for. Ps 7:13; 2 Thess 1:6.
- Illustrated. Matt 21:33-39.

Spirit of—Exemplified
- Pharaoh, etc. Ex 1:8-14.
- Saul. 1 Sam 26:18.
- Jezebel. 1 Kin 19:2.
- Zedekiah, etc. Jer 38:4-6.
- Chaldeans. Dan 3:8-30.
- Pharisees. Matt 12:14.
- Jews. John 5:16; 1 Thess 2:15.
- Herod. Acts 12:1.
- Gentiles. Acts 14:5.
- Paul. Phil 3:6; 1 Tim 1:13.

Suffering of—Exemplified
- Micaiah. 1 Kin 22:27.
- David. Ps 119:161.
- Jeremiah. Jer 32:2.
- Daniel. Dan 6:5-17.
- Peter, etc. Acts 4:3.
- Apostles. Acts 5:18.
- The Prophets. Acts 7:52.
- The Church. Acts 8:1.
- Paul and Barnabas. Acts 13:50.
- Paul and Silas. Acts 16:23.
- Hebrews. Heb 10:33.
- Saints of old. Heb 11:36.

PERSEVERANCE.

An evidence of reconciliation with God. Col 1:21-23.
An evidence of belonging to Christ. John 8:31; Heb 3:6,14.
A characteristic of saints. Prov 4:18.
To be manifested in
- Seeking God. 1 Chr 16:11.
- Waiting upon god. Hos 12:6.
- Prayer. Rom 12:12; Eph 6:18.
- Well-doing. Rom 2:7; 2 Thess 3:13.
- Continuing in the faith. Acts 14:22; Col 1:23; 2 Tim 4:7.
- Holding fast hope. Heb 3:6.

Maintained through
- The power of God. Ps 37:24; Phil 1:6.
- The power of Christ. John 10:28.
- The intercession of Christ. Luke 22:31,32; John 17:11.
- The fear of God. Jer 32:40.
- Faith. 1 Pet 1:5.

Promised to saints. Job 17:9.
Leads to increase of knowledge. John 8:31,32.
In well-doing
- Leads to assurance of hope. Heb 6:10,11.
- Is not in vain. 1 Cor 15:58; Gal 6:9.

Ministers should exhort to. Acts 13:43; 14:22.
Encouragement to. Heb 12:2,3.
Promises to. Matt 10:22; 24:13; Rev 2:26-28.
Blessedness of. James 1:25.
Want of
- Excludes from the benefits of the gospel. Heb 6:4-6.
- Punished. John 15:6; Rom 11:22.
- Illustrated. Mark 4:5,17.

PHARISEES, THE.

A sect of the Jews. Acts 15:5.
The strictest observers of the Mosaic ritual. Acts 26:5.
By descent, especially esteemed. Acts 23:6.
Character of
- Zealous of the law. Acts 15:5; Phil 3:5.
- Zealous of tradition. Mark 7:3,5-8; Gal 1:14.
- Outwardly moral. Luke 18:11; Phil 3:5,6.
- Rigid in fasting. Luke 5:33; 18:12.
- Active in proselytising. Matt 23:15.
- Self-righteous. Luke 16:15; 18:9.
- Avaricious. Matt 23:14; Luke 16:14.
- Ambitious of precedence. Matt 23:6.
- Fond of public salutations. Matt 23:7.
- Fond of distinguished titles. Matt 23:7-10.
- Particular in paying all dues. Matt 23:23.
- Oppressive. Matt 23:4.
- Cruel in persecuting. Acts 9:1,2.

Believed in the resurrection, etc. Acts 23:8.
Made broad their phylacteries. Matt 23:5.
Their opinions, a standard for others. John 7:48.
Many priests and Levites were of. John 1:19,24.
Many rulers, lawyers, and scribes were of. John 3:1; Acts 5:34; 23:9.
Had disciples. Luke 5:33; Acts 22:3.
Some came to John for baptism. Matt 3:7.
As a body, rejected John's baptism. Luke 7:30.

Christ
Often invited by. Luke 7:36; 11:37.
Condemned by, for associating with sinners. Matt 9:11; Luke 7:39; 15:1,2.
Asked for signs by. Matt 12:38; 16:1.
Tempted by, with questions about the law. Matt 19:3; 22:15,16,35.
Watched by, for evil. Luke 6:7.
Offended, by his doctrine. Matt 15:12; 21:45; Luke 16:14.
Declared the imaginary righteousness of, to be insufficient for salvation. Matt 5:20.
Declared the doctrines of, to be hypocrisy. Matt 16:6,11,12; Luke 12:1.
Denounced woes against. Matt 23:13-33.
Called, an evil and adulterous generation. Matt 12:39.
Called, serpents and generation of vipers. Matt 23:33.
Called, fools and blind guides. Matt 23:17,24.
Compared, to whited sepulchres. Matt 23:27.
Compared, to graves that appear not. Luke 11:44.
Left Judea for a time on account of. John 4:1-3.
Imputed Christ's miracles to Satan's power. Matt 9:34; 12:24.
Sent officers to apprehend Christ. John 7:32,45.
Often sought to destroy Christ. Matt 12:14; 21:46; John 11:47,53,57.

PHILISTINES.

Descended from Casluhim. Gen 10:13,14.
Originally dwelt in the land of Caphtor. Jer 47:4; Amos 9:7.
Conquered the Avims and took from them the west coast of Canaan. Deut 2:23.
Called
The Caphtorims. Deut 2:23.
The Cherethites. 1 Sam 30:14; Zeph 2:5.
Country of
Called Philistia. Ps 87:4; 108:9.
Divided into five sates of lordships. Josh 13:3; Judg 3:3; 1 Sam 6:16.
Had many flourishing cities. 1 Sam 6:17.
Given by God to the Israelites. Josh 13:2,3; 15:45,47.
Were a great people and governed by kings in the patriarchal age. Gen 21:22,34; 26:8.
Character of
Proud. Zech 9:6.
Idolatrous. Judg 16:23; 1 Sam 5:2.
Superstitious. Is 2:6.
Warlike. 1 Sam 17:1; 28:1.
Men of great strength and stature amongst. 1 Sam 17:4-7; 2 Sam 21:16,18-20.
Some of, left to prove Israel. Judg 3:1-3.
Always confederated with the enemies of Israel. Ps 83:7; Is 9:11,12.
Shamgar slew six hundred of, and delivered Israel. Judg 3:31.
Oppressed Israel after the death of Jair for eighteen years. Judg 10:7,8.
Oppressed Israel after the death of Abdon forty years. Judg 13:1.
Samson
Promised as a deliverer from. Judg 13:5.
Intermarried with. Judg 14:1,10.
Slew thirty, near Askelon. Judg 14:19.
Burned vineyards, etc. of. Judg 15:3-5.
Slew many, for burning his wife. Judg 15:7,8.
Slew a thousand, with the jawbone of an ass. Judg 15:15,16.
Blinded and imprisoned by. Judg 16:21
Pulled down the house of Dagon and destroyed immense numbers of. Judg 16:29,30.
Defeated Israel at Ebenezer. 1 Sam 4:1,2.
Defeated Israel and took the ark. 1 Sam 4:3-11.
Put the ark into Dagon's house. 1 Sam 5:1-4.
Plagued for retaining the ark. 1 Sam 5:6-12.
Sent back the ark and were healed. 1 Sam 6:1-18.
Miraculously routed at Mizpeh. 1 Sam 7:7-14.
Jonathan smote a garrison of, at Geba and provoked them. 1 Sam 13:3,4.
Invaded the land of Israel with a great army. 1 Sam 13:5,17-23.
Jonathan and his armour-bearer smote a garrison of, at the passages. 1 Sam 14:1-14.
Miraculously discomfited. 1 Sam 14:15-23.
Saul constantly at war with. 1 Sam 14:52.
Defied Israel by their champion. 1 Sam 17:4-10.
Defeated Israel at Ephesdammim and pursued to Ekron. 1 Sam 17:1,52.
David
Slew Goliath the champion of. 1 Sam 17:40-50.
Procured Saul's daughter for an hundred foreskins of. 1 Sam 18:25-27.
Often defeated during Saul's reign. 1 Sam 19:8; 23:1-5.
Fled to, for safety. 1 Sam 27:1-7.
Gained the confidence of Achish king of. 1 Sam 28:2; 29:9.
Distrusted by. 1 Sam 29:2-7.
Often defeated in the course of his reign. 2 Sam 5:17-23; 8:1; 21:15-22; 23:8-12.
Had a guard composed of. 2 Sam 8:18; Ezek 25:16; Zeph 2:5.
Gathered all their armies to Aphek against Israel. 1 Sam 28:1; 29:1.
Ziklag a town of, taken and plundered by the Amalekites. 1 Sam 30:1,2,16.
Israel defeated by, and Saul slain. 1 Sam 31:1-10.
Besieged in Gibbethon by Nadab. 1 Kin 15:27.
Sent by God against Jehoram. 2 Chr 21:16,17.
Defeated by Uzziah. 2 Chr 26:6,7.
Distressed Judah under Ahaz. 2 Chr 28:18,19.
Defeated by Hezekiah. 2 Kin 18:8.
Israel condemned for imitating. Judg 10:6; Amos 6:2; 9:7.
Prophecies respecting
Union with Syria against Israel. Is 9:11,12.
Punishment with other nations. Jer 25:20.
Dismay at ruin of Tyre. Zech 9:3,5.
Base men to be their rulers. Zech 9:6.
Hatred and revenge against Israel to be fully recompensed. Ezek 25:15-17; Amos 1:6-8.
Utter destruction by Pharaoh king of Egypt. Jer 47:1-4; Zeph 2:5,6.
Destruction and desolation of their cities. Jer 47:5; Zeph 2:4.
Their country to be a future possession to Israel. Obad 19; Zeph 2:7.
To help in Israel's restoration. Is 11:14.

PILGRIMS AND STRANGERS.

Described. John 17:16.
Saints are called to be. Gen 12:1; Acts 7:3; Luke 14:26,27,33.
All saints are. Ps 39:12; 1 Pet 1:1.
Saints confess themselves. 1 Chr 29:15; Ps 39:12; 119:19; Heb 11:13.
As saints they
Have the example of Christ. Luke 9:58.
Are strengthened by God. Deut 33:25; Ps 84:6,7.
Are actuated by faith. Heb 11:9.
Have their faces toward Zion. Jer 50:5.
Keep the promised in view. Heb 11:13.
Forsake all for Christ. Matt 19:27.
Look for a heavenly country. Heb 11:16.
Look for a heavenly city. Heb 11:10.
Pass their sojourning in fear. 1 Pet 1:17.
Rejoice in the statutes of God. Ps 119:54.
Pray for direction. Ps 43:3; Jer 50:5.
Have a heavenly conversation. Phil 3:20.
Hate worldly fellowship. Ps 120:5,6.
Are not mindful of this world. Heb 11:15.
Are not at home in this world. Heb 11:9.
Shine as lights in the world. Phil 2:15.
Invite others to go with them. Num 10:29.
Are exposed to persecution. Ps 120:5-7; John 17:14.
Should abstain from fleshly lusts. 1 Pet 2:11.
Should have their treasure in heaven. Matt 6:19; Luke 12:33; Col 3:1,2.
Should not be over anxious about worldly things. Matt 6:25.
Long for their pilgrimage to end. Ps 55:6; 2 Cor 5:1-8.
Die in faith. Heb 11:13.
The world is not worthy of. Heb 11:38.

God is not ashamed to be called their God. Heb 11:16.
Typified
Israel. Ex 6:4; 12:11.
Exemplified
Abraham. Gen 23:4; Acts 7:4,5.
Jacob. Gen 47:9.
Saints of old. 1 Chr 29:15; Heb 11:13,38.
David. Ps 39:12.
The apostles. Matt 19:27.

PILLARS.

The supports of a building. Judg 16:29.
Things raised up as memorials. Gen 31:51.
Made of
Marble. Esth 1:6.
Wood. 1 Kin 10:12.
Iron. Jer 1:18.
Brass. 1 Kin 7:15.
Silver. Song 3:10.
The vail and hangings of the tabernacle supported by. Ex 26:32,37; 36:36,38.
Two, placed in the temple porch. 1 Kin 7:15-21.
Of memorial
Sometimes of a single stone. Gen 28:18.
Sometimes of a heap of stones. Josh 4:8,9,20.
To witness vows. Gen 28:18; 31:13.
To witness covenants. Gen 31:52.
To mark the graves of the dead. Gen 35:20.
To commemorate remarkable events. Ex 24:4; Josh 4:20,24.
To perpetuate names. 2 Sam 18:18.
In honour of idols. Lev 26:1; Deut 7:5.
Often anointed. Gen 28:18; 31:13.
Often had inscriptions. Job 19:24.
The divine glory appeared to Israel in the form of. Ex 13:21,22; Num 12:5.
Lot's wife became a pillar of salt. Gen 19:26.
Illustrative of
Stability of the heavens. Job 26:11.
Stability of the earth. 1 Sam 2:8; Ps 75:3.
The church. 1 Tim 3:15.
Stability of Christ. Song 5:15; Rev 10:1.
Ministers. Jer 1:18; Gal 2:9.
Saints who overcome in Christ. Rev 3:12.

PLAGUE OR PESTILENCE, THE.

Inflicted by God. Ezek 14:19; Hab 3:5.
One of God's four sore judgments. Ezek 14:21.
Described as noisome. Ps 9:13.
Israel threatened with, as a punishment for disobedience. Lev 26:24,25; Deut 28:21.
Desolating effects of. Ps 91:7; Jer 16:6,7; Amos 6:9,10.
Equally fatal day and night. Ps 91:5,6.
Fatal to man and beast. Ps 78:50; Jer 21:6.
Sent upon
The Egyptians. Ex 12:29,30.
Israel for making golden calf. Ex 32:35.
Israel for despising manna. Num 11:33.
Israel for murmuring at destruction of Korah. Num 16:46-50.
Israel for worshipping Baal-peor. Num 25:18.
David's subjects for his numbering the people. 2 Sam 24:15.
Often broke out suddenly. Ps 106:29.
Often followed war and famine. Jer 27:13; 28:8; 29:17,18.
Egypt often afflicted with. Jer 42:17; Amos 4:10.
Specially fatal in cities. Lev 26:25; Jer 21:6,9.
Was attributed to a destroying angel. Ex 12:23; 2 Sam 24:16.
The Jews sought deliverance from, by prayer. 1 Kin 8:37,38; 2 Chr 20:9.
Predicted to happen before destruction of Jerusalem. Matt 24:7; Luke 21:11.
Illustrative of
God's judgments upon the apostasy. Rev 18:4,8.
The diseased state of man's heart. 1 Kin 8:38.

PLOUGHING.

The breaking up or tilling of the earth. Jer 4:3; Hos 10:12.
Noah the supposed inventor of. Gen 5:29.
Performed
By a plough. Luke 9:62.
With oxen. 1 Sam 14:14; Job 1:14.
During the cold winter season. Prov 20:4.
In long and straight furrows. Ps 129:3.
Generally by servants. Is 61:5; Luke 17:7.
Sometimes by the owner of the land himself. 1 Kin 19:19.
With an ox and an ass yoked together forbidden to the Jews. Deut 22:10.
Difficulty of, on rocky ground. Amos 6:12.
Followed by harrowing and sowing. Is 28:24,25.
Illustrative
Of repentance and reformation. Jer 4:3.
Of peace and prosperity. Is 2:4; Mic 4:3.
Of a severe course of affliction. Hos 10:11.
Of a course of sin. Job 4:8; Hos 10:13.
Of the labour ministers. 1 Cor 9:10.
(Attention and constancy required in,) of continued devotedness. Luke 9:62.

POMEGRANATE TREE, THE.

Egypt abounded with. Num 20:5.
Canaan abounded with. Num 13:23; Deut 8:8.
The Jews
Cultivated, in orchards. Song 4:13.
Often dwelt under shade of. 1 Sam 14:2.
Drank the juice of. Song 8:2.
The blasting of, a great calamity. Joel 1:12.
God's favour exhibited, in making fruitful. Hag 2:19.
Representations of its fruit
On the high priest's robe. Ex 39:24-26.
On the pillars of the temple. 1 Kin 7:18.
Illustrative
Of saints. Song 6:11; 7:12.
(An orchard of,) of the Church. Song 4:13.
(Fruit of,) of the graces of the Church. Song 4:3; 6:7.

POOLS AND PONDS.

Made by God. Is 35:7.
Made by man. Is 19:10.
Artificial, designed for
Supplying cities with water. 2 Kin 20:20.
Supplying gardens with water. Eccl 2:6.
Preserving fish. Is 19:10.
Water of, brought into the city by a ditch or conduit. Is 22:11; 2 Kin 20:20.
Filled by the rain. Ps 84:6.
Mentioned in Scripture
Bethesda. John 5:2.
Gibeon. 2 Sam 2:13.
Hebron. 2 Sam 4:12.
Samaria. 1 Kin 22:38.
Siloam. John 9:7.
The upper pool. 2 Kin 18:17; Is 7:3.
The lower pool. Is 22:9.
The king's pool. Neh 2:14.
The old pool. Is 22:11.
The land of Egypt abounded in. Ex 7:19.
Illustrative
Of Nineveh. Nah 2:8.
(In the wilderness,) of the gifts of the Spirit. Is 35:7; 41:18.
(Turning cities into,) of great desolation. Is 14:23.

POOR, THE.

Made by God. Job 34:19; Prov 22:2.
Are such by God's appointment. 1 Sam 2:7; Job 1:21.
Condition of, often results from
Sloth. Prov 20:13.
Bad company. Prov 28:19.
Drunkenness and gluttony. Prov 23:21.
God
Regards equally with the rich. Job 34:19.
Forgets not. Ps 9:18.
Hears. Ps 69:33; Is 41:17.
Maintains the right of. Ps 140:12.
Delivers. Job 36:15; Ps 35:10.
Protects. Ps 12:5; 109:31.
Exalts. 1 Sam 2:8; Ps 107:41.
Provides for. Ps 68:10; 146:7.
Despises no the prayer of. Ps 102:17.
Is the refuge of. Ps 14:6.
Shall never cease out of the land. Deut 15:11; Zeph 3:12; Matt 26:11.
May be
Rich in faith. James 2:5.
Liberal. Mark 12:42; 2 Cor 9:12.
Wise. Prov 28:11.
Upright. Prov 19:1.
Christ lived as one of. Matt 8:20.

Christ preached to. Luke 4:18.
Christ delivers. Ps 72:12.
Offerings of, acceptable to God. Mark 12:42-44; 2 Cor 8:2,12.
Should
  Rejoice in God. Is 29:19.
  Hope in God. Job 5:16.
  Commit themselves to God. Ps 10:14.
  When converted, rejoice in their exaltation. James 1:9.
  Provided for under the Law. Ex 23:11; Lev 19:9,10.
Neglect towards is
  A neglect of Christ. Matt 25:42-45.
  Inconsistent with love to God. 1 John 3:17.
  A proof of unbelief. James 2:15-17.
Rob not. Prov 22:22.
Wrong not in judgment. Ex 23:6.
Take no usury from. Lev 25:36.
Harden not the heart against. Deut 15:7.
Shut not the hand against. Deut 15:7.
Rule not, with vigour. Lev 25:39,43.
Oppress not. Deut 24:14; Zech 7:10.
Despise not. Prov 14:21; James 2:2-4.
Relive. Lev 25:35; Matt 19:21.
Defend. Ps 82:3,4.
Do justice to. Ps 82:3; Jer 22:3,16.
A care for
  Is characteristic of saints. Ps 112:9; 2 Cor 9:9; Prov 29:7.
  Is a fruit of repentance. Luke 3:11.
  Should be urged. 2 Cor 8:7,8; Gal 2:10.
Give to
  Not grudgingly. Deut 15:10; 2 Cor 9:7.
  Liberally. Deut 14:29; 15:8,11.
  Cheerfully. 2 Cor 8:12; 9:7.
  Without ostentation. Matt 6:1.
  Specially if saints. Rom 12:13; Gal 6:10.
  Pray for. Ps 74:19,21.
They who in faith, believe
  Are happy. Prov 14:21.
  Are blessed. Deut 15:10; Ps 41:1; Prov 22:9; Acts 20:35.
  Have the favour of God. Heb 13:16.
  Have promises. Prov 28:27; Luke 14:13,14.
By oppressing, God is reproached. Prov 14:31.
By mocking, God is reproached. Prov 17:5.
The wicked
  Care not for. John 12:6.
  Oppress. Job 24:4-10; Ezek 18:12.
  Vex. Ezek 22:20.
  Regard not the cause of. Prov 29:7.
  Sell. Amos 2:6.
  Crush. Amos 4:1.
  Tread down. Amos 5:11.
  Grind the faces of. Is 3:15.
  Devour. Hab 3:14.
  Persecute. Ps 10:2.
  Defraud. Amos 8:5,6.
  Despise the counsel of. Ps 14:6.
Guilt of defrauding. James 5:4.
Punishment for
  Oppressing. Prov 22:16; Ezek 22:29,31.
  Spoiling. Is 3:13-15; Ezek 18:13.
  Refusing to assist. Job 22:7,10; Prov 21:13.
  Acting unjustly towards. Job 20:19,29; 22:6,10; Is 10:1-3; Amos 5:11,12.
Oppression of—Illustrated. 2 Sam 12:1-6.
Care for—Illustrated. Luke 10:33-35.
Exemplified
  Gideon. Judg 6:15.
  Ruth. Ruth 2:2.
  Widow of Zarephath. 1 Kin 17:12.
  Prophet's widow. 2 Kin 4:2.
  Saints of old. Heb 11:37.
Regard for—Exemplified
  Boaz. Ruth 2:14.
  Job. Job 29:12-16.
  Nebuzaradan. Jer 39:10.
  Zacchaeus. Luke 19:8.
  Peter and John. Acts 3:6.
  Dorcas. Acts 9:36,39.
  Cornelius. Acts 10:2.
  Church at Antioch. Acts 11:29,30.
  Paul. Rom 15:25.
  Churches of Macedonia and Achaia. Rom 15:26; 2 Cor 8:1-5.

Power of Christ, The.

As the Son of God, is the power of God. John 5:17-19; 10:28-30.
As man, is from the Father. Acts 10:38.
Described as
  Supreme. Eph 1:20,21; 1 Pet 3:22.
  Unlimited. Matt 28:18.
  Over all flesh. John 17:2.
  Over all things. John 3:35; Eph 1:22.
  Glorious. 2 Thess 1:9.
  Everlasting. 1 Tim 6:16.
Is able to subdue all things. Phil 3:21.
Exhibited in
  Creation. John 1:3,10; Col 1:16.
  Upholding all things. Col 1:17; Heb 1:3.
  Salvation. Is 63:1; Heb 7:25.
  His teaching. Matt 7:28,29; Luke 4:32.
  Working miracles. Matt 8:27; Luke 5:17.
  Enabling others to work miracles. Matt 10:1; Mark 16:17,18; Luke 10:17.
  Forgiving sins. Matt 9:6; Acts 5:31.
  Giving spiritual life. John 5:21,25,26.
  Giving eternal life. John 17:2.
  Raising the dead. John 5:28,29.
  Raising himself from the dead. John 2:19-21; 10:18.
  Overcoming the world. John 16:33.
  Overcoming Satan. Col 2:15; Heb 2:14.
  Destroying the works of Satan. 1 John 3:8.
Ministers should make known. 2 Pet 1:16.
Saints
  Made willingly by. Ps 110:3.
  Helped by. Heb 2:18.
  Strengthened by. Phil 4:13; 2 Tim 4:17.
  Preserved by. 2 Tim 1:12; 4:18.
  Bodies of, shall be changed by. Phil 3:21.
Rests upon saints. 2 Cor 12:9.
Present in the assembly of saints. 1 Cor 5:4.
Shall be specially manifested at his second coming. Mark 13:26; 2 Pet 1:16.
Shall subdue all power. 1 Cor 15:24.
The wicked shall be destroyed by. Ps 2:9; Is 11:4; 63:3; 2 Thess 1:9.

Power of God, The.

Is one of his attributes. Ps 62:11.
Expressed by the
  Voice of God. Ps 29:3,5; 68:33.
  Finger of God. Ex 8:19; Ps 8:3.
  Hand of God. Ex 9:3,15; Is 48:13.
  Arm of God. Job 40:9; Is 52:10.
  Thunder of his power. Job 26:14.
Described as
  Great. Ps 79:11; Nah 1:3.
  Strong. Ps 89:13; 136:12.
  Glorious. Ex 15:6; Is 63:12.
  Mighty. Job 9:4; Ps 89:13.
  Everlasting. Is 26:4; Rom 1:20.
  Sovereign. Rom 9:21.
  Effectual. Is 43:13; Eph 3:7.
  Irresistible. Deut 32:39; Dan 4:35.
  Incomparable. Ex 15:11,12; Deut 3:24; Job 40:9; Ps 89:8.
  Unsearchable. Job 5:9; 9:10.
  Incomprehensible. Job 26:14; Eccl 3:11.
All things possible to. Matt 19:26.
Nothing too hard for. Gen 18:14; Jer 32:27.
Can save by many or by few. 1 Sam 14:6.
Is the source of all strength. 1 Chr 29:12; Ps 68:35.
Exhibited in
  Creation. Ps 102:25; Jer 10:12.
  Establishing and governing all things. Ps 65:6; 66:7.
  The miracles of Christ. Luke 11:20.
  The resurrection of Christ. 2 Cor 13:4; Col 2:12.
  The resurrection of saints. 1 Cor 6:14.
  Making the gospel effectual. Rom 1:16; 1 Cor 1:18,24.
  Delivering his people. Ps 106:8.
  The destruction of the wicked. Ex 9:16; Rom 9:22.
Saints
  Long for exhibitions. Ps 63:1,2.
  Have confidence in. Jer 20:11.
  Receive increase of grace by. 2 Cor 9:8.
  Strengthened by. Eph 6:10; Col 1:11.
  Upheld by. Ps 37:17; Is 41:10.
  Supported in affliction by. 2 Cor 6:7; 2 Tim 1:8.
  Delivered by. Neh 1:10; Dan 3:17.
  Exalted by. Job 36:22.
  Kept by, to salvation. 1 Pet 1:5.
Exerted in behalf of saints. 2 Chr 16:9.
Works in, and for saints. 2 Cor 13:4; Eph 1:19; 3:20.
The faith of saints stands in. 1 Cor 2:5.
Should be
  Acknowledged. 1 Chr 29:11; Is 33:13.
  Pleaded in prayer. Ps 79:11; Matt 6:13.
  Feared. Jer 5:22; Matt 10:28.
  Magnified. Ps 21:13; Jude 1:25.
Efficiency of ministers is through. 1 Cor 3:6-8; Gal 2:8; Eph 3:7.
Is a ground of trust. Is 26:4; Rom 4:21.
The wicked
  Know not. Matt 22:29.
  Have against them. Ezra 8:22.
  Shall be destroyed by. Luke 12:5.

The heavenly host magnify. Rev 4:11; 5:13; 11:17.

POWER OF THE HOLY SPIRIT, THE.

Is the power of God. Matt 12:28; Luke 11:20.
Christ commenced his ministry in. Luke 4:14.
Christ wrought his miracles by. Matt 12:28.
Exhibited in
  Creation. Gen 1:2; Job 26:13; Ps 104:30.
  The conception of Christ. Luke 1:35.
  Raising Christ from the dead. 1 Pet 3:18.
  Giving spiritual life. Ezek 37:11-14; Rom 8:11.
  Working miracles. Rom 15:19.
  Making the gospel efficacious. 1 Cor 2:4; 1 Thess 1:5.
  Overcoming all difficulties. Zech 4:6,7.
  Promised by the Father. Luke 24:49.
  Promised by Christ. Acts 1:8.
Saints
  Upheld by. Ps 51:12.
  Strengthened by. Eph 3:16.
  Enable to speak the truth boldly by. Mic 3:8; Acts 6:5,10; 2 Tim 1:7,8.
  Helped in prayer by. Rom 8:26.
  Abound in hope by. Rom 15:13.
Qualifies ministers. Luke 24:49; Acts 1:8.
God's Word the instrument of. Eph 6:17.

PRAISE.

God is worthy of. 2 Sam 22:4.
Christ is worthy of. Rev 5:12.
God is glorified by. Ps 22:23; 50:23.
Offered to Christ. John 12:13.
Acceptable through Christ. Heb 13:15.
Is due to God on account of
  His majesty. Ps 96:1,6; Is 24:14.
  His glory. Ps 138:5; Ezek 3:12.
  His excellency. Ex 15:7; Ps 148:13.
  His greatness. 1 Chr 16:25; Ps 145:3.
  His holiness. Ex 15:11; Is 6:3.
  His wisdom. Dan 2:20; Jude 1:25.
  His power. Ps 21:13.
  His goodness. Ps 107:8; 118:1; 136:1; Jer 33:11.
  His mercy. 2 Chr 20:21; Ps 89:1; 118:1-4; 136:1-26.
  His lovingkindness and truth. Ps 138:2.
  His faithfulness and truth. Is 25:1.
  His salvation. Ps 18:46; Is 35:10; 61:10; Luke 1:68,69.
  His wonderful works. Ps 89:5; 150:2; Is 25:1.
  His consolation. Ps 42:5; Is 12:1.
  His judgment. Ps 101:1.
  His counsel. Ps 16:7; Jer 32:19.
  Fulfilling of his promises. 1 Kin 8:56.
  Pardon of sin. Ps 103:1-3; Hos 14:2.
  Spiritual health. Ps 103:3.
  Constant preservation. Ps 71:6-8.
  Deliverance. Ps 40:1-3; 124:6.
  Protection. Ps 28:7; 59:17.
  Answering prayer. Ps 28:6; 118:21.
  The hope of glory. 1 Pet 1:3,4.
  All spiritual blessings. Ps 103:2; Eph 1:3.
  All temporal blessings. Ps 104:1,14; 136:25.
  The continuance of blessings. Ps 68:19.
Is obligatory upon
  Angels. Ps 103:20; 148:2.
  Saints. Ps 30:4; 149:5.
  Gentiles. Ps 117:1; Rom 15:11.
  Children. Ps 8:2; Matt 21:16.
  High and low. Ps 148:1,11.
  Young and old. Ps 148:1,12.
  Small and great. Rev 19:5.
  All men. Ps 107:8; 145:21.
  All creation. Ps 148:1-10; 150:6.
Is good and comely. Ps 33:1; 147:1.
Should be offered
  With understanding. Ps 47:7; 1 Cor 14:15.
  With the soul. Ps 103:1; 104:1,35.
  With the whole heart. Ps 9:1; 111:1; 138:1.
  With uprightness of heart. Ps 119:7.
  With the lips. Ps 63:3; 119:171.
  With the mouth. Ps 51:15; 63:5.
  With joy. Ps 63:5; 98:4.
  With gladness. 2 Chr 29:30; Jer 33:11.
  With thankfulness. 1 Chr 16:4; Neh 12:24; Ps 147:7.
  Continually. Ps 35:28; 71:6.
  During life. Ps 104:33.
  More and more. Ps 71:14.
  Day and night. Rev 4:8.
  Day by day. 2 Chr 30:21.
  For ever and ever. Ps 145:1,2.
  Throughout the world. Ps 113:3.
  In psalms and hymns, etc. Ps 105:2; Eph 5:19; Col 3:16.
Accompanied with musical instruments. 1 Chr 16:41,42; Ps 150:3,5.
Is a part of public worship. Ps 9:14; 100:4; 118:19,20; Heb 2:12.
Saints should
  Show forth. Is 43:21; 1 Pet 2:9.
  Be endued with the spirit of. Is 61:3.
  Render, under affliction. Acts 16:25.
  Glory in. 1 Chr 16:35.
  Triumph in. Ps 106:47.
  Express their joy by. James 5:13.
  Declare. Is 42:12.
  Invite others to. Ps 34:3; 95:1.
  Pray for ability to offer. Ps 51:15; 119:175.
  Posture suited to. 1 Chr 23:30; Neh 9:5.
Called the
  Fruit of the lips. Heb 13:15.
  Voice of praise. Ps 66:8.
  Voice of triumph. Ps 47:1.
  Voice of melody. Is 51:3.
  Voice of a psalm. Ps 98:5.
  Garment of praise. Is 61:3.
  Sacrifice of praise. Heb 13:15.
  Sacrifices of joy. Ps 27:6.
  Calves of the lips. Hos 14:2.
The heavenly host engage in. Is 6:3; Luke 2:13; Rev 4:9-11; 5:12.
Exemplified
  Melchizedek. Gen 14:20.
  Moses. Ex 15:1-21.
  Jethro. Ex 18:10.
  Israelites. 1 Chr 16:36.
  David. 1 Chr 29:10-13; Ps 119:164.
  Priests and Levites. Ezra 3:10-11.
  Ezra. Neh 8:6.
  Hezekiah. Is 38:19.
  Zacharias. Luke 1:64.
  Shepherds. Luke 2:20.
  Simeon. Luke 2:28.
  Anna. Luke 2:38.
  Multitudes. Luke 18:43.
  Disciples. Luke 19:37,38.
  The apostles. Luke 24:53.
  First converts. Acts 2:47.
  Lame man. Acts 3:8.
  Paul and Silas. Acts 16:25.

PRAYER.

Commanded. Is 55:6; Matt 7:7; Phil 4:6.
To be offered
  To God. Ps 5:2; Matt 4:10.
  To Christ. Luke 23:42; Acts 7:59.
  To the Holy Spirit. 2 Thess 3:5.
  Through Christ. Eph 2:18; Heb 10:19.
God hears. Ps 10:17; 65:2.
God answers. Ps 99:6; Is 58:9.
Is described as
  Bowing the knees. Eph 3:14.
  Looking up. Ps 5:3.
  Lifting up the soul. Ps 25:1.
  Lifting up the heart. Lam 3:41.
  Pouring out the heart. Ps 62:8.
  Pouring out the soul. 1 Sam 1:15.
  Calling upon the name of the Lord. Gen 12:8; Ps 116:4; Acts 22:16.
  Crying to God. Ps 27:7; 34:6.
  Drawing near to God. Ps 73:28; Heb 10:22.
  Crying to heaven. 2 Chr 32:20.
  Beseeching the Lord. Ex 32:11.
  Seeking to God. Job 8:5.
  Seeking the face of the Lord. Ps 27:8.
  Making supplication. Job 8:5; Jer 36:7.
Acceptable through Christ. John 14:13,14; 15:16; 16:23,24.
Ascends to heaven. 2 Chr 30:27; Rev 5:8.
Quickening grace necessary to. Ps 80:18.
The Holy Spirit
  Promised as a Spirit of. Zech 12:10.
  As the Spirit of adoptions, leads to. Rom 8:15; Gal 4:6.
  Helps our infirmities in. Rom 8:26.
An evidence of conversion. Acts 9:11.
Of the righteous, avails much. James 5:16.
Of the upright, a delight to God. Prov 15:8.
Should be offered up
  In the Holy Spirit. Eph 6:18; Jude 1:20.
  In faith. Matt 21:22; James 1:6.
  In full assurance of faith. Heb 10:22.
  In a forgiving spirit. Matt 6:12.
  With the heart. Jer 29:13; Lam 3:41.
  With the whole heart. Ps 119:58,145.
  With preparation of heart. Job 11:13.
  With a true heart. Heb 10:22.
  With the soul. Ps 42:4.
  With the spirit and understanding. John 4:22-24; 1 Cor 14:15.
  With confidence in God. Ps 56:9; 86:7; 1 John 5:14.
  With submission to God. Luke 22:42.
  With unfeigned lips. Ps 17:1.
  With deliberation. Eccl 5:2.
  With holiness. 1 Tim 2:8.

With humility. 2 Chr 7:14; 33:12.
With truth. Ps 145:18; John 4:24.
With desire to be heard. Neh 1:6; Ps 17:1; 55:1,2; 61:1.
With desire to be answered. Ps 27:7; 102:2; 108:6; 143:1.
With boldness. Heb 4:16.
With earnestness. 1 Thess 3:10; James 5:17.
With importunity. Gen 32:26; Luke 11:8,9; 18:1-7.
Night and day. 1 Tim 5:5.
Without ceasing. 1 Thess 5:17.
Everywhere. 1 Tim 2:8.
In everything. Phil 4:6.

For temporal blessings. Gen 28:20; Prov 30:8; Matt 6:11.
For spiritual blessings. Matt 6:33.
For mercy and grace to help in time of need. Heb 4:16.
Model for. Matt 6:9-13.
Vain repetitions in, forbidden. Matt 6:7.
Ostentation in, forbidden. Matt 6:5.
Accompanied with
Repentance. 1 Kin 8:33; Jer 36:7.
Confession. Neh 1:4,7; Dan 9:4-11.
Self-abasement. Gen 18:27.
Weeping. Jer 31:9; Hos 12:4.
Fasting. Neh 1:4; Dan 9:3; Acts 13:3.
Watchfulness. Luke 21:36; 1 Pet 4:7.
Praise. Ps 66:17.
Thanksgiving. Phil 4:6; Col 4:2.
Plead in the
Promises of God. Gen 32:9-12; Ex 32:13; 1 Kin 8:26; Ps 119:49.
Covenant of God. Jer 14:21.
Faithfulness of God. Ps 143:1.
Mercy of God. Ps 51:1; Dan 9:18.
Righteousness of God. Dan 9:16.
Rise early for. Ps 5:3; 119:147.
Seek divine teaching for. Luke 11:1.
Faint not in. Luke 18:1.
Continue instant in. Rom 12:12.
Avoid hindrances in. 1 Pet 3:7.
Suitable in affliction. Is 26:16; James 5:13.
Shortness of time a motive to. 1 Pet 4:7.
Postures in
Standing. 1 Kin 8:22; Mark 11:25.
Bowing down. Ps 95:6.
Kneeling. 2 Chr 6:13; Ps 95:6; Luke 22:41; Acts 20:36.
Falling on the face. Num 16:22; Josh 5:14; 1 Chr 21:16; Matt 26:39.
Spreading forth the hands. Is 1:15.
Lifting up the hands. Ps 28:2; Lam 2:19; 1 Tim 2:8.
The promises of God encourage to. Is 65:24; Amos 5:4; Zech 13:9.
The promises of Christ encourage to. Luke 11:9,10; John 14:13,14.
Experience of past mercies an incentive to. Ps 4:1; 112:2.

PRAYER, ANSWERS TO.

God gives. Ps 99:6; 118:5; 138:3.
Christ gives. John 4:10,14; 14:14.
Christ received. John 11:42; Heb 5:7.
Granted
Through the grace of God. Is 30:19.
Sometimes immediately. Is 65:24; Dan 9:21,23; 10:12.
Sometimes after delay. Luke 18:7.
Sometimes differently from our desire. 2 Cor 12:8,9.
Beyond expectation. Jer 33:3; Eph 3:20.
Promised. Is 58:9; Jer 29:12; Matt 7:7.
Promised especially in times of trouble. Ps 50:15; 91:15.
Received by those who
Seek God. Ps 34:4.
Seek God with all the heart. Jer 29:12,13.
Wait upon God. Ps 40:1.
Return to God. 2 Chr 7:14; Job 22:23,27.
Ask in faith. Matt 21:11; James 5:15.
Ask in the name of Christ. John 14:13.
Ask according to God's will. 1 John 5:14.
Call upon God in truth. Ps 145:18.
Fear God. Ps 145:19.
Set their love upon God. Ps 91:14,15.
Keep God's commandments. 1 John 3:22.
Call upon God under oppression. Is 19:20.
Call upon God under affliction. Ps 18:6; 106:44; Is 30:19,20.
Abide in Christ. John 15:7.
Humble themselves. 2 Chr 7:14; Ps 9:12.
Are righteous. Ps 34:15; James 5:16.
Are poor and needy. Is 41:17.
Saints
Are assured of. 1 John 5:15.
Love God for. Ps 116:1.
Bless God for. Ps 66:20.
Praise God for. Ps 116:17; 118:21.
A motive for continued prayer. Ps 116:2.
Denied to those who
Ask amiss. James 4:3.
Regard iniquity in the heart. Ps 66:18.
Live in sin. Is 59:2; John 9:31.
Offer unworthy service to God. Mal 1:7-9.
Forsake God. Jer 14:10,12.
Reject the call of God. Prov 1:24,25,28.
Hear not the law. Prov 28:9; Zech 7:11-13.
Are deaf to the cry of the poor. Prov 21:13.
Are blood shedders. Is 1:15; 59:3.
Are idolaters. Jer 11:11-14; Ezek 8:15-18.
Are wavering. James 1:6,7.
Are hypocrites. Job 27:8,9.
Are proud. Job 35:12,13.
Are self-righteous. Luke 18:11,12,14.
Are the enemies of saints. Ps 18:40,41.
Cruelly oppress saints. Mic 3:2-4.
Exemplified
Abraham. Gen 17:20.
Lot. Gen 19:19-21.
Abraham's servant. Gen 24:15-27.
Jacob. Gen 32:24-30.
Israelites. Ex 2:23,24.
Moses. Ex 17:4-6,11-13; 32:11-14.
Samson. Judg 15:18,19.
Hannah. 1 Sam 1:27.
Samuel. 1 Sam 7:9.
Solomon. 1 Kin 3:9,12.
Man of God. 1 Kin 13:6.
Elijah. 1 Kin 18:36-38; James 5:17,18.
Elisha. 2 Kin 4:33-35.
Jehoahaz. 2 Kin 13:4.
Hezekiah. 2 Kin 19:20.
Jabez. 1 Chr 4:10.
Asa. 2 Chr 14:11,12.
Jehoshaphat. 2 Chr 20:6-17.
Manasseh. 2 Chr 33:13,19.
Ezra. Ezra 8:21-23.
Nehemiah. Neh 4:9,15.
Job. Job 42:10.
David. Ps 18:6.
Jeremiah. Lam 3:55,56.
Daniel. Dan 9:20-23.
Jonah. Jon 2:2,10.
Zacharias. Luke 1:13.
Blind man. Luke 18:38,41-43.
Thief on the cross. Luke 23:42,43.
Apostles. Acts 4:29-31.
Cornelius. Acts 10:4,31.
The Christians. Acts 12:5,7.
Paul and Silas. Acts 16:25,26.
Paul. Acts 28:8.
Refusal of—exemplified
Saul. 1 Sam 28:15.
Elders of Israel. Ezek 20:3.
Pharisees. Matt 23:14.

PRAYER, INTERCESSORY.

Christ set an example of. Luke 22:32; 23:34; John 17:9-24.
Commanded. 1 Tim 2:1; James 5:14,16.
Should be offered up for
Kings. 1 Tim 2:2.
All in authority. 1 Tim 2:2.
Ministers. 2 Cor 1:11; Phil 1:19.
The Church. Ps 122:6; Is 62:6,7.
All saints. Eph 6:18.
All men. 1 Tim 2:1.
Masters. Gen 24:12-14.
Servants. Luke 7:2,3.
Children. Gen 17:18; Matt 15:22.
Friends. Job 42:8.
Fellow-countrymen. Rom 10:1.
The sick. James 5:14.
Persecutors. Matt 5:44.
Enemies among whom we dwell. Jer 29:7.
Those who envy us. Num 12:13.
Those who forsake us. 2 Tim 4:16.
Those who murmur against God. Num 11:1,2; 14:13,19.
By ministers for their people. Eph 1:16; 3:14-19; Phil 1:4.
Encouragement to. James 5:16; 1 John 5:16.
Beneficial to the offerer. Job 42:10.
Sin of neglecting. 1 Sam 12:23.
Seek an interest in. 1 Sam 12:19; Heb 13:18.
Unavailing for the obstinately impenitent. Jer 7:13-16; 14:10,11.
Exemplified
Abraham. Gen 18:23-32.
Abraham's servant. Gen 24:12-14.
Moses. Ex 8:12; 32:11-13.
Samuel. 1 Sam 7:5.
Solomon. 1 Kin 8:30-36.
Elisha. 2 Kin 4:33.
Hezekiah. 2 Chr 30:18.
Isaiah. 2 Chr 32:20.
Nehemiah. Neh 1:4-11.
David. Ps 25:22.
Ezekiel. Ezek 9:8.
Daniel. Dan 9:3-19.

Stephen. Acts 7:60.
Peter and John. Acts 8:15.
Church of Jerusalem. Acts 12:5.
Paul. Col 1:9-12; 2 Thess 1:11.
Epaphras. Col 4:12.
Philemon. Philem 22.

Prayer, Private.

Christ was constant in. Matt 14:23; 26:36,39; Mark 1:35; Luke 9:18,29.
Commanded. Matt 6:6.
Should be offered
At evening, morning, and noon. Ps 55:17.
Day and night. Ps 88:1.
Without ceasing. 1 Thess 5:17.
Shall be heard. Job 22:27.
Rewarded openly. Matt 6:6.
An evidence of conversion. Acts 9:11.
Nothing should hinder. Dan 6:10.
Exemplified
Lot. Gen 19:20.
Eliezer. Gen 24:12.
Jacob. Gen 32:9-12.
Gideon. Judg 6:22,36,39.
Hannah. 1 Sam 1:10.
David. 2 Sam 7:18-29.
Hezekiah. 2 Kin 20:2.
Isaiah. 2 Kin 20:11.
Manasseh. 2 Chr 33:18,19.
Ezra. Ezra 9:5,6.
Nehemiah. Neh 2:4.
Jeremiah. Jer 32:16-25.
Daniel. Dan 9:3,17.
Jonah. Jon 2:1.
Habakkuk. Hab 1:2.
Anna. Luke 2:37.
Paul. Acts 9:11.
Peter. Acts 9:40; 10:9.
Cornelius. Acts 10:30.

Prayer, Public.

Acceptable to God. Is 56:7.
God promises to hear. 2 Chr 7:14,16.
God promises to bless in. Ex 20:24.
Christ
Sanctifies by his presence. Matt 18:20.
Attended. Matt 12:9; Luke 4:16.
Promises answers to. Matt 18:19.
Instituted form of. Luke 11:2.
Should not be made in an unknown language. 1 Cor 14:14-16.
Saints delight in. Ps 42:4; 122:1.
Exhortation to. Heb 10:25.
Urge others to join in. Ps 95:6; Zech 8:21.
Exemplified
Joshua. Josh 7:6-9.
David. 1 Chr 29:10-19.
Solomon. 2 Chr 6:1-42.
Jehoshaphat. 2 Chr 20:5-13.
Jeshua. Neh 9:1-38.
Jews. Luke 1:10.
The Christians. Acts 2:46; 4:24; 12:5,12.
Peter. Acts 3:1.
Teachers and Prophets, at Antioch. Acts 13:3.
Paul. Acts 16:16.

Prayer, Social and Family.

Promise of answers to. Matt 18:19.
Christ promises to be present at. Matt 18:20.
Punishment for neglecting. Jer 10:25.
Exemplified
Abram. Gen 12:5,8.
Jacob. Gen 35:2,3,7.
Joshua. Josh 24:15.
David. 2 Sam 6:20.
Job. Job 1:5.
The Disciples. Acts 1:13,14.
Cornelius. Acts 10:2.
Paul and Silas. Acts 16:25.
Paul. Acts 20:36; 21:5.

Precious Stones.

Dug out of the earth. Job 28:5,6.
Brought from Ophir. 1 Kin 10:11; 2 Chr 9:10.
Brought from Sheba. 1 Kin 10:1,2; Ezek 27:22.
Called
Stones of fire. Ezek 28:14,16.
Stones to be set. 1 Chr 29:2.
Jewels. Is 61:10; Ezek 16:12.
Precious jewels. 2 Chr 20:25; Prov 20:15.
Of great variety. 1 Chr 29:2.
Of many colours. 1 Chr 29:2.
Brilliant and glittering. 1 Chr 29:2; Rev 21:11.
Mentioned in Scripture
Agate. Ex 28:19; Is 54:12.
Amethyst. Ex 28:19; Rev 21:20.
Beryl. Dan 10:6; Rev 21:20.
Carbuncle. Ex 28:17; Is 54:12.
Coral. Job 28:18.
Chalcedony. Rev 21:19.
Chrysolite. Rev 21:20.
Chrysoprasus. Rev 21:20.
Diamond. Ex 28:18; Jer 17:1; Ezek 28:13.
Emerald. Ezek 27:16; Rev 4:3.
Jacinth. Rev 9:17; 21:20.
Jasper. Rev 4:3; 21:11,19.
Onyx. Ex 28:20; Job 28:16.
Pearl. Job 28:18; Matt 13:45,46; Rev 21:21.
Ruby. Job 28:18; Lam 4:7.
Sapphire. Ex 24:10; Ezek 1:26.
Sardine or Sardius. Ex 28:17; Rev 4:3.
Sardonyx. Rev 21:20.
Topaz. Job 28:19; Rev 21:20.
Highly prized by the ancients. Prov 17:8.
Extensive commerce in. Ezek 27:22; Rev 18:12.
Often given as presents. 1 Kin 10:2,10.
Art of engraving upon, early known to the Jews. Ex 28:9,11,21.
Art of setting, known to the Jews. Ex 28:20.
Used for
Adorning the high priest's ephod. Ex 28:12.
Adorning the breastplate of judgment. Ex 28:17-20; 39:10-14.
Decorating the person. Ezek 28:13.
Ornamenting royal crowns. 2 Sam 12:30.
Setting in seals and rings. Song 5:12.
Adorning the temple. 2 Chr 3:6.
Honouring idols. Dan 11:38.
A part of the treasure of kings. 2 Chr 32:27.
Given by the Jews for the tabernacle. Ex 25:7.
Prepared by David for the temple. 1 Chr 29:2.
Given by chief men for the temple. 1 Chr 29:8.
Illustrative of
Preciousness of Christ. Is 28:16; 1 Pet 2:6.
Beauty and stability of the church. Is 54:11,12.
Saints. Mal 3:17; 1 Cor 3:12.
Seductive splendour and false glory of the apostasy. Rev 17:4; 18:16.
Worldly glory of nations. Ezek 28:13-16.
Glory of heavenly Jerusalem. Rev 21:11.
Stability of heavenly Jerusalem. Rev 21:19.

Preciousness of Christ.

To God. Matt 3:17; 1 Pet 2:4.
To Saints. Song 5:10; Phil 3:8; 1 Pet 2:7.
On account of his
Goodness and beauty. Zech 9:17.
Excellence and grace. Ps 45:2.
Name. Song 1:3; Heb 1:4.
Atonement. 1 Pet 1:19; Heb 12:24.
Words. John 6:68.
Promises. 2 Pet 1:4.
Care and tenderness. Is 40:11.
As the corner-stone of the Church. Is 28:16; 1 Pet 2:6.
As the source of all grace. John 1:14; Col 1:19.
Unsearchable. Eph 3:8.
Illustrated. Song 2:3; 5:10-16; Matt 13:44-46.

Presents.

Antiquity of. Gen 32:13; 43:15.
Were given
To judges to secure a favourable hearing. Prov 17:23; Amos 2:6.
To kings to engage their aid. 1 Kin 15:18.
By kings to each other in token of inferiority. 1 Kin 10:25; 2 Chr 9:23,24; Ps 72:10.
To appease the angry feelings of others. Gen 32:20; 1 Sam 25:27,28,35.
To confirm covenants. Gen 21:28-30.
To reward service. 2 Sam 18:12; Dan 2:6,48.
To show respect. Judg 6:18.
In token of friendship. 1 Sam 18:3,4.
As tribute. Judg 3:15; 2 Sam 8:2; 2 Chr 17:5.
On occasions of visits. 2 Kin 8:8.
On all occasions of public rejoicing. Neh 8:12; Esth 9:19.
At marriages. Gen 24:53; Ps 45:12.
On recovering from sickness. 2 Kin 20:12.
On restoration to prosperity. Job 42:10,11.
On sending away friends. Gen 45:22; Jer 40:5.
Considered essential on all visits of business. 1 Sam 9:7.
Not bringing, considered a mark of disrespect and disaffection. Is 10:27; 2 Kin 17:24.
Generally procured a favourable reception. Prov 18:16; 19:6.

When small or defective, refused. Mal 1:8.
Of persons of rank, of great value and variety. 2 Kin 5:2; 2 Chr 9:1.
Receiving of, a token of good will. Gen 33:10,11.
Things given as
Cattle. Gen 32:14,15,18.
Horses and mules. 1 Kin 10:25.
Money. Gen 45:22; 1 Sam 9:8; Job 42:11.
Food. Gen 43:11; 1 Sam 25:18; 1 Kin 14:3.
Garments. Gen 45:22; 1 Sam 18:4.
Weapons of war. 1 Sam 18:4.
Ornaments. Gen 24:22,47; Job 42:11.
Gold and silver vessels. 1 Kin 10:25.
Precious stones. 1 Kin 10:2.
Servants. Gen 20:14; 29:24,29.
Often borne by servants. Judg 3:18.
Often conveyed on camels. 1 Sam 25:18; 2 Kin 8:9; 2 Chr 9:1.
Sometimes sent before the giver. Gen 32:21.
Generally presented in person. Gen 43:15,26; Judg 3:17; 1 Sam 25:27.
Laid out and presented with great ceremony. Gen 43:25; Judg 3:18; Matt 2:11.

PRESUMPTION.

A characteristic of the wicked. 2 Pet 2:10.
A characteristic of Antichrist. 2 Thess 2:4.
Exhibited in
Opposing God. Job 15:25,26.
Wilful commission of sin. Rom 1:32.
Self-righteousness. Hos 12:8; Rev 3:17.
Spiritual pride. Is 65:5; Luke 18:11.
Esteeming our own ways right. Prov 12:15.
Seeking precedence. Luke 14:7-11.
Planning for the future. Luke 12:18; James 4:13.
Pretending to prophecy. Deut 18:22.
Pray to be kept from sins of. Ps 19:13.
Saints avoid. Ps 131:1.
Punishment for. Num 15:30; Rev 18:7,8.
Exemplified
Builders of Babel. Gen 11:4.
Israelites. Num 14:44.
Korah etc. Num 16:3,7.
Men of Bethshemesh. 1 Sam 6:19.
Uzzah. 2 Sam 6:6.
Jeroboam. 1 Kin 13:4.
Benhadad. 1 Kin 20:19.
Uzziah. 2 Chr 26:16.
Sennacherib. 2 Chr 32:13,14.
Theudas. Acts 5:36.
Sons of Sceva. Acts 19:13,14.
Diotrephes. 3 John 9.

PRIDE.

Is sin. Prov 21:4.
Hateful to God. Prov 6:16,17; 16:5.
Hateful to Christ. Prov 8:12,13.
Often originates in
Self-righteousness. Luke 18:11,12.
Religious privileges. Zeph 3:11.
Unsanctified knowledge. 1 Cor 8:1.
Inexperience. 1 Tim 3:6.
Possession of power. Lev 26:19; Ezek 30:6.
Possession of wealth. 2 Kin 20:13.
Forbidden. 1 Sam 2:3; Rom 12:3,16.
Defiles a man. Mark 7:20,22.
Hardens the mind. Dan 5:20.
Saints
give not away. Ps 131:1.
Respect not, in others. Ps 40:4.
Mourn over, in others. Jer 13:17.
Hate, in others. Ps 101:5.
A hindrance to seeking God. Ps 10:4; Hos 7:10.
A hindrance to improvement. Prov 26:12.
A characteristic
The devil. 1 Tim 3:6.
The world. 1 John 2:16.
False teachers. 1 Tim 6:3,4.
The wicked. Hab 2:4,5; Rom 1:30.
Comes from the heart. Mark 7:21-23.
The wicked encompassed with. Ps 73:6.
Leads men to
Contempt and rejection of God's word and ministers. Jer 43:2.
A persecuting spirit. Ps 10:2.
Wrath. Prov 21:24.
Contention. Prov 13:10; 28:25.
Self-deception. Jer 49:16; Obad 3.
Exhortation against. Jer 13:15.
Is followed by
Shame. Prov 11:2.
Debasement. Prov 29:23; Is 28:3.
Destruction. Prov 16:18; 18:12.
Shall abound in the last days. 2 Tim 3:2.
Woe to. Is 28:1,3.
They who are guilty of, shall be
Resisted. James 4:6.
Brought into contempt. Is 23:9.
Recompensed. Ps 31:23.
Marred. Jer 13:9.
Subdued. Ex 18:11; Is 13:11.
Brought low. Ps 18:27; Is 2:12.
Abased. Dan 4:37; Matt 23:12.
Scattered. Luke 1:51.
Punished. Zeph 2:10,11; Mal 4:1.
Exemplified
Ahithophel. 2 Sam 17:23.
Hezekiah. 2 Chr 32:25.
Pharaoh. Neh 9:10.
Haman. Esth 3:5.
Moab. Is 16:6.
Tyre. Is 23:9.
Israel. Is 28:1; Hos 5:5,9.
Judah. Jer 13:9.
Babylon. Jer 50:29,32.
Assyria. Ezek 31:3,10.
Nebuchadnezzar. Dan 4:30; 5:20.
Belshazzar. Dan 5:22,23.
Edom. Obad 3.
Scribes. Mark 12:38,39.
Herod. Acts 12:21-23.
Laodiceans. Rev 3:17.

PRIESTS.

First notice of persons acting as. Gen 4:3,4.
During patriarchal age heads of families acted as. Gen 8:20; 12:8; 35:7.
After the exodus young men (firstborn) deputed to act as. Ex 24:5; 19:22.
The sons of Aaron appointed as, by perpetual statute. Ex 29:9; 40:15.
All except seed of Aaron excluded from being. Num 3:10; 16:40; 18:7.
Sanctified by God for the office. Ex 29:44.
Publicly consecrated. Ex 28:3; Num 3:3.
Ceremonies at consecration of
Washing in water. Ex 29:4; Lev 8:6.
Clothing with the holy garments. Ex 29:8,9; 40:14; Lev 8:13.
Anointing with oil. Ex 30:30; 40:13.
Offering sacrifices. Ex 29:10-19; Lev 8:14-23.
Purification by blood of the consecration ram. Ex 29:20,21; Lev 8:23,24.
Placing in their hands the wave offering. Ex 29:22-24; Lev 8:25-27.
Partaking of the sacrifices of consecration. Ex 29:31-33; Lev 8:31,32.
Lasted seven days. Ex 29:35-37; Lev 8:33.
Required to remain in the tabernacle seven days after consecration. Lev 8:33-36.
No blemished or defective persons could be consecrated. Lev 21:17-23.
Required to prove their genealogy before they exercised the office. Ezra 2:62; Neh 7:64.
Garments of
The coat or tunic. Ex 28:40; 39:27.
The girdle. Ex 28:40.
The bonnet. Ex 28:40; 39:28.
The linen breeches. Ex 28:42; 39:28.
Worn at consecration. Ex 29:9; 40:15.
Worn always while engaged in the service of the tabernacle. Ex 28:43; 39:41.
Worn by the high priest on the day of atonement. Lev 16:4.
Purified by sprinkling of blood. Ex 29:21.
Laid up in holy chambers. Ezek 44:19.
Often provided by the people. Ezra 2:68,69; Neh 7:70,72.
Required to wash in the brazen laver before they performed their services. Ex 30:18-21.
Services of
Keeping the charge of the tabernacle. Num 18:1,5,7.
Covering the sacred things of the sanctuary before removal. Num 4:5-15.
Offering sacrifices. Lev 1:1-6:30; 2 Chr 29:34; 35:11.
Lighting and trimming the lamps of the sanctuary. Ex 27:20,21; Lev 24:3,4.
Keeping the sacred fire always burning on the altar. Lev 6:12,13.
Burning incense. Ex 20:7,8; Luke 1:9.
Placing and removing show-bread. Lev 24:5-9.
Offering firstfruits. Lev 23:10,11; Deut 26:3,4.
Blessing the people. Num 6:23-27.
Purifying the unclean. Lev 15:30,31.
Deciding in cases of jealousy. Num 5:14,15.
Deciding in cases of leprosy. Lev 13:2-59; 14:34-45.
Judging in cases of controversy. Deut 17:8-13; 21:5.

Teaching the law. Deut 33:8,10; Mal 2:7.
Blowing the trumpets on various occasions. Num 10:1-10; Josh 6:3,4.
Carrying the ark. Josh 3:6,17; 6:12.
Encouraging the people when they went to war. Deut 20:1-4.
Valuing things devoted. Lev 27:8.
Were to live by the altar as they had no inheritance. Deut 18:1,2; 1 Cor 9:13.
Revenues of
Tenth of the tithes paid to the Levites. Num 18:26,28; Neh 10:37,38; Heb 7:5.
First-fruits. Num 18:8,12,13; Deut 18:4.
Redemption-money of the firstborn. Num 3:48,51; 18:15,16.
Firstborn of animals or their substitutes. Num 18:17,18; Ex 13:12,13.
First of the wool of sheep. Deut 18:4.
Show-bread after its removal. Lev 24:9; 1 Sam 21:4-6; Matt 12:4.
Part of all sacrifices. Lev 7:6-10,31,34; Num 6:19,20; 18:8-11; Deut 18:3.
All devoted things. Num 18:14.
All restitutions when the owner could not be found. Num 5:8.
A fixed portion of the spoil taken in war. Num 31:29,41.
Thirteen of the Levitical cities given to, for residence. 1 Chr 6:57-60; Num 35:1-8.
Might purchase and hold other lands in possession. 1 Kin 2:26; Jer 32:8,9.
Special laws respecting
Not to marry divorced or improper persons. Lev 21:7.
Not to defile themselves for the dead except the nearest of kin. Lev 21:1-6.
Not to drink wine, etc. while attending in the tabernacle. Lev 10:9; Ezek 44:21.
Not to defile themselves by eating what died or was torn. Lev 22:8.
While unclean could not perform any service. Lev 22:1,2; Num 19:6,7.
While unclean could not eat of the holy things. Lev 22:3-7.
No sojourner or hired servant to eat of their portion. Lev 22:10.
All bought and home-born servants to eat of their portion. Lev 22:11.
Children of, married to strangers, not to eat of their portion. Lev 22:12.
Restitution to be made to, by persons ignorantly eating of their holy things. Lev 22:14-16.
Divided by David into twenty-four courses. 1 Chr 24:1-19; 2 Chr 8:14; 35:4,5.
The four courses which returned from Babylon subdivided into 24. Ezra 2:36-39; Luke 1:5.
Each course of, had its president or chief. 1 Chr 24:6,31; 2 Chr 36:14.
Services of, divided by lot. Luke 1:9.
Punishment for invading the office of. Num 16:1-35; 18:7; 2 Chr 26:16-21.
On special occasions persons not of Aaron's family acted as. Judg 6:24-27; 1 Sam 7:9; 1 Kin 18:33.
Were sometimes
Greedy. 1 Sam 2:13-17.
Drunken. Is 28:7.
Profane and wicked. 1 Sam 2:22-24.
Unjust. Jer 6:13.
Corrupters of the law. Is 28:7; Mal 2:8.
Slow to sanctify, themselves for God's services. 2 Chr 29:34.
Generally participated in punishment of the people. Jer 14:18; Lam 2:20.
Made of the lowest of the people by Jeroboam and others. 1 Kin 12:21; 2 Kin 17:32.
Services of, ineffectual for removing sin. Heb 7:11; 10:11.
Illustrative of
Christ. Heb 10:11,12.
Saints. Ex 19:6; 1 Pet 2:9.

Prisons.

Antiquity of. Gen 39:20.
Kinds of, mentioned
State. Jer 37:21; Gen 39:20.
Common. Acts 5:18.
Dungeons attached to. Jer 38:6; Zech 9:11.
Were under the care of a keeper. Gen 39:21.
Used for confining
Persons accused of crimes. Luke 23:19.
Persons accused of heresy. Acts 4:3; 5:18; 8:3.
Suspected persons. Gen 42:19.
Condemned persons till executed. Lev 24:12; Acts 12:4,5.
Enemies taken captive. Judg 16:21; 2 Kin 17:4; Jer 52:11.
Debtors till they paid. Matt 5:26; 18:30.
Persons under the king's displeasure. 1 Kin 22:27; 2 Chr 16:10; Mark 6:17.
Confinement in, often awarded as a punishment. Ezra 7:26.
Confinement in, considered a severe punishment. Luke 22:33.
Places used as
Court of the king's house. Jer 32:2.
House of the king's scribe. Jer 37:15.
House of the captain of the guard. Gen 40:3.
Prisoner's own house, where he was kept bound to a soldier. Acts 28:16,30; 2 Tim 1:16-18.
The king had power to commit to. 1 Kin 22:27.
Magistrates had power to commit to. Matt 5:25.
Persons confined in
Said to be in ward. Lev 24:12.
Said to be in hold. Acts 4:3.
Often placed in dungeons. Jer 39:6; Acts 16:24.
Often bound with fetters. Gen 42:19; Ezek 19:9; Mark 6:17.
Often chained to two soldiers. Acts 12:6.
Often fastened in stocks. Jer 29:26; Acts 16:24.
Often kept to hard labour. Judg 16:21.
Often subjected to extreme suffering. Ps 79:11; 102:20; 105:18.
Fed on bread and water. 1 Kin 22:27.
Clothed in prison dress. 2 Kin 25:29.
Sometimes allowed to be visited by their friends. Matt 11:2; 25:36; Acts 24:23.
Might have their condition ameliorated by the king. Jer 37:20,21.
Often executed in. Gen 40:22; Matt 14:10.
The king had power to release from. Gen 40:21.
Magistrates had power to release from. Acts 16:35,36.
Keepers of
Strictly guarded the doors. Acts 12:6.
Responsible for the prisoners. Acts 16:23,27.
Put to death if prisoners escaped. Acts 12:19.
Often used severity. Jer 37:16,20; Acts 16:24.
Sometimes acted kindly. Gen 39:21; Acts 16:33,34.
Sometimes entrusted the care of the prison to well-conducted prisoners. Gen 39:22,23.
Illustrative of
Deep afflictions. Ps 142:7.
Hell. Rev 20:7.
Bondage to sin and Satan. Is 42:7; 49:9; 61:1.

Privileges of Saints.

Abiding in Christ. John 15:4,5.
Partaking of the divine nature. 2 Pet 1:4.
Access to God by Christ. Eph 3:12.
Being of the household of God. Eph 2:19.
Membership with the Church of the firstborn. Heb 12:23.
Having
Christ for their Shepherd. Is 40:11; John 10:14,16.
Christ for their intercessor. Rom 8:34; Heb 7:25; 1 John 2:1.
The promises of God. 2 Cor 7:1; 2 Pet 1:4.
The possession of all things. 1 Cor 3:21,22.
All things working together for their good. Rom 8:28; 2 Cor 4:15-17.
Their names written in the book life. Rev 13:8; 20:15.
Having God for their
King. Ps 5:2; 44:4; Is 44:6.
Glory. Ps 3:3; Is 60:19.
Salvation. Ps 18:2; 27:1; Is 12:2.
Father. Deut 32:6; Is 63:16; 64:8.
Redeemer. Ps 19:14; Is 43:14.
Friend. 2 Chr 20:7; James 2:23.
Helper. Ps 33:20; Heb 13:6.
Keeper. Ps 121:4,5.
Deliverer. 2 Sam 22:2; Ps 18:2.
Strength. Ps 18:2; 27:1; 46:1.
Refuge. Ps 46:1,11; Is 25:4.
Shield. Gen 15:1; Ps 84:11.
Tower. 2 Sam 22:3; Ps 61:3.
Light. Ps 27:1; Is 60:19; Mic 7:8.
Guide. Ps 48:14; Is 58:11.
Law-giver. Neh 9:13,14; Is 33:22.
Habitation. Ps 90:1; 91:9.
Portion. Ps 73:26; Lam 3:24.
Union in God and Christ. John 17:21.
Committing themselves to God. Ps 31:5; Acts 7:59; 2 Tim 1:12.

Calling upon God in trouble. Ps 50:15.
Suffering for Christ. Acts 5:41; Phil 1:29.
Profiting by chastisement. Ps 119:67; Heb 12:10,11.
Secure during public calamities. Job 5:20,23; Ps 27:1-5; 91:5-10.
Interceding for others. Gen 18:23-33; James 5:16.

Procrastination.

Condemned by Christ. Luke 9:59-62.
Saints avoid. Ps 27:8; 119:60.
To be avoided in
- Hearkening to God. Ps 95:7,8; Heb 3:7,8.
- Seeking God. Is 55:6.
- Glorifying God. Jer 13:16.
- Keeping God's commandments. Ps 119:60.
- Making offerings to God. Ex 22:29.
- Performance of vows. Deut 23:21; Eccl 5:4.

Motives for avoiding
- The present the accepted time. 2 Cor 6:2.
- The present the best time. Eccl 12:1.
- The uncertainty of life. Prov 27:1.

Danger of illustrated. Matt 5:25; Luke 13:25.
Exemplified
- Lot. Gen 19:16.
- Felix. Acts 24:25.

Promises of God, The.

Contained in the Scriptures. Rom 1:2.
Made in Christ. Eph 3:6; 2 Tim 1:1.
Made to
- Christ. Gal 3:16,19.
- Abraham. Gen 12:3,7; Gal 3:16.
- Isaac. Gen 26:3,4.
- Jacob. Gen 28:14.
- David. 2 Sam 7:12; Ps 89:3,4,35,36.
- The Israelites. Rom 9:4.
- The Fathers. Acts 13:32; 26:6,7.
- All who are called of God. Acts 2:39.
- Those who love him. James 1:12; 2:5.

Confirmed by an oath. Ps 89:3,4; Heb 8:6.
Covenant established upon. Heb 8:6.
God is faithful to. Titus 1:2; Heb 10:23.
God remembers. Ps 105:42; Luke 1:54,55.
Are
- Good. 1 Kin 8:56.
- Holy. Ps 105:42.
- Exceeding great and precious. 2 Pet 1:4.
- Confirmed in Christ. Rom 15:8.
- Yea and amen in Christ. 2 Cor 1:20.
- Fulfilled in Christ. Acts 13:23; Luke 1:69-73.
- Through the righteousness of faith. Rom 4:13,16.
- Obtained through faith. Heb 11:33.
- Given to those who believe. Gal 3:22.
- Inherited through faith and patience. Heb 6:12,15; 10:36.
- Performed in due season. Jer 33:14; Acts 7:17; Gal 4:4.

Not one shall fail. Josh 23:14; 1 Kin 8:56.
The law not against. Gal 3:21.
The law could not disannul. Gal 3:17.
Subjects of
- Christ. 2 Sam 7:12,13; Acts 13:22,23.
- The Holy Spirit. Acts 2:33; Eph 1:13.
- The gospel. Rom 1:1,2.
- Life in Christ. 2 Tim 1:1.
- A crown of life. James 1:12.
- Eternal life. Titus 1:2; 1 John 2:25.
- The life that now is. 1 Tim 4:8.
- Adoption. 2 Cor 6:18; 7:1.
- Preservation in affliction. Is 43:2.
- Blessing. Deut 1:11.
- Forgiveness of sins. Is 1:18; Heb 8:12.
- Putting the law into the heart. Jer 31:33; Heb 8:10.
- Second coming of Christ. 2 Pet 3:4.
- New heavens and earth. 2 Pet 3:13.
- Entering into rest. Josh 22:4; Heb 4:1.

Should lead to perfecting holiness. 2 Cor 7:1.
The inheritance of the saints is of. Rom 4:13; Gal 3:18.
Saints
- Children of. Rom 9:8; Gal 4:28.
- Heirs of. Gal 3:29; Heb 6:17; 11:9.
- Stagger not at. Rom 4:20.
- Have implicit confidence in. Heb 11:11.
- Expect the performance of. Luke 1:38,45; 2 Pet 3:13.
- Sometimes, through infirmity, tempted to doubt. Ps 77:8,10.
- Plead in prayer. Gen 32:9,12; 1 Chr 17:23,26; Is 43:26.

Should wait for the performance of. Acts 1:4.
Gentiles shall be partakers of. Eph 3:6.
Man, by nature, has no interest in. Eph 2:12.
Scoffers despise. 2 Pet 3:3,4.
Fear, lest ye come short of. Heb 4:1.

Prophecies Respecting Christ.

As the Son of God. Ps 2:7.
Fulfilled. Luke 1:32,35.
As the seed of the woman. Gen 3:15.
Fulfilled. Gal 4:4.
As the seed of Abraham. Gen 17:7; 22:18.
Fulfilled. Gal 3:16.
As the seed of Isaac. Gen 21:12.
Fulfilled. Heb 11:17-19.
As the seed of David. Ps 132:11; Jer 23:5.
Fulfilled. Acts 13:23; Rom 1:3.
His coming at a set time. Gen 49:10; Dan 9:24,25.
Fulfilled. Luke 2:1.
His being born of a virgin. Is 7:14.
Fulfilled. Matt 1:22,23; Luke 2:7.
His being called Immanuel. Is 7:14.
Fulfilled. Matt 1:22,23.
His being born in Bethlehem of Judea. Mic 5:2.
Fulfilled. Matt 2:1; Luke 2:4-6.
Great persons coming to adore him. Ps 72:10.
Fulfilled. Matt 2:1-11.
The slaying of the children of Bethlehem. Jer 31:15.
Fulfilled. Matt 2:16-18.
His being called out of Egypt. Hos 11:1.
Fulfilled. Matt 2:15.
His being preceded by John the Baptist. Is 40:3; Mal 3:1.
Fulfilled. Matt 3:1,3; Luke 1:17.
His being anointed with the Spirit. Ps 45:7; Is 11:2; 61:1.
Fulfilled. Matt 3:16; John 3:34; Acts 10:38.
His being a Prophet like to Moses. Deut 18:15-18.
Fulfilled. Acts 3:20-22.
His being a Priest after the order of Melchizedek. Ps 110:4.
Fulfilled. Heb 5:5,6.
His entering on his public ministry. Is 61:1,2.
Fulfilled. Luke 4:16-21,43.
His ministry commencing in Galilee. Is 9:1,2.
Fulfilled. Matt 4:12-16,23.
His entering publicly into Jerusalem. Zech 9:9.
Fulfilled. Matt 21:1-5.
His coming into the temple. Hag 2:7,9; Mal 3:1.
Fulfilled. Matt 21:12; Luke 2:27-32; John 2:13-16.
His poverty. Is 53:2.
Fulfilled. Mark 6:3; Luke 9:58.
His meekness and want of ostentatious. Is 42:2.
Fulfilled. Matt 12:15,16,19.
His tenderness and compassion. Is 40:11; 42:3.
Fulfilled. Matt 12:15,20; Heb 4:15.
His being without guile. Is 53:9.
Fulfilled. 1 Pet 2:22.
His zeal. Ps 69:9.
Fulfilled. John 2:17.
His preaching by parables. Ps 78:2.
Fulfilled. Matt 13:34,35.
His working miracles. Is 35:5,6.
Fulfilled. Matt 11:4-6; John 11:47.
His bearing reproach. Ps 22:6; 69:7,9,20.
Fulfilled. Rom 15:3.
His being rejected by his brethren. Ps 69:8; Is 63:3.
Fulfilled. John 1:11; 7:3.
His being a stone of stumbling to the Jews. Is 8:14.
Fulfilled. Rom 9:32; 1 Pet 2:8.
His being hated by the Jews. Ps 69:4; Is 49:7.
Fulfilled. John 15:24,25.
His being rejected by the Jewish rulers. Ps 118:22.
Fulfilled. Matt 21:42; John 7:48.
That the Jews and Gentiles should combine against Him. Ps 2:1,2.
Fulfilled. Luke 23:12; Acts 4:27.
His being betrayed by a friend. Ps 41:9; 55:12-14.
Fulfilled. John 13:18,21.
His disciples forsaking him. Zech 13:7.
Fulfilled. Matt 26:31,56.
His being sold for thirty pieces silver. Zech 11:12.
Fulfilled. Matt 26:15.
His price being given for the potter's field. Zech 11:13.
Fulfilled. Matt 27:7.
The intensity of his sufferings. Ps 22:14,15.
Fulfilled. Luke 22:42,44.
His sufferings being for others. Is 53:4-6,12; Dan 9:26.
Fulfilled. Matt 20:28.

His patience and silence under suffering. Is 53:7.
Fulfilled. Matt 26:63; 27:12-14.
His being smitten on the cheek. Mic 5:1.
Fulfilled. Matt 27:30.
His visage being marred. Is 52:14; 53:3.
Fulfilled. John 19:5.
His being spit on and scourged. Is 50:6.
Fulfilled. Mark 14:65; John 19:1.
His hands and feet being nailed to the cross. Ps 22:16.
Fulfilled. John 19:18; 20:25.
His being forsaken by God. Ps 22:1.
Fulfilled. Matt 27:46.
His being mocked. Ps 22:7,8.
Fulfilled. Matt 27:39-44.
Gall and vinegar being given him to drink. Ps 69:21.
Fulfilled. Matt 27:34.
His garments being parted, and lots cast for his vesture. Ps 22:18.
Fulfilled. Matt 27:35.
His being numbered with the transgressors. Is 53:12.
Fulfilled. Mark 15:28.
His intercession for His murderers. Is 53:12.
Fulfilled. Luke 23:34.
His death. Is 53:12.
Fulfilled. Matt 27:50.
That a bone of him should not be broken. Ex 12:46; Ps 34:20.
Fulfilled. John 19:33,36.
His being pierced. Zech 12:10.
Fulfilled. John 19:34,37.
His being buried with the rich. Is 53:9.
Fulfilled. Matt 27:57-60.
His flesh not seeing corruption. Ps 16:10.
Fulfilled. Acts 2:31.
His resurrection. Ps 16:10; Is 26:19.
Fulfilled. Luke 24:6,31,34.
His ascension. Ps 68:18.
Fulfilled. Luke 24:51; Acts 1:9.
His sitting on the right hand of God. Ps 110:1.
Fulfilled. Heb 1:3.
His exercising the priestly office in heaven. Zech 6:13.
Fulfilled. Rom 8:34.
His being the chief corner-stone of the Church. Is 28:16.
Fulfilled. 1 Pet 2:6,7.
His being King in Zion. Ps 2:6.
Fulfilled. Luke 1:32; John 18:33-37.
The conversion of the Gentiles to him. Is 11:10; 42:1.
Fulfilled. Matt 1:17,21; John 10:16; Acts 10:45,47.
His righteous government. Ps 45:6,7.
Fulfilled. John 5:30; Rev 19:11.
His universal dominion. Ps 72:8; Dan 7:14.
Fulfilled. Phil 2:9,11.
The perpetuity of his kingdom. Is 9:7; Dan 7:14.
Fulfilled. Luke 1:32,33.

PROPHECY.

Is the foretelling of future events. Gen 49:1; Num 24:14.
God is the Author of. Is 44:7; 45:21.
God gives, through Christ. Rev 1:1.
A gift of Christ. Eph 4:11; Rev 11:3.
A gift of the Holy Spirit. 1 Cor 12:10.
Came not by the will of man. 2 Pet 1:21.
Given from the beginning. Luke 1:70.
Is a sure word. 2 Pet 1:19.
They who uttered
Raised up by God. Amos 2:11.
Ordained by God. 1 Sam 3:20; Jer 1:5.
Sent by God. 2 Chr 36:15; Jer 7:25.
Sent by Christ. Matt 23:34.
Filled with the Holy Spirit. Luke 1:67.
Moved by the Holy Spirit. 2 Pet 1:21.
Spoke by the Holy Spirit. Acts 1:16; 11:28; 28:25.
Spoke in the name of the Lord. 2 Chr 33:18; James 5:10.
Spoke with authority. 1 Kin 17:1.
God accomplishes. Is 44:26; Acts 3:18.
Christ the great subject of. Acts 3:22-24; 10:43; 1 Pet 1:10,11.
Fulfilled respecting Christ. Luke 24:44.
Gift of, promised. Joel 2:28; Acts 2:16,17.
Is for the benefit of after ages. 1 Pet 1:12.
Is a light in dark place. 2 Pet 1:19.
Is not of private interpretation. 2 Pet 1:20.
Despise not. 1 Thess 5:20.
Give heed to. 2 Pet 1:19.
Receive in faith. 2 Chr 20:20; Luke 24:25.
Blessedness of reading, hearing, and keeping. Rev 1:3; 22:7.
Guilt of pretending to the gift of. Jer 14:14; 23:13,14; Ezek 13:2,3.
Punishment for
Not giving ear to. Neh 9:30.
Adding to, or taking from. Rev 22:18,19.
Pretending to the gift of. Deut 18:20; Jer 14:15; 23:15.
Gift of, sometimes possessed by unconverted men. Num 24:2-9; 1 Sam 19:20,23; Matt 7:22; John 11:49-51; 1 Cor 13:2.
How tested. Deut 13:1-3; 18:22.

PROPHETS.

God spoke of old by. Hos 12:10; Heb 1:1.
The messengers of God. 2 Chr 36:15; Is 44:26.
The servants of God. Jer 35:15.
The watchmen of Israel. Ezek 3:17.
Were called
Men of God. 1 Sam 9:6.
Prophets of God. Ezra 5:2.
Holy prophets. Luke 1:70; Rev 18:20; 22:6.
Holy men of God. 2 Pet 1:21.
Seers. 1 Sam 9:9.
Were esteemed as holy men. 2 Kin 4:9.
Women sometimes endowed as. Joel 2:28.
God communicated to
His secret things. Amos 3:7.
At various times and in different ways. Heb 1:1.
By an audible voice. Num 12:8; 1 Sam 3:4-14.
By angels. Dan 8:15-26; Rev 22:8,9.
By dreams and visions. Num 12:6; Joel 2:28.
Were under the influence of the Holy Spirit while prophesying. Luke 1:67; 2 Pet 1:21.
Spoke in the name of the Lord. 2 Chr 33:18; Ezek 3:11; James 5:10.
Frequently spoke in parables and riddles. 2 Sam 12:1-6; Is 5:1-7; Ezek 17:2-10.
Frequently in their actions, etc. were made signs to the people. Is 20:2-4; Jer 19:1,10,11; 27:2,3; 43:9; 51:63; Ezek 4:1-13; 5:1-4; 7:23; 12:3-7; 21:6,7; 24:1-24; Hos 1:2-9.
Frequently left without divine communication on account of sins of the people. 1 Sam 28:6; Lam 2:9; Ezek 7:26.
Were required
To be bold and undaunted. Ezek 2:6; 3:8,9.
To be vigilant and faithful. Ezek 3:17-21.
To receive with attention all God's communications. Ezek 3:10.
Not to speak anything but what they received from God. Deut 18:20.
To declare everything that the Lord commanded. Jer 26:2.
Sometimes received divine communications and uttered predictions under great bodily and mental excitement. Jer 23:9; Ezek 3:14,15; Dan 7:28; 10:8; Hab 3:2,16.
Sometimes uttered their predictions in verse. Deut 32:44; Is 5:1.
Often accompanied by music while predicting. 1 Sam 10:5; 2 Kin 3:15.
Often committed their predictions to writing. 2 Chr 21:12; Jer 36:2.
Writings of, read in the synagogues every Sabbath. Luke 4:17; Acts 13:15.
Ordinary
Numerous in Israel. 1 Sam 10:5; 1 Kin 18:4.
Trained up and instructed in schools. 2 Kin 2:3,5; 1 Sam 19:20.
The sacred bards of the Jews. Ex 15:20,21; 1 Sam 10:5,10; 1 Chr 25:1.
Extraordinary
Specially raised up on occasions of emergency. 1 Sam 3:19-21; Is 6:8,9; Jer 1:5.
Often endued with miraculous power. Ex 4:1-4; 1 Kin 17:23; 2 Kin 5:3-8.
Frequently married men. 2 Kin 4:1; Ezek 24:18.
Wore a coarse dress of hair-cloth. 2 Kin 1:8; Zech 13:4; Matt 3:4; Rev 11:3.
Often led a wandering and unsettled life. 1 Kin 18:10-12; 19:3,8,15; 2 Kin 4:10.
Simple in their manner of life. Matt 3:4.
The historiographers of the Jewish nation. 1 Chr 29:29; 2 Chr 9:29.
The interpreters of dreams. Dan 1:17.
Were consulted in all difficulties. 1 Sam 9:6; 28:15; 1 Kin 14:2-4; 22:7.
Presented with gifts by those who consulted them. 1 Sam 9:7,8; 1 Kin 14:3.
Sometimes thought it right to reject presents. 2 Kin 5:15,16.
Were sent to
Reprove the wicked and exhort to repentance. 2 Kin 17:13; 2 Chr 24:19; Jer 25:4,5.

Denounce the wickedness of kings. 1 Sam 15:10,16-19; 2 Sam 12:7-12; 1 Kin 18:18; 21:17-22.
Exhort to faithfulness and constancy in God's service. 2 Chr 15:1,2,7.
Predict the coming of Christ. Luke 24:44; John 1:45; Acts 3:24; 10:43.
Predict the downfall of nations. Is 15:1; 17:1; Jer 47:1-51:64.
Felt deeply on account of the calamities which they predicted. Is 16:9-11; Jer 9:1-7.
Predictions of
Frequently proclaimed at the gate of the Lord's house. Jer 7:2.
Proclaimed in the cities and streets. Jer 11:6.
Written on tables and fixed up in some public place. Hab 2:2.
Written on rolls and read to the people. Is 8:1; Jer 36:2.
Were all fulfilled. 2 Kin 10:10; Is 44:26; Acts 3:18; Rev 10:7.
Assisted the Jews in their great national undertakings. Ezra 5:2.
Mentioned in Scripture
Enoch. Gen 5:21-24; Jude 1:14.
Noah. Gen 9:25-27.
Jacob. Gen 49:1.
Aaron. Ex 7:1.
Moses. Deut 18:18.
Miriam. Ex 15:20.
Deborah. Judg 4:4.
Prophet set to Israel. Judg 6:8.
Prophet sent to Eli. 1 Sam 2:27.
Samuel. 1 Sam 3:20.
David. Ps 16:8-11; Acts 2:25,30.
Nathan. 2 Sam 7:2; 12:1; 1 Kin 1:10.
Zadok. 2 Sam 15:27.
Gad. 2 Sam 24:11; 1 Chr 29:29.
Ahijah. 1 Kin 11:29; 12:15; 2 Chr 9:29.
Prophet of Judah. 1 Kin 13:1.
Iddo. 2 Chr 9:29; 12:15.
Shemaiah. 1 Kin 12:22; 2 Chr 12:7,15.
Azariah the son of Oded. 2 Chr 15:2,8.
Hanani. 2 Chr 16:7.
Jehu the son of Hanani. 1 Kin 16:1,7,12.
Elijah. 1 Kin 17:1.
Elisha. 1 Kin 19:16.
Micaiah the son of Imlah. 1 Kin 22:7,8.
Jonah. 2 Kin 14:25; Jon 1:1; Matt 12:39.
Isaiah. 2 Kin 19:2; 2 Chr 26:22; Is 1:1.
Hosea. Hos 1:1.
Amos. Amos 1:1; 7:14,15.
Micah. Mic 1:1.
Oded. 2 Chr 28:9.
Nahum. Nah 1:1.
Joel. Joel 1:1; Acts 2:16.
Zephaniah. Zeph 1:1.
Huldah. 2 Kin 22:14.
Jeduthun. 2 Chr 35:15.
Jeremiah. 2 Chr 36:12,21; Jer 1:1,2.
Habakkuk. Hab 1:1.
Obadiah. Obad 1.
Ezekiel. Ezek 1:3.
Daniel. Dan 12:11; Matt 24:15.
Haggai. Ezra 5:1; 6:14; Hag 1:1.
Zechariah son of Iddo. Ezra 5:1; Zech 1:1.
Malachi. Mal 1:1.
Zacharias the father of John. Luke 1:67.
Anna. Luke 2:36.
Agabus. Acts 11:28; 21:10.
Daughters of Philip. Acts 21:9.
Paul. 1 Tim 4:1.
Peter. 2 Pet 2:1,2.
John. Rev 1:1.
One generally attached to the king's household. 2 Sam 24:11; 2 Chr 29:25; 35:15.
The Jews
Require to hear and believe. Deut 18:15; 2 Chr 20:20.
Often tried to make them speak smooth things. 1 Kin 22:13; Is 30:10; Amos 2:12.
Persecuted them. 2 Chr 36:16; Matt 5:12.
Often imprisoned them. 1 Kin 22:27; Jer 32:2; 37:15,16.
Often put them to death. 1 Kin 18:13; 19:10; Matt 23:34-37.
Often left without, on account of sin. 1 Sam 3:1; Ps 74:9; Amos 8:11,12.
Were mighty through faith. Heb 11:32-40.
Great patience of, under suffering. James 5:10.
God avenged all injuries done to. 2 Kin 9:7; 1 Chr 16:21,22; Matt 23:35-38; Luke 11:50.
Christ predicted to exercise the office of. Deut 18:15; Acts 3:22.
Christ exercised the office of. Matt 24:1-25:46; Mark 10:32-34.

Prophets, False.

Pretended to be sent by God. Jer 23:17,18,31.
Not sent or commissioned by God. Jer 14:14; 23:21; 29:31.
Made use of by God to prove Israel. Deut 13:3.
Described as
Light and treacherous. Zeph 3:4.
Covetous. Mic 3:11.
Crafty. Matt 7:15.
Drunken. Is 28:7.
Immoral and profane. Jer 23:11,14.
Women sometimes acted as. Neh 6:14; Rev 2:20.
Called foolish prophets. Ezek 13:2.
Compared to foxes in the desert. Ezek 13:4.
Compared to wind. Jer 5:13.
Influenced by evil spirits. 1 Kin 22:21,22.
Prophesied
Falsely. Jer 5:31.
Lies in the name of the Lord. Jer 14:14.
Out of their own heart. Jer 23:16,26; Ezek 13:2.
In the name of false gods. Jer 2:8.
Peace, when there was no peace. Jer 6:14; 23:17; Ezek 13:10; Mic 3:5.
Often practised divination and witchcraft. Jer 14:14; Ezek 22:28; Acts 13:6.
Often pretended to dream. Jer 23:28,32.
Often deceived by God as a judgment. Ezek 14:9.
The people
Led into error. Jer 23:13; Mic 3:5.
Made to forget God's name by. Jer 23:27.
Deprived of God's word by. Jer 23:30.
Taught profaneness and sin by. Jer 23:14,15.
Oppressed and defrauded by. Ezek 22:25.
Warned not to listen to. Deut 13:3; Jer 23:16; 27:9,15,16.
Encouraged and praised. Jer 5:31; Luke 6:26.
Mode of trying and detecting. Deut 13:1,2; 18:21,22; 1 John 4:1-3.
Predicted to arise
Before destruction of Jerusalem. Matt 24:11,24.
In the latter times. 2 Pet 2:1.
Judgments denounced against. Jer 8:1,2; 14:15; 28:16,17; 29:32.
Involved the people in their own ruin. Is 9:15,16; Jer 20:6; Ezek 14:10.

Proselytes.

Described. Esth 8:17; Is 56:3.
Required
To give up all heathen practices. Ezra 6:21.
To give up all heathen associates. Ruth 1:16; 2:11; Ps 45:10; Luke 14:26.
To be circumcised. Gen 17:13; Ex 12:48.
To enter into covenant to serve the Lord. Deut 29:10-13; Neh 10:28,29.
To observe the law of Moses as Jews. Ex 12:49.
Unfaithfulness in, punished. Ezek 14:7.
From the Ammonites and Moabites restricted for ever from holding office in the congregation. Deut 23:3.
From the Egyptians and Edomites restricted to the third generation from holding office in the congregation. Deut 23:7,8.
Were entitled to all privileges. Ex 12:48; Is 56:3-7.
Went up to the feasts. Acts 2:10; 8:27.
Pharisees, zealous in making. Matt 23:15.
Many, embraced the gospel. Acts 6:5; 13:43.
Later called devout Greeks. John 12:20; Acts 17:4.

Protection.

God is able to afford. 1 Pet 1:5; Jude 1:24.
God is faithful to afford. 1 Thess 5:23,24; 2 Thess 3:3.
Of God is
Indispensable. Ps 127:1.
Seasonable. Ps 46:1.
Unfailing. Deut 31:6; Josh 1:5.
Effectual. John 10:28-30; 2 Cor 12:9.
Uninterrupted. Ps 121:3.
Encouraging. Is 41:10; 50:7.
Perpetual. Ps 121:8.
Often afforded through means inadequate in themselves. Judg 7:7; 1 Sam 17:45,50; 2 Chr 14:11.
Is afforded to
Those who hearken to God. Prov 1:33.

Returning sinners. Job 22:23,25.
The perfect in heart. 2 Chr 16:9.
The poor. Ps 14:6; 72:12-14.
The oppressed. Ps 9:9.
The Church. Ps 48:3; Zech 2:4,5.
Is vouchsafed to saints in
Preserving them. Ps 145:20.
Strengthening them. 2 Tim 4:17.
Upholding them. Ps 37:17,24; 63:8.
Keeping their feet. 1 Sam 2:9; Prov 3:26.
Keeping them from evil. 2 Thess 3:3.
Keeping them from falling. Jude 1:24.
Keeping them in the way. Ex 23:20.
Keeping them from temptation. Rev 3:10.
Providing a refuge for them. Prov 14:26; Is 4:6; 32:2.
Defending them against their enemies. Deut 20:1-4; 33:27; Is 59:19.
Defeating the counsels of enemies. Is 8:10.
Temptation. 1 Cor 10:13; 2 Pet 2:9.
Persecution. Luke 21:18.
Calamities. Ps 57:1; 59:16.
All dangers. Ps 91:3-7.
All places. Gen 28:15; 2 Chr 16:9.
Sleep. Ps 3:5; 4:8; Prov 3:24.
Death. Ps 23:4.
Saints
Acknowledge God as their. Ps 18:2; 62:2; 89:18.
Pray for. Ps 17:5,8; Is 51:9.
Praise God for. Ps 5:11.
Withdrawn from the
Disobedient. Lev 26:14-17.
Backsliding. Josh 23:12,13; Judg 10:13.
Presumptuous. Num 14:40-45.
Unbelieving. Is 7:9.
Obstinately impenitent. Matt 23:38.
Not to be found in
Idols. Deut 32:37-39; Is 46:7.
Man. Ps 146:3; Is 30:7.
Riches. Prov 11:4,28; Zeph 1:18.
Hosts. Josh 11:4-8; Ps 33:16.
Horses. Ps 33:17; Prov 21:31.
Illustrated. Deut 32:11; Ps 125:1,2; Prov 18:10; Is 25:4; 31:5; Luke 13:34.
Exemplified
Abraham. Gen 15:1.
Jacob. Gen 48:16.
Joseph. Gen 49:23-25.
Israel. Josh 24:17.
David. Ps 18:1,2.
Shadrach etc. Dan 3:28.
Daniel. Dan 6:22.
Peter. Acts 12:4-7.
Paul. Acts 18:10; 26:17.

Providence of God, The.

Is his care over his works. Ps 145:9.
Is exercised in
Preserving his creatures. Neh 9:6; Ps 36:6; Matt 10:29.
Providing for his creatures. Ps 104:27,28; 136:25; 147:9; Matt 6:26.
The special preservation of saints. Ps 37:28; 91:11; Matt 10:30.
Prospering saints. Gen 24:48,56.
Protecting saints. Ps 91:4; 140:7.
Delivering saints. Ps 91:3; Is 31:5.
Leading saints. Deut 8:2,15; Is 31:5; 63:12.
Bringing His words to pass. Num 26:65; Josh 21:45; Luke 21:32,33.
Ordering the ways of men. Prov 16:9; 19:21; 20:24.
Ordaining the conditions and circumstances of men. 1 Sam 2:7,8; Ps 75:6,7.
Determining the period of human life. Ps 31:15; 39:5; Acts 17:26.
Defeating wicked designs. Ex 15:9-19; 2 Sam 17:14,15; Ps 33:10.
Overruling wicked designs for good. Gen 45:5-7; 50:20; Phil 1:12.
Preserving the course of nature. Gen 8:22; Job 26:10; Ps 104:5-9.
Directing all events. Josh 7:14; 1 Sam 6:7-10,12; Prov 16:33; Is 44:7; Acts 1:26.
Ruling the elements. Job 37:9-13; Is 50:2; John 1:4,15; Nah 1:4.
Ordering the minutest matters. Matt 10:29,30; Luke 21:18.
Is righteous. Ps 145:17; Dan 4:37.
Is ever watchful. Ps 121:4; Is 27:3.
Is all pervading. Ps 139:1-5.
Sometimes dark and mysterious. Ps 36:6; 73:16; 77:19; Rom 11:33.
All things are ordered by
For his glory. Is 63:14.
For good to saints. Rom 8:28.
The wicked made to promote the designs. Is 10:5-12; Acts 3:17,18.
To be acknowledged
In prosperity. Deut 8:18; 1 Chr 29:12.
In adversity. Job 1:21; Ps 119:15.
In public calamities. Amos 3:6.
In our daily support. Gen 48:15.
In all things. Prov 3:6.
Cannot be defeated. 1 Kin 22:30,34; Prov 21:30.
Man's efforts are vain without. Ps 127:1,2; Prov 21:31.
Saints should
Trust in. Matt 6:33,34; 10:9,29-31.
Have full confidence in. Ps 16:8; 139:10.
Commit their works to. Prov 16:3.
Encourage themselves. 1 Sam 30:6.
Pray in dependence upon. Acts 12:5.
Pray to be guided by. Gen 24:12-14; 28:20,21; Acts 1:24.
Result of depending upon. Luke 22:35.
Connected with the use of means. 1 Kin 21:19; 22:37,38; Mic 5:2; Luke 2:1-4; Acts 27:22,31,32.
Danger of denying. Is 10:13-17; Ezek 28:2-10; Dan 4:29-31; Hos 2:8,9.

Prudence.

Exhibited in the manifestation of God's grace. Eph 1:8.
Exemplified by Christ. Is 52:13; Matt 21:24-27; 22:15-21.
Intimately connected with wisdom. Prov 8:12.
The wise celebrated for. Prov 16:21.
They who have
Get knowledge. Prov 18:15.
Deal with knowledge. Prov 13:16.
Look well to their goings. Prov 14:15.
Understand the ways of God. Hos 14:9.
Understand their own ways. Prov 14:8.
Crowned with knowledge. Prov 14:18.
Not ostentatious of knowledge. Prov 12:23.
Foresee and avoid evil. Prov 22:3.
Are preserved by it. Prov 2:11.
Suppress angry feelings. Prov 12:16; 19:11.
Regard reproof. Prov 15:5.
Keep silence in the evil time. Amos 5:13.
Saints act with. Ps 112:5.
Saints should especially exercise, in their intercourse with unbelievers. Matt 10:16; Eph 5:15; Col 4:5.
Virtuous wives act with. Prov 31:16,26.
The young should cultivate. Prov 3:21.
Of the wicked
Fails in times of perplexity. Jer 49:7.
Keeps them from the knowledge of the gospel. Matt 11:25.
Denounced by God. Is 5:21; 29:15.
Defeated by God. Is 29:14; 1 Cor 1:19.
Necessity for—Illustrated. Matt 25:3,9; Luke 14:28-32.
Exemplified
Jacob. Gen 32:3-23.
Joseph. Gen 41:39.
Jethro. Ex 18:19-23.
Gideon. Judg 8:1-3.
David. 1 Sam 16:18.
Abigail. 1 Sam 25:23-31; 2 Sam 15:32-34; 17:6-14.
Aged counsellors of Rehoboam. 1 Kin 12:7.
Solomon. 2 Chr 2:12.
Nehemiah. Neh 2:12-16; 4:13-18.
The poor wise man. Eccl 9:15.
The scribe. Mark 12:32-34.
Gamaliel. Acts 5:34-39.
Sergius Paulus. Acts 13:7.
Paul. Acts 23:6.

Publicans.

The collectors of the public taxes. Luke 5:27.
Suspected of extortion. Luke 3:13.
Often guilty of extortion. Luke 19:8.
Chiefs of, were very rich. Luke 19:2.
The Jews
Despised. Luke 18:11.
Classed with the most infamous characters. Matt 11:19; 21:32.
Despised our Lord for associating with. Matt 9:11; 11:19.
Often kind to their friends. Matt 5:46,47.
Often hospitable. Luke 5:29; 19:6.
Many of
Believed the preaching of John. Matt 21:32.
Received John's baptism. Luke 3:12; 7:29.
Attended the preaching of Christ. Mark 2:15; Luke 15:1.
Embraced the gospel. Matt 21:31.
Matthew the apostle was of. Matt 10:3.

Punishment of the Wicked, The.

Is from God. Lev 26:18; Is 13:11.
On account of their
Sin. Lam 3:39.
Iniquity. Jer 36:31; Ezek 3:17-18; 18:4,13,20; Amos 3:2.

Idolatry. Lev 26:30; Is 10:10,11.
Rejection of the law of God. 1 Sam 15:23; Hos 4:6-9.
Ignorance of God. 2 Thess 1:8.
Evil ways and doings. Jer 21:14; Hos 4:9; 12:2.
Pride. Is 10:12; 24:21; Luke 14:11.
Unbelief. Mark 16:16; Rom 11:20; Heb 3:18,19; 4:2.
Covetousness. Is 57:17; Jer 51:13.
Oppressing. Is 49:26; Jer 30:16,20.
Persecuting. Jer 11:21,22; Matt 23:34-36.
Disobeying God. Neh 9:26,27; Eph 5:6.
Disobeying the gospel. 2 Thess 1:8.
Is the fruit of their sin. Job 4:8; Prov 22:8; Rom 6:21; Gal 6:8.
Is the reward of their sins. Ps 91:8; Is 3:11; Jer 16:18; Rom 6:23; Heb 2:2.
Often brought about by their evil designs. Esth 7:10; Ps 37:15; 57:6.
Often commences in this life. Prov 11:31.
In this life by
Sickness. Lev 26:16; Ps 78:50.
Famine. Lev 26:19,20,26,29; Ps 107:34.
Noisome beasts. Lev 26:22.
War. Lev 26:25,32,33; Jer 6:4.
Deliverance to enemies. Neh 9:27.
Fear. Lev 26:36,37; Job 18:11.
Reprobate mind. Rom 1:28.
Put in slippery places. Ps 73:3-19.
Trouble and distress. Is 8:22; Zeph 1:15.
Cutting off. Ps 94:23.
Bringing down their pride. Is 13:11.
Future, shall be awarded by Christ. Matt 16:27; 25:31,41.
Future described as
Hell. Ps 9:17; Matt 5:29; Luke 12:5; 16:23.
Darkness. Matt 8:12; 2 Pet 2:17.
Death. Rom 5:12-17; 6:23.
Resurrection of damnation. John 5:29.
Rising to shame and everlasting contempt. Dan 12:2.
Everlasting destruction. Ps 52:5; 92:7; 2 Thess 1:9.
Everlasting fire. Matt 25:41; Jude 1:7.
Second death. Rev 2:11; 21:8.
Damnation of hell. Matt 23:33.
Eternal damnation. Mark 3:29.
Blackness of darkness. 2 Pet 2:17; Jude 1:13.
Everlasting burnings. Is 33:14.
The wrath of God. John 3:36.
Wine of the wrath of God. Rev 14:10.
Torment with fire. Rev 14:10.
Torment for ever and ever. Rev 14:11.
The righteousness of God requires. 2 Thess 1:6.
Often sudden and unexpected. Ps 35:8; 64:7; Prov 29:1; Luke 12:20; 1 Thess 5:3.
Shall be
According to their deeds. Matt 16:27; Rom 2:6,9; 2 Cor 5:10.
According to the knowledge possessed by them. Luke 12:47,48.
Increased by neglect of privileges. Matt 11:21-24; Luke 10:13-15.
Without mitigation. Luke 16:23-26.
Accompanied by remorse. Is 66:24; Mark 9:44.
No combination avails against. Prov 11:21.
Deferred, emboldens them in sin. Eccl 8:11.
Should be a warning to others. Num 26:10; 1 Cor 10:6-11; Jude 1:7.
Consummated at the day of judgment. Matt 25:31,46; Rom 2:5,16; 2 Pet 2:9.

PUNISHMENTS.

Antiquity of. Gen 4:13,14.
Power of inflicting, given to magistrates. Job 31:11; Rom 13:4.
Designed to be a warning to others. Deut 13:11; 17:13; 19:20.
Were inflicted
On the guilty. Deut 24:16; Prov 17:26.
Without pity. Deut 19:13,21.
Without partiality. Deut 13:6-8.
By order of magistrates. Acts 16:22.
By order of kings. 2 Sam 1:13-16; 1 Kin 2:23-46.
Immediately after sentence was passed. Deut 25:2; Josh 7:25.
By the witnesses. Deut 13:9; 17:7; John 8:7; Acts 7:58,59.
By the people. Num 15:35,36; Deut 13:9.
By soldiers. 2 Sam 1:15; Matt 27:27-35.
Sometimes deferred until God was consulted. Num 15:34.
Sometimes deferred for a considerable time. 1 Kin 2:5,6,8,9.
Secondary kinds of
Imprisonment. Ezra 7:26; Matt 5:25.
Confinement in a dungeon. Jer 38:6; Zech 9:11.
Confinement in stocks. Jer 20:2; Acts 16:24.
Fine, or giving of money. Ex 21:22; Deut 22:19.
Restitution. Ex 21:36; 22:1-4; Lev 6:4,5; 24:18.
Retaliation or injuring according to the injury done. Ex 21:24; Deut 19:21.
Binding with chains and fetters. Ps 105:18.
Scourging. Deut 25:2,3; Matt 27:26; Acts 22:25; 2 Cor 11:24.
Selling the criminal. Matt 18:25.
Banishment. Ezra 7:26; Rev 1:9.
Torturing. Matt 18:34; Heb 11:37.
Putting out the eyes. Judg 16:21; 1 Sam 11:2.
Cutting off hands and feet. 2 Sam 4:12.
Mutilating the hands and feet. Judg 1:5-7.
Cutting off nose and ears. Ezek 23:25.
Plucking out the hair. Neh 13:25; Is 50:6.
Confiscating the property. Ezra 7:26.
Inflicting of capital, not permitted to the Jews by the Romans. John 18:31.
Capital kinds of
Burning. Gen 38:24; Lev 20:14; Dan 3:6.
Hanging. Num 25:4; Deut 21:22,23; Josh 8:29; 2 Sam 21:12; Esth 7:9,10.
Crucifying. Matt 20:19; 27:35.
Beheading. Gen 40:19; Mark 6:16,27.
Slaying with the sword. 1 Sam 15:33; Acts 12:2.
Stoning. Lev 24:14; Deut 13:10; Acts 7:59.
Cutting in pieces. Dan 2:5; Matt 24:51.
Sawing asunder. Heb 11:37.
Exposing to wild beasts. Dan 6:16,24; 1 Cor 15:32.
Bruising in mortars. Prov 27:22.
Casting headlong from a rock. 2 Chr 25:12.
Casting into the sea. Matt 18:6.
Strangers not exempted from. Lev 20:2.
Were sometimes commuted. Ex 21:29,30.
For murder not to be commuted. Num 35:31,32.

PURIFICATIONS.

Of Israel at the exodus. Ex 14:22; 1 Cor 10:2.
Of Israel before receiving the law. Ex 19:10.
Of priests before consecration. Ex 29:4.
Of Levites before consecration. Num 8:6,7.
Of high priest on Day of Atonement. Lev 16:4,24.
Of things for burnt offerings. 2 Chr 4:6.
Of individuals who were ceremonially unclean. Lev 15:2-13; 17:15; 22:4-7; Num 19:7-12,21.
Of the healed leper. Lev 14:8,9.
Of Nazirites after vow expired. Acts 21:24,26.
Used by the devout before entering God's house. Ps 26:6; Heb 10:22.
Multiplied by traditions. Matt 15:2; Mark 7:3,4.
Means used for
Water of separation. Num 19:9.
Running water. Lev 15:13.
Water mixed with blood. Ex 24:5-8; Heb 9:19.
Was by
Sprinkling. Num 19:13,18; Heb 9:19.
Washing parts of the body. Ex 30:19.
Washing the whole body. Lev 8:6; 14:9.
Of priests performed in the brazen laver. Ex 30:18; 2 Chr 4:6.
Vessels in the houses of the Jews for. John 2:6.
Consequence of neglecting those prescribed by law. Lev 17:16; Num 19:13,20.
Availed to sanctifying the flesh. Heb 9:13.
Insufficient for spiritual purification. Job 9:30,31; Jer 2:22.
The Jews laid great stress on. John 3:25.
Illustrative of
Purification by the blood of Christ. Heb 9:9-12.
Regeneration. Eph 5:26; 1 John 1:7.

RAIN.

Occasioned by the condensing of the clouds. Job 36:27,28; Ps 77:17; Eccl 11:3.
God
Made a decree for. Job 28:26.

Prepares. Ps 147:8.
Gives. Job 5:10.
Causes, to come down. Joel 2:23.
Exhibits goodness in giving. Acts 14:17.
Exhibits greatness in giving. Job 36:26,27.
Sends upon the evil and good. Matt 5:45.
Should be praised for. Ps 147:7,8.
Should be feared on account of. Jer 5:24.
Impotence of idols exhibited in not being able to give. Jer 14:22.
Not sent upon the earth immediately after creation. Gen 2:5.
Rarely falls in Egypt. Deut 11:10; Zech 14:18.
Canaan abundantly supplied with. Deut 11:11.
Designed for
Refreshing the earth. Ps 68:9; 72:6.
Making fruitful the earth. Heb 6:7.
Replenishing the springs and fountains of the earth. Ps 104:8.
Promised in due season to the obedient. Lev 26:4; Deut 11:14; Ezek 34:26,27.
Frequently withheld on account of iniquity. Deut 11:17; Jer 3:3; 5:25; Amos 4:7.
The want of
Causes the earth to open. Job 29:23; Jer 14:4.
Dries up springs and fountains. 1 Kin 17:7.
Occasions famine. 1 Kin 18:1,2.
Removed by prayer. 1 Kin 8:35,36; James 5:18.
Withheld for three years and six months in the days of Elijah. 1 Kin 17:1; James 5:17.
Divided into
Great. Ezra 10:9.
Plentiful. Ps 68:9.
Overflowing. Ezek 38:22.
Sweeping. Prov 28:3.
Small. Job 37:6.
The former, after harvest, to prepare for sowing. Deut 11:14; Jer 5:24.
The latter, before harvest. Joel 2:23; Zech 10:1.
The rainbow often appears during. Gen 9:14; Ezek 1:28.
Often succeeded by heat and sunshine. 2 Sam 23:4; Is 18:4.
The appearance of a cloud from the west indicated. 1 Kin 18:44; Luke 12:54.
The north wind drives away. Prov 25:23.
Unusual in harvest time. Prov 26:1.
Thunder and lightning often with. Ps 135:7.
Storm and tempest often with. Matt 7:25,27.
Instances of extraordinary
Time of the flood. Gen 7:4,12.
Plague of, upon Egypt. Ex 9:18,23.
During wheat harvest in the days of Samuel. 1 Sam 12:17,18.
After long drought in Ahab's reign. 1 Kin 18:45.
After the captivity. Ezra 10:9,13.
Often impeded travelling in the east. 1 Kin 18:44; Is 4:6.
Often destroyed houses. Ezek 13:13-15; Matt 7:27.
Illustrative
Of the word of God. Is 55:10,11.
Of the doctrine of faithful ministers. Deut 32:2.
Of Christ in the communication of his graces. Ps 72:6; Hos 6:3.
Of spiritual blessings. Ps 68:9; 84:6; Ezek 34:26.
Of righteousness. Hos 10:12.
(Destructive,) of God's judgments. Job 20:23; Ps 11:6; Ezek 38:22.
(Destructive,) of a poor man oppressing the poor. Prov 28:3.

Raven, The.

Unclean and not to be eaten. Lev 11:15; Deut 14:14.
Called the raven of the valley. Prov 30:17.
Described as
Black. Song 5:11.
Solitary in disposition. Is 34:11.
Improvident. Luke 12:24.
Carnivorous. Prov 30:17.
God provides food for. Job 38:41; Ps 147:9; Luke 12:24.
Sent by Noah from the ark. Gen 8:7.
Elijah fed by. 1 Kin 17:4-6.
Plumage of, illustrative of the glory of Christ. Song 5:11.

Reaping.

Is the cutting of the corn in harvest. Job 24:6; Lev 23:10.
The sickle used for. Deut 16:9; Mark 4:29.
Both men and women engaged in. Ruth 2:8,9.
The Jews not to reap
The corners of their fields. Lev 19:9; 23:22.
During the Sabbatical year. Lev 25:5.
During the year of jubilee. Lev 25:11.
The fields of others. Deut 23:25.
Mode of gathering the corn for, alluded to. Ps 129:7; Is 17:5.
Corn after, was bound up into sheaves. Gen 37:7; Ps 129:7.
Persons engaged in
Under the guidance of a steward. Ruth 2:5,6.
Visited by the master. Ruth 2:4; 2 Kin 4:18.
Fed by the master who himself presided at their meals. Ruth 2:14.
Received wages. John 4:36; James 5:4.
A time of great rejoicing. Ps 126:5,6.
The Jews often hindered from, on account of their sins. Mic 6:15.
Often unprofitable on account of sin. Jer 12:13.
Illustrative of
Receiving the reward of wickedness. Job 4:8; Prov 22:8; Hos 8:7; Gal 6:8.
Receiving the reward of righteousness. Hos 10:12; Gal 6:8,9.
Ministers receiving temporal provision for spiritual labours. 1 Cor 9:11.
Gathering in souls to God. John 4:38.
The judgments of God on the antichristian world. Rev 14:14-16.
The final judgment. Matt 13:30,39-43.

Rebellion Against God.

Forbidden. Num 14:9; Josh 22:19.
Provokes God. Num 16:30; Neh 9:26.
Provokes Christ. Ex 23:20,21; 1 Cor 10:9.
Vexes the Holy Spirit. Is 63:10.
Exhibited in
Unbelief. Deut 9:23; Ps 106:24,25.
Rejecting his government. 1 Sam 8:7; 15:23.
Revolting from him. Is 1:5; 31:6.
Despising his law. Neh 9:26.
Despising his counsels. Ps 107:11.
Distrusting his power. Ezek 17:15.
Murmuring against him. Num 20:3,10.
Refusing to hearken to him. Deut 9:23; Ezek 20:8; Zech 7:11.
Departing from him. Is 59:13.
Rebellion against governors appointed by him. Josh 1:18.
Departing from his precepts. Dan 9:5.
Departing from his instituted worship. Ex 32:8,9; Josh 22:16-19.
Sinning against light. Job 24:13; John 15:22; Acts 13:41.
Walking after our own thoughts. Is 65:2.
Connected with
Stubbornness. Deut 31:27.
Injustice and corruption. Is 1:23.
Contempt of God. Ps 107:11.
Man is prone to. Deut 31:27; Rom 7:14-18.
The heart is the seat of. Jer 5:23; Matt 15:18,19; Heb 3:12.
They who are guilty of
Aggravate their sin by. Job 34:27.
Practise hypocrisy to hide. Hos 7:14.
Persevere in. Deut 9:7,24.
Increase in, though chastised. Is 1:5.
Warned not to exalt themselves. Ps 66:7.
Denounced. Is 30:1.
Have God as their enemy. Is 63:10.
Have God's hand against them. 1 Sam 12:15; Ps 106:26,27.
Impoverished for. Ps 68:6.
Brought low for. Ps 107:11,12.
Delivered into the hands of enemies on account of. Neh 9:26,27.
Cast out in their sins for. Ps 5:10.
Cast out of the church for. Ezek 20:38.
Restored through Christ alone. Ps 68:18.
Heinousness of. 1 Sam 15:23.
Guilt of
Aggravated by God's fatherly care. Is 1:2.
Aggravated by God's unceasing invitations to return to him. Is 65:2.
To be deprecated. Josh 22:29.
To be confessed. Lam 1:18,20; Dan 9:5.
God alone can forgive. Dan 9:9.
God is ready to forgive. Neh 9:17.
Religious instruction designed to prevent. Ps 78:5,8.
Promises to those who avoid. Deut 28:1-13; 1 Sam 12:14.

Forgiven upon repentance. Neh 9:26,27.
Ministers
Cautioned against. Ezek 2:8.
Sent to those guilty of. Ezek 2:3-7; 3:4-9; Mark 12:4-8.
Should warn against. Num 14:9.
Should testify against. Is 30:8,9; Ezek 17:12; 44:6.
Should remind their people of past. Deut 9:7; 31:27.
Punishment for. Lev 26:14-39; 1 Sam 12:15; Is 1:20; Jer 4:16-18; Ezek 20:8,38.
Punishment for teaching. Jer 28:16.
Ingratitude of—Illustrated. Is 1:2,3.
Exemplified
Pharaoh. Ex 5:1,2.
Korah, etc. Num 16:11.
Moses and Aaron. Num 20:12,24.
Israelites. Deut 9:23,24.
Saul. 1 Sam 15:9,23.
Jeroboam. 1 Kin 12:28-33.
Zedekiah. 2 Chr 36:13.
Kingdom of Israel. Hos 7:14; 13:16.

Rechabites.

Descended from Hemath. 1 Chr 2:55.
The head of, assisted Jehu in his conspiracy against the house of Ahab. 2 Kin 10:15-17.
Prohibited by Jonadab from forming settlements or drinking wine. Jer 35:6-8.
Obedience of, a sign to Israel. Jer 35:12-17.
Perpetuity to, promised. Jer 35:18,19.

Reconciliation with God.

Predicted. Dan 9:24; Is 53:5.
Proclaimed by angels at the birth of Christ. Luke 2:14.
Blotting out the hand-writing of ordinances is necessary to. Eph 2:16; Col 2:14.
Effected for men
By God in Christ. 2 Cor 5:19.
By Christ as High Priest. Heb 2:17.
By the death of Christ. Rom 5:10; Eph 2:16; Col 1:21,22.
By the blood of Christ. Eph 2:13; Col 1:20.
While alienated from God. Col 1:21.
Without strength. Rom 5:6.
Yet sinners. Rom 5:8.
While enemies to God. Rom 5:10.
The ministry of committed to ministers. 2 Cor 5:18,19.
Ministers, in Christ's stead, should beseech men to seek. 2 Cor 5:20.
Effects of
Peace of God. Rom 5:1; Eph 2:16,17.
Access to God. Rom 5:2; Eph 2:18.
Union of Jews and Gentiles. Eph 2:14.
Union of things in heaven and earth. Col 1:20; Eph 1:10.
A pledge of final salvation. Rom 5:10.
Necessity for—Illustrated. Matt 5:24-26.
Typified. Lev 8:15; 16:20.

Redemption.

Defined. 1 Cor 6:20; 7:23.
Is of God. Is 44:21-23; 43:1; Luke 1:68.
Is by Christ. Matt 20:28; Gal 3:13.
Is by the blood of Christ. Acts 20:28; Heb 9:12; 1 Pet 1:19; Rev 5:9.
Christ sent to effect. Gal 4:4,5.
Christ is made, to us. 1 Cor 1:30.
Is from
The bondage of the law. Gal 4:5.
The curse of the law. Gal 3:13.
The power of sin. Rom 6:18,22.
The power of the grave. Ps 49:15.
All troubles. Ps 25:22.
All iniquity. Ps 130:8; Titus 2:14.
All evil. Gen 48:16.
The present evil world. Gal 1:4.
Vain conversation. 1 Pet 1:18.
Enemies. Ps 106:10,11; Jer 15:21.
Death. Hos 13:14.
Destruction. Ps 103:4.
Man cannot effect. Ps 49:7.
Corruptible things cannot purchase. 1 Pet 1:18.
Procures for us
Justification. Rom 3:24.
Forgiveness of sin. Eph 1:7; Col 1:14.
Adoption. Gal 4:4,5.
Purification. Titus 2:14.
The present life, the only season for. Job 36:18,19.
Described as
Precious. Ps 49:8.
Plenteous. Ps 130:7.
Eternal. Heb 9:12.
Subjects of
The soul. Ps 49:8.
The body. Rom 8:23.
The life. Ps 103:4; Lam 3:58.
The inheritance. Eph 1:14.
Manifests the
Power of God. Is 50:2.
Grace of God. Is 52:3.
Love and pity of God. Is 63:9; John 3:16; Rom 6:8; 1 John 4:10.
A subject for praise. Is 44:22,23; 51:11.
Old Testament saints partakers of. Heb 9:15.
They who partake of
Are the property of God. Is 43:1; 1 Cor 6:20.
Are first-fruits to God. Rev 14:4.
Are a peculiar people. 2 Sam 7:23; Titus 2:14; 1 Pet 2:9.
Are assured of. Job 19:25; Ps 31:5.
Are sealed to the day of. Eph 4:30.
Are Zealous of good works. Eph 2:10; Titus 2:14; 1 Pet 2:9.
Walk safely in holiness. Is 35:8,9.
Shall return to Zion with joy. Is 35:10.
Alone can learn the songs of heaven. Rev 14:3,4.
Commit themselves to God. Ps 31:5.
Have an earnest of the completion of. Eph 1:14; 2 Cor 1:22.
Wait for the completion of. Rom 8:23; Phil 3:20,21; Titus 2:11-13.
Pray for the completion of. Ps 26:11; 44:26.
Praise God for. Ps 71:23; 103:4; Rev 5:9.
Should glorify God for. 1 Cor 6:20.
Should be without fear. Is 43:1.
Typified
Israel. Ex 6:6.
Firstborn. Ex 13:11-15; Num 18:15.
Atonement-money. Ex 30:12-15.
Bond-servant. Lev 25:47-54.

Red Heifer, The.

To be without spot or blemish. Num 19:2.
To be given to Eleazar the second priest to offer. Num 19:3.
To be slain without the camp. Num 19:3.
Entire body of, to be burned. Num 19:5.
Blood of, sprinkled seven times before the tabernacle. Num 19:4.
Cedar, hyssop, burned with. Num 19:6.
Ashes of, collected and mixed with water for purification. Num 19:9,11-22.
Communicated uncleanness to
The priest that offered her. Num 19:7.
The man that burned her. Num 19:8.
The man who gathered the ashes. Num 19:10.
Could only purify the flesh. Heb 9:13.
A type of Christ. Heb 9:12-14.

Repentance.

What it is. Is 45:22; Matt 6:19-21; Acts 14:15; 2 Cor 5:17; Col 3:2; 1 Thess 1:9; Heb 12:1,2.
Commanded to all by God. Ezek 18:30-32; Acts 17:30.
Commanded by Christ. Rev 2:5,16; 3:3.
Given by God. Acts 11:18; 2 Tim 2:25.
Christ came to call sinners to. Matt 9:13.
Christ exalted to give. Acts 5:31.
By the operation of the Holy Spirit. Zech 12:10.
Called repentance to life. Acts 11:18.
Called repentance to salvation. 2 Cor 7:10.
We should be led to, by
The long-suffering of God. Gen 6:3; 1 Pet 3:20; 2 Pet 3:9.
The goodness of God. Rom 2:4.
The chastisements of God. 1 Kin 8:47; Rev 3:19.
Godly sorrow works. 2 Cor 7:10.
Necessary to the pardon of sin. Acts 2:38; 3:19; 8:22.
Conviction of sin necessary to. 1 Kin 8:38; Prov 28:13; Acts 2:37,38; 19:18.
Preached
By Christ. Matt 4:17; Mark 1:15.
By John the Baptist. Matt 3:2.
By the apostles. Mark 6:12; Acts 20:21.
In the name of Christ. Luke 24:47.
Not to be repented of. 2 Cor 7:10.
The present time the season for. Ps 95:7,8; Heb 3:7,8; Prov 27:1; Is 55:6; 2 Cor 6:2; Heb 4:7.
There is joy in heaven over one sinner brought to. Luke 15:7,10.
Ministers should rejoice over their people on their. 2 Cor 7:9.
Should be evidenced by fruits. Is 1:16,17; Dan 4:27; Matt 3:8; Acts 26:20.
Should be accompanied by
Humility. 2 Chr 7:14; James 4:9,10.
Shame and confusion. Ezra 9:6-15; Jer 31:19; Ezek 16:61,63; Dan 9:7,8.
Self-abhorrence. Job 42:6.
Confession. Lev 26:40; Job 33:27.
Faith. Matt 21:32; Mark 1:15; Acts 20:21.
Prayer. 1 Kin 8:33; Acts 8:22.

Conversion. Acts 3:19; 26:20.
Turning from sin. 2 Chr 6:26.
Turning from idolatry. Ezek 14:6; 1 Thess 1:9.
Greater zeal in the path of duty. 2 Cor 7:11.
Exhortations to. Ezek 14:6; 18:30; Acts 2:38; 3:19.
The wicked
Averse to. Jer 8:6; Matt 21:32.
Not led to by the judgments of God. Rev 9:20,21; 16:9.
Not led to, by miraculous interference. Luke 16:30,31.
Neglect the time given for. Rev 2:21.
Condemned for neglecting. Matt 11:20.
Danger of neglecting. Matt 11:20-24; Luke 13:3,5; Rev 2:22.
Neglect of, followed by swift judgment. Rev 2:5,16.
Denied to apostates. Heb 6:4-6.
Illustrated. Luke 15:18-21; 18:13.
The Prodigal Son. Luke 15:17-19.
The Repentant Son. Matt 21:29.
Paul. Gal 1:23.
True—Exemplified
Israelites. Judg 10:15,16.
David. 2 Sam 12:13.
Manasseh. 2 Chr 33:12,13.
Job. Job 42:6.
Nineveh. Jon 3:5-8; Matt 12:41.
Peter. Matt 26:75.
Zacchaeus. Luke 19:8.
Thief on the Cross. Luke 23:40,41.
Corinthians. 2 Cor 7:9,10.
False—Exemplified
Saul. 1 Sam 15:24-30.
Ahab. 1 Kin 21:27-29.
Judas. Matt 27:3-5.

Rephaim, or Giants, The.

Subdued by Chedorlaomer. Gen 14:5.
Dwelt in Canaan. Josh 17:15.
Og the king of Bashan was of. Josh 13:12.
The valley of
A border of Judah. Josh 15:8.
Was exceedingly fruitful. Is 17:5.
David obtained victories over the Philistines in. 2 Sam 5:18,25.
The last of, destroyed by David and his warriors. 1 Sam 17:4,49,50; 2 Sam 21:15-22.

Reproof.

God gives, to his own children. 2 Sam 7:14; Job 5:17; Ps 94:12; 119:67,71,75; Heb 12:6,7.
God gives, to the wicked. Ps 50:21; Is 51:20.
Christ sent to give. Is 2:4; 11:3.
The Holy Spirit gives. John 16:7,8.
Christ gives, in love. Rev 3:19.
On account of
Impenitence. Matt 11:20-24.
Not understanding. Matt 16:9,11; Mark 7:18; Luke 24:25; John 8:43; 13:7,8.
Hardness of heart. Mark 8:17; 16:14.
Fearfulness. Mark 4:40; Luke 24:37,38.
Unbelief. Matt 17:17,20; Mark 16:14.
Vain boasting. Luke 22:34.
Hypocrisy. Matt 15:7; 23:13.
Reviling Christ. Luke 23:40.
Unruly conduct. 1 Thess 5:14.
Oppressing our brethren. Neh 5:7.
Sinful practices. Matt 21:13; Luke 3:19; John 2:16.
The Scriptures are profitable for. Ps 19:7-11; 2 Tim 3:16.
When from God
Is for correction. Ps 39:11.
Is despised by the wicked. Prov 1:30.
Should not discourage saints. Heb 12:5.
Pray that it be not be in anger. Ps 6:1.
Should be accompanied by exhortation to repentance. 1 Sam 12:20-25.
Declared to be
Better than secret love. Prov 27:5.
Better than the praise of fools. Eccl 7:5.
An excellent oil. Ps 141:5.
More profitable to saints, than stripes to a fool. Prov 17:10.
A proof of faithful friendship. Prov 27:6.
Leads to
Understanding. Prov 15:32.
Knowledge. Prov 19:25.
Wisdom. Prov 15:31; 29:15.
Honour. Prov 13:18.
Happiness. Prov 6:23.
Eventually brings more respect than flattery. Prov 28:23.
Of those who offend, a warning to others. Lev 19:17; Acts 5:3,4,9; 1 Tim 5:20; Titus 1:10,13.
Hypocrites not qualified to give. Matt 7:5.
Ministers are sent to give. Jer 44:4; Ezek 3:17.
Ministers are empowered to give. Mic 3:8.
Ministers should give
Openly. 1 Tim 5:20.
Fearlessly. Ezek 2:3-7.
With all authority. Titus 2:15.
With longsuffering, etc. 2 Tim 4:2.
Unreservedly. Is 58:1.
Sharply, if necessary. Titus 1:13.
With Christian love. 2 Thess 3:15.
They who give, are hated by scorners. Prov 9:8; 15:12.
Hatred of, a proof of brutishness. Prov 12:1.
Hatred of, leads to destruction. Prov 15:10; 29:1.
Contempt of, leads to remorse. Prov 5:12.
Rejection of, leads to error. Prov 10:17.
Saints should
Give. Lev 19:17; Eph 5:11.
Give no occasion for. Phil 2:15.
Receive kindly. Ps 141:5.
Love those who give. Prov 9:8.
Delight in those who give. Prov 24:25.
Attention to a proof of prudence. Prov 15:5.
Exemplified
Samuel. 1 Sam 13:13.
Nathan. 2 Sam 12:7-9.
Ahijah. 1 Kin 14:7-11.
Elijah. 1 Kin 21:20.
Elisha. 2 Kin 5:26.
Joab. 1 Chr 21:3.
Shemaiah. 2 Chr 12:5.
Hanani. 2 Chr 16:7.
Zechariah. 2 Chr 24:20.
Daniel. Dan 5:22,23.
John the Baptist. Matt 3:7; Luke 3:19.
Stephen. Acts 7:51.
Peter. Acts 8:20.
Paul. 1 Cor 1:10-13; 5:1-5; 6:1-8; 11:17-22; Gal 2:11.

Reptiles.

Created by God. Gen 1:24,25.
Made for praise and glory of God. Ps 148:10.
Placed under the dominion of man. Gen 1:26.
Unclean and not eaten. Lev 11:31,40-43; Acts 10:11-14.
Mentioned in Scripture
Chameleon. Lev 11:30.
Lizard. Lev 11:30.
Tortoise. Lev 11:29.
Snail. Lev 11:30; Ps 58:8.
Frog. Ex 8:2; Rev 16:13.
Horseleech. Prov 30:15.
Scorpion. Deut 8:15.
Serpent. Job 26:13; Matt 7:10.
Flying fiery serpent. Deut 8:15; Is 30:6.
Dragon. Deut 32:33; Job 30:29; Jer 9:11
Viper. Acts 28:3.
Adder or Asp. Ps 58:4; 91:13; Prov 23:32.
Cockatrice or basilisk. Is 11:8; 59:5.
Solomon wrote a history of. 1 Kin 4:33.
Worshipped by Gentiles. Rom 1:23.
No image or similitude of, to be made for worshipping. Deut 4:16,18.
Jews condemned for worshipping. Ezek 8:10.

Resignation.

Christ set an example of. Matt 26:39-44; John 12:27; 18:11.
Commanded. Ps 37:7; 46:10.
Should be exhibited in
Submission to the will of God. 2 Sam 15:26; Ps 42:5,11; Matt 6:10.
Submission to the sovereignty of God in his purposes. Rom 9:20,21.
The prospect of death. Acts 21:13; 2 Cor 4:16-5:1.
Loss of goods. Job 1:15,16,21.
Loss of children. Job 1:18,19,21.
Chastisements. Heb 12:9.
Bodily suffering. Job 2:8-10.
The wicked are devoid of. Prov 19:3.
Exhortation to. Ps 37:1-11.
Motives to
God's greatness. Ps 46:10.
God's love. Heb 12:6.
God's justice. Neh 9:33.
God's wisdom. Rom 11:32,33.
God's faithfulness. 1 Pet 4:19.
Our own sinfulness. Lam 3:39; Mic 7:9.
Exemplified
Jacob. Gen 43:14.
Aaron. Lev 10:3.
Israelites. Judg 10:15.
Eli. 1 Sam 3:18.
David. 2 Sam 12:23.
Hezekiah. 2 Kin 20:19.

Job. Job 2:10.
Stephen. Acts 7:59.
Paul. Acts 21:13.
Disciples. Acts 21:14.
Peter. 2 Pet 1:14.

Resurrection, The.

A doctrine of the Old Testament. Job 19:26; Ps 16:10; 49:15; Is 26:19; Dan 12:2; Hos 13:14.
A first principle of the gospel. 1 Cor 15:13,14; Heb 6:1,2.
Expected by the Jews. John 11:24; Heb 11:35.
Denied by the Sadducees. Matt 22:23; Luke 20:27; Acts 23:8.
Explained away by false teachers. 2 Tim 2:18.
Called in question by some in the church. 1 Cor 15:12.
Is not incredible. Mark 12:24; Acts 26:8.
Is not contrary to reason. John 12:24; 1 Cor 15:35-49.
Assumed and proved by our Lord. Matt 22:29-32; Luke 14:14; John 5:28,29.
Preached by the apostles. Acts 4:2; 17:18; 24:15.
Credibility of, shown by the resurrection of individuals. Matt 9:25; 27:53; Luke 7:14; John 11:44; Heb 11:35.
Certainty of, proved by the resurrection of Christ. 1 Cor 15:12-20.
Effected by the power of
God. Matt 22:29.
Christ. John 5:28,29; 6:39,40,44.
The Holy Spirit. Rom 8:11.
Shall be of all the dead. John 5:28; Acts 24:15; Rev 20:13.
Saints in, shall
Rise through Christ. John 11:25; Acts 4:2; 1 Cor 15:21,22.
Rise first. 1 Cor 15:23; 1 Thess 4:16.
Rise to eternal life. Dan 12:2; John 5:29.
Be glorified with Christ. Col 3:4.
Be as the angels. Matt 22:30.
Have incorruptible bodies. 1 Cor 15:42.
Have glorious bodies. 1 Cor 15:43.
Have powerful bodies. 1 Cor 15:43.
Have spiritual bodies. 1 Cor 15:44.
Have bodies like Christ's. Phil 3:21; 1 John 3:2.
Be recompensed. Luke 14:14.
Saints should look forward to. Dan 12:13; Phil 3:11; 2 Cor 5:1.
Of saints shall be followed by the change of those then alive. 1 Cor 15:51; 1 Thess 4:17.
The preaching of, caused
Mocking. Acts 17:32.
Persecution. Acts 23:6; 24:11-15.
Blessedness of those who have part in the first. Rev 20:6.
Of the wicked, shall be to
Shame and everlasting contempt. Dan 12:2.
Damnation. John 5:29.
Illustrative of the new birth. John 5:25.
Illustrated. Ezek 37:1-10; 1 Cor 15:36,37.

Resurrection of Christ, The.

Foretold by the prophets. Ps 16:10; Acts 13:34,35; Is 26:19.
Foretold by Himself. Matt 20:19; Mark 9:9; 14:28; John 2:19-22.
Was necessary to
The fulfilment of Scripture. Luke 24:45,46.
Forgiveness of sins. 1 Cor 15:17.
Justification. Rom 4:25; 8:34.
Hope. 1 Cor 15:19.
The efficacy of preaching. 1 Cor 15:14.
The efficacy of faith. 1 Cor 15:14,17.
A proof of his being the Son of God. Ps 2:7; Acts 13:33; Rom 1:4.
Effected by
The power of God. Acts 2:24; 3:15; Rom 8:11; Eph 1:20; Col 2:12.
His own power. John 2:19; 10:18.
The power of the Holy Spirit. 1 Pet 3:18.
On the first day of the week. Mark 16:9.
On the third day after his death. Mark 16:9.
On the third day after His death. Luke 24:46; Acts 10:40; 1 Cor 15:4.
The apostles
At first did not understand the predictions respecting. Mark 9:10; John 20:9.
Very slow to believe. Mark 16:13; Luke 24:9,11,37,38.
Reproved for their unbelief of. Mark 16:14.
He appeared after to
Mary Magdalene. Mark 16:9; John 20:18.
The women. Matt 28:9.
Simon Peter. Luke 24:34.
Two disciples. Luke 24:13-31.
Apostles, except Thomas. John 20:19,24.
Apostles, Thomas being present. John 20:26.
Apostles at the sea of Tiberias. John 21:1.
Apostles in Galilee. Matt 28:16,17.
About five hundred brethren. 1 Cor 15:6.
James. 1 Cor 15:7.
All the apostles. Luke 24:51; Acts 1:9; 1 Cor 15:7.
Paul. 1 Cor 15:8.
Fraud impossible in. Matt 27:63-66.
He gave many infallible proofs of. Luke 24:35,39,43; John 20:20,27; Acts 1:3.
Was attested by
Angels. Matt 28:5-7; Luke 24:4-7,23.
Apostles. Acts 1:22; 2:32; 3:15; 4:33.
His enemies. Matt 28:11-15.
Asserted and preached by the Apostles. Acts 25:19; 26:23.
Saints
Begotten to a lively hope. 1 Pet 1:3,21.
Desire to know the power of. Phil 3:10.
Should keep, in remembrance. 2 Tim 2:8.
Shall rise in the likeness of. Rom 6:5; 1 Cor 15:49; Phil 3:21.
Is an emblem of the new birth. Rom 6:4; Col 2:12.
The first-fruits of our resurrection. Acts 26:23; 1 Cor 15:20,23.
The truth of the gospel involved in. 1 Cor 15:14,15.
Followed by his exaltation. Acts 4:10,11; Rom 8:34; Eph 1:20; Phil 2:9,10; Rev 1:18.
An assurance of the judgment. Acts 17:31.
Typified
Isaac. Gen 22:13; Heb 11:19.
Jonah. Jon 2:10; Matt 12:40.

Reuben, the Tribe Of.

Descended from Jacob's first son. Gen 29:32.
Predictions respecting. Gen 49:4; Deut 33:6.
Persons selected from
To number the people. Num 1:5.
To spy out the land. Num 13:4.
Strength of, on leaving Egypt. Num 1:20,21.
Led the second division of Israel in their journeys. Num 10:18.
Encamped with its standard south of the tabernacle. Num 2:10.
Offering of, at the dedication. Num 7:30-35.
Families of. Num 26:5,6,8,9.
Obtained inheritance east of Jordan on condition of helping to conquer Canaan. Num 32:1-33; Deut 3:18-20.
Bounds of their inheritance. Deut 3:16,17; Josh 13:15-23.
Strength of, at the time of receiving their inheritance. Num 26:7.
Cities built by. Num 32:37,38.
On Ebal, said amen to the curses. Deut 27:13.
Dismissed by Joshua after the conquest of Canaan. Josh 22:1-9.
Assisted in building the altar of witness which offended the other tribes. Josh 22:10-29.
Did not assist against Sisera. Judg 5:15,16.
Some of, at David's coronation. 1 Chr 12:37,38.
Officers appointed over, by David. 1 Chr 26:32; 27:16.
Took land of the Hagarites. 1 Chr 5:10,18-22.
Invaded and conquered by Hazael king of Syria. 2 Kin 10:32,33.
Carried away by Tiglathpileser. 2 Kin 15:29; 1 Chr 5:6,26.
Remarkable persons of
Dathan, Abiram, and On. Num 16:1; 26:9,10.
Adina, etc. 1 Chr 11:42.

Revenge.

Forbidden by our Lord. Lev 19:18; Prov 24:17,29; Matt 5:39-41; Rom 12:17,19; 1 Thess 5:15; 1 Pet 3:9.
Christ an example of forbearing. Is 53:7; 1 Pet 2:23.
Rebuked by Christ. Luke 9:54,55.
Inconsistent with Christian spirit. Luke 9:55.
Proceeds from a spiteful heart. Ezek 25:15.
Instead of taking, we should
Trust in God. Prov 20:22; Rom 12:16.
Exhibit love. Lev 19:18; Luke 6:35.

Give place to wrath. Rom 12:19.
Exercise forbearance. Matt 5:38-41.
Bless. Rom 12:14.
Overcome others by kindness. Prov 25:21,22; Rom 12:20.
Keep others from taking. 1 Sam 24:10; 25:24-31; 26:9.
Be thankful for being kept from taking. 1 Sam 25:32,33.
The wicked are earnest after. Jer 20:10.
Punishment for. Ezek 25:15-17; Amos 1:11,12.
Exemplified
Simon and Levi. Gen 34:25.
Samson. Judg 15:7,8; 16:28-30.
Joab. 2 Sam 3:27.
Absalom. 2 Sam 13:23-29.
Jezebel. 1 Kin 19:2.
Ahab. 1 Kin 22:26.
Haman. Esth 3:8-15.
Edomites. Ezek 25:12.
Philistines. Ezek 25:15.
Herodias. Mark 6:19-24.
James and John. Luke 9:54.
Chief priests. Acts 5:33.
Jews. Acts 7:54,59; 23:12.

Reviling and Reproaching.

Forbidden. 1 Pet 3:9.
Of rulers specially forbidden. Ex 22:28; Acts 23:4,5.
The wicked utter, against
God. Ps 74:22; 79:12.
God, by opposing the poor. Prov 14:31.
Christ. Matt 27:39; Luke 7:34.
Saints. Ps 102:8; Zeph 2:8.
Rulers. 2 Pet 2:10,11; Jude 1:8,9.
Of Christ, predicted. Ps 69:9; Rom 15:3; Ps 89:51.
The conduct of Christ under. 1 Pet 2:23.
Saints
Endure. 1 Tim 4:10; Heb 10:33.
Endure for God's sake. Ps 69:7.
Endure for Christ's sake. Luke 6:22.
Should expect. Matt 10:25.
Should not fear. Is 51:7.
Sometimes depressed by. Ps 42:10,11; 44:16; 69:20.
May take pleasure in. 2 Cor 12:10.
Supported under. 2 Cor 12:10.
Trust in God under. Ps 57:3; 119:42.
Pray under. 2 Kin 19:4,16; Ps 89:50.
Return blessings for. 1 Cor 4:12; 1 Pet 3:9.
Ministers should not fear. Ezek 2:6.
Happiness of enduring, for Christ's sake. 1 Pet 4:14.
Blessedness of enduring, for Christ's sake. Matt 5:11; Luke 6:22.
Excludes from heaven. 1 Cor 6:10.
Punishment for. Zeph 2:8,9; Matt 5:22.
Exemplified
Joseph's brethren. Gen 37:19.
Goliath. 1 Sam 17:43.
Michal. 2 Sam 6:20.
Shimei. 2 Sam 16:7,8.
Sennacherib. Is 37:17,23,24.
Moabites and Ammonites. Zeph 2:8.
Pharisees. Matt 12:24.
Jews. Matt 27:39,40; John 8:48.
Malefactor. Luke 23:39.
Athenian philosophers. Acts 17:18.

Reward of Saints, The.

Is from God. Rom 2:7; Col 3:24; Heb 11:6.
Is of grace, through faith alone. Rom 4:4,5,16; 11:6.
Is of God's good pleasure. Matt 20:14,15; Luke 12:32.
Prepared by God. Heb 11:16.
Prepared by Christ. John 14:2.
As servants of Christ. Col 3:24.
Not on account of their merits. Rom 4:4,5.
Described as
Being with Christ. John 12:26; 14:3; Phil 1:23; 1 Thess 4:17.
Beholding the face of God. Ps 17:15; Matt 5:8; Rev 22:4.
Beholding the glory of Christ. John 17:24.
Being glorified with Christ. Rom 8:17,18; Col 3:4; Phil 3:21; 1 John 3:2.
Sitting in judgment with Christ. Dan 7:22; Matt 19:28; Luke 22:30; 1 Cor 6:2.
Reigning with Christ. 2 Tim 2:12; Rev 3:21; 5:10; 20:4.
Reigning for ever and ever. Rev 22:5.
A crown of righteousness. 2 Tim 4:8.
A crown of glory. 1 Pet 5:4.
A crown of life. James 1:12; Rev 2:10.
An incorruptible crown. 1 Cor 9:25.
Joint heirship with Christ. Rom 8:17.
Inheritance of all things. Rev 21:7.
Inheritance with saints in light. Acts 20:32; 26:18; Col 1:12.
Inheritance eternal. Heb 9:15.
Inheritance incorruptible. 1 Pet 1:4.
A kingdom. Matt 25:34; Luke 22:29.
A kingdom immovable. Heb 12:28.
Shining as the stars. Dan 12:3.
Everlasting light. Is 60:19.
Everlasting life. Luke 18:30; John 6:40; 17:2,3; Rom 2:7; 6:23; 1 John 5:11.
An enduring substance. Heb 10:34.
A house eternal in the heavens. 2 Cor 5:1.
A city which had foundation. Heb 11:10.
Entering into the joy of the Lord. Matt 25:21; Heb 12:2.
Rest. Heb 4:9; Rev 14:13.
Fulness of joy. Ps 16:11.
The prize of the high calling of God in Christ. Phil 3:14.
Treasure in heaven. Matt 19:21; Luke 12:33.
An eternal weight of glory. 2 Cor 4:17.
Is great. Matt 5:12; Luke 6:35; Heb 10:35.
Is full. 2 John 8.
Is sure. Prov 11:18.
Is satisfying. Ps 17:15.
Is inestimable. Is 64:4; 1 Cor 2:9.
Saints may feel confident of. Ps 73:24; Is 25:8,9; 2 Cor 5:1; 2 Tim 4:8.
Hope of, a cause of rejoicing. Rom 5:2.
Be careful not to lose. 2 John 8.
The prospect of, should lead to
Diligence. 2 John 8.
Pressing forward. Phil 3:14.
Enduring suffering for Christ. 2 Cor 4:16-18; Heb 11:26.
Faithfulness to death. Rev 2:10.
Present afflictions not to be compared with. Rom 8:18; 2 Cor 5:17.
Shall be given at the second coming of Christ. Matt 16:27; Rev 22:12.

Riches.

The true riches. Eph 3:8; 1 Cor 1:30; Col 2:3; 1 Pet 2:7.
God gives. 1 Sam 2:7; Eccl 5:19.
To God belongs this world's riches. Hag 2:8.
God gives power to obtain. Deut 8:18.
The blessing of the Lord brings. Prov 10:22.
Give worldly power. Prov 22:7.
Described as
Temporary. Prov 27:24.
Uncertain. 1 Tim 6:17.
Unsatisfying. Eccl 4:8; 5:10.
Corruptible. James 5:2; 1 Pet 1:18.
Fleeting. Prov 23:5; Rev 18:16,17.
Deceitful. Matt 13:22.
Liable to be stolen. Matt 6:19.
Perishable. Jer 48:36.
Thick clay. Hab 2:6.
Often an obstruction to the reception of the gospel. Mark 10:23-25.
Deceitfulness of, chokes the word. Matt 13:22.
The love of, the root of all evil. 1 Tim 6:10.
Often lead to
Pride. Ezek 28:5; Hos 12:8.
Forgetting God. Deut 8:13,14.
Denying God. Prov 30:8,9.
Forsaking God. Deut 32:15.
Rebelling against God. Neh 9:25,26.
Rejecting Christ. Matt 19:22; 10:22.
Self-sufficiency. Prov 28:11.
Anxiety. Eccl 5:12.
An overbearing spirit. Prov 18:23.
Violence. Mic 6:12.
Oppression. James 2:6.
Fraud. James 5:4.
Sensual indulgence. Luke 16:19; James 5:5.
Life consists not in abundance of. Luke 12:15.
Be not over-anxious for. Prov 30:8.
Labour not for. Prov 23:4.
They who covet
Fall into temptation and a snare. 1 Tim 6:9.
Fall into hurtful lusts. 1 Tim 6:9.
Err from the faith. 1 Tim 6:10.
Use unlawful means to acquire. Prov 28:20.
Bring trouble on themselves. 1 Tim 6:10.
Bring trouble on their families. Prov 15:27.
Profit not in the day of wrath. Prov 11:4.
Cannot secure prosperity. James 1:11.
Cannot redeem the soul. Ps 49:6-9; 1 Pet 1:18.
Cannot deliver in the day of God's wrath. Zeph 1:18; Rev 6:15-17.
They who possess, should
Ascribe them to God. 1 Chr 29:12.
Not trust in them. Job 31:24; 1 Tim 6:17.

Not set the heart on them. Ps 62:10.
Not boast of obtaining them. Deut 8:17.
Not glory in them. Jer 9:23.
Not hoard them up. Matt 6:19.
Devote them to God's service. 1 Chr 29:3; Mark 12:42-44.
Give of them to the poor. Matt 19:21; 1 John 3:17.
Use them in promoting the salvation of others. Luke 16:9.
Be liberal in all things. 1 Tim 6:18.
Esteem it a privilege to be allowed to give. 1 Chr 29:14.
Not to be high-minded. 1 Tim 6:17.
When converted, rejoice in being humbled. James 1:9,10.
Heavenly treasures superior to. Matt 6:19,20.
Of the wicked laid up for the just. Prov 13:22.
The wicked
Often increase in. Ps 73:12.
Often spend their day in. Job 21:13.
Swallow down. Job 20:15.
Trust in the abundance of. Ps 52:7.
Heap up. Job 27:16; Ps 39:6; Eccl 2:26.
Keep, to their hurt. Eccl 5:13.
Boast themselves in. Ps 49:6; 52:7.
Profit not by. Prov 11:4; 13:7; Eccl 5:11.
Have trouble with. Prov 15:6; 1 Tim 6:9,10.
Must leave, to others. Ps 49:10.
Vanity of heaping up. Ps 39:6; Eccl 5:10,11.
Guilt of trusting in. Job 31:24,28; Ezek 28:4,5,8.
Guilt of rejoicing in. Job 31:25,28.
Denunciations against those who
Get, by vanity. Prov 13:11; 21:6.
Get, unlawfully. Jer 17:11.
Increase, by oppression. Prov 22:16; Hab 2:6-8; Mic 2:2,3.
Hoard up. Eccl 5:13,14; James 5:3.
Trust in. Prov 11:28.
Receive their consolation. Luke 6:24.
Abuse. James 5:1,5.
Spend, upon their appetite. Job 20:15-17.
Folly and danger of trusting to—Illustrated. Luke 12:16-21.
Danger of misusing—Illustrated. Luke 16:19-25.
Examples of saints possessing
Abram. Gen 13:2.
Lot. Gen 13:5,6.
Isaac. Gen 26:13,14.
Jacob. Gen 32:5,10.
Joseph. Gen 45:8,13.
Boaz. Ruth 2:1.
Barzillai. 2 Sam 19:32.
Shunammite. 2 Kin 4:8.
David. 1 Chr 29:28.
Jehoshaphat. 2 Chr 17:5.
Hezekiah. 2 Chr 32:27-29.
Job. Job 1:3.
Joseph of Arimathea. Matt 27:57.
Zacchaeus. Luke 19:2.
Dorcas. Acts 9:36.
Examples of those truly rich. Matt 5:8; 8:10; 13:45,46; Luke 10:42; John 1:45; Phil 3:8; James 2:5; 1 Pet 2:7; Rev 3:18.
Examples of wicked men possessing
Laban. Gen 30:30.
Esau. Gen 36:7.
Nabal. 1 Sam 25:2.
Haman. Esth 5:11.
Ammonites. Jer 49:4.
People of Tyre. Ezek 28:5.
Young man. Matt 19:22.

RIGHTEOUSNESS.

Is obedience to God's law. Deut 6:25; Rom 10:5; Luke 1:6; Ps 1:2.
God loves. Ps 11:7.
God looks for. Is 5:7.
Christ
Is the Son of. Mal 4:2.
Loves. Ps 45:7; Heb 1:9.
Was girt with. Is 11:5.
Put on, as breastplate. Is 59:17.
Was sustained by. Is 59:16.
Preached. Ps 40:9.
Fulfilled all. Matt 3:15.
Is made to his people. 1 Cor 1:30.
Is the end of the law for. Rom 10:4.
Has brought in everlasting. Dan 9:24.
Shall judge with. Ps 72:2; Is 11:4; Acts 17:31; Rev 19:11.
Shall reign in. Ps 45:6; Is 32:1; Heb 1:8.
Shall execute. Ps 99:4; Jer 23:6.
None, by nature have. Job 15:14; Ps 14:3; Rom 3:10.
Cannot come by the law. Gal 2:21; 3:21.
No justification by works of. Rom 3:20; 9:31,32; Gal 2:16.
No salvation by works of. Eph 2:8,9; 2 Tim 1:9; Titus 3:5.
Unregenerate man seeks justification by works of. Luke 18:9; Rom 10:3.
The blessing of God is not to be attributed to our works of. Deut 9:5.
Saints
Have, in Christ. Is 45:24; 54:17; 2 Cor 5:21.
Have, imputed. Rom 4:11,22.
Are covered with the robe of. Is 61:10.
Receive, from God. Ps 24:5.
Are renewed in. Eph 4:24.
Are led in the paths of. Ps 23:3.
Are servants of. Rom 6:16,18.
Characterised by. Gen 18:25; Ps 1:5,6.
Know. Is 51:7.
Do. 1 John 2:29; 3:7.
Work, by faith. Heb 11:33.
Follow after. Is 51:1.
Put on. Job 29:14.
Wait for the hope of. Gal 5:5.
Pray for the spirit of. Ps 51:10.
Hunger and thirst after. Matt 5:6.
Walk before God in. 1 Kin 3:6.
Offer the sacrifice of. Ps 4:5; 51:19.
Put no trust in their own. Phil 3:6-8.
Count their own, as filthy rags. Is 64:6.
Should seek. Zeph 2:3.
Should live in. Titus 2:12; 1 Pet 2:24.
Should serve God in. Luke 1:75.
Should yield their members as instruments of. Rom 6:13.
Should yield their members servants to. Rom 6:19.
Should have on the breastplate of. Eph 6:14.
Shall receive a crown of. 2 Tim 4:8.
Shall see God's face in. Ps 17:15.
Of saints endures forever. Ps 112:3,9; 2 Cor 9:9.
An evidence of the new birth. 1 John 2:29.
The kingdom of God is. Rom 14:17.
The fruit of the Spirit is in all. Eph 5:9.
The Scriptures instruct in. 2 Tim 3:16.
Judgments designed to lead to. Is 26:9.
Chastisements yield the fruit of. Heb 12:11.
Has no fellowship with unrighteousness. 2 Cor 6:14.
Ministers should
Be preachers of. 2 Pet 2:5.
Reason of. Acts 24:25.
Follow after. 1 Tim 6:11; 2 Tim 2:22.
Be clothed with. Ps 132:9.
Be armed with. 2 Cor 6:7.
Pray for the fruit of, in their people. 2 Cor 9:10; Phil 1:11.
Keep saints in the right way. Prov 11:5; 13:6.
Judgment should be executed in. Lev 19:15.
They who walk in, and follow
Are righteous. 1 John 3:7.
Are the excellent of the earth. Ps 16:3; Prov 12:26.
Are accepted with God. Acts 10:35.
Are loved by God. Ps 146:8; Prov 15:9.
Are blessed by God. Ps 5:12.
Are heard by God. Luke 18:7; James 5:16.
Are objects of God's watchful care. Job 36:7; Ps 34:15; Prov 10:3; 1 Pet 3:12.
Are tried by God. Ps 11:5.
Are exalted by God. Job 36:7.
Dwell in security. Is 33:15,16.
Are bold as a lion. Prov 28:1.
Are delivered out of all troubles. Ps 34:19; Prov 11:8.
Are never forsaken by God. Ps 37:25.
Are abundantly provided for. Prov 13:25; Matt 6:25-33.
Are enriched. Ps 112:3; Prov 15:6.
Think and desire good. Prov 11:23; 12:5.
Know the secret of the Lord. Ps 25:14; Prov 3:32.
Have their prayers heard. Ps 34:17; Prov 15:29; 1 Pet 3:12.
Have their desires granted. Prov 10:24.
Find it with life and honour. Prov 21:21.
Shall hold on their way. Job 17:9.
Shall never be moved. Ps 15:2,5; 55:22; Prov 10:30; 12:3.
Shall be ever remembered. Ps 112:6.
Shall flourish as a branch. Prov 11:28.
Shall be glad in the Lord. Ps 64:10.
Brings its own reward. Prov 11:18; Is 3:10.
Tends to life. Prov 11:19; 12:28.
The work of, shall be peace. Is 32:17.
The effect of, shall be quietness and assurance for ever. Is 32:17.
Is a crown of glory to the aged. Prov 16:31.
The wicked
Are far from. Ps 119:150; Is 46:12.

Are free from. Rom 6:20.
Are enemies of. Acts 13:10.
Leave off. Amos 5:7; Ps 36:3.
Follow not after. Rom 9:30.
Do not. 1 John 3:10.
Do not obey. Rom 2:8; 2 Thess 2:12.
Love lying rather than. Ps 52:3.
Make mention of God, not it. Is 48:1.
Though favoured, will not learn. Is 26:10; Ps 106:43.
Speak contemptuously against those who follow. Ps 31:18; Matt 27:39-44.
Hate those who follow. Ps 34:21.
Slay those who follow. Ps 37:32; 1 John 3:12; Matt 23:35.
Should break off their sins by. Dan 4:27.
Should awake to. 1 Cor 15:34.
Should sow to themselves in. Hos 10:12.
Vainly wish to die as those who follow. Num 23:10.
The throne of kings established by. Prov 16:12; 25:5.
Nations exalted by. Prov 14:34.
Blessedness of
Having imputed, without works. Rom 4:6.
Doing. Ps 106:3.
Hungering and thirsting after. Matt 5:6.
Suffering for. 1 Pet 3:14.
Being persecuted for. Matt 5:10.
Turning others to. Dan 12:3.
Promised to the Church. Is 32:16; 45:8; 61:11; 62:1.
Promised to saints. Is 60:21; 61:3.
Exemplified
Jacob. Gen 30:33.
David. 2 Sam 22:21.
Zacharias. Luke 1:6.
Abel. Heb 11:4.
Lot. 2 Pet 2:8.

Righteousness Imputed.

Predicted. Is 56:1; Ezek 16:14.
Revealed in the gospel. Rom 1:17.
Is of the Lord. Is 54:17.
Described as
The righteousness of faith. Rom 4:13; 9:30; 10:6.
The righteousness of God, without the law. Rom 3:21.
The righteousness of God by faith in Christ. Rom 3:22.
Christ being made righteousness to us. 1 Cor 1:30.
Our being made the righteousness of God, in Christ. 2 Cor 5:21.
Christ is the end of the law for. Rom 10:4.
Christ called "The Lord our righteousness." Jer 23:6.
Christ brings in an everlasting righteousness. Dan 9:24.
Is a free gift. Rom 5:17.
God's righteousness never to be abolished. Is 5:16.
The promises made through. Rom 4:13.
Saints
Have, on believing. Rom 4:5,11,24.
Clothed with the robe of righteousness. Is 61:10.
Exalted in righteousness. Ps 89:16.
Desire to be found in. Phil 3:9.
Glory in having. Is 45:24,25.
Exhortation to seek righteousness. Matt 6:33.
The Gentiles attained to. Rom 9:30.
Blessedness of those who have. Rom 4:6.
The Jews
Ignorant of. Rom 10:3.
Stumble at righteousness by faith. Rom 9:32.
Submit not to. Rom 10:3.
Exemplified
Abraham. Rom 4:9,22; Gal 3:6.
Paul. Phil 3:7-9.

Righteousness of God, The.

Is part of his character. Ps 7:9; 116:5; 119:137.
Described as
Very high. Ps 71:19.
Abundant. Ps 48:10.
Beyond computation. Ps 71:15.
Everlasting. Ps 119:142.
Enduring for ever. Ps 111:3.
The habitation of his throne. Ps 97:2.
Christ acknowledged. John 17:25.
Christ committed his cause to. 1 Pet 2:23.
Angels acknowledge. Rev 16:5.
Exhibited in
His testimonies. Ps 119:138,144.
His commandments. Deut 4:8; Ps 119:172.
His judgments. Ps 19:9; 119:7,62.
His word. Ps 119:123.
His ways. Ps 145:17.
His acts. Judg 5:11; 1 Sam 12:7.
His government. Ps 96:13; 98:9.
The gospel. Ps 85:10; Rom 3:25,26.
The final judgment. Acts 17:31.
The punishment of the wicked. Rom 2:5; 2 Thess 1:6; Rev 16:7; 19:2.
Shown to the posterity of saints. Ps 103:17.
Shown openly before the heathen. Ps 98:2.
God delights in the exercise of. Jer 9:24.
The heavens shall declare. Ps 50:6; 97:6.
Saints
Ascribe, to him. Job 36:3; Dan 9:7.
Acknowledge, in his dealings. Ezra 9:15.
Acknowledge, though the wicked prosper. Jer 12:1; Ps 73:12-17.
Recognise, in the fulfilment of his promises. Neh 9:8.
Confident of beholding. Mic 7:9.
Upheld by. Is 41:10.
Do not conceal. Ps 40:10.
Mention, only. Ps 71:16.
Talk of. Ps 35:28; 71:15,24.
Declare to others. Ps 22:31.
Magnify. Ps 7:17; 51:14; 145:7.
Plead in prayer. Ps 143:11; Dan 9:16.
Leads God to love righteousness. Ps 11:7.
We should pray
To be led in. Ps 5:8.
To be quickened in. Ps 119:40.
To be delivered in. Ps 31:1; 71:2.
To be answered in. Ps 143:1.
To be judged according to. Ps 35:24.
For its continued manifestation. Ps 36:10.
His care and defence of his people designed to teach. Mic 6:4,5.
The wicked have no interest in. Ps 69:27.
Illustrated. Ps 36:6.

Rings.

Antiquity of. Gen 24:22; 38:18.
Made of gold and set with precious stones. Num 31:50,51; Song 5:14.
Were worn
On the hands. Gen 41:42.
On the arms. 2 Sam 1:10.
In the ears. Job 42:11; Hos 2:13; Ezek 16:12.
In the nose. Is 3:21.
Rich men distinguished by. James 2:2.
Women of rank adorned with. Is 3:16,21.
Of kings
Used for sealing decrees. Esth 3:12; 8:8,10.
Given to favourites as a mark of honour. Gen 41:42; Esth 3:10; 8:2.
Numbers of, taken from Midianites. Num 31:50.
Illustrative
Of the glory of Christ. Song 5:14.
(Put on the hands,) of favour. Luke 15:22.

Rivers.

Source of. Job 28:10; Ps 104:8,10.
Enclosed within banks. Dan 12:5.
Flow through valleys. Ps 104:8,10.
Some of
Great and mighty. Gen 15:18; Ps 74:15.
Deep. Ezek 47:5; Zech 10:11.
Broad. Is 33:21.
Rapid. Judg 5:21.
Parted into many streams. Gen 2:10; Is 11:5.
Run into the sea. Eccl 1:7; Ezek 47:8.
God's power over, unlimited. Is 50:2; Nah 1:4.
Useful for
Supplying drink to the people. Jer 2:18.
Commerce. Is 23:3.
Promoting vegetation. Gen 2:10.
Bathing. Ex 2:5.
Baptism often performed in. Matt 3:6.
Of Canaan abounded with fish. Lev 11:9,10.
Banks of
Covered with flags. Ex 2:3,5.
Planted with trees. Ezek 47:7.
Frequented by doves. Song 5:12.
Frequented by wild beasts. Jer 49:19.
Places of common resort. Ps 137:1.
Frequently overflowed. Josh 3:15; 1 Chr 12:15.
Peculiarly fruitful. Ps 1:3; Is 32:20.
Gardens often made beside. Num 24:6.
Cities often built beside. Ps 46:4; 137:1.
Often the boundaries of kingdoms. Josh 22:25; 1 Kin 4:24.
Mentioned in Scripture
Of Eden. Gen 2:10.
Of Jotbath. Deut 10:7.
Of Ethiopia. Is 18:1.

Of Babylon. Ps 137:1.
Of Egypt. Gen 15:18.
Of Damascus. 2 Kin 5:12.
Of Ahava. Ezra 8:15.
Of Judah. Joel 3:18.
Of Philippi. Acts 16:13.
Abana. 2 Kin 5:12.
Arnon. Deut 2:36; Josh 12:1.
Chebar. Ezek 1:1,3; 10:15,20.
Euphrates. Gen 2:14.
Gihon. Gen 2:13.
Gozan. 2 Kin 17:6; 1 Chr 5:26.
Hiddekel. Gen 2:14.
Jabbok. Deut 2:37; Josh 12:2.
Jordan. Josh 3:8; 2 Kin 5:10.
Kanah. Josh 16:8.
Kishon. Judg 5:21.
Pharpar. 2 Kin 5:12.
Pison. Gen 2:11.
Ulai. Dan 8:16.
Many, fordable in some places. Gen 32:22; Josh 2:7; Is 16:2.
Illustrative
Of the abundance of grace in Christ. Is 32:2; John 1:16.
Of the gifts and graces of the Holy Spirit. Ps 46:4; Is 41:18; 43:19,20; John 7:38,39.
Of heavy afflictions. Ps 69:2; Is 43:2.
Of abundance. Job 20:17; 29:6.
Of people flying from judgments. Is 23:10.
(Steady course of,) of peace of saints. Is 66:12.
(Fruitfulness of trees planted by,) of the permanent prosperity of saints. Ps 1:3; Jer 17:8.
(Drying up of,) of God's judgments. Is 19:1-8; Jer 51:36; Nah 1:4; Zech 10:11.
(Overflowing of,) of God's judgments. Is 8:7,8; 28:2,18; Jer 47:2.

Rocks.

Often composed of Flint. Deut 8:15; 32:13.
Described as
Hard. Jer 5:3.
Durable. Job 19:24.
Barren. Ezek 26:4,14; Amos 6:12; Luke 8:6.
Often sharp-pointed and craggy. 1 Sam 14:4.
Often had holes and clefts. Ex 33:22.
Were a defence to a country. Is 33:16.
Dreaded by mariners. Acts 27:20.
Inhabited by
Wild goats. Job 39:1.
Conies. Ps 104:18; Prov 30:26.
Doves. Song 2:14; Jer 48:28.
Eagles. Job 39:28; Jer 49:16.
The olive tree flourished amongst. Deut 32:13; Job 29:6.
Bees often made their honey amongst. Deut 32:13; Ps 81:16.
Used as
Altars. Judg 6:20,21,26; 13:19.
Places for idolatrous worship. Is 57:5.
Places of Observation. Ex 33:21; Num 23:9.
Places of safety in danger. 1 Sam 13:6; Is 2:19; Jer 16:16; Rev 6:15.
Places for shelter by the poor in their distress. Job 24:8; 30:3,6.
The shadow of, grateful to travellers during the heat of the day. Is 32:2.
Houses often built on. Matt 7:24,25.
Tombs often hewn out of. Is 22:16; Matt 27:60.
Important events often engraved upon. Job 19:24.
Mentioned in Scripture
Adullam. 1 Chr 11:15.
Bozez. 1 Sam 14:4.
Engedi. 1 Sam 24:1,2.
Etam. Judg 15:8.
Horeb in Rephidim. Ex 17:1-6.
Meribah in Kadesh. Num 20:1-11.
Oreb. Judg 7:25; Is 10:26.
Rimmon. Judg 20:45.
Seneh. 1 Sam 14:4.
Selahammahlekoth in the wilderness of Maon. 1 Sam 23:25,28.
Selah in the valley of salt. 2 Kin 14:7; 2 Chr 25:11,12.
Man's industry in cutting through. Job 28:9,10.
Hammers used for breaking. Jer 23:29.
Casting down from, a punishment. 2 Chr 25:12.
Miracles connected with
Water brought from. Ex 17:6; Num 20:11.
Fire ascended out of. Judg 6:21.
Broken in pieces by the wind. 1 Kin 19:11.
Rent at the death of Christ. Matt 27:51.
God's power exhibited in removing. Job 14:18; Nah 1:6.
Illustrative of
God as creator of his people. Deut 32:18.
God as the strength of his people. Ps 18:1,2; 67:2; Is 17:10.
God as defence of his people. Ps 31:2,3.
God as refuge of his people. Ps 94:22.
God as salvation of his people. Deut 32:15; Ps 89:26; 95:1.
Christ as refuge of his people. Is 32:2.
Christ as foundation of his church. Matt 16:18; 1 Pet 2:6.
Christ as source of spiritual gifts. 1 Cor 10:4.
Christ as a stumbling stone to the wicked. Is 8:14; Rom 9:33; 1 Pet 2:8.
A place of safety. Ps 27:5; 40:2.
Whatever we trust in. Deut 32:31,37.
The ancestor of a nation. Is 51:1.

Roe, The.

Clean and fit for food. Deut 12:15; 14:5.
Male of, called the roebuck. 1 Kin 4:23.
Described as
Cheerful. Prov 5:19.
Wild. 2 Sam 2:18.
Swift. 1 Chr 12:8.
Inhabits the mountains. 1 Chr 12:8.
Often hunted by men. Prov 6:5.
Illustrative of
Christ. Song 2:9,17.
The church. Song 4:5; 7:3.
A good wife. Prov 5:19.
The swift of foot. 2 Sam 2:18.

Roman Empire, The.

Called the world from its extent. Luke 2:1.
Represented by the
Legs of iron in Nebuchadnezzar's vision. Dan 2:33,40.
Terrible beast in Daniel's vision. Dan 7:7,19.
Rome the capitol of. Acts 18:2; 19:21.
Judea a province of, under a procurator or a governor. Luke 3:2; Acts 23:34,26; 25:1.
Allusions to military affairs of
Strict obedience to superiors. Matt 8:8,9.
Use of the panoply or defensive armour. Rom 13:12; 2 Cor 6:7; Eph 6:11-17.
Soldiers not allowed to entangle themselves with earthly cares. 2 Tim 2:4.
Hardship endured by soldiers. 2 Tim 2:3.
The soldier's special comrade who shared his toils and dangers. Phil 2:25.
Danger of sentinels' sleeping. Matt 28:13,14.
Expunging from the muster roll name of soldiers guilty of crimes. Rev 3:5.
Crowning of soldiers who distinguished themselves. 2 Tim 4:7,8.
Triumphs of victorious generals. 2 Cor 2:14-16; Col 2:15.
Different military officers. Acts 21:31; 23:23,24.
Italian and Augustus' band. Acts 10:1; 27:1.
Allusions to judicial affairs of
Person accused, examined by scourging. Acts 22:24,29.
Criminals delivered over to the soldiers for execution. Matt 27:26,27.
Accusation in writing placed over the head of those executed. John 19:19.
Garments of those executed given to the soldiers. Matt 27:35; John 19:23.
Prisoners chained to soldiers for safety. Acts 21:33; 12:6; 2 Tim 1:16; Acts 28:16.
Accusers and accused confronted together. Acts 23:35; 25:16-19.
Accused person protected from popular violence. Acts 23:20,24-27.
Power of life and death vested in its authorities. John 18:31,39,40; 19:10.
All appeals made to the emperor. Acts 25:11,12.
Those who appealed to Caesar, to be brought before him. Acts 26:32.
Allusions to citizenship of
Obtained by purchase. Acts 22:28.
Obtained by birth. Acts 22:28.
Exempted from the degradation scourging. Acts 16:37,38; 22:25.
Allusions to Grecian game adapted by
Gladiatorial fights. 1 Cor 4:9; 15:32.
Foot races. 1 Cor 9:24; Phil 2:16; 3:11-14; Heb 12:1,2.
Wrestling. Eph 6:12.
Training of combatants. 1 Cor 9:25,27.

Crowning of conquerors. 1 Cor 9:25; Phil 3:14; 2 Tim 4:8.
Rules observed in conducting. 2 Tim 2:5.
Emperors of, mentioned
Tiberius. Luke 3:1.
Augustus. Luke 2:1.
Claudius. Acts 11:28.
Nero. Phil 4:22; 2 Tim 4:22.
Predictions respecting
Its universal dominion. Dan 7:23.
Its division into ten parts. Dan 2:41-43; 7:20,24.
Origin of papal power in. Dan 7:8,20-25.

SABBATH, THE.

Instituted by God. Gen 2:3.
Grounds of its institution. Gen 2:2,3; Ex 20:11.
The seventh day observed as. Ex 20:9-11.
Made for man. Mark 2:27.
God
Blessed. Gen 2:3; Ex 20:11.
Sanctified. Gen 2:3; Ex 31:15.
Hallowed. Ex 20:11.
Commanded, to be kept. Lev 19:3,30.
Commanded to be sanctified. Ex 20:8.
Will have his goodness commemorated in the observance of. Deut 5:15.
Shows favour in appointing. Neh 9:14.
Shows considerate kindness in appointing. Ex 23:12.
A sign of the covenant. Ex 31:13,17.
A type of the heavenly rest. Heb 4:4,9.
Christ
Is Lord of. Mark 2:28.
Was accustomed to observe. Luke 4:16.
Taught on. Luke 4:31; 6:6.
Servants and cattle should be allowed to rest upon. Ex 20:10; Deut 5:14.
No manner of work to be done on. Ex 20:10; Lev 23:3.
No purchases to be made on. Neh 10:31; 13:15-17.
No burdens to be carried on. Neh 13:19; Jer 17:21.
Divine worship to be celebrated on. Ezek 46:3; Acts 16:13.
The Scriptures to be read on. Acts 13:27; 15:21.
The word of God to be preached on. Acts 13:14,15,44; 17:2; 18:4.
Works connected with religious service lawful on. Num 28:9; Matt 12:5; John 7:23.
Works of mercy lawful on. Matt 12:12; 13:16; John 9:14.
Necessary wants may be supplied. Matt 12:1; Luke 13:15; 14:1.
Called
The Sabbath of the Lord. Ex 20:10; Lev 23:3; Deut 5:14.
The Sabbath of rest. Ex 31:15.
The rest of the holy Sabbath. Ex 16:23.
God's holy Day. Is 58:13.
The Lord's day. Rev 1:10.
First day of the week kept as, by the church. John 20:26; Acts 20:7; 1 Cor 16:2.
Saints
Observe. Neh 13:22.
Honour God in observing. Is 58:13.
Rejoice in. Ps 118:24; Is 58:13.
Testify against those who desecrate. Neh 13:15,20,21.
Observance of, to be perpetual. Ex 31:16,17; Matt 5:17,18.
Blessedness of honouring. Is 58:13,14.
Blessedness of keeping. Is 56:2,6.
Denunciations against those who profane. Neh 13:18; Jer 17:27.
Punishment of those who profane. Ex 31:14,15; Num 15:32-36.
The wicked
Mock at. Lam 1:7.
Pollute. Is 56:2; Ezek 20:13,16.
Profane. Neh 13:17; Ezek 22:8.
Wearied by. Amos 8:5.
Hide their eyes from. Ezek 22:26.
Do their own pleasure on. Is 58:13.
Bear burdens on. Neh 13:15.
Work on. Neh 13:15.
Traffic on. Neh 10:31; 13:15,16.
Sometimes pretend to zealous for. Luke 13:14; John 9:16.
May be judicially deprived of. Lam 2:6; Hos 2:11.
Honouring of—Exemplified
Moses. Num 15:32-34.
Nehemiah. Neh 13:15,21.
The women. Luke 23:56.
Paul. Acts 13:14.
Disciples. Acts 16:13.
John. Rev 1:10.
Dishonouring of—Exemplified
Gatherers of manna. Ex 16:27.
Gatherers of sticks. Num 15:32.
Men of Tyre. Neh 13:16.
Inhabitants of Jerusalem. Jer 17:21-23.

SACKCLOTH.

Made of coarse hair. Matt 3:4; Rev 6:12.
Rough and unsightly. Zech 13:4.
Of a black colour. Rev 6:12.
Was worn
By God's prophets. 2 Kin 1:8; Is 20:2; Matt 3:4; Rev 11:3.
By persons in affliction. Neh 9:1; Ps 69:11; Jon 3:5.
Girt about the loins. Gen 37:34; 1 Kin 20:31.
Frequently next to the skin in deep afflictions. 1 Kin 21:27; 2 Kin 6:30; Job 16:15.
Often over the whole person. 2 Kin 19:1,2.
With ashes on the head. Esth 4:1.
With ropes on the head. 1 Kin 20:31.
In the streets. Is 15:3.
At funerals. 2 Sam 3:31.
The Jews lay in, when in deep affliction. 2 Sam 21:10; 1 Kin 21:27; Joel 1:13.
No one clothed in, allowed into the palaces of kings. Esth 4:2.
Illustrative
(Girding with,) of heavy afflictions. Is 3:24; 22:12; 32:11.
(Covering the heavens with,) of severe judgments. Is 50:3.
(Heavens becoming as,) of severe judgments. Rev 6:12.
(Putting of,) of joy and gladness. Ps 30:11.

SACRIFICES.

Divine institution of. Gen 3:21; 1:29; 9:3; 4:4,5; Heb 11:4.
To be offered to God alone. Ex 22:20; Judg 13:16; 2 Kin 17:36.
When offered to God, an acknowledgement of his being the supreme God. 2 Kin 5:17; Jon 1:16.
Consisted of
Clean animals or bloody sacrifices. Gen 8:20.
The fruits of the earth or sacrifices without blood. Gen 4:4; Lev 2:1.
Always offered upon altars. Ex 20:24.
The offering of, an acknowledgment of sin. Heb 10:3.
Were offered
From the earliest age. Gen 4:3,4.
By the patriarchs. Gen 22:2,13; 31:54; 46:1; Job 1:5.
After the departure of Israel from Egypt. Ex 5:3,17; 18:12; 24:5.
Under the Mosaic age. Lev 1:1-7:38; Heb 10:1-3.
Daily. Ex 29:38,39; Num 28:3,4.
Weekly. Num 28:9,10.
Monthly. Num 28:11.
Yearly. Lev 16:3; 1 Sam 1:3,21; 20:6.
At all the feasts. Num 10:10.
For the whole nation. Lev 16:15-30; 1 Chr 29:21.
For individuals. Lev 1:2; 17:8.
In faith of a coming Saviour. Heb 11:4,17,28.
Required to be perfect and without blemish. Lev 22:19; Deut 15:21; 17:1; Mal 1:8,14.
Generally the best of their kind. Gen 4:4; 1 Sam 15:22; Ps 66:15; Is 1:11.
Different kinds of
Burnt offering wholly consumed by fire. Lev 1:1-17; 1 Kin 18:38.
Sin offering for sins of ignorance. Lev 4:1-35.
Trespass offering for intentional sins. Lev 6:1-7; 7:1-7.
Peace offering. Lev 3:1-17.
To be brought to the place appointed by God. Deut 12:6; 2 Chr 7:12.
Were bound to the horns of the altar. Ps 118:27.
Were salted with salt. Lev 2:13; Mark 9:49.
Often consumed by fire from heaven. Lev 9:24; 1 Kin 18:38; 2 Chr 7:1.
When bloody, accompanied with meat and drink offering. Num 15:3-12.
No leaven offered with, except for peace offering. Ex 23:18; Lev 7:13.
Fat of, not to remain until morning. Ex 23:8.
The priests
Appointed to offer. 1 Sam 2:28; Ezek 44:11,15; Heb 5:1; 8:3.
Had a portion of, and lived by. Ex 29:27,28; Deut 18:3; Josh 13:14; 1 Cor 9:13.
Were typical of Christ's sacrifice. 1 Cor 5:7; Eph 5:2; Heb 10:1,11,12.
Were accepted when offered in sincerity and faith. Gen 4:4; Heb 11:4; Gen 8:21.

Imparted a legal purification. Heb 9:13,22.
Could not take away sin. Ps 40:6; Heb 9:9; 10:1-11.
Without obedience, worthless. 1 Sam 15:22; Prov 21:3; Mark 12:33.
The covenants of God confirmed by. Gen 15:9-17; Ex 24:5-8; Heb 9:19,20; Ps 50:5.
The Jews
 Condemned for not treating with respect. 1 Sam 2:29; Mal 1:12.
 Condemned for bringing defective and blemished. Mal 1:13,14.
 Condemned for not offering. Is 43:23,24.
 Unaccepted in, on account of sin. Is 1:11,15; 66:3; Hos 8:13.
 Condemned for offering, to idols. 2 Chr 34:25; Is 65:3,7; Ezek 20:28,31.
Offered to false gods, are offered to devils. Lev 17:7; Deut 32:17; Ps 106:37; 1 Cor 10:20.
On great occasions, very numerous. 2 Chr 5:6; 7:5.
For public use often provided by the state. 2 Chr 31:3.
Illustrative of
 Prayer. Ps 141:2.
 Thanksgiving. Ps 27:6; 107:22; 116:17; Heb 13:15.
 Devotedness. Rom 12:1; Phil 2:17.
 Benevolence. Phil 4:18; Heb 13:16.
 Righteousness. Ps 4:5; 51:19.
 A broken spirit. Ps 51:17.
 Martyrdom. Phil 2:7; 2 Tim 4:6.

Sadducees, The.

A sect of the Jews. Acts 5:17.
Denied the resurrection and a future state. Matt 22:23; Luke 20:27.
The resurrection a cause of dispute between them and the Pharisees. Acts 23:6-9.
Were refused baptism by John. Matt 3:7.
Christ
 Tempted by. Matt 16:1.
 Cautioned his disciples against their principles. Matt 16:6,11,12.
 Vindicated the resurrection against. Matt 22:24-32; Mark 12:19-27.
 Silenced. Matt 22:34.
Persecuted the Christians. Acts 4:1; 5:17,18,40.

Saints, Compared To.

The sun. Judg 5:31; Matt 13:43.
Stars. Dan 12:3.
Lights. Matt 5:14; Phil 2:15.
Mount Zion. Ps 125:1,2.
Lebanon. Hos 14:5-7.
Treasure. Ex 19:5; Ps 135:4.
Jewels. Mal 3:17.
Gold. Job 23:10; Lam 4:2.
Vessels of gold and silver. 2 Tim 2:20.
Stones of a crown. Zech 9:16.
Lively stones. 1 Pet 2:5.
Babes. Matt 11:25; 1 Pet 2:2.
Little children. Matt 18:3; 1 Cor 14:20.
Obedient children. 1 Pet 1:14.
Members of the body. 1 Cor 12:20,27.
Soldiers. 2 Tim 2:3,4.
Runners in a race. 1 Cor 9:24; Heb 12:1.
Wrestlers. 2 Tim 2:5.
Good servants. Matt 25:21.
Strangers and pilgrims. 1 Pet 2:11.
Sheep. Ps 78:52; Matt 25:33; John 10:4.
Lambs. Is 40:11; John 21:15.
Calves of the stall. Mal 4:2.
Lions. Prov 28:1; Mic 5:8.
Eagles. Ps 103:5; Is 40:31.
Doves. Ps 68:13; Is 60:8.
Thirsting deer. Ps 42:1.
Good fishes. Matt 13:48.
Dew and showers. Mic 5:7.
Watered gardens. Is 58:11.
Unfailing springs. Is 58:11.
Vines. Song 6:11; Hos 14:7.
Branches of a vine. John 15:2,4,5.
Pomegranates. Song 4:13.
Good figs. Jer 24:2-7.
Lilies. Song 2:2; Hos 14:5.
Willows by the water courses. Is 44:4.
Trees planted by rivers. Ps 1:3.
Cedars in Lebanon. Ps 92:12.
Palm trees. Ps 92:12.
Green olive trees. Ps 52:8; Hos 14:6.
Fruitful trees. Ps 1:3; Jer 17:8.
Corn. Hos 14:7.
Wheat. Matt 3:12; 13:29,30.
Salt. Matt 5:13.

Salt.

Characterised as good and useful. Mark 9:50.
Used For
 Seasoning food. Job 6:6.
 Seasoning sacrifices. Lev 2:13; Ezek 43:24.
 Ratifying covenants. Num 18:19; 2 Chr 13:5.
 Strengthening new-born infants. Ezek 16:4.
Partaking of another's a bond of friendship. Ezra 4:14.
Lost its savour when exposed to the air. Matt 5:13; Mark 9:50.
Often found
 In pits. Josh 11:8; Zeph 2:9.
 In springs. James 3:12.
 Near the Dead Sea. Num 34:12; Deut 3:17.
Places where it abounded barren and unfruitful. Jer 17:6; Ezek 47:11.
The valley of, celebrated for victories. 2 Sam 8:13; 2 Kin 14:7; 1 Chr 18:12.
Miracles connected with
 Lot's wife turned into a pillar of. Gen 19:26.
 Elisha healed the bad water with. 1 Kin 2:21.
Places sown with, to denote perpetual desolation. Judg 9:45.
Liberally afforded to the Jews after the captivity. Ezra 6:9; 7:22.
Illustrative
 Of saints. Matt 5:13.
 Of grace in the heart. Mark 9:50.
 Of wisdom in speech. Col 4:6.
 (Without savour,) of graceless professors. Matt 5:13; Mark 9:50.
 (Pits of,) of desolation. Zeph 2:9.
 (Salted with fire,) of preparation of the wicked for destruction. Mark 9:49.

Salutations.

Antiquity of. Gen 18:2; 19:1.
Were given
 By brethren to each other. 1 Sam 17:22.
 By inferiors to their superiors. Gen 47:7.
 By superiors to inferiors. 1 Sam 30:21.
 By all passers-by. 1 Sam 10:3,4; Ps 129:8.
 On entering a house. Judg 18:15; Matt 10:12; Luke 1:40,41,44.
Often sent through messengers. 1 Sam 25:5,14; 2 Sam 8:10.
Often sent by letter. Rom 16:21-23; 1 Cor 16:21; Col 4:18; 2 Thess 3:17.
Denied to persons of bad character. 2 John 10.
Persons in haste excused from giving or receiving. 2 Kin 4:29; Luke 10:24.
Expressions used as
 Peace be with thee. Judg 19:20.
 Peace to thee, and peace to thine house, and peace to all that thou hast. 1 Sam 25:6.
 Peace be to this house. Luke 10:5.
 The Lord be with you. Ruth 2:4.
 The Lord bless thee. Ruth 2:4.
 The blessing of the Lord be upon you, we bless you in the name of the Lord. Ps 129:8.
 Blessed be thou of the Lord. 1 Sam 15:13.
 God be gracious to thee. Gen 43:29.
 Art thou in health? 2 Sam 20:9.
 Hail. Matt 26:49; Luke 1:28.
 All hail. Matt 28:9.
Often perfidious. 2 Sam 20:9; Matt 26:49.
Given to Christ in derision. Matt 27:29; 15:18.
Often accompanied by
 Falling on the neck and kissing. Gen 33:4; 45:14,15; Luke 15:20.
 Laying hold of the beard with the right hand. 2 Sam 20:9.
 Bowing frequently to the ground. Gen 33:3.
 Embracing and kissing the feet. Matt 28:9; Luke 7:38,45.
 Touching the hem of the garment. Matt 14:36.
 Falling prostrate on the ground. Esth 8:3; Matt 2:11; Luke 8:41.
 Kissing the dust. Ps 72:9; Is 49:23.
The Jews condemned for giving, only to their countrymen. Matt 5:47.
The Pharisees condemned for seeking, in public. Matt 23:7; Mark 12:38.

Salvation.

Is of God. Ps 3:8; 37:39; Jer 3:23.
Is of the purpose of God. 2 Tim 1:9.
Is of the appointment of God. 1 Thess 5:9.
God is willing to give. 1 Tim 2:4.
Is by Christ. Is 63:9; Eph 5:23.
Is by Christ alone. Is 45:21,22; 59:16; Acts 4:12.
Announced after the fall. Gen 3:15.
Of Israel, predicted. Is 35:4; 45:17; Zech 9:16; Rom 11:26.
Of the Gentiles, predicted. Is 45:22; 49:6; 52:10.

Revealed in the gospel. Eph 1:13; 2 Tim 1:10.
Came to the Gentiles through the fall of the Jews. Rom 11:11.
Christ
The Captain of. Heb 2:10.
The Author of. Heb 5:9.
Appointed for. Is 49:6.
Raised up for. Luke 1:69.
Has. Zech 9:9.
Brings, with him. Is 62:11; Luke 19:9.
Mighty to effect. Is 63:1; Heb 7:25.
Came to effect. Matt 18:11; 1 Tim 1:15.
Died to effect. John 3:14,15; Gal 1:4.
Exalted to give. Acts 5:31.
Is not by works. Rom 11:6; Eph 2:9; 2 Tim 1:9; Titus 3:5.
Is of grace. Eph 2:5,8; 2 Tim 1:9; Titus 2:11.
Is of love. Rom 5:8; 1 John 4:9,10.
Is of mercy. Ps 6:4; Titus 3:5.
Is of the long-suffering of God. 2 Pet 3:15.
Is through faith in Christ. Mark 16:16; Acts 16:31; Rom 10:9; Eph 2:8; 1 Pet 1:5.
Reconciliation to God, a pledge of. Rom 5:10.
Is deliverance from
Sin. Matt 1:21; 1 John 3:5.
Uncleanness. Ezek 36:29.
The devil. Col 2:15; Heb 2:14,15.
Wrath. Rom 5:9; 1 Thess 1:10.
This present evil world. Gal 1:4.
Enemies. Luke 1:71,74.
Eternal death. John 3:16,17.
Confession of Christ necessary to. Rom 10:10.
Regeneration necessary to. John 3:3.
Final perseverance necessary to. Matt 10:22.
Described as
Great. Heb 2:3.
Glorious. 2 Tim 2:10.
Common. Jude 1:3.
From generation to generation. Is 51:8.
To the uttermost. Heb 7:25.
Eternal. Is 45:17; 51:6; Heb 5:9.
Searched into and exhibited by the prophets. 1 Pet 1:10.
The gospel is the power of God to. Rom 1:16; 1 Cor 1:18.
Preaching the word is the appointed means of. 1 Cor 1:21.
The Scriptures are able to make wise to. 2 Tim 3:15; James 1:21.
Now is the day of. Is 49:8; 2 Cor 6:2.
From sin, to be worked out with fear and trembling. Phil 2:12.
Saints
Chosen to. 2 Thess 2:13; 2 Tim 1:9.
Appointed to obtain. 1 Thess 5:9.
Are heirs of. Heb 1:14.
Have, through grace. Acts 15:11.
Have a token of, in their patient suffering for Christ. Phil 1:28,29.
Kept by the power of God to. 1 Pet 1:5.
Beautified with. Ps 149:4.
Clothed with. Is 61:10.
Satisfied by. Luke 2:30.
Love. Ps 40:16.
Hope for. Lam 3:26; Rom 8:24.
Wait for. Gen 49:18; Lam 3:26.
Long for. Ps 119:81,174.
Earnestly look for. Ps 119:123.
Daily approach nearer to. Rom 13:11.
Receive, as the end of their faith. 1 Pet 1:9.
Welcome the tidings of. Is 52:7; Rom 10:15.
Pray to be visited with. Ps 85:7; 106:4; 119:41.
Pray for the assurance of. Ps 35:3.
Pray for a joyful sense of. Ps 51:12.
Evidence, by works. Heb 6:9,10.
Ascribe, to God. Ps 25:5; Is 12:2.
Praise God for. 1 Chr 16:23; Ps 96:2.
Commemorate, with thanks. Ps 116:12.
Rejoice in. Ps 9:14; 21:1; Is 25:9.
Glory in. 1 Cor 1:31; Gal 6:14.
Declare. Ps 40:10; 71:15.
Godly sorrow works repentance to. 2 Cor 7:10.
All the earth shall see. Is 52:10; Luke 3:6.
Ministers
Give the knowledge of. Luke 1:77.
Show the way of. Acts 16:17.
Should exhort to. Ezek 3:18,19; Acts 2:40.
Should labour to lead others to. Rom 11:14.
Should be clothed in. 2 Chr 6:41; Ps 132:16.
Should use self-denial to lead others to. 1 Cor 9:22.
Should endure suffering that the elect may obtain. 2 Tim 2:10.
Are a sweet savour of Christ to God, in those who obtain. 2 Cor 2:15.
The heavenly host ascribe, to God. Rev 7:10; 19:1.
Sought in vain from
Idols. Is 45:20; Jer 2:28.
Earthly power. Jer 3:23.
No escape for those who neglect. Heb 2:3.
Is far off from the wicked. Ps 119:155; Is 59:11.
Illustrated by
A rock. Deut 32:15; 2 Sam 22:47; Ps 95:1.
A horn. Ps 18:2; Luke 1:69.
A tower. 2 Sam 22:51.
A helmet. Is 59:17; Eph 6:17.
A shield. 2 Sam 22:36.
A lamp. Is 62:1.
A cup. Ps 116:13.
Clothing. 2 Chr 6:41; Ps 132:16; 149:4; Is 61:10.
Wells. Is 12:3.
Walls and bulwarks. Is 26:1; 60:18.
Chariots. Hab 3:8.
A victory. 1 Cor 15:57.
Typified. Num 21:4-9; John 3:14,15.

Samaria, Ancient.

The territory of Ephraim and Manasseh properly so called. Josh 17:17,18; Is 28:1.
The whole kingdom of Israel sometimes called. Ezek 16:46,51; Hos 8:5,6.
Had many cities. 1 Kin 13:32.
Samaria the capital of
Built by Omri king of Israel. 1 Kin 16:23,24.
Called after Shemer the owner of the hill on which it was built. 1 Kin 16:24.
Called the mountain of Samaria. Amos 4:1; 6:1.
Called the head of Ephraim. Is 7:9.
Kings of Israel sometime took their titles from. 1 Kin 21:1; 2 Kin 1:3.
The residence of the kings of Israel. 1 Kin 16:29; 2 Kin 1:2; 3:1,6.
The burial place of the kings of Israel. 1 Kin 16:28; 22:37; 2 Kin 13:13.
Was a fenced city, and well provided with arms. 2 Kin 10:2.
The pool of Samaria near to. 1 Kin 22:38.
The prophet Elisha dwelt in. 2 Kin 2:25; 5:3; 6:32.
Besieged by Benhadad. 1 Kin 20:1-12.
Deliverance of, predicted. 1 Kin 20:13,14.
Deliverance of, effected. 1 Kin 20:15-21.
Besieged again by Benhadad. 2 Kin 6:24.
Suffered severely from famine. 2 Kin 6:25-29.
Elisha predicted plenty in. 2 Kin 7:1,2.
Delivered by miraculous means. 2 Kin 7:6,7.
Remarkable plenty in, as foretold by Elisha. 2 Kin 7:16-20.
Besieged and taken by Shalmaneser. 2 Kin 17:5,6; 18:9,10.
A mountainous country. Jer 31:5; Amos 3:9.
People of characterised as
Proud and arrogant. Is 9:9.
Corrupt and wicked. Ezek 16:46,47; Hos 7:1; Amos 3:9,10.
Idolatrous. Ezek 23:5; Amos 8:14; Mic 1:7.
Predictions respecting its destruction. Is 8:4; 9:11,12; Hos 13:16; Amos 3:11,12; Mic 1:6.
Inhabitants of, carried captive to Assyria. 2 Kin 17:6,23; 18:11.
Repeopled from Assyria. 2 Kin 17:24,25.

Samaria, Modern.

Situated between Judea and Galilee. Luke 17:11; John 4:3,4.
Had many cities. Matt 10:5; Luke 9:52.
Cities of, mentioned in Scripture
Samaria. Acts 8:5.
Sychar. John 4:5.
Antipatris. Acts 23:31.
Christ preached in. John 4:39-42.
Christ at first forbade his disciples to visit. Matt 10:5.
Christ after his resurrection commanded the gospel to be preached in. Acts 1:8.
Inhabitants of
Their true descent. 2 Kin 17:24; Ezra 4:9,10.
Boasted descent from Jacob. John 4:12.
Professed to worship God. Ezra 4:2.
Their religion mixed with idolatry. 2 Kin 17:41; John 4:22.

Worshipped on Mount Gerizim. John 4:20.
Opposed the Jews after their return from captivity. Neh 4:1-18.
Expected the Messiah. John 4:25,29.
Were superstitious. Acts 8:9-11.
More humane and grateful than the Jews. Luke 10:33-36; 17:16-18.
Abhorred by the Jews. John 8:48.
Had no intercourse or dealings with the Jews. Luke 9:52,53; John 4:9.
Ready to hear and embrace the gospel. John 4:39-42; Acts 8:6-8.
The persecuted Christians fled to. Acts 8:1.
The gospel first preached in, by Philip. Acts 8:5.
Many Christian churches in. Acts 9:31.

Sanctification.

Is separation to the service of God. Ps 4:3; 2 Cor 6:17.
Effected by
God. Ezek 37:28; 1 Thess 5:23; Jude 1:1.
Christ. Heb 2:11; 13:12.
The Holy Spirit. Rom 15:16; 1 Cor 6:11.
In Christ. 1 Cor 1:2.
Through the atonement of Christ. Heb 10:10; 13:12.
Through the word of God. John 17:17,19; Eph 5:26.
Christ made, of God, to us. 1 Cor 1:30.
Saints elected to salvation through. 2 Thess 2:13; 1 Pet 1:2.
All saints are in a state of. Acts 20:32; 26:18; 1 Cor 6:11.
The Church made glorious by. Eph 5:26,27.
Should lead to
Mortification of sin. 1 Thess 4:3,4.
Holiness. Rom 6:22; Eph 5:7-9.
Offering up of saints acceptable through. Rom 15:16.
Saints fitted for the service of God by. 2 Tim 2:21.
God wills all saints to have. 1 Thess 4:3.
Ministers
Set apart to God's service by. Jer 1:5.
Should pray that their people may enjoy complete. 1 Thess 5:23.
Should exhort their people to walk in. 1 Thess 4:1,3.
None can inherit the kingdom of God without. 1 Cor 6:9-11.
Typified. Gen 2:3; Ex 13:2; 19:14; 40:9-15; Lev 27:14-16.

Scapegoat, The.

Part of the sin offering on the day of atonement. Lev 16:5,7.
Chosen by lot. Lev 16:8.
The high priest transferred the sins of Israel to, by confessing them with both hands upon its head. Lev 16:21.
Sent into the wilderness by the hands of a fit person. Lev 16:21,22.
Communicated uncleanness to
The high priest. Lev 16:24.
The man who lead him away. Lev 16:26.
Typical of Christ. Is 53:6,11,12.

Sciences.

Architecture. Deut 8:12; 1 Chr 29:19.
Arithmetic. Gen 15:5; Lev 26:8; Job 29:18.
Astronomy. Job 38:31,32; Is 13:10.
Astrology. Is 47:13.
Botany. 1 Kin 4:33.
Geography. Gen 10:1-30; Is 11:11.
History and Chronology. 1 Kin 22:39; 2 Kin 1:18; 1 Chr 9:1; 29:29.
Mechanics. Gen 6:14-16; 11:4; Ex 14:6,7.
Medicine. Jer 8:22; Mark 5:26.
Music. 1 Chr 16:4-7; 25:6.
Navigation. 1 Kin 9:27; Ps 107:23.
Surveying. Josh 18:4-9; Neh 2:12-16; Ezek 40:5,6; Zech 2:2.
Zoology. 1 Kin 4:33.

Scorning and Mocking.

The sufferings of Christ by, predicted. Ps 22:6-8; Is 53:3; Luke 18:32.
Christ endured. Matt 9:24; 27:29.
Saints endure, on account of
Being children of God. Gen 21:9; Gal 4:29.
Their uprightness. Job 12:4.
Their faith. Heb 11:36.
Their faithfulness in declaring the word of God. Jer 20:7,8.
Their zeal for God's house. Neh 2:19.
The wicked indulge in, against
The second coming of Christ. 2 Pet 3:3,4.
The gifts of the Spirit. Acts 2:13.
God's threatening. Is 5:19; Jer 17:15.
God's ministers. 2 Chr 36:16.
God's ordinances. Lam 1:7.
Saints. Ps 123:4; Lam 3:14,63.
The resurrection of the dead. Acts 17:32.
All solemn admonitions. 2 Chr 30:6-10.
Idolaters addicted to. Is 57:3-6.
Drunkards addicted to. Ps 69:12; Hos 7:5.
Those who are addicted to
Delight in. Prov 1:22.
Are contentious. Prov 22:10.
Are scorned by God. Prov 3:34.
Are hated by men. Prov 24:9.
Are avoided by saints. Ps 1:1; Jer 15:17.
Walk after their own lusts. 2 Pet 3:3.
Are proud and haughty. Prov 21:24.
Hear not rebuke. Prov 13:1.
Love not those who reprove. Prov 15:12.
Hate those who reprove. Prov 9:8.
Go not to the wise. Prov 15:12.
Bring others into danger. Prov 29:8.
Shall themselves endure. Ezek 23:32.
Characteristic of the latter days. 2 Pet 3:3; Jude 1:18.
Woe denounced against. Is 5:18,19.
Punishment for. 2 Chr 36:17; Prov 19:29; Is 29:20; Lam 3:64-66.
Exemplified
Ishmael. Gen 21:9.
Children at Bethel. 2 Kin 2:23.
Ephraim and Manasseh. 2 Chr 30:10.
Chiefs of Judah. 2 Chr 36:16.
Sanballat. Neh 4:1.
Enemies of Joab. Job 30:1,9.
Enemies of David. Ps 35:15,16.
Rulers of Israel. Is 28:14.
Ammonites. Ezek 25:3.
People of Tyre. Ezek 26:2.
Heathen. Ezek 36:2,3.
Soldiers. Matt 27:28-30; Luke 23:36.
Chief Priests. Matt 27:41.
Pharisees. Luke 16:14.
The men who held Jesus. Luke 22:63,64.
Herod. Luke 23:11.
People and rulers. Luke 23:35.
Some of the multitude. Acts 2:13.
Athenians. Acts 17:32.

Scorpion, The.

Armed with a sharp sting in its tail. Rev 9:10.
Sting of, venomous and caused torment. Rev 9:5.
Abounded in the great desert. Deut 8:15.
Unfit for food. Luke 11:12.
Illustrative of
Wicked men. Ezek 2:6.
Ministers of Antichrist. Rev 9:3,5,10.
Severe scourges. 1 Kin 12:11.
Christ gave his disciples power over. Luke 10:19.

Scribes.

Antiquity of. Judg 5:14.
Wore an inkhorn at their girdles. Ezek 9:2,3.
Families celebrated for furnishing
Kenites. 1 Chr 2:55.
Zebulun. Judg 5:14.
Levi. 1 Chr 24:6; 2 Chr 34:13.
Generally men of great wisdom. 1 Chr 27:32.
Often learned in the law. Ezra 7:6.
Were ready writers. Ps 45:1.
Acted as
Secretaries to kings. 2 Sam 8:17; 20:25; 2 Kin 12:10; Esth 3:12.
Secretaries to prophets. Jer 36:5,26.
Notaries in courts of justice. Jer 32:11,12.
Religious teachers. Neh 8:2-6.
Writers of public documents. 1 Chr 24:6.
Keepers of the muster-rolls of the host. 2 Kin 25:19; 2 Chr 26:11; Jer 52:25.
Modern
Were doctors of the law. Mark 12:28; Matt 22:35.
Wore long robes and loved pre-eminence. Mark 12:38,39.
Sat in Moses' seat. Matt 23:2.
Were frequently Pharisees. Acts 23:9.
Esteemed wise and learned. 1 Cor 1:20.
Regarded as interpreters of Scripture. Matt 2:4; 17:10; Mark 12:35.
Their manner of teaching contrasted with that of Christ. Matt 7:29; Mark 1:22.
Condemned by Christ for hypocrisy. Matt 23:15.
Often offended at out Lord's conduct and teaching. Matt 21:15; Mark 2:6,7,16; 3:22.
Tempted our Lord. John 8:3.
Active in procuring our Lord's death. Matt 26:3; Luke 23:10.

Persecuted the Christians. Acts 4:5; 18:21; 6:12.
Illustrative of well instructed ministers of the gospel. Matt 13:52.

Scriptures, The.

Given by inspiration of God. 2 Tim 3:16.
Given by inspiration of the Holy Spirit. Acts 1:16; Heb 3:7; 2 Pet 1:21.
Christ sanctioned, by appealing to them. Matt 4:4; Mark 12:10; John 7:42.
Christ taught out of. Luke 24:27.
Are called the
- Word. James 1:21-23; 1 Pet 2:2.
- Word of God. Luke 11:28; Heb 4:12.
- Word of Christ. Col 3:16.
- Word of truth. James 1:18.
- Holy Scriptures. Rom 1:2; 2 Tim 3:15.
- Scripture of truth. Dan 10:21.
- Book. Ps 40:7; Rev 22:19.
- Book of the Lord. Is 34:16.
- Book of the law. Neh 8:3; Gal 3:10.
- Law of the Lord. Ps 1:2; Is 30:9.
- Sword of the Spirit. Eph 6:17.
- Oracles of God. Rom 3:2; 1 Pet 4:11.

Contain the promises of the gospel. Rom 1:2.
Reveal the laws, statutes, and judgments of God. Deut 4:5,14; Ex 24:3,4.
Record divine prophecies. 2 Pet 1:19-21.
Testify of Christ. John 5:39; Acts 10:43; 18:28; 1 Cor 15:3.
Are full and sufficient. Luke 16:29,31.
Are an unerring guide. Prov 6:23; 2 Pet 1:19.
Are able to make wise to salvation through faith in Christ Jesus. 2 Tim 3:15.
Are profitable both for doctrine and practice. 2 Tim 3:16,17.
Described as
- Pure. Ps 12:6; 119:140; Prov 30:5.
- True. Ps 119:160; John 17:17.
- Perfect. Ps 19:7.
- Precious. Ps 19:10.
- Quick and powerful. Heb 4:12.

Written for our instruction. Rom 15:4.
Intended for the use of all men. Rom 16:26.
Nothing to be taken from, or added to. Deut 4:2; 12:32.
One portion of, to be compared with another. 1 Cor 2:13.
Designed for
- Regenerating. James 1:18; 1 Pet 1:23.
- Quickening. Ps 119:50,93.
- Illuminating. Ps 119:130.
- Converting the soul. Ps 19:7.
- Making wise the simple. Ps 19:7.
- Sanctifying. John 17:17; Eph 5:26.
- Producing faith. John 20:31.
- Producing hope. Ps 119:49; Rom 15:4.
- Producing obedience. Deut 17:19,20.
- Cleansing the heart. John 15:3; Eph 5:26.
- Cleansing the ways. Ps 119:9.
- Keeping from destructive paths. Ps 17:4.
- Supporting life. Deut 8:3; Matt 4:4.
- Promoting growth in grace. 1 Pet 2:2.
- Building up in the faith. Acts 20:32.
- Admonishing. Ps 19:11; 1 Cor 10:11.
- Comforting. Ps 119:82; Rom 15:4.
- Rejoicing the heart. Ps 19:8; 119:111.
- Work effectually in them that believe. 1 Thess 2:13.

The letter of, without the spirit, killeth. John 6:63; 2 Cor 3:6.
Ignorance of, a source of error. Matt 22:29; Acts 13:27.
Christ enables us to understand. Luke 24:45.
The Holy Spirit enable us to understand. John 16:13; 1 Cor 2:10-14.
No prophecy of, is of any private interpretation. 2 Pet 1:20.
Everything should be tried by. Is 8:20; Acts 17:11.
Should be
- The standard of teaching. 1 Pet 4:11.
- Believed. John 2:22.
- Appealed to. 1 Cor 1:31; 1 Pet 1:16.
- Read. Deut 17:19; Is 34:16.
- Read publicly to all. Deut 31:11-13; Neh 8:3; Jer 36:6; Acts 13:15.
- Known. 2 Tim 3:15.
- Received, not as the word of men, but as the word of God. 1 Thess 2:13.
- Received with meekness. James 1:21.
- Searched. John 5:39; 7:52.
- Searched daily. Acts 17:11.
- Laid up in the heart. Deut 6:6; 11:18.
- Taught to children. Deut 6:7; 11:19; 2 Tim 3:15.
- Taught to all. 2 Chr 17:7-9; Neh 8:7,8.
- Talked of continually. Deut 6:7.
- Not handled deceitfully. 2 Cor 4:2.
- Not only heard, but obeyed. Matt 7:24; Luke 11:28; James 1:22.
- Used against our spiritual enemies. Matt 4:4,7,10; Eph 6:11,17.

All should desire to hear. Neh 8:1.
Mere hearers of, deceive themselves. James 1:22.
Advantage of possessing. Rom 3:2.
Saints
- Love exceedingly. Ps 119:97,113,159,167.
- Delight in. Ps 1:2.
- Regard, as sweet. Ps 119:103.
- Esteem, above all things. Job 23:12.
- Long after. Ps 119:82.
- Stand in awe of. Ps 119:161; Is 66:2.
- Keep, in remembrance. Ps 119:16.
- Grieve when men disobey. Ps 119:158.
- Hide, in their hearts. Ps 119:11.
- Hope in. Ps 119:74,81,147.
- Meditate in. Ps 1:2; 119:99,148.
- Rejoice in. Ps 119:162; Jer 15:16.
- Trust in. Ps 119:42.
- Obey. Ps 119:67; Luke 8:21; John 17:6.
- Speak of. Ps 119:172.
- Esteem, as a light. Ps 119:105.
- Pray to be taught. Ps 119:12,13,33,66.
- Pray to be conformed to. Ps 119:133.
- Plead the promises of, in prayer. Ps 119:25,28,41,76,169.

They who search, are truly noble. Acts 17:11.
Blessedness of hearing and obeying. Luke 11:28; James 1:25.
Let them dwell richly in you. Col 3:16.
The wicked
- Corrupt. 2 Cor 2:17.
- Make, of none effect through their traditions. Mark 7:9-13.
- Reject. Jer 8:9.
- Stumble at. 1 Pet 2:8.
- Obey not. Ps 119:158.
- Frequently wrest, to their own destruction. 2 Pet 3:16.

Denunciations against those who add to, or take from. Rev 22:18,19.
Destruction of, punished. Jer 36:29-31.

Sea, The.

The gathering together of the waters originally called. Gen 1:10.
Great rivers often called. Is 11:15; Jer 51:36.
Lakes often called. Deut 3:17; Matt 8:24,27,32.
God
- Created. Ex 20:11; Ps 95:5; Acts 14:15.
- Made the birds and fished out of. Gen 1:20-22.
- Founded the earth upon. Ps 24:2.
- Set bounds to, by a perpetual decree. Job 26:10; 38:8,10,11; Prov 8:27,29.
- Measures the waters of. Is 40:12.
- Does what he pleases in. Ps 135:6.
- Dries up, by his rebuke. Is 50:2; Nah 1:4.
- Shakes, by his word. Hag 2:6.
- Stills, by his power. Ps 65:7; 89:9; 107:29.

Of immense extent. Job 11:9; Ps 104:25.
Of great depth. Ps 68:22.
Rivers supplied by exhalations from. Eccl 1:7.
Replenished by rivers. Eccl 1:7; Ezek 47:8.
Called the
- Deep. Job 41:31; Ps 107:24; 2 Cor 11:25.
- Great waters. Ps 77:19.
- Great and wide sea. Ps 104:25.

The clouds the garment of. Job 38:9.
Darkness the swaddling band of. Job 38:9.
Sand the barrier of. Jer 5:22.
Inhabited by innumerable creatures great and small. Ps 104:25,26.
The wonders of God seen in. Ps 107:24.
Made to glorify God. Ps 69:34; 148:7.
Seas mentioned in Scripture
- The Adriatic or Sea of Adria. Acts 27:27.
- Mediterranean or Great Sea. Num 34:6; Deut 11:24; 34:2; Zech 14:8.
- Red Sea. Ex 10:19; 13:18; 23:31.
- Sea of Joppa or Sea of the Philistines. Ezra 3:7; Ex 23:21.
- Salt or Dead Sea. Gen 14:3; Num 34:12.
- Sea of Galilee. Matt 4:18; 8:32; John 6:1.
- Sea of Jazer. Jer 48:32.

Raised by the wind. Ps 107:25,26; Jon 1:4.
Caused to foam by Leviathan. Job 41:31,32.
The waves of
- Raised upon high. Ps 93:3; 107:25.
- Tossed to and fro. Jer 5:22.
- Multitudinous. Jer 51:42.
- Mighty. Ps 93:4; Acts 27:41.
- Tumultuous. Luke 21:25; Jude 1:13.

The shore of, covered with sand. Gen 22:17; 1 Kin 4:29; Job 6:3; Ps 78:27.

Numerous islands in. Ezek 26:18.
Passed over in ships. Ps 104:26; 107:23.
Sailing on, dangerous. Acts 27:9,20; 2 Cor 11:26.
Commercial nations
Often built cities on the borders of. Gen 49:13; Ezek 27:3; Nah 3:8.
Derived great wealth from. Deut 33:19.
Shall give up its dead at the last day. Rev 20:13.
The renewed earth shall be without. Rev 21:1.
Illustrative
Of heavy afflictions. Is 43:2; Lam 2:13.
(Troubled,) of the wicked. Is 57:20.
(Roaring,) of hostile armies. Is 5:30; Jer 6:23.
(Waves of,) of righteousness. Is 48:18.
(Waves of,) of devastating armies. Ezek 26:3,4.
(Waves of,) of the unsteady. James 1:6.
(Covered with waters,) of the diffusion of spiritual knowledge over the earth in the latter days. Is 11:9; Hab 2:14.
(Smooth as glass,) of the peace of heaven. Rev 4:6; 15:2.

Sealing of the Holy Spirit.

Christ received. John 6:27.
Saints receive. 2 Cor 1:22; Eph 1:13.
Is to the day of redemption. Eph 4:30.
The wicked do not receive. Rev 9:4.
Judgment suspended until all saints receive. Rev 7:3.
Typified. Rom 4:11.

Seals.

Called signet. Gen 38:18,25.
Precious stones set in gold used as. Ex 28:11.
Inscriptions upon, alluded to. 2 Tim 2:19.
Generally worn as rings or bracelets. Jer 22:24.
Impressions of
Frequently taken in clay. Job 38:14.
Used for security. Dan 6:17; Matt 27:66.
Attached to all royal decrees. 1 Kin 21:8; Esth 3:12; 8:8.
Attached to covenants. Neh 9:38; 10:1.
Attached to lease and transfers of property. Jer 32:9-12,44.
Set upon treasures. Deut 32:34.
Attached to the victims approved for sacrifice, alluded to. John 6:27.
Were given by kings as a badge of authority. Gen 41:41,42.
Illustrative of
Circumcision. Rom 4:11.
Converts. 1 Cor 9:2.
What is dear or valued. Song 8:6; Jer 22:24; Hag 2:23.
Secrecy. Dan 12:4; Rev 5:1; 10:4.
Security. Song 4:12; 2 Tim 2:19; Rev 7:2-8; 20:3.
Full approval. John 3:33.
Appropriation of saints to God by the Spirit. 2 Cor 1:22; Eph 1:13; 4:30.
Restraint. Job 9:7; 37:7; Rev 20:3.

Second Coming of Christ, The.

Time of, unknown. Matt 24:36; Mark 13:32.
Called the
Times of refreshing from the presence of the Lord. Acts 3:19.
Times of restitution of all things. Acts 3:21; Rom 8:21.
Last time. 1 Pet 1:5.
Appearing of Jesus Christ. 1 Pet 1:7.
Revelation of Jesus Christ. 1 Pet 1:13.
Glorious appearing of the great God and our Saviour. Titus 2:13.
Coming of the day of God. 2 Pet 3:12.
Day of our Lord Jesus Christ. 1 Cor 1:8.
Foretold by
Prophets. Dan 7:13; Jude 1:14.
Himself. Matt 25:31; John 14:3.
Apostles. Acts 3:20; 1 Tim 6:14.
Angels. Acts 1:10,11.
Signs preceding. Matt 24:3-51.
The Manner of
In clouds. Matt 24:30; 26:64; Rev 1:7.
In the glory of his Father. Matt 16:27.
In his own glory. Matt 25:31.
In flaming fire. 2 Thess 1:8.
With power and great glory. Matt 24:30.
As he ascended. Acts 1:9,11.
With a shout and the voice of the Archangel. 1 Thess 4:16.
Accompanied by angels. Matt 16:27; 25:31; Mark 8:38; 2 Thess 1:7.
With his saints. 1 Thess 3:13; Jude 1:14.
Suddenly. Mark 13:36.
Unexpectedly. Matt 24:44; Luke 12:40.
As a thief in the night. 1 Thess 5:2; 2 Pet 3:10; Rev 16:15.
As the lightning. Matt 24:27.
The heavens and earth shall be dissolved, etc. at. 2 Pet 3:10,12.
They who shall have died in Christ shall rise first at. 1 Thess 4:16.
The saints alive at, shall be caught up to meet him. 1 Thess 4:17.
Is not to make atonement. Heb 9:28; Rom 6:9,10; Heb 10:14.
The purposes of, are to
Complete the salvation of saints. Heb 9:28; 1 Pet 1:5.
Be glorified in his saints. 2 Thess 1:10.
Be admired in them that believe. 2 Thess 1:10.
Bring to light the hidden things of darkness. 1 Cor 4:5.
Judge. Ps 50:3,4; John 5:22; 2 Tim 4:1; Jude 1:15; Rev 20:11-13.
Reign. Is 24:23; Dan 7:14; Rev 11:15.
Destroy death. 1 Cor 15:25,26.
Every eye shall see him at. Rev 1:7.
Should be always considered as at hand. Rom 13:12; Phil 4:5; 1 Pet 4:7.
Blessedness of being prepared for. Matt 24:46; Luke 12:37,38.
Saints
Assured of. Job 19:25,26.
Love. 2 Tim 4:8.
Look for. Phil 3:20; Titus 2:13.
Wait for. 1 Cor 1:7; 1 Thess 1:10.
Haste to. 2 Pet 3:12.
Pray for. Rev 22:20.
Should be ready for. Matt 24:44; Luke 12:40.
Should watch for. Matt 24:42; Mark 13:35-37; Luke 21:36.
Should be patient to. 2 Thess 3:5; James 5:7,8.
Shall be preserved to. Phil 1:6; 2 Tim 4:18; 1 Pet 1:5; Jude 1:24.
Shall not be ashamed at. 1 John 2:28; 4:17.
Shall be blameless at. 1 Cor 1:8; 1 Thess 3:13; 5:23; Jude 1:24.
Shall be like him at. Phil 3:21; 1 John 3:2.
Shall see him as he is, at. 1 John 3:2.
Shall appear with him in glory at. Col 3:4.
Shall receive a crown of glory at. 2 Tim 4:8; 1 Pet 5:4.
Shall reign with him at. Dan 7:27; 2 Tim 2:12; Rev 5:10; 20:6; 22:5.
Faith of, shall be found to praise at. 1 Pet 1:7.
The wicked
Scoff at. 2 Pet 3:3,4.
Presume upon the delay of. Matt 24:48.
Shall be surprised by. Matt 24:37-39; 1 Thess 5:3; 2 Pet 3:10.
Shall be punished at. 2 Thess 1:8,9.
The man of sin to be destroyed at. 2 Thess 2:8.
Illustrated. Matt 25:6; Luke 12:36,39; 19:12,15.

Seed.

Every herb, tree and grass yields its own. Gen 1:11,12,29.
Each kind of, has its own body. 1 Cor 15:38.
Sowing of
Time for, called seed time. Gen 8:22.
Necessary to its productiveness. John 12:24; 1 Cor 15:36.
Required constant diligence. Eccl 11:4,6.
Often attended with great waste. Matt 13:4,5,7.
Often attended with danger. Ps 126:5,6.
Yearly return of time of sowing, secured by covenant. Gen 8:21,22.
The ground carefully ploughed, and prepared for. Is 28:24,25.
Often sown beside rivers. Eccl 11:1; Is 32:20.
Often trodden into the ground, by the feet of oxen. Is 32:20.
Required to be watered by the rain. Is 55:10.
In Egypt required to be artificially watered. Deut 11:10.
Yielded an abundant increase in Canaan. Gen 26:12; Matt 13:23.
Mosaic laws respecting
Different kinds of, not to be sown in the same field. Lev 19:19; Deut 22:9.

If dry, exempted from uncleanness though touched by an unclean thing. Lev 11:37.
If wet, rendered unclean by contact with an unclean thing. Lev 11:38.
The tithe of, to be given to God. Lev 27:30.
Not to be sown during the sabbatical year. Lev 25:4,20.
Not to be sown in year of jubilee. Lev 25:11.
Difference between, and the plant which grows from it, noticed. 1 Cor 15:37,38.
The Jews punished by
Its rotting in the ground. Joel 1:17; Mal 2:3.
Its yielding but little increase. Is 5:10; Hag 1:6.
Its increase being consumed by locusts. Deut 28:38; Joel 1:4.
Its increase being consumed by enemies. Lev 26:16; Deut 28:33,51.
Its being choked by thorns. Jer 12:13; Matt 13:7.
Illustrative of
The word of God. Luke 8:11; 1 Pet 1:23.
Spiritual life. 1 John 3:9.
Sowing, illustrative of
Preaching the gospel. Matt 13:3,32; 1 Cor 9:11.
Scattering or dispersing a people. Zech 10:9.
Christian liberality. Eccl 11:6; 2 Cor 9:6.
Men's works producing a corresponding recompence. Job 4:8; Hos 10:12; Gal 6:7,8.
The death of Christ and its effects. John 12:24.
The burial of the body. 1 Cor 15:36-38.

SEEKING GOD.

Commanded. Is 55:6; Matt 7:7.
Includes seeking
His Name. Ps 83:16.
His word. Is 34:16.
His face. Ps 27:8; 105:4.
His strength. 1 Chr 16:11; Ps 105:4.
His commandments. 1 Chr 28:8; Mal 2:7.
His precepts. Ps 119:45,94.
His kingdom. Matt 6:33; Luke 12:31.
His righteousness. Matt 6:33.
Christ. Mal 3:1; Luke 2:15,16.
Honour which comes from him. John 5:44.
Justification by Christ. Gal 2:16,17.
The city which God has prepared. Heb 11:10,16; 13:14.
By prayer. Job 8:5; Dan 9:3.
In his house. Deut 12:5; Ps 27:4.
Should be
Immediate. Hos 10:12.
Evermore. Ps 105:4.
While he may be found. Is 55:6.
With diligence. Heb 11:6.
With the heart. Deut 4:29; 1 Chr 22:19.
In the day of trouble. Ps 77:2.
Ensures
His being found. Deut 4:29; 1 Chr 28:9; Prov 8:17; Jer 29:13.
His favour. Lam 3:25.
His protection. Ezra 8:22.
His not forsaking us. Ps 9:10.
Life. Ps 69:32; Amos 5:4,6.
Prosperity. Job 8:5,6; Ps 34:10.
Being heard of him. Ps 34:4.
Understanding all things. Prov 28:5.
Gifts of righteousness. Hos 10:12.
Imperative upon all. Is 8:19.
Afflictions designed to lead to. Ps 78:33,34; Hos 5:15.
None, by nature, are found to be engaged in. Ps 14:2; Rom 3:11; Luke 12:23,30.
Saints
Specially exhorted to. Zeph 2:3.
Desirous of. Job 5:8.
Purpose, in heart. Ps 27:8.
Prepare their hearts for. 2 Chr 30:19.
Set their hearts to. 2 Chr 11:16.
Engage in, with the whole heart. 2 Chr 15:12; Ps 119:10.
Early in. Job 8:5; Ps 63:1; Is 26:9.
Earnest in. Song 3:2,4.
Characterised by. Ps 24:6.
Is never in vain. Is 45:19.
Blessedness of. Ps 119:2.
Leads to joy. Ps 70:4; 105:3.
Ends in praise. Ps 22:26.
Promise connected with. Ps 69:32.
Shall be rewarded. Heb 11:6.
The wicked
Are gone out of the way of. Ps 14:2,3; Rom 3:11,12.
Prepare not their hearts for. 2 Chr 12:14.
Refuse, through pride. Ps 10:4.
Not led to, by affliction. Is 9:13.
Sometimes pretend to. Ezra 4:2; Is 58:2.
Rejected, when too late in. Prov 1:28.
They who neglect denounced. Is 31:1.
Punishment of those who neglect. Zeph 1:4-6.
Exemplified
Asa. 2 Chr 14:7.
Jehoshaphat. 2 Chr 17:3,4.
Uzziah. 2 Chr 26:5.
Hezekiah. 2 Chr 31:21.
Josiah. 2 Chr 34:3.
Ezra. Ezra 7:10.
David. Ps 34:4.
Daniel. Dan 9:3,4.

SELF-DELUSION.

A characteristic of the wicked. Ps 49:18.
Prosperity frequently leads to. Ps 30:6; Hos 12:8; Luke 12:17-19.
Obstinate sinners often given up to. Ps 81:11,12; Hos 4:17; 2 Thess 2:10,11.
Exhibited in thinking that
Our own ways are right. Prov 14:12.
We should adhere to established wicked practices. Jer 44:17.
We are pure. Prov 30:12.
We are better than others. Luke 18:11.
We are rich in spiritual things. Rev 3:17.
We may have peace while in sin. Deut 29:19.
We are above adversity. Ps 10:6.
Gifts entitle us to heaven. Matt 7:21,22.
Privileges entitle us to heaven. Matt 3:9; Luke 13:25,26.
God will not punish our sins. Ps 10:11; Jer 5:12.
Christ shall not come to judge. 2 Pet 3:4.
Our lives shall be prolonged. Is 56:12; Luke 12:19; James 4:13.
Frequently preserved in, to the last. Matt 7:22; 25:11,12; Luke 13:24,25.
Fatal consequences of. Matt 7:23; 24:48-51; Luke 12:20; 1 Thess 5:3.
Exemplified
Ahab. 1 Kin 20:27,34.
Israelites. Hos 12:8.
Jews. John 8:33,41.
Church of Laodicea. Rev 3:17.
Babylon. Is 47:7-11.

SELF-DENIAL.

Christ set an example of. Matt 4:8-10; 8:20; John 6:38; Rom 15:3; Phil 2:6-8.
A test of devotedness to Christ. Matt 10:37,38; Luke 9:23,24.
Necessary
In following Christ. Luke 14:27-33.
In the warfare of saints. 2 Tim 2:4.
To the triumph of saints. 1 Cor 9:25-27.
Ministers especially called to exercise. 2 Cor 6:4,5.
Should be exercised in
Denying ungodliness and worldly lusts. Rom 6:12; Titus 2:12.
Controlling the appetite. Prov 23:2.
Abstaining from fleshly lusts. 1 Pet 2:11.
No longer living to lusts of men. 1 Pet 4:2.
Mortifying sinful lusts. Mark 9:43; Col 3:5.
Mortifying deeds of the body. Rom 8:13.
Not pleasing ourselves. Rom 15:1-3.
Not seeking out own profit. 1 Cor 10:24,33; 13:5; Phil 2:4.
Preferring the profit of others. Rom 14:20,21; 1 Cor 10:24,33.
Assisting others. Luke 3:11.
Even lawful things. 1 Cor 10:23.
Forsaking all. Luke 14:33.
Taking up the cross and following Christ. Matt 10:38; 16:24.
Crucifying the flesh. Gal 5:24.
Being crucified with Christ. Rom 6:6.
Being crucified to the world. Gal 6:14.
Putting off the old man which is corrupt. Eph 4:22; Col 3:9.
Preferring Christ to all earthly relations. Matt 8:21,22; Luke 14:26.
Becomes strangers and pilgrims. Heb 11:13-15; 1 Pet 2:11.
Danger of neglecting. Matt 16:25,26; 1 Cor 9:27.
Reward of. Matt 19:28,29; Rom 8:13.
Happy result. 2 Pet 1:4.
Exemplified
Abraham. Gen 13:9; Heb 11:8,9.
Widow of Zarephath. 1 Kin 17:12-15.
Esther. Esth 4:16.
Rechabites. Jer 35:6,7.

Daniel. Dan 1:8-16.
Apostles. Matt 19:27.
Simon, Andrew, James, and John. Mark 1:16-20.
Poor Widow. Luke 21:4.
The Christians. Acts 2:45; 4:34.
Barnabas. Acts 4:36,37.
Paul. Acts 20:24; 1 Cor 9:19,27.
Moses. Heb 11:24,25.

SELF-EXAMINATION.

Enjoined. 2 Cor 13:5.
Necessary before the communion. 1 Cor 11:28.
Cause of difficulty in. Jer 17:9.
Should be engaged in
With holy awe. Ps 4:4.
With diligent search. Ps 77:6; Lam 3:40.
With prayer for divine searching. Ps 26:2; 139:23,24.
With purpose of amendment. Ps 119:59; Lam 3:40.
Advantages of. 1 Cor 11:31; Gal 6:4; 1 John 3:20-22.

SELFISHNESS.

Contrary to the law of God. Lev 19:18; Matt 22:39; James 2:8.
The example of Christ condemns. John 4:34; Rom 15:3; 2 Cor 8:9.
God hates. Mal 1:10.
Exhibited in
Being lovers of ourselves. 2 Tim 3:2.
Pleasing ourselves. Rom 15:1.
Seeking our own. 1 Cor 10:33; Phil 2:21.
Seeking after gain. Is 56:11.
Seeking undue precedence. Matt 20:21.
Living to ourselves. 2 Cor 5:15.
Neglect of the poor. 1 John 3:17.
Serving God for reward. Mal 1:10.
Performing duty for reward. Mic 3:11.
Inconsistent with Christian love. 1 Cor 13:5.
Inconsistent with communion of saints. Rom 12:4,5; 1 Cor 12:12-27.
Especially forbidden to saints. 1 Cor 10:24; Phil 2:4.
The love of Christ should constrain us to avoid. 2 Cor 5:14,15.
Ministers should be devoid of. 1 Cor 9:19-23; 10:33.
All men addicted to. Eph 2:3; Phil 2:21.
Saints falsely accused of. Job 1:9-11.
Characteristic of the last days. 2 Tim 3:1,2.
Exemplified
Cain. Gen 4:9.
Nabal. 1 Sam 25:3,11.
Haman. Esth 6:6.
Priests. Is 56:11.
Jews. Zech 7:6.
James and John. Mark 10:37.
Multitude. John 6:26.

SELF-RIGHTEOUSNESS.

Man is prone to. Prov 20:6; 30:12.
Hateful to God. Luke 16:15.
Is vain because our righteousness is
But external. Matt 23:25-28; Luke 11:39-44.
But partial. Matt 23:25; Luke 11:44.
No better than filthy rags. Is 64:6.
Ineffectual for salvation. Job 9:30,31; Matt 5:20; Rom 3:20.
Unprofitable. Is 57:12.
Is boastful. Matt 23:30.
They who are given to
Audaciously approach God. Luke 18:11.
Seek to justify themselves. Luke 10:29.
Seek to justify themselves before men. Luke 16:15.
Reject the righteousness of God. Rom 10:3.
Condemn others. Matt 9:11-13; Luke 7:39.
Consider their own way right. Prov 21:2.
Despise others. Is 65:5; Luke 18:9.
Proclaim their own goodness. Prov 20:6.
Are pure in their own eyes. Prov 30:12.
Are abominable before God. Is 65:5.
Folly of. Job 9:20.
Saints renounce. Phil 3:7-10.
Warning against. Deut 9:4.
Denunciation against. Matt 23:27,28.
Illustrated. Luke 18:10-12.
Exemplified
Saul. 1 Sam 15:13.
Young man. Matt 19:20.
Lawyer. Luke 10:25,29.
Pharisees. Luke 11:39; John 8:33; 9:28.
Israel. Rom 10:3.
Church of Laodicea. Rev 3:17.

SELF-WILL AND STUBBORNNESS.

Forbidden. 2 Chr 30:8; Ps 75:5; 95:8.
Proceed from
Unbelief. 2 Kin 17:14.
Pride. Neh 9:16,29.
An evil heart. Jer 7:24.
God knows. Is 48:4.
Exhibited in
Refusing to hearken to God. Prov 1:24.
Refusing to hearken to the messengers of God. 1 Sam 8:19; Jer 44:16; Zech 7:11.
Refusing to walk in the ways of God. Neh 9:17; Ps 78:10; Is 42:24; Jer 6:16.
Refusing to hearken to parents. Deut 21:18,19.
Refusing to receive correction. Deut 21:18; Jer 5:3; 7:28.
Rebelling against God. Deut 31:27; Ps 78:8.
Resisting the Holy Spirit. Acts 7:51.
Walking in the counsels of an evil heart. Jer 7:24; 23:17.
Hardening the neck. Neh 9:16.
Hardening the heart. 2 Chr 36:13.
Going backward and not forward. Jer 7:24.
Heinousness of. 1 Sam 15:23.
Ministers should
Be without. Titus 1:7.
Warn their people against. Heb 3:7-12.
Pray that their people may be forgiven for. Ex 34:9; Deut 9:27.
Characteristic of the wicked. Prov 7:11; 2 Pet 2:10.
The wicked cease not from. Judg 2:19.
Punishment for. Deut 21:21; Prov 29:1.
Illustrated. Ps 32:9; Jer 31:18.
Exemplified
Simeon and Levi. Gen 49:6.
Israelites. Ex 32:9; Deut 9:6,13.
Saul. 1 Sam 15:19-23.
David. 2 Sam 24:4.
Josiah. 2 Chr 35:22.
Zedekiah. 2 Chr 36:13.

SERPENTS.

Created by God. Job 26:13.
Characterised as subtle. Gen 3:1; Matt 10:16.
Called crooked. Job 26:13; Is 27:1.
Unclean and unfit for food. Matt 7:10.
Infest
Hedges. Eccl 10:8.
Holes in walls. Amos 5:19.
Deserts. Deut 8:15.
Produced from eggs. Is 59:5.
Cursed above all creatures. Gen 3:14.
Doomed to creep on their belly. Gen 3:14.
Doomed to eat their food mingled with dust. Gen 3:14; Is 65:25; Mic 7:17.
Many kinds of poisonous. Deut 32:24; Ps 58:4.
All kinds of, can be tamed. James 3:7.
Were often enchanted or fascinated. Eccl 10:11.
Dangerous to travellers. Gen 49:17.
Man's aversion and hatred to. Gen 3:15.
Often sent as a punishment. Num 21:6; Deut 32:24; 1 Cor 10:9.
Miracles connected with
Moses' rod turned into. Ex 4:3; 7:9,15.
Israelites cured by looking at one of brass. Num 21:8,9; John 3:14,15.
Power over, given to the disciples. Mark 16:18; Luke 10:19.
Illustrative
Of the devil. Gen 3:1; 2 Cor 11:3; Rev 12:9; 20:2.
Of hypocrites. Matt 23:33.
Of the tribe of Dan. Gen 49:17.
Of enemies who harass and destroy. Is 14:29; Jer 8:17.
(Sharp tongue of,) of malice of the wicked. Ps 140:3.
(Poisonous bite of,) of baneful effects of wine. Prov 23:21,32.

SERVANTS.

Early mention of. Gen 9:25,26.
Divided into
Male. Gen 24:34; 32:5.
Female. Gen 16:6; 32:5.
Bond. Gen 43:18; Lev 25:46.
Hired. Mark 1:20; Luke 15:17.
Persons devoted to the service of another so called. Ps 119:49; Is 56:6.
The subjects of a prince or king so called. Ex 9:20; 11:8.
Persons of low condition so called. Eccl 10:7.
Persons devoted to God so called. Ps 119:49; Is 56:6; Rom 1:1.
The term often used to express humility. Gen 18:3; 33:5; 1 Sam 20:7; 1 Kin 20:32.

Hired
Called hireling. Job 7:1; John 10:12,13.
Engaged by the year. Lev 25:53; Is 16:14.
Engaged by the day. Matt 20:2.
Not to be oppressed. Deut 24:14.
To be paid without delay at the expiration of their service. Lev 19:13; Deut 24:15.
To be esteemed worthy of their hire. Luke 10:7.
To partake of the produce of the land in the sabbatical year. Lev 25:6.
If foreigners not allowed to partake of the Passover or holy things. Ex 12:45; Lev 22:10.
Anxiety of, for the end of their daily toil, alluded to. Job 7:2.
Hebrew slaves serving their brethren to be treated as. Lev 25:39,40.
Hebrew slaves serving strangers to be treated as. Lev 25:47,53.
Often stood in the market place waiting for employment. Matt 20:1-3.
Often well fed and taken care of. Luke 15:17.
Often oppressed and their wages kept back. Mal 3:5; James 5:4.
Slaves or bond
Called bondmen. Gen 43:18; 44:9.
By birth. Gen 14:14; Ps 116:16; Jer 2:14.
By purchase. Gen 17:27; 37:36.
Captives taken in war often kept as. Deut 20:14; 2 Kin 5:2.
Strangers sojourning in Israel might be purchased as. Lev 25:45.
Persons belonging to other nations might be purchased as. Lev 25:44.
Persons unable to pay their debts liable to be sold as. 2 Kin 4:1; Neh 5:4,5; Matt 18:25.
Thieves unable to make restitution were sold as. Ex 22:3.
More valuable than hired servants. Deut 15:18.
When Israelites not to be treated with rigour. Lev 25:39,40,46.
When Israelites to have their liberty after six years service. Ex 21:2; Deut 15:12.
Israelites sold as, refusing their liberty, to have their ears bored to the door. Ex 21:5,6; Deut 15:16,17.
Israelites sold to strangers as, might be redeemed by their nearest of kin. Lev 25:47-55.
All Israelites sold as, to be free at the jubilee. Lev 25:10,40,41,54.
Could not when set free demand wives or children procured during servitude. Ex 21:3,4.
To be furnished liberally, when their servitude expired. Deut 15:13,14.
When foreigners to be circumcised. Gen 17:13,27; Ex 12:44.
To be allowed to rest on the Sabbath. Ex 20:10.
To participate in all national rejoicings. Deut 12:18; 16:11,14.
Persons of distinction had many. Gen 14:14; Eccl 2:7.
Engaged in the most menial offices. 1 Sam 25:41; John 13:4,5.
Maimed or injured by masters to have their freedom. Ex 21:26,27.
Masters to be recompensed for injury done to. Ex 21:32.
Laws respecting the killing of. Ex 21:20,21.
Of others not to be coveted or enticed away. Ex 20:17; Deut 5:21.
Seeking protection not to be delivered up to masters. Deut 23:15.
Custom of branding, alluded to. Gal 6:17.
Sometimes rose to rank and station. Eccl 10:7.
Sometimes intermarried with their master's family. 1 Chr 2:34,35.
Laws respecting marriage with female. Ex 21:7-11.
Seizing and stealing of men for, condemned and punished by the law. Ex 21:16; Deut 24:7; 1 Tim 1:10.
Laws respecting, often violated. Jer 34:8-16.
Bond, illustrative
Of Christ. Ps 40:6; Heb 10:5; Phil 2:7,8.
Of saints. 1 Cor 6:20; 7:23.
Of the wicked. 2 Pet 2:19; Rom 6:16,19.
Christ condescended to the office of. Matt 20:28; Luke 22:27; John 13:5; Phil 2:7.
Are inferior to their masters. Luke 22:27.
Should follow Christ's example. 1 Pet 2:21.
Duties of, to masters
To pray for them. Gen 24:12.
To honour them. Mal 1:6; 1 Tim 6:1.
To revere them the more, when they are believers. 1 Tim 6:2.
To be subject to them. 1 Pet 2:18.
To obey them. Eph 6:5; Titus 2:9.
To attend to their call. Ps 123:2.
To please them well in all things. Titus 2:9.
To sympathise with them. 2 Sam 12:18.
To prefer their business to their own necessary food. Gen 24:33.
To bless God for mercies shown to them. Gen 24:27,48.
To be faithful to them. Luke 16:10-12; 1 Cor 4:2; Titus 2:10.
To be profitable to them. Luke 19:15,16,18; Philem 11.
To be anxious for their welfare. 1 Sam 25:14-17; 2 Kin 5:2,3.
To be earnest in transacting their business. Gen 24:54-56.
To be prudent in the management of their affairs. Gen 24:34-49.
To be industrious in labouring for them. Neh 4:16,23.
To be kind and attentive to their guests. Gen 43:23,24.
To be submissive even to the froward. Gen 16:6,9; 1 Pet 2:18.
Not to answer them rudely. Titus 2:9.
Not to serve them with eye-service, as men-pleasers. Eph 6:6; Col 3:22.
Not to defraud them. Titus 2:10.
Should be contented in their situation. 1 Cor 7:20,21.
Should be compassionate to their fellows. Matt 18:33.
Should serve
For conscience towards God. 1 Pet 2:19.
In the fear of God. Eph 6:5; Col 3:22.
As the servants of Christ. Eph 6:5,6.
Heartily, as to the Lord, and not to men. Eph 6:7; Col 3:23.
As doing the will of God from the heart. Eph 6:6.
In singleness of heart. Eph 6:5; Col 3:22.
With good will. Eph 6:7.
When patient under injury are acceptable to God. 1 Pet 2:19,20.
When good
Are the servants of Christ. Col 3:24.
Are brethren beloved in the Lord. Philem 16.
Are the Lord's freemen. 1 Cor 7:22.
Are partakers of gospel privileges. 1 Cor 12:13; Gal 3:28; Eph 6:8; Col 3:11.
Deserve the confidence of their masters. Gen 24:2,4,10; 39:4.
Often exalted. Gen 41:40; Prov 17:2.
Often advanced by master. Gen 39:4,5.
To be honoured. Gen 24:31; Prov 27:18.
Bring God's blessing upon their masters. Gen 30:27,30; 39:3.
Adorn the doctrine of God their Saviour in all things. Titus 2:10.
Have God with them. Gen 31:42; 39:21; Acts 7:9,10.
Are prospered by God. Gen 39:3.
Are protected by God. Gen 31:7.
Are guided by God. Gen 24:7,27.
Are blessed by God. Matt 24:46.
Are mourned over after death. Gen 35:8.
Shall be rewarded. Eph 6:8; Col 3:24.
The property of masters increased by faithful. Gen 30:29,30.
Characteristics of wicked servants
Eye-service. Eph 6:6; Col 3:22.
Men-pleasers. Eph 6:6; Col 3:22.
Deceit. 2 Sam 19:26; Ps 101:6,7.
Quarrelsomeness. Gen 13:7; 26:20.
Covetousness. 2 Kin 5:20.
Lying. 2 Kin 5:22,24.
Stealing. Titus 2:10.
Gluttony. Matt 24:49.
Unmerciful to their fellows. Matt 18:30.
Will not submit to correction. Prov 29:19.
Do not bear to be exalted. Prov 30:21,22; Is 3:5.
Shall be punished. Matt 24:50.
Good—Exemplified
Eliezer. Gen 24:1-67.
Deborah. Gen 24:59; 35:8.
Jacob. Gen 31:36-40.
Joseph. Gen 39:3; Acts 7:10.
Servants of Boaz. Ruth 2:4.
Jonathan's armour bearer. 1 Sam 14:6,7.
David's servants. 2 Sam 12:18.
Captive maid. 2 Kin 5:2-4.
Servants of Naaman. 2 Kin 5:13.
Servants of Centurion. Matt 8:9.

Servants of Cornelius. Acts 10:7.
Onesimus after his conversion. Philem 11.
Bad—Exemplified
Servants of Abraham and Lot. Gen 13:7.
Servants of Abimelech. Gen 21:25.
Absalom's servants [Absalom's servants obeyed a bad master; they were bad men rather than bad servants]. 2 Sam 13:28,29; 14:30.
Ziba. 2 Sam 16:1-4.
Servants of Shimei. 1 Kin 2:39.
Jeroboam. 1 Kin 11:26.
Zimri. 1 Kin 16:9.
Gehazi. 2 Kin 5:20.
Servants of Amon. 2 Kin 21:23.
Job's servants. Job 19:16.
Servants of the High Priest. Mark 14:65.
Onesimus before his conversion. Philem 11.

Sheep.

Clean and used as food. Deut 14:4.
Described as
Innocent. 2 Sam 24:17.
Sagacious. John 10:4,5.
Agile. Ps 114:4,6.
Being covered with a fleece. Job 31:20.
Remarkably prolific. Ps 107:41; 144:13; Song 4:2; Ezek 36:37.
Bleating of, alluded to. Judg 5:16; 1 Sam 15:14.
Under man's care from the earliest age. Gen 4:4.
Constituted a great part of patriarchal wealth. Gen 13:5; 24:25; 26:14.
Males of, called rams. 1 Sam 15:22; Jer 51:40.
Females of, called ewes. Ps 78:71.
Young of, called lambs. Ex 12:3; Is 11:6.
Places celebrated for
Kedar. Ezek 27:21.
Bashan. Deut 32:14.
Nebaioth. Is 60:7.
Bozrah. Mic 2:12.
Flesh of, extensively used as food. 1 Sam 25:18; 1 Kin 1:19; 4:23; Neh 5:18; Is 22:13.
Milk of, used as food. Deut 32:14; Is 7:21,22; 1 Cor 9:7.
Skins of, worn as clothing by the poor. Heb 11:37.
Skins of, made into a covering for the tabernacle. Ex 25:5; 36:10; 39:34.
Wool of, made into clothing. Job 31:20; Prov 31:13; Ezek 34:3.
Offered in sacrifice from the earliest age. Gen 4:4; 8:20; 15:9,10.
Offered in sacrifice under the law. Ex 20:24; Lev 1:10; 1 Kin 8:5,63.
Flocks of
Attended by members of the family. Gen 29:9; Ex 2:16; 1 Sam 16:11.
Attended by servants. 1 Sam 17:20; Is 61:5.
Guarded by dogs. Job 30:1.
Kept in folds or cotes. 1 Sam 24:3; 2 Sam 7:8; John 10:1.
Conducted to the richest pastures. Ps 23:2.
Fed on the mountains. Ex 3:1; Ezek 34:6,13.
Fed in the valleys. Is 65:10.
Frequently covered the pastures. Ps 65:13.
Watered every day. Gen 29:8-10; Ex 2:16,17.
Made to rest at noon. Ps 23:2; Song 1:7.
Followed the shepherd. John 10:4,27.
Fled from strangers. John 10:5.
Washed and shorn every year. Song 4:2.
Firstlings of, not to be shorn. Deut 15:19.
Firstlings of, not to be redeemed. Num 18:17.
Firstlings of, could not be dedicated as a free-will offering. Lev 27:26.
Tithe of, given to the Levites. 2 Chr 31:4-6.
First wool of, given to the priests. Deut 18:4.
Time of shearing, a time of rejoicing. 1 Sam 25:2,11,36; 2 Sam 13:23.
Were frequently
Given as presents. 2 Sam 17:29; 1 Chr 12:40.
Given as tribute. 2 Kin 3:4; 2 Chr 17:11.
Destroyed by wild beasts. Jer 50:17; Mic 5:8; John 10:12.
Taken in great numbers in war. Judg 6:4; 1 Sam 14:32; 1 Chr 5:21; 2 Chr 14:15.
Cut off by disease. Ex 9:3.
False prophets assume the simple appearance. Matt 7:15.
Illustrative
Of the Jews. Ps 74:1; 78:52; 79:13.
Of the people of Christ. John 10:7-26; 21:16,17; Heb 13:20; 1 Pet 5:2.
Of the wicked in their death. Ps 49:14.
Of those under God's judgment. Ps 44:1.
(In patience and simplicity,) of patience, of Christ. Is 53:7.
(In proneness to wander,) of those who depart from God. Ps 119:176; Is 53:6; Ezek 34:16.
(Lost,) of the unregenerate. Matt 10:6.
(When found,) of restored sinners. Luke 15:5,7.
(Separation from the goats,) of the separation of saints from the wicked. Matt 25:32,33.

Shepherds.

Early mention of. Gen 4:2.
Usually carried a scrip or bag. 1 Sam 17:40.
Carried a staff or rod. Lev 27:32; Ps 23:4.
Dwelt in tents while tending their flocks. Song 1:8; Is 38:12.
Members of the family both male and female acted as. Gen 29:6; 1 Sam 16:11; 17:15.
Had hired keepers under them. 1 Sam 17:20.
The unfaithfulness of hireling, alluded to. John 10:12.
Care of the sheep by, exhibited in
Knowing them. John 10:14.
Going before and leading them. Ps 77:20; 78:52; 80:1.
Seeking out good pasture for them. 1 Chr 4:39-41; Ps 23:2.
Numbering them when they return from pasture. Jer 33:13.
Watching over them by night. Luke 2:8.
Tenderness to the ewes in lamb, and to the young. Gen 33:13,14; Ps 78:71.
Defending them when attacked by wild beasts. 1 Sam 17:34-36; Amos 3:12.
Searching them out when lost and straying. Ezek 34:12; Luke 15:4,5.
Attending them when sick. Ezek 34:16.
An abomination to the Egyptians. Gen 46:34.
Illustrative
Of God as leader of Israel. Ps 77:20; 80:1.
Of Christ as the good shepherd. Ezek 34:23; Zech 13:7; John 10:14; Heb 13:20.
Of kings as the leaders of the people. Is 44:28; Jer 6:3; 49:19.
Of ministers of the gospel. Jer 23:4.
(Searching out straying sheep,) of Christ seeking the lost. Ezek 34:12; Luke 15:2-7.
(Their care and tenderness,) of tenderness of Christ. Is 40:11; Ezek 34:13-16.
(Ignorant and foolish,) of bad ministers. Is 56:11; Jer 50:6; Ezek 34:2,10; Zech 11:7,8,15-17.

Showbread.

Twelve cakes of fine flour. Lev 24:5.
Called hallowed bread. 1 Sam 21:4.
Materials for, provided by the people. Lev 24:8; Neh 10:32,33.
Prepared by Levites. 1 Chr 9:32; 23:29.
Placed in two rows on the table by the priests. Ex 25:30; 40:23; Lev 24:6.
Table of
Dimensions of. Ex 25:23.
Covered with gold. Ex 25:24.
Had an ornamental border. Ex 25:25.
Had staves of shittim wood covered with gold. Ex 25:28.
Had rings of gold in the corners for the staves. Ex 25:26,27.
Had dishes, spoons, covers, and bowls of gold. Ex 25:29.
Placed in the north side of the tabernacle. Ex 40:22; Heb 9:2.
Directions for removing. Num 4:7.
Pure frankincense placed on. Lev 24:7.
Was changed every Sabbath day. Lev 24:8.
After removal from the table given to the priests. Lev 24:9.
Not lawful for any but the priests to eat, except in extreme cases. 1 Sam 21:4-6; Matt 12:4.
Illustrative of
Christ as the bread of life. John 6:48.
The Church. 1 Cor 5:7; 10:17.

Shields.

A part of defensive armour. Ps 115:9; 140:7.
Frequently made of, or covered with
Gold. 2 Sam 8:7; 1 Kin 10:17.
Brass. 1 Kin 14:27.
Said to belong to God. Ps 47:9.
Kinds of
The buckler or target. 2 Chr 9:15; 1 Chr 5:18; Ezek 26:8.
The small shield. 2 Chr 9:16.
Often borne by an armour bearer. 1 Sam 17:7.
Before war
Gathered together. Jer 51:11.
Uncovered. Is 22:6.
Repaired. Jer 46:3.
Anointed. 2 Sam 1:21; Is 21:5.
Often made red. Nah 2:3.
Provided by the kings of Israel in great abundance. 2 Chr 11:12; 26:14; 32:5.
A disgrace to lose, or throw away. 2 Sam 1:21.
Of the vanquished, often burned. Ezek 39:9.
In times of peace were hung up in towers or armouries. Ezek 27:10; Song 4:4.
Were scarce in Israel in the days of Deborah and Barak. Judg 5:8.
Many of the Israelites used, with expertness. 1 Chr 12:8,24,34; 2 Chr 14:8; 25:5.
Illustrative of
Protection of God. Gen 15:1; Ps 33:20.
Favour of God. Ps 5:12.
Truth of God. Ps 91:4.
Salvation of God. 2 Sam 22:36; Ps 18:35.
Faith. Eph 6:16.

Ships.

Probably originated from the ark made by Noah. Gen 7:17,18.
Antiquity of, among the Jews. Gen 49:13; Judg 5:17.
Described as
Gallant. Is 33:21.
Large. James 3:4.
Strong. Is 23:14.
Swift. Job 9:26.
Solomon built a navy of. 1 Kin 9:26.
Mentioned in Scripture
Of Chittim. Num 24:24; Dan 11:30.
Of Tarshish. Is 23:1; 60:9.
Of Adramyttium. Acts 27:2.
Of Alexandria. Acts 27:6.
Of Chaldea. Is 43:14.
Of Tyre. 2 Chr 8:18.
Generally made of the fir tree. Ezek 27:5.
Sometimes made of bulrushes. Is 18:2.
The seams of, were caulked. Ezek 27:9,27.
Parts of mentioned
The forepart or foreship. Acts 27:30,41.
The hinder part or stern. Acts 27:29,41.
The hold or between the sides. Jon 1:5.
The mast. Is 33:23; Ezek 27:5.
The sails. Is 33:23; Ezek 27:7.
The tackling. Is 33:23; Acts 27:19.
The rudder or helm. James 3:4.
The rudder-bands. Acts 27:40.
The anchors. Acts 27:29,40.
The boats. Acts 27:30,32.
The oars. Is 33:21; Ezek 27:6.
Often the property of individuals. Acts 27:11.
Commanded by a master. Jon 1:6; Acts 27:11.
Guided in their course by pilots. Ezek 27:8,27-29.
Governed and directed by the helm. James 3:4.
Course of frequently directed by the heavenly bodies. Acts 27:20.
Worked by mariners or sailors. Ezek 27:9,27; Jon 1:5; Acts 27:30.
Generally impelled by sails. Acts 27:2-7.
Often impelled by oars. Jon 1:13; John 6:19.
Navigated
Rivers. Is 33:21.
Lakes. Luke 5:1,2.
The ocean. Ps 104:26; 107:23.
Soundings usually taken for, in dangerous places. Acts 27:28.
Usually distinguished by signs or figure heads. Acts 28:11.
Course of, through the midst of the sea, wonderful. Prov 30:18,19.
Employed in
Trading. 1 Kin 22:48; 2 Chr 8:18; 9:21.
Fishing. Matt 4:21; Luke 5:4-9; John 21:3-8.
War. Num 24:24; Dan 11:30,40.
Carrying passengers. Jon 1:3; Acts 27:2,6; 28:11.
The hinder part of, occupied by the passengers. Mark 4:38.
Endangered by
Storms. Jon 1:4; Mark 4:37,38.
Quicksands. Acts 27:17.
Rocks. Acts 27:29.
When damaged were sometimes undergirded with cables. Acts 27:17.
Were often wrecked. 1 Kin 22:48; Ps 48:7; Acts 27:41-44; 2 Cor 11:25.
Illustrative
Of industrious women. Prov 31:14.
(Wrecked,) of departure from the faith. 1 Tim 1:19.

Shoes.

Early use of. Gen 14:23.
Called sandals. Mark 6:9; Acts 12:8.
Soles of, sometimes plated with brass or iron. Deut 33:25.
Bound round the feet with latchets or strings. John 1:27; Acts 12:8.
Of ladies of distinction
Often made of badgers' skins. Ezek 16:10.
Often highly ornamental. Song 7:1.
Probably often adorned with tinkling ornaments. Is 3:18.
Loosing of, for another a degrading office. Mark 1:17; John 1:27.
Bearing, for another a degrading office, only performed by slaves. Matt 3:11.
The Jews
Put on, before beginning a journey. Ex 12:11.
Never wore, in mourning. 2 Sam 15:30; Is 20:2,3; Ezek 24:17,23.
Put off, when they entered sacred places. Ex 3:5; Josh 5:15.
Worn out by a long journey. Josh 9:5,13.
Of Israel preserved for forty years, while journeying in the wilderness. Deut 29:5.
Often given as bribes. Amos 2:6; 8:6.
Customs connected with
A man who refused to marry a deceased brother's wife disgraced by pulling off his shoes. Deut 25:9,10.
The right of redemption resigned by a man's giving one of his shoes to the next of kin. Ruth 4:7,8.
The Apostles prohibited from taking for their journey more, than the pair they had on. Matt 10:10; Mark 6:9; Luke 10:4.
Illustrative
Of the preparation of the gospel. Eph 6:15.
Of the beauty conferred on saints. Song 7:1; Luke 15:22.
(Having blood on,) of being engaged in war and slaughter. 1 Kin 2:5.
(Taken off,) of an ignominious and servile condition. Is 47:2; Jer 2:25.
(Thrown over a place,) of subjection. Ps 60:8; 108:9.

Sickness.

Sent by God. Deut 28:59-61; 32:39; 2 Sam 12:15; Acts 12:23.
The devil sometimes permitted to inflict. Job 2:6,7; Luke 9:39; 13:16.
Often brought on by intemperance. Hos 7:5.
Often sent as a punishment of sin. Lev 26:14-16; 2 Chr 21:12-15; 1 Cor 11:30.
One of God's four sore judgments on a guilty land. Ezek 14:19-21.
God
Promises to heal. Ex 23:25; 2 Kin 20:5.
Heals. Deut 32:39; Ps 103:3; Is 38:5,9.
Exhibits his mercy in healing. Phil 2:27.
Exhibits his power in healing. Luke 5:17.
Exhibits his love in healing. Is 38:17.
Often manifests saving grace to sinners during. Job 33:19-24; Ps 107:17-21.
Permits saints to be tried by. Job 2:5,6.
Strengthens saints in. Ps 41:3.
Comforts saints in. Ps 41:3.
Hears the prayers of those in. Ps 30:2; 107:18-20.
Preserves saints in time of. Ps 91:3-7.
Abandons the wicked to. Jer 34:17.
Persecutes the wicked by. Jer 29:18.
Healing of, lawful on the Sabbath. Luke 13:14-16.
Christ compassionate toward those in. Is 53:4; Matt 8:16,17.
Christ healed
Being present. Mark 1:31; Matt 4:23.
Not being present. Matt 8:13.
By imposition of hands. Mark 6:5; Luke 13:13.
With a touch. Matt 8:3.
Through the touch of his garment. Matt 14:35,36; Mark 5:27-34.
With a word. Matt 8:8,13.

Faith required in those healed of, by Christ. Matt 9:28,29; Mark 5:34; 10:52.
Often incurable by human means. Deut 28:27; 2 Chr 21:18.
The Apostles were endued with power to heal. Matt 10:1; Mark 16:18,20.
The power of healing
- One of the miraculous gifts bestowed on the early Church. 1 Cor 12:9,30; James 5:14,15.

Saints
- Acknowledge that, comes from God. Ps 31:1-8; Is 38:12,15.
- Are resigned under. Job 2:10.
- Mourn under, with prayer. Is 38:14.
- Pray for recovery from. Is 38:2,3.
- Ascribe recovery from, to God. Is 38:20.
- Praise God for recovery from. Ps 103:1-3; Is 38:19; Luke 17:15.
- Thank God publicly for recovery from. Is 38:20; Acts 3:8.
- Feel for others in. Ps 35:13.
- Visit those in. Matt 25:36.

Visiting those in, an evidence of belonging to Christ. Matt 25:34,36,40.
Pray for those afflicted with. Acts 28:8; James 5:14,15.
God's aid should be sought in. 2 Chr 16:12.
The wicked
- Have much sorrow, with. Eccl 5:17.
- Forsake those in. 1 Sam 30:13.
- Visit not those in. Matt 25:43.

Not visiting those in, an evidence of not belonging to Christ. Matt 25:43,45.
Illustrative of sin. Lev 13:45,46; Is 1:5; Jer 8:22; Matt 9:12.

Sidonians, The.

Descended from Sidon, son of Canaan. Gen 10:15; 1 Chr 1:13.
Formerly a part of the Phoenician nation. Matt 15:21,22; Mark 7:24,26.
Dwelt on the sea coast. Luke 6:17; Acts 27:3.
Cities of mentioned
- Zidon. Josh 11:8; 19:28.
- Zarephath or Sarepta. 1 Kin 17:9; Luke 4:26.

Governed by kings. Jer 25:22; 27:3.
Character of
- Careless and secure. Judg 18:7.
- Idolatrous. 1 Kin 11:5.
- Superstitious. Jer 27:3,9.
- Wicked and impenitent. Matt 11:21,22.

Engaged in extensive commerce. Is 23:2.
Were skilful sailors. Ezek 27:8.
Supplied the Jews with timber. 1 Chr 22:4; Ezra 3:7.
Supplied from Judea with provisions. Acts 12:20; Ezek 27:17.
Territory of
- Bordered on the land of Canaan. Gen 10:19.
- Given by God to Israel. Gen 49:13; Josh 13:6.
- Allotted to the tribe of Asher. Josh 19:24,28.
- Visited by our Lord. Matt 15:21.

Israel unable to expel. Judg 1:31; 3:3.
Hostile and oppressive to God's people. Judg 10:12; Ezek 28:22,24; Joel 3:5,6.
Solomon intermarried with. 1 Kin 11:1.
Ahab intermarried with. 1 Kin 16:31.
Israel followed the idolatry of. Judg 10:6; 1 Kin 11:33.
Predictions respecting
- Territory of, to be given to Nebuchadnezzar, king of Babylon. Jer 27:3,6.
- Partaking with the other nations of God's judgments. Jer 25:22-28; Ezek 32:20.
- All their helpers to be cut off. Jer 47:4.
- That God should be glorified in the judgments upon them. Ezek 28:21-23.
- Their spoiling and oppression of the Jews to be fully recompensed. Joel 3:4,8.

Many of, attended Christ's ministry. Mark 3:8.
Having revolted from Herod, were obliged to propitiate him. Acts 12:20.

Sieges.

Fenced cities invested by. 2 Kin 18:13.
Threatened as a punishment. Deut 28:52.
Described as
- Encamping against. 2 Sam 12:28; 2 Chr 32:1.
- Pitching against. 2 Kin 25:1.
- Compassing about with armies. 2 Kin 6:14; Luke 21:20.
- Setting in array against. Jer 50:9.
- Being against round about. Jer 51:2.

Often lasted for a long time. 2 Kin 17:5.
Great noise and tumult of, alluded to. Joel 2:5.
Those engaged in
- Built forts and mounts. Ezek 4:2; 26:8.
- Dug a trench round the city. Luke 19:43.
- Invested the city on every side. Ezek 23:24.
- Cut off all supplies. 2 Kin 19:24.
- Frequently laid ambushes. Judg 9:34.
- Called upon the city to surrender. 1 Kin 20:2,3; 2 Kin 18:18,20.
- Employed battering rams against the walls. Ezek 4:2; 26:9.
- Cast arrows and other missiles into the city. 2 Kin 19:32.
- Often suffered much during. Ezek 29:18.

The Jews forbidden to cut down fruit trees for the purpose of. Deut 20:19,20.
Extreme difficulty of taking cities by, alluded to. Prov 18:19.
Cities invested by
- Repaired and newly fortified beforehand. 2 Chr 32:5; Is 22:9,10; Nah 3:14.
- Supplied with water beforehand. Nah 3:14.
- The inhabitants of, cut off beforehand supplies of water outside, useful to besiegers. 2 Chr 32:3,4.
- Were strictly shut up. Josh 6:1.
- Walls of, defended by the inhabitants. 2 Sam 11:20,21; 2 Kin 18:26; 2 Chr 32:18.
- Sometimes used ambushes or sorties. Jer 51:12.
- Often suffered from famine. 2 Kin 6:26-29; 25:3; Ezek 6:12.
- Often suffered from pestilence. Jer 21:6; 32:24.
- Often demanded terms of peace. 1 Sam 11:1-3.
- Frequently taken by ambush. Judg 9:43,44.
- Frequently taken by assault. Josh 10:35; 2 Sam 12:29.
- Frequently helped by allies. 1 Sam 11:11; 23:5.
- Inhabitants of, exhorted to be courageous. 2 Chr 32:6-8.

Cities taken by
- Given up to pillage. Jer 50:26,27.
- Inhabitants of, often put to the sword. Josh 10:28,30,32,35; Jer 50:30.
- Frequently broken down. Judg 9:45.
- Frequently destroyed by fire. Josh 8:19.
- Sometimes sown with salt. Judg 9:45.
- Sometimes called after the name of the captor. 2 Sam 12:28.

Mentioned in Scripture
- Jericho. Josh 6:2-20.
- Ai. Josh 7:2-4; 8:1-19.
- Makkedah. Josh 10:28.
- Libnah. Josh 10:29,30.
- Lachish. Josh 10:31,32.
- Eglon. Josh 10:34,35.
- Hebron. Josh 10:36,37.
- Debir. Josh 10:38,39.
- Shechem. Judg 9:34,45.
- Thebez. Judg 9:50.
- Jabesh-gilead. 1 Sam 11:1.
- Keilah. 1 Sam 23:1.
- Ziklag. 1 Sam 30:1,2.
- Rabbah. 2 Sam 11:1; 12:26-29.
- Gibbethon. 1 Kin 16:15.
- Tirzah. 1 Kin 16:17.
- Samaria. 1 Kin 20:1; 2 Kin 6:24; 17:5.
- Ramoth-gilead. 1 Kin 22:4,29.
- Cities of Israel in Galilee. 2 Kin 15:29.
- Cities of Judah. 2 Kin 18:13.
- Jerusalem. 2 Kin 24:10,11; 25:1,2.

Illustrative of
- The omnipresence of God. Ps 139:5.
- The judgments of God. Mic 5:1.
- Zion in her affliction. Is 1:8.

Silver.

Veins of, found in the earth. Job 28:1.
Generally found in an impure state. Prov 25:4.
Comparative value of. Is 60:17.
Described as
- White and shining. Ps 68:13,14.
- Fusible. Ezek 22:20,22.
- Malleable. Jer 10:9.

Purified by fire. Prov 17:3; Zech 13:9.
Purified, called
- Refined silver. 1 Chr 29:4.
- Choice silver. Prov 8:19.

Tarshish carried on extensive commerce in. Jer 10:9; Ezek 27:12.
The patriarchs rich in. Gen 13:2; 24:35.
Used as money from the earliest times. Gen 23:15,16; 37:28; 1 Kin 16:24.
Very abundant in the reign of Solomon. 1 Kin 10:21,22,27; 2 Chr 9:20,21,27.

The working in, a trade. Acts 19:24.
Made into
- Cups. Gen 44:2.
- Dishes. Num 7:13,84,85.
- Bowls. Num 7:13,84.
- Thin plates. Jer 10:9.
- Chains. Is 40:19.
- Wires (alluded to). Eccl 12:6.
- Sockets for the boards of the tabernacle. Ex 26:19,25,32; 36:24,26,30,36.
- Ornaments and hooks for the pillars of the tabernacle. Ex 27:17; 38:19.
- Candlesticks. 1 Chr 28:15.
- Tables. 1 Chr 28:16.
- Beds or couches. Esth 1:6.
- Vessels. 2 Sam 8:10; Ezra 6:5.
- Idols. Ps 115:4; Is 2:20; 30:22.
- Ornaments for the person. Ex 3:22.

Given by the Israelites for making the tabernacle. Ex 25:3; 35:24.
Given by David and his subjects for making the temple. 1 Chr 28:14; 29:2,6-9.
Taken in war often consecrated to God. Josh 6:19; 2 Sam 8:11; 1 Kin 15:15.
Taken in war purified by fire. Num 31:22,23.
Often given as presents. 1 Kin 10:25; 2 Kin 5:5,23.
Tribute often paid in. 2 Chr 17:11; Neh 5:15.
Illustrative
- Of the words of the Lord. Ps 12:6.
- Of the tongue of the just. Prov 10:20.
- Of good rulers. Is 1:22,23.
- Of the Medo-Persian kingdom. Dan 2:32,39.
- Of saints purified by affliction. Ps 66:10; Zech 13:9.
- (Labour of seeking for,) of diligence required for attaining knowledge. Prov 2:4.
- (Reprobate,) of the wicked. Jer 6:30.
- (Dross of,) of the wicked. Is 1:22; Ezek 22:18.

Wisdom to be esteemed more than. Job 28:15; Prov 3:14; 8:10,19; 16:16.

Simeon, the Tribe Of.

Descended from Jacob's second son by Leah. Gen 29:33.
Predictions respecting. Gen 49:5-7.
Persons selected from
- To number the people. Num 1:6.
- To spy out the land. Num 13:5.
- To divide the land. Num 34:20.

Formed part of the second division of Israel in their journeys. Num 10:18,19.
Encamped under the standard of Reuben south of the tabernacle. Num 2:12.
Strength of, on leaving Egypt. Num 1:22,23; 2:13.
Offering of, at the dedication. Num 7:36-41.
Families of. Num 26:12-13.
Strength of, on entering Canaan. Num 26:14.
Plagued for following the idolatry, of Midian, which accounts for their decrease. Num 25:9,14; 26:14; 1:23.
On Mount Gerizim said amen to the blessings. Deut 27:12.
Inheritance of, within Judah. Josh 19:1-8.
Bounds of their inheritance with cities and villages. Josh 19:2-8; 1 Chr 4:28-33.
United with Judah in expelling the Canaanites from their inheritance. Judg 1:3,17.
Many of, at the coronation of David. 1 Chr 12:25.
Officer appointed over, by David. 1 Chr 27:16.
Part of, united with Judah under Asa. 2 Chr 15:9.
Josiah purged their land of idols. 2 Chr 34:6.
Part of, destroyed the remnant of the Amalekites, and dwelt in their land. 1 Chr 4:39-43.

Simplicity.

Is opposed to fleshly wisdom. 2 Cor 1:12.
Necessity for. Matt 18:2,3.
Should be exhibited
- In preaching the gospel. 1 Thess 2:3-7.
- In acts of benevolence. Rom 12:8.
- In all our conduct. 2 Cor 1:12.
- Concerning our own wisdom. 1 Cor 3:18.
- Concerning evil. Rom 16:19.
- Concerning malice. 1 Cor 14:20.

Exhortation to. Rom 16:19; 1 Pet 2:2.
They who have the grace of
- Are made wise by God. Matt 11:25.
- Are made wise by the word of God. Ps 19:7; 119:130.
- Are preserved by God. Ps 116:6.
- Made circumspect by instruction. Prov 1:4.
- Profit by the correction of others. Prov 19:25; 21:11.

Beware of being corrupted from that, which is in Christ. 2 Cor 11:3.
Illustrated. Matt 6:22.
Exemplified
- David. Ps 131:1,2.
- Jeremiah. Jer 1:6.
- The Christians. Acts 2:46; 4:32.
- Paul. 2 Cor 1:12.

Sin.

Is the transgression of the law. 1 John 3:4.
Is of the devil. 1 John 3:8; John 8:44.
All unrighteousness is. 1 John 5:17.
Omission of what we know to be good is. James 4:17.
Whatever is not of faith is. Rom 14:23.
The thought of foolishness is. Prov 24:9.
All the imaginations of the unrenewed heart are. Gen 6:5; 8:21.
Described as
- Coming from the heart. Matt 15:19.
- The fruit of lust. James 1:15.
- The sting of death. 1 Cor 15:56.
- Rebellion against God. Deut 9:7; Josh 1:18.
- Works of darkness. Eph 5:11.
- Dead works. Heb 6:1; 9:14.
- The abominable thing that God hates. Prov 15:9; Jer 44:4,11.
- Reproaching the Lord. Num 15:30; Ps 74:18.
- Defiling. Prov 30:12; Is 59:3.
- Deceitful. Heb 3:13.
- Disgraceful. Prov 14:34.
- Often very great. Ex 32:20; 1 Sam 2:17.
- Often mighty. Amos 5:12.
- Often manifold. Amos 5:12.
- Often presumptuous. Ps 19:13.
- Sometimes open and manifest. 1 Tim 5:24.
- Sometimes secret. Ps 90:8; 1 Tim 5:24.
- Besetting. Heb 12:1.
- Like scarlet and crimson. Is 1:18.
- Reaching to heaven. Rev 18:5.

Entered into the world by Adam. Gen 3:6,7; Rom 5:12.
All men are conceived and born in. Gen 5:3; Job 15:14; 25:4; Ps 51:5.
All men are shapen in. Ps 51:5.
Scripture concludes all under. Gal 3:22.
No man is without. 1 Kin 8:46; Eccl 7:20.
Christ alone was without. 2 Cor 5:21; Heb 4:15; 7:26; 1 John 3:5.
God
- Abominates. Deut 25:16; Prov 6:16-19.
- Marks. Job 10:14.
- Remembers. Rev 18:5.
- Is provoked to jealousy by. 1 Kin 14:22.
- Is provoked to anger by. 1 Kin 16:2.
- Alone can forgive. Ex 34:7; Dan 9:9; Mic 7:18; Mark 2:7.
- Recompenses. Jer 16:18; Rev 18:6.
- Punishes. Is 13:11; Amos 3:2.

The Law
- Is transgressed by every. James 2:10,11; 1 John 3:4.
- Gives knowledge of. Rom 3:20; 7:7.
- Shows exceeding sinfulness of. Rom 7:13.
- Made to restrain. 1 Tim 1:9,10.
- By its strictness stirs up. Rom 7:5,8,11.
- Is the strength of. 1 Cor 15:56.
- Curses those guilty of. Gal 3:10.

No man can cleanse himself from. Job 9:30,31; Prov 20:9; Jer 2:22.
No man can atone for. Mic 6:7.
God has opened a fountain for. Zech 13:1.
Christ was manifested to take away. John 1:29; 1 John 3:5.
Christ's blood redeems from. Eph 1:7.
Christ's blood cleanses from. 1 John 1:7.
Saints
- Made free from. Rom 6:18.
- Dead to. Rom 6:2,11; 1 Pet 2:24.
- Profess to have ceased from. 1 Pet 4:1.
- Cannot live in. 1 John 3:9; 5:18.
- Resolve against. Job 34:32.
- Ashamed of having committed. Rom 6:21.
- Abhor themselves on account of. Job 42:6; Ezek 20:43.
- Have yet the remains of, in them. Rom 7:17,23; Gal 5:17.

The fear of God restrains. Ex 20:20; Ps 4:4; Prov 16:6.

The word of God keeps from. Ps 17:4; 119:11.
The Holy Spirit convinces of. John 16:8,9.
If we say that we have no, we make God a liar. 1 John 1:10.
Confusion of face belongs to those guilty of. Dan 9:7,8.
Should be
Confessed. Job 33:27; Prov 28:13.
Mourned over. Ps 38:18; Jer 3:21.
Hated. Ps 97:10; Prov 8:13; Amos 5:15.
Abhorred. Rom 12:9.
Put away. Job 11:14.
Departed from. Ps 34:14; 2 Tim 2:19.
Avoided even in appearance. 1 Thess 5:22.
Guarded against. Ps 4:4; 39:1.
Striven against. Heb 12:4.
Mortified. Rom 8:13; Col 3:5.
Wholly destroyed. Rom 6:6.
Specially strive against besetting. Heb 12:1.
Aggravated by neglecting advantages. Luke 12:47; John 15:22.
Guilt of concerning. Job 31:33; Prov 28:13.
We should pray to God
To search for, in our hearts. Ps 139:23,24.
To make us know our. Job 13:23.
To forgive our. Ex 34:9; Luke 11:4.
To keep us from. Ps 19:13.
To deliver us from. Matt 6:13.
To cleanse us from. Ps 51:2.
Prayer hindered by. Ps 66:18; Is 59:2.
Blessings withheld on account of. Jer 5:25.
The wicked
Servants to. John 8:34; Rom 6:16.
Dead in. Eph 2:1.
Guilty of, in everything they do. Prov 21:4; Ezek 21:24.
Plead necessity for. 1 Sam 13:11,12.
Excuse. Gen 3:12,13; 1 Sam 15:13-15.
Encourage themselves in. Ps 64:5.
Defy God in committing. Is 5:18,19.
Boast of. Is 3:9.
Make a mock at. Prov 14:9.
Expect impunity in. Ps 10:11; 50:21; 94:7.
Cannot cease from. 2 Pet 2:14.
Heap up. Ps 78:17; Is 30:1.
Encouraged in, by prosperity. Job 21:7-15; Prov 10:16.
Led by despair to continue in. Jer 2:25; 18:12.
Try to conceal, from God. Gen 3:8,10; Job 31:33.
Throw the blame of, on God. Gen 3:12; Jer 7:10.
Throw the blame of, on others. Gen 3:12,13; Ex 32:22-24.
Tempt others to. Gen 3:6; 1 Kin 16:2; 21:25; Prov 1:10-14.
Delight in those who commit. Ps 10:3; Hos 7:3; Rom 1:32.
Shall bear the shame of. Ezek 16:52.
Shall find out the wicked. Num 32:23.
Ministers should warn the wicked to forsake. Ezek 33:9; Dan 4:27.
Leads to
Shame. Rom 6:21.
Disquiet. Ps 38:3.
Disease. Job 20:11.
The ground was cursed on account of. Gen 3:17,18.
Toil and sorrow originated in. Gen 3:16,17,19; Job 14:1.
Excludes from heaven. 1 Cor 6:9,10; Gal 5:19-21; Eph 5:5; Rev 21:27.
When finished brings forth death. James 1:15.
Death, the wages of. Rom 6:23.
Death, the punishment of. Gen 2:17; Ezek 18:4.

Sincerity.

Christ was an example of. 1 Pet 2:22.
Ministers should be examples of. Titus 2:7.
Opposed to fleshly wisdom. 2 Cor 1:12.
Should characterise
Our love to God. 2 Cor 8:8,24.
Our love to Christ. Eph 6:24.
Our service to God. Josh 24:14; John 4:23,24.
Our faith. 1 Tim 1:5.
Our love to one another. Rom 12:9; 1 Pet 1:22; 1 John 3:18.
Our whole conduct. 2 Cor 1:12.
The preaching of the gospel. 2 Cor 2:17; 1 Thess 2:3-5.
A characteristic of the doctrines of the gospel. 1 Pet 2:2.
The gospel sometimes preached without. Phil 1:16.
The wicked devoid of. Ps 5:9; 55:21.
Exhortations to. Ps 34:13; 1 Cor 5:8; 1 Pet 2:1.
Pray for, on behalf of others. Phil 1:10.
Blessedness of. Ps 32:2.
Exemplified
Men of Zebulun. 1 Chr 12:33.
Hezekiah. Is 38:3.
Nathanael. John 1:47.
Paul. 2 Cor 1:12.
Timothy. 2 Tim 1:5.
Lois and Eunice. 2 Tim 1:5.
The Redeemed. Rev 14:5.

Sin Offering.

Probable origin of. Gen 4:4,7.
Was offered
For sins of ignorance. Lev 4:2,13,22,27.
At the consecration of priests. Ex 29:10,14; Lev 8:14.
At the consecration of Levites. Num 8:8.
At the expiration of a Nazarite's vow. Num 6:14.
On the day of atonement. Lev 16:3,9.
Was a most holy sacrifice. Lev 6:25,29.
Consisted of
A young bullock for priests. Lev 4:3; 9:2,8; 16:3,6.
A young bullock or he-goat for the congregation. Lev 4:14; 16:9; 2 Chr 29:23.
A male kid for a ruler. Lev 4:23.
A female kid or female lamb for a private person. Lev 4:28,32.
Sins of the offerer transferred to, by imposition of hands. Lev 4:4,15,24,29; 2 Chr 29:23.
Was killed in the same place as the burnt offering. Lev 4:24; 6:25.
The blood of
For a priest or for the congregation, brought by the priest into the tabernacle. Lev 4:5,16.
For a priest or for the congregation, sprinkled seven times before the Lord, outside the vail, by the priest with his finger. Lev 4:6,17.
For a priest or for the congregation, put upon the horns of the altar of burnt offering by the priest with his finger. Lev 4:25,30.
In every case poured at the foot of the altar of burnt offering. Lev 4:7; 18:25,30; 9:9.
Fat of the inside, kidneys, burned on the altar of burnt offering. Lev 4:8-10,19,26,31; 9:10.
When for a priest or the congregation, the skin, carcass, burned without the camp. Lev 4:11,12,21; 6:30; 9:11.
Was eaten by the priests in a holy place, when its blood had not been brought into the tabernacle. Lev 6:26,29,30.
Aaron, etc. rebuked for burning and not eating that of the congregation, its blood not having been brought into the tabernacle. Lev 10:16-18; 9:9,15.
Whatever touched the flesh of, was rendered holy. Lev 6:27.
Garments sprinkled with the blood of, to be washed. Lev 6:27.
Laws respecting the vessels used for boiling the flesh of. Lev 6:28.
Was typical of Christ's sacrifice. 2 Cor 5:21; Heb 13:11-13.

Sins, National.

Pervade all ranks. Is 1:5; Jer 5:1-5; 6:13.
Often caused and encouraged by rulers. 1 Kin 12:26-33; 14:16; 2 Chr 21:11-13; Prov 29:12.
Often caused by prosperity. Deut 32:15; Neh 9:28; Jer 48:11; Ezek 16:49; 28:5.
Defile
The land. Lev 18:25; Num 35:33,34; Ps 106:38; Is 24:5; Mic 2:10.
The people. Lev 18:24; Ezek 14:11.
National worship. Is 1:10-15; Amos 5:21,22; Hag 2:14.
Aggravated by privileges. Is 5:4-7; Ezek 20:11-13; Amos 2:4; 3:1,2; Matt 11:21-24.
Lead the heathen to blaspheme. Ezek 36:20,23; Rom 2:24.
Are a reproach to a people. Prov 14:34.
Should be
Repented of. Jer 18:8; Jon 3:5.
Mourned over. Joel 2:12.
Confessed. Lev 26:40; Deut 30:2; Judg 10:10; 1 Kin 8:47,48.
Turned from. Is 1:16; Hos 14:1,2; Jon 3:10.
Saints especially mourn over. Ps 119:136; Ezek 9:4.
Ministers should
Mourn over. Ezek 10:6; Jer 13:17; Ezek 6:11; Joel 2:17.
Testify against. Is 30:8,9; 58:1; Ezek 2:3-5; 22:2; Jon 1:2.
Try to turn the people from. Jer 23:22.

Pray for forgiveness of. Ex 32:31,32; Joel 2:17.
National prayer rejected on account of. Is 1:15; 59:2.
National worship rejected on account of. Is 1:10-14; Jer 6:19,20; 7:9-14.
Cause the withdrawal of privileges. Lam 2:9; Amos 8:11; Matt 23:37-39.
Bring down national judgments. Matt 23:35,36; 27:25.
Denunciations against. Is 1:24; 30:1; Jer 5:9; 6:27-30.
Punishment for. Is 3:8; Jer 12:17; 25:12; Ezek 28:7-10.
Punishment for, averted on repentance. Judg 10:15,16; 2 Chr 12:6,7; Ps 106:43-46; Jon 3:10.
Exemplified
 Sodom and Gomorrah. Gen 18:20; 2 Pet 2:6.
 Children of Israel. Ex 16:8; 32:31.
 Nations of Canaan. Deut 9:4.
 Kingdom of Israel. 2 Kin 17:8-12; Hos 4:1,2.
 Kingdom of Judah. 2 Kin 17:19; Is 1:2-7.
 Moab. Jer 48:29,30.
 Babylon. Jer 51:6,13,52.
 Tyre. Ezek 28:2.
 Nineveh. Nah 3:1.

SLANDER.

An abomination to God. Prov 6:16,19.
Forbidden. Ex 23:1; Eph 4:31; James 4:11.
Includes
 Whispering. Rom 1:29; 2 Cor 12:20.
 Backbiting. Rom 1:30; 2 Cor 12:20.
 Evil surmising. 1 Tim 6:4.
 Tale-bearing. Lev 19:16.
 Babbling. Eccl 10:11.
 Tattling. 1 Tim 5:13.
 Evil speaking. Ps 41:5; 109:20.
 Defaming. Jer 20:10; 1 Cor 4:13.
 Bearing false witness. Ex 20:16; Deut 5:20; Luke 3:14.
 Judging uncharitably. James 4:11,12.
 Raising false reports. Ex 23:1.
 Repeating matters. Prov 17:9.
Is a deceitful work. Ps 52:2.
Comes from the evil heart. Matt 15:19; Luke 6:45.
Often arises from hatred. Ps 41:7; 109:3.
Idleness leads to. 1 Tim 5:13.
The wicked addicted to. Ps 50:20; Jer 6:28; 9:4.
Hypocrites addicted to. Prov 11:9.
A characteristic of the devil. Rev 12:10.
The wicked love. Ps 52:4.
They who indulge in, are fools. Prov 10:18.
They who indulge in, not to be trusted. Jer 9:4.
Women warned against. Titus 2:3.
Minister's wives should avoid. 1 Tim 3:11.
Christ was exposed to. Ps 35:11; Matt 26:60.
Rulers exposed to. 2 Pet 2:10; Jude 1:8.
Ministers exposed to. Rom 3:8; 2 Cor 6:8.
The nearest relations exposed to. Ps 50:20.
Saints exposed to. Ps 38:12; 109:2; 1 Pet 4:4.
Saints
 Should keep their tongue from. Ps 34:13; 1 Pet 3:10.
 Should lay aside. Eph 4:31; 1 Pet 2:1.
 Should be warned against. Titus 3:1,2.
 Should give no occasion for. 1 Pet 2:12; 3:16.
 Should return good for. 1 Cor 4:13.
 Blessed in enduring. Matt 5:11.
 Characterised as avoiding. Ps 15:1,3.
Should not be listened to. 1 Sam 24:9.
Should be discountenanced with anger. Prov 25:23.
Effects of
 Separating friends. Prov 16:28; 17:9.
 Deadly wounds. Prov 18:8; 26:22.
 Strife. Prov 26:20.
 Discord among brethren. Prov 6:19.
 Murder. Ps 31:13; Ezek 22:9.
The tongue of, is a scourge. Job 5:21.
Is venomous. Ps 140:3; Eccl 10:11.
Is destructive. Prov 11:9.
End of, is mischievous madness. Eccl 10:13.
Men shall give account for. Matt 12:36; James 1:26.
Punishment for. Deut 19:16-21; Ps 101:5.
Illustrated. Prov 12:18; 25:18.
Exemplified
 Laban's Sons. Gen 31:1.
 Doeg. 1 Sam 22:9-11.
 Princes of Ammon. 2 Sam 10:3.
 Ziba. 2 Sam 16:3.
 Children of Belial. 1 Kin 21:13.
 Enemies of the Jews. Ezra 4:7-16.
 Gashmu. Neh 6:6.
 Haman. Esth 3:8.
 David's enemies. Ps 31:13.
 Jeremiah's enemies. Jer 38:4.
 Jews. Matt 11:18,19.
 Witnesses against Christ. Matt 26:59-61.
 Priests. Mark 15:3.
 Enemies of Stephen. Acts 6:11.
 Enemies of Paul. Acts 17:7.
 Tertullus. Acts 24:2,5.

SOBRIETY.

Commanded. 1 Pet 1:13; 5:8.
The gospel designed to teach. Titus 2:11,12.
With watchfulness. 1 Thess 5:6.
With prayer. 1 Pet 4:7.
Required in
 Ministers. 1 Tim 3:2,3; Titus 1:8.
 Wives of ministers. 1 Tim 3:11.
 Aged men. Titus 2:2.
 Young men. Titus 2:6.
 Young women. Titus 2:4.
 All saints. 1 Thess 5:6,8.
Women should exhibit, in dress. 1 Tim 2:9.
We should estimate our character and talents with. Rom 12:3.
We should live in. Titus 2:12.
Motives to. 1 Pet 4:7; 5:8.

SPEAR.

An offensive weapon. 2 Sam 23:8,18.
First mention of, in Scripture. Josh 8:18.
Parts of, mentioned
 The staff of wood. 1 Sam 17:7.
 The head of iron or brass. 1 Sam 17:7; 2 Sam 21:16.
Probably pointed at both ends. 2 Sam 2:23.
Called the glittering spear. Job 39:23; Hab 3:11.
Different kinds of
 Lances. Jer 50:42.
 Javelins. Num 25:7; 1 Sam 18:10.
 Darts. 2 Sam 18:14; Job 41:26,29.
Those who used, called spearmen. Ps 68:30; Acts 23:23.
Frequently used by horse soldiers. Nah 3:3.
Furbished before war. Jer 46:4.
Pruning-hooks made into, before war. Joel 3:10.
Made into pruning-hooks in peace. Is 2:4; Mic 4:3.
The Israelites
 Acquainted with the making of. 1 Sam 13:19.
 Frequently used. Neh 4:13,16.
 Ill provided with, in the times of Deborah and Saul. Judg 5:8; 1 Sam 13:22.
Provided by the kings of Israel in great abundance. 2 Chr 11:12; 32:5.
Frequently thrown from the hand. 1 Sam 18:11; 19:10.
Often retained in the hand of the person using. Num 25:7; 2 Sam 2:23.
Stuck in the ground beside the bolster during sleep. 1 Sam 26:7-11.
Illustrative of the bitterness of the wicked. Ps 57:4.

STARS, THE.

Infinite in number. Gen 15:5; Jer 33:2.
God
 Created. Gen 1:16; Ps 8:3; 148:5.
 Set, in the firmament of heaven. Gen 1:17.
 Appointed to give light by night. Gen 1:16,14; Ps 136:9; Jer 31:35.
 Numbers and names. Ps 147:4.
 Established, for ever. Ps 148:3,6; Jer 31:36.
 Obscures. Job 9:7.
Revolve in fixed orbits. Judg 5:20.
Shine in the firmament of heaven. Dan 12:3.
Appear of different magnitudes. 1 Cor 15:41.
Appear after sunset. Neh 4:21; Job 3:9.
Called
 The host of heaven. Deut 17:3; Jer 33:22.
 Stars of light. Ps 148:3.
 Stars of heaven. Is 13:10.
When grouped together called constellations. 2 Kin 23:5; Is 13:10.
Exhibit the greatness of God's power. Ps 8:3; Is 40:26.
Made to praise God. Ps 148:3.
Impure in the sight of God. Job 25:5.
Mentioned in Scripture
 Morning star. Rev 2:28.
 Arcturus. Job 9:9; 38:32.
 Pleiades. Job 9:9; 38:31; Amos 5:8.
 Orion. Job 9:9; 38:31; Amos 5:8.
 Mazzaroth. Job 38:32.

One of extraordinary brightness appeared at Christ's birth. Matt 2:2,9.
Idolaters worshipped. Jer 8:2; 19:13.
The Israelites forbidden to worship. Deut 4:19; 17:2-4.
Punishment for worshipping. Deut 17:5-7.
False gods frequently worshipped under the representation of. Amos 5:26; Acts 7:43.
Astrology and star-gazing practised by the Babylonians. Is 47:13.
Use of, in navigation, alluded to. Acts 27:20.
Illustrative
 Of Christ. Num 24:17.
 Of angels. Job 38:7.
 Of ministers. Rev 1:16,20; 2:1.
 Of princes and subordinate governors. Dan 8:10; Rev 8:12.
 (Bright and morning star,) of Christ. Rev 22:16.
 (Morning star,) of glory to be given to faithful saints. Rev 2:28.
 (Shining of,) of the reward of faithful ministers. Dan 12:3.
 (Withdrawing their light,) of severe judgments. Is 13:10; Ezek 32:7; Joel 2:10; 3:15.
 (Setting the nest amongst,) of pride and carnal security. Obad 4.
 (Wandering,) of false teachers. Jude 1:13.

STEADFASTNESS.

Exhibited by God in all his purposes and ways. Num 23:19; Dan 6:26; James 1:17.
Commanded. Phil 4:1; 2 Thess 2:15; James 1:6-8.
Godliness necessary to. Job 11:13-15.
Secured by
 The power of God. Ps 55:22; 62:2; 1 Pet 1:5; Jude 1:24.
 The presence of God. Ps 16:8.
 Trust in God. Ps 26:1.
 The intercession of Christ. Luke 22:31,32.
A characteristic of saints. Job 17:9; John 8:31.
Should be manifested
 In cleaving to God. Deut 10:20; Acts 11:23.
 In the work of the Lord. 1 Cor 15:58.
 In continuing in the Apostles' doctrine. Acts 2:42.
 In holding fast our profession. Heb 4:14; 10:23.
 In holding fast the confidence and rejoicing of the hope. Heb 3:6,14.
 In keeping the faith. Col 2:5; 1 Pet 5:9.
 In standing fast in the faith. 1 Cor 16:13.
 In holding fast what is good. 1 Thess 5:21.
 In maintaining Christian liberty. Gal 5:1.
 In striving for the faith of the gospel. Phil 1:27; Jude 1:3.
 Even under affliction. Ps 44:17-19; Rom 8:35-37; 1 Thess 3:3.
Saints pray for. Ps 17:5.
Saints praise God for. Ps 116:8.
Ministers
 Exhorted to. 2 Tim 1:13,14; Titus 1:9.
 Should exhort to. Acts 13:43; 14:22.
 Should pray for, in their people. 1 Thess 3:13; 2 Thess 2:17.
 Encouraged by, in their people. 1 Thess 3:8.
 Rejoiced by, in their people. Col 2:5.
The wicked devoid of. Ps 78:8,37.
Principle of—Illustrated. Matt 7:24,25; John 15:4; Col 2:7.
Want of—Illustrated. Luke 8:6,13; John 15:6; 2 Pet 2:17; Jude 1:12.
Exemplified
 Caleb. Num 14:24.
 Joshua. Josh 24:15.
 Josiah. 2 Kin 22:2.
 Job. Job 2:3.
 David. Ps 18:21,22.
 Shadrach. Dan 3:18.
 Daniel. Dan 6:10.
 The Christians. Acts 2:42.
 Corinthians. 1 Cor 15:1.
 Colossians. Col 2:5.
 Those who overcame Satan. Rev 12:11.

STRANGERS IN ISRAEL.

All foreigners sojourning in Israel were counted as. Ex 12:49.
Under the care and protection of God. Deut 10:18; Ps 146:9.
Very numerous in Solomon's reign. 2 Chr 2:17.
Chiefly consisted of
 The remnant of the mixed multitude who came out of Egypt. Ex 12:38.
 The remnant of the nations of the land. 1 Kin 9:20; 2 Chr 8:7.
 Captives taken in war. Deut 21:10.
 Foreign servants. Lev 25:44,45.
 Persons who sought employment among the Jews. 1 Kin 7:13; 9:27.
 Persons who came into Israel for the sake of religious privileges. 1 Kin 8:41.
Laws respecting
 Not to practise idolatrous rites. Lev 20:2.
 Not to blaspheme God. Lev 24:16.
 Not to eat blood. Lev 17:10-12.
 Not to eat the Passover while uncircumcised. Ex 12:43,44.
 Not to work on the Sabbath. Ex 20:10; 23:12; Deut 5:14.
 Not to be vexed or oppressed. Ex 22:21; 23:9; Lev 19:33.
 Not to be chosen as kings in Israel. Deut 17:15.
 To be loved. Lev 19:34; Deut 10:19.
 To be relieved in distress. Lev 25:35.
 Subject to the civil law. Lev 24:22.
 To have justice done to them in all disputes. Deut 1:16; 24:17.
 To enjoy the benefit of the cities of refuge. Num 35:15.
 To have the gleaning of the harvest. Lev 19:10; 23:22; Deut 24:19-22.
 To participate in the rejoicings of the people. Deut 14:29; 16:11,14; 26:11.
 To have the law read to them. Deut 31:12; Josh 8:32-35.
 The Jews might purchase and have them as slaves. Lev 25:44,45.
 The Jews might take usury from. Deut 23:20.
 Might purchase Hebrew servants subject to release. Lev 25:47,48.
 Might offer their burnt offerings on the altar of God. Lev 17:8; 22:18; Num 15:14.
 Allowed to eat what died of itself. Deut 14:21.
Motives urged on the Jews for being kind to. Ex 22:21; 23:9.
Admitted to worship in the outer court of the temple. 1 Kin 8:41-43; Rev 11:2; Eph 2:14.
Were frequently employed in public works. 1 Chr 22:2; 2 Chr 2:18.
The Jews condemned for oppressing. Ps 94:6; Ezek 22:7,29.

STRIFE.

Christ, an example of avoiding. Is 42:2; Matt 12:15-19; Luke 9:52-56; 1 Pet 2:23.
Forbidden. Prov 3:30; 25:8.
A work of the flesh. Gal 5:20.
An evidence of a carnal spirit. 1 Cor 3:3.
Existed in the church. 1 Cor 1:11.
Excited by
 Hatred. Prov 10:12.
 Pride. Prov 13:10; 28:25.
 Wrath. Prov 15:18; 30:33.
 Frowardness. Prov 16:28.
 A contentious disposition. Prov 26:21.
 Tale-bearing. Prov 26:20.
 Drunkenness. Prov 23:29,30.
 Lusts. James 4:1.
 Curious questions. 1 Tim 6:4; 2 Tim 2:23.
 Scorning. Prov 22:10.
Difficulty of stopping, a reason for avoiding it. Prov 17:14.
Shameful in saints. 2 Cor 12:20; James 3:14.
Saints should
 Avoid. Gen 13:8; Eph 4:3.
 Avoid questions that lead to. 2 Tim 2:14.
 Not walk in. Rom 13:13.
 Not act from. Phil 2:3.
 Do all things without. Phil 2:14.
 Submit to wrong rather than engage in. Prov 20:22; Matt 5:39,40; 1 Cor 6:7.
 Seek God's protection from. Ps 35:1; Jer 18:19.
 Praise God for protection from. 2 Sam 22:44; Ps 18:43.
Saints kept from tongues of. Ps 31:20.
Ministers should
 Avoid. 1 Tim 3:3; 2 Tim 2:24.
 Avoid questions that lead to. 2 Tim 2:23; Titus 3:9.
 Not preach through. Phil 1:15,16.
 Warn against. 1 Cor 1:10; 2 Tim 2:14.
 Reprove. 1 Cor 1:11,12; 3:3; 11:17,18.
Appeased by slowness to anger. Prov 15:18.
It is honourable to cease from. Prov 20:3.
Hypocrites make religion a pretence for. Is 58:4.
Fools engage in. Prov 18:6.

Evidences a love of transgression. Prov 17:19.
Leads to
- Blasphemy. Lev 24:10,11.
- Injustice. Hab 1:3,4.
- Confusion and every evil work. James 3:16.
- Violence. Ex 21:18,22.
- Mutual destruction. Gal 5:15.

Temporal blessing embittered by. Prov 17:1.
Excludes from heaven. Gal 5:20,21.
Promoters of, should be expelled. Prov 22:10.
Punishment for. Ps 55:9.
Strength and violence of—Illustrated. Prov 17:14; 18:19.
Danger of joining in—Illustrated. Prov 26:17.
Exemplified
- Herdmen of Abram and of Lot. Gen 13:7.
- Herdmen of Gerar and of Isaac. Gen 26:20.
- Laban and Jacob. Gen 31:36.
- Two Hebrews. Ex 2:13.
- Israelites. Deut 1:12.
- Judah and Israel. 2 Sam 19:41-43.
- Disciples. Luke 22:24.
- Judaising Teachers. Acts 15:2.
- Paul and Barnabas. Acts 15:39.
- Pharisees and Sadducees. Acts 23:7.
- Corinthians. 1 Cor 1:11; 6:6.

Summer.

Made by God. Ps 74:17.
Yearly return of, secured by covenant. Gen 8:22.
Characterised by
- Excessive heat. Jer 17:8.
- Excessive drought. Ps 32:4.

Approach of, indicated by shooting out of leaves on trees. Matt 24:32.
Many kinds of fruit were ripe and used during. 2 Sam 16:1; Jer 40:10; 48:32.
The ancients had houses or apartments suited to. Judg 3:20,24; Amos 3:15.
The ant provided her winter food during. Prov 6:8; 30:25.
The wise are diligent during. Prov 10:5.
Illustrative of seasons of grace. Jer 8:20.

Sun, The.

Called the greater light. Gen 1:16.
God
- Created. Gen 1:14,16; Ps 74:16.
- Placed in the firmament. Gen 1:17.
- Appointed to rule the day. Gen 1:16; Ps 136:8; Jer 31:35.
- Appointed to divide seasons. Gen 1:14.
- Exercises sovereign power over. Job 9:7.
- Causes, to rise both on evil and good. Matt 5:45.
- Causes to know its time of setting. Ps 104:19.

Made to praise and glorify God. Ps 148:3.
The power and brilliancy of its rising alluded to. Judg 5:31; 2 Sam 23:4.
Clearness of its light alluded to. Song 6:10.
Compared to a bridegroom coming forth from his chamber. Ps 19:5.
Compared to a strong man rejoicing to run a race. Ps 19:5.
Diffuses light and heat to all the earth. Ps 19:6.
The rays of
- Pleasant to man. Job 30:28; Eccl 11:7.
- Produce and ripen fruits. Deut 33:14.
- Soften and melt some substances. Ex 16:21.
- Wither and burn up the herbs of the field. Mark 4:6; James 1:11.
- Change the colour of the skin. Song 1:6.
- Frequently destructive to human life. 2 Kin 4:18-20; Ps 121:6; Is 49:10.

Indicates the hours of the day by the shadow on the dial. 2 Kin 20:9.
The Jews
- Commenced their day with the rising of. Gen 19:23,24,27,28; Judg 9:33.
- Commenced their evening with the setting of. Gen 28:11; Deut 24:13; Mark 1:32.
- Expressed the east by rising of. Num 21:11; Deut 4:41,47; Josh 12:1.
- Expressed the west by setting of. James 1:4.
- Expressed the whole earth by, from rising of, to setting of. Ps 50:1; 113:3; Is 45:6.
- Forbidden to worship. Deut 4:19; 17:3.
- Made images of. 2 Chr 14:5; 34:4.
- Consecrated chariots and horses, as symbols of. 2 Kin 23:11.
- Worshipped. 2 Kin 23:5; Jer 8:2.

Worshippers of, turned their faces towards the east. Ezek 8:16.
Miracles connected with
- Standing still for a whole day in the valley of Ajalon. Josh 10:12,13.
- Shadow put back on the dial. 2 Kin 20:11.
- Darkened at the crucifixion. Luke 23:44,45.

Illustrative
- Of God's favour. Ps 84:11.
- Of Christ's coming. Mal 4:2.
- Of the glory of Christ. Matt 17:2; Rev 1:16; 10:1.
- Of supreme rulers. Gen 37:9; Is 13:10.
- (Its clearness,) of the purity of the church. Song 6:10.
- (Its brightness,) of the future glory of saints. Dan 12:3; Matt 13:43.
- (Its power,) of the triumph of saints. Judg 5:31.
- (Darkened,) of severe calamities. Ezek 32:7; Joel 2:10,31; Matt 24:29; Rev 9:2.
- (Going down at noon,) of premature destruction. Jer 15:9; Amos 8:9.
- (No more going down,) of perpetual blessedness. Is 60:20.
- (Before or in sight of,) of public ignominy. 2 Sam 12:11,12; Jer 8:2.

Swearing Falsely.

Forbidden. Lev 19:12; Num 30:2; Matt 5:33.
Hateful to God. Zech 8:17.
We should not love. Zech 8:17.
Fraud often leads to. Lev 6:2,3.
Saints abstain from. Josh 9:20; Ps 15:4.
Blessedness of abstaining from. Ps 24:4,5.
The wicked
- Addicted to. Jer 5:2; Hos 10:4.
- Plead excuses for. Jer 7:9,10.
- Shall be judged on account of. Mal 3:5.
- Shall be cut off for. Zech 5:3.
- Shall have a curse upon their houses for. Zech 5:4.

False witnesses guilty of. Deut 19:16,18.
Exemplified
- Saul. 1 Sam 19:6,10.
- Shimei. 1 Kin 2:41-43.
- Jews. Ezek 16:59.
- Zedekiah. Ezek 17:13-19.
- Peter. Matt 26:72,74.

Swearing, Profane.

Of all kinds is desecration of God's name and is forbidden. Ex 20:7; Matt 5:34-36; 23:21,22; James 5:12.
The wicked
- Addicted to. Ps 10:7; Rom 3:14.
- Love. Ps 109:17.
- Clothe themselves with. Ps 109:18.

Guilt of. Ex 20:7; Deut 5:11.
Woe denounced against. Matt 23:16.
Nations visited for. Jer 23:10; Hos 4:1-3.
Punishment for. Lev 24:16,23; Ps 59:12; 109:17,18.
Exemplified
- Son of Israelitish woman. Lev 24:11.
- Gehazi. 2 Kin 5:20.
- Peter. Matt 26:74.

Swine.

When wild inhabited the woods. Ps 80:13.
Unclean and not to be eaten. Lev 11:7,8.
Described
- Fierce and ungenerous. Matt 7:6.
- Filthy in its habits. 2 Pet 2:22.
- Destructive to agriculture. Ps 80:13.

Fed upon husks. Luke 15:16.
Sacrificing of, an abomination. Is 66:3.
Kept in large herds. Matt 8:30.
Herding of, considered as the greatest degradation to a Jew. Luke 15:15.
The Gergesenes punished for having. Matt 8:31,32; Mark 5:11,14.
The ungodly Jews condemned for eating. Is 65:4; 66:17.
Illustrative of
- The wicked. Matt 7:6.
- Hypocrites. 2 Pet 2:22.

Sword, The.

Probable origin. Gen 3:24.
Was pointed. Ezek 21:15.
Frequently had two edges. Ps 149:6.
Described as
- Sharp. Ps 57:4.
- Bright. Nah 3:3.
- Glittering. Deut 32:41; Job 20:25.
- Oppressive. Jer 46:16.
- Hurtful. Ps 144:10.

Carried in a sheath or scabbard. 1 Chr 21:27; Jer 47:6; Ezek 21:3-5.
Suspended from the girdle. 1 Sam 17:39; 2 Sam 20:8; Neh 4:18; Ps 45:3.

Was used
By the patriarchs. Gen 34:25; 48:22.
By the Jews. Judg 20:2; 2 Sam 24:9.
By heathen nations. Judg 7:22; 1 Sam 15:33.
For self-defence. Luke 22:36.
For destruction of enemies. Num 21:24; Josh 6:21.
For punishing criminals. 1 Sam 15:33; Acts 12:2.
Sometimes for self-destruction. 1 Sam 31:4,5; Acts 16:27.
Hebrews early acquainted with making of. 1 Sam 13:19.
In time of war, plough shares made into. Joel 3:10.
In time of peace made into plough shares. Is 2:4; Mic 4:3.
Sharpened and furbished before going to war. Ps 7:12; Ezek 21:9.
Was brandished over the head. Ezek 32:10.
Was thrust through enemies. Ezek 16:40.
Often threatened as a punishment. Lev 26:25,33; Deut 32:25.
Often sent as a punishment. Ezra 9:7; Ps 78:62.
Was one of God's four sore judgments. Ezek 14:21.
Those slain by, communicated ceremonial uncleanness. Num 19:16.
Illustrative
Of the word of God. Eph 6:17; Heb 4:12.
Of the word of Christ. Is 49:2; Rev 1:16.
Of the justice of God. Deut 32:41; Zech 13:7.
Of the protection of God. Deut 33:29.
Of war and contention. Matt 10:34.
Of severe and heavy calamities. Ezek 5:2,17; 14:17; 21:9.
Of deep mental affliction. Luke 2:35.
Of the wicked. Ps 17:13.
Of the tongue of the wicked. Ps 57:4; 64:3; Prov 12:18.
Of persecuting spirit of the wicked. Ps 37:14.
Of the end of the wicked. Prov 5:4.
Of false witnesses. Prov 25:18.
Of judicial authority. Rom 13:4.
(Drawing of,) of war and destruction. Lev 26:33; Ezek 21:3-5.
(Putting, into its sheath,) of peace and friendship. Jer 47:6.
(Living by,) of rapine. Gen 27:40.
(Not departing from one's house,) of perpetual calamity. 2 Sam 12:10.

SYNAGOGUES.

Places in which the Jews assembled for worship. Acts 13:5,14.
Early notice of their existence. Ps 74:8.
Probably originated in the schools of the prophets. 1 Sam 19:18-24; 2 Kin 4:23.
Revival of, after the captivity. Neh 8:1-8.
Service of, consisted of
Prayer. Matt 6:5.
Reading the word of God. Neh 8:18; 9:3; 13:1; Acts 15:21.
Expounding the word of God. Neh 8:8; Luke 4:21.
Praise and thanksgiving. Neh 9:5.
Service in, on the Sabbath day. Luke 4:16; Acts 13:14.
Governed by
A president or chief ruler. Acts 18:8,17.
Ordinary rulers. Mark 5:22; Acts 13:15.
Provided with a minister, who had charge of the sacred books. Luke 4:17,20.
Had seats for the congregation. Acts 13:14.
Chief seats in, reserved for elders. Matt 23:6.
The portion of Scripture for the day sometimes read by one of the congregation. Luke 4:16.
Strangers were invited to address the congregation in. Acts 13:15.
Christ often
Attended. Luke 4:16.
Preached and taught in. Matt 4:23; Mark 1:39; Luke 13:10.
Performed miracles in. Matt 12:9,10; Mark 1:23; Luke 13:11.
The Apostles frequently taught and preached in. Acts 9:20; 13:5; 17:1,17.
Often used as courts of justice. Acts 9:2; James 2:2.
Offenders were often
Given up to, for trial. Luke 12:11; 21:12.
Punished in. Matt 10:17; 23:34; Acts 22:19.
Expelled from. John 9:22,34; 12:42; 16:2.
The building of, considered a noble and meritorious work. Luke 7:5.
Sometimes several, in the same city. Acts 6:9; 9:2.
Each sect had its own. Acts 6:9.

SYRIA.

Originally included Mesopotamia. Gen 25:20; 28:5; Deut 26:5; Acts 7:2.
More properly the country around Damascus. 2 Sam 8:6.
Damascus the capital of. Is 7:8.
Abana and Pharpar rivers of. 2 Kin 5:12.
Governed by kings. 1 Kin 22:31; 2 Kin 5:1.
Inhabitants of
Called Syrians. 2 Sam 10:11; 2 Kin 5:20.
Called Syrians of Damascus. 2 Sam 8:5.
An idolatrous people. Judg 10:6; 2 Kin 5:18.
A warlike people. 1 Kin 20:23,25.
A commercial people. Ezek 27:18.
Spoke the Syriack language. 2 Kin 18:26; Ezra 4:7; Dan 2:4.
Israel followed the idolatry of. Judg 10:6.
David
Destroyed the army of, which assisted Hadadezer. 2 Sam 8:5.
Garrisoned and made tributary. 2 Sam 8:6.
Dedicated the spoils of. 2 Sam 8:11,12.
Obtained renown by his victory over. 2 Sam 8:13.
Sent Joab against the armies of, hired by the Ammonites. 2 Sam 10:6-14.
Destroyed a second army of. 2 Sam 10:15-19.
Asa sought aid of, against Israel. 1 Kin 15:18-20.
Elijah anointed Hazael king over, by divine direction. 1 Kin 19:15.
Benhadad king of, besieged Samaria. 1 Kin 20:1-12.
The Israelites
Under Ahab encouraged and assisted by God, overcame. 1 Kin 20:13-20.
Forewarned of invasion by, at the return of the year. 1 Kin 20:22-25.
Insignificant before. 1 Kin 20:26,27.
Encouraged and assisted by God overcame a second time. 1 Kin 20:28-30.
Craftily drawn into a league with. 1 Kin 20:31-43.
At peace with, for three years. 1 Kin 22:1.
Under Ahab sought to recover Ramoth-gilead from. 1 Kin 22:3-29.
Defeated by, and Ahab slain. 1 Kin 22:30-36.
Harassed by frequent incursions of. 2 Kin 5:2; 6:23.
Heard the secrets of, from Elisha. 2 Kin 6:8-12.
God smote with blindness those sent against Elisha by the king of. 2 Kin 6:14,18-20.
Besieged Samaria again. 2 Kin 6:24-29.
Army of, miraculously routed. 2 Kin 7:5,6.
Death of the king of, and the cruelty of his successor foretold by Elisha. 2 Kin 8:7,15.
Joram king of Israel in seeking to recover Ramothgilead from, severely wounded. 2 Kin 8:28,29; 9:15.
Israel delivered into the hands of, for the sins of Jehoahaz. 2 Kin 13:3,7,22.
A saviour raised up for Israel against. 2 Kin 13:5,23-25.
Elisha predicted to Joash his three victories over. 2 Kin 13:14-19.
Joined with Israel against Ahaz and besieged Jerusalem. 2 Kin 16:5; Is 7:12.
Retook Elath and drove out the Jews. 2 Kin 16:6.
Subdued and its inhabitants taken captive by Assyria. 2 Kin 16:9.
Prophecies respecting
Destruction of Rezin king of. Is 7:8,16.
Ceasing to be a kingdom. Is 17:1-3.
Terror and dismay in, occasioned by its invasion. Jer 49:23,24.
Destruction of its inhabitants. Jer 49:26.
Plundering of Damascus. Is 8:4.
Burning of Damascus. Jer 49:27; Amos 1:4.
Its calamities, the punishments of its sins. Amos 1:3.
Its inhabitants to be captives. Amos 1:3.
Its history in connection with the Macedonia empire. Dan 11:6-45.
Subdued and governed by the Romans. Luke 2:2.

Gospel preached and many churches founded in. Acts 15:23,41.

TABERNACLE.

Moses was commanded to make after a divine pattern. Ex 25:9; 26:30; Heb 8:5.
Made of the free-will offerings of the people. Ex 25:1-8; 35:4,5,21-29.
Divine wisdom given to Bezaleel to make. Ex 31:2-7; 35:30-35; 36:1.
Called the
  Tabernacle of the Lord. Josh 22:19; 1 Kin 2:28; 1 Chr 16:39.
  Tabernacle of testimony or witness. Ex 38:21; Num 1:50; 17:7,8; 2 Chr 24:6; Acts 7:44.
  Tabernacle of the congregation. Ex 27:21; 33:7; 40:26.
  Tabernacle of Shiloh. Ps 78:60.
  Tabernacle of Joseph. Ps 78:67.
  Temple of the Lord. 1 Sam 1:9; 3:3.
  House of the Lord. Josh 6:24; 1 Sam 1:7,24.
Was a moveable tent suited to the unsettled condition of Israel. 2 Sam 7:6,7.
Designed for manifestation of God's presence and for his worship. Ex 25:8; 29:42,43.
The boards of
  Made of shittim wood. Ex 26:15; 36:20.
  Ten cubits high by one and a half broad. Ex 26:16; 36:21.
  Had each two tenons fitted into sockets of silver. Ex 26:17,19; 36:22-24.
  Twenty on south side. Ex 26:18; 36:23.
  Twenty on north side. Ex 26:20; 36:25.
  Six, and two corner boards for west side. Ex 26:22-25; 36:27-30.
  Supported by bars of shittim wood resting in rings of gold. Ex 26:26-29; 36:31-33.
  With the bars, covered with gold. Ex 26:26-29; 36:34.
The door of, a curtain of blue and purple suspended by gold rings from five pillars of shittim wood. Ex 26:36,37; 36:37,38.
Coverings of
  The first or inner, ten curtains of blue, purple, etc. joined with loops and golden taches. Ex 26:1-6; 36:8-13.
  The second, eleven curtains of goats' hair. Ex 26:7-13; 36:14-18.
  The third of rams' skins dyed red. Ex 26:14; 36:19.
  The fourth or outward of badgers' skins. Ex 26:14; 36:19.
Divided by a vail of blue, purple, suspended from four pillars of shittim. Ex 26:31-33; 36:35,36; 40:21.
Divided into
  The holy place. Ex 26:33; Heb 9:2-6.
  The most holy place. Ex 26:34; Heb 9:3,7.
Had a court round about. Ex 40:8.
The table of show-bread, the golden candlestick, and the altar of incense were place in the holy place. Ex 26:35; 40:22,24,26; Heb 9:2.
The ark and mercy-seat put in the most holy place. Ex 26:33,34; 40:20,21; Heb 9:4.
Court of
  One hundred cubits long and fifty cubits wide. Ex 27:18.
  Surrounded by curtains of fine line suspended from pillars in sockets of brass. Ex 27:9-15; 38:9-16.
  The gate of, a hanging of blue, purple, etc. twenty cubits wide, suspended from four pillars, etc. Ex 27:16; 38:18.
  Contained the brazen altar and laver of brass. Ex 40:29,30.
  All the pillars of, filleted with silver, etc. Ex 27:17; 38:17.
  All the vessels of, made of brass. Ex 27:19.
First reared, on the first day of the second year after the exodus. Ex 40:2,17.
Was set up
  By Moses at Mount Sinai. Ex 40:18,19; Num 10:11,12.
  At Gilgal. Josh 5:10,11.
  In Shiloh. Josh 18:1; 19:51.
  In Nob. 1 Sam 21:1-6.
  Finally at Gibeon. 1 Chr 16:39; 21:29.
Anointed and consecrated with oil. Ex 40:9; Lev 8:10; Num 7:1.
Sprinkled and purified with blood. Heb 9:21.
Sanctified by the glory of the Lord. Ex 29:43; 40:34; Num 9:15.
The Lord appeared in, over the mercy-seat. Ex 25:22; Lev 16:2; Num 7:89.
The cloud of glory rested on, by night and day during its abode in the wilderness. Ex 40:38; Num 9:15,16.
The journeys of Israel regulated by the cloud on. Ex 40:36,37.
The priests
  Alone could enter. Num 18:3,5.
  Performed all services in. Num 3:10; 18:1,2; Heb 9:6.
  Were the ministers of. Heb 8:2.
The Levites
  Appointed over, and had charge of. Num 1:50; 8:24; 18:2-4.
  Did the inferior service of. Num 3:6-8.
  Took down, and put up. Num 1:51.
  Carried. Num 4:15,25,31.
  Pitched their tents around. Num 1:53; 3:23,29,35.
Free-will offerings made at the first rearing of. Num 7:1-9.
Free-will offerings made at the dedication of the altar of. Num 7:10-87.
All offerings to be made at. Lev 17:4; Deut 12:5,6,11,13,14.
Punishment for defiling. Lev 15:31; Num 19:13.
A permanent house substituted for, when the kingdom was established. 2 Sam 7:5-13.
Illustrative
  Of Christ. Is 4:6; John 1:14; Heb 9:8,9,11.
  Of the Church. Ps 15:1; Is 16:5; 54:2; Heb 8:2; Rev 21:2,3.
  Of the body. 2 Cor 5:1; 2 Pet 1:13.
  (The holy of holies,) of heaven. Heb 6:19,20; 9:12,24; 10:19.
  (The vail,) of Christ's body. Heb 10:20.
  (The vail,) of the obscurity of the Mosaic age. Heb 9:8,10; Rom 16:25,26; Rev 11:19.

TEMPLE, THE FIRST.

Built on Mount Moriah on the threshing-floor of Ornan or Araunah. 1 Chr 21:28-30; 22:2; 2 Chr 3:1.
David
  Anxious to build. 2 Sam 7:2; 1 Chr 22:7; 29:3; Ps 132:2-5.
  Being a man of war not permitted to build. 2 Sam 7:5-9; 1 Kin 5:3; 1 Chr 22:8.
  Told by the prophet that Solomon should build. 2 Sam 7:12,13; 1 Chr 17:12.
  Made preparations for building. 1 Chr 22:2-5,14-16; 29:2-5.
  Charged Solomon to build. 1 Chr 22:6,7,11.
  Prayed that Solomon might have wisdom to build. 1 Chr 29:19.
  Charged his princes to assist in building. 1 Chr 22:17-19.
  Free-will offering of the people for the building. 1 Chr 29:6-9.
Solomon
  Determined to build. 2 Chr 2:1.
  Specially instructed for. 2 Chr 3:3.
  Employed all the strangers in preparing for. 2 Chr 2:2,17,18; 1 Kin 5:15.
  Applied to Hiram for a skilful workman to superintend, etc. the building of. 2 Chr 2:7,13,14.
  Employed thirty thousand Israelites in the work. 1 Kin 5:13,14.
  Contracted with Hiram for wood, stone, and labour. 1 Kin 5:6-12; 2 Chr 2:8-10.
  Commenced second day of second month of fourth year of Solomon. 1 Kin 6:1,37; 2 Chr 3:2.
  Built without the noise of hammers, axe, or any tool. 1 Kin 6:7.
Divided into
  The sanctuary or greater house. 2 Chr 3:5.
  The oracle or most holy place. 1 Kin 6:19.
  The porch. 2 Chr 3:4.
Surrounded with three stories of chambers communicating with the interior on the right side. 1 Kin 6:5,6,8,10.
Surrounded with spacious courts. 1 Kin 6:36; 2 Chr 4:9.
Was three score cubits longs, twenty broad, and thirty high. 1 Kin 6:2; 2 Chr 3:3.
Was lighted by narrow windows. 1 Kin 6:4.
Was roofed with cedar. 1 Kin 6:9.
The greater or outer house
  Was forty cubits long. 2 Kin 6:17.
  Had folding doors of fir wood carved and golden. 1 Kin 6:34,35.
  Had door posts of olive wood carved and gilded. 1 Kin 6:33; 2 Chr 3:7.
The oracle or most holy place
  Was twenty cubits every way. 1 Kin 6:16,20.
  Two cherubims of gilded olive wood made within. 1 Kin 6:23-28; 2 Chr 3:11-13.

A partition of chains of gold between it and outer house. 1 Kin 6:21.
The doors and the posts of, of olive wood carved and gilded. 1 Kin 6:31,32.
Separated from the outer house by a vail. 2 Chr 3:14.
The floor and walls of, covered with cedar and fir wood. 1 Kin 6:15.
Cedar of, carved with flowers, etc. 1 Kin 6:18.
Ceiled with fir wood and gilt. 2 Chr 3:5.
The whole inside and outside covered with gold. 1 Kin 6:21,22; 2 Chr 3:7.
Garnished with precious stones. 2 Chr 3:6.
The porch of
Twenty cubits long and ten broad. 1 Kin 6:3.
One hundred and twenty cubits high. 2 Chr 3:4.
Pillars of, with their chapiters described. 1 Kin 7:15-22; 2 Chr 3:15-17.
Its magnificence. 2 Chr 2:5,9.
Was seven years in building. 1 Kin 6:38.
Was finished in the eighth month of the eleventh year of Solomon. 1 Kin 6:38.
Was called
The house of the Lord. 2 Chr 23:5,12.
The mountain of the Lord's house. Is 2:2.
House of the God of Jacob. Is 2:3.
Zion. Ps 84:1-7.
Mount Zion. Ps 74:2.
Appointed as a house of sacrifice. 2 Chr 7:12.
Appointed as a house of prayer. Is 56:7; Matt 21:13.
God promised to dwell in. 1 Kin 6:12,13.
All dedicated things placed in. 2 Chr 5:1.
The ark of God brought into with great solemnity. 1 Kin 8:1-9; 2 Chr 5:2-10.
Filled with the cloud of glory. 1 Kin 8:10,11; 2 Chr 5:13; 7:2.
Solemnly dedicated to God by Solomon. 1 Kin 8:12-66; 2 Chr 6:1-42.
Sacred fire sent down from heaven at its dedication. 2 Chr 7:3.
Was but a temple built with hands. Acts 7:47,48.
Complete destruction of, predicted. Jer 26:18; Mic 3:12.
Historical notices of
Pillaged by Shishak king of Egypt. 1 Kin 14:25,26; 2 Chr 12:9.
Repaired by Jehoash at the institution of Jehoiada. 2 Kin 12:4-14; 2 Chr 24:4-13.
Treasures of given by Jehoash to propitiate the Syrians. 2 Kin 12:17,18.
Defiled and its treasures given by Ahaz to the king of Assyria. 2 Kin 16:14,18; 2 Chr 28:20,21.
Purified and divine worship restored under Hezekiah. 2 Chr 29:3-35.
Its treasures given by Hezekiah to the Assyrians to procure a treaty. 2 Kin 18:13-16.
Polluted by the idolatrous worship of Manasseh. 2 Kin 21:4-7; 2 Chr 33:4,5,7.
Repaired by Josiah in the 18th year of his reign. 2 Kin 22:3-7; 2 Chr 34:8-13.
Purified by Josiah. 2 Kin 23:4-7,11,12.
Pillaged and burned by the Babylonians. 2 Kin 25:9,13-17; 2 Chr 36:18,19.
Illustrative of
Christ. John 2:19,21.
The spiritual church. 1 Cor 3:16; 2 Cor 6:16; Eph 2:20-22.
The bodies of saints. 1 Cor 6:19.

TEMPLE, THE SECOND.

Built on the site of the first temple. Ezra 6:2-12.
Cyrus
His decree for building, predicted. Is 44:28.
Gave a decree for building, in the first year of his reign. Ezra 1:1,2; 6:3.
Gave permission to the Jews to go to Jerusalem to build. Ezra 1:3.
Furnished means for building. Ezra 6:4.
Ordered those who remained in Babylon to contribute to the building of. Ezra 1:4.
Gave the vessels of the first temple for. Ezra 1:7-11; 6:5.
Divine worship commenced before the foundation was laid. Ezra 3:1-6.
Materials for building procured from Tyre and Sidon. Ezra 3:7.
Foundation of, laid the second month of second year after the captivity. Ezra 3:8.
Solemnities connected with laying the foundation of. Ezra 3:9-11.
Its dimensions. Ezra 6:3,4.
Grief of those who had seen the first temple. Ezra 3:12; Hag 2:3.
Joy of those who had not seen the first temple. Ezra 3:13.
The Samaritans
Proposed to assist in building. Ezra 4:1,2.
Their help refused by the Jews. Ezra 4:3.
Weakened the hands of the Jews in building. Ezra 4:4,5.
Wrote to Artaxerxes Smerdis to interrupt the building. Ezra 4:6-16.
Procured its interruption for fifteen years. Ezra 4:24.
The Jews reproved for not building. Hag 1:1-5.
The Jews punished for not persevering in building. Hag 1:6,9-11; 2:15,17; Zech 8:10.
The Jews encouraged to proceed in building. Hag 1:8; 2:19; Zech 8:9.
Resumed by Zerubbabel and Jeshua. Ezra 5:2.
Its completion by Zerubbabel foretold, to encourage the Jews. Zech 4:4-10.
Future glory of, predicted. Hag 2:7-9.
Tatnai the governor wrote to Darius to know if the building had his sanction. Ezra 5:3-17.
The decree of Cyrus found and confirmed by Darius. Ezra 6:1,2,6-12.
Finished the third of the twelfth month in the sixth year of Darius. Ezra 6:15.
Dedication of, celebrated with joy and thankfulness. Ezra 6:16-18.
Repaired and beautified by Herod, which occupied forty-six years. John 2:20.
The magnificence of its building and ornaments. John 2:20; Mark 13:1; Luke 21:5.
Beautiful gate of, mentioned. Acts 3:2.
Solomon's porch connected with. John 10:23; Acts 3:11.
Christ
To appear in. Hag 2:7; Mal 3:1.
Presented in. Luke 2:22,27.
Miraculously transported to a pinnacle of. Matt 4:5; Luke 4:9.
Frequently taught in. Mark 14:49.
Purified, and the commencement of his ministry. John 2:15-17.
Purified, at the close of his ministry. Matt 21:12,13.
Predicted its destruction. Matt 24:2; Mark 13:2; Luke 21:6.
The vail of, rent at our Lord's death. Matt 27:51.
Separation between the outer or Gentile court and that of the Jews alluded to. Eph 2:13,14.
No Gentile allowed to enter the inner courts of. Acts 21:27-30.
The Jews
Prayed without, while the priest offered incense within. Luke 1:10; 18:10.
Considered it blasphemy to speak against. Matt 26:61; Acts 6:13; 21:28.
Desecrated by selling oxen, etc. in. John 2:14.
Desecration of, foretold. Dan 9:27; 11:31.
Cleansed and rededicated by Judas Maccabaeus after its desecration by Antiochus Epiphanes. John 10:22.
Desecrated by the Romans. Dan 9:27; Matt 24:15.

TEMPTATION.

God cannot be the subject of. James 1:13.
Does not come from God. James 1:13.
Comes from
Lusts. James 1:14.
Covetousness. Prov 28:20; 1 Tim 6:9,10.
The devil is the author of. 1 Chr 21:1; Matt 4:1; John 13:2; 1 Thess 3:5.
Evil associates, the instruments of. Prov 1:10; 7:6; 16:29.
Often arises through
Poverty. Prov 30:9; Matt 4:2,3.
Prosperity. Prov 30:9; Matt 4:8.
Worldly glory. Num 22:17; Dan 4:30; 5:2; Matt 4:8.
To distrust of God's providence. Matt 4:3.
To presumption. Matt 4:6.
To worshipping the god of this world. Matt 4:9.
Often strengthened by the perversion of God's word. Matt 4:6.
Permitted as a trial of
Faith. 1 Pet 1:7; James 1:2,3.
Disinterestedness. Job 1:9-12.

Always conformable to the nature of man. 1 Cor 10:13.
Often ends in sin and perdition. 1 Tim 6:9; James 1:15.
Christ
  Endured, from the devil. Mark 1:13.
  Endured, from the wicked. Matt 16:1; 22:18; Luke 10:25.
  Resisted by the word of God. Matt 4:4,7,10.
  Overcame. Matt 4:11.
  Sympathises with those under. Heb 4:15.
  Is able to help those under. Heb 2:18.
  Intercedes for his people under. Luke 22:31,32; John 17:15.
God will not suffer saints to be exposed to, beyond their powers to bear. 1 Cor 10:13.
God will make a way for saints to escape out of. 1 Cor 10:13.
God enables the saints to bear. 1 Cor 10:13.
God knows how to deliver saints out of. 2 Pet 2:9.
Christ keeps faithful saints from the hour of. Rev 3:10.
Saints may be in heaviness through. 1 Pet 1:6.
Saints should
  Resist, in faith. Eph 6:16; 1 Pet 5:9.
  Watch against. Matt 26:41; 1 Pet 5:8.
  Pray to be kept from. Matt 6:13; 26:41.
  Not to occasion, to others. Rom 14:13.
  Restore those overcome by. Gal 6:1.
  Avoid the way of. Prov 4:14,15.
The devil will renew. Luke 4:13.
Has strength through the weakness of the flesh. Matt 26:41.
Mere professors fall away in time of. Luke 8:13.
Blessedness of those who meet and overcome. James 1:2-4,12.
Exemplified
  Eve. Gen 3:1,4,5.
  Joseph. Gen 39:7.
  Balaam. Num 22:17.
  Achan. Josh 7:21.
  David. 2 Sam 11:2.
  Jeroboam. 1 Kin 15:30.
  Peter. Mark 14:67-71.
  Paul. 2 Cor 12:7; Gal 4:14.

TENTS.

Origin and antiquity of. Gen 4:20.
Called
  Tabernacles. Num 24:5; Job 12:6; Heb 11:9.
  Curtains. Is 54:2; Heb 3:7.
Were spread out. Is 40:22.
Fastened by cords to stakes or nails. Is 54:2; Jer 10:20; Judg 4:21.
Were used by
  Patriarchs. Gen 13:5; 25:27; Heb 11:9.
  Israel in the desert. Ex 33:8; Num 24:2.
  The people of Israel in all their wars. 1 Sam 4:3,10; 29:1; 1 Kin 16:16.
  The Rechabites. Jer 35:7,10.
  The Arabs. Is 13:20.
  Shepherds while tending their flocks. Song 1:8; Is 38:12.
  All eastern nations. Judg 6:5; 1 Sam 17:4; 2 Kin 7:7; 1 Chr 5:10.
Separate, for females of the family. Gen 24:67.
Separate, for the servants. Gen 31:33.
Were pitched
  With order and regularity. Num 1:52.
  In the neighbourhood of wells, etc. Gen 13:10,12; 26:17,18; 1 Sam 29:1.
  Under trees. Gen 18:1,4; Judg 4:5.
  On the tops of houses. 2 Sam 16:22.
Sending persons to seek a convenient place for, alluded to. Deut 1:33.
Ease and rapidity of their removal, alluded to. Is 38:12.
Of the Jews contrasted with those of the Arabs. Num 24:5; Song 1:5.
Custom of sitting and standing at the door of. Gen 18:1; Judg 4:20.
Illustrative
  (Spread out,) of the heavens. Is 40:22.
  (Enlarging of,) of the great extension of the Church. Is 54:2.

THANKSGIVING.

Christ set an example of. Matt 11:25; 26:27; John 6:11; 11:41.
The heavenly host engaged in. Rev 4:9; 7:11,12; 11:16,17.
Commanded. Ps 50:14; Phil 4:6.
Is a good thing. Ps 92:1.
Should be offered
  To God. Ps 50:14.
  To Christ. 1 Tim 1:12.
  Through Christ. Rom 1:8; Col 3:17; Heb 13:15.
  In the name of Christ. Eph 5:20.
  In behalf of ministers. 2 Cor 1:11.
  In private worship. Dan 6:10.
  In public worship. Ps 35:18.
  In everything. 1 Thess 5:18.
  Upon the completion of great undertakings. Neh 12:31,40.
  Before taking food. John 6:11; Acts 27:35.
  Always. Eph 1:16; 5:20; 1 Thess 1:2.
  At the remembrance of God's holiness. Ps 30:4; 97:12.
  For the goodness and mercy of God. Ps 106:1; 107:1; 136:1-3.
  For the gift of Christ. 2 Cor 9:15.
  For Christ's power and reign. Rev 11:17.
  For the reception and effectual working of the word of God in others. 1 Thess 2:13.
  For deliverance through Christ from in-dwelling sin. Rom 7:23-25.
  For victory over death and the grave. 1 Cor 15:57.
  For wisdom and might. Dan 2:23.
  For the triumph of the gospel. 2 Cor 2:14.
  For the conversion of others. Rom 6:17.
  For faith exhibited by others. Rom 1:8; 2 Thess 1:3.
  For love exhibited by others. 2 Thess 1:3.
  For the grace bestowed on others. 1 Cor 1:4; Phil 1:3-5; Col 1:3-6.
  For the zeal exhibited by others. 2 Cor 8:16.
  For the nearness of God's presence. Ps 75:1.
  For appointment to the ministry. 1 Tim 1:12.
  For willingness to offer our property for God's service. 1 Chr 29:6-14.
  For the supply of our bodily wants. Rom 14:6,7; 1 Tim 4:3,4.
  For all men. 1 Tim 2:1.
  For all things. 2 Cor 9:11; Eph 5:20.
Should be accompanied by intercession for others. 1 Tim 2:1; 2 Tim 1:3; Philem 4.
Should always accompany prayer. Neh 11:17; Phil 4:6; Col 4:2.
Should always accompany praise. Ps 92:1; Heb 13:15.
Expressed in psalms. 1 Chr 16:7.
Ministers appointed to offer, in public. 1 Chr 16:4,7; 23:30; 2 Chr 31:2.
Saints
  Exhorted to. Ps 105:1; Col 3:15.
  Resolved to offer. Ps 18:49; 30:12.
  Habitually offer. Dan 6:10.
  Offer sacrifices of. Ps 116:17.
  Abound in the faith with. Col 2:7.
  Magnify God by. Ps 69:30.
  Come before God with. Ps 95:2.
  Should enter God's gate with. Ps 100:4.
Of hypocrites, full of boasting. Luke 18:11.
The wicked averse to. Rom 1:21.
Exemplified
  David. 1 Chr 29:12.
  Levites. 2 Chr 5:12,13.
  Daniel. Dan 2:23.
  Jonah. Jon 2:9.
  Simeon. Luke 2:28.
  Anna. Luke 2:38.
  Paul. Acts 28:15.

THEFT.

Is an abomination. Jer 7:9,10.
Forbidden. Ex 20:15; Mark 10:19; Rom 13:9.
From the poor specially forbidden. Prov 22:2.
Includes fraud in general. Lev 19:13.
Includes fraud concerning wages. Lev 19:13; Mal 3:5; James 5:4.
Proceeds from the heart. Matt 15:19.
Defiles a man. Matt 15:20.
The wicked
  Addicted to. Ps 119:61.
  Store up the fruits of. Amos 3:10.
  Lie in wait to commit. Hos 6:9.
  Commit, under shelter of the night. Job 24:14; Obad 5.
  Consent to show who commit. Ps 50:18.
  Associate with those who commit. Is 1:23.
  May, for a season, prosper in. Job 12:6.
  Plead excuses for. Jer 7:9,10.
  Repent not of. Rev 9:21.
  Destroy themselves by. Prov 21:7.
Connected with murder. Jer 7:9; Hos 4:2.
Shame follows the detection of. Jer 2:26.
Brings a curse on those who commit it. Hos 4:2,3; Zech 5:3,4; Mal 3:5.

Brings the wrath of God upon those who commit it. Ezek 22:29,31.
Excludes from heaven. 1 Cor 6:10.
They who connive at
Hate their own souls. Prov 29:24.
Shall be reproved of God. Ps 50:18,21.
Mosaic law respecting. Ex 22:1-8.
Saints
Warned against. Eph 4:28; 1 Pet 4:15.
All earthly treasure exposed to. Matt 6:19.
Heavenly treasure secure from. Matt 6:20; Luke 12:33.
Woe denounced against. Is 10:2; Nah 3:1.
Illustrates the guilt of false teachers. Jer 23:30; John 10:1,8,10.
Exemplified
Rachel. Gen 31:19.
Achan. Josh 7:21.
Shechemites. Judg 9:25.
Micah. Judg 17:2.

THEOCRACY, THE, OR IMMEDIATE GOVERNMENT BY GOD.

Lasted from the deliverance out of Egypt until the appointment of kings. Ex 19:4-6; 1 Sam 8:7.
Was established on
The right of redemption. Ex 6:6,7; 2 Sam 7:23; Is 43:3.
The right of covenant. Deut 26:17-19.
Consisted in his
Promulgating laws. Ex 20:1-23:33.
Directing the movements of the nation. Ex 40:36,37; Num 9:17-23.
Proclaiming war. Ex 17:14-16; Num 31:1,2; Josh 6:2,3; 8:1.
Appointing civil officers. Ex 3:10; Num 27:18,20.
Appointing ecclesiastical officers. Ex 28:1; 40:12-15.
Being the supreme judge. Num 9:8-11; 15:34,35; 27:5-11.
Exercise of the prerogative of mercy. Num 14:20; Deut 9:18-20.
Distribution of conquered lands. Josh 13:1-7.
Exacting tribute. Ex 35:4-29; Lev 27:30; Deut 16:16; 26:1-4.
The tabernacle designed as a royal residence for God during. Ex 25:8; Lev 26:11,12.
The emblem of the divine presence appeared over the tabernacle during. Num 9:15,16.
Guilt of Israel in rejecting. 1 Sam 2:17.

THRESHING.

The removing or separating corn, etc. from the straw. 1 Chr 21:20.
Was performed
By a rod or staff. Is 28:27.
By cart wheels. Is 28:27,28.
By instruments with teeth. Is 41:15; Amos 1:3.
By the feet of horses and oxen. Is 28:28; Hos 10:11; 2 Sam 24:22.
Cattle employed in, not to be muzzled. Deut 25:4; 1 Cor 9:9; 1 Tim 5:18.
Continued until the vintage in years of abundance. Lev 26:5.
The place for
Called the floor. Judg 6:37; Is 21:10.
Called the threshing floor. Num 18:27; 2 Sam 24:18.
Called the barn-floor. 2 Kin 6:27.
Called the corn-floor. Hos 9:1.
Was large and roomy. Gen 50:10.
Generally on high ground. 1 Chr 21:18; 2 Chr 3:1.
Sometimes beside the wine-press for concealment. Judg 6:11.
Used for winnowing the corn. Ruth 3:2.
Often robbed. 1 Sam 23:1.
The Jews slept on, during the time of. Ruth 3:7.
Fulness of, promised as a blessing. Joel 2:24.
Scarcity in, a punishment. Hos 9:2.
Followed by a winnowing with a shovel or fan. Is 30:24; 41:16; Matt 3:12.
Illustrative
Of the judgments of God. Is 21:10; Jer 51:33; Hab 3:12.
Of the labours of ministers. 1 Cor 9:9,10.
Of the church in her conquests. Is 41:15,16; Mic 4:13.
(Gathering the sheaves for,) of preparing the enemies of the Church for judgments. Mic 4:12.
(Dust made by,) of complete destruction. 2 Kin 13:7; Is 41:15.
(An instrument for, with teeth,) of the Church overcoming opposition. Is 41:15.

TIME.

The duration of the world. Job 22:16; Rev 10:6.
The measure of the continuance of anything. Judg 18:31.
An appointed season. Neh 2:6; Eccl 3:1,17.
Computed by
Years. Gen 15:13; 2 Sam 21:1; Dan 9:2.
Months. Num 10:10; 1 Chr 27:1; Job 3:6.
Weeks. Dan 10:2; Luke 18:12.
Days. Gen 8:3; Job 1:4; Luke 11:3.
Hours, after the captivity. Dan 5:5; John 11:9.
Moments. Ex 33:5; Luke 4:5; 1 Cor 15:52.
The heavenly bodies, appointed as a means for computing. Gen 1:14.
The sun-dial early invented for pointing out. 2 Kin 20:9-11.
Eras from which, computed
Nativity of the patriarchs during the patriarchal age. Gen 7:11; 8:13; 17:1.
The exodus from Egypt. Ex 19:1; 40:17; Num 9:1; 33:38; 1 Kin 6:1.
The jubilee. Lev 25:15.
Accession of kings. 1 Kin 6:1; 15:1; Is 36:1; Jer 1:2; Luke 3:1.
Building of the temple. 1 Kin 9:10; 2 Chr 8:1.
The captivity. Ezek 1:1; 33:21; 40:1.
Part of a period of, usually counted as the whole. 1 Sam 13:1; Esth 4:16; 5:1.
In prophetic language, means a prophetic year, or 360 natural days. Dan 12:7; Rev 12:14.
Shortness of man's portion of. Ps 89:47.
Should be redeemed. Eph 5:16; Col 4:5.
Should be spent in fear of God. 1 Pet 1:17.
Particular periods of, mentioned
The ancient time. Is 45:21.
The accepted time. Is 49:8; 2 Cor 6:2.
The time of visitation. Jer 46:21; 50:27.
The time of refreshing. Acts 3:19.
The time of restitution of all things. Acts 3:21.
The time of reformation. Heb 9:10.
The time of healing. Jer 14:19.
The time of need. Heb 4:16.
The time of temptation. Luke 8:13.
The evil time. Ps 37:19; Eccl 9:12.
The time of trouble. Ps 27:5; Jer 14:8.
All events of, predetermined by God. Acts 17:26.
All God's purposes fulfilled in due time. Mark 1:15; Gal 4:4.

TITHE.

The tenth of anything. 1 Sam 8:15,17.
Antiquity of the custom of giving to God's ministers. Gen 14:20; Heb 7:6.
Considered a just return to God for his blessings. Gen 28:22.
Under the law belonged to God. Lev 27:30.
Consisted of a tenth
Of all the produce of the land. Lev 27:30.
Of all cattle. Lev 27:32.
Of holy things dedicated. 2 Chr 31:6.
Given by God to the Levites for their services. Num 18:21,24; Neh 10:37.
The tenth of, offered by the Levites as an heave offering to God. Num 18:26,27.
The tenth of, given by the Levites to the priests as their portion. Num 18:26,28; Neh 10:38.
Reasonableness of appointing, for the Levites. Num 18:20,23,24; Josh 13:33.
When redeemed to a fifth part of the value added. Lev 27:31.
Punishment for changing. Lev 27:33.
The Jews slow in giving. Neh 13:10.
The Jews reproved for withholding. Mal 3:8.
The pious governors of Israel caused the payment of. 2 Chr 31:5; Neh 13:11,12.
Rulers appointed over, for distributing. 2 Chr 31:12; Neh 13:13.
The Pharisees scrupulous in paying. Luke 11:42; 18:12.
A second
Or its value yearly brought to the tabernacle and eaten before the Lord. Deut 12:6,7,17-19; 14:22-27.
To be consumed at home every third year to promote hospitality and charity. Deut 14:28,29; 26:12-15.

TITLES AND NAMES OF CHRIST.

Adam, Second. 1 Cor 15:45.
Almighty. Rev 1:18.
Amen. Rev 3:14.
Alpha and Omega. Rev 1:8; 22:13.
Advocate. 1 John 2:1.
Angel. Gen 48:16; Ex 23:20,21.

Angel of the Lord. Ex 3:2; Judg 13:15-18.
Angel of God's presence. Is 63:9.
Apostle. Heb 3:1.
Arm of the Lord. Is 51:9; 53:1.
Author and Finisher or our faith. Heb 12:2.
Blessed and only Potentate. 1 Tim 6:15.
Beginning of the creation of God. Rev 3:14.
Branch. Jer 23:5; Zech 3:8; 6:12.
Bread of Life. John 6:35,48.
Captain of the Lord's hosts. Josh 5:14,15.
Captain of salvation. Heb 2:10.
Chief Shepherd. 1 Pet 5:4.
Christ of God. Luke 9:20.
Consolation of Israel. Luke 2:25.
Chief Corner-stone. Eph 2:20; 1 Pet 2:6.
Commander. Is 55:4.
Counsellor. Is 9:6.
David. Jer 30:9; Ezek 34:23.
Day-spring. Luke 1:78.
Deliverer. Rom 11:26.
Desire of all nations. Hag 2:7.
Door. John 10:7.
Elect of God. Is 42:1.
Emmanuel. Is 7:14; Matt 1:23.
Eternal life. 1 John 1:2; 5:20.
Everlasting Father. Is 9:6.
Faithful witness. Rev 1:5; 3:14.
First and Last. Rev 1:17; 2:8.
First-begotten of the dead. Rev 1:5.
Firstborn of every creature. Col 1:15.
Forerunner. Heb 6:20.
God. Is 40:9; John 20:28.
God blessed for ever. Rom 9:5.
God's fellow. Zech 13:7.
Glory of the Lord. Is 40:5.
Good Shepherd. John 10:14.
Great High Priest. Heb 4:14.
Governor. Matt 2:6.
Head of the Church. Eph 5:23; Col 1:18.
Heir of all things. Heb 1:2.
Holy One. Ps 16:10; Acts 2:27,31.
Holy One of God. Mark 1:24.
Holy One of Israel. Is 41:14.
Horn of salvation. Luke 1:69.
I AM. Ex 3:14; John 8:58.
Jehovah. Is 26:4.
Jesus. Matt 1:21; 1 Thess 1:10.
Judge of Israel. Mic 5:1.
Just One. Acts 7:52.
King. Zech 9:9; Matt 21:5.
King of Israel. John 1:49.
King of the Jews. Matt 2:2.
King of Saints. Rev 15:3.
King of Kings. 1 Tim 6:15; Rev 17:14.
Law giver. Is 33:22.
Lamb. Rev 5:6,12; 13:8; 21:22; 22:3.
Lamb of God. John 1:29,36.
Leader. Is 55:4.
Life. John 14:6; Col 3:4; 1 John 1:2.
Light of the world. John 8:12.
Lion of the tribe of Judah. Rev 5:5.
Lord of glory. 1 Cor 2:8.
Lord of all. Acts 10:36.
Lord our righteousness. Jer 23:6.
Lord God of the holy prophets. Rev 22:6.
Lord God Almighty. Rev 15:3.
Mediator. 1 Tim 2:5.
Messenger of the covenant. Mal 3:1.
Messiah. Dan 9:25; John 1:41.
Mighty God. Is 9:6.
Mighty One of Jacob. Is 60:16.
Morning-star. Rev 22:16.
Nazarene. Matt 2:23.
Offspring of David. Rev 22:16.
Only-begotten. John 1:14.
Our Passover. 1 Cor 5:7.
Plant of renown. Ezek 34:29.
Prince of life. Acts 3:15.
Prince of peace. Is 9:6.
Prince of the kings of the earth. Rev 1:5.
Prophet. Luke 24:19; John 7:40.
Ransom. 1 Tim 2:6.
Redeemer. Job 19:25; Is 59:20; 60:16.
Resurrection and life. John 11:25.
Rock. 1 Cor 10:4.
Root of David. Rev 22:16.
Root of Jesse. Is 11:10.
Ruler of Israel. Mic 5:2.
Saviour. 2 Pet 2:20; 3:18.
Servant. Is 42:1; 52:13.
Shepherd and Bishop of souls. 1 Pet 2:25.
Shiloh. Gen 49:10.
Son of the blessed. Mark 14:61.
Son of God. Luke 1:35; John 1:49.
Son of the Highest. Luke 1:32.
Son of David. Matt 9:27.
Son of man. John 5:27; 6:37.
Star. Num 24:17.
Sun of righteousness. Mal 4:2.
Surety. Heb 7:22.
True God. 1 John 5:20.
True Light. John 1:9.
True Vine. John 15:1.
Truth. John 14:6.
Way. John 14:6.
Wisdom. Prov 8:12.
Witness. Is 55:4.
Wonderful. Is 9:6.
Word. John 1:1; 5:7.
Word of God. Rev 19:13.
Word of Life. 1 John 1:1.

Titles and Names of the Church.

Assembly of the saints. Ps 89:7.
Assembly of the upright. Ps 111:1.
Body of Christ. Eph 1:22,23; Col 1:24.
Branch of God's planting. Is 60:21.
Bride of Christ. Rev 21:9.
Church of God. Acts 20:28.
Church of the Living God. 1 Tim 3:15.
Church of the firstborn. Heb 12:23.
City of the Living God. Heb 12:22.
Congregation of saints. Ps 149:1.
Congregation of the Lord's poor. Ps 74:19.
Dove. Song 2:14; 5:2.
Family in heaven and earth. Eph 3:15.
Flock of God. Ezek 34:15; 1 Pet 5:2.
Fold of Christ. John 10:16.
General assembly of the firstborn. Heb 12:23.
Golden candlestick. Rev 1:20.
God's building. 1 Cor 3:9.
God's husbandry. 1 Cor 3:9.
God's heritage. Joel 3:2; 1 Pet 5:3.
Habitation of God. Eph 2:22.
Heavenly of Jerusalem. Gal 4:26; Heb 12:22.
Holy city. Rev 21:2.
Holy mountain. Zech 8:3.
Holy hill. Ps 15:1.
House of God. 1 Tim 3:15; Heb 10:21.
House of the God of Jacob. Is 2:3.
House of Christ. Heb 3:6.
Household of God. Eph 2:19.
Inheritance. Ps 28:9; Is 19:25.
Israel of God. Gal 6:16.
King's daughter. Ps 45:13.
Lamb's wife. Rev 19:7; 21:9.
Lot of God's inheritance. Deut 32:9.
Mount Zion. Ps 2:6; Heb 12:22.
Mountain of the Lord's house. Is 2:2.
New Jerusalem. Rev 21:2.
Pillar and ground of the truth. 1 Tim 3:15.
Sanctuary of God. Ps 114:2.
Spiritual house. 1 Pet 2:5.
Spouse of Christ. Song 4:12; 5:1.
Sought out, a city not forsaken. Is 62:12.
Temple of God. 1 Cor 3:16,17.
Temple of the Living God. 2 Cor 6:16.
Vineyard. Jer 12:10; Matt 21:41.

Titles and Names of the Devil.

Abaddon. Rev 9:11.
Accuser of our brethren. Rev 12:10.
Adversary. 1 Pet 5:8.
Angel of the bottomless pit. Rev 9:11.
Apollyon. Rev 9:11.
Beelzebub. Matt 12:24.
Belial. 2 Cor 6:15.
Crooked serpent. Is 27:1.
Dragon. Is 27:1; Rev 20:2.
Enemy. Matt 13:39.
Evil spirit. 1 Sam 16:14.
Father of lies. John 8:44.
Great red dragon. Rev 12:3.
Leviathan. Is 27:1.
Liar. John 8:44.
Lying spirit. 1 Kin 22:22.
Murderer. John 8:44.
Old serpent. Rev 12:9; 20:2.
Piercing serpent. Is 27:1.
Power of darkness. Col 1:13.
Prince of this world. John 14:30.
Prince of the devils. Matt 12:24.
Prince of the power of the air. Eph 2:2.
Ruler of the darkness of this world. Eph 6:12.
Satan. 1 Chr 21:1; Job 1:6.
Serpent. Gen 3:4,16; 2 Cor 11:3.
Spirit that works in the children of disobedience. Eph 2:2.
Tempter. Matt 4:3; 1 Thess 3:5.
The god of this world. 2 Cor 4:4.
Unclean spirit. Matt 12:43.
Wicked-one. Matt 13:19,38.

Titles and Names of the Holy Spirit.

Breath of the Almighty. Job 33:4.
Comforter. John 14:16,26; 15:26.
Eternal Spirit. Heb 9:14.
Free Spirit. Ps 51:12.
God. Acts 5:3,4.
Good Spirit. Neh 9:20; Ps 143:10.
Holy Spirit. Ps 51:11; Luke 11:13; Eph 1:13; 4:30.
Lord, The. 2 Thess 3:5.
Power of the Highest. Luke 1:35.
Spirit, The. Matt 4:1; John 3:6; 1 Tim 4:1.
Spirit of the Lord God. Is 61:1.
Spirit of the Lord. Is 11:2; Acts 5:9.
Spirit of God. Gen 1:2; 1 Cor 2:11; Job 33:4.

Spirit of the Father. Matt 10:20.
Spirit of Christ. Rom 8:9; 1 Pet 1:11.
Spirit of the Son. Gal 4:6.
Spirit of life. Rom 8:2; Rev 11:11.
Spirit of grace. Zech 12:10; Heb 10:29.
Spirit of prophecy. Rev 19:10.
Spirit of adoption. Rom 8:15.
Spirit of wisdom. Is 11:2; Eph 1:17.
Spirit of counsel. Is 11:2.
Spirit of might. Is 11:2.
Spirit of understanding. Is 11:2.
Spirit of knowledge. Is 11:2.
Spirit of the fear of the Lord. Is 11:2.
Spirit of truth. John 14:17; 15:26.
Spirit of holiness. Rom 1:4.
Spirit of revelation. Eph 1:17.
Spirit of judgment. Is 4:4; 28:6.
Spirit of burning. Is 4:4.
Spirit of glory. 1 Pet 4:14.
Seven Spirits of God. Rev 1:4.

Titles and Names of Ministers.

Ambassadors for Christ. 2 Cor 5:20.
Angels of the Church. Rev 1:20; 2:1.
Apostles. Luke 6:13; Eph 4:11; Rev 18:20.
Apostles of Jesus Christ. Titus 1:1.
Bishops. Phil 1:1; 1 Tim 3:1; Titus 1:7.
Deacons. Acts 6:1; 1 Tim 3:8; Phil 1:1.
Elders. 1 Tim 5:17; 1 Pet 5:1.
Evangelists. Eph 4:11; 2 Tim 4:5.
Fishers of men. Matt 4:19; Mark 1:17.
Labourers. Matt 9:38; Philem 1; 1 Thess 2:2.
Messengers of the church. 2 Cor 8:2,3.
Messengers of the Lord of hosts. Mal 2:7.
Ministers of God. 2 Cor 6:4.
Ministers of the Lord. Joel 1:17.
Ministers of Christ. Rom 15:16; 1 Cor 4:1.
Ministers of the sanctuary. Ezek 45:4.
Ministers of the gospel. Eph 3:7; Col 1:23.
Ministers of the word. Luke 1:2.
Ministers of the New Testament. 2 Cor 3:6.
Ministers of the Church. Col 1:24,25.
Ministers of righteousness. 2 Cor 11:15.
Overseers. Acts 20:28.
Pastors. Jer 3:15; Eph 4:11.
Preachers. Rom 10:14; 1 Tim 2:7.
Servants of God. Titus 1:1; James 1:1.
Servants of the Lord. 2 Tim 2:24.
Servants of Jesus Christ. Phil 1:1; Jude 1:1.
Servants of the Church. 2 Cor 4:5.
Shepherds. Jer 23:4.
Soldiers of Christ. Phil 2:25; 2 Tim 2:3.
Stars. Rev 1:20; 2:1.
Stewards of God. Titus 1:7.
Stewards of the grace of God. 1 Pet 4:10.
Stewards of the mysteries of God. 1 Cor 4:1.
Teachers. Is 30:20; Eph 4:11.
Watchmen. Is 62:6; Ezek 33:7.
Witnesses. Acts 1:8; 5:32; 26:16.
Workers together with God. 2 Cor 6:1.

Titles and Names of Saints.

Believers. Acts 5:14; 1 Tim 4:12.
Beloved of God. Rom 1:7.
Beloved brethren. 1 Cor 15:58; James 2:5.
Blessed of the Lord. Gen 24:31; 26:29.
Blessed of the Father. Matt 25:34.
Brethren. Matt 23:8; Acts 12:17.
Brethren of Christ. Luke 8:21; John 20:17.
Called of Jesus Christ. Rom 1:6.
Children of the Lord. Deut 14:1.
Children of God. John 11:52; 1 John 3:10.
Children of the Living God. Rom 9:26.
Children of the Father. Matt 5:45.
Children of the Highest. Luke 6:35.
Children of Abraham. Gal 3:7.
Children of Jacob. Ps 105:6.
Children of promise. Rom 9:8; Gal 4:28.
Children of the free-woman. Gal 4:31.
Children of the kingdom. Matt 13:38.
Children of Zion. Ps 149:2; Joel 2:23.
Children of the bride-chamber. Matt 9:15.
Children of light. Luke 16:8; Eph 5:8; 1 Thess 5:5.
Children of the day. 1 Thess 5:5.
Children of the resurrection. Luke 20:36.
Chosen generation. 1 Pet 2:9.
Chosen ones. 1 Chr 16:13.
Chosen vessels. Acts 9:15.
Christians. Acts 11:26; 26:28.
Dear children. Eph 5:1.
Disciples of Christ. John 8:31; 15:8.
Elect of God. Col 3:12; Titus 1:1.
Epistles of Christ. 2 Cor 3:3.
Excellent, The. Ps 16:3.
Faithful brethren in Christ. Col 1:2.
Faithful, The. Ps 12:1.
Faithful of the land. Ps 101:6.
Fellow-citizens with the saints. Eph 2:19.
Fellow-heirs. Eph 3:6.
Fellow-servants. Rev 6:11.
Friends of God. 2 Chr 20:7; James 2:23.
Friends of Christ. John 15:15.
Godly, The. Ps 4:3; 2 Pet 2:9.
Heirs of God. Rom 8:17; Gal 4:7.
Heirs of the grace of life. 1 Pet 3:7.
Heirs of the kingdom. James 2:5.
Heirs of promise. Heb 6:17; Gal 3:29.
Heirs of salvation. Heb 1:14.
Holy brethren. 1 Thess 5:27; Heb 3:1.
Holy nation. Ex 19:6; 1 Pet 2:9.
Holy people. Deut 26:19; Is 62:12.
Holy priesthood. 1 Pet 2:5.
Joint-heirs with Christ. Rom 8:17.
Just, The. Hab 2:4.
Kings and priests to God. Rev 1:6.
Kingdom of priests. Ex 19:6.
Lambs. Is 40:11; John 21:15.
Lights of the world. Matt 5:14.
Little children. John 13:33; 1 John 2:1.
Lively stones. 1 Pet 2:5.
Members of Christ. 1 Cor 6:15; Eph 5:30.
Men of God. Deut 33:1; 1 Tim 6:11; 2 Tim 3:17.
Obedient children. 1 Pet 1:14.
Peculiar people. Deut 14:2; Titus 2:14; 1 Pet 2:9.
Peculiar treasure. Ex 19:5; Ps 135:4.
People of God. Heb 4:9; 1 Pet 2:10.
People near to God. Ps 148:14.
People saved by the Lord. Deut 33:29.
Pillars in the temple of God. Rev 3:12.
Ransomed of the Lord. Is 35:10.
Redeemed of the Lord. Is 51:11.
Royal priesthood. 1 Pet 2:9.
Salt of the earth. Matt 5:13.
Servants of Christ. 1 Cor 7:22; Eph 6:6.
Servants of righteousness. Rom 6:18.
Sheep of Christ. John 10:1-16; 21:16.
Sojourners with God. Lev 25:23; Ps 39:12.
Sons of God. John 1:12; Phil 2:15; 1 John 3:1,2.
The Lord's freemen. 1 Cor 7:22.
Trees of righteousness. Is 61:3.
Vessels to honour. 2 Tim 2:21.
Vessels of mercy. Rom 9:23.
Witnesses for God. Is 44:8.

Titles and Names of the Wicked.

Adversaries of the Lord. 1 Sam 2:10.
Children of Belial. Deut 13:13; 2 Chr 13:7.
Children of the devil. Acts 13:10; 1 John 3:10.
Children of the wicked one. Matt 13:38.
Children of hell. Matt 23:15.
Children of base men. Job 30:8.
Children of fools. Job 30:8.
Children of strangers. Is 2:6.
Children of transgression. Is 57:4.
Children of disobedience. Eph 2:2; Col 3:6.
Children in whom is no faith. Deut 32:20.
Children of the flesh. Rom 9:8.
Children of iniquity. Hos 10:9.
Children that will not hear the law of the Lord. Is 30:9.
Children of pride. Job 41:34.
Children of this world. Luke 16:8.
Children of wickedness. 2 Sam 7:10.
Children of wrath. Eph 2:3.
Children that are corrupters. Is 1:4.
Cursed children. 2 Pet 2:14.
Enemies of God. Ps 37:20; James 4:4.
Enemies of the cross of Christ. Phil 3:18.
Enemies of all righteousness. Acts 13:10.
Evil doers. Ps 37:1; 1 Pet 2:14.
Evil men. Prov 4:14; 2 Tim 3:13.
Evil generation. Deut 1:35.
Evil and adulterous generation. Matt 12:39.
Fools. Prov 1:7; Rom 1:22.
Froward generation. Deut 32:20.
Generation of vipers. Matt 3:7; 12:34.
Grievous revolters. Jer 6:28.
Haters of God. Ps 81:15; Rom 1:30.
Impudent children. Ezek 2:4.
Inventors of evil things. Rom 1:30.
Lying children. Is 30:9.
Men of the world. Ps 17:14.
People loaded with iniquity. Is 1:4.
Perverse and crooked generation. Deut 32:5; Matt 17:17; Phil 2:15.
Rebellious children. Is 30:1.
Rebellious people. Is 30:9; 65:2.
Rebellious house. Ezek 2:5,8; 12:2.
Reprobates. 2 Cor 13:5-7.
Scornful, The. Ps 1:1.
Seed of falsehood. Is 57:4.
Seed of the wicked. Ps 37:28.
Seed of evil doers. Is 1:4; 14:20.
Serpents. Matt 23:33.

Servants of corruption. 2 Pet 2:19.
Servants of sin. John 8:34; Rom 6:20.
Sinful generation. Mark 8:28.
Sinners. Ps 26:9; Prov 1:10.
Sons of Belial. 1 Sam 2:12; 1 Kin 21:10.
Sottish children. Jer 4:22.
Strange children. Ps 144:7.
Stubborn and rebellious generation. Ps 78:8.
Transgressors. Ps 37:38; 51:13.
Ungodly, The. Ps 1:1.
Ungodly men. Jude 1:4.
Unprofitable servants. Matt 25:30.
Untoward generation. Acts 2:40.
Vessels of wrath. Rom 9:22.
Wicked of the earth. Ps 75:8.
Wicked transgressors. Ps 59:5.
Wicked servants. Matt 25:26.
Wicked generation. Matt 12:45; 16:4.
Wicked ones. Jer 2:33.
Wicked doers. Ps 101:8; Prov 17:4.
Workers of iniquity. Ps 28:3; 36:12.

TOWERS.

Origin and antiquity of. Gen 11:4.
Were built
  In cities. Judg 9:51.
  On the walls of cities. 2 Chr 14:7; 26:9.
  In the forests. 2 Chr 27:4.
  In the deserts. 2 Chr 26:10.
  In vineyards. Is 5:2; Matt 21:33.
Frequently very high. Is 2:15.
Frequently strong and well fortified. Judg 9:51; 2 Chr 26:9.
Were used as armouries. Song 4:4.
Were used as citadels in time of war. Judg 9:51; Ezek 27:11.
Watchmen posted on, in times of danger. 2 Kin 9:17; Hab 2:1.
Mentioned in Scripture
  Babel. Gen 11:9.
  Edar. Gen 35:21.
  Penuel. Judg 8:17.
  Shechem. Judg 9:46.
  Thebez. Judg 9:50,51.
  David. Song 4:4.
  Lebanon. Song 7:4.
  Of the furnaces. Neh 3:11.
  Meah. Neh 12:39.
  Jezreel. 2 Kin 9:17.
  Hananeel. Jer 31:38; Zech 14:10.
  Syene. Ezek 29:10; 30:6.
  Siloam. Luke 13:4.
Of Jerusalem remarkable for number, strength, and beauty. Ps 48:12.
Frequently thrown down in war. Judg 8:17; 9:49; Ezek 26:4.
Frequently left desolate. Is 32:14; Zeph 3:6.
Illustrative of
  God as the protector of his people. 2 Sam 22:3,51; Ps 18:2; 61:3.
  The name of the Lord. Prov 18:10.
  Ministers. Jer 6:27.
  Mount Sion. Mic 4:8.
  The grace and dignity of the church. Song 4:4; 7:4; 8:10.
  The proud and haughty. Is 2:15; 30:25.

TRAVELLERS.

Called way-faring men. Judg 19:17; Is 35:8.
Preparations made by, alluded to. Ezek 12:3,4.
Often collected together and formed caravans. Gen 37:25; Is 21:13; Luke 2:44.
Often engaged persons acquainted with the country as guides. Num 10:31,32; Job 29:15.
Friends of
  Often supplied them with provision. Gen 21:14; 44:1; Jer 40:5.
  Sometimes accompanied them a short way. 2 Sam 19:31; Acts 20:38; 21:5.
  Frequently commended them to protection of God. Gen 43:13,14; Acts 21:5.
  Frequently took leave of them with sorrow. Acts 20:37; 21:6.
  Often sent them away with music. Gen 31:27.
Generally commenced their journey early in the morning. Judg 19:5.
Generally rested at noon. Gen 18:1,3; John 4:6.
Halted at even. Gen 24:11.
Generally halted at wells or streams. Gen 24:11; 32:21,23; Ex 15:27; 1 Sam 30:21; John 4:6.
Carried with them
  Provisions for the way. Josh 9:11,12; Judg 19:19.
  Provender for their beasts of burden. Gen 42:27; Judg 19:19.
  Skins filled with water, wine, etc. Gen 21:14,15; Josh 9:13.
  Presents for those who entertained them. Gen 43:15; 1 Kin 10:2; 2 Kin 5:5; Matt 2:11.
Often travelled on foot. Gen 28:10; 32:10; Ex 12:37; Acts 20:13.
On foot, how attired. Ex 12:11.
After a long journey, described. Josh 9:4,5,13.
Of distinction
  Rode on asses, camels, etc. Gen 22:3; 24:64; Num 22:21.
  Rode in chariots. 2 Kin 5:9; Acts 8:27,28.
  Generally attended by running footmen. 1 Sam 25:27; 1 Kin 18:46; 2 Kin 4:24; Eccl 10:7.
  Often preceded by heralds, etc. to have the roads prepared. Is 40:3,4; Mark 1:2,3.
  Generally performed their journey in great state. 1 Kin 10:2; 2 Kin 5:5,9.
  Frequently extorted provisions by the way. Judg 8:5,8; 1 Sam 25:4-13.
  Before setting out gave employment, etc. to their servants. Matt 25:14.
Strangers civil to. Gen 18:2; 24:18,19.
Generally treated with great hospitality. Gen 18:3-8; 19:2; 24:24,32,33; Ex 2:20; Judg 19:20,21; Job 31:32; Heb 13:2.
The caravanserai or public inn for noticed. Gen 42:27; Ex 4:24; Luke 2:7; 10:34.
Were frequently asked whence they came and whither they went. Judg 19:17.
Protected by those who entertained them. Gen 19:6-8; Judg 19:23.
For security often left the highways. Judg 5:6.
Tesserae hospitales or pledges of hospitality, alluded to. Rev 2:17.
On errands requiring despatch
  Went with great speed. Esth 8:10; Job 9:25.
  Saluted no man by the way. 2 Kin 4:29; Luke 10:4.
Estimated the length of their journey by the number of days which it occupied. Gen 31:23; Deut 1:2; 2 Kin 3:9.
The Jews prohibited from taking long journeys on the Sabbath. Ex 20:10; Acts 1:12.
Ceasing of, threatened as a calamity. Is 33:8.

TREES.

Originally created by God. Gen 1:11,12; 2:9.
Made for the glory of God. Ps 148:9.
Different kinds of mentioned
  Of the wood. Song 2:3.
  Of the forest. Is 10:19.
  Bearing fruit. Neh 9:25; Eccl 2:5; Ezek 47:12.
  Evergreen. Ps 37:35; Jer 17:2.
  Deciduous or casting the leaves. Is 6:13.
Of various sizes. Ezek 17:24.
Given as food to the animal creation. Gen 1:29,30; Deut 20:19.
Designed to beautify the earth. Gen 2:9.
Parts of mentioned
  The roots. Jer 17:8.
  The stem or trunk. Is 11:1; 44:19.
  The branches. Lev 23:40; Dan 4:14.
  The tender shoots. Luke 21:29,30.
  The leaves. Is 6:13; Dan 4:12; Matt 21:19.
  The fruit or seeds. Lev 27:30; Ezek 36:30.
Each kind has its own seed for propagating its species. Gen 1:11,12.
Often propagated by birds who carry the seeds along with them. Ezek 17:3,5.
Planted by man. Lev 19:23.
Each kind of, known by its fruit. Matt 12:33.
Nourished
  By the earth. Gen 1:12; 2:9.
  By the rain from heaven. Is 44:14.
  Through their own sap. Ps 104:16.
Specially flourished beside the rivers and streams of water. Ezek 47:12.
When cut down often sprouted from their roots again. Job 14:7.
Were sold with the land on which they grew. Gen 23:17.
Often suffered from
  Locusts. Ex 10:5,15; Deut 28:42.
  Hail and frost. Ex 9:25; Ps 78:47.
  Fire. Joel 1:19.
  Desolating armies. 2 Kin 19:23; Is 10:34.
Afford an agreeable shade in eastern countries during the heat of the day. Gen 18:4; Job 40:21.
Were cut down
  With axes. Deut 19:5; Ps 74:5; Matt 3:10.
  For building. 2 Kin 6:2; 2 Chr 2:8,10.

By besieging armies for erecting forts. Deut 20:20; Jer 6:6.
For making idols. Is 40:20; 44:14,17.
For fuel. Is 44:14-16; Matt 3:10.
God increases and multiplies the fruit of, for his people. Lev 26:4; Ezek 34:27; Joel 2:22.
God often renders, barren as a punishment. Lev 26:20.
Early custom of planting, in consecrated grounds. Gen 21:33.
The Jews
Prohibited from planting in consecrated places. Deut 16:21.
Prohibited from cutting down fruit bearing, for sieges. Deut 20:19.
Often pitched their tents under. Gen 18:1,4; Judg 4:5; 1 Sam 22:6.
Often buried under. Gen 35:8; 1 Sam 21:13.
Often executed criminals on. Deut 21:22,23; Josh 10:26; Gal 3:13; Gen 40:19.
Considered trees on which criminals were executed abominable. Is 14:19.
Mentioned in Scripture
Almond. Gen 43:11; Eccl 12:5; Jer 1:11.
Almug or algum. 1 Kin 10:11,12; 2 Chr 9:10,11.
Apple. Song 2:3; 8:5; Joel 1:12.
Ash. Is 44:14.
Bay. Ps 37:35.
Box. Is 41:19.
Cedar. 1 Kin 10:27.
Chestnut. Ezek 31:8.
Cyprus. Is 44:14.
Fig. Deut 8:8.
Fir. 1 Kin 5:10; 2 Kin 19:23; Ps 104:17.
Juniper. 1 Kin 19:4,5.
Lign-aloes. Num 24:6.
Mulberry. 2 Sam 5:23,24.
Myrtle. Is 41:19; 55:13; Zech 1:8.
Mustard. Matt 13:32.
Oak. Is 1:30.
Oil-tree. Is 41:19.
Olive. Deut 6:11.
Palm. Ex 15:27.
Pine. Is 41:19.
Pomegranate. Deut 8:8; Joel 1:12.
Shittah or shittim. Ex 36:20; Is 41:19.
Sycamore. 1 Kin 10:27; Ps 78:47; Amos 7:14; Luke 19:4.
Teil. Is 6:13.
Vine. Num 6:4; Ezek 15:2.
Willow. Is 44:4; Ezek 17:5.
Solomon wrote the history of. 1 Kin 4:33.
Illustrative
Of Christ. Rom 11:24; Rev 2:7; 22:2,14.
Of wisdom. Prov 3:18.
Of kings, etc. Is 10:34; Ezek 17:24; 31:7-10; Dan 4:10-14.
Of the life and conversation of the righteous. Prov 11:30; 15:4.
(Green,) of the innocence of Christ. Luke 23:31.
(Good and fruitful,) of saints. Num 24:6; Ps 1:3; Is 61:3; Jer 17:8; Matt 7:17,18.
(Evergreen,) of saints. Ps 1:1-3.
(Duration of,) of continued prosperity of saints. Is 65:22.
(Casting their leaves yet retaining their substance,) of the elect remnant in the church. Is 6:13.
(Barren,) of the wicked. Hos 9:16.
(Shaking of the leaves off,) of the terror of the wicked. Is 7:2.
(Producing evil fruit,) of the wicked. Matt 7:17-19.
(Dry,) of useless persons. Is 56:3.
(Dry,) of the wicked ripe for judgment. Luke 23:31.

Trespass Offering.

Esteemed as a sin offering, and frequently so called. Lev 5:6,9.
To be offered
For concealing knowledge of a crime. Lev 5:1.
For involuntarily touching unclean things. Lev 5:2,3.
For rash swearing. Lev 5:4.
For sins of ignorance in holy things. Lev 5:15.
For any sin of ignorance. Lev 5:17.
For breach of trust, or fraud. Lev 6:2-5.
Was a most holy offering. Lev 14:13.
Consisted of
A she lamb or kid. Lev 5:6.
A ram without blemish. Lev 5:15; 6:6.
Two turtle doves by those unable to bring a lamb. Lev 5:7-10.
A meat offering by the very poor. Lev 5:11-13.
Being for minor offences was lessened for the poor, not so the sin offering. Lev 4:1-5:19.
Atonement made by. Lev 5:6,10,13,16,18; 6:7; 19:22.
Accompanied by confession. Lev 5:5.
Generally accompanied by restitution. Lev 5:16; 6:5.
To be slain where the sin offering and burnt offering were slain. Lev 14:13; Ezek 40:39.
Sometimes waved alive before the Lord. Lev 14:12,13.
Special occasions of offering
Cleansing of a leper. Lev 14:2,12-14,21,22.
Purification of women. Lev 12:6-8.
Purification of those with issues. Lev 15:14,15.
Purification of Nazirites who had broken their vow. Num 6:12.
For connection with a betrothed bondmaid. Lev 19:20-22.
Was the perquisites of the priest. Lev 14:13; Ezek 44:29.
Illustrative of Christ. Is 53:10; Ezek 46:20.

Tribes of Israel, The.

Were twelve in number. Gen 49:28; Acts 26:12; James 1:1.
Descended from Jacob's sons. Gen 35:22-26.
Manasseh and Ephraim numbered among, instead of Joseph and Levi. Gen 48:5; Josh 14:3,4.
Predictions respecting each of. Gen 49:3-27; Deut 33:6-29.
Each of
Under a president or chief. Num 1:4-16.
Divided into families. Num 1:2; 26:5-50; Josh 7:14.
Usually furnished an equal number of men for war. Num 31:4.
Each family of, had a chief or head. Num 36:1; 1 Chr 4:38.
Total strength of, on leaving Egypt. Ex 12:37; Num 1:44-46; 2:32.
Divided into four divisions while in the wilderness. Num 10:14-28.
Encamped in their divisions and by their standards round the tabernacles. Num 2:2-31.
Canaan to be divided amongst according to their numbers. Num 33:54.
Reuben, Gad and half Manasseh
Settled on east side of Jordan. Deut 3:12-17; Josh 13:23-32.
Were required to assist in subduing Canaan. Num 32:6-32; Deut 3:18-20.
Total strength of, on entering the land of Canaan. Num 26:51.
Canaan divided amongst nine and a half of, by lot. Josh 14:1-5.
Situation of, and bounds of the inheritance of each. Josh 15:1-17:18.
All inheritance to remain in the tribe and family to which allotted. Num 36:3-9.
Names of, engraved on the breastplate of the high priest. Ex 28:21; 39:14.
Divided on mounts Ebal and Gerizim to hear the law. Deut 27:12,13.
Remained as one people until the reign of Rehoboam. 1 Kin 12:16-20.

Tribute.

Sometimes exacted by kings from their own subjects. 1 Sam 8:10-17.
Exacted from all conquered nations. Josh 16:10; Judg 1:30,33,35; 2 Kin 23:33,35.
Often exacted in
Labour. 1 Kin 5:13,14; 9:15,21.
Produce of land, etc. 1 Sam 8:15; 1 Kin 4:7.
Gold and silver. 2 Kin 23:33,35.
The Jews required to pay half a shekel to God as. Ex 30:12-16.
Christ to avoid offence wrought a miracle to pay for himself and Peter. Matt 17:24-27.
Kings of Israel
Forbidden to levy unnecessary or oppressive. Deut 17:17.
Set officers over. 2 Sam 20:24; 1 Kin 4:6,7.
Often oppressed the people with. 1 Kin 12:4,11.
When oppressive frequently led to rebellion. 1 Kin 12:14-20.
Priests and Levites exempted from. Ezra 7:24.
Roman
Decree of Augustus for. Luke 2:1.
First levied in Judea when Cyrenius was governor. Luke 2:2.
Persons enroled for, in the native place of their tribe and family. Luke 2:3-5.

Collected by the Publicans. Luke 3:12,13; 5:27.
Was paid in Roman coin. Matt 22:19,20.
Was resisted by the Galilaeans under Judas of Galilee. Acts 5:37; Luke 13:1.
Christ showed to the Pharisees and Herodians the propriety of paying. Matt 22:15-22; Mark 12:13-17.
Our Lord falsely accused of forbidding to pay. Rom 13:6,7.
All saints exhorted to pay. Rom 13:6,7.

TRINITY, THE.

Doctrine of proved from Scripture. Matt 3:16,17; 28:19; Rom 8:9; 1 Cor 12:3-6; 2 Cor 13:14; Eph 4:4-6; 1 Pet 1:2; Jude 1:20,21; Rev 1:4,5.
Divine titles applied to the three persons in. Ex 20:2; John 20:28; Acts 5:3,4.
Each person in, described as
Eternal. Rom 16:26; Rev 22:13; Heb 9:14.
Holy. Rev 4:8; 15:4; Acts 3:14; 1 John 2:20.
True. John 7:28; Rev 3:7.
Omnipresent. Jer 23:24; Eph 1:23; Ps 139:7.
Omnipotent. Gen 17:1; Rev 1:8; Rom 15:19; Jer 32:17; Heb 1:3; Luke 1:35.
Omniscient. Acts 15:18; John 21:17; 1 Cor 2:10,11.
Creator. Gen 1:1; Col 1:16; Job 33:4; Ps 148:5; John 1:3; Job 26:13.
Sanctifier. Jude 1:1; Heb 2:11; 1 Pet 1:2.
Author of all spiritual operations. Heb 13:21; Col 1:29; 1 Cor 12:11.
Source of eternal life. Rom 6:23; John 10:28; Gal 6:8.
Teacher. Is 54:13; Luke 21:15; John 14:26; Is 48:17; Gal 1:12; 1 John 2:20.
Raising Christ from the dead. 1 Cor 6:14; John 2:19; 1 Pet 3:18.
Inspiring the prophets, etc. Heb 1:1; 2 Cor 13:3; Mark 13:11.
Supplying ministers to the Church. Jer 3:15; Eph 4:11; Acts 20:28; Jer 26:5; Matt 10:5; Acts 13:2.
Salvation the work of. 2 Thess 2:13,14; Titus 3:4-6; 1 Pet 1:2.
Baptism administered in name of. Matt 28:19.
Benediction given in name of. 2 Cor 13:14.

TRUMPET.

An instrument of music. 1 Chr 13:8.
Called the trump. 1 Cor 15:52.
Made of
Rams' horns. Josh 6:4.
Silver. Num 10:2.
Required to give an intelligible and understood sound. 1 Cor 14:8.
Used for
Regulating the journeys of the children of Israel. Num 10:2,5,6.
Calling assemblies. Num 10:2,3,7.
Blowing over the sacrifices on the feast day. Num 10:10; Ps 81:3.
Blowing at all religious processions and ceremonies. 1 Chr 13:8; 15:24,28; 2 Chr 5:13; 15:14.
Assembling the people to war. Judg 3:27.
Sounding for a memorial when the people went into battle. Num 10:9; 31:6,7.
Proclaiming kings. 2 Kin 9:13; 11:14.
Giving alarm in cases of danger. Ezek 33:2-6.
Moses commanded to make two, for the tabernacle. Num 10:2.
Solomon made a great many, for the service of the temple. 2 Chr 5:12.
The priests to blow the sacred. Num 10:8; 2 Chr 5:12; 7:6.
The feast of trumpets celebrated by blowing of. Lev 23:24; Num 29:1.
The jubilee introduced by blowing of. Lev 25:9.
Miracles connected with
Falling of the walls of Jericho. Josh 6:20.
Heard at Mount Sinai at giving of the law. Ex 19:16; 20:18.
Confusion produced in the camp of the Midianites by sound of. Judg 7:16,22.
The war-horse acquainted with the sound of. Job 39:24,25.
Sounding of, illustrative of
God's power to raise the dead. 1 Cor 15:52; 1 Thess 4:16.
The proclamation of the gospel. Ps 89:15.
The bold and faithful preaching of ministers. Is 58:1; Hos 8:1; Joel 2:1.
The latter day judgments. Rev 8:2,13.

TRUST.

God is the true object of. Ps 65:5.
The fear of God leads to. Prov 14:26.
Encouragements to
The everlasting strength of God. Is 26:4.
The goodness of God. Nah 1:7.
The lovingkindness of God. Ps 36:7.
The rich bounty of God. 1 Tim 6:17.
The care of God for us. 1 Pet 5:7.
Former deliverances. Ps 9:10; 2 Cor 1:10.
Should be with the whole heart. Prov 3:5.
Should be from youth up. Ps 71:5.
Of saints is
Not in the flesh. Phil 3:3,4.
Not in themselves. 2 Cor 1:9.
Not in carnal weapons. 1 Sam 17:38,39,45; Ps 44:6; 2 Cor 10:4.
In God. Ps 11:1; 31:14; 2 Cor 1:9.
In the word of God. Ps 119:42.
In the mercy of God. Ps 13:5; 52:8.
In Christ. Eph 3:12.
Through Christ. 2 Cor 3:4.
Grounded on the covenant. 2 Sam 23:5.
Strong in the prospect of death. Ps 23:4.
Fixed. 2 Sam 22:3; Ps 112:7.
Unalterable. Job 13:15.
Despised by the wicked. Is 36:4,7.
For ever. Ps 52:8; 62:8; Is 26:4.
Saints plead, in prayer. Ps 25:20; 31:1; 141:8.
The Lord knows those who have. Nah 1:7.
Exhortations to. Ps 4:5; 115:9-11.
Leads to
Being compassed with mercy. Ps 32:10.
Enjoyment of perfect peace. Is 26:3.
Enjoyment of all temporal and spiritual blessings. Is 57:13.
Enjoyment of happiness. Prov 16:20.
Rejoicing in God. Ps 5:11; 33:21.
Fulfilment of all holy desires. Ps 37:5.
Deliverance from enemies. Ps 37:40.
Safety in times of danger. Prov 29:25.
Stability. Ps 125:1.
Prosperity. Prov 28:25.
Keeps from
Fear. Ps 56:11; Is 12:2; Heb 13:6.
Sliding. Ps 26:1.
Desolation. Ps 34:22.
To be accompanied by doing good. Ps 37:3.
Blessedness of placing, in God. Ps 2:12; 34:8; 40:4; Jer 17:7.
Of the wicked
Is not in God. Ps 78:22; Zeph 3:2.
Is in idols. Is 42:17; Hab 2:18.
Is in man. Judg 9:26; Ps 118:8,9.
Is in their own heart. Prov 28:26.
Is in their own righteousness. Luke 18:9,12.
Is in vanity. Job 15:31; Is 59:4.
Is in falsehood. Is 28:15; Jer 13:25.
Is in earthly alliances. Is 30:2; Ezek 17:15.
Is in wealth. Ps 49:6; 52:7; Prov 11:28; Jer 48:7; Mark 10:24.
Is vain and delusive. Is 30:7; Jer 2:37.
Shall make them ashamed. Is 20:5; 30:3,5; Jer 48:13.
Shall be destroyed. Job 18:14; Is 28:18.
Woe and curse of false. Is 30:1,2; 31:1-3; Jer 17:5.
Of saints—Illustrated. Ps 91:12; Prov 18:10.
Of the wicked—Illustrated. 2 Kin 18:21; Job 8:14.
Of saints—Exemplified
David. 1 Sam 17:45; 30:6.
Hezekiah. 2 Kin 18:5.
Jehoshaphat. 2 Chr 20:12.
Shadrach etc. Dan 3:28.
Paul. 2 Tim 1:12.
Of the wicked—Exemplified
Goliath. 1 Sam 17:43-45.
Benhadad. 1 Kin 20:10.
Sennacherib. 2 Chr 32:8.
Israelites. Is 31:1.

TRUTH.

God is a God of. Deut 32:4; Ps 31:15.
Christ is. John 14:6; 7:18.
Christ was full of. John 1:14.
Christ spoke. John 8:45.
The Holy Spirit is the Spirit of. John 14:17.
The Holy Spirit guides into all. John 16:13.
The word of God is. Dan 10:21; John 17:17.
God regards, with favour. Jer 5:3.
The judgments of God are according to. Ps 96:13; Rom 2:2.

Saints should
- Worship God in. John 4:24; Ps 145:18.
- Serve God in. Josh 24:14; 1 Sam 12:24.
- Walk before God in. 1 Kin 2:4; 2 Kin 20:3.
- Keep religious feasts with. 1 Cor 5:8.
- Esteem, as inestimable. Prov 23:23.
- Rejoice in. 1 Cor 13:6.
- Speak, to one another. Zech 8:16; Eph 4:25.
- Meditate upon. Phil 4:8.
- Write upon the tables of the heart. Prov 3:3.

God desires in the heart. Ps 51:6.
The fruit of the Spirit is in. Eph 5:9.
Ministers should
- Speak. 2 Cor 12:6; Gal 4:16.
- Teach in. 1 Tim 2:7.
- Approve themselves by. 2 Cor 4:2; 6:7,8; 7:14.

Magistrates should be men of. Ex 18:21.
Kings are preserved by. Prov 20:28.
They who speak
- Show forth righteousness. Prov 12:17.
- Shall be established. Prov 12:19.
- Are the delight of God. Prov 12:22.

The wicked
- Destitute of. Hos 4:1.
- Speak not. Jer 9:5.
- Uphold not. Is 59:14,15.
- Plead not for. Is 59:4.
- Are not valiant for. Jer 9:3.
- Punished for want of. Jer 9:5,9; Hos 4:1.

The gospel as
- Came by Christ. John 1:17.

Christ bear witness to. John 18:37.
Is in Christ. Rom 9:1; 1 Tim 2:7.
John bears witness to. John 5:33.
Is according to godliness. Titus 1:1.
Is sanctifying. John 17:17,19.
Is purifying. 1 Pet 1:22.
Is part of Christian armour. Eph 6:14.
Revealed abundantly to saints. Jer 33:6.
Abides continually with saints. 2 John 2.
Should be acknowledged. 2 Tim 2:25.
Should be believed. 2 Thess 2:12,13; 1 Tim 4:3.
Should be obeyed. Rom 2:8; Gal 3:1.
Should be loved. 2 Thess 2:10.
Should be manifested. 2 Cor 4:2.
Should be rightly divided. 2 Tim 2:15.
The wicked turn away from. 2 Tim 4:4.
The wicked resist. 2 Tim 3:8.
The wicked destitute of. 1 Tim 6:5.
The church is the pillar and ground of. 1 Tim 3:15.
The devil is devoid of. John 8:44.

TRUTH OF GOD, THE.

Is one of his attributes. Deut 32:4; Is 65:16.
Always goes before his face. Ps 89:14.
He keeps, for ever. Ps 146:6.
Described as
- Great. Ps 57:10.
- Plenteous. Ps 86:15.
- Abundant. Ex 34:6.
- Inviolable. Num 23:19; Titus 1:2.
- Reaching to the clouds. Ps 57:10.
- Enduring to all generations. Ps 100:5.

United with mercy in redemption. Ps 85:10.
Exhibited in his
- Counsels of old. Is 25:1.
- Ways. Rev 15:3.
- Works. Ps 33:4; 11:7; Dan 4:37.
- Judicial statutes. Ps 19:9.
- Administration of justice. Ps 96:13.
- Word. Ps 119:160; John 17:17.
- Fulfilment of promises in Christ. 2 Cor 1:20.
- Fulfilment of his covenant. Mic 7:20.
- Dealings with saints. Ps 25:10.
- Deliverance of saints. Ps 57:3.
- Punishment of the wicked. Rev 16:7.

Remembered toward saints. Ps 98:3.
Is a shield and buckler to saints. Ps 9:14.
We should
- Confide in. Ps 31:5; Titus 1:2.
- Plead, in prayer. Ps 89:49.
- Pray for its manifestation to ourselves. 2 Chr 6:17.
- Pray for its exhibition to others. 2 Sam 2:6.
- Make known to others. Is 38:19.
- Magnify. Ps 71:22; 138:2.

Is denied by
- The devil. Gen 3:4,5.
- The self-righteous. 1 John 1:10.
- Unbelievers. 1 John 5:10.

Exemplified towards
- Abraham. Gen 24:27.
- Jacob. Gen 32:10.
- Israel. Ps 98:3.

TYPES OF CHRIST.

Adam. Rom 5:14; 1 Cor 15:45.
Abel. Gen 4:8,10; Heb 12:24.
Abraham. Gen 17:5; Eph 3:15.
Aaron. Ex 28:1; Heb 5:4,5; Lev 16:15; Heb 9:7,24.
Ark. Gen 7:16; 1 Pet 3:20,21.
Ark of the Covenant. Ex 25:16; Ps 40:8; Is 42:6.
Atonement, sacrifices offered on the day of. Lev 16:15,16; Heb 9:12,24.
Brazen serpent. Num 21:9; John 3:14,15.
Brazen altar. Ex 27:1,2; Heb 13:10.
Burnt offering. Lev 1:2,4; Heb 10:10.
Cities of refuge. Num 35:6; Heb 6:18.
David. 2 Sam 8:15; Ezek 37:24; Ps 89:19,20; Phil 2:9.
Eliakim. Is 22:20-22; Rev 3:7.
First-fruits. Ex 22:29; 1 Cor 15:20.
Golden candlestick. Ex 25:31; John 8:12.
Golden altar. Ex 40:5,26,27; Rev 8:3; Heb 13:15.
Isaac. Gen 22:1,2; Heb 11:17-19.
Jacob. Gen 32:28; John 11:42; Heb 7:25.
Jacob's ladder. Gen 28:12; John 1:51.
Joseph. Gen 50:19,20.
Joshua. Josh 1:5,6; Heb 4:8,9; Josh 11:23; Acts 20:32.
Jonah. Jon 1:17; Matt 12:40.
Laver of brass. Ex 30:18-20; Zech 13:1; Eph 5:26,27.
Leper's offering. Lev 14:4-7; Rom 4:25.
Man. Ex 16:11-15; John 6:32-35.
Melchizedek. Gen 14:18-20; Heb 7:1-17.
Mercy-seat. Ex 25:17-22; Rom 3:25; Heb 4:16.
Morning and evening sacrifices. Ex 29:38-41; John 1:29,36.
Moses. Num 12:7; Heb 3:2; Deut 18:15; Acts 3:20-22.
Noah. Gen 5:29; 2 Cor 1:5.
Paschal lamb. Ex 12:3-6,46; John 19:36; 1 Cor 5:7.
Peace offerings. Lev 3:1; Eph 2:14,16.
Red heifer. Num 19:2-6; Heb 9:13,14.
Rock of Horeb. Ex 17:6; 1 Cor 10:4.
Samson. Judg 16:30; Col 2:14,15.
Scapegoat. Lev 16:20-22; Is 53:6,12.
Sin offering. Lev 4:2,3,12; Heb 13:11,12.
Solomon. 2 Sam 7:12,13; Luke 1:32,33; 1 Pet 2:5.
Tabernacle. Ex 40:2,34; Heb 9:11; Col 2:9.
Table and show bread. Ex 25:23-30; John 1:16; 6:48.
Temple. 1 Kin 6:1,38; John 2:19,21.
Tree of life. Gen 2:9; John 1:4; Rev 22:2.
Trespass offering. Lev 6:1-7; Is 53:10.
Vail of the tabernacle and temple. Ex 40:21; 2 Chr 3:14; Heb 10:20.
Zerubbabel. Zech 4:7-9; Heb 12:2,3.

TYRE.

Antiquity of. Is 23:7; Josh 19:29.
Called
- The daughter of Zidon. Is 23:12.
- The daughter of Tarshish. Is 23:10.
- The joyous city. Is 23:7.
- The crowning city. Is 23:8.
- The renowned city. Ezek 26:17.

Insular position of. Ezek 26:17; 27:4,25.
Strongly fortified. Josh 19:29; 2 Sam 24:7; Ezek 26:17; Zech 9:3.
Governed by kings. 1 Kin 5:1; Jer 25:22.
Celebrated for
- Its beauty. Ezek 27:3,4.
- Its commerce. Is 23:2,3; Ezek 27:3,12-25.
- Its wealth. Ezek 27:33; 28:4,5; Zech 9:3.
- Strength and beauty of its ships. Ezek 27:5-7.

Soldiers of, supplied by Persia, etc. Ezek 27:10,11.
Inhabitants of
- Sea-faring men. Ezek 26:17.
- Mercantile men. Is 23:8.
- Proud and haughty. Is 23:9; Ezek 28:2,17.
- Self-conceited. Ezek 28:3-5.
- Superstitious. Jer 27:2,3,9.
- Wicked. Ezek 28:18.

Often confederated against the Jews and rejoiced in their calamities. Ps 83:7; Ezek 26:2; Amos 1:9.
David and Solomon formed alliances with. 1 Kin 5:1; 2 Chr 2:3.
Supplied
- Seamen for Solomon's navy. 1 Kin 9:27; 2 Chr 8:18.
- A master-builder for the temple. 2 Chr 2:7,13.
- Stones and timber for building the temple. 1 Kin 5:6,9; 2 Chr 2:8,9,16.
- Timber for rebuilding the temple and city. Ezra 3:7.

The Jews condemned for purchasing from the people of, on the Sabbath. Neh 13:16.
Christ
- Alluded to the depravity of. Matt 11:21,22.
- Visited the coasts of. Matt 15:21; Mark 7:24.

Was followed by many from. Mark 3:8; Luke 6:17.
Paul found disciples at. Acts 21:3,4.
Depended for provision upon Galilee. Acts 12:20.
Propitiated the favour of Herod. Acts 12:20.
Prophecies respecting
Envy against the Jews a cause of its destruction. Ezek 26:2.
Pride a cause of its destruction. Ezek 28:2-6.
To be destroyed by the king of Babylon. Is 23:13,14; Jer 27:3,6; Ezek 26:7-13.
Inhabitants of, to emigrated to other countries. Is 23:6,12.
To be scraped as the top of a rock, and to be a place for the spreading nets. Ezek 26:3-5,14.
The king of Babylon to be rewarded with the spoil of Egypt for his service against. Ezek 29:18-20.
To lie waste and be forgotten for seventy years. Is 23:15.
Its restoration to commercial greatness after seventy years. Is 23:16,17.
Its second destruction by the Macedonians. Ezek 27:32; 28:7,8,18; Zech 9:2-4.
The ruins of the first city to be employed in making a causeway to effect the destruction of insular Tyre. Ezek 26:12.
Never to recover its greatness. Ezek 26:21.
Its inhabitants to be sold as slaves, as a recompence for their selling the Jews. Joel 3:4-8.
All nations to be terrified at its destruction. Ezek 26:15-18; 27:29-36; Zech 9:5.
To participated in the blessings of the gospel. Ps 45:12; Is 23:18.

UNBELIEF.

Is sin. John 16:9.
Defilement inseparable from. Titus 1:15.
All, by nature, concluded in. Rom 11:32.
Proceeds from
An evil heart. Heb 3:12.
Slowness of heart. Luke 24:25.
Hardness of heart. Mark 16:14; Acts 19:9.
Disinclination to the truth. John 8:45,46.
Judicial blindness. John 12:39,40.
Not being Christ's sheep. John 10:26.
The devil blinding the mind. 2 Cor 4:4.
The devil taking away the word out of the heart. Luke 8:12.
Seeking honour from men. John 5:44.
Impugns the veracity of God. 1 John 5:10.
Exhibited in
Rejecting Christ. John 16:9.
Rejecting the word of God. Ps 106:24.
Rejecting the gospel. Is 53:1; John 12:38.
Rejecting evidence of miracles. John 12:37.
Departing from God. Heb 3:12.
Questioning the power of God. 2 Kin 7:2; Ps 78:19,20.
Not believing the works of God. Ps 78:32.
Staggering at the promise of God. Rom 4:20.
Rebuked by Christ. Matt 17:17; John 20:27.
Was an impediment to the performance of miracles. Matt 17:20; Mark 6:5.
Miracles designed to convince those in. John 10:37,38; 1 Cor 14:22.
The Jews rejected for. Rom 11:20.
Believers should hold no communion with those in. 2 Cor 6:14.
They who are guilty of
Have not the word of God in them. John 5:38.
Cannot please God. Heb 11:6.
Malign the gospel. Acts 19:9.
Persecute the ministers of God. Rom 15:31.
Excite others against saints. Acts 14:2.
Persevere in it. John 12:37.
Harden their necks. 2 Kin 17:14.
Are condemned already. John 3:18.
Have the wrath of God abiding upon. John 3:36.
Shall not be established. Is 7:9.
Shall die in their sins. John 8:24.
Shall not enter rest. Heb 3:19; 4:11.
Shall be condemned. Mark 16:16; 2 Thess 2:12.
Shall be destroyed. Jude 1:5.
Shall be cast into the lake of five. Rev 21:8.
Warnings against. Heb 3:12; 4:11.
Pray for help against. Mark 9:24.
The portion of, awarded to all unfaithful servants. Luke 12:46.
Exemplified
Eve. Gen 3:4-6.
Moses and Aaron. Num 20:12.
Israelites. Deut 9:23.
Naaman. 2 Kin 5:12.
Samaritan Lord. 2 Kin 7:2.
Disciples. Matt 17:17; Luke 24:11,25.
Zacharias. Luke 1:20.
Chief Priests. Luke 22:67.
The Jews. John 5:38.
Brethren of Christ. John 7:5.
Thomas. John 20:25.
Jews of Iconium. Acts 14:2.
Thessalonian Jews. Acts 17:5.
Ephesians. Acts 19:9.
Saul. 1 Tim 1:13.
People of Jericho. Heb 11:31.

UNICORN.

Generally had a single horn. Ps 92:10.
Sometimes found with two horns. Deut 33:17.
Described as
Intractable in disposition. Job 39:9,10,12.
Of vast strength. Job 39:11.
The young of, remarkable for agility. Ps 29:6.
Illustrative
Of God as the strength of Israel. Num 23:22; 24:8.
Of the wicked. Is 34:7.
(Horns of,) of the strength of the descendants of Joseph. Deut 33:17.
(Horns of,) of the strength of powerful enemies. Ps 22:21.
(The position of its horns,) of the exaltation of saints. Ps 92:10.

UNION WITH CHRIST.

As Head of the Church. Eph 1:22,23; 4:15,16; Col 1:18.
Christ prayed that all saints might have. John 17:21,23.
Described as
Christ being in us. Eph 3:17; Col 1:27.
Our being in Christ. 2 Cor 12:2; 1 John 5:20.
Includes union with the Father. John 17:21; 1 John 2:24.
Is of God. 1 Cor 1:30.
Maintained by
Faith. Gal 2:20; Eph 3:17.
Abiding in him. John 15:4,7.
His word abiding in us. John 15:7; 1 John 2:24; 2 John 9.
Feeding on him. John 6:56.
Obeying him. 1 John 3:24.
The Holy Spirit witnesses. 1 John 3:24.
The gift of the Holy Spirit is an evidence of. 1 John 4:13.
Saints
Have, in mind. 1 Cor 2:16; Phil 2:5.
Have, in spirit. 1 Cor 6:17.
Have, in love. Song 2:16; 7:10.
Have, in sufferings. Phil 3:10; 2 Tim 2:12.
Have, in his death. Rom 6:3-8; Gal 2:20.
Have assurance of. John 14:20.
Enjoy, in the Lord's Supper. 1 Cor 10:16,17.
Identified with Christ by. Matt 25:40,45; Acts 9:4; 8:1.
Are complete through. Col 2:10.
Exhorted to maintain. John 15:4; Acts 11:23; Col 2:7.
Necessary to growth in grace. Eph 4:15,16; Col 2:19.
Necessary to fruitfulness. John 15:4,5.
Beneficial results of
Righteousness imputed. 2 Cor 5:21; Phil 3:9.
Freedom from condemnation. Rom 8:1.
Freedom from dominion of sin. 1 John 3:6.
Being created anew. 2 Cor 5:17.
The spirit alive to righteousness. Rom 8:10.
Confidence at his coming. 1 John 2:28.
Abundant fruitfulness. John 15:5.
Answers to prayer. John 15:7.
They who have, ought to walk as he walked. 1 John 2:6.
False teachers have not. Col 2:18,19.
Is indissoluble. Rom 8:35.
Punishment of those who have not. John 15:6.
Illustrated
Vine and branches. John 15:1,5.
Foundation and building. 1 Cor 3:10,11; Eph 2:20,21; 1 Pet 2:4-6.
Body and members. 1 Cor 12:12,27; Eph 5:30.
Husband and wife. Eph 5:25-32.

Unity of God.

A ground for obeying him exclusively. Deut 4:39,40.
A ground for loving him supremely. Deut 6:4,5; Mark 12:29,30.
Asserted by
God himself. Is 44:6,8; 45:18,21.
Christ. Mark 12:29; John 17:3.
Moses. Deut 4:39; 6:4.
Apostles. 1 Cor 8:4,6; Eph 4:6; 1 Tim 2:5.
Consistent with the deity of Christ and of the Holy Spirit. John 10:30; 1 John 5:7; John 14:9-11.
Exhibited in
His greatness and wonderful works. 2 Sam 7:22; Ps 86:10.
His works of creation and providence. Is 44:24; 45:5-8.
His being alone possessed of foreknowledge. Is 46:9-11.
His exercise of uncontrolled sovereignty. Deut 32:39.
His being the sole object of worship in heaven and earth. Neh 9:6; Matt 4:10.
His being alone good. Matt 19:17.
His being the only Saviour. Is 45:21,22.
His being the only source of pardon. Mic 7:18; Mark 2:7.
His unparalleled election and care of his people. Deut 4:32-35.
The knowledge of, necessary to eternal life. John 17:3.
All saints acknowledge, in worshipping him. 2 Sam 7:22; 2 Kin 19:15; 1 Chr 17:20.
All should know and acknowledge. Deut 4:35; Ps 83:18.
May be acknowledged without saving faith. James 2:19,20.

Uprightness.

God is perfect in. Is 26:7.
God has pleasure in. 1 Chr 29:17.
God created man in. Eccl 7:29.
Man has deviated from. Eccl 7:29.
Should be in
Heart. 2 Chr 29:34; Ps 125:4.
Speech. Is 33:15.
Walk. Prov 14:2.
Judging. Ps 58:1; 75:2.
Ruling. Ps 78:72.
The being kept from presumptuous sins is necessary to. Ps 19:13.
With poverty, is better than sin with riches. Prov 28:6.
With poverty, is better than folly. Prov 19:1.
They who walk in
Fear God. Prov 14:2.
Love Christ. Song 1:4.
Countenanced by God. Ps 11:7.
Delighted in by God. Prov 11:20.
Their prayer delighted in by God. Prov 15:8.
Prospered by God. Job 8:6; Prov 14:11.
Defended by God. Prov 2:7.
Upheld in it by God. Ps 41:12.
Recompensed by God. Ps 18:23,24.
Find strength in God's way. Prov 10:29.
Obtain good from God's work. Mic 2:7.
Obtain light in darkness. Ps 112:4.
Guided by integrity. Prov 11:3.
Walk surely. Prov 10:9.
Direct their way. Prov 21:29.
Kept by righteousness. Prov 13:6.
Scorned by the wicked. Job 12:4.
Hated by the wicked. Prov 29:10; Amos 5:10.
Abominated by the wicked. Prov 29:21.
Persecuted by the wicked. Ps 37:14.
Praise is comely for. Ps 33:1.
A blessing to others. Prov 11:11.
The truly wise walk in. Prov 15:21.
The way of, is to depart from evil. Prov 16:17.
They who walk in, shall
Possess good things. Prov 28:10.
Have nothing good withheld. Ps 84:11.
Dwell in the land. Prov 2:21.
Dwell on high and be provided for. Is 33:16.
Dwell with God. Ps 15:2; 140:13.
Be blessed. Ps 112:2.
Be delivered by righteousness. Prov 11:6.
Be delivered by their wisdom. Prov 12:6.
Be saved. Prov 28:18.
Enter into peace. Ps 37:37; Is 57:2.
Have dominion over the wicked. Ps 49:14.
Have inheritance for ever. Ps 37:18.
A characteristic of saints. Ps 111:1; Is 26:7.
Saints should resolve to walk in. Ps 26:11.
The wicked
Have not, in heart. Hab 2:4.
Leave not the path of. Prov 2:13.
Do not act with. Mic 7:2,4.
Pray for those who walk in. Ps 125:4.
Reprove those who deviate from. Gal 2:14.

Urim and Thummim.

Placed in the breastplate of the high priest. Ex 28:30; Lev 8:8.
God to be consulted by. Num 27:21.
Instances of consulting God by. Judg 1:1; 20:18,28; 1 Sam 23:9-11; 30:7,8.
Sometimes no answer by, in consequence of the sin of those consulting. 1 Sam 28:6.
Were wanting in the second temple. Ezra 2:63; Neh 7:65.
Illustrative of the light and perfection of Christ, the true high priest. Deut 33:8; John 1:4,9,17; Col 2:3.

Usury or Interest.

The lending of money or other property for increase. Lev 25:37.
Those enriched by unlawful, not allowed to enjoy their gain. Ps 28:8.
The curse attending the giving or receiving of unlawful, alluded to. Jer 15:10.
The Jews
Forbidden to take, from brethren. Deut 23:19.
Forbidden to take, from brethren specially when poor. Ex 22:25; Lev 25:35-37.
Often guilty of taking. Neh 5:6,7; Ezek 22:12.
Required to restore. Neh 5:9-13.
Allowed to take, from strangers. Deut 23:20.
True and faithful Israelites never took, from their brethren. Ps 15:5; Ezek 18:8,9.
Judgments denounced against those who exacted unlawful. Is 24:1,2; Ezek 18:13.
Illustrative of the improvement of talents received from God. Matt 25:27; Luke 19:23.

Vail or Veil.

A covering for the head usually worn by women. Gen 38:14.
Was worn
As a token of modesty. Gen 24:65.
As a token of subjection. 1 Cor 11:3,6,7,10.
For concealment. Gen 38:14.
The removing of, considered rude and insolent. Song 5:7.
Removing of, threatened as a punishment to ungodly women. Is 3:23.
Moses put one on to conceal the glory of his face. Ex 34:33; 2 Cor 3:13.
Illustrative
Of the spiritual blindness of the Gentile nations. Is 25:7.
Of the spiritual blindness of the Jewish nation. 2 Cor 3:14-16.

Vail, the Sacred.

Moses commanded to make. Ex 26:31.
Made by Bezaleel for the tabernacle. Ex 36:35.
Suspended from four pillars of shittim wood overlaid with gold. Ex 26:32.
Hung between the holy and most holy place. Ex 26:33; Heb 9:3.
Designed to conceal the ark, mercy seat, and the symbol of the divine presence. Ex 40:3.
The high priest
Alone allowed to enter within. Heb 9:6,7.
Allowed to enter but once a year. Lev 16:2; Heb 9:7.
Could not enter without blood. Lev 16:3; Heb 9:7.
Made by Solomon for the temple. 2 Chr 3:14.
Was rent at the death of our Lord. Matt 27:51; Mark 15:38; Luke 23:45.
Illustrative
Of the obscurity of the Mosaic age. Heb 9:8.
Of the flesh of Christ which concealed his divinity. Heb 10:20; Is 53:2.
(Rending of,) of the death of Christ which opened heaven to saints. Heb 10:19,20; 9:24.

Valleys.

Tracts of land between mountains. 1 Sam 17:3.
Called
Vales. Deut 1:7; Josh 10:40.

Dales. Gen 14:17; 2 Sam 18:18.
Fat valleys, when fruitful. Is 28:1,4.
Rough valleys, when uncultivated and barren. Deut 21:4.
Watered by mountain streams. Ps 104:8,10.
Canaan abounded in. Deut 11:11.
Abounded with
Fountains and springs. Deut 8:7; Is 41:18.
Rocks and caves. Job 30:6; Is 57:5.
Trees. 1 Kin 10:27.
Lily of the valley. Song 2:1.
Ravens. Prov 30:17.
Doves. Ezek 7:16.
Of Israel well tilled and fruitful. 1 Sam 6:13; Ps 65:13.
Often the scenes of idolatrous rites. Is 57:5.
The heathen supposed that certain deities presided over. 1 Kin 20:23,28.
The Canaanites held possession of, against Judah. Judg 1:19.
Often the scenes of great contests. Judg 5:15; 7:8,22; 1 Sam 17:19.
Mentioned in Scripture
Achor. Josh 7:24; Is 65:10; Hos 2:5.
Ajalon. Josh 10:12.
Baca. Ps 84:6.
Berachah. 2 Chr 20:26.
Bochim. Judg 2:5.
Charashim. 1 Chr 4:14.
Elah. 1 Sam 17:2; 21:9.
Eshcol. Num 32:9; Deut 1:24.
Gad. 2 Sam 24:5.
Gerar. Gen 26:17.
Gibeon. Is 28:21.
Hebron. Gen 37:14.
Hinnom or Tophet. Josh 18:16; 2 Kin 23:10; 2 Chr 28:3; Jer 7:32.
Jehoshaphat or decision. Joel 3:2,14.
Jericho. Deut 34:3.
Jezreel. Hos 1:5.
Jephthah-el. Josh 19:14,27.
Keziz. Josh 18:21.
Lebanon. Josh 11:17.
Megiddo. 2 Chr 35:22; Zech 12:11.
Moab where Moses was buried. Deut 34:6.
Passengers or Hamongog. Ezek 39:11.
Rephaim or giants. Josh 15:8; 18:16; 2 Sam 5:18; Is 17:5.
Salt. 2 Sam 8:13; 2 Kin 14:17.
Shaveh or king's dale. Gen 14:17; 2 Sam 18:18.
Shittim. Joel 3:18.
Siddim. Gen 14:3,8.
Sorek. Judg 16:4.
Succoth. Ps 60:6.
Zared. Num 21:12.
Zeboim. 1 Sam 13:18.
Zephathah. 2 Chr 14:10.
To be filled with hostile chariots, threatened as a punishment. Is 22:7.
Miracles connected with
The moon made to stand still over Ajalon. Josh 10:12.
Ditches in, filled with water. 2 Kin 3:16,17.
Water in, made to appear to the Moabites like blood. 2 Kin 3:22,23.
Illustrative
Of the church of Christ. Song 6:11.
(Fruitful and well watered,) of the tents of Israel. Num 24:6.
(Dark,) of affliction and death. Ps 23:4.
(Filling up of,) of removing all obstructions to the gospel. Is 40:4; Luke 3:5.

Vanity.

A consequence of the fall. Rom 8:20.
Every man is. Ps 39:11.
Every state of man is. Ps 62:9.
Man at his best estate is. Ps 39:5.
Man is like to. Ps 144:4.
The thoughts of man are. Ps 94:11.
The days of man are. Job 7:16; Eccl 6:12.
Childhood and youth are. Eccl 11:10.
The beauty of man is. Ps 39:11; Prov 31:30.
The help of man in. Ps 60:11; Lam 4:17.
Man's own righteousness is. Is 57:12.
Worldly wisdom is. Eccl 2:15,21; 1 Cor 3:20.
Worldly pleasure is. Eccl 2:1.
Worldly anxiety. Ps 39:6; 127:2.
Worldly labour is. Eccl 2:11; 4:4.
Worldly enjoyment is. Eccl 2:3,10,11.
Worldly possessions are. Eccl 2:4-11.
Treasures of wickedness are. Prov 10:2.
Heaping up riches is. Eccl 2:26; 4:8.
Love of riches is. Eccl 5:10.
Unblessed riches are. Eccl 6:2.
Riches gotten by falsehood are. Prov 21:6.
All earthly things are. Eccl 1:2.
Foolish questions, etc. are. 1 Tim 1:6,7; 6:20; 2 Tim 2:14,16; Titus 3:9.
The conduct of the ungodly is. 1 Pet 1:18.
The religion of hypocrites is. James 1:26.
The worship of the wicked is. Is 1:13; Matt 6:7.
Lying words are. Jer 7:8.
False teaching is but. Jer 23:32.
Mere external religion is. 1 Tim 4:8; Heb 13:9.
Alms giving without charity is. 1 Cor 13:3.
Faith without works is. James 2:14.
Idolatry is. 2 Kin 17:15; Ps 31:6; Is 44:9,10; Jer 10:8; 18:15.
Wealth gotten by, diminishes. Prov 13:11.
Saints
Hate the thoughts of. Ps 119:113.
Pray to be kept from. Ps 119:37; Prov 30:8.
Avoid. Ps 24:4.
Avoid those given to. Ps 26:4.
The wicked
Especially characterised by. Job 11:11.
Though full of, affect to be wise. Job 11:12.
Love. Ps 4:2.
Imagine. Ps 2:1; Acts 4:25; Rom 1:21.
Devise. Ps 36:4.
Speak. Ps 10:7; 12:2; 41:6.
Count God's service as. Job 21:15; Mal 3:14.
Allure others by words of. 2 Pet 2:18.
Walk after. Jer 2:5.
Walk in. Ps 39:6; Eph 4:17.
Inherit. Jer 16:19.
Reap. Prov 22:8; Jer 12:13.
Judicially given up to. Ps 78:33; Is 57:13.
Fools follow those given to. Prov 12:11.
Following those given to, leads to poverty. Prov 28:19.
They who trust in, rewarded with. Job 15:31.

Vine, The.

Often found wild. 2 Kin 4:39; Hos 9:10.
Cultivated
In vineyards from the time of Noah. Gen 9:20.
On the sides of hills. Jer 31:5.
In the valleys. Song 6:11.
By the walls of houses. Ps 128:3.
Required to be dressed and pruned to increase its fruitfulness. Lev 25:3; 2 Chr 26:10; Is 18:5.
Canaan abounded in. Deut 6:11; 8:8.
Places celebrated for
Eshcol. Num 13:23,24.
Sibmah. Is 16:8,9.
Lebanon. Hos 14:7.
Egypt. Ps 78:47; 80:8.
The dwarf and spreading vine particularly esteemed. Ezek 17:6.
Of Sodom bad and unfit for use. Deut 32:32.
Often degenerated. Is 5:2; Jer 2:21.
Frequently injured by hail and frost. Ps 78:47; 105:32,33.
Foxes destructive to. Song 2:15.
The wild boar destructive to. Ps 80:13.
The fruit of
Called grapes. Gen 40:10.
Peculiarly sour when unripe. Jer 31:30.
Eaten fresh from the tree. Deut 23:24.
Eaten dried. 1 Sam 25:18; 30:12.
Sold in the markets. Neh 13:15.
Made into wine. Deut 32:14; Matt 26:29.
The wood of, fit only for burning. Ezek 15:2-5.
Young cattle fed on its leaves and tender shoots. Gen 49:11.
Probably produced two crops of fruit in the year. Num 13:20.
Perfumed the air with the fragrance of its flowers. Song 2:13; Hos 14:7.
God made, fruitful for his people when obedient. Joel 2:22; Zech 8:12.
Frequently made unfruitful as a punishment. Jer 8:13; Hos 2:12; Joel 1:7,12; Hag 2:19.
Sometimes cast its fruit before it came to perfection. Job 15:33; Mal 3:11.
Nazirites prohibited eating any part of. Num 6:3,4.
Illustrative
Of Christ. John 15:1,2.
Of Israel. Ps 80:8; Is 5:2,7.
(Its fruitful branches,) of saints. John 15:5.
(Of unfruitful branches,) of mere professors. John 15:2,6.
(Its quick growth,) of the growth of saints in grace. Hos 14:7.
(Its rich clusters,) of the graces of the church. Song 7:8.
(Pruning of,) of God's purifying his people by afflictions. John 15:2.

(Worthlessness of its wood,) of the unprofitableness, of the wicked. Ezek 15:6,7.
(Unfruitful,) of the wicked. Hos 10:1.
(Sitting under one's own) of peace and prosperity. 1 Kin 4:25; Mic 4:4; Zech 3:10.
Proverbial allusion to fathers eating the unripe fruit of. Jer 31:29,30; Ezek 18:2.

VINEYARDS.

Origin and antiquity of. Gen 9:20.
The design of planting. Ps 107:37; 1 Cor 9:7.
Frequently walled or fenced with hedges. Num 22:24; Prov 24:31; Is 5:2,5.
Cottages built in, for the keepers. Is 1:8.
Provided with the apparatus for making wine. Is 5:2; Matt 21:33.
The stones carefully gathered out of. Is 5:2.
Laws respecting
Not to be planted with different kinds of seed. Deut 22:9.
Not to be cultivated in the Sabbatical year. Ex 23:11; Lev 25:4.
The spontaneous fruit of, not to be gathered during the sabbatical year. Lev 25:5,11.
Compensation in kind to be made for injury done to. Ex 22:5.
Strangers entering, allowed to eat fruit of, but not to take any away. Deut 23:24.
The gleaning of, to be left for the poor. Lev 19:10; Deut 24:21.
The fruit of new, not to be eaten for three years. Lev 19:23.
The fruit of new, to be holy to the Lord in the fourth year. Lev 19:24.
The fruit of new, to be eaten by the owners from the fifth year. Lev 19:25.
Planters of, not liable to military service till they had eaten of the fruit. Deut 20:6.
Frequently let out to husbandmen. Song 8:11; Matt 21:33.
Rent of, frequently paid by part of the fruit. Matt 21:34.
Were often mortgaged. Neh 5:3,4.
Estimated rent of. Song 8:11; Is 7:23.
Estimated profit arising from, to the cultivators. Song 8:12.
The poor engaged in the culture of. 2 Kin 25:12; Is 61:5.
Members of the family often wrought in. Song 1:6; Matt 21:28-30.
Mode of hiring and paying labourers for working in. Matt 20:1,2.
Of the kings of Israel superintended by officers of the state. 1 Chr 27:27.
The vintage or ingathering of
Was a time of great rejoicing. Is 16:10.
Sometimes continued to the time of sowing seed. Lev 26:5.
Failure in, occasioned great grief. Is 16:9,10.
Of red grapes particularly esteemed. Is 27:2.
The produce of, was frequently destroyed by enemies. Jer 48:32.
The whole produce of, often destroyed by insects, etc. Deut 28:39; Amos 4:9.
In unfavourable seasons produced but little wine. Is 5:10; Hag 1:9,11.
The wicked judicially deprived of the enjoyment of. Amos 5:11; Zeph 1:13.
The Rechabites forbidden to plant. Jer 35:7-9.
Of the slothful man neglected and laid waste. Prov 24:30,31.
Illustrative
Of the Jewish Church. Is 5:7; 27:2; Jer 12:10; Matt 21:23.
(Failure of,) of severe calamities. Is 32:10.
(Cleaning grapes of,) of the elect. Is 24:13.

VISIONS.

God often made known his will by. Ps 89:19.
God especially made himself known to prophets by. Num 12:6.
Often accompanied
A representative of the divine person and glory. Is 6:1.
An audible voice from heaven. Gen 15:1; 1 Sam 3:4,5.
An appearance of angels. Luke 1:22,11; 24:23; Acts 10:3.
An appearance of human beings. Acts 9:12; 16:9.
Frequently difficult and perplexing to those who received them. Dan 7:15; 8:15; Acts 10:17.
Often communicated
In the night season. Gen 46:2; Dan 2:19.
In a trance. Num 24:16; Acts 11:5.
Often recorded for the benefit of the people. Hab 2:2.
Often multiplied for the benefit of the people. Hos 12:10.
Mentioned in Scripture
To Abraham. Gen 15:1.
To Jacob. Gen 46:2.
To Moses. Ex 3:2,3; Acts 7:30-32.
To Samuel. 1 Sam 3:2-15.
To Nathan. 2 Sam 7:4,17.
To Eliphaz. Job 4:13-16.
To Isaiah. Is 6:1-8.
To Ezekiel (See chapters 10, 40-48 of Ezekiel). Ezek 1:4-14; 8:2-14; 11:24,25; 37:1-10.
To Nebuchadnezzar. Dan 2:28; Dan 4:5.
To Daniel (See chapters 7, 8, and 10 of Daniel). Dan 2:19.
To Amos. Amos 7:1-9; 8:1-6; 9:1.
To Zechariah. Zech 1:8; 3:1; 4:2; 5:2; 6:1.
To Paul. Acts 9:3,6; 16:9; 18:9; 22:18; 27:23; 2 Chr 12:1-4.
To Ananias. Acts 9:10,11.
To Cornelius. Acts 10:3.
To Peter. Acts 10:9-17.
To John (See also Rev chapters 4 - 22). Rev 1:12.
Sometimes withheld for a long season. 1 Sam 3:1.
The withholding of a great calamity. Prov 29:18; Lam 2:9.
False prophets pretended to have seen. Jer 14:14; 23:16.
The prophets of God skilled in interpreting. 2 Chr 26:5; Dan 1:17.

VOWS.

Solemn promises made to God. Ps 76:11.
Were made in reference to
Devoting the person to God. Num 6:2.
Dedicating children to God. 1 Sam 1:11.
Devoting property to God. Gen 28:22.
Offering sacrifices. Lev 7:16; 22:18:22; Num 15:3.
Afflicting the soul. Num 30:13.
To be voluntary. Deut 23:21,22.
To be performed faithfully. Num 30:2.
To be performed without delay. Deut 23:21,23.
Danger of inconsiderately making. Prov 20:25.
Of children void without the consent of parents. Num 30:3-5.
Of married women void without consent of husbands. Num 30:6-8,10-13.
Of widows and women divorced from their husbands binding. Num 30:9.
Of wives, could only be objected to at the time of making. Num 30:14,15.
Might be redeemed by paying a suitable compensation. Lev 27:1-8,11-23.
Clean beasts the subjects of, not to be redeemed. Lev 27:9,10.
Recorded in Scripture
Of Jacob. Gen 28:20-22; 31:13.
Of Israelites. Num 21:2.
Of Jephthah. Judg 11:30,31.
Of Hannah. 1 Sam 1:1.
Of Elkanah. 1 Sam 1:24.
Of David. Ps 132:2-5.
Of mariners who cast out Jonah. Jon 1:16.
Of Jonah. Jon 2:9.
Of Lemuel's mother. Prov 31:1,2.
Of Paul. Acts 18:18.
Of certain Jews with Paul. Acts 21:23,24,26.
All things dedicated by, to be brought to the tabernacle. Deut 12:6,11,17,18,26.
Of things corrupt or blemished an insult to God. Lev 22:23; Mal 1:14.
The hire of a prostitute or price of a dog could not be the subject of. Deut 23:18.

WAITING UPON GOD.

As the God of providence. Jer 14:22.
As the God of salvation. Ps 25:5.
As the Giver of all temporal blessings. Ps 104:27,28; Ps 145:15,16.
For
Mercy. Ps 123:2.
Pardon. Ps 39:7,8.
The consolation of Israel. Luke 2:25.
Salvation. Gen 49:18; Ps 62:1,2.
Guidance and teaching. Ps 25:5.
Protection. Ps 33:20; 59:9,10.
The fulfillment of His word. Hab 2:3.
The fulfillment of His promises. Acts 1:4.
Hope of righteous by faith. Gal 5:5.

Coming of Christ. 1 Cor 1:7; 1 Thess 1:10.
Is good. Ps 52:9.
God calls us to. Zeph 3:8.
Exhortations and encouragements to. Ps 27:14; 37:7; Hos 12:6.
Should be
With the soul. Ps 62:1,5.
With earnest desire. Ps 130:6.
With patience. Ps 37:7; 40:1.
With resignation. Lam 3:26.
With hope in His word. Ps 130:5.
With full confidence. Mic 7:7.
Continually. Hos 12:6.
All the day. Ps 25:5.
Specially in adversity. Ps 59:1-9; Is 8:17.
In the way of His judgments. Is 26:8.
Saints resolve on. Ps 52:9; 59:9.
Saints have expectation from. Ps 62:5.
Saints plead, in prayer. Ps 25:21; Is 33:2.
The patience of saints often tried in. Ps 69:3.
They who engage in
Wait upon Him only. Ps 62:5.
Are heard. Ps 40:1.
Are blessed. Is 30:18; Dan 12:12.
Experience His goodness. Lam 3:25.
Shall not be ashamed. Ps 25:3; Is 49:23.
Shall renew their strength. Is 40:31.
Shall inherit the earth. Ps 37:9.
Shall be saved. Prov 20:22; Is 25:9.
Shall rejoice in salvation. Is 25:9.
Shall receive the glorious things prepared by God for them. Is 64:4.
Predicted of the Gentiles. Is 42:4; 60:9.
Illustrated. Ps 123:2; Luke 12:36; James 5:7.
Exemplified
Jacob. Gen 49:18.
Hannah. 1 Sam 1:2.
David. Ps 39:7.
Isaiah. Is 8:17.
Micah. Mic 7:7.
Joseph. Mark 15:43.

WALLS.

Designed for separation. Ezek 43:8; Eph 2:14.
Designed for defence. 1 Sam 25:16.
Mentioned in Scripture
Of cities. Num 13:28.
Of temples. 1 Chr 29:4; Is 56:5.
Of houses. 1 Sam 18:11.
Of vineyards. Num 22:24; Prov 24:31.
Frequently made of stone and wood together. Ezra 5:8; Hab 2:11.
Were probably often strengthened with plates of iron or brass. Jer 15:20; Ezek 4:3.
Of cities
Often very high. Deut 1:28; 3:5.
Strongly fortified. Is 2:15; 25:12.
Had towers built on them. 2 Chr 26:9; 32:5; Ps 48:12; Song 8:10.
Houses often built on. Josh 2:15.
Were broad and places of public resort. 2 Kin 6:26,30; Ps 55:10.
Were strongly manned in war. 2 Kin 18:26.
Kept by watchmen night and day. Song 5:7; Is 62:6.
Houses sometimes broken down to repair, and fortify. Is 22:10.
Danger of approaching too near to, in time of war. 2 Sam 11:20,21.
Were battered by besieging armies. 2 Sam 20:15; Ezek 4:2,3.
Adroitness of soldiers in scaling alluded to. Joel 2:7-9.
Sometimes burned. Jer 49:27; Amos 1:7.
Frequently laid in ruins. 2 Chr 25:23; 36:19; Jer 50:15.
Destruction of, a punishment and cause of grief. Deut 28:52; Neh 1:3; 2:12-17.
The falling of, sometimes occasioned great destruction. 1 Kin 20:30.
The bodies of enemies sometimes fastened on, as a disgrace. 1 Sam 31:10.
Custom of dedicating. Neh 12:27.
Idolatrous rites performed on. 2 Kin 3:27.
Instances of persons let down from. Josh 2:15; Acts 9:24,25; 2 Cor 11:33.
Small towns and villages were not surrounded by. Lev 25:31; Deut 3:5.
Of houses
Usually plastered. Ezek 13:10; Dan 5:5.
Had nails or pegs fastened into them when built. Eccl 12:11; Is 22:23.
Liable to leprosy. Lev 14:37.
Often infested with serpents. Amos 5:19.
Could be easily dug through. Gen 49:6; Ezek 8:7,8; 12:5.
The seat next, was the place of distinction. 1 Sam 20:25.
Hyssop frequently grew on. 1 Kin 4:33.
Miracles connected with
Falling of the walls of Jericho. Josh 6:20.
Handwriting on the wall of Belshazzar's palace. Dan 5:5,25-28.
Illustrative
Of salvation. Is 26:1; 60:18.
Of the protection of God. Zech 2:5.
Of those who afford protection. 1 Sam 25:16; Is 2:15.
Of the Church as a protection to the nation. Song 8:9,10.
Of ordinances as a protection to the Church. Song 2:9; Is 5:5.
Of the wealth of the rich in his own conceit. Prov 18:11.
(Brazen,) of prophets in their testimony against the wicked. Jer 22:20.
(Bowing or tottering,) of the wicked under judgments. Ps 62:3; Is 30:13.
(Of partition,) of separation of Jews and Gentiles. Eph 2:14.
(Daubed with untempered mortar,) of the teaching of false prophets. Ezek 13:10-15.
(Whited,) of hypocrites. Acts 23:3.

WAR.

Antiquity of. Gen 14:2.
Originates in the lusts of men. James 4:1.
A time for. Eccl 3:8.
God
Frequently ordered. Ex 17:16; Num 31:1,2; Deut 7:1,2; 1 Sam 15:1-3.
Taught His people the art of. 2 Sam 22:35.
Strengthens His people for. Lev 26:7,8.
Gives the victory in. Num 21:3; Deut 2:33; 3:3; 2 Sam 23:10; Prov 21:31.
Causes to cease. Ps 46:9.
Scatters those who delight in. Ps 68:30.
Large armies frequently engaged in. 2 Chr 13:3; 14:9.
Weapons used in. Josh 1:14; Judg 18:11.
Preceded by
Consultation. Luke 14:31; Prov 24:6.
Great preparation. Joel 3:9.
Rumors. Jer 4:19; Matt 24:6.
Frequently long continued. 2 Sam 3:1.
Frequently sore and bloody. 1 Sam 14:22; 1 Chr 5:22; 2 Chr 14:13; 28:6.
Often attended by
Famine. Is 51:19; Jer 14:15; Lam 5:10.
Pestilence. Jer 27:13; 28:8.
Cruelty. Jer 18:21; Lam 5:11-14.
Devastation. Is 1:7.
Records often kept of. Num 21:14.
Often sent as a punishment for sin. Judg 5:8.
The Jews
Were expert in. 1 Chr 12:33,35,36; Song 3:8.
Frequently engaged in (See Joshua chapters 6 through 11). 1 Kin 14:30; 15:7,16.
Illustrative of
Our contest with death. Eccl 8:8.
The contest of saints with the enemies of their salvation. Rom 7:23; 2 Cor 10:3; Eph 6:12; 1 Tim 1:18.
The contest between Antichrist and the Church. Rev 11:7; 13:4,7.
The malignity of the wicked. Ps 55:21.

WARFARE OF SAINTS.

Is not after the flesh. 2 Cor 10:3.
Is a good warfare. 1 Tim 1:18,19.
Called the good fight of faith. 1 Tim 6:12.
Is against
The devil. Gen 3:15; 2 Cor 2:11; Eph 6:12; James 4:7; 1 Pet 5:8; Rev 12:17.
The flesh. Rom 7:23; 1 Cor 9:25-27; 2 Cor 12:7; Gal 5:17; 1 Pet 2:11.
Enemies. Ps 38:19; 56:2; 59:3.
The world. John 16:33; 1 John 5:4,5.
Death. 1 Cor 15:26; Heb 2:14,15.
Often arises from the opposition of friends or relatives. Mic 7:6; Matt 10:35,36.
To be carried on
Under Christ, as our captain. Heb 2:10.
Under the Lord's banner. Ps 60:4.
With faith. 1 Tim 1:18,19.
With a good conscience. 1 Tim 1:18,19.
With steadfastness in the faith. 1 Cor 16:13; 1 Pet 5:9; Heb 10:23.
With earnestness. Jude 1:3.
With watchfulness. 1 Cor 16:13; 1 Pet 5:8.

With sobriety. 1 Thess 5:6; 1 Pet 5:8.
With endurance or hardness. 2 Tim 2:3,10.
With self-denial. 1 Cor 9:25-27.
With confidence in God. Ps 27:1-3.
With prayer. Ps 35:1-3; Eph 6:18.
Without earthly entanglements. 2 Tim 2:4.
Mere professors do not maintain. Jer 9:3.
Saints
Are all engaged in. Phil 1:30.
Must stand firm in. Eph 6:13,14.
Exhorted to diligence. 1 Tim 6:12; Jude 1:3.
Encouraged in. Is 41:11,12; 51:12; Mic 7:8; 1 John 4:4.
Helped by God in. Ps 118:13; Is 41:13,14.
Protected by God in. Ps 140:7.
Comforted by God in. 2 Cor 7:5,6.
Strengthened by God in. Ps 20:2; 27:14; Is 41:10.
Strengthened by Christ in. 2 Cor 12:9; 2 Tim 4:17.
Delivered by Christ in. 2 Tim 4:18.
Thank God for victory in. Rom 7:25; 1 Cor 15:57.
Armour for
Girdle of truth. Eph 6:14.
Breastplate of righteousness. Eph 6:14.
Preparation of the gospel. Eph 6:15.
Shield of faith. Eph 6:16.
Helmet of salvation. Eph 6:17; 1 Thess 5:8.
Sword of the Spirit. Eph 6:17.
Called armour of God. Eph 6:11.
Called armour of righteousness. 2 Cor 6:7.
Called armour of light. Rom 13:12.
Not carnal. 2 Cor 10:4.
Mighty through God. 2 Cor 10:4,5.
The whole, is required. Eph 6:13.
Must be put on. Rom 13:12; Eph 6:11.
To be on right hand and left. 2 Cor 6:7.
Victory in, is
From God. 1 Cor 15:57; 2 Cor 2:14.
Through Christ. Rom 7:25; 1 Cor 15:27; 2 Cor 12:9; Rev 12:11.
By faith. Heb 11:33-37; 1 John 5:4,5.
Over the devil. Rom 16:20; 1 John 2:14.
Over the flesh. Rom 7:24,25; Gal 5:24.
Over the world. 1 John 5:4,5.
Over all that exalts itself. 2 Cor 10:5.
Over death and the grave. Is 25:8; 26:19; Hos 13:14; 1 Cor 15:54,55.
Triumphant. Rom 8:37; 2 Cor 10:5.
They who overcome in, shall
Eat of the hidden manna. Rev 2:17.
Eat of the tree of life. Rev 2:7.
Be clothed in white raiment. Rev 3:5.
Be pillars in the temple of God. Rev 3:12.
Sit with Christ in his throne. Rev 3:21.
Have a white stone, and, in it a new name written. Rev 2:17.
Have power over the nations. Rev 2:26.
Have the name of God written upon them by Christ. Rev 3:12.
Have God as their God. Rev 21:7.
Have the morning-star. Rev 2:28.
Inherit all things. Rev 21:7.
Be confessed by Christ before God the Father. Rev 3:5.
Be sons of God. Rev 21:7.
Not be hurt by the second death. Rev 2:11.
Not have their names blotted out of the book of life. Rev 3:5.
Illustrated. Is 9:5; Zech 10:5.

WATCHFULNESS.

Christ an example of. Matt 26:38,40; Luke 6:12.
Commanded. Mark 13:37; Rev 3:2.
Exhortations to. 1 Thess 5:6; 1 Pet 4:7.
God especially requires in ministers. Ezek 3:17; Is 62:6; Mark 13:34.
Ministers exhorted to. Acts 20:31; 2 Tim 4:5.
Faithful ministers exercise. Heb 13:17.
Faithful ministers approved by. Matt 24:45,46; Luke 12:41-44.
Should be
With prayer. Luke 21:36; Eph 6:18.
With thanksgiving. Col 4:2.
With steadfastness in the faith. 1 Cor 16:13.
With heedfulness. Mark 13:33.
With sobriety. 1 Thess 5:6; 1 Pet 4:7.
At all times. Prov 8:34.
In all things. 2 Tim 4:5.
Saints pray to be kept in a state of. Ps 141:3.
Motives to
Expected direction from God. Hab 2:1.
Uncertain time of the coming of Christ. Matt 24:42; 25:13; Mark 13:35,36.
Incessant assaults of the devil. 1 Pet 5:8.
Liability to temptation. Matt 26:41.
Blessedness of. Luke 12:37; Rev 16:15.
Unfaithful ministers devoid of. Is 56:10.
The wicked averse to. 1 Thess 5:7.
Danger of remissness in. Matt 24:48-51; 25:5,8,12; Rev 3:3.
Illustrated. Luke 12:35,36.
Exemplified
David. Ps 102:7.
Anna. Luke 2:37.
Paul. 2 Cor 11:27.

WATCHMEN.

Soldiers generally acted as. Matt 27:65,66.
Citizens sometimes acted as. Neh 7:3.
Were stationed
On watch towers. 2 Kin 9:17; Is 21:5.
On the walls of cities. Is 62:6.
In the streets of cities. Ps 127:1.
Around the temple in Jerusalem on special occasions. 2 Kin 11:6.
Paraded the streets at night to preserve order. Song 3:3; 5:7.
In time of danger
Increase in number. Jer 51:12.
Vigilant night and day. Neh 4:9; Is 21:8.
Reported the approach of all strangers. 2 Sam 18:24-27; 2 Kin 9:18-20; Is 21:6,7,9.
Sounded an alarm at the approach of enemies. Ezek 33:2,3.
Vigilance of, vain without God's protection. Ps 127:1.
Were relieved by turns. Neh 7:3.
Danger of sleeping on their posts, referred to. Matt 28:13,14.
Neglecting to give warning punished with death. Ezek 33:6.
Often interrogated by passengers. Is 21:11.
Illustrative
Of ministers. Is 5:28; 62:6; Ezek 3:17; Heb 13:17.
(Blind,) of careless ministers. Is 56:10.
(Looking for the morning,) of anxious waiting for God. Ps 130:5,6.

WATER.

One of the elements of the world. Gen 1:2.
God originally
Created the firmament to divide. Gen 1:6,7.
Collected into one place. Gen 1:9.
Created fowls and fishes, etc. from. Gen 1:20,21.
Necessary to vegetation. Gen 2:5,6; Job 14:9; Is 1:30.
Some plants particularly require. Job 8:11.
Necessary to the comfort and happiness of man. Is 41:17; Zech 9:11.
Collected in
Springs. Josh 15:19.
Pools. 1 Kin 22:38; Neh 2:14.
Ponds. Ex 7:19; Is 19:10.
Fountains. 1 Kin 18:5; 2 Chr 32:3.
Wells. Gen 21:19.
Brooks. 2 Sam 17:20; 1 Kin 18:5.
Streams. Ps 78:16; Is 35:6.
Rivers. Is 8:7; Jer 2:18.
The sea. Gen 1:9,10; Is 11:9.
The clouds. Gen 1:7; Job 26:8,9.
Rises in vapour to the clouds. Eccl 1:7; Ps 104:8.
Drops from the clouds in rain. Deut 11:11; 2 Sam 21:10.
Described as
Fluid. Ps 78:16; Prov 30:4.
Unstable. Gen 49:4.
Penetrating. Ps 109:18.
Reflecting images. Prov 27:9.
Wearing the hardest substances. Job 14:19.
Cleansing. Ezek 36:25; Eph 5:26.
Refreshing. Job 22:7; Prov 25:25.
Congealed by cold. Job 38:29; Ps 147:16,17.
Was used by Jews
As their principal beverage. Gen 24:43; 1 Kin 13:19,22; 18:4; Hos 2:5.
For culinary purposes. Ex 12:9.
For washing the person. Gen 18:4; 24:32.
For legal purification. Ex 29:4; Heb 9:10,19.
Kept for purification in large waterpots. John 2:6.
Carried in vessels. Gen 21:14; 1 Sam 26:11; Mark 14:13.
Artificial mode of conveying, into large cities. 2 Kin 20:20.

Frequently brackish and unfit for use. Ex 15:23; 2 Kin 2:19.
The want of, considered a great calamity. Ex 17:1-3; Num 20:2; 2 Kin 3:9,10; Is 3:1.
In times of scarcity, sold at an enormous price. Lam 5:4.
Miracles connected with
- Turned into blood. Ex 7:17,20.
- Turned into wine. John 2:7-9.
- Brought from the rock. Ex 17:6; Num 20:11.
- Brought from the jaw-bone of an ass. Judg 15:19.
- Consumed by fire from heaven. 1 Kin 18:38.
- Divided and made to stand on heap. Ex 14:21,22; Josh 3:16.
- Trenches filled with. 2 Kin 3:17-22.
- Iron made to swim in. 2 Kin 6:5,6.
- Our Lord, etc. walking on. Matt 14:26-29.
- Healing powers communicated to. 2 Kin 5:14; John 5:4; 9:7.

The world and its inhabitants once destroyed by. Gen 7:20-23; 2 Pet 3:6.
The world not to be again destroyed by. Gen 9:8-15; 2 Pet 3:7.
Illustrative
- Of the support of God. Is 8:6.
- Of the gifts and graces of the Holy Spirit. Is 41:17,18; 44:3; Ezek 36:25; John 7:38,39.
- Of persecutors. Ps 124:4,5.
- Of persecutions. Ps 88:17.
- Of hostile armies. Is 8:7; 17:13.
- (Still,) of the ordinances of the gospel. Ps 23:2.
- (Deep,) of severe affliction. Ps 66:12; 69:1; Is 30:20; 43:2.
- (Deep,) of counsel in the heart. Prov 20:5.
- (Deep,) of the words of the wise of the wise. Prov 18:4.
- (Poured out,) of the wrath of God. Hos 5:10.
- (Poured out,) of faintness by terror. Ps 22:14.
- (Pouring, out of buckets,) of a numerous progeny. Num 24:7.
- (Spilled on the ground,) of death. 2 Sam 14:14.
- (Its instability,) of a wavering disposition. Gen 49:4.
- (Its weakness,) of faintness and cowardice. Josh 7:5; Ezek 7:17.
- (Difficulty of stopping,) of strife and contention. Prov 17:14.
- (Rapidly flowing away,) of the career of the wicked. Job 24:18; Ps 58:7.
- (Many,) of different nations and people. Rev 17:1,15; Jer 51:13.
- (Many,) of a variety of afflictions. 2 Sam 22:17.
- (Noise of many,) of the word of Christ. Rev 1:15.
- (Covering the sea,) of the general diffusion of the knowledge of God. Is 11:9; Hab 2:14.

WAVE OFFERING.

Placed in the hand of the priest and waved before the Lord. Ex 29:24; Lev 8:27.
Consisted of
- The fat, right shoulder, etc. of the priest's consecration ram. Ex 29:22,23; Lev 8:25,26.
- The breast of the priest's consecration ram. Ex 29:26; Lev 8:29.
- The breast of all peace offerings. Lev 7:30; 9:18,21; 6:17,20.
- Left shoulder, of Nazarite's peace offering. Num 6:17,19.
- The firstfruits of barely harvest. Lev 23:10,11.
- The firstfruits of wheaten bread. Lev 23:20.
- The Jealousy offering. Num 5:25.
- The leper's trespass offering. Lev 14:12,24.

Of the fat, etc. of the consecration ram burnt on the altar. Ex 29:25; Lev 8:28.
Was given to the priest as his due. Ex 29:26-28; Lev 7:31,34; 8:29; 10:15; 23:20; Num 18:11.
Was to be eaten in a holy place by the priest's family. Lev 10:14.

WEEKS.

A period of time consisting of seven days. Lev 23:15,16; Luke 18:12.
A space of seven years sometimes so called. Gen 29:27,28; Dan 9:24,25,27.
Origin of computing time by. Gen 2:2.
The feast of pentecost called the feast of weeks. Ex 34:22; Acts 2:1.

WEIGHTS.

Generally regulated by the standard of the sanctuary. Ex 30:24.
Sometimes regulated by the king's standard. 2 Sam 14:26.
Were frequently used in scales or balances. Job 31:6; Is 40:12.
Mentioned in Scripture
- Gerah. Ex 30:13; Ezek 45:12.
- Bekah or half shekel. Gen 24:22.
- Shekel. Ex 30:13; Ezek 45:12.
- Dram. Neh 7:70,71.
- Maneh or pound. Neh 7:71; Ezek 45:12.
- Talent. 2 Sam 12:30; Rev 16:21.

Value of money estimated according to. Gen 23:16; 43:21; Jer 32:9.
All metals were given by. Ex 37:24; 1 Chr 28:14.
Provisions were sold by, in times of scarcity. Lev 26:26; Ezek 4:10,16.
The Jews
- Forbidden to have various. Deut 25:13,14.
- Forbidden to have unjust. Lev 19:35,36.
- Frequently used unjust. Mic 6:11.

Illustrative
- Of sins. Heb 12:1.
- Of the restraints put on the elements. Job 28:25.
- (Heavy,) of the exceeding glory reserved for saints. 2 Cor 4:17.

WELLS.

First mention of. Gen 16:14.
Frequently made
- Near encampments. Gen 21:30; 26:18.
- Outside cities. Gen 24:11; John 4:6,8.
- In the courts of houses. 2 Sam 17:18.
- In the desert. 2 Chr 26:10.

Supplied by springs. Prov 16:22.
Supplied by the rain. Ps 84:6.
Surrounded by trees. Gen 49:22; Ex 15:27.
Names often given to. Gen 16:14; 21:31.
Canaan abounded with. Deut 6:11.
Many supplied from Lebanon. Song 4:15.
Mentioned in Scripture
- Beerlahairoi. Gen 16:14.
- Bethlehem. 2 Sam 23:15; 1 Chr 11:17,18.
- Beer (east of Jordan). Num 21:16-18.
- Beer-sheba. Gen 21:30,31.
- Elim. Ex 15:27.
- Esek. Gen 26:20.
- Hagar. Gen 21:19.
- Haran. Gen 29:3,4.
- Jacob. John 4:6.
- Rehoboth. Gen 26:22.
- Sitnah. Gen 26:21.

Often deep and difficult to draw from. John 4:11.
Often covered to prevent their being filled with sand. Gen 29:2,3.
Had troughs placed near for watering cattle. Gen 24:19,20; Ex 2:16.
Frequented by
- Women who came to draw water. Gen 24:13,14; John 4:7.
- Travellers. Gen 24:11,13,42; John 4:6.

Strangers not to draw from, without permission. Num 20:17.
Water of, frequently sold. Num 20:19.
Were a frequent cause of strife. Gen 21:25; 26:21,22; Ex 2:16,17.
Were often stopped up by enemies. Gen 26:15,18; 2 Kin 3:19,25.
Often afforded no water. Jer 14:3; Zech 9:11.
Illustrative
- Of the ordinances of the Church. Is 12:3.
- Of the Holy Spirit in saints. Song 4:15; John 4:14.
- Of the mouth of the righteous. Prov 10:11.
- Of wisdom and understanding in man. Prov 16:22; 18:4.
- (A fruitful bough by,) of Joseph's numerous posterity. Gen 49:22.
- (Drinking from one's own,) of enjoyment of domestic happiness. Prov 5:15.
- (Without water,) of hypocrites. 2 Pet 2:17.

WHIRLWIND.

Generally came from the south. Job 37:9; Is 21:1; Zech 9:14.
Sometimes came from the north. Ezek 1:4.
Called the whirlwind of God. Jer 23:19; 30:23.
Arose up from the earth. Jer 25:32.
Miracles connected with
- Elijah taken to heaven in. 2 Kin 2:1,11.
- God spoke to Job from. Job 38:1; 40:6.

Frequently continued for a long time. Jer 30:23.
Destructive nature of. Prov 1:27.

Illustrative of the
- Speed with which God executes his purposes. Nah 1:3.
- Velocity of Christ's second coming. Is 66:15.
- Velocity of the chariots in hostile armies. Is 5:28; Jer 4:13.
- Fury of God's judgments. Jer 25:32; 30:23.
- Sudden destruction of the wicked. Ps 58:9; Prov 1:27; Is 17:13; 40:24; 41:16; Jer 30:23.
- Unavoidable fruit of a life of sin and vanity. Hos 8:7.

Wicked, The, Are Compared To.

Abominable branches. Is 14:19.
Ashes under the feet. Mal 4:3.
Bad fishes. Matt 13:48.
Beasts. Ps 49:12; 2 Pet 2:12.
Blind, The. Zeph 1:17; Matt 15:14.
Brass and iron. Jer 6:28; Ezek 22:18.
Briars and thorns. Is 55:13; Ezek 2:6.
Bulls of Bashan. Ps 22:12.
Carcasses trodden under feet. Is 14:19.
Chaff. Job 21:18; Ps 1:4; Matt 3:12.
Clouds without water. Jude 1:12.
Corn blasted. 2 Kin 19:26.
Corrupt trees. Luke 6:43.
Deaf adders. Ps 58:4.
Dogs. Prov 26:11; Matt 7:6; 2 Pet 2:22.
Dross. Ps 119:119; Ezek 22:18,19.
Early dew that passes away. Hos 13:3.
Evil figs. Jer 24:8.
Fading oaks. Is 1:30.
Fiery oven. Ps 21:9; Hos 7:4.
Fire of thorns. Ps 118:12.
Fools building upon sand. Matt 7:26.
Fuel of fire. Is 9:19.
Garden without water. Is 1:30.
Goats. Matt 25:32.
Grass. Ps 37:2; 92:7.
Grass on the housetop. 2 Kin 19:26.
Green bay-trees. Ps 37:35.
Green herbs. Ps 37:2.
Heath in the desert. Jer 17:6.
Horses rushing into the battle. Jer 8:6.
Idols. Ps 115:8.
Lions greedy of prey. Ps 17:12.
Melting wax. Ps 68:2.
Morning-clouds. Hos 13:3.
Moth-eaten garments. Is 50:9; 51:8.
Passing whirlwinds. Prov 10:25.
Potsherds. Prov 26:23.
Raging waves of the sea. Jude 1:13.
Reprobate silver. Jer 6:30.
Scorpions. Ezek 2:6.
Serpents. Ps 58:4; Matt 23:33.
Smoke. Hos 13:3.
Stony ground. Matt 13:5.
Stubble. Job 21:18; Mal 4:1.
Swine. Matt 7:6; 2 Pet 2:22.
Tares. Matt 13:38.
Troubled sea. Is 57:20.
Visions of the night. Job 20:8.
Wandering stars. Jude 1:13.
Wayward children. Matt 11:16.
Wells without water. 2 Pet 2:17.
Wheels. Ps 83:13.
Whited sepulchres. Matt 23:27.
Wild ass's colt. Job 11:12.

Widows.

Character of true. Luke 2:37; 1 Tim 5:5,10.

God
- Surely hears the cry of. Ex 22:23.
- Judges for. Deut 10:18; Ps 68:5.
- Relieves. Ps 146:9.
- Establishes the border of. Prov 15:25.
- Will witness against oppressors of. Mal 3:5.

Exhorted to trust in God. Jer 49:11.

Should not be
- Afflicted. Ex 22:22.
- Oppressed. Jer 7:6; Zech 7:10.
- Treated with violence. Jer 22:3.
- Deprived of raiment in pledge. Deut 24:17.

Should be
- Pleaded for. Is 1:17.
- Honoured, if widows indeed. 1 Tim 5:3.
- Relieved by their friends. 1 Tim 5:4,16.
- Relieved by the Church. Acts 6:1; 1 Tim 5:9.
- Visited in affliction. James 1:27.
- Allowed to share in our blessings. Deut 14:29; 16:11,14; 24:19-21.

Though poor, may be liberal. Mark 12:42,43.

When young, exposed to many temptations. 1 Tim 5:11-14.

Saints
- Relieve. Acts 9:39.
- Cause joy to. Job 29:13.
- Disappoint not. Job 31:16.

The wicked
- Do no good to. Job 24:21.
- Send, away empty. Job 22:9.
- Take pledges from. Job 24:3.
- Reject the cause of. Is 1:23.
- Vex. Ezek 22:7.
- Make a prey of. Is 10:2; Matt 23:14.
- Slay. Ps 94:6.

Curse for perverting judgment of. Deut 27:19.

Woe to those who oppress. Is 10:1,2.

Blessings on those who relieve. Deut 14:29.

A type of Zion in affliction. Lam 5:3.

Were released from all obligation to former husbands. Rom 7:3.

Were clothed in mourning after the decease of husbands. Gen 38:14,19; 2 Sam 14:2,5.

Reproach connected with. Is 54:4.

Increase of, threatened as a punishment. Ex 22:24; Jer 15:8; 18:21.

Laws respecting
- Not to be oppressed. Ex 22:22; Deut 27:19.
- Raiment of, not to be taken in pledge by creditors. Deut 24:17.
- Bound to perform their vows. Num 30:9.
- Not to intermarry with priests. Lev 21:14.
- To be allowed to glean in fields and vineyards. Deut 24:19.
- To have a share of the triennial tithe. Deut 14:28,29; 26:12,13.
- To share in public rejoicings. Deut 16:11,14.
- When daughters of priests and childless to partake of the holy things. Lev 22:13.
- When left childless, to be married by their husband's nearest of kin. Deut 25:5,6; Ruth 3:10-13; 4:4,5; Matt 22:24-26.

Allowed to marry again. Rom 7:3.

Intermarrying with, of kings considered treason. 1 Kin 2:21-24.

Not to be deplored by, considered a great calamity. Job 27:15; Ps 78:64.

Were under the special protection of God. Deut 10:18; Ps 68:5.

Were frequently oppressed and persecuted. Job 24:3; Ezek 22:7.

Specially taken care of by the Church. Acts 6:1; 1 Tim 5:9.

Often devoted themselves entirely to God's service. Luke 2:37; 1 Tim 5:10.

Instances of great liberality in. 1 Kin 17:9-15; Mark 12:42,43.

Illustrative of
- A desolate condition. Is 47:8,9.
- Zion in captivity. Lam 1:1.

Wind, The.

Variable nature of. Eccl 1:6.

God
- Created. Amos 4:13.
- Restrains. Job 28:25; Ps 107:29.
- Brings forth, out of his treasuries. Ps 135:7; Jer 10:13.
- Raises. Ps 107:25; Jon 4:8.
- Changes. Ps 78:26.
- Assuages. Matt 8:26; 14:32.
- Gathers, in his hand. Prov 30:4.

Accomplishes the purposes of God. Ps 148:8.

Theory of, above man's comprehension. John 3:8.

Mentioned in Scripture
- North. Prov 25:23; Song 4:16.
- South. Job 37:17; Luke 12:55.
- East. Job 27:21; Ezek 17:10; Hos 13:15.
- West. Ex 10:19.
- Euroclydon. Acts 27:14.
- The simoom or pestilential wind. 2 Kin 19:7,35; Jer 4:11.
- The whirlwind. Job 37:9.

Drying nature of. Gen 8:1; Is 11:15.

Purifying nature of. Job 37:21; Jer 4:11.

When violent called
- Tempest. Job 9:17; 27:20; Jon 1:4.
- Storm. Job 21:18; Ps 83:15.
- Stormy wind. Ps 148:8; Ezek 13:11,13.
- Windy storm. Ps 55:8.
- Great and strong wind. 1 Kin 19:11.
- Mighty wind. Acts 2:2; Rev 6:13.
- Fierce wind. James 3:4.
- Rough wind. Is 27:8.

From the north drives away rain. Prov 25:23.

Frequently brings rain. 1 Kin 18:44,45; 2 Kin 3:17.

Often blighting. Ps 103:16; Is 40:7.

Movement of the leaves of trees, etc. by, noticed. Is 7:2; Matt 11:7; Rev 6:13.

Tempestuous
- Raises the sea in waves. Ps 107:25; John 6:18.
- Drives about the largest ships. Matt 14:24; Acts 27:18; James 3:4.
- Destroys houses. Job 1:19; Matt 7:27.

Miracles connected with
Locusts brought by. Ex 10:13.
Locusts removed by. Ex 10:19.
Red sea divided by. Ex 14:21.
Quails brought by. Num 11:31.
Rocks and mountains rent by. 1 Kin 19:11.
Raises on account of Jonah. Jon 1:4.
Calmed by casting out Jonah. Jon 1:15.
Calmed by Christ. Matt 8:26; 14:32.
Illustrative
Of the operations of the Holy Spirit. Ezek 37:9; John 3:8; Acts 2:2.
Of the life of man. Job 7:7.
Of the speeches of the desperate. Job 6:26.
Of terrors which pursue the soul. Job 30:15.
Of molten images. Is 41:29.
Of iniquity which leads to destruction. Is 64:6.
Of false doctrines. Eph 4:14.
(Chaff or stubble before,) of the wicked. Job 21:18; Ps 1:4.
(Without rain,) of one who boasts of a false gift. Prov 25:14.
(When destructive,) of the judgments of God. Is 27:8; 29:6; 41:16.
(Sowing,) of a course of sin. Hos 8:7.
(Feeding upon) of vain hopes. Hos 12:1.
(Bringing forth,) of disappointed expectations. Is 26:18.

WINE.

First mention of. Gen 9:20,21.
Was made of
The juice of the grape. Gen 49:11.
The juice of the pomegranate. Song 8:2.
First mode of making, notice. Gen 40:11.
Generally made by treading the grapes in a press. Neh 13:15; Is 63:2,3.
Refining of, alluded to. Is 25:6.
Improved by age. Luke 5:39.
Places celebrated for
Canaan in general. Deut 33:28.
Possessions of Judah. Gen 49:8,11,12.
Lebanon. Hos 14:7.
Helbon. Ezek 27:18.
Assyria. 2 Kin 18:32; Is 36:17.
Moab. Is 16:8-10; Jer 48:32,33.
Many kinds of. Neh 5:18.
Sweet, esteemed for flavour and strength. Is 49:26; Amos 9:13; Mic 6:15.
Red, most esteemed. Prov 23:31; Is 27:2.
Often spiced to increase its strength, etc. Prov 9:2,5; 23:30; Song 8:2.
Was used
As a beverage from the earliest age. Gen 9:21; 27:25.
At all feasts and entertainments. Esth 1:7; 5:6; Is 5:12; Dan 5:1-4; John 2:3.
For drink offerings in the worship of God. Ex 29:40; Num 15:4-10.
For drink offerings in idolatrous worship. Deut 32:37,38.
As a medicine. Luke 10:34; 1 Tim 5:23.
Firstfruits of, to be offered to God. Deut 18:4; 2 Chr 31:5.
With corn and oil, denoted all temporal blessings. Gen 27:28,37; Ps 4:7; Hos 2:8; Joel 2:19.
Given in abundance to the Jews when obedient. Hos 2:22; Joel 2:19,24; Zech 9:17.
The Jews frequently deprived of, as a punishment. Is 24:7,11; Hos 2:9; Joel 1:10; Hag 1:11; 2:16.
The Jews frequently drank, to excess. Is 5:11; Joel 3:3; Amos 6:6.
In times of scarcity, was mixed with water. Is 1:22.
Sometimes mixed with milk as a beverage. Song 5:1.
Characterised as
Cheering God and man. Judg 9:13; Zech 9:17.
Gladdening the heart. Ps 104:15.
Strengthening. 2 Sam 16:2; Song 2:5.
Making mirthful. Esth 1:10; Eccl 10:19.
Custom of presenting to travellers. Gen 14:18; 1 Sam 25:18.
Custom of giving to persons in pain or suffering, mixed with drugs. Prov 31:6; Mark 15:23.
Forbidden to the priests while engaged in the tabernacle. Lev 10:9.
Forbidden to Nazirites during their separation. Num 6:3.
The Rechabites never drank. Jer 35:5,6.
In excess
Forbidden. Eph 5:18.
Infuriates the temper. Prov 20:1.
Impairs the health. 1 Sam 25:37; Hos 4:11.
Impairs the judgment and memory. Prov 31:4,5; Is 28:7.
Inflames the passions. Is 5:11.
Leads to sorrow and contention. Prov 23:29,30.
Leads to remorse. Prov 23:31,32.
An article of extensive commerce. Ezek 27:18.
Was stored in cellars. 1 Chr 27:27.
Was kept in bottles. 1 Sam 25:18; Hab 2:15.
Consequence of putting (when new), into old bottles. Matt 2:22.
The love of Christ to be preferred to. Song 1:2,4.
Water miraculously turned into. John 2:9.
Illustrative
Of the blood of Christ. Matt 26:27-29.
Of the blessing of the gospel. Prov 9:2,5; Is 25:6; 55:1.
Of the wrath and judgments of God. Ps 60:3; 75:8; Jer 13:12-14; 25:15-18.
Of the abominations of the apostasy. Rev 17:2; 18:3.
Of violence and rapine. Prov 4:17.

WINTER.

God makes. Ps 74:17.
Yearly return of, secured by covenant. Gen 8:22.
Coldness and inclemency of, noticed. Prov 20:4; John 10:22.
Unsuited for
Travelling. Matt 24:20; 2 Tim 4:21.
Navigation. Acts 27:9.
Ships were laid up in port during. Acts 27:12; 28:11.
The Jews frequently had special houses for. Jer 36:22; Amos 3:15.
Illustrative of seasons of spiritual adversity. Song 2:11.

WISDOM OF GOD, THE.

Is one of his attributes. 1 Sam 2:3; Job 9:4.
Described as
Perfect. Job 36:4; 37:16.
Mighty. Job 36:5.
Universal. Job 28:24; Dan 2:22; Acts 15:18.
Infinite. Ps 147:5; Rom 11:33.
Unsearchable. Is 40:28; Rom 11:33.
Wonderful. Ps 139:6.
Beyond human comprehension. Ps 139:6.
Incomparable. Is 44:7; Jer 10:7.
Underived. Job 21:22; Is 40:14.
The gospel contains treasures of. 1 Cor 2:7.
Wisdom of saints is derived from. Ezra 7:25.
All human wisdom derived from. Dan 2:1.
Saints ascribe to him. Dan 2:20.
Exhibited in
His works. Job 37:16; Ps 104:24; 136:5; Prov 3:19; Jer 10:12.
His counsels. Is 28:29; Jer 32:19.
His foreshadowing events. Is 42:9; 46:10.
Redemption. 1 Cor 1:24; Eph 1:8; 3:10.
Searching the heart. 1 Chr 28:9; Rev 2:23.
Understanding the thoughts. 1 Chr 28:9; Ps 139:2.
Exhibited in knowing
The heart. Ps 44:21; Prov 15:11; Luke 16:15.
The actions. Job 34:21; Ps 139:2,3.
The words. Ps 139:4.
His saints. 2 Sam 7:20; 2 Tim 2:19.
The way of saints. Job 23:10; Ps 1:6.
The want of saints. Deut 2:7; Matt 6:8.
The afflictions of saints. Ex 3:7; Ps 142:3.
The infirmities of saints. Ps 103:14.
The minutest matters. Matt 10:29,30.
The most secret things. Matt 6:18.
The time of judgment. Matt 24:36.
The wicked. Neh 9:10; Job 11:11.
The works, etc. of the wicked. Is 66:18.
Nothing is concealed from. Ps 139:12.
The wicked question. Ps 73:11; Is 47:10.
Should be magnified. Rom 16:27; Jude 1:25.

WITNESS OF THE HOLY SPIRIT.

Is truth. 1 John 5:6.
To be implicitly received. 1 John 5:6,9.
Borne to Christ
As Messiah. Luke 3:22; John 1:32,33.
As coming to redeem and sanctify. 1 John 5:6.
As exalted to be a Prince and Saviour to give repentance, etc. Acts 5:31,32.
As perfecting saints. Heb 10:14,15.
As foretold by himself. John 15:26.
In heaven. 1 John 5:7,11.
On earth. 1 John 5:8.

The first preaching of the gospel confirmed by. Acts 14:3; Heb 2:4.
The faithful preaching of the Apostles accompanied by. 1 Cor 2:4; 1 Thess 1:5.
Given to saints
On believing. Acts 15:8; 1 John 5:10.
To testify to them of Christ. John 15:26.
As an evidence of adoption. Rom 8:16.
As an evidence of Christ in them. 1 John 3:24.
As an evidence of God in them. 1 John 4:13.
Borne against all unbelievers. Neh 9:30; Acts 28:25-27.

Wives.

Not to be selected from among the ungodly. Gen 24:3; 26:34,35; 28:1.
Duties of, to their husbands
To love them. Titus 2:4.
To reverence them. Eph 5:33.
To be faithful to them. 1 Cor 7:3-5,10.
To be subject to them. Gen 3:16; Eph 5:22,24; 1 Pet 3:1.
To obey them. 1 Cor 14:34; Titus 2:5.
To remain with them for life. Rom 7:2,3.
Should be adorned
Not with ornaments. 1 Tim 2:9; 1 Pet 3:3.
With modesty and sobriety. 1 Tim 2:9.
With a meek and quiet spirit. 1 Pet 3:4,5.
With good works. 1 Tim 2:10; 5:10.
Good
Are from the Lord. Prov 19:14.
Are a token of the favour of God. Prov 18:22.
Are a blessing to husbands. Prov 12:4; 31:10,12.
Bring honour on husbands. Prov 31:23.
Secure confidence of husbands. Prov 31:11.
Are praised by husbands. Prov 31:28.
Are diligent and prudent. Prov 31:13-27.
Are benevolent to the poor. Prov 31:20.
Duty of, to unbelieving husbands. 1 Cor 7:13,14,16; 1 Pet 3:1,2.
Should be silent in the Churches. 1 Cor 14:34.
Should seek religious instruction from their husbands. 1 Cor 14:35.
Of ministers should be exemplary. 1 Tim 3:11.
Good—Exemplified
Wife of Manoah. Judg 13:10.
Orpah and Ruth. Ruth 1:4,8.
Abigail. 1 Sam 25:3.
Esther. Esth 2:15-17.
Elizabeth. Luke 1:6.
Priscilla. Acts 18:2,26.
Sarah. 1 Pet 3:6.
Bad—Exemplified
Samson's wife. Judg 14:15-17.
Michal. 2 Sam 6:16.
Jezebel. 1 Kin 21:25.
Zeresh. Esth 5:14.
Job's wife. Job 2:9.
Herodias. Mark 6:17.
Sapphira. Acts 5:1,2.

Wolf, The.

Rapacious nature of. Gen 49:27.
Particularly fierce in the evening when it seeks its prey. Jer 5:6; Hab 1:8.
Destructive to flocks of sheep. John 10:12.
Illustrative
Of the wicked. Matt 10:16; Luke 10:3.
Of wicked rulers. Ezek 22:27; Zeph 3:3.
Of false teachers. Matt 7:15; Acts 20:29.
Of the devil. John 10:12.
Of the tribe of Benjamin. Gen 49:27.
Of fierce enemies. Jer 5:6; Hab 1:8.
(Taming of,) of the change effected by conversion. Is 11:6; 65:25.

Woman.

Origin and cause of the name. Gen 2:23.
Originally made
By God in his own image. Gen 1:27.
From one of Adam's ribs. Gen 2:21,22.
For man. 1 Cor 11:9.
To be an helpmeet for man. Gen 2:18,20.
Subordinate to man. 1 Cor 11:3.
To be the glory of man. 1 Cor 11:7.
Deceived by Satan. Gen 3:1-6; 2 Cor 11:3; 1 Tim 2:14.
Led man to disobey God. Gen 3:6,11,12.
Curse pronounced on. Gen 3:16.
Salvation promised through the seed of. Gen 3:15; Is 7:14.
Safety in childbirth promised to the faithful and holy. 1 Tim 2:15.
Characterised as
Weaker than man. 1 Pet 3:7.
Timid. Is 19:16; Jer 50:37; 51:30; Nah 3:13.
Loving and affectionate. 2 Sam 1:26.
Tender and constant to her offspring. Is 49:15; Lam 4:10.
To wear her hair long as a covering. 1 Cor 11:15.
Good and virtuous, described. Prov 31:10-28.
Virtuous, held in high estimation. Ruth 3:11; Prov 31:10,30.
Frequently
Fond of self-indulgence. Is 32:9-11.
Subtle and deceitful. Prov 7:10; Eccl 7:26.
Silly and easily led into error. 2 Tim 3:6.
Zealous in promoting superstition and idolatry. Jer 7:18; Ezek 13:17,23.
Active in instigating to iniquity. Num 31:15,16; 1 Kin 21:25; Neh 13:26.
Generally wore a vail in the presence of the other sex. Gen 24:65.
Generally lived in a separate apartment or tent. Gen 18:9; 24:67; Esth 2:9,11.
Submissive and respectful to husbands. 1 Pet 3:6; Gen 18:12.
Of distinction
Fair and graceful. Gen 12:11; 24:16; Song 1:8; Amos 8:13.
Haughty in their deportment. Is 3:16.
Fond of dress and ornaments. Is 3:17-23.
Wore their hair plaited and adorned with gold and pearls. Is 3:24; 1 Tim 2:9.
Of the poorer classes swarthy from exposure to the sun. Song 1:5,6.
Young
Called maids. Ex 2:8; Luke 8:51,52.
Called damsels. Gen 24:55; Mark 5:39.
Called virgins. Gen 24:16; Lam 1:4.
Gay and merry. Judg 11:34; 21:21; Jer 31:13; Zech 9:17.
Kind and courteous to strangers. Gen 24:17.
Fond of ornaments. Jer 2:32.
Required to learn from and imitate their elders. Titus 2:4.
Inherited parents' property when there was no male heir. Num 27:8.
Could not marry without consent of parents. Gen 24:3,4; 34:6; Ex 22:17.
Not to be given in marriage considered a calamity. Judg 11:37; Ps 78:63; Is 4:1.
Often taken captive. Lam 1:18; Ezek 30:17,18.
Punishment for seducing, when betrothed. Deut 22:23-27.
Punishment for seducing when not betrothed. Ex 22:16,17; Deut 22:28,29.
Often treated with great cruelty in war. Deut 32:25; Lam 2:21; 5:11.
Of distinction, dressed in robes of various colours. 2 Sam 13:18; Ps 45:14.
Were required to hear and obey the law. Josh 8:35.
Had a court of the tabernacle assigned to them. Ex 38:8; 1 Sam 2:2.
Allowed to join in the temple-music from the time of David. 1 Chr 25:5,6; Ezra 2:65; Neh 7:67.
Often engaged in
Domestic employments. Gen 18:6; Prov 31:15.
Agriculture. Ruth 2:8; Song 1:6.
Tending sheep. Gen 29:9; Ex 2:16.
Drawing and carrying water. Gen 24:11,13,15,16; 1 Sam 9:11; John 4:7.
Grinding corn. Matt 24:41; Luke 17:35.
Spinning. Prov 31:13,14.
Embroidery. Prov 31:22.
Celebrating the victories of the nation. Ex 15:20,21; Judg 11:34; 1 Sam 18:6,7.
Attending funerals as mourners. Jer 9:17,20.
Vows of, when married not binding upon the husband. Num 30:6-8.
Unfaithfulness of, when married found out by the waters of jealousy. Num 5:14-28.
Punishment for injuring, when with child. Ex 21:22-25.
To be governed by, considered a calamity by the Jews. Is 3:12.
To be slain by, considered a great disgrace. Judg 9:54.

Considered a valuable booty in war. Deut 20:14; 1 Sam 30:2.
Often treated with great cruelty in war. 2 Kin 8:12; Lam 5:11; Ezek 9:6; Hos 13:16.
Illustrative
(Gloriously arrayed,) of the Church of Christ. Ps 45:13; Gal 4:26; Rev 12:1.
(Delicate,) of backsliding Israel. Jer 6:2.
(Chaste and holy,) of saints. Song 1:3; 2 Cor 11:2; Rev 14:4.
(Lewd,) of the Roman apostasy. Rev 17:4,18.
(Wise,) of saints. Matt 25:1,2,4.
(Foolish,) of mere professors. Matt 25:1-3.
(At ease and careless,) of a state of carnal security. Is 32:9,11.
(Forsaken,) of Israel in her captivity. Is 54:6.

Works, Good.

Christ, an example of. John 10:32; Acts 10:38.
Called
Good fruits. James 3:17.
Fruits meet for repentance. Matt 3:8.
Fruits of righteousness. Phil 1:11.
Works and labours of love. Heb 6:10.
Are by Jesus Christ to the glory and praise of God. Phil 1:11.
They alone, who abide in Christ can perform. John 15:4,5.
Wrought by God in us. Is 26:12; Phil 2:13.
The Scripture designed to lead us to. 2 Tim 3:16,17; James 1:25.
To be performed in Christ's name. Col 3:17.
Heavenly wisdom is full of. James 3:17.
Justification unattainable by. Rom 3:20; Gal 2:16.
Salvation unattainable by. Eph 2:8,9; 2 Tim 1:9; Titus 3:5.
Saints
Created in Christ to. Eph 2:10.
Exhorted to put on. Col 3:12-14.
Are full of. Acts 9:36.
Are zealous of. Titus 2:14.
Should be furnished to all. 2 Tim 3:17.
Should be rich in. 1 Tim 6:18.
Should be careful to maintain. Titus 3:8,14.
Should be established in. 2 Thess 2:17.
Should be fruitful in. Col 1:10.
Should be perfect in. Heb 13:21.
Should be prepared to all. 2 Tim 2:21.
Should abound to all. 2 Cor 9:8.
Should be ready to all. Titus 3:1.
Should manifest, with meekness. James 3:13.
Should provoke each other. Heb 10:24.
Should avoid ostentation in. Matt 6:1-18.
Bring to the light their. John 3:21.
Followed into rest by their. Rev 14:13.
Holy women should manifest. 1 Tim 2:10; 5:10.
God remembers. Neh 13:14; Heb 6:9,10.
Shall be brought into the judgment. Eccl 12:14; 2 Cor 5:10.
In the judgment, will be an evidence of faith. Matt 25:34-40; James 2:14-20.
Ministers should
Be patterns of. Titus 2:7.
Exhort to. 1 Tim 6:17,18; Titus 3:1,8,14.
God is glorified by. John 15:8.
Designed to lead others to glorify God. Matt 5:16; 1 Pet 2:12.
A blessing attends. James 1:25.
The wicked reprobate to. Titus 1:16.
Illustrated. John 15:5.

Years.

The sun and moon appointed to mark out. Gen 1:14.
Early computation of time by. Gen 5:3.
Divided into
Seasons. Gen 8:22.
Months. Gen 7:11; 1 Chr 27:1.
Weeks. Dan 9:27; Luke 18:12.
Days. Gen 25:7; Esth 9:27.
Length of, during the patriarchal age. Gen 7:11; 8:13; 7:24; 8:3.
Commencement of, changed after the exodus. Ex 12:2.
Remarkable
Sabbatical. Lev 25:4.
Jubilee. Lev 25:11.
In prophetic computation, days reckoned as. Dan 12:11,12.
Illustrative
(Coming to,) of manhood. Heb 11:24.
(Well stricken in,) of old age. Luke 1:7.
(Being full of,) of old age. Gen 25:8.
(Acceptable,) of the time of the gospel. Is 61:2; Luke 4:19.
(Of the right hand of the Most High,) of prosperity. Ps 77:10.
(Of the redeemed,) of redemption by Christ. Is 63:4.
(Of visitation,) of severe judgments. Jer 11:23; 23:12.
(Of recompences,) of judgments. Is 34:8.

Zeal.

Christ an example of. Ps 69:9; John 2:17.
Godly sorrow leads to. 2 Cor 7:10,11.
Of saints, ardent. Ps 119:139.
Provokes others to do good. 2 Cor 9:2.
Should be exhibited
In spirit. Rom 12:11.
In well-doing. Gal 4:18; Titus 2:14.
In desiring the salvation of others. Acts 26:29; Rom 10:1.
In contending for the faith. Jude 1:3.
In missionary labours. Rom 15:19,23.
For the glory of God. Num 25:11,13.
For the welfare of saints. Col 4:13.
Against idolatry. 2 Kin 23:4-14.
Sometimes wrongly directed. 2 Sam 21:2; Acts 22:3,4; Phil 3:6.
Sometimes not according to knowledge. Rom 10:2; Gal 1:14; Acts 21:20.
Ungodly men sometimes pretend to. 2 Kin 10:16; Matt 23:15.
Exhortation to. Rom 12:11; Rev 3:19.
Holy—Exemplified
Phinehas. Num 25:11,13.
Josiah. 2 Kin 23:19-25.
Apollos. Acts 18:25.
Corinthians. 1 Cor 14:12.
Epaphras. Col 4:12,13.

Zebulun, the Tribe Of.

Descended from Jacob's tenth son. Gen 30:19,20.
Predictions respecting. Gen 49:13; Deut 33:18,19.
Persons selected from
To number the people. Num 1:9.
To spy out the land. Num 13:10.
To divide the land. Num 34:25.
Strength of, on leaving Egypt. Num 1:30,31.
Formed the rear of the first division of the army of Israel in its journeys. Num 10:14,16.
Encamped under the standard of Judah, east of the tabernacle. Num 2:3,7.
Offering of, at the dedication. Num 7:24-29.
Families of. Num 26:26,27.
Strength of, on entering Canaan. Num 26:27.
On Ebal said amen to the curses. Deut 27:13.
A naval and commercial people. Gen 49:13.
Furnished scribes or writers to Israel. Judg 5:14.
Bounds of their inheritance. Josh 19:10-16.
Unable to drive out the Canaanites from their cities, but made them tributary. Judg 1:30.
Praised for assisting Deborah and Barak in opposing Sisera. Judg 5:14,18; 4:10.
Aided Gideon against the army of the Midianites. Judg 6:35.
Furnished a judge to Israel. Judg 12:11,12.
Some of, at David's coronation. 1 Chr 12:33.
Officer appointed over by David. 1 Chr 27:19.
Only some of, assisted in Hezekiah's reformation. 2 Chr 30:10,11,18.
Country of, blessed with the presence and instruction of Christ. Is 9:1; Matt 4:13-15.

Read Through The Bible In a Year

JANUARY

Date	MORNING	EVENING
	MATT.	**GEN.**
1	1	1, 2, 3
2	2	4, 5, 6
3	3	7, 8, 9
4	4	10, 11, 12
5	5:1-26	13, 14, 15
6	5:27-48	16, 17
7	6:1-18	18, 19
8	6:19-34	20, 21, 22
9	7	23, 24
10	8:1-17	25, 26
11	8:18-34	27, 28
12	9:1-17	29, 30
13	9:18-38	31, 32
14	10:1-20	33, 34, 35
15	10:21-42	36, 37, 38
16	11	39, 40
17	12:1-23	41, 42
18	12:24-50	43, 44, 45
19	13:1-30	46, 47, 48
20	13:31-58	49, 50
		EX.
21	14:1-21	1, 2, 3
22	14:22-36	4, 5, 6
23	15:1-20	7, 8
24	15:21-39	9, 10, 11
25	16	12, 13
26	17	14, 15
27	18:1-20	16, 17, 18
28	18:21-35	19, 20
29	19	21, 22
30	20:1-16	23, 24
31	20:17-34	25, 26

FEBRUARY

Date	MORNING	EVENING
	MATT.	**EX.**
1	21:1-22	27, 28
2	21:23-46	29, 30
3	22:1-22	31, 32, 33
4	22:23-46	34, 35
5	23:1-22	36, 37, 38
6	23:23-29	39, 40
		LEV.
7	24:1-28	1, 2, 3
8	24:29-51	4, 5
9	25:1-30	6, 7
10	25:31-46	8, 9, 10
11	26:1-25	11, 12
12	26:26-50	13
13	26:51-75	14
14	27:1-26	15, 16
15	27:27-50	17, 18
16	27:51-66	19, 20
17	28	21, 22
	MARK	
18	1:1-22	23, 24
19	1:23-45	25
20	2	26, 27
		NUM.
21	3:1-19	1, 2
22	3:20-35	3, 4
23	4:1-20	5, 6
24	4:21-41	7, 8
25	5:1-20	9, 10, 11
26	5:21-43	12, 13, 14
27	6:1-29	15, 16
28	6:30-56	17, 18, 19
29	7:1-13	20, 21, 22

MARCH

Date	MORNING	EVENING
	MARK	**NUM.**
1	7:14-37	23, 24, 25
2	8:1-21	26, 27
3	8:22-38	28, 29, 30
4	9:1-29	31, 32, 33
5	9:30-50	34, 35, 36
		DEUT.
6	10:1-31	1, 2
7	10:32-52	3, 4
8	11:1-18	5, 6, 7
9	11:19-33	8, 9, 10
10	12:1-27	11, 12, 13
11	12:28-44	14, 15, 16
12	13:1-20	17, 18, 19
13	13:21-37	20, 21, 22
14	14:1-26	23, 24, 25
15	14:27-53	26, 27
16	14:54-72	28, 29
17	15:1-25	30, 31
18	15:26-47	32, 33, 34
		JOSH.
19	16	1, 2, 3
	LUKE	
20	1:1-20	4, 5, 6
21	1:21-38	7, 8, 9
22	1:39-56	10, 11, 12
23	1:57-80	13, 14, 15
24	2:1-24	16, 17, 18
25	2:25-52	19, 20, 21
26	3	22, 23, 24
		JUDG.
27	4:1-30	1, 2, 3
28	4:31-44	4, 5, 6
29	5:1-16	7, 8
30	5:17-39	9, 10
31	6:1-26	11, 12

APRIL

Date	MORNING	EVENING
	LUKE	**JUDG.**
1	6:27-49	13, 14, 15
2	7:1-30	16, 17, 18
3	7:31-50	19, 20, 21
		RUTH
4	8:1-25	1, 2, 3, 4
		1 SAM.
5	8:26-56	1, 2, 3
6	9:1-17	4, 5, 6
7	9:18-36	7, 8, 9
8	9:37-62	10, 11, 12
9	10:1-24	13, 14
10	10:25-42	15, 16
11	11:1-28	17, 18
12	11:29-54	19, 20, 21
13	12:1-31	22, 23, 24
14	12:32-59	25, 26
15	13:1-22	27, 28, 29
16	13:23-35	30, 31
		2 SAM.
17	14:1-24	1, 2
18	14:25-35	3, 4, 5
19	15:1-10	6, 7, 8
20	15:11-32	9, 10, 11
21	16	12, 13
22	17:1-19	14, 15
23	17:20-37	16, 17, 18
24	18:1-23	19, 20
25	18:24-43	21, 22
26	19:1-27	23, 24
		1 KIN.
27	19:28-48	1, 2
28	20:1-26	3, 4, 5
29	20:27-47	6, 7
30	21:1-19	8, 9

MAY

Date	MORNING	EVENING
	LUKE	**1 KIN.**
1	21:20-38	10, 11
2	22:1-20	12, 13
3	22:21-46	14, 15
4	22:47-71	16, 17, 18
5	23:1-25	19, 20
6	23:26-56	21, 22
		2 KIN.
7	24:1-35	1, 2, 3
8	24:36-53	4, 5, 6
	JOHN	
9	1:1-28	7, 8, 9
10	1:29-51	10, 11, 12
11	2	13, 14
12	3:1-18	15, 16
13	3:19-38	17, 18
14	4:1-30	19, 20, 21
15	4:31-54	22, 23
16	5:1-24	24, 25
		1 CHR.
17	5:25-47	1, 2, 3
18	6:1-21	4, 5, 6
19	6:22-44	7, 8, 9
20	6:45-71	10, 11, 12
21	7:1-27	13, 14, 15
22	7:28-53	16, 17, 18
23	8:1-27	19, 20, 21
24	8:28-59	22, 23, 24
25	9:1-23	25, 26, 27
26	9:24-41	28, 29
		2 CHR.
27	10:1-23	1, 2, 3
28	10:24-42	4, 5, 6
29	11:1-29	7, 8, 9
30	11:30-57	10, 11, 12
31	12:1-26	13, 14

JUNE

Date	MORNING	EVENING
	JOHN	**2 CHR.**
1	12:27-50	15, 16
2	13:1-20	17, 18
3	13:21-38	19, 20
4	14	21, 22
5	15	23, 24
6	16	25, 26, 27
7	17	28, 29
8	18:1-18	30, 31
9	18:19-40	32, 33
10	19:1-22	34, 35, 36
		EZRA
11	19:23-42	1, 2
12	20	3, 4, 5
13	21	6, 7, 8
	ACTS	
14	1	9, 10
		NEH.
15	2:1-21	1, 2, 3
16	2:22-47	4, 5, 6
17	3	7, 8, 9
18	4:1-22	10, 11
19	4:23-37	12, 13
		ESTH.
20	5:1-21	1, 2
21	5:22-42	3, 4, 5
22	6	6, 7, 8
23	7:1-21	9, 10
		JOB
24	7:22-43	1, 2
25	7:44-60	3, 4
26	8:1-25	5, 6, 7
27	8:26-40	8, 9, 10
28	9:1-21	11, 12, 13
29	9:22-43	14, 15, 16
30	10:1-23	17, 18, 19

Read Through The Bible In a Year

JULY

Date	MORNING	EVENING
	ACTS	**JOB**
1	10:24-48	20, 21
2	11	22, 23, 24
3	12	25, 26, 27
4	13:1-25	28, 29
5	13:26-52	30, 31
6	14	32, 33
7	15:1-21	34, 35
8	15:22-41	36, 37
9	16:1-21	38, 39, 40
10	16:22-40	41, 42
		PSS.
11	17:1-15	1, 2, 3
12	17:16-34	4, 5, 6
13	18	7, 8, 9
14	19:1-20	10, 11, 12
15	19:21-41	13, 14, 15
16	20:1-16	16, 17
17	20:17-38	18, 19
18	21:1-17	20, 21, 22
19	21:18-40	23, 24, 25
20	22	26, 27, 28
21	23:1-15	29, 30
22	23:16-35	31, 32
23	24	33, 34
24	25	35, 36
25	26	37, 38, 39
26	27:1-26	40, 41, 42
27	27:27-44	43, 44, 45
28	28	46, 47, 48
	ROM.	
29	1	49, 50
30	2	51, 52, 53
31	3	54, 55, 56

AUGUST

Date	MORNING	EVENING
	ROM.	**PSS.**
1	4	57, 58, 59
2	5	60, 61, 62
3	6	63, 64, 65
4	7	66, 67
5	8:1-21	68, 69
6	8:22-39	70, 71
7	9:1-15	72, 73
8	9:16-33	74, 75, 76
9	10	77, 78
10	11:1-18	79, 80
11	11:19-36	81, 82, 83
12	12	84, 85, 86
13	13	87, 88
14	14	89, 90
15	15:1-13	91, 92, 93
16	15:14-33	94, 95, 96
17	16	97, 98, 99
	1 COR.	
18	1	100, 101, 102
19	2	103, 104
20	3	105, 106
21	4	107, 108, 109
22	5	110, 111, 112
23	6	113, 114, 115
24	7:1-19	116, 117, 118
25	7:20-40	119:1-88
26	8	119:89-176
27	9	120, 121, 122
28	10:1-18	123, 124, 125
29	10:19-33	126, 127, 128
30	11:1-16	129, 130, 131
31	11:17-34	132, 133, 134

SEPTEMBER

Date	MORNING	EVENING
	1 COR.	**PSS.**
1	12	135, 136
2	13	137, 138, 139
3	14:1-20	140, 141, 142
4	14:21-40	143, 144, 145
5	15:1-28	146, 147
6	15:29-58	148, 149, 150
		PROV.
7	16	1, 2
	2 COR.	
8	1	3, 4, 5
9	2	6, 7
10	3	8, 9
11	4	10, 11, 12
12	5	13, 14, 15
13	6	16, 17, 18
14	7	19, 20, 21
15	8	22, 23, 24
16	9	25, 26
17	10	27, 28, 29
18	11:1-15	30, 31
		ECCL.
19	11:16-33	1, 2, 3
20	12	4, 5, 6
21	13	7, 8, 9
	GAL.	
22	1	10, 11, 12
		SONG
23	2	1, 2, 3
24	3	4, 5
25	4	6, 7, 8
		IS.
26	5	1, 2
27	6	3, 4
	EPH.	
28	1	5, 6
29	2	7, 8
30	3	9, 10

OCTOBER

Date	MORNING	EVENING
	EPH.	**IS.**
1	4	11, 12, 13
2	5:1-16	14, 15, 16
3	5:17-33	17, 18, 19
4	6	20, 21, 22
	PHIL.	
5	1	23, 24, 25
6	2	26, 27
7	3	28, 29
8	4	30, 31
	COL.	
9	1	32, 33
10	2	34, 35, 36
11	3	37, 38
12	4	39, 40
	1 THESS.	
13	1	41, 42
14	2	43, 44
15	3	45, 46
16	4	47, 48, 49
17	5	50, 51, 52
	2 THESS.	
18	1	53, 54, 55
19	2	56, 57, 58
20	3	59, 60, 61
	1 TIM.	
21	1	62, 63, 64
22	2	65, 66
		JER.
23	3	1, 2
24	4	3, 4, 5
25	5	6, 7, 8
26	6	9, 10, 11
	2 TIM.	
27	1	12, 13, 14
28	2	15, 16, 17
29	3	18, 19
30	4	20, 21
	TITUS	
31	1	22, 23

NOVEMBER

Date	MORNING	EVENING
	TITUS	**JER.**
1	2	24, 25, 26
2	3	27, 28, 29
3	**PHILEM.**	30, 31
	HEB.	
4	1	32, 33
5	2	34, 35, 36
6	3	37, 38, 39
7	4	40, 41, 42
8	5	43, 44, 45
9	6	46, 47
10	7	48, 49
11	8	50
12	9	51, 52
		LAM.
13	10:1-18	1, 2
14	10:19-39	3, 4, 5
		EZEK.
15	11:1-19	1, 2
16	11:20-40	3, 4
17	12	5, 6, 7
18	13	8, 9, 10
	JAMES	
19	1	11, 12, 13
20	2	14, 15
21	3	16, 17
22	4	18, 19
23	5	20, 21
	1 PET.	
24	1	22, 23
25	2	24, 25, 26
26	3	27, 28, 29
27	4	30, 31, 32
28	5	33, 34
	2 PET.	
29	1	35, 36
30	2	37, 38, 39

DECEMBER

Date	MORNING	EVENING
	2 PET.	**EZEK.**
1	3	40, 41
	1 JOHN	
2	1	42, 43, 44
3	2	45, 46
4	3	47, 48
		DAN.
5	4	1, 2
6	5	3, 4
7	**2 JOHN**	5, 6, 7
8	**3 JOHN**	8, 9, 10
9	**JUDE**	11, 12
	REV.	**HOS.**
10	1	1, 2, 3, 4
11	2	5, 6, 7, 8
12	3	9, 10, 11
13	4	12, 13, 14
14	5	**JOEL**
		AMOS
15	6	1, 2, 3
16	7	4, 5, 6
17	8	7, 8, 9
18	8	**OBAD.**
19	10	**JON.**
		MIC.
20	11	1, 2, 3
21	12	4, 5
22	13	6, 7
23	14	**NAH.**
24	15	**HAB.**
25	16	**ZEPH.**
26	17	**HAG.**
		ZECH.
27	18	1, 2, 3, 4
28	19	5, 6, 7, 8
29	20	9, 10, 11, 12
30	21	13, 14
31	22	**MAL.**

The Character of

GENUINE SAVING FAITH

2 CORINTHIANS 13:5

I. EVIDENCES THAT NEITHER PROVE NOR DISPROVE ONE'S FAITH

A.	Visible Morality:	Matt. 19:16-21; 23:27.
B.	Intellectual Knowledge:	Rom. 1:21; 2:17ff.
C.	Religious Involvement:	Matt. 25: 1-10
D.	Active Ministry:	Matt. 7:21-24
E.	Conviction of Sin:	Acts 24:25
F.	Assurance:	Matt. 23
G.	Time of Decision:	Luke 8:13,14

II. THE FRUIT/ PROOFS OF AUTHENTIC/TRUE CHRISTIANITY:

A.	Love for God:	Ps. 42:1ff; 73:25; Luke 10:27; Rom. 8:7
B.	Repentance from Sin:	Ps. 32:5; Prov. 28:13; Rom. 7:14ff; 2 Cor. 7:10; 1 John 1:8-10
C.	Genuine Humility:	Ps. 51:17; Matt. 5:1-12; James 4:6,9ff.
D.	Devotion to God's Glory:	Ps. 105:3; 115:1; Is. 43:7, 48:10ff.; Jer. 9:23,24; 1 Cor. 10:31.
E.	Continual Prayer:	Luke 18:1; Eph. 6:18ff.; Phil. 4:6ff.; 1 Tim. 2:1-4; James 5:16-18
F.	Selfless Love:	1 John 2:9ff, 3:14; 4:7ff.
G.	Separation from the World:	1 Cor. 2:12; James 4:4ff.; 1 John 2:15-17, 5:5
H.	Spiritual Growth:	Luke 8:15; John 15:1-6; Eph. 4:12-16
I.	Obedient Living:	Matt. 7:21; John 15:14ff.; Rom. 16:26; 1 Pet. 1:2,22; 1 John 2:3-5

If List I is true of a person and List II is false, there is cause to question the validity of one's profession of faith. Yet if List II is true, then the top list will be also.

III. THE CONDUCT OF THE GOSPEL:

A.	Proclaim it:	Matt. 4:23
B.	Defend it:	Jude 3
C.	Demonstrate it:	Phil. 1:27
D.	Share it:	Phil. 1:5
E.	Suffer for it:	2 Tim. 1:8
F.	Don't hinder it:	1 Cor. 9:16
G.	Be not ashamed:	Rom. 1:16
H.	Preach it:	1 Cor. 9:16
I.	Be empowered:	1 Thess. 1:5
J.	Guard it:	Gal. 1:6-8

Overview Of

THEOLOGY

THE HOLY SCRIPTURES

We teach that the Bible is God's written revelation to man, and thus the 66 books of the Bible given to us by the Holy Spirit constitute the plenary (inspired equally in all parts) Word of God (1 Cor. 2:7-14; 2 Pet. 1:20,21).

We teach that the Word of God is an objective, propositional revelation (1 Cor. 2:13; 1 Thess. 2:13), verbally inspired in every word (2 Tim. 3:16), absolutely inerrant in the original documents, infallible, and God-breathed. We teach the literal, grammatical-historical interpretation of Scripture, which affirms the belief that the opening chapters of Genesis present creation in six literal days (Gen. 1:31; Ex. 31:17).

We teach that the Bible constitutes the only infallible rule of faith and practice (Matt. 5:18; 24:35; John 10:35; 16:12,13; 17:17; 1 Cor. 2:13; 2 Tim. 3:15-17; Heb. 4:12; 2 Pet. 1:20,21).

We teach that God spoke in His written Word by a process of dual authorship. The Holy Spirit so superintended the human authors that, through their individual personalities and different styles of writing, they composed and recorded God's Word to man (2 Pet. 1:20,21) without error in the whole or in the part (Matt. 5:18; 2 Tim. 3:16).

We teach that, whereas there may be several applications of any given passage of Scripture, there is but one true interpretation. The meaning of Scripture is to be found as one diligently applies the literal, grammatical-historical method of interpretation under the enlightenment of the Holy Spirit (John 7:17; 16:12-15; 1 Cor. 2:7-15; 1 John 2:20). It is the responsibility of believers to ascertain carefully the true intent and meaning of Scripture, recognizing that proper application is binding on all generations. Yet the truth of Scripture stands in judgment of men; never do men stand in judgment of it.

GOD

We teach that there is but one living and true God (Deut. 6:4; Is. 45:5-7; 1 Cor. 8:4), an infinite, all-knowing Spirit (John 4:24), perfect in all His attributes, one in essence, eternally existing in three Persons—Father, Son, and Holy Spirit (Matt. 28:19; 2 Cor. 13:14)—each equally deserving worship and obedience.

God the Father

We teach that God the Father, the first person of the Trinity, orders and disposes all things according to His own purpose and grace (Ps. 145:8,9; 1 Cor. 8:6). He is the Creator of all things (Gen. 1:1-31; Eph. 3:9). As the only absolute and omnipotent ruler in the universe, He is sovereign in creation, providence, and redemption (Ps. 103:19; Rom. 11:36). His fatherhood involves both His designation within the Trinity and His relationship with mankind. As Creator He is Father to all men (Eph. 4:6), but He is Spiritual Father only to believers (Rom. 8:14; 2 Cor. 6:18). He has decreed for His own glory all things that come to pass (Eph. 1:11). He continually upholds, directs, and governs all creatures and events (1 Chr. 29:11). In His sovereignty He is neither author nor approver of sin (Hab. 1:13), nor does He abridge the accountability of moral, intelligent creatures (1 Pet. 1:17). He has graciously chosen from eternity past those whom He would have as His own (Eph. 1:4-6); He saves from sin all those who come to Him; and He becomes, upon adoption, Father to His own (John 1:12; Rom. 8:15; Gal. 4:5; Heb. 12:5-9).

God the Son

We teach that Jesus Christ, the second person of the Trinity, possesses all the divine excellencies, and in these He is coequal, consubstantial, and coeternal with the Father (John 10:30; 14:9).

We teach that God the Father created "the heavens and the earth and all that is in them" according to His own will, through His Son, Jesus Christ, by whom all things continue in existence and in operations (John 1:3; Col. 1:15-17; Heb. 1:2).

We teach that in the incarnation (God becoming man) Christ surrendered only the prerogatives of deity but nothing of the divine essence, either in degree or kind. In His incarnation, the eternally existing second person of the Trinity accepted all the essential characteristics of humanity and so became the God-man (Phil. 2:5-8; Col. 2:9).

We teach that Jesus Christ represents humanity and deity in indivisible oneness (Mic. 5:2; John 5:23; 14:9,10; Col. 2:9).

We teach that our Lord Jesus Christ was virgin born (Is. 7:14; Matt. 1:23,25; Luke 1:26-35); that He was God incarnate (John 1:1,14); and that the purpose of the incarnation was to reveal God, redeem men, and rule over God's kingdom (Ps. 2:7-9; Is. 9:6; John 1:29; Phil. 2:9-11; Heb. 7:25,26; 1 Pet. 1:18,19).

We teach that, in the incarnation, the second person of the Trinity laid aside His right to the full prerogatives of coexistence with God, assumed the place of a Son, and took on an existence appropriate to a servant while never divesting Himself of His divine attributes (Phil. 2:5-8).

We teach that our Lord Jesus Christ accomplished our redemption through the shedding of His blood and sacrificial death on the cross and that His death was voluntary, vicarious, substitutionary, propitiatory, and redemptive (John 10:15; Rom. 3:24,25; 5:8; 1 Pet. 2:24).

We teach that on the basis of the efficacy of the death of our Lord Jesus Christ, the believing sinner is freed from the punishment, the penalty, the power, and one day the very presence of sin; and that he is declared righteous, given eternal life, and adopted into the family of God (Rom. 3:25; 5:8,9; 2 Cor. 5:14,15; 1 Pet. 2:24; 3:18).

We teach that our justification is made sure by His literal, physical resurrection from the dead and that He is now ascended to the right hand of the Father, where He now mediates as our Advocate and High-Priest (Matt. 28:6; Luke 24:38,39; Acts 2:30,31; Rom. 4:25; 8:34; Heb. 7:25; 9:24; 1 John 2:1).

We teach that in the resurrection of Jesus Christ from the grave, God confirmed the deity of His Son and gave proof that God has accepted the atoning work of Christ on the cross. Jesus' bodily resurrection is also the guarantee of a future resurrection life for all believers (John 5:26-29; 14:19; Rom. 4:25; 6:5-10; 1 Cor. 15:20,23).

We teach that Jesus Christ will return to receive the church, which is His body, unto Himself at the Rapture and, returning with His church in glory, will establish His millennial kingdom on earth (Acts 1:9-11; 1 Thess. 4:13-18; Rev. 20).

We teach that the Lord Jesus Christ is the one through whom God will judge all mankind (John 5:22,23):

a. Believers (1 Cor. 3:10-15; 2 Cor. 5:10);
b. Living inhabitants of the earth at His glorious return (Matt. 25:31-46); and
c. Unbelieving dead at the Great White Throne (Rev. 20:11-15).

As the mediator between God and man (1 Tim. 2:5), the head of His body the church (Eph. 1:22; 5:23; Col. 1:18), and the coming universal King who will reign on the throne of David (Is. 9:6,7; Ezek. 37:24-28; Luke 1:31-33), He is the final judge of all who fail to place their trust in Him as Lord and Savior (Matt. 25:14-46; Acts 17:30,31).

God the Holy Spirit

We teach that the Holy Spirit is a divine person, eternal, underived, possessing all the attributes of personality and deity, including intellect (1 Cor. 2:10-13), emotions (Eph. 4:30), will (1 Cor. 12:11), eternality (Heb. 9:14), omnipresence (Ps. 139:7-10), omniscience (Is. 40:13,14), omnipotence (Rom. 15:13), and truthfulness (John 16:13). In all the divine attributes He is coequal and consubstantial with the Father and the Son (Matt. 28:19; Acts 5:3,4; 28:25,26; 1 Cor. 12:4-6; 2 Cor. 13:14; and Jer. 31:31-34 with Heb. 10:15-17).

We teach that it is the work of the Holy Spirit to execute the divine will with relation to all mankind. We recognize His sovereign activity in the creation (Gen. 1:2), the incarnation (Matt. 1:18), the written revelation (2 Pet. 1:20,21), and the work of salvation (John 3:5-7).

We teach that a unique work of the Holy Spirit in this age began at Pentecost when He came from the Father as promised by Christ (John 14:16,17; 15:26) to initiate and complete the building of the body of Christ. His activity includes convicting the world of sin, of righteousness, and of judgment; glorifying the Lord Jesus Christ and transforming believers into the image of Christ (John 16:7-9; Acts 1:5; 2:4; Rom. 8:29; 2 Cor. 3:18; Eph. 2:22).

We teach that the Holy Spirit is the supernatural and sovereign agent in regeneration, baptizing all believers into the body of Christ (1 Cor. 12:13). The Holy Spirit also indwells, sanctifies, instructs, empowers them for service, and seals them unto the day of redemption (Rom. 8:9-11; 2 Cor. 3:6; Eph. 1:13).

We teach that the Holy Spirit is the divine teacher who guided the apostles and prophets into all truth as they committed to writing God's revelation, the Bible (2 Pet. 1:19-21). Every believer possesses the indwelling presence of the Holy Spirit from the moment of salvation, and it is the duty of all those born of the Spirit to be filled with (controlled by) the Spirit (Rom. 8:9-11; Eph. 5:18; 1 John 2:20,27).

We teach that the Holy Spirit administers spiritual gifts to the church. The Holy Spirit glorifies neither Himself nor His gifts by ostentatious displays, but He does glorify Christ by implementing His work of redeeming the lost and building up believers in the most holy faith (John 16:13,14; Acts 1:8; 1 Cor. 12:4-11; 2 Cor. 3:18).

We teach, in this respect, that God the Holy Spirit is sovereign in the bestowing of all His gifts for the perfecting of the saints today and that speaking in tongues and the working of sign miracles in the beginning days of the church were for the purpose of pointing to and authenticating the apostles as revealers of divine truth, and were never intended to be characteristic of the lives of believers (1 Cor. 12:4-11; 13:8-10; 2 Cor. 12:12; Eph. 4:7-12; Heb. 2:1-4).

Man

We teach that man was directly and immediately created by God in His image and likeness. Man was created free of sin with a rational nature, intelligence, volition, self-determination, and moral responsibility to God (Gen. 2:7,15-25; James 3:9).

We teach that God's intention in the creation of man was that man should glorify God, enjoy God's fellowship, live his life in the will of God, and by this accomplish God's purpose for man in the world (Is. 43:7; Col. 1:16; Rev. 4:11).

We teach that in Adam's sin of disobedience to the revealed will and Word of God, man lost his innocence; incurred the penalty of spiritual and physical death; became subject to the wrath of God; and became inherently corrupt and utterly incapable of choosing or doing that which is acceptable to God apart from divine grace. With no recuperative powers to enable him to recover himself, man is hopelessly lost. Man's salvation is thereby wholly of God's grace through the redemptive work of our Lord Jesus Christ (Gen. 2:16,17; 3:1-19; John 3:36; Rom. 3:23; 6:23; 1 Cor. 2:14; Eph. 2:1-3; 1 Tim. 2:13,14; 1 John 1:8).

We teach that because all men were in Adam, a nature corrupted by Adam's sin has been transmitted to all men of all ages, Jesus Christ being the only exception. All men are thus sinners by nature, by choice, and by divine declaration (Ps. 14:1-3; Jer. 17:9; Rom. 3:9-18,23; 5:10-12).

Salvation

We teach that salvation is wholly of God by grace on the basis of the redemption of Jesus Christ, the merit of His shed blood, and not on the basis of human merit or works (John 1:12; Eph. 1:4-7; 2:8-10; 1 Pet. 1:18,19).

Election

We teach that election is the act of God by which, before the foundation of the world, He chose in Christ those whom He graciously regenerates, saves, and sanctifies (Rom. 8:28-30; Eph. 1:4-11; 2 Thess. 2:13; 2 Tim. 2:10; 1 Pet. 1:1,2).

We teach that sovereign election does not contradict or negate the responsibility of man to repent and trust Christ as Savior and Lord (Ezek. 18:23,32; 33:11; John 3:18,19,36; 5:40; 2 Thess. 2:10-12; Rev. 22:17). Nevertheless, since sovereign grace includes the means of receiving the gift of salvation as well as the gift itself, sovereign election will result in what God determines. All whom the Father calls to Himself will come in faith and all who come in faith the Father will receive (John 6:37-40,44; Acts 13:48; James 4:8).

We teach that the unmerited favor that God grants to totally depraved sinners is not related to any initiative of their own part nor to God's anticipation of what they might do by their own will, but is solely of His sovereign grace and mercy (Eph. 1:4-7; Titus 3:4-7; 1 Pet. 1:2).

We teach that election should not be looked upon as based merely on abstract sovereignty. God is truly sovereign but He exercises this sovereignty in harmony with His other attributes, especially His omniscience, justice, holiness, wisdom, grace, and love (Rom. 9:11-16). This sovereignty will always exalt the will of God in a manner totally consistent with His character as revealed in the life of our Lord Jesus Christ (Matt. 11:25-28; 2 Tim. 1:9).

Regeneration

We teach that regeneration is a supernatural work of the Holy Spirit by which the divine nature and divine life are given (John 3:3-8; Titus 3:5). It is instantaneous and is accomplished solely by the power of the Holy Spirit through the instrumentality of the Word of God (John 5:24), when the repentant sinner, as enabled by the Holy Spirit, responds in faith to the divine provision of salvation. Genuine regeneration is manifested by fruits worthy of repentance as demonstrated in righteous attitudes and conduct. Good works will be its proper evidence and fruit (1 Cor. 6:19,20; Eph. 5:17-21; Phil. 2:12b; Col. 3:12-17; 2 Pet. 1:4-11). This obedience causes the believer to be increasingly conformed to the image of our Lord Jesus Christ (2 Cor. 3:18). Such a conformity is climaxed in the believer's glorification at Christ's coming (Rom. 8:16,17; 2 Pet. 1:4; 1 John 3:2,3).

Justification

We teach that justification before God is an act of God (Rom. 8:30,33) by which He declares righteous those who, through faith in Christ, repent of their sins (Luke 13:3; Acts 2:38; 3:19; 11:18; Rom. 2:4; 2 Cor. 7:10; Is. 55:6,7) and confess Him as sovereign Lord (Rom. 10:9,10; 1 Cor. 12:3; 2 Cor. 4:5; Phil. 2:11). This righteousness is apart from any virtue or work of man (Rom. 3:20; 4:6) and involves the placing of our sins on Christ (Col. 2:14; 1 Pet. 2:24) and the imputation of Christ's righteousness to us (1 Cor. 1:2,30; 6:11; 2 Cor. 5:21). By this means God is enabled to "be just, and the justifier of the one who has faith in Jesus" (Rom. 3:26).

Sanctification

We teach that every believer is sanctified (set apart) unto God by justification and is therefore declared to be holy and is therefore identified as a saint. This sanctification is positional and instantaneous and should not be confused with progressive sanctification. This sanctification has to do with the believer's standing, not his present walk or condition (Acts 20:32; 1 Cor. 1:2,30; 6:11; 2 Thess. 2:13; Heb. 2:11; 3:1; 10:10,14; 13:12; 1 Pet. 1:2).

We teach that there is also by the work of the Holy Spirit a progressive sanctification by which the state of the believer is brought closer to the likeness of Christ through obedience to the Word of God and the empowering of the Holy Spirit. The believer is able to live a life of increasing holiness in conformity to the will of God, becoming more and more like our Lord Jesus Christ (John 17:17,19; Rom. 6:1-22; 2 Cor. 3:18; 1 Thess. 4:3,4; 5:23).

In this respect, we teach that every saved person is involved in a daily conflict—the new creation in Christ doing battle against the flesh—but adequate provision is made for victory through the power of the indwelling Holy Spirit. The struggle nevertheless stays with the believer all through this earthly life and is never completely ended. All claims to the eradication of sin in this life are unscriptural. Eradication of sin is not possible, but the Holy Spirit does provide for victory over sin (Gal. 5:16-25; Eph. 4:22-24; Phil. 3:12; Col. 3:9,10; 1 Pet. 1:14-16; 1 John 3:5-9).

Security

We teach that all the redeemed once saved are kept by God's power and are thus secure in Christ forever (John 5:24; 6:37-40; 10:27-30; Rom. 5:9,10; 8:1,31-39; 1 Cor. 1:4-9; Eph. 4:30; Heb. 7:25; 13:5; 1 Pet. 1:4,5; Jude 24).

We teach that it is the privilege of believers to rejoice in the assurance of their salvation through the testimony of God's Word, which however, clearly forbids the use of Christian liberty as an excuse for sinful living and carnality (Rom. 6:15-22; 13:13,14; Gal. 5:13,16,17,25,26; Titus 2:11-14).

Separation

We teach that separation from sin is clearly called for throughout the Old and New Testaments, and that the Scriptures clearly indicate that in the last days apostasy and worldliness shall increase (2 Cor. 6:14–7:1; 2 Tim. 3:1-5).

We teach that out of deep gratitude for the undeserved grace of God granted to us and because our glorious God is so worthy of our total consecration, all the saved should live in such a manner as to demonstrate our adoring love to God and so as not to bring reproach upon our Lord and Savior. We also teach that separation from any association with religious apostasy, and worldly and sinful practices is commanded of us by God (Rom. 12:1,2; 1 Cor. 5:9-13; 2 Cor. 6:14–7:1; 1 John 2:15-17; 2 John 9-11).

We teach that believers should be separated unto our Lord Jesus Christ (2 Thess. 1:11,12; Heb. 12:1,2) and affirm that the Christian life is a life of obedient righteousness demonstrated by a beatitude attitude (Matt. 5:2-12) and a continual pursuit of holiness (Rom. 12:1,2; 2 Cor. 7:1; Heb. 12:14; Titus 2:11-14; 1 John 3:1-10).

The Church

We teach that all who place their faith in Jesus Christ are immediately placed by the Holy Spirit into one united spiritual body, the church (1 Cor. 12:12,13), the bride of Christ (2 Cor. 11:2; Eph. 5:23-32; Rev. 19:7,8), of which Christ is the head (Eph. 1:22; 4:15; Col. 1:18).

We teach that the formation of the church, the body of Christ, began on the day of Pentecost (Acts 2:1-21,38-47) and will be completed at the coming of Christ for His own at the Rapture (1 Cor. 15:51,52; 1 Thess. 4:13-18).

We teach that the church is thus a unique spiritual organism designed by Christ, made up of all born-again believers in this present age (Eph. 2:11–3:6). The church is distinct from Israel (1 Cor. 10:32), a mystery not revealed until this age (Eph. 3:1-6; 5:32).

We teach that the establishment and continuity of local churches is clearly taught and defined in the New Testament Scriptures (Acts 14:23,27; 20:17,28; Gal. 1:2; Phil. 1:1; 1 Thess. 1:1; 2 Thess. 1:1) and that the members of the one scriptural body are directed to associate themselves together in local assemblies (1 Cor. 11:18-20; Heb. 10:25).

We teach that the one supreme authority for the church is Christ (Eph. 1:22; Col. 1:18) and that church leadership, gifts, order, discipline, and worship are all appointed through His sovereignty as found in the Scriptures. The biblically designated officers serving under Christ and over the assembly are elders (males, who are also called bishops, pastors, and pastor-teachers; Acts 20:28; Eph. 4:11) and deacons, both of whom must meet biblical qualification (1 Tim. 3:1-13; Titus 1:5-9; 1 Pet. 5:1-5).

We teach that these leaders lead or rule as servants of Christ (1 Tim. 5:17-22) and have His authority in directing the church. The congregation is to submit to their leadership (Heb. 13:7,17).

We teach the importance of discipleship (Matt. 28:19,20; 2 Tim. 2:2), mutual accountability of all believers to each other (Matt. 18:15-17), as well as the need for discipline for sinning members of the congregation in accord with the standards of Scripture (Matt. 18:15-22; Acts 5:1-11; 1 Cor. 5:1-13; 2 Thess. 3:6-15; 1 Tim. 1:19,20; Titus 1:10-16).

We teach the autonomy of the local church, free from any external authority or control, with the right of self-government and freedom from the interference of any hierarchy of individuals or organizations (Titus 1:5). We teach that it is scriptural for true churches to cooperate with each other for the presentation and propagation of the faith. Local churches, however, through their pastors and their interpretation and application of Scripture, should be the sole judges of the measure and method of their cooperation (Acts 15:19-31; 20:28; 1 Cor. 5:4-7,13; 1 Pet. 5:1-4).

We teach that the purpose of the church is to glorify God (Eph. 3:21) by building itself up in the faith (Eph. 4:13-16), by instruction of the Word (2 Tim. 2:2,15; 3:16,17), by fellowship (Acts 2:47; 1 John 1:3), by keeping the ordinances (Luke 22:19; Acts 2:38-42) and by advancing and communicating the gospel to the entire world (Matt. 28:19; Acts 1:8).

We teach the calling of all saints to the work of service (1 Cor. 15:58; Eph. 4:12; Rev. 22:12).

We teach the need of the church to cooperate with God as He accomplishes His purpose in the world. To that end, He gives the church spiritual gifts. First, He gives men chosen for the purpose of equipping the saints for the work of the ministry (Eph. 4:7-12) and He also gives unique and special spiritual abilities to each member of the body of Christ (Rom. 12:5-8; 1 Cor. 12:4-31; 1 Pet. 4:10,11).

We teach that there were two kinds of gifts given the early church: miraculous gifts of divine revelation and healing, given temporarily in the apostolic era for the purpose of confirming the authenticity of the apostles' message (Heb. 2:3,4; 2 Cor. 12:12); and ministering gifts, given to equip believers for edifying one another. With the New Testament revelation now complete, Scripture becomes the sole test of the authenticity of a man's message, and confirming gifts of a miraculous nature are no longer necessary to validate a man or his message (1 Cor. 13:8-12). Miraculous gifts can even be counterfeited by Satan so as to deceive even believers (Matt. 24:24). The only gifts in operation today are those non-revelatory equipping gifts given for edification (Rom. 12:6-8).

We teach that no one possesses the gift of healing today but that God does hear and answer the prayer of faith and will answer in accordance with His own perfect will for the sick, suffering, and afflicted (Luke 18:1-8; John 5:7-9; 2 Cor. 12:6-10; James 5:13-16; 1 John 5:14,15).

We teach that two ordinances have been committed to the local church: baptism and the Lord's Supper (Acts 2:38-42). Christian baptism by immersion (Acts 8:36-39) is the solemn and beautiful testimony of a believer showing forth his faith in the crucified, buried, and risen Savior, and his union with Him in death to sin and resurrection to a new life (Rom. 6: 1-11). It is also a sign of fellowship and identification with the visible body of Christ (Acts 2:41,42).

We teach that the Lord's Supper is the commemoration and proclamation of His death until He comes, and should be always preceded by solemn self-examination (1 Cor. 11:23-32). We also teach that whereas the elements of communion are only representative of the flesh and blood of Christ, the Lord's Supper is nevertheless an actual Communion with the risen Christ who is present in a unique way, fellowshiping with His people (1 Cor. 10:16).

Angels

Holy Angels

We teach that angels are created beings and are therefore not to be worshiped. Although they are a higher order of creation than man, they are created to serve God and to worship Him (Luke 2:9-14; Heb. 1:6,7,14; 2:6,7; Rev. 5:11-14).

Fallen Angels

We teach that Satan is a created angel and the author of sin. He incurred the judgment of God by rebelling against his Creator (Is. 14:12-17; Ezek. 28:11-19), by taking numerous angels with him in his fall (Matt. 25:41; Rev. 12:1-14), and by introducing sin into the human race by his temptation of Eve (Gen. 3:1-15).

We teach that Satan is the open and declared enemy of God and man (Is. 14:13,14; Matt. 4:1-11; Rev. 12:9,10), the prince of this world who has been defeated through the death and resurrection of Jesus Christ (Rom. 16:20) and that he shall be eternally punished in the lake of fire (Is. 14:12-17; Ezek. 28:11-19; Matt. 25:41; Rev. 20:10).

LAST THINGS (ESCHATOLOGY)

Death

We teach that physical death involves no loss of our immaterial consciousness (Rev. 6:9-11), that there is a separation of soul and body (James 2:26), that the soul of the redeemed passes immediately into the presence of Christ (Luke 23:43; 2 Cor. 5:8; Phil. 1:23), and that, for the redeemed, such separation will continue until the Rapture (1 Thess. 4:13-17) which initiates the first resurrection (Rev. 20:4-6), when our soul and body will be reunited to be glorified forever with our Lord (1 Cor. 15:35-44,50-54; Phil. 3:21). Until that time, the souls of the redeemed in Christ remain in joyful fellowship with our Lord Jesus Christ (2 Cor. 5:8).

We teach the bodily resurrection of all men, the saved to eternal life (John 6:39; Rom. 8:10,11,19-23; 2 Cor. 4:14), and the unsaved to judgment and everlasting punishment (Dan. 12:2; John 5:29; Rev. 20:13-15).

We teach that the souls of the unsaved at death are kept under punishment until the second resurrection (Luke 16:19-26; Rev. 20:13-15), when the soul and the resurrection body will be united (John 5:28, 29). They shall then appear at the Great White Throne judgment (Rev. 20:11-15) and shall be cast into hell, the lake of fire (Matt. 25:41-46), cut off from the life of God forever (Dan. 12:2; Matt. 25:41-46; 2 Thess. 1:7-9).

The Rapture of the Church

We teach the personal, bodily return of our Lord Jesus Christ before the seven-year tribulation (1 Thess. 4:16; Titus 2:13) to translate His church from this earth (John 14:1-3; 1 Cor. 15:51-53; 1 Thess. 4:15-5:11) and, between this event and His glorious return with His saints, to reward believers according to their works (1 Cor. 3:11-15; 2 Cor. 5:10).

The Tribulation Period

We teach that immediately following the removal of the church from the earth (John 14:1-3; 1 Thess. 4:13-18) the righteous judgments of God will be poured out upon an unbelieving world (Jer. 30:7; Dan. 9:27; 12:1; 2 Thess. 2:7-12; Rev. 16), and that these judgments will be climaxed by the return of Christ in glory to the earth (Matt. 24:27-31; 25:31-46; 2 Thess. 2:7-12). At that time the Old Testament and tribulation saints will be raised and the living will be judged (Dan. 12:2,3; Rev. 20:4-6). This period includes the seventieth week of Daniel's prophecy (Dan. 9:24-27; Matt. 24:15-31; 25:31-46).

The Second Coming and the Millennial Reign

We teach that after the tribulation period, Christ will come to earth to occupy the throne of David (Matt. 25:31; Luke 1:32,33; Acts 1:10,11; 2:29,30) and establish His messianic kingdom for a thousand years on the earth (Rev. 20:1-7). During this time the resurrected saints will reign with Him over Israel and all the nations of the earth (Ezek. 37:21-28; Dan. 7:17-22; Rev. 19:11-16). This reign will be preceded by the overthrow of the Antichrist and the False Prophet, and by the removal of Satan from the world (Dan. 7:17-27; Rev. 20:1-6).

We teach that the kingdom itself will be the fulfillment of God's promise to Israel (Is. 65:17-25; Ezek. 37:21-28; Zech. 8:1-17) to restore them to the land which they forfeited through their disobedience (Deut. 28:15-68). The result of their disobedience was that Israel was temporarily set aside (Matt. 21:43; Rom. 11:1-26) but will again be awakened through repentance to enter into the land of blessing (Jer. 31:31-34; Ezek. 36:22-32; Rom. 11:25-29).

We teach that this time of our Lord's reign will be characterized by harmony, justice, peace, righteousness, and long life (Is. 11; 65:17-25; Ezek. 36:33-38), and will be brought to an end with the release of Satan (Rev. 20:7).

The Judgment of the Lost

We teach that following the release of Satan after the thousand year reign of Christ (Rev. 20:7), Satan will deceive the nations of the earth and gather them to battle against the saints and the beloved city, at which time Satan and his army will be devoured by fire from heaven (Rev. 20:9). Following this, Satan will be thrown into the lake of fire and brimstone (Matt. 25:41; Rev. 20:10) whereupon Christ, who is the judge of all men (John 5:22), will resurrect and judge the great and small at the Great White Throne judgment.

We teach that this resurrection of the unsaved dead to judgment will be a physical resurrection, whereupon receiving their judgment (John 5:28,29), they will be committed to an eternal conscious punishment in the lake of fire (Matt. 25:41; Rev. 20:11-15).

Eternity

We teach that after the closing of the Millennium, the temporary release of Satan, and the judgment of unbelievers (2 Thess. 1:9; Rev. 20:7-15), the saved will enter the eternal state of glory with God, after which the elements of this earth are to be dissolved (2 Pet. 3:10) and replaced with a new earth wherein only righteousness dwells (Eph. 5:5; Rev. 20:15,21,22). Following this, the heavenly city will come down out of heaven (Rev. 21:2) and will be the dwelling place of the saints, where they will enjoy forever fellowship with God and one another (John 17:3; Rev. 21,22). Our Lord Jesus Christ, having fulfilled His redemptive mission, will then deliver up the kingdom to God the Father (1 Cor. 15:23-28) that in all spheres the triune God may reign forever and ever (1 Cor. 15:28).

Monies, Weights, and Measures

The Hebrews probably first used coins in the Persian period (500–350 B.C.). However, minting began around 700 B.C. in other nations. Prior to this, precious metals were weighed, not counted as money.

Some units appear as both measures of money and measures of weights. This comes from naming the coins after their weight. For example, the shekel was a weight long before it became the name of a coin.

It is helpful to relate biblical monies to current values. But we cannot make exact equivalents. The fluctuating value of money's purchasing power is difficult to determine in our own day. It is even harder to evaluate currencies used two- to three-thousand years ago.

Therefore, it is best to choose a value meaningful over time, such as a common laborer's daily wage. One day's wage corresponds to the ancient Jewish system (a silver shekel is four days' wages) as well as to the Greek and Roman systems (the drachma and the denarius were each coins representing a day's wage).

The monies chart below takes a current day's wage as thirty-two dollars. Though there are differences of economies and standards of living, this measure will help us apply meaningful value to the monetary units in the chart and in the biblical text.

Monies

Unit	Monetary Value	Equivalents	Translations
Jewish Weights			
Talent	gold—$5,760,000[1] silver—$384,000	3,000 shekels; 6,000 bekas	talent, one hundred pounds
Shekel	gold—$1,920 silver—$128	4 days' wages; 2 bekas: 20 gerahs	shekel
Beka	gold—$960 silver—$64	1/2 shekel; 10 gerahs	beka
Gerah	gold—$96 silver—$6.40	1/20 shekel	gerahs
Persian Coins			
Daric	gold—$1,280[2] silver—$64	2 days' wages; 1/2 Jewish silver shekel	daric, drachma
Greek Coins			
Tetradrachma	$128	4 drachmas	stater
Didrachma	$64	2 drachmas	two-drachma tax
Drachma	$32	1 day's wage	coin, silver coins
Lepton	$.25	1/2 of a Roman kodrantes	cents, small copper coin
Roman Coins			
Aureus	$800	25 denarii	gold
Denarius	$32	1 day's wage	denarii
Assarius	$2	1/16 of a denarius	cent
Kodrantes	$.50	1/4 of an assarius	cent

[1]Value of gold is fifteen times the value of silver

[2]Value of gold is twenty times the value of silver

Weights

Unit	Weight	Equivalents	Translations
Jewish Weights			
Talent	ca. 75 pounds for common talent, ca. 150 pounds for royal talent	60 minas; 3000 shekels	talent, one hundred pounds
Mina	1.25 pounds	50 shekels	maneh, mina
Shekel	ca. .4 ounce (11.4 grams) for common shekel ca. .8 ounce for royal shekel	2 bekas; 20 gerahs	shekel
Beka	ca. .2 ounce (5.7 grams)	1/2 shekel; 10 gerahs	half-shekel
Gerah	ca. .02 ounce (.57 grams)	1/20 shekel	gerah
Roman Weight			
Litra	12 ounces		pound, pint

Measures of Length

Unit	Length	Equivalents	Translations
Day's journey	ca. 20 miles		day's journey, day's walk
Roman mile	4,854 feet	8 stadia	mile
Sabbath day's journey	3,637 feet	6 stadia	a Sabbath day's journey
Stadion	606 feet	1/8 Roman mile	mile, stadion
Rod	9 feet (10.5 feet in Ezekiel)	3 paces; 6 cubits	measuring rod
Fathom	6 feet	4 cubits	fathom
Pace	3 feet	1/3 rod; 2 cubits	pace
Cubit	18 inches	1/2 pace; 2 spans	cubit, yards
Span	9 inches	1/2 cubit; 3 handbreadths	span
Handbreadth	3 inches	1/3 span; 4 fingers	handbreadth
Finger	.75 inches	1/4 handbreadth	finger

Dry Measures

Unit	Measures	Equivalents	Translations
Homer	6.52 bushels	10 ephahs	homer
Kor	6.52 bushels	1 homer; 10 ephahs	kor, measure
Lethech	3.26 bushels	1/2 kor	a homer and a half
Ephah	.65 bushel, 20.8 quarts	1/10 homer	ephah
Modius	7.68 quarts		peck-measure
Seah	7 quarts	1/3 ephah	measure, pecks
Omer	2.08 quarts	1/10 ephah; 1 4/5 kab	omer
Kab	1.16 quarts	4 logs	kab
Choenix	1 quart		quart
Xestes	1 1/16 pints		pitcher
Log	.58 pint	1/4 kab	log

Liquid Measures

Unit	Measures	Equivalents	Translations
Kor	60 gallons	10 baths	kor
Metretes	10.2 gallons		gallon
Bath	6 gallons	6 hins	measure, bath
Hin	1 gallon	2 kabs	hin
Kab	2 quarts	4 logs	kab
Log	1 pint	1/4 kab	log

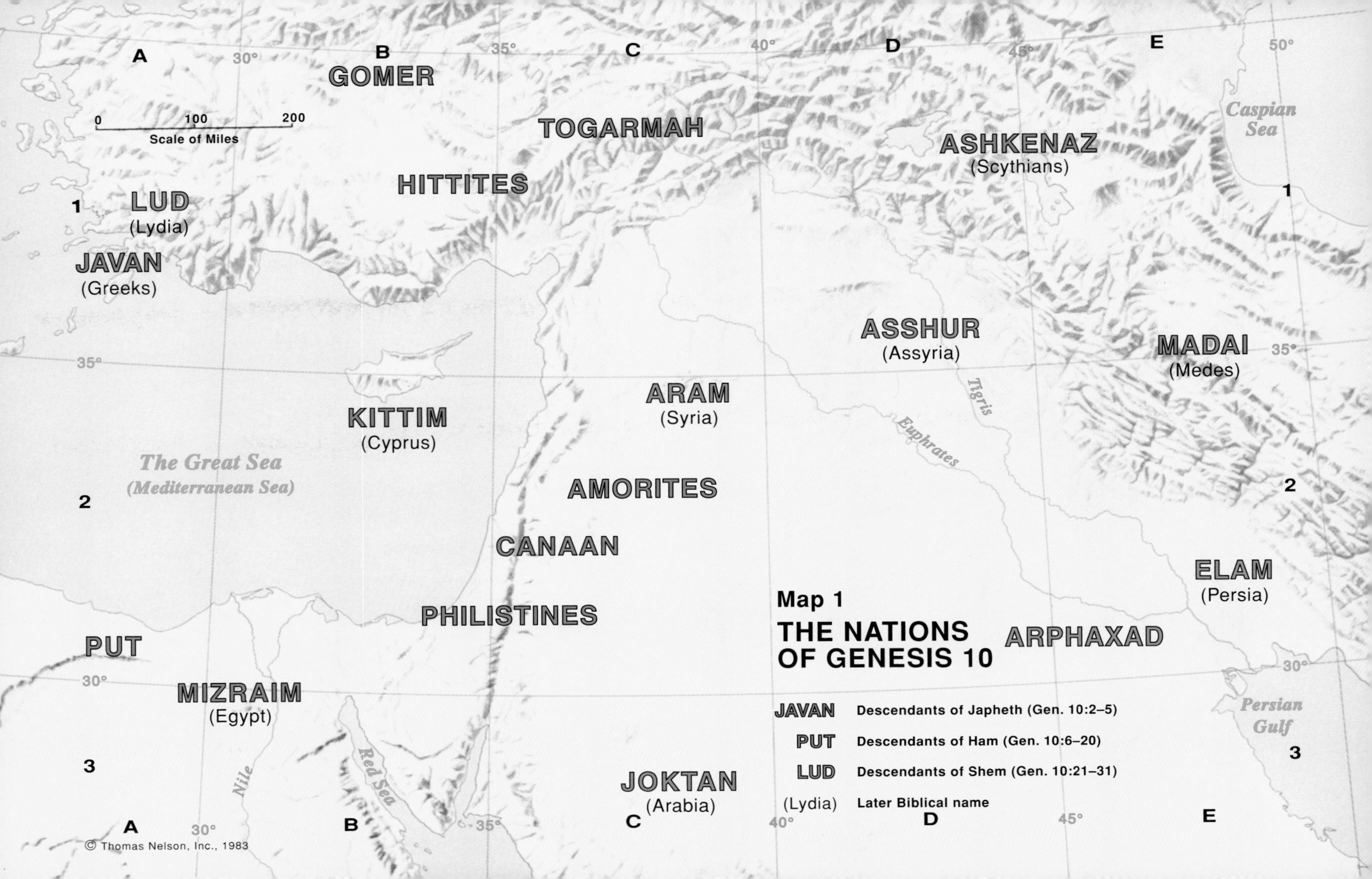
Map 1
THE NATIONS OF GENESIS 10
JAVAN Descendants of Japheth (Gen. 10:2–5)
PUT Descendants of Ham (Gen. 10:6–20)
LUD Descendants of Shem (Gen. 10:21–31)
(Lydia) Later Biblical name
GOMER
TOGARMAH
ASHKENAZ
(Scythians)
HITTITES
LUD
(Lydia)
JAVAN
(Greeks)
Caspian Sea
ASSHUR
(Assyria)
MADAI
(Medes)
ARAM
(Syria)
KITTIM
(Cyprus)
The Great Sea
(Mediterranean Sea)
AMORITES
CANAAN
ELAM
(Persia)
PHILISTINES
ARPHAXAD
PUT
MIZRAIM
(Egypt)
Persian Gulf
JOKTAN
(Arabia)
Tigris
Euphrates
Nile
Red Sea
Scale of Miles
0
100
200

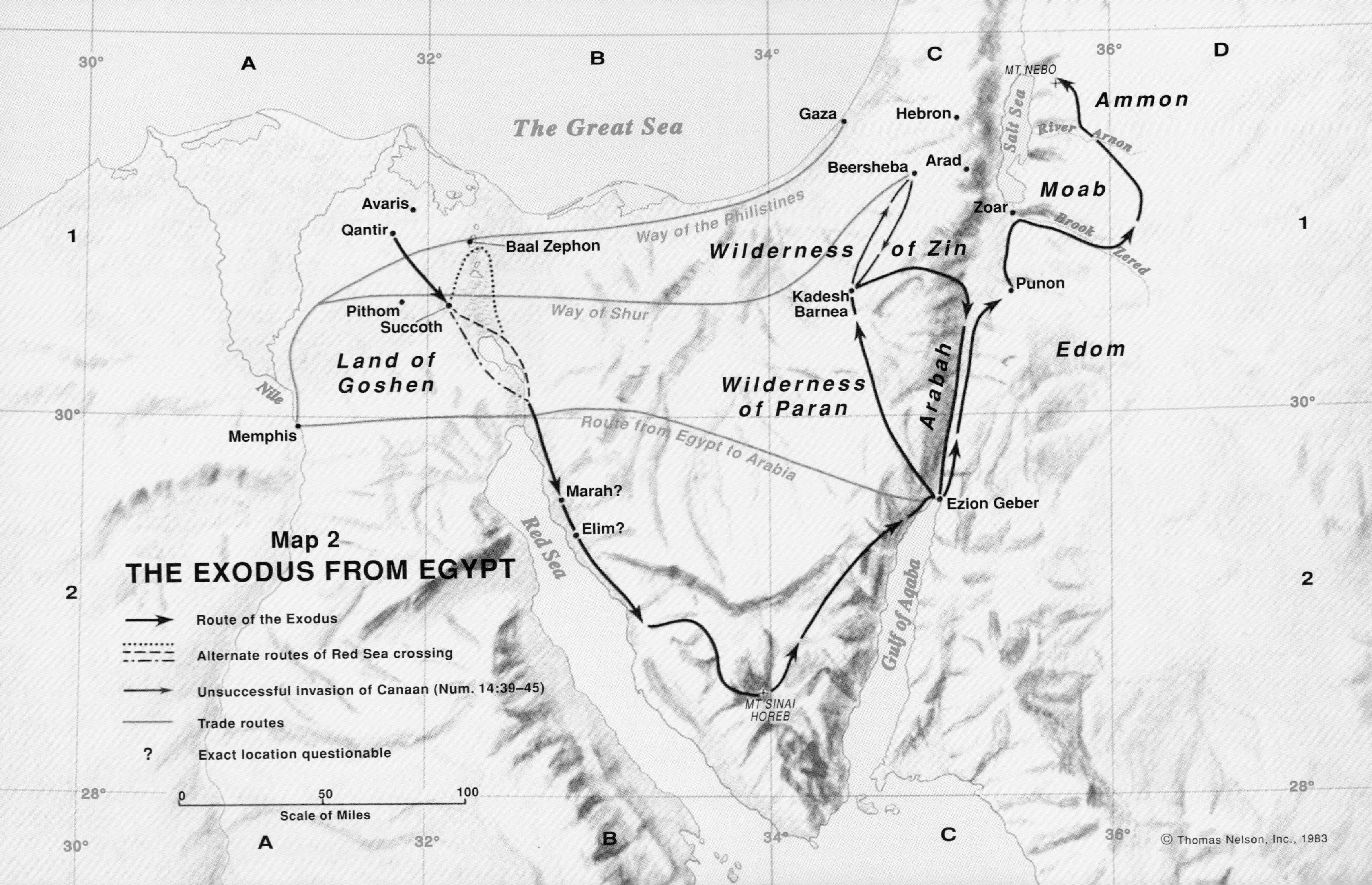

Map 2
THE EXODUS FROM EGYPT
Route of the Exodus
Alternate routes of Red Sea crossing
Unsuccessful invasion of Canaan (Num. 14:39–45)
Trade routes
? Exact location questionable
0
50
100
Scale of Miles
A
B
C
D
1
2
30°
32°
34°
36°
28°
The Great Sea
Avaris
Qantir
Baal Zephon
Pithom
Succoth
Land of Goshen
Nile
Memphis
Way of the Philistines
Way of Shur
Route from Egypt to Arabia
Marah?
Elim?
Red Sea
MT SINAI HOREB
Gulf of Aqaba
Wilderness of Paran
Wilderness of Zin
Kadesh Barnea
Gaza
Beersheba
Hebron
Arad
Arabah
Ezion Geber
Punon
Edom
Zoar
Moab
Salt Sea
MT NEBO
River Arnon
Brook Zered
Ammon

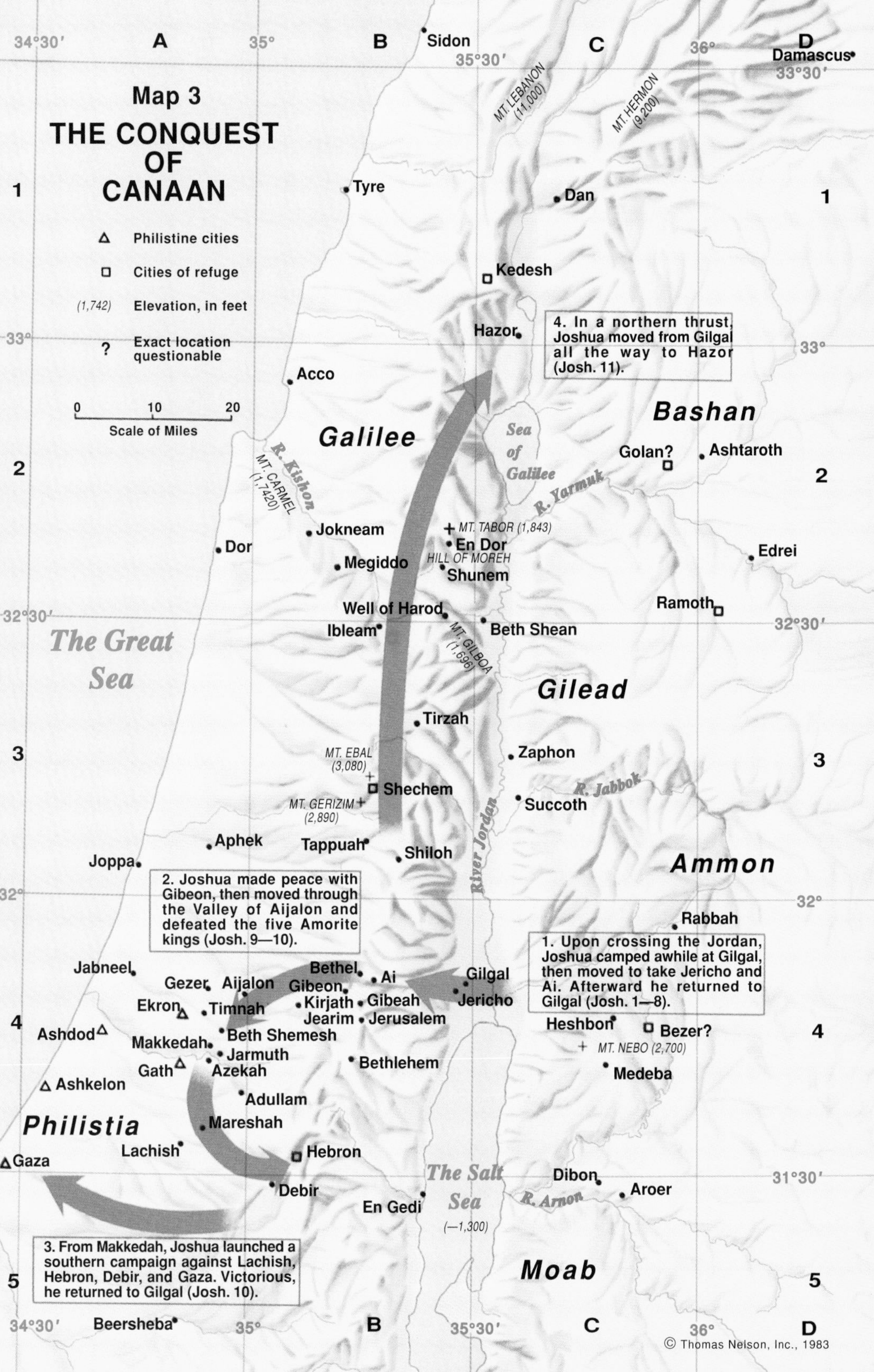

Map 3
THE CONQUEST OF CANAAN
Philistine cities
Cities of refuge
(1,742) Elevation, in feet
Exact location questionable
Scale of Miles
4. In a northern thrust, Joshua moved from Gilgal all the way to Hazor (Josh. 11).
2. Joshua made peace with Gibeon, then moved through the Valley of Aijalon and defeated the five Amorite kings (Josh. 9—10).
1. Upon crossing the Jordan, Joshua camped awhile at Gilgal, then moved to take Jericho and Ai. Afterward he returned to Gilgal (Josh. 1—8).
3. From Makkedah, Joshua launched a southern campaign against Lachish, Hebron, Debir, and Gaza. Victorious, he returned to Gilgal (Josh. 10).
Sidon
Damascus
MT. LEBANON (11,000)
MT. HERMON (9,200)
Tyre
Dan
Kedesh
Hazor
Acco
Galilee
Bashan
Sea of Galilee
Golan?
Ashtaroth
R. Kishon
MT. CARMEL (1,742)
R. Yarmuk
MT. TABOR (1,843)
Jokneam
En Dor
Dor
HILL OF MOREH
Megiddo
Shunem
Edrei
Well of Harod
Ramoth
Ibleam
Beth Shean
MT. GILBOA (1,696)
The Great Sea
Gilead
Tirzah
Zaphon
MT. EBAL (3,080)
Shechem
R. Jabbok
MT. GERIZIM (2,890)
Succoth
Aphek
Tappuah
Shiloh
River Jordan
Joppa
Ammon
Rabbah
Jabneel
Bethel
Ai
Gilgal
Gezer
Aijalon
Gibeon
Ekron
Timnah
Kirjath Jearim
Gibeah
Jerusalem
Jericho
Ashdod
Beth Shemesh
Heshbon
Bezer?
Makkedah
Jarmuth
MT. NEBO (2,700)
Gath
Azekah
Bethlehem
Medeba
Ashkelon
Adullam
Philistia
Mareshah
Lachish
Hebron
Gaza
The Salt Sea
(—1,300)
Dibon
Aroer
Debir
En Gedi
R. Arnon
Moab
Beersheba
© Thomas Nelson, Inc., 1983

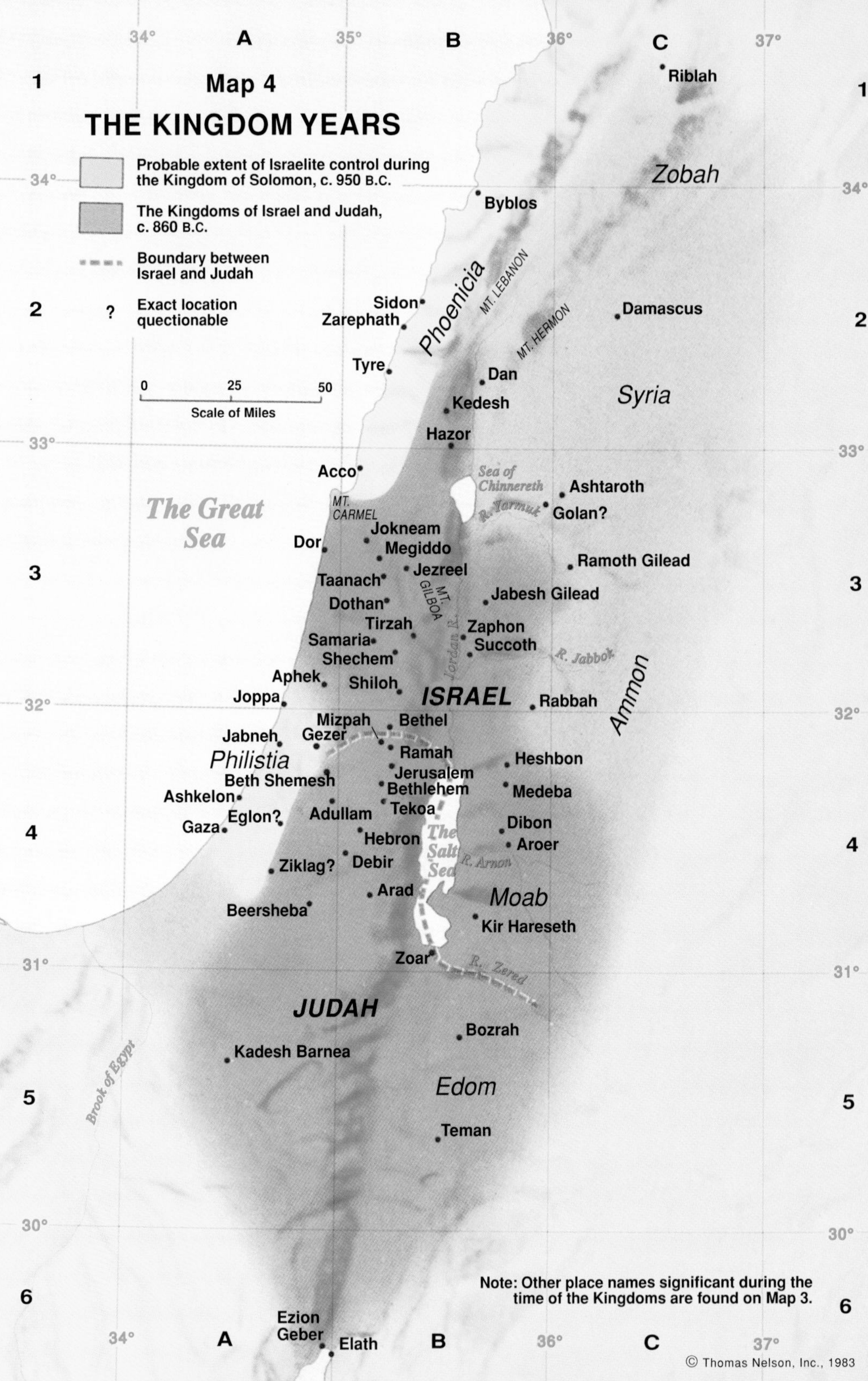
Map 4
THE KINGDOM YEARS
Probable extent of Israelite control during the Kingdom of Solomon, c. 950 B.C.
The Kingdoms of Israel and Judah, c. 860 B.C.
Boundary between Israel and Judah
? Exact location quectionable
0 25 50
Scale of Miles
A B C
1 2 3 4 5 6
34° 35° 36° 37°
33° 32° 31° 30°
Riblah
Zobah
Byblos
Phoenicia
MT. LEBANON
Sidon
Zarephath
Damascus
MT. HERMON
Tyre
Dan
Kedesh
Syria
Hazor
Acco
Sea of Chinnereth
Ashtaroth
MT. CARMEL
R. Yarmuk
Golan?
The Great Sea
Jokneam
Dor
Megiddo
Jezreel
Ramoth Gilead
Taanach
MT. GILBOA
Dothan
Jabesh Gilead
Tirzah
Zaphon
Samaria
Jordan R.
Succoth
Shechem
R. Jabbok
Aphek
Shiloh
Ammon
Joppa
ISRAEL
Rabbah
Mizpah
Bethel
Jabneh
Gezer
Ramah
Philistia
Heshbon
Jerusalem
Beth Shemesh
Bethlehem
Medeba
Ashkelon
Tekoa
Eglon?
Adullam
Dibon
Gaza
Hebron
The Salt Sea
Aroer
R. Arnon
Ziklag?
Debir
Arad
Moab
Beersheba
Kir Hareseth
Zoar
R. Zered
JUDAH
Bozrah
Kadesh Barnea
Brook of Egypt
Edom
Teman
Note: Other place names significant during the time of the Kingdoms are found on Map 3.
Ezion Geber
Elath

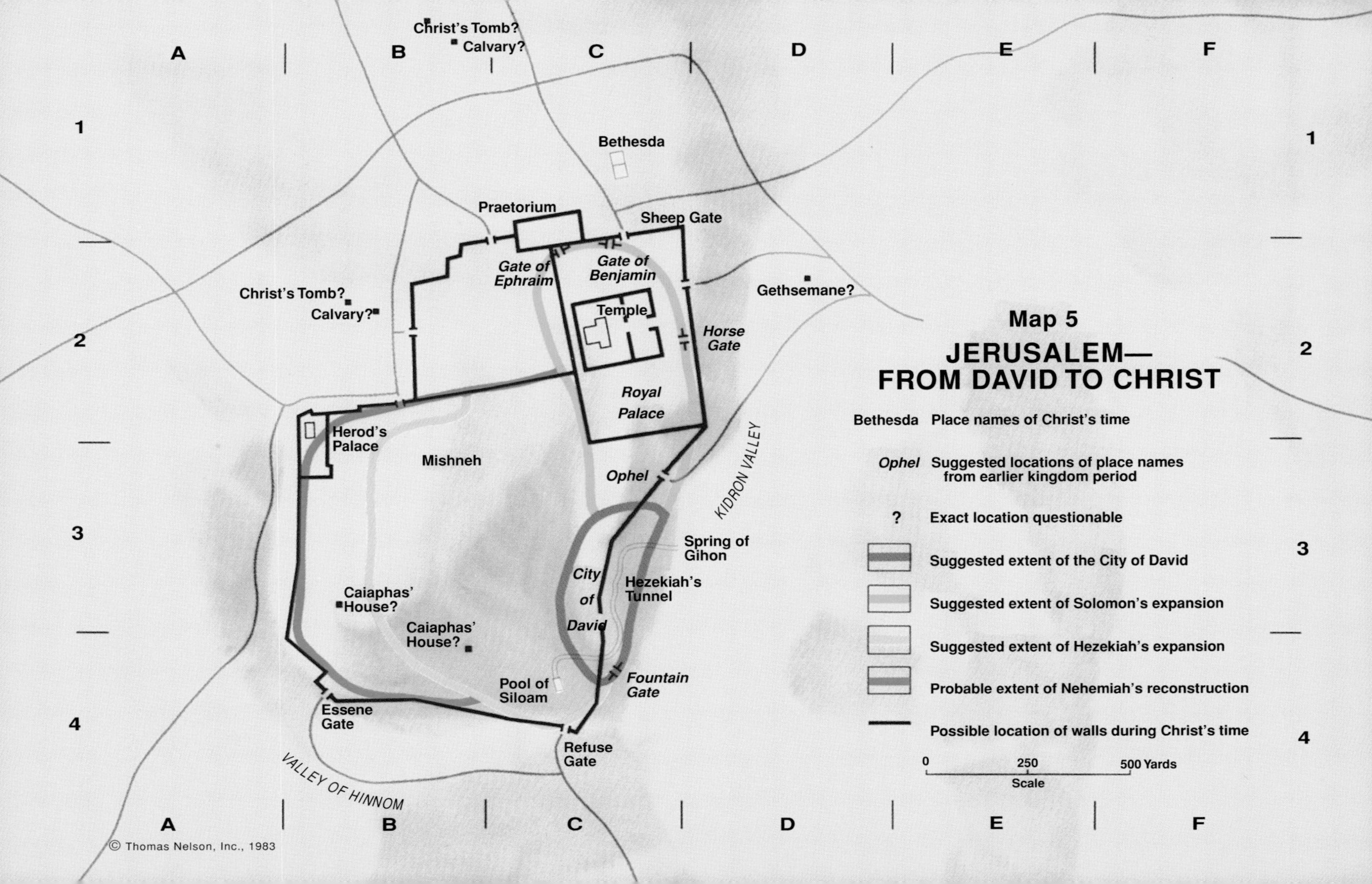

Map 5
JERUSALEM—
FROM DAVID TO CHRIST
Bethesda Place names of Christ's time
Ophel Suggested locations of place names from earlier kingdom period
? Exact location questionable
Suggested extent of the City of David
Suggested extent of Solomon's expansion
Suggested extent of Hezekiah's expansion
Probable extent of Nehemiah's reconstruction
Possible location of walls during Christ's time
0
250
500 Yards
Scale
A
B
C
D
E
F
1
2
3
4
Christ's Tomb?
Calvary?
Bethesda
Praetorium
Sheep Gate
Gate of Ephraim
Gate of Benjamin
Gethsemane?
Temple
Horse Gate
Royal Palace
Herod's Palace
Mishneh
Ophel
KIDRON VALLEY
Spring of Gihon
City of David
Hezekiah's Tunnel
Caiaphas' House?
Fountain Gate
Pool of Siloam
Essene Gate
Refuse Gate
VALLEY OF HINNOM

Map 6
PALESTINE IN CHRIST'S TIME
(1,742) Elevation, in feet
? Exact location questionable
0 10 20
Scale of Miles
34°30′
A
35°
B
35°30′
C
36°
D
33°30′
33°
32°30′
32°
31°30′
1
2
3
4
5
Sidon
Damascus
Zarephath
MT. LEBANON (11,000)
MT. HERMON (9,200)
Phoenicia
Tyre
Iturea
Panias (Caesarea Philippi)
Trachonitis
Galilee
Ptolemais
Chorazin
Bethsaida?
Capernaum
Magdala
Sea of Chinnereth
Gergesa
Cana
Tiberias
R. Kishon
MT. CARMEL (1,742)
R. Yarmuk
Nazareth
MT. TABOR (1,843)
Gadara?
Nain
Esdraelon
R. Jezreel
Scythopolis
MT. GILBOA (1,696)
Caesarea
The Great Sea
Decapolis
Samaria
Samaria
Gerasa
Sychar
R. Jabbok
MT. GERIZIM (2,890)
River Jordan
Antipatris
Joppa
Perea
Arimathea
Gadara?
Lydda
Ephraim
Philadelphia
Emmaus
Jericho
Kirjath Jearim
Bethabara
Jerusalem
Bethany
Azotus
Beth Haccerem
Qumran
Bethlehem
Medeba
Ashkelon
Herodium
Judea
Machaerus
Hebron
Gaza
The Salt Sea
R. Arnon
(—1,300)
Masada
Idumea
Beersheba

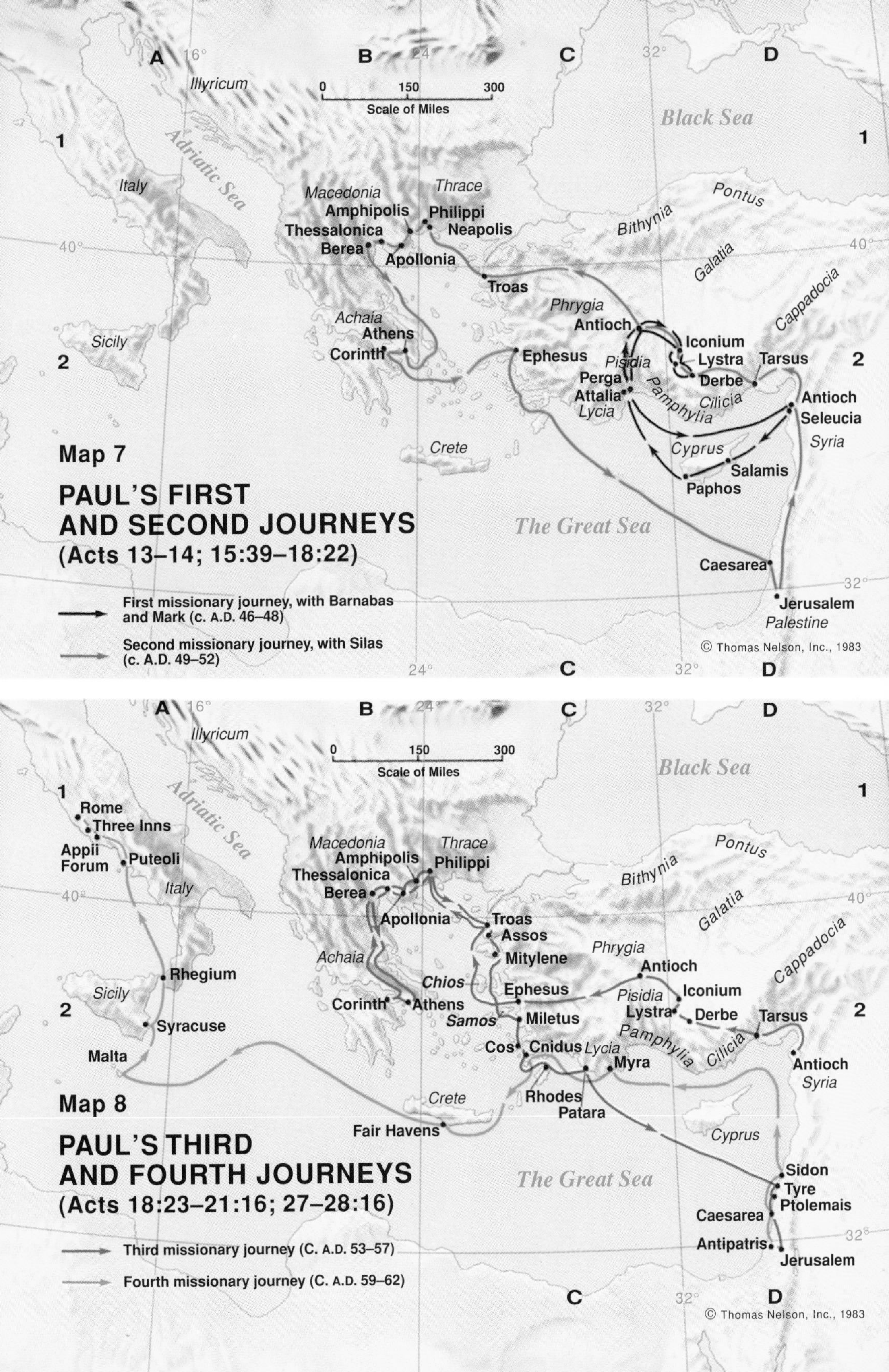
A
B
C
D
16°
24°
32°
40°
1
2
Illyricum
0
150
300
Scale of Miles
Black Sea
Adriatic Sea
Italy
Macedonia
Thrace
Amphipolis
Philippi
Thessalonica
Neapolis
Berea
Apollonia
Pontus
Bithynia
Galatia
Troas
Phrygia
Cappadocia
Achaia
Sicily
Athens
Corinth
Antioch
Iconium
Ephesus
Pisidia
Lystra
Tarsus
Perga
Derbe
Attalia
Lycia
Pamphylia
Cilicia
Antioch
Seleucia
Syria
Crete
Cyprus
Salamis
Paphos
Map 7
PAUL'S FIRST
AND SECOND JOURNEYS
(Acts 13–14; 15:39–18:22)
The Great Sea
Caesarea
Jerusalem
Palestine
First missionary journey, with Barnabas and Mark (c. A.D. 46–48)
Second missionary journey, with Silas (c. A.D. 49–52)
© Thomas Nelson, Inc., 1983
Rome
Three Inns
Appii Forum
Puteoli
Macedonia
Amphipolis
Thrace
Philippi
Thessalonica
Berea
Apollonia
Troas
Assos
Mitylene
Achaia
Rhegium
Chios
Ephesus
Corinth
Athens
Samos
Miletus
Syracuse
Cos
Cnidus
Lycia
Myra
Malta
Rhodes
Patara
Phrygia
Antioch
Pisidia
Iconium
Lystra
Derbe
Tarsus
Pamphylia
Cilicia
Antioch
Syria
Map 8
Crete
Fair Havens
Cyprus
PAUL'S THIRD
AND FOURTH JOURNEYS
(Acts 18:23–21:16; 27–28:16)
The Great Sea
Sidon
Tyre
Ptolemais
Caesarea
Antipatris
Jerusalem
Third missionary journey (C. A.D. 53–57)
Fourth missionary journey (C. A.D. 59–62)
© Thomas Nelson, Inc., 1983

Map 9
THE HOLY LAND IN MODERN TIMES
Area occupied by Israel since June, 1967
0 25 50
Scale of Miles
A
B
C
D
E
34°
35°
36°
37°
1
2
3
4
5
6
33°
32°
31°
30°
Tripoli
LEBANON
Beirut
BEKAA VALLEY
LEBANON MTS.
ANTI-LEBANON MTS.
Sidon
Damascus
Tyre
Dan
U.N. Buffer Zone
1973 Line
SYRIA
Qiryat Shemona
Quneitra
1967 Cease-Fire Line
Nahariyya
Safad
Akko
Sea of Galilee
Golan Heights
Haifa
Tiberias
Nazareth
Dera
Mediterranean Sea
Afula
Ramtha
Beth Shean
Hadera
Netanya
Tulkarm
Jordan River
Jarash
Nablus
Herzliyya
Tel Aviv
West Bank
Petah Tiqwa
Yafo
Rishon le Zion
Lod
Ramalah
Amman
Ramla
Ashdod
Jericho
Jerusalem
Bethlehem
Ashqelon
Madaba
Qiryat Gat
Gaza
Hebron
Dead Sea
En Gedi
Dhiban
Beersheba
Al-Arish
Karak
JORDAN
ISRAEL
EGYPT
Negev
Arabah
Sinai
Elat
Aqaba